THE 21ST CENTURY WEBSTER'S INTERNATIONAL ENCYCLOPEDIA

FIRST EDITION

THE 21ST CENTURY
WEBSTER'S
INTERNATIONAL
ENCYCLOPEDIA
FIRST EDITION

THE NEW ILLUSTRATED
REFERENCE GUIDE

Editor-in-Chief
Bart Drubbel

Trident Press International

2003 EDITION

THE 21ST CENTURY
WEBSTER'S
INTERNATIONAL
ENCYCLOPEDIA

◆ ◆ ◆

FIRST EDITION

2003 Edition published by Typhoon International Corp. and distributed exclusively by
Trident Press International, 801 12th Avenue South, Suite 400, Naples Florida 34102
www.trident-international.com • email: tridentpress@worldnet.att.net
+1 (239) 649-7077 • Toll Free 1-800-593-3662

Library of Congress Cataloging-in-Publication Data
The 21st Century Webster's International Encyclopedia, First Edition the new illustrated reference guide.
Summary: A concise, general-subject encyclopedia with color and black-and-white illustrations, maps and charts.

1. Children's encyclopedias and dictionaries. 2. Encyclopedias and dictionaries. [1. Encyclopedias and dictionaries.]

ISBN 1-58279-552-5 Standard Edition
ISBN 1-58279-553-3 Ten Volume Hardcover Edition
ISBN 1-58279-571-1 Ten Volume Hardcover Edition in Slipcase

Printed in Columbia

Table of contents

Foreword

We live in times dominated by information and communication technology. Information reaches us ever faster and in ever greater amounts. Each day we are flooded with a multitude of names and facts about which we yearn to learn more. We are not always able to place people, countries or events within their proper context. The first edition of **The 21st Century Webster's International Encyclopedia** contains thousands of biographies of politicians, artists, sportsmen and scientists. Faces you know from the news are given shape and thus come to life.

Science appears to have become science fiction. Technical developments border on the extreme. Mathematics oversteps the boundary with philosophy. This Encyclopedia gives a complete survey of the developments in science and technology from ancient times up until the present day, from AIDS to borderline personality disorder, from the greenhouse effect to the Kyoto Protocol, from the Space Shuttle to the International Space Station.

Various entries are not only instructive and educational, but are also well within the range of appreciation of any intelligent reader. Facts and interpretations of facts are presented directly and in a way which attempts to be objective. The aim is not to impose opinions but instead to provide facts and general theories. **The 21st Century Webster's International Encyclopedia** is a reference book that is not only visually attractive thanks to the hundreds of illustrations, maps and schedules, but one that will also arouse the reader's curiosity everyday, inciting him to read and discover.

Jan Van Miert, Ph.D

A, first letter of the English alphabet and others that can be traced back to Semitic roots. The letter was originally drawn to represent the head of an ox and given the name *aleph* (Phoenician 'ox'). In Greek this became *alpha*. The shape of the letter changed gradually as it passed into the Hebrew, Greek, and Roman alphabets. Our capital *A* is based on the Greek form. The lower-case *a* was first used in medieval manuscripts. From the first 2 letters of the Greek alphabet, alpha and beta, we derive the word *alphabet*.

Aachen, also Aix-la-Chapelle (pop. 247.000), city and spa in North Rhine-Westphalia, Germany. A major industrial center producing machinery, textiles, and chemicals, it is also the site of mineral springs frequented since Roman times. The emperor Charlemagne built a palace and cathedral in the city.

Aalto, Alvar (1898-1976), a Finnish architect and furniture designer. His functional, regularly shaped buildings harmonize in both form and material with the natural environment. Among his many works are National Pensions Institute, House of Culture, and Finlandia House - all in Helsinki - and Baker House, a dormitory at Massachusetts Institute of Technology. He also designed the furniture and lighting fixtures for many of his buildings. Aalto was born in central Finland and studied in Helsinki.

Aardvark (*Orycteropus afer*), nocturnal African mammal. Measuring up to 6 ft (1.8 m) in length and weighing up to 150 lbs (68 kg), the aardvark has a stout body with a plump, ratlike tail, elongated piglike snout, and large ears. It feeds on ants and termites, tearing open their nests with its powerful limbs and catching them with its long, sticky tongue.
See also: Anteater.

Aaron, elder brother of Moses and first Jewish high priest. In the Old Testament (Exodus) Aaron speaks for the Israelites and in the Egyptian court, after Jehovah has commanded Moses to lead his people out of Egypt.
See also: Moses.

Aaron, Hank (Henry Louis Aaron; 1934-), U.S. baseball player. He broke Babe Ruth's record in 1974 with his 715th career home run. He retired in 1976 with 755 homers. An outfielder with the Milwaukee (later Atlanta) Braves, Aaron also set a National League record with 2,297 runs batted in. He finished his career with the Milwaukee Brewers of the American League. He retired in 1976 and became a baseball executive. *I Had a Hammer* (1991) is his autobiography.

Abacá (*Musa textilis*), name of the plant, native to the Philippines, that yields Manila hemp.

Abacus, or counting frame, ancient calculating instrument still widely used in Asia. It consists of a wooden frame containing a series of parallel rods strung with beads and divided into upper and lower portions. Each of the rods represents a power of 10; each of the beads on the lower portion counts for a power of 1 and the 2 on the upper portion for a power of 5 apiece. It can be used to solve addition, subtraction, multiplication, and division problems.

Abacus

Abadan (pop. 470,000), Persian Gulf port city in Khuzestan province, southwestern Iran, on Abadan Island in the Shatt al Arab, the waterway formed by the confluence of the Tigris and Euphrates rivers. An important oil-refining center since 1909, Abadan was badly damaged by bombing during the Iraq-Iran war, which began in 1980 and ended in August 1988.

Abahai (1592-1643), ruler of the Manchus (since 1629), founder of the Manchu or Qing dynasty of China (until 1911). Korea (1636) and the territory of the Amur (1636-43) were also brought under his command and was thereby influenced by the Qing.

Abakanowicz, Magdalena (1930-), Polish artist; makes woven wall hangings, which are striking because of their great power of expression in particular their three-dimensional effect. Mankind became an important theme in her work during the 1970s.

Abalone, or ear shell, marine mollusk (genus *Haliotis*) harvested as a popular seafood and for the colorful lining of its shell, which is used for making buttons and costume jewelry. The abalone is found in most mild and tropical waters clinging to submerged rocks by means of a muscular foot.

Abbado, Claudio (1933-), an Italian conductor. Born in Milan, Abbado made his conducting debut in Trieste in 1958. He served as the musical director of La Scala in Milan from 1968 until 1986, when he was appointed musical director of the state opera in Vienna. In 1989, he replaced Herbert von Karajan as artistic director and principal conductor of the Berlin Philharmonic Orchestra.

Abbasid, dynasty of Arab caliphs (749-1258) descended from Abbas (d. 653), uncle of Muhammad. The early years of Abbasid rule were marked by prosperity and strong government; they reached their high-water mark with the reign of the fifth caliph, Harun-Rashid (764-809). The dynasty was finally overthrown by Hulagu Khan, grandson of Genghis Khan, who sacked Baghdad in 1258.
See also: Muslims.

Abbas the Great (1571-1629) Shah of Persia (since 1588) from the dynasty of Safawiden. He modernized the army following the example of the Turks and improved the infrastructure. He enlarged the empire and tried, through means of alliances (with India, Moskovia, and England, among others), to close in the Ottoman Empire. In Esfahan, the capital, arts and sciences flourished. His rule was seen as tolerant towards religion.

Abbe, Cleveland (1838-1916), U.S. meteorologist who inaugurated a system of scientific weather forecasting in the United States. After studying at the Pulkova Observatory in Russia, he became head of the Cincinnati Observatory and in 1869 began publishing official forecasts based largely on analyses of telegraphic reports on approaching storms.

Abbey, building of a monastic house or religious community, centered on a church. The cloistered life of medieval times grew out of the anchorite, or hermit, communities of Egypt and the Near East in the early Christian era. The first abbey in western Europe was established in France in 360, and the first in England, Bangor Abbey, in 560. Abbeys were centers of culture and the practical arts throughout western Europe.

Abbey Theatre, originally called Irish National Theatre. It was founded in 1902 by William Butler Yeats, Lady Gregory, and others to promote the work of Irish playwrights. The company moved to the Abbey Theatre in Dublin in 1904. It performs works in both English and Gaelic.
See also: Yeats, William Butler; Irish literature.

Abbey Theatre, established in Dublin in 1904, has played an important part in the Irish Revival.

A

Abbott, Robert Sengstacke (1868-1940), journalist, editor, and publisher and founder of the *Chicago Defender*, an important newspaper in the United States. The son of former slaves, Abbott graduated from Kent College of Law in 1899, but soon left the legal profession. Utilizing previous newspaper experience he published the first issue of the *Chicago Defender* on May 15, 1905. A leading proponent of equal rights for African Americans, Abbott used the paper to encourage Southern blacks to move to the North for better jobs and opportunities during the industrial boom of World War I.

A.B.C. Powers, loose entente between Argentina, Brazil, and Chile, initiated in 1906, taking its name from the countries' initials. The entente's mediation averted a U.S.-Mexican war in 1915. Its aims were cooperation and mutual nonaggression, but a treaty signed by the 3 countries in May 1915 had little real effect.

Abd-al-Latif (1162-1231) Arabic philosopher and natural scientist, traveled widely and provided precise descriptions of the plants and animals he ccame upon. He is known for his travel book of Egypt; the hippopotamus and the crocodile are described in detail. Abd-al-Latif is also known for his description of the structure of the skeleton. He worked and lived in Damascus and Cairo, where he taught medicine and philosophy.

Abdomen, in vertebrates, large body cavity between the chest and the pelvis. It contains the stomach, intestines, liver, gallbladder (which are covered by the peritoneum, the thin membrane lining the cavity), kidneys, spleen, adrenal glands, pancreas, and, in the female, reproductive organs. In invertebrates, *abdomen* refers to the part of the body behind the thorax.
See also: Intestine; Stomach.

Abdul-Hamid, name of 2 sultans of the Ottoman Empire. **Abdul-Hamid I** (1725-1789) succeeded his brother Mustafa III in 1774. Throughout his reign the power of Turkey was on the wane, weakened by internal revolt and continuing war with Russia. **Abdul-Hamid II** (1842-1918) succeeded his brother Murad V in 1876. The following year he began a disastrous war with Russia that resulted in Turkey's loss of control over her European provinces of Serbia, Montenegro, Bulgaria, Romania, Herzegovina, and Bosnia. After some initial gestures toward reform, he ruled harshly by decree. Sometimes called the Bloody Sultan, he roused world opinion against him and his government by the massacre of Armenians (1894-1896).The Young Turks, a reform-minded political organization, forced him to accept a constitution and deposed him the following year after he attempted a counter-revolution.
See also: Ottoman Empire.

Abdul-Jabbar, Kareem (Ferdinand Lewis Alcindor, Jr.; 1947-), U.S. basketball player. The 7-ft 2-in (218-cm) center is considered one of the greatest players of all time. Known for his 'sky hook' jump shot, Abdul-Jabbar holds records in regular season scoring (38,387 points) and games played (1,560) and received the league's most-valuable-player award 6 times. After a successful college career at UCLA, he played for the Milwaukee Bucks and Los Angeles Lakers of the NBA (1969-1989). Abdul-Jabbar legally changed his name in 1971 after adopting the Muslim religion.
See also: Basketball.

Abdullah bin Abd al-Aziz (1921-), heir to the throne of Saudi Arabia, one of the younger sons of Abd al Aziz ibn Saoud, founder of the kingdom. Abdullah has been commander of the National Guard since 1962 and Vice President and heir to the throne since 1982. In 1996, he partly took over the tasks of his half-brother King Fahd who was ill. Abdullah is known as a pious Muslim, wary of western influences.
See also: Saudi Arabia.

Abdullah bin Hussein (1962-), king of Jordan, succeeded his father in 1999 on the day he died. At first, Abdullah had no political ambitions. Instead, he pursued a military carreer, which eventually led to the rank of Major General and made him head of the National Guard. Being a military person, he was regarded as non-intellectual, but smart, charming and socially skilled. Abdullah was appointed heir to the throne only days before his father passed away. Before that, Hussein's brother Hassan was heir. After he was crowned, he promised to follow in his father's footsteps regarding the peace-policy. The new heir to the throne is Abdullah's half-brother Hamza.
See also: Jordan.

Abdul Rahman, Tunku (Tunku = prince; 1903-1990) Malaysian politician. Abdul Rahman was cofounder of the United Malays National Organization (UMNO) after the second World War and played an important role in acquiring independence from the Federation of Malaya in 1957. As prime minister (1957-70) he was able to form the Federation of Malaysia in 1963 and was nicknamed Bapak Malaysia (Father of Malaysia). He endeavored to bridge the differences between the Malaysian and Chinese communities, yet race riots in 1969 led to his resignation.

Abdur Rahman (1844-1901) Emir of Afghanistan. He succeeded in playing off the British and the Russians, who were both seeking influence in Afghanistan at the time, against each other. Abdur Rahman received powerful backing from the Russians after war broke out between England and Russia in 1878. He entered into an agreement with the English, who recognized him as Emir of Afghanistan (1880). Formally, he remained loyal to the English but in reality he turned out to be an ardent supporter of anti Western pan Islamism. He subdued a number of tribes in his country and arranged fixed borders for Afghanistan. His son Habib Ullah Khan succeeded him in 1901.

Abè, Kobo (1924-1993), a Japanese author. His works typically portray a world in which people experience bizarre events, struggle to create a personal identity, and seek a sense of belonging. Absurd elements combine with realistic details in his best-known novel *The Woman in the Dunes* (1962), in which a man on a weekend trip becomes the captive of a strange community of people who live in sandpits.
Abè was born in Tokyo but grew up in Japanese-occupied Manchuria where his father, who was a doctor, taught medicine. Abè graduated from Tokyo University in 1948 with a medical degree but never practiced medicine. Other works include: novels - *The Road Sign at the End of the Street* (1948); *The Ruined Map* (1967); *The Box Man* (1973); *Secret Rendezvous* (1977); plays - *Friends* (1967) and *The Man Who Turned into a Stick* (1969).

Abel, second son of Adam and Eve. His older brother, Cain, killed him in a fit of anger when God accepted Abel's offering but rejected Cain's. (Genesis 4.)
See also: Adam and Eve; Cain; Old Testament.

Abelard, Peter (1079-1142), leading medieval French scholastic philosopher and teacher. The school he founded in Paris would evolve into the University of Paris. The main thrust of Abelard's philosophy was that the power of human thinking or reason could achieve true knowledge in the natural and supernatural spheres. He excelled in his study of the nature of abstraction and in his search for the source of responsibility in human actions. The church condemned Abelard's original teachings as heretical. Abelard is probably best remembered for his love affair with Héloïse, one of his pupils. Following the birth of a child, Héloïse and Abelard married secretly, but Héloïse's vengeful uncle had Abelard castrated. After separating to take up monastic life, the couple exchanged a series of moving love letters.

Pierre Abelard (1079-1142).

Aberdeen (pop. 217,000), Scottish seaport and the most populous city of northern Scotland. Aberdeen is a shipbuilding and fishing center also known as the market center for the Aberdeen Angus cattle breed. In the 1970s it became the hub of the industries based on the exploitation of North Sea oil.

Abernathy, Ralph David (1926-1990), U.S. black civil rights leader and Baptist minister. In 1968 he succeeded the murdered Martin Luther King, Jr., as president of the Southern Christian Leadership Conference and led the Poor People's March on Washington D.C. that year.
See also: Civil rights; King, Martin Luther, Jr..

Aberration, optical, failure of a lens to form a perfect image of an object. The 2 types are chromatic aberration, where dispersion causes colored fringes to appear around the image, and spherical aberration, where blurring occurs because light from the outer parts of the lens is brought to a focus at a shorter distance from the lens than that passing through the center. Chromatic aberration can be reduced by using an achromatic lens; spherical aberration can be reduced by separating the elements of a compound lens.
See also: Lens.

Abidjan (pop. 2.9 million), largest city and former capital of the Ivory Coast, West Africa. Abidjan is a major port and railroad terminus, as well as one of the most modern cities of Africa. The city's main industries include canning, shipping, and the production of beer, margarine, and soap.

Abilene (pop. 107,000), agricultural city in central Kansas. Settled in 1856, Abilene was an important shipping point for Texas cattle brought north to the railroad over the Chisholm Trail. As marketing center for the surrounding farmlands, its chief industries are grain milling and the processing of dairy products. President Dwight D. Eisenhower lived in the town as a boy and chose it for his burial place and the site of a memorial museum.

Ability test, test to demonstrate a particular level of knowledge or skill. An individual general ability test consists of 8 small subtests: information test, analogies test, vocabulary, letter memory, number series, spatial relations, clock test, and sign language test.

Abkhazia (pop. 506,000), an autonomous republic in Georgia, 3,322 sq mi (8,600 sq km). The capital as well as the economic and cultural center is the seaport town of Sukhumi. The climate is subtropical, allowing the cultivation of tea, citrus fruits, tobacco, and grapes (wine). The area is rich in minerals, especially manganese and coal. Tourism is important along the coast (seaside resorts).
In 1989, Abkhazians (Muslims) formed 18% of the population; the Georgians (Christians) were the largest group with approximately 45%.
Abkhazia was an autonomous SSR within Georgia during the period when Georgia was still part of the Soviet Union. The republic declared itself independent from Georgia in 1990 but the decision was reversed by Georgian representatives in the parliament of Abkhazia in 1991. During 1990 and 1991 clashes between Abkhazians and Georgians took place quite regularly.

The Georgian President Gamsakhurdia cancelled the autonomy of the republic. The conflict escalated in 1992 when the Abkhazian parliament, headed by President Vladislav Ardzinba, again declared the republic independent and Georgian government troops were deployed to suppress the independence movement. Russia tried to mediate and sent troops to uphold the various truces, which were generally quickly broken. Initially the rebels could count on Russian sympathy because Georgia refused to become a member of the CIS. When they did so (1994) and Abkhazia supported their related Chechen rebels in their fight against Russia, the Georgian government could count on more Russian aid.
A couple of hundred thousand Georgians fled the battle zone, partly after they were attacked by Abkhazians. The area became a de facto independent state. Negotiations under the auspices of the UN led to a truce in 1994. Russian troops in CIS connection took up positions along the border between Abkhazia and Georgia. UN observers were also stationed there. In 1997 the Georgian government stated that it was willing to grant far-reaching autonomy to Abkhazia but stood by its demand that Georgia would remain a unified state, whereas the Abkhazian separatists stuck to their demand that Georgia would become a confederation of two sovereign states. Both parties decided to set up a council to coordinate the return of the more than 200,000 Georgian refugees to Abkhazia. However, conflict broke out again in 1998.

Abnormal psychology, sometimes called *psychopathology,* the scientific study of disorders of the mind. Treatment for these disorders includes medication, psychoanalysis (the technique developed by Sigmund Freud), psychotherapy, and behavior modification.
See also: Mental illness.

Abolitionism, movement in the United States and other countries that aimed at abolishing slavery. The *Liberator*, an antislavery paper edited by William Lloyd Garrison, began publication in 1831. In 1833 the American Anti-Slavery Society was founded in Philadelphia. Some abolitionists used their homes as stations for fugitive slaves on the underground railroad. The movement produced much literature, including Harriet Beecher Stowe's *Uncle Tom's Cabin*. After the outbreak of the Civil War, abolitionist demands led to President Lincoln's Emancipation Proclamation (1863). The 13th Amendment (1865) completed the abolition of slavery in the United States. William Wilberforce and others led the movement in Britain to abolish the slave trade (1807) and slavery (1833).
See also: Douglass, Frederick; Emancipation Proclamation; Slavery; Civil War, U.S.; Underground Railroad.

Abortion, ending of pregnancy before the fetus is able to survive outside the womb. It can occur spontaneously (miscarriage), or it can be artificially induced. Spontaneous abortion may occur as a result of maternal or fetal disease or faulty implantation in the

Ralph David Abernathy (1926-1990).

womb. Abortion may be artificially induced by surgical or medical means, depending on the stage of pregnancy and the patient's condition. Today, an early abortion performed in a modern facility by qualified health care professionals is relatively simple and safe. However, complications of abortion like uterine infection or injury can contribute to an inability to have children at a later time. Abortion has been long practiced in most cultures, but public opinion in the Western nations, combined with the opposition of religious leaders, led to restrictive legislation in the 19th century. By the second half of the 20th century, however, abortion was legalized in most of Europe, the USSR, and Japan. In 1973, the U.S. Supreme Court ruled in *Roe* v. *Wade* that abortions in the first or second trimester are legal, but the moral and legal controversy surrounding abortion continues.

Aboukir, village in Egypt situated on the Mediterranean coast between Alexandria and the Rosetta mouth of the Nile. The Battle of the Nile (Aug. 1798), in which British naval forces under Nelson defeated Napoleon's fleet, took place in Aboukir Bay. A second battle (1801) was fought on land at Aboukir, and Napoleon's forces were again beaten decisively by the British. The village is the site of ancient Canopus, a thriving port in Hellenistic times.

Abraham, first of the patriarchs (founding fathers) of the Jews; regarded as the founder of Judaism. God promised Abraham that his people would inherit Canaan through his son Isaac. As a test of faith and obedience, God commanded Abraham to slay Isaac. Abraham unquestioningly obeyed, and Isaac was spared. (Genesis 11-25.) Muslims consider Abraham an ancestor of the Arabs through another son, Ishmael.
See also: Jews; Judaism; Lot.

Abraham, Karl (1877-1925), German psychoanalyst whose most important work concerned the development of the libido, particularly in infancy. He suggested that various psychoses should be interpreted in terms of interruption of this development.

A

A

Abramovic, Marina (1946-) Yugoslavian (Montenegro) conceptual artist, initially engaged in 'body art', who gave many highly stylized performances. Since 1976 she and her partner Ulay (Uwe Laysiepen) achieved highly formal esthetics by using symmetrical and circular shapes. To her, form however, is subordinate to testing physical strength and opening up new reserves of spiritual energy. Since 1988 she has worked independently from Ulay with sculptures that use minerals in an attempt to influence the consciousness of the audience.

Abravanel (Abrabanel), Isaac (1437-1508), Jewish theologian and statesman. Born in Lisbon, he served King Alfonso V of Portugal in state and financial affairs. Forced after the king's death to flee to Spain, he was employed by Ferdinand and Isabella until the Jews were expelled from Spain in 1492. He then lived in various Italian cities, eventually becoming a minister of state in Venice, where he died. He is best known for his extensive commentaries on the Bible.

Absalom, third son of King David of Israel. Absalom fled his father's court after killing his brother Amnon. He later returned and was pardoned, but he then conspired against his father, proclaimed himself king, and was killed against David's wishes. (2 Samuel 13-19.)
See also: David.

Abscess, localized accumulation of pus, usually representing a response of the body to bacterial infection. The bacteria enter the skin via a natural opening or small cut, and they can pass into the intestinal mucous membrane or the respiratory system and be swept by the bloodstream to various organs of the body. The immune, or defense, system of the body possesses 2 mechanisms for destroying the penetrating bacteria: the leukocytes (white blood cells) and antibodies. If these defense mechanisms succumb to the bacteria, an abscess forms: The bacteria destroy a large number of cells, causing tissue death and the formation of an ulcer, which forms a pussy mass. Fortunately, the tissue is

The Great Temple at Abu Simbel (1301 B.C.), one of two temples built here by Ramses II.
1. four rock-hewn seated colossi of Ramses, each more than 19 metres high
2. concrete dome that protects the Temple from tons of rocks that are piled up
3. stepped walling behind the facade, reinforces the colossi
4. grid-like structure supports the ceiling blocks
5. inner chambers

Blue, Orange, Red (1961) by Russian-born American Mark Rothko (1903-1970).

usually capable of stopping the destructive work of the bacteria, forming a barrier to the spread of the bacteria by building a wall of cells and connective tissue. Such an abscess may drain spontaneously; otherwise it should be incised.
See also: Carbuncle.

Absinthe, common European wormwood (*Artemisia absinthium*); also, bitter, green, distilled liqueur principally flavored with an aromatic oil obtained from the wormwood. Allegation that absinthe is poisonous led to the drink's prohibition in many countries, including the United States and Canada.

Absolute zero, temperature (0°K [kelvin]/-273.15°C/-459.67°F) at which all substances have zero thermal energy and thus, theoretically, the lowest possible temperature. Originally conceived as the temperature at which an ideal gas at constant pressure would contract to zero volume, absolute zero is of great significance in thermodynamics and is used as the fixed point for the absolute, or kelvin, temperature scale. In practice the absolute zero temperature is unattainable, although temperatures within a few millionths of 0°K have been achieved in cryogenics laboratories.
See also: Gas; Temperature.

Absolution, in the Roman Catholic and some other churches, remission of sins pronounced by a priest in favor of a penitent.

Absolutism, form of government, such as a dictatorship, in which all power is held by an unchecked ruler. Monarchies in the ancient world were usually absolute. In England, in the 18th century, the Stuart attempt to rule by divine right failed, but elsewhere in Europe, especially France, absolutism flourished until the early 19th century. Examples of absolutism in the 20th century are the totalitarian governments of Adolf Hitler in Germany and Joseph Stalin in the Soviet Union.
See also: Dictatorship; Totalitarianism.

Absorption, taking in of energy or molecules by a material. While in *adsorption* molecules are attracted to the surface, in absorption the energy or molecules are distributed throughout the material.

Abstract expressionism, U.S. art movement of the 1940s and 1950s that explored the emotional, expressive power of nonfigurative painting. It was the first significant school of U.S. painting, influencing artists in other countries. Jackson Pollock, who dipped and spattered paint on the canvas, was called, along with some other members of the movement, an 'action painter.' Franz Kline, Willem de Kooning, Mark Rothko, Barnett Newman, and Arshile Gorky are considered leading abstract expressionists.
See also: Pollock, Jackson; Kline, Franz; Rothko, Mark; Newman, Barnett; Gorky, Arshile; De Kooning, Willem.

Abu Bakr (c. A.D. 573-634), first Muslim caliph of Arabia in 632, following Muhammad's death. He ordered incursions into Syria and Iraq, thus beginning the Muslim conquests. He was Muhammad's father-in-law, as well as his closest companion and adviser.
See also: Muslims.

Abu Dhabi (pop. 928,000), largest (25,000 sq mi/64,750 sq km) of the 7 emirates that make up the United Arab Emirates (UAE), located on the southern coast of the Persian Gulf. The land is mostly desert, with extensive oil deposits. The city of Abu Dhabi (pop. 243,000) is the capital of the UAE.
See also: United Arab Emirates.

Abu Jihad (Khalil al-Wazir; 1935-1988) Palestinian leader. Driven from his place of birth in 1948, Abu Jihad grew up in Gaza. He was already known as a Palestinian nationalist at his high school and in Egypt, where he studied law, he cofounded the resistance movement of al-Fatah at the end of the 1950s with Yasir Arafat and others. al-Fatah led an obscure existence to start with and only carried out its first military operation in Israel on 1st January 1965. Abu Jihad became the main military leader of al-Fatah and of the Palestine Liberation Organization (PLO), which was dominated by al-Fatah. As the brains behind many attacks in Israel, he was probably assassinated by Israeli commandos.
See also: al-Fatah; Palestine Liberation Organization.

Abu Simbel, archeological site of 2 temples commissioned by Ramses II (13th century B.C.) on the west bank of the Nile, 762 mi (1,226 km) south of Cairo. The Aswan High Dam construction threatened to submerge the site, but a UNESCO project, completed in 1966, saved the temples by removing them and reconstructing them above the future waterline.
See also: Aswan High Dam.

Abuya (pop. 480,000), capital of Nigeria since 1991. Abuya was built to replace Lagos, predominantly to combat further overpopulation and pauperization, and to create a more centrally located capital city. Construction began in 1980.
See also: Nigeria.

Abydos, Greek name for a religious center in Middle Egypt inhabited since the early dynastic period (3100-2686 B.C.) and con-

nected with the god Osiris. It is noted for its tombs of early dynastic kings and its 19th-dynasty temple (c.3100 B.C.).
See also: Osiris.

Acacia, any of a genus (*Acacia*) of mostly tropical trees and shrubs in the pea family. Various species produce catechu, gum arabic, and tannin. Acacia are characteristic of the savanna type of vegetation (grassland with some trees) in central and southern Africa. More than a dozen species grow in the United States. The flowers tend to be mostly yellow or white.

Academic freedom, right of members of the academic community to freedom of thought and expression.

Académie Française (French Academy), literary and linguistic society officially recognized in 1635. Membership is limited to 40, the so-called immortals, and includes prominent public literary figures. It has been criticized for electing individuals with personal influence, while ignoring those with real merit. Molière and Emile Zola were never elected. Over the centuries, the Academy has produced the *dictionnaire*, the official arbiter of the French language.

Academy Awards®, or Oscars®, annual awards given by the Academy of Motion Picture Arts and Sciences for outstanding achievement in various branches of filmmaking. The major awards are for best leading and supporting actor and actress, best direction, best screenplay, and best film. The awards were first presented in 1928, when the best picture award was presented to *Wings*.

Acadia, name given to Nova Scotia and neighboring regions of New Brunswick, Prince Edward Island, and parts of Quebec and Maine by the French colonists who settled there starting in 1604. All but Prince Edward Island and Cape Breton passed under British control by the Treaty of Utrecht (1713). The French colonists, dispersed by the British in 1755, are the subject of Henry Wadsworth Longfellow's poem *Evangeline*. Those who went to Louisiana are the ancestors of the present-day Cajuns.
See also: Cajuns; French and Indian Wars; Nova Scotia.

Acanthus, any of a genus (*Acanthus*) of mostly tropical shrubs and herbs in the acanthus family having large, spiny leaves. Acanthus also refers to a leafy ornament used in Greek and Roman architecture.

Acapulco (pop. 687,000), seaport and tourist center on the Pacific coast of southern Mexico. Founded in 1550 on a natural harbor, Acapulco was a base for Spanish explorers and an important trading port. Since the 1920s it has been chiefly noted as a winter resort.

Accelerometer, device used to measure acceleration, working on the principle expressed by Newton's law: $a = F/m$, where a = acceleration, F = force, m = mass. The accelerometer measures the force expressed on a spring by an object of known mass. When acceleration takes place, the object is forced back against the spring as passengers in a car are pressed against the back of their seats. The greater the acceleration, the more the object is forced back. The distance the object moves back, measured in an electrical circuit, is a measure of the acceleration.

Accent, vocal emphasis placed on a syllable in a word. In all languages there are two kinds of accent: (1) musical chromatic or pitch accent; (2) emphatic or stress accent.

Acclimatization, process of adjustment that allows an individual organism to survive under changed conditions in its environment. In a hot, sunny climate, for example, human beings acclimatize by eating less, drinking more, and wearing lighter clothes. At higher altitudes, humans adjust to the diminished oxygen by increasing production of red blood cells.
See also: Adaptation.

Accommodation, focusing. To see clearly, the eye must be accurately focused. When the eye views distant objects the crystalline lens is held in a rather flattened shape by the pull of the suspensory ligaments. When the eye looks at closer objects, the ciliary muscle contracts, reducing the pull of the suspensory fibers and permitting the lens to bulge at its middle. The thicker, rounder lens has a stronger focusing power, so the nearby objects come into sharp focus on the retina. This increase in focusing power, particularly necessary for near vision, is known as *accommodation*.
The ability to accommodate is slowly lost because of gradual hardening of the lens as a person grows older. A young child can normally focus on objects as close as 2 1/2 inches (6 cm), but by the time a person reaches the age of 45 the shortest distance at which he or she has distinct vision is normally about 10 inches (25 cm). Accommodation may gradually grow so difficult that eyeglasses become necessary for reading or other close work.

Acconci, Vito (1940-) American fine artist; engaged in body art during the late 1960s and the 1970s. He used his own body to express himself in front of a live audience and/or documented this using photography, film and video (activities). Subsequently, he set up certain installations in which he himself did not perform, but, instead, let the audience participate. In the 1990s, he also applied himself to public art and created brightly colored installations which refer to pop art.
See also: Pop art.

Accordion, portable reed organ used for jazz and folk music. Tuned metal reeds are set in vibration by air directed at them from a central bellows through valves operated by piano-type keys on the instrument's right-hand side. Buttons on the left produce chords. Although they were known in ancient China, the first modern accordions were built in 1829 in Vienna.

Accounting, analysis of financial records in order to reveal the financial position of an individual or firm.
A financial statement is audited-that is, checked for accuracy and fairness-by an accountant who was not involved in the preparation of the statement.
See also: Audit.

Accra (pop. 1,700,000), capital and largest city of Ghana, on the Gulf of Guinea. The seaport, founded in the 1600s, was a center of the African slave trade until the mid-1800s. It grew in commercial importance in the 20th century after a railroad linked it with the interior.
See also: Africa; Ghana.

Aceh (pop. 2,913,000), area and province on the Indonesian island of Sumatra; 21,395 sq mi (55,392 sq km), capital: Banda Aceh (Kutaradja). The inhabitants converted to Islam as early as in the 14th century. Agriculture (spices) and fisheries are their main means of existence. Aceh was a sultanate as early as the 13th century and succeeded in remaining independent until 1873. It has held a special status as a province (daerah istimewah Atjeh), and in 2002 the Indonesian government gave Aceh an autonomous status.

Acerola, commonly known as Puerto Rican, West Indian, or Barbados cherry, any of a group of subtropical and tropical trees and shrubs (genus *Malpighia*) indigenous to the West Indies, southern Texas, and parts of Mexico, Central America, and northern South America. The cherry-sized edible fruit, also called acerola, is tart, rich in vitamin C (ascorbic acid), and bright red when ripe.

Acetaminophen, common, over-the-counter pain-relieving and fever-reducing drug. It is sometimes taken instead of aspirin, which can irritate the stomach.
See also: Aspirin.

Acetic acid ($C_2H_4O_2$), colorless organic acid, the principal constituent of vinegar, used industrially in the synthesis of plastics. It was first isolated by George Stahl in 1700.
See also: Vinegar.

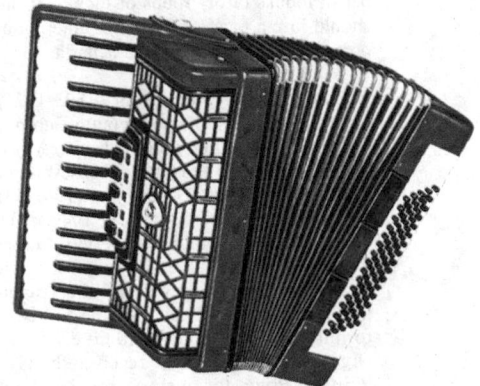

The accordion, invented in the 1920's. The right hand plays the melody on the keyboard, while the left hand operates the buttons for the accompanying chords.

Acetone (CH_3COCH_3), colorless, flammable chemical used in industry as a solvent. Because of its ability to dissolve cellulose, it is used to manufacture synthetic fibers. It is also used to make compounds. Acetone is found in large amounts in the blood and urine of diabetics. It is prepared commercially by removing the hydrogen from isopropyl alcohol or by fermenting starch.
See also: Acetylene.

Acetylene, or ethyne (C_2H_2), colorless gas that explodes on contact with air. Acetylene and oxygen are mixed and burned in the oxyacetylene torch, producing an extremely hot flame (up to 6,300°F/3,480°C) used for welding and cutting metals. Acetylene, used to make plastics, rubber, and explosive compounds, is poisonous if inhaled.
See also: Acetone; Calcium carbide.

Achaeans, people of ancient Greece identified by Homer as the Greeks who fought in the Trojan War. Some authorities believe that the Achaeans came to Greece in the 12th century B.C., briefly dominating Mycenae before being driven by the Dorians to a region in the northern Peloponnesus, which came to be known as Achaea. The Achaean cities formed the Achaean League, which opposed the Macedonians and the Romans, in the 4th century B.C. The Romans defeated the league in 146 B.C.
See also: Aeolians; Dorians; Iliad.

Achaemenids, Persian dynasty that dominated much of West Asia during the 6th-4th centuries B.C. The outstanding rulers were Cyrus the Great, Darius I, and Xerxes I. It ended when Alexander the Great defeated Darius III in 330.

Acharja (Sanskrit: master), usually another word for guru that is used in all Indian religions. In Hinduism acharja is the name of an initiate's future guru. The title is also used for the educated temple priest as opposed to the family priest (purohita). In Vishnuism: great thinker and theologist. Nathamuni (900) received this honorary title for the first time. It was added to the name of Ramanudsha. In Buddhism the acharja and the teacher (upadjaya) are the leaders of the newly ordained monk. In Jainism it is the rank of a monk: acharja is a leader of a number of monks or of groups of monks. If one should lose a hand or foot after entering an order, one cannot become an acharja.

Acheson, Dean Gooderham (1893-1971), U.S. diplomat who helped rebuild Europe's economic and military strength after World War II. He served Presidents Roosevelt and Truman in the State Department (1941-53), becoming secretary of state in 1949. After the war he promoted the recovery of Europe through the Marshall Plan and worked to curb Soviet expansion through the Truman Doctrine (both 1947). In 1949 he helped to formulate the North Atlantic Treaty Organization (NATO). He received the 1970 Pulitzer Prize for history for his book *Present at the Creation: My Years in the State Department*.
See also: Marshall Plan; North Atlantic Treaty Organization; Truman, Harry S..

Achilles, legendary Greek hero of the Trojan War and central figure in the *Iliad* of Homer. Dipped in the River Styx by his mother, Thetis, he was made invulnerable except at the point on his heel where she had held him. Achilles killed the Trojan hero Hector in revenge for the death of Achilles' friend Patroclus. Achilles was killed when the god Apollo guided an arrow from the Trojan warrior Paris into his heel.
See also: Trojan War; Iliad.

Achilles' tendon, tendon at the back of the ankle joining the bone of the heel to the muscles of the calf. It plays a critical role in the ability to walk, run, and stand on the toes. It is commonly injured in strenuous athletics. The name comes from the mythical Greek warrior, Achilles, who was vulnerable only in the heel.
See also: Achilles; Ankle; Tendon.

Acid, any of a class of organic or inorganic water-soluble chemical compounds that taste sour, redden vegetable substances, contain hydrogen, and readily accept electrons or give up protons. Many chemical reactions are speeded up in acid solutions, giving rise to important industrial applications. Strong acids (e.g., hydrochloric acid [HCl]), which break down easily in solution to yield hydrogen (H^+) ions, are good electrolytes (conductors of electricity). Amino acids, constitutive of proteins, are essential components of all living systems.
See also: Base.

Acidosis, medical condition in which the acid-base balance in the body fluids is disturbed in the direction of excess acidity. It can cause heavy breathing and weakness and lead to acidemia. Respiratory acidosis results from the underbreathing and consequent build-up of plasma carbon dioxide caused by lung disease, heart failure, and central respiratory depression. Metabolic acidosis may be caused by the ingestion of excess acids (as in aspirin overdose), ketosis (resulting from malnutrition or diabetes), heavy alkali loss (as from a fistula), and the inability to excrete acid (occurring in some kidney disorders).
See also: Alkalosis.

Acid rain, popular name for polluting rain or other precipitation caused by the combining of oxides of sulfur and nitrogen with atmospheric moisture. Although it is produced by naturally occurring combustion (volcanoes, forest fires), its serious increase is blamed on the burning of fossil fuels (oil, coal, natural gas) by automobiles and in industry. Acid rain may pollute water, kill vegetation, and erode buildings far from its point of origin and has thus become an international as well as a local issue.
See also: Air pollution; Environmental pollution.

Acne, common skin disease caused by inflammation of the sebaceous glands, resulting in pimples on the face and upper trunk. Acne occurs most frequently between the ages of 14 and 19 years, but cases at up to 40 years may occur. An inflamed acne lesion is preceded by a noninflamed lesion (a whitehead or blackhead), which is a plugged sebaceous gland. How these lesions form is uncertain. Blackheads become inflamed either because of local production of irritant fatty acids by bacteria or because of bacterial infection.

Patients with mild acne need only topical therapy, such as the application of a preparation containing either retinoic acid (a derivative of vitamin A) or benzoyl peroxide. Patients with more severe acne require antibiotic drugs as well as topical treatment.

Aconcagua, highest (22,834 ft/6,960 m) mountain in the Western Hemisphere, located in the Andes of northwest Argentina. It was first climbed by E.A. Fitzgerald's expedition in 1897.
See also: Andes.

Aconite, any of a genus (*Aconitum*) of flowering plants, commonly called monkshood or wolfsbane, belonging to the crowfoot family. The species *A. napellus* produces aconite, a poisonous drug.

Acorn, fruit of the oak tree, an oval nut partly encased in a hard, woody cup.
See also: Oak.

Acoustics, the science of sound, dealing with its production, transmission, and effects. Acoustics may be practically applied to, for example, the designing of auditoriums, where the audience must be able to hear the speaker or performer clearly and without echoes. This is achieved by attending to the geometry and furnishings of the hall and incorporating appropriate sound absorbing, diffusing, and reflecting surfaces.
See also: Sound.

ACP countries, group of countries in Africa, the Caribbean, and the Pacific (ACP). Former colonies and developing countries given preferential treatment by the European Union based on the Lomé Treaties. The first Lomé Treaty was signed by 46 ACP countries in 1975, the fourth by 71 developing countries in 1989. This convention continues until the beginning of 2000. Lomé 5 negotiations started in September 1998. The ACP secretariat is in Brussels.

The ACP countries are: Angola, Antigua and Barbuda, Bahamas, Barbados, Belize, Benin, Botswana, Burkina Faso, Burundi, Central-African Republic, Comoros, Congo, Congo-Brazzaville, Djibouti, Dominica, Dominican Republic, Equatorial Guinea, Eritrea, Ethiopia, Fiji, Gabon, Gambia, Ghana, Grenada, Guinea, Guinea-Bissau, Guyana, Haiti, Ivory Coast, Jamaica, Cape Verde, Cameroon, Kenya, Kiribati, Lesotho, Liberia, Madagascar, Malawi, Mali, Mauritania, Mauritius, Mozambique, Namibia, Niger, Nigeria, Papua-New-Guinea, Rwanda, Saint Kitts and Nevis, Saint Lucia, Saint Vincent and the Grenadines, Samoa, Sao Tomé a Principe, Senegal, Seychelles, Sierra Leone, Solomon Islands, Somalia, Sudan, Suriname, Swaziland, Tanzania, Togo, Tonga, Trinidad and Tobago, Chad, Tuvalu, Uganda, Vanuatu, Zambia, and Zimbabwe.

A

Acquired characteristics, modifications in an organism resulting from interaction with its environment. In 1801 Jean Baptiste Lamarck proposed an evolutionary theory in which the inheritance of acquired characteristics provided the mechanism for species divergence. In later editions of *The Origin of Species*, Charles Darwin moved toward accepting this explanation along with that of natural selection, but eventually the Lamarckian mechanism was entirely discounted. Geneticists currently believe that inheritance is determined by reproductive cells.

Acromegaly, rare disease associated with the overgrowth of bone, especially in the jaws, hands, and feet. An endocrinological disorder or chronic hyperpituitarism may be the cause.

Acropolis (Greek, 'high city'), fortified hilltop of an ancient Greek city, serving as its military and religious center. The most famous is the acropolis of Athens, with its many temples, including the Parthenon.
See also: Athens.

Acrylic, group of versatile and durable synthetic products manufactured from petroleum as fibers, plastics, and resins for use in fabrics, glass substitutes, and protective paints. The molecules of a petroleum-based synthetic chemical or substance, acrylonitrile or acrylate, are polymerized (combined in a long, repetitive chain) to form acrylic. Orlon, Lucite, and Plexiglas are trademark names for some common acrylic products.
See also: Polymer; Polymerization.

ACTH (adrenocorticotrophic hormone), or corticotropin, hormone produced by the pituitary gland that stimulates the cortex of the adrenal gland to produce corticosteroids, which regulate many biochemical reactions in the body. Too much ACTH induces growth of the adrenal glands and provokes increased secretion of hydrocortisone. Lack of ACTH gives rise to a wasting away of the adrenal cortex; skin pigmentation is reduced, and the function of other endocrine glands, such as the thyroid, testes, and ovaries, is inhibited. The secretion of ACTH is largely controlled by the release of chemicals to the pituitary gland by the brain.
See also: Gland; Hormone.

Actinide *See:* Rare earth; Element.

Actinium, chemical element, symbol Ac; for physical constants see Periodic Table. Actinium was discovered by André Debierne in 1899. It is radioactive and occurs naturally in minute amounts in uranium minerals. Actinium is synthesized by irradiating radium with neutrons. A reactive metal, it is obtained by reducing its fluoride with lithium vapor. It is about 150 times as active as radium and valuable in the production of neutrons. There are 26 known isotopes. Actinium- 227, a beta emitter and a powerful source of alpha rays, has the longest half-life (21.77 years). Chemically, actinium is similar to lanthanum. It is the first of the actinides, a series of homologous elements analogous to the lanthanide transition series.

Actinomycosis, chronic infectious disease caused by *Actinomyces israeli*, a microorganism often (and usually harmlessly) present on the gums, tonsils, and teeth. The characteristic lesion is a hard area of multiple small communicating abscesses surrounded by granulation tissue. Other similar bacteria are usually also present.

Action painting (gesture painting) Movement within the abstract expressionist movement whereby the artist tried to express his emotions on canvas in a very direct manner. Paint is applied or literally thrown on in thick daubs and fanciful streaks using broad gestures of the whole arm. Important representatives include Jackson Pollock and Willem de Kooning.
See also: Pollock, Jackson; De Kooning, Willem.

Actium, now Ákra Nikólaos, promontory on the west coast of Greece. In a great sea battle fought near it in 31 B.C., Octavian's naval forces crushed those of Marc Antony and Cleopatra. Victory gave mastery of the Roman world to Octavian, who later became the first Roman emperor, Augustus.

Act of Settlement, English parliamentary act of 1701 securing the succession of the Hanoverian line. It increased parliamentary control over the monarch, who was also required to belong to the Protestant Church of England.

Act of Union, 4 acts of the British Parliament uniting England with Wales (1536), Scotland (1707), and Ireland (1801) and uniting Upper and Lower Canada (1840).

Acton, Lord (John Emerich Edward Dalberg Acton, 1st Baron Acton; 1834-1902), English historian and moralist. Lord Acton introduced German research methods into English history and launched the monumental *Cambridge Modern History* (1899-1900). He is famous for the remark, 'All power tends to corrupt, and absolute power corrupts absolutely.'

Actors Studio, professional workshop for actors, established in New York City in 1947; Lee Strasberg became director in 1948. The school's training, often called the Method, is based on the teachings of Constantin Stanislavski, stressing an actor's psychological interpretation of a role and emotional identification with the personality of the character.

Acts of the Apostles, fifth book of the New Testament, the only history of the early

A

Acropolis
1. the Pelasgic wall
2. an old, never completed tempel for Athens
3. the marble entrance gate, the propylaea
4. the wings, in which the pinacotheca can be found, a reception hall with many paintings
5. the temple of Athena Nike
6. a bronze statue of Athena Promachus
7. the Erechtheion
8. the Hall of the Kariatides
9. the theater of Dionysos
10. the round temple of Rome and Augustus, from Roman times
11. the Odeion (music hall), which was built by Herod Atticus

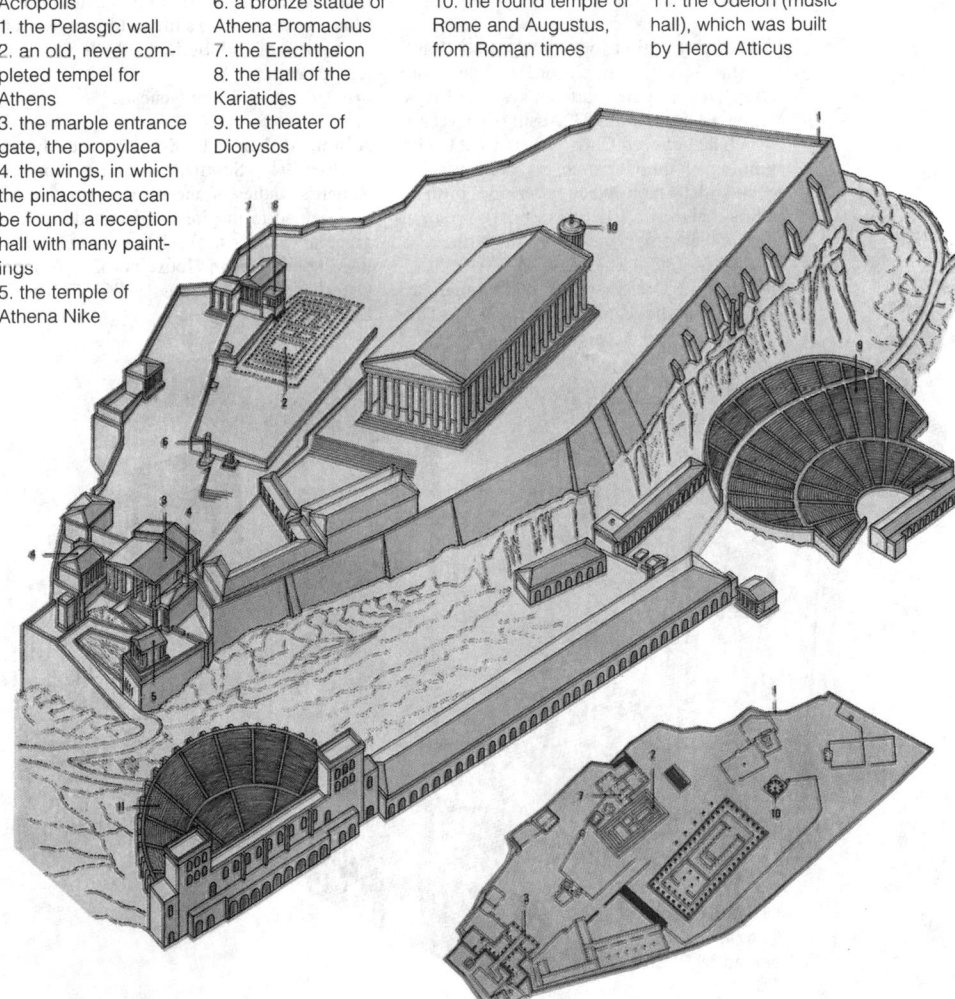

A

Christian Church. Probably written between A.D. 60 and 90 by the evangelist Luke, it is a continuation of St. Luke's Gospel and deals mainly with the deeds of the apostles Peter and Paul.
See also: Bible.

Acupressure (Japanese *shiatsu*), treatment system comparable to acupuncture. Pressure is applied to specific points on the surface of the body to eliminate fatigue and to stimulate natural curative abilities. Seven interrelated effects may stimulate the body to operate normally and help maintain good health: (1) invigoration of the skin, (2) stimulation of the circulation of body fluids, (3) promotion of function of striated muscles, (4) correction of disorders of the skeletal system, (5) promotion of harmonious functioning of the nervous system, (6) regulation of the operation of endocrine glands, and (7) stimulation of the normal function of internal organs.

Acupuncture, ancient Chinese medical practice in which fine needles are inserted into the body at specified points. It can be used as a pain reliever, an anesthesia, and a treatment for a variety of conditions, including arthritis, ulcers, and migraine. Research has shown that acupuncture has a specific effect on the release of certain chemical transmitters- natural painkillers known as endorphins-from nerve cells in the brain.
See also: Endorphins.

A.D., abbreviation for *anno Domini* (Latin, 'in the year of our Lord'). The monk Dionysius Exiguus started a system of reckoning years in A.D. 532, using the year in which he believed Christ was born at the beginning of the Christian era. A.D. refers to events that took place after the birth of Christ, and B.C. (before Christ) refers to events that took place before his birth.

Adam and Eve, first man and woman, according to the Bible (Genesis 2-3). They

The story of Adam and Eve from Charles the Bald's Bible (St. Paul's Outside the Walls, Rome, second half of the 9th century).

were created in God's image and placed in the Garden of Eden to care for the earth and its inhabitants. According to the story, Adam and Eve ate the fruit from the forbidden tree of knowledge of good and evil and were exiled from Eden by God to live a mortal life. Man was destined to a life of toil and woman to the pain of childbirth, and both were subject to death.
See also: Abel; Cain; Genesis.

Adam, Robert (1728-1792) and **James** (1730-1794), Scottish architect brothers. Robert's studies of ancient Roman architecture helped to inspire their joint designs of graceful interiors, furnishings, and buildings, notably Syon House (1762-1769) and Osterley Park House (1761-1780) in London.

Dining room in Osterley Park designed by Robert Adam.

Adams, Ansel (1902-1984), U.S. photographer known for his dramatic black-and-white photos capturing the beauty of California's Sierra Nevada and of the American Southwest. He founded the first college photography department in 1946 at the California School of Fine Arts (now the San Francisco Art Institute).

Adams, Gerard (Gerry) (1948-   ) Northern-Irish politician. Gerry Adams was one of the first members of the Northern Ireland Civil Rights Association. He was arrested several times on suspicion of terrorist activities from 1972 onwards. In 1983, he became chairman of Sinn Féin, the political wing of the IRA, as well as a British MP (until 1993). He played a key role in the conciliation between the British Government, the IRA, and Sinn Féin in 1994. To attract more attention for the Northern Ireland situation, (and to the annoyance of the British), Adams went to the US twice in 1994, where he had several meetings with President Clinton and various members of Congress. He also visited the United States in 1996, but this time Clinton refused to receive him in protest of the bombing campaign by the IRA in March that same year.
Peace talks, started in September 1997, resulted in the Good Friday Agreement of 1998. This agreement opted for a non violent approach to achieve a political goal. The people of Northern Ireland and the Republic of Ireland voted in favor of this agreement during a referendum (May 1998). From then on, one of the government's objectives has been to maintain durable peace between both religions in Northern Ireland.

Adams, Henry Brooks (1838-1918), U.S. historian, brother of Brooks Adams. His autobiography, *The Education of Henry Adams*, in which he attempted to show how ill- prepared his generation was for the 20th century, won a Pulitzer Prize in 1919. His other works include *Mount-Saint- Michel and Chartres* (1913) and the 9-volume *History of the United States* (1885-91).

Adams, John (1735-1826), second president of the United States (1797-1801) and father of the sixth president, John Quincy Adams. In 1776 he served on the committee that prepared the Declaration of Independence. Adams also served in various diplomatic posts, including Great Britain.
In 1782 he helped negotiate the Treaty of Paris, which marked formal British recognition of the former colonies' independence. In 1789 Adams became the nation's first vice president, serving under President George Washington for 2 terms. In 1796 he was elected president. During his presidency the United States became involved in a war between Britain and France. In 1799 Adams sent ministers to France in a successful attempt to negotiate a peace accord. Adams lost the support of his own party by seeking peace with France, and he angered the opposing party by allowing passage of the Alien and Sedition Acts, which limited the rights of both foreigners and U.S. citizens. As a result, Adams lost the 1800 election and was succeeded by Thomas Jefferson as president.

Adams, John Quincy (1767-1848), sixth president of the United States (1825-1829) and son of the second president, John Adams. Adams also served as diplomat, secretary of state, senator, and representative.
In 1794 Adams was appointed ambassador to the Netherlands. He later served in diplomatic posts in London, Lisbon, and Berlin.
In 1809 President James Madison appointed Adams the first U.S. ambassador to Russia, a post he held until 1814. Adams helped to negotiate the Treaty of Ghent (1814), which ended the War of 1812 between the U.S. and Britain. From 1815 to 1817, he was ambassador to England.
John Quincy Adams became secretary of state in 1817, under President James Monroe. He helped develop the Monroe Doctrine, which stated U.S. opposition to involvement by European countries in the Americas. He also negotiated the treaty with Spain (1819) that ceded Florida to the United States and established a border with Mexico.
As president (1825-1829), Adams advocated a strong national bank, protective tariffs, conservation of public lands, and protection of Native American tribes. Adams ran for reelection in 1828 but was defeated by Andrew Jackson.
In 1830 Adams was elected to the U.S. House of Representatives, where he served until his death in 1848. Known as Old Man Eloquent, he fought vigorously for the right of the people to petition for the redress of wrongs, as well as against the extension of slavery. He was one of the first to claim that the federal government could free slaves during time of war, an argument that later supported President Abraham Lincoln's Emancipation Proclamation of 1862.

Adams, Maude (1872-1953), U.S. actress best remembered for her leading roles at the turn of the century in plays by James Barrie, Edmond Rostand, and William Shakespeare.

Adams, Roger (1889-1971), U.S. chemist and teacher whose work included research on the molecular structure and laboratory synthesis of organic compounds. He contributed to medicine and industry by determining the organic composition of gossypol, the toxic cottonseed pigment; cannabinol, a compound in marijuana; and chaulmoogric, used in treating leprosy and by developing catalytic hydrogenation, a petroleum-refining process using a platinum oxide.

Adams, Samuel (1722-1803), American Revolutionary leader and signer of the Declaration of Independence. His oratory and writings increased colonial discontent with British rule. Adams opposed the Sugar and Stamp acts (1764-65), helped organize the Boston Tea Party (1773), and urged independence at the First Continental Congress (1774). He served as governor of Massachusetts from 1794 to 1797.
See also: Boston Tea Party; Stamp Act.

Adams, Samuel Hopkins (1871-1958), U.S. writer. As a newspaper and magazine journalist Adams attacked dishonesty in medicine, business, and government, and his collected articles, *The Great American*

Fraud (1906), furthered the passage of the Pure Food and Drug Act. His novels include *The Clarion* (1914) and *Revelry* (1926).

Adams-Onís Treaty, or Transcontinental Treaty, U.S.-Spanish agreement (1819) defining the western boundary of the United States, negotiated by Secretary of State John Quincy Adams and the Spanish minister to the United States, Luis de Onís. Spain ceded Florida to the United States in return for the abandonment of U.S. claims to Texas.

Adam's Peak, English name for the Samanalakanda mountain on Sri Lanka; 7,359 ft (2,243 m). Place of pilgrimage for Muslims, Buddhists, and Hindus (because of a footprint belonging to Adam, the Buddha, and Shiva respectively).

Adana (pop. 1,000,000), Turkey, the country's fourth largest city and the capital of Seyhan Province. It is on the Seyhan River, about 240 miles (385 km) south-southeast of Ankara. It is an agricultural trading center. Manufactured products include tobacco goods, cotton textiles, processed foods, and agricultural machinery.
Adana was an ancient Hittite town that flourished under the Romans and then declined. The city's vitality was restored under the Muslims, beginning in the late eighth century.

Adaptation, an organism's adjustment to its environment in order to survive, believed to arise from transmitted genetic variations preserved by natural selection. Successful and versatile adaptation in an organism leads to widespread distribution and long-term survival. Examples include the development of lungs in amphibians and of wings in birds and insects.
See also: Acclimatization; Evolution.

Adapter, a device to connect two pieces of equipment that do not have the same interface.

Addams, Charles Samuel (Chas) (1912-1988) American cartoonist. Addams decided to call a halt to his art education and start drawing cartoons when it became apparent that everyone who saw his drawings was inclined to either grin or smile. His first cartoon appeared in the New Yorker in 1935 and he remained faithful to this magazine. In his mostly macaber drawings, coffins, skeletons, and tombstones belonged to his favorite ob-

jects. Right from the start he introduced the members of the later-on well-known 'Addams family', which was later to become a television series, into his cartoons. He also favored the macaber in everyday life; he was once married at an animal cemetery.

Addams, Jane (1860-1935), U.S. social reformer. With Ellen Gates Starr she founded Chicago's Hull House (1889) to provide social and cultural activities for the neighborhood poor. An ardent pacifist, she served as president of the Women's International League for Peace and Freedom from 1915 to 1929 and was cowinner of the 1931 Nobel Peace Prize.

Addax (*Addax nasomaculatus*), North African desert antelope of the family Bovidae. The addax stands about 3.5 feet (1 m) at the shoulder and has spirally twisted horns and broad hoofs.

Adder, common name for several species of venomous and harmless snake found in different parts of the world. Examples are the European viper (*Vipera berus*) and the puff adder (*Bitis arietans*) of Africa, deadly members of the viper family, and the hognose snake (genus *Heterodon*), a harmless species found in North America.

Adder's tongue *See:* Dogtooth violet.

Addis Ababa (pop. 2,600,000), capital of Ethiopia (since 1889). The modern city, standing on an 8,000-ft (2,438-m) central plateau, is Ethiopia's center for trade, communications, and administration and houses the headquarters of the Organization of African Unity.
See also: Ethiopia.

Addison, Joseph (1672-1719), English writer and statesman, including service as secretary of state (1717-1718). Author of plays and poems, it was for his lasting contribution to the English essay form that he is best remembered, especially those essays published in the *Tatler* and the *Spectator*, which he co-founded with Sir Richard Steele.
See also: Steele, Sir Richard.

Addison, Thomas (1793-1860), English physician and teacher who described Addison's disease (atrophy of the adrenal cortex) and Addison's anemia (now *pernicious anemia*).
See also: Addison's disease; Anemia.

A

The common adder (*Vipera berus*) is a venomous snake of Europe and Asia. It feeds on rodents and birds, and its bite is painful to humans.

Addison's disease, progressive disease resulting from atrophy of the cortex (outer layer) of the adrenal glands. Deficient secretion of the hormones aldosterone or cortisol causes lowered blood volume and pressure, anemia, low blood sugar, gastrointestinal upsets, and brownish pigmentation of the skin. The cause is unknown. The disease, which occurs in all age groups and in both sexes, is often successfully treated today with adrenocortical hormones, reversing its previously fatal effects.
See also: Gland.

Adelaide (pop. 1,100,000), capital of the state of South Australia in Australia. Located near the mouth of Torrens River, the city is an industrial center for automobiles and textiles and the commercial hub of a large region, exporting wool, grains, and dairy products. Adelaide accounts for almost two-thirds of the state's population and has many notable buildings and parks.
See also: Australia.

Aden (pop. 401,000), former capital and chief port of the People's Democratic Republic of Yemen (Southern Yemen), on the Gulf of Aden. Sana became the capital upon the creation of the Republic of Yemen (May 22, 1990) which merged the two Yemens. Under British rule from 1839 to 1967, it became a coaling station for ships sailing between Europe and India with the opening of the Suez Canal in 1869. Chief trade center of southern Arabia, it is also the country's industrial center, with an oil refinery.
See also: Yemen.

Aden, Gulf of, arm of the Arabian Sea, 550 mi (885 km) long, lying between the Republic of Yemen on the north and Somalia on the south and connected with the Red Sea by the Strait of Bab-el Mandeb. It forms part of the sea route from the Mediterranean through the Suez Canal to the Indian Ocean.

Adenauer, Konrad (1876-1967), first chancellor of West Germany (1949-1963). A politician since World War I, he was twice imprisoned by the Nazis. He became leader of the Christian Democratic Union Party in 1947, and as chancellor he led West Germany through its postwar recovery into membership in the North Atlantic Treaty Organization (NATO) and the European Common Market.

Adenoids, or pharyngeal tonsils, mass of lymph tissue in the nasopharynx (above the soft palate in the back of the throat) that acts as a filter against disease. Adenoidal enlargement is the most common cause of nasal obstruction in the young and follows recurrent infections in that region.
See also: Tonsil.

Adhesion, force of attraction between surfaces of different substances, such as glue and wood or water and glass, due to intermolecular forces.
See also: Cohesion; Tissue.

Adi Granth, the holy book belonging to the Indian religion of the Sikhs, called literally 'first book' and also called Granth Sahib, 'the noble book'. It contains scriptures in six languages derived from the Sikh gurus, but also from Hindu and Islamic (Sufi)sources. For musical performance it makes use of Indian music (ragas). The Adi Granth was compiled by the fifth guru, Arjun (1563-1606) and by the tenth, Govind Singh (1666-1708), who was acclaimed as the eternal guru.

Adirondack Mountains, forested range in northeast New York, source of the Hudson River, and southern extension of the Laurentian (Canadian) Shield. Mt. Marcy (5,344 ft/1,629 m), the highest peak, towers over scenic lakes and millions of acres of woodland, all contributing to make this an important resort region.
See also: New York.

Adjutant, either of 2 species of scavenger storks of India and southeast Asia. The adjutant has a naked pink neck and head, a white body, and gray wings, back, and tail. The greater adjutant (*Leptoptilos dubius*) stands about 5 ft (1.5 m) high and has a respiratory pouch hanging from the throat. The lesser adjutant (*L. javanicus*) measures about 4 ft (1.2 m).
See also: Stork.

Adler, Alfred (1870-1937), Austrian psychiatrist who founded the school of individual psychology. Adler believed that feelings of inferiority account for the maladjustment of certain individuals to society. He saw the overcoming of these feelings as the basic human drive for power.
See also: Psychology.

Adler, Dankmar (1844-1900), German-born U.S. architect and engineer whose partnership with Louis Sullivan from 1881 helped to create the famous Chicago School of Architecture. Adler's first important work was the Chicago Central Music Hall (1879).
See also: Sullivan, Louis Henri.

Admiral, in several countries the highest rank in the navy. The term is derived from Arabic and in the 12th or 13th century was adopted by the Sicilians and the French.
See also: Rank, military.

Admiralty Islands, group of about 40 volcanic and coral-reef Melanesian islands in the South Pacific, some 200 mi (320 km) northwest of New Guinea, in the Bismarck Archipelago.
See also: Bismarck Archipelago; Pacific Islands.

Adobe, Spanish name for sun-dried clay and straw bricks of Mexico and the southwest United States; also, a structure made of adobe brick. Because the brick will crumble if exposed to excessive moisture or cold, it is used for building only in hot, dry climates. Material similar to adobe has been used in arid climates throughout the world since ancient times.

Adolescence, period of life between childhood and full adulthood (between 12 and 20 years of age). Its physical manifestation is puberty, the development of sex characteristics, making possible sexual union and reproduction. Physical changes include the development of breasts in girls, changes in voice in boys, and the appearance of pubic hair in both. Adolescence is of psychological interest because of the changes in attitudes, emotional responsiveness, and social behavior that accompany this sexual maturation.
See also: Developmental psychology; Growth.

Adonis, in Greek mythology, beautiful mortal beloved of Aphrodite and Persephone. In an effort to resolve the problem of who would keep Adonis, Zeus commanded that he spend 6 months of every year on earth with Aphrodite, during which crops flourished, and 6 months in the underworld with Persephone, during which the earth was barren. This myth was used by the Greeks to explain the changing of the seasons. In another myth, Adonis is killed by Aphrodite's husband who is disguised as a boar.
See also: Aphrodite.

Adoption, in law, the act of taking a child of other parents into one's family as a son or daughter. Adoption is a legal process, and permission of a court is necessary. Consent of the natural parents of the child's legal guardian is required, and if the child is of a certain age his or her consent also is required. The adopted child acquires the same rights and duties as children born in the family.

There are two types of adoptions - agency adoptions and private adoptions. In the former, adoptive parents work through a licensed agency; in the latter, they deal directly with the biological mother. A biological mother who consents to a child's adoption before birth may revoke consent to the adoption during a specified period after the child is born. Adoptions made after the birth of the child can be revoked only if there had been fraud or duress in the process. In *open adoptions*, adoptive parents agree to allow biological parents to have some contact with the child after the adoption.

Adoption records are usually sealed and can be opened only by court order.

A

In August 1961, Chancellor Konrad Adenauer (1876-1967) paid a visit to Berlin, and personally inspected the Berlin Wall that was erected that same year by the government of the German Democratic Republic, in an attempt to stop the great exit of refugees to the West.
In the background is Brandenburg Gate.

Adrenal glands, or suprarenal glands, small endocrine glands closely attached to the upper part of each kidney, each comprising a central medulla and a surrounding cortex. The adrenal medulla secretes the hormones epinephrine (adrenaline) and norepinephrine. Release of these hormones follows stress-related stimuli such as pain, emotional disturbance, hypotension (low blood sugar), exposure to severe cold, and muscular exertion. The adrenal medulla is not essential to life; a person can survive in good health after total removal of the glands if adequate substitution therapy is provided. The adrenal cortex secretes about 30 steroid hormones that are separated into 3 main groups. The glucocorticoids, including cortisol, enhance glucose formation in the tissues and cells. The mineralocorticoids, including aldosterone, are steroids that promote retention of sodium and excretion of potassium by the kidney. The androgens are sex hormones that have a weaker effect than those produced by the (male) testes and (female) ovaries. Disorders of the adrenal cortex, such as Addison's disease or Cushing's syndrome, may be due to either defective or excessive secretion of hormones.
See also: Epinephrine; Gland; Hormone.

Adrenalin *See:* Epinephrine.

Adrian IV (Nicholas Breakspear; 1100?-59), only Englishman to become pope (1154-59). He crowned Frederick Barbarossa as Holy Roman Emperor in 1155, but angered Frederick by his persistent demands for papal supremacy and also by excommunicating the crowned king of Sicily, William I the Bad. Adrian then invested William upon his pledge of allegiance and service to him. He also promised excommunication for Frederick when the latter declared himself ruler of northern Italy, but he died before carrying out his threat.

Adrianople, former (Roman) name for Edirne, a town in northwest Turkey.

Adriatic Sea, arm of the Mediterranean Sea between Italy and former Yugoslavia and Albania. The Adriatic extends for about 500 mi (800 km), with an average width of 110 mi (177 km) and a depth of up to 4,201 ft (1,250 m). The Strait of Otranto links it to the Ionian Sea to the south.

Adsorption, adhesion of molecules to a surface, to be distinguished from absorption.
See also: Absorption.

Adult education, or continuing educaton, learning undertaken by adults. Originally offering adults the educational opportunities missed in youth, adult education is now seen more as part of an ongoing process, enhancing the education already received.

Advent (from Latin *adventus*, 'arrival'), first season of the Christian church year. It begins on the Sun. nearest Nov. 30 (St. Andrew's Day) and ends on Christmas Eve. Advent has been observed since the 6th century as a period of meditative preparation for the celebration of Christ's birth and second coming.
See also: Christmas.

Adventists, members of Christian sects, mainly in the United States, who believe in the imminent second coming of Christ. Adventism grew from the teachings of William Miller (1782-1849). Members of the largest Adventist sect, the Seventh-Day Adventists, formally organized in 1863, observe Saturday as the Sabbath and support an extensive missionary program.
See also: Seventh-day Adventists.

Advertising, paid publicity designed to persuade people to buy a product or service or to adopt a viewpoint. Advertising in magazines, newspapers, radio, the internet, and television provides these media with most of their income. Advertisers pay advertising agencies to conduct market research, formulate advertising campaigns, buy the necessary time or space in the medium or media chosen, and produce the actual advertisements.

Adygea (pop. 432,000), autonomous republic in Russia, in the north of the Caucasus region; 2,936 sq mi (7,600 sq km). Capital: Majkop. Industry: machine building, food and timber processing. Cattle breeding.

Adzhubei, Alexei (1924-) Soviet Russian journalist who modernized the Komsomolskaya Pravda (official voice of the youth organization Komsomol) and became editor of the *Izvestiya* and a member of the Supreme Soviet in 1959. As Krushchev's son-in-law, he accompanied him at conferences. In 1963 Adzhubei was the first prominent Soviet representative to be received by a Pope. Krushchev's fall in 1964 meant the end of his editorship and membership of the Supreme Soviet. Following this, he became department manager of the monthly *The Soviet Union Today*.

Aegean civilization, collective term for the Bronze Age civilizations surrounding the Aegean Sea. These cultures, which flourished from 3000 to 1200 B.C., are the Mycenaean, or Helladic, culture of the Greek mainland; the Cycladic culture of the Cyclades; the Minoan culture of Crete; and the Trojan culture. Archeological work in the area was begun in the 1870s-80s by Heinrich Schliemann, who located Troy.
See also: Crete; Mycenae; Schliemann, Heinrich; Troy.

A

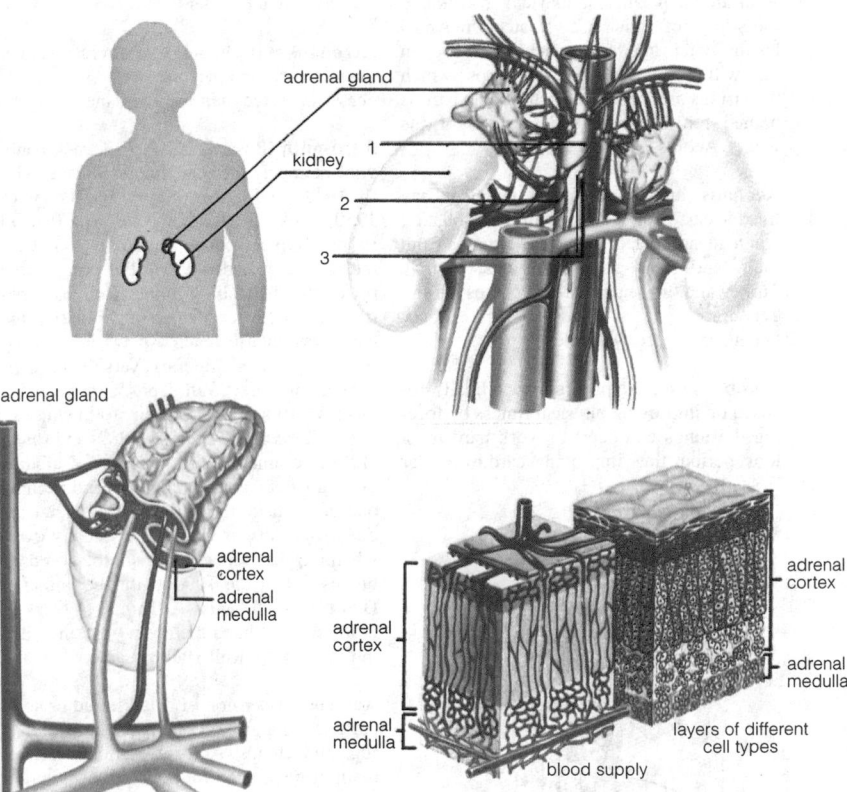

The adrenal glands, located on top of the kidneys, manufacture hormones that affect a person's reaction to stress, emergencies, and infection. Blood flows from the aorta (1) and renal arteries (2) into the extensive network of vessels, supplying the adrenal glands with nourishment and oxygen. Veins leaving these glands transport adrenal hormones throughout the body. The brain sends nervous impulses to the adrenal glands by means of nerves (3) of the sympathetic system. The two basic tissues of the adrenal glands, the cortex and the medulla, act as two different organs. The outer cortex, which is essential to life, comprises three layers of cells, each of which secrete several hormones that affect body metabolism. The inner medulla secretes epinephrine and norepinephrine, both of which perpare the body for 'fight or flight' in reation to ermergencies. During stress, these two hormones mobilize reserves, increase heart action, and direct the blood flow to muscles of the arms and legs.

A

Aegean Sea, arm of the Mediterranean Sea between mainland Greece and Turkey, the heart of the classical Greek world. About 400 mi (640 km) long and 200 mi (320 km) wide, its numerous islands, known as the Grecian Archipelago, include the Sporades, Dodecanese, and Cyclades groups. Islanders live by fishing and tourism; the Aegean also contains deposits of natural gas.
See also: Mediterranean Sea.

Aeneas, mythological Trojan prince, son of Venus and Anchises and hero of the Roman poet Vergil's *Aeneid*. After the fall of Troy he rescued his father and son and fled to Carthage and then to Italy. Rome was said to be founded by his descendants, Romulus and Remus.
See also: Aeneid; Vergil.

Aeneid, epic Latin poem, 12 books in length, depicting the life of the mythical Trojan hero Aeneas. The poem, written by Vergil between 30 and 19 B.C., describes the great achievements of Aeneas as he sought to create a new nation. Vergil selected his theme to bring glory to the emperor, Augustus, and to reconfirm the integrity of religious values in ancient Rome.

Aeolian harp, ancient musical instrument, the strings of which are vibrated ('played') by the wind. It is constructed of a wooden box with 2 low wood bridges, across which the strings are loosely stretched. The harp is named for the ancient Greek god of the winds, Aeolus.

Aeolians, an ancient Greek people. They lived in east-central Greece until c.1150 B.C., when invading Dorians forced many from their land. They moved to what is now Turkey and the nearby islands of Lesbos and Tenedos.
See also: Greece, Ancient.

Aerobics, exercise program specifically focused on improving physical fitness by forcing the lungs and heart to work hard for a long period, thus improving cardiovascular

functioning. Running, swimming, and cycling are common aerobic activities.

Aerodynamics, branch of physics dealing with the motion of air and other gases and their flow around a body in motion, used particularly in the development of the airplane and other aircraft. Aerodynamic forces depend on the body's size, shape, and velocity and on the density, compressibility, viscosity, temperature, and pressure of the gas. At low velocities flow around the body is streamlined and causes low drag; at higher velocities turbulence occurs, with fluctuating eddies, and drag is much greater. Additional drag is created by friction. Pressure impulses radiate at the speed of sound ahead of the moving body; at supersonic velocities these impulses pile up, producing a shock wave-the 'sonic boom.' In airplane design all of these factors must be considered. In normal cruising flight the lift provided by the wings must equal the aircraft's weight; the forward thrust of the engine must balance the forces of drag. Lift occurs because the wing's upper surface is more convex, and therefore longer, than the lower surface, creating a difference in air speed and thus pressure, according to Bernoulli's principle.
See also: Wind tunnel.

Aeronautics, technology of aircraft design, manufacture, and performance.
See also: Aerodynamics; Airplane.

Aerosmith (Boston, 1970), U.S. rock band, vital members are lead singer Steven Tyler (b 1948) and guitar player Joe Perry (b 1950), broke through in the early 1970s with its prototypical power ballad 'Dream On', but was overshadowed by the comparable rock band the Rolling Stones for a long period of time. After a lapse in popularity, the band was able to reach a new audience by recording a contemporary version of their former hit song 'Walk This Way' with the rapcrew Run-D.M.C. Their following albums, *Permanent Vacation* (1987) and *Pump* (1989) became the most successful albums of their career, after which the band became one of the favorites of the MTV-generation, due to spectacular videos and visually overwhelming live shows. Aerosmith scored its biggest hit of the 1990s with the ballad 'I Don't Want to Miss a Thing' (1998). In 2001, the five band members were included in the Rock 'n' Roll Hall of Fame.

Aerosol, suspension of small liquid or solid particles in a gas. Examples include smoke, fog, and clouds. Aerosol particles can remain in suspension for hours, or even indefinitely. Aerosols are also manufactured for the dispersion of insecticides, air fresheners, paints, cosmetics, etc. The use of the most common aerosol propellants, the fluorocarbons, has been curtailed because they have been implicated in the destruction of the ozone layer of the atmosphere.
See also: Fluorocarbon; Ozone.

Aertsen (Aertszen), Pieter (1508-1575), Dutch painter of finely detailed still-lifes and domestic interiors. He is regarded as one of the founders of genre painting.

Aeschylus (525-456 B.C.), earliest of the 3 great dramatists of ancient Greece, preceding Sophocles and Euripides. He is often regarded as the originator of tragedy. Only 7 of at least 80 plays survive, including *The Persians*, *Prometheus Bound*, and the *Oresteia*, which concerns the murder of Agamemnon by his wife, Clytemnestra, and the subsequent revenge of their son, Orestes. Aeschylus elaborated Greek dramatic form by adding a second actor (previously the poet had spoken all roles) and exploiting the dramatic possibilities of dialogue.

Aesculapius *See:* Asclepius.

Aesop, in tradition, Greek author of animal fables, said to have been a slave on 6th-century B.C. Samos, but perhaps a wholly legendary figure. Some fables attributed to Aesop are known in versions by La Fontaine and other writers.
See also: Allegory; La Fontaine, Jean de.

Affidavit, voluntary statement reduced to writing and sworn to or affirmed before an authorized magistrate or officer. Affidavits are not testimony in courts of law because the makers cannot be cross-examined, but a person who makes a false affidavit may be punished for perjury.

Afghan hound, breed of dog known for speed and agility, used as a hunter in Afghanistan for centuries. It stands 24-28 in. (61-71 cm) in height at the shoulder and weighs 50-60 lb (23-27 kg), has long ears, a slim body, large feet, and a coat of long silky hair. The breed originated in Egypt c. 3000 B.C., was perfected in Afghanistan to hunt the leopard and gazelle, and was discovered by Europeans in the 1800s and brought to England after World War I.

Afghanistan

Capital:	Kabul
Area:	251,825 sq mi (652,225 sq km)
Population:	27,750,000
Language:	Pashto, Dari Persian
Government:	Islamic republic
Independent:	1747
Head of gov.:	Prime minister
Per capita:	US$ 800
Monetary unit:	1 Afghani (AF) = 100 puls

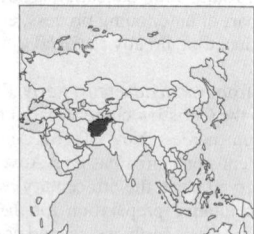

An aerosol can comprise a plunger cap (A) that is pressed to allow a highpressure mixture of liquefied gas and product (D) to flow through a plastic tube (E) and out of an exit orifice (C). A fine mist (B) of product results as the liquefied gas vaporizes at atmospheric pressure. The base (F) is domed at the bottom to withstand pressure.

A

Afghanistan, land-locked country in central Asia.

Land and climate. The high rugged mountains of the Hindu Kush cover three quarters of the country. The winters are extremely cold (as low as 15°F/-9°C) and the summers extremely hot (up to 120°F/49°C). There is very little rainfall, but the Hindu Kush is a major watershed containing fertile river valleys.

People. The majority of the people live in the fertile mountain valleys. About 2.5 million are nomadic. Islam is the most important factor in the everyday life of the country. The two principal languages are Pashtu and Dari.

Economy. Less than 15% of the country is good for cultivation. Main crops are wheat, corn, barley, rice, and fruits. Sheep are also raised. Fruits, wool, skins, and various handicrafts are important sources of foreign exchange. Coal and salt have been mined for some years, and the country has long been famous for its lapis lazuli. Iron ore is plentiful, and vast deposits of natural gas have been exploited. The lack of an infrastructure is a major obstacle to economic development; there are few paved roads, and there is no railroad.

History. Afghanistan was conquered by Alexander the Great in 330 B.C. and thrived as the Kingdom of Bactria (250-150 B.C.). The Arabs conquered Afghanistan in the 7th century, and Islam took root. Genghis Khan and Tamerlane invaded, and Babur (1143-1530) used Kabul as his base for establishing the Mogul Empire in India. Afghanistan became a united state under Ahmed Shah in 1747. Amanullah (1919-1929) seized control of foreign policy from the British, began modernizing, and proclaimed a monarchy in 1926. The last king, Mohammed Zahir Shah, was overthrown in 1973 by Lt. Gen. Sardar Mohammed Daud Khan, who became president and prime minister of the new republic. Daud was overthrown in 1978 and replaced by the pro-Soviet government of Noor Mohammed Taraki. Taraki was overthrown by Hafi-zullah Amon, who was in turn overthrown by Babrak Karmal. In 1979, some 100,000 Soviet troops invaded Afghanistan in order to contain the rebellion. Despite the withdrawal of the Soviet troops in 1989 and various steps towards a transition to a new government the fighting continued into the 1990s. At the beginning of the 2000s the Taliban (radical-islamic militia) was almost entirely in control of the country. Despite the international efforts of UNESCO, the two historic statues of Buddha in the Bamian valley were blown up by the Taliban. After

The Afghan capital of Kabul, with Mount Pagham (4699 me-   tres) in the background.

the terrorist attacks on the Twin Towers in New York, probably committed by the al-Qaida network (09-11-2001), American and British troops went to Afghanistan hoping to arrest the leader of the network, Osama bin Laden. Although they did not succeed, the operation did lead to the downfall of the Taliban regime. Hamid Karzai became leader of the government and the International Security Assistance Force (ISAF) was founded.
See also: Taliban.

Africa, world's second-largest continent, 11,672,639 sq m (30,232,135 sq km). Africa includes Madagascar and many smaller off-shore islands. With the completion of the Suez Canal in the 19th century, Africa was severed from Asia and is completely surrounded by water. Its coastline has few indentations, bays, or inlets, thus, few good harbors. From narrow coastal plains the land rises steeply to form the immense African plateau about 2,000 ft (610 m) above sea level. Apart from the coastal plains, the Congo Basin is the only sizable lowland region. The Atlas Mountains form the continent's major system, including Africa's highest peak, Mt. Kilimanjaro (19,340 ft/5,895 m) in Tanzania. The Great Rift Valley of East Africa is the continent's major geological feature, with its long narrow depressions forming some of the world's largest lakes: Lake Victoria (26,828 sq mi/69,485 sq km), third largest lake in the world; Lake Tanganyika (5,715 ft/1,742 m deep), the largest freshwater lake in the world; and Lake Nyasa (360 mi/579 km long and 50 mi/80 km wide). The great rivers of Africa include the Nile (4,157 mi/6,690 km), the world's longest; the Niger; the Congo; and the Zambesi, which has been dammed at the Kariba Gorge, where it forms a lake 120 mi (193 km) long. The great mass of Africa lies within the tropics, but contains a variety of climates. The equatorial rain forest of the Congo Basin, which receives up to 200 in. (508 cm) of rain per year, and the tropical rain forest along the Gulf of Guinea and in

west Central Africa account for 20% of the continent. The humid subtropical regions have up to 43 in (109 cm) of rainfall per year. Temperate grasslands known as savannah or veldt cover 40% of Africa and usually have one dry and one rainy season per year with 20-50 in (51-127 cm) annual rainfall. The deserts cover more than 40% of the continent and include the Sahara, the world's largest, in the north and the Kalahari in the south. Finally, Africa's Mediterranean coast and the area south and southwest of Cape Province enjoy the most moderate climate, with average annual rainfall of 15-30 in (38-76 cm), hot summers, and warm pleasant winters.

Falls in the Abbai (Blue Nile), Ethiopia.

Africa's richly varied animal life is largely preserved in national parks. Poaching, the increase in human populations, and economic development have reduced the animal population, leading to the extinction of many species and threatening more.
Africa's population consists of many distinct peoples and cultures. The northern part of the continent, from Morocco in the west to Egypt in the east, is primarily Arab, with minorities of Berbers and Tuaregs. South of the Sahara the population is overwhelmingly black. Excluding European languages intro-

A market in the town of Arusha in northern Tanzania.

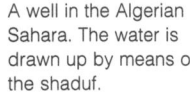

A well in the Algerian Sahara. The water is drawn up by means of the shaduf.

duced by colonizers, there are nearly 1,000 different languages or distinct dialects. Most people in North Africa speak Arabic; major languages in black Africa include Swahili, Hausa, Yoruba, Xhosa, and Amharic. Besides those who practice the native religions of the black African majority, there are more than 100 million African Muslims and about 35 million Christians, 5 million of them belonging to the ancient Coptic church of Egypt and Ethiopia.

African Americans, preferred term to designate Americans of African descent, who account for about 12% of the U.S. population, a major minority group in society. Most African Americans live in the South and in the large cities of the North, in many of which they constitute a large portion, or even a majority, of the population.
The first African Americans were brought to North America as indentured servants, under contract to work for a particular master for a specified period, after which they were free. But from the early 1600s, the expansion of the slave trade brought larger and larger numbers of Africans who were forced to work on the expanding plantations in the South.
The institution of slavery was recognized by the U.S. Constitution, and the importance of slaves increased after 1793, when the invention of the cotton gin gave southern plantations a new financial viability. Conflict between slave society in the South and industrial development in the North led eventually to the Civil War, which ended slavery in the United States. During the period of Reconstruction (1865-77), newly freed African Americans, despite extreme poverty, played a major role in political life, 16 serving in Congress. But Reconstruction was followed by the reimposition of discriminatory legislation and practices, denying African Americans the right to vote and segregating them socially. The system of segregation, sanctioned by the Supreme Court in its *Plessy* v. *Ferguson* decision of 1896, kept the African American population in conditions of social, economic, and political oppression. That system began to break down only after World War II. In 1954 the Supreme Court outlawed 'separate but equal' facilities in its historic *Brown* v.

Board of Education decision. The struggle for equal rights and the abolition of segregation soon took a new turn.
In the 1950s and 1960s African Americans developed a broad-based civil rights movement to end discrimination in education, jobs, public facilities, and voting rights. The successes of this movement eliminated most formal barriers to the incorporation of African Americans into U.S. society, but socioeconomic discrimination remained; the gap between white and black average incomes, for example, widened during the 1980s, despite the emergence of an African American middle class. African Americans have made major contributions to U.S. society in many areas. They fought in all the nation's wars, though in integrated units only after World War II. Notable African American historical figures include Frederick Douglass and George Washington Carver, who made significant contributions to politics and science in the 19th century. In the early 1900s, Booker T. Washington, W.E.B. DuBois, and Marcus Garvey were major political leaders. The towering figures of the 1950s and 1960s included Martin Luther King, Jr., and Malcolm X. More recently, African Americans have made their mark in the political sphere (Mayor David Dinkins in New York City), the military (General Colin Powell, Chairman of the Joint Chiefs of Staff), and as members of federal, state, and local legislatures. They have achieved nationwide recognition for outstanding contributions in literature, the arts, sports, entertainment, business, and education.

African Methodist Episcopal Church (A.M.E.), black Protestant denomination akin to, but separate from, white Methodist denominations. Founded in Philadelphia (1815) by the Rev. Richard Allen, it is the largest black Methodist body, with about 6,000 churches and 2,000,000 members.
See also: Allen, Richard.

African Methodist Episcopal Zion Church (A.M.E. Zion), independent Methodist denomination founded in New York City in 1796 by blacks disaffected by white prejudices. The church has over 1,000,000 members.

African National Congress, black African organization devoted to the 'creation of a united democratic South Africa' and the political empowerment of blacks. Founded in 1912 as the Native National Congress, the organization encouraged passive resistance to the 'pass' laws and other instruments of apartheid. After an outbreak of violence, it was banned in 1961 by the government of South Africa. Its leader, Nelson Mandela, was sentenced to life imprisonment, but he was released Feb. 1990 and the ban was lifted. The ANC won the majority of the votes in the first democratic elections in South Africa in 1994. Mandela became the first black president of South Africa. In 1997 Thabo Mbeki succeeded Mandela as chairman of the ANC. The ANC again won the elections in 1999 but the party did not get enough votes to change the constitution.

See also: Apartheid; Mandela, Nelson; South Africa.

African violet, any of a genus (*Saintpaulia*) of perennial herbs with velvety heart-shaped leaves and purple, pink, or white violetlike flowers, native to tropical East Africa.

Afrikaans, one of the 11 official languages of South Africa. Afrikaans evolved from the form of Dutch spoken by 17th-century Boer settlers, but incorporates Bantu, Khoisan, Malayo-Portuguese, and English words.

Afrikaners *See:* Boers.

Afterbirth *See:* Placenta.

Agadir (pop. 110,000), port in Southern Morocco, capital of the province with the same name (pop. 579,740), 2,283 sq mi (5,910 sq km). Seaport; vegetables and fruit exports. In 1960 Agadir was virtually destroyed by an earthquake.

Aga Khan, Spiritual leader of the Ismaili sect of Shi'te Muslims; a hereditary title. His millions of followers are dispersed through the Near East, India, Pakistan, and parts of Africa and are descended from 14th-century Hindus converted by Persian Ismails. **Aga Khan I** (Hasan Ali Shah; 1800-1881), a Persian provincial governor who emigrated to India in 1840, was invested as leader of the sect in 1866. **Aga Khan II** (Ali Shah) held the title from 1881 until his death in 1885. **Aga Khan III** (Sultan Sir Mahomed Shah; 1877-1957) represented British India at numerous conferences and as first president of the All-Indian Muslim League worked for Indian independence. **Aga Khan IV** (H.H. Shah Karim; 1936-) inherited the title in 1957.
See also: Islam.

Agamemnon, in Greek legend, son of Atreus and king of Mycenae who organized the expedition against Troy recounted in Homer's *Iliad*. Before setting sail he was forced to sacrifice his daughter Iphigenia. He was murdered on his return home by his wife Clytemnestra and her lover, his cousin Aegisthus. His death was avenged by his son, Orestes, and his daughter Electra.
See also: Iliad; Mycenae; Trojan War.

Agana (pop. 4,700), capital and political center of the island of Guam, a U.S. territory in the western Pacific Ocean.

Agar-agar, is a gelatinous substance derived from marine algae. Agar has many uses. It is used in laxatives, in materials on which dental impressions are made, in textile sizing, and in additives that thicken such foods as cheese, soup, and bakery products. Agar is also used as a gelling agent in cooking and, in laboratory work, as a medium in which bacteria are grown.

Agassi, Andre (1970-) American tennis player who turned professional at the age of sixteen. Success came rapidly and two years later he was in the top 10. His wilful character and eye-catching wear made him especially popular with young people. The Masters title of 1990 was his first major title

Andre Agassi (1970-).

followed by Wimbledon in 1992, the American Open in 1994, and the Australian Open in 1995. That same year he ousted Pete Sampras from the top of the ATP ranking. During the Olympic Games of 1996 in Atlanta (US) he won gold in the men's singles. The right-handed Agassi is known for his excellent return, the best on the professional tennis circuit. After a few bad years, in which he even disappeared from the ATP top one hundred, Agassi won the French Open tennis title at Roland Garros in 1999. It was the only Grand Slam title still missing from his role of honor. That same year, he also won the US Open and, in 2000 and 2001, the Australian Open.
See also: Sampras, Pete.

Agassiz, Louis (Jean Louis Rodolphe Agassiz; 1807-1873), Swiss-American naturalist, geologist, and educator who first proposed (1840) that large areas of the northern continents had been covered by ice sheets in the geologically recent past. He is also noted for his studies of fishes. He became a professor of zoology and geology at Harvard in 1848, where he founded the Museum of Comparative Zoology in 1859.

Lois Agassiz (1807-1873).

Agate, variety of the quartz chalcedony, found chiefly in Brazil and Uruguay. Agates form as layers in the cavities of older rocks, creating characteristic bands of colors. Semiprecious stones, they are used to make ornaments and grinding equipment.

Agave, any of a genus (*Agave*) of economically important U.S. tropical plants of the amaryllis family. Different species are used to produce soaps, foods, and drinks.

Agee, James (1909-1955), U.S. writer whose works include *Let Us Now Praise Famous Men* (1941), a portrayal of Depression-era white sharecroppers done in collaboration with photographer Walker Evans, and a partly autobiographical novel, *A Death in the Family* (1957), which won a Pulitzer Prize. Agee was an influential film critic and also wrote screenplays, including *The African Queen* (1951) and *The Night of the Hunter* (1955).

Agent Orange, herbicide used by the United States during the Vietnam War to defoliate the jungle. Agent Orange was contaminated with dioxin, a substance discovered to be toxic to human beings and animals. Use of the chemical was abandoned in the late 1970s. In postwar years, 60,000 veterans complained to the Veterans Administration that they had suffered lasting damage from Agent Orange poisoning. In 1984 the manufacturers of Agent Orange created a relief fund for the victims of Agent Orange.
See also: Vietnam War; Chemical and biological warfare.

Age of Reason, or the Enlightenment, a period in history in which accepted social, political, and religious doctrines were challenged by a new, rational view of the universe. Beginning in the 1600s and lasting until the late 1700s, the movement was led by such philosophers as, in France, René Descartes, Denis Diderot, Jean Jacques Rousseau, and Voltaire, and, in England, John Locke. Scholars of the period produced many breakthroughs in the fields of anatomy, astronomy, chemistry, mathematics, and physics. Their ideas about human dignity and progress influenced the future leaders of the French Revolution.
See also: Locke, John; Rousseau, Jean-Jacques.

Aggression, behavior characterized by physical or verbal attack. Aggression is defined by psychoanalysts as a manifestation of the will to have power over other people (Alfred Adler) or as a projection of the death impulse (Sigmund Freud). Unable to find a satisfactory explanation for the human readiness for hatred and aggression, Freud believed that it may be instinctual. Thus, the violent and strenuous behavior shown by infants may not be oriented toward a goal. Still, in many instances aggression that serves no apparent goal is associated with emotional disorder.
See also: Psychology.

Agincourt, now Azincourt, village in northwest France, scene of a decisive battle in the Hundred Years' War. On Oct. 25, 1415, English forces under Henry V routed the French under Claude d'Albret, demonstrating the power of the English longbow over a heavily armored enemy. The French lost over 7,000 men, the English only a few hundred.
See also: Hundred Years War.

Agio (premium), amount that newly issued shares or bonds realize above the nominal value. If the issue price is under 100%, it is referred to as discount. For instance: a company issues bonds worth USD 1 million; at the stock exchange the price is 103. The agio is then 3%, or U.S. $ 30,000.

Agitato (mus.) Agitated, restless.

Agnes, Saint, 4th-century virgin martyr of the Roman Catholic Church and patron saint of young girls. For refusing to sacrifice to pagan gods, she was disgraced, miraculously saved, and martyred. On her feast day, Jan. 21, the pope blesses 2 lambs in the church of St. Agnes; their wool is used to weave palla (items of ceremonial dress) for archbishops.

Agnew, Spiro Theodore (1918-1996), U.S. vice president under Richard Nixon (1969-1973). Agnew was elected Republican governor of Maryland (1966) and gained a reputation as a moderate liberal, though he later took a conservative stand toward civil rights demonstrations and urban unrest. He resigned from the vice presidency in 1973 following revelations of political corruption in his Maryland administration and pleaded no contest to a charge that he had failed to report income from payoffs by Maryland business people, for which he was fined $10,000. A Maryland court later fined him $248,000 for taking bribes while in office.
See also: Nixon, Richard Milhous.

Agnon, Shmuel Yosef (Samuel Josef Czaczkes; 1888-1970), Israeli writer remembered for his novels and stories of Jewish life in his native Galicia and in Palestine. In 1966 he shared the Nobel Prize for literature (with Nelly Sachs of Sweden) for works that include *The Bridal Canopy* (1937) and *The Day Before Yesterday* (1945).

Agnosticism, doctrine that one cannot know about things beyond the realm of one's experience, in particular about God. Unlike atheism, which is a rejection of divine order, agnosticism is a skeptical holding back of judgment in the absence of proof.
See also: Atheism.

Agnus Dei, in Christian churches, a term used in liturgy and symbolism. The words are Latin and mean 'Lamb of God,' a name for Jesus Christ used in John 1:29, 36. In the

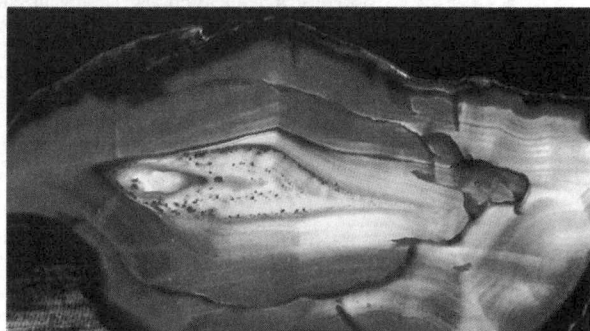

Agate is a semiprecious variety of   arranged in curved or circular transparent to translucent quartz,   bands of different colors.

A

A

Roman Catholic Mass the Agnus Dei is an invocation that comes between the Lord's Prayer and the communion. The Agnus Dei sounds the themes of sacrifice and adoration. Several other churches, including the Lutheran and Anglican (Episcopal), retain the Agnus Dei in the communion service.

In symbolism the Agnus Dei is an image of a lamb, usually with a halo and bearing a cross. In the Roman Catholic Church a wax medallion with the image of a lamb, also called Agnus Dei, is used as an object of devotion. These medallions are blessed by the pope in the first and in every seventh year of his pontificate.

Agoraphobia, pathological fear of big, open spaces. As with other forms of phobia it is a result of a neurotic projection of inner fears or of conflicts to concrete situations or objects.

Agostini, Giacomo (1942-) Italian racing driver. Contracted by MV Agusta in 1965 as a result of his national successes in the 250 cc class. Agostini won thirteen world titles for this team in the 350 and 500 cc classes between 1966 and 1973. Agostini became world champion later for Yamaha in the same classes (350 cc in 1974, 500 cc in 1975). Agostini was famous for his attractive driving style. After his active career he became team manager for Yamaha.

Agra (pop. 892,000), historic city in the northern Indian state of Uttar Pradesh, which is situated on the Jumna River, 110 mi (177 km) southeast of Delhi. An important military and commercial center, it produces cotton, grain, raw silk, sugar, and rugs. It was the capital of the Mogul empire during the late 16th and the first half of the 17th centuries. The city has several beautiful and important Mogul buildings, including the Taj Mahal, built by Shah Jahan.
See also: Taj Mahal.

Agribusiness, the business of agriculture, extended to include supply, management, information, and machine services, as well as processing and distribution.

Agricola, Gnaeus Julius (A.D. 37-93), Roman general. As proconsul of Britain (77-84) he defeated the Caledonians and extended Roman rule into Scotland. His son-in-law, the historian Tacitus, wrote the famous biography of Agricola.

Agricultural education, as an organized field of study began only at the end of the 18th century, when a number of agricultural societies grew up in the United States and Great Britain. In most developing countries, agricultural education is not as available as in developed countries. In general, emphasis is put on agricultural management instead of on technical instruction.

Agriculture, science and practice of farming, including the production of crops, the rearing of livestock, and the care of soil. The storing and sowing of seeds, central to agriculture, developed in the Neolithic period. Tools and techniques developed gradually over the centuries. The organization of farm-

ing, especially the ownership of land, was crucial in determining the prevailing social, economic, and political structures of civilizations as diverse as those of Egypt and Babylonia, China, Rome, and Japan. In medieval Europe the self-contained manorial system shaped the agricultural village. Late in the Middle Ages communal subsistence farming gave way to farms organized to produce salable surpluses. The agricultural revolution of the 16th and 17th centuries saw advances in horticultural techniques, and by the dawn of the industrial revolution, farming was concentrated in fewer hands and was geared to feeding the cities and supplying raw materials for manufactures. During the 19th century the United States led the world in agricultural development. The transportation revolution, the introduction of artificial fertilizers, and increased specialization all helped raise productivity. In the late 20th century agriculture in most indus-

This 15th-century Flemish miniature is a pictorial almanac of farming activities.

trialized countries is highly specialized and relies upon pesticides, growth-stimulating antibiotics for livestock, fertilizers, and artificial insemination. By contrast, agriculture in much of the Third World is not mechanized, crop yields are not high, and famine still occurs.

Beginning in the 1980's, advances in biotechnology furthered the progress of agriculture. For example, a variety of genet-

ic techniques were developed to increase the rate at which crops grow and decrease their vulnerability to insects, diseases, and harsh weather. Other genetic techniques were developed to produce desirable traits in livestock. In a process called cloning, genetically identical cattle (or other types of livestock) are produced. Although the use of insecticides and herbicides has greatly improved farmer's ability to cope with pests, the benefits of using these chemicals have been accompanied by groundwater contamination and potential health risks for humans, domestic animals, and wildlife. These problems have helped stimulate the passage of strict laws on pesticide use. Many farmers have turned to non-conventional, or alternative, agricultural practices. These farmers use practices that conserve soil, water, and other resources and they use integrated pest management, which has been developed as an ecological approach to pest control. Organic farming, an alternative form of agriculture in which only natural methods and materials are used to farm the land, became popular in some areas in the 1980's. It is popular because it avoids contaminating the crops and polluting the environment and helps to assure the continued productivity of the land. By the 1980's, to insure the protection and survival of as many plant species as possible, scientists throughout the world had established *plant gene banks*, where seeds of almost every species of plant are stored. These banks also provide a source of genetic diversity to allow farmers and breeders to produce cross-bred plants with the ability to better resist disease, insects, and the effects of adverse weather. In the mid-1990's, genetically engineered food products (food products obtained from organisms that have been genetically been manipulated) became available to consumers for the first time. Among these products were a tomato designed to resist spoilage and a squash designed to resist viral infection.

Agrimony, any of a genus (*Agrimonia*) of woodland plants of the rose family, native to Europe, Asia, North America, and the Andes Mountains of South America. The agrimony plant has featherlike hairy leaves and clusters of small yellow flowers on long spikes; the fruit is a cone-shaped burr.

Agrippa, Marcus *See:* Augustus.

Crop-dusting planes spread pesticide over an Arizona cotton field. To prevent the airdrifting of the pesticide, dusting can be carried out only in windless weather.

A

Agrippina The Younger (A.D. 15-59), mother by her first marriage, of Nero and second wife of the Roman emperor Claudius. Agrippina persuaded Claudius to adopt Nero as his son and heir and then poisoned the emperor. When she interfered with Nero's rule, he had her murdered.
See also: Claudius; Nero.

Agronomy, branch of agricultural science dealing with production of field crops and management of the soil. The agronomist studies crop diseases, selective breeding, crop rotation, and climatic factors and also tests and analyzes the soil, investigates soil erosion, and designs land reclamation and irrigation schemes.

Aguinaldo, Emilio (1869-1964), leader of the Philippine independence movement. After helping the United States capture the Philippines during the Spanish-American War (1898), he led Filipino guerilla warfare against U.S. occupation. He was defeated in 1901.
See also: Philippines.

Ahasueros, Hebrew name for Xerxes, king of Persia (reigned 486-464 B.C.), mentioned in the Bible in Ezra 4:6 and Ester 1:1. The Greek historian Herodotus describes Ahasueros as a volatile, cruel, and frivolous king. In the rabbinical tradition he is seen as a symbol of misery and disaster.

Ahmadabad, or Ahmedabad (pop. 2,900,000), capital of the state of Gujarat in northwest India, situated on the Sabarmati River, north of Bombay. One of the largest and most important cities of India in Mogul times, Ahmadabad was ceded to the British in 1818. The modern city is an important trade center, particularly for cotton textiles, and a railway junction.
See also: India.

Ahmad Shah (1724-1773), Afghan ruler who founded the Durrani dynasty. Through several successful invasions of India he acquired a huge empire. Although unable to hold his empire together, he succeeded in strengthening and uniting Afghanistan and is thus often thought of as founder of the modern nation.

Ahura Mazda *See:* Zoroastrianism.

Ahvaz, or Ahwaz (pop. 833,000), Iran, the capital of Khuzestan province. It is on the Karun River about 70 miles (113 km) north of the head of the Persian Gulf. Ahvaz lies in the midst of rich oil fields and has numerous petroleum-related industries. The city is a river port as well as a hub of southern Iran's highway, railway, and petroleum pipeline systems. As early as the 12th century Ahvaz flourished as an agricultural trade center. It became prominent after 1908 when oil was discovered.

AIDS (Acquired Immune Deficiency Syndrome) Sexually transmitted disease that gradually breaks down the immune system. AIDS is caused by HIV (human immunodeficiency virus), which is responsible for destroying T4-lymphocytes (T4-cells, a certain

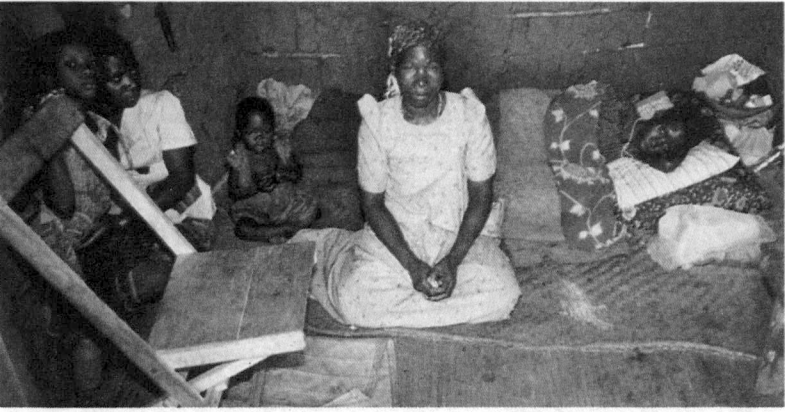
In a village in Uganda a grandmother takes care of her granddaughter, who suffers from AIDS. In many African countries hospitals can no longer cope with the enormous amount of AIDS patients.

type of white blood cells which are crucial to the immune system of humans and animals). The body's defense mechanism against infections is gradually broken down. HIV can only be transmitted through sexual intercourse or direct blood-to-blood contact. Children can be infected prenatally if the mother is a carrier of the virus or after birth, through breast-feeding. Contact with, or exposure to, the virus can be indicated with a test. If this is the case, antibodies against the virus are present in the blood (HIV-positive).
See also: Virus.

Aiken, Conrad Potter (1889-1973), U.S. writer. His *Selected Poems* (1929) won a Pulitzer Prize (1930). His critiques and essays on poetry were published in *A Reviewer's ABC* (1958). Other prose works include the novel *Great Circle* (1933) and his autobiography, *Ushant* (1952).

Aikido, was founded in Japan in 1925 as an adaptation of jujitsu. Meditation is stressed as much as physical training. Techniques include throwing and joint-locking, but these maneuvers are performed in a highly stylized manner that limits their value in self-defense.

Ailanthus, any of a genus (*Ailanthus*) of tropical-looking deciduous trees native to Asia and Australia but now widely cultivated in Europe and North America. The best-known species, *A. altissima*, grows up to 60 ft (18 m) high and thrives in polluted urban conditions in almost any kind of substrate.

Ailey, Alvin (1931-1989), U.S. dancer and choreographer. Ailey was a pupil of Lester Horton, with whom he made his debut in 1950. He began choreographing in 1953 and formed his own company, the Alvin Ailey American Dance Theater, in 1958. *Creation of the World* (1954), *Blues Suite* (1958), and *Revelations* (1960) are among his most noted works.

AIM *See:* American Indian Movement.

Ainu, Japanese aborigines, possibly of Caucasoid descent, distinguished by stockiness, pale skin, and profuse body hair. Most Ainu live on Hokkaido, the northernmost of Japan's major islands. Ainu speech, little used today, bears no relation to any other language. The Ainu are few in number, many having been assimilated into Japanese society.
See also: Japan.

Air, heterogeneous mixture of tasteless, odorless, colorless, and invisible gases surrounding the earth, consisting of about 78% nitrogen, 21% oxygen, and 1% argon, carbon dioxide, hydrogen, krypton, neon, helium, and xenon. Air is what we breathe and what is essential to all plant and animal life. It is kept close to the surface of the planet by the force of gravity.
See also: Air pollution; Climate; Gas; Nitrogen; Oxygen; Weather.

Air bag, safety device for car passengers, consisting of a bag that inflates automatically on collision and protects the passenger. The air bag can be built into the steering wheel, the dashboard, or the doors. The moment an accelerator-sensitive sensor registers a collision, a capsule containing sodium azide is ignited electrically, releasing a large quantity of nitrogen, which fills the balloon in around 50 milliseconds. As an alternative to the environmentally unfriendly and sometimes dangerous sodium azide, the use of ammonium nitrate or argon is being tested.

Airborne troops, or paratroops or sky soldiers, soldiers brought into a combat area by parachute drop or airplane. Airborne troops have been a part of military strategy since World War II, often figuring in surprise at-

Alvin Ailey (1931-89), the former artistic leader of the black ballet troupe Alvin Ailey American Dance Theatre, made an important contribution to the struggle for emancipation of American negroes.

A

tacks. After landing behind enemy lines, the troops may be used to destroy bridges, communications, and supplies or for hand-to-hand combat.
See also: Parachute.

Airbrush, pencil-like painting tool that uses compressed air to apply a fine spray. A smaller, more delicate version of the spray gun, the airbrush is often used to shade drawings, retouch photographs, or accent highlights in prints. The operator creates different effects by varying the air pressure passing through the brush.

A Phantom fighter-plane with a brake-parachute. Thanks to its large surface area, the brake-parachute experiences an enormous air resistence, by which the kinetic energy of the jet is converted into friction energy via the air pressure increased in the parachute.

Airbus, consortium of aerospace companies from Great Britain, France, Germany, Spain, Belgium, and The Netherlands which was formed in 1970. It developed the A300, a twin-engine passenger aircraft for medium distances with a capacity of almost 260 passengers, and the smaller A310 version. The A320 had a narrower body and like its predecessors, was a huge commercial success. The A330 (two engines) and the A340 (four engines) were designed following this success.

Air compressor, device used to compress air, which is then used to power air brakes, pneumatic tools, and other machinery. Commonly, air compressors work like a piston pump, with a cylinder moving within to compress air and force it into a closed chamber.
See also: Pump; Turbine.

Air conditioning, regulation of the temperature, humidity, circulation, and composition of the air in a building, room, or vehicle. In warm weather an air-conditioning plant, working like a refrigerator, cools, dehumidifies, and filters the air. In colder weather it may be reversed to run as a heat pump.

Aircraft *See:* Airplane; Airship; Balloon; Glider; Helicopter; Rocket; Autogiro.

Aircraft, military, airplanes, helicopters, and other flying machines used for military purposes: to attack enemy forces, transport troops and supplies, and defend territory. Aircraft range in size from small electronically powered devices to huge transport planes designed to carry tanks or trucks. Speeds can reach as high as 2,000 mph (3,200 kmph). Varieties include bombers, fighters, reconnaissance aircraft, transports, special-mission aircraft, and helicopters.

Aircraft carrier, warship equipped to launch and land airplanes. Planes are launched by steam catapults, and arresting cables are used to bring landing aircraft to a halt. Each ship is equipped with antiaircraft guns and missiles and is protected by its own planes and sister ships. The U.S. Navy's first aircraft carrier went into service in 1922. The U.S. Navy's first nuclear-powered aircraft carrier is the *Enterprise*, launched in 1961, which can carry about 50 airplanes.
See also: Navy.

Air cushion vehicle (ACV), or hovercraft or ground effect machine, vehicle that rides on a cushion of compressed air. ACVs have fans that pull air inside and then force it beneath the vehicle, trapping the air between the ground surface and a rubberized skirt on the ACV. This invisible, compressed air cushion enables the ACV to maneuver over rough terrain smoothly because it eliminates friction between the craft and the surface. Though some can reach speeds of over 100 mph (160 kmph), ACVs are designed for short distances. ACVs are most often used to transport passengers and heavy freight over land or water like the one in service across the English Channel.
See also: Ship.

Airedale terrier, breed of large terriers. Weighing from 50 to 60 lb (23 to 27 kg), the Airedale was first bred in England in the 1880s. Considered to be fearless and loyal to their owners, Airdales are commonly used as watchdogs.

Airline *See:* Airport; Aviation.

Air lock, mechanism that allows people to pass between areas of different atmospheric pressures. The air lock chamber has 2 airtight doors sandwiched between the 2 pressure regions. The atmosphere in the air lock is gradually adjusted to match the pressure of the next space to be entered. Air locks are used when transferring people between the outside air and compressed air spaces such as underground tunnels and pneumatic caissons (watertight chambers) and between space vehicles in outer space.
See also: Bends.

Airmail, the transporting of mail by aircraft. A revolutionary 20th-century postal development, airmail is used for almost all first-

The U.S.S. Enterprise (launched in 1960), one of the largest warships ever built, was the first nuclear-powered aircraft carrier. It weighs about 80.000 tons, has a crew of around 5.000, carries more than 100 aircrafts, and has a flight deck of more than 335 metres long. Its 8 nuclear reactors drive it at a cruise speed of 60 km/h, and are able to power the ship for several years of active service.

class mail traveling more than 200 mi (320 km). The first official U.S. airmail delivery was in 1911, from Garden City to Mineola, N.Y.; regular airmail service in the United States began in 1918. The first European regular service was the one between London and Paris in 1919. Airmail service between Europe and the United States started in 1924 and between London and Singapore in 1933. After the second World War airmail services expanded immensely, covering the entire world.

Airplane, powered heavier-than-air craft that obtains lift from the aerodynamic effect of the air rushing over its wings. Besides wings, the typical airplane has a cigar-shaped fuselage that carries the pilot and payload, a power unit to provide forward thrust, stabilizers and a tail fin for controlling the plane in flight, and landing gear for supporting it on the ground. The plane is piloted using the throttle and the 3 basic control surfaces: the elevators on the stabilizers, which determine *pitch* (whether the plane is climbing, diving, or flying horizontally), the rudder on the tail fin, which governs *yaw* (the rotation of the plane about a vertical axis), and the ailerons on the wings, which control *roll* (the rotation of the plane about the long axis through the fuselage). In turning the plane, both the rudder and the ailerons must be used to *bank* the plane into the turn. The airplane's control surfaces are operated by moving a control stick or steering column (elevators and ailerons) in conjunction with a pair of footpedals (rudder).
See also: Aerodynamics; Wright brothers; Aviation.

Air pollution, contamination of the atmosphere by harmful vapors, aerosols, and dust particles, resulting principally from the activities of humans, but to a lesser extent from natural processes. Natural pollutants include pollen particles, saltwater spray, wind-blown dust, and fine debris from volcanic eruptions. Pollution attributable to humans includes the products of fossil fuel combustion (from municipal, industrial, and domestic furnaces and automobiles): carbon monoxide, lead, oxides of nitrogen and sulfur dioxide, and smoke particles; crop spraying; and atmospheric nuclear explosions. Most air pollution arises in the urban environment, with a large portion coming from the automobile. Pollution control involves identifying the sources of contamination, developing improved or alternative technologies and sources of raw materials, and persuading industries and individuals to adopt these, if need be under the sanction of legislation. Key areas for current research are automobile emission control, the recycling and thorough oxidation of exhaust gases, the production of lead-free gasoline, and the development of alternatives to the conventional internal combustion engine.

Airport, site where airplanes and other aircraft take off and land. Consisting of passenger terminals, hangars, and cargo terminals, large-city airports also include related services such as shops, hotels, restaurants, movie theaters, police and fire-fighting forces,

medical facilities, and sewage plants.
See also: Air traffic control; Aviation.

Air rights, rights to the use of building space above a piece of property, especially railroad tracks, highways, and bridge and tunnel approaches. As urban land has grown scarcer, such rights have become increasingly valuable for housing developments and office construction.

Airship, or dirigible, lighter-than-air, self-propelled balloon whose buoyancy is provided by hydrogen or helium. The internal gas pressure causes the nonrigid type of airship, or blimp, to maintain its form. The first successful airship was designed by Henri Giffard, a French engineer, in 1852. In 1900 Count Ferdinand von Zeppelin of Germany built the first rigid airship. It used hydrogen, which is flammable, as the lifting gas and had a metal-lattice frame that held its shape. The vulnerability of rigid airships in storms and a series of spectacular fires, including the *Hindenburg* disaster in 1937, brought an end to their use.
See also: Zeppelin, Ferdinand von.

Air traffic control, system by which airplanes are monitored and guided. Relying on radar and other electronic equipment, air traffic controllers on the ground instruct pilots on landing and take-off patterns and on use of runways for taxiing.

Aisne River, northeastern French river that rises in the forests of Argonne near Vaubecort and flows northwest and west to join the Oise river near Compiègne. The Aisne is about 180 mi (290 km) long. The valley of the Aisne was the scene, during World War I, of prolonged trench warfare and was crossed in World War II by the U.S. Army during its Aug. 1944 offensive.
See also: World War I; World War II.

Aix-en-Provence (pop. 126,000), city in southern France, in the department of Bouches-du-Rhône, about 20 mi (32 km) north of Marseilles. As the Roman settlement Aquae Sextiae, it was colonized by the proconsul C. Sextius Calvinus in 123 B.C. Known from antiquity for its mineral baths, in medieval times Aix became the capital of the region of Provence, as well as a famous literary center. In 1536 it was the temporary residence of the Holy Roman Emperor Charles V. Present-day industries include the production of olive oil, food processing, the manufacture of textiles, and the milling of flour.

Aix-la-Chapelle *See:* Aachen.

Aix-la-Chapelle, Congress of, meeting (1818) of the rulers of Austria, Prussia, and Russia and representatives from Great Britain and France at Aachen (Aix-la-Chapelle), Germany, after the Napoleonic

A

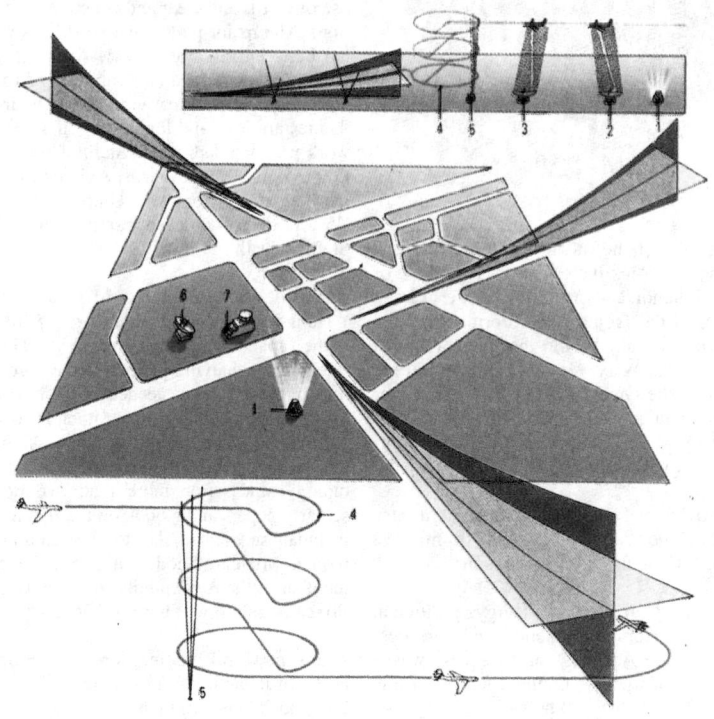

Air traffic often follows airways like a street plan, with navigation aids such as VOR beacons (1) at intersections, to give bearings and distances. At the destination, traffic plotted by a primary radar (2) will be called by a secondary surveillance radar (3), individually identified and guided to a holding stack (4), and a radio beacon (5), where inbound aircraft will fly a racetrack pattern at successively lower levels. From the bottom of the stack, each aircraft will capture the sloping glidepath of the landing runway, and it will land almost automatically, even at the worst degree of visibility. The airport surveillance radar (6) can oversee all moving vehicles on the airport, even in dense fog, and the aircraft control centre (7) will co-ordinates all these movements.

A

Wars. The nations sought to preserve the peace established by, and resolve problems arising from, settlements made at the Congress of Vienna (1814-15).
See also: Vienna, Congress of.

Ajanta, village in India, 248 mi (399 km) northwest of Bombay. Famous for its Buddhist cave temples and monasteries cut into the rock face in the area (1st century B.C.-7th century A.D.), the walls of which were sculpted in high relief during the Gupta era. The paintings on the inner walls, which are among the most beautiful in the world, were applied to dried plaster and depict the life of the Buddha.

The head of Akhenaton (1365-49/47 B.C.), the radical reformer of religion and society in Egypt, in the 14th century B.C.

Ajax, the name of 2 figures in Greek mythology. Ajax the Greater was the son of King Telamon and one of the greatest Greek heroes of the Trojan War. Informed that the arms of the slain Achilles had been awarded to Odysseus, Ajax went mad and committed suicide. The Greek warrior Ajax the Lesser also fought in the Trojan War. As punishment for raping Cassandra in Athena's temple, Ajax was shipwrecked and then killed.

Ajman (pop. 119,000), one of the emirates of the United Arab Emirates; 97 sq mi (250 sq km). Capital has the same name.

Akayev, Askar (1944-), Kyrgyz politician. Akayev, a prominent scientist and also president of the Academy of Sciences, was a member of the Communist Party in the Soviet Union. In 1990 he was elected president of Kyrgyzstan. One of his first acts was to draw up a declaration of independence for the Republic of Kyrgyzstan. He considered privatization an absolute necessity to make economic reforms and stimulate private entrepreneurship in the country. In 1996, however, he had to send out warning signals about the state of the economy and presented an economic program for the period until 2005 aimed at doubling the national income and bringing back inflation to 8%. Due to a

failing economic policy, Akajev forced the resignation of the government at the end of 1998. The new cabinet started an intensive battle against corruption and tax evasion and strove to promote industrial production. At the end of 2000, Akajev was re-elected president for the third time.

Akbar (1542-1605), greatest of the Mogul emperors of India (1556-1605). He extended Mogul power over most of Afghanistan and India. An excellent administrator, he pursued a policy of religious toleration and also improved social laws, commerce, and transportation.
See also: India.

Akhenaton, or Ikhnaton, title taken by Amenhotep IV, king of Egypt (c. 1379-50 B.C.). Akhenaton started the cult of the sun god Aton, despite the opposition of the priesthood of Amon-Ra. He moved the capital from Thebes, city of Amon, to Akhetaton (now Tell el-Amarna), where he fostered a naturalistic school of art and literature. After his death the old religion was reestablished. Akhenaton was married to Nefertiti.

Akhmatova, Anna (pseudonym of Anna Andreyevna Gorenko; 1889-1966) Russian poet. Together with her husband (1910-1918) Gumilyov, she belonged to the 'acmeists', a Russian literary movement between 1912-1922, which arose as a reaction to symbolism: the acmeists wanted logical use of words and clear and concrete descriptions. The major part of her work was written between 1912 and 1921. Although her style is characterized by simplicity of form, her poems reflect great virtuosity. The main themes are love and loneliness. In 1946 her work was branded by the Stalin administration as containing no ideas; Akhmatova was then expelled from the Union of Soviet Writers. Her work appeared again after Stalin's death.

Akihito (1933-), emperor of Japan (1989-). He is formerly called *Tenno Heisei*; Tenno is the Japanese title for emperor and Heisei (meaning 'achieving peace') is the name of his reign. Akihito succeeded to the imperial throne upon the death of his father, Hirohito. He is the 125th emperor of Japan. Akihito, like his father, became an expert in marine biology, and wrote more than two dozen scolarly papers and a book on the fish found in Japanese waters. Akihito married a commoner, Michiko Shodo, in 1959, the first member of the royal family to do so. Crown Prince Naruhito was born in 1960.

Akita, powerful hunting dog originating in northern Japan in the 17th century. Standing 20-27 in (51-69 cm) high at the shoulder and weighing 75-110 lbs (34-50 kg), the Akita possesses a solid body and a short, stiff coat. Sometimes called the royal dog of Japan, the Akita is considered a symbol of good health and has been designated a national treasure by the Japanese government.

Akiva Baer ben Joseph (c. A.D. 50-135), Jewish rabbi, one of the greatest compilers of Hebrew Oral Law, whose work later formed the basis of the Mishnah. The

Mishnah is part of the Talmud, a collection of writings constituting Jewish civil and religious law. After supporting a revolt against the Romans, he was executed as a rebel
See also: Talmud.

The famous emperor Akbar, taming a wild elephant on an illustration from the *Akbar-nama*. The emperor is sitting on a horse, an example of quietness among his somewhat frightened subjects.

Akron (pop. 223,000), industrial city, seat of Summit County, Ohio, located on the Cuyahoga River, 36 mi (58 km) south of Cleveland. Akron was settled early in the 19th century and incorporated in 1865. Among the city's historical buildings is the home of John Brown, the abolitionist. B.F. Goodrich founded his pioneer rubber factory in Akron in 1870. With the invention of the automobile, Akron developed some of the world's largest tire and automobile plants. In addition, the city manufactures aircraft, matches, plastics, and clay and wood products.

Akutagawa, Ryunosuke (1892-1927), Japanese writer of short stories, poetry, and plays. From medieval themes he turned to autobiographical subjects. His work's fantastic and morbid nature reveals susceptibilities that led to his suicide. His most famous story is *Rashomon* (1915).

Alabama (Heart of Dixie; pop. 4,400,000), state in the southeast of the U.S.; 51,725 sq mi (133,915 sq km). Capital: Montgomery. The largest cities are Birmingham and Mobile.
Its southern position makes the climate generally moderate.
Minerals: iron ore, bauxite, coal, petroleum, and natural gas. Agriculture: cotton, soya beans, peanuts, etc.; poultry farming. Industry: iron and steel industry (Birmingham), chemicals, food, paper and pulp, and other timber processing industry. Hydroelectric power stations (built by the

Tennessee Valley Authority). Mobile is an important seaport.

The Spaniards were the first Europeans to visit the area. At that time it had probably already been inhabited for 10,000 years. The Native Americans who lived there at the time (16th century) belonged mainly to the Creek, the Choctaw, and the Cherokee people. The state has been a member of the Union since 1819. Confederates organized themselves in Montgomery in 1861 (Civil War). A rigid segregation policy was carried out from 1870 and was only slowly dismantled in the 1960s. In 1965 African Americans were enfranchised after the state of Alabama had been the stage of civil rights activities headed by Martin Luther King.

Alabaster, soft, usually white, semitransparent variety of the mineral gypsum, used to make decorative objects. Gypsum is composed of calcium sulfate. The alabaster used in ancient times is composed of calcium carbonate and is harder than gypsum.
See also: Gypsum.

Aladdin, boy hero of one of the stories of the *Thousand and One Nights*, a collection of folk tales from the Middle East preserved in Arabic in the 16th century. Aladdin, the son of a poor widow, comes into possession of a magic ring and lamp. As the master of the lamp and of the 2 genies, or jinns, who reside within, Aladdin amasses great wealth and becomes a sultan.
See also: Arabian Nights.

Alai Mountains, range of mountains in Kyrgyzstan, part of the Tien Shan. Highest point is the Lenin Peak (23,407 ft, 7,134 m) in the Trans Alai Mountains.

Alain-Fournier (Henri Alban Fournier; 1886-1914), French writer whose one novel, *The Wanderer* (1913), is the haunting tale of a boy's attempt to rediscover the dreamlike setting of his meeting with a beautiful girl.

Alamo, Spanish mission fortress in San Antonio, Tex. It was the site of a heroic defense (1836) by fewer than 200 Texans in the struggle for independence from Mexico. All the defenders, including Davy Crockett and Jim Bowie, died in a lengthy siege by 4,000 Mexicans under Gen. Santa Anna. The famous phrase 'remember the Alamo' refers to the siege.
See also: Texas.

Alamogordo, (pop. 35,500), town in south-central New Mexico, seat of Otero County. It is the center of an agricultural, timber, and recreation area that includes the White Sands National Monument and Lincoln National Forest. The first atomic bomb was exploded near Alamogordo in a test on July 16, 1945.
See also: Nuclear weapon.

Alanbrooke, Lord (Alan Francis Brooke, 1st Viscount; 1883-1936), one of the leading British military strategists of World War II and chief of the Imperial General Staff (1941-46).

Alarcón, Pedro Antonio de (1833-1891),

Spanish regional writer best known for his novel *The Three-Cornered Hat* (1874). His work is distinguished by sharp realistic observation and picturesque effects.

Alaric, name of 2 Visigothic kings. **Alaric I** (c. A.D. 370-410) was commander of the Visigothic auxiliaries under the Roman Emperor Theodosius, upon whose death Alaric was proclaimed king of the Visigoths. After invading Greece and northern Italy, he captured and sacked Rome in 410. **Alaric II** (d. 507), ruled Spain and South Gaul from 484 and in 506 issued the Breviary of Alaric, a Visigothic code of Roman law, for his Roman subjects. He was slain in battle by Clovis I, king of the Franks.
See also: Goths.

Alaska (Last Frontier; pop. 627,000), largest state in the United States, located at the extreme northwest corner of North America, separated from the rest of the continental United States by northwest Canada; bordered by British Columbia and Yukon Territory in the west, the Pacific Ocean in the south, the Bering Sea in the west, and the Arctic Ocean in the north.
Alaska's general coastline is 6,640 mi (10,686 km) long, longer than the coastlines

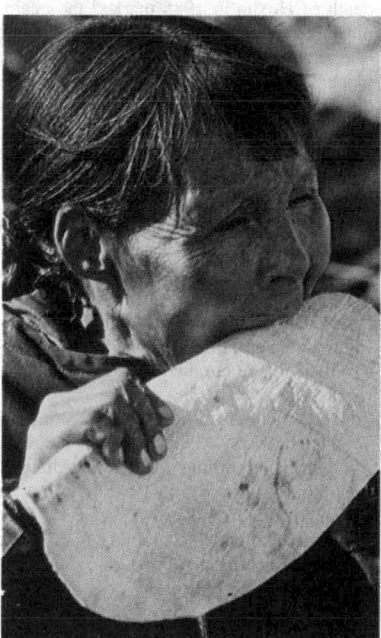

A woman from Alaska, chewing on a piece of seal skin, in order to make it sup-ple and soft. The skin will be used for the manufacturing of soles for boots.

of the other 49 states combined. In the southeastern part of the Alaskan mainland is the mountainous Panhandle region, which is paralleled by the Alexander Archipelago. The Alaska Range, in the south-central part of the state, contains the highest peak in North America, Mt. McKinley. Extending southwest from the Alaska Range are the Alaska Peninsula and the Aleutian Islands. The Aleutian Range, which extends over the peninsula to Attu Island, near the Asian continent, has many active volcanoes. Between the mountain chains along the Pacific Coast and the Brooks Range, an extension of the

Rockies, lies the central plateau of Alaska, crossed by the Yukon River. Alaska's northernmost settlement is Point Barrow, lying in the frozen tundra of the Arctic Coastal Plain. Southern Alaska has a relatively mild climate, with brief but hot summers. Winters are much colder in central Alaska. Principal cities are Anchorage, Fairbanks, and Juneau. Oil is Alaska's most valuable natural resource. Prudhoe Bay, on the Arctic Coastal Plain, is believed by engineers to be the largest oil field in North America. Alaska's other major mineral products are gold, sand and gravel, and natural gas. Alaska's fishing industry is the largest in the United States. Salmon is the most important catch. Alaska's leading manufactures are food, petroleum, and paper products. Furs were the original motive for Alaska's colonization and are still important.
Alaska's constitution was adopted in 1956. The governor is elected for a 4-year term. The state senate has 20 members elected for 4-year terms, and the house of representatives is composed of 40 members serving 2-year terms. Alaska sends 1 representative and 2 senators to the U.S. Congress.
Russia claimed Alaska after Vitus Bering sighted it in 1741. Gregory Shelikof founded the first permanent white settlement in 1784 on Kodiak Island. U.S. Secretary of State William H. Seward bought Alaska in 1867 for $7.2 million-about 2 cents an acre. Economic growth remained slow until the 1896 Klondike gold rush in the Yukon and after subsequent deposits were discovered in Nome in 1899 and Fairbanks in 1902. Alaska was established as a U.S. territory in 1912. World War II brought economic change to Alaska, with the United States sending thousands of workers to the territory to build defense installments and the Alaska Highway.In 1942 the Japanese occupied the Aleutian Islands of Agattu, Attu, and Kiska, the only part of North America to be invaded during the war. In 1968 the Prudhoe Bay oil field was discovered, transforming the economy. The Trans-Alaska Pipeline, which carries petroleum from Prudhoe Bay to the port of Valdez, was completed in 1977. In 1980 the federal government, which controls most of the state's land, set aside more than 104 million acres 42 million hectares) for wilderness areas, wildlife refuges, and national parks and preserves. In 1989 the *Exxon Valdez* accidentally discharged 10 million gal (39 million l) of oil into Prince William Sound, in North America's worst oil spill.

Alaskan malamute, strong sled dog developed by the Malemiut Eskimos. The malamute's thick coat is gray or black with white markings and a bushy tail curls across its back. Weight ranges from 75 to 85 lb (34 to 39 kg).

Alaska pipeline, oil pipeline running 789 mi (1,270 km) from Alaska's Prudhoe Bay to the port of Valdez. Finished in 1977, it was bitterly opposed by environmentalists for adversely affecting the ecology.
See also: Petroleum; Pipe and pipeline.

Ala-tau, name for various mountain ranges in Kyrgyzstan and Kazakhstan. Part of the

A

Tien Mountain. The ski resort Almaty is located in the southern part of the higher mountains; highest peak 17,717 ft (5,400 m).

Alawites, 1. An Islamic Shiite sect that originated in the 19th century and who consider Ali and not Abu Bekr to be the successor to Mohammed. The 'State of the Alawites' is located between the Orontes River and the Mediterranean Sea and has been a part of Syria since the second World War. After initial tension the Alawites have exercised great influence on the government since the Baath party assumed power in 1966.
2. Moroccan dynasty founded by Mulay Rashid (1666-1672). The Alawites succeeded the dynasty of Sadides and managed to survive despite enormous difficulties. Their position was acknowledged in 1912 when Morocco became a French protectorate.

Al-Azhar University, in Cairo, Egypt, one of the world's oldest universities (founded in c. A.D. 970) and a major center of Islamic learning. Women gained admittance in 1962.

Alba, Duke of *See:* Alva or Alba, Fernando Alvarez de Toledo, Duke of.

Alban, Saint (d. c. 304), first Christian martyr in Britain. Martyred during the persecutions of the Emperor Diocletian, he is said to have performed many miracles. A monastery was built in his memory in 795 by the king of Mercia, near the presumed place of his execution. St. Alban's feast day is celebrated on June 22 by Roman Catholics and on June 17 by the Church of England.

Albania

Capital:	Tirana
Area:	11,100 sq mi (28,748 sq km)
Population:	3,545,000
Language:	Albanian
Government:	Presidential republic
Independent:	1912
Head of gov.:	Premier
Per capita:	U.S. $3,800
Monetary unit:	1 Lek = 100 qindars

Albania, one of the smallest countries in the Balkans, 210 mi (338 km) long, and less than 100 mi (161 km) wide.
Land and climate. The country is mountainous, with isolated fertile basins and a narrow coastal plain. The climate is Mediterranean, but summers can bring prolonged droughts and winters can be harsh.
People. Albania's population is largely Muslim, with a Roman Catholic and Greek Orthodox Christian minority.
Economy. Albania is a poor country with slow development. Farming yields grapes and olives as well as grains, fruits, tobacco, and cotton. Albania is rich in chromium, copper, nickel, and coal, and mining provides most of the country's income. Industries produce food and petroleum products, textiles and building materials.
History. As part of ancient Illyria, Albania was successively under Greek, Roman, and Byzantine influence and control. In succeeding centuries it was invaded by Goths, Bulgars, Slavs, and Normans. Later, the national hero Scanderberg (1403?-1468) delayed but failed to stop Ottoman Turkish conquest. Turkish rule Islamized Albania and suppressed nationalist aspirations until the First Balkan War (1912). Occupied in World War I, ruled by the self-proclaimed King Zog I (1928-1939), then annexed by Italy and occupied in World War II, Albania regained independence under the antifascist guerila leader Enver Hoxha, a Communist, who proclaimed a republic in 1946. The death of Hoxha in 1985 marked the beginning of a period of political and economic liberalization. In 1991 free elections took place. During 1990, Albania began to restore diplomatic relations with the West. Shortly afterward a democratic constitution was adopted. Later that year, a nationwide strike forced the Communist-led government to resign and an interim government was formed. In the 1992 elections the Communists lost their majority in the People's Assembly. Antigovernment rioting broke out throughout the country in 1997, in part because of dissatisfaction with the government in dealing with the collapse of investment schemes to which a large number of citizens had contributed money.
Towards the end of the 1990s, tensions developed between Albania and its neighbor Yugoslavia, regarding the ethnic Albanian population of Kosovo. In 1999 thousands of Albanians fled from Kosovo because of Serb aggression, after which joining NATO and the European Union became one of the government's main objectives.

The small town of Gjirokaster. Despite the rugged terrain, the area is an important producer of olives, tobacco, and wheat.

Albany (pop. 102,000), capital of New York since 1797 and seat of Albany County, located on the west bank of the Hudson River about 145 mi (233 km) north of New York City. An important industrial center, Albany's products include chemicals, paper, and textiles. Many people are also employed in state and county government offices. The opening of the Erie and Champlain canals in the 1820s and the first railroad connection with Schenectady in 1831 established Albany's position as a commercial and shipping center.
See also: New York.

Al Basrah, or Basra (pop. 789,000), second-largest city in Iraq and an important port, lying on the Shatt al Arab River approximately 55 mi (90 km) from the Persian Gulf. Arabs founded Al Basrah in A.D. 636, after which it became a trade center. Under Ottoman rule (1534-1918) the city declined in importance. From 1918 to 1932, the years Great Britain ruled Iraq, Al Basrah served as a military center. Located near major oil fields, it became a center for oil refining and export. Because it was the site of heavy fighting, the city's importance as a port decreased during the Iran-Iraq War of 1980-88.
See also: Persian Gulf War.

Albatross, any of 14 species of large, long-winged, gliding, hook-billed seabirds forming the family Diomedeidae. Two species form the genus *Phoebetria*, the other 12 the genus *Diomedea*. Most albatrosses are white with darker markings on the back, wings,

Black-browed albatross (*Diomedia melanophris*), oceans of the southern hemisphere, wing span 210 centimetres.

and tail. The wandering albatross (*D. exulans*) has the broadest wingspan of any living bird-up to 12 ft (3.7 m).

Albee, Edward Franklin (1928-), U.S. playwright who gained international fame with *Who's Afraid of Virginia Woolf?* (1962), a penetrating look at contemporary American marriage. His other plays include *The Zoo Story* (1958) and *The American Dream* (1961), both one-act plays, and *Tiny Alice* (1964). He won Pulitzer Prizes for *A Delicate Balance* (1966), *Seascape* (1975) and *Three Tall Women* (1991).

Albéniz, Isaac (1860-1909), Spanish composer and pianist. He is best remembered for his later piano works, including the suite *Iberia* (1906-9), which is based on Spanish folk themes and popular music forms.

Alberta (pop. 2,697,000), a prairie province in Canada; 246,517 sq mi (638,233 sq km). Capital: Edmonton. Mount Columbia (12,294 ft, 3,747 m) is the highest point; the lowest point is in Wood Buffalo National Park (558 ft, 170 m). Cold winters and mild summers. In winter the warm chinook winds feed in from the Rockies. Canada's main supplier (> 80%) of petroleum and natural gas; in addition it supplies sulfur and coal (44%). Agriculture mainly includes cattle-breeding products and wheat. Petrochemical, metal, food, timber, paper, and machinery industry; tourism in the Banff National Park.
The majority the of 15% of the population born abroad is American or British. The province has 68,000 Native Americans and 40,000 Mestizos.
Europeans (French) entered the province for the first time in 1750 and from 1780 onwards furriers became active. Around 1900 the economy grew quickly and the population increased from 75,000 in 1901 to 375,000 in 1911. Since 1905, Alberta has been a member of the Canadian Confederation. The oil boom took place during World War II.
Named after a daughter of Queen Victoria who was married to the governor-general of Canada.

Albert, Prince (Francis Charles Augustus Albert Emmanuel; 1819-1861), prince consort of Great Britain, husband of Queen Victoria. German-born son of the Duke of Saxe-Coburg-Gotha, he married Victoria in 1840 and served as her trusted adviser. He was active in promoting fine arts.

Albert I (1875-1934), king of the Belgians (1909-1934); nephew and successor of Leopold II. During World War I Albert commanded the armed forces. He did much to improve conditions in the Belgian Congo, and he strengthened national defense and the merchant fleet and introduced social reforms in Belgium.

Alberti, Leon Battista (1404-1472), Italian Renaissance scholar, architect, painter, and art theorist. His architectural works include the Palazzo Rucellai in Florence and the church of San Francesco in Rimini. Alberti is noted for his literary contributions during the Italian Renaissance, including *Della pittura*, the first formulation of the aesthetic and scientific attitudes of Renaissance painting; it idealized the imitation of nature and served as a foundation for modern perspective. His architectural influence was presented in his treatise *De re aedificatoria*, which provided the Renaissance with an original program for architectural design. Alberti also wrote on a variety of subjects involving domestic animals, religion and the priesthood, jurisprudence, politics, government, mathematics, mechanics, literature, and language. He was the prototype of the Renaissance man.

Albert II (1934-), sixth king of Belgium. He succeeded his brother, King Baudouin, who died in 1993. Married Paola Ruffo di Calabria (1937-) in 1959. They have three children: Philip (1960-), Astrid (1962-), and Laurence (1963-).

Albertus Magnus, Saint (1206?-1280), German scholastic philosopher and scientist and teacher of St. Thomas Aquinas. He helped establish Aristotelianism and the study of the natural sciences in Christian thought, and he was possibly the first to isolate arsenic.

Albertus Magnus (1206-1280) in a fresco by Tommasso da Modena (1325-1379). Seminar of Treviso.

Albigenses, members of a heretical sect that flourished in the 12th and 13th centuries in southern France. The Albigenses believed that the principles of good and evil are in constant struggle and that matter is evil and only the human spirit is good. A crusade proclaimed by Pope Innocent III in 1208 broke the hold of the heresy, and a special inquisition was created in 1233 to convert the Albigenses.

Albino, organism lacking normal pigmentation. The skin and hair of albino animals (including humans) is uncolored, and the irises of the eyes appear pink. Albinism, which may be total or only partial, is generally inherited. Because albino plants contain no chlorophyll and thus are unable to perform photosynthesis, they rapidly die.

Albinoni, Tomaso (1671-1750) Italian composer, one of the last representatives of the Italian baroque. Composed instrumental works such as concerti grossi, triosonates, ballets, and over fifty operas.

Albion, other name for England. This term is probably derived from the Celtic name for Scotland (Alba) and interpreted by the Romans as 'the white island'-'albus' (Latin for 'white') refers to the white chalk cliffs of the English southeast coast. Since the French Revolution 'perfidious Albion' stands for England as a sly and unreliable superpower. This term was also used by the Nazis.

Albright, Ivan Le Lorraine (1897-1983), U.S. painter of microscopically detailed canvases that focus on decay and human dissolution. His works include *That Which I Should Have Done I Did Not Do* (1941) and a series of paintings for the film *The Picture of Dorian Gray* (1944).

Albright, Madeleine Korbel (1937-), U.S. politician, born in Czechoslovakia. At the age of 11 she and her family moved to the United States. A professor of international affairs, she started to work for the White House in 1978 where she dealt with foreign policy legislation. She is a former president of the Center for National Policy and a former member of the National Security Council staff. In 1993 she became ambassador to the United Nations. In 1997, she succeeded Warren Christopher as Secretary of State. Albright was the most highly placed woman in the American government. She retired in 2001.

Albumin, protein that occurs in its most well-known state in the white of an egg. Albumin appears in animal and plant tissues. It is the primary constituent of the protein in blood serum. Albumins are used in the dyeing industry and in making photographic chemicals.

Albuquerque (pop. 449,000), largest city in New Mexico and seat of Bernalillo County, situated on the Rio Grande. Founded in 1706, it is an important commercial and industrial city, a center for nuclear energy and defense research, and a transcontinental air and land route hub. Its dry, sunny climate and nearby mountains and Native American reservations have made it a popular tourist center.

Alcatraz, rocky island in San Francisco Bay, famous as the site from 1933 to 1963 of a federal maximum security prison, nicknamed 'the Rock.' It is now part of the Golden Gate National Recreation Area.

Alcazar (Arab.: al-kassr = the castle, fortress) palace or fortress built for the Moorish kings in Spain during the Moorish occupation. Characterized by a rectangular or square ground plan, a fortified wall with towers round an inner court with houses, and usually one fortified entrance. Well known alcazars are in Seville, Segovia, and Toledo.

Alchemy, blend of philosophy, mysticism, and chemical processing that originated before the Christian era. Practitioners sought the conversion of base metals into gold us-

A

A

ing the 'philosopher's stone.' Other goals were the prolongation of life and the secret of immortality. Alchemy began in Hellenistic Egypt and passed through the writings of the great Arab alchemists to the Latin West. In the early 16th century Paracelsus set alchemy on a new course toward chemical pharmacy, although other alchemists-including John Dee and Isaac Newton- continued to work along quasi-religious lines.
See also: Chemistry; Metallurgy.

Alcibiades (c. 450-404 B.C.), Athenian statesman and general, nephew of Pericles, and student of Socrates. He fell in and out of favor with the Athenian people during the era of the Peloponnesian War. He was eventually exiled and assassinated.
See also: Peloponnesian War.

Alcindor, Lew *See:* Abdul-Jabbar, Kareem.

Alcock and Brown, pioneer British aviators, who made the first nonstop flight across the Atlantic Ocean in 1919. Pilot Sir John William Alcock (1892-1919) and navigator Sir Arthur Whitten Brown (1886-1948) began their transatlantic flight near St. John's, Newfoundland, in a twin-engine, converted bomber, landing in a bog near Clifden, Ireland, the next day, having traveled 1,950 mi (3,138 km).

Alcohol, class of compounds containing a hydroxyl group bonded by a carbon atom. Alcohols occur widely in nature and are used as solvents and antifreezes and in chemical manufacture. They are obtained by fermentation, by oxidation or hydration of alkenes from petroleum and natural gas, and by reduction of fats and oils. The simplest alcohols are methanol and ethyl alcohol, or ethanol (the intoxicating constituent of alcoholic beverages); others include benzyl alcohol, ethylene glycol, and glycerol.
See also: Solvent.

A nineteenth-century American brand label, presenting a romanticized view of an old distillery. In 1776, the year in which America attained its independence, a distillery must have looked like that. The brew was distilled in a set of copper containers that were heated by a log fire. The alcohol, passing from the copper containers through a spout and copper tubing into a barrel, was cooled with cold water from an outside drainpipe. In the background, a black slave is busy stirring the fermentation containers.

Alcoholics Anonymous (A.A.), international organization founded in 1935 to help people suffering from alcoholism overcome their addictions. The practice of sharing recovery experiences among its members is a successful part of the treatment plan.

Alcoholism, chronic illness marked by compulsive drinking of alcohol, leading to physical and psychological addiction. Alcohol is a depressant that acts on the central nervous system to reduce anxiety and inhibition. It is a potent and addictive substance that impairs physical coordination, judgment, and perception and, in sufficiently high dosages, can cause unconsciousness or death. Alcohol is nearly unique among potent drugs in that moderate, self-induced levels of intoxication are socially acceptable. Because alcohol is so readily available and its use so generally accepted, its abuse remains by far the most serious drug problem in the United States. Alcohol abuse is the direct cause of crime, delinquency, and accidents that cost billions of dollars, as well as considerable physical and psychological suffering and loss of life. Prolonged alcohol abuse causes cirrhosis of the liver, damages other organs, including the brain and heart, and may contribute to cancer of the esophagus. Drinking during pregnancy is harmful to the fetus. For the severely addicted alcoholic, withdrawal from alcohol is more dangerous and potentially more life-threatening than withdrawal from heroin and must be done under medical supervision. Treatment most often includes individual or group psychological counseling, but may also include prescriptions of Antabuse (disulfiram), which causes unpleasant physical responses, such as nausea, in patients who drink alcohol while they are taking the drug. Research continues into the causes of alcoholism, including findings that indicate a genetic component in the disease suggesting heredity.
See also: Alcoholics Anonymous; Drug abuse.

Alcott, (Amos) Bronson (1799-1888), U.S. educator, philosopher, and author, father of

Louisa May Alcott. Founder of the progressive Temple School in Boston, his teaching methods were too advanced to be popular. A leading transcendentalist along with Ralph Waldo Emerson and Henry David Thoreau, his writings include *Concord Days* (1872) and *Table Talk* (1877).
See also: Transcendentalism.

Alcott, Louisa May (1832-1888), U.S. author; daughter of Bronson Alcott. Her best-known work is the autobiographical *Little Women* (1869). Another important work, *Hospital Sketches* (1863), was based on her experiences as a Union nurse in the Civil War.

Alcuin, or Albinus (c. A.D. 735-804), English prelate and educator whose scholarship influenced medieval teaching of the liberal arts. He supervised Charlemagne's program of ecclesiastical and educational reform.

Aldehyde, any of a class of highly reactive organic chemical compounds characterized by a CHO group; especially, acetaldehyde (C_2H_4O). Formaldehyde (CH_2O) is a pungent gaseous aldehyde used commonly as a disinfectant and preservative and in making resins and plastics.
See also: Formaldehyde.

Alder, any of a genus (*Alnus*) of shrubs and small trees of the birch family. Found in moist, temperate regions at high altitudes, they are indigenous to the Americas, Asia, and North Africa. One variety, the red alder (*A. rubra*), is used commercially as timber.

Aldridge, Ira Frederick (1805-1867), first African American to achieve fame as an actor in the Western Hemisphere. Because of limited opportunities in the United States due to racial prejudice, he was forced to go to Europe, where he became known for his bold interpretations of Lear, Othello, and Macbeth.

Aldrin, Buzz (Edwin Eugene Aldrin, Jr.; 1930-), U.S. astronaut. Aldrin was the second man to walk on the moon, during the Apollo 11 space flight in 1969. In 1966 he was the pilot of the Gemini 12 flight, which included rendezvous maneuvers and his record 5-hour space walks.

Aldus Manutius (Teobaldo Mannucci or Manuzio; 1450-1515), Venetian founder of the Aldine Press, whose scrupulous editions of Greek and Roman classics (including the works of Aristotle) advanced Renaissance scholarship. He was the first to use italic type (1501) to produce cheap, pocket-sized editions of the Latin classics.

Aleatory music (from Latin *alea*, 'dice'), music dependent on chance, applied to the post-1950 tendency of composers, such as John Cage, to leave elements in their work to the performer's decision or chance.

Alechinsky, Pierre (1927-) Belgian painter. Member of the Jeune Peinture Belge in 1947; joined the Cobra movement in 1949. Lived in Paris, Tokyo (1955) and New

The first men on the moon. Reflected in Edwin Aldrin's helmet are the lunar module and Neil Armstrong, the first man ever to walk on the moon, who took the picture.

York (1960), where he made a 'Hommage à Ensor'. He paints in a lyrically abstract style based on eastern calligraphy. His imaginary figures emanate from surrealism.

Aleichem, Sholem *See:* Sholem Aleichem.

Aleixandre, Vicente (1898-1984), Spanish poet. His collections of poetry include *Destruction or Love* (1935) and *Shadow of Paradise* (1944). He won the 1977 Nobel Prize for literature.

Alekhine, Alexander (1892-1946) Russian/French chess master; world champion from 1927-35 and 1937-46. Alekhine is generally regarded as the most allround chess genius ever to have existed. He possessed a near perfect technique, could attack swiftly, combine brilliantly but could also control positional play and the endgame. A very ambitious person, he pushed himself to the limit and of the 87 tournaments he participated in, won 62, sometimes by a large margin as happened in San Remo in 1930 (14 out of 15) and Veldes 1931 (20.5 out of 26). In 1927 he defeated world champion Capablanca (+6, -3, =25), held off Bogolyubov twice(in 1929 and 1934), but lost in 1935 to Euwe (+8, -9, =13). In 1937 he regained the title (+10, -4, =11). Alekhine also improved the world blindfold chess record, setting the record at 32 matches. He wrote many books and tournament books, in particular, about the big tournaments in New York during 1924 and 1927.

Alembert, Jean le Rond d' (1717-1783), French philosopher, physicist, and mathematician, a leading figure in the French Enlightenment, and coeditor with Denis Diderot of the *Encyclopédie*. His early fame rested on his formulation of d'Alembert's principle in mechanics (1743). His other works treat calculus, music, philosophy, and astronomy.

Jean Baptiste Le Rond d'Alembert (1717-1783) at the age of 36. Painting by Quentin de La Tour (1704-1788).

Aleppo (pop. 1,580,000), second-largest city of Syria. It flourished in Byzantine times as a trade center on the caravan route to Baghdad. An important manufacturing center, its industries include textile- and carpetmaking. The cultural center of Syria, Aleppo contains the National Museum, a medieval citadel, and numerous mosques with many fine examples of Islamic art.

Alesi, Jean (1964-), French racing driver, made his Formula One debut in the French GP in 1989 for Tyrrell. Alesi won his first Grand Prix (Canada) on his 31st birthday after he had competed in 90 GP races. He switched to Ferrari in 1990. His last Formula One race took place in 2001.

Aleut, native of the Aleutian Islands and western Alaska. Descended from an Eskimo people, Aleuts have their own language. Traditionally, Aleuts hunted land animals, such as caribou and bear, and sea animals, such as whales and seals. They traveled in skin-covered kayaks, made spears and fishhooks, and dressed in parkas made from animal furs. Under Russian domination, which began in the 18th century, the Aleutian population dropped dramatically, dropping further with Japanese occupation of the Aleutians during World War II. Through the Alaska Native Claims Settlement Act of the U.S. Congress (1971), the Aleuts won the rights to their homeland.

Aleutian Islands, chain of rugged Alaskan islands of volcanic origin, extending westward 1,200 mi (1,900 km) from the Alaska Peninsula and separating the Bering Sea from the Pacific. Fishing is the chief occupation. During World War II the Japanese occupied the islands Agattu, Attu, and Kiska.
See also: Alaska.

Alewife (*Alosa pseudoharengus*), fish in the herring family. Alewives travel in large schools along the Atlantic coastline of the United States. They grow up to 15 in (38 cm) in saltwater and, in the freshwater of the Great Lakes, up to 6 in (15 cm). After maturity, saltwater alewives travel from the Atlantic to freshwater, where they lay their eggs.

Alexander, name of 3 Russian tsars. **Alexander I** (1777-1825) succeeded his father, Paul I, in 1801. In 1805 he joined England and Austria against Napoleon. After French victories Napoleon proposed Franco-Russian domination of Europe, but mutual mistrust came to a head, and Napoleon invaded Russia in 1812. The French were defeated, and in 1815 Alexander formed a coalition with Austria and Prussia, the Holy Alliance. At his death, Russia faced economic ruin and rebellion. **Alexander II** (1818-1881) succeeded his father, Nicholas I, in 1855. He was responsible for the emancipation of the serfs in 1861, but he was assassinated when his domestic reforms did not satisfy populist groups. In foreign policies he was a moderate, making peace in the Crimea and extending Russian power in the Far East as well as in Central Asia. **Alexander III** (1845-1894) succeeded his father, Alexander II, in 1881. He discarded the latter's proposals for moderate reform in favor of rigid repression and persecution of minorities.

Russian Czar Alexander I, who initiated the Holy Alliance.

Alexander, Grover Cleveland (1887-1950), U.S. baseball player. One of the greatest right-handed pitchers in baseball history, in 1916 he set the major league record for shutouts in a season (16). Third on the career win list with 373, Alexander's 90 career shutouts are the second most in major league history. Alexander played with the Philadelphia Phillies, Chicago Cubs, and St. Louis Cardinals from 1911 to 1930. He was inducted into the National Baseball Hall of Fame in 1938.

Alexander Archipelago, group of more than 1,100 islands lying along the coastline of the Alaska Panhandle. They are the peaks of a submerged coastal range. Sitka, on the island of Baranof, was once capital of Alaska. The islands were discovered by Vitus Bering in 1741 and were acquired by the United States as part of the Alaska purchase in 1867. Fish, furs, gold, and timber are important items in their economy.

Alexander I (1888-1934), king of Yugoslavia from 1921 to 1934. Yugoslavia, which has been formed as a country in 1918, was home to several peoples, including Serbs, Croats, and Slovenes. To ensure Serb dominance, Alexander declared himself dictator in 1929. He was assassinated by a Croatian terrorist in 1934.

Alexander III (Orlando Bandinelli; ?-1181), pope (1159-1181). He continued a longstanding conflict with the Holy Roman Emperor Frederick I. Opposed also by 3 antipopes, he was victorious over Frederick at the Battle of Legano in 1176. He convened the Third Lateran Council (1179) and forced King Henry II of England to recognize papal supremacy.

Alexander IV (Rodrigo Borgia; 1431-1503), pope (1492-1503). The most notorious of the Renaissance popes, he directed his efforts at increasing the temporal power

A

of the papacy and creating great hereditary domains for his children, among them Cesare and Lucrezia Borgia.

Alexander of Tunis, 1st Earl (Harold Rupert Leofric George Alexander; 1891-1969), last British-born governor of Canada (1946-1952). He was known for his military achievements in both world wars and, in 1944, was named commander in chief of all Allied forces for Italy. Knighted (1942) and made Viscount Alexander of Tunis (1946), he then served as minister of defense for Britain (1952-1954).

Alexander the Great, or Alexander III (356-323 B.C.), king of Macedonia (336-323 B.C.). At 20 Alexander succeeded his father, Philip II of Macedon, and executed Philip's plans for freeing the Greeks of Asia Minor from Persian rule. After his defeat of the Persian king Darius III at Issus in 333, Alexander subdued Phoenicia and Egypt, founding Alexandria. In 331 Alexander again defeated Darius in the battle of Guagamela, after which the principal cities of the Persian Empire fell easily to his attack. He was proclaimed king of Asia and moved on eastward. He intended to conquer India, but his soldiers refused to follow him. Though he lived to be only 33, he conquered the greatest empire yet known in Western civilization and prepared the way for the Hellenistic Age.

Alexandria (pop. 3,328,000), chief port and second-largest city of Egypt. Founded by Alexander the Great c. 332 B.C., it was the capital of Ptolomaic Egypt and a center of trade and learning in the Hellenistic and Roman worlds. The city has grown into Egypt's principal channel for foreign trade. *See also:* Seven Wonders of the Ancient World.

A flushed Alexander in the Battle of Issus (333 B.C.) on a fragment from the famous mosaic, found in the 'House of the Faun' at Pompei (Naples, Museo Nazionale).

Alexandrian Library, in antiquity, the greatest collection of manuscripts, first assembled in the 3rd century B.C. The library, containing more than 400,000 scrolls, was housed in Alexandria, Egypt. It was probably destroyed in stages during sieges starting with Julius Caesar's in 47 B.C.; its destruction is thought to have been complete by 400 A.D.

Alexandrite, variety of the mineral chrysoberyl, discovered in 1833 and named for Tsar Alexander II. It has brilliant luster and is predominantly green, but changes col-

ors when viewed from different directions or in different light.

Alfalfa, or lucerne (*Medicago sativa*), legume widely grown for pasture, hay, and silage. The high protein content of this perennial makes it an excellent food for livestock, and the nitrogen-fixing bacteria on its roots are important in enriching depleted soil.

al-Fatah (Lit.: the victory) First and greatest Palestine liberation movement founded in 1956. Yasir Arafat, chairman of the Palestine Liberation Organization (PLO), was co-founder and has been its leader since then. Its main aim is to found a democratic Palestinian state. Its military wing, called al-Asifa (the storm), launched its first attack on Israel in 1965 and was incorporated in the PLO when al-Fatah joined the Palestine National Council (1968). Arafat's leadership was questioned when the party took the view that Arafat made too many concessions to Israel during the negotiations about occupied territories in the early nineties of the 20th century. At the elections for the Palestine Council (1996) al-Fatah received the most seats; the presidential election was won by Arafat.

Alfonso XIII (1886-1941), king of Spain from birth until 1931. Because of the unrest during his reign, Alfonso supported Primo de Rivera's establishment of a military dictatorship in 1923. The dictator fell from power in 1930, however, and the outcome of the elections in 1931 was so pro-republican that Alfonso, although not abdicating the throne, left Spain, and a republic was established. *See also:* Juan Carlos I.

Alfred the Great (A.D. 848-899), king of the West Saxons from 871. He halted the Danish invasions with his victory at Edington (878), making his kingdom of Wessex the nucleus of a unified England. He also introduced educational and legal reforms, translated Latin works into English, and began the *Anglo-Saxon Chronicle*, an important source for Anglo-Saxon history.

Algae, large and diverse group of nonvascular (rootless and stemless) aquatic plants that contain chlorophyll and carry on photosynthesis, including some of the simplest organisms known. They range in size from microscopic single-celled organisms to strands of seaweed several yards long. Most species of green algae, which are found mainly in freshwater, are microscopic. Brown algae include the familiar seaweeds found on rocky shores. Red algae, found mostly in warmer seas, include several species of economic importance. Algae are important as the basis of food chains. Many of the larger algae are used in foodstuffs, in medicine, and as manure. *See also:* Eutrophication; Seaweed.

Algebra, branch of mathematics in which relationships between known and unknown quantities are represented symbolically. For a relationship to satisfy the fundamental theorem of algebra it must consist of a finite number of quantities and must have a solution. An example of such a relationship taken from elementary alge-

bra is: $ax^n + bx^{n-1} + cx^{n-2} + \ldots + z = 0$

This is an 'n degree' polynomial equation (of order n). Here x is a variable denoting an unknown quantity to be found, and a, b, c...z represent known values. Elementary algebra, the algebraic system most familiar to the general public, uses operations of arithmetic to solve equations from sets of numbers. Abstract algebra developed from elementary algebra by mathematicians attempting to solve specific problems. Mathematical structures such as fields, rings, and groups were devised. Concepts of abstract algebra have been used by theoretical physicists in the development of quantum theory as well as by digital communications engineers in the development of coding theory. Linear algebra is used to solve simultaneous linear equations and is applied extensively in economics and psychology. Manipulations of equations are accomplished through the use of matrices and vectors. Boolean algebra is a symbolic representation of classical logic developed in 1854 by George Boole. Operations such as union and intersection are used. This algebraic system is used in computer science.

Gradual introduction of algebraic symbols occurred between 2000 B.C. and 1550 A.D. *Arithmetica*, regarded as the first treatise on algebra, was written by Diophantus of Alexandria in the 3rd century A.D. The Arabs became leaders in the field in about the 9th century. It was not until the 16th and 17th centuries in Europe that algebra underwent a complete transformation and became almost completely symbolic, much as it is today. Abstract algebra developed in the early 19th century, with major contributions by Niels Abel and Evariste Galois.

Algeria

Capital:	Algiers
Area:	919,595 sq mi
	(2,381,741 sq km)
Population:	32,278,000
Language:	Arabic
Government:	Republic
Independent:	1962
Head of gov.:	Prime minister
	(appointed by president)
Per capita:	U.S. $5,600
Monetary unit:	1 Algerian dinar (DA)
	= 100 centimes

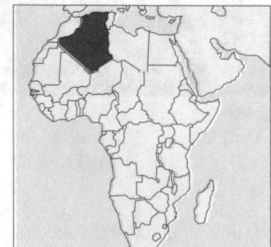

Algeria, country in northwest Africa; bordered by Mauritania, Morocco, and Western Sahara in the west, the Mediterranean Sea in the north, Tunisia and Libya in the east, and Niger and Mali in the south.
Land and climate. The Atlas Mountains divide the large country (919,590 sq mi/2,381,741 sq km) into the coastal region (Tell), the steppe, and the desert. Some 75% of the Algerians live in the narrow fertile coastal area.
People. Algeria's population is predominantly Arab and 99% follows the Sunni denomination of Islam. Berbers are an important minority. More than half of the population is literate. Most Algerians still live on their land, and farms yield citrus fruits, grapes, grain, and vegetables.
Economy. Algeria is an important oil-producing country and a primary exporter of liquified natural gas. However, the economy is burdened with high levels of debt repayment.
History. The Phoenicians settled North Africa around 1200 B.C. The area belonged to Carthage, then to Rome, and became the Roman province of Numidia in 201 B.C. Subsequently, Algeria was conquered by Vandals, Byzantines, and Arabs. From the 16th to the 18th centuries, Algeria was home to the Barbary pirates and the slave trade. The French took and colonized Algeria (1830-1909), governing until the nationalist revolt (1954-1962) led by the National Liberation Front (FLN), in which at least 100,000 Muslims and 10,000 French soldiers died. Algeria became independent on July 3, 1962. In the 1990s Algeria had to deal with severe economic problems. This situation was aggravated by the continuous assaults made by fundamentalist Muslims, in which more than half a million civilians lost their lives. Islamic fundamentalists had become a major political force. In 1992 the army cancelled part of the elections to prevent a fundamentalist takeover after the assassination of the newly chosen president Mohammed Boudiaf. A five-member High State Council was formed to temporarily replace the presidency; in 1994 it appointed a new president, Lamine Zeroual. In 1995 Zeroual was elected president. Revisions to the constitution, which were passed in 1996, included such changes as banning political parties based on religion and creating a two-chamber legislature. In 1997, multiparty elections for the new legislature were held; these were the first such elections since 1991. In the years following the cancelled elections of 1992, fundamentalists carried out a terrorist campaign of murder, targeting government, employees, intellectuals, Westernized citizens, and foreigners. The government retaliated with counterinsurgency measures. By 1997, more than 60,000 people had been killed in the conflict. In 1999 Abdelaziz Bouteflika became the new president. After massive Berber rebellions in 2001, their language, Tamazight, was acknowledged as an official language. The parliamentary elections of 2002 were won by the Front de Libération National (FLN), prime minister Ali Benflis's political party.

Algiers (pop. 1,500,000), capital, major port, and largest city of Algeria. Founded by Berbers in A.D. 935 on the site of the Roman settlement of Licosium, it was taken by the French in 1830. The modern city lies at the base of a hill overlooking the Bay of Algiers; higher up the slope is the old Moorish city, dominated by the Casbah, a citadel built by the Turks.

ALGOL (computers), Short for ALGOrithmic Language. High-level computer programming language used in particular to solve mathematical problems.

Algonquins, or Algonkins, North American Native Americans. They were driven out of their territory along the St. Lawrence and Ottawa rivers by the Iroquois in the 17th and 18th centuries.

Algren, Nelson (1909-1981), U.S. naturalistic novelist, best known for his fiction describing Chicago slum life. Among his works are *Never Come Morning* (1942), *The Man with the Golden Arm* (1949), and *A Walk on the Wild Side* (1956).

Alhambra (Arabic, 'The Red'), 13th-century citadel and palace dominating the city of Granada, the finest large-scale example of Moorish architecture in Spain.
See also: Moors.

Ali, Muhammad (Cassius Marcellus Clay; 1942-), U.S. boxer. Ali won an Olympic gold metal in 1960 and the heavyweight

Muhammad Ali, the flamboyant threetime heavyweight boxing champion, was known for his precise punching and great speed.

championship from Sonny Liston in 1964. He was stripped of this title in 1967 by the World Boxing Association while appealing a conviction for draft evasion, later overturned. One of the greatest and most outspoken heavyweights in boxing history, he defeated George Foreman for the title in 1974, lost it in 1978 to Leon Spinks, and won it back from Spinks later that year. Larry Holmes defeated Ali in 1980. Ali changed his name after adopting the Black Muslim religion in 1964. In 1998 Ali became a UN ambassador for peace. *Ali*, the movie about his life, premiered in 2002.

Ali Baba, main character in the story in *1,001 Nights*, 'Ali Baba and the Forty Thieves.' A poor woodcutter, he discovers that the magic words 'Open, Sesame' will open the door to a secret cave containing stolen treasure. The thieves plan to kill him but are outwitted by the slave girl Morgana.

Alibi, in law, a defense made by the accused in a criminal case. The word *alibi* is Latin for 'elsewhere'. The accused tries to establish that at the time the crime was committed he or she was at some place other than where it was committed.

Alienation, one's estrangement from society and from oneself. According to the 19th-century social and economic philosopher Karl Marx, the sale of labor power and the general conditions of production and exchange under capitalism deprive the individual of his or her essential humanity.

Alimentary canal, passage from the throat to the anus functioning in digestion and absorption of food.
See also: Digestive system.

Alkali, water-soluble compound of an alkali metal that acts as a strong base and neutralizes acids. Common alkalis are sodium hydroxide ($NaOH$), ammonia (NH_3), and sodium carbonate (Na_2CO_3). Alkalis are used to manufacture glass, soap, paper, and textiles.

Alkaloid, any of a group of organic alkali compounds found in certain plants and fungi, containing carbon, hydrogen, and nitrogen. Many alkaloids are poisonous; others, such as morphine, nicotine, and cocaine, can be addictive. Other alkaloids are caffeine and quinine. In small doses alkaloids are powerful medicines, used as analgesics, tranquilizers, and cardiac and respiratory stimulants.

Alkalosis, condition wherein the concentration of alkali in the body cells and tissues is higher than normal.
See also: Acidosis.

The oasis of El Goléa in the Algerian Sahara, with its houses that are made from dried clay.

A

A

Allah, Arabic name (*al-ilah*) for the supreme being, used by the prophet Muhammad to designate the God of Islam.

The Muslim name for God, Allah, in Arabic script and surrounded by ornamental designs, is used as a decorative emblem of Islam. Believing in Allah is the basis of the Muslim faith, and the naming of Allah is an affirmation of absolute submission to the benevolent and just rule of God.

Allahabad (pop. 885,000), city in the state of Uttar Pradesh, northern India. Situated at the confluence of the sacred rivers Ganges and Jumna, Allahabad is the goal of many Hindu pilgrims and the site of India's oldest universities.

Allegheny Mountains, central Appalachian range extending from southwest Virginia into north-central Pennsylvania. The Alleghenies average heights of 2,000 ft (610 m) in the north and more than 4,500 ft (1,372 m) in the south.

Allegory, literary work in which characters and concrete images are used to represent abstract philosophical or moral notions. John Bunyan's *Pilgrim's Progress* and Edmund Spenser's *Faerie Queene* are classic English-language allegories.

Allen, Mark (1958-) U.S. triathlete who gained his first international success in 1982 by winning the prestigious Nice triathlon. Allen is considered one of the world's strongest triathletes, which is evident from his victories at various distances. He managed to win the Nice triathlon a further eight times, followed by various other international competitions. In 1989 Allen won the Hawaii Ironman for the first time with a world recordbreaking time of 8 hours, 9 minutes and 14 seconds. He went on to win this competition from 1990 to 1993, which earned him the honorary title 'Lord of the Lava'.

Allen, Richard (1760-1831), first bishop and founder of the African Methodist Episcopal Church. Born a slave, he was raised on a plantation in Delaware, becoming a Methodist at age 17. He bought his freedom (1786) and moved to Philadelphia, where he organized an Independent Methodist Church to better serve black people. He was ordained a minister in the Methodist Church (1799) and later founded the African Methodist Episcopal Church (1816), the first black denomination in the United States.

Allen, Woody (Allen Stewart Konigsberg; 1935-), U.S. comedian, author, and film director. A self-effacing wit established him as a major comedic talent of the 1960s and 1970s. Following a nightclub career he broke into films (1965) and wrote, directed, and starred in successes like *Bananas* (1971), the Academy Award-winning *Annie Hall* (1977), *Crimes and Misdemeanors* (1989), *Scenes from a Mall* (1991), *Manhattan Murder Mystery* (1993) *Deconstructing Harry* (1997), *Small Time Crooks* (2000), and *Hollywood Ending* (2002).

Allenby, Edmund Henry Hynman, 1st Viscount (1861-1936), British field marshal who directed the campaign that won Palestine and Syria from the Turks in World War I. From 1919 to 1925 he was British high commissioner in Egypt.

Allende, Isabel (1942-) Chilean author who writes in Spanish, a cousin of the president of Chili who was murdered in 1973. A journalist at the time, she went into exile, first to Venezuela and later to the U.S. Her first novel written in 1982, *The House of the Spirits*, a wonderful family saga with a political and historical background, was immediately a worldwide success. The same applied to *Of Love and Shadows* (1984), *Eva Luna* (1987), an exotic chronicle about the passionate life of a woman, *The Stories of Eva Luna* (1990), and *The Infinite Plan* (1991). All her books contain autobiographical elements, which is particularly the case in *Paula* (1994), where she looks back on the period her daughter was in a coma.

Allende Gossens, Salvador (1908-1973), Marxist founder of the Chilean Socialist Party, president of Chile (1970-73). His radical reform program disrupted the economy; strikes and widespread famine led to a military coup and to his death, reportedly by murder or suicide.

Allergy, abnormal sensitivity to specific foreign material (an allergen). The allergy sufferer produces an antibody that combines with antigens, causing certain chemicals to be released, producing allergy symptoms. In the skin, this appears as eczema or urticaria (hives); in the nose and eyes, hay fever results; in the gastrointestinal tract, diarrhea may occur. In the lungs, there may be a spasm of the bronchi (airways), leading to the wheezing and breathlessness of asthma. Common allergens include drugs (penicillin, aspirin), foods (shellfish), plant pollens, animal furs or feathers, insect stings, and the house dust mite.

Alliance for Progress, program to aid the economic and social development of Latin America, instituted by President John F. Kennedy in 1961 and brought into being when 22 nations and the United States signed the Charter of Punta del Este. The Latin American countries drew up development plans and guaranteed the larger part of capital costs, the United States meeting the remainder. Most U.S. funds are administered by the Agency for International Development, and since 1970 the Organization of American States (OAS) has also reviewed and coordinated programs.
See also: Organization of American States.

Allies, during World War I, nations bound together in opposition to the Central Powers. The Allies included the members of the Triple Entente, as well as Serbia, Belgium, Japan, Italy, and, as an 'associated power,' the United States. During World War II 'Allies' was the popular term for some 25 nations that opposed the Axis powers. The major nations among the Allies were the United States, Britain, Russia, China, and later, the Free French. These 5 became the permanent members of the UN Security Council, established in 1945.

Alligator, either of 2 species of aquatic, carnivorous, lizardlike reptiles (genus *Alligator*) belonging to the crocodile family. The American alligator (*A. mississipiensis*), which lives in the southeastern United States, generally reaches a length of 9 ft (2.7 m), but the rare Chinese alligator (*A. sinensis*) is much smaller. An adult American alligator is gray and dark green in color, weighs about 500 pounds, and lives to 50 or 60 years old. The females make excellent mothers and protect the newborn for over a year. Alligators like to eat fish, frogs, turtles, birds, and small mammals.

Alliluyeva, Svetlana (1926-), daughter of Joseph Stalin and his second wife Alliluyeva. She defected from the USSR to the United States in 1966. Her *Twenty Letters to a Friend* (1967) described her life in Moscow and the reasons for her departure. *Only One Year* (1969) tells of her life after her defection. In 1984 she returned to the USSR.

Allopathy, standard form of medical practice, producing a condition incompatible with or antagonistic to the condition being treated; the opposite of homeopathy.
See also: Homeopathy.

Allotropy, occurrence of an element in 2 or more forms (allotropes) that differ in their crystalline or molecular structure. Allotropes may have strikingly different physical or chemical properties. Allotropy in which the forms are stable under different conditions and are reversibly interconvertible at certain temperatures and pressures is called anantiotropy. Notable examples of allotropy are diamond and graphite (allotropes of carbon) and oxygen and ozone.

Alloy, combination of metals with each other or with nonmetals, such as carbon or phosphorus, and formed by mixing the molten components. An alloy's properties can be adjusted by varying the proportions of the constituents. Very few metals are used today in a pure state. The most common alloys are the different forms of steel, all of which contain a large proportion of iron and small amounts of carbon and other elements. Brass and bronze, 2 well-known alloys of

copper, are still used in industry.
See also: Metallurgy; Permalloy.

Allspice, dried berry of the pimento, an evergreen tree (*Pimenta officinalis*) of the myrtle family, used as a spice and for medicinal purposes.
See also: Pimento.

Allston, Washington (1779-1843), U.S. painter. After studying in London and Rome, he lived in the Boston area. He was noted for paintings on biblical and classical themes, such as *Belshazzar's Feast* and *The Deluge*. He was one of the first romantics in the United States to show a preference for classical landscapes in the style of Claude Lorrain and Salvator Rosa.

Alluvial fan, fan-shaped deposit of sediment composed of gravels, sands, and silts. When a stream suddenly diminishes in speed before entering a large body of water or a valley, an alluvial fan is formed.

Alluvium, sand, mud, or other earthly material deposited by rivers and streams, especially in the lower parts of their courses. The deltas of some rivers, for example, the Ganges, the Nile, and the Mississippi, consist of great masses of alluvial deposits. The meadows or plains flanking many rivers have been built up of alluvium and often receive further accumulations during floods.

Alma Ata, or **Almaty**
(pop. 1,147,000), Kazakhstan, the nation's capital and largest city. It lies in the southeastern part of the country in the foothills of the Tien Shan. Almaty is a major rail hub and industrial center, with textile, food-processing, engineering, and printing industries. The Kazakh Academy of Sciences, the Kazakh State University, the National Library, the Central State Museum, and several performing-arts organizations are here. The city was founded as a Russian military post in 1854. It was known as Verny until 1921, when it acquired its present name. In 1929 Almaty became the capital of the Kazakh Soviet Socialist Republic, a part of the Soviet Union. After the collapse of the Soviet Union in 1991, the city became the capital of Kazakhstan.

Almagro, Diego de *See:* Pizarro, Francisco.

Almanac, originally, a calendar giving the position of the planets, the phases of the moon, etc., particularly as used by navigators (nautical almanacs), but now any yearbook of miscellaneous information, often containing abstracts of annual statistics.
See also: Banneker, Benjamin.

Almond, tree (*Prunus amygdalus*) of the rose family, native to Asia, the seed of whose fruit is used as food and flavoring and for medicinal purposes. It usually grows 10-20 ft (3-6 m) high and has spear-shaped, finely serrated leaves on thorny branches. The large flowers usually occur in pairs and are rose to white in color.

Aloe, any of the succulent plants (genus *Aloe*), of the lily family. Aloes are natives of warm climates and especially abundant in Africa. Some aloes are used medicinally for treatment of burns, as insect repellents, and for pigment.

Alpaca (*Lama pacos*), South American hoofed herbivorous mammal, closely related to the llama. It has a long body and neck, and is about 3 ft (1 m) high at the shoulder. Its long, thick coat of black, brown, or yellowish hair provides valuable wool. All alpacas are domesticated, living in the Andes above 13,000 ft (3,962 m).
See also: Llama; Vicuña.

Alphabet (from first 2 Greek letters, *alpha* and *beta*), set of characters intended to represent the sounds of spoken language. The chief alphabets of the world are Roman (Latin), Greek, Hebrew, Cyrillic (Slavic), Arabic, and Devanagari (used for Sanskrit). Alphabets probably originated around 2000 B.C. Hebrew, Arabic, and other written languages sprang from an alphabet that appeared around 1500 B.C. Greek was derived from the Phoenician alphabet, which appeared around 1700 B.C. Roman letters were derived from Greek and from Etruscan, also a descendant of the Greek. Most of the letters used in English are from the Latin alphabet. The Cyrillic alphabet, used for Slavic languages, also derives from the Greek.

Alpha Centauri, star 4.3 light-years (about 26 trillion miles) from the earth; only the sun is nearer. It is the brightest star in the constellation Centaurus and the third brightest star in the sky.

Alpha Orionis *See:* Betelgeuse.

Alpha particle (α-, or alpha ray), one of the particles emitted in radioactive decay. It is identical with the nucleus of the helium atom, consisting of 2 protons plus 2 neutrons bound together. A moving alpha particle is strongly ionizing and so loses energy rapidly in traversing through matter. Natural alpha particles will traverse only a few centimeters of air before coming to rest.
See also: Radiation; Radioactivity; Nuclear energy.

Alphonsus Liguori, Saint (1696-1787), Italian priest who founded the Congregation of the Most Holy Redeemer (Redemptorist Order), a society of missionary preachers working with the rural poor. He was canonized in 1839.

Alps, Europe's largest mountain system, 650 mi (1000 km) long and 30-180 mi (50-290 km) wide. Its fold mountains resulted from earth movements in the Tertiary period. The Western Alps run along the French-Italian border and include Mont Blanc, the highest Alpine peak at 15,771 ft (4,807 m). The Central Alps run northeast and east through Switzerland. The Eastern Alps extend through southern Germany, Austria, and northern Italy into Yugoslavia. Peaks are snowy and etched by ice action. The Alps are known for their many glaciers, glacially deepened valleys, and magnificent scenery.

Al-Qaida, Islamic fundamentalistic terrorist group, supposed to be established by Osama bin Laden in the late 1980s to bring together Arabs who fought in Afghanistan against the Soviet Union. Al-Qaida helped finance, recruit, transport, and train Islamic extremists for the Afghan resistance against the Soviets. In the 1990s al-Qaida came in the news by a number of spectacular terroristic attacks on western targets, culminating in the attacks of September 11, 2001, on the World Trade Center in New York and the Pentagon in Washington. After that the U.S. declared the `war against terrorism', specifically aimed at eliminating al-Qaida and Osama bin Laden.
See also: Osama bin Laden; Pentagon, The.

Alsace-Lorraine (pop. 4,000,000), region in northeast France occupying 5,608 sq mi (14,525 sq km) west of the Rhine. It produces grains and grapes; timber, coal, potash, and salt (Vosges Mts.); iron ore; and textiles. Metz, Nancy, Strasbourg, and Verdun are the chief cities. The people are of French and German origin. France and Germany have long disputed control of the area. In medieval times both Alsace and Lorraine were part of the Holy Roman Empire. France took Alsace after 1648 and Lorraine in 1766. Germany seized most of the region in 1871 in the Franco-Prussian War, lost it to France after World War I, regained control in World War II, then lost it again.

Alston, Walter Emmons (1911-1984), baseball manager. The low-keyed man of baseball, he led the Brooklyn (later Los

A

Cleft, in the Bossons glacier near Chamonix in the French Alps.

A

Angeles) Dodgers to 7 National League pennants and 4 World Series championships (1955, 1959, 1963, and 1965).

Altai Mountains, mountain system in central Asia stretching across part of the USSR and the Mongolian People's Republic. Consisting of a number of parallel ranges, the Altai region is similar in geological character to the Alps but covers a larger area. The highest peak is Mt. Belukha (15,157 ft/4,620 m). Rich in minerals (gold, silver, copper, tin, lead, zinc, iron), the Altai Mountains supply the Soviet Union with large quantities of metals, particularly lead and zinc.

Altamira, cave near Santander, northern Spain, inhabited during the Aurignacian, upper Solutrean, and Magdalenian periods (14,000 B.C.-10,000 B.C.). In 1879 the daughter of an amateur archaeologist discovered the striking cave paintings, believed to date from the Magdalenian period. They skillfully depict larger-than-life bulls, boars, and horses, among other paleolithic animals.

Altdorfer, Albrecht (1480?-1538), a German painter and engraver. He was one of the first artists to paint landscapes for their own sake, without human figures. *Landscape near Regensburg* is characteristic of his romantic interpretations of the Danube valley. In other works, such as *Battle of Alexander* and *St. George in the Forest*, he set small, detailed figures in elaborate landscape backgrounds. Altdorfer also did many drawings and etchings of the Bavarian forests. Little is known about his early life. He worked in Regensburg, where he was the city architect and a councilman.

Alternating current, electrical signal that reverses direction at regular intervals. The frequency of alternation is measured in cycles per second (hertz); U.S. household current is 60 hertz.

Alternation of generations, in many lower plants and animals, alternation of 2 distinct forms. One form reproduces sexually and gives rise to the other form, which reproduces asexually. The offspring of the generation that reproduces asexually usually reproduce sexually again, but under certain conditions several asexual generations may follow each other.
See also: Plant.

Altimeter, instrument used for estimating the height of an aircraft above sea level. Most are modified aneroid barometers and work on the principle that air pressure decreases with increased altitude, but these must be constantly recalibrated during flight to take account of changing meteorological conditions (local ground temperature and air pressure). Radar altimeters, which compute absolute altitudes (the height of the aircraft above the ground surface immediately below) by measuring the time taken for radar waves to be reflected to the aircraft from the ground, are essential for blind landings.
See also: Barometer.

Alum, class of double sulfates containing aluminum and such metals as potassium, ammonium, and iron.
See also: Salt, chemical.

Alumina, or aluminum oxide, chemical compound (Al_2O_3). Found in bauxite ore, it is used in the production of aluminum, and also as an abrasive in ceramics.
See also: Aluminum.

Aluminum, chemical element, symbol Al; for physical constants see Periodic Table. Aluminum in the form of its compounds has been used for hundreds of years. Potassium aluminum sulfate, the most common alum, continues to be used in medicine as an astringent, and as a mordant in dyeing. Aluminum was first isolated by Oersted in 1825 although in an impure form. It occurs primarily in the form of complex silicates, and is the third most abundant element on earth. The principal ore of aluminum is *bauxite*, a hydrated oxide. Aluminum is a soft, tin-white, reactive, metal, the most abundant metal in the earth's crust. Aluminum is prepared by electrolysis of *alumina* (aluminum oxide) in fused *cryolite*, a procedure known as the Hall-Héroult process. Aluminum oxide occurs naturally in other important and useful forms as ruby, sapphire, corundum, and emery. Aluminum has many valuable properties which account for its wide use. It is second in malleability and sixth in ductility of all metals. It is light and a good electrical conductor. Since aluminum is soft, it is almost always alloyed with small amounts of other elements. It is the second most important metal after iron.

Alva or Alba, Fernando Alvarez de Toledo, Duke of (1507?-1582), Spanish general who tyrannized the Netherlands. During his brutal campaign against rebellious Dutch Protestants (1567-73), he executed some 18,000 people. Hated for his atrocities and harsh taxes, and harassed by William the Silent's liberation army, Alva was recalled to Spain in 1573. In 1580 he conquered Portugal for Spain.

Alvarado, Pedro de (1485-1541), Cortés's chief lieutenant in the conquest of Mexico (1519- 21) and leader of the force that seized

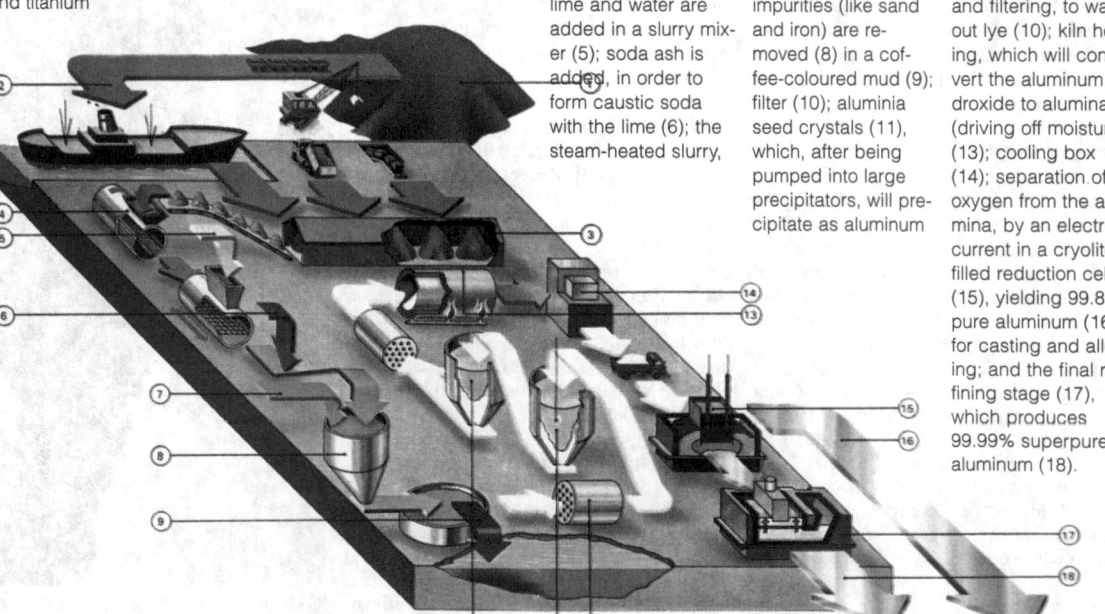

Aluminum is found naturally as an oxide in bauxite (a mixture of sand, aluminum, iron and titanium oxides). The illustration traces the many stages required in the processing of bauxite ore, in order to produce pure aluminum. The numbers indicate: a bauxite mine (1); transport of the ore (2); storage (3); a rod mill, to grind the ore (4); lime and water are added in a slurry mixer (5); soda ash is added, in order to form caustic soda with the lime (6); the steam-heated slurry, in which the alumina will dissolve in the caustic soda (7); the settling tanks, where impurities (like sand and iron) are removed (8) in a coffee-coloured mud (9); filter (10); aluminia seed crystals (11), which, after being pumped into large precipitators, will precipitate as aluminum hydroxide. This will follow a process of cooling and thickening, then settling (12) and filtering, to wash out lye (10); kiln heating, which will convert the aluminum hydroxide to alumina (driving off moisture) (13); cooling box (14); separation of oxygen from the alumina, by an electric current in a cryolite-filled reduction cell (15), yielding 99.8% pure aluminum (16) for casting and alloying; and the final refining stage (17), which produces 99.99% superpure aluminum (18).

what are now Guatemala and El Salvador (1523-24). As governor of Guatemala he instituted forced Indian labor and founded many cities.
See also: Cortés, Hernando.

Alvarez, Luis Walter (1911-1988), U.S. physicist awarded the 1968 Nobel Prize for physics for work on subatomic particles, including the discovery of transient resonance particles. He helped develop much of the hardware of nuclear physics. During World War II he worked on the development of radar and on the Manhattan (atomic bomb) Project.
See also: Bubble chamber.

Alzheimer's disease, progressive, incurable disease of the brain, the most common cause of premature senility. Its symptoms may include loss of memory, changes in personality, impaired language and motor skills, loss of control of bodily functions, and unresponsiveness. Currently it is difficult to diagnose and there is no specific treatment.
See also: Senility.

Amadís of Gaul, Spanish romance of chivalry. Garci Ordóñez de Montalvo is credited with the first known version, *The Four Books of the Virtuous Knight Amadís* (1508), although some evidence suggests that the story of Amadís, the medieval knight, may have been in circulation since the late 14th century. Cervantes' *Don Quixote* owes much to *Amadís*.

Amado, Jorge (1912-2001), Brazilian novelist, author of *The Violent Land* (1942), *Gabriela, Clove and Cinnamon* (1958), and *Doña Flor and Her Two Husbands* (English, 1969). His books are particularly concerned with the plight of the poor.

Amalfi (pop. 5,8000), seaport in the Campania region of Italy, on the Gulf of Salerno, near Naples. Built on a steep mountain slope and having a mild climate, it is a popular tourist center along the Amalfi Drive from Sorrento to Salerno. Amalfi became an important commercial and maritime center during the Middle Ages, for a time even rivaling Venice.

Amalgam, alloy of mercury with another metal, commonly used for tooth fillings.
See also: Metallurgy.

Amaranth, common name for plants of genus *Amaranthus*, including pigweed as well as plants grown as cereal and as ornamentals; also, a poetical name for a flower that never fades.
See also: Pigweed; Tumbleweed.

Amar Das (1479-1574), third guru of the Sikhs. The great organizer. Amar Das divided the land into 22 'dioceses' (regions). He maintained a casteless public eating-house. Amar Das reformed the Brahman ritual for marriage and death and banned pilgrimages. He opposed all kinds of excesses in Hindu society, such as the burning of widows. Many hymns of the Adi Granth are composed by him. His son Ramdas was his successor.

Amarna (Tell el Amarna, also: Akhetaton) Religious center in ancient Egypt founded by Amenhotep IV (ruled 1365-1349/47 B.C.) as part of a religious revolution to establish himself as an absolute ruler. Amenhotep stated that the sun god was the only god and banned all other forms of worship. By founding Amarna he tried to break the power of the priests in the traditional religious center of Thebe. His successor Tutankhamen restored the ancient customs.

Amaryllis, family of bulbous-rooted plants with lilylike flowers. Among the best-known of the 1,200 species are the true amaryllis, the narcissus, and the snowdrop.
See also: Narcissus.

Amasis II (569-525 B.C.), Egyptian pharaoh of the 26th dynasty. During his long reign, he developed strong ties with Greece, using mercenaries and maintaining relations with various Greek states. Egypt prospered under his enlightened rule and skilled diplomacy. He thwarted an invasion by Nebuchadnezzar, added Cyprus to his kingdom, and through marriage became very influential in Cyrene. He was the last great Egyptian ruler before the Persian conquest, which occurred soon after his death. Amasis (or Ahmose) is also the name of the lesser-known pharaoh (c.1580-87 B.C.) who rid Egypt of the Hyksos conquerors.

Amaterasu (Amaterasu Omikami = heavenly shining deity) Sun goddess, most important deity of Shintoism. According to myth, she was the daughter of the oldest pair of gods and born from the left eye of Izanagi. Appointed her grandson Ninigi to govern the earth. The first Japanese emperor, Jimmu Tenno, (whose reign probably began in 660 B.C.), came from his line. The temple of Amaterasu at Ise on Honshu is the most sacred shrine of Japan.

Amati, Nicola, the name of a family of violinmakers in Cremona, Italy. Their instruments rank with the Stradivari and Guarneri violins as the greatest ever made. Andrea Amati (1530?-1611?) is considered the designer of the modern violin. His amber-colored varnish came to be identified with the Amati violin. Other members of the family specialized in bass viols and cellos. Andrea's grandson, Niccolò (1596-1684), became the most famous member of the family. Antonio Stradivari and Andrea Guarneri were his pupils. Niccolò's son Girolamo (1649-1740) was the last famous Amati.

Amazonas (pop. 2,100,000), state in the north western part of Brazil; 604,266 sq mi (1,564,445 sq km). Capital: Manaus. Mainly covered with ancient forest. Population mainly spread along the Amazon. Production of rubber, timber, and nuts. Production of oil, coal, nickel, iron, and manganese.

Amazon River, world's second-longest river (3,900 mi/6,280 km). The Amazon rises in Andean Peru near the Pacific Ocean and flows east through the world's largest equatorial rain forest to the Atlantic Ocean. It is also the world's largest river in volume and drainage area. Its basin drains 40% of South America, and it has hundreds of tributaries. Most of the Amazon is navigable, and oceangoing vessels can travel 2,300 mi (3,700 km) to Iquitos in Peru. Other ports are Belém and Manaus in Brazil. The

Modern roads through the Amazonas cause discussion.

Amazon is important for commerce in hardwoods and other forest products.
See also: Brazil.

Amazons, in Greek mythology, race of warrior women living in the Black Sea area. Their name derives from the Greek word for 'breastless,' due to their alleged practice of removing the right breast to aid archery. For his ninth labor, Heracles (Hercules) was required to take the girdle of the Amazonian queen Hippolyta. Amazons fought on the side of Troy in the Trojan War.

Amber, fossilized resin from prehistoric evergreens. Brownish-yellow and translucent, it is highly valued and can be easily cut and polished for ornamental purposes. Its chief scientific importance is that fossil insects up to 20 million years old have been found embedded in it.
See also: Resin.

Ambergris, waxy solid formed in the intestines of sperm whales, perhaps to protect them from the bony parts of their squid diets. When obtained from dead whales, it is soft, black, and foul-smelling, but on weathering (as when found as flotsam) it becomes hard, gray, and fragrant, and is used as a perfume fixative and in the East as a spice. The heaviest piece of ambergris found in the intestine of a sperm whale weighed 1,003 lb (455 kg).
See also: Whale.

Amberjack (genus *Seriola*), large, elongated fish found in tropical oceans. The amberjack's superior swimming and fighting abil-

A

A

The Amazon River meanders without restriction through a wide flood plain. These flooded areas receive rich deposits of silt from the receding waters, leaving fertile ground.

The people of the Amazon have fished for centuries in these waters. The Amazon is a freshwater home for millions of fish. The pirarucu, catfish, and the ferocious piranha are but a few of the species in the Amazon.

A

Deforestation in the Amazon is a direct threat to many rare animals. The "slash and burn" method to claim farmland is an environmental disaster to the "green lungs" of South America.
Projects for reforestation (top right) of the tropical rainforest cannot undo the damage against which such original inhabitants as the Kaiapo (bottom left) protest in vain.

A

ities make it a popular game fish. Of the approximately 12 species of amberjacks, the greater amberjack (*S. dumerili*) is the largest, reaching a weight of more than 150 lb (68 kg) and a length of more than 5 ft (1.5 m).

Ambon (pop. 210,000), city in Indonesia on the island of the same name, capital of the province Maluku (Moluccas). Exports: spices and copra. The island of Ambon (Amboina; pop. 652,000, 294 sq mi,761 sq km) was conquered by the Dutch in 1605. In 1946 it became part of the state of East Indonesia. After the transfer of sovereignty to Indonesia, the South Moluccan Republic was proclaimed (1950). They waged a guerrilla war against Indonesia over a long period of time.

Ambrose, Saint (c. A.D. 340-397), important Father of the Latin Church. A Roman governor who became the influential bishop of Milan, he attacked imperial moral standards and strengthened the position of the Church amid the ruins of the Roman Empire by his preaching and writing. St. Augustine was one of his converts.

Ambrosia, fabled food of the ancient Greek gods, which conferred immortality on those who partook of it; hence, anything pleasing to the taste or smell.

Ameba, or amoeba, microscopic, one-celled organism that lives in moist earth, water, and parasitically in the bodies of animals. The ameba is a shapeless cell of jellylike materi-

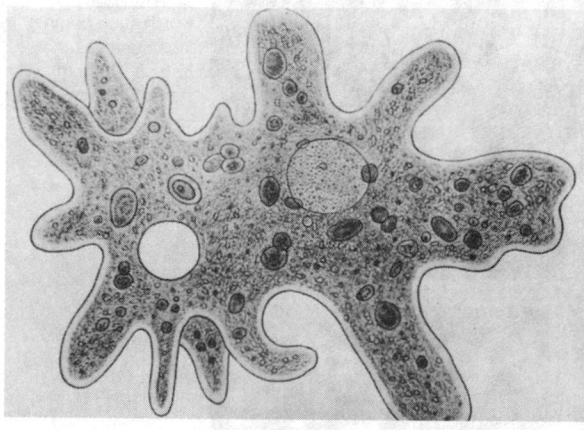

Ameba can take any shape by stretching would-be feet (pseudopodies), which help them to move and to feed. An amebe flows around his prey (phagocytose) and creates a feeding vacuole in which the digestion will take place.

al (protoplasm) encased in a thin membrane. It constantly changes shape by forming temporary projections called pseudopods (false feet) used for feeding and locomotion. The ameba reproduces by fission (splitting). Amebas are harmless to people, except for a type that inflames the lining of the large intestine, causing a disease called amebic dysentery.

Ameling, Elisabeth Sara (Elly) (1938-) Dutch vocalist (soprano). Made her debut in Amsterdam in 1961. Acquired international acclaim, in particular with her recitals. Also sings in oratorios and operas and performs as a soloist with orchestras. Her repertoire stretches from Händel to Gershwin. Received an Edison prize in 1965, 1970, and 1995. She stopped performing in 1996.

Amendment, in legislation, change in a bill or motion under discussion, or in an existing law or constitution.
See also: Parliamentary procedure; Constitution of the United States; Bill of rights.

America, the 2 major continents of the Western Hemisphere, North and South America (although the name is sometimes used to mean the United States). In 1507 the German geographer Martin Waldseemüller first gave the name to the area that is now Brazil in honor of the Italian navigator Amerigo Vespucci, who supposedly discovered much of South America.
See also: Vespucci, Amerigo.

American Academy and Institute of Arts and Letters, organization to promote literature, music, and the fine arts in the United States. Based in New York City, it was formed in 1976 from the merger of the National Institute of Arts and Letters (founded 1898) and the American Academy of Arts and Letters (founded 1904). The organization, consisting of 250 members who serve for life, makes awards to American writers, artists, and composers, sponsors exhibits of their works, and purchases works to donate to museums.

American Expeditionary Forces (AEF), name given to the U.S. forces serving in Europe during World War I. Its commander was General John Pershing. The first U.S. troops arrived in June 1917 and saw major action in May 1918, when they relieved the French at Château-Thierry and stopped a German advance. In June, some 6,000 U.S. marines were killed at Belleau Wood. U.S. forces were important in stemming the German counteroffensive in the second Battle of the Marne (July-Aug. 1918). By the end of the war the AEF held one-fourth of the line and had taken part in 13 battles, most of them major encounters. U.S. troops were at the front for a total of 200 days, with 1,993,000 men fighting at the end of the war. Over 100,000 members of the AEF were killed in action, a similar number died of disease (especially influenza), and more than 200,000 were wounded.
See also: Pershing, John Joseph; World War I.

American Indian Movement (AIM), civil rights organization in the United States and Canada, founded in 1968 to establish equal rights and improve living conditions of Native Americans. AIM has demanded the return of property rights as specified in U. S. and Canadian government treaties with various tribes, legal reform, and reform of education, employment, and health services for Native Americans.

American Library Association, society 'to extend and improve library service throughout the world.' Founded in Philadelphia (1876) by Melvil Dewey, it is the world's oldest and largest library association and has had great influence on library development in English-speaking countries, as well as in Scandinavia, the Netherlands, and Germany. With headquarters in Chicago, the organization has more than 50,000 members.

American literature, see: United States literature.

American Museum of Natural History, institution in New York City founded in 1869 and dedicated to research and public education in anthropology and natural science. It is noted for its mounted specimens of birds and other animals from all over the world, fossil collections including dinosaur skeletons, its gem collection, and the Hayden Planetarium.

American Philosophical Society, oldest surviving U.S. learned society, based in Philadelphia, where it was founded by Benjamin Franklin (1753). The U.S. counterpart of the Royal Society of London, it has nearly 600 U.S. and foreign members. It has an extensive library, much relating to Colonial science.

American Revolution *See:* Revolutionary War in America.

American Samoa, unincorporated U.S. territory in the South Pacific, about 2,300 mi (3,700 km) southwest of Hawaii, with a total area of 76 sq mi (197 sq km). The territory consists of 7 islands: Tutuila (site of the capital, Pago Pago), the Manua group (Aununu, Ofu, Tau, Olosega), Rose, and Swains. The region is mountainous and tropical. The native Polynesians speak Samoan and English, live in villages, and practice Christianity. The leading industry is tuna canning. Agricultural products include coconuts, bananas, and taro. Samoa was divided between the United States and Germany, by treaty, in 1899; the eastern portion was administered by the U.S. Navy until 1951, when it passed to the jurisdiction of the Department of the Interior. American Samoans are nationals, but not citizens of the United States. They elect a governor, a legislature, and a nonvoting delegate to the U.S. Congress.
See also: Pacific Islands.

American Society of Composers, Authors and Publishers (ASCAP), association that serves as a clearinghouse between creators and users of music. Founded in 1914, ASCAP grants licenses and collects fees to protect members from copyright infringement, covering performance as well as publication of music. The national headquarters are in New York City.

America's Cup, international yachting trophy. The cup, the oldest trophy in international sports, was held continuously by the United States from the first race in 1851 until 1983, when the *Australia II* defeated the U.S. yacht *Liberty*. The U.S. yacht *Stars & Stripes* defeated Australia's *Kookaburra* in 1987 to regain the cup. In 1988 controversy surrounded the U.S. use of a 60-ft (20-m) catamaran, *Stars & Stripes*, which defeated the challenger, the 133-ft (44.4-m) monohull *New Zealand*. *New Zealand*'s team claimed the catamaran was illegal, but after several U.S. court rulings *Stars & Stripes* was awarded the cup. To avoid controversy, all competitors had to use 75-ft (25-m) monohulls with a 110-ft (36.6-m) mast in the May 1992 America's Cup competition.

The 'Australia II' on its way to winning the America's Cup in 1983.

Americium, chemical element, symbol Am; for physical constants see Periodic Table. Americium was synthesized by Glenn Seaborg and co-workers in 1944 by bombardment of plutonium-234 with alpha particles at the wartime Metallurgical Laboratory of the University of Chicago (now the Argonne National Laboratory). It is produced in quantity by neutron irradiation of plutonium isotopes in a nuclear reactor. Americium is a reactive, radioactive, metal, obtained by reducing its trifluoride with barium vapor. It is a member of the actinide series. The element must be handled with special care because of its great alpha and gamma activity. Americium is used in gamma radiography, glass thickness gages, and in smoke detectors. Thirteen isotopes of americium are known.

Amerigo Vespucci *See:* Vespucci, Amerigo.

Amethyst, transparent violet or purple variety of quartz, thought to be colored by iron or manganese impurities. A semiprecious gem, it is used to make jewelry. Amethysts are mined in Brazil, Uruguay, North America, and the USSR.

Amiens (pop. 133,000), city in northern France, capital of the Somme department on the Somme River 80 mi (130 km) north of Paris. An important trade and manufacturing center, Amiens has been noted since the 16th century for its linens, woolens, silks, and velvets. Its Cathedral of Notre Dame, begun c.1220, is one of the finest examples of French Gothic architecture.

Amin Dada, Idi (1925-), president of Uganda (1971-1979). He led the military overthrow of President Milton Obote in 1971. A flamboyant and dictatorial ruler, he expelled Uganda's Asian middle class in 1972, called for the extinction of Israel in

1975, and purged many opponents. In 1975-1976 he was president of the Organization of African Unity. Insurrectionists, aided by Tanzanian forces, drove out Amin in 1979. After his exile to Saudi Arabia, his whereabouts were uncertain.

Amine, chemical compound formed from ammonia (NH_3) by replacing 1 or more hydrogen atoms of the ammonia molecule with a corresponding number of hydrogen-carbon groups.

Amino acids, class of organic acids containing a carboxyl group (COOH) and 1 or more (NH_2) groups. Amino acids are synthesized in cells and are the basis of proteins. Amino acids are white crystalline solids that are soluble in water; they can act as acids or bases depending on the chemical environment. All amino acids (except glycine) contain at least 1 asymmetric carbon atom to which are attached the carboxyl group, the amino group, a hydrogen atom, and a fourth group that differs for each amino acid and determines its character. Amino acids can exist in 2 mirror-image forms. Generally only L-isomers (left-turning) occur in nature, but a few bacteria contain D-isomers (right-turning). Organisms link amino acids in chains called polypeptides and proteins. Digestion breaks down these linkages. *See also:* Protein.

Amis, Kingsley (1922-1995), English novelist, poet, and critic. He emerged as a sharp satirist in *Lucky Jim* (1953), an attack on social and academic pretensions. Among his other works are *New Maps of Hell* (1960), *One Fat Englishman* (1964), *The Green Man* (1969), and *Jake's Thing* (1979).

Amis, Martin Louis (1949-) British author, son of Kingsley Amis. Amis describes the life of his generation though the use of cynical prose. His works include: *The Rachel Papers* (1973), *Success* (1978), *The Moronic Inferno: and Other Visits to America* (1986; a collection of morose travel accounts), *Einstein's Monsters* (1987), *London Fields* (1989), *Time's Arrow* (1991), *Visiting Mrs Nabokov and Other Excursions* (1993), *The Information* (1995), *Night Train* (1997), *Heavy Water* (1998), *Experience* (2000), and *Koba the Dread* (2002).

Amish, conservative group of the Mennonite sect, founded by Jacob Ammann in Switzerland in the 1690s. In the 18th century members settled in what are now Indiana, Ohio, and Pennsylvania. Their farm communities reject modern life, including electricity, telephones, and cars. *See also:* Mennonites.

Amman (pop. 1,700,000), largest city, capital, and commercial and industrial center of the kingdom of Jordan. Industries include food and tobacco processing, textiles, cement, and leatherware. It is a busy transport junction, with good rail and road connections to major Middle Eastern cities and an international airport. Arab refugees from Israel and Israeli-held territories of Jordan have greatly enlarged its population in recent years. Amman was the scene of heavy

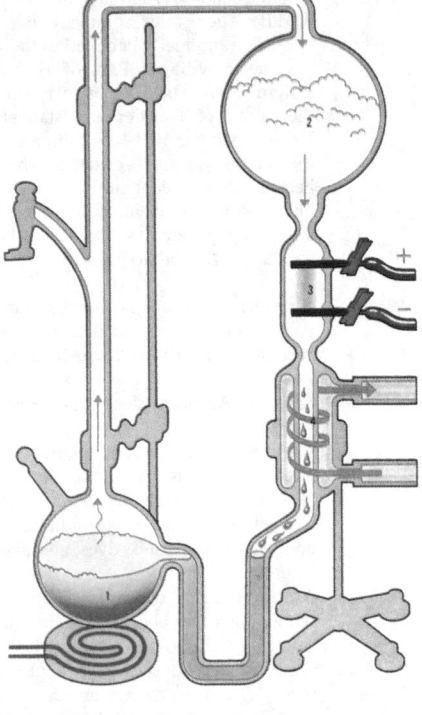

In 1953, the creation of the conditions for life was demonstrated by Stanley L. Miller, an American biochemist. He boiled a mixture of methane, ammonia, water, and hydrogen in a flask (1). The chemicals evaporated, and the vapors were mixed in another flask (2). These vapors were then subjected to electrical discharges (3), and condensed (4). The vapors and products were returned to the boiling flask. After several days of recirculation and reaction, the mixture was tested for newly synthesized chemicals. Miller found that several chemicals necessary for life, such as simple amino acids, sugars, and urea, were present in the flask. He hypothesized that primitive life was formed in the oceans of the world by a similar process, in which the chemicals were evaporated by the sun's heat, then exposed to electrical storms, and condensed by cold air currents.

fighting between government troops and guerilla forces of the Palestine Liberation Organization in 1970.

The modern city is built on the site of the Rabbath Ammon, the capital of the ancient Ammonites. Named Philadelphia in the third century B.C., it prospered under Greek,

Hexagonal (6-sided) amethyst ranked among the most precious of gems until the 18th century, after the discovery of large deposits in South America.

A

Roman, and Byzantine rule. During the Middle Ages, after coming under Muslim control, it gradually declined to the status of a caravan village. Part of the Ottoman Empire until World War I, Amman became the capital of Transjordan, established as a British mandate in 1920. Amman remained the capital and royal residence when Jordan became independent in 1946. Its extensive Greco-Roman ruins include baths, a fortress, a temple dedicated to Hercules, a huge theater, and a Byzantine basilica.

Ammeter, instrument for measuring amperes of electric current. The most commonly used ammeter is of the permanent-magnet moving-coil type.
See also: Ampere; Electromagnetism.

Ammonia, chemical compound (NH_3), colorless acrid gas. Ammonia is used as a cleaning fluid (with water), as a fertilizer, a refrigerant, and to make ammonium salts, urea, and many drugs, dyes, and plastics.

Ammonite, any one of a group of shelled sea animals that became extinct millions of years ago. Ammonites were mollusks whose shells ranged in size from about one-half inch (13 mm) to more than six feet (1.8 m) in diameter. They are known today only from the fossilized remains of their shells. Ammonite shells resemble the shells of the pearly nautilus, a living sea creature, in that they consist of a succession of chambers, with the animal occupying the outermost chamber. Ammonites flourished during the Triassic and Jurassic periods, and became extinct about 65 million years ago, at the end of the Cretaceous period.
The name 'ammonite' comes from the fact that many of the shells resemble the horns of the ancient Egyptian god Ammon, who sometimes was represented as a man with a ram's head.
Ammonites make up the suborder Ammonoidea of the class Cephalopoda, phylum Mollusca.

Amnesia, partial or complete loss of memory. It can result from concussions, senility, severe illness, or physical or psychological trauma, and is of varying duration.

Amnesty International, independant international organization founded in 1961 to aid political prisoners and others detained for reasons of conscience throughout the world. With thousands of members in the United States and around the world, it has advisory status with the UN and other international organizations. Amnesty International received the Nobel Prize for peace in 1977. Headquarters are in London.

Amniocentesis, procedure of sampling the amniotic fluid surrounding a fetus by puncturing the abdomen of the pregnant woman with a very fine, hollow needle. Cells and other substances shed into the amniotic fluid by the fetus are used for detecting the presence in the fetal genes of such disorders as Down's syndromė, Tay-Sachs disease, and spinal malformations.Amniocentesis also can be used to determine the sex of an unborn child with 98% accuracy.
See also: Genetic counseling.

Amoeba *See:* Ameba.

Amon, ancient Egyptian deity, sometimes depicted as a ram or a human with a ram's head. Chiefly worshipped in Thebes, he was identified with the sun god Re, and became known as Amon-Re, king of the gods. In Hellenistic times his temple and oracle were visited by many Greeks, who identified Amon with Zeus.

Amor, Asteroid no. 1221, discovered in 1932. Amor belongs to the group of asteroids known as Earth Crossers because their orbit brings them close to the earth. Amor makes a long drawn-out orbit around the sun with a revolution of 2,66 years. The perihelion of the orbit is approx. 7,460,000 mi (12 million km) outside the earth's or-

bit. Amor has a diameter of c. 0,310 mi (0.5 km).

Amos (8th century B.C.), Hebrew prophet; also, a book of the Old Testament containing his life and teachings. A shepherd from Judah, Amos proclaimed that there was one God for all peoples. In neighboring Israel, he denounced corruption until expelled by the king.

Ampere (amp or A), unit for measuring the rate of flow of an electric current. One ampere is defined as the current in each of 2 parallel wires when the magnetic force between them is 2×10^{-7} newtons per meter. It is named after André Marie Ampère, the French scientist.
See also: Ammeter; Ohm's law.

Ampère, André Marie (1775-1836), French mathematician, physicist, and philosopher best remembered for many discoveries in electrodynamics and electromagnetism. He expanded Hans Oersted's experiment on the interaction between magnets and electric currents and investigated the force set up between current-carrying conductors. He also made contributions in the fields of statistics, chemistry, optics, and crystallography.
See also: Ampere; Electromagnetism.

Amphetamine, any of a group of stimulant drugs, including Benzedrine and Methedrine, derived from the chemical compound amphetamine ($C_9H_{13}N$). Amphetamines counteract fatigue, suppress appetite, speed up performance (hence the slang 'speed'), and give the taker a false sense of confidence. Pronounced depression often follows use, encouraging psychological and then physical addiction. A paranoid psychosis resembling schizophrenia may result from prolonged use. Amphetamines have been used in the treatment of obesity and narcolepsy (a rare condition of abnormal sleepiness).

The ammonite, an extinct mollusk, probably had an internal anatomy that was similar to that of the present-day nautilus. The animal moved by rapidly ejecting water through a siphon tube. The shell was divided into air-filled chambers that were separated by septa, or walls. The animal lived in the outer open chamber, which could be closed with an operculum, or lid. A siphuncle, or tube connected all chambers, allowing air pressure regulation within. Thus, the animal could ei- ther sink or swim, by simply altering its buoyancy. The suture line, along which the septa joined the shell, had a characteristic pattern for each species. These patterns became more complex, as the ammonites evolved from the primitive Ceratites (A), through the intermediate Hildoceras (B), to the advanced Baculite forms (C). The blue arrows point to the head and siphuncle positions. The large variations in ammonite shell shapes indicate that some of them were active predators, others were drifters or bottom feeders.

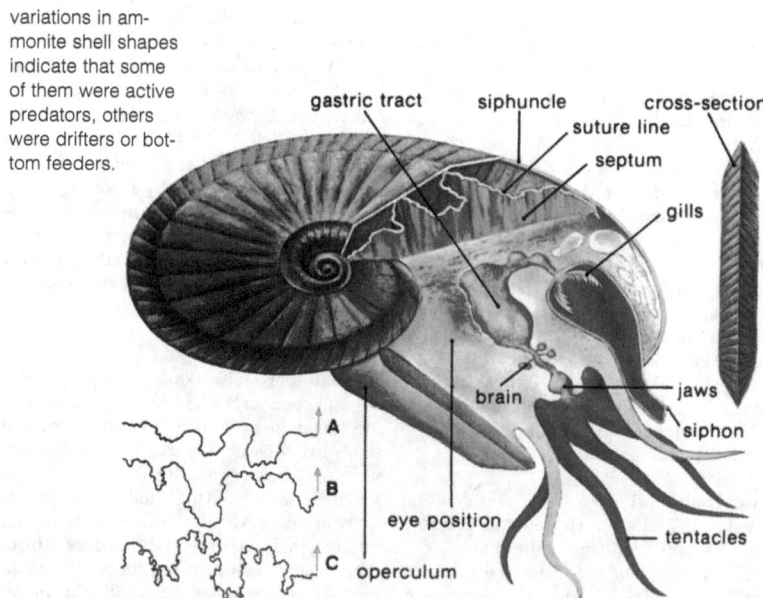

gastric tract | siphuncle | cross-section | suture line | septum | gills | brain | jaws | siphon | eye position | tentacles | operculum

Amphibian, class of cold-blooded vertebrates, including frogs, toads, newts, salamanders, and caecilians. Typically they spend part of their life in water, part on land. They are distinct from reptiles in that their eggs must be laid in moist conditions, and that their soft, moist skins have no scales. The larval amphibian is usually solely aquatic; the adult is partly or entirely terrestrial, generally 4-legged, and carnivorous.

Amphibious warfare, coordinated use of land and sea forces to seize a beachhead, an area from which to carry on further military action. Although naval and ground forces have often cooperated since the earliest days of warfare, the strategy of modern amphibious military operations did not develop fully until World War II. Specially outfitted ocean vessels were constructed, and landing craft were designed, capable of making long voyages to transport troops, weapons, and supplies, and then unload them ready for combat if they met concentrated enemy opposition. Allied operations against the Japanese in the Pacific and in the landings in Italy and Normandy during World War II were typical of this strategy.

Amphibole, any of a group of silicate minerals with similar chemical compositions and characteristic optical properties. Amphiboles are usually found in lava or very old rock strata. They form long slender crystals, which in asbestos become fine fibers. Hornblende is the most common amphibole.

Amphioxus, or lancet, a small, primitive, fishlike sea animal (genus *Branchiostoma*), important as a possible descendant of the evolutionary link between invertebrates and vertebrates.

Amphitheater, open edifice built in the Roman Empire for public viewing of contests and spectacles (e.g., the Colosseum in Rome). Usually oval in form, it comprises a central arena surrounded by ascending rows of seats. Gladiators and animals used in the spectacles were held under the arena. The term is now used loosely for any large auditorium.

Ampicillin, semisynthetic antibiotic that is a derivative of penicillin, used to treat a wide range of bacterial infections. Ampicillin can kill some bacteria not effectively killed by other forms of penicillin, and is used to treat severe ear and sinus infections, meningitis in children, and various infections of the urinary, respiratory, and intestinal tracts. Among the microorganisms susceptible to ampicillin are *Salmonella*, several species of which cause a type of food poisoning, and *Salmonella typhosa*, the cause of typhoid fever. Although penicillin is still widely prescribed, its effectiveness has decreased somewhat since its introduction in 1961, because certain bacteria have begun to develop resistance to it.
See also: Penicillin.

Amplitude, The maximum displacement of a vibrating point measured from its point of equilibrium. The amplitude of forced vibra-

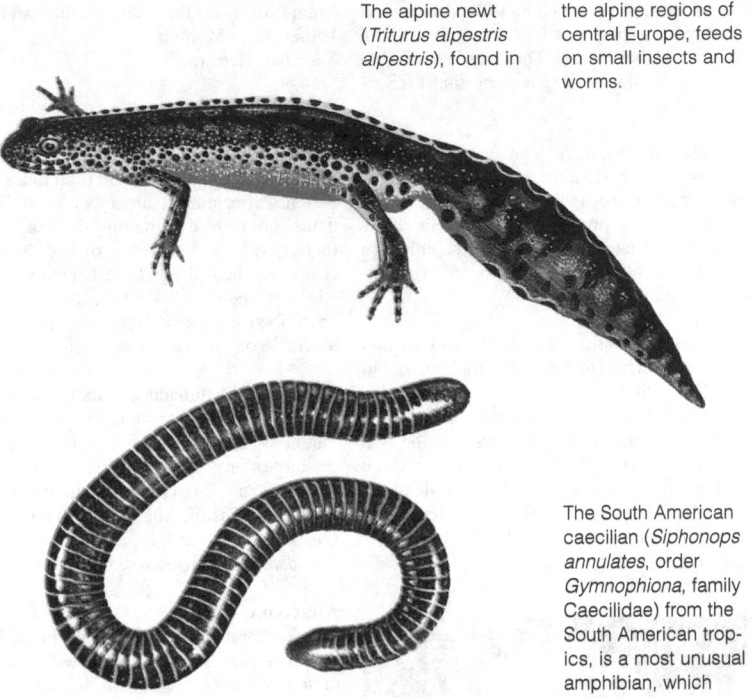

The alpine newt (*Triturus alpestris alpestris*), found in the alpine regions of central Europe, feeds on small insects and worms.

The South American caecilian (*Siphonops annulates*, order *Gymnophiona*, family Caecilidae) from the South American tropics, is a most unusual amphibian, which lives underground, probably feeding on earthworms. This caecilian is blind and his eyes are rudimentary. It incubates its eggs. Length about 46 cms.

tions has a constant value; the amplitude of damped vibrations steadily decreases and becomes almost zero.

Amritsar (pop. 767,000), city in Punjab state in northwest India. The center of the Sikh religion, it is the site of the *Amritsar* or sacred 'pool of immortality' in which Sikhs immerse themselves as an act of purification. The city is also an important industrial center, known for textiles and carpets. Amritsar was founded in 1577 by Ram Das, the fourth guru (leader) of the Sikhs. With the building of the temple, begun under Ram Das, the city grew, as a stronghold of Sikhism. Early in the 20th century it was the scene of many attacks against British authority. In 1919 British troops fired on a public meeting, killing 400 persons. The Amritsar Massacre, as it is sometimes called, spurred the nationalist movement throughout India.

Amsterdam (pop. 734,000), capital and largest city of the Netherlands, and one of Europe's great commercial, financial, and cultural centers. In the province of North Holland, it lies on the IJ and Amstel rivers, at the south end of Lake IJsselmeer. The city

center is built on a series of concentric semicircular canals. Other canals link it to the Rhine River and the North Sea and make Amsterdam one of Europe's major ports. It is also a major rail center and has an international airport. Amsterdam is a diamond-cutting center and produces chemicals, machinery, bicycles, electronics, beer, and textiles. It has an important stock exchange, two universities, and about 50 museums, and is home to major collections of works by Rembrandt and Van Gogh. Amsterdam grew from a medieval fishing village, becoming a major city by the 17th century. Amsterdam was under German occupation 1940-45.
See also: Netherlands.

Amu Darya, a river in Central Asia known as the Oxus in ancient times. It is formed by the Vakhsh and Pyandzh rivers, which flow from the Pamirs. The Amu Darya is about 1,600 miles (2,580 km) long. It flows generally northwestward, forming a delta near the Aral Sea. The Amu Darya marks part of

Amphioxus, found on sandy shores in temperate and tropical regions, length 5 cms.

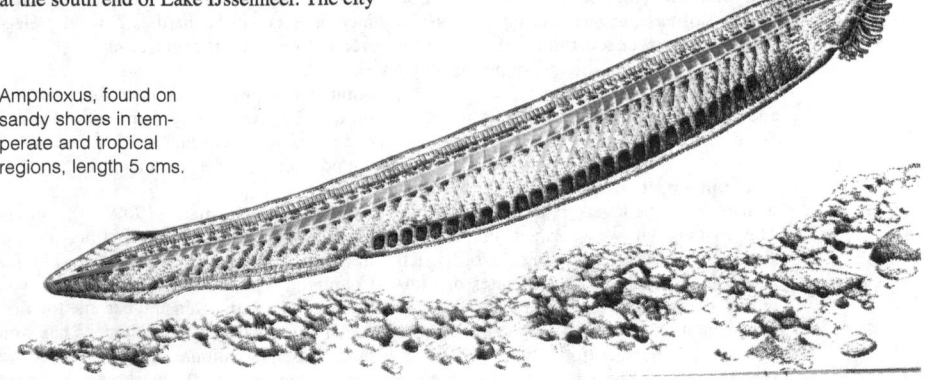

A

A

the Afghan-Tajik, Afghan-Turkmen, and Turkmen-Uzbek borders and all of the Afghan-Uzbek border. The river is navigable in its lower course and is important for irrigation.

Amulet, object carried on one's person to which special powers are attributed regarding (prevention) against illness, accidents, theft, and as protection in general. The amulet is related to the talisman, although the latter is also known as a power which attracts positive things.

Amundsen, Roald (1872-1928), Norwegian polar explorer. He was the first person to reach the South Pole (Dec. 14, 1911), his party beating the ill-fated Robert F. Scott expedition by one month. In the Arctic he was the first to navigate the Northwest Passage (1903-6), later crossing the North Pole in the dirigible *Norge* (1926). He was killed in the Arctic during an air search for the Italian explorer Umberto Nobile.
See also: Antarctica.

Roald Amundsen (1872-1928).

Amur, river in northeastern Asia. Formed by the Shilka and Argun rivers in Mongolia, it flows east through the USSR for 2,700 mi (4,300 km) to empty into the Pacific. For more than half its course it forms the boundary between the USSR and China.

Amyotrophic lateral sclerosis, or Lou Gehrig's disease, progressive fatal disease in which there is degeneration of the motor nerve cells of the brain and spine, resulting in progressive muscular atrophy, paralysis, and death from asphyxiation.
See also: Gehrig, Lou.

Anabaptism, movement advocating baptism of adult believers rather than infants. The first group was formed in 1523 at Zürich by dissatisfied followers of Ulrich Zwingli. Most stressed the dictates of individual conscience, and urged nonviolence and separation of church and state. Despite widespread persecution, their doctrines spread, forming the basis of belief for the

Mennonites in the Netherlands and the Hutterites in Moravia.
See also: Reformation.

Anabolic steroid, any of a group of steroids derived from the male sex hormone testosterone. They affect growth, muscle bulk, and protein buildup, and may be used in treating patients after major surgery or severe accidents or with debilitating disease, when there may be a breakdown of body protein. However, these drugs have been abused by athletes, and for this reason they are only prescribed by hospital doctors and are not available on normal prescriptions.

Anaconda, semiaquatic subfamily of the boa family. *Eunectes notaeus* is found in Paraguay and *Eunectes murinus*, probably the largest snake in the world-up to 25 ft (8 m) long and 3 ft (1 m) in circumference-throughout Brazil. Anacondas do not have a poisonous bite, but kill prey by constriction.
See also: Boa constrictor.

Anacreon (572-485? B.C.), Greek lyric poet who celebrated wine and love in mellow, simple verses. These were copied in the so-called Anacreontics, fashionable in the Hellenistic Age and again in 18th-century Europe. His main patrons were the tyrants of Samos and Athens.

Anagram, a word or group of words formed by transposing the letters of another word or group of words and bearing some relation in meaning to the original. For example, the sentence *Flit on, cheering angel* is an anagram of the name *Florence Nightingale*. (Nightingale was known as the 'Angel of the Crimea' for her work as a nurse during the Crimean War.)
The ancient Greeks believed that an anagram made from a person's name had some occult or mystical influence over that person's life and destiny. Anagrams were popular throughout Europe during the Middle Ages and later. King Louis XIII of France (1601-43) was so fond of them that he employed a court anagrammatist.

Anaheim (pop. 328,000), city in Orange County, southern California, southeast of Los Angeles. Settled in the 1850s by German immigrant grape growers, it became a prosperous center for handling the local citrus fruit. Now a tourist center, it is home to Disneyland (built 1955), the California Angels baseball team, and the Los Angeles Rams football team. Its diversified industry includes chemicals, hardware plants, electronics, and aircraft engineering.

Analog computer, computer that operates on data by representing them with physical quantities such as voltages. Most computers are now digital rather than analog.

Anand, Viswanathan (1969-   ), Indian chess prodigy, who had his first big success in 1984, when he won the Asian Junior Championship. The subsequent year he won the championship again and became the first Asian Grand Master. Since then, he has won numerous international, highly competitive tournaments all over the world. Anands most

succesful year was 2000, given the fact that he won the FIDE World Cup Barejev and the FIDE World Championship title in Teheran. His highest score was 2795 points in 1998.
See also: Chess.

Anarchism, political belief that government should be abolished and the state replaced by the voluntary cooperation of individuals and groups. Like socialists, anarchists advocate the abolition of the institution of private property. But unlike socialists, they believe that government is unnecessary and intrinsically harmful.
Pioneers of modern anarchism included England's William Godwin (1756-1836), France's Pierre Joseph Proudhon (1809-65), and the Russian revolutionary Mikhail Bakunin (1814-76). Emma Goldman (1869-1940) and Alexander Berkman (1870?-1936) were active U.S. anarchists who were deported for their actions (1919). After President William McKinley was assassinated by an anarchist in 1901, anarchists were barred from entering the United States.

December 9, 1893, anarchist Auguste Vaillant threw a bomb in the House of Representatives in France.

Although anarchism is now more important philosophically than politically, it has recently become linked with student radicalism in Europe and America.
See also: Nihilism.

Anastasia (1901-1918?), Russian grand duchess. Daughter of the last tsar, Nicholas II, she was probably murdered with her family during the Revolution. Several women later claimed to be Anastasia, but none could prove her identity.
See also: Russian Revolution.

Anatomy, study of the structure of plants and animals. The word is derived from a Greek verb meaning to cut up, since dissection was the main source of anatomical knowledge. Anatomy is closely related to physiology, the investigation of the functions and vital processes of living organisms. Gross anatomy is the study of the structures that can be seen with the naked eye, and mi-

croscopic anatomy, the investigation of minute parts of organs and tissues with the aid of a microscope. Comparative anatomy systematically compares the structures of different organisms.
See also: Human body.

Anaxagoras (500-428 B.C.), Greek philosopher of the Ionian school, resident of Athens, who taught that the elements were infinite in number and that everything contained a portion of every other thing. He also postulated a basic moving force of the universe, *Nous* or Mind. He was the teacher of Pericles, Euripides, and reputedly, of Socrates.
See also: Socrates.

Anaximander (611?-547? B.C.), Greek philosopher, first to give a naturalistic, rather than mythological, explanation to natural processes. He believed that the origin of all things was a formless matter, which he called 'indefinite.' His later works anticipated the theory of evolution and certain laws of astronomy.

ANC *See:* African National Congress.

Anchorage (pop. 226,000) Largest city in Alaska, America. Mining (gold and coal), salmon fishing and fur processing industry.
See also: Alaska.

Anchovy, small fish of the family Engraulidae, related to the herring family, exported from the Mediterranean for use as a seasoning and garnish. It is also found on the coast of Peru.

Ancien Régime (Fr: ancient regime) Period in French history between 1715 and 1789 and more generally the whole European political and social order in Europe before the French Revolution of 1789, which was characterized by absolutism.

Ancient civilization, term used to describe history and culture prior to the fall of the Roman Empire. Achievements in art, mathematics, literature, and architecture from those times still influence the modern world. The cultures of Egypt, Mesopotamia, Greece, and Rome are instances of ancient civilizations.

Andaman and Nicobar Islands (pop. 368,000), a union territory of India, consisting of two island groups. They lie south of Burma, between the Andaman Sea on the east and the Bay of Bengal on the west. The islands stretch generally northsouth for about 490 miles (790 km).
The Andamans have a total area of 2,500 square miles (6,475 sq km). Five of the largest islands - Baratang, Rutland, and North, Middle, and South Andaman - lie close together and are known as the Great Andamans. Another main island, Little Andaman, is separated from the cluster by the waters of Duncan Passage. There are also some 200 smaller islands in the Andaman group. The Nicobars, with a total area of 635 square miles (1,645 sq km), are separated from the Andamans by Ten Degree Channel. Two large islands, Great Nicobar and Little

Nicobar, and 16 smaller islands make up the group.
The rolling hills of the Andaman and Nicobar islands are the weathered crests of partly submerged mountains. The maximum elevation above sea level is 2,402 feet (732 m), on North Andaman. Tropical rain forests are widespread, and mangrove swamps fringe much of the coasts. The islands have a hot, humid climate. The mean annual temperature is 85? F. (29? C.). Rainfall measures as much as 138 inches (3,500 mm) annually; most of it falls during the southwest, or summer, monsoon (May to October).
Cultivated areas on the Andamans are used for growing rice, coffee, coconuts, and rubber trees. Timber is also a major product. Coconuts are the chief product of the Nicobars. Port Blair on South Andaman, with a population of about 26,000, is the territory's largest town; it is also the administrative center.
Both island groups were settled many centuries ago by primitive immigrants from Indochina: the Nicobars by people of Mongoloid stock and the Andamans by Negrito pygmies. There was little contact with the outside world until the mid-19th century, when the British took control of the islands. Until India became independent (1947), the Andamans were used as a penal colony. The Japanese held both island groups during World War II. Since 1951 the government of India has resettled peasant farmers from the mainland on the Andamans in an effort to develop agriculture.

Andersen, Greta (1928-), Danish-American swimmer, won Olympic gold in 1948 in the 100 m freestyle and silver in the 4 x 100 m freestyle relay. In 1950 she became European champion at the 400 m freestyle. She then specialized in marathon swimming and swam the Channel several times at the end of the 1950s and the beginning of the 1960s (she held the record for many years).

Andersen, Hans Christian (1805-1875), Danish writer, best remembered for his 168 fairy tales. Based on folklore and observation of people and events in Andersen's life, they have a deceptively simple, slyly humorous style and often carry a moral message for adults as well as children. Among his

The Danish author Hans Christian Andersen (1805- 1875) has become famous for his fairy-tales.

best known stories are 'The Ugly Duckling,' 'The Emperor's Clothes,' and 'The Red Shoes.'

Andersen, Hjalmar (1923-) Norwegian skater who was Norwegian champion several times. In 1950, 1951, and 1952 Andersen was both world and European champion. During the Winter Olympics of 1952 (Oslo) he acquired gold at the 1500 m, 5,000 m, and 10,000 m.

Anderson, Carl David (1905-1991), U.S. physicist who shared the 1936 Nobel Prize in physics for the discovery of the positron (1932). Later he was codiscoverer of the first meson.
See also: Dirac, Paul Adrien Maurice.

Anderson, Dame Judith (1898-1992), Australian-born actress who worked in the United States. She is best known for her tragic roles in the plays of Eugene O'Neill and Shakespeare and in Robinson Jeffers's version of *Medea* (1947).

Anderson, Elizabeth Garrett (1836-1917), one of the first English women to become a doctor (1865). She helped establish the place of women in the profession and founded a women's hospital and a medical school for women.

Anderson, Marian (1902-93), U.S. contralto. Overcoming the handicaps of poverty and discrimination, she became an international singing star in the 1930s. In 1939, Anderson was refused permission to perform in the DAR Constitution Hall, in Washington, D.C. Through the sponsorship of Eleanor Roosevelt and Secretary of the Interior Harold Ickes, Anderson sang from the steps of the Lincoln Memorial to a massive crowd of people of all races. She was awarded the Springarn Medal by the National Association of Colored People for the highest achievement by a black American (1939). In 1955 she became the first African American to sing a leading role with, and be named a permanent member of, the Metropolitan Opera. She also served as alternate delegate to the UN in 1958, and won the UN peace prize in 1977.

Anderson, Maxwell (1888-1959), U.S. playwright. After early realistic plays, he concentrated on the revival of verse drama, achieving some success with such plays as *Elizabeth the Queen* (1930), *Winterset* (1935), *High Tor* (1936), and *The Bad Seed* (1954).

Anderson, Sherwood (1876-1941), U.S. writer whose novels and short stories deal largely with the rebellion of individuals against contemporary industrial society. He is best remembered for the novel *Winesburg, Ohio* (1919), which details the frustrations of small-town Midwestern life, and such story collections as *The Triumph of the Egg* (1921) and *Horses and Men* (1923). Other novels include *Poor White* (1920) and *Dark Laughter* (1925).

Anderssen, Adolf (1818-1879) German chess master and mathematician, winner of

A

A

the first official international chess tournament (London 1851). Andersen was the best tournament player of his time. However, he was so engaged in teaching that he only participated in 16 tournaments. He won nine of them (among others London in 1862 and Baden-Baden in 1870) and was a three-time runnerup. He lost two unofficial matches for the world championship against Morphy in Paris 1858 (+2, -7, =2) and against Steinitz in London in 1866 (+6, -8).

Andes, South America's largest mountain system, 4,500 mi (7,200 km) long and averaging 200-250 mi (320-400 km) wide, near the west coast and running almost the entire length of the continent. Aconcagua (22,835 ft/6,960 m) is the highest peak in the Western Hemisphere. The Andes rose largely in the Cenozoic era (the last 70 million years), and volcanic eruptions and earthquakes suggest the range is still rising. The South Andes divide Chile and Argentina. The Central Andes form 2 ranges flanking the high Bolivian plateau (the Altiplano), once home to the Incan civilization. The North Andes divide in Colombia and form four ranges ending in the Caribbean area. Many high Andean peaks are jagged and snowy, and glaciers fill some southern valleys. The region is an important source of copper, silver, and tin, and oil has been found in the north.

Andhra Pradesh (pop. 73,000,000), state in India; 106,245 sq mi (275,068 sq km). Capital: Hyderabad. Religion: mainly Hindu. Language: Telugu. Approx. 22% forest (timber, bamboo, casuarina); agriculture (grain, sugar cane, cotton, oilseeds); cattle breeding (cattle, buffalo, goats, sheep). Production of manganese, mica, iron ore, coal. Sugar refining, textile and paper industry. Domestic industry: carpets, among other things. Main port: Vishakhapatnam.

The Cotopaxi (5.896 m), an active volcano in the Andes Mountains in Ecuador, is continually covered with snow at a height of 4.700 metres.

Andizan (Andijon) (pop. 293,000), industrial city in Uzbekistan. Place of residence of the khanates of Kokand, successors to Timur Lenk. Now flourishing industrial city, including petroleum refining and metal-related industries. The surrounding area has several irrigation projects to increase the harvest of cotton and silk.

Ando, Tadao (1941-), Japanese architect. At a young age, Ando became fascinated by western modernists such as Le Corbusier and Mies van der Rohe. He first attracted worldwide attention with his Azuma-house (1976) in Osaka. He confines himself to unambiguous forms such as rectangles and circles in his architecture and only uses 'authentic' material like reinforced concrete, untreated wood, steel and glass. Every part of a building is preferably made out of only one of these materials. Ando mostly built in Japan; mainly houses, museums and churches, but, he also built outside Japan: the Vitra Seminar House (Germany; 1989-1993) for example, and a place of worship for UNESCO (France; 1994-1995). In 1995 he received the Pritzker Price for Architecture. In 2002 his Museum of Modern Art in Fort Worth (Texas) was completed.
See also: Le Corbusier; Mies van der Rohe, Ludwig.

Andorra

Capital:	Andorra la Vella
Area:	180 sq mi (468 sq km)
Population:	68,400
Language:	Catalan
Government:	Parliamentary co-principality
Independent:	1278
Head of gov.:	President of gov.
Per capita:	US$ 19,000
Monetary unit:	euro = 100 eurocent

Andorra (pop. 67,600), tiny European principality (180 sq mi/465 sq km) in the eastern Pyrenees along the border between France and Spain. The Andorrans speak Catalan, French, and Spanish. The country attained autonomous status under Charlemagne, and since 1278 has been a co-principality, under the joint sovereignty of the Bishop of Urgel in Spain and, in modern times, the French chief of state. Andorra's terrain is extremely mountainous, pocketed by gorges and a few fertile valleys; the average altitude of the whole country is above 6,000 ft (1,810 m). The Valira River, flowing into Spain, has a sizable hydroelectric potential, still little exploited. Tobacco is Andorra's main money crop; rye and barley, grapes, potatoes, and

The bell tower of St. Miquel d'Engolasters in Encamp (Andorra).

sheep and cattle are also important. Other assets include iron and lead deposits, quarries, trout and lake salmon, and extensive pine woods. In recent decades tourism has brought new commercial affluence. The capital is the township of Andorra la Vella (Andorra-la-Vielle). In a national referendum in 1993 Andorra approved its first constitution, which made it a fully sovereign nation. Also that year Andorra became a member of the United Nations. The country's position as a tax haven is dependent on the attitude of the European Union.

Andrada é Silva, José Bonifácio de (1763-1838), Brazilian geologist and statesman, known as the father of Brazilian independence. He helped create an independent monarchy under Pedro I, whom he served as prime minister (1822-23) until exiled for his democratic views. He was later tutor to Pedro II.

Andrea, John de (1941-), U.S. sculptor, representative of hyperrealism. Especially known for his life-sized, polyester painted nudes.

Andre, Carl (1935-), U.S. conceptual artist. Representative of conceptual and minimalist art. Famous for objects that are formed by a sequence or piling up of the same elements, for instance woodblocks, square tiles, or metal sheets.

Andrea del Sarto (1486-1531), leading 16th-century Florentine painter, influenced by Michelangelo and Albrecht Dürer and renowned for delicately colored church frescoes. He rivaled Raphael's classicism but foreshadowed Mannerism through his pupils Jacopo da Pontormo, Il Rosso, and Giorgio Vasari. Two of his well-known paintings are *Madonna of the Harpies* and *Holy Family*.

Andrea Doria, Italian luxury liner that sank on July 26, 1956, following an inexplicable collision with the *Stockholm*, a Swedish liner, about 45 mi (72 km) south of Nantucket Island; 51 people died. In 1981 a salvage operation run by Peter Gimbel and his wife, Elga Andersen, raised the ship's safe; further work was abandoned because of dangerous conditions.

Andreotti, Giulio (1919-), Italian politician, lawyer, and publicist. Andreotti belonged to the right wing of the Democrazia Cristiana. In the 50s and 60s he was a minister several times and later headed seven cabinets (1972; 1972-1973; 1976-1978; 1978-1979; 1979; 1989-1991; 1991-1992). In 1993 an investigation was held regarding possible links between Andreotti and the Mafia and his involvement with Mafia murders in 1979. Andreotti denied these charges and partly at his own request has his parliamentary immunity removed by the Senate so he would be able to defend himself in court. In September 1995 Andreotti had to appear in court. In January 1996 Mafia boss Tomasso Buscetta reiterated that the Mafia had made regular requests for and had been granted special favors by the Christian Democratic leader. Another trial against Andreotti started in April 1996. This case centered around the murder of a journalist, Mino Pecorelli, in 1979. The Christian Democrat was suspected of being an accessory to the murder by using indirect sources to ask the Mafia to get rid of Pecorelli. At the beginning of 2001, he and union leader Sergio D'Antoni founded a new political party: Democrazia Europea. This party profiled itself as a centralist traditional party. In 2002, he was sentenced to 24 years imprisonment due to his involvement in the Pecorelli murder.

Andretti, Mario (1940-), Italian-born U.S. race car driver. His many achievements include winning the United States Auto Club national driving championship (1965, 1966, 1969) and the Grand Prix world driving championship (1978). Andretti also finished first in the Daytona 500 (1967) and Indianapolis 500 (1969). He became world champion in 1978. In 1980, he returned to Indy Car racing; he became champion in 1984. He ended his career in 1994.

Andrew, John Albion (1818-1867), U.S. statesman and antislavery proponent. A Unitarian, he became a staunch but moderate abolitionist and was active in organizing both the Free-Soil Party (1848) and the Republican Party (1854). He helped form the first regiment of free blacks in the North (54th Massachusetts) and ensured that black troops received the same pay as white soldiers. During Reconstruction he favored leniency toward the defeated Confederacy and opposed giving former slaves immediate citizenship.

Andrew, Saint (1st century A.D.), one of Jesus's 12 Apostles, formerly a fisherman and disciple of John the Baptist. He reputedly preached in what is now Russia and was martyred in Patras, Greece, on an X-shaped ('St. Andrew's') cross. He is the patron saint of Russia and of Scotland.
See also: Apostles.

Andrews, Roy Chapman (1884-1960), U.S. naturalist, explorer, and author. From 1906 he worked for the American Museum of Natural History (later becoming its direc-

tor, 1935- 41) and made important expeditions to Alaska, the Far East, and Central Asia. In Mongolia he discovered the first known fossil dinosaur eggs.

Andreyev, Leonid Nikolayevich (1871-1919), Russian novelist, short-story writer, and playwright. His work, including *The Seven That Were Hanged* (1908), reflects a basic pessimism and preoccupation with death.
See also: Russian literature.

Andric, Ivo (1892-1975), Yugoslav novelist who won the Nobel Prize for literature in 1961, largely for the epic quality of *The Bridge on the Drina*. His themes are humanity's insecurity and isolation in the face of change and death.

Androcles, in Roman legend, slave who was thrown to the wild animals in the Roman arena but was spared by a lion from whose paw he had once extracted a thorn. Amazed at the lion's behavior, the Roman officials pardoned Androcles and presented him with the lion.

Androgen *See:* Hormone.

Andromache, in Greek mythology, wife of Hector, prince and hero of Troy. After the fall of Troy, Achilles' son Neoptolemus took her as a slave to Epirus and later married her. After he divorced her, she became the wife of Hector's brother Helenus. Her farewell to Hector and mourning of his death are among the most celebrated passages in Homer's *Iliad*. Euripides also based a tragedy on her story.

Andromeda, spiral galaxy visible in the Andromeda constellation. The most distant object visible to the naked eye in northern skies, it is the nearest galaxy external to our own, but larger (120,000 light-years in diameter), and about 2 million light-years from earth.
See also: Astronomy.

Andromeda, in Greek mythology, daughter of Cassiopeia and Cepheus, king of Ethiopia. Her mother boasted that she was more beautiful than the Nereids (sea nymphs). Out of revenge for this insult, Poseidon inundated the land and sent a sea monster to ravage the shore. Andromeda was rescued by Perseus, whom she then married.
See also: Mythology.

Andropov, Yuri Vladimirovich (1914-1984), Soviet political leader, who became general secretary of the Communist party in 1982 after the death of Leonid Brezhnev and also, in 1983, chief of state. Earlier he had served as ambassador to Hungary (1954-1957) and as head of the KGB, the Soviet security service (1967-1982). In 1973 he became a full member of the Politburo, the governing body of the Communist party. As party leader, Andropov fought bureaucratic corruption, adopted a conciliatory attitude toward China, and tried to create a division between Western Europe and the United States on trade and military issues. After August 18, 1983, he was not seen in public.

Anemia, deficiency in the number of red blood cells or their hemoglobin content (the red substance that binds with oxygen), or both. Causes vary, but symptoms include pallor, fatigue, difficulty breathing, giddiness, heart palpitations, and loss of appetite.

Anemometer, instrument for measuring wind speed. The rotation type of mechanical anemometer estimates wind speed from the rotation of cups mounted on a vertical shaft. The sonic or acoustic anemometer depends on the velocity of sound in the wind. In laboratories, air flow is estimated from the change in resistance it causes by cooling an electrically heated wire.

Anemone, genus of wild or cultivated perennial herbs of the buttercup family (*Ranunculaceae*). Up to 3 ft (1 m) high, anemones have deeply cut, whorled leaves and white, pink, red, blue, or rarely, yellow flowers.

Anesthesia, loss of sensation, especially the sensation of pain. The loss of sensation following injury or disease is known as pathological anesthesia, but anesthesia, either general or local, can also be drug-induced. General anesthesia is a reversible state of unconsciousness accompanied by muscle relaxation and suppression of reflexes. It is indispensable for many surgical procedures. Injections of short-acting barbiturates such as sodium pentothal are frequently used to speed the onset of anesthesia; inhaled agents, including halothane, ether, nitrous oxide, trichlorethylene, and cyclopropane, are then used to induce and maintain general anesthesia. Local anesthesia is induced by the chemical action of cocaine derivatives like novocaine or lidocaine. Regional anes-

A

The well-known Andromeda nebula (M 31), with its two elliptical companions M 32 (below) and NGC 205 (above right). The two systems are approximately at an equal distance from the earth. They can be seen through a large number of stars belonging to our own Milky Way system. This photograph was taken with the 120 centimetres-Schmidt-telescope of the Hale Observatories. With a 5 metres-telescope, it is possible to discern individual stars in the system, and thus enabling detailed study.

thesia may be induced by blocking one or more large nerves or spinal nerve roots, as in epidural anesthesia for childbirth.
See also: Anesthesiology.

Anesthesiology, branch of medicine that deals with the administration before and during childbirth or surgery of anesthetics, drugs that dull or block sensation or anxiety. Anesthesiologists (physicians who administer anesthetics) use various techniques to anesthetize all or part of the patient's body during surgery, while monitoring and maintaining important body functions; their work may also involve resuscitation and intensive respiratory care.
See also: Anesthesia.

Aneurysm, localized dilation of a blood vessel, usually an artery, due to local fault in the wall through defect, disease, or injury, producing a pulsating swelling over which a murmur may be heard. Generally the structural integrity of the arteries enables them to resist the destructive effects of the repetitive hydraulic stress of circulation. Sometimes, however, the wall of an artery gives way, and a segment of the artery expands to form a balloon-like dilation: an aneurysm. If left untreated, the aneurysm may burst, causing death or grave disability. Even an unruptured aneurysm can lead to damage by interrupting the flow of blood or by impinging on and in some cases eroding nearby blood vessels, organs, or bone. The incidence of aneurysm rises with age.
See also: DeBakey, Michael Ellis; Stroke.

Angel, supernatural messenger and servant of the deity. Angels figure in Christianity, Judaism, Islam, and Zoroastrianism. In Christianity angels traditionally serve and praise God, but guardian angels may protect the faithful against the evil of the devil (the fallen angel, Lucifer). The hierarchy of angels is said to have 9 orders: cherubim, seraphim, thrones, dominions, virtues, powers, principalities, archangels, and angels.

Angel Falls, world's highest known waterfall (3,212 ft/979 m), on the Churín River in southeastern Venezuela, discovered by U.S. aviator Jimmy Angel in 1935. Its longest unbroken drop is 2,648 ft (807 m).

Angelfish, any of a group of freshwater tropical fish, and of several fish found in

warm seas (family Chaetodontidae). The colorful freshwater angelfish is native to the Amazon basin.

Angell, Sir Norman (1874-1967), English economist and internationalist, awarded the Nobel Peace Prize in 1933. A journalist most of his life, he argued in *The Great Illusion* (1910) that war was futile and best prevented by the mutual economic interest of nations.

Angeloú, Maya (1928-), U.S. author best known for her autobiographical books *I Know Why the Caged Bird Sings* (1970) and *Gather Together in My Name* (1974), which recount her struggles for identity as an African American in a hostile world. Other works include *The Heart Of A Woman* (1976), *All God's Children need Traveling Shoes* (1986), and *A Song Flung Up To Heaven* (2002).

Angevin, name of 2 medieval royal dynasties originating in the Anjou region of western France. The first ruled in parts of France and in Jerusalem and England. Henry II, son of Geoffrey of Anjou, became England's first Angevin (or Plantagenet) ruler in 1154. His descendants held power in England until 1485. The second branch, which began in 1266 when Charles, brother of Louis IX of France, became king of Naples and Sicily, ruled in Italy, Hungary, and Poland until the end of the 15th century.

Angina pectoris, severe but temporary attack of heart pain that occurs when the demand for oxygen by the heart muscle exceeds the ability of the coronary vessels to supply oxygen, due to narrowing or blockage of the vessels. The discomfort of angina pectoris, although highly variable, is most commonly felt beneath the sternum (breastbone). Pain may radiate to the left shoulder and down the inside of the left arm, straight through to the back, into the throat, the jaws, and the teeth. Anginal discomfort may be felt in the upper and lower abdomen, and occasionally in the right arm. Angina pectoris is characteristically triggered by physical activity and usually persists for no more than a few minutes, subsiding with rest.
See also: Heart.

Angiography, technique allowing visualization of blood vessels on X rays after injec-

tion of a radiopaque substance (one that shows up on X ray). It is usually performed on arteries or veins connected with organs such as the brain, heart, or kidneys, when a narrowing or blockage is suspected. Angiography is used to determine if deposits of substances such as cholesterol or calcium, known as plaque, are causing vessel narrowing, and has developed into a relatively safe and useful diagnostic technique. A typical angiographic procedure involves the passing of a catheter through the skin and into a vein or artery, where it is advanced to the structure being evaluated. Contrast material is injected into the area, making the section visible on X ray.

Angioplasty, set of techniques used in reconstructing damaged blood vessels, which may involve surgery, lasers, or tiny inflatable balloons. Usually, arteries that have become blocked by deposits of such substances as cholesterol or calcium-substances known as plaque-are reopened by inserting a catheter with an attached balloon into the diseased vessel where inflation of the balloon compresses or splits the deposits that clog the artery. Angioplasty is an important alternative to surgery for patients whose clogged coronary arteries predispose them to risk of a heart attack.

Angiosperm, member of a large class of seed-bearing plants (the flowering plants), its seeds developing completely enclosed in the tissue of the parent plant (rather than unprotected, as in the only other seed-bearing group, the gymnosperms). Containing about 250,000 species distributed throughout the world, from tiny herbs to huge trees, angiosperms are the dominant land flora. There are 2 subclasses: monocotyledons (with 1 leaf) and dicotyledons (with 2).

Angkor, extensive ruins from the ancient Khmer Empire in northwestern Cambodia, covering 40 sq mi (100 sq km). Dating from the 9th to the 13th century, the remains were found by the French in 1861. The city of Angkor Thom, with its temples and palace, is intersected by a canal system and lies within a perimeter wall. Angkor Wat, a massive complex of carved Hindu temples, is the foremost example of Khmer art and architecture.

Angle, in plane geometry, the figure formed by the intersection of two straight lines. The point of intersection is known as the vertex. If the two lines are viewed as radii of a circle of unit radius, the magnitude of an angle can be defined in terms of the proportion of the circle's circumference cut off by the two lines. Angles are measured in radians or degrees. One radian is the magnitude of an angle whose two sides cut off an arc of circumference equal in length to the radius. A degree is the magnitude of an angle whose two sides cut off 1/360 of the circumference. An angle of $\pi/2$ rad (90°), whose sides cut off one-quarter of the circumference, is a right angle, the two lines being said to be perpendicular. An angle of π rad, or 180°, whose sides cut off one-half of the circumference, is a straight angle or straight line. Angles less than 90° are termed acute; those greater than 90° but less than 180°, obtuse;

Angelfish are among the most colorful of all fish. Their exotic coloration facilitates territoriality by warning off intruders.

greater than 180°, reflex. Pairs of angles that add up to 90° are complementary; those that add up to 180°, supplementary. In solid geometry, angles have definitions that are specific to the solids.
See also: Geometry; Trigonometry.

Angles, Germanic tribe from which England derives its name. Coming from the Schleswig-Holstein area of northern Germany, the Angles, with the Saxons and Jutes, invaded England in the 5th century and founded kingdoms including East Anglia, Mercia, and Northumbria.
See also: Anglo-Saxons.

Anglicans, community of churches developed from the Church of England. The Church of England split from the Roman Catholic Church in the 1500s, during the Reformation. It was formed by King Henry VIII, who broke with the Roman Catholic Church because he was denied permission to divorce his second wife, Anne Boleyn. The Anglican Communion is made up of the Church of England, the Anglican Church of Canada, and the Episcopal Church in the United States.

Anglo-Saxons, collective name for the Germanic peoples who dominated England from the 5th to the 11th centuries. They originated as tribes of Angles, Saxons, and Jutes who invaded England after Roman rule collapsed, creating kingdoms that eventually united to form the English nation. In modern usage, Anglo-Saxons are the English or their emigrant descendants in other parts of the world.

Angola

Capital:	Luanda
Area:	481,354 sq mi
	(1,246,700 sq km)
Population:	13,100,000
Language:	Portuguese
Government:	Republic
Independent:	1975
Head of gov.:	Prime minister
Per capita:	U.S. $1,330
Monetary unit:	1 Kwanza (Kz) = 100 lwei

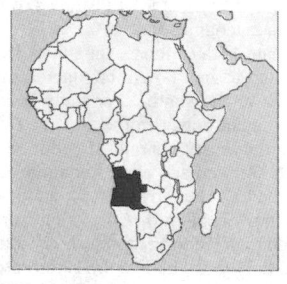

Land and climate. Angola is dominated by the Bié Plateau, some 4,000 ft (1,219 m)

above sea level, which occasionally rises to altitudes of 8,000 ft (2,438 m) or more. To the north are tropical rain forests; to the south, semiarid or desert regions. In the east, the plateau drops off to the basins of the Zambezi and Congo rivers. The narrow coastal plain to the west, though humid, receives little rainfall. Savanna wildlife is abundant.
People. The overwhelming majority of Angolans are Africans belonging to several Bantu tribes. More than half of the population are Christians (chiefly Roman Catholic) and a significant minority follows traditional religions.
Economy. Crude oil is Angola's principal export, followed by coffee, diamonds, and iron ore. There is also some light industry, including food processing and production of cotton, textiles, and paper.
History. Angola was a Portuguese colony from 1576 onward, and the export of slaves to Brazil caused severe depopulation. Portuguese colonization and economic development grew in the early 20th century, coupled with repression of the native peoples. Nationalists began the fight for independence in 1961, and by the 1970s some 50,000 Portuguese troops were engaged in fighting nationalist guerrillas. Angola became independent on November 5, 1975, and conflict erupted among three rival groups for control of the government. The Popular Liberation Movement (MPLA), backed by Soviet and Cuban troops, prevailed. UNITA, a pro-Western group, continued resistance against the MPLA. A truce was agreed to in 1991 ending the civil war. Elections that included UNITA candidates were held in 1992 and were won by the MPLA. UNITA resumed the civil war, but in 1994 agreed to a peace settlement with MPLA. A UN force was brought in to keep the peace, but UNITA resumed fighting in 1998. UNITA-leader Jonas Savimbi was killed on 22 February 2002 during fighting with the Angolan army. In April of the same year, a peace treaty was signed.

Angora *See:* Ankara.

Angora, term used for the long-haired varieties of goats, cats, and rabbits. Originally it referred to goats bred in the Angora (now Ankara) region of Turkey. The silky white hair of Angora goats has long been used for fine yarns and fabrics, especially for making mohair cloth.
See also: Ankara.

Angry Young Men, 'Angry Young Men' was a group of British authors that started in the 1950s. They had in common a need to rebel against the social and political values of their period and the middle-class mentality, which they felt to be worn out. Instead they stood up for the working class from which they generally originated. The most important authors of this group are: John Osborne (play: *Look Back in Anger*, 1952), Kingsley Amis, John Braine (*Room at the Top*, 1957), Alan Sillitoe (*Saturday Night and Sunday Morning*, 1958), John Wain (*Hurry on Down*, 1953), Keith Waterhouse, Colin Wilson (*The Outsider*, 1956), and Shelagh Delaney.

Ångström, Anders Jonas (1814-1874), Swedish physicist, one of the founders of spectroscopy (spectrum analysis) and the first to identify hydrogen in the solar spectrum (1862). The Ångström unit is named in his honor.
See also: Ångström (Å).

Ångström (Å), unit used to measure the length of light waves and other extremely small dimensions, named for Swedish physicist Anders Jonas Ångström. It is equivalent to one ten-millionth of a millimeter (1 x 10-10m).
See also: Ångström, Anders Jonas.

These magnificent waterfalls are located on the Malange Plateau, west of Luanda in Angola.

Anguilla (pop. 12,000), island in the West Indies, 35 sq mi (90 sq km), lying 150 mi (240 km) east of Puerto Rico. Local industries include cattle breeding, fishing, and tourism. Discovered by Columbus, it became a British colony in 1650. Anguilla was part of the West Indian Associated States of St. Kitts, Nevis, and Anguilla, but it seceded in 1967 and is again under British rule. The colony consists of the islands Anguilla and Sombrero. Main city: The Valley.

The Turkish Angora has a regal appearance accentuated by its long body, plume-like tail, and long, fine hair.

Anhinga, also called darter, snakebird, or water turkey, large bird of the anhinga family that feeds in waters from southeast and southcentral United States to Argentina. Measuring about 3 ft (91 cm) long, it is glossy black, with silver and brown markings. The anhinga is a strong swimmer and flier. It has webbed feet and swims mostly submerged, with its snakelike neck visible, spearing fish with its long, sharp beak. It perches in an upright position, often with wings and long fan-shaped tail spread.

A

A

The smooth-billed ani
(*Crotophaga ani*).

Similar species are the cormorant and the darters of the Eastern Hemisphere.

Anhui (pop. 60,700,000 province in Eastern China; 54,036 sq mi (139,900 sq km). Capital: Hefei. Industry (metalware, paper, cigarettes, ink, leatherwork, etc.) is increasing dramatically, reducing the share of agriculture (corn, tea, wheat, cotton, tobacco) in the economy to less than 50%.

Anhydride, oxide that forms an acid or base when it reacts with water. Metal oxides such as calcium oxide produce hydroxides (bases) and are termed basic anhydrides. Oxides of nonmetals such as phosphorus, carbon, and sulfur produce acids on being dissolved in water and are acid anhydrides. Organic anhydrides are used in the manufacture of solvents, paints, and dyes. Acetic anhydride is used in large quantities during the production of acetic acid and various plastics.

Anhydrous ammonia, dry or liquid form of ammonia, made by compressing pure ammonia gas (NH_3) and used as nitrogen fertilizer and as a refrigerant.
See also: Ammonia.

Ani, or tickbird, any of a genus (*Crotophaga*) of long-tailed black cuckoos native to the warm regions of the Americas. About 12 in (30 cm) in length and having flattened, blade-like beaks, anis live in flocks and build a single communal nest.

Aniakchack, volcano on the Alaska Peninsula, in the Aleutian mountain range. It is one of the largest craters in the world, with a diameter of about 6.5 mi (10.5 km). Thought to be extinct when discovered in 1922, it erupted in 1931 and is now classified as dormant.

Aniline, chemical compound ($C_6H_5NH_2$) obtained from indigo or other organic substances, or from benzol, and used in the production of dyes.
See also: Dye.

Animal, living organism distinguished from plants by locomotion, environmental reactivity, nutrient absorption, and cell structure. Animals move freely using a wide variety of mechanisms to do so, whereas plants are rooted to one place. Animals sense their environments and react to them. In the case of multicellular animals, they react by means of the nervous system; in more highly developed animals reactions to the environment are mediated by the nervous system combined with sense organs of touch, smell, taste, hearing, and sight. Plants may react to light, chemicals, and other stimuli, but such reactions are automatic and not nervous. Plants usually contain chlorophyll, which helps them build, from inorganic material, the organic substances of which they consist. Animals must consume organic food. And while both plants and animals are made up of cells, plants have a cell wall strengthened with cellulose (a woodlike substance), but animals contain no cellulose. Other minor distinctions include the ability of plants, lacking in animals, to periodically form new organs from undifferentiated cells.

Animation, cinematographic technique creating the illusion of movement by projection of a series of drawings or photographs showing successive views of an action. The first animated cartoons were made by Emile Cohl in France in 1907. Walt Disney pioneered in the use of sound and color and in producing cartoons that aimed at suspense and drama as well as broad humor. In classic animation, drawings on transparent celluloid (cels) are superimposed to form each picture; only cels showing motion are changed from frame to frame.
See also: Disney, Walt; Schulz, Charles Monroe.

Walt Disney (1901-1966), an American motion picture producer and animator, applies the finishing touches to a sketch of his most famous cartoon character, Mickey Mouse. Disney pioneered in the development of full-length animated films.

Animism, term first used by anthropologist E.B. Tylor in 1871 to designate a general belief in spiritual beings, which belief he held to be the origin of all religions. A common corruption of Tylor's sense interprets animism as the belief that all natural objects possess spirits. The psychologist Jean Piaget proposed that a growing child passes through an animistic phase.
See also: Piaget, Jean; Tylor, Sir Edward Burnett.

Anise, herb of the carrot family that yields seeds with a spicy, licorice flavor. The seeds, and the oil produced from them, are used to flavor foods, candy, and liquors like ouzo and Pernod. Anise is native to the eastern Mediterranean.

Ankara (pop. 2,900,000), capital of Turkey and of Ankara province in Asia Minor. It produces textiles, cement, flour, and beer, and trades in local Angora wool and grain. Ankara (formerly Ancyra or Angora), once a Hittite trade center, later became capital of a Roman province in 25 B.C. It replaced Istanbul as Turkey's capital in 1923.

Ankle, joint connecting the foot and the leg. Sprained ankle is a common acute injury, causing considerable discomfort and disability. The ankle joint may also be affected in rheumatoid arthritis. Pain is often due to inflammation of the sheaths of the peroneal tendon and of the bursa.
See also: Anatomy.

Anna, in the New Testament (Luke 2), Jewish prophetess, daughter of Phanuel of the tribe of Asher. Widowed at an early age, she served God in the temple by continual prayer and fasting. At the age of 84 she witnessed the presentation of Jesus in the temple.

Anna Ivanovna (1693-1740), empress of Russia from 1730. Elected puppet empress by the nobles' supreme privy council, she overthrew the council and, with German advisers, waged costly wars against the Poles and Turks and opened Russia's way to Central Asia.

Annam, a historic region on the eastern coast of Indochina, now central Vietnam. In the fourth century B.C., the ancestors of the Vietnamese were driven from southern China to the upper Indochinese Peninsula. The kingdom of Nam Viet was established about 207 B.C. In the following century, the Chinese overran the kingdom. The Vietnamese regained their independence in the 10th century A.D. and founded the kingdom of Dai Viet, although China's overlordship was recognized.
In the late 15th century, Annam, as Dai Viet had come to be known, conquered most of Champa to the south, eventually becoming the dominant power in the area. In 1802 the Nguyen dynasty gained the throne, with French aid, and soon the Annamite Empire controlled all the territory east and south of Siam (now Thailand). Attacks on European missionaries led to French military intervention in the second half of the 19th century. In 1884 Annam was made a French protectorate. In 1887 it became part of the French-supervised Indochinese Union (French Indochina), which included Tonkin, Cochin

China, Laos, and Cambodia. Unsuccessful revolts against French control occured in the decades that followed.

During World War II, Indochina was occupied by the Japanese. At the end of the war, France's attempt to reimpose its rule was resisted. An independent republic of Vietnam was proclaimed, and war with France resulted in 1946.

Annan, Kofi (1938-), a Ghanaian United Nations official. He became the seventh secretary general of the United Nations in 1997, succeeding Boutros Boutros-Ghali. Annan received a bachelor's degree in economics from Macalester College in 1961 and a master's degree in management from Massachusetts Institute of Technology in 1972. He began his UN career in 1962 as an administrative officer at the World Health Organization. In 1993 he was appointed UN undersecretary general for peacekeeping operations. In 2001, Annan was reappointed as secretary-general of the UN. In that same year, he was awarded the Nobel Peace prize, together with the UN.

Annapurna, Himalayan mountain in Nepal with the world's 11th-highest peak (26,391 ft/8,044 m). Its conquest in 1950 by Maurice Herzog's team was the first such success involving any great Himalayan peak.

Ann Arbor (pop. 109,500), city in southeastern Michigan, seat of Washtenaw County, and home of the University of Michigan since 1841. It is situated on the Huron River about 40 mi (65 km) west of Detroit. Once mainly a farming and fruit-growing center, Ann Arbor has also become a center of light industry since World War II. The city was settled in 1824, incorporated as a village in 1833, and given its city charter in 1851.

Anne (1665-1714), queen of Great Britain and Ireland (1702-14), last of the Stuart monarchs. Her reign was dominated by the War of the Spanish Succession, also known as Queen Anne's War in the colonies (1702-13). It also saw the Act of Union (1707), uniting England and Scotland to form the kingdom of Great Britain, and the growth of the parliamentary system.

Anne, Saint, mother of the Virgin Mary and wife of St. Joachim. Though not mentioned in Scripture, she was venerated in Early Christian times. According to an apocryphal writing of St. James, long after St. Anne had despaired of bearing a child, an angel appeared to her and foretold the birth of Mary. Often represented in art in such scenes as the Birth of the Virgin, St. Anne is the patron saint of women in labor. Her feast day is July 26.
See also: Sainte-Anne-de-Beaupré.

Anne of Austria (1601-1666), queen consort and regent of France. The daughter of King Philip III of Spain, Anne married King Louis XIII of France in 1615. Her position at court was precarious because of France's involvement in the Thirty Years' War against Spain and Austria. After her husband's death in 1643, Anne served as regent for her young son, King Louis XIV, relying on Cardinal Mazarin, the successor of Cardinal Richelieu, for guidance. In 1651 she had her 13-year-old son proclaimed of age, but she remained powerful until the death of Mazarin in 1661, when Louis personally took control of the state.
See also: Mazarin, Jules Cardinal.

Anne of Brittany (1477-1514), duchess of Brittany and queen of France. Anne was married to King Charles VIII of France in 1491 and after his death became the wife of his successor, King Louis XII. Through the marriage of her daughter to the future King Francis I of France, the duchy of Brittany, the last of the great feudally held territories of France, was permanently united to the crown of France.

Anne of Cleves (1515-1557), queen consort and fourth wife of England's Henry VIII. She was the daughter of a powerful German noble, and Henry married her (1540) on Thomas Cromwell's advice to forge international bonds, but 6 months later he had Parliament annul the marriage.
See also: Henry (England).

Annexation, acquisition by a country of a territory previously outside its jurisdiction. The term is generally used to refer to the extension of a country's sovereignty by conquest or threat of force, rather than by treaty.

Anno Domini *See:* A.D..

Annual, plant that completes its life cycle in one growing season, as contrasted with biennials (two seasons) and perennials (more than two). Annuals include garden flowers and food plants such as cornflowers and tomatoes. Preventing seeding may convert an annual to a biennial or a perennial.

Annual rings, rings of dark and light wood seen across the trunk of a tree that has been cut down. The lighter rings are formed during the spring and are made up of cells with large cavities. The darker rings are formed during the summer, when less new wood is laid down and the cells have smaller cavities. In hot countries the rings represent dry and wet seasons. The size of the rings tells a great deal about the conditions under which the tree was growing, and the number of rings can be used to measure the age of the tree. The science of dating things by counting annual rings is dendrochronology.

Annuity, yearly payment a person receives for life or for a term of years, the person usually being entitled to such payment in consideration of money advanced to those who pay.

Annulment, decree to the effect that a marriage was invalid when contracted. Grounds for annulment include fraud, force, and close blood links between the parties. The Roman Catholic Church recognizes annulment but not divorce.

Annunciation, in Christian belief, the archangel Gabriel's announcement to the Virgin Mary that she would give birth to the Messiah. The Roman Catholic Church celebrates the Annunciation on March 25. The Annunciation is the theme of many Christian paintings.

Annunzio, Gabriele d' *See:* D'Annunzio, Gabriele.

Anodizing, electrolytic method of producing a corrosion-resistant or decorative layer of oxide on a metal, usually aluminum. The metal to be coated is used as an anode (positive pole), suspended in an electrolyte (usually an aqueous solution of sulfuric, chromic, or oxalic acid). When an electric current is passed through this solution, a coating of oxide builds up on the anode.
See also: Electrolysis.

Anorexia nervosa, psychological disorder characterized by a disturbed sense of body image and exaggerated anxiety about weight gain, manifested by abnormal refusal to eat, leading to severe weight loss, and, in women, amenorrhea (loss of period). The onset is usually in adolescence, and the disorder affects females predominantly; only about 5% of the cases occur in males.

Anouilh, Jean (1910-1987), French playwright, whose highly theatrical dramas emphasize the dilemma of modern times, in which individuals are forced to compromise their dreams. His works include *Antigone* (1944), *The Lark* (1953), and *Beckett* (1959).

Anoxia, severe hypoxia (lowered oxygen levels in body tissues), whether due to lack of oxygen in air inhaled or lack of oxygen available in the blood or tissues. Anoxia can be of such severity as to cause permanent damage. Anemic anoxia, resulting from deficient amounts of hemoglobin in the blood, may be caused by hemorrhage or anemia or by poisoning with carbon monoxide, nitrites, or chlorates. Anoxic anoxia occurs when blood flowing through the lungs does not pick up enough oxygen, possibly caused by high altitudes or foreign gases or by abnormalities in pulmonary tissues. Stagnant anoxia, in which slow blood circulation results in loss of oxygen before the blood reaches tissues, is often associated with congestive cardiac failure or postoperative shock.

Anselm, Saint (1033?-1109), archbishop of Canterbury (from 1093), a founder of Scholasticism. He endured repeated exile for challenging the right of English kings to influence church affairs. Anselm saw reason as the servant of faith and was the author of an ontological 'proof' of God's existence: the human idea of a perfect being itself implies the existence of such a being. Saint Anselm's Day is celebrated on April 21.

Anselmo, Giovanni (1934-) Italian visual artist. Keywords for his work: contrasts and materials. He is seen as a representative of 'arte povera' and conceptual art.

Ansermet, Ernest (1883-1969), Swiss orchestral conductor who directed many premieres of Stravinsky ballets. He founded the

A

A

Orchestre de la Suisse Romande in 1918, conducting it until his death.

Ansky, Shloime (Solomon Samuel Rapoport; 1863-1920), Russian Yiddish author and playwright, best known for *The Dybbuk* (1916), a tragedy of demonic possession. He was active in Russian Jewish socialism, but left Russia after the Revolution and died in Poland.

Anson, Adrian Constantine (1851-1922), U.S. baseball player, also known as 'Cap' or 'Pop.' In 1939 he was elected to baseball's Hall of Fame as 'the greatest hitter and greatest National League player-manager of the 19th century.'

Ant, insect of order Hymenoptera (which also includes bees and wasps), family Formicidae, living in communities consisting of males, females, and infertile worker females. An ant colony may contain thousands and even millions of ants organized into a highly socialized community. The queen ant's function is to produce eggs. The female worker ant (there are no male worker ants) is responsible for food, protection, and building the nest. The male's singular function is to mate and die quickly. Ants are found in all parts of the planet but prefer warmer climates. An ant is usually under 1 inch (2.5 cm) in height and black, brown, or red in color. It usually lives in tunnels beneath the earth or mounds of its own making. The two antennae on the head provide the ability to hear, smell, touch, and taste, although other areas of the body can taste and touch. The ant has no ears. It has acquired a reputation for remarkable strength because it can lift 50 times its own weight. The ant produces a humming or buzzing sound capable of detection by the human ear.

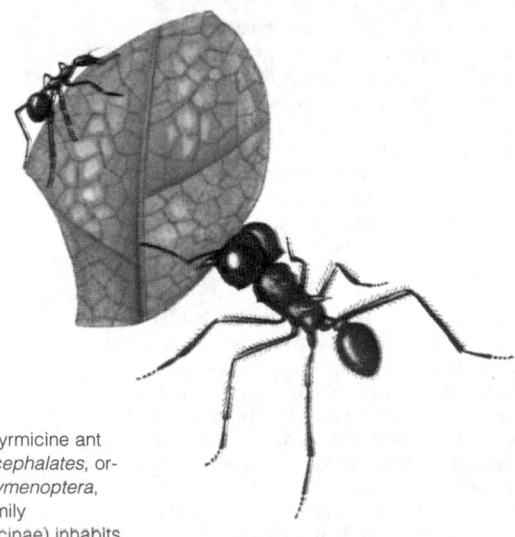

The myrmicine ant (*Atta cephalates*, order *Hymenoptera*, subfamily Myrmicinae) inhabits tropical and subtropical America. They have lengths from 4-18 mms, according to what type of worker it concerns. These ants cut up leaves and transport them to their underground place, where they are used as a medium to grow certain fungi. The ants themselves live on the protein-containing bodies of the fungal mycelia. The illustration shows a medium worker, carrying a freshly cut leaf, and a minor worker on the leaf, guarding against parasitic flies attempting to oviposit in the leaf.

Mount Erebus, one of Antarctica's five known active vulca-noes, dominates the coastal landscape along McMurdo Sound. The volcano was first sighted during the 1840s by the James Clark Ross expedition.

Antall, József (1932-1993) Hungarian politician. Antall is leader of the Hungarian Democratic Forum (MDF) and became prime minister (1990) of the first democratically elected government in Hungary since 1947. His center-right coalition opted for a gradual transition to the free market economy. In contrast to many other eastern European countries where disillusionment has often led to unrest, Hungary's political situation remained stable under Antall's leadership.

Antalya (pop. 503,000), capital of the Antalya Province, Turkey; 8,040 sq mi (20,815 sq km). Port on the Gulf of Antalya, exports semi tropical fruits. Attractive to tourists due to the favorable climate and historic sites. Visited by the apostles St. Paul and St. Barnabas during their travels.

Antananarivo, or Tananarive (pop. 1,200,000), capital and largest city of Madagascar. Located near the center of the island of Madagascar on a mountain ridge and linked to other areas by railroad, it is a manufacturing and communications center. The University of Madagascar and the 200-year-old palace of the Merina rulers are located in the city.

Antarctic *See:* Antarctica.

Antarctica, fifth largest continent, almost 6,000,000 sq mi (17,400,000 sq km). Antarctica is almost entirely covered by an ice cap up to 14,000 ft (4,267 m) thick except where the ice is pierced by mountain peaks.
The Vinson Massif is Antarctica's highest mountain (16,900 ft /5,150 m). The continent is circular, indented by the arc-shaped Weddell Sea (south of the Atlantic Ocean) and the rectangular Ross Sea (south of New Zealand). Pack ice virtually surrounds the rest of the continent. The western half of Antarctica, including the Antarctic Peninsula, is structurally related to the Andes; the eastern half geologically resembles Australia and South Africa. Antarctica is almost entirely within the Antarctic Circle (66°30' S) and the climate is intensely cold, with winter temperatures as low as -80° F (-62° C), and winds up to 100 mph (161 kmph).

Capt. James Cook was the first to attempt a scientific exploration of the region (1773). The mainland was probably first sighted in 1820 by the American sea captain, Nathaniel Palmer. The Englishman James Weddell led an expedition to the area in 1823 and another Englishman, James Clark Ross, discovered the sea later named for him. The Norwegian Roald Amundsen was the first to reach the South Pole on Dec. 4, 1911 and Admiral Richard Evelyn Byrd became the first to fly over the pole on Nov. 29, 1929. Since the International Geophysical Year (1957-58), international cooperation in Antarctica has increased. On Dec. 1, 1959, 12 nations signed the 30-year Antarctic Treaty reserving the area south of 60° S for peaceful scientific investigation. In 1985, 32 nations agreed to limit access of humans to Antarctica to specific research sites. Antarctica is home to over 25 scientific installations, three of which are from the United States. During the 1980s scientists began to detect a deterioration in the ozone level above Antarctica which created great environmental concern for the region and the planet. The ozone layer protects the planet from destructive sun rays. Because of this new awareness and increasing accessibility to the region, tourism to Antarctica is rising.

Antarctic Circle, imaginary boundary, 66°30' S lat., marking the northernmost latitude of the Antarctic region at which the sun remains above the horizon at least one day a year, the December solstice, and the southernmost latitude at which the sun is visible at the June solstice. Most of the continent of Antarctica lies within the circle.

Antarctic Ocean, ocean surrounding the Antarctic continent, also called the Southern Ocean; sometimes not considered to be a separate ocean but rather a part of the Atlantic, Indian, and Pacific oceans. Its width varies from 700 mi (1,100 km) at the tip of South America to 2,400 mi (3,860 km) off the tip of Africa. Pack ice and icebergs drift in the ocean's 29°F (-2°C) waters.

Antares, one of the brightest stars in the southern sky, in the constellation Scorpio. It is over 400 light years from earth. It is a visual binary, or double, star; the main star is a

While some of the seas and islands surrounding Antarctica were known in the 18th century, the mainland was not explored until the 19th century.

A

The young of the Weddell seal (*Leptonychotes weddelli*) are born on the sea ice.

The grey-headed albatross (*Diomedea chrysostoma*) lives on the island of South Georgia

Lowest on the Antarctic food chain are phytoplankton, which are eaten by zooplankton. Both are eaten by fish and baleen (toothless) whales, and fish are then eaten by birds, seals, and toothed whales.

A

red (thus, cool) giant, 480 times the size of the sun; its companion star is blue (hot) and too small to be visible without a powerful telescope.
See also: Astronomy.

Anteater, any of 3 genera of Central and South American mammals, family Myrmecophagidae, order Edentata, including the giant anteater and the tamandua. They have long snouts, tubular, toothless mouths, and long, sticky tongues with which they catch their food, chiefly termites.
See also: Aardvark.

Antelope, swift-moving hollow-horned ruminant of the family Bovidae, order Artiodactyla. Common features include a hairy muzzle, narrow cheek teeth, and permanent, backward-pointing horns. Distribution is throughout Africa and Asia. Antelopes range in size from the royal antelope, probably the smallest hoofed mammal, standing about 10 in (25 cm) high at the shoulders, to the giant eland, which may be as tall as 6 ft (1.8 m).

Antenna, or aerial, component in an electrical circuit that radiates or receives radio waves. A transmitting antenna is a combination of conductors that converts AC electrical energy into electromagnetic radiation. The simple dipole consists of 2 straight conductors energized at the small gap which separates them. It can be made directional by adding electrically isolated director and reflector conductors in front and behind. Other configurations include the folded dipole, the highly directional loop antenna, and the dish type used for microwave links. A receiving antenna can consist merely of a short dielectric rod or a length of wire for low-frequency signals. For VHF and microwave signals, complex antenna configurations similar to those used for transmission must be used.

Antennae, paired sensory appendage on the head of most insects, crustaceans, and other arthropods. Nerves on the antennae are sensitive to vibrations, heat, water vapor, or chemicals. Hairs on the antennae of male

mosquitoes pick up female sounds as far as one-quarter mi (0.4 km) away, while June bugs have pits in their antennae that help them smell. Most insects have 1 pair of antennae; crustaceans, such as lobsters and crabs, have 2 pairs.

Antheil, George (1900-1959), U.S. composer. He studied under Ernest Bloch and brought popular motifs into serious music in works such as *Jazz Symphonietta* (1926) and the opera *Transatlantic* (1928-29). In later work he was more traditional, and after World War II he developed a neoclassical style influenced by Igor Stravinsky.

Anthemius of Tralles (d. c.534), Byzantine architect, mathematician, and physicist. With Isidorus of Miletus, he designed the Hagia Sophia in Constantinople at the order of the Byzantine emperor Justinian. It is likely that he also designed the Church of Saints Sergius and Bacchus in the same city.

Anthony, Susan Brownell (1820-1906), major U.S. leader and organizer of the fight for women's rights. She cofounded the

National Woman Suffrage Association (1868) and served as president of the National American Woman Suffrage Association (1892-1900). She is the co-author of the first 3 volumes of *The History of Woman Suffrage*. In 1979, Anthony became the first woman to have her image on a coin of general circulation in the United States.
See also: Women's movement.

Anthony of Padua, Saint (1195-1231), Franciscan friar, theologian, and preacher. He was born near Lisbon but taught and preached in France and Italy. Patron saint of the poor, his feast day is June 13.

Anthony of Thebes, Saint (c.250-350), Egyptian hermit, considered the founder of Christian monasticism. He founded a desert community of ascetics near Fayum, then lived alone in a mountain cave near the Red Sea and died aged over 100. He supported St. Athanasius in the Arian controversy. His feast day is Jan. 17.

Anthrax, infectious disease affecting livestock and, more rarely, humans, causing skin

In order to protect the three very long claws on each hand, the giant anteater (*M. tridactyla*) (A) walks on its knuckles (B), moving at a clumsy gallop when disturbed. It takes to water readily and is able to swim wide rivers. The large bushy tail is meant to cover the animal's body when it curls up in a secluded place to sleep. Anteaters are found from Mexico to northern Argentina.

Anteaters are completely toothless and feed by ripping apart ant and termite nests with their long claws, and picking up eggs, cocoons and ants with their sticky, saliva-coated tongues.

The early predecessors of modern humans, Australopithecus africanus and A. robustus, belong to a species of prehuman creatures known as australopithecines, who lived in Africa 5.5 to 1.5 million years ago. They walked erect but had features similar to the chimpanzee. Peking man, a member of the species Homo erectus, lived in eastern Asia 500,000 to 250,000 years ago and probably used stone tools and fire. Steinheim man, usually classified as an early species of Homo sapiens, lived in Europe about 200,000 years ago. Neanderthal man, Homo sapiens neanderthalensis, who lived in Europe, Asia and Africa between 100,000 and 40,000 years ago, is considered to have had high intelligence, compared with that

Australopithecus

africanus   robustus

Peking man

Steinheim man

pustules and lung damage. Anthrax spores, which can survive for years, may be picked up from infected animals or bone meal. It was the first disease shown (by Robert Koch in 1876) to be caused by bacteria. A vaccine effective on sheep and cattle was developed by Louis Pasteur. Anthrax is now rare in developed countries. After the terrorist attacks on the United States of September 11, 2001, panic broke out for a short period of time due to anthrax. Spread by mail, it caused a number of deaths.
See also: Pasteur, Louis.

Anthropoid *See:* Primate.

Anthropology, study of the origins, evolution, and development of human beings and their various cultures and societies. Physical anthropology is concerned with human beings as physical organisms, the place of *Homo sapiens* in the framework of evolution, and the classification of early humans based upon the study of fossil remains. Cultural anthropology examines the specific knowledge, values, and behaviors that are characteristic of members of a particular society, emphasizing the uniqueness of cultures while attempting to compare them. Cultural anthropology shares with social anthropology an emphasis upon understanding behaviors within a particular context and rejects any attempt to classify or explain particular behaviors in the abstract. Social anthropology studies the structures of a society through the detailed and direct examination of patterns of relations among its classes, generations, and religious and political institutions. One of the major contributions of social anthropology has been to discredit the idea that preliterate societies are lacking in complexity or that the peoples in them lack the same intellectual abilities as peoples in industrialized societies.

Antiaircraft defense, method of protection from attack by enemy aircraft or missiles, involving early detection and interference and destruction. Radar is an early detector but can be foiled if the enemy confuses the radar by dropping metal strips called chaff.

Interference with incoming missiles is accomplished with chaff, decoys, and electronic jamming devices. Radar is also used in coordination with guns or missiles on ships or on the ground to destroy the attackers. Some antiaircraft missiles use homing devices attracted to heat from enemy planes, guiding the missiles to the target.
See also: Radar.

Anti-Ballistic Missile Treaty (ABM-treaty) Arms control treaty concluded in 1972 between the USA and the former Soviet Union, part of the SALT-I-agreement. The ABM-treaty limits the Soviet Union and the US in the development of their strategic defense systems against ballistic missiles. The treaty was set up at the insistence of the USA in order to guarantee mutually assured deterrence (MAD). The Strategic Defense Initiative (SDI), which was launched by American president Ronald Reagan in 1983, violated the stipulations of the ABM-treaty, which not only prohibits the deployment, but also the development of, and the experimentation with, a satellite defense against ballistic missiles. The Soviet Union refused to conclude an arms control treaty with the USA as long as the SDI was still in place. The SDI-program was delayed considerably due to technological and financial problems and was given low priority after the end of the Cold War. In the meantime, the USA was engaged in the development of the Global Protection Against Limited Strikes system. The developments after the attacks of September 11, 2001 and the new plans for the manufacture of a space shield, developed by the government under president George W. Bush, led to the unilateral American decision to withdraw from the ABM-treaty at the end of 2001. The cancellation came into effect in 2002.
See also: Strategic Arms Limitation Talks; Reagan, Ronald Wilson; Bush, George W..

Antibiotic, any of the substances, usually produced by microorganisms, that kill or prevent the growth of other microorganisms, especially bacteria and fungi. Louis Pasteur noted the effect in the 19th century, and in 1928 Alexander Fleming showed that the

mold *Penicillium notatum* produced penicillin, a substance able to destroy certain bacteria. Penicillin was the first antibiotic to be used on a large scale for treating human infections.Other early discoveries of antibiotics include the isolation of streptomycin (by Selman Waksman), gramicidin (by René Dubos), and the cephalosporins. Semisynthetic antibiotics, in which the basic molecule is chemically modified, have increased the range of naturally occurring substances. Each antibiotic inhibits specific microorganisms. Some antibiotics, such as penicillin, are effective against only a few types of microorganisms. Others, such as streptomycin and the tetracyclines, are effective against many different types. Some microorganisms are highly sensitive to small amounts of a given antibiotic, while others require larger amounts to be inhibited.
Some infectious microorganisms develop, through genetic changes, a resistance to particular antibiotics. Since the early 1980's, resistant strains of microorganisms have caused outbreaks of pneumonia, tuberculosis, and certain other diseases. Many health authorities believe the improper use of antibiotics has contributed to the development of these strains. They advise that dosages of antibiotics be taken as prescribed (even after syptoms disappear) to end an infection completely. They also advise that antibiotics be used only when necessary, since the more often microorganisms are exposed to an antibiotic, the greater is the chance that resistant microorganisms will develop. In some cases, an antibiotic can produce an allergic reaction. Some antibiotics can produce secondary diseases by inhibiting the growth of useful bacteria. Therefore, antibiotics should be taken only when prescribed by a qualified physician.
See also: Penicillin; Bacteria.

Antibody *See:* Immunity.

Antichrist, in Christian belief, the human antagonist of Christ. The term appears in the Epistles of St. John. While the concept is sometimes interpreted as a lawless but impersonal power, others consider the Antichrist a personal incarnation of evil. Roman Catholic writers commonly interpret the term to mean any adversary of Christ and of the Church's authority, specifically the last and greatest antagonist of the Christian Church, whose coming will precede the end of the world.

Anticoagulant, substance that interferes with blood clotting, used to treat or prevent strokes and embolism. The 2 main types are heparin, which is injected and has an immediate but short-lived effect, and the coumarins, which are taken orally and are longer lasting.
See also: Coagulant.

Antidote, remedy that neutralizes a poison or counteracts its effects. A chemical antidote unites with a poison to produce a harmless chemical, a mechanical antidote prevents the absorption of a poison, and a physiologic antidote produces effects contrary to those of the given poison. Most antidotes are effective against only one kind of poison, al-

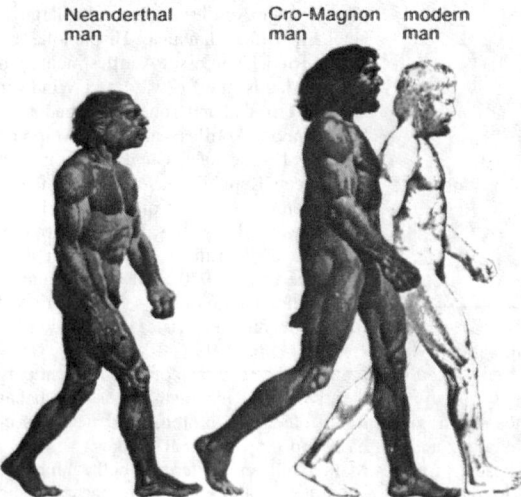

Neanderthal man Cro-Magnon man modern man

of his ancestors. Cro-Magnon man, Homo sapiens sapiens, whose fossils have been discovered at numerous European sites, first appeared about 40,000 years ago. This anatomically modern human developed a culture that included stone and bone toolmaking, paintings and carvings, and elaborate rituals associated with hunting, birth, and death.

A

though specific antidotes are available in less than 2% of poisonings.
See also: Antitoxin; Poison.

Antietam, Battle of *See:* Civil War, U.S..

Antifreeze, substance added to a solvent to prevent it from freezing in cold weather. Antifreeze used in the cooling system of automobiles is generally made of water mixed with ethylene glycol, methanol, ethanol, or other substances that lower the freezing point.
See also: Glycol.

Antigen, foreign substance introduced into an organism, stimulating the production of antibodies that combat the intruder. Antigens may be viruses, bacteria, or the non-living toxins they produce.

Antiglobalism, Somewhat undefined and heterogeneous movement that opposes the globalization of economy and culture. Among other things, antiglobalists take a stand against world trade that they claim is defined by the wealthy West, protecting its own economy against the import of goods from less developed countries and dumping its own glut of farm produce on Third World markets. They also oppose unregulated currency speculations which pose a threat to weaker currencies, multinational concerns creating genetically manipulated soy, exploitation of children and child labor which they believe play an important role in production activities in low-wage countries, global brand names which determine consumers' buying behavior, American fast food chains and anonymous large-scale activities. They alert people to the dangers of climatic change and global warming due to unbridled economic growth. According to anti-globalists, globalization strenghtens a small privileged group, but does nothing for the enormous mass of poor people, from Third World countries. They support small-scale activities, local markets and local communities. Unintentionally, the Canadian journalist Naomi Klein became the epitome of antiglobalization after the publication of her book *No Logo* in 2000, in which she berated the increasing economic and cultural dominance of multinationals. Anti-globalists form a heterogeneous group of individuals, who, although they have various convictions, motivations and backgrounds, turn against (the effects of) globalization out of various convictions, motivations and backgrounds. They mainly congregate during international meetings of political leaders.
See also: Globalization; Third World; Klein, Naomi.

Antigone, in Greek mythology, daughter of Oedipus and Jocasta. When her brothers Eteocles and Polynices killed each other in combat, Creon, king of Thebes and Jocasta's brother, refused to allow the burial of Polynices, whom he regarded as a traitor. When Antigone defied him, Creon sentenced her to death. She is the subject of tragedies by the ancient Greek playwright Sophocles and the modern French playwright Jean Anouilh.
See also: Mythology.

Antigonid dynasty, line of kings that ruled Macedonia (northern Greece) 294 B.C.-168 B.C. **Antigonus I**, a general under Alexander the Great, was the first of the dynasty to rule Macedonia (294-283 B.C.). He was succeeded by **Antigonus II** (r. 283-239) and grandson **Demetrius II** (r. 239-229). **Phillip V**, son of Demetrius II, challenged Rome but was defeated in 197 B.C. Antigonid rule ended 168 B.C. with the defeat and capture of Philip's successor, **Perseus**.

Antigravity, hypothetical force of repulsion described in science fiction but never scientifically observed. The opposite of gravity, antigravity would cause objects to repel one another rather than to be attracted to one another. Earth's gravity pulls objects toward the planet's center, antigravity would push objects away from earth's center.

Antigua, also called Antigua Guatemala (pop. 28,000), city in south central Guatemala, once the capital. After an earthquake and flood leveled an earlier capital, Antigua was founded in 1542, quickly becoming one of the richest cities in the New World, only to be destroyed itself by an earthquake in 1773. Today Antigua is a trading and tourist center in a coffee-growing area.

Antigua and Barbuda

Capital:	Saint John's
Area:	170.5 sq mi (442 sq km)
Population:	67,400
Language:	English
Government:	Parliamentary monarchy in the British Commonwealth
Independent:	1981
Head of gov.:	Prime minister
Per capita:	U.S. $10,000
Monetary unit:	1 East Caribbean dollar ($) = 100 cents

Antigua and Barbuda, island nation in the West Indies, largest and most developed of the Leeward Islands.
Land and climate. The islands of Antigua, Barbuda, and Redonda (uninhabited), are of volcanic origin. White sandy beaches fringe the coasts; few places rise to more than

1,000 ft (300 m) above sea level. The climate is tropical with a dry season July-Dec. *People and economy.* Pop. 67,000. The population is predominantly of African and British origins. St. John's is the largest town and chief port, and tourism is the principal economic activity. In the 19th century, cotton replaced sugarcane as the main crop, and some tropical fruits are also grown. The United States maintains large naval and army bases near Parham.
History. Antigua was named by Christopher

The marina of Antigua's English Harbour. In the foreground, we see the remains of the 18th-century harbour.

Columbus in 1493. The island passed from Spanish to French control in the 17th century and was taken over by the British in 1632. With Barbuda and Redonda as dependencies it became a self-governing West Indies Associated State in 1967 and independent in 1981. During recent years, the country has been accused of corruption and drug money laundering.

Antihistamine, drug used to neutralize the effects of histamine (an organic compound released by certain cells that causes tissue swelling, hives, and severe itching). It is used to relieve the symptoms of allergies.

Antilles, The, islands of the West Indies, with the exception of the Bahamas. Shaped like an arc that stretches from Cuba to the coast of South America, the Antilles separate the Caribbean Sea from the Atlantic Ocean. The Greater Antilles include the large islands of Cuba, Jamaica, Hispaniola, and Puerto Rico. The Lesser Antilles include the Virgin Islands, the Leeward and Windward Islands, Trinidad and Tobago, Barbados, the Netherlands Antilles, and the Margarita Islands of Venezuela. Cuba, Haiti, and the Dominican Republic have long been independent nations. Three of the large islands formerly held by the British-Barbados, Jamaica, and Trinidad-gained their independence in the 1970s. All other islands of the Antilles are colonies, self-governing affiliates, or integral parts of other nations.

Antimatter, material composed of antiparticles, which are identical in mass and behavior to electrons, protons, and neutrons but have opposite electrical charges.
Matter and antimatter are both annihilated when they collide, and other particles, such

A

as photons (quanta of energy) are released. Antimatter is rare and short-lived in our part of the universe, where matter predominates. The first antiparticle, the positron (antielectron), was discovered by Carl D. Anderson in 1932. In 1995, physicists created atoms of antihydrogen. The atoms, which existed only a fraction of a second, were the first known atoms of antimatter. In 1997 three scientists received the Nobel prize for developing a method to cool off antimatter using a laserbeam, in order to make particles more managable and to prevent annihilation. *See also:* Antigravity.

Antimony, chemical element, symbol Sb; for physical constants see Periodic Table. Substances containing antimony have been used for thousands of years as medicines and cosmetics. It was first characterized accurately by Nicolas Lémery in 1707. Its principal ore is stibnite, a sulfide. Antimony is obtained by roasting the sulfide to the oxide, which can be further reduced with carbon. It is an extremely brittle, bluish-white metalloid and a poor conductor of heat and electricity. Two allotropes of antimony are known. Antimony greatly increases the hardness and mechanical strength of lead. It is used in batteries, antifriction alloys, type metal, infrared detectors, diodes, and Hall-effect devices. Its compounds are used in safety matches, flameproofing agents, paints, ceramic enamels, glass, and pottery. Antimony and its compounds are toxic.

Antioch (pop. 141,000), ancient city in Asia Minor, now known as Antakya, in southern Turkey on the Orontes River. Founded by Seleucus I in 301 B.C., it became the capital of the Seleucid Empire and was one of the great commercial centers of the ancient world. In 64 B.C. control of the city passed to Rome, which made 'Antioch the Golden' capital of the empire in Asia, surpassed in splendor only by Rome and Alexandria. It was the most important center of early Christianity outside Palestine. After the decline of the Eastern Roman Empire, Antioch came under Arab and then Ottoman Turkish rule. After World War I, it was incorporated into French-administered Syria, but in 1939 it was restored to Turkey. The city is a trade and agricultural center.

Antipodes (Greek, 'foot-to-foot'), 2 places exactly opposite each other on the globe, so that a straight line connecting them would pass through the center of the earth. The region around Australia and New Zealand is the antipode of England, and is thus sometimes called the Antipodes.

Antique, object that has acquired value through a combination of age, rarity, craft, and historic interest. Generally, the term applies to objects over 100 years old, though by the 1980s even those of the 1890s and early 1900s, particularly in the art nouveau style, were becoming sought-after. The U.S. 1939 Tariff Act defined antiques as 'artistic antiquities' made before 1830. Certain categories of objects are favorites, notably furniture, china, rugs, and other useful and decorative articles.

Antirenters, group of tenant farmers in New York State who protested against paying rent to landlords (1839-1847). The tenant families had lived on the disputed land for generations and considered it theirs. When, in 1839, the heirs of the Dutch merchant Van Rensselaer tried to collect $400,000 in back rents. The Antirenters rose up in protest, rioting and terrorizing the landlords. In 1846, a new state constitution guaranteed ownership to the tenants.

Anti-Semitism, systematic hostility to Jews. Until the 19th century, antiJewish prejudice was basically religious in nature, stemming from the claim that the Jews were responsible for Christ's death. In the late 1800s, particularly in eastern Europe, religious hostility acquired a racist rationale, based on the idea that Jews were a distinct, and evil, race. In Tsarist Russia the Jewish population was subjected to brutal physical attacks (pogroms). Anti-Semitism became a cornerstone of the ideology of Nazi Germany under Adolf Hitler, culminating in the murder of some 6 million Jews during World War II. *See also:* Concentration camp; Holocaust; Jews; Racism.

Antiseptic, substance that kills or prevents the growth of microorganisms (particularly bacteria and fungi), especially used to avoid sepsis (infection) from contamination of body surfaces and surgical instruments. Vinegar and cedar oil have been used since early times to treat wounds and for embalming. Commonly used antiseptics and disinfectants include iodine, chlorine, alcohol, isopropanol, formaldehyde, and hydrogen peroxide. Heat, ultraviolet, and ionizing radiations also have antiseptic effects. *See also:* Disinfectant; Lister, Sir Joseph.

Antitoxin, antibody released into the bloodstream to counteract the poisonous products (toxins) of invading bacteria. When a small amount of a bacterial toxin is injected into the blood, the body produces its own antitoxins to combat infection. The body may also accept blood serum injected from another organism that has already formed the antitoxin. This technique is effective in fighting such diseases as diphtheria and tetanus.

Antitrust laws, legislation designed to protect competition among businesses. By preventing large firms from controlling the price or supply of goods and services, these laws work to ensure that smaller firms are not forced out of business. Antitrust legislation has recently been complicated by the growth of huge conglomerates that control businesses in many industries.

Anti-war movement, opposition to U.S. involvement in the Vietnam war. From a relatively small group of protesters during the Kennedy administration, the movement proliferated and gained a broad base, its popularity widely believed responsible for President Lyndon B. Johnson's decision not to run for a second term in 1968. Hundreds of thousands demonstrated their opposition in protest marches in 1968-1969. Anti-war pressure intensified under President Richard

M. Nixon and strongly influenced his decision to settle for peace without victory.

Ant lion, or doodlebug, larval form of any of several insects of the Myrmeleontidae family that traps ants and other prey in pits dug in sandy soil. It uses its plump, hairy body to dig by backing into the soil in a narrowing spiral path. When prey slides into the pit, the ant lion, hiding under sand at the bottom, kills the prey with its long sharp jaws, and sucks its nourishment from the victim.

Antofagasta (pop. 401,000), major Pacific seaport in northern Chile, capital of Antofagasta province. An important industrial center, it is also the shipping point for the copper, nitrates, and sulfur mined in the surrounding region, as well as being the crossroads for rail and highway connections to southern Chile and across the Andes to Bolivia and Argentina. Antofagasta was ceded to Chile by Bolivia after the War of the Pacific (1879-83).

Antoinette, Marie *See:* Marie Antoinette.

Antonioni, Michelangelo (1912-), Italian film director. His work includes *L'Avventura* (1959), *La Notte* (1961), *Eclipse* (1962), *The Red Desert* (1964), *Blow-Up* (1966), *Zabriskie Point* (1969), and *The Passenger* (1975). In 1995, he received an honorary Academy Award for his achievement in film.

Michelangelo Antonioni filming *Zabriskie Point* in an inhospitable area in the United States.

Antonius Pius (A.D. 86-161), Roman emperor (138-161), tolerant of Christians, the last to achieve relative stability in the empire. Chosen consul in 120, he adopted Marcus Aurelius and Lucius Verus as successors.

Antony, Marc (Marcus Antonius; 82-30 B.C.), Roman politician and general. A member of Caesar's family, he became a tribune in 50 B.C.; after Caesar's murder in 44 B.C., Antony, then consul, joined the Triumvirate, including his brother-in-law Octavian and Lepidus, dividing the empire among them.Antony controlled the east from the Adriatic to the Euphrates, but soon alienated Octavian by falling in love with the Egyptian queen, Cleopatra, and combining forces with her. As a result, the senate stripped Antony of his powers (32 B.C.), certain the insult would invite civil war.

A

Octavian attacked and defeated Antony in a naval battle at Actium; Antony returned to Egypt, pursued by Octavian, and committed suicide. Cleopatra, too, died by her own hand.
See also: Rome, Ancient.

Antwerp (pop. 445,600), city and leading port, on the Scheldt River in northern Belgium. It is the capital of Antwerp province, the commercial and cultural center of Flemish Belgium, and an important manufacturing city, with oil, metal, automobile, and diamond industries. It was the center of the great Flemish school of painting: artists like Brueghel, Rubens, and Van Dyck worked there in the 16th and 17th centuries.

Anubis, ancient Egyptian god of the dead, usually portrayed as having the head of a dog or jackal. In Egyptian belief, Anubis guided the dead to the underworld, where he symbolically weighed their hearts on the scales of justice.
See also: Mythology.

Anuradhapura (pop. 40,000), provincial capital of Sri Lanka, founded in the 6th century B.C.. Anuradhapura was the national capital from the 5th century B.C. until 600 A.D.. A contemporary of Emperor Ashoka built Buddhist monuments here in the 3rd century B.C. of which the 'pagoda of the golden sand' is particularly well-known. The Buddhist university competed with the University of Nalanda (India). A detailed description by the Chinese pilgrim Fa Hsien of the city from 411/12 has been preserved. The irrigation system from around 450 was unparalleled in the whole world. Around 750 the place was abandoned. Under British government a railroad and a small settlement were built.

Anxiety, unpleasant and disturbing emotion, ranging from ill-defined discomfort to panic or a profound sense of impending doom. Anxious people may be irritable, restless, and agitated, or have impulses for physical activity that may be purposeless and aimless. Physical symptoms may include an increase in heart rate and blood pressure, generalized or localized muscle tension, rapid and shallow breathing, sighing or shortness of breath, dizziness, or nausea. Anxiety may be acute, lasting a few minutes to a few hours, or chronic, with symptoms mild to moderate in intensity but almost constantly present. The chronic state may be intermittently and unpredictably accompanied by acute increases in the severity of the symptoms.
Anxiety is usually brought on by stress, which may be well defined and external or ill defined and internal. While it is often thought that anxiety is always undesirable and to be avoided, human personality development studies have demonstrated that tolerable levels of age-appropriate anxiety are largely responsible for individuals' gradual establishment of sophisticated, self-reliant behavior, attitudes, and values.
See also: Phobia.

Anzio (pop. 28,000), Italian fishing port and seaside resort about 30 mi (48 km) south of Rome. As ancient Antium, it was the birthplace of the emperors Caligula and Nero. Anzio was the site of Allied landings in Jan. 1944, during World War II, leading to a bloody battle in which casualties were high.

Anzus Pact, treaty signed Sept. 1, 1951, by Australia, New Zealand, and the United States for mutual defense in the Pacific. The name consists of the initials of the participating countries, which meet annually.

Aorta, the body's main artery, carrying blood from the left ventricle of the heart to the branch arteries that spread throughout the body.

Apache, Native American tribe of North America's Southwest (since c.1100), from Athabascan linguistic family. Nomadic hunting culture. Most present-day Apaches live on 3 million acres of federal reservations in Oklahoma, New Mexico, and Arizona, supported by income from timber, tourism, cattle, and mineral resources.

Apartheid (Afrikaans, 'apartness'), policy of racial segregation as employed by the Republic of South Africa, enforced by the dominant white minority. The system separates whites from nonwhites (i.e., Coloreds, or mulattoes; Asiatics; and Africans, or Bantu), nonwhites from each other, and each individual Bantu group. The policy also involves the 'separate development' of 10 Bantu homelands, where the majority of the population lives on a very small portion of poor land. Segregation and discrimination of nonwhite peoples is imposed by denying the rights to vote, own land, travel, or work without permits. In addition, workers are often separated from their families, which undermines family structure. Although dissent, led largely by the formerly outlawed African National Congress, is met with imprisonment, exile, or house arrest, resistance to apartheid continues, both inside the country (where thousands have been killed or imprisoned) and outside (in the form of nearly worldwide economic and political sanctions against South Africa). Since the 1970s and 1980s many apartheid laws have been repealed. In the early 1990s the system was completely dismantled, democratic structures were introduced, and a black majority rule was established in 1994.
See also: African National Congress; Mandela, Nelson.

Apatosaurus, see: Brontosaurus.

Ape, primate, family Pongidae, closely related to human beings. These forest dwellers, whose brain structure allows for fairly advanced reasoning, range in size from the gibbon (3 ft/0.9 m, 15 lb/6.8 kg) of southeast Asia to the gorilla (6 ft/1.8 m, 500 lb/227 kg) of Africa. The chimpanzee (5 ft/1.5 m, 150 lb/68 kg), also of Africa, is the animal most closely related to humans. It is a member of the ape family.

APEC *See:* Asia-Pacific Economic Cooperation.

Apennines, mountain chain forming the backbone of the Italian peninsula and extending into Sicily, about 800 mi (1,287 km) long and 25-80 mi (40-129 km) wide. The predominant rocks are limestone and dolomite; sulfur and cinnabar are mined in the volcanic area near Vesuvius. Olives, grapes, and grains are widely grown, although lack of fertile topsoil prevents intensive agriculture.

Apennine Tunnel, 11.5-mi (18.5-km) train tunnel in Italy on the Florence-Bologna line; one of the longest train tunnels in the world, built from 1920-34.

Aphasia, partial or total language impairment, in which the comprehension or expression of words is diminished as a result of injury to the brain. Reeducation is the only proven treatment.

Aphid, destructive sap-feeding insect of the aphid family, also known as greenfly or plant louse. Because of the damage caused by their piercing of plant tissue and because

Many of the sap-feeding Homoptera excrete a sugar-rich liquid, known as honeydew.
A number of them have developed a trophobiotic relationship with ants, which obtain the honeydew directly from the homoptera's anus. In return, the ants usually offer some protection against predators.

A. Aphids can reproduce sexually, but in spring, they give birth to live young without mating: a phenomenon known as parthenogenetic viviparity.
This allows the species to reach large numbers rapidly, during the most favourable season. Here, a female is giving birth to live young.

B. A worker ant of the species Formica is solliciting an aphid, by stroking it with its antennae. The aphid then raises its abdomen slightly, and a droplet of honeydew will be emitted slowly, which will be directly consumed by the ant.

many of the 4,000 species carry viruses, aphids are one of the world's greatest crop pests. They are an important food source for ants and other insects.

Aphrodite, in Greek mythology, goddess of love, fertility, and beauty. The daughter of Zeus and Dione in some versions, in others she is described as having risen from the sea. Her intensely sensual beauty aroused jealousy among other goddesses, particularly after the Trojan Paris chose her as the most beautiful over Hera and Athena. Wife of the crippled smith Hephaestus, she took both divine and mortal lovers, giving birth to Aeneas and Eros. The Greeks honored her with many major shrines. The Romans called her Venus.

Apia (pop. 35,000), capital and main port of Western Samoa, on the northern coast of Upolu Island. Apia's Government House was once the home of Robert Louis Stevenson, author of *Treasure Island*, who died there in 1894 and is buried nearby.

Apocalypse, prophetic revelation, usually about the end of the world and the ensuing establishment of a heavenly kingdom. Jewish and Christian apocalyptic writings appeared in Palestine between 200 B.C. and 150 A.D. and offered hope of liberation to a people under alien rule.

Apocrypha, appendix to the King James Version of the Old Testament. Protestants use the term mainly for books written in the 2 centuries before Christ and included in the Septuagint and the Vulgate, but not in the Hebrew Bible. These include Esdras I and II, Tobit, Judith, additions to Esther, the Wisdom of Solomon, Ecclesiasticus, Baruch, the Song of the Three Holy Children, Susanna and the Elders, Bel and the Dragon, the Prayer of Manasses, and Maccabees I and II.

Apollinaire, Guillaume (Wilhelm Apollinaris de Kostrowitzky; 1880-1918),

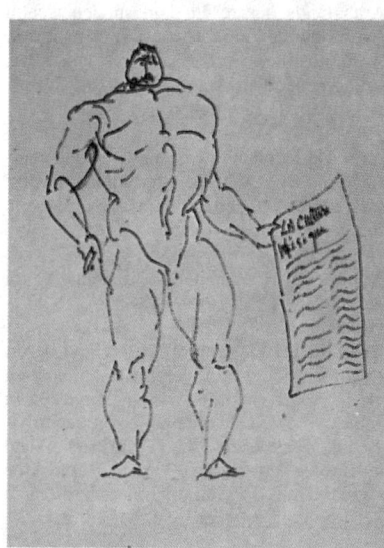

Pen drawing by Picasso (1915), depicting the French poet Guillaume Apollinaire (1880-1918) as an athlete.

influential French avant-garde poet and critic. The friend of Derain, Dufy, and Picasso, he helped to publicize Cubist and primitive art. In his lyric poems *Alcools* (1913) and *Calligrammes* (1918), he anticipated Surrealism with his use of startling associations and juxtapositions.

Apollo, in Greek mythology, the son of Zeus and Leto, twin of Artemis, and second only to Zeus in that he had the power of the sun as giver of light and life. He was the god of justice and masculine beauty, purifier of those stained by crime, divine patron of the arts, leader of the Muses, and god of music and poetry. Apollo was considered a healer who could also send disease. He spoke through the oracle at Delphi. The Romans adopted Apollo, honoring him as healer and sun god.

Apollo Project, U.S. space program initiated by President John F. Kennedy on May 25, 1961, to place a person on the moon by the end of the 1960s. The program's mission was accomplished (at a cost of over $24 billion) when the Apollo 11 Lunar Excursion Module (LEM) carrying astronauts Neil Armstrong and Buzz Aldrin touched down on the moon's surface on July 20, 1969. Subsequent flights allowed exploration of various areas of the moon. The program ended in 1972 with Apollo 17.
See also: National Aeronautics and Space Adminstration.

Apostles, the 12 disciples closest to Jesus, whom he chose to proclaim his teaching: Andrew, John, Bartholomew, Judas, Jude, the two Jameses, Matthew, Peter, Philip, Simon, and Thomas. When Judas died, Matthias replaced him. Paul and Barnabas became known as apostles for their work in spreading the gospel.
See also: Bible.

Apostles' Creed, statement of belief ascribed to Jesus's apostles and maintained in its present form since the early Middle Ages. The Roman Catholic Church uses it in the sacraments of baptism and confirmation. It is also used by various Protestant denominations.
See also: Apostles.

Apothecaries' weight, system of weights once widely used in Great Britain and the United States by druggists, now replaced by the metric system. Apothecaries' weight divides the pound into 12 ounces, the ounce into 8 drams, the dram into 3 scruples, and the scruple into 20 grains.
See also: Weights and measures.

Appalachian Mountains, mountain system of Northeastern America, about 1,800 mi (2,897 km) long and 120-375 mi (193-603 km) wide, stretching south from Newfoundland to central Alabama. In the northern part are the Green Mountains and White Mountains. The Allegheny Mountains and Blue Mountains are located in the southern part. The highest peak is Mt. Mitchell (6,684 ft/2,037 m) in North Carolina. Appalachian forests yield much timber, and there are rich deposits of coal and iron.

Appeal, in law, transfer of a case that has been decided in a lower court to a higher court for review.

Appeasement, in international relations, the act of yielding to a foreign government's demand in an effort to eliminate grievances that might lead to war. The most famous example of appeasement was the Munich agreement of 1938, which allowed Germany to annex parts of Czechoslovakia. Instead of satisfying the German leader Adolf Hitler, however, it encouraged him to take new steps of aggression. After World War II, the word *appeasement* was often used as a term of shame to condemn any concessions made by one country in negotiations with another.

Appel, Karel (1921-), Dutch painter, one of the founders of the Cobra group in 1948. He owes his great international fame to his later, abstract-expressionist work.
He also designs decors for theater and opera. He works both in France/Monaco and the United States. Appel has received numerous international prizes, including the Guggenheim Prize. His work, which had a major influence especially in The Netherlands and which initially led to fierce protests, has been bought by important museums across the world, especially in the United States.

Appellate court *See:* Court; Trial.

Appendicitis, inflammation of the appendix, often caused by obstruction to its narrow opening, followed by swelling and bacterial infection. Acute appendicitis can lead to rupture of the organ, formation of an abscess, or peritonitis. Symptoms include abdominal pain (usually in the right lower abdomen), nausea, vomiting, and fever. Early surgical removal of the appendix is essential; any abscess requires drainage of pus and delayed removal.
See also: Appendix.

Appendix, in biology small, hollow, closed tube located where the small and large intestines meet. While it aids digestion in certain rodents, it no longer has a function in humans and is considered a vestigial organ. The disease appendicitis results when the appendix becomes inflamed.
See also: Appendicitis.

Appia, Adolphe (1862-1928), Swiss stage designer whose ideas revolutionized early 20th-century theater. He stressed the use of 3-dimensional settings and of mobile lighting with controlled intensity and color.

Appian Way, oldest Roman road, constructed by the censor Appius Claudius Caecus in 312 B.C. At first stretching from Rome to Capua (about 130 mi/209 km), by the mid-third century B.C. the road had been extended to the site of present-day Brindisi, making it the main artery to southern Italy.

Apple, tree (genus *Malus*) of the rose family, widely cultivated in temperate climates; also, the fruit of the tree. Over 7,000 varieties are known, but only about 40 are com-

A

mercially important. There are 3 main types of apples: cooking, dessert, and those used in making cider.

Apple of Sodom (*Solanum sodomeum*), spiny plant of the nightshade family, native to Palestine, that bears yellow fruit resembling small apples. It is named for the biblical apple of Sodom, which looked tempting but turned to ashes in the mouth.

Appleton, Sir Edward Victor (1892-1965), English physicist who discovered the Appleton layer (now resolved as 2 layers, F_1 and F_2) of ionized gas molecules in the ionosphere. His work in atmospheric physics won him the 1947 Nobel Prize for physics and contributed to the development of radar. During World War II he helped develop the atomic bomb.
See also: Ionosphere.

Appolonius of Rhodes (3rd century B.C.), Greek poet, pupil of Callimachus, and later head of the library at Alexandria. In addition to shorter works, he wrote the epic *Argonautica*, describing the expedition of Jason and the Argonauts. The poem uses much of Homer's style and meter, and its portrayal of Medea is thought to have influenced the Roman poet Vergil in the creation of Dido, a character in the *Aeneid*
See also: Homer; Vergil.

Apprentice, person who works for an accomplished craftsperson to learn a trade. An apprentice normally works regular hours and earns a salary. The system of apprenticeship, begun in ancient times, reached its peak in medieval Europe with the organization of guilds representing individual crafts. Following the Industrial Revolution, guilds were gradually replaced by smaller, newer fields of apprenticeship, particularly among machine workers and electricians.
See also: Guild.

Apricot (*Prunus armeniaca*), tree of the rose family, native to China but grown throughout temperate regions; also, the orange-colored fruit of the tree. They are eaten fresh or preserved by drying or canning; the kernels are used to make a liqueur.

April Fools' Day, or All Fools' Day, Apr. 1, the traditional day for practical jokes. The custom probably began in France in 1564, when New Year's Day was changed from Apr. 1 to Jan. 1. Those continuing to observe Apr. 1 were ridiculed.

Apuleius, Lucius (C.A.D. 125-185), Latin writer. His *Metamorphoses* or *The Golden Ass* is the only complete extant Latin novel. The adventures of the novel's hero, who has been turned into an ass, provide insight into Imperial Roman society.

Aqaba, Gulf of, northeastern arm of the Red Sea, between the Sinai Peninsula and Saudi Arabia. Geologically part of the Great Rift Valley of Africa and Asia, it is about 110 mi (177 km) long and 5-17 mi (8-27 km) wide. At the northern end of the gulf stand the ports of Aqaba (Jordan) and Elat (Israel). The Egyptian blockade of Elat sparked the 1967 Arab-Israeli Six-Day War.

Aqsa Mosque, Al-, mosque in Jerusalem. The Al-Aqsa Mosque was built around 700 on the Temple Mount in Jerusalem and together with the nearby Qubbat as-Sakhrah, the Dome of the Rock, counts as one of the most sacred Islamic sites.

Aquaculture, controlled raising of marine animals and seaweed for harvest. Aquaculture takes place in enclosures built on land or in natural bodies of water. China has practiced aquaculture for 4,000 years and is still the leading world producer of cultivated freshwater fish. In addition to fish, Asian sea farmers cultivate seaweed, from which are produced agar, algin, and carrageenan, used in food thickeners and in drugs.

Aqualung *See:* Skin diving.

Aquamarine, transparent blue or pale blue-green semiprecious stone, a variety of the mineral beryl. The most important deposits are in Brazil, but aquamarine is also found in Siberia, Madagascar, and sections of the United States. Other bluish gemstones are sometimes incorrectly called aquamarine, including a blue variety of corundum called Oriental aquamarine.
See also: Beryl.

Aqua regia (Latin, 'royal water'), mixture of concentrated nitric and hydrochloric acids used since the Middle Ages to dissolve gold, the 'royal metal' and other substances that are difficult to get into solution.

Aquarium, tank, bowl, or pool in which aquatic animals and plants are kept. Aquariums originated in ancient Egypt and Asia. Romans used them not for decorative purposes, but as a source of fresh fish for the dinner table. The ornamental aquarium made its appearance in the West in the 18th century, when the goldfish became popular in France. The first public aquarium was opened in London in 1853; today they are found in many of the major cities of the world.

Aqueduct, artificial conduit for water. Ancient Rome was supplied with fresh drinking water from mountain springs by 14 aqueducts. In the south of France the Pont du Gard still stands. The longest aqueduct today is the California State Water Project aqueduct (826 mi/1,329 km), completed in 1974.

Aquinas, Saint Thomas (1225-1274), Italian scholastic theologian and philosopher. Known as the Angelic Doctor, St. Thomas reconciled Christian faith with Aristotelian reason. His teachings are basic to Roman Catholic theology. His greatest work is the *Summa Theologica* (1267-73).
See also: Scholasticism.

Aquino, Corazon (1933-), first woman president of the Philippines (1986-92). The widow of slain Philippine opposition leader Benigno Aquino, she was the major opposition candidate in the 1986 presidential elections. The National Assembly, controlled by supporters of President Marcos, declared Marcos winner of the election, although there were major signs of fraud. After rioting broke out, Marcos left the Philippines on board a U.S. plane, and Aquino was recognized as president. She was succeeded by Fidel Ramos in 1992.

Arab, one whose language is Arabic and who identifies with Arab culture. The term originally referred to inhabitants of the Arabian Peninsula, but the Arab world today includes the countries Algeria, Egypt, Iraq, Jordan, Lebanon, Libya, Morocco, Sudan, Syria, and Tunisia. Arab culture spread after the successful campaigns of Mohammed (c.A.D. 570). In the 7th century the Arabs extended their hegemony from northwestern Africa and Spain to Afghanistan and northern India, where many non-Arabic peoples were converted to the Arabic religion of Islam. Non-Muslim peoples who are also Arabs include Palestinian, Lebanese, and Syrian Christians. In the 20th century the discovery and exploitation of petroleum in Arab lands has resulted in sudden wealth and modernization for many Arab countries. Arab hostility to the state of Israel has strengthened Pan-Arab nationalism.
See also: Islam; Middle East; Muslims.

Arabesque, elaborate decorative style characterized by curved or intertwining shapes, with grotesque, animal, human, or symbolic forms and delicate foliage.

Arabia *See:* Arabian Peninsula; Saudi Arabia.

Arabian Desert, one of the greatest desert regions in the world, comprising almost all of the deserts of the Arabian Peninsula in southwest Asia. The desert covers approximately 900,000 sq mi (2,331,000 sq km) and is surrounded by the Syrian Desert, the Persian Gulf, the Gulf of Oman, the Arabian Sea, the Gulf of Aden, and the Red Sea.

Arabian Nights, or *The Thousand and One Nights*, collection of ancient Persian, Indian, and Arabian folktales, written in Arabic and arranged in its present form during the early

The Pont du Gard, an approximately 2000-year-old Roman aqueduct over the Gard river, north of Nimes, France.

16th century. The stories, which include the tales of Aladdin, Ali Baba, and Sinbad the Sailor, are linked by a framing story about Scheherazade. She marries a king who executes his wives on the second day of their marriage. Each night, she tells him part of a story but leaves the ending for the next night. The king must spare her for another day if he is to learn the ending. By the 1001st night, the king has learned to love his wife, and Scheherazade is spared.
See also: Burton, Sir Richard Francis.

Arabian Peninsula, vast land, largely desert, in southwest Asia, surrounded by the Red Sea, the Arabian Sea, and the Persian Gulf. Saudi Arabia takes up the greatest part of land. Other countries are the Republic of Yemen, Oman, United Arab Emirates, Qatar, and Kuwait. The arid area, approximately 1,162,000 sq mi (3,009,600 sq km), is economically and politically important because of its great petroleum resources.

Arabian Sea, northwestern sea of the Indian Ocean, between India and Arabia. It is connected with the Persian Gulf by the Gulf of Oman and with the Red Sea by the Gulf of Aden. Its ports include Bombay and Karachi.

Arabic, one of the Semitic languages. The Arabic alphabet comprises 28 consonants, vowels being expressed either by positioned points or, in some cases, by insertion of the letters *alif, waw,* and *ya* where they would not otherwise occur, thereby representing the long *a, u,* and *i* respectively. Arabic is written from right to left. Classical Arabic, the language of the Koran, is used occasionally in writing, rarely in speech; a standardized modern Arabic is used in newspapers. Arabic played a large part in the dissemination of knowledge through medieval Europe because many ancient Greek and Roman texts were available solely in Arabic translation.
See also: Semitic languages.

Arabic numerals, also called Hindu-Arabic numerals, the most common symbols for numbers. These basic symbols or digits (Latin, 'fingers') are: 0, 1, 2, 3, 4, 5, 6, 7, 8, and 9. The position of the digit determines its value. For example, in the Arabic numeral 846, the digit 8 has a value of 8 x 100, the digit 4 has a value of 4 x 10, and the digit 6 has a value of 6. Exactly how Arabic numerals originated is unknown. The Hindus in India probably developed 1 through 9 in about 200 B.C.; they developed zero after A.D. 600. Traders and merchants helped spread the Arabic numeral system into Europe.
See also: Numeration systems.

Arab-Israeli Wars, several conflicts between Israel and the Arabs. In 1948, when Israel was established as an independent state on what the Arabs regarded as Arab land, Egypt, Iraq, Transjordan (Jordan), Lebanon, and Syria attacked, but within a month Israel had occupied the greater part of Palestine. By July 1949, separate ceasefires were concluded with the Arab states.
On Oct. 29, 1956, with the Suez Canal and Gulf of Aqaba closed to its ships, Israel in-

vaded Egypt, which had nationalized the canal in July. British and French supporting troops occupied the canal banks but were replaced by a UN force after international furor. By Mar. 1957 all Israeli forces had left Egypt in exchange for access to the Gulf of Aqaba. In 1967 Egypt again closed the Gulf to Israel, and on June 5, at the start of the Six-Day War, Israeli air strikes destroyed the Arab air forces on the ground. Israel won the West Bank of the Jordan River, the Golan Heights, the Gaza Strip, the Sinai Peninsula, and the Old City of Jerusalem. A ceasefire was accepted by June 10. On Oct. 6, 1973, Yom Kippur, Egypt and Syria attacked Israel to regain the lost territories. A ceasefire was signed on Nov. 11, 1973. Talks between Egypt and Israel led to a peace treaty in 1979. In 1994 Jordan and Israel signed a peace agreement.

Arab League, organization promoting economic, cultural, and political cooperation among Arab states, founded in 1945. Its members include 21 of the Arab states and the PLO. In 1948 the members attacked the new state of Israel, which had been established on what the Arabs considered Arab land. The league broke with Egypt, an original member, in 1979 after the country signed a peace treaty with Israel. Egypt rejoined the league in 1989. In 2002 Libya left the league.

Arachne, in Greek mythology, mortal so expert in weaving that she challenged Athena to a contest. Arachne's tapestry, which depicted the foibles of the gods, angered the goddess, who tore it up. Arachne hanged herself in despair and was transformed into a spider.

Arachnid, insectlike arthropod of the class Arachnida. Spiders, mites, and scorpions are arachnids. While an insect's body consists of head, thorax, and abdomen, an arachnid's body has only 2 main parts: abdomen and cephalothorax, which combines head and thorax. Also unlike insects, arachnids have no wings or antennae, and they have simple rather than compound eyes.

Arafat, Yasir (1929-), Palestinian political figure. After organizing the anti-Israel Al Fatah guerrillas in the 1950s, Arafat became chairman of the Palestine Liberation Organization (PLO) in 1969. In 1974 Arafat opened a debate on Palestine at the UN, where he led the first nongovernmental delegation to take part in a General Assembly plenary session. It is generally believed that Arafat authorized terrorist actions to accom-

PLO chairman Yasir   to the European
Arafat during his visit   Union in 1993.

plish the goals of the PLO. In 1991, the PLO sided with Iraq in the Persian Gulf War which led to a weakening of its position. Arafat regained esteem when he signed an agreement (Oslo 1) with Israel regarding limited Palestinian autonomy in the Gaza Strip and Jericho (1993). This resulted in him being awarded the Nobel Peace prize, together with Yitzhak Rabin and Shimon Peres (1994). In 1995 Arafat and Rabin signed an agreement (Oslo 2) regarding the withdrawal in stages of the Israeli troops

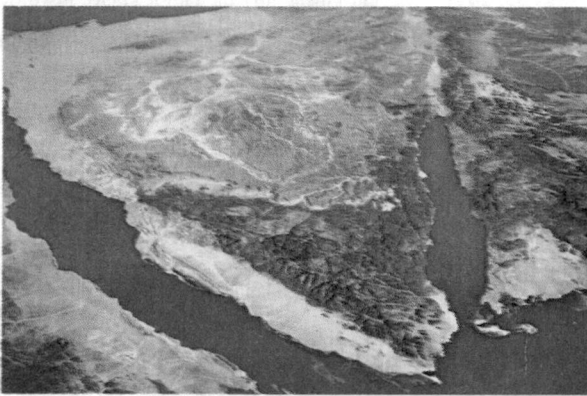

The Arab peninsula.

from six important cities on the West Bank. The agreement also provided for elections for a Palestinian council and a president. In 1996 Arafat was elected president of the council.
However, due to the Israeli settlement policy as well as the ongoing opposition of HAMAS (Islamic resistance movement) against the Oslo treaties, the peace process stagnated soon after Arafat was elected president. In Palestinian circles, Arafat was accused of corruption and a lack of respect for human rights. In 2000, negotiations between Arafat and Barak failed, and the beginning of a second Infitadah meant the end of the peace process. After Sharon came to power in 2001, Arafat was continuously forced into a corner. He was held hostage for months in his own headquarters and Sharon refused to negotiate with him. The Palestinian parliament on March 10th 2003, approved the new position of prime minister as part of reforms sought by the United States, Europe and Israel to curb Yasir Arafat's near absolute powers. President Bush has said the Palestinians have to choose new leaders as a precondition for Statehood. Mahmoud Abbas is Arafat's appointee for prime minister.
See also: Palestine Liberation Organization.

Aragón, historic region of northeastern Spain, stretching from the central Pyrenees to south of the Ebro River. The medieval kingdom of Aragón comprised what are now the provinces of Huesca, Teruel, and Saragossa, although the influence of the kings of Aragón was more extensive. King Ferdinand II of Aragón's marriage to Isabella of Castile (1479) laid the foundations of a unified Spain. Aragón's sovereignty was ended 1707-9 by Philip V during the War of the Spanish Succession (1701-14).

Aragon, Louis (1897-1982), a French author. He was prominent in the Dadaism and

A

Surrealism movements in the 1920's but after a visit to the Soviet Union in 1931 turned to social realism. *The Bells of Basel* (1936) and *The Century Was Young* (1941) are novels with a Marxist approach. *Holy Week* (1958) is a historical novel set in the Napoleonic era, and *Henri Matisse: A Novel* (1972), despite its title, is a biography. Aragon's verse includes *Red Front* (1931), *Le Crève-coeur* (1940), and *Les Yeux d'Elsa* (1942). Aragon was decorated for valor in World War I and served in the Resistance movement after the fall of France in World War II. He became a Communist in the 1930's and remained an active member of the party until his death.

Arakawa, Shusaku (1936-), Japanese visual artist who took up residence in New York in 1961. Makes 'blueprints' for paintings: monochrome maps with points, arrows, lines, and short texts. Representative of conceptual art.

Aral Sea, inland sea or saltwater lake covering 24,904 sq mi (64,501 sq km) in Kazakhstan and Uzbekistan. It is the fourth largest lake in the world and is fed by the Amu Darya and Syr Darya rivers. The sea is commercially important for its bass, carp, perch, and sturgeon. In the last 30 years, the irrigation needed for the extensive cultivation of cotton, has led to a considerable reduction of the water supply. This, together with pollution resulted in an environmental disaster which also threatened public health in the surrounding areas. In 1997, the Worldbank granted a loan for the construction of water pipes and water treatment plants.

Aramaic, Semitic language. It spread throughout Syria and Mesopotamia from the 8th century B.C. on, and was the official language of the Persian Empire. Aramaic was probably spoken by Jesus and the apostles, and parts of the Old Testament are in Aramaic. Aramaic survives only in isolated Lebanese villages and among some Nestorians of northern Iraq and eastern Turkey.
See also: Semitic languages.

Arapaho, North American tribe of the Algonquian family. They lived as nomadic buffalo hunters on the Great Plains. The Arapaho are divided into 3 groups: the Southern Arapaho, the Northern Arapaho, and the Gros Ventre. Less than 5,000 Arapaho remain, mostly on reservations.

Ararat, Mount, dormant volcanic mountain in eastern Turkey with 2 peaks, 16,950 ft (5,166 m) and 13,000 ft (3,962 m) high. According to the Bible, Noah's Ark landed on Mount Ararat (Genesis 8:4). The Armenians venerate the mountain as the 'Mother of the World.'
See also: Noah.

Araucanians, South American tribes famous for their resistance to the Spaniards, beginning with the 16th-century Spanish invasion of what is now central Chile. Many Araucanians crossed the Andes into Argentina on stolen Spanish horses. The tribes were defeated in the late 19th century.

Today over 200,000 Araucanians live in Chile.

Arawak, group of often culturally distinct South American tribes, now living mostly in Brazil, the Guyanas, and Peru. Arawak inhabited several West Indian islands when Columbus landed in 1492. The Caribbean Arawak were wiped out by the mid-16th century by a combination of disease and forced labor brought on by Europeans.

Arbitration, process for settling disputes in which the parties submit the controversy to an impartial arbitrator. In conciliation or mediation, the impartial person tries to persuade the parties to accept a settlement; in arbitration, by prior agreement the arbitrator imposes a final and binding decision, called an award. Experienced tribunals established by trade associations arbitrate commercial disputes between business organizations. Industrial arbitration settles disputes between labor and management. Collective bargaining agreements generally provide for an impartial arbitrator to settle conflicts arising from different interpretations of the agreement. Arbitration in international affairs is one of the oldest ways of settling disputes. It was used by the Greek city-states and is today included as a provision in many treaties between nations.

Arboretum, place in which trees and shrubs

This statue was found in Moravia (former Czechoslovakia) and is dated back to the Paleothic period (about 250,000 B.C.). It represents woman as mother and is known as the Venus of Dolni Vestonice.

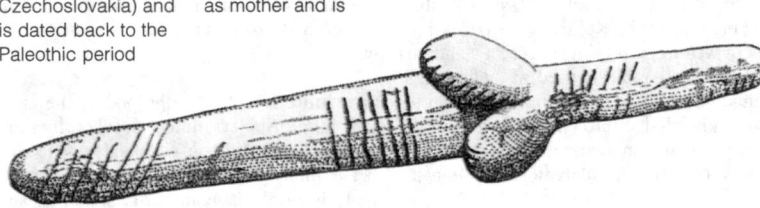

are cultivated for scientific or educational purposes.

Arbus, Diane (1923-1971) American photographer. Worked for *Vogue* and *Harper's Bazaar* among others. Very well known through her fascinating photographs of people who deviate from the norm, such as transvestites, junkies, mongols, nudists, etc.

Arcadia, ancient Greek region in central Peloponnesus, enclosed by mountains. The simple life of its rustic inhabitants was idealized by classical pastoral poets and later writers, notably the English poet Sir Philip Sidney, as the embodiment of innocent, virtuous living.

Arc, electric *See:* Electric arc.

Arc, Joan of *See:* Joan of Arc, Saint.

Arcaro, Eddie (George Edward Arcaro; 1916-1997), U.S. jockey. The first to have won the Triple Crown twice (1941,1948) and the Kentucky Derby 5 times, and the

third jockey to win more than 4,000 races. Arcaro's purses totaled more than $30 million during his career (1931-62).

Arc de Triomphe, Napoleon's triumphal arch in the Place Charles de Gaulle at the end of the Champs-Elysées, Paris. It was built 1806-36 and is 163 ft (49 m) high and 147 ft (45 m) wide. Inspired by Roman triumphal arches, it bears reliefs celebrating Napoleon's victories. The arch is also the site of the tomb of France's Unknown Soldier.

Arch, structural device to span openings and support loads. In architecture the simplest form of the arch is the round (semicircular), in which wedge-shaped stones, or voussoirs, are fitted together, receiving the stresses in the arch exerted outward onto them. Downward forces from the load combine with these to produce a diagonal force, or thrust. The voussoirs at each end of the arch are called springers; the one in the center, usually the last to be placed, is the keystone. Although the arch was known in ancient Egypt and Greece, it was not until Roman times that its use became popular.

Archaeopteryx, prehistoric feathered reptile the size of a crow, with 2 claws representing the thumb and forefinger projecting from its wing and about 20 tail vertebrae. *See also:* Prehistoric animal.

Archangel (pop. 419,000; Russian, *Arkhangelsk*), city in northwestern Russian Federation, near the mouth of the North Dvina River. Archangel is a major White Sea port. Major industry is wood processing. Established as a trading post called Novo-Kholmogory in 1584, it later became a leading Russian port, declining after 1703, when St. Petersburg was founded.

Archbishop, metropolitan bishop of the Roman Catholic, Anglican, or Eastern Orthodox church, or of the Lutheran churches of Finland and Sweden, having jurisdiction over the bishops of a church province, or archdiocese. The archbishop consecrates bishops and presides over synods.

Archeoastronomy, study of the astronomy of ancient peoples and its relation to other aspects of culture. The field includes the work of archeologists, astronomers, historians, and anthropologists. Archeoastronomers in Great Britain have studied the circles of large stones laid more than 5,000 years ago, and believe the circles may have been calendars

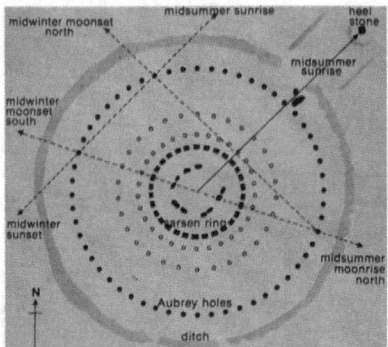

Stonehenge, a composite structure consisting of a ditch, 56 chalkfilled holes, and huge standing stones arranged in concentric circles, was built more than 4,000 years ago. Some of the stones are aligned with the rising Sun at the summer solstice; others line up with the rising or setting Sun and Moon on certain days of the year.

or a way of predicting eclipses. Also of interest are Mayan buildings, which were constructed in a direct line with Venus on the horizon.
See also: Archeology; Astronomy; Stonehenge.

Archeology, study of the past through identification and interpretation of the material remains of human cultures. Archeology uses the knowledge and techniques of such disciplines as anthropology, history, paleography, and philology. Its keystone is fieldwork. Archeology began in the early 18th century with excavations of Roman and other sites. The famous Rosetta Stone, which provided the key to Egyptian hieroglyphics, was discovered in 1799 and deciphered in 1818. In the 19th century archeology became a systematized science through the work of Heinrich Schliemann, Arthur Evans, C. L. Woolley, Howard Carter, and others. In the United States archeologists have studied the culture of early Native Americans as well as settlements of colonial America-an example of historic archeology, which deals with peoples who left behind written documents. Suitable sites may be revealed as a result of war damage or during construction of buildings and roads. Because unusually shaped hills or mounds are sometimes artificial, they are often investigated. Ancient writings may help in locating sites. Aerial photography has sometimes revealed the existence of buried structures. The archeological team then recovers objects or fragments lying loose on the ground or inside caves, or, more often, excavates (digs) to find the artifacts. Great care is required not to damage any object or trace of an object. Small hoes, spades, trowels, penknives, brushes, and fingers are used. Archeologists record the spatial relationships artifacts have to one another and to the layers in which they are found. Notes and drawings are made, each item is numbered, and photographs are taken.
Archeologists use 2 dating systems: absolute dating and relative dating. Early inscriptions, and especially, mention of an eclipse or other astronomical phenomena, make it easy to date a monument or site. Tree-ring chronology can help date wood remains.

Pollen, an extraordinarily durable organic substance, is also a useful date indicator. Radiocarbon dating uses the known half-life of radioactive carbon-14, found in all organic matter, as a yardstick. Stratigraphy, the most important method for relative dating, uses the principle that objects found near the surface are more recent than those found lower within the ground. Because pottery styles sometimes overlap on several sites, information gained from one site can be applied to another. Chemical changes in bones can also help differentiate younger ones from older ones.

Archerfish, any of several species of Indo-Pacific fishes of the family Toxotidae with the ability to eject water from their mouths to knock insect prey to the surface; especially, *Toxotes jaculator*. The archerfish has a flat, elongated body and inhabits both fresh and salt water.

Archery, competitive and recreational sport, using bows and arrows. The three major types of archery are target, field and flight. Target and field archery involve firing arrows at set targets, while flight archery is a contest of distance shooting. An Olympic event, archery's popularity worldwide led to the formation of the International Archery Federation (1931).

Archimedes (c.287-212 B.C.), Greek mathematician and physicist who spent most of his life in Syracuse, Sicily, where he was born. In mathematics he worked on the areas and volumes of conic sections, determined the value of π as lying between 3-1/7 and 3-10/71, and defined the Archimedean spiral.

He founded the science of hydrostatics with his enunciation of Archimedes' principle, that the force acting to buoy up a body partially or totally immersed in a fluid is equal to the weight of the fluid displaced. He is also credited with the invention of Archimedes' screw, a machine for raising water that is still used to irrigate fields in Egypt. In physics he was the first to prove the law of the lever.
See also: Calculus; Physics.

Archipelago (Greek, 'chief sea'), name originally applied to the Aegean Sea, which is studded with many small islands; by extension, any space of water interspersed with islands or the group of islands itself. The greatest archipelago is the 3,200-mile (5,100-km) crescent of more than 3,000 islands that form Indonesia.

Archipenko, Alexander (1887-1964), a U.S. sculptor. He was one of the first 20th-century sculptors to reintroduce color as a sculptural element. In his stylized representations of the human figure, he often combined a variety of materials, such as terracotta, papier-mâché, cement, and plastic. *The Bride* and *Woman Doing Her Hair* are characteristic of his cubist-abstract style. Archipenko was born in Kiev, Russia, and studied in Paris and in Berlin. He came to the U.S. in 1923 and became a citizen in 1928.

Architecture, art or science of designing and building structures. While the beginnings of architecture are traceable to areas around the Nile, Euphrates, and Tigris rivers, the Greeks and Romans created the

A

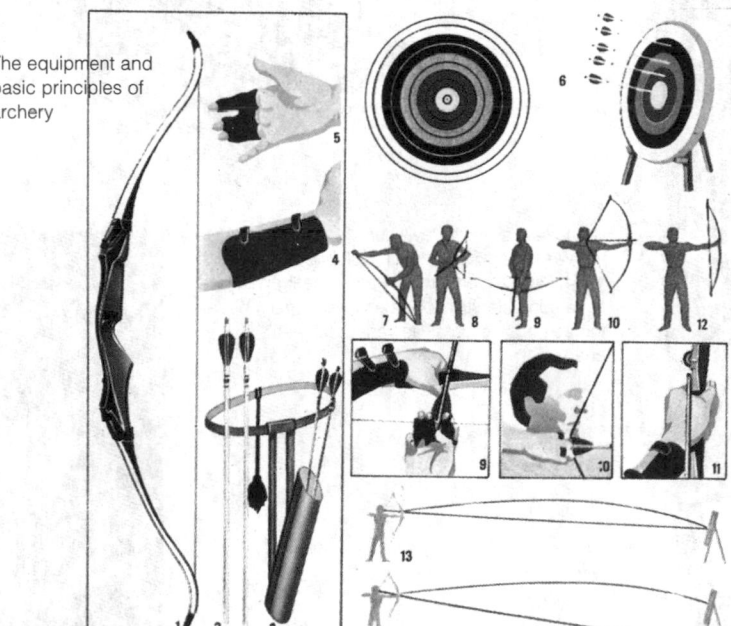

The equipment and basic principles of archery

1 typical modern bow of fibreglass and wood
2 arrows of tubular aluminum alloy
3 quiver, with waist-belt and tassel attached (to wipe the arrows clean)
4 arm bracer
5 tab
6 most commonly used targets are: the five-ring target (in which the gold has a value of 9, the red of 7, the blue of 5, the black of 3, and the white a value of 1), and the FITA target (in which each ring is divided into two, giving a scoring of 1-10)
7 stringing the bow
8/9 nocking the arrow and preparing to draw
10 drawing
11 aiming
12 loosing
13 two different methods of aiming: the line-of-sight method, and the point-of-aim method.

A

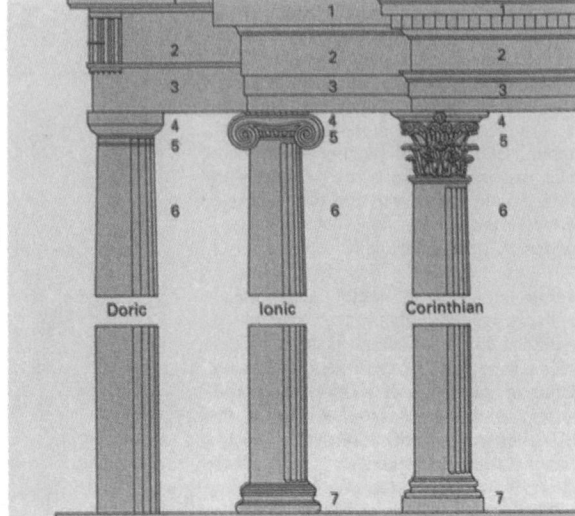

Doric, Ionic, and Corinthian columns. The Doric is the simplest and oldest of the three styles and evolved in the 7th century B.C. The Ionic style reached maturity in the 5th century B.C. and the Corinthian in the 4th century B.C. Shown are the following elements:
1. cornice
2. frieze
3. architrave
4. abacus
5. capital
6. columns with fluting
7. base

Pier Luigi Nervi's interior of the Turin Exhibition Hall.

Rome's Pantheon (c. A.D. 115-125) is the world's oldest building with its original roof intact. Shown are the following:
1. Corinthian columns of white marble
2. intermediate block leading to rotunda
3. rotunda
4. semi-domed exedra
5. marble and granite pavement
6. attic
7. hemispherical, brick and mortar dome with bronze tiles
8. central oculus, the only source of light.

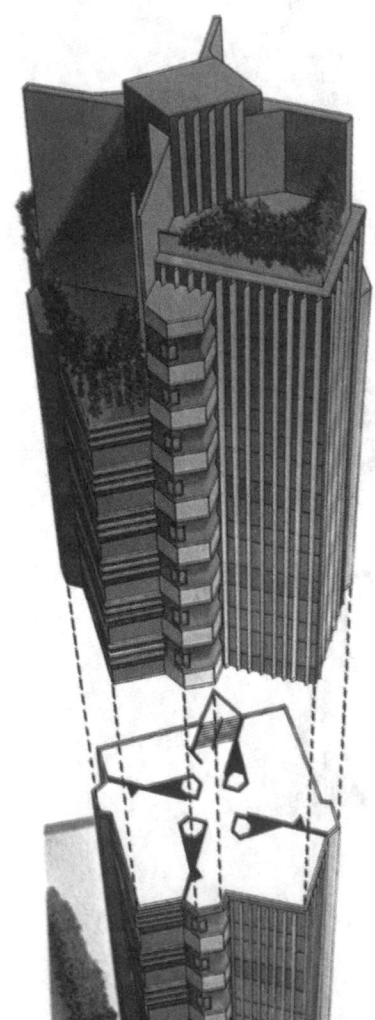

Bruno Taut's Glass Pavillion, which appeared at the Werkbund Exhibition in Cologne, Germany in 1914. Taut wrote that this was `...the lightest possible concrete structure, destined to demonstrate the use of glass in all its varied aesthetic charm....'

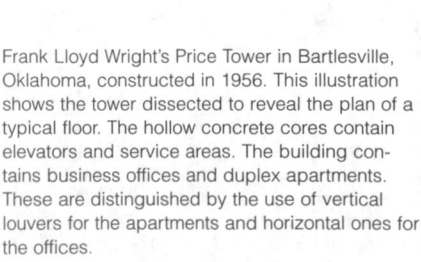

Frank Lloyd Wright's Price Tower in Bartlesville, Oklahoma, constructed in 1956. This illustration shows the tower dissected to reveal the plan of a typical floor. The hollow concrete cores contain elevators and service areas. The building contains business offices and duplex apartments. These are distinguished by the use of vertical louvers for the apartments and horizontal ones for the offices.

styles that we rely on today. Greek architecture used post-and-lintel construction: a rectangle formed by beams and columns. The Romans were the first to fully use the arch and to use concrete as a building material, making possible structures with enormous roof spans.

Byzantine architecture, which arose in the Eastern Roman Empire and later influenced Russia, introduced the dome. Islamic architecture featured interior courtyards surrounded by colonnades. At the end of the Middle Ages, European churches and monasteries were stoutly built, for defensive purposes. Starting at the end of the 12th century, stained glass, high pillars, and thin arches of Gothic architecture were held in equilibrium by exterior buttresses. The Renaissance brought a revival of classical (Greek and Roman) architecture. In the Baroque period, rich ornamentation and curves replaced the straight lines of the Renaissance. The 18th century saw a revival of classical architecture in Europe and America, and a Gothic revival began in the 19th century. Starting in the last half of the 19th century, the use of iron, steel, and reinforced concrete allowed skyscrapers to be built.

Archon, administrator of ancient Athens and other Greek city-states. Originally a life term open only to nobles, by 682 B.C. the archonship was shared by 9 members elected from the population for 1 year, and included a civil ruler, a religious head, a military commander, and 6 lawmakers. The archons lost influence with the rise of democracy.

Arc light, device in which electrical current flowing between poles or electrodes produces the electric arc, yielding an intensely bright light. Arc lights are used in searchlights and movie projectors. The mercury arc is the basis for modern fluorescent lamps.
See also: Electric light.

Arctic, region north of the Arctic Circle (66°30' N); alternatively, regions north of the tree line.
Land and climate. The Arctic comprises the Arctic Ocean, Greenland, Spitsbergen and other islands, extreme northern Europe, Siberia, Alaska, and northern Canada. The area's central feature is the Arctic Ocean, opening south into the North Atlantic Ocean and Bering Strait. The Arctic Ocean comprises 2 main basins and has a shallow rim floored by the continental shelves of Eurasia and North America. Much of the ocean's surface is always covered with ice.
The Arctic climate is cold. In midwinter the sun never rises and the mean Jan. temperature is -33° F (-57.6° C), far lower in interior Canada and Siberia. Snow and ice never melt in the high altitudes and latitudes of the Arctic, but elsewhere the short mild summer, with 24 hours of sunlight a day, thaws the sea and the topsoil. In spring, melting icebergs floating south from the Arctic Ocean endanger North Atlantic shipping. Vegetation in the Arctic is varied but confined mainly to shrubs, flowering herbaceous plants, mosses, and lichens. Wild mammals include polar bears, reindeer,

musk oxen, moose, wolves, weasels, foxes, and lemmings. Geese, ducks, gulls, cranes, falcons, auks, and ptarmigan all nest in the Arctic, and its seas harbor whales, seals, cod, salmon, and shrimp.
People. Inuits (Eskimos), Lapps, Russians, and others make up a human population of several million. Eskimos have lived in the Arctic for at least 9,000 years. Once exclusively hunters and fishers, Eskimos now also work in towns and on oil fields.
Economy. The Arctic is home to scattered agricultural, mining, and fishing industries, and the United States, Canada, and the Russian Federation maintain air bases and meteorological stations there. In 1978, oil production began at Prudhoe Bay, an inlet of the Arctic Ocean in northern Alaska, the oil moving south to Valdez, Alaska, through the Alaskan Pipeline.

History. Vikings were the first recorded Arctic explorers. Norwegians visited the Russian Arctic in the 9th century and the Icelander Eric the Red established a Greenland settlement in A.D. 982. In the 16th and 17th centuries exploration was encouraged by the search for a northwest passage (a water route along the northern coast of North America, between the Atlantic and Pacific oceans) and a northeast passage (a water route between the same oceans but along the northern coast of Europe and Asia). In the 16th century Martin Frobisher reached Baffin Island, and Willem Barentz explored Novaya Zemlya and saw Spitsbergen. Henry Hudson probed eastern Greenland and the Hudson Strait in the early 17th century. But the longed-for passages remained undiscovered, and interest in Arctic exploration declined until Canadian

and Russian fur traders revived it late in the 18th century. Early in the 19th century the British naval officers John and James Ross, W. E. Perry, John Rae, and Sir John Franklin traveled to unexplored areas, and James Ross discovered the north magnetic pole. N.A.E. Nordenskjöld of Sweden navigated the Northeast Passage (1878-79) and R. Amundsen the Northwest Passage (1906). In 1909 Robert E. Peary reached the North Pole. Richard E. Byrd and Floyd Bennett flew over the Pole in 1926, pioneering polar air exploration and transpolar air travel. The feasibility of using the shortest undersea route between the North Atlantic and North Pacific oceans, under the Arctic ice cap, was demonstrated by the voyage of the nuclear submarine USS Nautilus in 1958. In 1969 the United States tanker Manhattan navigated the Northwest Passage to demonstrate

that the route could be used for oil shipments. In 1977 the Soviet ship Arktika became the first surface vessel to reach the Pole.

Arctic Circle, imaginary circle at 66 30° N lat. roughly defining the tree line and marking the southernmost point of the polar area at which the midnight sun is seen. The sun never rises on the Arctic Circle at the winter solstice on or about Dec. 21.

Arctic fox (*Alopex lagopus*), tundra dweller of the family Canidae. In summer, it is brown or gray; in winter it is white or slate blue. The Arctic fox is about 2 ft (60 cm) long, with a long tail and short, rounded ears. A true scavenger, it eats any available food and follows polar bears to eat the remains of their kills.

A

The food chain of the ice cap. At the peak of the circumpolar ice cap's ecological pyramid, there are two main predators: the polar bear, Thalarctos maritimus, and the arctic fox, *Alopex lagopus*. The former feeds principally on seals and young walruses, the latter chiefly on carrion, left by the polar bear.
A. polar bear.
B. young walruses (*Odobenus rosmarus*), preyed on by polar bear.
C. ringed seal (*Pusa hispida*), also preyed on by polar bear.
Both of the above-mentioned species feed on molluscs and shellfish.
D. arctic fox, feeds on carrion (*seal carcasses*), left by a polar bear, which only eats the blubber.
E. polar bear, preyed on by the killer whale (*Orcinus orca*).

A

Arctic Ocean, the smallest ocean, centering on the North Pole and connecting with the Atlantic through the Greenland Sea and with the Pacific through the Bering Strait. It covers about 4 million sq mi (10.3 million sq km), has an average depth of 4,362 ft (1,330 m), and includes an abyss with a known depth of 17,880 ft (5,450 m) and a continental shelf extending up to 1,000 mi (1,600 km) from the coast. Most of the Arctic Ocean is frozen all year. It was probably discovered by Greek sailors around 400 B.C. and was sailed by Vikings in the 800s. Norwegian explorer Fridtjof Nansen conducted the first scientific study in 1893-96.

Fridtjof Nansen (1861-1930) was one of the great discoverers and explorers of the North Pole area. His instruments, sledge and cooking utensils set the example for modern North Pole equipment, while his methods are still used in modern Pole exploration. Most sensational, however, was his ship, the `Fram', which had specially reinforced sides to resist the pressure of the pack-ice.

Arctic tern (*Sterna paradisaea*), a coast-dwelling, long-distance migrant bird of the family Laridae. The Arctic tern winters in Antarctica, then flies north to breed on Atlantic coasts from New England to the northernmost islands of the Arctic Ocean. It is about 17 in (43 cm) long, with gray, black, and white feathers and a red bill and feet. *See also:* Tern.

Arcturus (*Alpha Bootes*), brightest and fourth-largest star, orange-red in color. It is located in the constellation Boötes. Arcturus is about 40 light-years from earth and is moving toward earth at 3 mi (5 km) per second. Its luminosity is about 100 times that of the sun.

Ardennes, forested plateau in southeastern Belgium, northern Luxembourg, and northern France. The area is sparsely populated, with some agriculture and quarrying. It was a major battleground in World War I and World War II.

Arendt, Erich (1903-1984), East German poet. In 1934 he went to Spain where he joined a republican division during the Civil War. In 1940 he fled via Marseilles to South America. From 1950 onwards he lived in the German Democratic Republic. The Spanish Civil War is the theme of a collection of ballads called *Bergwindballade* (1952). Later he dealt with his experiences as an emigrant in *Trug doch die Nacht den Albatros. Gedichte* (1951). Later poems are dominated by disappointment with topics such as international political development and focus on the theme of growing old: *Memento und Bild* (1976), *Zeitraum* (1978), and *Entgrenzen* (1981).

Arendt, Hannah (1906-1975), German-born U.S. political philosopher. In 1959 she became the first woman appointed a full professor at Princeton University; she later taught at the University of Chicago and the New School for Social Research in New York. In *The Origins of Totalitarianism* (1951) she traced Nazism and Communism back to 19th-century anti-Semitism and imperialism. Her controversial *Eichmann in Jerusalem* (1963), with its theory of the 'banality of evil,' analyzed Nazi war crimes and the 1960 trial of Adolph Eichmann by the Israeli government.

Areopagus, small hill northwest of the Acropolis in Athens, where the supreme council of the city passed judgment on matters of state, religion, and morality. The name came to refer to the council itself. The Areopagus tried homicide cases, and it had a legislative veto and powers of impeachment. *See also:* Solon.

Arequipa (pop. 621,000), city in southern Peru, capital of Arequipa department. Located at an altitude of 8,000 ft (2,400 m), between the Pacific Ocean and the Andes, Arequipa has a mild, dry climate. An important wool market and a crossroads of trade and transportation, its industries produce textiles, food, and shoes. Arequipa has frequently suffered severe damage from earthquakes.

Ares, in Greek mythology, the god of war. He was known to the Romans as Mars.

Argentina

Capital:	Buenos Aires
Area:	1,068,302 sq mi
	(2,780,400 sq km)
Population:	37,813,000
Language:	Spanish
Government:	Federal presidential republic
Independent:	1816
Head of gov.:	President
Per capita:	U.S. $12,000
Monetary unit:	1 Peso = 100 centavos

Argentina, second-largest country in South America (1,072,157 sq mi/2,776,889 sq km). Only Brazil is larger. Argentina borders on the Atlantic Ocean in the southeast; Uruguay, Brazil in the east, Paraguay in the northeast, Bolivia in the north, and Chile in the west.

Land and climate. The Andes Mountains form a natural border with Chile. The Gran Chaco region, in the north, is an extensive forested plain. Also in the north is the Paraná Plateau. The fertile Pampa in the heart of Argentina is the country's most important region economically. Semiarid Patagonia to the south yields oil. In the west, the Andes include Mt. Aconcagua (22,834 ft/6,960 m), the highest peak in South America. The climate of Argentina varies from damp and subtropical in the north to cool and dry in the south.

People. About 90% of the people are descended from Southern European immigrants, with a small Native American population. The national language is Spanish and about 90% of the population is Roman Catholic, with 87% living in urban areas like Buenos Aires.

Economy. Grain-growing and cattle-raising dominate the pampas, and agriculture is the basis of the country's wealth. Oil and other minerals come from the north and south. About 25% of the labor force works in the country's well-developed industrial sector, much of which is located in and around Buenos Aires. High inflation is chronic and persistent.

History. Colonized by the Spanish in the 16th century, Argentina won its independence in 1816. The 19th century saw increased European immigration, economic progress, and political instability and strife with repercussions well into the 20th century. In 1943, Col. Juan Perón seized power and ruled until 1955. His dictatorship was supported by nationalists, the army, and the Roman Catholic church. However, his rule depended in large measure upon the popularity of his wife, Eva Duarte de Perón, and her death (1952), combined with a bad economy, led to Perón's ouster (1955). The Perónist movement remained popular, and in 1973 Perón was restored to power. He died in 1974 and was succeeded by his wife, Isabel Perón, but the economy worsened and violence between left and right increased. Isabel Perón was overthrown in 1976 by military juntas. In reaction to terrorism from the left, the juntas, through their agents and surrogates, kidnapped and murdered some 20,000-30,000 Argentine citizens suspected of leftist sympathies. In 1982, Argentina occupied the Falkland Islands and was defeated by Britain in the subsequent war. Gen. Leopoldo Galtieri resigned and Raúl Alfonsin was elected president of a civilian government in 1983. Nine members of the juntas stood trial for murder and human rights abuses and were sentenced to long prison terms. Carlos Raúl Menem, a Perónist, was elected president in 1989 and started an austerity program to devitalize the economy. This program led to a decline of inflation, but at the same time increased unemployment. In 1995 Menem was reelected. Fernando de la Rúa succeeded Menem in 1999. The economic situation of the country

Stretching between the Codillera de los Andes and a coastal range (with altitudes of 2000 metres), Atacama Desert is situated at an altitude of 800 to 1000 metres, here and there intersected by rivers from the higher Cordillera.

continued to deteriorate. The peso was no longer pegged to the dollar. In 2001, the situation became dramatic: 5 presidents succeeded each other in only 2 weeks time.

Argon, chemical element, symbol Ar; for physical constants see Periodic Table. Argon was discovered by Lord Rayleigh and Sir William Ramsay in 1894. It is prepared by fractionation of liquid air, the atmosphere containing almost 1% of the element. Argon is a colorless, odorless, and chemically inert gas. It is not known to form chemical compounds, as do krypton, xenon, and radon. It is available in high purity, and is used in electric light bulbs, as a nonreactive shield in arc welding and in the production of reactive metals, and as a protective atmosphere for growing silicon, and germanium crystals.

Argonaut, or paper nautilus, small marine animal (genus *Argonauta*), a cephalopod which is native to the Mediterranean and other warm seas. Eggs are laid in a semitransparent, papery spiral shell that can be carried by the female. The male seldom reaches an inch in length, but the female may be as long as 6 in (15 cm) or more.

Argonauts, heroes of Greek mythology who set sail in the ship *Argo* under Jason to find the Golden Fleece. With many illustrious members (Orpheus, Hercules, Castor and Pollux, Theseus), they sailed for Colchis, where the fleece was guarded by a dragon. After averting many perils, they obtained the fleece and returned home.

Argus, or Argos, in Greek mythology, (1) the designer of the Argonauts' ship *Argo*; (2) the old dog who died after recognizing his master, Odysseus, returning in disguise to his home in Ithaca after an absence of 19

years; (3) the monster called Panoptes (the all-seeing) because of the great number of eyes in his head and over his body. He was ordered by Hera to watch Io, who had been transformed into a cow, but Hermes killed him, and by Hera's orders, Argus's eyes were sprinkled as decorations through the tail of the peacock.

Århus (pop. 280,000), port and Denmark's second largest city. Developed by the 9th century. Århus is a commercial and industrial center producing textiles, machines, beer, and timber. It is the site of the Cathedral of St. Clemens, built around 1100, and of the University of Århus, foundened in 1928.

Ariadne, in Greek mythology, daughter of Minos, king of Crete. She loved the hero Theseus and gave him thread that helped him find his way out of the labyrinth. After Theseus killed the Minotaur, he married Ariadne but later deserted her. The god Bacchus gave her a crown of seven stars, which became a constellation.

Arianism, 4th-century Christian heresy founded in Alexandria by the priest Arius. He taught that Christ was not coequal and coeternal with God the Father, for the Father had created him. To curb Arianism, the Emperor Constantine called the first Council of Nicaea (A.D. 325), and the first Nicene Creed declared that God the Father and Christ the Son were of the same substance.
See also: Nicene Councils.

Arias Sánchez, Oscar (1941-), Costa Rican politician. He served as the president's financial adviser (1970-72), minister of national planning (1972-77), and president (1986-90). Arias Sánchez denied U.S.-supported Nicaraguan contras operating bases in Costa Rica, and promoted peaceful regional negotiations, for which he was awarded the Nobel Peace Prize in 1987.

Ariosto, Ludovico (1474-1533), Italian poet best remembered for the epic *Orlando Furioso* (1532), which continued the Roland legend, depicting the hero as a love-torn knight. The work greatly influenced later poets such as Edmund Spenser and Lord Byron.

Aristarchus of Samos (310-230 B.C.), Alexandrian Greek astronomer who recognized that the sun is larger than the earth. According to Archimedes, he taught that the earth orbited a motionless sun.
See also: Archimedes.

Aristide, Jean-Bertrand (1953-), Haitian politician. Until he was elected president, Aristide was a priest with leftist ideals. He dedicated himself to the struggle against poverty. His party, the National Front for Change and Democracy (FNCD) won the elections in 1990 by a large majority. In 1991 Aristide left the country after a military coup led by General Raoul Cédras took place. Aristide only returned in 1994 after diplomatic intervention by Jimmy Carter. Previous attempts to mediate had failed, including efforts by the OAS since 1992. In the presidential elections of 1995 which

were boycotted by a number of opposition parties, Aristide's candidate from the Lavalas Party, former Prime Minister René Préval, won a landslide victory. He succeeded Aristide as president on 7th February 1996.

Aristides (530?-468? B.C.), called the Just, Athenian politician and general, a founder of the Delian League. He fought at the battle of Marathon (490 B.C.) and was elected archon for 489. Ostracized in 482, he was recalled in 480 and helped repulse the Persians. Later he fixed Greek cities' contributions to the Delian League.
See also: Themistocles.

Aristocracy (from Greek *aristos*, 'the best,' and *kratos*, 'rule'), originally, the ruling of a state by its best citizens in the interest of all; used by the philosophers Plato and Aristotle in this sense. The term later came to mean a form of government dominated by a small privileged class. Today the term refers to members of a class that has hereditary privileges.

Aristophanes (450-385 B.C.), comic dramatist of ancient Greece. His works feature political, social, and literary satire, witty dialogue, vigorous rivalry, cleverly contrived comic situations, and choral lyrics. Eleven of his 40 plays survive, notably *The Frogs* (satirizing Euripides), *The Clouds* (satirizing Socrates), *Lysistrata* (a plea for pacifism), and *The Birds* (a fantasy about a sky city).
See also: Greece, Ancient; Theater.

Aristotle (384-322 B.C.), Greek philosopher, one of the most influential thinkers of the ancient world. He studied at Plato's academy in Athens in 343 B.C. and became the tutor of the young Alexander the Great. In 335 Aristotle set up his own school at the Lyceum in Athens. His works, covering a vast range of subjects, include *Physics*, *Metaphysics*, *On the Soul*, *On the Heavens*, *Poetics*, *Politics*, *Nicomachean Ethics*, and works on biology, aesthetics, rhetoric, and other subjects. Aristotle's writings reached the West through Latin translations in the

Aristotle (384-322 B.C.), the versatile Greek thinker, whose works have had a major impact on philosophy (Museo Nazionale, Naples).

A

11th and 13th centuries, and had a prevailing influence on medieval and later thought. His emphasis on observation and analysis of the physical world, revolutionary for his time, underlies modern science. He developed the system of logic in use in the West until recent times.
See also: Greece, Ancient; Philosophy.

Arithmetic (Greek *arithmos*, 'number'), science of numbers. Until the 16th century arithmetic was viewed as the study of all the properties and relations of all numbers; in modern times, the term usually denotes the study of the positive real numbers and zero under the operations of addition, subtraction, multiplication, and division.
See also: Mathematics.

Ariyoshi, Sawako (1931-1984), Japanese writer of short stories, murder mysteries, and historical novels that explore the culture, traditions, social structure, and domestic problems of classical and modern Japan. Among her works are *Kokotsu No Hito, The Twilight Years, The River Ki, Compound Pollution, The Doctor's Wife, Diary of Princess Kazu,* and *The Curtain-Raising Bell Sounds Beautiful.*

Arizona (pop. 4,555,000; Grand Canyon State), state in the US, bordering states are: New Mexico, California, Nevada, and Mexico; 112,308 sq mi (290,765 sq km). Capital: Phoenix. Other important cities: Mesa, Glendale, Tucson.
The state mainly consists of a plateau cut by the Colorado River. This is the same river that has eroded the well known Grand Canyon to what it is today. The climate varies as a result of the different terrains. The dry Sonora Desert is hot in summer but regularly has frost in winter. The Colorado Plateau is hot in summer but windy and cold in winter. The Mexican Plateau has the coolest climate, and invariably has frost in winter.
Arizona is one of the fastest growing states in the US. Main products are cotton, grain, fruit, vegetables, and timber. The soil has rich layers of ore, especially copper, as well as gold, silver, lead, and zinc. Most important means of existence include mining, metal industry, food production, and timber processing.
Arizona became part of the US in 1912.

Ark, biblical vessel Noah built for protec-

Armadillos, together with sloths and anteaters, belong to an order of mammals, called Edentata. They can be found in South America and southern North America. They are covered with horny plates that are connected by flexible skin, allowing them to roll into a ball, in order to protect their soft underparts.

tion from the great flood (Genesis 6-9); also, the Ark of the Covenant, the sacred chest of the Hebrews representing God's presence (Exodus 25). The word can refer to a basket, box, or coffer, and in the United States, to the flat riverboats used for transport during western expansion.
See also: Noah.

Arkansas (Land of Opportunity; pop. 2,523,000), state in the U.S., bound by the Missouri and Mississippi rivers and the states of Texas, Louisiana, and Oklahoma; 53,124 sq mi (137,539 sq km). Capital: Little Rock. Other important cities are Fort Smith and North Little Rock.
Mountainous in the west and north, the rest of the state is alluvial plane in the Mississippi Basin. Climate is subtropical and humid.
Agriculture (Soya beans, cotton, rice), cattle breeding and industries connected to these are the most important sources of income. Furthermore coal mining, natural gas production, and bauxite (the latter contributes almost the entire national supply).
The state is named after the original inhabitants of the area, the Arkansa Native Americans (also called Quapaw). The Spaniard Hernando the Soto was the first European to visit the area. In 1803 the US bought it from the French (Louisiana Purchase). The battle for equal civil rights by the African American population led to serious conflicts in Arkansas (Little Rock, 1957).

Arkansas River, the longest tributary of the Mississippi-Missouri system, rising in the central Colorado Rocky Mountains and flowing SE 1,459 mi (2,339 km) to join the Mississippi near Greenville, Miss. The Arkansas is controlled by dams and reservoirs and is navigable to Tulsa, Okla.

Ark of the Covenant, wooden chest, overlaid inside and out with gold, containing the original Ten Commandments. The Ark was the most sacred religious object of ancient Israel, for the divine presence was believed to dwell within. It was installed in Solomon's temple but disappeared after the fall of Jerusalem and the destruction of the temple by Nebuchadnezzar in 586 B.C.

Arkwright, Sir Richard (1732-1792), English industrialist and inventor of cotton carding and spinning machinery. In 1769 he patented a spinning frame that was the first machine able to produce cotton thread strong enough to use in the warp. He was a pioneer of the factory system of production, building several water- and later steam-powered mills.

Arlington National Cemetery, U.S. national cemetery in northern Virginia, established in 1864. More than 175,000 U.S. war dead and public figures are buried here. Monuments include the Tomb of the Unknown Soldier and the grave of John F. Kennedy, with its eternal flame.

Armada, fleet of armed ships, in particular Spain's 'Invincible Armada,' 130 ships carrying 30,000 men sent by Philip II in 1588 to

seize control of the English Channel for an invasion of England. After battles with Charles Howard and Sir Francis Drake, the Spaniards took refuge off Calais. Driven out by fire ships, the surviving vessels battled storms as they attempted to return home. Only half of the ships survived.

Armadillo, armored mammals (family Dasypodidae) of the order Edentata, native to warm regions of the Western Hemisphere. There are 20 species, ranging in length from about 5 in. (12 cm) to about 5 ft (1.5 m). Largely insectivorous (insect-eating), they are usually nocturnal and live in burrows either excavated by themselves or deserted by other animals. Armadillos generally produce several identical offspring from a single fertilized egg.
See also: Edentate.

Armageddon, according to the Bible, the site of the world's last great battle, in which the powers of good will destroy the forces of evil (Revelation 16:16). The word derives from the name of an ancient city called 'Megiddo' because of the many battles fought on its soil.

Armagnac, hilly farming area of southwestern France noted for its brandy. Count Bernard VII of Armagnac was virtual ruler of France in 1413-18. Armagnac passed to the French crown in 1607. The chief city, Auch, is a commercial center.

Armenia

Capital:	Yerevan
Area:	11,500 sq mi (29,800 sq km)
Population:	3,330,000
Language:	Armenian
Government:	Republic
Independent:	1991
Head of State:	President
Per capita:	U.S. $3,350
Monetary unit:	1 Dram= 100 luma

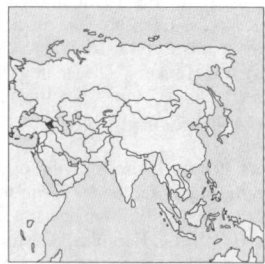

Armenia, republic in western Asia, bordered by Turkey, Azerbaijan, and Georgia.
Land and climate. Armenia is mountainous and the landscape extends from subtropical lowland to snow-covered peaks. Small mountain pastures provide rich grazing for sheep and cattle, and the valleys are fertile

when irrigated. The climate is continental, with cold winters and hot summers.

People. The population is mainly Armenian (90%) with minorities of Azerbaijanis, Kurds, Russians, Ukrainians, Greeks and Georgians. The majority of the inhabitants are Christians.

Economy. Armenia was highly industrialized during the Soviet period. The economy suffered severely as a result of the Nagorno-Karabach conflict with Azerbaijan.

History. Armenia was conquered in 328 B.C. by Alexander the Great and in 66 B.C. by Rome. In A.D. 301 it became the first country to make Christianity its state religion. Later it was successively under Byzantine, Persian, Arab, Seljuk, Mongol, and Ottoman Turkish control. An Armenian republic emerged after World War I but was swiftly absorbed by the USSR. In 1988 an earthquake killed about 25,000 people in Armenia. Also that year, fighting broke out between Azerbaijanis and Armenians living in Nagorno-Karabach, a predominantly Armenian region within Azerbaijan. After the Soviet Union collapsed in 1991, Armenia once again became independant. Also that year, Armenia joined the Commonwealth of Independant States. Fighting between the Azerbaijanis and Armenians over Nagorno-Karabach continued and in 1993 the Armenians captured all of the region. In the spring of 1994, a cease-fire agreement was negotiated. A definite agreement on Nagorno-Karabach has, however, not yet been reached. In 1995 Armenia adopted a new constitution. In 1999, an attack on the Parliament killed several people, including the prime minister. Armenia still refused to make further concessions in 2002 concerning Nagorno-Karabach, which led to an economic blockade by Turkey and Azerbaijan. Many impoverished Armenians were forced to emigrate.
See also: Union of Soviet Socialist Republics.

Armor, protective body covering used in armed combat. The earliest armor consisted of boiled and hardened animal skins, but Roman soldiers wore armor made of iron. By the end of the 11th century, chain mail, a fabric of interlocking metal rings, was the standard form of armor. It provided poor protection against heavy blows, however, and the Middle Ages saw the development of full suits of metal plates with chain mail joints for flexibility. Full armor was used in Europe only until the 16th century. Modern armor employs nylon, fiberglass, and other synthetic materials.
See also: Knights and knighthood.

Armory Show, officially the International Exhibition of Modern Art, the first show of its kind in the United States, held at the 69th Regiment Armory, New York City, Feb.-Mar. 1913. Comprising over 1,300 works, it included a large section of paintings by contemporary Americans and works by modern European artists, including Constantin Brancusi, Georges Braque, Paul Cézanne, Marcel Duchamp, Henri Matisse, and Pablo Picasso. The avant-garde paintings caused much controversy but also the acceptance of modern art in the United States.

Arms control *See:* Disarmament; Strategic Arms Limitation Talks.

Armstrong, Edwin Howard (1890-1954), U.S. electronic engineer who developed the feedback concept for amplifiers (1912), invented the superheterodyne circuit used in radio receivers (1918), and perfected FM radio (1925-39).
See also: Frequency modulation.

Armstrong, Henry (1912-1988), U.S. boxer. Nicknamed 'Perpetual Motion' for his aggressive style, he was the only fighter to hold 3 world championships (featherweight, welterweight, and lightweight) simultaneously (1938).

Armstrong, Lance (1971-), American racing cyclist. Won the world title in the professional league in 1993, followed by several places of honor in major routes. In 1995, he won the ephemerally classical Clasica San Sebastian and the American stage Tour DuPont. In 1996, he again established a record in the latter stage and he won the so-called Waalse Pijl. At the end of that year, he was diagnosed with cancer, but in 1998, Armstrong returned to the peloton. There he fought his way back to the top, experiencing the major victory of winning the Tour de France in 1999, 2000, 2001 en 2002.

Armstrong, Louis 'Satchmo' (1900-71), U.S. jazz musician renowned as a virtuoso trumpeter and singer. A master of improvisation, he was one of the most important figures in the early history of jazz. Satchmo grew up in New Orleans, moved to Chicago in 1922, and by the 1930s was internationally famous. In later life he played at concerts around the world as goodwill ambassador for the U.S. State Department.
See also: Jazz.

Louis Armstrong, affectionately known as `Satchmo', who was one of the greatest personalities in the history of jazz music, enjoyed a widespread reputation as a trumpet player and singer.

Armstrong, Neil Alden (1930-), U.S. astronaut, first human to set foot on the moon. He studied aeronautical engineering at Purdue University (1947-55) with time out on active service in the Korean War. He joined NASA in 1962, commanding *Gemini 8* (1966) and landing the *Apollo 11* module on the moon on July 20, 1969.
See also: Astronaut.

Armstrong, Samuel Chapman (1839-1893), U.S. educator and philanthropist. Colonel of a black regiment in the Civil War and agent of the Freedmen's Bureau (Virginia), Armstrong founded the Hampton Institute (1868), an industrial school for blacks and Native Americans.

Army, land fighting force of a nation; more narrowly, a large unit of ground forces under a single commander. Primitive armies consisted of raiding parties that waged individual combat using stones and clubs. Later, horses and chariots increased the mobility of

Lance Armstrong

armies, while the development of artillery extended their range. Formation tactics evolved with the Macedonian phalanx and Roman legion. The 20th-century army depends upon technology. Because of the ongoing development of weapons and detection systems, modern armies must be highly mobile, a need that has blurred the traditional distinctions between army, navy, and air force. Nuclear weaponry has taken the range of firepower to its limits, and the value of tactical formations has largely been eliminated by radar, making unconventional units (guerrillas, paratroops) increasingly important.

Army worm, any of several species of voracious caterpillars that travel in masses, causing severe crop damage; especially the common army worm (*Pseudaletia unipuncta*). The common army worm is the larva of a brown moth found in North America east of the Rocky Mountains. The eggs, laid in grass or on small grains, hatch into small worms that, if not controlled by parasites or pesticides, devour everything within reach and then migrate in armies to new feeding grounds.

Arnhem (pop. 141,000), capital of the province Gelderland in the east Netherlands, located on the north bank of the Rhine River, about 60 mi (100 km) east of Rotterdam. A major river port with shipyards and a large tin refinery, Arnhem produces textiles, furniture, leather goods, and synthetic fibers. The city was seriously damaged in September 1944, when it was the site of one of the largest Allied paratroop landings in World War II.

A

A

Arnica, genus of plants of which the flowers and rootstock are used for medicinal purposes. The horizontal, dark-brown, branched rootstock of the arnica sends up a slightly hairy simple or tightly branched stem that reaches a height of 1-2 ft (30-61 cm). The basal leaves are oblong-ovate with short stems.

Arnim, Ludwig Joachim (Achim) von (1781-1831) German romantic writer, married to Bettina Brentano, remains popular especially for the collection of German folk songs he wrote together with Clemens Brentano, which were published in *Des Knaben Wunderhorn* (1806-08).

Arnold, Benedict (1741-1801), general and traitor in the American Revolution. He fought outstandingly for the American cause at Ticonderoga (1775) and Saratoga (1777) and in 1778 received command of Philadelphia. In 1780 Arnold assumed the command of West Point and with John André plotted its surrender to the British in revenge for past criticisms. André's capture forced Arnold to flee to the British side, and in 1781 he went into exile in London.
See also: Revolutionary War in America.

Arnold, Matthew (1822-1888), English poet and literary critic. His poetry, as represented by *Empedocles on Etna* (1852) and *New Poems* (1867), is mainly introspective, though Arnold also achieved a classical impersonality. Both in his poetry and in his criticism-*Culture and Anarchy* (1869), *Literature and Dogma* (1873)-Arnold showed a keen awareness of the changing cultural climate of his time.

Arnold of Brescia (c.1100-1150), Italian religious reformer and political activist who strongly opposed the temporal power of the pope. He was a supporter of Peter Abelard, with whom he was condemned at the Council of Sens in 1140. In 1147 Arnold, a great orator, became leader of the rebellion that had suppressed papal authority in Rome and replaced it by a republic. On the collapse of the republic, Arnold fled to Campania but was captured, delivered to the pope by Emperor Frederick Barbarossa, and executed as a heretic.

Arno River, river in central Italy, about 150 mi (241 km) long. Its source lies in the Apennine Mountains, from which it flows through the city of Florence, emptying into the Ligurian Sea below Pisa. Much of its valley is a fertile plain where olives and grapes are grown.

Aron, Raymond (1905-1983), prominent French sociologist and political scientist particularly influenced by the German sociologist Max Weber. Aron was a militant opponent of Marxist views. Among other issues, his work concerned political systems, including conflicts in modern industrial societies and the history of sociology: *Paix et guerre entre les nations* (Peace and War; 1962), *Dix-huit leçons sur la société industrielle* (1962), *La lutte des classes* (1964), *Marxismes imaginaires* (1970), and *Plaidoyer pour l'Europe décadente*(1977). Erasmus Prize 1983.

Arpád, dynasty of Hungarian rulers founded by Arpád (c.840-907), around whose life countless heroic legends are woven. In 890 he became chief of the Magyars and 6 years later led the conquest of Hungary and proceeded to lay the foundations for a strong, centralized state. His successors ruled as dukes of Hungary and replaced the predominantly nomadic Magyar culture by one based on agriculture and firm central rule.

Arp, Jean (or **Hans**, 1887-1966), French sculptor, painter, and poet. Briefly associated with the expressionist art movement Der Blaue Reiter, he was a cofounder of Dada in Zürich (1916). He was also one of the best known exponents of the surrealist movement. Starting in the 1930s he created sculptures and reliefs notable for their elemental purity and strength.
See also: Dada; Surrealism.

Shortly after 1930, Jean Arp (1887-1966) began to make figures with flowing organic shapes, which he often gave the title *Concretion*. This *Human concretion* dates from 1934 (Paris, Musée National d'Art Moderne).

Arrabal, Fernando (1932-), Spanish author and filmmaker who generally publishes work in French. His work is classified as belonging to absurdism, but he himself calls it 'panic theatre': a ceremonial form of theater full of wild fantasies, blasphemy, obscenities, cruelty, and poetical tenderness. His pieces are full of shocking effects and have had an enormous influence on modern theatre. Arrabal's works include: *Picnic on the Battlefield* (1952), *The Architect and the Emperor of Assyria* (1967), *Garden of Delights* (1969), and *And They Put Handcuffs on the Flowers* (1969). *Long Live Death* (1970) is a movie written and directed by Arrabal.

Arraignment, appearance of a person in a court of law to plead guilty or not guilty to legal charges. Before or after entering this plea, the defendant may also enter various motions in his or her own behalf, such as requesting a change of venue (moving the place where the trial is to be held) or a continuance (allowing more time to prepare the case), and the defendant can even challenge the validity of the arrest and trial. If the defendant is not yet represented by a lawyer, the court may appoint one.

Arrau, Claudio (1903-1991), Chilean pianist. A child prodigy, he was noted throughout his long career mainly for his performances of the Romantic composers, such as Brahms.

Arrest, taking into custody of a person believed to have committed a crime. Most often an arrest is made by police or other law-enforcing officer on the strength of a warrant issued by a court and supported by evidence indicating that the named person or persons have probably committed a crime. As a general rule, and in most states, arrests may be made without a warrant only when the arresting officer has evidence that a felony (serious crime) has been committed; and on the basis of suspicious behavior, even when there is no evidence of an actual felony. A private person may sometimes make a 'citizen's arrest' for a crime he or she sees committed.

Arrhenius, Svante August (1859-1927), a Swedish chemist and physicist. In 1903 he received the Nobel Prize in chemistry for his theory of electrolytic dissociation. According to this theory, in a dilute solution a certain proportion of the molecules of electrolytes (acids, bases, and salts) break up, or dissociate, into electrically charged particles (ions).
Arrhenius was born near Uppsala, and studied at the university there. In 1895 he became professor of physical chemistry at the University of Stockholm. He directed the Nobel Institute for Physical Chemistry from 1905 until his death.

Arrhythmia, irregularity in rhythm of the heartbeat, either in time or force. Arrhythmias are often extra heartbeats that cause no serious problems, although sometimes the heart rhythm can become dangerously slow or fast or is disruptive to heart function.

Arrow *See:* Archery.

Arrow, Kenneth Joseph (1921-), U.S. economist, former professor at Harvard and adviser on economic affairs to the U.S. government. In 1972 he won the Nobel Prize in economic science.

Arrowroot, plant (genus *Maranta*) native to warm, humid regions of the Western Hemisphere; also, form of starch from the rhizomes (underground stems) of the arrowroot plant and various other tropical plants. Easily digested, arrowroot is valued as a food for children and people with delicate stomachs, and is used as a thickening agent in sauces.

Arroyo, Gloria Macapagal (1947-), Philippino politician and President (2001-). Arroyo became Vice-Secretary of Commerce and Industry under Corazón Aquino in 1986. In 1992, she became a member of the Senate and she was re-elected in 1995. She was very active as a senator and numerous laws, mainly economic, were passed on her initiative. In 1998, she was a ran for the Vice Presidency. Her presidential candidate, José de Venecia, lost the presi-

dency to Joseph Estrada but Arroyo herself had enough votes to become Vice President. Under Estrada she also fulfilled the ministerial office post for Social services and Development. In 2001 she was declared President after President Estrada was forced to resign after a revolt. Main issues of her policy are the economy and the unity of the multi-etnic archipelago.
See also: Aquino, Corazon.

Arsenic, chemical element, symbol As; for physical constants see Periodic Table. Arsenic has been known since ancient times. Elemental arsenic was first described by Albertus Magnus in the 13th century. Sometimes found native, it occurs widely in the form of arsenides, from which the element is obtained as a byproduct. Arsenic is a soft and brittle gray element with a metallic luster which sublimes without melting; several other allotropic forms have been reported. The metal conducts electricity moderately well. Arsenic is used in bronzing, hardening, and improving the sphericity of metal shot, and in pyrotechnics. Compounds of arsenic are used as agricultural insecticides and poisons. Arsenic in high purity is used as a doping agent in solid-state devices. Gallium arsenide is used as a laser material to convert electricity directly into coherent light. Arsenic and its compounds are poisonous.

Artagnan, Charles d' (1620-1673), French soldier whose name was immortalized by the swashbuckling character d'Artagnan in Alexandre Dumas's *The Three Musketeers*. The real d'Artagnan served bravely in the armies of Louis XIII and Louis XIV and rose to the rank of brigadier general before his death at the siege of Maastricht.

Art and the arts, skill of making or doing. The term can be used to define useful arts (beautiful objects that have functional value), decorative arts (beautiful objects that exist for their own sake), liberal arts (the study of humanities), applied arts (such as architecture), language arts (the related skills of reading, writing, speaking, and spelling), and graphic arts (such as printmaking and bookmaking). However, the term *art* is most often used to describe the fine arts, which consist of painting, sculpture, literature, dance, music, and film. Works of art can be classified as verbal (literature) or nonverbal (musical composition and visual design). Mixed arts, a combination of 2 or more basic arts, include dance, drama, and film. Theories of art which attempt to define its meaning, explain its effects, assess its worth, set guidelines for its execution, or provide a historical or social context for its interpretation have existed since the ancient Greeks and continue to be a subject of discussion among artists, scholars, and critics.

Artaud, Antonin (1896-1948) French theorist on theater, actor and author, whose progressive ideas met with ignorance during his life but who was later acknowledged as being innovative. Artaud wanted to go back to the mystery plays in order to show the primal fears and primitive urges of people. He was in favor of the so-called theater of cru-

elty, a shocking and revealing form of theater. Artaud also wrote surreal film scenarios, of which one: *La coquille et le clergyman* was filmed in 1927/28. The company he founded in 1933 ('Société Anonyme du Théâtre de la Cruauté') played the only piece of his which has been preserved: *Les Cenci*. It met with a lack of understanding from audiences and critics.

Art deco, style of design popular in the United States and Europe from the late 1920s through the 1930s. In its emphasis on geometrical shapes and simplified lines, art deco represented a radical reaction to the ornateness of Victorian design. The style was applied in architecture, interior decoration, furnituremaking, and the design of a wide range of objects from locomotives to salt-

A

Examples of furnishing accessories created in the Art Deco style early in the 20th century include:

1 Lamp of bronze and parchment, with a shade in the form of a parachutist.
2 `Senlis' vase, 1925, by René Lalique, smoked glass.
3 Vase by Fauré, its African gourd shape is embellished with a

triangle and stripe design, in turquoise and cobalt blue enamel.
4 Plastic imitation-amber scent bottle.
5 Crystal perfume flask, 1925, by Baccarat.

6 Pottery inkwell, French, late 1920s.
7 Marble clock by F. Priess, with silver-bronze face, mountings and figure of an Amazon.
8 Candlestick of plastic and chrome.

9 Teapot, 1937, by Jean Puiforcat, in streamlined silver-gilt verseuse with rock crystal handle and knob on lid.

A

and-pepper shakers. Prime examples are the Chrysler Building and the interior of Radio City Music Hall in New York City.

Artemis, in Greek mythology, virgin goddess of the hunt. Apollo's twin, the daughter of Zeus and Leto, Artemis is usually pictured carrying a bow and arrows or a torch. She presided over wild animals and is primarily known as the goddess of the hunt. Although Artemis was a stern protector of chastity, she also watched over women in childbirth. She was worshipped as goddess of the waters; fruit, grain, and domestic animals were sacrificed to her at harvest time. Artemis is also sometimes known as the moon goddess, probably through identification with the huntress Diana, Roman goddess of the moon.

Artherosclerosis is a common degenerative disease in which the structure of a healthy artery (A) hardens. A diseased artery (D) has an accumulation of fat, loses elasticity, and has less interior space than a normal artery. According to one theory, atherosclerosis is caused by cholesterol and animal fats (yellow dots) penetrating the artery wall (B). Another theory suggests that fibrin (blue dots) and fats accumulate around lesions (C). In cerebral and carotid arteries (1 and 2), atherosclerosis can result in a stroke; in cardiac arteries (3) it can cause several types of heart disease.

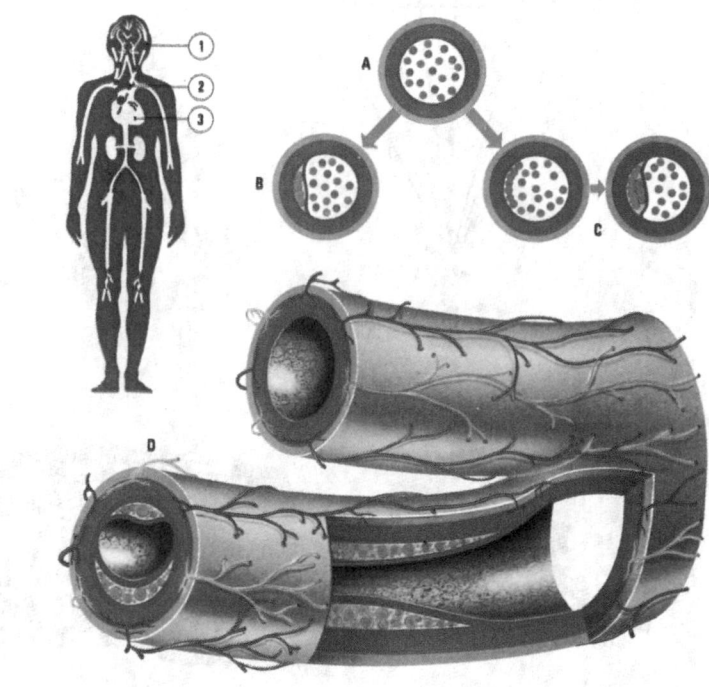

Arte Povera, name of a movement within conceptual art in Italy that started in the mid 1960s. The name is derived from the title of an exhibition held in Genoa in 1967. Its main aspect was to show processes of change by using 'poor' material: climatic changes, rotting processes, chemical reactions, etc. Materials such as wax, fat, soap, rags, steam, light, and earth did not produce static objects but changeable works. Representatives among others were: Mario Merz, Kounellis, Fabro, and Penone. After 1971 the group fell apart and the participants went their separate ways.

Arteriosclerosis, generic term for disease of the arteries in which their walls become thickened and rigid, and blood flow is hindered, often resulting in heart disease or stroke. The most common form of arteriosclerosis is atherosclerosis, in which fatty deposits accumulate on the artery walls, which then tend to harden. Research indicates that there probably is a connection between atherosclerosis and a bacterium

(Chlamydia pneumoniae). This bacterium allegedly accelerates the accumulation of fat in the artery and might be responsible for the development of small wounds in the artery walls.
See also: Artery.

Artery, blood vessel that carries blood away from the heart to other parts of the body. The two main arteries are the pulmonary artery and the aorta. The pulmonary artery carries blood from the right side of the heart to the lungs to be reoxygenated; the aorta, the main arterial vessel, carries oxygen-enriched blood to the body from the left side of the heart. The main arteries are quite large, the aorta being about the width of a garden hose (about 1 in/2.5 cm in diameter). Major arteries branch from the aorta to supply each

limb and organ, dividing repeatedly down to the arterioles, which in turn supply the capillaries, located in body tissue. The structure of artery walls accounts for their strength and elasticity and makes them well suited to resisting the stress of the pulsating flow of blood.
See also: Arteriosclerosis.

Artesian well, well in which water rises under hydrostatic pressure above the level of the aquifer (water-bearing layer of rock) in which it has been confined. True artesian wells (named for the French province of Artois, where they were first constructed) flow without assistance.
See also: Ground water.

Arthritis, inflammation of a joint, usually accompanied by pain and frequently by changes in structure. The two most widespread arthritic disorders, osteoarthritis and rheumatoid arthritis, are usually chronic problems for which there is no cure, though modern medicine can now do a good deal to control them. Two or three times more

women than men are affected by osteoarthritis, and women have the most serious form, rheumatoid arthritis, three times as often.
See also: Joint.

Arthropod, largest and most diverse phylum of the animal kingdom, containing insects, millipedes, centipedes, crustacea, arachnida, and king crabs. Arthropods are characterized by a segmented exoskeleton (external skeleton) with joined limbs that is shed at intervals, the animal emerging in a new, soft exoskeleton that has developed beneath; often this molting is followed by rapid growth. Molting may cease on attainment of adulthood, but many crustacea molt periodically throughout their lives.

Arthroscopy, technique used to visualize the interior of a joint. Using a fiber-optic endoscope (arthroscope) inserted into the joint through a small incision, a doctor can perform a thorough examination and certain surgical operations. Arthroscopy is most commonly used to treat torn cartilage in the knee, although arthroscopic procedures of the shoulder, elbow, and hip are also common. The low morbidity associated with this procedure makes it useful in a variety of joint disorders as an adjunct to diagnosis, to determine prognosis, and as a treatment.

Arthur, Chester Alan (1830-1886), 21st president of the United States (1881-1885). Republican. Arthur was vice president under James A. Garfield and became president on Garfield's assassination. Arthur was a protectionist.

Arthur, King, legendary British king, subject of tales and poems dating back to the 7th century. Although there are many variations of the story, which probably arose out of Irish heroic folktales, all of these have certain common elements: Arthur wins recognition as king by pulling a sword (Excalibur) from a stone; he reigns from his castle at Camelot; his Knights of the Round Table, including such heroes as Lancelot and Tristram, engage in heroic quests and illicit sexual unions.

The legendary King Arthur beheading an enemy. Late medieval miniature.

Artichoke (*Cynara scolymus*), tall, thistle-like perennial plant of the composite family;

also, its globe-shaped flower bud, the heart and spiny bracts of which are eaten as a vegetable. Native to the Mediterranean region, the artichoke is grown commercially in warm regions of the U.S.
See also: Jerusalem artichoke.

Articles of War, code adopted in 1775 by the Continental Congress to guide administration of justice and discipline in the Continental Army. The articles were based on British Army Code. Revised many times, they were replaced in 1950 by the Uniform Code of Military Justice.

Artificial insemination, introduction of sperm into the vagina by means other than copulation. The technique, widely used for breeding livestock as it produces many offspring from 1 selected male, has a limited use in treating human impotence and sterility. In humans, the procedure is timed to coincide with the woman's ovulation. If she has a regular 28-day menstrual cycle, insemination should be performed as many as 3 times between the 10th and the 14th days of the cycle.

Artificial intelligence (AI), use of computers to perform functions normally associated with human intelligence, such as reasoning, learning, and self-improvement. The term is also often used to refer to the study of how to design and construct such computers. A typical electronic computer generally follows a precise series of step-by-step instructions to solve a problem. A computer with artificial intelligence, on the other hand, generally solves problems by a *heuristic* approach, that is, by using rules of thumb that guide the computer in choosing the best way of solving a problem. Although the field of artificial intelligence is still largely experimental, advances have been made in a number of areas, as illustrated by the development of chess-playing computers that can win against high-rated players, and of *expert systems*, which provide advice and make judgements in specialized areas of expertise.

Artificial limb, device to replace missing hands, feet, arms, or legs. Prosthetics, the branch of medicine dealing with artificial limbs, has developed rapidly since World War I. Prosthetic devices are now complex mechanisms made of materials such as aluminum alloys, rubber, and plastics. Some of them are capable of mimicking the use of human limbs to a considerable extent.

Artificial organ, mechanical device designed to assume the functions of an organ of the body, particularly during surgical procedures. The 3 most commonly used artificial organs are the heart-lung machine, the artificial kidney, and (since 1985) the artificial heart, still in an experimental stage.

Artificial sweetener, synthetic substance, usually saccharin, aspartame, or acesulfame-K, used in place of sucrose (table sugar) to sweeten food and beverages.

Artificial turf, grasslike product of nylon or other synthetic material used to carpet athletic playing fields and also used in outdoor landscaping. It came into widespread use during the 1960s.

Artigas, José Gervasio (1764-1850), Uruguayan military leader who championed the cause of national independence. He joined the 1810 Argentine revolt against Spanish rule but later fought against both Portuguese and Argentine troops. He was forced into exile after Brazil occupied Montevideo in 1820. An independent Uruguay was achieved only in 1828.

Artillery, once the term for all military machinery, now applied to guns too heavy to be carried by one or two soldiers. Modern artillery had its origins in the 14th century, when weapons using gunpowder were first developed. Its use became more important as equipment became more mobile, accurate, and effective. World War II saw the development of antitank and antiaircraft guns and the first effective use of rockets. The most modern artillery is often made of light, tough alloys, and targeting systems draw on laser and radar technology.

Art nouveau, late 19th-century art movement that influenced decorative styles throughout the West. Its themes were exotic or decadent, its characteristic line sinuous

A

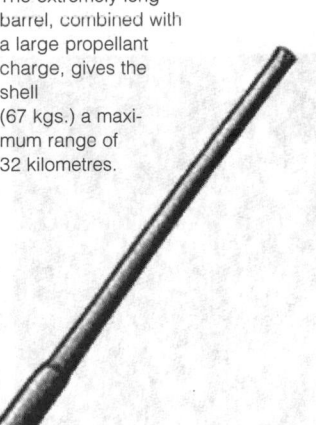

The M-107, an American 175 mm. self-propelled gun, which has been in service with the US army since 1962, was intended as a replacement for big towed guns. It is currently the largest-calibre self-propelled gun in service. The chassis was designed to be as light as possible, allowing for a maximum speed of 54 kilometres per hour, and a limited cross-country mobility, but sacrificing armour protection for the crew and necessitating the use of hydraulically-lowered spades at the rear, to absorb the recoil. The extremely long barrel, combined with a large propellant charge, gives the shell (67 kgs.) a maximum range of 32 kilometres.

A

The art nouveau 'Job' poster by Alphonese Mucha. The poster was origi-nally designed for a brand of cigarette paper.

Center: Wrought iron gate set in stonework at Castle Beranger, Paris (Hector Guimard, 1894-98). Right: Metal balustrade with leaf motif for a staircase (Louis Majorelle, 1900).

Below: fine metalwork and jewelry artifacts. Top: Brooch of gold and translucent enamels. It typifies the art nouveau ob-session with plant and insect forms (C. Dessosiers, 1901). Bottom: Silver pillbox decorated with translucent enamel.

Art nouveau light fixtures in the Hotel Solvay in Brussels, Belgium.

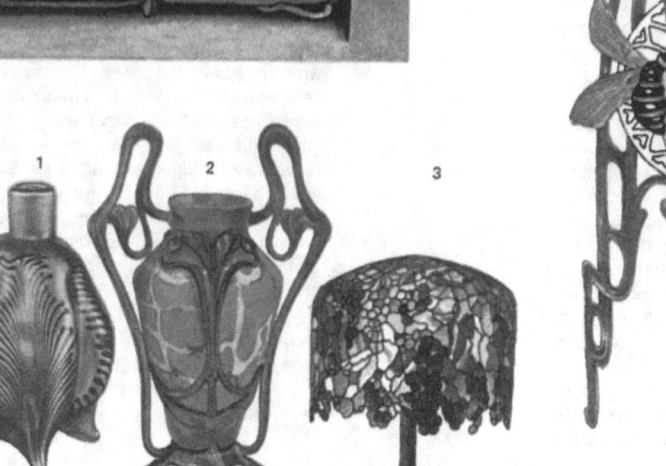

Left: Glass and ceramic artifacts.
1. Tiffany glass bottle
2. Vase of green glass encased in pewter tendrils which form handles
3. Tiffany lamp in a tree form bearing green and purple fruit
4. Tile work

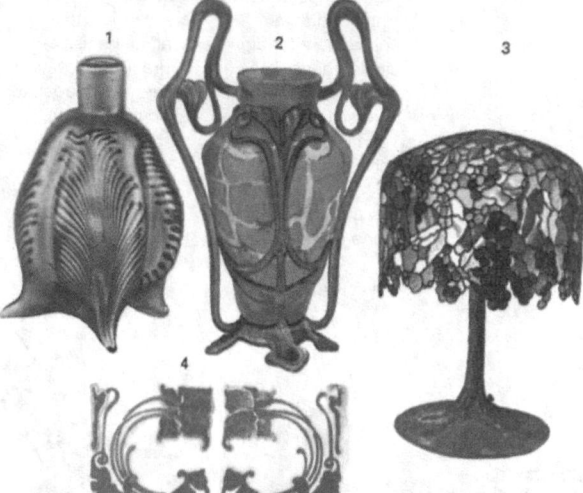

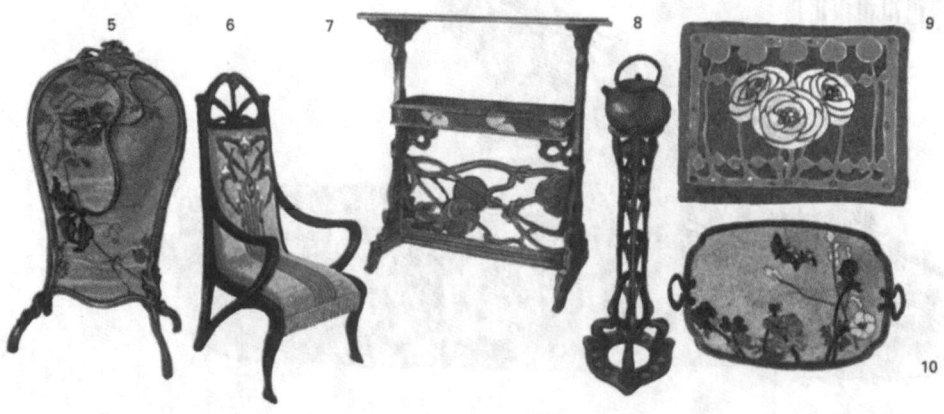

Furniture and furnishing artifacts.
5. Firescreen of ash (Emil Galle, 1900)
6. Armchair (Louis Majorelle, c.1900)
7. Inlaid work table of ash (Emile Galle, 1900)
8. Copper kettle and pedestal (Reynolds)
9. Embroidered and appliquéd cushion cov-er with rose motif (Ann Macbeth)
10. Inlaid tray with brass handles (Louis Majorelle, 1900)

and highly ornamental. The movement aimed to reunite art and life, and so to produce everyday objects of beauty. Some notable architecture, furniture, jewelry, and book designs were produced in this style. The graphic arts were much affected by art nouveau, as seen in the work of Aubrey Beardsley. Other notable artists were the painter Gustav Klimt, the architects Antonio Gaudi and Victor Horta, and applied artists Louis Comfort Tiffany and René Lalique.

Aruba

Capital:	Oranjestad
Area:	75 sq mi (193 sq km)
Population:	70,400
Language:	Dutch
Government:	internal autonomy within the Kingdom of the Netherlands
Independent:	1996 scheduled, postponed indefinitely
Head of gov.:	Prime minister
Per capita:	more than US$ 28,000
Monetary unit:	1 Aruban florin = 100 cents

Aruba (pop. 89,000), island off the Venezuelan coast, part of the Netherlands Antilles, about 19 mi (30.6 km) long and 4 mi (6.4 km) wide. Its capital is Oranjestad. Its chief industries are the refining of crude oil imported from Venezuela and tourism. On January 1, 1986, Aruba became a semi-independent state. It was agreed upon that in 1996 Aruba would gain complete independancy. In 1994 Aruba however declared it preferred to remain semi-dependant of the Netherlands which was acknowledged by the Dutch government in 1995. The Aruban florin fluctuates with the dollar exchange rate on the world market.

Arum, common name of certain plants of the Araceae family, including lily, philodendron, and elephant's ear.

Aryabhata (5th century A.D.), Indian astronomer and mathematician. Transcribed the mathematics of his period in his work 'Aryabathiya'. It contains a sine table, among other things. In 1874 a Sanskrit translation of this work was published in Leiden, The Netherlands. He was also active in fields such as astronomy and spherical trigonometry.

Aryan (Sanskrit, 'noble' or 'ruler'), name originally applied to peoples who invaded the Indus Valley in India about 1500 B.C. As a linguistic term, Aryan applies to speakers of Indo-European languages. As a racial category-used by the Nazis to designate Germans and other North Europeans-the term has no valid basis and has been discredited as an instrument of bigotry.

Arzú Irigoyen, Alvaro Enrique (1945-), Guatemalan politician, son of Basque immigrants. Arzú had a business career before he was elected Mayor of Guatemala City in 1982. Because of the military coup that year, he had to wait until 1986 before he could hold his position. In cooperation with other business people, entrepreneurs and young people from the higher middle class, he founded the rightwing Partido de Avanzada Nacional (PAN). In 1990 he was the PAN candidate for the presidential elections but lost to Jorge Serrano. He became minister of foreign affairs in Serrano's cabinet for a few months. Arzú became president on 14th January 1996 after he had won the elections with only a slight margin. Contrary to his predecessors, he was quite successful in imposing his will on the army. Headed by Arzú, the government signed a final peace accord with the URNG guerrillas on 29th December 1996 ending the country's 36-year civil war.

Asafetida, foul-smelling substance extracted from the roots of an Asian herb. Asafetida has long had a mystical significance and was often used in magical ceremonies or worn as an amulet to keep away evil spirits. It was also once used in medicine as a sedative. The plant belongs to the carrot family (Umbelliferae).

Asante *See:* Ashanti.

Asbestos, name for various fibrous minerals, such as chrysotile, used as noncombustible material. Canada and the USSR are the chief producers. It can be spun to make fireproof fabrics or molded to make tiles, bricks, and automobile brake linings. If inhaled, asbestos particles cause lung cancer and asbestosis, a serious lung disease.

ASCAP *See:* American Society of Composers, Authors and Publishers.

Ascari, Alberto (1918-1955), Italian racing driver. Initially involved in motorcycle racing, and in motor racing from 1940 onwards. Drove for Maserati and then Ferrari, for whom he became world champion in 1952 and 1953 respectively, and then for Lancia. Like his father, racing driver Antonio Ascari (1888-1925), he was killed in an accident.

Ascension, The, in Christian belief, the bodily ascent of Jesus Christ into heaven on the 40th day after his resurrection. Ascension Day is a major Christian festival.
See also: Jesus Christ.

Asceticism, self-denial or self-mortification in the interest of heightening spiritual powers. The term was first used by the ancient Greeks to describe the discipline of athletic training, but was later applied by Stoicists to the conquest of the body and its desires as a means to spiritual awareness. The practice is an essential means of escape from matter in Hindu and Buddhist belief
See also: Stoicism.

Asch, Sholem (1880-1957), Yiddish novelist and playwright. Born in Poland, he spent most of his life in the United States. His many books deal with Jewish life in both countries and with the relationship between Judaism and Christianity.

ASCII, acronym for American Standard Code for Information Interchange, the character code used for representing information by most non-IBM equipment.
See also: Computer.

Asclepius, in Greek mythology, the god of healing, who became so skilled that he attempted to resurrect the dead, thus angering Zeus, who struck him dead with a thunderbolt. The medical profession has adopted his symbol, a staff entwined by a snake.

Ascorbic acid *See:* Vitamin.

ASEAN *See:* Association of Southeast Asian Nations.

Asexual reproduction *See:* Reproduction.

Asgard, or Aesir, in Norse mythology, the realm of the gods. It contained many halls and palaces; chief of these was Valhalla, where Odin entertained warriors killed in battle. The only entry to Asgard was by the rainbow bridge called Bifrost.

Ash, tree or shrub (genus *fraxinus*) of the olive family. The hard, elastic wood of the white ash (*F. americana*) is used for items like mallets and baseball bats; that of the blue ash (*F. quadrangulata*) for barrel hoops, furniture veneers, and baskets.

A

The university for science and technology (1961) at Kumasi, Ghana, the administrative centre of the Ashanti region.

Ashanti, or Asante, region of central Ghana, in West Africa, inhabited by the people of the same name. From the 17th century to 1902, when Britain militarily took over the region, the powerful Ashanti Confederacy linked several kingdoms under one chief.

A

The symbol of their unity was the sacred Golden Stool.

Ashbery, John (1927-), U.S. poet of unconventional style, whose poems are experimental, fragmentary, and dreamlike. Associated with the poets of the 'New York School,' Ashbery is also an art critic. His *Self-Portrait in a Convex Mirror* won the Pulitzer Prize for poetry in 1975. Other works include *Some Trees* (1956), *The Tennis Court Oath* (1962), and *A Wave* (1984).

Ashcroft, Dame Peggy (1907-1991), British stage actress. She is best known for her roles in *Dear Brutus, Othello, The School for Scandal*, and *The Merchant of Venice*.

Ashe, Arthur (1943-1993), U.S. tennis player. As a student at UCLA, he won the NCAA singles and doubles titles (1966). He became the first African-American (and the first U.S. player since 1955) to win the U.S. Men's National Singles Championship (1968). He won the Australian Open (1970) and the men's singles title at Wimbledon (1975). Since 1983 he served as nonplaying captain of the U.S. Davis Cup team. He also wrote *A Hard Road to Glory: a History of the African American Athletes*.
In 1992 he founded the Ashe Foundation to fight AIDS. He was infected with this disease while being given a blood transfusion.

Ashkabad (Ashgabat; pop. 498,000), capital of Turkmenistan. Textile, glass, and food industry; university. Founded in 1889. It was completely rebuilt after the 1948 earthquake.

Ashkenazim, Jews whose medieval ancestors lived in Germany. Persecution drove them to spread throughout central and eastern Europe and, in the 19th and 20th centuries, overseas, notably to the United States. Their ritual and Hebrew pronunciation differ from those of Sephardim (Jews originally from Spain and Portugal). Most of the Jews in the United States and the majority of the world's Jews are Ashkenazim.

Ashkenazy, Vladimir (1937-), Russian pianist and conductor. Left the Soviet Union in 1963 and settled in England.
Ashkenazy belongs to the great pianists of this era and is especially known for his interpretations of Chopin and Liszt.

Ashkenazy also conducts from behind the grand piano and of late has been concentrating to a greater degree on conducting. He has been Musical Director of the Royal Philharmonic Orchestra since 1987 and Musical Director of the Berlin Radio Symphonic Orchestra since 1989.

Ashton, Sir Frederick (1906-1988), British dancer and choreographer. Among his influential works are *Façade* (1931) and *La Fille Mal Gardée* (1960). He was director of the Royal Ballet from 1963 to 1970.

Ashurbanipal, or Assurbanipal (d. 626? B.C.), last of the great kings of Assyria, ruled 669-633 B.C. over an empire that included Babylonia, Syria, and Palestine. Though troubled by numerous revolts, his reign was prosperous. He established the library of cuneiform tablets in Nineveh, discovered in the 1840s.
See also: Babylonia and Assyria.

Ash Wednesday, 40th weekday before Easter Sunday and the first day of the Christian fast of Lent. The name derives from the early practice of sprinkling penitents with ashes. Today the ash of burnt palms is used to mark the sign of the cross on the foreheads of believers.

Asia, Asia is the largest continent and is located east of Europe. It covers 16,994,979 sq mi (44,000,000 sq km), one-third of the earth's total land area.
The continent is only partially suitable for human settlement. The Himalayas play an important role in this respect, not only because of their high altitude but also because the mountain ranges prevent large areas of the interior from receiving rainfall. Other areas of the continent are too cold (Siberia) or too warm (the deserts in the middle and southwest) for permanent settlement.
The population was more than 3.1 billion in 1992 (excluding the inhabitants of the former Soviet Union) and is divided extremely unevenly across the area. People tend to concentrate especially in areas where soil and climactic conditions are most favorable, such as along the coasts and in the deltas of South and Southeast Asia.
Asia's soils can be divided from north to south into a number of main groups: in the far north are tundras, the ground is permanently frozen while only a thin part of the surface thaws in summer. South of the tundra are the so-called podsols in the area of

the Siberian coniferous forests: the taiga. Black earth (chernozem) and brown earth can be found between Saint Petersburg, Odessa, and Irkutsk; the area is rich in humus and was part of the agricultural triangle of the former Soviet Union. South of this region are the semiarid and arid soils. The Indian subcontinent and East and Southeast Asia are characterized by the so-called latosols, created under the influence of the tropical monsoon climate. The regur of the Deccan Plateau, one of the oldest soils in the world, is very fertile.
As nearly all terains are present in Asia, the animal and plant life shows great variation. The cold north has reindeer, ptarmigans, lemmings, and polar bears, among others; the taiga has elks, lynxes, wolves, and wolverines. In Central Asia antelopes, wolfs, camels can be found, and in the tropical rain forests and savannas are anthropoids, rhinoceroses, elephants, tigers, snakes, buffalo and various species of birds and insects. The giant panda and the common panda can be found in the bamboo forests of East Tibet and Southwest China, and yaks, snow panthers, and bears in the mountains.
With regard to the botany, Asia is the home of several plants imported from the West such as primrose, peach, apricot, cherry, fig, grape, hemp, grain, buckwheat and garlic.
Many tropical plants produce spices, such as ginger, cinnamon, nutmeg and pepper.
The three major races into which the world is divided are all present in Asia. The Caucasoid and Mongoloid are the main races. The Negroid race can only be found in parts of India, Sri Lanka, and Irian Jaya. The Turks, Arabs, Persians, Kurds, Afghans, Sikhs, Indians, and Singhalese belong to the Caucasoid race. Mongols, Tibetans, Chinese, Japanese, Malays, and Filipinos, for instance, all belong to the subraces of the Mongoloid race.
The ethnic composition of the Asian population is very complicated because many Asian peoples are a hybrid of one or more races. This is the result of the large-scale migrations that have taken place in the course of history.
The continent is also linguistically divers. In the Southwest they speak Semitic languages, chiefly Arabic and Hebrew. Turkish languages are spoken, for instance, in Turkey, the Asian part of the former Soviet Union and the Chinese Xinjiang province; Slavic languages in the north; Indo-European languages in India, Afghanistan, and Iran. Sino-Tibetan languages are spoken in China, Tibet, Burma, and the countries of Indo-China. In the southern parts of India there are the so-called Dravidian languages: Tamil, Telugu, and Malayalam. The languages of the Indonesian archipelago are classified as Austroasiatic; Japanese and Korean are difficult to categorize within one of the larger language families.
All the major world religions have taken root in Asia and influenced the shape of society in numerous countries. The most important religions are Islam, Hinduism, Buddhism, Confucianism, Taoism, Shintoism, the Jewish and Christian religions. In addition to these, there are many ethnic religions.
The vastness of the continent makes the term

Agriculture in Asia is very labour-intensive, because there is hardly any mechanization. In many countries, about 75% of the working population works the fields. However, there is a lot of hidden unemployment, and productivity is low.

of Asian art more a geographic than an artistic notion. Thousands of years before the Christian era there were already four major cultural centers in Asia: Mesopotamia, Persia, India, and China. Mesopotamia flourished during the reign of the Sumerians (starting around 3,000 B.C.) and the Assyrians and Babylonians (from 2,000 B.C.), until it was taken over by Persia for a couple of centuries B.C. After the heydays of the Persian empire, Hellenism became influential. A new period of prosperity began under the Sassanides (224-651 A.D.). With the rise of Islam, the Arabic sphere of influence also spread towards India and Indonesia. Around 300 B.C. Buddhism created a new development in art in India. This religion - and its art - spread across large parts of Asia, even as far as Japan. In India, Buddhist art was ultimately supplanted by Hinduism (with its own art). Islamic art began to have influence around 1200.

In other Southeast Asian countries Buddhism remained the most important religion and so Buddhist art remained the most important form of artistic expression. In China, where art dated from the last period of the stone age, cultural life already showed a high standard from around 2,000 B.C.. This standard remained almost uninterrupted until the 19th century, when outside influences (for instance, Buddhism) began to play a role. Japanese art was heavily influenced by Chinese art around 500 A.D., but became more independent in the course of time.

In the 19th century the influence of Western art was noticeable in nearly all Asian countries.

From a historic perspective this vast continent shows little cohesion. There were already several cultural centers in prehistoric times. From around 8000 B.C., some centers, such as Mesopotamia, had agriculture and cattle breeding as the main means of existence. Between 3000 and 2000 B.C., the oldest known civilizations in the world started up in the vicinity of these agricultural areas. These civilizations developed independently of each other in Mesopotamia, India, and China and also spread their influence gradually across the rest of Asia. From the 7th century A.D. Islam spread from the Arabic peninsula across Asia. This influence contradicted sharply with the Chinese civilization (Chang dynasty) and the Hindu states in India. About 1200 the swift Mongolian expansion under Genghis Khan began in central Asia and brought turmoil to almost all of Asia. New Mongolian empires (khanates) came into existence in the south of Russia, Persia, Central Asia, and China, while migrations and expeditions also brought important changes in southeast Asia and Japan. After the Mongolian dominance, the Turkish Empire emerged in southwest Asia, which was to remain the main political center from the 15th until the 20th century.

European explorers brought about close contacts between Asia and Europe in the 16th century. In the 17th century, and especially in the 18th and 19th century, the Dutch, Russians, French, and English formed their colonial empires. Only strong states such as the Turkish Empire, China, and Japan were spared from colonization.

Asian nationalism, which began in the 19th century, continued in the 20th century and was influenced by Western ideas. It led to political independence after WW I (Southwest Asia) and WW II (the 'Far East'). Nationalism often occurred with far-reaching social-economic changes, like in Japan, which became almost completely westernized and China, which became a Communist People's Republic. The Cold War between the USSR and the US also spread to Asia, where several bloody conflicts took place (for instance Korea, Vietnam).

Asia Minor, peninsula in southwestern Asia including most of modern Turkey, mountainous and surrounded on 3 sides by the Black and Mediterranean seas, bounded on the east by the upper Euphrates River. After the destruction of the Hittite empire c.1200 B.C., the land was occupied successively by the Medes, Persians, Greeks, and Romans. In the 5th century of the present era it passed to the Byzantine emperors. It was settled by Turks beginning in the 13th century and became part of the Ottoman Empire in the fifteenth. The modern Turkish state was founded in 1923.

Asian Games, sports competition for Asian countries following the model of the Olympic Games. The first Asian Games were organized under supervision of the IOC in New Delhi in 1951 as the Pan Asian Games. Since 1954 they have been held every four years.

Asian Tigers, name for the East-Asian economies of Taiwan, South Korea, Singapore, and Hong Kong; developing areas that began to carry out an export-driven industrial policy (for instance, clothes and electronics). In the course of the 20th century they became industrialized and achieved high figures of economic growth. China and the 'young tigers' of Malaysia, Vietnam, the Philippines, Indonesia, and Thailand are also undergoing a similar development. It is expected that these ten countries will become the leading centers of economic power in the world.

Asia-Pacific Economic Cooperation (APEC), informal consultation between countries along the so-called Pacific Rim, in particular, about trade policy, which started in 1989. Participants: Brunei, the Philippines, Indonesia, Malaysia, Singapore, Thailand, Australia, Canada, Chile, China,

The first Europeans to travel to the Far East during the Middle Ages, were members of the Venetian Polo family. Between 1271 and 1295 they made a journey during which the Polos - who were favoured by the Mongolian emperor - visited China, Tibet, Burma, Java and many other areas. Later, in prison in Genoa, Marco Polo dictated his account of this journey, from which this is an original illustration.

Hong Kong, Japan, Mexico, New Zealand, Papua-New Guinea, Peru, Russia, Taiwan, United States, Vietnam, and South Korea.

Asimov, Isaac (1920-1992), prolific (almost 400 books) U.S. author, biochemist, and educator, known for his science fiction works, including the *Foundation* trilogy (1951-53, 1982) and *The Gods Themselves* (1972), as well as for his many popular works on various fields of science and general knowledge.

Asita, Indian sage; in Hinduism the first to recognize the deity of Krishna. In Buddhism Asita is the one who descended from heaven after the birth of the Buddha and predicted his future. For this reason he is sometimes referred to as 'Buddhist Simeon'.

Askenase, Stefan (1896-1985), Polish-Belgian pianist. Askenase studied in Vienna, made his debut there in 1919 and was teacher at the school of music in Cairo from 1922-1925. In 1925 Askenase based himself in Brussels between his innumerable concert travels. Between 1954-1961 he taught at the schools of music in Brussels, Hamburg, and Cologne. He has lived in 'Bahnhof Rolandseck' a home for artists, which he founded near Bonn, since 1961. As a pianist Askenase was mainly known for his Chopin interpretations.

Chinese soldiers of the fourth Communist army corps, giving the official party salute (1946). Their faces show that, as far as they are concerned, the final victory over the Nationalists is not far away.

A

Asmara (pop. 358,000), capital of Eritrea. The city is situated on a plateau about 7,000 ft (2,134 m) above sea level and has road and rail connections to the interior and to the Red Sea port of Massawa, about 40 mi (64 km) away. Industrial centre with production of textiles, soap and food. Seized by Italy in 1889, the town became the administrative seat of the colony of Eritrea in 1900. Awarded to Ethiopia by the UN in 1952, Eritrea became a province in 1962. From the 1970s the Eritrean guerillas waged a war of independence and the control of Asmara has been contested. When Asmara was captured by the Eritreans in the early 1990s independence was on its way and formally achieved in 1993.

Asoka (d.232 B.C.), third emperor of the Maurya dynasty of India, whose acceptance of Buddhism as the official religion of his vast empire contributed to that faith's predominance in Asia. He was said to have been so repelled by a particularly bloody victory of his troops over what is now Orissa that he turned to nonviolence and the Buddhist way of righteousness, and sent missionaries into Burma, Ceylon (Sri Lanka), Syria, Greece, and Egypt.
See also: Buddhism.

Asp, Egyptian cobra (*Naja haja*) of the family Elapidae, an extremely poisonous snake up to 7 ft (2 m) in length. Considered sacred in ancient Egypt, it was, according to legend, the snake that killed Cleopatra. The name is also applied to several species of vipers.
See also: Cobra.

Asparagus, garden vegetable (*Asparagus officinalis*) of the lily family, a perennial plant cultivated for its tender stalks. A well-tended asparagus bed may yield heavy crops for as long as 20 years. One variety of asparagus is grown for its attractive foliage alone.

Aspartame *See:* Artificial sweetener.

Aspasia (5th century B.C.), learned woman from Miletus, mistress of the Athenian statesman Pericles, by whom she had a son, Pericles the Younger. Her house was the literary and social gathering place for intellectual Athenians. She was the target of many spiteful attacks, mainly by conservatives who did not dare confront Pericles himself. Pericles was compelled to defend her against a charge of 'impiety' in 432 B.C.

Aspen (pop. 20,000), town in south-central Colorado and seat of Pitkin County. In the late 19th century, Aspen (originally Ute City) was a flourishing silver-mining town, but its prosperity declined when ore deposits were exhausted.

Aspen, deciduous tree of the poplar genus widely distributed in north temperate regions, commercially valued as a source of pulp and matches.

Asphalt, tough black material made of heavy hydrocarbons and used in road paving, roofing, and canal and reservoir lining. Although natural deposits are still used, asphalt is now obtained mainly from petroleum refinery residues.

Asphodel, perennial herbaceous plant (genera *Asphodelus* and *Asphodeline*) of the lily family, with white or yellow flowers along the stalk. The yellow asphodel, or Jacob's rod, is often cultivated as an ornamental plant. Native to southern Europe and India, the asphodel was considered the flower of Hades by the ancient Greeks.

Asphyxiation, complex of symptoms resulting from a lack of oxygen or excess of carbon dioxide in the lungs. The commonest causes are drowning, suffocation or strangulation, inhalation of poisonous gases, and the obstruction of the larynx, trachea, or bronchi (as in severe cases of croup and asthma).

Aspidistra, perennial plant (*Aspidistra lurida*) of the lily family, with sturdy leaves, once a widely grown houseplant. Native to China, Java, and Japan, aspidistras bear small blue flowers close to the ground and have particularly attractive foliage.

Aspirin, or acetylsalicylic acid, effective painkiller that reduces fever and inflammation. It is useful in treating headache, minor fever, menstruation pain, rheumatic fever, inflammatory arthritis, and may help in the prevention of thrombosis (blood clots). Possible side effects include gastrointestinal irritation and hemorrhage.

Asquith, Herbert Henry, 1st Earl of Oxford and Asquith (1852-1928), English prime minister, 1908-16. His term as head of the Liberal Party was one of great activity and political reform, but his leadership foundered in Dec. 1916 over his conduct of World War I, coupled with the chaos brought about by the Easter Rising in Ireland. He resigned in favor of the rival Liberal leader, David Lloyd George.

Gatherers, working on a tea-plantation. Tea is Assam's principal export product.

Assad, Bashar al- (1965-   ), President of Syria (2000-   ), son of Syrian president Hafiz al-Assad. His elder brother Basil was predestined to succeed his father. Bashar went to Medical School were he studied ophtalmology. In 1992 he continued his studies in London. When Basil was killed in a car crash in 1994, Bashar was called back from England had to take over the role of successor. He became commander of an armored division in the Syrian army. In 1999, he attained the rank of colonel. One day after the death of his father, in 2000, the ruling Baath-party recommended him as the new president of the country and commander-in-chief of the army. That same day, a law was passed which stipulated that the minimum age of the president should be 34 in stead of 40, in order to enable the election of the 34-year-old Bashar. In July, the Syrian people voted via a referendum, which completed the succession. After his appointment, Bashar indicated that he wanted to continue the peace policy with Israel. During the conference of the Baath-party, of which Bashar became chairperson, 74 new officials, who shared Bashar's ideas on reform in Syria, were appointed to the organization of the party.
See also: Baath party.

Assad, Hafiz al- (1930-2000), politician and member of the Syrian military. After the Baath party came into power in 1963, Assad carved out a quick career for himself within the army. In 1965 he was made a general in the air force and minister of defense in 1966. As such he played an important part in the Syrian defeat during the Six Day War of 1967. As a minister, Assad belonged to the moderate wing within the Baath party. The moderates took control in November 1970. Assad became prime minister and has been president of Syria since March 1971. Two years after he took office, he introduced a new constitution containing socialist elements. After the Soviet Union ceased to be an important ally (and arms supplier), Assad focussed on improving the relationship with the West, and in particular with the US, during the 1990s. Assad withdrew his opposition to the peace negotiations with Israel and became willing to cooperate in the peace process. There was a cautious political and economic liberalization (for instance, regarding Syrian Jews). The peace process with Israel, however, arrived at an impasse in 1995. Attempts by the European Union in 1997 and by the American Foreign Secretary, Madeleine Albright, to get Syria and Israel back to the negotiating table, failed.
After a referendum in 1999, a new seven year term of presidential office was accepted. However, well over one year later, Assad died.
See also: Persian Gulf War; Syria.

Assam (pop. 23,500,000), state in India located in the extreme northeast of the country and connected to the rest of India by West Bengal. To the north it is bordered by Tibet and Bhutan and to the east by Burma. The rugged land is drained by the Brahmaputra River. The climate is subtropical and rainfall varies from 70 in (178 cm) to more than 400 in (1,016 cm) per year. Tea is the main commercial product, and about 90% of the population is engaged in agriculture. Assamese is one of the official languages of India.

Assassins, in the original sense, members of a Moslem secret order of fanatics. The name, from the Arabic *hash-shashin*, 'hashish eaters,' refers to the supposed practice of using the drug hashish to excite a religious fervor in members chosen to kill persons marked for death by the order's leaders. The order was founded in Persia about 1090 by Hasan ibn al-Sabbah, called 'The Old Man of the Mountains' by the Crusaders. It spread into Lebanon and Syria, and terrorized the Middle East for almost 200 years. At times, rival political factions used members of the order as paid murderers. In 1256 the Mongol invaders destroyed the order in Persia; the Syrian branch was stamped out in 1273.

Assault and battery, any threatening physical act that reasonably causes another person to fear bodily harm or offensive contact. If there is actual contact, the crime is called battery. One may have assault without battery, but any case of battery necessarily includes assault. Assault and battery may be either a felony or a misdemeanor, depending on the degree of seriousness.

Assaying, method of chemical analysis used to determine the presence, absence, or quantity of a particular component of ores or alloys, used since the 2nd millennium B.C. In modern assaying, the sample is fused with a flux containing lead oxide. This produces a lead button containing the material being sought (such as gold or silver), which is heated in oxygen to oxidize the lead and other impurities. This leaves a bead of the metal sought, which is then weighed.

Assembler, computer program that converts symbolic code into binary object (machine) code for execution.
See also: Computer.

Assembling, in computer terminology, automatic process by which a computer converts a symbolic-language program into a machine language, usually on an instruction-by-instruction basis.
See also: Assembler; Computer.

Assembly language, hardware-dependent symbolic language used in computers, usually characterized by a one-to-one correspondence of its statements with machine-language instructions.
See also: Computer.

Assembly line, production line of equipment, machinery, and workers along which successive operations are performed until the final product is complete. The modern assembly line, largely a result of innovations by Henry Ford in the automotive industry, also employs automation (machines run by machines).
See also: Mass production.

Assessment, value of property (most commonly homes, shops, and offices) for purposes of taxation, or the process of determining this value. The tax rate is generally stated as so many dollars per thousand dollars of assessed valuation. The term also refers to a demand made by a corporation for extra funds from its stockholders.

Assignment, in law, transfer of rights, especially intangible property rights: insurance policies, certificates of corporate shares, and rights to monies due or to become due. In bankruptcy, a debtor's assets may be assigned to a trustee for distribution among creditors.

Assimilation, the process by which food is appropriated as nourishment for the body, following digestion and absorption. The food is converted into living tissues by the cells.
See also: Cell; Digestive system.

Assiniboine, Sioux tribe of the North American plains who left the Yanktonai Sioux to spread out from Canada across the northwestern United States. A nomadic people who lived primarily by hunting, they were greatly weakened by the extinction of the buffalo as a result of European settlements, and were placed on reservations in 1884.

Assisi, Francis of *See:* Francis of Assisi, Saint.

Associated Press (AP), oldest and one of the largest U.S. news agencies (gatherers and distributors of news). Founded in 1848 by 6 New York City newspapers, it now has offices worldwide. The AP is a nonprofit organization financed by subscriptions from member newspapers, periodicals, and broadcasting stations.

Association, in psychology, mental linking of one item with others, by similarity, contiguity, opposition, or other principles. In association tests, subjects are presented with a word and asked to respond either with a specifically related word, such as a rhyme or an antonym, or with the first word that comes to mind.
See also: Learning.

Associationism, psychological school holding that the sole mechanism of human learning consists in the permanent association in the intellect of impressions that have been repeatedly presented to the senses. Originating in the philosophy of John Locke and developed through the work of John Gay, David Hartley, James and John Stuart Mill, and Alexander Bain, the 'association of ideas' was the dominant thesis in British psychology for 200 years.

Association of Southeast Asian Nations (ASEAN), alliance, founded on the 8th of August 1967 between the Southeast Asian countries of Malaysia, Singapore, Thailand, the Philippines and Indonesia. Brunei (1984), Vietnam (1995) and Cambodia (1999) also joined as members. Objective: to stabilize the Southeast Asian region and to stimulate economic growth, for instance by economic and cultural cooperation and mutual support to counterbalance China's growing influence.
In 1997 Burma (Myanmar) and Laos joined ASEAN despite Western pressure not to admit Burma because of its human rights abuses.

Assumption of the Virgin, Roman Catholic belief (declared as official dogma by Pope Pius XII in 1950) that the Virgin Mary was 'assumed into heaven body and soul' at the end of her life. Assumption Day is celebrated Aug. 15.

Assurbanipal *See:* Ashurbanipal.

Assyria *See:* Babylonia and Assyria.

Astaire, Fred (Frederick Austerlitz; 1899-1988), U.S. dancer, choreographer, and actor. First in partnership onstage with his sister Adele and later with Ginger Rogers in such films as *Top Hat* (1935) and *Swing Time* (1936), he became one of the most popular dancers and musical comedy stars, renowned for his originality and perfection. Later films, with other partners, included *Holiday Inn* (1942), *The Band Wagon* (1953), and *Funny Face* (1957).

Musical-stars Fred Astaire and Ginger Rogers were one of the famous romantic teams in the history of film (from *The Gay Divorce*, made in 1934 by Mark Rex Sandrich).

Astana (pop. 300,000), capital of Kazakhstan. Astana, formerly called Akmola, has only been the capital of Kazakhstan since 1997. For various reasons, the old capital, Almaty or Alma-Ata (1.2 million inhabitants) was thought to be less suitable as a capital city after independence in 1991.

Astarte, Phoenician goddess of love and fertility, corresponding to Babylonian Ishtar and Greek Aphrodite. In Syrian art Astarte is frequently represented with two curled ram's horns on her head.

Astatine, chemical element, symbol At; for physical constants see Periodic Table. Astatine was synthesized in 1940 by Corson, MacKenzie, and Segré at the University of California by bombarding bismuth with alpha particles. Minute quantities of astatine exist in nature as isotopes produced from uranium and thorium reacting with naturally produced neutrons. Astatine is radioactive and belongs to the halogen group of elements. It behaves chemically very much like them and is reported to be more metallic

A

A

than iodine. The longest-lived isotope, astatine-210, has a half-life of 8.1 hours. Twenty-eight isotopes of astatine are known.

Aster (genus *Aster*), also known as Michaelmas or Christmas daisy, perennial plant with blue, purple, white, or red flowers that bloom in autumn. The China aster (*Callistephus chinensis*), in the same family, produces bigger, almost chrysanthemum-like flowers in bright colors.

Asteria, in Greek mythology, daughter of Coeus, the Titan, and mother of Hecate. Courted by Zeus in the form of an eagle, she threw herself into the sea, where she was changed into an island, later called Delos.

Asteroid, planetoid, or minor planet of irregular shape, orbiting the sun. Ranging in diameter from a few feet (1 m) to Ceres's 470 mi (750 km), most (some 50,000 that are too small to yield to diameter measurements) lie in the asteroid belt between the orbits of Mars and Jupiter, their total mass estimated to be 0.001 that of the earth. Ceres was the first to be discovered (1801 by Giuseppe Piazzi), and Vesta is the only one visible to the naked eye. The Apollo asteroids have highly elliptical, earth-approaching orbits, and may have caused several of earth's meteorite craters. The Trojan asteroids share the orbit of the planet Jupiter.

Asthenosphere, the worldwide 'soft layer' underlying the rigid lithosphere, located some 43.5-155 mi (70-250 km) below the earth's surface. Considered part of the upper mantle, the zone is characterized by low seismic velocities, suggesting that it may be partially molten. In plate tectonic theory, rigid slablike plates of the lithosphere move over the asthenosphere.

Asthma, reversible obstruction of the airways that compromises the respiratory system. Asthma attacks are typically accompanied, by coughing and wheezing. Asthma is a chronic disorder that can be triggered by exposure to certain allergens or in response to physical or emotional stress. Therapy includes the use of steroids and bronchodilators.
See also: Allergy; Bronchitis.

Astigmatism, defect of vision caused by irregular shaping in the cornea or lens. In astigmatism, light rays do not converge evenly, some focusing behind the retina, some before it, others on it. It can be corrected by glasses or contact lenses.
See also: Eye.

Aston, Francis William (1877-1945), British physicist and chemist. At the Cavendish Laboratory, Cambridge, Aston accomplished the first artificial separation of isotopes. He was awarded the Nobel Prize for chemistry in 1922, chiefly for devising the mass spectrograph to study isotopes.

Astor, name of a prominent U.S. family in-

volved in fur trading, real estate, and finance, as well as in U.S. and British politics. **John Jacob Astor** (1763-1848), arrived in Baltimore from Waldorf, Germany, began as a baker's boy, became a fur trader and real estate investor, and eventually amassed the fortune of the Astors. **William Backhouse Astor** (1792-1875), John Jacob's son, doubled the family's wealth. His son, **John Jacob IV** (1864-1912), an inventor and science fiction writer, died in the sinking of the *Titanic*. **William Waldorf, 1st Viscount Astor** (1848-1919), John Jacob's great-grandson, was a financier who moved to England, where he was made baron and later viscount. **Nancy Witcher (Langhorne) Astor, Viscountess Astor** (1879-1964) was the first woman to serve in the British Parliament, as Conservative member for Plymouth.

Astrakhan (pop. 481,000), capital of Astrakhan Oblast in the RF. A port on the Caspian Sea at the mouth of the Volga River, Astrakhan handles trade in oil, fish, grain, and wood. Astrakhan became the capital of a Tatar khanate in the mid-15th century. In 1556 it was captured by Ivan IV and made part of Muscovy. The city began to grow as a port and trade center in the 17th century.

Astringent, substance that causes the organic tissues and canals of the body to contract, thereby checking or diminishing excessive discharges.

Astroarcheology *See:* Archeoastronomy.

Astrolabe, astronomical instrument dating from ancient times, used to measure the altitude and movements of celestial bodies. Before the introduction of the sextant, it served as a navigational aid.
See also: Sextant.

Astrology, system of beliefs based on the theory that movements of celestial bodies influence human events, which can therefore be predicted. The key factor in Western astrology is the position of the stars and planets, described relative to the 12 divisions of the zodiac, at the moment of an individual's birth.
See also: Zodiac.

Astronaut, term for U.S. test pilot or scientist chosen by NASA to crew space flights. Alan B. Shepard, Jr., made the first suborbital flight in 1961. John Glenn, Jr., orbited the earth in 1962, and Edwin E. Aldrin, Jr., and Neil Armstrong landed on the moon in 1969.

Astronautics, or astronautical engineering, scientific study of the principles of space flight, including astrodynamics, space communications, propulsion theory, astrobiology, astrogeology, and the design analysis of spacecraft.

Astronomy, science dealing with the universe and its celestial bodies. Research around the world is coordinated by the International Astronomical Union. Depending on the branches of research, it is

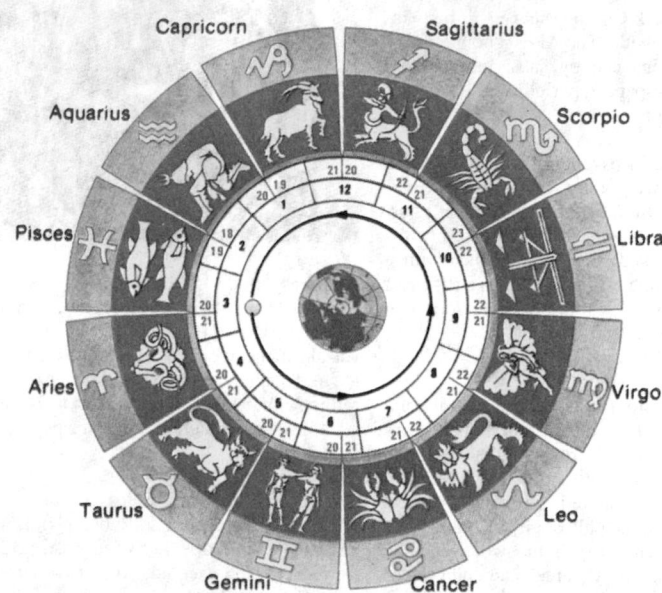

The year divided, according to the twelve Signs of the Zodiac. In the early days of astrology, the sun and the planets were thought to revolve round the earth. Each Sign corresponds with a different constellation in the Zodiac, of the heavens across which they appeared to pass in the course of a year. Passing outwards from the earth at the centre, the diagram shows the sun's imaginary orbit round the earth, the calendar months numbered from January (1) to December (12), the days of the month on which a Sign changes to the next, representations of the Signs, and in the outer circle the 'glyph' or astrological symbol for each sign. They are (beginning opposite the sun and going anti-clockwise through the year): Aries, Taurus, Gemini, Cancer, Leo, Virgo, Libra, Scorpio, Sagittarius, Capricorn, Aquarius, Pisces.

Johannes Kepler discovered the laws of planetary motion and deduced that the planets move in orbits around the Sun.

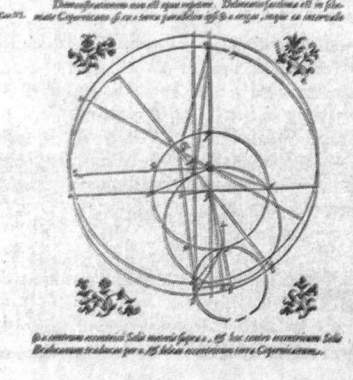

A print from an 18th- century atlas indicating the movement of the planets around the Sun. While this observation had been made two centuries earlier by Copernicus, political and intellectual acceptance of this fact was not easily accomplished.

A

The rings of the planet Saturn. The outer and inner rings are separated by a dark band called the Cassini division.

Drawing from Kepler's Astronomia nova which dates from 1609. In this work Kepler compared his observations with those of his former teacher Tycho Brahe.

Three views of planetary motion.
A. Hipparchus' view (150 B.C.): each planet (1) moves around in a small circle (epicycle), the center of which (2) makes a larger circle around the Earth (3). Although Hipparchus' view positioned the Earth at the center at of the solar system, his calculations about the position of the planets was correct.
B. Ptolemy's view (2nd century A.D.): In the Ptolemaic system each planet (1) travels in a circle whose center (2) moves around the Earth. Ptolemy placed the Earth (3) almost at the center (4) and introduced a fictitious opposite point (5) around which the planets move.
C. Copernican view (16th century): The Sun (6) is at the center with the planets moving around it. The known planets at this time were Mercury (7), Venus (8), Earth and Moon (9), Mars (10), Jupiter (11), and Saturn (12).

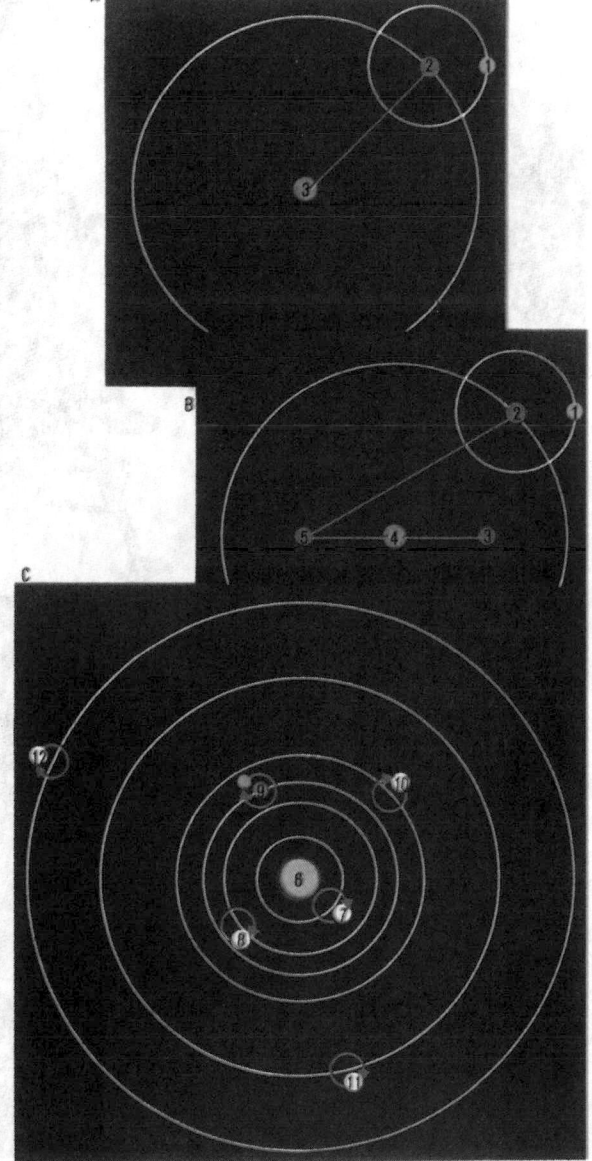

An ultraviolet photograph of the comet Kohoutek made by the crew of the Skylab space station on December 25, 1973. The different colors indicate regions of different temperatures. Photographs in ultraviolet light cannot be made from the Earth because of the screening influence of the atmosphere.

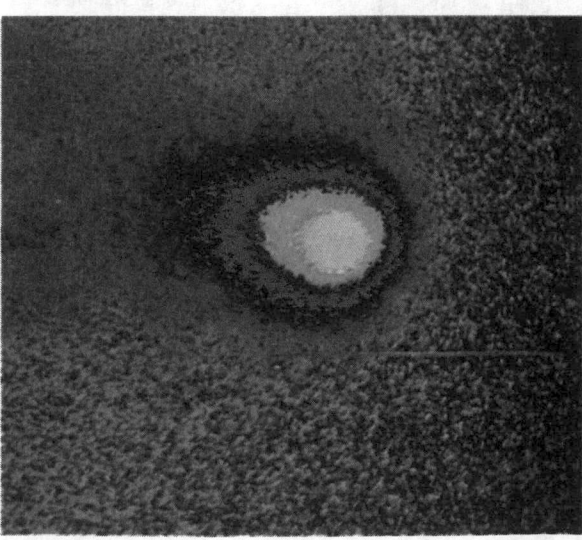

A

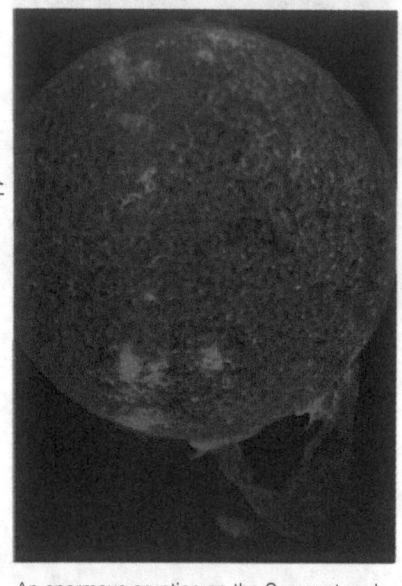

An enormous eruption on the Sun captured with ultraviolet photography by the crew of Skylab.

Photomicrograph of moon rocks brought back by the Apollo 12 mission. In order to reveal the structure, the photograph was taken with a polarization microscope. The colors are due to differences in thickness of the crystal layers.

The fully assembled combination of service module (1), Apollo capsule (2), and lunar lander (3).The lunar lander also carried a moon jeep (4) on the last three missions.

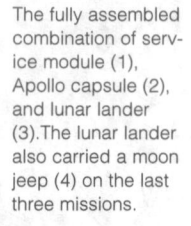

Photograph of Halley's Comet made in 1986 by the European space probe *Giotto*. Brown section (upper left) is part of the core of the planet. The various colors represent emissions of gas and dust.

Astrophysics is the study of the universe. A. Observations using gamma and X-rays of the solar corona must be made from the upper atmosphere by balloon or satellite. B. Studies of the Martian atmosphere may be made using ultra-violet radiation. Earth-based observato~ries or martian probes may perform the task. C. The visible spectrum. The Moon is observable from Earth.D. Infrared studies of Mars reveal surface detail. Observations may be made from telescopes on Earth or from space probes. E. Microwave radiation and radar wave lengths. Radar transmitters on Earth bounce radiation off the lunar surface to obtain profiles. F. Radio Waves. Radio telescopes map the powerful source, Centaurus A.

divided into: astrophysics, celestial mechanics, cosmology, astrophotography, astrophotometry, radio, radar, X-ray astronomy, and even more specialist research areas. The first real astronomers can be found among the Greeks (Hipparchus, Ptolemy). Their observations regarding, for instance, the solar system were discarded in the 17th and 18th century, especially after the introduction of the telescope (Galileo) and new physical theories (Newton). In the 19th century new planets were discovered and research into the Milky Way (Herschel) got underway. Modern physics (spectrum analysis, theory of relativity, and quantum theory) and radio astronomy have laid the foundation for the enormous theoretical rise in and expansion of possibilities for observation in the 20th century. Using space probes and interplanetary satellites in research has also drastically increased knowledge of the solar system.
See also: Cosmology.

Astrophysics, science dealing with the physical laws governing the nature of celestial objects and events, enabling astronomers to formulate theories of stellar evolution and cosmology.
See also: Astronomy; Cosmology.

Asturias, Miguel Ángel (1899-1974), Guatemalan writer and diplomat. He won the Lenin Peace Prize in 1966 and the Nobel Prize for literature in 1967. His books *The Cyclone* (1950) and *The Green Pope* (1954) attack the exploitation of Guatemalan Indians.

Asunción (pop. 500,000), capital and largest city of Paraguay. Situated on the Paraguay River, Asunción is the main port and the industrial, transportation, and administrative center of the country. Founded in 1537 by Spanish explorers searching for a short route to Peru, Asunción was the rival of Buenos Aires until the 18th century when it was weakened by conflict between the Jesuits and their enemies.

Aswan (Assouan; pop. 220,000), capital of the Egyptian Aswan Governorate; 262 sq mi (679 sq km). On the Nile River, north of Lake Nasser. Trade and tourist center. Fertilizer and metal industry. The first Aswan Dam was built around 1900 to allow for constant irrigation; the Aswan High Dam was completed in 1971 with Soviet assistance. There are remains of temples from the times of Ptolemy and of the Romans. The temples at Abu Simbel were removed in the 1960s so that the reservoir could be built.

Aswan High Dam, one of the world's largest dams, built on the Nile River in Egypt (1960-70), located 4 mi (6.4 km) south of the 1902 Aswan dam. The dam's hydroelectric generating station has a capacity of 10 billion kwh, and Lake Nasser, formed by the dam, has enough water to irrigate more than 7 million acres of farmland.

Asylum, sanctuary or place of refuge; an institution for receiving and maintaining persons suffering certain physical or mental diseases or defects.

Asyut (pop. 313,000), city in the eastern central region of Egypt, on the left bank of the Nile, about 250 mi (402 km) south of Cairo. A commercial and industrial center producing textiles, pottery, and ivory and wood carvings, Asyut is also the educational center of the Upper Nile Valley; its schools and institutions include the University of Asyut and the Technical and Trade School. A large community of Coptic Christians lives in the city. Asyut Barrage controls the flow of the Nile and provides water for the irrigation of Middle Egypt.

Atacama Desert, arid plateau extending from central Chile to southern Ecuador, some 600 mi (966 km) long and 2,000 ft (610 m) high. One of the driest regions on earth, it is a major source of nitrates and copper.

Atahualpa (1500-1533), last Inca emperor of Peru. After holding power only in Quito, Atahualpa deposed his half brother Huascar as heir of the Inca kingdom. In 1532 the Spanish conquistadors under Francisco Pizarro executed Atahualpa for refusing to accept Christianity.
See also: Inca.

Atalanta, in Greek mythology, beautiful, swift-footed huntress who promised to marry any suitor who outran her, but to kill any she could beat. She lost to (and married) Hippomenes, who, helped by the goddess Aphrodite, had dropped 3 golden apples that Atalanta paused to pick up.

Atatürk, Kemal (Mustafa Kemal; (1881-1938), founder of modern Turkey. An army officer who gained prominence during World War I, Atatürk headed a provisional government in Ankara that opposed the Allied regime in Istanbul established after the collapse of the Ottoman Empire. In 1923 he won European recognition of the new Turkish republic. His secular regime replaced the political power of Islam and modernized the Turkish economy.

Atavism, inheritance by an individual organism of characteristics not shown by its parental generation. Once thought to be throwbacks to an ancestral form, atavisms are now known to be primarily the result of the random appearance of recessive traits, though they may result also from aberrations in the development of the embryo or from disease.

Ataxia, impaired muscular coordination resulting in unsteady gait, difficulty in fine movements, and speech disorders. Usually caused by damage to the cerebellum or the spinal cord, ataxia occurs with multiple sclerosis, syphilis, and brain tumors.

Athabasca, river and lake in northern Alberta and Saskatchewan, Canada. The river rises in Jasper National Park and flows to the 3,120 sq mi (8,080 sq km) lake.

Athanasius, Saint (c.297-373), early Christian theologian and Greek Father of the Church. Athanasius was elected archbishop of Alexandria in 328. He was banished to

Trèves (Trier) in 335 by the emperor Constantine for his refusal to compromise with Arianism, but was restored by Constantius in 338. His writings include *On the Incarnation, Five Books Against Arius*, and *Life of St. Anthony*.

Atharva-Veda *See:* Vedas.

Atheism, denial of the existence of God, distinguished from agnosticism, which holds that the existence of God cannot be proved or disproved but does not necessarily take any position on belief.
See also: Agnosticism.

Athena (Pallas Athena), in Greek mythology, goddess of wisdom, war, and peace, who sprang fully grown from the head of Zeus. She was a patron of agriculture, arts, and the crafts of civilization. The Romans identified her with Minerva.

Athens (pop. 772,000), capital and largest city of Greece, in east central Greece. The center of ancient Greek civilization, Athens reached its political peak after the Persian wars (499-449 B.C.). Athens lost its supremacy to Sparta in the Peloponnesian War (431-404 B.C.) and later became a subject of Macedonia and then of Rome. Modern Athens, including the Aegean port of Piraeus, is the administrative, political, cultural, and economic center of Greece.

Atherosclerosis *See:* Arteriosclerosis.

Athlete's foot, popular name for a fungus infection of any area of the skin of the feet or toes, causing inflammation and itching. The fungus thrives in a warm, humid environment.
See also: Ringworm.

Athletics, refers to activities involving some form of contest or competition and depending on the skill, prowess, or stamina of the contestant - the *athlete*. In British usage the term refers specifically to track and field events. In American usage it includes many other kinds of physical contests, such as tennis, football, baseball, boxing, and weightlifting.
Popular athletic sports in ancient times included foot racing, wrestling, boxing, archery, and discus and javelin throwing. In Greece, such sports festivals as the Olympic Games, Pythian Games, and Isthmian Games had a religious significance. In the Middle Ages knights participated in tournaments that tested their ability to use weapons of war. Hunting was also popular with the nobility. Peasants played various kinds of ball games.
By the 19th century many sports had developed into their modern forms. Toward the end of the century, the introduction of standardized rules for most sports contributed to the growth of organized competition. The establishment of the modern Olympic Games as an international amateur sports festival in 1896 did much to establish sports as a spectator attraction.
Sports experienced a tremendous growth during the 20th century. Professional teams came into prominence, and women began to

A

A

participate in a wide variety of sports. Increased leisure time and the impact of television made sports more popular than ever before. There was an expansion of professionalism worldwide, and in the 1990's most sports in the Olympic Games were opened to professional athletes. The use of performance-enhancing drugs, especially *anabolic steroids* by athletes became a problem and most sports organizations banned them.

Athlone, Alexander Augustus Frederick William Alfred George Cambridge, 1st Earl of (1874-1957), British army officer and member of the royal family. After a military career during the Boer War and World War I, he was governor general of the Union of South Africa (1923-31) and governor general of Canada (1940- 46).

Atkinson, Rowan (1955-), British actor, graduated as an electrical engineer from Oxford University and started his career as a stand-up comedian at the Edinburgh Festival. He featured in television series such as *Monty Python* and *Blackadder*. He was also the deviser and co-writer of the latter. He was most renowned for his role of Mr Bean in the television series of the same name and the highly successful motion picture. Moreover, Atkinson featured in *The Witches* (1990), *Four Weddings And A Funeral* (1994), *Maybe Baby* (2000) and *Rat Race* (2001).

Atlanta (pop. 402,000), capital and largest city of the American state of Georgia.

Cultural and financial center; medical center for the southeast of the US. Motor vehicle industry; Coca-Cola factories; three universities; CNN. The city has one of the country's busiest airports (Hartsfield). Founded in 1837. Martin Luther King who was murdered in 1968, is buried here. In 1996 Atlanta hosted the Summer Olympic Games.
See also: Georgia.

Atlanta, Battle of *See:* Civil War, U.S..

Atlantic Charter, declaration of common objectives signed by U.S. President F. D. Roosevelt and British Prime Minister Winston Churchill on Aug. 14, 1941, before the United States entered World War II. It affirmed the determination of the 2 governments not to extend their territories and to promote human rights.

Atlantic City (pop. 40,000), seaside resort and convention center in southeast New Jersey. Its famous Boardwalk (built 1870) is lined by hotels, restaurants, casinos, and Convention Hall.

Atlantic Ocean, world's second-largest ocean (c.31.8 million sq mi/82.3 million sq km), separating the Americas from Europe and Africa. The North Atlantic carries the greatest proportion of the world's shipping, and about half of the world's fish come from the area.

Atlantikwall, defenses built by the Germans

during the second World War along the North-Atlantic coast, the North Sea, and the Channel. The Atlantikwall was built by the SS (Organization Todt) and by (forced) labor, but was not strong enough to resist the allied invasion in June 1944.

Atlantis, in Greek mythology, an island in the western sea (Atlantic Ocean?). Plato described it as an advanced civilization destroyed by volcanic eruptions and earthquakes. The legend has fascinated humanity since antiquity, and many have searched for the lost island. Some scholars identify Atlantis with the Mediterranean island of Thera (also called Santorini), a center of ancient Cretan civilization devastated by volcanic eruptions in 1625 B.C.

Atlas, in Greek mythology, a titan. After the titans were defeated by the Olympians, he was condemned to carry the sky on his shoulders for eternity.

Atlas Mountains, mountain system of northwest Africa. The highest peak, 13,671 ft (4,167 m), is Mount Toubkal in southwestern Morocco. The Atlas mountains are rich in coal, oil, iron ore, and phosphates.

Atmosphere, spheroidal envelope of gas and vapor surrounding a planet, retained by gravity. The composition of the earth's atmosphere and most of its physical properties vary with altitude. About 75% of the total mass of the atmosphere and 90% of its water vapor are contained in the troposphere, the lowest zone, which extends from the earth's surface to an altitude of about 5 mi (8 km) at the poles and 10 mi (16 km) at the equator. The stratosphere, where the ozone layer filters out the sun's ultraviolet radiation, extends from the troposphere to about 30 mi (50 km); the mesosphere ranges from there to about 50 mi (80 km); the ionosphere, containing electrically charged particles that reflect radio signals, goes to about 400 mi (640 km); finally, the exosphere merges into the interplanetary medium. Overall, the atmosphere is about 78% nitrogen by volume. Other major components include oxygen (21%), argon (0.93%), and carbon dioxide (0.03%).

Atoll, low-lying oval or circular coral reef, enclosing a lagoon, most prevalent in the western Pacific Ocean. Examples are the Maldive Islands, Whitsunday Island, and the Bikini Atoll.
See also: Coral.

Atom, classically, one of the minute, indivisible, homogeneous particles of which physical objects are composed; in 20th-century science, the name given to a relatively stable package of matter that is itself made up of at least 2 subatomic particles, and that defines an element. Every atom consists of a tiny nucleus (containing positively charged protons and electrically neutral neutrons) with which a number of negatively charged electrons are associated. The much smaller electrons occupy a hierarchy of orbitals that represent the atom's electronic energy levels and fill most of the space taken up by the atom. The number of protons in the nucleus

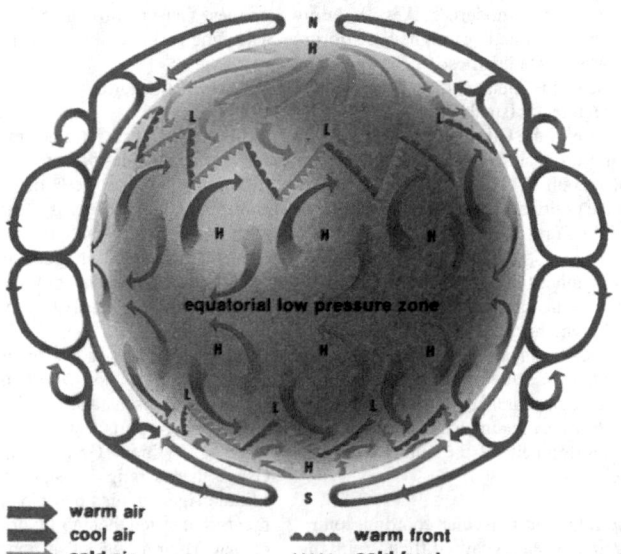

equatorial low pressure zone

➡ warm air
➡ cool air
➡ cold air

⌁⌁⌁ warm front
▲▲▲ cold front

The earth's atmosphere functions as a giant heat engine, in which the temperature differences between the poles and the equator provide a global driving force that can circulate air masses vertically and horizontally. When warm air rises at the equator and moves toward the poles at high altitudes, cold polar air will move toward the equator at low altitudes to replace it. Winds in any given area are set in motion by the movement of the air from high pressure cells (H), to low pressure cells (L). Prevailing wind directions at different latitudes, however, depend not only on pressure differences, but also on the Coriolis effect, a sideway drift that is caused by the earth's rotation. Thus, the winds (indicated by the curved arrows) tend to spiral out of high-pressure areas in clockwise direction in the northern hemisphere, and in counterclockwise direction in the southern hemisphere. Precipitation occurs where cold and warm fronts meet.

of an atom (the atomic number, Z) defines the chemical element of which the atom is an example. In an isolated neutral atom the number of electrons equals the atomic number, but an electrically charged ion of the same atom has either a surfeit or a deficit of electrons. The number of neutrons in the nucleus (the neutron number, N) can vary among different atoms of the same element. Atoms with the same number of protons but different numbers of neutrons are called isotopes of the element in question. Most stable isotopes have slightly more neutrons than protons. Although the nucleus is very small, it contains nearly all the mass of the atom-protons and neutrons having very similar masses, the mass of the electron (about 0.05% of the proton mass) being almost negligible. The mass of an atom is roughly equal to the total number of its protons and neutrons. This number, $Z + N$, is known as the mass number of the atom, A, the mass of a proton being counted as 1. In equations representing nuclear reactions, the atomic number of an atom is often written as a subscript preceding the chemical symbol for the element, and the mass number as a superscript following it. Thus an atomic nucleus with a mass number 16 and containing 8 protons belongs to an atom of oxygen-16, written $_8O^{16}$. The average of the mass numbers of the various naturally occurring isotopes of an element, weighted according to their relative abundance, gives the chemical atomic weight of the element. Subatomic particles fired into atomic nuclei can cause nuclear reactions that give rise either to new isotopes of the original element or to atoms of a different element. Such nuclear reactions emit alpha particles, or beta rays, sometimes accompanied by gamma rays.

Atomic clock, precise electric device for measuring time, indirectly controlled by atomic or molecular vibration.

Atomic energy *See:* Nuclear energy; Fission; Nuclear energy.

Atomic fusion *See:* Fusion; Nuclear energy.

Atomic number *See:* Atom.

Atomic particle *See:* Atom.

Atomic reactor *See:* Nuclear reactor.

Atomic theory *See:* Atom.

Atomic weight, mean of the masses of all the various isotopes of a given element. Atomic weight is normally given in atomic mass units; an atomic mass unit is defined as 1/12 of the mass of an atom of carbon-12. *See also:* Atom; Periodic table.

Atom smasher *See:* Particle accelerator.

Atonement, in Christian theology, reconciliation of humanity with God through the sacrificial death of Christ. In Jewish theology, one day of the year is designated as the Day of Atonement (*Yom Kippur*).

Atreus, in Greek mythology, king of Mycenae and the father of Agamemnon and Menelaus. His brother, Thyestes, seduced Atreus's wife, Aërope, and attempted to seize the throne of Mycenae. Atreus, pretending to forgive his brother, invited him to a banquet at which he served Thyestes the bodies of his 2 sons.

Atrium, unroofed or partially roofed interior court of a Roman house, with rooms extending around it; also, entrance court of early Christian churches.

Atrophy (Greek, 'not nourished'), decrease in size and function or wasting away of any organ, tissue, or part of the body as a result of disease, malnutrition, decreased work, or normal processes of growth or body function. Among the types of atrophy are acute yellow atrophy, massive necrosis of the liver associated with severe infection; toxemia of pregnancy or ingested poisons; and progressive muscular atrophy, a motor neuron disease characterized by loss of power and wasting in the arms and legs.

Atropine, crystalline alkaloid contained in plants such as jimsonweed and deadly nightshade (belladonna), used in many gastrointestinal and ophthalmic preparations. Its chief use is as an antispasmodic to relax smooth muscles.
See also: Belladonna.

Atsina *See:* Gros Ventre.

Attachment, seizure of property by legal process, to prevent a defendant from disposing of disputed property before trial, and to guarantee payment of any judgment against him or her.

Attainder, loss of civil rights (strictly, rights of ownership and disposition of property) by someone outlawed or sentenced to death. Attainder has been almost universally abolished except in cases of treason.

Attar, fragrant, essential oil, often made from various species of roses, that forms a valuable perfume.

Attica, a small, triangular peninsula on the Aegean coast of south-central Greece. It is historically famous as the district making up the ancient city-state of Athens; 'Attic' is used to mean ancient Athenian. Attica at that time was bounded on the northwest by Boeotia and on the west by Megaris. Modern Attica, including Megaris, is a prefecture of Greece, with Athens as its capital and Piraeus as its chief port.
Important historic sites in Attica include Mount Pentelicus, famous for its white marble, and Mount Hymettus, for its blue. Eleusis was the scene of the Eleusian Mysteries (religious rites), and a road known as the Sacred Way connected Eleusis with Athens. Cape Sunium (Colonna), at the

A

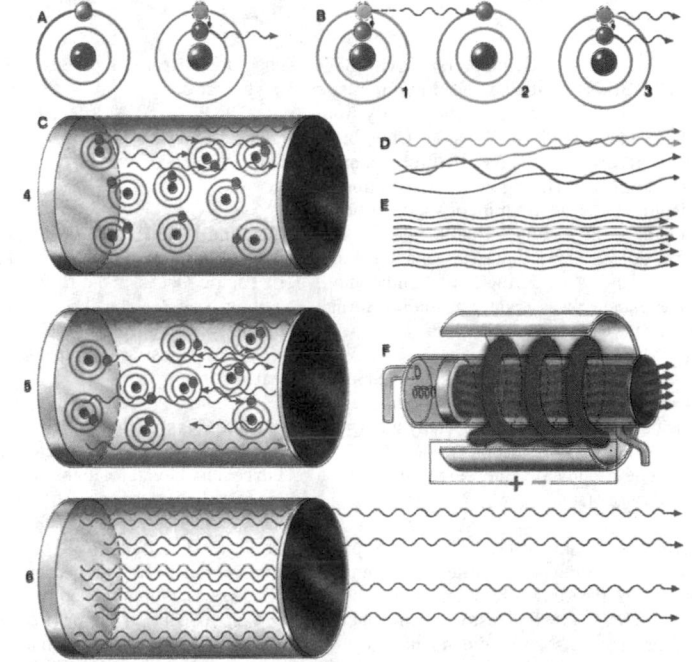

A laser is a device that produces an intense, highly concentrated beam of single-wavelength light. Most light is emitted by an exited atom (A) containing an electron in a higher-than-normal energy level. The electron soon returns spontaneously to its normal, or ground, state, releasing the excess energy in the form of light waves, or photons. In stimulated emission (B), a photon emitted from an atom (1) induces an electron in another excited atom (2) to fall immediately to a lower level and emit an photon indentical to itself (3). Stimulated emission can thus be used to increase the number of emitted photons. Energy is first pumped into a laser material (C), raising most of the electrons to a level just above the ground state. Initially (4), only a few atoms will spontaneously radiate photons. Two silvered end mirrors, one partially transparent, reflect the radiation back and forth repeatedly (5), inducing a chain reaction of photon emission. All the electrons return to the ground state almost simultaneously, and a powerful pulse of laser light (6) emerges from the partially transparent end. Whereas light waves from conventional sources have a wide range of wavelengths and move in various directions (D), laser light waves have a single wavelength and are unidirectional and exactly in step with one another (E). A ruby laser (F) comprises a ruby rod with silver-coated ends spring-mounted in a liquid-cooled chamber. Energy for raising the atoms to the high-energy state is supplied by a coiled gas-discharge tube surrounded by a focusing reflector.

A

southern tip of the peninsula, was the point from which, according to legend, King Aegeus watched for his son Theseus to return from battling the Minotaur in Crete. The silver mines of Mount Laurium, near Cape Sunium, financed the building projects of Athens' Golden Age. Marathon, the plain where the Persians were repulsed in 490 B.C., is also in Attica.

Attila (A.D. 406?-453), king of the Huns, who claimed domination from the Alps and the Baltic to the Caspian Sea. From 441 to 450 he ravaged the Eastern Roman Empire as far as Constantinople, and invaded Gaul in 451, this expedition earning him the title Scourge of God. He was defeated by the Romans, and subsequently invaded Italy (452), but retired without attacking Rome, apparently due to lack of supplies and sickness among his troops. He died of overindulgence at his wedding feast.
See also: Hun.

Attlee, Clement Richard, 1st Earl (1883-1967), British politician and prime minister (1945-51). Attlee led the Labour party from 1935 and served in Winston Churchill's wartime coalition cabinet before becoming prime minister. During his administration he instituted a broad program of social reforms, including the National Health Service, and nationalized many industries and the Bank of England. Also during his administration, independence was granted to India, Burma, Pakistan, Palestine, and Ceylon.

Attorney, one who is legally appointed in the place of another as an agent to transact any business for him or her; especially a lawyer.

Attorney general, chief law officer of a country or state.

Attucks, Crispus (c.1723-1770), U.S. patriot of African and Native American parentage who was the first of 5 men to die in the Boston Massacre. It is historic irony that one of the first persons to die in the cause of American independence was an individual whose personal rights were not secure at the time of his death.

Atwood, Margaret (1939-), Canadian poet and novelist. Atwood gained prominence with a collection of poetry, *The Circle Game* (1966). Among her other works are *Bluebeard's Egg* (1983), a collection of short stories, and the novels *Surfacing* (1972), *Lady Oracle* (1976), *The Handmaid's Tale* (1985), *Cat's Eye* (1989), *The Robber Bride* (1993), *Alias Grace* (1996), and *The Blind Assassin* (2000; Booker Prize).

Auckland (pop. 998,000), chief port, largest city, naval base, and industrial center of New Zealand, capital of Auckland province on North Island. Founded in 1840, Auckland was New Zealand's capital until 1865, when the government was transferred to Wellington. Important industries include shipbuilding, oil refining, food processing, and automobile manufacturing. The city's War Memorial Museum contains one of the finest collections of Maori art in the world.

Lithograph (1825) from the famous book *The Birds of America*, by John James Audubon (1785-1851). The wood duck (*Aix sponsa*) is depicted.

Auckland Islands, group of uninhabited islands, of volcanic origin, lying in the southern Pacific Ocean about 200 mi (320 km) south of New Zealand. They were used as a whaling station during the early 19th century. The islands are controlled by New Zealand.

Auden, W(ystan) H(ugh) (1907-1973), Anglo-American poet and major influence in 20th century literature. In the 1930s, when he also collaborated with Christopher Isherwood on verse plays (*The Dog Beneath the Skin*, *The Ascent of F6*, and *On the Frontier*), his poetry probed pre-World War II European culture. In 1939 Auden moved to the United States, where he became a citizen in 1946. His later work, which delves into religion, psychology, and politics, includes *The Double Man* (1941), *The Age of Anxiety* (1947, Pulitzer Prize), *The Shield of Achilles* (1955), and *About the House*. He also wrote opera librettos and literary criticism.

Audio, the audible frequency with a range between 20 hertz and 20,000 hertz. In electronics also referred to as LF, low frequency, as distinguished from the higher frequency ranges referred to as HF, high frequency. The term audio is often used nowadays as opposed to the term video: audio refers to sound, video to images.

Audiology, science of hearing; particularly, the study of hearing disorders and rehabilitation of individuals with hearing defects. Audiologists determine whether a person has a hearing deficiency by identifying and measuring hearing function loss and assessing the patient's ability to communicate. Corrective treatment may involve a hearing aid, learning to read lips, or improvement of listening skills.

Audit, in accounting, examination of ac-

counts or dealings with money or property, performed by persons not involved in the preparation of the accounts.
See also: Accounting.

Audubon, John James (1785-1851), U.S. artist and ornithologist famous for his paintings of North American birds, reproduced in *Birds of America* (1827-38). He collaborated with the Scottish naturalist William MacGillivray on an accompanying text, *Ornithological Biography* (1831-39).

Augeas, in Greek mythology, King Augeas of Elis had a herd of 3000 cattle. Hercules had to clean the extremely dirty stables. He did this by diverting a river to run through them. Augeas refused to reward Hercules, after which the hero killed him. Phyleus, Augeas' son, gave Hercules the 300 cattle he was promised.

Augsburg (pop. 261,000), capital of the administrative district of Swabia in Bavaria, Germany, on the Lech River about 35 mi (56 km) from Munich. Situated on the site of a Roman colony founded by Emperor Augustus (late 1st century B.C.), it became a free imperial city (1276) and flourished as an important trade center. Augsburg lost much in power and prestige during the Thirty Years War (1618-48) and eventually was annexed by Bavaria (1806). Today it is an important commercial and rail center for south Germany. Its medieval inner quarter includes the late Gothic church of St. Ulrich and the Renaissance-style Rathaus.
See also: Augsburg Confession.

Augsburg Confession, statement of Lutheran beliefs presented to the Diet of Augsburg on June 25, 1530. The Confession, largely the work of Philip Melanchthon, was an attempt to reconcile Luther's reforms with Roman Catholicism. It was rejected by Emperor Charles V, which sealed the break between the Lutherans and Rome.
See also: Luther, Martin.

Augur, in ancient Rome, official who derived signs (auguries) concerning future events from the flight or other actions of birds, certain appearances in quadrupeds, lightning, or other unusual occurrences. In an elaborate ceremony, the augur would choose a spot with a clear view to wait for any signs-from thunder in the skies to the squeak of a mouse-that might indicate the 'will of the gods.' No important business of state could be initiated without first consulting such a diviner.

Augustan Age *See:* Augustus; England; English literature; Latin literature.

Augustine, Saint (A.D. 354-430), bishop of Hippo, church father. Though raised as a Christian by his mother, St. Monica, in northern Africa, he embraced Manichaeism while in school at Carthage. Moving to Rome (383), he was influenced by Neoplatonism, but it was in Milan, where he met St. Ambrose, bishop of the city, that he was baptized a Christian (387) and took the vows of priesthood (391). In 396 he became bishop of Hippo (northern Africa). Generally acknowledged by Christians as the father of theology, he wrote many books, including the autobiographical *Confessions* and *De Civitate Dei* (*The City of God*), containing the great defense against paganism and the Christian philosophy of history. His feast day is Aug. 28.

Augustine, Saint (d. A.D. 604), Italian missionary and first archbishop of Canterbury (from 601). A Benedictine monk, he was sent to England by Pope Gregory the Great to convert the populace and bring the Celtic Church under Rome's control. He was given support by King Ethelbert of Kent. His feast day is May 27 (May 26 in England and Wales).

Augustus (63 B.C.-A.D. 14), honorific title given in 27 B.C. to Gaius Julius Caesar Octavianus, adopted great-nephew and heir of Julius Caesar. With Lepidus and Marc Antony he formed a triumvirate that avenged his great-uncle's murder by defeating and destroying the main conspirators, at Philippi (42 B.C.). The deposition of Lepidus (36 B.C.) and the suicide of Antony after his defeat at Actium (31 B.C.) left Augustus sole master of the Roman world. After the ravages of 50 years of civil war, he used his power to institute religious, legal, and administrative reforms and to promote literature, the arts, and agriculture. While nominally restoring the Republic, his control of the state's finances and armed forces made him the sole ruler. He is accounted first Roman emperor (Latin, *imperator*, 'commander'). He was succeeded by his stepson Tiberius. The month of August is named for him.
See also: Antony, Marc; Cleopatra; Caesar, (Gaius) Julius.

Auk, marine diving bird of the family Alcidae, including razorbills, puffins, and guillemots. Of the 22 species (including the extinct great auk) the smallest is the dovekie, or little auk (*Plautus alle*), which is about the size of a robin (lengths of other species are 6-30 in/15-76 cm). Auks, who seldom leave the water except to nest, usually breed in colonies, sometimes millions of individuals, and nest on high ledges or in burrows.
See also: Guillemot; Murre; Puffin.

Aung San, U (1915-1947), Burmese independence fighter, father of Aung San Suu Kyi. He was Secretary-General of the revolutionary Dobama Asiayone (1939-40), member of the executive council for the governor (1946-47) and head of the transitional government (1947). He and other members were assassinated prior to Burma's independence.

Aung San Suu Kyi, Daw (1945-), politician, leader of the human rights movement in Burma, and winner of the Sakharov Prize for Freedom of Thought (1990), the Nobel Peace Prize (1991), and the Simon Bolívar Prize (1992).
In her book *Freedom From Fear and Other Writings* she reflects on the early death of her father, U Aung San. This book is also the formulation of her nonviolent resistance.

Bishop Augustine (354-430) exerted great influence on the development of Christianity, with his writings against heretic movements. Here, he is on a fresco by Botticelli (1445-1510), In the Ognissanti Church in Florence, Italy.

After demonstrations for democracy had been savagely suppressed in 1988, she publically spoke out for democracy and co-founded the *National League for Democracy*. At the next elections the NLD won 80% of the parliamentary seats. The military government then placed her under house arrest and prevented the newly elected parliament from convening. This drew national and international attention. In 2002, the house arrest was terminated.

Aurangabad (pop. 573,000), city in India, in Maharashtra State. Textiles industry (cotton and silk). Aurangabad was the residence of Mughal Emperor Aurangzeb who is buried here. Ruins of his palaces can be found here and in the surroundings are Buddhist rock temples from the 7th century.

Aurangzeb (1618-1707), an Indian emperor of the Mogul dynasty, reigned 1658-1707. He was the third son of Shah Jahan, who built the Taj Mahal. Aurangzeb imprisoned his father and caused the deaths of his three brothers in order to gain the throne. He extended the territory of the Mogul empire during his reign. However, he was a fanatic Muslim, and his persecution of the Hindus led to armed rebellions and helped cause the decline of the Mogul dynasty.

Aurelius, Marcus *See:* Marcus Aurelius.

Aureole, heavenly crown around the head or body of Christ and saints. The body of Christ is often depicted with an almond-shaped aureole called mandorla. Nimbus refers to a red glowing disc behind the head.

Auric, Georges Abel Louis (1899-1983),

French composer. He was one of the group of composers who founded the famous 'groupe des six'; they distanced themselves from both Wagner and Debussy to strive for a greater simplicity. Auric composed mostly for film and theater including Cocteau's movies. The song he composed for the film *Le Moulin Rouge* (1952) brought international fame. He also wrote ballets (*Phèdre*, 1950), piano music, lieder, and chamber music. Auric was a critic for *Marianne* and *Paris-Soir*.

Aurobindho, Sri (also: Ghose Aurobindho; 1872-1950), Indian philosopher and mystic in the Vedanta tradition. Forerunner of India's independence. Founded an ashram in Pondicherry in 1909 and withdrew from political life. He tried to become spiritually one with the divine through use of yoga and to combine this with active participation in social life. His writings included *Essays on the Gita* (1926-44, 1950),

Aurora, display of colored lights and shimmering forms seen at night, most frequently during the equinoxes, in regions of high latitude. The aurora borealis, or northern lights, can be seen in northern Scandinavia, Canada, and Alaska, and the aurora australis, or southern lights, are seen on the borders of Antarctica in the Southern Hemisphere. Fast-moving electrons from the sun are attracted to the earth's magnetic poles, where they collide with oxygen and nitrogen ions in the ionosphere, causing them to give off energy in the form of light. The aurora most frequently appears following a major solar flare; the occurrence and intensity of the aurora is also related to the 11-year sunspot cycle.

Auschwitz, present-day Oswiecim in Poland, site of the infamous Nazi concentration camp in World War II where some 4 million inmates, mostly Jews, were murdered. The camp was opened in 1940 and run by Rudolf Hoess for 3 years. Its huge gas chambers were responsible for most deaths.

Austen, Jane (1775-1817), English novelist. Daughter of a clergyman, her novels, including *Sense and Sensibility* (1811), *Pride and Prejudice* (1813), and *Emma* (1816), vividly portray the provinciality of the English middle class of her time with ironic insight and vivid characterizations. She ultimately gave up writing, discouraged by her inability to find a publisher. Her novels were published many years after she wrote them; 2 were published posthumously. Today she is considered one of the greatest novelists in the English language, and her work is an inspiration and model for many writers.

Austerlitz (pop. 5,000), town in Moravia in the southern part of the Czech Republic. Currently an agricultural center, on Dec. 2, 1805 it was the site where Napoleon's army defeated the combined forces of Emperor Francis I of Austria and Tsar Alexander I of Russia in the 'Battle of the Three Emperors,' the beginning of Napoleon's mastery in Europe.
See also: Napoleon I.

A

A

Austin (pop. 541,000), capital of Texas and seat of Travis County on the Colorado River in south-central Texas. Founded in 1839 as Waterloo, it served as the capital of the Republic of Texas 1840-42 and was re-named in honor of Stephen F. Austin. It became state capital in 1870. Austin has seen great industrial development since the 1930s, currently is the site of extensive scientific and electronic research, and is also the center of an important agricultural, ranching, dairy, and poultry region.
See also: Texas.

Austin, Stephen Fuller (1793-1836), U.S. pioneer statesman, 'Father of Texas.' Upon bringing 300 families to Texas (1821), he was made the settlement's administrator. Between 1822 and 1830 he presented Texan demands for autonomy to the Mexican government, and was imprisoned for it. On his release in 1835, he joined the Texan rebellion against Mexico, and in 1836 was appointed secretary of state of the Republic of Texas.

Australia

Capital:	Canberra
Area:	2,966,151 sq mi
	(7,682,300 sq km)
Population:	19,547,000
Language:	English
Government:	Parliamentary monarchy in
	the British Commonwealth
Independent:	1901
Head of gov.:	Prime minister
Per capita:	U.S. $24,000
Monetary unit:	1 Australian dollar ($A) =
	100 cents

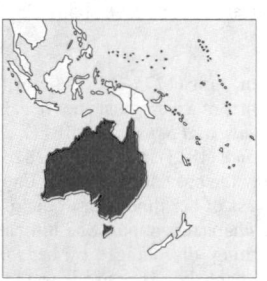

Australia, world's largest island and smallest continent, with a total area of 2,966,151 sq mi (7,682,000 sq km). It is the only continent occupied by a single nation, the Commonwealth of Australia, a federal union comprising 6 states (the island of Tasmania, Queensland, New South Wales, Victoria, South Australia, Western Australia), the Northern Territory, Jefferson Bay Territory and the Australian Capital Territory (Canberra).
Land and climate. Geologists believe that 120 million years ago Australia was part of a vast land mass that included India, Arabia,

Although gold-digging has decreased in importance, Australia is still the fourth largest producer of gold in the world, except for the former Soviet Union. Australia hopes to raise production by improving its mining and digging methods.

and parts of Africa and South America. Later land bridges to Australia were destroyed by geological upheavals, leaving the continent completely isolated. This isolation accounts for the development of various species of animal life peculiar to Australia. For example, the pouched mammals (marsupials) are found mainly in Australia and neighboring islands. Australia is the world's flattest continent. Approximately 75% of its area is covered by a plateau rarely higher than 1,500 ft (450 m) The outstanding physical feature of the continent is the Great Western Plateau, most of which is desert or semi-arid scrub country. The Great Barrier Reef, a mass of coral reefs and islands, extends for 1,250 mi (2,000 km) along its east coast. Australia has a moderate-warm climate, ususally dry and sunny.
People. Australia has a low population density, with about 17 million people living in a country almost as large as the United States. The people of Australia are mainly of European (particularly British) origin (95%), Asian immigrants (4%), or Aboriginals and others (1%). Most of the population is concentrated in the coastal cities, of which the largest is Sydney. The majority belongs to the Roman Catholic Church (26%) or to the Anglican Church (24%). Asians and Aboriginals have their own religions. The official language is English.
Economy. The Australian export products wheat, sugar, and wool are an important part of the world market. Australia is also an important exporter of raw materials.
History. Visited by the Dutch in the early 1600s, Australia was claimed for Britain by Capt. James Cook (1770). New South Wales, the first area settled, began as a penal colony (1788). But free settlement began in 1816, and no convicts were sent to Australia after 1840. The gold rushes (1851, 1892)

brought more people to Australia, and in 1901 the 6 self-governing colonies formed an independent commonwealth. In 1986 the last vestige of British control in Australia was removed when Queen Elizabeth II signed the Australia Act. In 1991 Paul Keating, at age 47, became the youngest prime minister in Australian history. In elections in 1996 the Labor Party, after 13 years in power, was defeated. John Howard, head of a coalition of conservative parties, became prime minister. In 1999, Australia voted in a referendum to keep the queen as head of state, and remained a republic. Australia turned out to be very attractive to Asian asylum seekers. The tightening of the asylum law in 2001 was received with much criticism and had many consequences, including a revolt in the asylum seekers' center of Woomera. After the attack by Islamic fundamentalists on the Indonesian island Bali in 2002, which killed many Australian citizens, the country became directly involved in the fight against international terrorism.

Australian Aborigines, earliest native inhabitants of Australia, racially distinguished by dark hair, dark skin, medium stature, broad noses, and narrow heads. Before European encroachment in the 18th and 19th centuries, they lived by well-organized nomadic food-gathering and hunting. Aborigines were enfranchised in 1962. The Australian government has attempted to integrate them into the European population, but they still face discrimination.

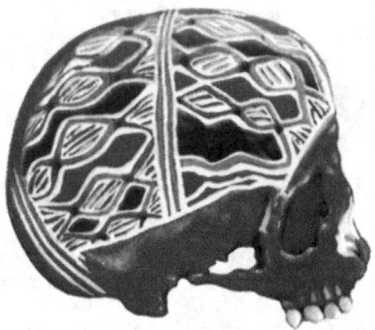

A painted skull from Arnhemland. The aboriginal peoples of this region used to decorate skulls. Relatives of the deceased were to wear the skull as a keepsake, as well as to attract the dead person's spirit.

Australian Desert, comprises 3 deserts that cover about one-third of Australia's western and central area. They are the Great Sandy Desert, about 160,000 sq mi (414,000 sq km); the Gibson Desert, 120,000 sq mi (311,000 sq km); and the Great Victoria Desert, 130,000 sq mi (337,000 sq km).

Austral Islands, group of islands of volcanic origin in the South Pacific, south of Tahiti. They have a combined area of about 70 sq mi (180 sq km). The largest of the island are Rurutu and Tubuai.

Australopithecus, or 'southern ape,' a genus of hominids whose fossilized bones, discovered in South Africa in 1924, date back about 3 million years.Australopithecines stood erect at about 4-5 ft (120-150 cm) and walked on 2 legs without the help of their arms. Their teeth were more human than apelike, their brains about one-third those of humans in size.

Austria

Capital:	Vienna
Area:	32,377 sq mi (83,858 sq km)
Population:	8,170,000
Language:	German
Government:	Federal republic
Independent:	Republic since 1918
Head of gov.:	Chancellor
	(chosen by the President)
Per capita:	U.S. $27,000
Monetary unit:	1 euro = 100 eurocents

Austria, federal republic in central Europe divided into 9 provinces: Vienna, Lower Austria, Burgenland, Upper Austria, Salzburg, Styria, Carinthia, Tyrol, and Vorarlberg.

Land. There are 4 geographic regions: the Austrian Alps to the West, including the country's highest mountain, Grossglockner (12,457 ft/3,797 m); the North Alpine foreland, a plateau cut by fertile valleys between the Danube and the Alps; the Austrian granite plateau, north of the Danube; and the Eastern lowlands, where the capital, Vienna, stands.

People. About 98% of today's Austrians are Germans ethnically and linguistically, although there are considerable differences in dialect among the provinces. About 75,000 Austrians speak Croatian, Slovene, Hungarian, or Czech only, or speak German only as a second language. The largest minority group are the Croatians, who mainly live in Burgenland. Austria's cultural contributions have been noteworthy. In the 19th century Vienna was a world center for musicians and composers. Wolfgang Amadeus Mozart, Franz Joseph Haydn, Franz Schubert, Anton Bruckner, and Gustav Mahler were all Austrians, while Ludwig van Beethoven, Johann Strauss, and Franz Lehar spent most of their lives in Vienna. Sigmund Freud, the father of psychoanalysis, studied and practiced in Vienna, along with many other psychologists.

Economy. Austrian farm crops include sugar beets, potatoes, grains, grapes, fruits, tobacco, flax, and hemp; wines and beers are produced in quantity. Almost 40% of the country is forested, so wood and paper are important products. Iron ore is the primary mineral resource, but there are also deposits of lead, magnesium, copper, salt, zinc, aluminum, silver, and gypsum. Vienna, Graz, and Linz are the chief industrial centers. Tourism has helped to stimulate economic growth in recent years.

History. Inhabited from prehistoric times, settled by the Celts, and subsequently part of the Roman Empire, starting in the third century A.D., Austria was devastated by invading Vandals, Goths, Alemanni, Huns, and Avars. In 788 Charlemagne conquered Austria. The Babenberg family inherited it in 976 and retained it as duchy until 1246. In 1247 the Habsburgs acquired Austria, which became a central part of their empire until 1918. By the Treaty of Versailles, independent states (Czechoslovakia, Hungary, and Yugoslavia) were created from the old empire, while Austria itself became a republic. In 1938 Austria was annexed by Hitler's Third Reich. After Germany was defeated in 1945, Austria was again declared a republic, but it was not independant. The United States, Great Britain, France and the Soviet Union divided the country into four zones, each occupied by one of the four Aliied powers. In 1955 the armies of the occupying powers withdrew, and the four zones were reunited into one fully independant nation. Austria agreed that it would not seek union with Germany and that it would be neutral in its foreign policy. In 1995, however, Austria became a member of the European Union. In 2000, a government coalition with the FPÖ received much criticism from other member states of the EU. During the elections of 2002, the FPÖ lost a large number of its supporters, partially because of the visit its leader Haider paid to Iraq

Austria-Hungary, empire formed by the union of the Kingdom of Hungary and the Austrian Empire in 1867. It was the assassination of the Archduke Francis Ferdinand, heir to the empire's throne, in 1914, by one of the many nationalist groups seeking independence that led directly to World War I. The empire, which was allied with Germany, ceased to exist at the end of World War I, and its lands were divided among the East European nations.

Austronesian languages, possibly the largest language family in the world; formerly called Malayo-Polynesian languages. These languages are spoken on a number of archipelago, viz. Indonesia and the Philippines, Micronesia, Melanesia, and Polynesia. People who speak these languages are called Austronesians.

Authoritarianism, political philosophy based on the principle of total submission of the population to a leader or elite group that is not constitutionally responsible to the people.

Autism, impairment in the perception of and response to environmental stimuli, accompanied by absorption in self-centered mental activity. In infantile autism, the development of speech is delayed; ritualistic behavior is usual and may include abnormal routines; resistance to change, attachment to odd objects, and stereotyped patterns of play are the norm. The capacity for abstract or symbolic thought and for imaginative play is diminished. Treatment is experimental, and performance has been found to be better on tasks involving rote memory than on those requiring symbolic or linguistic skills.

Autocracy, form of government in which an individual or group has absolute power, as in Russia under the tsars and France under Louis XIV.

Autogiro (or autogyro), rotary-wing aircraft that uses a conventional propeller to provide forward motion and an unpowered horizontal rotor for lift. Though it cannot hover or

land vertically, current technology permits almost vertical takeoffs.

Automatic frequency control (AFC), circuit used in electronic devices such as radio, television, and radar to help maintain and control the frequency. The AFC circuit corrects frequency drifts (e.g., from a particular radio station) by producing a voltage that automatically reverses the drift and holds it on frequency.

Automatic pilot *See:* Gyropilot.

Automation, automatically controlled operation of an apparatus, process, or system by mechanical or electronic devices (often computers) that replace constant human observation, effort, and decision.

Automobile, small, 4-wheeled vehicle that carries passengers. The 4 major components of an automobile are its power plant, drive system, control system, and body.

Power plant. Almost all automobiles are powered by internal combustion engines, usually with 4-8 cylinders attached to a crankshaft. In the internal combustion engine, gasoline from the fuel tank is mixed with air in the carburetor and fed to the cylinders. The highly explosive mixture is ignited by the spark plugs and, as it explodes, expands rapidly.The piston within the cylinder is forced downward, turning the

A village in the Salzkammergut district is illustrative of Austria's scenery. The region is noted for its picturesque alpine villages, ancient salt mines, and excavated Iron Ages sites.

A

A

crankshaft. The heavy metal flywheel attached to one end of the crankshaft moves the piston back up the cylinder to its original position. The order in which the spark plugs fire is controlled by the distributor. In most engines, the gasoline vapor simply enters the cylinder through a valve at the beginning of the downstroke, but some automobiles have fuel-injection systems that greatly increase efficiency.

Drive system. In most cars, the drive is supplied by the rear wheels. The motion of the crankshaft must therefore be transmitted by a driveshaft to the rear axle, where a system of cogs turns the wheels. The rotation of the crankshaft is transmitted to the driveshaft by the clutch, which consists of 2 circular plates, one attached to the driveshaft, the other to the crankshaft. When the plates are in contact, both rotate. When one plate is drawn back, the crankshaft rotates without affecting the driveshaft, and the engine can 'turn over' without moving the car. Gears alter the number of turns required from the engine to achieve a single turn of the drive wheels. The gear box also makes reverse movement possible. When cars are equipped with automatic transmission, manual control of the gears or clutch is not required.

The controls. Steering is controlled by a steering wheel, attached to horizontal track rods between the two front wheels. The movement of these rods turns the wheels. In heavy cars, power steering uses hydraulic pressure to assist the driver in turning the wheel. The pedal-operated brake system uses either the pressure of brake shoes against brake drums attached to the wheels or the more efficient disk brakes. The handbrake, which clamps onto the driveshaft or one set of wheels, is used as an emergency brake or for parking. The gas pedal is connected to the carburetor and controls the amount of gasoline vapor that enters the cylinders of the engine. The greater the quantity of vapor, the more powerful the explosion and the greater the speed of the automobile.

Body. The chassis of the car is the large steel frame that supports the engine and the control and running mechanisms. It may be a solid piece of stamped metal or a series of metal parts welded together. In cars that do not have a chassis, the body may simply be the framework that links the mechanical

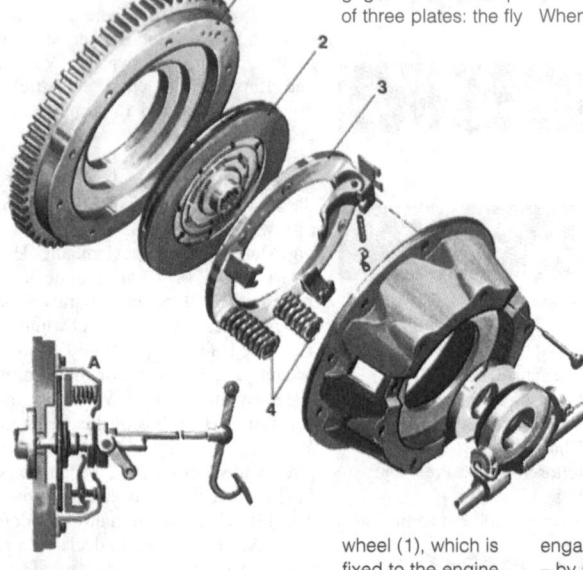

The clutch disconnects the engine from the gearbox, so that a new gear can be smoothly engaged. It is made up of three plates: the fly wheel (1), which is fixed to the engine shaft and rotates with it; the driven plate (2), which is connected to the gearbox shaft; and the pressure plate (3), which clamps the driven plate to the fly wheel.

Disengaging the clutch (A) will separate the three plates. The fly wheel and the driven plate now rotate independently. When the clutch is engaged – by releasing the pedal (B) – springs (4) will keep the driven plate clamped between the pressure plate and the fly wheel, so that they rotate together.

parts. The weight of the car is supported at the front and rear axles by metal springs, or sometimes by a hydraulic mechanism, to absorb shocks transmitted from the road and ensure a smooth ride.

Automobile racing, sport in which specially designed or adapted motor vehicles race indoor or outdoor courses. Dating from 1894 in France, races include the Grand Prix (worldwide series culminating in world-champion driver), stock car (special equipment on standard vehicles), midget car, sports car, and drag (acceleration competition).

Autonomic nervous system, certain sections of the brain, spinal cord, and nerve pathways that govern the activity of a number of organs, making them function largely independently of conscious control. The autonomic nervous system regulates the organs of the chest (heart and lungs), the abdomen (stomach, intestine, liver, etc.), the pelvis, and many other organs and tissues of the body, including the blood vessels and skin. By contrast, the somatic nervous system comprises those parts of the brain, spinal cord, and nerve pathways that respond to the external environment, and are under voluntary control. The autonomic nervous system governs the processes that serve to maintain the individual and the species: metabolism, growth, reproduction, respiration, nutrition and digestion, the functioning of the heart and blood vessels, the excretion of waste products, temperature control, etc. An intricate system of nuclei and nerve pathways in the brain regulates the workings of the various organs. In the hypothalamus lie dozens of nuclei and pathways that exert a controlling influence over such basic life functions as eating and drinking behavior, temperature regulation, and the percentage of sugars, fats, and water in the blood. The autonomic nervous system is also involved in emotional response. Emotions can give rise to quickening of the heartbeat, changes in breathing

1. driver in flame-proof suit
2. air box
3. wing of aerodynamic stability
4. foam rubber-lined fuel tank
5. oil cooler
6. monocoque chassis of aluminum alloy

The major operational features of a Tyrell Ford Formula One, a Grand Prix racing car. Formula One racers are built to the specifications established by the Fédération Internationale de l'Automobile (FIA), the governing body of Grand Prix racing. Drivers compete for the world championship by amassing points, awarded according to their order of finish in Grand Prix races.

patterns, increased secretion of gastric acid in the stomach, and alterations in the secretory pattern of the gallbladder. Malfunction of the autonomic nervous system can easily lead to serious disturbances in the functioning of an organ. Often a stomach ache is caused by the malfunction of one of the subsystems of the autonomic nervous system. The autonomic nervous system can be divided into the sympathetic and the parasympathetic systems, which in general produce opposite effects on various organs.
See also: Nervous system.

Autopsy, examination of the external structures and internal organs of a dead body for the purpose of determining the cause of death or for studying the damage done by disease; also called necropsy or postmortem examination. When the authorities are uncertain of the conditions leading to death, such as in a suicide or homicide, an autopsy may be indicated.

Auxin, any of several organic compounds that act as plant hormones to promote cell growth.

Avant-garde, term referring to those who experiment with new and original art forms. Used originally to describe a military unit that led the rest of the troops, *avant-garde* was first given its modern meaning by the French socialist Henri de Saint-Simon in 1825. During the 19th century, the avant-garde notion of art as a tool of social reform gave way to the idea of 'art for art's sake,' leading to the Dadaist and Surrealist movements of the early 20th century. Important avant-garde artists include U.S. composer John Cage (1912-92) and French painter Marcel Duchamp (1887-1968).
See also: Dada; Surrealism; Cage, John; Duchamp, Marcel.

Average, number that is typical of a group of numbers or quantities. The 3 kinds of averages-mean, median, and mode-have different statistical significance. The mean is derived by taking the sum of a group of quantities and dividing it by the number of quantities. The median divides a sampling in half; there are the same number of items above and below it. The mode is the most frequently occurring number in a group.

Avercamp, Hendrick Berentsz. (1585-1634), Dutch painter, nicknamed 'The Mute of Kampen' because he was deaf and mute and worked in Kampen (the Netherlands). He was influenced by Flemish landscape painting. He was especially known for his winter landscapes, which contained many brightly colored figures (such as Winter Landscape, Winter Scene, and Ice Pleasure.)

Averroës (Ibn-Rushd; 1126-1198), Spanish-Arabian philosopher, commentator on Aristotle and Plato who exerted a great influence on the development of Latin scholastic philosophy. For him, the source of philosophic truth was reason, not faith, though he believed there was no conflict between the two.

Avesta, collection of holy scriptures from the religion of Zarathustra (600 B.C.). Written in Avestan, and probably transcribed during the of Sassaniden dynasty (226-651 A.D.). Only a few fragments have been saved, yet these are still one and a half times as long as the New Testament. The four parts are: Yasna and Vispered (both liturgical), Vendidad (regulations), and Yashts (songs of praise). The translation into Pahlavi (Middle Persian) contains much commentary (Zend) on the original texts.

Aviation, term referring to all aspects of building and flying aircraft. Aviation has not only changed the face of long-distance travel, but affected medical accessibility, farming practices, and the way nations wage war. The aviation industry, which includes the manufacture of aircraft and the operations of airlines, involves the work of millions of engineers, mechanics, pilots and air traffic controllers, as well as many governmental agencies. The world's first successful airplane flight was made by Wilbur and Orville Wright in 1903. Within a few years Europe and the United States had several small airplane-producing factories. Interested in developing their own air forces, various governments around the world began to purchase airplanes for military purposes. The first solo, nonstop flight across the Atlantic Ocean was accomplished by Charles Lindbergh on May 21, 1927. The use of commercial airplanes in the late 1930s assured the growth of aviation as an industry. The jet airliner, developed in the 1950s, gave the industry a further boost. In recent years, criticism has increased due to worries about the environment.

Avicenna (Ibn-Sina; 980-1037), Persian physician and philosopher. Of his prolific writings on theology, logic, metaphysics, and mathematics, his greatest is considered to be *The Canon of Medicine*, which remained a standard medical text in Europe until the Renaissance.

Avignon (pop. 91,000), French city on the east bank of the Rhône River in southern France, capital of Vaucluse department. During the 'Babylonian Exile' (1309-78) Avignon was the papal seat. From 1378 to 1417, the city was the home of the 'antipopes,' rivals to the popes in Rome.

Avila Camacho, Manuel (1897-1955), Mexican soldier and statesman. As Mexico's president (1940- 46), he supported the U.S. and promoted Latin American opposition to the Axis powers.
See also: Mexico.

Avocado (*Persea americana*), tropical evergreen tree native to the United States, Mexico, and the West Indies. The fruit, also called avocado or alligator pear, has a dark green or purple rind, bright green flesh rich in protein, vitamins, iron, and oil, and a large central seed. Avocados are also grown as house plants.

Avocet, any of several long-legged wading birds (genus *Recurvirostra*). One species flourishes in Europe, Asia, and Africa. It uses its long curving beak to sweep the water in search of the small aquatic animals on which it feeds. It has black-and-white plumage. The related American avocet has a pinkish head and breast.

Avogadro, Amedeo (1776-1856), an Italian physicist and chemist. His research in molecular structure was one of the early steps leading to modern atomic theory. In 1811 he published the important hypothesis, now known as *Avogadro's Law*, that under the

A

same conditions of temperature and pressure, equal volumes of all gases contain the same number of molecules.
Avogadro was born in Turin. He was a professor of mathematical physics at the University of Turin, 1834-50.

Avoirdupois, English system of weight in which 1 lb contains 16 oz, in contrast to troy weight, another English system, in which 1 lb equals 12 oz. In the United States, commodities are generally weighed in avoirdupois. Most other countries use the metric system, to which Britain is gradually converting.
See also: Weights and measures.

Avon, name of 2 British rivers. The longer, the Upper Avon, arises in Northamptonshire and flows 96 mi (154 km) past Warwick and Stratford-upon-Avon to join the Severn at Tewkesbury. Stratford-upon-Avon was the birthplace of William Shakespeare.

AWACS, Airborne Warning And Control System (AWACS) which has a view of more than 250 mi (400 km) beyond the horizon with the aid of very powerful radar systems. A single AWACS can oversee 193,125 sq mi (500,000 sq km) and follow hundreds of moving objects at the same time. Specially made to spot the most modern and effective low- flying combat planes. AWACS airplanes play a crucial role in NATO's air defense. The NATO Airborne Early Warning Force (NAEWF) has 18 AWACS airplanes.

AWOL (Absent Without Leave) *See:* Desertion.

Axiom, any general statement accepted as true without proof as the basis for building a logical system of other statements that are proven. These proven statements are called theorems. The axioms of a system need not be self-evident, but they must be consistent with one another.
See also: Geometry.

Axis Powers, countries allied with Nazi Germany before or during World War II. The Rome-Berlin Axis, a diplomatic agreement

'The Haviland 16' was an aircraft, designed after the bomber DH 9a. This plane was used on many of the early European flights.

Orville and Wilbur Wright were responsible for the first controlled airplane flight on December 17,1903. Their observations of a bird's flight were invaluable in understanding balance in flying objects.

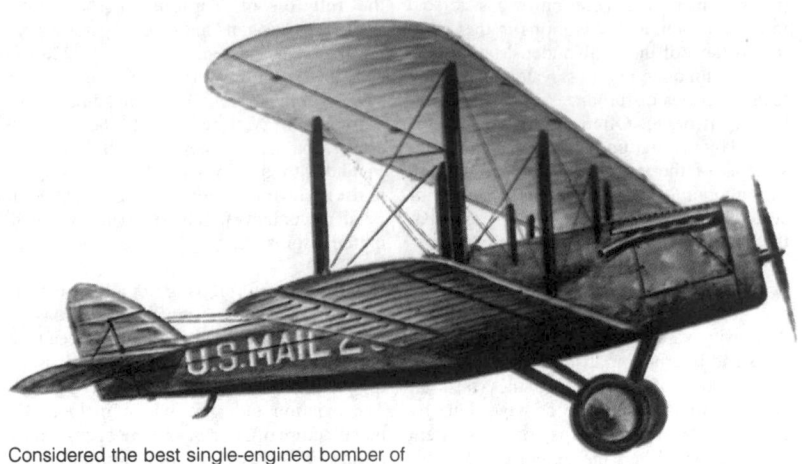

Considered the best single-engined bomber of World War I, Britain's De Havilland DH-4 was of wooden construction and covered with fabric. Its armaments included forward and rear guns with bombs under each wing. After the war, more than 60 different varieties were produced and used for civil aviation.

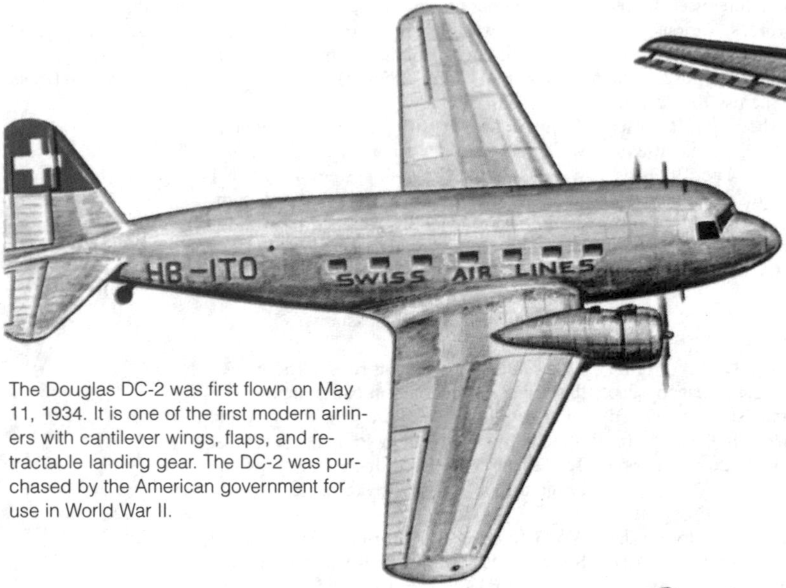

The Douglas DC-2 was first flown on May 11, 1934. It is one of the first modern airliners with cantilever wings, flaps, and retractable landing gear. The DC-2 was purchased by the American government for use in World War II.

The Junkers Ju 52/3m was one of the most reliable transport aircraft ever built. Its structure was made entirely of the light alloy duralumin. Its double wing flaps were patented and its landing gears were virtually indestructible. It also had the ability to land in water and snow. More than 90% of German Luftwaffe transports were of this variety. During the 1930s, it was the leading civil airliner in Europe.

Left: The Lockheed Constellation was designed to satisfy the need for a transcontinental aircraft which would offer the ultimate in speed and luxury. Production on a civil aviation model began in 1940 but was interrupted by World War II. Flown during the war as C-69, the Constellation made its first civil, trans-Atlantic flight for TWA on Dec. 3-4, 1945. The aircraft evolved into the L-1049 Super Constellation, with increased fuel capacity and more powerful engines.

Right: In 1952 the Boeing Corporation spent $20 million to build a turbojet transport. On July 15, 1954, the now-famous Boeing 707 made its first flight. The U.S. Air Force ordered large quantities of the 707 because of its great flexibility. Both Pan American Airways and American Airlines bought the 707 for long-distance routes.

A

The light-as-a-feather design of this U.S. aircraft, the Voyager, made possible its 1986 flight around the world. It remained aloft 111 hours without stopping or refueling, covering 11,600 mi (18,560 km). Its shell is less than one-half inch thick with panels of Hexcel honeycomb, a paperlike polymer, covered with graphite fibers. The panels weigh 4 oz. per square foot (1 kg/sq m) but possess incredible tensile strength– a 110 -ft (33- m) wing can flex up and down more than 30 ft (90 m). The benefit of such remarkable advances in aviation materials means diminished costs, reduced friction, greater speed, and less noise and pollution.

In 1956 Britain and France began research on a supersonic transport. In 1962 a joint agreement was signed for design, development, and production. In November 1970 the British-French Concorde achieved a speed of Mach 2 (twice the speed of sound). On May 24,1976 the Concorde's trans-Atlantic service began, with a flying time of 3 1/2 hours from New York to Paris.

The Airbus A340. It is part of a combined program with the A330 aircraft. This multinational venture (France, Germany, Spain, Great Britain) service long-range flights that carry as many as 440 people.

The 'Stealth' fighter was a 10-year-old Pentagon secret. In April 1990 the Defense Department released, for the first time, a video of this reconnaissance-fighter aircraft.

A

between Hitler and Mussolini, was formed in 1936 and reinforced by the Italian-German military pact of 1939. Japan joined the pact in 1940, and other countries followed: Hungary, Bulgaria, Romania, Slovakia, and Croatia. The Axis Powers were defeated by the Allies (or Allied Powers), led by the United States, Britain, and the Soviet Union.
See also: World War II.

Axolotl, a Mexican salamander that retains most of its larval characteristics, but which matures sexually and is able to reproduce. This ability to reproduce without attaining adult form is called *neoteny*. Axolotls were first known in the lakes around Mexico City, and were given their name by the Aztecs. They look like the larvae of the tiger salamander, a closely related species. Axolotls are sold in Mexican markets as food.
Neotenic tiger salamanders, often confused with axolotls, are occasionally found in Texas, Kansas, and Oklahoma, and in the Rocky Mountains. In most parts of the United States, however, the tiger salamander attains adult form.
The axolotl is *Ambystoma mexicanum;* the tiger salamander is *A. tigrinum*. Both belong to the family Ambystomatidae.

Aya Sofia (Greek: Hagia Sophia = Holy Wisdom) Church in Constantinople; unique example of Byzantine architecture. The

The interior of the Aya Sofia (building begun in 532) in Istanbul. Originally the main church of the city, the building was used as a mosque after the conquest of the Turks. Today, it is a museum.

original building was consecrated in 360, destroyed in 404 and rebuilt in 416. The church was destroyed again under the rule of Emperor Justinian I in 532 who ordered it to be rebuilt five years later. The huge central dome which is 180 ft (55 m) high and 101 ft (31 m) in diameter is flanked by half domes on the east and the west sides. These domes accentuate the length of the central structure. The church is decorated with a number of beautiful mosaics and holds a wealth of historical information. After 1453 the Turks used the church as a mosque. Today it accommodates a museum.

Ayatollah (Arabic: Sign of God) Shiite name for a prominent religious scholar who takes up a high rank in the hierarchy. The term became especially known in the West as a result of the Islamic Revolution in Iran in 1978-79 in which Ayatollah Khomeini played an important role.

Aycock, Alice (1946-), American conceptual artist. Her work mainly consists of large, semi architectural constructions, which through their structure, environment, and material are a challenge to the observer both mentally and physically. Aycock accompanies her work with texts, which are just as descriptive as the titles of her work.

Ayudhya (Ayutthaya; pop. 62,000), city in Thailand on the Chao Phraya River. It was capital of the country from 1350 until 1767 when it was conquered by Burma. There are still ruins of temples and palaces in Ayudhya which date from this period.

Azalea, number of species of a shrub (genus *Rhododendron*), cultivated principally for ornamental purposes. Best known in the United States are the pinxter (*R. nudiflorum*), the flame azalea (*R. calendulacea*), and the rhodera (*R. canadense*).
See also: Heath.

Azazel, evil spirit thought by the early Hebrews to inhabit the wilderness. On the Day of Atonement, a goat would be sent out to the Azazel bearing the discarded sins of the people; hence the word *scapegoat*.

Azerbaijan

Capital:	Baku
Area:	33,400 sq mi (86,600 sq km)
Population:	7,798,000
Language:	Azerbaijani
Government:	Republic
Independent:	1991
Head of gov.:	Prime minister
Per capita:	U.S.$3,100
Monetary unit:	1 Azerbaijan manat= 100 gepik

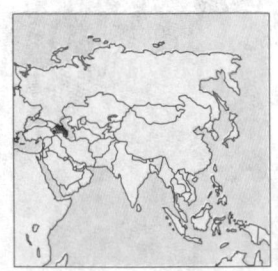

Azerbaijan, or Azerbaidjan, independent country on the westcoast of the Caspian Sea, bordered by Russia, Armenia and Iran. The capital and chief port is Baku, and Kirovabad and Sumgait are important cities. *Land and climate*. The republic consists mainly of lowlands surrounded by the Kura River and its tributary, the Araks, which forms the border with Iran. Near the Caspian coast is a fertile plain with an abundant water supply. Tea, citrus fruits, tobacco, and rice are produced there. Further inland the climate is arid, but extensive irrigation makes cultivation possible. *People*. The majority of the inhabitants are Azerbaijanis. The most important minority group consists of Armenians. Most Azerbaijanis are Muslims. The official language is Azerbaijani.
Economy. Cotton and sheep are the basis of a large textile industry. The region is rich in minerals, notably oil and natural gas from the long-established Baku oilfields; it is one of the oldest oil-producing areas in the world. The Caucasian hills provide iron ore. *History*. Settled by Medes as part of the Persian Empire, it was periodically dominated by Romans, Arabs, Mongols, and Turks, returning to Persia in the 16th century. The Russian Tsar Alexander I annexed northern Azerbaijan in 1813. An independent republic was formed in 1918, but was conquered by the Soviets in 1920. Ethnic and religuous diffirences between Azerbaijanis and Armenians led to tension between the two groups. Tensions rose in the late 1980's and fighting broke out in Nagorno-Karabach, a predominantly Armenian region within Azerbaijan. In 1990 Soviet troops were sent to the region to restore order. In 1991 the Soviet Union collapsed and Azerbaijan became independant. Also that year, Azerbaijan joined the Commonwealth of Independant States (CIS), a loose confederation of former Soviet republics. During 1992 fighting between Azerbaijanis and Armenians in Nagorno-Karabach intensified. During 1993 Azerbaijani forces suffered several disastrous defeats at the hands of rebel Armenians, who captured all of Nagorno-Karabach and parts of surrounding areas. In the spring of 1994, a cease-fire agreement was negotiated between the Azerbaijanis and the rebel Armenians. However, a definite agreement on Nagorno-Karabach has not yet been reached. In 2001, the country became a member of the Council of Europe. It is trying hard to become a democratic and secular state.
See also: Union of Soviet Socialist Republics.

Azimuth, in navigation and astronomy, the angular distance, measured from 0 to 360°, along the horizon eastward from an observer's north point to the point of intersection of the horizon and a great circle passing through the observer's zenith and a star or planet.

Azimuth circle *See:* Navigation.

Aziz, Tareq (1936-), Iraqi politician. Aziz worked as a journalist for a long period. In 1974 he was appointed minister of information. In 1977 he became regional leader of the Baath Party, in 1979 vice premier. From 1983 until 1991 Aziz was minister of foreign affairs and played an important role in the political crisis which ultimately led to the invasion of Kuwait in 1990 and the subsequent Gulf War. Aziz has been vice premier since 1991.

Aznar Lopéz, José María (1953-), Spanish politician. After studying at the University of Madrid he worked in trade and industry and as a tax inspector. In 1978 he became a member of the Alianza Popular, winning a seat in parliament in 1982. In 1987 he became premier of the autonomous region of Castilia and León. In 1990 he was elected chairman of the Partido Popular (PP) which succeeded the Alianza Popular. As party leader of the PP he beat Felipe González, who had held power since 1982, and in the parliamentary elections of 1996 became prime minister.

Aznavour, Charles (Varenagh Aznavourian; 1924-), French singer and composer of Armenian origin. After the success of *J'ai bu* (1946) he quickly made a name for himself and has since written hundreds of songs (including *La mamma* and *For me formidable*). He also played had parts in a few films such as *Tirez sur le pianiste* (1960). His autobiographies are *Aznavour par Aznavour* (1971) and *Sur ma vie* (1977).

Azores (pop. 253,000), 9 mountainous islands in the North Atlantic about 900 mi (1,448 km) west of Portugal. São Miguel is the largest and most populated. Colonized and under Portuguese rule since the mid-15th century, the islands enjoy considerable autonomy.

Azov, Sea of, arm of the Black Sea in southwest RF, joined to that sea by the Strait of Kerch. Maximum depth is only 50 ft (15 m); length is 200 mi (322 km), maximum width 80 mi (129 km). The Don River flows into the eastern end of the sea, known as the Gulf of Taganrog.

Aztec Ruins National Monument, site in northwestern New Mexico on the Animas River containing the excavated ruins of a 12th-century Pueblo Indian town. Mistaken for Aztec by European American settlers, the ruins include a 500-room building and many Pueblo artifacts. The monument was established in 1923.

Aztecs, Native American people who settled between many other tribes in central Mexico after the fall of the Toltec Empire in the 11th century. During the 15th century the Aztecs succeeded in conquering the major part of present-day Mexico. They developed a high level of civilization, which included mathematics, architecture, astronomy, and various art forms. The Spanish conquerors, headed by Hernan Cortés (1485-1547), supported by several tribes who had been displaced by the Aztecs destroyed the empire in 1521. They put the King of the Aztecs, Montezuma II to death and razed the capital, Tenochtitlan, - which the Spaniards themselves called 'the most beautiful city in the world' - to the ground. *See also:* Mexico.

Azurite, blue-colored crystalline mineral once used to make artist's pigment but now mainly used in jewelry. The crystals consist of copper carbonate and water and commonly occur near the surfaces of copper mines. Large deposits of azurite are found at Chessy, near Lyon in France, in Southwest Africa, and in smaller deposits in the western United States (Arizona, Utah).

B, second letter of the English alphabet, can be traced back to ancient Semitic roots. The letter is believed to derive from the Maobite Stone hieroglyph, found in the present state of Jordan, dating from the 9th century B.C. The Hebrew letter *beth*, meaning 'house,' and the Greek *beta* both come from this form. The Latin is virtually the same as the Greek, and it is this latter which is still used today. The lowercase *b*, a variant in which the upper loop has disappeared through the speed of writing, appeared in the Roman period.

Baal (Semitic, 'lord' or 'owner'), ancient Middle East fertility god. Canaanite tablets dating from 2500 B.C. represent him combating Mot, god of drought and sterility. In Babylonia, Baal was known as Bel, and in Phoenicia as Melkart. In the Old Testament the name is used pejoratively, the cult of Baal having been denounced by the Hebrew prophets.

Baalbek (pop. 15,000), Lebanon, a city in the Bekaa valley, some 40 miles (65 km) east-northeast of Beirut, the capital. Baalbek was one of the great cities of ancient times and today is primarily a tourist center, known for its magnificent ruins. The ruins

The religion of the Aztek god of Huitzilopochtli, depicted here as a hummingbird, demanded human offerings, whose blood would feed the sun. Slaves or prisoners-of-war were generally used for this goal. (National Museum, Mexico-City)

have served as the site of the Baalbek International Festival, with dance, drama, and classical music.

In early times Baalbek was probably a center for the worship of Baal. After its conquest by the Greeks, the city was called Heliopolis (City of the Sun). It later became a colony of the Romans, who built several temples dedicated to their gods. Largest was the Temple of Jupiter; only foundations, a staircase, and 6 of its 58 massive columns remain. The lovely Temple of Bacchus is almost entirely preserved. Other ruins include the Temple of Venus and remains of the ancient city walls.

Ba'al Shem Tov (Israel ben Eliezer; 1700?-1760), Jewish teacher and founder of the religious movement Hasidism. Ba'al Shem Tov (Hebrew: 'Master of the Good Name') was considered by his followers a miracle healer. He advocated the joyous worship of God in all activities, opposing fasting and other forms of self-denial. Hasidism is now practiced by some Jews in Europe, Israel, and the United States. *See also:* Hasidism.

Baath party, the actual name of this party is 'Hizb al-ba'th al arabi al-isjtiraki' (Socialist Party of the Arab Resurrection). The Baath party is a pan Arabic socialist party founded by Michael Aflaq in 1940. It consists of two wings, a military and a civil wing, which exercise their power in Syria and Iraq respectively. Despite its inter Arabic orientation, the party has been banned in some Arabic countries and only has a strong influence in Syria and Iraq.

Babangida, Ibrahim (1941-), Nigerian politician and military man. Babangida received his military training in Nigeria and India and progressed quickly within the army. As chief-of-staff in the army he was the military brain behind the coup of 1983 in which Major General Mohammed Buhari was promoted to head of state. Dissatisfaction with his government made Babangida decide to take control in 1985 and proclaimed himself president. Although Babangida soon built up international credit (by releasing political prisoners, for example), his regime was also characterized by cruelty. He had his opponents executed (in 1985 and 1990 there were coups against his regime). When free presidential elections were held in 1993 for the first time in ten years and Babangida was defeated, he initially postponed the announcement of the results. Two months later he finally resigned as president and commander-in-chief of the army. A temporary civil government came to power headed by Premier Ernest Shonekan, who had previously been chairman of the Transitional Council.

Babar (1483-1530), also spelled Babur or Baber, Turkish prince who founded the Mogul empire in India. A descendant of Genghis Khan and Tamerlane, Babar ruled 1526-30. He defeated the forces of the Afghan sultan near Delhi and went on to conquer most of northern India. *See also:* Akbar.

B

B

A part of the Difference Engine 1, designed by Charles Babbage. This was his first invention (1833) prior to the analytical engine. The Difference Engine was designed to calculate mathematical and astronomical ta- bles. Babbage's idea to construct a me- chanical device with which he would be able to work with numbers of up to twenty figures and which would also write down the results of the calculations, has never been real- ized. The calculator consists of three ver- tical columns that are subdivided into six partitions, each com- partment containing a wheel with the figures 0 to 9.

Babbage, Charles (1792-1871), British mathematician and inventor who devoted much labor and expense to an unsuccessful attempt to devise a mechanical calculator, his so-called 'analytical engine.' With J. Herschel and G. Peacock, he introduced the Leibnizian 'd' notation for calculus into British mathematical use in place of the less flexible 'dot' notation devised by Sir Isaac Newton.

Babbitt, Irving (1865-1933), U.S. scholar and noted opponent of Romanticism. He led the New Humanism movement in literary criticism, which stressed classical reason and restraint. His works include *The New Laokoön* (1910) and *On Being Creative* (1932).

Babbler, any of a large and varied group of birds of the Muscicapidae family found mainly in Africa, southern Asia, and Australia. Named for their loud, repeated calls, babblers are sometimes called bab- bling thrushes or chatterers.

Babel, Isaak Emanuilovich (1894-1941?), Russian short-story writer best known for his collections *Odessa Tales* (1923-24) and *Red Cavalry* (1926), the former describing Jewish life in the Ukraine, the latter his serv- ice with the Red Army during the Russian civil war (1918-20). Arrested in 1939, he died in a Siberian prison camp.

Babel, Tower of, in the Old Testament, a tower erected to reach heaven. God punished the builders for their presumption by making them speak many mutually unintelligible languages.
See also: Old Testament.

Babirussa (*Babirussa babirussa*), wild hog of Indonesia, about 27 in (69 cm) tall and weighing about 128 lb (58 kg). The males are notable for their long tusks. A docile, night-hunting member of the pig family, it forages for fruits and vegetables in the soil near rivers and swamps.

Babi Yar, ravine near Kiev, in the Ukraine. On Sept. 29 and 30, 1941, German SS troops executed and buried more than 33,000 Soviet Jews who had been brought to the ravine on a promise of resettlement. In 'Babi Yar' (1962) the Russian poet Yevgeni Yevtushenko indicted the Soviet leadership for failing to commemorate the massacre or to honor its victims.
See also: Holocaust.

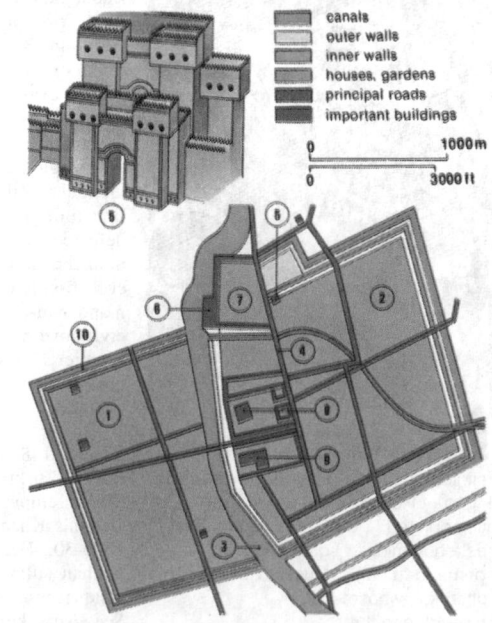

canals
outer walls
inner walls
houses, gardens
principal roads
important buildings

0 ————— 1000m
0 ————— 3000 ft

Early Babylon has been rebuilt many times. Its sophisticated layout was created mainly by Nebuchadnezzar II (604-561 B.C.).
1. old city
2. new city
3. Euphrates
4. ritual Processional Way
5. Ishtar Gate
6. fortress
7. main citadel complex
8. ziggurat (possibly that of Babel)
9. temple of Marduk
10. moat

Baboon, large primate monkey of the African savannas (genus *Papio*), distin- guished by long muzzle and great strength. Baboons move in groups of 20 to 150 indi- viduals. They are highly aggressive omni- vores with a complex social structure. Their bodies are covered with unusually long hair, except for parts of the face and the buttocks, which may be brightly colored.
See also: Mandrill; Monkey.

Baby, infant, newborn, neonate. Babies are classified as premature, full-term, or post- mature, depending on their gestational age (i.e. whether they are born early, on time, or late). Premature babies often have medical problems.

Baby boom, term often used for a steep in- crease in the birthrate of most Western coun- tries following World War II. Such an in- crease was caused by the expectations of a better future after the war.

Babylon, capital of the ancient kingdom of Babylonia, between the Tigris and Euphrates rivers (Babylon, 'gate of the god'), about 55 mi (88.5 km) south of mod- ern Baghdad. The reign of Nebuchadnezzar II (d. 562 B.C.) marked the height of Babylonian splendor. The city's Hanging Gardens were one of the Seven Wonders of the World. Cyrus of Persia captured Babylon in 538 B.C.
See also: Hammurabi; Nebuchadnezzar.

Babylonia and Assyria, ancient kingdoms of the Middle East in Mesopotamia, the fer- tile valley of the Tigris and Euphrates rivers. Assyria was in northern Mesopotamia, while Babylonia lay to the south. The Tigris- Euphrates Valley, along with the Nile, the Indus, and the Yellow rivers, was one of the cradles of world civilization. Agriculture and the raising of livestock may have begun in Mesopotamia earlier than anywhere else, about 8000-7000 B.C. The first urban econo- my was also established in Mesopotamia. About 3000 B.C. the Sumerian civilization began to emerge in southern Babylonia. The Sumerians built an irrigation system and in- vented cuneiform writing. Sumer was com- posed of the independent and frequently hostile city-states of Lagash, Ur (where the biblical Abraham was born), Kish, Erech, and Umma. Northern Babylonia was con- quered by a Semitic people from the west around 2500 B.C. and the kingdom of Akkad emerged. Its founder, Sargon (c. 2306- 2250), conquered Sumer areas to the east and west, a policy of expansion that was continued by his successors. Sumerian civi- lization survived for a time under the kings of Ur, under whom the earliest known code of laws was compiled and work started on the great ziggurat, a tiered pyramid-shaped temple.
Meanwhile an Amorite dynasty established itself in Akkad and made the town of Babylon its chief center. Southern Mesopotamia came to be called Babylonia. The sixth king of this dynasty, Hammurabi (c. 1792-1750), was an able ruler who or- ganized his territories on imperial lines. Hammurabi's famous code divided the peo- ple into 3 classes (citizens, commoners, and

slaves), and contained laws on property, inheritance, marriage, and the family. Punishments for criminal offenses were usually severe, and increased with the status of the victim. About 1594 a Hittite army sacked Babylon, and the country was conquered by the Kassites, who ruled for more than 400 years, adopting Babylonian culture. By 1171 a native Babylonian dynasty had taken over, but its authority was uncertain. The 11th and 10th centuries B.C. saw the influx of Aramaean tribes from the west and Chaldean infiltration along the Persian Gulf. The Middle Assyrian Empire began to emerge as a great military power in the 14th century B.C., reaching the height of its power around 1100. A period of decline followed, but a new Assyrian Empire rose in the 9th and 8th centuries B.C. Babylonia, Syria, and Israel fell to Assyrian arms; even Egypt was for a time under Assyrian rule. Sennacherib (705-682) made Nineveh his capital and transformed it into one of the most splendid cities of the time. During his reign Babylon revolted (689) and he destroyed the city and its inhabitants, but Babylon was in part restored by his successor, Esarhaddon.

The last great king of Assyria was Ashurbanipal (669-627?). An able general like his predecessors, he was also a devoted patron of the arts and literature. Some 25,000 tablets from the large library he assembled are now in the British Museum, London. During this period Assyria was the most powerful nation in the Middle East, but after Ashurbanipal's death it suddenly began to collapse. There was widespread revolt, and in 612 the Chaldeans of Babylonia, in alliance with the Scythians and Medes, captured and destroyed Nineveh. The last Assyrian forces were destroyed in 609.

The Assyrians decorated their buildings with glazed bricks and wall paintings. During the height of the empire the palace walls were covered with great stone reliefs that give a vivid impression of life of the time. Other remains include great statues of winged bulls and lions with human heads that once guarded the palaces.

The Neo-Babylonian Empire. After many years as a subject state of the Assyrian Empire, Babylonia recovered its independence under the Chaldean king Nabopolassar (626 B.C.). He devoted most of his reign to the destruction of Assyria, and after the fall of Nineveh brought the southern part of the empire, including Syria, Palestine, and part of southern Persia, under his control, despite the opposition of Egypt. This new Babylonian Empire, which was to enjoy immense power and prosperity, was consolidated by his son Nebuchadnezzar II (605-562).

Nebuchadnezzar continued the war against Egypt. Meanwhile, Tyre and Judah revolted. He twice captured Jerusalem, and on the second occasion (587) destroyed the city and deported most of the inhabitants of Judah to captivity in Babylon. Tyre surrendered after a siege lasting 13 years. Nebuchadnezzar made Babylon one of the most magnificent cities of ancient times. It was girdled by massive outer and inner walls with numerous gates, including the gate of Ishtar, which opened on to the great processional way that led to the temple of Marduk.

The terraced Hanging Gardens overlooking the Euphrates River were one of the seven wonders of the ancient world and formed part of the imposing palace. Assassination and civil war followed his death, but prosperity returned under Nabonidus and his son Belshazzar. In 539 B.C. the ambitious Cyrus II, king of the Medes and Persians, invaded Babylonia. The Book of Daniel tells how Belshazzar was warned of the final disaster by the 'writing on the wall' that mysteriously appeared during a feast the evening before Babylon fell. Babylonia now became a province of the Persian Empire, and Babylon the provincial administrative center.

Knowledge of Babylonian life comes largely from the thousands of clay cuneiform tablets that have been found at various sites, including legal and commercial records, literary and historical texts, and treatises on magic and astrology. The ancient Babylonians based their number system on 60. They separated the day into 12 double hours and the year into 12 months of 30 days each. They were the first to divide the circle into 360 degrees and the minute into 60 seconds. Their system was able to express fractions and squares and cube roots. The later Babylonians were noted astronomers, and the Chaldean priests could predict eclipses of the sun and moon.

Midway between the civilizations of the Indus and the Nile, the Babylonians acted as the great cultural intermediaries of the ancient world. Because Mesopotamia lacked such raw materials as metals, stone, and wood, the Babylonians became great merchants, trading as far as Armenia and the Red Sea. The Chaldeans, like the Assyrians before them, brought the area of the Near East known as the Fertile Crescent together under one rule, creating the first cosmopolitan society of peoples of many cultures and languages.
See also: Hammurabi; Nebuchadnezzar.

Babylonian Captivity, in Israeli history, period from the fall of Jerusalem to the Babylonians (586 B.C.) to the reconstruction of new Jewish Palestinian state (after 538 B.C.).

Baby's breath, or babies' breath, garden plant (*Gypsophila paniculata*), known for branched clusters of tiny white or pink flowers. Most are perennials; annuals are grown from seed. Ranging from 2 to 3 ft (61 to 90 cm) in height, baby's breath is frequently used in floral bouquets.
See also: Pink.

Bacchus, in Roman mythology, god of wine and revelry. The festivals in his honor, called *bacchanalia*, became orgies of drink and sex and were banned in 186 B.C.
See also: Dionysus.

Bach, Carl Philipp Emanuel (1714-1788), German composer and musician, known as the 'Hamburg Bach'; one of the sons of Johann Sebastian Bach. His *Essay on the True Art of Playing Keyboard Instruments* (1753) is still considered a valid guide to keyboard technique. From 1740 until his death he was court musician and harpsichordist to Frederick the Great.

Bach, Johann Christian (1735-1782), German composer and musician, often known as the 'English Bach'; youngest son of Johann Sebastian Bach. He spent many years in Italy, where he angered his family by converting to Catholicism and writing operas. He spent the last 20 years of his life in London, where he was music master to King George III.

Bach, Johann Sebastian (1685-1750), German composer. He composed preludes, passacaglias, toccatas, and fugues for the organ, perfecting the art of polyphony. The 48 preludes and fugues he wrote for the keyboard, published collectively as *The Well-Tempered Clavier*, are particularly renowned. Bach wrote much music for other solo instruments, notably the cello, as well as a number of concertos and orchestral suites. He also wrote hundreds of church cantatas. Among his religious compositions are the *St. John Passion*, the *Mass in B Minor*, and the *Christmas Oratorio*. His music is seen as the crowning achievement of the Baroque Age.
See also: Baroque; Cantata.

Bachelor's button, common name for several annual plants bearing small, button-shaped flowers. The cornflower is the best known.

Johann Sebastian Bach (1685-1750), the great German composer and organ virtuoso, brought baroque music to its peak.

Bachelor's degree *See:* Degree, academic.

Backbone *See:* Spine; Vertebrate.

Back swimmer *See:* Water bug.

Bacon, Francis (1561-1626), English philosopher and statesman who held various posts, finally becoming lord chancellor to James I in 1618. In 1621 he was banished from office for taking bribes and spent his last years writing. His most important contribution to philosophy was his advocacy of induction, the process of reasoning from the particular to the general, building theories on the basis of observed fact rather than making predictions from immutable general propositions. In this he was one of the founders of modern experimental science. His philosophical works were compiled in *Instauratio Magna* (1620).

B

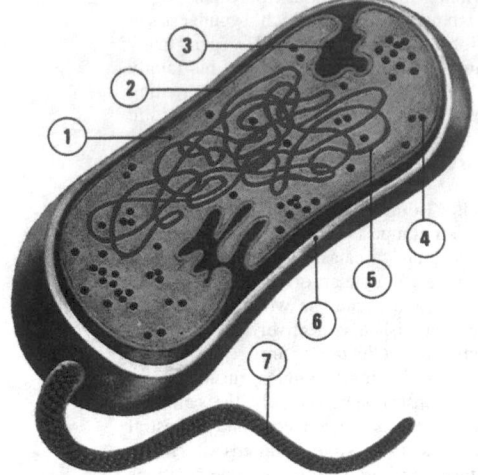

Bacteria are cellular micro-organisms that may appear as rod-shaped bacilli, spherical cocci, or corkscrew-shaped spirilla. They all consist of protoplasm (1), bounded by a cell membrane (2), which is invaginated, to form a mesosome (3). Embedded in the protoplasm, are ribosomes (4) and nuclear material (5), which has no surrounding membrane. Bacteria are bounded by a cell wall (6) and some of them have flagella (7).

Bacon, Francis (1909-1992), English painter. His unique style expresses the isolation and horror of the human condition, through distorted figures often conveying panic and menace.

Bacon, Roger (c.1214-1292), English Franciscan and scholastic philosopher renowned for his interest in science and his observation of natural phenomena. He is sometimes credited with many precocious discoveries (of the microscope, for example), but there is great doubt about the truth of these claims.

Bacteria, unicellular (one-celled) microorganisms of the class Schizomycetes, existing either as free-living organisms or as parasites. Bacteria may be divided into 3 groups: aerobes, which require atmospheric oxygen to live; anaerobes, which cannot live when exposed to it; and facultative anaerobes, which can live with or without it. They also come in 3 main shapes: rod, round, and spiral, called bacillus, coccus, and spirillum respectively. Generally a bacterium has an exterior cell wall within which a membrane encloses the soft *cytoplasm*, where enzymes digest and assimilate food. The DNA in which genetic information is encoded is in a portion of the cytoplasm, but unlike that of most other cells, is not separately enclosed in a nucleus. Bacteria reproduce asexually, by fission (*mitosis*), with each cell dividing evenly in two. In certain bacteria DNA is also sometimes transferred between 2 cells (*conjugation*). Bacteria cause many different chemical reactions in their hosts. Some aid in digestion and after processes within animals, and others break down dead plant and animal material in soil to provide nutrients for new growth. Bacteria that cause disease are called pathogens.
See also: Bacteriology; Cell; Leeuwenhoek, Anton van.

Bacteriological warfare *See:* Chemical and biological warfare.

Bacteriology, science that deals with the characteristics and activities of bacteria, as related to medicine, industry, and agriculture. Bacteria were discovered in 1676 by Anton van Leeuwenhoek. Modern techniques of study began to arise around 1870, with the use of stains and the discovery of methods of growing bacteria in laboratory dishes. Much pioneering work was done by Louis Pasteur and Robert Koch.
See also: Antibiotic; Bacteria; Immunity.

Bactria, ancient Greek kingdom in central Asia, lying between the Hindu Kush Mountains and the Amu Darya River, in what is now Afghanistan and Russian Turkestan. Bactria became part of the Persian Empire and fell to Alexander the Great in 330 B.C. It became independent in 256 B.C. but fell 150 years later.

Bad Aachen *See:* Aachen.

Baden-Baden (pop. 51,000), city and spa in the German state of Baden-Württemberg. It is situated at the edge of the Black Forest in the Rhine Valley, and is famous for its warm mineral springs.

Baden-Powell, Agnes *See:* Girl Scouts and Girl Guides; Baden-Powell, Robert Stephenson Smyth, Lord.

Baden-Powell, Robert Stephenson Smyth, Lord (1857-1941), British army officer and founder of the Boy Scouts (1908) and Girl Guides (1910). His sister, Agnes Baden-Powell, was cofounder of the Girl Scouts. His published works include *Scouting for Boys* (1908) and *Girl Guiding* (1917).
See also: Boy Scouts.

Badger, any of several medium-size (about 30 lb/13.6 kg), omnivorous, burrowing mammals of the weasel family Mustelidae, distributed throughout Eurasia, North America, and parts of Indonesia. Badgers are almost always nocturnal.

Badlands, region of southwestern South Dakota, about 100 miles (160 km) long and 40 miles (64 km) wide, characterized by an almost total lack of vegetation. Heavily eroded by wind and water, the area shows rugged hills, gullied slopes, steep buttes, fluted pinnacles, and layers of multicolored shales and sandstones. The term 'badlands' is also applied to similar regions in western North Dakota, eastern Arizona, northwestern Nebraska, and northern Wyoming.
See also: South Dakota.

Badminton, game played by 2 or 4 persons using lightweight rackets and a shuttlecock or bird (a feathered ball made of cork or rubber), which is hit back and forth over a 5-foot high net that divides the court at the center. Each player 'serves' by hitting the shuttlecock over the net to an opponent, who must return it before it hits the ground. The game probably originated in India.

Baeck, Leo (1873-1956), German rabbi and theologian of Reform Judaism. Baeck survived the Theresienstadt concentration camp. His *Essence of Judaism* (1905) interpreted Judaism as a religion devoid of mythology and concerned with the personal duty.

Badminton, a game that was introduced by British troops returning from India, grew popular in England, where the first set of rules was codified in 1895.

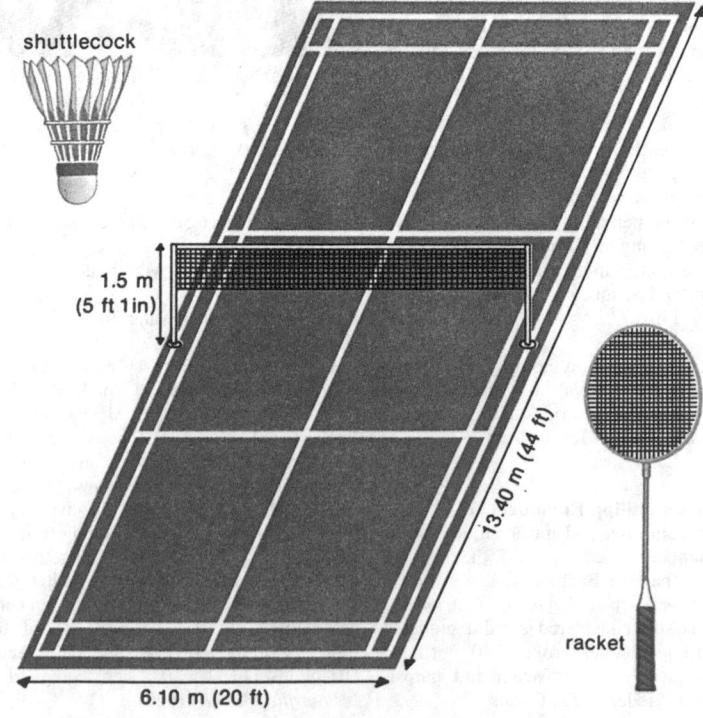

shuttlecock

1.5 m (5 ft 1 in)

13.40 m (44 ft)

6.10 m (20 ft)

racket

B

Baedeker, Karl (1801-1859) German book publisher. Started a bookshop in Koblenz in 1827. He published a handbook about the city of Koblenz in 1828. In 1832 he reprinted *Rheinreise* by Klein and renamed it *Rheinlande*. It was the first of the travel guidebooks that were later to become famous as 'Baedekers'. In 1839 he issued books about Belgium and Holland, in 1914 about India. In addition he published editions in French (1857) and English (1864).

Baekeland, Leo Hendrik (1863-1944), Belgian-born chemist who, after emigrating to the United States in 1889, devised Velox photographic printing paper (selling the process to Eastman in 1899) and discovered Bakelite, the first modern synthetic plastic.

Baer, Karl Ernst von (1792-1876), German founder of comparative embryology. He discovered the notochord and the mammalian egg in the ovary.

Baez, Joan (1941-), U.S. singer of folk ballads and popular songs, known for her clear, expressive voice and her involvement in social and political action. Baez achieved widespread fame during the height of the Vietnam War as a performer of protest songs.

Baffin, William (c. 1584-1622), English navigator and Arctic explorer. As pilot on a vessel seeking the Northwest Passage, he is credited with the discovery of Baffin Bay (1616). Baffin Island is named after him.

Baffin Island, world's fifth-largest island, between Greenland and Canada, part of Canada's Northwest Territories, a rugged, glaciated tract 183,810 sq mi (477,906 sq km) in area with a mountain range along its east coast. The largely Eskimo population lives by fishing, trading, and whaling.
See also: Baffin, William.

Baganda *See:* Ganda.

Baghdad (pop. 4,000,000), capital and largest city of Iraq, on both banks of the Tigris River, at a point where the Tigris is only 25 mi (40 km) from the Euphrates. Founded 762 A.D., the city became the center of Arab and Muslim civilization during its golden age, in the 9th and 10th centuries. In 1258 the city was sacked by the Mongols, and in 1638 it became part of the Ottoman Empire. In 1921 it became the capital of the newly formed kingdom of Iraq. After World War II Baghdad developed into a modern metropolis. The city is a shipping and industrial center and has an international airport. During Gulf War the city was damaged by allied bombing.
See also: Iraq; Persian Gulf War.

Bagpipe, musical wind instrument in which air is blown into a leather bag and then forced out through musical pipes. The melody is played on one or two pipes (the chanters), while drone pipes sound bass tones. The bagpipe originated in Asia but is best known as Scotland's national instrument.

Ahmadiyah Mosque in Baghdad. Ahmadiyah is the name of a Muslim sect, which started at the beginning of the 20th century.

Baguio (pop. 207,000), mountain resort city in Luzon in the Philippines. Baguio was developed as a modern city by William Howard Taft, then U.S. governor of the Philippines, when the country was under U.S. rule in the early 1900s. Nearly destroyed during World War II, the city was later rebuilt and is now an important gold-mining center.
See also: Philippines.

Bahadur Shah I (1643-1712), Indian Great Mogul, Mughal emperor (1707-12), second son of Aurangzeb. He was appointed governor of Kabul in 1669 by his father. After Aurangzeb's death he killed his two brothers in order to become emperor himself. During his reign he experienced conflict with the Mahratti and the Rajputs. The Sikhs were driven into the hills of the Punjab.

Bahadur Shah II (1775-1862), Indian Great Mogul, the last of the Mogul emperors (reigned 1837-1858). During his period of government, Bahadur no longer had any real authority (it resided with the British). Against his will, he was proclaimed leader of the Sepoy mutiny in 1857 by the rebel troops who had marched into Delhi. After the rebellion was put down by the British, Bahadur Shah II and his family were exiled to Burma.

Baha'i faith, religion founded by the Persian Mirza Husain Ali Nuri (1817-1892), known as Baha Ullah ('Glory of God'). The Baha'is believe in the unity of all religions and the equality of men and women. They advocate world government. The faith It has a worldwide following; its international center is in Haifa, Israel.

Among the various indigenous bagpipes existing today, are the Cretan mandoura (1), the Northumbrian bagpipe (2), the Italian zampogna (3), and, the most well-known of them all, the Scottish Highland bagpipe (4). Common to all these instruments are reed pipes —chanters and drones— which may be either double or single.

B

Bahamas

Capital:	Nassau
Area:	5,382 sq mi (13,939 sq km)
Population:	300,500
Language:	English
Government:	Parlementary monarchy in the British Commonwealth
Independent:	1973
Head of gov.:	Prime minister
Per capita:	US$ 16,800
Monetary unit:	1 Bahamian dollar = 100 cents

Bahamas, nation of some 700 subtropical islands and more than 2,000 islets, or cays, extending about 600 mi (970 km) from the coast of Florida, southeast toward Haiti. Nassau is the capital. The economy is based on tourism, fishing, and the export of wood products, cement, salt, and crayfish. Colonized by Britain in the 1640s, the islands became an independent state in the British Commonwealth in 1973. The Bahamas are a tax haven. The country has one of the world's largest flag of convenience shipping fleets.
See also: Nassau.

Bahasa Indonesia, the official designation of Malay as the common national language of Indonesia established by constitution in 1945. The vocabulary and structure of Bahasa Indonesia differ from the old literary Malay through, among other items, the addition of many new words. New spelling was introduced in August 1972.

Baha Ullah (Mirza Husain Ali Nuri; 1817-1892), Persian religious leader. A disciple of Babism, a sect that split off from Islam in 1848, he was exiled to Turkey by the Persian government in 1863. In that year he proclaimed himself the Promised One awaited by the Babists. He later founded the Baha'i faith, authoring its basic text, *Kitabi Ikan*, or *Book of Certitude*.
See also: Baha'i faith.

Bahrain

Capital:	Manama
Area:	267 sq mi (691 sq km)
Population:	656,000
Language:	Arabic
Government:	Absolute monarchy (emirate)
Independent:	1971
Head of gov.:	Prime Minister
Per capita:	US$ 13,000
Monetary unit:	1 Bahrain dinar = 1,000 fils

Bahrain, independent Arab emirate consisting of Bahrain Island and a number of smaller islands, in the Persian Gulf between the Saudi Arabian coast and the Qatar peninsula. The capital is Manama. The country has a desert climate, and the economy is based on oil drilling and refining. A trading center in ancient times, Bahrain became an emirate (monarchy) in 1783 and fell under British control in 1861. It attained independence in 1971.
Since the oil supply is slowly becoming exhausted, Bahrain is now developing the industrial sector and the services sector. In 2002, Bahrain became a constitutional monarchy. General elections will take place in 2003.
See also: Arab League; Manama.

Baikal, Lake, Lake in Siberia; 12,167 sq mi (31,500 sq km). The largest freshwater lake in Eurasia and the deepest in the world; 5,315 ft (1,620 m); 1,493 ft (455 m) above sea level. Influx chiefly through the Selenga River, outflow through the Angara River to the Yenisey. On its west bank is the Baikal Mountain Range (up to 8,531 ft, 2,600 m). There is an immense diversity of both plant and animal species. It is the habitat of about 1200 different living creatures, three-quarters of which are indigenous. There are about 600 species of plant life.

Baikonur, launching site in Kazakhstan. The launches of manned Russian space flights take place from Baikonur.

Bail, money or property security deposited to obtain a prisoner's freedom of movement, pledging that he or she will appear before the court when called.

Bailey, Liberty Hyde (1858-1954), U.S. botanist and educator whose studies of cultivated plants linked the practice of horticulture to the science of botany. He established (1888) the country's first horticulture laboratory at what is now Michigan State University. As a professor of botany and horticulture (1888-1903), and later as dean of the College of Agriculture at Cornell University (1904-1913), he pioneered agricultural education in the United States. His *Cyclopedia of American Horticulture* (1900-1902) was considered a major reference work.

Bailey Bridge, strong temporary or semi-permanent bridge constructed by a method suggested in 1941 by Sir Donald Bailey, then chief designer at the Royal Engineers Experimental Bridging Establishment in England. It consists of a series of mass-produced, lightweight girders that can be easily bolted together to produce the required length or to reinforce one another. Its immense flexibility and ease of construction made it immediately successful, particularly for military use. During World War II over 4,000 were built in Europe.

Baily's Beads, named for Francis Baily (1774-1844), the apparent fragmentation of the thin crescent of the sun just before totality in a solar eclipse, caused by sunlight

The construction of a 30 metre long bailey bridge, by 25 men, within a time frame of 46 minutes (see clock). The stages are: the men and the equipment are ready (1); assembly of the bridge and the 'nose' (2); the structure of the bridge is ready (3); the bridge is rolled across (4); the roadway is installed (5); the first vehicle can drive to the other side (6).

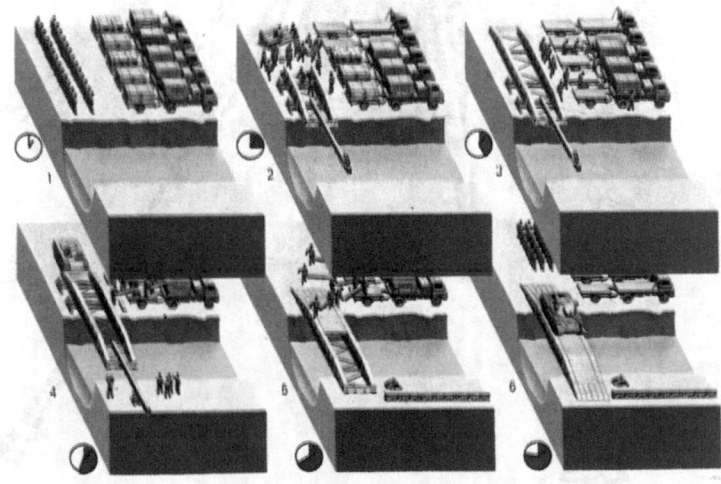

shining through mountains at the edge of the lunar disk.
See also: Eclipse.

Bainbridge, Beryl (1934-), British novelist, formerly an actress. Her work shows a masterly, yet barely uplifting description of working class life. Novels include *A Weekend with Claude* (1967), *The Dressmaker* (1973), *The Bottle Factory Outing* (1974), *Sweet William* (1975) and *Mum and Mr Armitage* (1985). *Young Adolf* (1978) is about the short stay of young Hitler in England in 1912. *Watson's Apology* is characterized by a preoccupation with crime and violence. *Filthy Lucre* (1986) is an extraordinarily melodramatic work which Bainbridge wrote when she was 13 years old. Novels published later include *An Awfully Big Adventure* (1989), *The Birthday Boys* (1991), *Something Happened Yesterday* (1993), *Every Man for Himself* (1996), *Master Georgie* (1998), and *According to Queenie* (2001).

Baja California, or Lower California, 761-mi (1,220-km) dry, mountainous peninsula in northwest Mexico. Separating the Pacific Ocean from the Gulf of California, it is 30-150 mi (48-241 km) wide. It is divided into the state of Baja California in the north and the territory of Baja California Sur in the south.

Baker, Josephine (1906-1975), U.S. born, French black singer and dancer of international fame. She was a film and stage artist, philanthropist, and social campaigner.

Bakhtaran (pop. 570,000; formerly Kermanshah), Capital of Bakhtaran province in Iran. The city is in Western Iran, lying in a basin of the Zagros Mountains. It is the trade center for an agricultural area producing grains, fruits, and sugar beets. The city dates from about the fourth century A.D. and was long a stop on major caravan routes. Nearby are the famed Behistun Inscriptions and Sassanian basreliefs.

Bakhtiar, Shapur (1916-1991), Iranian politician. After his studies in Paris, Bakhtiar started a lawyer's practice in Iran. He became one of the leaders of the secular opposition against the Shah's regime. At the beginning of 1979, when the Shah's position seemed untenable, he accepted the premiership at the latter's request, hoping to establish a democracy in Iran following the western model. After only 37 days this was brought to an end by Khomeini's return from exile. Bakhtiar fled to Paris, from where he continued to criticize the Iranian regime. He was probably murdered by agents of the regime.

Baking soda *See:* Soda.

Bakst, Leon-Nikolayevich (Lev Samoylovich Rosenberg; 1866-1924), Russian painter, draughtsman, costume and stage designer. Went to Paris in 1893. Belonged to the avant-garde Russian group of artists, which published the magazine *Mir Iskusstva* in Paris. He is especially known as a designer of the exotic costumes and stage settings for Diaghilev's Ballets Russes.

Baku (pop. 1,700,000), capital of Azerbaijan. On the southwest shore of the Apsheron peninsula in the Caspian Sea, Baku is an oil refining center as well as an important port, industrial center, and railroad center.
See also: Azerbaijan.

Balaklava, seaport village in the Crimean region, southwestern part of the former USSR, and site of the Crimean War battle (Oct. 25, 1854) commemorated by Alfred Lord Tennyson's 'The Charge of the Light Brigade' (1854).
See also: Crimean War.

Balalaika, usually 3-stringed musical instrument of ancient Slavic origin used in Russian and East European folk music. It has a triangular body and long fretted neck. Its six sizes may be combined in ensemble playing.

Balance, instrument for weighing; usually a bar with 2 matched pans suspended from each end, which pivots on a central point as weights are placed in the pans. If the weights are equal, the force of gravity on them is equal, and the balance swings level.
See also: Scale, weighing.

Balance of nature, concept of nature as a network of relationships and interdependencies between animals and plants, all of which support and control each other in a stable and unchanging equilibrium. The concept has been greatly modified since it was first suggested in the latter half of the 19th and early 20th centuries. It is now recognized that although a degree of balance does exist, it is a highly dynamic and unstable state. The main reason for this is that animals and plants depend not only on each other but on such external factors as climate and availability of food. Where food supplies are plentiful and the range of forms of life is large, a community may achieve a fairly high degree of stability. But where the 'food web' is simple, as in the northern tundras, there may be insufficient control mechanisms to prevent the periodic explosions of population that cause, for example, the self-destructive mass migration of lemmings. Many natural communities that were once stable have become unstable or have been destroyed by industry, agriculture, and disposal of sewage. Pesticides may kill beneficial insect parasites and thus lead to an uncontrollable increase in the pest population in succeeding years. Pesticides may also become concentrated in the bodies of predators at the top of the food chain. The death of hawks and owls from pesticides allows the population of rodent pests to increase. A small alteration in the balance of nature may produce unexpected consequences in some other part of the community.

Balance of payments, relation between payments in and out of a country. The figures that make up the balance of payments include trading (imports and exports), invisible earnings (insurance and banking), and capital movements (investment overseas or money from abroad). A country that persistently shows a deficit may have to devalue its

currency, borrow money, or adopt strict economies. A country with a large surplus is pressured by inflation.

Balance of power, system of international relations wherein nations alter their alliances to other nations so no single nation dominates. Sincer World War II, the United States and the former Soviet Union have emerged as superpowers, but Japan and China may, by virtue of size and military-industrial potential, demand a radically altered balance of power.
See also: International relations.

Balanchine, George (George Melitonovich Balanchivadze; 1904-1983), Russian-born choreographer, founder of the School of American Ballet (1934). He worked with Sergei Diaghilev in France in the 1920s and came to the United States in 1934. In 1948 he became artistic director of the New York City Ballet.
See also: Ballet.

Balboa, Vasco Núñez de (c.1475-1519), Spanish conquistador credited as first European discoverer of the Pacific Ocean. In 1510 he cofounded one of the first lasting European settlements on the American mainland, Antigua in Panama. Encouraged by Native American tales of a wealthy kingdom on 'the other sea,' in 1513 he led an expedition across the isthmus, saw the Pacific, and claimed it and all its coasts for Spain. He was later charged with treason and executed.
See also: Pacific Ocean.

Balch, Emily Greene (1867-1961), U.S. sociologist, economist, and humanitarian; joint winner of the 1946 Nobel Peace Prize. Cofounder of the Women's International League for Peace and Freedom, she was its secretary 1919-22 and 1934-35 and its honorary president from 1936.

Bald cypress, common name for a family (Taxodiaceae) of evergreens with wood cones and needlelike or scalelike leaves.

Bald eagle (*Haliaetus leucocephalus*), only native North American eagle, national bird of the United States since 1782. About 3 ft (90 cm) long, with a wingspan that may reach 7 ft (2 m), it is black, with white feathers on neck, tail, and head. A member of the hawk family, it preys on fish and is protected as an endangered species in all states.

Baldessari, John (1931-), American conceptual artist, his work is mainly photographic. He is considered the inventor of so-called narrative art but actually only uses storytelling to discuss abstract themes. In this sense he is also considered a representative of conceptual art. In 1969 Baldessari took part in an exhibition held in Chicago entitled *Art by Telephone* and in 1970 in New York he participated in two exhibitions on the themes 'information' (Museum of Modern Art) and 'software'. He also works with video.

Baldness, or alopecia, lack or loss of hair, usually from the scalp, due to disease of hair

B

follicles. Pattern baldness is an inherited tendency, often starting when a man is in his 20s. It is found in about 40% of the male population. Alopecia areata is a disease of unknown cause producing usually temporary patchy baldness, though it may be total. Prolonged fever, lupus erythematosus, ringworm, certain drugs, and poisons may lead to temporary baldness.

Baldpate *See:* Wigeon.

Baldwin I (of Jerusalem) (1058-1118; reign. 1100-1118) Youngest brother of Godfrey of Bouillon. Baldwin took part in the First Crusade and conquered Akko, Beirut, and Sidon as a result of which the Holy Roman Empire was expanded.

Baldwin II (of Jerusalem) (of Burgandy; d. 1131) Count of Edessa. He took over the army from his uncle Baldwin I and took part in the First Crusade. He succeeded Baldwin I as Count of Edessa in 1100. He was crowned King of Jerusalem in 1118.

Baldwin III (of Jerusalem) (1130-1162; reign. 1143-1162), grandson of Baldwin II. The Second Crusade (1147-1149) took place under his reign.

Baldwin IV (of Jerusalem) (1160-1185; reign. 1174-1183), son of King Amalric I (1135 1174; reign 1162-1174).

Baldwin V (of Jerusalem) (d. 1186) Nephew of Baldwin IV, King of Jerusalem in name only from 1183 until 1186.

Baldwin, James (1924-1987), African-American novelist, essayist, and playwright much of whose work deals with racial themes. His novel *Go Tell It on the Mountain*

A funeral procession in Bali. The increasing flow of tourists is leading to commercialization of various ceremonies and customs.

(1953) was based on his Harlem adolescence, while *Another Country* (1962) deals with sexual and racial identity. His best-known essays are collected in *Notes of a Native Son* (1955) and *The Fire Next Time* (1963). His book, *The Evidence of Things*

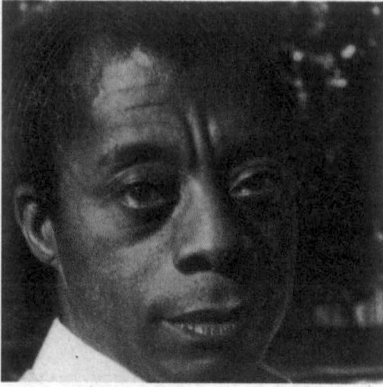

Important themes in the work of the American author James Baldwin (1924-1987) are racial problems and homosexuality.

Not Seen, about the Atlanta child murders (1985) is one of his most controversial works.

Baldwin, Stanley (1867-1947), British Conservative politician, 3 times prime minister (1923-24, 1924-29, 1935-37). He led the breaking of the General Strike of 1926 and was criticized for underestimating the dangers of the rise of fascism in Europe.

Balearic Islands, mediterranean archipelago off eastern Spain, under Spanish rule since 1349. The largest are Majorca, Minorca, and Ibiza. Products include grapes, olives, and citrus fruit.
See also: Majorca.

Baleen *See:* Whale.

Balfour, Arthur James Balfour, 1st Earl of (1848-1930), British statesman best known as author of the Balfour Declaration. He was a Conservative member of parliament 1874-1911; prime minister, 1902-05; and foreign secretary 1916-19.
See also: Balfour Declaration.

Balfour Declaration, statement of British policy issued in 1917 by Foreign Secretary Arthur Balfour. It stated British support for a Jewish national home in Palestine without prejudice to the rights of the non-Jewish population.

Bali, volcanic island and province of South Indonesia, 2,171 sq mi (5,623 sq km). It is a lush, densely populated island. Industries include food processing, tourism, and handicrafts. The largely Hindu Balinese are famous for dancing, music, and decorative arts.

Balikpapan (pop. 375,000), seaport on the Indonesian island Kalimantan (Borneo). Center of the most important oil region of the country, has a refinery; also the site of a coal deposit. In 1942 a Japanese-American sea battle took place here.

Baline, Israel *See:* Berlin, Irving.

Balka, Miroslaw (1958-), Polish conceptual artist. Around 1985 he made figurative sculptures of cement, clay, and wood, later on more abstract statues, combined with

neon. He subsequently made statues with a rectangular or cylindrical form chiefly from steel combined with unpretentious materials such as ashes, felt, salt, etc. They are placed on or just above the ground, or against a wall, and they are reminiscent of graves or gravestones. Their dimensions are based on Balka's own body measurements (6,23 ft, 1,90 m long). Rituals of the passage between life and death are a central theme.

Balkan Peninsula, mountainous land area in southeastern Europe, south of the Danube and Sava rivers, surrounded by the Adriatic, Ionian, Mediterranean, Aegean, and Black seas. It contains the nations of Bulgaria, Albania, Greece, European Turkey, and most of former Yugoslavia.

Balkan Wars, 2 wars in which the Ottoman Empire lost almost all its European territory. In the first war (1912-1913) Serbia, Bulgaria, Greece, and Montenegro conquered all of Turkey's European possessions except Constantinople. In the second war (1913) Bulgaria attacked Serbia, but was itself attacked by Rumania, Greece, and Turkey. In the ensuing Treaty of Bucharest (Aug. 1913) Bulgaria lost territory to each of its enemies.

Balkenhol, Stephan (1957-), German sculptor, pupil of Ulrich Rückriem at the Hamburg academy of art. In the late 1970s he photographed country folk. Since 1982 he has chiefly been making human and animal figures, roughly sculpted from wood and painted in just a few plain, bright colors. They have a frontal, static stance and are reminiscent of popular art. By devoting himself to a motif, Balkenhol wants to demonstrate the artist's freedom and to reject the compulsory necessity of innovation.
See also: Rückriem, Ulrich.

Balkhash, Lake, lake in Kazakhstan; 6952 sq mi (18,000 sq km). Fed by the Ili River. Fishing and salt extraction. On its north bank lies the industrial center of Balkhash (pop. 80,000).

Ballad, verse narrative, often meant to be sung, usually describing an event. Traditionally ballads celebrated folk heroes or related popular romances; they were developed by European minstrels in the Middle Ages. Romantic writers, such as Sir Walter Scott, William Wordsworth, and Samuel Taylor Coleridge, adapted the form. In modern popular music the term is used loosely to apply to any kind of sentimental song, but the United States has also produced ballads of the traditional type, ranging from the anonymous 'Frankie and Johnny' to the work of Bob Dylan and Joan Baez.

Ballade, verse of three 8-line stanzas concluding with a 4-line summary. The French poet François Villon (1431-63?) and the English poet Geoffrey Chaucer (c.1340-1400) used this form, which originated in 14th-century France.

Ballangrud, Ivar (1904-1969), Norwegian speed skater, holder of several Norwegian titles. World champion in 1926, 1932, 1936,

1938. European champion in 1929, 1930, 1933, 1936. Ballangrud won Olympic gold in 1928 in the 5000 m, in 1936 in the 500 m, 5,000 m, and 10,000 m.

Ball bearing *See:* Bearing.

Ballet, form of solo and ensemble dance meant for the stage. Ballet evolved from court entertainments of Renaissance Italy, where training in graceful movement was considered essential to a courtier's education. These entertainments were introduced into France by Catherine dé Medici, wife of King Henry II. In the courts of later kings, ballet became firmly established as an aristocratic pastime, and the kings themselves were skilled dancers. King Louis XIV established the first professional ballet school, the Royal Academy of Music and Dance, in 1661. Charles Louis (Pierre) Beauchamp, balletmaster of the Academy, originated the 5 basic foot positions and turnout of the feet that are still fundamental to ballet technique. Early-18th-century ballet was an adjunct to opera. By mid-18th century self-contained pantomime ballets began to appear, and virtuoso dancers modified their costumes to allow more freedom of movement. Jean Georges Noverre helped establish ballet as an integral art form in which plot, music, decoration, and dance were fused into an artistic whole. The 19th-century romantic movement introduced a new emphasis on lightness and grace. Ballerinas began to dance on their toes and adopted the short, full-skirted tutu. The center of European ballet shifted to Russia with the appointment of the French dancer Marius Petipa as balletmaster of the Imperial Ballet in the 1850s. Petipa brought new standards of technical perfection, and his use of Russian folk themes and music gave ballet a wider support among the public. With his assistant Lev Ivanov, he created such classical ballets as *Swan Lake*, *The Nutcracker*, and *The Sleeping Beauty*.
In 1907 the visit of the U.S. dancer Isadora Duncan to St. Petersburg spurred the Russian choreographer Michel Fokine to create a new, modern ballet. Fokine joined with the Russian impresario Sergei Diaghilev to form the Russian Ballet, which opened in Paris in 1909. Diaghilev's company included some of the greatest dancers in the history of ballet: Vaslav Nijinsky, Anna Pavlova, Léonide Massine, and George Balanchine. Many of these dancers went on to found new ballet companies, thus extending Diaghilev's influence throughout the world of the dance. For the Russian Ballet Fokine created *Les Sylphides*, *The Firebird*, and *Rite of Spring*. From 1909 until his death, Diaghilev was the most important figure in European ballet. England's first permanent ballet company, the Vic Wells (later Sadler's Wells), was formed in 1930. Renamed the Royal Ballet in 1957, it is noted for the choreography of Frederick Ashton, and featured dancers Margot Fonteyn and Rudolph Nureyev. After the Revolution, the Russian Ballet was devoted to experimental works on political and social themes, but then returned to the classical models of Petipa. Russian dancers are acknowledged masters of the traditional style.

In the U.S., contemporary ballet has evolved into a distinctive form combining the modern dance of Jerome Robbins, Martha Graham, and Ruth St. Denis with the tradition of the classical ballet as adapted by Massine and Balanchine. The Ballet Theater, established in 1940, encouraged the work of new U.S. composers and choreographers, and George Balanchine's New York City Ballet has continued to add new and unorthodox works to the repertoire. Professional ballet companies have been established throughout the U.S., and the popular tours U.S. companies have undertaken abroad have made this country among the most vital and influential in the dance world. Canada also has several major professional companies: Royal Winnipeg Ballet, National Ballet of Canada (Toronto), and Les Grands Ballets Canadiens (Montreal).
By the 1980's ballet's dancing and choreographic styes varied widely. The distinction between ballet and modern dance grew narrower as many companies fused the technical discipline of ballet with the freedom of modern dance.
See also: Ailey, Alvin; Balanchine, George; Baryshnikov, Mikhail; Diaghilev, Sergei Pavlovich; Pavlova, Anna; Dance; Nijinsky, Vaslav.

Ballistic missile *See:* Guided missile.

Ballistic Missile Early Warning System *See:* Radar.

Ballistics, science dealing with projectiles, traditionally divided into 3 parts: interior ballistics, relating to the progress of the projectile before it is released from the launching device; exterior ballistics, relating to the free flight of the projectile; and terminal ballistics, relating to the behavior of the projectile upon impact, at the end of its trajectory.

Balloon, nonpowered, nonrigid, lighter-than-air craft consisting of a bulbous envelope that holds the lifting medium and a payload-carrying basket, or 'gondola,' suspended below. Balloons may be captive (secured to the ground by a cable) or free-flying. Lift may be provided by a gas such as hydrogen or nonflammable helium or by heated air. Balloons are used in science (weather forecasting and astronomy), as well as for recreational purposes. In July 2002 Steve Fossett (U.S.) made the first solo flight around the world.
See also: Zeppelin, Ferdinand von.

Ballot, method of registering a vote. It can be a pre-printed list of people running for office or of issues to be decided by a popular vote (referendum). Elections can be held in a closed booth with a printed ballot mounted on a voting machine. Another type of balloting involves voters checking off their choices and depositing their ballots into a sealed box. After voting is over, the ballots are counted and the highest vote-getters are determined to be the winners.
See also: Voting.

Balm, any of various fragrant herbs of the mint family (genera *Melissa* or *Monarda*). Used in medicinal teas and wine drinks in ancient Greece and Asia, balm is now widely used as a scent in perfume and as a food and drink flavoring.
See also: Balm of Gilead.

Balmain, Pierre Alexandre Claudius (1914-1982), French fashion designer who started a fashion house in the Parisian Rue Francois in 1945 aided by Gertrud Stein. This was followed by branches in New York and Caracas. He was celebrated for simple, stylish, and classical collections.

Balm of Gilead, liquid resinous balsam derived from an evergreen tree (*Commiphora meccanesis*). The balsam had medicinal uses

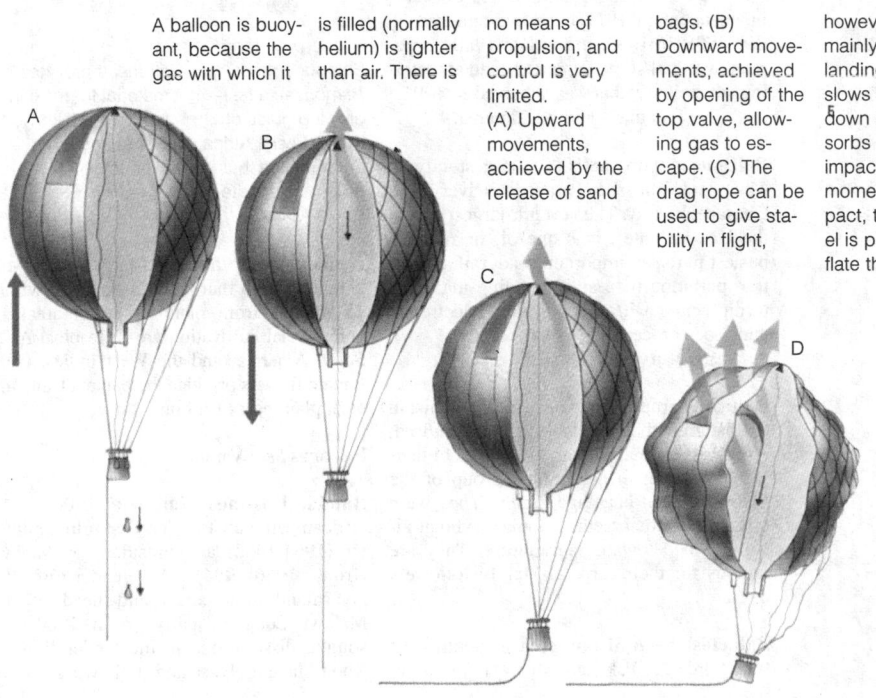

A balloon is buoyant, because the gas with which it is filled (normally helium) is lighter than air. There is no means of propulsion, and control is very limited. (A) Upward movements, achieved by the release of sand bags. (B) Downward movements, achieved by opening of the top valve, allowing gas to escape. (C) The drag rope can be used to give stability in flight, however, it is mainly useful as a landing aid: it slows the balloon down and absorbs part of the impact. (D) At the moment of impact, the rip panel is pulled to deflate the balloon.

B

Honoré de Balzac (1799-1850), a French novelist of the 19th century.

in ancient times. By extension, balm of Gilead may refer to anything that soothes or heals.

Balsa, or corkwood, tropical tree (*Ochroma lagopus*), known for its extremely light wood. Ecuador is a large producer of balsa wood, which is an effective insulating material and is also popular for making model airplanes and boats.

Balsam, aromatic resinous substance produced by certain plants and trees. Balsam is used in medicines, ointments, chewing gum, varnish, and perfumes.

Balsam poplar *See:* Poplar.

Baltic Sea, arm of the Atlantic Ocean, extending into northern Europe. Its 163,000 sq mi (422,170 sq km) are surrounded by Sweden, Finland, Estonia, Latvia, Lithuania, RF, Poland, Germany, and Denmark. It is linked to the North Sea by the Skagerrak, Kattegat, and Oresund straits.

Baltic States, Baltic coast republics of Estonia, Latvia, and Lithuania. They became independent in 1917 but were annexed by the USSR in 1940. In the late 1980s, separatist nationalist movements aimed at restoring sovereignty, this was achieved in 1991. *See also:* Estonia; Latvia; Lithuania.

Baltimore (pop. 680,000), largest city in Maryland, on the Patapsco River near Chesapeake Bay. The seventh-largest city in the United States, it is one of the nation's busiest ports, an important road, rail, and air transportation hub, and a leading manufacturing center with metallurgical, electronic, and food-processing industries. *See also:* Maryland.

Baluchi, group of tribes in Baluchistan (Pakistan) and the neighboring areas in Iran, Afghanistan, and India. The Baluchi languages belong to the Iranian group of the Indo-European language family. They were originally cattle breeding nomads who gradually turned towards agriculture. They are famous for their carpets. Mainly followers of Islam.

Baluchistan en Sistan, area in South-west Iran, bordering Pakistan. Mostly agriculture.

Named for the Baluchi, a nomadic people. In the 1970's, nationalist unrest among the Baluchis became a source of concern.

Balzac, Honoré de (1799-1850), French novelist noted for social observation and sweeping vision. *The Human Comedy*, his greatest work, is a collection of novels and stories that offer a comprehensive portrait of French society. Written over a period of two decades, its best-known novels are *Père Goriot* (1835) and *Cousin Bette* (1847).

Bamako (pop. 880,000), capital of Mali, located on the Niger River in West Africa. Bamako is a trade center linked by rail to Dakar, Senegal, on the Atlantic Ocean. Factories manufacture food, textiles, and metal goods. A former French colony, Mali became independent in 1960. *See also:* Mali.

Bamboo, woody plant (genus *Bambusa*) with hollow stems found in Asia, Africa, Australia, and the southern United States. Some species grow to 120 ft (27 m). In Asia the young shoots are a major foodstuff, while mature stems are used in building houses and furniture. Amorphous silica from stems is used as a catalyst in some chemical processes.

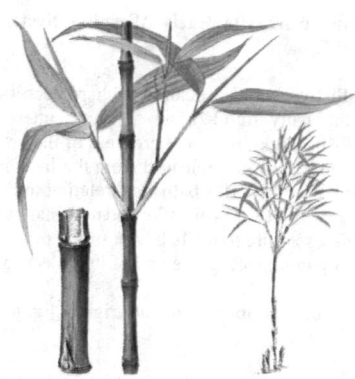

Bamboo (genus *Bambusa*), a fast-growing grass of tropical Asia, Africa, and America, has hollow, segmented stems. It provides material for making furniture, wickerwork, poles, and other products.

Banana, edible fruit of a large (30-ft/9-m) perennial herb that reaches maturity within 15 months from planting. Main areas of commercial cultivation are in tropical Asia, South America, and the West Indies. Only female flowers produce the banana fruit, and each plant bears fruit only once.

Banaras *See:* Varanasi.

Banda, Hastings Kamuzu (1906-1997), African nationalist leader, first prime minister (1964-1966) and president of Malawi (from 1966-1994). As leader of the Nyasaland nationalists and head of the Malawi Congress party (from 1960), he sought dissolution of the Federation of Rhodesia and Nyasaland. Following his de-

feat at the 1994 presidential elections he stepped down. *See also:* Malawi.

Bandaranaike, Sirimavo Ratwatte Dias (1916-2000), prime minister of Sri Lanka and the world's first woman premier. After the assassination of her husband, Prime Minister Solomon Bandaranaike, in 1959, she led his Sri Lanka Freedom party to victory in 1960, continuing his pro-Buddhist and pro-Sinhalese policies. She lost office in 1965 but returned in 1970 with a landslide victory for her left-oriented coalition. Conservatives defeated her in 1977. Her daughter, Chandrika Kumaratunga, who was elected President in 1994, reappointed her Prime Minister in that same year. *See also:* Sri Lanka.

Bandar Seri Begawan (formerly Brunei Town; pop. 56,000), capital of the Sultanate Brunei located on the mouth of the Brunei River on the island Kalimantan. A large harbor, trade center for rubber and agrarian products, shipbuilding, textile industry. Largely destroyed during WW II. University (1985). The most striking buildings are the mosque, one of the largest in Asia, and the royal palace.

Bandeira, Manuel Carneiro de Sousa (1886-1968),one of the greatest and most popular poets of modern Brazilian literature. Although his work is more traditional than that of most of his contemporaries, Bandeira is considered as belonging to the Brazilian 'modernismo', especially during its first phase.

Manuel Bandeira was strongly influenced by the poets surrounding the French periodical *Le Parnasse contemporain* , which is apparent from, among others, his debut work *Ashes of the Hours* (1917). In 1924 the first collection appeared which reflected the new, modernistic estheticism, *Dissolute Rhythm*. *Libertinism* (1930) is regarded as his best work and most representative collection. Bandeira made no secret in his work of the tuberculosis that gave his life a whole different direction. The theme of 'a life that might have been and never was' is recognized in

The banana family exhibits a wide variety of flower structures. This is the common, edible banana, *Musa*.

his poetry as a theme of death - yet a death shown as a familiar companion, a daily dinner companion.

Bandicoots, any of several genera of marsupials of the family Peramelidae found in Oceania, roughly rabbit-sized with tapering snouts. There are considerable reproductive differences from other marsupials, and their fossil history is problematic, so that their relationship to other marsupials is not fully understood.

Bandinelli, Baccio (Bartolommeo de'Brandini; 1493-1560), Florentine sculptor, pupil of Andrea Sansovino. Compromised himself by competing with Michelangelo. While working for the Medicis he made gravestones for Pope Leo X and Pope Clemens VII in the S. Maria sopra Minerva in Rome. His most famous works are the beautiful marble reliefs on the choir screen in the Florence Cathedral and the colossal Hercules and Cacus (1534) at the entrance of the Palazzo Vecchio in Florence.

Bandung (pop. 2,500,000), capital city of West Java province, Indonesia. The third-largest city in the country, Bandung is an important industrial, educational, and tourist center.

Baneberry, several herbaceous plants with poisonous red, white, or black berries. Two species known as cohosh are native to the United States. Native Americans used them as emetics and cathartics.

Banff (pop. 7,600), resort town in Alberta, Canada. Situated in the Bow River Valley of the Rocky Mountains at 4,538 ft (1,383 m) altitude, its attractions are hot springs, skiing, and an abundance of wildlife.

Banff National Park, oldest park in Canada, established in 1885, located on the eastern slopes of the Rocky Mountains in southwestern Alberta. The 2,564-sq-mi (6,640-sq-km) park is characterized by glaciers, deep valleys, and mountains. There are also dense forests, alpine meadows, and many animals, including bighorn sheep, bear, and deer.

Bangalore (pop. 3,302,000), capital city of Karnataka state, south central India. A major industrial city, it manufactures soap, telephones, machine tools, pharmaceuticals, and aircraft, along with cotton textiles and hand-loomed silk.

Bangka (pop. 400,000), Indonesian island, 4,376 sq mi (11,330 sq km); separated from Sumatra by the Bangka Strait. Hilly island with one of the largest tin ore reserves in the world; also has other minerals. Mining and processing of tin ore is controlled by the Indonesian government. Also cultivation of pepper. Important places: Pangkalpinang and Muntok.

Bangkok (pop. 6,700,000), capital city of Thailand. Situated on the Chao Phraya River, about 25 mi (40 km) inland from the Gulf of Siam, Bangkok is Thailand's main port. About three-fourths of Thailand's foreign trade passes through Bangkok; principal exports include rice, teak, rubber, tin, gold, and silver. The city is also a famous jewelry trading center. In addition, almost all of Thailand's higher education institutions are located in Bangkok. Among its numerous Buddhist temples (wats) is the Wat Phra Keo, located within the Grand Palace and containing the famed 'Emerald Buddha,' carved from jasper.
See also: Thailand.

Bangladesh

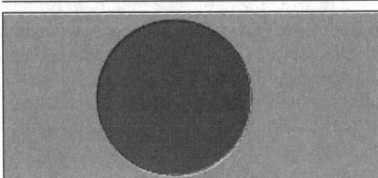

Capital:	Dhaka
Area:	55,598 sq mi (147,570 sq km)
Population:	133,377,000
Language:	Bengali
Government:	Republic
Independent:	1971
Head of gov.:	President
Per capita:	U.S. $1,750
Monetary unit:	1 Bangladesh taka = 100 poisha

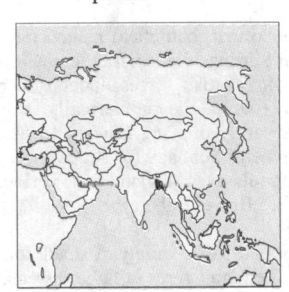

Bangladesh, People's Republic of Bangladesh, republic in the northeast of the Indian subcontinent, on the Bay of Bengal; formerly East Pakistan. Bangladesh is a low-lying land centered on the alluvial Ganges-Brahmaputra Delta. A tropical monsoon climate prevails, and because of heavy rains and severe cyclones, most of the country is subject to flooding. Overpopulation accentuates periodic famines and epidemics among the mainly Muslim Bengalis who constitute the great majority of the population. Bangladesh produces a large portion of the world's jute; tea is the other main cash crop, and sugarcane is also grown. Rice and wheat are the major subsistence crops. Natural gas is the only important mineral resource, and manufacturing is largely limited to the proceessing of raw materials. The region was created as East Pakistan (Pakistan's eastern province) in 1947. The province sought greater independence, but West Pakistan refused autonomy and troops crushed large-scale opposition in the ensuing civil war (March-Dec. 1971). Guerrilla fighting continued, Bengalis exiled in India proclaimed a Bengali republic, and Indian invasion forces overran the West Pakistani forces. A Bangladesh government was established in Dhaka in Dec. 1971. In September 1988 Bangladesh was devastated by the worst floods ever. About 30 million people lost their homes. In 1998 and 2001 Bangladesh again suffered from heavy floods. At the beginning of the 2000s Bangladesh is still one of the poorest countries in the world. In 2001, Begum Khaleda Zia (of the Bangladesh Nationalist Party) was appointed Prime Minister for the third time.

Bangui (pop. 600,000), capital city of the Central African Republic. On the Ubangi River, it is being developed as a tourist center for the country's wildlife preserves.
See also: Central African Republic.

Banja Luka (pop. 143,000), city in the republic of Bosnia-Hercegovina. In the early 1990s located in Serb-occupied territory. Varied industry (including textile and breweries). Used to have more than forty mosques, most of them almost completely destroyed due to earthquakes.

Banjarmasin, Banjermasin, or Bandjarmasin (pop. 481,000), capital of South Kalimantan province in Indonesia, located on an island between the Barito and Martapura rivers in southeastern Borneo. Exports include oil, diamonds, and lumber.

Banjo, stringed musical instrument with a long fretted neck and a circular frame covered by a skin resonator. Its 4 to 9 strings are played by plucking. The banjo originated among slaves in North America and may have been derived from West African instruments. It became popular in 19th-century minstrel shows, in early jazz bands, and in folk music.

Banjul (pop. 50,000), capital of Gambia in West Africa, located on St. Mary's Island where the Gambia River flows into the Atlantic Ocean. It is Gambia's only large city, its chief port and economic center. Exports include peanuts, clothing, and farm machinery. It was founded in 1816 (as Bathurst) as a British base for eliminating the slave trade. Gambia gained independence in 1965, and the city was renamed Banjul in 1973.
See also: Gambia.

Bank holiday, day on which banks are legally closed. In England, such days are fixed annual public holidays. In U.S. history, the term refers to the 4-day period in March

B

Festooned cattle, destined to be ritually slaughtered at a Muslim festival in Bangla Desh.

B

1933 when President Franklin D. Roosevelt ordered all banks closed to halt panic and to assess their financial condition. More than 1,900 banks had collapsed since the beginning of the Depression in 1929.

Banking, business of dealing with money and credit transactions. The services offered by banks fall into 4 categories: safe storage, interest-bearing deposit facilities, money transfer, and loans. The nature of safe storage has changed now that most money is held in the form of bank deposits rather than gold or silver coin. Bank branches keep cash available for customers. Most banks also have safe-deposit boxes for storing valuables other than cash. The second basic service arises from the first. Since money given to a bank for safekeeping effectively amounts to a loan to the bank, the bank pays interest on it. Rates vary, depending in part on how much notice the bank requires for withdrawals. The third category of bank services, transfer of money, is carried out mainly by means of checks and credit cards. In making out checks customers authorize the bank to transfer a specified sum from their own account to someone else's (or to pay them in cash). After the check has been handed in or mailed to the bank by the payee (the person to whom the money is to be paid) it is returned to the bank of the person who has writen the check (the payor). Credit cards, in widespread use since about 1970, allow the purchase of services and goods even in places where the bearer is not well known enough to be able to use a check. The final category of bank services, lending to customers, is the most highly developed. Although basic services are the same from one bank to another all around the world, the details and, in particular, the manner in which they are offered vary considerably. Banking and the financial services industry are now in a state of transition and restructuring to meet the financial demands of the 21st century.

Bank of England, central bank of the English government founded in 1694 by an Act of Parliament and Royal Charter. In 1946 it was nationalized and its stock was passed to the British Treasury. It advises the government on financial and economic conditions, facilitates the payment of government debt, services the foreign exchange markets, issues bank notes, and administers foreign exchange control.

The banyan tree (*F. benghalensis*), sacred to Hindus, may shade a huge area beneath its canopy. Supporting trunks are formed by aerial roots growing from the branches. It has paired, edible figs (bottom right).

Bankruptcy, legal status of a debtor whom the courts have declared unable to pay debts. Bankruptcy is regulated by laws that provide for an orderly adjustment when a person or business becomes insolvent. A person or business with more debts than assets and no means of meeting debt payment may declare bankruptcy. The interest of both creditors and debtor are given consideration by the court. Bankruptcy may be voluntary (filed by the debtor) or involuntary (filed by creditors). When a petition of bankruptcy is filed, the court assumes control over the assets of the debtor. A custodian or trustee is appointed to oversee the debtor's property to protect it from loss. This trustee has legal ownership of all assets of the bankrupt estate except those exempt under local law. The property of the debtor must be sold and the proceeds distributed to creditors on a percentage basis. The debtor is then legally discharged from all previous obligations.

Banneker, Benjamin (1731-1806), U.S. mathematician and astronomer, notable as the first African American to gain distinction in science. He was the author of many celebrated astronomical almanacs (1791-1802).

Bannister, Sir Roger Gilbert (1929-), British athlete, the first man to run a mile in less than 4 minutes, on May 6, 1954, in Oxford. His time was 3 min 59.4 sec.

Bannockburn, battlefield named for a village in Stirlingshire, central Scotland. Here, in 1314, Scottish forces under Robert the Bruce routed the numerically superior English army of King Edward II, assuring the throne of Scotland for Bruce and ending English rule over Scotland for a period. *See also:* Bruce, Robert the.

Bantam, any of a variety of small domestic fowl, often miniatures of larger breeds.

Bantam (Banten), Indonesian realm on northwest Java, first meeting place of the Dutch with the Archipel (1596). The English settled here in 1602. Jan Pieterszoon Coen moved the administrative center of the VOC (Dutch East India Company) to Batavia (= Jacatra, part of Bantam) in 1619.

Banting, Sir Frederick Grant (1891-1941), Canadian physiologist who, with C.H. Best, first isolated the hormone insulin from the pancreas of dogs (1921), thus providing a major breakthrough in the treatment of diabetes. For this he shared the 1923 Nobel Prize in physiology or medicine with J.J.R. Macleod, who developed the experimental facilities. *See also:* Insulin.

Bantu, linguistic group of central, east, and south Africa. Bantu languages include Swahili and Zulu. The term is often used in South Africa to denote black Africans.

Banyan tree, sacred tree (*Ficus bengalensis*) of India, related to the fig. It grows up to 100 ft (30 m) high, and its branches send down aerial roots that form new trunks on reaching the soil. An individual tree can thus become a dense thicket of intertwined stems

and secondary trunks covering an acre or more.

Bánzar Suarez, Hugo (1926-2002), Bolivian soldier and politician. Became president in 1971 as the result of a coup d'état, supported by the fascist Falangists and Brazil. Resigned in 1978 and was succeeded by Juan Pereda Asbun. He founded the right-wing nationalistic party Acción Democrática Nacionalista. In the 1980s, the former dictator contributed to the establishment of a democracy in Bolivia. In 1997, Bánzer Suarez was elected as President. He was forced to resign in 2001 due to health problems.

Baobab (*Adansonia digitata*), tree of tropical Africa and India with a remarkably thick trunk, reaching 30 ft (10 m) in diameter. The related Australian species is sometimes called the bottle tree for its unusual shape.

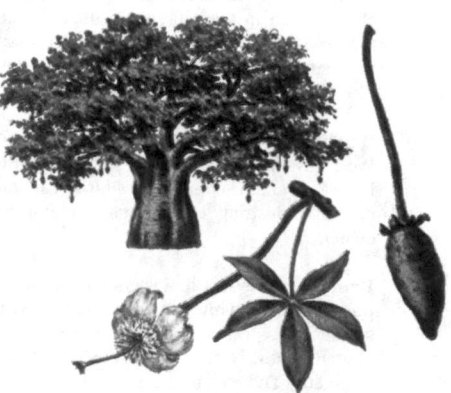

Baobab (*A. digitata*), one of the largest trees in the world, is one of the few trees found on the African savanna. It has compound leaves, fragrant flowers, and a woody, elongated fruit.

The branches bear dense masses of leaves, used for medicine and condiments, white flowers, and an edible gourdlike fruit, the juice of which is made into a beverage. The bark is used to make rope, cloth, and paper, and the hollowed trunks are used for dwellings.

Bao Dai (1913-1997), Vietnamese emperor during the French colonial period. He was the last emperor of Annam (1926-45), until overthrown by the Viet Minh. He was later made head of state of a unified Vietnam (1949-55) created by the French in a final bid to retain Indochina, but he was forced into exile. *See also:* Vietnam.

Baptism, rite of initiation into the Christian church. Some churches consider the ceremony the first step to salvation, as a symbolic purification of water. Others regard baptism as a confirmation of salvation through Christ. *See also:* Christianity; John the Baptist, Saint; Roman Catholic Church.

Baptists, members of a Protestant denomination who hold that baptism is for believers only, not simply those born into the faith. Baptism, often at age 12, is by immersion.

Total world membership is said to be more than 31 million, most of whom live in the United States, where they constitute the largest Protestant group. Individual churches have considerable autonomy. There is no single Baptist creed; beliefs range from fundamentalist to modernist. The evangelistic and revivalist tradition emphasizes the influence of the laity as well as ministers. The church originated with John Smyth, the leader of a group of English religious dissenters who sought refuge in Holland around 1608. The first U.S. church was founded in Providence, R.I. in 1639, by Roger Williams, and the new denomination evolved independently among the variety of Puritan dissenters. In the 19th century the Baptists founded more than 100 colleges and universities. By 1845 the denomination had become particularly influential in the Midwest and the South. In that year a great split occurred over the slavery issue, creating Northern and Southern Baptists. After the Civil War, black churches developed an independent grouping, the National Baptist Convention of America (1880). In 1915 a dispute within that membership created another major group, the National Baptist Convention, USA, Inc. In 1950 the interracial Northern Baptists formed the American Baptist Convention. The Southern Baptist Convention now includes churches beyond the borders of the historic South. U.S. Baptist are active in the World Council of Churches through the Baptist World Alliance, which was founded in 1905.
See also: Protestantism.

Bar, professional association of lawyers. Attorneys must be admitted to the bar before they can practice law.
See also: Law.

Barabbas, man described in the New Testament as a bandit condemned to crucifixion at the same time as Jesus. The Roman governor Pontius Pilate agreed to spare one prisoner, and a palace crowd chose Barabbas instead of Jesus.
See also: New Testament.

Baraka, Imamu Amiri (LeRoi Jones; 1934-), African-American author and political activist whose plays, especially *Dutchman* (1964), express revulsion at the oppression of black people in white society.

Barak, Ehud (1942-), Israeli politician. In 1995 Barak became Secretary of the Interior in the national government of Yitzhak Rabin. And, after Rabin's assassination in 1995, he became Secretary of State under Peres. In 1996, after the electoral defeat of Peres by Netanyahu, Barak was elected Chairman of the Labor party. In 1999, he succeeded Netanyahu as Prime Minister. Barak initiated peace-conferences with neighboring Arab countries and the PLO, but disappointing results and mounting violence between Israel and the PLO led to his political defeat. In the advanced elections of 2001, he lost his presidency to Ariel Sharon, leader of the right-winged Likud party.
See also: Rabin, Yitzhak; Peres, Shimon; Netanyahu, Benjamin; Palestine Liberation Organization; Sharon, Ariel.

Barbados

Capital:	Bridgetown
Area:	166 sq mi (430 sq km)
Population:	276,600
Language:	English
Government:	Parliamentary monarchy in the British Commonwealth
Independent:	1966
Head of gov.:	Prime minister
Per capita:	less than US$ 14,500
Monetary unit:	1 Barbados dollar = 100 cents

Barbados, densely populated small island in the Caribbean; a parliamentary state, part of the British Commonwealth.
About 21 mi (34 km) long and 14 mi (22.5 km) wide, Barbados lies surrounded by coral reefs 250 mi (400 km) northeast of Venezuela. Bridgetown is the capital and chief business center. Carlisle Bay on the southwest coast is the only harbor. The island has no real mountains and no rivers, and water supply is from artesian wells. The mild climate makes Barbados a popular resort, but it lies in a zone of tropical storms, and destructive hurricanes are not uncommon. The soil is fertile and the whole island is cultivated. Sugarcane, introduced in the 17th century, is still the main crop, though efforts are being made to diversify agriculture and to establish light industry. Chief exports are sugar, molasses, and rum. Nearly 90% of the very dense population is of African descent. Emigrants, mainly to other West Indian islands, are numerous, and money sent home forms a useful part of the economy, which is based on the tourist sector.
Barbados was claimed by the British in 1605 and remained a colony for more than 300 years. The representative assembly was established in 1639, giving the island one of the oldest constitutions in the Commonwealth. Slavery was abolished in 1834, and full adult suffrage was granted in 1950. In 1966 the island gained independence and was admitted to the United Nations. The language is English, the Anglican church is established, and the general outlook is much influenced by a traditional image of England, though many details of life reflect historical and family links

with North America. The present Prime Minister, Owen Arthur, wants Barbados to become a republic.

Barbarian, term originally used by ancient Greeks to denote any non-Greek-speaking people. As Greek culture spread with the conquests of Alexander the Great in Asia and the subsequent expansion of the Roman Empire in Europe, the word came to refer to peoples who lived beyond the borders of the Empire and therefore outside Greco-Roman civilization. It then took on a pejorative meaning and now refers to anyone considered uncivilized, primitive, or unsophisticated.
See also: Goths; Hun; Vandals.

Barbarossa (Khayr ad-Din; c.1483-1546), Turkish naval commander of the western Mediterranean. As high admiral of the Turkish fleet he captured Tunis and Algiers in 1518 and brought the Barbary states under Turkish sovereignty. In 1533 and 1544 he defeated Italian fleets and raided towns in Greece, Italy, France, and Spain.

Barbarossa *See:* Frederick.

Barbary ape, small tailless monkey (*Macaca sylvana*) of Algeria, Morocco, and Gibraltar. There is a legend that the British will lose the Rock of Gibraltar when its small colony of Barbary apes departs.

Barbary Coast *See:* Barbary States.

Barbary pirates *See:* Barbary Wars.

Barbary States, term historically applied to countries along the Mediterranean coast of North Africa, now Algeria, Tunisia, Libya, and Morocco.

Barbary Wars, 2 wars waged by the United States against African states. Barbary pirates had been attacking ships in the Mediterranean since the 16th century. In May 1801, the United States blockaded Tripoli in opposition to exorbitant payments to the Barbary States to protect its shipping. The United States won the war in 1805. The second Barbary War was fought in 1815 with Algiers. Treaties ending piracy were signed with Algiers, Tunis, and Tripoli.

Barbel *See:* Catfish.

Barber, Samuel (1910-1981), U.S. composer. Initially, he composed in a late romantic style. His music is generally tonal. Major

B

The Barbary ape (*M. sylvana*), the only wild monkey existing in Europe, was probably brought from Africa by Arabs during the Middle Ages.

B

Sortie de Forêt à Fontainebleau (Paris, Jeu de Paume) was painted by Théodore Rousseau (1812-1867), the most important representative of the Barbizon school, a group of landscape painters, who lived and worked in Barbizon between 1830 and 1870 and who often painted the woods near Fontainebleau.

works include two symphonies, *Adagio for Strings* (1936), and the cycle *Knoxville: Summer of 1915* (1947) for soprano and orchestra. He also wrote the operas *Vanessa* (1956) and *Anthony and Cleopatra* (1966).

Barberry, any of several mostly evergreen, usually spiny shrubs (genus *Berberis*) having globular yellow flowers and red berries. The sour berries of the common barberry make excellent preserves, and the bark yields a yellow dye used in leather manufacture.
See also: May apple; Oregon grape.

Barbirolli, Sir John (1899-1970), English cellist and conductor, famous for his interpretations of compositions by Sibelius and

View of the Plaza de Cataluña, the largest square in Barcelona, situated in the centre of the city and surrounded by hotels and banks. Underneath it, a large metro station has been built.

other late romantics. After conducting the New York Philharmonic Orchestra (1937-42), he began a lifelong association with the Halle Orchestra in Manchester, England, and conducted the Houston Symphony Orchestra (1961-67).

Barbiturate, any of a group of drugs, derived from bituric acid, that act as sedatives, anesthetics, or anticonvulsants in the central

nervous system by depressing nerve cell activity. Widely prescribed in the past for insomnia, their use is now discouraged because of high rates of addiction and the danger of overdose. Phenobarbital is used in the treatment of convulsions. Overdoses of barbiturates cause the deep and rapid onset of coma and can be fatal, especially when combined with alcohol.
See also: Drug.

Barbizon school, informal group of French painters of natural and rural subjects, active c.1830-70, who frequented the village of Barbizon, near Paris. It included Théodore Rousseau, Narciso Diaz de la Peña, Jean-Baptise Corot, Jean François Millet, Jules Dupré, Constant Troyon, and Charles Daubigny.

Barbuda, island in the West Indies (62 sq mi/160 sq km), located north of the Windward group and southeast of Puerto Rico. Antigua and Barbuda form an independent nation within the Leeward Islands. Barbuda's main product is sea-island cotton.

Barcarole, or barcarolle (from Italian for 'boat'), traditional boat song or musical composition of the 18th or 19th century written in that style. Barcaroles were originally sung by gondoliers in Venice. Many European composers, including Frédéric Chopin, adapted the style for their own works. Sung or played primarily in 6/8 time, barcaroles were composed as opera arias and instrumental pieces for pianos, orchestras, and choruses.

Barcelona (pop. 1,500,000), Spain's largest seaport and second largest city after Madrid. It is situated on the Mediterranean coast, in northeastern Spain, on a broad plain dotted with hills, between the Besos and Llobregat rivers. Barcelona's wide range of industries includes shipbuilding, metalworking, food processing, the manufacture of chemicals, textiles (including silk), leather goods, and glass. Agricultural commodities such as wine, olive oil, and cork are exported, and raw materials such as coal, grain, and textile fibers pass through its port. The city was founded in the 3rd century B.C. by Carthaginians. It flourished in the Middle Ages as an economic center. In 1137 it united with Aragon. Except for two brief periods of French rule (1640, 1808-14), Barcelona has been under Spanish rule ever since. Among the city's principal landmarks are the cathedral (begun 1298, completed 1498) and the Church of the Holy Family, by Antonio Gaudi, begun in 1882 and still unfinished. The center of Catalan nationalism in modern times, Barcelona was the stronghold of left-wing politics and Republican allegiance in the Spanish Civil War. It was the host city for the 1992 Summer Olympic Games.
See also: Spain.

Bar code, identifying code consisting of dark and light bars, designed to be read by an optical viewer. The bar code contains information about a particular product and is used primarily for inventory control.

Bard, ancient Celtic minstrel. First written

of around 200 B.C., the early bards were educated poets who wielded political power in Wales, Scotland, and Ireland. Through the Middle Ages they mainly composed eulogies to their noble patrons.

Bardeen, John (1908-1991), U.S. physicist noted for his studies of transistors and superconductors. He shared the 1956 Nobel Prize for physics with W. H. Brattain and W. Shockley, doing much of the research in solid-state physics that led to the development of transistorized electronic equipment. In 1972 he became the first person to win a second Nobel Prize in the same field, sharing the award with L.P. Cooper and J.R. Schrieffer for the development of their theory of superconductivity.
See also: Superconductivity.

Barenboim, Daniel (1942-   ), Argentine-born Israeli pianist and conductor known for his musical interpretations of Beethoven. He made his debut at the age of 7 in Buenos Aires. From 1975 to 1989 he was music director of the Orchestre de Paris and, from 1994, of the Chicago Symphony Orchestra. In 1992, he became artistic director of the Berlin State Opera.

Barents, Willem (c.1550-1597), Dutch navigator, for whom the Barents Sea is named. He made 3 voyages to the Arctic in search of a northeast passage to Asia.

Barents Sea, shallow arm of the Arctic Ocean north of Norway and European Russia, bounded by Svalbard (Spitsbergen) to the northwest, Franz Josef Land to the north, and Novaya Zemlya to the east. The southwestern portion is warmed by the North Atlantic Drift and remains ice-free in winter; on its southwestern coast lies the former Soviet port of Murmansk.
See also: Barents, Willem.

Barge dog *See:* Schipperke.

Bari (ancient Barium; pop. 335,000), southern Italian port on the Adriatic Sea, capital of Bari province and of the Apulia region. The city is an important agricultural, commercial, and industrial center and also has a university. Bari is the site of the Fiera del Levante, an annual trade fair highlighting the city's role as center for commercial exchanges with the Balkan countries and the Middle East. In the old quarter are the cathedral, the Church of St. Nicola (begun 1087), and the 13th-century castle of Frederick II.
See also: Italy.

Barite *See:* Barium.

Barium, chemical element, symbol Ba; for physical constants see Periodic Table. Barium, a soft, silvery white metal, was discovered by Sir Humphrey Davy in 1808. In nature it is found chiefly as *barite* or *heavy spar* (sulfate) or *witherite* (carbonate). Barium is produced by electrolysis of its chloride and is easily oxidized. Barium sulfate (*blanc fixe*) has good covering power and does not darken in the presence of sulfides. It is used in pigments and as a filler in paper, as well as in X-ray diagnos-

Barite (barium sulphate) from the Tunisian Sahara. Both barite and gypsum belong to the sulfate group. Both may, under arid conditions, form rose-shaped mineral aggregates: desert roses.

tic work and glassmaking. Other compounds of barium are used in fireworks and rat poison. Soluble barium compounds are poisonous.

Bark, outer covering of the stems and branches of woody plants. The protective outer bark usually consists of cork, while the inner bark contains food-conducting phloem and the reproductive cells of the cork cambium. Bark is usually formed in annual rings, the outer layers bursting and splitting with each new growth. Bark helps to protect the tree from extremes of climate and from various pests and diseases. Some varieties of bark have medicinal uses, others are sources of textile fibers and dyes.

Bark beetle *See:* Dutch elm disease.

Barker, Pat (1943-), British author. Barker won the Booker Prize in 1995 for *The Ghost Road*, the last part of a trilogy about the horrors on the western front in the first World War. The first two parts were *Regeneration* (1991) and *The Eye in the Door* (1993). Her other novels include *Union Street* (1982), which was turned into a movie as *Stanley and Iris*, *The Man Who Wasn't There* (1989), *Another World* (1998), and *Border Crossing* (2001).

Barlach, Ernst (1870-1938), German expressionist sculptor, graphic artist, and playwright whose figures in bronze and wood show Gothic and cubist influences. Barlach also produced many woodcuts and lithographs, some of them to illustrate his own writings. His war memorials and other works earned him fame in the 1920s, although he fell into disfavor under Hitler and his works were removed from museums.
See also: Gothic art and architecture.

Barley, adaptable and hardy cereal plants (*Hordeum vulgare* and *Hordeum distichon*), of the grass family, cultivated since ancient times. Russia is the largest producer, with Canada and the United States following. Over half of the world's crop is used for animal feed, and 10% is turned into malt.

Bar mitzvah, Jewish religious ceremony marking a boy's entrance into the adult community, traditionally performed at the age of 13. The initiate is usually called upon to read part of the weekly portion of the Pentateuch or the Prophets in the synagogue. The equivalent for girls, the bas (or bat) mitzvah, was established in 20th-century Reform and Conservative Judaism.
See also: Judaism.

Barnacle, marine crustacea of the subclass Cirripedia. The shell consists primarily of calcium carbonate. Adults attach themselves to solid surfaces (even the bodies of other sea animals) and trap plankton by means of feathery organs known as cirri. There are some 1,000 species.

Barnacle goose (*Branta leucopsis*), bird that breeds in the Arctic and winters in northern Europe and occasionally North America.

Barnard, Christiaan Neethling (1922-2001), South African surgeon who performed the first successful human heart transplant in Dec. 1967. His autobiography *One Life* was published in 1970.

Barnard, Edward Emerson (1857-1923),

The reunion, carved in 1926 in walnut by Ernst Barlach, is one of his many wood sculptures in the medieval German tradition he revived.
Barlach, a sculptor, graphic artist and playwright, was a major German expressionist (Ernst Barlach Haus, Hamburg).

U.S. astronomer who discovered Amalthea, the fifth satellite of Jupiter (1892). In 1916 he discovered Barnard's star, a red dwarf only 6 light-years from the earth, with the largest known proper motion.
See also: Jupiter.

Barnes, Djuna (1892-1982), U.S. poet, playwright, and novelist. Her works include a collection of stories and poems entitled *A Book* (1923) and the novels *Ryder* (1928) and *Nightwood* (1936).

Barney, Matthew (1967-), American fine artist. Since the 1990s he has been producing installations, sculptures, photos, videos and performances with a mythical character. Central issues are the American obsession with sports and health, bizarre sexual habits, travesty and androgyny. Odd rituals depict the same ancient as well as modern mythical creatures like, satyrs, made-up dandies, bikers and stewardesses, accompanied by attributes as dumbbells, fitness equipment and laboratory instruments. Barney is inspired by the body art of the 1970s.

Barn owl, common white owl (*Tyto alba*) useful as a destroyer of rodents. It grows to a length of about 18 in (46 cm), with a white face and cinnamon-dappled white breast. It nests in cliffs, hollow trees, and buildings. Its piercing scream is probably responsible for many tales of 'haunted houses.'

Barn swallow (*Hirundo rustica*), common North American bird. The upper parts of the wings and head are a metallic blue, the throat is chestnut brown, and the breast is white. Barn swallows eat insects harmful to crops.

Barnum, P(hineas) T(aylor) (1810-1891), U.S. impresario, showman, and publicist. The hoaxes, freaks, and curiosities exhibited in his American Museum (founded 1841) in New York included the original Siamese twins and General Tom Thumb. In 1871 he opened his famous traveling circus, which in 1881 merged with James A. Bailey's show to become Barnum and Bailey's 'Greatest Show on Earth.' Today there is a Barnum Museum in Bridgeport, Conn., the city of his birth.
See also: Circus.

Baroda (pop. 1,100,000; also Vadodara), city in Gujarat state, India. It is in western India near the Gulf of Cambay, about 230 miles (370 km) north of Bombay. Baroda lies at a railway junction and is a rapidly growing industrial city, producing such goods as foods, textiles, and chemicals. Oil and natural gas are produced nearby in the Gulf of Cambay. Attractions include old palaces and gardens, temples, museums, and an old city gate. Maharaja Sayajirao University is here. Baroda was the capital of the former princely state of Baroda from about 1734 until 1947.

Barometer, instrument for measuring air pressure, used in weather forecasting and for determining altitude. Most commonly encountered is the aneroid barometer, in which the effect of the air in compressing a thin

B

B

corrugated metal box is amplified mechanically and read off on a scale.
See also: Altimeter.

Baron, title of nobility in Europe, indicating a powerful man, especially a business magnate.

Baroque, European style of art and architecture, and by extension, music, that flourished from the early 17th to the mid-18th century. The style in art emphasized dramatic lighting, emotional portrayal of subjects, and the illusion of depth. The direct simplicity, apparent realism, and revolutionary painting technique of the Italian artist Michelangelo Caravaggio (1573-1610) helped to spread baroque art throughout Europe. The same effects were adapted to sculpture, as seen in the works of Giovanni Lorenzo Bernini (1598-1680). In Holland, where life was dominated by a prosperous Protestant middle class, religious and mythological subjects gave way to portraits, still lifes, interior scenes, and landscapes. Frans Hals (1580-1666), Rembrandt van Rijn (1606-69), and Jan Vermeer (1632-1675) explored techniques of light effects. In Flanders, high baroque art was epitomized in the art of Peter Paul Rubens (1577-1640). In France Caravaggio's influence can be seen in the works of Georges de la Tour (1593-1652), Louis le Nain (1593-1648), and Nicolas Poussin (1594-1665). After 1680 the impact of Rubens, who was employed at the French court, is evident. In Spain important painters of the Baroque included the court painter Diego Rodriguez de Silva y Velazquez (1599-1660) and Bartolome Esteban Murillo (1617-1682).
Music of the early Baroque was characterized by simplicity; the florid style often identified as baroque did not appear in music until around 1700. The Baroque also saw the cultivation of virtuoso instrumental writing and the development of the concerto by

Antonio Vivaldi (c.1675-1741). In France, Jean Baptiste Lully (1632-87) composed orchestral ballet music; in England, Henry Purcell (c.1659-95) wrote theater works and George Frideric Handel (1685-1759), oratorios. In Germany, church composer and organ and harpsichord virtuoso Johann Sebastian Bach (1685-1750) perfected the fugue.

Barquisimeto (pop. 680,000), capital of Lara state in northwestern Venezuela, about 220 mi (354 km) southwest of Caracas, founded in 1552. It is the commercial and agricultural center of central and western Venezuela.

Barracuda, predatory fish (family Sphyraenidae) found in warm seas. Barracudas have elongated, cigar-shaped bodies, long snouts, and sharp teeth. They strike automatically at any gleaming object.

Barras, Paul François Jean Nicolas, Vicomte de (1755-1829), French revolutionary. At first a Jacobin, in favor of Louis XVI's execution, he later became the most powerful member of the Directory (the revolutionary government) and aided Napoleon's rise to power. He was exiled after Napoleon's coup d'état of Brumaire (1799).
See also: French language.

Barrault, Jean-Louis (1910-1994), French actor, director, producer, and mime. He was with the Comédie Française 1940-46 and directed the Théâtre de France 1959-68. His most famous film role was that of the mime in *Les Enfants du Paradis* (1944).

Barrett, Elizabeth *See:* Browning, Elizabeth Barrett.

Barrichello, Rubens (1972-), Brazilian racing driver, initially successful in karting.

In 1990 he became European champion for Opel Lotus. After racing in the F3 (champion in 1991) and the F3000 (champion in 1992) he entered Formula One. Barrichello now drives for Jordan.

Barrie, Sir James Matthew (1860-1937), Scottish playwright and novelist best known for *Peter Pan* (1904), his play about a boy who will not grow up. His works-including *The Admirable Crichton* (1902), *What Every Woman Knows* (1908), and *Dear Brutus* (1917)-range in tone from whimsy and sentimentality to satire and pathos.

Barrier reef *See:* Coral; Great Barrier Reef.

Barrios, Justo Rufino (1835-1885), president of Guatemala from 1873 until his death in 1885. A dictator, Barrios dreamed of a united Central America. He died in El Salvador fighting to achieve that goal by force.
See also: Guatemala.

Barrios de Chamorro, Violeta (1939-), Nicaraguan politician. Chamorro, who was director of the family business, La Prensa (a conservative newspaper that was in opposition to Nicaragua's Sandinista government), became leader of the government in 1990 and president of Nicaragua. She was a candidate for the UNO, an electoral coalition of fourteen parties. In the early part of 1997 she was succeeded by the liberal, Arnoldo Alemán, who won the presidential election at the end of 1996.

Barrow, Point, northernmost point on the North American continent, at the tip of Point Barrow Peninsula on the Arctic coast of Alaska, named for Sir John Barrow, 19th-century British geographer. The city of Barrow lies some 12 mi (19 km) south.

Barry, Philip (1896-1949), U.S. playwright, best known for popular drawing room comedies such as *Holiday* (1928) and *The Philadelphia Story* (1939).

Barrymore, name of a noted Anglo-American theatrical family. The father was the British actor Herbert Blythe (1847-1905), who adopted the stage name **Maurice Barrymore** and came to the United States in 1875. **Lionel Barrymore** (1878-1954), their eldest child, became an outstanding stage, radio, and film actor. **Ethel Barrymore** (1879-1959) won an Academy Award for her supporting role in *None But the Lonely Heart* (1944). **John Barrymore** (1882-1942) was a distinguished interpreter of Shakespearean roles, particularly *Richard III* (1920) and *Hamlet* (1922). Later he became a popular and flamboyant film actor, nicknamed 'the great profile.'
His children **Diana Barrymore** (1921-1960) and **John Barrymore, Jr.** (1932-) also became actors. John Barrymore Jr.'s daughter **Drew Barrymore** (1975-) also became an actress.

Barter, exchange of goods or services instead of money. Many primitive economies work on this system, and barter agreements

A barograph is a device for measuring atmospheric pressure. It consists of an aneroid barometer that is connected to a recording instrument. The barometer (1), a flexible metal chamber controlled by a spring, responds to changes in air pressure by either contracting (A), or expanding (B).
A stylus (2) records these movements on a graph (3) that is mounted on a turning cylinder. Any fluctuation in pressure will immediately be registered (C). The cylinder completes one rotation a week.
A more sensitive microbarograph rotates once every 24 hours (D).

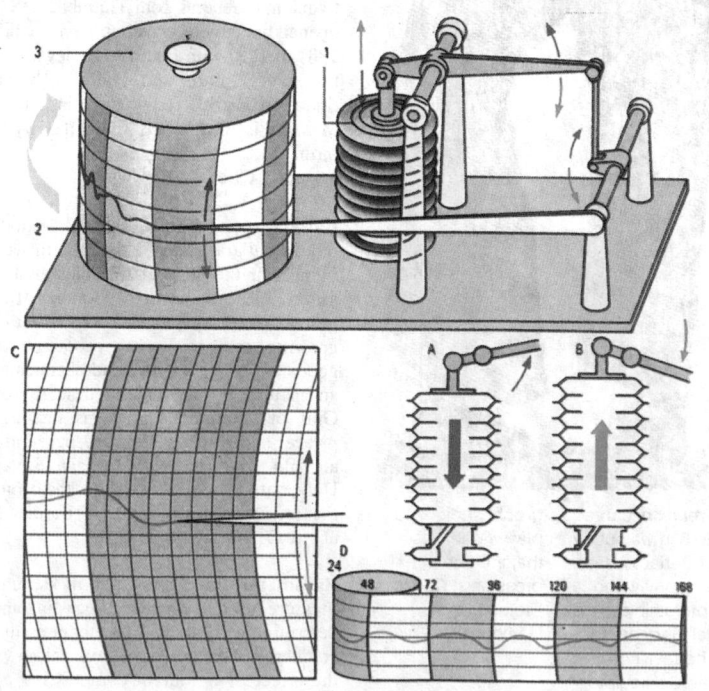

B

Interior of the Gesù in Rome: one of the very first Baroque churches, designed by Vignola (1507-1573) and Della Porta (around 1537-1602) The unity of architecture, sculpture and painting was very popular, as was the extravagant use of classic style elements.

Ensemble piece in the convent church of Rohr (Southern Germany). This Ascension of Mary clearly shows baroque's theatrical and dramatic nature. The smooth transitions from architecture to sculpture are a strong point; the figures really make use of the space with Mary rising towards the light from the skylight.

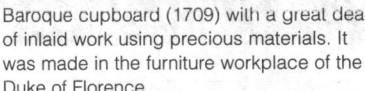

Baroque cupboard (1709) with a great deal of inlaid work using precious materials. It was made in the furniture workplace of the Duke of Florence.

Peter Paul Rubens (1577-1640) was one of the great Baroque painters. This is the Arrival of Maria de Médicis in Marseille.

B

The Immaculate Conception by the Italian Baroque painter Giovanni Battista Tiepolo (1696-1770).

Details of a ceiling fresco by Pietro da Cortona (1596-1669), a painter and architect who was famous for his illusionism.

are still common in international trade. During acute inflation when the value of money changes daily, a barter system may work better.

Barth, John (1930-), U.S. novelist known for his ironic style and use of comic and elaborate allegory. His best-known works include *The Sot-Weed Factor* (1960) and *Giles Goat-Boy* (1966). Other novels include *Sabbatical* (1982), *The Tidewater Tales* (1987), *Once Upon a Time* (1994), and *On With The Story* (1996).

Barth, Karl (1886-1968), Swiss theologian, one of the most influential voices of 20th-century Protestantism. He taught in Germany 1921-35, was expelled by the Nazis, and spent the rest of his life in Basel. In his 'crisis theology,' Barth stressed revelation and grace and reemphasized the principles of the Reformation, initiating a movement away from theological 'liberalism.'
See also: Protestantism.

Barthelme, Donald (1931-1989), U.S. short-story writer and novelist noted for his innovative techniques and surrealistic style. His works include the novels *Snow White* (1967) and *The Dead Father* (1975); the children's book *The Slightly Irregular Fire Engine or the Hithering Thithering Djinn* (1971), for which he won a National Book Award; and *Sixty Stories* (1981).

Barthes, Roland (1915-1980), French philosopher, literary critic, and theorist of semiology. His works include *Writing Degree Zero* (1953), *Mythologies* (1957), *A Lover's Discourse* (1978), and his autobiography, *Roland Barthes* (1975).

Bartholdi, Frédéric Auguste (1834-1904), French sculptor, creator of the Statue of Liberty. His other monumental works include *Lion of Belfort* at Belfort, France.

Bartholomew, Saint, one of the 12 apostles. According to tradition, he preached the Gospel in Asia Minor and India and was martyred in Armenia.
See also: Apostles.

Bartlett, John (1820-1905), U.S. editor and publisher, best known for his *Familiar Quotations*, which has gone through more than a dozen editions since its first appearance in 1855.

Bartók, Béla (1881-1945), Hungarian composer, one of the major figures of 20th-century music, also a virtuoso concert pianist and teacher at the Budapest Academy of Music (1907-34). In 1940 he emigrated to the United States. His work owes much to the rhythmic and melodic vitality of Eastern European folk music, on which he was an authority. Bartók's major works include his six string quartets (1908-39), *Music for Strings, Percussion*, and *Celesta* (1936), and *Concerto for Orchestra* (1943).

Barton, Clara (1821-1912), founder of the American Red Cross (1881) and its first president (until 1904). She began a lifetime of relief work by organizing care and sup-

plies for the wounded in the Civil War. On a trip to Europe (1869-73) she became involved in the activities of the International Red Cross, working behind German lines in the Franco-Prussian War. She was later influential in extending the range of the organization's relief work.
See also: Red Cross.

Baruch, Bernard Mannes (1870-1965), U.S. financier and presidential economic adviser. He was chairman of the War Industries Board in World War I, adviser to F. D. Roosevelt in World War II, and U.S. delegate to the UN Atomic Energy Commission in the 1950s, proposing the 'Baruch Plan' for international control of atomic energy.

Barye, Antoine Louis (1796-1875), French painter and sculptor who specialized in animal statues. His artwork is noted for its attention to detail. Barye also painted realistic landscapes.

Baryon, in particle physics, largest class of elemental particles, including protons, neutrons, and hyperons, also called 'heavy particles' because of their relatively high mass.
See also: Atom.

Baryshnikov, Mikhail (1948-), Soviet-born U.S. dancer and choreographer. He was a soloist with the Kirov Ballet, Leningrad, from 1966 until 1974, when he defected to the West, joining the American Ballet Theatre and appearing there and with other companies in modern and classical ballets. He served as director of the American Ballet Theatre 1980-89. In Philadelphia in 1990 he began his own company (the White Oak Dance Project). He starred in several films, including *The Turning Point* (1977), *White Nights* (1985), and *Giselle* (1987).

Mikhail Baryshnikov (1978) in Jerome (1948-), the Latvian Robbins's version of dancer, performs *Afternoon of a Faun.*

Barytes *See:* Barium.

Barzani, Idriss (d. 1987), Iraqi Kurdish leader. Barzani was a son of the legendary Kurdish leader Mustafa al Barzini. After his

father died in 1977, Idriss took over the leadership of the Kurdish Democratic Party (KDP) together with his brother Massoud. As a result of an agreement between the then Shah of Iran and President Saddam Hussein of Iraq, the KDP suffered a major defeat against the Iraqi army in 1975. Together with his brother he reorganized the party and entered into an alliance with the other opposition groups in Iraq. Thanks to the support given by Iran, the KDP managed to acquire large parts of the area in Iraq that is inhabited by the Kurds.

Barzani, Mustafa al- (1903-1979), Kurdish military leader, led revolts against Iraq (including in 1943) and became commanding officer of the troops of Mehabad, which was declared a republic by Qazi Mohammed in 1946. After his defeat, he took refuge in the Soviet Union. In 1961 Barzani led a revolt of the Pesh Merga ('Forward to Death') Kurdish forces against Kassem. In 1970 he entered into an agreement with Iraq that the autonomous state of Kurdistan would be established in 1974. Another war broke out when the Kurds refused to give up the oil-rich area in the Kirkuk province. This war resulted in another major defeat for the Kurds.

Basalt, dense rock formed by the solidification of lava. It underlies ocean floors and is the basis of most oceanic islands. Frequently dark in color, its main constituents are labradorite feldspar and pyroxene. Basalt strata usually consist of hexagonal columns produced by crystallization of the molten lava during a slow cooling process, as seen in the Palisades along the Hudson River, the Devil's Postpile National Monument, Calif., and the Giant's Causeway in Ireland.

Base, in chemistry, complement of an acid. Bases are often defined as substances that react with acids to form salts, or as substances that give rise to hydroxyl (OH⁻) in aqueous solutions.
See also: Chemistry.

Baseball, outdoor team sport which derives its name from the 4 bases on the playing field. Called the 'national pastime' in the United States, it is also popular in Japan, Latin America, and Canada. Invented, according to legend, by Abner Doubleday in Cooperstown, N.Y. in 1839, it appears rather to have evolved from the game of rounders which was played by New England colonists. Popular with Union troops during the Civil War, it was played nationally by the late 1880s.
Baseball is played on a large field between 2 opposing teams each consisting of 9 players: a pitcher, a catcher, 4 infielders, and 3 outfielders. The field consists of the infield, outfield, and foul territory. The infield is square, with a base at each corner-home plate, first, second, and third base. The foul lines extend from home plate past first base on one side and past third on the other, separating fair (infield and outfield) from foul territory. The pitcher's mound stands near the center of the infield. The outfield is the large area between the infield and the walls or fences farthest from home plate. While one team posi-

B

tions itself in the field, the other team bats. The pitcher, standing on the pitcher's mound, throws the small, hard ball (about 9 in/23 cm in circumference) over home plate, within an area between the batter's knees and shoulders (the strike zone)-sometimes at speeds over 90 mph (145 kmph). The batter attempts to hit the ball with the bat, a long rounded piece of wood or metal up to 42 in (107 cm) long and 2.75 in (7 cm) in diameter. A pitch outside of the strike zone is called a ball; 4 balls pitched to the batter allow the batter to 'walk' to first base. A pitch counts as a strike if the batter fails to swing at a good pitch, swings and misses, or hits the ball foul (except when there are already 2 strikes); 3 strikes and a batter is out. If the ball is hit into fair territory, the batter runs to first base. The batter is out if the ball is caught without a bounce (fly), if it is thrown to first base before the batter gets there, or if the batter is 'tagged' with the ball by a fielder. As new batters walk or get hits, earlier batters move around the bases. A batter reaching home plate scores a run. When 3 batters are out, the teams switch position. When each team has had a turn at bat, an inning is complete. A team wins by scoring the most runs within 9 innings. In the case of a tie, extra innings are added.

Players in the field wear padded leather gloves to catch the ball. All players wear shoes with spiked soles so they can start and stop quickly. Batters wear plastic batting helmets to avoid injuries. Catchers wear metal face masks, padded chest protectors, and shin guards. Most major league games have 4 umpires (game officials). The home plate umpire decides whether a pitch is a ball or a strike as well as whether runners attempting to reach home plate are safe or out. The other umpires rule on plays near as well as in the outfield.

There are 2 major baseball leagues; the American League (founded 1900), with 14 teams, and the National League (founded 1876), with 12. The teams in each league are divided into Eastern and Western Divisions. These teams play a 162-game schedule between April and September. The 2 divisional champions in each league meet in a playoff after the regular season, and the first team to win 4 games in each playoff is the league champion. The American and National League champions then play in the World Series. The first team to win 4 games in this series wins the world championship. In addition to major and minor leagues, the game is played in amateur leagues and college and high school associations, as well as by neighborhood teams of all age groups. Originally restricted to boys, baseball is now played by girls as well.

Basel (pop. 173,000), second largest city in Switzerland, capital of the half-canton of Basel Stadt. The city is Switzerland's only river port, located on the Rhine, its major trans-European railhead, and one of its most important commercial, industrial, and financial centers. Situated at the junction of the French and German borders, Basel is a key distribution center for raw materials and manufactured products between northern and central Europe. The most important industries are chemical, electrical, and machine engineering.
Founded by the Romans, Basel joined the Swiss confederation as a canton in 1501. It later became the center of the Protestant Reformation, Luther's writings being printed here. The city's ancient cathedral (founded 1019) housed the great ecumenical council of 1431-48, and Erasmus is buried there. Switzerland's oldest university, founded in 1459, is in Basel.
See also: Switzerland.

Baselitz, Georg (real name Georg Kern; 1938-), German painter, graphic artist, and sculptor who was trained in East (1955-1957) and West Berlin (1957-1964). Precursor of neo expressionism. His touch was initially heavy and he painted portions of landscapes and human limbs. From 1968-69 he turned the images upside down with the aim of studying the transition between abstract and figurative art, and to emphasize the actual art of painting. In this respect he consciously followed the conventional painting tradition. Since 1980 Baselitz has made large, roughly cut wooden sculptures based on the same concept of form.

Basenji, breed of dog, first bred in central Africa. The Basenji has short silky hair, pointed ears, and a wrinkled forehead. It weighs 22-24 lb (10-11 kg), and does not bark.

Bashkiria (also called Bashkortostan; pop. 4,100,000), Russian republic west of the Urals; 55,465 sq mi (143,598 sq km). Its capital is Ufa. Chemical and petrochemical industry, steel, electrotechnical, timber, and paper industry. Agriculture: grain, potatoes, and sugar beets. An oil pipeline runs to Omsk.
The population of Bashkiria consists of Bashkirs, Tartars, Russians, and Mari.
The first time Bashkiria's name is mentioned is in ninth and tenth century written sources. In 1557 the area was annexed by the Muscovite Empire, Russia. At the time, the population was mainly nomadic. Since the 17th century the exploitation of metallic ore has attracted many Russians. In 1919 the area became an autonomous Socialist Soviet Republic within the Soviet Union.

BASIC, Beginner's All-purpose Symbolic Instruction Code, easy-to-use, algebraic programming language developed at Dartmouth College in 1967 by John Kemeny and Thomas Kurtz. BASIC has a small repertory of commands and simple statement formats. For this reason, BASIC is widely used in programming instructions, personal computing, and business and industry.

Basie, Count (William Basie; 1904-1984), U.S. jazz pianist, composer, and bandleader. Count Basie's big band, which included some of the outstanding jazz musicians of the time, brought the ragged rhythm and improvisational verve of jazz into the smooth swing era of the late 1930s and 1940s.

Basil, annual aromatic herb of the mint family, native to Asia, whose leaves are used in cooking and in the preparation of Chartreuse liqueur. The most popular kinds are known as sweet basil (*Ocimum basilicum*).

Basilica, in its earliest usage, large public building of ancient Rome of characteristic rectangular layout, with a central area (nave) separated by rows of columns from 2 flanking side aisles with high windows. At one or both ends was a semicircular or polygonal apse. This design was adopted as a basic pattern for Christian churches from the time of Constantine (4th century A.D.). The term 'basilica' is also a canonical title for certain important Roman Catholic churches.

Basil the Great, Saint (c.330-379), one of the great Fathers of the Eastern Church, bishop of Caesarea, a founder of Greek monasticism and author of the *Longer* and *Shorter Rules* for monastic life.

Baskerville, John (1706-1775), English printer and type designer, whose elegant Baskerville type was the ancestor and inspiration of the 'modern' group of typefaces. He took great care in all aspects of his craft and produced many handsome editions.

Basketball, popular indoor team sport, the object of which is to score points by propelling a leather ball through a basket (hoop and net). Two baskets, 18 in (46 cm) in diameter and 10 ft (3 m) from the floor, are fixed on two backboards situated at either end of a court, the maximum dimensions of which are 94 x 50 ft (29 x 15 m). Basketball is played between 2 teams, each of 12 players and a coach, with 5 players from each team allowed on court at any one time (2 forwards, 2 guards, and a center, who is usually the tallest player on the team). The coach calls timeouts, advising the team on tactics and substituting players on the 'bench' for players who are tired, injured, off their stride, or disqualified. The ball is moved by *passing* from one player to another or by an individual player *dribbling* (bouncing) it, never by kicking or by carrying it more than one and a half steps. In addition to game violations involving illegal moves with the ball, there are *personal fouls*, involving bodily contact or unsportsmanlike conduct. Five fouls disqualify a player from the game. Basketball is a fast-moving game played within a relatively confined space.

The Basenji is one of the oldest breeds of dogs and was first raised to kill small predators.

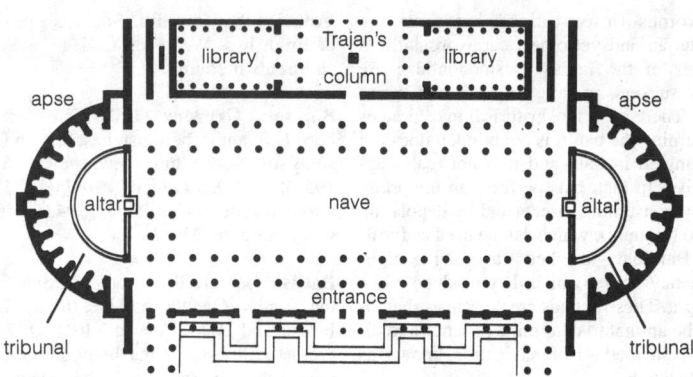

The Basilica Ulpia (98-112) in Trajan's Forum, Rome, was designed by Apollodorus of Damascus. The plan reveals a typical basilican structure with a wide central nave, double side aisles, and raised tribunals in semicircular apses with sacrificial altars at either end.

B

The game is split into 2 or 4 equal periods of play, with the actual playing time for the whole game varying between 32 minutes and one hour depending upon the level and whether U.S. or international rules govern the game. The game was originated by the American Dr. James A. Naismith in 1891. International interest in basketball was first kindled by an exhibition game played at the 1904 Olympic Games in St. Louis, Missouri. The game was once dominated by New York's Celtics (1915-28), the all-black New York Renaissance (1923-40s), and the all-black Harlem Globetrotters (formed 1928). Like the original New York Celtics, the Globetrotters became an exhibition team. Basketball is played in more countries than any other team ball game.

Basket making, popular handicraft dating back to prehistoric times. It uses flexible materials to make utensils, primarily for the preparation, transportation, or storage of food. Two kinds of material are used to make baskets: hard material including grasses, leaves, and wood, and soft material including cotton, wool, and jute fiber. Two different strands are woven together to produce the basket: the warp strand runs vertically, the weft horizontally.

Basking shark (*Cetorhinus maximus*), one of the largest living sharks, reaching a length of 45 ft (14 m). Found chiefly in temperate waters, the basking shark feeds only on plankton. The liver, a valuable source of oil, may account for a tenth of the total weight of the fish and provides the buoyancy that enables the shark to bask, motionless, on the surface. *See also:* Shark.

Bas mitzvah *See:* Bar mitzvah.

Basov, Nikolai Gennadievich (1922-), Russian physicist who, with his colleague Alexander Prokhorov, stated the principles of using molecular energy to amplify radio waves. They shared the 1964 Nobel Prize in physics with the U.S. physicist Charles H. Townes.

Basques, people of unique language and culture living mainly in the vicinity of the Pyrennees Mountains (about 100,000 in southwestern France and 600,000 in northeastern Spain). Research into their blood groups indicates a long separation from other Europeans. After the Spanish Civil War, in which many Basques fought against General Franco, an effort was made to subdue the region. A surge of Basque nationalism in recent years was marked by the assassination of Admiral Luis Blanco by the Basque resistance movement ETA in 1973. In 1980 the Basques were given limited political self-determination by Spain by allowing the 3 Basque regions of Spain a parliament and some control over police, education, taxes, and other administrative procedures.

Basra (pop. 620,000), city and major port in Iraq, situated on the Shatt-al-Arab River, about 75 mi (120 km) from the Persian Gulf. The actual port is the suburb of Al'Ashr, the old town of Basra being 2 mi (3 km) away. The third part of Basra is the modern port of Ma'quil, 4 mi (6 km) above Ashr and accessible to seagoing vessels. Oil is exported through the pipeline terminus at Fao, about 4 mi (6 km) downstream, where there is also a refinery. The other main industry is the packing and export of dates. Under the rule of the Abbasid family in the 8th century, and until its conquest by the Mongols in the 13th century, Basra was a center of Arabic culture noted for its mosques and library. The city was heavily damaged during the war with Iran in the 1980s and during Gulf War (1991). *See also:* Iraq.

Bas relief *See:* Relief.

Bass, fish of the Serranidae and Centrarchidae families. In Europe the name usually refers to saltwater fish of the family Serranidae, popular as game fish and food. Most of them grow to 2 ft (60 cm) or more, and the giant sea bass found in tropical waters may exceed 7 ft (2 m). The European bass is common around the Mediterranean and Atlantic coasts, but related species are found in shallow tropical waters and in fresh water. In the United States and Canada, the name is applied to freshwater fish of the Centrarchidae family. The black bass, one of the most popular of game fishes, is found in lakes and streams of eastern North America. Sunfish, the smaller members of the family, are often found in aquariums.

Bass, or double bass, largest instrument of the violin family. Its form is less standardized than the other string instruments, but it usually stands about 6 ft (2 m) high and has 4 strings 42 in (108 cm) long and tuned in fourths. To increase its range a fifth low string is sometimes added. The strings are made of thick copper wire or steel cable. They are played with a bow.

Bassae, site of one of the best-preserved temples of classical Greece, located near the ancient city of Phigalia in Arcadia. The temple of Apollo at Bassae was built at the end of the 5th century B.C. and its architect may have been Ictinus, builder of the Parthenon.

Bassano II (real name Jacopo da Ponte; 1510/19-1592), Italian painter, pupil of Veronese. Originally worked in the mannerist style: thin figures and flat compositions. Later turned to a more Baroque style. Talented artist who often transformed his religious works into genre pieces. Alternating warm and cold colors, free composition, and application of clair-obscure characterized his later work. His sons Francesco (1549-1592), who closely followed the style of his father (particularly as far as the genre element and the attention to landscape in his religious works was concerned), and Leandro (1553-1622), known mainly as a painter of religious portraits, also worked in his studio.

Bass drum *See:* Drum.

Basse-Terre (pop. 14,000), capital city of the French department of Guadeloupe in the Antilles islands in the Caribbean. Settled by the French in 1643, Basse-Terre is a transportation center exporting bananas, coffee, cocoa, and sugar. *See also:* Guadeloupe.

Basset hound, short-legged, long, heavy-bodied, long-eared dog. Averaging 12-14 in (30-36 cm) in height and 45-60 lb (20-27 kg) in weight, the basset is a scent hound originally bred for hunting by the abbots of St. Hubert in France.

Bassoon, musical instrument, bass of the woodwind family, an 8-ft (2.4-m) conical tube bent double, with a double-reed mouthpiece, 8 holes, 20-22 keys, and a range of 3.5 octaves. Irrational key placement and an unstable pitch make it difficult to play.

Basswood, or linden, tree (genus *Tilia*) of the linden family that grows to 120 ft (37 m) in height and 3.5 ft (107 cm) in diameter. The basswood tree is valued for ornamentation and shade as well as for its soft wood and tough bark.

Bastille, fortress in Paris built c.1370, destroyed during the French Revolution. It was first used to house political prisoners by Cardinal Richelieu, in the 17th century, but was almost empty by the time of the Revolution. It remained a symbol of oppression, however, and its capture on July 14,

B

1789, was the first act of the Revolution. Bastille Day, July 14, is a French national holiday.
See also: French Revolution.

Bastogne (pop. 13,400), small town on the Ardennes plateau in southeast Belgium. During the Battle of the Bulge, the German counteroffensive of 1944 in World War II, an American division under Gen. Anthony McAuliffe was surrounded here for some weeks before the Germans were driven back.
See also: World War II.

A fine example of a Roman medicinal bath survives in Bath, England. The Romans built health spas at the sites of hot mineral springs while occupying the area in the 1st century A.D. Today, Bath is still known as a fashionable spa and resort city.

Bat, nocturnal mammal, the only mammal capable of flight, a member of the order Chiroptera. There are almost 1,000 species of bats, accounting for about one-seventh of mammalian species. Bats generally live in caves, trees, roofs, and other enclosures, hanging upside down to sleep. Most are in-

sectivorous (insect-eating), but some are vegetarian and yet others carnivorous-the 3 species of the family Desmodontidae are blood suckers, preying on birds and mammals. There are a few historical inaccuracies concerning the bat. It is not blind, it does not get tangled in hair, and it is not really aggressive. In fact, bats perform an important job by consuming insects and by depositing guano (manure), which can be used as fertilizer. Bats navigate their travel using high-frequency noises which they produce while in flight. These sounds create echoes that allow the animal to determine distance and direction, a method of navigation known as echolocation.

Bataan Peninsula, province of southwestern Luzon, the Philippines. A mountainous jungle region historically known as the last stronghold of U.S. and Philippine troops who held out 3 months against Japanese forces in 1942, during World War II. The prisoners were sent on a 'death march' to a prison camp.
See also: Philippines; World War II.

Bataille, Georges (1897-1962), French writer, from 1922-1962 archivist at the Bibliothèque Nationale de Paris. In 1946 he founded the important literary magazine *Critique*. His work was influenced by surrealism and Nietzsche's pessimism. Bataille saw eroticism as a ray of hope in the somber human condition, for which reason it plays a central role in his work. Works include *On Nietzsche* (1945), *Literature and Evil* (1957), *Eroticism* (1957), *The Tears of Eros* (1961).

Batavia *See:* Jakarta.

Bates, Katharine Lee (1859-1929), U.S. author, best known for writing the lyrics of

'America the Beautiful.' She was a professor of English at Wellesley College and wrote children's literature.

Bateson, Gregory (1904-1980), British-born U.S. anthropologist, best known for his study of New Guinea, *Naven* (1936; rev. 1958), and *Ecology of Mind* (1972). He wrote *Balinese Character* (1943) with his wife, Margaret Mead.

Batfish, beautifully colored marine fish of the family Ogcocephalidae, found in the Indian and Pacific oceans. Its highly compressed, almost circular body and long fins give it the appearance of a bat when swimming.

Bath (pop. 80,000), city in southwest England, on the River Avon near Bristol. Bath was founded by the Romans, who were attracted by the mineral hot springs there. In the 1700s Bath became a resort for English high society. During World War II many government services were moved there.

Bath, Order of the, British honor, established by George I in 1725 (supposedly based on an order founded in 1399). There are two divisions, military and civil, with three classes in each: knight grand cross (G.C.B.), knight commander (K.C.B.), and companion (C.B.).

Baths and bathing, historically, primarily religious, social, or pleasurable functions more often than hygienic ones. The Egyptians, Assyrians, and Greeks all used baths, but the Romans developed bathing as a central social habit, constructing elaborate public buildings, often ornately decorated and of enormous size. A Roman bath contained several rooms for disrobing, exercise, and entertainment, as well as bathing. Men and women bathed at separate times, except for one brief period in the 1st century A.D. The baths were tended by slaves. After the fall of the Roman Empire bathing declined in popularity in Europe, though it did survive as a part of monastic routine, in Jewish ritual, and in Muslim countries. In Russia and Turkey the steam bath became popular. The crusaders brought steam bathing back with them from the Middle East, but an association with immorality caused it to fall into disrepute. In the 18th century it became fashionable to spend a season at a watering-place, such as Bath, England, but only 19th-century research into hygiene made a virtue of bathing, often with primitive and usually portable cold baths at schools and institutions. Only after World War I did plumbing and bathtub production allow the bath to become a permanent installation in the home.

Bathsheba, in the Bible, wife of King David and mother of Solomon. David married Bathsheba after arranging the death of her husband, Uriah the Hittite (2 Samuel 11, 12; 1 Kings 1-20).
See also: Bible.

Bathyscaph, submersible deep-sea research vessel, invented by Auguste Piccard in the late 1940s, comprising a small, spherical, pressurized passenger cabin suspended be-

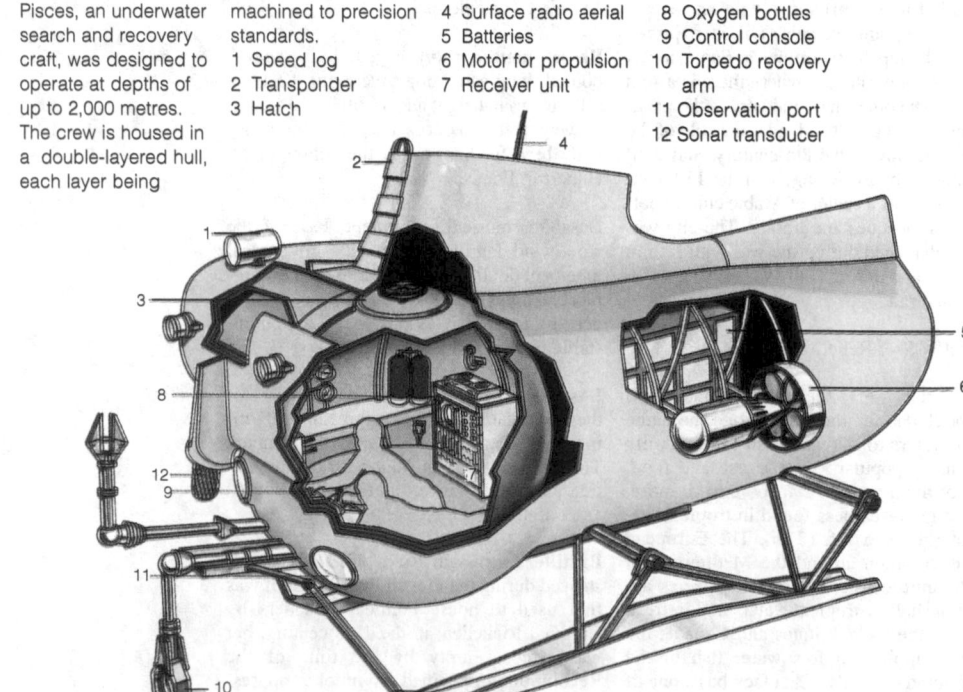

Pisces, an underwater search and recovery craft, was designed to operate at depths of up to 2,000 metres. The crew is housed in a double-layered hull, each layer being machined to precision standards.

1 Speed log
2 Transponder
3 Hatch
4 Surface radio aerial
5 Batteries
6 Motor for propulsion
7 Receiver unit
8 Oxygen bottles
9 Control console
10 Torpedo recovery arm
11 Observation port
12 Sonar transducer

neath a cigar-shaped flotation hull. Before dives most of the flotation tanks in the hull are filled with gasoline, the rest with air. For dives, the air is vented and seawater takes its place; seawater is allowed to enter the gasoline-filled tanks from the bottom, compressing the gasoline and increasing the density of the vessel. To begin descent, iron ballast is jettisoned. As the vessel rises, the gasoline expands, expelling water from the flotation tanks, thus lightening the vessel further and accelerating the ascent. Battery-powered motors provide the vessel with a degree of submarine mobility.

Batik, dyeing technique in which the portions of material not to be colored are covered with wax before the fabric is dipped into dye. After the dye is dry, the wax is removed by boiling and, if necessary, the procedure is repeated for each new dye. It is an ancient Indonesian technique, introduced into Europe by Dutch traders and now also used in Africa. Imperfections caused by the breaking or melting of the wax surface are responsible for much of the accidental effect that gives batik work its character.

Batista y Zaldívar, Fulgencio (1901-1973), Cuban military dictator. Becoming army chief of staff after the overthrow of the Machado government in 1933, he appointed and deposed presidents at will. He was himself president 1940-44, and took the title permanently in 1952. After his overthrow by Fidel Castro in 1959 he lived in exile in Spain.
See also: Cuba.

Bat mitzvah *See:* Bar mitzvah.

Baton Rouge (pop. 228,000), capital of Louisiana, situated on the Mississippi River. A deepwater port and regional trade center, the city also has major oil refineries and petrochemical and aluminum factories. Founded by the French in 1719, Baton Rouge was later transferred to the British and was occupied by the Spanish from 1779. U.S.-born citizens rebelled against Spanish rule and established their independence at the battle of Baton Rouge on Sept. 23, 1810. Acquired by the United States in 1815, the city was incorporated in 1817 and became the state capital in 1849.
See also: Louisiana.

Battenberg, name of princely family of Germany. **Prince Alexander of Battenberg** (1857-1893) was prince of Bulgaria 1879-1886. **Prince (Louis) Alexander of Battenberg** became a British subject, joined the Royal Navy, married the granddaughter of Queen Victoria, and changed his name to Mountbatten in 1917.

Battering ram, ancient war machine used to break down walls and doors. Used by the Assyrians and by Alexander the Great, it was made of a beam of heavy timber with a metal tip and survived as a weapon until the 1400s, when it was replaced by the cannon.

Battery, device for converting internally stored chemical energy into direct-current electricity. The term is also applied to various other electricity sources, including the solar cell and the nuclear cell, but is usually taken to exclude the fuel cell, which requires the continuous input of a chemical fuel for operation.
See also: Electric circuit; Fuel cell.

Battle of, Battles are listed under the key word, as in *Antietam, Battle of*.

Battleship, historically the largest of conventionally armed warships. Aircraft carriers superseded them during World War II as the largest fighting ships afloat. The largest battleship is the Japanese *Yamato* with 72,000 tons. The USS *Massachusetts* is now a floating marine museum in Fall River, Massachusetts. The most famous battleship is the German *Bismarck* with 41,000 tons.

Batu Khan (d. 1255 A.D.), Mongol conqueror of Russia, grandson of Genghis Khan. He ruled the westernmost part of the Mongol Empire and threatened eastern Europe from 1235 to 1242. He founded the khanate of the Golden Horde that ruled southern Russia for 200 years, isolating it from western European developments.
See also: Mongol Empire.

Baud, in computer technology, one bit per second. In general, the rate at which data is transmitted.
See also: Computer.

Baudelaire, Charles Pierre (1821-1867), French poet and critic, forerunner of the Symbolists. The poems in *Les Fleurs du Mal* (*The Flowers of Evil*, 1857), with their probing of even the most bizarre sensations, outraged public opinion and led to the poet's being tried for obscenity. His later prose poems were posthumously published in *Le Spleen de Paris* (1869). He was also a critic of music and fine art, and was renowned for his translations of Edgar Allen Poe.

Baudot, Emile *See:* Telegraph.

Baudouin (1930-1993), fifth king of the Belgians. He spent World War II with his family in Nazi internment, and succeeded his father, King Leopold III, who abdicated in 1951. In 1960 Baudouin proclaimed Congolese independence. He married a Spanish noblewoman, now Queen Fabiola. Succeeded by his brother Albert.
See also: Belgium.

Bauhaus, school of design and architecture in the 20th century. Founded by Walter Gropius in 1919 at Weimar, Germany, its teachers included some of the leading artists of the time. Gropius's ideal of uniting form with function is now a universal canon of design, and the dictum 'less is more' has influenced much U.S. design. The Bauhaus left Weimar in 1925 and was installed in new premises designed by Gropius in Dessau in 1927. The school was closed by the Nazis in 1933. Bauhaus teachers Gropius, Lyonel Feininger, and Ludwig Mies van der Rohe later moved to the United States.
See also: Gropius, Walter; Mies van der Rohe, Ludwig; Feininger, Lyonel.

A twelve-volt car battery has six two-volt cells, that are connected in series. A simple cell contains an anode (or electrically negative plate) of brown lead oxide, and a cathode (or positive plate) of porous grey lead, that are immersed in sulphuric acid. An electric current will flow when the plates are connected by an electric conductor. During discharge, the sulphuric acid will convert the anode to lead sulphate, thus reducing the strength of the acid. This process is being reversed during recharge. Each cell of a battery is made of several positive and negative plates, separated by porous insulators. The cells are housed in a hard rubber case and interconnected by lead bars.

Baum, Lyman Frank (1856-1919), U.S. children's writer, author of 14 Oz books, including *The Wonderful Wizard of Oz* (1900), a tale of a girl carried by a cyclone to a land of adventure. The 1939 film adaptation became a motion-picture classic.

Baum, Vicki (1888-1960), Austrian-born American novelist, settled in the U.S. in 1931. In her teens she studied music at the Vienna Conservatory, which was reflected in her novel *Der Eingang zur Bühne* (staged in 1920). Baum made her debut with heavy and serious novels like *Die Welt ohne Sünde* (1924), but after the worldwide success of *Menschen im Hotel* (People in a Hotel) (1929), she switched to more accessible prose full of local color (*Die Karriere der Doris Hart* (1936); *Marion lebt* (1941) and *Hier stand ein Hotel* (1944). She traveled widely to places such as East Asia and Mexico and her adventures are an important part of her literary oeuvre. Baum's works were prohibited in the Third Reich.

Baumfree, Isabella *See:* Truth, Sojourner.

Bausch, Pina (Philippines; 1940-   ), German dancer and choreographer. She studied at the Folkwang Schule in Essen and subsequently continued her study at the Juilliard School of Music in New York. In 1969 she was appointed Artistic Director of the Folkwang Tanzstudio which stemmed from the Folkwang Ballett and in 1973 she took up the management of the Wuppertal opera ballet. She renamed it into the

B

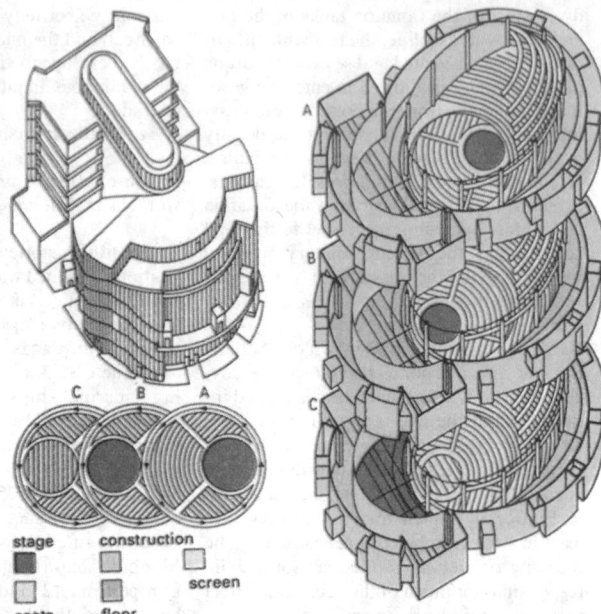

Bauhaus group picture showing (from left to right): Josef Albers, Hinnerk Scheper, Georg Musche, Laszlo Moholy-Nagy, Herbert Bayer, Joost Schmidt, Walter Gropius (with hat in center), Marcel Breuer, Vassily Kandinsky, Paul Klee, Lionel Feininger, Gunta Stolz, and Oskar Schlemmer.

Herbert Bayer, first a pupil and later a teacher of typography at the Bauhaus, designed this poster announcing a lecture by the German architect Hans Poelzig (New York, Museum of Modern Art).

Walter Gropius designed the Total Theater in 1927 to create a flexible theater in which the audience is drawn into the drama. The stage and the surrounding seats could be revolved, even during a performance, with stage settings created primarily by projection of film and lights. The three possible positions shown create (A) a central arena, (B) a classical Greek theater, and (C) a standard theater with the stage at one end.

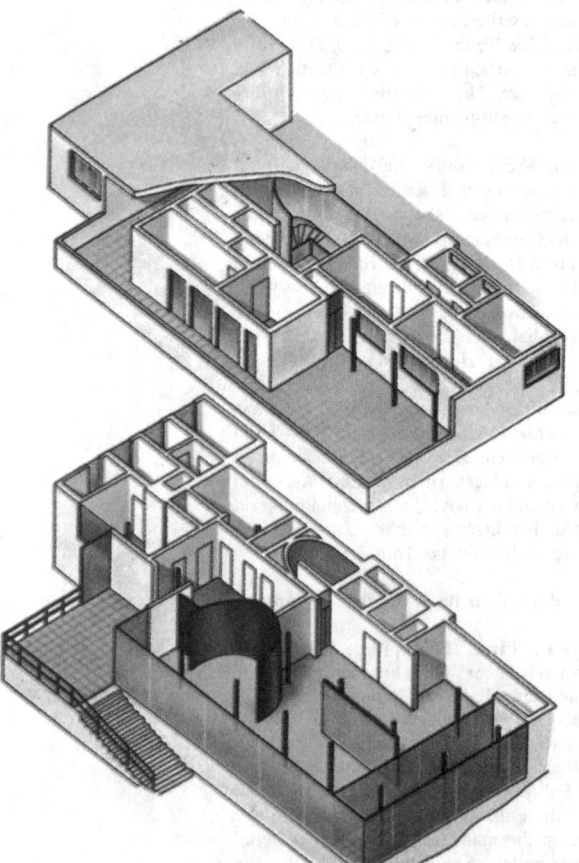

(Left) The concrete-surfaced Tugendhat House at Brno, Czechoslovakia (1930) was the last and most important European house designed by Mies van der Rohe.
It particularly illustrates the made-to-measure house, with an innovative large living room area partially subdivided to fulfill various functions.

(Right) Lionel Feininger, Woman in Mauve (1922, private collection, Lugano)

Wuppertaler Tanztheater and focused on dance. Although her choreographic work was initially very dance-oriented (Frühlingsopfer by Igor Stravinsky), in the course of time her productions became more static (more based on acting and mime) and also increasingly pessimistic. She based her works on the experiences of her dancers with whom she reminisced about the good old days during endless sessions, and from these discussions she eventually distilled her works at an average of one new production a year. Her husband, Rolf Borzik, was of great influence and provided her with his extraordinary decors: a thick layer of soil covered the stage for *Frühlingsopfer* in 1975, a high barrage in the background with people on top of it who were about to fall off for *Komm Tanz mit Mir* in 1977, and chairs all over the stage for *Cafè Müller* in 1978. With her works, Bausch influenced the dance scene of her time and, in particular, the dance scene in France.

Bauxite, ore consisting of hydrated aluminum oxide, usually with iron oxide; the main source of aluminum. It is a claylike, amorphous material formed by the weathering of silicate rocks, especially under tropical conditions. Bauxite is used as a lining for furnaces, and is an ingredient in some quick-setting cements. Leading bauxite-producing countries include Jamaica, Australia, the former USSR, Suriname, Guyana, France, and the United States.
See also: Aluminum.

Bavaria (German: *Bayern*), southwest state in Germany. Its area is 27,239 sq mi (70,549 sq km) and its population exceeds 12 million. Munich is the capital and administrative center, and the site of most of the state's industry. Forestry and agriculture are also important in Bavaria. The region's borders have often changed, and it has seen many rulers, including the Romans in the 6th century B.C. and Charlemagne in the 9th century A.D. Bavaria became a kingdom in 1805 and a part of Germany in 1871. Following World War I it was a short-lived republic and then part of Germany again. After World War II Bavaria was part of West Germany.
See also: Germany.

Bavarian Succession, War of the *See:* Succession wars.

Bay, inlet of water formed along the coastline of an ocean or lake. Examples include Hudson Bay, and the Bay of Bengal.

Bayberry (Myricaceae), any of a family of trees and shrubs found in temperate and subtropical climates. The waxy fruit of some species is used to make candles, scented soaps, sealing wax, and cosmetics.

Bay Colony *See:* Massachusetts.

Bayezid I (1360-1403), Turkish sultan. Oppressed rebellious vassals in Anatolia. In 1397-98 he conquered the principalities of Karamanoglu and Siva for the Ottoman Empire. After successful expeditions in Greece, Albania, and Bulgaria, he defeated the European princes who were allied against him - among others Jean Sans Peur - at Nicopolis in 1396. Bayezid I put great pressure on Constantinople but from 1399 onwards was threatened from the east by Timur. In 1402 he entered into battle with the latter at Angora in which he was defeated and taken prisoner. Bayezid I died in captivity.

Bayezid II (1447-1512) Turkish sultan. Took great interest in literature and mysticism. The victories gained during 1499-1502 by the reinforced Turkish fleet against the Venetians were the most important results of his active military reign. In 1511 his sons contested the succession. Aided by the Khan of the Crimea and the Janissaries, his son Selim forced Bayezid II to abdicate on the 25th April 1512.

Baylor, Elgin (1934-), U.S. basketball player and coach. Baylor, a 6 ft 5 in (196 cm) forward, played on the Los Angeles (formerly Minneapolis) Lakers of the National Basketball Association (NBA) from 1958 to 1971 and is considered one of the best all-around players in history. His achievements include being named NBA Rookie of the Year (1958-1959), and scoring 71 points in a game (1960). Baylor was head coach for the New Orleans Jazz (1976-1979), and is director of basketball operations for the Los Angeles Clippers (1986-).

Bay of Bengal, wide arm of the Indian Ocean between India and Ceylon on the west, and Burma on the east. In the north, along the coast of Bangladesh, the sea is shallow because vast quantities of silt are brought down by the rivers. Further south the depth increases to a maximum of 13,020 ft (3,968 m). The winds and surface sea currents vary with the prevailing monsoon: clockwise with the northeast monsoon and counterclockwise with the southwest monsoon. In October particularly, at the change of monsoon, very severe storms occur. The important rivers flowing into the bay are the Ganges, Brahmaputra, Godavari, Kistna, and Cauvery.
See also: Indian Ocean.

Bay of Biscay, section of the Atlantic Ocean adjoining northern Spain and part of the west coast of France. The name is a corruption of 'Vizcaya,' the term used by the Basques, an ethnic group populating northern Spain and southern France.
See also: Atlantic Ocean.

Bay of Fundy, funnel-shaped inlet of the Atlantic Ocean between New Brunswick and Nova Scotia in Canada. It is known for having the highest tides in the world, reaching up to 50 ft (15 m) in some parts.
See also: Atlantic Ocean.

Bay of Pigs, English name for Bahia de Cochinos (southwestern Cuba), scene of an abortive invasion of Cuba on April 17, 1961. The invaders were Cubans who had fled to the United States after Fidel Castro seized power. Although U.S. citizens were not directly involved, the CIA helped plan the invasion. The invasion was a political disaster for President Kennedy, who had approved the operation.

Bayonet, stabbing or thrusting weapon that may be fitted at the muzzle of a rifle without preventing normal firing. Usually consisting of a straight tapering blade, but sometimes a sabre or cutlass, it is used in close combat.

Bayou, shallow, slow-moving creek or water channel running into a lake or a river. The word is Louisiana French, probably derived from the Choctaw (Native American) *bayuk*.

Bayreuth (pop. 73,000), industrial city in northeastern Bavaria, Germany. It is famous as the last home of Richard Wagner and as the site of his opera house, the Festspielhaus. The Bayreuth festivals, held each summer since 1876, feature Wagner's music.
See also: Wagner, Richard.

Bazargan, Mehdi (1907-1995), Iranian politician. Bazargan studied thermodynamics in Paris and taught at the University of Teheran from 1937. From 1951 until 1953 he was director of the state oil company. He was imprisoned several times due to his activities in the National Front, which opposed the Shah, and the Iranian Liberation Movement, which he founded in 1961. After the Shah fled the country and the Ayatollah Khomeini assumed power in early 1979, Bazargan was appointed prime minister. His moderate views, however, constantly clashed with those of the fundamentalists. Six months later he stepped down in protest against the occupation of the American embassy in Teheran. Since then he has opposed Islamic rule.

Bazooka, portable rocket launcher constructed from a smooth-bore steel tube 5 ft (1.5 m) long and open at both ends. Two people operate it: The midpoint of the tube rests on the shoulder of one person, who aims and fires the weapon while the other person loads the rockets.

BBC *See:* British Broadcasting Corporation.

B.C., 'Before Christ' in the Christian (and now generally Western) system for dating events, developed by the monk Dionysius Exiguus and based on the time he believed Christ to have been born. The year of Christ's birth is considered the year 1, and the higher the number, the earlier the event. The year 100 B.C., for instance, was the year before 99 B.C. Events in the years after the birth of Christ are designated A.D. (for the Latin *Anno Domini*, 'in the year of our Lord'). The expressions B.C.E. ('Before the Common Era') and C.E. ('Common Era') are also used.

BCG, bacillus Calmette-Guérin, a vaccine used to immunize against tuberculosis.

Beach, Sylvia (1887-1962), U.S. expatriate bookstore owner whose Paris shop, Shakespeare & Co., was the center of expatriate literary life in Paris during the interwar period. James Joyce, Ernest Hemingway, and other important writers were frequent visitors. Beach published Joyce's *Ulysses* (1922).

B

B

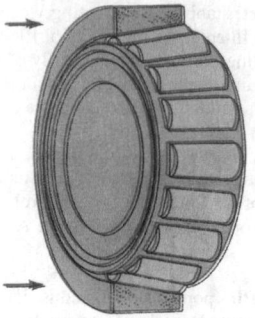

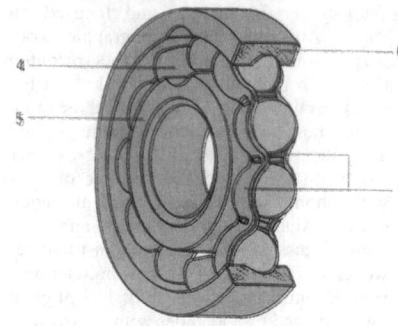

A roller bearing reduces friction because of the fact that each roller is only in line-contact with the housing. This line-contact also reduces axial movement, which gives this type of bearing an advantage over a normal ball bearing.

Ball bearings have wide applications in systems that involve circular motion. Friction is drastically reduced, because contact between moving parts is being made along the diameters of the steel balls. This particular bearing is designed to take lateral forces from one side: the outer ring (1) has a ledge on the right (3). The balls are kept in place by an extra inner ring (2).

In this caged ball bearing, friction is being further reduced by a smaller area of contact of the balls. The cage (7) prevents the balls from bunching, and also facilitates a reduced number of balls to keep the outer (6) and the inner ring (5) apart. Through the dimple (4) in the inner ring, the balls are placed inside the bearing.

Beach plum, wild shrub (*Prunus maritima*) of the rose family, found along the eastern coast of the United States from Virginia to Maine. It produces an edible fruit, resembling a small plum, used in sauces, preserves, jellies, and pies.

Beacon, originally a warning sign or signal, for example, a fire kindled at a prominent point on the coast to warn of the approach of hostile fleets.

Beaconsfield, Earl of *See:* Disraeli, Benjamin.

Beaded lizard (*Heloderma horridum*), poisonous lizard found in Mexico, close relative of the Gila monster. It is slow-moving, with small bead-like scales and markings of alternate black and pink-orange rings, and has hooked, grooved teeth. Glands along the inside of the lower lip secrete poison.

Beads, term derived from the Saxon word *biddan*, meaning to pray. Primitive beads were made of seeds, pierced shells, teeth, and stone; later materials ranged from semiprecious stones to gold and silver. Beads have been used by humans since before history. Magical properties were assigned to them, such as the promotion of fertility and the ability to guard against evil

Beans (*P. vulgaris*) are among the world's most important food crops. Shown (left to right) are the snap bean bush; flowers; green and yellow (or wax) snap beans, which are harvested when the pods are immature and soft; and the leaves and immature and mature pods of the shell, or horticultural, bean. The shell bean is harvested when the pod is hard and mature and the bean is dry with a somewhat nutty taste.

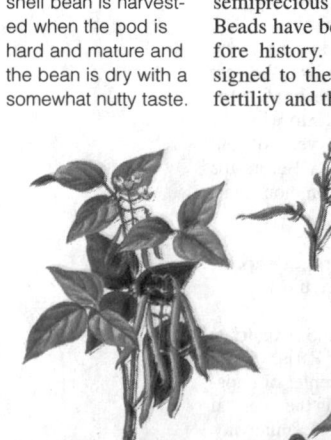

spirits. They were often exported over vast distances by explorers for trade.

Beagle, small, short-legged hound originally bred for hunting hares. They can grow up to 15 in (38 cm) tall. Beagles weigh from 20 to 40 lb (9-18 kg).

Beagle *See:* Darwin, Charles Robert.

Beaked whale, any of various medium-sized toothed whales whose snouts are narrow and pointed. They feed mainly on cuttlefish and generally have 2 or 4 teeth protruding from the lower jaw. There are 15 species living in all seas.

Bean, any plant of the pulse family (especially genus *Phaseolus*), also called legumes, cultivated for its edible seeds, immature pods, or shoots. The high protein content of beans, and especially of soybeans, make them a staple item in the diets of many peoples as well as an important animal feed. Soybeans are also used for a growing range of industrial products including adhesives, plastics, and firefighting foam.

Bean beetle, insect (*Epilachna varivestis*) of the order of beetles (Coleoptera), and the ladybug family (Coccinellidae). A serious pest to bean plants in Mexico, the bean beetle was accidentally introduced into Alabama

around 1920, and later spread through the central and eastern United States and southern Canada.

Bean curd *See:* Tofu.

Bear, large mammal (family Ursidae), usually omnivorous, characterized by heavy build, thick limbs, small tail, and small ears. All have coarse thick hair which is, with the exception of the polar bear, dark in color. Species include the brown bear, the North American black bear, the spectacled bear, the Asiatic black bear, the sun bear, and the sloth bear. The Kodiak, a brown bear, is the largest, up to 9 ft (2.7 m) tall and 1,600 lb (730 kg).

Beard, Charles and Mary, U.S. authors and historians who coauthored seven books, the best-known being *The Rise of American Civilization* (2 vols, 1927) and its sequels. **Charles Austin Beard** (1874-1948) was author of more than 70 books, his most controversial was *An Economic Interpretation of the Constitution* (1913), in which he argued that the U.S. Constitution reflected the economic interests of its authors. **Mary Ritter Beard** (1876-1958), an author and leader of the women's rights movement, focused on the historical role of women.

Bearded collie, breed of dog distinguished by a beardlike growth of hair around its mouth. Bred in Scotland as a sheep and cattle herder, the bearded collie is a popular farm pet. It stands 20-25 in (51-56 cm) tall and weighs about 60 lb (27 kg).

Beardsley, Aubrey Vincent (1872-1898), English illustrator and author. By 1894 Beardsley had become art editor of the *Yellow Book* magazine and a prolific artist. His graphic style was one of sharp black-and-white contrasts, with flowing lines and detailed patterning; his subject matter-for instance, Oscar Wilde's *Salomé*, or Aristophanes' *Lysistrata*-tended toward the decadent or erotic.

Beardtongue, any of a genus (*Pentstemon*) of

tubular flowers containing five stamens. The flower derives its name from the fifth stamen, whose strands of yellow filament give a beardlike appearance. These flowers are native to northeast Asia and North America and are widespread in the United States.

Bearing, device to minimize friction and provide support and guidance for the moving parts of a machine. There are 2 main types of bearings-plain or journal bearings, and ball or roller bearings. In the plain bearing, a sheath lined with a special metal is clamped around a turning or sliding axle or journal. Plain bearings are used in engines and industrial machines. In roller or ball bearings, small round balls or rollers are placed between the journal and the housing of the bearing case. Contact is made only at points (ball bearings) or along thin lines (roller bearings), thus reducing friction to a minimum. Ball bearings are used mainly with revolving axles such as those of cars. Roller bearings are used to carry heavy loads at relatively slow speeds. Bearings were first used in Egypt to move blocks of stone from quarries to build palaces and pyramids.

Bears and bulls, popular terms for stock and commodity investors of opposing views of market prospects. Bulls believe that stock prices will rise, bears that they will fall. Bulls therefore buy, where bears seek to sell, either to prevent a loss or to buy back at lower prices. Rising stock values are therefore referred to as a bullish market, while falling ones constitute a bearish market.
See also: Commodity exchange.

Beat generation, U.S. literary movement of the 1950s, exemplified by Jack Kerouac's *On the Road* (1956), the adventures of the original social dropout, Allen Ginsberg's long poem *Howl*, and work by such poets as Lawrence Ferlinghetti and Gregory Corso, and by novelist William S. Burroughs. The movement, a protest against complacent middle-class values, was short-lived, but influenced artistic experiments for the next 15 years.
See also: Kerouac, Jack; Ginsberg, Allen; Ferlinghetti, Lawrence.

Beatitudes, in the New Testament, 8 blessings pronounced by Jesus as a prologue to the Sermon on the Mount (Matthew 5:3-10), in which he calls 'blessed' those who are poor in spirit, the meek, those who mourn, those who seek after holiness, the merciful, the pure in heart, the peacemakers, and those who suffer persecution for righteousness' sake.
See also: New Testament.

Beatles, English rock music group that dominated popular music in the 1960s. Guitarists and composers **John Lennon** (1940-80), **Paul McCartney** (1942-), and **George Harrison** (1943-2001), and drummer **Ringo Starr** (Richard Starkey; 1940-), won fame in Britain with their recording 'Please Please Me' (1963). The 1964 song 'I Want to Hold Your Hand' introduced them to the United States, where their concerts became scenes of mass adulation. *Revolver* (1966) and *Sgt. Pepper's Lonely Hearts Club Band* (1967) are ranked among their finest albums. The

group disbanded in 1970. John Lennon's murder by a demented fan in New York City (December 1980) caused mourning around the world. In 1995, the other three members launched a new single 'Free as a Bird', using a demo tape with John Lennon's voice.
See also: Lennon, John; McCartney, (James) Paul.

Beaton, Sir Cecil Walter Hardy (1904-1980), English photographer and designer, known for his royal portraits, collections such as *Cecil Beaton's Scrapbook* (1937), and set and costume designs for shows and films such as *My Fair Lady* (stage, 1956; motion picture, 1964).

Beatrix (1938-), queen of the Netherlands (1980-), following the abdication of her mother, Juliana.
See also: Netherlands.

Beauchamp, Kathleen *See:* Mansfield, Katherine.

Beaufort scale, scale from 0 to 12 used to measure the force of wind. An 8 on the scale signifies a gale and a 12 a hurricane.
See also: Wind.

Beauharnais, Joséphine de (1763-1814), first wife of Napoleon I and empress of France. Her first husband, General Alexandre, Vicomte de Beauharnais, was guillotined in the Reign of Terror. Their son, Eugène de Beauharnais (1781-1824), was made viceroy of Italy by Napoleon. He distinguished himself in campaigns against Austria and Russia.

Beaumarchais, Pierre Augustin Caron (1732-1799), French dramatist and variously an artist, litigant, and political agent. His best-known plays, *The Barber of Seville* (1775) and *The Marriage of Figaro* (1784), the basis of operas by Rossini and Mozart, ridiculed the established order and the nobility. He was instrumental in furnishing the Americans with arms and money at the outbreak of their Revolution.

Beaumont, Francis (1584-1616), English Jacobean playwright. He is best known for his collaborations with John Fletcher, although Beaumont is probably the sole author of *The Woman Hater* (1607) and *The Knight of the Burning Pestle* (1607?). Beaumont and Fletcher's works include *Philaster* (1608), *The Maid's Tragedy* (1609), and *A King and No King* (1611).
See also: Fletcher, John.

Beaumont, William (1785-1853), U.S. army physician noted for his research on the human digestive system. He treated a trapper with a gunshot stomach wound; when the abdomen wouldn't close, Beaumont conducted experiments over several years to analyze the digestive process.
See also: Digestive system.

Beauvoir, Simone de (1908-1986), French writer and a leading exponent of Existentialism and the role of women in politics and intellectual life. Her best-known works are *The Second Sex* (1953) and *The*

French author (1908-1986), at the age of 64.
Simone de Beauvoir

Mandarins (1956). She also wrote an autobiographical trilogy, and a moving account of her mother's death, *A Very Easy Death* (1966). Jean-Paul Sartre was her close associate.
See also: Existentialism.

Beaver, large rodent (family Castoridae), weighing up to 100 lb (45 kg) or over, of northern lands. Beavers have thick, furry waterproof coats, powerful, web-footed hindlegs, and small forelimbs with dexterous, sensitive paws. Although lissencephalic (smooth-brained), they are the most intelligent rodents, building dams and lodges (domes up to 23 ft/7 m in diameter, in which they live) from logs and mud. They use their powerful incisor teeth to fell trees and gnaw logs into shape. Their large, heavy tails are used on land for balance and in the water as rudders. Their respiratory system enables them to remain underwater for up to 15 minutes.

Beaverbrook, William Maxwell Aitken, 1st Baron (1879-1964), Canadian-born British newspaper owner and Conservative cabinet minister under Winston Churchill. Among his mass-circulation newspapers were the *Daily Express*, *Sunday Express*, and *Evening Standard*.

Bebel, August (1840-1913), leading German socialist and cofounder of the Social Democratic Party (1869). A strong

The Beatles in their early years of success. From left to right: John Lennon, Ringo Star, George Harrison and Paul McCartney.

B

antimilitarist and fighter for women's rights, his *Women and Socialism* was published in 1879.

Bebop *See:* Jazz.

Becker, Boris (1967-), German tennis player. He was the youngest winner of the men's singles title at Wimbledon (1985) and he won it again the following year. In 1988 he helped West Germany win its first Davis Cup, while winning the Masters and World Championship the same year. In 1989 he won his third Wimbledon title. Among other victories were the U.S. Open in 1989, the Masters tournament (1992), and the Australian Open in 1991 and 1996. Becker ended his career in 1999.

Becker, Jurek (1937-1997), German writer. Becker, of Polish-Jewish origin, spent his early years in a ghetto in the town where he was born and in German concentration camps. After the war he relocated to East Berlin. His first novel *Jacob the Liar* (1969), about a person who lives in a ghetto and tries to keep up morale among the other ghetto occupants with radio messages he invents himself, was hailed as a masterpiece. In his later works like his novels *Sleepless Days* (1978) and *Bronstein's Children* (1986), the fate of the Jews before, during, and after the war plays an important role. From 1986 he became well known as scenario writer of the popular television series *Darling Kreuzberg*. By then he had lived in West Berlin for about decade, ever since he was expelled from the East German writers' union in 1976 for supporting the protests against Wolf Biermann being sent into exile.

Becket, Saint Thomas à (1118?-1170), martyr and archbishop of Canterbury. He first served as chancellor under Henry II, becoming a close friend. In 1162 he was ap-

Bee (*Hymenoptera*)

pointed archbishop of Canterbury. After years of dissension with the king, in 1170 he was murdered in the cathedral of Canterbury by four knights inspired by some rash words of the king.

Beckett, Samuel Barclay (1906-1989),

Irish dramatist and novelist, resident in France from 1937. His work, much of it written in French, deals with habit, boredom, and suffering, and is deeply pessimistic. His novels include *Murphy* (1938) and the trilogy, *Molloy*, *Malone Dies*, and *The Unnameable* (1951-53). Among his plays are *Waiting for Godot* (1952) and *Happy Days* (1961). Beckett won the 1969 Nobel Prize for literature.

Becquerel, Antoine Henri (1852-1908), French physicist, discoverer of natural radioactivity in uranium (1896). He shared the 1903 Nobel Prize for physics with Pierre and Marie Curie.
See also: Radioactivity.

Bedbug, blood-sucking insect of the order Hemiptera (bugs), family Cimicidae. Parasites on warm-blooded animals, bedbugs are about one-quarter in (6mm) long and may survive for a year without feeding.

Bede, Saint (673?-735), known as The Venerable Bede, Anglo-Saxon monk and scholar. His *Ecclesiastical History of the English Nation*, written in Latin, is a major source for the early history of England.

Bedlington terrier, long-legged, fleecy-coated breed of terrier first bred in Bedlington, England, in the 19th century. It stands about 16 in (41 cm) tall and weighs 22-24 lb (10-11 kg), and was bred to fight badgers.

Bedouin, nomadic peoples of the Middle East and North Africa, especially the Syrian, Arabian, and Sahara deserts. Many bedouins have adopted non-nomadic life styles as a result of 20th-century development.

Bed sore, ulceration of the skin on the back of a person who is bedridden. Pressure of the bed against the skin first restricts the blood supply and then, by friction, breaks down the tissues into an ulcer (sore).

Bedstraw, any of a group of wild plants (genus *Galium*) found in damp woods and swamps. They have slender, square stems and fine needle-shaped leaves arranged in whorls of four to eight. The clustered flowers may be white, brown, yellow, or green. The name is derived from their former use as mattress stuffing.

Bee, any of about 20,000 species of flying insects of the superfamily Apoidae. Bees cross-pollinate plants and convert nectar into honey. Social bees (honeybees and bumblebees) live in complex societies of 10,000-50,000 members. Headed by the queen (who lays up to 2,000 eggs a day), the colony also includes female workers, who collect pollen and build cells, and fertile male bees, or drones.
See also: Beeswax; Honey; Pollen; Bumblebee.

Beech, common name for a family (Fagaceae) of deciduous forest trees indigenous to the Northern Hemisphere. Featuring thin, smooth gray bark, oval leaves, and edible nuts, beech trees may grow up to 100 ft

(305 m) high. The European beech is ornamental; the American beech is used for furniture and flooring.

Beecham, Sir Thomas (1879-1961), English conductor, founder of the London Philharmonic and the Royal Philharmonic orchestras.

Beecher, Henry Ward (1813-87), U.S. clergyman, orator, lecturer, author, and abolitionist. The preacher of Plymouth Congregational Church (1847-87) in Brooklyn, N.Y., he was an advocate of women's suffrage and of the theory of evolution.

Bee-eater, any of various species of insect-eating birds (family Meropidae) living mainly in tropical Africa and Asia. They range in length from 6 to 14 in (15-36 cm), are usually green and yellow, and have long curved beaks.

Beef, the flesh of mature cattle slaughtered for food. Leading beef consuming and exporting countries include the United States, Argentina, Australia, Canada, and New Zealand.

Bee fly, insect of the family Bombyliidae that closely resembles a bee but has only one pair of wings and no stinger.

Beefwood, pine-like tree (*Casuarina equisetifolia*) native to Australia and commonly found in warm climates around the world. It thrives in sandy soil, grows to 50 ft (15 m), and is prized for its dense, hard wood.

Beekeeping, practice of cultivating bees dating back over 7,000 years. In prehistoric times, people and animals collected honey from the nests of wild bees. Today the main value of the domestic honey bee is the pollination of crops.

Beelzebub, in the Bible, one of the names for the devil.

Beer, alcoholic beverage known since ancient times, made by fermenting cereals. Ale, stout, porter, and lager are varieties of beer. Today beer is produced worldwide but the beers of Germany and Holland are especially popular. The alcohol content of beer can range from 2 to 6%.

Beerbohm, Sir Max (1872-1956), English critic, satirist, and caricaturist best known for his caustic but benign characterizations of eminent Victorian and Edwardian figures, his satirical novel about Oxford, *Zuleika Dobson* (1911), and his parody *A Christmas Garland* (1912).

Beersheba (pop. 140,000), chief city of the Negev Desert in southern Israel, 45 mi (72 km) southwest of Jerusalem. The city was closely associated with the biblical patriarchs Abraham and Isaac. After almost 2,000 years of somnolent existence, Beersheba was rebuilt by the Turks in the late 19th century. Since 1948 it has grown into a major industrial, trading, and transportation center.

B

Beeswax, yellow secretion of the glands on the abdomen of worker bees, who use it to make honeycombs. After the honey is removed, the honeycomb is melted in boiling water to yield the beeswax, which is used in such products as candles, chewing gum, cosmetics, and polishes.

Beet (*Beta vulgaris*), biennial or annual root vegetable. Red beets are edible; white-rooted sugar beets provide about one-third of the world's sugar supply; spinach beets, or chard, are used as herbs, and mangel-wurzel for fodder.

Beethoven, Ludwig van (1770-1827), German composer, recognized worldwide as one of history's greatest musicians. His progressive deafness, total by the time he reached his late 40s, never interfered with his creativity. Beethoven's work may be divided into 3 periods. During the first, ending about 1802, he was still influenced by Haydn and Mozart. The middle period, ending about 1816, was his most productive. His individual style was developed in such works as the Third (*Eroica*) and Fifth symphonies, the Fifth Piano Concerto (*Emperor*), the *Kreutzer* Violin Sonata, and his only opera, *Fidelio*. His later, more intense works include the Ninth (Choral) Symphony, the *Missa Solemnis* (Mass in D), and the late string quartets, including the Great Fugue.

Ludwig van Beethoven (1770-1827), as painted in 1815 by Willibrord Joseph Mahler (1778-1860) (Gesellschaft der Musikfreunde collection, Vienna).

Beetle, any of the more than 250,000 species of the insect order Coleoptera. Beetles are found worldwide except in oceans and have evolved adaptations to nearly all extremes of climate and environment. Beetle eggs hatch into soft, usually wormlike, larvae known as grubs. These grow and metamorphose into pupae, which are soft but resemble adult beetles in form. Pupae often live underground while they develop into adults. Adult beetles range from 1/32 in (1 mm) to over 6.5 in (16 m) in length. Their hard, protective wing cases enclose the fragile flight wings. Beetles are generally plant eaters. Many beetles, such as weevils and leaf beetles, are serious pests to crops, eating seeds

or boring into roots and stems. Ladybugs are helpful to humans, feeding on other insect pests.

Beggar-tick, or stick-tight, flowering plant of genus *Bidens* of the composite family, named for the hairy, barbed seeds of its yellow flowers, which adhere to clothing or animal fur. The name is often applied to the tick trefoil, a plant of a different family (Leguminosae) but with similar barbed seeds.

Beggarweed, tall (6 ft/1.8 m), fast-growing, flowering plant (*Desmodium tortuosum*), native to the West Indies and now found in many warm climates. Beggarweed is commonly cultivated as a natural fertilizer; its roots are a source of nitrogen-fixing bacteria.

Begin, Menachem (1913-1992), Israeli prime minister, 1977-1983. Begin was active in the Zionist Movement's effort to create a Jewish state in the 1930s and 1940s. He fought in the Arab-Israeli war of 1948. He was elected to the Knesset (parliament) in 1948, with Israel's independence, and was an opposition leader for most of the next 30 years, pressing Israel's claim to the West Bank of the Jordan River and refusing to consider sovereignty for the Palestinians. Begin signed a peace treaty with Egypt in 1979; in 1978 he shared the Nobel Peace Prize with Egyptian President Anwar Sadat. In 1982 Begin launched a much criticized invasion of Lebanon intended to destroy command and military units of the Palestinian Liberation Organization (PLO). Israeli forces succeeded in driving out the PLO but also occupied West Beirut, a move that was very unpopular in Israel and abroad. The Israelis withdrew most of their forces between 1983 and 1985.
See also: Israel.

Begonia, common name for a family (Begoniaceae) of perennial plants with about 900 species. Mostly succulent herbs, native to tropical regions, they are cultivated in houses and gardens for their colorful foliage.

Behan, Brendan (1922-1964), Irish playwright and author, noted for his vivid ribaldry and satire. His works *The Quare Fellow* (1956), the autobiographical *Borstal Boy* (1958), and *The Hostage* (1959) deal largely with his experiences in the Irish Republican Army and his subsequent imprisonment.

Behavioral sciences, sciences dealing with human behavior, individually or socially, as opposed to their physiological makeup. The term embraces anthropology, psychology, and sociology.
See also: Anthropology; Psychology; Sociology.

Behaviorism, school of psychology that studies behavior exclusively in terms of objective observations of reactions to environmental stimuli. Originating with Pavlov's animal experiments in conditioned reflexes, behaviorism in human psychology was introduced by J.B. Watson and championed by

B.F. Skinner.
See also: Pavlov, Ivan Petrovich; Watson, John Broadus; Skinner, B.F..

Behavior therapy, methods for changing undesirable habits through learning.

Behn, Aphra (1640-1689), dramatist, novelist, and poet, first professional female author in England. Her plays *The Rover* (1677) and *The Forced Marriage* (1670) and her novel *Oroonoko* (1688) show technical ingenuity and wit.

Behrens, Peter (1868-1940), German architect who pioneered a mode of functional design suited to industrial technology. His most influential work was the AEG turbine factory in Berlin (1908-09). He influenced Le Corbusier, Gropius, and Mies van der Rohe.

Behrman, Samuel Nathaniel (1893-1973), U.S. dramatist noted for his comedies of manners, including *Biography* (1932) and *No Time for Comedy* (1939). He also wrote film scripts and a biography of satirist Max Beerbohm (1960).

Beiderbecke, Bix (Leon Bismarck Beiderbecke; 1903-1931), U.S. jazz musician. An accomplished pianist and brilliant cornetist, he joined the renowned Paul Whiteman band in 1928. Despite his early death through alcoholism and general ill health, he was a major innovator in the development of jazz.
See also: Jazz.

Beijing (formerly Peking; pop. 7,000,000), capital of the People's Republic of China, lying within the Hebei province, but administered directly by the central government. It is the political, commercial, cultural, and communications center of the country, and embraces a massive industrial complex. The city's rectangular layout was the work of Kublai Khan in the 13th century, and its splendors were described by Marco Polo. It became the permanent capital of China in 1421. Its occupation by French and British troops from 1860 was a contributing cause of the Boxer Rebellion (1900). In 1928 Peking (renamed Peiping) was superseded by Nanking (Nanjing), but regained its capital status and its name with the Communist victory under Mao Zedong in 1949. Beijing has two historic districts: the Inner City, enclosing the Imperial Palace and the

The imperial palace museum in the Forbidden City in Beijing, with its white marble bridges, steps and terraces of the Southern Gate of the Supreme Harmony (Tai-ho-nan). Mao Zedong's mausoleum, built in the year of his death, 1976, on the Square of Heavenly Peace, has become another important tourist attraction.

B

Forbidden City, and the Outer City. In mid-1989 a massacre of demonstrators in Beijing's Tiananmen Square signaled the difficulty of China's democracy movement in the face of totalitarian authority.
See also: China.

Beirut (pop. 1,900,000), capital city and chief port of the Republic of Lebanon, situated on the Mediterranean Sea. During early Roman times the city became famous as a center of learning. The Arabs conquered the city in A.D. 635. In 1110 it was captured by the Crusaders, who held it for two centuries. It eventually became part of the Ottoman Empire. During World War I it came under French rule and was proclaimed the capital of Lebanon in 1920. Beirut has excellent railroad connections with other nearby cities, which have enlarged the region served by its harbor. Growth of the city during the 20th century was rapid until the Lebanese civil war of 1975-76 between Muslims and Christians caused severe damage and ended Beirut's success as a financial center and tourist resort. Much of the city was left in ruins following a siege by Israeli forces in 1982, which brought about the expulsion of thousands of PLO guerrillas.

Béjart, Maurice (1927-), French dancer and choreographer. He danced with various companies in Europe and organized his own company in 1954. The Ballet of the 20th Century in Brussels, Belgium, which he has directed since 1959, has an international reputation.
See also: Ballet.

Bekesy, Georg von (1899-1972), Hungarian-born U.S. scientist who was awarded the 1961 Nobel Prize for medicine for research into the mechanism of the inner ear. A senior research fellow at Harvard University since 1947, he made discoveries about the physical mechanisms of hearing, particularly with respect to discrimination of pitch.
See also: Ear.

The neo-classic City Hall on Donegal Square in Belfast, dates from the beginning of the 20th century.

Belafonte, Harry (1927-), U.S. singer and actor best known for his interpretations of West Indian calypso folksongs. Belafonte is also active in many human rights causes.

Belarus (formerly Byelorussia; also known as White Russia), independent country in eastern Europe, bordered by Russia, Ukraine, Poland, Latvia and Lithuania.
Country and climate. Though mainly a plain, Byelorussia has hilly regions and extensive marshes, particularly in the southwest. The climate is mild. There are extensive waterways, in which the Dnieper, Pripet, Berezina, and Western Dvina rivers are linked by canals. About a quarter of the country is forestland.
People. White Russians constitute 78% of the population; the largest minorities are Russians (13%), Poles (4%), and Ukranians (3%). 60% of the population belongs to the Russian Orthodox Church. The official language is White Russian, which is usually written in Cyrillic script.
Economy. Natural resources include peat, rock salt, phosphorite, limestone, and iron ore. The people are dependent on both agriculture and industry. Products include agricultural machinery, trucks, timber, wood products, and textiles. Minsk, the capital, produces heavy vehicles and tractors. Other cities and industrial centers include Vitebsk, Gomel, and Mogilev.
History. Byelorussia was originally inhabited by Slavic tribes, became part of Lithuania in the 14th century, and was made part of Poland in the 16th century. When Poland was partitioned in the late 18th century, Byelorussia became part of the Russian Empire. By the Treaty of Riga in 1921, the western part of Byelorussia was ceded to Poland. When the USSR (Soviet Union) was formed in 1922, Byelorussia became one of the 4 original constituent republics. The region was the scene of bitter fighting during World War II. The collapse of communism in the USSR resulted in the republic's independence in 1991. In the same year, Byelorussia joined the Commonwealth of Independent States. The Byelorussian Soviet Socialist Republic changed its name to Republic of Belarus. In 1992 the country signed the Non-proliferation treaty in which Belarus declared it would hand over its nuclear weapons to Russia. Belarus and Russia signed an agreement in 1996 establishing close political and economic ties. The former communist Aleksandr Loekasjenko was elected as president in 1994. He pursued an autoritarian policy and oriented strongly towards Russia. However, he still rejected a Russian proposal for unity with only one government and Parliament.
See also: Union of Soviet Socialist Republics.

Belau *See:* Palau Islands.

Belaúnde Terry, Fernando (1912-2002) Peruvian politician, president of Peru from 1963 until 1968, deposed by General Juan Velasco Alvarado. Once more president from 1980 until 1985. The pro Western Belaúnde Terry's activities included support for the farmers (land reform), improvement of the infrastructure, and the fight against illiteracy.

Belém (pop. 1,300,000), capital of the state of Pará in northern Brazil. Situated on the Pará River, about 90 mi (145 km) from the Atlantic coast, Belém is the commercial center of the mouth of the Amazon River basin. Among its industries are tourism, rubber, timber, cacao, and Brazil nuts.
See also: Brazil.

Belfast (pop. 297,000), seaport and capital of Northern Ireland, located at the mouth of the Lagan River, an inlet of the Irish Sea. The town was populated by about 2,000 English settlers in 1613, became a county borough in 1898, and was made capital of Northern Ireland in 1920. By the end of the 18th century Belfast had become the export center for the Irish linen trade and for the developing cotton industry. The city was long known for shipbuilding, but that industry has recently declined in importance. Although newer industries, including an aircraft factory, have been established, unemployment in the area is still the highest in the United Kingdom. For the past century, Belfast has been the scene of violent conflict between the Protestant majority and Catholic minority and, recently, of guerrilla fighting between the Irish Republican Army and British troops.
See also: Ireland.

Belgian Congo *See:* Congo (Zaïre).

Belgium

Capital:	Brussels
Area:	11,783 sq mi (30,528 sq km)
Population:	10,275,000
Language:	Dutch, French, German
Government:	Federal state with constitutional monarchy
Independent:	1830
Head of gov.:	Prime minister
Per capita:	U.S. $22,313
Monetary unit:	1 Belgian franc = 100 centimes

Belgium, kingdom of northwestern Europe, bordered to the west by France, to the east by Luxembourg and Germany, and to the north by the Netherlands.
Land and climate. The region called Flanders borders the North Sea and is mostly flat plain with sandy beaches; further in-

land, the country is intensively cultivated, and is drained by the Leie, Schelde, and Dender rivers. Central Belgium consists of a low plateau that is also a rich agricultural area. At the southern end of this plateau is the Sambre-Meuse valley, the main industrial and coal-mining region. About 25% of all Belgians live in this area of only 800 sq mi (2,000 sq km). The country has a generally temperate climate.

People. Belgium is linguistically, culturally, and politically divided. A line running from east to west, just south of Brussels, divides the Flemish-speaking Flemings in the north from the French-speaking Walloons in the south. Both languages are in official use. There also is a small German-speaking minority of some 70,000 in Wallonia.

Economy. Belgium is not rich in natural resources, except for the coal deposits of the Sambre-Meuse valley and the Kempenland region. Its high standard of living derives from successful manufacturing industries, which account for 30% of the gross national product. The chief commodities, include textiles, glass, chemicals, metal and machine goods, and diamonds; Antwerp is one of the world's leading diamond centers. Brussels (the capital), Bruges, and Mechelen are noted for lace. Belgium's numerous small farms provide about 80% of the country's food needs. Belgium's excellent system of transportation, including fine inland waterways and well-equipped ports at Antwerp and Ghent, facilitate the foreign trade that has made the country prosperous.

History. The kingdom emerged in the 1830s, when it seceded from the Netherlands, and in 1839 Belgium was recognized as a perpetually neutral sovereign state. In 1914 the Germans invaded and occupied the country for the next 4 years. In May 1940 Germany again violated Belgian neutrality, invading Belgium, the Netherlands, and Luxembourg simultaneously. Belgian forces capitulated in June 1940, but Belgian resistance forces fought alongside the Allies until the country was liberated in 1944. Belgium was a founding member of the United Nations in 1945 and a founding member of the North Atlantic Treaty Organization (NATO) in 1950. It also helped to establish the European Economic Community (EEC), which was to become part of the European Union (EU), with headquarters in Brussels. After 1995 several large-scale vice scandals and political scandals took place in Belgium. In 1999, a coalition under a liberal leadership came into power on a national level, which, for the first time in years, formed a government without Christian Democrats. The country was confronted with its colonial past: Burundi, Rwanda and Congo (Zaïre).
See also: Brussels.

Belgrade (pop. 1,168,000), capital and largest city of Yugoslavia, a port and industrial center at the junction of the Danube and Sava rivers. Important products include metals, chemicals, and textiles. Held in turn by the Romans, Byzantines, Bulgars, Serbs, and Ottoman Turks, the city became Yugoslavia's capital after World War I and kept it's status after the desintegration of former Yugoslavia in 1991. Belgrade is

known for its beautiful parks, churches, and museums.
See also: Yugoslavia.

Belisarius (c. 505-565 A.D.), Byzantine general under Justinian I. He crushed the Vandals in North Africa and the Ostrogoths in Italy, taking Rome in 536. In 559 Belisarius was called from retirement to repel the Huns and Slavs from the gates of Constantinople.
See also: Byzantine Empire; Justinian I.

Belitung (Billiton; pop. 200,000) Indonesian island in the Java Sea, between Sumatra and Kalimantan; 1,860 sq mi (4,816 sq km). Capital: Tanjungpandan. Export of rice, sago, nuts, and turtles. Main industry: tin mining. The Sultanate of Palembang ceded the island to the British in 1814, who, in turn, ceded it to the Dutch twelve years later. In 1958 the Dutch tin companies Bangka Tin and Billiton Company were nationalized.

Belize

Capital:	Belmopan
Area:	8,867 sq mi (22,965 sq km)
Population:	263,000
Language:	English
Government:	Parliamentary monarchy in the British Commonwealth
Independent:	1981
Head of gov.:	Prime minister
Per capita:	U.S. $3,250
Monetary unit:	1 Belizean dollar = 100 cents

Belize (British Honduras until 1973), independent nation since 1981, on the subtropical Caribbean coast of Central America, bordered by Mexico on the north and Guatemala on the southwest. The country is densely forested. The population consists of Creoles (of mixed African and European origin), descendants of the Carib and Maya tribes, and a small minority of Europeans. Most people live on the coast. Citrus fruits, bananas, and sugarcane are the mainstay of the export-oriented economy. Fishing and livestock industries are being developed. European settlement began in the 17th century, and in the 18th century African slaves

were brought in to cut mahogany. The country became a British colony in 1862 and achieved internal self-government in 1964. Disputes with Guatemala concerning the latter's claim that it had inherited Belize from Spain delayed the proclamation of independence until 1981. Guatemala officially recognized Belize's independence in 1991, and in 1993 the two countries signed a non-aggression pact. In the 1990s, the smuggling of narcotics and the tensions between Hispanic immigrants and the black creole population were the most important problems. In 2002, Belize and Guatemala concluded a concept-treaty in order to settle their border conflict.

Belize City (pop. 50,000), largest city and former capital of Belize, a country on the Caribbean coast. Though its proximity to the sea earned Belize City a reputation as a chief seaport, it also makes the city especially susceptible to hurricanes. Following a devastating hurricane in 1961 that destroyed the city, killed hundreds, and left thousands homeless, the capital was moved from Belize City inland to Belmopan, the current capital. For over 300 years, Belize City has been world renowned for its shipping of mahogany and logwood. The city also ships rosewood, cedar, coconuts, maize, bananas, and sugar. The British first settled Belize City in the 1600s. Now about 1 in 4 Belize citizens live in Belize City.

Bell, metal instrument rung by a metal clapper inside. Most bells are cup-shaped, with the bottom edges tapering outward, but as musical instruments they can be pipes of varying lengths (chimes) that create different tones when struck. Bells originated in China in the 800s B.C. and were introduced to Europe in the 6th century A.D. Commonly associated with churches, where they were rung to summon people to worship, bells have also signalled emergencies or momentous events.
See also: Big Ben.

Bell, Alexander Graham (1847-1922), Scottish-born U.S. scientist and educator who invented the telephone (1876), the wax-cylinder phonograph, and various aids for teaching the deaf. He also founded the Bell Telephone Company.
See also: Telephone.

Belladonna, or deadly nightshade (*Atropa belladonna*), poisonous herbaceous plant of the nightshade family whose dried leaves and roots produce a crude drug of the same name. Various medicinal alkaloids, such as the muscle relaxant atropine, are produced by refining belladonna.

Bellamy, Edward (1850-1898), U.S. author. His Utopian *Looking Backward 2000-1877* (1888) pictured a benevolent state socialism with worker-ownership and made him famous. His other novels include *Miss Ludington's Sister* (1884) and *Equality* (1897), a sequel to *Looking Backward*.

Bellarmine, Saint Robert Francis Romulus (1542-1621), theologian known for his opposition to Protestant Reformation

B

B

Saul Bellow (1915-).

doctrines. Saint Bellarmine was regarded by the Roman Catholic church as a key defender of the church's rights in an age when royal absolutism reigned. In 1560, he joined the Jesuit order. He became a cardinal (1599) and then archbishop of Capua (1602). Bellarmine was a prolific author. He gave all his money to those less fortunate, dying a pauper. Bellarmine was canonized in 1930. His feast day is May 17.
See also: Roman Catholic Church.

Bellbird, common name for a number of bird species whose songs resemble ringing bells. The *campañero* of the South American tropical rain forest is a well-known white bellbird.

Bellerophon, Greek mythological hero. Bellerophon tamed the winged horse Pegasus to aid him in the tasks set by King Iobates. He attempted to reach Olympus on his mount, but Pegasus, stung by a gadfly sent by Zeus, threw him, and Bellerophon was crippled and blinded.
See also: Mythology.

Bellflower, or bluebell, any of several species of annual, biennial, and perennial plants producing bell-shaped flowers, ranging from a few inches to more than 6 ft (1.8 m) tall, found in temperate and subtropical areas.

Bellini, family of Early Renaissance Venetian painters. **Jacopo** (c.1400-1470) evolved a much-imitated compositional technique of depicting small figures in vast, detailed architectural settings. **Gentile** (1429-1507), his elder son, is noted for his realistic portraits and his use of perspective to give a sense of spatial depth. **Giovanni** (1430-1516), the younger son, is considered the greatest Early Renaissance Venetian painter, famous for his use of light and col-

or. His pupils, Titian and Giorgione, continued and developed his style.
See also: Renaissance.

Bellini, Vincenzo (1801-1835), Italian opera composer of the bel canto school. His most popular works today are his last 3: *La Sonnambula* (1831), *Norma* (1831), and *I Puritani* (1835).
See also: Opera.

Belloc, (Joseph Pierre) Hilaire (1870-1953), French-born English poet, essayist, and historian. An ardent Roman Catholic polemicist, his first well-known work was *The Bad Child's Book of Beasts* (1896).

Bellow, Saul (1915-), Canadian-born U.S. novelist noted for his narrative skill and his studies of Jewish-American life. His best-known books are *The Adventures of Augie March* (1953) and *Herzog* (1964). Other novels include *Dangling Man* (1944), *Henderson the Rain King* (1959), *Humboldt's Gift* (1975), *The Dean's December* (1982), *More Die of Heartbreak* (1987), *The Actual* (1997), and *Ravelstein* (2000). He won the 1976 Nobel Prize in literature.

Bell's palsy, nerve disorder that causes paralysis of one side of the face. Thought to be due to a virus infection, Bell's palsy occurs most often in young men. It begins suddenly with a dull ache behind the jaw and weakened facial muscles. The paralyzed muscles usually begin to recover within ten days or so.

Belmopan (pop. 6,800), capital city of Belize, a country on the Caribbean coast. Belmopan, the capital since 1970, is a new city built approximately 50 mi (80 km) inland from Belize City, the former capital, which was plagued by devastating hurricanes. Many of the buildings in Belmopan are adorned with ancient Mayan designs. The country's most modern hospital and many government buildings are located in the city.
See also: Belize.

Belo, Carlos Filipe Ximenes (1948-), bishop of East Timor. In 1996 Belo received the Nobel Peace Prize together with José Ramos Horta for their support to the people of East Timor in their fight against systematic oppression by Indonesia. Belo has always advocated a peaceful settlement in the conflict over East Timor, which was annexed by Indonesia in 1975 and where resistance has so far been put down with a great deal of bloodshed.

Belo Horizonte (pop. 2,000,000), city in Brazil, about 220 mi (354 km) north of Rio

de Janeiro. It is a fast-growing city, with heavy industry and secondary products including furniture, textiles, and footwear. The capital of Minas Gerais state, Belo Horizonte was built in 1895-97 as Brazil's first planned city. It is a center of culture and tourism.
See also: Brazil.

Belorussia *See:* Belarus.

Belsen, German village in Lower Saxony, site of the infamous Nazi concentration camp called Bergen-Belsen, where over 115,000 people, mostly Jews, were killed.
See also: Holocaust.

Beluga, or white whale, small (13 ft/4 m) whale (*Delphinapterus leucas*) living in northern seas and prized for its skin. The sturgeon, largest Russian freshwater fish, source of caviar, is also called beluga.

Bemelmans, Ludwig (1898-1962), Austrian-American writer and illustrator of *Hansi* (1934), *My War with the United States* (1937), *Madeline* (1939), and other satiric and children's stories.

Benares *See:* Varanasi.

Benavente y Martínez, Jacinto (1866-1954), Spanish playwright. He wrote and staged 172 comedies and helped establish the modern theater in Spain. He was awarded the 1922 Nobel Prize for literature for such popular plays as *The Bonds of Interest* (1907) and *La Malquerida* (1913).

Ben Bella, Ahmed (1916-), Algerian revolutionary who helped plan the 1954 anti-French revolt. After the post-independence power struggle, Ben Bella became president in 1962. He was ousted during Col. Houari Boumedienne's 1965 coup. He was imprisoned until 1979 and returned from exile in 1990.
See also: Algeria.

Bends, also known as caisson disease or decompression sickness, dangerous physiological reaction resulting from a rapid decrease in atmospheric pressure that may release nitrogen bubbles into the body. These can obstruct small blood vessels, collect in the joints, and damage the nervous system. Symptoms involve painful joints and muscles, convulsions, double vision, and paralysis. Divers, airplane pilots, and others working in compressed-air situations are the usual victims.

Benedict, Ruth Fulton (1887-1948), U.S. cultural anthropologist whose extensive fieldwork helped illustrate the theory of cultural relativism-what is considered deviant in one culture may be normal in another. Her classic work was *Patterns of Culture* (1934).
See also: Anthropology.

Benedictine Orders, the 'Black Monks,' order of monks and nuns following the rule of St. Benedict of Nursia. They believe in a combination of prayer, choral office, study, and manual labor under an abbot's supervision.
See also: Benedict of Nursia, Saint.

The beluga, or white whale (*D. Leucas*) ranges throughout the Arctic Ocean and northern seas into Hudson Bay, Canada.

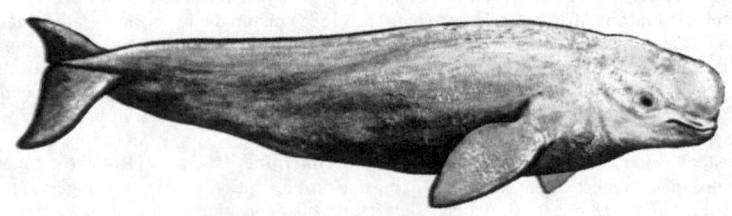

Benedict of Nursia, Saint (c.480-547), father of Western monasticism, whose 'rule' set the pattern of monastic life from the mid-7th century. He founded the first Benedictine monastery at Monte Cassino. *See also:* Benedictine Orders.

Benedict XV (Giacomo Della Chiesa; 1854-1922), Roman Catholic pope during the outbreak of World War I. Benedict was elected pope in 1914, 3 months after he was made a cardinal. His reign was punctuated by World War I and a conflict with Italy regarding Italian troops that were occupying Rome. Though Benedict tried to maintain and encourage strict neutrality, his papacy was plagued with war problems. The Allies eventually excluded him from peace negotiations. After the war, Benedict encouraged international reconciliation and endorsed the founding of the League of Nations. In 1917, he was credited with the issuance of the Code of Canon Law, a compilation of comprehensive church laws.

Benelux, customs union formed by Belgium, the Netherlands, and Luxembourg, in 1948. 'Benelux' is often used collectively for the countries themselves.

Benes, Eduard (1884-1948), co-founder, with Thomás Masaryk, of the Czechoslovak Republic. He held the posts of foreign minister (1918-1935), prime minister (1921-1922), president (1935-1938 and 1946-1948), and head of the government-in-exile (1940-1945). His appeals to Great Britain and France in 1938 failed to prevent Hitler's occupation of the Sudetenland. He died after the 1948 Communist coup. *See also:* Czechoslovakia.

Benét, Stephen Vincent (1898-1943), U.S. poet, novelist, and short story writer, whose works center on U.S. history and tradition. His epic poems *John Brown's Body* (1928) and *Western Star* (1943) won Pulitzer Prizes. Among his most famous short stories is 'The Devil and Daniel Webster' (1937).

Bengal, region including Bangladesh and northeastern India on the Bay of Bengal. Its chief city, Calcutta, was capital of British India 1833-1912, and it was an autonomous province from 1935 until the partition of India in 1947. At that time the western part became West Bengal State of India. The eastern part became a province of Pakistan, and in 1971, the independent nation of Bangladesh.

Bengal, Bay of *See:* Bay of Bengal.

Benghazi (pop. 500,000), seaport and second largest city of Libya. It is situated in northeastern Libya on the Gulf of Sidra about 600 mi (966 km) east of the capital, Tripoli. Benghazi markets and exports the products of a rich agricultural region: wool, grains, citrus fruits, dates, and olives. There is also considerable tuna and sponge fishing. Benghazi was the scene of fighting (changing hands several times) during World War II. *See also:* Libya.

Benguela Current, A relatively cold ocean current in the south-eastern part of the Atlantic Ocean. It flows from the Namibian coast to the Gulf of Guinea.

Ben-Gurion, David (David Grün; 1886-1973), Polish-born Israeli statesman and first prime minister of Israel. After World War I, he helped to found the Haganah, the underground Jewish army, and the Histadrut, the General Federation of Jewish Labor (1920). He became leader of the Mapai Labor Party (1930) and the World Zionist Organization (1935). As prime minister (1949-1953 and 1955-1963) he helped to mold the state of Israel. *See also:* Israel.

Ben-Hur *See:* Wallace, Lew.

Benin

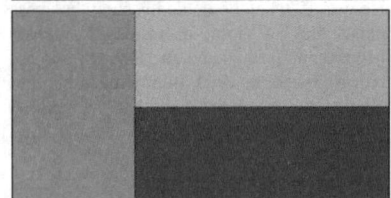

Capital:	Porto-Novo
Area:	43,450 sq mi (112,622 sq km)
Population:	6,788,000
Language:	French
Government:	Presidential republic
Independent:	1960
Head of gov.:	President
Per capita:	U.S. $1,040
Monetary unit:	1 CFA franc = 100 centimes

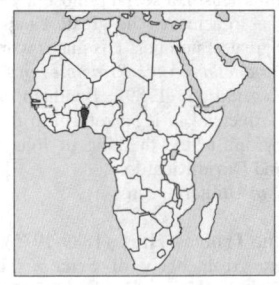

Benin (formerly Dahomey), republic in West Africa, flanked by Togo in the west, Burkina Faso (formerly Upper Volta) in the northwest, Niger in the north, Nigeria in the east, and the Gulf of Guinea in the south.
People. The population is concentrated in the south coastal region, where Cotonou, a major port city and commercial center, and Porto-Novo, the capital, are located. There are 4 major tribes: the Fon, Adja, and Yoruba in the south and the Bariba in the northeast and central regions. There is a small European community, mostly French.
Economy. Benin is one of the world's poorer countries. Its economy is principally agricultural with most people engaged in subsistence farming. The major cash crop is the oil palm. Other exports include hides and skins, cotton, peanuts, and coffee. Benin's position as a transit point for Nigeria and land-locked Niger has provided the impetus for an expanding transport sector. Manufacturing presently accounts for less than 13% of the country's economy.

Italian painter Spinello Aretino (1373-1410) painted a series of frescoes on the life of Benedict of Nursia (480-547). Here, Benedict meets Totila, king of the Eastern Goths (San Miniato, Florence).

History. The independent Fon Kingdom of Dahomey emerged in the 17th century and engaged in profitable trade with the Portuguese. Known as the Slave Coast, Dahomey became one of the main slave exporting regions of West Africa. King Gezo (1818-1858) raided the Yoruba for slaves and extended Dahomey's northern boundaries with the aid of its famous women soldiers. By 1850 the slave trade was declining and in 1851 the French established a trading station at Cotonou. By 1894 the French conquered the kingdom and in 1904 merged Dahomey into French West Africa. In 1960, after more than 50 years as a French colony, Dahomey became an independent republic and joined the United Nations. Plagued by economic and political instability, Dahomey witnessed a series of takeovers after independence. The first president, Herbert Maga, was toppled from power in 1963. Rivalry between President Sourow-Migan Apithy and the prime minister resulted in a coup in 1965. Following a series of unstable regimes, a 3-man Presidential Council was established in 1970 only to be overthrown

Benin's presidential palace is located in Cotonou, the capital of the Atlantique district. Since the construction of an artificial deep-water harbor on the Gulf of Guinea, Cotonou has become the leading port and commercial center of Benin (formerly Dahomey).

B

by Maj. Mathieu Kérékou in 1972. In 1975 Dahomey was renamed and became the People's Republic of Benin. As a result of the socio-economic crisis in the late 1980s Kérékou was forced to introduce economic and political liberalization measures and was replaced by Nicéphore Soglo in 1991. In 1996 Kérékou returned to power. He was reinstated as president in 2001. He had also been a government leader since 1998.

Benjamin, in the Old Testament, the youngest son of Jacob and Rachel. Benjamin founded the Israelite tribe called Benjamin. Its territory encompassed Jerusalem and towns to the north of the city, notably Jericho and Bethel. The Benjamites were warriors, known for their skill in archery. In the 10th century B.C., most of Benjamin joined the tribe of Judah to form the kingdom of Judah.

Ben Jelloun, Tahar (1944-), Moroccan writer, who pays a great deal of attention to the oppressed position of Moroccan women. He wrote the novels *Solitaire* (1976), *The Sand Child* (1985), *The Sacred Night* (1987; Prix Goncourt), *Silent Day in Tangier* (1990), *With Downcast Eyes* (1991). In 1995, his various poems were published.

Benn, Gottfried (1886-1956), German poet and essayist who was strongly influenced by expressionism and Nietzsche's views, such as his idea that culture is carried to the limit and thus to its downfall. He considered art the only remedy in a chaotic and nihilistic world. He was introduced to expressionism during his college years in Berlin. His first collections of verse entitled *Morgue* (1912) and *Söhne* (1913) are clear examples of expressionism: dynamic language and a direct expression of feelings. The fact that Benn was a physician played an important role in his works: he describes the sick and deformed human being.

Bennett, Arnold (1867-1931), English novelist, journalist, and playwright. He is famous for his novels set in the potteries of Staffordshire: *Anna of the Five Towns*

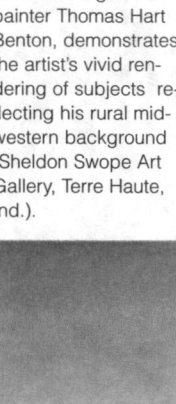

Threshing Wheat (1939) by the American regionalist painter Thomas Hart Benton, demonstrates the artist's vivid rendering of subjects reflecting his rural midwestern background (Sheldon Swope Art Gallery, Terre Haute, Ind.).

(1902), *The Old Wives' Tale* (1908), and *These Twain* (1916). He was influenced by Zola's naturalism.
See also: Zola, Émile.

Bennett, James Gordon (1795-1872), Scottish-born U.S. newspaper publisher and editor, pioneer of modern news reporting. In 1835 he launched the sensationalist *New York Herald*, the first to print stock market items and use the telegraph. His son, James Gordon Bennett (1841-1918), sent H. M. Stanley to find David Livingston (1869) and founded the *New York Evening Telegram* (1869) and the *Paris Herald* (1887).

Benny, Jack (Benjamin Kubelsky; 1894-1974), U.S. comedian. Benny was known for his radio and television routines about the hilarious experiences of a miserly man. He was 17 when he made his show business debut playing violin in vaudeville shows. More than 20 films and an 18-year radio career followed. In 1950, Benny made his first television appearance using the themes that made him famous-stinginess, condemning quiet stares, and his violin playing.

Bent grass, popular name for some grasses (genus *Agrostis*) of Europe, North America, and North Africa, widely grown for pasture cover and for hay. In the United States one widely grown species is redtop (*A. albot*). Some kinds of bent grass are suitable for lawns and golf greens.

Bentham, Jeremy (1748-1832), English philosopher, economist, and jurist, founder of Utilitarianism, a social philosophy whose aim was to achieve 'the greatest happiness of the greatest number.' His major work was *An Introduction to the Principles of Morals and Legislation* (1789). Bentham's ideas were influential in legal reform in the 19th century and in the thinking of John Stuart Mill and David Ricardo.
See also: Utilitarianism.

Benton, Thomas Hart (1889-1975), U.S. painter; greatnephew of Senator Thomas Hart Benton. He was a leader of the influen-

tial 1930s regionalist school of painting, devoted to depicting the life of rural America as in his *Threshing Wheat*.

Bentonite, type of fine-grained clay that greatly increases in volume when saturated with water. It is found in rocks formed from volcanic ash. Bentonite is used in ceramics, paper manufacture, and the sealing of dams and oil wells.

Benz, Karl (1844-1929), German engineer believed to have built the first automobile (1885) with an internal combustion engine. His earliest autos had tricycle carriages and electric ignitions. His company merged with Daimler in 1926, and Daimler-Benz became the manufacturer of the Mercedes-Benz.
See also: Automobile.

Benzedrine, trade name of a drug containing amphetamine.

Benzene, colorless, flammable, toxic liquid hydrocarbon (C_6H_6) produced from petroleum and from coal gas and coal tar. Benzene is used in the manufacture of plastics and as a fuel in some engines.
See also: Aniline; Faraday, Michael.

Benzine, flammable liquid distilled from petroleum. Clear, colorless, and lighter than kerosene, benzine is a volatile mixture consisting primarily of aliphatic hydrocarbons. Benzine is often used as a drycleaning solvent, motor fuel, and to dissolve fats and oils. Benzine boils between 95° and 175F° (35°- 79°C).
See also: Petroleum.

Benzocaine, crystalline ester, used as a local anesthetic, usually in an ointment or in lozenges. It reduces pain or itching in minor wounds.
See also: Anesthesia.

Benzol *See:* Benzene.

Ben-Zvi, Itzhak (1884-1963), Russian-born second president of Israel (1952-1963). Active in Jewish self-defense groups in Palestine from 1907, in 1929 he founded the National Council of Palestine Jews.

Benzyl alcohol (also called phenylcarbinol $C_6H_5CH_2OH$), colorless, aromatic alcohol found in the oils of many flowers. Ephedrine and adrenaline are derived from it. Benzyl alcohol is widely used in the perfume industry, in pharmaceuticals, and as a solvent in cellulose lacquers.

Beograd *See:* Belgrade.

Beowulf, anonymous heroic epic poem, probably composed in the 8th century, the greatest extant poem in Old English. Using elements of Germanic legend, it is set in Scandinavia and recounts the hero Beowulf's victories over the monster Grendel and Grendel's mother, his battle with a dragon, and his death and burial.
See also: English literature.

Berberian, Cathy (1928-1983) American singer (soprano) and composer of Armenian

origin. Berberian studied drama at Columbia University, dance and singing with Giorgina del Vigo in Milan, and was a soloist with the Armenian Folk Dance Group in New York. Although as a singer she mastered the classical repertoire very well, she mainly attracted attention as a performer of contemporary music. Stravinsky, Milhaud, Cage and, in particular, Berio, whom she married in 1950, all wrote special works for her. She had an unconventional singing style, in which impersonations and sound eruptions played a major role. Her voice contained a wealth of variety and, as a result, was most suitable for experimental music. Berberian was one of the most remarkable artists of her era.

Berbers, several culturally distinct North African peoples, usually Muslim, who speak the Hamitic Berber language or any of its main dialects. They live mainly in Algeria, Libya, Morocco, and Tunisia. Most are farmers or nomadic herders, but some are oasis-dwellers.

Berchtesgaden (pop. 8,200), small Alpine resort town in southeastern Bavaria. Nearby, Adolf Hitler built the Berghof, his fortified chalet retreat.

Berdyayev, Nikolai Aleksandrovich (1874-1948), Russian religious philosopher. A Marxist in his youth, he later turned to Christianity and created a highly individual Christian existentialism. Expelled from the USSR in 1922, he settled in Paris.

Berg, Alban (1885-1935), Austrian composer of expressive 12-tone music. A pupil of Schoenberg, he adopted his technique in such works as his violin concerto (1935) and his operas, *Wozzeck* (1925), and the unfinished opera *Lulu*.

Bergamot (*Citrus bergamia*), fruit whose rind yields an oil used in perfumes and essences. Related to the orange, it is pearshaped, pale-yellow or green in color, and has fragrant green pulp.

Bergen (pop. 225,000), seaport and second largest city in Norway, situated on the southwest coast on the By Fjord. From the 14th to the 16th centuries it was the northernmost member of the Hanseatic League. Several buildings from this period survive, most notably the Tyskebyggen (German House), now a museum. The central districts of the city have been destroyed by fire several times, notably in 1702, 1855, and 1916. Modern architects have used the 'open plan' to create wide streets and many parks. Bergen is a major commercial and communications center for western Norway. Its shipping industry is the third largest in the country. Processing and canning of fish, shipbuilding, paper manufacture, and metalworking are its important modern industries. Bergen was the birthplace of the composer Edvard Grieg. Playwright Henrik Ibsen was manager of the National Theater there (1851-57).
See also: Norway.

Bergen-Belsen *See:* Belsen.

Bergerac, Cyrano de *See:* Cyrano de Bergerac, Savinien de.

Berger, Gerhard (1959-), Austrian racing driver, made his debut during the Austrian Grand Prix in 1984 for ATS BMW. He subsequently drove for the racing teams of Arrows, Benetton BMW, Ferrari, McLaren-Honda, and for Ferrari again. Berger took part in more than 160 Grand Prix events, nine of which he won.

Bergman, Ingmar (1918-), Swedish film and stage director, producer, and writer. He combines realism with imaginative symbolism to explore themes such as good and evil, love, old age, and death. Motion pictures include *The Seventh Seal* (1956), *Wild Strawberries* (1957), *Persona* (1965), *Cries and Whispers* (1972), and *Fanny and Alexander* (1982).

Bergman, Ingrid (1917-1984), Swedish stage and screen actress. In 1936 she came to the attention of Hollywood with the film *A Woman's Face*. She went to the United States in 1939 and soon became a star. Her fresh style was shown to advantage in such films as *Intermezzo* (1939), *Gaslight* (1944), for which she won an Academy Award, and *Notorious* (1946). In 1950 her love affair with the Italian director Roberto Rossellini led to her ostracism from Hollywood. She married and later divorced Rossellini, returning to the United States with the film *Anastasia* (1956), for which she won a second Academy Award. Returning to the stage in the 1960s, Bergman was acclaimed for her performances in Turgenev's *A Month in the Country* in London and Eugene O'Neill's *More Stately Mansions* on Broadway.

Bergson, Henri-Louis (1859-1941), French philosopher. He viewed the world as containing a life-force (*élan vital*) in constant conflict with matter. Evolution, he wrote, is creative process energized by the *élan vital*, and time he saw not as a unit of measurement but as the duration of life experience. Bergson was awarded the Nobel Prize for literature in 1927.

Beriberi, disease caused by lack of vitamin B₁ (thiamine). Beriberi leaves the nerves and heart impaired. Treatment involves thiamine replacement.

Bering, Vitus Jonassen (1681-1741), Danish explorer. Sailing in the service of Russia, he explored northeast Siberia (in the 1720s) and Alaska (1741). The Bering Sea and the Bering Strait are named for him.

Bering Sea, extreme northern arm of the North Pacific Ocean, 885,000 sq mi (2,292,150 sq km) in area, bounded by East Siberia, Alaska, and the Aleutian Islands. It contains Nunivak Island, St. Lawrence Island, and the Komandorskiye Islands (former USSR). The international dateline crosses it diagonally.
See also: Bering, Vitus Jonassen.

Bering Strait, sea-channel linking the Arctic Ocean with the Bering Sea and separating Siberia from Alaska. The channel is shallow and 55 mi (90 km) wide, covered with drift-ice from November to June.
See also: Bering, Vitus Jonassen.

Berio, Luciano (1925-), an Italian composer. He became a leader of Italy's musical avant-garde in the 1950's, when he helped found the Studio di Fonologia Musicale, an electronic-music studio in Milan. Berio's works, which include music for convention-

Swedish film director Ingmar Bergman (born 1918).

al instruments as well as electronic music, often were composed with the use of the serial techniques of twelve-tone music and the random techniques of aleatory music. Among his many compositions are *Differences* (1959), *Visage* (1961), *Sinfonia* (1968), *Coro* (1976), *Entrata* (1980), and *La Vera Storia* (1982). Berio studied music at the Verdi Conservatory in Milan and with Luigi Dallapiccola. He taught at the Juilliard School in New York City, 1965-72, and for a number of years worked at the Institut de Recherche et de Coordination Acoustique/Musique in Paris.

Berkeley (pop. 105,000), California city on the east side of San Francisco Bay. Berkeley is the home of several renowned schools including the University of California's main campus. Incorporated in 1878, the city is named after George Berkeley, a bishop and philosopher. Its major industries include

Nomadic Berbers of the Tuareg tribe are still dependent on the camel for food and transportation. The Berbers, a lightskinned Hamitic people, are thought to have been the original inhabitants of Mediterranean Africa.

B

printing and chemical, equipment, and metal manufacturing. During the Vietnam War Berkeley was the site of major antiwar protests.
See also: California.

Berkeley, Busby (1895-1976), U.S. choreographer and film director who revolutionized the staging of musical production numbers in Hollywood films. He introduced lavish settings, revolving platforms, and giant staircases upon which hundreds of extras performed in such extravaganzas as *42nd Street* (1933), *Footlight Parade* (1933) and *The Gang's All Here* (1942).

Berkeley, George (1685-1753), Irish philosopher and bishop who, rejecting the views of Locke, argued that the apparent existence of material reality was merely a projection of the mind of God.
See also: Idealism.

Berkelium, chemical element, symbol Bk; for physical constants see Periodic Table. Berkelium was discovered in Berkeley, Calif., in 1949 by S.G. Thompson, Albert Ghiorso, and Glenn Seaborg. It was synthesized initially by bombarding americium-241 with helium ions. It is produced from plutonium by multiple neutron capture in a high-flux nuclear reactor. Berkelium is a metallic element and a member of the actinide series. Several compounds of berkelium have been made, and its chemistry is analogous to that of curium. Berkelium-247 is the longest-lived isotope. It is an alpha-emitter with a half-life of 1,400 years. Ten isotopes of the element are known.

Berlage, Hendrik Petrus (1856-1934), Dutch architect who was one of the major innovators of architecture in The Netherlands at the beginning of the 20th century. His concepts as well as his creations exerted considerable influence on modern architecture in The Netherlands. His design of the Koopmanbeurs (Commodity Exchange) in Amsterdam made him widely known both in The Netherlands and abroad.

Emile Berliner's gramophone. In 1887, this American-German inventor replaced the wax cylinder by a planar disc, and vertical modulation by transverse modulation: the gramophone record was to retain its form for almost 75 years, until the 1960s, when vertical modulation reappeared in stereo records.

Berle, Milton (Milton Berlinger; 1908-2002), U.S. comedian. Nicknamed 'Uncle Miltie' and 'Mr. Television,' Berle had successful careers in vaudeville, motion pictures, stage musicals, and radio before becoming host of the 'Texaco Star Theatre' on NBC (1948). For the next 6 years, his comedy show was the most frequently watched program on television and he is credited with popularizing the new medium.

Berlin (pop. 3,438,000), capital city of Germany located in the eastern part of the country on the Spree and Havel rivers. It covers 341 sq mi (883 sq km) and is at the center of a network of railroads and waterways. It was the capital of Germany from 1871-1945. After World War II, it was divided into East Berlin (which became the capital of the communist state of East Germany) and West Berlin (a state of West Germany). In August 1961 East Germany erected the Berlin Wall to separate the 2 parts of the city. On October 3, 1990, divided Berlin was officially reunited as East Germany ceased its independent existence and became part of a unified German state.The new German government appointed Berlin as the new capital city in 1991. The full transition to Berlin will take until the early 2000s.
See also: Germany.

Berlin, Congress of, international meeting of Russia, Turkey, and major European powers held in 1878 under the leadership of Otto von Bismarck to settle problems created by the 1877-78 Russo-Turkish War. The resultant Treaty of Berlin redrew boundaries in eastern Europe, generally to the advantage of Great Britain and Austria-Hungary.
See also: Bismarck, Prince Otto von.

Berlin Airlift, operation by the United Kingdom and the United States to fly essential supplies into West Berlin during the Russian land and water blockade (1948- 49). Its 250,000 flights and 2 million tons of supplies cost $224 million.
See also: Cold War.

Berlin, Irving (Israel Baline; 1888-1989), U.S. songwriter. He wrote over 900 popular songs, including 'Alexander's Ragtime Band' (1911), 'God Bless America' (1918), and 'White Christmas' (1942). His film scores include *Top Hat* (1935), *Annie Get Your Gun* (1946), and *Call Me Madam* (1950).

Berliner, Emile (1851-1929), inventor who contributed to early telephone and phonograph developments. A year following Alexander Graham Bell's invention of the telephone, Berliner developed a powerful transmitter that enhanced the telephone receiver. He also created the flat phonograph disc, or record, and a process that employed a needle moving horizontally, thus minimizing distortion of Thomas Edison's earlier method. Berliner later produced a method for mass-duplication of records from one master disc. Born in Hanover, Germany, Berliner moved to the United States in 1870.
See also: Phonograph; Telephone.

Berlin Wall, wall 26 mi (42 km) long built in 1961 dividing East and West Berlin. Before 1961, many people fled East Germany by crossing from East to West Berlin. The wall halted this emigration. Between 1961 and 1989 over 70 East Germans were killed attempting to get past the Berlin Wall. In November 1989 the wall began to be dismantled after demonstrations for political reform erupted in East Germany.
See also: Berlin; Cold War.

Berlioz, Louis-Hector (1803-1869), French romantic composer of dramatic, descriptive works. Major works include his *Symphonie Fantastique* (1830), *Requiem* (1837), the choral symphony *Romeo and Juliet* (1838-39), the oratorio *The Childhood of Christ* (1850-54), and the operas *Benvenuto Cellini* (1838), and *The Trojans* (1856-59).

Berlusconi, Silvio (1936-), Italian politician. In 1993 Berlusconi founded the moderately right of center party, Forza Italia, to counter domination by the former communists. After the laborious formation of a new cabinet in 1994, Berlusconi's prime ministership only lasted a week because he was almost immediately part of a corruption scandal. Berlusconi's party was among the greatest losers during the elections in 1996. In 1997 he was sentenced to 16 months imprisonment for bribing tax inspectors. He did not have to serve this sentence, however, due to an extreme shortage of cells. The parliamentary elections of 2001 brought triumph to the alliance of Forza Italia, Lega Nord and Alleanza Nazionale, led by Berlusconi. He promised his constituents tax reductions and less bureaucracy and was reappointed as Prime Minister.

Bermuda, British colony comprising about 150 coral islands of which 20 are inhabited, lying in the North Atlantic Ocean, 580 miles (933 km) east of North Carolina. The main island is Bermuda Island, with the capital, Hamilton. The climate is warm and the vegetation lush and tropical. Bermuda's first British colonists arrived in 1609. Some 60% of present inhabitants are descendants of African slaves, and the rest are mainly British. The economy depends on tourism and 2 U.S. military bases.

Bermuda Triangle, area of the Atlantic Ocean roughly bounded by Bermuda, the Greater Antilles, and the southeastern coast of the United States, in which many ships and planes are said to have vanished. Though supernatural causes have been proposed to explain the allegedly mysterious disappearances, there is no evidence of any unusual phenomena in the area at all.

Bern, or Berne (pop. 126,000), capital city of Switzerland and of Bern canton. It lies on the Aare River in German-speaking west-central Switzerland. It is an important commercial, industrial, and cultural center and the headquarters of some major international communications organizations. Bern was founded in 1191 and retains many old buildings.
See also: Switzerland.

The clock tower in the centre of Bern is built on the site of the old city wall.

The Bernese mountain dog, a working breed, was used by the merchants of Berne to pull wagons loaded with goods to market.

B

Bernadette, Saint (Marie-Bernarde Soubirous; 1844-1879), French peasant girl who claimed to have had 18 visions of the Virgin Mary in a Lourdes grotto in 1858. The grotto became a shrine, and she was beatified (1925) and canonized (1933). Her feast day is Feb. 18 in France, April 16 elsewhere.
See also: Lourdes.

Bernadotte, Jean Baptiste Jules (1763-1844), French general who founded Sweden's present royal dynasty. One of Napoleon's marshals (1804), he was elected Swedish crown prince in 1810. He fought Napoleon at Leipzig (1813) and ruled Sweden and Norway as Charles XIV (1818-44).
See also: Sweden.

Bernanos, Georges Louis (1888-1948), French Catholic writer. Religion plays an important role in his novels and essays, which are pertinant to our age. One of the recurring themes is the struggle between God and Satan. From 1906 until 1913 he studied law and liberal arts in Paris and managed the monarchist and reactionary paper *L'action française*. Despite having been declared unfit, he fought in the trenches during World War I. After his first novel *Sous le soleil de Satan* (1926) was a great success, he became a professional writer. In 1934 Bernanos moved to Majorca, but after the Spanish Civil War broke out he first settled in Paraguay and next in Brazil. In 1945 he returned to France. He joins François Mauriac and Julien Green as one of the greatest Catholic writers of 20th century France. His works include: *Le journal d'un curé de campagne* (The Diary of a Country Priest) (1936), *Monsieur Ouine* (Mr. Ouine) (written in 1940), published in 1943), *l'imposture* (The Imposter) (1927). *Le journal d'un curé de campagne* was filmed by Robert Bresson in 1951. *Les dialogues des Carmélites* (1948) is a stage play. Composer Francis Poulenc converted it into an opera (1957).

Bernard, Claude (1813-1878), French physiologist, one of the founders of experimental medicine. He studied the digestive process and the function of glycogen in the liver, and in 1851 he reported the existence of the vasomotor nerves.
See also: Digestive system.

Bernard of Clairvaux, Saint (1090?-1153),

French theologian and mystic who was the abbot of a Cistercian monastery and inspired the Second Crusade. Founder of the Clairvaux Abbey in 1115, he was adviser to popes, kings, and bishops and was instrumental in Abelard's condemnation (1140). He was canonized in 1174.
See also: Crusades.

Bernese mountain dog, Swiss breed of large, powerful dog. They have long black hair with russet brown spots on the legs and face and white feet and chests. The dogs typically weigh from 50-75 lbs (23-34 kg) and stand 21-27 in (53-69 cm) tall at the shoulders. Romans originally brought the breed to Switzerland more than 2,000 years ago.

Bernhard, Thomas (1931-1989), Austrian writer. When he was eighteen, Bernhard suffered from a serious lung disease. After a few collections of poetry, *Der Frost* was published in 1963, one of the first and most successful and controversial pieces of prose and stage plays. Central themes in his work were death and decay, illness, humiliation, and loneliness. In his stage plays in particular, he criticized the way Austria repressed the atrocities of World War II. He was considered a merciless critic of his own country. His work includes epic prose such as *Der Stimmenimitator* (The Voice Imitator) (1978) and *Wittgensteins Neffe* (Wittgenstein's Nephew)(1983); novels such as *Das Kalkwerk* (The Lime Works)(1970) and *Korrektur* (Correction)(1975); stage plays such as *Ein Fest für Boris* (1970), *Der Ignorant und der Wahnsinnige* (1972), *Die Jagdgesellschaft* (1974) and *Heldenplatz* (1988).

Bernhardt, Sarah (Henriette Rosine Bernard; 1844-1923), French actress. Renowned for her great emotional power, she was the leading performer in classical French theater, appearing in roles created by Victorien Sardou and Edmond Rostand, among others. She made several triumphant worldwide tours.

Until the outbreak of World War I, France had a dominant position in international film industry. An important part consisted of `film d'art', a kind of filmed theatre, with famous actors from the Comédie Française in the leading roles. Thus, legendary Sarah Bernhardt played in Louis Mercantor and Henri Desfontaine's *Queen Elisabeth* (1912). This photograph by the famous photographer Nadar, shows a young Sarah Bernhardt around 1862.

Bernier, Joseph Elzéar (1852-1934), Canadian explorer renowned for his arctic voyages. Bernier staked Canada's claim to all the North American arctic islands, captained a dozen voyages to the arctic, and journeyed around the world several times.

Between 1624 and 1633, Gianlorenzo Bernini (1598-1680) worked on an immense gilded bronze baldachin (Italian: baldacchino) over the main altar of Saint Peter's in Rome. The four pillars are striking: a motif from early Christian art (the old Saint Peter's had similar pillars), which became quite common during the baroque period, thanks to, among others, Bernini.

Bernini, Giovanni Lorenzo (1598-1680), Italian sculptor and architect who gave Rome many of its characteristic baroque features. He designed the tomb of Pope Urban VIII, the canopy over the high altar in St. Peter's, the Piazza S. Pietro, the fountain *Four Rivers* in the Piazza Navona, and the statue *St. Teresa in Ecstasy*.
See also: Baroque.

Bernoulli's principle, theorem of aerodynamics stating that the pressure of a moving gas will be lowest where its speed is highest, or that a moving fluid conserves energy. The theorem, named after Swiss mathematician Daniel Bernoulli (1700-82), explains how airplane wings create lift. Because the air flow is faster across the wing's curved top surface than across its flat underside, air pressure is greater under the wing than over, creating lift.
See also: Aerodynamics; Hydraulics.

Bernstein, Carl *See:* Watergate.

Bernstein, Leonard (1918-1990), U.S. con-

B

ductor and composer, best known for his musical *West Side Story* (1957). He rose to fame as conductor of the New York Philharmonic Orchestra (1958-69). His varied works include the symphony *The Age of Anxiety* (1949), the musical *On The Town* (1944), and *The Mass* (1971).

Berry, Chuck (Charles Edward Anderson Berry; 1931-), U.S. rock and roll singer, songwriter, and guitarist. An influential pioneer of rock and roll music, Berry gained notoriety with white audiences and shaped blues rock and roll into his own big-beat and melodic patterned style that later influenced the Beatles and the Rolling Stones. Born in St. Louis, Mo., Berry played the guitar as a teenager and had his first big hit, 'Maybellene,' in 1955. Other hits followed: 'Johnny B. Goode,' 'Roll Over Beethoven,' 'Sweet Little Sixteen,' and 'Rock and Roll Music.'

Berryman, John (1914-1972), U.S. poet, active from the 1930s. His reputation was solidified by the long poem *Homage to Mistress Bradstreet* (1956). Berryman's later work, distinguished by its black ironies and linguistic innovation, includes *His Toy, His Dream, His Rest* (1968) and *Dream Songs* (1969). He committed suicide, throwing himself off a bridge in Minneapolis.

Bertillon, Alphonse (1853-1914), French criminologist who devised a system for identifying criminals based on the body measurements. The system was adopted by the French police in 1888 and used until fingerprints became a method of identification.

Bertolucci, Bernardo (1940-), Italian filmmaker known for such films as *The Conformist* (1970), *Last Tango in Paris* (1972), *La Luna* (1979), *Tragedy of a Ridiculous Man* (1981), *The Last Emperor* (1985), *The Sheltering Sky* (1990), *Little Buddha* (1993), *Stealing Beauty* (1995), and *Besieged* (1998). His films are often controversial and provocative.

Beryl, beryllium and aluminum silicate ($Be_3AP_2Si_6O_{18}$), the most common ore of beryllium. It is a transparent or translucent mineral found mainly as hexagonal crystals in granite rocks. The gem emerald is a dark green beryl containing a small amount of chromium; aquamarine is a blue-green variety of beryl. The finest varieties are found in Brazil, Sri Lanka, Siberia, and New England.
See also: Aquamarine; Beryllium.

Beryllium, chemical element, symbol Be; for physical constants see Periodic Table. Beryllium was isolated as a free metal by Friedrich Wöhler and Antoine Bussy in 1828. *Beryl* (beryllium aluminum silicate) is the commercial source of the element. The element is prepared by the reduction of beryllium fluoride with magnesium metal. Beryllium is one of the lightest and strongest of all metals and greatly increases the strength of other metals when used in alloys. Beryllium copper is extensively used for springs, electrical contacts, and nonsparking tools. Beryllium is used as a moderator in

nuclear reactors. It is also used in gyroscopes, computer parts, and inertial guidance instruments. Beryllium and its salts are toxic and should be handled with the greatest of care.

Berzelius, Jöns Jakob, Baron (1779-1848), Swedish chemist who determined the atomic weights of nearly 40 elements before 1818, discovered cerium (1803), selenium (1818), and thorium (1829), introduced terms *protein*, *isomerism*, and *catalysis*, and devised the modern method of writing chemical formulas (1813).

Besant, Annie (Wood) (1847-1933), British theosophist and social reformer. Besant joined the Fabian Society and was an early advocate of birth control. She became international president of the Theosophical Society (1907-33) and championed independence for India, becoming president of the Indian National Congress (1917). She published many theosophical works.
See also: Fabian Society.

Bessarabia, historic region of southeastern Europe, northwest of the Black Sea, between the Dniester and Danube rivers. After various Russo-Turkish conflicts it was ceded to Russia in 1812. After the Crimean War it passed to Moldavia (1856) but was regained by Russia (1878). Romania controlled it almost continuously from 1918 to 1944, when it joined the USSR. In 1991 it became part of independent Moldavia and Ukraine.

Bessel, Friedrich Wilhelm (1784-1846), astronomer and mathematician. Born in Germany, Bessel made the first authentic measurement of a star's distance from the earth, also called a parallax. This discovery allowed astronomers to document the earth's movement. Bessel also established a class of mathematical functions known as Bessel functions.
See also: Parallax.

Bessemer process, process of making steel from pig iron. The pig iron is loaded into a specially designed furnace or Bessemer converter. A continuous blast of compressed air is forced through the molten metal to oxidize impurities, which are burned off or form slag. The result is molten steel. Since the 1950s, a modification of the Bessemer process, the basic oxygen process, has been in use. The Bessemer process was developed by the British inventor Sir Henry Bessemer (1813-98).
See also: Steel.

Best, Charles Herbert (1899-1978), Canadian physiologist. As a medical student at the University of Toronto, he and several colleagues isolated the hormone insulin from the pancreas and developed it as a treatment for diabetes (1921). Best's other discoveries include histaminase for the treatment of allergies, the blood-clotting agent heparin, and the vitamin choline.
See also: Insulin.

Beta-blocker, drug that affects the transmission of signals at beta-receptors, parts of the sympathetic nervous system located in the

heart, lungs, kidneys, and blood vessels. Beta-blockers (or beta-adrenergic blocking agents) interfere with the stimulation of the beta-receptors. They thereby lower blood pressure and heart rate. They are used in the treatment of hypertension and cardiac arrhythmia.
See also: Drug.

Betancourt, Rómulo (1908-1981), president of Venezuela (1945-1947 and 1957-1963) and founder of the left-wing Acción Democrática Party (1935). Betancourt spent 1948-1958 in exile after a military coup. He survived an assassination attempt in 1960.
See also: Venezuela.

Beta particle, one of the particles that can be emitted by a radioactive atomic nucleus. Most are high-speed electrons, with a mass off about $1/_{1837}$ and a negative charge. More rarely, a beta particle can be positively charged (positron). The emission of an electron entails the change of a neutron into a proton within the nucleus. The emission of a positron is similarly associated with the change of a proton into a neutron.
See also: Radioactivity.

Betatron, apparatus designed to accelerate electrons to high velocities. Electrons are injected into a ring-shaped vacuum tube where an electromagnet running on alternating current creates a magnetic field whose polarity changes at short intervals. The electrons are accelerated around the ring by the changing magnetic field. Large betatrons can accelerate particles to energies of several hundred million electron volts.
See also: Particle accelerator.

Betel, preparation made with the seeds of the betel palm. A masticatory, betel has been chewed as a stimulant by southern Asians and eastern Africans since ancient times. Betel is made by combining slices of the betel nut seeds with lime paste and other flavorings and spreading it on a betel pepper leaf. It is then rolled and chewed.

The betel palm *(A. catechu)* is cultivated for its nuts, which grow in clusters; chewed as a mild stimulant, they stain the teeth black.

Betelgeuse, or Alpha Orionis, second brightest star in the constellation Orion. The name was given to it by Arab astronomers (*bayt al-jawzaa*, 'house of twins' in Arabic). Betelgeuse is a regular variable first magni-

tude red giant with a diameter up to 420 times that of the sun. It is about 500 light-years from Earth.
See also: Orion.

Bethe, Hans Albrecht (1906-), German-born U.S. theoretical physicist who proposed the nuclear carbon cycle to account for the sun's energy output (1938). During World War II he worked on the Manhattan Project. He was awarded the 1967 Nobel Prize in physics for his work on the source of stellar energy.

Bethesda (pop. 63,000), city in Montgomery County, central Maryland, a residential suburb of Washington, D.C. The U.S. Naval Medical Center is located here, as are several noted medical research centers and institutes, including the National Cancer Institute.
See also: Maryland.

Bethlehem (Hebrew: *Bayt Lahm*; pop. 62,500), town in Israeli-occupied West Bank, 6 mi (9.7 km) south of Jerusalem, and sacred to Jews, Christians, and Muslims. According to the Bible, it is the city where David was annointed by Samuel and the birthplace of Jesus; the traditional tomb of Rachel is outside the town. A basilica built by the Emperor Constantine over the Grotto of the Nativity (326-333) and rebuilt by Justinian I now forms the Church of the Nativity, a major attraction for tourists and pilgrims. Long contested by Christians and Muslims, it was taken by Israel during the 1967 Six-Day War.
See also: Jesus Christ; West Bank.

Betjeman, Sir John (1906-1984), English poet laureate and architectural conservationist, often called a lyrical satirist. His works include *New Bats in Old Belfries* (1945), *Selected Poems* (1948), *Collected Poems* (1958), and *Victorian and Edwardian Architecture in London* (1969).

Bettelheim, Bruno (1903-1990), Austrian-born U.S. psychologist who drew on his personal experience as an inmate of Nazi concentration camps to write his famous article, 'Individual and Mass Behavior in Extreme Situations' (1943). His subsequent work mainly concerned the treatment of autistic and disturbed children.

Beuys, Joseph (1921-1986), German avant-garde sculptor who experimented with unorthodox materials such as fat, felt, and metal sheets. Due to his work as well as to his theories (he was strongly influenced by anthroposophy), he is considered to be of great importance to European avant-garde visual arts after 1960. Initially he studied natural science and had a great interest in zoology, microbiology, geology, and electronics. During World War II he was active as a fighter pilot in Eastern Europe. Both the natural sciences and his introduction to Eastern Europe strongly influenced the development of his later works. In the early 1960s Beuys was a prominent representative of the 'Fluxus' movement in Europe. This movement, which was joined by visual artists, poets, and musicians, organized events to involve the audience as well as the artist more closely in various artistic genres and thus to stimulate them to contemplate life more profoundly. To Beuys the connection between man and the arts is a central point in his works.

Bevatron, in physics, a 6 or more billion electron volt accelerator of protons and other atomic particles.
See also: Particle accelerator.

Beveridge, William Henry (1879-1963), British economist and social planner, director of London School of Economics (1919-37). In *Social Insurance and Allied Services* (1942), he proposed a social security system that became law. Beveridge became a knight in 1919 and a baron in 1946.

Beverly Hills (pop. 32,000), residential city in southern California, completely surrounded by Los Angeles. Formerly a Spanish ranch, it is now the home of wealthy film and television stars. The town extends into the foothills of the Santa Monica Mountains.
See also: California.

Bhadgaon (Bhatgaon, Bhaktapur; pop. over 60,000), town in central Nepal. Agricultural production: rice, vegetables, fruit, tobacco, and jute. Pilgrim center for Hindus with many temples, including the Najatapola Dewai (18th century), and a Shiva temple. Founded around 865; until 1500 the most important town in Nepal. In 1934 it was damaged heavily during an earthquake.

Bhagavad-Gita (*Song of God*), anonymous Sanskrit poem dating from c.200 B.C., incorporated into the Mahabharata epic, a classic work of Hinduism. It consists of a dialogue in 700 verses between Prince Arjuna and the god Krishna. The dialogue, held on the eve of a battle, covers many aspects of Hindu religious thought.
See also: Hinduism; Vishnu.

Bhagwan *See:* Bhagwan Shree Rajneesh.

Bhagwan Shree Rajneesh (real name Chandra Mohan Jain; 1931-1990), Indian spiritual leader. Because of his unorthodox ideas about religion, sexual freedom, and politics, his meditation techniques and his personal charisma, Bhagwan (Hindi: 'the godly') managed to attract many devotees in the West between 1974 and 1985. Thousands of devotees went to the center of meditation he established in Pune (Poona), India in 1974. In 1981 the Bhagwan, who was by then immensely wealthy, relocated to Oregon (U.S.) with a large number of devotees (sannyasins) and founded a new spiritual community, Rajneeshpuram. Scandals, an internal power struggle, and a conviction for breaking American immigration laws led to his return to Pune in 1985, where he accepted the new Buddhist title of Osho.

Bhaktivedanta Prabhupada (1896-1977), Indian spiritual leader and founder of the Hare Krishna movement. At an advanced age he resigned as director of a chemical plant in India to devote his full time to religious work. From 1965 his mission was to create 'Krishna consciousness' in the U.S. and Europe.

Bhopal (pop. c. 1,260,000), capital of Madhya Pradesh in central India. On December 3, 1984, a deadly cloud of toxic gas leaked from a Union Carbide plant, killing some 2,000 people and injuring about 200,000 others for the worst industrial accident in history. The Indian government filed lawsuits in the U.S. and in India, charging Union Carbide with negligence. Union Carbide offered a $350-million settlement over a period of 30 years, which the Indian government refused. The U.S. courts rejected the suit in 1986, but in 1989 the Indian Supreme Court ordered Union Carbide to pay $470 million in damages, which seemed to close the matter although many in India still felt the assessment was too low.
See also: India.

Bhubaneswar (historically: Bhuvaneshvara; pop. 508,000), capital of Orissa state, eastern India. The town is situated on the most important national highway between Calcutta and Madras. The town consists of the old city, containing about 30 ancient temples dating back to the 7th until the 16th century. The state government buildings and two universities are situated in the new town (1948). From the 5th until the 10th century A.D. it was the provincial capital of many Hindu dynasties and a center for the adoration of Shiva. The town is still a major center for pilgrimages.

Bhumibol, Adulyadej (also: Phumiphon Adunlayadet 1927-), king of Thailand, succeeded his murdered brother Ananda Mahidol as Rama IX in 1946. He is married to Princess Sirikit Kitiyakara and is a democrat.

Bhutan

Capital:	Thimphu (summer) /Phunakha (winter)
Area:	18,150 sq mi (46,500 sq km)
Population:	810,000
Language:	Dzongkha
Government:	Constitutional monarchy
Independent:	1949
Head of gov.:	Monarch
Per capita:	U.S. $1,200
Monetary unit:	1 Ngultrum = 100 chetrum

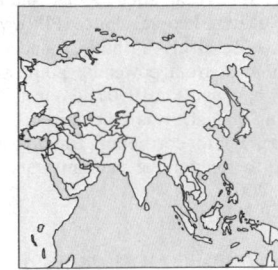

Bhutan, kingdom on the southern slopes of

B

the eastern Himalayas, between Tibet on the north and Bangladesh and India on the south. It is extremely mountainous, falling from 24,000 ft (7,315 m) on the northern border to 600 ft (183 m) on the frontier with India. Agriculture, limited to a few areas, is backward; terraced rice cultivation might be extended, but the cultivators lack capital. Corn, potatoes, wheat, millet, and buckwheat are grown. Fine handicrafts include wood carving, basketry, and swords and daggers with elaborately chased silver engravings. The country is slowly changing from an isolated barter system into a transitional market economy. Buddhism of the Tibetan Mahayana type mingles with propitiation of spirits.

During much of its history, Bhutan has been dominated by Tibet. The Bhutanese were

Peasants in the fertile Paro Valley haul firewood past the local dzong, a Buddhist monastery and administrative center. Paro, in west central Bhutan, is significant as a terminus of the nation's major highway.

frequently in conflict with the British in India until 1866, when they made peace in return for an annual subsidy. The hereditary monarchy was established in 1907. A 1910 treaty gave Britain control of external affairs. After becoming independent in 1947, India undertook to maintain Bhutan as a buffer state between itself and China. During the 1960's, Bhutan's King Jigme Dorji Wangchuk, with Indian assistance, began a vast program of modernization and development. Bhutan joined the United Nations in 1971. In 1972, the throne passed to 16-year-old Jigme Singhye Wangchuk. In 1998, a partially chosen legislative assembly came into being in Bhutan. Television was introduced a year later. Many Bhutans of Nepalese origin were forced to leave the country.

Bhutto, Benazir (1953-), prime minister of Pakistan (1988-1990, 1993-1996). She was the first female leader of an Islamic nation. Bhutto, a graduate of both Harvard and Oxford universities, went into exile in 1984, returned to Pakistan after 2 years, and headed the Pakistan People's Party (PPP), which her father, Zulfikan Ali Bhutto, founded. She was removed from power by political and military opponents in 1990 and reinstalled in 1993. In 2002, she was sentenced to 3 years imprisonment for corruption. Bhutto was not allowed to run for the parliamentary elections in 2002.
See also: Pakistan.

Bhutto, Zulfikar Ali (1928-1979), president and prime minister of Pakistan (1971-1977); father of Benazir Bhutto. He held several government posts under President

Mohammad Ayub Khan, but became one of his leading opponents and was imprisoned (1968-1969). He was deposed by Mohammad Zia ul-Haq in a military coup and executed 2 years later.
See also: Pakistan.

Biafra, name assumed by Nigeria's Eastern Region during its attempted secession (1967-70). Under the leadership of Colonel Ojukwu, the Ibo people of the Eastern Region declared their independence in May 1967, and the civil war, for which both sides had been preparing for some time, broke out. Outnumbered and outgunned, the Biafrans suffered heavy losses, with large numbers dying from starvation, before their final surrender. The former breakaway region was divided to form the East-Central, River, and South-Eastern states.
See also: Nigeria.

Biaggi, Massimiliano (1971-), Italian motorcycle racer, achieved his first international title in 1991 when he became European champion. In 1994 he won his first world title on an Aprilia in the 250 cc class and he won the same title again in 1995 and 1996. The following year Biaggi joined Honda, with which he also became world champion in the 250 cc class. In 1998 during his debut in the king's class, the 500 cc, he won the Grand Prix in Japan for Honda.

Bialik, Chaim Nachman (1873-1934), one of the greatest of modern Hebrew poets and novelists. Born in the Ukraine, he settled in Palestine in 1924. His poetry gave fiery expression to Jewish national aspirations. His publishing business in Odessa was a significant force in the revival of Hebrew language and literature.

Bialystok (pop. 260,000), town in northeastern Poland. Capital of Bialystok województwo (province) (pop. 680,000, 3,883 sq mi, 10,053 sq km). Mainly flax growing and sheep breeding. The capital, with textile industry and construction of agricultural machinery, is a major rail junction as well as the industrial and cultural center of northern Poland. Places of interest are the baroque town hall and the Branicki mansion.

Bible, name of the sacred writings of the Christian religion. The word 'bible' is derived from the Greek *biblia*, meaning 'books.' A collection of writings gathered into books, the Bible consists of two main parts, the Old Testament and the New Testament. The Old Testament, written in Hebrew and Aramaic centuries before the birth of Christ, is the Christian name for the Jewish Bible. It comprises 39 books, of which the most important are the five books of the Law (Pentateuch), the Jewish Torah: Genesis, Exodus, Leviticus, Numbers, and Deuteronomy. These are followed by the books of the Prophets (Joshua, Judges, the two books of Samuel, the twelve minor prophets, and others). Finally, the Writings (Hagiographa) include Esther, Job, Psalms, Proverbs, Ecclesiastes, the Song of Songs, Lamentations, and Daniel. The New Testament, the specifically Christian part of the Bible, was written in Greek in the first 2

centuries after Christ. Of its 27 books, the 4 Gospels-of Matthew, Mark, Luke, and John-occupy the hallowed central position. These describe aspects of the life and teachings of Jesus. The remaining 23 books consist of a selection of early Christian writings that were definitively selected as canonical in the 4th century A.D.. The English translation of the Bible in widest use is the King James version (1611). In Christian doctrine, the Bible is written under the guidance of God and contains the moral and historical bases of the Christian view of the world.
See also: Christianity.

Bibliothèque nationale, national library in Paris, France. Also a depository (a library that stores copies of most printed works, especially government documents), the Bibliothèque nationale is one of the largest libraries in Europe. Known more as a government archive than a public library, this expansive facility houses about 20 million printed volumes as well as numerous magazines, manuscripts, maps, engravings, coins, and medals. Many of the collections and manuscripts were once part of royal libraries.

Bicameral legislature *See:* Legislature.

Bicarbonate of soda ($NaHCO_3$), sodium bicarbonate, or baking soda, chemical compound used to relieve stomach acidity. It is also used in baking powder and fire extinguishers.

Bichat, Marie François Xavier (1771-1802), French anatomist and pathologist, founder of histology, the study of the small-scale structure of tissue. Although working without the microscope, Bichat distinguished 21 types of elementary tissues of which the organs of the body are composed.

Bicuspid *See:* Teeth.

Bicycle, 2-wheeled vehicle propelled by pedals. In the late-18th century, a device called a célérifère was demonstrated in Paris by Count Mède de Sivrac. By the early 19th century, an improved model, called a draisine, had been developed, with handlebars and a saddle. The design was further improved by Kirkpatrick MacMillan, a Scottish blacksmith, who introduced treadles that the rider moved back and forth to provide power to the rear wheels. The use of rotary pedals was incorporated by the Frenchman Ernest Michaux in his vélocipède. Popular in the 1870s was the 'penny-farthing,' which had a large front wheel and a much smaller rear wheel. The first bicycle with a chain-drive powering the rear wheel was made in England in 1885. Pneumatic tires were introduced soon after, and the bicycles of the 1890s were similar to those of today. Subsequent improvements include the use of gear-changing systems.

Bicycle racing, popular sport in many countries, especially in Europe. Races may take place on a special track or on open roads. Track events, which range from 140-500 m (459-1,640 ft), exercise the cyclists' tactical skills as well as testing their strength and en-

B

durance. Road races cover 50 mi (80 km) to several thousand miles. The most famous event is the Tour de France, an annual international competition that covers about 2,500 mi (4,000 km) and lasts three weeks.

Biedermeier, utilitarian middle-class style of furniture popular in Germany from about 1810 to 1850.

Bierce, Ambrose Gwinett (1842-1914?), U.S. short-story writer and satirical journalist. His works include *In the Midst of Life* (1891), *Can Such Things Be?* (1893), and *The Devil's Dictionary* (1906), a compilation of sarcastic definitions. An adventurer, he distinguished himself in the Union army during the Civil War. He disappeared without trace during the Mexican Revolution of 1913-14.

Biermann, Wolf (1936-), German poet-singer, settled in East Berlin in 1953. As a cabaret performer and protest singer he was one of those who adopted a critical attitude towards East German society, but nevertheless, considered himself a Marxist. After a visit to West Germany in 1976 Biermann was no longer allowed to return to the GDR. In 1995 he published *Alle Gedichte*.

Bierstadt, Albert (1830-1902), German-born U.S. landscape painter famous for his large, realistic Western scenes, including *Sierra Nevada* and *The Settlement of California*.

Bifocals *See:* Glasses.

Bigamy, in law, felony or misdemeanor of being married to 2 persons simultaneously. Ignorance of the fact that the first marriage is still valid is not an acceptable defense in most courts.

Big and Little Dippers, 2 constellations that each resemble a water dipper. The Big Dipper, located in the constellation of Ursa Major (the Great Bear), has 7 stars that are often used as reference points to find other stars. The Little Dipper, a smaller, similar grouping of stars, is fainter except for the North Star, which lies at the end of the Little Dipper's handle. The Little Dipper forms most of the constellation of Ursa Minor, the Little Bear.

Big bang, theory that all the matter and energy of the universe was concentrated in a compact, infinitely small volume that exploded some 15 to 20 billion years ago, giving rise to the present universe, still expanding from the initial explosion. The big bang theory is the most widely accepted cosmological theory today.
See also: Cosmology.

Big Ben, popular name for the tower clock of the Houses of Parliament in London. It is named for Sir Benjamin Hall, the commissioner of works at the time of its installation in 1856. The bell of the clock weighs 13 tons.

Big Five, the 5 permanent members of the UN Security Council: China, France, Great Britain, Russia, and the United States. Each of these countries has the right to veto Security Council resolutions.
See also: United Nations.

Bighorn, Rocky Mountain sheep (*Ovis canadensis*) inhabiting the higher mountain ranges of the western United States from New Mexico and southern California northward. The large horns of the male form a full circle; those of the female are smaller and upright. The bighorn stands about 3 ft (1 m) high at the shoulder.

Bighorn Mountains, range of the eastern Rocky Mountains, mainly in northern Wyoming, but extending into Montana east of the Bighorn River. The highest point is Cloud Peak (13,165 ft/4,013 m).
See also: Rocky Mountains.

Bighorn River, river in the Wind River Canyon in Wyoming and flowing through Montana, where it joins the Yellowstone River. Much of its 335 mi (539 km) course runs through deep canyons. Dams and reservoirs provide irrigation, flood control, and hydroelectric power.

The Bignonia Lorraine, a popular bignonia.

Bignonia, any of several hundred species of plants of the Bignoniaceae family, native to warmer parts of the Americas. They usually have creeping or climbing stems and may reach the top of even the highest trees. One of the best known in the United States is the cross vine, which has orange-red, trumpet-shaped flowers.
See also: Calabash.

Bihar (pop. 95 million), constituent state of India, bordering on Nepal; 67,159 sq mi (173,877 sq km). Capital, Patna. North Bihar is formed by the Gangetic Plane. The chief crops are barley, rice, maize, sugar cane, and wheat. South Bihar is formed by the Chota Nagpur plateau, rich in copper ore and iron ore, bauxite, mica and coal. In Muzaffapur (pop. 200,000) there is a university (1952). Buddha is supposed to have come to important insights in Buddh Gaya in 528 B.C.. In Bihar City (pop. 200,000) there is a 9th-century Buddhist monastery and many mosques. The official language is Hindi. Under British rule from 1765 until in-

dependence. Center of the resistance against British rule in 1857-1859.

Bihzad, Kamal ad-Din (1450-1537), Persian miniature painter, famous for illustrating manuscripts such as *Timur Namah*, *Gulistan*, and *Khamsa*. His paintings of battle scenes and nature scenes were admired throughout the world.

Bikila, Abebe (1932-1973), Ethiopian athlete who became famous for running barefoot to a record-setting victory in the marathon at the 1960 Olympics in Rome, then improved his own record at the 1964 Olympics in Tokyo. Bikila suffered serious back injuries in a car crash and ended up in a wheelchair. At the Paralympic Games he won a medal for archery.

Bikini, atoll in the Marshall Islands in the central Pacific Ocean. It was the site of U.S. nuclear bomb tests in the 1940s and 1950s. Inhabitants evacuated during the tests began to return in the early 1970s, but the island was again declared uninhabitable because of dangerously high radiation levels in 1978.
See also: Marshall Islands.

Bilbao (pop. 359,000), major seaport in

One of the Biedermeier painters of the Netherlands was Jan Adam Kruseman (1804-1862), who around 1835 produced this group portrait of the governors of the leper hospital in Amsterdam (Amsterdam, Rijksmuseum). The custom of painting a group portrait of the governors of institutions, dates from the 17th century.

The Maha-Bodhi temple is one of the many temples in Bihar.

B

northern Spain and former capital of a once autonomous Basque region. The town is built on both sides of the Nervión River, 8 mi (13 km) from the Bay of Biscay. The banks of the Nervión below the city are lined with shipyards, blast furnaces, and factories, for Bilbao is one of Spain's leading centers of heavy industry. The good harbor and rail connections have helped make the city the most important port on Spain's Atlantic coast. Iron ore, lead ore, and steel products rank high among its exports. Also important are wine, olive oil, and canned fish. The 14th-century city on the right bank has provisions for drainage, ventilation, and orderly pedestrian traffic that were advanced for their time.
See also: Spain.

Bile, yellow or greenish fluid secreted by the liver which aids in digestion and absorption, particularly of fatty foods. It contains water, lecithin, cholesterol, bile salts, and the pigments bilirubin and biliverdin. When needed, it is discharged through the common bile duct into the small intestine, where it breaks down fats and enables them to be absorbed

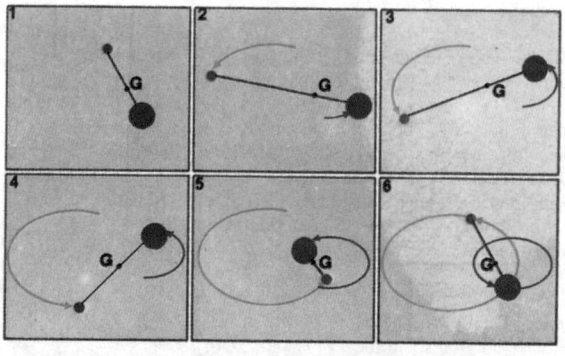

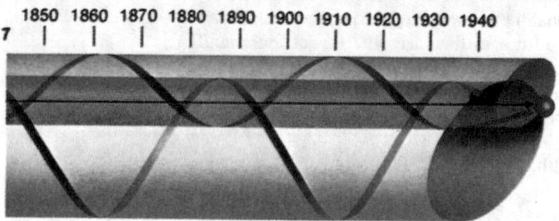

Binary stars revolve in different elliptical paths about a common center of gravity (G), or barycenter, so that the distance between them constant-ly varies (diagrams 1-6). The stars also move, so that a line between them will always pass through the barycenter. A more massive star re-mains closer to the barycenter, has a smaller elliptical orbit, and moves slower than a smaller one.

through the intestinal wall. Bile is also a route of excretion for cholesterol and various drugs.
See also: Digestive system.

Bilharziasis *See:* Schistosomiasis.

Bilirubin *See:* Bile; Jaundice.

Bill, term for various written documents in politics, law, banking, commerce, and so forth. In politics, it is the draft of a statute submitted to the legislature for debate and eventual adoption as law. In the courtroom it

was formerly applied to the written statement of a plaintiff's case, now usually referred to as a writ or statement of claim. In the commercial field, a bill of sale is a document transferring ownership of goods or property, sometimes used to secure a debt. In international trade, a bill of lading is a receipt given by a public carrier, agreeing to convey goods to a stated destination. In banking, a bill of exchange is a negotiable document, guaranteeing payment by the drawer to the payee, a form of promissory note or check. A bill of health is a document given to a ship's captain by a local authority, signifying absence of infectious or contagious disease on board.

Bill, Max (1908-1994), Swiss visual artist and architect. From 1927 until 1929 Bill studied at the Bauhaus in Dessau. In 1932 he met Mondrian who strongly influenced his work. From 1931 until 1936 he was a member of the Abstraction-Création group in Paris. Together with Van Doesburg and Vantongerloo he was one of the pioneers of concrete art in the 1930s, which entailed arranging shapes and colors according to particular patterns. His sculptures and paintings are entirely abstract and of an utmost precision as regards style and design. As an architect he designed a number of public buildings such as the Vidy theater in Lausanne. He also produced decors and posters.
See also: Mondrian, Piet; Doesburg, Theo van.

Billiards, any of several indoor games in which balls set on a felt-covered rectangular table with cushioned edges are struck by the end of a long tapering stick (the cue). Billiards was popular in France and England as early as the 14th century. In most forms of the game, the table has 6 pockets, one in each corner and one midway along each of the longer sides. The object is to sink balls into the pockets by playing one ball off another or, in games played without pockets, to hit the balls against each other successively. *Carom billiards* and *English billiards* feature 2 white cue balls and 1 red ball. *Snooker* has 1 white cue ball, 15 red balls, and 6 balls of other colors. *Pool* (or pocket billiards), as played in the United States, has 1 white cue ball and 15 numbered colored balls

Billings, William (1746-1800), first professional composer and musician born in the American colonies. He was noted for his simple, lively styles in hymns, psalms, and anthems.

Bill of exchange, negotiable instrument used in commerce that is drawn up and signed by one person to direct another person to pay a certain sum of money at a certain time to the bearer or to the party named on the bill. Parties involved in this transaction are frequently banks and businesses; the bill is a convenient means of transferring funds.

Bill of rights, constitutional document that defines the rights of a people, safeguarding them against undue governmental interfer-ence. In the United States these rights and safeguards are embodied in the first 10 amendments to the Constitution. After the American Revolution there was great popular demand for constitutionally defined rights to limit the power of the new government. On Dec. 15, 1791, Secretary of State Thomas Jefferson proclaimed the Federal Bill of Rights in full force. The bill guarantees freedom of speech, of the press, and of religion. It protects against arbitrary searches and self-incrimination. It sets out proper procedures for trials, giving to all the right to trial by jury and to cross-examination of witnesses. In addition to these rights, the 5th Amendment provides that no person shall 'be deprived of life, liberty, or property, without due process of law.'
See also: Constitution of the United States.

Billy the Kid (William H. Bonney; 1859-1881), U.S. outlaw. Notorious in New Mexico as a cattle thief, he was sentenced to hang. In 1878 he escaped from jail by killing 2 guards, and was tracked down and killed by Sheriff Pat Garrett.

Bimetallism, economic term for the use of 2 metals (usually gold and silver) to back a country's currency, making every coin and bill in circulation related to a definite value of both gold and silver. Nearly all countries now use currency based only on gold (monometallism).

Binary numbers, system of designating numbers using only the digits 0 and 1, widely employed in digital computers. Each digit in the binary system represents a successive power of 2, just as digits in the decimal system represent successive powers of 10. For example, in the binary system, the number 110 represents: $(1 \times 2^2) + (1 \times 2^1) + (0 \times 2^0)$, which equals (in the decimal system) $4 + 2 + 0$, or 6. While this system may appear cumbersome, it is easily adaptable to electronic circuits, where the 2 digits (0 and 1) can be represented by the 2 states of a switch: open or closed.

Binary star, or double star, pair of stars that orbit around their common center of gravity. Though some binaries can be observed separately without a telescope, in most cases the stars are so close together that they appear to be a single star. A great number of binaries are too close to be seen separately by even the most powerful optical telescopes and are detected by studying the spectral lines of the stars.
See also: Black hole; Nova; Pulsar.

Bindweed, common name for a weedy plant (genus *Convolvulus*) of the morning-glory family, Convolvulaceae. Bindweeds have long twining stems, arrow-shaped leaves, and white or pink funnel-shaped flowers that often open only in the morning.
See also: Morning-glory.

Binet, Alfred (1857-1911), French psychologist who pioneered methods of mental testing. He collaborated with Théodore Simon in devising the Binet-Simon tests, widely used to estimate intelligence.
See also: Intelligence quotient; Psychology.

Bing, Sir Rudolf (1902-1997), Austrian-born British opera impresario. An opera administrator in Germany, he emigrated to Britain when the Nazis came to power, headed the Glyndebourne Opera (1935-49), and helped organize the Edinburgh Festival (1947). As general manager of New York's Metropolitan Opera (1950-72), he introduced black singers and presided over the company's move to Lincoln Center.
See also: Opera.

Binoculars, optical instrument consisting of a pair of compact telescopes mounted side by side. Since both eyes are used, the magnified image of distant objects appears to be in 3 dimensions. The magnifying power of a pair of binoculars and the diameter of the object lens (front lens) are engraved on the instrument. Binoculars marked 10 x 50, for example, will make objects appear 10 times closer and have object lenses that are 50 mm (about 6 in) in diameter. Binoculars can be adjusted to focus the image, to move the two telescopes nearer or farther apart to fit the eyes, and to remove double images.

Biochemistry, study of the substances occurring in living organisms and the reactions in which they are involved. It is a science on the border between biology and organic chemistry. The main constituents of living matter are water, carbohydrates, lipids, and proteins. The total chemical activity of the organism is known as its metabolism. Landmarks in biochemistry include the synthesis of urea by Friedrich Wöhler (1828), the pioneering research of Von Liebig, Pasteur, and Bernard, and, more recently, the elucidation of the structure of DNA by James Watson and Francis Crick (1953).
See also: Biology; Chemistry; DNA.

Biofeedback, method of electronically monitoring various specific biological functions, such as blood pressure, with the aim of helping a person gain greater control of otherwise unconscious physiological processes. Biofeedback techniques have been used with some success in the treatment of hypertension, chronic headaches, epilepsy, and other disorders.

Biogenesis, origin and evolution of living forms. The law of biogenesis is the principle that all living organisms are derived from a parent or parents.
See also: Reproduction.

Biological clock, mechanism that controls the rhythm of various activities of plants and animals. Some activities, such as mating, migration, and hibernation, have a yearly cycle; others, chiefly reproductive functions (including human menstruation), follow the lunar month. But the majority have a period of roughly 24 hours, called the circadian rhythm. Although related to the day/night cycle, circadian rhythms are not directly controlled by it. Many organisms in unvarying environments will continue to show 24-hour rhythms, but the pattern can be changed and the clock 'reset.' In December 1997 a human clock gene 'rigui' was discovered, named after the ancient Chinese sundial.

Biological warfare, war waged with microorganisms and their toxins against people, animals, and plants. The United States, USSR, Great Britain, and more than 100 other countries signed an agreement in 1972 to prohibit the development, production, and stockpiling of biological weapons.

Biology, science of living things. The most important subdivisions of biology are zoology, the study of animals, and botany, the study of plants. Advances in scientific knowledge have led to an increase in the number of fields of biological study. Some biologists study subdivisions of the animal and plant kingdoms: entomology (the study of insects), mycology (fungi), paleontology (fossils), and microbiology (microorganisms). The they were mainly interested in anatomy, still an important field of study. As early biologists accumulated information about plants and animals, they noticed that some closely resembled others. Such observations were the basis for a system of classification. The Swedish naturalist Carolus Linnaeus devised a method of classifying living things, called taxonomy, in which each plant and animal is assigned a unique name. Physiology is the study of the workings of organs and how they are affected by disease. The study of diseases themselves is called pathology. Biology is also connected with other scientific disciplines. Biochemistry is the application of chemistry to biology, and biophysics is the application of physics to biology. The study of animal behavior often employs the techniques of psychology. Molecular biology studies biological processes at the level of the molecule. The study of genetics, dealing with heredity, has become increasingly important. Genetic engineering is now making possible the production of substances by means of intervention in genetic processes.

Bioluminescence, the production of non-thermal light by living organisms, such as fireflies, many marine animals, bacteria, and fungi. The effect is an example of chemiluminescence. In some cases its utility to the organism is not apparent, though in others its use is clear: In the firefly, the abdomen of the female glows, enabling the male to find her; similarly, luminescence enables many deep-sea fish to locate each other or to attract their prey. The glow in a ship's wake at night is due to luminescent microorganisms.

Biome, major ecological unit that is relatively stable, widespread, and well-defined. An example would be a savanna, a tropical grassland with a characteristic range of interlocking plant and animal forms.
See also: Ecology.

Biomedical engineering, application of principles of engineering to biology and medicine, usually involving collaboration between engineers and biological scientists. There are a number of specialty areas in the field. Bioinstrumentation is the use of electronic measuring devices to monitor, diagnose, and treat diseases; biomechanics is the study of effects of various forces on the body, such as gravity. The development of appropriate materials that can be implanted inside the human body is the province of biomaterials, and systems physiology aims at an integrated understanding of living organisms. Clinical engineering involves the development of computer instruments in hospitals, and rehabilitation engineering develops devices and procedures to expand the capabilities of disabled people.

Bionics, science of designing artificial systems that apply the principles that govern the functioning of living organisms. These may be simple imitations of nature or systems that embody laws learned from nature. An example of the latter would be radar, inspired by the echolocation systems of bats.

Biophysics, branch of biology in which the methods and principles of physics are applied to the study of living things. It has grown up in the 20th century alongside the development of electronics. Its tools include the electroencephalograph and the electron microscope. Its techniques include those of spectroscopy and X-ray diffraction. Its field of study deals with such questions as nerve transmission, bioluminescence, and materials transfer in respiration and secretion.
See also: Biology; Physics.

Biosphere, the part of the earth inhabited by living things. It forms a thin layer around the earth, including air, water, and land.

Biosynthesis, biochemical reactions by which living cells build complex molecules from simple ones.
See also: Biochemistry; Cell.

Biotechnology, industrial application of biological knowledge, in particular through the alteration of genes, called genetic engineering. Alteration of genes has been used to create new drugs, chemicals, and animal growth hormones, as well as therapies to repair genetic defects. Ethical and safety concerns about the uses of genetic engineering have generated many legal and moral conflicts in recent years.
See also: Genetic engineering.

Biotite *See:* Mica.

Birch, name for various deciduous trees and shrubs of the family Betulaceae, characterized by their smooth, white outer bark, which sometimes peels off in layers. The heart-shaped leaves have saw-tooth edges. Birch grows widely in the cooler parts of the Northern Hemisphere. The close-grained timber is used for furniture, the bark for tanning and thatching. Among the best-known species are the paper birch of North America, used by Native Americans to make canoes and tents; the silver birch, a native of Europe, widely used in the USSR for roofing material, containers, and in processing leather; and the yellow birch, which makes up some 75% of the American harvest of birchwood.

Bird, animal adapted for flight and unique in its body covering of feathers. There are more than 8,500 species. Birds are warm-blooded descendants of reptiles of the dinosaur group. They developed feathers from

B

scales (still evident on their legs) and became two-legged as their forelimbs became wings. Their teeth disappeared, replaced by a horny bill used for feeding and performing complicated tasks, such as nest-building. The bird's body has been adapted for flight. The feathers, an efficient and light body covering, streamline the body and extend the flight surfaces: wings and tail. The skeleton is light, and the bones are hollow. Large breast muscles provide power for flight. The heaviest flying bird is the trumpeter swan of North America, which can weigh up to 38 lb (17 kg). At the other end of the scale, the bee hummingbird is about 2.5 in (6 cm) long and weighs 1/10 oz (3 g). Flightless birds can be much larger. The ostrich stands up to 8 ft (2 1/2 m) and can weigh 300 lb (136 kg). Flightless birds are mainly adapted for running or swimming. Runners have strong

The magnificent bird of paradise (*Diphyllodes magnificus*) of the forests of New Guinea, has sickle-shaped feathers extending from its tail.

The earliest known bird is the primal bird (*Archaeopteryx lithographica*), which lived in the Jurassic era (180-135 million years ago).

legs, like the ostrich; swimmers have wings that are modified as flippers, as in penguins. But some flying birds are also powerful runners, or swimmers. All birds reproduce by laying eggs that must be kept warm for correct development.
In 1997 fossils were found in Patagonia, which belonged to a previously unknown dinosaur variety (*Unenlagia comahuensis*). Scientists put that this variety is the missing link between birds and dinosaurs. In 1998

scientists presented the *Rahona ostromi*, a primitive bird with claws that resemble those of carnivorous dinosaurs.

Bird, Larry (1956-), U.S. basketball player. Known for his excellence in all phases of the game, he is considered one of the best players of all time. The 6-ft 9-in (206-cm) forward joined the Boston Celtics of the National Basketball Association (NBA) in 1979 and was named the NBA Rookie of the Year. Bird's other achievements include winning 6 NBA Most Valuable Player (MVP) awards-3 regular season (1984, 1985, 1986), 2 playoff (1984, 1985), and 1 All-Star (1982)-and leading the Boston Celtics to 3 NBA Championships (1981, 1984, 1986).

Bird of paradise, any of more than 40 species of brilliantly colored, plumed birds of the family Paradiseidae, found in eastern Australia, the Moluccas, and New Guinea.

Bird of paradise, plant (*Strelitzia reginae*) named for the colorful bird which its flowers resemble. Native to South Africa, this perennial herb grows to a height of 3 to 4 ft (0.9 to 1.2m) and has long-stalked leaves. Several showy flowers, with orange sepals and blue-purple petals, rise from each of the boat-shaped bracts that tip the flowering stalks.

Birdseye, Clarence (1886-1956), U.S. inventor and industrialist who, having observed during fur-trading expeditions to Labrador (1912-1916) that many foods keep indefinitely if frozen, developed a process for freezing food. In 1924 he founded General Foods to market frozen produce.
See also: Food, frozen.

Birendra Bir Bikram Shah Deva (1945-2001), king of Nepal (1972-2001), succeeded his father Mahendra. He was officially crowned king in 1975.

Birmingham (pop. 1,000,000), second-largest city in England, about 200 mi (161 km) northwest of London. Birmingham is known as the steel city, producing everything from pins to automobiles. In ancient times a Saxon settlement existed in this area, and by 1166 the site had become a busy market village trading in small metal goods made in nearby Staffordshire, where iron and coal were plentiful. By the late 16th century the population was manufacturing metal products, from swords and cutlery to guns, buckles, jewelry, and plate. In the 17th century Birmingham became a center for scientific ideas and innovation in industry. Scientists and inventors established the Lunar Society there, its members including James Watt, Matthew Boulton, and Joseph Priestley. By 1800 Birmingham was one of the major industrial towns in Britain, but its rapid growth caused deplorable living and working conditions, resulting in riots (1839). The modern city is a center for the machine and tool industries; other products include armaments, toys, and electrical equipment.
See also: England.

Birmingham (pop. 266,000), largest city in

Alabama, situated in the Jones Valley and protected by mountains to the southeast and northwest. Located in a region rich in coal and iron, it manufactures numerous iron and steel products, including pipes, stoves, cotton gins, diesel engines, and electrical equipment. Birmingham was founded and incorporated in 1871, on a site where railroads from 4 directions met in a cotton field. It is now an important rail and air terminus and has a port of entry accessible from the Gulf of Mexico through a channel. The city is also an important educational center, being the site of Miles College, Howard College, Birmingham-Southern College, and the University of Alabama Birmingham (UAB).
See also: Alabama.

Birth, the climax of gestation (the development of a child or other baby mammal within its mother's body) and the beginning of an independent life. In humans, a normal birth proceeds in 3 stages. Mild labor pains caused by contractions of the muscles of the uterus are usually the first sign that a woman is about to give birth. The contractions push the baby downwards, usually head first, which breaks the membranes surrounding the baby, causing the amniotic fluid to escape. In the second stage of labor, stronger contractions push the baby through the cervix and vagina, or birth canal. This is the most painful part and usually lasts less than 2 hours. Anesthetics and analgesics are commonly administered at this time, and delivery is aided by hand or with obstetric forceps. In some cases, the baby must be delivered by a surgical procedure called cesarean section. As soon as the baby is born, its nose and mouth are cleared of fluid and breathing starts, whereupon the umbilical cord is cut and tied. In the third stage of labor, the placenta is expelled from the uterus and bleeding is stopped by further contractions.The exact mechanism by which labor is initiated remains unknown; however, recent research indicates that hormones both from the placenta and from the mother's pituitary gland play important roles in the onset of labor.
See also: Reproduction.

Birth control, prevention of conception in order to avert unwanted births. There are various contraceptive, or birth-control, devices, including condoms, spermicidal jellies, diaphragms, intrauterine devices, and pills taken by women. Surgical sterilization (for men: vasectomy; for women: tubal ligation) is also possible. Diverse methods of birth control have become increasingly widespread in the 20th century, especially in industrialized countries.

Birth defect, congenital anomaly; structural or severe functional defect present at birth. Birth defects cause about 10% of neonatal deaths. A major anomaly is apparent at birth in 3-4% of newborns; by the age of 5, up to 7.5% of all children manifest a congenital defect. The incidence of specific congenital anomalies varies with a number of factors: (1) Individual defect (common malformations such as cleft lip and cleft palate occur in 1 in every 1,000 births). (2) Geographical area (because of factors such as differences

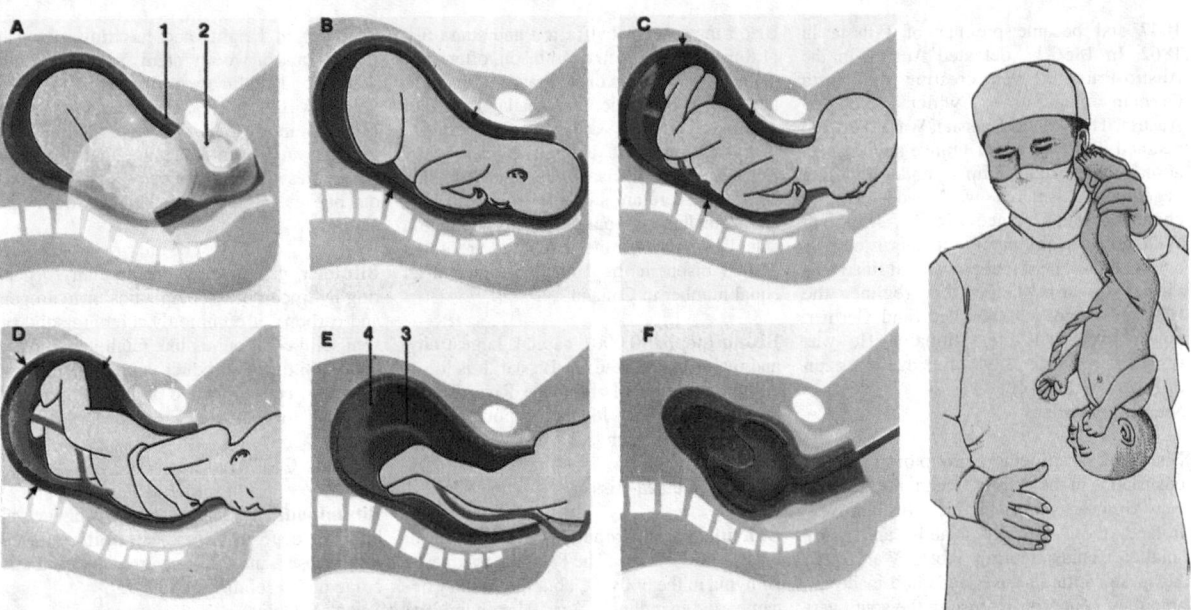

B

At completion of pregnancy (A) the fetus usually lies with its head toward the cervix, or neck of the uterus, and birth canal, or vagina; the pelvic girdle (2; transparent area) protects the lower part of the uterus, or womb (1). During the first stage of labor (B) the muscular walls of the uterus begin to contract, and the cervix dilates; this stage lasts an average of 12 to 14 hours in a woman's first pregnancy, 6 or 7 hours in subsequent pregnancies. During the next stage, contractions and the mother's voluntary efforts push the baby through the birth canal. The baby's head emerges (C) and rotates (D), often with the assistance of a doctor or midwife, and the rest of the body follows (E). The umbilical cord (3) is cut. The placenta (4), or afterbirth, separates from the uterus and is expelled in the third stage of labor (F). The newborn infant is usually held (G) with head lower than feet; this procedure drains fluids from its respiratory tract and stimulates breathing.

in the genetic pool or the environment). For example, the occurrence of spina bifida is 3-4 in every 1,000 births in areas of Ireland, but under 2 in 1,000 in the United States. (3) Cultural practices: where marriages between relatives are frequent, the incidence of certain defects increases. (4) Certain prenatal problems.

Birthmark, skin blemish, usually congenital. There are 2 main types: pigmented nevuses or moles, which are usually brown or black and may be raised or flat; and vascular nevuses or hemangiomas, local growths of small blood vessels, such as the 'strawberry mark' and the 'portwine stain.' Although harmless, they are sometimes removed for cosmetic reasons or if they show malignant tendencies.
See also: Mole.

Birthstone, gemstone associated with a month. The ancients allotted a birthstone to each month and believed that it would influence anyone born in that month. The stones and the qualities they were thought to impart are: *January*, garnet (loyalty); *February*, amethyst (sincerity); *March*, bloodstone (courage); *April*, diamond (innocence); *May*, emerald (love); *June*, moonstone (health); *July*, ruby (contentment); *August* sardonyx (married happiness); *September*, sapphire (clear thinking); *October*, opal (hope); *November*, topaz (faithfulness); *December*, turquoise (prosperity).

Biruni, al- (Arab.: in full Abu Ar-Rayhan Muhammad ibn Ahmad Al-Biruni; 973-1048), Arabic scientist. His work *Tarih al-Hind* is a description and history of India. In addition, he wrote about astronomy, arithmetic, physics, and the *Al-kanoen al-Mas'oedi*, an encyclopedia on astronomy. From 1017 onwards he was court astrologer to Sultan Mas'ud of Ghazna.

Bishkek (Frunze; pop. 626,000), capital of Kirgizstan, about 125 mi (201 km) southwest of Alma Ata. Until World War II mainly meat, grain processing, and tanning, currently mechanical engineering and metalworks. Cultural and educational center (including a university since 1951). Founded as Pishpek and for a long time named after the revolutionary and Red Army leader Mikhail Vasilyevich Frunze (1885-1925). After Kirgizstan became independent in 1991 it was renamed Bishkek.

Bishop, Elizabeth (1911-1979), U.S. poet and translator of Brazilian poetry, widely acclaimed for her succinct style and lyricism. Her books include the Pulitzer Prize-winning *North and South-A Cold Spring* (1955), *Questions of Travel* (1965), and *Geography III* (1976).

Bisitun (Behistun), village in Iran, 19 mi east of Kermanshah, known for the bas-relief of Persian King Darius the Great (521-486 B.C.), with a trilingual rock inscription below it, which records Darius' feats and a list of the peoples of the Persian Empire. Thanks to these inscriptions, H.C. Rawlinson was able to decipher the Babylonian cuneiform script.

Bismarck, one of the most powerful German battleships of World War II. It had a speed of 30 knots, carried eight 15-in (38.1-cm) guns, and displaced more than 45,000 long tons (45,700 m tons) of water. It was sunk in May 1941 after eight different British ships bombarded it about 600 mi (970 km) off the French coast. A 1989 inspection of the sunken ship by U.S. researchers indicated that the Germans might have caused it to go down themselves to prevent its capture.
See also: World War II.

Bismarck, Prince Otto von (1815-1898), German political leader who was instrumental in creating a unified German state. Born of Prussian gentry, he entered politics in

The title page of the satirical newspaper *Lustige Blätter* of March 28, 1899. Bismarck is astounded and annoyed at the fact that a citizen can be a member of his cabinet. The large Prussian representation in the cabinet of the empire was expressed in the great number of ministers from the army. In Prussia, the army was the focus of society, and its officers came from the Junker nobility.

B

1847 and became premier of Prussia in 1862. In 1866 he defeated Austria in the Austro-Prussian War, creating the North German Federation, which excluded Austria. The Franco-Prussian War (1870-71) resulted in the defeat of France and the creation of a German empire under Prussian hegemony. Bismarck was made imperial chancellor and prince (1871). Although Wilhelm I was nominally the kaiser (emperor), Bismarck held real power and ruled as a virtual dictator. Under his regime, the German economy flourished, and German power expanded internationally. He was forced to resign in 1890 after the accession of Kaiser William II.
See also: Germany.

Bismarck Archipelago, group of mountainous islands in the Pacific Ocean, northeast of New Guinea, comprising New Britain, New Ireland, the Admiralty Islands, and many smaller islands. During World War II the Japanese captured the islands and made the area their center of defense in the southwest Pacific. After the war the islands were handed back to Australia and are currently administered from New Guinea. Most of them are covered with jungle vegetation and some have active volcanoes.

Bismuth, chemical element, symbol Bi; for physical constants see Periodic Table. Bismuth was known to the ancients and in early times was confused with tin and lead. It was shown to be distinct from lead in 1753 by Claud J. Geoffroy. Bismuth is sometimes found native, as the minerals *bismite* and *bismuthinite*. It is obtained as a byproduct of the refining of lead, copper, and tin. Bismuth is a grayish-white, hard, brittle, low-melting metal. It is the most diamagnetic of all metals and has the highest Hall effect of any metal. It has a low thermal conductivity and a high electrical resistance. Bismuth forms low-melting alloys that are widely used in fire detection and fire extinguishing systems. Bismuth and its compounds are used in powerful magnets and, in medicine, as antisyphilitics and anti-infectives.

The massive American bison (*B. bison*) is aggressive and easily angered. Before combat, a bull will compete with other bulls. The one who can make the loudest roar, is the winner.

Bison, any of several species (genus *Bison*) of ox-like animals of the family Bovidae.

Bison may weigh half a ton and stand 6 ft (1.8 m) tall. The American bison, often miscalled the buffalo, once grazed the plains and valleys of Mexico to Canada in herds of millions and was economically vital to Native Americans. Hunted ruthlessly by European Americans, it was almost extinct by 1900. There are still a few herds in U.S. and Canadian national parks and population calculations determine that there are about 15,000 bison in the United States and an equal number in Canada.

Bissau (pop. 200,000), capital, largest city, and major port of Guinea-Bissau. It is located at the mouth of the Geba River on the West African coast. Its main exports include coconuts, rice, peanuts, hardwood, palm oil, and shellfish.
See also: Guinea-Bissau.

Bithynia, ancient country of Asia Minor, in what is now Turkey. The Persians conquered Bithynia in the 600s B.C., but the country became independent after Alexander the Great's destruction of the Persian empire. Bithynia was independent from the 3rd century B.C. until 74 B.C. when Rome annexed it. It declined in the 2nd century A.D.

Bitterling, minnowlike fish of the family Cyprinidae, found in the fresh waters of Europe and Asia Minor. It is remarkable for its association with freshwater mussels. In the breeding season the female develops a 2-in (5-cm) tube with which she deposits her eggs inside a mussel. The milt (sperm), deposited by the male near the mussel, is drawn in through the mussel's respiratory siphon to fertilize the eggs. Meanwhile the mussel releases its larvae, which cling to the skin of the female bitterling and are carried around before dropping to the bottom.

Bittern, any of several species of migratory birds of the heron family. The U.S. bittern (Botaurus lentiginosus) ranges from 2 to 3 ft (61 to 91 cm) tall. Its brownish color blends into marshland reeds, allowing it to feed upon its diet of fish, frogs, mice, and insects. There are three other kinds who all look similar; the Botaurus pinnatus (South America), the Botaurus poiciloptilus (Australia), and the Botaurus stellaris (Europe).

Bitternut, medium to large-sized tree (*Carya cordiformis*) of the walnut family, which grows mostly in low wet woods. Its name is derived from the tree's bitter-tasting nuts. Thin-shelled and cylindrical in shape, they contain a fat white kernel. Bitternut wood is used for making wooden crates and furniture.

Bitter root, any of several small perennial plants of the family Portulaceae, with long edible roots. It is also called tobacco root because of the tobacco odor generated when cooked. Bitter root has a fat stalk and produces a single rose-colored or white flower. It is the state flower of Montana.

Bittersweet, either of 2 unrelated woody vines: U.S. bittersweet (*Celastrus scandens*) and European bittersweet (*Solanum dulcamara*). The U.S. bittersweet grows up to 20

ft (6 m) in height, and has tiny greenish flowers and a woody stem. In late autumn yellow pods split open, displaying red and yellow waxen berries. European bittersweet is rarely more than 8 ft (2.4 m) high. Its flowers vary from violet to light blue and sometimes white. The vine produces poisonous berries and leaves. It is native to Europe and Asia.

Bitumen, general term for naturally occurring hydrocarbons (compounds of hydrogen and carbon). It commonly refers to solid or semisolid compounds like pitch, tar, and asphalt. Bitumen products are widely employed to coat timber to protect it from water, and to seal roofs, arches, walls and floors.
See also: Coal; Hydrocarbon.

Bituminous sands, sands containing natural bitumen deposits. The heavy oil extracted from these sands is converted to synthetic crude oil by refining.
See also: Coal.

Biya, Paul (1933-), Cameroonian politician. Biya worked for the government of Cameroon from 1962. In 1975 he became prime minister and in 1982 president (succeeding Ahidjo). In 1984 the office of prime minister was abolished and he became both head of state and leader of the government. In 1991 he introduced a number of political reforms under international pressure, such as reestablishing the office of prime minister and appointing Sadou Hayatou as leader of the new government. Biya was reelected with 40% of the votes during the presidential elections in 1992. The presidential elections in 1997 were boycotted by most parties because the government refused to set up an independent electoral committee. This time Biya was reelected with 92% of the votes.

Bizet, Georges (1838-1875), French composer, best known for his opera *Carmen* (1875), one of the most popular in history. He also wrote symphonies and incidental music for other operas.

Björk (Björk Gudmundsdóttir; 1965-), Icelandic singer. Björk experienced a minor breakthrough with the formation The Sugarcubes, but achieved her major success with her solo-albums *Debut* (1993) and *Post* (1995). On these albums, she produces an experimental sound with a strong dance influence. On *Homogenic* (1997) she was inspired by Icelandic folk music. In 2000 she recorded the soundtrack and played the leading part in Lars Von Triers's movie *Dancer in the dark*, which was awarded a Palme D'Or.
See also: Trier, Lars von.

Björling, Jussi (1911-1960), Swedish operatic tenor who specialized in Italian opera, especially works by Verdi and Puccini.
See also: Opera.

Bjørnson, Bjørnstjerne Martinius (1832-1910), Norwegian poet, critic, novelist, dramatist, and politician, winner of the Nobel Prize in literature (1903). Initially concentrating on themes of Norwegian history, he later wrote about modern social problems. Among his writings was the novel *Flags Are Flying in Town and Port* (1884).

Black, Davidson (1884-1934), Canadian anthropologist who discovered the early human species later known popularly as Peking man. He was professor at Peking Union medical college in China until his death.
See also: Anthropology.

Black, Joseph (1728-1799), Scottish physician and chemist. He investigated the properties of carbon dioxide, discovered the phenomena of latent and specific heats, distinguished heat from temperature, and pioneered the techniques used in the quantitative study of chemistry.
See also: Chemistry; Heat.

Black Americans *See:* African Americans.

Blackbeard (d. 1718), English pirate whose real name was probably Edward Teach or Thatch. A privateer in the War of the Spanish Succession, he later turned to piracy in the West Indies and along the Atlantic coast, until he was killed by the British.

Blackberry, prickly bramble (genus *Rubus*) of the rose family, native to north temperate regions of the world, that produces an edible fruit. Some varieties, including the loganberry and boysenberry, are cultivated to be sold fresh, frozen, or canned, and are used in beverages, liqueurs, and preserves.

Blackbird, any of several dark-colored perching birds of the family Icteridae, including the red-winged blackbird and the yellow-headed blackbird. Blackbirds may survive temperatures as low as 20°F (-6°C). They travel in huge flocks (as many as 5 million birds) and eat fruit, insects, and worms, and often do serious damage to crops.

Blackbuck (*Antilope cervicapra*), antelope of India and Pakistan. Once numbering millions, there are now only a few thousand left in the plains and woodlands where they live in herds. The females and young are yellow-fawn with a white eye-ring; the adult males are dark brown, stand about 32 in (81 cm) tall at the shoulder, and bear spiral horns up to 2 ft (60 cm) long. Blackbuck are very swift and used to be hunted with cheetahs.

Black Death, common name for an epidemic of bubonic plague that swept through Asia and Europe in the mid-14th century, perhaps halving the population of Europe. Caused by a bacterium, the disease was carried by flea-infected rats. Its economic effects were far-reaching, among other things fanning flames of superstition and religious prejudice.
See also: Bubonic plague.

Black-eyed pea *See:* Cowpea.

Black-eyed Susan, hardy annual or biennial coneflower (*Rudbeckia hirta*), the state flower of Maryland. Sometimes called yellow daisy, it bears 20 to 40 orange-yellow ray flowers around a group of darker brown florets.

Blackfish, common name given to any of various dark-colored fishes, including the black sea bass found along the Atlantic coast of the United States, the Alaska blackfish found in streams and ponds in Alaska and Siberia, and the tautog, found in the Atlantic Ocean from New Brunswick, Canada, to South Carolina.

Blackfoot tribes, North American plains tribes of the Algonquin linguistic family. The Blackfoot, named for their black-dyed moccasins, were originally hunters and trappers in what is now Montana and the Canadian provinces of Alberta and Saskatchewan. The disappearance of the bison (killed off by white settlers), a smallpox epidemic, and wars with whites reduced the Blackfoot population. Blackfoot today are farmers and ranchers in Montana and Alberta.
See also: Algonquins.

Black Forest, wooded mountain range in the province of Baden-Württemberg, southwestern Germany. An area of great scenic beauty, it is an important tourist attraction, with lumber, clock, and toy industries.

Black haw, small tree or shrub (*Viburnum prunifolium*) of the eastern and southern United States. It grows up to 15 ft (4.6 m) high. After a frost, its bluish-black berries can be eaten.

Blackhead *See:* Acne; Porc.

Black Hills, mountain range in South Dakota and Wyoming, famous for the Mount Rushmore National Memorial. Here, the heads of 4 past U.S. presidents are carved out of the mountainside. The Black Hills are rich in minerals, including gold. Their highest point is Harney Peak (7,242 ft/2,207 m).

Black hole, according to current astrophysical theory, the final stage of evolution for very massive stars following complete gravitational collapse. In theory, a star with a mass more than 3 times that of the sun could collapse to an indefinitely small size. The gravitational field of such an object would be so powerful that not even electromagnetic radiation (including visible light) could escape. Black holes, if they exist, would have to be detected by their gravitational effects on other bodies and by the emission of X- and gamma rays by objects falling into them. A black hole would therefore bear some resemblance to the initial state of the universe in the big bang theory.
See also: Astronomy; Star; Big bang.

Black Hole of Calcutta, prison cell in which 146 British captives were incarcerated on the night of June 20, 1756, after a battle between British and Indian troops during which the Indian forces captured a British fort. Some of the prisoners suffocated in the 14 ft (4.3 m) by 18 ft (5.5 m) room. John Holwell, a British survivor, alleged that 123 of the 146 had died, but subsequent research suggests that there were probably about 15 deaths.

Blacklist, list of persons, companies, or organizations who are disapproved of and are to be boycotted.

Black lung, disease caused by inhaled dust which collects in the lungs and may eventually destroy them. Black lung has two forms, simple and complicated, and is found among coal miners and sandblasters. Symptoms are wheezing, coughing, and a higher incidence of lung infection.

Black market, illicit dealing in scarce commodities or currencies, in defiance of rules for rationing and price restrictions. In many countries, black market operations did not appear on a large scale until World War II. A black market also operates in countries where there is a shortage of reliable foreign currencies such as dollars or marks and people are prepared to pay above the official exchange rate to obtain them.

Black Muslims, popular name of a U.S. black nationalist movement (originally called the Nation of Islam) founded in Detroit in 1930 by Wali Farad, who rejected racial integration and advocated thrift, hard work, and cleanliness. Under Elijah Muhammad (1934-75), the Black Muslims became a major force in the African-American community, demanding the formation of an independent Black nation in the United States. In the 1960s a split between Elijah Muhammad and Malcolm X, a Black Muslim minister and the group's most prominent leader, undermined the strength of the Nation of Islam. Malcolm X was assassinated in 1965, and when Wallace Muhammad succeeded his father as leader of the group in 1975, he turned the organization into a non-political association whose beliefs are closer to those of orthodox Islam, changing its name to the American Muslim Mission. A splinter group bearing the original name, the Nation of Islam, continues to uphold Elijah Muhammad's teachings.
See also: Malcolm X; Muhammad, Elijah.

Black Panther Party, U.S. black political movement founded in Oakland, Calif. in 1966, advocating self-defense of the African-American community and revolu-

Incandescent gas, streaming from the surface of a blue supergiant star (left), and spiraling into its companion black hole. The matter is heated to a million Kelvins by the release of gravitational energy, and it emits intense ultraviolet and X-radiation. Then it is lost forever, as it is sucked into the black hole, from which no matter or radiation can ever escape.

B

tionary change in the United States. Under the leadership of Eldridge Cleaver, Huey P. Newton, Bobby Seale, and others, the Panthers opened community centers and bookshops as well as doing legal battles with the authorities. Their often violent rhetoric was used to justify armed attacks that resulted in the death of many Panther leaders, such as Fred Hampton in Chicago. The influence of the party was weakened by internal factional disputes in the early 1970s, and by the 1980s its influence in the black liberation movement had ended.

Black Power, slogan coined in the mid-1960s by militant black activists, particularly Stokely Carmichael of the Student Non-violent Coordinating Committee (SNCC), to give voice to and inspire a growing black pride and aspiration for political power. A significant turning point in the history of Black Power occurred at the 1968 Summer Olympics when U.S. athletes receiving medals for their victory raised their fists in sympathy for this movement. It has evolved a multiplicity of meanings ranging from awareness of African-American economic potential to cultural and political organization.
See also: African Americans; Carmichael, Stokely.

Black Prince *See:* Edward the Black Prince.

Black Sea, tideless island sea between Europe and Asia, bordered by Turkey, Bulgaria, Romania, Ukraine, Russian Federation and Georgia and linked to the Sea of Azov and (via the Bosporus) to the Mediterranean. It covers 181,000 sq mi (468,790 sq km) and is up to 7,250 ft (2,210 m) deep. The Danube, Dniester, Bug, Don, and Dnieper rivers all flow into the sea. The chief ports are Odessa, Sevastopol, Batumi, Constanta, and Varna. The Black Sea coast is an important resort area.

Black September, name applied to various armed groups within the Palestine Liberation Organization. Named for the civil war in Jordan in Sept. 1970 that led to the expulsion of all Palestinian guerrilla groups from the country by King Hussein, groups called Black September claimed responsibility for or were implicated in many violent acts in the 1970s, including the killing of 11 Israeli athletes at the 1972 Olympic Games in Munich.
See also: Arafat, Yasir; Palestine Liberation Organization.

Black Shirts, nickname given to Fascist Party activists in Italy. They were organized by Benito Mussolini in 1919 and seized control of the Italian government in 1922, forcing King Victor Emmanuel III to appoint Mussolini as leader.
See also: Mussolini, Benito.

Blacksnake (*Coluber constrictor*), nonvenomous snake common in almost every part of the United States. One of the largest North American snakes, it is 4-7 ft (120-210 cm) long. The adult is a deep slate-black color, while the young are pale gray with grayish-brown patches. Sometimes known as the 'racer,' this snake can move along the ground as fast as a running human can run and can climb trees with ease. Its food consists mainly of lizards, frogs, mice, and birds. The eggs, usually a dozen or more, are encased in a leathery shell. Also referred to as blacksnakes are the pilot black snake (*Elaphe obsoleta*) of North America and various black snakes of Australia (genus *Pseudeschis*).

Black stone, holy stone Mecca. The black stone, set in a ring of silver, is bricked into one of the corners of the Kaaba, the holy shrine in Mecca. As the pilgrims complete their seven circles around the Kaaba, and if they are able to get close to it despite the crowds, they try to kiss the stone or at least touch it. The precise origin and composition of the stone is unclear. Some people say it is a piece of lava or basalt, while others believe it to be a meteorite. According to one Islamic tradition, the stone was in the Garden of Eden at the time of Adam and Eve. Initially white, it turned black when touched by original sin. There are many other stories concerning the stone, but by far not every Muslim attaches importance to such myths.
See also: Mecca.

Blackstone, Sir William (1723-1780), English jurist, author of *Commentaries on the Laws of England* (1765-1769). Educated at Oxford, Blackstone was admitted to the bar in 1746 and in 1758 became the first holder of the new chair in English law at Oxford. The *Commentaries*, whose influence was considerable in the United States as well as England, forms a compendium of English law up to the 18th century.

Black studies, in U.S. education, program of study of the culture, history, and literature of African Americans, initiated to correct the omission of such information from traditional scholastic disciplines. These courses were added to high-school and university curricula as a result of black protests of the 1960s.

Black widow, poisonous spider (genus *Latrodectus*) of the Americas. Adults are black and have red or orange hourglass-shaped marks on their abdomens. The adult

The venomous bite of the black widow spider (*Latrodectus mactans*) causes muscle spasms and breathing difficulty in humans and may be fatal. The female is distinguished by a red hourglass marking on its underside.

female is 0.5 in (1.3 cm) long and often devours the smaller male during mating. The bite of the black widow can cause considerable pain, swelling, and nausea, but is rarely fatal to healthy adults.

Bladder, muscular sac in the lower abdomen of all mammals that stores urine produced by the kidneys. Urine is carried to the bladder through 2 tubes called ureters and is emptied through the urethra by the contraction of a sphincter muscle. The term is also used to designate any similar organ in plants or animals; for example, the swim bladder in fish and the vesicles in some seaweeds.
See also: Kidney; Urine.

Bladder, gall *See:* Gall bladder.

Bladderwort, aquatic plant (genus *Utricularia*) found in tropical and temperate zones that traps insects, larvae, small worms, and protozoa in air-filled sacs attached to its stems and roots. In medical history, the plant has been used for the treatment of eczema and other allergic skin conditions.

Blair, Eric *See:* Orwell, George.

Blair, Henry (19th-century), U.S. slave and inventor. He became the first black to hold a patent when he obtained patents for a corn harvester (1835) and a cotton planter (1836). In 1858, however, it was ruled that slaves could not hold federal patents; this situation prevailed until after the Civil War.

Blair, Tony (Anthony Charles Lynton; 1953-), British politician and Prime Minister (1997-). Blair studied law, became a member of the Labour Party in 1976, and won a seat in Parliament in 1983. He rapidly became a prominent spokesman. He was elected leader of the Labour Party in 1994. He managed to modernize the party and to get rid of obsolete and dogmatic points of view (such as nationalization of companies). The Labour Party became a modern social-democratic movement. In 1997, after 18 years of opposition, Blair's Labour Party won the general elections by a landslide. Blair succeeded John Major, of the Conservative Party, as Prime Minister. Blair campaigned on forging stronger European ties and negotiated to find a Northern Irish peace settlement. In 1998, he gained a major victory when after lengthy negotiations, he succeeded in realizing a peace treaty (Good Friday-agreement) between the Northern-Irish parties. He was a loyal ally to the U.S. during the bombing of former Yugoslavia as well as in the war in Afghanistan that followed the terrorist attacks of September 11, 2001. Blair advocates military action against regimes which endanger western interests and human rights. In 2001, he was re-elected Prime Minister after his Labour Party again won the general elections.
See also: Northern Ireland; United Kingdom; Labour Party.

Blair House, official guest house of the U.S. government, on Pennsylvania Ave. in Washington, D.C. It was used as a temporary White House by President Truman (1948-52). The house, built in 1824, was named for its second owner, Francis Preston Blair, whose family sold it to the government in 1942.

Blake, Eubie (James Hubert Blake; 1883-

1983), African-American ragtime pianist and composer of the Broadway musical *Shuffle Along* (1921) and the songs 'I'm Just Wild About Harry' and 'Memories of You.' He was still performing publicly in his 90s.

Blake, William (1757-1827), English poet and painter. With the help of his wife, Catherine Boucher, he developed a printing process that he used to illustrate and publish his own works, including *Songs of Innocence* (1789) and *Songs of Experience* (1794), collections of lyrics that contrast natural beauty with humanity's material world. Blake was a revolutionary in both politics and religion, which is reflected in his art, particularly in the powerful 'Prophetic Books,' in which he created a mythology of his own. The most famous of his Prophetic Books are *The Marriage of Heaven and Hell* (c.1790) and the epic *Jerusalem* (1804-20). Blake's work was largely ignored by his contemporaries, and his reputation grew significantly after his death.

Blanc, Mont, highest peak (15,771 ft/4,807 m) in the European Alps, in southeastern France on the border with Italy. One of the world's longest vehicular tunnels (7.5 mi/12 km), exceeded in Europe only by the 10.2 mi (16.4 km) St. Gotthard (1980), was constructed through Mont Blanc's base in 1965.

Blanchard, Jean Pierre François (1753-1809), French balloonist who made the first aeronautical crossing of the English Channel (1785) and the first balloon ascent in America (1793). He also invented the parachute (1785).
See also: Parachute.

Bland, James A. (1854-1911), African-American composer. In the late 1800s he helped popularize 'minstrel music' and was an accomplished banjo player. Among the songs he wrote were 'Carry Me Back to Old Virginny' (1878), 'Oh, Dem Golden Slippers' (1879), and 'In the Evening by the Moonlight' (1879).

Blank verse, unrhymed verse in iambic pentameter (lines consisting of 5 short-long feet, totaling 10 syllables). The most common English meter, it was used to great effect by Marlowe, Shakespeare, and Milton.

Blarney stone, stone of Blarney Castle, Ireland. In legend it has the magical power to confer the gift of eloquence on those who kiss it.

Blasco Ibáñez, Vicente (1867-1928), Spanish antimonarchist politician and novelist. His naturalistic novels include *Reeds and Mud* (1902), *Blood and Sand* (1909), and the World War I novel *The Four Horsemen of the Apocalypse* (1916). He was imprisoned dozens of times for his political activities.

Blaue Reiter, Der, organization of artists, formed in 1912 in Munich. Named after a volume of essays on esthetics that was published that year and was co-edited by Franz Marc and Wassily Kandinsky. The drawing on the cover - a horseman - had been designed by Kandinsky. Members of the group included Klee, Von Javlensky, Feininger, Macke, Campendonck, and Schönberg, who became known as a composer. Two exhibitions were organized, which included works by members of 'Die Brücke' and 'Les Fauves'. Their style was expressionist, the colors they used were bright: red, yellow, green, and blue. With the outbreak of World War I, Der Blaue Reiter dispersed: Marc and Macke were killed in action, Von Jawlensky, Kandinsky, and Klee left Germany.

Blavatsky, Helena Petrovna (1831-1891), Russian founder of the Theosophical Society in New York City in 1875, together with H.S. Olcott. Madame Blavatsky was greatly influenced by Oriental religions. She taught that God is a boundless, impersonal spirit. Knowledge from God has been revealed through the ages by persons, called *Adepts*, or *Masters*, who are spiritually perfect. Every person is capable of gaining spiritual perfection through a series of transmigrations ending when the perfected soul merges with God. From 1882 she led the theosophic movement from Madras, India. Her works include *Isis Unveiled* (1877) and *The Secret Doctrine* (1888).

Blazing star, or gay feather, any of about 30 species of perennial North American wildflowers of the family Asteraceae, found in prairies and woodlands. The blazing star grows 1 to 6 ft (30 to 180 cm) high, with clusters of purple or pink blossoms surrounded by bracts (leaflike structures the same color as the flowers).

Bleaching, the process of whitening materials, usually with chemicals that reduce or oxidize color. Textiles, flour, oil, and sugar are often bleached.

Bleeding heart, garden plant (*Dicentra spectabilis*) with drooping, heart-shaped flowers, native to China and Japan. The bleeding heart vine of the verbena family is from West Africa.

Blenheim, Battle of, decisive battle in the War of Spanish Succession. On Aug. 13, 1704, troops of the Grand Alliance (England, Austria, and the United Provinces), commanded by the Duke of Marlborough and Prince Eugene of Savoy, triumphed over the Franco-Bavarian soldiers under Marshall Tallard. Fought on the Danube between the Bavarian villages of Blindheim and Hochstadt, Blenheim saved Vienna from the forces of King Louis XIV, consolidated the Grand Alliance, and ended French occupation of Germany.
See also: Spanish Succession, War of the.

Blériot, Louis (1872-1936), French pioneer aviator and inventor. In 1909 he became the first to fly a heavier-than-air machine across the English Channel.

Bley, Paul (1932-), Canadian jazz pianist. Professional in bop idiom since the early 1950s. Soon afterwards he became involved in Ornette Coleman's first free jazz attempts. Has ever since played a combination of harmonically restrained and 'free' improvizations. Used to work with Jimmy Giuffre (1961) and Sonny Rollins (1963). Major records: *Footloose* (1963) and *Diane* (with Chet Baker, 1985).

Bligh, William (1754-1817), reputedly cruel British naval officer, captain of the *Bounty* at the time of the now-famous mutiny (1789). In 1805 he became governor of New South Wales and was subsequently imprisoned by mutinous soldiers (1808-10).

B

William Blake's watercolor *The Beating of Achan* (c.1800) illustrates what Blake called the 'cruelties of Moral Law'. The first of the great English romantic poets, Blake proclaimed the primacy of imagination and freedom over reason and law (Tate Gallery, London).

Blindness, partial or complete loss of vision, caused by injury to the eyes, congenital defects, or diseases such as cataracts, diabetes, glaucoma, and hypertension. Infant blindness can result if the mother had rubella (German measles) early in pregnancy; malnutrition (especially vitamin A deficiency) may cause blindness in children. There are many ways for blind people to overcome their disability, including Braille (a method of reading with the fingers by touching raised dots), books on tape, and optical scanners generating speech. The use of a cane, guide dog, and sonar devices on glasses all contribute in assisting the blind.

Blindworm, legless European lizard (*Anguis fragilis*), found in meadows and woodlands. The adult is about 1 ft (30 cm) long, brownish in color, with smooth scales. The blindworm eats snails and slugs. It is believed to be blind.

Blitzkrieg (German, 'lightning war'), originally used to describe the sudden German mechanized warfare attacks on Poland and France in World War II, now applied to any rapid, forceful military advance, such as the 1944 sweep through France by the U.S. Army under Patton.
See also: World War II.

Blixen-Finecke, Karen *See:* Dinesen, Isak.

Blizzard, snowstorm with high velocity

B

Centrifugation of blood yields (A) a cell-free plasma zone (55% of total volume), (B) a white blood cell and blood platelets `buffy coat' (about 1-2%), and (C) a red cell zone (about 45%). The straw-coloured, slightly opaque fluid plasma contains various proteins, organic and anorganic materials, but 90% of plasma consists of water. Blood cells exist in a ratio of about 500:30:1 (red:platelets:white cells). There are 4.5-6.5 million red cells per mm3 blood. White blood cells (1-6) (here: x 1,200) are subdivided on the basis of their staining properties, into basophils (1), eosinophils (2), neutrophils (3), small (4) and large (5) lymphocytes, and monocytes (6). Platelets (7) (here: x 1,200) have no nuclei. Red cells are biconcave, disc-shaped cells without nuclei (8) (here: x 6,000). Various diseases and physiological disorders may produce changes in the shape and number of blood cells.

winds, temperatures well below freezing, and visibility less than 500 ft (152.4 m). Such storms are common on the Great Plains east of the Rockies in the United States and Canada, in polar regions, and in parts of Europe and Asia.
See also: Snow.

Bloch, Ernest (1880-1959), Swiss-American classical composer. He was greatly influenced by traditional Jewish music, as evidenced in his symphonic poem *Israel* (1916), *Sacred Service* (1930-33), and *Three Jewish Poems* (1913). He also wrote concertos, chamber music, and suites for piano and strings.

Bloch, Konrad Emil (1912-), U.S. biochemist. His studies of animal cells resulted in the discovery of cholesterol, a fatty substance produced from acetic acid. In 1964 he shared the Nobel Prize for physiology or medicine.
See also: Biochemistry; Cholesterol.

Blockade, maneuver normally imposed by means of seapower, designed to cut an enemy's supply routes and force a surrender. The objective may also be to capture an enemy port.

Blockhouse, small log or stone fortification, usually temporary and built to defend newly won territory. Common in frontier America, blockhouses were used by settlers as a gathering place to protect themselves from Native American attacks.
See also: Pioneer life in America.

Bloemfontein, capital of the Orange Free State and judicial capital of South Africa. First settled by Dutch farmers in 1846, it is now a rail and industrial center. Harvard University and the University of Michigan maintain astronomical observatories in the city.
See also: South Africa.

Blok, Aleksandr Aleksandrovich (1880-1921), a Russian poet and dramatist. He was a leader of the Russian Symbolist movement. Blok's poetry is evocative in a musical and magical sense, deeply confessional, and full of innovative rhythms. The collection of poems *Verses About the Beautiful Lady* (1904) illustrates the mystical and idealistic nature of his early work. Disillusioned by the failure of the 1905 Revolution and embittered by his collapsing marriage, Blok infused his later writings with motifs of loneliness and despair. His play *The Puppet Show* (1906) is a tragic farce mocking his earlier idealism. Blok's masterpiece, *The Twelve* (1918), is a verse epic depicting the chaos in the streets of St. Petersburg during the Revolution of 1917.

Blood, thick red fluid pumped by the heart and flowing throughout the body in the blood vessels of the circulatory system. The blood serves many functions in the body, but principally it carries nutrients to and waste away from individual cells and helps regulate the body's metabolism. It carries oxygen from the lungs to the tissues, and carbon dioxide from the tissues to the lungs. It transports hormones to tissues that need them, carries nutrients absorbed from the intestine, and bears away the waste products of metabolism to the organs of excretion-the lungs, the kidneys, the intestines, and the skin. Blood also defends the body against infection, and the clotting mechanism minimizes the loss of blood after an injury.
Seen with the naked eye, the blood appears opaque and homogeneous, but upon microscopic examination it is seen to consist of cells. The most numerous are red corpuscles (erythrocytes), which normally outnumber white cells (leucocytes) by 500 to 1. Also present in the blood are minute circular bodies known as platelets, or thrombocytes, necessary for clotting. The blood cells subsist in an intercellular liquid called plasma. The volume of cells and plasma is approximately equal. Blood plasma itself is a complex fluid; 90% of it is water, but the balance consists of proteins, electrolytes, other minerals, and nutrients needed by the body's cells.
Common blood disorders are leukemia (excess white blood cells or leucocytes) and anemia (a lack of red blood cells). For medical purposes, principally transfusion, blood is usually categorized into one of 4 groups, A, B, AB, and O.
See also: Blood transfusion; Blood type; Circulatory system.

Blood count, number of blood cells found in a standard volume of blood; also, the test used to determine that number.
See also: Blood; Hemoglobin.

Bloodhound, breed of dog of European origin, often used for tracking because of its acute sense of smell. Full-grown bloodhounds stand about 2 ft (0.61 m) high at the shoulder and weigh up to 110 lb (50 kg).

Bloodless Revolution *See:* Glorious Revolution.

Blood poisoning, or septicemia, invasion of the bloodstream by toxic microorganisms from a local infection. Symptoms include chills, fever, and prostration.
See also: Blood.

Blood pressure, pressure of the blood upon the walls of the arteries as it is pumped from the heart. The pressure is strongest at the left ventricle of the heart but can be felt pulsing at various points on the body. The pulsing corresponds to the force and rhythm of the heart's pumping action, and it can be measured to determine blood pressure. An instrument called a sphygmomanometer is used to ascertain the pressure at the brachial artery of the forearm, just above the elbow.
Blood pressure is recorded by 2 figures written as a fraction. The numerator indicates the systolic, or maximum, pressure pro-

duced by the heart; the denominator indicates the diastolic, or lower, pressure produced by the heart, which results in the least pressure upon the artery. '130/90,' for example, is read as '130 over 90.' Hypertension and stroke are disorders accompanied by high blood pressure.
See also: Blood.

Bloodroot (*Sanguinaria canadensis*), spring-flowering North American perennial. The blossom is white with 8 to 12 petals and is about 2 in (5 cm) across on a reddish stalk. Native Americans used the red sap as a paint and dye.

Bloodsucker *See:* Leech.

Blood transfusion, transfer of blood or components of blood from one person or animal to another. Transfusions are used to replace blood loss due to hemorrhaging, severe burns, or shock, and in such disorders as hemophilia. They are also used regularly in surgical procedures. Blood must be tested for compatible classification (blood group and Rh factor) to prevent rejection reactions by the recipient. Plasma, the fluid part of blood, is often given when whole blood is not needed or is unavailable.
See also: Blood; Plasma.

Blood type, classification of an individual's blood by group-A, B, AB, or O-and Rh-factor (negative or positive). People with blood group AB can receive blood from all other groups; those with group O can donate to all other groups.
See also: Blood.

Blood vessel *See:* Artery; Blood; Capillary; Vein.

Bloody Sunday *See:* Lenin, V.I.; Union of Soviet Socialist Republics.

Bloomfield, Leonard (1887-1949), U.S. linguist whose book *Language* (1933) was the chief text of the structuralist school of linguistics, the scientific study of the form and pattern of language. Bloomfield taught at Illinois and Ohio State universities and was Sterling professor of linguistics at Yale after 1940.
See also: Linguistics.

Bloomsbury group, influential coterie of writers and artists who met in Bloomsbury Square, London, in the early 20th century. Influenced by G. E. Moore, the group included Virginia Woolf, Leonard Woolf, Clive Bell, Vanessa Bell, E. M. Forster, V. Sackville-West, Roger Fry, Duncan Grant, J. M. Keynes, and Lytton Strachey.

Blow fly, any of various flies of the family Calliphoridae. The best known of these 2-winged flies is the bluebottle (*Calliphora vicina*). Blowflies lay eggs in carrion, excrement, or open wounds.

Blücher, Gebhard Leberecht von (1742-1819), Prussian general, made a field marshal after helping to defeat Napoleon in the Battle of Leipzig (1813). A year later he led Prussian troops into Paris, and in 1815 the timely intervention of his troops was important in Wellington's victory over Napoleon at Waterloo.
See also: Napoleonic Wars.

Blue baby, infant with a blueness of skin usually caused by a congenital heart defect leading to a mixture of venous and arterial blood.
See also: Cyanosis.

Bluebeard, villain of a traditional tale in which a rich man's seventh wife disobeys him and finds the murdered bodies of former wives. She is saved by her brothers. Maeterlinck based a play on the legend.

The English bluebell (*Endymion nonscriptus*) is a bulbous European woodland lily that flowers early (April to June). It is 0.5 metre in height.

Bluebell, any of various wild perennial plants with blue bell-shaped flowers. The term also refers to the Scottish bluebell or harebell of the bellflower family, most commonly the English bluebell, California bluebell, and Virginia bluebell.

Blueberry, any of several hardy deciduous shrubs (genus *Vaccinium*) bearing a blue-black fruit, many species of which are found in North America. The high-bush blueberry (*V. cerymbosum*), which may reach 15 ft (4.6 m) in height, and the low-bush blueberry (*V. augustifolium*) are the two most commonly cultivated. A popular component of jellies, jams, and pastry fillings, blueberries are frequently canned and frozen.

Bluebird, any of several species (genus *Sialia*) of migratory songbirds of the thrush family, related to the robin but with blue above a red breast. Bluebirds often nest near human habitations.

Bluebonnet (*Lupinus subcarnosus*), annually blooming, low-growing lupine (with edible, bean-like seeds). It is the state flower of Texas.

Blue crab, any of several edible, soft-shell crabs (*Callinectes sapidus* and *C. hastatus*) that inhabit Atlantic coastal shores and estuaries. The shell is green-brown and about 6 in (15 cm) wide; the legs are bluish. The blue crab is a scavenger, feeding on dead animals.

Bluefish (*Pomatomus saltatrix*), voracious fish of the family Pomatomidae, found in the Atlantic and Indian oceans and the Mediterranean Sea. It can grow to a length of about 4 ft (1.22 m) and attain a weight up to 30 lb (13.6 kg), though it normally averages 30 in (.75 m) in length and 10-12 lb (4.5-5.5 kg) in weight. A popular game fish resembling the pompano and related to the sea bass, the bluefish is caught commercially for food.

Bluegrass, traditional, instrumental country music, played on unamplified string instruments (banjo, fiddle, mandolin, and guitar). The style, highly improvisational with close harmonies, was developed in the late 1930s by Bill Monroe and his Blue Grass Boys and by the banjo player Earl Scruggs.

B

The bloodhound, whose name means 'blooded' or 'pure-bred', trails animals and humans by scent; it will not harm the person it is trailing.

B

Bluegrass State *See:* Kentucky.

Blue jay, crested bird (*Cyanocitta cristata*) widespread in the eastern half of the United States and Canada. The adult is 1 ft (30 cm) long with pale gray underparts and a black necklace. Upperparts are blue with black and white markings.

The blue jay (*C. cristata*) is large, loud, and agressive. It may eat the eggs of other birds during the nesting season.

Blue Nile *See:* Nile River.

Blue Ridge Mountains, eastern range of the Appalachians extending southwest 600 mi (960 km) from Pennsylvania to northern Georgia. Grandfather Mountain, at 5,964 ft (1,818 m), is the tallest peak. The Blue Ridge Mountains are pre-Cambrian metamorphic rock with igneous intrusions. Constituent ranges include the Great Smoky Mountains and the Black Mountains.
See also: Appalachian Mountains.

Blues, U.S. musical form derived from the work songs, spirituals, and 'field hollers' of African Americans of the South, characterized by the use of flattened 'blue notes.' The blues, which came to be the principal basis of the jazz idiom, has the characteristic pattern of a 12-bar structure, with distinctive harmonies, most probably of African origin. What began as songs, many about despair and cynicism, accompanied by guitar, harmonica, or piano, has expanded to include a purely instrumental form. The blues were first popularized by W.C. Handy ('Memphis Blues' and 'St. Louis Blues'); early blues artists include Ma Rainey, Bessie Smith, and Blind Lemon Jefferson.

The boa constrictor (*C. constrictor*) is a New World snake that kills rodents and other small animals by striking and coiling around them with incredibly fast movements. The boa constrictor tightens its coils, preventing the animal from breathing. Then the snake swallows the meal in one piece.

Bluet, North American wildflower (*Houstonia caerula*) having 4 bluish lobes with a yellow center.

Blue thistle *See:* Viper's bugloss.

Blue vitriol *See:* Sulfate.

Blue whale, member (*Balaenoptera musculus*) of the rorqual family of baleen whales. The blue whale is the largest animal that has ever lived-up to 100 ft (30 m) in length and 220 tons (200 metric tons) in weight. Baleen whales have no teeth. Instead, thin plates in their mouths (called baleen) strain out tiny organisms, called plankton, on which the whales feed. Blue whales live in all oceans, but breed in warm waters. Like other whales, they are mammals; they bear live young and suckle them on milk. A newborn blue whale may be over 20 ft (6.1 m) long and weigh 3 tons (2.7 metric tons). Today, the blue whale is an endangered species because of excessive whaling.

Bluford, Guion Stewart, Jr. (1942-), U.S. astronaut. In 1983, Bluford made a 6-day voyage on the space shuttle *Challenger*, becoming the first African American to travel in space.

Blum, Léon (1872-1950), creator of the modern French Socialist party, and the first socialist and the first Jewish person to become premier of France. As premier in 1936-37, he led the Popular Front, a coalition of Socialists and Radicals opposed to fascism. Blum was imprisoned by the Germans, 1940-45. He became premier again in 1946-47.

Blushing, sudden, brief redness to the face and neck that occurs when capillaries, tiny blood vessels in the skin, swell with blood.

Bly, Robert (1926-), U.S. poet and translator whose works deal with American themes. *Silence in a Snowy Field* (1962) explores his native state of Minnesota and concepts of solitude and silence. *The Light Around the Body* (1967) is an anti-Vietnam War statement. He has also translated and printed works of foreign poets including Rilke. He was the recipient of the National Book Award in 1968.

Boa constrictor (*Constrictor constrictor*), nonpoisonous snake of the family Boidae (which includes pythons and anacondas),

mostly found in the tropics of the Americas. The live-bearing boa constrictor, 10-18 ft (3-5 m) in length, suffocates its prey (birds and mammals) by squeezing.

Boadicea, or Boudicca (d. A.D. 61), British queen of the Iceni of Norfolk. In A.D. 60 she led a revolt against the Romans, sacking Camulodunum (Colchester), Londinium (London), and Verulamium (St. Albans) before being defeated. She took poison to avoid capture.

Boar, wild, either of 2 species of wild pig, the Eurasian *Sus scrofa* and the Indian *S. cristatus*. The wild boar stands about 3 ft (91 cm) at the shoulder and has stiff bristles over a short gray-black undercoat. It has 2 tusks in the lower jaw and broad feet, adaptations to the marshy areas it inhabits. The wild boar is omnivorous.
See also: Peccary.

Boas, Franz (1858-1942), German-born U.S. anthropologist and ethnologist, leader in establishing the cultural-relativist school of anthropology in the English-speaking world. One of the earliest to use statistical methods in his field, he was an authority on Native American languages, the first professor of anthropology at Columbia University (1899-1936), and the author of more than 30 books, including *The Mind of Primitive Man* (1911) and *Anthropology and Modern Life* (1928).
See also: Anthropology; Ethnography.

Boat *See:* Boating; Ship.

Boating, popular pastime using waterborne craft for pleasure. Boats can be propelled by small motors, sails, or paddles (oars). They vary from 1- and 2-person kayaks, canoes, and rowboats to yachts ranging from 30 to 120 ft (9 to 36.5 m).

Boat people, term for the Vietnamese who fled from their country in tiny boats following the communist North Vietnamese victory over South Vietnam in 1975. Many of them drowned or fell victim to pirates. The stream of refugees continued until well into the 1990s. The refugee camps in Hong Kong alone accommodated 35,000 Vietnamese boat people.

Bobcat (*Lynx rufus*), ferocious North American spotted lynx (wild cat), named for its short (6 in/15.2 cm) tail. A nocturnal animal, the bobcat grows to a length of about 3 ft (0.9 m) and has a brown and white coat with black spots and stripes.

Bobet, Louis (Louison) (1925-1983), French cyclist, has won the Tour de France three times (1953, 1954, 1955) and won the mountain classification in 1950. In addition, Bobet won various other classic races, the French road championship (twice) and the world road championship for professional cyclists (1954).

Bobolink (*Dolichonyx oryzivorus*), North American migratory songbird. Also called ricebird (for feeding on rice crops during southern migration), it has a dull plumage, except in spring, when the male acquires white and yellow patches. Once hunted but now protected, the bobolink breeds in the United States and southern Canada, migrating to South America for the winter.

Bobrowski, Johannes (1917-1965), German romanticist and poet. Johannes Bobrowski grew up in the German-Lithuanian border region and studied art history in Berlin. In 1939 he was drafted into military service. In 1949 he returned from Russian captivity and settled in East Berlin, where he worked as an editor with a publishing house. Bobrowski wrote prose and poetry. Aspects such as nature and landscape, myths, cultural tradition, and the history of the area where he was born all played an important role throughout his oeuvre. He evokes the relationship between the Germans and other peoples of Eastern Europe. Collections of verse include: *Schattenland, Ströme* (Shadowlands; 1962), and he wrote the novels *Levins Mühle* (Levin's Mill; 1965) and *Litauische Claviere* (Lithuanian Piano's; 1967).

Bobsledding, winter sport pitting 2- or 4-person sleds against each other down a steep incline. Capable of traveling at 90 mph (145 kmph), bobsleds negotiate a twisting course with steep embankments ranging from 1,312 yards (1,200 m) to 1,640 yards (1,500 m) long. The team posting the fastest times after 4 runs is the winner. Bobsledding was invented in Switzerland around 1890.

Bobwhite, any of several North American gamebirds (genus *Colinus*)of the pheasant family, often called quail or partridge. About 10 in (25 cm) long and reddish-brown in color, the bobwhite is named for the sound of its mating call and feeds on insects and seeds. Bobwhites travel and sleep in groups, called coveys.

Boccaccio, Giovanni (1313-1375), Italian writer and humanist, whose work had a lasting influence on European literature and was used as a source by such writers as Chaucer and Shakespeare. A classical scholar and friend and admirer of Petrarch, he is the author of *Amorous Fiammetta* (1343-1344), the first modern psychological novel, and the *Decameron* (1348-1353), a collection of 100 short and often ribald tales set against the background of a plague epidemic in Florence. The latter work was the first literary expression of Renaissance humanist realism. He also produced important works in mythology, anthropology, and biography. *See also:* Renaissance.

Boccherini, Luigi (1743-1805), Italian composer and cellist, noted for his chamber music. His more than 400 works, including string quartets and quintets and cello concertos, have been compared to those of Haydn, his contemporary. *See also:* Chamber music.

Boccioni, Umberto (1882-1916), Italian painter and sculptor. A pioneer of futurism, he tried to capture the movement, speed, and sensations of modern life by using dynamic forms. *See also:* Futurism.

Bode's law, or Titius-Bode law, a statement of the relative mean distances of the planets from the sun. The formula begins with the numbers of the series, 0, 3, 6, 12, 24 (each new number being twice the previous one). If each number is increased by 4 and divided by 10, the series becomes 0.4, 0.7, 1.0, 1.6, 2.8, 5.2, 10.0, 19.6, 38.8. The law holds that these numbers express the relative mean distances of the planets from the sun, the earth's distance being the standard: 1.0. The German mathematician Johann Titius discovered this relationship in 1766; the German astronomer Johann Bode published it in 1772. It holds fairly well for the planets known at the time and for Uranus and the asteroid belt (both discovered later), but not for Neptune and Pluto. *See also:* Astronomy.

Bodhisattva, in Mahayana Buddhism, spiritual being on the path to enlightenment. A bodhisattva delays entrance into the state of nirvana until all others have entered the same state. Bodhisattvas are worshiped and can respond to prayer; their exemplary lives are the subject of many Buddhist legends. *See also:* Buddha, Gautama; Buddhism.

Bodhi tree *See:* Bo tree; Buddha, Gautama.

Bodin, Jean (1530?-1596), French political philosopher who argued that stable government required a moderate absolutism founded on divine right but subject to divine and natural law. He advocated religious toleration as necessary in a just state. *See also:* Philosophy.

Bodleian Library, the library of Oxford University in Britain. It was established in 1602 by the English diplomat Sir Thomas Bodley to replace an earlier library, dating back to the 14th century, that had been destroyed. Its collection includes 2.5 million books, including many Oriental manuscripts. *See also:* Oxford University.

Bodoni, Giambattista (1740-1813), Italian printer. The Bodoni typeface, with its sharp contrast between thick and thin strokes, has been widely used in modern printing. *See also:* Printing.

Boehmeria, any of about 100 species of perennial plants of the nettle family. One variety, called *false nettle*, grows as a wild flower in the Eastern United States. Another kind, *ramie*, native to China and Japan, has been cultivated for fiber since prehistoric times. Ramie is used in industrial sewing thread, packing materials, and fishnet. *See also:* Ramie.

Boeing, William Edward (1881-1956), U.S. industrialist and founder of the Boeing Aircraft Company, a firm specializing in large commercial and military aircraft. Boeing helped carry the world's first international airmail in one of his planes in 1919. In the post-World War I and World War II periods, his company gained worldwide importance with the development of various kinds of military aircraft. The company currently produces some of the most widely used jet aircraft in commercial aviation, including the Boeing 707 and the famous jumbo jet, the Boeing 747.

Kamakura Daibutsu, a 15-meter-high bronze statue of the Buddha of Amida, a very popular bodhisattva (redeemer) in Japan, can be found in the Japanese town of Kamakura.

Boeotia, region of ancient Greece, north of the Gulf of Corinth in central Greece. The area of 1,100 sq mi (2,850 km) was rich farmland. The chief city, Thebes, dominated the Boeotian League, formed to protect the area from encroachment by other city-states. The home of the poets Hesiod and Pindar, Boeotia later became part of the modern Greek state. *See also:* Thebes.

Boers (Dutch, 'farmers'), term applied to South African inhabitants of Dutch, German, and French Huguenot descent who settled in the region beginning in 1652. Now called Afrikaners, they speak their own language (Afrikaans). Their racial attitudes were responsible for the rise of apartheid.

Unique Forms of Continuity in a Space by Umberto Boccioni (1882-1916) (private collection, Milan). Futurist Boccioni wished to represent movement, by letting space and movement flow into each other.

Boer War, or South African War, fought between the British and the Boers (settlers of Dutch descent) from 1899 to 1902. The Boers resented British territorial expansion from their Cape of Good Hope colony, while the British aimed at a united South Africa and complained of the harsh treatment of immigrant British gold prospectors by Boers. Well-equipped by Germany, the more numerous Boer forces took the offensive in 1899, but the arrival of British reinforcements turned the tide, and by late 1900 the Boers had to resort to guerrilla tactics. The war ended with the Treaty of Vereeniging in 1902, a British victory that shifted the conflict into the political arena.
See also: South Africa.

The army of King Dingaan, attacking a Boer encampment, consisting of wagons that are placed in a circle around the cattle.

Boethius, Anicius Manlius Severinus (c.480-525), Roman philosopher and statesman whose works profoundly influenced medieval thought. A high official under Theodoric the Great, he was accused of treason and executed. While in prison, he wrote his great work, *The Consolation of Philosophy*.
See also: Philosophy.

Bofill, Levi Ricardo (1939-), Spanish architect. Mainly known for his enormous

A view of the modern business centre of the Columbian capital of Bogotá. The walled-in complex in the foreground is the central cemetery. Bogotá has more than 6 million residents (1996), and lies at a height of over 2,600 metres above sea level, making it one of the highest capitals in the world.

housing projects, Palacio d'Abraxas and Le Théatre (Marne-la-Vallee, 1978-1982), where he created a mock classical language of shapes by means of prefabricated concrete panels.

Bog, spongy, waterlogged ground composed chiefly of decaying vegetation. Often formed in stagnant lakes, bogs are mainly produced by sphagnum (bog moss), from which peat is formed. Their acidity makes bogs good natural preservers, and in Europe and America they have yielded plant and animal remains from earlier ages.

Bogart, Humphrey DeForest (1899-1957), U.S. film actor, famous for his screen image as the cool, tough anti-hero. Among his most notable films are *The Maltese Falcon* (1941), *Casablanca* (1942), and *The African Queen* (1951), for which he won an Academy Award as best actor.

Boghazköy (also: Bogazkoy; Khattusas), village in central Turkey, where excavations were carried out in 1906, which gave more insight into the Hittite civilization. Texts of treaties between Hittite sovereigns and their allies and vassals were excavated. The formulation of the vassal treaties are strikingly similar to the prescriptions in the covenant between God and Israel as described in the Bible. In the neighborhood are the archaeological remains of Khattusas, the ancient capital of the Hittites.

Bogolyubov, Efiem Dmitrijevitsj (1889-1952), Russian/German chess master who was of great influence to the popularization of chess in Germany. Bogolyubov took part in more than one hundred major tournaments. His greatest successes were the major tournament in Moscow in 1925 (151/2 out of 20), where he beat Lasker and Capablanca, and Kissingen in 1928, where he snatched the trophy from Capablanca, Euwe, Nimzowitsch, and Réti, among others. Bogolyubov played two matches against Aljechin for the world championship title, but was beaten impressively in 1929 as well as in 1934.

Bogotá (pop. 6,000,000), capital and largest city of Colombia. Founded by the Spanish in 1538 on the site of Chibcha settlement, it is a commercial and cultural center, with several universities (the oldest from 1573). Its climate is mild because of its altitude of over 8,500 ft (2,591 m), at the edge of an Andean plateau.
See also: Colombia.

Bohemia, historic region in central Europe. It was once part of the Austro-Hungarian Empire. In 1918, after a war-torn history, it became a province in the republic of Czechoslovakia, of which its chief city, Prague, became the capital. In 1949 it lost its separate provincial status. The area is rich in minerals and fine agricultural land.

Bohr, Niels Henrik David (1885-1962), Danish physicist who proposed a model of the atom in 1913, suggesting that the hydrogen atom consisted of a single electron orbiting around a central proton (the nucleus), and that the electron could carry only certain well-defined quantities of energy. This theory accounted both for the atom's stability and for its characteristic radiation and absorption of energy. In 1927 Bohr proposed the complementarity principle to account for apparent paradoxes in the wave and particle approaches to describing subatomic particles. Although he helped develop the atomic bomb, he was always deeply concerned about implications for humanity. In 1922 he received the Nobel Prize in physics.
See also: Atom; Physics.

Boileau-Despréaux, Nicolas (1636-1711), French poet, satirist, and critic. His insistence on classical standards, expressed in the didactic poem *L'Art poétique* (1674), influenced literary taste in France and England in the 18th century.

Boiler, device for heating water to produce steam. The 2 main types of boiler are the fire-tube, in which hot gases are passed through tubes surrounded by water, and the water-tube, in which water is passed through tubes surrounded by hot gases. Fuels include coal, oil, gas, and nuclear energy.

Boito, Arrigo (1842-1918), Italian poet and composer. His own operas include *Mefistofele* (1868; revised 1875) and *Nerone* (1918), though he is best known as the librettist of Verdi's *Otello* (1887) and *Falstaff* (1893) and of Ponchielli's *La Gioconda* (1876).
See also: Opera.

Bokassa, Jean-Bédel (1921-1996), Central African dictator. After a career in the French armed forces, Bokassa became Chief of Staff of the army of the Central African Republic in 1963. At the end of 1965 he overthrew President David Dacko, dissolved parliament, and declared himself president of the republic. In December 1976 he renamed his country the Central African Empire and, subsequently, crowned himself Emperor Bokassa I in a lavish ceremony. He conducted a veritable reign of terror and did not hesitate to feed his political opponents to the crocodiles or, according to rumors, to canabalize them. After Bokassa had personally participated in a massacre of over 100 schoolchildren by his Imperial Guard in 1979, ex President Dacko carried out a military coup against him with the help of French paratroops. He fled to France, but returned to his country in 1986, where he was sentenced to death. Later his sentence was commuted from death to life imprisonment, and he was freed in 1993.

Bola (Spanish, 'ball'), weapon used for hunting by native South American tribes. It consists of round leather-covered stone or iron weights connected by cords or leather thongs up to 8 ft (2.4 m) long. There may be 2 or 3 such covered balls, each with its own cord connected to a common center. The bolas are whirled overhead to gain momentum and then hurled at quarry. On contact the balls wind around the animal's legs and prevent it from fleeing. Argentinean gauchos still use bolas for catching cattle, and Eskimos in the Arctic hunt with a similar weapon.

Bolero, type of Spanish folk dance and the music that accompanies it. The bolero is performed in 3/4 time. It is often accompanied by castanets, guitars, and tambourines. Dancers perform solo or as couples. *Bolero* (1928), a 1-act ballet composed by Maurice Ravel, helped popularize the dance and musical form.

Boleyn, Anne (1507-1536), second wife of Henry VIII and mother of Elizabeth I. Henry's first queen, Catherine of Aragon, had failed to produce a son, and he divorced her to marry Anne in 1533. Elizabeth was born later that year, but Anne bore no living son either. She was beheaded after being convicted of dubious charges of adultery and incest.
See also: Henry (England).

Bolingbroke, Henry St. John, 1st Viscount (1678-1751), English statesman and historian. A Tory, as secretary of state he successfully handled the negotiations for the Treaty of Utrecht (1713). He lost office on the death of Queen Anne, and sought exile in France (1715-25).
See also: Utrecht, Peace of.

Bolívar, Simón (1783-1830), South American soldier and statesman responsible for several liberation movements against Spanish authority. After several abortive attempts during the 1810s, he led the liberation of Venezuela in 1821 and created the federal state of Greater Colombia, including what is now Venezuela, Colombia, and Ecuador. He went on to liberate Peru (1824) and to form the republic of Bolivia (1825). Bolívar envisaged a united South America, but secessionist movements arose, and Peru and Bolivia turned against him in the 1820s. Venezuela and Ecuador seceded from Greater Colombia in 1829, and in the following year Bolívar resigned as president. Today he is regarded as the liberator of South America, one of the great heroes of its history.
See also: Venezuela.

Bolivia

Capital:	Sucre (official), La Paz (actual)
Area:	424,164 sq mi (1,098,581 sq km)
Population:	8,455,000
Language:	Spanish, Aymara, Quechua
Government:	Presidential republic
Independent:	1825
Head of gov.:	President
Per capita:	U.S. $2,600
Monetary unit:	1 Peso boliviano = 100 centavos

Bolivia, landlocked South American republic, bordered by Brazil in the north and east, Paraguay in the southeast, Argentina in the south, and Peru and Chile in the west.
Land and climate. The 3 distinct regions of Bolivia are the Oriente (east), the Montañas (center), and the Altiplano (west). The Oriente is a low alluvial plain containing tropical forest and extensive swamps. The Montañas consists of the Cordillera Oriental mountain range, whose eastern slopes shelter fertile valleys. It is Bolivia's largest cultivated area with peaks over 21,000 ft (6,400 m) high and valleys that fall to 6,000 ft (1,929 m). The windswept Altiplano, a broad plain between 2 high Andes ranges, is the most populous area and the highest in-

An experienced team of drillers prepares to extract ore from one of Bolivia's nationalized mines. Despite the nation's extensive mineral resources and the development of newly discovered petroleum deposits, Bolivia has one of the lowest per-capita incomes in South America.

habited area in the world, most of it over 12,000 ft (3,658 m). It is home to more than half the population. Lake Titicaca on the Peruvian border is the highest navigable lake in the world (12,507 ft/3,812 m). The climate varies from the steady cold of the Altiplano to jungle heat in the Oriente.
People. More than 40% of Bolivians are Native Americans, with another one-third being mestizo (Native American and Caucasian) and about 15% Caucasians of Spanish descent. Spain's colonial policy prevented Native Americans from learning Spanish, so less than 40% of the population speak it. Most Caucasians speak at least 1 Native American language. About 95% of the people are Roman Catholic. Sucre is Bolivia's capital, but La Paz is its major city and seat of government.
Economy. About two-fifths of Bolivians work subsistence farms and wheat and rice must be imported to meet basic needs. The animals of the highlands (llamas, alpacas, and vicuñas) furnish high-grade wool, a leading source of income in certain areas. Bolivia is leading world producer of tin and antimony. Oil has been a major export since 1967. Despite its mineral wealth Bolivia remains a comparatively poor country.
History. Before being conquered by Gonzalo and Hernando Pizarro (1538), Bolivia was home to an advanced Ayamará civilization around Lake Titicaca that was subjugated by the Incas. The Spanish exploited Bolivia's wealth with forced Indian labor. The country won its independence in 1825 after long campaigns led by José de Sucre, but over the next 100 years Bolivia lost much valuable territory in wars with Brazil, Chile, and Paraguay. The Nationalist Revolutionary Movement (MNR), a prominer organization, came to power in 1952 but was overthrown by the military in 1964. In 1980, after nearly 20 years of unstable military regimes, a civilian government came to power under President Hernán Siles Zuazo. Zuazo resigned in 1985 and was succeeded by Paz Estenssoro. Jaime Paz Zamora was elected president in 1989 and left his seat to Gonzalo Sanchez de Lozada in 1993. The latter was succeeded by Hugo Bánzer Suárez in 1997. In 2001, he resigned due to illness. At the end of 2002, Gonzalo Sanchez de Lozada was elected president. He experienced a great deal of opposition from the coca farmers. Many farmers suffered from the destruction of their coca crops.

Bolkiah, Hassanal (Haji Hassanal Bolkiah Mu'izzaddin Waddaulah; 1946-), Sultan of Brunei. Bolkiah succeeded his father in 1967 and in 1968 was crowned Sultan. He is the 29th Sultan of his family, which goes back to the 14th century. The Sultan of Brunei is also Prime Minister, Secretary of State for Defence, Chancellor of the Exchequer and head of the church. The profits of the oil and gas industry in Brunei, are used for the development of Health care, Social Services and Education. These services are free of charge for every inhabitant. In 1990 he introduced the *Malay Muslim Monarchy*, a new state-ideology.

Böll, Heinrich (1917-1985), German author

B

B

and winner of the Nobel Prize for literature in 1972. His books are bitterly satiric, exploring themes of despair and love in post-World War II Europe. Important among his works are *Billiards at Half Past Nine* (1959) and *The Clown* (1965).

Bologna (pop. 385,000), Italian city 51 mi (82 km) north of Florence at the foot of the Apennines. It is an ancient Etruscan and Roman city, with a university founded in 1088, many medieval buildings, and Renaissance paintings and sculptures. Capital of the Emilia Romagna region, it is an agricultural and industrial center.
See also: Italy.

Bolometer, in physics, instrument used to measure minute differences of radiant energy by changes in the electrical resistance of a *thermistor*, a form of conductor exposed to the energy. Biometers can measure the radiation from stars.
See also: Physics.

Bolsheviks, proponents of the wing of the Russian Social Democratic Labor Party (RSDLP) led by Lenin. The name originated in 1903 when the Central Committee of the RSDLP split over the criteria of party membership. Lenin called his followers *Bolsheviks* (from the Russian word for *majority*) and his opponents *Menshevik* (from the word for *minority*). The party seized state power in the revolution of Oct. 1917. In March 1918 the name was changed to Russian Communist Party. The Bolsheviks later founded the Third (Communist) International, while the Mensheviks remained affiliated to the Second (Socialist) International.
See also: Communism; Mensheviks; Lenin, V.I..

Bolshoi Ballet, the foremost ballet company of the former USSR. The Moscow company (established 1825) was overshadowed by the more traditional St. Petersburg companies until the early 20th century, when it was taken over by Alexander Gorsky, who reshaped the Bolshoi. It has been one of the world's leading companies since the late 1950s.
See also: Ballet.

Bolshoi Theater, Russian theater, ballet, and opera house, with one of the largest stages in the world. It is the home of the Bolshoi Ballet, and its productions have a worldwide reputation.
See also: Bolshoi Ballet.

Boltraffio, Giovanni Antonio (also Beltraffio; 1467-1516), Italian painter; student and disciple of Leonard da Vinci, who left his workshop under Boltraffio's care on leaving Milan. Due to his personal interpretation of Da Vinci's influence, he is one of the most important representatives of the renaissance in Lombardia. The sensitive portrait of the so-called 'La Belle Ferronnière' (Louvre, Paris) is considered to be his masterpiece. His works include reredos for the Casio family (1500; Louvre, Paris), portraits of Casio (Pinoacoteca di Brera, Milan) and of Borromeo (palace on Isola Bella).

Boltzmann, Ludwig (1844-1906), Austrian physicist who made fundamental contributions to thermodynamics, classical statistical mechanics, and kinetic theory. His Stefan-Boltzmann Law states that the total energy radiated from a body is proportional to the fourth power of the temperature.
See also: Thermodynamics.

Bomb, in computer technology, major failure in a program. A computer system is said to be 'bombed' when it is significantly disrupted by a faulty program.
See also: Computer.

Bomb, explosive weapon that injures and kills on detonation. World War I bombs dropped by aircraft weighed as much as 660 lb (300 kg). During the late 1960s, the United States built bombs weighing 15,000 lb (6,800 kg) for use in the Vietnam War. The development of the atomic bomb enormously increased explosive power. In 1952, the United States exploded an even more destructive (10.4 megaton) hydrogen bomb, with an explosive force equivalent to 10.4 million tons of TNT. Hydrogen bombs with an explosive power of up to 100 million tons of TNT have been built since then. The so-called 'smart bomb' was developed in the 1980s and used extensively in the Persian Gulf War of 1991. These bombs contain electronic mechanisms that guide the trajectory and have remarkable pinpoint accuracy. The use of cameras located in the 'nose' of the bombs have provided excellent photographs of such hits.
See also: Explosive.

Bombay (pop. 15 million), large seaport in western India, capital of Maharashtra state, on the Arabian Sea. Bombay was built on several small islands, now joined to each other and to the mainland, forming an area of 25 sq mi (65 sq km). Its large harbor deals with the bulk of India's imports, notably wheat and machinery, and exports such as cotton, rice, and manganese. Local industries include textiles, leather goods, and printing. Bombay is an important cultural center, with a university founded in 1857. The city is overcrowded, with a fast-growing, mainly Hindu population. The site was ceded to the Portuguese in 1534 and passed to Great Britain in 1661. The city was headquarters of the British East India Company (1668-1856).
See also: India.

Bonaparte, family name of the Emperor **Napoleon I**. The Italian spelling, Buonaparte, was general until Napoleon adopted the French form in 1796. The family emigrated to the island of Corsica in the 16th century, and Napoleon was born there in 1769. His older brother, **Joseph** (1768-1844), was king of Naples (1806-08) and of Spain (1808-13); his youngest brother, **Jérôme** (1784-1860), held the throne of Westphalia (1807-13). Napoleon's son by Empress Marie Louise of Austria was hailed by supporters as **Napoleon II** (1811-32) and king of Rome (1811-14), but he never reigned in France. **Napoleon III** (Louis Napoleon Bonaparte; 1808-73), the son of Napoleon I's brother Louis, became emperor of France after a coup in 1852, establishing the Second Empire. He was deposed in 1870.
See also: Napoleon I; Napoleon II; Napoleon III.

Bonaparte, Napoleon *See:* Napoleon I.

Bonaventure, Saint (1221-1274), Italian medieval scholastic philosopher and theologian. He taught at Paris and later became Master General of the Franciscan order. He distinguished between philosophy, based on humanity's natural knowledge, and theology, which attempts to under-

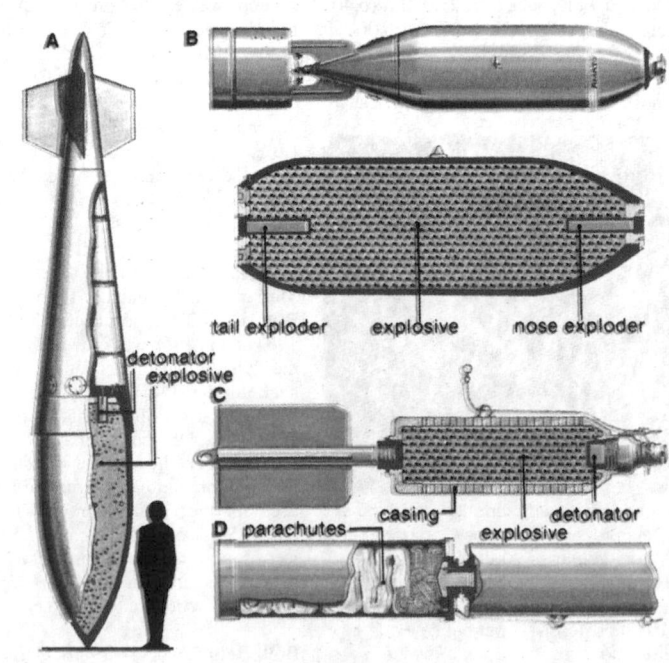

The 10-ton British Slam bomb (A) was the heaviest bomb used in World War II. Designed to destroy underground factories, heavily armored buildings, and U-boat pens, it could penetrate the earth up to 110 ft (30 m). A modern American 500 lb (227 kg) high explosive bomb (B) is used for the destruction of open targets. Fragmentation bombs (C and D) are antipersonnel weapons whose casings are designed to burst into jagged fragments. Parachutes are used to control descent.

tail exploder   explosive   nose exploder

detonator explosive

casing   detonator

parachutes   explosive

B

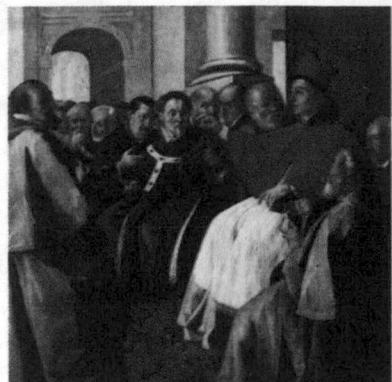

At the Council of Lyons (1274), a temporary unification of the Roman-Catholic Church with its Greek counterpart was achieved. Franciscan theologian, Cardinal Bonaventura (1221-1274), played an important role in this council. His conversation with the emissaries of the Byzantine emperor was depicted by Spanish painter Francesco de Zurburán (1598-1664).

stand the Christian mysteries.
See also: Scholasticism.

Bond, chemical, link that holds atoms together in compounds. The theory that atoms consist of electrons orbiting in shells around the nucleus led to an explanation of chemical bonding, which had first been noted in the nineteenth century. Atoms combine to achieve highly stable filled outer shells containing 2, 8, or 18 electrons, either by transfer of electrons from one atom to the other (ionic bond) or by the sharing of one electron from each atom such that both electrons orbit around both nuclei (covalent bond). The energy and length of chemical bonds, as well as the angles between them, may be investigated by spectroscopy and X-ray diffraction.
See also: Atom; Chemistry.

Bone, hard tissue that forms the skeleton. Bone supports the body, protects its organs, acts as an anchor for muscles and as a lever for the movement of limbs, and is the main reserve of calcium and phosphate in the body. Bones have a compact, hard shell surrounding a porous, spongy bone inner layer. Human bones are classified as long bones (mostly in the arms and legs) and short bones (e.g., the skull, pelvis, and vertebrae). A hollow cavity in long bones contains marrow, which helps to form blood cells. Broken bones (fractures) mend by the production of new cartilage and its gradual replacement by new bone. Insufficient calcium, phosphate, or vitamin D causes soft bones (rickets). Other disorders include osteoporosis (loss of bone density, common in old age) and osteoarthritis.
See also: Skeleton.

Bonefish, or ladyfish, herringlike fish (*Elops saurus*) named for the large numbers of fine bones that make it tedious to eat. A popular game fish nonetheless, the bonefish is found in the West Indies and along the coast of Mexico.

Boneset, perennial plant (*Eupatorium perfoliatum*) with hairy leaves, native to wet areas of the United States. This bitter herb grows from 2 ft to 6 ft (.5 m to 2 m) high and bears small white flowers in numerous heads. Tea made from the leaves makes people sweat and is used as a tonic.

Bongo, Albert-Bernard (Omar) (also Omar; 1935-), Gabonese politician and president (1967). Maintains close relations with France and ensured that Gabon became one of the richest countries in Africa by developing mining of mineral resources. After the multiparty system was introduced in Gabon in 1990, Omar Bongo was reelected with 51% of all votes during presidential elections in 1993. The opposition, however, complained about largescale fraud and challenged the outcome of the elections. This disagreement about the outcome resulted in a lengthy period of unrest and tension. The presidential elections of 1998 were the cause of many reports of irregularities. Bongo was re-elected receiving 66% of the votes, and he prolonged his term of office from 5 to 7 years.

Bonheur, Rosa (1822-1899), French artist famous for paintings of animals. She made her reputation with *The Horse Fair* (1853), a scene full of vigor and grace. Much of her work can be seen in England and America.

Bonhoeffer, Dietrich (1906-1945), German Lutheran pastor and theologian, author of many books on Christianity in a secular world. A prominent anti-Nazi, he was arrested in 1943 and executed two years later.
See also: Theology.

Boniface, Saint (c.672-754?), English missionary, called the Apostle of Germany. Backed by the Frankish rulers Charles Martel and Pepin the Short, he organized the German church, reformed the Frankish clergy, and advanced the conversion of the Saxons.

Boniface VIII (1235-1303), pope 1294-1303. He asserted papal authority over the political leaders of Europe. His bull (decree) *Unam Sanctam*, which called for the subjugation of political leaders to the pope, led to a clash with Philip IV of France. In 1303 the king's emissaries attacked Boniface in his

palace at Anagni, Italy. He died three weeks later in Rome and was succeeded as pope by Benedict XI.

Bonifácio, José *See:* Andrada é Silva, José Bonifácio de.

Bonington, Richard Parkes (1802-1828), English artist noted for his watercolor landscapes and genre subjects. He spent most of his brief career in France; among those he influenced were Delacroix and Corot.

Bonin Islands, group of volcanic islands about 500 mi (802 km) southeast of Japan. In all there are 27 islands with some 200 inhabitants. They were administered by the United States from 1945 to 1968, when they were returned to Japan.

Bonito, 3 types of fish resembling bluefin tuna, but rarely more than 30 in (76 cm) long. The striped bonito is found in all warm oceanic waters. The Atlantic bonito flourishes in the Mediterranean and warm sections of the Atlantic. The Pacific bonito is found in and near the Indian Ocean. They are strong swimmers and congregate in schools. Bonito, which average 6 lbs (2.7 kg), are valuable food fish.

Bonn (pop. 292,000), historic city on the Rhine River in North Rhine-Westphalia, founded in the 1st century A.D. by the Romans. It was the birthplace of Beethoven and from 1238 to 1794 served as the residence of the electors of Cologne. In 1949 it became the de facto capital of West Germany (Berlin was always considered the de jure capital). As such it served as the administrative center of the German Federal Republic. With the unification of the Federal Republic and the East German communist People's Democratic Republic in October 1990 into a single German state, Bonn lost it's status as capital to Berlin in 1991. The full transition to Berlin will take until the early 2000s.
See also: Germany.

Bonnard, Pierre (1867-1947), French artist whose style gave sparkling life and color to the sunny interiors he favored (*The Breakfast Room*). With Maurice Denis and Jean Vuillard, he formed the group known as the Nabis.

The Horse Fair is often considered Rosa Bonheur's masterpiece (Metropolitan Museum of Art, New York City).

B

Bonneville, Benjamin Louis Eulalie de (1796-1878), French-American soldier and pioneer. He explored the far west (1832-35) and fought in the Mexican War (1846-48). He is remembered largely because of Washington Irving's romanticized *The Adventures of Captain Bonneville* (1837). *See also:* Pioneer life in America.

Bonney, William H. *See:* Billy the Kid.

Bonsai, ancient Oriental art of growing dwarf trees. Trees are kept small by pruning roots and branches and by restricting growth in trays or pots. The modern enthusiast may spend many years cultivating a miniature tree. Plants that can be dwarfed include the cedars, myrtles, junipers, oaks, cypresses, pyracanthas, and pines.

Bonus Army March *See:* Hoover, Herbert Clark.

Booby, large fish-eating bird of the Sulidae family, so named because it is unwary and easily captured. Boobies have straight, sharp bills, long wedge-shaped tails, short, stout legs, and long tapered wings. Excellent fliers, boobies live mainly in tropical and subtropical regions.

Boogie-woogie *See:* Jazz.

Book, medium of communication consisting of written, printed, or blank sheets of a material, usually paper, bound together into a volume. Ancient Assyrian and Babylonian clay tablets, incised when wet, then baked until hard, are the earliest form of books. The Egyptians further developed books by changing their materials. From papyrus they made paper, which they inscribed with reed pens and ink. The ancient world adopted the Egyptian innovations, and portable rolls of sheets joined together to form scrolls were at one time the most common form of books. But animal skins were also used and eventually led to a new form. Sheets of animal skin were much stronger than papyrus; they could be sewn together and folded to form rectangular pages. Pressed tightly between wooden boards to make up a book or 'codex,' these were prototypes of modern books. The Chinese discovered the art of making paper in the 2nd century. Paper reached Europe in the 12th century, and by the 15th century it had almost entirely replaced all kinds of parchment in the making of books. Then, around 1436 or 1437, Johann Gutenberg of Mainz perfected movable type and produced the first mechanically printed books. The history of books since the 15th century is the story of innovations

The judgement of the dead. Top: judges, bottom: Anubis, who will lead the dead, Thor, who will pronounce the judgement, and Horus, who will introduce the dead to Osiris, after they have been accepted. Illustration from *Book of the Dead*, painted on papyrus (1300 B.C.).

This binding of the Codex Aureus of St. Emmeran, from the 9th century, is decorated with gold and gemstones (Bayerische Staatsbibliothek, Munich).

and advances in materials, techniques, and technology, which continues with today's computerized type setting, automated presses, and a wide variety of photographic and other reproduction processes.

Bookbinding, craft of gathering the pages of a book into a volume with a protective cover. Bookbinding began after papyrus gave way to parchment, sheets of which could be sewn together, glued, and secured with leather thongs and protective boards. Leather was used for bookbinding for many centuries but is now reserved for special editions. Printing and the use of paper made the production of smaller books possible. During the 19th century, new cover materials were introduced.

Bookkeeping, systematic recording of financial transactions. The single-entry system consists of a single account that shows the debts owed to and by the firm. The double-entry system, more detailed, enters debit and credit items in a journal and then classifies them in a ledger. In the monthly system, a number of separate daybooks are kept, and monthly totals are posted to the ledger accounts.
See also: Accounting.

Book of Changes *See:* I Ching.

Book of Common Prayer, name of the official liturgy of the Church of England, including the services of Morning and Evening Prayer and of Holy Communion, and the Psalter, Gospels, and Epistles.
See also: Church of England.

Book of Hours, collection of prayers to be said at canonical hours, widely used by laymen during the late Middle Ages. Illuminated editions were often masterpieces of the miniaturist's art. Famous are the Rohan and the de Berry Hours.

Book of Kells, illuminated manuscript of the Gospels dating from the late 8th or early 9th century, probably produced by monks of Kells in County Meath, Ireland. Its rich decoration makes it one of the finest examples of medieval manuscript decoration. It is exhibited in the library of Trinity College, Dublin.

Book of Mormon *See:* Mormons; Smith, Joseph.

Book of the Dead, collection of prayers, hymns, and spells brought into the object-laden tombs of the ancient Egyptians, the earliest of which dates to the 16th century B.C. These writings, which were either inscribed on the walls of the tomb or collected in a text, served as a guide for the soul's journey in the afterlife and a protection against evil.

Boomerang, throwing weapon developed in Australia. Precisely bent and balanced, it follows a curved path when thrown, such that it comes back to the thrower.

Boone, Daniel (1734-1820), American pioneer and hunter. Beginning in 1767 he made a series of trips into what is now Kentucky and in 1775 built a fort there, called Boonesboro. In 1778 he was captured by the Shawnee, who were allied with the British against the American revolutionaries. Boone escaped to warn settlers at Boonesboro of a planned attack, which they successfully resisted. He moved to Missouri in 1799, after his land titles in Kentucky were overturned. *See also:* Pioneer life in America.

Boötes, constellation of the Northern Hemisphere, easily recognizable because it contains Arcturus, one of the brightest orange stars in the sky. Boötes is also known as The Huntsman or the Bear Driver. *See also:* Arcturus.

Booth, John Wilkes (1838-1865), U.S. actor who assassinated Abraham Lincoln. A son of the actor Junius Brutus Booth, he was a Confederate sympathizer; eager to avenge the South's defeat, he shot President Lincoln during a performance at Ford's Theater, Washington, D.C., on April 14, 1865. Booth, breaking a leg, escaped but was finally trapped in a barn near Bowling Green, Va., where he either was shot or shot himself.

Bop, or bebop, style of jazz developed toward the end of World War II, so named in imitation of its basic rhythmic feature. Under the inspiration of musicians like Dizzy Gillespie and Charlie Parker, bop broke with the blues tradition, and carried jazz forward into new harmonic and rhythmic fields, opening the way for a more intellectual kind of jazz.

Bophuthatswana (pop. 1,450,000), former independent homeland in South Africa; 16,995 sq mi (44,000 sq km). The capital is Mmabatho. Bophuthatswana consisted of seven distinct territorial units located in the former Transvaal, the Cape Province, and the Orange Free State and was to be the homeland for the Republic of South Africa's Tswana people. It was declared an independent republic by South Africa (though never internationally recognized as such) on

6th December 1977. Lucas Lawrence Manyane Mangope was head of state until, under strong resistance, Bophuthatswana was dissolved and reincorporated into South Africa with its new government based on majority rule. As a result of the new provincial structures, various enclaves of Bophuthatswana became part of the newly created North West province and others of the Orange Free State province. The most important sources of income are mining and agriculture.

Boracic acid *See:* Boric acid.

Borax, common name for a hydrated form of sodium borate or sodium tetraborate, a white powder that becomes transparent and glasslike when heated. Borax is used in glazes and in the manufacture of ceramics and heat-resistant glass. In metallurgy it is used to remove oxide slags. Borax 'beads' are used as a test for metals in chemical analysis. Large quantities of borax in the form of the mineral tincal come from California, Nevada, and Tibet.
See also: Boric acid; Boron.

Bordeaux (pop. 215,000), city in southwestern France and capital of Gironde department, on the Garonne River. It is France's third-largest port and chief center for the French wine trade. Bordeaux also has canning and shipbuilding industries. The city dates from Roman times.
See also: France.

Borden, Sir Robert Laird (1854-1937), Canadian prime minister (1911-20) who helped his country gain an independent voice in world affairs. Borden became Conservative leader in 1901. He was a vigorous World War I prime minister, forming a Union Party government with pro-conscription Liberals in 1917, and securing separate representation for Canada at the peace conference and in the League of Nations.
See also: Canada.

Borg, Arne (1901-1987) Swedish freestyle swimmer, broke 32 world records of various lengths between 1921 and 1929. Became European champion five times and won five Olympic medals (participated in the 1924 and the 1928 Games). The duels between Borg, Andrew Charlton, and Johnny Weissmuller became legendary.

Borg, Björn (1956-), Swedish tennis player and the only player in modern tennis history to win the men's singles title at the Wimbledon Championships in five consecutive years, 1976-80. Earlier, as a 19-year-old, he led Sweden to its first Davis Cup victory. Borg retired from tournament tennis in 1983.

Borges, Jorge Luis (1899-1986), Argentine poet and prose writer. At first influenced by the metaphorical style of Spanish *ultraísmo*, he later developed a unique form between short story and essay, the 'fiction.' Some of the best examples are in his *Ficciones* (1944) and *El Aleph* (1949).

Borgia, powerful Italian family descended from the Borjan of Valencia in Spain. **Alfonso de Borja** (1378-1458) became Pope Calixtus III. By bribery, his nephew **Rodrigo Borgia** (1431-1503) became Pope Alexander VI in 1492 and worked to enrich his family by crushing the Italian princes. His son, **Cesare Borgia** (1476-1507), used war, duplicity, and murder to seize much of central Italy. Alexander's notorious daughter, **Lucrezia Borgia** (1480-1519), was probably a pawn in her family's schemes. As duchess of Ferrara, she generously patronized the arts and learning.

Cesare Borgia, shown in this Giorgione painting, was one of the major princes of Renaissance Italy.

Boric acid, white crystalline acid (H_3BO_3) occurring in nature or prepared from borax and used as a weak antiseptic.

Borlaug, Norman Ernest (1914-), U.S. agricultural scientist who was awarded the 1970 Nobel Peace Prize for his part in the development of improved varieties of cereal crops that are important in the green revolution in the developing nations of the Third World.

Borman, Frank (1928-), U.S. astronaut. After joining the Manned Spacecraft Center of NASA in 1962, Borman became command pilot on the 14-day orbital *Gemini 7* flight in December 1965. Along with James Lovell and William Anders, Borman participated in the *Apollo 8* flight, the first humans to voyage around the moon. In 1970, Borman retired from NASA and entered commercial aviation.
See also: Astronaut.

Bormann, Martin Ludwig (1900-1945), German Nazi politician, Hitler's deputy from 1941. Though he vanished in 1945, he was sentenced to death for war crimes at the Nuremberg Trials in 1946. It is now thought he was killed as Berlin fell.
See also: Nazism; Nuremberg Trials.

Born-again Christians, fundamentalist Christians who feel themselves regenerated through the experience of being 'born again' (John 3:3). Related to the Calvinist doctrine of election, the experience today assumes a revivalist character. In the late 1970s, citing a decline in morality, Born-again Christians became active in U.S. politics through such organizations as the Moral Majority, led by Rev. Jerry Falwell.

Born, Max (1882-1970), German theoretical physicist active in the development of quantum physics. His probabilistic interpretation of the Schrödinger wave equation provided a link between wave mechanics and the quantum theory. Sharing the Nobel Prize for physics with W. Bothe in 1954, he devoted his later years to the philosophy of physics.

Borneo, largest island of the Malay Archipelago and third largest in the world (280,100 sq mi/725,459 sq km). It contains the Indonesian province of Kalimantan, the sultanate of Brunei, and the Malaysian states of Sabah and Sarawak. Borneo is a mountainous equatorial island largely clad in tropical rain forest, and drained by several major rivers. Its highest point is Mt. Kinabalu (13,455 ft/4,101 m). The island suffered severely due to the forest fires in 1997-98.
See also: Brunei; Indonesia; Malaysia.

Borobudur (Barabudur), Buddhist relic in Jawa Tengah (central Java). Built in the shape of a stupa enclosing a small hill. Consists of six square terraces, three round platforms with a stupa in the center. At the center of the four sides are high steps; small-

Buddhism left only a few traces in Indonesia, in contrast to Hinduism and Islam. But the eighth-century Shailendra dynasty, the only important Buddhist dynasty in Java, did make some grand cultural contributions, which is climaxed by the Borobudur temple complex (800) on Djawa Tengah.

B

B

er stupas have been built on the platforms. Its construction started around 825 and lasted a number of decades. Various styles can be distinguished in the abundantly sculpted decorations.

Borodin, Aleksandr Porfirevich (1833-1887), Russian chemist and composer of the group known as the Five. His musical works include the opera *Prince Igor*, completed after his death by Aleksandr Glazunov and Nikolai Rimsky-Korsakov.

Boron, chemical element, symbol B; for physical constants see Periodic Table. Boron is not found free in nature, but its compounds have been known for thousands of years. The most important source of boron is the mineral *kernite* (sodium borate). A nonmetal, boron is prepared by the vapor phase reduction of boron trichloride with hydrogen on electrically heated filaments. It is similar to carbon in that it forms stable, covalently bonded molecular networks. Compounds of boron are used in the manufacture of fiberglass, bleach, laundry products, flame retardants, antiseptics, and borosilicate glasses. Boron-10 is used as a control in nuclear reactors. Filaments of boron are lightweight and strong and are used for aerospace structures.

Borotra, Jean (1899-1994), prominent French tennis player who won the singles at Wimbledon in 1924 and 1926. In addition, he won the doubles at Wimbledon in 1925. Borotra was one of the 'Four Musketeers', together with Jacques Brugnon, Henri Cochet, and René Lacoste. They were called the Four Musketeers because they won the Davis Cup for France for five straight years from 1927 to 1932. In 1940 Borotra became minister of sport under General Pétain, and he was imprisoned in Austria in 1942.

Borromini, Francesco (1599-1667), Italian architect; initially worked under Maderno, later under Bernini. He developed a very personal architectural style which strongly expressed his skills in the field of sculpting. He is now considered one of the greatest master builders specialized in the baroque architectural style and mainly worked in Rome. His major works are: S. Carlo alle Quattro Fontane (1634-1647), renovation of the interior of the S. Giovanni at Laterano (1646-1649) and completion of the S. Agnese in Agone in Piazzo Navona (1653-1657).

Borsippa (currently Birs Nimrud), old Babylonian city and an important religious center. Hammurapi (ruled 1792-1750 B.C.) built a religious temple here. The city blossomed under Nebuchadnezzar II (ruled 604-562), but was destroyed by the Persian king Xerxes I in the 5th century B.C.. Excavations were carried out by the German archaeologist Robert Koledeway around 1900. He uncovered a ziggurat which was thought to be the tower of Babel.

Bos, Jan (1975-), Dutch skater, excelled in short-distance skating. In 1998 he finally broke through by winning Dutch titles for the 500 m and 1000 m events and won the national sprint title. In the same year he won the world sprinting title. Bos won a silver medal for the 1000 m race at the 1998 Olympic Winter games in Nagano. In 1999 he once again acquired the national sprint title and became world champion of the 1000 m. During the sprinting world championship in Calgary in 1999 he ended second behind Jeremy Wotherspoon, but still broke a world record for the 1000 m at 1,08.55. In addition, Bos broke a number of Dutch records including the 500 m at 34.87.

Bosch, Hieronymus (c.1450-1516), Dutch painter whose work features grotesque fantasy. In paintings like the *Haywain* (1485) and *The Garden of Earthly Delights* (1500) he used part-human, part-animal, part-vegetable forms to express symbolically his obsessive vision of worldly sin and eternal damnation.

Bosch, Juan *See:* Dominican Republic.

Bose, Subhas Chandra (1897-1945), Indian radical nationalist politician, co-founder of the Swaraj Party and, together with Nehru, founder of the Independence Movement (1928). This movement refused to accept dominion status for India. Chairman of the Indian National Congress (1938). In World War II he proclaimed the establishment of a provisional independent Indian government with support of the Japanese in Singapore.

Bosnia and Hercegovina

Capital:	Sarajevo
Area:	20,452 sq mi (51,129 sq km)
Population:	3,964,000
Language:	Bosnian, Serbian, Croatian
Government:	Republic
Independent:	1992
Head of gov.:	2 (co)Prime ministers
Per capita:	less than US$ 1,800
Monetary unit:	marka

Bosnia and Hercegovina (Republic of), independent country in southeastern Europe, bordering Croatia and the Federal Republic of Yugoslavia, formerly one of the 6 states of Yugoslavia. The population of over 3,500,000 consists of Serbian Orthodox, Croatian Roman Catholics, and Turkish Muslims. Before the war that ensued independence, the economy was largely based on agriculture, with wheat, maize, sugar, meat and milk the most important products. However, the war caused an economic standstill in the early 1990s, and the population became almost completely dependent on foreign-relief aid. When Yugoslavia disintegrated, Bosnia-Hercegovina became an independent state. The Bosnian Serbs opposed independence from Serbian-dominated Yugoslavia and started to expand the area under their control. Despite international intervention, the war between the Muslims, Croatians and Serbs continued into the mid-1990s. In 1995 Bosnia was partitioned into two 'entities': the Muslim-Croatic Federation Bosnia-Hercegovina and the Bosnian Serbian Republic (Republika Srpska). In 1997 the first federal Bosnian government was formed. In 2001, the former president, Biljana Plavsic, voluntarily turned herself in to the Yugoslavia Tribunal and admitted to being guilty of war crimes during the civil war. Two other Serbian suspects, Radovan Karadzic and Ratko Mladic, had still not been arrested.
See also: Yugoslavia.

Fragment of the right panel of Hieronymus Bosch's perception of the torments of Hell (Prado, Madrid).

Boson, one of the 4 major classes of elementary particles (the others being the leptons, mesons, and baryons). The bosons have no mass. They include photons, gluons, and, hypothetically, the graviton. Bosons were named for the Indian physicist Satyendranath Bose, who with Albert Einstein developed a statistical theory of the behavior of these particles in the 1920s.
See also: Particle physics.

Bosporus, Turkish strait 19 mi (30.6 km) long and about 0.5-2.5 mi (0.8-3.6 km) wide connecting the Black Sea and the Sea of Marmara (which is connected to the Aegean arm of the Mediterranean by the Dardanelles strait). Historically important as the sole sea link between the Black Sea and the Mediterranean, it was bridged in 1973.
See also: Turkey.

Bossuet, Jacques Bénigne (1627-1704), French prelate and historian renowned for his eloquence as an orator, especially his *Funeral Orations* (1689). He was bishop of Condom (1669-71) and of Meaux (from 1681). He wrote the famous *Discourse on Universal History* (1681) and *Treatise of the Knowledge of God and One's Self* (1722).

The Boston Tea Party. White people, disguised as Indians, throwing a load of tea from their ships in Boston harbour, as a way of protest against the fiscal measures of the English government (1773).

Boston (pop. 2,900,000), capital and largest city of Massachusetts, seaport on Massachusetts Bay. It is the most populous state capital, New England's largest city, and the nearest major U.S. seaport to Europe. It is also a major commercial, financial, manufacturing, and cultural center. Boston's industries include shipbuilding, electronics, chemicals, plastics, rubber products, and printing. The city's wool market is the nation's largest. Historic buildings include the Old State House, Paul Revere House, Christ Church, and Faneuil Hall. Boston has many notable educational institutions, and nearby Cambridge has Harvard University and the Massachusetts Institute of Technology. Settled by English Puritans in 1630, Boston became the capital of Massachusetts Bay Colony. In the Boston Massacre and Boston Tea Party the city led colonial unrest that erupted into the Revolutionary War. Modern Boston shares the acute urban problems of most large U.S. cities.
See also: Massachusetts.

Boston Tea Party, incident at Boston on Dec. 16, 1773, in protest against the tea tax and British import restrictions. A party of colonial patriots disguised in Native American dress boarded three British East India Company ships and dumped their cargo of tea into the harbor.
See also: Revolutionary War in America.

Boswell, James (1740-1795), Scottish writer and lawyer, most famous for his *Life of Samuel Johnson* (1791). In his journals he recorded his life and times with great zest. From them he culled the accounts of his travels in Corsica and elsewhere, and the brilliant conversations that distinguish the portrait of his friend Samuel Johnson.
See also: Johnson, Samuel.

Botany, the study of plants. Botany has several closely related branches. *Plant morphology*, the study of plant structure, has 2 subdisciplines: (1) plant anatomy deals with the gross structure of the plant-the shapes of the roots, stems, and leaves and the organization of the flowers; (2) plant histology deals with the structure and arrangement of the cells and tissues inside the plant. *Plant physiology* is concerned with how the plant works-how it gets its water from the soil, how the water passes up the stem, how the plant grows and moves, how its flowers open, and so on. *Biochemistry* deals with the chemical reac-

tions going on in the plant. *Cytology* is the study of the cell protoplasm and its contents, including the nucleus. *Plant breeding* helps to produce bigger and better crops. Plants have been bred for thousands of years, but it was not until the present century, when Gregor Mendel's work in the 19th century was rediscovered, that scientists understood how characteristics are passed on from parent to offspring. By cross-pollinating selected plants, 2 or more desirable features can be combined into 1 variety. *Plant pathology* deals with plant diseases and their control. *Plant ecology* deals with the relationships between plants and their surroundings and is concerned especially with why plants grow where they do. *Plant taxonomy* deals with the naming and classification of plants. The Swedish naturalist Carolus Linnaeus (1707-78) put forward the idea of the species as the smallest unit and the genus as a group of closely related species, giving species a generic name and a specific name. For ex-

Carolus Linnaeus (1707-1778), founder of the modern system of binomial nomen-clature used for classifying plants and animals.

ample, the plant whose common name is ragwort is scientifically known as *Senecio jacobaea*. Taxonomy is designed to show the relationships between living things, drawing information from morphology, physiology, and other branches of botany. Species with many features in common are grouped into a genus, genera with common features are grouped into a family, and families with common features are grouped into an order. If relationships exist, they may be discovered by specialists in *paleobotany*, the study of fossil plants.

Botfly, family of flies (order Diptera) whose larvae are parasitic in the tissues and cavities of humans and other mammals. The name is generally given to the horse botfly, a yellowish-brown insect about 1/2 in (13 mm) long. It lays eggs in the mane and on the legs and belly of horses. When these are licked off and swallowed, they are carried to the stomach, where they hatch. The larvae attach themselves to the lining of the stomach. Within a year, the mature larvae are discharged in the feces; they pupate in the ground and change into flies. The flies have virtually no mouth parts and do not feed during their short adult life.

Botha, Pieter Willem (1916-), South African politician who became the first executive president under a new constitution (1984-1989). He entered Parliament in 1948, becoming defense minister in 1966 and prime minister in 1978. He came to recognize the importance of political change

and the need to win over the loyalty and cooperation of the country's black majority. In 1984 he became president of South Africa. He reformed apartheid policy, although not enough for the black majority of the population. In 1989 he abdicated and was succeeded by F. W. de Klerk.
See also: South Africa.

Bothwell, James Hepburn, 4th Earl of (1536-1578), Scottish nobleman who married Mary Queen of Scots in May 1567, after helping to murder her husband, Lord Darnley. In June he fled Scotland, and later died in a Danish prison.

Bo tree, or bodhi tree, Asian fig (*Ficus religiosa*), sacred to Buddhists as the tree under which Buddha received enlightenment. The Bo tree grows to 100 ft (30 m).
See also: Buddha, Gautama.

Botswana

Capital:	Gaborone
Area:	224,607 sq mi
	(581,730 sq km)
Population:	1,591,000
Language:	Setswana, English
Government:	Presidential republic
Independent:	1966
Head of gov.:	President
Per capita:	US$ 7,800
Monetary unit:	1 Pula = 100 thebe

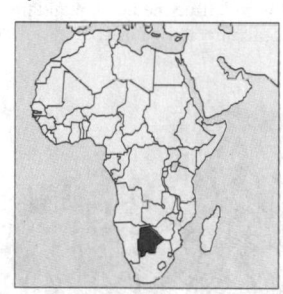

Botswana (formerly Bechuanaland), landlocked republic in southern Africa, enclosed by Namibia, Zimbabwe, and the Republic of South Africa. Its capital is Gaborone.
Land and climate. Botswana is divided into 3 main regions: the Okavango Swamp to the north, the Kalahari Desert in the south and southwest, and the mountainous areas to the east. Most of Botswana is an arid plateau some 3,000 ft (914 m) above sea level, and lack of water makes farming difficult.
People. The majority of the people are Tswana. Both English and Setswana are the official languages. Most of the people adhere to traditional African religions. About three-quarters of the population is literate.
Economy. Botswana is rich in mineral resources, principally diamonds, but also manganese, asbestos, copper, nickel, and coal. Because Botswana is landlocked, it is de-

B

The *Birth of Venus* (around 1485) is one of the most important paintings by Florentine Renaissance painter Sandro Botticelli (1445-1510) (Uffizi Gallery, Florence).

pendent upon its neighbors, South Africa, Namibia and Zimbabwe. Diamonds are the principal export. Botswana also exports its labor: considerable numbers of men move into South Africa for at least part of each year to work in the larger mines.

History. The San Bushmen, original inhabitants of Bechuanaland, were replaced by the Tswana in the 19th century. Under the leadership of King Khama in the early 1800s, the Tswana maintained their independence against invasions by Zulu and Ndebele warriors. By the mid-19th century Boers of the Transvaal sought to annex portions of Bechuanaland for its gold deposits. Bechuana sought British protection and by 1885 had become a British protectorate. On Sept. 30, 1966, the country was given complete independence as Botswana. Sir Seretse M. Khama, grandson of King Khama, was president from 1965 until his death in 1980. Khama was succeeded by Sir Ketumile Joni Masire. Masire abdicated in 1998. At the beginning of 2003, 40% of the sexually active population had been infected with the HIV-virus. President Festus Mogae made a promise to provide free medication and treatment for people infected with AIDS.

The bougainville (*B. glabra*) is a flowering vine or shrub commonly grown in warm climates.

Botticelli, Sandro (Alessandro di Mariano Filipepi; c.1444-1510), Florentine Renaissance painter. His work is noted for superb draftsmanship, the use of sharp yet graceful and rhythmic line, and exquisite coloring. Among his most famous works are the allegorical tableaux on mythological subjects, *Spring* and *The Birth of Venus*.
See also: Renaissance.

Bottle tree, Australian tree (*Brachychiton rupestris*) of the chocolate family, with a trunk resembling a round bottle. Although the main trunk is short and thick, the trees may grow to 60 ft (18 m). A related tree, the baobab of Africa, is also sometimes called a bottle tree.

Botulism, acute type of food poisoning, often fatal, caused by a toxin produced by the anaerobic bacteria *Clostridium botulinum* and *C. parabotulinum*, which normally live in soil but may infect poorly canned food. The toxin paralyzes the nervous system. Thorough cooking destroys both bacteria and toxin.
See also: Toxin.

Botvinnik, Mikhail Moiseyevitsj (1911-1995), Russian chess player. Botvinnik began playing chess at the age of twelve and within two years managed to defeat the world champion at the time during a demonstration match. In 1935 he became a grand master. During his career as chess player he became champion of the Soviet Union seven times (between 1931 and 1952) and continuously won the world championships from 1948 until 1963 with the exception of two years. In 1957 Botvinnik lost the title to Vasily Smyslov and in 1960 he was challenged successfully by Mikhail Tal. In 1963 he finally lost the world title to Tigran Petrosjan. Botvinnik was not only a great tournament player, but also a master strategist who applied a scientific approach to chess and developed new methods for chess strategies and training. He also occupied himself with designing computer chess programs. He was convinced that artificial intelligence would one day be superior to any chess player.

Boucher, François (1703-1770), a French painter. His art vividly expresses the light-hearted Rococo spirit of pre-Revolutionary France. Although he painted historical and *genre* (everyday life) scenes and portraits, Boucher is famous for his sensual pastoral and mythological paintings, such as *The Interrupted Sleep* and *Venus Consoling Love*.
Boucher lived most of his life in his native Paris. With the help of Mme. de Pompadour, Louis XV's mistress, he became first painter to the king and director of the Royal Academy and of the Gobelins tapestry works. Boucher's influence was enormous. He designed tapestries, prepared models for the porcelain works at Sèvres and Vincennes, and created theater and opera decorations.

Boudicca *See:* Boadicea.

Bougainville, largest of the Solomon Islands, a part of the independent nation of Papua-New Guinea. Bougainville produces cacao, copra, and gold.
See also: Solomon Islands.

Bougainvillea, ornamental tropical and subtropical flowering vine (genus *Bougainvillaea*) named for the French navigator and explorer, Louis Antoine de Bougainville. The flower clusters are white or creamy-colored, each surrounded by three large floral bracts that may range from crimson or purple to yellow or white.

Boulder Dam *See:* Hoover Dam.

Boulding, Kenneth Ewart (1910-1993), British-born U.S. economist who proposes a social science unifying economics, politics, and sociology. He is the author of more than 15 books, including *A Reconstruction of Economics* (1950), *Economics as a Science* (1970), *A Primer on Social Dynamics* (1970), *Stable Peace* (1978), and *Human Betterment* (1985).

Boulez, Pierre (1925-), French composer and conductor, noted for his extension of 12-tone techniques to rhythm and dynamics in such works as *Le Marteau sans maître* (1951) and *Pli selon pli* (1960). He was music director of the New York Philharmonic (1971-77), and has conducted many of the world's leading orchestras.

Bounty, Mutiny on the *See:* Bligh, William; Nordhoff and Hall.

Bourbon, powerful family that for generations ruled France, Naples and Sicily (the Two Sicilies), Parma, and Spain; named for the castle of Bourbon northwest of Moulins. Bourbons became part of the French ruling house when a Bourbon heiress married **Duke Robert**, Louis IX's sixth son, in 1272. In 1589 their descendant, **Henry of Navarre**, founded France's Bourbon dynasty as Henry IV. Bourbon rule in France was interrupted with Louis XVI's execution in 1793, was restored in 1814 under **Louis XVIII**, and finally ended with the deposition of **Charles X** in 1830. In Spain, Louis XIV's grandson came to the throne in 1700 as **Philip V**. In Italy, cadet branches of his family ruled Parma (1748- 1860) and Naples and Sicily (1759-1861). Bourbons ruled Spain until 1931, when Alfonso XIII abdicated. In 1947 Spain was again declared a monarchy, and in 1975 **Prince Juan Carlos** of Bourbon succeeded the head of state, General Franco.

Bourdelle, Antoine (1861-1929), a French sculptor. *Hercules the Archer* and *Le Fruit* are among his many expressive works that convey a sense of movement. Bourdelle first studied art in his native Montauban and in Toulouse. In 1884 he settled in Paris and enrolled in the Ecole des Beaux-Arts. For several years he was Rodin's chief assistant. About 1909 Bourdelle began reaching and his studio became a school. His home and studio, donated to the French government in 1948, is now the Musée Bourdelle.
Other works include *Apollo and the Muses,* a relief on the facade of the Théâtre des

Champs-Elysées; *Rodin at Work;* and portrait busts of Beethoven, Gustave Eiffel, and Anatole France.

Bourgeoisie *See:* Communism.

Bourguiba, Habib Ben Ali (1903-2000), Tunisian nationalist politician and Tunisia's first president (1957-87). He led the campaign for independence from the 1930s onwards and was imprisoned by the French several times. He was ousted in 1987.
See also: Tunisia.

Bourke-White, Margaret (1906-1971), U.S. photographer and war correspondent who covered World War II and the Korean War for Time-Life, Inc. Her coverage of India's independence movement and its leader, Mohandas Gandhi, is famous.

Bournonville, August (1805-1879), dancer and choreographer. Student of his father, Antoine, and of Auguste Vestris. Among other dancers, he partnered Marie Taglioni in Paris. He was best known, however, as a choreographer and directed the Royal Danish Ballet in Copenhagen (1830-1855), where he produced ballets such as: La Sylphide in 1836 (following the French version of 1832 by Filippo Taglioni and scored by Jean-Madeleine Schneitzhoeffer, with music by Severin Lövenskjold), Napoli in 1848, Konservatoriet in 1849, Bruges in 1851, and Flower Festival at Genzano in 1858. He also established a ballet academy where students from lower to higher classes had to dance solos from his ballets every day, so that they would know all ballets thoroughly and would be able to perform them by the time they joined a dance company. For over 100 years this system was the basis of the so-called Bournonville school. Since the 1960s these ballets have increasingly attracted interest at international level. As a result, Danish dancers like Harald Lander, Niels Kehlet, Peter Martins, Erik Bruhn, Peter Schaufuss, Henning Kronstam and the somewhat older Hans Brenaa studied these ballets with many dance companies in Europe and the United States.

Boutros-Ghali, Boutros (1922-), Egyptian diplomat and United Nations official. Boutros-Ghali was born in Cairo, into a prominent Coptic family. He obtained a doctorate from the University of Paris in 1949, and then served 28 years as a professor of international law and international relations at Cairo University. In 1977 Boutros-Ghali became Egypt's Minister of State for Foreign Affairs, and in 1991 deputy prime minister. He was the sixth secretary general of the United Nations, serving 1992-1997. He succeeded Javier Perez de Cuellar and, in turn, was succeeded by Kofi Annan.

Bouts The Elder, Dierick (Dirk) (1410-1475), Flemish painter of Dutch origin. One of the so-called Flemish primitives. Influenced by Rogier van der Weyden. Characteristic of his art are grouped figures in an interior, the three-dimensional effect, and scenic backgrounds. Best known work: *The last Supper* (1464-1467; St. Peter's Church, Leuven). His son Albert Bouts

(1456/1460-1549) was also a painter. His most important work is the triptych *The Ascension of Maria* (Royal Museum of Fine Arts, Brussels).

Bowen, Elizabeth (1899-1973), English-Irish novelist, whose works are distinguished by their meticulous style and emotional sensitivity. They include *The Death of the Heart* (1938), *The Heat of the Day* (1949), and *Eva Trout* (1969).

Bowerbird, forest-dwelling bird (family Ptilonorhynchidae) native to Australia and New Guinea that builds 'bowers' of sticks decorated with bones, shells, berries, and flowers. Males fight and court in the bowers; the birds mate in the bower, but nest in a nearby tree. The largest of these birds, the great or red-crested bowerbird, may grow 14 in (36 cm) long.

Bowfin, large freshwater fish (*Amia calva*) of eastern North America, also known as the grindle, mudfish, or freshwater dogfish. It is sometimes referred to as a 'living fossil' because it resembles a type of fish that can be traced back 130 million years. Its body may reach a length of 30 in (76 cm). Because it eats large numbers of valuable food fish, it is sometimes regarded as a pest.

Bowie, James (1796-1836), Kentucky-born frontier hero who reputedly invented the bowie hunting knife. He grew rich by land speculation and slave trading. Bowie joined the Texan fight for independence from Mexico and was one of the leaders at the Alamo, where he died.
See also: Alamo.

Bowles, Paul (1910-1999), U.S. author and composer living in Morocco. He is known for his exotic novels and short stories of alienation, despair, and psychological horror. His works include *The Sheltering Sky*

(1949), *Collected Stories: 1939-1976* (1979) and *Unwelcome Words* (1989). His wife, **Jane Auer Bowles** (1917-1973), was also a writer. Her works include the novel *Two Serious Ladies* (1943) and the play *In the Summer House* (1954).

Bowling, indoor sport that involves rolling a ball to knock down wooden pins. In tenpin bowling, the most popular form in the United States, players aim a large heavy ball down a long wooden lane at 10 pins set in a triangle. The number of pins felled determines the score. Bowling became popular in 14th-century Europe, and was brought to America by the Dutch in the 17th century. Tenpin bowling was standardized by the American Bowling Congress, founded in 1895.

Boxelder, or ash-leaf maple (*Acer negundo*), deciduous tree native to North America. It grows up to 70 ft (20 m) high and has compound leaves and grooved bark. The

Tooth billed bowerbird (*Scenopoeetes dentirostris*, order *Passeriformes*, family Ptiloriorhynchidae). Found in northeastern Australia. Length up to 9 in (23 cm).

B

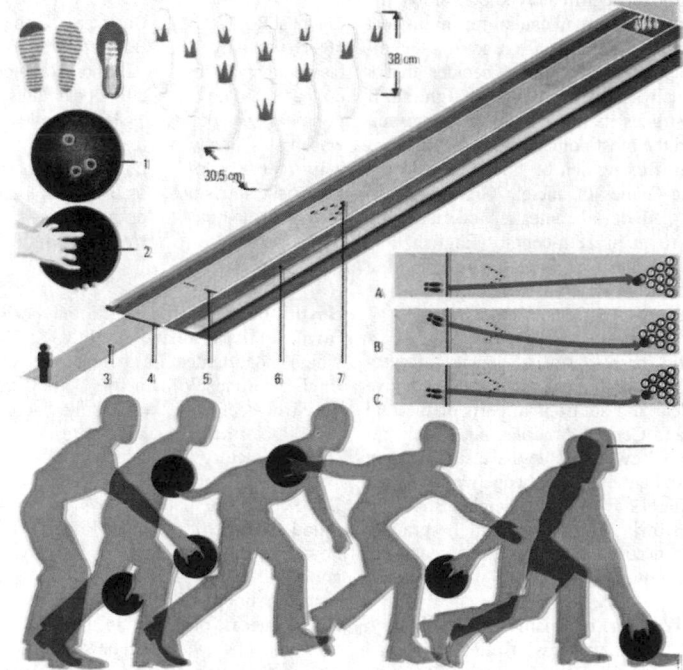

For bowling right-handed, the sole of the left shoe is made of leather, for sliding, and the sole of the right shoe is made of rubber. The ball (2) is made of hard rubber, it weighs between 4.5 and 7.3 kg, and it has three holes, for gripping (1). The lane has an approach of approximately 4.8 m (3), the distance between the foul line (4) and the number-1 pin is 18.28 m, and it is 1.066 m wide. On the alley, there are two sets of guide spots, (5) and (7), to help the bowler aim, beside the alley are two shallow gutters (6). Also shown are the delivery action, and three different methods of bowling: the straight ball (A), the curve ball (B) and the hook ball (C).

B

greenish-yellow flowers are unisexual and are borne on separate trees. The sap is sometimes tapped for its sugar.

Boxer, medium-sized dog first bred in Germany in the 1800s. The stocky, muscular dog has been used as a guide dog for the blind. Its short, shiny coat is sometimes striped or caramel-colored. It measures 21-24 in (53-61 cm) in height at the shoulder and weighs about 60-75 lb (27-34 kg).

Boxer Rebellion, violent uprising in China in 1900 directed against foreigners and instigated by the secret society 'Harmonious Fists' (called Boxers by the Europeans). Encouraged by the Dowager Empress Tz'u Hsi, the Boxers showed their dislike of growing European influence and commercial exploitation in China, attacking missionaries and Chinese converts to Christianity. Troops sent to protect European nationals at Peking were repulsed. The German minister in Peking was murdered and foreign legations were besieged for nearly 2 months until relieved by an international force. Boxer violence was the pretext for Russian occupation of South Manchuria. On Sept. 7, 1901, China was forced to sign the humiliating Boxer Protocol, in which it promised to pay a huge indemnity to the United States and the European powers concerned.
See also: China; Open-Door Policy.

Boxing, sport of skilled fist-fighting. Two contestants wearing padded gloves attack each other by punching prescribed parts of the body, while avoiding or blocking their opponent's punches. Boxing contests are arranged between opponents in the same weight division or class; there are 10 classes ranging from flyweight to heavyweight. Fights take place in a square roped-off ring and consist of a number of 2- or 3-minute rounds. Scoring is usually made by a referee and 2 judges. A win can occur by a knockout, if a boxer legitimately knocks down his opponent and the man cannot regain his feet in 10 sec. A fight may also end in a technical knockout if the referee decides that a boxer is physically unfit to go on fighting. If a contest goes its full length, the contestant awarded the most points or rounds wins by a decision. Boxing can be traced back to the Olympic Games of ancient Greece, and to Roman gladiatorial contests. Modern boxing has its roots in 18th-century English fairground fights between bare-knuckled pugilists, who battered each other for bets until one could no longer continue.

Boxwood, or box, several species of evergreen shrubs and trees (genus *Buxus*), native to tropical and subtropical parts of the Old World and Central America, but widely introduced elsewhere. They have small glossy leaves and are excellent hedge plants, rarely exceeding 12 ft (4 m) in height. Boxwood grows slowly. Its yellow, finely grained wood is used for musical instruments and wood engraving.

Boyd, William (real name Andrew Muray; 1952-), British writer who, after having had a Spartan upbringing at Gordonstoun board-

ing school and having studied at the Universities of Nice, Glasgow, and Oxford, taught English in the latter city. In 1981 he made his debut with the satirical novel *A Good Man in Africa* and the collection of stories *On the Yankee Station*. Other works by him include *An Ice-cream War* (1982) about the beginning of World War I in German southeast Africa, *Stars and Bars* (1985), *The New Confessions* (1987) modeled after the book by Rousseau about the trials and tribulations of a Scottish moviemaker during World War I, *Brazzaville Beach* (1990; James Tait Black Memorial Prize), *The Blue Afternoon* (1993), *The Destiny of Nathalie and other Stories* (1995), *Armadillo* (1998), and *Any Human Heart* (2002).

Boyle, Robert (1627-1691), British natural philosopher, often called the father of modern chemistry for his rejection of the theories of the alchemists and his espousal of atomism. He discovered what is called Boyle's Law for Gases: At a constant temperature the volume of a given quantity of gas varies inversely to the pressure to which the gas is subjected.
See also: Chemistry; Philosophy.

Scientist Boyle (1627-1691), unlike most of his contemporaries, concentrated on experiments, without wasting his time with interminable philosophical discussions on the way things ought to be. Chemistry owes Boyle the first correct definition of the concept of elements, while his significant experiments with the compression of gases produced the celebrated Boyle's Law: pV = constant.

Boyne, Battle of the, battle on the River Boyne in East Ireland on July 12, 1690, which ended James II's attempt to regain the English throne. William III's 35,000 troops decisively defeated the Catholic Jacobites' 21,000. Northern Ireland's Protestants celebrate the victory to this day.

Boy Scouts, international boys' organization founded in 1908 by Sir Robert Baden-Powell to develop character, initiative, and good citizenship. The organization is non-sectarian, nonpolitical, and nonmilitary. The Boy Scouts are organized in about 100 countries, and worldwide membership is approximately 8 million. Scouting emphasizes out-

door knowledge and skills, including nature lore and woodcraft. The Boy Scout program includes Cubs (8-10 years old), Scouts (11-13), and Explorers (14 years and older). Other senior scout groups are the Sea Scouts and Air Scouts. To achieve higher ranks, Scouts must pass tests for merit badges in various fields. The standard troop, led by a volunteer adult scoutmaster, has 32 members and is divided into 4 patrols of 8 Scouts. Boy Scouts have been active in safety campaigns, and conservation programs, and other community service.
See also: Baden-Powell, Robert Stephenson Smyth, Lord.

Boysenberry, variety of blackberry (*Rubus ursinus*) that grows on a trailing plant. The tart, dark-red to black fruits are made up of clusters of drupelets. Boysenberries grow best in mild climates and can be eaten fresh or in pies, jams, and jellies.

Bozeman Trail, route between Wyoming, and Montana used as a short-cut during the 1860s to reach gold fields in Montana and Idaho. The trail, named for John M. Bozeman, covered 600 mi (970 km). Native American attacks, protesting rampant European immigration, closed the trail in the late 1860s.
See also: Gold Rush.

Brabham, John Arthur (Jack) (1926-), Australian racing driver who became Formula One world champion three times. In 1955 he moved from Australia to England to drive for the Cooper team and won the world driving championship for them in 1959 and 1960. A year later Brabham set up his own engineering business. In 1966 he was the first Formula One world champion to drive a car developed and built by himself. He retired in 1970.

Braces *See:* Orthodontics.

Bradbury, Ray (1920-), U.S. science-fiction writer, whose short stories deal with moral dilemmas. Among his best-known science fiction works are *The Martian Chronicles* (1950) and *Fahrenheit 451* (1953).

Bradford (pop. 449,000), city and parliamentary borough of Yorkshire, England, in the Aire valley, 9 mi (14 km) from Leeds. It was concerned with the wool trade during the Middle Ages, and by the end of the 15th century had become an important center of the industry. The Bradford Exchange is a major international wool market, and the Bradford Institute of Technology is world famous for its textile design.
See also: England.

Bradford, William (1590-1657), Pilgrim Father who helped to establish Plymouth Colony and governed it most of his life (re-elected 30 times from 1621). He described the *Mayflower's* voyage and the colony's first years in his *History of Plymouth Plantation*.
See also: Pilgrims.

Bradley, James (1693-1762), British as-

tronomer. His 2 great discoveries were the aberration of light (1729) and the nutation (nodding motion) of the earth's axis (1748). Just before his death he published a catalog listing more han 60,000 stars.
See also: Astronomy.

Bradley, Omar Nelson (1893-1981), U.S. general. In 1944-1945 he led the 12th Army Group (1 million men in 4 armies) in Europe. He was chief of staff of the U.S. Army (1948-1949) and first chairman of the joint chiefs of staff (1949-1953).
See also: World War II.

Bradstreet, Anne Dudley (c. 1612-1672), English-American colonial poet. She began writing after her emigration to Massachusetts in 1630. Her poems deal with personal reflections on the Puritan ethic. Her collection, *The Tenth Muse Lately Sprung Up in America*, was published in England in 1650.

Brady, Mathew B. (1823-1896), U.S. photographer of historic events and eminent people, including 18 U.S. presidents. He spent his fortune in hiring 20 teams of photographers to take over 3,500 shots covering almost every big battle of the Civil War, a project that bankrupted him. His most famous photographs are those of Lincoln and of the battles of Bull Run and Gettysburg.

A photograph by Mathew B. Brady of General Grant with his staff.

Bragg, Sir William Henry (1862-1942), British physicist who shared the 1915 Nobel Prize in physics with his son, **Sir William Lawrence Bragg** (1890-1971), for the deduction of the atomic structure of crystals from their X-ray diffraction patterns (1912).
See also: Physics.

Brahe, Tycho (1546-1601), Danish astronomer, the greatest exponent of naked-eye positional astronomy. Johannes Kepler, who became his assistant in 1601, postulated an elliptical orbit for Mars based on his confidence in Brahe's data. Brahe's 'Tychonic system,' in which the planets circled the sun, which in turn orbited a stationary earth, was the principal 17th-century rival of the Copernican hypothesis. Brahe observed a supernova with the naked eye in 1872.
See also: Astronomy.

Brahmanism, Indian religion based on belief in Brahma. It developed about 500 B.C. from Dravidian and Aryan beliefs. Its ritual, symbolism, and theosophy came from the *Brahmanas*, sacred writings of the priestly caste, and from the Upanishads. It developed the 'divinely ordered' caste system and gave rise to modern Hinduism.
See also: Hinduism.

Brahmans *See:* Hinduism.

Brahmaputra River, river that rises in the Himalayas and flows about 1,800 mi (2,897 km) through Tibet, northeastern India, Bangladesh, and south to the Ganges, forming the Ganges-Brahmaputra delta on the Bay of Bengal. A holy river to the Indians, its name means 'son of Brahma.'

Brahmnananda Saraswati (Guru Dev; 1868-1953), Indian spiritual teacher, became known through his student Maharishi, leader of the Transcendental Meditation Movement, who calls him Guru Dev (divine teacher). His spiritual support is called upon during the Transcendental Meditation Movement's consecration ceremony.

Brahms, Johannes (1833-1897), major German Romantic composer. Though strongly influenced by Beethoven and the Romantic movement, he developed his own rhythmic originality and emotional intensity, while using classical forms. He lived largely in Vienna from 1863. His major works include four symphonies, two piano concertos, a violin concerto, a double concerto for violin and cello, piano and chamber works, songs, part-songs, and choral works-notably, *A German Requiem* (1868) and the *Alto Rhapsody* (1869).
See also: Schumann, Clara.

Braille, system of writing for the blind developed by Louis Braille, employing patterns of raised dots that can be read by touch. Braille typewriters and printing presses allow the mass production of books for the blind.
See also: Braille, Louis.

Braille, Louis (1809-1852), French inventor of braille. Accidentally blinded at the age of 3, he conceived his raised-dot system at 15, while at the National Institute for the Blind in Paris. In 1829 he published a book explaining how his system could be used, not only for reading but also for writing and musical notation.
See also: Braille.

Brain, complex organ coordinating nerve activity and responsible for thought in higher animal forms. Invertebrates have only a rudimentary brain, most highly developed in the octopus. Vertebrates have brains more fully differentiated, consisting of forebrain, midbrain, and hindbrain. In highly developed vertebrate animals, the forebrain has developed into a large and highly differentiated *cerebrum*. The human brain is composed of some billions of interconnecting nerve cells and many more supporting cells (neuroglia). Together with the spinal cord, the brain makes up the central nervous system (CNS), which governs and coordinates the operations of all tissues and organs and is the physical basis of all mental activities: consciousness, sensation, thought, speech, memory, emotion, character, and skill.

The nervous system carries information in the form of electric signals. All the outlying nervous pathways-the peripheral nervous system, or PNS-converge on the CNS. Nerve fibers conduct in 1 direction only: Those that carry information from the sensory organs to the CNS are called afferent, or sensory pathways; those that carry impulses outward from the CNS to the muscles and glands are called efferent, or motor, pathways. Nervous pathways are made up of separate units-nerve cells known as neurons. The main parts of the neuron are the cell body, the axon, and the dendrites. Dendrites generally carry an impulse toward the cell body, and the axon carries it away from the cell body to another cell. The ends of the axon lie adjacent to, but not quite touching, the dendrites or cell bodies of other neurons; the region where the 2 nearly touch is called a synapse. Electrical impulses cannot cross synapses; the transfer is made by chemical substances called neurotransmitters. These substances have become extremely important because of the part they play in the pharmacological treatment of some psychiatric and neurological conditions. The full-grown brain is described as having 3 parts. *(1)* The *brain stem* is chiefly a relay station for nervous pathways between the higher parts of the brain and the rest of the body; if it is damaged, sensory and motor functions are greatly impaired. It is also responsible for subvoluntary activities like digestion and respiration.

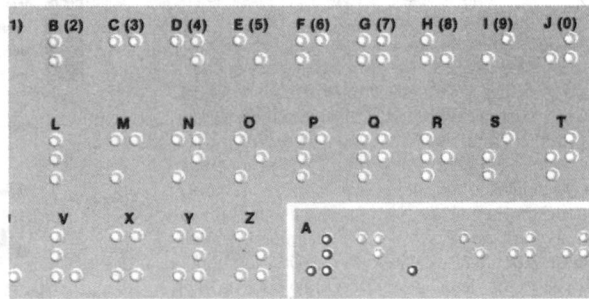

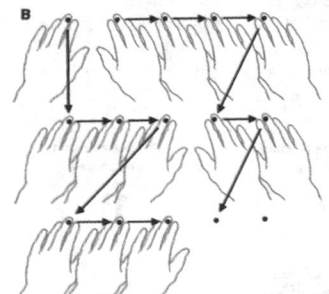

The braille alphabet, which consists of a different pattern of raised dots for each letter of the alphabet (the numerals corresponding to the letters A-J). (A) The numeral sign, to indicate that a number will follow, and then a 4, a comma, a 5 and two zeroes: the number 4,500 in braille. (B) Reading braille. Basically, the right hand picks up the message, using one or more fingers — according to the skill of the reader — while the left hand simultaneously scans down the column for the beginning of the next line.

B

B

(2) The *cerebellum*, divided into hemispheres, each controlling a side of the body, is responsible for the coordination of voluntary muscular movements and for posture.

(3) The *cerebrum*, the highest center of the brain and the latest in evolutionary development, is responsible for sensation, thought, and the initiation of voluntary motor activity. It, too, is divided into hemispheres, each consisting of 2 main parts: (1) the *basal ganglia*, made up of a complicated collection of bunches of gray matter that clusters about the top of the brain stem, and (2) the *cerebral cortex*, also made of gray matter, separated from the basal ganglia by tracts of white matter. The cerebrum is customarily divided into 4 lobes: (1) The *frontal lobe (lobus frontalis)* controls voluntary motor patterns, the organization of the motor units necessary for speech, original thinking, and the evaluation of ideas. (2) The *parietal lobe (lobus parietalis)* is mainly concerned with the reception of body sensations and memory in regard to language and learning. The region also has a role in spatial organization. (3) The *temporal lobe (lobus temporalis)* receives auditory sensations (the sense of hearing), participates in speech through auditory monitoring, plays a role in spatial organization, and is a memory mechanism. The temporal lobe has also been variously claimed to be concerned with memory and dreams. (4) The *occipital lobe (lobus occipitalis)*, in the back of the head, is the primary center for vision. The limbic system contains components of the frontal, parietal, and temporal lobes, and controls behavioral reactions to the external environment, possibly influenced by the internal environment, which may alter the excitability of the nervous system. It seems to operate in preserving the individual (feeding, fleeing, or fighting) or the species (reproduction).

The *corpus callosum*, a large white bundle of fibers that connects the cerebral hemispheres, appears concerned with the transfer of learning from 1 hemisphere to another. The functions of the *corpus callosum* include (1) correlation of images in the left and right halves of the visual field, (2) integration of sensations from paired limbs or for learning that requires motor coordination of the limbs, and (3) unification of cerebral processes of attention and awareness. The absence of a *corpus callosum* slows down the rate of learning.

Brainwashing, manipulation of an individual's will, generally without his or her knowledge and against his or her wishes. Most commonly, it consists of a combination of isolation, personal humiliation, disorientation, systematic indoctrination, and alternating punishment and reward.

Brake, device for slowing or halting motion, usually by conversion of kinetic energy into heat energy via the medium of friction. Most airplane, automobile, and railroad brakes are mechanical drum or disk brakes, applying friction directly to some portion of the wheel or of a drum rotating with the wheel. Mechanically operated brakes cannot always be used, as when a single control must operate on a number of wheels simultaneously and equally. Hydraulic, vacuum, and air brakes, which use different mediums to distribute the pressure, may be used in combination with mechanical brakes.

Bramante, Donato (1444-1514), Italian architect who developed the classical principles of High Renaissance architecture. In 1499, he moved from Milan to Rome, where his major designs included the Tempietto of S. Pietro in Montorio (1502) and the Belvedere Court at the Vatican (1505). His greatest project, the reconstruction of St. Peter's, was not realized.
See also: Renaissance.

Bramble, any of a genus (*Rubus*) of prickly shrubs of the rose family. Several of the more than 300 species produce edible berrylike fruits, including blackberries, raspberries, and boysenberries.

Bran, husk of cereal grains (e.g., wheat, rye, or corn), removed from the flour during milling. Bran is ground and used as cattle fodder and is also mixed with cereals and other foods for human consumption, to add roughage and some nutritional elements to the diet. Certain bran extracts are also used in cleaning and dyeing compounds.

Brancusi, Constantin (1876-1957), Romanian sculptor famous for his simple, elemental, polished forms. Living in Paris from 1904, he rejected Rodin's influence, turning to abstract forms and the example of primitive art. Among his best-known works are *The Kiss* (1908) and *Bird in Space* (1919).

Brandenburg, historic region in eastern Germany. Formerly the central province of Prussia, it was divided by the Allies at the end of World War II between Poland and East Germany. In 1952 the German state of Brandenburg was abolished and divided into the districts of Frankfurt, Potsdam, and Cottbus.
See also: Germany.

Brand name *See:* Trademark.

Brando, Marlon (1924-), U.S. stage and screen actor. Brando's first great success was his portrayal of Stanley Kowalski in the Broadway production of Tennessee Williams's *A Streetcar Named Desire*, the film version of which (1951) brought him international fame. Although widely acclaimed as one of the greatest actors of his time, he has appeared in relatively few parts, particularly in recent years. He won Academy Awards for *On the Waterfront* (1954) and *The Godfather* (1972). Other films include *Last Tango in Paris* (1972), *Apocalypse Now* (1979), and *Don Juan de Marco* (1995).

Brandt, Willy (Karl Herbert Frahm; 1913-92), social democratic chancellor of West Germany 1969-74, whose *Ostpolitik* (Eastern policy) marked a major step to-

Lower vertebrate animals, such as frogs, have the most primitive brain, with only a brain stem, a cerebellum, and an undeveloped cerebrum. The brain stem controls involuntary actions, such as breathing, digestion, and heart rate; and the cerebellum coordinates muscular activity. The most dramatic change in the course of brain evolution involves the development of the cerebrum. At the lower end of the evolutionary scale, the cerebrum is merely a center for the sense of smell, and small in size, relative to the other areas, such as the cerebellum. As complexity increases to its stage in primates, the cerebrum controls more senses, as well as perception, limited memory, and learned behavior. Primate brains contain cerebrums that have four lobes: frontal, parietal, temporal, and occipital. Development of the brain culminates in the highly organized brain of humans, which is capable of sophisticated reasoning.

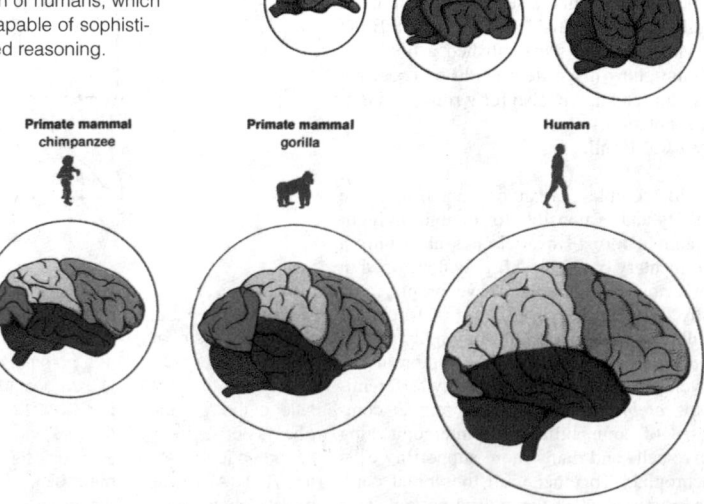

- cerebrum
- frontal lobe
- parietal lobe
- temporal lobe
- cerebellum
- occipital lobe
- brain stem

Reptile — frog

Amphibian — alligator

Bird — pigeon

Mammal — rabbit

Mammal — cat

Mammal — dolphin

Primate mammal — macaque

Primate mammal — chimpanzee

Primate mammal — gorilla

Human

wards East-West detente in Europe. He opposed Hitler, fleeing to Norway (1933) and returning after World War II to become mayor of West Berlin (1957- 66). As chancellor, he secured friendship treaties with Poland and the USSR (1970), with East Germany (1972), and with Czechoslovakia (1974). Brandt's initiative won him the 1971 Nobel Peace Prize. Forced to resign in 1974 over a spy scandal in his own administration, he returned to political life in 1975.
See also: Germany.

Brandy, alcoholic drink of distilled wine, usually matured in wood casks. Brandies include cognac, made from white grapes of the Charente district in France, kirsch (made from cherries), and slivovitz (made from plums).

Brant, any of several North American wild geese (genus *Branta*) which breed in the Arctic and fly southward to Eurasia and North America for the winter.

Braque, Georges (1882-1963), French painter and sculptor. From fauvism he went on, together with Pablo Picasso, to evolve cubism and to be among the first to use collage. Among his major works are *Woman with a Mandolin* (1937) and the *Birds* series (1955-63).
See also: Collage; Cubism; Fauves.

Brasília (pop. 1,820,000), federal capital of Brazil since 1960, located on the Paraná River, 600 mi (966 km) northwest of the old coastal capital, Rio de Janeiro. It was built to help open the immense Brazilian interior. Its cross-shaped plan was designed by Lúcio Costa, while such major buildings as the presidential palace and the cathedral are the work of Oscar Niemeyer.
See also: Brazil.

Brass, alloy of copper and zinc, known since Roman times and widely used in industry and for ornament and decoration. Up to 36% zinc forms 'alpha' α-brass, which can be worked cold; with more zinc a mixture of α and 'beta'-brass is formed, which is less ductile but stronger. Brasses containing more than 45% zinc (white brasses) are unworkable and have few uses. Some brasses also contain other metals: lead for machinability, aluminum or tin for corrosion resistance, and nickel, manganese, or iron for strength.
See also: Alloy.

Brassens, Georges Charles (1921-1981), French singer. Was discovered in 1952 by Patachou. Was awarded the Grand Prix de la Poésie of the Académie Française in 1967.

Bratislava (pop. 452,000), capital of Slovakia. Bratislava is a port city on the Danube River. Its industries include mechanical engineering, oil refining, petrolem products, and cloth.
See also: Slovakia.

Brattain, Walter Houser (1902-1987), U.S. physicist who helped invent the transistor. He shared the 1956 Nobel Prize in physics with William Shockley and John Bardeen for this invention, and for the research into the electrical properties of semiconductors that made it possible.
See also: Physics; Transistor.

Braun, Eva (1912-1945), mistress (from 1930) and later wife of Adolf Hitler. On April 29, 1945, a few days before Germany's defeat in World War II, they were married. The next day both Braun and Hitler committed suicide.
See also: Hitler, Adolf.

Braun, Wernher von (1912-1977), German-American rocket pioneer. He designed most of the rockets that powered the U.S. space program, including the Jupiter rocket that launched the first U.S. satellite, *Explorer 1*, in 1958. Von Braun was born in Wirsitz, Germany (now Wyrzysk, Poland). He studied engineering at Berlin and Zürich, and in 1936, became director of the Peenemünde rocket research station. During World War II he developed the V-2 rocket, more than 4,000 of which were fired against Britain. Von Braun surrendered to the U.S. forces at the end of the war, and went to work in the United States, becoming a U.S. citizen in 1955.
See also: Rocket.

Brazil

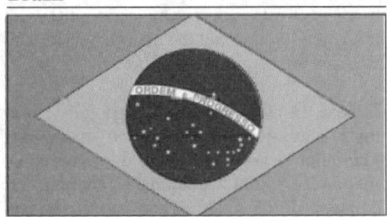

Capital:	Brasília
Area:	3,286,488 sq mi
	(8,547,400 sq km)
Population:	176,030,000
Language:	Portuguese
Government:	Federal presidential republic
Independent:	1822
Head of gov.:	President
Per capita:	U.S. $7,400
Monetary unit:	1 Real = 100 centavos

Brazil, fifth largest country in the world and largest in South America, constituting nearly half the continent's land area. Brazil shares borders with all South American countries except Ecuador and Chile. It is the only Latin American country whose official language is Portuguese.
Land and climate. Most of Brazil falls within 2 major geographical regions: the lowlands of the Amazon River system and the plateau. Drained by the Amazon River and its tributaries, the Amazonian lowlands form the world's most extensive tropical rain forests. The climate is not excessively hot, but rainfall is as much as 80 in (203 cm) annually. The Brazilian plateau, rising to 1,000 to 3,000 ft (305 to 914 m) above sea level, is studded with occasional mountain ranges. About 40% of the population lives in the southerly part of the plateau, known as the 'heartland,' which contains some of the country's most productive farmland and valuable mineral deposits.
Economy. Agriculture is the traditional mainstay of Brazil's economy. Exports include cattle, coffee, cotton, sugarcane, cocoa, tobacco, soybeans, citrus fruit, and bananas. Industry has also developed; particularly iron and steel, motor vehicles, textiles, and machinery. Brazil's vast natural resources have yet to be fully developed. Rich oil deposits have been found, as well as, iron, manganese, coal, chromium, quartz, uranium, and industrial grade diamonds. The exploitation of the Amazon basin has posed a threat to the tropical rain forest, creating a major point of controversy, within Brazilan politics.
History. Portuguese colonists under Pedro Alvarez Cabral claimed Brazil in 1500, and colonization began in 1532. Slaves were extensively used by plantation owners. The country remained a colony until winning its independence in 1822, as a monarchy. Slavery was abolished in 1888, and Brazil became a republic in 1889. Military regimes prevailed until the accession of President Getúlio Vargas in 1930. A military coup overthrew the leftist civilian government of João Goulart in 1964. Often accused of torture and other human rights violations, the military continued to rule through a succession of generals who served as president. The first presidential election with civilian candidates in 20 years was held in Jan. 1985. Civilian rule was restored in the late 1980s. From 1995 onwards, president, Cardoso tried to reform the corrupt political system. In 1999 Brazil experienced an economic crisis after it devaluated the national currency.
Luiz Inacio Lula da Silva, who once was a

A complex of falls and rapids in the river Iguaçú, on the border of Argentina and Brazil. Both countries have plentiful tourist facilities in this region.

B

shoe shine boy, won the elections of October 2002. He promised ending the famine would be his main political goal. He also promised that Brazil would honour its obligations to the International Monetary Fund.

Brazil nut, South American tree (genus *Bertholletia*) of the Amazon and Negro rivers. The tree grows to 160 ft (50 m), bearing very hard 6 in (15 cm) fruit containing 10 to 20 nuts. The nuts are used as food and for lubricating oil. The trees are also used for hardwood lumber.

Brazilwood, heavy wood of various trees (genus *Caesalpinia*). Extracts from this wood produce bright crimson and deep purple colors. Once an important source of dye, it is still used for making violins and in cabinetwork.

Brazzaville (pop. 760,000), river port and capital of the Republic of the Congo, situated below the Stanley Pool on the right bank of the Congo River. Kinshasa lies on the other side of the pool. Brazzaville was formerly the capital of the French Equatorial Africa. It was the headquarters of the Free French in Africa during World War II and gained independence in 1960. Brazzaville has always been primarily a center of government and education, although since 1945 industries such as brewing, matchmaking, and sugar refining have become established. Contributing to this industrial development is the hydroelectric plant at the nearby Djoué Falls. The Center for Administrative and Advanced Technical Studies is located in Brazzaville.
See also: Congo.

Bread, one of humanity's earliest and most important foods, made of baked dough-a mixture of flour and water. In developed western societies, wheat flour is most commonly used and the dough is leavened (i.e., increased in volume by introducing small bubbles of carbon dioxide throughout) using yeast.

Breadfruit (*Artocarpus altilis*), tree of the mulberry family, whose fruit is the staple diet in the South Pacific. Breadfruit trees are now seen in much of tropical America. The fruit is melonlike, 8 in (20 cm) across, and is protected by a thick rind that can be woven into cloth. The pulp, which tastes like potato meal, is eaten cooked, and may be ground to make a flour.

Breakbone fever *See:* Dengue.

An unusual 'fruit', the breadfruit (*Artocarpus altilis*), contains a high proportion of starch. A popular food in the Pacific area, but it has hardly spread beyond Southeast Asia.

Bertolt Brecht (1898-1956).

Breakwater, timber, masonry, or stone barrier constructed to give protection from heavy seas. Breakwaters built at right angles to the shore are called *jetties*; those built parallel with the shore (providing additional protection for a harbor), with a wharf on the sheltered side, are called *moles*.

Bream, any of a variety of European freshwater fishes of the carp family, growing up to 17 lb (8 kg). The freshwater sunfishes of the United States and the marine porgies and wrasses are also known as bream.

Breast, front of the chest; especially in female mammals, the modified cutaneous, glandular structure it bears-the mamma or mammary gland. In humans, each breast consists of 15 to 20 branching ducts surrounded by connective tissue that acts as a supporting framework. The larger partitions between the lobes form strands that extend from the skin to the underlying deep fascia. At puberty in the female, fat accumulates in the connective tissue of the breast and the overlying skin. The skin of the areola, the disk-shaped area surrounding the nipple, contains modified sweat glands and sebaceous glands. The breasts usually secrete a small quantity of fluid, or colostrum, from early pregnancy onwards, and for 2-3 days after childbirth. Milk begins about 3 days after childbirth, increasing to an average rate of about 28 fl oz (850 ml) per day. The principal constituents of breast milk are water, lactose, fat, and protein. The ejection of milk is stimulated by sucking and by the release of the pituitary hormone oxytocin.
See also: Mammary glands.

Breast cancer, malignant growth in the breast or mammary gland. Breast cancer-carcinoma of the breast-is the most common malignancy among women and has the highest fatality rate of all cancers affecting them. The annual mortality rate since 1950 has remained at about 25 in every 100,000 women. Breast cancer in men is rare and tends not to be recognized until late, thus the results of treatment are poor. In women, breast carcinoma is rarely seen before the age of 30, and the incidence rises rapidly after menopause.
See also: Cancer.

Brecht, Bertolt (Eugen Berthold Friedrich Brecht; 1898-1956), German Marxist playwright and poet, who revolutionized modern theater with his production techniques and concept of epic theater. He left Nazi Germany in 1933, returning to East Berlin in 1948 to found the Berliner Ensemble. His plays include *The Threepenny Opera* (1928), *The Life of Galileo* (1938), *Mother Courage* (1939), and *The Caucasian Chalk Circle* (1949).

Breckinridge, Sophonisba (1866-1948), U.S. pioneer teacher of social work. She wrote *The Delinquent Child and the Home* (1912) and *The Family and the State* (1934). She believed the government should play a key role in helping the needy.

Breed's Hill *See:* Bunker Hill, Battle of.

Brel, Jacques (real name Jacques Romain Georges Brel; 1929-1978), Belgian singer. Moved to Paris in 1953 and became well known with songs such as 'La valse à mille temps' (1959), 'Les bourgeois' (1961) and 'Amsterdam' (1965). He was a great success in the Parisian Olympia in 1961, 1964, and 1966. Subsequently, Brel increasingly focused on musicals and movies; he was the leading actor in the comedy *l'Homme de la Mancha* (Man of La Mancha) (1967-1968), which was adapted by him.

Bremen (pop. 683,000), city in northwest Germany, situated on the Weser River, 38 mi (61 km) from Bremerhaven on the estuary. Founded by Charlemagne in A.D. 787, Bremen became a major medieval trading center, controlling its own small state within the Holy Roman Empire (from which it broke free in 1646), and acting as a leading force in the Hanseatic League of city-states. From 1806 to 1815 Bremen was in French hands. After the Congress of Vienna, it became one of the independent German states, and in 1871 merged with Bismarck's Germany. Commercial fishing, truck farming, and cattle raising are the main occupations in the rural areas surrounding the city. In the city itself, which retains much of its medieval character, the main occupations are shipbuilding and import and export shipping.
See also: Germany.

Brendan, Saint (c.A.D. 484-c.578), Irish monk, founder of Clonfert and other monasteries. Tales of his travels are recorded in the 8th-century *Voyages of St. Brendan*, and he is sometimes honored as having reached America 900 years before Columbus.

Brendel, Alfred (1931-), renowned Austrian pianist. Brendel studied piano (student of Paul Baumgartner and Edwin Fischer) and composition (in Zagreb and Graz). He made his first appearance in 1948 in Graz. One year later he won the Busoni Concours at Bolzano. Brendel, who is mainly known for his performances of Mozart, Beethoven, and Schubert, also writes essays such as *Musical Thoughts and Afterthoughts* (1976). Together with P. Badura-Skoda and J. Demus, Brendel used to direct a piano course during the Wiener Festwochen for many years. Less known, but not less important, are Brendel's strong pleas for music from the first half of the 20th century. Legendary, for example, is his interpretation of Schönbergs piano concert (op. 42), once considered unplayable, which he recorded in 1952. Since 1954 Brendel has recorded over three hundred works varying from Bach to Bartók, from Schubert and Chopin to Schönberg and Stravinsky.

Brenner Pass, important pass across the Alps, in the Tyrol, linking Innsbruck in Austria with Bolzano in Italy. The first good road along this ancient route was completed in 1772, and the railroad was built from 1864 to 1867.
See also: Alps.

Brentano, Clemens (1778-1842), German poet and prosaist, one of the most important representatives of the early German romantic period. Together with Achim von Arnim he collected old German folk songs, *Des Knaben Wunderhorn* (3 volumes, 1805-1808). From this collection he derived the themes for his novella *Die Geschichte vom braven Kasperl und dem schönen Annerl* (1816). The magnificent epic poem *Romanzen vom Rosenkranz* (1804-1811), which Brentano considered to be his principal work, was never completed.

Breslau *See:* Wroclaw.

Bresson, Robert (1901-1999), French film director, noted for the austere, penetrating quality of his work. His films include *Diary of a Country Priest* (1950), *The Trial of Joan of Arc* (1962), and *Lancelot of the Lake* (1976). In 1994, he received a 'Felix' (European film prize) for his works.

Brest (pop. 153,000), seaport and naval station in Finistère department, northwest France. It is built on two hills overlooking an island harbor linked with the Atlantic Ocean by a natural 6-mi (9.7-km) channel. Brest is a commercial port, but important primarily as a naval base. During World War II the base was used by German submarines and was largely destroyed by Allied bombing.
See also: France.

Brest (formerly: Brest-Litovsk; pop. 295,000), capital of the province of Brest in Belorussia on the Bug River. Industries: timber, cotton, and foodstuffs. Railroad junction and river port with trade in timber, grain, and livestock. In 1918 the Treaty of Brest-Litovsk was signed between Germany and the Soviet government and put an end to the hostilities on the eastern front during World War I.

Breton, André (1896-1966), French poet and critic, a founder of surrealism. Associated at first with Dada, he broke with it and in 1924 issued the first of three surrealist manifestos, becoming the new movement's chief spokesperson. Among his works is the poetic novel, *Nadja* (1928).
See also: Surrealism.

Bretton Woods Conference, international gathering at Bretton Woods, N.H., in July 1944, at which 44 members of the United Nations planned to stabilize the international economy and national currencies after World War II. They also established the International Monetary Fund and the World Bank.
See also: United Nations; World Bank.

Breuer, Marcel (Lajos) (1902-1981), Hungarian-born U.S. architect. A student and teacher at the Bauhaus 1920-1928, in 1937 he moved to Harvard and continued working with Walter Gropius. A pioneer of the international style, he collaborated in the design of the UNESCO headquarters, Paris (1953-1958).
See also: Bauhaus.

Brewing, process of making beer from cereal grains, usually barley. Brewing is a major industry in the United States, with a total annual production of about 125 million barrels. In the first step of brewing, malting, cleaned barley is soaked in water 2-3 days, allowed to germinate, and dried in a kiln. The malt is stored for several weeks while the malt flavor develops and various enzymes are produced. In the next stage, mashing, the ground malt is mixed with water, maintained at a warm temperature, and stirred constantly. During this process the enzymes break down the insoluble starch into soluble carbohydrates. The liquor containing these substances is filtered out (the remaining solid mash is used as animal feed) and boiled to stop enzyme activity and sterilize the brew. Hops are added at this stage to impart their characteristic flavor. Yeast is then added for about 8 days of fermentation.
See also: Beer; Fermentation.

Breytenbach, Breyten (1939-   ), South African writer and visual artist. Stayed in exile in Europe (1959-1975) - mainly in Paris - because he was married to a Vietnamese woman, a marriage which was prohibited in South Africa, and because of his criticism of apartheid. After he returned to South Africa in 1975 he was sentenced to nine years' imprisonment. He was released in December 1982. His works include *Lotus* (1970; under the pseudonym of Jan Blom), and *True Confessions of an Albino Terrorist* (1984), about his experiences in a South African prison.

Brezhnev, Leonid Ilyich (1906-1982), USSR political leader, who became first secretary of the Communist Party and effective head of the Soviet government in 1964. He first became a member of the party central committee in 1952, and was chairman of the Presidium of the Supreme Soviet 1960-1964. Brezhnev, Aleksei Kosygin, and Nikolai Podgorny took control when Nikita Khrushchev was ousted in 1964. Brezhnev assumed the additional office of chief of state in 1977. He pursued a policy of détente with the West while overseeing a massive Soviet military buildup.
See also: Union of Soviet Socialist Republics.

Brian Boru (941-1014), king of Ireland from 1002. His reign marked the end of Norse domination, but unified rule ended when he was murdered after his victory against the Danes at Clontarf.
See also: Ireland.

Briand, Aristide (1862-1932), French politician, lawyer, and socialist leader who was 11 times premier of France. As foreign minister (1925-1932), he was the author of the Kellogg-Briand Pact (1928). He was awarded the Nobel Peace Prize in 1926.
See also: Kellogg-Briand Peace Pact.

Briar *See:* Brier.

The briard is known in France as berger de Brie, or 'the sheepdog of Brie'. It has been used to defend sheep against predators.

Briard, sheepdog first bred in France in the twelfth century. Used for herding and police work, the briard is strongly built and usually black, grey, or tawny in color. It stands 22 to 27 in (56 to 69 cm) and weighs about 70 to 80 lb (32 to 36 kg).

Brice, Fanny (Fannie Borach; 1891-1951), U.S. popular singer and performer of musical comedy. Acclaimed for her radio series in which she portrayed 'Baby Snooks,' she was also known for her satirical sketches and her long association with the *Ziegfeld Follies*.

Brick, building material made of clay, sometimes reinforced with straw, shaped into rectangles and hardened by heat. Sun-dried bricks were used as a building material at least 6,000 years ago in Mesopotamia. The discovery of the technique of firing clay in kilns enabled hard durable bricks to be made. Examples of fired bricks have been found in excavations at the city of Ur that are at least 5,000 years old. The Greeks used bricks, and the Romans made an art of brick masonry in their large-scale constructions. After the fall of Rome, bricks were not used again on a large scale until the 12th and 13th centuries.
Although bricks are important in the construction industry, concrete, plastics, and light alloys have taken over some of their functions. Modern bricks include: *common brick*, used for ordinary building purposes; *face brick,* used to resist erosion or for decoration; *firebrick* (refractory brick), which can withstand the high temperatures found in furnaces and kilns; *paving brick*, larger, harder, and more water-resistant than the common brick; and *insulating brick*, a porous type that insulates against extremes of temperature.

B

B

Three primary types of bridges: the beam bridge (A), the arch bridge (B) and the suspension bridge (C). The bascule bridge (D) is a special type of beam bridge. A beam bridge exerts a simple downward force onto its piers. Generally, the beam will consist of a lattice of steel work. An arch bridge exerts a diagonal force on its supports, and the roadway may be supported either above or below the arch. A suspension bridge utilises a cable in tension as a load-carrying member.

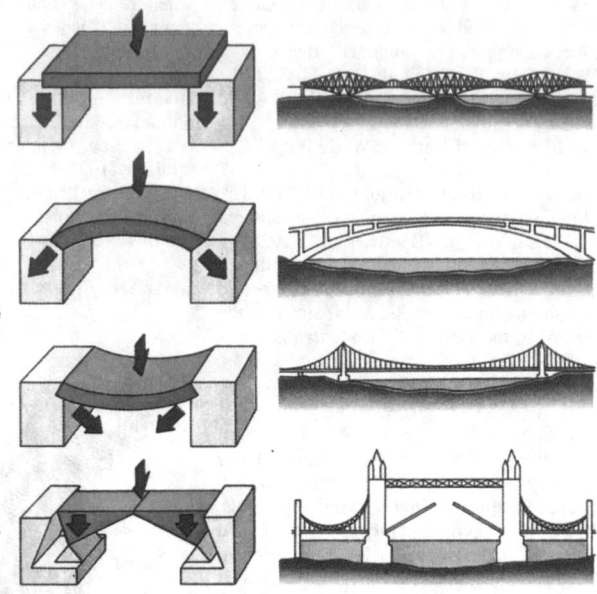

Bridge, card game developed from whist. Contract bridge, the form now universally adopted, was perfected by Harold S. Vanderbilt in 1925-1926. It is played by 2 pairs of partners, who make bids according to how many tricks (rounds of cards played) they calculate they can win. Demanding great skill, bridge has become immensely popular as a social and competitive game, with international championships controlled by the World Bridge Federation.

Bridge, structure that spans an obstacle and permits traffic across it. The *beam* (or girder) *bridge* consists of a rigid beam resting at either end on piers. A development of this is the *truss bridge*, with a metal framework designed for greatest strength at those points where the load has greatest moment around the piers. Where piers are impracticable, a *cantilever bridge* may be built on beams (cantilevers) extending from each side. An *arch bridge* consists of one or more arches. A *suspension bridge* comprises two towers that carry one or more flexible cables that are firmly anchored at each end; the roadway is suspended by means of vertical cables. *Movable bridges* include the *swing*

The Gladesville Bridge in Sydney, Australia. Columns located above its 1,000 ft (305 m) concrete arch span support a 72 ft wide (22 m) roadway and two footpaths.

bridge, pivoted on a central pier; the *bascule* (a descendant of the medieval drawbridge), whose cantilevers are pivoted inshore so that they may be swung upward; the *vertical-lift bridge*, a pair of towers between which runs a beam that may be winched vertically upward; and the *retractable bridge*, whose cantilevers may be run inshore on wheels. Temporary bridges include the pontoon or floating bridge, in which floating structures support a continuous roadway.

Bridge of Sighs, landmark bridge in Venice, Italy. Spanning the canal between the Doges' Palace and the state prison, its name derives from the 'sighs' of the unhappy prisoners who had to cross it. Renowned for its beauty, it was designed by Italian architect Antonio Contino and completed c.1600.

Bridgetown (pop. 8,000), capital and only port of Barbados. It is a crowded and attractive tourist center, with public buildings made of coral. It was founded in 1628, and then named Indian Bridge, from a crude structure over the creek. Its modernized port now handles sugar, molasses, and rum.
See also: Barbados.

Brier, shrubby plant (*Erica arborea*) of the heath family, known for its fragrant, white, globe-shaped flowers. Its thick roots are used in making pipes.

Bright, Richard (1789-1858), English physician who first identified the kidney disorder known as Bright's Disease, now called nephritis.
See also: Nephritis.

Brighton (pop. 132,000), popular English seaside resort on the south coast, 51 mi (82 km) south of London. The town first gained popularity when an 18th-century doctor claimed its seawater had curative power. In 1783 the Prince of Wales (later George IV) visited the town. The onion-domed Royal Pavilion was built to his orders. Originally in classical style, it was rebuilt in 1815 by John

Nash, in the exotic style of Indian Mogul architecture.
See also: England.

Brink, André Philippus (1935-), South African writer who usually first writes his novels in Afrikaans and then in English. He was a strong critic of apartheid and experienced censorship. For example, *Kennis van die Aand* was banned in 1973. His works include *A Dry White Season* (1979), *A Chain of Voices* (1982), *The Wall of the Plague* (1984), *An Act of Terror* (1991), *The First Life of Adamastor* (1993), *On the Contrary* (1993), *Imaginings of Sand* (1996), *Devil's Valley* (1998), and *The Rights of Desire* (2001). Brink also wrote stage plays and a theoretical work about literature.

Brisbane (pop. 1,422,000), city and seaport in eastern Australia, capital of the state of Queensland. The city is built on both banks of the navigable Brisbane River, about 15 mi (24 km) from the outlet to the Pacific Ocean. The area was a penal settlement in 1824, then in 1838 became a city. Queensland became a separate colony in 1859.
See also: Australia.

Bristlecone pine, evergreen tree (*Pinus aristata*) native to the Rocky Mountains of the United States. Some bristlecone pines are thought to be more than 4,000 years old, possibly the oldest living things on earth. The long life of the needles helps the tree survive years of harsh weather, when few new needles can grow.

A bristlecone, or hickory, pine (*P. aristata*) grows extremely slowly, and some bristlecones have lived to be more than 4,000 years old.

Bristol (pop. 399,000), large city and port in southwestern England, situated at the confluence of the Avon and Frome rivers, 6 mi (9.7 km) from the mouth of the Avon. First a Saxon settlement called Brycgstowe ('the place of the bridge'), by Norman times it had become a wool center and the chief port for trade with Ireland. The textile trade flourished and in 1540 Bristol became a city. In the 17th and 18th centuries, when new trade routes had been established, Bristol shipowners engaged in 'the triangular trade of the Atlantic,' dealing in sugar, slaves, and tobacco. Another source of prosperity in the 18th century was the development of the city as a fashionable spa, making use of the hot mineral springs. There are some fine historic

B

buildings and a famous suspension bridge (1864) that spans the precipitous Avon gorge.
See also: England.

Bristol Channel, inlet of the Atlantic Ocean between Wales and southwestern England. Extending 80 mi (130km) from the sea to the River Severn, it separates the heavily industrialized southwestern Wales from largely agricultural southwestern England.

Britain, modern form of the ancient name for the island now comprising England, Scotland, and Wales. The Romans referred to the 1st century B.C. Celtic inhabitants as Pritani, hence their own name for the island, Britannia.

Britain, Battle of, air battle of World War II from Aug. 8 to Oct. 31, 1940, between the British Royal Air Force (RAF) and the German Luftwaffe. The Germans intended to weaken British defenses and morale before invading the country. The Luftwaffe forces were much larger than those of the RAF, but the latter proved technically and tactically superior. The Germans bombed shipping and ports, then airfields and Midland industries, and finally, London. Daylight raids proving too costly, the Germans turned to night attacks. At the end the RAF had lost some 900 planes, the Germans over 2,300, causing Hitler to postpone his projected invasion indefinitely, thus tacitly admitted failure.
See also: Churchill, Sir Winston Leonard Spencer; World War II.

British Broadcasting Corporation (BBC), publicly financed company that runs all radio and 2 of the 3 television networks in Britain. The BBC first went on the air in 1922. Regular television programs, which began in 1936, were interrupted by World War II, but resumed in 1946. The BBC provides a wide range of news programs, documentaries, plays, comedies, concerts, and school programs, and is known for the excellence of its panel programs and educational broadcasts. The BBC has a considerable overseas audience.

British Cameroons, former UN trust territory on the west coast of Africa in what is now Nigeria and Cameroon. After World War I the former German colony of Cameroons was divided between France and Britain. After World War II both became UN trust territories. In 1960, French Cameroons became independent, and in 1961 the southern part of British Cameroons joined it to form the Republic of Cameroon. The northern part was incorporated into Nigeria.

British Columbia, westernmost of Canada's provinces, bordered by Alberta on the east, Montana, Idaho, and Washington on the south, the Pacific Ocean and Alaska on the west, and the Yukon and Northwest Territories on the north. Alberta is dominated by two mountain chains, the Coast Mountains in the west and the Canadian Rocky Mountains in the east. The 700-mi (1,127-km) coastline is broken by fjords. Vancouver Island and the Queen Charlotte Islands are the most important of the offshore chains. About 75% of the population lives in the relatively mild southwest corner of the province. Greater Vancouver alone accounts for about one-half of the total population. The provincial capital is Victoria. Forestry is the mainstay of British Columbia's economy and accounts for the province's major industries. Mining is second, including zinc, lead, silver, gold, and iron ore.
See also: Canada.

British Commonwealth of Nations *See:* Commonwealth of Nations.

British Guiana *See:* Guyana.

British Honduras *See:* Belize.

British Indian Ocean Territory, British dependency in the Indian Ocean, about 1,180 mi (1,900 km) northeast of Mauritius. Consisting of the Chagos Archipelago Island group, it covers a land area of about 30 sq mi (78 sq km) and has a population of about 2,500 people. The United States maintains a naval base on the main island, Diego Garcia.

British Isles, island group bounded by the English Channel, the Strait of Dover, the North Sea, and the Atlantic Ocean. The British Isles consist of the island of Great Britain (England, Scotland, and Wales), Ireland, and about 5,500 small islands and inlets.

British Library, national library of Great Britain, one of the largest research libraries in the world. Located in London, it was originally a part of the British Museum. Its collection of rare books and manuscripts includes *Beowulf* and the Magna Carta.
The library is also a depository for copyrights.

British Museum, national museum of antiquities and ethnography in London. Founded in 1753, when the British government acquired the art collection and library of Sir Hans Sloane, it opened to the public in 1759. Its present neoclassical premises were built 1823-1847 and its natural history section was separated 1881-1883. The museum has one of the world's foremost collections, including the Elgin Marbles.

British North America Act, act passed by the British Parliament in 1867 to create the Dominion of Canada, uniting Canada (Quebec and Ontario), New Brunswick, and Nova Scotia under a federal government. The act served as Canada's constitution until 1982; under it, amendments had to be submitted to the British Parliament for formal approval. The Constitution Act, 1982, superseded the earlier law (now also known as the Constitution Act, 1867), thus 'patriating' the constitution.

British thermal unit (BTU), quantity of heat required to raise the temperature of one pound of water 1°F at, or near, its point of maximum density (39.1°F). The BTU is equivalent to 0.252 kilogram-calorie.
See also: Calorie.

British West Indies, collective name for islands in the Caribbean Sea that are or have been dependencies of Great Britain, including Anguilla, the Bahamas, Barbados, Bermuda, Grenada, Jamaica, Trinidad and Tobago, and the British Virgin Islands. Although the British West Indies is not a political entity, the islands have formed such organizations as the West Indies Federation (1958-1962) and Caricom, or the Caribbean Community, an alliance based on foreign policy and economic cooperation (1973).

Brittany, breed of hunting dog with a short, thick coat, white with orange or red-brown markings. Brittanies average 35-40 lbs (16-18 kg) and stand 18-20 in (45-50 cm) at the shoulder. A breed with a long history in France and Spain, the Brittany has the build of a spaniel but points at its quarry.

Brittany (French: *Bretagne*), historic peninsular region of northwestern France. The Romans conquered the area in 56 B.C. and named it Armonica. It was settled about 500 A.D. by Celtic Britons fleeing the Anglo-Saxon invasion. After struggles for independence from the Franks and from Normandy, Anjou, England, and France in turn, it became a French province in 1532. The Bretons retain their own cultural traditions and language.

Britten, Benjamin (1913-1976), British composer. His works include the operas *Peter Grimes* (1945), *Billy Budd* (1951), *The Turn of the Screw* (1954), and *Death in Venice* (1973), as well as such instrumental and choral works as the *Variations on a Theme by Frank Bridge* (1937) and *War Requiem* (1962).
See also: Opera.

Brittle star, marine invertebrate (class Ophiuroidea), 5-armed relative of starfish found in seas all over the world. The button-shaped body grows up to 2 in (5 cm), and the flexible arms, which break off readily but are regrown, grow to 2 ft (60 cm). Brittle stars feed by trapping minute particles in mucus on the arms and passing them to the mouth on the underside of the disk, or by holding animals or carrion in an arm and pushing them into the mouth. Eggs are fertilized after being released into the sea or retained in the female, where larval development takes place, the young being released as small adults.

Brno (formerly Brünn; pop. 388,000), city in the eastern part of the Czech Republic, chief city of Moravia. It was founded in the 9th century, flourishing as a free city within the kingdom of Bohemia in the 13th-14th centuries. In the 18th-19th centuries its Spielberg castle was used as a Hapsburg prison. Situated on the Svratka and Svitava rivers, Brno is a manufacturing center for cars, machinery, textiles, and other products, and is the seat of the Czech supreme court.
See also: Czech Republic.

Broad bean, Windsor bean, or horse bean (*Vicia faba*), annual plant producing seed pods up to 1 ft (30 cm) long, containing large edible beans. An important food in ear-

English composer Benjamin Britten (1913-1976), who was also famous as a conductor and a pianist.

B

ly civilizations of North Africa and southwest Asia, it is one of the most widely cultivated beans in Europe and Latin America, and is also grown for fodder.

Broadcasting *See:* Journalism; Radio; Television.

Broadway, wide and 17 mi (27 km) long New York City thoroughfare that runs through Manhattan, with a very high concentration of theatres dating back to the mid 19th century between 42nd and 50th Street. As a result it has become synonymous with theater in New York. The area had its heyday in the 1920 and has been extremely commercialized ever since. Serious productions went to the smaller 'off Broadway' theatres.

Broccoli, form of cabbage, a branching cauliflower (*Brassica oleracea botytis*), grown for the immature flowers. Originating in Italy, it is grown in Europe and America, where green-sprouting broccoli is the most popular variety.

Brodski, Iosif Aleksandrovitsj (1940-1996; also Joseph Brodsky), Soviet-American poet. Brodsky's poetry is personal and humanistic, examining love, loss, aloneness, and redemptive hope. His writing is sensitive, vibrant, and often religious. The lack of political themes in his poetry antagonized Soviet authorities, and in 1964 Brodsky was sentenced to five years in a labor camp for being a 'social parasite'. In 1965 he gained international recognition with the publication in the West of *Short and Long Poems*. After 18 months he was released from the labor camp; he was exiled from the Soviet Union in 1972. Brodsky was born in Leningrad (now St. Petersburg). He became a United States citizen in 1977. Brodsky won the Nobel Prize for literature in 1987 and was named poet laureate of the United States in 1991. After his exile, Brodsky continued to write much of his poetry in Russian, then translated it into English.

Broglie, Louis Victor, Prince de (1892-1987), French physicist, awarded the 1929 Nobel Prize in physics for his suggestion that subatomic particles would display wave-like properties under appropriate conditions. The prediction was borne out experimentally, and de Broglie's theories led to the branch of quantum mechanics called wave mechanics.
See also: Physics.

Bromegrass, any of about 60 kinds of grass of genus *Bromus*, found mostly in the Northern Hemisphere and including both weed grasses and grasses valuable as pasturage and soil binders. Plants have flat thin leaves 12-40 in (30-100 cm) tall, often with drooping flower clusters. Rescue grass (*B. unioloides*) and smooth brome (*B. inermis*) are the most economically important varieties. Some weed varieties, such as ripgut grass (*B. rigidus*) and foxtail brome (*B. rubens*), have spines on the flower clusters that can cause serious internal and external injury to grazing animals.

Bromeliad, large family of tropical plants, mostly native to the Americas, including the pineapple and epiphytes (air plants) such as Spanish moss. Most bromeliads have spike-shaped leaves that form a tight cluster, with flowers in the cluster or on spikes; the cup-shaped cluster holds water, allowing the plants to survive droughts.

Bromide, salt of hydrobromic acid, especially potassium bromide, that acts as a depressant of brain function and the heart and is used in medicine as a sedative and a hypnotic.

Bromine, chemical element, symbol Br; for physical constants see Periodic Table. Bromine was discovered by Antoine J. Balard in 1826. It belongs to the halogen group of elements and is obtained from natural brines and sea water by displacement with chlorine. Bromine, a heavy reddish-brown liquid, is the only nonmetallic element that is liquid at room temperature. It produces irritating red fumes at room temperature and produces painful sores on skin contact. Bromine is less active than chlorine. The major use of bromine is in the production of ethylene dibromide, a lead scavenger used in making gasoline antiknock compounds. It is also used in making fumigants, flameproofing agents, water purification compounds, dyes, medicinals, sanitizers, and photographic chemicals.

Bronchitis, inflammation of the bronchi, the main branches of the windpipe, caused by viruses or bacteria or by the inhalation of smoke. Coughing, fever, and chest pains are common symptoms.

Brontë sisters, 3 English novelists and poets, daughters of an Anglican clergyman. The isolated life of the Yorkshire moors, their mother's early death, and the dissipations of their brother, Branwell, informed much of their work. **Charlotte Brontë** (1816-1855) published the partly autobiographical novel *Jane Eyre* (1847) under the name Currer Bell and met with immediate success. Together with *Shirley* (1849) and *Villette* (1853), it represents an important advance in the treatment of women in English fiction. **Emily Brontë** (1818-1848), using the name Ellis Bell, published a single nov-

The Brontë sisters Anne, Emily and Charlotte (from left to right), painted by their brother Branwell. (London, National Portrait Gallery)

el, *Wuthering Heights* (1847), a masterpiece of visionary power. **Anne Brontë** (1820-1849) published two novels, *Agnes Grey* (1847) and *The Tenant of Wildfell Hall* (1848), under the name Acton Bell.

Brontosaurus, large, plant-eating, four-legged dinosaur whose fossilized skeletons have been found in the western United States. With its long neck and tail, small head, and huge body (about 68 ft/28 m long, weighing 35 tons), the brontosaurus was probably the largest land animal in the earth's history.
See also: Dinosaur.

Bronx, The, one of the 5 boroughs of New York City, the only one situated on the mainland, separated from Manhattan Island by the Harlem River. Jonas Bronck purchased the area from the Native Americans in 1639.
See also: New York City.

Bronze, corrosion-resistant alloy of copper and tin, used for machine parts, marine hardware, and casting statues. Aluminum, iron, lead, zinc, and phosphorus are often added to bronze to harden it.
See also: Alloy.

Bronze Age, phase of history in which metal was first used to make tools and weapons. Copper and bronze were used interchangeably in the first stage, called the Copper Age. Bronze casting began in the Middle East about 3500 B.C. and in the Americas, about 1100 A.D.

Broodthaers, Marcel (1924-1976), Belgian visual artist, whose art is related to surrealism and conceptual art. Initially a journalist and poet (*Mon livre d'ogre* (1957), *La bête noire* (1961). Literature and literary themes played an important role in his work of visual arts. In 1968 he turned his house in Brussels into a museum, the so-called Musée d'Art Moderne, Département des Aigles, where he exhibited reproductions and empty crates with captions of famous 19th century paintings, which he also exhibited at other places. In this way, he countered so-called objective museum presentations.

Brook, Peter (1925-), British producer-director and one of the most versatile and significant directors of modern times. In 1962 Brook became comanager of the Royal Shakespeare Company. In addition, he has directed in the most important centers of theater in the world. He caused quite a stir by assisting with the parties of the Shah of Persia in Shiraz in 1971. At the age of 18 he had already directed *Doctor Faustus* by Marlowe in London. He produced his first Shakespeare productions in Stratford-upon-Avon when he was barely 20 years old. He made several world tours with the Royal Shakespeare Company, which created a profound impression wherever they were performed, in particular because of his modern vision of Shakespearean plays. He enjoyed great fame with his productions of contemporary drama such as Dürrenmatt's *Der Besuch der alten Dame* and the renowned *Marat-Sade* by Peter Weiss. Brook also became famous as a film director. He made movies like *The Beggar's Opera* (1952), *Lord of the flies* (1962), *King Lear* (1970), and *The Mahabharata* (1989).

Brooke, Rupert (1887-1915), English poet whose patriotic war sonnets were widely popular during World War I, author of *Poems* (1911) and *1914 and Other Poems* (1915).

Brooklyn, one of the 5 boroughs of New York City, situated at the southwest extremity of Long Island. First settled in 1636 by Dutch farmers, Brooklyn was chartered as a city in 1834 and gradually absorbed the surrounding communities until it became a borough of New York (1896). Though its large area is primarily residential, it also has a considerable business and industrial area and the port handles a great share of New York's oceangoing traffic. Brooklyn's facilities for higher education include Pratt Institute, Polytechnic University, Brooklyn College, and parts of Long Island University (LIU). The Brooklyn Museum, located on the edge of Prospect Park, has a fine collection of Egyptian and primitive art and a notable group of 18th-century and 19th-century American paintings. The Institute of Arts and Sciences, the Brooklyn Philharmonic Orchestra, and the Brooklyn Academy of Music have international reputations.
See also: New York City.

Brooklyn Bridge, world's first steel-wire suspension bridge. It spans 1,595 ft (486 m) over the East River and joins the boroughs of Brooklyn and Manhattan. Built 1869-1883 by J. A. Roebling and his son, W. A. Roebling, it was the largest suspension bridge in the world at the time of its completion.

Brookner, Anita (1938-) British author of novels that reflect the influence of French novels. She studied history of art, taught, in particular, the French art of painting at the Courtauld Institute of Art in London for a number of years and wrote, among other things, the studies *Watteau* (1968) and *Jacques-Louis David* (1980). She made her debut as a novelist with *A Start in Life* (1981), followed by works such as *Providence* (1982), *Look at me* (1983), *Hôtel du Lac* (1984; Booker Prize), *A Misalliance* (1986), *Brief Lives* (1990), *A Family Romance* (1993), *The Bay of Angels* (2001), and *The Next Best Thing* (2002). Women and problems with relationships are central to many of her novels.

Brooks, Gwendolyn Elizabeth (1917-   ), U.S. poet. She was the first African American to win the Pulitzer Prize (1949), for her semiautobiographical *Annie Allen* (1949). Her books of poems include *Bronzeville Boys and Girls* (1956), *Selected Poems* (1963), *In the Mecca* (1968), and *To Disembark* (1981).

Brooks, Van Wyck (1886-1963), U.S. critic. In *America's Coming of Age* (1915), he saw the 19th-century U.S. as torn between the idealistic and the materialistic. He wrote critical biographies of Mark Twain, Henry James, and Emerson. His series *Makers and Finders: A History of the Writer in America,* *1800-1915,* included the Pulitzer Prize-winning *The Flowering of New England* (1936).

Broom, any of various European and Asian leguminous shrubs with yellow flowers that 'explode' when bees land on them. The seeds develop in pods that twist open suddenly, throwing the seeds out with an audible crackle.

Broom, Robert (1866-1951), Scottish anatomist and paleontologist, discoverer of fossils of the humanlike *Australopithecus*. From 1903 he lived in South Africa, where he taught at Victoria College and studied the fossils, important for their bearing on human evolution. His writings include *Mammal-Like Reptiles of South Africa* (1932) and *The South African Fossil Apemen* (1946).
See also: Paleontology.

Brough, Althea Louise (1923-), American tennis player, who did not only have a very strong service, but also great tactical insight. Between 1942 and 1957 she won seventeen titles in the singles, women's doubles, and mixed doubles in the U.S. In 1950 she won the women's doubles in France four times, as well as the singles and doubles in Australia. In Wimbledon she triumphed four times in the singles (1948 to 1950 and in 1955) and nine times in the women's doubles and mixed doubles.

Browder, Earl Russell (1891-1973), U.S. Communist party secretary-general 1930-1944 and president of the Communist Political Association 1944-1945. He was also the Communist presidential candidate in 1936 and 1940, but was expelled from the party in 1946 for advocating greater cooperation between the Soviet Union and the West. **Brown, Charles Brockden** (1771-1810), one of the first U.S. professional novelists. Influenced by William Godwin, his *Alcuin: A Dialogue* (1798) and novel *Edgar Huntly* (1799) plead for social reform. *Wieland* (1799) is an outstanding Gothic novel.
See also: Communism.

Brown, Jim (1936-), U.S. football player. A running back for the Cleveland Browns (1957-1965), he was one of the greatest players in National Football League (NFL) history. Brown's achievements include winning a record 8 league rushing titles and placing second among all-time leading rushers (12,312 yards). Brown was inducted into the football Hall of Fame in 1971.

Brown, John (1800-1859), U.S. abolitionist. After supporters of slavery burned down the town of Lawrence, Kansas, Brown retaliated by murdering five proslavery men at Pottawatamie Creek. In October 1859 Brown seized the government arsenal at Harper's Ferry, Virginia, attempting to ignite a massive slave insurrection. Troops under Robert E. Lee stormed the arsenal and captured Brown. He was tried for treason and hanged on Dec. 2, 1859.
See also: Abolitionism.

Brown, Robert (1773-1858), Scottish physician and botanist. Brown discovered the natural continuous random movement of microscopic particles now known as Brownian motion (1827), and identified the nucleus as a constituent of nearly all living plant cells (1831). Brown studied and collected specimens of flora in Australia and Tasmania. He identified the two plant groupings of gymnosperms (conifers) and angiosperms (flowering plants), and otherwise elaborated the system of plant classification. He was also a pioneer in the microscopic examination of plant fossils.
See also: Botany.

Brown, Sir Arthur Whitten *See:* Alcock and Brown.

Brownian motion *See:* Brown, Robert; Einstein, Albert.

Brownie, in British folklore, small creature that lives with a household and helps with chores while a family sleeps. It looks like an ugly, shaggy man and usually dresses in a brown cloak. The brownie, who accepts no pay, may also cause mischief. The name is also used for the youngest group (6-8 years) of the Girl Scouts.

Brownies *See:* Girl Scouts and Girl Guides.

Browning, Elizabeth Barrett (1806-1861), English lyric poet best known for *Sonnets from the Portuguese* (1850), inspired by her husband, Robert Browning, who had 'rescued' her from illness and family tyranny in 1846. Other works include *Casa Guidi Windows* (1851) and *Aurora Leigh* (1857), a novel in verse.

Browning, Robert (1812-1889), English poet. He perfected the dramatic monologue in 'Andrea del Sarto' and 'My Last Duchess.' His masterpiece is *The Ring and the Book* (4 vols., 1868-1869), a 17th-century Roman murder story told from different viewpoints. His psychological insight and colloquial language profoundly influenced 20th-century poets.

Brown lung, or byssinosis, lung disease caused by inhaling of cotton dust. Symptoms include difficulty in breathing, a tight feeling in the chest, and coughing. Because cotton dust can permanently harm workers' health, the governments of many countries have set limits on their exposure to it.

Brown recluse, poisonous spider (*Loxosceles reclusa*) of the southern United States, member of the family of brown spiders (Loxoscelidae). It is about 3/8 in (1 cm) long, with a dark violin-shaped patch on its back and 6 eyes in 2 rows. The spider's poisonous bite, used to paralyze insects it eats, leaves a deep and long-lasting sore in humans, and may produce severe reactions, even death.

Brown-tail moth (*Nygmia phaeorrhoea*), member of the family of tussock moths (Liparidae, which also includes the gypsy moth), native to the northeastern United States, whose caterpillar is a serious pest to fruit and shade trees. The hairs of the caterpillars and female moths can be irritating to

B

human skin. The moth is white with a brown abdomen, and a wingspan of about 1.5 in (3.8 cm). The female lays about 300 eggs, which hatch into hairy brown caterpillars with orange, white, or other markings. All summer the caterpillars eat leaves, spinning silk tents to winter over and emerging in spring to continue eating. Grown caterpillars spin cocoons and pupate, maturing by July.

Brown thrasher (*Toxostoma rufum*), bird of the mockingbird family (Mimidae), of the eastern United States and Canada. It is about 11.5 in (29 cm) long, with red-brown head and back, white-and-brown striped breast, long tail, and yellow eyes. The thrasher lives in brush and shrubs and eats insects. Its musical song, like the mockingbird's, resembles that of a variety of other birds.

Brubeck, Dave (1920-　), U.S. pianist and composer in the classical and jazz idioms. He studied composition with Darius Milhaud and Arnold Schoenberg. His jazz quartet, founded in 1951 and active through the 1960s, featured alto saxophonist Paul Desmond. During the 1970s and 1980s Brubeck often performed with his three sons. His compositions, known for complex cross-rhythms and baroque counterpoint, include 'Blue Rondo a la Turk' and 'Take Five.'

Bruce, Robert the (1274-1329), claimant to the Scottish throne, which Edward I of England awarded to John de Baliol instead. In 1314 his forces defeated the English in the battle of Bannockburn, briefly interrupting English rule over Scotland.

Portrait of the Austrian composer Anton Bruckner (1824-1896), painted in 1889 by Ferry Bératon (1860-1900). (Vienna, Kunsthistorisches Museum)

Bruce, Sir David (1855-1931), British physician and bacteriologist, specialist in tropical diseases. Born in Melbourne, Australia, he studied in Edinburgh and Berlin. In Malta he discovered the bacillus causing brucellosis (1886) and its transmission in goat's milk; in Africa he discovered the organism causing sleeping sickness and its transmission by the tsetse fly (1903-1910). An expert on trench fever and tetanus, he also studied the connection between human and animal diseases.
See also: Bacteriology.

Brucellosis, undulant fever, or Malta fever, infectious diseases of vertebrate animals, caused by any of a genus (*Brucella*) of bacteria. Symptoms are chills, fever, profuse sweating, slow pulse and, finally, enlargement of the spleen. Cattle, sheep, goats, and swine can pass the disease on to humans

Hunters in the Snow (1565), by the Flemish painter Pieter Bruegel the Elder, is one of a series of paintings representing the months of the year. In a solemn January landscape, a band of hunters and their dogs trudge wearily toward their homes, where villagers skate on the frozen ponds (Kunsthistorisches Museum, Vienna).

through contaminated meat, milk, and cheese, or by direct contact.

Bruch, Max (1838-1920), German composer and conductor. His best-known works are his Violin Concerto No. 1 in G minor (1868), *Scottish Fantasy* for violin and orchestra (1880), and *Kol Nidrei* for cello and orchestra (1881), based on a traditional Hebrew liturgical melody and written for the Jewish community of Liverpool, England (although Bruch himself was Protestant). He taught at the Berlin Academy of Arts 1891-1910.

Brücke, Die, organization of expressionist artists, founded in 1905 in Dresden,

Ernst Ludwig Kirchner's *A group of Artists* (1926-1927) portrays some of the most important members of the expressionist group Die Brücke. The artistsm (left to right) are Otto Müller, Kirchner, Erich Heckel, and Karl Schmidt-Rottluff (Wallraf-Richartz Museum, Cologne).

Germany. Together with 'Der blaue Reiter' they initiated German expressionism in the art of painting. Kirchner, Schmidt-Rottluff, Heckel, Pechstein, and Otto Mueller formed the backbone of the group. Emil Nolde was also a member for a brief period. They abandoned the traditional esthetic standards laid down by the academy of arts and wanted to express their feelings by means of a substantial simplification of shapes and by using bright colors. They drew their inspiration from Van Gogh, Gauguin, and Munch, and were also influenced by the 'fauves'. Their graphic work and particularly their woodcuts are also of great importance. In 1910 the core of the organization moved to Berlin, where the theme of landscape gave way to the big city. In 1913 the group was dissolved as a result of a publication by Kirchner with which the other members disagreed.
See also: Blaue Reiter, Der; Expressionism; Kirchner, Ernst Ludwig; Schmidt-Rottluff, Karl; Van Gogh, Vincent; Gauguin, Paul Eugène-Henri; Munch, Edvard.

Bruckner, (Josef) Anton (1824-1896), Austrian composer, noted for his 9 sym-

phonies and his choral music-Masses in D Minor (1864), E Minor (1866), and F Minor (1867-1871). Richard Wagner greatly influenced Bruckner.

Bruegel, family of Flemish painters. **Pieter Bruegel the Elder** (c.1525-1569) was a great painter of landscapes and allegories: *Peasant Wedding, Fall of Icarus*. Influenced by Bosch (*The Fall of the Rebel Angels*), his works are profoundly marked by his views of the human condition. **Pieter Bruegel the Younger** (1564-1637), also called Hell Bruegel, worked in his father's manner, often with an emphasis on the grotesque. **Jan Bruegel** (1568-1625), also called Velvet Bruegel, the second son, painted landscapes and still lifes with great subtlety and delicacy. He often collaborated with Rubens.

Brugge, or Bruges (pop. 117,000), well-preserved medieval city in northwestern Belgium. Once a center for wool trade, in the 15th century it was home to a school of painting led by the van Eycks and Hans Memling. Its commercial interest revived in the 19th century when the Zeebrugge Canal to the North Sea was opened. It manufactures lace and textiles.
See also: Belgium.

Brugnon, Jacques (1895-1978) French tennis champion, who formed a part of the 'Four Musketeers' (the others being Jean Borotra, Henri Cochet, and René Lacoste). They were called the Four Musketeers because they won the Davis Cup for France from 1927 to 1932 without interruption. Brugnon won Wimbledon with Cochet in 1926 and with Borotra in 1932 and 1933. With the latter, Brugnon won the Australian doubles in 1928. He also won the French mixed doubles five times, playing with Suzanne Lenglen.

Bruhn, Erik (1928-1986), Danish ballet dancer. He debuted with the Royal Danish Ballet in 1947 and became a soloist in 1949. For his roles in *Giselle, Swan Lake*, and *La Sylphide*, Bruhn is considered one of the greatest classical dancers of his time.
See also: Ballet.

Brulé, Étienne (1592?-1633), French-born Canadian explorer. He came to Quebec around 1608, and was sent by Samuel de Champlain to live with the Algonquins (1610) and the Hurons (1611), studying their language and becoming an interpreter. On another mission for Champlain, he was the first European to reach Lake Ontario (1615), and also explored the valley of the Susquehanna River. When Quebec was seized by the English (1629) he fled to the Hurons; according to some accounts, he was later killed by the Hurons.

Brummell, Beau (George Bryan Brummell; 1778-1840), English dandy, friend of the Prince of Wales (later George IV), and an arbiter of fashion in Regency society. The 'Beau' window is named after him.

Brundage, Avery (1887-1975), American chairman of the International Olympic Committee from 1952 to 1972. Brundage

B

maintained the apolitical nature of the Olympic Games and was convinced of the need to preserve amateur competition in all its purity. He refused to boycott the 1936 Games in Nazi Germany and insisted that the 1972 Olympics in Munich would continue after 11 Israeli athletes were murdered by Palestinian terrorists. Brundage was also a very successful sportsman: as pentathlete and decathlete he participated in the 1912 Games in Stockholm and became champion of the U.S. in 1914, 1916, and 1918. Following his career in sport, he became a very successful businessman.

Brundle, Martin (1959-), British racing driver who initially drove in the FF2000 and Formula Three races. In 1984 he made his debut for Tyrrell in the Formula One Grand Prix in Brazil. In his spare time Brundle also entered other forms of motor racing. In 1990, for example, he became joint winner of the 24-Hour race at Le Mans in a Jaguar.

Brundtland, Gro Harlem (1939-), Norwegian politician. Brundtland, who studied medicine, joined the Norwegian Labor Party (DNA) at an early age. In 1974 she became minister of the environment, in 1975 vice party leader and in 1977 member of the Norwegian parliament. She was prime minister from 1981 to 1982, from 1986 to 1989, and from 1990 to 1996. Brundtland advocates Norway's entry into the EU, but, despite the fact that she argued in favor of Norway's entry, the majority of the Norwegian population voted against it during the most recent referendum on this subject. In 1994 Brundtland received the Charlemagne award. In 1998 she was appointed director-general of the World Health Organization (WHO).

Brunei

Capital:	Bandar Seri Begawan
Area:	2,226 sq mi (5,765 sq km)
Population:	351,000
Language:	Malay
Government:	Absolute monarchy (sultanate)
Independent:	1984
Head of gov.:	Sultan
Per capita:	US$ 18,000
Monetary unit:	1 Brunei dollar = 100 sen

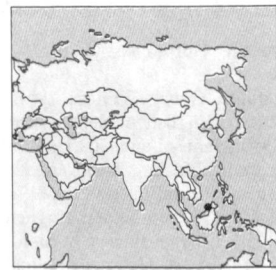

Brunei, sultanate on the north coast of the island of Borneo, on the South China Sea. It has a humid tropical climate that supports dense forests. Malay is the chief language, Islam the official religion. Rubber and timber were superseded as main products after petroleum was found in 1929. Petroleum and natural gas are now extracted both on and off shore. A local sultanate, established in the 15th century, controlled all of Borneo during the 16th century. It became a British protectorate in 1888, and a 1959 constitution gave it domestic autonomy. Brunei received full independence in 1984. At the end of the 1990s, the country suffered severely due to the forest fires on Borneo. Sultan Hassanal Bolkiah is acknowledged as one of the wealthiest people in the world.
See also: Borneo.

Brunel, Sir Marc Isambard (1769-1849), French-born British engineer and inventor who built the world's first underwater tunnel (Thames Tunnel, 1825). His son, **Isambard Kingdom Brunel** (1806-1859), a civil engineer, designed the Clifton suspension bridge at Bristol, England, and built ironhulled steamships, including the giant *Great Eastern* (1858).

Brunelleschi, Filippo (1377-1446), first great Italian Renaissance architect. One of the first practitioners of linear perspective, he was influenced by classical Roman and 11th-century Tuscan Romanesque architecture. His masterpiece is the dome of the Florence cathedral (1420-36).
See also: Renaissance.

Brunhild, Brünnehilde, or Brynhild, heroine of German and Scandinavian mythology dating back to A.D. 400. In the oldest Scandinavian version, Sigurd rescues her from a deep sleep imposed by Odin. In the medieval epic, she loves and is deserted by Sigurd, whose death she contrives, destroying herself on his funeral pyre. As Brünnhilde, the Valkyrie, she is the subject of German composer Richard Wagner's opera *Ring of the Nibelungs*.
See also: Nibelungenlied.

Bruno, Giordano (1548-1600), Italian philosopher. A Dominican who was expelled from the order for heresy, he held that the universe was infinite and that there is no absolute truth. He also defended the Copernican hypothesis. His major works were *On the Infinite Universe and Worlds* and *The Infinite* (both 1584). Brought to trial by the Inquisition, he refused to recant and was burned at the stake. His ideas later influenced Leibniz and Spinoza, making him an important philosophical influence on early modern science.
See also: Philosophy.

Brunswick (German: *Braunschweig*), descendants of the Wolf family. Great Britain's present line of monarchs are descendants of Brunswick dukes of Hanover, Germany. The duchy of Brunswick-Luneburg was established by Frederick II in 1235 and given to Otto, grandson of the Wolf family's founder, Henry the Lion. In 1714, Elector George Louis of Hanover succeeded to the throne of Britain as George I. A reduced duchy of Brunswick existed as a separate state and after 1735 was associated with Prussia under the House of Brunswick-Beven. Brunswick remained a constituent state of Germany from 1871 to 1946.

Brussels (pop. 134,000), Belgian capital city, headquarters of the European Common Market and NATO. First commercially important in the 12th century, it was granted a ducal charter in 1312. From the 16th to the 19th centuries it was subject successively to Spain, Austria, and France. It manufactures textiles, lace, and furniture and is a transport center.
See also: Belgium.

Brussels griffon, breed of toy dog developed in 19th-century Belgium. The Brussels griffon may be reddish brown, black, or a combination of the two. It comes in two varieties, one rough and wiry and the other, called Brabançon, having a smooth coat. Standing about 10-12 in (25-30 cm) and weighing 8-10 lb (3.6-4.5 kg), it is noted for its intelligent and affectionate nature.

Brussels sprouts, variety of cabbage first grown on the outskirts of Brussels. The edible buds on the stem are best eaten after being touched by frost.

Brussels sprouts (*B. oleracea*) are cool-weather vegetables derived from wild cabbage.

Brutus, Marcus Junius (85?-42 B.C.), Roman statesman who led the assassination plot against Julius Caesar. He committed suicide after being defeated by Mark Antony and Octavian at Philippi.
See also: Philippi; Caesar, (Gaius) Julius; Antony, Marc.

Bryan, William Jennings (1860-1925), U.S. political leader, orator, and lawyer. After serving in Congress in 1891-1895, he ran unsuccessfully as Democratic candidate for president in 1896, 1900, and 1908. He was secretary of state under Woodrow Wilson in 1913-1915. His famous 'Cross of Gold' speech at the 1896 Democratic convention defended free silver. A Christian fundamentalist, he assisted in the prosecution at the Scopes Trial in 1925, when John Scopes was convicted for teaching evolution in public schools in Dayton, Tenn. Bryan was also a supporter of the income tax and of women's suffrage.

B

Bryant, Paul 'Bear' (1913-1983), U.S. football coach. The all time winningest coach in Division I-A football, Bryant compiled a record of 323 wins, 85 losses, and 17 ties while coaching at Maryland (1945), Kentucky (1946-1953), Texas A & M (1954-1957), and Alabama (1958-1982). Bryant won or shared six national championships at Alabama (1961, 1964, 1965, 1973, 1978, 1979).

Bryant, William Cullen (1794-1878), U.S. poet and journalist. Editor of the New York *Evening Post* (1826) and later part owner (1829-1878), he campaigned against slavery and for free speech. He wrote the pastoral odes 'Thanatopsis' (1817) and translated the *Iliad* (1870) and the *Odyssey* (1872).

Bryce, James, 1st Viscount (1838-1922), British politician and historian. A professor of law at Oxford, he wrote *History of the Holy Roman Empire* (1864) and *The American Commonwealth* (1888). He was British ambassador to the U.S. 1907-1913.

Bryce Canyon National Park, area of 5,835 acres in southwest Utah, created as a park in 1924. Its extraordinary formations in limestone and sandstone are the result of erosion.

Brynhild *See:* Brunhild.

Bryophyte, most primitive division of land plants, including liverworts and mosses. The life-cycle of bryophytes has two stages: the gametophyte, a sexual stage, and its offspring, the sporophyte, an asexual spore-bearing stage.

Bryozoan, freshwater and marine moss animals living in colonies encrusting seaweeds, stones, or the hulls of ships and sometimes forming lacy fans. Each colony is made up of minute, tentacled polyps.

Brzezinski, Zbigniew (1928-), Polish-born U.S. political scientist and national security adviser (1977-1981), who advocated more vigorous anticommunist policies.

BTU *See:* British thermal unit.

Bubble chamber, device invented by

James Buchanan (1791-1868), 15th president of the United States (1857-1861).

Donald Glaser (1952) to observe the paths of subatomic particles. The particles are shot through pressurized liquefied gas; they create strings of tiny bubbles, leaving 'tracks' of their path.
See also: Wilson cloud chamber.

Buber, Martin (1878-1965), Jewish philosopher, born in Austria. Editor of a major German-Jewish journal, *Der Jude*, 1916-1924, he was a leading educator and scholar of Hasidism. He was forced to leave Germany in 1938 and moved to Jerusalem. His central philosophical concept, the direct relationship between God and the individual, is expressed in *I and Thou* (1923).
See also: Hasidism.

Bubka, Sergej (1963-), Ukrainian pole vaulter, broke the world record for the first time with 5.85 m in Bratislava. One year later he was the first pole vaulter to clear 6 m. Ever since, he has broken his own world record with clock-like regularity and eventually reached the 6.14 m in 1994. In 1985 he won the world cup, in 1986 he became European champion, world champion in 1983, 1987, 1991, 1993, 1995, and 1997, and Olympic champion in 1988. Bubka ended his sports career in 2001.

Bubonic plague, disease transmitted to humans by fleas from infected rats. One form of the plague called Black Death swept through Europe and parts of Asia in the 1300s, killing three-quarters of the population in 20 years. Symptoms include fever, chills, and enlarged, painful lymph nodes (buboes), particularly in the groin. In its black form, hemorrhages turn black. The antibiotics tetracycline and streptomycin as well as rat control and sanitation have greatly reduced the mortality rate.
See also: Epidemic.

Buchan, John, 1st Baron Tweedsmuir (1875-1940), Scottish author and politician. He wrote a four-volume history of World War I (1920-1921), biographies (of Julius Caesar, 1932), and classic adventure stories (*The Thirty-Nine Steps*, 1915). From 1935 he was governor-general of Canada.

Buchanan, James (1791-1868), 15th president of the United States (1857-1861). Buchanan held office during the years of mounting crisis that led up to the Civil War. The bitter divisions between North and South over the issue of slavery intensified during Buchanan's administration. When he left office in Mar. 1861, 7 slave states had already seceded from the Union and the nation was on the verge of war.
Initially a Federalist, Buchanan switched to the Democratic party after the Federalist party dissolved in the 1820s. After serving as U.S. minister to Russia (1832-1833), Buchanan became a U.S. senator (1834-1845). In 1845 President James K. Polk appointed him secretary of state, a position he held until 1849. In 853, he became minister to Great Britain. In 1854 Buchanan, along with the U.S. ministers to France and Spain, formulated the Ostend Manifesto, which stated that the United States should try to purchase Cuba from Spain but also suggest-

ed that the United States might be justified in using force to 'wrest' the island away from Spain.
In 1856 he won the presidential elections. Although he opposed slavery on moral grounds, Buchanan felt that it was an issue for each state or territory to decide. His attitude towards slavery and secession and the financial panic of 1857 weakened confidence in Buchanan's administration. In 1860 he lost the elections to Abraham Lincoln.

Bucharest (pop. 2,065,000), capital of Romania, on the Dîmbovita River. A medieval fortress, it became the residence of the princes of Walachia in 1459 and the capital when the new Romania was formed in 1861. It produces pharmaceutical and electrical goods, machinery, and automobiles. Bucharest was the site of violence during the 1989 overthrow of the communist government of Nicolae Ceausescu.
See also: Romania.

Buchenwald, Nazi concentration camp set up near Weimar, Germany in 1937 to hold political and 'non-Aryan' prisoners. More than 100,000 (mostly Jews) died there through starvation, extermination, and medical experimentation.
See also: Holocaust.

Buchman, Frank Nathan Daniel (1878-1961), evangelist and founder of the Moral Re-Armament movement (1938), commonly known as the MRA, an anticommunist grouping that grew rapidly and spread to over 50 countries.

Büchner, Georg (1813-1837), German dramatist, forerunner of expressionism. His *Danton's Death* (1835) and *Woyzeck* (1837) use colloquial language and sometimes sordid settings to trace the powerlessness of isolated individuals against historical forces of society. Woyzeck, for example, is a soldier pressured into murdering his unfaithful mistress. *Lenz*, an unfinished work, is about a dramatist on the verge of madness.

Buchwald, Art (1925-), U.S. political columnist. Known primarily for his satires, Buchwald began his column with the *International Herald Tribune* in 1949. Later syndicated, it appeared in more than 500 newspapers. Buchwald won a Pulitzer Prize in 1982. He remains an active columnist.

Buck, Pearl Sydenstricker (1892-1973), U.S. author. Most of her novels are set in China, where she lived until 1934. She won the Pulitzer Prize in 1932 for *The Good Earth* (1931), and the 1938 Nobel Prize in literature.

Buckeye *See:* Horse chestnut.

Buckingham, George Villiers, 1st Duke of (1592-1628), English nobleman whose influence over James I and Charles I inflamed antimonarchical feeling. He promoted costly and unsuccessful military ventures, notably the expedition to relieve the Huguenots of La Rochelle. Charles, however, shielded him from impeachment. He was eventually assassinated.

Buckingham Palace, London residence of the British royal family since 1837, built in 1703 and bought by George III from the Duke of Buckingham in 1761. Queen Victoria was the first monarch to use it as an official residence.
See also: London.

Buckthorn, common name for thorny shrub (*Rhamnus cathartica*) of the family Rhamnaceae. It has oval leaves and small, green flowers that grow in clusters. Its fruit resembles small black berries. Buckthorns are sometimes grown to form hedges and may reach a height of 12 ft (3.7 m). The bark is used to produce a yellow dye. Buckthorns are found in Europe and the United States.

Buckwheat, any of a genus (*Fagopyrum*) of common weeds, including dock and sorrel and a few tropical trees. The name applies particularly to species *F. esculentum* and *F. tartaricum*, cultivated for seeds used as cereal grain and cattle fodder.

Bucovina, or Bukovina a region of east-central Europe. It lies chiefly in the upper courses of the Prut and Siret rivers, and extends from the Dniester River in the northeast to the Carpathian Mountains in the southwest. Northern Bucovina, covering 1,708 square miles (4,424 sq km), is in Ukraine. Southern Bucovina, with an area of 2,322 square miles (6,014 sq km), is in Romania. Bucovina is heavily forested; the name means 'Land of the Beeches.'
Bucovina was first mentioned as a separate district in 1412. It was under Turkish rule from 1512 until 1769, when it was occupied by Russian armies. In 1774 Turkey was forced to cede Bucovina to Austria. In 1849 Austria set up Bucovina as a separate crown land. When Austria-Hungary broke up in 1918 after World War I, Bucovina became part of Romania. During World War II the Soviet Union took over northern Bucovina. In 1991, after the collapse of the Soviet Union, northern Bucovina became a part of the newly independent Ukraine.

Budapest (pop. 1,900,000), capital of Hungary, on the Danube River. Two settlements, Buda on the right bank and Pest on the left, date from Roman times but were destroyed by Mongol invaders in 1241. Buda became Hungary's capital in 1361. Both cities declined under the Turks but revived under the Hapsburgs and were united in 1873. Textiles are the main industry. The city was virtually destroyed in World War II. It was the center of the Hungarian uprising in 1956.
See also: Hungary.

Budd, Lanny *See:* Sinclair, Upton.

Buddha, Gautama (c. 563-c. 483 B.C.), founder of Buddhism. He was born Siddhartha Gautama, son of the raja of Kapilavastu, India, near Nepal. At the age of 29, confronting human misery for the first time, he set out to find the path to peace and serenity. For 6 years he studied under Brahman teachers, living as a hermit. Enlightenment came to him while seated under a *bodhi* or pipal tree. Thereafter he

preached and gathered disciples as Buddha ('The Enlightened One').
See also: Buddhism.

Buddhism, religion and philosophy originating in India in the 6th century B.C., based on interpretations of the teaching of Siddhartha Gautama, called the Buddha, or 'Enlightened One.' His first disciples became the Sangha, or original Buddhist monastic order, men (and later women) who gave up home and family, shaved their heads, dressed only in rags, and devoted their lives to practicing and spreading his philosophy of Enlightenment.
In the 5th century B.C. a council in Rajagaha resulted in the Pali Canon, a body of scriptures from the oral tradition of the Buddha's teaching, together with his rules for monastic life, a collection of his sermons, and a metaphysical analysis of his concepts. From a second council, held in Vesali in the 4th century B.C., there emerged 2 separate schools of thought, the Hinayana ('Small Vehicle,' surviving as Theravada, 'Doctrine of the Elders'), which elected to adhere to strict monastic rules, and the Mahayana ('Large Vehicle'), which adopted a more flexible approach. As a result of a third council, in the 3rd century B.C., called by the Indian emperor Asoka, an ardent convert to Buddhism, missionaries were sent throughout India, as well as to Syria, North Africa, Greece, and Ceylon (now Sri Lanka). From Ceylon, in the 4th century A.D., Buddhism reached Burma, and in the 7th century it reached Tibet, where it combined with existing beliefs to become Lamaism. It made a deep mark on Chinese thought in the 4th and 5th centuries A.D. In 630 an Indian Buddhist living in China, Bodhidarma, introduced his method of meditation and direct or 'spontaneous' enlightenment, which led to the dominant School of Ch'an (Zen, in Japanese). Buddhism spread to Korea in the 4th century A.D., and from there in the 6th century it entered Japan. Eventually Buddhism declined in China, but more from its ever-tolerant absorption of other philosophies, which often blurred its intrinsic character, than from the failure of its teaching. By the 7th century, Buddhism had begun to recede from India itself and, by the year 1000, except in Nepal, Buddhist sects had been al-

most entirely absorbed back into the Brahman religion.
Today the world of Buddhism has 2 main divisions, Theravada, the Southern School, covering Sri Lanka, Burma, Thailand, and Cambodia, and Mahayana, the Northern School, covering Nepal, Korea, China, and Japan. In the 2 schools can be counted 300-500 million followers, and there are many millions more who practice the teaching alone, for Buddhism has no service, ritual, or church in the Western sense. It is a lone process of self-awareness and self-development aimed at the ultimate enlightenment known as nirvana, a state beyond intellect, words, and form. This attainment, Buddhism

Monks form an essential part of Buddhism. Because all forms of property are forbidden to them, they are obliged to live from the offerings of the laity, which are collected in large pots.

The magnificent neo-Gothic parliament building of Hungary (built between 1884 and 1905), on the left bank of the Danube, on the Pest side of the river.

B

holds, is the sole means by which one can be liberated from the 'wheel of life,' the continual cycle of birth, death, and suffering. Human beings are bound to this cycle by the cause-effect of karma, in which present circumstances and experience are the result of past thoughts and actions, and present thoughts and actions are creating those of the future. Through Buddhist teaching and the use of meditation, one can begin to purify one's thoughts and thus improve one's destiny. Buddhist teaching uses the Pali Canon as its scriptural authority, Buddha's Four Noble Truths as its main premise, and the Noble Eightfold Path as its manual.
The Four Noble Truths are (1) suffering is omnipresent; (2) its cause is wrongly directed desire; (3) remove the wrong desire and the cause for suffering is removed; (4) the Noble Eightfold Path leads to the end of suffering. The Noble Eightfold Path consists of (1) right understanding, (2) right thought, (3) right speech, (4) right action, (5) right means of livelihood, (6) right effort, (7) right concentration, (8) right meditation.

Budge, Donald (1915-), U.S. tennis player. His team won the Davis Cup in 1937, and in 1938 he was the first player to win 4 top world championships (U.S., British, Australian, and French), now referred to as the Grand Slam.

Budget, document designed to estimate income and expenditures over a certain period of time, usually 1 year. The most important budget in the United States is the federal budget, prepared annually by the executive branch of government, and transmitted to the Congress, usually in January. Most aspects of the budget must be approved by Congress.

Budgie *See:* Parakeet.

Bueno, Maria Esther (1939-), Brazilian amateur tennis player who won the singles championships at Wimbledon three times (1959, 1960, 1964) and the women's doubles five times. In addition, she won the same titles four times in the U.S. (among others with Althea Gibson, Darlene Hard, and Billie Jean King). Her play was characterized by great accuracy and magnificent volleys.

Buenos Aires (pop. 3,000,000), capital of Argentina. On the Rio de la Plata, it is a port for Argentine agricultural products, meat, hides, wool, and cereals. It has several universities and an opera house (Teatro Colón), and is the world's leading Spanish-language publishing center. Industries include food processing, textiles, automobiles, and chemical manufacturing. Founded in 1536, it became the capital of Rio de la Plata viceroyalty in 1776. An impressive economic growth after 1850 attracted many immigrants.
See also: Argentina.

Buffalo, any of several humpbacked fishes (genus *Ictiobus*) of the sucker family. Related to the carp, buffalo are large freshwater fishes that inhabit the bottom of lakes and rivers and feed by sucking up tiny plant organisms. Some grow to 3 ft (91 cm) long and weigh 73 lbs (33 kg). Buffalo are fished for food.

Buffalo, any of several species of wild ox, members of the bovid family. The domesticated Indian water buffalo or carabao is used as a draft animal and for milk. It weighs about a ton, is 5 ft (1.5 m) high, and has large curved horns. Other types of Asiatic buffalo are the Philippine tamarau and the small anoa of Celebes. Cape buffaloes are dangerous big-game animals living in herds. The American bison is also incorrectly called a buffalo.

Buffalo (pop. 328,000), second largest city in the state of New York, situated at the eastern end of Lake Erie near Niagara Falls, in western New York. Buffalo was incorporated in 1832. Buffalo is at a natural junction point for lake, rail, and road transportation and is a hub of rail transport. The completion of the Erie Canal in 1825 was a turning point in the city's development. Buffalo is one of the United States' major centers of grain distribution and a leading flour-milling center and steel producer. Among the important institutions located in Buffalo are the Albright-Knox Gallery and one of the campuses of the State University of New York. *See also:* New York.

Buffalo Bill (William Frederick Cody; 1846-1917), U.S. scout and showman. He claimed to have killed 4,280 buffalo to feed the builders of the Kansas Pacific Railway. He rode with the pony express in 1860, and during the Civil War was a scout in Tennessee and Missouri for the Union army. From 1872 he toured the United States and Europe with his Wild West Show.

Buffalo Bill (1846-1917), who posed for this photograph in 1903, inspired colorful myths of the cowboy hero.

Buffalo grass, low-growing grass (*Buchloë dactyloides*) that was once abundant on the central plains of North America and a main food of the bison and pronghorn.

Buffet, Bernard (1928-1999), French painter and graphic artist, studied at the École des Beaux-Arts in Paris. Produced figurative work in somber colors. The rigid linear style emphasizes the ascetic nature of his work. In 1948 he was one of the founders of 'l'Homme témoin', a group that turned against the general tendency of abstract arts and propagated a return to the figurative style. His art is dominated by graphic elements which, with their elongated shapes, emphasize the austerity of his style. His works include *Les horreurs de la guerre* (1954) and his self-portraits. He illustrated, among other things, *Les chants de Maldoror* by Lautréamont (1952).

Buffon, Georges Louis Leclerc, Comte de (1707-1788), French naturalist who was the first modern taxonomist of the animal kingdom. He led the team that produced the 44-volume *Histoire Naturelle* (1749-1804).

Bug, name commonly given to all insects but properly applied to the order Hemiptera. These insects have pointed beaks with which they suck juice from plants or blood from animals, including humans.

Buganda *See:* Uganda.

Bugbane, any of several tall plants (genus *Cimicifuga*) of the buttercup family. They have broad leaves that divide into thin leaflets. Their small white flowers grow in branched clusters. Bugbanes are perennials that grow in mild climates. It was once thought that their unpleasant smell repelled bugs.

Bugging *See:* Wiretapping.

Bugle, wind instrument of the brass family, made of either copper or brass, with a conical bore and a cupshaped mouthpiece. The sound it produces is clear and penetrating. The bugle can produce only 7-8 different pitches; only 5 are needed in the military calls for which it is used. An instrument of great antiquity, it is mentioned in the Old Testament description of the siege of Jericho.

Buick, David Dunbar (1855-1929), Scottish-born U.S. plumber turned automobile maker. His Detroit manufacturing company produced the first Buick automobile in 1903. Money problems forced Buick to sell his interest in the company in 1906.

Building *See:* Architecture.

Bujumbura (until 1962 Usumbura; pop. 300,000), capital of Burundi on Lake Tanganyika. Mercantile port with a ferry to Kigoma, Tanzania, for the export of products such as coffee, cotton, fish and hides. Textile, steel, cement, pharmaceutical, and food industries. Airport; university (1960). Visited in 1871 by Stanley. In German hands from 1880 and a major German army town at the turn of the century. In 1923 the Belgians turned it into the capital of their mandated territory (and from 1945 UN trust territory) Rwanda-Urundi.

Bukhara, 1. former state (khanate) in West Turkistan (South Siberia), which was most prosperous in the 14th and 15th centuries. In 1369 Timur Lenk became Emir of Bukhara. He took up residence in Samarkand, the city which he also developed. He constructed a complex road system and boosted agriculture by improving irrigation methods. In 1917 the Emir of Bukhara was forced to draw up a constitution, whereupon he left the country in 1920. In 1924 the Soviet republics of Bukhara and Chiwa were replaced by Uzbekistan, Tajikistan, Turkmeniya, and the autonomous areas of Kara Kyrgyz and Karakalpak. This resulted in the republics of Uzbekistan, Tajikistan, Turkmenistan, and Kirghizstan in 1991/92.

2. (pop. 260,000), city in Uzbekistan, mainly Sunni Muslims. Seat of the highest mufti in Central Asia.

Bukovski, Vladimir (1943-), Soviet-Russian dissident. In 1971 Bukovski reported to the West that the Soviet Union was confining a large number of dissidents to psychiatric clinics. As a result, in 1972 he was sentenced to two years' imprisonment, five years of a strict regime in a labor camp, and five years of internal exile. At the end of 1976 Bukovski was transferred to Switzerland as part of an exchange with the Secretary-General of the Chilean Communist party, Luis Corvalan, who was imprisoned after the 1973 coup. Works by Bukovski include *My life as a Dissenter* (1978) and *The Peace Movement and the Soviet Union* (1982).

Bukowski, Charles (1920-1994) American writer. Bukowski led a nomadic life in the lowest stratum of American society. In his poems, stories, and novels he wrote about a life of alcohol abuse, drugs, and prostitutes in a very direct and crude manner. During the mid 1960s he started to gain recognition in the underground circuit and had a column in a hippie paper: *Notes of a Dirty Old Man*, compiled in 1969. He is mainly known for his novel *Post Office* (1971) and the scenario of the movie *Barfly* (1987). In 1981 his collection of stories *Erections, Ejaculations, and General Tales of Ordinary Madness* (1972) was made into a movie by Marco Ferreri. *Screams from the Balcony* (1994) consists of a selection of letters he wrote from 1960 to 1970. Other novels include: *Factotum* (1975), *Women* (1978) and *Ham on Rye* (1982).

Bulb, short, underground storage stem composed of many fleshy scale leaves that are swollen with stored food and an outer layer of protective scale leaves. Bulbs are a means of overwintering; in the spring, flowers and foliage are rapidly produced when growing conditions are suitable. Examples of plants producing bulbs are the daffodil, tulip, snowdrop, and onion.

Bulbul, any of various species of tropical songbirds of the family Pycnonotidae, native to Africa and southern Asia. About 7 to 10 in (18 to 25 cm) long, bulbuls have plain, fluffy feathers and a slim, notched beak designed for eating fruits and insects. They tend to travel in noisy flocks and can cause damage to orchards and crops.

Bulfinch, Charles (1763-1844), U.S. architect. He designed the Massachusetts statehouse, Boston (1800); University Hall, Harvard University (1815); and the east portico of the Capitol, Washington, D.C. (1818). He emphasized the neoclassical style in U.S. civic architecture.

Bulganin, Nikolai Alexandrovich (1895-1975), Soviet leader. With the support of Nikita Khrushchev, he succeeded Georgy Malenkov as premier in 1955. He was expelled from the central committee when Khrushchev became premier in 1958.

Bulgaria

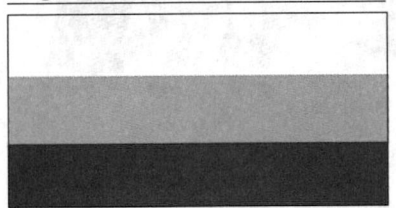

Capital:	Sofia
Area:	42,855 sq mi (110,994 sq km)
Population:	7,621,000
Language:	Bulgarian
Government:	Republic
Independent:	1908
Head of gov.:	Prime minister
Per capita:	U.S. $6,200
Monetary unit:	1 Lev = 100 stotinki

Bulgaria, country in eastern Europe, in the Balkan mountains; bordered on the east by the Black Sea, on the west by Yugoslavia and Macedonia, on the south by Greece and Turkey, and on the north by Rumania, the Danube River forming the border.

Land and climate. The climate is continental in the north, with cold winters and hot summers, temperate continental in the center, and mediterranean south of the Rhodope Mountains and along the Black Sea coast. The country's capital is Sofia.

People. Nearly 90% of Bulgarians are descendants of the Bulgars, a migratory people of Mongol origin. About a tenth of the population is ethnically Turkish. Bulgarian is a southern-Slavic language similar to Russian.

Economy. Though agriculture still employs the majority of the work force, it accounts for only 14% of the national income. Modern industries produce trucks, ships, transistors, chemicals, cement, porcelain, and glass. Lead, zinc, iron ore, copper, and manganese are mined. There are also deposits of oil and natural gas.

History. In the 7th century, the Eastern Bulgars conquered and merged with the Slavic population and adopted their language and customs. Between the 7th and 14th centuries, Bulgarian empires were major participants in Balkan political life, but in 1396 the country was occupied by the Ottoman Empire, which ruled Bulgaria for nearly 500 years. The Congress of Berlin (1878) restricted Turkish hegemony and in 1908 Bulgaria proclaimed its independence under Ferdinand I of Saxe-Coburg-Gotha. Bulgaria supported Germany in World War I and World War II. In 1944 the USSR occupied the country; in 1946 the monarchy was abolished and a republic proclaimed, under the control of the Communist party. In the late 1980's, discontent with the dictatorship of Todor Zhivkov, who had ruled Bulgaria since 1954, arose. Reformers within the Communist Party ousted Zhivkov's regime in 1989. In 1990 the National Assembly abolished the party's constitutional monopoly on political power and established a transitorial government. Later in 1990, Bulgaria held its first free elections since 1931, resulting in the election of a National Assembly dominated by the Socialist Party (formerly known as the Communist Party). The National Assembly elected Zhelyu Zhelev president, Bulgaria's first non-Communist president in more than 45 years. Because of economic difficulties, Bulgaria's Socialist government collapsed in late 1990. Shortly afterward a coalition government was established. In 1991 the National Assembly ratified a democratic constitution. Legislative elections in 1994 resulted in a victory for the Socialist Party. The popularity of the Socialists waned and in early 1997 protests and strikes occurred throughout the country. The government fell and new elections resulted in the defeat of the Socialists. After the elections of 2001, the former king of Bulgaria, Simeon ll, became prime minister. Bulgaria will not be one of the countries entering the European Union in 2004 (possibly 2007), but it has been accepted as a member of the NATO.

Bulge, Battle of the, last major western counteroffensive by the Germans in World War II. They planned to capture Liège and Antwerp, thus dividing the Allied armies. The German assault in the Ardennes began on Dec. 16, 1944, and create a huge 'bulge' in the Allied lines. Although suffering about 77,000 casualties, the Allies stopped the German advance by Jan. 16, 1945.
See also: World War II.

Bulimia, eating disorder characterized by insatiable appetite; eating binges are generally followed by self-induced vomiting. It is related to anorexia nervosa. Often observed in psychotics, it also commonly affects adolescent girls.
See also: Anorexia nervosa.

Bull, John *See:* John Bull.

Bulldog, medium-sized, low-slung dog originally bred in England for bullbaiting and related sports (outlawed in 1835). It has a massive head with an undershot jaw, broad shoulders, and strong legs. It weighs 40 to 50 lb (18 to 23 kg).

B

B

The main participants of bullfighting. Only after the mounted picador (left) has lanced the bull's neck and the banderillero (center) has placed darts in the animal's shoulders does the matador (right) confront his adversary. Armed with a sword and a muleta, a red cloth attached to a rod, the matador is expected to kill the bull with a single swordstroke.

Bullfighting, Spanish national sport and spectacle, also popular in Latin America. Probably developed by the Moors, it was taken over by aristocratic professionals in the 18th century. The modern bullfight stresses the grace, skill, and daring of the *matador*. After a procession, the bull is released. Two mounted *picadors* jab the bull's neck with lances to lower its head for the matador's capework. Then three *banderilleros* thrust decorated wooden goads into the bull's back. The matador, after using his cape to make daring and graceful passes at the bull, kills it with a swordthrust between the shoulders. In Portugal, the matador is on horseback and does not kill the bull.

Bullfinch, any of several species of small songbirds native to Europe and Asia, named for their short, stout bill. The common bullfinch (*Pyrrhula pyrrhula*) is a popular cage bird that can be taught to sing tunes. The bullfinch's diet is mostly berries and seeds.

Bullfrog, large North American frog (*Rana catesbeiana*) named for its booming call, which is made by passing air up and down the windpipe, the swollen airsacs acting as resonators. Bullfrogs grow up to 8 in (20 cm) long and live near water, where they feed on many kinds of animals, including small snakes and alligators. They hibernate under logs or in holes, emerging in spring to lay up to 25,000 eggs.
See also: Frog.

The bullfrog (*Rana catesbeiana*) is a common, long-lived aquatic frog known for its loud, raucous croaking.

Bullhead, North American freshwater catfish (genus *Ictalurus*) with broad head and tapering tail. Bullheads grow up to 1 ft (30 cm) long and weigh 2 lb (1 kg). Bullhead is also a name for a marine fish of the southern United States, and for the miller's thumb, a European freshwater fish.
See also: Catfish.

Bullmastiff, breed of dog obtained by crossing the bulldog and the mastiff. Standing about 24 to 27 in (61 to 69 cm) and weighing 100 to 130 lb (45 to 59 kg), this agile, powerful dog is used as a watchdog and bodyguard.

The bullmastiff is a working dog that was bred in England to protect game preserves and estates from poachers.

Bull Run, Battles of, 2 clashes in the American Civil War around Manassas Junction near Bull Run Creek, 25 mi (40 km) southwest of Washington, D.C. In the First Battle of Bull Run, July 1861, Union general Irvin McDowell was sent against Confederates led by P.G.T. Beauregard, but was repulsed by them. Gen. 'Stonewall' Jackson was so nicknamed for his tenacity in this battle. In the Second Battle of Bull Run, Aug. 1862, Jackson attacked Union general John Pope and forced his retreat.
See also: Civil War, U.S..

Bull terrier, muscular dog that combines the strength of the bulldog and the speed and intelligence of the white English terrier, the 2 breeds from which it was first developed in 1835. The bull terrier has an oval head,

pointed ears, a straight tail, a smooth white or brindled coat, and weighs 30-36 lb (13.5-16 kg).

Bulrush, any of a genus (*Scirpus*) of sedges growing in water or marshes, up to 6 ft (2 m) high, with narrow leaves and spiky flowers. Bulrushes grow from rhizomes, which help to anchor debris accumulating in the water, hastening the natural drying out of swamps. Bulrushes are used by Peruvian Indians to make boats.

Bulwer, Sir Henry *See:* Clayton-Bulwer Treaty.

Bulwer-Lytton, Edward George Earle Lytton, 1st Baron Lytton (1803-1873), English author and politician. His best-known works include the historical novels *The Last Days of Pompeii* (1834) and *Rienzi* (1835), and the utopian *The Coming Race* (1871).

Bumblebee, insect belonging to the family Apidae, subfamily Bombinae, having a hairy coat, typically black with orange or yellow stripes, and a sting. Bumble bees range in length from 0.6 to 1 in (1.5 to 2.5 cm). They are social insects, living in colonies consisting of a queen, workers (females), and drones (males). In spring the queen comes out of hibernation and finds a nesting place. She begins laying eggs that develop into worker bees. All summer the workers gather pollen and care for the hive. At the end of summer unfertilized eggs, produced by either the queen or the workers, develop into drones; the colony also rears new queens. Once mature, these queens leave the nest, mate, and find a place to hibernate, while the old colony dies out.

Bunchberry, common name for a low-growing woody perennial (*Cornus canadensis*) related to dogwood. Its clusters of yellowish flowers, surrounded by white bracts, develop into red berries. Bunchberry is found in North America, Greenland, and Asia.

Bunche, Ralph Johnson (1904-1971), U.S. diplomat. He entered the UN in 1946, and was undersecretary for political affairs 1958-1971. Having supervised the 1959 Arab-Israeli armistice, he became the first African American to win the Nobel Peace Prize (1950).

Bungee jumping, Recreational activity. One jumps of high buildings or bridges, equipped with elastic bands around waist and legs. Bungee jumping originates from Polynesia, where young men jumped from high trees, tied to lianas, as a token of courage. In so-called *base jumping*, *base* meaning *building, antenna, span, earth*, a parachute is used to jump from a building, antenna, bridge or high cliff.

Bunin, Ivan Alekseyevich (1870-1953), Russian novelist, short-story writer, and poet. He is best known for such short stories as *The Gentleman from San Francisco* (1916). He emigrated to France in 1919, and won the Nobel Prize in literature in 1933.

B

Bunker Hill, Battle of, one of the first engagements in the American Revolutionary War (June 17, 1775), involving some 2,300 British troops under generals Thomas Gage and Sir William Howe, and some 1,500 inexperienced American volunteers under Colonel William Prescott, Major-General Israel Putman, and General J. Warren. The British had planned to occupy Bunker Hill (near Charlestown, Mass.) as a good site for the defense of Boston. However, the rebels dug themselves into neighboring Breed's Hill under cover of night. Colonial troops opened fire on the arriving British troops, causing heavy casualties. Although the British eventually took Breed's Hill, the Americans, who had lost only about 450 men and proved their skills against seasoned troops, gained greatly in morale.
See also: Revolutionary War in America.

Bunraku, Japanese traditional puppet theater, named after the Bunraku theater in Osaka. Bunraku originated around the 16th century and consists of puppetry and recitation to the accompaniment of a small samisen (three-stringed Japanese lute). Founders were singer Takèmoto Gidajoe (1651-1714) and writer Chikamatsu Monzaèmon (1653-1724). In 1685 Takèmoto established the first large puppet theater in Osaka. The almost life-size Bunraku puppets are of the utmost perfection. The samisen player and the reciter sit in front of the stage where the puppet show takes place. The reciter speaks for all the puppets and sings narrative and descriptive passages.

Bunsen, Robert Wilhelm Eberhard (1811-1899), German chemist who conducted important work on organo-arsenic compounds and, with G.R. Kirchhoff, pioneered chemical spectroscopy, discovering the elements cesium (1860) and rubidium (1861). He also helped to popularize the gas burner known by his name.

Bunsen burner, gas burner consisting of a metal tube with a gas inlet and adjustable

Buntings are 4 to 5.5 in (11 to 14 cm) long and prefer to live in dry, open scrubland. (Left to right, male in foreground): the indigo bunting (*P. cyanea*), whose black feathers diffract bright light and appear indigo; the lazuli bunting (*P. amoena*); and the painted bunting (*P. ciris*) also called 'nonpareil' ('without equal') because it is one of the most colorful and unusually marked birds in North America.

openings for air near the lower end. The air and the gas mix before ignition, producing an extremely hot and smokeless flame. Developed by the German chemist Robert Wilhelm Bunsen (1811-1899), the Bunsen burner is used in scientific laboratories.
See also: Bunsen, Robert Wilhelm Eberhard.

Bunting, finchlike bird (especially, genus *Passerina*), with a conical seed-cracking bill. Buntings feed on seeds and live near the ground in woods or grasslands. They range from hot, humid forests of the tropics to polar regions. The snow bunting nests in northern Greenland, farther north than any other land bird.

Buñuel, Luis (1900-1983), Spanish-Mexican director of films marked by fierce realism, social criticism, and wry humor. Surrealist fantasy is evident in his work ever since his first film, *Un Chien andalou* (made with Salvador Dali in 1929).

Bunyan, John (1628-1688), English author. A tinker by trade, he became a Baptist preacher in 1657. While imprisoned for unlicensed preaching (1660-72; 1675) he wrote his most famous work, *The Pilgrim's Progress* (1678), an allegory in simple prose describing Christian's journey to the Celestial City.

Buonarroti, Michelangelo *See:* Michelangelo.

Burbank (pop. 100,000), city in southern California, 12 mi (19 km) north of Los Angeles in the San Fernando Valley. Incorporated as a town in 1911 and as a city in 1927, Burbank is famous today for its motion picture and television studios.
See also: California.

Burckhardt, Jacob Cristoph (1818-1897), Swiss historian. He was one of the founders of cultural history. His greatest work was *The Civilization of the Renaissance in Italy* (1860). In *Reflections on History* (1905) Burckhardt expressed pessimistic views about the effects of modern civilization on

human values. Burckhardt was born in Basel and was educated there. He visited Italy many times and spent most of his adult life teaching at the University of Basel.

Burdock, any of a genus (*Arctium*) of plants with hairy stems, heart-shaped leaves, and burrs. A North American biennial, also called beggar's-button, burr-bur, cockle button, and stickbutton, it grows to heights of 4 to 9 ft (1 to 3 m).

Buren, Daniel (1938-), French visual artist who formed the BMPT group together with Niele Toroni and others in 1965. Their ambition was to restore painting to its basic form. In doing so, he limited himself to producing paintings with straight, vertical 3.4 inch (8.7 cm) wide white lines alternating with colors. The initial painted stripes were soon replaced by ready-made striped canvas, printed paper or, since 1974, transparent plastic foil. His art is classified as conceptual art.

Burgas (pop. 205,000), port and town in Bulgaria on the Gulf of Burgas, an inlet on the Black Sea. Capital of the province with the same name; 2,972 sq mi (7,694 sq km). (administrative area: pop. 875,000). Shipbuilding industry, oil refining; chemical, steel, textile, and food industries. Fishing, seaside resort. Export of, among other things, tobacco and wool. Metals such as copper are mined in the province.

Burgess, Anthony (1917-1993), English writer, best known for *A Clockwork Orange* (1962), a bitter satire about a violent gang leader in a corrupt, violent society of the near future. His other works include *Inside Mr. Enderby* (1961), *Earthly Powers* (1980), *The Kingdom of the Wicked* (1985), and the critical study *Re Joyce* (1965).

Anthony Burgess (1917-1993).

Burghley, Lord (1520-1598), English statesman. He was chief advisor to Queen Elizabeth I (1558-98) and her spokesman in Parliament. A supporter of the Anglican Church, he repressed Catholic revolts and advocated the execution of Elizabeth's Catholic sister, Mary Queen of Scots.

In 1948, American politician Ralph Johnson Bunche mediated in the Palestinian conflict, on behalf of the United Nations. As a result of his efforts, Israel and the Arab states started negotiations for an armistice. For this and other work for the U.N., Bunche was awarded the Nobel Peace Prize in 1950.

B

Burgkmair the Elder, Hans (1473-1531), German painter and woodcut artist, student of Martin Schongauer, representative of the renaissance. The Venetian influence of Titian in particular is very obvious in his work. He produced Madonnas and many beautiful portraits. His reproduction of landscapes is very striking. He also made drawings and designs for woodcuts.

Burgoyne, John (1722-1792), British general in the American Revolutionary War. He fought in the Seven Years War (1756-1763), and became a playwright, socialite, and member of Parliament. Posted to America, he attempted to put into effect his plan to split off the New England colonies, but was forced to surrender by Gen. Horatio Gates at Saratoga (1777).
See also: Revolutionary War in America.

Burgundy (French: *Bourgogne*), historic region of eastern France, occupying what are now the departments of Côte-d'Or, Saône-et-Loire, Nièvre, and Yonne. It was named for the Burgundians, a Germanic tribe. A rich agricultural region, Burgundy is famous for its wines.
See also: France.

Burke, Edmund (1729-1797), Irish-born British statesman, political philosopher, and orator. He entered parliament in 1765, and advocated more just policies toward the American colonies, opposing the Stamp Act and (in 1775) arguing for conciliation. Concerned for justice in India, he promoted the impeachment of Warren Hastings (1786-1787). His famous *Reflections on the Revolution in France* (1790) presented his rational case against violent change.

Burke, Martha Jane *See:* Calamity Jane.

Burkina Faso

Capital:	Ouagadougou
Area:	105,869 sq mi
	(274,200 sq km)
Population:	12,603,000
Language:	French
Government:	Presidential republic
Independent:	1960
Head of gov.:	President
Per capita:	U.S. $1,040
Monetary unit:	1 CFA franc = 100 centimes

Burkina Faso, land-locked country in West Africa known as Upper Volta until 1984. It is bounded on the west and north by Mali, on the east by Niger and Benin, and on the south by Togo, Ghana, and the Ivory Coast. Burkina Faso is a broad expanse too dry to support much vegetation. Water is scarce.

In Upper Volta, sedentary agriculture can be found mainly in the southern part of the country, where there is sufficient rainfall and the soil is suitable for intensive farming.

Temperatures range from 68°F to 95°F (20°C-35°C). The largest ethnic group in Burkina Faso is the Mossi tribe, but well over half a million nomadic Fulanis and others live in the north. Traditional African religions predominate, but there are also about a million Muslims and a quarter of a million Roman Catholics. The capital is Ouagadougou. French is the official language. Burkina Faso is one of the poorest countries of Africa, and the majority of its work force is engaged in subsistence farming. The country exports cotton, animals, meat, oil seeds, and karite nuts. There are deposits of manganese, limestone, and bauxite, but they have not been fully exploited.
What is now Burkina Faso was once the heart of the great Mossi kingdoms, which dated back to the 1100s and lasted some 500 years. The French made the area a protectorate in 1896 and a colony in 1919. Upper Volta became independent in 1960. The country had a series of civilian and military regimes. Although a new constitution was introduced in 1978, the military continued to dominate the country's politics until 1991 when a multi party system was introduced. In 1993, the IMF acquitted part of the foreign debt.
During past years, the United Nations has threatened to apply sanctions, because the country has been suspected of illegal arms and diamond traffic with rebel forces in West-Africa.

Burleigh, Lord *See:* Burghley, Lord.

Burma *See:* Myanmar.

Burne-Jones, Edward Coley (1833-1898), a British painter, book illustrator, and designer of stained glass and mosaics. He was born at Birmingham, and attended Oxford. Before completing his work at the university he came under the influence of Dante Gabriel Rossetti, an English painter and poet of the Pre-Raphaelite Brotherhood. Burne-Jones turned his whole attention to art. His work is representative of the Romantic school that was dominant in England at that time. He painted in watercolors and oils. Among his works are *The Golden Stairs* (1880); *The Depths of the Sea* (1886); and *The Briar Rose* (1890).

Burnet, Sir Frank Macfarlane (1899-1985), Australian physician and virologist. He shared the 1970 Nobel Prize in physiology or medicine with P.B. Medawar for the suggestion that the ability of organisms to form antibodies in response to foreign tissues was acquired and not inborn.

Burnett, Frances (Eliza) Hodgson (1849-1924), English-born U.S. author. She is particularly famous for her children's stories, *Little Lord Fauntleroy* (1885-1886) and *The Secret Garden* (1910).

Burney, Fanny (Frances Burney; 1752-1840), English novelist and diarist. Her first novel, *Evelina* (1778), won her the respect of Samuel Johnson. She was a member of Queen Charlotte's household 1786-91. Her *Early Diary: 1768-1778* and *Diary and Letters: 1778-1840* provide interesting background to the period.

Burnham, Daniel Hudson (1846-1912), U.S. architect, a pioneer of city planning. He built some of America's early skyscrapers, including the Masonic Temple Building, Chicago (1892), and the Flatiron Building, New York City (1902). He also designed the plan for the Columbian Exposition in Chicago (1893). Much of his improvement plan for Chicago (1907-1909) was subsequently put into effect.

Burn-out, Condition caused by an overload of work pressure during a long period of time. Burnout is a form of stress, the difference being that it lasts longer, occurring mainly in the beginning and in the middle of one's career. Singles, childless couples and highly-educated people run a higher risk. This condition is characterized by 3 symptoms: emotional exhaustion, depersonalization and lack of self confidence. One feels extremely tired and listless and experiences a lack of initiative. Other symptoms that can occur are: lack of concentration, forgetfulness, touchiness, insomnia, physical symptoms such as headaches and tensed muscles, inferiority complexes and a dwindling sexual appetite.

Burns, Arthur Frank (1904-1987), Austrian-born U.S. economist. An expert on the business cycle, he served as presidential adviser on economics 1953-1956 and on labor management 1961-1966. Among his many books, the most influential was *Measuring Business Cycles* (1946), written with Wesley Clair Mitchell.

Burns, Robert (1759-1796), Scottish poet. The son of a poor farmer, he himself farmed for a living and later worked as a customs official. In 1786 he published *Poems, Chiefly in the Scottish Dialect* (enlarged 1787). His poetry, in Scots-English idiom, deals with rural life. He also wrote satirical poems such as 'The Twa Dogs' and 'The Jolly Beggars.' Influenced by Scottish folk tradition, he was a master at writing songs to traditional airs ('Auld Lang Syne'). At first taken up by fashionable society, he died neglected and in debt. Other poems are 'Tam O'Shanter,' 'To a Mouse,' and 'The Cotter's Saturday Night.'

Robert Burns, an 18th-century Scottish poet, painted by Alexander Nasmyth.

Burroughs, Edgar Rice (1875-1950), U.S. writer of adventure novels. He is most famous for *Tarzan of the Apes* (1914), whose characters have passed into comic strips, films, and television.

Burroughs, John (1837-1921), U.S. naturalist and author, known for his philosophical nature essays. His *Notes on Walt Whitman* (1867) was the first biographical study of the poet, who was his friend.

Burroughs, William (1855-1898), U.S. inventor, best known for his practical and commercially successful adding machine (1898). His firm, the American Arithmometer Company (1886), was later renamed Burroughs Adding Machine Company.

Bursa (pop. 1,017,000; formerly Brusa), city in the northwestern part of Turkey, 55 miles (90 km) south of Istanbul. Bursa is a railway terminal and a trade center for agricultural products. The city is noted for its silk production. Bursa's mineral springs and historic mosques attract many visitors The city was the capital of the Ottoman Empire from 1326 to 1366.

Bursitis, inflammation of a bursa (fibrous sac containing synovial fluid that reduces friction where tendons move over bones), commonly caused by excessive wear and tear or by rheumatoid arthritis, gout, or bacteria. It causes pain and stiffness, and may require cortisone injections and, if infected, surgical drainage.

Burton, Sir Richard Francis (1821-1890), English explorer, writer, and linguist. His interest in Muslim culture led him to secretly visit shrines in the holy city of Mecca (1853). In the 1880s, he translated the *Arabian Nights* into English. He was the first European to see Lake Tanganyika in central Africa (1858), and he also explored Santos, Brazil (1865). The motion picture *Mountains of the Moon* is based on his adventures.

Burundi

Capital:	Bujumbura
Area:	10,747 sq mi (27,834 sq km)
Population:	6,373,000
Language:	French, Kirundi
Government:	Presidential republic
Independent:	1962
Head of gov.:	Prime minister
Per capita:	U.S. $600
Monetary unit:	1 Burundi franc = 100 centimes

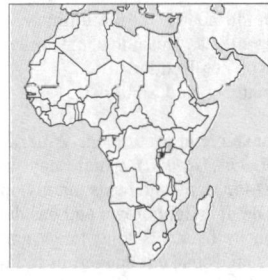

Burundi, one of Africa's smallest states, bordered on the east by Tanzania, on the west by Congo, on the north by Rwanda, and on the southwest by Lake Tanganyika. The capital, situated alongside the lake, is Bujumbura. The climate is tropical, with a rainy season from Oct. to April and a dry season in June, July, and Aug.
The Hutu and Tutsi are the country's main ethnic groups. There is a small minority of Twa, a pygmy people. The official language is French; the chief African language is Kurundi; Swahili is also widely spoken. About 30% of the people adhere to traditional beliefs, the rest being Christian, principally Roman Catholic. The economy is mainly agricultural. Principal exports are arabica coffee and cotton.
The earliest inhabitants seem to have been the Twa, who were succeeded by the Hutu, who came from the Congo Basin. The Hutu were later subjugated by the Tutsi, who may have originated in northeast Africa. In 1899

Germany claimed Burundi as part of German East Africa. After World War I, Belgium was granted control of the area. In 1962, following a referendum, Burundi became an independent monarchy. The monarchy was overthrown and replaced by a republic in 1966. Since independence Burundi has been the scene of recurrent fighting between the Tutsi minority (who dominated the government for a long time) and the Hutu majority (*e.g.* in 1972, 1987 and 1993). In 1996 the Tutsi army overthrew the Hutu-dominated government. An interim government was formed with a Hutu prime minister and vice president at the end of 2001. The Tutsi President Buyoya visited some EU-countries to gain financial support.

Buryatiya (pop. 1,040,000), republic of Russia in southeastern Siberia, 135,689 sq mi (351,298 sq km). The capital is Ulan-Ude. Mountainous area rich in mineral resources which include gold, coal, and various nonferrous metals. The Trans-Siberian and the Baikal-Amur railroads run through the republic. Lake Baika is also situated in this republic. The original inhabitants, the Buryats, make up about one third of the republic's total population. They are originally a nomadic, Buddhist people, related to the Mongols and they speak Buryat. Russian and Mongolian are also common languages. Until the 2nd century B.C. the area belonged to the Hun empire and was subsequently dominated by various Mongolian dynasties. A feudal, nomadic society evolved. After the Russians arrived in the 17th century, the first settlements originated and agriculture and mining were developed. In 1918 the country was occupied by the Japanese and whites; in 1922 the Bolsheviks came into power and founded the Buryat-Mongolian Autonomous Soviet Republic. In 1958 the area became an Autonomous Soviet Socialist Republic; since 1992 it has been a republic of the Federation of Russia.

Burying beetle, insect of the carrion beetle family (Silphidae). Averaging 1/2 in (12 mm) in length, the burying beetle digs around and beneath dead insects or animals, effectively burying them. Eggs are laid there, and the hatched larvae feed off the carrion until they reach maturity.

The Tarzan stories by E.R. Burroughs were made into a comic by Burne Hogarth.

Bush, George Herbert Walker (1924-), 41st president of the United States (1989-1993). American politician and diplomat, member of the Republican Party. From 1970 to 1976 Bush was active in diplomatic service and served as US Ambassador to the United Nations. From 1976 to 1977 he headed the CIA. In 1980 Bush was elected vice president in Ronald Reagan's team and was reelected in 1984. President of the United States from 1989-1993. In the presidential elections on 8th November 1988 he defeated the Democratic candidate Michael Dukakis and became president of the U.S. In 1993 Bush was succeeded by the Democratic candidate Bill Clinton.
See also: Persian Gulf War.

George W. Bush

Bush, George W. (George William; 1946-), American politician and 43rd President of the United States (2001-), son of President George Bush sr., who started his career in business but changed to politics in 1988. From 1995 to 2000 he was the Republican Governor of Texas. It is noticeable how much he was supported by the Spanish-speaking minority in Texas, who make up well over 25% of the total population. Bush presented himself as a moderate conservative. He supports the death penalty. In 2000 he ran for the presidential elections against democrat Al Gore and in the preambles to the party conventions, he managed to consolidate his position. Dick Cheney, who had been Secretary of State for Defense under his father, became his running mate. Their electoral battle was mainly focused on Bush's promise of tax reductions, while Gore gave priority to debt repayment and to secure old age provision. Furthermore he campaigned to uphold traditional family values and private social aid, as an alternative for social security. After the elections the final results turned out to be problematic: the difference in votes was so small that a recount was requested in Florida. The ballots appeared to be ambiguous and as a result, a number of voters elected the wrong candidate. And the ballots were not machine-readable. Only after the U.S. Supreme Court intervened, was Bush announced winner of the presidential elections. In the Senate, Republicans and Democrats were balanced, while in the House of Representatives, the Republicans only held a small majority. This meant that the President's mandate was very weak. Bush intended to increase defense spending and to develop a strategic shield de-

The bushmaster (*Lachesis muta*) is, among poisonous snakes, second in size only to the king cobra. In Greek mythology Lachesis is the goddess of fate, and determines the duration of human life.

fense system against enemy missiles. After the terrorist attacks of September 11, 2001, Bush declared war on international terrorism and he managed to form an international coalition against terrorism. Following the terrorist attacks against the Pentagon and World Trade Centers on September 11, Bush emerged as a powerful leader for all Americans in a time of crisis: most critics fell silent. Tax reductions were enforced and Homeland Security was introduced. Bush's power increased after the mid-term elections of 2002: Republicans gained control in the House of Representatives as well as in the Senate. At the end of 2002, Bush seemed to prepare the US and the rest of the world for a war against Iraq, which allegedly was still manufacturing weapons of mass destruction. According to UN-resolutions, Iraq is not allowed to posses or produce such weapons. Saying the 'danger is clear' that the Iraqi regime would provide terrorists with biological, chemical or nuclear weapons, on March 17th, 2003, Bush gave the Iraqi leader, President Saddam Hussein and his sons 48 hours to leave Iraq or face military action.
See also: Gore, Albert Jr. (Al); Clinton, William Jefferson (Bill); September 11, 2001; Sharon, Ariel; Arafat, Yasir; Bush, George Herbert Walker; Powell, Colin; Cheney, Dick; Rumsfeld, Donald Henry; Rice, Condoleezza.

Bushido (Japanese: Way of the Warrior), the code of conduct and ethical training method of the samurai, which developed into a national ideology. Fulfilling one's duty (giri) is demonstrated by loyalty towards one's master, brave defence of one's own status and honor, and strict abidance to daily duties. One should not shy at the ultimate, even if involves suicide. Bushido came under the influence of Zen Buddhism, Confucianism, and Shintoism.

Bushmaster, large tropical American pit viper (*Lachesis muta*), which may grow up to 12 ft (4 m) long and feeds mainly on small mammals. It is light brown and has dark patterns on its back. Its long fangs and large venom glands make it dangerous to humans.

Business cycle, periodic fluctuation in the economy of an industrialized nation, between prosperity and recession or depression, with marked variations in growth rate and employment levels. Recession may be caused by overproduction, declining demand, changes in money supply, and general loss of confidence. Government interventions to moderate the cycle have become common in recent years.
See also: Economics.

Business law *See:* Law.

Bussotti, Sylvano (1931-), Italian composer. Due to the artistic and intellectual background of his family he was able to travel widely and to meet many celebrities from all movements in art. As a result, he occupied himself with the fusion of music and visual arts throughout his life. He is not only renowned as a composer, but also as a painter, film producer, film director, and writer. Theater works include: *Le passion*

selon Sade (1965), *Lorenzaccio* (1972), *Bergkristall* (ballet, 1974); instrumental/vocal: *Due voci* for a soprano, Ondes Martenot and orchestra (1958), *Torso* (1963), *Rara Requiem* (1970), *I semi di Gramsci* (1971), *Opus Cygne* (for orchestra, 1979); movies: *Rara* (1971) and *Apology* (1973).

Bustamante, Jean-Marc (1952-), French visual artist. From 1978 to 1982 he mainly produced photographs ('Tableaux') of landscapes on the edge of town. From 1982 to 1987 he worked together with Bernard Bazile under the name BAZILEBUSTAMANTE. Their work varies from photographs to objects that look like furniture. It is characterized by decorative elements, references to indoor architecture, and a highly perfect finish. Concepts such as art and decor, usefulness and uselessness, and conventional ideas are negated. Since 1987 Bustamante has produced plain sculptures that also refer to pieces of furniture. The focus is on the place, desire, nostalgia, and memory.

Bustard, any of Otididae family of large-bodied, strong-legged birds of the Old World and Australia, usually with drab plumage but sometimes with ornamental plumes on the head and neck. They feed on seeds, leaves, and small animals and prefer to run rather than fly. The great bustard is the size of a turkey. Bustards are scarce in many places, as they have been killed for food.

The great bustard (*Otis tarda*, family *Otididae*) is found on the plains and steppes of Eurasia and North Africa. It has a height of 3 ft (1 m) and a weight of 44 lbs (20 kg).

Butane and propane, odorless, colorless, flammable gases. These hydrocarbons (compounds of hydrogen and carbon) are found in natural gas and crude petroleum, and can be produced by cracking, a chemical process by which gasoline is derived from heavy oil. In their liquid form (referred to as LPG, or liquified petroleum gas), they are used as fuels for industry and for isolated homes.

Buthelezi, Gatsha Mangosuthu (1928-), South African politician and Zulu chief. Buthelezi opposed apartheid and the creation of black homelands. He is also leader of the influential Inkatha Freedom Party of the Zulus. At the end of the 1970s he opposed the more radical ANC. Several times during the mid 1980s there were violent outbursts between the various contending organizations, such as the UDF and the Inkatha movement. In 1989 Buthelezi joined the ANC again, and was enraged to be kept out of most of the negotiations over the political future of South Africa between the ANC and the South African government. At the very last moment Buthelezi and his Inkatha Freedom Party (IFP) decided to participate in the first general elections for all citizens in April 1994. Buthelezi was appointed minister of home affairs in a coalition government formed by ANC leader Nelson Mandela.

Butler, Nicholas Murray (1862-1947), U.S. educator. President of Columbia College (1902-1945), he expanded it into Columbia University. He was president of the Carnegie Endowment for International Peace (1925-1945) and, in 1931, shared the Nobel Peace Prize with Jane Addams. He also served as president of the American Academy of Arts and Letters (1928-1941).

Butler, Samuel (1835-1902), English novelist. He considered Darwinism too mechanistic and satirized it in *Erewhon* (1872), his version of utopia. His major work is *The Way of All Flesh* (1903), an autobiographical novel satirizing Victorian morality.

Butler, Samuel (1612-1680), English poet, author of *Hudibras* (1663-1678), a mock-heroic, anti-Puritan satire. He attacked the hypocrisy and pedantry of the Puritans of the Commonwealth.

Butor, Michel (1926-), French novelist and philosopher, one of the most important representatives of the Nouveau Roman ('new novel'). His works focus on the time during which man is always traveling. His oeuvre is characterized by detailed descriptions of minutiae that impel the reader to become fully aware of the fictional situation. His works include *Passage to Milan* (1954) and *Degrees* (1960). He subsequently stopped writing novels and mainly published essays.

Butter, dairy product made by churning milk or cream, containing fat, protein, and water. Made in some countries from the milk of goats, sheep, or yaks, it is most often made from cow's milk. Continuous mechanized production has been general since the 1940s. After skimming, the cream is ripened with a bacterial culture, pasteurized, cooled to 40°F (4°C), and then churned, causing the butterfat to separate from the liquid residue, buttermilk. The butter is then washed, worked, colored, and salted.

Buttercup, any of 300 species of flower (genus *Ranunculus*), native to temperate North America; especially the familiar gold flower of meadows and pastures. Buttercups have five-petaled flowers and deeply notched leaves that give them the alternative name of crow foot. The common buttercup has an acrid taste and can be poisonous to cattle.

The different stages in the life of a European swallowtail butterfly (*Papilio machaon*). The egg was laid on a milk parsley plant (1). After a while, the caterpillar hatches (2), it eats the leaves and develops to its full size (3). After three weeks, it attaches itself to a stalk by a silk thread (4). It then sheds its skin (5), revealing a bright green pupa, or chrysalis (6). An adult swallowtail finally emerges from the chrysalis after weeks of metamorphosis (7).

Butterfish, any of several fish of the family Stromateidae. They have mucous-coated slippery skins and live in temperate seas around the world. The most common U.S. butterfish, found along the Atlantic Coast, is also known as the dollarfish (*Poronotus triacanthus*).

Butterfly, flying insect of the order Lepidoptera (which also includes moths), characterized by wide, brightly colored wings. The butterfly undergoes metamorphosis (change in form) several times during its life. The egg grows into a larva called a caterpillar, which feeds on vegetation. During the next stage, the pupa, it does not feed, but is protected by a shell or cocoon while developing into the adult butterfly. Most species of butterflies are members of one of the main family groups: (1) skippers, (2) blues, coppers, and hairstreaks, (3) brush-foots, (4) sulphurs and whites, (5) metalmarks, (6) satyrs and wood nymphs, (7) swallowtail, (8) milkweed butterflies, and (9) snout butterflies. Although butterflies are found worldwide in a variety of climates, the greatest number of species are native to the tropical rainforests. Migratory butterflies such as the monarch may travel thousands of miles to reach warm winter habitats.

Butternut, or white walnut, tree (*Juglans cinerea*) of the walnut family. This decidu-ous tree with pale gray bark and ridged leaves grows in the eastern and southern United States. Its light brown wood produces fine furniture.
See also: Walnut.

Butterwort, insect-eating plant (genus *Pinguicula*) that grows in damp places in Eurasia and the Americas. The yellow or violet flower grows on a 2 in (5 cm) stalk surrounded by a rosette of light green fleshy leaves that lie flat against the ground. At the slightest pressure, such as the weight of an insect, glands on the upper surfaces of the leaves secrete a sticky fluid and the insect becomes trapped. The fluid also contains a digestive juice that breaks down the insect's body and allows nitrogenous products to be absorbed.
See also: Carnivorous plant.

Buttress *See:* Architecture.

Buxtehude, Dietrich (1637?-1707), German composer and organist, possibly born in Denmark. His cantatas, organ toccatas, and chorale preludes influenced J.S. Bach.

Buzzard, any of a group of medium-sized hawks of the family Accipitridae, identifiable by their soaring flight, widespread wings, and broad tail. They prey on small mammals by swooping from the air or from

B

B

The common buzzard (*B. buteo*) is perhaps the most frequently sighted bird of prey in Europe. It nests in woodlands but hunts small rodents, reptiles, and amphibians in open country.

a perch. In North America they are called hawks, 'buzzard' being applied to vultures.

Byblos (Hebrew: Gebal), major Phoenician trading and seaport dating back from ancient times. Since 4000 B.C. one of the oldest continuously inhabited towns in the world and from 2700 a center of contact between Egypt and Syria. Prospered between 2000 and 1500 when the export of cedar wood was of great importance. In 332 B.C. it was conquered by Alexander the Great. Excavation during the 20th century revealed temples (Astarte) and sarcophagii with Phoenician inscriptions. The Bible owes its name to Byblos.

Byelorussia *See:* Belarus.

Bypass operation, an operation in which a section of artery (vein) from the leg is bypassed along closed coronary arteries or blocked leg arteries. Nowadays synthetic tubing is also used.

Byrd, Richard Evelyn (1888-1957), U.S. aviator and pioneer of exploration and research in Antarctica. He led the air unit with D. B. MacMillan's 1925 Arctic expedition and, with Floyd Bennett, overflew the North Pole (1926). In 1929 he flew over the South Pole. Beginning as a Navy flier, he rose to the rank of Rear Admiral in 1930. He made 5 important expeditions to Antarctica (1928-1956), established the Antarctic base camp Little America, and spent the entire winter of 1933-1934 alone at an advance camp. He was in charge of the U.S. Antarctic program from 1955.
See also: Antarctica.

Byrd, William (1652-1704) and **William II** (1674-1744), colonial Virginian father and son. The father attained wealth and influence after developing farmlands at Westover, now Richmond, Virginia. The son, like his father, joined the House of Burgesses (1692) and became a member of the Council of State (1709). William II amassed an impressive library and produced diaries and journals that give a detailed picture of aristocratic life in colonial Virginia.

Byrd, William (1543-1623), English composer. His choral music includes the Great Service for the Anglican Church, Roman Catholic mass settings, and *Cantiones Sacrae* (1589; 1591). He also wrote keyboard music and madrigals. He was closely associated with Thomas Tallis, and in 1575 they were granted a joint monopoly for the printing and sale of music.

Byron, George Gordon Byron, 6th Baron (1788-1824), English poet, a leading figure of European Romanticism. Lameness and an unhappy childhood bred morbidity, a scorn for authority, and hatred for oppression. A disastrous marriage and the strictures of English society drove him into exile in Italy (1816). He later joined the Greek revolt against the Turks and died of fever at Missolonghi, Greece. *English Bards and Scotch Reviewers* (1809), a savage riposte to his critics, brought overnight fame, and the first two cantos of *Childe Harold's Pilgrimage* (1812) established his European reputation. The 'Byronic' hero of the poetic drama, *Manfred* (1817) became a great Romantic theme. Major works include the incomplete satiric epic *Don Juan* (1819-24) and *The Vision of Judgement* (1812), satirizing the poet laureate Robert Southey and King George III.
See also: Romanticism.

Byssinosis *See:* Brown lung.

Byzantine art and architecture, aesthetic style that arose in the city of Byzantium (Constantinople) after it became the capital of the Roman Empire (330 A.D.), under Constantine the Great. The term also may be applied to art and architecture heavily influenced by Byzantine forms, which spread to Italy, Greece, Russia, and much of the Middle East. The greatest monument of the early phase is the cathedral of Hagia Sophia (Santa Sophia), built 532-537 in Constantinople. Mosaics, the principal form of decoration in Byzantine churches, were highly developed during this period.
The minor arts, including ivory carving, silverwork, illuminated manuscripts, and textiles, became very sophisticated. Stylized naturalistic motifs and lavish decorative color were used.
The period after 1204 saw a second great flowering of Byzantine art, known as the Second Golden Age. In church building the favored type, initiated by Basil I, was a plan based on a circle inscribed in a square, a three-aisled plan with five domes, the largest one in the middle. The most famous example of this type is Saint Mark's Venice (11th-13th century). Manuscript illumination also flourished, the most famous example being the Paris Psalter.
Constantinople was sacked by the Crusaders in 1204, and during the next 2 centuries Byzantine art underwent profound changes. Fresco became the most important form of decoration; by the late 14th century mosaics had virtually disappeared. Work in the minor arts was generally of a lower quality. During this late period it was in the outlying areas of the former empire-Russia, Sicily, and the Balkans-that Byzantine art flourished. In 1453 Constantinople was conquered by the Turks, marking the end of the Byzantine state. The style of art and architecture, however, continued to flourish in Russia, Greece, and Bulgaria for several centuries.
See also: Byzantine Empire.

Byzantine Empire, historical term for the successor state to the Roman Empire in the East. Its capital was Constantinople (now Istanbul), founded by Constantine I in 330 at the site of the ancient Greek Byzantium. The heartlands of the empire were Asia Minor and the Balkans, but at its height it ruled

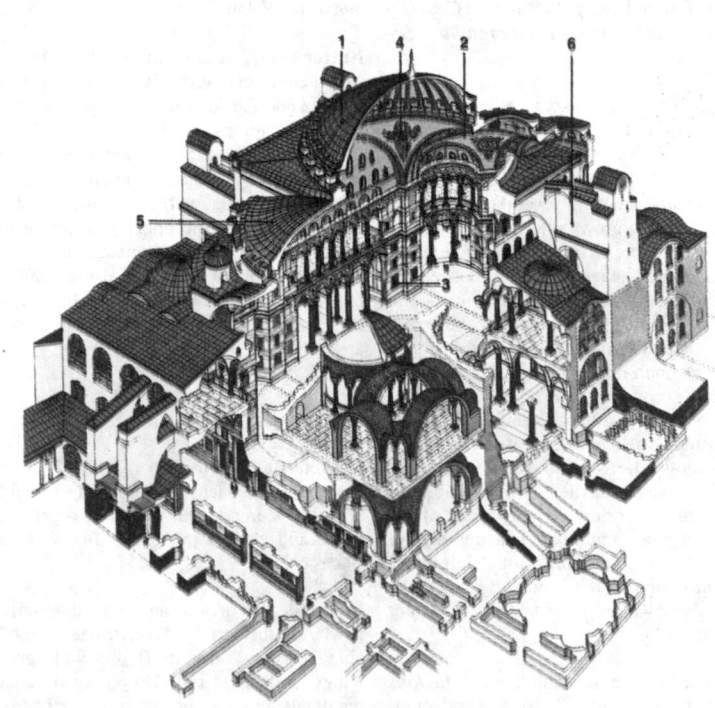

Hagia Sophia (532-37) in Istanbul, designed by Anthemius of Tralles and Isodorus of Miletus, incorporates: a huge central dome (1) supported by four large arches (2) that transfer the thrust to the main piers (3); pendentives (4), spherical triangles in the four corners that rise to the base of the circular dome; semidomes (5) flanking the main piers; buttresses (6) that absorb the dome's north and south thrust.

southern Spain, Italy, Sicily, northern Africa, Egypt, Syria, Palestine, the Crimean coast, Cyprus, and the Aegean islands. Its religion was Eastern Orthodox Christianity. Byzantine missionaries carried Christianity to Russia, and Byzantine theologians were among the chief Church Fathers.

The Roman Empire was divided after the death of Theodosius I in 395. By about 500 the Western Empire had fallen, Germanic invaders occupying Italy, Spain, and northern Africa. In the East, however, Roman institutions continued. However, after about 600, Roman institutions were replaced by typically Byzantine (Greek) ones. From the late seventh century onward, the Byzantine Empire was in frequent conflict both with the West and with the rising Muslim civilization in the East. Much of the empire's territory was lost, first to the Arabs, later to the Turks. The empire finally collapsed in 1453, when the Ottoman Turks captured Constantinople.

Byzantium *See:* Byzantine Empire; Istanbul.

C, third letter of the alphabet, derived from the letter *gimel* of the ancient Semitic alphabet and a rounded form of the Greek *gamma*. The Romans used *C* as an abbreviation for *Gaius*, and *Cn* for *Gnaeus* but also gave the letter a *k*-sound, which survives in modern English (*case, concrete,* etc.) *C* also has the 'soft' sound of *s*, as in *face* and *city*. When *C* is combined with the letter *H*, 2 further sounds may be represented (*church, loch*); the combination can also have the *K* sound (*ache, anchor, chronicle*). *C* can also be a superfluous letter, as in *thick*. In musical notation, *C* is a note of the scale. In chemistry, it is the symbol of the element *carbon*, in roman numbers, *C* = 100.

Cabal, secret group or organization engaged in intrigues; also applied to the intrigues themselves. The term was already used in the 17th century for a secret council of the king. The conduct of English king Charles II's ministers *C*lifford, *A*rlington, *B*uckingham, *A*shley, and *L*auderdale (whose initials spelled 'cabal') gave the word a sinister sense.

Cabala, or Kabbalah (Hebrew, 'tradition'), body of esoteric Jewish mystical doctrines dealing with the manifestations of and revelation of God. The Cabala attaches mystical significance to every detail in the Torah, the first 5 books of the Bible. Its chief books are the *Sefer Yezirah* (Book of Creation; 3rd-6th centuries) and the *Sefer HaZohar* (Book of Splendor; 13th century). The Cabala arose in France and Spain in the Middle Ages and was later a major influence on Hasidism.
See also: Hasidism.

Cabbage (*Brassica olearacea*), biennial vegetable from which other brassicas, such as kale, cauliflower, and broccoli, have been developed. The cabbage originated many centuries ago from the European wild cabbage. It has a characteristic tight 'head' of leaves. Cabbages can be boiled or pickled, or fermented in salt to give sauerkraut; also used as animal feed.

Cabbage palm, name used for various palm trees with edible leaf buds, especially, the palmetto (*Sabal palmetto*), a common fan palm ranging from North Carolina through Central America. It can grow up to 80 ft (24 m) and thrives in swampy country such as Florida everglades. The terminal buds and fruit are edible, the trunks can be used for fences and posts.
See also: Palm; Palmetto.

Cabell, (James) Branch (1879-1958), U.S. novelist, who combined an ironic, often antiromantic style with a strong element of fantasy in plots and settings. His best-known novel is *Jurgen* (1919).

Caber, trunk of a young tree, tossed in the Scottish sport of tossing the caber.

Cabeza de Vaca, Alvar Núñez (1490?-1557?), Spanish explorer. Shipwrecked off the coast of Texas and imprisoned by the Native Americans in 1528, he escaped and made his way to Mexico City (1530-1536). His account of southwestern United States, including descriptions of 'Seven Cities of Cíbola,' supposedly laden with riches, stirred Spanish interest in the area. He was made governor of Paraguay (1542-1544), but after a rebellion against him, he was recalled to Spain.

Cabinda (pop. 152,000), city and district in Angola. This coastal district, separated from the rest of Angola by the Congo River and Zaire, produces large quantities of oil. The city is an important seaport. When Angola fought for independence from Portugal (1961-1975), Cabinda fought unsuccessfully for its independence from Angola.
See also: Angola.

Cabinet, top-level advisory council to the head of state. Most countries have a cabinet which in principle is based on either the British cabinet or the American one. In the United States the cabinet is composed of the heads of the major executive departments. Normally the cabinet meets weekly with the president, though procedure varies. Members of the cabinet are individually appointed by and responsible to the president. They are not members of either house of Congress and may not address them, though they are often called to testify before committees. The British cabinet consists of those ministers who hold the most important portfolios and of some officials without responsibility. The prime minister chairs the meetings, the monarch does not attend. The ministers are responsible for the cabinet's policy.

Cable, electric, insulated conductor used to carry electric power or electric signals. A cable consists of a core conducting metal, usually of several wires twisted or stranded together, surrounded by insulating material. The conducting metal is usually copper, aluminum, or steel. The insulation is most often made of plastic or rubber. Multicore cables contain many cores, each insulated from the others, all contained inside a tube of plastic, rubber, copper, aluminum, or lead, which also serve to keep out moisture and heat. Telephone cables contain several thousand cores. Such cables run along the sea bed between the continents; however, satellite communications are replacing such long cables.

Electric power is distributed by power cables. Inside the home they carry electricity at low power (usually 110 volts). Electricity at high power is carried between cities by overhead cables slung from pylons. The cables do not need insulation around the cores

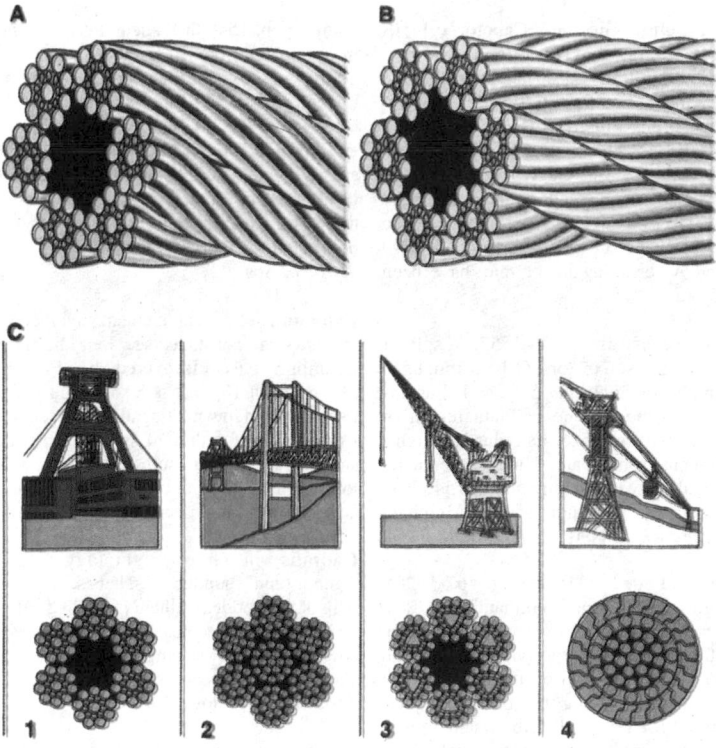

Wire cables are made from preformed wires, wound into strands and twisted together. Two common ways of winding wire rope are indicated by the lay of the rope. In lang lay (A), the wires in the strand and the strands themselves are laid in the same direction. In regular lay (B), the wires in the strand are laid in one direction and the completed strands are laid perpendicular to them. (C) Crosssections of typical cables:
1 Fibre core cable, for haulage and driver conveyors
2 Wire rope, for bridges and structural engineering
3 Steel core-triangular strand cable, for earth moving machinery
4 Locked coil cable, for aerial ropeways

C

as they are kept far enough apart for the air to act as an insulator and prevent sparking between them, but special glass or ceramic insulators are used to attach them to the pylons. Super-voltage power cables carrying currents at up to about 500,000 volts are usually buried underground and filled with oil or gas, such as nitrogen, to remove heat and increase insulation.

Radio, television, telephone, and other electronic equipment uses low-power signals with high frequencies, requiring a coaxial cable, which has a central core of wire surrounded by insulation, then a sheath of wire braid, and finally an insulating outer covering.

Cable, George Washington (1844-1925), U.S. author noted for his depiction of New Orleans and Creole life in works like *Old Creole Days* (1879) and *The Grandissimes* (1880).

Cable car, vehicle to carry passengers up steep gradients. The cable cars in San Francisco travel on rails like street cars, but they are pulled along by means of a continuous underground cable, to which the engineer can hook the car by pulling on a lever. Alpine cable cars are suspended from cables and usually operate on a funicular system, in which one car goes up a slope while another goes down, balancing each other, which demands much less power to operate.

Cable television, or CATV (community antenna television), broadcasting by means of coaxial cables rather than airwaves, used originally in areas where mountains or tall buildings made television reception poor or impossible, but now expanding throughout other areas because of the multiplicity of channels and programs it makes available. *See also:* Television.

Cabot, John (Giovanni Caboto; c.1450-c.1499), Italian navigator and explorer, probably the first European to reach the North American mainland. In 1497, after receiving permission from Henry VII to sail for England, Cabot sailed in search of a western route to Asia and reached the coasts of Nova Scotia and Newfoundland, where he planted the English and Venetian flags. On a second voyage (1498) Cabot may have reached America again, or may have been lost at sea.

Cabot, Sebastian (1476-1557), explorer and navigator, son of John Cabot. Appointed pilot-major of Spain in 1518, he led an expedition to the Rio de la Plata region of South America in 1526. Its failure led to his banishment from Spain. Though eventually reinstated, he went to England in 1548, and later became governor of the Merchant Adventurers Company.

Cabral, Pedro Alvares (1467-1520), Portuguese navigator. Commanding a fleet that was meant to sail from Lisbon to India, in 1500, Cabral went too far southwest and sighted Monte Pascoal on the east coast of Brazil. After exploring the coast and claiming Brazil for Portugal, Cabral sailed on to India, where he founded a small factory at the port of Calicut. Very little is known of his life after his return to Portugal in 1501.

Cacao (*Theobroma cacao*), tropical tree that produces cacao or cocoa beans. The raw material for chocolate is prepared by roasting, grinding, and pressing the dried seeds (or beans) from the woody cacao fruits. Pressing squeezes out cocoa butter and leaves a solid mass that is reground to make cocoa powder. The cacao tree has been cultivated since the time of the Aztecs, who used it for beverages and currency. Christopher Columbus introduced cocoa beans into Europe in 1502. *See also:* Chocolate.

Cactus, name for over 1,500 kinds of succulent prickly plant of the Cactaceae family nearly all native to America. Cacti are well adapted for desert life. They have no leaves, allowing them to conserve water. Photosynthesis takes place in the swollen stem, which may be 98% water and can swell to store the water collected by the long roots during rare desert showers. The spines that cover the stem may have 2 functions, protecting the cacti from being eaten and, where the spines form a dense mat, helping to retain moisture. The cacti produce flowers that may last for only a few hours, in some cases opening only at night. The flowers are pollinated by bees, moths, hummingbirds, and bats. Some cacti are edible. Cacti are grown for ornamental purposes and to form hedges. The peyote cactus is the natural source of the hallucinogenic drug mescaline.

Cadence, in musical harmony, successive chores that usually bring a passage of music to a close. One of the most common cadences consists of the chords traditionally sung to the word 'Amen' at the end of a hymn or psalm.

Cádiz (pop. 154,300), ancient city and port in southwest Spain, on the Atlantic coast northwest of Gibraltar. Founded by the Phoenicians in 1130 B.C. as Gadir, the city came under the rule of Carthage c.550 B.C. and became prosperous under Roman rule after 205 B.C. After the discovery of America it became important as the headquarters of the Spanish fleets. It is now a commercial port noted for sherry exports. *See also:* Spain.

Cadmium, chemical element, symbol Cd; for physical constants see Periodic Table. Cadmium was discovered by Friedrich Stromeyer in 1817. It is a soft, bluish-white metal, used in low melting alloys and solders. Compounds of cadmium are used in television tubes. Cadmium sulfide is used as a yellow pigment. Cadmium and its compounds are toxic and should be handled with care.

Cadmus, in Greek mythology, son of Agenor and founder of Thebes. With the help of the goddess Athena, he killed a dragon and sowed its teeth. Where the teeth were sown, soldiers sprang up and helped Cadmus build the city of Thebes. *See also:* Mythology; Thebes.

Caecilian, wormlike amphibian that lives in underground burrows. Caecilians are found in America, from Mexico southward, as well as Africa and Asia. The largest species grows to 4 ft (1.4 m).

Caedmon (7th century), illiterate herdsman, English poet who reputedly became a poet overnight after a stranger commanded him in a dream to 'sing of the beginning of created things.' Author of the Caedmon Hymn, he spent the rest of his life rendering Bible history into verse.

Caesar, (Gaius) Julius (c.100-44 B.C.), Roman general, politician, and writer. Although a member of the ancient patrician Julian clan, he supported the antisenatorial party. His early career through various public offices won him popularity, and in 60 B.C. he formed the First Triumvirate with Pompey, who supplied the army, and Marcus Licinius Crassus, who provided the money. With Caesar as consul they succeeded in controlling Roman politics. Caesar's successful Gallic Wars (58-51 B.C.) gained him great esteem and a loyal and well- trained army. After the death of Crassus, Pompey tried to force Caesar to lay down his command, but in 49 B.C. Caesar crossed the Rubicon River (the boundary between Caesar's Gaúl and Rome), and civil war began. Pompey was finally defeated at Pharsalus in 48 B.C., and by 45 B.C. Caesar had secured the defeat of all the Pompeian forces. In 44 B.C. he was made dictator for life, but on the Ides of March (March 15) he was murdered. *See also:* Rome, Ancient.

The Romans were masters of realistic portraits. They left us countless busts of their contemporaries, like this one of Julius Caesar, dating from the first century A.D., which can be found in the Museo Nazionale of Naples.

Caffeine, slightly bitter alkaloid used as a stimulant and diuretic and found in coffee, tea, cocoa, and other plants; poisonous when taken in large doses.

C

Cage, John (1912-1992), U.S. experimental composer and musical theoretician. He composed for 'prepared piano,' attaching objects to strings to alter tone and pitch and get percussive effects. Later work included prolonged silences, improvisation, aleatoric (chance) music, and electronic music.
See also: Aleatory music.

Cage, Nicolas (Nicolas Coppola; 1964-), American actor, cousin of film director Francis Ford Coppola. Cage made his debut on television in 1981. His first film was *Fast Times at Ridgemont High* (1982). In the 1980s he starred in movies such as *Rumble Fish* (1983), *The Cotton Club* (1984) and *Moonstruck* (1987). Thanks to David Lynch's *Wild at Heart* (1990), he became a star. In 1995 he received an Academy Award for his role as an alcoholic scriptwriter in Mike Figgis's *Leaving Las Vegas*. Cage developed from an offbeat actor to an action hero, due to high-adrenaline movies such as *Kiss of Death* (1995), *Face/Off* (1997), *Snake Eyes* (1998), *8 mm* (1998), *Gone in 60 Seconds* (2000) and *Windtalkers* (2002).

Cagney, James (1904-1986), U.S. film actor who played cocky, aggressive tough guys in such classic gangster movies as *The Public Enemy* (1931) and *The Roaring Twenties* (1939). He won an Academy Award for his portrayal of George M. Cohan in *Yankee Doodle Dandy* (1942).

Cahokia Mounds, group of prehistoric mounds, mostly in the form of truncated pyramids, near East St. Louis, Ill. The largest of these, Monks Mound, is about 1,200 ft (360 m) by 650 ft (200 m) at base and 100 ft (30 m) high, and is the largest mound in the United States. More than 300 of the mounds have in recent years been bulldozed to make way for agricultural and municipal expansion, but the 18 largest remain.

Cahow (*Pterodroma cahow*), bird in the petrel family (Procellariidae). This seabird, often referred to as the Bermuda petrel, was believed extinct for hundreds of years until its rediscovery in 1906. Cahows, of which there are only 100 or so alive today, are approximately 15 in (38 cm) long with dark tops and white undersides. They nest only in the Bermuda Islands.

Cain, in the Old Testament, eldest son of Adam and Eve (Gen. 4:1), a tiller of the ground. Because the offering of his brother Abel was accepted by God, and his own rejected, he murdered Abel, and was doomed to be a wandering fugitive. But God gave him a protective sign and promised sevenfold vengeance if he were slain. He built a city and named it Enoch for his son (Gen. 4:17).
See also: Old Testament.

Cain, James Mallahan (1892-1977), U.S. writer of crime novels admired for their accuracy of dialogue and characterization. His best-known works are *The Postman Always Rings Twice* (1934), *Serenade* (1937), *Mildred Pierce* (1941), and *Double Indemnity* (1943), which have been made into films.

Cairn terrier, breed of dog that originated in Scotland. Its name comes from its ability to dig under cairns (piles of stone) in order to hunt animals. It weighs 13-14 lb (5.9-6.4 kg). Its wiry topcoat is of various colors, but never white.

Cairo (Arabic: El Qahira; pop. 6,890,000), Egypt, the nation's capital and the largest city in Africa. It is one of the most densely populated cities in the world. Cairo is on the Nile River near the head of the delta, about 100 miles (160 km) south of the Mediterranean Sea. East of Cairo stretches the Eastern Desert, west of the city the Western Desert; both are part of the Sahara.

The Sphinx and the Pyramids of Giza are just southwest, beyond the Nile.

The Cairo area is Egypt's chief industrial and commercial center. Manufacturing plants, producing a great variety of industrial and consumer goods, are located mainly in the suburbs and other nearby cities, especially Helwan and Shubra el Kheima. In higher education, publishing, and filmmaking Cairo is the leading center in the Middle East. Tourism is an increasingly important part of the city's economy. Serving Cairo are an international airport, several railways, a subway, numerous roads and highways, and river craft on the Nile.

Cairo grew from three distinct settlements: Babylon, the Roman fort and settlement of the early Christian Era; the seventh-century Arab capital of El Fustat; and, most importantly, the walled Fatimid capital of El Qahira, founded in 969. The city prospered during the 200 years of Fatimid rule and especially under the Mamelukes, 1255-1517. Thereafter came almost two and one-half centuries of gradual decline under the Ottoman Turks.

In the 19th century Cairo recovered under Mohammed Ali, pasha of Egypt, and grew rapidly after the opening of the Suez Canal in 1869. In 1936, when Egypt became independent, Cairo became the national capital. Growth has been extremely rapid since the mid-20th century.

Most of Cairo lies on the eastern bank of the Nile; the rest occupies the western bank and several sizable islands in the river. Downtown Cairo is centrally located and extends eastward from the Nile. Found here in the modern section of the city are European-style buildings, broad boulevards, major government offices and public buildings, foreign embassies, and several large squares and gardens. Liberation Square and Ezbekiya Garden are among the more impressive places in the city. Nearby Gezira and Roda islands and part of the west bank are an integral part of the modern section of

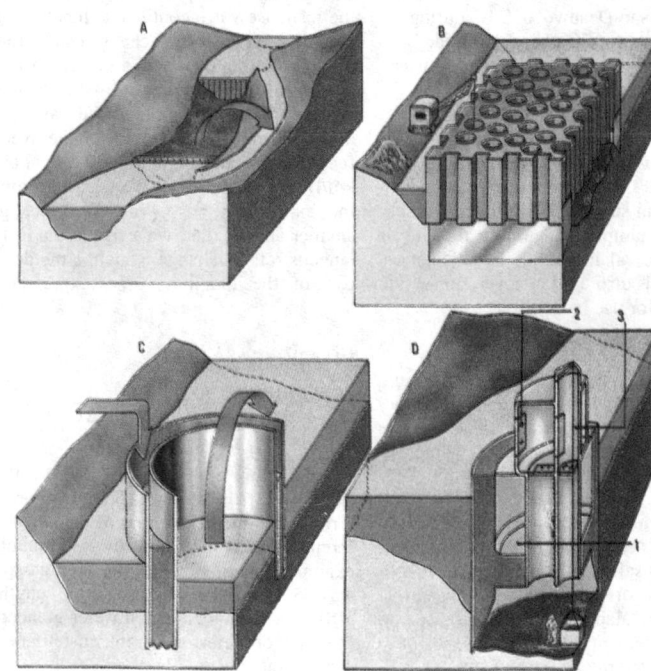

The simplest method of excavating foundations on a river bed, is to divert the river around two dams (A), thus exposing the bed. If the ground is soft, a heavy block (B) can be used. The block will sink, and can be excavated from the inside. In other cases, cofferdams (C) are used to pump the river bed dry. If the river flow is strong, two concentric cofferdams can be used, the annular space filled with concrete to provide rigidity. When the bed is very hard, a pneumatic caisson is used (D). Air under pressure will be pumped into the space below the deck (1) to prevent water from seeping under the cutting edge. The access for the working crew is gained through an airlock (2), the exit for the excavated material through another one (3).

Cairo. The better residential areas, large parks, sports facilities, and cultural institutions are here.

The old Muslim quarter, sometimes called Old Town, occupies much of eastern Cairo and centers on the walled area developed by the Fatimids and Mamelukes, beginning in the 10th century A.D. Streets are often narrow and winding; many are cobbled or unpaved. Congestion and overcrowding are common throughout the quarter. Along the eastern fringe are some of Cairo's worst slums. Landmarks in the Muslim quarter include the Citadel, a stronghold begun by Saladin in the 1170's; many historic mosques; and the bustling Bazaar, where diverse handicraft items and other goods have been sold for centuries. El Azhar University, founded in the 10th century as an integral part of El Azhar Mosque (970), is the oldest Muslim university in the world and one of Islam's chief theological schools. Cairo University (1908) and Ain Shams University (1950) are two of the largest universities in Egypt.

Old Cairo, in the southernmost part of the city, is an ancient section with ruins of a Roman fort and settlement called Babylon. Many Copts live in this part of Cairo, making it the chief Christian quarter. Nearby are the remains of Cairo's first Arab settlement, El Fustat.

Cairo's Egyptian Museum houses the world's finest collection of Egyptian antiquities, including the treasures of Tutankhamen. In the Museum of Islamic Art are masterpieces from throughout the Islamic world. Notable too are the Coptic Museum and the Museum of Modern Art.

In Ramses Square, in front of the central railway station, stands a giant, ancient statue of Ramses II, brought to Cairo from Memphis in 1955. The 19th-century Abdin Palace, part of which is preserved as a museum, is the residence of the president of Egypt. On Gezira Island, overlooking the Nile and the downtown area, is the Cairo Tower, which rises 614 feet (187 m) and is topped by an observatory.

A major earthquake struck the Cairo area in 1992. More than 425 people perished and many ancient monuments were damaged.
See also: Egypt.

Caisson, concrete or steel box, open at both ends, used in civil engineering when excavation or construction must be carried out underwater, particularly in sinking foundations for bridges. Caissons are sunk in the re-

An agglomeration of calcite crystals.

quired position and built up to keep the top above water. As the soil is dredged from the bottom, the caisson sinks. It is eventually filled with concrete and acts as part of the foundation of the bridge. Sometimes a pressurized, watertight chamber is built at the bottom of the caisson for workers.

Caisson disease *See:* Bends.

Cajuns (from 'Acadian'), descendants of expatriate French-Canadians, living in Louisiana. Cajuns were deported from Acadia (Nova Scotia) by the British in 1755. They have a distinctive patois: a combination of archaic French forms with English, Spanish, German, Native American, and African American idioms.
See also: Acadia.

Calabash (*Crescentia cujete*), tree of tropical America, the woody shell of whose gourdlike fruit is used as a waterproof container. The flowers of calabash trees grow close to the trunk and main limbs, not on the tips of the branches among the leaves. They are pollinated by nectar-drinking bats and develop into 12 in (30 cm) pulpy fruit.

Caladium, genus of tropical American plant in the Arum family *(Aracaea)*. Its large, arrow-shaped leaves have vividly colored markings. Caladiums are grown commercially as houseplants.

Calais (pop. 75,800), French seaport on the Pas de Calais (Strait of Dover), 170 mi (274 km) from Paris and 21 mi (34 km) from Dover. Calais is an important port, and the center of heavy passenger traffic between England and continental Europe. The city has fishing industries and textile and paper manufacturing.
See also: France.

Calamity Jane (Martha Jane Canary Burk; 1852-1903), frontier-town prostitute and campfollower who roamed the West in male garb. Famous in Deadwood, S.D., during the 1870s gold boom, she claimed she had been an army scout, a pony express rider, Custer's aide, and Wild Bill Hickok's mistress.

Calcination, process of heating used in chemistry and industry to convert salts containing oxides and to remove volatile constituents from substances. In making quicklime, for example, calcium carbonate is changed into calcium oxide by calcination. Calcination is also used to covert bones into phosphates for use in fertilizer.
See also: Chemistry.

Calcite, soft mineral, consisting of calcium carbonate ($CaCO_3$), found mainly in limestone. Most stalagmites and stalactites are made of calcite. Calcite is usually white, but impurities may give it other colors. Very pure calcite, such as Iceland spar, is often transparent and causes double refraction, so that objects seen through it appear double, making it useful in some optical instruments. Other forms of calcite include marble and Oriental alabaster. Calcite is used to make lime, cement, and fertilizers.
See also: Calcium carbonate; Lime.

Calcium, chemical element, symbol Ca; for physical constants see Periodic Table. It was first isolated in 1808 by Sir Humphry Davy. A member of the alkaline earth group, calcium is the fifth most abundant element in the earth's crust, occurring in numerous compounds. It is an essential constituent of plants and animals, neccessary for building bones and teeth.

Calcium carbide, crystalline compound (CaC_2) made from calcium and carbon. Produced by heating lime and coke, it is used in the manufacture of fertilizers and acetylene, a gas used to cut or weld metals.
See also: Acetylene.

Calcium carbonate, mineral ($CaCO_3$) abundant in nature. Limestone, marble, coral, calcite, and chalk have calcium carbonate as a main ingredient. Calcium carbonate is used in toothpaste, tooth powder, and stomach medicine. Stalactites and stalagmites that form in caves are made from water that deposited this white, crystalline mineral.
See also: Calcite; Chalk.

Calculator, mechanical or electronic machine for performing numerical calculations. Calculators have number keys (0 through 9) and additional keys for computing mathematical equations or functions, which are then displayed on a small screen. Calculators, first made available in the early 1960s, were miniaturized and marketed for consumers during the 1970s.

Calculus, branch of mathematics dealing with calculating rates of change (differential calculus) and determining functions from information about their rate of change (integral calculus).

Differential calculus is used to calculate accelerations, velocities, slopes of curves, and maximum and minimum values, based on experimental or theoretical relationships expressed as continuous equations. If a relationship can be expressed as $y = f(x)$, where the response y is a continuous function of x, then the average rate of change can be found by determining the change in $y(\Delta y = y_2 - y_1 = f(x_2) - f(x_1))$ and dividing it by the change in $x(\Delta x = x_2 - x_1)$. The average speed traveling in a car, 55 mph (88.5 kmph), or the average fuel efficiency during a trip, 30 mi/gal (12.8 km/l), are examples. If we take the limit of the expression $\Delta y / \Delta x$ as $\Delta x = x_2 - x_1$ gets smaller and smaller, we arrive at the instantaneous rate of change, which is the derivative of the function $y = f(x)$ expressed as

$$f'(x) = \frac{dy}{dx}:$$

$$f'(x) = \frac{dy}{dx} = \lim_{x_1 \to x_2} \frac{y_2 - y_1}{x_2 - x_1} = \lim_{\Delta x \to 0} \frac{\Delta y}{\Delta x}$$

'the derivative of the function $y = f(x)$ with respect to x.' The symbol dy and dx are referred to as the differential of y and the differential of x respectively. In the automobile example above, although the average speed was 55 mph (88.5 kmph) over the length of a trip, each moment the traveler glanced at the speedometer different instantaneous speeds (rates) were observed.

When the derivative of a function $f'(x)$ is known, the function itself can be determined. This process of finding the *antiderivative* is done with integral calculus. Just as differential calculus is concerned with changes and differences, integral calculus is concerned with summations. Rearranging the expression above, $dy = f'(x)dx$. Summing each side of this equation over a range gives the expression:

$$y = \int_a^b f'(x) \ dx$$

read 'y is the integral of f prime of x with respect to x.' The elongated s stands for 'sum' and is the symbol for integration. The range of summation indicated is from $x = a$ to $x = b$ and takes place over tiny intervals of x, dx. Integration is used to find lengths of curves, areas bounded by curves, volumes enclosed by surfaces, and centers of gravity of attracting bodies.

Many 17th-century mathematicians, astronomers, and physicists contributed to the development of calculus, predominant developers were Isaac Newton and Gottfried Wilhelm Leibniz .
See also: Newton, Sir Isaac; Leibniz, Gottfried Wilhelm von.

Calcutta (pop. 4.4 million), capital of West Bengal state, the leading transportation, industrial, financial, and commercial center of eastern India, and the largest city in India, situated on the Houghly River, in the Ganges delta, 80 mi (130 km) north of the Bay of Bengal. Calcutta is accessible to oceangoing vessels and has road and rail links with the whole of northern India, and an international airport. Calcutta was founded as a permanent settlement by the British East India Company in 1690. In 1756 the British were driven out by the nawab of Bengal, at the time of the infamous Black Hole of Calcutta incident. Robert Clive recaptured the town in 1757, and the British became virtual

More than half a million people leaving the Maidan in Calcutta, where they have attended a political meeting.

rulers of Bengal. In 1834 Calcutta became the capital of the British India empire. By 1900 it was the center of a strong nationalist movement, and the developing unrest continued. The capital of India was transferred to Delhi in 1912, but Calcutta's commercial importance continued to grow.With the partition of India in 1947, Calcutta lost most of its jute-producing hinterland to Pakistan, and was faced with an influx of thousands of Hindu refugees. The city has often been the scene of religious and political strife. In spite of the overcrowding and poverty, Calcutta has continued its development as a commercial city and a vitally important port. Among the principal exports are tea, jute, iron, manganese, and mica. Calcutta's factories produce iron and steel, textiles, shoes, rubber, leather, glass, and cement.
See also: India.

Calder, Alexander (1898-1976), U.S. abstract sculptor and creator of the mobile. His mobiles consist of flat metal shapes connected by rods, wire, or string, which are hung or balanced and moved by motors or by air currents.

Calderón de la Barca, Pedro (1600-1681), Spanish playwright and poet. He and Lope de Vega were the leading dramatists of Spain's Golden Age. He wrote over 200 plays, distinguished by their heightened style and poetic symbolism, many on religious themes. Among his most famous works are *The Constant Prince* (1629), *Life Is a Dream* (1635), and *The Surgeon of His Honor* (1635).

Caldwell, Erskine Preston (1903-1987), U.S. author noted for his portrayal of poor Southern whites in short stories and novels such as *Tobacco Road* (1932), *God's Little Acre* (1933), and *Trouble in July* (1940).

Caledonia, ancient Roman name for what is now Scotland. The area was invaded by Agricola, a Roman general, in A.D. 83. Roman artifacts have been found in present-day Scotland. Caledonia is still used as a poetic name for Scotland.
See also: Scotland.

Calendar, method of reckoning days and months of the year. The earliest calendars were based upon the phases of the moon. The first day of each month was the day of the new moon. When the moon had gone through its cycle of phases 12 times, a year was said to have passed. Unfortunately, the moon takes about 29 days to go through its phases, and consequently 12 lunar months (354 days, 8 hrs, 48 min) are 11 days short of a full year. Only by adding an extra month every 3 years or so could the calendar be kept roughly in line with the seasons. The Jewish and Muslim calendars are lunar calendars. The ancient Egyptians used a solar calendar with 12 months of 30 days each and added 5 feast days at the end of the year, making it one of the most accurate early calendars. But the length of the solar year is about 365 days, so that the Egyptian calendar got 1 day out of step with the seasons every 4 years. The Roman calendar, originally contained only 10 months and began

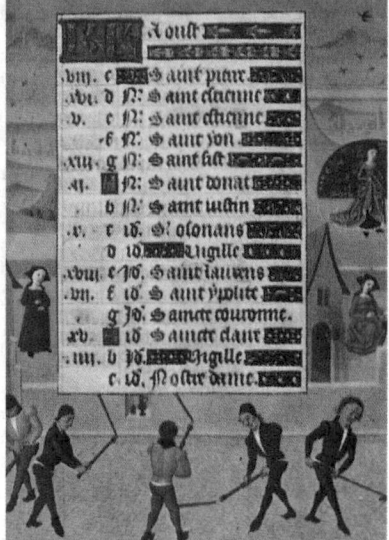

A page, containing a saints' calender, from the Breviary of the Duchess of Burgundy (around 1450). The calender shows half of the month of August, with the activities of that period (threshing), and the `mark' (the sign of Virgo). The Roman numerals at the left, refer to the calculation of the phases of the moon, the figures in the next column indicate the Sundays of that year, and the third column corresponds to the Roman calender.

with March. Later January and February were added to the end of the year, and the months received their odd numbers of days in an attempt to fit every day of the year into months of roughly equal length. In 46 B.C. Julius Caesar reformed the calendar, making January the first month and adding a leap year day to February in every fourth year to prevent the calendar from getting out of step. This system, the Julian calendar, continued to be used in Europe for over 1,500 years. Because a year is not exactly 365 days long, but slightly shorter (365 days, 5 hrs, 48 min, 46 sec), adding an extra day every 4 years proved too much. By the 16th century the calendar was 10 days out of step with the seasons. Pope Gregory VIII decided that Thursday, Oct. 4, 1582, would be followed by Friday, Oct. 15, thus wiping out the error. To prevent a recurrence, he ruled that a century year could be a leap year only if divisible by 400. The Gregorian, or New Style, calendar, though not perfect, is adequate for most practical purposes and is the calendar in widest use today.

Calendula, or pot marigold (*Calendula officinalis*), annual plant. Infusions of the leaves and yellow flowers are used medicinally for gastrointestinal problems, fever, abscesses, and vomiting.

Calgary (pop. 882,000), city in southern Alberta, Canada, at the junction of the Bow and Elbow rivers, at a height of 3,438 ft (1,048 m). Its name is Gaelic for 'clear running water.' Founded as a Northwest Mounted Police fort in 1875, it is a center of grain and livestock marketing, located in a good farming and ranch region. Related industries are milling and meatpacking.

C

Nearby coal, oil, and gas have resulted in a rapid expansion of the city. The city is famous for the annual Calgary Stampede, a 10-day rodeo that attracts cowboys from all over North America.
See also: Alberta.

Cali (pop. 1,9 mln), Colombia, the capital of Valle del Cauca department. It lies on the Cauca River, about 180 mi (290 km) southwest of Bogotá, the national capital. Cali is the center of manufacturing, commerce, and transportation for the Cauca Valley, a fertile farming region, and for much of Colombia. Products include processed foods, clothing, chemicals, construction materials, and tires. Two universities are in the city. Cali was founded in 1536. It remained small until the early 1900's, when railway linkage with the Pacific port of Buenaventura prompted its development.

California (Golden State; pop. 32,200,000), state in the U.S. on the Pacific Ocean; 158,767 sq mi (411,049 sq km), the most populous state (since 1962) of the U.S. Capital: Sacramento.

A fragment of the Egyptian Book of the Dead, written on papyrus in hieroglyphs.

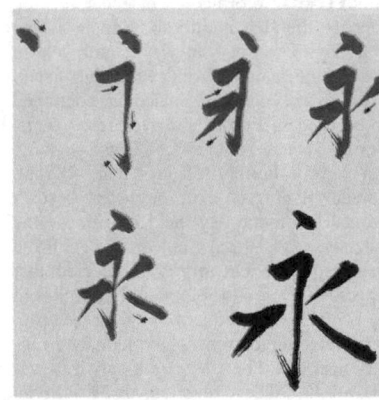

Generally accepted theory breaks Chinese characters down into eight basic strokes, all of which are to be found in the character 'yung', meaning 'eternity', which you can see in this diagram. Supposedly, Wang Hsi-chih, the celebrated fourth-century calligrapher, took fifteen years to perfect this character. The eight strokes composing 'yung' are basic to most exercises in calligraphy. Each character has its

correct sequence of strokes, which is generally from top to bottom, and from left to right. The diagram shows the sequence

of strokes by which the character 'yung' evolves. The arrows indicate the direction of the brushstroke.

An example of the work of Dutch calligrapher Jan I van de Velde (1568-1623).

The landscape is dominated by two mountain ranges: the Coastal Range and the Sierra Nevada (highest peak is Mt. Whitney, 14,495 ft (4,418 m) with the fertile Central Valley between them. The Death Valley desert, at 282 ft (86 m) below sea level, lies in the southeast and is the lowest-lying point on the continent. Predominantly subtropical climate.
Agriculture and mining are traditionally important, followed by rapid industrialization in the 20th century. No other state in the United States produces as many agricultural products. The most important include fruit, vegetables, potatoes, cotton, rice, and wine. Forestry (10% of the national timber production), fishing (4%), cattle-breeding and poultry-breeding. California is the United States' largest producer of petroleum, after Texas and Louisiana; other resources of which large quantities are found include natural gas, gold, mercury, lead, and salt. The main harbors are San Francisco and Los Angeles. Aircraft industry, electronics, food and chemical industry. Tourism and the film industry are important sources of revenue as well.
California entered the Union as the 31st state in 1850 after gold was discovered in 1848. Over one hundred Indian tribes originally lived here, all of which were hunters/gatherers, except for the Mojave and Yuma tribes who were farmers.
The name was given to the Mexican peninsula of Baja California by the Spanish conqueror Hernán Cortés and is derived from a Spanish mythological island. The Spaniards first came upon the area at the beginning of the 16th century, but it took until 1769 before they built settlements, missionary posts, and forts. The area was Mexican territory from 1822 to 1846, after which time it was conquered by the United States. The transcontinental railroad was completed in 1879. San Francisco was the largest city on the West Coast in 1890, and California accounted for a quarter of the global petroleum production in 1925. The population tripled between 1950 and 1990. The favourable climate and an abundance of military research institutions resulted in the rapid development of sophisticated technological industries following World War II, particularly in and around Silicon Valley.

California, University of, large U.S. state university system, founded 1868. It is housed on 9 campuses (Berkeley, Davis, Irvine, Los Angeles, San Francisco, Riverside, San Diego, Santa Barbara, Santa Cruz). It comprises a library with more than 10 million items, the Lawrence Radiation Laboratory, the Scripps Institute of Oceanography at La Jolla, and the Lick Observatory at Mt. Hamilton.
See also: California.

Californium, chemical element, symbol Cf; for physical constants see Periodic Table. Californium is a radioactive element that does not occur naturally. It was produced in 1950 by Glenn Seaborg and others, by bombarding curium-242 with helium ions in a cyclotron. Californium is metallic, a member of the actinide series. It is produced in nuclear reactors and is a source of neutrons.

Caligula (Gaius Caesar; A.D. 12-41), nickname (meaning 'little boots') of cruel and despotic Roman emperor (37-41). He believed he was a god. His demands that his statue be erected in Jerusalem's temple almost precipitated a revolt in Palestine.
See also: Rome, Ancient.

Calla, plant of genus *Calla* or *Zantedeschia* of the arum family *(Araceae).* Genus *Calla* includes water plants such as the arum lily of North America(*C. palustris*). Plants of genus *Zantedeschia* have showy white, yellow, or pink funnel-shaped leaves (spathes) that look like flowers. The white calla lily (*Z. aethiopica*), golden calla lily (*Z. elliottiana*), and red calla lily (*Z. rehmannii*) are found in South Africa.
See also: Arum.

Callaghan, (Leonard) James (1912-), prime minister of the United Kingdom 1976-1979. He was elected Labour party leader on the resignation of Harold Wilson and became prime minister immediately. Labour lost the 1979 general election to Margaret Thatcher's Conservatives.
See also: United Kingdom.

Callaghan, Morley Edward (1903-1990), Canadian novelist and short story writer influenced by the style of Ernest Hemingway. His books include the novel *They Shall Inherit the Earth* (1935) and a memoir, *That Summer in Paris* (1963).

Callao (pop. 590,000), Peruvian seaport located 8 mi (13 km) west of the capital city of Lima. As Peru's chief seaport, most of this nation's imports and exports pass through its harbor. The city, which is part of Peru's largest metropolitan area, has survived major earthquakes, tidal waves, and foreign attacks since its founding by Spaniards (1537).
See also: Peru.

Callas, Maria (Maria Kalogeropoulos; 1923-1977), leading Greek-American operatic soprano. She was famous for her expressive phrasing and acting ability in a wide variety of roles.
See also: Opera.

Calligraphy, art of penmanship. Combining beauty with legibility, it developed in the Far East, where it was a recognized art form as early as 250 B.C. In early medieval Europe calligraphy was practiced in monastic communities, which developed the Carolingian and Insular scripts. A high point was reached with the Book of Kells and the Lindisfarne gospels. The Italian Renaissance manuscripts provided models for the first printed books and for roman and italic types. Edward Johnston (1872-1944) and his pupil Graily Hewitt (1864-1952) began the modern revival of calligraphy in the early 1900s.

Calliope, keyboard instrument dating from 1855 and much used in circuses and amusement parks. The original version was operated by steam forced through whistles controlled by a keyboard, but later models have used compressed air.

C

Calms, Regions of, areas characterized by little or no wind. They include *horse latitudes*, *subpolar regions*, and the equatorial *doldrums*. Horse latitudes lie between 30 degrees north latitude and 30 degrees south. The calms of Cancer and of Capricorn both fall within the horse latitudes. Calms in the subpolar regions are caused by the sinking of the cold air over the North and South poles, which forms high-pressure centers. In the equatorial doldrums, air masses are forced upwards after being heated in the tropics, causing a belt of low pressure to form.
See also: Doldrums; Horse latitudes.

Calorie, amount of heat required to raise the temperature of one gram of water one centigrade degree (more precisely, from 14.5C to 15.5C). One kilocalorie is the amount of heat required to raise 1 kg of water through 1 centigrade degree and is therefore equal to 1,000 calories. The calorific value of foods is actually a measure of the number of kilocalories that can be obtained by the body, in the form of energy, when the foods are broken down.
See also: British thermal unit.

Calvary, or Golgotha, Jerusalem hill site of the crucifixion of Jesus. It is traditionally accepted to be the hill on which Constantine founded the church of the Holy Sepulcher in the 4th century.

Calvin, John (1509-1564), French theologian. After a 'sudden conversion' in 1533, Calvin became a leader of the Protestant Reformation, eventually systematizing his ideas with those of other reformers. His *Institutes of the Christian Religion* (1536) is one of the most important religious works ever written. Calvin's theology, which rejected the authority of the pope, focused on the faith of the individual and study of the Bible. Calvin also believed in predestination, the idea that God preordains some souls for salvation and others for damnation. His church organization became the model for Presbyterianism and the Reformed Churches. Calvin was active in politics, in 1541 establishing in Geneva a government based on his theology. The academy that he founded in 1559 later became the University of Geneva.
See also: Calvinism; Reformation.

Calvin, Melvin (1911-), U.S. biochemist who won the 1961 Nobel Prize for chemistry, having led the team that unraveled the details of the chemistry of photosynthesis.
See also: Calvin, John; Chemistry.

Calvinism, Protestant doctrine formulated by John Calvin and stated chiefly in his *Institutes of the Christian Religion* (1536). Its basic tenets are that God is omnipotent; His will is supreme and governs all actions; each person's life is predestined, the salvation or damnation of each soul determined by God before creation; God's elect will be saved and given eternal life, and those He has damned can find no release (justification) from the consequences of their sins except by dedicating themselves to His service. The strict Calvinist maintains that God

sees humankind as loathsome and corrupt, with feeble delusions of virtue and worth. Calvinism preaches that the Bible is the only source of God's laws and refers more often to the Old Testament than the New, emphasizing the judgment of sinners more than the love and compassion of God.

Calvino, Italo (1923-1985), Italian writer notable for his use of fantasy. Calvino has written in several genres, including science fiction and historical allegory, but he received his greatest acclaim for *Italian Folktales* (1956) and the experimental *If on a Winter's Night a Traveler* (1979; trans. 1981).

Calypso, West Indies musical style notable for its lyrics, which are usually improvised and often humorous or ironic. The music is typically played on steel drums, which carry the tune as well as provide the beat.

Cambodia

Capital:	Phnom Penh
Area:	69,898 sq mi
	(181,035 sq km)
Population:	12,775,000
Language:	Khmer
Government:	Constitutional monarchy
Independent:	1953
Head of gov.:	Prime minister
Per capita:	US$ 1,500
Monetary unit:	1 Riel = 100 sen

Cambodia (formerly Kampuchea) republic in Southeast Asia, bordered on the north by Thailand and Laos, on the east and southeast by Vietnam, on the southwest by the Gulf of Siam, and on the west and northwest by Thailand. The capital is Phnom Penh.
Land and climate. Mainly a broad plain, Cambodia occupies 69,898 sq mi (181,035 sq km), and is separated from Thailand by the Dangrek Mountains in the north and the Cardamom Mountains in the west. The Mekong, one of the most important rivers in southern Asia, enters Cambodia from Laos and crosses the country from north to south. A large, shallow lake, the Tônlé Sap, occupies central Cambodia. Annual inundations caused by the overflow of the Mekong River create excellent conditions for rice cultivation. The climate is tropical and humid, with

a rainy season lasting from May to Oct. Rainfall is plentiful, reaching as high as 250 in (635 cm) per year in the Cardamom Mountains. Temperatures range from 68° to 97°F (20° to 36°C).
Wildlife is abundant, particularly in the forests, and includes elephants, water buffaloes, tigers, leopards, honey bears, crocodiles, and snakes. Elephants are often domesticated. There are abundant freshwater fish. Plant life is also rich. The country produces tropical hardwood trees, as well as rubber, coconut, mango, orange, banana, and kapok trees.
People. About 90% are Khmers. The Chinese and Vietnamese are minorities and there are Chams, Europeans, Indians, Thai, and primitive tribes. The modern official language is Khmer, spoken by about 60% of the population, and French is used by a sizable minority. Numerous other languages are found among the hill peoples. Theravada Buddhism is practiced, and most Cambodian males spend at least a short time in Buddhist monasteries, many of which are also educational establishments. There are several technical schools, and the Buddhist University and the former Royal Khmer University are located in Phnom Penh. The literacy rate is about 40%.
Located at the confluence of the Mekong and Tônlé Sap rivers, Phnom Penh is the principal city of the country. Other towns are generally much less than 50,000 in population. The majority of Khmers live in villages in the Mekong and Tônlé Sap basins. Their houses, often of bamboo and thatch, are built on stilts in preparation for the rainy season. Most Cambodians are skilled in art, music, and dancing, and their many temples are elaborately carved.
Economy. Small and often primitive rice farms on the plains around the Tônlé Sap are the basis of Cambodia's economy. Rice is the most important export product. Rubber is the second most important. In addition, corn, livestock, sugar, pepper, tobacco, cotton, coffee, and soybeans are raised. Deep-sea fishing in the Gulf of Siam is an important commercial activity, while the Tônlé Sap and the Mekong rivers provide one of the greatest concentration of freshwater fish in southeast Asia. The extensive forests are largely untouched and, because of transport problems, high-grade iron ore deposits in the north are also unexploited.

Houses in this village along the Mekong River, like many throughout Cambodia, are supported on stilts several feet above the water. These villages permit farmers to maximalize cultivable land for rice, the nation's staple food crop, on fertile riverbank property.

C

History. Mythology claims that the country was founded by a Hindu king, Kambu, who gave the country the name Kambuja. In the 1st century A.D., Hindu people established the flourishing kingdom of Funan, which ruled large areas. Toward the end of the 6th century, the territory was split up among rival groups. The most powerful of these, the Khmer, founded the great Angkor Dynasty between 800 and 850. This Khmer kingdom reached its greatest power about 1100 and attained a high level of civilization. Much of Thailand, Laos, and Vietnam were part of the Khmer empire, which began its decline in the late 14th century. By the middle of the 19th century the country was approximately its present size and in 1863, to prevent its complete conquest, King Norodom asked for the protection of the French. In 1887, Cambodia became part of the French Union of Indochina.

In the 1930s, a Cambodian nationalist movement gained strength and by 1940 anti-French feeling was running high. In 1953 Cambodia achieved full independence. Norodom Sihanouk became prime minister after the elections of 1955 and remained so for 5 years. In 1960 Sihanouk was made head of state, without the title of king. A member of the United Nations since 1955, Cambodia proclaimed a policy of neutrality. Aid from both communist and Western countries was used to develop the economy: to build roads, air-transport facilities, and irrigation systems. In 1963, Sihanouk refused further economic and military aid from the United States, and in 1965 diplomatic relations were broken off. The military coup d'etat of 1970, when Sihanouk was deposed in his absence, together with incursions of North Vietnamese troops, precipitated internal crises. General Lon Nol established a military government (the Khmer Republic) in Phnom Penh, but the new and inexperienced Cambodian army proved a poor match for the Vietcong. U.S. and South Vietnamese forces crossed the border to clear out enemy 'sanctuaries' in April 1970, but American troops soon withdrew.

The Cambodian communists (Khmer Rouge) emerged in 1970 as a powerful political group. In alliance with the Khmer Rouge, Sihanouk formed an exile government in Peking. Civil war raged between Lon Nol's government forces and the Khmer Rouge, who were gaining control of the country despite intensive U.S. bombing. In Apr. 1975 Phnom Penh was besieged and surrendered to the Khmer Rouge. 'The Royal Government of the National Union of Cambodia (Kampuchea)' returned from exile under Sihanouk. Following the resignation of Sihanouk in 1976, Pol Pot became prime minister of the newly named Democratic Kampuchea. The regime enacted harsh measures, evacuating all cities and suppressing opposition. Hundreds of thousands of people died or were killed. In 1978 Vietnam launched attacks against Kampuchea, and in 1979 Vietnamese troops captured Phnom Penh and proclaimed the People's Republic of Kampuchea. Pol Pot, as commander-in-chief of the Khmer Rouge forces, continued to fight the Vietnamese from unoccupied parts of the country. In 1983, Vietnam launched major offensives against the rebel forces and by Feb. 1985 had overrun all Khmer Rouge bases. In 1989 the Vietnamese forces withdrew and the name Kampuchea was changed into Cambodia.

The U.N. established a preliminary government in 1991, which prepared free elections to be held in 1993, combined with the restauration of the monarchy. Sihanouk became King, and his son Ranarridh and Hun Sen were installed as co-prime ministers. In 1997 however, Ranarridh was deposed by Hun Sen. In July 1998, parliamentary elections were held that were won by Hun Sen, although the results were disputed by the opposition. Meanwhile, with the desertion of Khmer Rouge leader Yeng Sary to the army and the death of another Khmer leader, Pol Pot, in 1998, the power of Khmer Rouge rapidly diminished. In 1999 Cambodia joined ASEAN.

At the beginning of 2003, negotiations with the UN were resumed in order to establish an international tribunal to try the war crimes committed by the Khmer Rouge.

Cambrian, earliest period of the Paleozoic Era, dated roughly 570-500 million years ago, immediately preceding the Ordovician period. Cambrian rocks contain the oldest fossils that can be used for dating.
See also: Paleozoic.

Cambridge (pop. 100,000), English market town, 51 mi (32 km) from London, and home of the Cambridge University. The town grew up in the 9th century at a ford on the Cam River, near what had been a Roman camp. The first university college, Peterhouse, was founded in 1284. Since then the growth of city and university have been closely linked.
See also: England.

Cambridge (pop. 96,000), city in Massachusetts on the Charles River opposite Boston; seat of Middlesex County. Since the establishment of Harvard University in 1636, the city has been an important educational center. In 1639 the first printing press in the American colonies was established there. In 1879, Radcliffe College for Women was opened, followed by the Episcopal Theological Seminary (1867) and the Massachusetts Institute of Technology (relocated from Boston in 1916). Principal industries include printing and publishing, baking, and the manufacture of light machinery.
See also: Massachusetts.

Cambridge University, one of the world's leading universities, at Cambridge, England. Its history dates from 1209, and its first college, Peterhouse, was established in 1284. Today the coeducational university has about 9,000 students and 29 colleges and approved societies.

Camcorder *See:* Video camera.

Camel, 2 species of haired, cud-chewing animals with humped backs, long necks, and hooves. The 1-humped Arabian camel or dromedary (*Camelus dromedarius*) of Africa and the Middle East is a widely kept domestic animal. The 2-humped Bactrian camel (*C. bactrianus*) is found from Asia Minor to Manchuria, and a few still live wild in the Gobi Desert. Domesticated in Babylonia about 1100 B.C., camels are invaluable in the desert. They can carry enor-

The Burgess Shales of British Columbia (disc. 1910), contain a large number of fossils from the Middle Cambrian Period (540 to 515 million years ago). This totally marine fauna was dominated by arthropods, including primitive malacostracan crustaceans (2); Burgessia (3), Sidneya (4), a trilobite-like animal with well-developed limbs, a tail, and sensory organs; Waptia (5), with its flattened swimming organ at the end of a long thorax; Agnostus (6), a small trilobite with a reduced thorax; Marrella (8), with a distinctive four-horned head shield; Emeraldella (9), an animal that was similar to a trilobite, but shaped like a shrimp; Naroia (11), with a shell consisting of two segments; Olenoides (13), a typical trilobite with a small pygidium, or posterior section; and Ogygopsis (15). Other fossils from the Burgess Shale fauna include arrowworms (1), which were similar to present-day members of the phylum Chaetognatha; jellyfishes (7); sponges (10); Aysheia (12), an onychophoran that was similar to the present-day Peripatus; and Canadia (14), a free-moving annelid worm. Scientists believe that the sudden release of an accumulation of toxic gases killed these organisms, and that preserved them in the resulting bacteria-free environment.

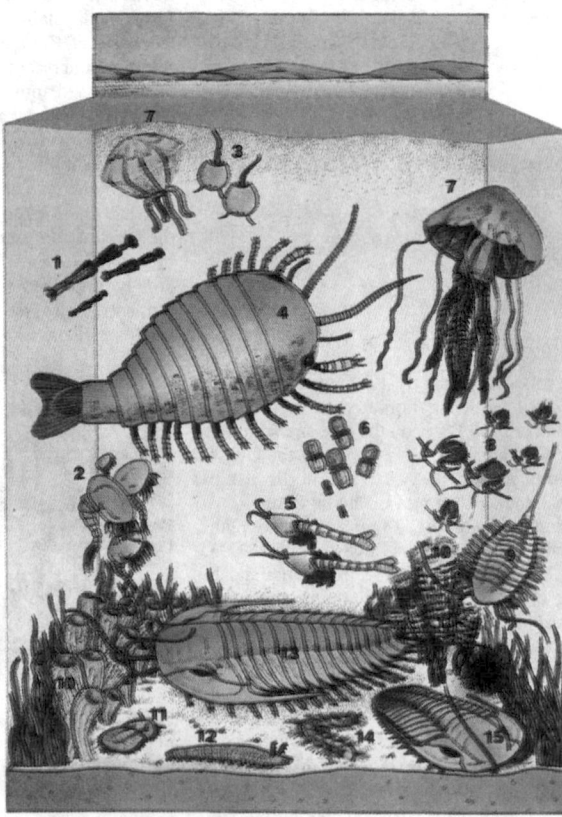

mous loads and are able to withstand the loss of about one third of their body fluid without danger. Their humps are fatty tissue, not water storage vessels. Their use as bearers has been greatly reduced by the use of motor vehicles.

Camellia, any of a genus *(Camellia)* of evergreen trees and shrubs of Asia that have large fragrant red, pink, or white flowers. The most important of the many cultivated varieties is the tea plant *(Co sinensis)*.

Camelot, in Arthurian legend, court of King Arthur and the Knights of the Round Table. It has been identified variously with Caerleon (Wales), Camelford (Cornwall), and South Cadbury (Somerset). *See also:* Arthur, King.

Cameron, Julia Margaret (1815-1879), Indian-born British pioneer photographer, best known for her portraits of such Victorians as Alfred, Lord Tennyson and Ellen Terry. Believing that a photograph should capture the spirit of its subject, Cameron put less emphasis on technique, and the blurred quality of some of her photographs is a distinction of her style. A revised edition of her book *Victorian Photographers of Famous Men and Women* appeared in 1973.

The Bactrian, or two-humped camel *(Camelus bactrianus)* is shorter than the dromedary, and is used as a domestic pack and riding animal in central Asia. The dromedary, or one-humped camel *(Camelus dromedarius)* can be trained to carry heavy loads on long journeys. Adapted to life in the desert, it has horny pads on its knees, thigh joints, and chest, on which it rests.

C

Cameroon

Capital:	Yaoundé
Area:	183,570 sq mi (475,442 sq km)
Population:	16,185,000
Language:	English, French
Government:	Presidential republic
Independent:	1960
Head of gov.:	Prime minister
Per capita:	U.S. $1,700
Monetary unit:	1 CFA franc = 100 centimes

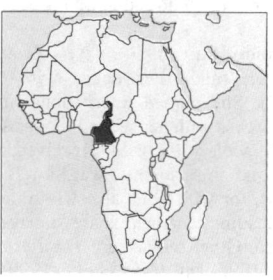

Cameroon, republic in West Africa. Cameroon is bordered by the Gulf of Guinea (west and southwest), Nigeria (northwest), Chad (northeast), the Central African Republic (east), and the Congo, Gabon, and Equatorial Guinea (south).

The narrow coastal plain of swamps and dense jungle rises to a plateau of savannah and forest some 2,000 ft (610 m) above sea level. The country's highest peak is the volcanic Great Cameroon (13,354 ft/ 4,070 m). The interior plateau covers about two-thirds of the country. The coast is tropical, the north, near Lake Chad, is semiarid. The central region receives about 30-40 in (76-102 cm) of rainfall annually. The country's capital is Yaoundé.

Cameroon's population consists of some 150 different tribes and ethnic groups. The official languages are English and French. Most of the people are Christian, but sizeable minorities follow traditional African beliefs or Islam.

The economy is based mainly on agriculture and forestry. Cameroon is mostly self-sufficient in food and exports coffee, cocoa, and timber as well as bananas, rubber, and aluminum. Aluminum smelting is Cameroon's largest industry.

The Sao people, who produced a distinctive kind of art and cast objects in bronze, settled near Lake Chad around 900 A.D. The Portuguese arrived in 1472 and established the slave trade. In 1884, Germany established a protectorate in the Cameroon area. British and French troops occupied the area in World War I and afterwards the League of Nations mandated the larger part (Cameroun) to France and the remainder (Southern and Northern Cameroons) to the British. In 1946 they became UN trust territories. In 1960, Cameroun became an independent republic after several years of guerrilla warfare. After plebiscites in 1961, the Northern Cameroons joined Nigeria, and the Southern Cameroons joined Cameroun to form the Federal Republic of Cameroon. In 1972, a unified republic replaced the federal system. In 1980, Ahmadou Ahidjo, president since independence, was reelected. President Paul Biya was elected unopposed in 1984 for his first full 5-year term and was reelected in 1988 and 1992.

Cameroon became the 52nd member state of the British Commonwealth in 1995. President Biya was reelected in 1997 with a 92% majority of the votes. Opposition parties had boycotted the elections. In 1996 and 1997, there were a few skirmishes between

A village near Maroua, a city in the north of Cameroon. This type of home with its conical roof and the clay-covered walls is common in Cameroon.

C

Cameroon and Nigerian troops at the controversial estuary of the Cross River, particularly on the Bakassi peninsula. After mediations on the part of Togo and the United Nations, both countries reached a ceasefire. The International Court of Justice, to which both countries had brought their dispute in 1994, held hearings in 1998, but it did not reach a final decision. Irritation and tension about the border dispute continued. At the beginning of 1999, Nigeria accused Cameroon of preparing for war in the controversial border region.

In October 2002, the authority of the oil-rich Bakassi peninsula was assigned to Cameroon in spite of Nigeria's protests.

Camoës, Luis Vaz de (1524?-1580), the most famous poet of Portugal. His masterpiece is the national epic *The Lusiads* (*Os Lusíadas*, 1572). Its central action is the discovery of the sea route to the East Indies by the Portuguese navigator Vasco da Gama. Through the incorporation of the history of Portugal, however, the poem becomes an exaltation of the achievements of the entire nation. Camoës is also noted for his lyric poetry.

Camoës' family was poor but of high social standing. At the court of Lisbon he was known as a gifted poet. He became a soldier and lost his right eye while fighting in North Africa. He returned to Lisbon and was jailed in 1552 for his part in a street brawl. A year later he was released on the condition that he serve in the Portuguese army in India. His shipboard experiences on the voyage to India provides Camoës with much background material for *The Lusiads*. He returned to Lisbon in 1570.

Camomile, also spelled chamomile, any of a genus (*Anthemis*) of various strong-scented herbs with daisylike flowers. The bitter-tasting flowers and leaves have had uses in folk medicine ranging from malaria cure to mouthwash.

Camorra, Italian secret society started in the Kingdom of Naples (1830). Although it specialized in extortion, smuggling, robbery, and assassination, it was often used by the authorities, and it became very powerful. After Italian unification in 1861, attempts were made to suppress the society, but it survived until 1911.

Campanella, Roy (1921-), one of the most popular and successful catchers in baseball history. He signed with the Negro leagues in 1936, joining the Brooklyn Dodgers in 1948. Campanella's 10-year major league career was cut short by an automobile accident in 1958 that left him paralyzed. He won the National League's Most Valuable Player award 3 times (1951, 1953, and 1955) playing for the Dodgers.

Campanile, bell tower, usually adjacent to a church. The first campaniles appeared in Italy about the 7th century. As in the round campanile of Sant' Apollinare Nuovo in Ravenna, Italy, the earliest examples probably contained not bells, but semantra, planks of wood or metal that sounded when struck. In the following century, the square cam-

panile became the standard. The campanile has been revived as an element of modern church architecture.

Campanula, plant genus of the family Campanulaceae containing some 700 species of mostly herbaceous (nonwoody) plants. Campanula is often called bellflower, and many of the species have showy, bell-like flowers.

Camp, Walter Chauncey (1859-1925), father of American football. As a player and coach at Yale and Stanford universities, he helped initiate, implement, and develop changes (such as the first down system and the line of scrimmage) that turned European rugby into the American game. Camp authored numerous books on athletics and physical fitness.

Campbell, Donald Malcolm (1921-1967), English speedboat racer. The first man to break the 200 mph (320 kmph) barrier and survive, Campbell's run, on Ullswater Lake, Cumberland, England in 1955, established a watercraft speed record of 202.32 mph (325.602 kmph). Campbell died in an accident in 1967, while exceeding 300 mph (480 kmph) in his jet-propelled boat.

Campbell, Malcolm (1885-1948), British businessman and racing driver (father of Donald Campbell). Obsessed with speed sports, he started racing on a Rex motorcycle, but later switched to motor racing. Campbell got off to a flying start by setting his first world speed record of 137.7 mi/h (221.6 km/h) over one mile in a Sunbeam in 1923. Afterwards, he broke this record (with the 'Blue Bird') another eight times, the last time being in 1937 on the salt plain of Bonneville (U.S.) with 301.2 mi/h (484.6 km/h). He also set the world speed record on water three times with boats that were also called 'Blue Bird'. Campbell, an officer in both world wars, was knighted in 1931.

Campbell, Mrs. Patrick (1865-1940), English actress. Popular on stage for over 40 years, she created many classic roles, including Eliza Doolittle in George Bernard Shaw's *Pygmalion* (1914), a part written for her.

Campbell-Bannerman, Sir Henry (1836-1908), British prime minister 1905-1908 and leader of the Liberal party from 1899. A member of the House of Commons from 1868 until his death, he championed progressive causes.
See also: United Kingdom.

Camp David, woodland camp in the Catoctin Mountains in Maryland near Washington, D.C., that has been used by U.S. presidents since Franklin D. Roosevelt as a retreat, workplace, and environment to receive foreign dignitaries.
See also: Maryland.

Camp David Agreement, peace treaty formulated in 1979 at Camp David by Egyptian President Anwar Sadat and Israeli Prime Minister Menachem Begin with the assistance of U.S. President Jimmy Carter. It in-

cluded a timetable for Israel's phased withdrawal from the Egyptian Sinai by 1982, mutual diplomatic recognition, and a framework for attempting to solve the Palestinian question.

Campeche, state in southeastern Mexico, on the Yucatán Peninsula. Although forest products yield a significant portion of the state's income, commercial fishing is also important. About a third of the inhabitants of Campeche are descended from the Mayas.
See also: Mexico.

Camphor, white, crystalline compound ($C_{10}H_{16}O$) distilled from the wood of a species of laurel tree (*Cinnamonum camphora*). It has a strong odor that repels insects and is used medicinally-internally as a pain-killer and antispasmodic, and externally in linaments.

Campin, Robert (1375?-1444), Flemish painter best known for his religious works. His art reflects the influence of manuscript illumination, though with a keener sense of plasticity in rendering the forms. One of his major works is the triptych of the Annunciation (c.1428) known as the *Mérode Altarpiece*. Depicting in realistic detail the daily life of the rising bourgeoisie, Campin became a founder of the Netherlandish School, influencing Jan Van Eyck and Rogier Van Der Weyden, among others.
See also: Van Eyck, Jan; Weyden, Rogier van der.

Campinas (pop. 1,7,000,000), city in state of São Paulo situated in the São Paulo highlands. The city is the center of coffee cultivation, sugar refining and textile, metal, machinery, chemical and food industries. The archbishop resides in Campinas and the city also has a university and a cathedral. The houses are in colonial style. Founded in the 18th century, Campinas grew rapidly during the coffee boom which took place around 1900.

Campion, plant of genera *Lychnis* or *Silene* grown for showy flowers. Many have escaped from gardens and grow wild. Descriptive names include ragged robin, Maltese cross, and mullein pink.

Campion, Jane (1954-), New Zealand film director, made her debut with *Sweetie* (1988). She gained international appraisal and success with her second movie *An Angel At My Table* (1990). She received a Palme D'Or and an Academy Award for *The Piano* (1993), for which she also wrote the script. Her leading characters are always strong women. Other movies are *The Portrait of a Lady* (1996) and *Holy Smoke* (1999).

Camus, Albert (1913-1960), French writer and philosopher. He communicated a vision of humanity in an absurd universe and felt that the only possibility for freedom and dignity lay in the awareness of this absurdity. His works include the essay 'The Myth of Sisyphus' (1942), which elucidated the philosophical basis of his novel *The Stranger* (1942); the novels *The Plague* (1947) and *The Fall* (1956); the essay 'The

Rebel' (1951); and the play *Caligula* (1945). He won the Nobel Prize in literature in 1957. *See also:* Philosophy.

Canaan, early name for Palestine. The region was inhabited from the 2nd millennium B.C. by Semitic peoples, mainly Amorites, whose script provides the earliest known alphabet. During the 13th century B.C. Canaan was occupied by the Israelites. In the next century its coasts were taken by the Philistines but later, King David (1000-961 B.C.) extended Israelite rule over all Canaan. *See also:* Palestine.

Canaanites, people who settled Canaan, the biblical name for Palestine, c.3000 B.C. The chief inhabitants of this land until the Israelites defeated them c.1200 B.C., the Canaanites spoke a Semitic language whose writing system influenced the development of the ancient Hebrew alphabet. *See also:* Canaan; Semites.

Canada

Capital:	Ottawa
Area:	3,849,675 sq mi
	(9,970,610 sq km)
Population:	31,902,000
Language:	English, French
Government:	Parliamentary democracy
	in the British
	Commonwealth
Independent:	1931
Head of gov.:	Prime minister
Per capita:	U.S. $27,700
Monetary unit:	1 Canadian dollar = 100 cents

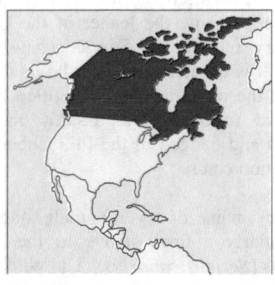

Canada, independent nation in North America, encompassing a land mass of 3,851,809 sq mi (9,976,185 sq km), making it the largest country in the Western Hemisphere and the second largest country in the world after Russia. Canada is an autonomous federation with 10 provinces and 2 federally administered territories. It is formally a constitutional monarchy under the British Crown and a member of the Commonwealth of Nations. English and French are the official languages. The federal capital is Ottawa.

Land and climate. Canada is divided into 7 regions. (1) The Appalachian region (New Brunswick, Nova Scotia, Prince Edward Island, and Newfoundland and the Gaspé peninsula) is a geological extension of the Appalachian mountain chain that runs along the eastern United States. The region is a source of varied farm products, timber, coal, and iron ore, and with numerous natural harbors, a major commercial fishing center. (2) The St. Lawrence lowlands, adjacent to the desolate Canadian Shield in the north and bordering on the Great Lakes and the St. Lawrence River in the south, is one of its most productive agricultural belts, containing about half of the total population. The Hudson Bay lowlands, embracing the southwest shore of Hudson Bay and James Bay, are situated in an Arctic zone, the region's swampy subsoil, consisting mostly of clay and sand, frozen the year round. Most of the region's inhabitants are fur trappers and fishers. (3) The Canadian Shield, almost 50% of the country, is a horseshoe-shaped region encircling Hudson Bay and including large portions of the provinces of Quebec, Ontario, Manitoba, and Saskatchewan, the northeastern corner of Alberta, the Labrador portion of Newfoundland, and much of the Northwest territories. The area is characterized by rocky hills and ridges, numerous lakes, and muskeg (a type of bog). Though unsuitable for agriculture, the region is rich in natural resources; forests, mineral deposits, and water power. (4) The Interior Plains reach from the Rocky Mountains to the Canadian Shield and include southern Manitoba and Saskatchewan, almost all of Alberta, and part of British Columbia and the Northwest Territories. The northern half of the Interior Plains is heavily forested, and there is some muskeg and tundra. The southern half includes fertile prairies and also contains rich deposits of natural gas, oil, and coal. (5) The Cordilleran region, between the Pacific Ocean and the Interior Plains of western Canada, is a 500-mi- (800- km-) wide strip of mountainous terrain that includes most of British Columbia, the Yukon territory, and part of western Alberta. Second to the Canadian Shield in wealth of mineral deposits, the region has extensive forests, water resources for hydroelectric plants, fertile soils particularly suited to fruit production, and important commercial fishing areas along the Pacific coast.

(6) With very limited animal life and vegetation, the Inuitian region in the Arctic Archipelago includes the 800-mi- (1,300-km-) long and 300-mi- (480-km) wide mountainous region extending from northernmost Ellesmere Island south and west to Melville Island. The Arctic lowlands and plateaus include most of Banks Island, southern Ellesmere Island, and eastern Baffin Island. (7) Though rugged and virtually uninhabitable, the Arctic Archipelago possesses rich deposits of coal, salt, gypsum, oil, and natural gas. About 70% of Canadian soil is useless for agriculture, but most of the nonarable soils support vast expanses of forests, and some are suitable for cattle raising. Covering about 40% of the country from coast to coast, the northern forests form Canada's largest belt of natural vegetation. The tundra extending across northern Canada can support only moss, lichens, and grass and flowers during the summer, when the surface layer is frost-free. Ever-frozen subsoil, or permafrost, prevents greater vegetation.

The government has created several game reserves; the land set aside for national parks totals about 29,500 sq mi (76,405 sq km). The largest of the national parks are Jasper, Wood Buffalo, Prince Albert, and Riding Mountain. Each province has also established its own provincial parks.

People. Canada's population is predomi-

nantly of British or French stock, though it includes many of German, Italian, Ukrainian, Dutch, and other origins. Native Americans number about 370,000 and Inuit (Eskimos) about 26,000. Population is concentrated in the southern part of the country, the most populous provinces being Ontario, Quebec, and British Columbia. About 76% of Canadians are urban.

Government. Canada has a parliamentary system of government, with executive power vested in a prime minister and cabinet. The federal legislature comprises a Senate of 105 appointed members and a House of Commons whose 301 members are elected for a 5-year term. Each of the 10 provinces has its own premier and elected legislature. The Yukon and Northwest Territories are governed by federally appointed commissioners and elected councils, and each sends 1 representative to the federal parliament.

Economy. Agriculture is responsible for 3% of Canada's employment and provides around 10% of Canada's total exports. One of the world's chief wheat producers, Canada grows other grains, oilseeds, fruit (especially apples), vegetables, and tobacco. Beef and dairy cattle, hogs, sheep, and poultry are reared. Forestry and fisheries are ma-

Most Canadian farms are large — the average size is 200 ha. The lotting is regular and completely adapted to mechanized tillage and combine harvesting.

La Puce River by Thomas Davies (1737-1812) is one of the many Canadian landscape paintings that flourished in the 18th century.

C

jor industries, and Canada remains a leading source of furs, both farmed and trapped. Mineral resources include petroleum and natural gas, molybdenum, platinum, copper, nickel, iron ore, zinc, lead, silver, gold, asbestos, elemental sulfur, and coal. Most manufacturing plants are located in Ontario and Quebec. Manufacturing accounts for about 25% of all employment. Products include nonferrous metals, machinery, chemicals, plastics, electrical equipment, and textiles.

History. Visited by 11th-century Vikings, Canada was later penetrated by explorers such as John Cabot, Jacques Cartier, and Samuel de Champlain. The French founded Quebec in 1608 and made Canada the royal colony of New France (1663). Anglo-French rivalry culminated in the cession of New France to Britain (Treaty of Paris, 1763). French rights were guaranteed by the Quebec Act (1774). Only 1 serious revolt against British rule took place (1837-1838), consisting of separate uprisings led by W.L. Mackenzie in Upper (English-speaking) Canada and Louis Papineau in Lower (French-speaking) Canada. The British North America Act (1867) established Canada as a dominion, the 4 founding provinces being Quebec, Ontario, Nova Scotia, and New Brunswick. The others entered later: Manitoba (1870), British Columbia (1871), Prince Edward Island (1873), Saskatchewan (1905), Alberta (1905), and Newfoundland (1949). The Northwest Territories, formerly administered by the Hudson's Bay Company, became a federal territory in 1870, and the Yukon was made a separate territory in 1898. Separatist tensions, particularly in French-speaking Quebec, developed during the 1960s and have continued. Efforts begun in 1978 to amend the British North America Act in order to 'patriate' the Canadian constitution resulted in the Constitution Act (1982). In 1994 Canada, the United States, and Mexico formed a free trade association, NAFTA. In 1995 Quebec voters narrowly rejected an independence referendum. In 1999 the Inuit were granted their own province, Nunavut.

In 2001, representatives of 34 American countries met in Quebec in order to discuss the establishment of a hemisphere-wide free

trade zone in 2005. After the terrorist attacks of September 11, Canada and the US decided to harmonize the protection of their borders.

Canada goose (*Branta canadensis*), large migratory bird common to North America, Greenland, and parts of Asia. It has a long black head and neck and distinctive white cheek bars, and flies in group formations.

Canada thistle (*Cirsium arvense*), weed native to Europe and Asia and now widespread in the northern United States and southern Canada. The weed is difficult to control because new thistle can grow from bits of the old roots.

Canadian literature, body of literary works reflecting the English and French heritage of Canada, often focusing on national identity and duality. Since 1945 French-language Quebecois fiction has evolved into an intense and experimental body of writing, while English-Canadian literature has tended to be marked by well-crafted novels of life in the various regions of the country. Robertson Davies, many of whose widely praised novels are set in Ontario towns, and Margaret Atwood, a poet and novelist whose work often has a strong feminist component, are two of the leading figures of contemporary Canadian literature.
See also: Atwood, Margaret.

Canadian Mounted Police *See:* Royal Canadian Mounted Police.

Canadian Shield, or Laurentian Plateau, geologic designation of that area of North America (including the eastern half of Canada and small portions of the United States) that has remained more or less stable since Precambrian times.

Canal, artificial waterway used for transportation, drainage, and irrigation. In 521 B.C. a precursor of the Suez Canal joined the Nile to the Red Sea. In China, the Ling Ch'u canal was completed during the 3rd century B.C. and the Grand Canal, joining the Paiho, Yellow, and Yangtze rivers, had sections in use by the 7th century A.D.. The Romans built many canals to supply their cities with

water and canalized a number of European rivers to create an empirewide transportation system. The lock, a device for raising boats from one land level to another, was invented in the 15th century. Although one of the great engineering projects of the 19th century, the Suez Canal to the Red Sea, was built entirely without locks, the other great international waterway, the Panama Canal, would not have been possible without them. There are various types of canals. A shipping canal is constructed for the purpose of sea navigation or inland navigation. The first is called a seaway (connection between the ocean and inland ports); the second is called an inland waterway (connection between inland areas). A lateral canal is a canal that is constructed parallel to an existing river in cases where this is more economical than making the river section in question navigable by means of canalization. A bilateral canal or connecting canal is usually used to connect two seas, such as the Panama Canal (51 mi, 82 km, 1920), the Suez Canal (100 mi, 161 km, 1869), the North Baltic Sea Canal (originally the Kaiser Wilhelm Canal: 61 mi / 98 km, 1895), the Korinthe Canal (3.9 mi / 6.3 km, 1893). In addition to shipping purposes, canals are also constructed to supply and drain water. The depth is determined based on the largest types of ships that can be expected. A depth of 13 to 15 ft (4 to 4.5 m) is sufficient for river vessels weighing 2,000 tons; seaways may be over 66 ft (20 m) deep. As transportation by water is often 50% less expensive than by train or automobile, cannels are of great economic significance.

The longest canalized system is the Volga-Baltic Canal (1965), which runs 1,850 mi (2,977 km), from Astrakhan up the Volga, via Kuybyshev, Gorkiy, and Lake Ladoga, to St. Petersburg, Russia.

Canal Zone *See:* Panama Canal Zone.

Canaris, Wilhelm (1887-1945), German admiral, became the leader of the German Military Intelligence Service (Abwehr) in 1938. It is uncertain whether he totally supported the resistance against Hitler. He was arrested following the assault on Hitler (1944) and hanged in the Flossenbürg concentration camp.

Canary, name of several small song birds, particularly a finch native to the Canary Islands (*Serinus canarius*). The wild canary is usually gray or green in color, but tame birds have been bred to produce the characteristic 'canary yellow.' Canaries have been bred in Europe since the 16th century and are valued for their song.

Canary, Martha Jane *See:* Calamity Jane.

Canary Islands, group of islands in the Atlantic Ocean off the northwest coast of Africa that make up 2 Spanish provinces. The main islands are Tenerife, Palma, Gomera, Hierro, Grand Canary, Fuerteventura, and Lanzarote; their land area is nearly 3,000 sq mi (7,770 sq km).

Canberra (pop. 279,000), capital city of the Commonwealth of Australia and the coun-

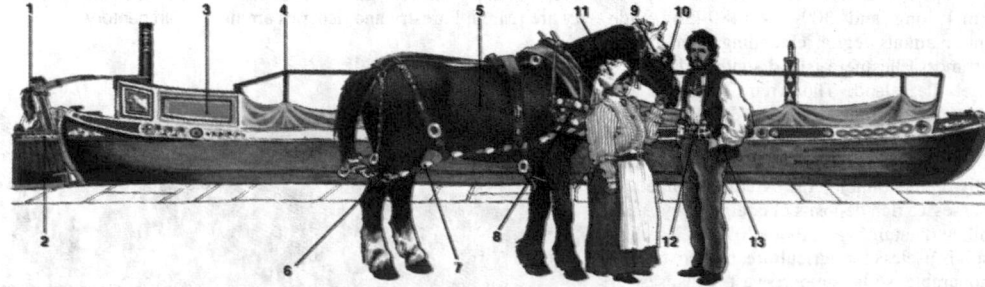

Freight-carrying narrow boat, used on the English canals, to fit the original locks designed by Brindley.
1. Grey horse's tail, believed to bring luck to the boat
2. Ornamental ropework
3. Decorated panels
4. Decorated top plank supports
5. Canal horse in traditional harness
6. Swingletree, or towing bar
7. Coloured bobbins
8. Decorated nose can
9. Crocheted ear protectors
10. Blinkers with brass company plates
11. Lady's bonnet with deep neck ruffle, to give protection in all weathers
12. Embroidered crochet `spider web' belt
13. Moleskin waistcoat

try's largest inland city. The Australian parliament first met there in 1927. The economy rests mainly on the public service and governmental departments.
See also: Australia.

Cancer, group of diseases in which some body cells change their nature, start to divide uncontrollably, and may revert to an undifferentiated type. They form a malignant tumor that enlarges and may spread to adjacent tissues or through blood and lymph systems to other parts of the body. The American Cancer Society has listed 7 warning signals: (1) change in bowel or bladder habits, (2) a sore that does not heal, (3) unusual bleeding or discharge, (4) thickening or lump in a breast or elsewhere, (5) indigestion or difficulty in swallowing, (6) obvious change in a wart or mole, and (7) nagging cough or hoarseness. Every diagnosis of cancer made by a doctor is subject to confirmation by a biopsy, in which a small piece of tissue is cut into very thin slices, stained with special dyes, and examined under a microscope. Routine periodic physical examinations are important, since the most successfully treated cancers are those that have not progressed to the stage of producing symptoms. The doctor feels, or palpates, parts of the body for unusual lumps or thickenings. A cervical smear is taken from adult women. The rectum and large intestine can be examined by means of a lighted tube, called a proctosigmoidoscope. Periodic self-examination of the skin, mouth, and genital organs is also important. Women should examine their breasts once a month after their menstrual cycles, and men should examine their testicles.

Successful treatment of cancer requires complete removal or destruction of the tumor by surgery, radiation, or drugs (chemotherapy). Some tumors cannot be destroyed by safe amounts of radiation, and some cannot be entirely removed surgically without destroying a vital organ, so surgery, radiation, and drugs may be combined.

Cancer is tenacious, sometimes subsiding but reappearing years after the patient has presumably been cured. For some cancers, even 5 years is not a long enough period; an indefinite length of time with frequent examinations is recommended. Physicians are increasingly reluctant to speak of '5-year cures,' preferring more the realistic expression of '5-year survival without clinical evidence of disease.'

Causes of cancer.
Chemical compounds.
Chemists have manufactured several hundred pure chemicals that produce cancer in animals. In humans, however, research has not found a relationship between chemical structure and cancer-producing activity. Some chemical carcinogens produce cancers at the site of contact, others at distant sites. Some are incomplete or weak in their action and need the action of other chemicals in order to induce tumors. The simultaneous injection of a chemical carcinogen and a closely related inactive compound (anticarcinogen) can prevent or retard the action of the carcinogen. This line of investigation may eventually uncover chemicals to prevent the development of cancer in individuals who are unavoidably exposed to certain cancer-producing hazards.

Environmental hazards.
Molds and bacteria growing naturally on food products may represent a source of environmental carcinogens. The human cancers due to industrial exposure include the following: (1) bladder cancer in aniline dye workers who handle betanaphtylamine, (2) bone cancer due to swallowing radium, (3) lung cancer caused by inhalation of chromium compounds, radioactive ores, asbestos, arsenic, and iron, (4) cancer of nasal sinuses and the lung in nickel mine workers, and (5) skin cancer from the handling of some products of coal, oil shale, lignite, and petroleum. Excessive or continuous exposure to inhaled impurities brings about changes in the bronchial linings and the lungs that may eventually result in disability and illness. If the impurities contain cancer-producing substances, prolonged exposure can lead to cancer.

During the past 40 years, cancer of the lung in the United States has shown the greatest increase of any cancer type. At least 80% of the total increase can be attributed to cigarette smoking. An additional important factor is air pollution caused by industrial wastes, car exhausts, and household sources.

Radiation.
The cancer-producing effects of the ultraviolet rays of sunlight appear to be limited to the skin. Related to the cancer-causing effects of sunlight are those of ionizing radiation from radium and X-rays. Ionizing radiation can cause several forms of cancer in humans and animals. Radiologists and others exposed to increased doses of radiation are more likely to develop leukemia than are people who are not exposed. Radium salts, which are deposited in bone, give rise to cancers of the bone.

Cancer-causing viruses.
Cancer-causing viruses penetrate the cells of victims and become part of the structure of the chromosomes. The presence of the virus in the genetic mechanism of the cell may make the cell behave immediately as a cancer, or the virus can remain dormant until activated by another stimulus. Scientists have identified several dozen types of cancer that are caused by viruses, in many species of animals, including cats, monkeys, chickens, and rodents. It is inevitable that some human cancers will be found to be caused by viruses and that such discoveries may lead to the development of protective vaccines.

Hormones.
Large doses of the female hormone estrogen given over long periods will lead to the development of leukemia and tumors of the testes, uterus, and pituitary in some strains of mice. The increasing use of hormones as treatment for various human conditions does not seem to have led to an increase in the incidence of any specific type of cancer in women or men. However, some girls born of mothers who took large doses of a synthetic estrogen, diethylstilbestrol (DES), during their pregnancy have developed cancer of the vagina. Widespread use of 'the pill' (the collective term for a variety of oral contraceptives containing progestogen, often estrogen, and sometimes other hormones) has increased the number of younger women receiving additional hormones. Carefully controlled, long-term observations of 'pill' users

C

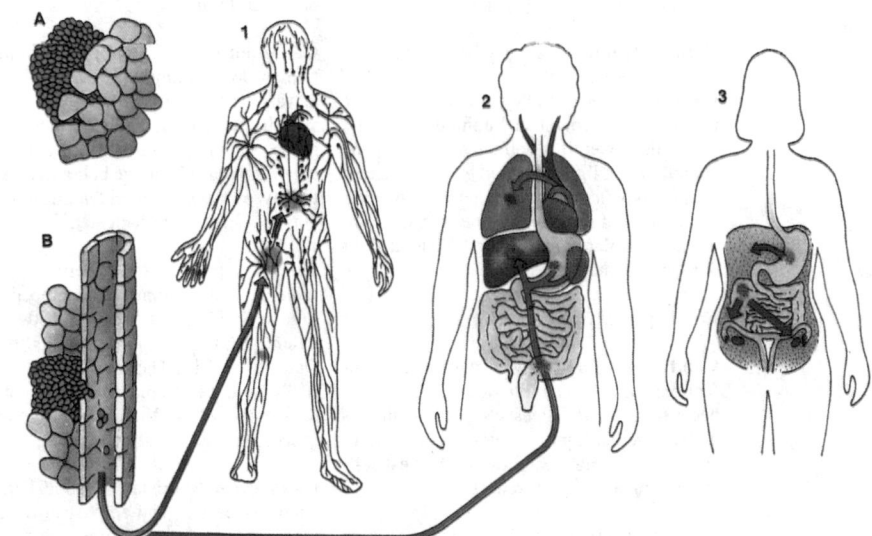

Cancer may spread by direct extension (A), the direct invasion of adjacent tissue. Bone, soft connective tissue, and the walls of veins and lymphatic vessels are easily penetrated by cancer cells (green), but cartilage, artery walls, tendons, and ligaments resist this invasion. Metastasis (B) may occur when one or more cancer cells separate from the main tumor, then penetrate a vessel wall, and travel to another part of the body, resulting in secondary growths. The lymphatic system (1) is the most common route of metastasis, with tumors frequently developing at regional nodes. Cancers of the connective tissues and of the gastrointestinal and urogenital tracts may spread to other organs through the veins (2). Cancer cells may also travel across body cavities (3), e.g. from the stomach or colon, into the abdominal cavity and perhaps to other organs.

C

are necessary to assess increased risks for cancer of the breast, uterus, or ovary.

Established tumors in both humans and laboratory animals have shown varying degrees of hormone dependency. For example, removal of the ovaries in some women with advanced breast cancer or removal of the testes in men with prostate cancer often leads to temporary regression of the tumors.

Nutrition.

There is no diet known to prevent cancer in humans. There is some evidence, that vitamin deficiency in humans plays a role in the occurrence of cancers of the mouth and the esophagus. However, such a deficiency is probably only 1 of a number of factors. The consumption of dietary fiber has been associated with reduced risk of colon cancer.

Heredity.

The limited data available suggest increased familial risk of developing cancer of the same site for cancers of the breast (female), stomach, large intestine, endometrium (lining of the uterus), prostate, lung, and possibly ovary. However, it is not known to what extent the tumors that have been observed to run in some families are due to genetic characteristics or to environmental factors such as diet or occupation that may remain the same from one generation to the next. Brain tumors and sarcomas seem to occur more frequently than expected in brothers and sisters of children with these tumors. When an identical twin has childhood leukemia, the probability that the other twin will develop the disease within 1 or 2 years of the date of diagnosis of the first twin is about 1 in 5. In addition, retinoblastoma, a rare form of cancer of the eye, is known to be due to inherited mutation.

Cancer, Tropic of *See:* Tropic of Cancer.

Candela, or new candle (symbol: cd), basic unit of measurement of luminous intensity, or candle power. It is defined as equal to one sixtieth of the light reflected by one sq cm of a blackbody (a theoretically perfect absorber and emitter of radiation) at the freezing temperature of platinum (1,769° C) and at standard atmospheric pressure.

Candlepower *See:* Candela.

Candy, any of a great variety of sweet confections. Candy can provide quick energy because the body digests sugar, usually its main ingredient, more rapidly than any other food. Chocolate candies are the best selling among all the different types.

Candytuft, any of several species of a genus (*Iberis*) of low-growing, Old World plants of the mustard family. Often cultivated as a rock garden or border plant, candytuft has variously colored blossoms.

Canetti, Elias (1905-1994), Bulgarian-born author of prose and plays in the German language. Major works include the novel *Auto da Fé* (1935) and the political study *Crowds and Power* (1960). He received the 1981 Nobel Prize for literature.

Canine *See:* Teeth.

Canis Major, constellation of stars visible in the Southern Hemisphere. It contains the brightest star in the sky, Sirius, (the Dog Star). Canis Major is visible on winter evenings.
See also: Sirius.

Canis Minor, constellation appearing north of Canis Major in the Southern Hemisphere. Procyon in Canis Minor is one of the brightest stars in the sky.

Cankerworm, or measuring worm, any of various larvae of insects, especially moths. Cankerworms feed on foliage and can seriously damage fruit and shade trees.

Canna, any of a genus (*Canna*) of tropical plants of the family Cannaceae. Widely cultivated in the United States, canna is bred in hybrid varieties.

Cannabis, tops and leaves of the female plant of Indian hemp (*Cannabis sativa*), from which marijuana, a mood-altering substance, is obtained.
See also: Marijuana.

Cannae, ancient town in southern Italy, site of Hannibal's decisive defeat of the Romans (216 B.C.). The encircling technique he perfected, regarded as a masterpiece of tactics, won him the battle and 10,000 prisoners.
See also: Hannibal; Italy; Punic Wars.

Cannes (pop. 69,300), French resort and seaport on the Mediterranean coast. Its superb climate makes it a center for tourism and festivals, notably the annual International Film Festival.
See also: France.

Cannibalism, consumption by humans of human flesh, common throughout the world at various times in the past and still occasionally practiced, though now generally taboo. Among primitive peoples, the motive appears to have been the belief that eating an enemy or a respected elder transferred that person's strength to the eater.

Canning, process of preserving foods in sealed metal containers, developed by the French chef Nicolas Appert in 1809 and first patented in the United States by Ezra Daggett in 1815. The fragile glass jars originally used were replaced by tin-coated iron cans after 1810. Today a production line process is used.

Cannizzaro, Stanislao (1826-1910), Italian chemist, teacher, and activist in Garibaldi's movement for Italian unification. Cannizzaro found that benzaldehyde treated with a concentrated alcoholic hydroxide produced equal amounts of benzyl alcohol and the salt of benzoic acid. This became known as the Cannizzaro reaction. In 1858 he differentiated between atomic and molecular weights, a discovery that won him the Copley medal from the Royal Society of London.
See also: Chemistry.

Cannon, large firearm with a barrel, breech, and firing mechanism. First used in warfare around the middle of the 14th century, early cannons were cast of bronze and wrought iron. The term gradually came to refer to any gun that was fired from a carriage or fixed mount and had a bore greater than 1 inch in diameter.

Cannon-ball tree, South American tree (*Couroupita guianensis*) noted for its spherical woody fruit, which resembles a rusty cannon ball. Related to the Brazil-nut tree, the cannon-ball tree sheds its leaves more than once a year.
See also: Brazil nut.

Cano, Juan Sebastián del (1476-1526), Basque sailor who succeeded Ferdinand Magellan as commander of the expedition that completed the first circumnavigation of the globe (1522).
See also: Magellan, Ferdinand.

Canoe, long, narrow, lightweight boat used primarily for fishing and recreational activities on lakes and rivers. Originally canoes were made by hollowing out logs and were used for combat as well as transport. Now they are made from canvas, thin wood, and aluminum. In contrast to kayaks, canoes have an uncovered top.

A team of canoers   during a slalom race.
negotiates a gate

Canon, form or procedure of contrapuntal musical composition in which one voice or instrument starts to sing or play a theme and other voices or instruments follow at a specified interval of time, all singing or playing the same theme according to the same rule (canon). The composer might specify that later voices enter at different pitches, or even execute the theme upside down or backwards (*cancrizans*, crabwise). In the best-known form of canon, the round, the theme is sung (played) identically by all voices, which enter at regular intervals. This very old musical form originated in the church music of the Middle Ages.

Canonization, process by which a Christian church declares a deceased person to be a saint. In the Roman Catholic Church the process involves a long and careful investigation of the individual's life for sanctity, heroic virtue, and orthodoxy.
See also: Saint.

Canopus, second brightest star in the sky. It

lies in the constellation of Carina, the Keel, visible in the Southern Hemisphere. Canopus is used as a guide star for navigating spacecraft.

Canova, Antonio (1757-1822), Italian sculptor, a leading exponent of neoclassicism. His works include *Cupid and Psyche* (1787-1792), several statues of his patron Napoleon, and a famous statue of Pauline Bonaparte Borghese as the reclining *Venus Victrix* (1808).

Cantaloupe *See:* Muskmelon.

Cantata (from: Italian *cantare*, 'to sing'), musical composition for solo voice or choir, usually with an instrumental accompaniment. One of the earliest composers of cantatas was Giacomo Carissimi, who wrote such works both for entertainment and for the church. Another important composer in this field was Alessandro Scarlatti, some of whose cantatas were almost as elaborate as opera. J.S. Bach wrote hundreds of cantatas as part of his normal duties as a church choirmaster.
See also: Bach, Johann Sebastian.

Canterbury (pop. 34,000), city and county borough of Kent, on the Stour River 55 mi (89 km) southeast of London. It has been England's ecclesiastical capital since A.D. 597. The archbishop of Canterbury is primate of all England.
See also: England.

Canterbury bell, any of several biennial flowering plants with bell-shaped flowers, in particular the *Campanula medium*. Found wild in woods and stony places, the canterbury bell does not flower until the second (and final) summer of its life. The plant may grow to 3 ft (91 cm) and has hairy, oval leaves.

Canterbury Tales, best-known work of English poet Geoffrey Chaucer, written between 1387 and his death in 1400. In 17,000 lines (mostly heroic couplets) it describes a party of 30 pilgrims going to the shrine of St. Thomas à Becket, and their plan to tell 4 tales each on the journey. Only 24 tales were written, 4 of them unfinished, but the work presents a vivid cross section of medieval society and the tales cover most medieval literary genres.
See also: Chaucer, Geoffrey.

Canticle, piece of religious music, similar in character to a psalm, but using a passage from the Bible other than the psalms themselves. Some canticles actually date from biblical times and are therefore very ancient. More recently the word has come to be used for shorter choral works with any kind of religious or semi-religious basis.

Canticles *See:* Song of Solomon.

Canton *See:* Guangzhou.

Canute (995?-1035), king of England, Norway, and Denmark. The younger son of Sweyn of Denmark, Canute invaded England with his father in 1013. He with-

drew in 1014, when Sweyn died, but invaded again in 1015 and became king in 1016 on the death of Edmund II. In 1019 he succeeded his brother as king of Denmark, and in 1028 he conquered Norway, ousting Olaf II. Canute is noted in English history for having brought peace and codifying English law. Anglo-Saxon rule was reestablished in England in 1042, when Edward the Confessor became king.

Canvasback (*Aythya valisneria*), diving duck found in coastal and inland waters of North America. About 2 ft (0.6 m) long and 3 lb (1.4 kg) in weight, it feeds on aquatic plants, shrimps, and small fish.

Canzoniere *See:* Petrarch.

Capablanca y Graupera, José Raoul (1888-1942), Cuban chess master, world champion from 1921-1927. When he was virtually unknown as a chess player, Capablanca won the tournament in San Sebastian in 1911, defeating Rubinstein, and with that began a major and successful chess career. Capablanca participated in 35 tournaments, twenty of which he won, and obtained second place in the other ten. His biggest successes were London 1922 (13 out of 15, defeating Aljechin), New York 1927 (14 out of 20, defeating Aljechin), Moscou 1936 (13 out of 18, defeating Botvinnik) and Nottingham 1936 (10 out of 15, together with Botvinnik). In 1921, Capablanca became world champion following a victory over Lasker in Havana (+4, -0, = 10), but he lost his title to Aljechin in 1927 (+3, -6, = 25). Capablanca was above all a positional player and his great capacity to assess rendered him virtually impossible to defeat.

Capacitance, ability of a system to store an electric charge, measured by the charge that must be communicated to a body to raise its potential 1 unit. Electrostatic unit capacitance is that which requires 1 electrostatic unit of charge to raise the potential 1 electrostatic unit. The farad = 9×10^{11} electrostatic units. A capacitance of 1 farad requires 1 coulomb of electricity to raise its potential 1 volt. A conductor charged with a quantity Q to a potential V has a capacitance $C = Q/V$. The capacitance of a spherical conductor of radius r is $C = Kr$. The capacitance of 2 concentric spheres of radii r and r' is $C = K [rr'/(r-r')]$. The capacitance of a parallel plate condenser, the area of whose plates is A and the distance between them d, is $C = KA/4\pi d$. Capacitances are given in electrostatic units if the dimensions of condensers are substituted in cm. K is the dielectric constant of the medium.

Capacitor, or condenser, electrical component used to store electric charge and to provide reactance in alternating current circuits. In essence, a capacitor consists of 2 conducting plates separated by a thin layer of insulator. When the plates are connected to the terminals of a battery, a current flows until the capacitor is 'charged,' with 1 plate positive and the other negative. The ability of a capacitor to hold charge, its capacitance C, is the ratio of the quantity of electricity on its

A life-sized marble statue (1808) of Pauline Borghese-Bonaparte (1780-1825), Napoleon's sister, in the guise of a classical Venus. The sculptor is the Italian Antonio Canova (1757-1822), whose work was frequently commissioned by the Bonaparte family.

plates, Q, to the potential difference between the plates, V. The electric energy stored in a capacitor is given by CV^2. The capacitance of a capacitor depends on the area of its plates, their separation, and the dielectric constant of the insulator. Small fixed capacitors are commonly made with metal-foil plates and paraffin-paper insulation; to save space, the plates and paper are rolled into a tight cylinder. Some small capacitors have a mica dielectric. Variable capacitors used in radio tuners consist of intermeshing metal vanes separated by an air gap. In electrolytic capacitors, the dielectric is an oxide film formed on the plates by the action of a solid electrolyte.

Cape Breton Island, island in northeast Nova Scotia, 110 mi (177 km) long, up to 75 mi (121 km) wide, separated from the Canadian mainland by the Strait of Canso (since 1955 joined by a causeway).
See also: Nova Scotia.

Cape Canaveral, promontory on the eastern coast of Florida, site of the John F. Kennedy Space Center called Cape Kennedy 1963-1973. It became famous with the launching of the first U.S. satellite, *Explorer 1*, in 1958, and the first manned lunar exploration in 1969. The cape was established as a national seashore in 1975.
See also: Florida; National Aeronautics and Space Adminstration.

Cape Cod, peninsula in Barnstable County, southeast Massachusetts, surrounded by the Atlantic Ocean and Cape Cod Bay. It is 65 mi (105 km) long and up to 20 mi (32 km) in width. Site of the first Pilgrim landing in 1620, shipping, whaling, fishing, and salt production were early industries. Today the cape is famous for its cranberries and its summer resorts.
See also: Massachusetts.

Cape Hatteras, promontory lying 30 mi (48 km) off the North Carolina coast and long

C

known as 'the graveyard of the Atlantic' because of its rocky shoals.
See also: North Carolina.

Cape Horn, southernmost tip of South America, known for its cold, stormy climate. Part of Chile, the cape's bare headland lies well south of the Strait of Magellan on Horn Island.
See also: Chile.

Capek, Karel (1890-1938), Czech writer whose works, known for their humor and antiauthoritarian stand, include the plays *R.U.R. (Rossum's Universal Robots*, 1920) and *The Insect Play* (1921) and the novel *The War with the Newts* (1936).

Cape Kennedy *See:* Cape Canaveral.

Capella, brightest star of the constellation Auriga, the charioteer. It is a yellow star, about 10 times the diameter of our sun. In midnorthern latitudes Capella appears overhead in winter.

Cape of Good Hope, rocky promontory near the southern tip of Africa, 30 mi (48 km) south of Cape Town, chief navigational hazard in rounding Africa. It was discovered by Bartholomeu Dias in 1488, who named it Cape of Storms. Vasco da Gama first sailed around it in 1497 into the Indian Ocean.
See also: South Africa.

Cape Province, former province of South Africa, 278,465 sq mi (721,224 sq km) in area. The capital and chief city is Cape Town. A Dutch colony from 1652, the cape became British in 1806. Many Dutch settlers (Boers) migrated north and west to found independent states. Self-governing after 1872, Cape Colony joined the Union of South Africa in 1910. In the early 1990s the province was subdivided into three new provinces.
See also: South Africa.

Caper (genus *Capparis*), prickly Mediterranean shrub cultivated for its tender aromatic buds, which are pickled for use in sauces such as tartare sauce.

Capet, Hugh *See:* Hugh Capet.

Capetians, ruling house of France (987-1328) that laid the basis for the French state by consolidating and extending its power. Hugh Capet, founder of the dynasty, was elected king in 987. Though his rule and territory were limited, his successors gradually increased their land and control. Under the Capetian dynasty many basic administration characteristics of the French monarchy were established, including the parliaments (courts) and the States-General (national assembly).
See also: Louis; Philip; Hugh Capet.

Cape Town (pop. 2,700,000), legislative capital of South Africa and capital of WestCape Province. Founded by the Dutch East India Company in 1652, it has a pleasant climate, excellent beaches, attractive scenery, and the country's largest harbor. Exports are gold, diamonds, fruits, wines, skins, wool, mohair, and corn.
See also: South Africa.

Cape Verde

Capital:	Praia
Area:	1,557 sq mi (4,033 sq km)
Population:	409,000
Language:	Portuguese
Government:	Republic
Independent:	1975
Head of gov.:	Prime minister
Per capita:	U.S. $1,500
Monetary unit:	1 Cape Verde escudo = 100 centavos

Cape Verde (Republic of), independent nation in Africa, lying in the Atlantic Ocean some 400 mi (644 km) west of Senegal. The area is about 1,550 sq mi (4,015 sq km). Cape Verde consists of 10 islands and 5 islets, forming a horseshoe. The islands are volcanic, only about 10% of the land is cultivable. The climate is tropical, with a rainy season, although recently there has been

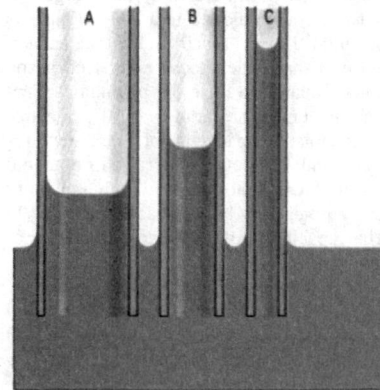

The cohesion between a liquid and a solid, results in the liquid surface curving near the solid, to meet it at a definite angle. Water curves upward against glass, and the force of cohesion is exerted along the water surface, tending to lift it. The lifting force is proportional to the circumference of the water surface. In a wide tube (A) the lifting force isn't very strong. When the tube gets more narrow (B,C) it becomes more powerful, compared with the weight of the liquid, and a correspondingly tall column of water will be lifted.

cyclical drought. Over half of the population is of Portuguese and African extraction. Living standards and the rate of literacy are low. Despite a paucity of fertile land, the country is primarily agricultural. However, most food must be imported. The fishing industry provides the major source of exports. Canned fish, salt, bananas, and frozen fish are the primary exports, most going to Portugal. The Portuguese discovered the island in the 15th century. Cape Verde became a supply station for ships and a transit point during the Atlantic slave trade. Blacks from Guinea were taken to the islands to work on Portuguese plantations. Portugal ruled the islands until 1975, when they became independent. Since the 1991 elections, the Movimento para Democracia (MpD) was in power until the elections of 2001. Pedro Verona Rodrigues Pires, opposition candidate, became the new President. .

Cap-Haitien (pop. 75,000), seaport on the north coast of Haiti and the country's second largest city. Under French rule it was the capital of the colony ('the Paris of the Antilles'). Today it has less than 10% of the population of Port-au-Prince, the capital.
See also: Haiti.

Capillarity, or capillary action, rise or fall of a liquid within a narrow tube (less than 0.02 m/0.5 mm in diameter) when one end is placed beneath the surface of a liquid, caused by its surface tension, which is due to the forces of attraction between the molecules of the liquid. Where, in the case of adhesion, these forces are weaker than the attraction of the molecules for the walls of the tube (as with water surrounded by a glass tube), a concave meniscus is formed (that is, the water level is higher wherever the water touches the tube). Surface tension pulls the rest of the surface upwards, and the level rises until the weight of the column balances the surface tension. In the case of cohesion, with a liquid like mercury, where the molecules of the liquid are more strongly attracted to each other than to the walls of the vessel, the reverse takes place and the level falls. Plants obtain food and water from the soil by capillary action, and it also helps the flow of sap up the stem. Blotting paper, towels, and sponges soak up moisture by capillarity.

Capillary, minute blood vessel that connects the arteries and veins. In general, the capillaries comprise fine tubes, approximately 0.004 in (0.1 mm) in diameter, the same order of size as the red blood corpuscles. The capillary walls are one cell thick and arranged in a network throughout every tissue of the body. Here, the primary functions of the circulation-the exchange of gases, nutrients, metabolites, and heat-take place.
See also: Circulatory system.

Capital, in economics, those goods that are used in production, such as plant and equipment (fixed capital) and raw materials, components, and semifinished goods (circulating capital), as opposed to goods intended for immediate consumption. To classical economists, 3 main factors of production were capital, labor, and land. Modern economists add management skill and human capital (education and training). The decision to invest in capital is determined by the cost and availability of labor and natural resources and the cost of capital (e.g., interest on the money used to buy equipment). Modern industrial countries are highly capitalized, but among the less developed countries the lack of capital is often acute.

Capitalism, economic system in which goods and services are provided by the efforts of private individuals and groups (firms) who own and control the means of production, compete with one another, and aim to make a profit. The concept has several overlapping senses, but the idea of private ownership of the means of production and their employment in the search of profit are common to all of them. Capitalism is usually regarded as having developed through a number of stages, beginning with *commercial capitalism*, under which large merchants came to dominate trade. This was succeeded by *industrial capitalism*, dominated by the owners of factories and mines, and then by *finance capitalism*, in which control passed into the hands of bankers and financiers, who exerted indirect control over industries they did not manage in person. Reference is sometimes made to a fourth form—*state capitalism*—defined by Lenin as a system under which the State owns and uses the means of production in the interests of the class that controls the State. A fifth term, *welfare capitalism*, is used to describe capitalist economies in which there is an increased element of state intervention, either by welfare programs or by taking responsibility for maintaining full employment. Socialists criticize the system on the grounds that in practice it produces luxuries for the rich rather than necessities for all. Capitalism is defended by the argument that an economic system based on private ownership and investment, if left to operate with a minimum of state interference, will be the most efficient method of raising production, distributing scarce resources rationally, and balancing supply with demand.

Capital punishment (from Latin *caput*, 'head'), originally, death by decapitation; now, execution in general. Historically, there has been a wide variety of death penalties, but in the United States electrocution is the most common, followed by lethal gas and hanging. It has long been debated whether capital punishment deters serious crime or is only a form of revenge. Its use has been declining recently as belief in rehabilitation has grown. In most civilized countries, capital punishment has been discontinued. But those who believe that capital punishment is necessary as a deterrent see their argument supported by recent statistics showing that violent crime has been increasing. In the U.S. it is the state government that determines the use of capital punishment.

Capitol, U.S., building in Washington, D.C. that houses the Congress of the United States. The U.S. Senate occupies the north wing of the Capitol, and the U.S. House of Representatives the south.

The Capitol is a brilliant white structure in the classical style. William Thornton designed the Capitol in 1792 and construction began in 1793 when President George Washington laid the cornerstone.

Capitol Hill *See:* Washington, D.C..

Capone, Al (1899-1947), U.S. gangster. He became head of a lucrative Chicago crime syndicate in the 1920s, and was involved in many gang murders, including the St. Valentine's Day Massacre. Because of the difficulty in securing evidence against him, he was eventually convicted only of income-tax evasion (1931).

Capote, Truman (1924-1984), U.S. writer. His best-known works are *Breakfast at Tiffany's* (1958) and *In Cold Blood* (1965). His earlier works include *Other Voices, Other Rooms* (1948) and *The Grass Harp* (1951). He was also coauthor of the motion picture *Beat the Devil*, cowrote the screenplay for *The Innocents*, and adapted some of his stories for television.

Cappadocia, region in central Turkey, between the Black Sea and the Taurus Mountains. It became significant for the first time during the rule of the Hittites (14th century B.C.; among others, the ruined city of Boghazköy), later a Persian satrapy with Mazaca (currently Kayseri) as its capital. An independent kingdom at the time of the Seleucids and a Roman province in the 1st century A.D..
Soft tuff layers can be found here in which caves have been hacked out for religious purposes and for housing. The stone churches with paintings stemming from the period of the iconoclasm (726-843) are historically significant.

Rock houses in the conical limestone formations south of Kayseri in Cappadocia, a region with a very rich history.

Capra, Frank (1897-1991), U.S. film director and 3-time Academy Award winner. With

The docile capybara (*Hydrochoerus capybara*) which may grow to the size of a sheep, is the largest rodent in the world.

a gift for gentle satire and comic improvisation, he directed *Mr. Deeds Goes to Town* (1936), *Lost Horizon* (1937), *You Can't Take It with You* (1938) and *It's a Wonderful Life* (1946).

Capri (pop. 8,000), Italian island resort in the Bay of Naples, site of the Villa Iovis of Roman Emperor Tiberius. Capri produces olive oil and wine, but its main industry is tourism. Anacapri, at the island's western end, is approachable from the sea by hundreds of steps, called the 'Phoenician Stairs.' *See also:* Italy.

Capricorn, Tropic of *See:* Tropic of Capricorn.

Capsicum, genus of the nightshade family, cultivated in warm climates for its fruit (pepper); also, pod of the cayenne pepper plant, which, when dried and prepared, is used in medicine as an irritant and a stimulant.

Captain Kidd *See:* Kidd, William.

Capuchin (*Cebus capucinus*), small tree-dwelling monkey with a long, prehensile tail. Native to South America, capuchins are popular as pets in North America and Europe because of their great intelligence. They are the traditional organ-grinder's monkey. Capuchins live in troops and feed on fruit, shoots, and small animals.

Capuchins, Roman Catholic order of friars and an independent branch of the Franciscans. Founded (1525) by Matteo di Basico, a Franciscan who sought a return to the simplicity of St. Francis's life, the order is distinguished by the pointed hood, or *capuccino*.
See also: Franciscans.

Capybara (*Hydrochoerus capybara*), world's largest rodent. It looks like a large guinea pig, weighing up to 120 lb (54 kg) and standing 21 in (53 cm) at the shoulder. The fur is coarse and grey-brown. Capybaras are found in wet areas of northern South America where they live a largely aquatic life, swimming with only their high-set nose, eyes, and ears showing.

Car *See:* Automobile; Railroad.

Caracal, or desert lynx (*Felis caracal*), medium-sized cat of Africa and southern Asia that is distinguished by a fawn coat, long legs, and long black ear tufts. It lives in grassland, bush, or rocky country and feeds on small animals.

The caracal (*Felis caracal*) is a fast, savage cat that has been called Simba kali ('fierce lion') in the Swahili language. Native to Africa and southern Asia, it preys on hares, birds, and gazelles.

Caracara, any of a variety of long-legged South American hawks with long narrow wings, related to the falcon. The patch of bare skin at the base of the bill, a characteristic shared with vultures, is an adaptation for carrion-eating, but caracaras also hunt for live prey and will eat fruit. They rob other birds of their food, and the red-throated caracara raids wasps' nests. The Guadeloupe caracara was exterminated before 1911.

Caracas (pop. 3,500,000), Venezuelan capital, near the Caribbean Sea at an altitude of 3,020 ft (920 m). Founded in 1567 by Diego de Losada, it was the birthplace of Simón Bolívar (1783). Independence from Spain was achieved in 1821, as part of the Republic of Gran Colombia. In 1829 Caracas became the capital of independent Venezuela. After World War II and the discovery of oil in Maracaibo, Caracas greatly expanded. Industries include textiles, cement, steel products, paper, leatherwork, and furniture.
See also: Venezuela.

Caramanlis, Constantine (1907-1998), Greek premier (1955-1963, 1974-1980) and president (1980-1985, 1990-1995). Following a dispute with then King Paul, he resigned as premier and went into exile in Paris (1963). He returned 11 years later when the military junta ruling Greece fell because of the Cyprus crisis. He helped restore constitutional government and his party, New Democracy, won a big victory in 1975. The republican form of government he advocated was also approved, and in 1980 he was elected president.
See also: Greece.

Carat, measure of the weight of gems and pearls or of the purity of precious metals. The name comes from the dried seeds of the carob tree, which were used to weigh gold in Africa and diamonds in India. The value of the carat varied from 190 mg to almost 210 mg until 1913, when a standard carat of 200 mg was adopted. As a measure of purity, 1 carat represents 1 part in 24 of the precious metal. Thus 22-carat gold contains 22 parts of gold and 2 of other metal.

Caravaggio, Michelangelo Merisi da (1573-1610), Italian Baroque painter who achieved startling and dramatic effects with a technique of shadow and light called *chiaroscuro*. Among his finest works are the *Death of the Virgin*, the *Fortune Teller*, and *Supper at Emmaus*.
See also: Baroque.

Caraway (*Carum carvi*), biennial or perennial plant of the carrot family, the seed of which is used for flavoring medicinal purposes. The hollow, furrowed, angular, branched stem grows in the second year from a white, carrot-shaped root. The leaves are deeply incised, the small white or yellow flowers form a flat, round cluster, and the fruit is dark brown, oblong, flattened, and 2-seeded.

Carbide, any chemical compound of carbon and a metal. Calcium carbide is one of the important ones, a source of acetylene, while carbides of silicon, tungsten, and other elements are known for being hard, strong, and resistant to high temperatures.
See also: Calcium carbide.

Carbine, short, lightweight rifle most useful to soldiers fighting from tanks and other cramped spaces. It fires ammunition heavier than a pistol's but lighter than the larger assault rifles.

Carbohydrate, any of a group of chemical compounds-including sugars, starches, and cellulose-containing carbon, hydrogen, and oxygen only, with the ratio of hydrogen to oxygen atoms usually 2:1. Carbohydrates provide the chief source of energy in most diets; about 50% of the total calories in the diet of a prosperous industrial community come from carbohydrates. In a poor agricultural community, living largely on cereals, the proportion is higher and may be as much as 85%. The chief dietary carbohydrate is starch, which is present in all cereal grains, roots, and tubers.

Carbolic acid, or phenol (C_6H_5OH), first chemical to be used as an antiseptic. Though poisonous and corrosive to the skin, in dilute form it is lethal to microorganisms, without many undesirable side effects on the patient.
See also: Antiseptic.

Carbon, chemical element, symbol C; for physical constants see Periodic Table. Carbon is nonmetallic and was discovered in ancient times. It occurs in 3 allotropic forms: amorphous (as in coal or charcoal), graphite, and diamond. All living things contain carbon, which forms more compounds than any other element. Organic chemistry, the study of carbon compounds, is therefore a major field in biology and medicine.

Carbon 14 *See:* Radiocarbon.

Carbonate, salt of carbonic acid that contains the carbonate ion $CO_3=$. They are produced by reacting a base, such as metal oxide or hydroxide, with carbonic acid, which is formed by dissolving carbon dioxide in water. Calcium carbonate is very abundant in nature, occurring as limestone, chalk, and marble. The mineral dolomite is a mixture of calcium and magnesium carbonates. Commercially, the most important carbonate is sodium carbonate, also called soda ash and washing soda. Carbonates are decomposed by acids, carbon dioxide being given off. Heating carbonates also drives off carbon dioxide, leaving the metal oxide.

Carbon bisulfide *See:* Carbon disulfide.

Carbon black *See:* Carbon.

Carbon dating *See:* Radiocarbon.

Carbon dioxide, a colorless, odorless gas composed of carbon and oxygen. Carbon dioxide does not burn nor does it support the combustion of most other substances. The gas is soluble in water, with which it forms carbonic acid. Carbon dioxide is about 11/2 times as heavy as air and makes up about 0.03 per cent of the atmosphere by volume. Carbon dioxide is needed by photosynthetic organisms (most plants and algae, and some bacteria) to manufacture food. In unusually high concentrations, such as sometimes occur in mines, carbon dioxide can cause death by asphyxiation.

Carbon dioxide is formed by the respiration of plants and animals; by the fermentation and decay of organic matter; and by the combustion of fuels containing carbon, such as fossil fuels and wood. Carbon dioxide is also formed when certain carbonates are treated with an acid or heated. Since the middle of the 19th century, the burning of fossil fuels in ever greater amounts has gradually increased the amount of carbon dioxide in the atmosphere. The increase, though small, may eventually raise the average atmospheric temperature of the earth, because the carbon dioxide traps infrared (heat) radiation that would otherwise escape from the earth into space.

For commercial use, carbon dioxide is obtained primarily from gas wells and ad a by-product of fermentation, the manufacture of ammonia, or the combustion of fossil fuels. For some uses, carbon dioxide is liquefied or solidified.

Carbon dioxide is used to carbonate beverages. In baking, it leavens dough. A major use or carbon dioxide is in *enhanced oil recovery;* the gas is pumped into largely exhausted petroleum deposits to force petroleum to the surface. Carbon dioxide is also used in extinguishing fires and in the manufacture of a number of chemical products.

Liquid carbon dioxide is used in processes that involve chilling; it is used, for example, to achieve cooling of certain plastics in molds and rapid freezing of foods.

Solid carbon dioxide (dry ice) is used for refrigeration, especially when transporting perishable items.
Chemical formula: CO_2.
See also: Photosynthesis.

Carbon disulfide (CS_2), clear, inflammable liquid chemical compound, composed of 1 carbon atom and 2 sulfur atoms, used in the manufacture of viscose rayon and cello-

phane, as a solvent for fats, rubber, resins, waxes, and sulfur, and in matches, fumigants, and pesticides. It is a typical toxic industrial chemical. The principal route of exposure in humans is by inhalation; skin contact is much less significant, and other routes are of negligible importance. Carbon disulfide is distributed in an organism through the bloodstream. Readily soluble in fats and lipids and binding to amino acids and proteins, it disappears rapidly from the bloodstream and has a high affinity for all tissues and organs. Hyperactive poisoning caused by massive short-term exposure to high concentrations of carbon disulfide is characterized by sudden coma and eventual death. Cases of poisoning due to relatively short exposures to concentrations of 3,000-5,000 mg per cubic meter are predominantly associated with psychiatric and neurological symptoms: (1) extreme irritability, (2) uncontrolled anger, (3) rapid mood changes, (4) hallucinations, (5) paranoia and suicidal tendencies, and (6) manic delirium. Other symptoms include: (1) memory defects, (2) severe insomnia, (3) nightmares, (4) fatigue, (5) loss of appetite, and (6) gastrointestinal problems. Exposure over many years may produce chronic damage to the brain at first associated with psychological and behavioral changes, later with neurological changes, both in the brain and peripheral nerves. Changes in the blood vessels due to exposure are similar to those of atherosclerosis and mainly affect the arteries supplying the brain and heart muscle. Incidence of coronary heart disease is disproportionately high in exposed workers.
See also: Sulfide.

Carboniferous, collective term used mainly in Europe for the combined Mississippian and Pennsylvanian periods of the geological time scale, 345-280 million years ago.

Carbon monoxide (CO), colorless, odorless, very poisonous gas that burns with a pale blue flame and is a component of coal gas, exhaust fumes, and most smoke (including cigarette smoke). Inhalation of carbon monoxide causes dizziness, headache, and convulsions, and can lead to brain damage, paralysis, and death.

Carbon tetrachloride (CCl_4), colorless liquid with a distinctive smell, used mainly as a solvent. It dissolves fats and oils, and can be used as a dry-cleaning fluid. Widely used in industry to dissolve resins, rubber, and many other organic chemicals, it must be handled carefully. It is not inflammable, but forms highly poisonous substances when heated in a flame. Breathing the fumes over a long period can itself cause kidney and liver damage, so carbon tetrachloride should be used only in well-ventilated places. Carbon tetrachloride is manufactured by passing chlorine gas over red-hot coke.

Carborundum, commercial name for silicon carbide (SiC), widely used abrasive and one of the hardest substances known. Carborundum has a very high melting point (about 4,892F/2,700C) and is used in the manufacture of heat-resistant materials. It conducts electricity and is used in electronic equipment. Carborundum is found in a variety of colors, ranging from blue-black to green, all with a lustrous sheen. A very pure colorless form also exists. Carborundum is widely found over the earth's surface and has also been found in meteorites that have landed on earth. It was first synthesized in 1891 by the American chemist Edward Acheson, who heated coke and clay in a furnace at very high temperatures.

Carbuncle, infection under the full thickness of the skin caused by the pus-forming germ *Staphylococcus*. It produces a large infected area from which the pus escapes by making numerous openings for itself through the skin, producing a sieve-like appearance.

Carburetor, device that mixes air and gasoline in the correct proportion for efficient combustion (about 15:1 by weight) in internal combustion engines (as in automobiles). In its simplest form a carburetor is a tube that is constructed at one point into a narrow throat or venturi. As air flows through the venturi, it speeds up and its pressure decreases. Gasoline from a reservoir (the float chamber) is piped to the venturi and sucked into the airstream. The fuel mixture then passes through a 'butterfly' throttle valve into the engine cylinders. The throttle valve controls the rate at which the fuel mixture enters the engine and therefore the engine speed. A butterfly choke valve is fitted in the air intake to the carburetor to cut off the air supply when the engine is started from cold.

See also: Gasoline engine.

Carcassonne (pop. 45,000), city in southern France, southeast of Toulouse. Carcassonne is divided by the Aude River into the old town (Cité) and the newer Ville Basse. The old town is a medieval walled city whose architecture has made Carcassonne a tourist attraction.
See also: France.

Carcinogen *See:* Cancer.

Carcinoma, malignant tumor or new growth (neoplasm) derived from epithelial and glandular tissues, a form of cancer.
See also: Cancer.

Cardamom (*Elettaria cardamomum*), perennial plant the seed of which is used as a spice and for medicinal purposes. The simple erect stem of the plant grows to a height of 6-10 ft (1.8-3 m) from a thumbthick, creeping rootstock. The leaves are lanceolate (spear-shaped) and dark green. The small, yellowish flowers grow in loose groups on prostrate flower stems. The fruit is a 3-celled capsule holding up to 18 seeds. These are useful in controlling flatulence, but they are usually used to increase the efficacy of other remedies.

Cárdenas, Lázaro (1895-1970), Mexican soldier and politician. He joined the Mexican revolutionary forces in 1913, rising to the rank of general. President from 1934 to 1940, he initiated many radical reforms,

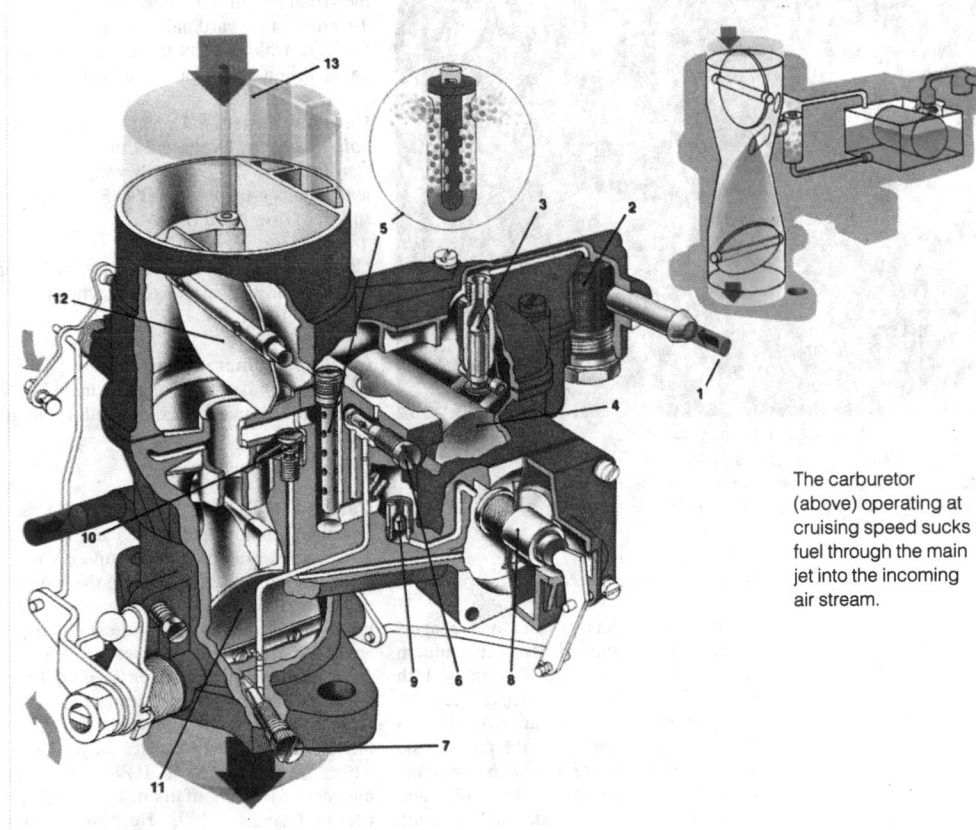

The carburetor (above) operating at cruising speed sucks fuel through the main jet into the incoming air stream.

C

including the expropriation of land and nationalization of foreign-owned oil companies.
See also: Mexico.

Card games, games played with rectangular cards marked with number (rank) and symbol (suit). Playing cards probably developed from small stones, scratched with various symbols, used in early cultures for religious ceremonies and magical purposes. These pebbles were eventually used for competitive games, often involving gambling. Cards were used in China in the 10th century A.D. By about the 13th century they had been introduced in Europe by travelers and gypsies from the East. Early cards varied greatly in design. The 14th century Italian tarocchi or tarot deck had 78 cards that included 22 picture cards bearing mainly religious illustrations, and 4 suits each of 14 plain cards. Today, many different decks exist, but the most popular contains 52 cards divided into 4 suits. First used in 14th-century Europe, this 52-deck was introduced to Britain, modified, and eventually popularized by the invention of games requiring such a deck. As games became more sophisticated, it became desirable to have written rules. The English writer Edmond Hoyle (1672-1769) produced a rule book giving details of many games.

This painting, *Les petits joueurs des cartes* is ascribed to Antoine Le Nain (1588-1648), and can be seen at the Louvre in Paris.

Cardiac *See:* Heart.

Cardiff (pop. 315,000), city and seaport near the mouth of the Taff River in southern Wales. The town was established in the 11th century around a Norman castle. Development was gradual until the discovery of coal in the valleys to the north made Cardiff a natural outlet for the export of coal, iron, and steel. Shipping of coal, coke, and steel is still the major industry; there are massive iron and steel works, and copper and tin are also produced. Flour milling and manufacture of chemicals and paper are valuable secondary industries. The city is the administrative center for Wales, and has important educational and cultural institutions including the National Museum of Wales.
See also: Wales.

Cardigan Welsh corgi, breed of dog first raised in Wales. The name derives from the Welsh words for 'dwarf dog'. The Cardigan Welsh corgi stands about 12 in (30 cm) high. Used for centuries to herd sheep, the corgi makes an affectionate and spirited pet.

Cardinal, or redbird (*Cardinalis cardinalis*), familiar songbird of the finch family, found in North America. It is about 9 in (23 cm) long, with a pointed crest and red beak. The male is scarlet with a black bib and face; the female is a dull brown.
See also: Roman Catholic Church.

Cardinal, hierarchically high-ranking official of the Roman Catholic Church, whose principal duties include the election of the pope, counseling the papacy, and administrating Church government. Cardinals are chosen by the pope and have the title of Eminence. Their insignia consists of scarlet cassock, sash, biretta (skullcap) and hat, and ring. There are three orders: cardinal bishops of the sees near Rome; cardinal priests (cardinal archbishops) with responsibilities outside the district of Rome; and cardinal deacons, who have been titular bishops since 1962. Cardinal bishops and cardinal deacons are members of the Curia, the central administrative body of the Church. They head the tribunals, or the courts of the Church. Together, the cardinals form the Sacred College, which elects the pope. The cardinalate originated in early 6th-century Rome.

Cardinal flower, tall plant (*Lobelia cardinalis*) native to North and Central America. Cardinal flowers thrive in wet soil. Their leafy stems grow up to 5 ft (1.5 m) and bear spikes of bright red flowers.

Cardiology, science of the heart, including the study of its diseases and functions.
See also: Heart.

Cardiopulmonary resuscitation (CPR), restoration of heartbeat and breathing by external cardiac massage and mouth-to-mouth breathing.
See also: First aid.

Cardoso, Fernando Henrique (1931-), Brazilian scientist and politician. In the 60s, as a professor of sociology, Cardoso wrote a few standard works concerning the economic (under)development of Latin America and he remained in Europe as an exile until the end of the 70s. He returned to Brazil in 1978, where he then entered politics. Cardoso went on to become senator (1983) for the PMDB opposition party and for the PSDB Social Democratic party PSDB, which he established in 1988. He became minister of foreign affairs in 1992, and minister of finance in 1993. He won the presidential elections in 1994 as a candidate from a left of center coalition and he was reelect-ed president in 1998. During his term as minister of finance and his presidency, he managed to reduce inflation and to reorganize government finances.
Cards *See:* Card games.

Carducci, Glosuè (1835-1907), Italian scholar and patriotic poet. His *Hymn to Satan* (1863) is an anticlerical political satire; the *Barbarian Odes* (1877-1889) are perhaps his best work. He won the 1906 Nobel Prize for literature.

CARE (Cooperative for American Relief to Everywhere, Inc.), charity founded in 1945, initially for aid to Europe but now operating worldwide. MEDICO (Medical International Cooperation Organization), a medical relief agency, became part of CARE in 1962.

Caribbean Sea, warm oceanic basin off Central America, partly enclosed by islands. The waters of the Caribbean flow into the Gulf of Mexico and thence into the Atlantic Ocean through the narrow strait of Florida. They create the warm current known as the Gulf Stream, which reaches Europe. The lands bordering the Caribbean have a warm and humid climate, with almost continuously high temperatures. The Caribbean was the route taken by the Spanish treasure ships, and became known as the 'Spanish Main.' It was an area overrun with buccaneers and fiercely disputed by France, England, Spain, and later the United States. At the end of the 19th century U.S. control over the Caribbean area was officially recognized. The building of the Panama Canal increased the importance of this 'Mediterranean of the West.'

Caribou (*Rangifer tarandus*), the only member of the deer family (Cervidae) in which both sexes bear antlers. They were at one time essential food animals for Native Americans of Canada. They live wild in Canada and Siberia, while the semi-domesticated reindeer, a subspecies, live in Greenland and Scandinavia. They can travel over boggy or snow-covered ground and live on lichen, dry grass, and twigs.

Caribs, Native American tribe encountered by the Spanish conquerors of America in the 16th century. They inhabited the islands of the Lesser Antilles in the Caribbean (which was named after them) and parts of the South American mainland, notably the Guianas. The Caribs grew a variety of crops and hunted with clubs, spears, bows, and blowguns. They were strongly independent and formed no political bonds between their own groups. Their raids on other tribes-including the more peaceful Arawaks-whom they dispossessed of their land, were made in large dugout canoes, and their conquests were celebrated by killing and eating the male captives. After Spanish settlement of the Antilles in 1527, most Caribs were exterminated except for some on the island of Aruba.

Caricature, sketch exaggerating or distorting characteristics of its subject for satirical purposes. It became an established form by the 18th century, in the hands of Francisco de Goya in Spain and William Hogarth in England, followed by Thomas Rowlandson, the Cruikshanks, and John Tenniel, and the savagely witty Honoré Daumier in France. Today, artists such as David Levine and Albert Hirschfeld continue the tradition in the United States.

Carillon, musical instrument, usually permanently set in a bell-tower, consisting of a series of bells on which melodies and simple harmonies are played from a keyboard and pedal console much like that of an organ. Some carillons are played automatically by a pegged rotating drum that operates the bell clappers or hammers. Modern instruments are electrically operated, and some do not have cast bells, but are completely electronic. Carillons originated in the Low Countries, and the old cities of Belgium and Holland have many notable examples, the oldest being the 24-bell carillon (1554) at the Rijksmuseum, Amsterdam.

Carl Gustaf (1946-), king of Sweden (Charles XV Gustavus) from 1973. Carl Gustaf's father died when his son was less than a year old, and Carl Gustaf therefore succeeded his grandfather, Gustavus VI (Gustaf Adolf).
See also: Sweden.

Carlos, Juan *See:* Juan Carlos I.

Carlota, Empress *See:* Maximilian.

Carlsbad Caverns National Park, national park in southeastern New Mexico. Its major site is a series of limestone caves about 60 million years old, among the largest caverns in the world. The caverns have spectacular stalagmite formations. The Big Room is a single chamber 1,800 ft (550 m) long, 1,100 ft (335 m) wide, and 225 ft (78 m) at its highest point. Several million bats still inhabit the caverns, which were designated a national park in 1930.

Carlyle, Thomas (1795-1881), Scottish essayist and historian. His writings greatly influenced literature and political and religious thought in mid-19th-century Britain. Carlyle was much influenced by Johann Wolfgang von Goethe, whose *Wilhelm Meister* he translated (1824). In 1826 he married Jane Welsh, who greatly helped his literary career. At her farm near Dumfries he wrote *Sartor Resartus* (The Tailor Retailored, 1833-1834). Moving to London (1834), he wrote his famous *French Revolution* (1837), which won him immediate recognition. Carlyle believed that progress was due to 'heroes' in history. He scorned the idea of democratic equality, exaggerated the importance of individual great men (*On Heroes, Hero-Worship and the Heroic in History*, 1841), and failed to realize the dangers inherent in hero-worship. His capacity for throwing new light on familiar subjects was shown by *Cromwell's Letters and Speeches* (1845), which many regard as his historical masterpiece, and *Frederick the Great* (1858-1865), his largest work.

Carmelites, friars of Our Lady of Mount Carmel, a religious order of the Roman Catholic Church. It is named for Mount Carmel, in Israel, where it originated about 1150. The Carmelites' strict rule was based on silence and solitude, but it was slightly relaxed by the English prior, Saint Simon Stock. The order's typical clothing consists of a brown habit and scapular, with a white mantle and black hood.
See also: Roman Catholic Church.

Carmichael, Hoagy (Hoagland Howard Carmichael; 1899-1981), U.S. songwriter. His 1929 ballad 'Star Dust' became a popular classic. Other compositions include 'Georgia on My Mind' (1930), 'Lazybones' (1933), and 'The Nearness of You' (1940). He appeared as a pianist in several films including *To Have and Have Not* (1944), and his song 'In the Cool, Cool, Cool of the Evening' won an Academy Award in 1951.

Carmichael, Stokely (1941-1998), U.S. Black Power leader. Prominent in the civil rights movement in the 1960s, he then advocated violent revolution and spent some time in exile in Algeria. He later argued for the use of political and economic power to attain African American demands.

Carmina Burana (Lat.: carmina = poems), a collection of Latin and German songs written by itinerant scholars in around 1200 and named after the place where it was found, namely the south German abbey Benediktbeuren. It contains serious songs on political, social, and religious subjects, sometimes critical in nature. It also contains love songs, drinking, and play songs, the latter of which are exuberant and sensual. The songs rhyme at the end of each line. In 1937, Carl Orff adapted them for choirs, soloists, and orchestras. The best known song: the wanderer's confession.

Carnap, Rudolf (1891-1970), German-U.S. logician and philosopher of science, a leading figure in the Vienna Circle and founder of logical positivism, who later turned to studying problems of linguistic philosophy and the role of probability in inductive reasoning.
See also: Positivism.

Carnarvon, George Edward Stanhope Molyneux Herbert, 5th Earl of (1866-1923), English Egyptologist. His excavations with Howard Carter in the Valley of Kings area revealed tombs of the 12th and 18th dynasties and, in Nov. 1922, the tomb of Tutankhamen.
See also: Tutankhamen.

Carnation, flower popular for buttonholes and in horticulture, subspecies of pink (*Dianthus caryophyllus*). Each carnation has a cluster of flowers, which are pink in the wild state. They have been cultivated since the time of ancient Greece, and their cultivation has become such a popular pastime that the American Carnation Society was established in 1891.

Carneades (213?-129? B.C.), Greek philosopher who rejected the notion of an absolute standard of truth. He founded and led the New Academy at Athens, and although he left no writings, his teachings were preserved by the philosopher Cleitomachus.
See also: Philosophy.

Carnegie, Andrew (1835-1919), U.S. steel magnate and philanthropist. A Scottish emigrant, Carnegie rose from bobbin-boy in a cotton factory to railroad manager and then steel producer at a time of great demand. He believed that the duty of the rich is to distribute their surplus wealth, and in 1900 he began to set up a vast number of charitable foundations and educational institutions.

Carnegie, Dale (1888-1955), U.S. author and lecturer whose *How to Win Friends and Influence People* (1936) became the best-selling nonfiction work of modern times, second only to the Bible. He offered courses in effective speaking and human relations in more than 750 U.S. cities and 15 foreign countries.

Carnelian, or cornelian, one of the chalcedony group of crystalline quartz forms. Carnelian is typically red, but is sometimes yellow or brown, the latter kind being the most precious and known as sard. Used in jewelry, the stones are often artificially colored by heating and dyeing with iron compounds.
See also: Chalcedony.

A caricature of Louis Philippe, for which the artist, Charles Philippon (1806-1862), was sued.

Carnival, term for any festive season with processions and masquerades, and particularly for the period preceding Lent. Historically, carnival can be traced back at least to the Dionysian festivals of Athens in the 6th century B.C., when a float dedicated to the god was escorted through the city, and to the Saturnalia of ancient Rome. The word *carnival* may have been derived from the Latin *carnem levare* (to put meat aside), a reference to Lenten abstinence. The Christian Church, unable to suppress the traditional pagan festivals, had to adapt and recognize them. Italy, Rome, Venice, and Florence have long been famed for their car-

C

C

The coronation of Charles the Bald, depicted in the Sacramentarium (a prayer book of the sacraments of the church) of Metz (end 9th century). The king is standing between the archbishops of Reims and Trier.

nivals. Rio de Janeiro in Brazil, Nice in France, and Cologne in Germany are still noted carnival centers.

The festivities traditionally reach their climax on the last night, Mardi Gras (Shrove Tuesday).

Carnivore, order of flesh-eating mammals with daggerlike canine teeth, cutting cheek teeth, and sharp claws.

Bears, dogs, cats, hyenas, foxes, and racoons are land carnivores; seals, sea lions, and walruses are fin-footed aquatic carnivores.

Carnivorous plant, or insectivorous plant, term used for plants that have mechanisms for trapping and digesting insects. Over 500 known species of these plants are divided into 6 unrelated families. The diverse group ranges in size from microscopic fungi to the large Pitcher Fungi.

Dionaea muscipula (Venus Fly Trap), found in the coastal swamplands of Carolina, has specialised its leaves for trapping insects. Flies are attracted by a sweet-smelling fluid. Then, triggering one of the sensitive bristles (A) by touch, will cause the two halves of the leaf to close within seconds, trapping the insect inside. Glands in the leaf then produce a colourless acid juice, which digests the insect's body, and after eight to fourteen days, depending on the size of the insect, the fluid is reabsorbed and the trap will reopen.

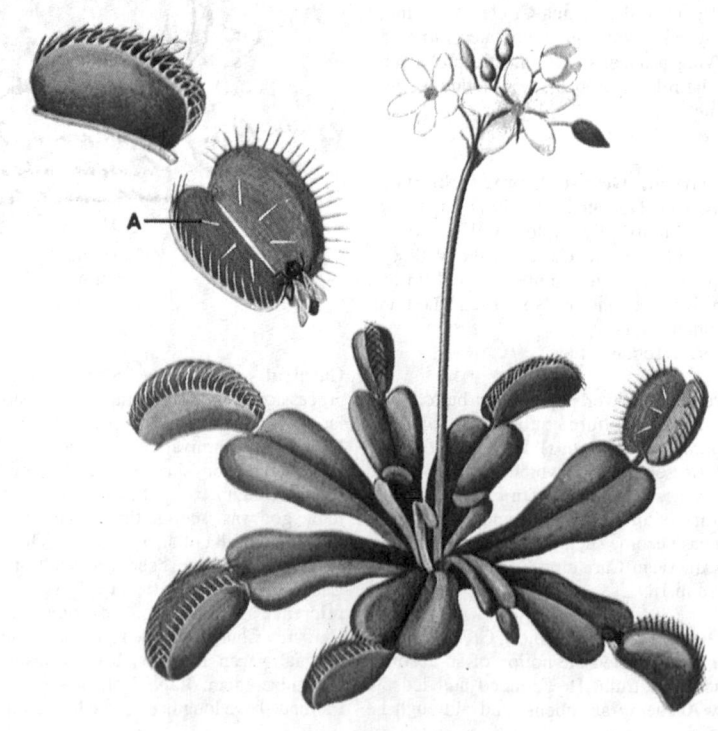

Carnot, Lazare Nicolas Marguerite (1753-1823), French soldier and politician, 'Organizer of Victory' for the Revolutionary armies. He later served as minister of war under Napoleon I, resigning in 1800.

Carnot, Nicolas Léonard Sadi (1796-1832), French physicist. Seeking to improve the efficiency of the steam engine, he devised the Carnot cycle (1824), on the basis of which Lord Kelvin and R. J. E. Clausius formulated the second law of thermodynamics. The Carnot cycle demonstrates that the efficiency of a heat engine working at maximum thermal efficiency does not depend on its mode of operation, but only on the temperatures at which it accepts and discards heat energy.

Carnotite, yellow mineral found in sandstone and limestone deposits in the Colorado Plateau. Carnotite is a valuable source of radium, uranium, and vanadium.

Caro, Anthony (1924-), British sculptor, important to modern sculpture because of the completely abstract, totally colored sculptures that he made from iron, steel, and aluminum. He influenced numerous young artists, partly due to the lessons he gave at various art academies.

Caro, Joseph ben Ephraim (1488-1575), Jewish Talmudist and philosopher whose codification of Jewish law, the *Shulhan Arukh* (1565), became the standard authority. Caro's family were Spanish Jews who settled in Constantinople; in later life he became a leader of the Jewish community in Palestine.
See also: Philosophy; Talmud.

Carob, evergreen tree (*Ceratonia siliqua*) native to the Mediterranean but also cultivated elsewhere. The carob, a member of the pea family, has pods that contain a sticky pulp that tastes similar to chocolate. Roasted and ground, it can be used as a chocolate substitute. Untreated carob pods are used as feed for cattle and horses.

Carol, name of 2 kings of Romania. **Carol I** (1839-1914), Romania's first king, brought economic development but no solution to political problems. **Carol II** (1893-1953) became king in 1930. He established a royal dictatorship to counter the growing Fascist movement, but after losing territory to the Axis powers in World War II, he abdicated in 1940 and went into exile.
See also: Romania.

Carol, cheerful song sung at Christmas, but once also performed (as a dance song) at other festive seasons. Some carols have pagan origins, and some of the older carols such as 'The Holly and the Ivy' (c.1710) have a folklore element. Certain 19th-century Christmas hymns now rank as carols. Among the oldest is the 'Boar's Head Carol,' in the collection printed by Wynkyn de Worde (1521). The German *Weihnachtslieder* (Christmas Eve Songs) and French *Noëls* have also provided carols.

Caroline Islands, volcanic islands in the Pacific Ocean, administered as a trust territory by the United States. The 900 islands are inhabited mainly by Malays, with some Japanese, Chinese, and Americans. The Spanish claimed the islands in 1696 and in 1899 sold them to Germany. After World War I they became a Japanese mandate and were invaded by U.S. troops in World War II.

Carolingian, Frankish dynasty founded in the 7th century by Pepin of Landen, whose successors ruled as mayors under the Merovingians until A.D. 751, when Pepin III made himself king. His son Charlemagne, crowned emperor in 800, reigned in the golden age of the Carolingians. His son Louis (814-840) and the Treaty of Verdun (843) partitioned the empire.
See also: Charlemagne; Pepin the Short.

Carolingian art, style created in France and western Germany in the late 8th and 9th centuries. The style, named for Charlemagne, who was crowned emperor of the restored Holy Roman Empire in 800, was an attempt to revive the arts of antiquity. Instead of the abstract geometric patterns and mythical animals used by artists of this region in the preceding centuries, Carolingian artists reintroduced the human figure in natural settings. Carolingian church architecture adopted the basilican plan of the early Christian era, adding towers, chapels, and crypts. Abbots built monasteries in which the church and living and working quarters were joined by covered walks. Artists also worked in metal, manuscript illumination, and ivory carving, combining the ornamental motifs of Anglo-Saxon and Irish art with figures from antiquity. Among the era's most important works still in existence are Charlemagne's chapel in Aachen, West Germany, built in 805, and the Utrecht Psalter, a religious manuscript written in France about 830.
See also: Charlemagne.

C

Carp (*Cyprinus carpio*), freshwater, bottom-feeding fish native to Asia but now found in Europe and America. It grows up to 3 1/3 ft (1 m) and 60 lb (27 kg) in weight and has a long dorsal fin and 4 barbels (whiskers) around the mouth.

Carpaccio, Vittore (c.1460-1526), Venetian Renaissance narrative painter, influenced by Gentile Bellini. A major work is the cycle of 9 paintings of the *Legend of St. Ursula* (1490-1495), typical in its atmospheric use of color and meticulous detail to create fantasy settings.
See also: Renaissance.

Carpal tunnel syndrome, sensation of pins-and-needles or numbness in the thumb and first two fingers, plus pain in the wrist, in the palm, or in the forearm. The carpal tunnel is the part of the wrist that encloses all the wrist tendons and the median nerve, one of the main nerves supplying the hand. This syndrome results from the compression of the median nerve when the fibrous tunnel becomes swollen. This may occur during pregnancy when the tissues are more likely to swell. The syndrome is relatively common, and is seen more often in women. A mild condition that usually responds rapidly to treatment, it can become chronic, and then surgery to remove swollen or damaged tissue may have to be considered. The condition is common among typists and keyboarders.

Carpathian Mountains, European mountain range, about 900 mi (1,448 km) long, an extension of the Alps running from Czechoslovakia through Poland, the USSR, and Rumania. Gerlachovka (8,737 ft/2,663 m) is the highest point.
See also: Alps.

Carpenter, M. Scott (1925-), second U.S. astronaut to circle the earth in a spacecraft. He made a 3-orbit flight in the Aurora 7 on May 24, 1962.
See also: Astronaut.

Carpentier, Alejo (1904-1984), Cuban writer of Russian-French descent, Carpentier spent some time in Paris during his youth where he was exposed to the influence of the surrealists. His native country Cuba plays an important role in his work, particularly the history and the cultural and sociological phenomena.
His work includes, among others *Eucué-Yamba-O* (1931), *El reino de este mundo* (1949), *Los pasos peridos* (1953), *Guerra del tiempo* (1956), *El acoso* (1958), and *El siglo de las luces* (1962).

Carpentier, Georges (1894-1975), French boxer, was the light heavyweight world champion from 1920 to 1922. He won the European title in the welterweight class in 1911, in the middleweight in 1912, in the light heavyweight in 1913 and 1922 and in the heavyweight class in 1913, 1919, 1923, and 1924. The duel between Carpentier and Jack Dempsey for the world heavyweight title in 1921, which Dempsey won, involved an amount exceeding one million dollars for the first time in the history of boxing. A stylish technique and hard blows were characteristic of Carpentier.

Carpentry, craft of laying floors, building stairways, and erecting ceiling joists and roof rafters of wood using traditional tools such as the hammer, chisel, pincers, plane, square, plumb line, and tape measure. Modern building techniques have created new applications for carpentry, most notably, the development of wooden molds for casting concrete.
See also: Woodworking.

Carpet beetle (*Anthrenus scrophulariae*), destructive household insect whose larvae feed on carpets, rugs, furniture, fur, and clothing. The tiny (under 0.2 in/5 mm long), wormlike larvae, which do more damage than the adult, are the only beetle larvae covered with hair. Adult carpet beetles, which are brownish-black or marked with red or yellowish-white spots, are discovered in infested houses during spring, and are usually found on windowsills attempting to get out to feed on pollen.

Carrà, Carlo (1881-1966), Italian painter and graphic artist; cosigned the Futurist Manifesto in 1909. After 1916, one of the most important representatives of metaphysical painting. His work is characterized by an ominous motionlessness, with which he attempted to illustrate the deeper meaning of reality.
He later went on to produce figurative, realistic paintings under the influence of Giotto.

Carracci, family of Bolognese painters. **Lodovico Carracci** (1555-1619), a painter of the Mannerist school, founded an academy of art in Bologna. **Agostino Carracci** (1557-1602) is famous primarily for his prints and *Communion of St. Jerome* (c.1590). **Annibale Carracci** (1560-1609) is considered the greatest painter of the family. Much influenced by Correggio, his work, particularly the vast decorations for the Farnese palace (1597-1604), introduced a strong classical element into a basically Mannerist style.

Carrageen *See:* Irish moss.

Carranza, Venustiano (1859-1920), Mexican political leader. He overthrew General Huerta in the Mexican revolution and became president (1914). The new constitution he supported established basic reforms in land ownership and national control of natural resources. Carranza fled an uprising led by General Obrégon, but was assassinated.
See also: Mexico.

Carrel, Alexis (1873-1944), U.S. surgeon and biologist who received the 1912 Nobel Prize in physiology and medicine for his work in suturing blood vessels, in transfusion, and in organ transplantation. During World War I he developed a treatment for wounds (the Carrel-Dakin method) that reduced the necessity for amputations.
See also: Biology.

Carreras, José Maria (1946-), Spanish singer (tenor). Quickly rose to prominence after winning the International Verdi Competition (1971: Italian debut in Parma; 1972: American debut at the New York City Opera; 1974: debut Metropolitan Opera and Covent Garden; 1975: debut at the Scala in Milan). Celebrated tenor, performer of classical opera repertoire, including film and video versions. Resumed performing in 1987 after being treated for leukaemia. Established the José Carreras International Leukaemia Foundation in 1988. Sang with Domingo and Pavarotti during the World Cup Soccer Finale in Rome in 1990. Published the autobiography *El placer de cantar: Un retrato autobiográfico* (Singing with the Soul) (1989).

Carrier pigeon, breed of show pigeon derived from the rock pigeon. Although this breed is not used for message carrying, the name is also used for the message carrying homing pigeon.
See also: Pigeon.

Carrington, Lord Peter (1919-), British politician. Carrington received training at the Sandhurst Royal Military College. He played a very important role in the British Conservative Party; as Leader of the House (1963-1970 and 1974-1979) and as minister of defence (1970-1974). Due to the Falklands war, he resigned from his position as minister for foreign affairs (1979-1983) in 1982. After that, he was active as Secretary-General of NATO (1984-1988) and negotia-

All members of the carp family (Cyprinidae) are conventional bony fish. They are widely distributed throughout the world. The most important species economically is *Cyprinus carpio*, the common carp. Fully scaled, lean, long-bodied (top). Cultivated carp: fully scaled with short body, and (bottom right) Mirror carp: body partially scaled.

The ceiling of the gallery of the Palazzo Farnese in Rome, by the Baroque painter Annibale Carracci (1560-1609), with scenes from Ovid's *Metamorphoses*. In the centre you can see *The Triumph of Bacchus*.

C

tor for the EC in former Yugoslavia, where he brought about the first of many brief ceasefires in 1992.

British illustrator Sir John Tenniel (1820-1914) obtained international fame for his illustrations of *Alice's Adventures in Wonderland* by Lewis Carroll (1832-1898).

Carroll, Lewis (Charles Lutwidge Dodgson; 1832-1898), English mathematician best known for his children's books, *Alice in Wonderland* (1865) and *Alice Through the Looking Glass* (1872), built on mathematical illogic and paradox.

Carrot (*Daucus carota*), biennial vegetable of the parsley family with a swollen, edible root, grown extensively in America and Europe. Its carotene is changed by the body to vitamin A, an essential chemical in the process of vision.

Carson, Kit (Christopher Carson; 1809-1868), American frontiersman. Carson worked as a trapper, hunter, and guide throughout the Southwest and accompanied John C. Fremont on his Western expeditions

The ruins of Roman Carthage with today's Tunis in the background.

(1842-1846). In 1854 he became an Indian agent in New Mexico. He was a Union general in the Civil War.
See also: Pioneer life in America.

Carson, Rachel Louise (1907-1964), U.S. marine biologist and science writer whose *Silent Spring* (1962) first alerted the U.S. public to the dangers of environmental pollution.
See also: Marine biology.

Cartagena (pop. 168,000), city and seaport on the Mediterranean coast in southeastern Spain. The Carthaginians, attracted by the gold and silver ores there, founded the city about 225 B.C. During the Civil War of 1936-1939, Cartagena was a naval base for General Franco.
See also: Spain.

Cartel, formal organization of producers in a particular industry, designed to set prices, control levels of production, and divide markets. Cartels normally attempt to gain sufficient control over supply, demand, and price to produce higher profits for their members. Cartels are illegal in the United States, though U.S. firms are permitted to join international associations. The best known international cartel of the 1970s and 1980s was the Organization of Petroleum Exporting Countries (OPEC).

Carter, Don (1926-), U.S. bowler. Voted the best bowler in history in a 1970 poll of bowling writers, he achieved the sport's first grand slam by winning the 4 major competitions of his day-the World Invitational All-Star, Professional Bowlers Association (PBA) National, and American Bowling Conference (ABC) Masters. He continued to win bowling championships throughout the 1950s and early 1960s. He was named to the ABC Hall of Fame in 1970 and to the PBA Hall of Fame in 1975. He was a founder and first president of the PBA.

Carter, Elliott Cook (1908-), U.S. composer, Pulitzer Prize winner (1960, 1973). Marked by unusual instrumentation and structure, his work is complex and highly contrapuntal, sometimes employing *metric modulation*, a technique he developed for creating subtle shifts in tempo. Among his best-known works are a ballet *The Minotaur* (1947), the *Double Concerto* (1961), and *Concerto for Piano and Orchestra* (1965).

Carter, Howard (1873-1939), English Egyptologist, famous for excavations in the Valley of the Kings at Luxor, Egypt, with Lord Carnarvon that discovered the tomb of Tutankhamen in 1922.
See also: Tutankhamen.

Carter, James (1969-), American jazz musician, plays a great number of saxophones and clarinets. Famous for his enthusiastic, robust marathon improvizations fusing swing, bebop, and free jazz. His record *Conversin' with the Elders* (1996), on which he plays together with older swing musicians such as Harry Edison, but also records work by the avant-garde Anthony Braxton, is characteristic of his work.

Carter, Jimmy (1924-), 39th president of the United States (1977-1981). Jimmy Carter followed a career in the navy, where he received training in nuclear physics. Returned to his parents' peanut farm in 1953, which then prospered under his management. He was elected to the Senate for the Democratic Party in 1962 and was governor of Georgia from 1970 until 1974. He was elected president in 1976. His most important achievements in foreign politics include: emphasis on human rights (resulting in friction with the Soviet Union), the 'Camp David' agreements between Egypt and Israel, political pressure on white minority regimes in Africa, seeking rapprochement with the Republic of China, and the ratification of SALT II (treaty concerning nuclear arms). The most important aspects of his domestic policy included expanding social security (among other things, increasing the minimum wage), and an energy policy. Despite the reproaches concerning his indecisive leadership and the strong economic opposition of Edward Kennedy, Carter was still nominated during the Democratic Convention in August 1980 as the only Democratic candidate for the presidential election at the end of 1980, which was won by Ronald Reagan. In 1994, there were a few occasions on which Carter acted as an intermediary on behalf of the American government: he reached an agreement with North Korea concerning international control of the North Korean nuclear power plants, in Haiti he managed only just in time to prevent the military regime from resisting the American invasion troops, and at the end of December, partly due to his efforts, a truce was brought about between the Bosnian government troops and the Bosnian Serbs. He was regularly called upon to act as intermediary in the years thereafter as well. In 2002, Carter was awarded the Nobel Peace prize owing to his 'decades of untiring effort to find peaceful solutions to international conflicts, to advance democracy and human rights, and to promote economic and social development.'

Cartesian philosophy *See:* Descartes, René.

Carthage, ancient North African city established in 814 B.C. by the Phoenicians, traders of the Mediterranean. Carthage colonized new lands and became the prominent center of the Phoenician world.
See also: Hannibal; Punic Wars.

Carthusians, contemplative and austere Roman Catholic monastic order founded in France in 1084 by St. Bruno. Each monk spends most of his life in solitude in his private cell and garden. Lay brothers prepare the Chartreuse liqueur for which the order is known.
See also: Roman Catholic Church.

Cartier, Jacques (1491-1557), French explorer who discovered the St. Lawrence River while in search of a Northwest Passage in Canada. Between 1534 and 1542 he made 3 voyages, discovering the Magdalene Islands and Prince Edward Island.
See also: Saint Lawrence River.

Cartier-Bresson, Henri (1908-), international French documentary photographer who rose to fame with his coverage of the Spanish Civil War. He has published many photographic books, including *The Decisive Moment* (1952), *China in Transition* (1956), and *Henri Cartier-Bresson, Photographer* (1979), and has also made films, as *Southern Exposures* (1970).

Cartilage, tough, flexible connective tissue found in all vertebrates, consisting of cartilage cells in a matrix of collagen fibers and a firm protein gel. The skeleton of the vertebrate embryo is formed wholly of cartilage; in most species much of this is replaced by bone during growth. There are 3 main types of cartilage: (1) hyaline, which is translucent and glossy and found in the joints, nose, trachea, and bronchi; (2) elastic, which is found in the external ear, Eustachian tube, and larynx; and (3) fibrocartilage, which attaches tendons to bone and forms the disks between the vertebrae.
See also: Bone.

Cartoon, originally, preparatory sketch in the fine arts; since the mid-19th century, humorous or satirical drawing. Today the term also includes the comic strip, the political cartoon, and cartoon animation.

Cartwright, Edmund (1743-1823), English inventor of a mechanical loom (1785) that was the ancestor of the modern power loom. He also invented a woolcombing machine (1789).

Caruso, Enrico (1873-1921), Italian operatic tenor famous for his voice and his artistry. Caruso sang over 50 roles in Europe, the United States, and Latin America, excelling in works by Puccini and Verdi. His recordings brought him worldwide fame.
See also: Opera.

Cary, Joyce (1888-1957), English novelist most famous for 2 trilogies: the first on art-*Herself Surprised* (1941), *To Be a Pilgrim* (1942), and *The Horse's Mouth* (1944), and the second on politics-*Prisoner of Grace* (1952), *Except the Lord* (1953), and *Not Honour More* (1955).

Casaba (*Cucumis melo*), type of muskmelon, also called winter melon because it ripens in fall and is available in winter. The casaba is round or oval, with a pointed stem, and weighs 2-9 lbs (1-4 kg). Its hard outer skin, which ripens from green to yellow, is smooth but wrinkled. Rich in vitamin C and potassium, its flesh is sweet and juicy and ranges in color from green to white. The casaba, which originated in Iran and the Transcaucasia, is named for the town in southwest Turkey (Kasaba) from which it was introduced in the United States in 1871. It is now grown in California and the Southwest. It is a member of the gourd family and grows on vines.

Casablanca (pop. 3,200,000), largest city in Morocco and the country's leading port. Casablanca handles most of Morocco's foreign trade, exporting grain and phosphates.

In 1907 the French occupied the port, and remained in control until 1956.
See also: Morocco.

Casals, Pablo (1876-1973), virtuoso Spanish cellist and conductor, brilliant interpreter of the music of J.S. Bach. In 1919 he founded an orchestra in Barcelona to bring music to the working classes. An outspoken antifascist, he left Spain after the Spanish Civil War to settle in Prades, France, and then (1956) in Puerto Rico, organizing music festivals in both places.

Casanova (De Seingalt), Giovanni Giacomo (1725-1798), Venetian author and adventurer whose name became a synonym for seducer. His memoirs, both sensual and sensitive, show him as a freethinking libertine; they also give an excellent picture of his times.

Cascade Range, mountain range extending 700 mi (1,127 km) from northern California to British Columbia. Its highest peak is Mt. Rainier (14,410 ft/4,392 m). There are 4 dormant volcanos and the recently active (1980) Mt. Saint Helens.

Cascade Tunnel, longest railroad tunnel in North America, cutting across 7.79 mi (12.5 km) of the Cascade range in the central part of Washington. The tunnel was completed in 1929 at a cost of 25 million dollars.
See also: Cascade Range.

Cascara sagrada, small buckthorn tree of the Western United States whose bark is used in making a laxative. It is also known as coffeeberry, as its berries were used by the pioneers to make a substitute coffee.

Casehardening, treatment of mild steel to give it an extremely hard surface. The steel is heated for several hours in carbon-containing material, such as powdered charcoal. During this process carbon is slowly absorbed to a shallow depth, converting this part to high-carbon steel. On quenching with cold water this 'case' becomes hard. An even harder case is produced by 'nitriding,' in which the steel is heated in gaseous ammonia, from which the surface absorbs nitrogen. Casehardening is commonly used on gears, roller bearings, and crankshafts to produce a wear-resistant surface.
See also: Steel.

Casein, important protein that accounts for 80% of the protein content of milk. It occurs as calcium caseinate. It coagulates to form curds when acted upon by certain acids and by the enzyme rennet. The curds are used to make cheese. Casein also has many industrial uses, especially as paper coatings, adhesives, paints, plastics, and synthetic fibers.

Case method, system of teaching law by the study of actual cases. Introduced in 1870 by Christopher C. Langdell, a professor at Harvard Law School U.S. By the early 1900s the case method was adopted by most law schools.
See also: Law.

Cashew (*Anacardium occidentale*), tropical American tree of the sumac family cultivated in Africa and India. It grows up to 40 ft (12 m) high and bears a kidney-shaped nut in a hard covering underneath a fleshy edible 'pear,' which can be made into 'cajee' wine. The nuts are roasted, and the oil surrounding each nut can be used in cooking.

Cashmere, very fine natural fiber, the soft underhair of the Kashmir goat, bred in India, Iran, China, and Mongolia. Cashmere is finer than the best wools, although the name may be applied to some soft wool fabrics.

Caslavska, Vera (1942-), Czech gymnast, originally a very promising female skater. Discovered at the age of fifteen to have a great talent for gymnastics and - having received training from Eva Bosakova - debuted in 1958. During her career, she won a total of 22 medals in European and world championships and during the Olympic Games. She went on to become a trainer.

Caslon, William (1692-1766), English typefounder, inventor of Caslon type, for many years the standard typeface in the 18th century. Although superseded by the 'new-style' faces of John Baskerville and others, versions of it are much in use today.

Caspian Sea, world's largest lake located in the European-Asian border region; 143,606 sq mi (371,795 sq km), of which 38,6% lies in Iran. Length 760 mi (1,223 km), greatest depth 3,215 ft (980 m); the water level lies 92 ft (28 m) below sea level. Volume 89,695 cubic mi (373,670 cubic km) of salt water. Reduced in size by 10,042 sq mi (26,000 sq km) and located 62 ft (19 m) lower since 1930. The coastal line has shifted 10 mi (16 km) in some places. Most abundant in fish at the mouth of the Volga, which supplies the largest amount of water. High salt levels in the bays along the east coast, for example, in the Gulf of Kara-Bogaz. In 1996, an agreement was reached between Russia, Kazakhstan, Turkmenistan, and Iran concerning the status of the Caspian Sea. The agreement provided for joint economic ownership from 47 mi (75 km) off the coast. The largest supplies of oil and natural gas of Azerbaijan, which refused to cosign the agreement, are located there.

Cassandra, in Greek mythology, prophetess of doom whose warnings were never heeded. The daughter of Trojan King Priam, she was taken prisoner by Agamemnon after the Trojan War and later murdered with him by his wife, Clytemnestra.
See also: Mythology; Troy.

Cassatt, Mary (1845-1926), U.S.-born impressionist painter who lived mainly in Paris. Strongly influenced by her friend Edgar Degas, she painted domestic scenes, especially mother-and-child studies: 'The Cup of Tea' (1879), 'The Bath' (1891), 'The Boating Party' (1893).
See also: Impressionism; Degas, (Hilaire Germain) Edgar.

Cassava, or manioc (genus *Manihot*), potato-like tuber plant, staple in its native

C

Central and South America and in West Africa and southeastern Asia. After being peeled to remove most of the poisonous prussic acid, the tubers are soaked. Lumps of cooked tuber form tapioca, which can be ground to make a flour.

Cassette *See:* Tape recorder; Videotape recorder.

Cassia, genus of tropical plants. Sennas, best known as medicinal plants, are a common species.

Cassino (pop. 33,000), Italian town about 75 miles southeast of Rome, site of Monte Cassino, a Benedictine monastery founded in A.D. 529. During World War II, Cassino was strategically important to the German defense of Rome, and the town and abbey were nearly destroyed in heavy fighting. Both have since been rebuilt.
See also: Italy.

Cassiopeia, w-shaped constellation of the northern hemisphere, which appears between the North Star and the Big Dipper, directly north of the constellation Andromeda. An exploding star (supernova) was observed in Cassiopeia in 1572 by the Danish astronomer Tycho Brahe.

Cassirer, Ernst (1874-1945), German-born philosopher. His work, based on the ideas of Immanuel Kant, examines the ways in which a person's symbols and concepts structure his or her world. He fled Nazi Germany in 1933 and taught at Oxford, in Sweden, and, from 1941, in the United States.
See also: Philosophy.

Cassiterite, or tinstone, principal ore of tin. The brown-to-black-colored mineral is found in veins, along with granite and

quartz, and in riverbeds as pebbles. It is mined commercially in Malaysia, China, Bolivia, Indonesia, Thailand, the Congo, and Nigeria.
See also: Tin.

Cassius Longinus, Gaius (d. 42 B.C.), Roman general, conspirator to assassinate Julius Caesar in 44 B.C. He fled to Syria and joined Brutus to fight Octavian and Mark Antony at Philippi. Despairing of victory, he committed suicide.
See also: Rome, Ancient.

Cassowary, large, flightless bird of northern Australia and New Guinea. The largest species is nearly 5 ft (1.5 m) tall. The plumage is coarse. The head and neck are naked and brightly colored with wattles and a bony helmet. The legs are strong, and cassowaries can run at 30 mph (48 km per hour), but they are shy and hide in thick cover. Cassowaries have large, sharp claws on their 3 toes that can be formidable weapons. The eggs are incubated by the male, who also cares for the chicks. They feed on insects and fruit.

Castagno, Andrea del (1423-1457), Florentine painter of church frescoes, portraits, and murals. Best known for his *Last Supper* (1445-1450), he stressed perspective and a stark, dramatic illumination. He is notable for the vigor and strength of his figure rendering.

Castanets, small percussion instrument consisting of 2 shell-shaped halves, usually made of wood or ivory. They are held in the palm of the hand and tapped by the fingers to produce a clicking sound. Castanets have been used for hundreds of years in Spanish flamenco dancing. More recently some composers have included a part for castanets in their music, especially to suggest a Spanish flavor.

Caste system, division of society into closed groups, primarily by birth, but usually also involving religion and occupation. The most caste-bound society today is that of Hindu India; its caste system, dating from 3000 B.C., was not discouraged until recently.

Castiglione, Comte Baldassare (1478-1529), Italian courtier, diplomat, and author. His *Il Cortegiano* (The Courier) (1528), a portrait of the ideal courtier and his relationship with the prince he serves, greatly influenced Renaissance mores and inspired writers like Edmund Spenser, Sir Philip Sidney, and Miguel Cervantes.
See also: Renaissance.

Castile and Aragón, 2 kingdoms of Spain, united in 1479 by Isabella of Castile and her husband, Ferdinand V. Aragón is in the northeast of Spain, bordering France; Castile, in central and northern Spain, surrounds the city of Madrid. The union of Castile and Aragón formed the core of the modern Spanish state and served as Ferdinand and Isabella's base in their struggle, eventually successful, to drive the Moors from southern Spain (Andalusia).
See also: Spain.

Castilla, Ramón (1797?-1867), president of Peru, 1845-1851 and 1855-1862. He joined the Peruvian independence movement in 1821 and fought the Spaniards alongside José de San Martín and Simón Bolívar. When he assumed the presidency, he ended a period of anarchy and is credited with bringing peace, stability, and economic improvements. Slavery and the taxation of Indians were abolished under his administration.
See also: Peru.

Casting, production of a desired form by pouring the raw material (alloys, fiberglass, plastics, steel) in liquid form into a suitably shaped mold. In *die casting*, molten metal is forced under pressure into a die; in *centrifugal casting*, used primarily for pipes, molten material is poured into a rapidly rotating mold; in *continuous casting*, material is poured into water-cooled, open-ended molds; in *sand casting* fine sand is packed tightly around each half of a permanent pattern, which is removed, after which the 2 halves of the mold are placed together.

Castle, Vernon (1887-1918), and **Irene** (1893-1969), couple who revolutionized ballroom dancing. They introduced the one-step and the Castle walk and popularized the hesitation waltz and tango during a meteoric career that began in 1912 and ended with Vernon's death in an air crash.

Castle, fortified dwelling, built to dominate and guard a region. The term derives from the Roman *castellum* (fort or frontier stronghold). In Western Europe, most of the extant castles were built between 1000 and 1500, often on an artificial mound, with a palisaded courtyard. Later, the stockade was replaced by masonry keeps, or dungeons; defensive outer walls; and frequently a moat and drawbridge. With the decline of feudalism, the castle evolved into the Renaissance

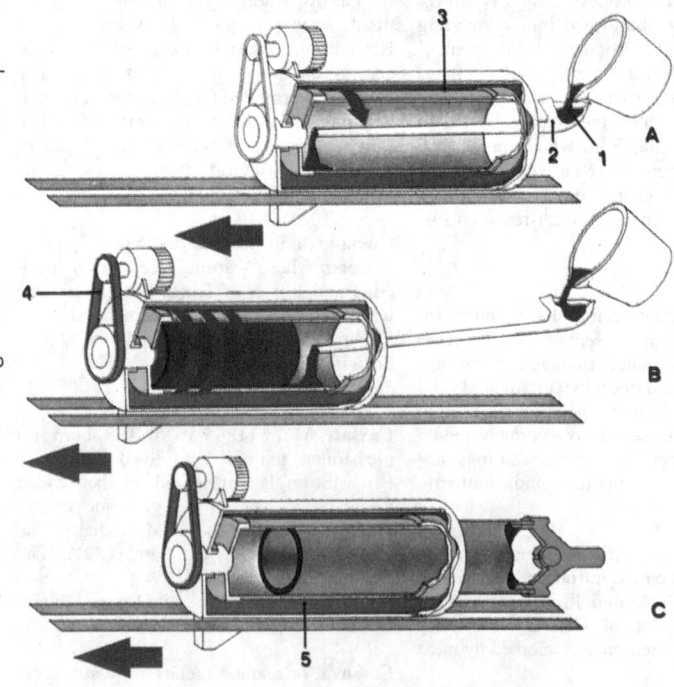

The cutaway diagrams show stages in the process by which large-diameter iron pipe is cast. (A) Molten iron (1) is poured into a trough (2) leading into a mold (3), which is mounted inside the centrifugal caster. (B) A motor-driven belt (4) causes the entire assembly to revolve. The centrifugal force thus generated forces the molten iron to conform to the mold. To ensure that the iron flows along the entire length of the mold, the casting assembly is moved away from the trough. (C) The molten metal is quickly cooled by a water-filled jacket (5) surrounding the mold.

château, with its emphasis on splendor rather than on fortification.

Castlereagh, Robert Stewart, 2d Viscount (1769-1822), Irish born British statesman, creator of the Quadruple Alliance that defeated Napoleon. As secretary for Ireland, he suppressed the 1798 rebellion and forced the Act of Union through the Irish Parliament (1800). He was war minister (1805-1806, 1807-1809), and as foreign secretary (1812-1822), played a major role in the organization of Europe at the Congress of Vienna (1814). Much maligned in his time, he committed suicide.
See also: Vienna, Congress of.

Castor and Pollux, in Greek mythology, twin heroes, called the Dioscuri. Castor the horseman was the son of Leda and Tyndareus; Pollux the boxer was the son of Leda and Zeus.
See also: Mythology.

Castor oil, thick oil obtained from the castor bean, used as a purgative and a lubricant.

Castries (pop. 55,000), capital and largest city of the Caribbean island nation of St. Lucia. Bordered by a deep-water harbor on the island's northwest coast, Castries is the chief port, exporting bananas, sugarcane, molasses, cacao, and other tropical products. Colonized by France in 1651, St. Lucia was fought over by the French and British until 1814, when Great Britain took control. Britain ruled St. Lucia until 1979, when it became an independent nation.
See also: Saint Lucia.

Castro, Fidel (1927-   ), Cuban premier (1959-   ) and revolutionary. He led an abortive revolution in 1953 against dictator Fulgencio Batista, and was imprisoned and exiled. In 1956 he invaded Cuba with 81 men and overthrew the regime, establishing himself as premier in 1959. He nationalized industry and collectivized agriculture, becoming increasingly dependent on the USSR for financial support. The U.S. has attempted to isolate Cuba both economically and politically but has not achieved success. After the collapse of the Soviet Union in 1991, many Cubans advocated free-market refoms. Castro, however, who was reelected in 1993, remained adamant in his commitment to Communism. Only in recent years did he allow gradual economic liberalization.
See also: Cuba.

Cat, hunting carnivore of the family Felidae, varying in size from the small domestic cat and the small wild cats (lynx and ocelot) to the great cats (lion, tiger, leopard, and cheetah). Cats have short snouts, large eyes, sensitive whiskers, and sharp claws and teeth.
See also: Lion; Tiger.

CAT (computerized axial tomography) scan, painless, quick diagnostic procedure in which hundreds of X-ray pictures are taken as a camera revolves around a body part. A computer integrates the pictures to reveal structures within the body. The CAT scan has created a new era in the history of diag-nostic medicine. It is especially effective in the diagnosis of neurologic disorders and cancers.

Catacombs, underground cemeteries of the early Christians, who did not follow the Greek and Roman practice of cremation. The best known and most extensive are outside Rome, built from the 1st to the 5th century A.D.

Catalepsy, condition of loss of voluntary motion in which the arms and legs remain in any position they are placed in. Causes may be organic or psychological. Catalepsy is often associated with severe cases of schizophrenia.
See also: Schizophrenia.

Catalonia, region in northeastern Spain, comprising the provinces of Lérida, Gerona, Barcelona, and Tarragona. It was occupied by the Romans and Goths, who called it Gothalonia. It maintained its own customs and language after its union with Aragon in 1137. There is also a rich body of Catalan literature. It is now the chief industrial area of Spain, and is dependent on the interior for grain and protected markets. It experienced a brief period of independence during the 1930s. In 1980 the Spanish government handed over certain limited functions to a Catalan regional government with its own parliament and premier.
See also: Spain.

Catalpa, genus of ornamental shade tree of the bignonia family, growing naturally in eastern Asia, the West Indies, and the southern United States. Its tubular white or yellow flowers have purple or brown markings.

Catalysis, change in the rate of a chemical reaction by an additive (a catalyst speeds up reactions; an inhibitor slows down reactions) that is itself unchanged at the end of the reaction. Catalysts are widely used in industry. All living organisms are dependent on the complex catalysts called enzymes, which regulate biochemical reactions.

Catamaran, boat with 2 narrow, identical hulls connected by a flat bridge deck. They are driven by sail or power and are extremely fast and stable. Trimarans are similar, but have 3 hulls, the center 1 being longer than the outer 2.

Catamount, folk name for the puma and the lynx. The word is a shortened form of *cata-mountain*, a form of *cat of the mountain*.

Cataplexy, condition of abrupt and temporary loss of voluntary muscle control brought on by some extreme emotional stimulus, especially fear, anger, or mirth. An attack may last from a few seconds to several minutes, and symptoms may range in severity from a mild weakening to paralysis of most of the muscles of the body.

Catapult, ancient military weapon used for hurling missiles. Some catapults were large crossbows, with a lethal range of over 400 yd (366 m), while others (*ballistas*) used giant levers to hurl boulders. In the Middle Ages catapults were an important part of siege artillery, but they were made obsolete by the cannon. A modern steam-powered version of the catapult launches jets from aircraft carriers.

Cataract, opacity of the lens of the eye, causing a progressive loss of vision. Aging is the most common cause, but cataracts may be hereditary or due to disease, such as diabetes. Cataracts are treated by lens extraction, followed by wearing corrective lenses or having a plastic lens implant.
See also: Blindness.

Catarrh, mild inflammation of a mucous membrane, associated with a copious secretion of mucus. Medically speaking, this refers to any mucous membrane in the body, but popularly it refers to nasal or bronchial catarrh.
See also: Sinus; Cold, common.

Catbird (*Dumetella carolinensis*), songbird of the thrush family, named for the mewing notes in its imitative song. Catbirds, which are gray with a black cap, live in the United States and in Canada, migrating in winter to Central America or to the West Indies.

Catechism, manual of religious instruction arranged in question-and-answer form. First appearing in the 8th and 9th centuries, catechisms were widely used during the Middle Ages. The Anglican catechism is included in the Book of Common Prayer, and the Baltimore Catechism (1885) is used by Roman Catholics.
See also: Book of Common Prayer.

Catechu, strong, astringent substance prepared from the wood of various tropical Asiatic plants and used in medicine with prepared chalk to treat diarrhea.

Caterpillar, larva of a moth or a butterfly, with 13 segments, 3 pairs of true legs, and up to 5 pairs of soft false legs.
See also: Butterfly.

Catfish, freshwater, bottom-feeding fish (suborder Nematognathi) with barbels, or whiskers, around the mouth, tough scaleless

Egyptian statue from the Saitic period (6th century B.C.), when cats were worshipped as a god.

C

C

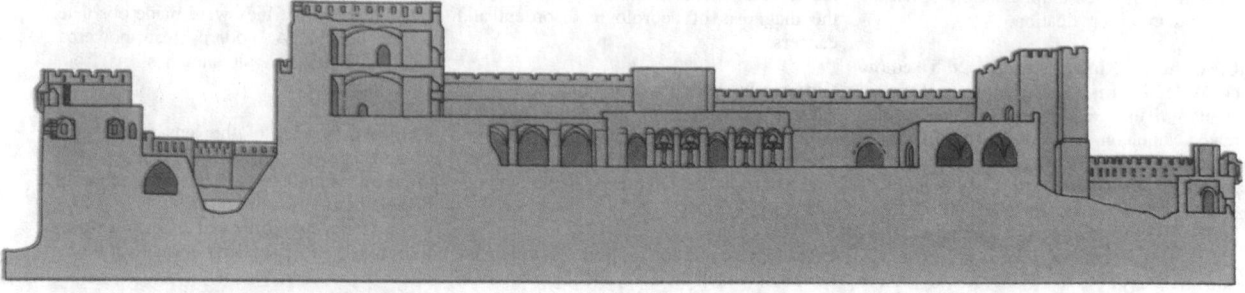

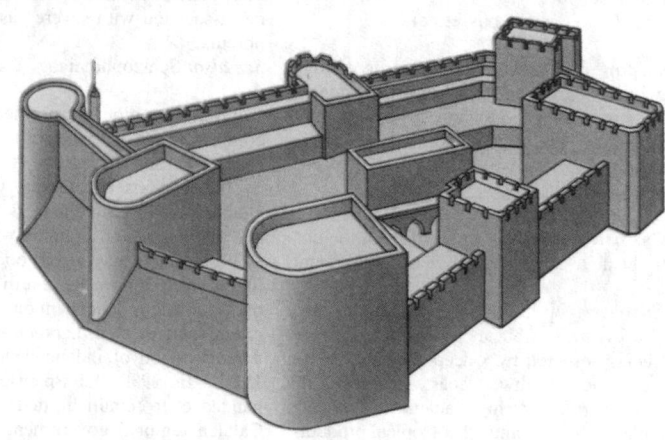

Schematic plan of a concentric castle built in Syria in the 13th century. The diagram at right shows the castle without its outer wall and defensive moat. (The moat doubles as a reservoir.) The inner courtyard, terraced and extensively vaulted, contains a romanesque chapel and the great hall and cloister.

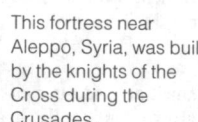

This fortress near Aleppo, Syria, was built by the knights of the Cross during the Crusades.

Motte-and-bailey earthworks originated in Gallic lands under Teutonic domination and spread throughout Europe during the eleventh and twelfth centuries. Invariably built in arable land near towns and villages, they were the forerunners of the great stone castles of the Middle Ages. The stockaded motte or mound (1), containing the tower or hall (2), must be small enough to be held by a few defenders. Stables and other outbuildings (3) were therefore kept in a stockaded bailey, connected to the motte by an inclined bridge (4). The entire castle was surrounded by a ditch (5) and counterscarp.

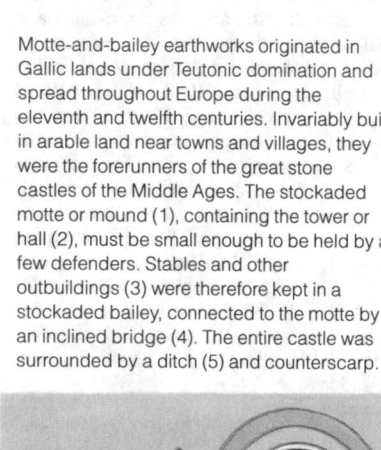

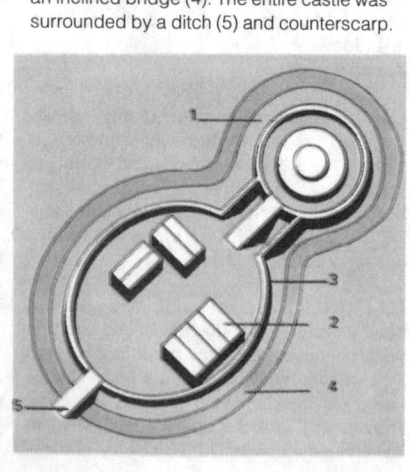

C

Doornenburg Castle (c. 1500) near Nijmegen, Netherlands, with a keep that expanded into a main castle with a moat and outworks (lower foreground) as extra protection.

Marksburg Castle, on the Rhine River, Germany

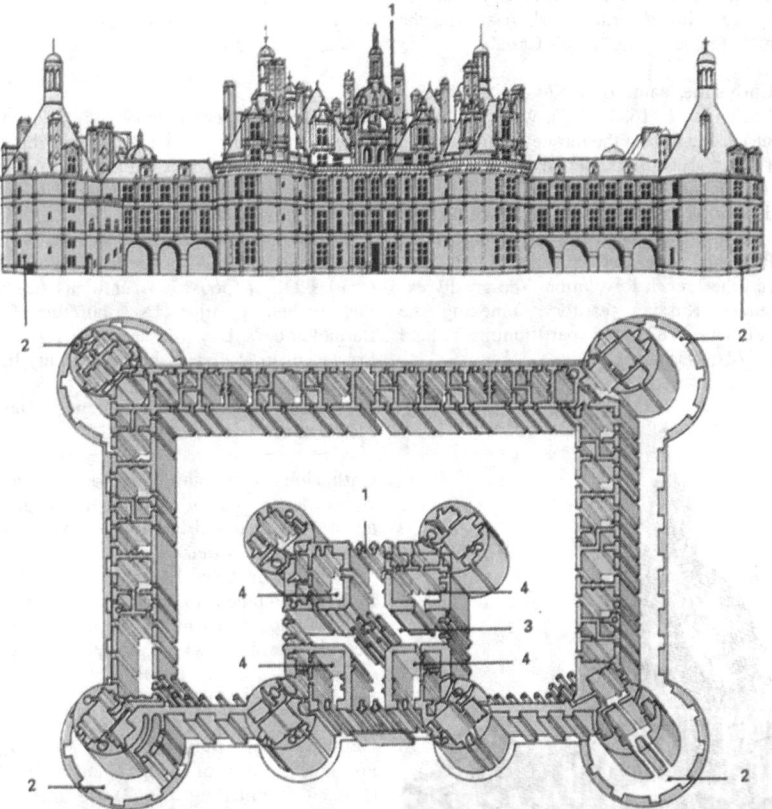

Illustration of the Château de Chambord (1519-47) is ascribed to Italian architect Domenico da Cortona. Its plan remains essentially that of a medieval concentric castle: a dungeon (1), surrounded on three sides by a courtine with massive conical towers (2), its facade (3) aligned with that of the courtine. The arms of the dungeon form a Greek cross and lead from the entrances to a double spiral staircase (4) connecting all floors. Corner suites of rooms—an Italian innovation—form appartements, the earliest French instance of what became the regular French domestic arrangement for two centuries. The vertical and ornate outline is basically French, clad in Italian decorative detail.

Photograph of the Château de Chambord in the Loire valley, France

C

Equestrian portrait of Catherine the Great, by the court painter Vigius Erichsen (1722-1782). (Musée des Beaux-Arts, Chartres)

skin, and sharp spines. Catfish are an important food source.

Catharsis, in psychoanalysis, bringing into the open of a previously repressed memory or emotion, in the hope of releasing and eliminating stress.

Cathay, name by which China was known in medieval Europe. The word derives from the Khitai, a seminomadic people of southern Manchuria whose rule extended to northern China in the 10th century A.D.
See also: China.

Cathedral, principal church of a diocese, in which the bishop has his *cathedra*, his official seat or throne. A cathedral need not be particularly large or imposing, though its importance as a major center led to the magnificent structures of the Gothic and Renaissance periods. By its prominent position and size, a cathedral often dominated a city and served as the focus of its life. In Europe, most of the older cathedral cities were already important centers in Roman and early Christian times.
See also: Architecture.

Cather, Willa Sibert (1876-1947), U.S. novelist noted for her psychologically-astute portrayals of the people of Nebraska and the Southwest. Her works include *O Pioneers!* (1913), *My Antonia* (1918), and *Death Comes for the Archbishop* (1927). She was also a brilliant writer of short stories, the most famous being 'Paul's Case.'

Catherine, name of 2 Russian empresses. **Catherine I** (1684-1727), wife of Peter I, succeeded him to the throne on his death in 1725. **Catherine II, the Great** (1729-1796) married the future Peter III in 1745. After his deposition and murder in 1762, she became empress. Her liberalism was quenched by Pugachev's peasant uprising (1773-1774) and the French Revolution. She greatly extended Russian territory, annexing the Crimea (1783) and partitioning Poland (1772-1795).

Painting by Jacopo da Empoli (1554-1640), of the marriage of Catherine and — Henry II (Palazzo Medici-Riccardi, Florence).

Catherine de' Medici (1519-1589), daughter of Lorenzo de' Medici, Duke of Urbino; wife of King Henry II of France; and mother of 3 kings of France. After the death of her eldest son, King Francis II (r.1559-1560), she acted as regent of France (until 1563) and was adviser to her son, King Charles IX, (r.1560-1574) until his death. She helped Charles IX plan the St. Bartholomew's Day Massacre against the Protestants in 1572. Her third son, Henry III, ruled from 1574 to 1589.
See also: Saint Bartholomew's Day, Massacre of.

Catherine of Aragon (1485-1536), first wife of Henry VIII of England. The daughter of Ferdinand and Isabella of Spain, she married Prince Arthur (1501) and, after his death, his brother, Henry VIII (1509). Henry's annulment of the marriage (1533) without papal consent led to the English Reformation. She was the mother of Mary I of England.
See also: Henry (England).

Catherine of Braganza (1638-1705), Portuguese wife of King Charles II of England. The marriage (1662) was intended to promote the Anglo-Portuguese alliance, but she produced no heir. After Charles's death, she returned to Portugal (1692), serving as regent (1704-1705).

Catherine of Siena, Saint (1347-1380), Italian religious and mystic known for her visions, charity, and diplomatic skill. Her influence over Pope Gregory XI (1331-1378) led him to leave Avignon in 1377 and return the papacy to Rome, thus ending the 'Babylonian captivity' of the papacy. Her feast day is Apr. 30.

Catherine the Great *See:* Catherine.

Cathode ray, stream of electrons that flows from a cathode (negative electrode) to an anode (positive electrode) in a vacuum tube when a potential of 4,000-10,000 volts is applied across them. Cathode rays were first detected when a glowing light was seen to emanate from a cathode; this is a secondary

St. Paul's Cathedral, designed by Sir Christopher Wren, was built between 1675 and 1710, on the site of a medieval cathedral that was destroyed in the Great Fire of 1666. It has a Latin-cross plan with a vast central space at the crossing, contained within the eight piers that support the dome. The interior of the dome was painted by Sir James Thornhill. On the facades, Wren used both Corinthian and composite orders. The two-storeyed central portico of the west facade is flanked by two elegant steeples.

C

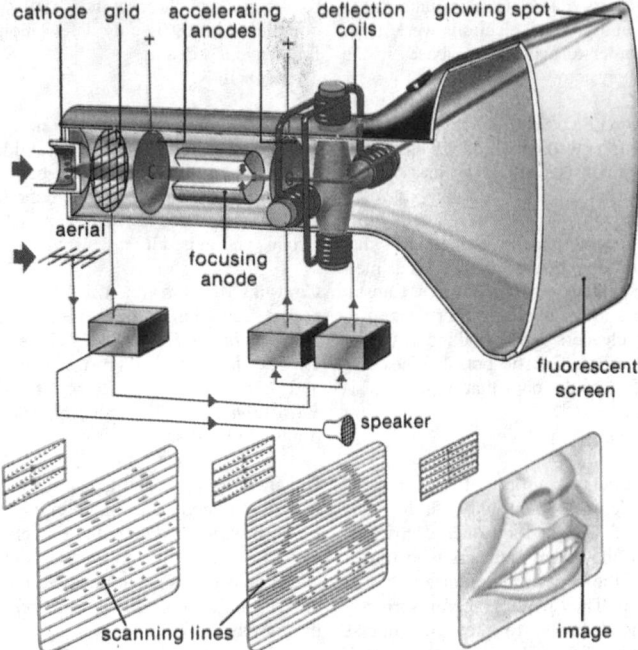

cathode grid accelerating deflection glowing spot
                  anodes   coils

aerial

focusing
anode

fluorescent
screen

speaker

scanning lines   image

The cathode ray tube of a television receiver contains a coated screen that fluoresces, or glows, when struck by electrons emitted by a cathode and	accelerated and focused into a beam by anodes. The electron velocity, and thus the intensity of each glowing spot, is controlled by a grid	synchronized with a signal transmitted from a camera. Signals also regulate two sets of coils that move the beam across and down the screen,	creating a picture of closely spaced horizontal lines. Color tubes use independent cathodes.

effect the rays produce only when traces of certain gases are present.
See also: Electrolysis; Electronics; Vacuum tube.

Catholic Church, Roman *See:* Roman Catholic Church.

Catholic Emancipation Act, British law enacted on Apr. 13, 1829, removing most of the civil disabilities imposed on British Roman Catholics from the time of Henry VIII. A controversial measure, it was introduced by Sir Robert Peel after considerable pressure from Irish campaigners headed by Daniel O'Connell.

Catiline (c.108-62 B.C.), Roman aristocrat who tried to seize power in 63 B.C. He was trapped and killed in battle at Pistoria. Cicero attacked him in a series of 4 celebrated orations.

Catkin, reproductive organ of many common trees. Each catkin bears a cluster of primitive flowers that lack petals and sepals. Instead, the stamens and pistils are protected by small leaves called bracts. 1 Catkin bears either male or female flowers. Plants bearing catkins include beech, birch, walnut, and willow families.

Catlin, George (1796-1872), U.S. artist, noted for his paintings of U.S. Native American life based on his trips to the American West. His books include *Notes on the Manners, Customs, and Conditions of*

the North American Indians (1841). A large portion of his work is in the Catlin Gallery of the National Gallery of Art in Washington, D.C.

Catnip, or catmint (*Nepeta cataria*), Eurasian mint naturalized in North America. It is grown for its aromatic leaves, which are stimulating to cats.

Cato, name of 2 Roman statesman. **Marcos Porcius Cato the Elder** (234-149 B.C.), was an orator and prose writer. He became consul in 195 B.C. and censor in 184 B.C. His only surviving work is a treatise on agriculture. **Marcus Porcius Cato the Younger,** (95-46 B.C.), great-grandson of Cato the Elder, was a model stoic and defender of Roman republicanism. He supported Pompey against Gaius Julius Caesar in the Civil War, but after the final defeat of the republican army at Thapsus (46 B.C.), he killed himself at Utica. *See also:* Rome, Ancient.

Cat's eye, any of several gemstones that, when cut to form a convex surface, resemble the eye of a cat. Common cat's eye is chalcedony, a form of quartz. The most kind is a variety of chrysoberyl.

Cattail, wild plant (genus *Typha*) that grows in marshes and other wetland areas. Also called clubrushes and, on the Pacific Coast, tule-reeds, cattails have long, slender leaves and a single tall stem. The female flowers form long brown spikes. The roots, which contain starch, are edible. The soft down

produced by cattails is sometimes used for furniture upholstery.

Cattle, large ruminant mammal of the family Bovidae, most of which have been domesticated, including bison, buffalo, yak, zebu, and European cattle. By 2500 B.C. the Egyptians had several breed of cattle, which may have been used as draft animals and for leather . Their dung served as fuel and manure. Today, beef cattle (like Aberdeen Angus or Hereford) are square and heavily built commonly kept on poor grazing land, whereas dairy breeds (like Holstein or Guernsey) have good grazing. Recent breeds are mixed beef and dairy animals. A dairy cow can give as much as 14,000 lb (6,350 kg) of milk in 1 year.

Cattle tick, brown parasitic insect (*Boophilus annulatus*) that lives on cattle. It carries an infectious cattle disease known as Texas fever, which in the mid-1800s threatened cattle throughout the U.S. Southwest. Control measures have all but eliminated cattle ticks in the United States, but they are still common in Mexico.

Catullus, Gaius Valerius (c.84-54 B.C.), Roman lyric poet influenced by Hellenistic Greek poetry. He wrote passionate lyrics, epigrams, elegies, idylls, and vicious satires, of which only 116 survive. He influenced the later Roman poets Horace and Martial.

Caucasia, oil-rich region that straddles the Caucasus Mountains in the southwest of the Russian Federation. After the Russian Revolution the southern part, called Transcaucasia, was organized as the re-

Hereford (beef)

Holstein-Friesian
(dairy products)

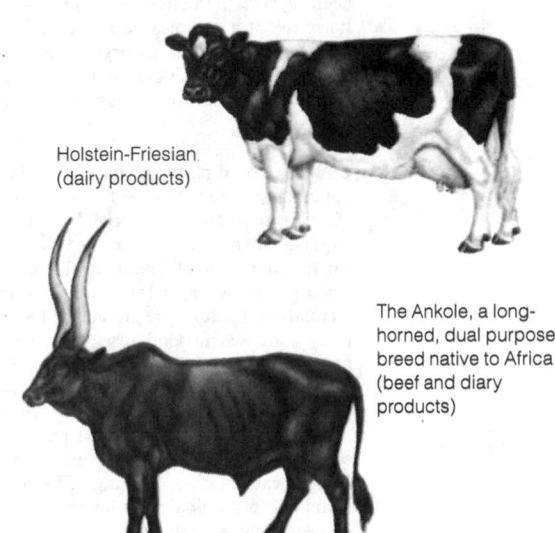

The Ankole, a long-horned, dual purpose breed native to Africa (beef and diary products)

C

publics of Georgia, Armenia, and Azerbaijan. In 1922, they became the Transcaucasian Soviet Federated Socialist Republic, but in 1936 they were again reorganized as 3 distinct republics of the Soviet Union and gained independence in 1991. *See also:* Union of Soviet Socialist Republics.

Caucasus, or Caucasia, a historic region between the Black and Caspian seas. In the north, the basins of the Kuban and Kuma rivers in Russia mark its approximate limit. The southern limit is set by Armenia's border with Turkey and Azerbaijan's border with Iran. The portion south of the Greater Caucasus Mountains is sometimes called Transcaucasia.
The people of the Caucasus are varied in ethnic background because the region was continuously invaded over the centuries by peoples who left behind settlers and elements of their culture. Parts of the Caucasus were conquered in ancient times by Scythians, Persians, Greeks, and Romans. Later invaders included Arabs, Mongols, and Turks. However, many of the native Caucasian tribes - such as the Circassians and Chechens - preserved their own languages and cultures. In the early 19th century, the German anthropologist J. F. Blumenbach gave the name 'Caucasian' to the white race because he thought certain peoples of Transcaucasia best typified the race.
During the 18th century the Ottoman Empire, Persia, and Russia struggled for control of the Caucasus. Russia gradually won supremacy, but mountain tribes held out against Russian forces until late in the 19th century. Following the 1917 Russian Revolution, Cossack groups in the North Caucasus fought the Bolsheviks until 1924. The Caucasus was again the site of battles during World War II when German forces invaded the region in an attempt to gain the oil fields on the Caspian coast.
See also: Union of Soviet Socialist Republics.

Cauchy, Augustin Louis (1789-1857), French mathematician and theoretical physicist. Cauchy is mainly known for his pioneering work in the field of the theory of the functions of a complex variable. He is seen as the father of this theory. He also contributed to strengthening the foundations of the analysis and to making the evidence more exact.

Caucus, closed party meetings to decide on policy or select candidates for public office. The term, possibly derived from the Algonquian *Kaw-Kaw-was* (to talk), originated as the name of a political club in 18th-century Boston. From 1800 until 1824 presidential candidates were nominated by the 2-party caucuses in Congress. Although the national convention system replaced the Congressional nominating caucus, party caucuses are important forums for deciding legislative policy, and they fill party posts such as floor leader and whip. A special form of caucus is the meeting of local party members to nominate candidates for office or elect delegates to party conventions. In the late 19th century political 'bosses' and

their followers came to dominate these meetings, and primary elections were introduced in order to avoid such abuses in the nominating system.

Cauliflower, *(Brassica oleracea)*, variety of cabbage similar to broccoli, in which the edible portion consists of a large mass of unopened flowers.

Caustic, general name for chemicals that burn or corrode other materials such as metal, plastics, and organic substances. Caustic soda, also known as lye, is used in household drain cleaners and in making soap, paper, and textiles. Caustic potash is used in the manufacture of soaps that dissolve easily in water.
See also: Lye.

Cavalier Poets, a group of 17th-century English lyric poets identified with the court of Charles I. Except for Robert Herrick, a clergyman, they were courtiers who fought against the Parliamentarians, or Roundheads. They wrote graceful, sprightly verses, mostly on love themes. Thomas Carew (1594/95-1639), Robert Herrick (1591-1674), Richard Lovelace (1618-1656/57) and John Suckling (1609-1642) were famous Cavalier Poets.

Cavalry, military force that fights on horseback. It played a key role in warfare from about the 6th century B.C. to the end of the 19th century, when the development of rapid-fire rifles began to reduce its effectiveness.

Cave, natural hollow or cavern found in rock. The most spectacularl caves are found in limestone rocks beneath the earth's surface. These caves were formed thousands of years ago by water erosion.
See also: Speleology.

Cavefish, common name of several varieties of small, blind, cave-dwelling fish of the family Amblyopsidae. Also known as blindfish, they navigate with the help of rows of small projections on their skin.

Cavell, Edith Louise (1865-1915), British nurse who became a World War I heroine. She was responsible for updating nurses' training in Belgium and eventually was executed by the Germans for helping some 200 Allied soldiers escape.

Cavendish, Henry (1731-1810), English chemist and physicist who showed hydrogen to be a distinct gas, water to be a compound - not an elementary substance, and the composition of the atmosphere to be constant. He also used a torsion balance to measure the density of the earth (1798).
See also: Chemistry; Hydrogen.

Cavour, Count Camillo Benso of (1810-1861), Italian statesman largely responsible for the unification of Italy. Cavour, under Victor Emmanuel II, became premier of Piedmont in 1852 and sought to unite the country by making piecemeal additions to Piedmont. A subtle diplomat, he secured the central Italian states. The unification, except

for Venice and the province of Rome, was completed in 1861, only a few months before Cavour's death.
See also: Italy.

Cavy, any of a number of related South American rodents (family Caviidae), of which the guinea pig is the best known. Cavies typically have short hair and legs and thick bodies. They are social animals, vegetarians, and generally nocturnal.

Caxton, William (c.1422-1491), English printer, trained in Cologne. He produced *The Recuyell of the Historyes of Troye* (Bruges, c.1475), the first book printed in English, and *Dictes and Sayenges of the Philosophers* (1477), the first dated book printed in English.

Cayenne (pop. 42,000), capital of French Guiana, situated on an island in the Cayenne River. It was founded by the French in 1643 and from the late 17th century until 1946 was a notorious French penal colony. Gold, hides, rum, cocoa, and cayenne pepper pass through the port.
See also: French Guiana.

Cayley, Sir George (1773-1857), British inventor who pioneered the science of aerodynamics. He built the first man-carrying glider (1853) and formulated the design principles later used in airplane construction.
See also: Aerodynamics.

Cayman, crocodilian of South America, notably of the Amazon basin. The dwarf cayman is up to 4 ft (1 m) long but the black cayman may grow to 15 ft (4-1/2 m). Similar to alligators, caymans can be distinguished by bony plates on the underside.
See also: Crocodile; Alligator.

Cayman Islands, British dependency in the Caribbean Sea, about 200 mi (320 km) northwest of Jamaica, consisting of 3 islands: Grand Cayman, Little Cayman, and Cayman Brac. Georgetown, on Grand Cayman, is the capital and largest city. Tourism is the main industry, but low taxes and banking secrecy laws have attracted a variety of companies.

Cayuga, Native American tribe, member of the Iroquois League. They inhabited the area of Cayuga Lake, N.Y., until the American Revolution. Favoring the British, many then moved to Canada, while others dispersed.

CB radio *See:* Citizens band radio.

CD *See:* Compact disc (CD).

CD-ROM, Compact Disc Read Only Memory, disk storage that works according to the same principle as the ordinary music CD. The disk, which may contain software, reference material, pictures and/or sound, can only be read. There are also versions that can be erased or written on (CD-e).

Ceausescu, Nicolae (1918-1989), president of Romania from 1967 until 1989, when he was overthrown and executed. First elected member of the Romanian Communist Party

C

Central Committee in 1948, he became head of the committee in 1965. As president, he instigated a policy of independence within the Soviet bloc.
See also: Romania.

Cebu, densely populated Philippine island with a narrow coastal plain and interior mountains. The city of Cebu is the main port and commercial center for the surrounding islands. It was the first permanent Spanish settlement in the Philippines (1565).
See also: Philippines.

Cecilia, Saint, early martyr of the Christian church, in 2nd or 3rd century Rome. According to legend, she converted St. Valerian and his brother Tiburtius. The Roman prefect Almachius ordered her burned to death for distributing goods to the poor. Tradition says that she was beheaded when her body would not burn. Though her authenticity is doubted, she continues to be popular and is represented on the church calendar (Nov. 22). She is considered the patron saint of music.
See also: Christianity.

Cedar (genus *Cedrus*), evergreen, cone-bearing tree with fragrant wood. The timber trade calls several unrelated trees 'cedar' but the true cedars are species found in the mountains of North Africa and Asia. They are distinguished by being the only evergreen conifers with needles in tufts along the branches.

Cela, Camilo José (1916-2002), a Spanish author. Cela's experimental and dramatic writing regenerated interest in the Spanish novel and greatly influenced 20th-century literature. *The Family of Pascual Duarte*

(1942), his first novel, portrays a murderer shaped by a twisted society and invokes both compassion for the criminal and revulsion at his actions. Vivid scenes of violence, emotionally grotesque characters, and social chaos are typical elements of Cela's writing. Cela was born in Galacia. His dissatisfaction with the Franco regime influenced the themes of his writing. He won the Nobel Prize for literature in 1989.
Other novels include: *The Hive* (1951), *San Camilo, 1936* (1969), *Mazurka for Two Dead People* (1983), *Cristo versus Arizona* (1988).

Celan, Paul (Paul Anczel; 1920-1970), German-speaking writer. He was initially strongly influenced by French symbolism and surrealism, but quickly surpassed these movements, as is obvious from his compilations *Der Sand aus den Urnen* (Sand from the Urns; 1948) and *Mohn und Gedächtnis* (1952). He later slid into the 'poésie pure' and his language became more and more mysterious. His compilations *Von Schwelle zu Schwelle* (1955) and *Sprachgitter* (1959) among others are evidence of this.
Celan was also an exceptional translator of poetry, including works by Cocteau, Rimbaud, Valéry, Shakespeare, and Mandelsjtam. His melancholic nature and mental instability drove him to his death: he drowned himself in the Seine in 1970.

Celandine (*Chelidonium majus*), low-growing biennial of the poppy family with yellow flowers that are open for most of the spring and summer.

Celebes *See:* Sulawesi.

Celery, biennial vegetable (*Apium grave-*

olens) related to parsley and carrots, eaten either raw or cooked. The seeds are used for seasoning. Celery grows best in cool weather and consists of long stalks topped with feathery leaves. It was first cultivated in France in the early 1600s.

Celery cabbage *See:* Chinese cabbage.

Celesta, keyboard musical instrument that looks like a miniature upright piano. The hammers strike metal bars, producing a delicate, bell-like sound. Introduced during the late 19th century as an improvement on the glockenspiel, the celesta is often used in orchestral compositions.

Celibacy, voluntary abstinence from marriage and sexual intercourse. Celibacy of Roman Catholic church clergy was instituted by Pope Siricius (386), but abandoned by Protestants during the Reformation. In the Eastern Church, married men can be ordained as priests, though bishops must be celibates or widowers.

Céline, Louis-Ferdinand (Louis-Ferdinand Destouches, 1849-1961), French novelist. His first novels, *Journey to the End of Night* (1932) and *Death on the Installment Plan* (1936), made his vivid, hallucinatory style notable.

Cell, in biology, smallest unit that possesses all the essential properties of a living organism: metabolism, reproduction, differentiation, regeneration, and excitability (response to stimulus). A living cell can also be described as having a flow of matter: Chemicals come into the cell; they are broken down or transformed into other chemicals that then leave the cell. There is also a

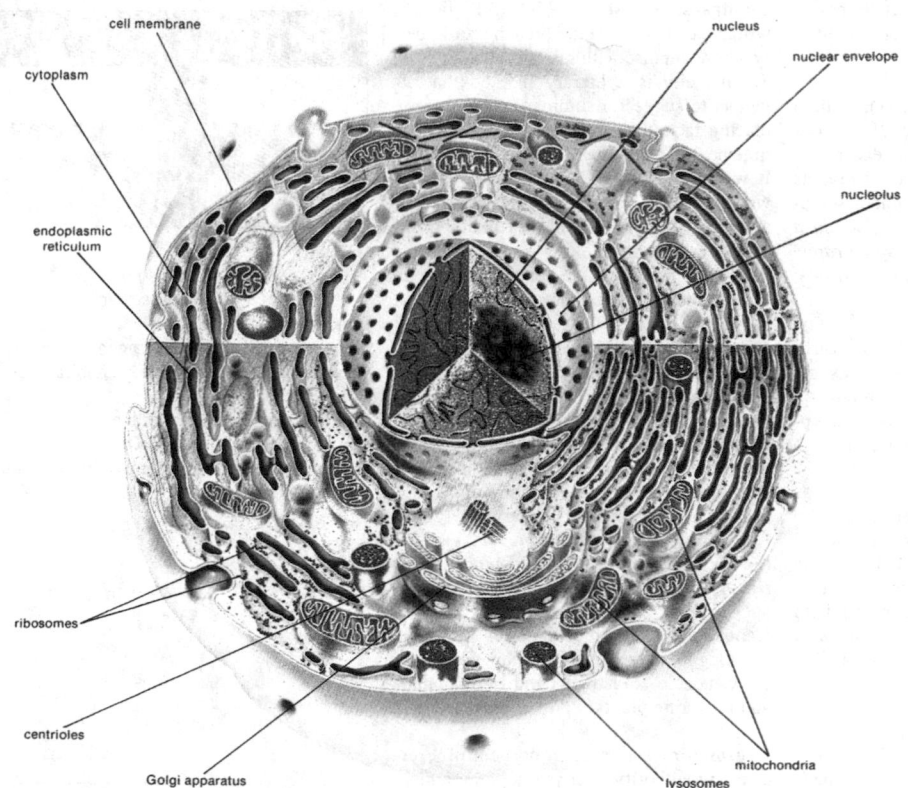

cell membrane
cytoplasm
endoplasmic reticulum
ribosomes
centrioles
Golgi apparatus
nucleus
nuclear envelope
nucleolus
mitochondria
lysosomes

The generalized human cell (drawn at a magnification of about 5,000 times) is, like all cells, surrounded by a cell membrane through which all food, wastes, and other substances involved in cell functions must pass. The cyptoplasm is the fluid medium in which the organelles are suspended, including the endoplasmic reticulum, a network of sacs and tubules that act as channels for material passing through the cell. Ribosomes are the sites where proteins are assembled from amino acids. Certain molecules synthesized in the cell or absorbed from outside are hollow cylinders that move to opposite poles of the cell during cell division. The largest structure in the cell is the nucleus, which controls the cell's overall activity. Bounded by a porous membrane called the nuclear enveloppe, the nucleus contains at least one nucleolus that is involved in formation of the ribosomes; it also carries DNA, the basic genetic material, in the chromosomes.

C

flow of energy: Energy comes into a living system either as chemical energy or as radiant energy from the sun. However, a third element is crucial: information. A living system is a directed and responsive system in which there is control and regulation of chemical reactions. The cell contains a specific information system: the nucleic acids and the proteins, DNA (deoxyribonucleic

A small statue, 1.7 in (4.5 cm), of a man with a battle-axe on his shoulder. This Celtic statue from the La Tène period (around 450 to 50 B.C.) was found near an oppidum in Bohemia (Narodni Museum, Prague).

acid) and RNA (ribonucleic acid). These molecules contain and transmit the genetic information of the cell. All cells have an outer membrane, or cell boundary, cytoplasm (the contents of the cell excluding the nucleus), a cell nucleus, more or less spherical, containing specific molecules, a nucleolus, and organelles (cytoplasmic structures) to which the diverse functions are attributed.
See also: Biology.

Cellini, Benvenuto (1500-1571), Italian metalsmith, sculptor, and writer. Of his work in precious metals little survives except the gold and enamel saltcellar made for Francis I of France in 1543. His most famous sculpture is *Perseus with the Head of Medusa* (1545-1554). His celebrated *Autobiography* (1558-1562) is colorful and vigorous, though somewhat exaggerated.

Cello, or violoncello, second largest instrument of the violin family, with 4 strings and a range starting 2 octaves below middle C. Dating from the 16th century, it is the deepest-toned instrument in the string quartet.
See also: Violin.

Cellophane, transparent, nonpenetrable film of cellulose used in packaging, first developed by J. E. Brandenburger (1911). Wood pulp is soaked in sodium hydroxide, shredded, aged, and mixed with carbon sulfide to form a solution of viscose. After an acid bath, the cellulose is regenerated as a film, dried and waterproofed.
See also: Cellulose.

Celluloid, first commercial synthetic plastic, developed by J. W. Hyatt (1869), made

by treating nitrocellulose with camphor and alcohol. It is tough, strong, and resistant to water and oils. Used in dental plates, combs, billiard balls, lacquers, and spectacle frames, celluloid is highly inflammable and has been largely replaced by newer plastics.
See also: Plastic.

Cellulose, main constituent of the cell walls of plants. Cellulose is a complex carbohydrate with a structure similar to that of starch. Processed cellulose is used in the manufacture of many goods, among them, paper, explosives, fibers, plastics, and adhesives.

Celsius scale, system for measuring temperature in which the interval between the freezing point and boiling point of water is divided into 100 equal degrees. In the Celsius scale, also called the centigrade scale, water freezes at 0 degrees and boils at 100 degrees. Invented by the Swedish astronomer Anders Celsius in 1742, the Celsius scale is widely used in scientific work and is the common system of measuring temperature in most of the world.

Celts, prehistoric people speaking Indo-European dialects, whose numerous tribes occupied much of Europe between 2000 and 100 B.C. They grouped together in small settlements. Their social unit, based on kinship, was divided into a warrior nobility and a farming class. Their priests or druids were recruited from the nobility.

Cement, most important modern construction material, notably as a constituent of concrete. Cement generally is composed mostly of limestone, clays, gypsum, and crushed rock.

Cendrars, Blaise (1887-1961), French writer. Cendrars gave the French art of poetry a new impulse with his 'simultaneity'. Simultaneity is a literary method that attempts to suggest a summarizing image by placing facts that are separated in place or time next to each other.
It was also always Cendrars' aim that his writing should keep up with the latest technological findings that have a major influence on human thinking (among others, film). His position as a renewing force in French literary history is mainly thanks to his poetry. Because of the literary renewal it presented, he and his friend Apollinaire became one of the most important precursors of surrealism. He also wrote adventure stories and a number of autobiographies that show evidence of a cosmopolitan mind. After an adventurous life, in which he occupied himself with both literature and films, he died in Paris, on 21st January 1961.
His work includes: *Les Pâques à New York* (Easter in New York) (1912), *Du monde entier* (1919), *l'Or* (1925), and *Rhum* (1930).

Cenozoic Era, third and current geologic era. Beginning about 65 million years ago, the Cenozoic is characterized by mammals and flowering plants.

Censorship, supervision or control exercised by authority over public communica-

tion, conduct, or morals. Early censorship in the Greek city-states curbed conduct considered insulting to the gods or dangerous to public order. In Rome the censor dictated public morality. Censorship of books was not widespread (although some books were publicly burned) until the invention of printing in the 15th century. The first *Index of Prohibited Books* was drawn up by the Roman Catholic Church in 1559 in an effort to stop the spread of subversive literature. Similar tactics were employed by Protestants and secular authorities. In the United States, freedom of the press is protected from federal interference by the First Amendment to the Constitution.
See also: Bill of rights.

Census, enumeration of persons, property, and other items within a community, state, or country. For example, manufacturing, mining, and business censuses.
See also: Population.

Centaur, in Greek mythology, a creature with the torso, arms, and head of a man and the body of a horse. Most centaurs were considered savages, but a few, such as Chiron, a son of Cronus, the titan, were wise teachers of humans.
See also: Mythology.

Centipede, long-bodied member of the class Chilopoda, phylum Arthropoda with 2 legs to each of their 15 to 100 segments. They are usually 1-2 in (2.5-5 cm) long, though in the tropics some reach 1 ft (30 cm). Normally insectivorous they paralyze their food by injecting poison through a pair of pincers located near the head. Centipedes live in moist places under stones or in soil.

Central African Republic

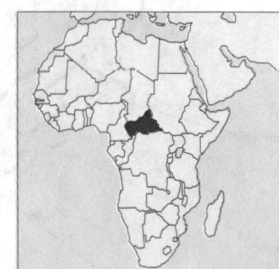

Capital:	Bangui
Area:	240,535 sq mi (622,984 sq km)
Population:	3,643,000
Language:	Sangho, French
Government:	Presidential republic
Independent:	1960
Head of gov.:	Prime minister
Per capita:	U.S. $1,300
Monetary unit:	1 CFA franc = 100 centimes

Central African Republic, landlocked country in equatorial Africa, bordered by Chad, Sudan, Congo, Congo-Brazzaville and Cameroon.

Land and climate. The republic lies north of the equator and is a rolling plateau at about 2,500 ft (763 m). In the east the Fertit Hills rise to 4,200 ft (1,280 m), and in the northeast the Ouanda-Djale Hills reach 3,750 ft (1,143 m). A dense tropical rainforest covers the southern part of the country; the rest is grassland, becoming drier and treeless toward the northern border. Jungle wildlife is abundant. Rain is abundant in the south, but mainly confined to the season from June to October in both central and northern areas. The chief rivers are the Ubangi and the Shari.

People. The Central African Republic has a population density of 5 persons per sq mi (2 per sq km). Ethnic groups include the Zandé, the Banda, and the Mbaka. The small European group is mainly French. French is the official language, but Sangho is the language most commonly spoken. Religion is mainly animism, but a growing number of Muslims live near the Chad border. Illiteracy is high, but school attendance is rising. There are technical schools, but no university.

Economy. The country's poor economy is based on farm crops for home consumption and cotton and diamonds for export. The tsetse fly prevents significant expansion of the cattle industry. There are plans to exploit the deposits of iron, limestone, silver, and uranium. The one large industrial complex is the textile plant at Bouali, which uses hydroelectric power. The country's economy suffers from the lack of a seaport and the absence of railways. The capital, Bangui, is a river port, located on the Ubangi, a tributary of the Congo River.

History. The first French outposts were established in 1886. In 1894 the area was called the territory of Ubangi-Shari. In 1910 it was incorporated into French Equatorial Africa. After World War II demands for independence were led by M. Barthélemy Boganda, resulting in the inclusion of Ubangi-Shari in the French Community in 1958. Two years later, on August 13, the country became an independent nation as the Central African Republic. In 1960 David Dacko became the independent nation's first president. He was overthrown in 1965 by a military coup, led by Colonel Jean-Bedel Bokassa, who assumed the presidency and had the nation's sole political party appoint him president for life in 1972. In 1979 Dacko regained control with support from the French, and Bokassa went into exile. Dacko, elected to a 6-year term in 1981, was ousted in a military coup later that year. The country returned to a civilian government in 1993 when Ange-Felix Pattassé was democratically elected as the new president. His policy is aimed at a socio-economic reconstruction of the country.

2001 and 2002 were boisterous years with several attempts at a Coup d'Etat.

Central America, North America southeast of Mexico, land bridge to South America, separating the Pacific Ocean from the Caribbean Sea. Its north and south land boundaries, about 1,100 mi (1,770 km) apart, are the Isthmus of Tehuantepec in Mexico and the valley of the Atrato in Colombia. Within this area are the republics of Guatemala, Honduras, El Salvador, Nicaragua, Costa Rica, Belize, and Panama. Most of the people are of Spanish or Native American ancestry, living as farmers in the mountain valleys or working in the forests or mines. The dominant feature of the region is a string of mountain ranges characterized by great volcanic activity and earthquakes. They are part of the same mountain system as the islands of the Greater and Lesser Antilles. Most of the mountains are no more than 6,000 ft (1,829 m), though some volcanoes are higher than 10,000 ft (3,048 m), with Mt. Tajumulco in Guatemala rising to 13,845 ft (4,220 m). The volcanic deposits in the northwest have produced very fertile highlands. Relatively level tracts of land occur on the Yucatán Peninsula and along the coast. These limestone plains of the peninsula are the most extensive in Central America, and support dense tropical forests. The rolling coastal lowlands appear insignificant by comparison, broadening to a width of only 90 mi (145 km) along the Mosquito Coast (on the Caribbean) and never exceeding 30 mi (48 km) along the Pacific coast. A trough, the Nicaraguan Depression, divides the northern part of the isthmus from the narrower southern part and encloses lakes Nicaragua (3,000 sq mi/7,770 sq km) and Managua (386 sq mi/1,000 sq km), the largest in Central America. The climate is basically tropical, but is drier on the Pacific side. The considerable variations in temperature and rainfall are due mainly to differences in elevation. The 2 early civilizations of the region were the Mayan and the Toltec. The Maya reached their highest cultural state between A.D. 300 and 900. They were familiar with mathematics, astronomy, and agricultural techniques; they built cities of stone, erected fine monuments, and developed intricate handicrafts. The Toltec of central and southern Mexico spread their influence to the Yucatán Peninsula and into Guatemala. The Spanish conquerors arrived in the early 1500s to destroy what were already dying civilizations. Hernando Cortes completed the conquest of the whole area by 1525, and it remained a Spanish colony for nearly 300 years. Foreign rule ended in 1821, when a sympathetic Spanish governor was elected the first head of the independent United Provinces of Central America. The union was dissolved in 1838, and the 5 states (Costa Rica, El Salvador, Guatemala, Honduras, and Nicaragua) became independent. Subsequent attempts to reestablish the confederation have failed. A looser form of cooperation was begun with the creation of the Organization of Central American States in the 1950s. Costa Rica is politically the most stable country; the others have suffered from external conflicts, dictatorships, and revolutions.

Central Intelligence Agency (CIA), U.S. government agency established in 1947 by the National Security Act to coordinate, evaluate, and disseminate intelligence from other U.S. agencies and to advise the president and the National Security Council on security matters. The CIA has done much to further the interests of the United States and its allies, but such fiascos as the Bay of Pigs invasion of Cuba, as well as concern over possible misuse of its considerable independence in the wake of 'Watergate,' led to a major investigation and internal reorganization in 1975.
See also: Intelligence service.

Central Park *See:* New York City.

Central Powers *See:* World War I.

Centrifugal and Centripetal Forces, forces acting on a body as it moves along a curved path. If a stone is whirled in a circular path on a piece of string, it is acted on by a force pulling it toward the center of the circle (centripetal force). The stone also appears to be acted upon by an equal and opposite force pulling it outward (centrifugal force). An example of centripetal force is the force of gravity exerted on the moon by the earth to keep it in orbit. The value of the centripetal force (F) is given by the equation $F=mv^2/r$ where m equals the mass of the body, v is its velocity, and r is the radius of curvature of its path.
See also: Inertia; Newton, Sir Isaac.

Centrifuge, machine for separating mixtures of different densities by rotating them in a container at high speed. The centrifugal force experienced in a rotating frame causes the heavier elements to sink. Centrifuges are used in drying clothes, in separating milk from cream, in chemical analysis, and in atomic isotope separation.

Dugout canoes line the banks of the Ubangi River, a major tributary of the Congo River and a vital artery of the Central African Republic's commercial transport.

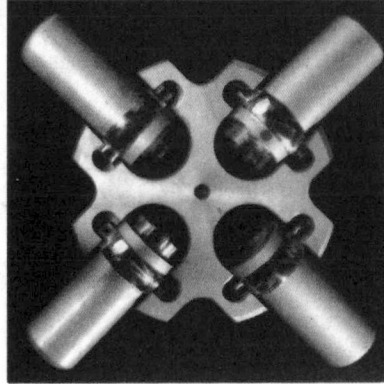
This ultracentrifuge contains four steel cylinders in which solutions and mixtures can be spun at extremely high speeds and subjected to acceleration forces hundreds of thousands of times greater than that of gravity. Such forces can separate large biological molecules from colloidal solutions or liquids from solids of nearly equal density.

C

C

Century plant, any of several desert plants (genus *Agave*) native to warm climates in the Americas. The name arose from the misconception that the plant bloomed only once every 100 years. The century plant, also known as the American aloe, has thick fleshy leaves and produces a yellow flower spike. In Mexico, the sap of some agaves is used to make beverages, and the long tough fiber is formed into cord and rope.

Cephalopoda, class of predatory mollusks including the cuttlefish, octopus, and squid. They swim by forcing a jet of water through a narrow funnel near the mouth. Cephalopods have sucker-bearing arms and a horny beak. The shell, typical of most mollusks, is absent or reduced.

Cephalosporins, group of broad-spectrum antibiotics, most of which are derived from the penicillinlike cephalosporin C that was discovered in sewage in Sardinia. They act against the same bacteria as natural penicillin and can produce allergic reactions.
See also: Antibiotic.

Cepheid variables, yellow giant stars whose brightness varies regularly with a period of 1 to 50 days. The length of their cycle is directly proportional to their brightness, making them useful mileposts for computing large astronomical distances.

Ceram *See:* Indonesia.

Ceram (pop. 132,000), Indonesian island, part of the Maluku province, one of the South Moluccas; 6, 663 sq mi (17,148 sq km). Capital: Amahai. Densely forested mountain country; infertile soil due to heavy rainfall. Primitive agriculture and coconut growing. Fishing. Oil extraction on the north coast at Bula.

Ceramics, materials produced by treating nonmetallic, inorganic substances (originally clay) at high temperatures. Modern ceramics include such diverse products as porcelain and china, furnace bricks, electric insulators, ferrite magnets, rocket nosecones, and abrasives. In general, ceramics are hard, are chemically inert under most conditions, and can withstand high temperatures in industrial applications. Primitive ceramics in the form of pottery date from the 5th millennium B.C.
See also: Pottery and porcelain.

Cerar, Miroslav (1939-   ), Yugoslavian gymnast, specialist in pommel-horse vaulting. Gained world titles in 1962, 1966, and 1970, and Olympic gold in 1964 and 1968.

Cerar was known for his immaculate style (particularly his scissor kicks) and his opinions on training.

Cerberus, in Greek mythology, huge multi-headed dog, with a mane and tail of snakes, that guarded the entrance to Hades.
See also: Hades.

Cereal, generic name for annual plants of the grass family, including wheat, rice, corn, barley, sorghum, millet, oats, and rye. Cereal is richer in carbohydrates than any other food, and also contains protein and vitamins. About 1,757 million acres of the world's arable land are sown with cereal crops each year.

Cerebellum *See:* Brain.

Cerebral hemorrhage, bleeding from a broken blood vessel in the brain, with damage to or destruction of surrounding tissues. The interruption of circulation also causes damage to tissue elsewhere in the brain. Cerebral hemorrhages are often fatal, and can leave victims suffering from various disabilities, including loss of speech and loss or impairment of muscle control.
See also: Stroke.

Cerebral palsy, diverse group of conditions caused by brain damage around the time of birth and resulting in a variable degree of nonprogressive physical and mental handicap. The condition is often accompanied by abnormalities of muscle control, loss of sensation, and some degree of deafness. Speech and intellectual development can also be impaired but may be entirely normal.

Cerebrospinal fluid, serum-like fluid produced in the lateral ventricles of the brain; it bathes the brain and spinal cord.
Lumbar puncture (spinal tap) between the third and fourth lumbar vertebrae is performed to obtain a specimen of cerebrospinal fluid for diagnostic study of brain and spinal cord disease.
See also: Human body.

Cerebrum *See:* Brain.

Ceres, in Roman mythology, goddess of grain, agriculture, and the harvest. A daughter of Saturn, she was the counterpart of the Greek Demeter. She was honored annually with a festival called Cerealia. The word 'cereal' is derived from her name.
See also: Mythology.

Ceres, largest and first discovered (1801) of thousands of asteroids, or minor planets, that orbit the sun between Jupiter and Mars.

It is named after the Roman goddess of grain.

Cerium, chemical element, symbol Ce; for physical constants see Periodic Table. A malleable metal, cerium is the most abundant of the rare-earth metals. Cerium was discovered in 1803 by Jons Berzelius and Wilhelm van Hisinger. It is found in various minerals monazite, being the most important source. Cerium and its compounds are used for decolorizing and polishing glass, in incandescent gas mantles, in carbon-arc lighting, and as catalysts.

Cermet, or ceramal, composite material made from mixed metals and ceramics. Cermets combine the hardness and strength of metals with a high resistance to corrosion, wear, and heat, qualities that make it invaluable in jet engines, cutting tools, brake linings, and nuclear reactors.

CERN *See:* European Organization for Nuclear Research.

Cervantes Saavedra, Miguel de (1547-1616), Spanish novelist, poet, and playwright, a major figure of Spanish literature. In 1585 he wrote *La Galatea*, a pastoral novel in verse and prose. In 1605 he published the first part of *Don Quixote de la Mancha*, his masterpiece. A debunking of pseudo-chivalric romance and a rich tragi-comic novel, it was an immediate success. He also wrote about 30 plays, of which 16 survive, a volume of short stories, and the second part of *Don Quixote* (1615). His last work was the prose epic *Persilas and Sigismunda* (1617).
See also: Don Quixote.

Cesarean section, surgical incision through the abdominal wall and uterus, performed to deliver a baby. Usually done when a vaginal delivery is considered dangerous because the woman's pelvis is too narrow or the baby is in an abnormal position.
See also: Birth.

Cesium, chemical element, symbol Cs; for physical constants see Periodic Table. Cesium was discovered spectroscopically by Robert Bunsen and Gustav Kirchhoff in 1860. It is a metal belonging to the alkaline group. Elemental cesium is silvery-white, soft, and ductile; it is one of the three metallic elements that is liquid at room temperature. Cesium is used in ion propulsion systems and in atomic clocks, as well as in optical instruments and in glass and ceramic production.

Cetacean, any of the mammalian order (Cetacea) comprised of whales, porpoises, and dolphins. Cetaceans have fishlike bodies with virtually no hair and thick layers of blubber to keep them warm. They bear their young alive and live entirely in water.

Cetewayo, or Cetshwayo (1826-1884), fourth and last Zulu king (1873-1879). In 1879 he declared war on British and Boer settlers in the Transvaal, but was captured and deposed.
See also: Zulu.

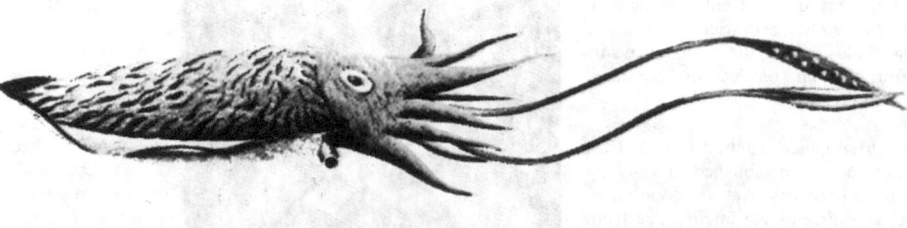

The cuttlefish is a marine mollusc belonging to the group Cephalopods.

Ceulemans, Raymond (1937-), Belgian billiards player, brilliant at every type of game. Participated for the first time in a Belgian championship in 1949 and since then won innumerable national and international titles and championships. His specialty is three-cushion billiards. Since 1978, Ceulemans is also referred to as 'Mister Hundred', because he won his 100th title in that year. Up until mid 1996, Ceulemans has won 34 world titles, 48 European and 60 Belgian championships. In 1985, he was one of the driving forces behind the foundation of a professional league for three-cushion billiards, including a World Cup competition.

Ceylon *See:* Sri Lanka.

Cézanne, Paul (1839-1906), French painter. His early work is impressionist in style, but he later abandoned that mode to develop an approach of his own, lyrical and vibrantly colorful, as in the *Grandes Baigneuses* (1905). Cézanne sought to suggest depth through the use of color and to give his paintings structural strength and formal integrity. He became a prime innovator of modern art, anticipating Cubism and other movements.

Les joueurs de cartes is a subject Paul Cézanne (1839-1906) painted several times. This version, dating from 1886/90, can be found at the Musée d'Orsay, Paris.

Chabrier, Alexis Emmanuel (1841-1894), French composer best remembered for orchestral works such as *España* (1883) and various piano pieces. His work influenced Claude Debussy, Maurice Ravel, and Erik Satie.

Chabrol, Claude (1930-), French film director. Chabrol ranks as one of the most productive filmmakers of the 'nouvelle vague'. Together with Jean-Luc Godard, Eric Rohmer, and François Truffaut, he is the most important representative of this movement. He chose the form of a thriller for most of his films, while the content often concerns the - often sexual - frustrations of the French bourgeoisie and the related feelings of guilt.
Before directing his first film, *Le Beau Serge* (1957-1958), he and Eric Rohmer wrote an important book on the subject of Alfred Hitchcock, which would later continue to inspire him in terms of form (suspense, police film) and content (the question of who is guilty). As a staff member of Cahiers du Cinéma (French film magazine that was

published as of 1953 and contributed greatly to the 'nouvelle vague'), Chabrol wrote a large number of remarkable film studies. His second wife, Stéphane Audran, played the leading role in many of his films.
His work includes the following films; *Les Cousins* (1959), *A Double Tour* (1959), *Que la Bête Meure* (1969), *Le Boucher* (1969), *Juste Avant la Nuit* (1971), *Les Noces Rouges* (1973), *Violette Nozière* (1978), *Madame Bovary* (1991), and *La Cérémonie* (1995).

Chad

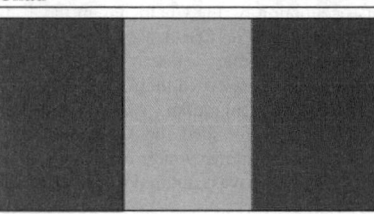

Capital:	N'Djamena
Area:	495,755 sq mi
	(1,284,000 sq km)
Population:	8,997,000
Language:	French, Arabic
Government:	Presidential republic
Independent:	1960
Head of gov.:	Prime minister
Per capita:	U.S. $1,030
Monetary unit:	1 CFA franc = 100 centimes

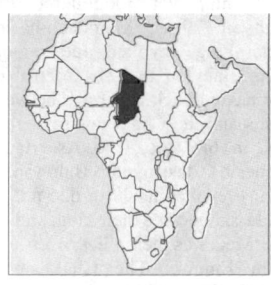

Chad (Republic of), landlocked state in north-central Africa bordered by 6 states, including Libya to the north and the Central African Republic to the south.
Land and Climate. Its northern part extends into the Sahara desert, where the Tibesti highlands rise to 11,000 ft (3,353 m). The southern part consists largely of semiarid steppe with wooded grasslands (savannas) near Lake Chad, watered by the Shari and Logone rivers.
People. Northern and central Chad are inhabited chiefly by nomadic Arab-influenced tribes, who are predominantly Muslim; many speak Arabic as well as their tribal language. In the savanna regions the black population speaks tribal languages and includes chiefly animists, although small groups have adopted Islam. Fewer than 5,000 Europeans, mainly French, live in Chad. French and Arabic are the official languages.
Economy. Chad's economy is very poorly developed. The great majority of the population is engaged in subsistence farming. The chief export crop is cotton; some rice, peanuts, meat, hides, and smoked fish are also exported. A major obstacle to economic development is the lack of adequate roads, along with the absence of railroads. Chad

depends on air and river transport, but the Shari River is navigable only 4 months of the year from Fort Lamy to Fort Archambault, and other rivers are even less reliable in the dry season.
History. Chad was penetrated by Arab traders and Berbers from the Sahara in the 7th century. The black kingdoms of Wadai and Baguirmi suffered from these incursions, but later became powerful sultanates. The Muslim empire of Kanem controlled most of the area around Lake Chad in the 16th century. The Chad area, lying in the heart of Africa, was not affected by the slave trade. Lake Chad was reached by British explorers in 1823. In 1850 the first German explorer mapped the area between Lake Chad and the Nile. By 1890 the French were arriving in considerable numbers, and by 1900 the French conquest of the whole area was completed. When French Equatorial Africa was formed in 1910, Chad was part of Ubangi-Shari-Chad and, 10 years later became the separate territory of Chad. In Aug. 1960 Chad became an independent republic within the French Community, with François Tombalbaye as the first president. Tombalbaye was killed in a coup in 1975. A new coalition government took power in 1979, but civil war soon broke out between rebels backed by Libya's Muammar Qadhaffi and government forces supported by France. In 1982 a faction led by Hissene Habre seized control, and gradually extended rule over most of Chad, except for the Aouzou region, an area in the far north that Libya claimed and occupied. In 1990 Habre was overthrown by Idriss Deby. In 1994 Libya surrendered the Aouzou region to Chad. In 1993 oil was found in the south of Chad.
Oil is expected to start flowing in 2003. The IMF was not satisfied with financial policies and removed Chad from the list of countries that qualify for mitigation of their foreign debt.

Chadwick, Sir James (1891-1974), English physicist who was awarded the 1935 Nobel Prize in 1932 for his discovery of the neutron. *See also:* Physics.

Chagall, Marc (1887-1985), Russian painter. His style is characterized by dream-

I and My Village (New York, Museum of Modern Art), as painted by Marc Chagall (1887-1985) in 1911.

C

C

like, lyrical fantasy and bright but never harsh colors. His subjects are often derived from the traditions of folklore and Jewish life in Russia before World War I. Chagall also illustrated a number of books and created memorable works in stained glass. Two large murals (1966) are in the Metropolitan Opera House, New York City.

Chagres, river in eastern Panama that was dammed during construction of the Panama Canal, thus forming Gatun Lake.

Chaikovsky, Peter Ilich *See:* Tchaikovsky, Peter Ilich.

Chailly, Riccardo (1953-), Italian conductor. After receiving lessons from his father, composer Lucian Chailly, he attended the Academy of Music in Milan, where he made his debut in 1970. Claudio Abbado selected him to be his assistant at the Scala, where he made his official debut (with Verdi's *I Masnadieri*). In 1982, he became the resident conductor of the Berlin Radio Symphony Orchestra, and in 1988 he succeeded Bernard Haitink as Chef d'Orchestra of the Royal Concert Hall Orchestra. He joined the Royal Academy of Music in 1996. In 2004, he will become Chef d'Orchestra of the Gewandhaus Orchestra in Leipzig.
See also: Abbado, Claudio.

Chain, Sir Ernst Boris (1906-1979), German-born English biochemist who helped develop penicillin for clinical use. He shared with Howard W. Florey and Alexander Fleming the 1945 Nobel Prize for physiology or medicine.
See also: Biochemistry; Penicillin.

Chain reaction *See:* Nuclear energy.

Chair, everyday piece of furniture that in early civilizations was reserved for persons in high authority. This historical significance is reflected in the term 'chairman.' A skilled craft became an art in the hands of English makers Thomas Chippendale (1718-1779) and George Hepplewhite (d.1786); and U.S. cabinetmakers William Savery (1721-1787) and Duncan Phyfe (c.1786-1854). Wood remains a favorite material, but steel and plastics are also now used. Modern chairs are designed on ergonomic principles; to conform to the structure of the body, thus providing support at anatomically correct points.

Chalcedon (current Turkish Kadiköy), in ancient times an important city on the Asia Minor bank of the Bosporus, established in 685 B.C. by Megara. Known for the Council of Chalcedon (451).

Chalcedony, mineral consisting of microcrystalline silica (silicon dioxide) with a glassy or waxy luster, sometimes translucent. Chalcedony occurs in a wide range of colors, some forms valued as gems and ornamental stones. Bloodstone (heliotrope), a dark green variety with red spots, was often used in the Middle Ages in sculptures showing martyrdom. Other chalcedonies are jasper, carnelian, agate, and onyx.

Chalcocite, sulfide mineral (Cu_2S) that is an important ore of copper. Shiny gray in color, chalcocite is formed at fairly low temperatures.
See also: Copper.

Chalcopyrite, most important copper ore. It contains iron and sulfur as well as copper, and has the formula $CuFeS_2$. Chalcopyrite has a yellowish coloration with a metallic luster, though it easily tarnishes to produce iridescent colors. It is found worldwide.
See also: Copper.

Chaldea, name for southern Babylonia after its occupation by the Chaldeans in the 10th century B.C. The Chaldeans were accomplished astronomers and astrologers, and ancient writers often used their name as a synonym for 'magician.' In 626 B.C. Nabopolassar founded the Chaldean Neo-Babylonian Empire, which held sway over the area until it was captured by the Persians in 539 B.C.

Chaldeans, an ancient Semitic people originally from the desert of Arabia. During the 11th century B.C., they began to settle in Babylonia at the head of the Persian Gulf. The 'Ur of the Chaldees' mentioned in the Bible may actually have been an earlier Babylonian city.
The Chaldeans, one of several Aramaic-speaking peoples who established kingdoms in Babylonia, were conquered by the Assyrians in 729 B.C. Merodach-baladan, a Chaldean king, revolted and retook the throne of Babylon in 721. Control of the country passed back and forth between the Assyrians and the Chaldeans several times. Finally, in 689 B.C., the Assyrian king Sennacherib destroyed Babylon. The Chaldeans revolted again in 626 B.C., when Nabopolassar became their king, and in 612, with the Medes as their allies, overthrew the Assyrian Empire. The Chaldeans then founded the Neo-Babylonian, or Chaldean, Empire.

Chaliapin, Feodor Ivanovich (1873-1938), Russian operatic bass. Famous for his acting as well as for his voice, he settled in France after the Russian Revolution. His main successes were as Mussorgsky's *Boris Godunov* and Boito's *Mefistofele*.
See also: Opera.

Chalid ibn al-Walied (d. approx. 642), Arabic general during the Omayyad dynasty who vehemently turned against the prophet Mohammed, but later became one of his most loyal generals as the 'Sword of Allah'. He led the invasion in Iraq (as of 633) and achieved important victories over the Byzantines and the Persians.

Chalk, soft, white rock composed of calcium carbonate, $CaCO_3$, a type of fine-grained, porous limestone containing the shells of minute marine animals. Widely used in lime and cement manufacture and as a fertilizer, chalk is also used in cosmetics, plastics, crayons, and oil paints.
See also: Calcite; Calcium carbonate.

Challenger, one of NASA's space shuttles. On Feb. 3, 1984, it began a spectacular flight (its fourth mission) during which 2 astronauts became the first human beings to fly freely in space. On Jan. 28, 1986, Challenger exploded shortly after lift-off with a crew of 7 aboard. The Nasa space program was suspended until 1988.

Chamberlain, family name of 3 prominent British statesmen, **Joseph Chamberlain** (1836-1914) entered Parliament in 1876 as a Liberal. He fought for integration of the Empire through preferential tariffs. His son, **Sir Joseph Austen Chamberlain** (1863-1937), entered Parliament as a Conservative in 1892, and held various government offices from 1902. As foreign secretary (1924-1929), he helped secure the Locarno Pact, which encouraged stability and good will in Europe following World War I, and shared the 1925 Nobel Peace Prize. Austen's half-brother, **Arthur Neville Chamberlain** (1869-1940), was a Conservative member of Parliament from 1918. He became prime minister in 1937. In his efforts to avert war with Germany, he followed a policy of appeasement and signed the Munich Pact (1938), which surrendered part of Czechoslovakia to Hitler.

Chamberlain, Wilt (1936-), U.S. basketball player. The 7-ft 1-in (216-cm) center, is regarded as one of the most dominant players of all time. Chamberlain holds National Basketball Association (NBA) records for most points in a season (4,029), in a game (100), and most rebounds per season (2,149), and is second on the all-time regular season scoring list (31,419 points). He played for the Philadelphia (now Golden State) Warriors, Philadelphia 76ers, and Los Angeles Lakers of the NBA (1959-1972). He was inducted into the Basketball Hall of Fame in 1978.

Chamber music, musical composition intended for a small ensemble. Originally the term meant domestic music, written by a house composer for a patron. It became established as a special genre during the 17th and 18th centuries. The instrumental combinations are varied, usually with not more than 15 instruments. Chamber music is characterized by an intimacy of communication between the performers. The principal form of composition is the string quartet (2 violins, viola, and cello), which was developed by Franz Joseph Haydn and Wolfgang Amadeus Mozart, and expanded to new dimensions by Ludwig van Beethoven.

Chamber of Commerce, association of businesspeople set up to improve business conditions and practices, and to protect business interests.

Chameleon, lizard of the family Chamaeleonidae, found in Africa and Madagascar, that is well adapted to living in trees. Its tail is prehensile, and its eyes can turn independently in all directions. It feeds on insects that it catches with its long, sticky tongue, and the color of its skin alters swiftly in response to changes of emotion or temperature. There are over 80 species, ranging in length from 2 in to 2 ft (5 cm to 0.6 m).

Chamois (*Rupicapra rupicapra*), goatlike mammal of the family Bovidae found in the mountain forests of Europe and Asia Minor. Famous for their agility, chamois are capable of leaps of over 20 ft (6 m). They have thick brown coats and stand about 3 ft at the shoulder. Their hides were used for making the original chamois leather.

Chamomile *See:* Camomile.

Chamoun, Camille (1900-1987), Lebanese politician. Chamoun was one of the most important political leaders after Lebanon obtained its independence, and president of Lebanon (1952-1958). His explicit pro Western disposition resulted in an uprising of pan Arabic- oriented Muslims in 1958. He requested the help of Americans, who remained for six months. During the civil war, the charismatic and canny Maronite Christian continued to play a significant role as the leader of the Christian coalition, The Lebanese Front. He lost the struggle for the leadership of the Christian community in 1980 to the Gemayal clan, the Phalangists. He held a seat in the government of national unity, but continued to resist any Syrian influences.

Champa, kingdom in south and central Annam (central Vietnam) - mentioned in Chinese sources as early as the 2nd century - populated by the Cham, an Indian people of Indonesian origin, experienced seafarers and pirates, trading in spices, precious stones, and slaves with Funan, Indonesia, and China. Champa was in continual strife with its northern neighbors. The capital Indrapura, which had been built in the 9th century, was destroyed by the Vietnamese in 982. In 1471 the new capital Vijaya was also destroyed by the Vietnamese, who later annexed the whole of Cham.

Champagne, historic province in northwestern France, famous for the effervescent sparkling white wines from vineyards between Reims and Epernay. The ruling counts of Champagne were especially powerful during the 12th and 13th centuries, and the region had a central role in French history. *See also:* France.

Champassak (current name Xédôn, Sédone; pop. 475,000) province in South-Laos; 1004 sq mi (2600 sq km). Capital Pakxé (Pakse), (pop. 50,000), inhabitants (Lao, related to the Thai) primarily make a living from growing rice, corn, cardamom, tea, and cinchona (for quinine). Nonexploited copper deposits.
Established as a kingdom in 1713. The Prince of Champassak devolved his sovereign rights to the King of Laos in 1946.

Champlain, Samuel de (1567-1635), French explorer, first governor of French Canada. He explored the St. Lawrence Gulf and River (1603) as far as the Lachine Rapids. He explored much of what is now Nova Scotia, founded Quebec in 1608, discovered Lake Champlain in 1609, and was named commandant of New France in 1612. When Quebec surrendered to the English in 1629, Champlain was imprisoned in England; on his release in 1633 he returned to Canada as governor.
See also: Lake Champlain; Quebec.

Champollion, Jean François (1790-1832), French linguist and historian. Professor of history at Grenoble University (1809-1816), he was the first to effectively decipher Egyptian hieroglyphics, a result of his research on the Rosetta stone.
See also: Rosetta stone.

Champs Élysées *See:* Paris (city).

Chan, Jackie (Kwong-sang Chan; 1954-), Chinese actor, director, producer and scriptwriter. He practiced mime, acrobatics and martial arts and became a superstar in Asia thanks to kung fu-comedies such as *Drunken Master* (1978), *Project A* (1983), *Armor of God* (1986), *Dragons Forever* (1988) and *Who Am I?* (1998). Chan performs all of his spectacular stunts himself, and his movies always end with a couple of takes of him injuring himself on set. After he left for Hollywood, he became famous in the western world as well. Some of his other movies are *Rumble in the Bronx* (1985), *First Strike* (1996), *Rush Hour* (1998) and *Shanghai Noon* (2000).

Chandannagar (pop. 575,000), joint capital of the Indian states Punjab and Haryana. The construction of the city began in 1950 in accordance with a design by an international group under supervision of the French architect Le Corbusier, and was for the most part completed in 1956. As of 1966, Chandannagar, along with the surrounding area, is union territory that is administrated by the central government (44 sq mi, 115 sq km). Haryana was to be given a new capital in 1986, but due to political conflicts concerning its exact details, this is yet to be realized.

Chandler, Raymond Thornton (1888-1959), U.S. detective novelist whose works combine wit and pace with strong characterization, particularly of their hero, Philip Marlowe, a tough but honest private detective. Among Chandler's best- known works are *The Big Sleep* (1939) and *The Long Goodbye* (1953).

Chandler, Zachariah (1813-1879), U.S. politician, a founder of the Republican Party. Elected to the Senate in 1857, he firmly opposed slavery and the Confederate cause. He was secretary of the interior, 1875-1877.
See also: Republican Party.

Chandragupta, Maurya (4th century B.C.), Indian emperor c.321-297 B.C., founder of the Maurya dynasty. He rose to power after Alexander the Great's withdrawal from India, extending his realm into Afghanistan. His grandson was the emperor Asoka.
See also: Maurya Empire.

Chandrasekhar, Subrahmanyan (1910-1995), Indian-American theoretical astrophysicist. In 1936, he settled in the U.S. where he became an assistant professor at the Yerkes observatory. He was appointed as professor in 1942; he was chief editor of the Astrophysical Journal from 1952 until 1971. Among others, Chandrasekhar conducted fundamental research in the field of the atmosphere and the interior of stars, and the dynamic characteristics of star clusters and star systems. He was known for his strictly mathematical approach to problems and for the enormous number of scientific publications to his name.
A very important discovery on his part was that the mass of white dwarfs cannot be limitlessly small. White dwarfs are stars that represent one of the last stages in the evolution of a star. The specific gravity of the matter that makes up such a star is on average a few million times heavier than that of the interior of the sun. It was Chandrasekhar's opinion that the mass of such stars could not exceed 1.4 to 1.5 times that of the sun: the Chandrasekhar limit. This limit led to the question of how the evolution of stars with a larger mass progresses. These stars could not simply evolve to the stage of a white dwarf. This problem led to the theory of neutron stars (stars that are thousands and thousands of times more compact than dwarfs) and, latterly, to the theory of black holes.
His work includes *Radiative Transfer* (1950), *An Introduction to the Study of Stellar Structure* (1939), *Principles of Stellar Dynamics* (1942), *Plasma Physics* (1961), *Hydrodynamic and Hydro-magnetic Stability* (1961) and *Ellipsoidal Figures of Equilibrium* (1969).

Chanel, Coco (1883-1971), Parisian female fashion designer. In the period between the two world wars, Coco Chanel was one of the most important couturiers who promoted the garçon (waiter) fashion - a boyish fashion

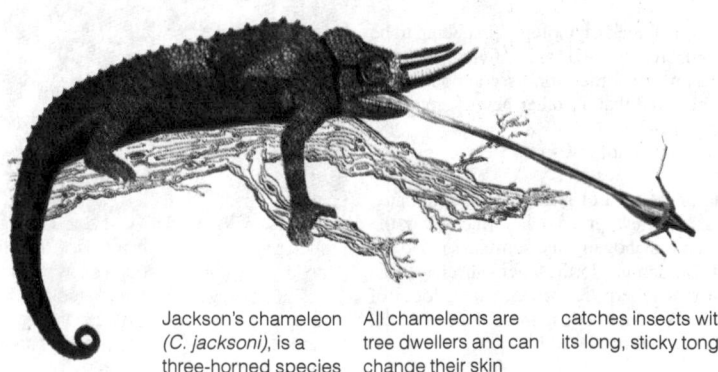

Jackson's chameleon (*C. jacksoni*), is a three-horned species that is found in Africa. All chameleons are tree dwellers and can change their skin colour. This one catches insects with its long, sticky tongue.

C

C

with closely cropped hair, flat chests, and chemises. She used supple material, such as jersey, for sophisticated simple straight dresses and woman's suits. Characteristic of Chanel's designs is the use of sombre colors, such as black, gray, and beige for pullovers with white piqué collars and cuffs. In addition to her designs, Coco Chanel was also famous for the production of perfumes such as No. 5.

One of her best-known designs is the *Chanel suit*. It consists of a smooth pleated skirt made from wool or a mixture of materials (often tweed), and a coat of the same material with gold-colored buttons or a buttonless jacket that is held together by the famous Chanel pin. The jackets are often trimmed with an edging in a contrasting color. A silk blouse is worn under the jacket, often with a bow. The suit is then adorned with many long pearl or gold-plated necklaces. Following her death on 10th January 1971, Gaston Berthelot continued with the production of these suits.

In 1969, a musical was performed on Broadway entitled *Coco*, which was based on her life story. Katharine Hepburn played the leading role.

Chang, Jung (1952-   ), Chinese-British writer. Jung Chang immediately became widely known following publication of her autobiographical book *Wild Swans* (1991). It is a moving history of China in the 20th century, reflected in the destiny of her grandmother, her mother, and herself. For many, this acquaintance with life in China before and during the communist regime was a shock.

Changamire Empire *See:* Zimbabwe.

Saint Peter Port, the harbour capital of Guernsey. In the background, you can see Cornet Castle, which was built in the 13th century.

Changchun (pop. 1,800,000), China, the capital of Jilin province in Manchuria. It lies on the fertile Manchurian Plain in northeastern China. Changchun is an industrial city known especially for the making of trucks and other transportation equipment. Jilin University, a branch of the Chinese Academy of Sciences, and several research institutes are here. Many motion pictures are made in studios in the city.

Changchun was a small settlement until the 20th century. Growth was aided by the completion of railways into the city in the early 1900's and by the opening of Manchuria to Chinese settlement after 1912. During 1933-

1945 Changchun was the capital of Manchukuo, the puppet state Japan created out of Manchuria. Industrial development was greatly spurred by the Chinese Communists after 1949. In 1954 Changchun replaced Jilin as the provincial capital.

Changsha (pop. 1,600,000), capital of the Chinese province Hunan. River harbor on the Xiang and located on the railroad to Peking, making it one of the most important container ports for agricultural products (including rice and tea). Also a center of culture and industry: machine industry, aluminum, textile, food, glass, fertilizer, and ceramic industry. Also paper production and embroidery. Mining center (including antimony). University (1959).

Changsha was established in the third century before Christ and was called Qingyang. The city is surrounded by a wall with seven gates. Changsha was opened for foreign trade in 1904. From 1913, Mao, who was twenty at the time, spent eight years here. During World War II, the city was the scene of four battles that resulted in heavy damage to the city. The city became an important center of industry after 1949.

Channel bass *See:* Redfish.

Channel Islands, archipelago totaling 75 sq mi (194 sq km) in area, in the English Channel off northwestern France. Dependencies of the British crown since 1066, they are administered according to their own local constitutions. The main islands are Jersey, Guernsey, Sark, and Alderney.

Channing, William Ellery (1780-1842), U.S. theologian, writer, and philanthropist, leader of the Unitarian movement in New England. Active in antislavery, temperance, and pacifist causes, he believed that moral improvement was humanity's prime concern. He influenced Emerson, Holmes, and Bryant.
See also: Unitarianism.

Chansons de Geste, medieval French epic poems written from the 11th through the 13th centuries. Most deal with the legendary exploits of the Emperor Charlemagne and his knights. The best known is the *Chanson de Roland*, composed c.1098-1100.
See also: Charlemagne.

Chanukah *See:* Hanukkah.

Chaos, in Greek mythology, first being to be created, represented as a living creature made up of all the world's components. It was believed that all other beings emanated from Chaos.
See also: Mythology.

Chaparral, area of plant growth dominated by shrubs, evergreen oaks (including the mountain mahogany and scrub oak), and the chamiso scrub. North American chaparrals exist in southern California, some slopes of the Rocky Mountains, the Sierra Nevada, and Baja California, in Mexico.

Chapel, place of Christian worship, usually

located in a chamber within a church. Chapels originated after the early Middle Ages because the increase of relics and altars devoted to certain saints required them. The Sistine Chapel in the Vatican is probably the best known.

Chaplin, Charlie (Sir Charles Spencer Chaplin; 1889-1977), English film actor and director, great comedian of the silent cinema. A vaudeville player, he rose to fame in Hollywood, 1913-1919 in a series of short comedies, in which he established his Little Tramp character. After 1918 he produced his own feature-length films, including *The Gold Rush* (1925) and, with sound, *Modern Times* (1936) and *the Great Dictator* (1940).

Chapman, George, (1559?-1634), English poet and dramatist. His translations of Homer (1598-1616), although imprecise and full of his own interjections, long remained standard, and they are still recognized as masterpieces. His plays include *Bussy d'Ambois* (1607).

Chapultepec, historic hill near Mexico City, site of an Aztec royal residence and religious center in the 14th century. American forces stormed the Spanish- built fort in the Mexican War of 1847. It is now a museum and state residence.
See also: Aztecs; Mexico.

Char, or brook trout, North American member of the trout family, (genus *Salvelinus*) prized for its flesh.

Charcoal, form of amorphous carbon produced when wood, peat, bones, cellulose, or other carbonaceous substances are heated with little or no air present. A highly porous residue of microcrystalline graphite remains. Charcoal as a fuel was used in blast furnaces until the advent of coke. A highly porous form, activated charcoal, is used for adsorption in refining processes and in gas masks.
See also: Carbon.

Charcot, Jean Martin (1825-1893), French neurologist whose researches advanced knowledge of hysteria, multiple sclerosis,

French psychiatrist Jean Martin Charcot (1825-1893), giving a clinical lecture on hysterics, in the famous Salpêtrière (an institution for the   mentally ill) in Paris. For a short period, Freud studied with Charcot and he had a copy of this picture in his study.

locomotor ataxia, asthma, and aging. Freud was one of his many pupils.
See also: Neurology.

Chard *See:* Swiss chard.

Chardin, Jean-Baptiste-Simeon (1699-1779), French painter. He is best known for his still-lifes and for his middle-period genre paintings, affectionate depictions of the everyday life of the bourgeoisie (*The Kiss, The Grace*). His work is characterized by a straightforward realism, with atmospheric use of light and color.

Chardonnet, Hilaire (1839-1924), French chemist, industrialist, and physiologist who did pioneering work on synthetic fiber, developing what later became known as rayon, first shown to the public at the Paris Exposition of 1889.
See also: Chemistry; Rayon.

Charkov *See:* Kharkiv.

Charlemagne (Charles the Great; 742?-814), King of the Franks, founder of the Holy Roman Empire. He waged war against the Saxons for 32 years, eventually compelling them to adopt Christianity. Crowned Emperor in Rome by Pope Leo III (800), Charlemagne ruled over a kingdom that included most of the lands that are now France, West Germany, Austria, Switzerland, the Netherlands, Belgium, and Luxembourg. It also included about half of Italy. The establishment of his reign sealed the break between the remnants of the Roman Empire and Byzantium, and thus the split between Roman Catholicism and the Greek Orthodox church. Charlemagne fostered a rich culture that inaugurated the Carolingian Renaissance.
See also: Holy Roman Empire.

Charles, name of 7 rulers of the Holy Roman Empire, starting with Charlemagne.

Charles, name of 10 kings of France. **Charles I** was Charlemagne. **Charles II** (the Bald; 823-877) reigned as king of the West Franks from 843 and as emperor of the West from 875. Numerous revolts and invasions troubled his reign, culturally the last flowering of the Carolingian renaissance. **Charles III** (the Simple; 879-929), grandson of Charles II, reigned (893-923). **Charles IV** (the Fair; 1294-1328) reigned from 1322. **Charles V** (the Wise; 1337-1380) reigned as regent 1356-1360 and as king from 1364. In poor health, he nevertheless put down a peasant uprising and various plots by his nobles. He declared war upon England in 1369 and before his death had regained most French territory occupied by the English. **Charles VI** (the Mad; 1368-1422) reigned from 1380. Corrupt advisers often ruled in his stead. England overran most of northern France, and Charles was forced to make Henry V of England his heir. **Charles VII** (1403-1461) reigned from 1422. Early in his reign he was unwilling to challenge the English occupation of France, and he allowed Joan of Arc to be burned as a heretic. Later Charles introduced tax reforms, rebuilt his army, and regained all oc-

cupied territory except Calais. **Charles VIII** (1470-1498) reigned from 1483. **Charles IX** (1550-1574), who reigned 1560-1598, was dominated by his mother, Catherine de Médici. **Charles X** (1757-1836) reigned 1824-1830. He returned to France from exile after the restoration of the monarchy, becoming king on the death of his brother Louis XVIII. He was exiled again after the 1830 revolution.

Charles, Stuart kings of England, Scotland, and Ireland. **Charles I** (1600-1649), a Catholic, came to the throne in 1625. His reign is most notable for his continual conflicts with the mainly Puritan Parliament. From 1629 to 1640 he ruled without a parliament, having dissolved it. Civil and religious liberties were eroded, leading to widespread emigration to America and finally, in the 1640s, to a civil war. In 1646-1648 the king's supporters were defeated. Charles I was executed. His son, **Charles II** (1630-1685) took refuge in France in 1646. In 1651 he returned to Scotland and was crowned king. He attempted to retake England, but was defeated by Oliver Cromwell and fled to France again. In 1660, 2 years after the death of Cromwell, Charles II took the throne again in the Stuart Restoration. Despite his dissolution of Parliament in 1681, that institution's power increased during his reign. Political parties were born, and colonization flourished.

Charles, Philip Arthur George (1948-), Prince of Wales and Duke of Cornwall, heir apparent to the British throne. The first child of Queen Elizabeth II and Prince Philip, he was educated at Cheam, Gordonstoun, and Cambridge. In 1981 he married Lady Diana Spencer, whom he divorced in 1996. They had two sons: William and Harry. In 1997 Prinses Diana died in a car crash in Paris.

Charles, Ray (Ray Charles Robinson; 1930-), U.S. singer, composer, and pianist, credited with synthesizing aspects of gospel, blues and country, and jazz to create a new form of music known as soul. He lost his eyesight at age 6 to untreated glaucoma. Charles's first popular successes were 'Baby Let Me Hold Your Hand' (1951) and 'I've Got a Woman' (1955). His albums include *Ray Charles* (1957), *Modern Sounds in Country and Western Music* (1962), and *Wish You Were Here Tonight* (1983).

Charles I (1887-1922), last emperor of Austria and King of Hungary (1916-1918). When coming to the throne, during World War I, he made peace overtures to the Allies, which provoked opposition in Germany. He abdicated after Austria's defeat in the war, going into exile in Switzerland. Three years later he unsuccessfully tried to regain the throne of Hungary.

Charles Martel (A.D. 688-741), Frankish ruler who, as mayor of the palace (chief minister) from 714, ruled in place of the weak Merovingian kings. The son of Pepin II, he received his surname Martel (the Hammer) after his victory against Muslim invaders in 732. His policies assured Frankish preeminence in northern Europe,

In his capacity as a court painter at the British court, Anthony van Dyck (1599-1641) made many portraits of the royal family. This picture, showing King Charles I of England, dates from about 1640 (Madrid, Prado).

which culminated in his grandson Charlemagne's coronation as emperor (800).
See also: Merovingian.

Charles the Great *See:* Charlemagne.

Charleston (pop. 96,600), capital of South Carolina and major regional port. The oldest and largest city in the state, Charleston is a tourist center famous for its 18th-century buildings and monuments. It is also a producer of chemicals and steel. In 1861 it was the scene of the first military incident of the Civil War, the firing on Fort Sumter.
See also: South Carolina.

Charlotte (pop. 416,000), largest city in North Carolina, seat of Mecklenburg County. A flourishing commercial, industrial, and railroad center, it produces textiles, manufactures chemicals and cottonseed oil, and is the central market for the region's agricultural products. Johnson C. Smith University, Queens College, and a campus of the University of North Carolina are located there.
See also: North Carolina.

Charlotte Amalie (pop. 15,000), capital of the U.S. Virgin Islands, located on St. Thomas. Founded by Danish colonists in 1673, it was purchased by the United States in 1917.
See also: Virgin Islands.

Charon, in Greek mythology, son of Erebus (the belt of darkness between Earth and Hades) and Nyx (night). His task was to ferry dead souls across the rivers Acheron and Styx to Hades, the underworld.
See also: Mythology.

Charteris, Leslie (real name: Leslie Charles Bowyer Yin; 1907-1993), British-American writer. In 1928, Charteris created the famous detective/crime fighter Simon Templar, alias 'the Saint', who then played the leading role in some 54 detective novels and detective

C

stories. The television series dating from the end of the 50s and based on this character, with Roger Moore as 'the Saint' was also very successful. Charteris' books have been translated into many languages.

Chartism, radical and unsuccessful attempt by voteless British laborers to gain economic and social equality, 1838-1848. It was one of the first working-class political movements in Britain. William Lovett of the London Workingmen's Association drafted the 'People's Charter.'

Chartres (pop. 45,000), historic city in northwestern France, capital of Eure-et-Loire department and commercial center of the Beauce region. It is famous for its Gothic Cathedral of Notre Dame, built in the 12th and 13th centuries.
See also: France.

Chartres Cathedral *See:* Chartres.

Charybdis *See:* Scylla and Charybdis.

Chase, William Merritt (1849-1916), U.S. painter and art teacher known for his portraits and still lifes. Chase taught in New York City and on Long Island. Among his students were Sheeler, Hopper, and O'Keeffe.

Chat, any of several singing birds. The yellow-breasted chat (*Icteria virens*) is the largest wood warbler and is common in thickets over much of the United States.

Château, French term for castle, often applied to any stately mansion; originally a well-fortified medieval castle with a moat, used for defense rather than residence. The 16th century château contained outbuildings and were of a more residential nature. Elegant châteaus in the Loire valley in France are Chenonceaux and Chinon.
See also: Castle.

Chateaubriand, François René, Vicomte de (1768-1848), French writer and diplomat, a founder of the Romantic movement in 19th-century French literature. His works include the North American romance *Atala* (1801), *René* (1802), and *Mémoires d'outre-tombe* (1849-1850).
See also: French language.

Chatham, Earl of *See:* Pitt.

Chattanooga, Battle of *See:* Civil War, U.S..

Chatterton, Thomas (1752-1770), English poet who at the age of 12 wrote poems in pseudomedieval English that he presented as the work of a 15th-century monk, Thomas Rowley. Despite the success of a burlesque opera, *The Revenge* (1770), he remained destitute and poisoned himself at age 17.

Chatwin, Bruce (1940-1989), British writer. Chatwin began working at the auction house Sotheby's in London in 1958. In 1965 he became the youngest director that Sotheby's had ever had. He later studied archeology in Edinburgh. However, traveling and writing for the Sunday Times became increasingly important. Besides numerous articles for newspapers and magazines, Chatwin also published a body of work that was small, yet highly appreciated by the public and the critics: *In Patagonia* (1977), *The Viceroy of Ouidah* (1980), *On the Black Hill* (1982), *The Songlines* (1987) en *Utz* (1988). In 1989, a collection of essays was published posthumously, entitled *What am I Doing Here?*.

Chaucer, Geoffrey (c.1340-1400), English poet. His early writing, including an incomplete translation of *Le Roman de la Rose*, shows strong French influence. In the 1370s, growing familiarity with Boccaccio and Dante influenced *The Parliament of Fowls* and *Troilus and Criseyde*, a powerful love poem. His masterpiece was *The Canterbury Tales*, a 17,000-line poem, in which pilgrims on their way to the shrine of St. Thomas à Becket pass the time by telling stories ranging from the serious to the comedic and ribald. Apart from creating vivid characters, the tales portray contemporary attitudes toward religion, love, and sex. The language of *The Canterbury Tales* is Middle English, sufficiently different from modern English to require translation to be understood. Changes in the language, particularly the emergence of Early Modern English less than a century after Chaucer's death, vastly reduced the popularity of his work, but since the 18th century, he has come to be regarded as one of the masters of world literature.
See also: Canterbury Tales.

Chausson, Ernest (1855-1899), French composer. Chausson studied with Massenet and Franck after having initially studied law. Although Chausson was highly appreciated by his colleagues, his music remained fairly unknown due to his timidity and aversion to publicity. It is partly due to this that his oeuvre is limited, although it was significant for the development of French music, as it clearly anticipates the impressionist movement. It includes a symphony (1890), symphonic poems (among which *Viviane*, 1882), *Poème* (1896) for the violin and orchestra, motets, stage music, choir, chamber and piano music, songs and a number of unpublished operas. Chausson died as a result of an unfortunate fall while cycling.

The site of Chartres has been a place of pilgrimage and worship since pre-Christian times. The first cathedral at Chartres was built in Carolingian times, and part of it is still existent in the present crypt. In 1020, this building was destroyed by fire. It was replaced with Bishop Fulbert's cathedral, which boasted a chevet with three chapels and an ambulatory. This church too was destroyed by fire in 1194, with the exception of the just recently added West front. The present Gothic structure was then built on the existing foundations, incorporating the surviving West front, and with the addition of transepts. By 1220, the new cathedral was all but complete. This was the first of the great cathedrals to dispense with the usual gallery above the aisle, allowing for a higher vault to the aisle itself, and extending the clerestory into the main vault.

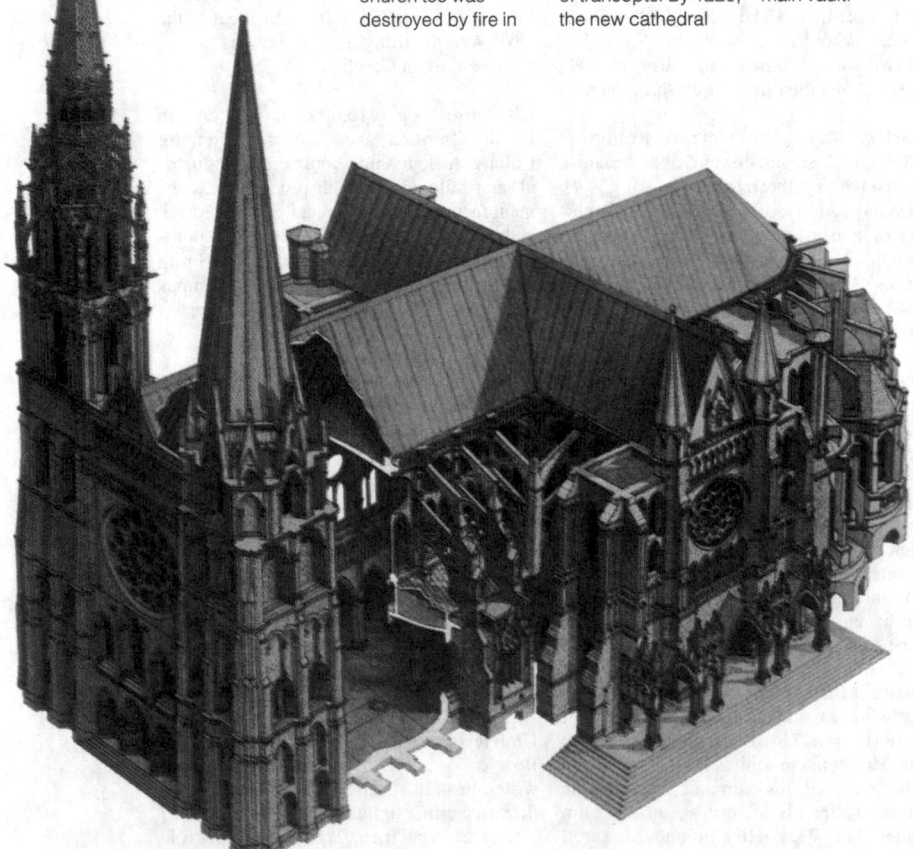

C

Chavez, Carlos (1899-1978), Mexican composer who founded the Symphony Orchestra of Mexico (1928), which he conducted until 1949. His compositions include the ballet *El fuego nuevo* (1921), the ballet-symphony *H. P.* (1926-27), and *Invention*, for string trio (1965).

Chavez, Cesar Estrada (1927-1993), Chicano (Mexican-American) labor leader, founder of the United Farm Workers (UFW), an affiliate of the AFL-CIO. The early history of the UFW was marked by bitter strikes and violent clashes with both growers and the Teamsters. In the 1960s and 1970s, Chavez was instrumental in organizing national boycotts of table grapes and lettuce in solidarity with the struggle of the farm workers.

Chávez, Hugo (1954-), Venezuelan soldier and politician. Chávez won the presidential elections of 1998 after a failed Coup d'Etat in 1992 resulting in an imprisonment of two years. His political aim was to break down the existing political system and the power of the corrupted elite. Constitutional reforms resulted in an increase in his power. During his presidency, he antagonized many Venezuelans with his unconventional behavior and ideas. His close relations with dictators like Fidel Castro of Cuba and Saddam Hussein of Iraq attracted a great deal of attention from other countries. In 2002 he was temporarily deposed. However, the Coup d' Etat was not sufficiently supported; he was able to return as the president after only three days.

Chayote, climbing vine of the gourd family cultivated chiefly for its pear-shaped, round fruit, which is used in puddings, pies, and salads. The plant is also used as livestock feed.

Chechnya (pop. 790,000), area in the Caucasus, in the southern regions of the Russian Federation; 6,064 sq mi (15,700 sq km). Capital, Grozny. Chechens are Sunni muslims related to the Turks. Agriculture is the most important means of existence. Up until it was destroyed in the 1990s, Grozny was the economic center, with an oil refinery. The region became part of the Russian Empire in the middle of the 19th century. It received autonomy, together with Ingushetia, in the Russian republic of Terek. From 1936 to 1992 Checheno-Ingus was an Autonomous Soviet Socialist Republic within the Russian Federation, but between 1944 and 1957 this status was withdrawn. Tension between the Chechens on the one hand and the Russians and the Ingus on the other became more pronounced with the political and economic reforms introduced by the Soviet leader Gorbachev at the end of the 1980s. After the Moscow coup in August 1991, the air force general Dzhokhar Dudayev carried out a coup in Grozny; he declared independence. In 1992 the Ingus Republic was created by Russia, an implicit recognition of Chechnya. Agreeing to secession would, however, have created a precedent for other regions in Russia that wanted independence. Moreover the area was rich in oil. At the end of 1994 Russian troops invaded Chechnya. Around 20,000 people died in the ensuing war, mainly Chechen civilians. Around 600,000 people were displaced by the violence. Dudayev was killed in 1996. Later that year President Yeltsin imposed a treaty that provided for the withdrawal of Russian troops and free elections. No agreement was made about the status of the republic; after the elections, intense war broke out again. Lebed, Yeltsin's special envoy, managed to reach a more lasting peace treaty, which provided for the withdrawal of Russian troops and a transitional period of five years before a definitive decision be taken on the status of the republic. The new government introduced Islamic law, known as Sharia. In 1997, the commander of the resistance army, Aslan Maskhadov, who had also led the peace negotiations with the Russians, was elected president.

Checkers, or draughts, game played by two people on a board of 64 alternating light and dark squares. Each player begins with 12 red or black checkers placed on the 12 dark squares nearest him or her. Taking turns, players advance their checkers diagonally in a forward direction. Once the last row of the board is reached, checkers are crowned, becoming kings, which may move forward or backward and can jump backwards over their opponents. The game became popular in Europe in the 16th century, but its origins go back to ancient times.

Checks and balances, term that describes the powers of the 3 branches of government: the legislature, which makes laws; the executive, which enforces them; and the judiciary, which interprets them. Each branch acts independently and participates in the realms of the other 2, thus limiting potential abuse of power.
See also: Government.

Cheese, food made from the milk of cows, sheep, or goats, with a high content of protein, calcium, and vitamins. Hard cheeses include Cheddar and Parmesan, soft cheeses may be unripened (cottage cheese) or ripened (Brie, Camembert) to develop flavor.

Cheetah, tawny-coated, black-spotted cat (*Acinonyx jubatus*), native to Africa and southwest Asia, the fastest land animal, capable of running at speeds of up to 70 mi (113 km) per hr. The average adult weighs 100 lb (45 kg). Hunting has greatly reduced their numbers.

Cheever, John (1912-1982), U.S. author. Noted for his irony and poetic style in portraying the lives of the upper middle classes in suburbia, he was awarded the Pulitzer Prize for fiction (1978) for *The Stories of John Cheever*. His novels are *The Wapshot Chronicle* (1957), *The Wapshot Scandal* (1964), *Bullet Park* (1969), *Falconer* (1979), and *Oh What a Paradise It Seems* (1982).

Cheju Do (pop. 510,000), South Korean island and province in the East China Sea; 705 sq mi (1,825 sq km). The capital is Cheju, a fishing port with over 210,000 inhabitants; woven materials, bamboo products, potassium, and iodine are produced here. The city dates back to 1955 and was a penal settlement until that time.
Highest point Halla-san 6,398 ft (1,950 m). Mountainous and woody. The island is being developed as a tourist resort (soft climate) and produces grain, soybeans, citrus fruits, sweet potatoes, and cotton.
In 1273, the Mongolian Kublai Khan built ships here with which to invade Japan. In the 17th century European geographers named the island Quelpart. At the time of the Japanese oppression (1910-1945), the Japanese called the island Saishu.

Cheka, Russian abbreviation of 'Extraordinary Commission for Combatting Counter-Revolution, Speculation, Sabotage, and Misuse of Authority,' the secret police set up by the Bolsheviks in 1917 to eliminate their opponents. Reorganized by Lenin in 1922 and renamed the GPU (State Political Directorate), it was the ancestor of the modern KGB.
See also: KGB.

Chekhov, Anton Pavlovich (1860-1904), Russian dramatist and short story writer. The

Thousands of demonstrants demanded Chávez's return after his deposition.

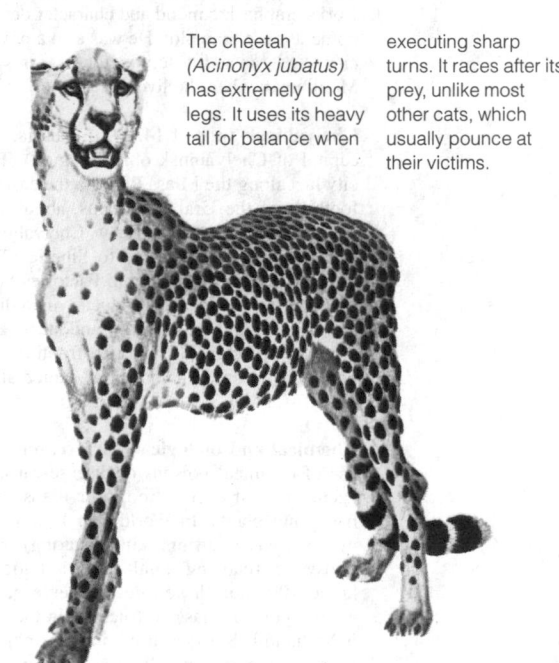

The cheetah (*Acinonyx jubatus*) has extremely long legs. It uses its heavy tail for balance when executing sharp turns. It races after its prey, unlike most other cats, which usually pounce at their victims.

C

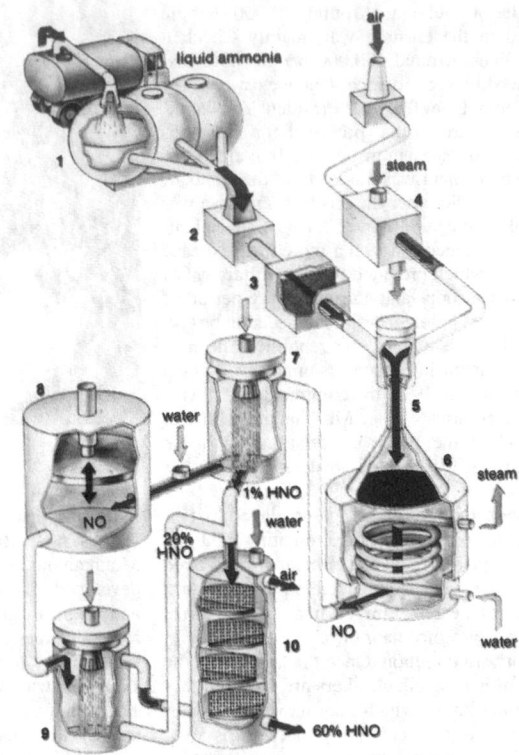

The production of nitric acid illustrates the complexity of many of the processes used by the chemical industry. Nitric acid is produced by the oxidizing of ammonia into nitrogen dioxide, which is then combined with water from the acid. The process begins with liquid ammonia (1), which is heated and vaporised into ammonia gas (2) and filtered (3). Air is heated in a steam jacket (4). In a converter (5), the heated air and gaseous ammonia are mixed and passed over a heated, platinum-rhodium wire-gauze catalyst (6), oxidizing the ammonia to the gas, nitrogen dioxide. The heat in the converter is also used to generate steam from powering the compressor (8). The nitrogen dioxide enters a water spray cooler (7), where a portion is removed as a 1% nitric acid solution, and the remainder, mixed with water, is led to the compressor (8), which heats the gas to 150° C (302° F). Compressed and heated, the gas is cooled again (9), forming a condensate of 20% nitric acid. This condensate enters the absorption tower (10), together with the weaker acid from the first cooler. Here, the acid and water are combined as they are led over a series of bubble trays. The end product is 60% nitric acid solution.

C

Moscow Art Theatre produced his 4 major plays, depictions of Russian rural upper- and middle-class life: *The Seagull* (1898), *Uncle Vanya* (1899), *The Three Sisters* (1901), and *The Cherry Orchard* (1904). Chekhov's works emphasize mood and character development more than plot. He was also a physician, and ran a free clinic for peasants in Melikhovo, where he lived.

Chelyabinsk (pop. 1,143,000), Russia, the capital of Chelyabinsk oblast (region). The city lies along the Miass River in the eastern foothills of the Ural Mountains, about 930 mi (1,500 km) east of Moscow. Chelyabinsk is known as 'the Gateway to Siberia.' The city is a major rail junction. Factories here produce a variety of products, including tractors, chemicals, and iron and steel. The city was founded in 1648 as a frontier outpost and became an industrial center after World War I.

Chemical and biological warfare, military use of chemical poisons or disease-causing agents against enemy troops, civilians, animals, and plants. In World War I chlorine, mustard gas (causing skin blistering), and phosgene (causing fatal lung irritation), killed 100,000. Newer, deadly nerve gases are weapons of mass destruction. In the war in Vietnam U.S. forces used riot-control gases and chemical defoliants with carcino-genic effects. The Iraqi regime of Saddam Hussein used poison gas against the Kurdish population in Iraq and against Iranian troops during the Iran-Iraq War (1980-1988).

Chemical bond *See:* Chemistry; Mineral.

Chemical element *See:* Element.

Chemical engineering *See:* Engineering.

Chemical reaction, process whereby 1 substance is changed chemically into another through the formation or destruction of bonds between atoms. Chemical equations, consisting of formulas and symbols representing elements and compounds, express the events of chemical reactions.
See also: Chemistry.

Chemical warfare *See:* Chemical and biological warfare.

Chemistry, science dealing with the composition of substances and the changes that occur when they react with one another. All chemical changes take place by the linking-up of atoms into molecules, a molecule being the smallest particle of a chemical compound that has that compound's characteristic properties. Chemical reactions may involve elements themselves, elements and compounds, or compounds and other com-pounds. Atoms themselves remain fundamentally unchanged in chemical reactions. It is the grouping of the atoms into molecules that is altered. Some chemical changes are relatively simple, while others, such as those that occur during the chemical processes of living matter, are highly complex, involving molecules that may consist of thousands of atoms. Organic chemistry deals with the chemistry of compounds of carbon (the chemical processes of life take place between substances in which carbon plays a major role). Inorganic chemistry is concerned with all the remaining elements. Apart from that broad division, there are other specialized fields. Physical chemistry deals with the physical properties and behavior of chemicals. Analytical chemistry develops laboratory methods of determining the chemical structure of materials. Chemotherapy is the treatment of diseases with chemical drugs; biochemistry is concerned with living processes; chemurgy deals with agricultural products; electro-chemistry studies the electrical effects of chemical change.

Chemotherapy, use of nonantibiotic chemical substances to treat disease, most often cancer. The drug destroys rapidly spreading cancer cells without significantly affecting normal cells in the body.
See also: Cancer.

Cheney, Dick (Richard Cheney; 1941-), American politician. Cheney studied politics and worked as a financial advisor for several years, before he was appointed 'White House Chief of Staff' in 1974 under President Ford. He was congressman from 1977 to 1989. During this period he became one of the leading figures of the Republican Party concerning foreign policies.
In 1989, Cheney became Secretary of Defense under President Bush. He was closely involved in decision-making during the Golf War and he played and important part in the invasion of Panama, during which general Noriega was deposed. In 2001, President Bush jr. appointed Cheney Vice President.

Chengdu (or **Chengtu**) (pop. 2,600,000),

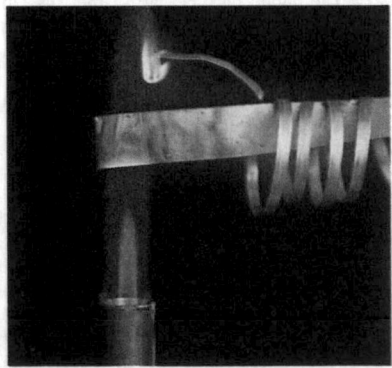

The reaction rates of different materials vary considerably. Iron, for example, reacts so slowly with oxygen that it can be heated red hot without showing any appreciable change. A heated strip of magnesium, however, burns rapidly to form an oxide.

China, one of the nation's largest cities and the capital of Sichuan province. It is on a branch of the Min River in the Sichuan Basin, south-central China.

For centuries Chengdu has been the center of one of the nation's richest agricultural regions, where wheat, rice, and many subtropical crops are grown. Since 1949, when the Communists gained control of China, the city has become increasingly industrialized and now manufactures a wide range of goods. Chengdu is a river port and has railway and air service.

Buddhist and Taoist temples and a shrine to the poet Du Fu are among the city's landmarks. The Sichuan Opera, Sichuan Union University, University of Electronic Science and Technology of china, and several specialized schools are here.

Chengdu is an ancient city, dating back to at least 400 B.C. During the Three Kingdoms period it was the capital of the Kingdom of Shu (221-263 A.D.).

Chénier, André Marie de (1762-1794), French poet. His work forms a bridge between classicism and romanticism: *Le Jeune Captive* (1795), *Elégies* and *Bucoliques* (1819). He was guillotined during the French Revolution for writing pamphlets against the Reign of Terror.

Chen Kaige (1952-), Chinese film director, son of director Chen Huaikai. In 1978 he enrolled at the film academy in Peking. Together with his fellow students, who would become known as the 'fifth generation', Chen went on to bring about a boom in the appreciation of Chinese films. His debut *Yellow Earth* (1984) immediately attracted attention all over the world, and films such as *The Big Parade* (1985) and *King of Children* (1987) also found their way to the West despite problems with censorship. He was awarded a Golden Palm for *Farewell to my Concubine* (1993). Chen is a master at working with color. He is capable of combining an overwhelming film image with the expression of refined human emotions. Other movies are *The Emperor and the Assassin* (1999), *Ten Minutes Older* (2002), and *Killing Me Softly* (2002).

Cheops *See:* Khufu.

Cherbourg (pop. 29,000), seaport and naval station in France, on the English Channel. The harbor is a base for French fishing fleets and a port of call for oceangoing vessels. *See also:* France.

Cherimoya (*Annona cherimola*), tropical tree native to Peru and Ecuador. It grows to about 25 ft (7.5 m), bearing oval, deciduous alternate leaves about 10 in (25 cm) long. Its round or conical edible fruit is pale green, 5 in (13 cm) long and weighing 1 lb (.45 kg), with an inner white pulp tasting of pineapple and banana. The cherimoya is cultivated in California and Florida.

Chernenko, Konstantin Ustinovich (1911-1985), leader of the Communist Party of the Soviet Union (1984-1985). He joined the Communist Party in 1931 and became a protege of Leonid Brezhnev, thus rising in the

hierarchy of the party. In 1978, Chernenko was elected a full member of the Politburo, the policymaking body of the Communist Party. He became general secretary of the Communist Party in Feb. 1984. As its leader, Chernenko renewed arms control talks with the United States. He was succeeded by Mikhail Gorbachev.
See also: Union of Soviet Socialist Republics.

Chernobyl, city in the Ukraine on the Pripyat River, approximately 65 miles (100 km) north of Kiev. Became the focal point of world news when the most serious nuclear disaster to date occurred there. On 26th April 1986 the nearby 1000 megawatt reactor, one of the four reactors at the Chernobyl complex, was damaged by explosions and fire, and for many weeks there was danger of a meltdown. Large amounts of radioactivity escaped and were spread by the wind over Europe, which was covered with radioactive rainfall. The area most affected was nearby Belarus, where large areas have been permanently evacuated. Of the 350,000 people who were involved in the evacuation and treatment of the contaminated area, more than 80% have suffered from radiation sickness. More than 10,000 of them have since died. The government of the Soviet Union initially tried to keep the accident secret, and would only confirm that 'an irregularity' had occurred when alarmingly high amounts of radioactivity were measured in Sweden. The reactor that exploded (no. 4, a so-called high-pressure water reactor) was entombed in a concrete sarcophagus, which however soon began to crack. In 1998 sufficient funds were collected in order to build a new sarcophagus. The Ukrainian government intends to close the entire complex in 2000.

Cherokees, once the largest Native American tribe in the southeast United States. The Iroquis-speaking Cherokees were decimated by smallpox and by conflicts with European settlers in the 18th century. They were deprived of their lands, and thousands of them died on a march west in 1838, an event known in Cherokee history as the 'trail of tears.' Today nearly 45,000 Cherokees live in Oklahoma. Several thousand remain in N. Carolina.

Cherry, any of several trees (genus *Prunus*) best known for their red, fleshy fruits with hard pits. Varieties of sweet and sour cherries are grown widely in the United States. Cherry blossom trees are also grown as ornaments and for their fine-grained timber.

Cherry laurel (family Rosaceae, genus *Prunus*), any of various evergreen shrubs native to southeastern Europe and the Orient. The cherry laurel is grown for ornamental use in the United States. Reaching to 18 ft (5.4 m), the shrub bears small, glossy, poisonous leaves, fragrant clusters of small white flowers, and dark purple, foul-tasting friut.

Cherubini, Maria Luigi (1760-1842), Italian composer who spent most of his life in France. He wrote operas: *Medea* (1797) and *Les Deux journées* (1800), which influ-

enced Beethoven, and sacred works, such as the *Requiem in D minor* (1836).
See also: Opera.

Chesapeake Bay, large inlet of the Atlantic Ocean on the east coast of the United States, an important trade route for oceangoing vessels. About 200 mi (320 km) long and 30 mi (48 km) wide, the bay separates the Delmarva Peninsula from sections of Maryland and Virginia.
See also: Atlantic Ocean.

Chesapeake Bay retriever, medium-sized breed of water-loving hunting dogs of the sporting group. The dog stands 21-26 in (53-66 cm) at the shoulder and weighs 55-75 lbs (25-34 kg), and possesses yellowish eyes. Its short, thick, oily coat ranges from dark brown to light tan in color, resists cold, and easily sheds water. The breed was developed in the United States when two English-stock puppies were found shipwrecked off the Maryland coast (1807) and were bred with local retrievers.

Chess, sophisticated board game for 2 players probably invented in India in ancient times. It was introduced into Persia in the 6th century A.D. and was brought to Europeans by the Arabs, probably at the time of the Crusades. By the 13th century, the game was widespread in Europe, and the rules of the modern version were definitively stabilized in the 16th century. The first modern world championship was held in 1851, and world champions have been recognized continuously since then. The game board has 64 squares in 8 rows of 8, and each player has 16 pieces. Each piece moves in specific ways, and the players alternate moves. The object of the game is to capture the opponent's king. If neither player is able to do this, the game is drawn. At the highest levels of international play, draws are common.

A miniature from a thirteenth-century book, showing King Alfonso X the Wise (1221-1284) of Spain (at the right), playing a game of chess (El Escorial, Madrid). Originating in the East, the game of chess initially only reached the countries of southwestern Europe, where it was often played, particularly at the courts.

Chesterfield, Philip Dormer Stanhope, 4th Earl of (1694-1773), English politician and author chiefly remembered for his posthumously published *Letters to His Son* (1774), which offer vivid, amusing insights into the morality of the age.

Chesterton, G(ilbert) K(eith) (1874-1936), English author and critic, noted for his lyrical style and delight in paradox. He wrote poetry, stories (the Father Brown detective stories, 1911-1935), novels (*The Napoleon of Notting*

C

C

The statue of the rain god Chac-Mool near the Temple of the Warriors (12th century) at Chichén-Itzá.

Hill, 1904), literary criticism (on Browning, 1903, and Dickens, 1906); and essays, collected in *Tremendous Trifles* (1909).

Chestnut, any of various deciduous trees (genus *Castanea*) of the beech family, with edible nuts. The American chestnut is rare, having been nearly wiped out by a fungus, 'chestnut blight,' introduced from Asia in 1904 and spread by woodpeckers. The related chinquapin of the southeastern states appears to be immune. Chestnuts are highly valued for their timber, nuts, and bark.

Chevalier, Maurice (1888-1972), French singer and film star. He gained international fame in the 1920s and 1930s as the embodiment of French charm and light-heartedness. His films include *The Love Parade* (1930), *Gigi* (1958), and *Can-Can* (1959).

Chevrolet, Louis (1879-1941), Swiss-born U.S. automobile racer and designer; in 1911 he designed and built (with William C. Durant) the first Chevrolet, a 6-cylinder car produced to compete with the Ford. He later designed the racers that won the 1920 and 1921 Indianapolis 500-mile race.
See also: Automobile.

Chewing gum, confection made from chicle, other resins and waxes, sugar, and corn syrup. For centuries Native American tribes chewed chicle (gum from the juice of the sapodilla tree) or spruce resin. Early European settlers adopted the habit, and chewing gum has been made commercially in the United States since the 1860s.

Mountain chickadee (*Parus gambeli*, order *Passiformes*, family Paridae). Found along the westcoast of the U.S. Lives at altitudes between 5,906 to 10,827 ft (1,800 to 3,300 m) above sea level.

Cheyenne, North American tribe speaking an Algonquian language. By the mid 19th century the Cheyenne had become nomadic hunters on the Great Plains, and after 1860 their fierce battles against encroaching whites culminated in the defeat of General Custer in 1876 by an alliance of Sioux and northern Cheyenne forces. Eventually the Cheyenne were resettled in Oklahoma and Montana.

Chiang Ching-kuo (1910-1988), leader of the Nationalist Chinese government on Taiwan (1975- 1988). The son of Chiang Kai-shek and his first wife, he was born in Zhejiang province. He attended Chinese schools before going to the Soviet Union to study in 1925, where he graduated from the military-political institute in Leningrad. In 1937 Chiang returned to China, where he advanced rapidly in the Nationalist government, becoming defense minister in 1965, prime minister in 1972, and president in 1978. Chiang was popular for his efforts in eliminating corruption in government.
See also: Taiwan.

Chiang Kai-shek (1887-1975), Chinese Nationalist leader. After Sun Yat-sen's Revolution (1911), Chiang joined the Kuomintang, the governing party, organized the nationalist army, and rose rapidly to power. After Sun's death (1925), Chiang made an alliance with the Communists, but in 1927 he reversed course, initiating a 22-year-long civil war against them. Chiang became president of the Nationalist government in 1928, and he commanded Chinese and later (1942) Allied forces in the war against Japan. In 1949, with the victory of the Communists in the civil war, Chiang withdrew from the mainland to Taiwan, where he became president of Nationalist China (1950).
See also: China.

Chiang Mai (pop. 170,000), capital of the province in North Thailand with the same name on the Ping River. A center of trade in an area with forestry (teakwood) and agriculture (rice, corn, tobacco, cotton). Domestic industry in silver processing, earthenware, and other luxury items. Tourism is also a significant source of income. End point of the northern railroad. Thirteenth century city center with 13th and 14th century temple ruins. University (1964). The population is mainly Lao. The city was Burmese from 1558 up to 1775 and subsequently semi autonomous for two centuries before becoming part of modern Thailand (Siam).

Chibcha, inhabitants of the plateau of Bogota in central Colombia. Their highly developed society was based on farming and the worship of the Sun God. The Spaniards destroyed their culture in the 16th century. Over a million descendants survive in the area today.

Chiburdanidze, Maia (1961-), Georgian chess player, became the youngest ladies' grandmaster at the age of 12. After she became the champion of the Soviet Union in 1977, she won her first world title the very next year. Chiburdanidze won the world

championship again in 1981, 1984, 1986, and 1988.

Chicago (pop. 3,554,000), third-largest city in the United States, on Lake Michigan in Illinois, hub of the U.S. road, rail, and air systems. Industry is diverse, including the famous meatpacking plants, grain elevators, and chemical, metal, and printing industries. Chicago grew as a French trading post in the 1700s, but it was not until after the Black Hawk War (1832) that the city began to grow rapidly. Even the Great Fire of 1871, which destroyed 2,000 acres of property, could not end Chicago's vitality. Downtown Chicago has some of the world's tallest buildings. The North Side, along the lake, is residential. The West Side is a largely white mixture of various ethnic groups, while the South Side is home to most of the city's African-Americans, who constitute nearly 40% of the population.
See also: Illinois.

Chicago, University of, private, nondenominational, coeducational institution in Chicago, Ill, incorporated in 1890. It has about 7,500 students and over 1,000 faculty members. The Pritzker School of Medicine, the Enrico Fermi Institute for Nuclear Studies, and the department of education are among its best-known facilities.

Chicano, person of Mexican-American descent. Chicanos first came to the United States as seasonal field workers. Over 8 million Chicanos now live in mainly southern U.S. cities. A Chicano labor leader, Cesar Chavez, organized the United Farm Workers (1962) and achieved bargaining power for Chicano field workers after years of bitter struggle.

Chicester, Francis (1901-1972), English publisher and writer, became famous by sailing around the world in 226 days in 1966-1967 on the Gipsy Moth IV. He emigrated to Australia in 1919, obtained his pilot license, and conducted a number of long-distance flights during the 30s. Following a bankruptcy, Chicester returned to England where he established a map publishing company following World War II. He repeatedly won major ocean-sailing competitions in the 60s.

Chichén Itzá, archeological remains of a Maya city in Yucatan, Mexico. Founded c.514 by the Itzá, abandoned (692), reoccupied (c.928), and finally abandoned in 1194, the city connected two great periods of Maya civilization. Its astronomical observatory and temples show Toltec influence.
See also: Yucatán Peninsula.

Chickadee, any of various common small songbirds of the family Paridae (genus *Penthestes* or *Parus*), with dark caps and bibs and white faces. They are noted for their tameness and agility.

Chicken, domesticated bird raised for its meat and eggs, originating in northern Asia from the jungle fowl. Chickens raised for meat are marketed as broilers and fryers when under three months old (weighing 2-4 lb/1-2 kg) and as roasters when 4-8 months old (weighing up to about 7 lb/3 kg).

Chickenpox, or varicella, contagious disease caused by a virus and affecting mainly children, usually in epidemics. Its characteristic blister-like, itching rash appears two to three weeks after infection.

Chickpea, or garbanzo bean (*Cicer arietinum*), bushy annual legume cultivated from antiquity in southern Europe, India, and the Middle East, and grown for its edible seeds. The chickpea plant grows to 1-2 ft (30-60 cm) and bears rectangular pods containing 1 or 2 3/8 in (9.5 mm), seeds, which may be white, light yellow, red, brown, or near-black. The chickpea is a good source of protein and carbohydrates.

Chicle, latex of the sapodilla tree, a tropical American evergreen, and the raw material of chewing gum. Obtained by cutting grooves in the bark, the latex is boiled to remove excess water, then molded into blocks.

Chicory, blue-flowered perennial herb (*Cichorium intybus*) of the Composite family, native to the Mediterranean. Its leaves are used in salads, and its roasted roots are sometimes added to coffee. Endive is a type of chicory used in salads.

Chigger, larva of the harvest mite, a small arachnid. Chiggers burrow beneath the skin of mammals and can produce troublesome ulcers. *See also:* Mite.

Chihuahua, small terrierlike dog. It stands about 5 in (13 cm) high at the shoulder and weighs about 1-6 lbs (0.5-2.7 kg), and possesses a smooth or a long coat of any color or markings. The chihuahua has a friendly and loyal temperament. Native to Mexico, it is named for the Mexican state of Chihuahua, and is called the 'royal dog of the Americas.'

Chihuahua (pop. 520,000), capital of the Mexican state of the same name. Founded as a mining community in northern Mexico in 1707, the city is still a center of silver mining, and of ranching as well. Father Miguel Hidalgo y Costilla, a hero of the Mexican independence struggle, was executed in Chihuahua in 1811. The city was later headquarters for Pancho Villa during the Mexican revolution of 1910- 1915.
See also: Chihuahua.

Chihuahua, geographically largest state 95,376 sq mi (247,086 sq km) in Mexico, bordering both Texas and New Mexico. With extensive forests, deep canyons, mineral deposits, and rich grasslands, Chihuahua is the leading cattle-raising and mining state in Mexico.
See also: Mexico.

Chilblain, reaction to cold with pain and itching that can lead to the formation of blisters and ulcers. The blue-red lesions are particularly common on fingers, toes, shins, nose, and ears.

Child abuse, physical, emotional, or sexual injury caused to a child under age 16 by an adult. It is often manifested in cuts, abrasions, bruises, and burns. Incidents of abuse are often detected by an inconsistency between an injury and the explanation of how it occurred. Emotional manifestations of abuse are less easily discovered. Small children who have been abused may be distrustful, passive, and overly concerned with pleasing adults. The emotional impact on children usually becomes obvious at school age, when difficulties in forming relationships with teachers and other children arise.

Child labor, employment of children in industrial or agricultural work, a practice common in the 19th century. Young children had to work hard in often unhealthy circumstances. In the 19th century, industrialized countries adopted laws which ended this kind of labor. In underdeveloped countries, child labor is still common.

Children's home, or orphanage, place where foundlings and homeless children live. Children may live in one of these institutions because both parents are deceased or because one or both parents are unable to care for them properly.

Children's literature *See:* Literature for children.

Child welfare, any of various programs, services and, institutions designed to administer to the well-being of children. They strive to ensure that children who are suffering from poverty, from the inability of parents to care properly for them, or from neglect or abuse, are provided with food, shelter, medical care, education, and other social services.

Chile

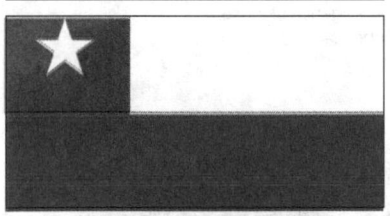

Capital:	Santiago (de Chile)
Area:	292,135 sq mi (756,626 sq km)
Population:	15,499,000
Language:	Spanish
Government:	Presidential republic
Independent:	1818
Head of gov.:	President
Per capita:	U.S. $10,000
Monetary unit:	1 Chilean peso = 100 centavos

Chile, country on the Pacific coast of South America, stretching 2,650 mi (4,264 km) from its northern borders with Peru and Bolivia to Cape Horn at the tip of the continent. Chile is narrow, sandwiched between the Pacific Ocean to the west and Argentina to the east; the average distance across the country is only 110 mi (177 km). The Andes Mountains run along the eastern length of the country, and Cerro Ojos del Salado, in

A salt pan at the edge of the Altiplano.

The central valley is the most fertile and most densely populated region in Chile.

the north, is the second-highest peak in the western hemisphere. Most Chileans live in the central part of the country, nearly a third of them in Santiago, the capital and main industrial city. About 80% of Chileans are Roman Catholic. The national language is Spanish. Chile is a major mining and manufacturing nation (a leading exporter of copper). Colonized by Spain in the 16th century, the country won its independence in 1818. In the 20th century Chile was one of Latin America's most stable democracies. In 1970, the election of Salvador Allende, a Marxist, led to a period of political polarization and economic and civil conflict. It ended in 1973, with a bloody military coup that established the right-wing dictator Pinochet in power and during which Allende died. Pinochet restored order but banned political parties and disbanded the legislature. A new constitution, allowing a gradual return to democracy, came into effect in 1981; elections were not held until 1989. Patricio Aylwin, a Christian Democrat, was elected president, but Pinochet remained head of the military. The 1993 presidential election was won by another Christian Democrat, Eduardo Frei Ruiz-Tagle, the son of the former president.
However, the conservatives won in the various chambers of the National Congress, making the president dependent on conservative votes for the implementation of his policy. An attempt to restrain the power of the military failed due to conservative opposition in the House of Representatives. In 1995, the government reached an agreement

C

C

with the rightwing opposition: in exchange for a drastic curtailment of the investigations into violations of human rights, a number of remnants of the military dictatorship were removed from the constitution. The amnesty proclaimed by Pinochet for violations of human rights dating from before 1979 continued to apply.

In March 1998, Pinochet retired from the military and became a senator-for-life according to the custom of former presidents. His assumption of this post met with wide opposition, however, since Pinochet had taken the presidency by force. In October 1998, Pinochet was arrested in a British hospital and accused of genocide, torture, and terrorism. He was brought to trial in Chile as well, but in 2002 the Supreme Court ruled that Pinochet was mentally unfit to stand trial.

A bronze chimera, found in Arezzo, dating from the 5th/4th century B.C. (Museo Archeologico, Florence).

Chilung (formerly Kirun; pop. 359,500), city in the north of Taiwan. The deep, natural harbor is also the export harbor of the capital Taipei; fishing port. Shipbuilding, agricultural industry, canned fish, and fertilizer industry. Coal, gold, and silver can be found in the vicinity. Occupied by the Spaniards in 1626, conquered by the Dutch in 1642, and transferred to the control of the Chinese Manchu dynasty in 1683. Opened for foreign trade in 1860. Modernized and expanded during the Japanese occupation (1895-1945) when coal was exported to Japan from this location.

Chimborazo, inactive volcanic mountain in the Cordillera Occidental of the Andes, located in central Ecuador about 120 mi (193 km) from the Pacific Coast. The peak is 20,561 ft (6,267 m) above sea level and Ecuador's highest mountain.

Chimera, in Greek mythology, fire-breathing female monster with a lion's head, goat's body, and serpent's tail. By extension, the word is applied to any imaginary being of incongruous parts, or to any unrealizable plan or scheme. In biology, the term is used for any individual or organ that is composed of tissue of varying genetic origin (e.g. from transplantation).
See also: Mythology.

Chimpanzee, black-haired ape (genus *Pan*) native to central and west Africa. Adult chimpanzees stand up to 5 ft (1.5 m) tall and may weigh 150 lb (68 k). They are the primates most closely related to humans genetically and are considered the most intelligent apes. They eat mainly fruit, leaves, nuts, and termites.

Chimu, ancient Indian culture of coastal northern Peru, developed c.1200. Its capital was the great city of Chan Chan. The Chimu built many cities and had efficient military and social systems, but were overcome by the Inca (c.1400- 1460).

China

Capital:	Beijing
Area:	3,695,500 sq mi
	(9,572,400 sq km)
Population:	1,284,304,000
Language:	Chinese (Mandarin)
Government:	People's republic
Independent:	1949 (people's republic)
Head of gov.:	Premier
Per capita:	US $4,300
Monetary unit:	1 Renminbi (yuan)= 10 jiao
	= 100 fen

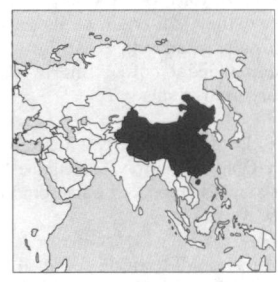

In many parts of Africa, wild chimpanzees have learnt how to 'fish' for termites. They break off twigs or grass stems near a termite mound, strip the leaves from the twigs, and then push these tools into holes in the mound. Termites will then attack the twigs, fastening their jaws to them. When the chimpanzees withdraw the twig, some of the termites will remain clinging to it. The chimpanzees then pick off the termites with their lips and eat them; an example of the advanced intelligence of these apes.

China, officially the People's Republic of China, world's most populous country and the third-largest in area. Located in the heart of Asia, China is bordered by the Russian Federation and Mongolia to the north; by North Korea and the Pacific Ocean (East China Sea and South China Sea) to the east; by Vietnam, Laos, Burma, Nepal, and India and Pakistan to the south; and by Afghanistan, Kazakhstan, Kyrgyzstan and Tajikistan to the west.

Land and climate. The country is made up of 3 large geographic regions. Western China is dominated by the high Tibetan Plateau, the mountain ranges that radiate from it, and a great belt of steppe and desert. North China contains lowland areas, dusty highlands, and part of the Gobi Desert. South China is a maze of hills and valleys. The chief rivers are the Yangtze in central China and the Huang He (Yellow) in the north. The capital is Beijing (formerly spelled Peking). The largest city is Shanghai, with a population of over 13 million. Other large cities are Tianjin (Tientsin), Harbin, Shenyang, Lüda (Lüta), Xi'an (Sian), Qingdao (Tsingtao), Taiyuan, Wuhan, Canton, Chongqing (Chungking), Chengdu (Chengtu), and Nanjing (Nanking).

People. The Han ethnic Chinese constitute nearly 95% of the population, but there are 56 officially recognized minority groups. The national language Putonghua, previously called Mandarin, is based on the spoken form of the Chinese language prevalent in the north, principally Beijing. Different spoken dialects persist in the south, including Cantonese, Wu, and Hakka. The written language, however, is the same everywhere. Traditional Chinese religions were Taoism,

Interior view of the Summer Palace in Beijing, a vast complex of countless structures, large and small, most of which were built during the 19th century.

and Confucianism. There are substantial minorities of Catholics and Protestants.

History. China has one of the world's oldest civilizations, dating back some 3,500 years. Though ravaged by floods, famines, and wars, it remained politically intact through the centuries, often enjoying levels of civilization unparalleled in the world. The first historic dynasty that ruled the country, the Shang (or Yin) dynasty, arose about 1500 B.C. and lasted for some 500 years. It was under this dynasty that the Chinese writing system developed. The next dynasty, the Chou (c.1027-256 B.C.), saw the rise of clas-

The Chinese considered the 1949 victory over the regime of Chiang Kai-shek as a victory over American imperialism. In this cartoon, we see U.S. President Truman and his foreign secretary Dulles being driven into the sea; a symbol for Chiang Kai-shek's ouster from the mainland.

sical Chinese philosophy, including such thinkers as Confucius and Lao-Tze. Under a later dynasty, the Han (202 B.C.-A.D. 220) Confucianism became the official state philosophy, but Buddhism also began to be introduced, and Taoism also grew in influence.

Other major dynasties include the T'ang (618-906), an age of great achievements in poetry and painting; the Sung (960-1279), during which gunpowder was first used for military purposes; and the Yüan (1260-1368), the Mongol dynasty founded by Kublai Khan, the grandson of Jenghiz Khan. It was during the Yüan dynasty that Marco Polo visited China, beginning a period of contact with the West.

The last Chinese monarchy was the Manchu (or Ch'ing) dynasty (1644-1912), founded by the Manchus, a non-Chinese people from Manchuria. It was in the later years of this dynasty that Chinese power gradually weakened, the country losing much of its territory to European, especially British, encroachments.

The monarchy was overthrown in 1912, and a republic was established under Sun Yatsen. After his death in 1916, China was fragmented among various warlords. In 1927, Chiang Kai-shek (leader of the Nationalist Party) gained control of the government and launched a civil war against the Chinese Communist Party, led by Mao Zedong. The Communists and Nationalists briefly cooperated to resist the Japanese invasion during World War II, but in 1945 civil war broke out again, leading to the victory of the Communists in 1949. The Communist Party established the People's Republic of China. From 1966 to 1969 Mao Zedong, supported by paramilitary groups known as the Red Guard, led the Cultural Revolution, which was an effort to purge the society and government of counterrevolutionary and bourgeois tendencies. During this period many government officials were removed from office, violent demonstrations took place in many cities, and all universities were closed. The late 1980s and early 1990s saw the rise of popular unrest, millions of citizens demanding democratic reforms in the political system. In 1989 student demonstrations were crushed by force, by order of Deng Xiaoping. The government then attempted to eliminate all political dissent. It also began to curtail the growth of private enterprise, but the economy began to stagnate and in 1992 Deng reversed that policy, allowing private enterprise to expand and reducing government control over the economy. By the late 1990's China had one the world's fastest growing economies, and the standard of living of many Chinese had risen dramatically. When Deng Xiaoping died in 1997, he was succeeded by Jiang Zemin, whom Deng had chosen to be his successor in 1989. In 1997 China gained control of Hong Kong, a former British Colony, in accordance with a 1984 agreement with Great Britain. Following the transfer of power, Hong Kong officially became Hong Kong Special Administrative Region of China. A legislature appointed by the Chinese government replaced the democratically elected legislative council established by the British. According to the terms of the agreement with Great Britain, Hong Kong's capitalist system will remain in effect for 50 years. In 1998 the economy suffered due to continuous floods.

In 1999, the Portugese overseas territory of Macau was returned to China. It became a formal WTO member in 2001 and at the end

of 2002 Vice President Hu Jintoa was appointed Communist Party Secretary General.

China Sea, western part of the Pacific Ocean, bordering the east coast of China. Taiwan divides it into the East China Sea to the north, 485,300 sq mi (1,256,927 sq km), maximum depth 9,126 ft (351 m), and the South China Sea to the south, 895,400 sq mi (2,319,086 sq km), maximum depth 15,000 ft (4,572 m). Major seaports are Canton and Hong Kong.

Chinch bug (*Blissus leucopterus*), small insect found in the United States, Canada, Central America, and the West Indies. The adult, about one-fifth in (5 mm) long, is black with red legs and white wings. In spring adults lay eggs on roots and stems in grain fields.

Chinchilla, rodent (genus *Chinchilla*) noted for its soft gray fur. Wild chinchillas were once common in the Andes from Peru to Argentina, but extensive hunting has made them rare. Now reared on fur farms, 100 chinchillas provide the pelts for a single coat.

Chin dynasty, First Chinese dynasty, ruled from 221 to 206 B.C., and from 280 to 315 A.D.. China takes its name from this dynasty. Until 221 B.C., China was made up of independent principalities constantly at war with one another. The rulers of the western state, Chin, eventually won a decisive final victory over the other principalities and unified China. The prince, Shi Huangdi (ruled 247-210 B.C.), was the first emperor and radically changed the way in which China was governed. The principalities were dissolved and the empire was divided into provinces and districts that fell under the direct rule of the emperor. A standard system of weights and currency was introduced and a proper infrastructure was created. Palaces were built and a part of the Chinese Wall was built too. Under the Chin dynasty China expanded,

Every Chinese child is entitled to education. However, since it is considered very important not to loose touch with practical experience, schooling is alternated with periods of work in a commune or factory. Only those who excell in their work, will be admitted to a university.

C

C

but after the death of the first emperor, the empire was torn apart by rebellion. In its second reign (280-315), the Chin dynasty was only able to reunify China for a short period.

Chinese, major language of the Sino-Tibetan family, with more native speakers (over 800 million) than any other language in the world. Most Chinese speak Mandarin, a form based on the speech of the educated classes of northern China, particularly the city of Beijing (Peking). Since the early 1950s, this has been called the national language. Other dialects include Cantonese, Hakka, Wu, Fukienese, and Amoy-Swatow. In written form, all these dialects are the same, but the pronunciation may be mutual-

The statute of the Chinese Communist Party said: 'Comrade Lin Piao (here next to Mao Zedong) is the closest comrade-in-arms of Comrade Mao, and his successor.' But Lin Piao (1908-1971) suddenly disappeared from the scene. There were rumours that he had planned to murder Mao. He was killed when trying to escape to the Soviet Union by plane.

ly incomprehensible. Chinese is a tonal, monosyllabic language. The writing system uses an individual character for each syllable, every character representing a word or idea rather than a sound. The characters range from one stroke to as many as 32, but the average is about 11. The earliest witten records in Chinese date back to about 1400 B.C., making Chinese one of the world's oldest, continuously written languages.

Chinese cabbage, common generic name for *pak-choi*, *pe-tsiao*, and *wong bok*, cabbagelike vegetables of the mustard family with wide, thick leaves on a celerylike stalk used raw in salads and cooked in casseroles and Chinese-style dishes. It is an annual or biennial crop grown in many cool areas of eastern Asia and northern United States.

Chinese-Japanese Wars, 2 wars between China and Japan (1894-1895 and 1937-1945). The first war began after both countries sent troops to quell a rebellion in Korea and ended April 17, 1895 with the Treaty of Shimonoseki granting Korea independence, but giving Japan Taiwan and the Liadong Peninsula. Weakened, China became vulnerable to increased foreign imperialism. Japan seized territory from China (1931-1935) resulting in an undeclared war (1937-1941). After China declared war on Japan, German,

and Italy, and Japan attacked the United States and Great Britain in 1941, the war became part of World War II. When Japan surrendered to the Allies in 1945 the second war ended.
See also: World War II.

Chinese literature, among the world's oldest and greatest, Chinese literary works can be traced back almost 3,000 years. Literature was not considered a separate art form and all cultured people were expected to write with style. As a result, literary topics include history, politics, philosophy, religion, and science.
Historically, government service was the most prestigious vocation in China and most government appointments were made on the basis of an examination which tested the ability to compose both poetry and prose.
Much of Chinese literature deals with moral lessons or the expression of political philosophy. Two early works were *The Book of Songs*, a collection of poems, and *The Book of Documents*, a prose work. Together with *Spring and Autumn Annals*, the *Book of Changes* and the *Book of Rites*, they form the Five Classics as the basis for Confucianism and the ideals of duty, moderation, proper conduct and public service.
Taoism, founded by the Laozi during the 300's B.C., was partly a reaction to Confucianism. In contrast to the Confucians, Taoists avoided social obligations and lived simple lives close to nature. *The Classics of the Way and the Virtue* and *The Zhuangzi* are the two literary masterpieces of Taoist thought.
The T'ang dynasty (A.D. 618-907) was the era of four great masters of poetry: Wang Wei, Li Bo, Du Fu and Bo Juyi. Wang Wei's four line poems describe nature. Li Bo wrote of his dreams, fantasies and his love of wine. Du Fu surpassed all others in his range of writing styles and subject matter. Some of his earliest works deal with his disappointment over failing a government service examination. Bo Juyi used satire to protest against numerous government policies.
Both drama and fiction evolved as important forms of Chinese literature in the 1200s. Two famous plays, *The Western Chamber*, by Wang Shifu, and *Injustice to Tou O*, by Guan Hanqing, were written in this period. Tang Xianzu, one of the greatest Chinese playwrights, wrote *Peony Pavillion*, his most notable work, around 1600. Luo Guanzhong wrote in a style resembling the novels of Western writers. In *Romance of the Three Kingdoms*, he describes a power struggle among 3 rival states in the A.D. 100 and 200s. In *The Journey to the West*, also called *Monkey*, Wu Cheng'en uses allegory to relate the adventures of a Buddhist monk on a pilgrimage to India. *Dream of the Red Chamber*, written by Cao Xueqin in the 1700, describes the decline of an aristocratic family. It is perhaps the greatest Chinese novel.
By the 1800, the Chinese had been exposed to Western culture and this influence was evident in the works of Chinese authors in the 1900. With the coming to power of the Communists in 1949 under the leadership of Mao Zedong, literature changed and was directed towards peasants, soldiers and indus-

trial workers. The Cultural Revolution of 1966-1968 set even greater limits to artistic expression. For a while all entertainment was banned. Traditional frction and poetry were denounced. In the years after the Cultural Revolution, restrictions were relaxed. China developed a new literature, called 'the literature of the wounded', dealing with the abuses of power that took place during the late 1960's and early 1970's. Literature, however, remained more political and didactic than expressive of individual creativity. In the late 1970's, after Deng Xiaoping came to power, there was much greater literary freedom. Writers such as Wang Meng, Lu Wenfu, and Ba Jin, who did little or no writing during the Cultural Revolution because they were forced to work as laborers or were imprisoned or exiled, started to write again. Other writers who were popular before the Cultural Revolution, including Lao She, a master of social criticism, and Ding Ling, China's foremost champion of women's rights, had their works republished. In the 1980's, writers such as Zhang Jie and Gua Hua became interested in portraying reality and emotion, and in using new techniques.

Chinese Revolution (1923-1949), battle between the Chinese Communists and the Nationalists for control over China. The Nationalists, united in the Kwoh-min-tang under Sun Yat-sen (1866-1925), overthrew the imperial regime in 1911. However, they did not manage to establish any central authority in chaotic China. Following the death of the moderate Sun Yatsen in 1925, Chiang Kai-shek (1887-1975) won the struggle over the succession; he established a government in 1927. The Chinese Communist Party under the direction of Mao Zedong (1893-1976), who had briefly worked with the KMT in 1924, opposed Chiang's conservative government. The communists retreated to north China and formed a guerilla movement with the support of the farming population. Both parties fought together against the Japanese conquest of China between 1937 and 1945, but once the Second World War ended and after a brief attempt at mediation on the part of the U.S., civil war broke out with great intensity. The Communists, who won over the farming population through land reform, quickly gained the upper hand. The Nationalists could eventually only hold their position in Taiwan, despite support from America. On 1st October 1949, the People's Republic of China was proclaimed, while the (National) Republic of China was proclaimed on Taiwan.

Ching dynasty, Manchu dynasty that ruled China from 1636-1911. Despite their non Chinese descent, the Ching dynasty governed in the manner of their Chinese predecessors, the Ming. They saw themselves as the protectors of the Chinese culture. Emperor Chen Lung (ruled 1736 -96), for example, ordered a complete collection of all Chinese literature, totaling 36,000 volumes, to be compiled. Under the Ching dynasty the empire went through its biggest period of expansion: Manchuria, Outer Mongolia, Tibet, and Formosa were added to the empire. In the 19th century China fell under the increasing domination of Western powers and Japan. In 1911 the last Chinese dynasty fell and a Chinese Republic was introduced.

Chinook, Native American tribe of the Pacific Northwest. The Chinook lived along the mouth of the Columbia River, trading, fishing, and gathering berries, nuts, and roots. Religion centered on a ritual welcoming the annual salmon run. Epidemics and contact with European American civilization destroyed Chinook culture in the 1800s. Modern Chinook live in Washington and Oregon making a living by ranching and fishing.

Chinook, warm, dry, westerly wind occurring in winter and spring on the Rocky Mountain eastern slopes. Pacific air condensing moisture on the mountains' western slopes result in air that increases in temperature 1°F for every 180 ft (1°C for every 99 m) as it descends the eastern slope. Chinooks, called snow eaters, rapidly melt and evaporate ground snow. The wind was named by settlers who thought it came from the direction of the Chinook Indian camp along the Columbia River. Similar winds blowing elsewhere are called *foehns*.

Chip, integrated circuit on which a large number of different circuits are combined to make up one complete arithmetic unit. Has since been perfected to such an extent that a chip suffices for virtually all of the electronic functions of pocket calculators, microprocessors, etcetera. The chip is the result of the continuing development of the integrated circuit (IC). An IC involves attaching a large number of electronic components (transistors, diodes, resistors, capacitors, and the like) next to each other on a carefully manufactured small plate of semiconductor material by using photographic and chemical techniques. Modern chips contain over 100,000 active components (transistors) (VLSI). The name 'chip' did not arise until the 70s, when it became possible to combine virtually all kinds of electronic components on a semiconductor plate.

Chipmunk, any of various small, striped ground-living rodents (genera *Tamias* and *Eutamias*) of the squirrel family. There are 16 species in North America and 1 in Asia. They feed on fruits and nuts, which they carry in their cheek pouches. Though they do not hibernate, they sleep for long periods in winter.

Chippendale, Thomas (1718-1779), English cabinetmaker whose elegant, individual style blended aspects of Gothic, Rococo, and Chinoiserie. Much 18th-century English furniture is given his name. His catalog *The Gentleman and Cabinet-Maker's Director*, first published in 1754, helped establish the English rococo style. Chippendale was born in Yorkshire. Little is known of his early life. By 1749 he had his own workshop in London. His son, Thomas Chippendale II (1749-1822), carried on his business.

Chippewa, or Ojibwa, one of the largest Algonquian-speaking tribes of Native Americans, traditionally living in woodland areas around Lakes Superior and Huron, and to the west. They fought frequently with the Sioux. Longfellow's *The Song of Hiawatha* was based on Chippewa mythology. Today Chippewa live in both the United States and Canada.

Chirac, Jacques (1932-), French political leader, president of the republic since 1995. A Gaullist, he was in the cabinets of four premiers before serving as Premier (1974-1976). He resigned over differences with President Giscard d'Estaing, formed his own party, and was elected mayor of Paris (1977-1986). Premier from 1986-1988 under President Mitterand. He succeeded Mitterand as president in 1995. After taking office, Chirac made a few radical decisions. For example, he allowed a final series of nuclear tests to be conducted in the Pacific Ocean in 1996, just before an international ban on nuclear testing became effective. Chirac also decided to fundamentally reorganize the armed forces, which involved, among other things, doing away with compulsory military service. With his aggressive statements on the subject of the Bosnian crisis and his fierce and constant criticism of the Dutch drug policy, Chirac soon created the image of being an impulsive and undiplomatic politician. In 1997, Chirac called for snap parliamentary elections in order to gain support for drastic reforms that would make it possible to enter the European Economic and Monetary Union. Contrary to his intentions however, the Socialists, led by Lionel Jospin, won the elections and so Chirac was forced to proceed with a cabinet that was led by the opposition (cohabitation). In May 2002, he won the presidential elections again. During the parliamentary elections of June 2002, the right-wing Union pour la Majorité Présidentielle (UMP) obtained absolute majority, which meant the end of the cooperation.

Chirico, Giorgio de (1888-1978), Greek-born Italian painter who founded 'metaphysical painting' and influenced surrealism. His works depict desolate, harshly hued scenes and solitary figures that might be seen in a nightmare: *The Soothsayer's Recompense* (1913), *Melancholy and Mystery of a Street* (1914), and *The Poet and His Muse* (c.1925).

Chiron, in Greek mythology, wisest centaur, famous for his knowledge of healing. He taught many Greek heroes, including Achilles. Wounded by Hercules' arrow, he gave up his immortality to Prometheus and was placed in the heavens as the constellation Sagittarius.
See also: Mythology.

Chiropractic, medical therapy based on the theory that disease results from misalignment of the vertebrae, which causes nerve malfunction. Manipulation of the spinal column, massage, and dietary adjustments are the principal methods used.

Chissano, Joaquim Alberto (1930-),

After 1800, European interest (the British in particular) in the vast Chinese market increased rapidly. Depicted here are European tea-merchants at a tea-auction in Hong Kong at the beginning of the 19th century.

Mozambican politician. As one of the founders of the Liberation Front, Frente de Libertaçao de Moçambique (Frelimo), Chissano was an important individual in the struggle for independence. He was the minister of foreign affairs between 1975 (the year in which the Portuguese left Mozambique) and 1986. When president Samora Machel was killed as a result of a plane crash, he was succeeded by Chissano. Chissano did away with the one party system and endeavored to end the internal struggle with the guerrilla movement Resistencia Nacional Moçambicana (Renamo), which operated with the support of South Africa. His efforts resulted in a peace agreement between Renamo and Chissano's party, Frelimo. Among other

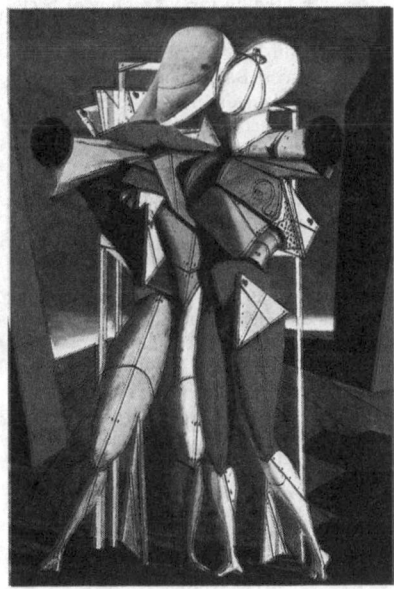

Giorgio de Chirico (1888-1978) painted *Hector and Andromeda* in 1917 (Matteoli Collectoin, Milan).

C

things, a general elections was called for in 1994 under the supervision of the UN. Frelimo won the elections and Chissano, having acquired 55% of the votes, was re-elected. With 52% of the votes, he was also re-elected during the elections of 1999.

Chiton, any of an order (Polyplacophora) of primitive mollusks with shells of light overlapping plates and a muscular foot that clings to rocks. Found on shores worldwide, chitons feed on algae scraped from the rocks. They range in length from 1/2 in (1.2 cm) to 1 ft (28.8 cm).

Chittagong (pop. 2,600,000), Bangladesh, a city on the Karnaphuli River near the Bay of Bengal, in the southeastern part of the country. Chittagong is the country's chief port and is an important center for exporting tea and jute. It is also a major rail terminus and has an international airport. Steel, plywood, paper, tea, refined oil, and textiles are produced in the city and nearby areas. The Jama Masjid, built in the 17th century, is one of the city's oldest mosques. The University of Chittagong was founded in 1966. Chittagong dates from the ninth century. The city was seriously damaged by a cyclone in 1991.

Chivalry, knightly code of conduct in medieval Europe combining Christian and military ideals of bravery, piety, honor, loyalty, and sacrifice, virtues valued by the Crusaders. Chivalry flourished in the 12th to 14th century and declined in the 15th century although it continues to be the basis for gentlemanly behavior. Examples of chivalric literature are the Arthurian legends and the Chansons de Geste.
See also: Knights and knighthood.

Chive, perennial plant (*Allium schoenoprasum*) of the lily family, of the same genus as the onion. Found wild in Italy and Greece, its leaves are used in salads.

Chlamydia, infectious sexually transmitted disease, caused by various strains of bacteria. Symptoms may include inflamed eyes (conjunctivitis) and pelvic inflammation disease in women. Babies born to mothers with untreated chlamydia may develop pneumonia or the infection itself. One of the most widespread sexually transmitted diseases, chlamydia, is treated with antibiotics. When contracted by women and not treated, chlamydia can cause infertility.
See also: Venereal disease.

Chloride, chemical compound of chlorine with another element or radical.
See also: Salt; Salt, chemical.

Chlorine, chemical element, symbol Cl; for physical constants see Periodic Table. Chlorine was discovered by Karl Scheele in 1774. It is a highly reactive, greenish-yellow poisonous gas that combines directly with nearly all elements. It is one of the top 5 industrial chemicals and is used throughout the world to make drinking water safe. It is also used in manufacturing products for sanitizing, bleaching, and disinfecting. Chlorine is a severe respiratory irritant; has been used as a weapon in war.

Chloroform, or trichloromethane, dense, colorless, volatile liquid ($CHCl_3$) produced by chlorination of ethanol or acetone. One of the first anesthetics to be used in surgery, it has since been replaced by less toxic anesthetics, such as ether. It is used in cough medicines and as an organic solvent.

Chlorophyll, green pigment of plants that gives them their color and traps and stores the energy of sunlight required for photosynthesis. The energy is used to convert water and carbon dioxide into sugars.
See also: Photosynthesis.

Chocolate, confection made from cacao beans, used to make candy and beverages. Fermented beans are roasted and ground, then mixed with cacao butter, sugar, and milk solids. The process for making chocolate was perfected in Switzerland around 1876.

Cholera, acute infectious disease involving the small intestine, characterized by diarrhea, vomiting, muscular cramps, and severe loss of body fluid. The disease is caused by a toxin produced by the bacillus *Vibrio cholerae* and is spread by ingestion of water and of foods contaminated by the excrement of infected persons. Cholera can be fatal if untreated. Outbreaks still occur in regions of Africa and Asia where sanitation is poor.

Cholesterol, basic component of fats or lipids, a steroid found in nearly all tissues. Cholesterol is present in large quantity in the nervous system, where it is a compound of myelin, the greasy substance that acts as a sheath around nerve fibers. It is a precursor of bile salts and of adrenal and sex hormones. Large amounts are synthesized in the liver, intestines, and skin. Since abnormal depositing of cholesterol in the arteries is associated with aterio-arteriosclerosis, some doctors advise avoiding high-cholesterol foods and substituting unsaturated for saturated fats. Cholesterol is also a major constituent of gallstones.
See also: Arteriosclerosis.

Chomsky, Noam (1928-), U.S. linguist that revolutionized the study of language structure with his theory of generative grammar, first outlined in *Syntactic Structures* (1957). He was also an influential critic of U.S. foreign policy both during and after the Vietnam War.

Ch'ongjin (pop. 911,000), port in the Northeast of North Korea, on the Sea of Japan. Capital of the province North Hamgyong. Important ice-free port. Very important center for the steel industry (metal processing, shipbuilding, and machine building, manufacturing of railway equipment) and important textile industry and chemical industry (synthetic fibers). A small fishing village up until the 20th century, after that developed by the Japanese (1910-1945) into a marine base, and then into an industrial center by the North Koreans.

Chongqing (Chungking, or Ch'ung-ch'ing; pop. 3,500,000), city in Sichuan province, Southwest China, on the Jialing and Yangtze rivers. It is a densely populated political and industrial center. Products such as tung oil, tea, and silk are exported and machines are imported by way of important waterways, highways, and railroads. The city is also the main industrial center of Southwest China with iron/steel industry, textile, chemical and food industry, and important crafts. The soil in the area surrounding the city is fertile; moreover, large amounts of coal and iron ore are found here. It became part of China in 220 B.C., served as a treaty port (1891-1943), and was capital of the Nationalist government (1937-1946) under Chiang Kai-shek. During the Chinese Revolution, the city served as a final refuge for the Nationalists before they left for Taiwan. In 1997, the People's Congress granted Chongqing its provincial status, just like Peking, Shanghai, and Tianjin. In addition to the city itself, the cities of Wanxian and Fuling, along with the Qianjiang district, also belong to Greater Chongqing (31,672 sq mi, 82,000 sq km). With that, it became the city with the largest population in the world: 30 million people.
See also: China.

Chopin, Frédéric François (1810-1849), Polish composer and pianist. In 1831 he moved from Poland to Paris. His chief works are for the piano and include piano concertos in E minor (1833) and F minor (1836), 24 preludes (1838-1839), and many waltzes, mazurkas, and polonaises that were inspired by his Polish nationalism. In 1837 he began his friendship with the novelist George Sand. Their relationship ended unhappily in 1847. Chopin died 2 years later of tuberculosis.

Chorale, type of hymn tune developed in Germany during the Reformation. Chorales formed the basis of the new Protestant church music. J.S. Bach harmonized many of these chorale tunes for the Lutheran Church, and used them as a basis for many organ and choral compositions.
See also: Reformation.

Choral music, unaccompanied choral music sung in monasteries during the early Christian era, known as plainsong. Choral music without accompaniment continued through the 16th century. The development of instrumental accompaniment in the 17th and 18th centuries culminated in J. S. Bach's orchestrated cantatas and passions and the oratorios of Handel. Beethoven's inclusion of a choir in the finale of his *Ninth Symphony* (1817-1823) marks a turning point in the history of music. Notable among 20th-century choral works are Elgar's *Dream of Gerontius* (1900) and Stravinsky's *Symphony of Psalms* (1930).

Chordate, animal possessing a primitive backbone-like structure (notochord) at some stage in its development. Grouped in the phylum Chordata, chordates include all vertebrates and many small aquatic invertebrates such as the tunicates.

Chorea, disease of the central nervous system causing abnormal, involuntary movements of the limbs, body, and face. Sydenham's chorea (St. Vitus' dance) is a

childhood illness associated with rheumatic fever; Huntington's chorea is a rare, fatal hereditary disease of adulthood associated with progressive dementia.
See also: Nervous system.

Chorus, in ancient classical Greek drama, group of actors who commented upon the action. The origin of the chorus is probably the dithyramb, a hymn to the god Dionysus. By the 6th century B.C. the formal dramatic chorus was an integral part of the performance. Gradually the size and role of the chorus was reduced as the actor's role grew. It disappeared by the 2nd century B.C.

Chorzów (German: Königshütte; pop. 129,000), city in Southeast Poland (Silesia). Iron and steel works, metal, chemical, and glass industry. Developed in the 18th century thanks to the extraction of coal. Municipality in 1868.

Chou En-lai (1898-1976), first prime minister of the People's Republic of China, 1949-1976. A founder of the Chinese Communist Party, in 1926 he organized the Shanghai Strike for Chiang Kai-shek and escaped when Chiang betrayed the communists. Director of military affairs for Mao Tsetung's guerrilla forces, he commanded the first stage of the Long March (1934-1935). He won support for China in the Third World and was a major force in taking China into the United Nations (1971) and reestablishing contact with the West in the 1970s.
See also: China.

Chow chow, breed of nonsporting dog believed to have come from China, with a thick, soft coat, and a unique blue-black tongue. The chow chow stands 18-20 in (46-51 cm) at the shoulder and weighs 50-60 lb (23-27 kg).

Chrétien de Troyes (1135-1183), French poet who wrote romances rooted in Arthurian legend. His work, including *Erec et Enide, Cligès,* and *Perceval,* influenced French and English literature through the next 2 centuries.

Christ, Jesus *See:* Jesus Christ.

Christchurch (pop. 325,000), New Zealand's third largest city, located on South Island near the east coast. A tourist and commercial center, it produces clothing, electrical goods, and fertilizers, and is served by an international airport, railroads, and tunnels linking the city with Lyttelton, the chief port. An Anglican church group settled Christchurch in 1850 and established the University of Canterbury there in 1873.

Christian *See:* Christianity.

Christian, Charlie (1919-1942), influential jazz guitarist who pioneered the use of electrically amplified instruments. While playing in the Benny Goodman orchestra (1939-1941), Christian joined with Dizzy Gillespie and Thelonious Monk to create bebop, a modern style of jazz. Christian's career ended when he contracted tuberculosis in 1941.
See also: Jazz.

Christianity, religion founded on the life and teachings of Jesus, acknowledged by all Christians to be the Son of God. Christianity had its beginnings when a small band of Jews recognized Jesus of Nazareth, who died about A.D. 33, as the Messiah, or Christ. Immediately after the crucifixion of Jesus, Christianity counted only a few hundred members, among them the Apostles, who followed Christ's teachings and preached his Gospel, particularly as it concerned the life, sufferings, death, resurrection, and divine nature of Jesus. The Christian community had its center in Jerusalem but soon spread into Asia Minor, Syria, Macedonia, and Greece. While St. Peter was the leader of the Jewish Christian community, Saul of Tarsus (later known as Paul the Apostle) was preeminent in the task of converting the Gentiles and establishing churches in the Greco-Roman world. As the faith spread, an ecclesiastical structure evolved. Bishops replaced the Apostles as celebrants of the ritual of the Eucharist. They were assisted by presbyters, or elders, who were given the right to perform the sacred duties connected with the Eucharist, while the bishops retained the right of consecrating the presbyters and of confirming the faithful. Various regions were organized into dioceses and provinces. Within 3 centuries, despite persecutions, the Christian religion had become firmly established; in A.D. 324 the emperor Constantine established Christianity as the official religion. In order to settle doctrinal disputes and establish basic tenets, Constantine called the first ecumenical council at Nicaea in 325. The Nicene Creed, adopted at this council, stated the basic truths of the Christian Church; departures from this statement of faith were thereafter regarded as heresy. From earliest times the preeminence of the bishop of Rome was recognized by the entire Western Church. However, the Eastern Church, headed by the patriarch of Constantinople, had traditionally retained jurisdiction over organizational and doctrinal matters in its own sphere. The question of papal authority led to the Great Schism (1054), when the Eastern Church broke its ties with the West. The popes emerged as influential rulers in western Europe during the Middle Ages, contending with the Holy Roman emperors for temporal power as well as spiritual authority. Disputes arose concerning papal succession, and popes and antipopes, supported by rival kings and princes, fought for the right to rule with the authority of the Holy See.

The entire structure of the Church was shaken by this dissension, and abuses such as simony and the sale of indulgences also cried out for reform. In the 14th century reform was advocated by John Wycliffe in England and Jan Hus in Czechoslovakia. The Reformation of the 16th century was led by Martin Luther, who denied the supreme authority of the pope and rejected all but 2 of the 7 sacraments, Baptism and the Eucharist. He affirmed the supreme authority of the Bible in all matters of faith. The Catholic Church responded to the Reformation with the Counter-Reformation, during which abuses were corrected, several new religious orders were formed, and a spirit of Christian mission was fostered among the faithful. It

A medieval church choir accompanied by vielle (a bowed lute), bells, and psaltery. With the beginning of polyphonic music in the 9th century, instruments were often used to reinforce the vocal parts, and were frequently used on major feast days.

was a highly active era for proselytizing the faith and a period of great creativity in religious art. Since the 16th century there have existed 2 main currents of western Christianity: Protestantism and Roman Catholicism. In Switzerland the Reformation was led by Huldreich Zwingli in Zürich and John Calvin in Geneva. Calvinism, which teaches the predestination of the elect and was adopted by the French Huguenots, forms the basis of modern Presbyterianism and the Reformed churches. During the 18th century John Wesley, who turned from Calvinism to a more traditional Christian view, founded the Methodist church in England.

After the pope refused to annul his first marriage, King Henry VIII declared the Church of England to be free of papal jurisdiction. Under Edward VI and Elizabeth I, the Anglican church became truly Protestant; its tenets were set forth in the Thirty-nine Articles of 1576. The Puritans considered these doctrinal reforms inadequate, however, and sought a form of worship based strictly on the Scriptures. Puritan sects later gave rise to the Baptist and Congregational churches and to the Religious Society of Friends, or Quakers. The settlements founded throughout the American colonies by dissenting members of Protestant churches gave impetus to the development of independent American church bodies, such as the Protestant Episcopal Church, an offshoot of the Church of England. Some distinctly American churches sprang up, among these the Church of Jesus Christ of Latter-Day Saints (Mormons), founded in 1830, and the Church of Christ Scientist (Christian Science), founded in 1882. In all there are more than 200 branches of the Christian Church in the United States.

One of the most significant developments in the continued growth of the Christian church in the 20th century is the ecumenical movement. Although still in an early phase, with its progress often slowed by organizational and doctrinal difficulties, ecumenicism has caught the imagination of a majority of the clergy and the faithful, who envision a future in which the Christian Church will again be one universal body, as it was established by Christ.
See also: Jesus Christ.

C

Christian IV (1577-1648), king of Denmark and Norway 1588-1648, longest reigning Danish monarch. He involved Denmark in wars with Sweden (1611-1613, 1643-1645), and helped Protestants fight Roman Catholics in Germany (1625-1629) during the Thirty Years' War. These wars left Denmark bankrupt.

Christian IX (1818-1906), king of Denmark 1863-1906. During his reign, Denmark acquired the territory of Schleswig in 1863, but in 1864 Prussia and Austria invaded, gaining control of Schleswig and Holstein. Although against democracy, in 1901 he recognized a democratic parliament.

Christian Science, religion based on belief in the power of Christian faith to heal sickness. It was founded by Mary Baker Eddy, who organized the first Church of Christ, Scientist at Boston, Mass., in 1879.

Christian X (1870-1947), king of Denmark (1912-1947), king of Iceland (1912-1944), symbol of Danish resistance to German occupation during World War II. In 1915, he granted a new constitution ending privileges of upper classes and admitting to women's rights. After the German invasion of Denmark in 1940 he continued to occupy the throne, but was under house arrest 1943-1945 for refusing to cooperate with the Germans.

Christie, Dame Agatha (1891-1976), British writer of popular detective novels and plays. Her works, which include *The Murder of Roger Ackroyd* (1926), *The Mousetrap* (1952), and *The Pale Horse* (1962) feature her 2 central characters, the egotistical Hercule Poirot and the elderly Miss Jane Marple.

In the polytene chromosome of *Drosophila hydei* (shown here), a relative of the fruitfly (*Drosophila melanogaster*), a terminal puff is visible in the centre of the photograph. This puff has been artificially induced in the laboratory by way of thermal treatment. Apparently, this environmental change calls for an adaption of the genes. Artificial puff formation can also be induced chemically.

Christmas (Christ's Mass), annual Christian festival observed on Dec. 25 to commemorate the birth of Jesus Christ. The exact date of Christ's birth is unknown. The origin of the Christmas story is based on the Gospels of Luke and Matthew in the New Testament. The first reference to the celebration of Christmas occurred in a Roman calendar of A.D. 336. By the Middle Ages, Christmas had become the most significant religious holiday in Europe, with Saint Nicholas as a symbol of giving. In the 19th century Christmas trees and Christmas cards became customs of the holiday. In the United States, Santa Claus replaced Saint Nicholas as the great gift giver.
See also: Christianity; Jesus Christ; Santa Claus.

Christmas Island *See:* Kiritimati Atoll.

Christmas Tree *See:* Christmas.

Christo (Christo Javacheff; 1935-), American visual artist of Bulgarian origin; associated himself with the 'nouveau réalisme' in Paris. Since 1968, he has wrapped up a wide variety of buildings, items, and objects using paper, string, jute, canvas, and textile. His work includes *Valley Curtain* (1972, Colorado); *Running Fence* (1976), a curtain 24 mi (39 km) in California; 11 small islands in Biscayne Bay (1983, Florida); the Pont Neuf in Paris (1985); the Reichstag in Berlin (1995); and 160 trees in a park near Basel (1998). Christo has been collaborating with his wife Jeanne since 1994.

Christ of the Andes, statue of Christ created by Mateo Alonzo, in Uspallata Pass on the Argentine-Chile border in the Andes Mountains. It was dedicated on March 13, 1904 to commemorate treaties for perpetual peace between Argentina and Chile.

Christophe, Henri (1767-1820), king of North Haiti. A freed black slave, he became president of Haiti in 1806, after plotting the assassination of Dessalines. After 1811 he ruled North Haiti, as King Henri I. Faced with a revolt, he shot himself.

Christopher, Saint (3rd century A.D.), Christian martyr and patron of travelers. According to legend, he carried the Christ child across a river. The Roman Catholic Church removed his feast day (July 25) from its liturgical calendar for lack of historical evidence as to his existence.

Christopher, Warren (1925-), American laywer and politician (Democrat). Christopher was active in the legal profession from 1950 until 1976. As of 1961, he has acted as advisor and negotiator for, among others, President Kennedy. He was the Assistant Secretary of Foreign Affairs under Carter, in which capacity he carried out the negotiations concerning the release of the American hostages in Iran. In 1993, he was appointed minister of foreign affairs under President Clinton. He made significant contributions to the peace process in the Middle East during 1995/96. His shuttle diplomacy proved successful in April 1996, when he managed to convince Israel, Syria,

and Lebanon to sign a truce during a (sixteen-day) 'war' between Israel and the radical Shiite movement, Hezbollah (Party of God). Following Clinton's reelection on 5th November 1996, Christopher resigned as minister of foreign affairs. He was succeeded by Madeleine Albright.

Christus, Petrus (fl. c.1442-1473), Flemish painter, early Netherlandish school. His work, strongly influenced by Jan van Eyck, was important in the 15th-century development of realistic perspective: *Madonna with S. S. Francis and Jerome*, *Lamentation*, and *Nativity*.

Chrome *See:* Chromium.

Chromic acid, common name for chromium trioxide (H_2CrO_4), an industrial compound used in chromium plating and the manufacture of fire resistant chemicals. Poisonous and caustic, most chromic acid takes the form of bright red crystals.

Chromium, chemical element, symbol Cr; for physical constants see Periodic Table. Chromium was discovered by L.N. Vauquelin in 1797. It is a steel-gray, lustrous, hard metal. Elemental chromium is prepared by reduction of its oxide with aluminum. It is used in the production of stainless steel, in plating, and in the production of other metal alloys. Many compounds of chromium are used to color glass, as pigments, and as mordants in the textile industry.

Chromosome, threadlike body in the cell nucleus, composed of genes, which carry genetic information responsible for the inherited characteristic of all organisms. Chromosomes consist of deoxyribonucleic acid (DNA), a sequence of nucleotides composed of 4 different bases, allowing over 500 million alternatives. The basic proteins are found in a complex with DNA in the cells of human organs and tissues; in general, these are called histones. The microscope shows that the chromosome is a coiled structure. This coiling should not be confused with the structure of the DNA molecule-a double helix- because there is a difference of several orders of magnitude in the scale. Mitosis is the normal process by which a cell divides, each new cell ending up with the same number of chromosomes as the original cell. Mitotic division occurs in somatic cells (i.e., not sex cells) during periods of growth, when the total number of cells is increasing, or during repair processes, when lost or damaged cells are being replaced. In the resting cell (interphase of mitosis) the chromosomes cannot be detected inside the nucleus as discrete structures. As a cell approaches mitosis, the chromosomes become visible as threads within the nucleus (prophase of mitosis). At the same time, cytoplasmic bodies, the centrioles, divide, and the 2 new centrioles move to opposite poles of the cell. The protein fibers that control the separation of the chromosomes radiate from these bodies. The chromosomes line up in the equatorial plane of the cell (metaphase of mitosis) and separate to form the chromosomes of the 2 new nuclei (anaphase of mitosis). A cleavage furrow begins to divide

the cytoplasm of the cell, the chromosomes elongate, and a nuclear membrane re-forms around them. This stage (telophase of mitosis) results in the reconstruction of 2 nuclei that are genetically identical with the parent nucleus.
See also: Genetics; Heredity.

Chronicles, 2 Old Testament books summarizing Jewish history from Adam through the Babylonian Captivity.
See also: Old Testament.

Chronometer, extremely accurate clock, used especially in navigation. The chronometer invented by John Harrison (1759) allowed navigation to determine longitude accurately for the first time. The mechanical chronometer is spring-driven, like a watch, but its parts are larger and devices in the spring minimize effects of temperature changes and the ship's rolling movements.

Chrysalis, pupa of certain insects, especially butterflies and moths at the state between caterpillar or larva and fully developed imago (winged adult).

Chrysanthemum, genus of popular flowering annual or perennial herbaceous plants of the daisy family (Compositae). The national flower of Japan, chrysanthemums are usually white, yellow, pink, or red and are native to temperate and subtropical areas.

Chrysler, Walter Percy (1875-1940), U.S. industrialist who produced the first Chrysler car (1924) and established the Chrysler Corporation (1925), which became a major auto producer in the United States.

Chrysostom, Saint John (c.347-407 A.D.), Greek Father and Doctor of the Church. He was called Chrysostom ('golden mouthed') for his powers of oratory. He was patriarch of Constantinople (398-404) and became its patron saint.

Chub, any of several small, freshwater carp (family Cyprinidae) found in flowing waters, common to Europe and North America. The chub, 4-12 in (10-31 cm) long, has a large head and wide mouth and is usually a gray-brown or blue and silver color. Being a generally coarse and bony fish, it is not much valued as food, but is popularly used for bait and is caught for sport.

Chuckwalla (*Sauromalus obesus*), lizard of the North American desert. Stoutly built and 1 ft (30 cm) long, it ranges from Arizona and Utah to northern Mexico, feeding on the flowers and leaves of desert plants. During the summer it lives below ground, and when alarmed it retreats into crevices, wedging itself by blowing up its body.

Chun Doo Hwan (1931-), South Korean general and politician. He became head of the military security forces in 1979. He was the acting head of the Korean Central Intelligence Service (KCIA) from April to June of 1980. Chun was promoted to general in August 1980 and resigned from the armed forces shortly afterwards. In September 1980, following a coup, he was installed as president of the Republic of South Korea as the successor of President Park Chung Hee, who was murdered in 1979, and Interim President Choi Kyu Hak. In the years 1986-1987, the protests against Chun and his party, the Democratic Party of Justice, saw a significant increase. He unexpectedly called for new elections which, partly due to the fact that the opposition was strongly divided, were won by his party. He was succeeded in 1988 by Roh Rae Woo. In December 1995, he was arrested and imprisoned for his part in the coup of 1979 and for violently suppressing the students' revolt in Kwangju in 1980. In January of 1996 he was officially indicted for corruption during his administration. He was sentenced to life imprisonment, but was pardoned in 1997 by President Kim Young Sam, following consultations with the newly-elected president, Kim Dae Jung.

Church, Frederick Edwin (1826-1900), U.S. landscape painter noted for his portrayal of light on large canvases. He was a student of Thomas Cole and the most famous member of the Hudson River School. Among his best known works are *Niagara* and *Heart of the Andes*.
See also: Hudson River School.

Church and state, phrase that refers to the relations between organized religion and organized government. This question, which for centuries has been a source of controversy, is whether the religious and political powers in a society should be kept clearly separate from one another.

Churches of Christ, evangelical Protestant Christian body that teaches strict adherence to principles and practices set forth in the New Testament. Formerly one with the Church of the Disciples of Christ, believed to have been founded at Pentecost and refounded by Thomas Campbell (1763-1854), this conservative church is one of the largest denominations in the United States.
See also: Protestantism.

Churchill, Jennie Jerome *See:* Churchill, Sir Winston Leonard Spencer.

Churchill, John *See:* Marlborough, Duke of.

Churchill, Sir Winston Leonard Spencer (1874-1965), British statesman, soldier, and writer. The son of Lord Randolph Churchill and his U.S. wife, Jennie Jerome, he was educated at Harrow and Sandhurst. He fought in India (1897), the Sudan (1898), and South Africa. A Conservative member of Parliament (1900), he changed to the Liberal party in 1905 and became first lord of the admiralty by 1911, in which office he was held accountable for the failure of the Dardanelles campaign during World War I. Churchill left government and saw active service in France until he was recalled by Lloyd George to serve in several cabinet positions (1917-1922). In 1924 he regained a seat in Parliament and was chancellor of the exchequer in Stanley Baldwin's Conservative government (1924-1929). Out of favor with his own party, he held no office for the next

Kyphosus sectatrix (top), a sea chub, is unrelated to the freshwater chubs, such as *Leuciscus cephalus* (bottom). The latter is a game fish prized more for its spirit than for its palatability.

10 years, during which time he voiced strong warnings regarding Hitler's activity in Germany. When World War II broke out (1939), Chamberlain appointed him first lord of the admiralty. Upon Hitler's invasion of the Low Countries, Churchill was made prime minister (1940) and minister of national defense. His persuasive oratory and unswerving confidence were instrumental assets in Allied resistance, as were his contributions to military strategy. He was coauthor, with President F.D. Roosevelt, of the Atlantic Charter, and played a key role in the diplomatic conferences that were to shape postwar Europe (e.g., Yalta Conference). In 1951 Churchill returned to power as prime minister for the second time, serving until his retirement from politics (1955). His extensive writings, for which he received the Nobel Prize (1953), include an autobiography, *My Early Life* (1930), *The Second World War* (6 vol., 1948-1953), and *A History of the English-Speaking Peoples* (4 vol., 1956-1958).
See also: World War II.

Churchill Downs *See:* Kentucky; Kentucky Derby; Louisville.

Sir Winston Churchill's expression in this famous portrait (1941) by Yousef Karsh suggests the determination with which the wartime leader pledged his 'blood, toil, tears, and sweat' to the task of defeating Nazi Germany.

C

Churchill River, formerly Hamilton River, river rising in Ashuanipi Lake in southwestern Labrador and flowing about 600 mi (970 km) through Newfoundland in eastern Canada to Lake Melville on the Atlantic Ocean. A large hydroelectric power plant, with a capacity of more than 5 million kilowatts of electricity, was completed in 1974 on the river at Churchill Falls.

Church of Christ *See:* Churches of Christ.

Church of Christ, Scientist *See:* Christian Science.

Church of England, national church of England and parent church of the Anglican Communion. Its doctrine is basically Protestant and its hierarchy and ceremony are rooted in Catholic tradition. The church broke with Rome in 1534 when Henry VIII assumed the title of the head of the church. In the 16th and 17th centuries the church was troubled by Puritan agitation and later by nonconformity. But it remains the established state church and its 26 senior bishops (lords spiritual) sit in the House of Lords, led by the archbishop of Canterbury. *See also:* Anglicans.

Church of Jesus Christ of Latter-Day Saints *See:* Mormons.

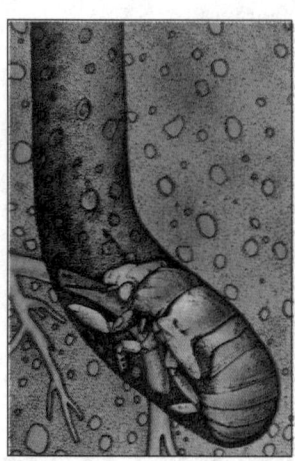

Cicadas are known for their characteristic loud, high-pitched sounds, produced by the males with their pair of tymbals - ribbed, platelike organs on the abdomen. Eggs are laid in trees. When these hatch, the nymphs will burrow into the ground and feed on sap sucked from roots (left). They will remain underground until just before the final molt. For *Magicicada septendecim* of eastern North America, this means as much as 17 years! The nymph then crawls out of the soil, climbs onto a tree, digs its claws into the bark, and finally molts into a fully winged adult (right).

Churriguera, José Benito (1665-1725), Spanish architect and sculptor who gave his name to the Spanish Baroque style featuring extravagant design, Churrigueresque (1650-1740). Churriguera designed grandiose theatrical altars and the entire urban complex of Nuevo Baztán in Madrid. He was also the architect for the cathedral of Salamanca. His style influenced the Spanish missions of colonial North America.

Chu Teh (1886-1976), Chinese Communist leader. He helped form the Chinese Red Army and joined Mao Tse-tung (1927). As commander in chief, he led the Long March (1934-1935) and defeated the Nationalists (1949). He held various high posts in the Communist government including chairman of the National People's Congress in 1959. *See also:* China.

Chuwarizmi, al- (Mohammad ibn Musa; approx. 780-approx. 830) Arabic mathematician. The term 'algebra' is derived from the title of his book *Hisab al djabr we al mukabalah* (regroup and set against). He wrote an elementary arithmetic that contributed to the distribution of the decimal position system. The term 'algorithm' is derived from the latin form of his name.

CIA *See:* Central Intelligence Agency (CIA).

Cibber, Colley (1671-1757), English actor-manager and dramatist who introduced sentimental comedy to the theater. He wrote over 30 plays including *Love's Last Shift* (1696) and *Apology* (1740) which offers a vivid depiction of the contemporary theater. He was made poet laureate in 1730.

Cibola, Seven Cities of, golden cities reported in the North American Southwest in the 16th century. The legend attracted Spanish exploration, notably by Francisco Coronado and his 300 Spanish cavalry and 1,000 Native American allies (1540).

Cicada, large insect (order Homoptera) known for its monotonous whining song produced by the rapidly vibrating, drumlike membranes on the male's abdomen (the female is mute). The larvae develop in the soil, feeding on roots; the periodical cicada (genus *Magicicada*) spends 17 years underground and live for 1 week above it.

Cicero, Marcus Tullius (106-43 B.C.), Roman orator, statesman, and philosopher. As consul (63 B.C.) he crushed the Catiline conspiracy. His refusal to submit to the First Triumvirate resulted in banishment in 58 B.C., but he was recalled the next year by Pompey, with whom he sided in the civil war. Cicero's tacit approval of Caesar's murder and his defense of the Republic against Mark Antony in his first and second *Philippics* led to his execution after Octavian took Rome. A master of Latin prose, his great works include personal letters and orations (57 extant). *See also:* Rome, Ancient.

Cid, El (Rodrigo Díaz de Bivar; 1040?-1099), Spanish soldier and hero. His name comes from the Arabic *El Sayyid*, which means 'the Lord.' El Cid led the forces of Sancho II of Castile and Alfonso VI of Leon until banishment by Alfonso (c.1081). He then fought for the Arab kings of Saragossa, capturing Valencia (1094), where he remained as ruler until his death. His romanticized exploits appear in literature, notably *The Song of the Cid* (c.1140) and Corneille's *Le Cid* (1636).

Cilia, hairlike projections, often part of a fringe, that provide locomotion for 1-celled organisms, and move fluid within higher forms of life. Cilia protruding from the lining of the upper respiratory tract move to pass on dust, germs, and mucus. *See also:* Protozoan.

Ciliate *See:* Protozoan.

Çiller, Tansu (1945-), Turkish politician and economist. Her conservative True Path Party was elected to Parliament in 1991. She became leader of the True Path Party and Prime Minister in 1993. Her political course was pro-western. After the electoral defeat and the subsequent failed partnership with Yilmaz's Motherland Party, she decided to form a coalition with the Islamic Welfare Party (Refah Partisi). She was Foreign Secretary from 1996 to 1997. After the fall of the cabinet she returned to Parliament. After 1997, her position was weakened by allegations of corruption. Relations between the True Path Party and Yilmaz's party were heavily damaged as a result of these accusations. *See also:* Yilmaz, Mesut.

Cimabue, Giovanni (Cenni di Pepo or Peppi; c.1240-c.1302), Italian painter. His work shows the transition from the formal Byzantine style of painting to the more lyrical Florentine school of the 14th century. His best known work, *Madonna and Child Enthroned with Angels and Prophets*, is now at the Uffizi Gallery in Florence, Italy.

Cimarosa, Domenico (1749-1801), prolific Italian composer famous for his comic operas, notably *Il Matrimonio Segreto* ('The Secret Marriage'; 1792). He was court composer to Catherine the Great of Russia, 1787-1791.

Cimmerians, ancient nomads of the Crimea and Asia Minor. First mentioned in Homer's *Odyssey*, they lived from about 1200 B.C. to 700 B.C., in an area of the Caucasus Mountains, near the Black Sea in what is now the southern USSR. The Cimmerians were warriors who rode horses and used bows and arrows. According to the Greek historian Herodotus, they were driven into Asia Minor by the Scythians. About 700 B.C. the Cimmerians battled the Assyrians, and plundered and destroyed the Phrygian dynasty.

Cimon (c.507-c.449 B.C.), Athenian statesman and military leader in the Greco-Persian Wars. He became the leader of the aristocrats, those opposing the democrat Pericles and his reform-minded followers. He was exiled by Pericles, but returned to Athens in 451 B.C., and eventually effected a reconciliation between Sparta and Athens. *See also:* Athens; Greece, Ancient.

Cinchona, or chinchona, genus of evergreen tree of South and Central America, cultivated for its bark, which yields quinine and other antimalarial alkaloids.

Cincinnati (pop. 364,000), city in southwest Ohio, on a height overlooking the Ohio River. First settled in 1788, the city grew

C

rapidly after the War of 1812. Manufacturing industries today include chemicals, automobile parts and bodies, soap, machine tools, and engines. Publishing and printing industries also contribute to the economy. The city is a major river and rail transportation center and inland port. Cincinnati's cultural life offers museums (including the Taft Museum; Cincinnati was the birthplace of William Howard Taft and Robert A. Taft), its symphony orchestra, opera, and conservatory.
See also: Ohio.

Cincinnatus, Lucius Quinctius (c.519-c.439 B.C.), statesman and Roman patriotic hero. Cincinnatus was named dictator by the Senate in 458 B.C. When Rome was threatened by the Aequians, he left his farm, defeated the enemy, resigned, and returned to his farm all within 16 days of taking office.
See also: Rome, Ancient.

Cinema *See:* Motion pictures.

Cinnabar, bright-red mercuric sulfide mineral (HgS), an important source of mercury and used in the pigment vermillion. Large deposits are found in Spain, Yugoslavia, Italy, China, and southern California.
See also: Mercury (element).

Cinnamon (genus *Cinnamomum)*, tree or shrub of the laurel family. The inner bark of the Ceylon cinnamon (*C. zeylanicum*) is used as a spice; in medicine, *C. camphora* serves as a digestion stimulant and to treat dyspepsia.

Cinquefoil, low-growing plant (genus *Potentilla*) of the rose family, named for its 5-fingered leaves. The bright yellow and white flowers are widespread over North America and the Pacific coast.

Circadian rhythm *See:* Biological clock.

Circe, in Greek mythology, daughter of Helios (the Sun), enchantress who transformed Odysseus' men into swine; Odysseus himself escaped her spell. Later legends say she had 3 sons by Odysseus, including Telegonus, doomed to slay his father.
See also: Mythology.

Circle, closed plane curve every point of which is at equal distance from a fixed point (center). A line segment between the center and the curve is called a *radius* (r); the word is also used for the length of that segment. A line segment whose 2 ends lie in the curve is a *chord*, and a chord passing through the center point is called the *diameter* (d). The distance around the edge is known as the *circumference* (C); $C = \pi d$. The area of a circle (A) is given by $A = \pi r^2$. The circle has been used to symbolize eternity, the universe, or heaven.

Circuit, electric *See:* Electric circuit.

Circuit breaker, electric device, like a fuse, that will automatically interrupt an electrical circuit (by separating the contacts) when the current exceeds a desired value. Circuit breakers may be reset by hand

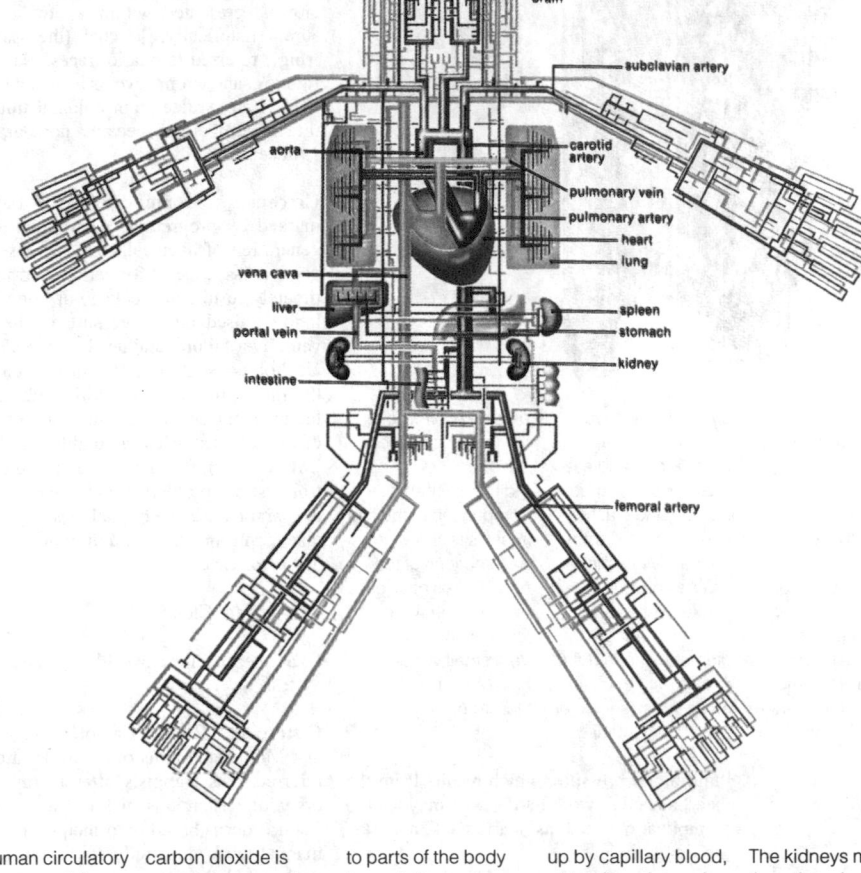

or automatically, whereas a fuse has to be replaced.
See also: Electricity.

Circulation *See:* Circulatory system.

Circulatory system, system of organs that carries blood throughout the body. It consists chiefly of a pump (the heart) and a network of blood vessels (arteries, veins, and capillaries). The circulatory system provides the body with essential food and oxygen while eliminating carbon dioxide and other wastes. In addition, as blood circulates, white blood cells help protect the body from disease by engulfing harmful invaders, and body temperature is regulated by absorbing heat from the cells' production of energy. Disease or injury may damage the circulatory system, possibly affecting blood flow. Arterioscleroisis, an accumulation of fatty deposits in the arteries, is one such condition. This disease may be associated with

The human circulatory system, comprising the heart, arteries, and veins, is divided into the pulmonary and the systemic systems. The pulmonary system starts with pulmonary arteries that circulate oxygen-poor blood (blue) from the heart to the lungs, where carbon dioxide is released as a waste product. Oxygen is absorbed from the lungs, and pulmonary veins carry oxygen-rich blood (red) back to the heart. The systemic system carries blood to all parts of the body. Oxygen-rich blood travels from the heart to parts of the body through the aorta, which is the largest artery. The blood travels through smaller arteries to capillaries from which oxygen and nutrients pass from the blood to the body tissues. Cellular waste products and carbon dioxide are poicked up by capillary blood, which flows into veins. The vena cava, the largest vein of the body, carries the blood back to the heart. Blood vessels absorb nutrients from the stomach and intestines, and the liver and spleen act as blood reservoirs and filtering systems. The kidneys maintain the salt and water balance in the body and filter toxic wastes from the blood. The heart, brain, and lungs receive a large blood supply in order to maintain their vital functions. The carotid artery carries blood to and from the brain.

Creeping cinquefoil (*P. reptans*) grows in cool climates as a spreading ground cover. Cinquefoil produces five-parted leaves, from which it got its (French) name, and small yellow flowers.

C

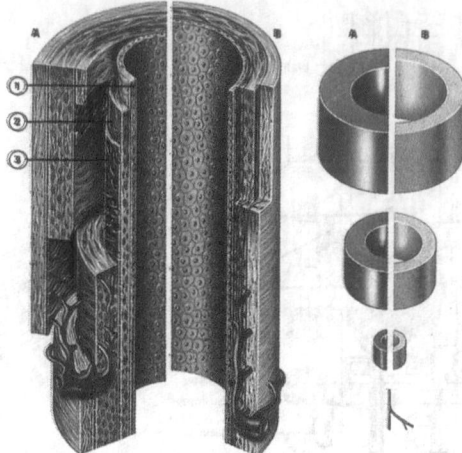

Arteries (A) and veins (B) both conduct the blood through the body. They have a common structure, consisting of an inner avascular coat, a vascular middle and outer coats. The inner coat is composed of (1) a cellular lining with (2) associated basement membrane, surrounded by (3) an elastic tissue/layer with longitudinal fibres. The middle coat contains smooth muscle and elastic fibres, and collagen connective tissue. Arteries have much thicker walls and a smaller channel diameter, the middle coat is very thick and gives the arteries their elastic, muscular properties. In veins, the inner coat layers are often indistinguishable. A comparison of the two vessels is shown in half-sections of the actual sizes of arteries and veins that are found in the body. Very small vessels have a similar structure.

high blood pressure, which results from the heart's need to work harder, and may lead to complications such as heart attack, a stroke, or kidney failure.

Circumcision, removal of the foreskin covering the glans of the penis, as a religious requirement (among Jews and Muslims) or as a surgical measure for sanitary reasons. In ancient Egypt circumcision was regarded as an initiation into puberty. For Jews it symbolizes a male's induction into the covenant between God and Abraham, usually 8 days after birth. In some tribes of Africa and South America, and in Islam, female circumcision, involving removal of all or part of the clitoris, is practiced.

Circumference *See:* Circle.

Circumstantial evidence *See:* Evidence.

Circus, form of entertainment featuring trained animals and performances by acrobats, trapeze artists, horseback riders, and clowns, presented within a circular enclosure. Historically, 'circus' (the Latin for 'ring') referred to chariot races, gladiatorial fighting, and animal events in ancient Rome. U.S. circuses date from colonial times, but the modern circus became popular in the 19th century.

Cirrhosis, chronic disease of the liver marked by progressive destruction and regeneration of liver cells and increased connective tissue (scar) formation. Cirrhosis ultimately results in blockage of portal circulation, raised blood pressure in the portal vein, liver failure, and death. Causes include alcohol consumption (Laennec's cirrhosis, the most prevalent), hepatitis and other infections, and severe malnutrition in children of tropical countries (a condition known as kwashiorkor). Results include jaundice, gastrointestinal problems, and edema. Though irreparable, treatment includes vitamin intake, controlled diet, and diuretics.
See also: Liver.

Cirrus *See:* Cloud.

CIS *See:* Commonwealth of Independent States.

Cistercians, Roman Catholic monastic order. Monks and nuns of this order are often referred to as Trappists, after a 17th-century order of Cistercians in La Trappe, France. Their order is based on principles of prayer, manual work, and study. Its followers often lead secluded lives.
See also: Trappists.

Citadel, fortress protecting or dominating a town.

Cities of refuge, 6 cities of ancient Palestine. People accused of murders, committed by accident or in self-defense remained safe in these cities until they were tried. If found innocent, they continued to live in the cities of refuge. If found guilty, they were returned to the place of the crime for punishment.
See also: Palestine.

Citizens band radio (CB), radio with a short range. These radios operate on frequencies reserved for private use and transmit signals from 5 mi (8 km) in the city to 20 mi (32 km) in rural areas. Frequencies used for CB radios also operate remote controlled devices, such as garage doors and model airplanes.
See also: Radio.

Citizenship, legal relationship between an individual and the country of nationality, usually acquired by birth or naturalization. Though laws regarding citizenship by birth vary from country to country, such citizenship is generally based on place of birth or the nationality of one or both parents. Some countries grant citizenship by marriage, adoption, long residence, land purchase, entrance into public service, or annexation of territory. It is possible for an individual to be a citizen of more than 1 country or to possess no citizenship at all. Citizenship implies both rights (to a passport, to the protection of the government when appropriate, to constitutional rights) and duties (to pay taxes, to serve in the armed forces) between the citizen and the country.

Citrange, hybrid orange produced by crossing the sweet orange and the trifoliate orange. It is stronger and hardier than the sweet orange plant. Citrange is used for cooking and flavoring beverages.

Citric acid, tricarboxylic acid ($C_6H_8O_7$) derived from lemons and similar fruits or obtained by fermentation of carbohydrates; used as a flavoring and to condition water.

Citrin, one of a group of chemicals known as flavinoids. Also referred to as vitamin P and used in medicine, citrin helps control bleeding within capillary (tiny blood vessels) walls. Citrin is often formulated from a mixture of lemon peel and paprika.

Citron, *(Citrus medica)*, fruit tree in the citrus family (Rutaceae); also its fruit. The citron is a large yellowish fruit with a thick white rind and a small pulpy though acidic center. It was the first of the citrus fruits to be introduced into Europe from India and Asia. The rind is crystallized as candy, while the juice flavors syrups and beverages.

Citrus, genus of tropical trees of the rue family, providing such edible fruits as the orange, lemon, citron, grapefruit, lime, tangerine, and shaddock, all of which are rich in vitamin C, sugars, and citric acid.

City, large center of population, often distinguished from a town or village by the diversity of its economic and cultural activities; also, a center officially designated as a city for purposes of local government.

City government, government that manages affairs for cities and various other communities. Most cities are incorporated municipalities, that is, corporations defined and empowered by the state through charters. An elected council or commission forms the legislature. The executive branch may be headed by an elected mayor, an appointed city manager, or elected commis-

Most fruits belonging to the genus *Citrus* originated in China and Southeast Asia. They are commercially important throughout the world. A number of hybrids have been created, to increase the number of varieties available.
A Orange
B Lemon
C Grapefruit
D Ugly

sioners. Larger cities also have their own court system. The branches of government, its related agencies, and the individual city workers (civil servants) make up a bureaucracy governed by city laws, also known as municipal ordinances. These ordinances cover day-to-day needs of city residents. Property taxes and state or federal grants-in-aid generate most of the money on which cities run.
See also: City.

City planning, planning for the growth of a city or town, taking into consideration the economic, physical, social, and aesthetic needs of its populace and government. Examples of such planning range from the grid-iron organization of ancient Roman cities to the grandiose planning of the Renaissance, usually intended to glorify a ruler or to strengthen his military position; to the piecemeal development of the Industrial Revolution, chaotic due to the enormous population movement; to Pierre L'Enfant's design for Washington, D.C. (1791) and Frederick L. Olmsted's city park designs. Today's city planners, many dealing with housing projects and city-center renewal projects, take into account such factors as existing roads and traffic patterns; availability of sanitation service, police and fire protection, employment; zoning regulations; location of schools, hospitals, and recreational facilities.

City-state, independent political community (particularly in ancient Greece) made up of a city and its surrounding countryside, from which it draws food and labor. The Greek city-state, or *polis*, which emerged around 700 B.C., ranged in size from Athens (1,000 sq mi/2,590 sq km) to minute states less than one-hundredth of its size, and ranged in government from monarchies to democracies. The Greeks colonized much of the Mediterranean, spreading the city-state form of organization until Rome became the nucleus of an empire that turned all the city-states into subunits of its administration. City-states have flourished during 3 major periods of Western civilization: the ancient civilizations of the Middle East, the classical period of Greece, and in Europe from the 11th to the 16th centuries.

Ciudad Bolívar (pop. 250,000), commercial center and port of eastern Venezuela, located on the Orinoco River. It was originally founded by Spaniards and called Angostura (1764). Here Simon Bolívar, known as the liberator of South America, claimed independence for Colombia and Venezuela (1819). It was subsequently named after him (Spanish: *ciudad*, city). Exports such as latex, animal skins, and lumber are shipped through Ciudad Bolivar.
See also: Venezuela.

Civet, weasel-like carnivorous mammal of the family Viverridae, found in Africa and South Asia. The African civet, (*Civettictis civetta*), is reared for the musky-smelling oily substance, used as a base for perfumes, that is produced by glands under its tail.

Civil code *See:* Code Napoléon.

Civil defense, nonmilitary measures taken to protect a nation's civilian population and its resources in case of enemy attack. Organized civil defense programs began shortly before World War II, when it was realized that powerful air forces greatly increased the wartime danger to civilians. Civil defense efforts include warning systems, the construction and stocking of shelters, and survival planning.

Civil disobedience, form of political action involving intentional violation of the law in order to force concessions from a government or to draw attention to alleged injustices. Henry David Thoreau, in his 19th-century essay *On Civil Disobedience*, expounded on these methods, which were essential to Mohandas Gandhi's 20th-century struggle for India's independence and which have been employed by the suffragettes, the civil rights movement, and Vietnam War protesters. Martin Luther King, Jr. was an advocate of civil disobedience and used it successfully during his career.
See also: Thoreau, Henry David; Gandhi, Mohandas Karamchand.

Civilization (Latin *civis*, 'citizen of a city'), stage of societal development in which complex economic, social, and governmental systems arise. Civilizations first arose as farming on permanent sites replaced the nomadic life of hunters and gatherers. In these new, permanent groups, inventions such as metal tools led to advances in the lives of people, and complex economic, social, and political structures evolved. The Tigris-Euphrates River valleys of the Middle East, the Nile River Valley of Egypt, the Indus River Valley in India, and the Huang He River Valley of China are sites of early civilizations.

Civil law, body of law based on Roman law, dealing with private rights claims between individuals, as opposed to criminal law (offenses against the state). After the fall of the Roman Empire, the customs of the ruling tribes developed into customary law throughout most of continental Europe, including England. Roman law was rediscovered in the 12th century, and European jurists began to codify the existing legal systems with Roman additions. The *Corpus Juris Civilis* of Justinian I (6th century) was of special importance for these evolving legal systems. The development of civil law was further enhanced by the Code Napoleon (1804), which gave France a unified national code. Other countries, mainly in continental Europe and Latin America, followed the French lead. Codes of civil law countries state general legal principles that courts must interpret in the light of particular cases. In common law countries such as Great Britain, Canada, and the United States (excluding Louisiana), the courts are bound by previous decisions (the rule of precedent). Trial by jury and the law of evidence are key features of legal practice in common law countries; they have no counterpart in civil law.

Civil liberties *See:* Civil rights.

Civil rights, rights and privileges enjoyed by citizens. A distinction is sometimes made between civil rights and civil liberties: Civil rights must be granted by the government (for example, the right to vote), while civil liberties are inalienable individual freedoms the government may be prohibited from restraining.
The concept of civil rights arose in the Roman Empire, whose courts protected the rights of Roman citizens against arbitrary acts by the government. In the Middle Ages nobles issued charters to their followers to protect against other nobles and the king. The rise of absolute monarchs in France, Spain, and other European nations ended many of the civil rights of their subjects. In England, however, the nobles, and later the House of Commons and the common law courts, defended and extended the rights of the people against the crown. The Magna Carta of 1215, under which the king granted specific rights to his lords in return for their support, and the Bill of Rights in 1689 established a basis in common law for the inviolable liberties of individual citizens. Many U.S. and Canadian concepts of civil rights and individual liberty derive from the English example. The so-called natural law theorists of the 17th and 18th centuries, such as Jean-Jacques Rousseau and John Locke, taught that the natural law, reflecting divine law, confers certain rights upon the individual that cannot be legitimately taken away by governments.
The international movement to secure civil rights for all people has been strengthened by the work of many agencies, including UNESCO, the International Labor Organization, the European Commission on Human Rights, the Inter-American Commission on Human Rights, the International Commission of Jurists, and the International League for the Rights of Man. The Universal Declaration of Human Rights, endorsed by the General Assembly of the United Nations (1948), includes a list of basic civil rights that should be available to all persons. In December 1965 the General Assembly approved the convention on the elimination of all forms of racial discrimination.

Civil service, body of civilian (non-military) employees of a government, excluding elected officials. Civil service dates from ancient China, where officials were chosen through competitive exams. It was also found in ancient Rome, and in France after Napoleon I.

Civil War, U.S. (1861-1865), conflict between 11 Southern states (Confederate States of America) and the U.S. federal government (Union). Because the 11 states had attempted to secede from the Union, in the North the conflict was officially called the War of the Rebellion. Since the war was a sectional struggle, North against South, it is sometimes also known as the War Between the States.
Origins. The economy of the South was based on the plantation system of agriculture, which absolutely depended on slave labor. Great staple crops- cotton, tobacco, sugar, and rice-were grown largely for export. The North had no need for slavery; its agri-

C

The 18 Union states and 11 Confederate states were well matched in land area. The 3 border states were critical in the balance of strength.

C

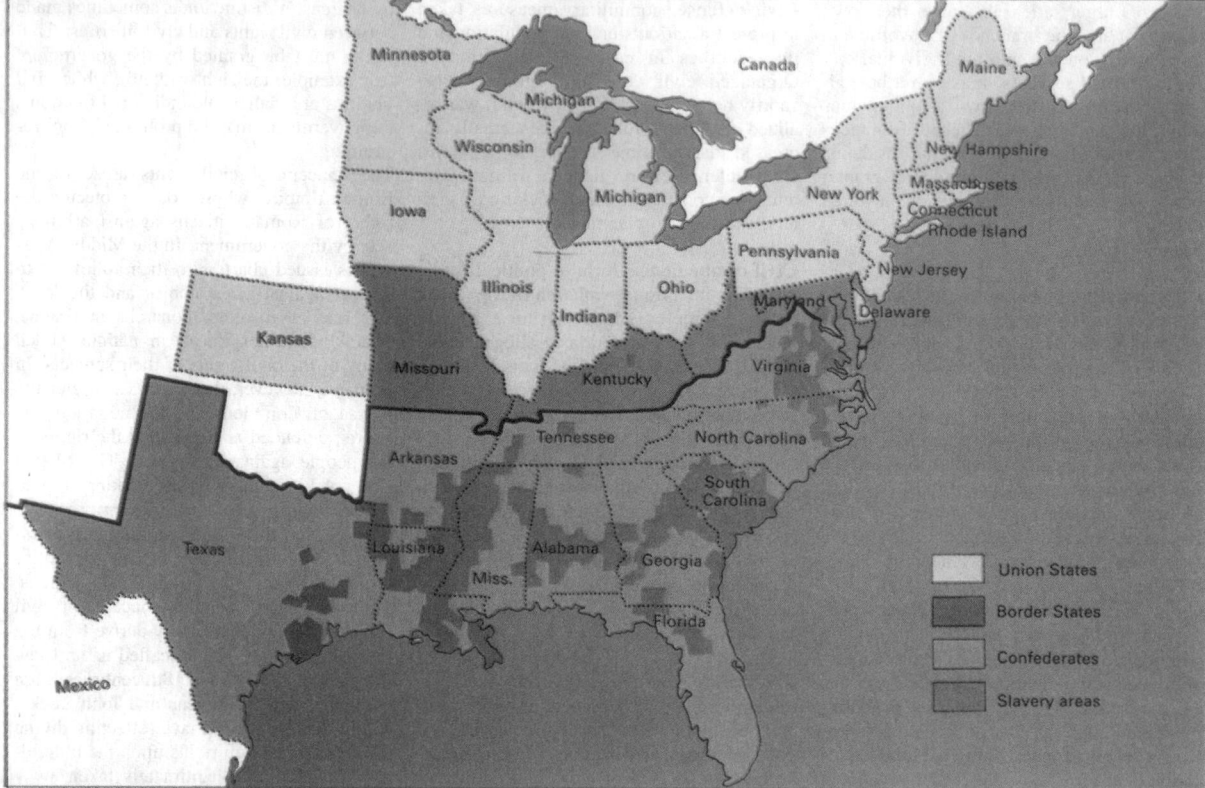

Union States

Border States

Confederates

Slavery areas

The victory of the Union fleet on the Mississippi River, Apr. 24, 1862, under Admiral David Glasgow Farragut (Currier & Ives, Museum of the City of New York)

A selection of the weapons in use at the Battle of Gettysburg (1863):
1. Springfield rifle musket
2. Bayonet
3. Sharps carbine
4. Spencer carbine
5. Cavalry sabre
6. Colt third model Dragoon
7. Remington new model revolver
8. Whitney revolver 9. Lefaucheux pinfire revolver
10. 3-inch rifled Ordnance Gun 11. Napoleon smooth-bore gun-howitzer

President Abraham Lincoln paid regular visits to the Union troops at the front.

The artillery of General McClellan in Yorktown, ready for transport

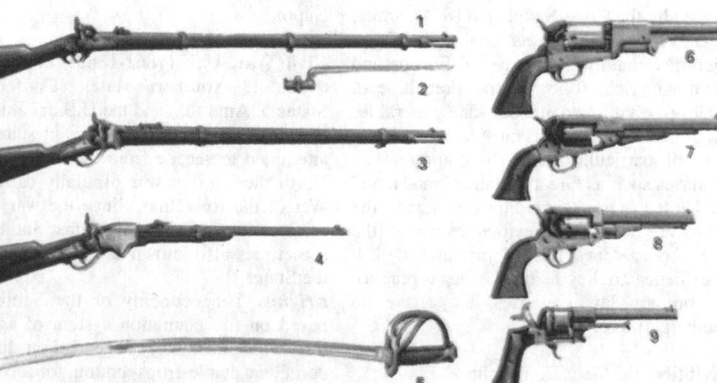

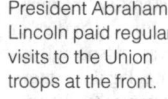

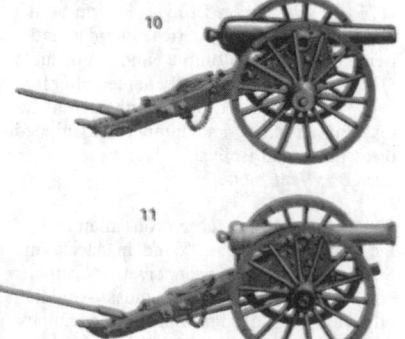

Far left: Ulysses S. Grant

Left: A Southern and a Northern ship engaged in battle (1862).

C

Below: Robert E. Lee

Top: General W. Sherman, General U.S. Grant, President A. Lincoln, and Admiral D.G. Farragut, in George Healy's The Peace-Makers, painted in 1894

Bottom: The Battle of Antietam (or Battle of Sharpsburg; 1862) was the bloodiest battle of the war. Approximately 5,000 soldiers died and 19,000 were wounded. It was considered a victory for the Union forces.

Left: Union General William Sherman, portrait by George Healy

C

A clam, class *Bivalvia*, is a shallow-water marine mollusk represented by more than 12,000 species, most of which are edible. A clam has two shells that open and close by muscle action; a muscular foot; and gills that filter oxygen and food from water.

culture, which produced corn and wheat largely for subsistence and internal consumption, was based on small family farms; its industry and towns were expanding rapidly, and it welcomed European immigrants in large numbers to supply its growing labor needs. Political differences came to a head over the question of whether slavery would be permitted in the newly settled western territories, soon to become states. The Missouri Compromise (1820) was the first attempt to ease North-South tensions by admitting Missouri as a slave state and Maine as a free state and forbidding slavery in the Louisiana Territory north of latitude 30°30'. As a long-term solution it failed because expansion continued westward, raising the issue again and more acutely, and also because of the growth of abolitionism in the North.

The admission to the Union of the huge slave state of Texas (1845) and the resultant Mexican War renewed the fears of Southern political dominance and the possible extension of slave territory. The Compromise of 1850 seemed to solve the problem, but it was nullified by the Kansas-Nebraska Act of 1854, which gave the residents of those territories the right to vote on whether or not slavery would be permitted. This opened the way for opponents and supporters of slavery to begin a virtual civil war in 'Bleeding Kansas.' The Dred Scott Decision (1857) further inflamed the problem as the Supreme Court's decision had the effect of declaring the Missouri Compromise unconstitutional. The presidential election of 1860 raised the fears of the South as Abraham Lincoln, the candidate of the newly formed Republican party, was known to be opposed to the further extension of slavery. Lincoln declared: 'My paramount object is to save the Union,

and not either to save or destroy slavery,' but South Carolina voted to secede from the Union (Dec. 20, 1860) and was followed by 6 more states by Feb. 1861. Representatives met at Montgomery, Ala., to draw up a constitution for these Confederate states and elected Jefferson Davis provisional president. When Lincoln announced he was sending supplies to the federal garrison of Fort Sumter, in Charleston harbor, Confederate guns opened fire on the fort (Apr. 12), which surrendered 2 days later. The outbreak of hostilities drove 4 more slave states (North Carolina, Virginia, Arkansas, and Tennessee) into the Confederacy.

First phase of the war-Union defeats. The capture of the Confederate capital seemed the natural objective, and the first rallying cry of the North was 'On to Richmond.' This simple aim of frontal attack led to the first major encounter, at Bull Run (July 21, 1861), and the Federals were routed. In the meantime the North blockaded the South, but chances of capturing a Southern blockade runner were rated at 1 in 10 and 800 vessels got through in the first year. The blockade, however, became increasingly effective. In Apr. the Union fleet under David Farragut took New Orleans, the first of many essential ports to fall to the North. Northern General George McClellan's Peninsular Campaign (1862) nearly reached Richmond but ended in defeat in the Battles of the Seven Days, and Southern General Robert E. Lee was again victorious at the second Battle of Bull Run. This opened the way for a Confederate invasion of Maryland that was thwarted by a Union victory at Antietam, and Lincoln seized the political initiative by issuing the preliminary Emancipation Proclamation (Sept. 1862) promising freedom to slaves held in the Confederacy. The year closed with a shattering defeat for the Union at Fredericksburg, Va.

Second phase-the Confederacy crushed. The first Union victories had come in the West in 1862, when General Ulysses S. Grant took forts Henry and Donelson, opening the Tennessee River. After the bloody battle of Shiloh, the Federals commanded nearly the entire length of the Mississippi. In 1863 Lee defeated the North at Chancellorsville, but General Stonewall Jackson, one of the ablest Confederate generals, was mortally wounded. Lee struck north into Pennsylvania, but Union forces won the decisive battle of the war after 3 days of costly fighting at Gettysburg (July 1863). On the following day Grant took Vicksburg, which finally gave the Union forces control of the Mississippi, cutting the Confederacy in two and opening the way for the invasion of Tennessee. Grant's attempt to capture Richmond in 1864 was halted in the Wilderness Campaign, but soon after he began the 9-month siege of Petersburg. Sherman meanwhile moved east from Chattanooga to take Atlanta in September 1864. His army marched through Georgia to the sea, leaving behind it a trail of devastation. The capture of Petersburg and Richmond on Apr. 2, 1865, led to Lee's surrender to Grant at Appomattox Court House a week later. Although Confederate forces in the South and West fought on for several weeks, the war was effectively over.

Cixous, Hélène (1937-), French female author, representative of a French movement that emphasizes typically feminine elements in its work. She in particular, had a typically female use of words. Cixous actively participated in the students' revolt in 1968 and largely contributed to the modernization of the education system at the University of Nanterre. Her work includes: *Inside* (1968), *The Book of Promethea* (1983), and *First Days of the Year* (1990; theater).

Clair, René (René Chomette; 1898-1981), French film director, producer, and writer, especially of screen comedies. Born in Paris, he worked on both silent and sound films, including *Sous les Toits de Paris* (1929).

Clam, name given to many edible marine bivalve mollusks that live in sand or mud, including the jacknife clam, the quahog or cherrystone clam, and the pismo clam; also refers to some freshwater bivalves. The giant clams of Indian Ocean and Pacific Ocean coral reefs may reach a diameter of 4 ft (2.4 m) and weigh one-quarter ton (0.27 metric tons).

Clan, social group claiming descent from a common ancestor. Clans have existed all over the world, from primitive societies to the famous Highland clans of Scotland (said to have originated in the 11th century). Some clans have expressed their unity in the symbol of the totem (an object, animal, or plant revered as the ancestor of the group). Most, but not all clans, are exogamous, requiring marriage outside of the clan (marriage within being regarded as incest). Several clans may organize into a larger social structure known as phratry.

Clapton, Eric (1945-), British guitarist and singer, who became famous with bands such as The Yardbirds, John Mayall's Bluesbreakers, Cream, Blind Faith and the one-time-only collaboration Derek & the Dominos (known for their world-wide hit *Layla*), before embarking on his own successful solo career. His most famous albums are: *461 Ocean Boulevard* (1974), *Money And Cigarettes* (1983) and *Journeyman* (1989). He received six Grammy Awards for, among other things, best pop singer and best album (*Unplugged*, 1992) in 1993.

Clarendon, Edward Hyde, 1st earl of (1609-1674), English statesman and historian. He originally opposed King Charles I, but supported him in 1642 when civil war started. Although Clarendon favored religious toleration, Parliament made him enforce the Clarendon Code, which strengthened the position of the Church of England. In 1667 Charles II made him a scapegoat for failures in the second Dutch War. He was forced into exile, from which he wrote the 10-volume *History of the Rebellion*, defending Royalist activities during the civil war.

Clarinet, single-reed woodwind instrument comprising a cylindrical tube (usually wooden) with a flared bell and tapered mouthpiece, played vertically. Tones are produced by opening and closing holes (some covered by keys) in the tube while

The clarinet is a versatile, single-reed wind instrument equally adaptable for use by orchestras, jazz ensembles, and dance bands. The B-flat clarinet (left) is the most common member of the family; less common is the alto clarinet (right).

blowing air through the mouthpiece. The clarinet, developed in Germany from the chalumeau by Johann Christoph Denner early in the 18th century, features in dance bands, military bands, woodwind groups, symphony orchestras, and as a solo instrument.

Clark, (Charles) Joseph (1939-   ), Canadian prime minister (1979-1980). After election to the House of Commons in 1972, he was elected leader of the Progressive Conservative party in 1976, and prime minister in 1979, replacing Pierre Trudeau and marking the beginning of western Canada's political importance.
See also: Canada.

Clark, Gordon Matta (1945-1978), English visual artist; engaged himself in architecture in a most unusual way. He cut buildings in half and sawed geometric forms out of floors and walls, making unexpected spatial views possible. By breaking open closed spaces, he wanted to literally break through the suffocating isolation of society.

Clark, James (Jim) (1936-1968), Scottish racing driver, became the Formula One world champion for Lotus in 1963 and 1965 and won the Indianapolis 500 in 1965. Clark won 25 Grand Prix races between 1962 and 1968, one more than the record at that time, which was held by Fangio. He was killed in

an accident on the wet circuit at Hockenheim during a Formula Two race.

Clark, Mark Wayne (1896-1984), U.S. general, commander of Allied ground forces in North Africa and Italy in World War II and commander of UN operations in the Korean War (1952-1953). He led the invasion of Italy in 1943.
See also: World War II.

Clark, William (1770-1838), U.S. explorer, a leader of the Lewis and Clark Expedition, 1804-1806, and brother of George Rogers Clark. He was superintendent of Indian affairs and governor of Missouri Territory, 1813-1821.
See also: Lewis and Clark expedition.

Clarke, Arthur C(harles) (1917-   ), British science fiction and science writer. Clarke is best known as co-author of the screenplay for the film *2001: A Space Odyssey* (1968) and for his detailed design for communications satellites in 1945. His novels include *Childhood's End* (1953) and *The Fountains of Paradise* (1979). In 1996 Clarke was awarded a Sri Lankan prize for his 'contributions to the development and realization of communications satellites'.

Class, level of social stratification (e.g., upper, middle, and lower class). Classes lack the rigid boundaries characterizing caste, so that mobility between classes is possible.

Classical music, or art music, music composed by individuals and written for instruments, for voices, or for combinations of voices and instruments. Classical music is more complex than *popular music* (country, folk, rock, jazz). Christianity helped spread Western classical music, which began in ancient times. Instrumental music includes solo, chamber, and orchestral music. Perhaps the most popular chamber group is the string quartet, consisting of 2 violins, a viola, and cello. Opera combines a large orchestra with soloists and chorus, and tells a story. Nonwestern classical music includes the music of the highly developed cultures of India, China, and Japan.

Classicism, in painting, sculpture, architecture, literature, and music, the emulation of classical antiquity, emphasizing harmony, order, and clarity of form, rather than subjectivity, heightened emotion, and the uncanny. The aims of the artists in the Italian Renaissance (literally, the 'rebirth' of classical culture) were rejected in the 16th and 17th centuries by the mannerist and baroque artists. Classicism was revived in the 18th-century movement known as neoclassicism (also called the Enlightenment). Important artistic figures include Samuel Johnson and Alexander Pope (English literature), Pierre Corneille and Jean Racine (French literature), and Franz Joseph Haydn and Wolfgang Amadeus Mozart (music). The 19th-century romantic movement in art was partly a reaction to perceived overreliance on reason and order in neoclassicism.

Classification, in biology, systematic

arrangement of the world's organisms into categories based on their characteristics. This science, sometimes called taxonomy, is often aimed at establishing evolutionary relationships. The system of classification comprises 7 major categories. These are, from most to least inclusive: kingdom; phylum (called division in botany); class; order; family; genus; species. Traditionally, there were only 2 kingdoms, plants and animals. Today, however, most biologists would recognize 3 others: the Protista (1-celled organisms and some forms of algae), the Monera (bacteria and blue-green algae), and the Fungi (mushrooms and molds). The species is the basic unit of classification. As a rule of thumb, 2 animals belong to the same species if they are capable of mating to produce fertile offspring.
See also: Biology.

Claudel, Paul (1868-1955), French dramatist, poet, and diplomat. Influenced by Arthur Rimbaud and intensely religious, he drew inspiration for his sensuous, lyrical verse from nature and Oriental thought.

Claude Lorrain (Claude Gelée; 1600-1682), a founder of French romantic landscape painting who lived and worked mostly in Rome. His canvases usually show a biblical or classical scene dominated by an idyllically lit landscape (*The Expulsion of Hagar*, 1668; *The Trojan Women Setting Fire to the Greek Fleet*; *Seaport at Sunset*). His later works are almost visionary in their intensity and inspired such painters as Poussin and Turner.

Claudius, name of 2 Roman emperors. **Claudius I** (Tiberius Claudius Drusus Nero Germanicus; 10 B.C.-A.D. 54) reigned 41-54. A sickly nephew of the emperor Tiberius, he was a scholar and writer. He invaded Britain (A.D. 43), annexed Mauretania, Lycia, and Thrace (41-46), improved Rome's legal system, and encouraged colonization. He was poisoned by his second wife, Agrippina, Nero's mother. **Claudius II** (Marcus Aurelius Claudius Gothicus; 214-270 A.D.) reigned 268-270. An army officer, he succeeded Gallienus.
See also: Rome, Ancient.

Clausewitz, Karl von (1780-1831), Prussian general, strategist, and military historian. His book *On War* (1833) revolutionized military thinking after his death. Defining war as an extension of diplomacy, he urged the destruction of enemy forces, morale, and resources, and has thus been called the prophet of total war, although he favored defensive fighting.

Clausius, Rudolf Julius Emmanuel (1822-1888), German theoretical physicist. He was first to state the second law of thermodynamics (1850), that heat never flows from a colder to a hotter body without work, and proposed the term *entropy* (1865). He also contributed to kinetic theory and the theory of electrolysis.
See also: Entropy; Thermodynamics.

Clavichord, keyboard musical instrument popular in the 16th to 18th centuries. The

C

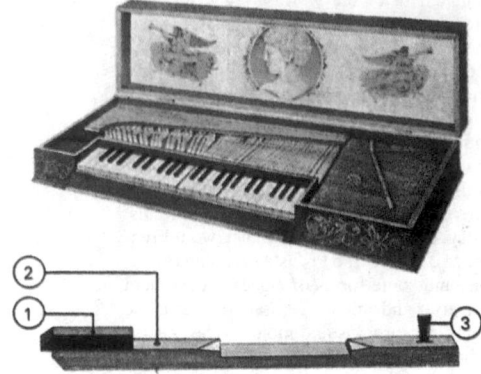

The clavichord, an ancient keyboard instrument, in which the strings are struck - like on a piano - not plucked - like on a harpsichord. The earliest examples date from about the middle of the 15th century. The clavichord remained a standard domestic keyboard instrument, until the piano replaced it at the end of the 18th century. The mechanism consists of a key (1), pivoted at (3), and fitted at the end furthest from the player, with a metal 'tangent' or striker (2), which hits a string when the key is depressed. On early instruments, known as 'fretted clavichords', the same string was sounded by two or more keys, striking it at different places along its length.

strings were struck with metal wedges (a piano uses felt hammers), and the sound was quiet and delicate.

Clay, 1 of 3 main types of earth, found in layers under the earth's crust and often at river mouths. Most clays consist of very small particles of hydrated aluminum silicates (kaolinites) that are usually produced by the weathering of rocks. Clay is easily malleable when wet and retains its shape when dried. If it is fired (baked) in a high-temperature oven or kiln it becomes extremely hard and, if first coated with a glaze, nonporous. Electrical insulators, sewage pipes, cement, kitchen tiles, chinaware, bricks, and paper manufacture all require clay. Clay is essential to the soil, holding moisture and preventing organic material from being washed away.

Clay, Cassius *See:* Ali, Muhammad.

Clayton, John Middleton (1796-1856), politician who served 3 terms as U.S. senator from Delaware. His greatest achievement was the Clayton-Bulwer Treaty of 1850.

Clayton-Bulwer Treaty, agreement signed by the United States and Great Britain in 1850, giving the 2 countries an equal role in protecting a canal to be built through Central America, the 2 countries agreeing to maintain the neutrality of the canal and the land on either side of it. John Clayton, U.S. secretary of state, and Sir Henry Bulwer (1801-1872), British minister to the United States, negotiated the treaty, which was replaced in 1901 by the Hay-Pauncefote Treaty, giving the United States the exclusive right to build and manage the canal.
See also: Hay-Pauncefote Treaties.

Clearinghouse, institution or system for exchanging checks among banks for the purpose of collection. The clearinghouse allows the banks in each city to settle their accounts among themselves on a daily basis.

Cleaver, (Leroy) Eldridge (1935-1998), U.S. black militant, a leader of the Black Panther party. His autobiographical *Soul on Ice* (1968) deals with his own experience of racial hatred and of the U.S. penal system.
See also: Black Panther Party; Black Power.

Cleft palate, congenital malformation in which the tissues that form the palate do not unite in the fetus, leaving a longitudinal gap in the upper jaw. It is often an accompaniment of harelip. The deformity needs surgical repair.

Cleisthenes (6th century B.C.), statesman of ancient Athens who instituted democratic reforms. The noble clan, Alcmaeonid, which Cleisthenes led, had a prophet persuade Cleomenes, king of Sparta, to overthrow Hippias, who had held complete power until 510 B.C. As a result, Cleisthenes was able to set up a democratic form of government, ending the political control of the noble clans.
See also: Athens; Greece, Ancient.

Clematis, genus of vines and free-standing plants whose flowers bear 4 sepals but no petals. They are best known as garden plants, but wild species include the *virgin's bower* of eastern states, whose seeds are buried in a fluffy ball called old-man's beard.

Clemenceau, Georges (1841-1929), French statesman and journalist. Known as 'the Tiger,' he was founder of the Third Republic and twice French premier (1906-1909, 1917-1920). He worked with Léon Gambetta (1870) for the overthrow of the Second Empire, supported the writer Emile Zola in the Dreyfus Affair, and headed the French delegation to the Paris Peace Conference at Versailles after World War I.
See also: World War I.

Clemens, Samuel Langhorne *See:* Twain, Mark.

Clemente, Roberto (Walker) (1934-1972), Puerto Rican-born U.S. baseball player. A star outfielder for the Pittsburgh Pirates (1954-1972), he amassed 3,000 hits with 240 home runs, compiled a .317 lifetime batting average, and was a 5-time National League batting champion. He was elected to the Baseball Hall of Fame in 1973, soon after his death in an airplane crash while helping Nicaraguan earthquake victims.

Clementi, Muzio (1752-1832), Italian composer and pianist, known as 'the father of the piano.' His compositions include more than 100 sonatas, as well as symphonies and his studies for the piano, *Gradus ad Parnassum* (1817). He enjoyed a successful concert career throughout Europe. In London he became a partner in one of the first firms to manufacture pianos (1799).

Clement I, Saint, or Clement of Rome (d. c.101 A.D.), citizen of Rome, elected pope c.29 A.D. Third in succession to Saint Peter as bishop of Rome, he is most famous for a letter to the church in Corinth c.96 A.D., condemning pride and arrogance in the church. The letter, which, except for the scriptures, is the oldest surviving Christian text, clarified the order of succession from bishop to presbyter (elder) to deacon (assistant). His feast day is Nov. 23.

Clement of Alexandria (c.150-215), Titus Flavius Clemens, Greek theologian of the early Christian Church. His most important work is the trilogy *Exhortation of the Greeks*, the *Tutor*, and *Miscellanies*. In his work he attempted to merge Platonic and Christian ideas.

Clement VII (1478?-1534), pope (1523-1534), reigning ineffectively during a difficult time in European political and religious affairs. Clement was born in Florence, Italy, into the powerful Medici family. When the Holy Roman Empire and France struggled for dominance in Italy, Clement formed an alliance with France. Troops of the Holy Roman emperor Charles V sacked Rome in 1527 and captured Clement. In 1529 Clement accepted peace and recognized Charles as emperor. Because of these preoccupations, Clement vacillated in responding to the Protestant Reformation, which spread in Germany and Scandinavia. The Reformation took hold in England partly because of Clement's unwillingness to grant King Henry VIII of England an annulment of his marriage to Catherine of Aragón.

Clement VII (1342-1394), one of the so-called antipopes. In 1309 Pope Clement V moved the seat of the papacy from Rome to Avignon, France, where it was subject to French control. In 1378 Pope Gregory XI returned the papacy to Rome, but died soon after the move. Urban VI was elected his successor, but he alienated the cardinals, who elected Robert of Geneva (Clement VII) pope in his stead. Clement acted as pope in Avignon, while Urban VI was pope in Rome. This period is known in Catholic history as the Great Schism. For 40 years (1378-1418) there were 2 rival lines of popes, until the Council of Constance settled the matter in favor of Rome. Since then, the Church has regarded the line of Avignon popes begun with Clement VII as illegitimate.

Clement VIII (1536-1605), pope (1592-1605). Clement fasted extensively, practiced devotions, and traveled on foot to Rome's pilgrimage churches. Reversing a papal policy, he allied himself with France instead of Spain and recognized Henry of Navarre, a Protestant convert who reverted to Catholicism, as King Henry IV of France.

Cleopatra (69-30 B.C.), queen of Egypt, daughter of Ptolemy XI. When her father died (51 B.C.) she was supposed to share the throne with her young brother-husband, Ptolemy XII, but his advisers drove her out of Egypt (49 B.C.). She won the support of Julius Caesar (48 B.C.), who had come to Alexandria in pursuit of Pompey. She became his mistress, bearing him a son,

Caesarion (later Ptolemy XIV). With Caesar's help she recovered her throne. The accidental death of Ptolemy XII was followed by her marriage to a younger brother, Ptolemy XIII, whom she later had murdered (44 B.C.). After the battle of Philippi, Mark Antony summoned her to Tarsus, where she made him her lover. They were married in 37 B.C., but the marriage was not legal in Rome, where she was feared and hated. Antony helped restore Ptolemaic power in Syria, and war with Octavian (later Emperor Augustus) became inevitable. In the sea and land battle at Actium (31 B.C.) the forces of Antony and Cleopatra were routed. Antony killed himself, and Cleopatra, fearing humiliation in Octavian's triumph in Rome, also committed suicide.
See also: Antony, Marc; Caesar, (Gaius) Julius.

Cleopatra's needles, 2 large stone pillars called obelisks, originally erected in 1460 B.C. by Thutmose III before a sun temple at Heliopolis. Sent by Ismail Pasha as gifts (1878, 1880), one currently stands in Central Park, New York City, and the other on the Thames Embankment in London.

Cleopatra, queen of ancient Egypt, appears as the goddess Isis in this Egyptian bas-relief. Although Cleopatra passionately strove to retore Egypt's power and to preserve its independence from Rome, she ultimately undermined her own efforts. The Ptolemaic dynasty was extinguished, and Egypt fell under Roman domination.

Cleveland (pop. 560,000), Ohio's largest city, situated on Lake Erie at the mouth of the Cuyahoga River. Founded in 1796, City by law in 1836.
It is a major port and railway center and an important manufacturer of steel, automobile parts, chemicals, paints, plastics, precision machinery, petroleum products, trucks and tractors, machine tools, and electrical products. Cultural centre (Cleveland Cultural Gardens, Cleveland Natural History Museum, Cleveland Museum of Arts, Cleveland orchestra) as well as educational centre (three universities). Airport: Hopkins airport.
See also: Ohio.

Cleveland, (Stephen) Grover (1837-1908), 22nd and 24th president of the United States (1885-1889; 1893-1897), the only president to have served 2 non-consecutive terms. Cleveland was first Democratic chief executive after 24 years of Republicans. In 1887 he began campaigning for lower tariffs. This was a major issue in the 1888 election, which Cleveland lost to Republican Benjamin Harrison, although Cleveland actually won more votes. In the election of 1892, Cleveland defeated Harrison by a comfortable margin. Shortly after Cleveland's second inauguration, a severe economic depression broke out (the 'panic of 1893'). In 1894 Cleveland used federal troops to break a strike at the Pullman works in Illinois. In 1896, with Cleveland's popularity at its lowest ebb, the Democratic party nominated William Jennings Bryan for the presidency.

Cliburn, Van (Harvey Lavan Cliburn, Jr; 1934-), U.S. concert pianist and conductor. He became world famous after winning the International Tchaikovsky Piano Competition in Moscow in 1958. An international event of the same kind is now held annually in his name in the United States.

Click beetle, long-bodied, short-legged beetle (family Elateridae) that can throw itself over with a 'click' if placed on its back. On the underside of the first segment of its thorax is a spine that rests in a groove in the second segment. When upside down, the beetle bends its head back, pulling the spine out of the groove. This is then thrust sharply back, making an audible click and throwing the beetle into the air. The larvae of click beetles are wireworms, serious agricultural pests.

Cliff dwellers, prehistoric Native American people who built elaborate houses, some with hundreds of rooms, sheltered beneath overhanging cliffs in the southwestern United States. The earliest of these multistoried dwellings dates from about A.D. 1000. They were a peaceful agricultural people whose inaccessible communities protected them from roving tribes such as the Apaches. In the 16th century the Spanish found the settlements mysteriously abandoned. Archeologists classify the cliff dwellers as members of the pueblo culture, ancestors of the tribes that built the large pueblo villages on the plains. The ruins of the cliff dwellings, well preserved in the dry desert climate, are found in Mesa Verde National Park, Colo., and in national monuments in Arizona, New Mexico, and Utah.

Climate, sum of weather conditions, or the characteristic weather, of any area. Weather conditions include temperature, rainfall, sunshine, wind, humidity, and cloudiness. One method of studying climate is to use average figures, but these often conceal wide variations; for example, mean temperatures are of little value in regions of extreme cold or heat. Climatology was developed by the ancient Greeks. Around 500 B.C. Greek philosopher Parmenides suggested that 5 climatic zones encircle the earth: a tropical zone on either side of the equator, 2 temperate zones in the middle latitudes, and 2 cold

zones around the poles. This classification was based on latitude, the most important factor affecting climate.
Long after the ancient Greeks, climatologists recognized that many factors besides latitude influence climate, for example, elevation, ocean currents, and variations in atmospheric pressure. In the early 1900s a German meteorologist, Vladimir Köppen, classified the world's climatic zones, combining temperature and rainfall boundaries with vegetation boundaries. He suggested 5 basic regions: tropical rainy climates with no cool season, dry climates, middle latitude rainy climates, northern forest climates, and polar climates with no warm season. Many other classifications exist, and each has its uses, but none takes into account all the features of climate. Paleoclimatologists, who study past climates through the record of rocks and fossils, have shown that climates have changed considerably during the earth's history. For example, coal seams in northern Canada show that swampy tropical forests once grew there. Several theories have been advanced to explain climatic change over time. The theory of continental drift suggests that the continents have moved in relation to the poles. Other theories include sunspots, variations in solar radiation, and changes in the earth's orbit or tilt. Climatologists have observed small changes in climate in the past 100 years. Their findings have raised speculation about our ability to influence climatic change.
See also: Weather.

Clinical psychology, scientific and applied branch of psychology concerned with the study, diagnosis, and treatment of individuals with emotional or behavioral disorders. The disorders which may be brief and minor or more prolonged and serious in nature, such as neuroses and psychoses, are diagnosed through testing and treated through psycho therapy. Research serves as a means of discovering or improving on the various methods of diagnosis and treatment.
See also: Psychology.

Clinton, William Jefferson (Bill) (1946-), 42nd president of the United States (1993-2001). Born as William Jefferson Blythe III, after his father who died in an automobile accident before he was born. He later adopted the name of the man with whom his mother remarried. After studying law, Bill Clinton taught at a university. He married Hillary Rodham, a lawyer, in 1975. They

Remnants of an old southwest Cliff dwellers' civilization in the state of Colorado. The Indians built houses like these into the rock walls.

Monsoons: During the summer large areas of the mainland of Asia are heated by the Sun. The air over these regions expands and rises forming regions of low pressure. Wet winds from the sea then blow into these areas giving the summer monsoons. In the winter the situation is reversed and regions of high pressure are formed over the land. Dry winter monsoon winds then blow out to the sea. The paths of these winds are deflected due to the coriolis effect.

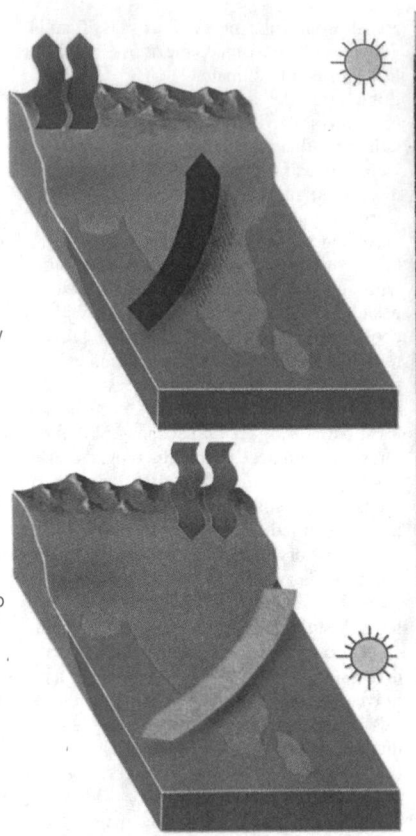

High temperature and plentiful rainfall in the tropics cause abudant vegetation and vast swampy regions.

The colors on the globe show the areas of the planet receiving the greatest (red) and least (violet) amounts of radiation from the Sun. The distribution of radiation on the Earth's surface is determined chiefly by the angle of incidence of the Sun's rays and the diffuse radiation of atmosphere and clouds. Though the Sun is high in the sky in the area around the equator, the total radiation received by the Earth's surface is limited by the protective cloud cover, and thus much smaller than the radiation received in the subtropics, where the cloud cover is absent. Similarly, on average there is less cloud cover above the South Pole, and it therefore receives more radiation than the North Pole.

During the day the temperature of the land rises more than that of the sea, causing the air above it to expand and rise. Cooler air is carried in from the sea to take its place. During the night the reverse is true and a breeze from the land is created.

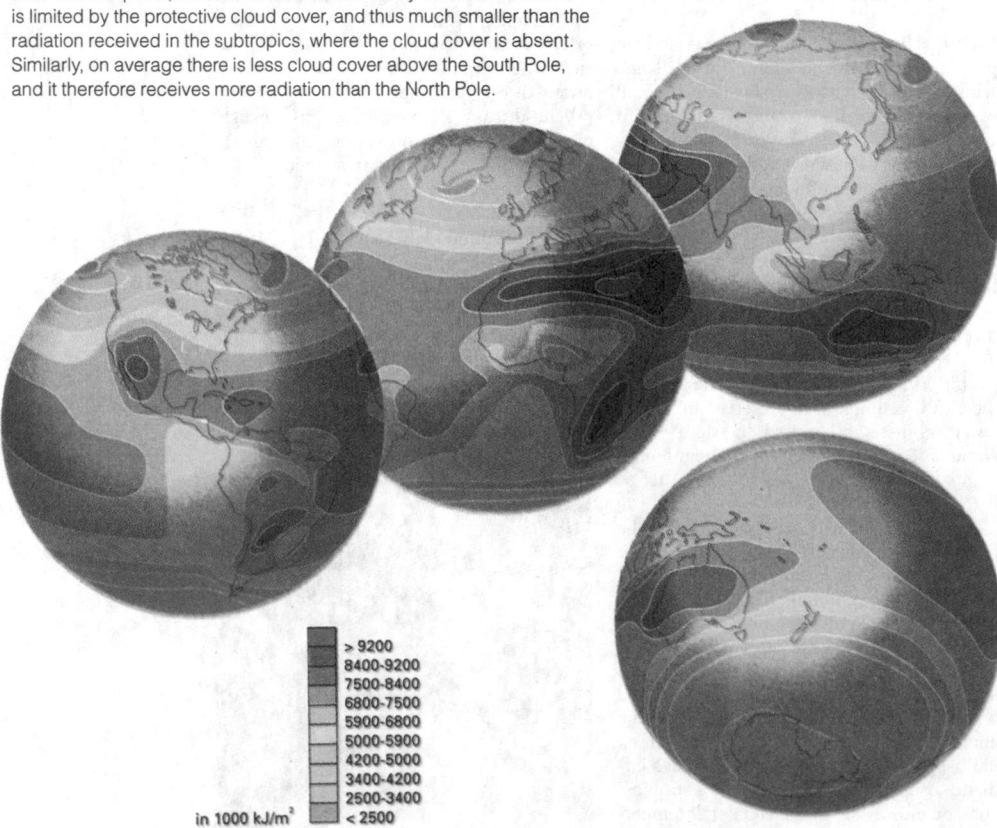

	in 1000 kJ/m²
	> 9200
	8400-9200
	7500-8400
	6800-7500
	5900-6800
	5000-5900
	4200-5000
	3400-4200
	2500-3400
	< 2500

Under conditions of an arid climate one of the two processes usually predominates: evaporation if there is water, wind erosion if there is no water. Here, in the Dead Sea region, the two are combined. Strong evaporation results in the extremely high salt content of the Dead Sea, while the wind, bearing sand and dust, scours the rocks into fantastic shapes.

have one daughter. Clinton was elected governor of Arkansas in 1978, making him the youngest governor ever known in the United States. He ran again for governor in 1980 and lost, but was returned as governor in 1983. Clinton became the presidential candidate for the Democratic Party in 1992. The presidential elections presented him with an unthreatened victory. At the beginning of 1993, he became the first Democratic president in twelve years. As early as his first year of government, Clinton's plans met with a lot of resistance; tax deduction for the middle classes did not take place and there were serious doubts concerning the necessity of economic reforms (the economy was already recovering slightly). Reforms were introduced in the health sector. Clinton's position was undermined in the course of 1994 due to an investigation into financial transactions dating from the time he was governor of Arkansas (Whitewater affair). Although two business partners and his successor were convicted, the case against Clinton did not amount to anything. The accusations of misconduct continued to pursue him during his second term of office, which began in 1997. In 1998, he admitted to having had a sexual relationship with Monica Lewinsky, a trainee at the White House. Clinton had previously denied the relationship. The affair undermined Clinton's authority, but did not result in his resignation, nor in the predicted election defeat during the elections for the Senate in 1998. The House of Representatives began an impeachment procedure against Clinton at the end of 1998, but Clinton was eventually acquitted. Clinton was succeeded by George W. Bush at the beginning of 2001.

Clipper ship, 19th-century sailing ship, the fastest ever built. Clippers evolved from the Baltimore clippers. They were built in the United States and later in Britain. They had a very large area of sail, relied on a good crew, and traded with China and Australia, where speed paid off. Two famous ships were Donald McKay's *Lightning* and the British *Cutty Sark* (now at Greenwich, England).

Clive, Robert, Baron Clive of Plassey (1725-1774), British soldier and administrator, twice governor of Bengal, who established British power in India. He defeated both the French at Arcot (1751) and the Bengal nawab, Siraj-ud-Daula, at Plassey (1757), thus securing all of Bengal for the East India Company. He reformed administrative corruption in Bengal. Investigated by Parliament on the charge of dishonesty when in office, he was acquitted, but afterward committed suicide.

Clock, device to indicate or record the passage of time. Generally a clock relies on a source of regular oscillation, such as a swinging pendulum or an electric current. Christiaan Huygens invented what was probably the first pendulum clock in the mid-17th century. The electric clock, commonly found in the home, was invented in the 19th century, and the quartz clock, utilizing the vibrations of a quartz crystal, in the early 20th. The atomic clock, invented in

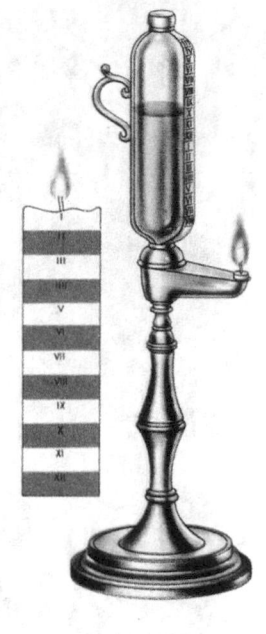

Water clocks, or clopsydrae, were first used in the ancient Greek law courts, for the timing of speeches. Here, we see an Egyptian water clock, from the 4th Century B.C. Water is supplied to the funnel (1) and passes to the cylinder, in which floats a piston (2), connected to a rack and pinnion, which actuates the hour hand. As the day was divided into twelve equal hours between sunrise and sunset, it was necessary to take account of the varying day length, according to the time of the year and the latitude. This was achieved by varying the rate of water flow by means of the stopper, which could be raised or lowered by a previously determined ammount marked on the stopper rule (3). The excess water would escape through the waste tube in the funnel.

As a means of recording time, the marked candle was used during the 9th century. King Alfred used 12 inch long candles (left), graduated with marks an inch apart and which burnt for four hours exactly. A more elegant and accurate applicaton of the principle was used in the 16th century. A glass reservoir was filled with oil, which was slowly consumed by the flame, the level dropping and thus showing the time on the scale at the side, while at the same time, the flame served to illuminate the scale (right).

C

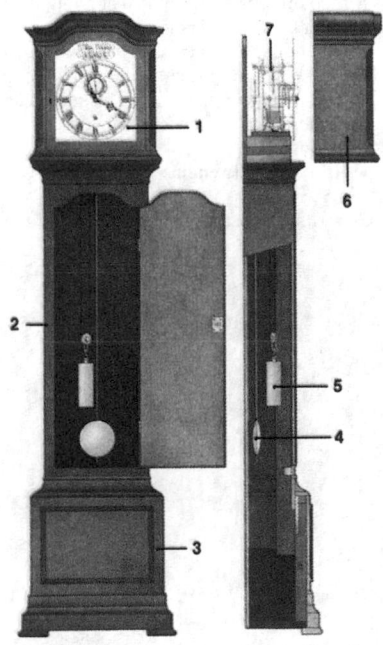
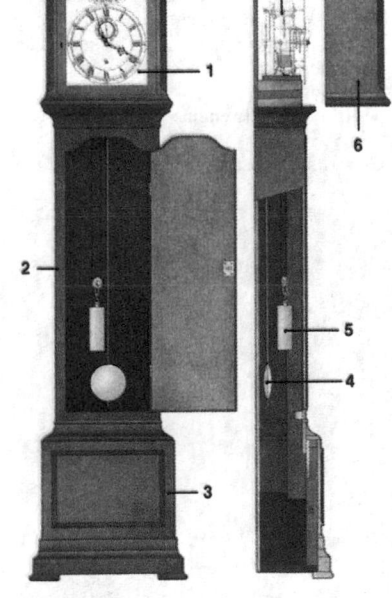

This long-case Grandfather's Clock is an early 19th century English clock. Made in London. It had an eight-day mechanism (7)

1 Clock face
2 Trunk
3 Plinth
4 Pendulum
5 Counterweight
6 Sliding-forward top
7 8-day clock mecanisme

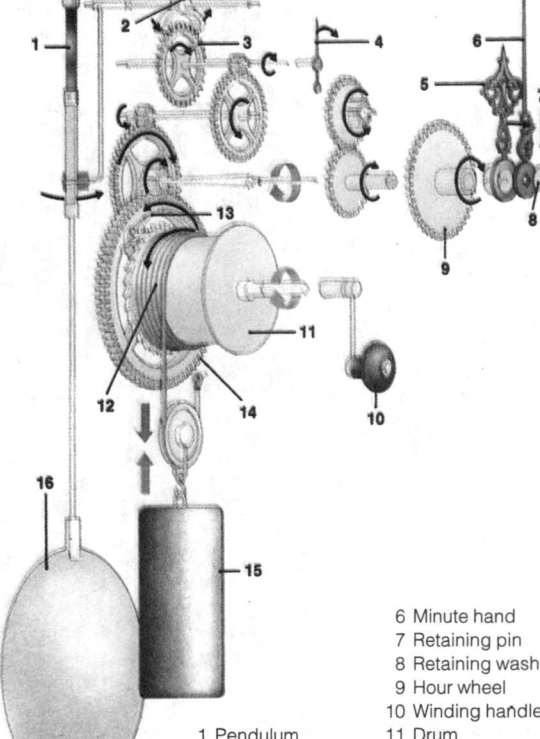

1 Pendulum suspension spring
2 Anchor
3 Escape wheel
4 Second hand
5 Hour hand
6 Minute hand
7 Retaining pin
8 Retaining washer
9 Hour wheel
10 Winding handle
11 Drum
12 Ratchet
13 Spring
14 Main wheel
15 Weight
16 Pendulum

C

The creeping species white clover (*Trifolium repens*) is an important fodder crop, often planted together with a variety of low-growing grass species. Livestock and poultry can all be fed with white clover, which has a protein content of between 15 and 30%.

An upright species, Alsike (*Trifolium hybridum*) often persists for two years. It will tolerate poorly drained soils. Though originally from Europe, it is now firmly established as a natural vegetation in many countries. It is grown by farmers as a forage crop and·for hay.

1948, is accurate to within 1 second in 3 million years. The most common way to display time has been the analogue, with clock hands sweeping over a face, in imitation of the sundial. The most recent type of display is the digital clock, which uses integrated circuits to show the time in changing figures.

Cloisonné, artistic process by which metal objects are decorated with enamel. Metal strips are soldered edgewise onto the surface of the object, creating compartments (*cloisons*) to be filled with colored enamel. When the object is heated, the enamel fuses with the surface. Originally a Persian technique, cloisonné was perfected by the Chinese, Japanese, and French.

Cloister, courtyard surrounded by vaulted and arcaded passageways supported by columns. Usually adjoining an abbey or church, the cloister served as a sheltered access to the surrounding buildings and was mainly used for recreation and exercise. An essential feature of Romanesque and Gothic churches and monasteries since the 11th century, cloisters are found throughout Europe.

Clone, cell or organism genetically identical to the cell or organism from which it has been derived. Clones are produced by asexual reproduction, for example through cell division in bacteria, cell budding in yeast, or vegetative duplication. Monoclonal systems (systems derived from a single cell) are used for the production of diagnostics and medicines. In 1997, scientists succeeded in cloning a sheep. In 1998, South Korean scientists announced that they had succeeded in cloning a human cell. It was the first known attempt to clone a human being. After the cloned cell had developed into an embryo of four cells, the experiment was terminated because the law prohibits tests using cells that are at a later embryonic stage.
At the beginning of 2001, Great Britain allowed the cloning of human embryos stem cells for medical use. The cloned cells may only be used for therapeutic purposes. In 2002, scientists demonstrated that the cloning of adult cells is possible, but is in fact too difficult to presume that it might develop into a full technology.
In the coming decades, cloning will probably play an important role, mainly in biotechnology with animals. This means another step is taken towards commercial applications.
See also: Genetic engineering.

Closed shop, establishment where the employer accepts only members of a specified union as employees and continues to employ them only if they remain union members.

Clothing, one of humanity's most important needs, including the various garments, accessories, and ornaments people throughout the world wear for decoration and protection. People probably began to wear clothing more than 100,000 years ago. By the end of the Old Stone Age (25,000 years ago) the needle had been invented, enabling people to sew skins into clothes. They learned to make yarn from plants and animal fur and to weave yarn into cloth. The advent of sewing machines and other machinery about 200 years ago ushered in the clothing industry, now a major business in many countries.

Cloture, or closure, in parliamentary procedure, closing of debate to ensure an immediate vote on a measure before the legislative body. In most parliamentary bodies, members cannot debate a cloture motion, but the motion must receive more than a majority vote. The main purpose of cloture is to check the *filibuster*, endless debate by a minority of the members to keep a motion from being voted upon. In the U.S. Senate a 60% majority is needed to invoke cloture.

Cloud, visible collection of water droplets suspended in the atmosphere. Clouds whose lower surfaces touch the ground are usually called fog. The water droplets are very small, indeed of colloidal size; they must coagulate or grow before falling as rain or snow. There are 3 main cloud types. Cumulus (heap) clouds, formed by convection, and often mountain- or cauliflower-shaped, are found from about 2,000 ft (610 m) up as far as the tropopause, even temporarily into the stratosphere. Cirrus (hair) clouds are composed almost entirely of ice crystals. They appear feathery, and are found at altitudes above about 20,000 ft (6,100 m). Stratus (layer) clouds are low- lying, found between ground level and about 5,000 ft (1,524 m). Other types of cloud include cirrostratus, cirrocumulus, altocumulus, altostratus, cumulonimbus, stratocumulus, and nimbostratus.
See also: Weather.

Cloud chamber, Wilson *See:* Wilson cloud chamber.

Cloud seeding *See:* Rainmaking.

Clove (*Syzygium aromaticum* or *Eugenia caryophyllata*), tropical evergreen tree of the myrtle family; also, its dried, unopened flower. Originally grown in the Moluccas (Spice Islands), the Philippines, and islands nearby, cloves were first appreciated by the Chinese for perfuming the breath. They are now grown in the West Indies and Mauritius. Their main use nowadays is as flavoring and in medicine.

Clover, familiar small plant (genus *Trifolium*) that grows wild in lawns and pastures and along paths and roads. Some U.S. clovers are natives, others have been introduced from Europe. The red clover, a native of Europe, is the state plant of Vermont.

Clouds are formed as a result of virtual suspension of large quantities of water droplets or ice crystals in the atmosphere. The forms of clouds vary from the towering cumulonimbus (1) to the smaller cumulus clouds (2). Other varieties are (in order of increasing altitude): stratus (3); nimbostratus (4); stratocumulus (5); altostratus (6); altocumulus (7); cirrostratus (8); cirrocumulus (9); and cirrus (10).

Clover leaves are normally divided into 3 parts, although more divisions are known; 4-leafed clovers are said to bring good luck. Clover is grown as forage and for hay. It is particularly valuable because, like other members of the pea family, its root contains nitrogen-fixing bacteria, so it enriches the soil if plowed back in.

Clovis I (A.D. 466-511), Frankish king (481-511), founder of the Merovingian monarchy. He amassed a huge kingdom from the Rhine River to the Mediterranean, defeating the Romans at Soissons (486) and the Visigoths under Alaric II of Spain at Vouillé (507). He became a Christian c.498 and compiled the code of Salic law.
See also: Merovingian.

Clown, comedy figure of the pantomime and circus. Modern clowns possibly derived from the vice figures of medieval miracle plays and jesters in medieval courts. They later figured as harlequins in the commedia dell'arte; but their grotesque makeup, baggy clothes, and slapstick developed fully only in the 1800s.

Clubfoot, deformity in which there is an abnormal relationship of the foot to the ankle; most commonly the foot is turned inward and down.

Club moss, or ground pine, primitive plant of the order Lycopodiales with small mosslike leaves, related to ferns. Many club mosses have creeping or climbing stems covered with leaves. Their distribution is mainly tropical, but some live in the United States, where they are used for Christmas decorations. Some are used in the manufacture of medicines and of fireworks.

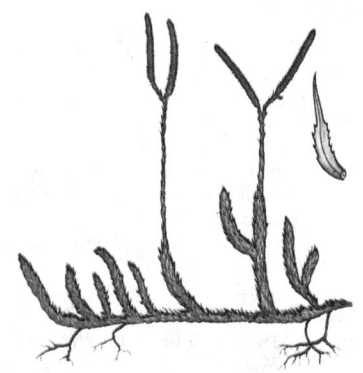

Club moss (*Lycopodium clavatum*) with roots, cones of sporophylls (spore-bearing leaves), and a leaf (enlarged).

Clumber spaniel, short, heavy hunting dog originally bred in France but developed in England in the 1800s. The Clumber has long, straight, white hair, stands 16-18 in (41-46 cm) high, and weighs 55-70 lb (25-31.5 kg). The Clumber is a small game hunter and family dog.

Clyde, most important river of Scotland and one of Britain's major commercial waterways. It rises on the Lanarkshire-Dumfriesshire border in southwest Scotland

and flows some 106 mi (171 km) to its estuary, the Firth of Clyde. Its upper valley, Clydesdale, is noted for its fruit and market garden crops. Near Lanark, at the Falls of Clyde, the river is harnessed for hydroelectricity. From Lanark on, its valley is occupied by heavy industry. At the head of navigation is the city-seaport of Glasgow, Scotland's chief commercial center. To the west, on the northern bank, is Clydebank, with large engineering interests and shipyards.
See also: Scotland.

Clytemnestra, in Greek mythology, daughter of Leda and Tyndareus, twin sister of Helen of Troy, wife of Agamemnon, and mother of 3 daughters and a son, Orestes. Clytemnestra, along with her lover, killed her husband after he had sacrificed one of their daughters to the gods. She and her lover were both then killed by her son to avenge the death of his father.
See also: Agamemnon; Mythology; Trojan War.

Cnut *See:* Canute.

Coagulant, any substance that causes or stimulates a liquid to change to a thickened curdlike or solidified state.

Coahuila, state in northern Mexico. Industries include livestock, agriculture, mining, and manufacturing. One of the original Mexican states, Coahuila included Texas until 1836.
See also: Mexico.

Coal, hard, black mineral, predominantly carbon, the compressed remains of tropical and subtropical plants, especially those of the carboniferous and Permian geological periods, burned as a fuel. With its by-products coke and coal tar, it is vital to many modern industries. Coal formation began when plant debris accumulated in swamps, partially decomposing and forming peat layers. A rise in sea level or land subsidence buried these layers below marine sediments, whose weight compressed the peat, transforming it under high-temperature conditions to coal; the greater the pressure, the harder the coal. Coals are classified according to their fixed-carbon content, which increases progressively as they are formed. Lignite, or brown coal, which weathers quickly, may ignite spontaneously, and has a low calorific value. Subbituminous coal is mainly used in generating stations; bituminous coal is the commonest type, used in generating stations and the home, and often converted into coke; anthracite is a lustrous coal that burns slowly and well and is the preferred domestic fuel.
Coal was burned in Glamorgen, Wales, in the 2nd millennium B.C. and was known in China and the Roman Empire around the time of Jesus. Coal mining was practiced throughout Europe and known to Native Americans by the 13th century. The first commercial coal mine in the United States was at Richmond, Va. (opened 1745), and anthracite was mined in Pennsylvania by 1790. The Industrial Revolution created a huge and increasing demand for coal. This

slackened in the 20th century as coal faced competition from abundant oil and gas, but production is again increasing. Annual world output is about 3 billion tons, 500 million tons from the United States. World coal reserves are estimated conservatively at about 7 trillion tons, enough to meet demand for centuries at present consumption rates.
See also: Diamond.

Coalition, combination or alliance of political groups having mutual interests. In countries with parliamentary systems, governments may be composed of coalitions when no single party has a majority.

Coal oil *See:* Kerosene.

Coal tar, heavy, black, viscous liquid liberated during the distillation of coal, the source of a number of valuable chemicals. Light oil, phenol (or medium oil), heavy oil, and anthracene oil (asphalt) are used as fuels, solvents, preservatives, lubricants, and disinfectants. The chemical products that can be extracted include benzene, toluene, xylene, phenol, pyridene, naphthalene, and anthracene, on which are based several important chemical industries, particularly pharmaceuticals, dyes, and explosives. Coal tar itself is commonly used for street-paving; coal-tar creosote is an important wood preservative.
See also: Coal.

Coanda, Henri Marie (1885-1972), Romanian-born French aeronautics engineer and inventor, who designed an aircraft based

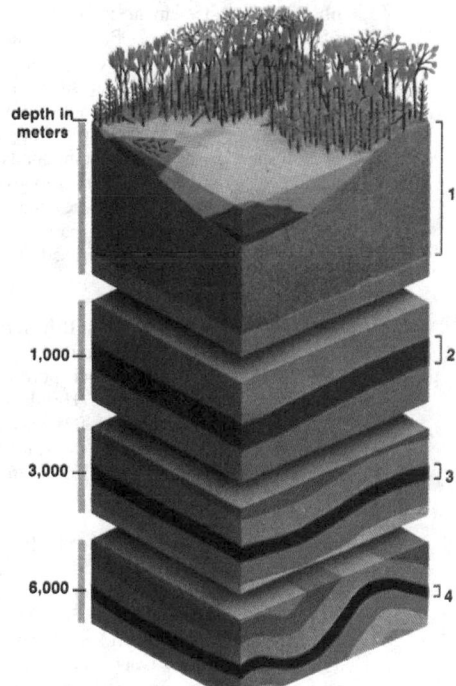

The formation of coal begins as thick deposits of partly decomposed plant material, or peat (1), accumulate on swamp bottoms. Compression increases with dept, and the peat succesively becomes lignite (2) at about 3,280 ft (1,000 m), bituminous coal (3) at about 10,000 ft (3,000 m), and anthracite (4) at about 20,000 ft (6,000 m).

C

C

on the jet-propulsion system. It crashed in 1912. Coanda also developed a dish-shaped aircraft and invented a device able to convert salt water to fresh water using solar energy.

Coast Ranges, string of mountain ranges along the Pacific coast of North America, running from Kodiak Island in Alaska to southern California. These include the Los Angeles Ranges and the California Coast Range (in southern California); the Klamath Mountains (northern California and southern Oregon); the Oregon Coast Ranges and the Olympic Mountains (Oregon and Washington); the Vancouver Range and the Queen Charlotte Islands (British Columbia); and the Kodiak, Kenai, Chugach, and St. Elias ranges and the Alexander Archipelago (Alaska). These mountains are of widely varying geological origin and composition, the highest peak being Canada's Mt. Logan (19,850 ft/6,050 m).

Coati (*Nasua nasua*), small, carnivorous mammal related to the raccoon. Its long tail is held vertically above its back. It ranges from Arizona to South America. Coatis live in small bands made up of females and young, the males being solitary except in the breeding seasons. They roam through the forest, feeding on small animals and fruit and climbing trees.

Coaxial cable, cable consisting of 2 conductors, one within the other, separated by an insulator. The inner is usually a small copper wire; the outer, usually copper braid. Coaxial cables are used in the transmission of TV, telephone, and telegraph signals.

Cobalt, chemical element, symbol Co; for physical constants see Periodic Table. Cobalt was discovered by Georg Brandt in 1735. Cobalt is a gray-white, lustrous, hard and brittle magnetic metal. It is alloyed with other elements to make powerful magnets and high speed cutting tools. Compounds of cobalt have been used for centuries to give a blue color to ceramic materials. Radioactive cobalt-60, an artificial isotope, is a powerful source of gamma rays and is used in the treatment of cancer.

Cobbett, William (1763-1835), British radical writer and reformer, best known for his book *Rural Rides* (1830), which portrayed the misery of rural workers. His *Weekly Political Register* (founded 1802) was the major reform newspaper of its day. He was elected to Parliament after the 1832 Reform Act.

Cobden, Richard (1804-1865), British politician and reformer, leader of the Manchester School. A textile merchant, he was known as 'the Apostle of Free Trade.' With John Bright and Robert Peel, he founded the Anti-Corn-Law League (1838-1839), and was its chief spokesman in Parliament (1841-1846). In 2 pamphlets, *England, Ireland, and America* (1835) and *Russia* (1836), he surveyed international relations and argued against British interventionist policies.

Cobra, venomous snake (family Elapidae)

that rears up and spreads the ribs of the neck to form a 'hood' when alarmed. Cobras are found in Africa and southern Asia. The ringhals, or spitting cobra, of Africa defends itself by spitting venom over a distance of 10-12 ft (3-3.7 m). If venom enters the eye it can cause blindness. The king cobra (*Ophiophagus hannah*) is the longest of all poisonous snakes, reaching a length of 18 ft (5.5 m). The Egyptian (*Naja haja*) and Indian (*Naja naja*) cobras are the traditional snakes of the snake charmer. Like all snakes, they are deaf to airborne sounds and are reacting to the snake charmer's swaying movement, not to the music.

Coca (*Erythroxylon coca*), shrub whose leaves contain various alkaloids. Native to the Andes, it is cultivated in Sri Lanka, Java, and Taiwan. South American Indians chew the leaves mixed with lime, which releases the drug cocaine. Cocaine-free coca extracts are used in making cola drinks.
See also: Cocaine.

Cocaine, colorless or white crystalline alkaloid, member of a broad group of plant substances that includes nicotine, caffeine, and morphine. In nature, cocaine is found in significant quantities in the leaves of 2 species of the coca shrub that grow throughout the eastern highlands of the Andes in Ecuador, Peru, and Bolivia and along the Caribbean coast of South America. In medicine it is used as a local anesthetic. Cocaine is used as a 'recreational' drug to produce euphoria and a feeling of energy. Such use is illegal in most countries although cocaine was legal for a long time (it was an ingredient in the early years of the Coca-Cola soft drink). The drug-induced euphoria is most pronounced shortly before the blood concentration has begun to fall, and it disappears several hours before the blood concentration returns to zero. Technically, cocaine is not addictive, as repeated use does not result in tolerance for it (i.e., repeating the same dose causing a diminishing response). There are withdrawal signs (particularly depression, which may be severe), but they are milder than withdrawal syndromes associated with opiates (e.g., heroin), barbiturates, or alcohol. On the other hand, cocaine is severely habit-forming. Chronic use of the drug can cause nervous system disorders and delusions, weight loss, and lessening of physical well-being. During the 1980s and 1990s use of a cocaine-derivative, called crack, has increased in many urban areas.
See also: Drug abuse; Narcotic.

Cochet, Henri Jean (1901-1987), French tennis player, belonged to the legendary 'four musketeers' together with René Lacoste, Jean Borotra, and Jacques Brugnon, who made France the most important tennis nation from 1927 through 1932. During that time, France won the Davis Cup six times. Cochet himself won the French Open Tennis Championships five times, the US Open once and Wimbledon twice.

Cochin China (Nam Bo), the Mekong delta area in the south of what is currently Vietnam; the most important cities include Ho Chi Minh City, Can Tho, Bien Hoa, and

My Tho. As of 1787, the French continued to extend their influence in this area. They reached a treaty with the ruler of Cochin China in that year, in which they agreed to help him conquer the rest of what is currently Vietnam; this goal was achieved in 1802. Cochin China was part of the Vietnamese Empire until 1866; it was annexed by the French in 1867 and by 1887 belonged to the French colony of Indo-China. Following the occupation during World War II by the Japanese, Cochin China was an independent republic for a brief period of time (1946-1949), before being united with Vietnam. Following the defeat of the French in 1954, Cochin China became part of South Vietnam. It joined the reunited Vietnam in 1975.

Cochise (1815-1874), chief of the Chiricahua Apache tribe. Aroused by the unjust execution of relatives by soldiers, he began a violent campaign against European Americans in Arizona in 1861 and effectively drove them from the area. In 1862 he was driven back by troops to the Dragon Mountains, which he held until his capture by Gen. George Crook in 1871. He escaped but gave himself up when the Chiricahua Reservation was formed in 1872. After his death, his people were removed from the reservation.

Cochran, Jacqueline (1912-1980), U.S. pilot. She obtained her pilot's license in 1932 after only 3 weeks' flying. First woman to fly in a Bendix transcontinental race (1934), she won it in 1938. She organized and headed the Women's Airforce Service Pilots (WASP) in World War II, was the first civilian woman to win the Distinguished Service Cross, and was the first woman to fly faster than sound.

Cockatiel, gray bird (*Nymphicus hollandicus*) found in Australia. It is about 12.5 in (32 cm) long, has a crown of feathers, a long tail, and a heavy beak.

Cockatoo, parrot with erectile crest (especially, genus *Kakatoe*). Its plumage is usually white, sometimes black, pink, or yellow. Cockatoos live in Australia and neighboring parts. They are good talkers.

Cockcroft, Sir John Douglas (1897-1967), English physicist who first 'split the atom.' With E.T.S. Walton, he built a particle accelerator and in 1932 initiated the first artificial nuclear reaction by bombarding lithium atoms with protons, producing alpha particles. For this work Cockcroft and Walton received the 1951 Nobel Prize for physics.
See also: Atom; Walton, Ernest Thomas Sinton.

Cocker spaniel, popular breed of dog in the United States, bred from the English spaniel. They weigh 22-28 lb (10-13 kg) and stand 15 in (38 cm) at the shoulder.

Cockle, bivalve mollusk (order Eulamellibranchia) with cupped shell ornamented with radiating grooves. Cockles live buried in mud or sand, in shallow water, and dig themselves in by means of a muscular foot that can be protruded between the shells. There are numerous species along the coasts of North America ranging in size from the 4-in (10.2-cm) giant Pacific egg cockle to 1/4-in (0.6-cm) cockles. The common cockle of Europe is edible.

Cocklebur, any of several weeds (genus *Xanthium*) of the composite family. This plant grows throughout Europe and parts of the United States. It has spiny burs that usually contain 2 seeds, 1 of which germinates a season before the other. The seedlings are poisonous to grazing animals.

Cock-of-the-rock, bird of genus *Rupicola*, of the cotingas family, native to South American forests. Cocks-of-the-rock have ornate orange or red plumage and helmetlike crests.

Cockroach, or roach, flat-bodied insect of the family Blattidae with long antennae and hardened forewings that protect the hind-wings, as in the beetle. Cockroaches feed on fungi and on plant and animal remains but also come indoors to eat exposed food, book bindings, and even wood. Sizes range from 0.5 in (0.6 cm) to 3 in (7.6 cm). There are about 70 species in the United States. Some species can fly.

The cockroach, *Blaberus gigantieus*, Central America. Wing span male: 2,7 in (7 cm), female 3,1 in (8 cm)

Cockscomb, tropical Asiatic flower (*Celosia argentea*) of the amaranth family. The cockscomb grows in tropical America, Asia, the East Indies, and the United States. The rooster's-comb-shaped flowers have been developed into varying shapes and colors.

Coconut palm (*Cocos nuerfera*), tropical tree. Its origin is obscure because coconuts can survive prolonged immersion in the sea, and they have been spread around the world by ocean currents. The height of the coconut palm ranges from 60 to 100 ft (18 to 30 m). The trunk, which often tilts over, bears a cluster of long fronds at the top. A single palm can produce over 400 nuts in the course of a year. The husk surrounding the 'nut' (seed) is used for mats and ropes. The nut is at first filled with a jelly. This liquefies when the nut is about 7 months old to become 'coconut milk.' Over the next 2 to 3 months the liquid solidifies to a white flesh used to make desiccated coconut. Finally, when a year old, the fruit falls of its own accord. The nuts are then cut out and split in two, and the flesh is allowed to dry. Then called copra, it yields an oil used in margarine, synthetic rubber, soap, and other items. Coconut palm fronds are used for thatching, and the copra, without its oil, is used as cattle feed. The tree is also a source of wood.

Cocoon, protective covering enclosing the larvae or pupae of insects. The larva prepares the cocoon as a shelter. While inside the cocoon, the larva becomes a pupa, which in turn develops into an adult insect.

Cocteau, Jean (1889-1963), French author, artist, and film director. He first rose to fame with poetry, ballets such as *Parade* (1917), and the novel *Thomas l'Imposteur* (Thomas the Imposter; 1923). After overcoming opium addiction, he produced some of his most brilliant work, such as the play *Orphée* (1926) and *La Machine Infernale* (The Infernal Machine; 1934). Prolific in many fields, he also made several films, including *Le Sang d'un Poete* (The Blood of a Poet; 1932), *Beauty and the Beast* (1945), *Orpheus* (1949), and *Les Enfants Terribles* (1950).

Cod, bottom-feeding fish (family Gadidae) of the northern Atlantic and the Pacific. The record weight is 211 lb (95.7 kg) for an Atlantic cod (*Gadus morrhua*), but the usual range is 2 to 25 lb (0.9 to 11.3 kg). Females lay up to 6 million eggs at a time. Cod fishing has been important in Europe since the 16th century, and Europeans soon discovered the New England and Newfoundland 'cod banks,' which played an important part in the colonization of the new continent. The cod were salted, their livers yielding an important vitamin-rich oil (cod liver oil), and the swimbladder was used for isinglass, a very pure form of gelatin.

Code, set of laws or rules arranged systematically and put in writing. Legal codes have existed for perhaps as long as writing. One of the earliest known codes is that of Hammurabi, the king of Babylonia, 18th century B.C. Roman law was codified in the form of the Twelve Tables around 450 B.C. By A.D. 534 its principles had been refined into the Code of Justinian, which had an enormous influence on later European law. The code Napoléon, formulated in 1804, served as the basis for the legal system of France and its colonies, including Quebec and Louisiana. In communications, code is a set of symbols made to yield information via specified operations. An example is the Morse code in telegraphy, a system of short and long signals in combinations that indicate letters of the alphabet. Codes whose rules are not revealed are often used for secret messages. Decoding these messages is called cryptography.

Code Civil *See:* Code Napoléon.

Codeine, mild but addictive narcotic alkaloid, analgesic, and cough suppressant derived from opium. It also reduces bowel activity, causing constipation, and is used to cure diarrhea.
See also: Narcotic.

Code Napoléon, French legal code, officially the *Code Civil*. Napoleon I, as first consul, appointed a commission to devise a replacement for the confused and corrupt local systems formerly in force. The code, made up of 2,281 articles arranged in 3 books, was enacted in 1804 and, although much altered, is still in force today.

Codes and ciphers, set of characters or signals, with prearranged meanings as letters or numbers, used for secrecy and brevity in transmitting messages, especially in wartime.

Codex (Lat., caudex = treetrunk), oldest form of the book, which was developed in the 2nd century B.C. It initially consisted of two wax tablets, the so-called *diptychon*, then of papyrus. Parchment, which was less fragile and could be easily folded, was then discovered. Around the 4th century A.D., papyrus codices (and the scroll) had been virtually replaced by codices made of parchment. The study of codices is referred to as codicology.

Codling moth, or codlin moth, small, nocturnal moth (*Laspeyresia pomonella*) whose caterpillars live in apples and pears. Infestations of codling moths can cause the destruction of entire orchards.

Cod-liver oil, pale yellow substance obtained from the liver of cod and related fish. Cod-liver oil is rich in vitamins A and D, and was formerly used by people with deficiencies of these vitamins.

Cody, John Patrick Cardinal (1907-1982), archbishop of Chicago 1965-1982. Cody served on the Vatican staff in the 1930s. He was appointed archbishop of New Orleans in 1964, and became a cardinal in 1967.

Cody, William Frederick *See:* Buffalo Bill.

Coeducation, education of both sexes in the same schools and classes. While coeducation in the primary grades became common in Protestant Europe after the Reformation, it was not introduced at higher educational levels until much later.

Coelacanth, lunged, bony fish of the family Coelacanthidae. Coelacanths were thought to be extinct until 1938, when one species (*Latimeria chalumne*) was discovered live off the South African coast. They are about 5 ft (150 cm) long, with circular overlapping scales. They were known as predecessors of the amphibians until in 1997 it was discovered that lungfish are more closely related to amphibians than coelacanths are.

Coelenterate, phylum of primitive, invertebrate animals, now renamed the *Cnidaria* (the *C* is silent). It includes anemones, corals, jellyfish, the freshwater hydra, and many others. The basic body form is a two-layered sac, with a mouth at one end surrounded by a ring of tentacles. Food is captured and poisoned by means of *nematocysts*, or 'stinging cells,' in the tentacles. Coelenterates exist in two forms. Anemones, corals, and hydra are *polyps*, which are anchored and tubular. Jellyfishes are *medusae*, or free-swimming.

Coelom, major body cavity in vertebrates and higher invertebrates. In vertebrates, the coelom is partitioned into the pericardial, pleural, and abdominal cavities, which house the stomach, liver, digestive tract, and other body organs.

Coetzee, John M. (1940-), South African author, his work discusses the dilemma with which former colonists in Africa are faced. Made his debut in 1974 with *Dusklands*, followed by *In the Heart of the Country* (1977)

C

The silver groat of Jan van Arkel, bishop of Utrecht (1342-64). On the reverse, there is a cross with a dual legend, which was very widespread in the Late Middle Ages in Europe.

and *Waiting for the Barbarians* (1980). Coetzee received various literature awards, including the Booker prize of 1983 and the Prix Fémina étranger 1985 for *The life and Times of Michael K* (1983). Other works include *Foe* (1986), a semi historical novel in which the female main character is washed ashore on the island where Robinson Crusoe and Friday are, *Age of Iron* (1990), *Disgrace* (1999; Booker Prize), and *Youth* (2002).

Coffee, evergreen shrub or tree (genus *Coffea*) from whose seeds the drink of the same name is made. The plant was first discovered in Ethiopia, where its fruit was used for wine and food before A.D. 1000 The hot drink made of ground and roasted coffee beans was first made in the Arabian peninsula in the 15th century. It reached Europe in the 17th century and then spread, with European settlers, to the Americas. The shrub is now grown in many hot, humid areas of Asia, the Americas, and Africa. The highest quality coffees are varieties of Arabian (*Coffea arabica*). Coffee of Liberian (*C. liberica*) and Congolese (*C. robusta*) origin are also commercially significant. Brazil is the world's largest coffee producer. Other major producing countries are Costa Rica, El Salvador, Guatemala, Honduras, Mexico, Colombia, Ecuador, Cameroon, Ethiopia, Ivory Coast, Uganda, India, and Indonesia. The red, cherry-like berries of the coffee plant generally contain 2 seeds per berry. These seeds are harvested, cleaned, and roasted. It is the heat of the roasting process that creates the flavor and aroma. The roasting also causes the formation of caffeine, a stimulant that may be harmful in large doses.

Coffee is a major beverage. The seeds or beans are taken from the plant, dried, roasted and finally ground.

Coffee house, variety of commercial establishment that arose in London in the mid-17th century. Coffee houses became centers of business, cultural, political, and religious information exchange. The first English newspapers arose as broadsheets distributed in coffee houses.
The institution died away in London in the 19th century, but cafes remain widespread in most European, Mediterranean, and Latin American countries.

Cohesion, attractive force holding the atoms or molecules of a single substance together. Cohesion is generally contrasted to adhesion, the attractive force between different substances.

Cohn, Ferdinand Julius (1828-1898), German botanist, one of the founders of bacteriology. He also contributed to the understanding of heat production by plants.
See also: Botany.

Coin, piece of stamped metal, of a fixed value and weight, issued to serve as money. Until banknotes came into use, coins were the only form of money. The principal metals used in coinage are gold, silver, and copper. They were originally used in their pure state, but were later alloyed (combined) with other substances to make the coins cheaper and more resistant to wear. Coins have presented a constant temptation to engage in monetary trickery. From the time of the Romans, when rulers had large debts, they reduced the amount of precious metals in coins and passed them off on their creditors at the old value; this process is called debasement.
The first known coins were struck in Lydia, Asia Minor, in the 8th century B.C. These coins, called *staters* (a unit of weight), were made of a natural combination of gold and silver and ornamented with crude animal likenesses. The Greek island of Aegina issued better-made silver *staters* about 700 B.C., and the use of coins soon spread throughout the Mediterranean world. The Athenian silver *tetradrachma* was the main coin from the 6th to the 4th centuries B.C., when the coinage of Alexander the Great replaced it. The Chinese independently developed coins about the same time as the Greeks. The first Roman coins, made of bronze (an alloy of copper and tin), date from the 4th century B.C.; during later Roman times, silver and gold coins were used. During the early Middle Ages, only silver coins were struck in western Europe. The breakup of the Roman Empire decreased the volume of trade, and the use of money diminished. In the 12th and 13th centuries, Genoa and Venice led the commercial revival, and their gold coins became a leading international medium of exchange. In modern times, gold replaced silver throughout most of the world. All monies were defined in terms of gold and bore a definite and fixed relationship to the value of gold. World War I and the Great Depression caused this system to break down, and most nations now no longer use gold coins.

Coin collecting, or numismatics, popular hobby throughout the world. Collecting involves the acquisition of coins of any particular grouping. Coins may be considered desirable for various reasons, including origin, history, rarity, and value. They are commonly graded according to quality. Categories of quality include: poor (features are mostly obliterated); good (worn, but with features mostly visible); very good (evenly worn, but with clear details); very fine or uncirculated (in newly minted condition); proof (specially struck from a highly polished die).

Coke, form of amorphous carbon that is left when bituminous coal is burned in special furnaces to remove volatile constituents. Coke is used primarily as a fuel in metallurgy, especially in blast furnaces to extract metal from ores.
See also: Carbon.

Coke oven gas, hydrogen and methane mixture produced when coal is heated to about 2000°F (1100°C) in an airtight chamber.

Coke oven gas is burned as an industrial fuel and for home heating.

Colbert, Jean Baptiste (1619-1683), French diplomat and finance superintendent. He became chief finance minister to King Louis XIV in 1661 and held that post for 22 years, supporting French industry and commerce and building a powerful navy.
See also: Louis.

Colchicum, poisonous flowering plant (*Colchicum autumnale*) of the lily family, also known as autumn crocus or meadow saffron. Found on the British Isles and in mid- to southern Europe, these plants have crocus-like flowers, whose autumnal blooms range from purple to white. From the underground stems a substance (colcherine) is extracted that is used in the treatment of rheumatism and gout.

Cold, common, viral infection of the mucous membrane of the nose and throat, marked by discharge of mucus, sneezing, and watering of the eyes. More than 100 specific viruses have been identified as causes of the common cold. There is no known cure, but symptoms can be treated. Drinking fluids prevents dehydration. Pain relievers can lower fever. Decongestants may shrink mucous membranes.

Cold-blooded animal, or poikilotherm, animal that cannot maintain a constant internal body temperature and therefore attains a temperature close to that of its environment, making it dangerously subject to climatic changes. Cold-blooded animals include fish, amphibians, and reptiles.

Cold sore, skin lesion, generally of the lips or nose, caused by the Herpes simplex virus. Often characterized by blisters filled with a clear liquid, cold sores may be triggered by infections such as the common cold or pneumonia. The virus frequently becomes dormant, persisting in the skin between attacks.
See also: Herpes.

Cold War, expression used to characterize the conflict after World War II between the Western powers led by the United States and the Communist bloc led by the USSR. The term arose to describe conditions of hostility and military build-up short of actual armed conflict. The 2 largest wars during the Cold War era were in Korea in the 1950s and in Indochina in the 1960s and early 1970s. The period was also characterized by the division of Europe into antagonistic military blocs: the North Atlantic Treaty Organization (NATO) in the West, the Warsaw Pact in the East. Most analysts would argue that the upheavals in Eastern Europe and the USSR in 1989 led to the end of the Cold War.

Cole, Thomas (1801-1848), English-born U.S. landscape painter. He studied painting at Pennsylvania Academy of Fine Arts and gained fame beginning in 1825 for his Hudson River Valley paintings. Some of his works which had moral themes included *The Course of Empire* (1839) and *The Voyage of Life* (1840).
See also: Hudson River School.

A workman is helping to build the Berlin Wall, August 1961. This would become the most tangible symbol of the Cold War. The Wall was meant as a physical barrier to stop the large numbers of people trying to flee from Eastern Germany to the West.

C

НАРОДЫ МИРА ЖДУТ!

An example of propaganda used during the Cold War. Both parties blame each other for the arms race. 'The people await peace' says Ivan (the Soviet Union) to Uncle Sam (the United States), and he offers him a disarmament agreement. The look on his face says it all.

A broken statue of Stalin lying in the street during the Hungarian Riots in 1956. The Soviet troops forcibly repressed the riots against the Soviet-minded Rákosi regime. They invaded Budapest on November 4 and re-instated the Communist government. This made a big impression on the West and tempered the high expectations they had of Khrushchev, the new Soviet leader.

C

American air photograph of rocket launching installations in Cuba. The Cuba Crisis (1962), 'the hottest moment of the Cold War', broke out after American espionage planes spotted launching pads for Russian rockets being built in Cuba. Tensions did not ease until the Soviet Union withdrew its weapons.

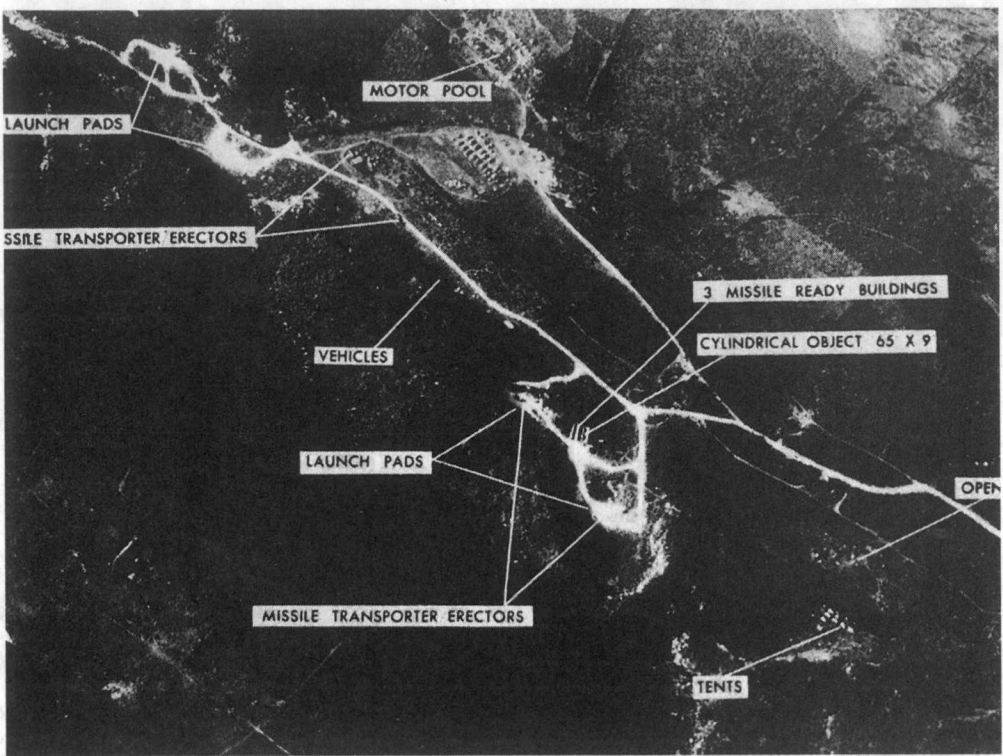

LAUNCH PADS

MOTOR POOL

SSILE TRANSPORTER ERECTORS

3 MISSILE READY BUILDINGS

VEHICLES

CYLINDRICAL OBJECT 65 X 9

LAUNCH PADS

OPEN

MISSILE TRANSPORTER ERECTORS

TENTS

Female Vietcong soldiers patrolling during the Vietnam War (1959-1975). After colonist France had left Vietnam, the United States took over France's position with the idea to stop the advance of communism in South-East Asia. This was part of the containment politics, which America was applying all over the world. In spite of America's efforts in the war, the intervention was a fiasco: besides great military losses, the United States also had to accept the introduction of the Socialist Republic of Vietnam in 1976.

Citizens of Prague demobilizing a Russian tank. The countries in the Warsaw Pact ended the Prague Spring (January-August 1968), a short period of liberalization of the Communist rule in the country then known as Czechoslovakia, using military force. This invasion was justified by the argument that the re-instatement of the Communist regime was in the best interests of 'Socialist Spirit'.

C

Coleridge, Samuel Taylor (1772-1834), English poet, philosopher, and critic. His works include the poems 'Kubla Khan,' 'Christabel,' and 'The Rime of the Ancient Mariner,' all 3 of which were included in the volume *Lyrical Ballads* (1798), a collection Coleridge produced with William Wordsworth. The book is one of the major works of English Romanticism.

Colette (Sidonie Gabrielle Colette; 1873-1954), French author noted primarily for her sensual style and her themes of women, love and jealousy. Among her many novels are *Cheri* (1920), *The Ripening* (1923), *The Cat* (1933), and *Gigi* (1945).

Coleus, tropical plant (genus *Coleus*) of the mint family. Native to the African and Indian tropics, the coleus plant grows to a height of 3 ft (91 cm) and is cultivated as a house-plant.

Colic, acute pain focused in an internal organ, frequently the colon or other component of the digestive tract.

Coliseum *See:* Colosseum.

Colitis, disease characterized by inflammation of the colon (large intestine). Symptoms include abdominal pain, cramps, and diarrhea. If ulcers develop in the walls of the intestine, the condition can become chronic, with fever and complications. Colitis sometimes follows attacks of dysentery, but causative microorganisms have not been traced. There is probably a psychosomatic component, anxiety bringing on attacks of the disease. In severe cases a section of the colon may have to be removed by surgery. *See also:* Colon.

Collage, 20th-century art form in which various objects and materials are glued onto a canvas or board, sometimes covered with paint. The term comes from the French word for pasting. The earliest experiments with collage were done by Pablo Picasso and Georges Braque in 1910-11. The technique was further developed by Henri Matisse and by the Dadaists, particularly Kurt Schwitters, who made entire compositions consisting of ticket stubs and other evocative remnants of paper. Later artists, like Jasper Johns, created more elaborate collages of wood, metal, and fabric.

Collagen, major component of connective tissue, constituting 70% of its dry weight. Collagen is an insoluble protein, whose fibers form a mesh. Collagen is also present in bones.

Collarbone, or clavicle, horizontal bone that connects with the breastbone (*sternum*) and the shoulder blade (*scapula*) to support the shoulder and to hold the arm in proper position. It is present in upright-walking mammals and in bats. *See also:* Bone.

Collard (*Brassica oreracea*), headless cabbage of the mustard family commonly grown in the southern United States. Both a summer and winter crop, the collard plant reaches 2-4 ft (60-120 cm), and is a dietary source of vitamins A and C.

Collective bargaining *See:* Labor movement.

Collective behavior, sociological term for human behavior in crowds and other large, unorganized, temporary groups. Instances of collective behavior include riots, panics, fashions, cults, and revolutionary movements. U.S. sociologists Robert E. Park and Ernest W. Burgess introduced the concept in their book *Introduction to the Science of Sociology* (1921). *See also:* Group dynamics.

Collective farm, agricultural enterprise operated cooperatively. The farm's land and equipment may be owned by members of the cooperative group or by the government, which controls production. Stalin introduced collectivization to the USSR in 1929, and it has been widely used in Communist countries and in Israel.

Collectivism, political doctrine that places control of economic activity in the hands of the community or the government, as opposed to individuals, as in the case under capitalism. The term may cover a wide variety of economic systems and structures, but will typically exclude private ownership of major means of production and distribution. *See also:* Communal society; Socialism.

Collie, 2 types of sheepdog, rough-coated and smooth-coated, originating in Scotland in the 1600s and brought to the United States by British colonists a century later. The collie stands 2 ft (60 cm) at the shoulder and may be sable and white, blue, tan, or all white, though early breeds were black. There is also a miniature variety.

Collins, (William) Wilkie (1824-1889), English novelist, often considered the originator of the detective novel in English. His works include *The Woman in White* (1860) and *The Moonstone* (1868).

Collodi, Carlo (Carlo Lorenzini; 1826-1890), Italian journalist and author of humorous adult fiction and moral children's stories, of which the best known is *The Adventures of Pinocchio* (1883).

Colloid, mixture in which particles of one substance are dispersed in another. Colloids are similar to solutions and suspensions. What determines the difference is the size of the particles of the substance that is distributed. In a solution, the particles are molecules. In a suspension, they are much larger, visible either with the naked eye or a microscope. A colloid has particles larger than molecules but too small to be seen with a normal microscope. Colloids can be categorized according to whether the substances mixed together are solids, liquids, or gases. For instance, a gas may be dispersed in a liquid to form foam. A liquid dispersed in another liquid forms an emulsion. A liquid dispersed in a solid is a gel.

Collor de Mello, Fernando (1950-   ), Brazilian politician. He began his political career in 1979 as the Mayor of Maceió and became the governor of the state Alogas. Due to his dissatisfaction with his party, the Brazilian Democratic Movement (PMDB), he established a new party, the Partido da Reconstruçao Nacional (PRN). As the leader of this party, he managed to defeat Lula, the Marxist candidate for the 1989 presidential elections with a slight majority of votes. Fighting inflation, social injustice, and corruption were important items on his agenda. However, Collor de Mello was forced to resign in 1992 when a parliamentary investigation was conducted into his own involvement in corruption. He was acquitted by the Supreme Court in 1994 due to lack of evidence.

Colobus, or guerza, genus of thumbless, long-tailed, African monkey of the family Cercopithecidae. The colobus is vegetarian, diurnal (active in the daytime), and lives in trees, though it may travel on the ground. Colobus species are divided by color and may be black and white, red, or olive. Young are white at birth. Colobus live in groups of 3 to 80. Some species are aggressively territorial.

Cologne (pop. 1,000,000), river port and industrial city in western Germany, on the Rhine River. Its products range from heavy machinery to toilet water (eau de cologne). The prosperity of Cologne (Köln in German) dates from its membership in the Hanseatic League in the 15th century. *See also:* Germany.

Colombia

Capital:	Bogota
Area:	440,831 sq mi
	(1,141,748 sq km)
Population:	41,008,000
Language:	Spanish
Government:	Presidential republic
Independent:	1819
Head of gov.:	President
Per capita:	U.S. $6,300
Monetary unit:	1 Colombian peso =
	100 centavos

Colombia (Republic of), fourth largest country in South America. It extends over 440,831 sq mi (1,141,748 sq km) of the ex-

C

treme northwest of South America, bounded on the northwest by Panama, on the northeast by Venezuela, on the southeast by Brazil, and on the south by Peru and Ecuador. It is the only South American country that has both an Atlantic and a Pacific coastline.

Cartagena's cobbled streets wind through the old section of the city, founded as a Spanish port more than 400 years ago.

Land and climate. Nearly half of the country is mountainous; more than half is comparatively uninhabited lowland plain. There are 4 major regions. By far the most important is the Andean region, where 3 great ranges branch out northward from the Pasto knot near the Ecuadorian border: the western, central, and eastern Cordilleras. Some 80% of the population lives in the narrow mountain valleys and basins of this region. Between the central and eastern Cordilleras, the Magdalena (Colombia's chief river) flows for 1,000 mi (1,609 km) to the Caribbean at the port of Barranquilla. A third of the population lives in the eastern cordillera (mountain chain), where the seat of government has been located since Chibcha times. Bogotá, the capital and largest city of Colombia, stands on a plateau at an altitude of 8,661 ft (2,640 km). The Caribbean coastal lowlands are the home of about 17% of the population; the chief centers are the ports of Barranquilla, Cartagena, and Santa Marta. The rivers draining the Caribbean lowlands-the Magdalena, Cauca, San Jorge, and César-form a maze of swamps and lagoons. The Pacific lowlands are a rainy, marshy littoral. Buenaventura and Tumaco are Colombia's chief Pacific ports. The Pacific lowlands and the eastern plains beyond the eastern Cordillera account for only 5% of the population. The northern section of the eastern region is part of the *Ilanos* (tropical grasslands) of northern South America; the southern section is almost impenetrable jungle. Although most of Colombia lies in the north tropical zone, the climate varies with topography. An excessively high rainfall prevails in the Pacific lowlands. Altitude modifies the climate of the highlands: the semitropical *tierra caliente* (hot land) extends to about 3,000 ft (914 m), where it is succeeded by the *tierra templada* (temperate land) coffee belt (to about 6,500 ft/2,000 m), the *tierra fria* (cold land) (6,500-10,000 ft/2,000-3,000 m)

where grain and potatoes are grown, and the almost polar *páramos* (grazing lands) below the snowline. The vast eastern plains are subject to successive wet and dry seasons, while in the Caribbean lowlands a hot, dry climate predominates.

People. More than half of Colombians are mestizos (of mixed European and Native American ancestry); there are about 20% whites, with minorities of mulattoes, blacks, and Native Americans.

Economy. Colombia is a major world coffee producer. It also grows cotton, bananas, sugar, tobacco, cocoa, rice, sorghum, corn, wheat, and barley. The country has the largest coal reserve in Latin America and substantial reserves of uranium. Other resources include oil, gas, and precious metals. Transportation is hindered by mountain ranges, but cities are joined by road, rail, or river and an advanced air network. Tourism is becoming an important source of foreign exchange.

History. Chibcha Native Americans of the eastern cordilleras had a highly developed culture when the Spanish arrived in the early 16th century. Spain ruled the area until independence, which followed Simón Bolívar's Boyacá victory over Spanish colonial forces (1819). At the end of the 19th century thousands died in fighting between liberals and conservatives, Colombia's 2 main political parties. Another civil war between liberals and conservatives, with about 200,000 casualties, lasted from 1948 until 1958, when a democratic government was reestablished. In the mid-1980s the government began battling the large and well-organized drug cartels that traffic in cocaine, which is processed from coca grown in Peru. In 1989 the United States supplied military personnel to help combat the increasing related violence. In spite of several arrests, and settlements between government and guerrilla movements, the violence continues. In 1999 northwest Colombia was devastated by an earthquake. More than a thousand people were killed, many became homeless.

The government tried to reach an agreement with the left-wing rebel group FARC, with no success. The new President, Alvoro Uribe, declared state of emergency in August, 2002.

Colombo (pop. 615,000), capital, chief port, and largest city of Sri Lanka (Ceylon), located on the southwest coast of the island, in the Indian Ocean. The city's harbor, built in 1875 and modernized in the 1950s, is one of the world's largest. Tea, cinnamon, rubber, and coconut products are the chief exports. *See also:* Sri Lanka.

Colombo Plan, cooperative program for economic development in South and Southeast Asia, inaugurated in 1951 at Colombo, Ceylon (now Sri Lanka). The first participants were members of the British Commonwealth, joined by the United States, Japan, and several Southeast Asian countries.

Colon, large intestine from the cecum (the pouch into which the small intestine empties) to the rectum, about 60 in (1.5 m) long.

The colon is divided into 4 segments: the ascending, transverse, descending, and the sigmoid, or pelvic.
See also: Intestine.

Colón (pop. 140,000), third largest city of Panama, established in 1850 at what is now the Atlantic terminus of the Panama Canal. Originally named Aspinwall, the city was renamed to honor Christopher Columbus in 1890. As a duty-free trade zone, Colón is an important commercial port and tourist center.
See also: Panama.

Colonialism, The politics of various European powers oriented towards establishing settlements outside Europe for the purpose of serving the economic and/or military interests of the mother country. The term dates from after World War II. The era of colonialism began at the beginning of the 16th century when Spain and Portugal conquered large parts of Central America and South America. The Dutch, French, English, and Danes followed shortly afterwards, not only in America, but in Africa, Asia, and the Pacific as well. The colonial forces were initially interested in luxury articles, spices, and gold, and the armed forces were in control. Merchants later became dominant and commercial enterprises became active (companies), often with the support of the colonial power. The colonies were often harshly conquered and repressed, and then exploited for the benefit of the mother country (for example, by means of slavery in South American mines and on plantations throughout the American

In 1913, an attempt was made to kill Viceroy Lord Harding, which was a sign for the English that their 'carefree' colonial days were over.

continent). The nature of colonialism changed at the end of the 19th century. All of the areas outside Europe that were not yet occupied were quickly conquered by the

C

colonial powers and a few newcomers (Germany, Belgium and Italy). Only a few areas, such as Persia and China, were not added to the colonial empire of a European country. The exploitation of the mineral resources in these areas was however completely controlled by Western countries, along with the construction of railroads, telegraph connections, and the like. After World War II, most of the colonies became politically independent. In an economic sense, and various other ways, they have often remained more or less dependent.

Colonial period, American, nearly 170 formative years of settlement and adventure before U.S. independence. The first colonies were established by chartered trading companies, groups of commercial speculators who shared the profits of the colony in return for putting up the capital necessary for its establishment. The first permanent English settlement in America, at Jamestown (1607), was the project of the London Company, which failed to exploit its new colony of Virginia and surrendered its charter to the crown in 1624. The Pilgrim settlement at Plymouth (1620) merged with the later Puritan settlement at Boston, and the 2 were governed by the charter of the Massachusetts Bay Company until 1691, when it, too, became a royal province under an appointed governor. Connecticut (1662) and Rhode Island (1663) were established by settlers from Massachusetts. New York, originally New Amsterdam, was founded by the Dutch West India Company in 1625 and captured by the English in 1664. Delaware, founded by a Swedish company in 1638, later fell under the control of the Penn family. Under the system of proprietorship, the crown also granted huge tracts of land to individuals or groups. Of the 13 colonies, 7 were founded as proprietorships: Maryland, New Hampshire, New Jersey, the Carolinas, Pennsylvania, and Georgia. All except Pennsylvania and Maryland became royal provinces before 1776.

Economic life. Despite rocky soil and a short growing season, many crops were raised on the small farms of New England. Fishing employed 10,000 people by 1765, and some 300 vessels were engaged in whaling. Shipbuilding was the main industry, though woolen textiles, leather goods, and iron tools and utensils were also produced. In the 18th century the distillation of rum from West Indian molasses became the second most important industry. The Middle Atlantic colonies-New York, New Jersey, and Pennsylvania-supplied New England and Europe with food and raw materials. Manufactures consisted of textiles, paper, glass, and iron. In the 17th century an important fur trade was carried on through the Iroquois country from Albany. In the Plantation Provinces, from Maryland south to Georgia, production became increasingly concentrated on great staple crops-tobacco, rice, and indigo. By the 1770s tobacco exports were around 50 million pounds a year, rice half a million. The forests of the Carolina uplands also furnished lumber for shipbuilding and 'naval stores' (pitch, tar, and turpentine), which were vital for the British navy.

Scarcity of labor was a problem common to all the colonies, for the ease with which land could be acquired meant that industrious colonists quickly became landlords in their own right. One solution was the employment of 'indentured' servants who were obliged to serve for a fixed period of years, in return for payment of their passage across the Atlantic or sometimes as a punishment for political or religious offenses or crimes.

From Virginia southward, African slaves were employed. The first shipload arrived as early as 1619; by 1760 there were 400,000 blacks in the English colonies. Migration from countries other than England brought new cultural influences to the colonies. King Louis XIV's revocation of the Edict of Nantes (1685) compelled many French Protestants to flee to America, where they became prominent in trade and industry. Germans, mostly peasant farmers, settled in Pennsylvania, the Shenandoah Valley, and the Piedmont region of Virginia and North Carolina. Scotch-Irish from Ulster also settled in Pennsylvania and the colonies to its south. By 1775 there were probably 200,000 Germans and 300,000 Scotch-Irish in America as well as Swiss, Welsh, and Dutch. Nevertheless, the English inheritance was predominant: English was the main language and also the basis of a shared literature, legal system, and political outlook. In the free and vigorous atmosphere of colonial America the British tradition of personal liberty was to culminate in revolution and independence.

Colony, area and people controlled by a foreign power. Types of colony defined by social or economic characteristics include settlement, trade, missionary, penal, and protectorate. Since World War II, the trend toward reorganization of empire has allowed many colonies to obtain independence or to be placed under the supervision of the United Nations' General Assembly or Trusteeship System.

Color, visual effect caused by the eye's ability to react differently to different wavelengths of light. Color is a sensation rather than a property of a thing. An object that reflects light of a certain wavelength will ap-

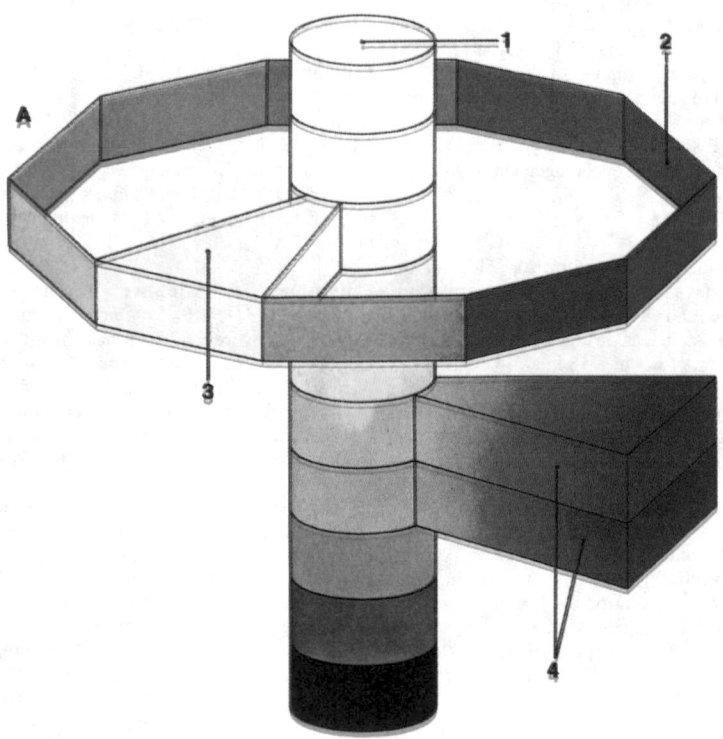

The Munsell color system (A) describes colors in terms of value, hue, and chroma. The value scale denotes a color's degree of darkness. It is measured along a cylinder (1) in steps of ranging from perfect black to perfect white. Hues are indicated on a band (2). Chroma, the extent to which a color differs from gray, is represented by its distance from the cylinder (3). The band shows different hues with the same value and chroma. Wedges (4) show the same hue with two different values and varying chroma. Ten colors represent the basic hues (B).

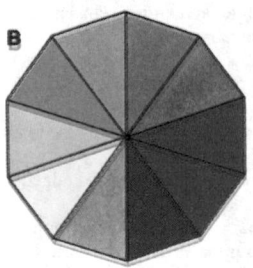

C

pear to be a certain color. The 3 primary colors-red, blue, and yellow-can be combined to form all other colors. Two colors whose light, when combined, produces white, are called complementary. In white light, an object that reflects all wavelengths will appear white, while one that absorbs all wavelengths will appear black.

Colorado (Centennial State; pop. 3,893,000), state in the United States, in the Rocky Mountains; 104,131 sq mi (269,595 sq km). Capital: Denver. Average height over 6,562 ft (2,000 m; Mt. Elbert, 14,433 ft, 4,399 m), making it the highest state in the U.S. The Colorado, Arkansas, and Rio Grande rivers, among others, find their source in Colorado. Cattle-breeding (cows, sheep, and pigs), agriculture (including corn, wheat, potatoes and sugar beet) and mining (petroleum, natural gas, coal, sand and gravel, and a number of metals). The largest molybdenum mine in the world is found near Climax. Industry (equipment, electronics, machines, graphic industry, and food) especially in the cities in the eastern part of the state. Tourism is significant (including winter sports in Aspen).
First establishments date from 1858; admitted to the Union in 1876. The construction of health resorts, a national park, and hotels began around the turn of the century in an attempt to promote tourism, a course that was continued in the 60s in Aspen and Vail. The electronics industry and aviation industry were developed here in the 70s.

Colorado River, major U.S. river, rising in the Rocky Mountains of northern Colorado and flowing 1,450 mi (2,333 km) in a generally southwesternly direction to enter the Gulf of California. The river has formed many canyons, including the Grand Canyon, one of the world's largest.
See also: Hoover Dam.

Colorado Springs (pop. 280,000), city in central Colorado, second-largest in the state and seat of El Paso County. Situated at the base of Pikes Peak, Colorado Springs is a popular resort, as well as an industrial center manufacturing chemicals, tools, airplane parts, and plastics. The United States Air Force Academy is 7 mi (11.3 km) to the north.
See also: Colorado.

Color blindness, inability to tell certain colors apart. An inherited trait, color blindness is caused by a disorder of the cones in the retina of the eye. The commonest form is a difficulty in distinguishing red from green. It is usually found in males. Total color blindness, which is rare, causes a person to see only black, white, and various shades of gray.
See also: Spectrum.

Colorfield painting, movement within abstract expressionism in the 50s and 60s, in which large fields of color are placed alongside each other. The boundary between the fields is often very sharp: 'hard edged'.

Colosseum, or Coliseum, oval amphitheater in Rome, built c.75-80 A.D., with seats for about 45,000 spectators on 4 tiers. Begun by

the Flavian Emperor Vespasian and completed by his son Titus, the Colosseum was used for gladiatorial combat and other events up to the 5th century. Though damaged by earthquakes, much of it still stands.

Colossians, Epistle to the, book of the New Testament written by St. Paul to the Christians of Colossae in southwest Asia Minor. Like Ephesians, it deals with the doctrine of the body of Christ.
See also: Bible; New Testament.

Colossus of Rhodes, one of the Seven Wonders of the World, statue of Helios, the sun god, erected c.290-280 B.C. by the sculptor Chares of Lindos in the harbor of Rhodes. The statue, made of bronze and 100 ft (30 m) high, commemorated the island's successful defense against an invasion in 304 B.C. There is no truth to the medieval legend that the statue straddled the harbor. The Colossus broke off at the knee in an earthquake in 224 B.C. and lay in ruins until A.D. 672, when Arab raiders broke it up and sold it for scrap.
See also: Seven Wonders of the Ancient World.

Colt, Samuel (1814-1862), U.S. inventor and industrialist who devised the revolver, a single-barreled pistol with a revolving multiple bullet chamber, in the early 1830s. His factories pioneered mass-production techniques and the use of interchangeable parts.
See also: Revolver.

Coltrane, John (1926-1967), U.S. musician and composer. A saxophonist, he was one of the leading artists of African-American jazz in the 1950s and 1960s, performing with such gifted players as Dizzy Gillespie, Miles Davis, and Thelonious Monk. In the early 1960s he formed his own group, which soon became the most innovative in U.S. music. As a saxophonist, Coltrane was known for his distinctive tone and superlative technique. As a composer, he introduced the 'sheets of sound' style and explored the possibilities of modal compositions, based on unusual scales. In his later years, he was also famous for his encouragement of younger musicians.
See also: Jazz.

Coltsfoot, *(Tussilago farfara)*, wild plant of the daisy family Compositae native to Europe and Asia. Dandelion-like yellow blossoms appear in spring before leaves. Coltsfoot grows to 6-18 in (15-45 cm).

Colum, Padraic (1881-1972), Irish poet and dramatist associated with the Celtic renaissance and the Irish National Theater; cofounder of the *Irish Review* (1911) and writer of several plays for Dublin's Abbey Theater including *The Fiddler's House* (1907) and *Thomas Muskerry* (1910). Colum moved to the United States in 1914 and was president of the Poetry Society of America. Other works are *Orpheus* (1929), *The Frenzied Prince* (1943), *Collected Poems* (1953), and *The Poet's Circuits* (1960).

Columbia (pop. 99,300), capital and largest

city of South Carolina; seat of Richland County. Columbia was purchased in 1786 by the South Carolina legislature as the site for the state capital, established there four years later. An industrial and agricultural center, Columbia produces textiles, lumber, corn, and cotton. The University of South Carolina and five other colleges are located in the city.
See also: South Carolina.

Columbia River, large river arising in the Canadian Rockies in southeast British Columbia, and flowing south into the northwest United States, where it turns west and forms the border between Oregon and Washington and empties into the Pacific Ocean. It is 1,150 m (1,850 km) long, and its volume is the largest of any North American river except the Mississippi.
See also: British Columbia.

Columbia University, one of the major private U.S. universities. Founded as King's College in 1754, it was renamed Columbia College in 1784 and became a university in 1896. Its schools and facilities, mostly in New York City, include important research institutes for international relations and schools of journalism, business, medicine, law, and social work.

Columbine, plant (genus *Aquilegia*) related to the buttercup, with tall, slender stems, lobed leaves, and intricate flowers.

Columbite, dense oxide mineral composed of manganese, niobium, and iron, general chemical formula $(Fe,Mn)Nb_2O_6$. The element tantalum sometimes wholly or partially replaces niobium. When the mineral contains more tantalum than niobium, it is called tantalite. Both are black, often iridescent, and are found in granite rocks called pegmatites.
See also: Niobium; Tantalum.

Columbium *See:* Niobium.

Columbus (pop. 179,000), second-largest city in Georgia, seat of Muscogee County. Situated on the Chattahoochee River in the western part of the state, Columbus is a cotton and textile center and an important industrial city.

Columbus, Christopher (Cristoforo Colombo; 1451-1506), commonly credited as the discoverer of America. Born in Genoa, Italy, he was the son of a wool weaver. An experienced sailor and student of navigation, Columbus was convinced that he could pioneer a new route to the treasures of the Far East by sailing West across the Atlantic. In 1484 he tried to win financial support for his plans from King John II of Portugal, but the king's advisers estimated the distance (surprisingly accurately) at 10,000 nautical miles, which would require a sailing time of 1 year, considered impossible. Columbus presented his plan to Queen Isabella and King Ferdinand of Spain, who, after years of negotiations, agreed to finance his voyage. Three small ships, the *Niña*, the *Pinta*, and the *Santa María*, were equipped with provisions for 1 year. With a crew of 90 men they set sail from Palos on Aug. 3, 1492. On Oct. 12, 1492, when the crew was on the verge of mutiny, Columbus landed on the east coast of one of the Bahama Islands, now called Watling Island. He spent the next 3 months sailing from one Caribbean island to another in search of the eastern Grand Khan, to whom he had a letter of introduction. He wrecked the Santa María and left 39 men in Hispaniola (now the Dominican Republic). On March 15, 1493, he returned to Spain and was welcomed with honors. In Sept. 1493 Columbus left again for the Caribbean with a fleet of 17 ships, this time intending to set up trading posts and colonies, still believing he had discovered India. He explored Puerto Rico. The men he had left in Hispaniola had been wiped out, so he established a colony further east, named it Isabela, left his brother Bartholomew in charge, and set off in search of the mainland of India. He explored Jamaica and a number of the Lesser Antilles and explored the coast of Cuba, which he thought was an extension of the mainland. He wanted to take 500 natives back to Spain as slaves, but 200 died during the voyage. In 1498 he embarked on a third voyage. He sailed farther south this time, explored Trinidad and reached the South American mainland at the mouth of the Orinoco River, mistaking it for a new continent south of India. When he reached Santo Domingo, he found that there had been bloody uprisings because the colonists had established free towns and divided much of the best land among themselves, and he was forced to make compromises in order to prevent a full-scale rebellion. The disorders continued, however, and Francisco de Bobadilla was sent by Spain to take over the government of the colony. He deposed the Columbus brothers, put them in chains, and shipped them back to Spain, where they were immediately released but remained in disgrace. In 1502, after promising King Ferdinand not to enslave the natives, Columbus set out on his fourth voyage. He sailed to Central America, explored Honduras, and coasted along Nicaragua and Costa Rica to Panama. His ships were worm-eaten and in such poor condition that he had to stop at Jamaica, where he and his crew were stranded for more than a year. Finally, he chartered a ship to bring him back to Spain, where he arrived a few days before the death of Queen Isabella in 1504. King Ferdinand refused to grant him the reinstatement as viceroy and governor. Rich, honored, but ill and cripple he died on May 20, 1506.

Column, in architecture, vertical structural support, usually cylindrical, consisting of a base, shaft, and capital. Columns support the entablature on which the roof rests. Apart from their utilitarian functions, columns are also decorative, the various types forming the classical orders of architecture. *See also:* Architecture.

Coma, state of unconsciousness from which a person cannot be roused by sensory stimulation. Body functions continue but may be impaired, depending on the cause of the co-ma. Poisoning, head injury, diabetes, and brain dysfunctions (including strokes) are the most common causes.

Comanche, native North Americans of the Southwest, closely related to the Shoshone. Brilliant horsemen and fierce warriors, they were dominant among the southern Great Plains peoples, ranging into Mexico and stubbornly defending the buffalo hunting grounds against white incursions until the 1870s. Some 3,000 Comanche still live in western Oklahoma.

Comaneci, Nadia (born Gheorghe Gheorghiu-Dei 1962-), Rumanian gymnast, made her debut in 1969 and won four gold medals during the European championships six years later. She became the star of the 1976 Olympic Games in Montreal, at which she was given a score of 10 for the first time for her horizontal bar exercise. During her career, she won nine Olympic medals, 5 of which were gold, including that of the general gymnastics title of 1976. She took up residence in the U.S. at the end of the 1980s. Comaneci was an extremely elegant gymnast.

Combine harvester, farm machine that cuts, threshes, and cleans grain. The latest, self-propelled models cut a swath 20 ft wide. Practically all kinds of grain, including rice, can be harvested by the combine, as can soybeans and other legumes. Combines were first developed in Michigan as long ago as the 1830s, but they came into widespread use only in the 1920s.

Combustion, rapid oxidation (or burning) of fuel in which heat and usually light are produced. In slow combustion (for instance, a glowing charcoal fire) the solid fuel may react directly with atmospheric oxygen; more commonly the fuel is first volatilized, and combustion occurs in the gas phase.

Comedy, literary work that aims primarily to amuse, often through ridicule, exaggeration, or satire of human nature and institutions, usually ending happily. Comedy was considered one of the two main dramatic categories in ancient Greece, the other being tragedy.

Comenius, John Amos (Jan Amos Komensk; 1592-1670), Czech educational reformer and Protestant theologian, last bishop of the old Moravian church (from 1632). *The Great Didactic* (1628-1632) was his best-known work. He advocated teaching in the vernacular instead of in Latin and favored a universal system open to women as well as men. His *Visible World* (1658) was probably the first children's picture book.

Comet, a celestial body that when seen from earth usually resembles a fuzzy star with a glowing tail. Comets are members of the solar system and are made up largely of dust and frozen gases loosely held together by gravitational attraction.

A comet typically travels in an elliptical orbit that is very elongated. At one end of its orbit, the comet swings around the sun. It is during this part of its orbit that a comet can be seen from the earth. Five or 10 or more comets typically appear each year, but most are too faint to be seen without a telescope. Some comets become very bright. The brightest comet remain visible in the nighttime sky for many months and may be visible even in the daytime.

A *periodic comet* is one that reappears at regular intervals, ranging from a few years for some comets to thousands of years for others. Astronomers believe that most comets come from the Oort cloud, a vast spherical cloud of material that extends as far as 5,000,000,000,000 miles (8,000,000,000,000 km) from the sun. (It is named after Jan Oort, a Dutch astronomer who first proposed its existence.) Other comets, particularly comets that orbit the sun in 200 years or less, probably come from an area much closer to the sun - the Kuiper belt, a disk-shaped region beyond the orbit the Neptune. (It is named after Gerard Kuiper, a Dutch-American astronomer who investigated it.)

Records of comets were made as long as 2,000 years ago by the Chinese, the Chaldeans, and the Egyptians. Many peoples have assigned special importance to major comets, often regarding them as omens.

In 1910, when the earth passed through the tail of Halley's comet, fears arose concerning its possible effect on the earth, but there

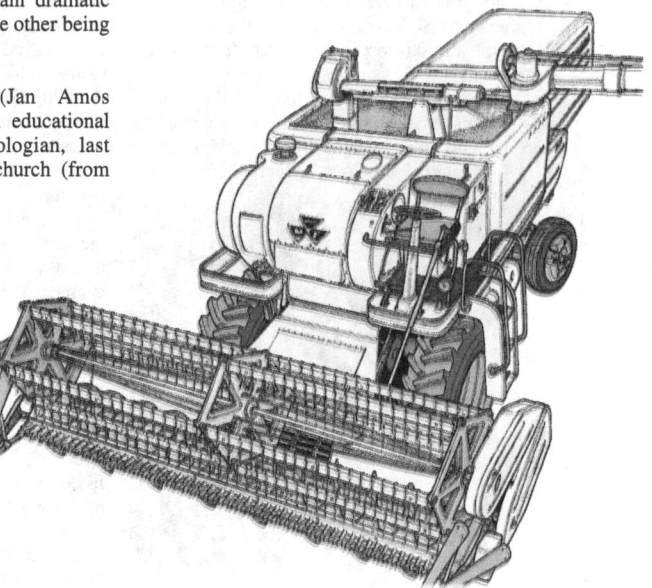

A self-propelled combine harvester cuts and threshes the crop, in order to separate the grain from the straw.

C

C

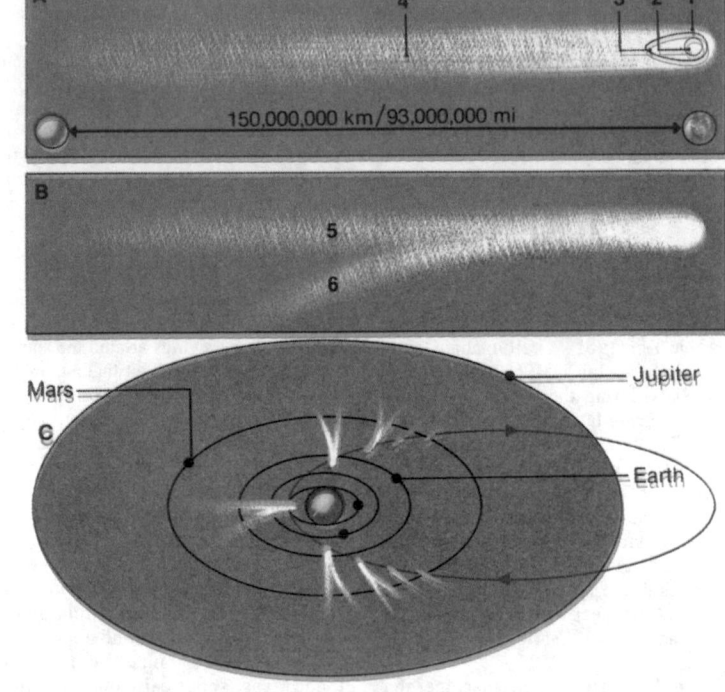

150,000,000 km/93,000,000 mi

Mars

Jupiter

Earth

C

Although all comets are part of the solar system, most of them orbit far from the sun. A comet (A) in the sun's vicinity consists of a bright, starlike nucleus (2) and a hazy, luminous coma (1), which together form the head (3). In addition, a tail (4) is usually formed, often reaching lengths comparable to the distance from the earth to the sun. As comets approach the sun (B), they often develop both a straight, ionized gas tail (5) and a curved, dusty tail (6). Throughout the comet's orbit (C), these tails will point away from the sun.

was little remarkable about the passage. If the main body of a comet were to enter the earth's atmosphere, some scientists believe it would disintegrate into thousands of meteors before striking the earth. Other scientists, however, believe that it might cause an explosion of great magnitude. In 1994, astronomers observed the collision between a comet and a planet for the first time when Comet Shoemaker-Levy 9 collided with Jupiter. The resulting explosions in Jupiter's atmosphere produced large, dark blotches that remained visible for several months.

When a comet is a great distance from the sun, it is a frozen mass of ice, dust, and other material. This body, called the *nucleus*, is typically 0.6 to 6 miles (1 to 10 km) in diameter.

As a comet approaches the sun, the nucleus begins to be warmed by the sun. Some of the ice and other material in the nucleus begins to change into gases, which then expand.

Ultraviolet radiation from the sun causes the gases to glow. The round, nebulous body of glowing gases that forms around the nucleus is called the *coma*, and it can reach a diameter of 60,000 miles (100,000 km) or more. The coma and nucleus are together known as the head of a comet.

As a comet continues to approach the sun it develops a *tail*. Comet tails always extend from the coma in the general direction away from the sun, because of the action of sunlight and other solar radiation on the tiny particles that make up the tail. Often there are two tails: one tail, composed of ionized atoms of gas, points directly away from the sun; the second tail, composed of dust, tends to be curved because of gravitational effects. Comet tails have reached a length of more than 90,000,000 miles (145,000,000 km).

Halley's comet was the first to be recognized as periodic. After calculating the comet's orbit, the English astronomer Edmund Halley concluded that the bright comets that had been seen in 1531, 1607, 1682 were really the same comet, and predicted - correctly - that it would reappear in 1758. It was seen again in 1835, 1910, and 1985-1986; it will next be seen in 2061. In early 1986, several spacecraft were sent past Halley's comet to study it. One came within 400 miles (640 km) of the nucleus and transmitted images to earth that showed the nucleus to be some 9 miles (15 km) long and 5 miles (8 km) wide.

In addition to Halley's comet, other prominent comets that have appeared in the 20th century include Comet Arlend-Roland (1957), Comet Ikeya-Seki (1965), Comet West (1976), and Comet Hale-Bopp (1997).

The brightest of these comets was Ikeya-Seki.
See also: Astronomy.

Comics, also known as comic strips, series of drawings, usually accompanied by captions or dialogue, telling a continuous story. The text, if any, is often conveyed by means of speech 'balloons.' The first comics were explicitly humorous, but the term is now applied to anything presented in the comic-strip style. Although comics may actually have originated with the English social satirists Thomas Rowlandson and George Cruikshank, they grew in popularity in the late 19th and early 20th century. At first devoted purely to farce and slapstick, the comics soon moved into the adventure market and then into science fiction, illustrated classics, social satire, and serious social criticism. Comics have added words to the American language and influenced dress habits. In 1954 the industry responded to criticism of the violence and horror by issuing a code for conduct.

Cominform (Communist Information Bureau), international organization set up in 1947 to coordinate among Communist parties in the Soviet Union, eastern Europe, and some capitalist countries. Essentially an agency of the Soviet government, it was disbanded by Nikita Khrushchev in 1956.
See also: Communism.

Comintern (Communist International), organization founded by the Russian Communist Party and composed of national Communist parties from all parts of the world. The Russian revolutionary leader V.I. Lenin called for the formation of a world revolutionary organization after the outbreak of World War I in 1914, but the first meeting of the Comintern was held only in 1919. Also known as the Third International (to distinguish it from the Second, or Socialist, International, a world organization of Social Democratic parties), the Comintern attempted during the 1920s to foster workers' revolution on a world scale. During the 1930s, however, it became essentially an organ of the Soviet government. Stalin dissolved it in 1943 as a gesture to his Western Allies during World War II.
See also: Communism.

Comitia, in ancient Rome, assemblies of people summoned in groups to vote on proposals presented by magistrates. Dating from c.500 B.C., comitia performed different functions during various periods of Roman history. The earliest such institution, the Comitia Curiata, confirmed the selection of Roman kings. Later comitia, such as the Comitia Centuriata (organized according to wealth) and Comitia Tributa (organized by tribe) voted on laws, established titles of authority, and judged criminals. By 100 A.D. the comitias' legislative and judicial powers had been abrogated.

Commando, military unit trained for swift, guerrilla-like raids into enemy territory. The British army adopted the word and the practice after the Boer War (1899-1902), and battalion-strength units were organized dur-

With the help of the science-fiction comic *Superman*, designed in 1938, the public could escape reality.

ing World War II. The U.S. army Special Forces and Ranger units are modeled after the British commandos.
See also: Guerrilla warfare.

Commedia dell'arte, form of Italian comedy that flourished in the 16th-18th centuries. Traveling professional actors (often wearing masks) improvised action and dialogue around outline plots with stock characters. The commedia had a lasting influence on the theater throughout Europe.

Commercial art, general term for any of the visual arts used in business, especially advertising, such as designing, drawing, and lettering for illustrations and advertisements, design and preparation of posters, billboards, display cards, packages, etc. The commercial arts are often distinguished from the fine arts in that their basic aim is to sell a product or service. But a more significant difference is that the products of commercial art have to be able to be reproduced by such techniques as zinc, steel, and halftone engraving; rotogravure; lithography; etching; electrotyping; and photography.

Commercial paper, generic term for various business documents involving the payment of money. Such documents include drafts, promissory notes, and bills of exchange. In a strict sense, the term denotes a short-term promissory note issued by a corporation. The note is redeemable for its full value, plus interest, on a given date.

Commission, military, written order and oath of service granting an individual the rank and authority of an officer in the armed services. A commission is accepted voluntarily and need not be renewed, though it may be resigned if allowed by law.

Committee for State Security *See:* KGB.

Committee of the whole, committee including the entire membership of an organization. It is convened to discuss matters whose disposition is not delegated to a smaller group.

Commodity exchange, formal market in which participants buy and sell contracts providing for the delivery of certain products at future dates. The world's major commodity exchanges are in New York, Chicago, and London. Prices set in these markets largely determine prices in other parts of the world. Commodities (metals, crops, livestock, etc.) tend to fluctuate in value depending on availability. Since contracts calling for future delivery set the price in advance, commodity exchanges allow for speculation in a rising market and hedging in a falling market.

Common carrier, person or company that transports people, goods, or messages for the public at large. Examples of common carriers are bus lines, railroads, airlines, express companies, telephone and telegraph companies, and pipelines.

Common law, body of laws based on court decisions and customs. It is usually contrasted to statute law, which is made by legislatures. Common law grew out of English custom and became established mainly by the adherence of judges to precedents, or previous decisions-a principle known as *stare decisis* (stand on things as decided). The decisions of earlier judges became the law of later ones. As new conditions arose, the body of the common law was expanded, and outdated principles fell into disuse, even if never actually abolished. Thus experience, rather than theorizing, furnished the basis for the development of common law. The body and concept of common law passed from England to the United States (except the state of Louisiana, which made the Code Napoléon the basis of its law), Canada (except Quebec), and other areas of the world that have been ruled or influenced by England. No organized body of law existed in England prior to the Norman conquest in 1066, but the Normans brought many new principles and greatly expanded legal institutions. The term *common law* itself came into general use during the reign of Edward I (1272-1307), who was responsible for a great deal of new legislation. Since by its very nature common law is relatively inflexible and not subject to change or adaptation to suit the needs of a particular case, the system of equity developed to permit judges to resort to the general principles of justice when existing law was inadequate to resolve a case fairly. Eventually, equity was merged with the common law. During the Middle Ages, Italian jurists pioneered the rediscovery of the principles of Roman law. These doctrines were accepted by many European countries, in which they then displaced the customary or common law. But the English legal system withstood the attempts of advocates of Roman law to establish their doctrine. The fight to maintain the authority of the common law, led by great lawyers such as Edward Coke, became part of the constitutional struggle of the 17th century between Parliament and the kings. When the English colonies in North America framed their legal systems after declaring their independence of the mother country, they either kept the English common law as a guide to judges or formally adopted its principles in their statutes and constitutions. There is no federal common law, though precedents in federal cases are very important in later decisions.

Common Market, European (EEC) European Economic community, established by the Treaty of Rome of on 25th March 1957, effective as of 1st January 1958, between the Benelux countries, France, Germany, and Italy as member states. Great Britain, Ireland, and Denmark joined the EEC in 1973, followed by Greece in 1981, and Spain and Portugal in 1986. In 1995, Sweden, Finland, and Austria entered the European Union, and with that, these countries automatically joined the European Communities. The objective of the EEC is to pursue steady and stable growth, to improve the standard of living, and to establish closer relationships between the participating countries. This is to be achieved by creating a single, large market and by means of a common policy in a number of areas. The

One of the stock characters of the Commedia dell'Arte is the greedy Venetian merchant Pantalone.

C

goal is complete economic union. Although the first stages have been completed, economic union is yet to be established. The internal market did, however, become effective on 1st January, 1993. As of 1st July 1967, the EEC, together with Euratom and the European Coal and Steel Community (ECSC), formed the European Communities. The EEC became a part of the European Union in 1992, at which time the name EEC was officially changed to European Community, as the official name for the pursuit of complete economic and monetary integration.
See also: European Community.

Commons, House of *See:* House of Commons.

Commonwealth, from the phrase 'common wealth' (public good), form of government based on the power and consent of the people. In the United States, the states of Massachusetts, Pennsylvania, Virginia, and Kentucky were historically known as commonwealths, as is Puerto Rico. The federated states of Australia are known as the Commonwealth of Australia, and various other nations are associated with Britain in the Commonwealth of Nations. In English history, the Commonwealth is the period of republican government (1649-1660) that followed the execution of Charles I.

Commonwealth Games, sports competition among amateur athletes from British Commonwealth countries, first held in Hamilton, Ontario, in 1930 under the name of British Empire Games. The games are held in a different Commonwealth city every four years. They include track and field events, badminton, swimming and diving, boxing, wrestling, and weightlifting.

Commonwealth of Independent States (CIS), a loose confederation of independent states that were once Soviet republics. The CIS was founded in 1991 by Russia, Ukraine, and Belarus, a few weeks before the Soviet Union collapsed. Other members are Armenia, Azerbaijan, Georgia,

C

Kazakhstan, Kyrgyzstan, Moldova, Tajikistan, Turkmenistan, and Uzbekistan. The Commonwealth's main purpose is to promote cooperation among members in political, economic, and military affairs. Particularly important are agreements to keep long-range nuclear weapons under unified control and to eventually destroy all such weapons or transfer them to Russia. Since its founding, conflict between members has been a major problem and the CIS has had little success in fostering political and military cooperation. Several members refused to sign a collective security agreement and some members formed independent national armies. In economic matters, however, the CIS has had some sucess. In 1993 most members signed an economic union pact, agreeing to eventually establish a customs and currency union.

Commonwealth of Nations, association of Britain and over 40 former colonies, now independent states, and their dependencies. Although not governed by a constitution or specific treaty, member states are linked by economic and cultural interests. The British monarch is recognized as the symbolic head

of the commonwealth. Commonwealth prime ministers and other officials meet at periodic conferences and exchange views on international, economic, and political affairs of mutual interest. Member states range in size from Canada, Australia, and India to Tonga and Fiji. Ireland has withdrawn from the commonwealth.

Communal society, cooperative group formed on the basis of shared interests (e.g., religious or political) and emphasizing the needs of the community above those of the individual. Communal societies usually forbid private possession of land and often restrict members' contact with the rest of society. Examples of communal societies are collective farms (kibbutzim) in Israel and Hutterite groups in Montana, South Dakota, and Canada.

Commune, term for small, locally governed territorial districts in France and some other countries. The commune's government structure resembles that of a township in the United States and includes a mayor and a council. The term was originally used to designate towns in medieval western Europe

During la semaine sanglante ('bloody week') of May 21-28, 1871, the Parisian communards resisted the troops of the Versailles government by barricading the streets and burning several buildings, including the Tuileries Palace (shown) and the Hôtel de Ville. The battle for Paris ended with 33,000 people dead. Harsh reprisals followed.

that had gained self-government through rebellion, treaty, or charter.

Communication, flow of information from one point (the source) to another (the receiver). The term is also used to describe the act of transmitting or making known.

Communications satellite, artificial earth-orbiting object used to relay radio signals between points on earth. The orbits of most such satellites are above the equator at a height of 22,300 mi (35,900 km). At that altitude a satellite orbits the earth at the same rate as the earth turns; it thus remains over a fixed point on the surface. The satellite carries a number of transponders that receive radio beams from the earth and retransmit them. The satellite is powered by solar cells. Communications satellites carry television programs, telephone calls, and business data.

Communion, in Christian churches, name for the sacrament of the Lord's Supper. Communion, from the Latin word for 'participation,' is a ritual repetition of the Last Supper before Christ's crucifixion, when he told his disciples, 'Take, eat. This is my body... This is my blood... This do in remembrance of me.' In most Christian churches, the rite of communion involves the eating of a wafer of unleavened bread and the drinking of wine.
See also: Christianity.

Communism, ideal economic order in which property and the means of production are held in common in a classless society. Elements of communism are as old as the Golden Age described by Greek poets and philosophers as a time long ago when people shared all things equally and lived simply. Primitive forms of communism are also discernible in the communities of early Christians and in the teachings and practices of certain groups considered heretical in the Middle Ages. The *Utopia* of Thomas More (1478-1535) also exerted a powerful influence on Western culture and politics, adding to that body of writings which inspired attempts to create a more perfect society. But

Intelsat satellites orbit above the equator over the Pacific (1), Atlantic (2), and Indian (3) oceans. Each satellite's orbital velocity is synchronized with the rotation of the Earth. They thus remain in fixed positions relative to the surface and can relay messages among most of the world's inhabited areas.

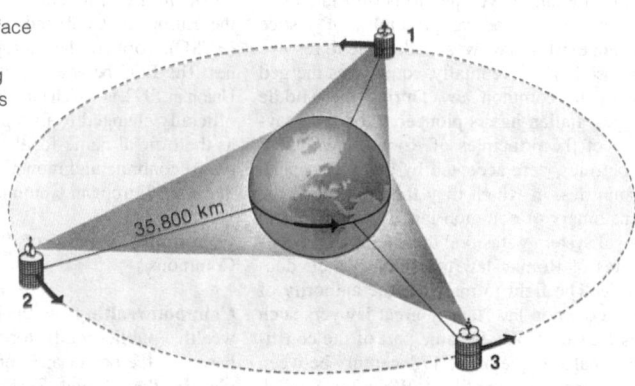

35,800 km

The Intelsat IV series of communications satelites, which were launched in 1971, were 17 ft (528 cm) high and could relay more than 4,000 twoway telephone calls or 12 television programs simultaneously. Included among the satellite's major components were a spot beam communications antenna (1), wide beam transmitting and receiving antenna (2), telemetry and command antenna (3), solar panels (4) and apogee motor for the satellite's final placement in orbit (5).

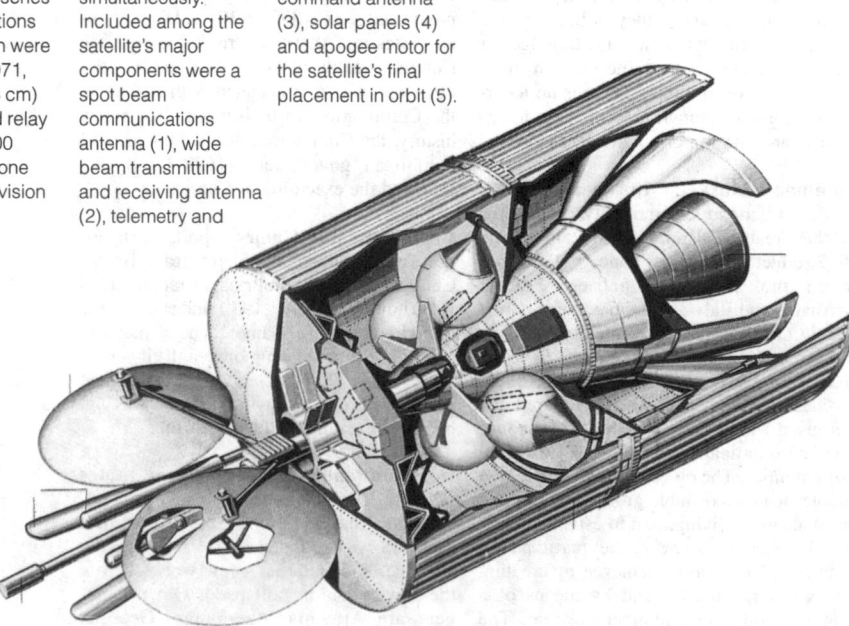

modern communism, as developed by Karl Marx and Friedrich Engels through their writings in the mid to late 19th century, is radically different from its predecessors.

As set forth in their seminal work, the *Communist Manifesto* (1848), the economic progress that accompanied the rise of modern capitalism divided society into 2 hostile camps, the bourgeoisie, who controlled capital and the means of production, and the proletariat or working class, who must sell their labor in order to live. This division was not seen as static but rather as dynamic. It was, in fact, a conflict central to understanding historical events, the development of cultures and civilizations, and the evolution of society. Marx and Engels repeatedly pointed out in their writings that their argument was based upon a study and analysis of actual political and economic developments, especially contemporary events, and was not filtered through or distorted by metaphysical abstraction. They argued that their analyses and conclusions rested on a scientific basis and, according to their analyses, the destruction of the bourgeois social and economic order and the rise and spread of a communist order throughout the world was historically inevitable. These ideas were more fully developed in the succeeding decades culminating in Marx's major work, *Das Kapital*.

Marx and Engels were careful to distinguish communism from socialism. As Engels explained in the preface to the English edition of the *Manifesto* (1888), they could not have called their work a *Socialist Manifesto* because the socialists were either followers of Utopian visionaries like Robert Owen or Charles Fourier, or mere 'social quacks' trying to remedy specific working class grievances rather than undertake full-scale revolution.

Communist parties were founded to advance the practical and effective cause of the proletariat and achieve communism through political action based upon strict party discipline. V. I. Lenin's Bolshevik party originally split from its fellow communists by espousing the violent overthrow of established regimes. In 1917, it adopted the title of Communist Party, and, thanks to the success of the Russian Revolution, enjoyed nearly unchallenged authority over international communism until 1948, when Yugoslavia rejected Soviet influence. In the 1960s, China under Mao Tse Tung would create a deeper and much more serious rift among communists.

In the more than 70 years since the Russian Revolution, communist regimes have proliferated, particularly in the Third World. Politically, they have been characterized by one-party rule, corrupt and inefficient bureaucracies, brutal and repressive secret police organizations, forced labor camps, strict censorship and thought control, the systematic murder of political opponents and entire groups of people considered dangerous to the state or the party and numbering in the millions. Economically, even the larger powers, the former Soviet Union and China, though they have succeeded in creating huge military establishments, have failed to provide for basic needs for their people, including food. Beginning in 1987, major commu-

nist regimes, led by Russia, openly admitted the failures of communism and have been looking to capitalist and pluralist systems in restructuring their governments, economies, and societies.

Communist Manifesto *See:* Communism; Marx, Karl.

Communist Party *See:* Communism.

Community, term used in the social sciences to designate a group of people within a larger society sharing similar customs, interests, characteristics or beliefs. Biologists define communities as ecological entities consisting of interdependent populations of flora (plants) and fauna (animals).

Community property, legal system of property ownership by husband and wife. Under the system, any property acquired by either spouse after marriage, except by gift or inheritance, is considered as being owned by both. Generally, each spouse may dispose by will of only a part of his or her half of the community property and is powerless to affect the other's half. In case of divorce the property is divided.

Comoros

Capital:	Moroni
Area:	719 sq mi (1,862 sq km)
Population:	614,000
Language:	Arabic, French
Government:	Islamic republic
Independent:	1975
Head of gov.:	Prime minister
Per capita:	US $710
Monetary unit:	1 Comorian franc = 100 centimes

Comoros, officially Federal Islamic Republic of the Comoros, an independant island-state in the Indian Ocean off the east coast of Africa, between Mozambique and Madagascar. Its area is 719 sq mi (1,862 sq km) and occupies three of the four main islands of the Comoros group, Grand Comore (or Njazidja), Anjouan (or Nzwani) and Moheli (or Mwali). The fourth, Mayotte, though claimed by the republic, remains under French administration: it chose to do so in 1975. The islands are volcanic in origin

The Chinese People's Army plays an important role. Many of its leaders wield considerable influence over the eleven military regions into which the country is divided. The army is not only a military apparatus, it also serves educational purposes. Here, soldiers are given education during a mass meeting.

and are hilly to mountainous. The climate is tropical with distinct wet and dry seasons. The Comoros is an extremely poor country. The main occupations are farming and fishing. Moroni, on Grande Comore, is the capital. In 1992 the first free elections (since 1975) were held, but invalidated. Troubles continued. In 1997 separatistic movements on the islands Anhouan and Moheli announced they wanted to rejoin France. However, France refused and in 1998 the two islands declared themselves independent. In 2002, the three islands were re-united

Compact disc (CD), optical rotating disc, for the reproduction of music (CD audio); also used for large amounts of information and images on screen: CD-ROM (Compact Disc Read Only Memory). Silver-colored plate with a diameter of 12 cm, developed by Sony in cooperation with Philips. The recording techniques and reproduction techniques are based on the following principle: the analogue recording of a sound signal, created by means of a pulse code modulation (PCM), is repeatedly measured at very small intervals, digitally recorded, and converted into a binary code, which is applied to the surface of the plate in the form of small pits. These are scanned by means of a laser in the compact disc player and then converted from digital back to analogue. The plate is covered with an invisible plastic layer to protect it from damage. The memory capacity is huge: one CD can contain 300,000 typed A4 pages (640 MB)`. The CD has a large number of variations for various purposes, such as CD-i, CD-e, CD-WORM and CD-s.

Comparative psychology, branch of psychology concerned with the study of animal (including human) behavior at different stages of development to discern similarities and differences in species. A single activity (for example, mating) performed by different species may be investigated, or the be-

C

C

havioral pattern of 2 or more related species may be studied, either in their natural environment or in controlled surroundings. The principal behavioral patterns studied by comparative psychologists include communication, learning, migration, orientation, reproductive behavior, and social behavior.
See also: Psychology.

Compass, instrument used to indicate direction. Navigators on ships and aircraft use a compass to determine the direction in which they are heading. There are 2 main kinds of compasses: magnetic compasses and gyrocompasses. Magnetic compasses point to the magnetic north pole; adjustments must be made to determine the true north.
See also: Navigation.

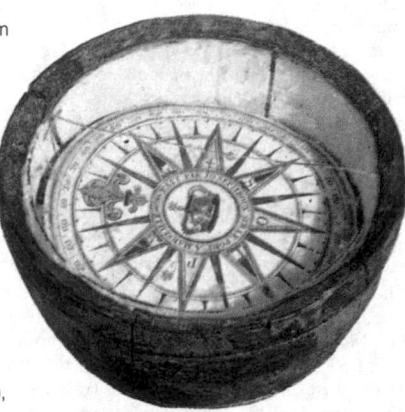

A liquid compass from about 1775, made by Joseph Rou from Marseilles. Here, the fact is being used that liquid in a pan always remains horizontal. On the points of the compasscard one can read (in Italian) the initials of the most important quarters: G-greco (Northeast), S-sirocco (Southeast), O-ostro (South), L-libeccio (Southwest), P-penete (West), M-maestro (Northwest).

Compass plant, or pilotweed, prairie plant (*Silphium laciniatum*) of the family Compositae. Its name comes from the tendency of its lower leaves to line up in a north-south direction. The compass plant has a tall stalk, up to 12 ft (3.5 m), covered with short, rough hairs and large solitary flowers.

Competency-based education, teaching programs requiring students to attain specified levels of achievement in designated courses or skills. Some programs focus on the fundamental skills of reading, writing, and mathematics, while others include such disciplines as science and social studies.

Compositae, largest family of flowering plants, including more than 20,000 species. Their characteristic feature is that what appears to be a single flower is actually a flower head made up of a large number of florets. Those in the center, closely packed and resembling the pile of a rug, are simple tubular flowers having both stamens (the male part) and pistils (the female part). Surrounding them is a ring of ray flowers, often mistaken for petals, which have flattened corollas and are sterile or bear only pistils.

Compound, in chemistry, any substance composed of atoms of more than one element chemically bonded to form a fixed structure with distinctive properties. Compounds may be separated into two groups: organic (containing carbon atoms)

and inorganic (all other compounds). Any compound may be described by a chemical formula that indicates the composition of one of its molecules, the molecule being the smallest unit of that compound to have the characteristics of that compound. The chemical formula for water, for example, is H_2O, which indicates that a molecule of water is made up of two atoms of hydrogen and one atom of oxygen.
See also: Chemistry.

Compound eye, organ of vision consisting of many tiny, closely packed lenses. The number of lenses varies from fewer than 100 to more than 20,000, depending on species. Compound eyes differ from the camera-type eye of only one lens. They apparently produce 'mosaics' of light and color rather than clear images. Members of the phylum Arthropoda (spiders, insects, crustaceans, etc.) have compound eyes.
See also: Insect.

Compton, Arthur Holly (1892-1962), U.S. physicist, Nobel Prize winner for physics (1927), for his discovery of the *Compton effect* (x-rays increase in wavelengths when they collide with electrons). At the University of Chicago Compton also contributed to the development of the atomic bomb during World War II.
See also: Physics.

Compton-Burnett, Ivy (1892-1969), English novelist. Her many novels, including *Pastors and Masters* (1925), *Parents and Children* (1941), and *Mother and Son* (1955), often feature crime and violence in English upper middle-class society at the turn of the century.

Computer, automatic device capable of carrying out calculations according to a predetermined set of instructions. First developed in the 1940s, their technological development has been rapid. Computers have taken over routine commercial calculations and are used in scientific research and technology design. Computers are usually classified according to their mode of operation: analog, digital, or a combination of the two. *Analog computers* use some measurable quantity to represent physically the calculation being carried out. They can perform simulations, such as the outcome of a missile launch or the effects of wind and rain on the flight of an aircraft. cold war*Digital computers* (such as the personal computer) contain 4 basic units: an input/output device, an arithmetical unit to perform basic math operations, a memory, and a control unit to interpret instructions and supervise operations. The applications of digital computers include forecasting, management, and preparation. Computers in the 1990s are becoming faster, smaller, and more powerful. Engineers are working to make computers more sophisticated, user-friendly, and accessible to all aspects of life.

Computer graphics, use of a computer for drawing lines, graphs, designs, and pictures. With the proper programs, computers are capable of displaying shapes as they would look from any angle. This has revolutionized

the process of drafting and has also given rise to new art forms.
See also: Computer.

Computerized axial tomography *See:* CAT.

Computervirus *See:* Virus (computer).

Comstock Law, U.S. legislation, passed in 1873 and named for anti-vice crusader Anthony Comstock. The law prohibited the mailing of obscene materials, defined at one time to include information on birth control and abortion. Comstock personally was responsible for the destruction of tons of literature and pictures that he considered objectionable.
See also: Obscenity and pornography.

Comstock Lode, enormously rich vein of gold and silver discovered near what became Virginia City in Nevada during the late 1850s. The lode, which eventually earned over $500 million, was named after one of its many claimants, Henry Comstock. The Virginia City mines brought settlers to Nevada, establishing a boom town and overnight fortunes. The lode was abandoned by the turn of the century.

Comte, Auguste (1798-1857), French philosopher and sociologist. His best-known work is *The Course of Positive Philosophy* (1830-1842), which introduced the philosophy that later came to be called positivism. Comte believed that human society had 3 phases of development, which he called theological, metaphysical, and positive. Society is ruled by rational science only when it reaches the last stage. Comte invented the term 'sociology' and influenced such thinkers as John Stuart Mill and Herbert Spencer.
See also: Positivism.

Conakry (pop. 1,500,000), capital and largest city of Guinea in West Africa. Located on Tombo Island on the Atlantic coast, Conakry is a modern port and a commercial center.
See also: Guinea.

Concentration camp, prison for the detention of political or military suspects, frequently found in totalitarian countries and sometimes in democratic nations during time of war. Concentration camps differ sharply from other prisons in the absence of regular judicial proceedings and the fact that prisoners may be held indefinitely. Camps have often served to confine large segments of the population felt to be dangerous to the government. During World War II the United States placed several thousands of its Japanese-American citizens in camps until the end of the war. The most notorious concentration camps were those maintained by the Nazi regime in Germany before and during World War II. Jews and a minority of nationals from occupied countries performed hard manual labor in a semistarved state. Those unwanted or unfit to work were sent to extermination centers to be gassed and afterward burned in incinerators. Sadism and torture were practiced in these camps. More than 6 million men, women, and children

died in the German concentration camps, of which the largest were at Auschwitz, Dachau, Buchenwald, and Belsen.
See also: Auschwitz; Belsen; Buchenwald; Dachau; Holocaust.

Concepción (Chile) (pop. 318,000), Chile, the capital of Concepción Province. It lies on the Bío-Bío River near the Pacific Ocean; its port is at Talcahuano. Concepción is a commercial and transportation center serving Chile's major agricultural region, the Central Valley. It is also an industrial city. The University of Concepción is here.
Concepción was founded as a Spanish outpost against Araucanian Indians in 1550 and remained a frontier settlement for several centuries. Throughout its history, the city has been devastated periodically by earthquakes, most recently in 1939 and 1960.

Conceptual art, an art trend dating from the middle of the 1960s up to the beginning of the 1970s, in which the abstract idea, the concept, is emphasized and not its visualization. Ideas, which often concern intangible projects and strongly appeal to the understanding and imaginative powers of the viewer, were presented by means of spoken, written, or printed texts. Representatives included, among others, Sol LeWitt, Joseph Kosuth, Jan Dibbets, and Lawrence Weiner. Though many returned to a form of presentation that was visually more appealing (LeWitt, Dibbets), it is impossible to imagine art without the influence of this particular trend.

Concerto, musical composition in which unequal musical forces play in opposition to each other, usually 1 solo instrument against a large orchestra. The 3- movement orchestral form was elaborated by J.S. Bach out of the *concerto da camera*, a type of chamber music. George Friedrich Handel added the *cadenza* (improvised or written out musical interlude for the soloist) as a regular feature. Wolfgang Amadeus Mozart set the style for the modern concerto: The orchestra announces an opening subject with a *tutti* (a passage for full orchestra), then takes a subordinate position when the solo instrument enters, thus establishing the pattern of interchanges.

Conch, name once applied to all mollusks-hence the term 'conchology'-but now restricted to certain marine gastropod mollusks with large spiral shells. The shells have been used by primitive people throughout the world as trumpets. Conches are also prized as ornaments and for their meat. They live in warm waters.

Concord (pop. 35,000), capital of the American state of New Hampshire, on the Merrimack River. Center of trade, industry, financial services, and transport for an extensive agricultural area. Graphic industry, production of electronic equipment, and insurance agencies.
In 1659, white immigrants established a trading post here in Native American territory. In 1725, Massachusetts Bay Colony gave its permission to establish Penacook Plantation at this location. It became the town of Rumford 8 years later. Violent conflict between the states of Massachusetts and New Hampshire, which lasted over 20 years, was resolved in 1762, three years before the town was given its current name.
The world's largest factory for stagecoaches, which played a very important role in opening up the West, could be found here in the 19th century.
The white granite that was used to build the Library of Congress originated from here. A place of interest is the State House (1816-1819).
See also: Massachusetts.

Concordat, treaty concluded between the pope and the secular government of a state to regulate religious affairs within the state and deal with such questions as the appointment of bishops and the status of church property. The most notable concordat was the Concordat of 1801 between Napoleon and Pope Pius VII which reestablished the Roman Catholic Church in France. The best-known recent concordat (1929) is the Lateran Treaty, arranged between Pius XI and Victor Emmanuel III of Italy which established Vatican City as a sovereign state.

Concrete, versatile structural building material made by mixing broken stone or gravel with sand, cement, and water. Initially moldable, the cement hardens into a solid mass. Concrete is often reinforced by embedding steel bars in it to bear the tension. It is used for all building elements and for bridges, dams, canals, and highways, often as precast units.
See also: Cement.

Concussion, temporary malfunction of brain activity, often including unconsciousness, due to a blow to the head causing the brain to jolt against the inner skull, injuring the brain's outer surface. Treatment usually consists of rest and close observation.

Condé, Louis II de Bourbon, Prince de (1621-1686), also called the Great Condé, an outstanding French general of the Thirty Years' War, related to the Bourbon royal family. He turned against Mazarin, led troops in the Fronde rebellion, and served with Spain; but was pardoned and fought for Louis XIV in the Dutch Wars.

Condensation, in physics, change of a substance from the gaseous (vapor) to the liquid state. Condensation occurs when warm air meets cold surfaces or mixes with cold air. Dew, fog, and clouds are the result of condensation of water vapor in the atmosphere.
See also: Physics.

Condensed-matter physics *See:* Solid-state physics.

Condominium, in real estate, individual ownership in property, such as an apartment, that is part of a larger complex owned in common. A cooperative building differs from a condominium in that tenants do not actually own their apartments; they hold shares in a corporation entitling them to a long-term 'proprietary' lease.
See also: Real estate.

Condor, one of two species of vultures and the largest flying birds in existence. They have broad wings with a span of 10 ft (3 m) and weigh up to 25 lb (11 kg). The Andean condor (*Vultur gryphus*), the larger of the two, is still fairly common in the Andes, but the numbers of the California condor (*Gymnogyps californianus*) have been greatly reduced.

Condorcet, Marie Jean Antoine Nicolas de Caritat, marquis de (1743-1794), French mathematician and philosopher. A brilliant thinker, he wrote biographies of Voltaire and Turgot, important essays on integral calculus and the theory of probability, and works in political science. He is best known for his *Sketch for a Historical Picture of the Progress of the Human Mind* (1795), which sets forth his belief in the perfectibility of mankind.

Cone, three-dimensional geometric figure whose base is a closed curve, such as a circle or an ellipse, and whose dimensional sides meet at a single point called the vertex.
See also: Geometry.

Conestoga wagon, large covered wagon used by North American pioneers. Originating about 1725 in Pennsylvania, it became the chief means of transporting settlers and freight across the Alleghenies until about 1850. It had big, broad-rimmed wheels and a canvas roof supported by wooden hoops, and was pulled by 4-6 horses.
See also: Pioneer life in America.

Confederate States of America, government formed by the Southern states (first seven, then eleven states) that seceded from the United States of America between Dec. 1860 and May 1861, which was the immediate cause for the American Civil War [1861-1865].
See also: Civil War, U.S..

Confession, in Christianity, admission of sin, an aspect of repentance. General confession may be made in a congregation; private confession may be made to God or to a priest. The latter form, a sacrament of the Roman Catholic and Eastern churches, is

Linear transmission is possible between two gears of different shapes, e.g. with the hyperbolic gears that are shown here. Such a gear wheel has a hyperbolic cross section in the axial plane, and a circular cross section in the plane that is perpendicular to the axis. The teeth become increasingly smaller towards the centre, which is difficult to realize technically, so that only part of the surfaces in the model shown is toothed, nevertheless, they are a practical gear-pair. Such systems can be recognized by their appearance: they are like bevel gears whose axes do not intersect, but cross each other.

C

C

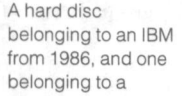

A hard disc belonging to an IBM from 1986, and one belonging to a camera from 2001. The featherweight disc contains more electronic memory than the apparatus –weighing 30 kilos– from 1986!

Reconstruction of one of the computer's predecessors, the 'Difference Engine I', designed by Charles Babbage (1792-1871). This machine was able to do simple differential calculus.

The production of microchips is a mainly mechanical process. The human factor means that sterility is of the utmost importance: one hair or flake of skin can have all kinds of effects on the chip's workings.

A LCD monitor. The basis of a Liquid Crystal Display is a layer of film between two thin glass plates, that come equipped with transistors, crystals, and color and polarization filters. The computer instructs the transistors to make the crystals lighter or darker, and to use the filters to change the color. This invention enables us to produce much flatter and lighter monitors than we could using traditional techniques, and they also use forty percent less energy.

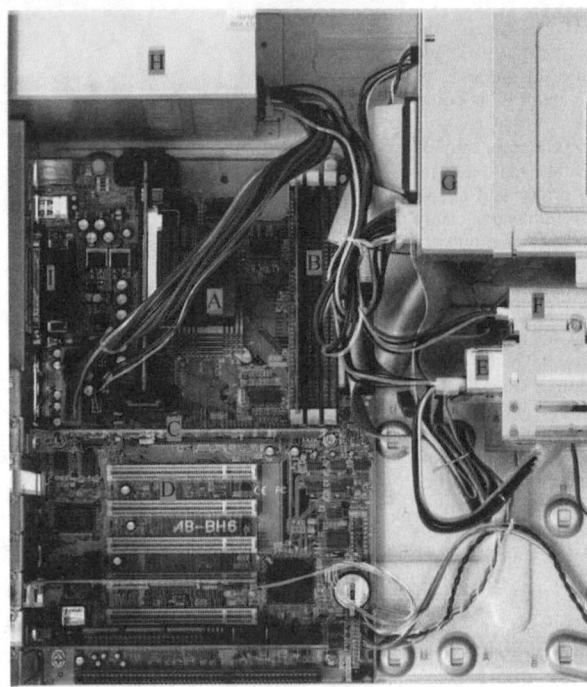

The interior of a modern fighter plane. Computer technology has made warfare largely 'electronic'. Radar systems, armament, the flight paths of a fighter plane can be calculated by on board computers; the pilot interprets the computer's data and uses it to his best advantage.

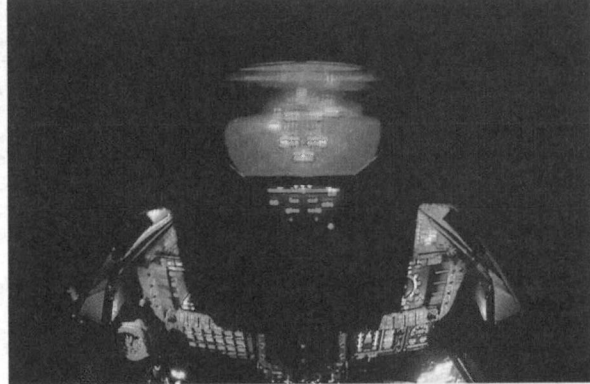

Interior of a personal computer (PC). The most important components are:
A- Processor with cooler
B- Memory (RAM)
C- Video card (graphic adaptor)
D- PCI port (for extension cards)
E- Hard disc
F- Floppy drive
G- CD-ROM drive
H- Power supply
I- Printer port

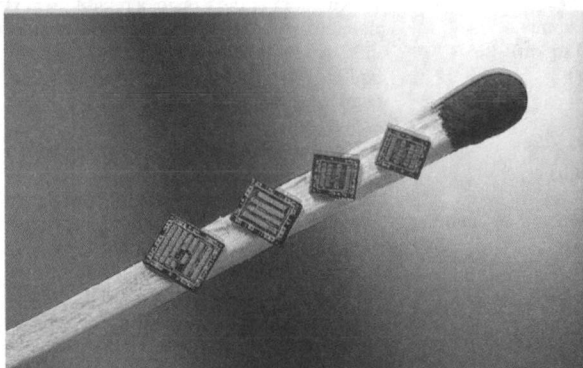

The development of the microchip has played an important role in the power and compactness of modern computers. A large number of different circuits are joined on the carefully fabricated plates to form a complete calculation unit that can empower all the electronic functions in a computer. The size of the plates has decreased spectacularly over the years.

Enlarged picture of a chip.

C

also observed in some Lutheran and Episcopalian churches.

Confirmation, rite of certain Christian churches, usually administered in adolescence. The candidates confirm the promises made at their baptism, and the bishop lays his hands on them, invoking the Holy Spirit upon them. In the Roman Catholic and Eastern churches confirmation is a sacrament. *See also:* Christianity.

Conflict of interest, situation in which an employee, part owner, officer or director of an organization has a financial or other interest in another organization that could cause him or her to favor one at the expense of the other.

Confucianism, philosophy based on the thinking of Confucius, the great Chinese philosopher and moralist. Confucianism teaches a moral and social philosophy and code of behavior based on certain abstract qualities and strengths, such as love, peace, harmony, order, humanity, wisdom, courage, and fidelity, without appealing to any ultimate higher authority or God. Heaven is the highest state one can attain, although no actual God-personality exists. One arrives at this perfect state by cultivating virtues such as curiosity, knowledge, patience, and sincerity, and by developing a personality based on the harmony of emotions and the harmony between the self and the universe. Thus people take their place in the universal pattern of creation, and immortality is won by those whose good name lives after them. Confucianism also has a strong social and political message. It teaches that individuals must not only cultivate themselves but must also enrich other people's lives. *See also:* Confucius.

Confucius (551-479 B.C.), Chinese philosopher and sage, founder of Confucianism, the great moral and religious system of China. He began teaching at age 20, gathering

The Chinese philosopher Confucius on an illustration from an early seventeenth-century Chinese encyclopaedia.

about him a group of disciples. During the next 30 years he evolved the code of 'right living' that was the basis of his philosophy. The ruling prince of the state of Lu appointed him magistrate of the city of Chang-tu, where Confucius put his principles into effect with great success. But he fell out of favor with the succeeding prince and for 13 years wandered with his followers, vainly seeking a patron and someone he could train as his 'model ruler.' Confucius's sayings and the most reliable information about his life are preserved in the *Confucian Analects*, compiled by his disciples shortly after his death. Although Confucius takes his place beside Gautama Buddha, Jesus, and Mohammed as founder of one of the world's great religions, he differs from them in being a rationalist who takes no account of mysticism or spirituality. His philosophy of human relationships, based on the golden rule 'What you do not wish done to yourself, do not do to others,' is essentially an appeal to reason and humanity.

Congenital defect *See:* Birth defect.

Conglomerate, corporation that has expanded into the production and sale of products quite different from those with which it was initially involved. Thus, a company identified with the extraction of metals may become conglomerate by moving into retail food, automobile accessories, and motion pictures.

Congo

Capital:	Brazzaville
Area:	132,047 sq mi
	(342,000 sq km)
Population:	2,958,000
Language:	French
Government:	Republic
Independent:	1960
Head of gov.:	Prime minister
Per capita:	US $900
Monetary unit:	1 CFA franc = 100 centimes

Congo, Republic of the Congo (also: Congo-Brazzaville), formerly part of French Equatorial Africa. It lies on the equator, with Gabon and the Atlantic Ocean to the west and Congo (Zaïre) to the east.

Land. A low, treeless plain extends from the

Dugout canoes are still used as vehicles of transportation along the Congo (Zaire) River in west-central Africa. This stretch of the Congo forms the boundary between Zaire and the Congo.

coast inland for about 40 mi (64 km). The land then rises to the mountainous area of the Mayombé Escarpment, with its series of sharp ridges, a region of dense tropical rain forest. To the north is a plateau covered with grassland. The (Congo River basin in the northeast is an area of numerous rivers and dense, tropical forests. The Congo and its tributary, the Ubangi River, form most of the border between Congo and DR Congo.

People. Some 60% of the population is rural, but there has been a major drift to the towns. Most people are Bantu speakers. French is the official language. The government has placed an emphasis on education, but the rate of illiteracy is still high.

Economy. Although the Congo has rich oil resources, a varied manufacturing sector, and ports providing it and its neighbors with vital outlets to the world market, it has had serious economic setbacks, mainly due to political instability and poor economic planning and management. The agricultural sector is underdeveloped.

History. The Congo was originally part of the Kingdom of the Kongo, a region first explored by the Portuguese in the 15th century and later broken up into smaller states and exploited by European slave traders. It became a French colony in 1891, an overseas territory of France in 1946, and an independent republic in 1960. Periodic civil strife from 1963 onward led to an army takeover in 1968. Following a presidential assassination in 1977 and subsequent martial law, the Congolese Labor Party, the sole legal party since 1970, confirmed a military head of state, Col. Denis Sassou-Nguesso, in 1979. Democratization in the early 1990s was accompanied by trouble and violence which eased off after a while. In 1997 the capital was largely destroyed as a result of the power struggle between Saessou-Nguesso (supported by Angolese troops) and the Congo government. Sessou-Nguesso ousted the democratically chosen president Pascal Lissouba (elected in 1992) and reinstalled himself as president. Shortly afterwards, the country was closely involved in the power struggle in the neighboring country Congo (Zaïre).

In 1997 a civil war broke out. With the peace agreement a new constitutional law was accepted in 2001, but the following year, the goverment had to fight the rebels once again.

Congo (Kinshasa) *See:* Congo (Zaïre).

Congo River, or Zaire River, second-longest river in Africa. It flows north and west 2,700 mi (4,345 km) from its source in the Chambezi River, Zambia, to the Atlantic Ocean in western Zaire. In volume of water, it is second only to the Amazon. The Congo River was renamed the Zaire by Zaire's former President Mobutu in 1971.

Congo (Zaïre)

Capital:	Kinshasa
Area:	905,446 sq mi
	(2,344,885 sq km)
Population:	55,225,000
Language:	French
Government:	Presidential republic
Independent:	1960
Head of gov.:	Prime minister
Per capita:	US$ 530
Monetary unit:	1 Congolese franc =
	100 centimes

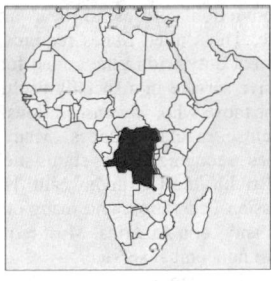

Congo (Zaïre) (formerly Zaïre, the Belgian Congo, the Democratic Republic of the Congo), officially Democratic Republic Congo since 1997, nation in west-central Africa. With an area of 905,446 sq mi (2,345,095 sq km), Congo is bordered by Angola on the southwest; Congo on the west; the Central African Republic and Sudan on the north; Uganda, Rwanda, Burundi, and Tanzania on the east; and Zambia on the southeast.
Land and climate. Central Congo, which straddles the equator, is a large, low plateau covered by rain forest. There is a higher, drier plateau in the southeast. In the east, on the border with Uganda, are the mountains of the Ruwenzori Range and lakes Albert, Edward, and Tanganyika. The Congo River, one of the largest in Africa, flows west to the Atlantic, where the country narrows to a 25-mi (40-km) wide coastline. Congo has a hot, rainy climate.
People. The population is divided among many groups, among which the Kongo are the most numerous. Other important peoples include the Mongo, Luba, and Zande. There are Nilotic-speaking peoples living primarily in the north, and Pygmies live in the east. About 200 languages are spoken, most of them in the Bantu family of languages.

French is the official language, but Lingola and Swahili are common. Most of the people are Christians, but sizable minorities adhere to traditional African religions. The capital of the country is Kinshasa.
Economy. The mainstay of Congo's economy is mining. The country has 65% of the world's reserves of cobalt and copper, the principal exports. Congo is also a leading diamond producer. The country has a diversified industrial sector including food processing, chemicals, cement, and textiles. Its farms produce cash crops of coffee, rubber, palm oil, cocoa, and tea.
History. First Pygmies and later Bantus were the original black African inhabitants of the region. The first Europeans in the area were Portuguese following in the wake of Diogo Cão, who came in 1482. In 1885 King Leopold II of Belgium took control of an area he called the Congo Free State; in 1908 it became the Belgian Congo and was a rich and profitable colony. The Belgian Congo became independent in 1960 and, as the Republic of the Congo, had Joseph Kasavubu as president and Patrice Lumumba as premier. The fledgling state was unable to maintain either stability or unity, and shortly after independence Moise Tshombe urged the secession of the mineral-rich province of Katanga (now Shaba). Before Katanga rejoined the nation in 1963, the UN and Belgium sent troops and both the United States and the USSR had taken sides in the conflict. In 1965, following continuing unrest, Maj. Gen. Joseph Mobutu, later Mobutu Sese Seko, took control and has been president since 1970. The Democratic Republic of the Congo was renamed Zaïre in 1971 and adopted its current constitution in 1978. Although Zaïre is rich in mineral resources, mismanagement and decreases in world-market prices have led to severe economic problems. In 1990 Mobutu pledged to establish a democratic system of government but took no concrete action, and unrest continued. In 1996 an armed rebellion broke out in eastern Zaire. The following year Mobutu was driven from office and rebel leader Laurent Kabila took control of the government, renaming the country Democratic Republic of the Congo. Kabila pledged to institute democratic reforms but instead ruled as a dictator. In 1998 a rebellion was launched against the Kabila government with the support of Rwanda, which was dissatisfied by Kabila's reluctance to crack down on anti-Rwandan militias operating in eastern Congo. The Rwandan-backed group was close to taking the capital in August when the armies of three other neighboring countries, Angola, Namibia, and Zimbabwe, intervened, forcing a rebel retreat to their stronghold in the eastern part of the country.
In January 2001, Kabila was shot and killed by a body-guard. He was succeeded by his son Joseph. According to refugee organizations, approximately 2.5 million people were killed in the war. In the course of 2002, peace was concluded with the surrounding countries and the rebels. During the war an important part of the conflict was formed by the fight for control of the production of the mineral coltan, which is used for the production of mobile phones, computer chips, etc.

Congregational Church, Protestant church

that holds that each local congregation should have complete autonomy, though congregations may form loose associations. In the 16th century Robert Browne first stated Congregational doctrine. In the 17th century Congregationalists established churches in the New England colonies and founded Harvard and Yale universities.
See also: Protestantism.

Congress of the United States, legislative branch of the U.S. federal government. Congress consists of 2 houses: the Senate, composed of 2 members from each state, and the House of Representatives, in which seats are appointed to the states on the basis of population. House membership, which was 65 in 1789, has grown with the nation's population but is now permanently fixed at 435. Membership is in proportion to state population as determined every 10 years by the census, but every state has at least 1 representative. The whole House is elected every 2 years. The U.S. Senate is composed of 100 members, 2 from each state. Since the Senate was created to represent the interests of the states, senators were elected by the state legislatures, rather than by popular vote, until 1913. The Senate is a continuing body; its members serve 6-year terms and only one-third of them are elected every 2 years. If a senator dies in office, the governor of the state names a replacement to serve until the next election.

Congreve, William (1670-1729), English Restoration dramatist, known for his comedies of manners. Among his comedies are *The Old Bachelor* (1693), *Love for Love* (1695), and his masterpiece, *The Way of the World* (1700).

Conifer, any cone-bearing tree or shrub. Examples include the yews, pines, redwood, cypress, and araucarias. Conifers are found in the drier parts of the world, particularly in cold regions. They usually have needle- or scale-like leaves that reduce the loss of water from the plant. Except for the larches and bald cypress, conifers are evergreen, retaining their leaves all year round.

Conjunctivitis, inflammation of the conjunctiva of the eye (the mucous membrane that lines the inner surface of the eyelids); also called pink-eye. Viruses and allergies are the most common causes of this condition. Mixed or unidentifiable disease-causing microorganisms may be present, and irritation of the conjunctiva by wind, dust, smoke, and other types of air pollution is often responsible. Conjunctivitis may also accompany the common cold, infections involving skin rashes (especially measles), and irritation of the eye's cornea resulting from intense electric light, sunlamps, and reflections from snow.

Connecticut (Constitution State, Nutmeg State; pop. 3,277,000), a state in the U.S., on the Atlantic Ocean, in New England; 5,018 sq mi (12,997 sq km). Capital: Hartford. Hilly and woody area. Poultry breeding and dairy cattle, cultivation of, among others, tobacco, corn, and fruit. Minerals, mainly for road construction. Strongly industrialized with,

C

C

among others, manufacturing of helicopters, submarines, ball bearings, and firearms. A large number of insurance companies have their seat in the capital, while many multinationals have their main offices in Greenwich-Stamford. Tourism. The well known Yale University (1701) is located in New Haven. The Dutch explorer Adriaen Block was the first European to step ashore (1614), after which his fellow countrymen constructed a number of fortifications along the coast. The British established the first white settlement, Windsor, in 1635. The Pequot, one of the Native American tribes in the region, revolted one year later when the immigration of

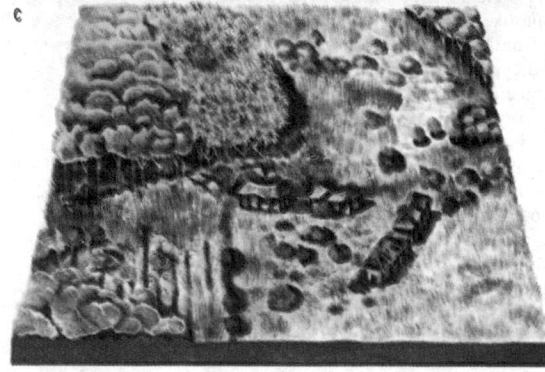

For hundreds of years, the forests of West Africa have been pushed back, as man attempted to grow crops in order to survive. This has resulted in a diminishing of the timber reserves and a reduced water content of the soil, which in turn caused

soil erosion and a reduced rainfall.

A 'Slash and burn' techniques, applied to a West African temperate forest of doum and deleb palms, banana trees, and vegetation such as lianas, mosses, ferns and epihytes.

B Crops such as millet, maize, groundnuts, plantain and cassava, growing on the cleared land at the edge of a forest.

C Abandoned land, which has become unproductive savannah and scrubland.

whites sharply increased. They were exterminated within a year.

Connecticut was one of the thirteen states to sign the Constitution in 1788; during the Revolutionary War that preceded this, the British had burned down or looted various cities.

The Connecticut River is the longest in New England (407 mi, 655 km). Its source lies in Vermont and it flows out into the Atlantic Ocean.

Connective tissue, basic tissue that constitutes the connective and supporting element of the body. Forms of connective tissue include fibrous bands, fat, blood, and bone. All forms of connective tissue consist of cells separated by a medium that has differentiated into matrix (amorphous elements) and fibers (formed elements). The matrix is a jellylike mass containing a variable number of fibers. Young cartilage is composed of a large number of cells surrounded by a firm matrix that contains a small number of fibers. Blood comprises a liquid matrix containing cells and fibers in a soluble form. The development of supporting tissue, such as cartilage and bone, results in cells being enclosed in a matrix that has a firm or hard composition.

Connelly, Marc(us Cook) (1890-1980), U.S. playwright, best known for his Pulitzer Prize-winning play *The Green Pastures* (1930). He collaborated with George S. Kaufman on several plays, including *Beggar on Horseback* (1924).

Connery, Thomas (Sean) (1930-), British (Scottish) film actor, known for his role as secret agent James Bond, among others in *Dr. No* (1962), *From Russia with Love* (1963), and *Thunderball* (1965). After playing James Bond in six films, he had had his share and went on to play heroes in other types of films, such as *Robin and Marian* (1976), *A Bridge too Far* (1977), *Meteor* (1979), *The Name of the Rose* (1986), *The Untouchables* (1987), *Indiana Jones and the Last Crusade* (1989), *The Hunt for Red October* (1990), and *Rising Sun* (1993). In 1983, he took on the role of James Bond for one last time in *Never Say Never Again*. Afterwards he played in the films *The Avengers* (1998) and *Entrapment* (1999).

Connolly, Maureen Catherine (1934-1969), American female tennis player, the first woman to win the Grand Slam (the championship of Australia, France, the U.S., and Wimbledon, all in one season) (1953). Connolly won the American championship when she was only 17 years old; a title that she also won in 1952 and 1953. She won the Wimbledon championship three times in succession: 1952, 1953, and 1954. She was also a strong doubles player: she won both the ladies' doubles and the mixed doubles in France in 1954 (while also winning the singles title), and the ladies' doubles in Australia in 1953. Her endless mental preparation prior to a game were legendary. Her career was cut short in 1954 due to an accident while horseback riding.

Connors, Jimmy (James Scott Connors; 1952-), U.S. tennis player. He was the top-ranked

player in the world through most of the 1970s. Known for his left-handed, two-fisted backhand, he won the U.S. Open (1974, 1976, 1978, 1982, 1983) and Wimbledon (1974, 1982).

Conquistadors, 16th-century military adventurers who founded Spain's empire in the Americas. Most famous among them were Hernán Cortes and Francisco Pizarro.

Conrad, Joseph (1857-1924), English novelist of Polish birth. His years at sea, during which he acquired a remarkable command of the English language, provided backgrounds for many of his novels. His lasting concern was the individual in isolation, struggling against adversity, moral degradation, and the forces of nature. His early novels include *Almayer's Folly* (1895) and its powerful sequel *An Outcast of the Islands* (1896), both set in Borneo. *The Nigger of the 'Narcissus'* (1897), *Lord Jim* (1900), and *Typhoon* (1903) are examples of his skill in creating atmosphere and character. The novella *Heart of Darkness* (1902) takes place on the Congo River, and the book Conrad considered his masterpiece, *Nostromo* (1904), is a story of revolution and corruption in South America.

Conscientious objector, person opposed to war in any form or in the specific form it is then taking, who by reason of conscience and conviction refuses to bear arms in wartime. The United States requires either noncombat duty within the armed forces or alternative service in a socially useful category for those who, as conscientious objectors, refuse regular services. Many other countries recognize this status-including Great Britain, the Commonwealth Nations, the Russian Federation, and many others in Europe and Latin America. Most require alternative noncombat service.
See also: Pacifism.

Conscription *See:* Draft, military.

Conservation, management and protection of the earth's natural resources to assure adequate supplies for future generations. Conservation aims to provide an environment free from pollution of air, water, and land, and to protect the welfare of plants, animals, and humans.

Conservatism, term for social and political philosophies or attitudes that stress traditional values and continuity of social institutions and that reject sudden radical change,while maintaining ideals of progress. It was first used in the early 19th century to describe the policies of the British Tory party. Modern conservative political parties include the British Conservative and Unionist Party, the Canadian Progressive-Conservative Party, and, in the United States, the Republican Party.

Conservative Party, one of the two major political parties in Great Britain. The second major political party is the Labor Party. The Conservative Party succeeded the Tory Party that appeared in the late 1600s. Benjamin Disraeli, a founder of the Conservative Party, strongly supported imperialism and

advocated rights for the working class. In recent history, the Conservative Party has been in control of the British government since 1979. As head of the Conservative Party 1979-1990, Margaret Thatcher became the first woman prime minister in British history. She was succeeded by Conservative John Major. At the general elections in 1997 the Conservative Party achieved the worst loss of seats since 1832. As a result, Major resigned as party leader.
See also: Disraeli, Benjamin.

Considérant, Victor Prosper (1808-1893), French socialist. He promoted the doctrines of Charles Fourier, edited *La Phalange*, and published *Social Destiny* (1834-1838) and *Principles of Socialism* (1847). He tried unsuccessfully to establish a communistic community in Texas (1855-1857).

Conspiracy, in U.S. law, agreement between two or more people to commit an unlawful act. The act of conspiracy is in itself a crime; the unlawful act does not have to be committed. Conspiracy is punishable by fines or imprisonment.

Constable, John (1776-1837), English painter. He and J.M.W. Turner were England's 2 greatest landscapists. Believing that painting should be pursued scientifically, he explored techniques of rendering landscape from direct observation of nature under different effects of light and weather.

Constance Missal, one of the earliest books printed in Europe. Believed to be printed by the inventor of movable type, Johannes Gutenberg c.1450, Constance Missal was a book of masses for the German diocese of Constance.

Constanta (pop. 351,000), Romanian Black Sea seaport city. An industrial center with a modern harbor, Constanta exports petroleum and grain and is Romania's primary Air and naval base Founded by the Greeks (7th century B.C.), Constanta became part of Romania in 1878.

Constantine (pop. 440,000), trading center in Algeria about 50 mi (80 km) from the Mediterranean Sea. A natural fortress, the city is on a plateau nearly surrounded by a steep gorge. Named for its patron, the Roman emperor Constantine the Great, it was built in A.D. 313 on the site of Cirta, a city destroyed by war.

Constantine, 2 kings of Greece. **Constantine I** (1868-1923) reigned 1913-1917 and 1920-1922. During World War I he opposed the Allies and was forced to abdicate the throne to his second son, Alexander. Brought back into power after Alexander's death, he abdicated again after the Greeks were defeated in a war with the Ottoman Empire. **Constantine II** (1940-) was king of Greece 1964-1974. As a result of his unsuccessful attempt to overthrow the military junta ruling Greece at the time, Constantine II was forced into exile in Italy. In 1974 the Greek people voted to replace the monarchy with a republican form of government.
See also: Greece.

Constantine I, The Great (c.280-337), first Emperor of Rome to convert to Christianity. After his father, Constantius, died in 306, there was a struggle for the succession. In 312 on the eve of the decisive Battle of Milvian Bridge, near Rome, Constantine, who was already sympathetic to Christianity, is said to have seen a vision of a flaming cross in the sky. He won the battle and became emperor in the West, while his brother-in-law, Licinius, was emperor in the East. In 324 war broke out between them, and in 325 Licinius was killed. Constantine thus became the sole ruler of the Roman world. In 325 he convened the Council of Nicaea, which settled various disputes in church doctrine. He made Christianity the official religion of the empire and moved the capital to the city of Constantinople, named for him and dedicated to the Virgin Mary. Constantine reigned as an absolute ruler until his death.
See also: Christianity; Rome, Ancient.

Constantinescu, Emil (1939-), Rumanian politician. Constantinescu followed an academic career, holding the post of professor of geology. He became a member of the Communist Party in 1965. After the fall of the dictator Ceausescu, Constantinescu became the Rector of the University of Bucharest in 1991. He stood as a presidential candidate in 1992, but was defeated by Ion Iliescu. Following this defeat, he became the leader of the opposition against the neo-communist government. In 1996, Constantinescu succeeded in getting a majority of the Rumanian voters to support him. Together with the new premier, Victor Ciorbea, Constantinescu formed the first noncommunist government team since the end of the Second World War. In 2000, Illiescu won the elections again and succeeded Constantinescu as President.

Constantinople *See:* Istanbul.

Constellation, group of stars that appear to lie in the same area of the sky. Constellations figure prominently in the mythology and folklore of ancient civilizations. The Greeks, for instance, saw the shape of Orion the hunter, who, with a shield and club, is facing Taurus the bull. Many of the characters in adjoining constellations are related. Cepheus was the husband of Cassiopeia, whose daughter Andromeda was rescued from the sea monster Cetus by Perseus. Many of the star divisions and names were originated by the Greeks.

Constipation, decrease in the frequency of bowel actions from the norm for an individual; also increased hardness of stool. Often precipitated by inactivity or changed diet or environment, it is sometimes due to gastrointestinal tract disease.

Constitution, system of fundamental principles or rules for the government of a nation, society, labor union, or other group that establishes basic guidelines and a framework of orderly procedure. While most Western countries have written constitutions, it is important to distinguish between written and unwritten constitutions. The written consti-

tution of the United States specifically catalogs the powers of the federal government and the rights of the citizens and states. Great Britain has an unwritten constitution in which common law and tradition play a greater part in the framework of the country's political and legal system than any single written document.
There are also 'hard' and 'soft' constitutions. A 'hard' constitution is difficult to alter, thus rendering it unresponsive to short-term political change. With a 'soft' constitution alteration can be achieved relatively easily, for example, by a simple vote of the legislature. The constitution of the United States is a fairly 'hard' document, since constitutional amendments require lengthy and involved procedures.

Constitutional law, U.S., section of the law that interprets and enforces the provisions of the U.S. Constitution. Although the Constitution, with its 7,000 words, launched the fledgling Union as a sovereign, democratic nation, it refrained from specifying too precisely the limits of governmental power or the roles of its institutions. A closer definition of these was left to history and experience. Constitutional law studies this historical development and pronounces on the contemporary status of its many concepts, concentrating on 3 topics: judicial review, the separation of powers, and the federal system. Judicial review deals with the powers of the U.S. courts-ultimately the Supreme Court-to pass judgment on the constitutionality of laws or specific acts of government. The U.S. Constitution did not provide for judicial review, but the Supreme Court has claimed, and exercised, the right to decide on constitutionality ever since Chief Justice John Marshall's famous decision in *Marbury* v. *Madison* (1803). His reasoning was simple: The Constitution is the supreme law of the land and it is the function of the courts to uphold the law; consequently, the courts are duty-bound to declare invalid any government law or action in conflict with the basic provisions of the Constitution. The Supreme Court exercises its power of review with restraint, and the burden of proof rests on the party challenging the law's constitutionality, not on the legislation. The Court assumes that the leg-

John Constable (1776-1837) was one of the foremost nineteenth-century landscape painters. He frequently chose motifs from his own native region. *Boatbuilding near Flatford Mill* (1815) can be found in the collection of the Victoria and Albert Museum, London.

C

C

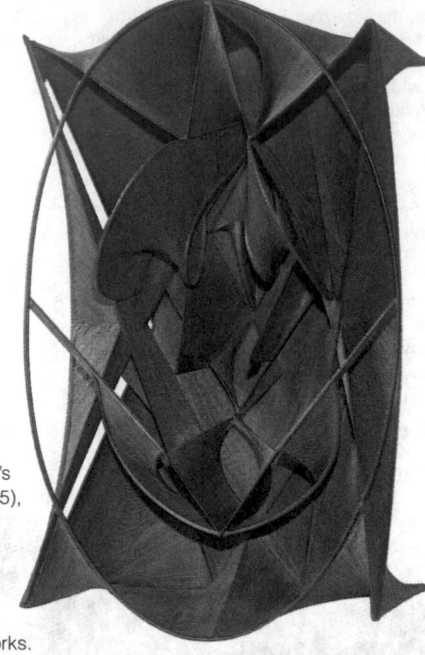

Antoine Pevsner's *Oval fresco* (1945), an abstract assemblage of bronze and oxidized tin, is typical of his constructivist works.

islation does not enact measures intended to violate the Constitution.

The doctrine of separation of powers maintains that despotism is best prevented by dividing the powers of government among several branches that 'check and balance' one another. The Constitution confers the legislative power upon Congress, the judicial authority upon the courts, and executive power upon the president. The federal system divides the powers of government between the national, or federal, government and the state administrators. The powers of the national government are enumerated in the Constitution, all other powers being reserved to the state governments. However, provisions like the clause that gives Congress the power to make all laws 'necessary and proper' to carry out its Constitutional function and the right to regulate interstate commerce have greatly increased federal power.

Constitution of the United States, supreme law of the nation. Written in Philadelphia in the summer of 1787, the Constitution was approved by the 55 delegates representing the 13 original states and went into effect on March 4, 1789, after ratification by the re-

quired 9 states. The actions of the virtually autonomous states and the failure of the country's first constitution, the Articles of Confederation, convinced the delegates that a strong executive and a powerful federal government were needed if the United States were to survive as a cohesive entity. The conflicting desires of large and small states resulted in a bicameral legislature, one house based on population size, the other house with an equal number of seats for each state. Most important was the eventual recognition by all stats that a strong central government would be needed if the United States was to be more than just a loose confederation. The states allayed their fears by constructing a separation of powers to limit governmental power. In 1791 a Bill of Rights to guarantee personal freedoms was added as the first 10 amendments to the Constitution. Only 16 amendments have been added since 1791.

Constructivism, artistic movement developed in Russia 1913-1920 by Vladimir Tatlin, Naum (Pevsner) Gabo, and Antoine Pevsner. Partly influenced by cubism and futurism, it was related to technology and industrial materials. Gabo and Pevsner went into exile in 1921 when Soviet authorities moved against all modern art movements.

Consul, official appointed by one country to look after its commercial and cultural interests in another country. Not to be confused with ambassadors, whose primary purpose is to further political understandings with the country to which they are appointed, consuls attend primarily to business and cultural matters. The term *consul* was originally given to the highest magistrates of ancient Rome. At the beginning of the 19th century, the consular system developed universally. Consuls are ranked in importance as consul general, consul, vice or honorary consul.

Consumer Price Index, index number indicating how the price of an item or items is in proportion to the price at an earlier point in time. The latter is usually set at 100; a price index number of 110 corresponds to an increase in price by 10%. Of particular importance is the price index figure for a standard package of products, for example, the average consumption of a family with two children. This is used, among other things, to determine price compensation and a government's pricing policy, inflation policy, and monetary policy.

Consumer protection, state, federal, and local laws that set standards for goods and services for consumers and the regulatory agencies that maintain these standards, as well as the efforts of consumers themselves to organize against misleading or unfair marketing practices. Scientific and technological advances have led to increasingly sophisticated goods, but modern sales methods, advertising, prepackaging, and self-service make it increasingly difficult for the consumer to know from personal experience the quality and value of the goods offered. The consumer may also need protection from artificial price-fixing by monopolies and from deliberate fraud. The federal gov-

ernment sets standards covering definition of weights and measures, packaging, the composition and purity of food and drugs, and descriptions of products in advertisements and brochures.

Consumer protection laws, laws as they relate to consumer protection.

Consumers' organization, a group of consumers attempting to arm themselves against their weakening position on the market: it is becoming increasingly difficult for consumers to determine the quality and applicability of the items offered. The emphasis generally lies on comparative commodities research: testing a number of brands of a certain article, in which special attention is paid to the price/quality ratio.

Consumption, in economics, use of goods and services. Wearing clothes, eating food, and washing with soap are examples of consumption. Patterns of consumption are related to size of income. Higher income families tend to spend larger portions of their earnings on nonessentials such as education and entertainment, while lower income families spend the greater part of their income on essentials such as food and housing.

Contact lens, small lens worn directly on the cornea of the eye under the eyelid to correct defects of vision. Generally made of transparent plastic, contact lenses sometimes give better results than glasses and are less noticeable.

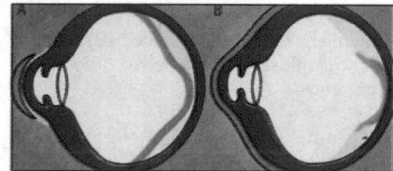

Contact lenses are made of hard or soft plastic, glass or a glass-plastic laminate. There are two main types, which can be either convex, concave, or cylindrical, depending on the type of eye-defect. There are also other types of lenses, for less common defects. The form of the lens constrains the front surface of the eye and may possess no other optical properties at all.
(A) Corneal lenses are relatively small and float on a film of tears, directly over the cornea of the eye.
(B) Scleral lenses fit over the cornea of the eye, and rest on the scleral surface surrounding the cornea.

Containerization, method of shipping freight in large containers usually made of aluminum, steel, fiberglass, or plywood. Developed in the mid-1950s, containerization helps prevent damage to freight. It is widely used by the air, shipping, railroad, and trucking industries.

Contempt of court, action that detracts from the dignity or authority of a court or that tends to obstruct the administration of justice. Such actions may be punished by

The most modern method of handling freight in ports, is the container system.

fine or imprisonment, or both, but can generally be appealed. Contempt can be classified as civil or criminal. Civil contempt is failure to obey a court order issued for the benefit of a third party; an example would be failure to produce books for creditors to look at. Criminal contempt is a direct offense to the dignity or authority of a court, such as the use of vulgar language, refusal to obey instructions, or bribery of a juror.

Continent, any of the largest land masses of the earth's surface. The number of continents is popularly reckoned to be 7: the 3 'Old World' continents (Europe, Africa, and Asia), those of the 'New World' (North America and South America), and the island continents (Australia and Antarctica). The division between Europe and Asia is purely arbitrary; they are therefore sometimes regarded as one continent, Eurasia.

Continental divide, imaginary line that divides a continent at the point where its rivers start flowing in opposite directions and empty into different oceans. In North America it follows the Rocky Mountains, in South America the Andes.

Continental drift, theory that the continents change position over time, moving very slowly. The theory was first suggested in 1912 by Alfred Wegener, a German meteorologist, who believed that the earth's land masses had once been joined in one supercontinent, Pangaea, which broke apart about 200 million years ago, forming the earth's continents. The theory was controversial for a long time, and it has since been revised by the modern concept of plate tectonics, which also incorporates continental drift.
See also: Geology.

Continental shelf, submarine rim around most of the earth's continents, extending on average about 50 mi (80 km) beyond the shoreline before dropping steeply to the ocean floor. They are relatively flat and shallow, between 300 ft (90 m) and 600 ft (180 m) below the ocean surface, although some are cut by deep submarine canyons. They are covered with layers of fine sediment. The shallower portions of the continental shelf were at one time dry land, since the sea level has risen about 300 ft (90 m) from the time of the Ice Ages.

Continental System, attempted economic blockade of England instituted in 1807 by Napoleon I. A counterblockade of the continent by England's superior seapower nullified it. The British blockade, because it interfered with American trade with the continent, was a major cause of the War of 1812.
See also: Napoleon I.

Contraband, trade forbidden by law. The term usually refers to goods that may not be shipped to an enemy during wartime, because those goods may serve a military purpose. In 1908-1909, 10 naval powers met in London to create a code to classify contraband and define terms for its seizure. The Declaration of London classified goods in terms of absolute contraband (military equipment), conditional contraband (other

goods when being shipped to an enemy), and free goods.

Contraception *See:* Birth control.

Contract, promise or agreement enforceable by law. Contracts are usually written, but they may be merely understood or oral. Some types of contracts, particularly for the sale of real estate or covering a long period of time, must be in writing. Even written contracts, however, often give rise to misunderstandings or disagreements that become the subject of lawsuits. A contract is a bargain between two or more persons, firms, or other organizations, in which there is an offer and an acceptance. Once the offer has been made and accepted, the law enforces the terms agreed to. A *breach of contract* occurs when either party to a contract fails to fulfill promises. The court will then award damages to the other party, usually in the form of a sum of money, sometimes equivalent to what the party has actually lost, or else according to terms specified in the contract.

Contract bridge *See:* Bridge.

Contrail, line of cloud that forms behind aircraft flying at high altitudes. Contrails form when water vapor from the exhaust or in the air condenses into droplets or freezes into ice crystals. Ice crystals from contrails may precipitate rain or snow.

Convent, monastic community of monks, friars, or nuns. Today the term usually applies to the residences of nuns, or, in the case of 'convent schools,' to girls' schools that are closely associated with convents.
See also: Nun; Religion.

Convertibility, in economics, financial arrangement under which currencies of different countries can be exchanged for each other. Under complete convertibility, all currencies can be exchanged for all others. Under partial convertibility, only certain currencies can be exchanged for certain others. The rate of exchange can be either fixed or floating (changing from day to day). After World War II, the lack of foreign exchange caused many European countries to restrict convertibility, but at the present time all major currencies are freely convertible with each other.

Convertiplane *See:* V/STOL.

Conveyor belt, device that mechanically conveys material. Principally used in factories and on large farms, the conveyor belt is looped over two pulleys, one of which is the drive pulley and is powered by an electric motor. The belt travels over a series of rollers. In factories, materials move along a conveyor belt to be worked on by workers standing along the line. In this way, the conveyor belt plays a major role in such mass-produced goods as automobiles. Other uses for conveyor belts include carrying material into mines and carrying cargo to and from ships, trucks, and railway cars.

Convoy, fleet of merchant or other unarmed

vessels sailing under the protective escort of a warship. Since the 17th century, international law has attempted to issue a 'right of convoy' mandate to protect neutral shipping from search and seizure on the high seas during time of war.

Convulsion, involuntary contraction of the muscles of the body. Such contractions may be tonic or clonic, according to whether they are continuous or spasmodic, and of either cerebral or spinal origin. Convulsions may be caused by lack of oxygen (e.g., convulsions during some bouts of fainting), toxic conditions (e.g., convulsions due to the poison strychnine), psychological factors (e.g.,

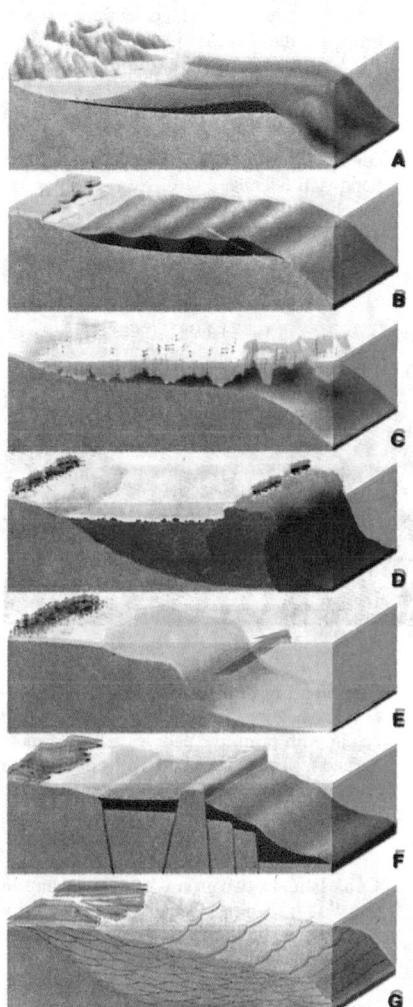

Structural features of continental shelves and slopes vary according to climate, oceanographic conditions, and the nature of the adjacent land masses. A shelf gouged out by glaciers consists of deep troughs at right angles to the coastline (A). A shelf near a glacier-free area generally has a series of low and sand ridges parallel to the coast (B). The grinding action of floating ice forms smooth, flat, shallow shelves (C). Shelves in tropical seas may be composed of land sediments deposited between the shore and a damlike coral reef at the edge of the continental slope (D). Shelves with steeper than normal slopes (E) are found in areas where strong currents constantly erode the seafloor. Fault-controlled shelves (F) are formed from sedimentation behind offshore fault barriers. Wide-layered shelves (G) are the result of river-discharged sediments that accumulate near large delta areas.

C

C

hysterical convulsions), or epilepsy. The term 'convulsion' now usually refers to discontinuous muscular contractions, either brief contractions repeated at short intervals or longer ones interrupted by intervals of muscular relaxation.
See also: Epilepsy.

Cony *See:* Hyrax.

Cook, Frederick Albert (1865-1940), U.S. explorer who claimed to have climbed Mt. McKinley in 1906 and to have discovered the North Pole in 1908, before Peary. Neither claim was widely believed.

Cook, James (1728-1779), English navigator and explorer. He led 3 celebrated expeditions to the Pacific Ocean (1768-1771, 1772-1775, 1776-1780), during which he charted the coast of New Zealand (1770), showed that if there were a great southern continent it could not be as large as was commonly supposed, and discovered the Sandwich Islands (1776). He died in an attack by native Hawaiians.
See also: New Zealand.

The death of James Cook in Kealakekua Bay (Hawaii), by James and John Cleveley.

Cooking, preparation of food for consumption, by heating. It is believed that cooking began with primitive peoples who ate meat burned in forest fires. Later the cooking fire was moved indoors, cooking utensils were invented, and the art of preparing foods arose.

Cook Islands, two groups of coral islands in the South Pacific Ocean, discovered by British captain James Cook in 1773. They were made a British protectorate in 1888, and are now self-governing but linked to New Zealand. The islanders are Polynesians, related to the Maoris of New Zealand. Their chief exports are citrus fruits, jewelry, copra, pearl shell, and tomatoes.

Cooley's anemia *See:* Thalassemia.

Coolidge, (John) Calvin (1872-1933), 30th president of the United States (1923-1929). American Republican politician and laywer. As the governor of Massachusetts, he became a national figure as a result of his forceful action against the police officials on strike in Boston. Coolidge became vice president in 1921 and succeeded Harding, who passed away, as president in 1923. Coolidge was reelected in 1924. As a confirmed believer in laissez-faire politics, he abstained

as much as possible from legislative work and from interfering in matters of economics. His politics were oriented towards achieving a budget that was as stable as possible. Coolidge was succeeded by his fellow party member Hoover in 1929, after refusing to stand for reelection. Coolidge was much more a calm and steady administrator than an inspired president; in 1924, he campaigned with the slogan 'Keep Cool with Coolidge'.

Cooper, Gary (1901-1961), U.S. film actor. He portrayed laconic, romantic heroes in such films as *A Farewell to Arms* (1933) and *For Whom the Bell Tolls* (1943), and won Academy Awards for roles in *Sergeant York* (1941) and *High Noon* (1952).

Cooper, James Fenimore (1789-1851), one of the first important U.S. novelists, who created a number of colorful and enduring characters of the early American frontier. His famous series of *Leatherstocking Tales*, which include *The Pioneers* (1823), *The Last of the Mohicans* (1826), *The Prairie* (1827), *The Pathfinder* (1840), and *The Deerslayer* (1841), centered around the adventures of an intrepid woodsman called Natty Bumppo. Cooper achieved popularity in Europe, where he wrote for several years. Cooper also wrote several works of social criticism.

Cooperative, association of producers and consumers for the purpose of sharing among the members profits that would otherwise go to intermediate businesses and individuals. The organized cooperative movement dates from the first half of the 19th century. Social reformers such as Claude Saint-Simon, Louis Blanc, Robert Owen, and Charles Fourier protested the exploitation of the workers associated with the Industrial Revolution and urged collective self-help. The first successful consumer cooperative was the Rochdale Society of Equitable Pioneers, founded in England in 1844. The Rochdale principles, still basic to many cooperatives, call for open membership, democratic control, education of members, and service at cost.
The founding of the National Grange in the United States in 1867 stimulated small-scale efforts to form cooperatives, and it promoted the adoption of the Rochdale principles throughout the country.

Cooperative education, method of combining classroom and practical work experience. Typically, formal written agreements between schools and employers allow students to hold jobs, usually for pay, related to their field of study.

Coop Himmelb(l)au, Austrian architectural firm run by Wolf Dieter Prix and Helmut Swiczinsky and established in Vienna in 1968. In the 70s, they mainly operated within the sphere of visual art, with installations, exhibitions, and 'actions', which could be considered sculptures; the spatial experience. They began creating real buildings at the beginning of the 80s, including the café The Red Angel (1980-1981) and an apartment complex (1986) in Vienna. They de-

signed a pavilion in the Groninger Museum, Groningen, which was otherwise designed by Mendini (1990-1996). In addition to other projects, they designed the film palace in Dresden (1997), which is shaped like an angular diamond.

Coot (genus *Fulica*), common member of the rail family of water birds. The American coot ranges from southern Canada to northern South America and is found on stretches of fresh water, where it is distinguished by its contrasting black plumage and white bill and tail. It paddles with its lobed feet and often skitters over the surface of the water. Other coots found around the world include the giant coot and horned coot of the Andes. The nest of a coot usually floats on the water, and the chicks have surprisingly bright colors.

Copenhagen (pop. 1,360,000), seaport capital of Denmark, on Sjaelland and Amager islands. It handles most of Denmark's trade, exporting ham, bacon, porcelain, silverware, and furniture. Its main industries are shipping, shipbuilding, brewing, and light manufacturing. Landmarks include Christianborg Palace, Rosenborg Palace, Tivoli amusement park, the National Museum, and several art museums. The city was occupied by the Germans from 1940 to 1945.
See also: Denmark.

Copepod, small crustacean of subclass Copepoda. Of great ecological importance, copepods serve as food for many species of fish. Although there are freshwater copepods, most of the 7,500 known species are marine forms. They are found both at the surface and at great depths of the sea. While most copepods reproduce sexually, some do so by parthenogenesis (the female's eggs produce new copepods without being fertilized).
See also: Plankton.

Copernicus, Nicolaus (1473-1543), Polish astronomer who put forward the theory that the earth and other planets orbit the sun. Until the time of Copernicus, Ptolemy's theory that the earth was the center of the universe and that heavenly bodies, with the exception of the 'fixed' stars, rotated around it, was generally accepted.
Copernicus studied mathematics and astronomy at the University of Krakow, and completed his education in Italy, He returned to Poland to become a canon in Frauenberg cathedral.
Many of the astronomers of Copernicus's day were dissatisfied with Ptolemy's theory, which was becoming more and more complex in order to take account of new discoveries about the universe. Copernicus tried to account for the observed motions of the planets by assuming that the earth and planets orbited the sun. He found that his system was much simpler than Ptolemy's complex picture of the universe. Afraid of a hostile reaction to his ideas, Copernicus began to circulate his theory anonymously until a pupil, Georg Joachim Rheticus, published a popular version of it in 1540. This version was enthusiastically received and Copernicus finally published his book *On*

C

the *Revolutions of the Celestial Spheres*. *See also:* Astronomy.

Copland, Aaron (1900-1990), U.S. composer. His lyrical and exuberant music incorporates jazz and folk tunes in a distinctively American idiom. His works include the ballet scores *Billy the Kid* (1938) and *Appalachian Spring* (1944), the song cycle *Twelve Poems of Emily Dickinson* (1950), the opera *The Tender Land* (1954), symphonies, piano and chamber works, and film scores. His many awards include the 1945 Pulitzer Prize and Presidential Medal of Freedom in 1964.

Copper, chemical element, symbol Cu; for physical constants see Periodic Table. Copper was discovered in prehistoric times. It is a metallic element occasionally occurring in pure form. The most important ore is chalcopyrite. Copper is a reddish metal, malleable and ductile, a good conductor of heat and electricity. Brass, bronze, monel metal, and gun metal are all important alloys of copper. Most copper is used in the electrical industry. Some copper compounds are used as pesticides.

Copperhead (*Agkistrodon contortrix*), pit viper of hilly country in the eastern United States. It ranges from 2 to 4 ft (0.6 to 1 m) in length and is distinguished by its characteristic copper-colored head and coppertoned markings on a chestnut background. The copperhead strikes without warning, and its bite can cause considerable discomfort, although it is seldom fatal to healthy adults. It feeds mainly on small, warm-blooded animals but will eat frogs and insects when driven by hunger.

Copperheads, Northern Democrats who advocated peace with the Confederacy during the Civil War and who opposed President Lincoln's war policy. The epithet originated in an article in the *New York Tribune* in July 1861 that depicted the antiwar Northerners as venomous copperhead snakes that strike without warning.

Coppi, Fausto (1919-1960) Italian racing cyclist, due to his allround performance one of the greatest cyclists history has known. Coppi won the Round of Italy in 1940, 1947, 1949, 1952, 1953 and the Tour de France in 1949 and 1952. He also excelled in 1-day classic races: he won the Milan-San Remo (1946, 1948, 1949), the Round of Lombardy (1946, 1947, 1949, 1953), the Walloon Arrow (1950) and Paris-Roubaix (1950). He also became world road racing champion in 1953. As a racer in a time trial, Coppi was virtually impossible to defeat, as is obvious from his many victories in the Grand Prix des Nations and the Trofeo Angelo Baracchi. Coppi was also a successful track racer: he established a world hour record on the Vigorelli track in Milan (28.509 m/h, 45.871 km/h) in 1942 and became pursuit world champion in 1947 and 1949. He died as a result of an infection, which he acquired in North Africa.

Coppola, Francis Ford (1939-), American film director. Best known for *The Godfather*

(1972) en *The Godfather II* (1974). Personal vision and technical perfection make his films stand out. Other films are: *Apocalypse Now* (1979), *The Outsiders* (1982), *Rumble Fish* (1983), *The Cotton Club* (1984), *Gardens of Stone* (1987), *The Godfather III* (1990), *Dracula* (1992) and *Don Juan de Marco* (1995).

Copra, dried kernel (endosperm) of the coconut fruit, from which oil is extracted. Copra is prepared by drying the exposed coconut meat and then pressing the coconut oil out. Copra yields 50-60% of its weight in oil.

Coptic Church, Christian church that derives from the church of Alexandria in pre-Muslim Egypt. The Copts were descended from ancient Egyptians, and spoke their own, now 'dead,' language. Early in the history of the church doctrinal disputes arose between the Roman Church and Coptic-speaking Christians. Following the Council of Chalcedon in A.D. 451, which condemned the view held by the Copts about the nature of Christ, the Copts broke away from Rome.

After the Arab conquest of Egypt in A.D. 640, many Copts became Muslims. The religious head of the church is the Coptic Patriarch of Alexandria, who lives in Cairo. The liturgy of the church is derived from the ancient Greek liturgy and church services are celebrated in Coptic and Arabic. The Coptic church is important in Ethiopia.

Copyright, exclusive right of an author or other creator to publish or sell his or her works. When a work has been copyrighted, other firms and individuals must have permission from the holder of the copyright in order to reproduce the work. If they do so without permission, the holder of the copyright may sue for damages and for an order to stop publication or distribution. Most published books are copyrighted. Other types of works that may be copyrighted include plays, musical compositions, periodicals (including newspapers), motion pictures, photographs, prints, reproductions, works of art, speeches and lectures, and maps and charts. A notice of copyright will usually appear on such published material.

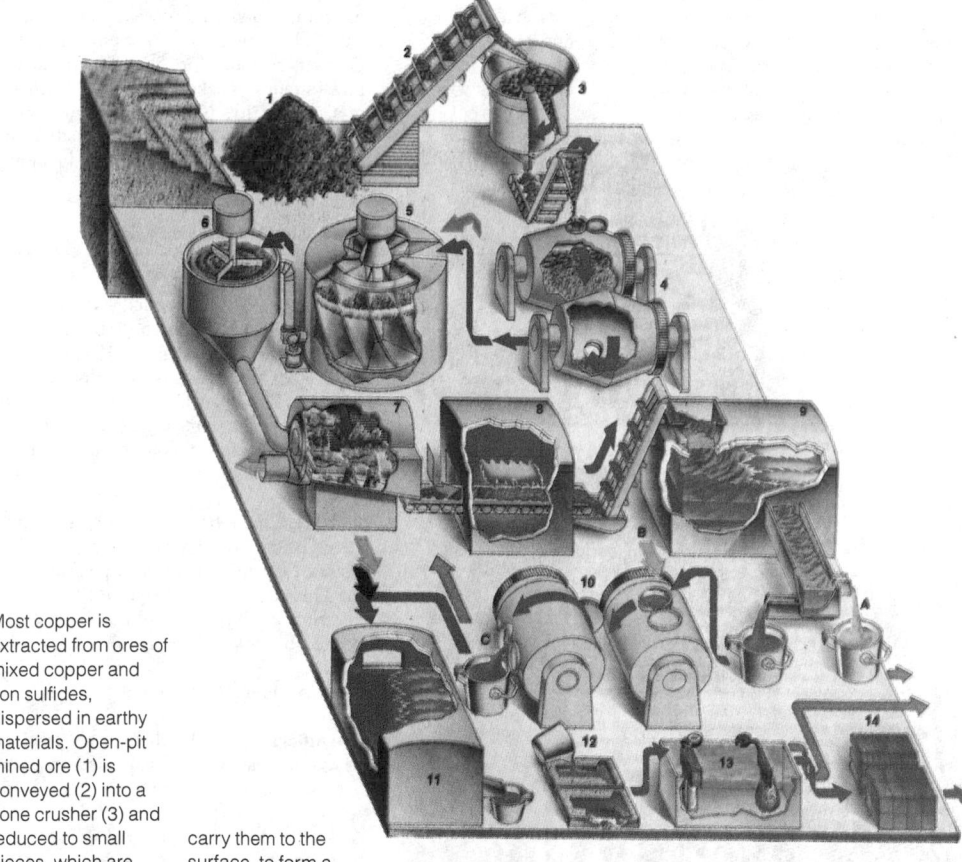

Most copper is extracted from ores of mixed copper and iron sulfides, dispersed in earthy materials. Open-pit mined ore (1) is conveyed (2) into a cone crusher (3) and reduced to small pieces, which are mixed with water and pulverized to a powder in ball mills (4). The powdered ore is mixed with frothing agents and more water in a flotation machine (5), and air is blown through the mixture. The air bubbles adhere to the sulfide minerals and carry them to the surface, to form a froth, whereas the waste matter settles out. Most of the water in the froth is removed in a thickening tank (6) and by way of a rotary suction filter (7). The filtered cake of ore is then heated in a roasting oven (8), where some of the sulfides are changed into oxides, then in a smelting furnace (9), in which fluxing agents form an iron oxide slag that floats to the surface and is removed (a). The melt is transferred to a converter furnace (10), and air (b) is blown through it, to remove sulfur as the dioxide, and to convert residual iron oxide into a slag, which is poured off (c). The slightly impure copper that remains, is first fire-refined with air and reducing agents in a reverberatory furnace (11), then cast in slabs (12), and used as anode plates in an electrolytic unit (13), for electrodeposition of copper on thin copper cathodes. Periodically, the almost pure copper cathodes that build up, are removed and cast in bars (14) for various applications.

C

The Universal Copyright Convention, which is adhered to by many nations, does not specify the minimum of copyright protection, so long as there is no favoritism.
See also: Patent.

Coral, small, sedentary marine invertebrate of the class Anthozoa. Most corals join to-

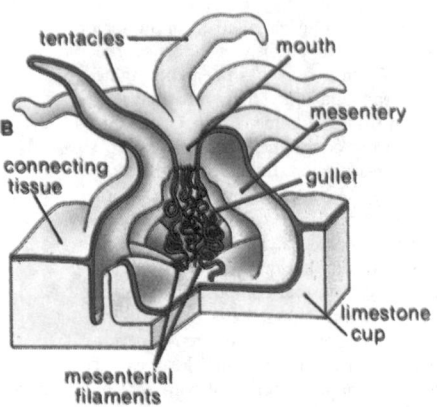

Stony, or true coral (order *Scleractinia*), builds the reefs that so spectacularly enhance warm seas of the world. The staghorn coral (genus *Acropora*) is composed of hundreds of tiny polyps. In a crossection of an individual polyp, tentacles, which capture prey, surround a mouth that leads to the gullet. The polyp embeds itself in a limestone cup it built, and connecting tissue extends between polyps of a colony.

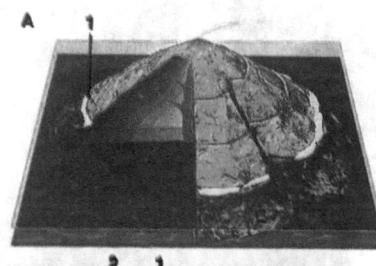

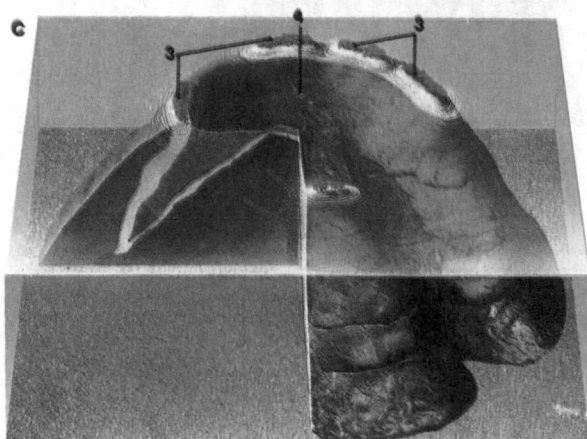

Atolls, the most prominent product of coral growth, are ring-shaped chains of low-lying islands enclosing a lagoon. Found only in tropical seas, atolls are believed to have started with the development of a fringing reef (1) around the shallow shores of a volcanic island (A). At some point, the volcano began subsiding (B), and corals grew upward and outward, creating a barrier reef (2). Eventually, the island's summit sank below sea level (C), and only barrier reef islands (3) circling a lagoon (4) remained.

gether in colonies and secrete external limestone skeletons that form coral reefs and islands in warm seas.

Coral Sea, part of the southwestern Pacific Ocean, between the northeast coast of Australia and the Solomon Islands. The sea floor is dominated by coral atolls and reefs, among them the Coral Sea Plateau, Osprey and Swain reefs, the Coral Sea Basin, and the Great Barrier Reef, which extends 1,200 mi (1,930 km) along the northeast Australian coast.
See also: Pacific Ocean.

Coral snake, slender poisonous snake (genus *Micrurus*) of the Western Hemisphere. Rings of black, yellow, or white and red cover its body. Two species are found in the southern U.S. states. Coral snakes feed on small reptiles and insects. In many parts of the world there are false coral snakes that have patterns of color similar to coral snakes but are harmless.

Corbett, James John (1866-1933), U.S. boxer. Known as 'Gentleman Jim', he became the first man to hold the world heavyweight title under Marquess of Queensberry Rules, beating John L. Sullivan (1892). Corbett reigned for 5 years, until Bob Fitzsimmons knocked him out in 14 rounds in Carson City, Nev. After his retirement from the ring in 1903, Corbett made a successful career on the stage and in motion pictures.

Corbusier *See:* Le Corbusier.

Corcoran Gallery of Art, art museum in Washington, D.C. Founded by the banker William Wilson Corcoran (1869) and chartered by the U.S. Congress (1870), the museum exhibits paintings, sculptures, and drawings that span U.S. history from colonial to modern times. The museum also presents changing exhibitions and offers educational courses.

Corday, Charlotte (1768-1793), French assassin of the French revolutionary Jean Paul Marat. Objecting to Marat's persecution of the Girondins, she stabbed him to death in his bath on July 13, 1793. She was guillotined by order of the revolutionary tribunal.
See also: French Revolution.

Cordillera (Spanish 'chain'), geographical description applied to extended mountain

systems in western North America, from Alaska to Nicaragua, including the Rocky Mountains and the Andes.

Cordite, smokeless gunpowder. Composed of 30% nitroglycerin, 65% nitrocellulose, and 5% petrolatum, cordite burns with a great deal of heat. Its name refers to the cordlike lengths in which it is made.
See also: Gunpowder.

Cordoba, monetary unit of Nicaragua, equal to 100 centavos. It is named after the Spanish explores Francisco Fernandez de Cordoba.

Córdoba (pop. 302,100), or Córdova, ancient Moorish city in Andalusia, southern Spain. The capital of Cordoba province, it is located 86 mi (146 km) northeast of Seville. Córdoba was a famous center of Moorish art and culture that reached its peak in the 10th century A.D. A great mosque was built as a Muslim house of worship in the 700s. Made into a Roman Catholic cathedral in 1238, Córdoba's chief landmark is supported by over 1,000 pillars of granite, onyx, marble, and jasper. Today, Córdoba's industries include brewing and metallurgy.
See also: Spain.

Córdoba (pop. 1,200,000), second-largest city in Argentina, Located on the Rio Primero in north central Argentina. Founded in 1573, Córdoba is an industrial center and home to Argentina's oldest university, the National University of Córdoba.
See also: Argentina.

Corelli, Arcangelo (1653-1713), Italian composer. During Corelli's lifetime the violin, together with the viola and cello, gradually replaced the older stringed instruments called viols. He did much to encourage this change by his own brilliance as a violinist and by his many compositions for the new stringed instruments. He was also a key figure in the development of the concerto grosso as an important new form of orchestral music.

Coreopsis, genus of summer-blooming plant also known as tickseed. This genus is a member of the family Asteraceae, which include about 100 species of herb native to North America. Coreopsis plants can grow to a height of 4 ft (120 cm). They bear yellow, red, or maroon flowers that resemble daisies.

Corgi *See:* Cardigan Welsh corgi.

Coriander (*Coriandrum sativum*), small annual plant of the carrot family, the seeds of which are used as a spice and for medicinal purposes. Coriander leaves, also called cilantro or chinese parsley, are used to flavor food.

Corinth (pop. 30,000), ancient city of Greece situated on the isthmus between the mainland and Peloponnesus. The old city is dominated by the Acrocorinthus, a rock that rises to 1,886 ft (575 m).
Corinth was conquered by the Dorians c.1100 B.C. By the 6th century B.C. it was the

leading mercantile city of Greece, a center of culture, commerce, and entertainment. It fought against Athens during the Peloponnesian War and emerged a weaker power. Later it was controlled by Macedonia. Corinth was destroyed by Rome in 146 B.C., but was rebuilt under Julius Caesar in 44 B.C. and became the capital of the Roman province of Achaea. St. Paul founded a Christian community there, to which he wrote his Epistles to the Corinthians. New Corinth was built 3.5 mi (5.6 km) from its ancient site, after the Hellenic city was destroyed by an earthquake. The modern town exports currants, olive oil, and silk.
See also: Greece.

Corinthians, Epistles to the, two letters written by St. Paul to the Christians of Corinth and forming the 7th and 8th books of the New Testament. The First Epistle, believed to have been written at Ephesus (c. A.D.55), is the longer, and is important for the light it throws on the problems, discipline, and organization of the early Church. The letter was prompted not only by questions raised by the Corinthians, but by Paul's awareness of divisions among them. The Second Epistle, according to modern scholars, may be a combination of two letters written at different times. It is an impassioned defense of Paul's work and authority as an apostle.
See also: Bible; New Testament.

Coriolanus, Gaius Marcius (fl. 5th century B.C.), Roman general. Capturing the town of Corioli from the Volscians, Roman enemies, Coriolanus won both a reputation for bravery and his last name. During a famine in 491 B.C., Coriolanus proposed that grain be given to the poor only if they surrendered their right to elect representatives. To express their indignity, the people exiled Coriolanus, who responded by joining the Volscians. According to legend, he led their army to the gates of Rome, where he was stopped from seizing the city only by the pleading of his wife and mother. The betrayed Volscians then killed Coriolanus. The story is told in Shakespeare's tragedy *Coriolanus*.
See also: Rome, Ancient.

Coriolis force, apparent curvature of the path of a moving object due to the rotation of the earth. Because the earth rotates from west to east, any object moving in a straight line in any direction other than due east or due west appears to follow a curved path in relation to the earth's surface: to the right in the Northern Hemisphere and to the left in the Southern Hemisphere. This effect, named for the French physicist Gaspard Gustave de Coriolis (1792-1843), is most apparent in the movement of the winds and the sea. Allowances for this effect must also be made in ballistics in order to be able to calculate where a missile will land.

Cork (pop. 450,000), second largest city in Ireland (after Dublin) situated at the mouth of the Lee River, in the southwest of the republic. Through its fine harbor at Cobh, Cork exports dairy products, leather, iron,

and glass. The city has large distilleries and breweries.
See also: Ireland.

Cork, spongy tissue in the bark of trees that acts as an insulation and protection to the delicate growing tissues. It also forms a seal over the wound where a leaf has been shed. Commercial cork, used for insulation, bottle stoppers, engine gaskets, and floor linings, comes from the cork oak (*Quercus suber*) of southern Europe and North Africa. The cork oak has a layer of cork several inches thick that can be stripped every 10 years. The operation has to be carefully performed so that the delicate underlying tissues are not harmed.

Corm, thick underground stem used by certain plants (e.g., crocus, gladiolus) to store food over the winter to get them ready for flowering in the spring. Corms are very similar to bulbs, but the food is stored in the thickened stem and not in fleshy underground leaves.

Cormorant, any of a number of long-necked seabirds (family *Phalacrocoracidae*). Cormorants feed on fish, diving from the surface of the water. Their nests are built in colonies on rocks or in trees and they can often be seen perching with wings outstretched to dry. Northern cormorants have black plumage, but many of those of the Southern Hemisphere have white underparts; all have patches of naked colored skin on the head. Cormorants have been trained to catch fish for people in Britain, China, and Japan. A ring is usually placed around the neck to prevent fish from being swallowed.

Corn, (*Zea mays*), family of grasses. Agricultural crop with broad leaves positioned along an erect stem, male flowers in a panicle at the end of the stem, female blossoming cobs (corncobs) in the axil of the leaves of the middle stem. Originated in America; nowadays often grown for its yellow or brown fruit: grains of corn. These are mainly used as cattle feed, but are also consumed by humans as a vegetable, boiled on the cob, ground and baked as cornbread, popped as popcorn, or processed into corn flakes. When preparing cornstarch, edible corn oil is squeezed from the corn germs. The corn harvest in the U.S. is threatened by corn borer, (*Pyrausta nubilalis*), a small butterfly originally from Europe that eats away at the stem of the plant. Global produce: approx. 420 million tons, of which almost half is produced in the U.S. China and Brazil hold second and third place.

Corn borer, caterpillars of a moth, especially the Old World maize moth, that feeds on a variety of plants, including beet, beans, and corn. It attacked the Indian corn that was introduced to Europe, and was transported to North America about 1907 to become a serious pest in the Corn Belt and elsewhere. The use of pesticides is effective, but complicated by the need to keep the crop free from contamination. The corn borer still destroys several million bushels of corn every year.

Common Cormorant (*Phalacrocorax carbo*). Coasts of northern Europe, Iceland, western Greenland, Africa, Asia, Australia and New Zealand. Length: 39 in (100 cm).

Cornea *See:* Eye.

Corneal transplant *See:* Eye bank.

Corn earworm, larval stage of moth (*Heliothis zea*) in the owlet moth family (Noctuidae). The corn earworm breeds on and attacks corn, tomatoes, alfalfa, and beans; it is called a bollworm when it attacks cotton. Insecticides such as carbaryl are used on some crops to protect them from the corn earworm.

Corneille, Pierre (1606-1684), French dramatist, creator of French classical verse tragedy. His masterpiece, *Le Cid* (1637), though controversial in its time, was a great popular success. His many other plays include *Horace* (1640), *China* (1640), and *Polyeucte* (1643). His popularity faded with the rise of his younger rival, Jean Racine.
See also: Racine, Jean.

Cornering the market, investment term for a speculator conspiracy to drive up stock prices. An investor or group of investors will buy all or most of the available shares in a company, forcing other buyers to pay higher prices for their shares and thus reaping maximum profits. The practice is now outlawed by the U.S. Securities and Exchange Commission.

Cornet, trumpetlike valved brass wind instrument. It has a mellow tone controlled by lip vibration at the cupped mouthpiece and a two-and-a-half octave range. It is usually tuned to B flat. Cornets have traditionally been used in brass bands but rarely in symphony orchestras. They have, however, found an important place in jazz.

The instruments of a brass band all belong to the saxhorn family, and have conical tubes (as opposed to trumpets and trombones, which have cylindrical tubes). The cornet has the highest sound of the group. It derives originally from the posthorn that was used on coaches, to which valves were added.

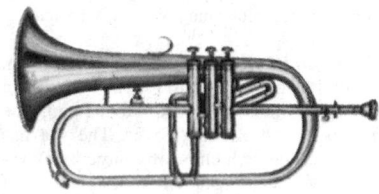

C

C

Cornflower (*Centaurea cyanus*), annual herb whose flowers are used for medicinal purposes. The large, blue flowers (white or rose-colored in some varieties) appear from June to August and are popular in U.S. gardens.

Corn laws, various laws regulating English import and export of grain from the 14th century to 1849. After the Napoleonic Wars the corn price was raised to offset agricultural depression. But protests from the poor and from manufacturers objecting to agricultural subsidy helped Cobden and Bright, leaders of the Anti-Corn Law League (1839-1846), persuade Prime Minister Sir Robert Peel to repeal the Corn Laws (1846 and 1849).

Corn oil, vegetable oil derived from the kernel of the corn plant. In processing, machines separate the germ (or embryo) from the rest of the corn kernel. Then the oil is extracted from the rest of the kernel. Corn oil is made up of about 55% polyunsaturated fat, which many nutritionists consider an essential element in a healthy diet. It is used in cooking and as a salad oil, as well as in margarine and potato chips.

Cornstarch, fine white flour extracted from corn. Ground and refined after the seed-bearing portion (germ) has been removed from the kernels, cornstarch is formed after a wet milling and drying process. It is a key ingredient in baking powder and is used in the manufacture of explosives, paints, and textiles.

Corn syrup, syrup prepared from cornstarch and containing glucose combined with dextrin and maltose. Corn syrup adds a smooth texture to creams such as those used in candies. It is used to sweeten baked goods, candies, canned fruit, ice cream, and soft drinks, and is sometimes added as a flavoring to peanut butter, catsup, salad dressings, processed meats, and other foods.

Cornucopia, or horn of plenty, curved goat's horn symbolizing nature's abundance. Fruit and grain overflow from the mouth of the cornucopia. It is often used as a decorative motif. Legend presents the cornucopia as the horn of the Greek nymph Amalthea that could always be filled with its possessor's desires.

Cornwallis, Charles Cornwallis, 1st Marquis of (1738-1805), British general whose surrender to Washington at Yorktown (Oct. 19, 1781) ended the Revolutionary War. Earlier, he had defeated Nathanael Greene in the Carolinas. He later gave important service as governor-general of India (1786-1793 and 1805), and as viceroy of Ireland (1798-1801).
See also: Revolutionary War in America.

Coromandel Coast, part of the Indian coast, on both sides of Madras (Chennai), from Point Calimere to False Divi Point, the mouth of the Krishna River. The sea has high breakers, which is why large breakwaters have been installed in the harbor of Madras.

The Dutch established factories here in the middle of the 17th century, with Negapatnam as the center, which was conquered by the British in 1781.

Coromandel wood is hard wood that grows, among other places, on Sulawesi (Celebes) and Maluku; it is chocolate brown with black stripes and is used for sculpting and decorative arts.

Corona, outer atmosphere of the sun or other stars. The term is used also for the halo seen around a celestial body due to diffraction of its light by water droplets in thin clouds of the earth's atmosphere, and for a part appended to and within the corolla of some flowers. Around high-voltage terminals there appears a faint glow due to the ionization of the local air. The result of this ionization is an electrical discharge known as corona discharge, the glow being called a corona.
See also: Star.

The corona of the sun, photographed from a height of more than 8530 ft (2600 m), during the total solar eclipse of 7 March, 1970. The corona consists of a highly tenuous gas with a temperature of over a million degrees Celsius.

Coronado, Francisco Vásquez de (1510-1554), Spanish explorer. Coronado was the first European to explore the southwestern United States. Searching for the legendary, gold-laden Seven Cities of Cibola in 1540, he set out from Mexico, traveling through areas that are now Kansas, Oklahoma, Texas, New Mexico, and Arizona. Though Coronado found no riches, he introduced the Spanish to the Pueblo and pioneered colonization in the southwestern United States.
See also: Cibola, Seven Cities of.

Coronary thrombosis, myocardial infarction, or heart attack, one of the commonest causes of serious illness and death in Western countries. The coronary arteries, which supply the heart with oxygen and nutrients, may become diseased with atherosclerosis that reduces blood flow. Significant narrowing may lead to the clotting of blood (thrombosis) in the artery, which can cause sudden, complete obstruction and resulting damage to a substantial area of heart tissue. This may end in sudden death, usually due to abnormal heart rhythm that prevents effective pumping. Characteristic changes may be seen in the electrocardiograph following myocardial (heart muscle) damage,

and enzymes appear in blood from the damaged heart muscle.
See also: Heart.

Coronation, ceremony of crowning a sovereign, usually consisting of a solemn ritual of religious as well as secular significance. It generally includes the anointing of the sovereign, investiture with special garments and symbols of royalty such as a crown, pronouncement of the coronation oath, enthronement, and, in Christian countries, taking of Communion. The actual authority of the new sovereign usually commences with the death of the predecessor. The kings and queens of England have been crowned in Westminster Abbey since 1066.

Coroner, public official who investigates sudden, suspicious, or violent death, sometimes with the aid of a jury. Coroners are also responsible for protecting the property of the deceased person until it is relinquished to the person(s) legally entitled to inherit it. A coroner may order an inquest if the death is considered suspicious. In some communities in the United States, medical examiners, who must be physicians, are appointed to serve as coroner, although public prosecutors are assigned to the legal aspects of the investigation. In some states, laymen are permitted to serve as coroner, but they must hire a physician to perform any necessary autopsies.

Corot, Jean Baptiste Camille (1796-1875), French landscape painter. He is best known for the subtly atmospheric paintings that made him popular in the 1850s. While studying in Rome, he broke from the classical tradition and began to achieve sensitive effects of light by painting directly from nature. After his return to France he began to develop the soft, gray-green landscapes that made his reputation. His influence on his fellow artists of the Barbizon School was considerable, and the impressionists learned a great deal from him, though he never shared their views. Most of the world's major art galleries have examples of Corot's work.
See also: Barbizon school.

Corporation, group of persons regarded as a legal entity apart from the individuals owning or managing it. As a legal person, a corporation can hold property and sue and be sued. Corporations may be either private or public.

Corps, unit of a military force, usually a tactical division consisting of 2 or more subdivisions. Corps are commanded by lieutenant generals and are usually organized for a specialized function.

Corpus Christi (pop. 257,000), city in southeastern Texas situated on the Corpus Christi Bay of the Texas Gulf Coast, seat of Nueces County. Corpus Christi was founded in 1839 and played an active role in the Mexican War and the Civil War. The city is the second largest port in Texas, and one of the centers of the vast Texas oil and gas industry. Corpus Christi also refines aluminum and manufactures fertilizers, cotton and corn products, cement, and chemical products. *See also:* Texas.

Corpuscle, in biology, isolated cell, usually one that can move freely in fluid and is not fixed in tissue. The term corpuscle is often used to refer to red and white blood cells, and to the nerve endings in the skin. *See also:* Biology; Blood.

Correggio (Antonio Allegri; 1494-1534), Italian Renaissance painter who influenced the Baroque style. His works (including most of his Parma frescoes) are primarily devotional, and are noted for softness and use of chiaroscuro (dramatic light and shadow). *See also:* Baroque; Renaissance.

Corregidor, fortified island near the entrance to Manila Bay and the Philippines. During World War II, Corregidor, was occupied by United States and Filipino troops who defended the island but eventually surrendered in 1942 to Japanese troops after extensive bombing. U.S. military forces reclaimed the island in 1945 and later dedicated the historic fortress as a national shrine to the World War II troops who died there. *See also:* World War II.

Corrosion, gradual destruction of a substance, usually a metal, by chemical action. Oxidation is the most common form of corrosion. Rusting of structures made of iron is a familiar example. Corrosion can dangerously weaken structures. The simplest precaution consists of coating the metal with protective layers of paint. Sometimes iron is coated with another metal, notably zinc, to produce *galvanized* iron. Plastic coatings have recently been developed to prevent corrosion. In jet engines and nuclear devices corrosion is a particularly difficult problem, since the metals used are subjected to high temperatures and stresses in circumstances where mechanical failure through corrosion could be disastrous. Radiation may also increase susceptibility to corrosion and also change the mechanical properties of the metal. Special alloys have been developed to overcome these difficulties. *See also:* Oxidation; Reduction.

Corsica, Mediterranean island and French department north of Sardinia, off the coast of western Italy, occupying 3,352 sq mi (8,682 sq km). It is largely mountainous, with Mediterranean scrub and forest. Its products include olive oil, wine, and citrus fruits. Its rulers have included Carthaginians, Romans, Vandals, Goths, Saracens, and (1347-1768) the Genoese, who sold it to France. There is strong nationalist feeling on the island. Napoleon Bonaparte was born here.

Cortázar, Julio (1914-1984), an Argentine author. Cortázar gained international attention with his novel *Rayuela* (1963; English translation: *Hopscotch*, 1966). This unconventional work emphasizes the structure of the novel itself, uses absurdist humor, and depicts a character who goes insane searching for meaning in a bizarre world. Cortázar attended Buenos Aires University, taught at the high school and college levels, and later worked as a translator in France. Other works include: novels - *Modelo para armar* (1968; *A Model Kit*, 1972), *Libro de Manuel* (1973: *A Manual for Manuel*, 1978); short-story collections - *Bestiario* (1951), *Todos los fuegos el fuego* (1966; *All Fires the Fire*, 1973).

Cortés, Hernando (1485-1547), Spanish explorer, conqueror of Mexico. In 1504 he settled in Hispaniola (Santo Domingo) and in 1511 joined the conquest of Cuba, becoming mayor of Santiago. Sent to explore the Yucatan, in 1519 he marched on the Aztecs' capital Tenochtitlán, where Montezuma greeted him as the white god Quetzalcoatl. Cortez took Montezuma prisoner, and the latter was killed in an uprising against the Spaniards. Cortez retreated, but returned in 1521 and conquered the capital, ending the Aztec Empire. He later explored Honduras and lower California.

Cortex, cerebral *See:* Brain.

Corticosteroid *See:* Cortisone.

Cortisone, one of the group of hormones secreted by the cortex of the adrenal glands. Cortisone was first isolated in 1935 and synthesized in 1944. It proved to be of immense value in treating diseases caused by malfunctioning of the adrenal cortex, such as Addison's disease, and in the treatment of arthritis, some forms of allergy, leukemia, and many other diseases. However, cortisone and the closely related hydrocortisone have undesirable side effects. As a result the drug is used with caution or replaced by a synthetic substitute. The secretion of cortisone is controlled by ACTH (adrenocorticotropic hormone), which is itself secreted by the anterior lobe of the pituitary gland. *See also:* Hormone.

Corundum, mineral consisting of alumina (aluminum oxide, Al_2O_3) and second in hardness only to diamond. It forms precious stones, such as rubies, sapphires, topaz, amethyst, and emerald; the 'jewels' in watches and instrument bearings are often made of corundum. Because of its hardness, corundum is widely used in emery and other abrasives. Corundum is found in many countries, often in association with quartz.

Cosby, Bill (William Henry Cosby, Jr.; 1937-), U.S. entertainer. Known mainly as a comedian, he is also an actor, producer, and author. He was the first African-American actor to star in a televison series ('I Spy', 1965-1968). He produced and starred in the award-winning television series *Cosby Show* (first aired in 1984). *Uptown Saturday Night* (1974) is one of his movie credits. He is the author of a number of books, including *Fatherhood* (1986), a collection of witty essays.

Cosimo de' Medici *See:* Medici.

Cosmetics, preparations applied to the human body to beautify or alter appearance. Cosmetics are used primarily to cleanse, color, condition, or protect the skin, hair, lips, nails, eyes, and teeth. Though cosmetics have been used since ancient times for reli-

Among the foremost works of the north Italian painter Correggio (1489/94-1534), is this decoration of the Cupola of the S. Giovanni Evangelista in Parma (1520-23). The fresco shows Jesus' ascension from a most unusual perspective, as if the spectator is looking up into the sky.

C

gious and ornamental rituals, since the early 1900s they have grown into what is now a billion dollar industry. Examples of commonly used cosmetics are lipsticks, eye shadows, blushes, deodorants, perfumes, lotions, shampoos, nail polishes, and some toothpastes.

Cosmic rays, highly penetrating radiation that strikes the earth, assumed to originate in interstellar space. They are classed as primary, coming from the assumed source, and secondary, induced in upper atmospheric nu-

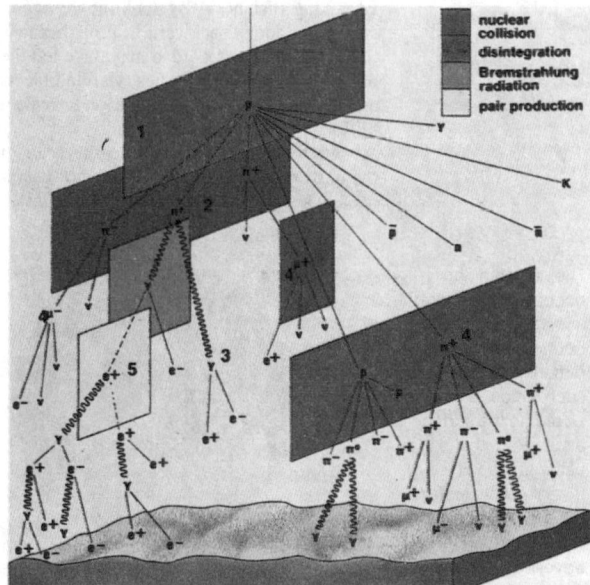

Cosmic rays are high-energy particles, entering the atmosphere from all directions. When primary cosmic rays, mainly high-speed protons, collide with the molecules of the air, a shower of smaller subatomic particles (1) is produced. Among these secondary particles are neutrons (n), protons (p), neutral π mesons ($\pi°$), positively and negatively charged mesons (π^+ and π^-), antiprotons ($\bar{p}$), heavy mesons (K), and hyperons (Y). A neutral $\pi°$ meson is highly unstable and rapidly decays (2) into electromagnetic gamma rays (γ). Gamma rays, approaching atomic nuclei may form positive and negative electrons (3). Charged mesons may strike other atmospheric nuclei (4) or decay into mu mesons (μ^+ and μ^-) and neutrinos (ν). Electrons passing through strong electric fields of nuclei will radiate part of their energy as Bremsstrahlung radiation, such as gamma rays (5). Few of these secondary cosmic rays will actually reach the earth's surface.

C

clei by collisions with primary cosmic rays. *See also:* Radiation.

Cosmology, study of how the universe originated and how it has evolved. There are 2 main theories. The first, known as the *evolutionary theory*, pictures the universe as having been born, and as evolving and eventually dying. The popular name for this theory is the 'big bang' theory, because it assumes that all the material in the universe was at one time packed tightly together and was then flung outward by an enormous explosion. This theory was first put forward in the 1920s by the Belgian astrophysicist and priest Georges Lemaître. It rested on the discovery by Edwin Hubble that the universe seemed to be expanding, like a balloon being blown up. Hubble showed that the galaxies are receding from each other with velocities increasing to nearly half the speed of light as they get farther away. After World War II, Hermann Bondi and Thomas Gold put forward the opposing *steady state* theory, which says that new material is continuously created to fill the space between the galaxies. Although the universe is expanding, the matter in it was never concentrated. New galaxies and old galaxies would exist side by side, and the universe would always look the same. The theory was later developed by the English astronomer Fred Hoyle. Observational tests for these theories rest on the fact that radiation takes time to cross very long distances. By looking deep into space, one looks backward in time, because the radiation now recorded may have left the object long ago. The farthest visible objects are so far away that their radiation has taken billions of years to reach earth.

As one looks back in time, the character of the universe seems to alter. Instead of galaxies one sees quasars, which may be galaxies

in the process of formation. At distances past 8 billion light-years, the number of objects seems to decrease, indicating a time when the universe was just forming, which seems to support the evolutionary theory.

Another piece of evidence against the steady state theory is that radio astronomers record a faint radiation from all over the universe. This so-called 'background' radiation, discovered in 1965 by Arno Penzias and Robert Wilson, may be the heat left over from a 'big bang' explosion. Though it still has adherents, the steady state theory has now largely been abandoned.

See also: Astronomy.

Cosmonaut *See:* Astronaut.

Cosmos, term for the universe and all its components. The ancient Greeks used the term to describe a total universe characterized not by chaos but by systematic harmony. Cosmos is an all-inclusive description of existence consisting of everything from tiny atoms to huge planets and galaxies.

See also: Universe.

Cosmos, genus of tropical fall-blooming flowers of the Compositae family. Cosmos, native to U.S. and Mexican tropics, are tall, brightly-colored annuals and may have either single-stemmed flowers or clustered blooms. Cosmos grow well in full sunlight and moderate soil.

Cossacks, Slavic warrior peasants living on the Ukrainian steppe and famed for horsemanship. Self-governing under leaders like Bohdan Chmielnicki (1595-1657), they resisted outside authority, but served the czars as irregular cavalry, pioneered in Siberia, and fought the Bolsheviks from 1918 to 1921. Collectivization broke up their com-

munities in the 1930s, but Cossack cavalry served in World War II.

Costa, Lúcio (1902-1998), Brazilian architect and urban developer. In his capacity as director of the Escola Nacional de Belas Artes in Rio de Janeiro, he greatly influenced contemporary architecture. Built, among others, together with Oscar Niemeyer, the Ministry of Education and Health in Rio de Janeiro (1937), the Brazilian pavilion at the 1939 World Exhibition in New York, and the housing complex Parque Guinle (1948-1954) in Rio de Janeiro. Later mainly known for his design for the new capital Brasília (commenced in 1957), for which he received an award.

Costa Rica

Capital:	San José
Area:	19,730 sq mi (51,100 sq km)
Population:	3,835,000
Language:	Spanish
Government:	Presidential republic
Independent:	1838
Head of gov.:	President
Per capita:	US $8,500
Monetary unit:	1 Costa Rican colón = 100 céntimos

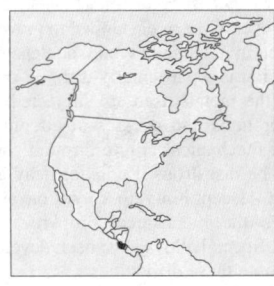

Costa Rica, republic in the southern part of Central America, between Nicaragua and Panama. Costa Rica is the second smallest of the Central American republics, measuring between 75 and 175 mi (121 and 282 km) from the Caribbean to the Pacific coasts.

Land and climate. Costa Rica consists of tropical coastal plains, chains of mountain ranges running in a northwest-southeast direction through the interior, and a central plateau. The mountains begin near the Nicaraguan border, split into 2 major ranges curving around the plateau, and continue into Panama. The highest peaks are in the south (Chirripó Grande, 12,533 ft/ 3,820 m) and in central Costa Rica, where 4 volcanic cones reach altitudes from 9,000 to 12,000 ft (2,743 to 3,658 m) above sea level. The central plateau is the most densely populated section of Costa Rica and the center of coffee cultivation. It lies at an elevation of 3,000-4,000 ft (914-1,219 m) in the climatic

The universe can occupy a finite volume, and yet have no boundaries. A two-dimensional analogy of such a closed universe would be the surface of a sphere, with the sum of the angles of a large triangle on its surface (A) greater than 180C°. A spacecraft (B) traveling in a straight line, would fly completely around this universe and return to its original launching point. Subsequently, a triangle of astronomical dimensions in the universe, with angles totaling more than 180C° (C), would reveal a closed universe. Similarly, a spacecraft from earth, traveling along a straight-line course (D) would, after a finite time, return to its launching point from the opposite direction.

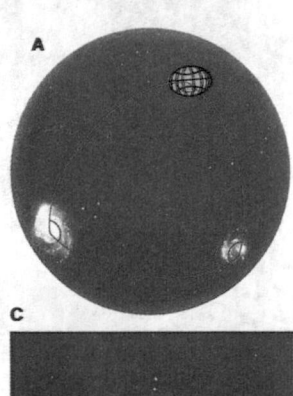

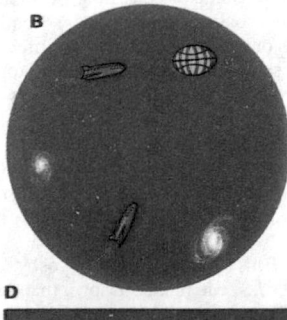
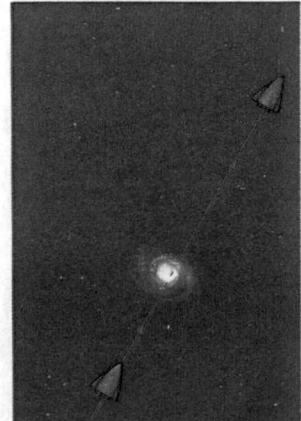

This coffee finca (plantation) lies in the Meseta Central of Costa Rica, which is favored with extremely fertile volcanic soil. Although various crops are cultivated in the central plateau, the region is best known for its high-grade coffee, the country's most valuable export crop.

zone known as *tierra templada* (temperate land). In the lowlying coastal areas the annual temperature averages close to 80° F (26.6° C). At elevations of more than 5,900 ft (1,800 m), year-round averages drop below 62° F (16.6° C). Rainfall is heaviest along the Caribbean coast, feeding the several short rivers that rise in the mountains. Broadleaf evergreens cover more than half the land, cleared in places for banana plantations. Grasslands cover the Meseta Central.

People. Unlike the peoples of the other Central American countries, most Costa Ricans are of direct Spanish descent, though most also claim to have some Native American blood. A large part of the population is made up of mestizos, people of mixed Spanish and Native American ancestry. About half of the people live in rural areas, frequently on small farms that they own and work. With the exception of a few Native American tribes, all inhabitants speak Spanish. Costa Rica has one of the lowest rates of illiteracy in Central America. School attendance is free and compulsory for children between the ages of 7 and 14. The University of Costa Rica is located at San José.

Economy. Though some gold and silver is mined in western Costa Rica, the country's volcanic soil is its most important natural resource. The principal cash crop and export product is high-grade coffee, which is in constant demand on world markets. Bananas, which rival coffee in importance as an export product, are raised on the humid plantations along the Pacific coast, where rubber trees also thrive. Local industry is mainly confined to sugar refining, food processing, and the manufacture of a limited range of consumer products. The discovery of large sulfur deposits has led to the construction of several processing plants. Despite the modest resources and the almost total lack of fuel, Costa Rica is being industrialized at a fairly rapid pace.

History. Columbus discovered Costa Rica in 1502, but because of its lack of resources the region escaped the ravages of the conquistadors. Since few Native Americans survived, the white farmers worked their own land, establishing a significant middle class and avoiding the semifeudal peonage system so destructive in other Latin American countries. In 1821 Costa Rica declared independ-

ence from Spain, joining first the Mexican Empire and then the Central American Federation, which dissolved into anarchy in 1838. Despite internal strife in 1919 and 1948, the country's history has been peaceful and its politics democratic. Its welfare system, dating from 1924, is one of the most advanced in the hemisphere. The country has had traditionally good relations with the United States. José Figueres Ferrer, head of a provisional government (1948-1958 and 1970-1974), long dominated Costa Rica. Under his leadership, numerous social welfare programs were adopted and banking and other institutions were nationalized. The country experienced rampant inflation in the early 1980's. In 1987 Costa Rica's president at that time, Oscar Arias, was awarded the Nobel Peace Prize for a plan he had devised to resolve civil wars in neighboring countries.

In 1995, a free trade agreement with Mexico took effect.

Eco-tourism became increasingly important for the economy of the country. In 2002, Abel Pacheco won the Presidential Elections.

Cost-benefit analysis, comparison study of costs versus benefits. Used often for planning, budgeting, or altering societal programs, a cost-benefit analysis measures the relationship between actual prices paid and benefits received. If an analysis identifies that the benefits outweigh the costs, the program is deemed cost-effective. The drawbacks to this economic study lie in the difficulty of determining future costs and placing monetary value on intangible benefits.

Costello, John Aloysius (1891-1976), Irish prime minister (1948-1951, 1954-1957). Costello's first term was marked by the withdrawal of Ireland from the Commonwealth of Nations (Republic of Ireland Act) and his second term was punctuated by terrorist acts of the Irish Republic Army (IRA).

See also: Ireland.

Coster, Roger Englebert Ghislain de (1944-), Belgian motorcycle racer, world champion in the motocross 500 cc event in 1971, 1972, 1973, 1975, 1976. Moreover, De Coster has claimed ten national titles since his debut in 1961: three in the 250 cc and seven in the 500 cc. He raced for Jawa, CZ, Suzuki, and Honda respectively.

Cost-of-living index, number or device showing how the cost of living compares at a certain time with the cost at a given time in the past, called the *base period*. Many governments compute such a monthly or quarterly index in order to detect and measure inflationary influences in the economy. Many wage contracts have features that automatically raise or lower wages by a given amount as the cost of living changes. The base period is usually recent enough to make the types of goods bought roughly comparable with those offered for sale at the present time. Economists then compute what the basic collection of goods and services chosen for the base period would cost at the time of the survey. If the cost of these goods and

services is set at 100 in the base period, and if the same things now cost 10.2% more, then the cost of living is now 110.2.

See also: Consumer Price Index.

Côte d'Azur, resort area along the eastern Mediterranean coast of France. Part of the French Riviera, the Côte D'Azur includes the coastal villages and cities of Nice, Cannes, Antibes, and Monte Carlo, Monaco. Named for its characteristically deep blue seas and skies and possessing a mild Mediterranean climate, the Côte d'Azur attracts tourists from all over the world.

Cotonou (pop. 537,000), city in the south of Benin, on the Bight of Benin. The country's most important city and port, railway junction and port for Niger, with the export of palm oil products, peanuts, coffee, cacao, and cotton. The port is manmade and was completed in 1965. Cement industry and textile industry, processing of forestry, fishery, and agricultural products. International airport. University (1970). The French established a military post here in 1851, from which they slowly proceeded to occupy the area.

Cotopaxi, highest active volcano in the world. It is located in the Andes Mountains of Ecuador, 40 mi (64 km) from Quito. The volcano towers 19,344 ft (5,896 m) above sea level and its crater is 2,600 ft (792 m) across. The last recorded eruption was in 1942.

Cottage industry, term used to describe the structure of industry, particularly the spinning and weaving industry in Britain, before the Industrial Revolution. Typically, a trader distributed supplies of wool, and later, cotton, among a series of peasant homes, where spinning and weaving provided a part-time occupation for the women and children of the household. Although the earlier technical advances of the 18th century-James Hargreaves's spinning jenny, for example-were not incompatible with this cottage industry, the introduction of Richard Arkwright's spinning frame (patented in 1769) encouraged mass production and the transfer of spinning to factories. Weaving remained largely a cottage industry until the 1820s, when the factories began to take over in this area as well.

Cotton, subtropical plant (genus *Gossypium*) grown for the soft white fibers attached to its seed, which can be woven into fabric, also called cotton. Cotton is grown all over the world although the United States, Russia, and China own the largest portion of the world market. Examples of woven cotton cloth dating to 3000 B.C. have been found at Mohenjo-Daro, in what is now Pakistan. Samples of prehistoric cotton have also been found in Pueblo ruins in Arizona (U.S.), and some cotton fabric made before the Inca civilization still is in existence. Despite competition from synthetic fibers, cotton is one of the world's most important crops. Cotton requires about 200 days of warm, sunny weather and 25-30 in (63.5-76 cm) of rain. It is generally cultivated as an annual plant. When the pods, or bolls, burst

C

C

Longfibred cotton, of which Sudan is — after Egypt — the world's largest producer, is grown mainly in the Gezira Region, inbetween the White and the Blue Nile.

to reveal the white fibers (lint) within them, the cotton is ready for harvesting. Since the bolls burst at different times, a field may have to be picked several times during the season.

Each cotton fiber is an elongated plant cell made up of 90% cellulose. Unlike other natural fibers, the cotton fiber has 200-400 twists per inch (500-1,000 twists per cm) along its length. These give it excellent spinning characteristics. The quality of cotton is measured in terms of the length and fineness of the lint. Egyptian-type cotton, grown mainly in Egypt, the Sudan, and Aden, is the finest, producing long fibers (more than 1 1/8 in/2.9 cm) that are strong and silky. It commands the highest prices, but constitutes only about 5% of world production. Cotton is prone to many pests and diseases that cause enormous damage to the crop. The main insect pests are the boll weevil in the United States and the pink boll worm in India and Egypt. Destructive fungus diseases that attack the plant include fusarium and verticillium wilt and Texas root rot.

Cotton gin, machine that separates cotton fibers from the seeds, leaves, and other unwanted matter. Invention of the cotton gin in 1793, attributed to Eli Whitney, revolutionized the cotton industry in the South. Within 50 years cotton production had increased a thousand-fold. The original machines were of very simple design. A rotating drum with fine wire spikes, turned by hand, drew the fibers through narrow slots in a wire grid. The grid allowed the cotton fibers through, but not the seeds. A set of revolving brushes removed the fibers from the drum to prevent matting and clogging. The basic design of cotton gins has changed little since the 18th century. Modern mechanized versions use blasts of air to remove the fibers

and are capable of producing a 500-lb (227-kg) bale of compressed cotton in little more than 10 min.
See also: Whitney, Eli.

Cottonmouth *See:* Water moccasin.

Cottonseed oil, edible oil extracted from cottonseeds. Used chiefly as a salad and cooking oil, cottonseed oil can also be hydrogenated to make shortening and margarine. The hull (outer seed covering), is removed and the seeds are soaked in a solution to extract the oil. Further refining, purifying, and bleaching is necessary to make the oil palatable.

Cottontail *See:* Rabbit.

Cottonwood, tree (genus *Populus*) of the willow family with windblown seeds surrounded by tufts of cottonlike hairs. There are nearly 40 species around the Northern Hemisphere, most of which are called aspens and poplars.

Cotyledon, first leaf developed by a seed plant's embryo. Cotyledons are formed in seeds and function primarily to absorb stored food. Plants with single cotyledon embryos are called monocots; dicots are embryos with 2 cotyledons; and gymnosperms have more than 2 cotyledons.

Coubertin, Pierre baron de (1863-1937), French pedagogue and promoter of sports, founder of the Olympic Games. Studied philosophy, literature, and sociology and traveled to, among other countries, England and the United States where he set about to reinstate the Olympic Games. Fourteen countries agreed to that effect on 23th June 1894 during a meeting in the Sorbonne, after which the first modern Olympic Games were held in Athens in 1896. De Coubertin was also the initiator of the Olympic Winter Games, which were held for the first time in Chamonix in 1924. He was chairman of the International Olympic Committee from 1896 until 1925, and honorary president thereafter. He has the following works to his name: *Notes sur l'éducation publique* (1901), *La gymnastique utilitaire* (1912), *La pédagogie sportive* (1923).
See also: Olympic Games.

Cougar *See:* Mountain lion.

Coulee Dam *See:* Grand Coulee Dam.

Coulomb (coul or C), unit of electricity, the quantity of electricity that must pass through a circuit to deposit .0000394 oz (0.0011180 g) of silver from a solution of silver nitrate. It is named for French physicist Charles Augustin de Coulomb. An ampere is 1 coulomb per second. A coulomb is also the quantity of electricity on the positive plate of a condenser of 1-farad capacity when the electromotive force is 1 volt.
See also: Ampere.

Coulomb, Charles Augustin de (1736-1806), French physicist noted for his researches into friction, torsion, electricity, and magnetism. Using a torsion balance, he

established Coulomb's Law of electrostatic forces.
See also: Physics.

Counterpoint, in music, art of combining 2 or more different melodic lines simultaneously in a composition.

Counter-Reformation, reform movement in the Roman Catholic Church during the 16th and 17th centuries. It arose in part as a reaction against the Reformation, which attacked the Church and in the end offered as an alternative the independent Protestant churches founded by Luther and Calvin. The Counter-Reformation, on the other hand, proposed to reform the Church from within. One of the first moves toward religious reform was the founding of the Oratory of Divine Love in 1516, an assembly of pious churchmen intent upon official and authoritative action toward reform. The movement gained impetus with the founding of several new religious orders that emphasized simplicity and austerity. The most important new order was the Society of Jesus (Jesuits), founded by Ignatius Loyola in 1540. The spirit and methods of the Counter-Reformation were enunciated by the Council of Trent (1545-1547, 1551-1552, 1562-1563), which reaffirmed the doctrines of the faith, reorganized ecclesiastical administration, set educational requirements and moral standards for the clergy, and condemned simony (the buying and selling of church offices). In moves to combat heresy, Pope Paul III revived the medieval institution of the inquisition in Italy and Spain and Pope Paul IV authorized the *Index of Forbidden Books*. The spiritual revival was particularly intense in Spain, where Teresa of Ávila and John of the Cross combined a profound mysticism that renewed the spiritual life of the Church with active contributions toward reform of the religious orders.
See also: Reformation; Roman Catholic Church; Trent, Council of.

Country, political nation with geographic boundaries. Independent countries often have distinguishable topographical or cultural features and can vary drastically in size. Countries may be as small as several hundred acres or as large as 1 million sq mi (2.6 million sq km or more).

Country and western music, broad category of popular music that has its roots in rural American music of the 18th and 19th centuries, particularly in the South where black music, religious music, and British folk music fused into a unique American musical genre. Most songs are deeply personal and deal with themes of love, loneliness, and separation, but maintain a strong sense of faith in the human spirit. Songs can be quite festive and funny. Musical instruments often include guitar, banjo, fiddle, horns, drums, pianos, and electric instruments.
With the advent of radio broadcasts of this music in the 1920s and 1930s, the genre gained nationwide recognition. The 'Grand Ole Opry,' the national center of country and western music located in Nashville, Tenn., began radio broadcasts in 1925. The stars of the 1930s and 1940s included Tex Ritter,

Jimmy Rodgers, Ernest Tubb, and Gene Autry. In the 1950s, Hank Williams achieved fame with 'Your Cheatin' Heart' and 'Cold, Cold Heart.' The sound of the 1960s and 1970s combined elements of pop music and thus added to the popularity of the music. By the 1980s, country and western performers had achieved superstar status and became active in television and film. Some of the notable performers are Johnny Cash, Loretta Lynn, Dolly Parton, Willie Nelson, the Judds, Reba McEntire, and Randy Travis.

County, territorial division of local government. In the United States, the county is the largest division for local government within a state. County functions differ from state to state, but counties generally administer judicial, educational, and political functions and make physical improvements. County boundaries are determined by each state's legislature and funds are raised by real estate and property taxes. Most counties are governed by an elected board of commissioners who serve from 2 to 4 years. The county system is also used in England, Scotland, Ireland, New Zealand, and Canada.

Coup d'état (French, 'stroke of state'), sudden and unlawful takeover of a government, usually the result of a country's unsteady and unbalanced politics. Notorious coups in the past include those effected by the Bolsheviks in Russia in 1917 and by the Communists in Czechoslovakia in 1948.

Couperin, François Le Grand (1668-1733), French composer, organist, and harpsichordist, of a family of musicians that included Louis Couperin (1626-1661), his uncle. He acted as teacher to King Louis XIV's children, and often exhibited his skill on the harpsichord before the royal court at Versailles. His compositions include 27 suites for harpsichord that make up the *Pieces de clavecin*, as well as church and chamber works. Students of the harpsichord still employ his instruction manual, *L'art de toucher le clavecin*.

Courbet, Gustave (1819-1877), 19th-century French painter, an early realist. *The Funeral at Ornans* and *The Stone Breakers* are 2 of his sympathetic depictions of ordinary life.

Coureurs de bois, French-Canadian adventurers, who in the late 1600s and early 1700s, traded furs with the Native Americans. Through their extensive trading contracts with the Native Americans they were able to assist the French in forming strong military pacts against the English in the French and Indian wars.

Courier, Jim (1972-   ), American tennis player, broke through in 1991 by winning the Wimbledon championship. He won the Open Championships in Australia, France, and Italy in 1992, and that of Australia and Italy in 1993. He also won numerous Grand Prix tournaments. Courier is known as a 'hard hitter', who strikes the ball as if slugging a baseball bat. He retired from competitive tennis in 2000.

Courrèges, André (1923-   ), French fashion designer, worked from 1950 until 1961 with his master, the Spaniard Balenciaga, who ran a fashion house in Paris from 1937 until 1968. Presented his first own fashion collection in 1964 and within months his name became as well known as that of Dior or Chanel. Courrèges mainly thanks his fame to his beautifully cut mini dresses, worn with boots without heels, and to his pantsuits, which may remind one of space clothing, because of the cut, color (often white) and accompanying helmet-like headwear. He is regarded as one of several fashion designers that strongly influenced the look of the years 1965-1970.

Courser, any of a genus (*Pluvianus*) of long-legged, short-winged, desert birds, particular to Australia, India, and Africa. They are primarily known for their quick running. The courser rarely flies unless it is bothered or disquieted, and even then, it is only for brief spaces. There are 9 different species, most of which share a distinctive brown and white marking.

Court, judicial portion of government, responsible for the administration of justice. The term also refers to the building in which courts sit and to the proceedings themselves. As a formal institution with definite rules of procedure, the court emerged during the late Roman Empire. Christians, however, were not allowed to participate in courts 'of this world,' so bishops and ecclesiastical courts ruled on cases involving Christians and developed a body of canon law. After the Norman Conquest (1066), England pioneered in the development of a complex national court system, and the royal courts were soon administering justice to all the king's subjects. Justices of the peace acted as inferior (lower) courts to deal with minor offenses. These courts gradually established a system based not on the power of the king but upon the power of the law. In their decisions, the British courts were in effect creating law by setting judicial precedents that were followed by succeeding courts. As Parliament (originally established as a court to reach decisions in the name of the king) grew in power and the legal precedents set up in earlier courts expanded and became accepted, the courts judged cases according to their merits under this body of common law.
International disputes brought about a movement in the latter part of the 19th century to establish courts to rule on international issues .The First Hague Conference (1899) established the Permanent Court of Arbitration. The League of Nations included a Permanent Court of International Justice. At present, the International Court of Justice functions as an organ of the United Nations. These courts, however, have exercised only marginal influence on international law, for they do not have the power to compel nations and individuals to submit to their jurisdiction.

Court-martial, court for the trial of offenses against military rules and regulations.

Court reporter, stenographer who records the proceedings in a court of law. Court reporters use shorthand or a stenography machine to note all testimony word for word (except what the judge or the attorneys deem 'off the record'), and later converts it into a typewritten official transcript.

Court-Smith, Margaret (1942-   ), Australian female tennis player, won the singles competition three times (1963, 1965, 1970) and the Wimbledon ladies' doubles and mixed doubles several times, titles which she also claimed in the U.S., France, and Australia. In 1970, she added the Grand Slam to her name. The best characteristics of her game wee her running ability and her strong service.

Cousteau, Jacques-Yves (1910-1997), French oceanographer who pioneered underwater exploration. In 1943 he co-invented the scuba (self-contained underwater breathing apparatus); later he developed an underwater television system. His popular films and television programs made him world famous.

Cousy, Bob (Robert Joseph Cousy; 1928-   ), U.S. basketball player. Known for his dribbling and passing, he is considered one of the greatest playmakers of all time. As a guard for the Boston Celtics (1950-1963) of the National Basketball Association (NBA), Cousy led the league in assists eight consecutive seasons (1952-1960) and helped his team win the NBA championship 6 times. After leaving the Celtics, he coached both college and professional teams for 10 years. Cousy was inducted into the National Basketball Hall of Fame in 1970.

Covenanters, 16th- and 17th-century Scottish Presbyterians pledged by covenants to defend their religion against Anglican influences. They were suppressed both by Oliver Cromwell and by the Stuart kings. Their savage persecution after the Restoration was known as the 'killing time.' *See also:* Presbyterianism.

Coventry (pop. 306,000), cathedral city in England, southeast of Birmingham. Coventry was formerly a small market town but is now an important center for the British automobile industry. It was founded in 1043, and by the 14th century was the fourth largest commercial town in England, famous for its wool and hides. In late 1940, Coventry was the first British town to suffer 'saturation' bombing. After 1945 the city was rebuilt in modern style. New buildings include the Belgrade Theater (1958) and the very modern Cathedral of St. Michael (1962).
See also: England.

Covered wagon *See:* Conestoga wagon.

Coward, Sir Noel Pierce (1899-1973), English actor, playwright, and composer. He is famous for his witty comedies of manners, such as *Private Lives* (1930) and *Blithe Spirit* (1941), revues, musicals, and serious plays such as *The Vortex* (1924). Their prevailing cynicism is offset by patriotic works such as the film *In Which We Serve* (1942).

C

C

Cowbird, bird of the blackbird family (Icteridae), so named because it follows cattle and feeds on the insects they stir up. Two species live in the United States, but most are South American. Most lay eggs in the nests of other birds, which hatch and raise the cowbird young.

Cowboy, person who handles cattle on horseback. The U.S. cowboy has become a legendary folk hero, celebrated in innumerable films and novels. In the early 1800s in areas such as Texas (then part of Mexico), settlers took over the Spanish practice of using the plains for grazing cattle. At the same time they borrowed from the Spanish the typical equipment and methods of the cattle herder: broad-brimmed sombrero hat, bandanna worn around the neck, high-heeled boots that went with heavy 'western' saddle and covered stirrups, leather chaps to protect the legs, and lariat with which to rope cattle. To this was added the 'six-shooter' revolver. The cowboy was really created by the 'long drive.' As the frontier moved westward after the Civil War and the Plains Indians were driven off the open lands into reservations, large herds of cattle, tended by cowboys, were driven every year from the southern plains to the new railheads in the north-central plains. By the 1880s and 1890s the settlement of the central plains and their enclosure with barbed wire put an end to the long drive, but the cowboy continued to be employed in ranch work and even today is known for his riding and roping skills in rodeos.

Cowell, Henry Dixon (1897-1965), U.S. composer. Like John Cage, he sought to explore new sonorities in his music, as with 'tone clusters,' produced on the piano by striking groups of keys with the forearm.

Cowley, Abraham (1618-1667), English poet and essayist of the metaphysical and neoclassical periods. His *Miscellanies* (1656) and *The Mistress* (1647) reflect the themes and motifs of the metaphysical poets. *Davideis* (1656), an unfinished epic in couplets, and the *Pindarique Odes* (1656) are neoclassical in their restraint, and his *Essays in Verse and Prose* (1668) reflect the influence of Montaigne's essays. Cowley sided with the Royalist cause during the English Civil War. Later he studied medicine at Oxford, and helped found the Royal Society, dedicated to the promotion of the physical sciences.
See also: Metaphysical poets.

Cow parsnip (*Heracleum maximum*), large perennial plant of the carrot family. Generally considered a weed, it can serve as a fodder. It thrives in damp soil. Cow parsnip can reach a height of 13 ft (4 m); it bears a white flowers that grow in clusters up to 20 in (50 cm) in diameter.

Cowpea, or black-eyed pea (*Vigna sinensis*), member of the pea family, cultivated widely in warmer climates for its edible beans. One variety is native to India and another, with very long pods, is native to China. In the United States, the cowpea is grown extensively in the South, where it is valued both for its beans and for the plant itself, which is used as manure and hay.

Cowper, William (1731-1800), 18th-century English poet. He wrote about nature and rural life in the English countryside. A strict Calvinist, he wrote the *Olney Hymns* (1779), which contained 'Oh! for a Closer Walk with God' and 'God Moves in a Mysterious Way.' Other works of Cowper's include 'The Diverting History of John Gilpin' (1782), *The Task* (1785), and 'Yardley Oak' (1791).

Cowpox *See:* Jenner, Edward.

Cowrie, any of a variety of mollusks (family *Cyprocidae*) with shells that have spirals like those of snails but that are obscured by the final dome-shaped twist. Unlike other mollusk shells, these are covered by a layer of flesh and are shiny. Most cowries are found in warm seas. Their shells have been used as money and as ornaments since the earliest times.

Cowslip, or marsh marigold (*Caltha palustris*), marsh plant with large yellow flowers, related to the buttercup. Virginia cowslip, also found in wet places, has blue flowers and grows in the eastern United States. The original cowslip is a yellow-flowered primula of Europe and Asia.

Coyote, or prairie wolf (*Canis latrans*), wild dog of North America. It is well known for its characteristic howl. Once confined to the plains of western North America, the coyote has spread to the Atlantic coast. It feeds mainly on rabbits and small rodents but has become more of a scavenger. Coyotes sometimes interbreed with dogs.

Coysevox, Antoine (1640-1720), French sculptor. In 1679 he was commissioned by Louis XIV to work on the Palace of Versailles, where he carved the equestrian marble relief of the king, in addition to 2 ornate sculptures for the gardens- 'Renown' and 'Mercury.' He also carved sculptures for the Cathedral of Notre Dame, as well as the tombs of finance minister Jean Baptiste Colbert and Cardinal Mazarin in Paris.

Cozzens, James Gould (1903-1978), U.S. novelist. His books, such as *By Love Possessed* (1957) and *Ask Me Tomorrow* (1940), deal with moral conflicts of the professional classes, seen by Cozzens as the custodians of social stability. *Guard of Honor* (1948) won him a Pulitzer Prize.

CPR *See:* Cardiopulmonary resuscitation (CPR).

Crab, crustacean with 10 pairs of legs, the first pair usually modified as pincers. Crabs start life as small, swimming larvae that look more like lobsters. After molting several times the larva settles on the bottom and becomes an adult crab, with the typical rounded shell protecting the body. Most crabs are marine or live in brackish water, feeding on small animals and carrion that are torn up with the pincers. The smallest is the pea crab, which lives in the shells of bivalve mollusks. The giant crab of the Pacific is a spider crab with a shell measuring over 1 ft (.03 m) across; like all spider crabs, it has very long legs, the record being a 12-ft (4-m) span. Some crabs spend a considerable amount of time out of water. The fiddler crab, with one large, colored claw, lives in holes on mudflats. Robber crabs climb trees but, contrary to belief, do not appear to be able to open coconuts. Hermit crabs, which shelter in the disused shells of mollusks, are a separate group of crustaceans.

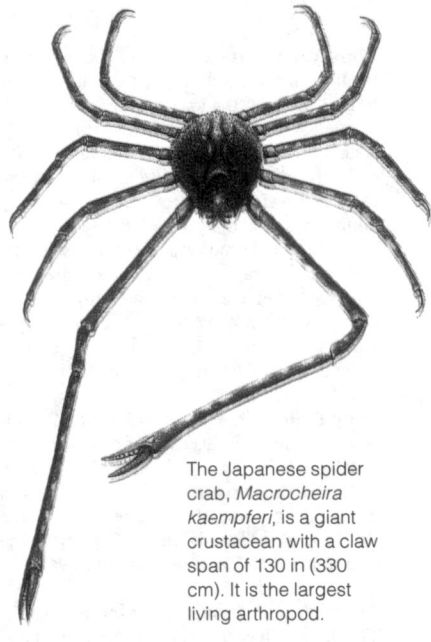

The Japanese spider crab, *Macrocheira kaempferi*, is a giant crustacean with a claw span of 130 in (330 cm). It is the largest living arthropod.

Crab apple (genus *Malus*, family Roseceae), tree that bears small tart-tasting apples, and has fragrant white or pink flowers. It grows in northern Asia and in North America, where the fruit is used for making pies, jellies, and condiments. The tree is usually about 20 ft (6 m) tall.

Craft *See:* Handicraft.

Craft union *See:* Labor movement.

Cragg, Tony (1949-), British sculptor, residing in Wuppertal (Germany) since 1978. Following his education in natural sciences, he studied painting and sculpture. From around 1980, he placed brightly colored pieces of plastic or objects that he found, separately on the floor or attached them to the wall, to make a silhouette. He also made stacks of angular forms, such as suitcases, blocks and the like, on which he then applied a pattern of scratches. After around 1985, his sculptures took on the form of large plastic bottles, retorts, distilling flasks, etcetera, and became more organic in form. He also cut stencil plates from rusty iron, bronze, plaster and wood and turned them into images. His sculptures often have a pattern of holes or ripples.

Cramp, painful contraction of muscle-often in the legs. The cause is usually unknown. It may be brought on by exercise or lack of salt. It also occurs in muscles with inadequate blood supply.

C

Lucas Cranach the Elder (1472-1553) had a clear personal ideal of female beauty. In this picture he shows a nude woman with her children (Royal Museum of Visual Art, Antwerp).

Cranach, Lucas, The Elder (1472-1553), German painter and engraver. As court painter to the electors of Saxony (1505-1553), he lived and worked most of his life in Wittenberg. A supporter of the Reformation, he was a close friend of Martin Luther, for whom he did a number of woodcuts. Among his many portraits are those of *Luther* (1553) and *Henry the Pious of Saxony* (1514). Influenced by Albrecht Dürer, his mature style is characterized by highly finished and emotionally expressive figures set in a dreamy and luxuriant landscape.
See also: Dürer, Albrecht.

Cranberry, berry-bearing shrub (genus *Oxycoccus*) found in wet bogs or heaths or in flooded areas known as cranberry bogs. The small cranberry grows in arctic and subarctic regions of Europe and America, while the large American cranberry is native to the northern United States and Canada. The red or bluish-black berries are edible, though somewhat acid in flavor, and are used in sauces, jellies, pies, preserves, and in making cranberry juice.

Crane, long-necked, long-legged bird of the family Gruidae. Its plumage is generally white or gray; some species have patches of colored skin around the head. The windpipe is even longer than the neck because it is coiled up in the breast. This long windpipe is responsible for the crane's remarkable trumpeting calls. There are 14 species spread around the world, most of them now rare. Their courtship includes graceful dances in which the birds leap into the air and drift down on outstretched wings. The two cranes of North America are the sandhill crane, common in the prairies, and the whooping crane, which, in 1967, numbered only 48 birds in one flock. Although strictly protected, the whooping cranes have a long, vulnerable migration route from Canada to Texas.

Crane, machine designed to lift loads and move them horizontally. Despite their great variety, all cranes have certain features in common: a winding mechanism, or *winch*, to operate a rope (usually of steel wire), attached to a *pulley block* on which there is a *hook* to pick up the load. In some cranes the rope is looped over a pulley at the top of a boom or *jib*; in others it is suspended from a horizontal beam or girder.

Crane, Hart (Harold Crane; 1899-1932), U.S. poet. One of the earliest 'modern' poets, Crane is best known for his long poem, 'The Bridge' (1930). The poem was inspired by the Brooklyn Bridge as a symbol of the direction and aspirations of American life, much in the way that an earlier midwestern poet, Walt Whitman, saw America through the flat, plowed prairie in *Leaves of Grass*. It is a difficult, mystical, and heavily symbolic work that was to exert an important influence on later poets such as Ezra Pound and Wallace Stevens.

Crane, Stephen (1871-1900), U.S. author. He wrote one of the earliest of naturalist novels, *Maggie: A Girl of the Streets* (1893), the story of a prostitute driven to despair. Although Crane's short poems anticipated the modern style and he wrote some fine short stories, like 'The Open Boat' (1898), he is best known for his fiction, and particularly for *The Red Badge of Courage* (1895), a sensitive study of a soldier during the Civil War that conveys the confusion and fear of battle and the vastness of the conflict. Crane himself had never seen war, but he went on to work as a journalist in New York and then actually became a war correspondent before dying of tuberculosis at the age of 28.

Crane, Walter (1845-1915), English artist and book illustrator. He is best known for illustrating popular nursery rhymes and fairy tales such as *Sing a Song of Sixpence* (1866), *Beauty and the Beast* (1874), *Little Red Riding Hood* (1875), and *Aladdin* (1875). Other children's works include *The Baby's Opera* (1877) and *The Baby's Bouquet* (1878). Crane also illustrated Edmund Spenser's *The Faerie Queene* (1895-1897).

Cranko, John (1927-1973), South African dancer, choreographer, and lead ballet dancer. Made his first choreography for Stravinsky's l'Histoire du Soldat at the early age of fifteen. He joined Sadler Well's Ballet in London in 1946. He enjoyed international fame as a choreographer for, among others, the Ballet Rambert, the Ballet of the Parisian Opera, and the New York City Ballet. Became artistic director of the Ballett der Würtembergischen Staatstheater in Stuttgart in 1961, which developed into a world-famous, travelling ballet company under his supervision. His greatest productions include: Romeo and Juliet (1962 Prokofjev), Onegin (1965 Tsjaikovski), and The Tamed Shrew (1969 Scarlatti). He died in an airplane crash.
Following his death, Marcia Haydée, his leading ballerina, took over his work in Stuttgart until 1996, during which time his choreographic works continued to function as the backbone of the company's repertoire.

The unloading of a wine-ship in sixteenth-century Bruges. The all-wooden crane was powered by men in a treadmill. The scene was painted in 1530 by Simon Bening

Cranko proved to be an excellent teacher and example, as his company produced no less than three choreographers who later became world famous: Jiri Kylian (Nederlands Dans Theater), William Forsythe (Ballett Frankfurt), and John Neumeier (Ballett Hamburg Staatsoper).

Cranmer, Thomas (1489-1556), first Protestant archbishop of Canterbury and English martyr. He was an outstanding scholar and one of the leaders of the English Reformation. He obtained the favor of Henry VIII by proposing to refer the question of the annulment of the king's marriage to Catherine of Aragon to the European universities rather than to the pope. He became the king's chaplain and in 1530 was sent on a mission to the pope to discuss the divorce. In 1533 he was appointed archbishop of Canterbury. In conformity with his belief in the ascendancy of the state over the church, he annulled Henry's marriages to Catherine

The crowned crane (*Balearica pavonina*), with its gold feather crown and contrasting white and black face and body, is a distinctively coloured species, found in central and southern Africa. Unlike other cranes, the crowned crane sometimes nests in low trees.

C

(1533) and Anne Boleyn (1536). As counselor to Edward VI Cranmer became increasingly Protestant, and compiled the Book of Common Prayer (1549), his most enduring achievement, but suffered impeachment and imprisonment under the Catholic queen, Mary Tudor. After several recantations he stood by his beliefs and met death at the stake at Oxford with great courage.
See also: Book of Common Prayer.

The battle near Crecy in 1346, was one of the last field battles involving (mainly French and English) knights. Miniature from the *Chronicle of Froissart* (British Museum, London).

Crappie, any of a genus (*Pomoxis*) of freshwater sunfishes that have been spread across the United States from the east because of their popularity with anglers. The black crappie prefers clear water, the white crappie turbid water.

Crassus, Marcus Licinius (112-53 B.C.), Roman general and political leader. He and Pompey crushed the slave revolt of Spartacus in 71 B.C. Eleven years later, Crassus, Pompey, and Julius Caesar formed the First Triumvirate, an alliance that governed Rome. In 53 B.C., Crassus went to war against the central Asian empire of Parthia and was killed in battle.
See also: Rome, Ancient.

Crater, depression on the surface of the earth or other celestial body. Craters are caused by volcanic activity or the impact of heavy objects from space (meteorites). Most craters on earth are volcanic. Craters are numerous on the moon, which lacks an atmosphere capable of burning out meteorites before they crash into the surface.

Crater Lake National Park, national park in the Cascade Mountains of southwest Oregon. The major feature is the crater lake, which is volcanic and covers 20 sq mi (52 sq km), reaching a depth of 1,932 ft (589 m).

Crawfish *See:* Crayfish.

Crawford, Joan (1908-1977), U.S. film actress noted for her roles as self-made, tough-minded women. Her best-known movies were *Rain* (1932), *A Woman's Face* (1941),

and *Mildred Pierce* (1945), for which she won an Academy Award.

Crayfish, or crawfish, edible freshwater crustacean found in ponds and streams in most parts of the world except Africa.

Crazy Horse (c.1849-1877), Native American leader, chief of the Oglala Sioux. He spent his life defending his tribe's territory in South Dakota and Wyoming. In 1876, he allied with Sitting Bull and annihilated General George Custer's cavalry at the Little Bighorn River, but a year later he was starved into surrender. He was stabbed to death while attempting to escape.

Creationism, also known as Creation Science, theory held by fundamentalist Christians that the Earth and living things were created as described in Genesis rather than through a process of evolution.

Crécy, Battle of, key battle in the Hundred Years War between England and France, fought in 1346. The English army under King Edward III was heavily outnumbered by a French force under King Philip VI at the village of Crécy in Normandy. After suffering serious losses from English archery attacks, the French retreated. The battle made an English national hero of the king's son, Edward, the 'Black Prince.'
See also: Hundred Years War.

Credit, delivery of goods, services, or money with a promise of payment in the future, usually with an interest charge.

Credit Union, cooperative bank formed by the members of a company, church, labor union, or other organization. Members buy shares with their savings and may borrow money at low interest rates. Any profits are distributed to members periodically in the form of dividends. Credit unions, like other banks, are closely supervised by the government.

Cree, Native American tribe originating in Manitoba. One group of Cree later moved southwest, becoming Plains Cree. Another, the Woodlands Cree, remained in Canada, where they had a deer-based (as opposed to bison-based) culture. Both Cree tribes were ravaged by serious epidemics during the 18th and 19th centuries. The survivors now live on reservations in Canada.

Creek, Native American confederation of tribes and settlements in Alabama and Georgia. The Creek had a stable, agricultural society centered on rivers and creeks. In 1813-1814 they lost most of their land in a war led by U.S. general Andrew Jackson. By 1840 the entire tribe had been transported to Oklahoma, where most of their descendants now live.

Creeley, Robert (1926-), U.S. poet and author. Along with Robert Duncan and Charles Olson, Creeley was one of the leading Black Mountain poets. While teaching at Black Mountain College in North Carolina, he was the editor of the *Black Mountain Review,* a literary magazine that pioneered modern forms of poetry and short prose. Creeley's best-known works are compiled in *Collected*

Poems: 1945-1975 (1983) and *The Collected Prose of Robert Creeley* (1984).

Creeper, any of several small brown birds of the treecreeper family, found in most parts of the world. Creepers use their pointed bills to probe for insects in bark. They get their name from their 'creeping' up a tree in a quick, hopping movement.

Creole, term used to describe the descendants of Spanish, Portuguese, and French settlers in the West Indies, Latin America, and parts of the United States. French- and Spanish-based patois are known as Creole languages.

Creosote, thick, oily liquid made by distilling coal or wood tar. Almost colorless, it has a powerful, smoky smell and can be used to protect wood from rot, insects, and marine organisms.
See also: Tar.

Creosote bush (*Larrea divaricata*), evergreen shrub that grows in the deserts of Mexico and southwestern United States. Growing to a height of 5-8 ft (1.5-2.5 m), the creosote bush produces a resin and tiny yellow flowers. Its berries are round and white and have a feltlike texture. Creosote bushes often grow in circles, and botanists believe that some of these colonies are thousands of years old.

Cresol, or hydroxytoluene, group of organic chemical compounds. Cresols are a major component of creosote oil, which is applied as a preservative to railroad ties, fence posts, and other wooden outdoor structures. Obtained from coal tar or a petroleum base, cresols are also used in antiseptic soaps and disinfectants.

Cress, any of various plants of the mustard family. They include watercress, bitter cress, rock cress, and penny cress.

Cretaceous period, geological period from about 140 to 65 million years ago. It is one of the 3 periods of the mesozoic era, the age of reptiles. The separation of Africa and South America occurred during the Cretaceous period, as did the disappearance of the dinosaurs and emergence of snakes and lizards.

Crete, mountainous island in the eastern Mediterranean Sea, about 3,235 sq mi (8,380 sq km). Part of Greece, Crete relies on agriculture and tourism. The island was the home of the ancient Minoan civilization (c.1600 B.C.), with its capital of Cnossus.
See also: Greece.

Cretinism, type of dwarfism characterized by mental retardation. It is caused by a failure of thyroid gland function during fetal development.
See also: Thyroid gland.

Creutzfeldt-Jakob disease, rare, degenerative disease of the nervous system. It was thought that the Creutzfeldt-Jakob disease was caused by a slow virus that incubated in the body for months or years before symptoms appeared. Nowadays it is suspected to

C

be a prion disease. The disease generally afflicts individuals during middle age. Earliest symptoms are memory loss or peculiar behavior, followed by visual disturbances and loss of muscular coordination. Death usually occurs within a year. There is no treatment or cure for this disease. Creutzfeldt-Jakob disease was first described in separate accounts in the early 1920s by 2 German neuropsychiatrists, Hans G. Creutzfeldt and Alfons M. Jakob. In 1996 a variation of the disease was discovered which is probably a human variant of the mad cow disorder.

Crèvecoeur, Michel-Guillaume Jean de (1735-1813), 18th-century French essayist. He chronicled rural life in early America under the pen name J. Hector St. John. The 12 essays that make up his *Letters from an American Farmer* (1782) were influential in persuading many Europeans to settle in America. He sided with the British during the American Revolution, and his *Sketches of Eighteenth Century America* (published posthumously in 1925) was critical of the rebellious colonists. He was French consul to the United States 1783-1790.

Crewel, type of woolen yarn as well as a form of embroidery crafted from the yarn. The yarn consists of twin threads twisted together. Most crewelwork is done from patterns stitched on a plain cloth background. As an art form, crewel dates back to the ancient Hebrews and was popular during the Middle Ages.

Cribbage, card game played with standard deck of cards and a special board with pegs for marking the score.

Crib death *See:* Sudden infant death syndrome.

Crick, Francis Harry Compton (1916-), English biologist who shared the 1962 Nobel Prize in physiology or medicine with Maurice Wilkins and James Watson, for establishing the function and structure of DNA, the key substance in transmitting hereditary traits.
See also: Biology.

Cricket, bat and ball game played extensively in Great Britain and the Commonwealth countries. The opposing teams have 11 players on a side. The rules are complex, and a match may take 3 days to complete.

Cricket, chirping, hopping insect of the Gryllidae family. Its familiar song is produced by the male, rubbing special parts of its front wings together.

Crime, violation of rules of behavior as laid down in a code of law. *Violent crimes* are directed against people; they include murder, assault, rape, and robbery. *Property crimes* include burglary, theft, and other violations of ownership laws.

Crimea, peninsula, 10,425 sq mi (25,900 sq km), on the northern side of the Black Sea, part of the Ukraine. Its population today is about 70% Russian and 20% Ukrainian. It was the scene of the Crimean War (1853-1856) and was also a battleground during World War I and World War II. There are three natural regions: the flat northern steppe lands, which make up about four-fifths of the total area; the southern mountains; and the subtropical coast. Mineral resources include phosphorous iron ores on the Kerch Peninsula, low-grade goal north of Yalta, and some oil and natural gas near Kerch. Extensive salt deposits are worked in the north. Fisheries operate along the entire coast. High-grade wheat is grown in the north. Other crops include cotton, tobacco, and fruits and vegetables. There are also vineyards. Because of its temperate climate, especially in the south, the Crimea is a popular tourist area. The majority of the people of the Crimea are Russians; most of the remainder are Ukrainians. The leading cities are the ports of Sevastopol and Kerch and the administrative center, Simferopol. The Khanate of Crimea, a Tatar dependency of the Ottoman Turks, was conquered by Russia in 1783. Much of the region was then settled by Russians and Ukrainians. A dispute between Russia and the Ottoman Empire resulted in the Crimean War, 1853-1856. In 1921 the Crimea became an autonomous republic of the Soviet Union. During World War II the Crimean Tatars, who numbered some 200,000 were accused of collaboration with the Germans and deported to Central Asia. The republic was dissolved and the peninsula became part of the Russian Federated Socialist Republic. The area was transferred to the Ukrainian S.S.R. in 1954. In 1967 the Tatars were cleared of the colloboration accusation. Several thousand Tatar families eventually returned to the Crimea. After Ukraine became independant in 1991, many Crimeans wanted their region to become an independant country or unite with Russia. Also, ownership of the former Soviet Black Sea fleet, which was based in Sevastopol, became a source of conflict between Ukraine and Russia. In 1997 Ukraine and Russia reached an agreement.
See also: Union of Soviet Socialist Republics.

Crimean War (1853-1856), war between Russia and an alliance of England, France, Turkey, and Sardinia. A chief cause was conflict over Russia's attempt to gain access to Mediterranean warm-water ports. The war ended when the city of Sevastopol, headquarters of the Russian fleet, was captured after a long, destructive siege.

Crime laboratory, law enforcement investigative facility that examines evidence gathered at a crime scene for clues. Forensic pathologists use crime labs to conduct autopsies on the bodies of crime victims, and ballistics experts use them to draw conclusions on weapons used in crimes. Crime labs are also used to isolate fingerprints, determine causes of suspicious fires, and test for substance abuse.

Criminal law, that part of the law that defines criminal offenses, establishes procedures for trying accused persons, and fixes penalties for those convicted of criminal offenses. Many offenses once punished as crimes now come under the civil law. These offenses, which usually grow out of carelessness or accidents, are called *torts*. The penalty is likely to be the payment of damages to the party that has been injured. Generally, crimes are willful acts considered dangerous to society. The modern criminal law of England, the United States, and Canada originated in the English common law of crimes, which grew over hundreds of years from judicial decisions applied throughout the realm and therefore 'common.' Legislation has supplemented these decisions, particularly in the past two centuries, when types of crime such as embezzlement that were almost unknown to the common law began to occur with frequency. The common law system has established some general principles of criminal law. One of these is that nothing can be treated as a crime unless there is a law against the conduct in question (in Latin, *nulla crimen sine lege*). A corollary of this is that no punishment can be imposed unless it is provided for by law (*nulla poena sine lege*). Another essential principle is that the crime must be accompanied by *mens rea*, a guilty mind. The criminal had to know what he or she was doing wrong. This principle has led to the difficult question of responsibility for criminal acts. Persons suffering from mental instability or disorder are not responsible for acts that, committed by others, would be crimes. But the legal criterion of mental responsibility, or competence, has long been a matter of controversy. In general, the British and U.S. courts have followed the so-called McNaghten (M'Naghten) Rule: Insanity is a valid defense if the accused was, at the time of the action, suffering from mental disease such that he or she did not know the nature of the act that he or she was committing, or did not know that it was wrong. Other grounds for diminished criminal responsibility include extreme youth and intoxication. There are also complicated questions of procedure involving arrests, confessions, searches, the right to have a lawyer, the right to confront witnesses, the right not to in-

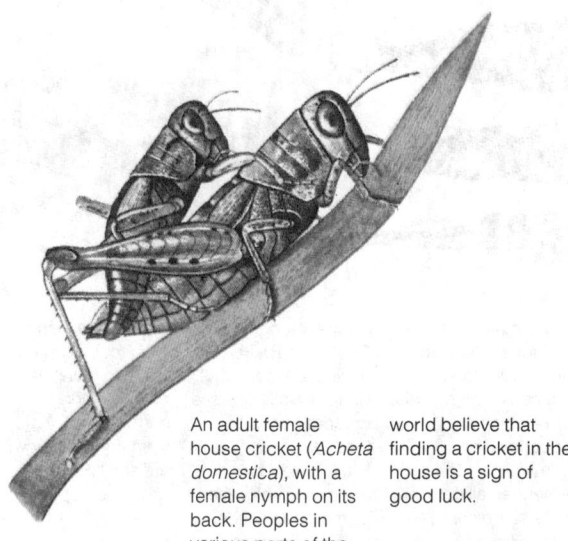

An adult female house cricket (*Acheta domestica*), with a female nymph on its back. Peoples in various parts of the world believe that finding a cricket in the house is a sign of good luck.

In Plitvicka Jezera national park in eastern Croatia, there are sixteen lakes that are connected by waterfalls. The region is considered one of the most beautiful in Yugoslavia.

C

criminate oneself, and other means of protecting the individual. Criminal law is not only a means of punishing wrongdoers; it is also a method of dealing with conflict, and as such reflects the weaknesses as well as the ideals of a society.
See also: Crime.

Criminology, scientific study of the causes of criminal behavior, its development, and its treatment. Belgian statistician Adolphe Quételet (1796-1874) introduced the correlation of crime and social or environmental conditions, and Italian scholars continued what was known as the positivist study of crime in the late 19th and early 20th centuries. Cesare Lombroso (1836-1909) advanced a now-discredited theory representing criminals as reversions to a more primitive stage of human development. His work

was followed by that of Enrico Ferri (1856-1929) and Raffaele Garofalo, both of whom stressed social factors.

Critical mass, minimum mass of material necessary to maintain a spontaneous fission chain reaction. For pure U^{235} it is computed to be about 20 lb (9.1 kg).

Criticism, act of analyzing and evaluating any object or activity, often unfavorably. The term is applied most often to the examination and evaluation of works of art and literature. Critical writings may take the form of prose verse, essays, reviews, or long books. In philosophy, criticism may be defined as an approach to problems in which the thinker weighs the evidence in the manner of a judge. The term *critical philosophy* is used to describe the theories of Immanuel Kant, whose *critiques* offer critical examinations of various ideas.

Croaker, any of a family (Sciaenidae) of medium-sized fish found in shallow tropical and temperate seas. They are renowned for their calls, a drumming, croaking chorus produced by special muscles that make the swim bladder vibrate.

Croatia

Capital:	Zagreb
Area:	21,829 sq mi (56,538 sq km)
Population:	4,391,000
Language:	Croatian
Government:	Republic
Independent:	1991
Head of gov.:	Prime minister
Per capita:	US $ 8,300
Monetary unit:	1 Kuna = 100 lipa

Croatia, republic on the east coast of the Adriatic Sea, bordered on the north by Slovenia, on the north east by Hungary and the Federal Republic of Yugoslavia, on the east by Bosnia, and on the south east by Montenegro.
Land and climat. Croatia has a diverse landscape, with flat plains, low mountains, a coastline, and several offshore islands. The interior has a continental climate, the coast has a Mediterranean climate.
People. The majority of the population is Croatian, a Slavic people who speak a

Serbo-Croatian language. Serbs form an important minority. Roman Catholicism is the predominant religion.
Economy The eastern plain is fertile, and crops like sugar beets, maize, and wheat are produced there. Croatia is a major supplier of coal, petroleum, bauxite, and timber, and industry is reasonably developed.
History United with Hungary in 1102, ruled by the Turks (16th-18th centuries) and then by the Habsburgs (until 1918), Croatia became part of Yugoslavia after World War I. In World War II the Germans ruled it as an Axis satellite. In 1946 Yugoslavia adopted a federal constitution, and Croatia became one of its 6 constituent republics. Beginnning in the 1970s, Croatia agitated for greater autonomy; however, by the end of the 1980s demands for autonomy changed to demands for independence, which was attained in 1991. Armed conflict soon arose between Croats and Serbs living in Croatia. When the Yugoslav army began to support Serbian rebels in Croatia, a bloody civil war ensued. By 1992 representatives from the United Nations negociated a cease-fire and UN peacekeeping troops were sent to Croatia. In two offensives during the spring and summer of 1995 Croatian forces recaptured most of the territory held by the Serbian rebels. In December 1995, the Serbian rebels agreed to return the remaining areas under their control to Croatia.
President Tudjman governed the country authocratically until 1999. After the constitutional change in 2000, Croatia became a parliamentary democracy. Prime Minister Racan tried to direct the country towards the EU and the NATO.

Croce, Benedetto (1866-1952), Italian philosopher and writer. A leading exponent of the modern Idealist school, Croce was the founder and editor of *La Critica*, a scholarly journal devoted to literature, history, and philosophy. Between 1902 and 1917, he produced his best-known work, *Philosophy of the Spirit*. Espousing liberal and intellectual causes, he opposed Mussolini and his Fascist government.

Crochet (from French *croche*, 'hook'), method of making fabrics, garments, lace, and even rugs, from threads or yarn, using a hook (made of steel, ivory, bone, or wood). The crochet stitch links each loop of thread to another to produce a foundation *chain*, into which additional rows of stitches are added. Single and double crochet are the basic forms from which all other stitches and patterns have developed.

Crockett, Davy (David Crockett; 1786-1836), U.S. frontiersman, representative from Tennessee (1827-1831, 1833-1835), and folk hero. Known for his amusing stories and sharpshooting, Crockett failed in his final bid for reelection in 1835, joined the Texan forces in the war of independence from Mexico, and died in the defense of the Alamo.
See also: Alamo.

Crocodile, carnivorous reptile (order Crocodilia) found in both fresh and salt water in tropical and subtropical regions.

The crocodile family includes crocodiles (top), alligators, caimans, and gavials, all of which are aquatic and carnivorous. The American alligator (*A. mississippiensis*) (A), differs from the African crocodile (*C. Niloticus*) (B), in having a wider snout. Unlike an alligator's, a crocodile's fourth tooth (from the front) in the lower jaw remains visible when its mouth is closed. A gavial (*G. gangeticus*) (C), a small member of the crocodile family, found in India, has an extremely long, narrow snout. Caimans (not shown) are small South American reptiles, resembling alligators most closely.

C

Crocodiles range in size from 3 ft 9 in (1.14 m; the dwarf crocodile), to 8 ft (2.4 m; the Nile), to 12 ft (3.7 m; the American), to 20 ft (6.1 m; the Orinoco), and are distinguished from the alligator by a narrower snout, greater aggressiveness, and a long protruding fourth tooth.

Crocodile bird (*Pluvianus aegyptius*), African plover that enters the mouth of a crocodile to feed on leeches and scraps of food. The crocodiles, which normally prey on birds, tolerate this behavior.

Crocus, genus of perennial herb of the iris family, originally from Asia and the Mediterranean, usually bearing a solitary blue, yellow, or white flower. The yellow dye, saffron, is produced from the dried flowers of one species. The wild crocus is a member of the buttercup family.

Croesus (d. c.547 B.C.), last king of Lydia (r.560-546 B.C.), and last of the Mermnadae dynasty. Known for his wealth and generosity, he ruled a large part of Asia Minor until he was overthrown by Cyrus the Great of Persia. Legend suggests he became an honored courtier of Cyrus.
See also: Lydia.

Cro-Magnon, race of primitive humans (*Homo sapiens*), indistinguishable biologically from modern human beings. Remains dating from the upper Paleolithic era (40,000-35,000 years ago) were first found in southern France. Cro-Magnon people, like the Neanderthals who preceded them, had high foreheads, developed chins and large brains, and stood erect (males about 6 ft/180 cm). Their advanced culture produced ivory jewelry, bone and flint tools, and sophisticated cave art (especially rock carvings and paintings).

Crompton, Samuel (1753-1827), English inventor. He devised a weaving machine that produced superior cotton fibers for commercial use. By combining the best features of the 2 existing weaving machines, Crompton created the 'mule' in 1779. By the early 1800s, more than 4.5 million mules were in use in England, making it the world's leading textile producer of that time.

Cromwell, Oliver (1599-1658), lord protector of England. As a Puritan and member of Parliament (from 1628) Cromwell joined the Puritan opposition to Charles I. During the first civil war he showed a remarkable ability for military strategy and leadership, and organized the Parliamentary forces in the eastern counties. His famous Ironsides regiment (cavalry) was instrumental in the victory of Marston Moor (1644), and in 1645, under Fairfax, he led the New Model Army to rout Charles's forces at Naseby. In the second part of the civil war, after Charles's flight, Cromwell defeated the Scottish royalists at Preston (1648). His political power was increased by the eviction of the Presbyterians from Parliament (Pride's Purge, 1648), and he was highly influential in bringing Charles I to trial and execution. Following the establishment of the Commonwealth, he ruthlessly punished

Ireland (1649), routed the Royalist Scots at Dunbar (1650), and quelched the forces of Charles II at Worcester (1651). He replaced the Rump Parliament with the short-lived Barebones Parliament, but this too accomplished very little. Finally, the army officers drew up the instrument of government that made Cromwell lord protector (1653). Although he ruled largely without Parliament, he refused the crown when it was offered (1657). His peace with the Dutch (1654) and treaties with Sweden and Denmark fostered trade, necessary to prevent the return of the Stuarts to power. Although he dreamed of a great Protestant League in Europe, he pragmatically formed an alliance with Catholic France against Spain (1655-1659), which he fought over trade rights. The Protectorate did not long survive his death.
See also: Puritans.

Cromwell, Richard (1626-1712), son of Oliver Cromwell. He served as lord protector of England (1658-1659) until he was deposed by military coup. He lived in France as John Clarke for the next 20 years, and then in England, still under an assumed name.

Cromwell, Thomas, Earl of Essex (1485?-1540), English statesman under Henry VIII. A ruthless administrator and the main agent for destroying papal power in England, he supervised the king's break with Rome under the Act of Supremacy (1534) and the dissolution of the monasteries (1536-1539), many of whose properties he was eventually rewarded. He arranged the king's marriage with Anne of Cleves, and on its failure was executed without trial on charges of heresy and treason trumped up by his many enemies. He died in the Catholic faith.

Cronin, A.J. (1896-1981), British novelist. After quitting the practice of medicine because of ill health, he began to write novels, many of which were turned into films, including *Hatter's Castle* (1931), *The Citadel* (1937), and *The Keys of the Kingdom* (1941). Cronin also wrote an autobiography based on his years of medical practice, entitled *Adventures in Two Worlds* (1952).

Cronkite, Walter Leland, Jr. (1916-), U.S. broadcast journalist. He was anchorperson for the Columbia Broadcasting System (CBS) nightly evening television news (1962-1981).

Cronus, in Greek mythology, king of the Titans and ruler of earth. He deposed his father, Uranus, with the help of his mother, Gaea. Cronus married his sister, Rhea, and their children were Zeus, Poseidon, Demeter, Hera, Hades, and Hestia. He was overthrown by Zeus, who succeeded him as king of the gods. Cronus's Roman counterpart was Saturn.
See also: Mythology.

Crookes, Sir William (1832-1919), British scientist and inventor. He is credited with the discovery of the element thallium and experimented with an electronic vacuum tube. The Crookes tube, developed in the 1870s,

was the forerunner of the modern cathode ray picture tube used in television sets. He also founded and edited *Chemical News* (1859), a scientific journal.
See also: Thallium.

Crookes tube, tube developed by English scientist Sir William Crookes to demonstrate the properties of cathode rays. A current, passed between metal electrodes in the tube, produces a glowing discharge, which disappears as the pressure is lowered. Cathode rays (beams of electrons) are then produced, striking the walls of the tube and causing it to glow. Experimenting with such a tube, Wilhelm Roentgen discovered X-rays.
See also: Cathode ray; Crookes, Sir William.

Cropping system, any of a number of methods of replenishing soil after crops have been harvested. This can be done with fertilizers or insecticides or by rotation, a system of planting crops that replenish nutrients in the soil the previous crop removed. Chemical analysis of the soil often determines which crops might best replace lost nutrients.

Croquet, lawn game of French origin (17th century) in which players hit wooden balls with wooden mallets through a series of iron hoops (wickets) stuck in the ground. To win, a player must hit the posts at both ends of the field. Croquet is popular in the United States and Britain.

Crosby, Bing (Harry Lillis Crosby; 1904-

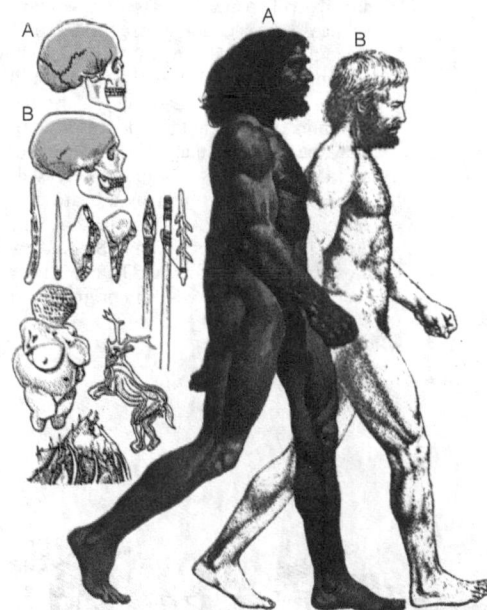

The first representatives of modern Homo sapiens are known as Cro-Magnon man (A), named for the cave in France where their fossil remains were discovered in 1868. Various Cro-Magnon populations of seminomadic tool-making hunters inhabited parts of Europe, Asia, and North Africa from about 50,000 to 10,000 B.C. The comparative illustration — based on reconstructed skulls and skeletal remains — suggests that the Cro-Magnons closely resembled modern humans (B); Cro-Magnon man was slightly taller and had broader facial features.

1977), U.S. singer and film actor. A big-band singer known for crooning, he performed on radio, records, and in films, including the *Road* series with Bob Hope and Dorothy Lamour. He won an Academy Award for his performance in *Going My Way* (1944). His rendition of 'White Christmas' was the best selling record until 1997, when Elton John rerecorded 'Candle in the Wind.'

The siege of Jerusalem, which was the culmination of the First Crusade, was preceded by more than a month of preparations by the depleted force that was encamped outside the city's walls. Captured in July 1099, the city remained in the hands of the crusaders until its reconquest by Sultan Saladin, in 1187.

Cross, cultural symbol, often consisting of an upright and a crosspiece. The cross appeared in cultures of Egypt, ancient India, and North America. Used by ancient Romans for execution by crucifixion, it became the principal symbol of the Christian religion. There are 4 basic forms of the Christian cross: the Latin cross, the most common, in which the upright is longer than the transom that crosses it near the top; the Greek cross, an upright crossed at right angles at its center by a beam of the same length; the tau, or St. Anthony's cross, in the form of a T; and St. Andrew's cross in the form of an X. The other forms, such as the papal cross, an upright crossed

by 3 bars, are mainly inventions for ecclesiastical or hierarchical purposes.

Crossbill, finch (genus *Loxia*) whose mandibles are so strongly curved that they cross each other. This specialized bill is used for splitting open seeds from the cones of pines and other conifers. Crossbills are found in the Northern Hemisphere.

Crossbow, medieval weapon consisting of a small, powerful bow fixed transversely on a stock, which is grooved to take the missile. Its bowstring is latched onto a trigger mechanism, often by a lever or winch, and fires a shaft (a bolt or quarrel, about 19 in/48 cm long). It has less range and accuracy than the longbow and is slower to load.

Cross-country, long-distance running sport. Cross-country is not confined to a track, but instead uses a mapped-out course over a variety of terrains. High school and collegiate courses may range from 1.5 to 7 mi (2.4 to 11 km), and teams generally consist of 6 to 9 members. Points are assigned to the place runners finish in the race, and the team with the lowest point total is the winner.

Cross-eye *See:* Strabismus.

Croton, shrub (genus *Codiaeum*) of the spurge family. Native to Southeast Asia, it is often used in parks in warm U.S. cities, and its multicolored leaves make it an attractive potted plant. One species, the purging croton, is a source of croton oil, a useful resin.

Croup, condition, common in children 6 mos. to 3 years old, due to allergy or virus infection of the larynx and trachea, causing difficulty in breathing and a hoarse cough due to spasm of the larynx.
See also: Diphtheria.

Crow, glossy black bird (family Corvidae), one of the most intelligent of birds, related to ravens, magpies, and jays. The crow has a harsh, croaking call and can imitate sounds, even the human voice. The American, or common, crow (19 in/49 cm long) feeds and nests in small colonies, killing small animals

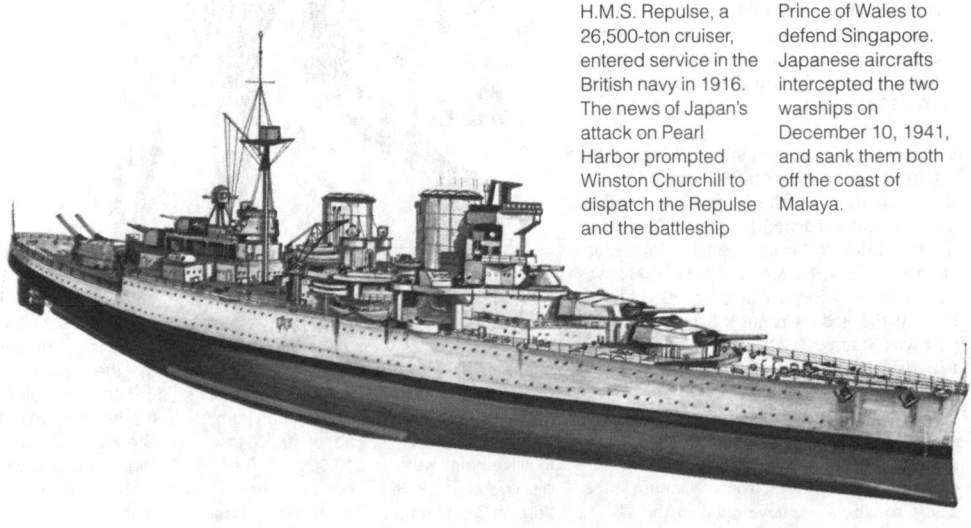

H.M.S. Repulse, a 26,500-ton cruiser, entered service in the British navy in 1916. The news of Japan's attack on Pearl Harbor prompted Winston Churchill to dispatch the Repulse and the battleship Prince of Wales to defend Singapore. Japanese aircrafts intercepted the two warships on December 10, 1941, and sank them both off the coast of Malaya.

and grubbing for insects in the soil. It thus destroys farm pests, but is itself a pest, eating grain crops.

Crow, Native American tribe of the Siouan linguistic group, from the North American plains of Montana and Wyoming. Originally they broke away from the Hidatsa tribe into 2 groups, the Mountain Crow and the River Crow. They hunted bison, cultivated tobacco, and had a highly developed social system. Most Crows now live in southern Montana, supported by income from mineral leases, ranching, and tourism.

Crude oil *See:* Petroleum.

Cruijff, Hendrik Johannes (Johan) (1947-), Dutch association football player. Cruijff played for AFC Ajax, the club where he made his debut when he was 17 years old and with which he won the national championship six times, the Europe Cup I three times (1971, 1972, 1973), and the World Cup for clubs in 1972; FC Barcelona (1973-1978, national champion in 1974); Los Angeles Aztecs (1979); Washington Diplomats (1980); Levante (1981). In 1987, he accepted the position of technical director at FC Barcelona which, under his supervision, won the Europe Cup 2 in 1989 and the Europe Cup 1 in 1992. From 1990-1994, Barcelona became the national champion four times in a row under Cruijff's supervision. Following his dismissal in 1996, he became a sports commentator on television. Cruijff was voted European football player of the year in 1971, 1973, and 1974 and was proclaimed best tournament player during the World Championships in 1974. He was not present at the 1978 World Championships. He drew attention because of his beautiful technique, speed, and tactical insight and is regarded by many as one of the best football players ever known. He was voted best European football player of the century in 1999.

Cruikshank, George (1792-1878), English artist and illustrator famous for his caricatures. Among his best-known works were illustrations for such classics as *Oliver Twist*, *Robinson Crusoe*, *Tom Jones*, and *Don Quixote*.

Cruiser, warship designed for speed and long-range attack, in size between the destroyer and aircraft carrier. Used as a small battleship in World War II, its function has been to maintain lines of sea communication and to defend carriers against air attack. The first cruiser with nuclear power, the USS *Long Beach*, was launched in 1959.

Crusades, under papal authority, wars waged in the Middle Ages (11th-13th centuries) by European Christians against the Muslims to recover the Holy Land, particularly Jerusalem. The initial impetus for the Crusades was a revival of religious fervor, as urged by Pope Urban II at the Council of Clermont (1095); however, conquest of territory, the attraction of riches, and the possibility of expanded trade with the East were also vital elements. At the end of the **First Crusade** (1095-99) Jerusalem was retaken and the Latin kingdom of Jerusalem was established, as were the orders of the Knights Templars and the Knights Hospitalers. The **Second Crusade** (1147-1149), a response to the loss of Edessa (1144) to the Turks, ended in failure. The **Third Crusade** was an attempt to recapture Jerusalem, lost to Saladin in 1187. Holy Roman Emperor Frederick I, Richard I of England, and Philip II of France led this crusade, but were only able to achieve a 3-year truce that gave Christians access to the holy city. During the **Fourth Crusade** (1202-1204) the Crusaders seized Constantinople. In 1212 the tragic **Children's Crusade** was waged. Thousands of children died of hunger or disease or were sold into slavery as they headed toward the Holy Land. The goal of the **Fifth Crusade**, another failure, was Egypt. There was a **Sixth Crusade** (1228-1229) in which another short-lived truce was arranged with the Muslims, and then 3 additional crusades, but Muslim gains held steady. The last Christian stronghold, Akko (Acre), fell in 1291.

Crustacean, invertebrate animal (phylum Arthropoda) with a bilaterally symmetrical segmented body, including crabs, shrimps, lobsters, and barnacles. A few live on land and are parasitic, but most are aquatic, breathing by gills or through the skin, their heads covered with a protective shell and bearing paired series of antennae, 3 paired sets of biting mouth parts, and 2 lateral eyes (plus 1 medial). Periodically they shed their exoskeleton (external skeleton).

Cryobiology, the study of the effects of extremely low temperatures on living organisms, generally for the purpose of preserving living material for future use. Cryobiologists use liquid nitrogen to achieve temperatures far below normal freezing temperature, allowing cells to cease working but to remain alive and unchanged for long periods; once thawed, the cells resume their normal work almost instantly. Frozen tissues, including skin, eye corneas, and blood, are stored in banks, allowing ready access to physicians in need of performing a skin graft, for example.

Cryogenics, or low-temperature physics, science that studies the production, maintenance, and effects of very low temperatures. A substance's temperature can be lowered by cooling with liquefied gases, removing energy from it, or successively magnetizing and demagnetizing it. The study of superconductivity and superfluidity, conditions which prevail at very low temperatures, are part of cryogenics.
See also: Cryobiology; Absolute zero.

Cryotron, miniature switch used in computers, consisting of a short wire around which is wound a fine control coil, kept at the temperature of liquid helium so that the wire and coil are superconducting. A signal in the coil produces a magnetic field that causes the wire to lose its superconductivity and become resistant to electric current. This action stores or produces a 'bit' of information. Cryotron computers may contain 100 billion components to the cubic inch, and can obtain a required bit of information from a

store of 300,000 in less than a 10-millionth of a second.
See also: Superconductivity.

Crystal, solid substance in which the individual molecules, atoms, or ions are arranged in a geometrical form. Almost all pure substances (chemical elements, compounds, mixtures) can form solid crystals. Substances that do not crystallize are called amorphous. Crystals may be formed from solutions, as salt crystals form when a pool of sea water evaporates in the sun; when liquids solidify, as when water freezes to ice or when molten rocks have solidified and have formed crystals; or when vapors solidify (iodine crystals can easily be made by heating some solid iodine in a closed container). Crystals form into definite shapes because the atoms in the substance always arrange themselves in a specific array called a *lattice*. The lattice consists of rows of atoms at various angles. The shapes of the crystals depend on the angles of the rows. The kind of lattice a crystal possesses can be found by passing X rays through the crystal. The lattice affects the X rays so that they emerge from the crystal with a pattern that can be recorded on photographic film, indicating the kind of crystal being studied. The study of crystals is called crystallography. Since crystals often form with corners missing from the basic shape, crystal systems are best described in terms of their axes, rather than their faces. The axes are imaginary lines across the crystals that join opposite faces. Cubic crystals have 3 equal axes at right angles. Salt and alum are cubic crystals, but whereas a salt crystal looks like a cube, an alum crystal has corners missing and is an 8-sided pyramid, or octahedron. Cubic crystals are also called isometric crystals. Tetragonal crystals also have 3 axes at right angles, but 1 axis is longer than the other 2, so the side faces are rectangular. Tin forms tetragonal crystals. In orthorhombic crystals, the 3 axes are at right angles but of different lengths. Sulfur forms orthorhombic crystals. Monoclinic crystals have 3 unequal axes, only 2 of which meet at right angles. Gypsum forms monoclinic crystals. Triclinic crystals have 3 unequal axes that do not meet at right angles. Copper sulfate forms triclinic crystals. Hexagonal crystals have 4 axes, 3 in one plane, equal in length and at 60° to each other, the fourth longer or shorter and at right angles to the others. Beryl forms hexagonal crystals. Trigonal crystals also have 4 axes, but only 3 basic side faces instead of 6. Quartz is a trigonal crystal. Several electrical effects occur in crystals. Piezoelectric crystals produce an electric signal when they are twisted out of shape and return to their original shape. Rochelle salt crystals can produce electric signals with the frequency range of sound waves and so are used in phonograph pickups, microphones, and hearing aids. Quartz crystals produce signals at only one frequency and so can be used in oscillators, electronic filters, and radio tuners. The electronic properties of a transistor depend on the arrangement of atoms in the lattice of the crystal. The crystals have to be very pure and are made with extreme care by a crystallization process called zone refining.

Crystals also have interesting optical properties. Certain types can be used, for example, to produce polarized light.

Crystal Night, name given to the night of November 9, 1938, when the nazi government organized a pogrom against the Jews in Germany, lead by Joseph Goebbels. The murder of a German diplomat in Paris by a seventeen-year-old Jewish boy was given as the reason. Throughout the country Jews were abused, synagogues were set on fire and shops were destroyed. Approximately 26,000 Jews were locked up in concentration camps within a brief period of time. Crystal Night marked the start of a more radical stage in Hitler's anti-Semitic policy, which reached the level of mass murder during the Second World War.

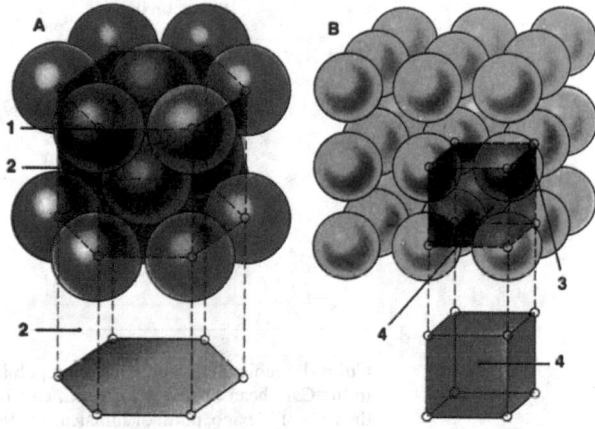

Geometrical and X-ray diffraction studies of crystals have shown them to comprise a number of regularly repeating stacks of submicroscopic building blocks, or unit cells. Each unit cell is composed of atoms, ions or molecules arranged in one of seven different systems. In the case of quartz, or silico dioxide, crystals (A), hexagonal groups of atoms in the same plane (1) are stacked above each other to form a hexagonal unit cell (2). Ions (3) in halite, or sodium chloride, crystals (B) are fixed at the corners of a cubic unit cell (4).

Ctenophore, or comb jelly, marine invertebrate (phylum Ctenophora) having 8 radially arranged combs of ciliated plates (ctenes) on its body used for swimming. Ctenophores are bioluminescent, carnivorous, usually transparent, and resemble jellyfish.

Cuauhtémoc (c.1495-1525), last Aztec emperor of Mexico, nephew and son-in-law of Montezuma. Cuauhtémoc defended the Aztec capital, Tenochtitlán, in a 4-month siege led by the Spanish conqueror Hernando Cortez. The subsequent capture of the city, in 1521, led to its destruction and massive Aztec casualties. Cuauhtémoc was captured and tortured to get him to reveal the location of supposed Aztec treasure. He refused to speak, and several years later he was hanged on the order of Cortez. Many modern Mexicans honor Cuauhtémoc as a national hero.

Cuba

Capital:	Havana
Area:	42,804 sq mi (110,860 sq km)
Population:	11,224,000
Language:	Spanish
Government:	Socialist republic
Independent:	1902
Head of gov.:	President
Per capita:	US$ 2,300
Monetary unit:	1 Cuban peso = 100 centavos

Cuba (Republic of), tropical island republic in the Caribbean Sea, west of Haiti, east of the Gulf of Mexico, north of Jamaica, and 90 mi (145 km) south of Key West, Fla. Cuba is the largest island in the West Indies, occupying 42,804 sq mi (110,860 sq km), including the Isle of Pines and other offshore islands. The capital is Havana.

Land and climate. Cuba has 3 main mountain ranges: the Sierra de los Organos in the west, the Sierra de Trinidad in the center, and the Sierra Maestra in the southeast. Cuba's upland areas generally go from east to west, cover only about 25% of the island, and are so spaced as to break up its surface into a series of clay and limestone plains, separated by gently rolling slopes. Over half of Cuba is flat or slightly undulating. Because Cuba is narrow, it has few big rivers; the longest is the 155-mi (249-km) Cauto, which rises in the Sierra Maestra and flows west across the lowlands of Oriente Province. It has deep bays on the coast that serve as fine natural harbors. Lying just south of the Tropic of Cancer, Cuba has a

warm climate with temperatures between 71° and 82° F (22° and 28° C), though frosts occur in winter on some mountains. Rainfall is generally plentiful, and Cuba is prone to severe hurricanes.

Forests of pine, cedar, oak, ebony, and mahogany still clothe much of the mountains, though only scattered royal palms and silk-cotton trees remain in the lowlands, now largely cleared for farming. Grasses and shrubs grow in sub-soil savanna areas, covering about a quarter of the island, and mangrove forests fringe some of the coast.

People. Around three-quarters of the population is of European, chiefly Spanish, descent. About one-sixth of the population is mulatto, and one-eighth black, a legacy of the West African slave trade. The aboriginal Native Americans are extinct. The distinction between blacks and Cubans of European extraction remains a divisive force in society despite the government's proclaimed policy of equality of opportunity of all. The Cuban blend of racial and ethnic elements has produced a rich national culture renowned for the rhythmic vitality of such dances as the conga, habanera, mambo, and rumba.

Economy. Cuba is dependent upon one crop, sugar; tobacco is the second most important export. The island's agriculture has been further diversified by the production of coffee, citrus fruit, and rice crops. The largest mineral resource is iron ore, and there are also deposits of nickel, cobalt, copper, and manganese. Before 1959 industrialization was limited; after a period of rapid development (1959-1963) it has progressed slowly. Neglected for almost 20 years, tourism began to grow in the late 1970s. All trade, commerce, and industrial production is nationalized, and most of the cultivated land has been reorganized as state cooperatives.

History. Christopher Columbus discovered Cuba in 1492, and it became important as the base for Spanish exploration of America and as a harbor for Spanish treasure ships. The Native Americans, decimated by ill treatment and disease, were replaced as a work force by West African black slaves, particularly in the 18th century, when the sugar plantations developed rapidly. In the 19th century Spain's colonial policy led to a series of nationalist uprisings, and after the Spanish-American War (1898) Cuba became an independent republic, though under U.S. military occupation (1899-1902, 1906-1909). Between 1924 and 1959 Cuba was under virtually continuous dictatorship. Fulgencio Batista, who had come to power in 1940, was overthrown by Fidel Castro,

Tobacco is Cuba's second-largest agricultural export product.

aided by Ernesto 'Che' Guevara in 1959. Castro, as premier, established a socialist state and instituted sweeping land, industrial, and educational reforms. After U.S. firms had been nationalized, the United States supported the abortive Bay of Pigs invasion and enforced an economic blockade. Thereafter, the USSR and the communist bloc replaced U.S. trade and provided great economic support. In 1962 Cuba's acceptance of Soviet nuclear missiles led to a major confrontation between the United States and USSR until the missiles were withdrawn. The Organization of American States (OAS) expelled Cuba in 1962 but lifted its sanctions in 1975. Despite many setbacks, the social policies have in general benefited the island. Castro became president in 1976. In the late 1970s a certain rapprochement between Cuba and the United States took place, and reestablishment of diplomatic ties seemed close. Cuban involvement in Africa and in Latin American revolutionary movements, however, strained the relations in the 1980s. Following the collapse of the Soviet Union in 1991, Soviet support fell away and Cuba had to face a severe economic crisis. In the 1990s many Cubans left the country, either legally or illegally. Foreign investors and economic liberalization have helped Cuba gradually recover. In 1993 the first direct general elections were held since the beginning of Communist rule but they were not considered by the world as free or democratic; Fidel Castro retained power.

The United States used their naval base Guantanamo on the eastern point of the island to hold prisoners, many members of al-Qaida, who had been arrested in Afghanistan, in anticipation of an interrogation. Russia closed its last military base and Jimmy Carter was in May 2002 the first former American president to visit Cuba since 1959.

Cube and cube root, terms in geometry. A cube is a closed solid figure with 6 equal square faces; adjoining faces are at right angles to each other. If the edge of a cube is of length a, then its volume is a^3. Conversely, if we start with a cube a^3, then a is called its *cube root*.

See also: Geometry.

Cubeb, dried, berrylike fruit of a climbing plant (*Piper cubeba*) of the pepper family. Cubeb is used as a spice and in many pharmaceutical preparations.

Cubism, art movement that began c.1907, Paris, as an intellectual response to the emotional and sensual art of previous times, primarily as represented in painting. In the analytic period (1907-1912) fragmented 3-di-

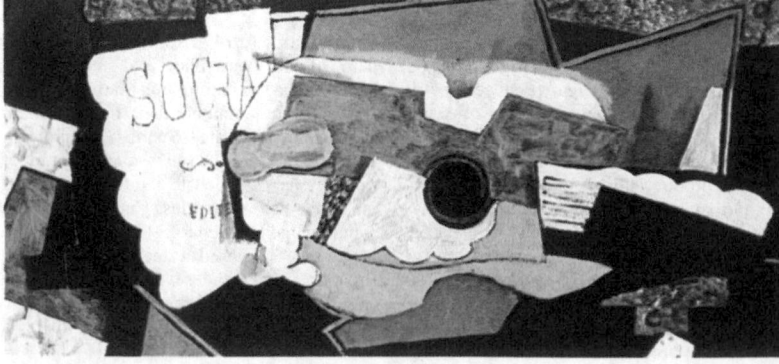

Still Life with Erik Satie Score by Georges Braque (1882-1963). To be seen in the Musée d'Art Moderne in Paris.

C

mensional subjects were explored from varying points of view simultaneously, art that came to be called conceptual realism because it portrayed its object as perceived by the mind, not the eye. In the synthetic phase (1913 through the 1920s) the cubists used brighter colors and fewer forms, and added the texture and construction of collage (for a *trompe l'oeil* effect) in their creations. Important figures in the analytic period were Pablo Picasso and Georges Braque. Other major cubists include Juan Gris, Fernand Léger, and Jean Metzinger.

Cub Scouts *See:* Boy Scouts.

Cuchulainn, great hero of the Ulster cycle of Irish epic mythological literature. Son of the Celtic god Lugh, Cuchulainn was known for his large size and great strength. He had 7 fingers on each hand, 7 toes on each foot, and was capable of superhuman exploits comparable to those of Achilles, the Greek hero. *The Cattle Raid of Cooley* records his single-handed defense of Ulster against the forces of Queen Mave of Connaught.
See also: Mythology.

Cuckoo, bird of the family Cuculidae, found in the tropics and in temperate regions. The common cuckoo of Europe, Asia, and Africa, a slender bird with long tail and dull-colored plumage, lays its eggs in other species' nests, where they are reared by their foster parents. The North American species, the black-billed and the yellow-billed (*Coccyzus americanus*), raise their own broods. The roadrunner (*Geococcyx californianus*), also of the Cuculidae, is found in the deserts of the Southwest and can run up to 15 mph (24.1 kmph).

Cuckoo-shrike, any of several species (genus *Coracina*) of songbirds of the family Campephagidae. Indigenous to Africa, Asia, Australia and the Pacific Islands, most species have long wings and tails and white and black or gray feathers. Most live in tropical woodlands and eat insects and fruit.

Cucumber, common garden vegetable (*Cucumis sativus*) of the gourd family. The creeping vines and triangular leaves produce yellow or white flowers and bear cylindrical fruit 1 to 36 in (2.5 to 91 cm) long. Cucumbers grow rapidly in warm weather and are easily killed by frost. The fruits are popular eaten raw or pickled.

Cuenca (pop. 200,000), city in the Andes Mountains of south central Ecuador. Founded in 1557 by Spanish colonists, Cuenca is a commercial center for agricultural products, animal hides, and gold.

Cuernavaca (pop. 282,000), capital of the state of Morelos in south central Mexico. Founded in 1521 by Hernando Cortez, the city is an agricultural and industrial center. Local crops include corn, beans, and wheat. Bottling plants and flour and textile mills are among its industries. The semitropical climate and beautiful scenery have made the city a popular resort.
See also: Mexico.

Cuisenaire method, teaching system by which students are introduced to mathematical concepts by manipulating 10 rods of different colors that vary proportionately in length. They can be used to teach addition, subtraction, multiplication, division, factoring, and fractions.

Cullen, Countee (1903-1946), African-American poet and member of the Harlem Renaissance of the 1920s. Among his works are *Color* (1925) and *Copper Sun* (1927), both poetry, and a novel, *One Way to Heaven* (1931).

Cult, religious worship of a supernatural object or of a representation of it. Although any religion may be called a cult, the term is used today primarily to refer to minority groups whose practices set them off from the rest of society in obvious ways. Sun Myung Moon's Unification Church would be an example. There are approximately 3,000 such cults claiming a membership of about 3 million in the world today.

Cultural lag, term developed in the 1920s by U.S. sociologist William F. Ogburn to refer to the unequal rate of development in various facets of culture. Technological change, for example, may produce unemployment and social problems that cause a cultural lag as workers adjust and acquire new skills.

Cultural Revolution *See:* China.

Culture, in biology, a colony of living microorganisms, such as bacteria or fungi, grown in a prepared medium (a watery solution of chemicals that supplies the microorganisms with nutrients). Pure cultures are obtained by introducing the organism into a sterile medium and permitting it to reproduce. Bacterial cultures are used commercially in the preparation of food products such as cheese, yogurt, sour cream, and vinegar. Cultures are also useful in the production of antibiotics, vaccines, and other medical compounds, and in the identification of disease-producing bacteria.
See also: Biology.

Culture, term for the general way of life of a human society, including ways of thinking, beliefs, customs, language, technology, art, music, literature, and traditions.

Cumberland Mountains, or Cumberland Plateau, part of the Appalachian Mountain Range. It extends 450 mi (725 km), forming the boundary between Virginia and Kentucky. The plateau contains hardwood trees, rich deposits of limestone, coal fields, and fine-grained sandstones used in construction.
See also: Appalachian Mountains.

Cumberland River, major tributary of the Ohio River, originating in the Cumberland Plateau and flowing 687 mi (1,106 km) before joining it. Flooding is frequent in winter and spring, whereas in late summer the river shrinks to become a mountain stream. Nashville and Clarksville, Tenn., are the major cities along the river.

Cummings, E.E. (Edward Estlin Cummings; 1894-1962), U.S. poet whose verse is known for its deliberate violation of grammatical rules, unusual words, and idiosyncratic punctuation and typography. One of the most individualistic writers of his time, cummings produced 12 volumes of verse, collected after his death into his *Complete Poems* (1968).

Cumulus *See:* Cloud.

Cunard, Sir Samuel (1787-1865), British shipowner, founder of the Cunard line. He introduced iron steamers and pioneered regular transatlantic crossings (as of 1840) after winning a contract to carry the mail between England and North America.

Cuneiform, system of writing developed in the ancient Middle East during the 4th millennium B.C. The characters were wedge-shaped strokes that represented words and syllables rather than letters, as in an alphabet. Cuneiform originated with the Sumerian people of the Tigris and Euphrates valley, but was later used to write other languages, including Babylonian and Assyrian.

Cunningham, Merce (1919-), U.S. dancer and choreographer noted for his abstract dances incorporating pure, isolated movements without emotional overtones. As a soloist with Martha Graham's company (1939-1945), he created several important roles. He began his choreographic career in 1942, creating dances for the music of modern composers. He formed his own company in 1953. He published in 1970 *Notes on Choreography*.

Cupid, or Amor, in Roman mythology, the god of love, the son and companion of Venus, identified with the Greek god, Eros, son of Aphrodite and Ares. He is usually depicted as a small boy, winged, naked, and armed with bow and arrow, capable of causing those wounded by his arrows to fall in love.
See also: Mythology.

Cuquenán Falls, also called Kukenaam, one of the world's highest waterfalls, on the Cuquenán River along the Guyana-Venezuelan border. The falls drop 2,000 ft (610 m).

Curaçao, island (178 sq mi/461 sq km) in the West Indies, an autonomous part of the Netherlands. Willemstad is the capital. Curaçao is the largest of the islands that make up the Netherlands Antilles. Its income derives largely from tourism and oil refining, the refineries being supplied with crude oil from nearby Venezuela. Settled by Spain in 1527, the island was conquered by Holland in 1634. Today's population is mainly descended from the African slaves imported in the early years of rule.
See also: Netherlands Antilles.

Curare, any of a number of alkaloid plant extracts originally used by South American tribes to make poison arrow tips. Curare paralyzes by blocking the transmission of nerve impulses in skeletal muscle. It is used med-

C

Marie (1867-1934) and Pierre Curie (1859-1906) in their laboratory.

ically as a relaxant before the administering of anesthesia, enabling the dose of anesthetic to be as low as possible.

Curassow, large forest-dwelling bird (especially genus *Crax*) with dark plumage and a crest of curved feathers. The curassow ranges from Texas to Argentina. Currasow are pheasantlike, with strong legs and heavy tails, and spend their time running along branches and fluttering clumsily from tree to tree. Curassow feed on fruit, leaves, and small animals and are hunted as gamebirds.

The great curassow (*Crax rubra*, order *Calliformes*, family Cracidae), length 37 in (95 cm), found in South America, from southern Mexico to Ecuador. All seven species of curassow inhabit forests. For some reason, their name is derived from the island of Curaçao in the Dutch West Indies, though none of them can be found there.

Curia Regis, in England, the King's Council, also called King's Court, a medieval council of nobles and church officials who met to advise the king on state issues such as legislation and taxation. The Curia Regis was the forerunner of the House of Lords, one of the branches of Parliament.

Curie, in physics, unit that measures radioactivity. One curie equals precisely 3.7 x 10^{10} nuclear disintegrations per second. The unit is named after the French-Polish physicist Pierre Curie.
See also: Physics.

Curie, Marie Sklodowska (1867-1934), Polish-born French physicist and two-time winner of the Nobel Prize (in physics, 1903, and chemistry, 1911). An early investigator of radioactive elements, including uranium, Curie and her husband, Pierre, discovered the elements polonium and radium in 1898, also determining their atomic weights. The Curies shared the 1903 prize with Antoine Becquerel, for their work on radioactivity. In 1911 Marie Curie became the first person to win a second Nobel Prize, for her study of the chemical properties of radium. She died of leukemia, probably radiation-related.
See also: Radioactivity.

Curie, Pierre (1859-1906), French physicist, professor at the Sorbonne, and winner, with his wife, Marie, and A. H. Becquerel, of the 1903 Nobel Prize for physics. Curie's early work concerned the electrical and magnetic properties of crystals and metals.
See also: Physics.

Curitiba (pop. 2,300,000), Brazil, the capital of the state of Paraná. It is located 65 miles (105 km) west of the port of Paranagua. Curitiba is an industrial city and is the center of an agricultural region that produces a tea (maté (the main export), coffee, bananas, and sugar. The city's manufactured products include paper, textiles, and cement. The Federal University of Paraná and the Pontifical Catholic University of Paraná are here.
Curitiba was founded in 1654. During the late 19th and early 20th centuries large numbers of immigrants, mainly from Germany, Italy, and Poland, settled here. Since 1940, when Curitiba was a city of 100,000, it has experienced tremendous growth, largely as a result of the development of the Paraná hinterland.

Curium, chemical element, symbol Cm; for physical constants see Periodic Table. Curium is a synthetic, radioactive element, discovered in 1945 by Glenn Seaborg and his co-workers. They produced it by bombarding plutonium-239 with alpha particles. Curium is a silvery, hard, brittle, reactive metal. It is toxic, accumulating in bones, where it injures red blood cells.

Curlew, migratory wading bird of pastures and marshes (especially genus *Numenius*), characterized by a long, down-curving bill. Curlews have become rare as their habitat is turned over to agriculture and building. The Eskimo curlew was once shot in vast numbers as it migrated from Labrador to Argentina. It was thought to have become extinct, but one was seen in Texas in 1959. The first nest of the bristlethighed curlew was found in 1948 near the Yukon River.

Curling, game introduced from Scotland and played in the United States and Canada for over 150 years. Granite stones of up to 3 ft (0.9 m) in circumference are propelled along 'rinks' of ice 138 ft (42 m) long, with the object of hitting, or getting nearest to, a tee or target stone at the other end. World championships were introduced in 1959, with Canada and the United States winning all but 1 of the first 11. Curling is also popular in Scandinavia, Switzerland (which has several curling 'schools,'), and, of course, Scotland, where a curling stone dated 1551 has been preserved.

Curly coated retriever, hunting dog with a black or liver-colored coat of tight curls, which enables it to endure thorny bushes, challenging terrain, and cold-water temperatures when retrieving shot game.

Currant, bushy plant (genus *Ribes*) of temperate regions; also, the fruit of the plant. Some varieties, such as the golden currant of the West, are native to North America. The fruits of European currants, such as the black and red currants, are cooked or used in jellies. They are very rich in vitamin C. Britain is the chief grower of currants, but both cultivated and wild currants are discouraged in parts of the United States where they are alternate hosts for white pine blister rust.

Currency *See:* Money.

Curry, Jabez Lamar Monroe (1825-1903), U.S. educator who promoted the education of both black and white children in the South. He represented the Peabody Fund for public education and the Slater Fund for the establishment of black schools after 1890. He served in the U.S. House of Representatives (1857-1861) and was president of Howard College (1865-1868).

Curry, John Steuart (1897-1946), U.S. painter best known for his striking portrayals of rural Midwestern life. His works include *Baptism in Kansas* (1928) and *Tornado Over Kansas* (1929).

Curtis, Cyrus Hermann Kotzschmar (1850-1933), U.S. founder of a publishing empire. From the age of 12 he started or bought magazines and newspapers including *The Saturday Evening Post*, *The Ladies' Home Journal*, and the *New York Evening Post*.

Curtiss, Glenn Hammond (1873-1930), U.S. pioneer in aviation, who made the first public flight in the United States (1908), opened the first pilots' school (1909), built engines for the first U.S. dirigibles, and built the first planes for the U.S. Navy (1911). He also invented ailerons, movable flaps on wings for better control. His 2 hr 51 min flight from Albany, N.Y., to New York City in 1910 made a spectacular impact.
See also: Aviation.

Curzon, George Nathaniel (1859-1925), first Marquess of Kedleston, a British statesman. Curzon was the eldest son of a British baron and was educated at Oxford. He was a Conservative member of the House of Commons, 1886-1898. Upon his appointment as viceroy of India in 1898, Curzon was made an Irish peer. In India, Lord Curzon made notable reforms in education and government administration, but aroused the opposition of Indian nationalists by the partition of Bengal. He resigned in 1905 when the home government failed to support his demand for civilian control of the army. Curzon became chancellor of Oxford University, and took a seat in the House of Lords. During World War I he was leader of the Lords and, as a member of Lloyd George's coalition cabinet, helped direct Britain's war effort. Curzon was foreign secretary from 1919 to his resignation in 1924. He proposed the Curzon Line in a Polish-Russian border dispute; presided over the Lausanne Conference to conclude peace between Greece and Turkey (1923); and strongly opposed French occupation of the Ruhr to extract war damages from Germany. Curzon was made a marquess in 1921. His books on eastern affairs include *Lord Curzon in India* (1906) and *British Government in India* (1926).

Curzon Line, boundary between Poland and the Soviet Union, proposed by the Allies in 1919, after World War I. It was named after British diplomat Lord George Curzon. The Curzon Line lost significance after the Russo-Polish War of 1920, but at the Yalta conference (1945) it was officially recognized as the Soviet- Polish border.

Cusco, or Cuzco (pop. 275,000), city in the Andes Mountains of southern Peru. Once the capital of the Inca empire, the city was captured in 1533 by the Spanish colonist Francisco Pizarro, who destroyed many of its palaces and temples. Parts of the old walls remain, however, and there are ruins of an Inca fortress. A cathedral, completed in 1654 on the site of the Inca palace, along with other significant colonial buildings, draws tourists to the city today.
See also: Peru.

Cush *See:* Kush.

Cuspid *See:* Teeth.

Custer, George Armstrong (1839-1876), controversial U.S. cavalry officer. Custer proved himself an outstanding Union cavalry leader during the Civil War. Appointed as a lieutenant colonel in 1866, he joined General Hancock's successful expedition against the Cheyenne. He was killed in the famous battle of Little Bighorn.

Custom, accepted practice or manner of doing things, established by tradition. Customs are handed down from one generation to another and often remain unchanged, especially in isolated communities. Customs vary from group to group, and interaction with other cultures causes changes.

Customs, the department of the inland revenue service (IRS) that inspects whether or not one observes the regulations concerning import, export, and transit duties of goods.

Customs union, agreement between two or more countries aimed at reducing tariffs to encourage trade.

Cutlassfish, long, silver-colored saltwater fish (*Trichiurus lepturus*) found in the western Pacific Ocean and the Caribbean Sea. It has a large mouth and doglike teeth. Adults reach 5 ft (1.5 m) in length and are caught for food in some areas.

Cuttlefish, small cephalopod (family Sepiidae) of Old World coastal waters. Its head is attached to 8 short arms and a pair of long tentacles for catching prey. Inside the body there is a flat, chalky cuttlebone that is used as a support and a buoyancy mechanism. The cuttlefish is a good swimmer. When alarmed, it protects itself by shooting out a jet of inky fluid and jerking violently backwards.

Cutworm, any of more than 20,000 species of caterpillars of the owlet moth or miller family, with the capacity to destroy field crops and fruit trees. Crops such as corn, wheat, beans, tomatoes, cotton, and tobacco are killed or damaged when the cutworm severs the roots and stems near the ground.

Cuvier, Baron (Georges Léopold Chrétien Frédéric Dagobert Cuvier; 1769-1832), French scientist known for his pioneer work in comparative anatomy. He deduced the structures of the soft tissues of fossils from their skeletal remains. His book *The Animal Kingdom* was an important authoritative reference in zoology. He was also the originator of the theory of catastrophism, which claimed that living things were eliminated by volcanic eruptions and other natural catastrophes and then supplanted by completely different species. This theory was later abandoned by scientists in favor of the theory of evolution.
See also: Anatomy.

Cuzco (or **Cusco**) (pop. 275,000), Peru, the capital of Cuzco Department. It is 365 miles (585 km) southeast of Lima in a deep Andean valley, at an elevation of 11,200 feet (3,400 m). Cuzco is a trading center with textile mills and other light industries. It is noted for its many old buildings in which Inca and Spanish architecture are blended. Cuzco was a small village when, in 1250, it was conquered by the Incas, who made it their capital. When Pizarro and his Spanish forces captured the city in 1533, they partially destroyed it. They then rebuilt, using some of the Inca foundations and walls. A Dominican convent incorporates parts of the Inca Temple of the Sun. There are a 17th-century cathedral and a university founded in 1598. Cuzco was severely damaged by earthquakes in 1650 and 1950.

Cyanides, group of compounds containing the cyanide radical, CN (a carbon atom linked to a nitrogen atom). Organic cyanides, which occur in nature, as in some poisonous plants, are called nitriles. Though extremely poisonous, cyanides have great commercial importance in recovery of gold and silver from their ores, in case-hardening iron and steel, in fumigation and pest control, and in electroplating. The cyanides of potassium, sodium, barium, and calcium must be handled with extreme care because they liberate prussic acid (HCN), a weak acid that prevents the body cells from reacting with oxygen and quickly causes death.

Cyanosis, bluish discoloration of skin and mucous membranes. Central cyanosis results from a lack of oxygen in the blood flowing in the arteries from the lungs. Peripheral cyanosis occurs when there is insufficient oxygen in the haemoglobin of the venous blood, as a result of extensive oxygen extraction at the level of the capillaries.

Cybernetics, branch of learning that deals with control mechanisms and the transmission of information. Cybernetics seeks to integrate the theories and studies of communication and control in machines and living organisms.
See also: Wiener, Norbert.

Cycad, tropical plant of the cycas family, one of the most primitive living seed-bearing plants. They grow in warm climates. Many are cultivated for their ornamental foliage. The leaves grow from the top of a stem that may be underground, giving a palmlike appearance, and some cycads have been incorrectly called palms. The leaves of cycads are poisonous and fatal to livestock. The sago palm is a cycad whose stem provides the sago that is used in puddings. In South Africa the seeds of the bread palm are used to make a meal.

Cyclamen, genus of cultivated plant of the primrose family native to the Mediterranean. After pollination the flower stalk coils down to bring the fruit near the ground.

Cyclone, closed system of winds revolving around a low-pressure area. The air rotates counterclockwise in the Northern Hemisphere and clockwise in the Southern Hemisphere. In the tropics, particularly in the Indian Ocean (where they are sometimes known as *typhoons*), cyclones bring severe tropical storms with winds of 200-300 mph (320-480 kmph). In temperate regions, where they are more common, they are often known as lows, or depressions, and generally bring rain, snow, or strong winds. A cyclone develops when a mass of warmer and lighter tropical air meets a mass of colder and heavier polar air (a polar front). The two masses flow in opposite directions and roughly parallel to each other, but under certain conditions the disturbance of the front may develop into a more serious turbulence. The rotating masses of cold and warm air mutually reinforce their circular movements, giving rise to winds of 30-40 mph (48-64 kmph) toward the center, and producing widespread clouds and rainfall.
See also: Hurricane; Tornado.

Cyclops (plural Cyclopes), in Greek mythology, shaggy giant with a single large eye in the center of his forehead. Homer's Cyclopes were lawless Sicilian herdsmen, one of whom, Polyphemus, was met by Odysseus. Other mythological Cyclopes include 3 blacksmith sons who were imprisoned in Tartarus by their father, Uranus, and who, in return for their freedom, helped Hephaestus make Zeus's thunderbolts in his forge under Mt. Etna; and the Cyclopes who built the great walls of Tiryns and Mycenae.
See also: Mythology.

C

C

Cyclosporine, drug used to prevent rejection of tissues and organs in transplant patients. It is produced from cultures of the fungus *Tolypocladium inflatum*. Cyclosporine suppresses the functioning of the immune system, most likely by inhibiting the production of a type of white blood cell-the T- helper cell-that is responsible for attacking foreign substances. Cyclosporine is also showing promise in the treatment of certain immunologic diseases. It is a potent compound with the potential for side effects, the most serious of which include hypertension, reduced kidney function, liver damage, and abnormal growth of hair.

Cyclotron, magnetic resonance particle accelerator. It is used to impart very great velocities to heavier nuclear particles without the use of excessive voltages.
See also: Particle accelerator.

Cygnus, the Swan, large constellation visible in the Northern Hemisphere sky. Because of its shape, it is sometimes called the Northern Cross. It is high in the sky during summer.

Cylinder, 3-dimensional figure consisting of a curved lateral surface and equal parallel ends, or *bases*. The bases may be either circles or ovals. A right circular cylinder is a common shape used for tin cans and automobile cylinders.

Cymbal, percussion instrument of very ancient origin. When 2 of these shallow concave metal discs are clashed together, swept by each other, or hit with a drumstick they produce a variety of sound effects. Today cymbals are made in many different sizes to produce sounds of varying pitch and intensity. The cymbal is a basic instrument in the military band, and is frequently used in modern orchestral music. Cymbals used in jazz or dance bands, mounted in pairs and operated by a foot pedal, are called choke cymbals.

Kyrenia (Girne in Turkish), a resort city and the chief seaport of Turkish Cyprus, is located on the northern coast of Cyprus.

Cynic philosophy, ancient Greek school of philosophy characterized by the unconventional way of life of its adherents. Its

founder, Antisthenes, a 4th century B.C. follower of Socrates, held ordinary social conventions in contempt and argued that virtue was the only good and that it could be attained only through independent and austere living conditions.
See also: Philosophy.

Cypress, family of cone-bearing trees, including arborvitae, juniper, and cedar. They have fragrant wood and small, scalelike leaves. Cypresses grow in North America, Europe, and Asia. Red cedar is used for pencils, chests, and closets and white cedar for fencing, shingles, and boats. The bald cypress, which is not a true cypress but kin of the sequoia, often grows in water.

Cyprus

Capital:	Nicosia
Area:	3,572 sq mi (9,251 sq km)
Population:	767,000
Language:	Greek, Turkish
Government:	Presidential republic
Independent:	1960
Head of gov.:	President
Per capita:	Greek part: US$ 15,000; Turkish part: US$ 7,000
Monetary unit:	1 Cyprian pound = 100 cents/1 Turkish lira or pound =100 kurus

Cyprus (Republic of) island republic situated in the northeastern Mediterranean Sea, about 40 mi (60 km) south of Turkey and 60 mi (97 km) west of Syria. Cyprus, 3,572 sq mi (9,251 sq km) in area, is the Mediterranean's third largest island. The capital is Nicosia (called Lefkosia in Greek Cyprus).
Land and climate. Two main mountain ranges dominate the island: the Kyrenia ridge in northern-central Cyprus and the Troödos Mountains in the southwest, including Mt. Olympus (6,403 ft/1,952 m). Between these rugged ranges lies the fertile Mesaöia plain. The island's climate is predominantly dry, with mild winters and hot, sunny summers. The remains of ancient forests of evergreen oak, Aleppo pine, and cypress cling to the rocky mountain slopes, but centuries of timber cutting have almost stripped Cyprus of its native forest cover, which has been largely replaced by poor pasture.

People. About 80% of Cypriots are of Greek extraction; the rest are predominantly Turkish in origin. Each group clings to its own cultural traditions; there are 2 official languages (Greek and Turkish), 2 main faiths (the Orthodox Church of Cyprus and Islam), and even separate schools for Greek and Turkish Cypriots.
History. Neolithic farmers lived on the island as early as 6000 B.C. Around 1200 B.C. Greek-speaking traders arrived, followed by the Phoenicians. Both peoples set up city-states, and Cyprus developed a cosmopolitan Eurasian culture. In 709 B.C., however, Cyprus submitted to Assyria, and from then on was largely dominated by foreign states. The Ottoman Turks (1570-1878) established their own Muslim culture alongside the Christian one that had flourished since A.D. 45. After Britain gained Cyprus in 1878 (making it a crown colony in 1925), conflict between Turkish and Greek Cypriots became a major issue, especially in the 1950s, when Archbishop Makarios led a powerful movement for *enosis*, political union with Greece. Also in the 1950s, Col. Giorgios Grivas headed EOKA, a guerrilla movement aimed at forcibly freeing Cyprus from Britain. In 1960 Britain granted Cyprus its independence. The new republic tried solving its Greco-Turkish problem by constitutional compromise, which failed. Fierce intercommunal fighting and the threat of intervention from both Greece and Turkey led to the arrival of a UN peacekeeping force in 1965. Subsequent talks between President Makarios and Turkish leaders were frequent but fruitless. In 1974 a military group organized by Greek army officers ousted Makarios, whereupon Turkey invaded the island, setting up a 'Turkish Federated State of Cyprus' under Turkish occupation in the northeastern third of the island. Negociations to reunite the island were held between the Turks and Greeks in the late 1970's and early 1980's. Meanwhile, in 1983 the Turkish state declared itself independant as the Turkish Republic of Northern Cyprus. In 1985 the republic adopted a constitution. Reunification talks continued in the late 1980's and early 1990's but no progress was made. In 1996 clashes between Greek Cypriots and Turkish Cypriot soldiers occurred along the partition line. At the end of the 1990s, negotiations regarding membership of the European Union commenced, resulting in Cyprus being allowed to become a member state of the EU in 2004. However, the EU and the UN are both of the opinion that the island should be reunited.

Cyrano de Bergerac, Savinien de (1619-1655), French author. He gave up a military career to write plays and prose. A free-thinker, influenced by Pierre Gassendi (1592-1655), he satirized contemporary society in ingenious fantasies about voyages to the sun and moon. Edmond Rostand, in his play *Cyrano de Bergerac*, made him into a flamboyant romantic hero, handicapped in love because of an unusually large nose.

Cyril of Alexandria, Saint (378?-444), Christian theologian and bishop, known primarily for his campaign against Nestorius, the bishop of Constantinople, who denied

that the Virgin Mary was the mother of God. When Cyril succeeded his uncle, Archbishop Theophilus, he attacked Christian heretics, pagans, and Jews. He was instrumental in expelling Jews from Alexandria. In 1882 the Roman Catholic church declared Cyril a doctor of the church, a special title granted to saints whose theological writings have particular authority. His feast day is Feb. 9.
See also: Christianity.

Cyrus the Great (c. 590-529 B.C.), founder of the Persian empire. He conquered Media (c.559), Lydia (c. 547), and Babylonia (c. 539), building an empire whose territory extended from the Black and Caspian seas to the Arabian Desert and Persian Gulf. He allowed the Jews to return from Babylonia to Palestine and did not suppress the religions of the various parts of the empire.
See also: Persia, Ancient.

Cyst, abnormal, sac-like growth in the body. Often surrounding a foreign body, oil gland, or hair follicle, cysts are formed by cells within the sac walls.

Cystic fibrosis, CF, or mucoviscidosis, hereditary disease, usually appearing in early childhood, characterized by an abnormality of the exocrine or mucus-screting glands. An excess of thick, sticky mucus accumulates particularly in the lungs and the pancreas, seriously affecting breathing and the digestion of food. CF patients may be identified by large amounts of salt in their perspiration. As the disease progresses the mucus-secreting glands are replaced by fibroid tissue and cysts. Individuals who are carriers of the CF trait are not afflicted with the disease, although the offspring of 2 carriers may inherit the disease. The control of pulmonary infection is critical to survival in CF patients; antibiotics are routinely used to prevent or treat respiratory infections, and physical therapy and the use of certain inhalants are encouraged to help remove the accumulation of mucus in the lungs.

Czechoslovakia, former nation in central Europe, consisting of the present Czech Republic and Slovakia. With the disintegration of Austria-Hungary at the end of World War I, the Czechs and Slovaks proclaimed the independent republic of Czechoslovakia (1918), which developed as a Western-style democracy. Seized by Nazi Germany (1938-1939), Czechoslovakia came under Russian domination after World War II, and a communist regime took power. In 1968-1969 an attempt by the Communist Party leader Alexander Dubcek to liberalize the country was crushed by invading Soviet and other Warsaw Pact troops. Dubcek and other moderates were purged and the staunchly pro-Soviet Gustáv Husák put in control. In 1989 the pro-Soviet regime collapsed during the widespread upheavals in Eastern Europe. In the first free elections since 1948, the former dissident playwright Vaclav Havel became president. The new government embarked on a program of democratization and the introduction of a free-market economy. Under pressure of Slovak political leaders, the Czech and Slovak federation was dissolved, and the republics became independent in 1993.

Czech Republic

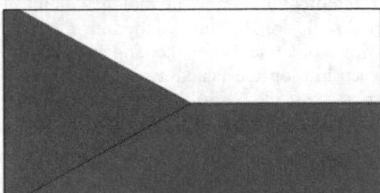

Capital:	Prague
Area:	30,450 sq mi (78,864 sq km)
Population:	10,257,000
Language:	Czech
Government:	Republic
Independent:	1993
Head of state:	Prime minister
Per capita:	US$ 14,400
Monetary unit:	1 Koruna = 100 haleru

Czech Republic, independent country in central Europe, bordering Germany on the west and northwest, Poland on the north and northeast, Slovakia on the southeast, and Austria on the south
Land and people. There are 2 main natural and historical regions. (1) Bohemia, in the west, comprises the Bohemian Massif, the Ore Mountains, and the Giant Mountains, which serve as natural boundaries between the republic and neighboring countries. Valleys carved out by rivers break through the mountains, notably the Labe (Elbe) valley linking northwestern Czech Republic with Germany. In north-central Bohemia rivers have carved the lowlands on which Prague stands. (2) Moravia, east of Bohemia, includes a lowland area featuring the fertile valleys of the southward-flowing Morava River and the northward-flowing Odra (Oder).The majority of the population (94%) is Czech, and Slovakians form the largest minority (3%). The population is Christian and the official language is Czech.
Economy. The Czech government continued the economic reforms that were started by the government of Czechoslovakia. After the fall of communism tourism became a major source of trade and employment. Other important economic activities are manufactruing (metallurgy), trade, and services. Important agricultural products include wheat, barley, sugar beets, and hops.
History. Bohemia and Moravia formed a separate entity until 1918. It was successively ruled by the Premysl dynasty, Austria, the Hussites, and the Habsburg dynasty. With the collapse of the Habsburg dynasty during World War I, Bohemia, Moravia, and Slovakia formed the new republic

Czechoslovakia. The Czech and Slovakian republics formed a federation in 1968. A Communist government was installed, which ruled until 1989 when it again became a democracy. The Czech Republic and Slovakia agreed by referendum to split into separate nations in 1993 and Václav Havel, who was president of Czechoslovakia during 1989-1992, was elected president of the Czech Republic. In 1997, in response to the Czech Republic's desire for a stronger relationship with Western Europe, the republic was invited to join NATO in 1999. In 1993 the Czech Republic had joined the UN. Since Czech independance there has been economic liberalization.
In 2004, the Czech Republic will become one of the ten new member states of the European Union. In 2002, the country was afflicted by the worst floods in 200 years.
See also: Czechoslovakia.

Czechs, Slavic people who settled in Bohemia and Moravia in central Europe in the early Middle Ages and accounted for about two-thirds of Czechoslovakia's population. The city of Prague, center of Czech culture, became one of the great political and artistic capitals of Europe between the 14th and 17th centuries.

Czerny, Karl (1791-1857), Austrian musician and teacher. He studied with Ludwig van Beethoven (1800-1803) and became the mentor of Hungarian pianist and composer Franz Liszt. Czerny is well known for his études, compositions for the piano which embody some point of technique but are intended for performance.

Czestochowa (pop. 275,000), capital of the Wojwodstwo (province) of Czestochowska in Poland, which was established in 1975; prov. 2388 sq mi (6182 sq km), (pop. 800,000). Heavy industry due to sources of coal and iron ore; blast furnaces, iron and steel; also textile industry, chemical, cement, and glass industry, among others. Railway junction. The portrayal of the Virgin Mary of Byzantine origin in the monastery Jasna Góra (the 'Black Madonna') attracts approx. one million Roman Catholic pilgrims each year.

Landscape of the Low Tatra mountains (highest peak: Dunbier, 6703 ft (2,043 m)).

C

D

D, fourth letter of the English alphabet. It is derived from the Phoenician *daleth* and Greek *delta*. It occupied the same position in those alphabets. Thought to originate from a pictorial representation of a door, it may have some connection with the Egyptian hieroglyph for door. In Roman numerals, D represents the number 500.

Dacca *See:* Dhaka.

Dachau, concentration camp in Germany where many thousands, mostly Poles and Jews, were murdered by the Nazis. The camp operated from 1933 until its liberation by U.S. soldiers in 1945.
See also: Concentration camp; Holocaust.

Dachshund, small (5-9 in/13-25 cm), short-legged dog with a long body, long ears, and a smooth, bronze (or black and bronze) coat.

Dacko, David (1930-), politician from the Central Africa Republic, premier and president from 1960-1965. He was deposed by a coup carried out by his nephew Bokassa (December 1965), but became Bokassa's advisor in 1976 following a lengthy house arrest. He regained power in September 1979 following a coup against Bokassa, during which France supported him. After once again being deposed by a coup (in September 1981), he was succeeded by Kolingba.

Dada, artistic movement born in Zurich and later spreading to New York, Berlin, and Paris, 1915-1922. The poet Tristan Tzara (*Vingtcinque Poèmes*, 1918), the artists Jean Arp (*Two Heads*, 1929) and Marcel Duchamp (*Why Not Sneeze, Rose Sélavy?*, 1921), and the writers Hugo Ball and Richard Huelsenbeck were deliberately provocative Dadaists, aiming at the destruction of aesthetic preconceptions. Favorite techniques of Dada included nonsense poetry, collage, anarchic typography, and outrageous theater events.

Daddy longlegs, or harvestman, relative of the spider with a small rounded body and 8 extremely long and delicate legs. Daddy lon-

glegs are nocturnal, eating plant juices and insects and other small invertebrates.
See also: Arachnid.

Daedalus, in Greek mythology, architect and sculptor. He built a labyrinth for King Minos of Crete. When the king attempted to keep him on the island against his will, he tried to escape by fashioning wax wings for himself and his son Icarus. Daedalus

Frenchman Louis Jacques Mandé Daguerre (1787-1851) did not invent photography, as is often alleged. It is true, however, that he was the first to develop photographic techniques that could be applied in practice, and at the same time, he was also the one who realized their commercial significance.

reached Sicily, but Icarus flew too close to the sun; the wings melted, and he fell into the sea.
See also: Mythology.

Daffodil, any of several bulbous, perennial plants (genus *Narcissus*) of the amaryllis family, having yellow trumpet-shaped flowers. Native to Europe and North Africa, daffodils are now grown worldwide as ornamental flowers.

Da Gama, Vasco (1469?-1524), sea captain from Portugal, the first to open sea routes for trade between Europe and Asia. Upon request from King Manuel I of Portugal, da Gama set out to establish trade with India by sailing east around southern Africa. He began his journey July 8, 1497, and reached Calicut, India, May 20, 1498. Muslim merchants resented da Gama's attempts to establish trade, and India's ruler found his gifts unacceptable. His return to Portugal included only limited Indian goods, but King Manuel was satisfied with this initial voyage. He sailed again in 1500, better prepared to conquer the Muslim control and increase trade. He succeeded and the Portuguese became a major trading power in the Indian Ocean.

Dagger, short, knifelike weapon for stabbing, with a sharp-edged, pointed blade.

Daghestan, autonomous republic in southeast Russia, in the Russian Federation, bounded by the Caspian Sea on the east, inhabited by Russians, Azerbaijanis, and various tribes of the Caucasus Mountain region.
See also: Union of Soviet Socialist Republics.

Daguerreotype, early photographic process in which a light-sensitive silver-coated copperplate was treated with iodine vapor. The method was perfected in the 1830s by the French physicist Louis J.M. Daguerre (1789-1851).
See also: Photography.

Dahl, Roald (1916-1990), British author of Norwegian origin. Dahl first made a name for himself with humorous/macaber stories, which usually had a very surprising dénouement, published in, among others, *Someone Like You* (1953) and *Kiss, Kiss* (1959). However, he became world famous due to his children's books, in which he conspires with the children against the adults. His best known work includes *James and the Giant Peach* (1961), *Charlie and the Chocolate Factory* (1964), *Danny, the Champion of the World* (1975), *The Twits* (1980), *The BFG* (1982), *The Witches* (1983), and *Matilda* (1988).

Dahlia, any of several perennial plants (genus *Dahlia*) of the composite family, having tuberous roots and red, purple, yellow, or white flowers. Over 7,000 varieties have been developed from the original Mexican stock; the largest now have blooms 1 ft (30 cm) across.

Dählie, Björn (1967-), Norwegian cross country skier, claimed a total of seven gold and four silver medals for various distances during the Olympic Winter Games in 1992 (Albertville), in 1994 (Lillehammer), and in 1998 (Nagano). He excelled in both classic and freestyle skiing.

Dahomey *See:* Benin.

Dahrendorf, Ralf Gustav (1929-), German sociologist and politician; one of the most important representatives of conflict sociology. Famous for his book *Class and Class Conflict in Industrial Society* (1959), a critique and supplement to the work of Marx and a new theory concerning class conflict and social change. Other publications include, among others *Homo Sociologicus* (1959), *The New Liberty: Survival and Justice in a Changing World* (1975), *Law and Order* (1985), and *Morals, Revolution and Civil Society* (1997).

Daimler, Gottlieb Wilhelm (1834-1900), German engineer who devised an internal combustion engine (1885) and used it in building one of the first automobiles, about 1886.

Dairy farming, all the processes producing milk and milk products. Dairy farming in-

The harvestman (*Phalangium africanum*, order *Opiliones*) lives in North Africa, feeding as a scavenger, 0.31-0.47 in (8-12 mm) long.

cludes the breeding, selection, and management of cattle (and sometimes goats and domesticated buffaloes) to ensure a regular output of good milk. Processing into butter and cheese is generally undertaken in factories.

Fresh milk is the single most nutritionally complete food.

Daisetz Teitaro Suzuki (1870-1966), Japanese philosopher, who greatly contributed to the promotion of (Rinzai) Zen Buddhism in America and Europe. Taught at Colombia University and other American universities and wrote approx. one hundred books. Adjustment of Zen to the West by emphasizing immediate enlightenment, contrary to the Buddhist principles of reincarnation and karma.

Daisy, any of various common wild plants of the composite family. The English daisy (*Bellis perennis*), with white, pink, or red flowers, is widely cultivated in the United States. Other species include the oxeye daisy and the yellow daisy, or black-eyed Susan.

Dakar (pop. 1,800,000), capital and largest city of Senegal, on the far western tip of Africa. The modern city originated in a fort built by French colonists in 1857. Dakar is a cultural center and one of West Africa's main commercial hubs. Its port is the most heavily trafficked in the region.
See also: Senegal.

Dakota *See:* North Dakota; South Dakota; Sioux.

Daladier, Édouard (1884-1970), French premier (1933-1934, 1938-1940) who, with British Prime Minister Neville Chamberlain, signed the 1938 Munich Agreement abandoning Czechoslovakia to Hitler. Ousted after failing to aid Finland against the USSR, he was imprisoned by the Vichy government after the fall of France. After the war, he served as a member of the National Assembly (1946-1958), as a representative of the Radical Party.
See also: Munich Agreement.

Dalai Lama, title of the head of the Tibetan Buddhists. When a Dalai Lama dies, his successor is chosen from among young boys born within two years of his death. Each Dalai Lama is considered by Tibetan Buddhists to be an incarnation of the Bodhisattva Avalokiteshvara, the founder of this branch of Buddhism.
The present Dalai Lama, the fourteenth, born Tenzin Cryatso in 1935, took refuge in India in 1959, when the Chinese government put down a rebellion in Tibet against Chinese rule. Since then he has traveled widely throughout the world. In 1989 he received the Nobel Peace prize.
See also: Buddhism; Tibet.

Dalat (Da Lat; pop. 600,000), city in the southern Lam Dong-province of Vietnam, to the northeast of Ho Chi Minh City (Saigon). Regional center for the production of tea, coffee, and rubber; connected to the port of Phan Rang by highways and railroads. Established as a health resort by the French

in 1920 due to its altitude; the surroundings include coniferous forests, lakes, and waterfalls. The city was a summer capital during the French period and therefore has many large villas in addition to a sanatorium. The city is currently expanding due to the government's policy to stimulate the migration from over-populated areas to new economic zones.

Dale, Sir Henry Hallet (1875-1968), British biologist who discovered and described the properties of acetylcholine, an agent in the chemical transmission of nerve impulses. In 1936 he shared the Nobel Prize in physiology or medicine with Otto Loewi.
See also: Biology.

Dali, Salvador (1904-1989), Spanish painter, one of the masters of surrealism. Dali sought to portray the life of the unconscious by juxtaposing incongruous elements and emphasizing rich fantasy, combined with a refined draftsmanship. Among his major paintings are *The Persistence of Memory* (1931), *Agnostic Symbol* (1932), *Geopoliticus* (1943).

Dallapiccola, Luigi (1904-1975), Italian composer of vocal works and operas who adapted the 12-tone technique to his own emotionally expressive and melodic style.

Dallas (pop. 1,050,000), second-largest city in Texas, founded in 1841 on the Trinity River. In the 1870s the railroads made Dallas a cotton center. By the 1930s, it had become a major oil center. It is now the banking and insurance capital of the Southwest, as well as a manufacturing city and convention center.
See also: Texas.

Dallas, George Mifflin (1792-1864), U.S. vice president (1845-1849) under James Polk. He served as U.S. senator from Pennsylvania (1833-1835), minister to Russia (1837-1839), and minister to Great Britain (1856-1861).

Dalmatia, mountainous region and province of Croatia, bordering the Adriatic Sea and including about 300 islands. Historically, the area has been dominated by the Romans (1st century B.C.-5th century A.D.), Venetians (1420-1797), and Austrians (1815-1918). Parts have also been dominated by Hungary and Turkey. The present population lives on tourism, fishing, and farming, producing wine, olive oil, and cotton. There is also shipbuilding, bauxite mining, and limestone quarrying.
See also: Yugoslavia.

Dalmatian, sturdy, medium-sized dog thought to have originated in Dalmatia (on the Adriatic Sea) many centuries ago. The dalmatian is born white and develops black or brown spots when just a few weeks old. It is used as a watchdog, for hunting, and is traditionally depicted as a companion on fire engines and coaches.

Dalton, John (1766-1844), English scientist who originated the modern chemical atomic theory. In 1801 Dalton discovered his *Law of*

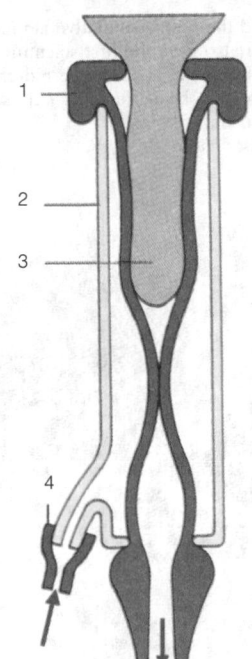

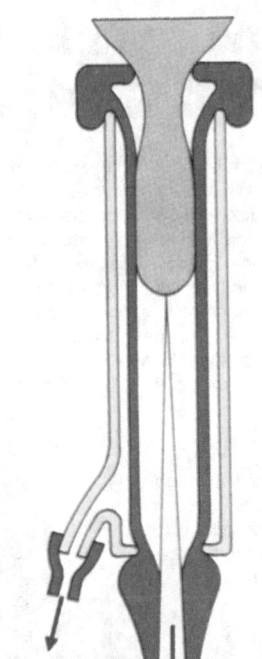

With the atmosphere in the outer chamber of the teat cup (A), the continuous vacuum in the inner chamber (2) will cause the rubber liner (1) to compress onto the cow's teat (3). When a vacuum is applied to the outer chamber (4) (B), the liner will relax and the massaging effect will cause milk release.

Partial Pressures, which states that the pressure exerted by a mixture of gases equals the sum of the partial pressures of the components. (The partial pressure of a gas is the pressure it would exert if it alone filled the volume.) In 1803 he published the first table of comparative atomic weights, which inau-

D

D

gurated the new quantitative atomic theory. Dalton also gave the first scientific description of color blindness. The red-green type from which he suffered is still known as Daltonism.
See also: Atom.

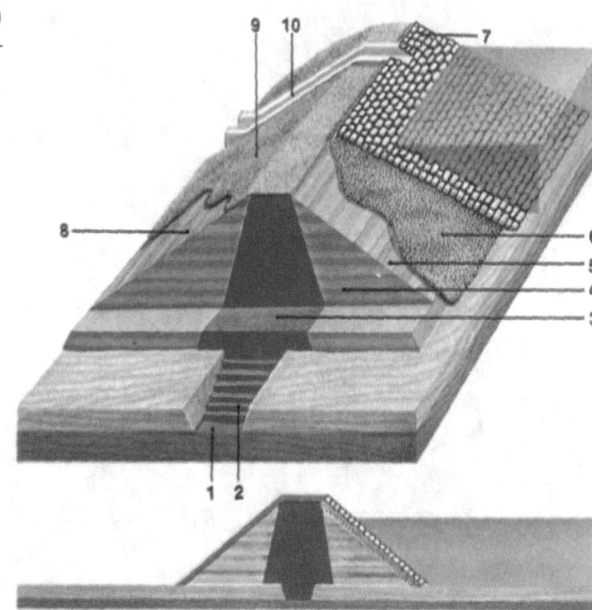

An earth-filled dam is begun by digging a trench (1) in a firm bedrock foundation and laying down the initial waterproof layer of compressed clay. Successive layers of compacted clay are laid until the trench is filled (2). A broad-based core (3) of compressed clay is built on this foundation, reaching above high-water level and supported on both sides by soil (4). The upstream slope (5) is covered with gravel (6) and surfaced with rock slabs (7). The downstream slope (8) is turfed (9), and a spillway (10) is added, to handle overflow during a flood.

In building a dam, a temporary, or coffer dam is constructed (1), and the river is diverted around the dam site through tunnels (2) in the riverbank. The area behind the coffer dam is then filled with an inclined layer of thoroughly compacted rocks (3). The steep, concave upstream face (4) is covered with carefully graded crushed rock (5), and then with a layer of impervious material (6), which is grouted into the bedrock (7) to prevent seepage underneath the dam. Finally, a spillway (8) is added to the downstream slope.

Dam, barrier built across a river to hold back the water. Dams are built to control flooding, to store water for drinking and irrigation, to improve navigation, or to produce hydroelectric power. The artificial lakes or reservoirs formed behind the dams provide a refuge for wild life and are often used for recreation.

Damascus (pop. 2,100,000), capital and largest city of Syria, founded c.2,000 B.C. and possibly the oldest continuously inhabited city in the world. From its origin until A.D. 635 it was ruled by a succession of all the major powers of the Middle East, including the Egyptians, Israelites, Greeks, Romans, and Byzantines. In 635 it was taken by the armies of the new Muslim state expanding out of the Arabian peninsula. It has been Islamic ever since. During the Umayyad dynasty (661-750), Damascus was the capital of an Arab empire extending from Spain to Persia. After 750 it was held by many rulers, mostly Arab and Turkish. Its major architectural landmark is its Great Mosque.
See also: Syria.

D'Amboise, Jacques (1934-   ), U.S. dancer and choreographer. He became a soloist with the New York City Ballet and was recognized for his outstanding performance in the ballet *Apollo* by George Balanchine. He is known for his roles in *Western Symphony* (1954), the film *Carousel* (1956), and his own ballet, *Irish Fantasy* (1964). D'Amboise is also known for his work with young people and dance.

Damien, Father (Joseph de Veuster; 1840-1889), Belgian Roman Catholic missionary who worked in the leper colony of Molokai Island, Hawaii, which he turned from a mere refuge into a thriving community. He died of leprosy himself.

Damon and Pythias, 2 youths from Greek legend whose commitment, friendship, and faithfulness to each other was demonstrated when Dionysius, leader of the city of Syracuse, condemned Pythias to death. Pythias was permitted to leave Syracuse briefly to put his affairs in order while Damon offered to die in his place if his friend did not return. Pythias returned in time to save Damon, and Dionysius chose to pardon Pythias upon seeing the youths' demonstration of loyalty and friendship.
See also: Mythology.

Damp, in mining, name given to various dangerous gases. *Firedamp* is methane, a colorless compound of hydrogen and carbon that forms a highly explosive mixture with air. *Afterdamp* (mainly carbon dioxide and nitrogen), and *chokedamp* and *blackdamp* (mainly carbon dioxide) are other noxious mine gases.
See also: Methane.

Dampier, William (1652-1715), English explorer. After sailing the Atlantic and Pacific as a buccaneer, he was commissioned by the British Admiralty to explore the southwest Pacific. The first Englishman to reach Australia, he wrote *A New Voyage Round the World* (1697) and other books.

Damping-off, disease of new plants caused by fungi in the soil. There are 2 types: pre-emergence, causing seeds to sprout and rot in the soil, and post- emergence, in which newly developed seedlings suddenly die. Seeds can be treated with fungicides before planting, or can be planted in fungus-free soil.

Damrosch, name of a father and 2 sons, German-born musicians active in U.S. music education. **Léopold Damrosch** (1832-1885), violinist and conductor, established the New York Symphony Society and was the orchestra's conductor until he died. **Frank Damrosch** (1859-1937) was a choral conductor and founder of the Institute of Musical Art (later a part of the Juilliard School of Music). **Walter Johannes Damrosch** (1862-1950), conductor and composer, conducted the New York Symphony during its first radio broadcast (1925) and was the music advisor for the 'Music Appreciation Hour' on NBC radio. He composed operas and incidental music for theater, and published an autobiography.

Danaë *See:* Perseus.

Da Nang, or Tourane (pop. 428,000) large port city in southern Vietnam on the South China Sea. Its accessible harbor and its location near North Vietnam made it a key city during the Vietnam War. After 1965, the United States built a major air base there. The city has a modern textile mill and also produces soap.

Dance, art of moving the body rhythmically, usually to music. Among primitive peoples a belief in the magical potency of dance found expression in fertility and rain dances, in dances of exorcism and resurrection, and in dances preparatory to hunting or fighting. Communal dance as a powerful symbol of group cooperation and mutual regard underlies enduring traditions in folk dancing. Classical ballet had its origins in the court dances in 15th and 16th-century Italy and France. The 19th century saw the development of the waltz, in which social dancing reached the height of popularity. Twentieth-century dance styles, promoted by the syncopated rhythms of popular music, have become vehicles of individual self-expression.

Dandelion, perennial herb (genus *Taraxacum*) of the composite family. Dandelions are common weeds producing a rosette of toothy, edible leaves and a yellow flower with a round head of white down.

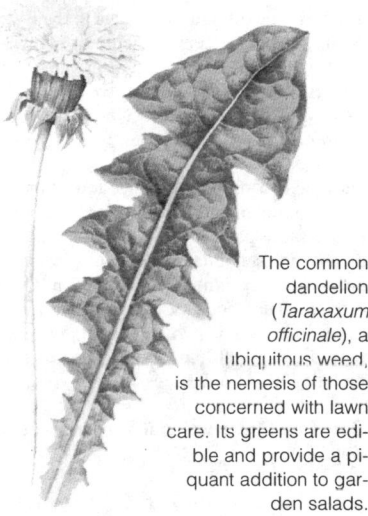

The common dandelion (*Taraxaxum officinale*), a ubiquitous weed, is the nemesis of those concerned with lawn care. Its greens are edible and provide a piquant addition to garden salads.

Dandie Dinmont terrier, short-legged dog originating in Scotland and England, weighing 18 to 24 lb (8 to 11 kg) and standing 8 to 11 in (20 to 28 cm) tall at the shoulders. It has large eyes, a curved body, and a silky tuft of hair on top of its head. It was named after a character in Sir Walter Scott's novel, *Guy Mannering* (1815).

Dandruff, thin, dry scales of skin that flake off the scalp. Severe dandruff- seborrhea, caused by overly secretive oil glands-must be treated by a dermatologist.

Daniel, Book of, Old Testament book, relating events in the life of the prophet Daniel, who was brought to Nebuchadnezzar's court during the Babylonian Captivity of the Jews, during the 6th century B.C. Daniel is most widely known for his reading of the writing on the wall and his miraculous escape from the lion's den. There is a different version of the book in the Apocrypha.
See also: Bible; Old Testament.

Danilova, Alexandra (1904-1997), Russian-born U.S. ballerina. She studied in Leningrad and rose to fame in Paris in Sergei Diaghilev's *Ballets Russes*.

D'Annunzio, Gabriele (1863-1938), Italian writer and adventurer, initially famous for his poetry, whose sensuous imagery reflect-

ed his own life-style. His many novels include *The Flame of Life* (1900), an account of his affair with the Italian stage actress Eleonora Duse. His nationalist speeches helped bring Italy into World War I on the Allies' side. Later his armed supporters occupied the Dalmatian port of Fiume, where D'Annunzio ruled as dictator until 1921. He was a supporter of Mussolini's fascists from the early days of the movement.

Dante Alighieri (1265-1321), Italian poet, regarded as among the greatest Italian writers in history. A descendant of an old Florentine family, he mastered the art of lyric poetry at an early age. His first major work, *The New Life* (c.1292), describes his love for his lifelong inspiration, Beatrice Portinari, who died in 1290. His masterpiece, *The Divine Comedy* (probably written between 1308 and 1320), consists of more than 14,000 lines, divided into three books: *The Inferno* (Hell), *Purgatory*, and *Paradise*. It criticizes the corruption Dante saw in the world around him and codifies the Catholic view of the world. It was also responsible for standardizing what became the modern Italian language.

Danton, Georges Jacques (1759-1794), French revolutionary political leader. A Parisian lawyer and member of the Cordeliers, a club that supported the French Revolution, Danton struggled to reconcile the opposing radical revolutionary factions, the Girondins and Jacobins. After the execution of Louis XVI in 1793, he emerged as the head of the Committee of Public Safety, but failed to take positive steps against the growing threat of civil war. Losing power to the militant Robespierre, Danton was unable to stop the Reign of Terror. He was accused of treason and executed by Robespierre's Jacobins.
See also: French Revolution; Marat, Jean Paul; Robespierre, Maximilien Marie Isidore.

Georges Jacques Danton (1759-1794), who was among the prominent politicians of the first years of the Revolution, was deposed as a member of the Committee of Public Safety on July 10, 1793, and was jailed for his large-scale corruption. He was eventually guillotined.

Dantzig, Rudi van (1933-), internationally known Dutch lead ballet dancer and chore-

ographer. He received the greater part of his education from Sonia Gaskell and worked at Ballet Recital, the Dutch Ballet, the Dutch Theater of Dance, and the National Ballet. He was the artistic leader of the National Ballet from 1971 until 1991. Human relationships, emotions, and conflicts are an important aspect of his choreographic works and he emphasizes past, present and future misunderstandings in society. His style is symbolic and expressionistic rather than dance purely based on music. His best ballets include his very first, *Nachteiland* (1955, Claude Debussy), *Monument for a Dead Boy* (1965, to the electronic music of Jan Boerman) and *Vier Letzte Lieder* (1977, Richard Strauss) which he produced when his mother passed away.

Danube River, second longest river of Europe. From southwest Germany it flows 1,750 mi (2,816 km) east through Austria, Slovakia, Hungary, Croatia, Yugoslavia, Romania, Bulgaria and Ukraine before emptying into the Black Sea. With its more than 300 tributaries, the Danube drains almost one-tenth of Europe and provides a major highway for European trade.

Danzig *See:* Gdansk.

Daoism *See:* Taoism.

Daphne, in Greek mythology, nymph who wished to remain chaste but was pursued by Apollo. She was changed into a laurel bush to escape from him. After that the laurel was sacred to Apollo, who wore the leaves for his crown.
See also: Mythology.

Darboven, Hanne (1941-), West German visual artist. Is considered a conceptual artist. She went to New York in 1966 and began her series of so-called constructions: large sheets of paper squared by the millimeter are arranged horizontally and vertically and divided by diagonal lines of varying lengths into planes that symmetrically repeat themselves. As of 1967, she no longer expressed the measuring units in drawn lines, but in numbers or numbers written in words. She then replaced the random order of the numbers by the calendar system: she added the numbers of the days and months to the year, for example 8.1.74 = 30. After 1971, she used phrases derived from literature and as of 1979, she used notes of music.

Dardanelles, narrow strait 40 mi (60 km) long in northwestern Turkey, separating Asia Minor from Europe, called the Hellespont in ancient times. It links the Sea of Marmara with the Aegean Sea and is part of the waterway leading from the Black Sea to the Mediterranean. Together with the Bosporus, the Dardanelles control the access of vessels from the former Soviet Union to the Mediterranean.
See also: Hellespont.

Dar es Salaam (pop. 2,100,000), former capital and largest city of Tanzania. Located on a natural harbor of the Indian Ocean, it is also Tanzania's main port and economic center. Founded by the Sultan of Zanzibar in

D

D

1866, Dar-es-Salaam, which means 'House of Peace' in Arabic and Swahili, became the capital of German East Africa in 1891 and of the British Colony of Tanganyika after World War I. Tanganyika won independence in 1961, and merged with newly independent Zanzibar in 1964 to form the new state of Tanzania.
See also: Tanzania.

Darío, Rubén (Félix Rubén García Sarmiento; 1867-1916), Nicaraguan poet. He introduced *modernismo*, which revolutionized Spanish and Spanish- American literature. His best-known works are *Profane Hymns* (1896) and *Songs of Life and Hope* (1905).

Darius, Persian kings of the Achaemenid dynasty. **Darius I** (r. 521-486 B.C.), the Great, is regarded as one of the greatest rulers of the ancient Middle East. In 512 he subjugated Thrace and Macedonia and temporarily expelled the Scythians from the Danube region. He then led a series of punitive expeditions into Greece, ultimately leading to the Persian defeat at Marathon in 490. **Darius II** (r. 423?-404 B.C.), seized the throne from his half-brother, beginning a reign marked by corruption and revolts. **Darius III** (r. 336-330 B.C.) was the last ruler of an independent Persian empire, which fell to Alexander the Great.
See also: Persia, Ancient.

Darjeeling (pop. 73,000), city on the lower slopes of the Himalayas, summer capital of West Bengal state, India. Its altitude is 7,100 ft (2,160 m), and the well-known Darjeeling tea thrives in the cool climate on large tea plantations near the city. There are teakwood forests, parks, gardens, museums, hospitals, a zoo, a race course, and colleges, including a medical school. Copper, iron ore, dolomite, and limestone are mined, and major crops include rice, corn, cardamon, and wheat. Mountain ranges and low valleys define 2 distinct regions in the Darjeeling district with a total area of 1,160 sq mi (3,005 sq km).
See also: India.

Dark Ages, popular term for the period in European history from the 5th to the 15th centuries. Beginning with the fall of Rome, the Dark Ages saw the establishment of Feudalism and the spread of Christianity through most of Europe. The term 'Dark Ages' refers to the relative stagnation of science and culture, now thought to be exaggerated. The period ended with the Renaissance and the transition to the modern world.
See also: Middle Ages; Renaissance.

Dark matter, most of the invisible material existing in galaxies and clusters of galaxies. Dark matter does not produce, cast, or absorb light, and is 10 times more prevalent than visible matter. Astronomers have determined the amount of dark matter in a galaxy by finding the orbital speed of gas clouds and stars. They conclude that amounts of dark matter were always greater than amounts of visible matter in both galaxies and clusters of galaxies.
See also: Galaxy.

Darling, Grace Horsley (1815-1842), English heroine, daughter of a lighthouse keeper. In 1838 she and her father rowed a small boat a mile through storm-tossed seas to rescue five survivors of a shipwreck.

Darling River, Australia's longest river. Originating in the Great Dividing Range in Queensland, it flows across the state of New South Wales and into the Murray River, which empties into the Indian Ocean. In winter the Darling is dry along most of its course, but in summer it is an important source of water for the Murray River.

Darnley, Henry Stuart, Lord (1545-1567), second husband of Mary Queen of Scots. Their son became James VI of Scotland and James I of England.

Darter *See:* Anhinga.

Darts, game of skill in which small wooden and metal feathered darts are thrown at a bull's-eye target. Singles, doubles, and team games can be played.

Darwin (pop. 78,000), largest city, administrative center, and chief port of the Northern Territory of Australia, on the Timor Sea. Originally called Palmerston, the city was renamed Darwin in 1911.
See also: Australia.

Darwin, Charles Robert (1809-1882), English naturalist who formulated and elaborated the theory of evolution by natural selection. Darwin sailed around the world on the H.M.S. *Beagle* (1831-1836), collecting data on the variability of species.

When his portrait was painted by John Collier, Darwin had been ill for a number of years, and was living a retired and solitary life at Down House.

In 1858 Darwin and Alfred Russel Wallace, working independently, published outlines of their concepts of natural selection. His greatest books were *The Origin of Species* (1859) and *The Descent of Man* (1871),

which advanced overwhelming evidence for his theories.
See also: Natural selection; Social Darwinism.

Darwin, Erasmus (1731-1802), English biologist and poet, grandfather of Charles Darwin. His *Zoonomia* (1794-1796) presented an early view of the doctrine of evolution.

Darwish, Mahmud (1941-), Palestinian poet, grew up in Israel and published his first collection of poems *Asafir bila ajniha* (Wingless Bird) in 1960. He became a member of the Israeli Communist Party in 1961. After serving a number of prison sentences, he fled Israel and lived in Paris and Beirut. He became an active member of the PLO in the 1970s, but resigned from the Executive Committee in protest against the Oslo Treaties. The difficult resistance to the Israeli occupation is the central theme of his work. Other collections are *Awraq al-Zaytun* (Olive Leaves, 1964), *Uhibbuki aw la Uhibbuki* (I Love You, I Love You Not, 1972) and *Qasidat Bayrut* (Ode To Beirut, 1982).

Database, a structured collection of data in which the elements are arranged according to the same pattern. Examples include: address database, a database with information concerning paintings by van Van Gogh, etcetera. The data in a database is arranged in records, each of which consists of one or more fields. Well known database programs include DBase and Access.

Date Line, International *See:* International Date Line.

Date Masamue (1565-1636), Japanese dignitary (daimio). He sent a delegation to the pope in 1613, which arrived there via the Cape of Good Hope and Lisbon. Portuguese missionaries had been previously welcomed, especially by Hideyoshi (governed from 1577-1598). The Christian mission was considerably successful in Japan during this period, though the success proved to be superficial and fleeting.

Date palm, date-producing tree (*Phoenix dactylifera*) of hot, dry climates. The many products of the date palm include: food and beverages, timber, materials for baskets and other artifacts, rope, fuel, animal feed, and packing material. In some areas the date palm is also grown as an ornamental tree, and it plays a role in religious ceremonies of Muslims, Christians, and Jews.

Datong (also Tatung or Ta-t'ung) (pop. 1.6 mln), China, a city in the northern part of Shanxi Province. It is the center of a large coal-mining area and produces coke, locomotives, and mining machinery. Datong is on the main railway line to Mongolia and is an important trading center.

Datura, genus of plants of the nightshade family, having large, funnel-shaped flowers and yielding the strong narcotics atropine and hyoscamine.

Daudet, Alphonse (1840-1897), French writer noted for his stories of his native

Provence, in southern France. He wrote with humor and compassion about the poor and is best remembered for *Letters from My Mill* (1866) and *Le Petit Chose* (1868).

Daumier, Honoré (1808-1879), French caricaturist, painter, and sculptor. In some 4,000 lithographs, he satirized the bourgeoisie and contemporary politicians, especially in the series *Parliamentary Idylls* and *The Representatives Represented* (1830-1870). In 1832, his cartoon of King Louis-Philippe earned him six months in jail.

Davao (pop. 1,000,000), capital of Davao province in the Philippines, situated on the southeast coast of Mindanao Island. The city is a port and produces Manila hemp, copra, and lumber, and has pearl fisheries.

David (c.1012-c.972 B.C.), king of ancient Israel, successor of Saul, and reputed author of many psalms. David is known as the killer of the Philistine giant Goliath. Chosen king of Judah on Saul's death, he seized Jerusalem, making it the religious and political capital of Israel. He was also known for his close friendship with Saul's son Jonathan and for his adultery with Bathsheba, wife of Uriah the Hittite. His reign lasted about 40 years.
See also: Israel.

David, name of 2 kings of Scotland. **David I** (1084-1153), who ruled 1124-1153, unsuccessfully fought England in support of his niece Matilda's claim to the English crown. But he was successful in obtaining Northumberland for his son. **David II** (David Bruce; 1324-1371) became king in 1329, but fled to France when England invaded Scotland in 1332. In 1346 he invaded England with French allies. The English captured and held him for 11 years, after which he was ransomed and returned to Scotland.

David, Gerard (1460-1523), last master of the Bruges school of painting. He is noted for his emotional power and accomplished technique, as in the altarpieces *Rest on the Flight into Egypt* and *Madonna with Angels and Saints*.

David, Jacques Louis (1748-1825), French painter and leader of the neoclassical movement. His style, combining formal perfection with romantic feeling and didactic purpose, is exemplified in his *Oath of the Horatii* (1784), *Death of Socrates* (1787), and *Death of Marat* (1793). He was Napoleon's official painter.

David, Saint (c.520-600), patron saint of Wales. He founded many monasteries and churches in the 6th century. His feast day is March 1.

Davidson, Jo (1883-1952), U.S. sculptor who lived in Paris. Among famous sitters for his portrait busts were Gertrude Stein, Will Rogers, Franklin Roosevelt, and Mahatma Gandhi.

Da Vinci, Leonardo (1452-1519), Florentine artist and scientist, whose creative and intellectual talents made him the supreme genius of the Italian Renaissance. One of the greatest painters of the period, he was also an architect, engineer, astronomer, anatomist, botanist, inventor, poet, and musician. Few completed works survive; scholars attribute this to Leonardo's restless movement from one project to another, his dissatisfaction with many of them, which were then left unfinished or were destroyed, and his habit of experimenting with new materials, some of which eventually decayed. Leonardo studied art under Andrea del Verrocchio. His mature style is first glimpsed in the unfinished *Adoration of the Magi* (1481), with its subtle tones of light and shade and its dynamic figures, and comes to full development in *The Madonna of the Rocks* (c.1482), painted when Leonardo was already in the service of the duke of Milan. He worked for the duke for 16 years, designing statuary and fortifications and sketching plans for new towns and cathedrals. He also completed *The Last Supper*, in the monastery of Santa Maria delle Grazie in Milan (c.1498), now badly decayed due to his inexperience with fresco techniques. Leonardo's drawings, which constitute most of his surviving work, display fine shading and delicacy. He used various media-colored chalk, pen, and metal points-and his subject range was enormous, reflecting his interest in nature and including comparative studies of youth and old age and a series on the cataclysmic movements of water. Leonardo returned to Florence in 1500 and painted 'Mona Lisa,' or *La Gioconda*, a landmark in portraiture. While still in the service of the duke of Milan, Leonardo designed a canal system with locks that is still in operation. For Cesare Borgia he planned fortifications (1502-3), drew excellent maps, and designed a tanklike armored vehicle and a breech-loading cannon. He may have joined (c.1513) Donato Bramante, Raphael, and Michelangelo in Rome to work on the Vatican and, possibly, plans for the new St. Peter's. Leonardo's notebooks, filled with ideas and sketches on anatomy, hydraulics, aeronautics, and machinery, are the best evidence of his genius; many of his inventions were centuries ahead of their time.

Davis, Angela Yvonne (1944-), Prominent African American activist and a member of the Communist Party. Davis was active in the Black Panthers movement as from 1967.

She lost her job at the University of Los Angeles due to her membership of the Communist Party. In 1970, she was accused of complicity in a hostage situation that was carried out by the 'Soledad Brothers', and during which, among others, a judge was killed. Davis was not present, but a few of the weapons that were used were registered in her name. She was also charged with murder. Protest actions against the trial, which was postponed many times, were held across the world. She was finally acquitted in June 1972. Following a journey through a number of socialist countries, she became the driving force behind the 'National Alliance Against Racist and Political Repression'.

Davis, Benjamin Oliver (1877-1970), first African-American general in the U.S. Army (1940). He later supervised the desegrega-

Honoré Daumier (1808-1879) gained great fame with his lithographic caricatures. He was also a painter and did this scene of *Crispino and Scapino* (1858-1860), two characters from the *Comedie Italienne* (Paris, Louvre).

D

King David, with the head of the giant Goliath at his feet. Bronze sculpture by Andrea del Verrocchio (1435-1488, Bargello, Florence).

D

tion of troop units. His son, Benjamin Oliver, Jr. (1912-   ), became the first African-American general in the Air Force.

Davis, Bette (1908-1990), U.S. film actress who won Academy Awards for her roles in *Dangerous* (1935) and *Jezebel* (1938). In the 1960s she won new fame in psychological thrillers. Other major films of hers include *Dark Victory* (1939), *The Little Foxes* (1941), and *All About Eve* (1950).

Davis, Dwight Filley (1879-1945), American lawyer and tennis player, known for the Davis Cup, which he founded. This cup, thirteen inches (33cm) in height and weighing 14.85 pounds (6.75kg), was at stake during the international match between the US and Great Britain (outcome 3-0) at the beginning of 1900. Davis was a credible tennis player: he was the winner of the US men's doubles from 1899-1901. He held a variety of high official positions following his sports career.

The Davy lamp was developed in 1815 by chemist sir Humphry Davy. It was used in the mines. The flame was unable to set fire to an explosive gas mixture (e.g. firedamp, which contains the highly flammable methane). It was screened off with one or more metal wire gauzes.

Davis, Jefferson (1808-1889), president of the Confederate States of America during the Civil War. U.S. Senator from Mississippi (1847-1851, 1857-1861) and secretary of War (1853-1857), Davis resigned from the Senate after Mississippi's secession from the Union in 1861. In 1862 Davis was inaugurated president of the Confederacy. His war measures weakened states' rights and distanced him from his Congress. Davis served 2 years in federal prison after the surrender of the South in 1865, but was released without being prosecuted.
See also: Confederate States of America; Civil War, U.S..

Davis, John (c.1550-1605), English navigator and early Arctic explorer. He discovered the Davis Strait between Greenland and

Baffin Island (1587) as well as the Falkland Islands (1592).
See also: Falkland Islands.

Davis, Miles Dewey (1926-1991), U.S. jazz musician, one of the pioneers of 'bebop' in the 1940s and of 'cool' jazz, with its restrained, clear sounds, in the 1950s. A renowned trumpeter, Davis played with many outstanding musicians, including Charlie Parker and John Coltrane. In the late 1960s he produced a new sound, based on a fusion of jazz and rock, and after a period of retirement, he reemerged in the 1980s as one of the major innovators in U.S. music.
See also: Jazz.

Davis, Richard Harding (1864-1916), U.S. writer, journalist, and war correspondent. He also wrote novels, short stories, and plays.

Davis, Stuart (1894-1964), U.S. abstract painter, illustrator, and lithographer. His style is characterized by brilliant colors, the use of printed words, and interlocking shapes.

Davis Cup, international men's tennis trophy, first contested in 1900. Sixteen qualifying nations are divided into 4 zones, and their teams compete for the annual award.

Davis Strait *See:* Northwest Passage.

Davy, Sir Humphry (1778-1829), English chemist who pioneered the study of electrochemistry. Electrolytic methods allowed him to isolate the elements sodium, potassium, magnesium, calcium, boron, and barium (1807-1808). He recognized the elemental nature of and named chlorine (1810). His early work on nitrous oxide was done at Bristol under Thomas Beddoes, but his later career centered on the Royal Institution, where he was assisted by Michael Faraday. He also invented a miner's safety lamp, known as the Davy lamp.
See also: Electrochemistry.

Dawes, Charles Gates (1865-1951), U.S. politician who shared the 1925 Nobel Peace Prize for the plan named after him. Vice president under Calvin Coolidge (1925-1929), he was later ambassador to Great Britain (1929-1932).
See also: Dawes Plan.

Dawes Act *See:* Native Americans.

Dawes Plan, program presented by Charles Gates Dawes in 1924 to enable Germany to pay off World War I reparations by means of an international loan and mortgages on German industry and railways.

Day, 24-hour period during which the earth completes one rotation on its axis as it rotates around the sun. The day is divided into 2 equal parts: from midnight (the beginning of the new day) to noon is designated as a.m. and from noon to midnight is p.m. The term day commonly refers to the time that the sun actually shines during the 24-hour period (the term night refers to the time it doesn't shine). The amount of daylight varies greatly in different parts of the world.

Day, Clarence (1874-1935), U.S. writer of essays, sketches, reviews, and stories. His best-known works are *Life with Father* (1935) and *Life with Mother* (published posthumously in 1937), which poked affectionate fun at upper-class family life in New York City c.1900.

Dayaks *See:* Dyak.

Dayan, Moshe (1915-1981), Israeli military and political leader. Active in Israel's War of Independence (1948), he commanded the Israeli forces during the 1956 Sinai Campaign. He was minister of defense during the Six Day War of June, 1967 and from 1969 to 1974, when he resigned after being blamed for Israel's unpreparedness in the Yom Kippur War of October 1973. He was foreign minister 1977-1979.
See also: Israel.

Dayfly *See:* Mayfly.

Day-Lewis, Cecil (1904-1972), English author. *The Magnetic Mountain* (1933) is his best-known volume of verse from the 1930s, but his style matured fully after 1945. He wrote novels under his own name and detective novels as Nicholas Blake. He was poet laureate (1968-1972).

Daylight saving time, method of making better use of daylight by setting clocks 1 hour ahead of standard time. Daylight saving time came into use in the United States and other countries during World War I, in an effort to conserve electricity by having business hours correspond more closely to the hours of natural daylight. It was again put into effect on a national scale during World War II, after which the matter was left to the discretion of local authorities. Daylight saving time in the United States now extends from the second Sunday in April to the last Sunday in October.

Day lily, any of several plants (genus *Hemerocallis*) of the lily family, growing 3-5 ft (91-150 cm) high. The day lily has sword-shaped leaves and yellow or orange, funnel-shaped flowers, which live only from sunrise to sunset.

Day of Atonement *See:* Yom Kippur.

Dayton (pop. 180,000), city in southwestern Ohio, seat of Montgomery County. The birthplace of the Wright brothers, who established an aviation research plant there after their historic first flight, Dayton became an industrial research center and producer of precision products.
See also: Ohio.

Daytona Beach (pop. 62,000), city in northeastern Florida, 90 mi (145 km) southeast of Jacksonville. Founded in 1870, it is made up of the former communities of Daytona, Daytona Beach, and Seabreeze, which were consolidated and incorporated as Daytona Beach in 1926. Tourism is the area's principal industry. Its hard, flat 23-mi (37-km) long beach has been used for automobile speed trials since 1903.
See also: Florida.

D

Dayton, Jonathan (1760-1824), U.S. soldier and politician, youngest signer of the Constitution (1787). He was a congressional representative (1791-1799), Speaker of the House (1795-1799), and U.S. senator from New Jersey (1799-1805). An associate of Vice President Aaron Burr, Dayton was charged with treason in 1807 but was never brought to trial.

DC *See:* Electric current.

D-Day, in World War II, June 6, 1944, the day Allied troops landed in Normandy, France, thus launching the last major campaign in Western Europe, under the command of General Eisenhower. Over 5,000 ships were used, delivering some 90,000 troops, primarily British, U.S., and Canadian. Some 20,000 more were delivered by parachute and glider. By June 11 the forces had linked up in a solid front. The invasion, code-named Overlord, was one of the most complex feats of organization and supply in military history.
See also: World War II.

DDT (dichloro-diphenyl-trichloroethane), powerful insecticide. Because of concern about the persistence of its toxic residues, DDT is no longer marketed for commercial use in the United States.
See also: Insecticide.

DEA *See:* Drug Enforcement Administration.

Deacon (Greek *diakonos*, 'servant'), assistant to the clergy in a Christian church. Deacons form a minor holy order in the Roman Catholic church and an important class of clergy in the Orthodox church. In Protestant churches deacons are usually laymen given special church responsibilities. Some Protestants maintain the office of deaconess, women who undergo religious training and devote themselves to serving the church.
See also: Christianity.

Deadly nightshade *See:* Belladonna.

Dead Sea, salt lake in the Great Rift Valley, on the Israel-Jordan border. About 390 sq mi (1,010 sq km) in area, the Dead Sea extends some 50 mi (80 km) south from the mouth of the Jordan River and is up to 11 mi (17.7

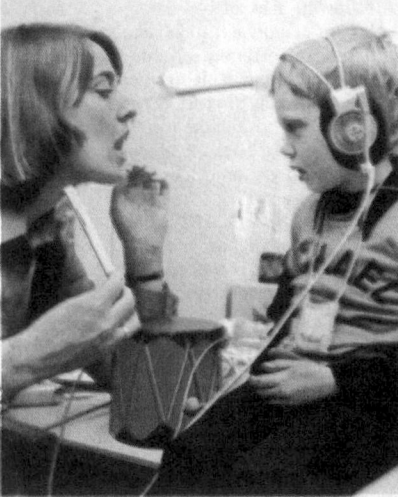

km) wide. Much of it is more than 1,000 ft (305 m) deep; at surface 1,292 ft (394 m) below sea level, it is the lowest point on earth. Its high salt content (over 20%) results from the rapid evaporation in the area's hot climate and prevents any aquatic life from surviving.

Dead Sea Scrolls, group of Hebrew and Aramaic manuscripts discovered in caves near the northwestern coast of the Dead Sea in 1947 and later. The scrolls, preserved in clay jars, were written between the 1st century B.C. and about A.D. 50. Many of the scrolls are books of the Old Testament, the most important of these being 2 complete texts of the Book of Isaiah, at least a thousand years older than any known copy. Among the non-biblical texts is one describing the 'war of the sons of light against the sons of darkness,' believed to be an allegory on political events of the time. Another important work is the *Manual of Discipline*, of a group of Jewish ascetics usually identified with the Essenes. Because many of their beliefs were similar to those of the early Christians, it has been suggested that they had some connection with or influence on early Christianity.
See also: Bible.

Deadwood (pop. 1,380), city in the Black Hills of South Dakota; the seat of Lawrence County. A gold rush in 1876 brought a huge

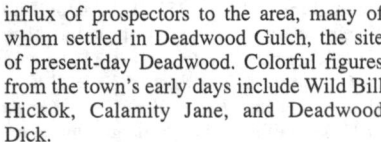

influx of prospectors to the area, many of whom settled in Deadwood Gulch, the site of present-day Deadwood. Colorful figures from the town's early days include Wild Bill Hickok, Calamity Jane, and Deadwood Dick.
See also: South Dakota.

Deafness, partial or total impairment of the sense of hearing. Hearing loss is of 2 basic types. In *conductive* deafness, the eardrum cannot make the bones of the inner ear vibrate. The nerve endings deep inside the ear are not stimulated, and the brain receives no message. This may be caused by blockage of the ear canal by wax or a foreign body; infections and perforation of the eardrum are other causes. This form of deafness can usually be corrected by surgery, antibiotics, hearing aids, or other techniques. *Nerve* (perceptive) deafness, on the other hand, stems from damage to the hearing nerve itself, which prevents the nerve from transmitting to the brain the message it receives from the vibrating eardrum and bones. The most common cause is atherosclerosis of the blood vessels supplying the nerve or injury due to excessive noise. This form of deafness is often permanent.

Educating deaf children with the audiological method at the Joh.C. Amman School in Amsterdam. Amman (1669-1724) was a Swiss physician, who worked in Amsterdam. He was perhaps the first to teach a deaf girl to speak, making use of lip reading. This method was later rediscovered and it then replaced sign-language, which had long been the only method in the education of the deaf. Later, the lip reading method was elaborated and refined, until it grew into the audiological method. This method makes use of technical aids such as earphones, to completely utilize any remnants of the hearing ability to the fullest.

Deák, Ferenc (1803-1876), Hungarian statesman who negotiated the 1867 Compromise that gave Hungary internal autonomy within Austria-Hungary. He entered the Diet in 1833. In the 1848 revolution he became minister of justice but resigned in disagreement with the revolutionary Lajos Kossuth the same year. He returned to the Diet in 1861, becoming the country's acknowledged leader.

Dean, Dizzy (Jay Hanna Dean; 1911-1974), U.S. baseball pitcher. He played for the St. Louis Cardinals (1930-1937), Chicago Cubs (1938-1941), and pitched one game for the St. Louis Browns (1947). Dean's achievements include winning the Most Valuable Player award (1934), and in the same season leading the St. Louis Cardinals to a World Series victory by winning 30 games in the regular season, and 2 in the World Series. Dean was inducted into the National Baseball Hall of Fame in 1953.

Spontaneous formation of salt pillars in the Dead Sea. Because of the high concentration of salt, the lake no longer contains any organic life.

D

James Dean, the brooding youth hero of the 1950s, shown here in a scene from *Rebel Without a Cause* (1955).

Dean, James (1931-1955), U.S. actor. Elia Kazan recognized his talent in the New York stage play *The Immoralist* (1954) and cast him in the film *East of Eden* (1955). His next film, *Rebel Without a Cause* (1955), established him as the romantic, rebellious antihero of a generation, but his career ended tragically when he was killed in a car crash.

De Angeli, Marguerite Lofft (1889-1987), U.S. author and illustrator of children's books. Many of her stories feature children of minority groups, such as the Quaker girl in *Thee Hannah* (1940), the Pennsylvania Dutch boy in *Yonie Wondernose* (1944), and the African-American girl in *Bright April* (1946). *The Door in the Wall* (1949), about English life in the 1300s, won the Newbery Award in 1950.

Dearborn (pop. 89,000), city in southeast Michigan, on the River Rouge 10 mi (16 km) west of Detroit. Dearborn grew rapidly after World War I. It is the center of the Ford motor company. It now also produces aircraft parts, farm machinery, metal goods, and air-conditioning equipment. Among its attractions are the Edison Institute of Technology and the Henry Ford Museum.
See also: Ford Motor Company; Michigan.

Death, complete and irreversible cessation of life in an organism or part of an organism. The moment of death is conventionally accepted as the time when the heart ceases to beat, there is no breathing, and the brain shows no evidence of function. Since it is possible to resuscitate and maintain heart function and to take over breathing mechanically, the brain may suffer irreversible death while 'life' is maintained artificially. In 'brain death,' reversible causes have been eliminated, and there is no spontaneous breathing, no movement, and no specific reflexes seen on 2 occasions; artificial life support systems can then be reasonably discontinued. After death, enzymes begin the process of *autolysis* (decomposition), which later involves bacteria. In the hours following death, changes occur in muscle that cause rigidity (*rigor mortis*). Death of part of an organism (*necrosis*), such as occurs

following lack of blood supply, consists of loss of cell organization, autolysis, and gangrene. The part may separate or be absorbed, but infection is liable to spread to living tissue. Cells may also die as part of the normal turnover of a structure (for example, skin or blood cells), because of compression (for example, by a tumor), or as part of a degenerative disease.
Criteria of death. The entire body does not die at the same rate; breathing and heart action may stop, but other functions may continue. In humans, for example, the kidneys, skin, bone, liver, pancreas, cornea, and heart have been transplanted into needy recipients and may continue to function for a long period. When on an artificial respirator, an individual may maintain a heartbeat. But is that person truly alive? If the respirator were turned off, how long would the person remain alive? What happens to the brain of a person maintained on a respirator? These questions have serious ethical, religious, and legal implications. The sequence of events toward the cessation of life suggests 4 stages: (1) a time of impending death, (2) a period of reversibility, with or without residual change, (3) a period of irreversibility, (4) absolute death, as set forth in the current legal definition, and (5) murder.
Causes of death. Natural death is often assumed to be due to coronary thrombosis ('heart attack'); the most common cause is ischemic (blood-starved) heart disease, though not necessarily the result of thrombosis. Other common causes of death are acute hypersensitive heart failure (that is, due to very high blood pressure), pulmonary embolism (a clot that has traveled to the lung), and subarachnoid or cerebral hemorrhage (stroke).
The principal causes of unnatural deaths are (1) mechanical violence, including traffic accidents, industrial mishaps or disasters, sexual and other forms of assault, and homicide, (2) physical agencies, such as heat, cold, electricity, or radiation, (3) deprivation involving the complete or partial lack of basic essentials, such as water, food, or warmth, and (4) poisoning (chemicals and drugs, anesthetics, intravenous infusions, and blood transfusions).

Death penalty *See:* Capital punishment.

Eugene V. Debs, a founder of and spokesman for the U.S. Socialist Party, ran five times as its candidate for the presidency, receiving nearly 920,000 votes in 1920.

Death's-head moth, large moth (*Acherontia atropos*) of the family Sphingidae. Found in Africa and Europe, it has a thick, hairy body with relatively small wings and feeds on flowers and honey.

Death Valley, arid valley in southeast California and southern Nevada. The United States' highest recorded air temperature-134°F (56°C)-was recorded here in 1913. Death Valley is 140 mi (225 km) long and up to 15 mi (24 km) wide. The lowest point in the Western Hemisphere, Badwater (282 ft/86 m below sea level), is at the heart of the valley. In 1933 it was made the Death Valley National Monument.

Deathwatch, any of several beetles belonging to the family Anobiidae. They bore through wood and furniture by knocking their heads against it, making a clicking sound. An old superstition held that the sound foretold death.

DeBakey, Michael Ellis (1908-), U.S. heart surgeon who developed the pump for the heart-lung machine (1932), devised a new surgical procedure to treat aneurysm, and successfully implanted a mechanical device to help restore a diseased heart (1967).

Debate, formal and regulated discussion of a given proposition. Platform debates, popular at many high schools and colleges, have precise rules and procedures. Legislative debates are more flexible.

Deborah, prophet and judge in the Old Testament. A member of the tribe of Ephraim, she enlisted the Israelite leader in the fight against the Canaanites, led by Sisera. After the battle at Mt. Tabor, in which the Canaanites were routed, she sang a song of victory (Judges 5), 'The Song of Deborah,' dedicated to the God of Israel.
See also: Bible; Old Testament.

Debrecen (pop. 214,000), city in Hungary, 120 m (193 km) east of Budapest. A market for surrounding farms since the Middle Ages, it is also a religious, political, cultural, and educational center. In the 1500s it was a stronghold of Protestantism.
See also: Hungary.

De Broglie, Prince Louis Victor (1892-1987), French physicist who received the 1929 Nobel Prize in physics for his discovery that the behavior of electrons, like that of light, could be explained in terms of wave motion. De Broglie's theory led to the development of wave mechanics, an important part of quantum mechanics.
See also: Quantum mechanics.

Debs, Eugene Victor (1855-1926), U.S. labor organizer and socialist political leader. A national leader of the Brotherhood of Locomotive Firemen, he founded the American Railway Union in 1893. Debs was jailed in 1895 for defying a federal court injunction during the Pullman railroad strike. Five times the Socialist party's candidate for the presidency, he waged his last and most successful campaign in 1920, while still imprisoned under the Espionage Act (1917) for his political opposition to World War I. He was released in 1921.

Debt, something owed, whether money, services, or goods. The debtor usually pays interest to the creditor (to whom the debt is owed). If the debtor fails to pay the debt, the creditor can take court action to try to acquire some of the debtor's property. Laws determine what may be seized.

Deburghgraeve, Frederik (1973-), Belgian swimmer, was the first Belgian to achieve a world record in Bastenaken in 1996: the 100 m breaststroke (in a 25 meter pool) in 59.02 s. The Olympic Games in Atlanta brought a second world record that year in a series of the 100m breaststroke with 1.00,60 (50 meter pool). Deburghgraeve won Olympic gold during the finals of that competition. He became the 100m world champion for breaststroke in Perth in January 1998. He improved his world record in December of that year (58.79).

Debussy, Claude Achille (1862-1918), French composer. Although influenced by Wagner in his early years, he later developed a highly original style of musical impressionism, based on his own revolutionary thinking about harmony and his studies of Asian music. *Prelude to the Afternoon of a Faun* (1894), the three *Nocturnes* (1899), and *La Mer* (1905) are among Debussy's most imaginatively scored orchestral works. *Pelléas et Mélisande* (1902) is a landmark in operatic history. His pieces for piano include *Reflets dans l'eau, Jardins sous la pluie, Poissons d'or*, 2 sets of preludes, and 12 études.

Debye, Peter Joseph William (1884-1966), Dutch physical chemist chiefly known for the Debye-Hückel theory of ionic solution (1923). He was awarded the 1936 Nobel Prize in chemistry and was head of the chemistry department of Cornell University (1940-1950).
See also: Chemistry.

Decalogue *See:* Ten Commandments.

Decameron, The, collection of 100 stories (written 1348-1353) by the Italian author Giovanni Boccaccio. Amusing and often bawdy, the tales are considered among the masterpieces of Italian and world literature. They also provide a shrewd commentary on 14th-century Italian life.
See also: Boccaccio, Giovanni.

Decathlon, 10-event track-and-field contest consisting of the 100-meter dash; the 400-meter and 1,500-meter flat races; the 110-meter hurdle race; pole vaulting; discus throwing; shot putting; javelin throwing; and the broad and high jumps. The decathlon has been an Olympic event since 1912.
See also: Track and field.

Decatur, Stephen (1779-1820), U.S. naval hero. He was responsible for many victories in the Barbary Wars (1804) and later in the War of 1812, when he commanded the *United States*. He served as a U.S. navy commissioner until his death in a duel. He is famous for saying: 'Our country, right or wrong.'

Decembrist revolt, unsuccessful uprising against the tsarist government in Russia organized by army officers in December 1825. The sudden death of Alexander I led to uncertainty and turmoil, and the Decembrists - many of whom had absorbed liberal ideals while serving in West Europe during the Napoleonic Wars - took the opportunity to rise up against Alexander's successor, Tsar Nicholas I. The rebellion was crushed, and 5 of the leaders were hanged. Many others were exiled to Siberia.

Decemvirs *See:* Twelve Tables, Laws of the.

Decibel (dB), measurement of sound intensity; one-tenth of a bel. The human ear can distinguish sounds at a level of 10 dBs and can tolerate sounds up to 120 decibels.

Deciduous tree, any of those trees that shed their leaves each year, usually in the fall. The tree reabsorbs food material from the leaves before they fall, and their loss greatly reduces the amount of water that evaporates from the tree, thus helping survival in bad weather. Trees that retain their leaves all year are called evergreens.

Decimal system, system of computation based on the number 10 (Latin *decem*). Almost all countries use the decimal system. The system uses 10 numerals - 0, 1, 2, 3, 4, 5, 6, 7, 8 and 9 - to represent any number as the sum of powers of 10. The *units* place indicates multiples of 10^0 (defined as 1), the *tens* place indicates multiples of 10^1, the *hundreds* place indicates multiples of 10^2, and so forth. Thus the number 4,256 means $(4 \times 10^3) + (2 \times 10^2) + (5 \times 10^1) + (6 \times 10^0)$. The system is also used to represent numbers between 0 and 1. Thus 1.345 means $(1 \times 10^0) + (3 \times 10^{-1}) + (4 \times 10^{-2}) + (5 \times 10^{-3})$. A decimal

Claude Debussy was the foremost innovative French composer of the late 19th century. He experimented with harmony and created new and strikingly original sounds in his orchestral compositions.

point is used to separate the part between 0 and 1 from the rest of the number; 4,256.345.

The decimal system was invented by the Hindus c.600 A.D. They introduced the concept of *zero* or 0. The system was spread throughout North Africa and Europe by the Arabs in the next few centuries.

Declaration of Independence, document in which representatives of the 13 American colonies set forth the reasons for their break with Britain. July 4, the day in 1776 on which the Continental Congress adopted the Declaration of Independence, is observed as Independence Day, a U.S. national holiday. A royal proclamation of Aug. 1775 held the colonies to be in a state of rebellion, and in Nov. the British instituted a naval blockade. Prolonged hostilities seemed inevitable, and formal independence was advocated to help the colonies gain assistance from France and Spain. The case for independence was strongly reinforced by the publication of Thomas Paine's *Common Sense* (Jan. 1776). Acting on instructions from the Virginia legislature, Richard Henry Lee introduced a resolution to the Continental Congress on June 7, 1776, stating that 'these United Colonies are, and of right ought to be, free and independent States.' Congress appointed a committee to draw up a formal declaration of independence for consideration. Thomas Jefferson was assigned to draft the document. On July 2, 12 of the 13 colonies approved Lee's resolution, with New York temporarily abstaining. Debate on the Declaration began on July 3, and after a few alterations, it was adopted the following day. Southern sensitivities over slavery caused the most important change: A clause censuring the king for aiding and abetting the slave trade was struck out. Another section that had placed blame on the people of England as well as the king was also eliminated. Only John Hancock, the president of the Congress, and Charles Thompson, the secretary, signed the document on July 4. On Aug. 2, 50 members signed, with another 6 putting their signatures to it later.

Declaration of the Rights of Man and the Citizen, key philosophical document of the French Revolution, adopted by the National Assembly on August 26, 1789. It reflects the French Enlightenment's rejection of the rule of absolute monarchy in favor of natural rights. These included equality, popular sovereignty (i.e. rule of the people), and individual rights to liberty, property, and freedom from arbitrary government abuse. It was made the preamble to the 1791 Constitution.
See also: French Revolution.

Declaratory Act *See:* Revolutionary War in America.

Declination, in astronomy, one of two coordinates used to specify the position of an object in the sky under the equatorial coordinate system. Declination in the sky is roughly equivalent to latitude on earth. An object north of the celestial equator (an extension of the earth's equator) is said to have a positive declination, written with a plus sign. An

D

D

object south of the celestial equator has a negative, or minus, declination.
See also: Astronomy.

Decode, in information science, the translation or determination of the meaning of a coded set of data. A *decoder* is a matrix of switching elements that selects one or more output channels according to the combination of input signals present.

Decomposition, chemical, reduction of a compound to simpler substances, or to its elemental components. The materials obtained after the chemical breakdown differ in their properties both from each other and from the original substances. Heat is the simplest agent of decomposition. Reducing metallic ores to separate out the pure metal uses heat along with other chemicals. Water can be decomposed into hydrogen and oxygen by electrolysis. The decomposition of organic matter is known as putrefaction.
See also: Compound.

Decompression sickness *See:* Bends.

Decoration Day *See:* Memorial Day.

Decorations, medals, and orders, awards acknowledging exceptional civil or military service, acts of bravery, and notable achievements in the arts and sciences. In the United States the highest civil decoration is the *Presidential Medal of Freedom*. The highest military decoration 'for conspicuous gallantry at the risk of life' is the *Congressional Medal of Honor*. The *Purple Heart* is awarded to service people wounded by enemy action. Britain's highest military decoration is the *Victoria Cross*, which, like other British decorations, may also be awarded to nationals of Commonwealth countries such as Canada. France awards the *Médaille Militaire* and the *Croix de Guerre*, and also recognizes outstanding civil or military service by membership (in various grades) in the *Legion of Honor*. There were also dif-

ferent grades of Germany's most famous decoration, the *Iron Cross*, which was awarded up through World War II. The highest award of the former German Federal Republic was the *Order of Merit*. The former Soviet Union had many orders, but its highest honor was the *Heroes of the Soviet Union* medal. China has such honors as *Hero of the Army of the People's Liberation*. Japan has the *Order of the Chrysanthemum*.

Decorative arts, term covering a variety of artistic activities (including woodworking, glass handicrafts, textiles, and metalworking) not traditionally included in the fine arts, which include painting, sculpture, and architecture. The aim of the decorative arts is to beautify surroundings. Decorative artisans create furniture, porcelain, jewelry, and fabrics, as well as embellishments of buildings, such as gilding and molded plasterwork.

Decoupage (from French *découper*, 'to cut out'), decorative art form in which paper shapes are glued onto other items and covered with coats of varnish. Used first in 17th-century France to embellish furniture, giving it the appearance and texture of enamel, decoupage became popular throughout Europe. A resurgence of interest occurred in the U.S. in the 1960s.

Deductive method, the process of reasoning by which conclusions are drawn by logical inference from given premises. The Aristotelian syllogism is an example of deductive logic. Conclusions reached by deductive reasoning are called valid rather than true to distinguish that which follows logically from that which is the case.

Dee, John (1527-1628), English philosopher and mathematician accused of sorcery against Queen Mary. He was tried and acquitted by the Star Chamber (1555). Dee created special reports for Queen Elizabeth detailing the geographical and aquatic characteristics of newly discovered regions. He also wrote several treatises on alchemy, navigation, and mathematics.

Deed, legal document transferring the ownership of property.

Deep, ocean area with a depth in excess of 18,000 ft (5,490 m). More than 100 deeps have been identified in ocean floors. Mariana Trench, located 200 mi (320 km) southwest of Guam, is the deepest ocean deep with an ocean floor at 36,498 ft (11,033 m) below the surface. The Milwaukee Deep, north of Puerto Rico, has the greatest depth in the Atlantic Ocean at 28,374 ft. (8,648 m).

Deer, any of about 40 species of cloven-hoofed mammals of the family Cervidae, found in Europe, Asia, and the Americas. Their most remarkable characteristic is the antlers of the males. Only the musk deer and the Chinese water deer lack antlers, while both sexes of the caribou and the reindeer are antlered. The smallest deer is the South American pudu, 13 in (33 cm) at the shoulder; the largest is the North American moose, up to 7 ft (2.1 m) and over 1000 lb

(454 km) in weight. Though many species are abundant, some, such as the axis deer of India and Sri Lanka, are fast becoming rare. The Chinese Pere David's deer survives mainly in zoos but is gradually being re-introduced to the wild in preserves.

Deere, John (1804-1886), U.S. inventor who developed and marketed the first steel plows.

Deer fly, insect belonging to the horsefly family, found throughout North America. They bite both large animals and people and sometimes carry disease-causing germs.

Deerhound, Scottish breed of dog skilled at hunting deer by sight. Deerhounds have coarse, wiry coats of gray or tan. They measure 28 to 32 in (71-81 cm) and weigh 75 to 110 lb (34-50 kg).

De facto segregation *See:* Segregation.

De Falla, Manuel *See:* Falla, Manuel de.

Defenestration of Prague *See:* Thirty Years' War.

Defense mechanism, term in psychoanalysis referring to involuntary or unconscious measures adopted by individuals to protect themselves against painful emotions associated with some disagreeable physical or mental situation of frequent occurrence. Defense mechanisms include repression, which prevents painful ideas from entering the conscious mind; displacement, in which impulses are released through disguised actions; and sublimation, the redirection of impulses into socially acceptable channels.
See also: Psychoanalysis.

Deflation, a contraction in the availability of money and credit, resulting in a downward movement in prices. Deflation can be caused intentionally by the government or be the result of a decrease of economic activity. When prices are declining, creditors gain (if their claims are paid) while debtors lose. Persons on fixed incomes gain (if they continue to receive their income). Businesses generally lose because they have difficulty in reducing their costs in proportion to the drop in their income from sales. People are afraid to spend their money, business declines, and workers lose their jobs.
See also: Inflation.

Defoe, Daniel (1660?-1731), English author, one of the originators of the English novel. Originally a merchant, he later took to writing essays and pamphlets, including *The Shortest Way with Dissenters* (1702), a satire parodying the leaders of the Anglican High Church (for which he was fined and pilloried). He was nearly 60 when he began writing the realistic novels for which he is best known, including *Robinson Crusoe* (1719), *Moll Flanders* (1722), and *A Journal of the Plague Year* (1722).

De Forest, Lee (1873-1961), U.S. inventor of the triode (1906), an electron tube with three electrodes that could operate as a signal amplifier as well as a rectifier. The triode

Fallow deer (*Dama dama*) during mating season. Seven to eight months after mating, the beautifully spotted young will be born.

was crucial to the development of radio and intercontinental telephony.
See also: Vacuum tube.

Degas, (Hilaire Germain) Edgar (1834-1917), French painter and sculptor associated with impressionism. His favorite subjects were ballet dancers and racetrack scenes. From the 1880s, Degas worked regularly in pastel and produced small bronze sculptures of dancers and horses. Among his best-known paintings are *The Bellelli Family* (1859), *The Rehearsal* (1882), and *The Millinery Shop* (c.1885).
See also: Impressionism.

De Gasperi, Alcide (1881-1954), Italian statesman. Active in political life from 1911, he was twice imprisoned for his opposition to the fascist regime. He clandestinely organized the Christian Democratic Party during World War II and, as its leader, became the first premier (1945-1953) of the new Italian Republic.
See also: Italy.

De Gaulle, Charles (1890-1970), French soldier and political leader, president 1945-1946 and 1958-1969. When France fell to Germany in 1940, De Gaulle launched the Free French movement in England. In 1944, his provisional government took power in liberated France. After resigning in 1946, he returned the following year leading a new party, but met with little success and retired in 1953. On June 1, 1958, at the height of the Algerian crisis, he was named premier and assumed new and wider powers, effectively ending the fourth republic. In 1959 a new constitution was adopted, inaugurating the fifth republic, with De Gaulle as president. He was nearly overthrown by worker-student struggles in 1968 and resigned in 1969 upon the defeat of a referendum designed to give him further powers for constitutional reforms.
See also: France.

Degree, academic, title conferred by a university as a recognition of academic competence. Degrees were originally awarded after the candidate had successfully passed a vigorous oral examination, but abuse of this system (particularly in the 18th century at Oxford and Cambridge) led to the gradual adoption of the written examination, at least for the lower (bachelor) degrees. *Master's* and *doctor's* degrees are usually awarded for research work undertaken after passing a first degree examination. *Honorary degrees* are now awarded to distinguished diplomats or artists, without regard to their academic standing. Special achievement in the bachelor's degree is recognized by the Latin terms (in ascending order of excellence) *cum laude, magna cum laude,* and *summa cum laude.*
The most commonly awarded degrees are B.A. (Bachelor of Arts), B.S. (Bachelor of Science), M.A. (Master of Arts), M.S. (Master of Science), Ph.D. (Doctor of Philosophy), LL.B. (Bachelor of Laws), LL.M. (Master of Laws), LL.D. (Doctor of Laws) or J.D. (Doctor of Jurisprudence), M.D. (Doctor of Medicine), and B.D. (Bachelor of Divinity).

De Groot, Hugo *See:* Grotius, Hugo.

Dehydrated food, food that has been preserved by drying. More than 90% of the water is removed in drying, making dehydrated food light in weight and compact. Food selected for drying must be fresh, clean and at the proper stage of ripeness.

Dehydration, removal of water from substances, usually as part of an industrial process or in the preservation of food. Water may be removed in drying chambers through which hot air or gases are passed. A vacuum may be used instead of hot air or gas to evaporate the water at lower temperatures. In chemical processes, gases are dried by passing them through tubes containing drying agents such as calcium chloride. Substances can be dried and kept away from moisture by placing them in a *desiccator*-an airtight chamber containing a drying agent such as silica gel. Dehydration is an important method of food preservation. Since most food spoilage is caused by bacteria, which can only function in the presence of moisture, dehydration inhibits their activity. Freeze drying, in which foods are frozen and ice removed by sublimation in a vacuum, is increasingly used as it does less damage to the texture and flavor of the food. *Dehydration* also refers to a serious physiological condition in which the body's tissues

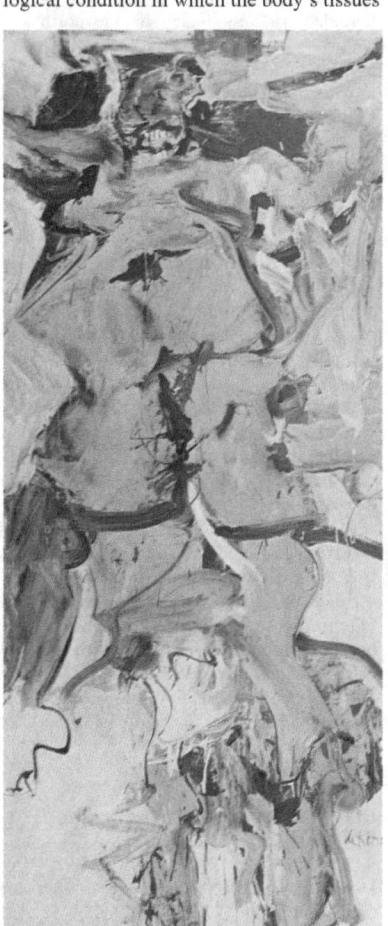

The American painter Willem de Kooning (1904-1997) gained international fame with his series *Women*. This *Woman* was painted in 1964.

L'absinthe, the 1876 painting of an absinthe drinker, by Edgar Degas (1834-1917) in the Musée d'Orsay, Paris.

lose too much water. It is caused by repeated vomiting, diarrhea, bleeding, or exposure to a hot environment without an adequate water supply.

Deism, religious system developed in the 17th and 18th centuries and championed by such thinkers as Voltaire and Jean Jacques Rousseau. Deists held that the rational nature of the universe was evidence of the existence of a Creator God, but they opposed organized religion and rejected supernatural explanations and religious revelation. Some of the leaders of the American Revolution were deists, among them Thomas Jefferson and Benjamin Franklin.
See also: Atheism; Theism.

De jure segregation *See:* Segregation.

Dekker, Thomas (c. 1570-c. 1632), English dramatist and pamphleteer. On many plays he collaborated with Philip Massinger, Thomas Middleton, John Ford, and John Webster. His most famous work is the comedy *The Shoemaker's Holiday* (1600), though he is also known for *Old Fortunatus* (1600) and *Satirot* (1602).

De Kooning, Willem (1904-1997), Dutch-born U.S. painter, among the founders of abstract expressionism. Influenced by Arshile Gorky, Joan Miró, and Pablo Picasso, he painted abstract, highly colored pictures with thickly applied pigment. His series entitled *Woman*, including, for instance, *Woman I* (1952), contains some of his most famous works.
See also: Abstract expressionism.

Delacroix, Ferdinand - Victor - Eugène (1798-1863), French painter whose themes

D

are typical of Romanticism. Such early works as *The Massacre of Chios* (1824) were influenced by Gericault, but his mastery of rich color schemes and handling of paint were largely learned from Rubens, as shown by *Death of Sardanapalus* (1827), *The Justice of Trajan* (1840), and the many official decorative schemes he undertook. His frescoes for Saint-Sulpice, Paris, influenced impressionism.

De la Madrid Hurtado, Miguel (1934-), Mexican political leader. He was budget minister (1976-1982) under President José López Portillo, whom de la Madrid succeeded as president in 1982. His technocratic administration, which held power until 1988, faced grave economic problems, including a huge foreign debt. He was a leader in Latin American efforts to end the strife in neighboring Central American countries.
See also: Mexico.

De La Mare, Walter John (1873-1956), English poet and novelist. His work, much of which was intended for children, is characterized by its evocation of the atmosphere of dreams and the supernatural. His best-known works are the novels *Henry Brocken* (1904) and *Memoirs of a Midget* (1921), and the children's poetry collection *Peacock Pie* (1913).

De la Roche, Mazo (1879-1961), Canadian writer best known for a series of 16 novels that chronicle the Whiteoak family from 1852 to 1954. The first novel, *Jalna*, was published in 1927, the last, *Morning at Jalna*, in 1960. De la Roche wrote plays, short stories, children's stories, travel books, and an autobiography, *Ringing the Changes* (1957).

Delaunay, Robert (1885-1941), French abstract painter. With his wife, Sonia, he founded the Orphist movement in 1910. His pictures comprise forms of brilliantly contrasting color.

Robert Delaunay's (1885-1941) *Fenêtres simultanées* (1911, Kunsthalle, Hamburg). In this painting, which has colour as its subject, Delaunay ignored the distinction between canvas and frame.

Delaunay-Terk, Sonia (1885-1979), French female painter of Russian origin. Initially influenced by Gauguin. Later, a representative of 'orphism', as was her husband Robert Delaunay. Designer of material, settings and costumes (for Diaghilev, among others), and ceramics. Illustrated works by Apollinaire and Majakovski. After 1935, she chose to devote herself solely to painting and lithography. She greatly contributed to the development of abstract art following WW II.

Delaware (First State, Diamond State; pop. 732,000), one of the mid-Atlantic states of the United States. Almost all of the state is part of the Atlantic Coastal Plain, which stretches from New Jersey to southern Florida. Delaware's mean elevation above sea level is the lowest of all 50 states. One third of the area is wooded. Delaware's climate is temperate but humid. It's capital is Dover. Wilmington and Newark are major cities.
The most important economic activity in Delaware is manufacturing. Chemical production is the major industry. Broiler chickens account for more than half of the state's farm income. Soybeans and corn are the 2 leading cash crops. Tourism is also important. The major religions are methodism and Roman Catholicism.
The first settlers were the Dutch (1613) who were later elbowed out by the Swedish (1638).
Delaware was one of the thirteen states to ratify the Constitution (1787).

Delaware Bay, inlet of the Atlantic Ocean, bounded by New Jersey on the north and Delaware on the south and west. It is approximately 50 mi (80 km) long and varies in width from about 4 mi (6 km) to 30 mi (48 km); it ranges from 30 to 60 ft (9 to 18 m) in depth. The ocean entrance into the bay is formed by a channel 12 mi (19 km) wide, leading to the Delaware River.
See also: Atlantic Ocean.

Delaware River, major waterway (about 410 mi/660 km long) in the eastern United States. Originating in the Catskill Mountains of New York, the river flows southeast, forming part of the Pennsylvania-New York border, then southward through the Delaware Water Gap, forming the boundary between New Jersey and Pennsylvania. It empties into Delaware Bay. It is connected to Chesapeake Bay on the west by the Chesapeake and Delaware Canal.

Delbrück, Max (1906-1961), German-born U.S. biologist whose discovery of a method for detecting and measuring the rate of mutations in bacteria opened up the study of bacterial genetics. Along with Alfred Hershey and Salvador Luria, he won the 1969 Nobel Prize for physiology and medicine for work with bacteriophages (viruses that attack bacteria).
See also: Biology.

Del Cano, Juan Sebastián *See:* Magellan, Ferdinand.

Deledda, Grazia (1871-1936), Italian author, daughter of a large landowner on Sardinia, which played a dominant role in her first novels. She was awarded the Nobel prize in 1926 for her literary qualities and the penetrating description of Sardinian society. Her work includes the novels *Elias* *Portolu* (1903), *Ashes* (1904), and *The Mother* (1920). In addition to novels, Deledda also wrote many collections of short stories.

De León, Juan Ponce *See:* Ponce de León, Juan.

De Lesseps, Ferdinand Marie (1805-1894), French engineer and diplomat, builder of the Suez Canal. He first conceived of the project while serving as a diplomat in Egypt. He supervised its construction (1859-1869) and later headed a French company formed to construct the Panama Canal. When this failed through lack of capital (1888), he was ruined mentally and financially.
See also: Suez Canal.

The most famous one of the many kinds of pottery that are made in Delft since the 17th century, is delftware. This is white glazed pottery with blue decorations. The motifs were frequently derived from Chinese designs.

Delft (pop. 96,000), Netherlands, a city in the province of Zuid (South) Holland. It is eight miles (13 km) northwest of Rotterdam and five miles (8 km) southeast of The Hague. Faïence pottery and ornamental tiles produced here are known as *delftware*. Delftware, with its blue and white or polychrome decorations, was first manufactured during the 17th century in imitation of Oriental porcelains. Other products include tobacco, glassware, machinery, leather goods, yeast, and metal goods. Cattle and sheep are raised in the surrounding area.
The city's old buildings include the Renaissance town hall, several Gothic churches, and the East India House. The tomb of William the Silent, who was assassinated in Delft in 1584, is in one of the city's churches. The Delft University of Technology was founded here in 1905. The painter Jan Vermeer was born in Delft.

Delgado, José Matías (1767-1832), Salvadoran priest and patriot. He led El Salvador's fight for independence from Spain (1811) and its resistance movement to annexation by Mexico (1822).
See also: El Salvador.

Delhi (pop. 10,300,000), city in northern India, on a plain that has always been strategically important for control of the whole

Indian subcontinent. In 1638 it became the capital of the Mogul Empire, and it had previously been the center of the Delhi Sultanate (1192-1398). The city fell to the British in 1803. In 1912 the administrative center of New Delhi was built immediately adjacent to it, and was designated the capital of British India. The old city, however, has a larger population.
See also: India.

Delhi sultanate, first Muslim empire in India (1192-1398). Established by Qutb ud-Din, a general serving Muhammad of Ghor, the ruler of Afghanistan, the sultanate reached its height in the early 1300s, when it dominated the subcontinent. The sultans constantly battled rival Hindu and Buddhist kings and successfully shielded India from Mongol invasion until 1398, when Delhi was sacked by Tamerlane. That ended the empire, although a sultan continued to rule in Delhi until 1526, when Babur, a descendant of Tamerlane, ousted the sultan and founded the Mogul Empire.

Delian League, confederacy of Greek states formed by Athens in 478 B.C. to follow up the Hellenic League's victories against Persia. It was nominally governed by a council in which each member state had one vote but was in fact dominated by Athens. After success against Persia, Athens began to turn the league into an empire, subjugating reluctant states such as Naxos. The league endured until 404 B.C., when Athens was defeated by Sparta in the Peloponnesian War. A second Delian League was founded in 378 B.C. It was crushed by Philip II of Macedon in 338 B.C.
See also: Athens; Greece, Ancient.

Delibes, (Clément Philibert) Léo (1836-1891), French composer. Initially known for his lighter works and operettas, some written in collaboration with Offenbach, he set new standards for ballet music with *Coppélia* (1870) and *Sylvia* (1876), and wrote the grand opera *Lakmé* (1883).

Delilah, Samson's Philistine mistress in the Old Testament. When Samson, an Israelite judge, told her that his long hair was the secret of his strength, she cut his hair, delivering him to the Philistines, who blinded him. When his strength returned, he tore down the Philistine temple, killing himself along with his enemies.
See also: Bible; Old Testament.

Delinquency, juvenile *See:* Juvenile delinquency.

Delirium tremens, specific condition of confusion, violent shaking, fever, and hallucinations caused by alcohol withdrawal.
See also: Alcoholism.

Delius, Frederick (1862-1934), English composer. He studied in Leipzig, where he met and was influenced by Edward Grieg. He is best known for orchestral pieces such as *Florida* (1886-1887) and *Brigg Fair* (1907), and for tone poems such as *Summer Night on the River* (1911) and *Sea Drift* (1903). His best-known opera is *A Village*

Romeo and Juliet (1907). In old age he became blind and paralyzed, but continued to compose by dictation.

Della Francesca, Piero *See:* Piero della Francesca.

Della Robbia, Luca (1399?-1482), Italian Renaissance sculptor and ceramicist known for his glazed terra cottas. His works include the *Cantoria* (1431-1438), 10 panels in relief sculpture depicting children with musical instruments; and *Madonna and Child*. His nephew Andrea and Andrea's sons Luca II, Giovanni, and Girolama continued Della Robbia's work.
See also: Renaissance.

Delphi, Greek town located on the lower slopes of Mt. Parnassus. In ancient times, it was the site of the most important oracle in Greece. The oracle was in a temple to Apollo built in the 6th century B.C. The messages were delivered by a priestess, usually in cryptic form, and were interpreted by a priest.
See also: Greece.

Delphinium *See:* Flower; Larkspur.

Delta, alluvial plain at the mouth of a river, often projecting into a sea or lake and crossed by many water channels. Deltas are generally formed of fertile mud dumped by a slow-flowing river. Often the river divides into two or more streams that thread their way through the delta to reach the sea or lake in different places, producing a tree-shaped pattern when seen from the air. The best-known deltas include the Mississippi Delta, the Nile Delta, and the Ganges-Brahmaputra Delta.

Deluge, in biblical tradition, great flood sent by God to punish humanity, described in Genesis 6-8. Noah, on divine instruction, built the Ark to save human and animal life from the flood.
See also: Bible; Noah.

Delvaux, Paul (1897-1994), Belgian painter and artist. Delvaux grew up in Brussels. In the 30s, partly under the influence of De Chirico, his art evolved from a late form of expressionism to surrealism, of which he became an important representative. He was partial to mysterious objects in a dreamy atmosphere: cool, partially naked women portrayed in settings that seem unreal, such as deserted antique cities. From the 50s onwards, trains and stations played an important role in his work. A Delvaux museum was opened in Sint-Idesbald (Koksijde, Belgium) in 1982. Known works include, among others *The Encounter* (1938: Museum of Modern Art, New York) and *Sleeping Venus* (1944).

Demand *See:* Supply and demand.

Demarcation, Line of *See:* Line of Demarcation.

De Maupassant, Guy (1850-1893), French writer noted for his short stories. He wrote simple, realistic stories and novels that bear the influence of his godfather, Gustave

The sanctuary of Athena-Pronaia, the Marmaria, is among the few fairly well-preserved temples gracing this center of ancient Greek religion, in Delphi.

Flaubert. De Maupassant's short stories, more than 250 in all, include 'The Diamond Necklace,' 'The Piece of String,' and 'Ball-of-Fat.' Among his novels are *A Woman's Life* (1883) and *Bel-Ami* (1885). He stopped writing in 1891, when he was committed to a mental asylum, where he died.

Dem Chuk dong Grup (1902-   ), Mongolian sovereign, who was the leader of a movement for the autonomy of Inner Mongolia, a part of China, in the 20s. He is known in China under the name Te Wang (De Wang). As the leader of an Inner Mongolia that was only autonomous in name, he collaborated with the Japanese during the Second World War. In 1945, there seemed to be no place for him in postwar Inner Mongolia; he sought solace in Peking, which was controlled by the nationalists at the time, but had to flee the city in 1948 due to the communist threat. He eventually fell into communist hands in 1952 and was tried as a war criminal. He was released during the Chinese New Year celebration in 1964 as a result of a general amnesty. He became a teacher at the University of Huhehot (Hohhot), the capital of Inner Mongolia, shortly afterwards.

Dementia, a condition characterized by deteriorated mental abilities. Symptoms include changes in personality and impairment of such intellectual functions as memory, judgment, and abstract thinking. A person with dementia becomes easily confused and has difficulty in performing ordinary activities. In most cases, the onset of dementia is gradual. It can occur at any age, but mainly affects elderly persons. Dementia is caused by disorders that result in brain damage or brain dysfunction. The most common cause is Alzheimer's disease.
Dementia is rarely reversible, even when the underlying disorder is cured. Persons with dementia need a stable, familiar environment in which they are protected from accidentally harming themselves.

Demeter, in Greek mythology, the goddess of grain, agriculture, harvest, and fertility. She is credited with teaching humans how to

D

farm. The Greeks honored her and her daughter Persephone in the rituals of the Eleusinian Mysteries. The ancient Romans identified Demeter with Ceres.
See also: Mythology.

De Mille, Agnes George (1909-1993), U.S. dancer and choreographer; niece of Cecil B. De Mille. She pioneered the combination of ballet and folk music. Her ballets include *Rodeo* (1942) and *Fall River Legend* (1948). Her choreography for the Rodgers and Hammerstein musical *Oklahoma!* (1943) revolutionized dance in musical comedy by using ballet as an integral part of the plot.

De Mille, Cecil Blount (1881-1959), U.S. motion picture producer and director, noted for his use of spectacle; uncle of Agnes George De Mille. He directed such epics as *The Ten Commandments* (1923 and 1956), *The Sign of the Cross* (1932), *Samson and Delilah* (1949), and *The Greatest Show on Earth* (1952).

Demirel, Süleyman (1924-   ), Turkish politician, leader of the Conservative Party for Justice. Was premier four times: 1965-1971, 1975-June 1977, July-December 1977 and 1979-1980, when he was deposed by a coup. Demirel became president in 1993.

Democracy, system of government under which all members of society have a say in making political decisions, either directly or indirectly. Direct democracy, in which political decisions are made by citizens meeting together, has generally been superceded by representative democracy, under which the population elects members of a decision-making body. Historically, the portion of the population permitted to participate in the voting process has expanded over time, racial, religious, and sexual restrictions being removed. Many political theorists argue

The goddess Demeter is venerated in the Eleusinian mysteries. She taught people agriculture and is therefore usually depicted with a wreath of wheat around her head (5th century, museum of Eleusis).

As a child, Demosthenes stuttered, but he trained himself so intensively that he became one of the most famous orators of Greek antiquity. His political aim was to preserve Greece's freedom from the Macedonian threat.

that other rights (besides voting) are equally essential if a system is to be democratic. These include freedom of speech and the press, freedom of assembly, freedom to organize politically, and so on. The concepts of natural rights and political equality expressed by such philosophers as John Locke in the 17th century, Voltaire and Jean Jacques Rousseau in the 18th century, and Jeremy Bentham and J.S. Mill in the 19th century are vital to the theory of representative democracy.

Democratic Party, one of the 2 major political parties in the United States. Democrats trace their history back to the Democratic Republican Party (1792) of Thomas Jefferson, who favored popular control of the government. In about 1830 the Democratic Republican Party became the Democratic Party. By comparison with the Republic Party, the Democratic Party is in favour of reform, tolerant of the left, centralist, and aimed at the lower income groups. Democratic presidents after the second World War were Truman, Kennedy, Carter and Clinton.

Democritus (460?-370? B.C.), Greek philosopher who theorized that reality is separated into atoms and the void. According to his theory, atoms make up all existing things and after a period of time, these atoms break apart and are drawn into

the void. Democritus also believed true knowledge is derived not from sensory input but from the native intellect.
See also: Philosophy.

Demography, study of the distribution, composition, and changes of human populations. Its prime concerns are birth and death rates, emigration and immigration patterns, and marital patterns.
See also: Census; Population.

De Molay, Order of, international organization of boys and young men between the ages of 13 and 21. Each local chapter is affiliated with a group of Masons. The membership is dedicated to upholding seven virtues: filial love, reverence for God, courtesy, friendship, fidelity, cleanliness, and patriotism. Founded in 1919, the Order is named for Jacques de Molay (1243-1314), the last Grand Master of the Knights Templars, a group of French Crusaders.

Demosthenes (384-322 B.C.), Athenian orator and speech writer, best known for his attempts to rouse Athens to resist the encroachment of Philip of Macedon, the father of Alexander the Great. Demosthenes' series of speeches against Philip were called the *Philippics* (351-341 B.C.). In the same cause he delivered a set of speeches known as the *Olynthiacs* (349 B.C.). In the end, however, Philip conquered Greece, and in 324 B.C. Demosthenes was exiled. He returned after the death of Alexander in 323 B.C., but failed to free Greece from Macedonian rule. He fled, was pursued, and took poison to avoid capture by the Macedonian general Antipater.
See also: Greece, Ancient; Philip II.

Dempsey, Jack (William Harrison Dempsey; 1895-1983), U.S. boxer. He won the world heavyweight championship from Jess Willard in 1919 and held it until 1926, when he lost a decision to Gene Tunney. Dempsey's loss to Tunney in the 1927 rematch was known for the 'long count' in the 7th round. Dempsey knocked Tunney down but refused to go to a neutral corner, thus delaying the start of the referee's count. Tunney, actually down for more than the normal 10 count, got up at the count of 9 and went on to win by decision.

Dempster, Arthur Jeffrey (1886-1950), U.S. physicist, developer of the first mass spectrometer (1918), an instrument that measures the mass of atomic nuclei, thereby providing a way to analyze chemical compositions and to distinguish isotopes. Dempster discovered uranium 235, which is used in atomic bombs and nuclear reactors.
See also: U-235.

Demuth, Charles (1883-1935), U.S. watercolorist and illustrator. Influenced by both cubism and expressionism, Demuth worked in a number of styles, but is best known for his precise and delicate studies of flowers and his stark, simple shapes inspired by the machine age. He is also noted for his illustrations of works by Edgar Allan Poe, Emile Zola, and Henry James.

Dendrochronology, or tree-dating, is a method used by archaeologists to determine the age of ancient wood objects. A growing tree produces one ring each year, which means that it can be dated by counting its rings. Trees of the same species grown in the same area produce matching ring sequences; thus rings in a tree stump of known cutting date (1) allow determination of the age of an older stump (2) by matching the ring patterns. The older stump can, in turn, be matched with a wood beam to determine its age (3). This cross-matching process can be continued with still older beams (4, 5), which are then used to date a prehistoric stump (6).

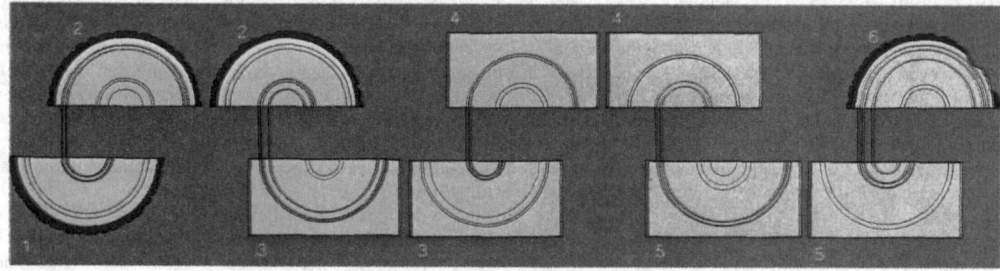

D

Dendrochronology, dating of past events by the study of tree rings. A hollow tube is inserted into the tree trunk and a section from bark to center removed. The annual rings are counted and compared with rings from dead trees so that the chronology may be extended further back in time.

Deneb, or Alpha Cygni, blue-white star, brightest star in the constellation Cygnus and one of the brightest in the sky.
See also: Cygnus; Star.

Dengue, or breakbone fever, infectious disease characterized by sudden onset of headache, fever, prostration, severe joint and muscle pain, and swollen glands. A rash appears with a second temperature rise following a period without fever. The disease is caused by a virus transmitted by the mosquito *Aedes aegypti*.

Deng Xiaoping (1904-1997), Chinese Communist leader. A strategist during the civil war, he became vice premier of the People's Republic of China in 1952 and a member of the Communist Party Politburo in 1955. Purged during the Cultural Revolution in 1967, he was rehabilitated in 1973, then purged again in 1976 and rehabilitated in 1977, after the death of Mao Zedong. Since then he has been the central figure in the Chinese government, directing both foreign and domestic policy, often from behind the scenes.
See also: China.

De Niro, Robert de (1943-), American film actor. De Niro grew up in Little Italy, New York. He received acting lessons from Stella Adler and Lee Strasberg and used to play in small theatres and low-budget films. In 1973 he appeared in two major movies for the first time: *Bang the Drum Slowly* and *Mean Streets*. He received Oscars for his roles in *The Godfather Part II* (1974) and *Raging Bull* (1980). He also played in *Taxi Driver* (1976), *The King of Comedy* (1982), *Goodfellas* (1990), *Cape Fear* (1991), *Sleepers* (1996), *Ronin* (1999), *Meet the Parents* (2000). He directed *A Bronx Tale* (1993), and set up a production house called Tribeca Centre.

Denktash, Rauf (1924-), Turkish-Cypriot politician. Denktash became vice president of Cyprus in 1973. When the conflict between the Greek Cypriots and the Turkish Cypriot minority escalated in 1974 and the negotiations between the two parties appeared to be fruitless, Denktash proclaimed a Turkish federal state on Cyprus in the Turkish zone in 1975, which was renamed the Turkish Republic of North Cyprus in 1983. He is the president of this republic, which is only recognized by Turkey. In 2002, Denktash and Klerides, leader of Greek Cyprus, agreed to start searching actively for a solution to the Cyprus issue.

Denmark

Capital:	Copenhagen
Area:	16,638 sq mi (43,094 sq km)
Population:	5,369,000
Language:	Danish
Government:	Parliamentary monarchy
Independent:	1849 (constitutional monarchy)
Head of gov.:	Prime minister
Per capita:	US$ 28,000
Monetary unit:	1 Danish krone = 100 ore

Denmark, country in northwest Europe consisting of the Jutland Peninsula and 483 islands, of which about 100 are inhabited. The Faeroe Islands, north of Scotland, form a self-governing community within the Kingdom of Denmark; Greenland, the largest island in the world, is a former Danish county that received Home Rule on May 1, 1979. The Jutland Peninsula contains the country's only land frontier, the 42-mi (68-km) long boundary with Germany. The capital of Denmark is Copenhagen.

Land and climate. Denmark is a low-lying country. The average elevation is 100 ft (31 m) above sea level; the highest point, Yding Skovhj (Forest Mountain), in Jutland, is 568 ft (173 m) above sea level. The prevailing climate is maritime, with cool summers and mild to cold winters.
People. The modern Danes are believed to be descended from early migrant hunters and farmers of northern Europe. The Danish language belongs to the Scandinavian group of Germanic languages, with many direct loan words from German and English. Since

The remains of Denmark's earliest history (rune stones), a stone's throw from Aalborg's modern industry.

the late 19th century, English has been the most important secondary language in the country. About 90% of the people are members of the Evangelical Lutheran Church, which is supported by grants from the state.
Economy. Agriculture was the mainstay of the economy until World War II, but manufacturing now accounts for more than 60% of Denmark's total exports. Among the major products are foodstuffs (particularly dairy products), furniture, glass, silverware, leather goods, and clothing. There are important shipbuilding and agricultural engineering industries, and fishing and tourism also contribute to the economy.
History. Denmark was a center of Viking expansion from the 9th to the 11th centuries. Under the Kalmar Union (1397-1523), with Norway and Sweden, it was the dominant partner. Norway remained under Danish rule until it was taken by Sweden in 1814. Prussia and Austria wrested Schleswig-Holstein from Denmark in 1864, but North

D

Schleswig was restored to Denmark after a plebiscite in 1920. Denmark was occupied by Germany during World War II. The country is governed as a constitutional monarchy. Queen Margaret II ascended the throne in 1972. From 1993 to 2001, Denmark was governed by a center left coalition. The welfare state has been slimmed down and the economy is developing favourably.

The Danes rejected the euro by way of a referendum in 2000. The right-wing cabinet under Fogh drastically tightened up the asylum law. At the Treaty of Copenhagen, under the chairmanship of Denmark, ten new countries were admitted to the EU.

Denominator *See:* Fraction.

Density, ratio of mass of a substance to its volume. By extension, the term is also applied to properties other than mass, e.g., charge density refers to the ratio of electric charge to volume.

Dental hygiene, study and practice of techniques designed to maintain good oral health. These techniques include cleaning and polishing teeth, flossing, the application of fluoride or protective sealants to prevent gum disease and cavities, and more complicated procedures involving surgery.

Dentistry, profession that deals with the diagnosis, prevention, and treatment of malformations and diseases affecting the teeth and their related structures, such as gums and oral bones.

Denver (pop. 498,000), capital and largest city of Colorado, situated in the Rocky Mountains foothills, a mile above sea level. Its location has made it the commercial center for the Rocky Mountain region. The Denver Union stockyards include the largest sheep market in the country and one of the largest cattle markets. Other industries include aerospace, food processing, printing and publishing, electronics, textiles and metal and mineral processing. The city maintains the world's largest municipal park and recreation system.
See also: Colorado.

Deoxyribonucleic Acid *See:* DNA.

Depreciation, loss in the value of an asset brought about by age, use, or both. Over the economic life of an asset, depreciation can be considered equal to the difference between the price of the asset when new and its scrap value. In accountancy, the amount needed to compensate for depreciation can be estimated through the course of the asset's economic life. A depreciation reserve can then be built up. Depreciation is allowed for in calculating corporate taxes for items such as equipment, furniture, real estate, and cars.

Depressant, any of various drugs that slow physical, mental, or emotional activity.
See also: Sedative; Tranquilizer.

Depression, in economics, major decline in business activity involving sharp reductions in industrial production, a rise in bankruptcies, increased unemployment, and a general loss of business confidence. Although less serious downturns, called recessions, occur regularly in industrial nations, the most serious and widespread depression was the Great Depression that began in 1929 and lasted worldwide through most of the 1930s. *See also:* Business cycle.

Depression, emotional state characterized by sadness, despondency, apathy, and sometimes a deep sense of loss; in psychiatry, clinical depressive illness is more intense and lasts longer than common depressed feelings. Seriously depressed people feel isolated and hopeless and often reproach or blame themselves for exaggerated faults and shortcomings. Fatigue and disturbed sleep are common, while some depressed people sleep more than usual. Crying spells, whether or not there is something to cry about, are also characteristic. Some depressive illness masks itself in physical discomfort or by contributing to alcoholism or drug addiction. Chronic fatigue and boredom, as well as habitual underachievement, may be unrecognized forms of depression. The hyperkinetic (overly active) child, conversely, may be compensating for an underlying depression; drugs that relieve depression in adults seem to help hyperactive children. Not all those suffering from depressive illness attempt suicide, nor are all those who attempt suicide necessarily suffering from depressive illness, but the relationship is striking. It is estimated that as many as 75% of those who attempt suicide are seriously depressed, and other studies indicate that people hospitalized for depression at some time in their lives are about 36 times more likely to commit suicide than are nondepressed people, with the greatest risk being during or immediately following hospitalization. After the age of 40, the possibility of suicide increases in severely depressed persons. Almost twice as many women as men suffer from depressive illness and almost twice as many women attempt suicide, but 3 times more men than women succeed.
Psychogenic (or *reactive*) depression, the most common form of depressive illness, is brought on by a stressful situation. Even in this milder form of depressive illness, suicide is a serious possibility. Often the person can be helped by the comforting of family or friends. Many who suffer the illness, however, require professional assistance. *Endogenous* depression is far more serious. *Unipolar* depression may show itself in severely withdrawn and uncommunicative behavior or agitated activity, such as pacing the floor, wringing the hands, and a rapid stream of talk about feelings and fear. *Bipolar* (or *manic-depressive*) illness shows itself in up-down swings. The manic-depressive is the victim of a cycle of moods, with a phase lasting from several days up to several years. Unlike the psychogenic depressive, these more severely afflicted persons have delusions about being unworthy, condemned, and criticized and often think they are physically altered. The very real danger of suicidal outcome makes hospitalization a usual requirement in treatment.
Involutional depression describes a category of mental illness found in persons in their middle years, due to disturbances of metabolism, growth, nutrition, or endocrine (hormone) function. Recent evidence, however, has cast strong doubts as to whether a special kind of depression actually affects this age group. There is wide agreement that both heredity and environmental factors play an important part in depressive illness. Depression is more likely to occur in a person with a family history of depressive illness. Some investigators have found that nearly 25% of patients had mentally ill mothers and more than 15% had depressed fathers.

Depth charge, explosive weapon used against submarines and other submerged targets. The charge detonates when it is subjected to a predetermined water pressure, and the resulting shock waves destroy the target.

De Quincey, Thomas (1785-1859), English essayist and critic, author of *Confessions of an English Opium Eater* (1822), which established his literary reputation. His output, affected by lifelong opium addiction, was erratic, but included penetrating essays and powerful descriptions of drug-inspired dreams.

Derain, André (1880-1954), French painter, one of the original fauves. He was also attracted to cubism for a time. Later, rejecting nonrepresentational extremes, he returned to a more traditional style.

Derby, annual horse race begun at Epsom, England, in 1780 by the 12th earl of Derby.

Derby, Kentucky *See:* Kentucky Derby.

Dermaptera *See:* Earwig.

Dermatitis, inflammation of the skin, accompanied by moderate to severe itching, with redness, swelling, and sometimes blisters. The causes are not known for sure, but many cases are provoked by chemical irritants.
See also: Eczema.

Dermatology, subspeciality of medicine concerned with the diagnosis and treatment of skin diseases: a largely visual speciality, but aided by skin biopsy in certain instances.

Dermis, or corium, the inner layer of skin beneath the epidermis. It comprises a layer of connective tissue 1 to 4 millimeters thick, that is thicker on the back than on the front of the body. The cells are most numerous just beneath the epidermis, the tissue being more fibrous in its deeper part. The boundary between dermis and epidermis is undulating, the waves being most pronounced where the skin is thick. The dermis contains many nerves, blood vessels, and seat glands. The raised parts of the dermis are called *papillae* and at some sites, such as the fingertips, these are arranged linearly and produce characteristic patterns responsible for individual fingerprints.

Dervish, Muslim mystic, member of a Sufi brotherhood. Members serve a period of ini-

Dancing dervishes, members of a mystic Islamic order in Konya, Turkey. The whirling dance may go on for hours, the accompanying drums, flutes and chants undoubtedly help to attain a mood of mystic ecstasy.

tiation under a teacher, and each order has its own ritual for inducing a mystic state that stresses dependence on the unseen world. The best known are the 'whirling' and 'howling' dervishes, who use forms of dancing and singing.

DES (diethylstilbestrol), synthetic hormone having the properties of estrogen, the main female sex hormone. It was formerly administered to pregnant women to prevent miscarriages, but in the 1970s it was linked to vaginal cancer in women whose mothers had taken the hormone. Men whose mothers took DES frequently have genital defects. A movement against the drug during the 1970s raised awareness about this problem. It is still used as a growth accelerator in beef cattle, but such use is controversial because of the possible carcinogenic effects of DES.
See also: Hormone.

Desai, Morarji (1896-1995), Indian political leader. A disciple of Mahatma Gandhi and a devout Hindu, he held cabinet posts under Jawaharlal Nehru and was deputy prime minister for Indira Gandhi (1967-1969) before breaking with her. He served as prime minister (1977-1979).
See also: India.

Desalination *See:* Water.

Descartes, René (1596-1650), French mathematician, scientist, and philosopher, often referred to as 'the father of modern philosophy.' A dualist who believed the world was composed of 2 basic substances (matter and spirit), he ignored accepted scholastic philosophy and stated a person should doubt all sense experiences; but if a person can think and doubt, he or she therefore exists. Descartes stated this belief in his famous phrase, *cogito, ergo sum* ('I think, therefore I am.') This skeptical philosophy is called Cartesianism and is detailed in Descartes's *Meditations on First Philosophy* (1641). His other major works include the *Discourse on Method* (1637) and *Principles of Philosophy* (1644). Descartes also attempted to explain the universe in terms of matter and motion and invented analytic geometry.
See also: Philosophy.

Desegregation *See:* Segregation.

Desert, dry region where life has extreme difficulty surviving. There are 2 types. In cold deserts, which cover about one-sixth of the earth's land area, water is unavailable during most of the year because it is trapped in the form of ice. Cold deserts include the Antarctic polar icecap and the barren wastes of Greenland. Warm deserts, which cover about one-fifth of the earth's surface, typically lie between latitudes 20° and 30° north and south, although they exist also farther from the equator in the centers of continental landmasses. They can be described as areas with annual rainfalls of 10 in (25 cm) or less. Plants may survive by being able to store water, like the cacti; by having tiny leaves to reduce evaporation loss, like the paloverde; or by having extensive root systems to capture maximum moisture, like the mesquite. Animals may be nomadic or spend the daylight hours underground. The best-known and largest warm desert is the Sahara.

Desertion, in military law, the abandonment by a soldier of his or her post without the intention of returning. Under the code of military justice, this is a much more serious offense than merely failing to return on time or being absent without leave (AWOL). In civil law, desertion is the act committed by a husband or wife who leaves the other and stays away for a certain statutory period. Desertion is grounds for divorce in many jurisdictions.

Desert Shield, Operation *See:* Persian Gulf War I.

Desert Storm, Operation *See:* Persian Gulf War I.

Desgrange, Henri (1865-1940), French (sports) journalist, established the weekly magazine *l'Auto* (the current *l'Equipe*) together with Victor Goddet and was the founder of cycling classics such as Bordeaux-Paris (1891), Paris-Brussels (1893), Paris-Roubaix (1896), and the Tour de France (1903). Desgrange wrote a book about competition tactics: *La tête et les jambes* (The head and the legs). Desgrange was a fairly successful runner (he claimed the world's first hour record in 1893 with 21.954 mi/h (35.325 km/h).

De Sica, Vittorio (1901-1974), Italian film director. His earlier films, such as *Shoeshine* (1946) and *The Bicycle Thief* (1948), are noted for their compassionate treatment of social problems in the neorealist style. Later films, made in more commercially viable style, include *Marriage, Italian Style* (1964) and *The Garden of the Finzi Continis* (1971).

Prolonged drought and high temperatures often lead to the development of deserts, places where vegetation is hardly possible anymore. In sand deserts (here in Venezuela near Coro, Estado Falcon), the predominant direction of the wind may blow the sand into sickle dunes (barchanes). The wind makes them 'move' forward, sometimes completely covering the already rare oases.

Deserts lack the sloping land produced by regular rainfall. Instead, they are characterized by angular, wind-buffeted rock outcroppings (1). Flat, steep-sided mesas (2), isolated buttes (3), and elongated trough formations resulting from wind abrasion (4) are typical of desert topography. The minimal desert rainfall — less than 4 in (10 cm) per year — generally comes as flash floods, rapidly eroding rocky surfaces and forming steep valleys, known as arroyos, or wadis (5). Sediments carried by the rushing streams are deposited at the mouths of these canyons, where the water decreases in velocity as its spreads from its course. The resultant alluvial fans (6) may occur in a sequence, constituting a bajada slope (7). Fine mud and dissolved salts may be carried into large flat areas, to form shallow lakes or salt pans (8) that will evaporate within a few days. Sand or sand dunes cover only 30 percent of desert land.

D

Design, purposeful arrangement of the elements in a creative work or process. Design is evident in the fine arts, industrial arts, engineering, and architecture, and in systems and processes. Broadly speaking, the aim of design is to unify function and aesthetics in a harmonious whole. Design in the fine arts refers to composition: how color, shape, and line create pattern and visual rhythm. In the applied arts, design also encompasses the product's function, the physical capabilities of the material, and the method of manufacture. Design of a process or system refers to the overall plan: how materials are utilized and coordinated with movement to achieve a purpose. Here criteria are efficiency, economy, and simplicity.

De Sitter, Willem (1872-1934), Dutch astronomer and cosmologist who examined the age, size, and structure of the universe. His greatest achievement was his recognition that distant galaxies are receding at greater speeds than nearer ones, which showed that the universe is expanding.
See also: Astronomy; Cosmology.

Desktop Publishing, the creation of newsletters, promotional materials, annual reports, and other publications with a computer, in particular a microcomputer. The documents typically have a variety of elements that are prepared separately and then assembled with the use of a desktop publishing program. For example, the text of the document may be typed and edited using a word-processing program, and illustrations may be created with a drawing program or copied with a scanner, a device that can convert photographs or other images into computer data.
A desktop publishing program has features for formatting and designing the document, making it possible, for example, to arrange the text into columns; size and position illustrations; add borders, boxes, and other design elements; and select typefaces. Most desktop publishing programs will display pages so that they closely resemble the way they will appear when printed. This capability is called WYSIWYG ('what you see is what you get').

Desna, River in Russia, ca. 740 mi (1,190 km) It rises east of Smolensk and empties into the Dnepr at Kiev. The river is navigable from Br'ansk.

De Soto, Hernando (1500?-1542), Spanish explorer, discoverer of the Mississippi River. He served as second in command in Pizarro's conquests in Peru (1531-1535), and supported the Inca emperor Atahualpa. He returned to Spain with a fortune and set out again to explore the Florida region. He landed in 1539 at Charlotte Harbor and spent 2 years exploring what is now the southeastern United States. He reached the Mississippi River in May 1541. Turning back in 1542, he died of illness.
See also: Mississippi River.

Despotism, absolute government by one person who rules without any constitutional controls. A despot need not necessarily be a tyrant. Indeed, in the 18th century, the concept of 'benevolent' or 'enlightened' despotism came into fashion. The theory was that people were not capable of governing themselves and needed a ruler who would look after their interests. Frederick the Great of Prussia considered himself an enlightened despot.

Desprez, Josquin (1440?-1521), Flemish composer who wrote both secular and sacred music for voice. He excelled at the canon, a composition in which a single melody is sung by several voices starting at different times, and the motet, an unaccompanied choral piece in which several voices sing different pitches to produce chords.

Dessalines, Jean Jacques (1758-1806), first black ruler of Haiti. Brought to Haiti as a slave, he took part in the rebellion against the French in the 1790s. After the final expulsion of the French in 1803 he became governor-general. In 1804 he proclaimed an independent country and took the title of Emperor Jacques I. His rule, characterized by extreme hostility to whites, ended when he was killed in a mulatto revolt.
See also: Haiti.

Destouches, Henri-Louis *See:* Céline, Louis-Ferdinand.

Destroyer, small, fast naval warship that evolved in the 1890s out of British torpedo boats. In the 2 world wars destroyers were used principally as escorts for convoys and for attacking submarines. Some of the modern destroyers are nuclear-powered and

many carry guided missiles. Some carry 1 or 2 helicopters.

De Sucre, Antonio José *See:* Sucre, Antonio José de.

Detective story, popular form of fiction in which a detective solves a crime, usually a murder, by discovering and interpreting clues. The detective is often an amateur and may appear in a series of mysteries. Sherlock Holmes, introduced in 1884 by Arthur Conan Doyle, is a prime example. The detective story and its conventions originated with Edgar Allan Poe's short story 'Murders in the Rue Morgue' (1841). Wilke Collins' *Moonstone* (1868) is one of the first important detective novels. In the 1920s, the hard-boiled detective story emerged. This style features a tough detective, snappy dialogue, and quick action. Its leading practitioners were Dashiell Hammet, Raymond Chandler, and Ross Macdonald. Other masters of the detective story include Agatha Christie, P. D. James, Ellery Queen, Georges Simenon, Rex Stout, Ruth Rendell, and John le Carré.

Détente (French, 'relaxation'), name given to the policy of easing tensions between the United States and the USSR that occurred in the late 1960s and 1970s. It was particularly associated with President Richard Nixon (and his adviser Henry Kissinger) during whose presidency the Strategic Arms Limitation Treaty (SALT) I was signed (1972). It was continued by President Ford, who signed the Helsinki Accords (1975). In the last years of the 1970s, however, tensions between the United States and the USSR rose again, and SALT II and détente were temporarily abandoned with the Soviet invasion of Afghanistan in 1979. The reforms made by Gorbachev in the second half of the 1980s improved the relationship between the superpowers, so that the name became obsolete. In 1990 the Cold War was officially ended.
See also: Cold War.

Detergent, synthetic chemical that has the same cleaning action as soap but does not form a scum when used in hard water. Most stains are caused by oily films holding dirt particles. Detergent molecules surround a particle of dirt and carry it into suspension in the water. Detergents are made with chemicals obtained from petroleum. Biological or enzyme detergents contain enzymes that digest organic matter and are very good at removing marks such as coffee stains, but they have been known to cause skin problems. Detergents are mostly used in water, but they may also be dissolved in other liquids. Hydrocarbons containing detergents are used in dry cleaning, and automobile engine lubricants use detergents to reduce buildup of carbon deposits.

Determinism, philosophical theory that all events are determined (inescapably caused) by preexisting events that, when considered in the context of inviolable physical laws, completely account for the subsequent events. The case for determinism has been variously argued from the inviolability of the

The Yukikaze, a 2,000-ton (2,032,000 kg) Japanese destroyer that was constructed in 1940, participated in most of the major naval engagements that were fought in the Pacific during World War II. Of the 18 destroyers built to similar specifications (the Kagero class), this was the only one afloat at the end of the war.

laws of nature and from the omniscience and omnipotence of God. Determinism is often taken to be opposed to the principles of free will and indeterminacy.
See also: Philosophy.

De Tocqueville, Alexis *See:* Tocqueville, Alexis de.

Detonator, device used to set off a high-explosive charge. A high explosive such as dynamite is not sensitive to small shocks and can therefore be handled safely. The detonator sets off a minor explosion to produce a shock large enough to initiate the main explosion. Alfred Nobel, the inventor of dynamite, also produced the first effective detonator.
See also: Explosive.

Detroit (pop. 1,000,000), Michigan, fifth-largest city in the United States, often called the 'Motor City' because it produces over a quarter of all the nation's cars and trucks. Detroit fronts on the Detroit River, which connects Lake Erie with Lake St. Clair. A bridge and 2 tunnels link Detroit with Windsor, Ontario. Almost since its founding (1701) Detroit has been a major lake port, and with the construction of the St. Lawrence Seaway (opened 1959) it has become an intercontinental port of considerable importance. The city sprawls over 140 sq mi (363 sq km), with the principal streets radiating from Grand Circus Park near the riverfront. The rapidly growing suburbs to the north and west contain many of the automobile factories that have made the city's fortune, as well as some of the most handsome residential areas in the country.
See also: Michigan.

Deucalion, in Greek mythology, son of the Titan Prometheus. Deucalion and his wife, Pyrrha, were the sole survivors of a flood visited on humanity by Zeus. After the flood, Deucalion and Pyrrha cast stones that turned into men and women who repopulated the earth. Deucalion and Pyrrha's own son, Hellen, is regarded as the ancestor of the Greeks.
See also: Mythology.

Deus ex machina (Latin: god from the machine), person or matter that suddenly appears on stage as a ministering angel; a dramatics term, first used by Plato. When Greek dramatists could not solve the conflicts they themselves evoked, they often called upon a deity for a solution. This deity (deus) was suspended from above using a type of crane (machina). The term is now metaphorically used when a play has a dénouement that does not logically result from a certain action or from the characters involved.

Deuterium, or heavy hydrogen (D or H_2), isotope of hydrogen in which the atomic nucleus contains a neutron as well as a proton, giving it an atomic weight of approximately 2. Deuterium was discovered by H.C. Urey in 1932 and is used as a tracer in biological research, in experiments for particle accelerators, and in the hydrogen bomb.
See also: Hydrogen.

Deuteron *See:* Deuterium.

Deuteronomy, fifth book of the Old Testament and last book of the Pentateuch. Supposedly a testament left by Moses to the Israelites about to enter Canaan, it is primarily a recapitulation of moral laws and laws relating to the settlement of Canaan. Much of it was written long after Moses, parts being added during the reforms under King Josiah (621 B.C.). It may have been the 'Book of the Law' discovered by Hilkiah in the Temple in Jerusalem at that time.
See also: Bible; Old Testament.

Deutschland über Alles, or 'Germany Above All Else,' the German national anthem from 1922 until the division of Germany after World War II. In 1952 the Federal Republic of Germany adopted the song's third stanza as its anthem. 'Deutschland über Alles' was composed by Hoffmann von Fallersleben in 1841.

Deutzia, genus of shrubs having clusters of white, pink, or purple, 5-petalled flowers and serated, fuzzy leaves. Native to Asia, deutzias are grown widely in gardens.

De Valera, Eamon (1882-1975), Irish statesman; prime minister 1932-1948, 1951-1954, and 1957-1958; and president of Ireland 1959-1973. Born in New York City, he was raised in Ireland, and became an ardent republican. Only his U.S. citizenship saved him from execution after the 1916 Easter Rebellion. He was imprisoned by the Irish Free State for refusing to recognize the Anglo-Irish treaty of 1922; in 1924 he organized the Fianna Fáil Party, which won power in 1932. As prime minister he declared Ireland independent of Britain (1937), and preserved Irish neutrality during World War II.
See also: Ireland; Sinn Féin.

De Valois, Dame Ninette (Edris Stanus; 1898-2001), Irish dancer and choreographer. She founded the ballet company at Sadler's Wells, which in 1956 became the Royal Ballet, and was its director (1931-1963).
See also: Ballet.

Devaluation, reduction of the official value of a currency, the opposite of revaluation. Aimed at reducing imports and stimulating exports that have become uncompetitive as a result of internal inflation, it has been used by many countries when their monetary reserves are threatened by a balance-of-payments crisis.

Deve Gowda, H.D. (1933-), Indian politician. Despite his parents' relatively high caste, Hardanahalli Doddagowda Deve Gowda grew up surrounded by poverty in the southern federal state of Karnataka. As a farmer's son, he was later given the nickname 'dharti ke lal', meaning 'the son of the soil'. He had a political career in Karnataka, where he became very popular. He became a member of the national parliament for the center left Janata Dalpartij (Peoples' Party) in 1991. He returned to Bangalore in 1994 to become the premier of the government of Karnataka. Quite unexpectedly, he was charged with forming a new government in 1996 and then appointed prime minister of India on 1st June.

Developing country, term used for any nation with a weak industrial base, a low per capita income, and low gross national product.

Developmental psychology, study of behavioral changes that occur during the years from birth to early childhood. In particular, developmental psychologists will examine the process by which a child acquires skills of language, reasoning, and interaction with others.
See also: Psychology.

Devers, Gail (1966-), American female athlete, specialized in the 100m and the 100m hurdles. She broke through at an international level after winning the 100m during the Pan American Games of 1987. Devers won the 100m during the Olympic Games of 1992 in Barcelona and in 1996 in Atlanta. She was the fastest at both the 100m and the 100m hurdles during the World Championships Athletics of 1993, held in Stuttgart (Germany). During the world Championship Athletics of 1995, held in Athene (Greece), and of 1999, held in Sevilla (Spain), she again claimed gold for the 100m hurdles.

Devil, in Western religions and sects, chief spirit of evil and commander of lesser evil spirits or demons. Dualistic systems-notably Zoroastrianism, gnosticism, and Manichaeism-have regarded the devil as the uncreated equal of God, engaged in an eternal war for evil against good. Such beliefs have appeared sporadically in connection with the occult and devil worship. In Judaism, Christianity, and Islam, the devil, Satan, is a fallen angel, powerful but subordinate to God, who opposes God and tempts humanity, but is to be utterly defeated and bound at the Last Judgment.

Devil's Island, small island off the coast of French Guiana, the site of a French penal colony (1852-1951) for political prisoners, among them Alfred Dreyfus.

Devil's paintbrush, plant with orange-red flowers on a leafless stem up to 28 in (71 cm) long, with oblong leaves growing from the base. The row of bristles on the seed lends the plant its name. Devil's paintbrush is found in Europe and eastern North America.

Devil's Triangle *See:* Bermuda Triangle.

Devil worship, worship of Satan, demons, or evil spirits. Its rituals may take the form of a mockery of the Christian mass and include elements of witchcraft and black magic.

Devolution, War of (1667-1668), conflict between Spain and France over the right of succession to the Spanish Netherlands. Louis XIV of France claimed that by an old law the territory should have reverted to France. Although his military campaign was successful, he was forced to withdraw in the face of the Triple Alliance of England, the United Provinces, and Sweden.

D

Devonian Period, fourth period of the Paleozoic Era, beginning about 400 million years ago and lasting 55 million years. During this period the oceans covered much of what is now dry land, and fish were the dominant life form.
See also: Paleozoic.

De Vries, Hugo (1848-1935), Dutch botanist who developed the theory of mutation, suggesting that new plant and animal species are the result of sudden transformations that occur spontaneously and are continued for generations. His findings stimulated advances in the study of heredity, and he was one of the first to introduce the experimental method in the investigation of the mechanisms of evolution.
See also: Botany.

Dew, layer of water droplets that forms at night on or near the ground. Dew may form in two ways: First, water vapor may rise out of the ground by capillary action and form droplets on reaching cooler surfaces (leaves, rocks) near ground level. Second, and more commonly, moisture from the air may condense in contact with relatively cool objects. In arid and semiarid areas, dew is an important source of moisture for plants.

Dewar, James (1842-1923), a Scottish chemist and physicist. He was the first to liquefy and solidify hydrogen. Dewar was born in Scotland, and studied at Cambridge

University. He was appointed professor of natural experimental philosophy at Cambridge in 1875 and was appointed to the Royal Institution, London, in 1877. He was knighted in 1904.
With Sir Frederick Abel, Dewar invented cordite, a smokeless gunpowder, in 1889. While investigating the properties of matter at low temperatures in 1898, Dewar liquefied hydrogen. The next year he solidified hydrogen at -399.82? F. (-239.9? C.). Until helium was solidified in 1908, this was the lowest temperature ever achieved. Dewar also invented the double-walled Dewar flask, forerunner of today's vacuum (thermos) bottle.

Dewberry, trailing bramble (genus *Rubus*) with blackberry-like fruit, the only U.S. member of the blackberry group that is cultivated. Loganberries arose from a chance crossing of dewberry and raspberry.

Dewey, George (1837-1917), U.S. naval hero promoted to admiral of the navy (the highest rank) for his victory at the Battle of Manila Bay and the capture of the Philippines from Spain. On May 1, 1898, during the Spanish-American War, Dewey led the Asiatic squadron into Manila Bay and, without losing a man, destroyed the Spanish eastern fleet. In Aug., aided by Filipino rebels and U.S. army forces, he received the surrender of Manila; the Philippines then fell to the United States. Dewey later served as president of the gen-

eral board of the Navy Department.
See also: Spanish-American War.

Dewey, John (1859-1952), U.S. philosopher and educator. Dewey founded the philosophical school known as instrumentalism (or experimentalism) and was the leading promoter of educational reform in the early years of the 20th century. Profoundly influenced by the pragmatism of William James, Dewey developed a philosophy in which ideas and concepts were validated by their practicality. He taught that 'learning by doing' should form the basis of educational practice, though in later life he came to criticize the 'progressive' movement in education, which, in abandoning formal tuition altogether, he felt had misused his educational theory.
See also: Pragmatism.

Dewey, Thomas Edmund (1902-1971), U.S. lawyer and politician. As Republican presidential candidate he was defeated in 1944 by Franklin D. Roosevelt and in 1948 by Harry S. Truman, although his election had been thought a foregone conclusion. In the 1930s, as U.S. attorney for the southern district of New York state and then as special prosecutor in New York City, Dewey gained a national reputation for successful campaigning against organized crime. He was governor of New York from 1943 to 1955. He declined the post of chief justice under Richard M. Nixon (1968).

Dewey decimal system, devised by Melvil Dewey (1851-1931) for classification of books in libraries, based on the decimal system of numbers. Dewey divided knowledge into 10 main areas, each of these into 10 subdivisions, and so on. Thus a book could fall into one of a thousand categories, from 000 to 999. Extensions of this system added further classificatory numbers after the decimal point.

De Witt, Jan (1625-1672), Dutch statesman. He was grand pensionary (ruler) of Holland (1653-1672) and republican opponent of the House of Orange. In 1667 he made peace with England, and in 1668 he negotiated the Triple Alliance with England and Sweden against Louis XIV of France to end the War of Devolution.
See also: Devolution, War of.

Dew point, air temperature at which water vapor turns to liquid. Through a process called condensation, moisture (dew) forms on plants and outdoor surfaces when the relative humidity in the air is 100% and a cooling process occurs around the exposed surfaces. Excessive condensation attained at dew point results in the formation of fog. Water formed at dew points below freezing temperature (32°F, 0°C) yields frost.

Dextrin, chemical substance formed when starch is broken down by the body during digestion. Dextrin can also be produced artificially for commercial or industrial use. It is used in manufacturing the glue for postage stamps and to stiffen paper and textiles.
See also: Starch.

Dextrose, chemical name for pure glucose

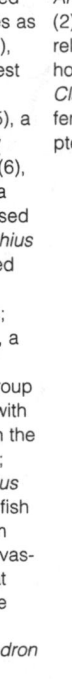

The Upper Devonian lakes of the northern hemisphere supported such vertebrates as *Ichthyostega* (4), one of the earliest amphibians; *Moythomasia* (5), a ray-finned bony fish; *Fleurantia* (6), a lungfish with a deep, compressed body; *Holoptychius* (7), a lobe-finned fish with large, rounded scales; *Bothriolepis* (8), a placoderm, or member of a group of bony fishes with bony shields on the head and trunk; and *Xenacanthus* (9), a sharklike fish with a long, slim body. Primitive vascular plants that grew near these lakes included *Protolepidodendron* (1), a lycopsid, or club moss, with recurved branches; *Archaeocalamites* (2), a giant, treelike relative of the horsetails; and *Cladoxylon* (3), a fernlike plant, or pteropsid.

sugar. It is produced commercially by subjecting starch to a pressurized heating process that converts it into a solid form of glucose. The final product usually takes the form of fine white granules. Dextrose is used to bake candy and pastries and as a base in high-fructose corn syrup, a soft-drink sweetener.
See also: Glucose.

Dhaka (formerly Dacca; pop. 9,000,000), capital of the independent state of Bangladesh (formerly East Pakistan). Located on the Burhi Ganga River in the Ganges-Brahmaputra Delta, the city is a marketing and processing center for the products (mainly jute) of the surrounding agricultural region. Since the 18th century it has been noted for is delicate hand-woven muslins. The city became an important commercial, political, and cultural center under India's Mogul emperors, and has many fine examples of Mogul art and architecture. Under British rule it was the capital of a province from 1905 to 1911. In 1971 Dacca was involved in the fighting betweeen West Pakistan forces and the Indian and guerrilla forces that led to the creation of the independent state of Bangladesh.
See also: Bangladesh.

Dharma, concept of the eternal truth or law in Hinduism, Buddhism, and Jainism. To Hindus, it denotes the universal law ordaining religous and social institutions, the rights and duties of individuals, or, simply, virtuous conduct. Buddhists consider it the universal truth proclaimed to all people by Buddha. In Jainism, it also represents an eternal substance.
See also: Buddhism; Hinduism.

Diabetes, or diabetes mellitus, disease characterized by the absence or inadequate secretion of insulin. Normally, sugars and starches (carbohydrates) in food are processed by digestive juices into a form of sugar called glucose, or blood sugar, which is the fuel used by the body. Insulin, a hormone produced by the pancreas, is a major regulator of this process. In the diabetic individual, either the body does not produce enough insulin, or the available insulin is somehow blocked or inactivated by other substances and is prevented from performing its primary function. Because of this impairment, excessive amounts of glucose accumulate in the blood and tissues and overflow into the urine. In juvenile-onset diabetes, there is a total or substantial lack of insulin, and daily injections of the hormone are necessary for survival. Juvenile-onset diabetes usually begins in the early years, from infancy to young adulthood. In adult-onset diabetes, which accounts for 85-90% of all cases, most individuals do not require insulin treatment and can maintain their blood sugar at relatively normal levels by controlling their weight and adhering to a prescribed diet. In general, women are more susceptible to this type than men, and the disease tends to occur most frequently in certain 'high-risk' groups: close relatives of individuals who have diabetes, people who are overweight or over 40, and women who have given birth to large infants.

The early symptoms of diabetes stem from the increased amount of sugar in the blood and urine. Since the kidneys excrete excessive amounts of water along with the excess sugar, uncontrolled diabetics are likely to urinate frequently and to be constantly thirsty. Because the sugar in the blood is not being converted to energy, they will be weak, tired, and hungry. Because of the calories lost in the urine, they will lose weight, no matter how much they eat. Treatment may include diet, exercise, and insulin. Diabetics must generally cut down on sugar and sugar-rich foods, and on fats found in fatty meats, most cheese, butter, margarine, and nuts. Regular exercise increases the ability of the body to use food. All juvenile-onset and a few adult-onset diabetics must take insulin in order to use blood sugar in a comparatively normal manner. 'Hypo' attacks, due to *hypoglycemia* (too little sugar in the blood), may result when the diet-exercise-insulin balance is disrupted. Symptoms include tremor, hunger, sweating, headache, nausea, blurred vision, and eventually, if not promptly treated, loss of consciousness (diabetic coma). Prompt relief can usually be obtained by taking sugar in water. *Hyperglycemia* (too much sugar in the blood) can occur when a diabetic fails to take sufficient insulin or to follow a meal plan; other contributory causes can be infection and illness. In this condition, fat is burned to supply energy, producing an increasingly acid condition of the blood and other body fluids (*acidosis*) due to the accumulation of so-called ketone substances, including acetone. Usual symptoms are nausea, drowsiness, extreme thirst, headache, blurred vision, abdominal pains, and rapid breathing. Acetone and high blood sugar levels can be detected in routine urine tests. As diabetics are more susceptible to infections than other individuals, even minor wounds should receive careful attention. Serious infections are frequently a precipitating factor in acidosis and diabetic coma. Despite satisfactory control of blood sugar levels through diet and the administration of insulin, in many cases long-term complications of diabetes develop, primarily those affecting blood vessels, nerves, kidneys, and eyes. In general, the juvenile diabetics are more severely affected.

Diaghilev, Sergei Pavlovich (1872-1929), Russian impresario and founder (Paris, 1909) of the Ballets Russes, which inaugurated modern ballet. His magazine *World of Art* (1899-1904) led a movement for Russian involvement in Western European arts. He moved to Paris in 1906. The Ballets Russes broke with the formalism of classical choreography and aimed to unify music, dance, and stage design. Its productions included the dancers and choreographers Michel Fokine, Anna Pavlova, Vaslav Nijinsky, and Léonide Massine, the composers Igor Stravinsky and Sergei Prokofiev, and the designers Aleksandr Benois and Léon Bakst. Matisse, Picasso, Debussy, Ravel, and many others also worked for Diaghilev.
See also: Ballet.

Dialectic *See:* Hegel, Georg Wilhelm Friedrich.

Dialectical materialism *See:* Materialism; Philosophy.

Dialysis, separation process by means of a semi permeable membrane, used for solutions that contain both compounds with small molecules and compounds with macro molecules (proteins, nucleic acids, etcetera) or colloidal particles. The solution to be processed is placed on one side of the membrane, while a constantly refreshed solvent is placed on the other side. The smaller molecules are then transported to the solvent through the membrane by means of diffusion; the larger molecules and the colloidal particles cannot penetrate the membrane. If one wants to prevent all of the small molecules from being removed from the solvent, one can add the types of molecules that are to remain in the solvent.

Dialysis machine *See:* Kidney.

Diamond, mineral allotrope (molecular form) of carbon forming colorless cubic crystals (the other forms being graphite and the recently discovered fullerene). Diamond is the hardest known substance, with a Mohs hardness of 10, which varies slightly with the orientation of the crystal. Thus diamonds can be cut only by other diamonds. They do not conduct electricity, but conduct heat extremely well. Diamonds occur naturally in the mineral kimberlite, notably in South Africa (Orange Free State and Transvaal), Tanzania, and in the United States at Murfreesboro, Ark. They are also mined from secondary (alluvial) deposits, especially in Brazil, Zaire, Sierra Leone, and India.

Ballet-impresario Serge Diaghilev (1872-1929), who caused a revolution in the world of Western dance with his company the Ballet Russes. Drawing by Pablo Picasso (1881-1973).

D

D

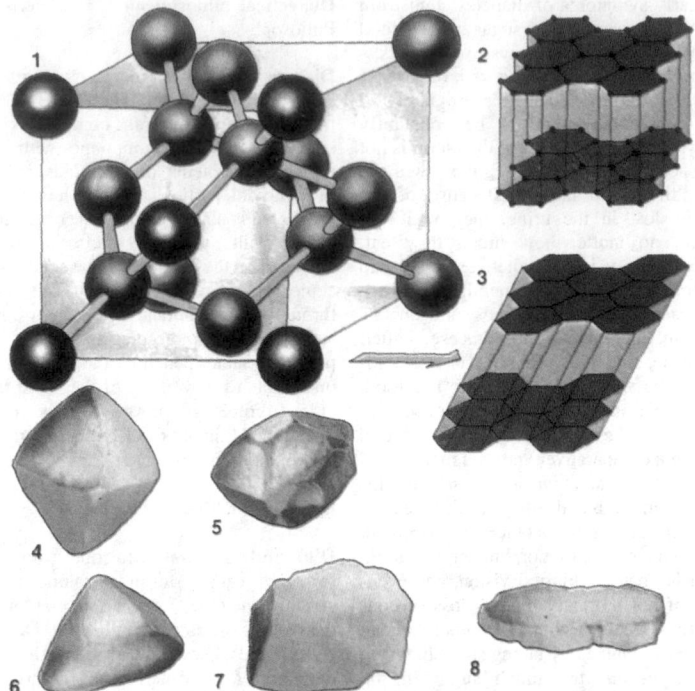

Diamonds and graphite are different forms of carbon. The carbon atoms in a diamond are linked in a rigid tetrahedral arrangement (1), resulting in a hard material. Graphite, which is extremely soft, consists of hexagonal rings of carbon atoms in weakly bonded, parallel layers (2) that can slide (3) easily over one another. Depending on its shape, a mined diamond is classified as a regular unbroken stone (4), a less regular unbroken shape (5), a twinned, roughly triangular macle (6), an irregular broken cleavage (7), or an irregular parallel-sided flat (8).

The diamonds are separated by mechanical panning, and those of gem quality are cleaved (or sawn), cut, and polished. Inferior, or industrial, diamonds are used for cutting, drilling, and grinding. Synthetic industrial diamonds are made by subjecting graphite to very high temperatures and pressures, sometimes with fused metals as solvents.
See also: Carbon.

Diana, in Roman mythology, goddess of the moon and the hunt, later identified with the Greek goddess Artemis. The sister of Apollo, she was the protectress of slaves and the lower classes and a special goddess of women and childbirth. The most famous Greek temple for the worship of Diana (Artemis) was at Ephesus in Asia Minor. There were also temples of Diana at Aricia on the shores of Lake Nemi, Italy, and on the Aventine Hill in Rome. Diana is usually represented as a huntress, carrying a quiver and accompanied by a hound or a deer.
See also: Mythology.

Diana Spencer, Princess of Wales (1961-1997), British princess, married Prince Charles in 1981. The couple had two children: William (1982) and Harry (1984). The marriage ended in divorce (1996). Diana, who was admired for her warm personality and charity work, died in a car crash in Paris. The funeral ceremony in London was watched by millions all over the world.

Diaphragm, in anatomy, dome-shaped, muscular partition separating the chest cavity from the abdominal cavity in humans and mammals. It plays an important role in respiration. By contracting when a person inhales, the diaphragm helps to pull air into the lungs. When a person exhales, the muscle relaxes, forcing air out of the lungs.
See also: Respiration.

Diarrhea, abnormally frequent evacuation of watery stools. *Choleraic diarrhea* refers to acute diarrhea with watery stools, resembling the major symptoms of cholera. A specific type of diarrhea runs in certain families; called *familial chloride diarrhea*, it is characterized by severe watery diarrhea with an excess of chloride in the stools, beginning in early infancy, and marked by a distended abdomen, lethargy, and retarded growth and mental development. *Parenteral diarrhea* is due to infections outside the gastrointestinal tract. 'Summer diarrhea' is an acute form that was formerly found in children during the intense heat of summer but now tends to occur at other times of the year as well; it may be caused by the *E. coli* microbe. *Traveler's diarrhea* occurs particularly in those visiting tropical or subtropical areas where sanitation is not optimal; it too may be due to infection with *E. coli*.

Diary, book containing a daily record of events and personal observations. Diaries are often of great value to historians and biographers, especially those written for private personal gratification rather than for later publication. The Romans kept daily records of various kinds, and there are fascinating Japanese diaries of the 10th and 11th centuries. The earliest known English diaries were written by the astrologer John Dee (1527-1608) and Edward VI. The 17th century produced famous literary diarists such as John Evelyn and Samuel Pepys. In the 18th century John Wesley kept a journal for 66 years. Fanny Burney (Madame D'Arblay) recorded her meetings with George III, Samuel Johnson, and other notables. Queen Victoria's monumental diary spans her entire life from the age of 13.

Diaspora *See:* Jews.

Diathermy, therapeutic use of high-frequency electric current to induce heat within deep tissues of the body that cannot be reached by surface heat. Deep heat can promote rapid healing by increasing the circulation of the blood, and it alleviates the pain of rheumatic conditions, joint dislocations, and sprains and fractures.

Diatom, single-celled alga plant (class Bacillariophyceae) of fresh and salt water. Their delicately sculptured cell walls contain silica, and the two halves fit together like the halves of a pill box. Diatoms are important as food for many small animals, and when they die their siliceous skeletons sink to the bottom. In some parts of the world deposits many feet thick have formed over a period of millions of years. These deposits (there is one over 1,000 ft/305 m thick in California) are excavated as *fuller's* or *diatomaceous earth*. The fine silica grains are used in metal polishes and toothpaste, as they scour but do not scratch. Diatoms are also connected with the formation of petroleum deposits.

Diaz, Bartholomeu (or Dias; 1450?-1500), a Portuguese explorer. He discovered the Cape of Good Hope, near the southern tip of the African continent. Dias, who had been sent by King John II of Portugal to circumnavigate Africa, reached the cape in 1488 after a storm had carried his ships off course. Rounding the cape, he discovered open sea - the long-south sea route around Africa to India. Although Dias was forced to turn back when near the Indian Ocean, another Portuguese explorer, Vasco da Gama, followed the route to India in 1497. Dias accompanied da Gama on this expedition as far as the Cape Verde Islands. Later, Dias sailed with Pedro Alvares Cabral on the expedition that discovered Brazil in 1500. Dias's ship was lost in a storm on the return journey.

Díaz, Porfirio (1830-1915), Mexican general and president. Renowned for his part in the war against the French (1861-1867), he came to oppose Benito Juárez and gained power in 1877. President until 1880 and again from 1884, he was politically ruthless. His policies and foreign investment brought stability and prosperity, while peasant conditions were wretched. He was overthrown in 1911 and died in exile in Paris.
See also: Mexico.

Dibbets, Jan (1941-), Dutch visual artist;

enjoys international fame. Stopped painting in 1967: 'My Last Painting' consists of unpainted canvasses stacked on top of one another. Since then, he has mainly worked as a photographer. His work can be divided into a number of themes. He produced what he termed 'corrections of perspective' from 1969-1970: black-and-white photographs of meadows or sandy plains, on which he applied lines that seem to correct the image. After 1970, recording the passage of time became an important theme. This work can be considered conceptual art. After that, his work consisted mainly of assembled photographic works of interiors and ceilings, becomes more expansive and picturesque in nature. He also designed church windows.

Dice (singular: die), two 6-sided cubes with sides numbered from 1 to 6. They are used in gambling games and in many board games. Dice in games of chance go back at least 5,000 years, the earliest such cubes found in the Sumerian royal tombs of Ur, date to the third millennium B.C.

Dick, Philip Kendrid (1928-1982), U.S. science fiction author whose works illustrate his philosophical ideas and concentrate on the characters instead of action or technology. Dick's most popular novel is *The Man in the High Castle* (1962); other works include *Do Androids Dream of Electric Sheep?* (1968), the basis for the movie *Bladerunner* (1982); and *Dr. Bloodmoney* (1965).

Dickcissel (*Spiza americana*), small bird of the prairies of the central United States, named for its song. A finch, it resembles a colorful sparrow. It feeds on insects and migrates to South America in the winter.

Dickens, Charles (1812-1870), English novelist. His brief childhood experience in a debtor's prison and work in a blacking factory shaped his future imagery and sympathies. Trained as a stenographer and lawyer's clerk, he began his literary career in London as a magazine contributor, under the pseudonym 'Boz,' publishing *Sketches by 'Boz'* in 1836. His comic work *The Pickwick Papers* (1837) made him famous. His chief concern was the effect of moral evil, crime, and corruption on society. He created some memorable comic characters, as in *David Copperfield* (1850), which was based on his own experiences. His works include *Oliver Twist* (1838), *Bleak House* (1853), *Little Dorrit* (1857), *Great Expectations* (1861), and *Our Mutual Friend* (1865). Dickens's novels were dramatized, and he made successful reading tours of England and the United States.

Dickey, James Lafayette (1923-1997), U.S. poet, novelist, and critic. Dickey is best known for his novel *Deliverance* (1970), which was made into a movie in 1972. His collection of poems *Buckdancer's Choice* (1965), which, like his novel, explores themes of violence, won a National Book Award in 1966. Another poetry volume was *The Zodiac* (1976).

Dickinson, Emily (1830-1886), U.S. poet. She spent most of her life secluded in her father's home in Amherst, Mass. Her concise lyrics, witty and aphoristic in style, simple in expression, and notable for metrical variations, are chiefly concerned with immortality and nature. Of 1,775 poems, only 7 were published during her lifetime.

Dickinson, John (1732-1808), U.S. statesman. Opposed to British colonial policy but against separation from Britain, he wrote *Letters from a Farmer in Pennsylvania* (1767-1768) and, while a member of the Continental Congress (1774-1776), probably drew up the *Declaration... Setting Forth the Causes and Necessity of Their Taking Up Arms* (1775). He wrote the first draft of the Articles of Confederation.

Dictatorship, form of government in which one person holds absolute power and is not subject to the consent of the governed. The term derives from the Roman dictator who was a magistrate appointed to govern for a 6-month period, following a state emergency. Both Lucius Sulla and Julius Caesar, however, abolished the constitutional limits to their dictatorial power. In the 20th century, Adolf Hitler and Josef Stalin assumed dictatorial powers and committed hideous atrocities; there have also been dictatorships in Portugal, Spain, and Greece, and in many South American and African countries. Current dictators include Col. Muammar Qadhaffi of Libya and Saddam Hussein of Iraq.

Dictionary, listing of the words of a language, usually in alphabetical order, with the meaning of each word, as well as information on pronunciation and etymology and examples of usage, with synonyms and antonyms. Foreign language dictionaries generally list only the translations of words without their definitions. Specialized or technical dictionaries define terms used in a particular field. The term 'dictionary' is sometimes applied to reference works arranged alphabetically, such as a dictionary of biography or *Grove's Dictionary of Music and Musicians*. The term 'dictionary' (Latin: *dictionarium*, from *dicere*, 'to say') first appeared c.1225 as the title of a book by the Englishman John Garland, a manuscript of Latin words to be learned by heart, arranged by subject rather than in alphabetical order. Some scholars consider Richard Huloet's *Abcedarium Anglico-Latinum pro Tyrunculis* (English-Latin Lexicon for Young Beginners; 1552) the first English dictionary, since it defined each English word in English before giving the Latin equivalent. Others give the honor to Robert Cawdrey's *The Table Alphabeticall of Hard Words* (1604), which contained about 2,500 words defined in 'plaine English [for] Ladies, Gentlewomen, or any other unskilfull persons.' Nathaniel Bailey's dictionary (1721) gave the etymology of each entry and was among the first works to indicate pronunciation. Samuel Johnson's *A Dictionary of the English Language* (1755) was the outstanding lexicon of its century and remained the authority until well into the 19th century. Noah Webster's *An American Dictionary of the English Language* (1828) quickly became the most authoritative U.S. dictionary.

Charles Dickens (1812-1870) is the most widely read English author, aside from Shakespeare. Robert William Buss (1804-1875) painted him in his study at Gad's Hill. In the background are a number of famous characters from his novels.

Although Webster died in 1843, many modern dictionaries still bear his name. The first (1890) and second (1934) editions of *Webster's International Dictionary* were considered authoritative. The third edition (1961) was attacked by some for its 'permissive' policy of description, rather than prescription, of usage.

The most comprehensive English-language dictionary project was probably the *New English Dictionary on Historical Principles*, later known as the *Oxford English Dictionary* (OED). Hundreds of scholars from Great Britain and the United States worked on this great lexicon, begun in 1858; the last section appeared in 1928 (a supplement appeared in 1933). The OED lists and defines every English word that has appeared from the 7th century to the 20th, with all known variants, as well as etymologies, quotations, usages, and pronunciation.

Diderot, Denis (1713-1784), French encyclopedist, philosopher, and writer. His versatility as a novelist, playwright, and art critic made him prominent in the Enlightenment. His fame rests on the *Encyclopédie* (1751-

French author and philosopher Denis Diderot (1713-1784), on a portrait by Louis-Michel van Loo (1707-1771, Louvre, Paris).

D

1771), which he edited with Jean d'Alembert. The *Encyclopédie*, attempting a comprehensive presentation of human thought and knowledge, presented the scientific discoveries and more advanced thought of the time. As a result, the French government tried to suppress it in 1759. Diderot's works include the play *Le Père de Famille* (1761) and the novel *Jacques le Fataliste* (1796).

Didion, Joan (1934-), U.S. writer concerned with the 'atomization' of post-World War II society. Her work includes the essay collections *Slouching Towards Bethlehem* (1968), *The White Album* (1979) and *Political Fictions* (2001), and the novels *Play It As It Lays* (1970) and *A Book of Common Prayer* (1977).

Diebenkorn, Richard (Clifford, Jr.) (1922-1993), a United States painter. He became known for both abstract and representational paintings that are marked by large areas of glowing color and broad, textured brushstrokes. Diebenkorn first gained recognition for such abstract expressionist works

as *Berkeley No. 32*. In the mid-1950's he began painting representational works. *Man and Woman in a Large Room* and *Girl Looking at Landscape* are typical examples. He returned to abstract painting in the late 1960's and created such works as *Ocean Park No. 132*.
Diebenkorn was born in Portland, Oregon. He studied art at Stanford University, the University of California at Berkeley, and the California School of Fine Arts. In 1948 his first one-man exhibition was held in San Francisco. Diebenkorn taught at several schools, including the University of California, Los Angeles.

Diefenbaker, John George (1895-1979), Canadian prime minister, 1957-1963. Becoming leader of the Progressive Conservative Party in 1956, he headed a minority government in 1957, after 22 years of Liberal rule. The 1958 election produced a record government majority. He instituted agricultural reforms, but the economic recession, the Cuban missile crisis, and the nuclear arms debate, which aggravated rela-

tions with the United States under President John F. Kennedy, brought on his defeat in 1966 by Lester Pearson and the Liberals. He served in the Commons until his death.
See also: Canada.

Diego Garcia, island in the Indian Ocean southwest of Sri Lanka. It is the site of a strategic communications center for U.S. and British naval troops and a refueling stop for military ships and aircraft. Diego Garcia is administered as a dependency of the British Indian Ocean Territory.

Diemaking *See:* Dies and diemaking.

Diem, Ngo Dinh *See:* Ngo Dinh Diem.

Dien Bien Phu, military outpost in North Vietnam where in 1954 France was finally defeated in the Indochina War. During the 56-day siege the French army lost 15,000 men in its bid to resist the onslaught of Gen. Vo Nguyen Giap's Vietminh forces. France formally withdrew from Indochina at the Geneva Conference (1954).
See also: Vietnam.

Dies and diemaking, tools and procedures for casting molds to shape metal in industrial processes. Raw materials-usually metals or plastics-are cast into uniform shapes and sizes by dies that may be used many times for the same purpose. The dies are made from rubber, metal, or plastic and require constant maintenance.

Diesel, Rudolf (1858-1913), German engineer and developer of the oil-fueled internal-combustion engine that is named after him. After working as a mechanic, parts designer, and thermal engineer, Diesel began work on his design in 1885, patented it in 1892, and had a working model by 1897.
See also: Diesel engine.

Diesel engine, internal combustion engine patented in 1892 by the German engineer Rudolf Diesel (1858-1913). Unlike the gasoline engines used in most modern automobiles, the diesel engine does not ignite the fuel with an outside source of heat such as a spark plug, but uses the heat generated by compression to ignite the fuel-air mixture in its cylinder. To achieve the necessary high temperatures diesel engines must have a high compression ratio. Compression ratios of 16:1 are most commonly used. At this ratio, the temperature within the cylinder reaches 940°F (504°C) and the pressure equals 546 lb (248 kg) per sq inch. (Ordinary gasoline engines have compression ratios between 4:1 and 10:1.)
See also: Diesel, Rudolf.

Diet, customary or specified kind of food and drink taken daily. Doctors, nurses, and dieticians must be skilled in dietetics (the science of diet and nutrition) so that they can advise on the selection, preparation, and presentation of food for patients. A balanced diet includes proteins, fats and carbohydrates, minerals, and vitamins. Special diets for weight loss or gain are designed according to the intake of calories, which measure energy yielded by food. Other diets may in-

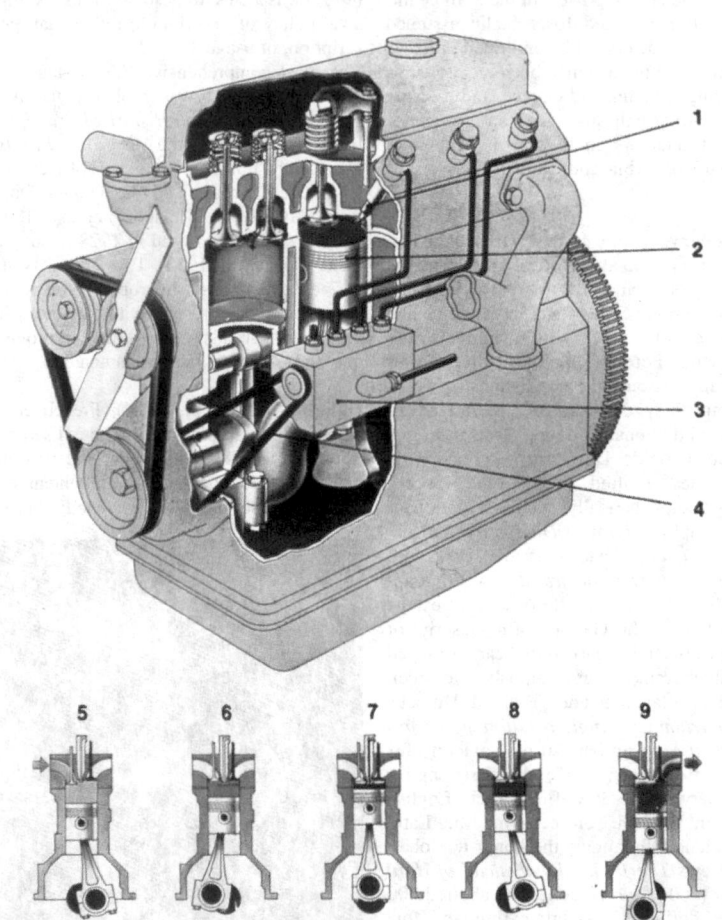

Diesel engines work after the principle of fuel injection, unlike most conventional internal combustion engines. Under high pressure, diesel fuel is being sprayed from an injector (1) into the combustion chamber. The increased temperature, caused by the compression of air in the chamber, will ignite the fuel (8). The accelerator controls the amount of fuel delivered by the pump (3), and hence the power of the engine. (2 = piston in combustion chamber, 4 = chain drive from crankshaft to pump, 5 = inlet valve pens, air is drawn into chamber, 6 = both valves are closed, piston compresses air, 7 = just before maximum compression, fuel is injected into the chamber, where it vaporises, 9 = exhaust valve opens and piston clears the chamber).

volve restriction of salt (for heart disease) or sugar (for diabetes).

Dietitian, one who applies the principles of nutrition to the feeding of an individual or a group of individuals.
See also: Nutrition.

Dietrich, Marlene (Maria Magdalene von Losch; 1904-1992), German-born U.S. actress and cabaret artist. Early in her career she studied acting with Max Reinhardt and acted on the Berlin stage. Her 'femme fatale' image originated with her first major film role, the dance-hall girl in *The Blue Angel* (1930). Her other well-known films include *Morocco* (1930) and *Shanghai Express* (1932). She became a U.S. citizen in 1937.

Dietrich of Bern *See:* Theodoric.

Diffraction, deviation and spreading of waves (such as electromagnetic radiation, sound or water waves) from a straight line, occurring when waves encounter an obstacle. Diffraction effects place the limit on the resolving power of optical instruments, radio telescopes, and the like. In a spectrograph, light passed through or reflected from a diffraction grating, a series of very accurately ruled slits or narrow parallel mirrors, produces a series of spectra by the interference of light from the different slits or mirrors.

Diffusion, gradual mixing of different substances placed in mutual contact, due to the random thermal motion of their constituent particles. Most rapid with gases and liquids, it also occurs with solids. Diffusion rates increase with increasing temperature; the rates at which gases diffuse through a porous membrane vary as the inverse of the square root of their molecular weight (gases of low molecular weight diffuse more quickly than those of high molecular weight). Gaseous diffusion is used to separate fissile uranium-235 from nonfissile uranium-238, the gas used being uranium hexafluoride (UF_6).

Digestive system, organs in the body that play a major role in the digestion of food, including the mouth, esophagus, stomach, and bowels. The pancreas and liver secrete juices that assist in the digestive processes. The muscular activity of the digestive tract disturbs the daily existence of humans. Hunger and the desire to defecate may arise from awareness of the movement of a part of the tract. Hunger contractions are a stimulus for food intake and arise when the stomach is empty. A few minutes after a meal, food, broken down by enzymes (digestive juices) into chyme, begins to leave the stomach, which is usually empty within 3 hours. On leaving the stomach, the food passes fairly rapidly through the small intestine, where it is further broken down, and within 3-4 hours the unabsorbed remnants begin to reach the colon, the residues of the various meals taken every day lying in the descending colon until expulsion. Defecation usually takes place once a day, but it is not abnormal for it to occur 3 times daily or to be withheld for up to 3 days. The muscle of the digestive

tract regulates the passage of the contents to allow adequate time for digestion and absorption. Mastication (chewing) is a voluntary movement, and swallowing can be initiated voluntarily, so the muscles of the mouth and pharynx are all striated, and the esophagus contains both striated and smooth (involuntary) muscle. From the stomach to the anus there is only smooth muscle, except for the external anal sphincter, which is again striated.

Digital computer *See:* Computer.

Digitalis, drug prepared from leaves of the foxglove plant (genus *Digitalis*). Its main effect is cardiotonic, causing the heart muscle to pump more forcefully and effectively, thereby improving the circulation of the blood and promoting the normal elimination of excess fluid. Digitalis is often used to treat heart failure because it can relieve one of the early effects of the condition-buildup of fluid in the body tissues.
Digitalis and its derivates (digitoxin and digoxin) are the most frequently used cardiotonic drugs; other examples are ouabain and strophanthus.

Dijkstra, Sjoukje Rosalie (1942-), Dutch figure skater, won the Dutch Championship six times between 1959 and 1964, the European championship 5 times, became world champion three times and claimed the Olympic gold medal (1964). Moreover, she won the Richmond Trophy three times.
She performed in the ice show *Holiday on Ice* from 1964-1972. Dijkstra is known for her great jumping ability and athletic capacity.

Dijon (pop. 151,636), France, the capital of Côte-d'Or Department. The city is in the historic region of Burgundy at the junction of the Ouche and Suzon rivers, 160 miles (260 km) southeast of Paris. Dijon is a major transportation hub and an industrial and cultural center, renowned for its wine and mustard. Other products include electric appliances, leather goods, and electronic equipment. Dijon University was founded in 1722. Although first settled in Roman times, the city did not become important until the 11th century, when it became the capital of the duchy of Burgundy. Under the dukes, Dijon flourished for nearly five centuries. It was during this period that many of its outstanding buildings were constructed, including the ducal palace, which now houses the Fine Arts Museum. After 1477, when Louis XI of France seized Burgundy, Dijon's importance declined.

D

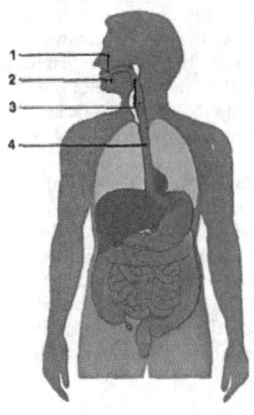

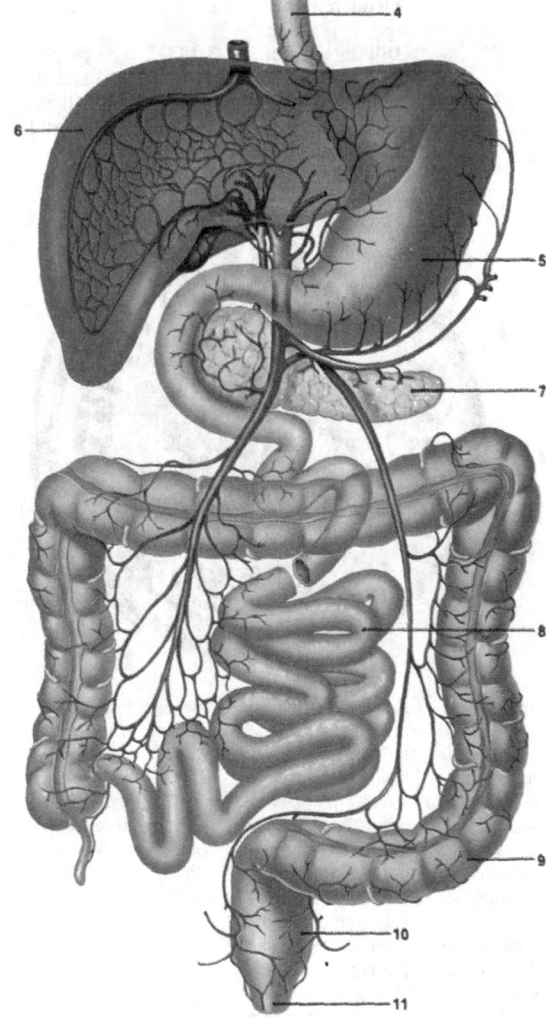

The digestive tract is a continuous muscular tube of about 33 ft (10 m) long, extending from the mouth to the rectum. Food enters the mouth, where it is chopped up by the teeth (1) and tasted by the tongue (2). Then, it is pushed into the pharynx (3) and is carried down the oesophagus (4), into the stomach (5). Through peristalsis, the muscular action of the stomach, the food is churned. Digestive juices supplied by the liver (6) and the pancreas (7) emulsify the food and convert it into a semi-liquid mass. The small intestine (8) absorbs digested food into the blood circulatory system as nutrients for the body. The large intestine (9) condenses unused food matter and expels it through the rectum (10) and anus (11).

Dik-dik, small African antelope (genus *Madoqua*), standing only 14 in (36 cm) high at the shoulder. The male has short, spiky horns.

Dike, artificial embankment for controlling water flow. Made of rock, clay, or cement, dikes are shaped in the form of a mound high enough to prevent an overflow of water. Often they are equipped with gates in order to permit irrigation of farmland. Dikes are a common feature in the Dutch landscape, since most of the Netherlands is below sea level. The term originally referred to a trench dug into the earth as a defensive measure. As water naturally collects in such trenches, *dike* also came to mean a natural or artificial water channel.

Dili (pop. 80,000), principal town of Loro Sae, the former Portuguese East Timor. Trading center and port with the export of, among other things, cotton, coffee and sandalwood. After the country became independent from the Portuguese in 1975, it was invaded by Indonesian forces. Dili was the scene of battle. This conflict has cost an estimated 200,000 lives.

Dill (*Anethum graveolens*), annual or biennial of the carrot family cultivated for its leaves and seeds, which are used as flavorings. Dill originated around the Mediterranean.

Dillinger, John (1903-1934), U.S. gangster who terrorized the Midwest in 1933 after escaping from jail. Responsible for 16 killings, he was the FBI's Public Enemy Number 1. FBI agents killed him in Chicago in 1934.

A portrait of Diocletian on an Antoninian coin. The inscription reads: imp(erator) c(aesar) c (abbreviation of Gaius) val(erian) diocletianus p(ontifex) m(aximus) aug(ustus). The Antoninian coin was struck and named after emperor Caracalla (Mark Aurelius Antoninus, 186-217), and until the time of Diocletian, it was the most common Roman coin. It originally contained a large percentage of silver, but eventually, it became a bronze coin with a very thin layer of silver (still partly present here). This devaluation of the coin had a negative effect on the economy of the empire. Diocletian handled this by reorganizing the monetary system and abolition of the Antoninian coin.

Dilthey, Wilhelm (1833-1911), German philosopher. He sought to achieve for the human sciences (law, religion, history, psychology, and the arts) a methodology free of the influence of the natural sciences. *See also:* Philosophy.

Diluvium *See:* Pleistocene Epoch.

DiMaggio, Joseph Paul (1914-1999), U.S. baseball player. Nicknamed 'the Yankee Clipper,' DiMaggio is considered one of the greatest outfielders of all time, and set a major league record by hitting safely in 56 consecutive games (1941). He won the American League's most valuable player award 3 times (1939, 1941, and 1947), and in 1948 he led the league in home runs (39) and runs batted in (155). DiMaggio, who played for the New York Yankees (1936-1951) and led them to 10 World Series appearances, played in 11 All-Star games and was inducted into the National Baseball Hall of Fame (1955).

Dimitrov, Georgi Michailovic (1882-1949), Bulgarian communist politician, immigrated to the Soviet Union in 1923, where he was employed in the Comintern. Detained by the nazis on suspicion of setting fire to the Reichstag (1933), Dimitrov became world famous as a result of his defense, which led to his acquittal. He was the Secretary-General of the Comintern from 1935-1943 and also a member of the Supreme Soviet (1937-1945). He returned to Bulgaria in 1946 and became prime minister. He became the Secretary-General of the Bulgarian Communist Party in 1948.

D'Indy, (Paul Marie Théodore) Vincent (1851-1931), French composer. A pupil of César Franck and cofounder (1894) of the Schola Cantorum academy in Paris, he admired the German classics and Renaissance polyphony and urged a renovated French style derived from folk idioms. His works include *Symphony on a French Mountain Air* (1886).

Dine, Jim (James Dine; 1935-), U.S. artist. His work makes use of 'found' objects, such as old shoes or tools, which he attaches to his canvases.

Dinesen, Isak (Baroness Karen Blixen; 1885-1962), Danish author of romantic tales of mystery, such as *Seven Gothic Tales* (1934) and *Winter's Tales* (1942). Dinesen wrote in both English and Danish. The autobiographical *Out of Africa* (1937) was based on her 20 years in East Africa.

Dinka, plains tribe of southern Sudan, in Africa. The Dinka are primarily farmers and cattle herders who supplement their diet with fish. Their religion centers around a single god and many spirits.

Dinoflagellate, single-celled organism that occurs in vast numbers in fresh and salt water. Each one is covered by a layer of cellulose that is a distinctive, and often elaborate, shape. Some contain chlorophyll while others do not, so they may be classed as animals or plants. Dinoflagellates are important as food for many animals, but some are poisonous. Swarms of one form, the 'red tide' of tropical waters, kill fish and damage beaches. Certain dinoflagellates create the phosphorescence of the sea.

Dinosaur (Greek, 'terrible lizard'), extinct reptile that flourished between about 220 and 63 million years ago and then suddenly disappeared. Dinosaurs dominated the land life during most of this period and occurred in a wide variety of forms, some no bigger than a chicken and others weighing many tons. The dinosaurs arose in the Triassic Period (early Mesozoic Era) from a group of small reptiles called *thecodonts*. They evolved into 2 great groups, or orders, the Saurischia, or 'lizard-hipped,' and the Ornithischia, or 'bird-hipped.' Saurischian dinosaurs include 2-legged carnivores-the theropods and 4-legged herbivores-the sauropods. The sauropods were the giant dinosaurs, including such types as the apatosaurus (brontosaurus) and the diplodocus, with tiny heads, very long necks and tails, and pillar-like legs. The theropods ranged from the fast-running coelurosaurs, which fed on insects and perhaps on eggs, to the carnosaurs like the Tyrannosaurus and allosaurus, which had enormous skulls and dagger-like teeth and could grow to a height of 20 ft (6m). Ornithischians diversified into many types, some producing strange body armor. All were herbivorous. Four-legged forms include the stegosaurs, which had triangular bony plates along the back, the armadillo-like ankylosaurs, and the ceratopsians, such as the triceratops, which carried 3 horns and a bony frill on the skull. The 2-legged ornithischians included the duck-billed dinosaurs. At the end of the Cretaceous Period (about 65 million years ago) dinosaurs disappeared. The reason for their extinction is unknown. It has been suggested that disease killed them off or that mammals preyed excessively on their eggs. Climactic and other changes caused by the impact of a huge asteroid have also been proposed.

Diocletian (Gaius Aurelius Valerius Diocletianus; A.D. 245-313), Roman emperor A.D. 284-305. He reformed the army and administration, dividing the empire into 4 regions (293), ruled by 2 emperors and 2 caesars. Much of his great palace at Split, Yugoslavia, survives. In 303 he initiated the last universal persecution of the Christians. He abdicated in 305. *See also:* Rome, Ancient.

Diode *See:* Electronics.

Diogenes (412?-323 B.C.), Greek philosopher. Contemptuous of his contemporaries and their values, he was nicknamed 'the Dog' and his followers the *cynics* (Greek: *kynikos*, 'doglike'). He abandoned all his possessions, begged his living, and reputedly lived in a tub. Supposedly, when Alexander the Great asked what he could do for him, Diogenes answered, 'Just step out of my light.' *See also:* Cynic philosophy.

Dionaea *See:* Venus's-flytrap.

D

The Tarbosaurus was a large thero-pod dinosaur over 45 ft (14 m) long. It was an asian relative of the North American Tyrannosaurus.

The Ceratosaurus was a fierce carnivo-rous dinosaur which lived in parts of North America dur-ing the Jurassic peri-od. It was a bipedal (two-legged) preda-tor with clawed forelegs that it used for grasping its prey, which probably in-cluded herbivorous dinosaurs such as the Stegosaurus and water-dwelling Sauropods.

The Oviraptor (egg-stealer), one of the os-trich-like dinosaurs of the Cretaceous period, is thought to have fed on the eggs of other reptiles. It was bipedal, and able to run fast.

The Scolosaurus was one of the anky-losaurian dinosaurs of the Upper Cretaceous period, characterized by their squat shape and armor. The Scolosaurus was about 20 ft (6 m) long and had 2 prominent spikes on its tail.

The Brontosaurus was one of the largest of the giant herbivorous di-nosaurs that lived in the Mesozoic era. Evidence suggest that it led an am-phibious existence in order to overcome the difficulties of sup-port and locomotion posed by its 35 ton body weight.

D

Dionysius the Elder (430?-367 B.C.), Greek soldier who distinguished himself in battle against Carthage and thus got himself elected sovereign general of Syracuse (in 405 B.C.). He converted the office into a tyranny, raising a large army of mercenaries.
See also: Greece, Ancient.

Dionysus, in Greek mythology, god of wine and fertility, generally thought of as a son of Zeus. He founded the art of vine cultivation. In early times his devotees, notably the Maenads, practiced an orgiastic cult of divine possession. Greek drama developed from the celebrations in honor of Dionysus. The Romans identified their wine god Bacchus with Dionysus.
See also: Mythology.

Diopside, mineral of the silicate family. Rich in calcium and magnesium, it is occasionally used as a gemstone. It has a glassy surface and can range in color from white to light green. Diopside is a metamorphic rock formed by intense heat and pressure on limestone-based dolomite. It can also be formed when molten rock (magma) crystalizes.

Dior, Christian (1905-1957), French fashion designer. Dior helped reestablish Paris as the leader in fashion after World War II. His salon, opened in 1946, branched out into subsidiary companies to manufacture perfume and clothing accessories. Known worldwide, Dior was the undisputed leader of fashion until his death.

Dioxin, toxic chemical produced in some chemical-manufacturing processes, contaminating various herbicides. The effects on human health of long-term exposure to dioxin are disputed, although it is generally accepted that dioxin causes chloracne. U.S. chemical workers have filed suits against employers for serious health problems, and Vietnam veterans also claimed damages for exposure to Agent Orange, a defoliant contaminated by dioxin. There were cleanups in the 1980s of dioxin deposits on sites in Missouri and New Jersey.
See also: Agent Orange.

Diphtheria, acute contagious disease caused by *Corynebacterium diphtheriae*, characterized by the formation of a soft crust (pseudomembrane) that forms in the inflamed throat, and by tissue damage in the heart and nervous system, a result of poisons produced by the bacteria. An effective vaccine prevents diphtheria.

Diplodocus *See:* Dinosaur.

Diplomacy, conduct of negotiations and maintenance of relations in time of peace between sovereign states. A diplomatic mission is generally headed by an ambassador, supported by attachés, chargés d'affaires, and other officials specializing in economic, political, cultural, administrative, and military matters. An embassy building is considered to have extraterritoriality (to be outside the jurisdiction of the receiving state). Accredited diplomats are immune from prosecution and customs regulations. Abuse of this privileged diplomatic immunity can lead to a diplomat being asked to quit the host country as *persona non grata*. The most common abuse is espionage. The whole body of diplomats in a capital is known as the diplomatic corps, and its spokesperson is the longest-serving ambassador. The first permanent residential missions were established by the Italian city-states c.1400. Diplomatic protocol and the forms of accreditation owed much to the practice of papal missions from the Vatican. Latin was the official language of diplomacy until the 17th century, when it was superseded by French, later joined by English. The Congress of Vienna (1815) further clarified diplomatic procedure. The traditional formulas of diplomatic exchange allow sharp expressions of protest without ruptures in international dealing. Improved communications have strengthened direct links between governments, and diplomacy is now often conducted at summit conferences between heads of state.

Dipper, small wrenlike bird (genus *Cinclus*) that dives under water. The American dipper (*C. mexicanus*) is slate-gray and lives along mountain streams in the western United States. It has a thick underplumage and large oil glands to keep the plumage waterproof.

Dirac, Paul Adrien Maurice (1902-1984), English theoretical physicist. He shared the 1933 Nobel Prize in physics with E. Schrödinger for their contributions to wave mechanics. Dirac's theory (1928) took account of relativity and implied the existence of the positive electron, or positron, later discovered by C.D. Anderson. Dirac was also the codeveloper of Fermi-Dirac statistics.
See also: Quantum mechanics.

Direct current *See:* Electric current.

Director *See:* Motion pictures; Theater.

Dirigible *See:* Airship.

Dirksen, Everett McKinley (1896-1969), U.S. legislator. Illinois Republican representative (1933-1948) and senator (1950-1969), Dirksen was Senate minority leader from 1959 until his death. He delivered conservative Republican support of major bipartisan legislation, most notably in the case of the landmark Civil Rights Act of 1964.

Disarmament, procedure for abolishing, limiting, regulating, or reducing a nation's military forces or weapons arsenal. Widespread or universal disarmament has been a long-sought goal of many. After World War II, the existence of nuclear weapons and the split of the world into 2 hostile camps lent a new urgency to curbing the destructive power of nations. Several treaties (Nuclear Test Ban Treaty, 1963; Nuclear Non-Proliferation Treaty, 1968, a non-binding treaty under UN auspices) were negotiated in the 1950s and 1960s. The Strategic Arms Limitation Talks (SALT) were unsuccessful in the 1970s, but the Strategic Arms Reduction Talks (START) between the United States and the USSR went on throughout the 1980s. With the end of the Cold War in Europe in 1989-90 and the dismantling of the Warsaw Pact Alliance, major reductions in military personnel and materiel throughout Europe and Russia became feasible, and are currently being planned and executed. In 1993 the Chemical Weapons treaty was signed and Russia and the United States signed START II, providing for further reductions in nuclear arms.
See also: Nuclear weapon; Non-proliferation Treaty; Strategic Arms Limitation Talks.

Disciple *See:* Apostles.

Disciples of Christ (The Christian Church), now the International Convention of Christian Churches, U.S. religious body founded (1832) by followers of Alexander Campbell. It has no formal ministry or creed, teaching personal faith in the Bible and the gospel of Christ. It has missions all over the world.

Discrimination, in science, perception of difference or of differential response, or ability to perceive slight differences. A discrimination experiment tests the presence of the ability to discriminate under certain conditions. A discrimination reaction is a variation between 2 or more stimuli before reacting; the time that is needed is the discrimination time.

Discus, disk thrown in athletic competition. The wooden disk has a smooth metal rim and brass plates set flush within its sides. Discus throwing was popular in classical times as a form of exercise and for athletic contests. The discus, then made of stone or metal, was thrown for distance, with a combination of strength, skill, and grace. The discus thrown by men in modern competition weighs not less than 4 lb 6.5 oz (2 kg). The women's discus weighs 2 lb 3 oz (1 kg).

Disease, disturbance of normal body function in an organism. Disease is usually brought to a person's attention by symptoms of an abnormality of, or change in, body function: pain, headache, fever, cough, shortness of breath, dyspepsia, constipation, diarrhea, loss of blood, lumps, paralysis, or numbness, or loss of consciousness. Diagnosis is made on the basis of symptoms and from signs on discovered physical examination and from laboratory and X-ray investigations.
Trauma (injury) may cause skin lacerations and bone fractures as well as disorders specific to the organ involved. Congenital diseases include hereditary conditions and diseases beginning in the fetus, such as those due to drugs or maternal infection during pregnancy. Infectious diseases caused by viruses, bacteria, and parasites are usually communicable; insects, animals, and human carriers may be important in their spread, and epidemics may occur. Inflammation is often the result of infection, but inflammatory disease can also result from disordered immunity and other causes. In vascular diseases, organs become diseased as a result of disease in their blood supply; examples are atherosclerosis, aneurysms, thrombosis, and embolism. In tumors, including benign

growths, cancer, and lymphoma, abnormal growth of a structure occurs and leads to a lump, causing pressure or spreading to other organs. In degenerative disease, death or premature aging of parts of an organ or a system lead to a gradual impairment of function. Deficiency diseases result from inadequate intake of nutrients; resulting disorders, including hormonal disorders, can lead to metabolic disease. An increasingly recognized side- effect of industrialization is occupational disease caused by chemicals, dust, or molds encountered at work. An iatrogenic disease is one produced by medical intervention in an attempt to treat or prevent another disease. Finally, psychiatric disease, including psychoses (schizophrenia and severe depression) and neuroses, are functional disturbances of the brain; they may represent disturbances of brain metabolism.

The characteristics of acute disease may be exemplified by acute infections. The onset of the condition is frequently sudden, and there may be almost total prostration, but there is the prospect of a limited period in this state. Most acute diseases, because of their finite duration, pose a minimal threat to the subject. The onset of chronic disease, on the other hand, is usually slow; there may be a progression of symptoms, or more permanent problems may develop as the sequel to a number of acute episodes.

Disinfectant, chemical substance or other agent, such as ultraviolet light, used to disinfect inanimate objects, with the aim of destroying or inhibiting the activity of disease-producing microorganisms.

Disler, Martin (1949-1996), Swiss painter. The self-taught Disler made large, very expressive drawings, paintings, and murals, in which he sought to confront himself and to express deeply, human emotions such as fear, pain, and ecstasy as irrationally and harshly as possible. Many of his works, which were often created during exhausting, all night painting sessions, are characterized by purposefully unesthetic, aggressive use of lines and, only partially recognizable, figurative elements, such as twisted faces, (hermaphrodite) naked bodies, and heads of animals.

Dislocation, movement of an organ, bone, or other body part away from its normal position, in particular the displacement of the bones of a joint. Dislocations are said to be simple (bearing no external wound) or complex (involving a wound that breaks the skin).

Disney, Walt (Walter Elias Disney; 1901-1966), U.S. pioneer of animated film cartoons. Starting in the 1920s, the Disney studios in Hollywood created the cartoon characters Mickey Mouse, Pluto, Donald Duck, and Goofy. Disney produced the first full-length cartoon feature, *Snow White and the Seven Dwarfs* (1938), which was followed by *Pinocchio* (1940), *Fantasia* (1940), and *Bambi* (1942), among others. The company he founded continues to make movies in his tradition, such as *The Fox and the Hound* (1981), *The Little Mermaid* (1989), and *Beauty and the Beast* (1991). Disney also produced many popular nature films. He opened the first of his theme parks, Disneyland, in Anaheim, Calif., in 1955. The park now includes over 160 acres of elaborate mechanized amusements and re-creations based on Disney movie features. Built on a permanent World's Fair scale, the park is one of the major tourist attractions in the United States. A similar, far larger park opened in 1971 on a 27,400-acre site near Orlando, Fla.; it was joined by the futuristic Epcot Center in 1982. The Tokyo Disney World also opened in 1982 and a European Disney World was opened in 1991.
See also: Cartoon.

Dispersion, optical phenomenon whereby a beam of white light is broken up into its component colors when it passes through a triangular glass prism. Each color has a different index of refraction; that is, it bends at a characteristic angle when passing from one medium to another (air to glass, for instance). Since white light is made up of all the colors of the spectrum, the colors separate when they pass through glass prisms. Rainbows are formed by the refraction and dispersion of sunlight through raindrops.

Displaced person *See:* Refugee.

Disraeli, Benjamin, 1st earl of Beaconsfield (1804-1881), British Conservative statesman, prime minister 1868 and 1874-1880. Baptized a Christian, Disraeli was the first British prime minister of Jewish ancestry. A member of Parliament from 1837, he was chancellor of the exchequer 1852, 1858-1859, and 1866-1868. His influence was crucial in the passing of the 1867 Reform Bill, which enfranchised some 2 million working-class voters. His brief first ministry ended when the Liberals under William Gladstone won the 1868 elections. His second period of office included domestic reforms: slum clearance, public-health reform, and improvement of working conditions. Abroad, Disraeli fought imperial wars, bought control of the Suez Canal (1875), had Queen Victoria proclaimed Empress of India (1876), and annexed the Transvaal (1877). In the confrontation between Russia and Turkey (1877-1878), he forced concessions on Russia in the Congress of Berlin. A prolific writer, he published many books, notably the novels *Coningsby* (1844) and *Sybil* (1845), both on social and political themes.

Dissection *See:* Anatomy.

Distemper, term applied to several animal diseases, but particularly referring to a specific viral disease of dogs. It commonly occurs in puppies, with fever, poor appetite, and discharge from mucous membranes; bronchopneumonia and encephalitis may be complications. Vaccination is protective.

Distillation, method of separating the parts of mixtures of liquids or of separating liquids from solids. The mixture or solution is heated so that the liquid vaporizes. The va-

D

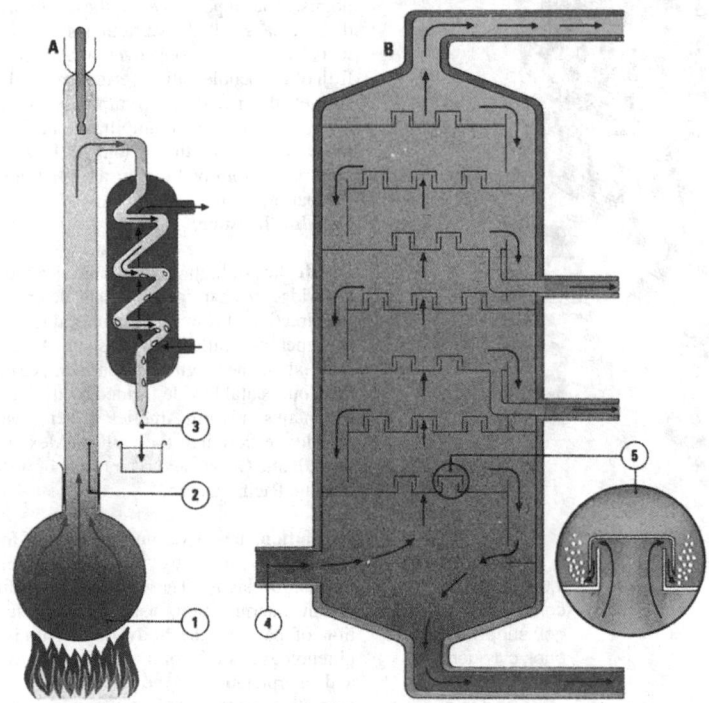

In (A), the liquid to be distilled (1) is heated until its molecules have enough energy to leave the liquid as a gas (2). When they encounter a colder surface, they will coalesce and form droplets (3). (B) shows a crude-oil fractionating column, which is hotter at the bottom, than it is at the top. As heavy oil enters (4), the heavier portion will sink, the lighter portion will rise as vapour, which the bubble caps (5), force to pass through a layer of liquid fractions. The less volatile constituents will condense, and join the liquid. When the liquid level will reach a certain depth, it will overflow. Hence, the vapour contains more volatile components as it travels up the column.

D

por is then condensed to form a liquid, called the distillate. The distillate is a purified form of the original solution, since the less volatile components are left behind as residue. Distillation is used in industry to separate and purify petroleum products, alcohols, and benzene hydrocarbons. It is also used in making alcoholic drinks. Distillation is carried out in a *still* consisting of a boiler, where the liquid is heated; a condenser, where the vapors are condensed; and a receiver to collect the distillate. Distillation can be carried out under high pressure or under reduced pressure or a vacuum to raise or lower the boiling points of the liquids involved.

Distilling, the manufacture of *spirits*, which are alcoholic beverages produced by fractional distillation. Spirits are distilled from a liquid or mash (pulpy mixture) that is obtained from fruit, grain, or some other plant product and then fermented. Spirits have a higher proportion of alcohol than wine, beer, and other alcoholic beverages made by fermentation alone. Although spirits retain the flavor of the liquid or mash from which they are made, they are colorless immediately after distillation. They acquire color as a result of aging in wooden casks or the addition of

A pressure-resistant deep-sea diving suit allows a diver to carry an air supply, so that he can breathe air at a normal atmospheric pressure. Thus, a diver can return rapidly to the surface without having to fear 'bends' or other pressure-related ailments. The suit is designed to withstand water pressures at depths up to 1,000 ft (305 m) and carries a 20-hour oxygen supply in back pack cylinders. Although cumbersome and heavy, the suit has jointed legs and arms, allowing limited movement. Hand-controlled external metal fingers can be used to manipulate various tools.

artificial coloring matter. Distilling was known to the Moors as early as 1000 A.D. The process became widespread in Europe during the 15th century.

District of Columbia (D.C.) *See:* Washington, D.C..

Disulfiram, sulphur-based drug used to treat alcoholism. Discovered in 1948 by two Danish physicians, Jens Hald and Erik Jacobsen, disulfiram makes alcohol unpalatable to the user. Mixing alcohol with the drug causes dizziness, nausea, and possible vomiting.
See also: Alcoholism.

Dittersdorf, Karl Ditters von (1739-1799), Austrian composer and violinist. He composed light operas, establishing the singspiel form. Among his works are the operas *Doktor und Apotheker* (1786), *Hieronymus Knicker* (1789), and *Das Rote Käppchen* (1790).
See also: Opera.

Diuretic, drug that increases urine production by the kidneys, removing excess sodium and water from the body. Alcohol and caffeine are mild diuretics. Thiazides and other diuretics are commonly used in treatment of heart failure, edema, high blood pressure, and liver and kidney diseases.

Diverticulitis, disease of the intestine involving inflamation of diverticula, pouches or sacs that sometimes appear in the surface of the colon, causing it to bulge out in weak points. The appearance of these abnormal diverticula is called diverticulosis, which affects 5 to 10% of people over 40. About one-fifth of the people with diverticulosis will also get diverticulitis. Symptoms include fever, spasms, and cramplike pain in the lower left part of the abdomen. Treatment may range from bed rest to drug therapy to combat infection.
See also: Intestine.

Divide, line of high ground, such as a mountain ridge or chain of hills, that determines the direction of flow of streams and rivers. It is sometimes called a watershed. A divide may extend the length of a continent, as does the Continental Divide formed by the Rocky Mountains in North America. Rivers east of this divide flow into the Gulf of Mexico or the Atlantic Ocean, and rivers west of it flow into the Pacific Ocean.

Divination, any of various methods of foretelling the future by means of oracles, omens, or signs. These methods include dream interpretation, astrology, investigation of parts of the body (e.g., palmistry, phrenology), study of the animal entrails, and interpretation of the cries of birds and animals (augury). Divination is one of the most ancient of practices, and has been found in almost all societies.

Diving *See:* Swimming and diving.

Diving, deep-sea, descent by divers to the seabed, usually for extended periods, for purposes of exploration, recreation, or sal-

vage. In 1715 John Lethbridge devised the forerunner of the armored suits used today in deepest waters. In 1802 William Forder devised a suit into which air is supplied by a pump. The diving suit today has a metal or fiberglass helmet with viewports and inhalation and exhalation valves, joined by an airtight seal to a metal chestpiece, itself joined to a flexible watertight covering of rubber and canvas; weights, especially weighted boots, provide stability and prevent the diver from shooting toward the surface. Air or, more often, an oxygen/helium mixture is conveyed to the diver via a thick rubber tube. Nowadays, self- contained underwater breathing apparatus (scuba diving), where the diver has no suit but carries gas cylinders and an aqualung, permits great mobility. In all diving great care must be taken for proper decompression to avoid the bends, a dangerous condition in which gas bubbles enter the blood and tissue during overly rapid ascent to the surface.

Divining rod, forked stick used by diviners, or dowsers, to find buried objects or water. Diviners believe that if they hold the forked end of the rod and pass over an area where water is located, the pointed end will be attracted to the water and pull downward. Diviners often officially refer to their skill as rhabdomancy. Although dowsers have claimed remarkable success on many occasions, tests and experiments have not been able to demonstrate more than a chance relationship to results.

Division, army unit consisting of a number of brigades and support troops; a lieutenant general or a brigadier general is the commander. A division can operate independently, but is usually grouped with one or more other divisions to form an army. One differentiates between the armored division (including tanks etcetera) and the less heavily armed, infantry division.

Divorce, legal dissolution of a valid marriage, as distinguished from separation, in which the partners remain married but live apart, and annulment, in which the marriage is deemed to be invalid. In most cases, divorce leaves the partners free to remarry, sometimes after a set period. Divorce has existed in most cultures, but its availability and the grounds for it have varied widely. Christianity regards marriage as a sacrament that may not lightly be set aside, and this view has affected the Western concept of divorce. The Roman Catholic Church still does not allow divorce, but most other churches do. Adultery is the most widely accepted ground for divorce; others include cruelty, alcoholism, insanity, desertion, and conviction of a serious crime. A modern trend is to make irreparable breakdown of the marriage another ground, without involving the misconduct of either party.
See also: Marriage.

Dix, Otto (1891-1969), German painter and leader of the 'new objectivity' school of social realism. His most famous work is the cycle of 50 etchings entitled *The War* (1924) that depicts the horrors of World War II. He was jailed (1939-1945) by the Nazi government. In later years his work reflected religious mysticism.

Otto Dix' (1891-1969) 1926 (Musee d'Art portrait of journalist Moderne, Paris). Sylvia von Harden,

Dixie, popular term for the southern states of the United States, particularly those that formed the Confederacy. There are a number of explanations of the origin of the term. One is that 'Dixie' derives from the pre-Civil War issue of 10-dollar notes by the Citizens Bank of New Orleans. The notes carried the French word *dix* ('ten') on the reverse side for the benefit of the area's many French-speaking people, so Louisiana and later the whole South became known as the land of 'Dixies.' Other stories connect the name with a slaveowner named Dixie or with the Mason-Dixon line. 'Dixie' is also the name of a popular song written in 1859, often regarded as the national anthem of the Confederacy.
See also: Confederate States of America.

Diyarbakir (pop. 381,000), capital of the province of the same name in Eastern Turkey, located on the Tigris; (province 4,533 sq mi, 11,735 sq km, pop. 942,000). Industrial center and trade center for a region with cattle breeding and grape cultivation and the cultivation of grain and cotton. Extraction of copper and petroleum in the near vicinity. Known in the past for its gold and silver filigree work. The city is surrounded by walls of black basalt, with a citadel, which probably originates from the 4th century B.C.. Originally a Roman colony called Amida; Turkish as of 1515. University (1966).

Dizziness, sensations of whirling, giddiness, and vertigo caused by abnormal stimulation of receptors of balance or by rapid movements of the visual field, sometimes accompanied by nausea and nystagmus (rapid, jerky eye movements). It can also be caused by psychological disorders.

Djakarta *See:* Jakarta.

Djibouti (pop. 473,000), capital of the Republic of Djibouti. A port city located on the Gulf of Aden, it is the country's only economic center. Founded by the French in 1888 and developed as a colonial capital, the city has since grown rapidly and is now plagued by poverty and inadequate housing. *See also:* Djibouti.

Djibouti

Capital:	Djibouti
Area:	8,950 sq mi (23,200 sq km)
Population:	473,000
Language:	Arabic, French
Government:	Presidential republic
Independent:	1977
Head of gov.:	Prime minister
Per capita:	less than US$ 1,400
Monetary unit:	1 Djibouti franc = 100 centimes

Djibouti (official name Republic of Djibouti), formerly French Somaliland, republic in northeastern Africa, situated where the coast of Africa approaches the Arabian peninsula, bounded by Ethiopia, Eritrea and Somalia. Its area is about 8,950 sq mi (23,200 km). The languages are Arabic and French. The official religion is Muslim.
Land and economy. Most of the country is stony desert. The climate is hot. Rainfall is usually scant, but in some years torrential rainfall causes flooding. Agricultural activity is limited. There are no known mineral resources, and industry is negligible. Hides and skins and live animals are the main exports.
People. The population is almost evenly divided into 2 ethnic groups: the Afars (from Ethiopia) and the Issas (from Somalia). The Issas are more urbanized than the Afars. The nation's government is carefully balanced between the two groups, but historical rivalries persist. The capital, also called Djibouti, is the economic and political hub of the country, with a port and a railway terminus.
History. In 1896 France signed treaties with Britain, Italy, and Ethiopia to define the boundaries of French Somaliland. In 1967 the colony voted to remain a French possession and became the French Territory of the Afars and Issas. It became independent in 1977. Djibouti has remained neutral during strife between its neighbors, Somalia and

Ethiopia, despite close ethnic ties. Thousand of refugees have streamed into Djibouti, creating serious economic problems. Djibouti was among the African countries severely affected by drought in 1984-1985. At the beginning of the 1990s there were considerable tensions in Djibouti, caused by a border dispute with Somalia and the increasing internal demands for democratization. From 1991-1994, an Afar movement waged war against the national army. A multi-party system was introduced in 1992. Nevertheless, the 'Rassemblement Populaire pour le Progrès' was the only party with any power. In 1999, the first President, Hassan Gouled Aptidon, was succeeded by Ismail Omar Guelleh. In 2002, a multi-party system came into being. The party of Guelleh won the first democratic elections in 2003.

Djilas, Milovan (1911-1995), Yugoslav communist leader and writer. He was a leading World War II partisan alongside Marshal Tito, and became a vice-president after the war. But because of his outspoken criticisms of the regime and his general indictment of communism as a form of government, he was imprisoned 1956-1966. Among his works are *The New Class* (1957), *Conversations with Stalin* (1962), and *Tito* (1980).
See also: Yugoslavia.

Djojopuspito, Suwarsih (1912-1977), Indonesian female prose writer, educated in the West. She was a protagonist of the independence of Indonesia from The Netherlands. A writer for the magazine *Kritiek en opbouw*, written in Dutch. Began writing in Indonesian after 1945. Prose: *Buiten het gareel* (1940).

Dmitri (d. 1606), tsar of Russia. The real Dmitri, son of Ivan the Terrible, is thought to have been murdered in childhood. The false Dmitri enlisted the aid of the Polish and Lithuanian nobility and invaded Russia, defeating Boris Godunov. On Boris's death in 1605, he was crowned tsar. Although he had the support of the peasantry, the boyars (nobles) opposed his Western ideas and had him murdered.
See also: Tsar.

DNA (deoxyribonucleic acid), informational molecules contained in the nucleus of every living cell that, along with ribonucleic acid (RNA), transmit all genetic information. The instructions of the nucleic acids are finally expressed by proteins, which form many of the structural and mechanical components of living systems and act as catalysts in the chemical activity of cells. The DNA molecule is an extremely long chemical thread made up of 2 strands that are held as a pair forming a spiral, or double helix. Each strand consists of a long chain of the sugar deoxyribose and phosphate residues. Two purines-adenine (A) and guanine (G)-and 2 pyrimidines-thymine (T) and cytosine (C)-are also commonly found in DNA. In the DNA thread the purine and pyrimidine bases lie opposite one another in the structure, and the pattern is always one in which a T on one strand is faced by an A, and a G by a C.

D

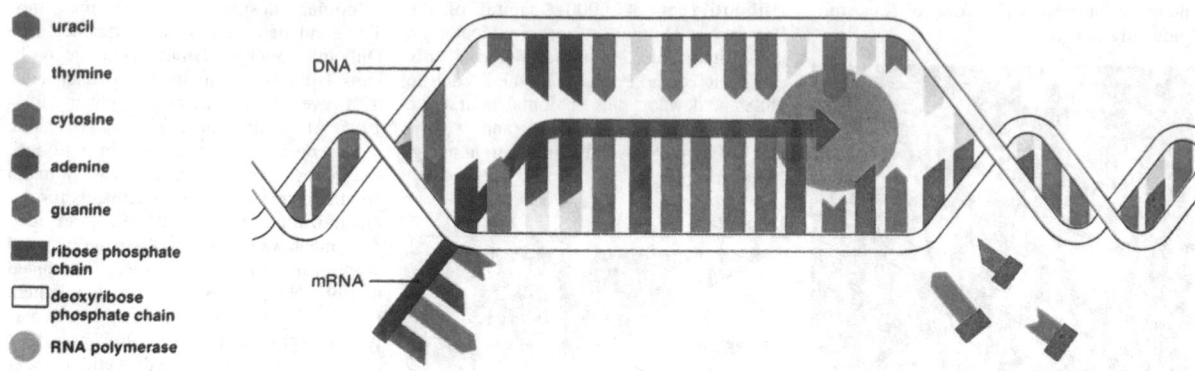

uracil

thymine

cytosine

adenine

guanine

ribose phosphate chain

deoxyribose phosphate chain

RNA polymerase

DNA

mRNA

For protein synthesis, the coded information in the DNA of the cell nucleus is tran-scribed into a mole-cule of messenger-ri-bonucleic acid (m-RNA) which, like DNA, has a linear se-quence of four basic groups. The m-RNA carries the message into the cytoplasm of the cell, where pro-tein synthesis will take place.

There is always one molecule of A to every molecule of T and one G for every C. The base pairs are stacked on top of one another like a pile of pennies. One millimeter of DNA contains about 5 million base pairs. The DNA of a human cell is about 16 in (41 cm) long. Owing to the fact that DNA pat-terns are unique, they can be used to trace and identify people.
See also: Genetics.

Dnepropetrovsk (pop. c. 1,200,000), city in Ukraine, on the Dnepr River. It is a major center of rail and water-transport and a lead-ing producer of iron, steel, and chemicals. Founded in 1787 as Ekaterinoslav, the city took its present name in 1926.
See also: Ukraine.

Dnepr River, or Dnieper River, river in Russia, Byelarussia and Ukraine, about 1,400 mi (2,253 km) long, navigable for nearly its whole length. Rising in the Valdai Hills, it flows in a southwestern direction to empty in the Black Sea east of Odessa. Leading tributaries are the Desna, Pripyat, Berezina, and Sozh. It is a major water trans-port route and also has many hydroelectric plants.

Dniester River, river in the former Soviet Union, about 875 mi (1,408 km) long. Rising in the Carpathian Mountains, in the western Ukraine, it flows southeast through the Ukraine and Moldavia, and empties into the Black Sea southwest of Odessa. The riv-er's water is used for irrigation and to gener-ate electricity.

Doberman pinscher, breed of dog originat-ing in Germany. Developed by Louis Dobermann in the late 1800s, it is prevalent in guard and police work because of its alert-ness, intelligence, loyalty, and excellent sense of smell. Dobermans average 24-28 in (61-71 cm) shoulder height and are general-ly black with rust-colored markings.

Döblin, Alfred (1878-1957), German-French physician and author. Particularly known for his novels that display traits of expressionism and of the 'new realism'. Döblin was born in Stettin as the son of a Jewish merchant and lived in Berlin as of 1888. It was here that he studied neurology and psychiatry from 1902-1905. He helped to establish the expressionist magazine, *Der Sturm* , in 1910. He served as an army doc-tor during the First World War. After the war, Döblin, using the pseudonym Linke Poot, expressed harsh criticism towards the reac-tionary nature of the Weimar Republic. He fled from Germany in 1933, adopted French nationality and returned in 1945 as a cultur-al worker associated with the French occu-pying forces. He wrote, among others, *Berlin Alexanderplatz; Die Geschichte von Franz Biberkopf* (Berlin Alexanderplatz; The Story of Franz Biberkopf) (1929, filmed in 1931), and *Hamlet oder die lange Nacht nimmt ein Ende* (Tales of a Long Night) (1956).

Dobson fly *See:* Hellgrammite.

Dobzhansky, Theodosius (1900-1975), U.S. biologist, famed for his study of the fruit fly, *Drosophila*. His work demonstrated that a wide genetic range can exist even in a well-defined species and that the greater the 'gentetic load' of unusual genes in a species, the better equipped it is to survive in changed circumstances.
See also: Biology; Fruit fly.

Dock, large-leafed plant (genus *Rumex*), of the buckwheat family with clusters of small green flowers. There are many species throughout the world, some of which are weeds, although the spinach dock is eaten. Sorrel is a dock but appears distinct from the others at first sight.

Doctor *See:* Medicine; Degree, academic.

Doctorow, E(dgar) L(aurence) (1931-), U.S. novelist. His books include *The Book of Daniel* (1971), a historical novel about Julius and Ethel Rosenberg and their chil-dren, *Ragtime* (1975), which interweaves fictional portraits of Sigmund Freud, C.J. Jung, Harry Houdini, and Henry Ford, among others, *Loon Lake* (1980), set during the Great Depression, *Billy Bathgate* (1989), *The Immortals* (1994), *The Waterworks* (1994), and *City of God* (2000).

Documenta, international exhibition of con-temporary visual art. Since 1955, it is organ-ized every four to fives years in Kassel, Germany.

Dodder, parasitic plant (genus *Cuscuta*), that bears no leaves and gains all its nour-ishment from the host plant. There are near-ly 200 species around the world. As each dodder plant develops, it reaches out for a host plant into which it sends suckers that penetrate the living tissues. Eventually the host plant becomes smothered in straggling stems of the dodder.

Dodecanese, group of about 20 Greek is-lands in the southeastern Aegean Sea off Turkey. Except for Rhodes and Kos, the 12 main islands are largely rocky and infertile. In 1912 Italy seized the group from the Turks, but after World War II they were ced-ed to Greece.
See also: Greece.

Doderer, Heimito von (1896-1966), Austrian author, particularly known for his novels *Die Strudlhofstiege* (The Strudlhof Steps; 1951) and *Die Dämonen* (The Demons; 1956), which are situated in and around Vienna. They provide a sharp image of the life of the inhabitants of that city during the second and third decade of the 20th century. Doderer was taken as a prisoner of war by the Russians during the First World War. He did not return to Vienna until 1920. He stud-ied history at the University of Vienna from 1921 until 1925. He became a member of the NSDAP in 1933, he later labeled this a 'theoretical mistake' and burned his party book in 1939. Despite this, Von Doderer served as a pilot during World War II and he returned to Vienna in 1946.

Dodge, family name of two early developers of the automobile. Both **John Francis Dodge** (1864-1920) and **Horace Elgin Dodge** (1868-1920) were born in Michigan and began working with cars in Detroit in 1901. At first they built car parts in their ma-chine shop for the Ford and Olds motor companies, but later they began developing their own automobile. In 1914 they pro-duced a car with an all-steel body. They founded the Dodge Company, which merged with the Chrysler Corporation in 1928.
See also: Automobile.

Dodge, Mary Elizabeth Mapes (1831-1905), U.S. children's author who founded and edited the magazine *St. Nicholas* (1873). She is best known for *Hans Brinker, or The Silver Skates* (1885), a classic of children's literature.

Dodgson, Charles Lutwidge *See:* Carroll, Lewis.

Dodo (*Raphus cucullatus*), extinct turkey-sized flightless bird with strong legs and a big bill, formerly found on the island of Mauritius. The last dodo died around 1681, but a few stuffed birds and skeletons can be seen in museums.
See also: Tanzania.

Dodoma (pop 204,000), capital of Tanzania, located in the central part of the country. It is a marketing and transportation center whose industries include brick manufacturing and clay processing. In 1973 it was selected to replace Dar es Salaam as the capital city, but that move has not yet been effected.

Doenitz, Karl (1891-1980), German admiral, head of the World War II U-boat service and later commander in chief of the German navy (1943-1945). On Hitler's death in 1945 he became head of state and subsequently surrendered to the Allies. He was tried for war crimes at Nuremberg and served 10 years in prison.
See also: World War II.

Doesburg, Theo van (1883-1931), Dutch painter and author. A leader of the de Stijl group, he turned to abstract art in 1916, influenced at first by Piet Mondrian. He taught at the Bauhaus (1921-1923).

A poster for a Dada soirée, designed by Theo van Doesburg (1833-1931). Dada soirées (with the collaboration of Dada artists) were first held in Germany, in 1922. Later, at Van Doesberg's request, they were also held in the Netherlands, in Amsterdam, Drachten, The Hague, Haarlem, Leiden, Utrecht and Rotterdam.

Dog, carnivorous mammal of the family Canidae. The wild dog, usually with long legs, long muzzle, and bushy tail, lives by chasing its prey. Many live in packs. Wild dogs include the raccoon dog of Asia and several South American forms, such as the bush dog and the maned wolf. Domestic dogs are members of the species *Canis fa-miliaris*. There are more than 200 known breeds of highly variable appearance, classified as sporting dogs, nonsporting dogs, working dogs, toy dogs, hounds, and terriers. The dog may have been the first domesticated animal.

Dogbane, plant (genus *Apocynum*), with clusters of small pinkish-white flowers and poisonous leaves and stems. Plants related to dogbane are used in the manufacture of poison for arrows.

Dogfish, any of various small sharks of the family Squalidac. Dogfish rarely reach 5 ft (1.5 m). They have the ugly heads and rough skins of the typical sharks and feed on the bottom of the sea, catching worms, shrimps, fish, and mollusks. The eggs are laid in horny cases. Dogfish are sold as grayfish for human consumption, and their flesh is used as a fertilizer. At one time an oil was extracted from them. They are now best known as subjects for dissection classes.

Dog racing, spectator sport in which people gamble on dogs chasing a mechanical hare (or other lure) around a track which is generally .25 mi (.4 km) in diameter. Greyhounds, the most common racing dog, can reach speeds of over 40 mph (64 kph). Each year over $3 billion is bet on dog-racing.

Dog Star *See:* Sirius.

Dogtooth violet (*Erythronium dens-canis*), also known as adder's tongue or trout lily, wildflower of eastern North America belonging to the lily family. Unrelated to true violets, its flowers are bell-shaped and bear no resemblance to a dog's tooth.

Dogwood, or cornel, name for any tree or shrub of the genus *Cornus*. The bunchberry (*C. canadensis*) is a herbaceous wildflower, and the flowering dogwood (*C. florida*) is a small tree. Some dogwoods are grown as ornamental plants.

Doha (pop. 400,000), or Ad Dawhah, capital of the Middle Eastern state of Qatar. Once a small fishing village, it developed into a major port of the Persian Gulf and important commercial center when Qatar's oil production began in the 1950s. Doha contains the majority of the country's people.
See also: Qatar.

Dohnanyi, Ernst von (1877-1960), Hungarian composer and pianist, conductor of the Budapest Philharmonic Orchestra (1919-1944). His music, influenced by Brahms, includes the lighthearted *Variations on a Nursery Song* (1913) and *Ruralia Hungarica* (1924), both for piano and orchestra.

Doldrums, narrow belt of light, variable winds located between the trade winds near the equator. Calm weather predominates in this low-pressure area; sailing ships can be stranded here for days without wind.
See also: Calms, Regions of.

Dolin, Sir Anton (1904-1983), English cho-

Through the ages, dolls have had several functions. For example, as an 'actor' in a puppet theatre, as an ornament on a musical instrument, or as a model, demonstrating a new fashion trend. In later years, dolls were mainly made for children to play with. Here, we see mechanical puppets from the 1950s, from southern Germany (Puppet Theatre, Munich).

reographer and dancer. He worked closely with dancer Alicia Markova, as her partner, choreographer, and cofounder of several companies. Among the ballet companies he founded were the Royal Ballet and the American Ballet Theater. Among the works he choreographed was *Le Pas de Quatre*. Dolin also wrote several books on dance.
See also: Ballet.

Doll, miniature representation of the human form, used as a toy or, in some societies, a sacred object. The practice of making dolls is an ancient one. Some of the earliest examples, made from a wide range of substances including wood, bone, ivory, and clay, have been found in Pakistan at Mohenjo-Daro (3000 B.C.), and on Babylonian, Egyptian, and Aztec sites. In ancient societies dolls were often entombed with the dead. In America, they are still used in Hopi and Zuni rites. The modern doll has its origin in medieval doll nativity scenes and in the 14th-century fashion dolls of France and England. During the 16th century, Germany became a major center of doll making, noted particularly for its figures carved from wood. Papier-mâché and wax were used in the 19th century as materials for fashioning dolls' heads. Present-day dolls are made from a variety of synthetic materials, their designs incorporating such sales gimmicks as 'voices,' working limbs, and moving eyelids.

Dollar, monetary unit originating in the 16th century as the German thaler, named after the Joachimsthal silver mines in Bohemia. It was used widely in the West Indies and the American mainland in the colonial period because of its standard weight and purity. Divided into 100 cents, it now is the basis of currency of many countries worldwide.

D

Since World War II, the U.S. dollar has become the basic currency unit of the international monetary and economic system. During the 1980s and 1990s the economic success of Germany and Japan has lifted the value of their currency - the German Mark and Japanese yen - to a level that rivals the dollar in international importance.
See also: Money.

Dollar Decade *See:* Roaring Twenties.

Dollar diplomacy, U.S. foreign policy that attempts to protect the nation's political and financial interests through diplomacy. First in use during the presidency of William Howard Taft (1909-1913) in such areas as the Caribbean, it has since been practiced by many U.S. administrations.
See also: Taft, William Howard.

Dollarfish *See:* Butterfish.

Dollinger, Johann Joseph Ignaz von (1799-1890), German Roman Catholic historian and theologian, excommunicated (1871) for rejecting the doctrine of papal infallibility. A professor of ecclesiastical history and law at Munich University (1826-1871), his books include *The Pope and the Council* (1869), which criticizes papal authoritarianism. He was an early leader of the Old Catholics.
See also: Roman Catholic Church.

Dolmen, a crude structure consisting of several standing stones capped by a flat stone.

Dolmens are found in the British Isles (especially Ireland), France (where there are more than 3,400 of them), Algeria, Scandinavia, the Netherlands, Germany, the Middle East, Madagascar, Australia, and Japan. Dolmens were set up in prehistoric times for religious purposes, as places of burial, or as memorials of some important event.

Dolomite, calcium magnesium carbonate mineral; chemical formula $CaMg(CO_3)_2$. There are large deposits of dolomite in the Alps, England, and the United States. It is similar to limestone and is used chiefly as a building material.

Dolomites, mountain range in the eastern Alps, northeastern Italy. The mountains are composed mainly of vividly colored dolomitic limestone. The highest peak is Marmolada (10,965 ft/3,342 m). The Dolomites are a popular tourist and climbing resort. The region's main center is Cortina d'Ampezzo.
See also: Italy.

Dolphin, Pacific spout fish (genus *Coryphaena*), of the family Coryphaenidae. It has a blunt head and forked tail and can swim at great speed. It is a popular food fish in Hawaii, where it is called dorado, or mahi mahi.

Dolphin, any of a family (Delphinidae) of small-toothed whales living in schools and feeding mainly on fish. The largest, the

killer whale (*Orcinus orcat*), also feeds on seals. The best-known is the bottle-nosed dolphin (genus *Tursiops*), a highly intelligent mammal with an amazingly developed system of echolocation for finding food and avoiding obstacles. A second family of dolphins (Platanistidae) lives in fresh water, and includes the Chinese lake dolphin and the blind susu, or Ganges dolphin. The dolphin has been threatened by reckless tuna fishers whose nets entangle the fish.

Domagk, Gerhard (1895-1964), German pharmacologist who discovered the antibacterial action of the dye prontosil red, which led to the discovery of other sulfa drugs. In recognition of this, Domagk was offered the 1939 Nobel Prize for physiology or medicine, but the Nazi government did not allow him to accept it at the time. He received the Nobel Prize medal in 1947.
See also: Pharmacology; Sulfa drug.

Dome, in architecture, oval or hemispherical vault, used to roof a large space without interior supports. The first domes were built around 1000 B.C. by the Persians and Assyrians, but these were small, and the dome did not become architecturally significant until the time of the Romans. The Pantheon in Rome (2nd century A.D.), in which the dome rests on a drum-shaped building, is an outstanding example of the large-scale dome. The Byzantine architects of Hagia Sophia (A.D. 532-537) in Constantinople developed the *pendentive*, a device enabling the construction of a great dome over a square central area. Brunelleschi's dome on the cathedral in Florence has an inner and an outer shell; Sir Christopher Wren's dome for St. Paul's, London, has 3 shells. Modern techniques and lightweight materials permit the spanning of vast areas, as in the case of the Houston Astrodome.
See also: Architecture.

Domenichino (Domenico Zampieri; 1581-1641), Italian Baroque painter noted for the landscape settings of his pictures. He painted large frescoes, notably *The Life of St. Cecilia* (1613-1614), in palaces and churches in Rome.
See also: Baroque.

Dome of the Rock *See:* Jerusalem.

Domesday Book, inventory of most of the land and property in England compiled by order of William the Conqueror (completed in 1086), giving the Norman overlords of the newly conquered country a basis for local control and taxation. Today it is an important source for historians interested in the period before and after the Norman Conquest. The book records not only the value of the land, but also the number of livestock and serfs in each locality.
See also: Norman Conquest; William.

Domingo, Placido (1941-), Spanish operatic tenor. In 1961 he made his Mexican debut as Alfredo in *La Traviata* and his U.S. debut with the Dallas Civic Opera. He sang in Israel (1963-1965) and with the N.Y. City Opera (1965-1967) before joining the

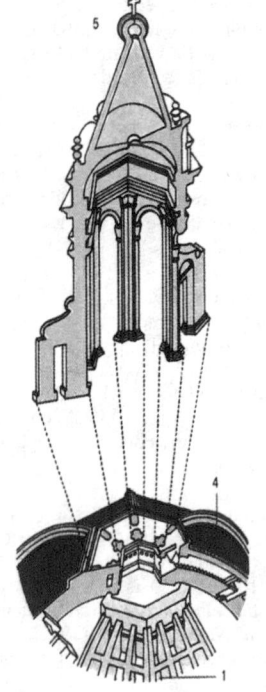

In 1401, Brunelleschi was consulted on the problem of covering an octagonal crossing, the largest since the Pantheon. A pointed dome was adopted, the side thrust being less than a hemispherical dome. Eight major ribs (1) spring from the angles of the octagon, sixteen minor ribs lie between them (2). Tied by horizontal ribs (3) to absorb the main thrust, the lightest filling was inserted between them. The first Renaissance use of a double shell dome — the outer tiled layer is to keep out the damp (4) — clearly shows the major ribs. A passage leads between the two layers to the base of the lantern (5).

Metropolitan Opera (1968). He sings over 60 parts and is one of the most popular tenors of this day.

See also: Opera.

Dominica

Capital:	Roseau
Area:	290 sq mi (750 sq km)
Population:	70,000
Language:	English
Government:	Republic
Independent:	1978
Head of gov.:	Prime minister
Per capita:	US$ 3,700
Monetary unit:	1 East Caribbean dollar = 100 cents

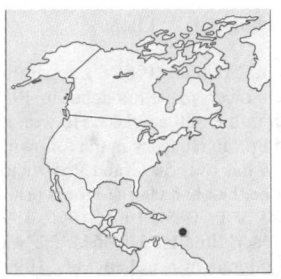

Dominica (official name, Commonwealth of Dominica), independent state, the largest island in the Windward Islands of the Lesser Antilles group, between Guadeloupe and Martinique. Its area is 290 sq mi (751 sq km). The population is largely descended from slaves brought to the island from Africa in the 18th century. The rich volcanic soil produces bananas, coconuts, citrus fruits, and cinnamon. Dominica also exports pumice. Discovered by Columbus in 1493, Dominica was colonized by France in the early 17th century, acquired by Britain in 1805, and became internally self-governing in 1960. In 1978 the island achieved full independence within the British Commonwealth. The capital city is Roseau. During 1979 and 1980, Dominica was hit by three hurricanes that devastated the island. Coups attempted by the military in 1980 and 1981 were unsuccessful. In the 1990's Dominica, Grenada, Saint Lucia, and Saint Vincent and the Grenadines agreed to work toward increased political and economical integration. After 1999, the export of bananas to the EU suffered severely due to restrictive measures. Many steps were taken in order to promote eco-tourism.

Dominican Order, Roman Catholic religious order founded by Saint Dominic and confirmed by Pope Honorius III in 1216. Officially known as the Order of Preachers (O.P.) and sometimes unofficially as the Black Friars, for the black cloak they wear when preaching, the Dominicans grew from a band of priests sent to combat the Albigensian heresy. Priests make up the first order of Dominicans, cloistered nuns the second order, and regular nuns and laymen and women the third order. Throughout their history the Dominicans have been noted for their scholarship and intellectual activity. Thomas Aquinas, Albert the Great, Vincent Ferrer, Catherine of Siena, and Rose of Lima were Dominicans, as were Savonarola and Fra Angelico. As guardians of scholastic theology, Dominicans took part in the Inquisition; in recent centuries they have been in the vanguard of theological and biblical studies.

See also: Dominic, Saint.

Dominican Republic

Capital:	Santo Domingo
Area:	18,704 sq mi (48,422 sq km)
Population:	8,722,000
Language:	Spanish
Government:	Presidential republic
Independent:	1844
Head of gov.:	President
Per capita:	US$ 5,800
Monetary unit:	1 Dominican peso = 100 centavos

Dominican Republic, country in the Caribbean Sea, occupying the eastern two-thirds of the island of Hispaniola. (The western third is Haiti.)

Santo Domingo, founded in 1496 by Bartholomew Columbus, has both modern buildings, and structures that are reminiscent of the old colonial period.

Land and climate. Parallel mountain chains cross the country from northwest to southeast. Between them are the Cibao and Vega Real lowlands, the country's main agricultural areas. The climate is subtropical, with lowland temperatures averaging 70°F (21°C). Annual rainfall averages over 50 in (127 cm), with hurricanes common between Aug. and Nov. Apart from the capital, Santo Domingo, the greatest concentration of people is in and around the rich agricultural valleys. Other major cities include Santiagi and Puerto Plata.

People. The official language of the country is Spanish, and most of the population professes the state-supported religion, Roman Catholicism.

Economy. The economy of the Dominican Republic is agricultural, with sugar the major export. Tourism is also a major source of foreign currency. In addition, the country produces coffee, cocoa, tobacco, and bananas. Industry is concentrated around the capital and, apart from agricultural processing, includes cement, plastic, and textile manufacturing. There is some mining of bauxite and nickel, and tourism is also important.

History. After centuries of turmoil, including conflict between the local population and Spain and Haiti, the independent Dominican Republic emerged in 1844. The new country was long troubled by political strife and economic instability. From 1916 to 1924, it was occupied by U.S. Marines. In 1930, an army revolt brought the dictator General Rafael Trujillo Molina to power. Free elections followed Trujillo's assassination in 1961, but the newly elected left-wing government of Juan Bosch was overthrown by a military coup in 1963. An attempt to reinstate Bosch led to armed intervention by the U.S. in 1965. Joaquín Balaguer served as president from 1966 to 1978 and from 1986 to 1996; he and his successors focused on improving the economy. Under Balaguer's leadership, the Dominican Republic became politically stable and developed one of the strongest economies in Latin America. However, poverty caused many Dominicans to leave the country and emigrate illegally to the United States. In 1998 the Dominican Republic was hit by hurricane Georges. Despite the hurricanes,

D

tourism has become increasingly important. The problem, however, is that the economy of the Dominican Republic is highly dependent on the U.S. In 2002, Joaquín Balaguer, who had controlled politics for over 40 years, died at the age of 95.

Dominic, Saint (1170?-1221), Spanish-born founder of the Dominican order. Sent by Pope Innocent III in 1205 to Languedoc (southern France) to convert the Albigensian heretics, Dominic and his band of priests were successful, and in 1216 he was given papal support for the new order he had established. His feast day is Aug. 4.
See also: Dominican Order.

Dominoes, game for 2 to 4 people, played with flat rectangular blocks usually made from wood, ivory, or bone. The game, introduced to Europe, probably from China, in the middle of the 18th century, is normally played with a set of 28 pieces. The face of each piece is divided into 2 sections, each of which either is blank or has up to 6 dots. The set of dominoes contains every possible combination of numbers from 0-0 (double blank) to 6-6 (double six). During play, each player in turn must attempt to match a number on one of the dominoes or 'bones' in his or her hand with one of the two exposed ends on the table. Failing to do so, the player must draw a further piece from the central pool, or boneyard. Play stops when a player has disposed of all his or her dominoes. A number of variations on the game have been developed, and the number of pieces may also vary.

Domitian (A.D. 51-96), Roman emperor (81-96), son of Vespasian and brother of Titus, whom he succeeded. He governed efficiently but harshly, his last years amounting to a reign of terror. He was assassinated at the instigation of his wife.
See also: Rome, Ancient.

Domus Aurea *See:* Rome.

Donatello (Donatello di Niccolo di Betto Bandi; c.1386-1466), Florentine sculptor, a major figure of the Italian Renaissance. He trained as a metalworker with Lorenzo Ghiberti and as a marble sculptor. His many commissions for the cathedral of Florence include the famous *putti* for the singing gallery. Other major works are *St. George Slaying the Dragon* (1415-1417), the bronze *David* (1432) in the Bargello, Florence, and the equestrian statue known as the Gattamelata Monument (1447-1453) in Padua.
See also: Renaissance.

Donetsk (also Donets'k; pop. c 1,100,000), capital of the Ukrainian province of the same name. Donetsk is located in the Donets River basin. Formerly a small mine settlement, it is now one of the most important industrial and administrative centers in the former USSR. The rich coal deposits of the region are used in the production of iron, steel, and machinery. Also, chemical, construction materials, textile, and leather industry, and food products. It has a university and other institutions for university training and an international airport. Severely damaged during

WW II. Founded in the 1870s, it became Stalino in 1935, but its name was changed back to Donetsk in 1961. The river of the same name (630 mi, 1015 km) is the most important tributary of the Don.
See also: Ukraine.

Donizetti, Gaetano (1797-1848), Italian opera composer. Influenced by Gioacchino Rossini, he developed the traditions of serious and comic opera. His operas include *The Elixir of Love* (1832), *Lucia di Lammermoor* (1835), and *Don Pasquale* (1843). He was an important influence on Giuseppe Verdi.
See also: Opera.

Donjon *See:* Castle.

Don Juan, legendary libertine of Spain, often the subject of dramatic and literary works in which, after a dissolute life, he is led off to hell. The earliest-known dramatization is Tirso de Molina's *The Rake of Seville* (1630). Other versions are by Molière, W.A. Mozart (*Don Giovanni*), Byron, and G.B. Shaw (*Man and Superman*).

Donkey, herbivorous (plant-eating), hoofed mammal (*Equus asinus*), domesticated form of the wild ass. The donkey is related to the horse, but it is smaller and has long ears, a large head and short mane, a tuft of hair at the end of the tail, and no callosities (hardened skin) on the hindlegs. A dark band usually runs along the back and another over the shoulder. Several species of wild asses are found in Africa (*E. asinus*) and Asia (*E. hemonius*), particularly in northeastern India, where large herds wander about the desert regions. The donkey is descended from the African wild ass of Ethiopia. It is much used as a pack animal, and shows tremendous powers of endurance. It is surefooted and intelligent, well adapted to heavy loads over rough terrain. Crossbreeding with a horse produces the mule or the hinny, which are sterile.

Donleavy, J(ames) P(atrick) (1926-), U.S. novelist and playwright. He is known for his black humor vision of life in such works as *The Ginger Man* (1955), *A Singular Man* (1963), *Shultz* (1979), and *That Darcy, that Dancer, that Gentleman* (1991). *The History of the Ginger Man* (1994) is his autobiography.

Donne, John (1572-1631), English metaphysical poet and clergyman. His love poems and religious verse and prose are characterized by sophisticated argument, complex metaphors, and a passionate and direct tone. His imagery relies upon both scholastic philosophy and 17th-century scientific thought. After a long period of exclusion from court life, he took religious orders in 1615 and became dean of St. Paul's, London, where he gave many sermons. His most famous writings are the love-lyrics *Songs and Sonnets*, and the religious works *Holy Sonnets*, *Sermons*, and *Devotions*.
See also: Metaphysical poets.

Don Quixote, classic novel by Spanish author Miguel de Cervantes. Published in two

parts (1605 and 1615), its titular character is a bored landowner whose fantasies of knighthood lead him to perform deeds he sees as courageous but are merely comic. Accompanied by his attendant, Sancho Panza, the two characters represent the practical and the ideal in life.
See also: Cervantes Saavedra, Miguel de.

Don River, river in the Soviet Union, about 1,220 mi (1,930 km) long. Rising in the central Russian upland, about 100 mi (160 km) south of Moscow, it flows generally southward, passes through the 100-mi-(160-km-)long Tsimlyansk Reservoir and empties into the Sea of Azov. A canal, built in 1952, connects the Don with the Volga River. Most of the Don is navigable by barges, except in winter, and it can accommodate oceangoing vessels as far upstream as Rostov, at the head of the river's delta outlet. Leading tributaries are the Donets, Khoper, and Voronezh rivers. The Don's water is used to generate electricity and for irrigation.

Doodlebug *See:* Ant lion.

Doohan, Michael (1965-), Australian motorcycle racer, made his debut in 1989 on a Honda in the 500 cc class. He won his first Grand Prix in Hungary in the following year. He now has over 50 Grand Prix victories to his name. Doohan claimed the world title in the 500 cc in 1994, 1995, 1996, 1997, and 1998, each time on a Honda. He was seriously injured in a fall in May 1999 while training for the Spanish Grand Prix.

Dooley, Thomas Anthony (1927-1961), U.S. physician, author, and a founder (1957) of Medico, an international medical aid organization for underdeveloped countries. In *Deliver Us from Evil* (1956), he tells how he supervised care for 600,000 Vietnamese refugees in Haiphong in 1954-1955.

Doolittle, Hilda (1886-1961), U.S. poet who lived in Europe after 1911. She wrote under the pseudonym H.D. H.D. was one of the first imagists in the United States, and she continued to develop the imagist style in her poetry. Works include *Sea Garden* (1916), *The Walls Do Not Fall* (1944), and a novel *Bid Me to Live* (1960).

Doomsday Book *See:* Domesday Book.

Doping, substances of which it is assumed that they increase one's performance. An innocent form is coffee, due to the presence of stimulating caffeine. Doping has long been a part of sports and, in the course of time, has developed from substances that 'merely' shift one's limit concerning fatigue, to muscle strengthening substances (anabolic steroids), growth inhibitors, etcetera. Anti doping tests involve testing the saliva, urine, and blood of sportsmen and sportswomen after a game or during training; the difficulty with such tests is the fact that the list of forbidden drugs and methods that is commonly used is usually not in keeping with medical developments. In addition to ethical aspects (unfair competition), there are also medical objections to doping: lengthy and

D

excessive use may lead to addiction, paralysis, and even death.

Doppler effect, apparent change in frequency of waves of light or sound due to the motion of an observer relative to the source. If either source or observer is approaching the other, the waves are bunched together, like the folds of a squeezed accordion. The observer encounters more waves in a given period of time than would be the case if both observer and source were stationary, so the observed frequency of the waves increases. Waves of high frequency have a shorter wavelength than waves of low frequency. In the case of light, a shortening of the wavelength makes the object seem bluer than normal, because blue light has the shortest wavelength. In the case of sound, the pitch, as of the whistle of an approaching train, will seem higher. When the source and the observer are moving apart, the waves are stretched out, like the folds of an extended accordion. Because the speed of the whole wave train is constant-the speed of light or the speed of sound-the waves pass less frequently. The distance between waves (the wavelength) seems to increase. If the waves are of light, the object appears redder than normal. If the waves are of sound, the note changes to a lower pitch. Named after its discoverer, the Austrian physicist Christian Johann Doppler (1803-1853), the effect has proved of particular use to astronomers in analyzing the light of distant objects in space. The light of these objects is reddened by the Doppler effect, from which it follows that the universe is expanding.

Dorado *See:* Dolphin.

Doré, Gustave (1832-1883), French engraver, illustrator, and painter. He created dreamlike, grandiose scenes in a fantastic, bizarre style and is known especially for line engravings of unusual power in editions of Balzac's *Contes Drolatiques* (1855), Dante's *Inferno* (1861), Cervantes's *Don Quixote* (1863), and the Bible (1866).

Dorians, people of ancient Greece. Originating from the lower Balkans, they probably defeated the Achaeans and conquered the Peloponnese between 1100 and 950 B.C., subsequently extending their influence to the Aegean Islands, Crete, Sicily, and parts of Asia Minor, Africa, and Italy. *See also:* Achaeans; Peloponnesus.

Dormancy *See:* Germination.

Dormouse, squirrel-like, nocturnal rodent of the family Gliridae that feeds on seeds, shoots, and small animals. There are several species scattered over Europe, Asia, and Africa. All hibernate. The common dormouse (*Muscardinus avellanarius*) of Europe and western Asia grows as large as 4 in (10 cm) long. The Romans fattened dormice for eating.

Dos Passos, John (Roderigo) (1896-1970), U.S. novelist and writer of social history. His trilogy, *U.S.A.* (1937), depicts 20th-century life up to 1929, making use of innovative, collage-like reportage techniques. Other

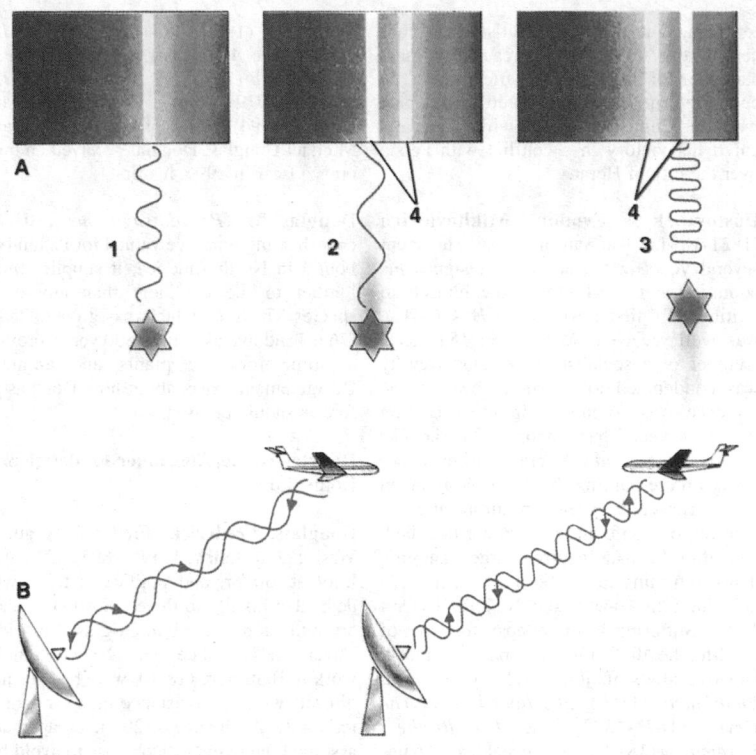

As the speed of light is great, the speed of the movement of source or observer should be quite large, for the Doppler effect to be detected. In 1842, Doppler predicted that, as all wavelengths that are emitted by a receding star are lengthened to a terrestial observer, the colour of such a star must be redder than that of an approaching star. This theory proved to be untrue, as for the approaching star, the infrared radiation would be shifted into the red, and the blue into the ultraviolet. However, the shift in wavelengths may be observed as a shift in the spectral lines. A star approaching an observer will seem to have a shorter wavelength (blue shift), a receding star will have a shorter wavelength (red shift) (A). The Doppler shift is also used to measure aircraft speed (B), by measuring the length of the radar wave that is reflected by a moving aircraft, and comparing this with the original wave.

works include *Manhattan Transfer* (1925), *District of Columbia* (a trilogy; 1952), and *Midcentury* (1961).

Dos Santos, José Eduardo (1942-), Angolan politician. Up until 1970, when Dos Santos joined the independence movement in Angola, he worked in the Russian oil industry. Following the declaration of independence (1975), he developed into an influential figure within the MPLA (Popular Movement for the Liberation of Angola). He succeeded Neto as president in 1979 and expanded his power in the years after that. In practice, Dos Santos was also the leader of the government. A multiparty system was introduced in the 90s. Ever since independence, there has been a civil war between supporters of the MPLA and UNITA (National Union for the Total Independence of Angola), which became even more violent when Dos Santos won the elections in 1993 and UNITA refused to acknowledge the outcome. International pressure led to new negotiations, in which Congo, Namibia, and Zimbabwe participated. In 1995, the negotiations led to peace and the leader of UNITA was included in the cabinet as Vice President. However, at the end of 1995, the civil war flared up again and the battle between the MPLA and UNITA continued.

Dost Mohammad (1793-1863), Amir (= ruler) of Kabul, whose conquests resulted in Afghanistan's present borders and who was the first to establish a central government by defeating the autonomous chieftains. He established the Barakzay dynasty, after conquering Kabul, the capital of Afghanistan in 1826 and Qandahar in 1834. The English conquered Afghanistan during the First Afghan War and banished Dost Mohammed

The common, or fat dormouse (*Myoxus glis*) looks for food at night, and dozes in a tree during the day. It has a reputation of being one of the sleepiest of all animals.

D

to India. The general dissatisfaction concerning this state of affairs resulted in mass slaughter of the English, after which he could return. He even entered into a pact with the English in 1855, which later secured his victory in a conflict with Persia over the city of Herat.

Dostoyevsky, Fyodor Mikhaylovich (1821-1881), Russian novelist. He spent several years in the army but resigned his commission in 1844 to devote himself to writing. His first novel, *Poor Folk* (1846), was well received. Arrested in 1849 as a member of a socialist circle, Dostoyevsky was condemned to be shot; however, the sentence was commuted in the execution yard to 4 years' hard labor in Siberia. *The House of the Dead* (1862) tells of his experiences there. During the 1860s he founded two journals and traveled in Europe after his consumptive wife and his brother had died, and after he had incurred large gambling debts, returning to Russia in 1871. In 1876 he edited his own monthly *The Writer's Diary*. Suffering from epilepsy for most of his life, he died after an epileptic attack. Dostoyevsky's major novels, *Crime and Punishment* (1866), *The Idiot* (1868), *The Devils* (1871-1872), and *The Brothers Karamazov* (1879-1880), reveal his deep understanding of psychology and the problems of sin and suffering.

Dou, Gerard (1613-1675), Dutch painter. A pupil of Rembrandt (1628-1631), Dou developed the tradition of small, minutely finished pictures with enamel-like surfaces, painting portraits, still lifes, landscapes, and scenes from everyday life.

Douala (pop. 1.3 mln.), largest city and major port of Cameroon, west central Africa, on the Wuori River, near the Gulf of Guinea. A commercial and transportation center, its chief economic activities are shipping and related businesses. Developed as a center of slave trade after the Portuguese arrived in 1472, it was later ruled by the Germans and then by the French.
See also: Cameroon.

Double star *See:* Binary star.

Doughnut, small cake made of sweetened and flavored leavened dough, shaped as a 'nut,' or ring, deep-fried in fat, and sprinkled lightly with sugar. Friedcake and cruller, despite traditional differences, are alternative names.

Doughty, Charles Montagu (1843-1926), English traveler and author. *Travels in Arabia Deserta* (1888), written in Elizabethan style, describes his experiences living and traveling with the Bedouins in the 1870s.

Douglas *See:* Man, Isle of.

Douglas, Kirk (Issur Danielovitch Demsky; 1916-), American film actor and film producer, performer of bold character roles. Films include *Out of the past* (1947), *Detective Story* (1951), *Lust for Life* (1956), *Gunfight at the OK Corral* (1957),

Spartacus (1960), *Seven Days in May* (1964), *The Arrangement* (1969), *Once is Not Enough* (1975), *The Fury* (1978), *The Villain* (1979), *Tough Guys* (1986), and *Greedy* (1994). Father of actor and producer Michael Douglas. Douglas received an honorary Oscar in 1996, his first.

Douglas fir (*Pseudotsuga menziesii*), a cone-bearing pine tree valued for its lumber. Found in North America, it supplies more lumber to the continent than any other species. The trees, which may grow to 250 ft (76 m) and live as long as 800 years, provide a home for rare plants and animals. Disagreement exists about how Douglas fir forests should be used.

Douglas-Home, Alexander Frederick *See:* Home, Lord.

Douglass, Frederick (Frederick Augustus Washington Bailey; 1817?-1895), U.S. abolitionist, orator, and political activist who dedicated his life to the eradication of slavery and support for black rights. Born into slavery in Tuckahoe, Md., he was sent to work in Baltimore (1826), were he educated himself with the assistance of a slave master's wife. At the age of 20, he escaped and assumed the name of Douglass to avoid being identified. In 1841 Douglass began lecturing for the Massachusetts Antislavery Society and throughout the 1840s protested against segregation. He spoke on trains and in churches, and, in some cases, had to be physically removed from passenger trains. His autobiography, *Narrative of the Life of Frederick Douglass* was published in 1845 (he later revised this work in two addional publcations - *My Bondage and My Freedom* (1855) and *Life and Times of Frederick Douglass* (1881). Fearing reprisal for the publication, Douglass moved to England where he continued his struggle against prejudice. In 1847 he returned to the United States and established the anti-slavery newspaper, North Star, in Rochester, N.Y. His home in Rochester became a stop on the Underground Railroad, among the network of homes and hiding places that aided slaves in their escape to freedom. During the Civil War (1861-1865), he encouraged blacks to join the Union Army. He also had several meetings with President Abraham Lincoln to discuss the issue of slavery. He later served as a U.S. minister to Haiti (1889-1891).
See also: Abolitionism.

Doukhobors, pacifist religious sect of Russian origin. They derive their name from the Russian word meaning 'spirit wrestlers.' Nonconformist peasants formed the first Doukhobor communities in Russia in the 18th century; they held that all men are equal and should be treated as brothers. Therefore they refused to fight or kill. The sect was repeatedly persecuted by the Russian government and the Orthodox clergy. Under Nicholas II the Doukhobors were driven from their farms. They went first to Cyprus in 1898 and then in 1899 to Canada, where about 7,500 immigrants settled.

Doum palm, or doom palm, fruit-bearing tree of the palm family found in the Middle

East and northern and central Africa. The tree has an oval fruit about the size of an apple. The Ancient Egyptians often put large quantities of the fruit in the tombs of their pharoahs.

Dove, name sometimes given to a small member of the pigeon family, for example, the rock dove (*Columba livia*). There is no real difference between pigeons and doves, and species are labeled arbitrarily.

Dove, Arthur Garfield (1880-1946), U.S. abstract painter. Recognized as an early proponent of abstract expressionism, he painted fluid, poetic compositions based on natural forms and created constructions similar to collages. Never a popular success, he was supported by photographer and art dealer Alfred Stieglitz.
See also: Abstract expressionism.

Dover (pop. 35,000), seaport in Kent, England. It is situated on the Strait of Dover, the narrowest part of the English Channel. The first settlement on the site was the Roman town of Dubris. The Saxons built fortifications on the cliffs above the town, later replaced by the Norman castle that stands on the chalk cliffs. In the Middle Ages, Dover became one of the privileged Cinque Ports, a group of channel ports given seafaring power in return for their contribution to England's sea defense. The main center for the evacuation from Dunkirk during World War II, it was heavily damaged by bombardment.
See also: England.

Dover (pop. 32,000), city, capital of Delaware and seat of Kent County, situated in central Delaware on the St. Jones River, 40 mi (64.4 km) south of Wilmington. Surrounded by a rich farming area, Dover serves as a marketing, shipping, and processing center. Among its industries are hosiery, rubber goods, and plumbing supplies. William Penn, the founder of Pennsylvania, planned the town in 1683, and it was laid out in 1717. In 1777 Dover replaced New Castle as the state capital. Dover is the site of Wesley Junior College and the Delaware State College.

Dover, Strait of, narrow passage separating southeastern England from northern France, connecting the English Channel with the North Sea. It is about 19 mi (30 km) across at its narrowest point. The chief ports are Dover and Folkestone in England, Calais and Boulogne in France. Of great strategic importance, the strait was the scene of the first repulse by the English of the Spanish Armada (1588), the Dover (antisubmarine) Patrol of World War I, and the evacuation from Dunkirk (1940). The strait is frequently crossed by long-distance swimmers.

Dow, Herbert Henry (1866-1930), pioneer in the U.S. chemistry industry. In 1897 Dow founded the Dow Chemical Company in Midland, Mich. At first Dow focused on deriving the maximum value from brines (concentrated solutions of salt and water), developing insecticides and pharmaceuticals. The first important producer of iodine, Dow was

eventually granted more than 100 patents and became one of the world's largest chemical companies.
See also: Chemistry.

Dow Jones Industrial Average, most frequently cited gauge of U.S. stock market performance. Compiled since 1884, the Dow Jones Average is a composite of the prices of 30 leading industrial stocks. In addition, Dow Jones compiles a Transportation Average (20 stocks), a Utility Average (15 stocks), and a Combined Average (all 65). Other key market indicators are Standard and Poor's 500 and the New York Stock Exchange Price index (all stocks traded on the exchange). On April 17, 1991 the Down Jones Industrial Average broke the 3000 mark with a record 3004.06.
See also: Stock exchange.

Dowland, John (1563-1626), English composer and lutenist, best known for his songs and the collection of lute pieces *Lachrimae* (1604). He traveled to France, Italy, Germany, and Denmark in the service of various kings and princes. From 1612 he served in the court of James I.

Down's syndrome, formerly called mongolism, chromosomal aberration resulting in mental retardation and physical abnormalities. In about 95% of cases of Down's syndrome, there is an extra chromosome 21, making 3 in all, hence its technical name trisomy 21. The overall incidence is about 1 in every 700 live births, but there is a marked variability depending on maternal age: In the early childbearing years, the incidence is about 1 in every 2,000 live births; for mothers over age 50, it rises to about 1 in every 45 live births. The cause of this genetic disorder is unknown. Infants tend to be placid, rarely cry, and have flabby muscles. Physical and mental development are both retarded and the mean IQ is about 50. Down's syndrome children have smaller than average heads and moon-shaped faces. Their eyes are slanted, usually with epicanthal folds above the eyelids. The bridges of their noses are flattened, and their mouths are often held open because of their large, protruding, furrowed tongues. Their hands are short and broad, with a single crease across the palm, and short fingers. Their feet have wide gaps between the first and second toes, and there is a furrow on each sole. The life expectancy of these children is decreased by heart disease and by susceptibility to acute leukemia. Most of those without a major defect survive to adulthood, but the aging process seems accelerated, with death occurring in their 40s and 50s.

Dowser *See:* Divination.

Dowson, Ernest Christopher (1867-1900), English poet, one of the Decadents of the 1890s. From a life of misery and squalor he produced a delicate, lyrical poetry on themes of love and lost childhood.

Doyle, Roddy (1958-), Irish author of a number of novels that are comical on the surface, but hold deep tragedy and a great compassion for all those who live on the fringes of Irish society. After *Your Granny is a Hunger Striker* (1982), *The Commitments* (1987; filmed by Alan Parker in 1991), *The Snapper* (1990) and *The Van* (1991), Doyles made his great breakthrough with *Paddy Clarke Ha Ha Ha* (1993), about a ten-year-old street boy in a working class area in Dublin, which was awarded the prestigious Booker Prize. This was followed by *The Woman Who Walked Into Doors* (1996), which is told by an abused woman, and *A Star Called Henry* (1999), on the subject of the Irish struggle for freedom.

Doyle, Sir Arthur Conan (1859-1930), British writer, creator of the detective Sherlock Holmes, featured in many short stories and 4 novels. A doctor, soldier, and campaigner for law reform, he also wrote historical novels like *Micah Clarke* (1889) and science fiction like *The Lost World* (1912). In later life he became an adherent of spiritualism.

D'Oyly Carte, Richard (1844-1901), English impresario. He produced Gilbert and Sullivan's first operetta, *Trial by Jury*, in 1875. He founded the D'Oyly Carte Opera Company (1878) and built the Savoy Theatre, London, as a stage for works by Gilbert and Sullivan (1881).
See also: Gilbert and Sullivan.

Drabble, Margaret (1939-), an English author. She is noted for her strong and complex female characters who are intelligent and witty. Often they are seeking a balance between maternal desires, career demands, and emotional independence. Drabble gained popularity with the novel *The Garrick Year* (1964), which depicts a woman beginning to discover and define herself after her husband becomes engrossed in his acting career. Drabble was born in Sheffield. She graduated from Cambridge in 1960. Other works include: *The Ice Age* (1977) and *The Gates of Ivory* (1991).

Draco (fl. c.621 B.C.), lawgiver in Athens. His code made serious and trivial crimes alike punishable by death-hence the term 'draconian' to describe any harsh legal measure. Solon later repealed all the laws except those dealing with homicide.
See also: Greece, Ancient.

Dracula, novel (1897) by English writer Bram Stoker about a Transylvanian vampire count. Dracula became the subject of many horror films. The name, meaning 'dragon,' was applied to Vlad IV the Impaler, the cruel 15th-century Walachian prince upon whom Stoker based the character.

Draft, military, or conscription, system of raising armed forces by compulsory recruitment. The modern practice is more aptly described as selective service. Obligatory military service dates back to ancient times, but modern conscription began in the late 18th century when Napoleon I imposed universal conscription of able- bodied males. Peacetime conscription became standard practice in Europe in the 19th century, except in Britain, where it was not imposed until just prior to World War II (wartime conscription was practiced in both Britain and the United States during World War I). In Israel the draft is applied to unmarried women as well as to men.

Dragon (Greek: *drakon*, 'serpent'), legendary monster, usually represented as a firebreathing, winged serpent or lizard with crested head and large claws. Apart from the wingless Chinese and Japanese dragons, which are considered beneficent, dragons have usually been regarded as symbols of evil, and dragon-slayers, for example Saint George, as saints and heroes.

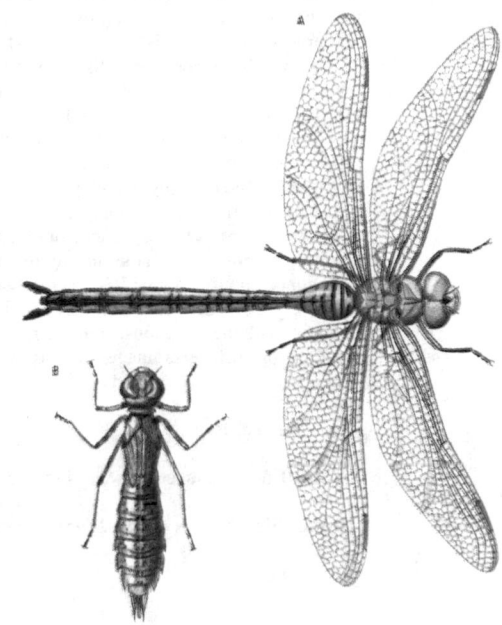

A common European dragonfly (A), *Anax imperator*, like other species, flies as fast as 35-60 m/h (56-97 km/h). Its two sets of netlike wings cannot be folded and remain outstretched continually. Dragonflies have long, brightly colored bodies and huge compound eyes that contain 20,000 to 30,000 facets. A dragonfly nymph (B) lives on river bottoms, never emerging until it becomes an adult.

Dragonfly, insect of the order Odonata, indentifiable by its long, slender, abdomen, 2 pairs of transparent wings, each covered in a network of veins, and large compound eyes, which may contain 30,000 separate facets. Dragonflies are superb fliers, some being credited with speeds of 60 mph (97 kmph), and can dart forward, hover, then shoot forward again. Each dragonfly patrols an area, usually near water, where it feeds on insects. The eggs are laid in water, and the nymphs (larvae) live underwater for a year or more. They have gills inside the intestine and can shoot water out of the rectum in a form of jet propulsion. The largest living dragonfly, from Borneo, has a 7-in (18-cm) wingspan, but fossilized remains have been found of a crow-sized dragonfly with a 27-in (68.6-cm) wingspan.

Drainage, removal of surplus water from land. Without drainage, successful crop pro-

D

D

duction and retention of soil fertility would be impossible. Wet lands are difficult to work with modern machinery, and most crops suffer from root injury if grown on water-logged ground. Undrained soils are structureless, with tightly packed subsoils full of stagnant water. Buildings and houses benefit from drainage, which is essential for sanitation and good health. Roads are not passable in wet weather unless provided with drains. Undrained swamps afford breeding grounds for malaria-carrying mosquitoes, and accumulated sewage becomes a source of disease epidemics. Early drainage consisted mainly of open ditches, often using natural watercourses. During the 18th century farmers began to employ patterns of underground channels covering whole fields, which collected and discharged surplus water into several outfalls. The invention and mass production of U-shaped clay or concrete drain tiles in England in the mid-19th century opened the way for the wide adoption of tile draining. On clay land, *mole draining* is effective: A mole plow moves over the surface of the ground, drawing a cylindrical mole through the subsoil, making a channel about 3-4 in (7.5-10 cm) wide, some 2 ft (60 cm) below the surface. This method, with the variations, comes under the heading of surface drainage. Excess water can also be pumped off land.

Draisine *See:* Bicycle.

Drake, Edwin Laurentine *See:* Petroleum.

Drake, Sir Francis (1543-1596), English admiral, the first English explorer to sail around the world (1577-1580). During his circumnavigation aboard the Golden Hind, Drake seized a fortune in booty from Spanish settlements along the South American Pacific coast. He was knighted on his return by Queen Elizabeth I. In 1587 he destroyed a large part of the Spanish fleet at anchor in Cadiz harbor. The following year he was joint commander of the English fleet that, with the help of a storm, dispersed and destroyed the Spanish Armada (1588).

Dram *See:* Apothecaries' weight.

Drama *See:* Theater.

Dramamine, brand name of the drug dimenhydrinate, used to prevent motion sickness and to control the nausea and vomiting associated with certain illnesses. An antihistamine, Dramamine may act as a mild sedative; it can cause drowsiness.

Draughts *See:* Checkers.

Dravidian, member of a subgroup of the Hindu race, including some 100 million people of (mainly) southern India. They are fairly dark-skinned, stocky, broad-nosed, and commonly dolichocephalic (longheaded). The **Dravidian languages** are a family of some 22 languages, perhaps the most important from a philological point of view being Tamil, texts which date back to at least the 1st century B.C.

Drawbridge *See:* Bridge; Castle.

Drawing, pictorial representation by means of line on any surface. An artistic expression, drawing has developed in 3 main directions: as the independent, preparatory sketch for work in another medium; as the preliminary sketch eventually incorporated into another medium (for example, as the basic outline for a painting, fresco, or mural); and as an independently conceived and executed work. Little is known of the early history of drawing in European cultures. With the advent of the Renaissance and the emphasis on perspective and detailed rendering, drawing became the object of serious study. The availability of good-quality paper by the end of the 15th century also influenced the development of drawing. Drawing was the subject of several treatises by Renaissance theoreticians, and around the end of the 16th century the collection of drawings became a hobby of the rich. In the 18th century drawing became a prerequisite for the study of painting and sculpture in the academies. In England the art of caricature and political cartooning was brought to a high level in the satirical drawings of William Hogarth and Thomas Rowlandson, as it was in France by Honoré Daumier and in Spain by Francisco de Goya. The 19th-century neoclassicist Jean Ingres, the romanticist Théodore Géricault, and the early-modern masters Paul Cézanne, Vincent van Gogh, Henri Toulouse-Lautrec, Auguste Renoir, Edgar Degas, and Georges Seurat were eminent. Great draftsmen of the 20th century include Pablo Picasso, Joan Miró, Paul Klee, and Vasili Kandinsky. Drawing plays a great

A cutter dredge uses a two-legged bracing system, to resist the action of the cutter. A suction pipe, situated close to the cutter, takes care of the debris and discharges it, away from the vessel.

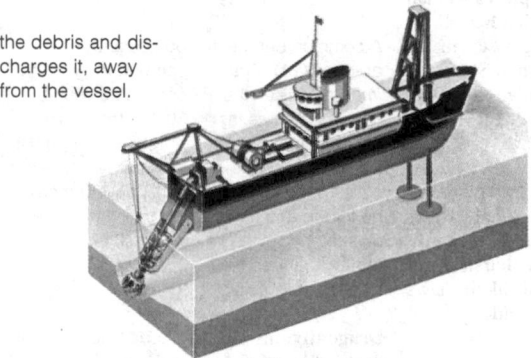

A dipper dredge uses four legs to brace the vessel against the cutting action of the shovel.

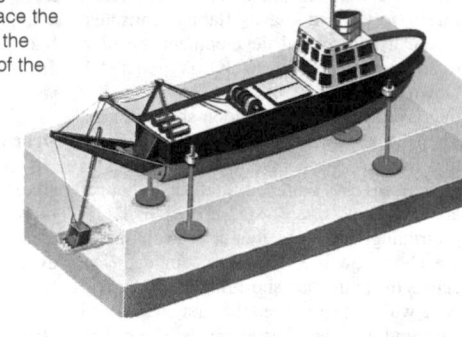

A bucket dredge uses an endless chain of buckets. The debris is discharged into a barge.

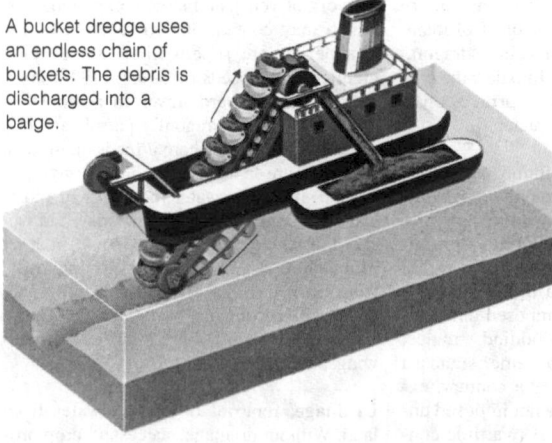

A dragline dredge draws a toothed bucket along the sea bed.

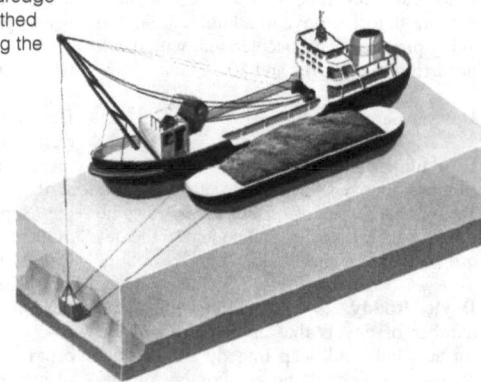

part in commercial art, illustrating advertisements, textbooks, brochures, and articles in magazines and periodicals. The availability of high-grade materials and the development of media have widened the modern graphic artist's choice of technique.

Dreadnought, British battleship (built 1906) whose design became the model for warships of the first half of the 20th century. Weighing 18,000 tons and capable of traveling at 21 knots (24 mph/38 kmph), the *Dreadnought* carried ten 12-in (30.5-cm) guns. At the time of its completion there was nothing afloat to match its speed and firepower. By the outbreak of World War I 9 *Dreadnought*-class ships and 12 other big-gun battleships were in service in the British navy.
See also: Battleship.

Dream, mental activity that occurs during sleep. Dreaming occurs during the REM (rapid-eye movement) period of sleep. Dreams are often quite vivid, though research indicates that most people forget the majority of their dreams. The interpretation of dreams has played an important part in pre-modern cultures, and major theories of dreams and their significance have been put forward by Sigmund Freud, Carl Jung, and others. In the latter 20th century, scientific thinking about dreams has focused on research into the physiological characteristics and mechanisms of sleep and the activity of the brain while in the sleeping state.

Dredging, removal of silt, mud, and sand from harbors and navigation channels to keep them open for shipping. Of the 3 kinds of dredging vessels, the *bucket dredger* is the most widely used: A continuous moving chain of buckets extends down beneath the keel into the mud to be dredged. The *grab dredger* is a floating crane that drops a heavy scoop, or grab, into the mud and then hauls it to the surface. A more modern type is the *suction*, or *hydraulic dredger* which sucks up the mud through a pipe that is lowered to the seabed. The biggest hydraulic dredgers can dredge and discharge 20,000 tons or more in an hour. Dredgers may discharge their 'spoil' into their own holds; into hopper barges moored alongside; or by means of a floating pipeline, directly onto the land. Dredgers are also used for mining deposits of heavy minerals that occur in alluvial gravels (deposited by running water). Tin, gold, platinum, and diamonds are often mined in this way.

Dred Scott case, suit brought by Dred Scott, a slave from Missouri, on the grounds that temporary residence in a territory in which slavery was banned under the Missouri Compromise had made him free. The majority opinion of the U.S. Supreme Court in 1857, read by Chief Justice Roger Taney, held that Scott could never be a citizen of any state and therefore could not sue his owner in federal court. Taney also declared the Missouri Compromise was unconstitutional. This decision inflamed and divided the nation, making the Civil War all but inevitable.
See also: Slavery; Civil War, U.S..

Dreiser, Theodore (1871-1945), U.S. novelist whose naturalistic fiction is concerned with the dispossessed and criminal. He wrote about the impersonal social and economic forces that compel behavior, and generally with grimmer realities of U.S. life. His novels include *Sister Carrie* (1900) and *An American Tragedy* (1925).

Dresden (pop. 474,000), historic German city on the Elbe River, administrative center of the district of Dresden, in southeastern Germany. Products include porcelain, chemicals, various light-engineering products, and beet sugar. Its river location and site on a network of railroads link Dresden with other major eastern German cities. It is also famous as a cultural center and contains world-famous art museums. Dresden originated as a Slav fishing village. The town developed during the 13th century and became the residence of the Saxon sovereigns in 1485. In the late 17th and early 18th centuries many rococo and baroque buildings were constructed. It survived the Battle of Dresden (1813), Napoleon's last great victory, but many historic buildings were destroyed in a devastating air raid in World War II which claimed thousands of lives and razed the city. The city has since been largely restored.
See also: Germany.

Dresden china, or Meissen ware (after the town near Dresden where china has been made since 1710), Europe's first true porcelain. The process of its manufacture was discovered by Johann Friedrich Böttger in 1707.

Dreyfus, Alfred (1859-1935), Jewish French army official who became the center of a bitter political quarrel known as the Dreyfus affair.
See also: Dreyfus Affair.

After having been falsely sentenced for high treason, Alfred Dreyfus (1859-1935) was reduced to the ranks in front of his soldiers in 1895.

Dreyfus Affair, French political scandal of the Third Republic. In 1894, Alfred Dreyfus (1859-1935), a Jewish army captain, was convicted of betraying French secrets to the Germans. Further evidence pointed to a

Major Ferdinand Walsin Esterhazy as the traitor, but when tried (Jan. 1898), Esterhazy was acquitted on secret, forged evidence. Dreyfus's conviction had aroused anti-Semitism, and although evidence against him had been forged, the army was reluctant to admit the error. As public interest in the case was aroused, it became known that the Roman Catholic Church supported the conviction. After Esterhazy's acquittal, the French novelist Émile Zola published an attack on the army's integrity, *J'accuse* ('I accuse'), which roused intellectual and liberal opinion to a furor. With the suicide of an army officer who had acknowledged the forgeries and with Esterhazy's flight from France, a new court-martial began, but Dreyfus was found 'guilty with extenuating circumstances' (Aug. 1899). Public opinion was outraged, and in Sept. the government gave him a pardon. He served in World War I and retired a lieutenant-colonel. The scandal had thrown government, army, and church into disrepute. Legislation followed that led to separation of church and state (1905). The original verdict against Dreyfus was quashed in 1906.
See also: Dreyfus, Alfred.

Drill, tool for cutting or enlarging holes in hard materials. *Rotary drills* are commonly used in the home for wood, plastic, masonry, and sometimes metal. In metallurgy the mechanical drilling machine, or drill press, operates one or several drills at a time. Most metallurgical drills are of high-speed steel. Dentists' drills rotate at extremely high speeds, powered by an electric motor or by compressed air; their tips (of tungsten carbide or diamond) are water-cooled. Rotary drills are also used for deeper oil well drilling: A cutting bit is rotated at the end of a long, hollow drill pipe, new sections of pipe being added as drilling proceeds. The *percussive drills* are used for rock-boring, for concrete and masonry, and for shallower oil well drilling. Rock drills are generally powered by compressed air, the tool rotating after each blow to increase cutting speed. The pneumatic drill familiar in city streets is also operated by compressed air. Ultrasonic drills are used for brittle materials; a rod attached to a transducer is placed against the surface, and to it are fed abrasive particles suspended in a cooling fluid. It is these particles that actually perform the cutting.

Drill, planting implement consisting of 4 parts: a hoe or opener that digs a row, a hopper that holds the seed, a seed meter that ensures even spacing of seeds in the furrows, and a chain or press wheel that covers the seed with soil.

Drive-in, U.S. marketing and service innovation designed to allow people to use the services provided without leaving their cars. At various times, the concept has been applied to restaurants, banks, movies, and churches.
See also: Restaurant.

Drought, excessively dry climatic conditions, generally due to absence of rainfall. Permanent drought conditions prevail over approximately one-third of the world's land

D

D

Gaseous drugs, such as anesthetics, nicotine, and opium, are absorbed through the lungs by inhalation (1). Drugs like steroids, which are easily inactivated by digestion or liver metabolism, can be absorbed by the mouth (2). Medicines may be absorbed by the stomach (3), or — in case of drugs that will be destroyed by stomach acid — given as capsules, which will dissolve in the small intestine (4). In both cases, the drugs will pass through the liver, before reaching the bloodstream. Injection (5) is the most direct route into the bloodstream; this way, the drug does not pass through the liver first. Rectal administration (6) is another path, avoiding inactivation by the liver.

surface, the sand deserts alone covering a total area more than twice as large as the United States. A region is classed as arid or drought-stricken when the annual precipitation is below 10 in (25.4 cm). Under such conditions, farming becomes extremely difficult. Recently, however, progress has been made in dry land reclamation by means of new irrigation schemes. Experiments for inducing artificial rainfall through cloud-seeding techniques have also been promising.
See also: Climate.

Drowning, death caused by suffocation due to immersion in water or any other liquid. In most cases of drowning, the heart continues to beat for several minutes after loss of consciousness. This means that mouth-to-mouth resuscitation can save the victim's life by renewing the flow of oxygen.

Drug, substance affecting the body and that may be used to treat illness or alleviate symptoms. Antibiotics, antitoxins, sulfa drugs, insulin, narcotics, contraceptives, stimulants, depressants, the special drugs used in chemotherapy to treat cancers are just a few of the many drugs that have transformed medical practice.
Drugs may be derived from organic substances, they may be manufactured through chemical modifications of natural products, or they may be synthetic. Some can be purchased over the counter, while others require a doctor's prescription. Drug research and the manufacture of new drugs has become a highly complex, technologically sophisticated, and highly capitalized industry. The modern pharmacopeia is so large that spe-

cialists must keep abreast of new developments through constantly revised standard references.
Side by side with scientific progress in the development of new drugs and their applications to medicine, there has been an increase in the manufacture, trade, and use of various narcotics. As a result, social, political, and religious institutions have tried to formulate responses to substances that, in one form or another, raise far-reaching ethical, moral, and legal questions.

Drug abuse, non-medical use of certain chemical substances that can induce unusual states of consciousness, relieve pain, increase endurance, or heighten sensation. The use of such substances very likely predates the historical record, and cultures and civilizations have taken varying attitudes to prohibition or legalization of various substances. In modern times, drug abuse refers to dependence upon any of a range of narcotics (marijuana, hashish, morphine, opium, and their derivatives), stimulants (cocaine and amphetamines), depressants (alcohol, barbituates, and sedatives), and many hallucinogenic agents.
See also: Drug.

Drug addiction, physical rather than psychological dependence upon an intoxicating substance, such that deprivation causes the addict to experience withdrawal. Common drugs that can produce addictions include alcohol, nicotine (in tobacco), caffeine, barbiturates, and opiates (opium, morphine, heroin). Not all who take dependence-producing drugs become dependent on them.

Withdrawal from addictive drugs such as alcohol can itself be dangerous, and detoxification is often medically supervised.
See also: Drug; Narcotic.

Drug Enforcement Administration (DEA), U.S. government agency that enforces federal laws against narcotics. Through 19 divisional offices in the U.S., the DEA also governs the manufacture and distribution of controlled substances. Established in 1973 as part of the U.S. Department of Justice, the DEA cooperates with the Federal Bureau of Investigation to prevent drug trafficking, and with state and local law enforcers and the agencies of other nations to combat illegal drug abuse and trade.
See also: Drug; Narcotic.

Druids, ancient Celtic priestly order in Gaul (France), Britain, and Ireland, respected for their learning in astronomy, law, and medicine, for their gift of prophecy, and as lawgivers and leaders. Little is known of their religious rites, though human sacrifice may have been involved. Because of their power, they were banned by the Romans.

Drum, musical instrument of the percussion family, common to most cultures. It consists of a shell, cylindrical or conical, with a membrane, or skin, stretched over one or both ends. The skin is struck with the hand or with sticks. The principal drum in the symphony orchestra is the kettledrum, or tympanum, whose pitch can be adjusted by the tightening or loosening of the membrane. Other orchestral drums include the tenor, snare, and bass drums and the tamborine. Snares are important in popular maintaining rhythm in popular marching music.

Drum, any of about 200 species of fishes of the family Sciaenidae. Some species produce a deep sound by means of an air bladder in the abdomen.

Drumlin *See:* Glacier.

Drummond de Andrade, Carlos (1902-1987), Brazilian poet and writer of prose, important representative of the second phase of Brazilian modernism. He is regarded by many as one of the greatest modern poets and intellectuals of Brazil.
He initially worked as a journalist and belonged to the modernist group of the city Belo Horizonte, which was established around 1925. He reputation as one of the greatest innovators of Brazilian poetry followed publication of his first collection, *Alguma poesia* in 1930. Since then, Drummond de Andrade has created an oevre of poetry and prose of great thematic wealth and inimitable style, which made him the intellectual 'mentor' of an entire generations of Brazilian writers and students. He also wrote, among others, the collection *A rosa do povo* (1945).

Druses, or Druzes, Islamic sect living in Lebanon, Syria, Israel, and the United States. They form a closed community, and most of their doctrines are kept secret. They have their own scriptures, and profess monotheism and the divinity of al-Hakim, sixth caliph (996-1021) of the Egyptian Fatimid dynasty.

Dry cleaning, use of liquids other than water to clean fabrics. In the United States, perchlorethylene is used in addition to petroleum solvents. Trichlorethylene is favored in other countries. The garments are placed in a washer along with the solvent, which removes grease and oil. Dust, dirt, lint, and other insoluble particles are removed by agitation and are carried away in the cleaning fluid, which is filtered and recycled. Solvent is removed in a centrifuge, and the fabric is dried. Spots and stains are removed by a specially trained 'spotter,' who uses chemicals appropriate for the type of fabric and stain. Finally, the garments are pressed with a steam press.

Dryden, John (1631-1700), English poet, dramatist, and literary critic. Dryden's career began around the time of the Restoration (1660). He became poet laureate in 1668 and historiographer royal in 1670. His plays include *Marriage à la Mode* (1672) and *All for Love* (1677). *Essay of Dramatick Poesie* (1668) did much to establish the primacy of Shakespeare and to promote English dramatic approach in place of the academicism of the Continent. Among his many great poems are *Absalom and Achitophel* (1681) and *Mac Flecknoe* (1682) brilliant satires, and *Religio Laici*, setting forth his religious credo. After the ascension of William of Orange, Dryden no longer the English laureate, worked on translations, notably of Vergil (1697).

Dry farming, type of agriculture without irrigation used in areas where less than 20 in (50 cm) rainfall per year prevents the use of traditional methods of farming. After harvest the land is tilled and kept free of weeds to reduce loss of moisture. Where crops are sown in spring, stubble of the previous year's crop is often allowed to stand over winter to trap snow. In very dry areas ground is left fallow in alternate years, allowing it to store up moisture. Fields are contoured and clods of dead vegetable matter are kept in the fields to prevent water runoff and make possible more efficient use of rainfall. Dry farming is frequently practiced in the U.S. and Canadian West, the Great Plains, the Mediterranean basin, the former Soviet Union, and interior areas of Australia and Asia. Among the crops appropriate for dry farming are corn, sorghum, and wheat. Crops grown this way are usually small in size and are quicker to mature than those grown in more moist areas.
See also: Agriculture.

Dry ice, common name (originally a trade name) for solid carbon dioxide (CO_2). Since it does not melt, but sublimates (turns directly into a gas), dry ice is a more efficient coolant than ordinary ice and does not corrode containers. It is much used in long-distance transportation of perishable products such as ice cream and meat. Because dry ice is usually at a temperature of -110°F (-43.3°C) or lower, it damages the skin on contact
See also: Carbon dioxide.

Eight Hausa instrumentalists from northern Nigeria combine in playing the shantu (5), a horn instrument, the sarewa (6), or bamboo flute, the duma (1), a gourd drum and the goge (4), a stringed instru ment. The silver flute (7), the obodo (2), or talking drum, and the gangi drum (3) are also played.

D

Two or more kettledrums have been in every standard orchestra since the 18th century. Brought to Europe from the Middle East in the 13th century, at first, they were just used in cavalry bands. Once in the orchestra, they became the only drums tuned to a specific pitch. The pitch is determined by the size of the brass or copper bowl, and, more importantly, by the tightness of the calfskin head. In the 18th century drum (top right), the four tuning screws had to be hand-turned individually, but the modern drum (left and bottom right) has a mechanical pedal, allowing the pitch to be changed easily during performance.
1 head
2 collar
3 tuning rods, attached to the pedal
4 bowl
5 external tensioning
6 pedal
7 castors

D

Dry rot, wood decay caused by a fungus that feeds on wood, making it lighter, weaker, and more brittle. It is sometimes found in houses. Dry rot does not attack living trees. Despite its name, dry rot cannot live in dry wood, and a good way of avoiding it is to use well-seasoned timber and ensure that there is good ventilation around the structure.

Dry Tortugas, group of 7 coral islands about 50 mi (80 km) west of Key West, Fla. They were discovered in 1513 by Juan Ponce de León, who gave them the Spanish name for the turtles with which the islands abound. The largest of the group, Loggerhead Key, is approximately 1 mi (1.6 km) in length.

DT's *See:* Delirium tremens.

Dualism, any religious or philosophical system characterized by a fundamental opposition of two independent or complementary principles. Among religious dualisms are the unending conflict of good and evil spirits envisaged in Zoroastrianism and the opposition of light and darkness in Gnosticism and Manichaeism. The Chinese complementary principles of *yin* and *yang* exemplify a cosmological dualism, while the mind-body dualism of René Descartes is the best-known philosophical type. Dualism is often opposed to monism and pluralism.

Duarte, José Napoleón (1925-1990), president of El Salvador 1980-1982 (appointed) and 1984-1988 (elected). His nation suffered from a civil war and attendant economic crises throughout his public life. A Christian Democrat, he promoted democracy and reconciliation as his nation's only hopes, but his efforts were in vain. Terminally ill, he declined to run again for office in 1989. *See also:* El Salvador.

Du Barry, Marie Jeanne Bécu, Countess (1743-1793), last mistress of Louis XV of France. Her years as mistress (1769-1774) were marked by her generosity and good nature but little political influence. She was executed in Paris for aiding royalist émigrés during the French Revolution.

The Hare's Path (1964) represents a change in Dubuffet's work. From 1962 on, it was more colourful, and it took on the effect of a jigsaw puzzle, with its patterns of irregular lines (Stedelijk Museum, Amsterdam).

Dubayy (pop. 674,000), one of the emirates of the United Arabic Emirates; 1506 sq mi (3900 sq km). Capital of the same name (pop. 300,000).

Dubcek, Alexander *See:* Czechoslovakia.

Dublin (Baile Atha Cliath; 1,057,000), city capital of the Republic of Ireland (Eire) and of County Dublin. Located at the mouth of the Liffey River and Dublin Bay on the Irish Sea, Dublin is the political and cultural center of Ireland. Its fine buildings include Four Courts, the Custom House, Trinity College, the National Library, Museum and Gallery, and the Royal Irish Academy. There is also a famous medical center and zoological gardens dating from 1830, as well as the Abbey Theatre and University College. English rule, which severely restricted Dublin's commercial development, was finally removed after the Easter Rebellion (1916) and the establishment of the Irish Free State (1921).
Dublin is an industrial seaport, and the city manufactures stout, whiskey, and textiles. There is a direct rail and steamer link to London.
See also: Ireland.

Dubois, Eugène (1858-1941), Dutch anatomist and physical anthropologist who in 1891-92, in Java, discovered the fossilized bones of a human-like creature who walked erect. Dubois named his discovery *Pithecanthropus erectus*. It led to the theory that there was a single 'missing link' in the chain of evolution joining apes and human beings. It is now generally believed that there were various intermediary forms in human evolution, of which *Pithecanthropus erectus* was one.
See also: Anthropology; Prehistoric people.

Du Bois, W(illiam) E(dward) B(urghardt) (1868-1963), African American educator and author. He was a proponent of equality for blacks, and later for Pan-Africanism, a movement to coordinate the struggle for equal rights of all people of African descent around the world. Professor of economics and history at Atlanta University (1897-1910), and head of its sociology department (1934-1944), his many works include *The Philadelphia Negro* (1899), *The Souls of Black Folk* (1903), and *Black Reconstruction* (1935). He also edited *The Crisis*, the magazine of the NAACP until 1932. Increasingly alienated from the United States, he joined the Communist Party in 1961 and moved to Ghana, where he died in self-imposed exile.
See also: African Americans.

Dubos, René Jules (1901-1982), French-born U.S. microbiologist who developed tyrothricin (1939), the first antibiotic to be used clinically. He wrote more than 30 books, including *So Human an Animal* (Pulitzer Prize, 1969), and founded the René Dubos Center for Human Environments.
See also: Antibiotic; Microbiology.

Dubrovnik (pop. 49,000) city in Croatia, on the Dalmatian coast of the Adriatic Sea. It is a major tourist center; the chief attractions are the medieval walled section, called Old

Town, and an annual music, drama, and dance festival. Dubrovnik was founded by Romans in the seventh century A.D. and was later inhabited by Slavs. It became a strong merchant republic and remained virtually independent under successive Byzantine, Venetian, Hungarian, and Turkish rule. Napoleon I abolished the republic in 1808. Dubrovnik was made a part of Austria in 1815. In 1918 it was incorporated into what became Yugoslavia. During 1991-1992, the city suffered severe damage as a result of the war that occurred when Croatia broke away from Yugoslavia.

Dubuffet, Jean (1901-1985), French artist influenced by spontaneous primitive amateur art, known as *art brut* (raw art). He used gravel, tar, and other unusual materials to produce fantastic impasto paintings that constitute fierce protests against conventional aesthetic criteria.

Duccio di Buoninsegna (1255?-1319?), Italian painter, first great master of the Siennese school. Combining Byzantine austerity with French Gothic grace, Duccio's work strongly influenced the development of Renaissance painting. The altarpiece *Maestà* is regarded as his masterpiece.

Duchamp, Marcel (1887-1968), French artist, a pioneer of dadaism, cubism, and futurism, initially influenced by Paul Cézanne. Duchamp often used common objects as art. This is the so-called 'ready-made' art, which includes the well-known controversial *Fountain*-nothing more than an ordinary toilet. The motive behind such displays was to propel the viewer into examining his or her

Marcel Duchamp's 'ready-made' *Bicycle Wheel* (1913) anticipated Dadaism in its rejection of traditional artistic subject matter.

criteria for art. His *Nude Descending a Staircase, No. 2* (1912), made up of superimposed images to suggest movement rather than to represent a figure, shocked the U.S. public. Having settled in New York in 1915, he became a U.S. citizen in 1955.
See also: Dada; Surrealism.

Duck, aquatic bird, any of the smaller members of the family Anatidae, which also contains the geese and swans. The word is properly used to describe the females of many members of the Anatidae, the term for the male being *drake*. Ducks are, broadly, of 3 types: surface-feeding (dabbling), diving, and fish-eating. The most familiar are the dabblers such as the mallard, which is found throughout the Northern Hemisphere and is the ancestor of the domestic duck. Many ducks are killed for sport and food. Their down (soft layer of feathers), particularly that of the eider duck, is of commercial importance.

Duckbill *See:* Platypus.

Duck hawk, name used in the United States for the peregrine falcon, a bird that can fly at speeds of more than 200 mi (320 km) per hour. Peregrines range from 13 to 19 in (33 to 48 cm) long. They fly high and dive at tremendous speeds, killing their prey (ducks and shorebirds) upon impact. The peregrine falcon was the first animal in the United States declared an endangered species.

Duckweed, aquatic plant (genus *Lemna*) with small round leaves, no stem, and a few rootlets, and simple flowers. Duckweeds float on the surface of still water, forming an almost continuous layer, and sink in winter.

Ductility, plastic property of certain substances, notably metals, which allows them to be drawn into the form of wires or extruded through an aperture without rupturing or returning to their original shape. Gold is the most ductile of all metals, but silver, platinum, copper, aluminum, and iron also exhibit a high degree of ductility. Hot glass can be drawn into very fine threads, though it is very brittle at ordinary temperatures.

Dudayev, Dzokhar (1944-1996), Chechen military leader and politician. General Dudayev, who received an education at the military aviation school, was an air force officer of the Soviet Union until 1990. He was a member of the Communist Party from 1968 until 1991. In October 1991, Dudajev seized power in the Russian republic and unilaterally declared independence. President Jeltsin sent troops to Chechen in December 1994 to support the pro Russian opposition in order to keep the rebellious Dudayev under control, a decision that ignited a violent war between the Russian national army and Dudayev's supporters. Dudayev was killed near the Chechen capital Groznyy during Russian bombardments in April 1996.

Duel, prearranged armed combat between 2 persons, usually in the presence of witnesses, for the purpose of deciding a quarrel, avenging an insult, or vindicating the honor of one of the combatants or a third party. While the purpose in modern times was seldom to kill the opponent, deaths did occur, and public outrage resulted in the banning of duels in most modern nations. The earliest form of duel was trial by battle, which probably originated among the Germanic tribes and became established in Europe in the early Middle Ages. The accuser threw down a gauntlet (glove) in the presence of a judge, and the opponent picked it up as a sign of acceptance of the duel. The belief was that God defended the right cause. Judicial duels died out in France in the 16th century but took place in England as late as 1818. Private duels or duels of honor were particularly common in France, and participants were often killed. Henry IV's edict of 1602 declared persons fighting unauthorized duels guilty of treason, but dueling remained popular, and duels for political reasons were frequent during the 19th century.

Dufay, Guillaume (1400?-1474), French composer. Attached to Cambrai Cathedral from 1445, he was an early master of counterpoint and wrote church music and songs, developing the mass in a graceful style.

Dufy, Raoul (1877-1953), French painter. He was influenced by fauvism, cubism, and the works of Cézanne. He is best known for lively sporting scenes in brilliant colors.

Dugong, or sea cow, (*Dugong dugong*) seal-like aquatic mammal found around the coasts of the Indian Ocean from Madagascar to Australia. Dugongs live in family groups, feeding on the leaves and roots of sea plants, which they root up with their thick, bristly lips. Hunted for their hide, meat, and oil, their numbers have been greatly reduced.

Duisburg (pop. 535,000), trading and manufacturing city in western Germany. The largest inland port in Western Europe, Duisburg is located where the Ruhr and Rhine rivers meet. It is a major producer of iron and steel.
See also: Germany.

Duisenberg, Willem Frederik (1935-), Dutch economist and politician (Dutch Labour Party). Duisenberg was a staff member of the International Monetary Fund in Washington (1965-1969) and Professor of Macro Eeconomics in Amsterdam (1970-1973). As minister of finance (1973-1977), he aimed to reduce the financial deficit and to control the public sector. For this reason, he came into conflict with his party on a regular basis. He became the managing director of the Dutch National Bank in 1981, president of the European Monetary Institution in 1997, the predecessor of the European Central Bank, and one year later, on 1st July 1998, the first president of that same European Central Bank. Duisenberg resigned his post at the European Central Bank in 2003.

The mallard (*Anas platyrhynchos*) is a dabbling duck, feeding in ponds and marshes. The male (rear) has a green head and brown breast separated by a white neck ring.

Following a series of political maneuvers and insults directed against him, Vice-President Aaron Burr challenged Alexander Hamilton to a duel of honor, which took place July 11, 1804. Hamilton refused to fire but was fatally wounded by Burr's shot.

D

D

Alexandre Dumas achieved fame with such historical adventure novels as *The Three Musketeers, The Count of Monte Cristo* and *The Man in the Iron Mask.*

Dukas, Paul Abraham (1865-1935), French composer and critic. Best known for *The Sorcerer's Apprentice*, written in 1897 in the lively symphonic form known as *scherzo*, Dukas also composed the opera *Ariadne and Bluebeard* (1907) and the ballet *The Peri* (1912).

Duke, Geoffrey (1923-), English motorcycle racer, became world champion six times at the beginning of the 50s. Duke began his career at Norton and claimed three world titles (both the 350 and the 500 cc in 1951). He transferred to Gilera in 1953, and went on to become the 500 cc world champion three more times. Duke was known for his virtually immaculate style of driving.

Dukenfield, William Claude *See:* Fields, W.C..

Dulcimer, musical instrument consisting of a set of strings stretched across a thin, flat soundbox and struck with mallets. Of ancient origin, it is still used in the folk music of central Europe, where it is called the cimbalom. The Kentucky dulcimer, a U.S. folk instrument, is plucked.

Dulles, name of 2 prominent U.S. lawyers and statesmen. **John Foster Dulles** (1888-1956) was U.S. secretary of state under President Dwight D. Eisenhower (1953-1959), employing a strong foreign policy to block Communist cold war expansion. He was legal counsel at the World War I peace conference, worked on the UN charter during World War II, and negotiated the Japanese peace treaty (1951). His brother, **Allen Welsh Dulles** (1893-1969), an intelligence official, negotiated the Nazi surrender in Italy in World War II. He directed the Central Intelligence Agency 1953-1961, considerably influencing foreign policy, as in the U.S.-backed Bay of Pigs invasion of Cuba.

Duma, name for several elected assemblies in tsarist Russia in 1906. The first 2 dumas (1906 and 1907), instituted by Nicholas II, were radical and were swiftly dissolved by Nicholas. The third and fourth (1907-1912 and 1912-1917), though restricted, introduced some reforms. Revolution in 1917 did away with the institution.

Dumas, name of two 19th-century French authors, a father and his illegitimate son. **Alexandre Dumas père** (1802-1870) wrote the famous historical novels *The Three Musketeers* (1844) and *The Count of Monte Cristo* (1845). **Alexandre Dumas fils** (1824-1895), his son, won fame with his tragic play *La Dame aux Camélias* (*Camille*; 1812), which formed the basis of Verdi's opera *La Traviata*. He also wrote moralizing plays aimed at the reform of social evils.

Du Maurier, name of 2 English novelists. **George Louis Palmella Busson du Maurier** (1834-1896), caricaturist, illustrator, and novelist, is best known for his novels *Peter Ibbetson* (1891) and *Trilby* (1894). **Daphne Du Maurier** (1907-1989), his granddaughter, wrote romantic novels. Her most famous work is *Rebecca* (1938).

Dumbarton Oaks Conference, meeting of diplomats of the 'Big Four' (China, United States, USSR, and England), held Aug. 24-Oct. 7, 1944, at the Dumbarton Oaks estate in Washington, D.C. Its discussions were the first major step toward establishing a postwar international security.
See also: United Nations.

Dunant, Jean Henri (1828-1910), Swiss businessman, writer, and philanthropist. In 1859, French and Sardinian troops defeated Austrian forces in the Battle of Solferino in northern Italy. The fighting cost 40,000 casualties, including thousands of wounded left helpless on the field. Dunant, with the help of volunteers, gave aid to as many battle victims as possible. In 1862 he published *A Memory of Solferino*, and traveled through Europe urging creation of volunteer committees to care for war-wounded. His idea led to a conference in Geneva in 1863, where the Permanent International Committee for Relief to Wounded Combatants was organized. This committee, later called the International Committee of the Red Cross, recommended that volunteer societies be formed in every country. In honor of Switzerland, where the conference was held, the symbol of the societies was designed as a white flag with a red cross, the reverse of the Swiss flag. In 1901 he received the Nobel Peace Prize.
See also: Red Cross.

Dunbar, Paul Laurence (1872-1906), African American poet and novelist. His poems about black rural life were influenced by the sentimental dialect poems of James Whitcomb. His works include *Lyrics of Lowly Life* (1896) and the novel *The Sport of the Gods* (1902).

Dunbar, William (c.1460-1520), Scottish poet. He became a priest and was employed by James IV on court business. His poems show great satiric power, originality, versatility, and wit.

Duncan, Isadora (1878-1927), U.S. pioneer of modern dance. Encouraging a sponta-neous personal style, she danced in a loose tunic, barefoot, to symphonic music. After European concert successes, she founded schools of dancing in Germany, the USSR, and the United States. She was strangled by a scarf caught in a car wheel.

Dundee (pop. 165,700), major industrial center and seaport on the east coast of Scotland. An important trading center since the Middle Ages, Dundee developed the world's largest jute industry during the 1800's. When the jute industry declined, workers turned to light engineering industries.
See also: Scotland.

Dung beetle *See:* Scarab.

Dunham, Katherine (1910-), U.S. choreographer, dancer, and anthropologist known for her interpretations of Afro-Caribbean dance forms. She toured extensively with her own company and also worked as choreographer on Broadway musicals and motion pictures. She is the author of *Katherine Dunham's Journey to Accompong* (1946) and also wrote an autobiography and numerous articles.

Dunkerque, or Dunkirk (pop. 71,000), seaport in northern France, on the English Channel, 10 mi (16 km) from Belgium. It is a shipbuilding, oil-refining, and food-processing center and railway terminus. In World War II some 1,000 vessels evacuated 337,000 trapped British and Allied troops from the town (May 27-June 4, 1940).
See also: France; World War II.

Dún Laoghaire, seaport town on the east coast of Ireland, 7 mi (11 km) southeast of Dublin. Dun Laoghaire was named in 1920 after an Irish king who lived in the 400s. Once a fishing village, it grew into a large residential town serving Dublin after the construction of a harbor was begun in 1817.
See also: Ireland.

Dunning, John Ray (1907-1975), U.S. physicist whose research on the discharge of neutrons from uranium fission contributed to the development of the atomic bomb. Using a *cyclotron*, Dunning produced high energy particles for changing one kind of atom into another.
See also: Physics.

Dunsany, Lord (1878-1957), Irish author and dramatist who created a credible fantasy world in such plays as *The Gods of the Mountain* (1911) and *A Night at an Inn* (1916). His more than 50 books include verse plays, novels, and memoirs.

Duns Scotus, John (1265?-1308?), Scottish philosopher and theologian. He joined the Franciscans in 1280, was ordained in 1291, and taught at Cambridge, Oxford, Paris, and Cologne. His system of thought, embodied chiefly in his commentary on Peter Lombard's *Sentences*, was adopted by the Franciscans and was highly influential. Typical of his scholasticism, and contrary to the thought of St. Thomas Aquinas, he asserted the primacy of love and the will over

reason. He was the first in the West to defend the Immaculate Conception.
See also: Scholasticism.

Duodenum, first part of the small intestine, extending from the pylorus valve of the stomach to the jejunum. The human duodenum is horseshoe-shaped and about 10 in (25 cm) long.
See also: Intestine.

Duong Van Minh (1916-2001), South Vietnamese general and politician. He led the struggle against a few Buddhist sects under President Ngo Dinh Diem. Duong remained neutral during the first coup against Diem (1960), but he was one of the leaders during the second (1963). However, he was not politically ambitious and did not gain much influence, reaching retirement age and leaving for Thailand. President Thieu requested his return in 1968. Duong became a crystallization point for the 'Third Force' between Thieu and the communists. Following the ceasefire (1973), Duong demanded that Thieu resign from the presidency and that the 'Third Force' participate in the negotiations. Following the January offensive by the communists, Thieu withdrew (April) and Duong became president. He capitulated after the evacuation of the Americans (30th April). He was released a few days later.

Duplicator, any of various machines that make copies of two-dimensional materials from a master copy. Three of the most common duplicating machines are the spirit, the stencil, and the offset duplicator. As distinct from a photocopier, all three require the preparation of a master copy, a special form from which the copies are made.

Du Pont, U.S. industrial family of French origin. **Pierre Samuel du Pont de Nemours** (1739-1817), French economist and statesman, publicized the Physiocrats' doctrines. He was a reformist member of the Estates General (1789) and secretary general of the provisional government (1814). He fled to the United States in 1799 and, having returned to France in 1802, fled again in 1815. His son **Éleuthère Irénée du Pont** (1771-1834) established a gunpowder factory near Wilmington, Del., in 1802. The company expanded enormously during the Mexican, Crimean, and Civil wars under Éleuthère's son **Henry du Pont** (1812-1889), who in 1872 organized the 'Gunpowder Trust' that soon controlled 90% of explosives output. **Alfred Irénée du Pont** (1864-1935), **Thomas Coleman du Pont** (1863-1930), and **Pierre Samuel du Pont** (1870-1954) reorganized the firm in 1902, and after World War II it exploited the valuable dye-trust patents confiscated from Germany. Under Pierre's brothers **Irénée du Pont** (1876-1963) and **Lamont du Pont** (1880-1952) the firm built up an immensely powerful synthetic chemicals industry, developing rayon, cellophane, neoprene, nylon, and other materials.

Du Pont Company, one of the world's largest manufacturers and marketers of chemicals and chemical products. Founded in 1802 by Éleuthère Irénée du Pont, the company began by producing gunpowder; in 1880 it began to produce high explosives, and later expanded into applications of cellulose in lacquers, adhesives, and plastics. Since the early 20th century, Du Pont has expanded its list of products, of which there are now over 40,000. Du Pont manufactured plutonium during World War II, and since 1950 it has operated a plant in South Carolina for the Atomic Energy Commission. The company pioneered the development of such widely used synthetic fibers as Orlon acrylic and Dacron polyester, as well as Teflon, a utensil coating that prevents sticking.

Duralumin, any of a group of aluminum-copper alloys. Typically made of 95% aluminum, 4% copper, 0.5% magnesium, and 0.5% manganese, duralumin is widely used in the aircraft industry because of its lightness and hardness.
See also: Alloy.

Durand, Asher Brown (1796-1886), U.S. painter and engraver, a founder of the Hudson River School. He made his reputation by engraving John Trumbull's painting *The Signing of the Declaration of Independence*. He painted realistic landscapes and portraits, and also designed banknotes.
See also: Hudson River School.

Durant, William Crapo (1861-1947), U.S. automobile executive. He founded the General Motors Corporation in 1916 with the aid of Louis Chevrolet (1879-1941), but lost control of General Motors in 1920.

Durant, Will(iam James) (1885-1981), U.S. educator and popular historian. He wrote the lively bestseller *The Story of Philosophy* (1926) and, with his wife **Ariel** (1898-1981), the 11-volume *Story of Civilization* (1935-1975).

Duras, Marguerite (1914-1996), French writer, associated with the New Wave in France during the 1950s and 1960s. Her works include the novels *The Sea Wall* (1950), *Moderato Cantabile* (1958), *La Douleur* (1985), and *C'est Tout* (1995), and the film scripts *Hiroshima Mon Amour* (1959) and *The Lover* (1984).

Duras, Oldrich (1882-1957), Czech chess master, active merely from 1903-1914. Though Duras was a gifted master, he withdrew once World War I began. His name lives on in a number of theoretical variations of opening moves. In 1908, he shared first place with Maróczy and Schlechter in Vienna, and with Schlechter in Prague. In 1912, he shared first place with Rubinstein in Breslau.

Durban (pop. 1,1 mln.), city in the Republic of South Africa, province of Natal. It is the third-largest city in southern Africa and South Africa's biggest seaport, providing a major outlet to the Indian Ocean, equipped with ship-repair yards and floating docks. Exports include coal, mineral ores, and agricultural products; imports include petroleum, grain, and timber. Durban's manufactures include fertilizers, textiles, and metalware, along with sugar and petroleum refining. Durban's beaches and parks and African and Indian markets have made it one of the country's leading tourist resorts, and it is also a cultural center.
See also: South Africa.

Dürer, Albrecht (1471-1528), German painter and engraver. He introduced the Italian Renaissance outlook and style to Germany, tempering it with the Gothic tradition. Dürer visited Venice (1494-1495 and 1505-1507) and was influenced by Jacopo Bellini, Andrea Mantegna, and Leonardo da Vinci. He became court painter to the emperors Maximilian I (1512) and Charles V (1520). Dürer produced a huge output of masterly, vividly detailed drawings, engravings, woodcuts, and paintings. His themes include religious subjects, plant and animal studies, and evocative landscapes in watercolor. His woodcuts include the 16 subjects of *The Apocalypse*; among his well-known engravings are *Death and the Devil* and *St. Jerome in His Cell*; his paintings include *Adam and Eve* and *Four Apostles*.
See also: Gothic art and architecture.

Albrecht Dürer (1471-1528) painted this water colour of a clump of grass in 1503. The painting shows his accurate observation of nature (Albertina, Vienna).

Durham (pop. 27,000), fortress town in northern England. A natural defensive site, Durham is located on a peninsula formed by an incised meander of the River Wear. The site was chosen by William I the Conqueror (r. 1066-1087) as a bulwark against the Scots to the north. The peninsula was fortified by a wall early in the 12th century, and most of the wall has been preserved. Durham Cathedral was built (in the 11th and 12th centuries) on the site of a shrine to the 7th-century ecclesiastic St. Cuthbert. Many tourists visit Durham Cathedral and the Norman castle that houses the University of Durham.
See also: England.

Durham, John George Lambton, 1st Earl of (1792-1840), British statesman. He authored Durham's Report, which laid down the basic principles of British colonial administration. A radical Whig, he was lord privy seal (1830-1833) and helped draft the

D

A bark beetle of the genus *Dendroctonus* bores through tree bark (1) until it reaches the outer sapwood. There, the male excavates a nuptial chamber (2) and mates with the female. The female beetle continues digging, occasionally making a materials chamber (3), where she dumps the debris. She burrows vertically into the wood, creating a birth chamber (4), and lays her eggs. Each larva then tunnels perpendicularly (5) away from the birth chamber and stops to develop into a pupa. It finally emerges from the tree as a mature beetle.

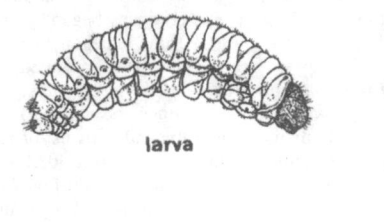

larva

pupa

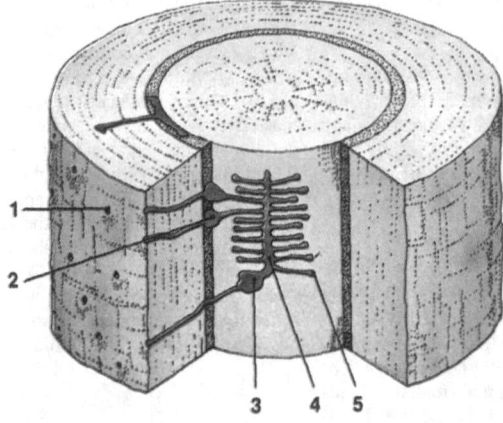

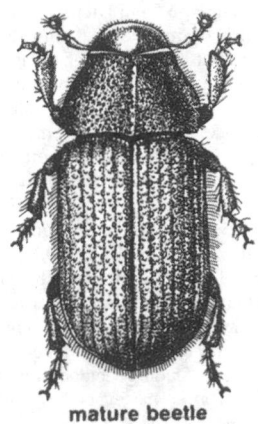

mature beetle

Reform Bill of 1832. Governor general of Canada (1838), he was criticized for his leniency toward rebels and resigned.

Durkheim, Émile (1858-1917), pioneer French sociologist. He advocated the synthesis of empirical research and abstract theory in the social sciences and developed the concepts of 'collective consciousness' and the 'division of labor.' His works include *The Rules of Sociological Method* (1895) and *Elementary Forms of Religious Life* (1912).
See also: Sociology.

The Swiss dramatist Friedrich Dürrenmatt has attracted international interest with his darkly comedic plays about the corrupting influence of power.

Durocher, Leo (1905-1991), U.S. baseball player and manager. He began his major league career in 1925. A brilliant defensive shortstop, he played for the New York Yankees, St. Louis Cardinals, Cincinnati Reds, and Brooklyn Dodgers. He went on to manage the Brooklyn Dodgers and New York Giants, winning the world championship with those teams in 1941, 1951, and 1954, and became manager of the Chicago Cubs in 1966. Also known as 'Leo the Lip,' Durocher is famous for his colorful, argumentative personality and fiercely driving team spirit. He shocked the sports world with his motto, 'Nice guys finish last.'

Durrell, Lawrence George (1912-1990), English novelist and poet, known for the lyricism and vitality of his style. His works include *The Alexandria Quartet-Justine* (1957), *Balthazar* (1958), *Mountolive* (1958), and *Clea* (1960)-and several volumes of poetry and travel literature.

Dürrenmatt, Friedrich (1921-1990), Swiss playwright and novelist. His often bizarre tragicomedies, which employ biting satire, include *The Visit* (1956) and *The Physicists* (1962). He also wrote crime novels.

Duse, Eleonora (1859-1924), Italian dramatic actress, rivaling Sarah Bernhardt as the greatest actress of her period, notably in plays by Henrik Ibsen and by Duse's lover, Gabriele D'Annunzio.

Dushanbe (pop. 580,000), capital and largest city of Tajikistan in central Asia. Established in 1926 when 3 small villages merged, Dushanbe is an important transport junction and accounts for a third of the Tajik Republic's industrial output, which includes textiles, automatic looms, electric cable, and refrigerators.
See also: Tajikistan.

Düsseldorf (pop. 572,000), city in Germany, 25 mi (40 km) northwest of Cologne. It is the capital of the state of North Rhine-Westphalia. Düsseldorf is an important Rhine River port, a road and railroad junction for the industrial Ruhr region, a West European air terminal, and a leading manufacturing and financial center. Iron and steel, chemicals, textiles, and machinery are among its main products. The city has study centers for medicine, metallurgy, and art.

Dust Bowl, area of some 50 million acres (20 million hectares) in the southern Great Plains region of the United States that, during the 1930s, suffered violent dust storms owing to accelerated soil erosion. Grassland had been plowed up in the 1920s and 1930s to plant wheat. A severe drought then bared the fields, and high winds blew the topsoil into huge dunes.

Dust storm, heavy winds carrying fine particles of earthy materials such as clay and silt for long distances. In the United States, a dust storm is declared when blowing dust reduces visibility below 5/8 mi (1 km). One of the factors causing soil erosion, dust storms occur where the ground has little vegetation to protect it.

Dutch, western Germanic language spoken in the Netherlands and (as Flemish) in North Belgium, as well as in Suriname and the Dutch Antilles. Afrikaans, spoken in South Africa, is derived from Dutch. Dutch evolved largely from the speech of the

Franks, who settled in the Low Countries in the 4th-5th centuries. About 20 million people speak Dutch.

Dutch Antilles *See:* Netherlands Antilles.

Dutch East India Company, trading company chartered by the Netherlands States General in 1602 and given a monopoly on all Dutch trade east of the Cape of Good Hope and west of the Strait of Magellan. The company functioned almost as an independent state, conquering territory and competing with other colonial countries. It was dissolved in 1798, its possessions coming directly under the authority of the Dutch state.

Dutch East Indies *See:* Indonesia.

Dutch elm disease, severe fungal disease of the elm tree. First identified in Holland in 1919, it was observed in America in 1930, in an area close to New York City. It now afflicts trees nationwide. The fungus, carried by certain beetles, can kill a tree within four weeks. Cutting and burning affected trees is one way to control the spread of the disease; another is the use of fungicides. But there is no safe cure for dutch elm disease.

Dutch Guiana *See:* Suriname.

Dutchman's-breeches, perennial plant (*Dicentra cucullaria*) of the Fumariaceae family. Native to eastern and midwestern North America, it is most often found in woodland areas. The yellow-tipped white flowers, resembling pantaloons hanging upside down, inspired the plant's name.

Dutch West India Company, trading and colonizing company chartered by the Netherlands States General in 1621 to compete with Portuguese and Spanish colonies in North America and Africa. The company founded posts in the West Indies, Guiana, and parts of Brazil, as well as establishing the cities of Fort Orange (now Albany) and New Amsterdam (New York) in what is now New York State. The charter was dissolved in 1674.

Dutch West Indies *See:* Netherlands Antilles.

Duvalier, François (1907-1971), president of Haiti (1957-1971), nicknamed 'Papa Doc.' A physician turned politician, he was elected to power as a reformer but ruled as dictator, helped by a political police force, the Tonton Macoutes. He made himself president for life in 1964. After his death his son, Jean-Claude Duvalier ('Baby Doc'), succeeded him as dictator.
See also: Haiti.

Duvoisin, Roger Antoine (1904-1980), Swiss-born U.S. author and illustrator of children's books. Duvoisin won the 1948 Caldecott Medal, a major U.S. award for children's book illustration for *White Snow, Bright Snow,* written by Alvin Tresselt. He wrote and illustrated the popular *Petunia* and *Veronica* series, and illustrated the series

Happy Lion, written by his wife, Louise Fatio.

Dvina River, name of 2 rivers in the former USSR. The Western Dvina or Daugava rises west of Moscow and flows 633 mi (1,019 km) east, to the Gulf of Riga in Latvia. The Northern Dvina flows 455 mi (732 km) northwest to the port of Archangel on the White Sea.

Dvořák, Antonín (1841-1904), Czech composer and violist. With composer Bedrich Smetana, he developed a Czech national style. His lyrical music began to win him acclaim in the 1870s. He spent 1892-95 in the United States, as director of the National Conservatory of Music, New York City. His works include 9 symphonies (including *From the New World*), 10 operas, concertos, the Slavonic dances and other orchestral compositions, choral works, and chamber music.

The Bohemian composer Antonín Dvořák became prominent at a time when many Bohemians were advocating independence from the Austrian Empire.

Dwarf, person with an underdeveloped skeleton caused by cartilage cells that fail to grow and divide properly. Chondrodystrophic dwarfism exists when certain cartilage cells are defective. Chromosome-related dwarfism occurs when all of the cells are defective. Hormonal dwarfism occurs when a hormone deficiency interferes with the growth of normal cartilage cells. Nonhormonal dwarfism results when disease or severely impaired nourishment blunts the normal growth of cartilage cells.

Dwarf star *See:* Star.

Dyak, or Dayak, indigenous people of Sarawak, largest state in Malaysia on the island of Borneo. Living by fishing and hunting, the Dyak have been little affected by modern civilization. There are two groups: Iban, who live along the seacoast and rivers, and Land Dyak, who live inland and call themselves by the name of their village or locality. The Dyak live in longhouses and grow crops communally. They practice the religious cults of shamanism and animism.

Dye, chemical compound used to color material or food. Natural dye comes from plants, animals, and minerals. Since the 19th century, manufacturers have brought synthetic dyes into wide use. There are several kinds of synthetic dyes, as well as methods to get them to bond to fibers and materials.

Dylan, Bob (Robert Allen Zimmerman; 1941-), U.S. folksinger and composer. His distinctive blues style and lyrics were influenced by Woody Guthrie. His songs, at times sharply protesting social injustice, at times densely surreal and elusive, had a strong influence on popular music in the 1960s. He later turned to country and ballad music.
See also: Guthrie, Woody.

Dynamite, high explosive invented by Alfred Nobel (1866), consisting of nitroglycerin absorbed in an inert material such as kieselguhr (a chalky earth) or wood pulp. Unlike nitroglycerin itself, it can be handled safely, and does not explode without a detonator. In modern dynamite sodium nitrate replaces about half the nitroglycerin. Gelatin dynamite, or gelignite, also contains some nitrocellulose.
See also: Explosive; Nobel, Alfred Bernhard; TNT.

Dysentery, group of diseases characterized by inflammation of the colon resulting in pain, spasm of the rectum, intense diarrhea, and the frequent passage of small amounts of mucus and blood, with symptoms of generalized poisoning of the body. Amoebic dysentery is caused by amoebas and treated with amoebicides. Bacillary dysentery is caused by bacteria and is treated with antibiotics.

Dyslexia, difficulty in learning to read when intelligence, vision, and available education are not limiting factors. The ophthalmologist W.P. Morgan described dyslexia in 1896 as 'word blindness.'
See also: Learning disabilities

Dyspepsia, or indigestion, abnormal visceral sensation in the upper abdomen or lower chest, often of a burning quality. Heartburn from esophagitis and pain of peptic (gastric or duodenal) ulcers are usual causes. Antacids and milk are used for relief.

Dysprosium, chemical element, symbol Dy; for physical constants see Periodic Table. Dysprosium, a metallic element, was discovered by Lecoq de Boisbaudran in 1886. The most important natural source of the element is the mineral monazite. It is a member of the lanthanide series of elements and is prepared by the reduction of the trifluoride with calcium metal. Ion-exchange and solvent extraction techniques have led to much easier isolation of the so-called 'rare-earth' elements. Dysprosium and its compounds are used in nuclear control rods, laser materials, and as a source of infrared radiation, as well as special glasses and enamels.

Dystrophy, muscular *See:* Muscular dystrophy.

D

E

E, fifth letter in the English alphabet. While it is the same letter as in the Greek and Latin alphabets, the ancient Phoenician letter from which it is derived was a smooth *h* sound, which it has retained in the Semitic alphabets. It is thought that the letter was originally a pictorial representation of a window or a fence. Pronounced variously in English, the most common uses are a short vowel as in *met*, a long vowel as in *feet*, or a silent *e* at the end as in *bite*. In musical terms, *E* represents the sound of *mi* in the scale of C.

Eagle, large bird of prey of the hawk family. Eagles have large eyes with extremely keen eyesight, hooked beaks for tearing their prey, and strong feet and talons (claws) for grabbing, killing, and carrying prey. Their size and noble attitude have led to their use in national and other emblems. The bald eagle (*Haliaetus teucocephalus*), named for its white head and neck, is the emblem of the United States of America, and the golden eagle was the emblem of the Roman legions. The largest eagles are the harpy eagle of South America and the Philippine eagle, whose wingspans reach 8 ft (2.4 m). Eagles spend much of their time perching on trees or rocky crags or soaring at great heights. Eagles generally feed on small mammals and birds, usually caught by pouncing from a height. The golden and bald eagles also eat carrion, although the latter is mainly a fish eater. Sea eagles and African fish eagles are fish eaters, the snake and harrier eagles eat mainly reptiles, and the black eagles rob other birds of their eggs.

Eakins, Thomas (1844-1916), U.S. realist painter. Eakins studied in Philadelphia and abroad, and went on to teach at the Philadelphia Academy. His teaching influenced the painters William Glackens, Robert Henri, and John Sloan. Considered a master portraitist, his most famous portraits include *Walt Whitman*, *The Thinker*, and the group portraits *The Clinic of Dr. Gross* and *The Clinic of Dr. Agnew*. Eakins placed great emphasis on the study of anatomy and perspective. Among his most famous paintings of sporting events are *Max Schmitt in a Single Hull* and *Between Rounds*. Eakins, who was also a sculptor, helped develop photographic techniques for studying the human body in motion.

Max Schmitt in a Single Scul (1871) by Thomas Eakins (Metropolitan Museum, New York City).

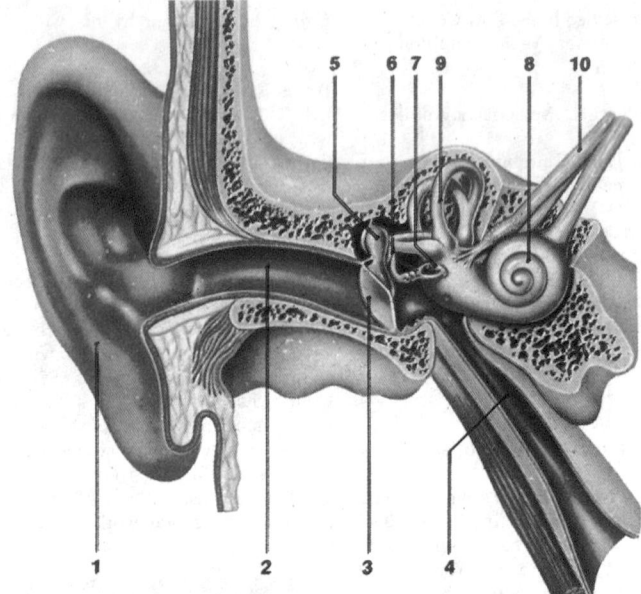

Structurally, the human ear is divided into an outer, middle, and inner ear. The pinna (1) of the outer ear receives sound waves, which travel through the auditory canal (2) to the middle ear. The eardrum (3), a thin membrane separating the outer from the middle ear, vibrates from the impact of the sound waves. The middle ear is filled with air that comes from the mouth through the eustachian (4). This chamber contains three tiny bones — the hammer (5), the anvil (6), and the stirrup (7) — that extend from the eardrum to the inner ear. The inner ear includes the cochlea (8), which contains the organ of Corti, and the vestibule (9), which maintains balance. The auditory nerve (10) sends messages from the inner ear to the brain.

Eames, Charles (1907-1978), U.S. designer who influenced contemporary furniture design. He created plywood and fiberglass form-fitting chairs and the upholstered 'Eames chair.'

Ear, organ of hearing and of balance. The ears convert the vibrations of air produced by sound into minute electrical impulses that can be sensed by the brain. They also contain a delicate and vital mechanism that enables the body to maintain its balance. In humans and many other higher animals, the visible part of the ear, or *auricle*, acts as a funnel for sound waves, directing them into the *auditory canal*. The auricle and the auditory canal together constitute the outer ear. The vibrations caused by sound waves first strike the eardrum, or *tympanum*, a membrane across the auditory canal that separates the outer ear from the middle ear. From the eardrum the vibrations are then transmitted to the 3 bones, or auditory ossicles, of the middle ear-the hammer (*malleus*), the anvil (*incus*), and the stirrup (*stapes*). These bones hinge on each other and act like a system of levers, transforming the relatively large but feeble vibrations of the eardrum into finer but much stronger vibrations of the same frequency. These enter the spiral-shaped *cochlea* of the inner ear via a small opening called the oval window. Within the fluid-filled cochlea the vibrations are converted into nerve signals and transmitted to the brain. Also within the inner ear are 3 semicircular canals and 2 saclike organs at the base where they meet. The canals are at right angles to each other. Two are vertical, one is horizontal, and they are filled with fluid. These organs send signals to the brain indicating the position and movement of the head. The signals are essential for keeping balance.

Earhart, Amelia (1898-1937), U.S. pioneer aviator. She was the first transatlantic woman passenger (1928) and the first solo transatlantic woman pilot (1932), and made the first solo flight from Hawaii to the U.S. mainland (1935). She disappeared over the Pacific Ocean during an around-the-world flight in 1937.
See also: Aviation.

Earl, Ralph (1751-1801), American portrait and landscape painter. His distinctively rugged portraits were influenced by John Singleton Copley. He is noted for his Revolutionary War battle scenes.

Early human being *See:* Prehistoric people.

Earp, Wyatt Berry Stapp (1848-1929), U.S. frontier lawman and folk hero. He was deputy sheriff and U.S. marshal in several Kansas and Arizona 'cow towns.' He is most famous for taking part in the gunfight at O.K. Corral in Tombstone, Ariz. (1881).

Ear shell *See:* Abalone.

Earth, only planet in the solar system on which the presence of living things is definitely known. It is the third planet outward from the sun, the fifth largest in the solar system. Together with its single moon, it travels around the sun at an average distance

E

of 92,960,000 mi (149,600,100 km). The earth also spins on an axis that is tilted at 23.5° from a line perpendicular to its path around the sun. This spinning motion makes the sun appear to travel across the sky from east to west, and it also causes day and night. The tilt of the earth's axis and its movement around the sun causes the change of seasons. The moon affects the earth's path around the sun and, together with the sun, causes tides. According to the most recent estimate, the earth is 4.55 billion years old. The first signs of life on the planet are some fossilized bacteria found in rocks estimated to be 3.3 billion years old.

The earth consists of 3 main zones: the atmosphere; the hydrosphere, including all the bodies of water and ice on earth; and the lithosphere, the rocks that form the earth's crust, mantle, and core. The atmosphere provides the air for breathing, shields plants and animals from excess heat from the sun, and filters out the lethal shorter ultraviolet rays that would otherwise destroy life. The hydrosphere is also essential for life. Water and ice cover more than 70% of the earth's surface, making possible the hydrologic cycle by which water is evaporated from the oceans and precipitated as rain or snow, moistening the land and then returning to the oceans. Finally, the lithosphere makes up the land masses or continents, sea beds, and the inner mass of the planet. The earth's crust varies in thickness from between an average of 20 mi (32 km) under the continents to 5 mi (8 km) under the oceans. Beneath the crust, the distinct zone called the mantle is some 1,800 mi (2,900 km) thick. Within the mantle lies the earth's core, with a diameter of about 4,300 mi (6,900 km). Seismic data suggest that the core may consist of a solid center surrounded by a liquid outer core.
See also: Solar System.

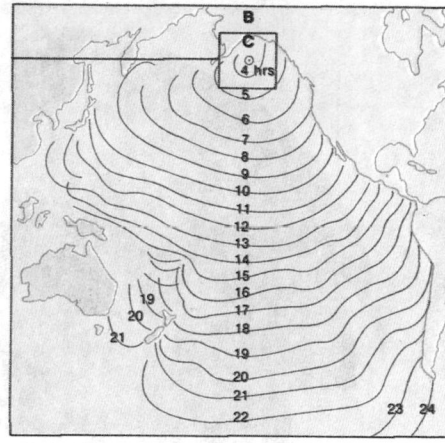

Earthquake, vibration or series of vibrations in the earth's crust. Earthquakes are the result of sudden vertical or horizontal movements along faults, or fractures, in the earth's crust. Some faults, such as the 600-mi (966-km) San Andreas fault in California, can be seen on the earth's surface, but most of the faults associated with earthquakes are underground. Scientists have recently suggested that the origin of many earthquakes is linked with continental drift. Many earthquakes also occur under the oceans. Underwater earthquakes or earthquakes that occur near coastlines may cause destructive waves called *tsunamis*, which may travel vast distances at speeds approaching 500 mph (805 kmph). Seismologists have studied earthquakes by recording the seismic waves that travel through the earth. Information from several seismographic stations makes it possible to locate the point of origin, or focus, of an earthquake, and also the epicenter, the point on the earth's surface directly above the focus. The most common and most destructive earthquakes are shallow-focus, that is, their focus lies within about 30 mi (48 km) beneath the epicenter. Intermediate and deep-focus earthquakes, which may occur as deep as 400 mi (644 km) below the surface, are less destructive. The magnitude of an earthquake is a measure of the strength of the

On March 27, 1964, one of the strongest earthquakes of the 20th century occurred, just under Prince William Sound in Alaska, with its epicenter located about 75 mi (120 km) southeast of Anchorage. The shock, originating from where the Pacific Plate thrusts beneath the Alaskan landmass, had a magnitude of about 8.5 on the Richter scale. Extensive changes in elevation were caused around the Gulf of Alaska (A), some sections subsiding over 7 ft (2 m), others rising over 26 ft (8 m). In some coastal areas (B), large blocks of alluvial deposits were loosened by the vibrations and slid down steep slopes. Devastating ocean waves, or tsunamis, that were generated by these slides and by 49 ft (15 m) movements of the sea floor during the earthquake, caused great damage, as far away as California. Successive hourly positions of the tsunamis (C) reveal that the waves had reached the tip of South America in 24 hours. At Anchorage (D), most of the damage was caused by the fluid movements of weak clays underlying the city, which caused the ground to break up into chaotic piles of slabs.

seismic wave it generates. It is usually measured on the Richter scale, devised by U.S. seismologist C.F. Richter in 1935. The scale ranges from 0 to 8.4, with higher numbers signifying greater magnitude. The intensity of an earthquake is a measure of its effect in a particular area and varies with the distance from the epicenter. The Modified Mescalli scale, which ranges from 1 (not felt) to 12 (nearly total damage), is normally used. Although scientific knowledge about earthquakes has greatly increased, there is still no effective way of forecasting them.
See also: Seismology.

Earth science, study of the origin, development, and makeup of the planet earth. A broad field that includes geology, meteorology, oceanography, and physical geography, earth science focuses on the forces that have formed and altered the earth's surface.

Earthworm, name of a large number of common worms of the Lumbricidae family with simple tubular bodies made up of a series of rings. The body tapers toward the head end, where there is a mouth. Earthworms move by extending and contracting these rings, anchoring them by means of short bristles. They feed on plant material in the soil. Some species eject the indigestible remains on the surface as worm casts, thereby improving the soil. The population of earthworms in the soil varies widely, but in some grazing lands it may reach 5 million per acre. A few species climb trees and are found under bark. Each earthworm is both male and female but mates with another

E

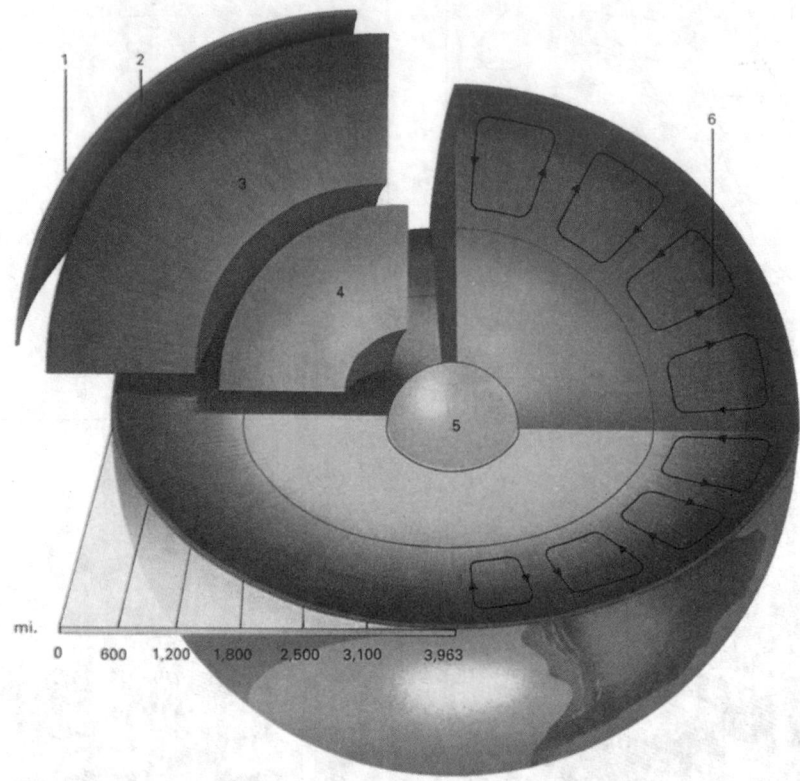

mi.

0   600   1,200   1,800   2,500   3,100   3,963

The Earth is composed of several distinct layers. The crust (1) is the top layer and ranges in thickness from 3 miles (5 km) to 25 miles (40 km). Under the crust is the Mohorovicic (Moho) discontinuity (2), which forms the base of the crust and occurs at an average depth of 20 miles (35 km). The Moho separates the crust from the mantle (3), which achieves a thickness of 1,800 miles (2,900 km) and dominates the composition of the Earth. The liquid outer core (4) is 1,400 miles thick (2,200 km) and the solid inner core (5) is 1,600 miles (2,500 km). Convection currents (6), perhaps created by the heat emanating from the liquid core, are responsible for the shifting sections, or plates, which in turn cause earthquakes, and the creation of new mountains.

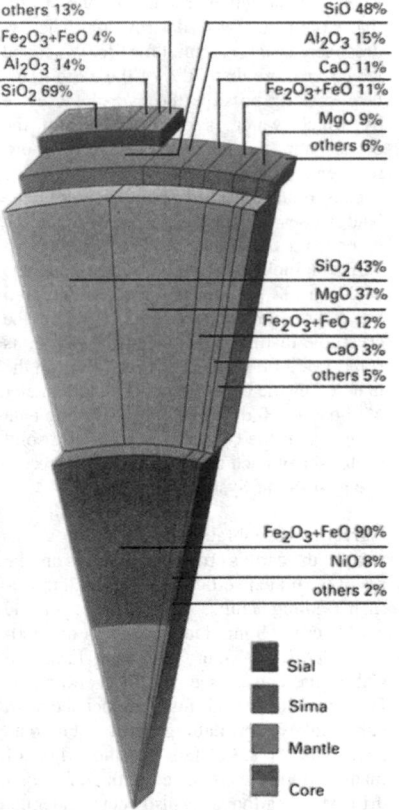

others 13% · SiO 48%
Fe_2O_3+FeO 4% · Al_2O_3 15%
Al_2O_3 14% · CaO 11%
SiO_2 69% · Fe_2O_3+FeO 11%
MgO 9%
others 6%

SiO_2 43%
MgO 37%
Fe_2O_3+FeO 12%
CaO 3%
others 5%

Fe_2O_3+FeO 90%
NiO 8%
others 2%

■ Sial
■ Sima
■ Mantle
■ Core

The chemical composition of the Earth changes from layer to layer. The continental crust is mostly granite, filled with silicon (Si) and aluminium (Al), while the oceanic crust is composed of silicon (Si) and magnesium (Mg). The mantle is mostly magnesium and iron silicates, while both cores are iron and nickel oxides.

The Earth as seen from outer space.

earthworm before laying eggs. These are deposited in a cocoon which is secreted by the *clitellum*, the broad band near the front of the worm. Size varies, with some species as small as 1/25 in (1 mm) long, and one Australian species growing to 11 ft (3 m).

Earwig, insect of the order *Dermaptera* distinguished by the pair of pincers at the tip of the abdomen. The short forewings act as covers for the membranous hindwings. Earwigs are nocturnal, hiding by day in crevices. They eat plant material, and the introduced European earwig is a pest in greenhouses in the United States. The female guards and cleans the eggs. The insect is named from the mistaken belief that it crawls into the ears of sleeping persons.

Easement, right of a property owner to use the adjacent property of another for a specified purpose. For instance, 2 homeowners may use a common driveway, half of which belongs to each. Each would then have an easement on the other's property 'of necessity' in the law. The right of easement may be established through necessity, contract, or custom.

East Berlin *See:* Berlin.

East China Sea *See:* China Sea.

Easter, chief festival of the Christian church year, celebrating the Resurrection of Jesus Christ, associated with spring and subsuming the Jewish Passover. Easter has been observed by the Western Church since the Council of Nicaea (325), on the Sunday after the first full moon following the vernal equinox. Easter is celebrated at a later date by the Eastern churches.

Easter Island, easternmost island of Polynesia in the South Pacific, about 2,000 mi (3,200 km) west of Chile, which annexed the island in 1888. This small, grassy, volcanic island features hundreds of colossal stone statues up to 40 ft (12 m) high, carved and raised on burial platforms, which have been the subject of much speculation by the explorer Thor Heyerdahl and others. Easter Island was discovered on Easter Sunday, 1722, by the Dutch admiral Jacob Roggeveen.

Easter lily, tall plant of the lily family bearing large, white, fragrant, trumpet-shaped flowers (especially *Lilium longiflorum*). Grown and cultivated throughout the world, the Easter lily has become a symbol of Easter.

Eastern Hemisphere *See:* Hemisphere.

Eastern Orthodox Church, one of the 2 major branches of the Christian Church. From the apostolic age a natural distinction arose between the Greek-speaking church of the eastern Roman empire and the Latin-speaking church of the west. The Eastern Church developed its own liturgical traditions. It became a family of orthodox churches, finally breaking with Rome in the Great Schism of 1054.
See also: Christianity.

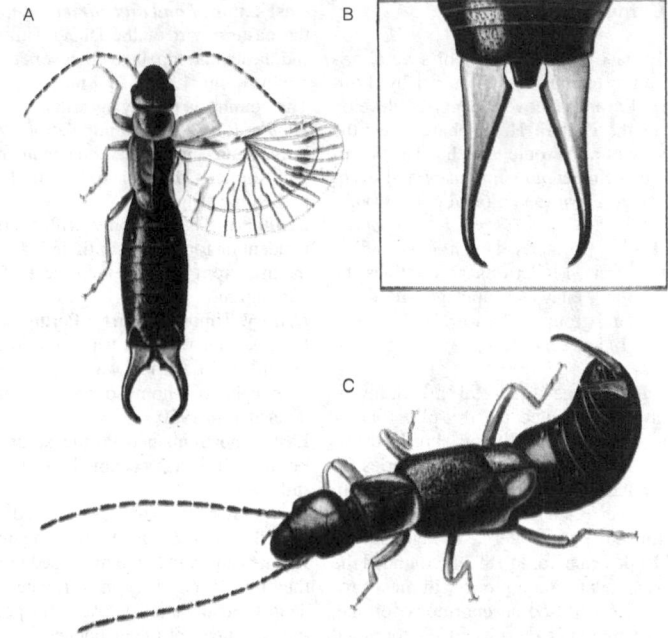

E

A male earwig (A), *Forficula auricularia*, differs from a female (C) by having wings, one pair of which is short and leathery and the other pair veined and delicate. Both male and female have forcepslike pincers on their abdomens (B), which are used for defense. The female is shown in a defensive posture, with pincers raised.

Eastern question, international political problems raised in the 19th century by the decline of the Ottoman Empire. The ambitions of Russia, Austria-Hungary, Britain, and France in the East Mediterranean led to the Crimean War (1854-1856) and Balkan Wars (1912-1913) and were partly responsible for the outbreak of World War I.

Eastern Star, organization associated with the men's fraternal society of the Masons. With 3 million members (chiefly women) throughout the world, Eastern Star supports charitable projects and sponsors social activities. There are several groups of Eastern Star, among which the General Grand Chapter is the largest, comprising 56 grand chapters in the United States. The title of the woman who is the executive officer of the General Grand Chapter is Most Worthy Grand Matron.
See also: Masonry.

Easter Rebellion, rebellion in Dublin, Ireland, in April 1916, in an attempt to secure Irish independence from Britain. Led by Patrick Pearse of the Irish Republican Brotherhood and James Connolly of the Sinn Fein nationalist movement, the rebellion began on Easter Monday. It grew out of a long opposition to British rule in Ireland. The rebels, who called themselves the Irish Republican Army (IRA), were about 1,000 strong. They seized the Dublin General Post Office and other public buildings. There was serious street fighting and loss of life; British forces quickly suppressed the rebellion, and Pearse and Connolly were executed, along with a number of other leaders. With nationalist feelings strengthened by this episode, the rebels continued to carry on guerrilla warfare throughout the 20th century, including the assassination of General Montgomery.
See also: Irish Republican Army; Sinn Féin.

The famous ancestral statues (moai) on Chile's Pacific Ocean Isla de Pascua (Easter Island). There are more than a thousand of them. The statues were proba- bly not erected by the present population, but by some other people of unknown origin. There are indications that they were related to the also unknown Andes sculp- tors from the first millennium A.D. The moai have an average height of 13-16 ft (4-5 m), but some of them (including several unfinished ones) are as high as 66 ft (20 m). The Easter Island statues were probably carved somewhere between the 10th and the 14th century.

E

East Germany *See:* Germany.

East India Company, name of several private trading companies chartered by 17th-century European governments to develop trade in the Eastern Hemisphere, after the discovery of a sea route to India. They competed for commercial supremacy and eventually aided European colonial expansion.

East Indies, formerly Dutch East Indies, now Indonesia. Modern usage confines the term to the Malay Archipelago. It is the largest island group in the world.
See also: Indonesia.

Eastman, George (1854-1932), U.S. inventor. Eastman invented the dry-plate photographic process in 1880 and shortly thereafter established one of the first factories for the production of photographic supplies. In 1884 he perfected a flexible paperbacked roll film, and 4 years later he brought out the small Kodak camera. In 1892 he founded the Eastman Kodak Co., a pioneer in mass production. He amassed an enormous fortune, most of which he gave away. He committed suicide in 1932.
See also: Photography.

Eastman, Max Forrester (1883-1969), U.S. poet and influential critic. His *Enjoyment of Poetry* (1913) proved a popular introduction to the subject. A Marxist, Eastman edited the left-wing journals *The Masses* (1911) and *The Liberator* (1918), but later rejected communism. His collected verse appeared in *Poems of Five Decades* (1954).

East Pakistan *See:* Bangladesh.

East Roman Empire *See:* Byzantine Empire; Rome, Ancient.

East Timor

Capital:	Dili
Area:	5,645 sq mi (14,609 sq km)
Population:	953,000
Language:	Tetum, Portugese
Government:	republic
Independent:	2002
Head of gov.:	Prime minister
Per capita:	US$ 500
Monetary unit:	US$

East Timor, *Land and climate.* Republic on the eastern part of the island Timor in the Indonesian archipelago. It covers an area of 5,645 sq. mi /14,609 sq. km.
The country is mainly agrarian.
People. It has a mixed population: Malayan, Polynesian and Papuan. Its main religions are Roman Catholicism, Islam, Hinduism and ethnic religions.
Economy. The economy will be fully dependent on foreign aid until, in 2005, its own income from oil will increase to $130mln per annum.
History. Timor was first a Portugese colony (1520), after which it was colonized by the Dutch. West Timor was handed over to Indonesia to whom sovereignty had been delegated in 1950.
East Timor remained Portugese until 1975, but in 1976 it was occupied and annexed by Indonesia.
Independence struggles headed by the guerilla organzation Fretilin againstt the Indonesian army led to increased violence in the 1990's causing an estimated 20,000 deaths. Finally almost 80% of the population voted in favor of independence.
Violence increased and the Indonesian army and police intervened, causing an estimated 20,000 deaths in the 1990s alone. Finally the Indonesian government agreed to a UN peacekeeping force presence. At the constitutional elections in August 2001, former guerilla organization Fretilin gained an absolute majority. The democratic government and Prime Minister Mari Alkatiri were sworn in. Jose Gusmao became the first East Timorese President, and on May 20, 2002, East Timor finally became independent.

Eastwood, Clint (1930-), U.S. film actor, director and producer. He starred in some of Sergio Leone's Spaghetti Westerns (*The Good, the Bad and the Ugly*, 1966, a.o.) and after that, in a number of mainly violent films such as *Dirty Harry* (1971), *Escape from Alcatraz* (1979) and *City Heat* (1984). He was the director of *Play Misty for Me* (1971), *Heartbreak Ridge* (1986) and the Charlie Parker biography *Bird* (1988). Some of his other well-known films include *Unforgiven* (1992; 5 Academy Awards), *The Bridges of Madison County* (1995), *Space Cowboys* (2000), and *Blood Work* (2002). He received a Golden Lion Lifetime Achievement Award in Venice in 2000.

EBCDIC, in computer technology, acronym for Extended Binary Coded Decimal Interchange Code. The 8-bit code is used to encode specific character sets. Based on the original punched card code, it encodes essentially the same characters as ASCII, but in a different numerical order.

Eberhart, Richard (1904-), U.S. poet and founder of the Poet's Theatre, Cambridge, Mass. Eberhart published his first book of poems, *A Bravery of Earth*, in 1930. His poetry makes use of the surprise effects of mixed abstractions and outcry, rough meters, inverted word orders, and sudden, striking lyricism. Eberhart served as Poetry Consultant and Honorary Consultant in American Letters to the Library of Congress. He won the Bollingen Prize in poetry in 1962, the Pulitzer Prize in 1966 for his *Selected Poems* (1930-1965), and the National Book Award in 1977 for *Collected Poems, 1930-1976.*

Ebola, the Ebola virus is a deadly virus that owes its name to the Congolese (mainly Zaire) river that flows through the valley where the first epidemic broke out in 1976. People who become infected with the Ebola virus show signs of fever, shivering, headaches, and muscle aches after a few days. Symptoms include nausea, vomiting, stomach ache, and diarrhea. If the illness intensifies, internal bleeding occurs, leading to the deterioration of all kinds of organs, including the liver, spleen, and kidneys. At this point, there is no hope for the patient.
The Ebola virus, together with HIV, is the most deadly virus known to man. However, contrary to what is generally believed, both types of viruses are not very contagious and can only spread through the blood and sperm, not by means of saliva. Most infections of Ebola are caught in hospitals in developing countries. A shortage of syringes and operating gloves, or of clean water, facilitates the spreading of the virus. Not surprisingly, more than half of the known cases of infection (less than 1000 throughout the world since the virus was discovered) concern hospital employees.
After 1976, three more epidemics of the Ebola virus broke out in Congo: in 1979, 1995 and 2001. They drew attention all over the world, but compared to other epidemics, such as measles and meningitis, which claim tens of thousands of victims every year, the number of casualties was small.

Ebony, hard, heavy heartwood of several trees (family Ebonaceae, genus *Diospuros*) native to equatorial Africa, southern Asia, and North and South America. Ebony can be highly polished and is used for small statues, cabinet work, golf clubs, and the black keys of pianos. The genus also includes persimmon trees.

E-Business, initiating electronic networks in order to facilitate business processes. E-Business is applicable in various cases, such as communication between suppliers and clients, invoicing and payment. As for potency, it introduces certain advantages which are closely connected to the speed and transparency of business associations: rapid exchange of information, maintaining small stock levels, it enables swift adjustments to business processes and immediate payment. In practice, certain difficulties may arise, such as language problems and compatibility issues, automation problems, safety leaks in used networks and an overestimation of the willingness of people to abandon familiar processes.
See also: Internet.

EB virus *See:* Epstein-Barr (EB) virus.

Eça de Queirós, José Maria (1845-1900), Portuguese author and lawyer. Entered consular employment and stayed abroad almost permanently as from 1872. As a writer, he joined the 'generation of 1870', which desired to renew society on the basis of utopian socialism and to develop a new literature along the lines of Flauberts realism. In keeping with the example of Balzac, Eça de Queirós wanted to point out the shortcomings of Portuguese society in a cycle of novels, but he only completed three novels, *The Sin of Father Amaro* (1875), *Cousin Bazilio* (1878), and *The Maias* (1888).

Ecclesiastes, 21st book of the Old Testament. It consists of about 40 aphorisms, including the famous phrase, 'vanity of vanities, all is vanity.' Pessimistic in tone, Ecclesiastes opposes the view that virtue is always rewarded and sin punished. Nevertheless, it exhorts people to fear God and keep his commandments, even without hope of reward in this or future life. It has traditionally been attributed to the Hebrew King Solomon, but was probably written as late as the 2nd or 3rd century B.C.
See also: Bible; Old Testament.

Ecevit, Bülent (1925-), Turkish politician, left wing leader of the Republican's People Party (RPP). He was Prime Minister three times (1974-1977, 1978-1979, and from 1999 onwards). During his Prime Ministry, the Turkish army occupied Northern Cyprus. For a long period of time, Ecevit was silenced under the military government, but in 1987, he was allowed to return to politics. In 1997, he became Vice Prime Minister in Mesut Yilmaz's cabinet. The arrest of PKK leader Öcalan increased his popularity and he won a landslide victory in the 1999 parliamentary elections. A government crisis resulted in snap in 2002.
See also: Yilmaz, Mesut; Öcalan, Abdullah.

ECG *See:* Electrocardiogram.

Echegaray y Eizaguirre, José (1832-1916), a Spanish dramatist. In 1904 he shared the Nobel Prize for literature with Frédéric Mistral. Echegaray wrote melodramatic tragedies about love and honor, reviving the Romantic tradition. He often chose current rather than historical settings, however, and dealt with contemporary social concerns, as in his bestknown plays, *Madman or Saint* (1877) and *The Great Galeoto* (1881).
Echegaray was born in Madrid. He was a mathematician and engineer, then served as minister of education (1872-1873) and of finance (1874-1875). His first play was produced in 1874. He wrote about 70 thereafter, some in prose and others in verse.

Echeverria, Luis (1922-), Mexican political leader. After holding several political and academic posts, he was president of Mexico (1970-1975). Rapid population growth in cities, inflation, and unemployment burdened his administration.

Echidna, or spiny anteater (*Tachyglossus aculeatus*), nocturnal hedgehog-like animal of Australia, Tasmania, and New Guinea. Like the platypus, it is an egg-laying mammal, or *monotreme*. It has fur as well as spines and uses its beaklike snout to root out termites, which it licks up with a long tongue. A single egg is laid into a pouch, in which the young echidna hatches and is fed

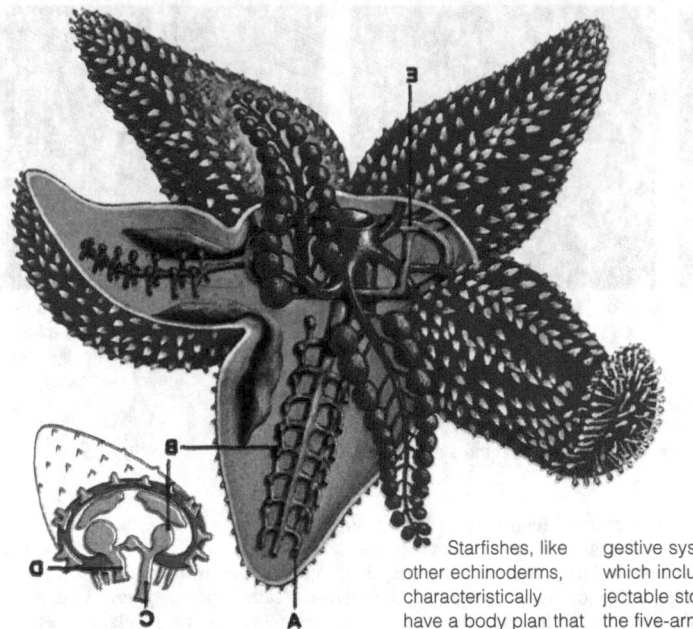

on milk from 'milk patches' that open into the pouch from the mother's body. The young echidna is later placed in a burrow, where it is visited by its mother for feeding.

Echinoderm, member of a large group, or *phylum*, of marine invertebrates with an external skeleton of plates just under the skin. Some live fixed on the ocean floor; others move slowly by means of arrays of tube-feet. Many classes of echinoderms are extinct, but 5 are still in existence and are very abundant: Crinoidea (sea lilies and feather stars), Asteroidea (starfishes), Ophiuroidea (brittle stars), Echinoidea (sea urchins and sand dollars), and Holothuroidea (sea cucumbers).

Echo, in Greek mythology, mountain nymph who helped Zeus carry on his affairs by distracting Hera with her endless chatter. She was punished by being able to speak only when spoken to. Later she fell in love with Narcissus, and when her love was not returned, she faded away to a mere voice.

Echo, sound reflected or reverberated from a distant surface, with at least a 0.1-sec time lag, allowing the reflection to be distinct from the original sound; or, in computer technology, a character received from the keyboard and fed back to the printer or cathode ray tube for display.

Eck, Johann (1486-1543), German scholar and theologian. Though advocating church reform, he was a bitter opponent of Martin Luther and the Reformation. He openly disputed with Luther at Liepzig in 1519, influenced the 1520 papal bull against Luther, and presented the Roman Catholic case at the Diet of Augsburg (1530).
See also: Luther, Martin; Reformation.

Eckhart, Meister (Johannes Eckhart; 1260?-1328?), German theologian and preacher. He taught that to unite with God, one must conquer basic human nature and

Starfishes, like other echinoderms, characteristically have a body plan that includes an internal calcium-carbonate skeleton; a watervascular system (blue), used for locomotion and suction; and a digestive system (red), which includes a projectable stomach. In the five-armed starfish, the watervascular system consists of a central, hollow ring with five branched tubes, one for each arm. At the end of each branch is a tube-foot (A), with a bulblike ampulla (B) at its top, and a sucker disk at the bottom. When the ampulla makes a contact, fluid is forced into the tube-foot, lengthening it (C). When the extended tube-foot touches an object, the center of its sucker disk is pulled up, and then shortened (D), forcing fluid back into the ampulla, while simultaneously either drawing the starfish forward or exerting a pulling force on its prey. Although a sieve plate (E) leads from outside to the central ring, it is not certain whether the plate provides water for the watervascular system. Starfishes feed by everything their stomachs reaches.

withdraw from sin. Then, a divine spark within one's soul can form a mystical bond with God. In 1329 Pope John XXII condemned many of Eckhart's ideas as heresy.
See also: Theology.

Eclampsia *See:* Toxemia of pregnancy.

Eclipse, blocking off of light from the Sun from one celestial body by another. An eclipse of the Moon (lunar eclipse) occurs when the Moon enters the shadow of the Earth. An eclipse of the Sun (solar eclipse) occurs when the Earth enters the shadow of the Moon. Other planets can also eclipse their own moons, and in the case of a double star, one star can eclipse the other. There are usually 2 or 3 lunar eclipses each year. Shadows have a central dark part called the *umbra*, and a less dark outer region called the *penumbra*. In the penumbra of the Earth's shadow, part of the light from the Sun is cut off from the Moon. In the umbra, all the Sun's light is cut off. Since the Earth's umbra is much wider than the diameter of the Moon, a total lunar eclipse can last up to 1 3/4 hours from the time the Moon first enters the umbra at one side to the time it moves out again at the opposite edge of the shadow. More often, the Moon moves through only part of the Earth's umbra, and the eclipse is somewhat shorter. The umbra of the Moon's shadow on the Earth is never wider than 170 mi (274 km), and the maximum diameter of the penumbra is 4,000 mi (6,437 km). Inside the umbra there is a total eclipse of the Sun, which can never last longer than 7 min and is usually less than half this duration. In the penumbra a partial eclipse is visible. Because of the Moon's motion, the track of a solar eclipse sweeps across the surface of the Earth at over 1,000 mph (1,600 kmph). An *annular* or ring

E

E

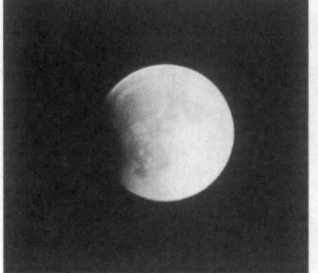  

The various stages of the total lunar eclipse of August 6, 1971, photographed with a 2.4 in (600 mm) telelens in Yalta (Soviet Union). The moon moves from right to left (from west to east) through the umbra (shadow cone) of the earth. Because of the breaking of the sunlight in the atmos-phere, this umbra is not sharply defined, but somewhat irregu-lar, and the moon — though entirely ob-scured — neverthe-less emits a red-brownish light, as can be seen in the middle picture (directly after the total eclipse).

eclipse occurs when the Moon is at its far-thest from Earth. At this distance it is not big enough in appearance to completely obscure the Sun, and a ring of light remains sur-rounding the shadow. Eclipses of the Sun, particularly total eclipses, have provided a lot of information about the outer layers of the Sun (the *corona* and the *chromosphere*), and about the Earth's upper atmosphere.

Ecliptic, in astronomy, the plane, passing through the center of the sun, that contains the orbit of the earth. All the planets orbit the sun in approximately the same plane, so that they are always seen near the ecliptic.
See also: Astronomy.

Eco, Umberto (1932-), Italian semiologist, medievalist, essayist and novelist. Was co-founder of the avant-garde literary move-ment 'Gruppo 63', and gave voice to their theories. In the interesting scientific paper *Opera aperta* (The Open Work; 1962), he argues in favor of the 'openness' and multi-formity of a creative creation, making a wide range of interpretations possible. He pub-lished clever dissertations about mass com-munication and the various (cultural) mani-festations of the consumer society, among others in *Diario minimo* (1963) and *Il supe-ruomo di massa* (1976). His first novel was published in 1980: *Il nome della rosa* (The Name of the Rose) and became a worldwide bestseller. It is an historical detective novel in which all kinds of other aspects (semi-otics, among others) are discussed. It was al-so filmed (by J.-J. Annaud in 1985). Other novels include: *Il pendolo di Foucault* (Foucault's Pendulum; 1988), *L'isola del giorno prima* (The Island of the Day Before; 1994), and *Baudolino* (2001).

École des Beaux-Arts (École Nationale Supérieure Des Beaux-Arts), school of de-sign and architecture established in Paris in 1648. In the early 1900s it influenced archi-tecture in the United States and elsewhere by promoting ancient Greek and Roman mod-els. The school today offers courses in archi-tecture, drawing, engraving, lithography, mosaics, and sculpture to students entering after a highly competitive enrollment proce-dure.

Ecology, study of the relationships between living organisms and their environment. The earth is covered from pole to pole with a thin, intricate web of interdependent living organisms called the *biosphere*. Within the biosphere there are many clearly defined subunits, or *ecosystems*. Ecosystems (for ex-ample, ponds, forests, fields of grass, deserts, or oceans) vary greatly in size, but in each case the animals and plants within them have a pattern of feeding relationships called a food chain or web. The ultimate foundation of the food chain is plant life and the process of photosynthesis, by which en-ergy from the sun is converted to organic material. Within an ecosystem, every species occupies a distinct ecological niche. The na-ture of the niche is determined by the space required by the species to survive, and the nature and availability of its food. Over a pe-riod of time, the numbers and types of ani-mals and plants in the system change. This change is actually a process of succession and is accompanied by continually increas-ing complexity. The process begins with an elementary ecosystem and culminates in what is called a climax community, an ecosystem capable of supporting an enor-mous number of species. Climax communi-ties, such as tundra, forests, or deserts, are stable until humans or natural geological up-heaval destroys them, thereby starting an en-tirely different ecosystem. The growth and stability of ecosystems depend entirely on the cycles that expand and renew the chemi-cals that are essential to life. Among the most common of these are the carbon and ni-trogen cycles and photosynthesis. Any seri-ous or prolonged disturbance of these vital cycles threatens the existence of an ecosys-tem and of the species it contains. The envi-ronment, left to itself, can continue to sup-port life for millions of years. The single most unstable and potentially disruptive ele-ment in the scheme is the human species. Human beings with modern technology have the capacity to bring about, intentionally or unintentionally, far-reaching and irreversible change. In addition to studying nature, ecol-ogy also considers the effects upon the envi-ronment and particular ecosystems of vari-ous human activities. The body of knowl-edge and insights unique to ecology are not only significant in their own right, but are al-so important in the development of environ-mentalism.

Econometrics, branch of economics that us-es statistical methods to describe economic phenomena and thus discover how they af-fect each other. Econometrics came into use during the 1930s when many governments wanted to obtain empirical information to solve the problems of the Depression. Econometricians are concerned primarily with the construction of mathematical mod-els of the economy in order to test them against reality. Such a model is basically a system of national accounts that record, from empirical data, the flow of goods and services among the various sectors of the economy.

Economic and Monetary Union (EMU), Economic collaboration between the mem-ber states of the European Union, consisting of a collective currency (the euro) and the coordination of the economic, monetary, and social policies.
Although the decision to form an economic and monetary union was taken as early as 1969, there was little headway due to the economic crisis of the 70s. It wasn't until the second half of the 80s that the discussion re-sumed, in the hope of realizing an internal market. The Delors report, which concerned the implementation of the EMU in three phases, was accepted in 1989. The EMU was included in the Treaty of Maastricht (1991). It was agreed to gradually imple-ment the collective currency in (some of) the EC member states by 1999. The United Kingdom and Denmark have insisted that they be regarded as exceptional cases; they are not obligated to participate.
Only the countries that complied with the so-called convergence criteria (low inflation, a reasonable government deficit, having been in the exchange rate of the European Monetary System for at least two years, and having an interest rate that is comparable to that of other member countries) can partici-pate.
The eleven member states that were found to comply with the criteria at the beginning of 1998 introduced EMU on 1st January 1999, with a collective currency and a European Central Bank. Greece did join in 2001; Sweden (entered the EU after 'Maastricht') chose not to participate in the EMU for the time being. On 1st January 2002 the euro was introduced as common currency.

Economic determinism, theory, first fully developed by Karl Marx in the mid-1800s, that a society's basis is determined by its economic structure. Fundamental changes in a society are produced not by educational or religious theories, but by alterations in that society's ability to manufacture and distrib-ute goods. The ruling class of a society is that which controls material production. Only by changing its influence on the eco-nomic system is a class able to gain strength in the political system of a society.
See also: Marx, Karl.

Economics, study of how goods and servic-es are produced and how they are distrib-uted. Resources are scarce or limited and not all needs can be met. Economics is con-cerned with how to distribute scarce resources in the most efficient, equitable way. Macroeconomics is the study of an entire economic system. Microeconomics deals with economic activity in the individual case.

ECOSOC (Economic and Social Council), one of the main organs of the United Nations, with 54 members (as of 1973) who are chosen by the General Assembly. Tasks and authorities are provided for in articles 61-72 of the charter. Object: increasing the standard of living of the global population, working towards improving health conditions and achieving universal respect for fundamental human rights. The main task is the coordination of the activities of the specialized organizations of the UN (for example WHO). Five regional economic committees have been appointed by the ECOSOC: the Economic Committee for Europe (ECE), for Africa (ECA), for Latin America (ECLA), for Asia and the Far East (ECAFE), and for West Asia (ECWA).

In addition, there are also eight specialized, functional committees: the Committee for Social Development, the Committee for Human Rights, the Committee for Narcotics and Drugs, the Committee for the Status of Women, the Population Committee, the Committee for Statistics, the Committee for Sustainable Development, and the Committee for the Prevention of Crime and for Justice.

Ecosystem *See:* Ecology.

Ectoplasm, in biology, outer portion of the cytoplasm of a cell; in spiritualism, glowing substance that resembles the face or hand of a dead person, through which communication with the dead is possible.
See also: Biology.

Ecuador

Capital:	Quito
Area:	105,037 sq mi (272,045 sq km)
Population:	13,447,000
Language:	Spanish
Government:	Presidential republic
Independent:	1830
Head of gov.:	President
Per capita:	US$ 3,000
Monetary unit:	1 Sucre = 100 centavos

Ecuador, republic in northwestern South America. It lies south of Colombia, west and north of Peru, and east of the Pacific Ocean. Its territory includes the Galapagos Islands, 650 mi (1,046 km) off the Ecuadorian coast. The country takes its name from the equator (Spanish, *ecuador*), which runs through the north. The capital is Quito and the country's largest city and main trading center is Guayaquil.
Land and climate. Ecuador is dominated by 2 chains of the Andes traversing the center of the country from north to south. These ranges contain some of the highest peaks in South America and many volcanoes. The area is also subject to disastrous earthquakes. Between the 2 Andean chains lies a string of 10 high plateaus or basins some 7,000-9,000 ft (2,100-2,700 m) above sea level. The area is the most densely populated in the country. Ecuador's ports are situated on the coastal lowlands to the west. Lowlands in the east are covered with equatorial forests and are sparsely populated. The climate of both the eastern and western lowlands is equatorial, with heavy rainfalls in the east. The Andean areas have a more temperate climate that varies with the altitude.
People. Though the official language is Spanish, Quechua or Jarvo and other Native American dialects are also spoken. The majority of the people are Roman Catholic.
Economy. Agriculture was the basis of Ecuador's economy until 1972, when exploitation of petroleum began. Ecuador is now a leading producer of oil in Latin America. Exports also include bananas, coffee, cocoa, and fish products. Economic growth in the 1980s led to industrial development in textiles, food processing, cement, and pharmaceuticals.
History. Following the conquest of the Incas by Pizarro in 1533, Ecuador became part of the Spanish Empire. Liberated from Spain in 1822, it has been an independent republic since 1830, but has always suffered from political instability marked by conflict among the conservative landed bourgeoisie of the Andean region and the Roman Catholic Church, the liberal mercantile interests centered in Guayaquil, and, more recently, the urban working classes. Military coups have been endemic-the most recent successful one in January 1976. A civilian government was installed in 1979 under a new constitution providing for an elected executive and legislature and, to date, has proven to be stable. During the early 1980's several border clashes between Ecuador and Peru erupted in the interior over access to the Amazon River. A decline in world oil prices during the 1980's severely weakened the economy. Each successive regime instituted austerity programs, such as price increases in fuel and other essential commodities, and caused widespread unrest. The country was beset by labor strikes, rioting, and terrorist bombings. In 1995 there was another border clash with Peru. In 1998 negotiations with Peru led to a peace treaty regarding the border dispute. The majority of the population did not profit from the extraction of oil and, in 2002, a revolt by poor native citizens nearly brought the oil production to a halt. In 2001, an oil tanker stranded on one of the Galapagos

Potatoes, bananas, onions, vegetables and local fruits are sold in the market by Indian women in Equador. Potatoes are the main source of food for a large part of the population.

Islands; an environmental disaster was fortunately prevented.

Ecumenical council, general council of the leaders of the entire Christian Church. The first was at Nicaea (325) and there have been 20 since; the most recent being the Second Vatican Council (1962-1965). Roman Catholics recognize all 21 councils; the Orthodox Church recognizes only the first 7 councils.
See also: Christianity.

Ecumenical movement, modern movement among the Christian churches to encourage greater cooperation and eventual unity. Organizations such as the International Missionary Council and the Life and Work and the Faith and Order conferences studied the churches' doctrinal differences. But substantial progress was not made until 1948, when representatives of 147 world churches agreed to form the World Council of Churches. Most Protestant Orthodox churches have since joined the council, and the Roman Catholic Church, though not a member, participates in some joint studies.
See also: Christianity.

Eczema, collective term for many inflammatory noncontagious conditions of the skin. The term *dermatitis*, often used incorrectly as a synonym for eczema, means any inflammation of the skin. Eczema causes one or more of the following physical changes to the skin: erythema (blood congestion), infiltration of plasma into the tissues, vesicles (blisters), and papules (pimples). Secondary changes include erosion of tissue, exudation of fluid onto the skin, crusts, lichenification (thickened areas of itchy skin), and scaling.

E

The annual festivities at Edinburgh, connected with the International Festival of Music and Drama, seen against the background of the castle on Castle Hill.

Edberg, Stefan (1966-), Swedish tennis player, became European youth champion in 1982. He won his first major title three years later, that of Australia, a title he also claimed in 1987. Edberg won Wimbledon in 1988 and 1990, and the Masters tournament in 1989. He won the US Open in 1991 and 1992. Edberg is a typical service-and-volley player, who, halfway through the 90s, found it increasingly difficult to cope with the power tennis of the new tennis generation.

Edda, name for 2 Icelandic collections about the exploits of heroes and gods: *Saemund's Edda*, or the *Poetic Edda*, and *Snorri's Edda*, or the *Prose Edda*. The Prose Edda was compiled by Snorri Sturluson (1179- 1241) as a handbook for the numerous allusions to mythology in poetry. The Poetic Edda, named by the Icelandic Bishop Brynjólf Sveinsson, who discovered the 13th-century manuscript in 1643, is a heterogeneous collection of poems celebrating the old heroes and gods, probably dating in part from the 9th century. Eddic poetry is generally written in short, rhythmical lines.

Eddington, Sir Arthur Stanley (1882-1944), English astronomer and physicist. He conducted significant research on the interiors of stars: how they transmit light and heat and how the mass of a star is related to its luminosity. Eddington supported the theory of relativity early on when he found that light rays are bent in a gravitational field. He wrote *The Internal Constitution of the Stars* (1926) and *The Expanding Universe* (1933). *See also:* Astronomy; Star.

Eddy, Don (1944-), American visual artist, representative of hyperrealism. His subjects are derived from the consumer society.

Eddy, Mary Baker (1821-1910), U.S. founder of Christian Science. In 1875 she published *Science and Health with Key to the Scriptures*. In 1877 she married Dr. Asa Gilbert Eddy, one of her earliest followers, and 2 years later she organized the First Church of Christ, Scientist, in Boston. She also founded the newspaper *The Christian Science Monitor*. *See also:* Churches of Christ.

Edelweiss, small flowering herb (genus *Leontopodium*) that grows high in the mountains of the European Alps, Asia, and South America. It is the national flower of Switzerland. The name means 'noble white,' referring to the plant's clusters of white flowers, a symbol of purity.

Edema, or dropsy, swelling of bodily tissues due to the accumulation of fluid. It most commonly affects the lower parts of the body, such as the ankles and lower part of the abdomen. Edema is generally the sign of a serious disease. A failing heart may cause edema because it cannot pump blood fast enough to carry away body fluids efficiently. Edema may be a sign of liver or kidney disease or of preeclampsia (toxemia that may occur late in pregnancy). The potbellies of starving children are also cases of edema. The basic cause of the edema must be removed to cure it, but the physician may also prescribe diuretic drugs to rid the body of excess water.

Eden, Garden of, in the Old Testament (Genesis), the first habitation of humans. Eden was created for Adam and Eve. It is described as being watered by the Euphrates, the Tigris, and 2 lesser-known streams, the Gihon and the Pishon, thus its location was probably in ancient Mesopotamia (modern Iraq). However, it is more important as a symbol of a natural state of perfection before sin. Its name is often synonymous with paradise. *See also:* Bible; Old Testament.

Eden, Robert Anthony, Earl of Avon (1897-1977), British diplomat and prime minister. Eden became foreign secretary in 1935 but resigned in 1938 in protest against Prime Minister Neville Chamberlain's appeasement of the Axis dictators Adolf Hitler and Benito Mussolini. He served again in the foreign office 1940-1945 and 1951-1955. As prime minister (1955-1957) he promoted an ill-advised invasion of Egypt (1956) to restore Anglo-French control of the Suez Canal after the Egyptians had nationalized it. He resigned the next year because of ill health.

Edentate, member of an order of mammals (*Edentata*) that have no teeth or only primitive, rootless teeth without enamel. Sloths, anteaters, and armadillos are the only members of the group. They are found mainly in tropical and subtropical climates.

Ederle, Gertrude Caroline (1906-), U.S. swimmer, the first woman to swim the English Channel. She broke all previous records, crossing the 35 mi (56.3 km) from France to England on Aug. 6, 1926, in 14 hr 39 min.

Edgerton, Harold Eugene (1903-1990), U.S. electrical engineer. He revolutionized photography with the invention of the electronic or stroboscopic flash. This light flashes at a fraction of a second's duration, enabling photographs to be taken of an object moving at high speed. Night aerial and oceanographic depth photography were made possible by Edgerton's invention. *See also:* Photography.

Edgeworth, Maria (1767-1849), Anglo-Irish novelist. Her gifts for social observation and colorful, realistic portrayal of Irish domestic life and youth influenced later novelists including Sir Walter Scott. Among her works are *Tales of Fashionable Life* (1809-1812).

Edinburgh (pop. 448,000), capital of Scotland since 1437 and the nation's second-largest city. The city is in southeastern Scotland south of the Firth of Forth and north of the Pentland Hills. Edinburgh Castle, crowning Castle Hill (the neck of an extinct volcano), dominates the city and separates the so-called Old Town (dating from the 11th century) to the east from the New Town (planned in 1767) to the north. The wide thoroughfare of Princess Street in the New Town is one of Europe's best-known streets. Other landmarks include the nearby extinct volcano called Arthur's Seat and many fine parks and gardens. Edinburgh has long been famous as a center of Scottish culture. Its university dates from 1583, and famous figures including James Boswell and Sir Walter Scott had links with the city. Edinburgh is known for public art galleries and, since 1947, its annual international arts festival. The city is also a leading government, banking, and insurance center. Its industries include brewing, distilling, printing, publishing, and electrical and chemical engineering.

Edirne (pop. 116,000), formerly Adrianople, ancient city in northwest Turkey near the Greek and Bulgarian borders where the Maritsa, Arda, and Tunca rivers converge. It is a regional trade and agricultural center producing *peynir* (white cheese), cotton, and grains. The architect Sinan built its Selimiye Mosque in the 1500s. Originally called Uskudama, it was renamed Hadrianopolis (c.A.D. 125) by the Roman emperor Hadrian, became the Ottoman Empire capital (1413-1458), and was occupied by Russians, Bulgarians, and Greeks before being restored to Turkey (1922). *See also:* Turkey.

Edison, Thomas Alva (1847-1931), U.S. inventor, the 'Wizard of Menlo Park.' The *New York Times* calculated when he died that the total value of commercial enterprises derived from his inventions was $25,683,544,343, thus crediting his brain with the highest cash value of all time. Edison had only 3 months of formal schooling; his teacher said he was 'addled.' He received the rest of his education from his mother. From 16 to 21 he roamed the United States and Canada as an itinerant telegraph operator. Arriving in New York penniless, he borrowed a dollar, found work with a company controlling stock-ticker apparatus, invented an improved ticker system, and sold it for $40,000. He opened a small factory to produce the device and continued inventing. In 1876 Edison moved to Menlo Park, N.J., where he set up the world's first industrial research laboratory. There he developed a carbon transmitter for the new but impractical Bell telephone, and sold it for $100,000. Further experimentation produced the phonograph (1877). Edison then turned to the problem of electric lighting, creating the filament and vacuum bulb that enabled an incandescent light to be steadily maintained (Dec. 31, 1879). His company, the Edison Machine Works, a forerunner of the giant modern utilities, was moved in 1886 to Schenectady, N.Y., which then became a major technological and manufacturing center. Edison moved his laboratories the following year to West Orange, N.J. His next great invention was the kinetoscope, or motion picture viewer. He also experimented with the concept of talking pictures. Among his many productions were a kiln for Portland cement, a synthetic substitute for carbolic acid, and a high-efficiency automobile battery. He also established the first electric power station at Pearl Street in New York City. His best-known remark was that genius is '1% inspiration and 99% perspiration.'

Edmonds, Walter Dumaux (1903-), U.S. writer of historical fiction. His novels, which focus on the area of upstate New York, include *Drums Along the Mohawk* (1936) and *Chad Hanna* (1940). For *Bert Green's Barn* (1975), he won the 1976 National Book Award for children's literature.

Edmonton (pop. 616,000), capital of the Canadian province of Alberta, situated on the North Saskatchewan River. Edmonton was founded in 1795 by the Hudson's Bay Company on the traditional boundary between Cree and Blackfoot territories. A railroad link with Calgary, completed in 1891, helped the town to develop as a supply center and starting point for the Klondike gold rush (1898) and as a market town for farmers settling the rich surrounding agricultural region. The city is the leading transportation and marketing center for northern Alberta and is served by transcontinental railroads, the Alaska Highway, and a major airport. It is a leading oil-refining center, using the by-products in chemicals and plastics, and also produces building materials and agricultural products. Edmonton is also a cultural center, with the University of Alberta (founded 1906), a symphony orchestra, and 2 museums. Elk Island National Park lies east of the city. Industrialization has been rapid since the local discovery of oil in 1947.
See also: Alberta.

Edom, ancient kingdom in what is now southern Jordan, between the Dead Sea and Gulf of Aqaba. Edomites, who were, according to the Old Testament, descendants of Esau, occupied the area around the 13th century B.C. and had frequent conflicts with Hebrews. Between 1200 and 700 B.C. Edom prospered because of its strategic trade route location and copper industry. Between 500 and 400 B.C. Edom was invaded by the Nabateans, an Arab people, and Edomites migrated to southern Judaea, where they established the territory of Idumea.

EDP, in computer technology, acronym for Electronic Data Processing, data processing performed largely by electronic digital computers.

Education, the process of establishing habits of critical and independent appraisal of information for the purpose of intellectu-

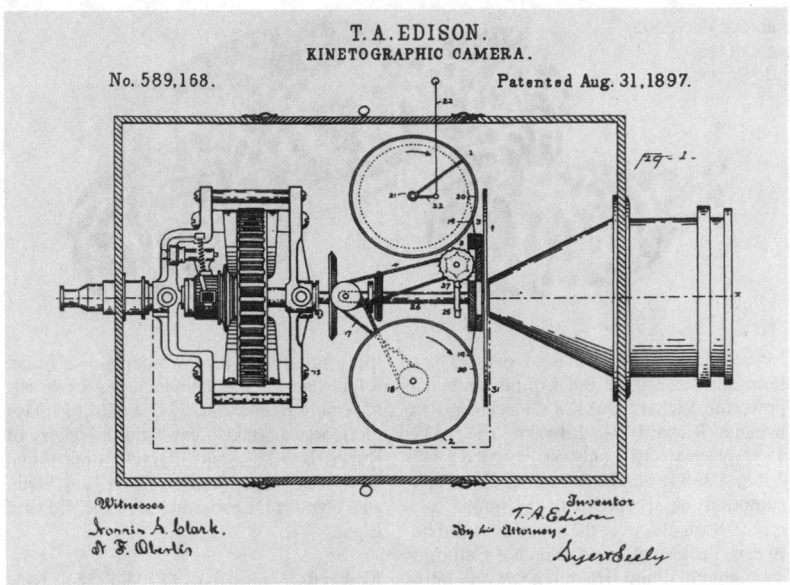

T. A. EDISON.
KINETOGRAPHIC CAMERA.
No. 589,168.   Patented Aug. 31,1897.

The patent registration form of Edison's cinematographic camera.

ally developing the whole person. Socrates held that the beginning of real learning was the realization that we do not know. Education can take place formally in schools with teachers, students, courses, books and activities. It can also take place informally in homes, streets, or meeting places when ideas and information are exchanged.

Educational measurement *See:* Testing.

Educational psychology, application of psychology to education, especially to problems of teaching and learning. By ascertaining typical student behavior at various stages, teaching methods for different age groups can be refined and developed. The German philosopher Johann Friedrich Herbart (1776-1841) is considered the pioneer of the application of psychology to the art of teaching. Since then many others have contributed, notably William James, (often

The most well-known example of a medieval legislative assembly, is the English parliament. Originally, it was not a representation of elected people, but first and foremost a Royal Council. Its present function the parliament attained much later, during the 18th and 19th centuries. This medieval miniature shows King Edward I (r.1272-1307) presiding over a meeting of his parliament.

considered the first theorist of American educational psychology), and John Dewey, founder of the liberal philosophy known as instrumentalism.
See also: Herbart, Johann Friedrich.

Education, vocational *See:* Vocational education.

Edward, 11 kings of England. There were 3 Saxon kings: Edward the Elder (A.D. 870-924), Edward the Martyr (963-978), and Edward the Confessor (1002-1066). Since the Norman Conquest in 1066, there have been 8 English kings named Edward. **Edward I** (1239-1307) reigned 1272-1307. He subjugated Wales and, inconclusively, Scotland, centralized the national administration, and reduced baronial and clerical power. He also summoned the Model Parliament (1295). **Edward II** (Edward of Caernarvon; 1284-1327), first heir apparent to be created prince of Wales (1301), reigned 1307-1327. He spent his reign resisting his barons. His poorly directed Scottish campaigns were highlighted by his defeat at Bannockburn (1314) by Robert Bruce. In 1326 he was unseated in a revolt led by his wife, Queen Isabella, and her paramour Roger de Mortimer. Edward was imprisoned and forced to abdicate in favor of his son, and was probably murdered. **Edward III** (1312-1377) reigned 1327-1377. Edward's claim to part of Guienne in France was one of the causes of the Hundred Years War. Despite decisive victories at Crécy (1346) and Poitiers (1356), he had lost most French territory by the end of his reign. In 1348-1349 the Black Death decimated the population, resulting in major economic and social upheavals. **Edward IV** (1442-1483) reigned 1461-1470 and 1471-1483 during the Wars of the Roses. A Yorkist, Edward deposed the Lancastrian Henry VI in 1461 and again in 1471 after the latter had been restored in 1470 by the Earl of Warwick. Edward reestablished the power of the monarchy, improved administration and law enforcement, and increased England's trade and prosperity. **Edward V** (1470-1483?), who reigned April-June 1483, was one of the

E

Moray eels, *Gymnothorax undulatis* (left) and *G. favagineus* (right), are plentiful in the rock outcrops and coral reefs of the Indo-Pacific.

E

The eggs of birds and reptiles are a self-sufficient environment that fills all the needs of the developing embryo, as is shown in this cross section of a chicken egg. The embryo (A) is surrounded by a membrane called the amnion, which forms the amniotic cavity and contains a saline solution to protect the embryo against mechanical and thermal shocks. The allantois collects and stores toxic waste products. The yolk sac contains sufficient yolk to provide nutrition until the egg hatches. The chorion (B), an outer protective membrane, develops on the inside of the shell (C). Through the shell, oxygen is taken in and carbon dioxide is released.

'princes in the tower.' He is believed to have been murdered at the order of his uncle and protector, Richard Duke of Gloucester, who became Richard III. **Edward VI** (1537-1553), Henry VIII's only son, reigned 1547-1553. A sickly child who was to die of consumption, he succeeded to the throne as a minor. Struggles over the succession and between Protestants and Roman Catholics soon engulfed him. His reign saw the introduction, under Archbishop Cranmer, of the first *Book of Common Prayer* (1549). **Edward VII** (1841-1910), king of Great Britain and Ireland 1901-1910, had a reputation as a *bon vivant*. He was concerned with Britain's role in Europe and helped to promote ententes with France and Russia and to defuse the rivalry with Germany. **Edward VIII** (1894-1972), king of Great Britain and Ireland Jan. 20-Dec. 11, 1936, had enjoyed great popularity as prince of Wales and heir, but his association with U.S. divorcée Wallis Warfield Simpson was treated as a scandal by the press and met stern opposition from government and Church. To avoid a constitutional crisis, Edward abdicated, becoming duke of Windsor. He married Mrs. Simpson in 1937 and thereafter lived mainly in France.

Edwardian era, in English history, period from the accession of Edward VII to the outbreak of World War I, 1901-1914. Apart from general peacefulness, opulence, and elegance, it was characterized by a growing awareness of social problems, questioning of established authority, and disregard for traditions. In politics the era was dominated by the Liberal Party (led by Herbert Asquith), the rise of the Labour Party, and

the agitation for women's suffrage. Representative literature included the novels of Arnold Bennett and H.G. Wells, the plays of George Bernard Shaw, and the poetry of Rupert Brooke. Major figures in the visual arts were Walter Sickert, P. Wilson Steer, and Wyndham Lewis, and in music, Edward Elgar.

Edwards, Jonathan (1703-1758), New England theologian and philosopher. A Calvinist in the Puritan tradition, he furthered the Great Awakening by his preaching. He was dismissed by his church in 1749 for his opposition to the taking of the sacrament of the Lord's Supper by those who had not experienced conversion. In 1757 he became president of the College of New Jersey. Influenced by John Locke, he wrote many works of philosophical theology, most notably *Religious Affections* (1746) and *The Freedom of the Will* (1754).
See also: Calvinism.

Edward the Black Prince (1330-1376), Prince of Wales and eldest son of Edward III of England. When only 16 he fought bravely at the Battle of Crécy (1346), his father's great victory, supposedly wearing black armor, which gave rise to his name. In 1356, at the Battle of Poitiers during the Hundred Years War, he defeated and captured King John II of France. In 1361 he married his cousin Joan, 'the fair maid of Kent,' and the following year was put in charge of the English possessions of France. After further fighting in Castile and in France, he gave up his military career but continued to play an important part in the political struggles of England. He died before his father and thus never became king. He was considered a model of medieval chivalry.
See also: Crécy, Battle of; Hundred Years War.

Edward the Confessor, Saint (1002?-1066), king of the English 1042-1066. Brought up in Normandy, he was respected for his piety. During most of his reign the government was dominated by the powerful Earl Godwin. Edward alienated the country by attempting to exile Godwin and introduce Normans into the government. He had named William of Normandy as his heir, but on his deathbed chose Harold, Godwin's son, precipitating the Norman Conquest. His feast day is Oct. 13.

Eel, long slender fish of the order Anguilliformes, without pelvic fins and with dorsal and ventral fins joining the tail fin. The order includes the conger, moray, snake,

snipe, and freshwater eel families. Some eels are covered in slime, and some have tiny scales on the skin. Moray eels live in warm water and are a danger to divers because of their bite. American and European freshwater eels spawn in the Sargasso Sea. The leaflike larvae cross the ocean and enter rivers as young eels, or elvers. When adult, they swim back to the Sargasso Sea to spawn and die.

Eelgrass (*Zostera marina*), grasslike plant of brackish estuaries and lagoons. It bears 3-ft (1-cm) narrow leaves that float in the water. In very salty water eelgrass reproduces by budding, but in fairly fresh water it produces flowers. Eelgrass is an important food for geese, manatees, and marine turtles.

Eelworm, any of the minute nematode worms, the largest being less than 1/50 in (0.5 mm) long. They are found in vast numbers in soil, in fresh water, and on the seashore. Many attack plants and insects and some are serious pests. The *stem and bulb eelworm*, for instance, stunts or kills a wide variety of crops, such as cereals, bulbs, and strawberries. They may be transmitted by plant-sucking bugs and themselves transmit diseases such as tobacco mosaic.

Efficiency, ratio of the useful work derived from a machine to the energy put into it. The mechanical efficiency of a machine is always less than 100%, some energy being lost as heat in friction. A typical gasoline engine may have a thermal efficiency of only 25%, a steam engine, 10%.
See also: Energy.

Effigy mounds, prehistoric Native American burial mounds in northeastern Iowa. Located west of the Mississippi River, the mounds were probably constructed about A.D. 1000. There were probably about 100,000 mounds, many in the form of birds or animals, but many have been destroyed by farming.

Efflorescence, in chemistry, loss of water from crystals. If the pressure of the water vapor produced by the crystals is greater than the pressure of water vapor in the atmosphere, the crystals will lose water and develop a crumbly appearance. The opposite of efflorescence, absorbtion of moisture from the atmosphere, is called *deliquescence*.

Eft *See:* Newt.

EFTA *See:* European Free Trade Association.

Egbert (A.D. 775?-839), king of Wessex in England (802-839). After being driven into exile by the king of Mercia, he gained the West Saxon throne. He conquered Cornwall, Kent, Surrey, and Sussex, also dominating Mercia, East Anglia, and Northumbria, thus expanding Wessex and making it the dominant kingdom of England.

Egg, or ovum, in biology, female gamete or germ cell, found in all animals and in most plants. Popularly, the term is used to describe those animal eggs that are deposited by the female either before or after fertiliza-

amniotic cavity · yolk sac · oxygen · allantois · carbon dioxide

In the oases, which are found throughout Egypt, there are approximately six million date trees, yielding an average of 320,000 tons (325,120,000 kg) of dates annually.

E

tion and develop outside the body, such as the eggs of reptiles and birds. The egg is a single cell that develops into the embryo after fertilization by a single sperm cell, or male gamete. In animals, it is formed in a primary sex organ, or gonad, called the ovary. In fishes, reptiles, and birds there is a food store of yolk enclosed within its outer membrane. In plants called angiosperms, the female reproductive organs form part of the flower. The egg cell is found within the ovules, which upon fertilization develop into the embryo and seed.
See also: Reproduction.

Eggplant (*Solanum melongena*), plant of the nightshade family, native to India but now grown around the world. It has lobed leaves and grows egg-shaped fruit up to 12 in (30.5 cm) long. These are eaten boiled, baked, stewed, or fried.

Eglantine, or sweetbrier, fragrant, branching rose originating in England, especially *Rosa eleganteria*. It grows wild in the eastern United States, and is used in landscaping. The shrub has curved stems with sharp thorns, small, dark green leaves, pink flowers, and bright red or orange fruit.

Eglevsky, André (1917-1977), Russian-born U.S. virtuoso ballet dancer and teacher. He was a member of the Ballet Russe de Monte Carlo (1939-1942) and the New York City Ballet (1951-1958).
See also: Ballet.

Ego (Latin: 'I'), psychological concept, first proposed by Sigmund Freud, referring to a part of the human personality that mediates between the *id*, or instinct, and the *superego*, or conscience. The ego represents what may be called reason and common sense.
See also: Psychoanalysis.

Egret, name of a group of small herons (family Ardeidae), wading birds with long necks, long legs, and pointed bills, with lacy, usually white, plumage, found around the world. The great, or common, egret (*Casmerodius albus*) ranges from Europe to New Zealand and throughout the Americas.

Other American species include the snowy egret (*Egretta thula*) and reddish egret (*E. rufescens*). The cattle egret (*Bubulcus ibis*) feeds on insects, often following cattle to catch insects which they flush from the grass. At one time the plumes of the egret were highly valued as items of ceremonial or fashionable dress, and the birds were nearly hunted to extinction. They are now protected by law and numbers are increasing once again.

Egypt

Capital:	Cairo
Area:	385,229 sq mi
	(997,739 sq km)
Population:	70,712,000
Language:	Arabic
Government:	Presidential republic
Independent:	1922
Head of gov.:	Prime minister
Per capita:	US$ 3,700
Monetary unit:	1 Egyptian pound
	= 100 piastres

Egypt, Arab republic in northeast Africa, bounded on the north by the Mediterranean Sea, on the east by Israel and the Red Sea, on the south by the Sudan, and on the west by Libya.

Land and climate. The Sinai peninsula, which is the northeast corner of Egypt, is divided from the rest of the country by the Suez Canal, linking the Mediterranean and the Red Sea. Most of the country's territory is in the western desert, which is the edge of the Sahara. Nearly all the population, however, lives in a narrow band around the Nile, the world's largest river, which runs north from Africa for more than 4,000 mi (6,500 km) and empties into the Mediterranean. The vast, triangular Nile delta, a rich plain of river mud about 150 mi (241 km) across, is known as lower Egypt, and is the major population center. Cairo, Africa's largest city and the capital of Egypt, stands at the head of the Nile delta. Alexandria, a Mediterranean port at the western edge of the delta, is Egypt's second-largest city. Although there has been considerable industrialization since World War II, the country is still predominantly agricultural, dependent on the highly fertile land along the river. The climate is generally dry, hot, and sunny. Only the Mediterranean coast and parts of southern Sinai receive more than 2 in (5 cm) of rain a year.

People. Arabic is the national language. Most Egyptians are Sunni Muslims, but there is a minority (5-10%) of Christians called Copts, who use a form of the ancient Egyptian language in their religious ritual.

Economy. Agriculture is based mainly on irrigation. The amount of available farmland was increased appreciably by the Aswan Dam. The principal export crop is cotton, but Egypt also raises wheat, corn, millet, and rice. Mineral resources include iron ore, salt, natural gas, petroleum, and phosphates. The production of textiles and processed foods dominate the industrial sector. Tourism and the Suez Canal are important sources of foreign currency.

History. Egypt's history goes back thousands of years, but the modern roots of the country begin with the Arab invasion of A.D. 641, when the majority of the people embraced Islam and were integrated into Arab civilization. For about 500 years the country was ruled by caliphs based in Damascus, Baghdad, and other cities. In 1250 power was taken by a Turkish dynasty, the Mamelukes, and in 1517 it became part of the Ottoman Empire. The modern Egyptian state was formed in 1805 by Muhammad Ali, a soldier of Turkish origin. In the late 19th century Egypt fell under British influence, and during World War I London proclaimed the country a British protectorate. In 1937 a formally independent state was created, with King Farouk as monarch. He was overthrown in 1952 by a group of army officers who proclaimed a republic with Gamal Abdel Nasser as president. During Nasser's reign, Egypt was the center of Arab nationalism. There were two wars with Israel, in 1956 and 1967, during which Egypt lost much territory, including the entire Sinai peninsula.

On Nasser's death in 1970, Anwar al-Sadat became president. He joined Syria and Iraq in the War against Israel in October 1973. Shortly after that, Sadat broke Nasser's alliance with the USSR and sought closer ties with the United States. In 1979 Sadat and Menachem Begin of Israel signed a peace

From approximately 5000 to 500 B.C., the
elongated valley and the Nile delta were the
home of a civilization that has fascinated
and intrigued people for centuries. Although
ancient Egypt, with its gigantic structures
and extraordinary death cult has inspired researchers for years, the first real systematic
study did not take place until 1822, when
the Frenchman Jean François Champollion
deciphered its hieroglyphics. The excavations that followed led to sensational discoveries (Tutankhamen's tomb, 14th century
B.C.).

E

Pharaoh Horemheb (14th century B.C.)
makes a sacrifice to the Goddess Isis. The
Egyptian religion worshipped a large number of gods and Isis, the wife and sister of
the God of the Kingdom of the Dead, Osiris,
was one of the most important. A Pharaoh
was also seen as a god.

Sphinx with ram's head, one of a series of
forty identical statues in the temple complex
Karnak, built in worship of the god Amon-
Re. Every little statue belonging to Pharaoh
Ramses II is protected by the holy animals.

Gallery from Ptolemaic times (301-30 B.C.). The architecture and designs
form an image of heaven (the ceiling is covered with paintings of gods) and
earth (the plant motifs on the pillars).

Pharaoh Djoser's tomb (around 2700 B.C.) with stair pyramid, the oldest complex built out of hewn stone known to man. Pyramids were first built during the period of the Old Kingdom (around 2700-2160 B.C.).

E

Egyptians believed in an afterlife with a physical identity; this is why (highly placed) people and honored animals, like cats, were mummified. This is a picture of the mummy of the great Pharaoh Ramses II (1304-1237 B.C.).

Painting on a tomb in Tebe (around 400 B.C.). Agriculture was the foundation of the Egyptian economy and therefore the power of the Kings. Because land could only be owned by Kings, agriculture was seen as a state affair.

After the Six-Day War (1967), the Suez Canal was closed to all shipping. It was not until after the October War (1973) that Egypt began clearing the canal and preparing it for maritime traffic. It was officially re-opened in June 1975.

treaty and Israel began a phased withdrawal from the Sinai. In 1981 Sadat was assassinated by Muslim fundamentalists. He was succeeded by his vice president, Hosni Mubarak, who has continued Sadat's general policies, both foreign and domestic. In 1993, Mubarak won the presidential elections for the third time. Muslim fundamentalists are posing a threat to the country's stability. In 1995 fundamentalists attempted to assassinate Mubarak. At the end of the 1990s, Egypt was dominated by the regime's battle against radical fundamentalist organizations, such as the Gama'at al-Islamiyya. In November 1997, this Gama'at committed an assault on 58 tourists in Luxor. In 1999, Mubarak was re-elected President for the fourth time. In 2002, the relations with Israel deteriorated due to the Israeli'sattitude towards the Palestinian leader, Arafat.

Ehrenburg, Ilya Grigoryevich (1891-1967), Russian author, poet and journalist. Went to Paris in 1909 and was a correspondent for Muscovite newspapers, including during WW I. In 1923 he decided to support the politics of the Soviet Union. His work, which was influenced by the Western approach to life, became very popular, partly due to his ability to adapt to the fluctuations in the party line. After Stalin's death, he anticipated the coming changes in the social climate in his novel *The Thaw* (1954) and dedicated himself to the rehabilitation of

Albert Einstein (1879-1955) physicist and Nobel Prize winner.

previously condemned writers. His work, which was also well read outside of Russia, includes *The Extraordinary Adventures of Julio Jurenito and His Disciples* (1922), *The Fall of Paris* (1941), *The Storm* (1947), *The Ninth Wave* (1952), and *People, Years, Life* (memoires, 1960-1965).

Ehrlich, Paul (1854-1915), German bacteriologist and immunologist, founder of chemotherapy and an early pioneer of hematology. His discoveries include a method of staining and hence identifying the tuberculosis bacillus (1882); the reasons for immunity in terms of the chemistry of antibodies and antigens, for which he shared the 1908 Nobel Prize for physiology or medicine with Élie Metchnikoff; and the use of the drug salvarsan to cure syphilis, the first drug to be used in treating the root cause of a disease (1911).
See also: Bacteriology.

Ehrlich, Paul Ralph (1932-), U.S. ecologist. Ehrlich first became aware of the consequences of overpopulation on a visit to India. In 1967 he forecast massive worldwide famines within the next 2 decades. He has suggested that all U.S. aid to foreign countries be made conditional upon stringent birth control and that the United States itself should discourage population growth by taxation. He wrote *The Population Bomb* in 1968.

Eich, Günter (1907-1972), German author, became famous especially after World War II for his poems and radio plays. His poetry possesses a great deal of expressive capacity and although sometimes melancholic, is always in search of the meaning of life. His work includes, among others, the following volumes: *Gedichte* (1930), *Botschaften des Regens* (1955), and *Anlässe und Steingärten* (1966).
In his radio plays he put the specific possibilities and the stimulating power of each word to use. By using flashbacks and inserting individual words and sentences, he was able to express much of the human experience of memories, needs, and fears, for example, in *Allah hat hundert Namen* (1957), *Die Brandung vor Setubal* (1958) and bundled: *Träume* (1953, revised in 1959), *Stimmen* (1958) and *Fünfzehn Hörspiele* (1966).

Eichmann, Adolf (1906-1962), German lieutenant-colonel in the Nazi Gestapo, head of the Jewish Division from 1939. He was responsible for the deportation, maltreatment, and murder of European Jews in World War II. He escaped to Argentina but was abducted, tried, and executed in Israel.
See also: Holocaust.

Eider, name of several species of diving ducks of northern latitudes. The common eider is famed for the soft, insulating down of its breast, which it plucks to line its nest. Of commercial value, the down is collected to fill eiderdowns (comforters). In Iceland and Norway, eiders are encouraged to nest on 'eider farms' for this purpose.

Eiffel, Alexandre Gustave (1832-1923), French engineer best known for his design and construction of the Eiffel Tower, Paris (1887-1889), from which he carried out experiments in aerodynamics. In 1912 he founded the first aerodynamics laboratory.

Eiffel Tower, famous tower dominating the skyline of Paris, designed by Alexandre Gustave Eiffel as the focal point of the Universal Exposition of 1889. From masonry piers, 4 iron columns, connected by delicate arches, sweep gracefully inward and upward. At 620 ft (189 m) they converge to form one column and continue to a height of 984 ft (289 m; now 1,056 ft/321 m including the television antenna). Elevators and staircases give visitors access to 3 observation platforms.

Eight Trigrams rebellion, in North China a number of religious communities rose against the ruling Manchu dynasty in the autumn of 1813; they called themselves the 'Religion of the Eight Trigrams' (pa-kwa tjiau) or 'Religion of the Heavenly Principle' (t'ièn-li tjiau). Their religious concepts were related to those of the White Lotus movement and they thought that their rebellion would be the start of an Empire of Peace. The actions of their leaders were poorly coordinated and an attempt to enter the Forbidden City (in Peking) using force failed. After three months of fighting the government troops succeeded in defeating the over 100,000 strong rebel force once and for all. The rebellion, however, marked the beginning of a period of social unrest, which ultimately culminated in the Taiping Rebellion (1851-1864).

Eijkman, Christiaan (1858-1930), Dutch pathologist. He discovered that beriberi results from a thiamine (vitamin B_1) deficiency. He was awarded (with Sir F.G. Hopkins) the 1929 Nobel Prize for physiology or medicine.
See also: Beriberi; Pathology.

Eilat *See:* Elat.

Einstein, Albert (1879-1955), German-born U.S. physicist, one of the greatest scientific figures. He received the Nobel Prize in physics in 1921 for his services to theoretical physics, especially the discovery of the law of the photoelectric effect. While still a youth he taught himself calculus and science. In 1896 he entered the Swiss Federal Polytechnic School in Zurich, where he trained as a teacher of physics and

mathematics. He became a Swiss citizen on receiving his diploma in 1900. Unable to find an academic position, Einstein worked for the Swiss Patent Office while studying for the Ph.D. degree, which he received from the University of Zurich in 1905. In 1905 he published 4 scientific papers, each containing a great discovery: (1) the first presentation of the special theory of relativity; (2) the statement of the equivalence of mass and energy (the famous $E=mc^2$ equation, stating that energy equals mass times the velocity of light squared), which later provided the theoretical basis for the atom bomb; (3) a theoretical explanation of Brownian motion, the incessant erratic movement of tiny particles suspended in a fluid; and (4) his application of Planck's quantum hypothesis to the investigation of the nature of light, in which he showed that light behaved as if it were composed of independent quanta (tiny units) of energy called photons, and not simply of waves. In 1914 he became professor at the University of Berlin and director of the Kaiser Wilhelm Physical Institute, resuming his German citizenship. In 1916 he published his general theory of relativity. Much of the rest of his life was spent in an unsuccessful effort to produce a *unified field theory*, that is, to show that both gravitational and electromagnetic phenomena derive from the geometrical properties of space-time. The task has still not been completed. With the rise of the Nazis, Einstein, a Jew, found his position in Germany impossible, and in 1932 he resigned from his post at Berlin. In 1933 he moved to the Institute for Advanced Study at Princeton, N.J. He became a U.S. citizen in 1940. Just before World War II, Einstein wrote a letter to President Franklin D. Roosevelt, pointing out the theoretical possibility of a nuclear bomb and warning of the danger that Germany might develop the bomb first. This resulted in the establishment of the Manhattan Project. He retired from the institute in 1945 but continued to work there until his death in 1955.
See also: Relativity; $E=mc^2$.

Einsteinium, chemical element, symbol Es; for physical constants see Periodic Table. Einsteinium was discovered in 1952 in the debris of the first thermonuclear explosion by Albert Ghiorso and co-workers at Berkeley, Calif. A special magnetic-type balance was used to weigh the amount of einsteinium-253 obtained, about 0.01 g. The element is prepared by irradiation of plutonium isotopes in a high flux reactor. It is a metallic element and a member of the actinide series. All of its 14 known isotopes are radioactive.

Einstein theory *See:* Relativity.

Einthoven, Willem (1860-1927), Dutch physiologist, awarded the 1924 Nobel Prize for physiology or medicine for his invention of, and investigation of heart action with, the electrocardiograph. In 1903 he devised the string galvanometer, a single fine wire placed under tension in a magnetic field. Current passed through the wire causes a deflection that can be measured, for greater accuracy, by a microscope. This galvanometer

was sensitive enough for him to use it to record the electrical activity of the heart.

Éire *See:* Ireland.

Eisenhower, Dwight David (1890-1969), 34th president of the United States (1953-1961). American general, Republican. Eisenhower gained a reputation as Commander-in-Chief of the Allied Forces during World War II. In that capacity, he was the highest commander during the invasion of North Africa in 1942 and the invasion of Normandy in 1944. His political ingenuity in reaching compromises and reconciling opponents in particular, made him suitable for this position. He became the first commander-in-chief of NATO in 1950. He became immensely popular in the U.S. due to his military successes. This was also expressed by his election to the presidency.

Eisenstein, Sergei Mikhailovich (1898-1948), Soviet film director. A major influence on the development of the cinema, he extended editing techniques, especially the use of montage. His films, notably *The Battleship Potemkin* (1925), *Ten Days That Shook the World* (1927), *Alexander Nevsky* (1938), and *Ivan the Terrible* (1944-1946), are undisputed classics.

Eishi, Hosoda (1756-1829), Japanese painter and artist, a member of the Samurai family, court painter who enjoyed his education at the Kano school. His portraits of courtesans, often painted against a neutral background, evoke a somewhat unreal world. He published an album in 1800, *The Thirty-Six Immortal Women Poets*, which is one of his finest works in terms of composition. He later intentionally exaggerated the height of the slim women in his prints, until they became fanciful apparitions. Around 1790, he produced a series of triptychs that displayed fashionably dressed girls in scenes from the famous novel *Genji monogatari* (The Tale of Genji), which dates from the 10th century.

Eisler, Johannes (Hanns) (1898-1962), German composer. A teacher in Berlin from 1924-1933; he left Germany due to the nazis and emigrated to the US in 1938. He returned in 1948 and took up residence in the GDR in 1950, where he became managing director of a new conservatory, which is currently named after him. He originally wrote dodecaphonic works, but complied with the socialist criterion after 1950; he left a sizeable and very varied oeuvre, including the melody of the East-German national anthem.

Ekaterinburg (formerly Sverdlovsk; pop. 1,367,000), industrial city in the eastern Ural Mountains of Russia. The western terminus of the Trans-Siberian railroad, Ekaterinburg is a major industrial center, with over 200 factories producing machinery, turbines, diesels, and a variety of engineering products. The city was founded in 1721 and called Ekaterinburg, after Tsarina Catherine I. It was renamed in 1924 after Sverdlov, a Bolshevik leader. It was in Sverdlovsk that Tsar Nicholas II and his family were execut-

ed in 1918, during the Russian civil war. The city was renamed Ekaterinburg in 1991. The inhabitants of the area want more autonomy, but so far Yeltsin has refused.
See also: Union of Soviet Socialist Republics.

EKG *See:* Electrocardiogram.

El Aaiun, also Aiun (pop. 94,000), Laayoune, or Ayun, city in Western Sahara (territory in northwest Africa occupied by Morocco), about 10 mi (16 km) from the Atlantic Ocean. It is an important shipping center for phosphates. The area was controlled from the early 1900s by Spain, who founded the city in 1940. El Aaiun was capital of the province of Spanish Sahara until Spain withdrew in 1976, at which time it was incorporated by Morocco.

El Alamein, Egyptian city 65 mi (105 km) east of Alexandria. The city is linked by coastal railroad to Alexandria, and an oil field is in operation nearby. During World War II Britain defeated Germany in 2 decisive battles at El Alamein (1942), preventing the conquest of Egypt. The battles at El Alamein are noted for the brilliant commanders facing each other-Montgomery for the British defeated Rommel of Germany.
See also: World War II.

Eland, largest antelope (6 ft/180 cm), belonging to the family Bovidae, with spiral horns and a short mane. Found in central and southern Africa, elands live in herds of up to 100. Attempts have been made to domesticate elands, because they can survive in very dry conditions and give excellent milk and meat.

Elat, or Eilat (pop. 26,000), town at the southern tip of Israel on the Gulf of Aqaba. It is Israel's only port, with direct access to East Africa and South Asia via the Red Sea. Established in 1948, it began to grow after 1956 when the Egyptian blockade on the Gulf of Aqaba was lifted. The blockade's re-

The common eland (*T. oreyx*), the world's largest antelope, can go for months without drinking, by obtaining moisture from the plants that it eats.

E

sumption in 1967 precipitated the Six-Day Arab-Israeli War. Exports include textiles, citrus fruit, and manufactured goods; lumber and crude petroleum are among the major imports. Its warm, dry climate has made Elat a winter resort with the additional attraction of the nearby Red Sea and its tropical fish and corals.

Elba, Italian island in the Mediterranean, 6 mi (9.7 km) off the west coast of central Italy. At various times under the rule of Pisa, Spain, and Naples, it was the site of Napoleon I's exile, 1814-1815. The island is about 20 mi (32 km) long and less than 10 mi (16 km) wide and is very mountainous. Industries include iron mining, marble quarrying, fishing, and agriculture.
See also: Italy.

Elbe River, major river in central Europe. It rises in the northwestern part of the Czech Republic and flows 725 mi (1,167 km) north through Germany into the North Sea beyond Hamburg. The river is navigable for some 525 mi (845 km). It is connected to the Weser river, the Oder river and the Rhine river and by a canalsystem to the Baltic Sea. Important cities on the Elbe include Hamburg, Dresden, and Magdeburg.

El'brus, mountain in the south of Russia, in the Caucasus mountains; 18,482 ft (5,633 m). Highest peak in Europe.

Elder, or elderberry, tree or shrub (genus *Sambucus*) of the honeysuckle family, native to temperate and subtropical regions. The plant bears white flowers that mature to juicy purple or red berries, used in pies and wines.

Elderberry *See:* Elder.

El Dorado (Spanish, 'the gilded one'), legendary South American king who was reputed to cover himself with gold dust at festivals and then, as a sacrifice, wash it off in a lake into which his subjects also threw gold; also, legendary kingdom on the Amazon River, sought for its reputed wealth by Spanish explorers of the 16th century.

Eleanor of Aquitaine (1122-1204), daughter and heir of William X, duke of Aquitaine; queen consort first to Louis VII of France (marriage annulled 1152) and then to Henry II of England. Her marriage to Henry in 1152 brought almost all of western France under English domination. In 1173 she supported her sons (later kings Richard I and John) in unsuccessful rebellion against their adulterous father and was afterward kept in captivity until Henry's death in 1185. She was subsequently active in politics in support of her sons.

Elecampane (*Inula helenium*), large coarse herb with yellow flowers, native to Europe and Asia as far east as the Himalayas. It was introduced to North America, where it now grows wild. The thick, fleshy roots are used medicinally.

Election, selection of public officeholders by vote. Elections may be direct or indirect.

In direct elections the voters themselves choose among the candidates for office or proposals in a referendum. In indirect elections voters choose delegates who cast the final and decisive votes. Elections may be based on the plurality system or on proportional representation. Under the former system, which is used in most English-speaking countries, the candidate who receives the largest number of votes in a district, not necessarily a majority, is the winner. The legislature is then composed of the winners of the individual contests. Under proportional representation, each party nominates a slate of candidates in each district, usually equal in number to the total number of seats to which that district is entitled. The parties are then allocated seats based on the percentage of the total vote they win in the district, with some minimum, such as 5%, required for any representation at all.
The idea that representative democracy requires the participation of all adults developed only slowly in the 19th century. Religious and property qualifications disappeared gradually. By 1920, most Western nations had adopted universal suffrage.

Election campaign, period before an election when candidates and political parties carry out actions to win votes. A campaign organization plans strategies to announce the candidacy, develop support, win the nomination, and get out the vote. Modern campaigning makes great use of broadcast media, targeting potential voters with demographic surveys and canvassing.
See also: Election.

Electra, in Greek mythology, daughter of Agamemnon and Clytemnestra, and the older sister of Orestes. To avenge the murder of Agamemnon, she helped Orestes slay the murderers, Clytemnestra and her lover, Aegisthus. This theme was the subject of tragedies by Aeschylus, Sophocles, and Euripides, as well as by Eugene O'Neill in his trilogy *Mourning Becomes Electra* (1931), and by composer Richard Strauss in his opera *Elektra* (1909).
See also: Mythology.

Electra complex, in psychoanalysis, the attraction of a daughter to her father, named for Electra, daughter of Agamemnon in Greek mythology.
See also: Psychoanalysis.

Electrical engineering *See:* Engineering.

Electric arc, area of intense light and heat produced by the passage of electricity across a small gap between 2 electrodes. Electricity is able to span the gap because it ionizes the surrounding air, which then serves as a conductor. The arc light, which uses carbon electrodes, is commonly used as a spotlight in the theater and as a floodlight. The heat produced by an arc is used in welding to melt metal rods, which solidify to provide a strong joint between 2 metal surfaces.

Electric battery *See:* Battery.

Electric car, automobile powered by electricity. Electric cars were in use in the 1870s

and remained in production until 1930, when they were displaced by the gasoline engine. Recently the electric car has been under reexamination because it is quiet, cheap to run, requires no oil or water, and emits no pollutants. A rechargeable battery or bank of batteries drives an electric motor that turns the wheels. The range of electric cars on single charge is still very limited, up to about 40 mi (64.4 km). Higher capacity silver/zinc and sodium/sulfur storage batteries under development promise a longer range. Fuel cells similar to those used to power spacecraft systems have also been applied to electric car propulsion, giving a theoretical range of about 150 mi (242 km). But many serious problems remain to be solved before family-sized electric cars become practical.

Electric circuit, path followed by an electric current. It consists of 3 basic parts: an energy source (e.g., battery or generator) that converts nonelectric energy into electric energy, an output device (e.g., motor or lamp) that uses electric energy to do work, and a connection (e.g., wire or cable) that allows electric current to flow between the source and output device. Circuits can be switched on and off. An open circuit has gaps, preventing the current from completing its path, while a closed circuit has no gaps.
See also: Electricity.

Electric current, flow of electric charges. Protons, part of every atom's nucleus, have a positive charge; electrons surrounding the nucleus have a negative charge. Substances that freely give up electrons, such as aluminum, copper, and silver, are good *conductors*, allowing electric current to flow freely. Poor conductors, such as lead and tin, are more resistant to electric current. Substances that do not conduct electricity, such as glass and rubber, are insulators. Direct current (DC), used to power automobiles, always flows in 1 direction, while alternating current (AC), used in homes and for many electronic devices, reverses direction periodically.
See also: Alternating current.

Electric eel (*Electrophorus electricus*), eel-like species of fish of the family Electrophoridae that can produce an electric discharge, found in northern South America. Electricity, generated by electric organs composed of modified muscle cells or electroplaques, is used to detect and stun prey, repel enemies, and communicate with other electric eels. These long, narrow fish can grow to 8 ft (2.4 m), are colored olive brown, and can produce 350-650 volts of electricity.

Electric eye, or photoelectric cell, electronic device either producing current or allowing current to flow when light shines on it, used for controlling such devices as lights and burglar alarms, and for measuring light for photographic and video equipment. They react rapidly to light changes and respond to visible as well as invisible (infrared and ultraviolet) light waves. Phototubes, solar cells, and photoconductive cells are types of electric eyes.
See also: Electronics.

Electric field, field that surrounds an electric charge and exerts force on any nearby electric charges. The concept of field considers one charge as central. The force is an attractive force between unlike charges and repellent between like charges. In empty space, unit charges 1 cm apart produce a force of 1 dyne. The force is reduced when a medium, or dielectric, separates the charges. *See also:* Electricity.

Electric fish, any of various fishes having the ability to generate electric currents for stunning prey or enemies or for locating nearby objects. The electric currents are generated in specialized muscles. Fish that stun their prey or their adversaries include the Mediterranean electric ray, which delivers a charge of 200 volts, the marine stargazers, the electric catfish of Africa, and the electric eel of the Amazon. The last is not a true eel; its body organs are squeezed into the head end, and most of the eellike body is given over to an electric organ that discharges 500 volts. The electric eel also discharges a very weak current in the form of continuous pulses, forming an electromagnetic field, allowing the fish to detect disturbances in this field. The elephant-snout fish and the knifefish of Africa also have this faculty.

Electric furnace, furnace powered by electricity and used for melting, alloying, and heat-treating steel alloys and for manufacturing high-speed tools. The chamber, salt bath, arc, and induction furnaces produce temperatures up to 1500°C and can melt 100 tons of steel.
See also: Furnace.

Electric fuse *See:* Fuse.

Electric generator, or dynamo, machine producing electricity most often by converting mechanical energy into electrical energy. They are used for factory machines, lighting, and home appliances. They can be either direct current (DC), producing electric current flowing in one direction, or alternating current (AC), producing electric current that reverses direction periodically. Some scientific instruments use midget generators while larger generators can supply electricity for entire cities.
See also: Electricity.

Electric heating *See:* Heating.

Electric induction *See:* Induction, electric.

Electricity, phenomenon of charged subatomic particles at rest or in motion. Electricity provides a highly versatile form of energy. *Electric charge* is an inherent property of matter. Electrons carry a negative charge and protons carry a positive charge. For each electron in the atom, there is normally 1 proton. When this balance is disturbed, a net charge is left on an object; the study of such isolated charges is called *electrostatics*. Like charges repel and unlike charges attract each other with a force proportional to the 2 charges and inversely proportional to the square of the distance between them (the inverse-square law). This

force is normally interpreted in terms of an *electric field* produced by one charge with which the other interacts. Pairs of equal but opposite charges separated by a small distance are called *dipoles*; the product of charge and separation is called the *dipole moment*. The amount of work done in moving a unit charge from one point to another against the electric field is called the electric *potential difference*, or voltage, between the points; it is measured in volts. The ratio of a charge added to a body to the voltage produced is called the *capacitance* of the body. The presence of an electric field in a conductor produces a steady flow of charge in the direction of the field; such a flow constitutes an *electric current*, measured in amperes. Electric sources such as batteries and generators convert chemical, mechanical, or other energy into electrical energy and pump charge through conductors much as a water pump circulates water in a radiator heating system. Batteries create a constant voltage, producing a steady, or direct, current (DC). Many generators, on the other hand, provide a voltage that changes in direction many times a second and so produces an alternating current (AC), in which the charges move to and fro instead of continuously in one direction. The latter system has advantages in generation, transmission, and application and is now used almost universally for domestic and industrial purposes. Static electricity was known to the ancient Greeks. The 18th century saw the initiation of many experiments with conduction and other aspects of electricity. The inverse square law was hinted at by J. Priestley in 1767 and later confirmed by H. Cavendish and C.A. Coulomb. G.S. Ohm formulated his law of conduction in 1826, although its essentials were known before then. The common nature of all the 'types' of electricity then known was demonstrated in 1826 by M.

Faraday, who also originated the concept of electric field lines.

Electric light, device using electric energy to produce visible light. Incandescent lamps have 3 basic parts: the filament, a wire through which electricity flows; the bulb, which protects the filament; and the base, which holds the lamp connecting it to an electric circuit. Gaseous-discharge lamps (fluorescent, neon, metal halide lamps) use pressurized gases instead of filaments. Light-emitting diodes (LEDs), used in computers and digital watches, and electroluminescent panels, used as night lights and on instrument panels, produce dim light directly from electric energy, and do not require a bulb, electric discharge, or filament. Thomas Edison developed the first incandescent light (1879).
See also: Edison, Thomas Alva.

Electric measurement, measurable, observable effects (heat, force, magnetism) of electric current. Electric current is measured in *amperes* (1 ampere is roughly 6 billion electrons per sec). The quantity of electricity carried by current is measured in *coulombs* (quantity transmitted by 1 ampere in 1 sec). Units of electric force are measured in *volts* (difference in potential energy between 2 points on a wire carrying 1 ampere, producing 1 watt). A *kilowatt-hour* is the power produced by 1,000 watts in 1 hr. Resistance (opposition of material to electric current) is measured in *ohms* (resistance of a conductor carrying 1 ampere when the potential difference across the conductor is 1 volt).
See also: Ampere; Coulomb.

Electric meter, instrument for measuring the consumption of electricity. Domestic electric meters register the quantity of electricity used in the home in kilowatt-hours

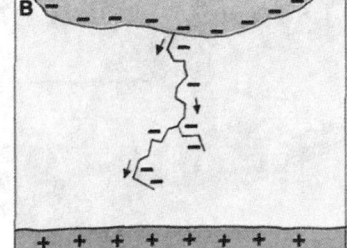

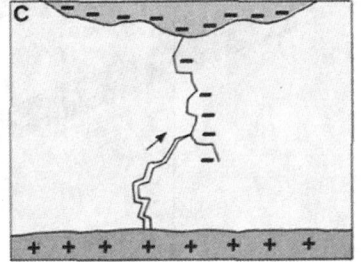

Lightning, an awesome display of natural electricity, is the result of a potential difference between a cloud and the ground (A). A stroke starts with a small lightning discharge called a step leader, which moves toward Earth in a series of steps (B). When the leader reaches the ground, the negative discharge moves back up the path followed by the step leader (C). The return stroke is the thunderbolt that is actually seen and heard; it is estimated to produce about 10,000 amperes.

E

(KwH). The meter contains a metal disk that rotates in a magnetic field produced by an electromagnet inside the meter. The greater the rate at which power is consumed, the faster the disk rotates. The disk is connected to the dials of the meter through a train of wheels. The amount consumed is periodically read by an official of the electricity company. Other electric meters used to measure the various factors of an electric current, such as ammeters, voltmeters, wattmeters, and ohmmeters, depend mostly on electromagnetism. Some electric meters combine all these instruments in one large instrument that can be switched from one kind of measuring operation to another.

Electric motor, machine for converting electric energy into mechanical energy. Appliances such as refrigerators and dishwashers, and power tools such as electric drills all use electric motors. Alternating current (AC) motors are ordinarily used in household appliances. The direct current (DC) motors are commonly used by machinery in factories.
See also: Alternating current.

Electric power, electric energy used for work, measured in units called watts. Electric power plants create mechanical energy that is converted via a generator into electricity. Fossil-fueled steam electric power plants produce electricity by burning fossil fuels (coal, oil, natural gas), and hydroelectric power plants use the energy of falling water. Nuclear power plants use heat produced by nuclear fission (splitting nuclei of atoms of uranium or other heavy elements in a nuclear reactor). While fission is a highly efficient form of power, it yields dangerous

radioactive wastes. Other sources of power valued for being nonpolluting and for not depleting natural resources include geothermal power, using heat from the earth, and plants using wind and solar energy. Electricity is distributed to consumers using a system of transmission lines to carry current and transformers to change voltage. Electric utilities are the organizations generating, transmitting, or distributing electric power.
See also: Electricity.

Electric railroad, fast, quiet, non-polluting, electrically powered, high-speed railway system including passenger and freight trains, subways, and elevated systems. Electricity is received by the train through an overhead wire (catenary) or electrified third rail. A framework (pantograph) atop the train conducts electricity from the catenary to a propulsion system moving the train, or a metal device (shoe) slides along an electrified third rail conducting electricity to the propulsion system. Only 1% of U.S. track is electrified, but electric railroads are common in Europe and Japan.
See also: Railroad.

Electric ray *See:* Torpedo.

Electric shock *See:* Shock treatment.

Electric switch, device used to open and close an electric circuit. The most common type is the snap-action toggle switch. A circuit is completed when the switch is turned on, and broken when it is turned off.

Electric train *See:* Electric railroad.

Electric wiring, system of wires that carries

electric current through a building. Faulty wiring is a common cause of fire. Most homes use 120-volt circuits of 15 amperes, although large appliances and machinery use 240-volt circuits with greater amperage.

Electrocardiogram (ECG or EKG), measurements of the wave patterns produced by the electrical currents generated by the contractions of the heart muscles. The electrocardiogram is the main diagnostic technique of electrocardiography, which is the science of measuring and interpreting the electrical activity of the heart. During an EKG electrodes are attached to the hands, feet, and chest, and the electrical currents are recorded on light-sensitive film. Deviations from the normal shape of the electrical waves point to various disorders of the heart.
See also: Heart.

Electrochemistry, branch of physical chemistry dealing with the effect of electricity on chemical charge and the interconversion of electrical and chemical energy. To produce electrochemical reactions, 2 *electrodes* or conductors are placed in liquid medium or *electrolyte*, producing an environment allowing the free flow of electrons.
See also: Chemistry; Electricity.

Electrocution, usually fatal effect of passing a high-energy electrical current through a body. Electricity passing through the body fluid, which acts as a resistor, causes burns at sites of connection and along the electrical pathway. Convulsions and rhythm disturbances in the heart are usual; the latter are the cause of immediate death. Artificial respiration with cardiac massage must be started immediately if resuscitation is to be successful.

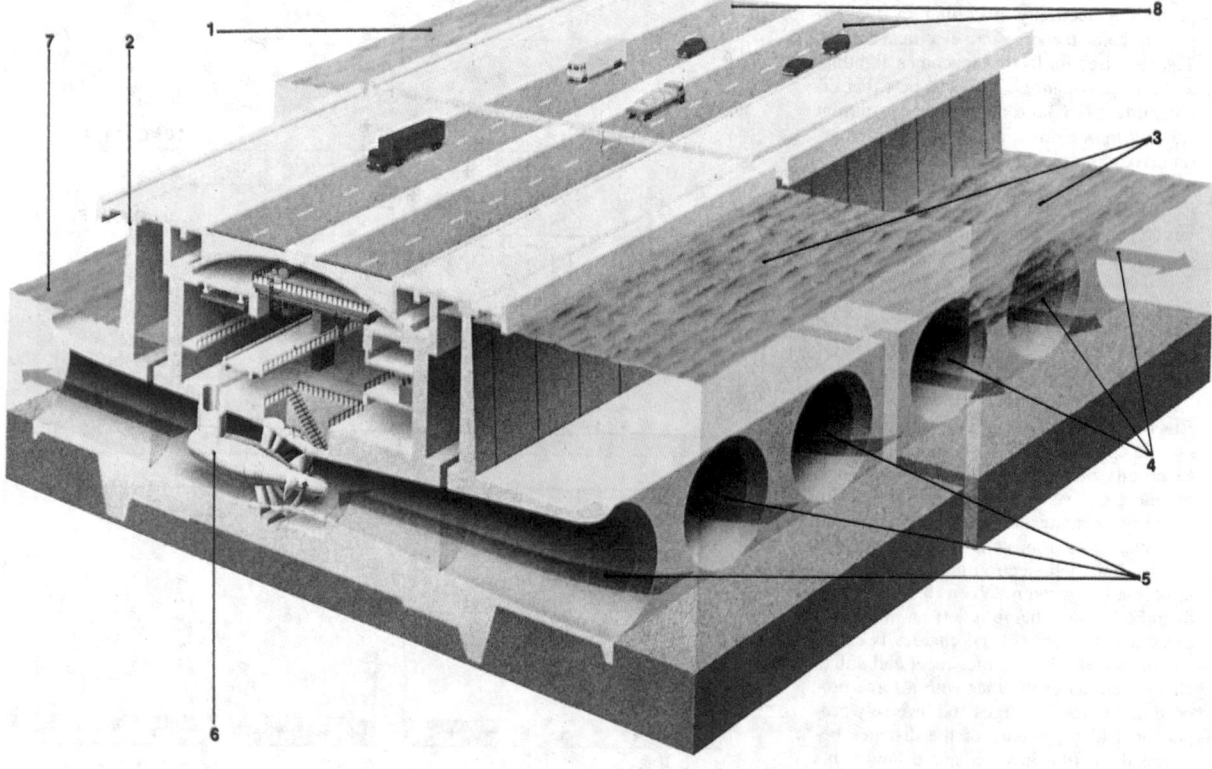

A tidal power station in an estuary of a river. The tides may reach heights of more than 33 ft (10 m). As the tide rises (1) against the low dam (2), water is channeled through 24 tunnels (4), containing turbine generator bulbs (6), which convert the force of the flowing water into electricity. At low tide (7), the seawater that is held in the storage basin (3) is channeled back through the turbines (5), in order to produce additional energy. The roof (8) serves as a bridge over the estuary.

Electrode, electric conductor that supplies current. Electrodes are used in electrolytic cells, and electric furnaces contain electrodes between which an electric arc forms for heating. Electronic tubes and discharge tubes contain electrodes for the transmission of an electric current through gas at low pressures. The anode is the electrode carrying a positive charge, and the cathode has a negative charge.

Electroencephalograph, instrument for recording the brain's electrical activity using several small electrodes on the scalp. Its results are produced in the form of an electroencephalogram (EEG). The EEG is a convenient method for the investigation of brain disturbances and disease (benign and malignant tumors, disturbances in blood vessels, epilepsy, inflammation, metabolic changes). The German psychiatrist Hans Berger began to record electrical activity in human brains in 1929. There are certain normal patterns for 'brain waves' in the alert and the sleeping individual. In a normal person, several varieties of rhythmic activity appear in different circumstances. The most prominent rhythm, noticeable when a healthy subject closes his or her eyes, shows a period of 8-13 cycles per sec that is chiefly present at the occipital pole of the cerebral hemispheres. This is the *alpha rhythm.* Sleep removes this rhythm and may substitute others in its place. *Theta rhythm,* with a frequency of 4-7 cycles per sec, occurs typically in the parietal and temporal regions of the brain and is associated with childhood and with emotional stress in some adults. *Beta rhythm,* with frequencies higher than 15 cycles per sec, is generally associated with activation and tension.
See also: Brain.

Electrolysis, process of changing the chemical composition of a conducting material (electrolyte) by sending an electric current through it.

Electrolyte, electrical conductor in which the current is in the form of ions-atoms with an electric charge-rather than free electrons, as is the case with a wire. Electrolytes are usually liquids, usually water solutions of acids, bases, or salts.

Electromagnet, device that produces a temporary magnetic field when an electric current flows through it. It contains a core, usually of iron, around which a coil of wire is wound. Electromagnets are used to produce strong magnetic fields in generators and motors, electric relays, and bells. They are also used to lift heavy metal loads.
See also: Henry, Joseph; Magnetism.

Electromagnetic force *See:* Grand unified theories.

Electromagnetic waves, patterns of electric and magnetic force. Gamma rays, X-rays, ultraviolet light, visible light, infrared rays, microwaves, and radio waves are different kinds of electromagnetic radiation, all of which behave as waves. In 1865 the Scottish scientist James Clerk Maxwell published his equations describing the behavior of electromagnetic waves. These equations have proven to be one of the most successful theories of modern science.
See also: Magnetism.

Electromagnetism, in physics, relation between electricity and magnetism based on the facts that electric currents produce magnetic fields and magnetic fields produce electric fields. These discoveries were made in the 1820s by physicists Hans Oersted (Denmark) and André Marie Ampère (France), working independently. Their work led to the development of the electromagnet, the basis of the electric motor, the telephone, and the loudspeaker, among other devices. *Electromagnetic induction* is the production of an electric current as a conductor moves in a magnetic field, or is situated in a magnetic field that is changing in strength. This effect was discovered by physicists Michael Faraday (England) and Joseph Henry (U.S.) in 1831, again independently. It is the basis of the electric generator and the transformer.

Electromotive force (emf), loosely, voltage produced by a battery generator or other source of electricity; more precisely, unit of measure of electrical energy per unit of electricity from a generator.

Electromotive series, or electromechanical series, ranking of metals according to their tendency to lose electrons in chemical reactions. Metals that lose electrons more easily will generally react more easily with other elements.

Electron, elementary particle circling the nucleus of an atom. By convention, an electron is one negative charge. The flow of electrons is an electrical current. Joseph John Thomson demonstrated the existence of the electron in 1897.
See also: Atom.

Electron gun, device that produces and aims a beam of electrons to produce a visual pattern on a phosphorescent screen. Electron guns are used in televisions, X-ray machines, and electron microscopes.

Electronic game, game generally featuring lights and sounds on a screen, controlled by microprocessors or tiny computers. Themes for the games vary enormously, and players can compete against the computer itself or against one another.

Electronic Mail (or **E-Mail**), a message (such as a letter, announcement, or report) that is transmitted between computers or computer terminals for retrieval by the person to whom the message is addressed. The ability to send and receive electronic mail is a common feature of personal computer networks, which are formed by interconnecting two or more personal computers.
Some companies and other organizations provide electronic mail services by telephone. Subscribers reach such a service with a device called a modem. Callers can either retrieve messages left for them or leave messages for other subscribers.
The term 'electronic mail' came into use in the late 1970's. By the early 1990's, following rapid growth in the use of personal computers and computer telecommunications services, it became an important form of communication.

Electronic music, music composed of sounds and manipulated, created solely on electronic equipment. Concrete music uses recordings of natural sounds as the basis for composition, and works mixing both approaches are called 'tape music.' Experiments with electronic composition began as early as the 1890s, but widespread production began only after World War II, as universities and broadcasting authorities in

E

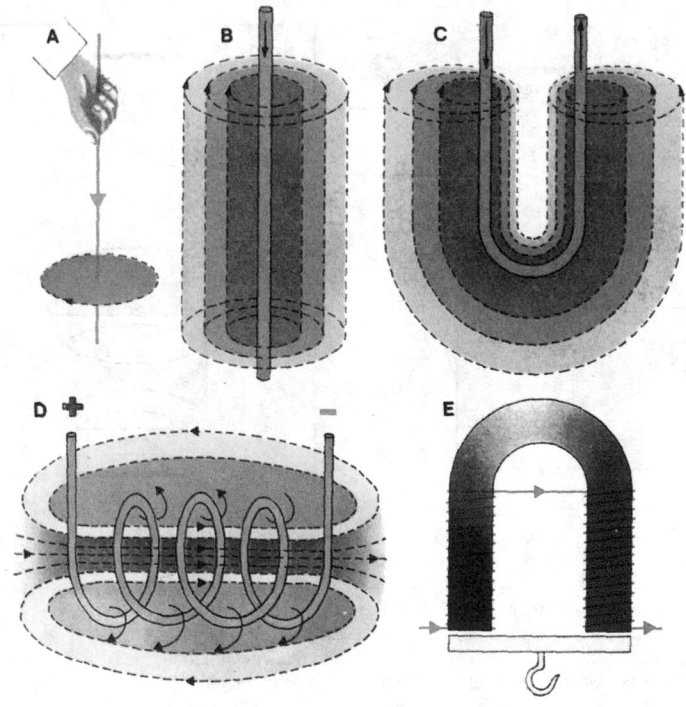

A magnetic field exists around a wire carrying an electric current. If the wire is held in the right hand (A) with the thumb pointing in the current's direction, the fingers curl in the field's direction. The field is symmetrical, whether the wire is straight (B) or curved (C). Its strength is increased if the wire is wound in a spiral, or solenoid (D). An electromagnet (E) with a strong magnetic field is obtained if the coil is wrapped around an iron core.

E

many countries began setting up studios to encourage this use of modern technology. Edgard Varèse, John Cage, and Karlheinz Stockhausen have produced important works in this field.

Electronics, applied science dealing with the development and behavior of devices in which the motion of electrons is controlled. It covers the behavior of electrons in gases, vacuums, conductors, and semiconductors. Its theoretical basis lies in the principles of electromagnetism and solid-state physics discovered in the late 19th and early 20th centuries. Electronics began to grow in the 1920s with the development of radio. During World War II, the United States and Britain concentrated resources on the invention of radar and pulse transmission methods, and by 1945 they had enormous industrial capacity for producing electronic equipment. The invention of the transistor in 1948 as a small, cheap replacement for vacuum tubes led to rapid development in such areas as computers, radio and TV receivers, and sound production and reproduction. Now, with the widespread use of integrated circuits, electronics plays a vital role in communications and industry. All electronic circuits contain both active and passive components and transducers (e.g., microphones), which change energy from one form to another. *Passive components* are normally conductors and are characterized by their properties of resistance, capacitance, and induc-

tance. *Active components* are electron tubes or semiconductors; they contain a source of power and control electron flow. Semiconductor diodes and transistors, which are basically sandwiches made of 2 different types of semiconductor, now usually perform the general functions once done by tubes, being smaller, more robust, and generating less heat. Demands for increased cheapness and reliability of circuits have led to the development of microelectronics. In printed circuits, printed connections replace individual wiring on a flat board to which about 2 components per cu cm are soldered. Integrated circuits assemble tens of thousands of components in a single structure, formed directly by evaporation or other techniques as films about 0.03 mm thick on a substrate.

Electron microscope, microscope that uses beams of electrons to produce extremely high magnifications. The optical microscope cannot produce images of objects smaller than the wavelength of the light used. But when the French physicist Victor De Broglie discovered in 1924 that electrons could behave like waves, it became apparent that streams of electrons could be manipulated to produce magnified images. A wavelength 100,000 times shorter than that of green light could be produced, making enormous magnifications possible. In 1935 an instrument was produced that exceeded the resolution of the optical microscope. An electron gun, consisting of a hot tungsten filament

and electrodes carrying up to 100,000 volts, generates a stream of high-velocity electrons. This electron beam is controlled by a system of magnetic fields generated by circular coils that are analogous to the lenses in ordinary microscopes. The beam has to travel in a high vacuum (about 1/10,000,000 atm) to avoid scattering the electrons and blurring the image. The object to be examined must be extremely thin to allow the passage of the electrons. On passing through the specimen, the electrons are scattered to varying extent by the different atoms in it. The scattered electrons produce contrast in an image either on a photographic plate or on a fluorescent screen. Further magnification can be obtained by enlarging the photograph. Instrumental magnifications up to 200,000 are common, and with photographic enlargements, magnifications exceeding 2 million can be made.

Electron tube, device used for amplifying electrical signals or currents. It consists of electrodes sealed in a glass tube that may contain a vacuum, but usually includes traces of gas. Once widely used in radio, television, and computers, electron tubes have been largely replaced by the transistor.

Electrophoresis, process by which components of large biological molecules are separated by being subjected to electric fields. An electric current causes positively and negatively charged molecules to move in opposite directions, thus separating them.

Electroplating, process by which a metal coating is produced by the action of an electric current. The object to be plated is placed in a solution of the metal it is to be coated with. The metal's atoms are ions-that is, electrically charged. The immersed object is negatively charged by an applied electric current, and the ions of the metal are attracted, affixing themselves to the object. A variety of metals, from gold to cadmium or nickel, are used in electroplating. Most coatings are quite thin, from 0.001 to 0.002 in (0.03 to 0.05 mm).

Electroscope, instrument for detecting electrostatic charge. It works on the principle that 2 bodies having the same charge will repel each other. In the *gold leaf electroscope* the 2 bodies are a rod and a piece of gold leaf, or two pieces of gold leaf. If the electroscope can be used to measure the charge, it is also known as an *electrometer*. The *quadrant electrometer* consists of a hollow circular box divided into 4 quadrants. A hollow plate inside the box is deflected by the quadrants when a charge is applied, and the amount of deflection gives the quantity of electrostatic charge. Other kinds of electrometers include instruments that depend on the deflection of a quartz fiber in an electrostatic field and modern instruments containing electronic amplifiers. Electroscopes can detect and measure the intensity of ionizing radiations such as X-rays.

Electrostatic precipitator, device that removes smoke and other particles from in-

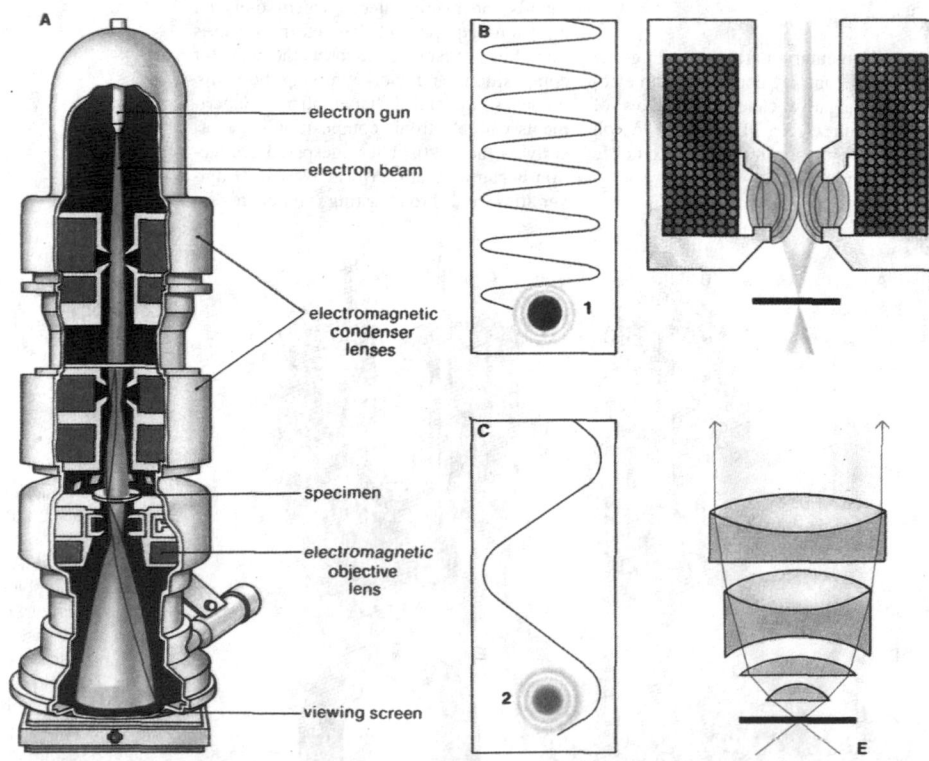

An electron microscope (A) produces an enlarged image of a small object, the same way an optical microscope does. However, it uses an electron beam (B), instead of a light beam (C), and electromagnets instead of lenses. The degree of magnification depends on the diffraction at the viewing aperture. Diffraction theory shows that the larger the wavelength, the fainter the rings will be around the image. The wavelength of light is about 12,500 times that of an elec-tron beam. With a larger degree of magnification, the rings become visible, and the image is blurred. The maximum magnification of a light microscope lies around 2,000, that of an electron microscope may be as much as 1,000,000.

dustrial fumes. The fumes pass through a chamber that is hung with steel tubes or plates, within or between which are suspended thin rods. A high-voltage current is fed to the rods, producing a negative charge on the particles in the fumes. The particles are then attracted by electric forces to the plates and precipitated from the fumes. The plates are shaken or knocked to dislodge the resulting deposits, which fall into a hopper and are removed. Up to 97% of particles in fumes can be captured in a precipitator. Frederick G. Cottrell built the first practical precipitator in 1904.

Electrotyping, method of creating reproductions of type, engravings, or etchings. The process was initially publicized in St. Petersburg by M.H. von Jacobi in 1838. Electrotyping was widely used until the 1960s, when more advanced techniques became available.

Elegy, in classical poetry, lyric poem of alternate 2-line stanzas written in a distinctive meter. In English, an elegy is a poem expressing sorrow, particularly about death, such as John Milton's 'Lycidas' (1637), Thomas Gray's 'Elegy Written in a Country Churchyard' (1750), and Percy Bysshe Shelley's 'Adonais' (1821).

Element, in chemistry, substance that cannot be broken down into simpler substances by normal chemical processes. Elements are generally mixtures of different isotopes. The elements are classified by physical properties as metals, metalloids, and nonmetals, and by chemical properties and atomic structure according to the periodic table. Most elements exhibit allotropy (more than one elemental form), and many are molecular. The elements have all been built up in stars from hydrogen by complex sequences of nuclear reactions.
Robert Boyle (1627-1691) was the first to distinguish between elements and compounds. The first scientific list of elements was prepared by Antoine Lavoisier in 1789. He listed 33 substances, mistakenly including heat and light. By the mid-1800s it became apparent that certain elements had similar properties and could be grouped together. The first periodic tables were produced and stimulated the search for the undiscovered elements that would fill the gaps in the table. By 1925 all the naturally occurring elements had been discovered. Now, 109 elements are known, although elements 104 through 109, created within the past 30 years, have not been officially recognized by the International Union of Pure and Applied Chemistry. Sixteen of these have been produced artificially. In 1996, scientists stated that they had created a new element. However, element 112 disintegrated within one-thousandth of a second. Element 112 is seen as a steppingstone to the creation of element 114.
See also: Boyle, Robert; Chemistry.

Element 104 (unnilquadium), chemical element, symbol (Unq); for physical constants see Periodic Table. The name of this element is temporary, proposed by the International Union of Pure and Applied Physics. In 1964,

Soviet workers at the Joint Institute for Nuclear Research at Dubna (USSR) produced what they claimed was isotope ^{260}104, by bombarding plutonium-242 with neon-22 ions. In 1969, scientists working under Albert Ghiorso at the University of California at Berkeley reported that they were unable to reproduce the work of the Dubna group but had produced isotopes of element 104, with mass numbers 257 and 259104 among them, by bombarding californium-249 with carbon-12 and carbon-13 ions. The names kurchatovium and rutherfordium have been proposed.

Element 105, chemical element; for physical constants see Periodic Table. In 1967, Georgii N. Flerov and his associates at the Joint Institute for Nuclear Research at Dubna (USSR) reported producing element 105 with mass numbers 260 and 261 by bombarding americium-243 with neon-22. In Oct. 1971, element 105 with mass number 261 was reported to have been synthesized by Albert Ghiorso and his co-workers by bombarding californium-250 with nitrogen-15, and by bombarding berkelium-249 with oxygen-16. Element 105 with mass number 262 was produced by bombarding berkelium-249 with oxygen-18.

Element 106, chemical element; for physical constants see Periodic Table. In June 1974, workers at the Joint Institute for Nuclear Research at Dubna (USSR) reported producing element 106 by bombarding lead-206, 207, and 208 with chromium-54. In Sept. 1974, Albert Ghiorso and co-workers bombarded californium-249 with oxygen-18 to produce element 106 with mass number 263. In 1984, Peter J. Armbruster and his co-workers in West Germany at the Heavy Ion Research Laboratory (GSI) at Darmstadt produced element 106 with mass number 261. It was seen to be a decay product of element 108 at this time.

Element 107, chemical element; for physical constants see Periodic Table. In 1976, Soviet scientists at the Joint Institute for Nuclear Research at Dubna (USSR) produced what they claimed was element 107 with mass number 261, by bombarding bismuth-204 with chromium-54. In 1981, Peter J. Armbruster and his co-workers in West Germany at the Heavy Ion Research Laboratory (GSI) at Darmstadt produced element 107 with mass number 262 by bombarding bismuth-209 with chromium-54 nuclei as well. The recoiling product atom was separated by a newly developed velocity filter. The new element decayed by three consecutive alpha-particle emissions to element 105 in 165 ms to lawrencium in 1.2 sec. and to mendelevium in 18.1 sec. It then became fermium by electron capture and emitted an alpha-particle to become californium.

Element 108, chemical element; for physical constants see Periodic Table. Peter J. Armbruster and his co-workers in West Germany at the Heavy Ion Research Laboratory (GSI) at Darmstadt produced element 108 with mass number 265 by bombarding lead-208 with iron-58 nuclei. The

recoiling product atom was separated by a newly developed velocity filter. The new element decayed by three consecutive alpha-particle emissions to element 106 in 2.4 ms and then to element 104 in 360 ms, and finally to nobelium in 9.8 seconds.

Element 109, chemical element; for physical constants see Periodic Table. Peter J. Armbruster and his co-workers in West Germany at the Heavy Ion Research Laboratory (GSI) at Darmstadt produced element 109 and confirmed its existence by four independent measurements on Aug. 29, 1982. It was produced by bombarding bismuth-209 with iron-58 nuclei. The recoiling product atom was separated by a newly developed velocity filter. The new element decayed by consecutive alpha-particle emissions to element 107 in 5 ms and then to element 105 in 22 ms. element 105 became element 104 by electron capture and this decayed by spontaneous fission.

Element 110, chemical element; for physical constants see Periodic Table. Yuri T. Oganessian and co-workers in Dubna in the USSR claimed discovery of element 110. It is a spontaneous fissioning nuclide with a mass of 272 and a half-life of 10 ms.

Elementary Particles, in physics, the basic components of matter and energy. The study of elementary particles is known as elementary particle physics, or particle physics. Elementary particles are also referred to as fundamental particles. They belong to a class of particles called subatomic particles - that is, particles smaller than an atom.
Physicists learn about elementary particles primarily through experiments with devices called particle accelerators. Particle accelerators provide the high energy needed to probe the structure of matter.
Particle physicists classify elementary particles into three main groups: quarks, leptons, and gauge bosons.
Quarks are the basic constituents of the subatomic particles called *hadrons*. Two of the most important kinds of hadrons are *protons* and *neutrons*, which make up the nuclei of atoms. There are a number of different kinds of quarks, and each possesses a type of charge called 'color'. For each kind of quark there also exists an antiparticle - that is, a particle with certain properties (such as electrical charge) opposite those of the ordinary particle.
Quarks and antiquarks always occur combined in pairs or groups of three. The combination of a quark and antiquark forms short-lived subatomic particles called *mesons*, which include *kaons* and *pions*. Combinations of three quarks form subatomic particles called *baryons*, which include protons and neutrons.
Leptons include *electrons*, several kinds of *neutrinos*, and their respective antiparticles.
A gauge boson is an elementary particle that carries energy between other elementary particles (including other gauge bosons), exerting a force in the process. Quarks (and antiquarks) create and absorb gauge bosons called *gluons*. Quarks (and antiquarks) are bound together, forming mesons and baryons, through a continuous exchange of

E

E

gluons. The *photon* is a gauge boson that is exchanged between leptons.

Before the discovery of the electron by the British physicist J. J. Thomson in 1897, scientists believed that the fundamental units of matter were atoms (the name 'atom' comes from the Greek word for 'indivisible.'). By the 1950's, physicists had discovered a large number of different subatomic particles, both through studies of cosmic rays (high-energy radiation from space) and through experiments with particle accelerators.

In 1964 Murray Gell-Mann and George Zweig, both physicists from the United States, independently proposed that protons and most other subatomic particles are composed of much smaller particles, which Gell-Mann called quarks. By the 1980's strong experimental evidence had been obtained for the existence of quarks, and a theory called quantum chromodynamics had been developed that explained their properties and interactions.

In the mid-1980's some physicists proposed that elementary particles are stringlike, not dotlike as had been previously believed. Through the 1980's and early 1990's, particle physicists sought to further unify the mathematical theories describing elementary particles and their interactions.

Elementary school, Schooling for children with a view to preparing them for secondary education by introducing them to elementary cultural skills such as reading, writing, arithmetic, and general education.
See also: Education.

Elephant, largest living land animal, of which there are 2 species, the African (*Loxodonta africana*) and the Indian (*Elephas maxima*). The African elephant is the larger of the 2, standing up to 11 1/2 ft (3.5 m) and weighing 6 tons (5,400 kg). It has larger ears and tusks, a sloping forehead and 2 'lips' at the end of the trunk, compared with the Indian elephant's 1 'lip.' The trunk is a long, flexible snout with nostrils at the tip, and the sense of smell is very acute. The trunk is also used for carrying food and water to the mouth and for spraying water during bathing. The African elephant is found over most parts of Africa south of the Sahara, usually in open country. It uses its large ears as radiators to keep cool. The Indian elephant lives from India to Sumatra and stays mainly in dense cover. The habits of the 2 species are similar. They live in herds that are led by an elderly cow, the old bulls being solitary. They feed on grass, foliage, and twigs and in some places destroy woodland by pushing over trees and bushes. The Indian elephant is used as a beast of burden. African elephants were once trained for use in warfare. Elephants are the major source of commercial ivory, and uncontrolled hunting considerably reduced their number, particularly in Africa. Since the 1970s international wildlife organizations have worked to prohibit sale of tusks and ivory products.

Elephant bird, extinct, flightless bird (genus *Aepyornis*) of Madagascar. Elephant birds were like massive ostriches, up to 10 ft (3 m) tall, with eggs over 1 ft (0.3 m) long. They may have been the origin of the legend of the giant roc bird.

Elephantiasis, chronic disease characterized by gross thickening of the skin or swelling of the lower limbs and external genital organs. The most common form is a tropical disease due to filariae (parasitic worms) entering the lymph channels and causing obstruction.
See also: Filaria.

Elephant's ear, plant of the arum family, especially *Colocasia antiquorum*, grown for its large ornamental leaves, which spring from a rhizome (underground stem). Two species, *dasheen* and *taro*, are grown in Southeast Asia for their edible rhizomes.

Eleusinian mysteries, secret religious rites in ancient Greece. They were originally performed in honor of Demeter, goddess of agriculture, at Eleusis, near Athens, dramatizing the descent of her daughter Persephone into the underworld and her inevitable return from the land of the dead, symbolizing the endless seasonal cycles. Later the rites were performed in Athens.
See also: Greece, Ancient.

Elevator, device that transports people or goods from one floor to another in a building. Elisha Otis's invention of an elevator with an automatic safety device (1840s) permitted the construction of tall buildings and skyscrapers. Most elevators use an electric traction system that lifts the elevator car with steel cables. Geared traction elevators can travel up to 450 ft (137 m) per min, while gearless ones can travel up to 2,000 ft (600 m) per min.
See also: Otis, Elisha Graves.

Eleventh Amendment *See:* Constitution of the United States.

Elgar, Sir Edward William (1857-1934), English composer. Elgar followed the German orchestral and choral traditions of the 19th century, but his *Enigma Variations* (1899) and *Pomp and Circumstance* marches (1901-1930) reflect a distinct English style. Other important works include the oratorio *The Dream of Gerontius* (1900), 2 symphonies, violin and cello concertos, and the concert overture *Cockaigne* (1901).

Elgin Marbles, ancient sculpture (mostly from the Acropolis) that Thomas Bruce, 7th Earl of Elgin and British envoy at Constantinople (1799-1802) shipped from Athens, Greece (then a Turkish possession), to London. They were bought by the government (1816) for half the cost of their transportation and are preserved in the British Museum, London. They include a

There are two types of living elephants, one in Southern Asia, the other in Africa. Both have skulls that are much shorter and higher than their ancestral elephants. They have two upper incisors, forming two long tusks, and the nose is extended to form the trunk. The African elephant (*Loxodonta africana*) with its large ears and high skull is relatively rare. It is larger than its Asiatic cousin. The Indian or Asiatic elephant (*Elephas maxima*) is found throughout India and the East Indies, and is readily distinguished from the African form by its relatively small ears and less domed forehead. The trunk is much smoother than that of the African elephant, and it ends in one fleshy lobe instead of two.

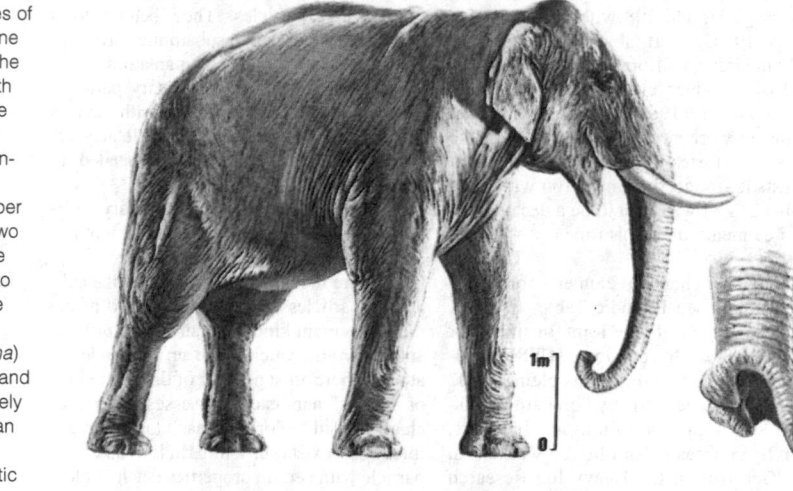

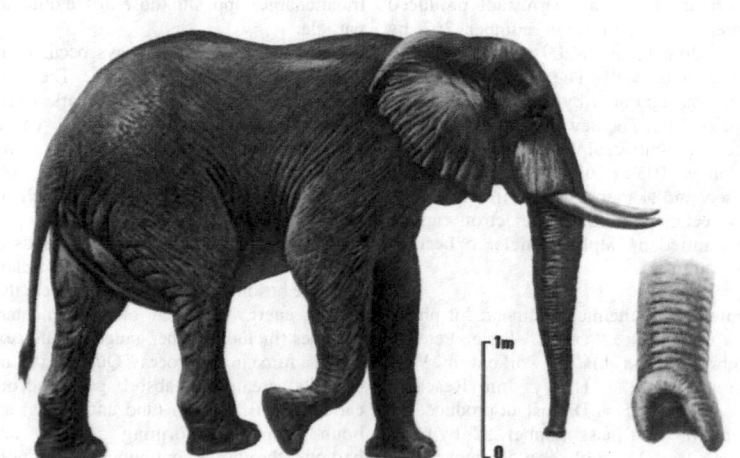

frieze from the Parthenon by Phidias and parts of the temple known as the Erechtheum.

El Greco *See:* Greco, El.

Elhuyar, Fausto and Juan José de *See:* Tungsten.

Elijah, or **Elias** (9th century B.C.), Hebrew prophet who, according to the Book of Kings of the Old Testament, resisted pagan idol worship during the reign of Israel's King Ahab. An outspoken enemy of Queen Jezebel, he was instrumental in thwarting her attempts to introduce the worship of Baal into Israel. During his own lifetime a number of supernatural events were ascribed to him, including restoring a dead child to life. The Bible recounts that he ascended to heaven in a fiery chariot.
See also: Bible; Old Testament.

Elijah Muhammad *See:* Muhammad, Elijah.

Eliot, George (Mary Ann Evans; 1819-1880), English novelist. Her writing was distinguished by a subtle style and compassionate understanding of character. Through her work for the *Westminster Review* she met writer George Henry Lewes, who recognized her talent and encouraged her to write. They lived together from 1854 till his death in 1878. From 1858 to 1866 she published *Scenes of Clerical Life, Adam Bede, The Mill on the Floss, Silas Marner, Romola,* and *Felix Holt the Radical. Middlemarch* (1871-1872) is generally considered her finest work.

Eliot, T(homas) S(tearns) (1888-1965), U.S.-born poet, dramatist, and critic. His learned, ironic, witty (and sometimes obscure) poetry and criticism influenced the literature of an entire generation. His first important poem, 'The Love Song of J.

English novelist George Eliot, painted at the age of 23 by Charles Bray.

Alfred Prufrock,' appeared in 1915, and *The Waste Land* appeared in 1922. These early poems, critical of the shallowness and squalidness of modern life, are in marked contrast to the later religiously colored poetry, such as *Ash Wednesday* (1930), and *Four Quartets* (1943). In 1927 he became a British citizen, declaring himself an 'Anglo-Catholic in religion, royalist in politics, and classicist in literature.' Reviving verse drama, he wrote *Murder in the Cathedral* (1935), *The Family Reunion* (1939), *The Cocktail Party* (1950), and *The Confidential Clerk* (1953). He was awarded the Nobel Prize for literature in 1948.

Elisha (9th century B.C.), Hebrew prophet, disciple of and successor to Elijah, whose life is described in II Kings of the Old Testament. Like Elijah, he acted as the conscience of the Hebrew king. He engineered the downfall of the dynasty of Omri and the rise of the house of Jehu. He was reputedly gifted as a soothsayer and healer.
See also: Old Testament.

Elixir, liquor sought by alchemists of the Middle Ages for turning metals into gold or prolonging life. In medical practice of today, the term is used to describe a tincture composed of various aromatic substances held in solution by alcohol in some form.

Elizabeth, name of 2 queens of England. **Elizabeth I** (1533-1603) was queen of England and Ireland (1558-1603) and the last Tudor monarch. A daughter of Henry VIII, who had broken with the Catholic Church to marry Anne Boleyn, her mother, her initial task as queen was to reestablish her supremacy over the English Church after the reign of her Catholic sister, Mary I. The defeat by her navy of the Spanish Armada (1588) established England as a major European power. At home, industry, agriculture, and the arts (especially literature) throve under conditions of relative peace and financial stability, and colonization of the New World was encouraged. The reign was plagued by the question of the Protestant succession as Elizabeth was unmarried and childless. After the execution of her Catholic cousin, Mary Queen of Scots, a possible heir, Elizabeth finally acknowledged the succession of James VI of Scotland, Mary's son, thus securing the peaceful union of England and Scotland. **Elizabeth II** (1926-) is queen of the United Kingdom of Great Britain and Northern Ireland (from 1952) and head of the Commonwealth of Nations. One of the world's few remaining monarchs, she is extremely popular at home and abroad and has traveled extensively as her country's representative. She married Philip Mountbatten, Duke of Edinburgh, in 1947 and has 4 children: Prince Charles, Princess Anne, Prince Andrew, and Prince Edward.

Elizabeth (1709-1762), empress of Russia (1741-1762), daughter of Peter the Great. She staged a coup against her cousin, Ivan VI, to gain the throne. She rid the court of German influence, founded Moscow University, and pursued the Seven Years War against Prussia.

Elizabethan Age *See:* Elizabeth.

Elizabeth, Queen Mother of England *See:* George.

Elizabeth, Saint, mother of St. John the Baptist and kinswoman of Mary. According to Luke I, the angel Gabriel predicted the birth of John to Elizabeth and her husband Zechariah. Nov. 5 is the feast day for St. Elizabeth.
See also: Bible; New Testament.

Elk, large member of the deer family. It inhabits some of the forest areas of northern Europe and Asia and is closely related to the larger American moose (*Cervus candensis*). The American elk (*Alces americana*) is also called the wapiti.

Ellesmere Island, Canadian Arctic island off northwest Greenland, occupying about 80,000 sq mi (207,200 sq km) and consisting of ice-capped plateaus and mountains flanked by a coastline pierced by deep fjords. Cape Columbia is North America's northernmost point.
See also: Baffin, William; Peary, Robert Edwin.

Ellice Islands *See:* Tuvalu.

Ellington, Duke (Edward Kennedy Ellington; 1899-1974), U.S. composer, pianist, and orchestra leader, one of the giants of jazz music. After a formal musical education, Ellington formed his first band in 1918 and by the 1930s enjoyed an international following. His superbly disciplined orchestra remained the envy of the jazz world for several decades, playing music composed by its leader for its well-known instrumental soloists. Ellington wrote such hit songs as 'Mood Indigo,' 'Sophisticated Lady,' and 'Satin Doll,' suites such as *Black, Brown and*

One of the few portraits of queen Elizabeth I of England. Under Elizabeth's authoritative leadership, England became a major European power with prospering commerce and a great navy.

E

In the 1960s, Duke Ellington (1899-1974) emerged as an extremely original solo pianist. In the solos he played with his orchestra, and in his own compositions, his music attained an outstanding quality, despite a lack of innovation in it.

Beige (1943), and late in life, considerable sacred music. He was awarded the Presidential Medal of Freedom in 1969.
See also: Jazz.

Ellipse, geometrical figure shaped like a circle viewed at an angle. There are 2 focal points in an ellipse, and the sum of the radii from them to any point on the curve is constant. It follows that an ellipse can be drawn with the help of 2 thumbtacks stuck in a piece of paper at the 2 foci with a loop of string attached to them. If the string is kept taut by a pencil, an ellipse will be generated as the pencil is moved along the string. The orbits of planets and their satellites are elliptical.

Ellis, (Henry) Havelock (1859-1939), British writer known for his studies of human sexual behavior and psychology. His major work was *Studies in the Psychology of Sex* (1897-1928).
See also: Psychoanalysis.

Ellis Island, island of about 27 acres (10.9 hectares) in upper New York Bay, within the boundaries of New York City. Bought by the government in 1808, it was the site of a fort and later an arsenal. From 1892 to 1954 it was an immigration station through which some 20 million immigrants entered the United States. It is now a national monument.
See also: Immigration.

Ellison, Ralph Waldo (1914-1994), African-American writer. His novel *Invisible Man* (1952), a story of black alienation in a hostile white society, won a National Book Award. *Shadow and Act* (1964) and *Going to the Territory* (1986) are collections of his essays and speeches.

Ellora, town in the Indian state Maharashtra, near Aurangabad. Known for its temples dating from the Gupta period (6th-8th century) that have been carved from rock. The most impressive is the Kailasanatha temple, devoted to Shiva; an important place of pilgrimage for Hindus.

Ellsberg, Daniel (1931-), American political scientist, entered the employment of the Rand Corporation in 1959, the 'thinking tank' of the American government. Ellsberg contributed to the policies on Vietnam and

visited the country many times. However, he became more and more convinced that the American political direction was incorrect and he passed along confidential documents belonging to the Rand Corporation to the New York Times. In June 1971, this newspaper published a number of these documents, which became known as the Pentagon Papers throughout the world. Ellsberg was indicted, but acquitted in 1973. He has been a professor at the Center for International Studies at the Massachusetts Institute of Technology since 1969 and, together with Sacharov, was awarded the Eleanor Roosevelt Peace Prize in 1974.

Ellsworth, Lincoln (1880-1951), U.S. explorer and scientist. In 1925 he made the transpolar flight with the Amundsen expedition. The following year he flew from the Spitsbergen archipelago in the dirigible *Norge* across the North Pole to Alaska. In 1936 Ellsworth made the first flight across Antarctica, traveling 2,300 mi (3,700 km) in a single-engine airplane.
See also: Antarctica.

Elm, deciduous tree (genus *Ulmus*) common to North America, Europe, and parts of Asia. It has toothed leaves and the seeds are carried on the wind by a wing. Elms, which grow to 160 ft (50 m) have tough wood, used in furniture and barrels. They are often grown as shade trees. The American, or white, elm (*U. americana*) is rapidly being killed off by Dutch elm disease, a fungus disease that is carried by the elm bark beetle. The disease, first identified in the Netherlands, appeared in the United States in the 1930s, spreading rapidly from New England. Other less valuable elms are immune to the disease.

Elman, Mischa (1891-1967), Russian-born U.S. violinist. He made his international debut in Berlin (1904), and first performed in the United States in 1908. He became a U.S. citizen in 1923.

El Misti, 19,101-ft (5,822-m) dormant volcano located in the Western Cordillera mountain range in Peru. El Misti had religious significance for the Incas and has inspired many Peruvian legends and poems.

El Niño, an ocean phenomenon of the Pacific Ocean. El Niño occurs when the southeast trade winds slacken or cease, preventing cool, nutrient-rich water within the Peru Current from moving up from moderate depths to replace warm surface water. With the absence of nutrient-rich water plankton, a major source of food for fish, dies off, resulting in a major disruption of the ecosystem. El Niño causes several other disturbances, among which is an altering of the path of the jet stream in the Northern Hemisphere, causing an unusual increase in precipitation in many areas. El Niño occurs irregularly, about 14 times in a century, causing various ecological and climatic disturbances for about a year. It is named El Niño ('the Child', referring to the baby Jesus) because it usually begins around Christmas. In 1997 El Niño caused droughts in Indonesia and heavy rain and floods in

East Africa. In the southeast of Africa there was less rain than usual, in the desert of Peru it rained, and Argentina and Paraguay experienced floods

Elodea, any of several underwater plants of the genus *Elodea*, some living in salt water, others in fresh water. They are sometimes used to help maintain the oxygen balance in aquariums.

Elohim, most common name for God used in the Old Testament. Although it is a plural form in Hebrew, the Canaanite root is singular. The Hebrews believed that the name of God should not be spoken, and therefore used substitutes such as Elohim and Adonai ('my Lord').

El Paso (pop. 544,000), city in western Texas and the seat of El Paso County. It is the largest city on the U.S.-Mexico border, situated on the Rio Grande, opposite Ciudad Juárez in Mexico. Copper smelting and refining are the major industries. Tourism, oil refining, lead smelting, meat packing, cement manufacture, brewing, and cotton processing also figure in its economy. Prior to the Texan declaration of independence (1836), which preceded the territory's annexation, the area was part of Mexico. The present site, settled in 1827, was named El Paso in 1859; it was incorporated in 1873.

El Salvador

Capital:	San Salvador
Area:	8,260 sq mi (21,041 sq km)
Population:	6,354,000
Language:	Spanish
Government:	Presidential republic
Independent:	1841
Head of gov.:	President
Per capita:	US$ 4,600
Monetary unit:	1 El Salvador colón = 100 centavos

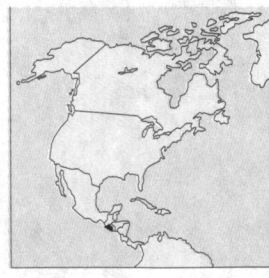

El Salvador, republic in Central America, bordered by Guatemala to the west, Honduras to the north and east, and the Pacific Ocean to the south.
Land and climate. El Salvador is the only country in Central America with no Caribbean coastline. Two parallel mountain ridges cross the country from east to west

enclosing generally fertile plateaus and valleys. The Lempa River (200 mi/322 km), Central America's largest, cuts across western and central El Salvador.

Economy. El Salvador has a high population density and a weak economy. Agriculture is the principal means of livelihood, and coffee is the major export. The land also yields food crops such as corn, rice, and beans, but El Salvador must import food to meet its needs. About 15% of the labor force is involved in the processing of food products and the production of a limited range of consumer goods.

History. El Salvador was colonized by Spain in 1524. After unsuccessful uprisings in 1811 and 1814, independence was won in 1821. The country was briefly part of a Mexican Empire (1821-1823), and joined the United Provinces of Central America in 1825. Following the breakup of the federation, El Salvador became an independent republic in 1839. During much of the 19th century the neighboring states of Guatemala and Nicaragua largely dominated the country's leadership. The development of the coffee crop led to the concentration of land ownership and wealth, and social and economic inequality generated deep divisions in society. The failure of land reforms led to armed violence between leftists and rightists throughout the 1970s and 1980s, with the United States backing various right-wing regimes, while Cuba and Nicaragua under the Sandinistas gave some help to the left-wing guerrillas. Between 1980 and 1986 some 56,000 people, most of them noncombatants, died in the bitter civil war, which ended in 1992. Economic recovery still depends on foreign aid. In 1994, in the first postwar election, Armando Calderón Sol of the Arena party was elected president. In 1998, the country was struck by hurricane Mitch and, in 2001, by a number of very severe earthquakes, which claimed approximately 1200 victims.

Elssler, Franziska (Fanny) (1810-1884), Austrian ballet dancer, educated in Vienna and Naples. Made her debut in Berlin in 1830, was associated with the Parisian Opera (1834-1840). Toured the US (1840-1842) and then Europe, giving many performances. Known for her creations of stylized folk dances. Ended her career in 1851.

Eltingh, Jacco (1970-), Dutch tennis player, formed, together with Paul Haarhuis, one of the strongest men's doubles in the world. They claimed the world title in 1993 and 1998, the Australian Open and US Open in 1994, and the French title in 1995. In 1998, Haarhuis and Eltingh also won Wimbledon, making them the first doubles team to win all four Grand Slam tournaments in the history of tennis. In November 1998, they became world champions once again. Eltingh then ended his tennis career.

Éluard, Paul (Eugène Paul Grindel; 1895-1952), French poet, became acquainted with the surrealists in 1920 and became one of their greatest poets. His work is very melodious (many poems were set to music) and is mainly oriented towards the love for one person. He wrote beautiful resistance poetry during the Second World War, collected in *Poésie et vérité* (1942; including the famous 'Liberté') and *Au rendez-vous allemand* (1944). Other collections include *Capitale de la douleur* (Capital of Pain) (1926), *l'Amour, la poésie* (1929), and *Pouvoir tout dire* (1951).

Elytis, Odysseus (Odysseus Alepoudhèlis; 1911-1996), Greek poet. Elytis owes his nickname 'the Singer of the Aegean Sea' to the numerous tributes to the Greek landscape in his poems, which initially were mainly in keeping with the tradition of surrealism. His style became more personal from 1940 onwards, including *Prosanatolismi* (Orientations) (1940) and *Ilios o Protos*; 1943). His masterpiece, *To axion esti*; 1959), brought him widespread fame, also due to the fact that part of this work was set to music by Mikis Theodorakis. In this poem, he expresses in words the Greek sorrow during the German occupation in WW II. Of his later works, *Maria Nefeli* (1978), on the subject of modern, urban Greece, is particularly worthy of mention. He was awarded the Nobel Prize for Literature in 1979.

E-Mail *See:* Electronic Mail.

Emancipation Proclamation, decree issued by President Abraham Lincoln on Jan. 1, 1863, abolishing slavery in the rebelling Confederate states. A shrewd military and political maneuver designed principally to deprive the Confederacy of its economic base, slavery, the proclamation also boosted the abolitionist cause, and 3 years later the 13th Amendment brought slavery in the U.S. to an end.
See also: Lincoln, Abraham.

Embalming, artificial process by which a corpse is prevented, at least temporarily, from decomposing. Embalming first appeared in ancient Egypt. Modern embalming began after William Harvey's discovery of the blood circulation in 1628. Embalming fluid is injected into an artery (arterial fluid) while blood is drained from a vein; then a stronger fluid (cavity fluid) is injected into the body's orifices and hollow organs. The most commonly used embalming fluid is formaldehyde.

Embargo, government detention of ships to prevent their departure from a port. A civil embargo applies to the ships and goods of the state issuing the order, while a hostile or political embargo is one imposed on ships and goods of another state, frequently involving war materials.

Embezzlement, crime involving someone legally entrusted with property belonging to another who takes it for personal use. Complicated bookkeeping and accounting procedures make detecting embezzlement difficult.

Embolism, presence of substances other than liquid blood in the blood circulation, causing obstruction in arteries or interfering with the pumping of the heart. The common causes of embolism are the breaking-away of fatty material from the wall of an artery, and thrombosis (blood clot formation) in a blood vessel or on the heart walls, where a fragment of clot breaks away. Fat globules from bone marrow may form emboli after major bone fractures. Emboli may also consist of bacteria, air bubbles, or amniotic fluid. Stroke (transient cerebral episodes), pulmonary embolism (in the lung), coronary thrombosis, and obstruction of the blood supply to a limb or organ with consequent cell death are common results, some of them fatal. Some emboli may be removed surgically, but prevention is preferable.
See also: Stroke.

Embossing, mechanical reproduction, by pressure, of designs and patterns in relief on various materials, such as metal, leather, fabrics, cardboard, and paper. The process involves passing the material between suitable dies or plates that impress the design from the back. Fabrics are embossed by passing them between copper cylinders, one engraved with the design, the other covered with felt and acting as the countercylinder, providing enough pressure to force the fabric into the hollows of the die-cylinder.

Embroidery, decorations on fabric produced by stitching with a needle and colored thread. A variety of threads and backing material are used. The basic stitches are flat, knotted, chained, or looped. This form of ornamentation has been used to decorate household items, peasant clothing, and the apparel of royalty for thousands of years, in many cultures around the globe.

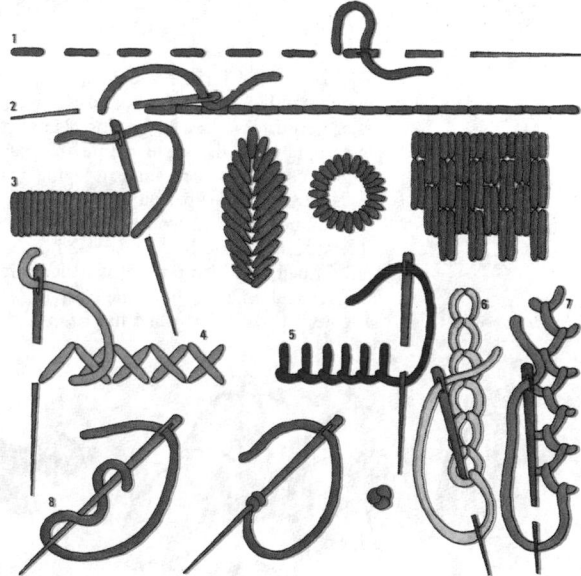

The basic stitches for 'surface embroidery'. The running stitch (1) and the back stitch (2) are simple lines of straight stitching. In the satin stitch (3), straight stitches are worked close together at any angle, to fill or create a shape; three uses of this versatile stitch are shown. The cross stitch (4) can also be used to fill designs. In the buttonhole stitch (5), the chain stitch (6) and the feather stitch (7), the thread is looped around the needle as it makes the straight stitch to form the distinctive shapes. For the French knot (8), the thread must be looped twice to achieve the compact result.

E

E

After three weeks of development (A), the embryo has a rudimentary, tubelike heart that starts to beat and a head swelling that contains the beginnings of the brain and spinal cord. By the fourth week (B), 40 pairs of tissue blocks, called somites, appear, which will later develop into muscle, bone, and connective tissue. After 5 weeks (C), limb buds are visible, and the eyes have developed. By the sixth week (D), the limbs will have enlarged and the tail will begin to recede. After 7 weeks (E), the head is enlarged and eyes, ears, fingers, and toes are well defined. By the end of the eighth week (F), most organs have developed, and the embryo is now called a foetus. The silhouettes indicate the actual size of the developing embryo.

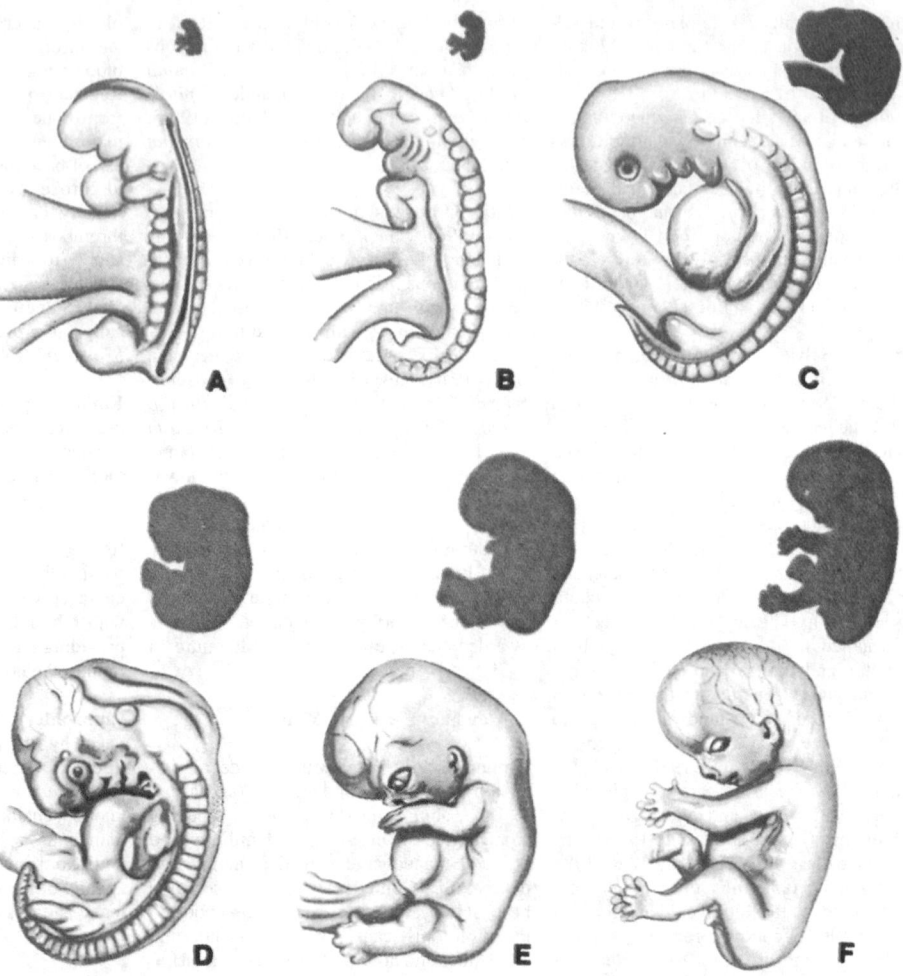

Embryo, name for the young of plants or animals at the earliest stage of development, after fertilization. In seed-bearing plants, the term applies to the stage before the plant emerges from its seed. In egg-laying animals, it refers to the period before hatching. In mammals, the embryonic stage lasts until the creature's basic body shape and organs are formed, at which point it is called a fetus. Animal embryos have their origin in a zygote, an ovum (egg) that has been fertilized by a sperm. By the process of cell division, the ovum forms a small solid cluster called the morula. In the next stage, a hollow cavity one-cell thick called a blastula develops. A second layer of cells develops, forming a 2-layered gastrula. In higher animals there is a third cell layer. The outermost layer, the ectoderm, develops into skin, feathers, or scales, and the nervous system. The innermost layer, the endoderm, gives rise to the lining of the alimentary canal and certain internal organs. The middle layer, the mesoderm, becomes the skeleton, muscular system, heart and circulatory system, kidneys, and reproductive organs. Exactly how a set of virtually identical cells develops into a great variety of specialized tissues remains one of biology's mysteries.
See also: Birth.

Embryology, study of the development of embryos of animals and humans, based on

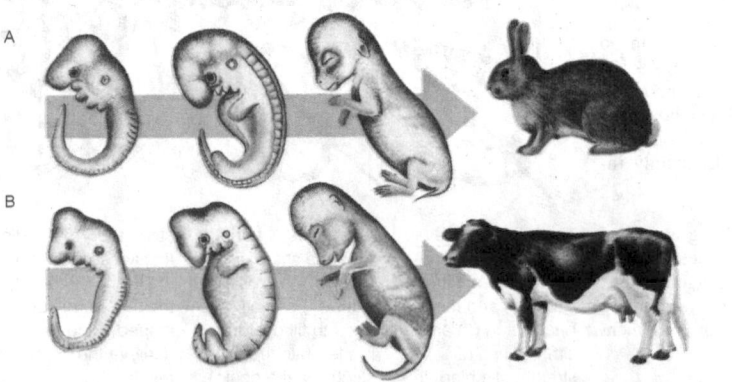

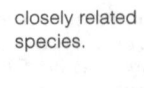

Comparative embryology shows that the early stages of vertebrate embryos resemble one another more closely than later stages, a fact that is seen as evidence for a common ancestor. Young embryos of (A) a rabbit, (B) a cow, and (C) a human are difficult to distinguish. They each have a fishlike tail and gill slits. As the development proceeds, distinctive features of each group become evident, first among the distantly related groups, and later among the more closely related species.

anatomical specimens of embryos at different periods of gestation, obtained from animals or from human abortion. Embryology aids in the study of anatomy and of the development of organ systems and the origins of congenital defects. It may reveal the basis for the separate development of identical cells and for control of growth.
See also: Embryo.

Emerald, valuable green gemstone, a variety of the mineral beryl. Its beautiful color is attributed to the presence of a small amount of chromium. The best emeralds are mined in Muzo, Colombia. Good quality emeralds are also found in South Africa, Brazil and in the Ural Mountains in Russia.

Emerald Isle, poetic name for Ireland, probably based on the predominant green color of the Irish landscape. The term was coined in the poem 'Erin' (1795) by William Drennan (1754-1820).

Emerson, Ralph Waldo (1803-1882), U.S. philosophical essayist, poet, and lecturer. He resigned a Unitarian pastorate (1831) and, after traveling in Europe, settled in Concord, Mass. His *Nature* (1836) was the strongest motivating statement of U.S. transcendentalism. After 1837 he became nationally renowned as a public speaker, and after 1842 as editor of the transcendentalist journal, *The Dial*. He later adjusted his idealistic view of the individual, expressed in essays and addresses like 'The American Scholar' and 'Self-Reliance,' to accommodate the U.S. experience of humanity's historical and political limitations, especially over the issue of slavery.
See also: Transcendentalism.

Emery, naturally occurring impure form of corundum containing iron oxides and other minerals. It has long been used as an abrasive. A layer of finely ground emery is coated onto grinding wheels, paper, or cloth. Though synthetic abrasives have replaced it in many applications, it is still used to polish precious stones and in the manufacture of lenses, prisms, and optical equipment. The major source of emery is the island of Naxos in the Aegean Sea.

Emetic, substance used to induce vomiting. Emetics are of 2 main types. *Centrally acting emetics* stimulate the nerve center that controls vomiting. Apomorphine and picrotoxin are the best examples. *Reflex-action emetics*, including copper sulfate, mustard, ipecac, and solutions of common salt, irritate the mucous membrane of the stomach. Emetics are used primarily as emergency measures in cases of serious poisoning and acute indigestion.

Eminem (Marshall Bruce Mathers; 1972-), American rapper, alias Slim Shady. Not only his white skin color, but his harsh humor and sharp lyrics make him stand out. He started his career as a member of various rap groups, such as Outsidaz and D-12. In 1997, he made his solo debut with the album *Infinite*. In 1999, he made his worldwide breakthrough with the album *The Slim Shady LP*. Other albums by his name are *The Marshall Mathers LP* (2000), *Devils Night* (with D-12; 2001) and *The Eminem Show* (2002).

Emin Pasha (Eduard Schnitzer; 1840-1892), physician and explorer. Emin Pasha became a surgeon in the Turkish and Sudan armies. He was appointed governor of a Sudan province in 1873, and in 1887 he was created a pasha by Egypt. He was rescued from a Mahdi uprising in 1889 but was murdered by Arab slave traders while engaging in explorations for the German East Africa Company.

Emotion, state of both body and mind consisting of a subjective feeling that is either pleasant or unpleasant but never neutral, accompanied by expressive behavior or posture and by physiological changes.

Empedocles (c.495-c.435 B.C.), Greek philosopher who lived in Sicily. He invented the theory that the universe was composed of 4 fundamental elements: earth, air, fire, and water. In medicine he taught that good health consisted of a balance of the 4 bodily 'humors,' corresponding to the 4 elements.

Emphysema, disease marked by the enlargement of the air sacs in the lungs, which interferes with breathing. Emphysema is probably caused by chronic bronchitis, genetic factors, smoking, air pollution, or various combinations of these factors. Lung infections are common side effects. The disease is generally chronic.

Empire State Building, office building in New York City. Rising 1,250 ft (381 m), it is one of the highest buildings in the world. It is one of the most popular tourist attractions in New York, and on a clear day there is a 50 mile (80.5 km) view from the top of its 102 stories. It was built in 1930-1931 and designed by the architectural firm Shreve, Lamb and Harmon.

Empire style, French neoclassical style in architecture, interior decoration, and furniture design that peaked during the Napoleonic empire (1804-1814). In architecture, Roman grandeur was imitated; mahogany and gilt were favored materials for furniture; and costume design was inspired by classical drapery.

Empiricism, philosophical theory that regards experience, mental or physical, as the only source of knowledge. With its emphasis on experimentation and its opposition to the concept of innate ideas, empiricism arose parallel to the development of experimental science during the 17th and 18th centuries, especially in England. Its major originators were John Locke (1632-1704) and David Hume (1711-1776).

Employee benefits *See:* Pension; Profit sharing.

Employment agencies, privately or publicly owned organizations that help workers find employment and employers to find workers. Private employment agencies receive a fee for their services usually based on the salary to be paid.

Emu, flightless, ostrichlike bird (*Dromiceius novaehollandiae*) of Australia, having long, coarse feathers that hide its wings. Emus are large (up to 6 ft/1.8 m tall) and are fast runners. The male incubates the eggs and guards the chicks.

EMU *See:* Economic and Monetary Union.

Emulsion, preparation of minute drops of one liquid dispersed evenly throughout another liquid. Each liquid is called a *phase*. One phase is usually water or an aqueous solution, and the other phase is usually an oil or other immiscible liquid. An emulsion consisting of oil droplets dispersed in water, called an *oil-in-water* emulsion, has properties like those of water, although an oil-in-water emulsion may contain so much oil that it is a semi-solid paste in consistency. If water droplets are dispersed in oil, the emulsion is a *water-in-oil* emulsion and has the properties of an oil. An emulsion is made by shaking or stirring the 2 liquids together, or beating them in a homogenizer. Unless the emulsion is very dilute, it requires an emulsifying agent such as a soap to prevent the dispersed droplets from coagulating together. Milk, butter, and mayonnaise are all emulsions. Emulsions are used in pharmaceutical preparations, cosmetics, paints, asphalt, and lubricants. The word *emulsion* is also used to describe the light-sensitive coating on a photographic film.

Enabling act, legislation giving special powers to individuals or groups. It was by an enabling act in 1933 that the German National Socialists (Nazis), with Nationalist and Catholic Center support, obtained dictatorial powers. Enabling acts have been used in the United States to set up governments in the territories before they were joined to the Union as states.

Enamel, vitreous (glasslike) glaze fused on metal for decoration and protection. Silica, potassium carbonate, borax, and trilead tetroxide are fused to form a glass (called flux) which is colored by metal oxides; tin

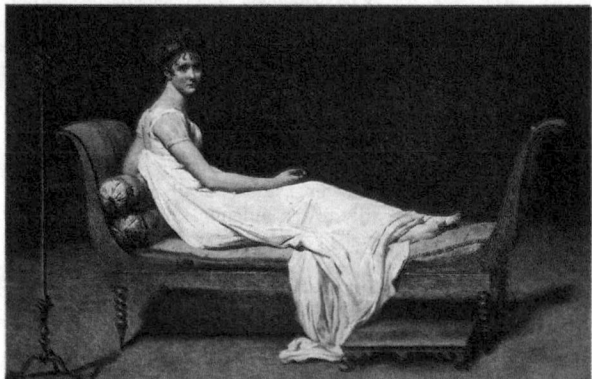

This portrait of madam Récamier, painted in 1800 by Jacques Louis David (1748-1825), clearly demonstrates the characteristics of the Empire style: the couch with its boat-shaped rests, and the high-waisted dress and curled hairstyle of the woman in the picture (Louvre, Paris).

E

E

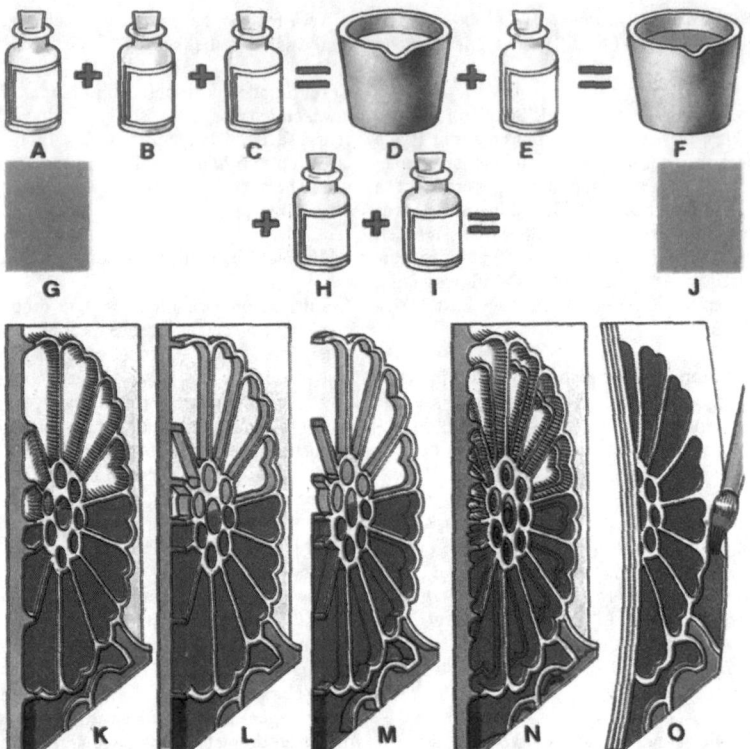

Enameling fuses powdered glass to a metallic base through firing. Enamel consists of 50% silica (A), 35% lead (B) and 15% potash (C), which, when fused, yield a neutrally colored flux (D). The addition of metallic oxide (E) creates colored enamel (F). Transparent enamel (G) is produced by adding tin oxide (H). Lead oxide (I) creates opaque enamel (J).
Five enameling methods are: champlevé (K); cloisonné (L); plique-à-jour (M), which is a backless, translucent form of cloisonnné; basse taille (N); and painted enamel (O).

oxide makes it opaque. The enamel is powdered and spread over the cleaned metal object, which is then fired in a furnace until the enamel melts.

Encephalitis, inflammation of the brain and spinal cord. It may be a specific disease due to an insect-borne virus, or it may occur as a result of influenza, measles, German measles, chicken pox, or other diseases. Symptoms include headache, listlessness, and convulsions.
A large number of organisms may invade the nervous system or its coverings (meninges), thus causing many forms of encephalitis or meningitis or a combination of both. When the disorder is described as meningitis, damage to the brain or spinal cord is secondary to the inflammation of the coverings. In encephalitis, if the coverings or meninges suffer at all, they do so secondarily to the inflammation of the brain and spinal cord.

Encephalograph *See:* Electroencephalograph.

Encomienda, labor system imposed by the Spanish in South America in the 16th century. Native Americans were required to pay tribute for their lands in return for Spanish protection. The system destroyed much of Indian culture.

Encounter group *See:* Sensitivity training.

Encyclical, letter from the Pope to the bishops of the Roman Catholic Church. Papal encyclicals set out guidelines for the application of theological and social Church teachings. Among the best-known encyclicals are *Rerum Novarum* (1891), on the condition of the working classes, by Leo XIII; *Pacem in Terris* (1963), on relationships between the Church and state, by John XXIII; and the controversial *Humanae Vitae* (1968), on birth control, by Paul VI.

Encyclopedia, reference work that summarizes all knowledge or a particular branch of knowledge in a series of articles arranged alphabetically or by subject. The original aim of the encyclopedia was to provide a general education. The word *encyclopedia* is of Greek origin, meaning instruction in the complete circle (*en kykloi*) of learning (*paideia*). While fragments of earlier works are known, the earliest extant encyclopedia is that of Pliny the Elder (1st century A.D.). Its 37 volumes concentrate on the natural sciences and are arranged by subject (rather than alphabetically). In the early Middle Ages, Isidore of Seville (6th-7th centuries) wrote encyclopedias based on 4 organizational principles: history, biography, arts, and words or subjects. His *Etymologiae* (also called *Origines*) in 20 books was an attempt to cover all knowledge, including the liberal arts, law, medicine, God, the Church, society, humanity, geography, food and drink, and tools. The most famous medieval encyclopedia was the *Speculum Majus* (Great Mirror) of Vincent of Beauvais (13th century), whose goal was to reflect 'all things of all times.' One of the earliest encyclopedias in English was the *Mirror of the World*, a translation of Beauvais, issued in 1481 by William Caxton. The 18th century inaugurated the great age of encyclopedias. The first English alphabetical encyclopedia, John Harris's *Lexicon Technicum* (1704), which emphasized the sciences, was soon superseded by Ephraim Chambers's *Cyclopaedia* (1728), which was among the first works to use articles written by specialists and to employ cross-references. The most important of the several German encyclopedias issued in this period was J.H. Zedler's *Great Complete Universal Lexicon*, issued in 64 volumes, 1732-1750. The French *Encyclopédie*, the most famous and perhaps the most influential encyclopedia of all time, was edited by the philosopher Denis Diderot and Jean d'Alembert, 1751. The work promoted rationalism and scientific truth in the name of enlightenment. The *Encyclopaedia Britannica* began with a modest 3 volumes (1768-1771) published by a 'Society of Gentlemen in Scotland.' Though it covered a great many subjects, it was mainly the work of a few men. Modern encyclopedias employ lots of specialists and large editorial staffs.

Endangered species *See:* Wildlife conservation.

Enderby Land, western region of Antarctica extending from Ice Bay to Edward VIII Bay. It was first explored by John Biscoe (1831), an English navigator employed by the Enderby Brothers whaling company. Today it is the site of a Soviet research base.

Enders, John Franklin (1897-1985), U.S. microbiologist who shared the 1954 Nobel Prize for physiology or medicine with F.C. Robbins and T.H. Weller for their cultivation of the poliomyelitis virus in non-nerve tissues, an achievement that prepared the way for the development of polio vaccines.
See also: Microbiology.

Endive, leafy plant (*Cichorium endivia*) of the composite family, of the same genus as chicory. Used as a salad green or cooking vegetable, endive comes in curly-leaf and narrow-leaf varieties.

Endo, Shusaku (1923-1996), Japanese author. Endo was baptized as a Roman Catholic as a young child. This determined his later life and work, in which the Japanese attitude towards Christianity and the issues of sin and guilt were the main themes. His most famous novel *Chinmoku* (Silence) (1966), is an account of a number of missionaries who managed to sneak on land at the beginning of the 17th century when Christianity was prohibited in Japan, and who were then tortured to death or forced to renounce their faith.

Endocrine gland *See:* Gland; Hormone.

Endocrine system, ductless glands that se-

crete chemicals called hormones, which regulate body functions. These organs and their general location are: pituitary gland in the brain, thyroid gland in the neck, parathyroid glands in the neck, adrenal glands in the abdomen, pancreas in the abdomen, ovaries in the abdomen (in females), and testes in the scrotum (in males). The hormones produced by the endocrine glands are extremely potent chemical substances that are effective in very minute quantities. They are secreted directly into the bloodstream and transported throughout the body.
See also: Hormone.

Endometriosis, condition in which tissue resembling the mucous membrane of the uterus-the endometrium-is present abnormally in various locations in the pelvic cavity. The endometrium normally builds up and flushes out periodically, but in endometriosis endometrial cells break off into cysts that move freely through the abdomen, attaching themselves to the ovaries and other organs and irritating surrounding tissue. The disease can cause infertility.

Endorphins, proteins produced by the pituitary gland (at the base of the brain) inhibiting certain brain cells from transmitting impulses and thereby blocking or reducing the sensation of pain. Endorphins were discovered in the 1970s, after it was realized that morphine and other opium-derived drugs inhibited pain by attaching to particular receptor sites in the brain. Endorphins are chemically similar to the opiates and function as natural painkillers.
See also: Pituitary gland.

Endymion, in Greek mythology, youthful lover of the goddess Selene. Various myths explain the eternal sleep and youth of the immortal Endymion. In one, Selene herself casts the spell; in another, Zeus offers eternal sleep and youth as an alternative to death. A poem named after Endymion was written by the English poet John Keats (1818).
See also: Mythology.

Energy, in physics, the capacity to do work. There are various forms of energy. Kinetic energy is the energy of motion, and is equal to one-half the mass of the moving body multiplied by the square of its velocity ($\frac{1}{2}mv^3$). Potential energy is the energy a body possesses by virtue of its position. A body raised to a certain height, h, for example, has a potential energy equal to its mass multiplied by h multiplied by the force of gravity. If the body were dropped, it would fall, and its potential energy would become kinetic. Other forms of energy include heat energy (the vibration of the molecules or atoms that make up substance), electrical energy (the motion of electrons), chemical energy (released by chemical reactions). Nuclear energy is produced when the nuclei of atoms disintegrate or combine, producing both heat and atomic and subatomic particles. One of the consequences of Einstein's theory of relativity is that mass and energy are mutually convertible. The relation between the 2 is described by the formula $E=mc^2$, where E is energy, m is mass, and c

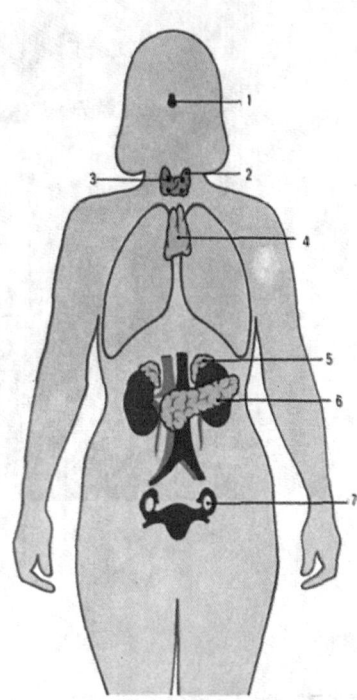

The pituitary (1) makes growth hormone. The thyroid (2) produces thyroxine, triiodothyronine, and thyrocalcitonin; the four parathyroid glands (3) make parathormone. The thymus (4) produces thymosin during childhood. Each adrenal gland (5) has two endocrine sites: the cortex, which makes aldosterone, corticosteroids, and cortisol; and the medulla, which makes epinephrine and norepinephrine. The pancreas (6) produces insulin and glucagon. Ovaries (7) makes estrogen, and the testes (8) make testosterone and androgen.

is the velocity of light. Since c^2 is a very large number, the transformation of even a small amount of matter (mass) into energy yields great quantities of energy. This is what happens in the explosion of a hydrogen bomb. Although matter can be transformed into energy and vice versa, and one form of energy can be transformed into another, neither mass nor energy can be created or destroyed. This is known as the law of conservation of mass-energy.
See also: Nuclear energy; Physics.

Energy supply, total amount of energy available, from all sources, including fossil fuels (coal, oil, natural gas), water power, nuclear energy, solar energy, wind power, etc. Currently, fossil fuels supply the great majority of energy used in industry. The pollution caused by these fuels has stimulated the search for alternate sources of energy that would be clean, practical, and renewable.

Enesco, Georges (1881-1955), a Romanian violinist, composer, and conductor. He won fame as a violinist for his interpretations of Bach. His most popular compositions, including *Romanian Rhapsodies* (1903) and the opera *Oedipe* (1936), are based on Romanian folk music. The tone poem *Vox Maris*, written shortly before his death, was first performed in 1964. Enesco studied at the Vienna conservatory and under Massenet and Fauré in Paris. He made frequent tours as a violinist and conductor.

Enewetak, or Eniwetok, atoll in the central Pacific Ocean, at the northwestern end of the Marshall Islands, a U.S. Trust Territory. It was used as a test site for nuclear weapons in the late 1940s and early 1950s.

Engels, Friedrich (1820-1895), German socialist, philosopher, and associate of Karl Marx, with whom he founded modern communism. Born into a wealthy family, he went to England in 1842 to work in his father's textile mill. There he wrote his first major work, *The Condition of the Working Class in England* in 1844 (published 1845). Engels became a socialist as a result of his exposure to the negative effects of capitalism, and in 1844 he and Marx began a collaboration that lasted until Marx's death. In 1848 they published *The Communist Manifesto*, setting forth the principles of communism. After being active in revolutionary groups in France, Belgium, and Germany during the unsuccessful revolutions of 1848, Engels returned to England in 1850. He supported Marx financially while Marx worked on writing his greatest work, *Das Kapital*, and after Marx's death, he completed the second and third volumes of that work. Among his other works are *The Origins of the Family, Private Property, and the State* (1844) and *Anti-Dühring* (1878), a philosophical polemic that laid the basis for Marxism's claim to be a 'scientific,' as opposed to utopian, socialism.
See also: Communism; Marx, Karl.

E

E

One of the differences between modern humans and animals is that humans use more energy than they need for their primary necessities of life. In the pre-industrial era man mainly used animal, wind and water power, and fuel that was ready to hand, like wood. During recent centuries, a spectacular increase in the use of fossil fuels has taken place, as has the introduction of nuclear energy. The fossil fuel supply is not endless, however, and the burning of fossil fuels on the scale we do today probably contributes to the greenhouse effect, causing temperatures on earth to rise. Nuclear energy, on the other hand, does not add to the greenhouse effect. With the environment in mind, the usage of energy sources like wind and water power was re-instated in the second half of the 20th century. The importance of energy for our modern society can be derived from the enormous extent of the transport and storage systems on our land (harbors, pipelines, warehouses, etc.).

James Watt's (1736-1819) steam machine played an important role in the Industrial Revolution. One of the characteristics of this time was that in the manufacture of goods, human and animal power was replaced by steam power.

Modern fuel motor. If there is one invention that has changed everyday life dramatically, this is it. Motorized transport has made the world smaller, changed street life, and, in heavily populated areas, had a negative impact on the environment.

Raw petroleum is subjected to all kinds of processes in oil refineries before finished products such as petrol and diesel are ready for consumer use.

A roofer finishing off a solar paneled roof. The panels convert solar energy to 220-volt mains voltage. This energy can be linked directly to an electricity supply or it can be stored in a battery for use on less sunny days.

Windmill park near Lelystad (the Netherlands). The energy that the 35 wind turbines generate can supply 4000 homes with electricity. Research into the positioning of wind turbines on platforms in the North Sea has shown that the yield is 20% higher per turbine.

E

The chimneys of a French nuclear reactor. The reactor can generate a chain reaction of fissions (nuclear fuels such as uranium-235, plutonium-239). The generated warmth produces steam from water, which is then turned into electricity in a steam turbine.

Just off the coast of Stavanger, Norway, lays Troll, the largest production platform for natural gas in the world. Troll drills from a gas bubble that stores 1300 billion cubic meters of gas. It is Europe's largest gas field in a seabed.

Steel factory in the German Ruhr Area. Its position and the ready availability of coal and iron ore have resulted in the area developing from an agricultural region in 1850 to the industrial heart of Germany today. Especially the heavy (steel) industry has left its mark on the environment and the landscape.

E

The chalk cliffs that form a large part of the southern coast of England, are the reason the country was given the sobriquet 'Albion'.

Engine, machine that transforms energy into useful mechanical work. The most familiar engines are heat engines, which transform heat energy, obtained by burning fuel, into a force that turns wheels, propellers, turbines, and so on. Other types of engines include hydroelectric plants, which use the energy of falling water to spin rotors that generate electricity, and windmills, which harness the energy of the wind. Engines may be classified by the fuel they use (gasoline engine), by the way they burn their fuel (internal or external combustion), and by the way they produce motion (reciprocating, rotary, or reaction). In internal combustion engines combustion takes place inside the engine cylinders. The gaseous products of combustion press against pistons in the cylinders to produce reciprocating, or back-and-forth, motion. Jet and rocket engines work on the principle of reaction. They burn fuel in a combustion chamber to produce hot gases that leave the engine at high velocity through a nozzle. Reaction to the backward stream of gases thrusts the engine forward. Jet engines take in oxygen from the atmosphere to burn their fuel; rockets carry their own oxygen supply as well as their fuel and are thus independent of the atmosphere. The industrial equivalent of the jet engine is the gas turbine in which a turbine drives a shaft. Gas turbines are used mainly to drive generators, but they also power locomotives, ships, and even some experimental automobiles. Steam engines and steam turbines are external combustion engines, since they burn their fuel in a furnace outside the engine itself. The heat is used to produce steam in a boiler, and the steam drives a piston back and forth or spins the blades of a turbine. Steam turbines, which are highly effi-

cient, are the major propulsion units in ships and the most widely used engines in the world's electricity-generating stations.
See also: Combustion; Steam engine; Turbine.

Engine analyzer, instrument that analyzes the performance of an automobile engine. Specific information about the engine's condition is obtained with oscilloscopes (instruments that measure electric current for the ignition system), tachometers (instruments that measure idling speed), and other devices that form part of the engine analyzer.

Engineering, applied science devoted to the design and construction of machinery and transportation and communications networks. Engineering is divided into many specialties (aeronautical, civil, chemical, electrical, mechanical, and so on), though the branches naturally overlap. Until the 19th century, the term *engineer* signified a military engineer, responsible for fortifications, tunnels, and explosives, or a civil engineer, responsible for designing and building such structures as dams and bridges. The industrial revolution, however, opened up the fields of mechanical, chemical, and electrical engineering. The entry to engineering may be a 3-year or longer course at a university, engineering school, or technical institute, followed by practical experience in working on actual projects.

England, largest of the four countries that make up the United Kingdom of Great Britain. The others are Northern Ireland, Scotland, and Wales. England is governed by a constitutional monarchy. Queen Elizabeth II is the head of state but a cabinet of government ministers rule the country. England (pop. 48 mil.) is an urban country, with 95% of its citizens living in cities. London (pop. 7,6 mil.) is the capital and largest city. The major industries are manufacturing, mining, agriculture, and fishing. The official church is the Church of England (Anglican Church).
See also: Northern Ireland; Scotland; United Kingdom; Wales.

English Channel, arm of the Atlantic Ocean separating Great Britain and France. About 300 mi (483 km) long, it varies in width from about 112 mi (180 km) to about 21 mi (34 km) at the Strait of Dover.

English cocker spaniel, breed of sporting dog, most popular as a pet. The average English cocker spaniel stands 16 in (41 cm) tall at the shoulder, weighs from 26 to 34 lb (12 to 15 kg), and comes in a variety of colors.

English foxhound, breed of hound dog with a short, glossy coat, bred to follow the scent left by a fox. They are white with black or tan patches, stand 23 in (58 cm), on average, at the shoulder, and weigh 60 to 75 lb (27 to 34 kg).

English horn, musical instrument, in the oboe family, somewhat larger than a standard oboe. Its 'bell' is pear-shaped, and its mouthpiece is a double reed.

English language, native language of more than 400 million people in the United States, the British Isles, Canada, Australia, New Zealand, and South Africa. English belongs to the Germanic branch of the Indo-European family of languages and is most closely related to Dutch, Flemish, and German. Old English originated when the languages of the Angle and Saxon tribes replaced those of the native Britons in invasions from the 6th to the 8th century. Only about one-fifth of modern English vocabulary comes from Old English, but this includes many words in frequent use, such as, *eat, drink, child,* and *house.* Scandinavian invasions from the 8th to the 11th centuries contributed Norse elements to the language. Old English evolved into Middle English largely as a result of the Norman invasion of 1066. The old inflectional endings of words began to disappear, and many thousands of French words were introduced. Early modern English began to emerge in about 1500, with major shifts in the pronunciation of vowels and drastic changes in the verb system. Greek and Latin words were absorbed into the language, partly as a result of the influence of the Renaissance, and spelling began to be made uniform. By the early 17th century, the language had attained something like its present form. American English evolved from the language of the early settlers, which varied according to their origin and social status. In some cases English words took on a new meaning; in others, Americans continued to use words no longer in use in England. Mostly because of its varied origins and international influences, the English language today has the largest vocabulary of any language. It has the second-highest number of native speakers (after Chinese), and the widest geographical influence.

English literature, poetry, prose, and drama written by authors from the British Isles, primarily England, Scotland, and Wales, and, to a certain extent, Ireland. English literature mirrors the development of the English language and is inextricably bound up with the country's history, politics, and social developments.
Old English literature (500-1100). Old English (OE) is the form of English spoken by the tribes of Angles, Saxons, and Jutes who settled in the British Isles in the 400s and 500s. The epic poem *Beowulf* is the first significant piece of English literature; its author is unknown. OE poetry is characterized by the use of alliteration (the repetitive use of words beginning with the same sound) and by its use of elaborate metaphoric phrases called kennings. The sea, for instance, may be referred to as 'the whale-road.' Caedmon (fl. 670) is the first known English poet, and the only work ascribed to him (by the Venerable Bede in 731) is a nine-line 'Hymn of Caedmon.' Prose works of that time comprised mostly histories and religious writings, Bede's *Ecclesiastical History of the English Nation* being the first and most important.
Middle English literature (1100-1485). The mixture of Latin (from the Catholic Church) and French (from the Norman invaders), overlaid on the earlier OE and local dialects,

John Donne (1572-1631).

created Middle English (ME). ME literature developed the romances (primarily adventure stories told mostly in verse). The cycle of legends about King Arthur and the Knights of the Round Table is a major example of this genre. The most complete version (*Le Morte d'Arthur*, or *The Death of Arthur*) was written in the late 1400s by Sir Thomas Malory. The most important English author of ME literature was the poet Geoffrey Chaucer (c. 1340-1400). His *Canterbury Tales* (late 1300s) employed end rhymes and a five-beat line (iambic pentameter) that is still a mainstay of English poetry.

Development of modern English. During the 1400s, changes in the language brought about modern English; for example, by the late 1500s, people were writing and speaking in a language we can recognize today. During the reign of Queen Elizabeth I (1558-1603), England experienced a golden age of poetry and drama. William Shakespeare (1564-1616) is the greatest figure of English drama, but contemporaries included Ben Jonson (*Volpone, Bartholomew Fayre*) and Christopher Marlowe (*Tamburlaine the Great, The Tragical History of Doctor Faustus*).

In poetry, longer narrative verse was written by William Shakespeare (*Venus and Adonis*) and Edmund Spenser (*The Faerie Queene*). Both also wrote sonnet sequences (a series of sonnets on a single topic or person) which were a popular verse form of the time.

The Later Renaissance and the Commonwealth (1600-1660). James I, a Stuart, ascended the throne after Elizabeth I. In 1648 the Puritans under Cromwell overthrew the monarchy and established a Commonwealth. The theater continued under James, but it took on a darker tone. Known as Jacobean drama, these plays often concentrated on action, violence, and the theme of revenge. John Webster's *Duchess of Malfi* (c. 1612-1614) is a prime example of Jacobean tragedy. Other playwrights included Francis Beaumont and John Fletcher (*The Maid's Tragedy*), and John Ford (*The Witch of Edmonton*). The Puritans closed the theaters in 1648. John Donne was the leading *metaphysical* poet (a school of poetry that used vivid, common speech together with complex metaphorical allusions called *conceits*). Others in the group included Henry Vaughan

and George Herbert. The Cavalier poets, on the other hand, concentrated on lighter verse. They are typified by the works of Robert Herrick and Richard Lovelace. The greatest poet of the era was John Milton, whose epic *Paradise Lost* (1667) was based on the Bible story of Adam and Eve. Perhaps the most enduring, influential prose work of the era was the King James version of the Bible (translated in 1611).

The Restoration (1660-1700). After the monarchy was restored in 1660, drama returned principally in the form of Restoration comedy, a comedy of manners that concentrated on the amorous pursuits of the upper class. Chief among the Restoration playwrights was William Congreve, whose *The Way of the World* (1700) is still a repertory staple. Others included William Wycherley, and Colley Cibber. Prose works of the era included John Bunyan's *Pilgrim's Progress* (1678). Serious drama and poetry were served by the outstanding poet John Dryden, as exemplified in his play *All for love* (1678) and his satire *MacFlecknoe* (1682).

The Augustinians (1700-1750). The early 18th century saw a revival of classical, mainly Roman, aesthetics with an emphasis on reason, proportion, and elegance. This was especially manifest in the poetic satires of Alexander Pope, most notably in *The Rape of the Lock* (1712), and in the prose writings of the powerful satirist Jonathan Swift, author of *Gulliver's Travels* (1726). The novel came into its own in this period, with such writers as Henry Fielding, Tobias Smollett, Samuel Richardson, and Daniel Defoe. From mid-century to about 1785, criticism reached new heights with the works of Samuel Johnson and his circle, which included James Boswell, biographer, and Edward Gibbon, historian, and the playwright/poet Oliver Goldsmith.

Romantic literature (1785-1837). Pre-romantics, principally the poet William Blake, began the shift in emphasis from reason to feeling and emotion, as exemplified in his *Songs of Innocence* (1789) and *Songs of Experience* (1794). Other pre-romantic poets of the era included Thomas Gray, William Cowper, and the great Scottish poet Robert Burns.

The great romantic poets of the early 19th century were William Wordsworth and Samuel Taylor Coleridge. Their joint effort *Lyrical Ballads* (1798) heralded a change to elemental human emotions and a deep, personal tone. Later, the extraordinary group of Lord Byron, Percy Bysshe Shelley, and John Keats brought romantic poetry to its heights. The novel was also well-served by Jane Austen, *Pride and Prejudice* (1813), and Sir Walter Scott, *Ivanhoe* (1819). The Gothic novel (horror story) was created by Horace Walpole with the *Castle of Otranto* (1754) and was taken up by Mary Shelley, *Frankenstein* (1818).

The Victorian Age in literature (1837-1901). In 1837, Victoria was crowned Queen and inaugurated the longest reign in England (till 1901) and one of its most illustrious literary eras. The novel is the jewel in the crown of Victorian literature. Charles Dickens created worlds of vivid, memorable characters in works like *The Pickwick Papers* (1836-1837) and *Oliver Twist* (1837-

1839) and, later, the grimmer side of Victorian life in *Bleak House* (1852-1853) and *Hard Times* (1854). Major novelists of this period also included: William Makepeace Thackeray (*Vanity Fair*, 1847-1848), Emily Brontë (*Wuthering Heights*, 1847), and Charlotte Brontë (*Jane Eyre*, 1847). Later Victorian novelists include such important figures as George Eliot (pen name of Mary Ann Evans), Thomas Hardy, and George Meredith. Late 19th-century poets often assumed a darker, more problematic tone, as in Lord Alfred Tennyson (*In Memoriam*, 1850), Matthew Arnold ('Dover Beach,' 1867), and Robert Browning (*The Ring and the Book*, 1868-1869). Drama came back after something of a hiatus for most of the century. By 1900, Oscar Wilde (*The Importance of Being Earnest*, 1895), and George Bernard Shaw (*Man and Superman*, 1901-1903; *Major Barbara*, 1905) were producing witty comedies and socially trenchant dramas.

Twentieth-Century literature. Joseph Conrad (*Heart of Darkness*, 1902) wrote penetrating psychological novels while John Galsworthy (*The Forsyte Saga*, 1906-1921, a series of three works) wrote realistic novels and plays. Virginia Woolf, largely forsaking normal plot and character development, wrote novels to describe inner reality using a technique called 'stream of consciousness,' as in *To the Lighthouse*, 1927. D.H. Lawrence brought a mystical approach to social ideas and sex. E.M. Forster, a craftsman highly respected by other writers, outlined the clash between Western and Eastern ideas in *A Passage to India* (1924). The Irish novelist James Joyce broke new ground in writing highly stylized, literary works that

D.H. Lawrence (1885-1930).

utilized interior monologues and random associations in ways not tried before, as in *Ulysses* (1922).

Several novelists were prominent both before and after World War II. These include Elizabeth Bowen, delicate explorar of the feminine mind, and Graham Greene. Greene wrote both 'thrillers' and novels in which the main conflict is with sin or a sense of guilt. Joyce Cary became widely known for *The Horses Mouth* (1944), third book of a trilogy dealing with conflict of cultures. C.P. Snow studied the interrelationship of individual attitudes and social action in a series of 11 novels, 'Strangers and Brothers' (1940-1970). J.B. Priestley, Rebecca West,

E

E

and Ivy Compton-Burnett are other writers with significant works both the prewar and postwar eras. In the postwar period many writers turned to new themes, but avoided experimenting with new forms. George Orwell dealt with Communism in a satire, *Animal Farm* (1946), and in the grim *1984* (1949). A group of young writers who criticized society in bitter terms became known as the 'angry young men'. John Wain in *Hurry on Down* (1953) and Kingsley Amis in *Lucky Jim* (1954) introduced the movement; John Osborne became its leader with his play *Look back in Anger* (1956). John Braine contributed *Room at the Top* (1957). Some writing was more experimental. William Golding used schoolboy characters in *Lord of the Flies* (1954) to show the basic destructive drive found in human nature. Iris Murdoch infused her writing with symbolism, as in *The Bell* (1958), and with her theory of the novel, as in *The Black Prince* (1973). Muriel Spark's *The Prime of Miss Jean Brodie* (1961) and later novels are concerned with the inner identities of individuals. Lawrence Durrell's *The Alexandria Quartet* (1957-1960) consists of four novels, each presenting characters and events form different viewpoints in an attempt to make literary use of the 'the four dimensions' of relativity. Angus Wilson dealt with contemporary themes in novels such as *The Old Men at the Zoo* (1961). Doris Lessing concerned herself with racial conflict, women's liberation, and, in *Memoirs of a survivor* (1975), the disintegration of human society. Anthony' Powell 's 'A Dance to the Music of Time' is a 12-volume sequence of novels that chronicle English life from World War I through the mid-1960's. It was concluded with *Hearing Secret Harmonies* (1975). J.R.R. Tolkien wrote immensely popular books about creatures calles hobbits (1937-1955). The best-selling novel *Watership Down* (1972), by Richard Adams, had rabbits as protagonists.

A Clockwork Orange (1962) by Anthony Burgess is a notable satire with black humor. Former professors, Malcolm Bradbury, David Lodge, John Fowles, and Murdoch, wrote novels that often were self-conscious in manner. Aspects of sexuality and selfhood are explored in Margeret Drabble's *The Needle's Eye* (1972) and Angela's Carter's *Nights at the Circus* (1984).

Through both World Wars and up to today, literature in the British Isles has made major contributions to world culture. Other significant novelists include Aldous Huxley, Evelyn Waugh, Doris Lessing, and John LeCarré. Early postwar drama included comedies of manners by Noel Coward, problem plays by Terence Rattigan, and the verse plays of Christopher Fry, which revitalized the London theater. Plays of social criticism began with Osborne. The Theatre of the Absurd was represented by Harold Pinter and others. Edward Bond's plays deal with indifference to inhumanity. Joe Orton turned the outrageous and horrifying into farce in *Entertaining Mr. Sloane* (1964) and *Loot* (1966). Tom Stoppard and Peter Schaffer wrote notable plays during the last half of the century. Playwrights include: Christopher Fry, Tom Stoppard, and David Hare.

William Butler Yeats, A.E. Housman, Robert Bridges, John Masefield, Alfred Noyes, and Wilfrid Gibson were prominent poets during the early years of the century. Rupert Brooke's promising career was cut short by his death in World War I. T.S. Eliot, an American who became a British subject, influenced many poets and critics. In the 1930's some poets concerned themselves with social and economic questions. Foremost of these were W.H. Auden, Stephen Spender, and C. Day Lewis. They continued to write after World War II, but shifted to more personal concerns. Dylan Thomas was admired for his lyricism.

A group known as the 'Movement', which rejected Romanticism and stressed simplicity of verse form and vocabulary, included Robert Conquest, Philip Larkin, Joan Halloway, and Elisabeth Jennings. Thomas Gunn also wrote in everyday language. John Betjeman's light touch and underlying melancholy made him Britain's most popular poet. He was named poet laureate in 1972. Another group, one which tended toward the metaphysical, included Roy Fuller, Norman MacCaig, and Ted Hughes, generally considered the most important poet of his generation and named poet laureate in 1984. New poets who received attention in the 1970's and 1980's included Geoffrey Hill and Tony Harrison.

English setter, breed of sporting dog, with silky coats and long hairs (feathers) on their legs and tails. Setters stand, on average, 25 in (64 cm) at the shoulder and weigh from 50 to 70 lb (23 to 32 kg). Their strong sense of smell enables them to discover game for hunters.

English sparrow, or house sparrow, bird (*Passer domesticus*) of the weaverbird family. English sparrows were introduced into the United States from Europe in 1852 and have since become abundant both in cities and the countryside. About 6 in (15 cm) long, with reddish-brown streaked feathers, they are omnivorous.

English springer spaniel, breed of sporting dog, the original hunting spaniel, popular with Renaissance hunters. Springer spaniels stand, on the average, 18 to 21 in (46 to 53 cm) at the shoulder and weigh 37 to 55 lb (17 to 25 kg). They have long, thick, protective coats.

English toy spaniel, small dog, originally bred in Asia, which became popular with the English aristocracy in the 17th century. On the average, toy spaniels stand 10 in (25 cm) at the shoulder and weigh from 9 to 12 lb (4.1 to 5.4 kg). The King Charles is black and tan; the Prince Charles is black, tan, and white; the Blenheim is red and white; and the Ruby is red.

Engraving, art of cutting lines in wood, metal, or some other material to produce writing, ornamental designs, or illustrations. Most often, engraving means incising designs or illustrations onto a block or plate for reproduction by printing. The prints obtained by this process are also called engravings. In relief engraving, the background is cut away, leaving a raised design as the printing surface, while the more common intaglio process involves cutting the design into the block or plate, leaving concave traces that hold the ink. Various metals have been used as plates. Because of its durability, steel was fashionable in the 19th century. Copper, although subject to rapid wear, gives higher-quality results. The design may be cut into the metal with a sharp tool or with acid.

Eniwetok *See:* Enewetak.

Enlightenment *See:* Age of Reason.

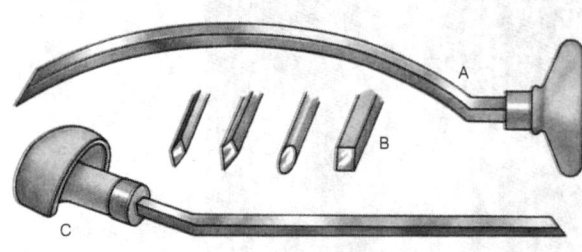

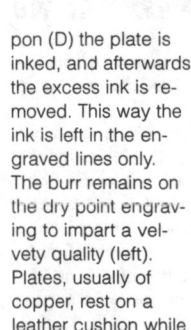

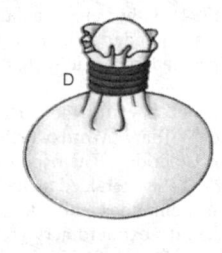

Engraving techniques require precisely angled tools to incise furrows of varying width or subtlety (above). A stipple graver (A) creates a dot, or stipple. Differing geometric points (B) of the burin (C) produce lines of corresponding delicacy or breadth. With a tampon (D) the plate is inked, and afterwards the excess ink is removed. This way the ink is left in the engraved lines only. The burr remains on the dry point engraving to impart a velvety quality (left). Plates, usually of copper, rest on a leather cushion while being incised.

Ennius, Quintus (239-169 B.C.), classical Roman poet. His most important work was the epic *Annales*, a literary history of Rome beginning with the fall of Troy. It was the national poem of Rome until Vergil's *Aeneid*.

Ensor, James (1860-1949), Belgian painter whose bizarre, sometimes macabre canvases were influenced by Hieronymus Bosch and Pieter Bruegel and anticipated surrealism. Among his best-known works are *Entry of Christ into Brussels* (1888) and *The Temptation of St. Anthony* (c. 1888).

Entente, Triple *See:* Triple Entente.

Entomology, study of insects, of which there are more species than of any other animal. Entomology is important not only as an academic discipline, but also because insects are among the most important pests and transmitters of disease.
See also: Insect.

Entropy, in thermodynamics, the amount of disorder in a system. The second law of thermodynamics states that as any process goes on, the entropy of the system concerned either remains the same or rises. Disorder, in this sense, is mathematically defined as randomness. In everyday language, this means, roughly, that any physical system, left to itself, will tend to become increasingly chaotic.
See also: Thermodynamics.

Environment, total of affecting or influencing circumstances surrounding an organism's growth and development. Temperature, other people, and food supply are some of the components of a person's environment. A flower's environment includes soil, animals that feed on it, and sunlight.

Environmental pollution, contamination of the air, land and water caused by human products. The sources of pollution include chemicals released by industrial processes, exhaust from gasoline-powered vehicles like automobiles, refuse and gases emitted by factories, sewage and garbage disposed of by cities, and pesticides used in agriculture.

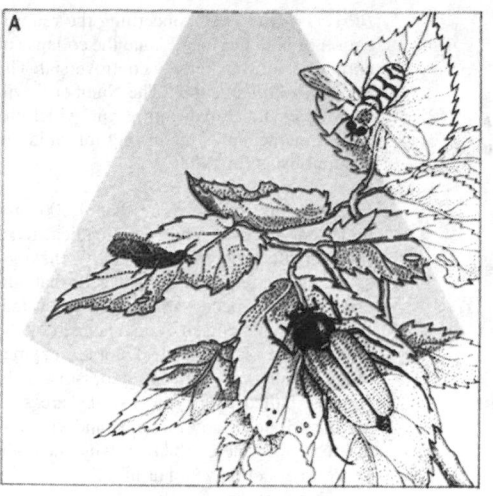

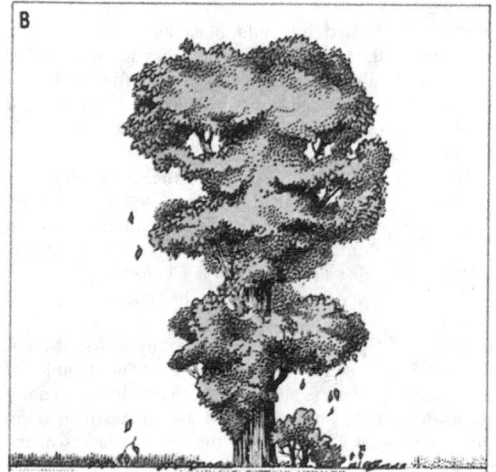

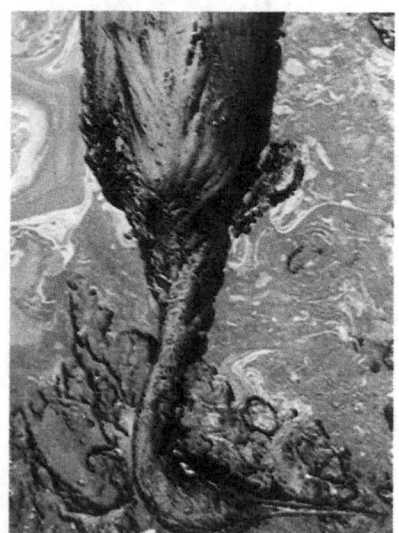

A victim of an oil spill.

Pesticides, which cannot be broken down by living organisms, accumulate as they reach higher levels of the food chain. Concentrations may increase 1,000 fold, as each organism in its lifetime eats a mass of food that is far larger than itself, retaining much of any pesticide it takes in, while the food itself is metabolised.
A. Insecticide reaches plants, as well as insects, when an area is sprayed to control pests.
B. With leaf fall insecticide-bearing vegetation reaches the soil.
C, D, E. Worms eating decaying leaves, small birds feeding on worms, and predators preying on birds, successively accumulate higher concentrations of insecticides.
F. The extremely high levels of pesticide in the peregrine, affect its metabolism, so that it lays extremely thin-shalled eggs. These are fragile and accordingly, there is a high mortality of embryos and fledglings.

Greater awareness of health and environmental hazards has created pressure for laws that control the amount of released pollutants. Conservation efforts, such as recycling, also help to reduce pollution, and new technologies allow industry to release fewer pollutants into the environment. The long-term effects of pollution are not yet precisely known, but it is widely believed by scientists that global warming-the heating of the earth's atmosphere as a result of the green-house effect-is a threat to most forms of life on the planet.

Enzensberger, Hans Magnus (1929-   ), West German philosopher, publicist, and publisher. Traveled through, among other countries, the U.S., Norway, Cuba, and the Soviet Union; held various posts as a guest lecturer. His non conformist, skeptical poems express a virtuoso command of language and use of editing techniques.

E

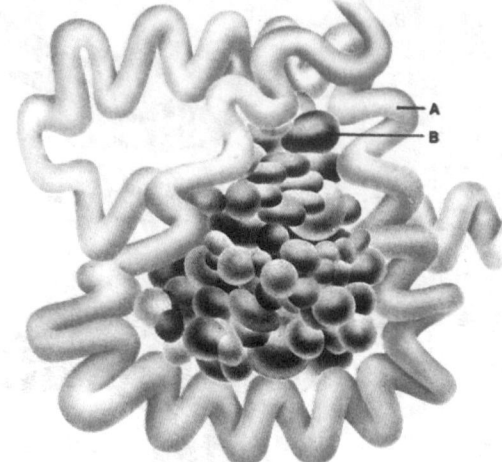

Enzymes are protein molecules that catalyse chemical reactions. They are composed of a long chain of amino acids, folded into a complex three-dimensional structure (A). Each enzyme catalyses a specific reaction, involving a particular molecule, known as a substrate molecule (B). A reaction commences with the disruption of the three-dimensional structure of the enzyme, in such a way that the correct alignment and orientation of the catalytic and binding positions of the enzyme will form around the substrate molecule. This 'induced-fit' phenomenon is essential for a reaction to occur. Hence, molecules of the 'wrong' shape will not combine with the enzyme.

Bürgerkrieg (1993), concerning the reunification of both Germanies and the collapse of communism, was fiercely controversial. The book *Der Zahlenteufel*, (The Number Devil: A Mathematical Adventure) in which he makes mathematics interesting for children, was published in 1998.

Enzyme, any of the more than 1,000 proteins that act as catalysts in chemical reactions in life processes. Generally, enzymes speed up chemical reactions in cells that otherwise would occur too slowly to sustain life. The enzyme itself is not changed by the reaction that it stimulates. Some enzymes cannot function without accessory substances, called coenzymes, which are supplied by food. Many minerals and vitamins act as coenzymes, which is why their absence in a diet may be harmful.
See also: Protein.

Ephedrine, mild, nonaddictive drug used in the treatment of asthma, hay fever, and other allergies. Originally obtained from a plant, it is now made synthetically. Its structure and effects are similar to those of adrenalin.

Ephesians, Epistle to the, New Testament book attributed to the apostle Paul. Probably written during Paul's first imprisonment in Rome, A.D. 60, its main theme is the universality and unity of the Church.
See also: Bible; New Testament.

Ephesus, ancient Greek city in Asia Minor, in what is now Turkey. The temple of Artemis, built in Ephesus in the 6th century B.C. and excavated by archaeologists in 1869, was one of the seven wonders of the ancient world. A major Greek seaport, Ephesus was later the Asian capital of the

Publisher of the magazines *Kursbuch* (since 1964) and *Transatlantik* (1980). After 1968, he mainly published essays that were critical of the social structure and the mass media. His work includes *Der Untergang der Titanic* (The Sinking of the Titanic: A Poem) (1978). His work *Aussichten auf den*

Roman Empire, before becoming a Christian center. It was destroyed in the early 15th century.
See also: Seven Wonders of the Ancient World.

Epic, long narrative poem concerned with heroism. *Gilgamesh*, the earliest known epic, dates from 2000 B.C. Many epics, such as the *Odyssey*, the *Iliad*, and *Beowulf*, existed as oral tradition before being written down. Literary epics, such as Vergil's *Aeneid*, Edmund Spenser's *Faerie Queene*, and John Milton's *Paradise Lost*, depict the eras of their heroes.

Epictetus (C.A.D. 55-135), Greek Stoic philosopher. An educated Roman slave, he held that virtue lies within oneself regardless of external conditions. His teachings were recorded by his pupil Arrian in the *Discourses* and the *Encheiridion*.

Epic theater, form of revolutionary theater developed in the late 1920s by Erwin Piscator and Bertolt Brecht, emphasizing the narrative and political aspects of staged events. Brecht's theories stressed the arousal of a critical response by alienating the spectator from the staged action: *Man is Man* (1926), *The Threepenny Opera* (1928), and *Mother Courage and Her Children* (1941).

Epicurus (341-270 B.C.), Greek philosopher, founder of epicureanism, which is named after him. Reviving the atomism of Democritus, he preached a materialist philosophy that argued that happiness was the goal of life. He saw happiness not as the pure indulgence of pleasure, but as the attainment of honesty and social justice.
See also: Philosophy.

Epidaurus, ancient Greek city about 40 mi (54 km) southwest of Athens. The 4th-century B.C. temple of Asclepius, the Greek god of healing, and the 3rd-century B.C. outdoor theater are 2 of the major ruins found in Epidaurus today.

Epidemic, outbreak of a disease in a given area affecting a large number of people.

Epidemiology, study of epidemics, diseases that affect large numbers of people. Epidemiology uses statistical and other methods to discover the cause of a disease, determine the elements affecting rate of incidence and degree of severity, and establish the means of control. AIDS is one of the most devastating epidemics in the 1980s and 1990s.

Epigram, short, pithy saying in verse or prose, often with a satirical turn. Originating in ancient Greece as a monument inscription, the English epigram is associated with Ben Jonson, John Dryden, Jonathan Swift, and the most famous of all, Alexander Pope. Modern epigrammatists include Oscar Wilde, W.B. Yeats, and Hilaire Belloc.

Epilepsy, brain disorder characterized by susceptibility to seizures and convulsions that can cause loss of consciousness and muscle control. The causes of epilepsy are

During an epilepsy attack, there are certain episodes of disorganised activity in parts of the brain with characteristic electroencephalogram (EEG) abnormalities.
A petit-malseizure, is a brief loss of consciousness, with a spike and wave in the EEG. It is idiopathic, as no lesion of the brain is involved. A grand mal seizure may be preceded by a brief 'aura', locating the attack, followed by convulsions, loss of consciousness and a brief cessation of breathing. In this case, EEG abnormality is widespread and synchronous in both hemispheres. It may be idiopathic or symptomatic of a cerebral lesion. Both forms of seizures may originate from the diencephalon. Psychomotoric epilepsy results from a lesion in or near one of the temporal lobes, and may take many forms, such as sensory hallucinations, disordered awareness, perceptual illusions, or abnormal emotions. In some cases, normal complex activities may be carried out unconsciously.

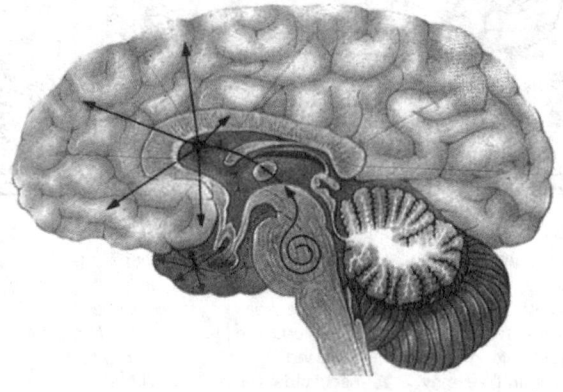

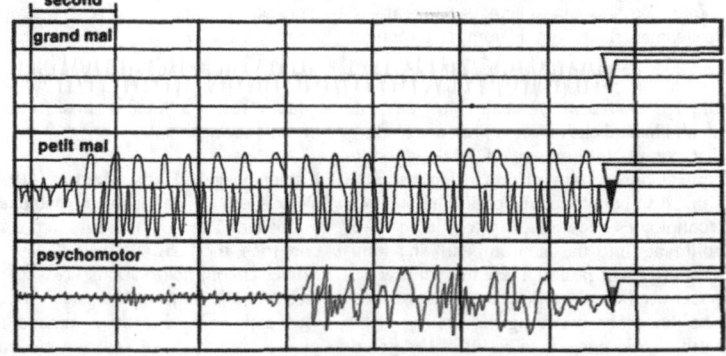

second									
grand mal									
petit mal									
psychomotor									

not well understood. Among children it may be a result of brain injuries during birth or of abnormalities in fetal development. In adults it can be caused by head injuries and tumors. It is normally treated with drugs that prevent or inhibit seizures.

Epinephrine, or adrenalin, hormone secreted by the adrenal glands. The release of epinephrine causes a rise in blood pressure, an increase in the heart rate, and a rise in muscle strength. Emotions like fear and anger, typically associated with 'fight or flight' situations, trigger the release of this hormone.
See also: Hormone.

Epiphany (from Greek *epiphania*, 'manifestation'), Christian feast held annually on Jan. 6 to celebrate Jesus's baptism, the visit of the 3 wise men to the manger in Bethlehem, and the transformation of water into wine at Cana. The night before Epiphany, 12 days after Christmas, is called the Twelfth Night.
See also: Christmas.

Epiphyte, or airplant, plant that grows on another but that does not obtain food from it. Various lichens, mosses, ferns, and orchids are epiphytes, usually living on trees. Epiphytes thrive in warm, wet climates.

Epistemology (from Greek *episteme*, 'knowledge'), branch of philosophy that inquires about the sources of human knowledge, its possible limits, and to what extent it can be certain or only probable. Epistemology is connected with psychology and logic.
See also: Philosophy.

Epistle, special, formal letter in the New Testament of the Bible. There are 21 epistles-14 are attributed to Paul, 2 to Peter, 3 to John, 1 to James, and 2 to Jude. Those ascribed to Paul are known as Pauline epistles, while the others are called Catholic, or general, epistles.
See also: New Testament.

Epithelioma, tumor of the epithelium. Although epithelioma can be benign or malignant and can occur in any part of the body, the term most often refers to basal cell carcinoma, a common form of skin cancer that rarely metastasizes (spreads through the blood or lymph system) and is treatable by surgery. Basal cell tumors can result from prolonged exposure to the sun, X-rays, or carcinogens like tar.
See also: Epithelium.

Epithelium, tissue covering external surfaces of the body, such as the skin, and lining various bodily tubes and cavities. It consists of one or more layers of cells variously modified to provide protection or aid in excretion of waste products and the assimilation of nutrients. The epithelium that covers the surface of the skin consists of one or more layers of adjoining cells. Often strands of cells grow from the epithelium into deeper-lying layers and differentiate to form glands. Some sensory organs are specialized forms of epithelium.

E pluribus unum ('out of many, one'), Latin

motto referring to the unification of the original 13 American colonies. Chosen for the Continental Congress by John Adams, Benjamin Franklin, and Thomas Jefferson, it is now inscribed on the Great Seal of the United States and on many U.S. coins.

Epsom salts, common name for magnesium sulfate, so called because it was first found at Epsom, England. The bitter-tasting substance has long been used as a laxative.

Epstein, Sir Jacob (1880-1959), U.S. sculptor, living in London, whose controversial early work was influenced by African sculpture, Constantin Brancusi, and Auguste Rodin. After 1915 he turned to religious subjects and portraiture. His works include the Oscar Wilde Memorial (1911), *Rock Drill* (1913), and *Ecce Homo* (1935).

Epstein-Barr (EB) virus, herpes virus that causes several diseases in humans. The virus, identified in 1964 by British scientists Michael A. Epstein and Y. M. Barr, is associated with infectious mononucleosis (common in the United States), Burkitt's lymphoma (a skin cancer in Africa), and a nasopharyngeal (nose-throat) cancer (in China). The EB virus, which can remain dormant in the body for long periods, infects certain white blood cells and reproduces in mucous membranes.

Equation, statement of equality. Mathematical equations are often expressed in algebraic notation, where known and unknown quantities can be represented by symbols. Notations of branches of mathematics such as differential calculus or logic can also be used to represent relationships of equality. Other disciplines have created shorthand notations representing equalities, as in chemistry, where chemical equations represent chemical reactions. One of the most familiar forms of equations in mathematics is the n *degree polynomial equation* (of order n):
$$ax^n+bx^{n-1}+cx^{n-2}+\dots z =0$$
Here x is a variable denoting an unknown quantity and a, b, c ... z represent known values.
If $n=2$, the generalized form reduces to a *quadratic equation*: $ax^2+bx+c=0$. Such equations have 2 solutions or *roots*:
$$x =\frac{- b + \sqrt{b^2 - 4ac}}{2a} \text{ and}$$
$$x =\frac{- b - \sqrt{b^2 - 4ac}}{2a}$$
Because these examples have only one unknown variable, solutions can be found. Equations can have more than one unknown. In such cases there must be as many equations as there are variables in order to solve for the unknowns. Consider the equation: $2x+xy+3=0$. Without additional information it is impossible to determine either x or y explicitly. However, with the additional information of another equation such as: $x+2xy=0$, finding values for both variables x and y that simultaneously satisfy each equation of the system is possible. By mathematical manipulation the solution to the system made up of the 2 equations is: $x=-2$ and $y=-{}^1/_2$. the formulation and solving of sys-

tems of equations are used extensively in operations analysis, economics, psychology, and the sciences.

Equator, imaginary great-circle line around the earth equidistant from the North and South poles. The equator divides the globe into the northern and southern hemispheres and forms the zero axis of latitude.

Equatorial Guinea

Capital:	Malabo
Area:	10,831 sq mi (28,051 sq km)
Population:	498,000
Language:	Spanish, French
Government:	Presidential republic
Independent:	1968
Head of gov.:	Prime minister
Per capita:	US$ 2,100
Monetary unit:	1 CFA franc = 100 centimes

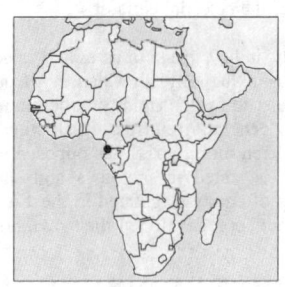

Equatorial Guinea, republic in west-central Africa, formerly a Spanish colony, independent since 1968. The country consists of the mainland province of Río Muni, bounded on the north by Cameroon and on the east and south by Gabon, and several islands off the Atlantic coast. Bata (on the mainland) is the largest city. Main products include cocoa, coffee, bananas, palm oil, and timber. The main ethnic groups are the Fang in Río Muni and the Bubi in Bioko. Spanish is the official language.
Portugese explorers discovered Fernando Po in 1472. It passed to the Spanish in 1778 and remained in their control except for a brief period of British occupation in the early 1800's. Claims to Río Muni were disputed by several European powers in the 19th century, but Spain finally gained the territory in 1900 and named it Spanish Guinea. Independance was granted in 1968 and the name was changed to Equatorial Guinea. Under the brutal dictatorship of Francisco Macias Nguema, the country's first president, some 50,000 Guineans were killed and more than 100,000 forced into exile. His economic policies caused the country's economy to collapse, and his foreign policy brought Equatorial Guinea under the influence of the Soviet Union. In 1979 Nguema was overtrown by his nephew, Lieutenant Colonel Obiang Nguema, and executed. Nguema, who made himself president in

E

E

1982, reestablished links with the West, receiving aid from Spain and France. In 1985 the country's currency was linked to France's currency. As a result, France's influence has increased and French has become the second language. According to various human rights organizations democratization has stagnated and human rights are constantly being violated. In 2002, Nguema was re-elected. Before that, he summoned the members of the opposition, who had been in exile, to return. However, they had opted out of the elections.

Equatorial Islands *See:* Line Islands.

Equilibrium, chemical, condition in which a chemical reaction and its reverse reaction are taking place at equal velocities, so that the overall concentrations of reacting substances remain constant.

Equinox (1) either of the 2 times each year when day and night are of equal length. The spring, or vernal equinox occurs in Mar., the autumnal equinox in Sept., (2) either of the 2 intersections of the ecliptic and equator on the celestial sphere. In other words, the equinoxes are the points at which the Sun crosses the celestial equator.

Equity, in law, group of rules and principles arising in the English Chancery Court to compensate for the rigidity of common law. Equity generally referred to that which was considered morally right as opposed to that which is stated in the laws and statutes. Courts of equity originated in the 17th century, but soon developed their own body of rules.

Erasistratus (3rd century B.C.), Greek physician of the Alexandrian School of Medicine, credited with the foundation of physiology as a separate discipline. He studied brain convolutions, named the trachea, and distinguished between motor and sensory nerves.

Erasmus, Desiderius (1466?-1536), Dutch Roman Catholic humanist and advocate of

Portrait of Erasmus, by his friend Hans Holbein the Younger (1466?-1543).

church and social reform. One of the leading scholars of the Renaissance, he did the first Latin translation of the New Testament from the original Greek and edited the works of the Church fathers. His works include *The Christian Soldier's Handbook* (1503) and *In Praise of Folly* (1509), a witty satire on Church corruption. Although he advocated church reform, he opposed the Protestant Reformation. He had a bitter debate with Martin Luther on the issue of predestination and free will.
See also: Humanism.

Erastus, Thomas (1524-1583), Swiss theologian. Erastianism, his doctrine, held that the state should have complete control over the affairs of the Church. An adherent of Zwingli, he clashed with the Calvinists, particularly over the practice of excommunication, which he opposed in his *Explicatio gravissimae quaestionis* (1589).

Eratosthenes (c.275-c.195 B.C.), Greek mathematician and astronomer. Postulating that the earth was round and that the sun's rays were parallel, he measured the lengths of shadows in different locations and used geometrical reasoning to estimate the circumference of the earth with remarkable accuracy. He also determined the size and distance of the sun and moon. The sieve of Eratosthene is a practical method for identifying prime numbers.

Erbakan, Necmettin (1926-), Turkish engineer and politician, fundamentalist Muslim. Erbakan founded the National Salvation Party (Milli Selamet Partisi; MSP) in 1970 and was Vice Prime Minister for three short stints in the 1970s. In 1981, he founded the Islamic Welfare Party (Refah Partisi), a fundamental Islamic party like the MSP. The Welfare Party became the largest party during the elections of 1995; in 1996, Erbakan became Prime Minister. He was the first Islamic-oriented Prime Minister in the history of secular Turkey. Under pressure of the Turkish army, which feared further damage to the secular character of the state, the Erbakan government resigned. In 1998, the Welfare Party was forbidden by the Constitutional Court. As for Erbakan, he was forbidden to hold any political function for 5 years.

Erbium, chemical element, symbol Er; for physical constants see Periodic Table. Erbium was discovered in 1843 by Carl G. Mosander. It occurs in the minerals *xenotime, gadolinite, euxenite, fergusonite*, and is obtained commercially from *monazite*. It is prepared by reducing anhydrous chloride with calcium metal. Erbium is a silvery, soft, reactive metal, belonging to the series of elements known as the rare-earth metals. Ion-exchange and solvent extraction techniques have led to much easier isolation of the rare-earth elements. Erbium and its compounds are used in carbon-arc lighting applications, special glasses and enamels, and refractory materials.

Erdogan, Recep Tayyip (1954-), Turkish politician, founder and leader of the AK party. Erdogan experienced an exceptional ca-

reer from shoeshine boy to mayor (1994) of the Turkish city Istanbul, with over a million citizens. However, he had to resign in 1998 because he was convicted of inciting religious hatred. He had publicly read an Islamic poem including the lines: 'The mosques are our barracks, the domes our helmets, the minarets our bayonets and the faithful our soldiers...' He spent four months in prison. After his release, he founded the conservative-Islamic AK party, which joined the battle against corruption. AK means Adalet ve Kalkinma (Justice and Development), but it also means ' clear' and ' clean'. The AK denies being ' Muslim-fundamentalist'. The AK experienced a landslide victory at the parliamentary elections of 2002. However, because of his criminal record, he was barred from becoming Prime Minister. At the end of 2002, the Turkish parliament decided to make an amendment to the constitution, which made it possible for Erdogan to fulfil the post of Prime Minister after all.

Erebus, Mount, an active volcano in Antarctica. It rises to a height of 12,450 feet (3,795 m) on Ross Island in the Ross Sea. It was discovered in 1841 by Sir James Clark Ross, a Scottish explorer, who named it after one of his ships. Members of Ernest Shackleton's expedition ascended the peak in 1908.

Ergonomics (human engineering), the science concerning the study of human labor conditions, based on the assumption that optimum circumstances for a laborer result in higher efficiency. One of the most important aspects of ergonomics is trying to find the most favorable correspondence between man and his tools and machines; another aspect is the fact that ergonomics focuses on the psychological stress resulting from the task, which often depends on the circumstances under which the task is to be carried out. As such, various sciences and techniques play an important part in ergonomics, such as industrial design, anatomy and physiology, cybernetics, information theory, and psychology. Ergonomics not only focuses on professional tasks in, for example, factories and offices, but also on the design and layout of houses, household equipment, etcetera.

Ergot, disease of grasses and cereals caused by a fungus of the genus *Claviceps*. The word is also used to apply to the dark purple spots on the heads of rye caused by the disease. Ergots contain toxic alkaloids that are poisonous to animals and humans. The alkaloid ergotamine, also contained in ergots, is used in the treatment of migraine headaches.

Erhard, Ludwig (1897-1977), West German economist and political leader. In 1949 he became economics minister under Konrad Adenauer; he was the prime architect of West Germany's post World War II revival. He succeeded Adenauer as chancellor from 1963-1966.

Eric the Red, 10th-century Norse explorer who founded the first colonies in Greenland c.985. According to the Icelandic sagas, he

was born in Norway but emigrated to Iceland. Arrested for manslaughter, he sailed westward in quest of a strange land sighted in 876 by the Norse searover Gunnbjorn Ulfsson; Eric named the place Greenland. His son, Leif Ericson, was also an adventurer. It is beleived that he landed in North America in 1000.
See also: Vikings.

Erie Canal, artificial U.S. waterway completed 1825, connecting Buffalo on Lake Erie with Albany on the Hudson River, thus providing a route to the Great Lakes from the Atlantic Ocean. It was replaced in 1918 by the New York State Barge Canal.
See also: Great Lakes; Lake Erie.

Erikson, Erik Homburger (1902-1994), German-born U.S. psychoanalyst who defined 8 stages, each characterized by a specific psychological conflict, in the development of the ego from infancy to old age (*Childhood and Society*, 1950). He also introduced the concept of the identity crisis.
See also: Psychoanalysis.

Erin *See:* Ireland.

Eritrea

Capital:	Asmara
Area:	46,774 sq mi
	(121,144 sq km)
Population:	4,466,000
Language:	Tigrinya, Arabic
Government:	Republic
Independent:	1993
Head of gov.:	President
Per capita:	US$ 740
Monetary unit:	1 Nakfa = 100 cents

Eritrea, independent state in East Africa, bounded by the Red Sea, Sudan, Ethiopia and Djibouti. A hot, dry, mountainous region, Eritrea is populated partly by nomadic herders, but there are also areas of agriculture and several cities, including Asmara, the capital. After several hundred years under the Ottoman Empire, Eritrea became an Italian colony in 1890. In 1962 it was annexed by Ethiopia. The Eritreans fought a war of independence since the 1960s. Two years after the installation of a more autonomous Eritrean government, the republic

became independent in 1993. Towards the end of the 1990s, the conflict with Ethiopia flared up again. Although a peace treaty was signed in 2002, the countries continued to harbor mutual feelings of distrust. One year later, a demilitarized buffer zone was established, which was supervised by a UN peacekeeping force.
See also: Ethiopia.

Ermine, term for any weasel that turns white in winter. In the Middle Ages ermine fur was used only by royalty; later it was associated with high court judges.

Ernst, Max (1891-1976), German-born artist, leader of the dada and surrealism movements in Paris. He developed the expressive techniques of *collage* and *frottage* (rubbing on paper placed over textured surfaces). He also painted in oil and produced graphics and sculpture. Two well-known paintings are *Woman, Old Man, and Flower* (1923-1924) and *The Eye of Silence* (1943-1944).
See also: Dada; Surrealism.

Eros, in Greek mythology, the god of sexual love. The Romans identified him with Cupid, son of Venus and Mars. The name was used by psychiatrist Sigmund Freud to personify the life-force and the sexual instincts.

Erosion, gradual wearing away of the land by natural forces. The main agents of erosion are weathering, running water, ice, winds, waves, and ocean currents. Natural erosion is an extremely slow process. For example, an average of 1 ft (0.3 m) of land is worn away from the surface of the United States every 900 years. But this rate is accelerated if the natural vegetation that covers and protects the surface is stripped away. Natural erosion is a continuous process, beginning as new land masses are uplifted and continuing until they are worn down.

Ershad, Hussein Mohammed (1930-), Bengalese military and politician. Ershad received military training and was stationed in West Pakistan for many years. After

Bangladesh had extricated itself from Pakistan (1971), Ershad continued his career within the armed forces. He became Chief of Staff in 1978, after which he seized power in 1982. He had himself elected as president in 1986. But the number of opponents to his regime increased steadily. Students in particular, along with the two largest opposition parties (the Nationalist Party and the Awami League) demanded that Ershad step down. When resistance towards his administration reached a climax in 1990, Ershad was forced to step down. He was arrested on the charge of corruption and was succeeded by the acting president, Ahmed. He was released on bail in 1997, after which he became actively involved in politics again.

Erving, Julius (1950-), U.S. basketball player. Erving, nicknamed 'Dr. J.,' stood 6'6" (198 cm) and played forward and guard. Known for his leaping ability and high-flying style of play, Erving ushered in the age of dunking and 'playing above the rim.' After attending the University of Massachusetts (1968-71), he played for the Virginia Squires (ABA, 1971-1973), the New York Nets (ABA, 1973-1976), and the Philadelphia 76ers (NBA, 1976-1987). He retired in 1987, having been named Most Valuable Player by the ABA (1974, 1975) and NBA (1981).

Erysipelas, contagious skin infection caused by streptococci bacteria, which generally enter through a small wound. The area affected becomes red and slightly swollen; the patient often has a fever and feels tired. If not treated, erysipelas can spread to deeper tissues, causing serious complications. Treated with antibiotics.

Erythema, redness of the skin resulting from dilation of the capillaries of the skin to allow extra blood to flow. It has many causes, from blushing and sunburn to infection.

Erythromycin, antibiotic synthesized by the soil bacterium *Streptomyces erythreus*. Discovered in 1952, erythromycin is used to treat staphylococcus and streptococcus infections, meningitis, scarlet fever, and

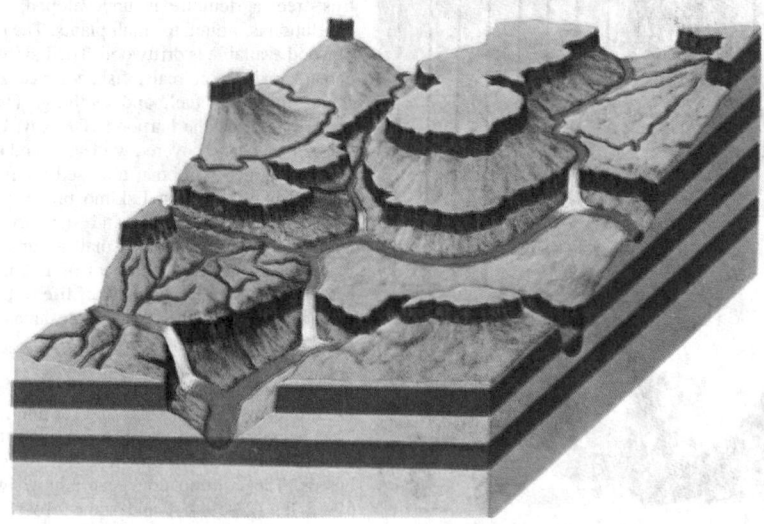

River erosion in hilly areas, built up of horizontal layers of weak (yellow) and resistant (green) rocks, results in steep-sided, flat-topped plateaus, or mesas, and in smaller separated remnants, or buttes. In dry regions, flash floods are common after a rainfall, because no vegetation exists to impede the flow. The erosive action of floods is great and leads to formation of steep-sided canyons, waterfalls, and badlands, or networks of gullies separated by narrow ridges.

E

Legionnaires' disease. It is also helpful in treating patients who are allergic to penicillin.

Erzurum (pop. 240,000), capital of the province of the same name in Northeast Turkey. (province 9,708 sq mi (25,133 sq km), pop. 875,000). Situated 6,398 ft(1,950 m) above sea level. Center of an agricultural area with cattle trade. Domestic industry: iron, copper, leather, and carpets. Atatürk university (1957); a number of mosques (including the Great Mosque dating from the 12th century) and two mausoleums. City fortified with forts and earthen walls. Narrow streets and dwellings made of gray volcanic rock. Due to its strategic location, it was already important in ancient times. Occupied by the Russians in the past two centuries in 1828, 1878, and 1916. The first conference of Turkish 'nationalists was held here in 1919.

Esaki, Leo (1925-), Japanese physicist, employed at Sony Corporation (1956-1960) and IBM. Nobel prize in 1973 for his research into semiconductors. Discovered that the tunnel effect of electrons can be used in very small and fast electronic circuits (tunnel diode).

Esau, or Edom, in the Bible (book of Genesis), son of Isaac and Rebecca, elder twin brother of Jacob. Esau was tricked by Jacob into selling his birthright. Esau's descendants, the Edomites, were consistently hostile to the Israelites, descendants of Jacob.

Escalator, moving stairway used in public buildings to transport passengers from one level to another. The steps move on a continuous belt and fold flat at the top and bottom to allow passengers to step on and off easily. An average-size escalator can carry over 5,000 passengers an hour.

Escape velocity, speed an object must reach in order to break free from the gravitational pull of a massive body, such as the earth,

An Eskimo woman preparing a seal skin. Seal skins are used to manufacture clothing, footwear, kayaks, tents and toys.

moon, or sun. The escape velocity depends upon the mass of the body and the distance of the moving object from it. The escape velocity from the earth's surface is about 7 mi/sec (11.3 km/sec).
See also: Astrophysics.

Escorial, monastery and palace in central Spain, 26 mi (42 km) northwest of Madrid. One of the most imposing buildings in Europe, it was built (1563-1584) by Philip II and houses a church, palace, college, and mausoleum in which many Spanish kings are buried. Its art collection contains works by Velásquez, El Greco, and Tintoretto, among others.

Esdraelon, or plain of Jezreel or of Megiddo, plain in northern Israel, about 200 sq mi (520 sq km), stretching along the coast near Mt. Carmel and the Jordan River valley. This plain, referred to in the Book of Revelation as Armegeddon, was often the site of battle. Though Esdraelon was formerly a low ground filled with water, sponge, and fungus, it has since been drained, and has grown to become one of Israel's most populous and fruitful lands.

Esfahan *See:* Isfahan.

Eshkol, Levi (1895-1969), Israeli political leader, one of the founders of the state, prime minister, 1963-1969. Born in the Ukraine, he moved to Palestine in 1914. He helped create the Mapai (Jewish Labor Party) and served as minister of agriculture and minister of finance under David Ben-Gurion. He was prime minister during the June 1967 war with Egypt, Jordan, and Syria.
See also: Israel.

Eskimo, European name for the Inuit people, indigenous inhabitants of the Arctic regions of northeast Asia, North America, and Greenland. Probably of Asian origin, the Eskimos speak languages of the Aleut group. Anthropologists believe that the Eskimos came to North America by crossing the Bering Strait land-bridge from Asia c.2000 B.C. Their traditional way of life was strongly influenced by the severity of the Arctic climate. Since the ground is seldom frost-free, agriculture is undeveloped, and vegetation is limited to small plants. The only wood available is driftwood. The Eskimos depend mainly on seals, fish, walrus, and shales for food, fuel, and clothing. Their main weapon is the harpoon. The *kayak*, a one-person canoe covered with skin, and the *umlak*, a larger skin boat, are used for fishing and hunting. Most Eskimo property is traditionally communal, and the people tended to live in relatively small groups. In recent years growing numbers of Eskimos have left their traditional way of life to take jobs and settle in the less remote areas of Alaska and Canada.

Eskimo dog, large, wolflike Arctic dog, used in teams to draw sleds and for hunting. The name is often used to include the Alaskan malamute and Siberian husky breeds. The Eskimo dog generally weighs 50-85 lbs (23-39 kg) and stands 16-18 in

(40-45 cm). Its long, coarse coat and oily undercoat protect it from cold and dampness.

Eskisehir (pop. 413,000), capital of the province of the same name in Northwest Turkey. (province 5,205 sq mi, 13,477 sq km, pop. 597,000). One of the most important industrial centers of Turkey: chemical industry, sugar, construction materials, and textile industry. Extraction of meerschaum (sepiolite), which is mainly used to manufacture tobacco pipes. Hot, sulfurous springs. University (1973). Established on the site of the Frygian city, Dorylaeum. The crusaders conquered the Seljuks at this location in 1097.

Esophagus, thin muscular tube leading from the pharynx to the stomach. Food passes down it by means of gravity and peristalsis.
See also: Alimentary canal; Digestive system.

ESP *See:* Extrasensory perception.

Esperanto, artificial language designed by Dr. Ludwig Lazarus Zamenhof (1859-1917) of Warsaw, Poland, and first proposed to the public in 1887. Based upon the main European languages, Esperanto is simple and easily learned. Pronunciation is phonetic, and its rules of grammar have no exceptions. Esperanto is one of various artificial languages meant to facilitate international communication. It is the most widely used.

Espionage, systematic secret gathering of information about the plans and activities of foreign governments or competing businesses. Espionage is as old as war itself, but modern military intelligence gathering developed under Frederick the Great of Prussia in the 18th century. Extensive espionage networks were developed during World War II, and since then intelligence agencies have become significant components of the state apparatus in many countries.

Esposito, Phil (1942-), Canadian hockey player. He is fourth on the all time regular season scoring list (1,590 points) and is among the top goal scorers in National Hockey League (NHL) history (with 717 goals). Esposito led the league in scoring for five seasons (1969, 1971-1974) and won the Hart Memorial Trophy as most valuable player in 1969. Esposito played center for the Chicago Black Hawks (1963-1967) and the Boston Bruins (1967-1975), where he led the Bruins to 2 Stanley Cup championships (1970, 1972). He finished his career with the New York Rangers (1975-1981) and was inducted into the Hockey Hall of Fame in 1984.

Esquivel, Adolfo Perez (1931-), Argentinean sculptor and architect. A professor of architecture at the University La Plata in Buenos Aires until 1974. Afterwards, a leader of a Christian ecumenical movement for human rights in Latin America (Servicio Paz y Justicia). He was repeatedly arrested and was imprisoned for more than a year (1977-1978) as a result of his nonviolent actions for Indians and other minorities.

Esquivel was awarded the Nobel Peace Prize in 1980.

Essay, literary composition in which the writer deals with a single topic or attempts to convert the reader to a point of view. The informal essay, often humorous, was mastered by Mark Twain. The formal essay, as written by Matthew Arnold, is opinionated and informative.

Essen (pop. 616,400), city in western Germany, on the Ruhr River. Established in the 9th century around a convent, it became an industrial center in the 19th century. The Krupp steelworks company, located in Essen, was a major arms manufacturer during both world wars, and much of Essen was destroyed by Allied bombings during World War II.
See also: Germany.

Essene, member of an ascetic Jewish sect that flourished in Palestine around the time of the birth of Jesus. Living in their own communities, the Essenes generally withdrew from public life, appearing only occasionally to warn others that the end of the world was at hand. Some scholars believe that the Dead Sea Scrolls belonged to an Essene group.
See also: Dead Sea Scrolls.

Essex, Robert Devereux, 2nd Earl of (1567-1601), English courtier, a favorite of Queen Elizabeth I. He acquired fame in European military campaigns, was knighted in 1589, and made lord lieutenant of Ireland in 1599, a post he lost by failing to crush the Earl of Tyrone's rebellion.

Established Church *See:* Church of England.

Estates-General, or States-General, French national assembly (first summoned in 1302) composed of representatives from the 3 'estates' or social classes: clergy, nobility, and commoners. During most of its existence it was an advisory body with little legislative power, and in fact it did not meet between 1614, when it was dismissed by King Louis XIII, and 1789, when it was called into session by King Louis XVI on the eve of the French Revolution. Traditionally each estate met and voted as a separate house, but in 1789 the 3rd estate declared itself a national assembly, each member having one vote. It was this decision that inaugurated the revolution.
See also: French Revolution.

Esters, organic compounds formed by condensation of an acid (organic or inorganic) and an alcohol, water being eliminated. This reaction, esterification, is the reverse of hydrolysis. Esters of low molecular weight have fruity odors and are used in flavorings and perfumes and as solvents; those of higher molecular weight are fats and waxes.

Estes, Richard (1936-), American painter, representative of hyperrealism. Using only painting materials and means, he produces works that can scarcely be distinguished from a photograph. Themes are derived from

(big) city life: shop windows, restaurants, movie theaters, billboards, etcetera.

Esther, book of the Old Testament. It tells of Esther (also called Hadassah), a Jewish queen of the Persian king Ahasuerus, who prevented the king's favorite, Haman, from massacring Persian Jews. The story is the origin of the feast of Purim.
See also: Bible; Old Testament.

Estivation, dormant state entered into by some animals in hot, dry climates, to conserve moisture during the summer. The slowing of body processes permits survival. Animals that estivate include many reptiles, amphibians, insects, snails, and fish.
See also: Hibernation.

Estonia

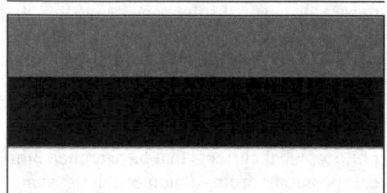

Capital:	Tallinn
Area:	17,462 sq mi (45,227 sq km)
Population:	1,415,000
Language:	Estonian
Government:	Republic
Independent:	1991
Head of state:	Prime minister
Per capita:	US$ 10,000
Monetary unit:	1 Estonian kroon = 100 senti

Estonia (Republic of), independent country on the east coast of the Baltic Sea, bordered by Russia in the west, and Latvia in the south. The largest cities are Tallinn, Tartu and Pärnu.
Land and climate. A third of the land, which consists of plains and low plateaus, is forested. The climate is temperate.
People. Estonians are ethnically and linguistically related to the Finns. The population largely consists of Estonians (64%). Russians are the most important ethnic minority (29%). Estonian is the official language. 60% of the population is Evangelical-Lutheran
More than half the population is urban.
Economy. Agriculture, especially dairy farming, is the chief industry. After independence was proclaimed, the economy was swiftly modernized, particularly the industry: machinery, electronics, and textile.
History. Estonia became an independent state in 1918, but was annexed by the USSR

in 1940 (along with Latvia and Lithuania) under the terms of a secret agreement between the Soviet Union and Nazi Germany. The country was occupied by Germany during World War II and again taken over by the USSR in 1945. An independence movement gained massive support in the late 1980s, and independence was attained in 1991. In 1994 Russian troops, that had been stationed in Estonia since 1944, were withdrawn from Estonia. Estonia aimed at joining western institutions, such as NATO and the EU. In 2002, the country was asked to join the NATO and, at the Treaty of Copenhagen (Dec. 2002), the decision was made to allow the country to become a member of the EU in 2004.

Estrogen, any of a group of female sex hormones that regulate the menstrual cycle and control the development of secondary sex characteristics. After the menopause, production of estrogen decreases.
See also: Hormone.

Estrous cycle, in most female mammals, periodic readiness for mating, regulated by environmental signals and the release of hormones. The length of the cycle and of estrus (the period of fertility and receptivity to mating) varies among species. The female is sexually receptive during estrus, and most female mammals will not mate at any other time.
See also: Reproduction.

ETA (Euzkadi Ta Azkatasuna), militant separatist movement in the Basque area of northern Spain. By means of terrorist activities, ETA seeks to force the reinstatement of Euzkadi, the republic that the Basques proclaimed in 1936. This republic only existed for a short period of time. ETA was very active at the beginning of the 70s. Despite concessions on the part of the Spanish government, such as the appointment of a Basque chamber of representatives in 1980, ETA continues its acts of terror. The support of the Basque population definitely decreased in the 80s, but the movement remains popular with many youngsters. The 90s saw many terrorist attacks as well, but the police also managed to arrest a number of ETA leaders. Millions of people in the major cities demonstrated against ETA's violence in 1997. The entire administration of the Herri Batasuna party, the political branch of the ETA, was sentenced to seven years for supporting ETA. In 1998 ETA announced a cease-fire.
The Spanish government was asked to start the negotiations on possible permanent peace in the Basque Country. However, at the end of 1999, the ETA announced that they no longer wanted to observe the truce. They claimed that not enough initiatives had been shown to realize the full independence of the Basque Country. After this, many more attacks followed.

Etching, method of engraving in which acid is used to carve the lines into a metal plate; also, the print obtained from such a plate. Modern plates are usually copper or zinc. The plate is covered with an 'etching ground,' an acid-resistant film of mixed

E

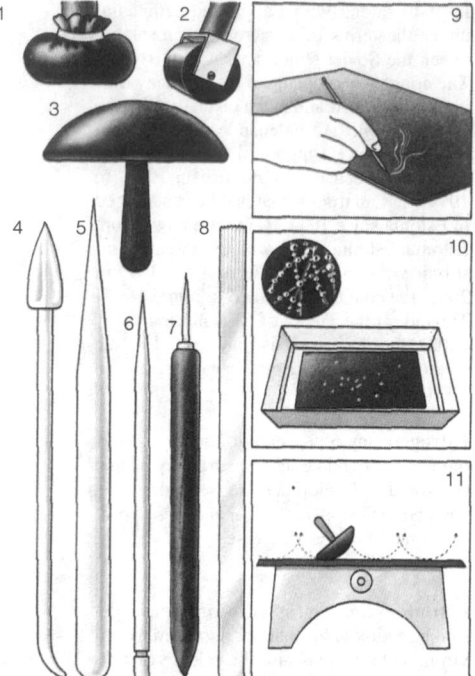

When making an etching, the plate is cleaned, then heated, to facilitate application of the ground, that is applied with a silk-covered cabber (1) or a hard roller (2). A mushroom-shaped dabber (3) then applies ink to this. Also shown here are a scraper (4), a burnisher (5), and etching needles (6, 7, 8). After the design is completed (9), the plate will be immersed in an acid bath (10), where the acid will bite into the exposed lines on the plate. When the process is completed, the plate is cleaned, inked with a dapper (11), and then printed.

waxes and resins, on which the etcher draws. The plate is then submerged in an acid bath until the faintest lines have been bitten. It is then removed, and these lines are 'stopped out' (protected) with varnish. The process is successively repeated until the darkest lines (those exposed longest to the acid) have been bitten.

Ethane, hydrocarbon (C_2H_6) of the paraffin series of chemical compounds. Ethane is a colorless, odorless, flammable gas that boils at -127°F (-89°C). A constituent of natural gas, it has a high fuel value.
See also: Hydrocarbon.

Ether, or aether, in physics, hypothetical substance that was once believed essential for transmission of light waves through space. Scientists assumed that waves required some medium. Observations of stars had suggested that the ether must be stationary in space, and that the earth therefore moved through it. In 1887 the U.S. scientists Albert A. Michelson and Edward W. Morley tried to measure the effect of the 'ether wind,' but found no sign of it. The theory of ether was finally abandoned when Albert Einstein's theory of relativity showed that electromagnetic radiation is not a mechanical distortion of a medium, but a type of energy that travels through a vacuum.

Ether ($C_2H_5)_2O$, flammable liquid that causes unconsciousness when inhaled. It was widely used as an anesthetic during the 19th and early 20th centuries. But its uncomfortable side effects and flammability led to its being replaced by other anesthetics. *See also:* Anesthesia.

Etherege, Sir George (c.1634-1691), English dramatist, writer of restoration comedy, who influenced both William Congreve and William Wycherley. His three plays are *The Comical Revenge* (1664), *She Wou'd If She Cou'd* (1668), and *The Man of Mode* (1676).

Ethics, branch of philosophy devoted to the consideration of the moral principles of human behavior and social organization. Over the centuries, various theories have been put forward to explain how it is that people develop awareness of and opinions about what is right and wrong. Some have argued that these values are absolute and/or innate, others that they are dependent on individual expertise or historical circumstances. Historically, ethics has been closely tied to religion, but in Europe and America, in the 19th and 20th centuries, there have been philosophical currents that have argued ethical positions from a non-religious standpoint.

Ethiopia

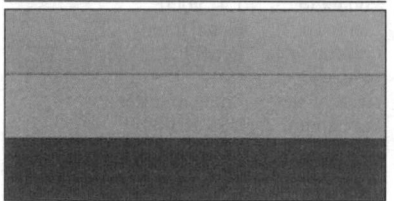

Capital:	Addis Abeba
Area:	436,233 sq mi
	(1,133,380 sq km)
Population:	67,673,000
Language:	Amharic
Government:	Federal republic
Independent:	1896 (republic since 1975)
Head of gov.:	Prime minister
Per capita:	US$ 700
Monetary unit:	1 Ethiopian birr = 100 cents

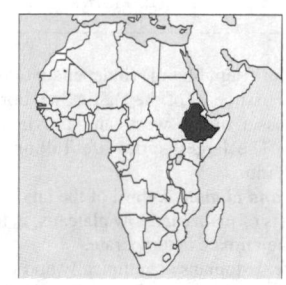

Ethiopia, formerly Abyssinia, country on the eastern edge of Africa, bordered by Eritrea on the north, the Sudan on the west, Kenya and Somalia on the south, and Somalia and Djibouti on the east.
Land. Geographically, Ethiopia consists of two great plateaus, separated by part of the Great Rift Valley. The Ethiopian plateau, to the west of the Great Rift Valley, is the most fertile and most densely populated part of the country. East of the Great Rift Valley is the Somali Plateau, which slopes eastward

Falls in the Awash River near the Koka Dam, south of Addis Ababa in Ethiopia.

to the Ogaden Plateau and reaches over 14,000 ft (4,267 m) in the Urgoma Mountains. The Great Rift Valley separating the plateaus is a long, narrow cleft dotted with lakes and broadening in the north to form the Danakil Depression, a desert. Lake Tana in the northwest is the country's largest lake and the source of the Blue Nile, one of the main components of the Nile River. The capital of Ethiopia is Addis Ababa.
People. The Amhara and Tigray ethnic groups constitute about one-third of the population and have traditionally accounted for most of the ruling class. Most of them are Coptic Christians. Amharic, a Semitic language, is the official language of the country, although English is widely spoken. The Galla, most of whom are Muslims, are the largest single ethnic group, accounting for 40% of the population. About one-tenth of the population practices tribal religions.
Economy. Ethiopia's economy is based upon agriculture and about 75% of the population is directly dependent upon farming and livestock raising. Coffee is the chief cash crop and principal export.
History. Traditionally, the kings of Ethiopia claimed descent from Menelik, the son of King Solomon and the Queen of Sheba, but the first Ethiopian kingdom to have left any historical record dates from the 1st century A.D. Coptic Christianity was introduced in the 4th century A.D. Throughout most of the Middle Ages Ethiopian power was weakened by internal political conflict and armed clashes with neighboring Somalis. In modern times, Menelik II reconsolidated the old empire in 1889. In 1895 Italy invaded Ethiopia but was defeated by Menelik's troops in 1896 at Aduwa. In 1936 Mussolini's Italian Fascist government invaded again. The country was liberated from occupation in 1941 when Emperor Haile Selassie, who had first come to power in 1930, was restored to the throne. His rule lasted until 1974, when army officers ousted him and inaugurated a one-party state that nationalized most of the economy. The military government has continued a war against the forces struggling for the independence of Eritrea, a territory annexed by Ethiopia in 1962, and there have been repeated armed clashes with Somalia over a territorial dispute. Compounding the country's troubles, reduced rainfall in the early 1970s led to se-

rious drought and famine; and severe famine again occurred in 1985. The civil war with the Eritreans ended in 1991 and Eritrea became independent in 1993. In 1998 a border dispute between the two countries led to a war. In 1995, the Ethiopian government adopted a new constitution providing for a federal form of government, and held democratic elections. The war with Eritrea ended in 2000. A year later, a UN peacekeeping force was formed to guard the border. At the end of that year, Prime Minister Zenawi warned of a famine, which would be worse than the famine of 1984, which took the lives of nearly a million people.

Ethnic group, collection of individuals united by ties of culture and/or heredity who are conscious of forming a subgroup within society. Due to migration and incorporation into larger groups, in many countries different ethnic groups can be found.

Ethnocentrism, belief that the characteristics of one's own culture or race are superior to those of other groups or races. The differences in other cultures are seen as deviations from the correct approach taken by one's own culture.

Ethnography, branch of anthropology concerned with the investigation of contemporary culture, particularly treating ethnic groups one by one.

Ethology, branch of zoology dealing with animal behavior. Ethologists try to determine the reasons behind such things as mating rituals, social structures, and care of offspring in various animals.
See also: Frisch, Karl von; Zoology.

Ethyl alcohol *See:* Alcohol.

Ethylene (C_2H_4), colorless, flammable organic gas. Ethylene is one of the most important industrial chemicals. Found in both petroleum and natural gas, it is obtained in large quantities by heating ethane and propane with steam. Ethylene is polymerized (combined into large molecules) to form polyethylene, a plastic widely used in packaging and other manufactures. Ethylene is also used to make styrene for other plastics. Converted to ethylene oxide, it is used to make ethylene glycol (antifreeze), and in various solvents and detergents. Ethylene occurs in plants, acting as a growth regulator; it is used commercially to help ripen fruit.

Etiquette, formal system of rules to guide human social behavior. The word originated in the 17th century to refer to the elaborate ceremonial rules of the royal court in France. By extension, it refers to the recognized ways of proper behavior in any given setting.

Etruria *See:* Etruscan.

Etruscan, name for the people whose civilization flourished in Italy before the rise of Rome. The Etruscans seem to have migrated from Asia Minor to Italy in the 12th century B.C. A distinctive culture had emerged by the 8th century, reaching its peak in the 6th. The early governments were monarchical and changed subsequently to republican states that were controlled by oligarchies. The Etruscans carried on extensive maritime trade with the Greeks and Phoenicians and had colonies in Sicily, Corsica, Sardinia, the Balearic Islands, and Spain. After the 5th century B.C. the Etruscan cities were absorbed by the expanding Roman state.
See also: Rome, Ancient.

Etymology, study of the origin and evolution of words. The history of language was first seriously studied in the 19th century. This led to the comparative analysis of languages that turned out to be related. Etymologists began to concentrate on the evolution of words within families of languages, especially examining changes in meaning according to context.
See also: Linguistics.

EU *See:* European Union.

Eucalyptus, any of a genus (*Eucalyptus*) of tall evergreen trees of the myrtle family, indigenous to Australia. The leaves of some species are used for medicinal purposes. The blue gum (*E. globulus*) is the best-known eucalyptus grown in the U.S.

Eucken, Rudolf Christoph (1846-1926), a German philosopher. He was awarded the Nobel Prize in literature for 1908. Eucken stressed the spiritual aspects of existence, and taught that people can by constant striving overcome to nonspiritual side of their nature. His books were inspirational and widely read. Eucken was born in Aurich and educated at Göttingen and Berlin. He taught at Basil, 1871-1874, and at Jena, 1874-1920. He was exchange professor at Harvard University in 1912-1913.
His works include *The Life of the Spirit* (1888); *The Meaning and Value of Life* (1908); *Can We Still Be Christians?* (1911).

Euclid (c.300 B.C.), Greek mathematician of Alexandria whose major work, the *Elements*, still constitutes a basis of many courses in geometry. Euclid was most notable for introducing the method of logically deducing theorems from axioms and other theorems.
See also: Geometry.

Etruscan clothing resembled Greek dress, and, in turn, had a stylistic influence on Roman fashion. Both sexes wore a tunic and a loose cloak, or tebenna, bordered by a band. The tebenna later evolved into the Roman toga, and the band, or clavus, became a mark of rank.

Eudoxus of Cnidus (400-350 B.C.), Greek mathematician and astronomer who proposed a system of homocentric crystal spheres to explain the movements of the planets; this system was adopted in Aristotle's cosmology. He was probably responsible for discovering parts of geometry detailed in Euclid's *Elements*.

Eugenics, study of techniques to improve the genetic endowment of human populations. Basically it consists of the recommendation that those with 'good' traits should be encouraged to have children, while those with 'bad' traits should be discouraged or forbidden from having children.
See also: Genetics.

Eugénie (Marie de Montijo; 1826-1920), empress of the French 1853-1870 as wife of Napoleon III. The daughter of a Spanish noble, she was a major influence on her husband and on three occasions was regent in his absence. After his downfall during the Franco-Prussian War, she escaped to England.
See also: Napoleon III.

The name of Euclid (about 300 B.C.) is inextricably connected with geometry. He summarized the geometrical knowledge of his time into a number of books ('Elements'). The first printed publication (in Latin) appeared in 1482. Starting from a number of assumptions (axioms, postulates), he developed geometry into an imposing logico-deductive system. For ages, Euclidean geometry served as the classical example of a deductive science. It was not until the end of the 19th century, that it was realized that the foundations of this system badly needed renovation and reinforcement. Euclid's system of axioms could not support the whole system of Euclidean geometry.

E

E

Eugenius III (d. 1153), pope 1145-1153, promoter of the Second Crusade. In 1146 Rome revolted against papal rule, and Eugenius was driven from the city. He lived in France and Germany and returned to Rome only in 1153.

Eugenius IV (1383-1447), pope (1431-1447). He fought with the Council of Basel (1431-1449) to affirm the pope's supreme authority over church councils. He also succeeded in obtaining a temporary reunification with the Greek Orthodox and other Eastern churches (1438). He reigned from Florence 1434-1443 because of civil disturbances in Rome.

Euglena, any of several microscopic, one-celled organisms found mainly in stagnant water. Euglenas show both plant and animal characteristics. Like plants, they can manufacture their own food and are capable of photosynthesis; like animals, they can move about freely, propelled by their whiplike flagella. They possess a red-pigmented 'eyespot' that is sensitive to light.

Eulachon, saltwater fish (*Thaleichthys pacificus*) of the smelt family, native to the North Pacific. The 8-in (20-cm) fish are harvested with nets when they swim up rivers to

The harvesting of grapes in the Monferrato province, in the northwestern region of Piedmont, Italy. The farms there are too small for mechanization. The supply of cheap Italian wines on the French market, caused a wine-war when, contrary to EEC agreements, France applied a 12% tariff on Italian wine imports.

The Ruhr River valley in West Germany, the single largest industrial complex in Europe incorporating several major cities, developed in an area with extensive deposits of coal and iron ore.

spawn. West Coast Native Americans dried the fish to use as candles.

Eulenspiegel, Till, Brunswick trickster hero of a group of German tales originally published 1515. His pranks demonstrated peasant cunning triumphing over establishment figures of his day. He was the subject of a tone poem by Richard Strauss in 1895.

Euler, Leonhard (1707-1783), Swiss mathematician who worked in St. Petersburg, Russia, and Berlin. He contributed to nearly all fields of mathematics, making major contributions to algebra and calculus in particular.
See also: Algebra; Calculus.

Euphrates River, Western Asia's longest river, over 2,200 mi (3,540 km). It rises in northeastern Turkey, crosses that country, then flows southeastward over the Syrian plateau and through Iraq, where it flows together with the Tigris River to form the 120-mi (193-km) long Shatt al Arab, which empties into the head of the Persian Gulf. The Euphrates has had great historical significance above all for its lifegiving waters, which irrigated the crops supporting great civilizations in Mesopotamia from pre-Babylonian times. It is still an important source of irrigation for Iraq and Syria.
See also: Tigris River.

Euripides (c.480-406 B.C.), ancient Greek playwright, writer of tragedies. He is thought to have written 92 plays, of which 19 have survived. The best known include *Medea*, *The Trojan Women*, *Electra*, *Orestes*, and *The Bacchae*.

Euro *See:* Economic and Monetary Union.

Europa, in Greek mythology, daughter of King Agenor of Phoenicia. Zeus fell in love with her and came to her in the form of a gentle white bull, enticing her to climb onto his back. He then carried her away to Crete, where she bore him three sons, Minos, Rhadamanthus, and Sarpedon.
See also: Mythology.

Europe, the continent of Europe is part of the Eurasian continent and has a surface of almost 3,862,495 sq mi (10 million sq km). Not counting the countries that formerly made up the Soviet Union and Turkey (the larger part of which lies in Asia), Europe is made up of 36 states, with a population of 498.4 million. Europe is highly developed in an economic sense, but is vulnerable due to the meager sources of raw materials, especially where the supply of energy is concerned.
More than half of Europe consists of lowlands: the Russian Lowlands cover virtually all of European Russia and extend out to the west to form the North European Lowlands, which can be divided into the Polish Lowlands, the North German Lowlands, the Lower Rhine Lowlands, and the French Lowlands. The second European topographical feature is the South European Highlands, consisting of the Alps, the Carpathian Mountains, the Balkan Mountains, and the Appennini Mountains.

The Dutch region of the grazing grounds in the peat moors, lies in the western-most part of the Lower Rhine Plain.

The Iberian Peninsula is separated from the rest of Europe by the Pyrenees and is largely made up of a plateau, the Spanish Meseta. The Scandinavian peninsula is made up of an old mouton complex, as can also be said of parts of Great Britain.
The influence of the Atlantic Ocean stretches into the mainland, so that a moderate maritime climate is found in the greater part of Western Europe. This gradually changes into a continental climate as one proceeds to the east, which particularly reveals itself in the significant differences in temperature between summer and winter. A zone along the Mediterranean is characterized by warm, dry summers and cool, humid winters.
The European tundra, situated above the pole circle, is characterized by arctic fauna and flora. The treeless tundra houses reindeer, lemmings, grouse, arctic foxes, etcetera. The natural coniferous forests are limited to Scandinavia, Russia, and Central Europe; elk, bears, and lynxes, live here. Original broadleaf forests can still be found in East-Europe. Oak and birch woods, sometimes mixed with beech trees, can be found in the western part of Europe. The Central European forests house red deer, roe, swine, and foxes. The vegetation around the Mediteranean Sea consists of evergreen broadleaf woods and the maquis: shrub with thick, leather-like leaves and fragrant blossoms. Citrus fruits, figs, olives, and cork oak grow here. European birds vary from water birds to bee-eaters and snake eagles. The magot, the only ape that can be found in Europe, lives on the Rock of Gibraltar.
The population of Europe is not evenly distributed; there are significant differences in the population density. Large parts of Iceland and Norway are (virtually) inhabited, while capital metropolitan conglomerates such as London and Paris house over 2,500 inhabitants per sq mi (1000 per sq km), as can also be said of the Dutch Randstad and the German Ruhrgebied.
A phenomenon that was typical of Western Europe for a long time is that of the immigrant worker, which developed mainly in the 60s. Laborers from the countries around the Mediterranean were contracted in order to solve the shortage of laborers (particularly for less appealing professions). In addition, the states with a colonial background were

faced with a stream of immigrants from their (former) overseas regions.

A majority of the languages that are spoken in Europe belong to the European language family and can be divided into three main groups; the Germanic, Romanic, and Balto-Slavonic languages. The Germanic languages include English, Dutch, Fries and the Scandinavian languages. The Romanic languages include French, Spanish, Portuguese, Italian, and Rumanian. The Balto-Slavonic languages can be divided into Slavonic languages (Russian, Czech, Slovakian, Slovenian, and Bulgarian) and the Baltic languages (Lithuanian and Latvian). In addition, the Celtic languages of Brittany, Ireland, and Northern Scotland belong to the Indo-European language family, along with Greek and Albanian.

The major European religious movements include Roman Catholicism, Protestantism, and the Eastern Orthodox religions. Roman Catholicism is mainly propagated on the Iberian peninsula, in Italy, Belgium, France, Ireland, and in eastern Europe, and Protestantism in northern and northwest Europe, central Germany and Great Britain. The Eastern Orthodox Churches can be found in Greece, the Balkans, and the European part of the former Soviet Union.

The economic significance of Europe on a global scale is greater than one might expect when considering its size and population in proportion to the earth's surface and population. For example, Western Europe accounts for around 20% of the total petroleum refining capacity. Particularly the United States and Japan, which developed into an economic world power after WW II, have meanwhile surpassed West Europe as an industrial power. With the far-reaching integration of the European countries in the European Union, Europe hopes to remain an economic power of significance.

In prehistoric times, Europe remained in Africa's and Asia's shadow for a long time. West European cultures did not come to the fore until the paleolithic period. Man distributed himself throughout Europe during the mesolithic period; he lived mainly by hunting, fishing, and gathering. This nomadic lifestyle was gradually replaced by sedentary means of existence in the neolithic such as agriculture and cattle breeding, which resulted in the first permanent settlements. Characteristic of the final phase of this era are the large rock formations (megalithic tombs, Stonehenge). Copper processing developed into the most important industry in Southeast Europe around 3000 B.C.. The bronze age (2000-800) not only saw a rapid increase in the European population, but also saw new cultures and trading over great distances. The prehistoric era ended with the iron age, the time of the great Celtic cultures, followed by the growth of the Roman Empire. From the beginning of our era up to approx. 400 AD, this empire controlled virtually all of Western Europe, from the northern part of The Netherlands and Great Britain to what is currently Israel. The eastern part continued as the Byzantine Empire, whereas the western part broke up into numerous small unrelated empires, a situation that did not change until the Carolingian Empire came about in the 9th century. This

On September 7, 1860, Garibaldi entered Naples. He conquered the kingdom of Naples with a group of about 1000 volunteers, the 'redshirts'.

After the Communist regime had established itself, the arts too were put at the service of the new society. This painting by Kartov, *Friendship of the Nations*, glorifies life under the hammer and sickle.

Left: 'Reichsparteitag' in Nuremberg (1938).

empire led to the West Frankish and East Frankish empires, leading to the Kingdom of France and the Holy Roman Empire respectively. The various empires did however have one thing in common: the Roman Catholic faith, which left its mark on every aspect of Medieval life. This continued to be the case until the Reformation (1517).

The European population saw a steady increase up until the 14th century, after which the situation was reversed due to famines, epidemics, and numerous wars, both dynasty-related and religion-related.

While the Holy Roman Empire fell apart into countless small states in the 17th century, the absolutist French rulers managed to maintain unity. Although the French Revolution ended this absolutist regime, Napoleon proclaimed himself emperor a short time later. By the end of the 19th century, Germany had developed into an economic and military power under the leadership of Bismarck. The major concentrations of power that resulted from this were released during the First World War, from which Germany emerged as the major loser. The financial bankruptcy, the political instability, and the crisis of the 20s proved to be an excellent breeding ground for national socialism, which unleashed World War II via the Third Reich. The map of Europe looked completely different once the horrors of the war were over: large states had lost land and relatively smaller states had gained land. Moreover, the allied dissension led to a dichotomy between the western part of Europe (influenced by the US) and the eastern part of Europe (influenced by the Soviet Union). The idea of a united Europe (expressed as early as in the 19th century) was given shape

in the form of various cooperative ventures, which eventually led to the establishment of the European Community in 1958.

At the end of the 80s, under the influence of the reforms of the Russian head of state Gorbatsjov, one could observe overtures between the two Europes. An official end was made to the strict separation between capitalist Western Europe and communist Eastern Europe at the beginning of the 90s, partly as a result of the disintegration of the former Soviet Union.

European Common Market *See:* European Community.

European Community (EC), one of the three branches of the European Union. During 1967-1993 European Community was the common name for all three branches of what is now the European Union.
See also: European Union.

European Economic Community *See:* Common Market, European.

European Free Trade Association (EFTA), an economic organization of European nations. Its purpose is to maintain free trade in industrial products and to expand trade in agricultural goods among its members, which are Iceland, Liechtenstein, Norway and Switzerland.

EFTA was formed in 1960. In 1973 two of its members, Great Britain and Denmark, withdrew from EFTA and joined the European Community (EC). (The EC became the European Union in 1993). Also that year, a free-trade zone in industrial goods was established between EFTA and

On January 1, 1973, Great Britain, Denmark and Ireland were added to the European Economic Community. On January 15 of that year, the European Commission met for the first time in its new, expanded form.

the EC, and during 1973-1984 trade barriers were abolished. In 1986 Portugal withdrew from EFTA and joined the EC. In 1994 members of EFTA, with the exception of Switzerland, joined with the EC members in integrating their markets into a single free-trade zone. In 1995 Austria, Finland, and Sweden left EFTA and joined the European Union.

European Organization for Nuclear Research, or CERN (Conseil Européen pour la Recherche Nucléaire), research center for particle physics (the study of subatomic particles), funded by 14 European members and located near Geneva, Switzerland. Established 1952, it has a staff of more than 3,500, and its facilities, including large particle accelerators, are available to researchers from any country. Its members are Austria, Belgium, Denmark, France, Great Britain, Greece, Italy, the Netherlands, Norway, Portugal, Spain, Sweden, Switzerland, and Germany.

European Recovery Program *See:* Marshall Plan.

European Space Agency (ESA) European Organization for Space Research, established in 1973 and effective as of 1975. The ESA is the result of the merger between the ESRO (European Space Research Organization) and the ELDO (European Launcher Development Organization). The ESA's member states are Sweden, Denmark, The Netherlands, Belgium, Norway, Austria, Great Britain, Germany, France, Ireland, Spain, Switzerland, and Italy. It was within this scope that artificial moons were launched for the purpose of pure space research and earth research, weather satellites and communication satellites. In addition, the ESA developed and built its own booster, the Ariane. Seeking to establish the autonomy of European space travel, the ESA has developed a new version of the Ariane booster, the Ariane 5, which was successful-

ly launched from the launch site Kourou in French Guinea in 1997. The ESA is also working on a manned module (Columbus), which is to be part of the future international space station. The ESA headquarters are located in Paris. It also has research centers in Germany, Italy, and The Netherlands, along with a ground station in Spain.

European Union (EU), an international organization that functions as a coordinating agency and central authority for certain economic, political, and social policies of member countries. The EU consists of 15 members: Belgium, Germany, France, Italy, Luxembourg, the Netherlands, Great Brittain, Ireland, Denmark, Greece, Spain, Portugal, Finland, Austria and Sweden. The most important branch of the European Union is the European Community. Its purpose is to maintain tariff-free trade among members in all goods and services and to advance economic unity among members.
In 2002, an agreement was reached on the entry of Malta, Cyprus, Estonia, Latvia, Lithuania, Hungary, Poland, Slovenia, the Czech Republic, Slovakia, Bulgaria and Romania in 2004. The entry of Turkey, with whom an association treaty had already been concluded in 1963, will be discussed further in 2004. In 2002, the euro was introduced in twelve EU-member states, which meant the end of the national currencies in those countries.
See also: European Community.

Europium, chemical element, symbol Eu; for physical constants see Periodic Table. Europium was discovered in 1901 by Eugène Demarcay. The element occurs in the minerals monazite and bastnasite, the two principal sources of the rare-earth elements. It is prepared by heating the oxide with excess lanthanum metal under high vacuum in a tantalum crucible. Europium is a silvery-white, soft metal, and the most reactive member of the elements known as the rare-earth metals. Ion-exchange and solvent extraction techniques have led to much easier isolation of the rare-earth elements. Europium and its compounds are used in laser materials, as neutron absorbers in nuclear reactors, and in color phosphors for TV tubes.

Europol, European police organization; cooperation between the police authorities of the member states of the European Union. Europol, with its seat in The Hague, is concerned with collecting information on drug trafficking and, since the end of 1994, with counteracting trade in human beings, car theft, trading in nuclear material, and money laundering. Europol also concerns itself with the prevention of crime at a European level.

Eurydice, in Greek mythology, nymph who married the musician Orpheus but died on her wedding day. Orpheus descended to the underworld in search of her. Hades and Persephone, rulers of the underworld, agreed to release Eurydice to follow Orpheus if he promised not to look back at her. But he was unable to resist, and Eurydice was taken back to the underworld forever.

Eustachian tubes, narrow tubes running from the middle ear to the back of the throat. They are vital in regulating pressure within the ears.
See also: Ear.

Euthanasia, practice of hastening or causing the death of a person suffering from an incurable disease. Its moral and legal implications are highly controversial in most cultures, and it is illegal in the majority of countries.

Eutrophication, increasing concentration of plant nutrients and fertilizers in lakes and estuaries, partly by natural drainage and partly by pollution. It leads to excessive growth of algae and aquatic plants, with oxygen depletion of the deep water.

Euwe, Machgielis (Max) (1901-1981), Dutch mathematician and chess master. Euwe was the Dutch champion from 1921 until 1958, with the exception of short interludes. He became the world champion by winning from Alyechin (15.5-14.5) in 1935, but lost the title to Alyechin in 1937 (9.5-15.5). Euwe remained internationally active until 1962. He was the managing director of the the foundation known as Study Center for Administrative Computerization from 1958 until 1965, and an associate professor from 1964 until 1971. Euwe was the director of the World Chess Association (FIDE) from 1970 until 1978. He has a number of different publications on chess to his name.

Evangelicalism, Protestant theological movement that emphasizes personal conversion and biblical authority. Among the denominations using the name are the Evangelical Lutherans; the Evangelical and Reformed Church, which joined the Congregational Christian Churches in 1961 to form the United Church of Christ; the Evangelical Covenant Church of America; and the Evangelical United Brethren. The name was also applied to the movement led by John Wesley in the 18th century that eventually separated from the Church of England to become the Methodist Church.
See also: Protestantism.

Evangeline (1847), long narrative poem by U.S. poet Henry Wadsworth Longfellow. The poem tells of the ill-fated love affair of 2 French citizens expelled by the British from their home in Acadia (now eastern Canada) during the French and Indian Wars. The form of the poem is modeled on such classical epics as Homer's *Odyssey*.

Evans, Mary Ann *See:* Eliot, George.

Evans, Sir Arthur John (1851-1941), English archeologist famous for his discovery of the Minoan civilization from excavations at Knossos in Crete. He was curator of the Ashmolean Museum, Oxford (1884-1908) and professor of prehistoric archeology at Oxford from 1909.
See also: Archeology.

Evans, Walker (1903-1975), U.S. photographer best known for documenting the effects of the Depression in the southern United

States. His photographs were an important part of *Let Us Now Praise Famous Men* (1941), written by James Agee. His work also appeared in *Fortune* magazine, of which he was an editor.
See also: Photography.

Evaporation, escape of molecules from the surface of a liquid such that they attain a gaseous state. Only those molecules with sufficient kinetic energy (i.e., heat) are able to overcome the cohesive forces holding the liquid together and escape from the surface. This leaves the remaining molecules with a lower average kinetic energy and hence a lower temperature. In an unenclosed space, the entire body of the liquid can eventually evaporate, which means that the matter will have changed from a liquid to a gas.

Eve *See:* Adam and Eve.

Evelyn, John (1620-1706), English writer and humanist whose *Diary* (1818) is one of the most important historical sources for English life in the 17th century.

Evening primrose, any of various wildflowers of family Onagraceae, native to North America. These annual, biennial, or perennial plants are 1-6 ft (30-180 cm) high, with hairy leaves and saucer-shaped white, yellow, or pink flowers. The name refers especially to *Oenothera biennis*, a biennial 3-5 ft (90-150 cm) tall, with yellow flowers 1-2 in. (3-5 cm) in diameter that open in the evening.

Evening star, general term for a bright planet (most often Venus) that appears in the western sky at sunset or in the early evening. Planets do not give off their own light, but the light they reflect from the sun makes them appear bright, and they were thought at one time to be wandering stars.
See also: Planet.

Everglades, swampy region of southern Florida covering an area of about 5,000 sq mi (12,950 sq km), extending from Lake Okeechobee in the north to the southern tip of the Florida peninsula. In 1947 the Everglades National Park was established.

Evergreen, plant that retains its leaves the year round; the leaves are continually shed and replaced. The term is usually applied to coniferous, or cone-bearing, trees.

Evert, Chris(tine) (1954-), U.S. tennis player. Known for her strong two-handed backhand, she set a record by winning 4 consecutive U.S. Opens (1975-1978); she won again in 1980 and 1982. Evert also captured 3 Wimbledon titles (1974, 1976, 1981) and 2 Australian Opens (1982, 1984).

Evidence, in law, that which is advanced by parties to a legal dispute to prove, or contribute to the proof of, their case. To be admissible in court evidence must conform to various rules designed to ensure its clear and fair presentation to the judge and jury. Evidence may consist of the oral testimony of witnesses summoned by either side or of

documents or physical objects. Evidence may be direct, supporting the facts of the case, or circumstantial: information from which facts may reasonably be deduced. An eyewitness account of an auto accident is direct evidence; unaccountable damage to the defendant's auto may be circumstantial evidence. In a criminal case, the burden of proof rests with the prosecution, whose evidence must demonstrate the guilt of the defendant. In a civil suit, both sides must present evidence to support their claims.
See also: Crime laboratory.

Evolution, process by which organisms have changed and species have arisen and disappeared since the origin of life. The formulation of the theory of evolution in its modern form is credited to Charles Darwin and Alfred Russel Wallace, 19th-century British scientists who proposed that the central mechanism of evolution was natural selection. In essence, this theory states that life forms with certain characteristics tend to reproduce in larger numbers and survive environmental changes better than other, similar life forms that lack these characteristics. These forms then tend to become dominant within the population, and the characteristics are inherited by subsequent generations. Integral to the theory is the notion that all species of life on earth are interrelated, ultimately having common ancestry.

Today, the evidence for evolution is overwhelming and comes from many branches of science, including biology, anatomy, embryology, paleontology, biochemistry, genetics, and other fields. The discovery of the phenomenon of genetic mutation and the increased understanding of the structure of genes has helped to answer many of the questions about the mechanisms of the changes that life forms undergo. The field of ecology has given new insight into how different species of plants and animals interrelate with and affect one another. Although the theory of evolution has undergone various important changes since the 19th century, it still rests basically on the foundations laid down by Darwin and Wallace and has been one of the most successful and influential theories in the history of science.
See also: Darwin, Charles Robert.

Ewe *See:* Sheep.

Examinations *See:* Testing.

Excalibur, in Arthurian legend, the name of King Arthur's sword. In Thomas Malory's 15th-century version, Arthur came into possession of the sword as a boy, when he alone was able to remove it from the stone in which it was lodged. In another version of the legend, the sword was given to Arthur by the Lady of the Lake.
See also: Arthur, King.

Darwin's finches, which were observed by Darwin on the Galapagos Islands in 1835, illustrate adaptive radiation from a common ancestor. The different beak shapes reflect their divergent food preferences. The warblerlike *Certhidea olivacea* (A) feeds on small insects in bushes. Most species of the tree finch, *Camarhynchus* (B), eat insects. Most ground finches, *Geospiza* (C and D), have heavy beaks that are specialized in crushing seeds. Those that feed largely on cactus have longer and more pointed beaks.

E

E

Excess-profits tax, tax levied on profits above a legislated level, generally enacted during wars to raise state revenue at a time when some businesses make 'windfall profits.' U.S. and British corporations were subject to such taxes during and after World War I (1917-1921), and during World War II (1940-1945). U.S. excess- profits taxes were imposed during the Korean War (1950-1953). Some countries maintain an excess-profits tax in peacetime. The U.S. 'windfall profits' tax on oil companies in 1980 was technically an excise tax, imposed on a specific product rather than on profits.
See also: Taxation.

Exchange rate, the price at which one country's currency can be exchanged for that of another. The exchange rate is determined by the supply of the currency for which an exchange is sought and the demand for the currency being changed. Economic conditions and governmental fiscal policies further affect exchange rates.
If there is a greater demand for the products of one country, say Japan, in relation to demand for United States goods, the Japanese yen would rise in price in relation to the dollar.
Banks and brokerage firms buy and sell foreign currency and offer exchange to their customers; some charge a fee for converting currency. Exchange rates are published in many newspapers.

Excommunication, expulsion of a person from a religious group. This practice exists in most Christian churches, most notably Catholicism. In the Roman Catholic Church an excommunicate may not attend mass or receive the sacraments and is denied a Christian burial. Excommunication was important in the Middle Ages as a punishment meted out by ecclesiastical courts. It was sometimes used to force temporal rulers to submit to papal authority.

Excretion, or elimination, removal of waste material from the body, including the undigested residue of food and the waste products of metabolism. The main organs responsible for elimination in humans are the kidneys and large intestine, which process liquid and solid wastes respective. Wastes such as water and salt are also eliminated through the skin in the form of sweat, and through the lungs, which expel water vapor and carbon dioxide.

Executive, the part of government that implements laws; also, the head of that part. The term is also used generally for that part of a private organization or company that manages and controls its business.
See also: President of the United States.

Executor, person appointed to administer the estate of a deceased person. The testator (one who makes a will) has the right to make his or her own choice of executors. If a person fails to name executors, the court may appoint administrators. Executors' duties involve the paying of debts and distribution of the property in the estate according to the terms of the will. The executors' position is

therefore one of trust, and they may be sued if they fail in their duties.
See also: Will.

Exeter (pop. 101,000), port city on the Exe River and capital of Devonshire, England. The center of transportation and trade for southwestern England, it is an area of much historic interest, containing ancient Roman ruins as well as the Norman Cathedral, built in the 12th century. Parts of the city were restored after severe damage during World War II.
See also: England.

Exile, expulsion or voluntary prolonged absence from one's homeland. In ancient Palestine, Greece, and Rome, exile was commonly used as a form of criminal punishment. During the 18th century, Great Britain exiled prisoners to provide labor in Australian and North American colonies. In the 20th century, the Soviet Union has exiled citizens to work camps in Siberia. The only form of exile now permitted in the United States is the deportation of noncitizens to their country of origin.

Eximbank *See:* Export-Import Bank of the United States.

Existentialism, 20th-century philosophical current that stresses personal responsibility and the relation of the individual to the universe or to God. In general, existentialists emphasize the fear and despair that isolated individuals feel. An important precursor of existentialism was Søren Kierkegaard, who held that one's sense of dread and despair arose from one's responsibility for one's own decisions and for one's relationship with God. Theologians influenced by Kierkegaard include Karl Barth, Martin Buber, Karl Jaspers, Reinhold Niebuhr, and Paul Tillich. Edmund Husserl and Martin Heidegger are often considered existentialists, but the only major philosopher to accept that designation was Jean-Paul Sartre, who argued that there was no God and that human nature was infinitely variable: humans were free to make their own destiny and therefore responsible for their own lives.

Exobiology, or xenobiology, study of possible life forms elsewhere than on earth. Drawing on many other sciences (e.g., biochemistry and physics), exobiology deals in hypotheses, since no extraterrestrial life has yet been found.

Exocrine gland *See:* Gland.

Exodus, second book of the Old Testament and of the Torah (Pentateuch). It describes the liberation of the Israelites from slavery in Egypt and the covenant made at Mt. Sinai between God and Moses. The Ten Commandments are given in Exodus.
See also: Bible; Old Testament.

Exorcism, ritual expulsion or casting out of malignant spirits and demons by incantations, prayer, and ceremonies.

Expansion, in physics, increase in the volume of a substance due to a rise in tempera-

ture. Virtually all substances expand when heated, whether in a gaseous, liquid, or solid state. Conversely, they contract when cooled. Water, an exception, expands on cooling below 4°C (39°F), which is why ice floats on water. Expansion occurs because molecules move further apart as they vibrate more violently under the influence of heat. The increase in the length of a solid when it is heated by 1°C is called the *coefficient of expansion*. A bimetallic strip made of 2 metals with different coefficients of expansion is used in the thermostat. The expansion of mercury or alcohol is used to measure temperature in thermometers. Engineers must allow space for expansion when they build bridges, highways, buildings, railways, and any other structure subject to temperature changes.
See also: Physics.

Exploration, discovery and surveying of unknown parts of the world and the universe. Among the purposes of exploration are settlement, commerce, conquest, and increase of scientific knowledge. The earliest records of exploration in the Western world go back to about 3000 B.C. Many early explorations were undertaken in search of trade routes, as in the case of the Phoenician and Greek seamen who explored the Black Sea and the Mediterranean, and even ventured into the Atlantic.

Explosive, substance that decomposes suddenly, but controllably, forming gas and releasing heat in the process. The resultant shock wave has many applications, including mining, demolition, missile propulsion, and warfare (bombs). Most explosives contain nitrogen, hydrogen, carbon, and oxygen in an unstable molecular configuration which, as the result of a spark, blow, or other small explosion, react extremely rapidly to produce carbon dioxide, steam, and nitrogen, with some carbon monoxide and hydrogen. Explosives may be solid, liquid, or gas. They are generally classified as low explosives, primary explosives (also called initiators or primers), and high explosives.

Export-Import Bank of the United States (Eximbank), U.S. government agency set up in 1934 to assist foreign exports. It makes loans to foreign borrowers who wish to buy U.S. goods and services. Eximbank helped develop trade with Latin America and the Allied countries after World War II. It is now active in supporting U.S. exports to developing countries.

Exports and imports, goods shipped out of or into a country. A country exports products it can produce cheaply or plentifully; it imports products it cannot produce or can produce only at high cost. Imports may compete with domestically produced goods, and a country may protect its own producers by levying import tariffs (taxes) on specific foreign products, or by limiting imports. Governments encourage exports by providing subsidies making it profitable for producers to export, or by granting tax exemptions to export industries. Governments may also control exports and imports by manipulating currency exchange rates. The ratio of

the value of a country's imports and exports is called the balance of trade.
See also: Trade.

Ex post facto, in law, retroactive legislation, most commonly to make illegal actions that were legal when committed. The expression comes from the Latin phrase meaning 'after the fact.' The U.S. Constitution prohibits *ex post facto* criminal laws. In English law they are permitted but rare.

Expressionism, early 20th-century movement in art and literature that held that art should be the expression of subjective feelings and emotions. Expressionist painters preferred intense coloring and primitive simplified forms, in that these seemed to convey emotions directly. Vincent Van Gogh and Edvard Munch influenced the movement, which developed in both France and Germany after 1905. In France the style was represented by the fauvists Henri Matisse and Georges Rouault, and in Germany by Die Brücke and the Blaue Reiter artists like Wassily Kandinsky, Ludwig Kirchner, and Franz Marc. Expressionist writers include August Strindberg, Frank Wedekind, and Franz Kafka.

Extension program, usually a non-degree educational program offered by a college or university, generally off campus. Extension students may take courses to advance their careers or for personal enjoyment or development. Some extension courses are now offered for college credit and can be counted toward degree requirements. Early extension programs were developed by Cambridge University in England (1873) and the University of Chicago (1892). Programs are now common in the U.S.

Extinct species, in biology, species of which no living individuals remain. Extinction is most often the result of changes in food supply, habitat, or climate. Massive environmental changes may result in the mass extinction of many species at once. Rapid changes in environment caused by humans since industrialization have resulted in the extinction of many species of plants and animals.

Extract, concentrated essence of plant or animal material, used as food flavoring, in drugs, and in cosmetics. Food extracts may be produced by a combination of crushing and cooking to extract oil and other flavorings. Some extracts, like vanilla, are prepared in a solution of alcohol; others may use glycerol or propylene glycol. Morphine is an extract of the opium poppy. Common cosmetic extracts include musk and balsam.

Extraction, selective removal of a substance or substances from a mixture by use of carefully selected solvents. The solvent is chosen so that the desired material dissolves more readily than the rest of the mixture. When the mixture is composed of solids, the process is known as leaching. Salt can be removed from a mixture of sand and salt by leaching with water, and metals can be separated from their ores by leaching with other solvents. Extraction can also be used to separate liquid and gaseous mixtures. The technique is widely used in the petroleum and chemical industries and in metallurgy. It is also used to obtain oil from oil seeds and sugar from sugar beet.

Extradition, surrendering of a person wanted for trial of a criminal offense by 1 state or country to another. International extradition only operates where a treaty has been signed by both countries involved. A country may refuse the extradition if the offender is to be tried for a political offense. Extradition is allowed only if an offense is punishable in both countries.

Extrasensory perception (ESP), communication or perception without use of sight, hearing, taste, touch, or smell. ESP includes telepathy (perception of the thoughts of others), clairvoyance (knowledge of distant objects), and precognition (foreknowledge of events). Although research into ESP continues through the field of parapsychology, most scientists feel that no convincing evidence of it has ever been offered.

Extraterrestrial intelligence, intelligent life originating outside the earth and its atmosphere. While none has been discovered, scientists engaged in the search for extraterrestrial intelligence (SETI) have been scanning the sky for radio frequencies that cannot be accounted for by natural phenomena and might indicate the existence of such life.
See also: Exobiology.

Extraterritoriality, privilege granted by a country to resident foreign nationals, allowing them to remain under the jurisdiction of the laws of their own country only. It is generally extended only to diplomatic agents.
See also: Diplomacy.

Extrovert, term used by Swiss psychiatrist Carl G. Jung to describe a person who prefers being surrounded by other people and much activity, as opposed to an introvert, who is happier with solitude and contemplation. While most people combine tendencies of both, Jung believed that one tendency or the other is generally predominant.
See also: Jung, Carl Gustav.

Extrusion, process for shaping materials-especially metals, but also such nonmetals as rubber, plastic, and glass-by forcing them through a small orifice or die. Hydraulic or mechanical rams are employed to apply pressure to a billet (square chunk) of the material to be shaped. Some metals, such as copper and steel, must be kept hot during extrusion, aluminum may be extruded cold. In extruding plastics, the raw material, in the form of tiny pellets, is heated and forced through dies by a long feed screw. In the extrusion of nylon, rayon, and other synthetic fibers, filaments of the material are extruded by centrifugal force from tiny dies called *spinnerets*. They may then be spun and woven into cloth in the same way as natural fibers.

Exxon Corporation, one of the world's largest petroleum company, founded 1882, by the Rockefeller family, as the Standard Oil Company of New Jersey. The company is involved in exploration, production, refining, and distribution of oil and natural gas. It owns wells, refineries, petrochemical plants, pipelines, and tanker fleets, and operates in nearly 100 countries. The company was responsible for the largest oil spill in U.S. history, when the tanker *Exxon Valdez* ran aground in the Bay of Alaska (1989).

Eyck, Aldo Ernest van (1918-1999), Dutch architect, known for his revolutionary ideas concerning the development of old city centers. Became internationally famous due to his design for the Burgerweeshuis (civilian orphanage) in Amsterdam (1959). Van Eyck was awarded the Wolf Prize for Architecture in 1996. He shared this annual Israeli prize with the German architect Frei Otto.

Eyck, Jan Van *See:* Van Eyck, Jan.

Eye, organ of vision possessed by all vertebrate and most invertebrate animals. Eyes vary widely in complexity. Many invertebrates have simple cup-shaped eyes containing light-sensitive cells that merely perceive the intensity of light. Insects and crustaceans have compound eyes comprising many hundreds of units that build up a picture composed of minute light and dark spots like a newspaper photograph. Vertebrates and a few invertebrates (such as the squid) have eyes with lenses that focus images onto a light-sensitive surface.

The human eye is roughly spherical and is moved in its socket by 6 muscles. The wall of the eyeball has 3 main layers. The outermost layer is the tough and fibrous *sclera*, which merges at the front into the *cornea*, a hard transparent layer. Beneath the sclera is the *choroid*, which contains a dark pigment to prevent scattering of light within the eye. Toward the front, the choroid forms the *ciliary body*, whose muscles control the lens. The ciliary body merges with the *iris*, the colored part of the eye, whose muscles respond to varying light intensity by widening and closing the *pupil*, the opening in the iris through which lights enters. The innermost layer of the eye is the *retina*, which contains light-sensitive nerve endings that send signals to the brain through the *optic nerve*. Since the nerve itself is not sensitive to light, there is a blind spot where it leaves the eye. The blood vessels supplying the retina enter the eye through the center of the optic nerve and spread out over the retina.

Light entering the eye first passes through a thin transparent layer of skin, the *conjunctiva*, which is lubricated by the tears, secreted by a gland above the eye. The *lens* lies behind the pupil and focuses an image on the retina. Spread over the surface of the retina are some 130 million minute light-sensitive nerve endings. About 7 million of these, shorter than the others, are called *cones*. The other nerve endings, called *rods*, are spaced out much more evenly. The cones are responsible for color vision, but function well only in fairly bright light. The rods operate at much lower levels of lighting, but their image is only in shades of gray. The optic nerve carries the signals via the *optic chiasma*, a major nerve junction, to the visual part

E

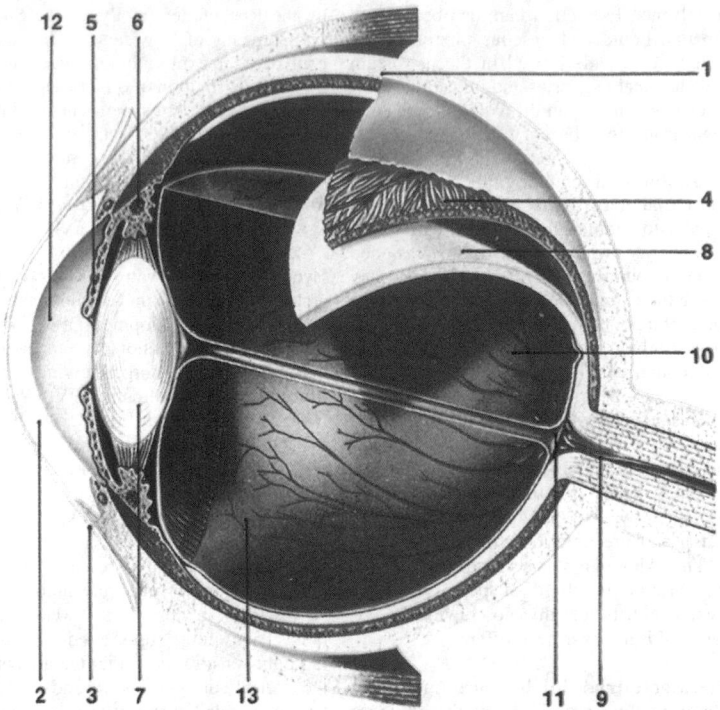

The eye is composed of three membrane layers. The outer white layer, or sclera (1), helps the eye keep its spherical shape. The transparent part of the sclera, or cornea (2), is protected by the conjunctiva (3). The middle layer, the choroid (4), supplies the eye with blood. The iris (5), which is colored, and the ciliary body (6), which holds the lens (7) in position, are part of this layer. The inner layer, or retina (8), receives the light and sends messages to the brain by way of the optic nerve (9). The fovea (10), or focal point, and the blindspot (11) are located on the inner surface. The aqueous humor (12), a fluid, and the vitreous humor (13), a jelly, fill the cavities of the eye.

Accomodation involves the unconscious adjustment of the eye, in order to be able to see far away and near objects, by changing the curvature of the lens. In order to focus onto a far away object (A), the ciliary body, to which the lens is attached, relaxes and flattens the lens. The eye focuses on a closer object (B) by contracting the ciliary body, through which the highly elastic lens becomes more curved. In both cases, the upside-down images of the objects are sharply focused against the retina, and are later reversed by the brain into the correct visual pictures.

of the brain, the *occipital lobe*, where the information from the two eyes is combined to give a stereoscopic image.

Eye bank, place where corneas removed from newly dead persons are stored until needed for transplantation to restore the sight of those with corneal defects.

Eyeglasses *See:* Glasses.

Ezekiel, Book of, book of the Old Testament of the Bible, named after the early 6th-century B.C. Hebrew priest and prophet. The book prophesizes disastrous consequences for the people of Jerusalem because of their sinful lives. Ezekiel, Jeremiah, and Isaiah are considered the major interpreters of the Babylonian Exile, the era following the Babylonian conquest of Palestine (587-586 B.C.).
See also: Bible; Old Testament.

Ezra, Book of, book of the Old Testament of the Bible, named for the 5th-century B.C. Babylonian Jewish priest and religious leader. Ezra advocated an exclusive and legalistic doctrine prohibiting marriages between Jews and gentiles. In Jewish editions of the Bible, the books of Ezra and Nehemiah are combined in Writings.
See also: Bible; Old Testament.

E=mc2, formula that relates mass (matter) and energy. Albert Einstein announced the formula in 1905, and it laid the basis for the application of nuclear energy. *E* stands for energy, *m* stands for mass, and *c* is a constant factor equal to the velocity of light. The formula states that large quantities of energy can result from tiny amounts of mass, if that mass is completely transformed into energy. In the 1930s scientists found a way to split the atoms of certain heavy elements into atoms of lighter elements. Reasoning that the lost mass turned into energy, they were able to use E=mc^2 to calculate the amount of mass changed into energy.

F, sixth letter in the English alphabet. It occupies the same place in the Latin alphabet and in the early Greek alphabet, although it is omitted in the classical Greek alphabet. F is derived from the Phoenician *vav* or *waw*, which was the symbol for a hook or peg. In Latin, the *v* sound was represented by *u* and thus *f* acquired its present sound. In musical terminology, it represents *fa* in the scale of C. It is also the sign for Fahrenheit in measurement of temperature.

Faber, Eberhard (1822-1879), founder of the first large-scale pencil factory in the United States. The family business began when Eberhard's great-grandfather, Kasper Faber, began making pencils in Bavaria, now Germany, in 1761. Eberhard's brother, Lothar von Faber, established branches of the business in Europe and the United States. In 1861, partly to avoid an import tariff, Eberhard Faber established a pencil factory in New York City. He later expanded the business to include other stationery products. The international business remains under family control.

Fabergé, Peter Carl (1846-1920), Russian goldsmith famous for the jewelry he made for the Russian tsars and other royalty, especially the jeweled and enameled Easter eggs. He went into exile in Switzerland in 1917.

Fabian Society, English society for the propagation of socialism. Established 1883-1884, it took its name from the Roman general Fabius Cunctator, who delayed fighting Hannibal in order to avoid defeat. Fabians rejected violent revolution, seeking to change society gradually. They helped form the Labour Representation Committee, which became the Labour Party in 1906. Leading Fabians were Sidney and Beatrice Webb and George Bernard Shaw.
See also: Labour Party; Socialism.

Fable, short story that usually teaches a moral. The characters are generally animals with human characteristics; they illustrate human follies humorously. The earliest collection is the *Fables of Aesop* 4th century B.C. As a literary form the fable flourished in France, particularly in the 17th century with Jean de la Fontaine.
See also: Aesop; Allegory; Folklore; La Fontaine, Jean de.

Fabre, Jean Henri Casimir (1823-1915), French entomologist who used direct observations of insects in their natural environments in his pioneering researches into insect instinct and behavior.
See also: Entomology.

Fabro, Luciano (1936-), Italian visual artist. He made images of pieces of clothing that had been dipped in plaster, works that are regarded as 'arte povera'. He worked on the series 'Italy' from 1968-1975, in which he created work based on the geographic shape of Italy in various materials, including glass, metal, and animal skin. The series 'Feet' dates from the same period, huge feet made from glass, bronze, and marble, stuck in long frills of material. The method of presentation was always an important aspect of Fabro's work; for example, he used rolls of paper and silk to cover the walls and floors of the spaces that housed the objects. The 'valley of the egg', which stands for the relationship of culture versus nature, is a motif that is repeatedly used in his sculpture.

Face fly (*Musca autumnalis*), insect that feeds on the body fluids of livestock. It is speculated that the first face flies, discovered in Nova Scotia in 1952, came from Europe. The face fly can transmit diseases to horses, donkeys, and cattle. Resembling the common house fly, the face fly is different in that the larvae (maggots) develop faster than house fly maggots and are yellowish instead of white.

Facsimile, precise reproduction of an original document; in modern usage, a reproduction transmitted over telephone lines. The image is scanned at the transmitter ('fax' machine), reconstructed at the receiving station, and duplicated on paper.

Factor, in mathematics, whole number (in-

teger) that may be divided into another number a whole number of times without remainder. Thus the factors of 12 are 1, 2, 3, 4, and 6.

Faeroe Islands, group of 18 Danish islands (540 sq mi/1,399 km) in the North Atlantic, northwest of the Shetland Islands and southeast of Iceland. The largest of these volcanic islands are Strömö and Österö. The main economic activities are fishing and sheep raising. The islands have been under Danish control since the 14th century but were granted a large degree of self-government in 1948.

Fahd ibn Abdul Aziz (1922-), king of Saudi Arabia (1982-). Fahd, a son of Ibn Saud, was interior minister from 1962 to 1975, when his half-brother, King Khalid, named him crown prince. He succeeded upon the death of Khalid, whose cautious policies he generally followed. He was deeply involved in discussions and decisions which led to the presence of allied forces on Saudi Arabian soil during operation Desert Shield, which would later become operation Desert Storm. He supported the peace process between Israel and the Arabic countries. When Israel and the PLO signed a treaty in 1993, Fahd provided the PLO with political and financial support. In 1995 he suffered from a stroke but did not abdicate. Crown prince Abdullah replaced him temporarily to cover the affairs in hand.
See also: Persian Gulf War; Saudi Arabia.

Fahrenheit, Gabriel Daniel (1686-1736), German-born Dutch physicist and instrument maker. He introduced the mercury-in-glass thermometer and discovered the varia-

tion of boiling points with atmospheric pressure, but is best remembered for his Fahrenheit temperature scale. This has 179 divisions (degrees) between the freezing point of water (32°F) and the boiling point (212°F). Although still commonly used in the United States, elsewhere the Fahrenheit scale has been superseded by the Celsius scale.

Fairbanks, Douglas, Jr. (1909-2002), U.S. movie actor and the son of the silent film star Douglas Fairbanks. Fairbanks, Jr., made his film debut in 1923. His best-known movies include *The Prisoner of Zenda* (1937), *Gunga Din* (1939), and *Sinbad the Sailor* (1947). The autobiographical book *The Salad Days* (1988) covers his early years.

Fairbanks, Douglas, Sr. (1883-1939), U.S. film actor famous for his romantic and swashbuckling roles in films such as *Robin Hood* (1922) and *The Black Pirate* (1926). In 1919 he founded United Artists Studio with his wife Mary Pickford, Charlie Chaplin, and D.W. Griffith.

Fairchild, Sherman Mills (1896-1971), U.S. inventor of aerial mapping photography. Already the inventor of several cameras, he developed his Fairchild Flight Analyzer Camera in 1953. The first camera capable of taking distortion-free aerial pictures in a continuous sequence of action, it has been used to track guided missiles and to study takeoffs and landings of missiles and planes.
See also: Photography.

Fair housing laws *See:* Open housing.

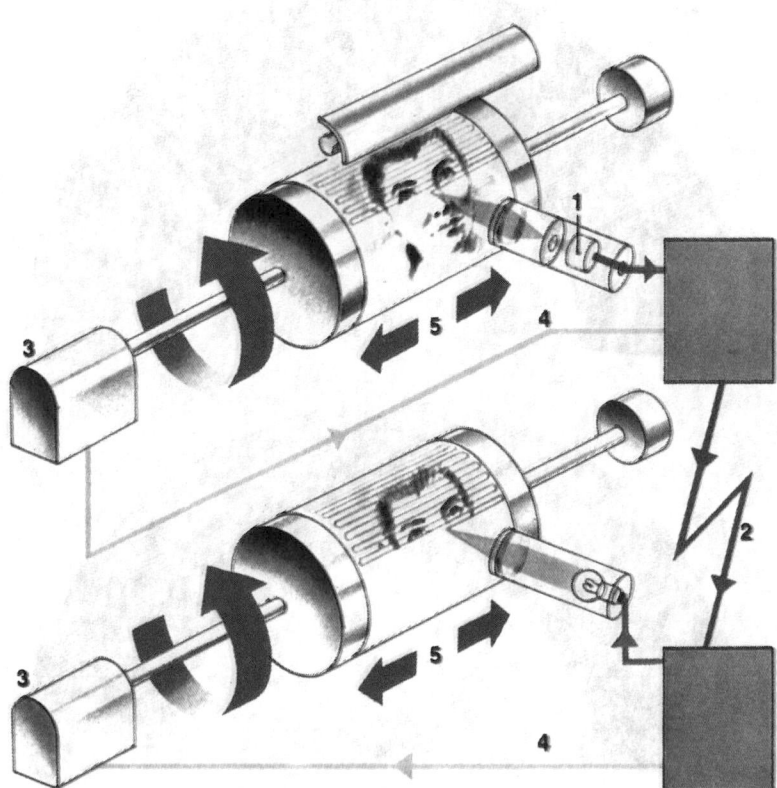

In the transmission of facsimiles an illuminated picture is wrapped around a rotating drum (5) and scanned by a traversing lens-photocell (1). The output current is transmitted along a telephone line (2) to a focused, variable light beam that reproduces the image on photographic paper wrapped on a rotating drum. Drive motors (3) and scanning traverses (4) are synchronized electronically.

F

F

Fairy tale, tale involving fantastic events and characters, not necessarily fairies. Many originate in myth and folklore, but an equal number have been written for adults, among them those by Charles Perrault, the brothers Grimm, Johann Wolfgang von Goethe, and Hans Christian Andersen. Modern writers J.R.R. Tolkien and C.S. Lewis incorporated fairy-tale elements in their works.
See also: Folklore.

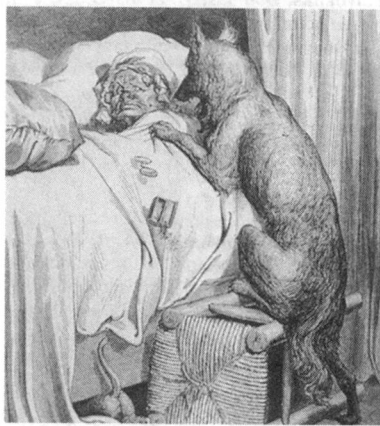

An illustration by the French artist Gustave Doré (1832-1883) for the fairy tale *Little Red Ridinghood* by Charles Perrault (1628-1703).

Faisal, or **Feisal**, name of 2 kings of Iraq. **Faisal I** (1885-1933) took part in the Arab revolt against the Ottoman Turks in 1915 and was king 1921-1933. **Faisal II** (1935-1958) reigned 1939-1958. His uncle, Abdul Ilah, ruled Iraq as regent till 1953. In 1958 they were both murdered in a revolution.
See also: Iraq.

Faisal, or **Feisal** (Faisal ibn Abdul Aziz al Faisal al Saud; 1905-1975), king of Saudi

Arabia from 1964, when his brother, King Saud, was forced to abdicate. A pious, moderate, and able ruler, Faisal instituted a far-ranging program of social reform. Friendly to the West, he nevertheless joined the campaign against Israel and supported the Arab oil cartel. He was assassinated by a nephew in Mar. 1975.
See also: Saudi Arabia.

Faisalabad (pop. 1.9 mln.; formerly Lyallpur), Pakistan, a city in Punjab province, in the northeastern part of the country. It is in a major wheat-and cotton-producing area and is known for its production of textiles and processed foods. The University of Agriculture, founded in 1909, is here. The city was settled in the 1890's. It was originally named for Charles James Lyall, lieutenant-governor of Punjab.

Faith *See:* Religion.

Falange Española, recognized as the only legal political party in Spain under dictator Francisco Franco. Founded by José Antonio Primo de Rivera in 1933, the fascist Falange joined the Nationalist forces of Franco during the Spanish Civil War (1936-1939). Franco assumed control of the party in 1937, and in 1945 the Falange became known as the National Movement. It was outlawed by the democratic government of Spain in 1977, after Franco's death, but is still active.

Falcon, name generally applied to about 60 species of hawk, though the true falcons of the family Falconidae number about 35 species. They are birds of prey, feeding mainly on other birds, which they kill in the air. They inhabit most parts of the world,

making their nests on rocky ledges or tree forks. Falcons in the United States include the prairie falcon and the sparrow hawk.

Falkland Islands, or Islas Malvinas, self-governing British colony, also claimed by Argentina, consisting of 200 islands totaling 4,700 sq mi (12,200 sq km) in the South Atlantic about 480 mi (770 km) northeast of Cape Horn. The capital is Stanley. In 1982 Argentina seized them, but British forces retook them. The inhabitants are mostly of British descent. The economy is largely dependent on sheep raising.

Falla, Manuel de (1876-1946), Spanish composer. He studied in Madrid and Paris, and his work was heavily influenced by Maurice Ravel and by native Andalusian folk music. His works include the ballets *El Amor Brujo* (1915) and *The Three-Cornered Hat* (1917), the opera *La Vida Breve* (1905), and *Nights in the Gardens of Spain* (1916), for piano and orchestra.

Fallaci, Oriana (1930-), Italian reporter and writer. Grew up in a militant, anti fascist environment. Employed as a war reporter in Vietnam, the Middle East, and South America, during which time her main interest was in reporting on social wrongs. Famous for her aggressive style of interviewing. She published her various interviews with important politicians in *Intervista con la storia* (Interview With History; 1974). She was awarded the Premio Viareggio for her novel *Un uomo* (A Man; 1979). Other works include: *Penelope alla guerra* (Penelope at War; 1962), *Lettera a un bambino mai nato* (Letter to a Child Never Born; 1975), *Insciallah* (Inshallah; 1990), about the civil war in Lebanon, and *La rabbia e l'orgoglio* (Fury and Pride; 2002).

Falling bodies, Law of, group of rules that tell what an object does when it falls freely to the ground. The force of gravity acts on all bodies in the same way, regardless of their shape, size, or density. Distance, velocity, and acceleration are the 3 factors to be considered when studying the laws of falling bodies. The velocity of a falling body is determined by how much the air resists it, which may in turn be determined by its shape. Acceleration is the rate at which a body's speed increases as it falls. The 16th-century scientist Galilei was instrumental in proving the laws of falling bodies.
See also: Galileo Galilei; Physics.

Fallout, radioactive debris produced by the explosion of nuclear weapons. Local fallout rains down over an area up to about 50 mi (80 km) downwind of the explosion for several hours afterwards. The radiation produced by the fallout causes severe radiation sickness and possibly death to any people living within this area. More fallout rises into the lower atmosphere (the *troposphere*) and is washed down with rain over a wider area over the next few months. Still more rises even higher, into the *stratosphere*, where it may be blown around the globe for months or years before it descends to the ground. Some isotopes in fallout keep pro-

This eighteenth-century French brisé fan (Felix Tal Fan Cabinet, Amsterdam) has a finely carved ivory frame. The side that should be turned towards the audience, is covered with mother-of-pearl panels, painted with gallant scenes in Rococo style. The reverse side portrays a romantic image of pastoral life.

ducing radiation for a long time and become absorbed by plants, animals, and human beings.
See also: Nuclear weapon; Radiation.

Fallout shelter, building or underground structure whose purpose is to protect people from the effects of fallout, or radiation. Buildings with thick layers of brick, concrete, or stone may serve as fallout shelters, and well-protected underground areas might also serve. Home fallout shelters, which need to be supplied with basic provisions, are usually underground buildings with thick walls.
See also: Civil defense; Fallout.

Falun Gong (also: Falun Dafa) Religious sect founded in 1992 by Li Hongzhi. According to the sect itself, it has 70 million followers inside and 30 million outside China. Falun Gong unites Buddhist and Taoist principles and connects these to physical exercises and meditation.
From the end of the 1990s onward, the Chinese authorities took strong action against this movement, which they regarded as a threat to the state. After a mass demonstration against intimidation and harassment by the authorities that took place in Peking in 1999, the sect was forbidden in China. Since then, Falun Gong has become a resistance movement.

Famine, acute food shortage resulting in widespread starvation. It is usually caused by natural disasters such as drought, floods, or plant diseases causing crop failure. Famines have often dramatically influenced the course of history. In the Irish famine (1846-1847), caused by potato blight, millions died and around 1.5 million emigrated, mostly to the U.S. Recently there have been crippling famines in Bangladesh and Africa.

Fan, instrument that excites a current of air by the agitation of a broad surface, vanes, or disks. In computer terminology the term *fan-in* is used to denote an electrical load presented to an output by an input. A *fan-out* is an electrical load that an output is capable of driving, usually expressed as the number of inputs that can be driven from a given output signal.

Fangio, Juan Manuel (1911-1995) Argentinean racing driver, one of few who managed to win more than one world title in Formula One. He won 24 of the 51 Grand Prix races in which he participated. He claimed his first world title in 1951 in an Alfa Romeo, followed by world titles in 1954, 1955, 1956, and 1957. He won the latter 4 titles for Maserati, Mercedes-Benz, Ferrari and, once again, Maserati. Although Fangio was a more than excellent driver, he was convinced that driving skills contributed a mere 25% to the degree of success; the rest could be accounted to the car and luck. He ended his career during the French Grand Prix on the Reims circuit on 6th July 1958, when he came in 4th place in a Maserati.

Fanon, Frantz Omar (1925-1961), French black psychoanalyst and social philosopher. He condemned racism in his book *Black Skin, White Masks* (1952). In *The Wretched of the Earth* (1961) he advocated extreme violence against whites as a cathartic expression for black people.
See also: Psychoanalysis.

Fantin-Latour, Ignace Henri Jean Théodore (1836-1904), French painter known for his flower paintings, his illustrations of the works of Robert Wagner and Louis-Hector Berlioz, and his group portraits of artists, such as *Homage to Delacroix* (1864) and *A Studio at Batignolles* (1870).

Fan Wen-Cheng (Fan Wencheng; 1597-1666), descendent of a prominent Chinese family of civil servants who was captured by the Manchu during the latter days of the Ming dynasty (1368-1636); as of that moment, he became the most important advisor to the Manchu rulers, who wanted to establish a machinery of government according to Chinese tradition. When the Ming capital, Peking, was taken over by rebels in 1644, he urged his bosses to invade China. In compliance with his recommendations, the Manchu restrained from murder and plundering and they gave the last Ming emperor a fitting funeral. The fall of Peking marks the beginning of the Ching dynasty (1636-1911). After providing the Manchu emperors with advice for several more years (concerning, among other things, taxes and examinations), he withdrew from the public eye in 1654.

FAO *See:* Food and Agriculture Organization.

Farad (F), unit of electrical capacitance. A 1-volt-per-sec change in voltage across a 1-farad capacitor will require 1 ampere of current flow. The farad is named for English physicist Michael Faraday.
See also: Electric current.

Faraday, Michael (1791-1867), English chemist and physicist, pupil and successor of H. Davy at the Royal Institution. He discovered benzene (1825), first demonstrated electromagnetic induction and invented the dynamo (1831), and, with his concept of magnetic lines of force, laid the foundations of classical field theory later built upon by J. Clerk Maxwell. He discovered the laws of electrolysis that bear his name and demonstrated a connection between light and magnetism. The *Faraday effect* is the rotation of the plane of polarization produced when plane-polarized light is passed through a substance in a magnetic field, the light traveling in a direction parallel to the lines of force. For a given substance, the rotation is proportional to the thickness traversed by the light and to the magnetic field strength. Faradays' laws state that in the process of electrolysis changes, equal quantities of electricity charge or discharge equivalent quantities of ions at each electrode.
See also: Electrolysis; Electromagnetism.

Farce, comedy based on exaggeration and broad visual humor. Its traditional ingredients are improbable situations and characters developed to their limits. Farcical elements are present in the plays of Aristophanes, Plautus, Shakespeare, Molière, and many others; such 19th-century writers as Georges Feydeau and W.S. Gilbert helped establish farce as a respected theatrical form.

Far East, term often used for eastern Asia, comprising China, Japan, Korea, Taiwan, and eastern Siberia in the Russian Federation. Sometimes the term extends to include the nations of Southeast Asia: Brunei, Myanmar (Burma), Indonesia, Cambodia (Kampuchea), Laos, Malaysia, the Philippines, Singapore, Thailand, and Vietnam. The term Far East was originated by the Europeans to describe an area of Asia far to the east of them.

Fargo, William George (1818-1881), cofounder of Wells and Company (later Wells-Fargo), the pioneer express service, in 1844.

Michael Faraday (1791-1867) was not only a physicist, but also a chemist. Harriet Moore made a drawing of him, sitting among the beakers and bottles in his laboratory.

F

F

In 1850 it merged with other companies to become the American Express Company, of which he was president until his death.

Farina, Giuseppe (Nino) (1906-1966), Italian racing driver, studied engineering. Farina became the Italian champion in 1937, 1938, 1939, and the first official world champion in 1950 (with Alfa Romeo).

Farm and farming, setting and activity of the cultivation of crops and the raising of livestock. Since the 1800s scientific advances have made farms increasingly productive. Farms can be either specialized or mixed. Scientific techniques have been developed to help crop farmers nourish their soil, irrigate dry areas, control pests (such as insects), and plant and cultivate their crops. Livestock farmers must feed, shelter, and provide grazing land and health care for their animals, as well as breed and finish (or fatten) them. Farm management includes everything a farmer does to make farming profitable.

Farmer *See:* Farm and farming.

Farming *See:* Agriculture; Farm and farming.

Faroe Islands *See:* Faeroe Islands.

Farouk I *See:* Faruk I.

Farquhar, George (1678-1707), English dramatist. His most successful plays, *The Recruiting Officer* (1706) and *The Beaux' Strategem* (1707), are characterized by vigorous language and pungent satire, and more realism than was then fashionable.

Farrell, James Thomas (1904-1979), U.S. writer. He is known for his social novels, particularly the *Studs Lonigan* trilogy (1932-1935), which depicts the often harsh life of the Irish on Chicago's South Side.

Farsightedness, or hyperopia, defect of vision in which light entering the eye from nearby objects comes to a focus behind the retina instead of on it. Near objects are blurred; far objects are seen clearly. The condition may be corrected by wearing eyeglasses with convex lenses.

Faruk I, or **Farouk I** (1920-1965), king of Egypt (1936-1952). He was considered weak and incompetent, and his rule was marked by corruption, alienation of the military, and many internal rivalries. This led to a military coup by Gamal Abdal Nasser, which forced Faruk's abdication.
See also: Egypt.

Fascism, originally, political system of Italy under Benito Mussolini 1922-1945; more broadly, authoritarian and antidemocratic political philosophy placing the state above the individual, and stressing absolute obedience to a glorified leader. Adolf Hitler's Nazi Party is generally considered fascist. Under facism, industry is privately owned but under government control. Nationalism, racism, and militarism are logical products of facism.
See also: Mussolini, Benito; Neofascism.

Fashion, prevailing style of dress, particularly new designs representing changes from previous seasons. Fashion in both dress and interior design is believed to have originated in 14th-century Europe and was set by monarchs and other prominent persons, with descriptions conveyed by travelers, in letters, and by exchange of the fashion doll. The first fashion magazine is thought to have originated in late 16th-century Germany. Paris has been the leading arbiter of fashion since the Renaissance. By the mid-19th century, designer-dressmakers became prominent in the fashion world for the first time. Other important fashion centers have been London, New York, and Rome.

Fassbinder, Rainer Werner (1946-1982), West German film director, established an anti-theater group in Munich in 1969. In addition to theater productions and television productions, he made films at a great pace that, in their intensely melodramatic form, were influenced by the work of Douglas Sirk and often provided a critical outlook on postwar Germany, such as *Katzelmacher* (1969), *Warnung vor einer Heiligen Nutte*

A European farm, with extensions added over time, so different architectural styles can be found. Most buildings exist of two levels. The lower level used to be a stable, and the upper level was used as living quarters for farmhands. Nowadays the upper level is mostly used for storage or as a hay-barn.

1. modern storehouse
2. modern cattle barn
3. main residence
4. outbuilding
5. stables for small stock
6. orchard
7. hay-barn with corrugated iron roof
8. calf stable and grain storage
9. milk storage
10. passage with modern milking equipment
11. pig stock
12. plow
13. cow shed
14. cattle feed storage
15. vegetable garden

(Beware of a Holy Whore; 1971), *Die Bitteren Tränen der Petra von Kant* (The Bitter Tears of Petra von Kant; 1972), *Die Ehe der Maria Braun* (The Marriage of Maria Braun; 1979), *Lili Marleen* (1981) and *Querelle* (1982). In 1980, he made the television series *Berlin Alexanderplatz*, based on the novel of the same name by Alfred Döblin (1929). Fassbinder had a stable of permanent staff workers gathered around him, including composer Peer Raben, camera people Xaver Schwarzenberger and Michael Ballhaus, and many male and female actors, such as Hanna Schygulla, Irm Hermann, Margit Carstensen, Kurt Raab, Karlheinz Böhm, Volker Spengler, Udo Kier, etcetera.

Fat, compound of carbon, hydrogen, and oxygen found in certain parts of the body, an important constituent of diet. Fat is the most concentrated source of food energy, supplying 9 calories per gram; protein and carbohydrate, the other 2 sources of food energy, supply only 4 calories per gram. Fats are the chief sources of essential fatty acids (EFAs), as well as carriers of vitamins A, D, E, and K. Three molecules of fatty acid combined with one molecule of glycerol constitute 1 molecule of fat, the chemical name of which is a triglyceride. A fatty acid is *saturated* if its chain of carbon atoms contains all the hydrogen it can hold, or if there are no double bonds between carbon atoms. Saturated fats are usually solid at room temperature; they occur in both animal and vegetable fats, but chiefly in the former. A fatty acid is *unsaturated* if its chain of carbon atoms has 1 or more double bonds where hydrogen could be added. The process of adding hydrogen to a double bond in an unsaturated fatty acid to make it more saturated is called *hydrogenation*. *Monounsaturated* fatty acids have only 1 double bond where hydrogen could be added. *Polyunsaturated* fatty acids have 2 or more double bonds where hydrogen could be added. Polyunsaturated fats are usually oils and are most abundant in plant and fish oils. Nearly all fats from plant sources are unsaturated; the only major exception is palm (or coconut) oil, which is highly saturated. The utilization of fat in humans is affected diet and state of nutrition, the endocrine system, degree of activity, age, heredity, and diseases that may interfere with the absorption and metabolism of fat. Diets high in fat can lead to above-normal amounts of lipids (triglycerides, fatty acids, cholesterol, and other fat-like substances) in the blood, associated with atherosclerosis. Changes in dietary habits to reduce the risk of coronary heart disease in later life include adjusting caloric intake to maintain an optimum weight, reducing fat intake so that fat supplies less than 35% of the total number of calories (of which less than 10% should be from saturated fats and up to 90% from polyunsaturated fats, with the remainder supplied by monounsaturated fats) and limiting the daily intake of cholesterol to fewer than 10.6 oz (300 mg).

Fates, in Greek and Roman mythology, goddesses of destiny, called *Moirai* by the Greeks and *Parcae* by the Romans. Three Fates rule human lives: Clotho, who spins the web of life; Lachesis, who measures its length; and Atropos, the inevitable, who cuts it.
See also: Mythology.

Father of Medicine *See:* Hippocrates.

Father of the Constitution *See:* Madison, James.

Fathometer, underwater device used on ships to measure the depth of water. As the speed of sound in water is known, the fathometer works by sending a sound down through the water, to be returned by echo. The fathometer dispatches sound through a submarine oscillator and receives it through a hydrophone echo receiver. First manufactured in 1927, the fathometer is the trade name for a refined sonic depth finder. The first sonic depth finder was developed in 1919 by the U.S. Navy.
See also: Sonar.

Fatimids, Muslim dynasty that ruled a North African empire from its conquest of Egypt in A.D. 969 until 1171. The first rulers claimed descent from Fatima, Muhammad's youngest daughter. In 969 al-Mu'izz established his capital at Cairo, bringing a religious and cultural renaissance to the city. At one time all of North Africa, Sicily, and Syria were under Fatimid rule, but the dynasty was overthrown in 1171 by Saladin.

Faulkner, William (1897-1962), U.S. writer, known for his vivid characterization and complex, convoluted style in novels and short stories set in fictional Yoknapatawpha County, based on the area of his hometown, Oxford, Miss. His works include the novels *The Sound and the Fury* (1929) and *Light in August* (1932) and the short story 'A Rose for Emily.' He painted a vivid picture of the decadent and dying South, seeing in it a microcosm of human destiny. He explored stream-of-consciousness techniques in his writing. He was awarded the Nobel Prize for literature in 1949 and won 2 Pulitzer prizes (1955 and 1963). He also worked as a Hollywood scriptwriter.

Fault, fracture in the earth's crust along which there has been relative movement and displacement of the rocks on each side. *Dip-slip faults* involve movement up or down an inclined fault plane. *Reverse* or *thrust faults* involves relative displacement upward of the overlying rocks and results from compressive stress. *Strike-slip faults* such as the San Andreas Fault in California, involve horizontal displacement and result from shearing stress.

Faun, in Roman mythology, woodland spirit, usually portrayed as having a human upper body and goat legs. Faunas, god of nature and fertility, was the Roman equivalent of the Greek god Pan.

Fauré, Gabriel Urbain (1845-1924), French composer. He was director of the Paris Conservatory (1905-1920), where his pupils included Maurice Ravel. His works include the *Requiem* (1887), the orchestral suite *Pelléas et Melisande* (1898), and the song cycle *La bonne chanson* (1894).

Faust, legendary German enchanter, based on a 16th-century charlatan, who sold his

F

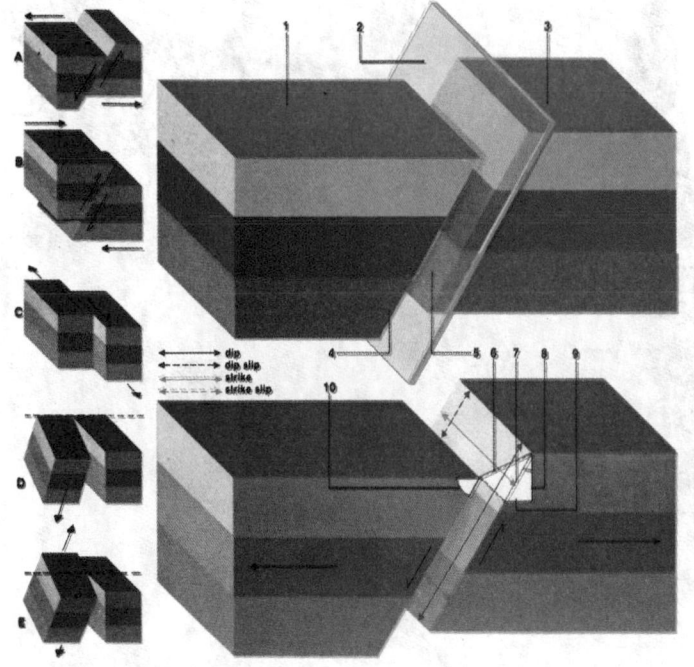

A normal fault (A) results from crustal tension forces, pulling apart blocks. A thrust fault (B) results from compressional forces, pushing one block over another. In strike-slip faults (C), crustal compression causes the blocks to move apart horizontally. Hinge faults (D), or pivotal faults (E), result when one end of a block moves downward on an axis at right angles to the fault, and another end remains level, or moves upward. The terms describing the movements of fault blocks include: a downthrown block (1), which moves down along a fault plane (2), relative to an upthrown block (3); a hanging wall (4); and a footwall (5). The net slip is the total distance that a block has moved (6); the hade is the angle between the fault plane and the vertical plane (7); the throw is the vertical displacement of the blocks (8); and the heave is their horizontal displacement (9). The angle of dip lies between the fault plane and the horizontal direction (10).

Labels in figure: dip, dip slip, strike, strike slip

F

The use of bright, pure colours is typical of the work of the Fauvists. Spatial representation was of less importance, as may be noted in this painting by Maurice de Vlaminck of 1904: *Street Scene in Marly-le-Roi* (Musée National d'Art Moderne, Paris).

soul to the devil Mephistopheles for knowledge and pleasure. Christopher Marlowe made the tale a tragedy of human presumption *Dr. Faustus* c.1590, while Johann Wolfgang von Goethe (*Faust*, 1808, 1832) made Faust a Romantic idealist whose sins are forgiven because of his continual striving after good.
See also: Goethe, Johann Wolfgang von; Marlowe, Christopher.

Fauves (French, 'wild beasts'), group of French painters whose style emphasized intense color, often applied directly from the paint tubes, and vigorous brush strokes. Although the term was originally used deri-

sively, the artists adopted it and their movement became known as fauvism. Led by Henri Matisse, fauvism flourished from 1903 to 1907, and its members included Raoul Dufy and Georges Rouault. Although the painters evolved other styles after 1907, fauvism influenced other movements, particularly German expressionism.

Fawkes, Guy (1570-1606), Roman Catholic Englishman, hired by the Gunpowder Plot conspirators as an explosives expert while he was serving in the Spanish army. Arrested while setting explosives beneath the House of Lords, he was tortured and hanged. In England he is burnt in effigy on Guy Fawkes Day, Nov. 5.

Feather, covering of a bird's body, made up of a central *shaft*, with the hollow *quill* at the tip, and the vane on each side, consisting of rows of fine threads called *barbs*, which are held together by hooked *barbules* to form a web. Feathers keep birds warm and enable them to fly.

Feather star *See:* Sea lily.

Federal Bureau of Investigation (FBI), investigative branch of the U.S. Department of Justice. Established in 1908, the FBI is responsible for the investigation of possible violations of all federal laws except those for which enforcement is specifically assigned to another agency. The bureau is also concerned with internal security, counterespionage, organized crime, and corruption. FBI history was dominated by J. Edgar Hoover, director 1924-1972, a conservative

figure who held the post until his death. Its first permanent director after Hoover was Clarence M. Kelley, who served 1973-1978 and modernized the bureau's procedures. William H. Webster, ex-federal judge and FBI director (1978-1987), restructured the bureau in the light of revelations that its agents had committed illegal acts during Hoover's tenure. His tenure was followed by appointment in 1987 of William Sessions.

Federal court *See:* Court; United States, government of the.

Federal government *See:* Federalism.

Federalism, system of government in which states form a union by granting a central government supreme power in common or national affairs, while retaining their independent existence and control over local affairs. Federations today include the United States, Canada and Australia. In the United States, the federal government is supreme in defense, foreign affairs, the postal and monetary systems, and interstate and foreign commerce. All levels of government may levy taxes and spend money, but the federal government accounts for the vast majority of public spending.

Federal system *See:* Federalism.

Federal Trade Commission (FTC), U.S. agency established (1914) to prevent unfair business practices, particularly monopolies, and to maintain a competitive economy. The FTC studies the effects of business mergers and price agreements, issuing cease and desist orders when necessary; it also attempts to prevent misleading advertising and to protect public health. Its 5 commissions are appointed by the president for 7-year terms.

Feiffer, Jules Ralph (1929-), American cartoonist and author, studied at the Art Students League in New York, among other places, and also gained experience working on a number of comics. He became known when his comic strips, which were critical of society, were first published in The Village Voice (Greenwich) and afterwards developed into one of the most prominent political cartoonists, whose work was also published abroad. His comics were published collectively in *Sick, Sick, Sick* (1958), *Passionella and Other Stories* (1959), *Boy, Girl, Boy, Girl* (1961), *Hold Me* (1962) and *The Unexpurgated Memoirs of Bernard Mergendeiler* (1965). He also wrote plays, including *Little Murders* (1966), *The White House Murder Case* (1970), *Feiffer's America* (1985) and *Carnal Knowledge* (1988), and novels, including *Harry, the Rat with Women* (1963), *Pictures at a Prosecution* (1971), *Ackroyd* (1978), *Jules Feiffer's America: From Eisenhower to Reagan* (1982), *Marriage is an Invasion of Privacy* (1984), *Feiffer's Children* (1986), *Ronald Reagan in Movie America* (1988) and *Elliott Loves* (1990), and film scripts, such as that of *Carnal Knowledge* (1971), *Popeye* (1980) and *I Want to Go Home* (1989).

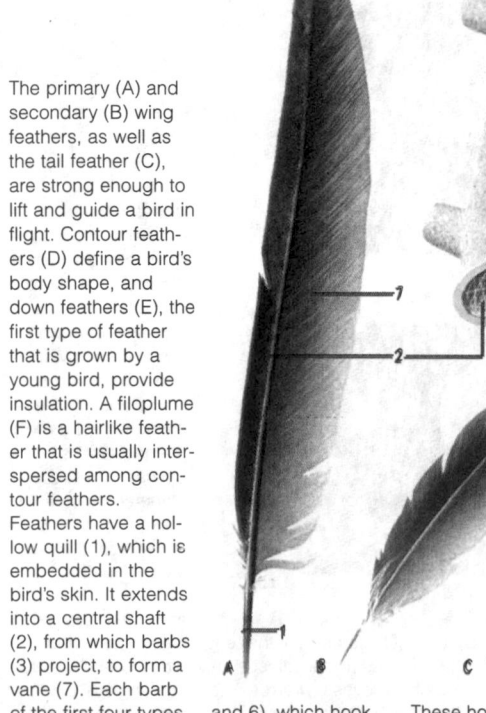

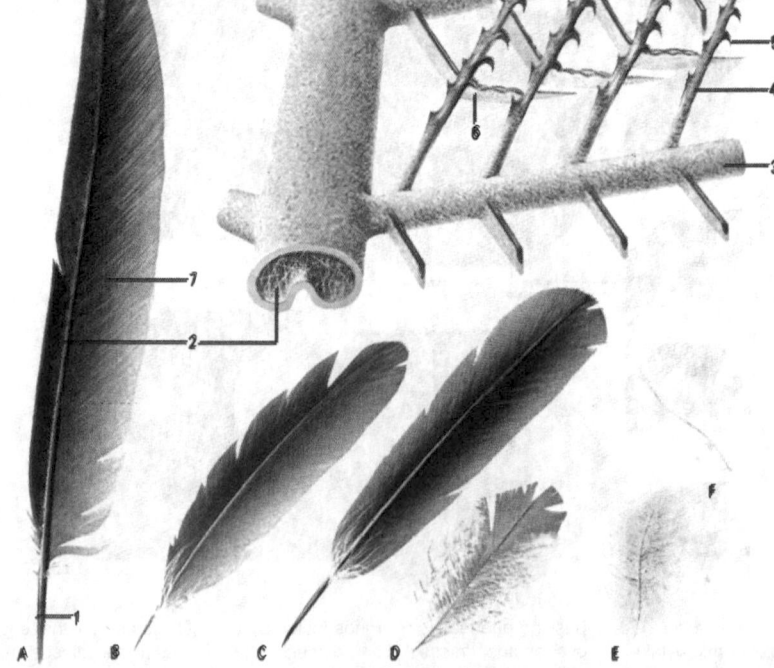

The primary (A) and secondary (B) wing feathers, as well as the tail feather (C), are strong enough to lift and guide a bird in flight. Contour feathers (D) define a bird's body shape, and down feathers (E), the first type of feather that is grown by a young bird, provide insulation. A filoplume (F) is a hairlike feather that is usually interspersed among contour feathers. Feathers have a hollow quill (1), which is embedded in the bird's skin. It extends into a central shaft (2), from which barbs (3) project, to form a vane (7). Each barb of the first four types of feathers has numerous barbules (4, 5 and 6), which hook onto the barbules of adjacent barbs.

These hooked barbules strengthen the feather for flight. The down and filiplume feathers appear fluffy, because they lack the hooked barbules. The fluffy down feathers provide warmth.

Feininger, Lyonel (1871-1956), U.S. artist. Influenced by cubism, his style is based on planes of color that create geometric designs. He lived in Germany (1887-1936), teaching at the Bauhaus (1919-1932). Also a caricaturist, he produced a comics page for the *Chicago Tribune* (1906-1907).
See also: Bauhaus; Cubism.

Feisal *See:* Faisal.

Feldspar, abundant mineral consisting of potassium-, sodium-, and calcium-aluminum silicates. Feldspars make up 60% of the earth's crust. They form a leading raw material for porcelain and ceramic glazes; some, such as moonstone, are used as gems.

Feller, Bob (Robert William Andrew Feller; 1919-), U.S. baseball star, pitcher with the Cleveland Indians (1936-1956). In 1946 he set a season record of 348 strikeouts (a record broken in 1973 by Nolan Ryan). He was elected to the Baseball Hall of Fame in 1962.

Fellini, Federico (1920-1993), Italian film director. His first major success was *La Strada* (1954), a film starring Anthony Quinn and Fellini's wife, Giulietta Masina. His early films, such as *La Dolce Vita* (1960), portray human disillusionment in a corrupt society. Later films such as *8 1/2* (1963) and *Satyricon* (1970) are often dreamlike and fantastic. In 1992 he received an Oscar for his complete works.

Fellini during the filming of *Amarcord* in his home town of Rimini (1973).

Felony, criminal offense more serious than a misdemeanor; the distinction between the two is generally the severity of the prescribed penalty. In U.S. law homicide, robbery, burglary, theft, and rape are the main felonies, punishable by imprisonment for more than one year or, under special circumstances that vary from state to state, by death.
See also: Crime.

Feminism, 19th- and 20th-century movement for women's political, economic, and social equality with men. Early feminists fought for women's rights to own property and enter the professions. U.S. women obtained the right to vote in 1920; in Great Britain women were enfranchised in 1928. Feminism had a major resurgence in the 1960s; current issues in the movement are equal pay and employment opportunities, abortion rights, and freedom from sexual harassment.
See also: Women's movement.

Fencing, sport of combat using a blunted sword (foil, epee, or saber), descended from the duel. In fencing the object is to touch, not wound, one's opponent. Fencers wear protective clothing and masks. Only the tip of the flexible foil and the stiffer epee may be used to score hits.

Fénelon, François de Salignac de la Mothe (1652-1715), French theologian, archbishop of Cambrai from 1695. His reform writings, especially those on education, were in advance of their day. For the duke of Burgundy, heir of Louis XIV, he wrote *Fables: Dialogues of the Dead* (1690) and the novel *Telemachus* (1699).
See also: Theology.

Feng Yu Lan (1895-1990), Chinese philosopher. Following an education in Chinese philosophy, Feng Yu Lan studied western philosophy at the Columbia University in New York (1919-1923). His work is an attempt to integrate both conceptual worlds. *The History of Chinese Philosophy* (1931-1934) ranks as his standard work. He was often in conflict with the Communist regime due to his ideas and views.

Fenian movement, movement for Irish independence from Great Britain in the mid- to late 1800s. Named after warriors from Irish mythology, the Fenians organized both in the United States and England. Also known as the Irish Republican Brotherhood, they directed raids in Ireland, England, and Canada. Later Irish republican movements advanced the goal of independence for Ireland and, after years of skirmishes and guerilla warfare, independence was won for southern Ireland (1921), northern Ireland remaining under British control.

Fennec (*Fennecus zerda*), small desert fox with long ears. A nocturnal hunter, it lives in the deserts of North Africa and Arabia and can go for long periods without water.

Fennel (*Foeniculum vulgare*), perennial herb of the parsley family native to southern Europe and cultivated widely for its licorice-flavored foliage and seeds.

Ferber, Edna (1887-1968), U.S. author, noted for her novels about 19th-century life, including *So Big* (1924), for which she won a 1925 Pulitzer Prize, *Show Boat* (1926), *Cimarron* (1930), and *Giant* (1952). Ferber also coauthored plays with George S. Kaufman, including *Dinner at Eight* (1932).

Fer-de-lance (*Bothrops atrox*), large, poisonous snake of the viper family, found on the eastern coast of South America and on some West Indian islands.

Lionel Feininger's (1871-1956) *Woman in Mauve* (1922, private collection, Lugano, Switzerland).

Ferdinand, name of 3 Holy Roman Emperors. **Ferdinand I** (1503-1564), emperor 1558-1564, was king of Bohemia and Hungary from 1526. The Peace of Augsburg ended religious conflict in Germany and his capable administration stabilized the unwieldy empire. **Ferdinand II** (1578-1637) reigned as emperor 1619-1637. His attempts to enforce Catholicism in Protestant Bohemia led to a revolt in 1619, which began the Thirty Years' War. **Ferdinand III** (1608-1657) succeeded his father Ferdinand II as emperor in 1637. A capable ruler, he compromised with Protestant powers in the Peace of Westphalia (1648).
See also: Holy Roman Empire.

Ferdinand, Spanish kings. **Ferdinand V** (1452-1516), also known as Ferdinand II of Aragon and Ferdinand III of Naples, married Isabella I of Castile in 1469, thus unifying Aragon and Castile. In 1492 he conquered Granada, becoming king of Spain. A supporter of the Spanish Inquisition, he expelled the Jews from Spain. **Ferdinand VI** (1713-1759) became king in 1746. A capable ruler and patron of the arts, he carried out administrative reforms and kept Spain neutral during the Seven Years' War. **Ferdinand VII** (1784-1833) acceded in 1808 but was deposed by Napoleon 2 months later and imprisoned until his restoration in 1814. A cruel and repressive absolutist, he revoked the new, liberal constitution twice; in 1823 he was backed by the French military. He was unable to prevent the complete loss of Spain's American possessions.
See also: Spain.

Ferdinand, Archduke *See:* World War I.

Ferlinghetti, Lawrence (1919-), U.S. poet who was at the center of the 'beat generation' writers of the 1950s. Ferlinghetti's

F

work reflects the movement's condemnation of commercialism and middle-class values. His poetry is written in a colloquial free-verse style, and he is most known for the satiric criticism of U.S. culture in *A Coney Island of the Mind* (1958). More recent publications include the fiction work, *Love in the Days of Rage* (1988). Ferlinghetti is also the publisher and founder of City Lights, an avant-garde publisher and bookstore in San Francisco.

Fermat, Pierre de (1601-1665), French mathematician, founder of modern number and probability theories. Fermat's Last Theorem, which was not proven until 1993, states that there is no whole number solution of $x^n+y^n=z^n$, where x, y, and z are nonzero integers and n is an integer greater than 2. Fermat's Principle states that light (or other waves) will follow the path with the shortest travel time between 2 points.
See also: Mathematics.

Pierre de Fermat (1601-1665).

Fermentation, chemical reaction that involves degradation of a carbohydrate (organic) material without the presence of oxygen. Agents of fermentation include bacteria, molds, and yeasts. Products of fermentation include alcohols, acids such as lactic acid, and gases such as carbon dioxide. Fermentation has been used in making bread, alcoholic beverages, and cheese for thousands of years.

Fermi, Enrico (1901-1954), Italian atomic physicist who won the 1938 Nobel Prize for physics for his experiments with radioactivity. He showed that neutron bombardment of most elements produced their radioisotopes. Fermi emigrated to the United States to escape the fascists, becoming professor at Columbia University (1939) and at University of Chicago (1942), where he built the world's first nuclear reactor (1942).
See also: Atom.

Fermium, chemical element, symbol Fm; for physical constants see Periodic Table. Fermium was discovered by Albert Ghiorso and co-workers in 1952 from the debris of a thermonuclear bomb exploded in the Pacific. It is a metallic element and a member of the actinide series. It has been pro-

duced by intense irradiation of plutonium and other lower elements with neutrons as well as by bombarding uranium-238 with oxygen-16 ions in a cyclotron. All of its 16 known isotopes are radioactive. The chemical identification of fermium-250 as a decay product is confirmation of nobelium-254.

Fern, green, nonflowering plant of the class Filicineae having creeping or erect rhizomes (rootstocks) or an erect aerial stem and large conspicuous leaves. Ferns may have appeared on earth more than 350 million years ago. The fern as it is commonly recognized is in its asexual *sporophyte* stage. Spores are produced on the underside of the leaf and germinate to form the sexual *gametophyte* stage of the life cycle. Ferns are widely distributed throughout the world and range in height from 1 in (2.5 cm) to 65 ft (20 m).

Fernandel (Fernand Joseph Désiré Contandin; 1903-1971), French film actor who performed on stage at the early age of five and who performed in music halls and variety show theaters until around 1930. He began a film career in the 30s and became one of the most popular French actors, especially thanks to the six films in which he played the Italian priest Don Camillo, in among others *The Little World of Don Camillo* (1951). Other films include *Forbidden Fruit* (1952), *The Sheep Has Five Legs* (1955), *Pantaloons* (1956) and *Around the World in Eighty Days* (1956).

Ferrari, Enzo (1898-1988), Italian racing driver and racing car designer, initially raced for Alfa Romeo, later a technical staff member. Head of the Scuderia (= racing stable) Ferrari since 1929, his own company that was involved in racing for Alfa Romeo. The cooperation with Alfa came to an end in 1939, after which he began building cars according to his own designs. The first sports car under his name was completed in 1940 and Ferrari's first Grand Prix car was launched in 1946. With drivers such as Juan

Enrico Fermi (1901-1954), 'father of the nuclear reactor', holding a scale model of uranium. The radioactive substances causing nuclear ex-

plosions, were expected to explode spontaneously when they had attained the size that is shown here.

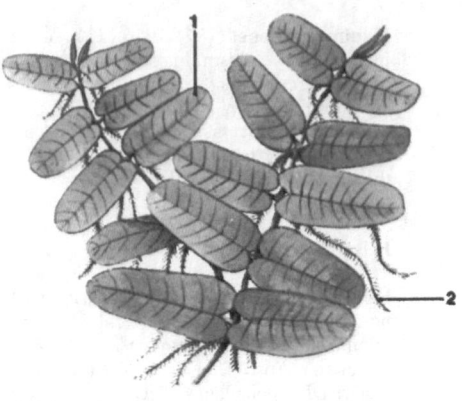

Salvina natans is a small, floating fern of Europe.
Water ferns of the genus *Salvinia* bear three leaves at each

node, or stem joint: two floating, or air leaves (1), and one finely divided water leaf (2), which may function as a root.

Fangio, John Surtees, Niki Lauda, Jody Scheckter, and Michael Schumacher (1996), it has been virtually impossible to beat Ferrari since the beginning of the 50s. Fiat currently owns a majority of the shares.

Ferrari, Luc (1929-), French composer, studied in Paris with Alfred Cortot, Arthur Honegger, and Olivier Messiaen. One of the founders of the 'Groupe de Recherches Musicales' in 1958. Active in the world of radio, theater, and film since 1964. In addition to many electronic compositions, he also wrote works in which the audience played an active role: best described as musical happenings. His electronic works include *Hétérozygote* (1964), *Music Promenade* (1969), *Unheimlich schön* (1971). Instrumental or vocal works are a variety of visages, societies, and tautologisms.

Ferraro, Geraldine Anne (1935-), U.S. politician. She served 3 terms (1979-1984) as Democratic congressional representative of New York's 9th district in Queens. In 1984 she became the first woman nominated for the vice presidency by a major U.S. political party (as Walter Mondale's running mate).

Ferret, small mammal of the weasel family. One species, the domesticated polecat of Europe and Asia (*Mustela putorious*), is kept to catch rabbits, mice, and rats. The black-footed ferret (*M. nigripes*) is an endangered species native to North America.

Ferrier, Kathleen Mary (1912-1953), British female singer (alt). Ferrier was initially a piano instructor, but focussed on a singing career after 1937, when she won a prize at the Carlisle Festival. She studied with Roy Henderson, among others, in London. She became world famous thanks to the beautiful timbre of her voice, her deeply felt interpretations, and her performances during the Second World War for the troops and factory workers. Her opera roles were limited to Lucrecia in Brittens *The Rape of Lucrecia* (1946) and Orfeo in Glucks opera of the same name (1947). Famous performances of this great singer of songs include: the oratorio arias by Händel, Mahler's *Kindertotenlieder* and *Das Lied von der Erde*, and British folk songs.

Ferrous sulfate (FeSO$_4$), iron salt of sulfuric acid consisting of light-green crystals that turn dark when exposed to air. In industry, ferrous sulfate is used to purify water, make ink, dye fabric, and preserve wood.

Ferry, Jules François Camille (1832-1893), French statesman. As minister of education (1879-1880, 1882) he organized the modern French educational system. He sought to exclude the clergy from education. As premier (1880-1881, 1883-1885), he directed the acquisition of many colonies.

Fertile Crescent, historic area in the Middle East, birthplace of the Sumerian, Phoenician, and Hebrew civilizations. It extends in an arc, or crescent, from the north coast of the Persian Gulf to the east coast of the Mediterranean Sea, with the Nile river to the west and the Tigris and Euphrates rivers to the east. Natural irrigation made this semi-arid land fertile.

Fertilization, in biology, union of 2 unlike gametes (sex cells: female egg and male sperm) in the sexual reproductive process, involving fusion of the 2 nuclei that combines hereditary traits of both parents to produce new individuals. The sperm may swim to the egg through fluid in the female or through an external medium, as in certain lower plants and animals, or pollination may facilitate contact, as in some higher plants. In humans and many other animals, fertilization takes place inside the female's body (internal fertilizaton) following copulation.

Fertilizer, material added to soil to provide essential plant nutrients. Fertilizers increase crop yields and, when used properly, add to the efficiency of farming and gardening. They include both organic materials, such as farmyard manure, compost, and activated sewage sludge, and inorganic chemical salts, known as artificial fertilizers, which contain phosphorus, nitrogen, and potassium as needed in a particular crop. Fertilizers may be used to change the mineral, vitamin, and protein contents of the produce. There is evidence that prolonged and overintensive use of fertilizers may damage the fertility of the soil by disrupting the communities of microorganisms in the soil, and that fertilizers that enter rivers and lakes contribute to the process of *eutrophication* (deficiency of dissolved oxygen and overabundance of dissolved nutrients, e.g., phosphates) that has polluted many bodies of water.

Fès *See:* Fez.

Fescue, tufted perennial grass (genus *Festuca*) common in meadows of temperate zones, used for pasture and hay crops.

Festival of Lights *See:* Hanukkah.

Fetish, inanimate object, such as a stone or a tree, worshipped for its magical powers. A fetish is often thought to be inhabited by a

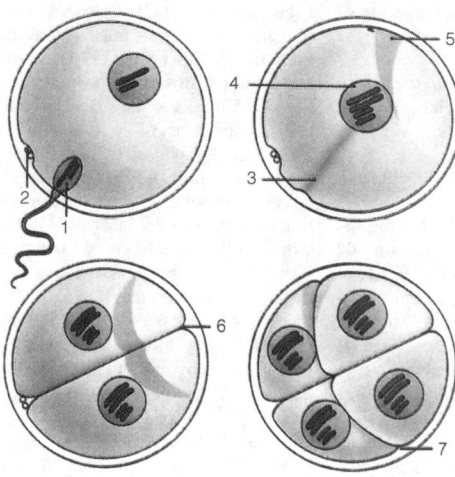

spirit. In psychiatry, a sexual fetish is not in itself erotic but it may be stimulating to certain people-a foot or a shoe, for example.

Fetus, unborn or unhatched vertebrate whose basis structural plan is in place; in humans, the period from 3 months' gestation to birth. The fetus lives in a sac of amniotic fluid that protects it and allows it to move about. Blood circulation takes place via the *placenta* and the *umbilical cord*-the sources of oxygen and nutrients and the means for waste excretion. During fetal life, organ development is consolidated so that function may be sufficiently mature at birth.
See also: Reproduction.

Feudalism, system of social, economic, and political relationships that shaped society in medieval Europe. It originated in the 9th century and flourished from the 10th to the 13th centuries. The system rested on the obedience and service of a vassal to his lord in return for protection, maintenance, and, most particularly, a tenancy of land (a *fief*). The duty owed by a vassal included military service, counsel and attendance at court, and contribution towards the lord's extraordinary expenditures, such as ransoms or dowries. At the apex of the social pyramid was the king, vassal only to God. His vassals were his great nobles, holding land or some other source of income in fief from him. They in turn invested, or *enfeoffed*, their own vassals, the lords of the manor (*seigneurs* or *suzerains*). At the base of the pyramid were the serfs, or villeins, permanently tied to the land. They worked both for the lord and for themselves, unpaid. Serfdom offered a degree of security in that, if a serf could not leave the land, neither could it be taken from him. In effect feudalism tended to allow vassal lords unrestricted freedom, at least in their own holdings. With the tendency towards centralized government this liberty was curbed. The system assumed a subsis-

tence economy; the growth of trade and of economically powerful towns attacked. By the 15th century the system was dying out, although many feudal institutions persisted into the 19th century.
See also: Middle Ages.

Feuerbach, Ludwig Andreas (1804-1872), German philosopher. A student of G.W.F. Hegel's, he eventually rejected idealism for a naturalistic materialism (which greatly influenced Karl Marx's development of dialectical materialism). Feuerbach attacked orthodox religion, analyzing the Christian concept of God as an illusory outward projection of human inward nature.

Fever, rise of body temperature above normal (98.6°/37°C), but varying from 97° to 99°F (36° to 37.2°C). Fever arises due to infection or to allergic or toxic reaction, and moderate fever is actually helpful in that it speeds up the body's chemical processes and

Fertilisation of a frog's egg takes place after the female frog has deposited it into the water. One of the sperms (1) shed by the male, will penetrate the egg and induce a second meiotic division and extrusion of a second polar body (2). Travelling along the copulation path (3), the sperm nucleus will fuse with the female nucleus, and a zygote is formed (4). The act of penetration will cause an influx of pigment and water, opposite the point of entry, which results in the formation of a grey crescent (5). This crescent will help determine the position of the first line of cleavage (6), which divides the zygote into two cells. Before this division is completed, the second has already begun, at right angles to the first (7). This division will continue until a ball of cells is formed.

An African statue, to which magical properties are attributed. This fetish prevents the birth of twins, which is considered a great sin among the Bayaka tribe in Central Africa (Ethnological Museum, Berlin).

F

mobilizes its immunological defenses against infectious organisms.

Feverfew (*Chrysanthemum parthenium*), small hardy plant with daisylike flowers, once thought to cure fever.

Feydeau, Georges (1862-1921), French playwright, very productive in the genre of the vaudeville (variety show). Following his death in 1921, he was ignored and dismissed as a clever producer of farces for a quarter of a century. He has since been generally recognized as the author of technically superior comedies. Feydeau's many comedies can be divided into two categories: the largescale spectacles, similar to a revue, such as *Occupe-toi d'Amélie* (Keep An Eye On Amélie; 1908) and *La dame de chez Maxim* (The Lady from Maxim's; 1899) and the smaller chamber comedies, based on one virtuoso idea.
Both categories are included in the genre of the vaudeville, a light-hearted comedy, often with a satiric undertone. Other works by Feydeau that are still performed today include *La puce à l'oreille* (A Flea in Her Ear; 1907).

Feynman, Richard Phillips (1918-1988), U.S. physicist. He shared the 1965 Nobel Prize for physics for work on quantum electrodynamics. He worked on the development of the atomic bomb, developed a system of notation (the Feynman diagram) for recording and calculating subatomic reactions, and, with Murray Gell-Mann, explained the interactions of weak nuclear force.
See also: Quantum electrodynamics.

Fez, traditional Turkish headgear first made in Fez, Morocco. A tall, red, brimless cap with a colored tassel, the fez was once colored only by a dye made from the juice of red berries found in Morocco.

Fiber, thin thread that may be spun into yarn. Natural fibers may be of vegetable, animal, or mineral origin. Artificial fibers combine compounds to make synthetics, such as nylon and rayon. Fibers are used for textiles.

Fiberglass, flexible fibers made of glass. Molten glass is forced through a platinumplate 'sieve,' producing durable, chemical- and temperature-resistant fibers that can be wound onto a spindle before being used to make glass wool, yarns, textiles, insulation, and automobile and boat bodies.
See also: Glass.

Fiber optics, branch of physics based on the transmission of light pulses along hair-thin glass fibers. Fiber optics is used in telecommunications; information is coded as a series of light pulses and thus can be transmitted over distances of up to 100 mi (160 km). There are 2 types of optical fibers: single-mode and multi-mode. Single-mode fibers are used for long-distance transmissions and require the use of a laser as a light source, while multi-mode fibers can use more types of light sources but cannot be used over long distances. Fiber optics is also used in instruments like the gastroscope, allowing physicians to view internal body parts without performing surgery, and aiding in surgery.
See also: Optics; Physics.

Fibonacci, Leonardo (Leonardo Pisano; 1189?-1250), Italian mathematician whose *Liber Abaci* (1202) was the first European account of Indian and Arabian mathematics. He created the Fibonacci sequence, used in higher mathematics, in which each term is the sum of the 2 preceding terms (0, 1, 2, 3, 5, 8, 13, 21, ...).
See also: Mathematics.

Fibrin, insoluble fibrous protein that enables the blood to clot. *Fibrinogen*, a protein synthesized in the liver, dissolves in the blood and circulates in the body. If the body is wounded, the fibrinogen is converted by the action of the enzyme thrombin into fibrin, which builds up a spongy, fibrous network joining the edges of the wound by trapping red blood cells that form a clot to prevent further bleeding.
See also: Protein.

Fichte, Johann Gottlieb (1762-1814), German philosopher and metaphysician. At first a disciple of Kant, he became an early exponent of ethical idealism and set forth a science connecting practical reason with pure reason and the individual ego with an absolute ego (moral will of the universe). His work, including *The Vocation of Man* (1800), influenced G.W.F. Hegel, Arthur Schopenhauer, and Freidrich Schelling, among others. His political theories, including his concept of the nation as a manifestation of divine order and as expressed in his *Address to the German People* (1808), stimulated German nationalism and won him great respect among the revolutionaries of 1848.
See also: Metaphysics; Philosophy.

Fiction, division of literature consisting of

narrative prose works with invented characters and incidents.
See also: Novel; Short story.

Fiddler crab, small tropical crab (genus *Uca*) that burrows in mud. The males have one oversized colored claw, which they wave to warn off other males and to attract females.

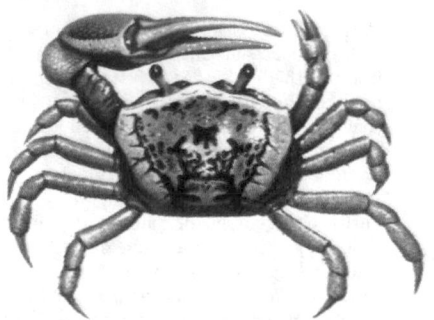

A male fiddler crab (*Uca*) waves its enlarged 'fiddle claw' as part of its courtship display; the movements vary from species to species.

Fiedler, Leslie A(aron) (1917-), U.S. social historian and literary critic, noted for *An End to Innocence: Essays on Culture and Politics* (1955), *The Jew in the American Novel* (1959), *Being Busted* (1969), and *Collected Essays* (1971). He has also written stories, novels, and poetry.

Field glasses *See:* Binoculars.

Field hockey, team game played with a stick and a leather ball. Two teams of 11 players each play on a field measuring 90-100 yds (82-91 m) long by 50-60 yds (46-55 m) wide. Players advance the ball by hitting it with a stick toward their goalpost at the end of the field. Only the goalkeeper may kick the ball.
See also: Hockey.

Fielding, Henry (1707-1754), English novelist and dramatist. His satirical comedies and farces, especially *Tom Thumb* (1730), a burlesque on the popular playwrights of the day, angered the government of Robert Walpole, provoking the enactment of a law to censor the stage. Fielding abandoned writing for the stage and turned to novels. *Joseph Andrews* (1742) and his masterpiece, *Tom Jones* (1749), are boisterous, picaresque works with strong, moral content.

Field-ion microscope *See:* Ion microscope.

Field Museum of Natural History, Chicago museum housing one of the largest and best-known natural history collections in the world. Founded by the merchant and philanthropist Marshall Field I in 1893, the museum currently has more than 13 million objects in the fields of anthropology, botany, geology, and zoology.

Fields, W.C. (William Claude Dukenfield; 1880-1946), U.S. comedian and actor who often played a cantankerous, drunken, witty misogynist and child-hater. His movies in-

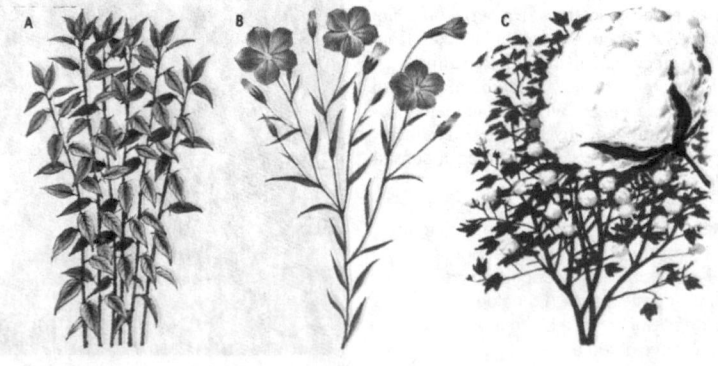

The most important fibre plants in the world today are (A) jute (*Corchurus sp.*), used for ropes and sacking; (B) flax (*Linum usitatissimum*), for textiles; and (C) cotton (*Gossypium sp.*), for textiles and thread.

clude *It's a Gift* (1934), *My Little Chickadee* (1940), and the classic farce, *The Bank Dick* (1940), which he wrote.

FIFA, Fédération Internationale de Football Association, the worldwide organization for soccer (also known as association football), established in Paris in 1904.

Fifth Column, term describing agents working within a country for the overthrow of the government, through their activities of spying, sabotage, and distributing propaganda.

Fig, any of over 600 species of shrubs, trees, and vines (genus *Ficus*) of the mulberry family, particularly the common fig (*F. carica*) native to the Mediterranean. The edible fruits, which, when dried, can be used medicinally as laxatives and poultices, are in fact a mass of female flowers enclosed in a fleshy receptacle. The rubber tree (*F. elastica*) and the weeping fig (*F. benjamina*) are popular house plants.

Fightingfish, small, brilliantly colored, long-finned freshwater fish (genus *Betta*) of southeastern Asia. The Siamese fightingfish, in confinement with another male, will battle to the death. Bets are often placed on the outcome.

Figure skating *See:* Ice skating.

Figwort family, or *Scrophulariaceae*, group of about 3,000 species of plants growing mainly in temperate regions. Members of the family have bell-shaped flowers and thin stems, and the leaves often grow in pairs. The wild mullein and the cultivated snapdragon are figworts. Some figworts are used in medicine, including a species of foxglove from which the heart medication digitalis is produced.

Fiji

Capital:	Suva
Area:	7,095 sq mi (18,376 sq km)
Population:	856,000
Language:	Fiji, English
Government:	Republic
Independent:	1970
Head of gov.:	Prime minister
Per capita:	US$ 5,200
Monetary unit:	1 Fiji dollar = 100 cents

Fiji, or Viti, independent republic in the southwest Pacific Ocean, comprising about 320 islands (about 105 inhabited) and about 7,095 sq mi (18,376 sq km). Viti Levu (capital city Suva) and Vanua Levu are the 2 largest islands, volcanic in origin. Discovered by Dutch navigator Abel Tasman (1643), the islands were visited by Capt. James Cook (1774) and settled by Europeans in 1804. Britain annexed Fiji in 1874, and over the course of time, brought many indentured servants from India; they eventually came to outnumber the native population (Melanesian and Polynesian in origin). Fiji became independent in 1970 and became a republic in 1987. Chief crops include sugarcane, ginger, and copra; exports include fish and gold; tourism is another major source of income. In 1997 Fiji was again admitted to the Commonwealth. In May 2000, businessman George Speight staged a coup in order to bring the native Fijians back to power. At the elections of 2001, the democracy was restored. A year later, Speight was sentenced to death. The government of Qarase refused to admit ethnic Indians to the government.

Filaria, parasitic roundworm (class Nematoda) that can live in the bodies of human beings or animals. The larvae (young worms) are born alive, and can be seen in the blood near the skin of their host (animal or human in which they live). When an insect bites the host, it takes the filaria with it, then releases the filaria into whatever host it bites next. In this way, the filaria continues to infect new hosts. Commonly found in tropical and subtropical countries, the filaria can cause inflammation and disease in the animal and human tissues in which it settles.

Filbert, any of various trees and shrubs of (genus *Corylus*) belonging to the birch family. The plant may grow 60 ft (18 m) tall. Native to the north temperate zone, filberts thrive in the U.S. Pacific Northwest and in southern Europe. Filberts (particularly *C. avellana*) are cultivated for their edible nuts (called filberts, hazelnuts, or cobnuts).

Filibuster, practice of prolonging debate to prevent the adoption of a measure or procedure, especially in the U.S. Senate. Opponents of a measure can organize a continuous succession of long speeches; however, two-thirds of the senators present can vote to end the filibuster.

Filipinos *See:* Philippines.

Fillmore, Millard (1800-1874), American politician, a member of Congress (1833-1835; 1837-1843) for the Whigs. Became vice president under Zachary Taylor in 1849 and the 13th president (1850-1853) after Taylor's death. The Fugitive Slave Act (which gave states the authority to transport runaway slaves back to their owners) cost him a great deal of his popularity. In 1856, Fillmore was an unsuccessful presidential candidate for the Know Nothing Party, which took action against the increasing influence of immigrants in the North.

Film *See:* Motion pictures; Photography.

Finance *See:* Banking; Budget; Economics; Money.

Finch, songbird of the family Frangillidae, typified by stout, conical bills adapted for opening seeds. Found year round and worldwide, except Australia, these highly developed birds are classified as triangular-billed (sparrow, canary, bullfinch, goldfinch); cross-mandibled (crossbill); or round-billed (cardinal).

Fine arts, art, such as painting, sculpture, architecture, music, literature, and theater, created with an esthetic goal rather than with functional application.

Fine, Rueben (1914-1993), American chess master and repeat national champion. In the 30s, Fine was rated as one of the strongest chess players in the world, which he emphasized by winning countless tournaments, including Hastings 1935, Zandvoort 1936, and Stockholm 1937. He shared first place with Keres in the famous AVRO candidate's tournament. After WW II, he lost interest and in 1948, he refused to compete against Botvinnik, Smyslov, Keres, Reshevsky, and Euwe for the world championship. He withdrew from chess after 1950, though he did publish a number of books on chess afterwards.

Fingerprint, impression of the underside tip of the finger or thumb, which has patterns of ridges unique to each person, used as a means of identification since ancient times. The first police system employing dactyloscopy (fingerprinting) was developed (1888) by Jean Vucetich in Argentina. English scientist Sir Francis Galton and others in the late 19th century developed the methods upon which current systems are based, systems extensively employed in the armed services, criminal investigations, government employment, and banking. The U.S. Federal Bureau of Investigation maintains a national fingerprint file.

Suva, the capital and chief port of Fiji, is located near the mouth of the Rewa River on the southeastern coast of Viti Levu, the largest of the nation's islands.

Finland

Capital:	Helsinki
Area:	130,559 sq mi
	(338,145 sq km)
Population:	5,184,000
Language:	Finnish, Swedish
Government:	Republic
Independent:	1917
Head of gov.:	Prime minister
Per capita:	US$ 25,800
Monetary unit:	1 Markka = 100 penni

Finland (Finnish: *Suomi*; Republic of), independent republic of northern Europe, east of the Scandinavian peninsula. This 'land of thousands of lakes' is bounded by 2 arms of the Baltic Sea in the southwest and south, Russia in the east, and Norway and Sweden in the north and northwest. About one-fourth of Finland lies inside the Arctic Circle, and about one-tenth consists of inland waters. Cessions to the former Soviet Union cost the Finns about one-tenth of their pre-World

One of the most important sources of income for Finland, is forestry. Extensive forests cover the hilly landscape.

War II area. The principal cities are the capital, Helsinki; Tampere, a major industrial city on the southwestern rim of the lake district; and Turku, a leading port on the southwest coast and Finnish capital until 1812. Finland has one important natural resource: timber. Forestry and allied industries in wood products are successful.

Land and climate. Finland has tens of thousands of lakes, linked in many cases by rivers and canals. Around the lakes are extensive areas of swamps and forests. Most of the rivers are short and swift, and rapids render navigation difficult. The longest river is the Kemi (340 mi/547 km). The coastal plain extends to about 80 mi (130 km) in width and includes most of the larger cities and the bulk of the farming land. The plateau region is heavily forested and ranges from 300 to 600 ft (90 to 180 m) above sea level. In the third region (Lapland), the uplands in the north rise to 1,500 ft (450 m) and contain the highest point in Finland, Mount Haltia (4,343 ft/1,324 m) on the Norwegian border. Wildlife includes large numbers of seabirds and waterfowl. The reindeer is disappearing from the northern forests, but bears, wolves, lemmings, and lynxes can be found. Salmon, trout, and whitefish are plentiful in the rivers, and seals and herring are caught off the coasts. The Gulf Stream helps keep the climate relatively mild in the south and central areas, with short, warm summers and long, cold winters. The north has a subarctic climate, with long, severe winters and the famous 'midnight sun' from May to the end of July.

People. The Finns are related directly to the Estonians and, more distantly, to Hungarians and Russians. Most live on farms or in small villages; only 6 cities have a population over 100,000. There is a Swedish minority of and a Lapp minority (largely nomads). The Swedes, who controlled Finland from the 13th century to the beginning of the 19th, have had a marked cultural influence on the nation. Both Finnish and Swedish are official languages. Finnish is not a Scandinavian language, but is a member of the Finno-Urgic group, which includes Hungarian and Estonian.

Economy. About 10% of the work force is in agriculture, 30% in industry, and 60% in other sectors. The government exercises considerable control over economic activities, operating the rail system and communications. It also monopolizes trade with the former USSR. Paper, pulp, and wood-working products account for over half of total exports. Other exports include dairy products, copper, and furs and hides.

History. Finland was colonized from the south and by the 9th century formed 3 tribal states, Karelia, Tavastenland, and Suomi. Sweden progessively colonized the area, and after the 14th century Finland became a Swedish grand duchy. In 1809 Sweden was forced to cede it to Russia. Tsar Alexander I maintained the country as a grand duchy but allowed it considerable autonomy under a governor-general. This period saw the rise of nationalism: The Swedish language was replaced by Finnish, particularly after the publication of the national folk-epic, the *Kalevala* (1835). Under Alexander III a policy of 'Russification' was adopted and gen-

erally bitterly resisted until World War I. In 1917 the parliament declared independence from the new regime in Russia, and Bolshevik forces were defeated in a brief civil war. In 1919 a republic was declared. In 1939, in breach of a nonaggression pact, the USSR invaded Finland, but was stalled by fierce resistance. For the German aid Finland received during World War II, it was made to pay massive postwar reparations to the USSR and lost southern Karelia. During the postwar period the Finnish government sought a peaceful rapprochement with the USSR, despite much Soviet interference in Finnish affairs. In 1995 Finland joined the European Union. Unlike Sweden and Denmark, Finland did introduce the euro as a national currency in 2002. It has been nominated as the least corrupted country in the world. Finland's economy is modern and highly industrialized.

Finlay, Carlos Juan (1833-1915), Cuban physician who first proposed (1881) that yellow fever is transmitted by the mosquito. Experiments by Walter Reed in 1900 proved his theory.
See also: Yellow fever.

Finnish, most important of the Finno-Urgic languages, spoken by around 5 million people in Finland. It has a written tradition dating from the 16th century but achieved official status only in the 19th century.

Finns *See:* Finland.

Fiord, or fjord, coastal inlet characterized by sheer parallel walls. Deep bays and inlets along the mountainous coastline of Norway, fiords were probably formed by rivers and deepened by glaciers millions of years ago. Norway's fiords are noted for their size: Sognafiord is 4,000 ft (1,220 m) deep and over 100 mi (160 km) long. The terms *sea loch* and *firth* are used for similar inlets in Britain.

Fir, common name for various evergreen members of the pine family, including 9 true firs (genus *Abies*) native to the United States. The fragrant balsam fir (*A. balsainea*) is a popular Christmas tree. The *Douglas fir* (*Pseudotsuga menziesii*), valued for its timber, is not a true fir.

Firbank, (Arthur Annesley) Ronald (1886-1926), English novelist known for his eccentric, innovative style and his verbal wit. Among his best-known works are *Vainglory* (1915), *Inclinations* (1916), and *Valmouth* (1919), which influenced Evelyn Waugh and Aldous Huxley.

Firdausi (Abul Qasim Mansur; 940?-1020?), Persian epic poet, author of the *Shah Namah* (*Book of Kings*), Persia's first great literary work. The poem, 60,000 verses long, recounts the story of Persia, legendary and historical, until the Muslim conquest (A.D. 641).
See also: Persia, Ancient.

Fire *See:* Combustion.

Fire ant, omnivorous ant (genus *Solenop-*

sis), primarily of the tropics, that inflicts an extremely painful sting. Two species, one introduced from Argentina, are found in the southern United States and are pests in fruit plantations.

Firearm, weapon from which a missile, as a bullet, is projected by firing explosive charges. Firearms, are classified as either artillery (heavy firearms) or small arms. *See also:* Gun.

Firecracker flower (*Dichelostemma idamaia*), perennial plant belonging to the amaryllis family and native to California. It is named for its bright red tubular blossoms, which grow on a slender stalk up to 3 ft (91 cm) high.

Firedamp *See:* Damp.

Fire extinguisher, portable appliance for putting out small fires. Extinguishers work either by cooling or by depriving the fire of oxygen (as typified by the simplest, a bucket of water or sand), and most do both. The *soda-acid extinguisher* contains a sodium bicarbonate solution and a small, stopped bottle of sulfuric acid. Depression of a plunger shatters the bottle, mixing the chemicals so that carbon dioxide (CO_2) gas is generated, forcing the water out of a nozzle. *Foam extinguishers* employ a foaming agent (usually animal protein or detergent) and an aerating agent. They are effective against oil fires, as they float on the surface. *Carbon dioxide extinguishers* provide a smothering blanket of CO_2. *Dry chemical extinguishers* provide a powder consisting mainly of sodium bicarbonate, from which the fire's heat generates CO_2.

Firefly, any of various soft-bodied, carnivorous, nocturnal beetles of the family Lampyridae that produce an intermittent greenish light in their abdominal organs. The light is created by the oxidation of luciferin under the influence of an enzyme, luciferase. In some species females are without wings and are known as *glowworms*. The lights serve to attract mates.

Firestone, Harvey Samuel (1868-1938), U.S. industrialist, founder of one of the largest rubber companies in the world, the Firestone Tire & Rubber Company. His million-acre rubber plantation in Liberia played a large role in that country's economic development starting in 1926. *See also:* Rubber.

Fireweed, or willow herb (*Epilobium angustifolium*), tall perennial plant of temperate regions of the Northern Hemisphere. The fireweed, so named because it springs up quickly after a forest fire, grows 3 to 6 ft (0.9 to 1.8 m) high and bears rose-purple flowers.

Fireworks, combustible or explosive preparations used for entertainment, probably first devised in ancient China to frighten off devils. Their initial European use was as weaponry, and not until after about 1500 were they employed for entertainment. Compounds of carbon, potassium, and sulfur are the prime constituents in fireworks,

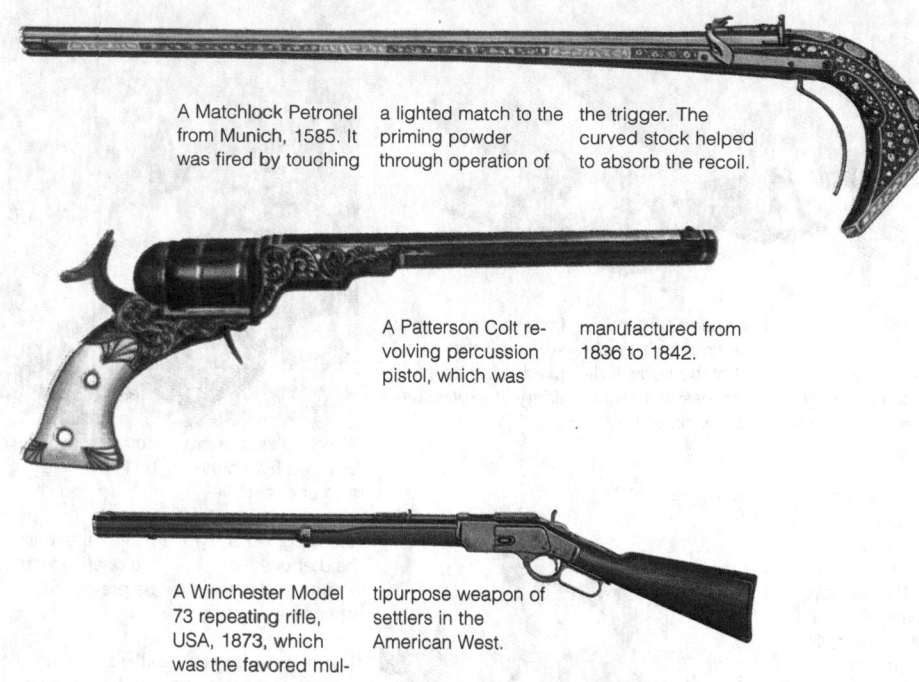

A Matchlock Petronel from Munich, 1585. It was fired by touching a lighted match to the priming powder through operation of the trigger. The curved stock helped to absorb the recoil.

A Patterson Colt revolving percussion pistol, which was manufactured from 1836 to 1842.

A Winchester Model 73 repeating rifle, USA, 1873, which was the favored multipurpose weapon of settlers in the American West.

F

colors being produced by metallic salts (e.g., blue, copper; yellow, sodium; red, lithium or strontium; green, barium), and sparks and crackles by powdered iron, carbon, or aluminum, or by certain lead salts. *See also:* Explosive.

First aid, treatment that can be given by minimally trained people for accident, injury, and sudden illness, until more skilled persons arrive or the patient is transferred to a hospital. Recognition of the injury or the nature of the illness and its gravity are crucial first measures, along with prevention of further injury to the patient or helpers. Clues such as medical bracelets or cards, evidence of food, drink, or drugs, and evidence of external injury should be sought and appropriate action taken. Cessation of breathing should be treated as a priority by clearing the airway of dentures, gum, vomit, and other foreign material and by the use of artificial respiration. Cardiac massage may be needed to restore blood circulation if major pulse cannot be felt. In traumatic injury, fractures must be recognized and splinted to reduce pain; the possibility of injury to the spine must be considered before moving the patient, to avoid unnecessary damage to the spinal cord. External hemorrhage should be arrested, usually by direct pressure on the bleeding point; tourniquets are rarely needed and may be dangerous. Internal hemorrhage may be suspected if shock (depression of vital signs) develops soon after collapse or trauma without obvious bleeding. Burns and scalds should be treated by immediately cooling the burned surface to reduce the continuing injury to skin due to retained heat. The use and, if necessary, improvisation of simple dressings, bandages, splints, and stretchers should be known; simple methods of moving the injured, should this be necessary, must also be understood. Accessory functions such as contacting ambulances or medical help, direction of traffic, and different aspects of resuscitation should be delegated by the most experienced person present. The inquisitive should be kept away and a calm atmosphere maintained. Prevention as a part of first aid includes due care in the home: avoiding highly polished floors and unfixed carpets, obstacles on or near stairs, loose cords, over-

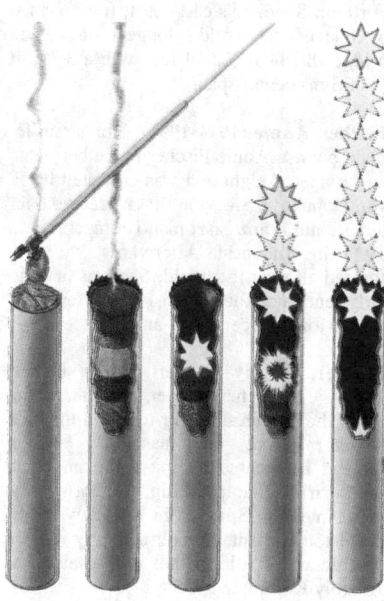

A Roman Candle is the basic example of a flare signal. It consists of a sealed cardboard cylinder that is packed with several layers of fuses, metal salt pellets, and gunpowder. A burning taper is used to light a slow-burning fuse, which lies above a salt pellet and a gunpowder charge. When the burning fuse reaches the salt pellet, the pellet begins to burn, igniting the gunpowder. The gunpowder charge then ejects the flaring pellet as a sparkling ball of color and ignites a fuse below it. The entire cycle is then repeated again.

F

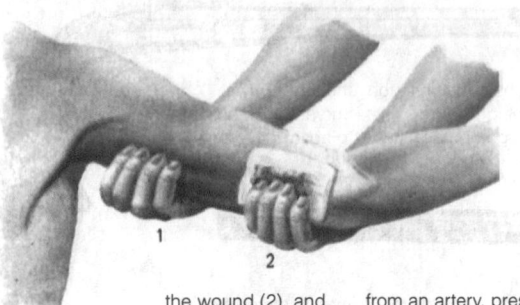

1

2

Severe bleeding can be treated by applying direct pressure to the wound (2), and elevating the injured part of the body. If direct pressure fails to stop the bleeding from an artery, pressure may also be applied to the supplying artery at a 'pressure point' (1).

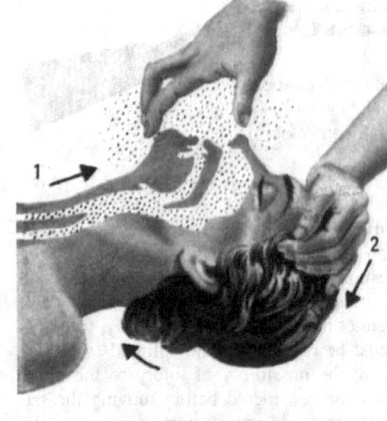

A

1

2

(A) In order to administer mouth-to-mouth artificial respiration, lie the victim on the back. Then remove any foreign matter from the mouth, tilt the victim's head back (2) and push the chin up (1) to open the airway. Then place your mouth tightly over the victim's mouth, while keeping the victim's nostrils closed (3), and blow air into the mouth and lungs until the chest rises, then pause and watch the chest fall. This procedure should be repeated until the victim resumes breathing.

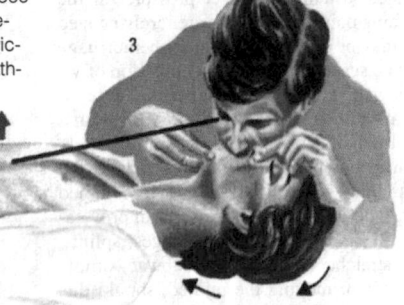

3

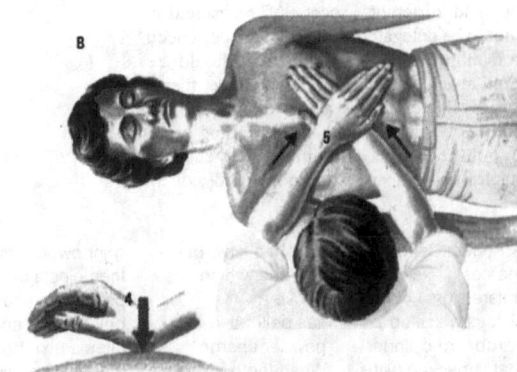

B

5

4

(B) If the heart is not beating, you should apply external cardiac compression (4 and 5) on the lower sternum (breastbone), alternating this with mouth-to-mouth respiration.

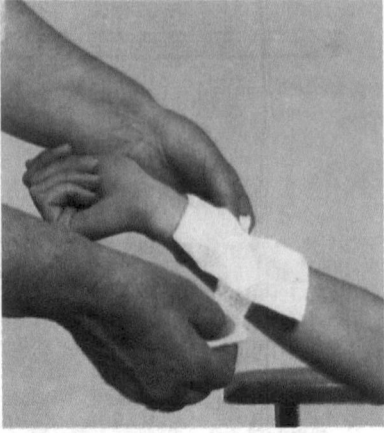

A wound should be covered by a bandage under sterile conditions. The dressing, which is held above the wound and then opened by pulling both rollers, should be immediately placed upon the wound. Thus, penetration of germs in the open wound can be prevented.

hanging saucepan handles, and unlabeled bottles of poison; drug cupboards accessible to children also present significant dangers. Effective first aid depends on prevention, recognition, organization, and, in any positive action, adherence to the principle of 'do no harm.'

Firth, arm of the sea or the opening of a river into the sea. Firths are similar to fiords but distinguished from them by lower walls. The term is used for such inlets in Scotland, including those of the rivers Forth, Clyde, and Tay.
See also: Fiord.

Firth of Clyde, bay-like mouth of the River Clyde in southwest Scotland 50 mi (80 km) long and 30 mi (50 km) wide. The term *firth*, used largely in Scotland, denotes an arm of the sea or an estuary (a river mouth that empties into the sea).

Firth of Forth, broad mouth of the River Forth on Scotland's east coast. It is spanned by one of the world's longest suspension bridges-8,244 ft (2,514 m), with a 3,300-ft (1,006-m) center span.

Fischer, Annie (1914-1995), Hungarian female pianist. Annie Fischer made her debut at the age of eight and was educated by E. von Dohnányi. She won first prize at the international Franz Liszt piano competition in 1933 in Budapest. Afterwards, she performed all over the world. She was particularly renowned for her sensitive performances of Mozart, Beethoven, and Schubert.

Fischer, Bobby (Robert James Fisher; 1943-), U.S. chess player, In 1958, he became the youngest player to attain the rank of international grand master. In 1972 in Iceland, he became the first American to win the world championship, defeating the Russian Boris Spassky in a widely publicized tournament. He subsequently refused to defend his title, which was awarded to Anatoly Karpov in 1975.

Fischer, Edwin (1886-1960), Swiss pianist and music teacher. Fischer studied in Basel and Berlin, where he was a teacher from 1905-1914. In 1931, he succeeded Artur Schnabel as a teacher at the Academy of Music of Berlin. He also worked as a conductor as of 1926. He was the leader of a master class in Luzern from 1945 until 1958. Fischer excelled in Bach, Mozart, and Beethoven. Many known pianists studied under him and he published many works on music education: *Musikalische Betrachtungen* (1950), *Von den Aufgaben des Musikers* (1960). Fischer also reintroduced the combination of conductor and performing soloist in the concert hall.

Fischer-Dieskau, Dietrich (1925-), German baritone. He achieved international fame in the 1950s as an opera singer and an interpreter of German lieder, notably those of Brahms, Schubert, and Wolf.
See also: Opera.

Fischer von Erlach, Johann Bernhard (1656-1723), Austrian baroque architect, educated in Rome (1670-1686). Designed the Kollegienkirche (1694-1699), among other things, and the Dreifaltigkeitskirche (1694-1707) in Salzburg, and Schloss Schönbrunn (1692-1713; altered later), the famous Karlskirche (1716-1739) and the Hofbibliothek (1723-1726; currently the Nationalbibliothek in the Hofburg) in Vienna.

Fish, cold-blooded aquatic vertebrate that breathes by means of gills. Typically, a fish's body is streamlined and covered by a layer of scales. Fish swim by means of fins, especially a vertical tail fin. All fish possess a 2-chambered heart. Fish are found wherever there is natural water, unless it is poisoned. Some fish, such as the African lungfish, spend some time out of water, breathing by means of a lunglike air bladder. Modern fish can be divided into 2 main groups: the cartilaginous fish (sharks, skates, and rays) and the bony fish. There are over 20,000 species of bony fish, ranging in size from the 1/2-in (1.3-cm) freshwater goby of the Philippines to the 20-ft (6-m) sturgeon of the former USSR. The largest of all fish, the 50-ft (15-m) whaleshark, is a cartilaginous fish. Most fish reproduce by shedding eggs into the water at the same time as the sperm and allowing fertilization to take place in the water. Perhaps 1 or 2 eggs in 10,000 grow to maturity. The female mouthbreeder, however, keeps the eggs and later the young in her mouth, and the discus, after carefully tending the eggs, secretes a special mucus in its skin to feed the young. These fishes do not need to lay thousands of eggs, as chances of survival improve with care. There must be, overall, a delicate balance between the number of eggs laid and the amount of care taken. Fish's eyes are adapted to underwater vision. Some, like the archer fish, which catches flying insects, can see well in air. The four-eyed fish can see out of the water and under water at the same time as it cruises just under the surface. The upper part of the eye focuses light in air and the lower half focuses in water. The sense of smell is developed variously, and some fish can taste as well as feel with barbels or other fleshy protuberances that trail in the water or along the bottom to detect food. Fish's ears are poorly developed, but a special sense organ, the lateral line system, enables fish to detect and identify many kinds of vibrations in the water. Some fish survive if blinded, but have great difficulty both in catching food and in escaping enemies without their lateral line system. Fish have bodies denser than water and would have to swim constantly to keep from sinking if it were not for the swimbladder, a sac that contains air or some gas secreted by the fish. The fish regulates the amount of gas by secreting more or by expelling some of it and thus keeps itself at its preferred depth. A few species of fish are able to generate electricity. Specially developed muscles build up a charge of electricity that is emitted to repel possible enemies. The South American electric eel is the most powerful, emitting up to 550 volts, enough to kill fish and even possibly a human.

Fisher *See:* Marten.

Fisher, Saint John (1469-1535), English cardinal. As bishop of Rochester (1504-1534), he refused to recognize the divorce of Henry VIII from Catharine of Aragon, was imprisoned in the Tower, and later beheaded. Canonized in 1935, his feast day is June 22.

Fishes, Age of *See:* Devonian Period.

Fish hawk *See:* Osprey.

Fishing, form of recreation that is probably the world's most popular participant sport; it is also one of the oldest. People fished for food in prehistoric times, probably first by using the 'tickling' method of catching fish by hand. Today there are millions of people who fish for pleasure or in competition; they are called anglers. There are more than 20 million fishing licenses issued annually. Competitively, the modes of fishing are almost as numerous and varied as the types of fish to be caught in fresh or salt water. World records by weight, length, and girth exist for every type of fish from albacore to yellowtail. The bait itself is subject to strict rules and regulations for competitive fishing, and skill in accuracy and length of casting is the subject of national and world championships.

History of the sport. References to fishing as a sport go back at least as early as Roman times, when Ovid, Martial, and Ausonius all remarked upon it in their writings. Even the specialized branch of flycasting was the subject of a work by Aelian in the 2nd century A.D. However, the best research on the subject came in 3 books published in England within the space of 40 years in the 17th century: John Denny's *Secrets of Angling* (1613), Thomas Barker's *Art of Angling* (1651), and Izaak Walton's *Compleat Angler* (1653).

Modes of angling. The 3 main types of modern angling are pan angling, game angling, and sea angling. Pan anglers stick mainly to angling for fish in slow and deep rivers or canals; game anglers go for trout,

Cichlids are perch-like fish of Central America, Africa and tropical South America. They can be distinguished from true perches by the presence of a single nasal opening on each side of the head. They show an exceptional degree of parental care in bringing their young to a free-swimming stage. (top) A male (right) and a female

Jack Dempsey cichlid (*Cichlasoma biocellatum*). Once the egg-laying is complete, both sexes take turns at guarding and fanning the eggs. They have a

command-and-response relationship between parent and fry. A fin signal from the alarmed parent will cause the fry to group below the parent. (bottom) The ci-

chlid *Tilapia* is a mouth brooder: eggs and fry are kept in the mouth. Fry are allowed to swim free only to forage for food.

salmon, and other fish that populate fast-running streams or mountain rivers and can only be caught by accurate casting of the appropriate lure; and sea anglers generally fish for the larger catches, such as shark, tuna, tarpon, and barracuda. In the modern era, sea angling has been the fastest of all in de-

veloping and has opened up wide areas of fishing off the coasts of Florida, Hawaii, California, the Carribbean, Australia, New Zealand, and England.

Fishing industry, worldwide economic activity that includes the production, market-

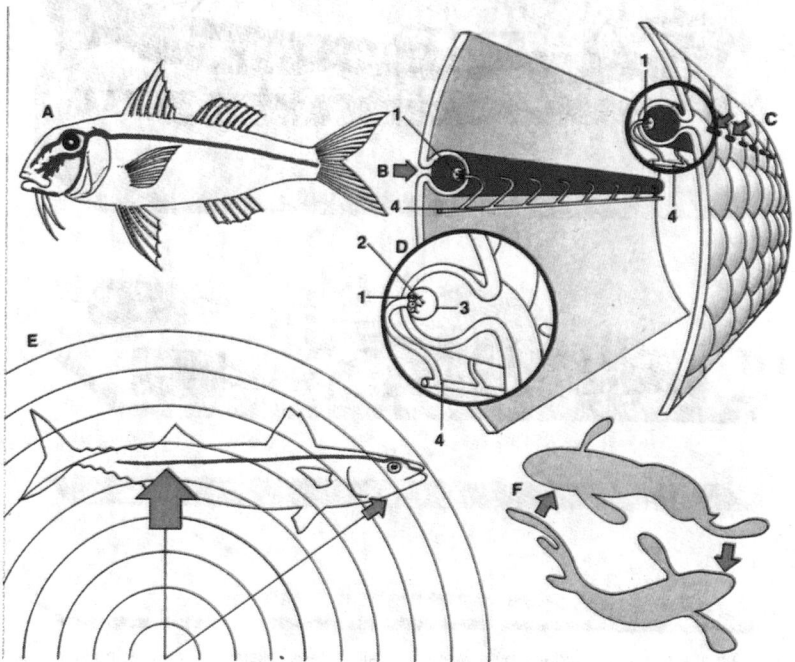

The lateral line system (red) of a red mullet (A) is located in the head and along the sides of the body. It consists of fluid-filled canals (B) under the skin, which open through small

pores (C). Within the canals (D) are groups of sensory cells (1) with projecting hairs (2), surrounded by a gelatinous cap (3). They send continuous trains of impulses along nerves (4) to

the brains. Pressure waves in the water stimulate the sensory cells, changing the frequency of the nerve impulses and allowing the fish to detect objects and other fishes. By com-

paring the pressure waves that reach different parts of its body (E), a fish can locate an object. Fighting fish (F) respond to pressure waves, caused by body movements.

F

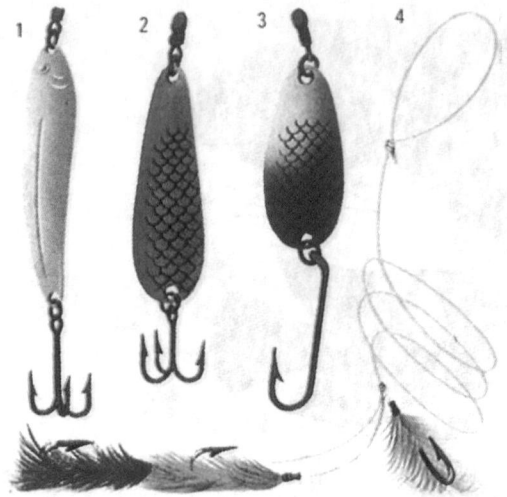

Examples of artificial baits for spinning and 'jigging'. The principle of the lure (1, 2 and 3) is that when drawn through the water, it revolves or flutters, giving an impression of bulk. One of the methods of catching mackerel is with feathers (4), fixed on dropper links and fished from anchored or moving boats.

ing, and conservation of fish, shellfish, and related products, such as seaweeds. Fish are an important source of protein, and two-thirds of the world's catch is used for human consumption; one-third is used in making animal feed and industrial products. Oceans supply most of the world's catch; rivers and lakes supply a small percentage, and fish farms-enclosed areas on land or in the natural bodies of water-supply a still smaller portion. Ocean fish include herring, sardines, and tuna, which are caught near the surface, and flounder, cod, and pollack, which are found near the ocean floor. Freshwater fish, which are found in lakes and rivers, include carp and catfish. To control overfishing and enforce conservation laws, in the 1970s most countries that border the sea established fishery conservation zones that extend 200 mi (320 km) from a country's coast.

Fission, nuclear reaction in which the atom is split into 2 approximately equal masses. Fission is accompanied by the emission of extremely high quantities of energy, since the sum of the masses of the 2 new atoms is less than the mass of the parent heavy atom.

The energy released is expressed by Einstein's equation $E=mc^2$.
See also: Atom; Nuclear energy; Uranium.

Fitch, John (1743-1798), U.S. inventor and engineer. Fitch built the first practical steamboat (1787), larger vessels being launched in 1788 and 1790. All were paddle-powered; his later attempt to introduce the screw propeller was a commercial failure.
See also: Steamboat.

Fitch, (William) Clyde (1865-1909), U.S. playwright known for his social satires and character studies. After graduating from Amherst College in 1886, he moved to New York City and began writing short stories for magazines. During his career he wrote and produced 30 plays and 22 adaptations of novels, including *Beau Brummel* (1890), *Captain Jinks of the Horse Marines* (1901), *The Girl With the Green Eyes* (1902), and *The City* (1909).

Fitness, collective name for a number of activities which are focused on improving the physical condition. The most popular forms are aerobics, aqua jogging, body shape, callanetics, spinning, step aerobics and TAE BO. Aerobics exercises consist of jumping movements in time to music. The term aqua jogging can be defined as exercises in the water. Body shape exercises are focused on abdominal, back and leg muscles, the main goal being to burn the fat in these areas. Callanetics are intensive exercises focused on specific muscle groups. Spinning is a term for bicycle exercises on a home trainer in time to music. Step aerobics involves moving on and off a step. TAE BO (short for total awareness, excellence, body, obedience) is a combination of aerobics and techniques that are based on martial arts, such as kicking and punching.
See also: Aerobics.

Fittipaldi, Emerson (1946-), Brazilian racing driver, began as a motorcycle racer, but switched to car racing at the age of eighteen. During his debut, he won the Grand Prix, beating Watkins Glen, for Lotus in the Formula One in 1971. Fittipaldi became the world champion the following year, a title that he also claimed in 1974. He won a total 14 Grand Prix races.

FitzGerald, Edward (1809-1883), English poet and scholar, translator of Omar Khayyam's *Rubaiyat*. FitzGerald's version of this Persian poet's quatrains (4-line rhymes) is not a literal and exact translation, but instead captures the spirit of the original to create a masterpiece of English poetry. The *Rubaiyat*, FitzGerald's only significant work, first appeared in 1859, and its tone of gentle melancholy had an important influence on later English poets.

Fitzgerald, Ella (1918-1996), U.S. jazz singer. She began her career in New York in 1935, singing in Chick Webb's orchestra. After that she toured widely abroad and was internationally known as one of the most original interpreters of jazz.

Fitzgerald, F(rancis) Scott (Key) (1896-

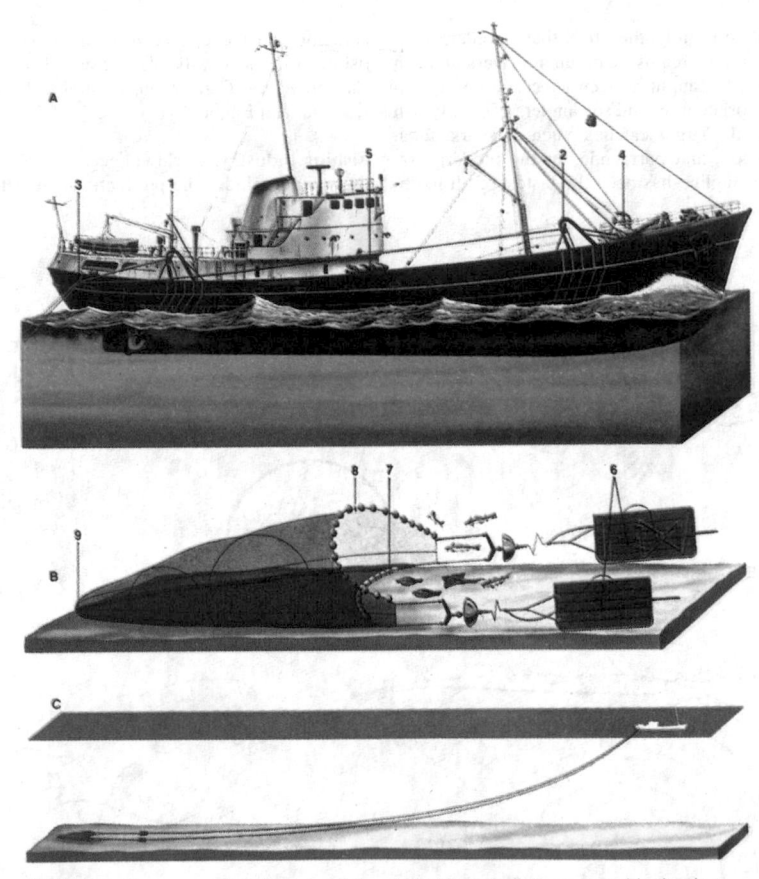

Otter trawling is a very important form of commercial fishing. The otter trawl is a dredge net that catches fish, living on or near the bottom. On the side trawler (A), the warp cables pass through fore and aft gallows (1 and 2) that are mounted on one side of the ship, then through a towing block (3). A third gallows (4) is rigged with a spare trawl, that can be used if the first trawl is damaged. When full, the trawl is hauled to the surface by powerful winches (5). On the trawl itself (B), the towing cables are attached to otter boards (6), iron-shod wood panels that pull sideways as they are dragged forward, keeping the trawl mouth open horizontally. Heavy rollers on the net's bottom lip (7), and floats along the top (8), keep the mouth from collapsing vertically. The trawl net tapers to a narrow end that is laced closed (9). When the trawl is hoisted on deck, the end-lacing is released and the catch is dropped into the ship. Otter trawling requires great lengths of cable (C). It is difficult to maneuver a side trawler with a large catch in its trawl.

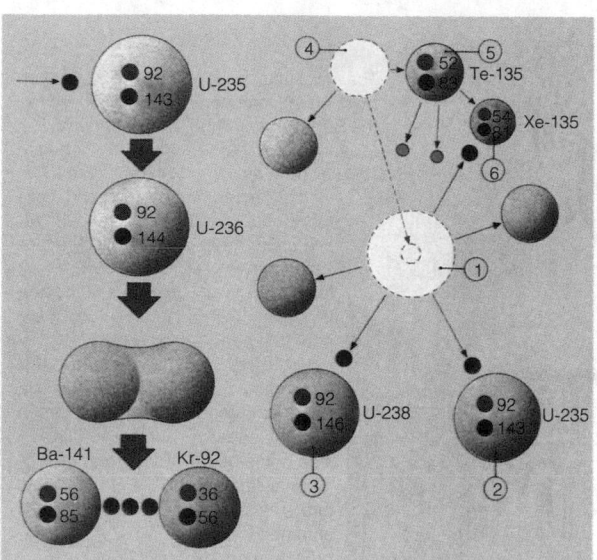

When a Uranium-235 nucleus is hit by a thermal (slow) neutron, it may split into two smaller nuclei, releasing neutrons and an amount of energy. This process occurs in a series of stages. In the left diagram, the numbers of protons (red) and neutrons (black) in the nuclei are shown at each stage. The absorption of the neutron causes the resulting Uranium-236 nucleus to become unstable. It will distort and then split into two nuclei (for example, Barium-141 and Krypton-92, but there are many other possibilities), plus two or three neutrons. On the right, you see how neutrons from a fissioned nucleus (1) may either strike another Uranium-235 (2), causing it to fission in turn and leading to a chain reaction, or they may be lost by absorption in a (non-fissionable) Uranium-238 nucleus (3), or in a nucleus created in a previous fission (4, 5, 6). A quite frequent fission product is Tellurium-135 (5), which will decay by electron-emission into Xenon-135 (6), absorbing neutrons. In nuclear physics, elements like Xenon-135 are called poisons.

F

1940), U.S. novelist and short-story writer. The 'spokesman' of the Jazz Age in the 1920s, he wrote about the frenetic life-style of the post-World War I generation and the spiritual bankruptcy of the so-called American Dream. His celebrated novel *The Great Gatsby* (1925) explores the ruthless society of the 1920s. *Tender Is the Night* (1934) draws upon the experience of American expatriates in Paris and upon the schizophrenic gaiety and breakdown of his wife, Zelda. *The Last Tycoon* (1941) is an unfinished work concerning Fitzgerald's final years, which were spent as a Hollywood scriptwriter.

Five Books of Moses *See:* Pentateuch.

Fjord *See:* Fiord.

Flag, piece of cloth or other material, usually rectangular, bearing a distinctive design. It is usually displayed as a symbol or signal of a country or organization.

Flagstad, Kirsten (1895-1962), Norwegian singer, one of the greatest Wagnerian sopranos. She made her New York debut as Sieglinde in *Die Walküre* in 1935 and retired from public singing in 1953, though she continued making records.

Flaherty, Robert Joseph (1884-1951), U.S. pioneer documentary filmmaker. He is chiefly famous for *Nanook of the North* (1922), a study of Eskimo life, and *Man of Aran* (1934), about life on the Aran Islands of Ireland.

Flamenco, folk music of Andalusia in southern Spain. Like most folk music traditions, flamenco combines singing and dancing. The influence of Moorish music has helped to create one of the most distinctive, colorful, and exciting of all folk music styles. True flamenco singing and dancing requires a considerable amount of training and skill, and professional flamenco groups are admired throughout the world.

Flamingo, several species of colorful water birds of the family Phoenicopteridae, related to herons. Flamingos have long spindly legs and necks, and large bills with bristles that they use to sift their food from the water. Their plumage is white, pink, and black. They live in large flocks on alkaline lakes in America, Africa, and southern Eurasia.

Flanagan, Barry (1941-), British sculptor. Began producing images around 1966 in which the characteristic qualities of sculpture, such as stability, spaciousness, mass and proportion, are revised in an untraditional manner. For example, by filling linen sacks with sand or plaster, he created forms that expressed an inversion. The mould and the image are not separated, but presented together. This work is regarded as conceptual art. In his later works, Flanagan attempted to give new meaning to the traditional techniques of sculpture, such as casting and carving in stone. The series of hares cast in bronze, which he created at the end of the 70s, is evidence of his return to figurative. The representative effect is, however, tarnished by the pointlessness of the actions undertaken by the hares, such as boxing and dancing.

Flanders, medieval county on the coast of northwestern Europe, largely corresponding to northern Belgium, with smaller portions in the Netherlands and France. In the 14th and 15th centuries, wealth from trade and textile manufacture enriched the chief towns (Antwerp, Ypres, Bruges, and Ghent) and made Flanders a major cultural center. Its famous artists included the Bruegel family, Peter Paul Rubens, and Anthony Van Dyck.

Flatfish, any of an order (Hetero somata) of plate-shaped fish with both eyes on one side of the head. A flatfish starts life as a normal-looking fish, but after a few days, one eye starts moving around the head, the dorsal fin grows along the head, and the mouth becomes twisted. The fish then lies on its side on the bottom. The underside stays pale, and the top becomes pigmented and can change color to match the background. Some of the 500 species are important food fishes, including flounder, halibut, sole, and turbot.

Flatworm, major group of simple animals that includes the parasitic flukes and tapeworms and the free-living flatworms. Flatworms have long, unsegmented, extremely thin bodies. The largest free-living species grow 1 ft (30 cm) long, though parasitic species may attain 40 ft (12 m). They are found under bark, in fresh water, and in the sea. Freshwater planarian flatworms are often used in biological research.

Flaubert, Gustave (1821-1880), French novelist. He was a scrupulous observer and stylist whose work influenced much subsequent French writing. His first work, *Madame Bovary* (1856-1857), brought him immediate fame. The vividly naturalistic tragedy of a provincial wife who attempts to live out her fantasies, it was unsuccessfully prosecuted as an offense against public morality in 1857. The exotic Carthaginian setting of *Salammbô* (1862) showed an equal mastery of romantic style. His *Three Tales* (1877), set in modern, medieval, and ancient times, combined both romanticism and realism.

Flax (genus *Linum,* especially *L. usitatissimum*), plant of temperate and subtropical areas grown for its fiber, which is spun into linen, and for linseed oil. Flax was first cultivated in the Mediterranean basin, and has been an important crop for thousands of years.

Flea, wingless insect (order Siphonaptera) with legs developed for jumping and a laterally compressed body. It sucks the blood of host animals, and can carry such diseases as typhus and the bubonic plague. The flea survives its early stages in unsanitary conditions; when newly emerged, adults leap onto passing hosts.

Fleabane, any of 200 species of an aster-like flowering plant (genus *Erigeron*) that grows in temperate climates around the world. So named because it was thought to repel or kill fleas, fleabane is often planted in rock gardens; some varieties grow as common weeds. A Canadian variety known as horseweed or bloodstanch yields a drug called erigeron, or fleabane, which is used to treat diarrhea and control bleeding. Mosquito repellents often contain oil of fleabane.

Fleet Prison, historic London jail in use from the 1100s, when it was the king's jail, until the 1800s, when it was torn down. Named for the nearby Fleet stream, the prison in turn gave its name to secret marriages called 'Fleet marriages,' which were performed in the jail by the clergy during the 1600s and 1700s.

Fleming, resident of Flanders (northern Belgium). Flemings, who make up about 55% of Belgium's population, are descended from the Franks and speak Dutch. The French-speaking Walloons, who live in Wallonia (southern Belgium), are descended from the area's original inhabitants, the Celts. When the Franks invaded what is now Belgium during the 3rd and 4th centuries, they pushed the Celts southward to the present north-south division between the 2 regions. When the newly independent country declared French its official language in 1830, the Flemings protested. Dutch was given official recognition in the late 1800s, but frictions have continued. In 1980 the government granted limited independence to Flanders and Wallonia. The Flemings dominated European commerce in the Middle Ages, and today are primarily involved in the manufacture of textiles. From the 1400s to the 1600s Flanders produced some of the world's most famous painters, including Pieter Brueghel the Elder and Jan van Eyck. *See also:* Flanders.

Fleming, Ian Lancaster (1908-1964), British author and creator of the James Bond series of spy thrillers. His novels, which won international fame, include *Casino Royale* (1953) and *Goldfinger* (1959). In the late 1920s and early 1930s Fleming worked as a journalist in Moscow. During World War II he did espionage work for British Naval Intelligence.

Fleming, Sir Alexander (1881-1955), British bacteriologist, discoverer of lysozyme (1922) and penicillin (1928). Lysozyme is an enzyme present in many body tissues and lethal to certain bacteria; its discovery prepared the way for that of antibiotics. His discovery of penicillin was largely accidental, and penicillin was developed as a therapeutic drug later, by Howard Florey and Ernst Chain. All 3 scientists received the 1945 Nobel Prize for physiology or medicine for their work.
See also: Bacteriology; Penicillin.

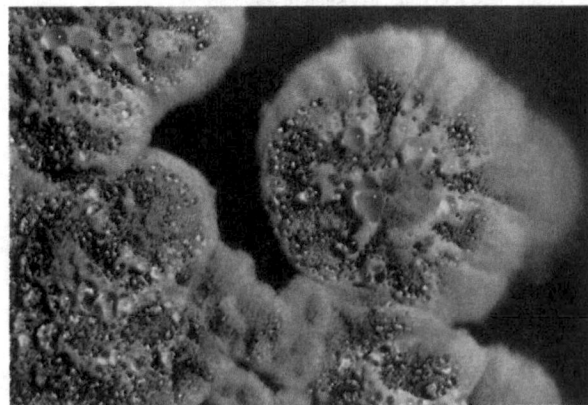

The mould *Penicillium notatum.* In 1928, Sir Alexander Fleming discovered that this mould produces a substance that can kill bacteria: namely penicillin.

The oldest surviving building in Florence, the Baptistery of San Giovanni, possible dates from as early as the 5th century. The distinctive green and white marble facing however, is of the 11th and 12th centuries. There is a rectangular apse, projecting from the western side of the octagonal structure. The south entrance has bronze doors by Andrea Pisano, dating from 1330-38. The north and east doors are by Lorenzo Ghiberti. These famous *Gates of Paradise* date from 1425-52. The interior of the cupola, concealed from the outside by a pyramidal roof, is covered with mosaics of the late 13th century. The attic, added to the earlier structure in the 13th century, is clad with slabs of green and white marble from Prato.

Flemish, form of Dutch traditionally spoken in North Belgium. Given official equality with French in 1898, it became the official language of North Belgium in 1934. Approximately 5 million people in Belgium and another 200,000 in France speak Flemish.

Flesh-eating animal *See:* Carnivore.

Fletcher, John (1579-1625), English author of plays. Primarily known for his collaborations with the playwright Francis Beaumont (1584?-1616), Fletcher wrote many of his own dramas before and after the active period of their partnership. Popular along with other great playwrights in his time, he also collaborated with Shakespeare on *Henry VI-II* and *The Two Noble Kinsmen*.
See also: Beaumont, Francis.

Flicker (*Colaptes auratus*), woodpecker of North America, known for its colorful plumage and loud calls. Its main food is ants.

Flickertail state *See:* North Dakota.

Flint, or chert, sedimentary rock composed of microcrystalline quartz and chalcedony. Found as nodules in limestone and chalk and as layered beds, it is mainly formed from marine sediments, and preserves many fossil outlines. A hard rock, flint may be chipped to form a sharp cutting edge, and it was used by Stone Age people for their characteristic tools.

Flood, flow of water from a river, lake, or ocean over normally dry land. Most floods are destructive to homes and other property, and can leave the land barren by carrying off topsoil. Some can be helpful: the annual floods of the Nile River in Egypt made the desert land of the Nile Valley fertile by depositing rich soil carried from far upstream. River floods, which are the most common type, are usually caused by heavy rains and sudden melting of ice and snow. Ocean floods are most often caused by hurricanes or other strong storms that raise the height of waves and push water far inland. Floods also occur when wave heights are raised by earthquakes or volcanoes. Abnormally high tides can also occasionally cause flooding. Lakeshore flooding is also usually caused by strong storms.

Flora, term used to refer to the plant life of a region or a particular time. *Fauna* is the corresponding term for animal life. The word *flora* comes from the Roman goddess of flowering plants.

Florence (Italian: *Firenze*; pop. 380,000), historic city of central Italy, capital of Firenze province, on the Arno River at the foot of the Apennines. A town on the Cassian Way during Roman times, it grew to become a powerful medieval republic, dominating Tuscany. Florence was a major commercial and artistic center during the Renaissance. It retains many architectural and other art treasures which, together with the proximity of the Apennines, serve to make the city an important tourist center. The great art museums of Florence include the Uffizi Gallery, the Pitti Palace, and the Accademia. Famous figures associated with Florence include Brunelleschi, Dante, Giotto, Machiavelli, Masaccio, Michelangelo, and Savonarola. Glass and leatherware, pottery, furniture, and precision instruments are among its products. In 1966 floods seriously damaged many of Florence's art treasures.
See also: Italy.

Flores (pop. 1.6 million), island belonging to the Indonesian province Nusa Tenggara Timur (Lesser Sunda Islands); 5504 sq mi (14,250 sq km). Capital: Ende. Very mountainous, with over 10 active volcanoes and peaks reaching to 6,989 ft (2,130 m). (Pearl)fishing and export of mother-of-pearl, copra and sandalwood. Agricultural products include corn, rice, coconuts, cinnamon, coffee, cotton, tobacco, beeswax, meat, and chicken.

Flores Island, westernmost island of the Portuguese Azores, in the North Atlantic. Named for its lush flora, the 55 sq mi (143 sq km) island is volcanic in origin and has many crater lakes that offer good fishing. Santa Cruz is the chief town, and cattle raising and dairy farming are the island's main industries.

Florey, Howard Walter (1898-1968), Baron Florey of Adelaide, Australian-born British pathologist. He worked with E.B. Chain and others to extract penicillin from *Penicillium notatum* mold for use as a therapeutic drug (1934-1944). He shared with Chain and Alexander Fleming the 1945 Nobel Prize for physiology or medicine. *See also:* Pathology; Penicillin.

Floriculture, cultivation of flowers and ornamental plants for commercial business. Scientific research has provided floriculturists with techniques for controlling the blooming of flowers, so that, for example, poinsettias bloom with red leaves at Christmas. Research has also produced such new varieties as thornless roses and the double snapdragon. Floriculturists work in public and private gardens, nurseries, seed companies, and landscape design companies.

Florida (Sunshine State; pop. 14,654,000), state in the United States on the Atlantic Ocean and the Gulf of Mexico; 58,686 sq mi (151,939 sq km); the fourth most populous state in the US. Capital: Tallahassee. Lowlands (highest peak 344 ft 105 m) with marshes and lakes. Humid subtropical climate with many, forests. The Florida Keys, a chain of approx. 50 coral islands, are located along the south coast.
The most important source of income is tourism, including the Everglades National Park and places such as Miami, Daytona Beach, and Fort Lauderdale. Florida produces 80% of the citrus fruits in the US and is the most important producer of vegetables, with the exception of California. Electronics industry, food, defense, chemical, metals, and paper industry. The population tripled between 1960 and 1990, particularly as a result of the influx of pensioners.
The first European to visit Florida was the Spaniard Juan Ponce de Leon (1513). St Augustine, the oldest permanently inhabited European settlement in North America dates back to 1565. The Spanish handed over Florida to the British in 1763, but it was not until 1819 that Florida was definitively handed over to the US. Florida entered the Union in 1845.
The name is Spanish for 'covered with flowers'.

Florida, Strait of, or Florida Strait, channel between the Florida Keys and the northern coast of Cuba. About 110 mi (177 km) wide, it links the Gulf of Mexico with the Atlantic Ocean and is the channel by which the Gulf Stream flows into the Atlantic.

Florida Keys, chain of about 20 small coral islands off southern Florida. Their arc curves

southwest from Biscayne Bay south of Miami to Key West. Causeways bearing some 160 mi (257 km) of highway link most of the islands, which support fishing and farming and attract vacationers.

Florin, solid-gold coin introduced in Florence, Italy, in 1252 and made until the early 1500s. Florins have a lily, symbol of Florence, on one side and an image of Saint John the Baptist, patron saint of Florence, on the other. Britain, one of many countries to produce versions of the coin, first introduced a silver florin in 1849.

Flotation, industrial process used to separate valuable mineral compounds from low-grade ores. The ore is pulverized into minute particles and mixed with water. Then special chemicals, called flotation reagents, are added to prevent the water from wetting those substances to be extracted. When air is sprayed into the mixture a foam develops and carries to the surface the dry particles, which are then easily removed. The waste materials sink to the bottom of the mixture.

Flotsam, jetsam, and lagan, terms in maritime law relating to goods lost at sea. Goods thrown overboard (to lighten a ship) and that float are *flotsam*; those that sink are *jetsam*, but if they sink and are flagged to indicate ownership, they are *lagan*. These goods are subject to the law of salvage whereby the finder is entitled to reward.
See also: Salvage.

Flounder, any of a group of edible saltwater flatfish (families Pleuronectidae and Bothidae) of the Pacific and Atlantic. The halibut and turbot belong to the group.
See also: Flatfish.

Flour, fine powder ground from the grains or starchy portions of wheat, rye, corn, rice, potatoes, bananas, or beans. Plain white flour is produced from wheat; soft wheat

halibut
Hippoglossus hippoglossus

(blind side)

flounder
Platichthys flesus

dab
Limanda limanda

turbot
Scopthalmus maximus

produces flour used for cakes, and hard wheat, with a higher gluten content, makes flour used for bread. Flour is made from the endosperm, which constitutes about 84% of the grain; the remainder comprises the bran, which is the outer layers of the grain, and the germ, which is the embryo.

Adult flounders, such as *Platichthys flesus*, have both eyes located on one side of the head (top); the lower, colorless side is blind.

Flour beetle (*Tribolium confusum*), small (1/7 in/4 mm long), dark-red beetle that feeds on dried foods, flour, and other grain products. Found throughout the world, flour beetles are more common in warm, dry climates. Remains of flour beetles were discovered in a grain jar in an Egyptian tomb dating to about 2500 B.C.

Flower, part of a plant that is concerned with reproduction. Each flower is borne on a stalk or *pedicel*, the tip of which is expanded to form a receptacle that bears the floral organs. The *sepals* are the first of these organs and are normally green and leaflike. Above the sepals there is a ring of *petals*, which are normally colored and vary greatly in shape. The ring of sepals is termed the *calyx*, and the ring of petals, the *corolla*. Collectively the calyx and corolla are called

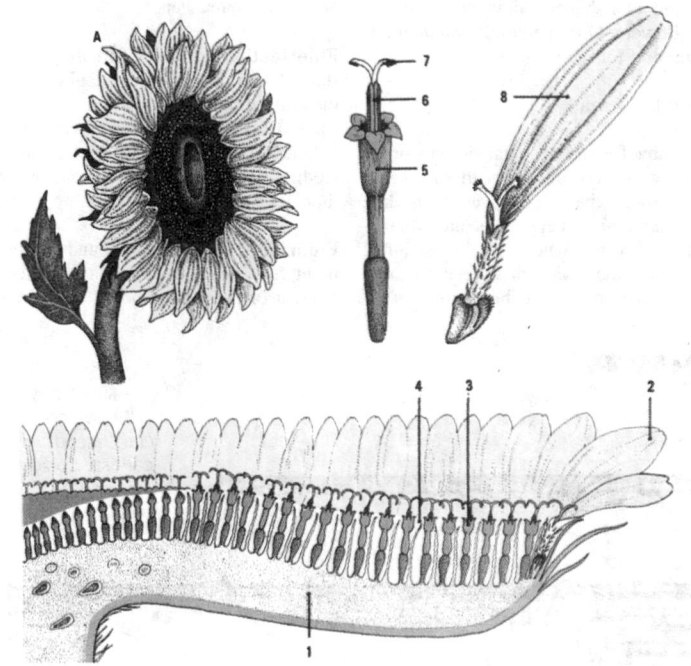

The sunflower *Helianthus annus* (A) is not a single flower, but a group of flowers, or inflorescence. This inflorescence consists of a receptacle (1) with an outer ray of florets (2) and a densely packed row of inner florets (3). Between each floret, there are modified petals, called pappus scales (4). Disc florets are composed of a tube of fused corolla (5), enclosing male anthers (6) and a female stigma (7), which leads to a style and the ovary. The ray florets have the same basic structure, but the corolla (8) is expanded, and has large petals around the outside of the flower.

F

F

the *perianth*. Above the perianth are the reproductive organs comprising the male organs, the *stamens* (collectively known as the *androecium*) and the female organs, the *carpels* (the *gynoecium*). Each stamen consists of a slender stalk, or filament, that is capped by the pollen- producing *anther*. Each carpel has a swollen base, the *ovary*, that contains the *ovules* that later form the seed. Each carpel is connected by a *style* to an expanded structure called the *stigma*. Together, the style and the stigma are sometimes termed the *pistil*. There are 3 main variations of flower structure. In hypogynous flowers (e.g., the buttercup) the perianth segments and stamens are attached below a superior ovary, while in perigynous flowers (e.g., the rose) the receptacle is cup-like, enclosing a superior ovary, with the perianth segments and stamens attached to a rim around the receptacle. In epigynous flowers (e.g., the dandelion) the inferior ovary is enclosed by the receptacle and the other floral parts are attached to the ovary. In many plants, the flowers are grouped together to form an *inflorescence* (flower cluster). Pollen produced by the stamens is transferred either by insects or the wind to the stigma, where pollination takes place. Many of the immense number of variations of flower form are adaptations that aid either insect or wind pollination.

Flowering maple, or Chinese bell flower, name for a number of trees and shrubs of the mallow family, and not, in fact, maples. Flowering maples come from southern Asia and South America. Some are now naturalized in North America. One, the velvetleaf, is cultivated for its fibers, called 'China jute,' used in rugmaking.

Flowering tobacco, any of several species of plants (genus *Nicotiana*) in the nightshade family that grow wild or are cultivated for their sweet-smelling flowers. Flowering tobacco plants are native to the South American tropics. They have hairy, sticky leaves and tube-shaped red, white, yellow, or purple flowers. One species, *N. tabacum*, is the source of tobacco.

Flu *See:* Influenza.

Fluke, name for various parasitic flatworms, some of which are important disease carriers. The sheep liver fluke lives in the bile duct of mammals. Its eggs pass out of the intestine into water, where the larvae infect water snails, then wait on vegetation to be eaten by mammals. The blood fluke (bil-

harzia) is responsible for the disease schistosomiasis, which is thought to affect 250 million people throughout the world.

Fluorescence, property of emitting visible radiation as the result of absorption of radiation from some other source. The emitted radiation persists only as long as the fluorescent material is subjected to radiation, which may be either electrified particles or waves. The fluorescent radiation generally has a longer wavelength than does the absorbed radiation. If the fluorescent radiation includes waves of the same length as that of the absorbed radiation, it is termed *resonance* radiation.
See also: Radiation.

Fluorescent lamp, tube-shaped electric light from which light is emitted by the process of fluorescence. Fluorescent lamps produce about one-fifth the heat of light bulbs (incandescent lamps), use one-fifth the electricity, and lasts far longer. Fluorescent lamps, first introduced at the N.Y. World's Fair in 1938-1939, are used largely in offices, schools, and factories. Inside a fluorescent lamp's glass tube is a small amount of mercury and a chemically inactive gas such as argon. The surface of the inside of the tube is coated with chemicals called phosphors. On each end of the tube is an electrode, which is a coated coil of tungsten wire. A *ballast* provides voltage to start the lamp and also regulates the flow of current. When a fluorescent lamp is turned on, electricity flows through the electrodes, heating it so that it gives off electrons. Some of these electrons hit the argon atoms and *ionize* them, giving them a positive or negative charge. Once ionized, the argon can conduct electricity. A current flowing through the gas from electrode to electrode forms a stream of electrons, exciting the electrons in the mercury. As the electrons in the mercury return to their normal state, they emit ultraviolet rays, which in turn cause the phosphors to glow (fluoresce).
See also: Fluorescence.

Fluoridation, addition of small quantities of fluorides to public water supplies, bringing the concentration to 1 part per million, as in some natural water. It greatly reduces the incidence of tooth decay by strengthening the teeth. Despite some opposition, many authorities now fluoridate water.

Fluoride, chemical compound of the element fluorine, and an important trace constituent of the human body. The bones and

teeth contain most of the body's fluoride. Sea fish and tea are rich sources, but intake is mainly from drinking water. Fluoridation of water that contains the ideal level of 1 part per million (ppm) significantly reduces the incidence of dental decay (caries). Excess accumulation of fluoride (called fluorosis) occurs in teeth and bone in proportion to the level and duration of intake, and communities in which the level in drinking water exceeds 10 ppm are commonly affected.

Fluorine, chemical element, symbol F; for physical constants see Periodic Table. Fluorine was discovered in 1886 by Henri Moisson. It occurs chiefly in the form of the minerals fluorspar (calcium fluoride) and cryolite (sodium aluminum fluoride). It is obtained by electrolyzing a solution of potassium hydrogen fluoride in anhydrous hydrogen fluoride. Compounds of fluorine were used for years before the element was finally isolated. Fluorine is a member of the halogen family of elements. Fluorine is a pale yellow, corrosive, and poisonous gas and is the most electronegative and reactive of all elements. Commercial production of the element began only after World War II for preparing uranium hexafluoride. Fluorine and its compounds are used for glass etching, production of fluorocarbons, and in drinking water to prevent dental cavities. Fluorine and the fluoride ion are highly toxic.

Fluorite, or fluorspar, common mineral composed mainly of calcium fluoride. Fluorite is mined in many parts of the world and is important as a flux in the iron and steel industries. It is sometimes used in making optical lenses and as a catalyst in the manufacture of high-octane fuels. Fluorite is found in a wide range of colors, including light green, yellow, blue-green, purple, and, rarely, pink and red.

Fluorocarbon, organic compound in which hydrogen atoms are replaced by fluorine atoms. Fluorocarbons are often similar to hydrocarbons, but because of the stability of the carbon-fluorine bond, they are unreactive and do not break down with heating. Fluorocarbons are used as lubricants in conditions where hydrocarbon lubricants would be attacked by chemicals or by heat. They are also used in the chemical industry as a corrosion-resistant and insulating coating. Polytetrafluoroethylene (*Teflon*) is a solid fluorocarbon that is used to make artificial joints and plates for surgical implantation. Its lack of reactivity makes it safe to use in the body. It is also the basis of the coatings on nonstick frying pans and the heatshields of spacecraft. Liquid fluorocarbons such as **freon** are used as refrigerants.

Fluoroscope, device used in medical diagnosis and engineering quality control that allows the direct observation of an X-ray beam that is being passed through an object under examination. It contains a fluorescent screen, which converts the X-ray image into visible light, and, often, an image intensifier.
See also: X ray.

Flute, musical instrument belonging to the woodwind group, although most modern or-

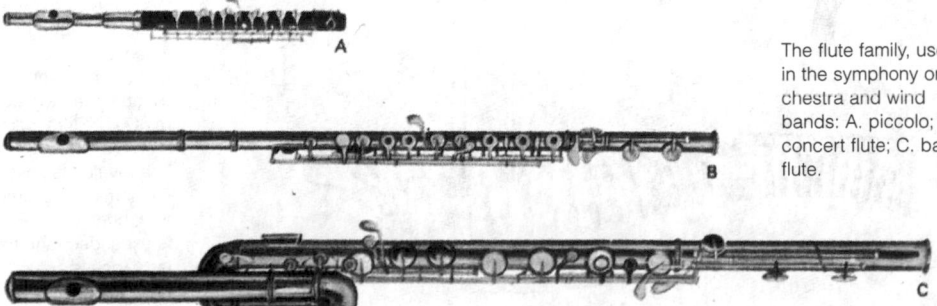

The flute family, used in the symphony orchestra and wind bands: A. piccolo; B. concert flute; C. bass flute.

A

B

C

chestral flutes are made of metal. The flute differs from most other woodwind instruments in that it is played in a sideways position. For this reason it was once often called the transverse flute, to distinguish it from similar instruments like the recorder. It is also distinguished in that the sound is produced by blowing directly across the mouthpiece instead of into it as in the bassoon, oboe, and clarinet.

Flutes, often made of clay, existed in ancient Sumer, Egypt, and Israel, as well as the Americas. In Europe technical improvements made the wooden flute an important solo instrument from the 17th century. Throughout the 18th century, from Bach to Mozart, the flute was very popular, both in orchestral and chamber music, and it remains an important member of the orchestra today. A much smaller version of the flute is the *piccolo* (Italian, 'little'), which has a correspondingly higher range of notes and a shriller tone. It came into orchestral use during Beethoven's lifetime and is regularly included in military bands.

Fluxus, a music and visual art movement that came about at the beginning of the 60s for the purpose of integrating art and daily life. Here, the artist is regarded as one who releases the creative abilities in man, and not as someone who produces art objects by virtue of his/her profession. Festivals, happenings, and publications were used to give shape to this idea. For reasons of an organizational nature, the world was divided into two zones, each with its own coordinator. Ken Friedman fulfilled this position for West Fluxus (America), while the German Joseph Beuys did so for East Fluxus (Europe). The registers include the names of artists from various movements, such as pop art, minimal art and conceptual art, but also those of critics, architects, philosophers, and interested parties with various backgrounds.

Fly, insect of the order Diptera, characterized by the presence of only 1 pair of wings. Well-known species include the common house fly, mosquitoes, and gnats. Many flies are known to transmit diseases such as malaria and dysentery, while others are beneficial as pollinators and as laboratory specimens in genetic studies. Approximately 100,000 varieties are found worldwide, ranging in size from 1/20 in (1.3 mm) to 3 in (7.6 cm).

Flycatcher, or tyrant flycatcher, family of birds found throughout the Americas, including kingbirds, phoebes, and pewees. They have broad bills with stiff bristles around the base. Their food usually consists of insects that they catch by flying out from a perch. Larger species, such as Kittlitz's ground tyrant, feed on lizards, mice, and small birds. The flycatchers of the Old World belong to a different family but have similar feeding habits.

Flying buttress, arch of brick or stone on the exterior of a building, spanning the roof of an aisle of a church or cathedral, or a half-arch issuing from the upper part of a wall. The flying buttress helped make possible the tall, light churches of Gothic architecture.

Flying dragon, tree-dwelling lizard (genus *Draco*) of southeastern Asia and the East Indies. The flying dragon's body is about 8 in (20 cm) long and has thin folds of skin along each side. By spreading these 'wings,' the lizard can glide from tree to tree.

Flying fish, tropical food food fish of the family Exocoetidae, that propels itself out of the sea by an elongated lobe of the tail. It can glide on its fins, but the flights are usually 180 ft (55 m) or less. The flight allows the fish to escape predatory fish.

Flying fox, or fruit bat, large bat of the family Pteropidae, found in tropical regions, especially Australia and the Philippines. The largest has a 5-ft (1.5-m) wingspan. Flying foxes roost in large groups in trees and fly out in the evening to feed on flowers and fruit of trees.

Flying lemur, or colugo, nocturnal mammal (genus *Cynocephalus*) of the East Indies and Philippines, similar in appearance but unrelated to the lemurs. It has flaps of skin running between fore- and hindlimbs that enable it to glide 150 yd (137 m) from one tree to another. Its food consists of leaves, buds, and flowers.

Flying saucer *See:* Unidentified flying object.

Flying squirrel, omnivorous, nocturnal squirrel that glides on a web of skin between its legs. Flying squirrels use their tails for balance and as a rudder. They are found in Asia, Europe, and North America. The 2 North American species are genus *Glaucamys*.

FM *See:* Frequency modulation.

Fo, Dario (1926-), Italian playwright and actor who owes his fame to his revolutionary stagings, which are inspired by 'commedia dell'arte'. Fo began writing satirical pieces for radio and television and established his own theater company together with his wife, the actress Franca Rame in 1959. Its name: Compagnia Dario Fo-Franca Rame, which existed until 1968. After this, they established the theater collective La Comune in Milan in 1970, which mainly performed for laborers in factories. Fo's plays express a strong leftist commitment and are often controversial; irony, satire, and the grotesque predominate. Of the more than 70 works he wrote, the most famous include *Archangels Don't Play Pinball* (1959), *Mistero Buffo* (1969), *The Accidental Death of an Anarchist* (1970) and *Can't Pay, Won't Pay!* (1974). He was awarded the Nobel Prize for Literature in 1997 for his 'many-sided oeuvre that manages to open the public's eye to the injustices in society by combining humor and earnestness'.

Foch, Ferdinand (1851-1929), French army marshal. His courageous stand against the

A typical flying fish, *Cypselurus opisthopus*, uses its enlarged pectoral fins to produce its gliding flight above the ocean's surface. It is found throughout the open waters of the Pacific.

Two-winged flies belong to the insect order of *Diptera*. They have only one pair of wings, the hind wings being reduced to small balancer organs, called 'halteres'. 1. Hover fly, *Volucella pellucens*, British Isles, body length 0.6 in (15 mm). 2. Blowfly, *Mesembrina meridiana*, British Isles, body length 0.4 in (11 mm). 3. Moth fly, *Pericoma palystris*, British Isles, body length 0.1 in (3 mm). 4. Mosquito, *Theobaldia annulata*, British Isles, body length 0.3 in (7 mm). 5. Beefly, *Bombylius major*, Europe to Japan, body length 0.5 in (12 mm).

F

F

Germans at the Marne in 1914 led to further commands, and he became chief of the French general staff in 1917. He commanded the Allied armies in France from Apr. to Nov. 1918, launching the Aisne-Marne offensive that ended World War I.
See also: World War I.

Fog, cloud near the earth's surface. It is generally formed when the air has cooled so much that it cannot hold all its water vapor, and the excess is precipitated in the form of water droplets. Fog may also form from the addition of water vapor to already saturated air. Fog is most common near large inland bodies of water and along the coasts in temperate zones.
See also: Cloud.

Fokine, Michel (1880-1942), Russian-born U.S. dancer and choreographer, a founder of modern ballet. Influenced by the work of Isadora Duncan, he stressed the total effect of expressive dancing, costume, music, and scenery. He worked in Paris as chief choreographer of Sergei Diaghilev's Ballets Russes (1909-1914), and from 1925 directed his own company in the United States.
See also: Ballet.

Fokker, Anthony Herman Gerard (1880-1939), Dutch pilot and pioneer in aircraft design. In World War I he designed pursuit planes for Germany, developing a synchronizer mechanism by which guns could be fired from directly behind a plane's propeller blades. In 1922 Fokker emigrated to the United States, where he designed for the Army Air Corps and build transport planes like the Fokker T-2, which in 1923 made the first nonstop flight across the United States.
See also: Aircraft, military.

Folk art, paintings, sculptures, or crafts created by individuals according to local needs, tastes and traditions. Folk art is most often functional and representative of everyday life. In the United States folk artists have designed shop signs, weather vanes, and decoys. Craftworkers have made kitchen utensils, dishes, quilts, and furniture according to the needs of the community. The portrayal of everyday life in the objects of folk art makes it a valuable source of history.

The gallery of King Francis I at Fontainebleau, with its frescoes and stucco decorations by Italian artists Rosso Fiorentino and Francesco Primaticcio (approximately 1530 to 1544).

Folk dancing, traditional popular dancing of a nation or region. Folk dances derive variously from ancient magic and religious rituals and also from the sequences of movement involved in certain forms of communal labor. Famous national dances include the Irish jig, the Italian tarantella, and the Hungarian czardas. The American Folk Dancing Society popularizes American folk dances, notably the square dance, in which an expert 'caller' gives rhyming instructions. Many U.S. dances have European origins, but the barn dance setting is authentically American.

Folk literature *See:* Folklore; Literature for children.

Folklore, traditional beliefs, customs, and superstitions of a culture, handed down informally in fables, myths, legends, proverbs, riddles, songs, and ballads. Folklore studies were developed in the 1800s, largely through collection and collation of material by the Grimm brothers in Germany, and folklore societies were set up in Europe and the United States. Folktale themes are echoed and paralleled among distinct and isolated cultures. One of the major studies of this phenomenon is Sir James Frazer's *Golden Bough* (1890).

Folk music, traditional popular music of a regional or ethnic group. Compositions are usually anonymous and, being in the main orally transmitted, often occur in several different versions. Among classical composers influenced by folk music are Béla Bartók, Zoltán Kodaly, Aaron Copland, and Ralph Vaughan Williams.

Fonda, family of U.S. actors. **Henry Fonda** (1905-1982), appeared in over 80 films, notably *The Grapes of Wrath* (1940), *The Ox-Bow Incident* (1943), and *Twelve Angry Men* (1957). He won an Academy Award for his performance in *On Golden Pond* (1981), in which his daughter, **Jane Fonda** (1937-), also appeared. She won Academy Awards for her performances in *Klute* (1971) and *Coming Home* (1978). She is also known for her political activism. Her brother, **Peter Fonda** (1940-), coproduced and starred in *Easy Rider* (1969), a film that made him a popular antihero of a generation.

Fontainebleau (pop. 18,000), town in the department Seine-et-Marne, France, 27 mi (60 km) southeast of Paris. The town did not develop until the 19th century. Fontainebleau is primarily a recreation and tourist town. The magnificent palace of the French kings, built in the 16th century on the site of a royal hunting lodge, stands just outside the town. It was the scene of Napoleon's farewell to his army after his abdication in 1814. Fontainebleau forest, once a royal hunting ground, was a favorite subject for the 19th-century landscape painters known as the Barbizon school.
See also: France.

Fontana, Lucio (1899-1968), artist, born in Argentina. Fontana spent most of his life in Italy and was an enormous influence on the development of visual art after 1960. In

1946 his 'Spatial Manifesto' was published, in which he proposed to drop the traditional distinctions between different forms of art. Fontana claimed that these distinctions did not belong in the twentieth century. Instead, a form of art had to be created in which light, color, movement, sound, and space were the key elements. Fontana is known especially for the perforated monochrome paintings he made from 1949 onwards. The perforations were meant to create a connection between the canvas and the surrounding space.

Fontane, Theodor (1819-1898), German author known for his novels about Prussian society. Most of Fontane's stories involve Berlin's upper class in the 1800s, their social lives, morals, and personal conflicts. Fontane's works include *Trials and Tribulations* (1888), *Jenny Treibel* (1892), and his masterpiece, *Effi Briest* (1895).

German novelist and poet Theodor Fontane (1819-1898).

Fonteyn, Dame Margot (1919-1991), English prima ballerina of the Royal Ballet. Before World War II she had danced leads in *Giselle*, *Swan Lake*, and *The Sleeping Beauty*, and Frederick Ashton had begun choreographing works for her. She retired from the Royal Ballet in 1959 but continued to appear as a guest star, and in 1962 she formed a dance partnership with Rudolf Nureyev that won new international fame for both of them.

Food, frozen, food that is kept at a constant temperature of 0°F (-18°C). A widely used method of food preservation, freezing inhibits the growth of organisms that cause spoilage. Foods can be frozen slowly in home freezer compartments or quickly in commercial processing. Clarence Birdseye developed a quick-freezing method in 1925 to produce frozen foods commercially. Today foods are quick-frozen using blasts of cold air, refrigerator-cooled plates, and freezing with nitrogen, dry ice, or liquid freon. These methods cause little structural change in food, therefore resulting in a higher quality product.
See also: Birdseye, Clarence.

Food and Agriculture Organization (FAO), agency of the UN, established in

1945, with headquarters in Rome. It provides member nations with information on food and agricultural problems and with technical and financial aid.
See also: United Nations.

Food for Peace, federal program (Public Law 480), established 1954, regulating the donation and distribution of food to developing or underdeveloped countries.

Food poisoning, disease resulting from ingestion of unwholesome food, usually resulting in colic, vomiting, diarrhea, and general malaise. While a number of viruses, contaminants, and irritant and allergic factors may play a part, 3 specific microorganisms are commonly responsible: *Staphylococcus*, *Clostridium*, and *Salmonella* bacteria. Inadequate cooking, allowing cooked food to stand for long periods in warm conditions, and contamination of cooked and uncooked food by bacteria from humans are usual causes. Staphylococci may be introduced from a boil or from the nose of a food handler; they produce a toxin if allowed to grow in cooked food. Sudden vomiting and abdominal pain occur 2 to 6 hours after eating. Clostridium poisoning causes colic and diarrhea 10 to 12 hours after ingestion of contaminated meat. Salmonella enteritis causes colic, diarrhea, vomiting, and often fever, starting 12 to 24 hours after eating; poultry and human carriers are the usual sources. Botulism, caused by a toxin produced by Clostridium bacteria, is an often fatal form of food poisoning. In general, food poisoning is mild and of limited duration, and only the treatment of symptoms is needed; antibiotics rarely help.

Food preservation, techniques used to delay the spoilage of food. The most common forms of preservation are heating, sealing, refrigeration, and freezing. Heating destroys enzymes that over-ripen food and bacteria that are responsible for decay. Sealing in sterile cans or bottles isolates food from airborne bacteria. Refrigeration and freezing slow the enzyme action and the reproduction of the bacteria, and freezing preserves flavor better. Dehydration, irradiation, and preservatives are also used. Traditional means of preservation include smoking, salting, and pickling.

Fool's gold *See:* Pyrite.

Foot, anatomical structure, part of the lower extremity, bearing weight and providing locomotion. The bones that make up the foot and their arrangement are designed to form a stable structure, somewhat limited in range of movement.

Foot, Michael (1913-), British political leader. A member of Parliament for 30 years, Foot served as secretary of state for employment (1974-1975), Speaker of the House of Commons (1976-1979), and leader of the Labour Party (1980-1983).

Foot-and-mouth disease, or hoof-and-mouth disease, highly contagious viral disease affecting cattle, hogs, sheep, and other animals with cloven (split) hoofs. The disease is spread directly from animal to animal or indirectly by contaminated food, soil, or water. Symptoms include blisters in the mouth and in the split in the hoof, fever, and loss of appetite. Epidemics cause severe losses, and although vaccines are available, they provide only short-term protection and are expensive.

Football, American, in the United States and Canada, team sport in which the object is to deliver a ball over a goal line and to prevent the opposing team from reaching its own goal line at the opposite end of a demarcated field. Teams include 11 men. The field is 100 yd (91.4 m) long by 53 1/3 yd (48.7 m) wide. Lines are marked across the field at 5-yd (4.6-m) intervals. Behind each goal line is an area 10 yd (9.1 m) deep called the end zone, at the end of which is the goal post. A touchdown-running or passing the ball (to a receiver) over the goal line-is worth 6 points. The field goal, or place-kick over the crossbar and between the goalpost uprights, is worth 3 points. A safety, where a man in posession of the ball is downed in back of his own goal line, is 2 points. A conversion kick, allowed after each touchdown, is worth 1 point; an alternative in college play is the 2-point conversion, which allows the ball to be run or passed over the goal line. Officials may penalize a team by moving the ball closer to its goal line when it violates a rule. Minor fouls cost 5 yd (4.6 m). Major fouls are penalized 15 yd (13.7 m).

Forbes, Esther (1891-1967), U.S. author of historical novels. In 1943 she won the Pulitzer Prize in American history for her biography *Paul Revere and the World He Lived In.* In 1944 she won the Newbery Medal for her young adult novel *Johnny Tremain,* about a young apprentice during the time of the American Revolution.

Forbidden City, walled enclosure in Beijing (Peking), China, containing the imperial palace, its grounds, reception halls, and state offices. In imperial times, the Forbidden City was closed to the public.
See also: Beijing.

Force, in mechanics, physical quantity that, when acting on a body, either causes it to change its state of motion (i.e., imparts to it an acceleration), or tends to deform it (i.e., induces in it an elastic strain). Dynamical forces are governed by Newton's laws of motion, from the second of which it follows that a given force acting on a body produces in it an acceleration proportional to the force, inversely proportional to the body's mass, and occurring in the direction of the force. Forces are thus *vector* quantities with direction as well as magnitude. Four naturally occurring forces are gravity, electromagnetism, and the strong and weak nuclear forces within atoms.
See also: Mechanics.

Ford, Ford Madox (Ford Madox Hueffer; 1873-1939), English author. His novels *The Good Soldier* (1915) and the tetralogy *Parade's End* (1924-1928), describe the decline of the English upper classes before World War I. As first editor of *The English Review* (1908-1911), he encouraged such writers as Joseph Conrad (with whom he also collaborated), Ezra Pound, Robert Frost, and D.H. Lawrence.

Ford, Gerald Rudolph, Jr. (1913-), 38th president of the United States (1974-1977). Ford succeeded Richard M. Nixon as president after one of the gravest traumas in U.S. political history forced Nixon to resign.
Ford was christened Leslie King, Jr. When his parents were divorced, his mother's second husband, Gerald Rudolph Ford, adopted and renamed the boy. Ford worked his way through Yale University Law School and received his law degree in 1941.
Ford became known as a hard- working member of Congress and of his party. In 1953 he was named to the House Appropriations Committee and, in 1963, to the Warren Commission (set up to investigate the assassination of President John F. Kennedy). He became House minority leader in 1965.
In Oct. 1973 Spiro T. Agnew resigned as vice president and President Nixon nominated Ford to replace him. The Senate approved the nomination, making Ford the first appointed vice president in U.S. history. After Nixon's involvement in the Watergate scandal led to his own resignation in Aug. 1974, Ford was thrust into the presidency.
In world affairs, he continued the widely endorsed policies of his predecessor. He reaffirmed U.S. commitment to traditional allies and announced plans to visit China and the Soviet Union. Ford made the nation's serious economic problems a top priority. He worked to establish a broad-ranging program that would generate more economic activity and reduce unemployment, continue efforts against inflation, and help reduce U.S. dependence on foreign sources of energy. Ford experienced a serious setback when in 1975 the U.S. lost the wars in Vietnam and Cambodia.

Ford, Henry (1863-1947), U.S. automobile production pioneer. He produced his first automobile in 1896 and established the Ford Motor Company in Dearborn, Mich., in 1903. By adopting mass-assembly methods, and introducing the moving assembly line in 1913, Ford revolutionized automobile production. Ford saw that mass-produced cars could sell at a price within reach of the average U.S. family. Between 1908 and 1926 he sold 15 million Model T's. Ford was a para-

F

Henry Ford (1863-1947) in his first automobile in 1896.

F

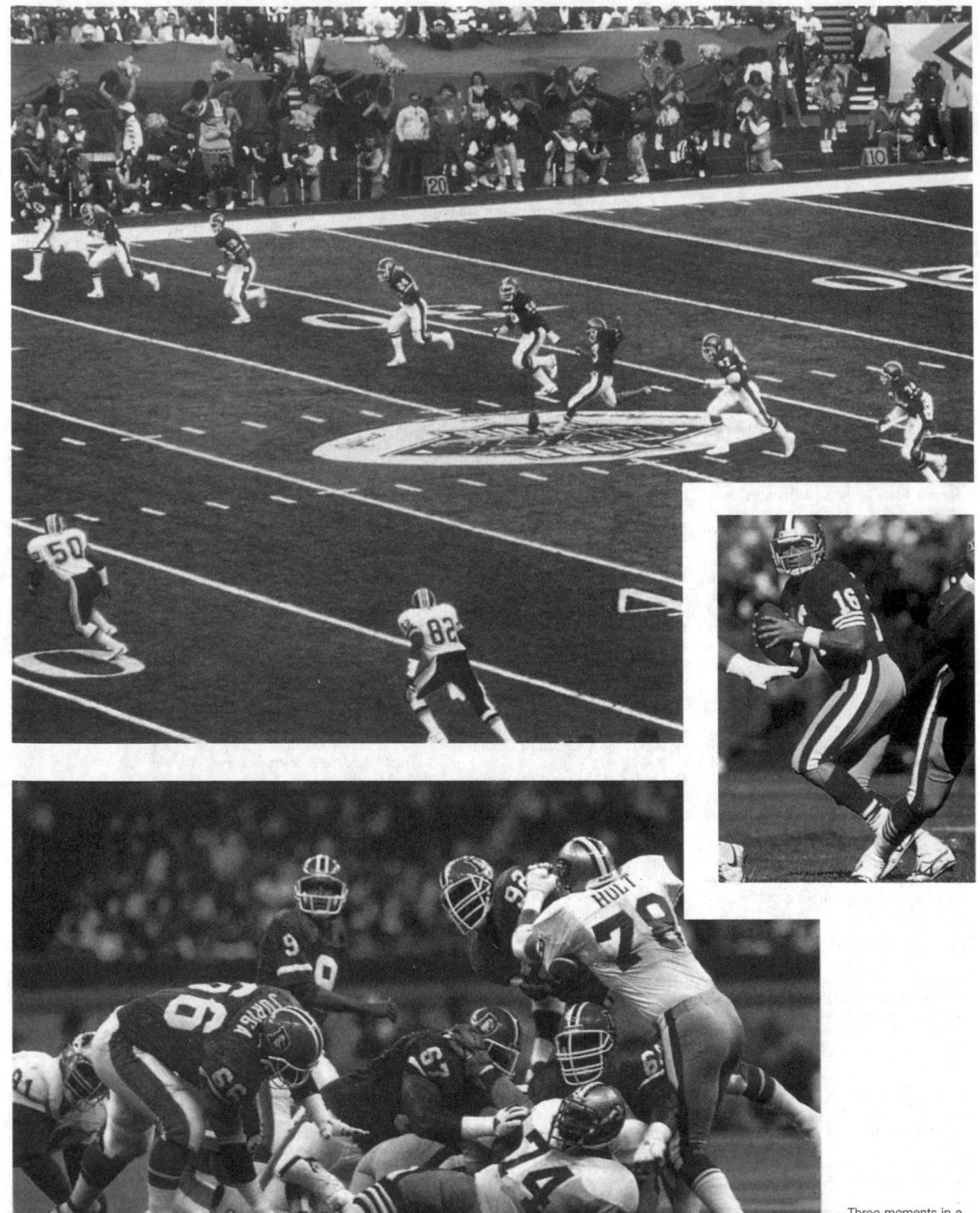

Three moments in a game: the kickoff, run and tackle, and the pass

doxical and often controversial character. Although a proud anti-intellectual, he set up several museums and the famous Ford Foundation. A violent antiunionist, he reduced the average working week, and introduced profit sharing and the highest minimum daily wage of his time. In 1938 he accepted a Nazi decoration and became a leading isolationist. At the outbreak of war, however, he built the world's largest assembly plant, to produce B-24 bombers.

Ford, John (1586-1640), English dramatist. Three tragedies, *'Tis Pity She's a Whore* (c.1627), *The Broken Heart* (c.1629), and *Love's Sacrifice* (1630), are his best-known works. Considered decadent by earlier critics because of his lack of moral comment, in the 20th century Ford is admired for his insight into human passion.

Ford, John (1895-1973), U.S. motion picture director. One of the great masters of his craft, he began directing the first of his more than 125 films in 1917. He won Academy awards for *The Informer* (1935), *The Grapes of Wrath* (1940), *How Green Was My Valley* (1942), and *The Quiet Man* (1952). In later years, his principal output consisted of Westerns, a form he had pioneered with such early films as *The Iron Horse* (1924) and *Stagecoach* (1939).

Ford Foundation, philanthropic corporation founded by Henry Ford in 1936. With assets of over $3 billion, it is the world's largest philanthropic trust. The foundation uses its funds for educational, cultural, scientific, and charitable purposes in the United States and abroad.

Ford Motor Company, one of the U.S. automotive industry giants, established in 1903 by Henry Ford. The Ford Motor Company has about 75 assembly and manufacturing plants in the United States, the largest of which is near Detroit, Mich. Manufacturing subsidiaries are Canada, Mexico, South America, Europe, and Australia. Ford is also a joint owner with companies in Asia, South Africa, and Turkey. Production of the Model N began in 1906, followed by the Model T in 1908 and the Model A in 1928. The company now builds Ford, Mercury, and Lincoln automobiles, trucks, tractors, and other farm and industrial machinery.

Ford's Theatre *See:* Lincoln, Abraham.

Foreign Legion, mercenary army created in 1831 by the French to save manpower in Algeria. The legion fought mainly outside France, in Morocco, Madagascar, Spain, Mexico, the Crimea, and Indochina, until Algerian independence (1962).

Foreign Service, diplomatic and consular employees of a country. They staff embassies and consulates, promote friendly relations between their country and countries in which they serve, advise on political and economic matters, protect and aid their country's citizens abroad, and deal with aliens seeking entry to a country.

Foreman, George Edward (1948-), U.S. boxer, world heavyweight champion from Jan. 1973 to Oct. 1974. He won the gold medal in the heavyweight competition in the 1968 Olympic Games in Mexico and turned professional in 1969. He had won 40 consecutive bouts when defeated by Muhammad Ali in 1974. Foreman retired in 1977, but returned to boxing 10 years later. In April of 1991, he once again fought for the championship against Evander Holyfield but lost a 12-round decision. In 1994 he won the world championship by knocking out Michael Moorer in the tenth round, thereby becoming the oldest heavyweight champion ever. He ended his boxing career in 1997.

Forensic science *See:* Crime laboratory.

Forest, area of land covered by trees. Forests are important for their economic, environmental, and recreational uses, and as habitats for plants, insects, birds, and other animals. As ecosystems, forests are classified as tropical rain forests, tropical seasonal forests, temperate deciduous forests, temperate evergreen forests, boreal forests, and savannas. They may also be classified by dominant tree type, such as needleleaf, coniferous, or deciduous.

Forest fire *See:* Forestry.

F

In the coniferous forest zone of northern Eurasia and North America, low temperatures keep the ground frozen for most of the year. Only hardy trees like spruce, fir and pine can tolerate the lack of water. In the Urals, the land is characterized by lakes and swamps. The region is known as 'taiga': swamp forest. Many of the animals are especially adapted to endure the long cold winters, and some of them migrate to this region for the summer only.

1. siberian jay (*Perisoreus infaustus*), nests in trees and feeds on caterpillars
2. red crossbill (*Loxia curvirostra*)
3. elk (or moose) (*Alces alces*)
4. black woodpecker (*Dryocopus martius*) with young
5. great grey owl (*Strix nebulosa*), feeds on small rodents
6. bohemian waxwings (*Bombycilla garrulus*)
7. goshawk (*Accipiter gentilis*) carrying a squirrel
8. eurasian red squirrel (*Sciurus vulgaris*), feeds on cones
9. nun moth (*Lymatria manacha*)
10. nun moth caterpillars
11. redshank sandpipers (*Tringa totanus*)
12. chipmunk (*Tamias sibericus*), being eaten by a
13. sable (*Martes zibellina*)
14. capercaillie (*Tetrao urogallus*)
15. blue throats (*Erithacus svevicus*)

Forest products, products derived from trees that since prehistoric times have provided food, shelter, clothing, and fuel. Most forest products are classified as wood, fiber, chemical, or fuel. From these, such things as lumber, paper, acetate, and charcoal are produced. About 1.5 million people are employed in the forest products industry in the United States. They produce about $120 billion worth of forest products annually.

Forestry, management of forests for productive purposes. The most important aspect of forestry is the production of lumber. Because of worldwide depletion of timber stocks, it has become necessary to view forests as renewable productive resources, and because of the time scale and area involved in the growth of a forest, trees need more careful planning than any other crop. Forestry work plans for a continuity of timber production by balancing planting and felling. Foresters also work to prevent and extinguish forest fires. Other important functions are disease, pest, and flood control. The forester must control the density and proportions of the various trees in a forest and ensure that people do not radically disturb a forest's ecological balance. Only 20% of the world's forests are being renewed, and timber resources are declining.

Forgery, in law, the making or altering of a written document with intent to defraud. Imitations of works of art, literature, and signatures are common forgeries. Counterfeit refers to forgery of objects, such as bills, coins, and gems.

Forget-me-not, any of various annual or perennial wild and garden flowers (genus

During the first planting and replantings of forests (after the trees have been cut), the forest soil must be well taken care of. As many stumps and loose roots as possible should be removed and the soil should be levelled, a task for which bulldozers are used.

Myosotis), native to North America, Europe, and Asia. Most have pink flower buds that become blue as the flower opens. It has long been a symbol of constancy. Yellow forget-me-not is a plant of western deserts.

Forging, shaping metal by hammering or pressing, usually when the workpiece is red

hot (about 400°-700°C) but sometimes when it is cold. Unlike casting, forging does not alter the granular structure of the metal, and hence greater strength is possible in forged than in cast metals. The most basic method of forging is that of the blacksmith, who heats the metal in an open fire (forge) and hammers it into shape against an anvil. Today, metals are forged between two dies, usually impressed with the desired shape. Techniques include *drop forging*, where the workpiece is held on the lower, stationary die, the other being held by a massive ram that is allowed to fall; *press forging*, where the dies are pressed together; and *impact forging*, where the dies are rammed horizontally together, the workpiece between.

Formaldehyde (HCHO), colorless, acrid, toxic gas; the simplest and most reactive aldehyde. Formaldehyde was discovered by A.W. von Hofmann in 1867. It is made by catalytic air oxidation of methanol vapor or of natural gas. Formaldehyde gas is unstable, and is usually stored as an aqueous solution, formalin, used as a disinfectant and preservative for biological specimens. Formaldehyde is used in the manufacture of pharmaceuticals, dyes, and plastics. Formaldehyde gas causes severe symptoms of the respiratory tract, and may be a carcinogen.
See also: Aldehyde.

Formalin *See:* Formaldehyde.

Formic acid (CH_2O_2), industrial chemical used to process textiles, leather, rubber, and other products. Produced from carbon monoxide and sodium hydroxide, formic acid is a strong-smelling, corrosive, colorless liquid.

A 19th-century blacksmith. A bellows (1) blew in air to increase the furnace temperature. An anvil comprised a tool hole (2), a punch hole (3), a face (4), and a pointed beak (5). The anvil body (6) was set on an elm block (7). A hot-coal rake (8) lay with other tools on a tool rail (9). After the hot iron was shaped by the smith (10) and the striker (11), it was cooled in the water trough (12). A floor mandrel (13) held other tools in use near the furnace.

Formosa *See:* Taiwan.

Forster, E(ward) M(organ) (1879-1970), English writer and critic, whose works reflected his sharp wit and graceful style. His most famous novels are *Howards End* (1910) and *A Passage to India* (1924), which illustrate Forster's interest in personal relationships and the racial and psychological impediments to these relationships. His other works include *Where Angels Fear to Tread* (1905), *The Longest Journey* (1907), *A Room with a View* (1908), and *Maurice* (1913-1914).

Forsythia, or golden bell, shrub (genus *Forsythia*) native to eastern Europe and Asia as far east as Japan. It is widely grown in the United States for ornamental purposes. It has slender, arching branches and yellow flowers that open in spring before the leaves.

Fortaleza (pop. 2,700,000), Brazil, the capital of the state of Ceará. Fortaleza is a port on the Atlantic Ocean. The city has cotton mills and sugar refineries. The main exports are sugar, coffee, cotton, hides, and carnauba wax. The Federal University of Ceará is here. Fortaleza was founded by the Portuguese in 1609.

Fort Knox, U.S. military reservation in Hardin County, north central Kentucky. Established in 1917 as a training camp, it was named for Major General Henry Knox, first secretary of war. It is now the site of the U.S. Army Armor Center, which includes the U.S. Gold Bullion Depository, and covers 110,000 acres (44,500 hectares).

Fort Lauderdale (pop. 150,000), city in southeastern Florida. Located 25 mi (40 km) north of Miami, it is a popular winter resort and tourist area. Although it is the site of a fort established in 1838, its development dates to 1906, when the draining of the mangrove swamps began. Crossed by a large number of waterways and canals, it is sometimes called the Venice of America. Port Everglades, the deepest harbor south of Norfolk and east of New Orleans, is located there.
See also: Florida.

Fort Sumter, fort in Charleston Harbor, S.C., where the first shots in the Civil War were fired on Apr. 12, 1861. When South Carolina seceded from the Union (1860), U.S. Major Robert Anderson received a rebel summons to surrender his garrison. He refused, Sumter was fired upon, and the war began. The fort was retaken when Confederates evacuated Charleston in Feb. 1865.

Fort Worth (pop. 454,000), city in northern Texas, seat of Tarrant County. Located on the Trinity River about 30 mi (48 km) west of Dallas, Fort Worth was founded in 1849 as an outpost against Native American attacks. The city became a major trading center during the cattle drives of the 1870s and was known as the place 'Where the West Begins.' It was incorporated in 1873 and has a council-manager government. Fort Worth

English writer and   (1879-1970).
critic E.M. Forster

is one of the major grain-storage and flour-milling centers in the southwest. It lies in the heart of one of the most important oil-producing regions of Texas and is the headquarters of numerous oil companies. One of the biggest aircraft factories in the country, and the largest stockyards and meat-processing plants in the South, are also major elements in Fort Worth's economy. The city is the home of Southwestern Baptist Theological Seminary, Texas Christian University, and Texas Wesleyan College. Its symphony orchestra and opera association are known throughout the nation.
See also: Texas.

Forty-Niners, name given to those who flooded into California following the gold strike of 1848. News of the gold discovery by James Marshall at Sutter's Mill started a migration from all over the world. By the end of 1849 California's population had swelled from 20,000 to over 107,000.
See also: Gold Rush.

Forum, public meeting or meeting place used for open discussion of current topics of general interest. In modern usage a forum may be a radio or TV program in which such current matters are discussed by leading personalities and authorities. The forum was the principal public square or marketplace in any ancient Roman city, where citizens gathered to discuss important issues, and where judicial and other public business was transacted. The forum contained colonnades, shops, temples, and other important buildings. The city of Rome had several forums, the oldest and best known being the Roman Forum below the Capitoline Hill.

Foscolo, Ugo (1778-1827), Italian author. His books include the novel, *The Last Letters of Jacopo Ortis* (1802) and the ode *The Sepulchers* (1806-1807). He left Italy in 1815 and spent the rest of his life in England, writing essays and teaching Italian.

Foss, Lukas (Lukas Fuchs; 1922-), German-born U.S. composer who developed a method of simultaneous improvisation and experimented with electronic effects, the use of prerecorded tape, and avant-garde composition, as in *Echoi* (1961-1963), *Cello Concerto* (1966), and *Fanfare* (1973). He conducted the Buffalo Philharmonic (1963-

1971) and was appointed music director of the Brooklyn Philharmonia in 1971.

Fossey, Dian (1932-1985), U.S. zoologist. A graduate of San Jose State College, Fossey went to Africa in 1963 to study the wild mountain gorilla. In 1966 she was selected by British anthropologist Louis Leakey to conduct a long-term study of the gorilla. Fossey studied the animals daily, learning their habits. When some of the gorillas were killed, she directed her work toward the protection of the animals from poachers and the preservation of their habitat. She founded the Karisoke Research Center in Rwanda, where she lived for 18 years. She was murdered in 1985. Her book *Gorillas in the Mist* (1983) and the movie with the same title (1988) tell her story.
See also: Zoology.

Fossil, evidence of ancient plant or animal life preserved in sediment or rock. Preservation of an organism in its entirety (i.e., unaltered hard and soft parts together) is exceptional. Entire mammoths have been preserved in Siberian permafrost. Unaltered hard parts are common in post-Mesozoic sediments but become increasingly scarce further back in geologic time. *Petrification* describes 2 ways in which the shape of hard parts of the organism may be preserved. In *permineralization* the pore spaces of the hard parts are filled by certain minerals (e.g., silica, pyrite, calcite) that infiltrate from the local groundwater. The resulting fossil is thus a mixture of mineral and organic matter. In many other cases substitution or replacement occurs, in which the hard parts are dissolved away but the form is retained by newly deposited minerals. Where this has happened very gradually, even microscopic detail may be preserved, but generally only the outward form remains. Often the skeletal materials are dissolved entirely, leaving either internal or external *molds*. The filling of a complete mold may also occur, forming a *cast*. The complete filling of a hollow shell interior may form a *core* or *steinkern* such as the corkscrewlike filling of a coiled snail shell. In the process of *carbonization* the tissues decompose, leaving only a thin residual carbon film that shows the outline of the organism's flattened form.

When this fish died and fell onto the calcareous floor of the sea, it was rapidly covered with new calcareous mud. In this material, the organic substance of the fish was rapidly dissolved, but its skeleton has been beautifully preserved.

Fossil fuel *See:* Energy supply.

Foster, Norman Robert (1935-), British architect, established Team 4 in 1964, together with his wife Wendy and Richard Rogers, called Foster Associates from 1967

F

F

onwards. Representative of 'high tech' architecture. Designed, among other things, the modern, glass-walled office building Willis, Faber, and Dumas in the old city of Ipswich (1972) and the Sainsbury Centre for the Visual Arts in Norwich (1975-1978). His skyscraper for the Hong Kong and Shanghai Banking Corporation in Hong Kong (1979-1985) drew attention. Other known works: the Stansted airport (1981-1991) near London, the tele communications building Torre de Collserola in Barcelona (1992), and the museum for contemporary art in Nîmes, Carré d'Art (1992). Also urban development, among others, the reconstruction of the Wilhelmina Pier in Rotterdam. Also furniture, including desk and desk chair *Nomos*. The largescale reconstruction of the Reichstag in Berlin, which was carried out in accordance with his design and includes a glass dome, was completed in 1999.

Foster, Stephen Collins (1826-1864), U.S. composer of over 200 songs and instrumental pieces. His 'Oh! Susannah,' 'My Old Kentucky Home,' and 'Old Black Joe' and other Southern dialect songs are essentially so simple and so popular that they are often mistakenly considered folk music.

Foucault, Jean Bernard Leon (1819-1868), French physicist. He is best known for showing the rotation of the earth with the Foucault pendulum, for inventing the gyroscope, and for accurately determining the velocity of light.
See also: Gyroscope; Pendulum.

Fouda, Farag (1915-1992), Egyptian author. Fouda was a great champion of Egypt's becoming a secular state, in which politics and religion are strictly divided, and he fiercely opposed Muslim fundamentalism. He mercilessly ridiculed and criticized fundamentalism in his newspaper articles and books. Much of his work was prohibited. He was murdered by a fundamentalist.

Foujita, Tsugouharu Tsuguji (1886-1968),

French painter, of Japanese origin. He painted very subtle still lives, portraits, and nudes. Became Roman Catholic in 1959 and called himself Léonard from then on. His subsequent work is mystical in nature.

Founding Fathers, statesmen of the American Revolution, in particular writers of the Constitution of the United States. They included George Washington, Benjamin Franklin, Alexander Hamilton, and James Madison.
See also: Constitution of the United States.

Foundry, metal casting plant. Founding is a process of pouring metals such as iron, aluminum, or lead into molds made with clay and sand. From this process, objects ranging from toy soldiers to automobile engine blocks are created.
See also: Casting; Forging.

Fouquet, Jean (c.1420-1480), French painter who helped bring the Italian Renaissance style to France. His miniatures, panels, portraits, and manuscript illuminations are realistic and precisely detailed. Among his finest works are the *Melun Diptych* (c.1450), and an illuminated Book of Hours for Étienne Chevalier.
See also: Renaissance.

Four Horsemen of the Apocalypse, allegorical biblical figures (Revelation 6:1-8). The red horse's rider represents war; the black's, famine; and the pale horse's, death. The rider on the white horse is usually taken to represent Christ.

Fourier, François Marie Charles (1772-1837), French Utopian socialist. Rejecting capitalism, he devised a social system based on cooperative, primarily farming communes of about 400 families. Fourierism gained considerable following in France and the United States, but attempts to put his theories into practice, as at Brook Farm, Mass., were short-lived.
See also: Socialism.

Fourier, Jean Baptiste Joseph, Baron (1768-1830), French mathematician best known for his equations of heat transmission and for showing that all periodic vibrations can be reduced to a series of simple, regular wave motions.

Fourteen Points, war objectives for the United States, proposed by President Woodrow Wilson in Jan. 1918, incorporated in the armistice of Nov. 1918. The points were that there should be open covenants of peace, freedom of the seas, abolition of trade barriers, general disarmament, settlement of colonial claims, evacuation of conquered Russian territories, evacuation and restoration of Belgium, return of Alsace-Lorraine to France, readjustment of Italian frontiers, autonomy for the subject peoples of Austria and Hungary, guarantees for the integrity of Serbia, Montenegro, and Romania, autonomy for the subject peoples of the Ottoman Empire, an independent Poland, and a general association of nations. These points formed the basis of the Treaty of Versailles and the League of Nations.
See also: Wilson, Woodrow; World War I.

Fourth of July *See:* Independence Day.

Fowl *See:* Chicken; Poultry farming.

Fowler, Henry Watson (1858-1933), English lexicographer, best known for his *A Dictionary of Modern English Usage* (1926). Fowler collaborated with his brother, Francis G. Fowler, on several reference works, including *The Concise Oxford Dictionary of Current English* (1911).

Fowles, John Robert (1926-   ), English novelist. His works include *The Magus* (1966; rev. version, 1978), *The French Lieutenant's Woman* (1969), *Daniel Martin* (1977), *Mantissa* (1982), and *A Maggot* (1995).

Fox, any of various small, bushy-tailed members of the dog family. Foxes feed mainly on small mammals and live alone or in pairs. The common red fox (*Vulpus fulva*) of the Northern Hemisphere is the quarry of British fox hunts; American foxes include the gray fox (*Urocyon cinereoargenteus*) and the desert kit fox (*Vulpus velox*). The Arctic fox (*Alopex lagopus*) lives in northern tundras and has a white winter coat. The insect-eating, bat-eared fox (*Otocyon megalotis*) is native to Africa.

Foxglove, plant (genus *Digitalis*) of Europe and Central Asia grown for its tall stem of hanging tubular flowers. The drug digitalis is extracted from its leaves and is used as a heart stimulant.

Foxhound, medium-sized hound originally used to hunt foxes. Standing 21-25 in (53-64 cm) at the shoulder and weighing 60-70 lb (27-32 kg), the foxhound, which has short, glossy black, white, or tan hair, is recognized as a breed by the American Kennel Club.

Fox terrier, breed of small dog developed in England in the mid-1800s to flush out

There is a rain of sparks, when molten casting iron is drained from the furnace. The molten iron is drained into a casting pan, which is brought to the casting site with the aid of pulleys. The fluid mass is then poured into a mold, by simply tilting the pan with a geared wheel. The draining hole in the furnace is stoppered with a plug of moist clay, pushed into the hole with a long pole. Later, when casting is again desired, this plug of baked clay will be pushed through the opening.

foxes during hunts. It measures about 15 in (38 cm) at the shoulder and weighs about 18 lb (8 kg). Two separate breeds have been developed: the wire fox terrier, with a rough, wiry white coat, often with black and brown patches, and the smooth fox terrier, with similar coloring but a smooth coat.

Foxx, James Emory (1907-1967), U.S. baseball player. In a 21-season career with the Philadelphia Athletics (1925-1935), the Boston Red Sox (1936-1942), the Chicago Cubs (1942-1944), and the Philadelphia Phillies (1945), Jimmy Foxx hit 534 home runs. His usual position was first base. He was elected to the Baseball Hall of Fame in 1951.

Fra Angelico (Guido di Pietro; 1400-1455), Italian painter and Dominican friar. His church frescoes (Convent of San Marco, Florence) and altarpieces combined traditionally bright, clear colors with the new use of perspective settings. His Tuscan backgrounds are among the great Renaissance landscapes.

Fraction, in mathematics, expression representing the ratio of 2 numbers. In the fraction $^3/_4$, 4, the number after or below the bar (the *denominator*) may be thought of as the total number of equal parts into which the unit has been divided, and 3, the number before or above the bar (the *numerator*) how many parts are being considered. In decimal fractions, the division of the numerator by the denominator is computed: $^3/_4=0.75$.
See also: Mathematics.

Fracture, break of a a bone. Diagnosis is made by X ray, which shows the breakline in a bone, and the identification of swelling and localized tenderness to pressure or percussion (tapping). Depending on the size and type of the fracture, strapping, an elastic bandage, a plaster cast, or metal fixation may be necessary for healing. In *simple* fractures the bone is completely broken but there is no wound through the skin. In *compound* fractures one end of the broken bone has penetrated and torn the skin. (This type is particularly dangerous, as it allows microorganisms to enter the wound.) In *comminuted* fractures the bone has broken into several smaller pieces. In *greenstick* fractures, common in the pliable bones of the young, the break only runs part of the way across the bone. The *stress* fracture is a gradually developing fault in bone caused by repetitions of a force. This common condition has been found in practically every bone in the body and often occurs in people who take unaccustomed prolonged exercise.
See also: Bone.

Fragonard, Jean-Honoré (1732-1806), French painter. An artist who worked in the rococo style, he was a noted portraitist. His work is characterized by a lightness of touch and a use of radiant color. Among his masterpieces are *The Swing* (1766) and *Fête at St Cloud* (1775), which convey the atmosphere of erotic playfulness and gaiety cultivated at the court of Louis XV.

France

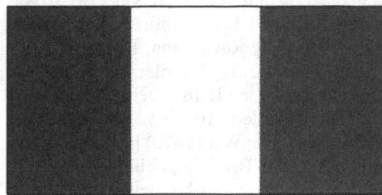

Capital:	Paris
Area:	210,026 sq mi
	(543,965 sq km)
Population:	59,766,000
Language:	French
Government:	Republic
Independent:	1871 (republic)
Head of gov.:	Prime minister
Per capita:	US$ 25,400
Monetary unit:	1 French franc
	= 100 centimes

France (official name République Française), republic of Western Europe, the third largest country of Europe (in area) after Germany and the Russian Federation.
Land and climate. Roughly square, France extends for about 600 mi (966 km) from Flanders to the Spanish border, and for about the same distance west to east. It borders the sea in 3 directions and has a coastline of almost 1,900 mi (3,058 km). Beyond the mainland the French Republic includes the Mediterranean island of Corsica and the overseas departments of Réunion, Guyana, Martinique, and Guadeloupe. In general, the western and northern parts of France are

Until the 19th century, small insular communities subsisted on cattle-raising and home industry in very isolated valleys. These sources of income have been replaced by services for tourism, work in the cities along the foot of the mountain chains, and in industries, utilizing hydroelectricity.

composed of low-lying plains and plateaus, while the eastern and southern sections are characterized by hilly or mountainous terrain. The 3 major mountain ranges are the Pyrénées, the Alps, and the Massif Central. There are 4 major river systems. The Rhône rises in the Swiss Alps and flows swiftly south through Provence to empty into the Mediterranean, west of Marseilles. The Garonne rises in the Pyrenees and flows through the Aquitaine Basin to empty into the Bay of Biscay through a long estuary known as the Gironde. The Seine drains most of the large Paris Basin, flowing through Paris, then goes on to Rouen and finally joins the English Channel at Le Havre. It is the most navigable of French rivers. The Loire, the longest river of France, flows from the southeastern portion of the Massif Central north to Orléans, then west to the Atlantic at St. Nazaire. Except for the Mediterranean coast, the climate is mild. The north and west have warm summers, mild winters, and a moderate rainfall. The Mediterranean coast has mild winters and hot summers; some areas have fewer than 50 days of rain a year.

In the northern and central regions there are forests of oak and beech, with smaller numbers of poplars and pines. The high hills south of the Loire grow heather and gorse. The roads in much of France are often planted with long lines of poplars and other trees. Oak and chestnut are common in the west and alluvial valleys. In the Massif Central area are forests of beech and chestnut. In the south the vegetation is mainly evergreen. Among forest animals are deer, martens, and badgers. The many field animals include foxes, hedgehogs, mice, rats, rabbits, and moles. Mountain species include the chamois, marmot, and ibex. Birdlife is also plentiful. The rivers and mountain streams contain many kinds of fish. Lobsters and crayfish are among the products of the Mediterranean, Biscay, and the English Channel. Among the main mineral resources of France are coal, iron ore, and bauxite (for aluminum); the bauxite reserves of central France are among the richest in the world.
People. The accessibility of France brought many invasions and a broad mingling of racial and national types including Celtic, Roman, Germanic, Scandinavian, and Basque. After about the 9th century A.D., large-scale migrations ceased, and the many peoples gradually combined to become one nation with a single language. Among the many dialects, that of the Ile de France (in which Paris is located) came to dominate, and became the official language in the 16th century. There are minority groups speaking other languages, including Breton in Brittany, Basque and Catalan in the southwest, Italian in Corsica and the Nice area, German in Alsace and Lorraine, and Flemish in the Dunkirk region. A great number of castles, churches, cathedrals, parks, libraries, museums, and other cultural attractions are scattered throughout France. The nation is highly conscious of its cultural heritage, and national laws protect the more important monuments of the past. Among the best known of such institutions are the Louvre Museum and the Bibliothèque Nationale (National Library) in Paris. The

F

F

The Dordogne River flows through a fertile agricultural area. The landscape is characterized by maize and wheat fields and clusters of high trees.

theater flourishes, and many of the principal ones are subsidized by the state, for example, the Comédie Française, the Opéra Nationale, and the Opéra Comique.

Economy. France is a major agricultural and industrial country. Leading crops include wheat, oats, rye, corn, sugar beets, rice, and all kinds of fruits. Millions of beef and dairy cattle, sheep, and hogs are reared. France is an important silk producer, and it leads in the production of high-quality wines. About 30% of the land is forested. Industry includes iron and steel production, oil refining and petrochemicals, aircraft, automobiles, and textiles. Paris is the chief manufacturing center. Tourism is important, and so is the production of high-fashion clothing, gloves, perfume, jewelry, and watches.

History. Greeks founded Marseilles about 600 B.C. The country was progressively settled and unified under the Gauls, Romans, and Franks. On Charlemagne's death (A.D. 814) the Frankish Empire disintegrated and feudal rulers became powerful. Their territories were increasingly welded together under the Capetians (987-1328), and the Hundred Years War (1338-1453) saw the eviction of the English. Under Louis XI (1461-1483) and later monarchs, royal power was strengthened, reaching its zenith with Louis XIV (1643-1715). Continuing royal extravagance culminated in the French Revolution (1789), the execution of Louis XVI, and the establishment of the First

During grape harvesting time, the heaviest work is done by the strongest man. He collects the grapes from the pickers and throws his load into a large vat, having to climb a small ladder to do so.

Republic. The Bourbon restoration following the downfall of Napoleon (1815) was short-lived, and Louis Philippe was put on the throne (July Revolution, 1830). After his deposition, Louis Napoleon headed the Second Republic (1848), then made himself Emperor Napoleon III (1852). Defeat in the Franco-Prussian War (1870) led to his downfall and to the Third Republic. World War I left France victorious but devastated, and in World War II the country was occupied by Germany (1940). The Fourth Republic (1946) proved unstable and Gen. Charles de Gaulle was recalled to head the Fifth Republic (1958). He established a strong presidential government and gave independence to most French possessions (notably Algeria, 1962). He pursued conservative policies at home and stressed greater independence from the United States in foreign policy. After de Gaulle resigned over a constitutional issue (1969), his conservative policies were maintained by his successors Georges Pompidou and Valéry Giscard d'Estaing. In 1981 François Mitterand, a Socialist, was elected president and instituted substantial changes in French domestic policy. In 1986 Conservatives won control of the Parliament, putting Jacques Chirac in office as prime minister, but Mitterand regained control in the 1988 elections. Chirac became president in 1995. In the same year, after nearly 30 years, France began to reintegrate itself back into the North Atlantic Treaty Organization (NATO) by sending a representative to NATO's military committee and by taking part in meetings of NATO defense ministers. Also that year proposed cuts in government pensions led to widespread strikes. The strikes lasted more than three weeks and severly disrupted the French economy. During 1995-1996 France came under international criticism for conducting a series of underground nuclear tests in French Polynesia. In 1997 the Socialists won the parliamentary elections. Jospin became Prime Minister. In spite of the fact that Chirac had been involved in a corruption scandal, he was re-elected President in 2002. When his party won the parliamentary elections in a landslide victory, it meant the end of the 'cohabitation' period (in which the government and the President are from different parties). The Front National of the right-wing Le Pen did not obtain a single seat at these elections.

France, Anatole (Jacques Anatole François Thibault; 1844-1924), French novelist and critic. Though he believed in and worked for social justice, his work is deeply pessimistic. Among his best-known books are *Penguin Island* (1908) and *The Revolt of the Angels* (1914). He won the 1921 Nobel Prize in literature.

Francesca, Piero della *See:* Piero della Francesca.

Francis, 2 kings of France. **Francis I** (1494-1547), king from 1515, strengthened royal power at the expense of the nobility. Failing in his candidacy for Holy roman emperor (1519), he conducted costly wars against the Habsburg emperor Charles V, including abortive Italian campaigns. Although he su-

ppressed Protestantism, he fostered Renaissance ideals and was a great patron of arts and letters. He was also a great builder of palaces. **Francis II** (1544-1560), king from 1559 and first husband of Mary Queen of Scots, was dominated by the House of Guise and his mother, Catherine de Medicis.

An equestrian portrait of King Francis I (reigned from 1515 to 1547), by court painter François Clouet (approximately 1520-1572).

Francis, Richard Stanley (Dick) (1920-), English jockey and writer. His father owned a racing stable, so he grew up around horses. He served in the Royal Air Force during World War II, after which time he became an amateur jockey and then a professional jockey in 1948. During the 1953-1954 season, he won more races than any of his colleagues, and in 1956, he almost won the Grand National on one of the British Queen Mother's horses. He withdrew in 1957 and became a sports reporter for the Sunday Express. His first detective novel, *Dead Cert*, was published in 1962. It takes place against a background of horse racing, as do all of his subsequent novels. Francis' books excel due to their authentic descriptions of the environment rather than their intrigues, which mainly depend on exciting events. Other novels include *Flying Finish* (1966), *Rat Race* (1970), *In the Frame* (1977), *Reflex* (1980), *Comeback* (1991), and *Field of Thirteen* (1998). *The Sport of Queens* (1957) is his autobiography.

Franciscans, largest order in the Roman Catholic Church. The order was founded by St. Francis of Assisi between 1209 and 1224. Franciscans were called Gray Friars for the color of their habits (modern habits are dark brown). Dissension within the First Order divided it into 3 main branches, the Observants (Friars Minor), Conventuals (Friars Minor Conventual), and Capuchins. The Second Order are nuns, known as Poor Clares for their foundress St. Clare. The Third Order is mainly a lay fraternity, though some members live in community under vows.

Francis de Sales, Saint (1567-1622), Fren-

F

ch nobleman, Roman Catholic bishop of Geneva-Annecy from 1603. Author of popular works such as *Introduction to the Devout Life* (1608), he was respected even by the Calvinists for his good nature and humility. He helped found the Order of the Visitation (1610). He was canonized in 1665. His feast day is Jan. 29.

Francis Ferdinand (1863-1914), Austrian archduke and heir apparent of the Austro-Hungarian throne. The assassination of the archduke and his wife, Sophie, in Sarajevo, Yugoslavia by the Serbian Gavrilo Princip precipitated the outbreak of World War I. *See also:* World War I.

Francis II (1768-1835), last emperor of the Holy Roman Empire and ruler of Austria. A member of the royal Habsburg family, he was crowned on the death of his father, Leopold II (1792). Francis II was a conservative monarch who opposed ideas of the French Revolution and political reform. Upon Napoleon's victory in Austria (1806), the Holy Roman Empire came to an end. For political reasons, Francis II allowed his daughter, Marie-Louise, to marry Napoleon (1810), although he aligned himself with those who eventually defeated Napoleon. *See also:* Holy Roman Empire.

Francis Joseph I, or Franz Josef I (1830-1916), emperor of Austria-Hungary (1848-1916) and king of Hungary from 1867. A member of the Habsburg family. He came to the throne in a year of revolutions and was at first highly absolutist. He suppressed a Hungarian revolt in 1849, but in 1867 further unrest forced him to create the dual (Austro-Hungarian) monarchy, giving Hungary internal autonomy. Alliance with Germany (1879) and Italy (1882) created the Triple Alliance. His harsh policies against Serbia were among the causes of World War I. He was a conservative autocrat and a patron of arts and learning. His only son, Rudolph, committed suicide in 1889, and his wife Elizabeth and grand nephew and heir apparent, Francis Ferdinand, were both assassinated (1898 and 1914 respectively). *See also:* Austria-Hungary; Habsburg, House of.

Francis of Assisi, Saint (1182?-1226), Italian Roman Catholic mystic, founder of the Franciscans. In 1205 he turned away from his extravagant life and wealthy merchant family and entered a religious life of utter poverty. He was given oral sanction by Pope Innocent III to form an order of friars in 1209. With his many followers Francis preached and ministered to the poor in Italy and abroad, stressing piety, simplicity, and the love of all living things. Eventually the order expanded beyond the control of its founder; Francis relinquished the leadership in 1221. His feast day is Oct. 4. *See also:* Franciscans.

Francis Xavier *See:* Xavier, Saint Francis.

Francium, chemical element, symbol Fr; for physical constants see Periodic Table. Francium was discovered by Marguerite Perey in 1939. It is found in uranium miner-

als and is formed by the decay of actinium. Francium can also be produced by bombarding thorium with protons. It is the heaviest member of the alkali metal series and the most unstable of the first 101 elements. The longest lived isotope, francium-223, has a half-life of 22 minutes.

Franck, César Auguste (1822-1890), Belgian-French composer. Organist of St. Clothilde, Paris, from 1858, he became a professor at the Paris Conservatory in 1872. Though at first little appreciated, his compositions greatly influenced French Romantic music. Among his famous works are the tone poem *The Accursed Hunter* (1882) and the *Symphony in D minor* (1888).

Franco, Francisco (1892-1975), Spanish general, dictator of Spain from 1939. Franco commanded Spanish troops in Spanish Morocco 1912-1927, helping to suppress rebellion against colonial domination. In 1934 he helped put down a leftist revolt in Spain. After leftists won national elections in 1935, the military plotted to overthrow the government. Civil war broke out in 1936, and Franco became commander in chief and dictator of the right-wing Nationalists, supported by the fascist governments of Italy and Germany. In the post-World War II period his rule became less totalitarian, but he retained power. In the late 1960s increasing unrest caused him to harden the regime once more; he remained in control until shortly before his death, when he named Prince Juan Carlos to rule as king and successor. *See also:* Spain.

Franco-Prussian War (July 1870-May 1871), war arising from Prussian premier Otto von Bismarck's desire to unify the German states against a common enemy and Napoleon III's fear of an alliance against him if a Prussian prince succeeded to the Spanish throne. Provoked by the 'Ems dispatch' (Bismarck's version of French demands concerning the Spanish question), France declared war; the more efficient Prussians trapped a large French army at Metz, and in Sept. 1870 captured the main

Francis of Assisi had a great love of nature and 'spoke' with animals. Here we can see him on a painting, that resembles the fresco from the famous series painted by Giotto (1267-1337). To be seen in the Louvre in Paris.

French army and Napoleon himself at Sedan. The Second Empire fell, and Paris was besieged; despite vigorous resistance led by Léon Gambetta, the city capitulated in Jan. 1871. William I of Prussia was declared German emperor at Versailles, and Germany was thus unified. In the treaty, France lost Alsace-Lorraine and incurred crushing indemnities. *See also:* Bismarck, Prince Otto von; Germany.

Frank *See:* Franks.

Frank, Anne (1929-1945), German born Dutch Jew who with her family lived in hiding from the Nazis in Amsterdam (1942-1944). Betrayed and sent to a concentration camp, she died there of typhus. Her diary, published in 1947, provided the material for a popular play and film. In 1998, five previously unpublished pages were published. They had been withheld by her father Otto Frank. *See also:* Holocaust.

Frankenstein, novel by Mary Shelley (1818). In an attempt to recreate life, its title character makes a hideous, suffering creature who seeks to torment its creator. The name has become attached to the creature, particularly as portrayed in film versions more or less loosely related to the novel. *See also:* Shelley, Mary Wollstonecraft.

Frankenthaler, Helen (1928-), U.S. painter whose work is considered transitional between abstract expressionism and color-field painting. She often uses stains and diluted paints to achieve her effects.

Frankfurt (pop. 651,000), city in central Germany, on the Main River. A major transportation center, it is one of the busiest European inland ports, with a large airport and a sophisticated network of highways and railroads. It was the original home of the Rothschild family and remains a banking and commerce center. A Roman fort, it became a Frankish settlement in A.D. 500, and flourished under the Holy Roman Empire. It was rebuilt after being heavily bombed by

A grenadier of the French imperial guard (left), sharing a drink with a franc-tireur (right), one of the guerrilla, or partisan soldiers that helped with the defence of France during the Franco-Prussian War. Because francs-tireurs were not affiliated with the national army of France, they were considered spies and were executed when captured.

F

Allied forces in World War II. The birthplace of Goethe, it is a center of cultural and intellectual activity.
See also: Germany.

Frankfurter, Felix (1882-1965), U.S. Supreme Court justice (1939-1962), legal adviser to presidents Woodrow Wilson and Franklin D. Roosevelt. He advocated the doctrine of judicial restraint, minimizing the judiciary's role in the process of government; he was equally opposed to attempts to obstruct 'progressive' legislation and to attempts to further it by undue interpretation.
See also: Supreme Court of the United States.

Franklin, Benjamin (1706-1790), U.S. printer, publisher, writer, politician, economist, scientist, statesman, and diplomat. At the start of his career he made his fortune as a publisher and printer and derived substantial revenue from writing his famous Poor Richard's almanacs (published annually between 1732 and 1757). As a writer, however, he is best revealed in his personal letters, journals, and autobiography, where he appears the most pragmatic of idealists, the most haphazard of scientists, and, most particularly, a witty and cynical observer of society. As a scientist, Franklin had practical ingenuity and produced bifocals and the Franklin stove. His famous experiment with the key and kite during an electrical storm, which confirmed that lightning was actually electricity, is typical of his genius. He served on the committee that drafted the Declaration of Independence. In 1778 he was appointed minister to France. Returning to Philadelphia in 1787, he was an influential figure in the drafting of the Constitution.

Franklin, John Hope (1915-), black U.S. historian, educator, and author of books on African American history, including *From Slavery to Freedom* (1947), *The Emancipation Proclamation* (1963), and *Racial Equality in America* (1976).

Franklin, Rosalind Elsie (1920-1958), British chemist and biologist. Her contributions, including information leading to the construction of a deoxyribonucleic acid (DNA) model (1953), made use of X-ray diffraction technique.
See also: Biology.

Franklin, Sir John (1786-1847), British rear admiral and Arctic explorer. In expeditions during 1819-1822 and 1825-1827 he charted territory from Hudson Bay North to the Arctic. He set out in 1845 with 2 ships to find the Northwest Passage; trapped in the ice, the entire expedition perished and was not traced until 1859.
See also: Northwest Passage.

Franklin's gull (*Larus pipixcan*), insect-eating land-based bird. It spends summers on the prairies of North America and winters in Louisiana and South America. The Franklin's gull is about 14 in (36 cm) long and is white and gray.

Franks, Germanic tribes, originally living east of the Rhine. In the 3rd-5th centuries

A.D. they repeatedly invaded Gaul and finally overran it (486). Clovis I united the disparate tribes under his rule, founding the Christian Merovingian dynasty; this was weakened by internal conflict, and finally deposed by the Carolingians in the 8th century. Under the rule of Charlemagne the Franks reached the height of their power. France and Franconia in Germany are named for them.

Franz Josef Land, group of 85 islands in the Arctic Ocean. Northernmost land in the Eastern Hemisphere, these islands, which were discovered in 1873, were claimed by the Soviet Union in 1926. They cover about 8,000 sq mi (21,000 sq km), and are uninhabited. Temperatures range from an average of 10°F (-12°C) or more in the summer to an average of -22°F (-30°C) in the winter.

Fraser, Dawn (1937-), Australian female swimmer, made a name for herself by winning the 100m freestyle at the Olympic Games in 1956, 1960, and 1964. She also won Olympic gold in the 4 x 100m freestyle relay race (1956). Fraser was the first woman to swim the 100m freestyle within one minute: 59.9 seconds in 1962.

Fraser, John Malcolm (1930-), Australian prime minister (1975-1983). First elected to Parliament in 1955, he served in various posts in Liberal Party governments, 1966-1971. In 1975 he became Liberal leader and later prime minister. His party easily won re-election in 1977. He pursued a policy of cutbacks in public expenditures in order to halve the inflation rate; however, a high unemployment rate continued in the country.

Fraser, Malcolm (1930-), Australian politician, a member of the lower house for the Liberal County Party since 1955. Belongs to the right wing of his party. Held a variety of ministerial posts; premier as of 1975; succeeded by the Labor politician Bob Hawke in 1983. His foreign policy in particular, was more traditional than that of the previous Labor government.

Fraser River, river in British Columbia, 850 mi (1,370 km) long, named for Simon Fraser, who explored it in 1808. It is famous for its salmon fisheries, and is an important shipping route. The Fraser rises in the Rocky Mountains, flows between the Rocky and Caribou ranges, then turns south and west to empty into the Georgia Strait south of Vancouver. It is navigable for about 90 mi (145 km) from its mouth.

Fraud, in law, any willful action intended to cheat another person by false pretenses or misrepresentation. The remedy granted to someone who can prove fraud is either compensatory damages or cancellation of the fraudulent contract.

Fraunhofer, Joseph von (1787-1826), a German optician and physicist. He was the first to make a careful study of the dark lines that appear in the solar spectrum, and these lines (and similar ones from other sources) were named in his honor. By analyzing Fraunhofer lines, scientists later learned to

identify elements in the sun and other astronomical bodies. Fraunhofer began work as a journeyman in an optical workshop in 1806, and quickly advanced as he made original contributions to optical science and developed technically superior telescopes, microscopes, and other optical instruments In 1814, he devised a diffraction grating for measuring wavelengths of rays of light. In 1823 he became director of the Physics Museum of the Bavarian Academy of Sciences.

Frazer, Sir James George (1854-1941), British social anthropologist. In *The Golden Bough: A Study in Magic and Religion* (1890; enlarged 1907-1915) he proposed a parallel evolution of thought in all peoples, from magic through religion to science, each mode of thought with its distinct notion of cause and effect.
See also: Anthropology.

Frazier, Joe (1944-), American boxer, became Olympic heavyweight champion in Tokyo in 1964. After becoming a professional in 1965, he claimed the world title for heavyweights from Jimmy Ellis on 2nd February 1970. Frazier lost his title to George Foreman in 1973. Characteristics of his game were the many victories owing to his powerful left-hook knockout punch.

Freckle, small area of skin pigmentation, usually occurring on the face, arms, and hands. Freckles are most frequently found in fair-skinned blonds and redheads because the pigment cells in their skin respond only slightly and irregularly to sunlight. The tendency to form freckles is often inherited.

Frederick, name of 3 Holy Roman Emperors. **Frederick I Barbarossa** (1123?-1190) was elected king of Germany in 1152. Having pacified Germany, where he promoted learning, primary and secondary educational systems, and economic growth, he occupied Lombardy and was crowned king of Italy in 1154 and Holy Roman emperor in 1155. He was drowned while leading the Third Crusade, and passed into legend as Germany's savior. **Frederick II** (1194-1250) became king of Sicily in 1198 and of Germany in 1211. He was crowned Holy Roman emperor in 1220. Made titular king of Jerusalem in 1227, he acquired territory in the Holy Land and was crowned in 1229. He was continually at odds with the papacy and was excommunicated 3 times. A capable administrator, scholar, and patron of the arts, he went into a decline after a serious defeat at Parma in 1248. **Frederick III** (1415-1493) was chosen king of Germany in 1440 and obtained election as Holy Roman emperor in 1452 by making concessions to the papacy, weakening the empire.
See also: Holy Roman Empire.

Frederick (Prussia), name of 3 kings of Prussia. **Frederick I** (1657-1713), elector of Brandenburg from 1688, sought the title of king from the Emperor Leopold I. In 1700 he obtained it in exchange for military assistance and in 1701 he crowned himself king of Prussia, which was the major part of his domain. **Frederick II (the Great)** (1712-

F

The sympathy for French culture of Frederick the Great was evident from the way he dressed (print by C. Townley of a painting by Bock).

1786) was one of the most influential 18th-century monarchs. As a boy his inclinations were artistic rather than military. He succeeded his father Frederick William I, in 1740. He almost immediately used his father's strong army to win Silesia from Austria, thus precipitating the War of the Austrian Succession. There followed a period of peace, which he used to strengthen Prussia, encouraging both arts and commerce. Fearing attack by an alliance of Austria, Russia, and France, he made a pre-emptive attack on Saxony in 1756, beginning the Seven Years War, from which Prussia emerged unscathed but exhausted. Frederick rebuilt the economy at considerable personal expense. Through the partition of Poland and the War of the Bavarian Succession he made further territorial gains for Prussia. By the end of his reign he had doubled the country's area and left it rich, powerful, more humanely governed, and dominant in Germany. **Frederick III** (1831-1888), son of Emperor William I, was cultivated and liberal. A distinguished army commander, he was a determined opponent of Bismarck's imperial policies. He died of cancer only 3 months after his coronation. *See also:* Prussia.

Frederick the Great *See:* Frederick (Prussia).

Frederick William (1620-1688), elector of Brandenburg from 1640, known as the Great Elector. By skillful shifting of alliances in an attempt to establish a balance of power, he was able to shield his country from the worst of the Thirty Years War and add Prussia to Brandenburg (1660). This and the modern army he created laid the foundations for the country's future predominance in Germany.

Frederick William I (1688-1740), king of Prussia from 1713. He centralized and radically reformed his administration. He spent freely on building up a powerful army but was otherwise frugal to the point of miserliness.
See also: Prussia.

Frederik, or **Frederick**, name of Danish kings, including 2 of the House of Schleswig-Holstein-Sonderburg-Glücksburg. **Frederik VIII** (1843-1912) was born in Copenhagen and ruled from the time of his father's death in 1906 until his own death. His sister was Queen Alexandra of England and his brother was King George I of Greece. **Frederik IX** (1899-1972) was married to Princess Ingrid of Sweden, spent 35 years as a crown prince, then ruled as king of Denmark from 1947 until his death.

Free enterprise system *See:* Capitalism.

Freemasonry *See:* Masonry.

Free-piston engine, engine that produces hot gas, which is used to run turbines. It was invented in the 1920s by the Spanish engineer, Pateras Pescara. Able to burn almost any liquid fuel, this engine has facing pairs of pistons that move back and forth from the fuel ignition and resulting air compression.

Freesia, sweet-scented flowering plant (genus *Freesia*) of the iris family, originating in South Africa. The flowers, which are most often white, yellow, or purple, grow in clusters on long stalks.

Freethinker, person who does not accept religious dogma. The English philosopher Anthony Collins used the word in *Discourse of Freethinking* (1713), an argument against the authority of the church. Freethinking movements were active in 18th-century England, Germany, and France. The necessity for such movements diminished with the establishment of freedom of religion.

Freetown (pop. 1,300,000), capital of Sierra Leone on the Atlantic Ocean. Largest city and port in the country, situated on one of the best natural ports of West Africa; marine base. Trade center for, among other things, palm oil, cola nuts, cocoa, ginger, diamonds and other minerals. Shipbuilding, clothing industry, paint, leather, fish processing, and soap industry; petroleum refinery. University (1967) and airport. Established by the British in 1787 as a place of residence for freed slaves. Re-established in 1792, after the population died out within a few years due to illness. The plan to turn this area into a country for freed American slaves did not get off the ground. The peninsula was proclaimed a British colony in 1808. Buildings dating back to the beginning of the colony include the Fourah Bay College (1827) and the Anglican St George's cathedral (1827).

Free trade, international commerce, free from tariffs, quotas, or other legal restriction, except nonrestrictive tariffs levied for revenue only. The opposite of free trade is protectionism. Among early advocates of free trade were the physiocrats, Adam Smith, David Ricardo, and J.S. Mill. Modern economists generally accept free trade but advocate varying degrees of protection to safeguard employment and developing industries, as in the theories of J.M. Keynes. The United States had traditionally been protectionist but after World War II became committed to free trade.

Free verse (from French *vers libre*), verse without conventional rhythm or meter, relying instead upon the cadences of the spoken language. It was first developed in 19th-century France as a reaction to the extreme formality of accepted styles. Among its exponents in English are Walt Whitman, D.H. Lawrence, Ezra Pound, and T.S. Eliot.

Freeze-drying, or lyophilization, process that removes water from foods, drugs, and other substances, preserving the items for later use. Unlike other food-drying processes, the costly freeze-drying method freezes the items, then changes any frozen moisture into water vapor in refrigerated vacuum chambers. Freeze-dried substances retain most of their original characteristics, do not shrink, and are easily dissolvable.

Frege, Gottlob (1848-1925), German logician, father of mathematical logic. Inspired by the earlier work of Leibniz, he tried to show that all mathematical truths could be derived logically from a few simple axioms. After criticism that his system contradicted itself, he wrote little more. However, his work did influence later philosophers such as Bertrand Russell and Ludwig Wittgenstein.
See also: Logic.

French *See:* French language.

French Academy *See:* Académie Française.

French, John Denton Pinkstone, 1st Earl of Ypres (1852-1925), British field marshal, commander of the British Expeditionary Force at the beginning of World War I. He was relieved of his command after the costly retreat from Mons and the battles of Ypres and Loos (1914-1915).

French, Marilyn (1929-), American female author, literary spokeswoman for the women's protest in the US. Made her debut with the novel *The Book As World; James Joyce's 'Ulysses'* (1976). Her feministic novel *The Women's Room* (1977) became a worldwide bestseller. She also wrote, among others, *The Bleeding Heart* (1980), *Beyond Power. On Women, Men, and Morals* (1985), *Her Mother's Daughter* (1987), *The War Against Women* (1992), *Our Father* (1993), *Season in Hell* (1998), and *Women's History of the World* (2000).

French and Indian Wars, conflict over control of North America that erupted into a series of wars involving England and its North American colonies against France and the colony of New France: King William's War (1689-1697), Queen Anne's War (1702-1713), King George's War (1744-1748), and the French and Indian War (1754-1763). In Europe these wars are known, respectively, as the War of the League of Augsburg, the War of the Spanish Succession, the War of

F

the Austrian Succession, and the Seven Years War, but Americans generally use these names only for the European phase of each war. All of these wars combined the struggle for specific North American territories between France and Britain with their battle for world power. In each struggle the French lost some territory, and in the last war they were forced entirely out of the North American mainland.

Both French and English fur trading was expanding, and territories were not clearly marked, so disputes became increasingly frequent.

French Canada *See:* Canada; Quebec.

French Canadians *See:* Canada; Canadian literature; Quebec.

French Equatorial Africa, 4 territories in Central Africa that were colonized by France in 1839 and became the independent countries of Gabon, Chad, Congo, and Central African Republic in 1960. Covering an area of about 969,000 sq mi (2.5 million sq km), these countries are rich in timber, minerals, farming, and livestock.

French Foreign Legion *See:* Foreign Legion.

French Guiana, French overseas department on the northeast coast of South America. It is bounded by Surinam on the west and Brazil on the east and south, and consists of a strip of lowland along the 200-mi (322-km) Atlantic coastline and a hilly interior stretching about 225 mi (363 km) inland. Its economy rests on the timber trade from its massive forests and on shrimp fishing. It was made an overseas department in 1947. The chief city is Cayenne. The European space station where the Ariane rockets are launched is in Kourou.

French Guinea *See:* Guinea; French West Africa.

French horn, musical horn instrument. Its circular shape, created by coiled brass, opens into a bell. Musical notes are created as the musician blows into the mouth piece, presses one or more of the three valves with one hand while the other hand creates sound effects by its placement in the bell. This horn was introduced into orchestras shortly after its invention in the mid-17th century. The original, valveless version of this horn was used for hunting.

French language, Romance language spoken in France and parts of Belgium, Switzerland, Canada, and former French and Belgian colonies. It is the official language of 21 countries. It developed from Latin during and after the Roman occupation of Gaul and also from Celtic and Germanic elements. By the 11th century 2 dialects had developed: in the south the *langue d'oc*, in the north the *lange d'öil*. From the latter came *francien*, the Paris dialect that became modern French, spoken and written since the 17th century.

French literature, poetry, prose, and drama

French writer Marcel Proust (1871-1922) has been the innovator of a new trend, with the publication of his series of novels *A la recherche du temps perdu* (*Remembrance of Things Past*, 1913-27). Now, more emphasis was placed upon the role that was played by the unconscious in human thought and behaviour, and less upon the description of external factors.

written by authors of France in standard modern French, as well as works in the medieval French dialects, in Breton, and in Provençal. French literature has exerted a strong influence on the writers of many nations, right up to the present.

Medieval French literature. Provençal, the language of the south of France, seems to be the first vernacular language used in French commerce and literature. It drew on elements of Latin and Arabic and flourished during the 11th and 12th centuries, when troubadours (musicians/poets) composed love songs. The form traveled to northern France, where it was imitated by the *trouvères*. In addition, *jongleurs* (itinerant poets and entertainers) popularized such songs throughout France and Norman England. François Villon (b.1431?) was the most remarkable medieval lyric poet.

The *jongleurs* and *trouvères* also developed epics and romances. The *chansons de geste* were epics that concentrated on a particular hero, the best known being the *Song of Roland* (c.1100). Romances were based on classical themes (e.g., the Trojan War) or on the Celtic legends of Breton (the Arthurian cycle). Chrétien de Troye's *Lancelot* (late 12th century) is a prime example. The allegorical romance, a symbolic story, also developed about this time. The greatest of these is the *Romance of the Rose* (c.mid-12th century). Prose was confined to historical chronicles, while drama developed in the mystery plays (depicting scenes from Scripture), miracle plays (about the saints and the Virgin Mary), and morality plays (meant to educate).

Renaissance French literature. The outstanding writer of the French Renaissance

was François Rabelais (c.1490-1553). His 2 great prose narratives, *Gargantua* and *Pantagruel* (1532-1552), are large, sprawling, often ribald works that satirize and comment on serious questions pertaining to education, politics, religion, and certain social institutions of the day. *La Pléiade* (c.1553) were a group of 7 poets, led by Pierre de Ronsard, who encouraged writing poetry in French rather than Latin and sought to create a French literature equal to other literatures. Michel Montaigne (1533-1592) was the last of the major French renaissance writers. He wrote several books of essays on a wide range of subjects. They are written in an informal, conversational style, but they reveal a sophisticated, skeptical, urbane mind. They have been widely read since their publication (late 16th century), and they greatly influenced English literature.

Classical French literature. During the 17th century, French literature enjoyed a golden age. French classicism was manifest in the 3 great dramatists, Pierre Corneille (*Polyeucte*, 1642), Jean Racine (*Andromaque*, 1667), and Molière (*Tartuffe*, 1664-1669). The works of these playwrights still hold the stage today in France and in many other countries as well.

The philosophers René Descartes (*Discourse on Method*, 1637) and Blaise Pascal (*Pensées*, 1670) wrote clear, elegant prose that typified classical thought. Descartes was influential in furthering rationalist thinking while Pascal examined closely his deep commitment to the Christian religion, especially as embodied in the Jansenist sect. Pascal was also a mathematician and scientist (Pascal's Law on the properties of liquids). Madame de La Fayette's *The Princess of Cleves* (1678) was one of the first French novels; it is still read for its psychological analysis and its fine style.

Classical French poetry began with the poet/critic François de Malherbe. His critical works, especially, influenced French literature, as he was a consistent advocate of precise language, objectivity, and serious intent in all literary endeavor, all of which became the hallmarks of French classicism. Other writers of this period include the historian Jacques Boussuet, La Rochefoucauld, La Fontaine, Madame de Sévigné, and La Bruyère. In addition, during this period Richelieu founded the Académie Français (1634).

French literature and the Age of Reason. The Age of Reason (18th century) saw some of its most influential political and philosophical writing come from France. The rationalist satires of Voltaire (*Candide*, 1759) and the enormous *Encyclopédie* (1751-1772), compiled under Denis Diderot, are prime examples of the period's sense that truth could be obtained mainly through reason. Other notable writers of the time included Charles Montesquieu, whose social commentaries affected the makers of the American Revolution; the playwrights Pierre Beaumarchais and Pierre Marivaux; and the novelists Alain René Lasage and the Abbé Prévost.

French literature and romanticism. Towards the end of the 18th century, a new sensibility took hold, due in part to the upheavals of the French Revolution. Jean Jacques Rousseau (*Confessions*, 1764-1770) was a precursor of the movement in that he emphasized the primacy of feeling over reason and valued spontaneity over self-discipline. François René de Chateaubriand and Madame de Staël also heralded the romantic emphasis on feeling and self by the end of the century. The great figures of 19th-century French romantic literature were Victor Hugo (*Les Misérables*, 1862), a poet, dramatist, and novelist, and the poet Alphonse de Lamartine (*Poetic Meditations*, 1820). Other major romantic writers included Alfred de Vigny, Alfred de Musset, and Alexandre Dumas *père* (*The Three Musketeers*, 1844) and Dumas *fils* (*Camille*, 1852).

Some writers of the period mixed romantic sensibility with a more realistic depiction of the human condition. Among them were Honoré de Balzac (*The Human Comedy*, 1842-1848, a collection of almost 100 novels and stories); George Sand, (*The Haunted Pool*, 1846); and Stendhal (*The Red and the Black*, 1831).

French literature and realism/naturalism. By the mid-19th century, the movement toward depicting life realistically, honestly, and objectively had begun to supplant the romantic sensibility. The novels of Gustave Flaubert (*Madame Bovary*, 1857), Émile Zola, and the brothers Goncourt are major examples. Other writers included Guy de Maupassant, Prosper Mérimée, and Alphonse Daudet; playwrights Eugène Scribe and Henri Becque; and critics Charles Sainte-Beuve and Hippolyte Taine.

French literature and symbolism. Late in the 19th century, a group of poets turned against both romanticism and realism/naturalism to write prose whose aim was to suggest meaning through impressions and intuition rather than by objective description. Known as *symbolists*, these poets included Charles Baudelaire (*Flowers of Evil*, 1857), Stéphane Mallarmé (*Afternoon of a Faun*, 1876), Paul Verlaine (*Songs Without Words*, 1874), and Arthur Rimbaud (*A Season in Hell*, 1873).

French literature in the 20th century. Early-20th-century French literature was dominated by 4 figures: André Gide, Paul Claudel, Marcel Proust, and Paul Valéry. Also important at this time was the development of surrealism, an ill-defined movement that placed emphasis on randomness and unconscious thought processes. Surrealism was manifest notably in the poetry of Guillaume Apollinaire and, later, in that of René Char and Louis Aragon.

During World War II a school of philosophy called *existentialism* became a rallying point for French writers, especially Jean-Paul Sartre (*No Exit*, 1944). Allied with him were several writers who also emphasized involvement with the moral and social problems of the day. These included Albert Camus (*The Stranger*, 1942), Simone de Beauvoir (*The Mandarins*, 1955), and, to a certain extent, Jean Genet, who wrote plays (*The Maids*, 1948) and autobiographical prose works. Both Sartre and Camus wrote plays as well as novels. Other significant playwrights of the mid-20th century included Jean Anouilh, Jean Giraudoux, and Jean Cocteau. Later in the century came Theater of the Absurd, primarily evidenced in the works of Samuel Beckett and Eugène

Ionesco, neither of whom were French-born but wrote in the language. The New Novel (*nouveau roman*) turned away from traditional concerns of the novel with plot and character to depictions of the characters' internal reactions to the outside world. Writers of these experimental novels included Alain Robbe-Grillet, Nathalie Sarraute, Michel Butor, and Claude Simon. Recent feminist writers include Marguerite Duras and Hélène Cixous.

In the mid-1980's writers began turning away from literary theory and, while not reverting to traditional fiction, started to bring back some of the elements, such as plots, that the *nouveau roman* writers had abandoned. Yann Queffelec's *The Wedding* (1987) and Patrick Besson's *Dara* (1987) are examples of this return. In 1981 the French Academy for the first time elected a woman, Marguerite Yourcenar-known for her historical novels-to join its ranks.

French Morocco *See:* Morocco.

French Polynesia, French territory in the South Pacific that includes Tahiti, one of the Society Islands. The island groups in the territory include the Austral, Gambier, Marquesas, Society, and the Tuamotu. The capital city in the territory is Papeete, Tahiti. The peoples of these islands, which lie 2,800 mi (4,500 km) south of Hawaii, are mainly Polynesian. The economy of the islands is based on farming, fishing, and tourism. The official language is French. In 1995 France carried out some nuclear tests in the area.

French Quarter *See:* New Orleans.

French Revolution, first European revolution in modern times, (1789-1799). Through its wars, the revolution spread the explosive ideas of the sovereignty of the people, liberty of the individual, and equality before the law. By 1788 in a time of the rise of the middle classes, the country was still ruled by the privileged nobility and clergy, the 2 upper Estates of the States-General. The tax burden fell on the Third Estate, made up of the middle classes and the landowning peasantry; it was further increased by the corruption of the fiscal system. When the nobility thwarted attempts by the royal ministers such as the popular director of finances, Jacques Necker, to reform government finance, the king was

forced to summon the Estates-General; when the Third Estate, which outnumbered the other 2 chambers, was not given a majority, it declared itself the National Assembly (June 20, 1789). When Louis XVI accepted the National Assembly but dismissed Necker, crowds stormed the Bastille prison on July 14 and pillaged the nobility's country estates. The royal family

fled in June, hoping to join their sympathizers, who had fled abroad, but they were arrested at Varennes and returned to Paris. On Aug. 4 the Assembly abolished the feudal system and approved the Declaration of the Rights of Man; the royal family was threatened by mobs; the Church, disestablished and largely suppressed. In Oct. 1791 the Legislative Assembly convened under a new constitution and became increasingly radical. Threat of attack from abroad by émigrés and their foreign supporters precipitated the French Revolutionary Wars. In the face of this crisis the mob again threatened the king, forcing him to replace the Assembly with the radical National Convention, elected in Sept. 1792, during mob massacres of jailed royalists. The First Republic was established, and the king was tried for treason and executed in Jan. 1793. In the face of royalist insurrection and foreign hostility the Jacobins seized power from the more moderate Girondins, transferring power from the Convention to arbitrary bodies such as the Committees for Public Safety and General Security. Dominated by Georges-Jacques Danton

A transitional phase to outright dictatorship, occured during the French Revolution at the time of the Consulate, when executive power rested with a triumvirate (Cambarceres, Napoleon and Lebrun). The Consulate was soon completely dominated by the First Consul, Napoleon.

While farmers suffered from heavy taxes and other oppressive feudalistic obligations, the nobility and clergy paid almost no taxes at all. This fact is usually regarded as one of the causes of the French Revolution.

F

and Maximilien Robespierre, these brought about the Reign of Terror, during which France became a police state and all were threatened with execution for the mere suspicion of disloyalty. This ended with Robespierre's execution by the Convention in July 1794. The Conven-tion then introduced a new constitution, setting up the Directory, which proved ineffectual and corrupt. In 1799 it was overthrown by the army, led by the popular general Napoleon Bonaparte. He established the Consulate, effectively ending the revolu-tionary period.

French Somaliland *See:* Djibouti.

French Southern and Antarctic Territo-ries, island possessions of France in the Indian Ocean and along a coastal portion of Antarctica. Covering an area of 3,300 sq mi (7,770 sq km), the territories include the Kerguelen and Crozet archipelagos, the is-lands of Saint Paul and Amsterdam, and the Adélie Coast of Antarctica. The area is in-habited by penguins, seals, and whales. Scientists live in the region to conduct re-search.

French West Africa, federation of 8 French overseas territories, 1895-1959. Its members were Dahomey (now Benin), French Guinea (now Guinea), Ivory Coast, Mauritania, Niger, Senegal, Sudan (now Mali), and Upper Volta (now Burkina Faso), now inde-pendent countries.

French West Indies, Caribbean islands of Martinique and Guadeloupe, French colonies until 1946.

Freneau, Philip (1752-1832), U.S. journal-ist and poet. His poem 'The British Prison Ship' (1781) was inspired by his experiences after being captured while running the British blockade. Other poems included 'The Wild Honeysuckle' (1786) and 'The Indian Burying Ground' (1788). Freneau was also the editor (1791-1793) of *National Gazette*, an anti-Federalist Party newspaper.

Freon *See:* Fluorocarbon.

Ceiling fresco in the Palazzo Berberini in Rome (1633-39), as created by Italian baroque painter Pietro da Cortona (1597-1669).

Sigmund Freud with his daughter Anna in 1929.

Frequency band, or waveband, radio fre-quency range assigned to a broadcasting sta-tion by the Federal Communications Commission. TV and AM and FM radio sta-tions, as well as those for commercial or government (e.g., police, amateur, and air-plane radio), are given specific numerical frequency ranges in *kilohertz* (1,000 cycles per second) to prevent stations from interfer-ing in each other's broadcasts.
See also: Radio.

Frequency modulation, one of two chief methods of sending sound signals on radio waves. More commonly referred to as FM, the frequency of a radio wave is adjusted higher or lower to match sound vibrations. This kind of signal may also be transmitted along two paths, or channels, to provide stereo broadcasting to a listener who has the appropriate radio receiver. Invented by Edwin H. Armstrong in 1933, FM is also used in television and long-distance tele-phone systems.
See also: Radio.

Fresco, painting dry earth pigments mixed with water on fresh, wet lime plaster. Fresco painting began with the Etruscans and Romans and was used extensively in Europe during the Middle Ages and the Renaissance. Michelangelo's fresco decora-tion of the Sistine Chapel is a famous exam-ple of the technique. Among modern masters it has been used in Mexico by José Orozco and Diego Rivera.

Fresnel, Augustin Jean (1788-1827), a French physicist and engineer who special-ized in the study of optics. His experiments firmly established the wave theory of light. He also performed experiments on the polar-ization and diffraction of light. As an engi-neer, he developed a type of lens, now known as the Fresnel lens, to replace mirrors in lighthouse lamps. The lens, which has a series of concentric, curved ridges instead of the usual smoothly curved face, is still used in lighthouses and is also used in the view-ing systems of many 35-mm cameras. Fresnel was admitted to the French Academy in 1823.

Freud, Anna (1895-1982), Austrian-born British pioneer of child psychoanalysis. Her book *The Ego and Mechanisms of Defense* (1936) is a major contribution to the field. After escaping with her father, Sigmund Freud, from Nazi-occupied Austria (1938),

she established an influential child therapy clinic in London.
See also: Psychoanalysis.

Freud, Sigmund (1856-1939), Austrian neurologist, author, psychiatrist, and founder of almost all the basic concepts of psychoanalysis. He graduated with an M.D. from the University of Vienna in 1881, and for some months in 1885 he studied under J.M. Charcot, whose work in hysteria con-verted Freud to the cause of psychiatry. Dissatisfied with hypnosis and electrothera-py as treatment techniques, he evolved the psychoanalytic method, founded on dream analysis and free association. Because of his belief that sexual impulses lay at the heart of neuroses, he was reviled professionally for a decade, but by 1906 disciples like Alfred Adler and Carl Gustav Jung were gathering around him (both were later to break away from the International Psychoanalytic Association, dissenting with Freud's views on infantile sexuality). For some 30 years he worked to establish the truth of his theories, and these years were especially fruitful. Fleeing Nazi anti-Semitism, he left Vienna for London in 1938 and there spent the last year of his life.
See also: Psychoanalysis.

Frey, in Scandinavian mythology, god of fertility, sunshine, and rain. Like his sister Freya, the goddess of love, he was associat-ed with the return of spring. Particularly venerated by the Swedes, his chief temple was at Uppsala.
See also: Mythology.

Friars Minor *See:* Franciscans.

Friction, resistance to motion arising at the boundary between two touching surfaces. As the force applied increases, equal force of static friction opposes it, reaching a maxi-mum limiting friction just before sliding be-gins. Lubrication is used to overcome fric-tion in machine bearings.

Friedan, Betty (1921-), U.S. feminist leader and author. Her book *The Feminine Mystique* (1963) challenged attitudes that had led women to become housewives and mothers at the expense of more ambitious careers. She was founding president of the National Organization for Women (1966-1970) and helped organize the National Women's Political Caucus (1971). *It Changed My Life* (1976) concerns her par-ticipation in the women's movement; *The Second Stage* (1981) charts the movement's course.

Friedman, Milton (1912-), U.S. econo-mist, proponent of the monetarist theory, which regards the money supply as the cen-tral controlling factor in economic develop-ment. A professor at the University of Chicago from 1946, he has written *A Monetary History of the U.S.: 1867-1960* (1963) and *Free to Choose* (1980; with Rose Friedman), a defense of free market capital-ism. He was awarded the 1976 Nobel Prize in economic science.

Friedrich, Caspar David (1774-1840), one

of the greatest German romantic painters. Caspar David Friedrich became famous for his landscape paintings, in which man, a small, lonely and mortal being, is seen in contrast to overwhelming nature. Moreover, he was one of the first to illustrate the landscape of his native region - northern Germany - with such conviction.

Friedrich's earliest work consists of a number of sepia drawings, drawings in brown watercolor aquarelle. He did not make his first oil painting until 1807: *The Cross in the Mountains*, which was intended as an altarpiece (currently in the Gemäldegalerie in Dresden).

Friends, Society of *See:* Quakers.

Frigatebird, any of a family (Fregatidae) of large seabirds with long pointed wings, forked tails, and weak legs. They are superb fliers and spend most of their lives in the air, feeding by snatching fish from the water, picking up baby turtles from the beach, and stealing the food of other birds. They breed in tropical seas. During the mating season, the male has a red throat pouch that may be inflated, for display, to the size of a human head.

Friml, (Charles) Rudolf (1879-1972), Czech-born U.S. composer of operettas and film scores. His best-known works include *The Firefly* (1912), *Rose Marie* (1924), and *The Vagabond King* (1925).

Fringe tree, tree of the olive family named for its fringe-shaped, white flower petals. This tree, which reaches a height of 35 ft (11 m), grows wild from the east coast of the United States to Missouri, and in China.

Frisch, Karl von (1886-1984), Austrian zoologist best known for his studies of bee behavior, perception, and communication, discovering the 'dance of the bees.' With Nikolaas Tinbergen and Konrad Lorenz, he was awarded the 1973 Nobel Prize for physiology or medicine for his work.
See also: Zoology.

Frisch, Max (1911-1991), Swiss architect, journalist, and playwright best known for his play *The Firebugs* (1958) and the novels *I'm Not Stiller* (1954), *Homo faber* (1957), and *Man in the Holocene* (1980). His dominant theme is the destructive effect of modern society upon individuals.

Frisch, Ragnar (1895-1973), Norwegian economist. He and Jan Tinbergen of the Netherlands were the first winners of the Nobel Prize in economics (1969). Frisch won the prize for his pioneering work in *econometrics*, the statistical analysis of economic problems. He was professor of economics at Oslo University and a founder of the Econometric Society (1930).
See also: Econometrics.

Fritillary, genus of herbs of the family Liliaceae that includes about 80 species of hardy perennials native to the north temperate zone. Fritillaries have bell-shaped flowers and are spring blooming.

Frobisher, Sir Martin (1539-1594), English navigator and explorer. In search of a northwest passage to the Pacific, he led 3 expeditions to northern Canada (1576-1578), landing at Labrador and Frobisher Bay and at Greenland, mistaking them for Cathay.

Froebel, Friedrich Wilhelm August (1782-1852), German educator noted as the founder of the kindergarten system. He believed in play as a basic form of self-expression and in the importance of spiritual development.
See also: Kindergarten.

Frog, jumping, tailless amphibian. Strictly, the name applies only to true frogs, members of the family Ranidae, but other members of the order Anura (which also includes the toads) are sometimes called frogs. True frogs are characterized by shoulder girdles that are fused down the midline. They are found throughout the world except in the southern parts of South America and Australia.

Froissart, Jean (1337?-1410?), French poet and chronicler. He traveled widely in search of material for his *Chronicles of France, England, Scotland and Spain*, which present a colorful, if not scrupulously accurate or objective, picture of events between 1325 and 1400. His poetry ranges from light verse to the romance *Meliador*.

Fromm, Erich (1900-1980), German-born U.S. psychoanalyst. He combined the ideas of Sigmund Freud and Karl Marx for the analysis of human relationships and development in the context of social structures and for proposed solutions to the problems of the modern industrial world, such as alienation. His books include *Escape from Freedom* (1941), *The Art of Loving* (1956), and *The Anatomy of Human Destructiveness* (1973).
See also: Psychoanalysis.

Fronde, series of uprisings against the French crown, 1648-1653. At first largely popular uprisings against heavy taxation, they were later fomented by the *parlements* and discontented members of the aristocracy, such as Louis II, prince de Condé, against the autocratic chief minister, Cardinal Mazarin, whose decisive intervention in 1652 finally crushed the Fronde.

Front, in meteorology, boundary between air masses. A cold front occurs when a cold air mass pushes a warm air mass ahead of it. A warm front occurs when a warm air mass pushes a cold air front. An occluded front occurs when a warm and a cold front meet; the warm air in between then rises.
See also: Meteorology.

Frontier, in U.S. history, boundary between the settled and unsettled areas of the country. It was constantly changing as the descendants of the original settlers of the 13 colonies spread out north, south, and especially, west. In the early days expansion was slow, consisting largely of migrations into the Appalachian area and into what is now Pennsylvania. By the time of Independence, Kentucky had been settled and the frontier

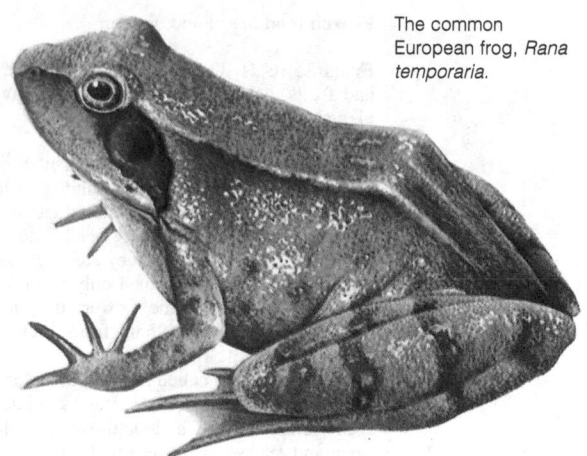

The common European frog, *Rana temporaria*.

F

was in Tennessee. The new government provided for surveying, settlement, and administration of new areas. The frontier moved steadily westward, and new states were formed in quick succession until, by 1848, Mexico was forced to cede the Southwest, and settlement began on the west coast. Native Americans suffered badly under the government's policy of moving them to make way for settlers and struggled to resist it. After the Civil War, wars with Native Americans broke out again, but by the 1870s and 1880s the growth of cities and the enclosure of much of the land meant that the settlers were firmly established. In 1890 the Bureau of the Census officially declared the frontier closed; its way of life and the peculiar mythology it created have had a great influence on U.S. culture.

Frost, frozen atmospheric moisture formed on objects whose surface temperature is below 32°F (0°C), the freezing point of water. Hoarfrost forms in roughly the same way as dew, but owing to the low temperature, the water vapor sublimes from gaseous to solid state to form ice crystals on the surface. The delicate patterns often seen on windows are hoarfrost. Glazed frost usually forms when rain falls on an object below freezing; it can be seen, for example, on telegraph wires. Rime occurs when supercooled water droplets contact a surface that is also below 32°F; it may result from fog or drizzle. The first frost of the year signifies the end of the growing season.

Frost, Robert Lee (1874-1963), U.S. poet. For most of his life he supported himself by farming and part-time academic work. His first volumes of poetry, *A Boy's Will* (1913) and *North of Boston* (1914) were published during a stay in England. His reputation grew in the United States, and he won many honors, including 4 Pulitzer prizes. Outwardly colloquial and concerned with commonsense rural wisdom, his poetry is also richly symbolic. Frost's complete poems were published in 1967.

Frostbite, damage occurring in skin and adjacent tissues caused by freezing. Extreme cold causes blood vessels in the hands, feet, ears, or nose to constrict, depriving tissues of nutrients. Warming and measures to maximize blood flow may reduce tissue loss.

Frozen food *See:* Food, frozen.

Fructose ($C_6H_{12}O_6$), sugar found in honey and fruits, used as a fluid and nutrient replenisher.

Fruit, ripe ovary of a flowering plant containing the seed or seeds. The fruit begins to develop after fertilization; its main functions are to protect the developing seeds and to help to scatter them when they are ripe. The majority of fruits are formed only from the carpel or carpels of the flower; they are known as true fruits. Some fruits include other parts of the flower, especially the receptacle; these are called false, or accessory, fruits. True fruits include dry fruits and juicy fruits. The dry fruits include those that split open and release their seeds (dehiscent) and those that do not split open (indehiscent). Juicy fruits also fall into 2 main groups. The drupes are the stone fruits: The inner layer, which is hard and woody, is the stone; the single seed is inside it. Berries are juicy fruits with many seeds in them, but without stones around the seeds.

Fruit bat *See:* Flying fox.

Fruit fly, small winged insects of the families Tephritidae and Drosophilidae that feed on decaying vegetation and ripe fruit, sometimes causing great damage to crops. Some species, such as the vinegar fly (*Drosophila melanogaster*), are used for genetics experiments because they breed rapidly.

Fry, Christopher (1907-), English verse dramatist and film writer. His plays, often in ancient settings, deal with contemporary themes. His best-known play, *The Lady's Not for Burning* (1949), is a dry comedy centering on witchcraft hysteria. His screenplays include *Ben Hur* (1959, Academy Award) and *The Bible* (1966). Other works include *Can You Find Me. A Family History* (1978; autobiography), and

One Thing More, or Caedman Construed (1986).

Fry, Elizabeth Gurney (1780-1845), British Quaker philanthropist whose inspections of prisons throughout Britain and Eu-rope led to great advances in the treatment of the imprisoned and the insane. Her proposed reforms of London's notorious Newgate prison, including segregation of the sexes and the provision of employment and religious instruction, were largely accepted.
See also: Quakers.

Fu-chou *See:* Fuzhou.

Fuchs, Klaus (1911-1988), German-born physicist and convicted spy. During World War II, Fuchs-a British citizen and Soviet agent-worked on the top-secret, atomic bomb project in the United States (1943-1945). He supplied the Russians with designs for the uranium and plutonium bombs. Released from a British prison in 1959, he returned to East Germany, where he directed the Institute for Nuclear Physics (1959-1979).
See also: Espionage; Manhattan Project.

Fuchsia, tropical plant (genus *Fuschia*) of South America and New Zealand, named for the German botanist Leonhard Fuchs. From a few species, over 2,000 varieties have been produced, some of which can be grown out of doors. The hanging flowers have a tubular calyx that flares out into wings, and from this dangle 4 petals and a group of stamens. The word also names the reddish purple hue associated with the flowers.

Fuel cell, device that produces electricity through the chemical reaction between 2 substances. The most common type is powered by the reaction between hydrogen and oxygen. Two porous electrodes are immersed into an electrolyte (usually an alka-

li). Through oxidation, hydrogen is supplied to the anode, and oxygen is allowed to diffuse through the cathode. At the anode, hydrogen gives up electrons to form hydrogen (H^+) ions, which react with hydroxyl (OH^-) ions in the solution to give water. The electrons pass around the external circuit to the cathode, where they react with oxygen and water to form more hydroxyl ions. The overall reaction is therefore the combination of hydrogen and oxygen to form water. The electric potential created is up to 1 volt. An ordinary battery is a type of fuel cell, but its electrodes are eaten away during use, whereas true fuel cells have an extremely long life and provide more power relative to their weight than other sources of electricity. Though fuel cells are theoretically more efficient than other generators, they are still very expensive and are only used for special purposes. The Apollo spacecraft use fuel cells to supply electricity. Scientists are working to produce fuel cells that can used low-cost fuels, such as gasoline or diesel fuel, which would make them practicable for domestic use.

Fuel-injection system, method of supplying fuel to internal combustion engines. It has always been used in diesel engines, where fuel is sprayed into the cylinder; when the inlet valve or port closes, the high pressure developed as the piston moves up the cylinder ignites the fuel. In gasoline engines there is a separate fuel injection line for each cylinder. Fuel is injected into a port, not into the cylinder. Electronic or mechanical devices ensure that each cylinder receives the correct mixture of fuel and air for efficient combustion. A fuel-injection system thus replaces the carburetor in gasoline engines. First used on aircraft and racing car engines, since 1957 it has been used on some automobiles.
See also: Engine.

Fuentes, Carlos (1928-), Mexican author of novels, essays, and short fiction. His works emphasize the elusive nature of time, historical truth, and personal identity, and tend to be unconventionally structured. Among his best known novels are *Terra Nostra* (1975) and *The Hydra's Head* (1977). Later works include *Gringo Viejo* (1985), *Cristobal Nonato* (1987), and

Fruit flies belong to the family of Trypetidae, insect order *Diptera*. The species that infest fruit, cause severe damage to crops. Here, we see the life cycle of the fruit fly, *Drosophila phalcrata*, body length 0.1 in (3 mm).
A. Adult flies deposit their eggs in the skin of fruit that is still hanging on a tree.
B. Hatched larvae develop and grow in the fruit, which begins to rot. The infested fruit usually drops to the ground and fully grown larvae enter the ground, where they pupate.
C. A newly emerged adult.

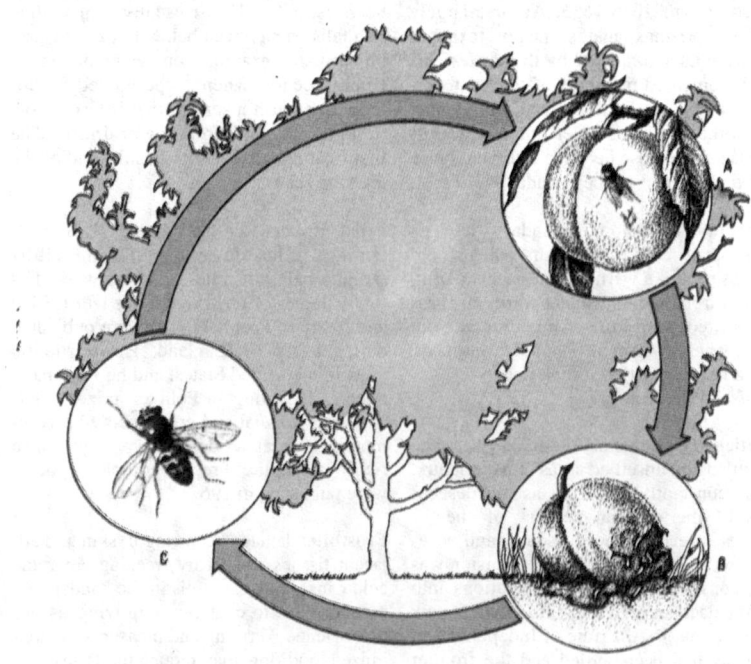

Mexican writer Carlos Fuentes (1928).

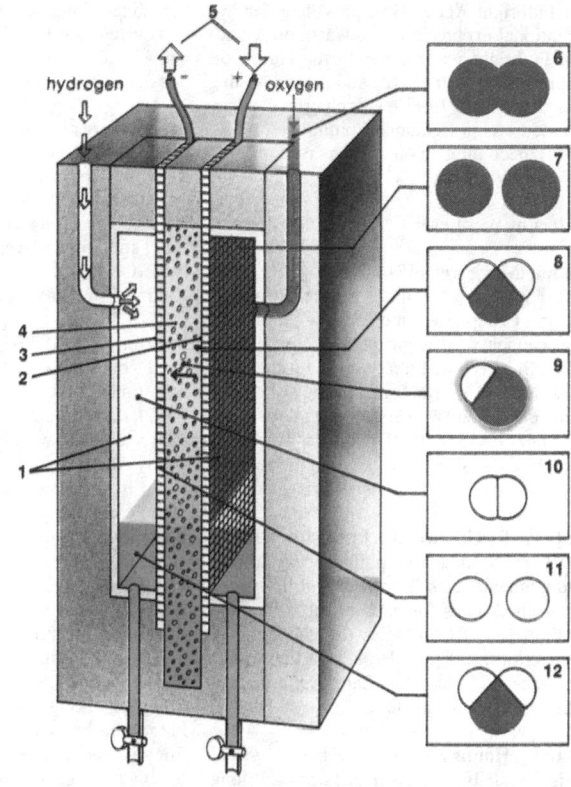

A fuel cell produces electricity from a chemical reaction of hydrogen and oxygen. The chemical reaction forms water as a by-product. This cell is made up of two gas chambers (1), a platinum-coated wire cathode (2) and anode (3), and a very thin electrolyte-saturated membrane (4), which can pass ions, but not atoms or molecules. As molecular oxygen entering the cell (6) contacts the cathodic platinum, it is split into atoms (7), which combine with electrolyte water (8) and cathode electrons, to form hydroxyl ions (9), which move to the anode. At the anode, molecular hydrogen (10) is split into atoms (11) similarly. These atoms combine with the hydroxyl ions to produce water (12), which is drained periodically, and electrons, which flow out through the external circuit (5) as an electric current.

Constancia y Otras Novelas para Virgenes (1989). Fuentes served as ambassador to France 1975-1977.

Fugard, Athol (1932-), South African playwright of Dutch descent known for his political dramas. A passionate opponent of apartheid, his plays reflect the ways in which blacks, coloreds, and disenfranchised whites are damaged by South Africa's racist policies. Among his best known works are *The Blood Knot* (1961) and *Master Harold ... and the Boys* (1981).

Fugger, Augsburgian family of merchants and bankers; very influential in the 15th and 16th century, financiers of the German emperors. It owned the copper monopoly in Europe; branches in Antwerp, Lisbon, and Rome. The family's role was largely over by the 17th century. Important representative: Jacob II the Wealthy (1459-1525), raised to the peerage after supporting Maximilian financially, and promoted Karol V as emperor.

Fugue (Italian, 'flight'), musical form in which 2 or more parts (voices) enter successively in imitation and combine in developing a theme. The classic fugue begins with the *exposition* of the theme or *subject* in successive voices. This is followed by variations on the subject, with *episodes* linking full statements. The subject may undergo various contrapuntal transformations, such as the *stretto*, in which it is stated in rapid, overlapping entrances. The fugue dates from the 16th-century canon and round. The greatest achievements in the fugue are by J.S. Bach (1685-1750).
See also: Counterpoint.

Fuji, Mount *See:* Mount Fuji.

Fujimori, Alberto (1939-), Peruvian politician. Fujimori was trained as an agricultural engineer. He stood for the presidential elections in 1990 as a candidate for the independent party Cambio '90 without any political experience, and to everyone's surprise, beat the famous author Vargas Llosa in the second election round. However, the rapid deterioration of the economy resulted in protests and strikes only a few months later. Fujimori expanded his power in 1992 by dissolving congress in order to, as he put it, be better equipped to crusade against the resistance movement, the Shining Path, and corruption. His autocratic style of government has met with increasing opposition since 1996. In 2000, he was re-elected President. A few months later, Fujimori called new elections as a result of a scandal, which concerned the head of the secret service, Vladimir Montesinos. He was an important advisor of Fujimori, who had bribed dozens of members of the opposition. Fujimori fled to Japan and sent a fax from this location giving notice of his resignation; the parliament enforced this decision by deposing him. Fujimori is wanted for the renunciation of his office. In 2001, the Peruvian parliament discontinued Fujimori's diplomatic immunity, in order to be able to charge him with crimes against humanity.

Fujiwara Mitjinaga (governed from 966-1028), most powerful ruler of the Japanese Fujiwara clan. Japanese classic literature reached its peak during his regime: *Genji monogatari* (The Tale of Genji) and *Makura no soshi* (Pillow Book). Fujiwara managed to suppress the growing power of the Taira clan and the Minamoto clan.

Fujiwara Mototsune (836-891), first kampaku in Japan (highest advisor to the emperor). In this position, which was reserved for the head of the Fujiwara clan until well into the 12th century, he was able to control the government.

Fujiwara period, period named after the famous noble lineage in Japan, which had virtually the entire state government in its hands between the 9th and 12th centuries. The Fujiwara had their daughters wed emperors, had them resign prematurely, and then acted as regents of the minor emperors. They gained control of practically every official position of significance. Japanese architecture reached a peak of subtlety during the Fujiwara period - or late Heian period. Nature and architecture were allowed to melt into a cultivated whole by constructing ponds, waterfalls, rock formations, and wonderfully trimmed trees whose growth was stunted. Buddhism saw two new sects emerge: Tendai and Sjingon, which proved to add a new impulse to the visual arts.

Fujiwara Tadahira (880-949), Japanese statesman from the Fujiwara clan, a regent in 930 and kampaku in 941. Riots broke out in the provinces during his regime, which then led to an increase in the power of the provincial military class.

Fujiwara Tokihira (871-909), Japanese statesman who sabotaged the attempts of Emperor Uda to break the power of the Fujiwara clan. Though he did not assume the title of kampaku, he was in fact the ruler of Japan. He attempted to increase the power of the central government in the provinces by introducing tax measures, among other things. The Engi-shiki, a collection of regulations, was drawn up by him.

Fujiyama *See:* Mount Fuji.

Fukuda, Takeo (1905-1995) Japanese politician. Fukuda was the minister of finance (1965-1966; 1986-1971), Secretary-General and president of the Liberal Democratic Party (1966-1968), minister of foreign affairs (1971-1972), vice premier in Takeo Miki's cabinet (1974-1976) and premier (1976-1978). He authored the Fukuda doctrine, the vow that Japan will never again become a military power, as well as the peace treaty with China, which was entered into in 1978. Ohira unexpectedly beat him at the end of 1978 during the elections for a new party leader.

Fukui, Ken'ichi (1918-1998), Japanese chemist, professor at the University of Kyoto. The first Japanese to be awarded the Nobel Prize for Chemistry, together with Roald Hoffman, in 1981. They were awarded the prize for their theories concerning the

F

F

course of chemical reactions, which they developed independently from one another.

Fukuoka (pop. 1,3 million), city in the northwest of the Japanese island Kyushu. Old fortified city of feudal nobility since 1601; across the Naka River lies the twin city Hakata, with the business district. Of the larger ports in Japan, it is the closest to the Asian mainland. Production and export of machines, silk, porcelain, paper, and dolls. In the 13th century, the armies of the Mongolian Kublai Khan attempted to invade Fukuoka, attempts that were in part sabotaged thanks to the high defense wall of nearly ten feet (3m); parts of the wall still exist. The Imperial University of Kyushu dates back to 1911, whereas the Fukuoka University dates back to 1934.

Fulani, people of West Africa living throughout a wide area from Senegal to Cameroon. They include nomadic pastoralists as well as settled communities. The Fulani have a deep-rooted culture based on Islam and have strong ties with the Hausa.

Fulbright, James William (1905-1995), U.S. political leader and lawyer, initiator of

Although most mushrooms are edible, there are a number of species that cause serious poisoning. The fly agaric, *Amanita muscaria*, contains the poison muscarine, which may cause slowed heart rate, delirium, and convulsions; its red or orange cap bears white scales.

A young specimen of the giant fungus (*Meripilus giganteus*) on an old deciduous tree. When this pore fungus gets the chance to develop it can attain an enormous size (up to 28 in/70 cm wide). When damaged, and during the process of ageing, the borders of the fungus become black and its — at first still rather succulent — substance becomes increasingly tough. The wood on which the fungus parasitizes, will be slowly broken down to a whitish substance. This phenomenon is called white rot.

the Fulbright Act (1946), providing for international exchange of students and teachers. Fulbright was elected to the House of Representatives in 1942, and served in the Senate (1944-1975). He was chairman of the Senate Foreign Relations Committee (1959-1974), becoming an outspoken critic of U.S. policy in Vietnam.

Fulcrum *See:* Lever.

Fuller, Margaret (1810-1850), U.S. critic and advocate of female emancipation. A friend of Ralph W. Emerson, she edited the transcendentalist magazine *The Dial*, 1840-1842. She became literary critic for the *New York Tribune* in 1844 and in the following year published *Woman in the Nineteenth Century*. In 1848-1849, with her husband, the Marchese Ossoli, she served the revolutionary cause in Italy under Mazzini.

Fuller, R(ichard) Buckminster (1895-1983), U.S. inventor, philosopher, author, and mathematician. He was a prolific source of original ideas for maximizing efficiency in numerous technologies (he called it the Dymaxion principle). He is best known for his concept 'Spaceship Earth' and for designing the geodesic dome.

Fulton, Hamish (1946-), British visual artist, initially a painter. Undertakes long journeys on foot through virgin landscapes since the end of the 1960s, as does Richard Long. This work is regarded as land art. Series of black-and-white photographs constitute a timeless document of the journey that was experienced as a piece of art. These photographs, which are accompanied by a simple text, do not portray any humans, and every labored effect common to conventional landscape photography has been avoided. Since the end of the 1980s Fulton also produces murals with landscape motifs and texts.

Fulton, Robert (1765-1815), U.S. inventor who improved both the submarine and the steamboat. His submarine *Nautilus* was launched at Rouen, France (1800), with the aim of using it against British warships: in fact, the British repeatedly escaped, and the French lost interest. His first steamship was launched on the Seine River (1803). After this success he returned to the United States, launching the first commercially successful steamboat, the *Clermont*, from New York (1807). He built several other steamboats and the *Demologus*, the first steam warship (launched 1815).
See also: Steamboat.

Fundamentalism, movement within various religions that adheres to the 'fundamental truths'. Originally a Protestant movement based on the literal inspiration of the Bible which therefore adhered to the virginal birth, the substitution, and the Resurrection and Second Coming of Christ in a literal sense. The movement emerged in the U.S. between 1870 and 1880; in 1919, the World's Christian Fundamental Association. Resistance against the establishment of the World Council of Churches (1948) led to the establishment of the International Council of Christian Churches.

In ordinary language, the term fundamentalism currently refers to Islamic fundamentalism.
See also: Protestantism.

Fundamental painting, movement that originated in the first half of the 1970s and in which the basic principles of painting dominate. Artists that practice this form of art research issues such as size, color, texture and form. Representatives include Robert Ryman, Robert Mangold, Rob van Koningsbruggen and Jaap Berghuis.

Fundin, Ove (1933-), Swedish motorcycle racer, became speedway world champion five times (1956, 1960, 1961, 1963 and 1967). After Fundin left for Australia to gain experience, he was discovered as a great talent by Aub Lawson, who included him in his team. In addition to his world titles, Fundin also claimed numerous European and Swedish championships.

Fungi, subdivision (phylum Eumycota or Eumycophyta) of the plant kingdom that comprises simple plants that reproduce mostly by means of spores and that lack chlorophyll. Fungi are now often considered a separate kingdom, not part of the plant kingdon. The majority of true fungi produce microscopic filaments (hyphae) that group together in an interwoven weft, called the *mycelium*. Reproduction is sometimes by budding (yeasts) but more normally by the production of asexual and sexual spores. Some fungi produce large fruit bodies; these are the structures commonly associated with fungi. Eumycota includes the myxomycetes, or slime molds. The true fungi are classified as the chytridomycetes, which produce motile gametes, or zoospores, with a single flagellum; the oomycetes, which have biflagellate zoospores and produce dissimilar male and female reproductive organs and gametes; zygomycetes, which do not produce motile zoospores and reproduce sexually by fusion of identical gametes; the ascomycetes, including yeasts, which reproduce asexually by budding or by the production of spores (conidia) and sexually by the formation of ascospores within saclike structures (asci) that are often enclosed in a fruiting body, or ascocarp; the basidiomycetes, in which sexual spores are produced or there are enlarged cells (basidia) that often occur on large fruiting bodies; and the deuteromycetes, or imperfect fungi, which are known to reproduce asexually, although sexual forms are often classified as ascomycetes and basidiomycetes.

Fungicide, substance used to kill fungi and so to control fungal diseases in humans and plants. In medicine some antibiotics, sulfur, carboxylic acids, and potassium iodide are used. In agriculture a wide variety of fungicides are used, both inorganic (e.g., Bordeaux mixture and sulfur) and organic (generally containing sulfur or nitrogen). They are applied to the soil before planting or around seedlings, or they are sprayed or dusted onto foliage.

Funj Sultanate, Muslim empire that ruled the Sudan of east Africa from c.1500 to

1821. Under `Amarah Dunqas, who founded the capital at Sennar (1504-1505), and throughout the 16th century, the Funj people, a group of uncertain origin, extended their dominion northward and over most of the area between the White Nile and the Blue Nile. They established supremacy by 1608 and reached the summit of their power c.1650 under Badi II Abu Daqn. By 1744 they had subdued the Kordofan region and Ethiopia. The Funj dynasty declined following the reign of Badi II, chiefly because of internal conflict between the ruler and the Funj aristocracy. In 1821 the Turkish government of Egypt invaded and conquered the Funj state.
See also: Muslims.

Funny bone, point at the bend of the elbow where the ulnar nerve passes over the ulna (1 of the 2 long bones of the forearm), and if struck, causes pain or tingling in the arm and fingers.

Fur, dense hair covering the skin of many mammals. Fur is an excellent heat insulator and protects against cold. It consists of a soft undercoat, generally interspersed with longer and stiffer guard hairs that form a protective outer coat and prevent matting. Fur clothing has long been valued for its beauty and warmth, and was an aristocratic luxury until the discovery of America, in whose exploration and economic development trapping and fur trading played a major role. Demand is still high, threatening some fur-bearing species with extinction; this has led to fur-farming of suitable animals such as mink and to the development of artificial furs made of synthetic fibers. The anti-fur consumer movement and groups for the humane treatment of animals have led to the banning of certain cruel forms of trapping and seal hunting in some countries.

Furchgott, Robert F. (1916-   ), American professor (ret.) of chemistry and biochemistry. Taught at several universities in the United States, including the University of North Carolina and the State University of New York, where he carried out research into cardiac and vascular pharmacy. He has been awarded several honorary degrees, including two from the universities of Gent and Madrid. He was awarded the Nobel Prize for medicine in 1998, together with L. Ignarro and F. Murad, for their discovery of nitrogen monoxide and their research into the cardiovascular system. Their research contributed much to the development of the Viagra pill.

Furfural ($C_5H_4O_2$), organic chemical belonging to the aldehyde family, used commonly in industry. A colorless liquid with irritating fumes, it is used in the manufacture of synthetics such as plastics, rubber, and nylon; as an insecticide and germicide; and in the refining of petroleum.

Furies, in Roman mythology, goddesses of vengeance. Known as Erinyes in Greek mythology, they were often depicted as 3 old women with snakes in their hair. In his tragedy *The Eumenides,* Aeschylus tells of how they punished Orestes for killing his mother by driving him insane.

Furnace, insulated structure in which high temperatures can be produced and controlled. In most furnaces the heat is produced by burning a fuel such as coal, oil, or gas, though some use the heating effect of electricity. In the so-called atomic furnaces (nuclear reactors), the heat comes from the splitting or fission of atoms and is used to generate electricity. In solar furnaces the heat is produced by concentrating the rays of the sun. Simple furnaces are used in the home to heat water for the heating system. Much larger ones are used in industry to heat, melt, and vaporize all kinds of materials. Metallurgical furnaces, massive structures that produce temperatures of thousands of degrees, are lined with refractory (heat-resistant) bricks that may also be water-cooled. In blast furnaces, used for reducing iron from its ore, fuel (coke) is burned in a blast of hot air inside a vertical cylindrical furnace. In the open hearth, or reverberatory furnace, the heating flame passes over the charge to be melted, and heat reflected from the low roof melts the charge; since there is no contact with the fuel, the charge does not receive any impurities. In the converter type of furnace, such as the Bessemer converter, which is used for refining pig iron, air or oxygen is blown through molten metal to burn out impurities; no fuel is necessary since the 'blow' itself generates heat. The electric furnace heats the charge externally and so does not contaminate the product.

Furniture, movable objects and accessories that add to the comfort, beauty, usefulness, and storage capacity of a dwelling. The development of furniture and increasing sophistication is closely allied to that of architecture. Furniture may be classified as *supporting* pieces (for example, chairs, tables, beds) and *storage* pieces (for example, chests, cupboards, and other boxlike containers). Accessories like rugs, drapes, and mirrors may also be considered furniture.

Furtwängler, Adolf (1853-1907), German archeologist, participated in excavations in Olympia; employed at the Antiquarian of Berlin from 1880 until 1894; later became a professor at the University of Munich and director of its library's glyptics center. He headed excavations in Aegina around 1900, from which location many sculptures were transferred to the glyptics center in Munich. He wrote many treatises on archeology, like *Die Bronzen von Olympia* (1890), *Meisterwerke der Griechischen Plastik* (1893), *Neuere Fälschungen von Antiken* (1899), *Die antiken Gemmen* (3 dln. 1900) and *Aegina, das Heiligtum der Aphapaia* (1906).

Furtwängler, Wilhelm (1886-1954), a German conductor. His command of the orchestra and musical knowledge brought him wide recognition. Furtwängler was born in Berlin. In 1922 he was named conductor of the Leipzig Gewandhaus concerts and Berlin Philharmonic Orchestra. As guest conductor of European orchestras, he was noted for interpretations of Wagner and Beethoven. He conducted the New York Philharmonic, 1925-1927.

Furze, whin, or gorse (*Ulex europaeus*), thorny shrub of the pea family native to Europe and Africa. Furze has yellow flowers on dark green stems. It is valuable for holding soil in place and is sometimes cultivated as winter fodder.

Fuse, safety device placed in an electric circuit to prevent overloading. It usually comprises a wire of low-melting-point metal mounted in or on an insulated frame. Current passing through the wire heats it, and excessive current heats the wire to the point that it melts, breaking the circuit. In most domestic plugs, the fuse consists of a cylinder of glass capped at each end by metal, with a wire running between the metal caps. Similar, but larger, cartridge fuses are used in industry.

Fushun (pop. 1,600,000) China, a city in Liaoning province. It is on the Hun River, about 25 miles (40 km) east of Shenyang. Fushun is the center of China's largest coal mining operation-an integral part of the vast iron and steel industry at nearby Anshan. Among the city's manufactured products are machinery, cement, chemicals, and steel.

Fusion, in physics, collision of 2 highly accelerated atomic nuclei to form the single nucleus of a heavier element. Fusion reactions (also called thermonuclear reactions) require extreme heat and release large amounts of energy. They occur naturally in space but are human-made phenomena on earth. Hydrogen bombs use the fusion process.
See also: Atom; Nuclear energy.

Fusion bomb *See:* Nuclear weapon.

Fu Teng (Fudeng, 1540-1613), 'Buddha lamp' (religious name), a Buddhist monk and architect of the Chinese Ming dynasty (1368-1644). During a largescale prayer meeting, which he organized, he was asked to pray for the birth of a successor to the throne by the empress mother. This prayer was successful and he could afterwards always appeal to imperial finances for an astonishing series of construction activities: particularly temples and pagodas, but bridges as well. His use of unorthodox materials is striking, such as iron, bronze, and brick; he was considered a specialist in building barrel vaults of brick. A large number of the so-called 'beamless brick' temples dating from the late Ming period can be attributed to his activities (beamless brick = brick construction without the use of wooden support beams and pillars).

Futures *See:* Commodity exchange.

Futurism, Italian 20th-century art movement. It was based on the 'Manifesto of the Futurist Painters' (1910) issued by the Italian publicist and poet F.T. Marinetti with a group of like-minded Italian artists, emphasizing speed and the dynamic forces of a mechanical age. The manifesto declared that 'a roaring motor car is more beautiful than

F

F

the *Winged Victory of Samothrace*.' It glorified war and violence and called for the destruction of all museums, libraries, and ancient monuments. This first general manifesto was followed by 2 further manifestos on futurist painting, also obsessed with the idea of universal dynamism. A typical futurist painting shows, for example, a dog with many legs to give the impression of movement. Futurist sculpture emphasizes sharp angles and jagged profiles. Futurism also exerted some influence on architecture and decorative art, particularly in the field of theatrical design. As a literary movement, futurism was never a major force.

Fuzhou, also Foo-chow or Fu-chou (pop. 1,600,000), port on the Min River, capital of Fujian province, southeastern China. Occupying both an ancient walled town and a modern city, Fuzhou is an industrial center known for electronics, chemicals, lacquerware, and food processing. It was a 'treaty port' following the Opium War (1839-1842) and was occupied by the Japanese in World War II. *See also:* China.

G, seventh letter of the English alphabet. Like the *c*, it developed from the Semitic *ghimel* and Greek *gamma*. The Romans, who used the same letter for the *k* sound and the hard *g* sound (as in go), added a small line to the *c*. English has a soft *g* sound (gelatin) in front of the vowels *e*, *i*, and *j* in words of French, Latin, or Greek origin.

G (gravitational constant), symbol that stands for the force of gravity. Newton's law of gravitation states that the gravitational attraction between any 2 bodies is directly proportional to the product of their masses and inversely proportional to the square of the distance between them. In other words, the greater the mass of 2 bodies, the greater the force of attraction between them; the further apart 2 bodies are, the less the force of attraction between them is. The gravitational constant, G, is the constant of proportionality in these equations. *See also:* Gravitation.

Gaberones *See:* Gaborone.

Gable, Clark (1901-1960), U.S. film star. Gable won a 1934 Academy Award for a comedy role in *It Happened One Night*. His most famous role was Rhett Butler in *Gone with the Wind* (1939). Called 'the King,' he was a leading box-office draw for more than 2 decades.

Gabo, Naum (Naum Pevsner; 1890-1977), Russian sculptor, pioneer of constructivism. With his brother, Antoine Pevsner, he issued the *Realist Manifesto* (1920). After he left Russia, he taught at the Bauhaus in Germany (1922-1932). In 1946 he emigrated to the United States. He is noted for his kinetic sculptures and geometrical constructions in metal, plastic, and nylon.

Gabon

Capital:	Libreville
Area:	103,347 sq mi
	(267,667 sq km)
Population:	1,233,000
Language:	French
Government:	Presidential republic
Independent:	1960
Head of gov.:	Prime Minister
Per capita:	US$ 5,500
Monetary unit:	1 CFA franc = 100 centimes

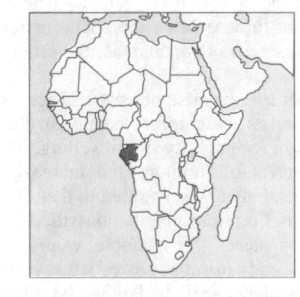

Gabon (officially Gabonese Republic), independent state in West Africa straddling the equator. It is bordered by the Atlantic Ocean on the west, Equatorial Guinea and Cameroon on the north, and the Republic of the Congo on the east and south.
Land and climate. The Atlantic coastline is backed by a narrow coastal plain that rises to rolling hills, leading to plateaus and mountains cut by the Ogooué River and its tributaries. The climate is tropical, with heavy, daily rainfall.
People. The largest ethnic groups are the Fang and Eshira; other groups include the Bateke, and Omyéné. The official language is French, but tribal languages are also spoken. The largest city and capital is Libreville. Port Gentil is the other major center. Lambaréné, in the interior, is renowned as the site of a hospital established in 1913 by Dr. Albert Schweitzer and run by him until his death in 1965.
Economy. Gabon is rich in timber and oil. The latter accounts for 80% of export earnings, but other minerals, including manganese and gold, are also exported. Cocoa is also an important cash crop. Gabon is an associate member of the European union.
History. Gabon was a center of the slave trade from the arrival of the first Portuguese navigators in the late 15th century until the 1880s. Libreville was established in 1849 by slaves freed from a slaving ship. By the end of the century, the French had taken over most of the territory that is now Gabon. In 1910 the area officially became a French colony. Following World War II, Gabon became an overseas territory, and in 1958 it became a self-governing member of the French Community. Two years later Gabon proclaimed its independence and became a member of the United Nations. Close relations have been maintained with France, while rising living standards have contributed to relative political stability. In 1990 a multiparty system was introduced. President Omar Bongo, who has held power since 1967, was re-elected for a 7 year term in 1998. In 2001 and 2002, some cases of the deadly Ebola virus were reported.

Gabor, Dennis (1900-1979), Hungarian-born British physicist who invented holography, for which he was awarded the 1971 Nobel Prize for physics. He had developed the basic technique in the late 1940s, but practical applications had to wait for the invention of the laser (1960) by C.H. Townes. *See also:* Holography.

Gaborone (pop. 135,000), capital of Botswana, an independent state in southern Africa. Gaborone is a governmental, cultural, and educational center and is served by an international airport and railroad. *See also:* Botswana.

Gone With the Wind (1939) was shown to packed houses throughout the world. Audiences were often moved to tears by this very romantic production. This photograph shows its two leading actors, Vivian Leigh (1913-1967) and Clark Gable (1901-1960).

The developing countries of Africa mainly export unprocessed raw materials towards the developed countries. In Gabon, timber is being transported by river from the inland areas to the sea, where it is loaded onto ocean-going ships. Fine wood is an important export article for Gabon, as are petroleum and manganese.

G

Gabriel, archangel in the Bible and the Koran. In St. Luke's gospel, Gabriel, meaning man of God in Hebrew, appeared to Zacharias, to Daniel, and then announced to Mary that she had conceived Jesus. In the Koran, Gabriel is the medium of revelation to Muhammad.

Gadda, Carlo Emilio (1893-1973), Italian novelist. Gadda became known for his novel *Quer pasticciaccio brutto de via Merulana* (That Awful Mess on Via Merulana; 1957). His work, which was often about life under a fascist dictatorship, attracts attention thanks to the original way in which the Italian language is used. He uses a great deal of regional expressions (dialect), initially when illustrating the words of certain characters, later in a 'monologue intérieur' as well, and even in passages that are purely descriptive in nature. Gadda made his debut in 1926 in the Florentine literary magazine Solaria. His work *l'Adalgisa*, in which Gadda portrays an image of his place of birth Milan in a humorous and clever fashion, was published in 1944. His novels *La cognizione del dolore* (Acquainted With Grief, 1962; awarded the Prix Formentor in 1963) and *Quer pasticciaccio brutto de via Merulana* were published serially in the magazine *Letteratura*. Gadda's other work includes *La madonna dei filosofi* (1931), *Il castello di Udine* (1934) and *La meccanica* (1970).

Gaddis, William (1922-1998), American novelist, made his debut in 1955 with *The Recognitions*, a novel that has become a classic in certain circles. This was followed by *JR* in 1976, a lengthy novel about the 'American dream': schoolboy becomes a rich businessman. It exposes the American world. After a lengthy silence, Gaddis published *Carpenter's Gothic* in 1985, in which he describes American society after the Vietnam war with stinging irony, followed by *A Frolic of His Own* in 1993, which was awarded the National Book Award in 1994.

Gadhafi, Muammar Muhammad al- *See:* Qadhafi, Muammar Muhammad al-.

Gadolinium, chemical element, symbol Gd; for physical constants see Periodic Table. Gadolinium, a rare-earth metal, was discovered by J.C.G. de Marignac in 1880. It occurs in bastnasite and monazite, which are the principal sources of the element. The metal is prepared by reducing the anhydrous fluoride with calcium. Gadolinium is silvery-white, soft, malleable, and ductile. It has the highest neutron capture cross-section of any element. Gadolinium is strongly magnetic but loses this property on heating. Gadolinium and its compounds are used in microwave applications and as color TV phosphors.

Gadsden Purchase, Mexican territory bought by the United States in 1853, to add to lands acquired in the war of 1848. The extra land, some 30,000 sq mi (77,700 sq km) cost $10 million. It provided a rail route through the conquered land to the Pacific. The purchase was negotiated by James Gadsden, U.S. minister to Mexico.

Gadwall, grayish-brown duck (*Anas strepera*), of the family Anatidae. Gadwalls are about 20 in (51 cm) long and weigh about 2 lbs (0.9 kg). They have white spots on their wings.

Gaea, or Ge, Mother Earth personified as a goddess. According to Greek myth, Gaea emerged out of Chaos and produced the sky, sea, and mountains. By her union with Uranus (heaven), she brought forth the Titans, Cyclopes, and Giants.
See also: Mythology.

Gaelic, group of Celtic languages, a subfamily of the Indo-European languages, native to Ireland (Irish Gaelic), the Isle of Man (Manx), and the Scottish Highlands (Scottish Gaelic).

Gaelic literature, writings in the Gaelic language. Irish Gaelic has 3 periods: Old Irish (up to 10th century), Middle Irish (up to mid-15th century), and Modern Irish. The early literature consists chiefly of lyric verse and sagas, of which the *Ulster Cycle* is a famous example. Scottish Gaelic diverged from the Irish tradition in 1300 and developed particularly in the area of poetry.

Gaels, or Goidels, Gaelic-speaking Celtic peoples of Ireland, Scotland, and the Isle of Man, as opposed to the Celtic peoples of Wales, Cornwall, or Brittany, who speak Brythonic.

Gagarin, Yuri Alekseyevich (1934-1968), Soviet cosmonaut, first human in space. His capsule, *Vostok 1*, was launched on Apr. 12, 1961, and orbited the earth once. A deputy to the Supreme Soviet from 1962, he died in a plane crash.
See also: Astronaut.

Soviet cosmonaut Yuri Alekseyevich (1934-68).

Gaillardia, any of several species of flowers (genus *Gaillardia*) of the composite family. Native to the central and western U.S., they are also called blanketflowers and fire wheels. They resemble daisies, with tubular disk flowers surrounded by ray flowers. Depending on the species, gaillardias have purple or crimson disk flowers and yellow, red, orange, or white ray flowers.

Gainsborough, Thomas (1727-1788), English portraitist and landscape painter. He painted numerous society portraits, and in 1780 he was commissioned to portray George III and Queen Charlotte. The landscapes in which many of his portraits are set were his primary interest. His work influenced John Constable and English landscape painting in the 19th century. Perhaps his most famous painting is *The Blue Boy*.

Galago, any of several species of small mammals (genus *Galago*) of the loris family, native to African forests. They can leap great distances between trees by using their long hind legs. Galagos range in size between large squirrels and chipmunks. They have soft, woolly fur, and large eyes and ears. Active at night, they feed on insects as well as small birds, eggs, lizards, and fruit.

Galahad, Sir, in British medieval legends, one of King Arthur's knights. He was the son of Sir Lancelot, one of the bravest of Arthur's knights, and of Elaine of Astolat, daughter of King Pelses. Noble and pure, he led other knights in a search for the Holy Grail. Galahad's story is told in *Le Morte d'Arthur* (1470), by Sir Thomas Malory, and in a poem by Alfred Lord Tennyson.
See also: Arthur, King.

Galapagos Islands, or Archipiélago de Colón, group of volcanic islands in the Pacific, on the equator west of Ecuador and belonging to that country. They were named for the giant tortoises found there in 1535 by the Spaniard Thomas de Berlanga. The islands have unique vegetation and wildlife. In 1835 Charles Darwin studied this wildlife, finding in it confirmation for his theory of evolution. There are large marine and land iguanas, scarlet crabs, penguins, a flightless cormorant, unique finches, and the giant tortoises, which are now rare. The main islands in the archipelago are Isabella, Santa Cruz, Fernandina, San Salvador, and San Cristobal; they are now a national park and wildlife sanctuary.
See also: Ecuador.

Galatia, ancient territory of central Asia Minor overrun by Gauls in the 3rd century B.C. Subjugated by Rome in 189 B.C., it became part of the Roman province of Galatia (which extended south) in 25 B.C.; by A.D. 200 it had merged with Anatolia.

Galatians, Epistle to the, 9th book of the New Testament, a letter written by St. Paul to the Christians in Galatia (now central Turkey) to counter the influence of those who taught that Christians must observe Jewish law. It sets forth the basis of Christian freedom, the union with Christ through faith.
See also: Bible; New Testament.

Galaxy, aggregation of stars, dust, and gas. The earth's galaxy is average sized: It contains approximately 100 billion stars, a beam of light would take approximately 100,000 years to cross from 1 side to the other, and it is shaped like a disk, with arms spiraling out from the bright nucleus. At the edge of the galaxy is the bright band of stars called the

From the earth, the Milky Way, which lies along the plane of the galaxy, appears as a circular band of light around the sky, containing dust and gas, as well as stars (A). The dust is sufficiently dense to prevent visual observations of the galaxy's center (1) in Sagittarius. A view of the galaxy from above (B) reveals a spiral-shaped structure with the sun (2) about 30,000 light-years from the center.

An edge-on view shows a hubbed disc (3), surrounded by a spherical halo region (4) containing globular clustres (5) and high-velocity stars, and by an intermediate region (6) containing planetary nebulae.

G

Milky Way. The sun, a star, lies about two-thirds of the way to the edge of the galaxy and takes about 250 million years to circle the galaxy once. The galaxy, often referred to simply as the Milky Way, has 2 small companion galaxies, called the Magellanic Clouds after the explorer Ferdinand Magellan. Other galaxies may be round or elliptical in shape, with no arms. Others are S-shaped. The nearest large galaxy, the Andromeda Nebula, is named after the constellation of Andromeda, inside whose borders it appears. The term *nebula* describes its cloudlike appearance. When the Andromeda Nebula was named, it was thought to be a cloud of gas in the earth's galaxy. In 1923 the astronomer Edwin Hubble found that it was a separate galaxy over a million light years away. Later studies showed that the 2 galaxies are near-twins, both in size and appearance. Galaxies tend to congregate in groups, linked by gravity, suggesting a common origin; they may have condensed out of 1 giant cloud of gas. The Milky Way is in a group including the Andromeda Nebula and about 20 other galaxies. Perhaps a billion galaxies are visible in the telescopes operating today.

Galaxies emit radio waves. The strongest emitters, known as radio galaxies, seem to have suffered internal explosions. There are often radio-emitting areas on either side of a galaxy. Quasars, star-like objects that emit strong radio waves, may be galaxies in the making. A quasar quiets down as it gets older, becoming a radio galaxy. Seyfert galaxies, discovered by Carl Seyfert, are galaxies with quasar-like characteristics and may be another stage of a galaxy's growth.

Galbraith, John Kenneth (1908-), Canadian-born U.S. economist and author, ambassador to India 1961-1963. A Harvard professor (1949-1975) and an activist in the liberal wing of the Democratic Party. Galbraith has been a consistent advocate of Keynesian economics, supporting active state intervention into the economy and urg-

ing government efforts to fight poverty and unemployment. His major books include *The New Industrial State* (1967; rev. ed. 1978), *Money* (1975), *The Age of Uncertainty* (1977), *Affluent Society* (1958; rev. ed. 1985), and *Economics and the Public Purpose* (1973).

Galen (A.D. 129-c. 200), Greek physician at the court of the Roman emperor Marcus Aurelius. His writings drew together the best of classical medicine and provided the form in which the science was transmitted in the West through the Middle Ages and Renaissance. He himself contributed many original observations in anatomy and physi-

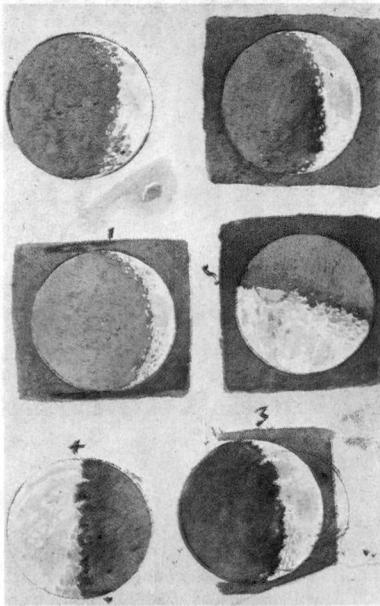

Drawings of the moon from the diary of Galileo. They proved that the moon was not a crystal, but that it was covered with mountains and valleys, like the earth. At the time, his ideas were considered very sensational.

ology, employing dissections of mammals to establish the field of comparative anatomy. *See also:* Anatomy; Physiology.

Galicia, historic region in east-central Europe, now part of Poland and Russia's Western Ukraine. It is rich in minerals and agriculture. Part of Poland since the 14th century, it was annexed by Austria in the 18th century, but was again Polish after World War I. After World War II its eastern portion passed to the USSR.

Galilee, in ancient Roman times, hilly region of northern Palestine between the Sea of Galilee and the Jordan River (now part of Israel). It was the homeland of Jesus, who was sometimes referred to as the Galilean, and a center for Jewish learning after the Roman destruction of the temple in Jerusalem in A.D. 70.

Galilee, Sea of, lake in northern Israel, also called Lake Tiberias. Fed and drained by the Jordan river, it contains many fish, and its water is used for irrigation. Many Bible stories, such as Jesus's transformation of water into wine, are set along this sea. Ruins of ancient cities lie along its northern shores.

Galileo Galilei (1564-1642), Italian mathematician and physicist who discovered the laws of falling bodies and the parabolic motion of projectiles. The first to turn the newly invented telescope to the heavens (1609), he was among the earliest observers of sunspots and the phases of Venus. A talented publicist, he helped to popularize the pursuit of science. However, his quarrelsome nature led him into an unfortunate controversy with the Roman Church. His most significant contribution to science was his provision of an alternative to Aristotelian dynamics, expressed in his *Dialogue Concerning the Two Chief World Systems* (1632). The motion of the earth thus became a conceptual possibility, and scientists at last had a genuine criterion for choosing between the Copernican and Tychonic hypotheses in astronomy. In 1633, the Vatican condemned Galileo as a heretic for claiming that the earth revolved around the sun. He was forced to recant the Copernican theory. Pope John Paul II started the move toward a reconciliation when he conceded in a 1979 speech that the astronomer had suffered at the hands of the Church. In January 1998, the archives of the papal inquisition, until 1902, were made accessible to researchers. It was expected that the archives would provide new insights regarding the trial against Galileo.

Galili, Itzik (1961-), Israeli dancer and choreographer He started out as a folk dancer and worked for Bat Dor and Batsheba. In 1991 - just before the beginning of the Gulf War - he came to the Netherlands, where he created several ballets for a number of companies. He is regarded as one of the most gifted choreographers of his time.

Gall (c. 1840-1894), Sioux chief who aided Sitting Bull in defeating General Custer at the Battle of the Little Bighorn (1876). After a subsequent battle in 1881, he surrendered and settled in a reservation in the Dakota Territory, where he worked to improve relations between Native Americans and white settlers.

Gall, abnormal growth on trees caused by parasites such as fungi and insects. Fungal galls are usually irregular in shape, whereas insects produce galls that are often spherical, like the oak apple. The adult insect lays its eggs in the plant's tissue, and the larvae cause the growth of the gall. They then feed on the deformed tissues and eventually bore their way out as adults. Gall insects include certain small flies and many small wasps. It is often possible to identify the insect by the shape of its gall. Galls are often a serious nuisance and destroy many acres of valuable crops. Some, however, are useful. The oak apple, for example, is a source of tannin, which is used in tanning leather.

Gall bladder, muscular sac in many vertebrate animals that stores the bile created by the liver. In humans the pear-shaped sac lies in its own depression, or foss, under the liver. It is about 3.5 in (9 cm) long, 1 in (2.5 cm) wide, and holds about 35 cu cm of fluid. Arising from the gall bladder is the cystic duct, which is connected to the liver by the common hepatic duct, and to the first part of the small intestine, the duodenum, by the common bile duct. In the presence of fatty foods in the small intestine, a hormone, cholecystokinin, produced by the cells of the small intestine, causes the gall bladder to contract and empty its contents into the duodenum. Cholecystitis (inflammation of the gall bladder resulting from infection by bacteria) can be acute or chronic. In most instances, acute cholecystitis is caused by a gallstone blocking the cystic duct. Chemical irritation and the digestive activities of certain enzymes can also play a contributing role. A sharp pain in the right upper part of the abdomen is a prominent symptom. The condition may require surgical removal of the gall bladder. The chronic condition is sometimes associated with cancer of the gall bladder.

Gallegos, Rómulo (1884-1968), Venezuelan novelist and statesman. Elected president of Venezuela in 1947, he was almost immediately overthrown by a military coup. His short stories and novels, of which the best known is *Doña Bárbara* (1929), are primarily didactic and ideological works concerned with social reform.
See also: Venezuela.

Galleon, sailing vessel with 3 or 4 masts and 2 to 4 decks. Most ships of this type were clumsily built, with projecting forecastles and square sterns. Used in the 16th and 17th centuries as warships and for carrying cargo, galleons were capable of relatively fast speeds. But they had to be handled with care, as their heavy superstructure made them subject to capsizing. Galleons varied greatly in size, the largest having displacements of about 1,200 tons (1,100 metric tons).

Galley, early seagoing warship, propelled by oars, sometimes with auxiliary sails. The

galleys that made up the ancient Greek and Roman navies were classified according to the number of banks of oars on each side: *uniremes* (1 bank), *biremes* (2 banks), and *triremes* (3 banks). There were usually about 25 oars per bank. The oars were 40-50 ft (12-15 m) long and as many as 7 slaves were required to work each oar. Galleys were long and narrow. Though fast, they were difficult to handle in rough seas. They were equipped with catapults and carried archers and soldiers who would board an enemy ship that had been rammed. Galleys were used in the Mediterranean and other seas until the late 17th century.

Gallfly *See:* Gall.

Gallic Wars, series of military campaigns (58-51 B.C.) by Julius Caesar. As governor of Transalpine Gaul, Caesar drove out invading German tribes while occupying more territory in Gaul, until almost the whole country was in Roman hands (55 B.C.). In 53-52 B.C. he put down revolts by the chieftains Ambiorix and Vercingetorix. Caesar wrote *Commentaries on the Gallic War* (c.50 B.C.).
See also: Gaul; Rome, Ancient.

Gallienus, Publius Licinius Valerianus

Egnatius (A.D. 218?-268), Roman emperor (253-268). He ruled with his father, Valerian, until Valerian's capture by the Persians in 260. Under pressure from German, Persian, and Gothic invasions and provincial revolutions, Gallienus reorganized the army and reduced the power of the Senate. He also ended official persecution of the Christians. Gallienus was assassinated in Milan while quelling a revolt.

Gallinule, any of several species of water birds (genus *Gallinula*) of the rail family. About 12 to 18 in (30 to 45 cm) long, gallinules have brightly colored feathers and long, thin toes. They are poor fliers but excellent swimmers.

Gallipoli Peninsula, 50 mi (80 km) strip of land in European Turkey between the Aegean Sea and the Dardanelles. A strategic point of defense for Istanbul, it was fought over during the Crimean War and World War I. In 1915 an Allied expedition of British, Australian, French, and New Zealand forces failed to dislodge Turkish troops in an effort to gain control of the Dardanelles.

Gallium, chemical element, symbol Ga; for physical constants see Periodic Table.

The galleon first appeared in the 16th century, replacing the carrack. Distinguished from the latter by her slimmer more graceful lines, and by the fact that the forecastle is built well inboard, behind a ramlike projection, called the beak head, which housed the crew's latrines; hence the term 'heads'. A powerful ship, used for both commerce and war, the galleon incorporated all the major innovations in square rig building, and was the direct ancestor of the ship of the line and the clipper. The English galleon was superior, both in design and gunnery to the Spanish galleon.

G

G

Gallium was discovered spectroscopically by P.E. Lecoq de Boisbaudran in 1875. The element occurs in the minerals diaspore, sphalerite, germanite, bauxite, and coal. It can be produced by electrolysis of a solution of the hydroxide in KOH. Gallium is a silvery, amphoteric metal that can be liquid near room temperature. It wets glass and has a long liquid range and low vapor pressure even at high temperatures. Gallium and its compounds are used in phosphors, semiconductors, solid-state devices, and low-melting alloys.

Gallon, a measure of capacity used in the United States and, formerly, in most other English-speaking countries. It contains four *quarts*. The quart is divided into two *pints*, the pint into four *gills*. There are 128 fluid ounces in a gallon.
The United States gallon contains 231 cubic inches. It is based on the English wine gallon of Queen Anne's reign, originally a cylinder seven inches in diameter and six inches high. The United States gallon equals 3.7854 liters.
The traditional British, or *imperial*, gallon contains 277.42 cubic inches, or 1.20095 United States gallons. Thus, five imperial gallons are approximately equal to six United States gallons. The imperial gallon equals 4.546 liters.

Gallstone *See:* Gall bladder.

Gallup, George Horace (1901-1984), U.S. pollster. In 1935 he established the American Institute of Public Opinion, which undertakes the Gallup polls, periodic samplings of public opinion on current issues. His several books include *The Pulse of Democracy* (1940) and *The Gallup Poll: Public Opinion, 1935-1971* (1972).

Gallup Poll *See:* Gallup, George Horace; Public opinion poll.

Galsworthy, John (1867-1933), English novelist and playwright. His novels of the Forsyte family, grouped in trilogies-*The Forsyte Saga* (1922), *A Modern Comedy* (1928), and *End of the Chapter* (1934)-depict the life and attitudes of the English upper-middle classes, typical of the 'man of property' Soames Forsyte. Galsworthy was awarded the Nobel Prize for literature in 1932.

Galtieri, Leopoldo Fortunato (1926-), Argentinean military and politician. Galtieri succeeded general Viola as president in 1981, but was forced to resign in 1982 following the military failure on the British Falkland islands. After civilians had regained the government of the country in 1983, Galtieri was called to account for his actions as military president. He was acquitted in 1985 on charges of violating human rights; in 1986 he was sentenced to twelve years in prison for 'negligence' in the Falkland war and lost his military rank. In 2002, Galtieri was arrested for alleged kidnapping and violations of human rights in the 1980s.

Galton, Sir Francis (1822-1911), British scientist, author of *Hereditary Genius* (1869). The founder of eugenics (talent is inherited) and biostatistics (the application of statistical methods to animal populations), Galton developed one of the first systems for identifying fingerprints.

Galvani, Luigi (1737-1798), Italian anatomist who discovered 'animal electricity' (c.1786). This discovery resulted from the observation of the twitching of a frog's leg when touched by 2 metals in a moist environment. A controversy with Alessandro Volta over the nature of animal electricity stimulated research in electrotherapy.
See also: Anatomy.

Galvanizing, industrial process for coating iron or steel with a thin layer of zinc to prevent rusting. It was discovered in 1742 but only named in 1830 after Luigi Galvani (1737-1798), who demonstrated that 2 unlike metals in contact produce an electric current, though he did not know why. There are several stages in galvanizing. The metal is thoroughly cleaned with solvents and acid, and a zinc ammonium flux is applied. The article is dipped into a bath of molten zinc kept at about 842°F (450°C), and a coating of layers of iron-zinc alloys or pure zinc forms. Finally, the article may be quenched in cold water to remove the flux and freeze the coating. Small items like nails are galvanized in wire baskets; sheet and wire are treated continuously in an automatic process. The sheet is widely used in building, automobile manufacture, and outdoor structures. In an alternative process, electrogalvanizing, a flow of electricity through a zinc sulfate solution causes a layer of zinc to adhere to steel.
See also: Electroplating.

Galvanometer, instrument used for measuring minute electrical currents. The modern instrument consists of a coil of wire delicately suspended by a thin conducting filament between the poles of a permanent magnet. The galvanometer is connected to a circuit, and when an electrical current flows, the coil is deflected at an angle directly proportional to the strength of the current. A small mirror attached to the coil reflects a spot of light onto a scale that indicates the current's strength.
See also: Electric current.

Galveston (pop. 59,000), city in southeastern Texas and seat of Galveston County. Located on the Gulf of Mexico, the city is an important seaport, commercial fishing center, and the world's largest cotton-shipping port. Meat packing, shipbuilding, oil refining, and the manufacture of wire, nails, textiles, and chemicals are important industries. Michel Menard, a Canadian civil engineer, laid out the town in 1836. That same year the city became the temporary capital of the Republic of Texas. During the Civil War it was a major supply port for the Confederacy, although it was occupied by the Union troops for several months.
See also: Texas.

Galway (pop. 57,000), port city and commercial center in western Ireland. Industries include clothing, foods, electrical equipment, and furniture. Many other Irish products, such as wool, marble, china, and metals are exported from Galway.
See also: Ireland.

Galway, James (1939-), Irish flutist. Galway began his career at the age of 14 as a bar violinist and flutist. Thanks to a scholarship he left to study in London (Royal College of Music) a few years later, and then went to Paris to complete his studies with the famous Jean-Pierre Rampal. Galway initially worked in various renowned opera orchestras, then in English symphony orchestras, and as solo flutist of the Berliner Symfoniker between 1969 and 1975. Galway's fame is owed mainly to his many studio recordings. As a concert flutist he travels the world and often performs on radio and television.

Gama, Vasco Da *See:* Da Gama, Vasco.

Gambia

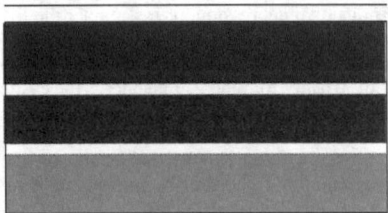

Capital:	Banjul
Area:	4,361 sq mi (11,295 sq km)
Population:	1,456,000
Language:	English
Government:	Presidential republic
Independent:	1965
Head of gov.:	President
Per capita:	less than US$ 1,770
Monetary unit:	1 Dalasi = 100 butut

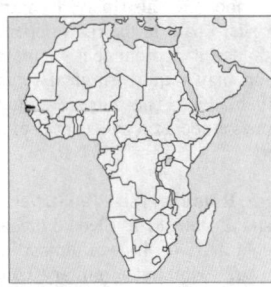

Gambia (officially Republic of The Gambia), independent country in West Africa.
Land and climate. Gambia is a narrow strip of land 7-20 mi (11-32 km) wide, stretching inland from the Atlantic Ocean, for about 200 mi (322 km) along the Gambia River. It is surrounded on three sides by Senegal.
People. The Mandingo ethnic group accounts for about 44% of the population. Other groups include the Fulani, Wolof, Jola, and Serahuli. More than 80% of the people are Muslim, the rest being animist or Christian. English is the official language, but tribal languages are also spoken.
Economy. The economy is largely agricultural, peanuts being the main cash crop. Millet, corn, and rice are grown for domestic consumption.

History. Portuguese navigators explored the mouth of the Gambia River in the 15th century, trading in gold and slaves. In 1588 the British obtained control of the trade on the Gambia River. During the following centuries the slave trade flourished, even after its official abolition by Britain in 1807. In 1843 the area around St. Mary's Island was made a British colony, and the interior settlements along the river were declared a British protectorate in 1894. In 1963 Gambia became self-governing, and in 1965 it became an independent member of the British Commonwealth. Relations with Senegal were close, and in 1981 a confederation called Senegambia was declared, linking the two economies while maintaining formal separate sovereignty. The confederation was dissolved in 1989. Lt. Yahya Jammeh became President in 1994, having ousted Dawda Jawara in a military coup and winning the parliamentary elections of 2001. Tourism flourished, as did transit trade. Gambia is aspiring to become the 'Singapore of West Africa'.

Gamblers Anonymous (G.A.), international organization designed to help people with an uncontrollable urge to gamble. G.A. consists of people who have quit or want to quit gambling. Regular meetings are held at which members support one another's efforts to quit gambling by discussing and sharing their experiences.
See also: Gambling.

Gambling, betting money or valuables on the outcome of some future event that is more or less unpredictable. Gambling is at least as old as recorded history. Dice games were popular in ancient Rome, and loaded dice found among the ruins of Pompeii indicate that some, at least, were rigged. The Roman historian Tacitus tells of Romans and Germans gambling themselves into social disgrace, financial ruin, and slavery. At the height of the West African slave raids in the 18th century, there were instances of Africans gambling away their families and even themselves. In China, there are reasonably authenticated cases of people staking their limbs and hacking them off when they lost.

The criminal underworld is closely connected with most forms of gambling, and bribery and corruption of officials is common. In most courts, games of skill are distinguished from games of chance, the latter being illegal when played for money. This kind of legislation eliminates organized gambling clubs but permits friends to play games of skill for money. Unfortunately, it is not easy to determine the relative effects of chance and skill in most games. Betting on horses may be a skillful exercise for some, although most people talk of good or bad 'luck'.

Horse racing is one of the most popular sports with gamblers. The bettor can place bets with the parimutuel, a computer-operated pooling system. A proportion of the total money staked is retained, and the rest paid out to winning bettors. The payout on any horse depends on the total amount in the pool and the number of winning bettors.

Game, contest or sport played by rules.

In the eastern and central parts of the country, along the Gambia River as well as along its left tributary, the Bintang, rice is the main crop.

G

Games may test mental and/or physical skills, and may be played by one or more persons. They range from crossword puzzles, card, and board games to organized sporting events played by competing teams. Some rely on skill and practice, others involve luck.

Gamelan, general term for the traditional orchestra in Java and Bali. It virtually always consists of percussion instruments alone (gongs, metallophones, drums, xylophones), but the rebab (two-stringed violin) and the suling (bamboo flute) are also used under special circumstances. Both the number of performers (ca. 20 to 50) and therefore the size may vary greatly. The gamelan orchestra fulfils a significant social function, e.g. at wayang presentations, religious parties, and marriage and funeral ceremonies.

Gamete, male or female reproductive cell, whether in animals, humans, or plants. In human beings, the female ovum and the male sperm are the gametes.
See also: Reproduction.

Game theory, branch of mathematics concerned with a mathematical process of selecting an optimum strategy in the face of an opponent's strategy. The term was initially used to describe the strategy of winning at poker. It has applications in such areas of competition as military and economic planning.
See also: Von Neumann, John.

Gamma globulin, portion of blood protein containing antibodies. Several types of gamma globulin are recognized. Although they share basic structural features, they differ in size, site, behavior, and response to different antigens. Absence of all or some gamma globulins causes disorders of immunity, increasing susceptibility to infection, while the excessive formation of one type is the basis for myeloma, a disease characterized by bone pain, pathological fractures, and liability to infection. Gamma globulin is available for replacement therapy, and a type from highly immune subjects is sometimes used to protect against certain diseases (e.g., serum hepatitis, tetanus).
See also: Immunity; Plasma.

Gamma rays, electromagnetic wave energy similar to, but of much higher energy than, ordinary X rays. The energy of a quantum is equal to hv ergs, where h is Planck's constant (6.6254×10^{-27} erg sec) and v is the frequency of the radiation. Gamma rays are emitted by the nuclei of uranium and other

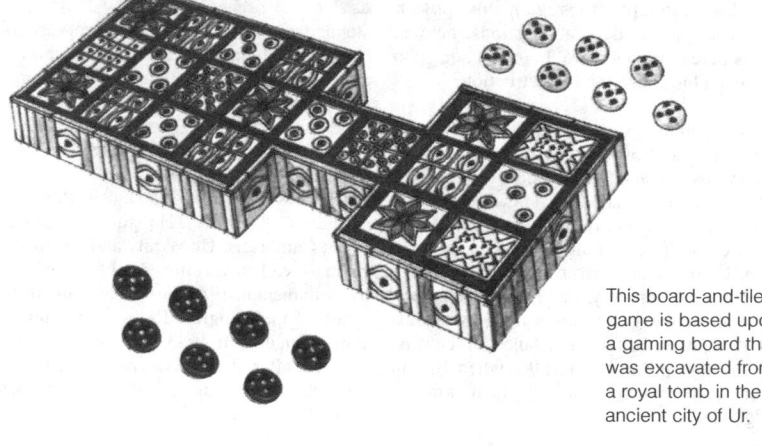

This board-and-tile game is based upon a gaming board that was excavated from a royal tomb in the ancient city of Ur.

The board, which dates from the third millennium B.C., is believed to be the forerunner of backgammon.

G

Indira Gandhi (1917-1984), was prime minister of India from 1966 to 1977 and from 1980 to 1984. She was the only child of Jawaharlal Nehru. In June 1975, she declared the state of emergency, thus suspending parliamentary democracy indefinitely. One of the events leading to this, was her conviction in an electoral corruption scandal, which was later revoked in a court of appeal.

radioactive elements. They are highly penetrating, an appreciable fraction being able to traverse several cm of lead. In large amounts they can be harmful to body tissue, but small quantities are used in radiation treatments for cancer.
See also: Radioactivity; X ray.

Gamow, George (1904-1968), Russian-born U.S. physicist and science writer, best known for his work relating to the evolution of stars and for his support of the 'big bang' theory of cosmology. In genetics, he did significant research on cell structure.
See also: Cosmology; Genetics.

Gamsakhurdia, Zviad (1939-1993), Georgian politician. Gamsakhurdia spent two years in prison as a dissident; only after 1989 did he succeed in making himself popular in Georgia with his extreme nationalism. He was elected president in April 1991 with an astonishing 85% majority of votes. However, he soon revealed himself as a true despot who took control of everything. This situation met with great resistance and he fled to the Chechen capital of Grozny in early 1992, from where he made a few more unavailing attempts to regain his power. Because of his ideas and actions, he was considered by many to be a lunatic who plunged his country into destruction.

Ganda, ethnic group living in Uganda, constituting about 30% of the population. Also known as Waganda or Baganda, they speak a Bantu language called Luganda. The Ganda have adopted many aspects of modern Western culture and are successful in farming, business, and government. In the early 1800s their territory, called Buganda, was one of the most powerful kingdoms of East Africa. With British assistance, it became even more powerful in 1896, when Britain added more kingdoms to it, making it Uganda.

Gander *See:* Goose.

Gandhi, Indira Priyadarshini (1917-1984), first woman prime minister of India. Daughter of Prime Minister Jawaharlal Nehru, she became president of the Congress Party in 1959. As prime minister (1966-1977) she improved relations with the USSR and helped India to become the dominant power in the region. In 1975 she was found guilty of electoral malpractice. During the ensuing constitutional crisis she declared a state of emergency and jailed nearly 700 political opponents. The Indian Supreme Court overruled the verdict against her and upheld her electoral and constitutional changes; however, she was briefly turned out of office (1977). She regained the premiership in 1980. She was assassinated by her Sikh bodyguards in 1984.
See also: India.

Gandhi, Mohandas Karamchand (1869-1948), nationalist leader of India. He was called the *Mahatma* ('Great Soul'). After studying law in London, he went to South Africa, where he lived until 1914, becoming a driving force in the Indian community's fight for civil rights. During this campaign he developed the principle of *satyagraha*, nonviolent civil disobedience to achieve economic, political, and social change, and held to it despite persecution and imprisonment. When he returned to India, he had achieved substantial improvements in civil rights and labor laws. In India he became leader of the Congress Party, initiating the campaign that led to the independence of India after World War II. He was assassinated by a Hindu fanatic who disapproved of his tolerance of Muslims. Gandhi wrote an autobiography, *My Experiment With Truth*, and edited the newspaper *Indian Opinion*.
See also: India.

Mohandas—Mahatma—Gandhi, an Indian political and spiritual leader, developed the tactics of nonviolent disobedience that forced Great Britain to grant independence to India in 1947.

Gandhi, Rajiv (1944-1991), prime minister of India (1984-1987). He studied engineering at Cambridge University and returned to India to work as a commercial pilot. Elected to Parliament in 1981, he was appointed secretary of the Congress Party by his mother, Indira Gandhi, in 1983, and became prime minister after she was assassinated. During the election campaign of 1991 he was assassinated.

Gandhi, Sonia (Sonia Maino; 1946-), Indian female politician of Italian origin. In 1968 Sonia Gandhi married Rajiv Gandhi, who then became premier in 1984. After her husband was killed as a result of bombings by the Tamil separatists on 21 May 1991, party leaders of the Congress Party urgently appealed to her to assume the leadership of the party, as they believed that only a member of the Nehru-Gandhi dynasty could be able to put the Congress Party back on the political stage. She finally accepted in 1998, and the party subsequently scored a major victory in three Indian states during the elections in December 1998. However, in 1999, her party suffered a defeat in the parliamentary elections.

Gang, group of people who come together for social purposes, often criminal. A gang may be tightly organized, with a definite leadership, or it may be a loose grouping. Some juvenile gangs have been known to be involved in delinquent behavior. In the 1920s and 1930s, crime organizations in the United States, such as the one led by Al Capone, were known as gangs.

Ganges River, in India, the most sacred Hindu river, believed to be the reincarnation of the goddess Ganga. It rises in the Himalayas and flows through northern and northeastern India, following a southeastern course across the plain of India. It joins the Brahmaputra River in Bangladesh, then continues through the vast Ganges delta to empty through several mouths (Meghna, Tetulia, Hooghly) into the Bay of Bengal. The river waters irrigate a populous agricultural area. Many cities line the river's banks, including the holy Indian cities Varanasi (Benares), Allahabad, and Calcutta, and the Bangladesh city of Dacca.

Gang of Four, group of supporters of China's Mao Tse-tung who, after Mao's death, were tried and convicted for the excesses of the Cultural Revolution of the late 1960s. Principal charges included planning a coup. Mao's widow, Jiang Qing, was identified as the group's leader; the others were Wang Hongwen, Yao Wenyuan, and Zhang Qunqiao. Imprisoned in 1976, their sentences (1981) ranged from death to 20 years in prison.
See also: China; Mao Zedong.

Gangrene, death of tissue following loss of blood supply, often after obstruction of arteries by injury, thrombosis (clot formation on a damaged artery wall), or embolism (blockage by an air bubble, clot, or other debris). Dry gangrene is seen when arterial blockage is followed by slow drying, blackening, and finally separation of dead tissue from healthy. Its treatment includes improvement of the blood flow to the healthy tissue and prevention of infection and further obstruction. Wet gangrene occurs when the dead tissue is infected with bacteria. Gas gangrene involves infection with gas-forming organisms (e.g., *Clostridium welchii*), and its spread is particularly rapid. Antibiotics, hyperbaric chambers (in which oxygen is kept at high pressure), and early amputation are often required.

Annually, masses of Hindu pilgrims visit the holy cities along the Ganges (of which Varanasi is one of the most important ones), in order to undergo a ritual cleansing.

Gannet (*Morus bassanus*), large, white seabird of the North Atlantic. It nests on isolated islands, as in the Gulf of St. Lawrence and the British Isles, and feeds on fish that it catches by spectacular vertical dives into the sea. Related species are found off South Africa, Australia, and New Zealand.

Gansu (pop. 23,140,000), province in central China; 175,357 sq mi (454,000 sq km). Capital: Lanzhou. Mountainous area with fertile valleys (of e.g. the Huang He), where soybeans, tobacco and millet are grown. Extraction of coal, petroleum, iron and copper. This area functions as the link to central Asia since the 3rd century B.C.; among others, the Silk Route ran through it. Center of the Muslim revolt (1862-1878). Somewhat industrialized due to the introduction of the railway in the 1950s.

Gantwarg, Anatoli (1948-), Russian checkers player, became the Russian champion for the first time at the age of 21. Gantwarg claimed his first world title in 1979, when he beat Harm Wiersma in Arco di Trento. He then lost the title to Wiersma in October, won it back in 1980, and lost it again a year later. Gantwarg became world champion again in 1984 and 1985, but lost the title to his fellow countryman Aleksandr Dibmann in 1986. He also won other major tournaments.

Ganymede, in Greek mythology, a young Trojan prince. Zeus, the ruler of the Gods, was fascinated by the prince's beauty and brought Ganymede to Mt. Olympus to be his cupbearer.

Gao Xingjian (1940-), Chinese prose writer and playwright. His international polemical plays such as *Signal d'alarme* (1982), *l'Arrêt de Bus* (1983) and *l'Homme Sauvage* (1985) are partly inspired by Brecht, Artaud en Beckett. In 1986, *l'Autre Arrive* was censored and from then on, none of his plays were performed in China. He settled in France as a political refugee in 1988. After the publication of *La Fuite* (1989), which is set against

Federico García Lorca (1898-1936), as drawn by Spanish painter and illustrator Gregorio Prieto.

the background of the massacre on the Square of Heavenly Peace, he was declared persona non grata by the Chinese government. His other works include *La Montagne de l'âme* (1999) and *Le Livre d'un Homme Seul* (2000). He was awarded the Nobel Prize of Literature in 2000.

Gaprindashvili, Nona (1941-), Russian female chess player, became world champion in 1962, a title she maintained until 1978. Gaprindashvili beat many strong opponents in various tournaments and was the first woman to be awarded the title of international master in 1979.

Gar, freshwater fish of the family Lepisosteidae with long, thin bodies, long jaws, and an armor of diamond-shaped scales. Gars are usually found in shallow, weedy

water from Canada to Costa Rica, but the alligator gar (*Lepisosetus spatula*), which can reach 10 ft (3 m) in length, may be found in saltwater.

Garamond, Claude (1480-1561), French type designer and publisher. He created typefaces that helped establish Roman type in place of Gothic or black letter as standard type. His royal Greek and italic types were also influential.

Garand rifle, single-shot, semiautomatic weapon. Also known as the M1, this .30-caliber gas-operated rifle was the standard rifle of the U.S. Army from 1936 to 1960. *See also:* Rifle.

Garbage, generally, refuse consisting of organic (animal or vegetable) or other matter. In computer science, the term describes inaccurate or useless data from a computer program, usually resulting from equipment malfunction, a mistake in a computer program, or unwanted or meaningless data carried in storage.

Garbo, Greta (Greta Lovisa Gustafsson; 1905-1990), Swedish-born U.S. film actress. She was a talented actress known for her aura of glamor and her passion for privacy; her 24 films include *Anna Christie* (1930), *Camille* (1937), and *Ninotchka* (1939). She retired in 1941.

García Lorca, Federico (1898-1936), Spanish poet and dramatist. Inspired by his native Andalusia and by gypsy folklore, he made his reputation with *Gypsy Ballads* (1928) and the surrealism-influenced *Poet in New York* (published 1940). He returned to folk themes in the plays *Blood Wedding* (1933), *Yerma* (1935), and *The House of Bernarda Alba* (1936). He was also a musician and theater director. He was murdered by Franco's Nationalists in the Spanish Civil War.

García Márquez, Gabriel (1928-), Colombian novelist. Winner of the 1982 Nobel Prize in literature, he first achieved world prominence in 1967 with *One Hundred Years of Solitude*. Set in the imaginary jungle town of Macondo, this novel tells of the decline of the town and the Buendía family. It perpetuates and brings to its fullest literary expression a literary style known as magical realism. Macondo was also the setting for two earlier works, *Leaf Storm* (1955) and *No One Writes to the Colonel* (1968). Later novels include *The Autumn of the Patriarch* (1975), a portrait of an aged and isolated dictator; *Chronicle of a Death Foretold*, a story of love, jealousy, and murder; *Love in the Time of Cholera* (1988), a love story; *The General in His Labyrinth* (1989), a novel about the South American 19th-century revolutionary Simón Bolívar, which generated great controversy; *Of Love and Other Demons* (1994); and *News of a Kidnapping* (1996).

Garcilaso de la Vega (1503-1536), became famous as the first Renaissance poet of Spain. As an innovator, his name is still as-

G

G

sociated before anything else with the 'lira', a form of poetry that later became very popular and which he first used in his poem 'A la flor de Gnido'. The lira is made up of eleven-syllable and seven-syllable lines of poetry combined in five-line strophes. The name 'lira' (lyre) is derived from the first line of the poem: 'Si de mi baja lira' (If From My Humble Lyre).

Garcilaso de la Vega was courtier and participated in the crusades of Charles V. In 1529 he traveled in the retinue of the emperor to Italy. He fell into disfavor in 1531, at which time he decided to remain in Naples and join a circle of humanists in that city.

Together with his friend Juan Boscán y Almogáver (1490-1542), he applied himself to the art of poetry in the Italian style and introduced it in Spain. The main examples include Petrarca and the classics. His work consists of 38 sonnets, a 'letter in poetic form', two elegies or mourning poems, three eclogues or pastoral poems and some minor works.

Gardenia (genus *Gardenia*), evergreen flowering shrub native to subtropical Asia and Africa that bears waxy, fragrant white flowers and has dark green, glossy leaves. It grows outdoors in the southern United States and blooms from May to September. In colder climates it is grown in greenhouses.

Gardening, process of cultivating plants, often as a hobby to beautify homes, sometimes to produce herbs, vegetables, and fruits for consumption.

Garden of Eden *See:* Eden, Garden of.

Gardiner, John Eliot (1943-), English conductor. Studied history and Arabic in Cambridge, music at King's College in London with Thurston Dart and in Paris with Nadia Boulanger (1967-1968), and conducting with George Hurst. Made his debut as a conductor in 1966, and as an opera conductor in 1969 - both in London. Founder and artistic director of the Monteverdi Choir (1964) and its accompanying orchestra (1968), the English Baroque Soloists (1978) and the Orchestre Révolutionaire et Romantique (1990). He was the conductor of the CBC Vancouver Orchestra from 1980 to 1983, and was associated with the Opera in Lyon from 1983 to 1988. Permanent guest conductor of the NDR Symphony Orchestra since 1991.

Gardner, Erle Stanley (1889-1970), U.S. mystery writer, creator of lawyer-detective Perry Mason. Gardner wrote over 140 novels under his name and the pseudonym A. A. Fair.

Gardner, Wayne (1959-), Australian motorcycle racer, made his debut in 1977. He claimed his first Grand Prix victory in 1986 in the 500 cc category on Honda at the Jarama racetrack. Gardner became world champion on Honda in 1987.

Garfield, James Abram (1831-1881), 20th president of the United States (Mar. 1881-Sept. 1881). Fatally wounded by an assassin

In the eighteenth-century garden of Blenheim Palace (Oxfordshire), designed by Lancelot (Capability) Brown (1716-1783), the link between the house and the garden was severed again. This carefully composed informality intended to enhance the beauty of nature as much as possible and to convey a romantic feeling onto the visitor.

less than four months after his inauguration, Garfield served only 199 days in office.

A supporter of the newly founded antislavery and antisecessionist Republican party, Garfield was elected to the Ohio state senate in 1859. In 1862 he was elected to the House of Representatives. On Reconstruction, a critical postwar issue, he sided with the radical Republicans, voting for the impeachment of President Andrew Johnson and favoring the continued presence of federal troops in the former Confederacy. Garfield was elected to the Senate in 1880. Later that year the Republican presidential convention was deadlocked between two frontrunners, James G. Blaine and former president Grant. Blaine's supporters eventually voted for Garfield as a compromise candidate. Support for Garfield grew, and he won the nomination and the elections. On July 1, 1881, Charles J. Guiteau, a disappointed office-seeker, shot Garfield at the Washington, D.C., train station. The assassination caused Congress to begin reforms to abolish the 'spoils system' of distribution of federal jobs and set up competitive examinations in the civil service to ensure fairer political appointments.

Garfish *See:* Gar.

Gargoyle, decorative waterspout on a building, used to throw rainwater clear of the walls. Though sometimes of plain geometric form, in medieval buildings of the 13th-16th centuries gargoyles were fanciful or grotesque images of demons or animals, with the water pouring out of the open mouths. Although gargoyles are to be found on many ancient buildings, including the

Parthenon in Athens, they are mostly associated with medieval structures such as the cathedrals of Milan, Italy, and Notre Dame in Paris.

Garibaldi, Giuseppe (1807-1882), Italian patriot and general. After fighting in a republican uprising in Genoa in 1834, he fled to South America, leading guerrilla revolutions in Brazil and Uruguay. In 1848 he returned to Italy to fight against Austrian, French, and Neapolitan armies in support of Mazzini's short-lived Roman Republic. On its collapse, Garibaldi fled to the United States. Returning to Italy in 1854, he led guerrilla campaigns (1859-1862) against Austria and captured Sicily and Naples with a volunteer army, his famous 'Red Shirts', in the most decisive campaign of the Risorgimento. He surrendered the territories to King Victor Emmanuel, effectively unifying Italy. In 1862 and 1867 Garibaldi unsuccessfully tried to capture Rome from the pope. Subsequently he fought for the French against Prussia (1870). In 1874 he was elected to the Italian parliament.

Garland, (Hannibal) Hamlin (1860-1940), U.S. writer. His fiction portrays pioneering midwestern farm life with bitterness and realism. Among his work is the story collection *Main-Travelled Roads* (1891) and his autobiographical 'Middle Boarder' stories (4 vols., 1917-1928). He won the 1921 Pulitzer Prize for biography for *A Daughter of the Middle Border*, about his wife and her family.

Garland, Judy (Frances Gumm; 1922-1969), U.S. singer and movie actress. Garland was the daughter of vaudeville performers. She costarred with Mickey Rooney in 9 films, and starred in *The Wizard of Oz* (1939), *Meet Me in St. Louis* (1944), and *A Star Is Born* (1954).

Garlic (*Allium sativum*), perennial plant of the lily family; also, its edible bulb. Garlic is rich in calcium, potassium, phosphorus, and other nutrients. It is claimed to have a beneficial effect on the digestive system and the mucous membranes and to be helpful in treating high blood pressure, respiratory diseases, and other disorders.

Garnet, group of common silicate minerals, including some gemstones and some varieties used as abrasives. They are transparent to translucent, red, brown, green, yellow, and white, and have a glassy luster. The most highly valued garnet gem is *demantoid*, an emerald green variety found in the former USSR and Italy. Perhaps the most popular is a ruby red *pyrope* found in South Africa, Bohemia, Arizona, and New Mexico. Crushed garnet is used as an abrasive for sand-blasting, dental wheels, lens grinding, and sandpaper.
See also: Gem.

Garrett, Pat (1850-1908), U.S. frontier sheriff. He arrested Billy the Kid in 1880. After 'the Kid's' escape from jail in New Mexico, Garrett pursued and shot him in 1881.
See also: Billy the Kid.

G

Garrick, David (1717-1779), English actor, manager, and dramatist. He introduced a more natural acting style to the English stage in roles such as Hamlet and partially restored the original versions of Shakespeare's plays. He managed the Drury Lane Theatre, 1747-1776.

Garrincha (Manoel Francisco dos Santos; 1933-1983), Brazilian soccer player, played outside right in the Brazilian national team a total of 54 times between 1955 and 1966. He played together with Didi, Vava and Pelé in the team that became world champion in 1958 (in Sweden) and in 1962 (in Chile). Garrincha, with the nickname 'Mané' (small bird), was a player who used inimitable diversions. The once so highly-gifted soccer player ended in the gutter at the end of his life due to his drinking.

Garrison, William Lloyd (1805-1879), leader of the U.S. abolitionist movement. From 1831-1865 he published *The Liberator*, an influential crusading journal that opposed slavery, war, and capital punishment and supported temperance and women's rights. He was president of the American Anti-Slavery Society (1843-1865), which he helped found in 1833.
See also: Abolitionism.

Garter, Order of the, highest order of British knighthood, established in 1348 by King Edward III. It consists of the sovereign, the Prince of Wales, 25 knights, and such foreign rulers and others as the monarch may name. Its patron is St. George.
See also: Knighthood, Orders of.

Garter snake, any of the harmless snakes of the genus *Thamnophis*. Garter snakes are the most common snakes of North America, growing to a length of 20-30 in (50-70 cm) and feeding on frogs or salamanders. Some are aquatic or semiaquatic and kept as pets.

Garuda, creature from Hindu mythology, with the body of a human and the beak and legs of a bird of prey; ruler of birds and enemy of snakes. Transports the god Vishnu. Symbol of the Sun.

Gary, Romain (Roman Leibovitch Kacev; 1914-1980), French author and diplomat, married to the actress Jean Seberg for a number of years. His first novel, *l'Éducation européenne* (Forest of Anger/Nothing Important Ever Dies, 1945) is set in the Polish resistance during WW II. The main character seeks some form of dignity amidst the violence, one of the main motifs in Gary's work. Other books include *Le grand vestiaire* (1946), *Les racines du ciel* (The Roots of Heaven, 1956; Prix Goncourt), *Gloire à nos illustres pionniers* (1962), *Chien blanc* (White Dog, 1970), *Clair de femme* (1977), *Les cerfs-volants* (1980). In addition, Gary wrote a few novels under the pseudonym Emile Ajar, including *La vie devant soi* (1975, Prix Goncourt), which would later be filmed, and *Les angoisses du roi Salomon* (King Solomon, 1978). This novel describes the loneliness and isolation of the weak and vulnerable groups of society against the background of a Parisian work-

ing-class district. The mystery surrounding the identity of Emile Ajar was not solved until Gary had died.

Gas, form of matter having no fixed shape or volume, as distinct from a solid, which has a distinct shape and volume, or a liquid, with distinct volume. Boyle's law, Charles' law, and Avogadro's law describe the relationship between the pressure, temperature, volume, and number of particles of gas in a given container.

Gas, gaseous fuel, not to be confused with gasoline, which is a liquid fuel often referred to as gas. An important energy source for homes, institutions, and industries, gas is used to heat and cool buildings, cook, heat water, and create steam. Chemicals in gas are used to produce plastics, drugs, and cleansers. Gas is used to create many products, such as metals, paper, fabrics, glass, and cement. Two kinds of gas exist: *natural* and *manufactured*. Natural gas is found by drilling into a gas deposit in the earth; manufactured gas is created by processing coal or petroleum. The U.S. is a leading natural gas producing country and has nearly 2 million miles (3,200,000 km) of gas pipeline through which gas is transmitted and distributed. Because the use of gas does not create much air pollution, scientists are trying to develop ways in which it can be used as a transportation fuel to power cars, trucks, and ships.

Gas meter, device that measures the volume of gas delivered to a consumer. Meters usually have several measuring chambers. As one chamber is being emptied, the other is being filled. This provides a steady flow of gas to the consumer. The total volume of gas used is determined by counting the number of times each chamber is filled and emptied.

Gasohol, fuel made by mixing 90% unleaded gasoline with 10% alcohol made by fermenting farm crops such as potatoes and grains. Used in automobile and truck engines, gasohol produces less air pollution than gasoline.

Gas oil, one of several liquids obtained by distilling petroleum. Heavier than gasoline, it has a very high boiling point. It is used as diesel fuel for train, truck, and bus engines, and is the source from which heating fuel and lubricating oils are produced.

Gasoline, liquid fuel, a mixture of hydrocarbons produced by refining petroleum. It is known as petrol in Britain and various other countries. Used to power engines in cars, trucks, airplanes, and motorboats, it is an important transportation fuel. It is also used as a cooking fuel.

Gasoline engine, engine that uses gasoline as fuel. Gasoline engines are internal-combustion engines because the fuel, mixed with air, is burned inside the engine itself to produce hot gases that cause parts of the engine to move. These movements in turn cause other mechanical parts of the vehicle to operate. Gasoline engines power most transportation vehicles, such as cars, trucks, air-

planes, and motorcycles, as well as lawn mowers, snowmobiles, and small tractors.
See also: Gasoline.

Gas poisoning *See:* Chemical and biological warfare; First aid.

Gass, William (Howard) (1924-   ), a U.S. author. Gass was born in Fargo, North Dakota, and served in the U.S. Navy in World War II. After graduating from Kenyon College and receiving a Ph.D. from Cornell University, he taught philosophy at several universities. *Omensetter's Luck* (1966), his best-known novel, deals with life and death in a small town in Ohio. *In the Heart of the Country* (1968) is a collection of short stories on the theme of loneliness. *Fiction and the Figures of Life* (1971) is a collection of essays. Other work includes: *Willie Master's Lonesome Wife* (1971), *The First Winter of My Married Life* (1979), and *Habitations of the World* (1985).

Gastritis, inflammation of the stomach lining, which can be either acute or chronic. Symptoms include sensation of dullness in the upper abdomen, loss of appetite, fever (in acute gastritis), nausea and vomiting (in acute gastritis), diarrhea, general aches and pains, intolerance to certain foods (in chronic gastritis), and anemia (in chronic gastritis). The acute condition may be caused by dietary indiscretion, specific food intolerances, chemical irritants (such as alcohol and aspirin), or food poisoning or many types of inflammation caused by bacteria or other microorganisms. Chronic gastritis, less common, can be associated with gastric ulcer, cancer of the stomach wall, and pernicious anemia. Diagnosis is established with the chemical and histological analysis of gastric secretions, gastroscopy, and X rays. For acute gastritis, treatment usually consists of removal of irritants and resting of the stomach.
See also: Stomach.

Gastropod *See:* Mollusk.

Gastroscope, tubelike instrument for visual examination of the inside of the stomach. The instrument employs fiber optics to light the stomach wall and transmit the image back to a lens. The gastroscope's flexible tube reaches the stomach via the mouth and esophagus.
See also: Stomach.

Gas turbine *See:* Turbine.

Gates, Bill, (William Henry Gates; 1955-), U.S. businessman, founder and chairman of the Microsoft Corporation, by far the largest producer of software. He developed a version of BASIC for the first microcomputer (MITS Altair), when he was a student at Harvard. Gates co-founded Microsoft in 1975 with his friend Paul Allen.
In 1981, Microsoft released the operating system MS-DOS (MicroSoft Disk Operating System) for IBM, which soon became the worldwide standard system. IBM developed its own system, OS/2, but was unable to compete with MS-DOS.
Gates, who had become one of the wealthi-

G

est men in the world, described his vision for the future of the information society in *The Road Ahead* in 1995. In that same year, Microsoft, which had become the world's largest software producer with sales figures of over $6 billion, was subjected to an investigation by anti-trust authorities. Gates ran into difficulties when an American judge sentenced him for misusing his monopoly position on the computer market. Gates resigned as chairman and was succeeded by Steve Ballmer. Gates still remained connected to the company, in an advisory capacity and as Chairman of the Board of Directors. He is also interested in bio technical research.
See also: Computer.

Gatling, Richard Jordan (1818-1903), U.S. inventor. After improving upon numerous agricultural techniques and inventing such equipment as the wheat planting machine in the early 1850's, Gatling patented his most famous invention, the Gatling gun, in 1862. A crank operated, multibarrel machine gun, the Gatling gun fired 600 rounds per minute. It was used in the Spanish-American War.

GATT *See:* General Agreement on Tariffs and Trade.

Gatun Lake, artificial lake in Panama Canal Zone created in 1912 by the damming of the Chagres River. Its water makes up part of the Canal route and is used to operate the canal's locks.
See also: Panama Canal Zone.

Gaucher's disease, rare, sometimes hereditary, disorder of lipid metabolism resulting in an abnormal accumulation of fats and fat-like substances (lipids) in the liver and spleen, greatly enlarging those organs, as well as jaundice, skeletal lesions, and anemia. The disease is the result of the body's inability to produce enzymes to break down fats. It is incurable, although surgical removal of the spleen can relieve some of the symptoms.

Gaucho, cowboy of the South American pampas (prairies). Gauchos flourished in the 18th and 19th centuries; they were skilled riders, usually employed to herd cattle. Their function ceased with the fencing of the pampas and reorganization of the cattle industry, but like the U.S. cowboys they survived as local folk heroes.

Gaudí, Antonio (Antoni Gaudí i Cornet; 1852-1926), Spanish architect. His fluid, intricate, and bizarre designs express Art Nouveau. He used glazed tiles to color his sculpted architecture. He worked mostly in Barcelona, creating the Casa Milá, the Park Güell, and his masterpiece, the Church of the Holy Family (1882-1930).
See also: Art nouveau.

Gauguin, Paul Eugène-Henri (1848-1903), French postimpressionist painter noted for his pictures of Polynesian life. After painting in a symbolist style at Pont-Aven, Brittany, and working with Vincent van Gogh, he went to Tahiti (1891-1893; 1895-1901) and the Marquesas (1901-1903) in the South Pacific. He painted scenes in brilliant colors and flattened, simplified forms. His concept of primitivism in art influenced expressionism.

Gaul, name given by the ancient Romans to the 2 regions inhabited by the Celts: Gallia Cisalpina, or northern Italy, and Gallia Transalpina, the area roughly equivalent to modern France, including parts of modern Belgium, Germany, Switzerland, and the Netherlands. Northern Italy was conquered by Celtic invaders in the 5th century B.C.; they in turn were subjugated by the Romans in the 3rd century B.C. Julius Caesar gave Roman citizenship to the Cisalpine Celts, and in 42 B.C. Augustus Caesar incorporated Cisalpine Gaul into Italy. Transalpine Gaul came under Celtic control in the 5th century B.C., and from about 400 B.C. Rome and the Greek colony of Massilia (Marseilles) were allied. In the late 2nd century B.C. the Romans took more decisive control of this region. At the same time Germanic tribes were crossing the Rhine River and pushing southward into Gaul. The Romans fully occupied southern Gaul around 121 B.C., and during the Gallic Wars (58-51 B.C.) Julius Caesar repulsed the Germanic tribes and conquered the whole of Gaul. Under Roman rule, Gaul was divided into a number of provinces that adopted Roman laws and customs. Cities were founded, roads built, and the area prospered. It remained under Roman rule until the 5th century A.D., when it was overrun by various Germanic tribes.

Gauntlet, protective glove worn by medieval knights. Early ones were made of very small chain links. Later ones were of leather covered with hinged steel plates.

Gauss, Johann Friedrich Carl (1777-1855), German mathematician who discovered the method of least squares (for reducing experimental errors), made many contributions to the theory of numbers, and discovered a non-Euclidean geometry. He directed the astronomical observatory at Göttingen (1807-1855). In 1833 he invented, with Wilhelm Weber, the electric telegraph.
See also: Geometry; Telegraph.

Gaudí's Casa Milá in Barcelona (1905-10), known locally as 'the stone quarry' or 'La Pedrera', is a brilliant feat of engineering, as well as one of the most unusual buildings in Europe. It was designed as a sculptural organism, in which all surfaces and supports blend together, without recourse to distinctions between columns and beams. It is constructed from stone, and the undulating bands of stonework wrapped around the façades, are broken only by the explosions of ironwork around the window openings. Internally, the building opens up into two enormous sources of light. The roof level is broken up by a motley collection of sculptured chimneys, light sources, roofs, etc., many of which have human facial characteristics.

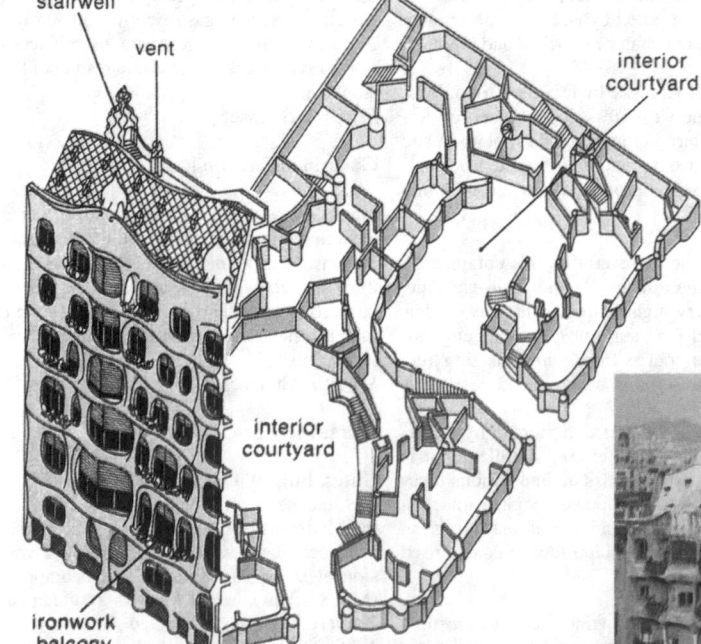

stairwell
vent
interior courtyard
interior courtyard
ironwork balcony

Casa Milá apartment house in Barcelona.

Gautama *See:* Buddha, Gautama.

Gautier, Théophile (1811-1872), French poet, novelist, and critic. He was a supporter of the aesthetic movement calling for 'art for art's sake,' which he explained in the preface to his novel *Mademoiselle de Maupin* (1835-1836). He wrote art, drama, and ballet criticism. His volumes of verse include *Enamels and Cameos* (1852).

Gavial (*Gavialis gangeticus*), harmless, slender-nosed relative of alligators and crocodiles. It is found in Indian rivers, where it grows to a maximum of 20 ft (6 m) on a diet of fish. The false gharial is a crocodile of southeastern Asia.

Gaviría Trujillo, César (1947-   ), Colombian politician. Gaviría, originally an economist, was minister of Finance and Foreign Affairs from 1986 to 1989. The 1990 elections were won by the Liberal Party, and Gaviría, as the presidential candidate of that party, became the new leader of Colombia. His policy focused on counteracting drug-related terrorism, something he tried to achieve with economic and politic means. His attempts proved to have little results; the popularity of the Liberal Party rapidly dropped due to economic decline and violence on the part of the guerrilla and drug traffickers. Despite these problems, the Liberal Party still managed to maintain its majority in parliament during the 1994 elections. Presidential elections took place as well: Gaviría was succeeded by his fellow party member Ernesto Samper Pizano. In 1994, Gaviría was appointed Secretary-General of the Organization of American States (OAS).

Johann Carl Friedrich Gauss (1777-1855) was not only a mathematician with a thorough insight into theoretical problems (the number theory), but he was also an extremely active investigator of nature. From 1807 on, he was the director of the astronomical ob-servatory at Gottingen. His land surveys for the Kingdom of Hannover, led to the development of a general theory of curved surfaces. Differential geometry developed from this, and has grown into a rich theory with many applications.

French poet Théophile Gautier (1811-1872), immortalized by his famous contemporary, photographer Félix Nadar (1820-1910).

Gawaine, Sir *See:* Round Table.

Gay, John (1685-1732), English poet and dramatist, author of *The Beggar's Opera* (1728). Using English ballads, he satirized Italian operatic forms and contemporary politics in this comedy of highwaymen, thieves, and prostitutes, on which Brecht based his *Threepenny Opera*.

Gay-Lussac, Joseph Louis (1778-1850), French chemist and physicist. He is best known for Gay-Lussac's law (1808), which states that when gases combine to give a gaseous product, the ratio of the volumes of the reacting gases to that of the product is a simple, integral one. He also showed that all gases increase in volume by the same fraction for the same increase in temperature, $1/273.2$ for $33.8°F$ ($1°C$), and made 2 balloon ascents to investigate atmospheric composition and the intensity of the earth's magnetic field at altitude. His many important contributions to inorganic chemistry include the identification of cyanogen gas (1815).

Gay Nineties, common name for the 1890s in U.S. history. Although the early years of the decade were marked by economic expansion, there was a serious depression from 1893 to 1897, millions of industrial workers lost their jobs. Farmers suffered too. Many had gone into debt to purchase machinery that would increase their production, and falling prices left the farmers with too little money to repay their debts. The depression ended only with the Spanish-American War, which marked the emergence of the United States as a world power. The term 'Gay Nineties' came into use in the 1930s, when the worldwide economic crisis made people nostalgic for what they chose to remember about the 1890s: the victorious war, the prosperity experienced by some, and the simpler charm of life.

Gay Rights *See:* Homosexuality.

Gaza Strip, narrow piece of land in the former southwestern Palestine, about 26 mi (42 km) long, 4-6 mi (6.4-8 km) wide. After the Arab-Israeli war of 1948, it was granted to Egypt, and many Arab refugees fled there. Israel occupied the area as a result of the 1967 Arab-Israeli war. Although the Israeli-Egyptian peace treaty (1979) provided for negotiations on self-rule in Gaza, the area has continued to be a subject of acrimonious disagreement, with violence occurring between protesting Palestinian Arabs and Israeli troops. In 1994, the strip was given limited autonomy under the Palestinian National Authority.
See also: Palestinian National Authority.

Gazelle, slender, graceful antelope (genus *Gazella*) of Asia and Africa. Males are horned; females may have short spikes. They are usually 2-3 ft (60 to 90 cm) high at the shoulder, swift, and light-footed. They inhabit dry open country. Thompson's and Grant's gazelles live in Africa; the goitered gazelle, so called from a swelling in the throat, in Asian deserts.

Gazelle hound *See:* Saluki.

Gaziantep (formerly: Aintab; in ancient times, Doliche; pop. 603,000), capital of the homonymous province in Southern Turkey, situated in a valley at a height of 1000 m (province 3096 sq mi / 8015 sq km, pop. 954,000). Market town with textile, copper and leather industries. Medieval fort and archeological museum. Cultivation of nuts, cotton, tobacco and grain in the vicinity.

Gdansk (pop. 465,000; formerly Danzig), large Polish industrial city and port on the Baltic Sea, with some of the world's largest shipyards. Its economy rests on mechanical engineering and chemical industries. Once a major city in the Hanseatic League, since 1772 Gdansk has alternately been a free city and a city under German or Polish control. The German invasion of Poland in 1939, on the pretext of reestablishing the city as German territory, precipitated World War II. The city became a center of the workers' rights movement led by Lech Walesa during the 1970s and 1980s.
See also: Poland.

Gdynia (pop. 252,000), city and a major seaport on the Gulf of Gdansk, an arm of the Baltic Sea. Gdynia is in northern Poland just northwest of the port of Gdansk. Together the two cities handle most of Poland's foreign trade. Gdynia is also a naval base and a manufacturing city with shipbuiliding and ship-repairing facilities. Gdynia was a fishing village until after World War I, when the Polish government developed it as a port. During the German occupation in World War II it was called Gotenhafen.

Gê, group of Native American tribes in east central Brazil. The Gê traditionally had a sophisticated social structure with intricate rituals and ceremonies. For food, the men hunted animals and the women gathered wild plants and raised potatoes and yams.

Gears are toothed wheels that are used to transmit motion from one shaft to another. Spur gears (A) have teeth cut parallel to the axis of rotation and connect shafts that are parallel to each other. Cone-shaped bevel gears (B) have straight teeth and are used to transmit power between shafts whose axes intersect. Hypoid gears (C), or bevel gears with straight teeth cut to an angle to the shaft axis, can transmit power between shafts whose axes cross each other in different planes. Spiral bevel gears (D) have teeth cut in a spiral, resulting in a larger area of contact between meshing teeth and permitting larger torques to be transmitted. In a worm gear (E) a spirally threaded worm drives a spiral-toothed gear at right angles to its own axis. Double helical gears (F) have two opposing helices cut in the same gear in order to cancel the sideways thrust generated by single spiral gears and thus reduce gear wear.

G

Although modern times have changed their lives, several Gê tribes still practice some of their traditions.

Gear, toothed wheel forming part of a system by which motion is transmitted between rotating shafts. By selecting gear wheels with different numbers of teeth, the shafts can be made to rotate at different speeds from each other, as in an automobile gearbox.

Gebrselassie, Haile (1973-), Ethiopian runner, specialized in long distances. He became world champion for the 10 km during the junior championships in 1992. A year later he claimed his first world record for the 5 km: 12.56,96. He has since achieved victories in countless competitions, as well as world records for the 3, 5 and 10 km. Gebrselassie became Olympic champion for the 10 km in 1996, with an Olympic record and a world record of 27.07,34. He was the world champion for the 10 km in 1993, 1995 and 1997. Gebrselassie reclaimed 'his' world record for the 10 km on June 1, 1998

Certain animals periodically shed their skin. This photo was taken at the exact moment a gecko was crawling out of its old skin.

with a time of 26.22,75; no less than two weeks later he also managed to reclaim 'his' world record for the 5 km in Helsinki: 12.39,36. He won the 10 km at the Olympics in Sydney. Afterwards he declared that he wanted to apply himself to marathons. At his debut at the World Championship half-marathon in 2001, he won the title first go. In 2002, he made his debut running a whole marathon in London. He came in third in 2.06,35.

Gecko, any of more than 400 species of small harmless lizards found in warm climates. The gecko's name is derived from the sound of the cry of on species. Geckos are most numerous in southeastern Asia, Africa, and Australia. The largest gecko is the tokay of Malaysia, 10 to 14 inches (25 to 36 cm) long. The gecko's tapering head and short, flat body are covered with tiny scales that give the skin a soft appearance. Many species have brittle tails that break off easily. The leaf-fingered gecko is among the many species that have clinging pads at the tips of their toes, enabling them to run on walls and ceilings. Geckos move about only at night, feeding mainly on insects.

Gedda, Nicòlai (Nicolai Ustinov; 1925-), Swedish singer (tenor), studied in Stockholm, where he also made his debut in 1952. Gedda has since become one of the most prominent singers of his generation, with a very extensive repertoire. He mainly sings operas in German or French, both classical and contemporary. In addition, he sings light operas and gives song recitals.

Geesink, Anton (1934-), Dutch judoka (heavyweight), two-time all categories world champion (1961, 1965), European champion more than 20 times (between 1952-1967) and Dutch champion countless times. His all categories Olympic title, which he won in Tokyo in 1964, was a peak in his career. At this last event Geesink proved himself to be a true shihan (grand master): after his victory, while still lying on the mat, he sent away the supporters who had rushed up on to the 'holy' tatami (judo mat), something which made a deep impression in Japan. After his judo career he was successful in catch-as-catch-can competitions. Geesink was the first European to achieve the 9th dan degree. He became a member of the executive board of the International Judo Federation in 1985 as Head of Training and Development; he was chosen as a member of the International Olympic Committee (IOC) two years later. In 2000, Geesink received an honorary degree from the Kokushikan University in Tokio.

Gehrig, Lou (Henry Louis Gehrig; 1903-1941), U.S. baseball player. As first baseman for the New York Yankees (1923-1939) he set a record by playing 2,130 consecutive games. He had a .361 batting average in 7 world series, a lifetime average of .341, and 493 home runs. He died of a rare muscle-wasting disease, amyotrophic lateral sclerosis, called Lou Gehrig's disease. Gehrig was inducted into the National Baseball Hall of Fame in 1939.

Gehry, Frank Owen (1929-), American architect, with an office in Los Angeles since 1962. He made sketches of buildings that appeared to be not entirely finished and in which he used cheap materials such as gauze, corrugated iron and plywood, giving each component a different 'skin', for example the California Aerospace Museum and Theatre (1982-1984). Famous buildings in Europe include the Vitra Design Museum (1986-1989) in Weil am Rhein and the much talked-about Guggenheim Museum in Bilbao (1991-1997), with the eye-catching metal rolling roof that would be unthinkable without sophisticated computer programs. Gehry also designed furniture, including chairs made of cardboard and later from curved wooden planks.

Geiger counter, or Geiger-Müller tube, instrument for detecting the presence of and measuring radiation, such as alpha particles, and beta, gamma, and X rays. It can count individual particles at rates up to about 10,000/sec and is used widely in medicine, in industries that use radioactive materials, and in prospecting for radioactive ores. A fine wire anode runs along the axis of a metal cylinder that has sealed insulating ends, contains a mixture of argon or neon and methane at low pressure, and acts as the cathode, the potential between them being about 1 kV. Particles entering through a thin window cause ionization in the gas; electrons build up around the anode, and there is a momentary drop in the interelectrode potential, which appears as a voltage pulse in an associated counting circuit.
See also: Radiation.

Geisel, Theodor *See:* Seuss, Dr..

Geisha, a Japanese entertainer who sings, dances, and provides lighthearted talk. Originally, geisha were men, but since 1800 only women and girls have become geisha. Geisha perform in white make-up and kimonos before male audiences in bars, teahouses, and establishments called geisha houses. By tradition geisha must remain unmarried or leave the profession. Geisha learn their skills at special schools; while learning, they are considered apprentice geisha, or maiko.

Geissler tube, tube lamp invented by Heinrich Geissler in 1858. It consists of a glass tube containing gas and air under low pressure, with metal electrodes at each end. When electricity is applied to the electrodes, a current passes through the tube and causes the gas within to glow.

Gelasius, Saint (?-496), Roman Catholic pope elected 492, noted for his 494 letter to Byzantine emperor Anastasius I setting forth the relationship between spiritual authority and secular power. He contended that the power of the popes stood above that of secular leaders.

Gelatin, colorless protein substance obtained from heating collagen, which is extracted from the skin, connective tissue, and bones of cattle and hogs, in boiling water or acid. Gelatin is used as an ingredient in jellies and baked goods, to form capsules around pills, and to coat photographic film.

Geldof, Bob (1954-), rock musician who launched a musical mobilization to aid starving people in Africa. In 1984 a single record by a group of British rock stars ('Band Aid') organized by Geldof raised $11 million. The Live Aid concert, held in London and Philadelphia in July 1985 and broadcast around the world, brought in an additional $72 million.

Gell-Mann, Murray (1929-), U.S. physicist. He was awarded the 1969 Nobel Prize for physics for his work on the classification of subatomic particles (notably K-mesons and hyperons) and their interactions. He (and independently George Zweig) proposed the quark as a basic component of most subatomic particles.
See also: Particle physics.

Gelsemium, any of various climbing shrubs belonging to the family Loganieaceae, with sword-shaped, glossy leaves, clusters of flowers, and fruit containing winged seeds. The flowers, roots and leaves are poisonous.

Gem, mineral or stone prized for its beauty and rarity and durable enough to be used in jewelry and for ornaments. Most types of gem are found in igneous rocks. The chief ones have a hardness of 8 or more on the Mohs' scale and are relatively resistant to cleavage and fracture, though some are fragile. They are identified and characterized by their specific gravity and optical properties, especially the refractive index. Gems of high refractive index show great brilliancy and prismatic dispersion ('fire'). Other attractive optical effects include chatoyancy (changeable color or luster), dichroism (different color in different light), opalescence (reflection or iridescence), and asterism (a star-shaped gleam caused by regular intrusions in the crystal lattice). Since earliest times gems have been engraved. Somewhat later cutting and polishing were developed, the cabochon (rounded) cut generally being used. In the late Middle Ages faceting, now

the commonest cutting style, arose. The most valuable gems are diamonds, rubies, sapphires, and emeralds. Other materials-such as aquamarine, garnet, jade, opal, turquoise-are considered semiprecious stones. Amber, coral, and pearls are gems of organic origin.

Gemayel, Amin (1942-), president of Lebanon (1982-1988), elected after the assassination of his brother, president-elect Bashir Gemayel. He worked to suppress factional strife between his Christian Phalange party and Druze, Palestinian, and Lebanese Muslims and to secure the withdrawal of Syrian and Israeli forces from the country.

Gemayel, Bechir (1947-1982), Lebanese Christian politician, succeeded his father as leader of the Falangists during the civil war of 1975-1976. Gemayal dealt summarily with all of his competitors when a united front of Christian groupings was formed under the leadership of former President Chamille Chamoun and managed to gain control of the Christian militias. During the Israeli invasion of 1982, the military forces of the Falange worked together with the Israelis. When the Palestinian troops were forced to retreat from Beirut in 1982, Gemayel was chosen as president, but was killed in a bombing before his term of office even began.

Gemayel, Pierre Amine (1905-1984), in 1936 co-founder and later leader of the Lebanese nationalist youth organization of Falangists (Kata'ib movement), which rejected Lebanon's affiliation to any other Arabic powers. Between 1958 and 1969

Gemayal fulfilled various ministerships for the movement, which was renamed as a political party in 1952 - a party that many regarded as fascist because its ideology was derived from the German national-socialists.

Gemini missions, series of American orbital space flights using the 2-person Gemini capsule. Gemini 3 was launched by the 2-stage Titan 2 rocket on Mar. 23, 1965. The Gemini 4 mission in June 1965 lasted 97 hrs and 56 mins, carrying astronauts James A. McDivitt and Edward H. White II; White walked in space for over 20 min. The last mission, Gemini 12, was in Nov. 1966.
See also: Space exploration.

Gender, in grammar, the designation of nouns and nounlike words as belonging to distinct categories. (The word comes from *genus*, the Latin word for 'kind.') Many languages divide nouns into the 2 genders of animate and inanimate, but more common are the classifications masculine, feminine, and neuter. These three genders exist in Russian and German, there are remnants of them in English ('he', 'she', and 'it'.). Other languages-such as French, Spanish, Italian, and Portuguese-have only 2 genders, masculine and feminine. Nouns that refer to males and females are often assigned their 'natural gender' (French, *le fils*, 'son', is masculine), but the gender of most nouns is independent of sexual class (French, *une proposition*, 'suggestion', is feminine; German, *das Mädchen*, 'girl', is neuter). Usually, gender depends on the spelling or derivation of the word. The spelling of a word's ending often indicates the gender. Many but not all languages classify words by gender.

The propulsion of rockets requires extremely powerful chemical reactions, as is evident from this photograph of the launching of Gemini 7. However, the energy that is released here (from reactions between electron clouds from atoms) is incomparably smaller than the energy that is being produced during nuclear reactions.

G

Gene, smallest particle of hereditary information that is passed from parent to offspring. Genes consist of chainlike molecules of nucleic acids: DNA in most organisms and RNA in some viruses. The genes are normally located on the chromosomes found in the nucleus of each cell. The genetic information is coded by the sequences of the 4 bases present in nucleic acids, with a differing 3-base code for each amino acid, such that each gene contains the information for the synthesis of 1 protein chain.
See also: Heredity; Genetic engineering.

Genealogy, study of family origins and history involving the compilation of lists of ancestors showing the line of descent. Apart from its value to the general historian, genealogy represents both a highly skilled professional activity and a widespread amateur preoccupation. In modern times, the main purposes of genealogy are to gain historical information to settle legal questions, such as inheritance, and to gain membership in certain patriotic and hereditary organizations. Although genealogies existed in ancient times among the Babylonians and the Hebrews, they were passed on by oral tradition and cannot be historically verified. In medieval Europe, family names were used only by the upper classes, and genealogical records for the other classes are nonexistent. In England, parish records were instituted for the general public in the 16th century.

Gene mapping, delineation of the genes on a cell's chromosomes, implying the identification of the complete sequence of the DNA, the material that makes up a gene. One current method of gene mapping is to isolate the DNA by cleaving the chromosome. Cleavage is achieved by the introduction of a restriction enzyme, which digests DNA at a specific recognition site. The recognition site also serves as a location marker, and by using a series of restriction enzymes, researchers can investigate a small segment of a chromosome. Other mapping techniques involve the use of radioactive DNA or RNA, which isolates a specific sequence in the gene, and molecular cloning, which allows the artificial generation of genes with a known composition. The genes of some simple organisms (like viruses) have been completely mapped. A vast project to map the human genome is now underway.
See also: Gene.

General Agreement on Tariffs and Trade (GATT), agreement signed in 1947 by 23 nations. It created an organization, also called GATT, to foster world trade. It served individual nations as well as international associations, such as customs unions, and free trade associations, by providing a set of rules and procedures for the conduct of international trade. It also sponsored international negotiations ('GATT trade rounds'), which led to lower tariffs and reductions of other trade restrictions.
GATT negotiations begun in 1987 and concluded in 1994 resulted in an agreement, signed by 125 nations, to reduce tariffs significantly and to create new international trade regulations. The agreement also provided for GATT to be superseded by a permanent body overseeing international trade law-the World Trade Organization (WTO)-in 1995.

General Assembly, branch of the United Nations (UN) where all member nations are represented and have a vote. The Assembly convenes annually or in special sessions and has some elements of control over all the other organs of the UN. Its functions are financial, supervisory, and deliberative and include control of the UN budget, admitting new members, advising the Security Council, and selecting the UN secretary general.
See also: United Nations.

General Motors Corporation, major U.S. manufacturer of motor vehicles and auto parts. Founded in 1908 to consolidate companies producing the Buick, Oldsmobile, Cadillac, and other cars, it also became producer of the Pontiac, the Chevrolet, and GMC trucks. General Motors now has factories and distribution facilities throughout the world.
See also: Automobile.

Generator *See:* Electric generator.

Genesis, first book of the Old Testament and first of the Five Books of Moses (the Pentateuch), the oldest part of the Old Testament. Its name comes from the Greek for 'birth' or 'beginning,' a translation of the first word in the original Hebrew text. The Book of Genesis begins with the creation of the world, and includes the stories of Adam and Eve, Cain and Abel, and Noah. Chapters 12-36 deal with the origins of the Hebrew people and the accounts of the patriarchs, Abraham, Isaac, and Jacob. Genesis ends with the story of Joseph and the arrival of Jacob and his sons in Egypt (Chapters 36-50).

Genet, Jean (1910-1986), French playwright and novelist. Pardoned from life imprisonment for repeated burglary convictions in 1948, Genet wrote of the homosexual underworld of France and the borderline between acceptable and unacceptable social behavior. His works include *Our Lady of the Flowers* (1943), *The Thief's Journal* (1948), and the plays *The Balcony* (1956) and *The Blacks* (1958).

Gene therapy, method for treating genetic diseases, by attempting to recover or replace disfunctional genes in (a part of) the cells, which are responsible for hereditary disorders, with functional genes. Gene therapy is especially suitable for treating defects in accessible organs that are caused by one single gene.

Genetic code *See:* Cell.

Genetic counseling, advice sought by couples concerned about the possibilities of passing inherited defects to children. Counselors can calculate the probabilities of a child being born with the hereditary defect.

Genetic Engineering, changing the genetic properties of an animal or plant, is not new. Humans have been doing this to suit their wishes for years. Until well into the 20th century, the only way to change anything was to crossbreed individual plants or animals. By crossing two different plants or animals that each have desirable qualities, a descendant that has both qualities may be produced. This method has two disadvantages: the first one is that only a few of the descendants turn out to posses the desired combination of traits, and the second one is that only closely-related plants or animals can be crossed. Increased scientific knowledge and the technical developments of the past years have enabled us to change the properties of plants and animals faster and in a more purposeful manner. We now know which part of the DNA, the carrier of all of a plant or animal's traits, we need to use, and it is now technically possible to move this part from one cell to another. This means we can add a property from one plant (or animal) to another plant (or animal), even if they are not related. Taking it one step further is producing a complete copy of a plant or animal, so-called cloning. In cloning, the descendant has exactly the same characteristics as the parent. We have been able to do this for while with plants, by taking cuttings or grafts. In 1997, the very first cloned animal, Dolly the sheep was produced. The DNA of an adult sheep was transferred to an empty egg and placed in a surrogate mother, where it grew into a new sheep. Genetic engineering of plants and animals is subject of discussion. Advocates point at the possibilities of the production of cheaper and better food, the production of drugs and possible cures for hereditary diseases. Opponents underline the dangers of the uncontrolled dissemination of hereditary properties in nature and overstepping ethical limits.

Genetics, study of the inheritance of biological characteristics from parent to offspring. The smallest unit of inheritance is the gene, which is contained within the gametes, or germ cells, that unite at fertilization. Genetics as a science arose at the end of the 19th century when Gregor Mendel's theories of certain basic laws determining some inherited characteristics were rediscovered. It has developed rapidly in the 20th century, spurred on by the growth of physics, chemistry, statistics, and biochemistry. The greatest advance was the discovery (1953) of the chemical nature of the genetic material, deoxyribonucleic acid (DNA), which carries the information necessary for the growth and development of the new individual.
See also: Gene; Heredity.

Geneva (pop. 172,000), city and capital of Geneva canton, Switzerland, on Lake Geneva at the Rhône River outlet. It is the headquarters of the World Health Organization, the International Labor Organization, and the International Red Cross. It is an important cultural, scientific, theological, industrial, and banking city and the center of the Swiss watchmaking industry. The College de Genève was founded (1559) by John Calvin.
See also: Switzerland.

Geneva accords, agreements reached during a series of conferences held in Geneva,

Schematic account of the way Dolly the sheep was cloned. The transplantation of the genetic material was done by taking the heart of a cell from an udder cell and transporting it to an egg. The udder cell was from a ewe (Dolly's mother); the egg was taken from another sheep. Dolly grew from embryo to lamb in the womb of a third sheep (the surrogate mother). The nuclei of regular body cells are made in such a way that they only produce new body cells if they are divided. The method used in this case shows that culturing them and then putting a stop to their cell division cycle can reprogram the nuclei of body cells.

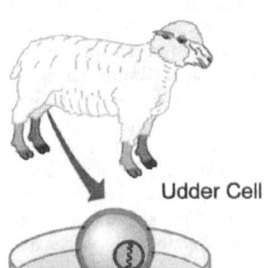

Udder Cell

1a. A cell is taken from the ewe's udder.

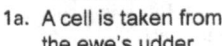

1b. The cell is multiplied.

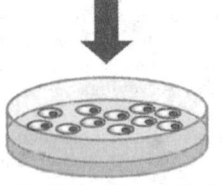

1c. The cells are put into a dormant state through lack of nutrition.

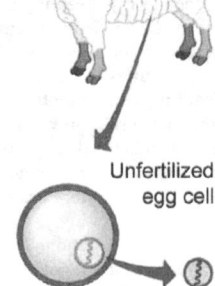

Unfertilized egg cell

The nucleus is removed

2. An unfertilized egg cell is taken from a different sheep. The nucleus is removed.

udder cell   unfertilized egg cell

electric current

3. Egg cell without nucleus and udder cell are fused using electric current, which means the DNA in the nucleus of the new cell is from the udder cell.

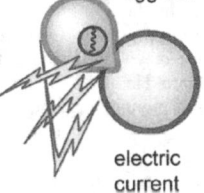

4. After a number of divisions, the fused cell is implanted in the uterus of a surrogate sheep.

surrogate sheep

6. 'Dolly' is born. The lamb has almost exactly the same genetic traits as the sheep the udder cell was taken from.

5. Embryo grows into a sheep.

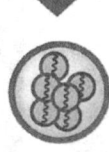

Dolly the sheep with her surrogate mother. Dolly made all the headlines in February 1997. Scottish scientists were the first to successfully grow a viable clone from a cell of an adult mammal. The method that had been used caused a great deal of concern, because it seemed the cloning of human cells was now also possible. An important point was, however, that before Dolly was born, 276 transplantation attempts had failed, and the scientists did not really know why it had worked with Dolly. This made it clear that cloning was not as simple as everyone assumed. Dolly died in February 2003.

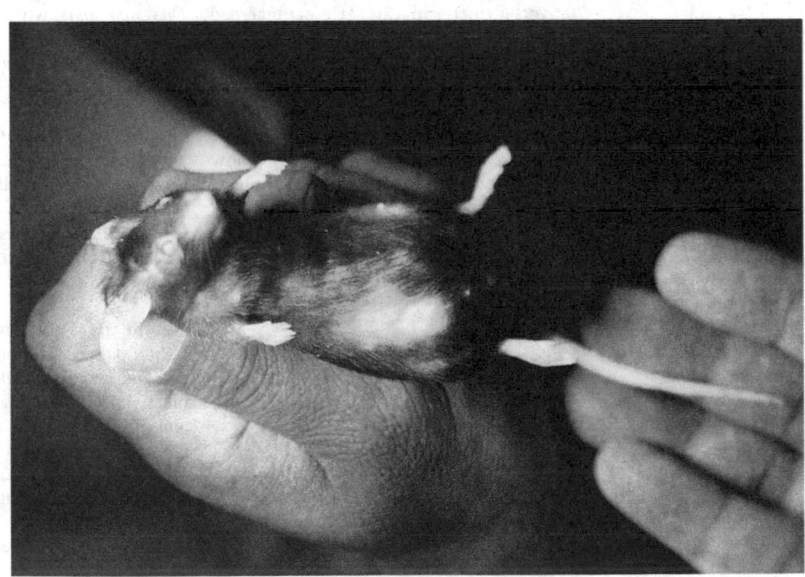

A genetically engineered mouse that glows in the dark. Japanese scientists achieved this effect in 1997 by placing the DNA of fluorescent jellyfish in a mouse's fertilized eggs. The in-your-face color was not the main aim: the green mice could be used for medical research. For example: when a regular mouse is injected with the cancer cells of a green mouse, the development of the cancer cells in the regular mouse can be documented step by step, enabling us to find out more about the disease and, if necessary, adjust medication.

G

G

Switzerland, Apr.-July 1954, to settle the conflict in Indochina, which was then a French colony. The negotiations were attended by delegates from the United States, the Soviet Union, Great Britain, France, China, and several of the contending forces in Indochina, especially Vietnam. The pacts provided for cease-fires in Laos and Cambodia and the temporary division of Vietnam along the 17th parallel. Control of northern Vietnam was ceded to the revolutionary forces led by Ho Chi Minh; southern Vietnam was controlled by the government of the Emperor Bao Dai, supported by France. Nationwide elections were supposed to be held by July 20, 1956 to unify the country. Bao Dai's government refused to hold the elections, the division of North and South Vietnam become frozen, and the stage was set for the next Vietnam war; which began in 1960.

Geneva Conventions, 4 international agreements signed by a large majority of sovereign nations for the protection of soldiers and civilians from the effects of war. Convention I derived from a conference in 1864, in which the work of Jean Dunant, founder of the Red Cross, led to an agreement to improve conditions for sick and wounded soldiers in the field. Convention II (1906) dealt with armed forces at sea, Convention III (1929) with treatment of prisoners of war, and Convention IV (1949) with protection of civilians.
See also: Prisoners of war; Red Cross.

Genghis Khan (Temujin; 1167?-1227), Mongol ruler of one of the largest empires in world history. After 20 years of tribal warfare he was acknowledged Genghis Khan ('universal ruler') in 1206. He campaigned against the Chin empire in North China (1213-1215), and in 1218-1225 he conquered Turkestan, Persia, Afghanistan, and South Russia. His empire stretched from the Caucasus Mountains to the Indus River and from the Caspian Sea to Peking (now Beijing). Genghis Khan was not only a fearsome warrior but also a skilled political leader.
See also: Mongol Empire.

Genghis Khan, the Mongol leader who conquered a vast Asian territory that stretched from the Pacific in the east to the Black Sea in the west.

Genie, or Jinni, good or evil supernatural spirit in Muslim and Arab folklore; an invisible body made from smokeless flame and possessing the power to assume human or animal form. In the *Arabian Nights* the spirit of Aladdin's lamp is a genie.

Genoa (pop. 725,000), capital of Genoa province and of the region of Liguria, northwestern Italy, 71 mi (114 km) southwest of Milan. Italy's largest port, it is second only to Marseilles on the Mediterranean. In ancient times it was the headquarters of the Roman fleet. In the 12th and 13th centuries it was an independent republic with its own fleet and possessions on the eastern Mediterranean. The city's principal industries include shipbuilding, iron and steel making, and oil and sugar refining.
See also: Italy.

Genocide, deliberate extermination by a government of a national, ethnic, or religious group. The term originated in 1944 with references to the German Nazi systematic killing of Jews. In 1948 the UN drew up a convention defining, ratified by the United States in 1986, the crime of genocide.

Genroku, the name of the Japanese era (1688-1703) that formed the peak of the culture of emancipated merchants, particularly in Kyoto and Osaka. Major developments were achieved in the sphere of literature (haiku poetry), Confucianism and the puppet theater.

Gent *See:* Ghent.

Gentian, any of the herbs of the family Gentianacea (genera *Gentiana* and *Dasystephana*), with intense blue or yellow flowers, common in the Northern Hemisphere and often a feature of high mountain slopes.

Gentile, word used in the Bible to refer to people who are not Jewish. In modern times the term is often used, incorrectly, to mean 'Christian.' Muslims and members of the Church of Jesus Christ of Latter Day Saints also refer to nonmembers of their faith as gentiles.

Gentile da Fabriano (c. 1370-1427), an Italian painter. The brilliant colors, rich ornament, and careful detail seen in his altarpiece *Adoration of the Magi* (1423) are typical of his work. The *Adoration*, considered his masterpiece, is an outstanding example of the International Gothic style. His work influenced many painters throughout Italy.

Genus *See:* Classification.

Geochemistry, study of the chemistry of the earth (and other planets). Chemical characterization of the earth as a whole relates to theories of planetary formation. Classical geochemistry analyzes rocks and minerals.
See also: Chemistry.

Geode, hollow mineral formation that is found in limestone areas, usually having an outer layer of chalcedony and an interior lining of crystals, usually quartz. Geodes are

generally between 1 in (2.5 cm) and 12 in (30 cm) in diameter.

Geodesic dome *See:* Fuller, R(ichard) Buckminster.

Geodesy, in geophysics, specialty that seeks to determine the precise size and shape of the earth. The ancient Greeks attempted to measure the earth, and Eratosthenes (3rd century B.C.) obtained a very accurate figure for the circumference. Geodesy began, however, in the 18th century, when surveyors found that they needed accurate reference points. Geodetic work consists of refining previous estimates of the shape of the earth. The earth is approximately an *oblate spheroid*-that is, it bulges somewhat at the equator because of its rotation and is correspondingly somewhat flattened at the poles (by about 13 mi/ 21 km). But topographical irregularities cause the curvature of the earth to vary from point to point. Such bulgings and flattenings are noted by geodesists carrying out surveys over great arcs of the globe. Since 1957 satellites have provided information about the earth's shape.
See also: Geophysics; Surveying.

Geoduck (*Panope generosa*), edible clam of the Pacific coast that may weigh over 5 lb (2.3 kg).

Geoffrey of Monmouth (1100?-1154?), British bishop and chronicler whose *History of the Kings of Britain* (c.1135), a romantic and fictional account of early Britain, introduced the Arthurian legends to the continent.
See also: Arthur, King.

Geography, study of all phenomena associated with the earth's surface, including the forces that act upon it. Geography also includes the study of the interaction between the earth and plant, animal, and human life. Some of the matters geographers deal with are the measurement of the earth, navigation, surveying, photogrammetry (mapping

The *Adoration of the Magi* (1423), by Gentile da Fabriano, an Italian master of the International Gothic style, was painted for the church of Santa Trinità in Florence (Uffizi, Florence).

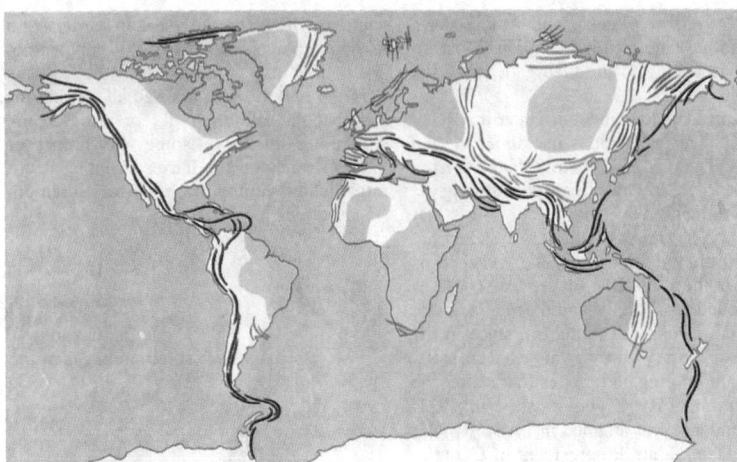

Inbetween the earth's precambrian (crypto-zoïd) shields, which have been stable for a long time, a large number of mountain ranges can be found. All major fold moun-tains, which are younger than the pre-cambrian shields, have been formed during only four rela-tively short periods. Alpine mountains (black), Mesozoic mountains (blue), Hercynic mountains (green), Caledonian mountains (orange) and Precambic shields (pink).

from aerial photographs), and cartography (including the study of map projections). Physical geography includes the study of landforms, the relationship between land-forms and rocks in the earth's crust, the evo-lution of landforms, climatology, meteorolo-gy, oceanography, and the origin and distri-bution of soils. Human geography studies human responses to and effects upon an en-vironment, including the location, develop-ment, and use of natural resources.

Geology, scientific study of the physical history and structure of earth. Branches of geology include geomorphology (the study of how natural forces shape and alter land forms), petrology (the study of rocks), and mineralogy (the study of minerals). Geochemistry bridges geology and chem-istry, investigating the chemical composi-tion of the earth and the origin and distribu-tion of the elements within it. Structural ge-ology studies mountain-building processes and the folding, jointing, and fracturing of rocks. Geophysics bridges geology and physics, applying the law of physics to the study of the earth's interior, atmosphere, and oceans; it includes the study of earth-quakes (seismology), volcanoes (volcanolo-gy), radioactivity, geomagnetism, and geo-electricity. One of the newest branches of geology is the investigation of plate tecton-ics, which accounts for the shifting of great land masses that used to be called continen-tal drifts.

Geomagnetic North Pole *See:* North Pole.

Geomagnetic South Pole *See:* South Pole.

Geometry, branch of mathematics con-cerned with spatial figures, their relation-ships, and deductive reasoning concerning these figures and relationships. Different geometric systems exist, each based on its own rules (axioms or postulates), compo-nents (objects), and self-consistent conclu-sions (theorems).
Euclidean geometry, the most familiar type of geometry, was developed by the Greek mathematician Euclid in 300 B.C. It was the first formalized deductive mathematical sys-tem, serving as a model for later systems. The axioms it is based on describe points, lines, and circles in a flat surface (plane). They also describe relationships among these objects. According to Euclidean geom-etry, a straight line may be drawn between any 2 points; a circle may be drawn with a point as its center and any given radius; and through any point outside a line 1 and only 1 parallel line can be formed. *Non-Euclidean* geometries are based on axioms and objects that differ in part or completely from those of Euclidean geometry. Euclidean geometry was the predominant geometric description for centuries. It was not until the 19th centu-ry that Nikolai Lobachevski, Janos Bolyai, and G.F.B. Riemann verified the existence of self-consistent systems based on all of Euclid's axioms except the one concerning parallel lines. Through deductive logic, Lobachevski proved the existence of geo-metric systems where more than one parallel line can be drawn. Riemann's non-Euclidean geometry is a system where no parallel lines exist. Navigation, based on a geometrical system concerned with relationships on the surface of a sphere rather than in a plane, is an example of Riemannian geometry. In it a straight line is defined as a 'great circle' (a circle with its center and radius being the same as that of the sphere), and no 2 great circles are parallel. Other geometries exist. *Analytic* geometry, established in 1637 by René Descartes, significantly enhanced the development of geometry by generalizing it through the application of algebra. As a re-sult, figures can be specified relative to co-ordinate systems by sets of numbers or equations and problems can be solved using algebraic and geometric methods. *Projective* geometry, developed around 1820 by Jean-Victor Poncelet, was a modification of Euclidean space by including points at infin-ity. Perspective drawing uses these concepts. *Topology*, the most recent branch of geome-try (dating from 1911 with the work of Dutch mathematician L.E.J. Brouwer), deals with geometric objects that remain un-changed upon deformation.

Geomorphology, study of the shape of the earth's surface and the way that landforms are produced.
See also: Tectonics.

Geophysics, physics of the planet earth, in-cluding studies of the lithosphere (seismolo-gy, geomagnetism, gravitation, radioactivity, electric properties, and heat flow) and stud-ies of the atmosphere and hydrosphere. Geophysical techniques are used extensively in the search for mineral deposits, an area known as exploration geophysics, or geo-physical prospecting.

Geopolitics, study of politics in relation to geography and demography. The term was originally applied to the theories of the biol-ogist and geographer Friedrich Ratzel (1844-1904), who sought to apply evolu-tionary theory to the rise and fall of nations. In the 1900s the British geographer Sir Halford Mackinder extended these, seeing the international struggle for survival as hanging on control of the heartlands, or inte-rior lands, of the world's great landmasses, particularly the 'world island' of Eurasia. The German geographer Karl Haushofer combined these theories to preach the even-tual regeneration of Germany through its in-evitable demand for *Lebensraum* (German: 'living space,' space for expansion), which would require sacrifice by the seaboard countries to the more dynamic countries of the heartland. Haushofer's theory was seized upon by Adolf Hitler and became a corner-stone of Nazi doctrine.

George, 6 kings of Great Britain and Ireland. **George I** (1660-1727; r. 1714-1727), great-grandson of James I. Of German origin, he was the first king of the House of Hanover (1698). Unable to speak English, he was unpopular and isolated. **George II** (1683-1760; r. 1727-1760), son of George I, was preoccupied with military adventures and relied heavily on the advice of Queen Caroline and his ministers. **George III** (1738-1820; r. 1760-1820) was the grandson and successor of George II. His reign saw the American revolution, the ex-pansion of the British Empire in Asia, and the beginning of the industrial revolution. **George IV** (1762-1830; r. 1820-1830), son of George III, was despised for his personal extravagances. **George V** (1865-1936; r. 1910-1936), son of Edward VII, changed the name of the royal house to Windsor during World War I. **George VI** (1895-1952; r. 1936-1952), younger son of George V, came to the throne upon the abdication of his brother Edward VIII. **Queen Elizabeth II** is the older daughter of George VI.

George, 2 kings of Greece. **George I** (1845-1913; r. 1863-1913), a Danish prince, was elected king of Greece after Otto I was de-posed in 1862. During George I's reign, which ended with his assassination, Greece increased its territory and adopted a demo-cratic constitution (1864). **George II** (1890-1947; r. 1922-1923, 1935-1947) went into exile (1923) when the country became a re-public. He was restored to the throne in 1935 and instituted a dictatorship run by General John Metaxas. Upon the German invasion of

Greece (1941), George fled, spending the war in exile. He returned in 1946, during the civil war, and in 1947 was succeeded by his brother Paul.

George, David Lloyd *See:* Lloyd George, David.

George, Saint, patron saint of England. Possibly a Christian convert martyred in 303, George became connected with many medieval legends, including his rescue of a maiden from a dragon. His feast day is Apr. 23.

George, Stefan (1868-1933), German poet. His symbolist and formally rigorous poems appeared in such volumes as *Algabal* (1892), *The Soul's Year* (1897), and *The New Kingdom* (1928). He was leader of a circle of intellectuals who shared his belief that art should shun the everyday and his devotion to German language and culture.

Georgetown (pop. 200,000), capital and largest city of Guyana, on the north (Atlantic) coast of South America, at the mouth of the Demarara River. The Dutch settled the city in the 1600s and named it Stabroek; in 1812 it came under British control and acquired its current name.
See also: Guyana.

Georgia

Capital:	Tbilisi
Area:	26,900 (69,700 sq km)
Population:	4,961,000
Language:	Georgian
Government:	Presidential republic
Independent:	1991
Head of gov.:	President
Per capita:	US$ 3,100
Monetary unit:	1 Lari = 100 tetri

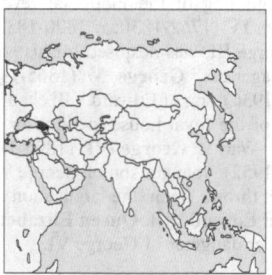

Georgia (Republic of), independent country in the Caucasus region, bordered by Russia, Azerbaijan, Turkey, Armenia, and the Black Sea.
Land and climate. The Caucasus Mountains run across the north of the republic. Georgia has a subtropical climate.
People. Georgians form the majority of the population (70%), and with the remainder comprised of Armenians, Russians, Azerba-

ijani, Ossetians, Greeks, and Abkha-zians. The official language is Georgian. Most inhabitants belong to the Georgian Orthodox Church.
Economy. The lowland areas near the Black Sea produce tea, fruit, wine, tobacco, and cereals. There is much heavy industry, iron, steel, textiles, and chemicals constituting the main products.
History. The ancient kingdom of Georgia, dating from the 4th century B.C., reached its height in the 12th and 13th centuries but was partitioned by Turkey and Persia in 1555. Georgia fell under Russian influence in the late 18th century and was annexed in 1801. An attempt to regain independence after the Revolution of 1917 was crushed in 1921. Independence was attained in 1991. In 1992, Zviad Gamsakhurdia, president of Georgia, was overthrown and replaced by a ruling council. In the same year, Eduard Shevardnadze was elected head of the ruling council. In 1995 he was elected president.
See also: Union of Soviet Socialist Republics.

Georgian architecture, 18th-century architectural style in Britain and the British North American colonies. In Britain it refers to the classically formal and elegant style, influenced by the Italian Renaissance architect Andrea Palladio and the English Palladian Inigo Jones, popular during the reigns of the first 3 Georges. In the United States it refers to the style prevailing between 1700 and the Revolution, deriving more from Christopher Wren and the Baroque; Palladian influences entered later. Fine examples are Independence Hall, Philadelphia (1745), and King's Chapel in Boston (1754).

Georgia (U.S.) (Peach State, Empire State of the South; pop. 7,486,000), state in the Southeast of the United States, on the Atlantic Ocean; 58,932 sq mi (152,576 sq km). Capital: Atlanta. Coastal plain with marshes (Okefenokee, approx. 657 sq mi, 1700 sq km) and forests, the Appalachian mountains in the north. The most important river is the Savannah. Sub-tropical climate. Forestry with products like turpentine, cultivation of corn, tobacco, peanuts and cotton, fruit farming (peaches), poultry breeding. Extraction of kaolin, marble, bauxite. Textile is the most important industry. Tourism. 67 higher education institutions, including the University of Georgia (1785) and Wesleyan College, the oldest women's college in the U.S.
In 1566 the Spaniards established the Santa Catalina mission, which was conquered in 1680 through an alliance of the British and the Indians. Georgia was established as the thirteenth colony in 1733 and became the fourth state of the Union in 1788.
The African American population was deprived of its right to vote in 1908; the struggle of the African American civil rights movement that took place in the 50s and 60s proceeded relatively smoothly here.

Geothermal power *See:* Energy supply; Volcano.

Geranium, any of the cosmopolitan, hardy perennial herbs of the family Geraniaceae,

some of which are cultivated in gardens and as house plants, especially the popular pot and bedding plants of the genus *Pelargonium*. Common, or zonal, geraniums have white, salmon, pink, or red flowers, single or semidouble, some with bronze or maroon zones on the leaves. Another decorative-leafed variety is the ivy-leaf geranium (*P. peltatum*).

The large, naked-soled gerbil (*Tater indica*).

Gerbil, or sand rat, small rodent of the family Cricetidae found in desert or semidesert regions of Africa and Asia. It has fine, dense fur and a long tail and can move fast by hopping. Gerbils live in burrows and eat seeds, flowers, and roots. As they are easy to keep, needing little water and simple food, they are popular as laboratory animals and as pets.

Geriatrics, branch of medicine specializing in the care of the elderly. Although concerned with the same diseases as the rest of medicine, the different susceptibility of the aged and a tendency for these people to have a number of disorders at the same time make its scope different. In addition, the psychological problems of old age differ markedly from those encountered in the rest of the population and require special management.

Géricault, (Jean Louis André) Théodore (1791-1824), French painter. His style combined a massive, dynamic romanticism with a minutely detailed realism. In his studies of lunatics, his horse paintings, and the *Raft of the Medusa* (1818-1819), Géricault's revolutionary approach helped eclipse the classical school in French art.

Germ *See:* Bacteria; Disease; Virus.

German, official language of Germany and Austria and an official language of Switzerland and Luxembourg, native tongue of more than 100 million people. Modern German is descended from 2 main forms. Low German, spoken mainly in the north, is the ancestor of both Dutch and Flemish. High German, spoken in central and southern Germany is, historically, the classical German. A large part of medieval German literature, such as the 12th and 13th century epics, is in Middle High German. Today the written language is standardized, but there are still great differences between spoken northern and southern German. Modern German is a highly inflected language with 3 genders and 4 cases, and requires agreement in number, gender, and case, as in Latin. Many words are formed by compounding.

German Democratic Republic *See:* Germany.

Germanium, chemical element, symbol Ge; for physical constants see Periodic Table. Germanium was discovered in 1886 by Clemens Winkler. It occurs in the mineral germanite, in zinc ores, and in coal. It is produced by reducing its dioxide with hydrogen. Germanium is a crystalline, brittle metalloid. It is used extensively in semiconductors. Germanium and its compounds are used in transistors, alloys, and phosphors and as catalysts.

German literature, literature of the German-speaking peoples in Europe, primarily the Germans, Austrians, and Swiss. The German language, like its literature, has strong regional characteristics. The language of southern and central Germany is considered High German, while the language of the northern regions is called Low German. Almost without exception, the great works of German literature have been written in High German.

Early German literature. The earliest works in German literature date from the 9th Century A.D. and were inspired by the growth of monasteries. The monks disseminated Christian thought through literature. As a result, poems and stories based on biblical sources were popularized. The first known German author of this period was a monk, Otfried von Weissenberg, who wrote *The Book of Gospels* in rhyme. In addition, the monks chronicled some of the more ancient heroic sagas and invented new ones. One of the classics of this era is the story *Lay of Hildebrand*, whose author is anonymous.

The golden ages of German literature. The first great, or golden, age of German literature occurred in the 12th century and was inspired by the Crusades and chivalry. Many of the great works were epics written by knights, who through the literature expressed love, courage, and a belief in God. Wandering minstrels, or minnesingers, composed poems of love and adventure. Perhaps the most famous minnesinger was Walther von der Vogelweide. One of the great works of this era is the epic poem *Song of the Nibelungs*. Another major influence on the German literature of this period is the legend of King Arthur, which came to Germany from France. The German poet Hartmann von Aue, inspired by these Arthurian tales, composed an important work of this period in Germany: *Poor Henry*. The greatest work of the German Middle Ages, however, was a poem about a knight's search for God written by Wolfram von Eschenbach: *Parzival*. Another major work of this golden age is *Tristan and Isolde* (early 13th century), written by Gottfried von Strassburg.

The highest literary expression during the Renaissance (16th century) was influenced by the events of the Reformation and the development of humanism. It is, however, in the 18th century that the second golden age began and the greatest cultural achievement was accomplished in Germany. During this era the works of Johann Wolfgang von Goethe in drama (*The Sorrows of Young Werther, Faust*); Friedrich Schiller in drama, poetry, and history (*The Robbers, Wallenstein, William Tell*); Immanuel Kant in metaphysics (*Critique of Pure Reason, Critique of Practical Reason*); and the brothers Grimm in folk literature (*Fairy Tales*) were all created.

German literature of the late 19th and early 20th centuries. The late 19th and early 20th centuries were characterized by a literature of naturalism characterized by social concern exemplified in the works of Karl Marx (*Communist Manifesto, Capital*) and Friedrich Nietzsche (*Thus Spake Zarathustra*). Also from this era are the works of more impressionistic writers whose focus was more idealistic, including Thomas Mann (*Buddenbrooks, The Magic Mountain*), Herman Hesse (*Demian, Steppenwolf, Siddartha*), and Arthur Schnitzler (*The Reckoning, Anatol*). In poetry, the works of Rainer Maria Rilke and Stefan George are most notable. The literature after World War I is often referred to as expressionistic, but shares with the naturalistic literature an emphasis on social concerns. Its unique characteristic, however, is the often terrifying and horrific dimension of the works. Its most important author is Frank Kafka (*The Trial, The Castle, Amerika*). Two of his short stories deserve particular distinction because they have become classics of world literature: 'The Metamorphosis' and 'A Country Doctor.'

German literature after 1945. The literature immediately following World War II dealt mostly with the war and its impact on German spirit and civilization. Most notable are the works of Heinrich Böll (*Group Portrait with Lady*), Günter Grass (*The Tin Drum*), and Siegfried Lenz, whose works continued into the 1970s and 1980s.

German measles, or rubella, infectious viral disease causing rash and fever. Although physical symptoms are usually mild, it is dangerous if contracted by a woman during the first 3 months of pregnancy, since it can then seriously harm the fetus, causing birth defects. There is a vaccine, which is usually given to children and to women of childbearing age who have not had the disease. Those who have already had it are immune to getting it again.
See also: Measles.

German shepherd dog, breed of dog developed in Germany in the early 1900s to be a herder. Also called a German police dog, it is now used in police and military work and as a guide dog. German shepherds are muscular, with large, pointed ears, long snouts, and dense black, gray, or tan coats. They stand about 24 in (61 cm) and weigh 60-85 lb (27-39 kg).

German short-haired pointer, dog used by hunters for pointing, following game, and guarding. It stands 24 to 25 in (62 to 64 cm) tall, weighs 55 to 70 lbs (25 to 32 kg), and has a keen sense of smell.

German wirehaired pointer, hunting dog and retriever, first bred in Germany in the mid-1800s by crossing the German short-haired pointer and the poodle-pointer. The German wirehaired pointer stands 24 to 26 in (61 to 66 cm) at the shoulder and weighs 55 to 65 lb (25 to 29 kg). Its coat may be brown or brown and white with liver-colored spots.

Germany

Capital:	Berlin (Bonn = seat of gov.)
Area:	137,854 sq mi (357,022 sq km)
Population:	83,252,500
Language:	German
Government:	Federal republic
Independent:	divided in two after Word War II; reunited in 1990
Head of gov.:	Chancellor
Per capita:	US$ 26,200
Monetary unit:	1 Deutsche mark = 100 pfennige

Johann Wolfgang von Goethe, one of the principal figures in German literature, influenced the development of the late 18th-century Sturm und Drang period and the classicism of the early 19th century. Goethe, whose work encompassed such fields as science, music, art, and philosophy, as well as literature, has been called the last 'universal man'.

G

Germany, country of central Europe that was divided into 2 nations after World War II. In 1990 the Federal Republic of Germany (West Germany) joined with the German Democratic Republic (East Germany) to form a single German state. Germany is bordered by Austria and Switzerland in the south; France, Luxembourg, Belgium, and the Netherlands in the west; the North and Baltic seas and Denmark in the north; and the Czech Republic and Poland in the east.

Land and climate. The northern part of Germany is a lowland area, while the south and central parts contain highlands. The western section has the Black forest. The eastern part is mostly flat, but it contains the Thuringian, the Bohemian, and the Oberfalz forests. Germany's climate is temperate with mild summers and cool winters and moderate precipitation in all seasons.

People. Essentially, the Germans are of 2 distinct types: the Nordic people, usually tall, fair-skinned, and blue-eyed, and the stockier Alpine type of the south, who are often dark-haired and brown-eyed. More than 80 percent of the German people live in urban areas; the area around the Rhine and Ruhr rivers is one of the most heavily populated sections of Europe. The language is German, divided into 2 distinct forms: High German, spoken in the north, and Low German, spoken in the south. In addition, there are numerous dialects confined to certain regions and cities.

Economy. Germany (at least the former western part) has one of the strongest economies in Europe. It is a world leader in manufacturing and heavy industry, due mainly to its large coal deposits, which provide the necessary energy for these enterprises. It is also a major producer of chemicals, for industrial use and for use in medicines, plastics, fertilizers, and synthetic fabrics. Its optics and electronics industries are world leaders in these technologies, and their products are noted for their quality and dependability. Its financial and banking network is one of the most powerful in the world. The smaller part that formerly made up East Germany suffered from 40 years of mismanagement under its communist government, and its economy lags far behind the highly developed west both in quantity and quality of its output. The new German government has made it clear it will raise the backward economy of the east to the level of the rest of the country. In the first ten years of unification this has proved to be extremely difficult.

History. The Romans succeeded in conquering the west bank of the Rhine (1st century B.C.-1st century A.D.) but they could not bring the Teutonic tribes of the area into the empire. It was the Romans who named the tribes' land *Germania*. In A.D. 768, Charlemagne, the great Frankish ruler, came to power and united most of the territory of modern France and Germany into the Frankish empire. In 843, the empire was divided among Charlemagne's 3 grandsons, with the area east of the Rhine going to Louis the German. Louis's kingdom subsequently was divided into independent duchies, and efforts to create a single state remained unsuccessful until the 19th century. The modern state of Germany was first created in the late 19th century by Otto von Bismarck. In a successful series of wars, he brought much of Germany under Prussian domination, and in 1871 he saw King Wilhelm I of Prussia crowned kaiser (emperor) and hereditary monarch of the empire. In 1890, Kaiser Wilhelm II (grandson of Wilhelm I) dismissed Bismarck as chancellor and embarked on a policy of nationalistic expansionism that brought Germany repeated conflict with other European states. In 1914 the strains proved too much, and Europe plunged into World War I. Germany was defeated, and in 1919 it gave up both empire and king and became the Weimar Republic. Throughout the 1920s and 1930s the republic suffered severe economic crises and social unrest, partly due to the harsh treatment of the Treaty of Versailles that ended World War I. As a result, in 1933 Adolf Hitler became chancellor of Germany and set about establishing a dictatorship (the

Former East Berlin's Alexander Platz.

Third Reich) that fostered extreme military aggression, nationalism, and racial violence. Hitler's expansionism (reoccupation of the Rhineland in 1936, annexation of Austria in 1938, and the takeover of Czechoslovakia in 1939) alarmed other European powers. Finally, Germany's invasion of Poland in Sept. 1939 triggered World War II. In 1945, the Allies defeated the Third Reich, ending World War II in Europe. Germany was occupied by the 4 victorious powers (United States, Soviet Union, France, and England) and in 1949 was divided into 2 sectors: East Germany (which became a communist state under Soviet influence) and West Germany (which became a republic allied with the western democracies and the United States). West Germany flourished economically while East Germany stagnated. In 1990, following the collapse of the Soviet-led alliance of eastern European nations, Germany was reunified, this time as a republic firmly rooted in the democratic, free-enterprise European Economic Community. Following reunification there were numerous economic and social problems, mainly in the eastern states. Among those problems were a high rate of unemployment and increasing incidents of crime, including attacks by right-wing extremists on foreigners. The costs associated with reunification plagued the German economy during the early 1990's. In national elections in 1994, the Christian Democratic Union and allied parties, who had governed Germany since 1982, were narrowly returned to power: Helmut Kohl was reelected by the Bundestag as chancellor and became Germany's longest serving chancellor of the 20th century (1982-1998). Meanwhile, during 1992-1994 German military forces were sent to Somalia and the Adriatic Sea as part of UN missions. Controversy arose within Germany concerning the use of German armed forces in international military missions outside the jurisdiction of the North Atlantic Treaty Organization (NATO). In 1994 Germany's highest court ruled that, with Bundestag approval, German forces could be used in missions outside NATO ar-

The small villages in the low mountain range of Germany are located in the midst of agricultural fields and meadows. On the slopes there are beeches, oak trees and spruce firs. The red color of the soil is caused by colored sandstone, which is often found in these regions.

eas. In 1998 Kohl was defeated by Gerhard Schröder, a member of the center-left Social Democratic Party. A so-called 'red-green' coalition was formed, consisting of the SPD (socialistic party) and Die Grünen (left wing party). This coalition also won the 2002 parliamentary elections in spite of the deteriorating economic situation. The unemployment figure exceeded 10%.

Germicide *See:* Antiseptic; Disinfectant.

Germination, resumption of growth of a plant embryo contained in the seed after a period of reduced metabolic activity or dormancy. Conditions required for germination include an adequate water supply, sufficient oxygen, and a favorable temperature. Rapid uptake of water followed by increased rate of respiration are often the first signs of germination. During germination, stored food reserves are rapidly used up to provide the energy and raw materials required for the new growth. The embryonic root and shoot that break through the seed coat are termed the radicle and plumule, respectively. In hypogeal germination the seed leaves, or cotyledons, remain below the ground. In epigeal germination they grow above the ground and become the first photosynthetic organs.

Germ theory *See:* Medicine.

Germ warfare *See:* Chemical and biological warfare.

Geronimo (1829-1909), greatest war leader of the Apache tribe of Arizona. When his tribe was forcibly removed to a barren reservation, he led an increasingly large band of hit-and-run raiders (1876-1886). Twice induced to surrender by Lt. Col. George Crook, he was driven to escape again by maltreatment. Persuaded to surrender a third time by Gen. Nelson Miles, he was summarily exiled to Florida and resettled in Oklahoma, where he became a successful farmer.

Gershwin, George (1898-1937), U.S. composer. From an immigrant background, he rose to fame first as a songwriter and then with musical shows like *Lady, Be Good!* (1924), his first Broadway success, and the Pulitzer Prize-winning satire *Of Thee I Sing* (1931), among many others. He also wrote highly regarded orchestral pieces, *Rhapsody in Blue* (1924), *Piano Concerto* (1925), and *An American in Paris* (1928), and an opera, *Porgy and Bess* (1935), noted for its lyricism and emotional power. Many of his songs, as well as *Porgy and Bess*, were written in collaboration with his lyricist brother, **Ira Gershwin** (1896-1983). His work shows the influence of Maurice Ravel, Igor Stravinsky, and, especially, U.S. jazz.

Gerulaitis, Vitas (1954-1994), American tennis player. Gerulaitis learned to play tennis from his father, who was national champion of Lithuania at the time. He became a professional tennis player at an early age and won his only Grand Slam tournament in 1977 in the singles competition: the Australian Open championship. As of that year he remained in the top ten until 1982. The right-handed Gerulaitis was an all-round player with great stamina. He was known for his flamboyant lifestyle.

Gessler *See:* Tell, William.

Gestalt psychology, school of psychology concerned with the tendency of the human (and even primate) mind to organize perceptions into 'wholes'-for example, to hear a symphony rather than a large number of separate notes of different tones-due to the mind's ability to complete patterns from the available stimuli. Its main proponents were Max Wertheimer, Kurt Koffka, and Wolfgang Köhler. Focusing on the patterns formed by a subject in order to deal with experience, the school provides an alternate to the structuralist approach.
See also: Koffka, Kurt; Köhler, Wolfgang; Psychology; Wertheimer, Max.

Gestapo, abbreviated form of *Geheime Staatspolizei* (secret state police), the executive arm of the Nazi police force, 1936-1945, possessing almost unlimited authority. Under the control of Heinrich Himmler, it shared responsibility for internal security and administered the concentration camps. The Gestapo arrested and sent to the camps thousands of Jews, intellectuals, clergy, homosexuals, and other 'undesirables.' It was declared a criminal organization at the Nuremburg Trials (1945-1946).
See also: Himmler, Heinrich; Nazism.

Gethsemane (Hebrew: *gat semanim*, 'oil press'), the garden across the Kidron valley, on the Mount of Olives, east of the old city of Jerusalem, where Jesus prayed on the eve of his crucifixion and was betrayed. Gethsemane was probably an olive grove; its precise location is disputed.

Getty, J(ean) Paul (1892-1976), U.S. business executive and one of the richest men in the world. He inherited his father's oil company, vastly expanded its wealth, and became an important art collector, founding and endowing the J. Paul Getty Museum in Malibu, Calif. (1954). From the early 1950s Getty lived in England. At his death, he left the museum $750 million.

Gettysburg, Battle of, central conflict of the U.S. Civil War, fought July 1-3, 1863. In a daring maneuver, Confederate general Robert E. Lee struck deep into Union territory, reaching Pennsylvania in June 1863. He and the Union Army of the Potomac, under Gen. George G. Meade, converged upon Gettysburg, Pa. There were many inconclusive attacks and counterattacks but eventually Lee retreated. Union losses were over 23,000, around 25%; Confederate losses were around 25,000, a similar percentage. The costly battle marked a reversal in the fortunes of the Confederacy, paving the way for the eventual Union victory.
See also: Civil War, U.S.

Gettysburg Address, speech delivered by President Abraham Lincoln at the dedication of the national cemetery at Gettysburg, Pa., on Nov. 19, 1863. A brief masterpiece of oratory, it combined the themes of grief for the dead with the need for maintenance of the principles they had died to uphold.

Getz, Stan(ley) (1927-1991), U.S. jazz musician. He played the saxophone under bandleaders Stan Kenton, Benny Goodman, and Woody Herman, before forming his own smaller groups. Influenced by jazz saxophonists Lester Young and Charlie Parker, during the 1950s Getz evolved his distinctive, intimate and reflective, 'cool' jazz style.
See also: Jazz.

Geyser, hot spring, found in currently or recently volcanic regions, that intermittently jets steam and superheated water into the air. It consists essentially of a system of underground tubelike fractures leading down to a heat source. Groundwater accumulates in the tube, that near the bottom being kept from boiling by the pressure of the cooler layers above. When the critical temperature is reached, bubbles rise, heating the upper layers, which expand and well out of the orifice. This reduces the pressure enough for substantial steam formation below, with subsequent eruption. The process then recommences. The famous Old Faithful in Yellowstone National Park used to erupt every 66.5 min, but has recently become less reliable.

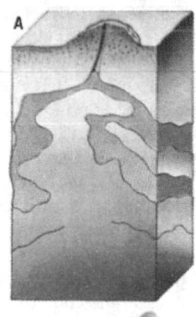
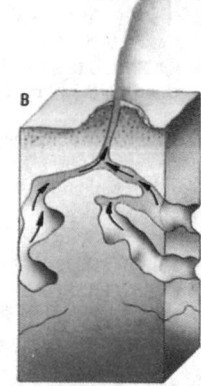
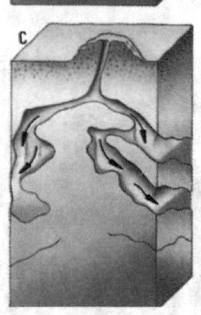

A geyser results from the superheating of pressurized water that comes into contact with hot volcanic rocks in deep, interconnecting chambers (A). As the superheated water expands, it drives out some of the water above it, thus reducing the pressure. The superheated water immediately flashes into steam, which violently drives out a column of water and steam through the surface opening (B). The groundwater then flows back into the chambers (C), and the process will be repeated.

G

Ghana

Capital:	Accra
Area:	92,098 sq mi (238,533 sq km)
Population:	20,244,000
Language:	English
Government:	Presidential republic
Independent:	1957
Head of gov.:	President
Per capita:	US$ 1,980
Monetary unit:	1 Cedi = 100 pesewa

Ghana, in West Africa, independent country bordered by the Atlantic Ocean (Gulf of Guinea) on the south, by the Ivory Coast on the west, by Togo on the east, and by Burkina Faso on the north.

Land and climate. Ghana is generally a low-lying country. Beyond the narrow coastal plain, the Kwahu Plateau extends inland, giving way to rolling savanna in the north. A belt of tropical rainforest covers much of the plateau. The Volta River system with its tributaries, the Black and White Voltas and the Oti, covers much of the country and forms a delta with lagoons and swamps at its mouth, east of Accra. With the completion of Akosombo Dam in 1965, about 70 mi (113 km) from the sea, the Volta formed a lake of over 3,000 sq mi (7,770 sq km) for hydro-electric power and irrigation.

People. Ghana has many ethnic groups, the most numerous being the Akan family, which includes the Fanti and Ashanti tribes. Other large groups are the Ga, the Ewe, and the Mole-Dagbani. The official language is English, though tribal languages are also used. About 40% of the people are Christian and about 16% are Muslim. The rest practice

A barrage dam near Akosombo, Ghana, which is 371 ft (113 m) high and 2,133 ft (650 m) long. The energy it produces, is very important for the development of the industry.

traditional African religions. The education system is highly developed. Institutions of higher learning include the University of Ghana, the University of Science and Technology at Kumasi, the University College of Cape Coast, and many technical schools. Though most of the population still depend directly on agriculture, urbanization is developing rapidly.

Economy. Cocoa is Ghana's biggest export, but coffee and tobacco are also grown, and there are mineral exports of gold, industrial diamonds, manganese, and bauxite. Local industries include aluminum, timber, and food processing.

History. Before colonialism, Ghana had a number of independent kingdoms, mainly the Ashanti Federation and Fanti states along the coast. The first European colonizers were the Portuguese, who arrived in 1482. The French, Danes, Dutch, and British all competed in the slave and gold trade, and in the 19th century the Ashanti organized a resistance. They were defeated by the British in 1874, and in 1901 Ghana formally became a British colony, called the Gold Coast. Ghana was a center of African nationalism, and it was one of the first African countries to win independence, in 1957. Kwame Nkrumah became premier. In 1960 he declared the country a republic, with himself as president for life. While he made reforms in education, transportation, and other social services, during his rule many political opponents were jailed, and government became increasingly inefficient and corrupt. In 1966 Nkrumah was deposed. After political instability throughout the 1970s, civilian rule was restored in 1979. But economic conditions did not improve, and at the end of 1981 the military, under Jerry Rawlings, again took control. Following the adoption of a new constitution in 1992, Rawlings was elected president. John Kufuor succeeded him in 2001. Due to its poor economic situation, Ghana became eligible for HIPC (Heavily Indebted Poor Countries), part of the World Bank, hoping to bring the country's debt burden to a sustainable level.

Ghana, Ancient Empire of, former empire in West Africa, centered between the Niger and the Senegal rivers. At the height of its power, the empire stretched from the Atlantic Ocean nearly as far as Timbuktu. Probably founded about the 4th century A.D., it reached its height in the 10th century. In the 11th century the invasions of the Muslim Almoravids of North Africa greatly weakened the empire. The empire regained its independence but never recovered its power. It was eclipsed by the rise of the Mali Empire in the 13th century and became part of that empire. Ghana carried on a flourishing trade with Morocco and was a highly organized state, with a powerful military force. *Ghana* was the title of the ruler and also the name of some of the various capitals. The name has been taken by the modern African state of Ghana.

Ghazali, Abu Hamid Mohammed al- (1058-1111), biblical scholar, theologian, philosopher and mystic. Al-Ghazali was born in Tus (Northeast Iran) and made a career as a scientist under the protection of Nizaam al-Mulk, the influential vizier of the

Seljuks in Baghdad; was strongly influenced by the ideas of al-Ashari. A psychosomatic disorder made his further career difficult, but he was a man of such standing that he went back to teaching a few years before he died. His influence on Sunnite Islam was very significant. He saw himself as a innovator and largely contributed to the synthesis between the mystical and theological traditions. His most famous work is *Ihya 'Ulum ad-Din* (The revival of the Religious Sciences), a bulky manual for believers.

Ghent (pop. 224,700), historic city in western Belgium, at the junction of the Lys (Leie) and Scheldt rivers. Former capital of Flanders, it was the textile center of medieval Europe. Its textile industry is still important, along with paper, chemical, and metal production. It also has a major port. In the 16th and 17th centuries it was a center of Flemish art.
See also: Belgium.

Ghetto, in European history, street or section of a city once set aside for the compulsory residence of Jews. The word itself is probably derived from the name of the area of Venice to which the Jews of that city were confined in 1516. Ghettos spread throughout Italy during the Counter-Reformation (the late 16th century) and had already been in existence in northern Europe for hundreds of years. The ghetto was surrounded by walls, and it was illegal for a Jew to remain outside its gates after the curfew hour. The French Revolution and reform movements of the 19th century removed legal discrimination against Jews in Western Europe and the ghettos were abolished. However, the practice was revived by fascist governments in World War II. Today the term refers to slum areas of inner cities in which minority groups are compelled to live, not by law, but by the forces of discrimination and poverty.

Ghibellines *See:* Guelphs and Ghibellines.

Ghiberti, Lorenzo (1378-1455), Italian sculptor. A Florentine, he was a leading figure of the early Renaissance, famous for his second pair of bronze doors, *Gates of Paradise* (1425-1452), for the Florence baptistery.

Ghirlandajo, or **Ghirlandaio, Domenico** (Domenico di Tommaso Bigordi; 1449-1494), Florentine Renaissance painter said to have taught Michelangelo. His frescoes include *St. Jerome* (1480) and the *Last Supper* (1480), both in the Church of the Ognissanti, Florence. He also helped decorate parts of the Sistine Chapel, and is noted for his portraits, among them *Grandfather and Grandson*.

Ghost dance, ceremonial ritual of a religion originated by the Paiute Indians in Nevada c.1870. It was led by the mystic prophet Wovoka, who prophesied the rebirth of the dead and the restoration of the Indians to their lands. The ritual took place over several days and was characterized by hypnotic trances. The Sioux performed the ritual prior or to their massacre at Wounded Knee in 1890 in the belief that they would be protected from the bullets.

Giacometti, Alberto (1901-1966), Swiss-born sculptor and painter who lived in Paris. He is best known for his elongated and skeletal human figures, which convey a sense of extreme spiritual isolation-*Man Pointing* and *Man Walking* (1947). His early work was influenced by primitive art and surrealism (*The Palace at 4 A.M.*, 1932).

Giant, in myths, human creature of great size and strength; survivor of races that lived before humanity. The Greek giants, the Titans, warred against the gods of Olympus. Other giants, such as the biblical Goliath, are probably exaggerated memories of large, fierce men.
See also: Mythology.

Giant panda *See:* Panda.

Giant schnauzer, largest dog of the schnauzer breed, standing about 25 in (65 cm) and weighing about 76 lb (35 kg). The giant schnauzer was developed in southern Germany in the 1700s by crossbreeding standard schnauzers with German sheepdogs. It is highly regarded as a watchdog.

Giant sequoia *See:* Sequoia.

Gibberellin, any of a group of chemical compounds that stimulate plant growth. Some gibberellins are plant hormones. Gibberellins cause dwarf varieties of peas, beans, corn, and coffee to grow as high as tall varieties, induce dormant seeds to germinate, and make sugarcane longer, thus increasing its yield of sugar. They may also be useful for stimulating growth of pastures and lawns during winter. The gibberellins were first noticed by a Japanese plant pathologist, E. Kurosawa, in 1926, during his investigations of a fungus disease of rice that caused elongation of the plant.

Gibbon, smallest of the apes, distinguishable by its very long arms. It is the only ape to walk upright with ease. Six species live in Southeast Asia. They can leap over 30 ft (9 m) and swing nimbly through the trees.

Gibbon, Edward (1737-1794), English historian, author of *The History of the Decline and Fall of the Roman Empire* (6 vols., 1776-1788), the greatest historical work of the 18th century and a literary masterpiece. Gibbon served somewhat unsuccessfully as a member of Parliament (1774-1783).

Gibbs, Josiah Willard (1839-1903), U.S. physicist best known for his pioneering work in chemical thermodynamics and his contributions to statistical mechanics. In *On the Equilibrium of Heterogeneous Substances* (1876, 1878) he states Gibbs's Phase Rule for chemical systems. In the course of his research on the electromagnetic theory of light, he made fundamental contributions to the art of vector analysis.
See also: Thermodynamics.

Gibraltar, self-governing British colony, 2.3 sq mi (6 sq km) in area, on the rock of Gibraltar at the southern tip of the Iberian peninsula. The population is mixed; natives are of English, Genoese, Portuguese, and Maltese descent. The economy rests on light industry, shipping, and tourism, and on the important British naval and airbases. Gibraltar was captured from Spain in 1704. A 1967 referendum showed overwhelming opposition to a return to Spanish rule. The inhabitants currently demand autonomy and entry into the European Union.

Gibraltar, Strait of, narrow body of water between Spain and North Africa, connecting the Mediterranean Sea with the Atlantic Ocean. It is the only natural waterway between the Mediterranean and any ocean. Through this narrow strait (only about 8.5 mi/13.7 km wide) a strong current flows into the Atlantic. The strait gives access from Northern Europe and North America not only to the Mediterranean basin, but also to the Black Sea and, via the Suez Canal, to East Africa, the Persian Gulf, and south Asia.

Gibran, Kahlil (1883-1931), Lebanese essayist and philosopher-poet who blended elements of Eastern and Western mysticism. Influenced by Blake and Nietzsche, he published *The Prophet*, his best-known work, in 1923; *The Garden of the Prophet* appeared in 1934.
See also: Philosophy.

Gibson, Althea (1927-), U.S. golf and tennis player, the first black to enter the United States women's tennis championship singles. She won that tournament in 1957-1958, along with the Wimbledon women's singles championship. She then turned professional and began competing in golf tournaments.

The lar gibbon of the montane forests of Southeast Asia (*Hylobates lar*) is about 3 ft (1 m) in height.

This portrait of French writer André Gide (1869-1951) was painted in 1912 by the fashionable artist Jacques-Emile Blanche (1861-1942).

G

Gide, André (1869-1951), French writer. His relentless examination of his own standards and assumptions and the resulting inner conflicts made him one of the foremost figures in French literature in the first half of the 20th century. In 1947 he was awarded the Nobel Prize for literature. Among his best-known works are the novels *The Immoralist* (1902) and *The Counterfeiters* (1926), and 4 volumes of *Journals* (1889-1949).

Gideon, in the Bible (Judges), leader and judge of Israel who, by his exploits in repelling the desert raiders, the Midianites, became a national hero. Having put the invaders to flight with a small force of 300 of his clan, Gideon was offered the crown. Though he declined it, his son Abimelech briefly asserted the authority his father had earned and became king.
See also: Bible.

Gielgud, Sir (Arthur) John (1904-2000), British actor, producer, and director, noted early in his career for his Shakespearean roles, especially Hamlet and Richard III. Highly versatile, he created many modern roles in his maturity in numerous stage, film, and television performances.

Gierek, Edward (1913-), first secretary of the Polish Communist Party (1970-1980). He was appointed to improve the standard of living following food riots in late 1970. A failing economy and labor unrest led to his fall from power in 1980.
See also: Poland.

Gigli, Beniamino (1890-1957), Italian singer (tenor). Gigli, who studied in Rome, made his debut in 1914 - he won first prize in a competition in Parma. He sang for the first time under Toscanini at La Scala in Milan in 1918. He was the most famous tenor of his generation, regarded by some as the successor to Caruso. He performed at the Metropolitan Opera in New York from 1920-1932 and 1938-1939 as well as in every major European and American opera center. Gigli's repertoire included more than 60 roles and during his career he was undisputedly the most celebrated tenor in the world.

Gila monster (*Heloderma suspectum*), stout-bodied lizard, up to 2 ft (61 cm) long. It and the related beaded lizard (*H. hor-*

G

ridum) are the only poisonous lizards. Both live in the deserts of the southwestern states and in Mexico. The gila monster is so rare that it is protected by law.

Gila River, river in Arizona and New Mexico, flowing westward and joining the Colorado River near Yuma, Calif. Over 600 mi (960 km) long, the river provides irrigation water for the surrounding farmland. Coolidge Dam is situated on the Gila River.

Gilbert and George, the name under which the two English artists Gilbert Proesch (1943-) and George Passmore (1942-) give performances. As a duo, they began presenting themselves as living statues in 1969, preferably in everyday situations, painted in bronze. After 1977 they limited their performances to appearing in photographic works in which nature is the main theme (conceptual art). The 'photo pieces' became very large in the 80s, with bright colors. Themes include life on the street in major cities.

Gilbert and Sullivan, English theater collaborators who wrote lighthearted musical satires of Victorian England and the British Empire. Sir William Schwenck Gilbert (1836-1911) wrote the words and Sir Arthur Seymour Sullivan (1842-1900) the music. Their major operettas include *H.M.S. Pinafore* (1878), *The Pirates of Penzance* (1879), *Patience* (1881), *Iolanthe* (1882), *Princess Ida* (1884), *The Mikado* (1885), *Ruddigore* (1887), and *The Gondoliers* (1889). Both enjoyed independent success as well, Gilbert as a journalist and playwright and Sullivan as a composer.

Gilbert, William (1544-1603), English sci-

entist. Regarding the earth as a giant magnet, he investigated its field in noted studies of magnetism and electricity.
See also: Magnetism.

Gild *See:* Guild.

Gilgamesh, Epic of, earliest known epic poem, written in the Akkadian language and originating in Mesopotamia in the 3rd millennium B.C. The fullest surviving text, preserved on clay tablets, was found in 1872 in a library at Nineveh from the 7th century B.C. The poem tells of the semidivine Gilgamesh (a historical 3rd-millennium king of Uruk), who seeks the secret of eternal life after the death of his friend Enkidu. At the end of his quest he hears the story of an ancient worldwide flood that closely parallels the story of Noah.
See also: Epic.

Gill, thin-walled, external respiratory organ of many aquatic animals. They take in oxygen from the water, and give off waste carbon dioxide. Usually either thin flat plates or finely divided feathery filaments, gills may take on the transport of food and the excretion of excess salt.

Gillespie, Dizzy (John Birks Gillespie; 1917-1993), U.S. jazz musician. With Charlie Parker he led the jazz movement of bop in the 1940s, playing the trumpet.
See also: Jazz.

Gillyflower *See:* Wallflower.

Gilman, Charlotte Perkins (1860-1935), U.S. writer and women's rights activist. Opposed to traditional marriage, Gilman urged women to gain economic independence

by working outside the home. She promoted her ideas through her books, *The Yellow Wallpaper* (1890), *Women and Economics* (1898), *Concerning Children* (1900), and *The Home* (1903), and through her monthly magazine, *Forerunner* (1909-1916).
See also: Women's movement.

Gin, cotton *See:* Cotton gin.

Ginger, herb of the family Zingiberaceae, grown in Japan, the West Indies, South America, and West Africa; also, the spice derived from the root, or rhizome, of the plant. The 4 principal varieties of the species are preserved, dried, black, and white. Ginger is used to season baked goods, meats, vegetables, and beverages.

Gingivitis, inflammation of the gums. Symptoms include swelling, redness, and tenderness of the gums, which may bleed with chewing and toothbrushing. Daily use of dental floss and prompt care by a dentist to clean the plaque from the teeth is the best treatment, before increasing inflammation leads to loosening of the teeth and periodontitis.

Ginkgo, or maidenhair tree (*Ginkgo biloba*), tree with fan-shaped leaves that is often grown in cities because of its tolerance for smoke, low temperatures, and mineral water. A 'living fossil,' the ginkgo is the remnant of a group of trees that flourished over 100 million years ago.

Ginsberg, Allen (1926-1997), U.S. poet of the beat generation. He has been active in protesting U.S. conformity and politics. His writings show the influence of his studies of religions of the East and West. His works include the poem 'Howl' (1956) and 'Kaddish' (1961) and *The Yage Letters* (1963).

Ginseng (genus *Panax*), small perennial plant that grows in damp woodlands in Korea and in the United States. The Chinese esteem ginseng root for its medicinal value.

Ginzburg, Natalia (Natalia Levi; 1916-1991), Italian author, once married to Leone Ginzburg (d. 1944), who established a publishing company together with Giulio Einaudi and Cesare Pavese. From 1940-1943 her family was banned by the fascists to the Appennini mountains, where her husband was arrested and tortured to death. Her novels and short stories have a strong autobiographic streak. She became a member of the communist party after the war and held a seat in the Italian parliament for many years. She has received a number of awards for her work. It includes the novels *The Dry Heart* (1947), and *Valentino* (1957), the collections of short stories *The Road to the City* (1942) and *Dead Yesterdays* (1962), the collections of essays *The Little Virtues* (1963) and *Never Must Ask Me* (1971), the plays *I Married You for the Fun of It* (1966) and *The Advertisement* (1968), and the memories *Family Sayings* (1963).

Giorgione (1478?-1510), Renaissance Venetian painter, student of Giovanni Bellini.

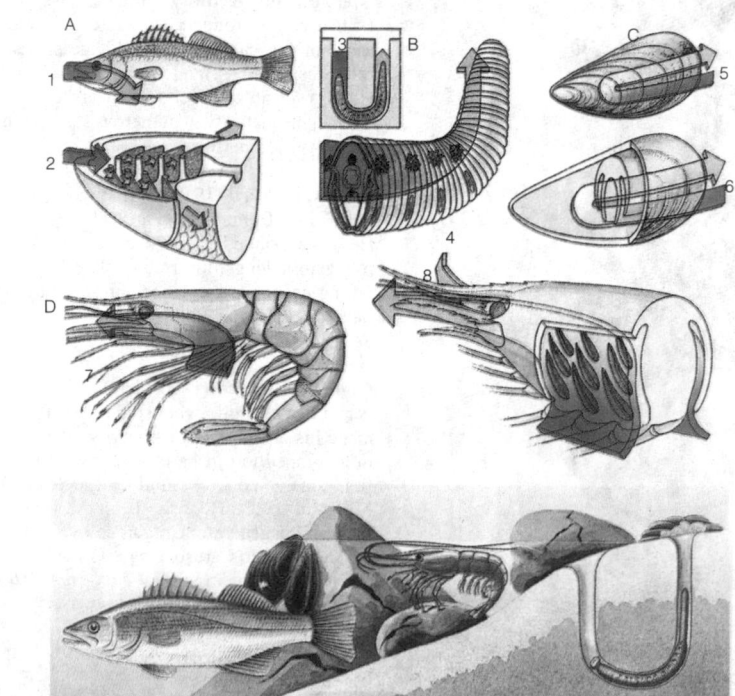

Gills, which are respiratory organs, allow many aquatic animals to breathe in oxygen from water. In a teleost fish (A), water flows into the mouth and through four pairs of arched gills. These gills have an abundance of capillaries, picking up the oxygen from the water, and releasing carbon dioxide. A lugworm (B) uses paired gills, located on either sides of the body, in a similar manner to a fish's gills. A mussel (C), like many bivalve mollusks, has a siphon that sucks water into internal gills, and another one for expelling water from its shells. A prawn (D) has five sets of featherlike gills, located near its thoracic legs. Water moves into the body through the gills, and is forced out through the prawn's mouth.

Subordinating line to light and color, he achieved a unity of human figures with landscape that influenced Titian. Among his works are *The Tempest* (1501), *Madonna and Child Enthroned* (1504), and *The Three Philosophers* (1510).
See also: Renaissance.

Giotto (Giotto di Bondone; c.1266-c.1337), Florentine painter and architect. Profoundly influential for many generations, he painted monumental figures dramatically and emotionally, giving the vast fresco scenes a sense of movement and spatial depth. Among his famous works are frescoes in Padua (*Life of the Virgin*, 1303-1306), and Florence (*St. John the Baptist*, and *Life of St. Francis*, c.1320).

Giovanni, Nikki (Yolande Cornelia Giovanni, Jr.; 1943-), African American poet. Her collections include *Black Feeling, Black Talk* (1968), *My House* (1972), *Cotton Candy on a Rainy Day* (1978), *Those Who Ride the Night Winds* (1983), *Sacred Cows and Other Edibles* (1988), *Our Traditions* (1994), and *Love Poems* (1997).

Gipsie *See:* Gypsy.

Giraffe (*Giraffa camelopardalis*), tallest mammal, native to Africa, reaching 18 ft (5.5 m), with extremely long neck (up to 7 ft/2.1 m) and legs. Its buff-colored coat is spotted with red-brown patches. A short, bristly mane runs along its spine from head to tail. Giraffes live by grazing on trees. They are speedy runners.

Giraudoux, (Hippolyte) Jean (1882-1944), French playwright. Known for his imaginative, satirical dramas, his major works include *Tiger at the Gates* (1935) and *Electra* (1937), both based on Greek mythology, and *The Madwoman of Chaillot* (1945).

Girl Scouts and Girl Guides, association promoting fitness, citizenship, outdoor living, and community service among girls. The movement was founded in England in 1909 by Lord Baden-Powell, who also founded the Boy Scouts. There are now about 14 million Girl Scouts in over 80 countries.
See also: Baden-Powell, Robert Stephenson Smyth, Lord.

Girondists, group of middle-class republicans in the French Revolution. The Girondists came into power under the 1791 Constitution but lost ground to the Jacobins. In June 1793, 29 Girondists were expelled from the National Convention; many were guillotined in the Reign of Terror.
See also: French Revolution.

Giscard d'Estaing, Valéry (1926-), president of France 1974-1981. A member of the national assembly from 1955, he was minister of finance under Presidents de Gaulle (1962-1966) and Pompidou (1969-1974). As president his austerity program failed to solve problems related to inflation, unemployment, and the balance of payments. He was defeated in his bid for reelection by Socialist candidate François Mitterand. In

From approximately 1305-08 Giotto painted a series of frescos on the lives of Christ and Mary, in the Arena chapel at Padua. In the painting depicting *Judas' kiss*, the monumentality of the figures is evident.

2001, he was appointed as chairman of the Convention which deals with the future of the European Union. In 2003, it should have formulated the answers to questions concerning the future organization and operating procedures of the Union.
See also: France.

Gish sisters, U.S. actresses best known for silent films, especially in the pioneering epics of D. W. Griffith. In *The Birth of a Nation* (1915), **Lillian Diana** (1896-1893) won world fame; with **Dorothy** (1898-1968), she starred in *Orphans of the Storm* (1921). Lillian later appeared in plays, including *All the Way Home* (1960) and *Uncle Vanya* (1973).

Gissing, George Robert (1857-1903), English novelist. His most famous novel, *New Grub Street* (1891), depicts much of the hardship he himself experienced as an aspiring writer. Influenced by Dickens, he is noted for his starkly realistic studies of late Victorian lower- and middle-class life, as in *The Private Papers of Henry Ryecroft* (1903).

Giulini, Carlo Maria (1914-), Italian conductor. Giulini studied viola and composition at Santa Cecilia Academy in Rome and orchestral direction with B. Molinari. He started conducting the orchestra of the RAI in 1946. In 1948 he made his debut at the opera with *La Traviata* and was a conductor at La Scala in Milan from 1953-1956. He made his first U.S. tour in 1960, where he accepted an appointment as first conductor of the Chicago Symphony Orchestra in 1969. He then became conductor of the Wiener Symphoniker (1973-1976) and chief conductor of the Los Angeles Philharmonic (1978). Giulini is not only an opera specialist, he also conducts many orchestral works: Mozart, the major 19th-century choral works, the German symphonies. Giulini's performances excel thanks to his subtleties and precision. He prefers to conduct from memory.

Giza (pop. 2,000,000), or Al Jizah, Egypt's third largest city, a suburb of Cairo, and the site of the 3 largest pyramids and the Great Sphinx. Its luxurious houses and apartments are homes to many wealthy Egyptians, diplomats, and business people. Unskilled workers arrive in Giza daily looking for factory work and hoping to settle there. Factory products include bricks, chemicals, cigarettes, and machine tools. Dozens of motion picture films are made in Giza each year.

Gizzard, thick-walled, muscular part of the stomach of birds that uses gravel to help digest grains and other partly digested food.

Gjellerup, Karl Adolph (1857-1919), Danish poet, novelist and playwright. He first wanted to be a minister, but after completing his studies he chose literature. Partly under the influence of Darwin's evolutionary theory, he became a confirmed freethinker and supporter of Georg Brandes' naturalism. In the 1880s Gjellerup broke with naturalism and chose German humanism. He settled in Dresden in 1892, where he studied Buddhism under the influence of Schopenhauer. He was awarded the Nobel Prize together with his fellow countryman Henrik Pontoppidan in 1917, which many regarded as too high an honor. Gjellerup left a very extensive oeuvre which quickly lost its significance. His novels include *Antigonos* (1880), *Germanernes laerling* (The Teutons Apprentice, 1882), *Minna* (1889), and *Pilgrimmen Kamanita* (Pilgrim Kamanita, 1906).

Glaciation *See:* Ice age.

Glacier, mass of ice that flows outward from ice caps or down from above the snow line. Glaciers cover about one-tenth of the earth's land area. They are classified as continental glaciers or ice caps, valley glaciers, and piedmont glaciers. The largest ice caps occur in Antarctica and Greenland. Almost all of Antarctica and about 85% of Greenland are buried by ice. Smaller ice caps occur in the islands of northern Canada and in Iceland and Norway. Valley glaciers occur in mountain ranges on every continent. Piedmont glaciers form when glaciers flow out from their valleys to form an ice sheet at the foot of a mountain range. Glaciers originate in areas above the permanent snow line, that is, above the level where snow does not melt completely during the summer. In Antarctica the permanent snow line is at sea level, but around the equator it is about 17,000-18,000 ft (5,200-5,500 m) above sea level. Snow that accumulates on gentle slopes forms snowfields, in which the snow is compacted into a white, spongelike substance called firn or névé. Under pressure, the névé is gradually transformed into hard, clear, blue ice, which consists of interlocking crystals. Pressure causes molecules of water to be released in the ice, lubricating the crystals, allowing them to glide over each other. Most valley glaciers move a few feet a day. They may produce rounded hollows called cirques, or turn the valleys into U-shaped troughs with steep sides. Glaciers cease to flow at a point where melting, evaporation, or the breaking away of icebergs balances the rate of accumulation of ice at the source. The surfaces of glaciers are pit-

G

ted with crevasses. Lines of rock fragment called moraines are also trapped within the ice, and some rocks are torn from the ground by the ice and frozen into the base and sides of the glacier. As the ice moves, this debris acts like sandpaper and wears away the bedrock over which it passes. It produces smooth land surfaces and may turn valleys into U-shaped troughs with steep sides. A moraine is deposited at the snout of the glacier as the ice melts. Sometimes streams form and transport eroded debris beyond the end of the glacier and deposit it over a wide area. Such deposits are called glacial drift. Among the types of glacial drift are drumlins, which are oval-shaped hills, and eskers, which are long ridges of sand and gravel.

Gladiator (Latin: *gladius*, 'short sword'), warrior-entertainer of ancient Rome. Gladiators fought each other and wild beasts in public arenas with a variety of weapons, including swords, for the favor of the crowds. They were recruited from prisoners of war, slaves, criminals, and sometimes freemen. The tradition survived into the 5th century A.D.

Gladiolus, genus of tall erect plants of the iris family with sword-shaped leaves and large flowers, native to South Africa and the Mediterranean area, popular in American and European gardens.

Gladstone, William Ewart (1809-1898), British statesman, Liberal Party; 4 times prime minister (1868-1874; 1880-1885; 1886; 1892-1894). A powerful orator, dedicated social reformer, and deeply religious man, he introduced the secret ballot, the extension of the franchise, the abolition of sales of army concessions, the first Education Act, the Irish Land Act, and the disestablishment of the Anglican Church in Ireland.
See also: Liberal Party.

William Ewart Gladstone (1809-1898).

Gland, in animals, organ that secretes essential substances. *Endocrine glands* (thyroid, adrenals, and pituitary) secrete hormones into the bloodstream. *Exocrine glands* secrete substances (perspiration, tears, mucus, saliva) via ducts into internal organs or onto body surfaces.
See also: Hormone.

Glanders, fatal contagious, bacterial disease of horses, donkeys, and mules that can be transmitted to humans. The nasal membranes, the lungs, and the skin are infected with lumps that release germ-spreading pus. Animals with glanders must be destroyed.

Glandular fever *See:* Mononucleosis.

Glasgow (pop. 616,000), Scotland's largest city and principal port, on the River Clyde. It is a major commercial and industrial center for shipbuilding, metal working, and manufacturing. A cultural center, it is home to the Scottish Opera, the Scottish National Orchestra, the Citizens Theatre, and 2 important museums: the Burrell Collection and the Kelvingrove Museum. The University of Glasgow, Scotland's second oldest university, was founded in 1451. Glasgow was founded in the 6th century. It became an important center with the unification of Scotland and England (1707) and by the late 18th century was the second-largest city in the British Empire (after London).
See also: Scotland.

Glasnost (Russian: publicity), part of the reform policy, the perestroika, of party leader and President Michail Gorbachov, introduced in the Soviet Union in 1985 for the purpose of transforming the rigid Soviet society into a society that was capable of solving the problems of the Soviet Union (particularly in the economic sphere). Glasnost manifested itself in e.g. more freedom of speech, resulting in a great deal of criticism with regard to the past (the terror of Stalin), the present (economic problems) and the future (Communism as an utopia is finished).

Glass, hard, brittle, transparent substance composed mainly of silicates. A natural black glass called obsidian occurs when the molten rock from an erupting volcano cools rapidly, and rock crystals, made of quartz, are another type of naturally occurring glass. The ancient Egyptians and Romans manufactured glass, and stained glass became important in medieval art and architecture in Europe. The mass production of glass is carried out in long 'tank' furnaces that may hold over 100 tons. The raw materials are melted and fused at high temperatures, then poured into molds or drawn into shape. For glassware of the highest quality, handblowing is still practiced. The glassblower dips a long blowpipe into the furnace and withdraws a 'gob' of molten glass that is blown down the pipe and inflated like a balloon. By deft manipulation of the pipe, shapes are formed. Bottles are blown mechanically. Ordinary window glass, or sheet glass, is made by drawing a wide ribbon of glass upwards from the furnace and through tall cooling towers, at the top of which it is cut into sheets. After glass has been shaped, it usually has to be reheated and cooled at a carefully controlled rate in a special oven called a leer. This process, called annealing, reduces the stress produced in the glass by uneven cooling.

Glass, Philip (1937-), U.S. composer. He was strongly influenced by rock, African and, through his studies with Ravi Shankar,

Indian music. He composed music in a style called minimalism and he played combinations of classical Western, rock, and African and Indian music on his electronic keyboards. His best known operas are *Einstein on the Beach* (1976) and *Satyagraha* (1980). He also composed music for films.

Glasses, or spectacles, lenses mounted in a frame and worn in front of the eyes to correct defects of vision. Converging lenses have been worn to correct farsightedness (hyperopia) since the late 13th century and diverging lenses for nearsightedness (myopia) since the 16th. Glasses with cylindrical lenses are used to correct astigmatism, and those having bifocal lenses (2 different powers in the upper and lower areas of each lens) or even trifocals (3 powers) may be worn for presbyopia (loss of elasticity of the eye's lens).
See also: Lens.

Glass lizard, or glass snake (genus *Ophisaurus*), legless, snakelike lizard. Unlike snakes, it has moveable eyelids, ear openings, a breakable tail, and nonexpandable jaws. It lives in loose soil or under roots and rocks. It reaches about 2 ft (61 cm) in length.

Glassware *See:* Glass.

Glasswort (*Salicornia*), plant belonging to the goosefoot family. It grows 4 to 20 in (10 to 51 cm) tall and has jointed bright green stems with small flowers growing at the joints.

Glastonbury (pop. 6,800), town in Somerset County, England. Archeologists have discovered artifacts from prehistoric Iron Age dwellings just north of Glastonbury and have found numerous types of pottery there dating from 60 B.C. According to legend, England's first Christian church was established in Glastonbury by St. Joseph of Arimathea, who was thought to have brought the chalice from the Last Supper to this site. It was also reputed to contain the graves of King Arthur and Queen Guinevere of the Arthurian legends. The town's economy is now supported by tourism and light industry.
See also: Arthur, King; England.

Glauber's salt, trade name of a drug containing sodium sulphate, used as a laxative.
See also: Salt, chemical.

Glaucoma, eye disease characterized by an increased pressure on the retina within the eyeball, caused by an excess of watery fluid. Symptoms range from blurred vision to loss of peripheral vision and even blindness.
See also: Eye.

Glauconite, or greensand, greenish iron-silicate mineral that resembles tiny flake-like particles or little lumps of clay. Large deposits have been found in Colorado, New Jersey, and Wisconsin. Glauconite is used as a water softener. Its natural content of silicate of potassium and iron makes it invaluable to geologists in dating rocks and fossils.

Glazunov, Aleksander Konstantinovich (1865-1936), Russian composer, among his teachers was Rimski-Korsakov; started conducting in 1888 and became a teacher at the conservatory in Saint Petersburg in 1899, where he was director from 1906-1912. He reorganized the conservatory after the revolution, but left the Soviet Union in 1928, became a conductor in Spain, the U.S. and England, and settled down in Paris. Although Glazunov was befriended with Balakirev, his music is strongly influenced by the West (Brahms), though his brilliant instrumentation clearly goes back to Rimski-Korsakov. Much of Glazunov's work, which includes 8 symphonies, orchestral pieces, concerti, 7 string quartets, piano music and songs, is scarcely played outside the former Soviet Union anymore, except for a few works like the *Violin Concerto* (1904), the first *Concert Waltz*, the ballets *Raymonda* (1897) and *The seasons* (1898), and the *Saxophone Concerto* (1934).

Glenn, John Herschel, Jr. (1921-), U.S. astronaut and senator. On Feb. 20, 1962, in the space capsule *Friendship 7*, he orbited the earth 3 times. Active in Ohio politics after retiring from the U.S. Marines as a colonel, he was first elected a Democratic senator in 1974. He was an unsuccessful candidate for the 1984 presidential nomination. In October 1998, Glenn again joined an astronaut team for a one-off flight in a space shuttle, making him the oldest astronaut ever.

Glider, nonpowered airplane launched by air or ground towing and kept aloft by its light, aerodynamic design and the skill of the pilot in exploiting rising air currents. Gliding is a popular sport throughout the world.
See also: Airplane.

Gligorov, Kiro (1917-), Macedonian politician. Gligorov, who studied law in Belgrade, fulfilled a prominent role in the resistance against the German fascist oppression during World War II. He became vice-minister of Finance under Tito in 1947. Afterwards he was instrumental in determining the political face of Yugoslavia; he became, among other things, the minister of Finance (1962-1967) and the Speaker of the parliament (1974-1978). Following the disintegration of Yugoslavia he became president of the republic of Macedonia in 1991 (officially, the Former Yugoslavian Republic of Macedonia). During the first years of his term in office, Gligorov made strong efforts to gain international recognition for the Republic of Macedonia. He was reelected as president as a candidate for a coalition of progressive parties in 1994.

Glinka, Mikhail Ivanovich (1804-1857), Russian composer. His 2 operas, *A Life for the Tsar* (1836) and *Russlan and Ludmilla* (1842), started a nationalistic Russian school of music.
See also: Opera.

Gliwice (pop. 216,000), city in the Polish province of Katowice, on the Klodnica. One of the oldest centers of heavy industry in Europe: blast furnaces, metal, construction materials and foodstuffs industries. Extraction of coal. Technical Academy. Established in 1246, a trading post for wood and hop in the Middle Ages.

Globalization (also: mondialization) a more progressive and complex form of internationalization which started in the 1970s. Internationalization is characterized by the phenomenon of large organizations expanding their production on a more international scale. However, internationalization is not a new phenomenon, whereas globalization is. It remains to be seen to what extent the state's autonomy is damaged by globalization: as multinationals become more and more powerful.
See also: Antiglobalism.

Globe Theatre, London open-air public theater where most of Shakespeare's plays were first performed. Built on the Thames River in 1598, it was destroyed in 1644 by the Puritans.
See also: Shakespeare, William.

Globulin, large family of proteins distributed in plants and animals, insoluble in water but soluble in dilute saline solutions. In humans, blood globulins resist disease.

Glockenspiel, or bells, pitched percussion instrument, originally a set of graduated bells, but now 2 rows of tuned steel bars on a frame. The bars are hit with hard mallets made of rubber, brass, or steel. The instrument originated in the Netherlands between 1650 and 1700. It became part of the orchestra during the 18th century.

Glomerulonephritis *See:* Nephritis.

Glorious Revolution, events of 1688-1689 that led to the deposition of King James II of England. When the birth of James's son threatened to turn England into a Catholic monarchy, the Whigs and Tories united and invited the Dutch prince William III and his wife Mary (James's daughter) to rule. In 1689, Parliament restricted royal powers in the Bill of Rights.

Glowworm *See:* Firefly.

Gloxinia (*Sinningia speciosa*), Brazilian plant prized for its colorful, velvety leaves and bell-shaped flowers. A new plant can be grown from a single leaf stuck in the soil.

Gluck, Christoph Willibald von (1714-1787), German operatic composer. In *Orpheus and Euridice* (1762) he introduced a new kind of opera combining drama, music, and emotion. His *Alceste* (1767) considerably influenced Mozart. His greatest work is *Iphigenia in Tauris* (1779).

Glucose ($C_6H_{12}O_6$), simple sugar found in certain foods, especially fruits. The chief

G

The glockenspiel has two rows of steel bars, laid out like a piano keyboard. The soft bell-like tone is produced by striking the bars with a pair of hammers, whose heads may be made of wood, rubber or plastic.

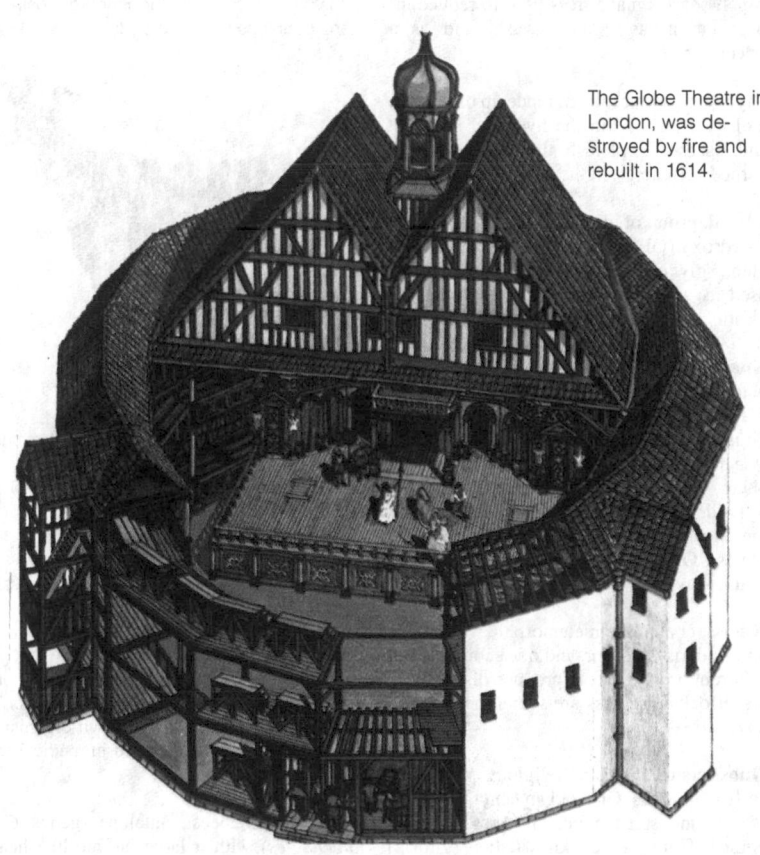

The Globe Theatre in London, was destroyed by fire and rebuilt in 1614.

source of energy for living organisms, it is absorbed directly into the bloodstream. Excess glucose is converted into glycogen and stored in the liver and muscles; beyond that, it is converted to fat. Glucose in urine may be a symptom of diabetes.

Glue, adhesive material produced from vegetable (starch, gum, soybeans) or animal (bones, hides, oil) substances. Glues dry to a strong film that bonds paper, wood, leather, and similar porous materials.

Gluon, elementary subatomic particle that holds the parts of protons and neutrons together. Gluons have no mass, move at the speed of light, and multiply themselves so rapidly that they intensify their force. The theory of gluons, first presented by U.S. physicists H. David Politzer, David J. Gross, and Frank A. Wilczek in 1974, is called quantum chromodynamics (QCD). *See also:* Physics.

Gluten, mixture of 2 proteins, gliadin and glutenin, found in wheat, rye, and other cereal flours. When bread rises, gluten forms an elastic network that traps carbon dioxide. The high gluten content of hard wheat is right for bread and pasta, while soft wheat (low gluten) is used for biscuits and cakes.

Glutton *See:* Wolverine.

Glycerin *See:* Glycerol.

Glycerol, or glycerin, colorless, sticky, sweet-tasting liquid alcohol. Its fatty-acid esters constitute natural fats and oils, from which soap is made. It is used to reduce inflammation, as a mouthwash, and as a sweetener.

Glycogen, animal starch made up of glucose molecules, stored in the liver and muscles, and used to replenish the glucose levels burned for energy in the body.

Glycol, group of alcohols, all of which have 2 hydroxy (OH) groups. The simplest is ethylene glycol (CH_2OH, CH_2OH), widely used as an antifreeze. Glycols are used as plasticizers and solvents.

Gnat, small biting fly such as a mosquito, belonging to the order Diptera.

Gnatcatcher, genus (*Polioptila*) of small, insect-eating birds of the Western Hemisphere, from the Old World warbler family, Sylviidae. Two species, the blue-gray and the black-tailed, are found in the United States. Others are found in Central and South America.

Gneiss, crystalline metamorphic rock, made up of quartz, feldspar, and mica combined in different proportions to produce distinct layers. Blocks of gneiss are sometimes used to pave streets.

Gnosticism, dualistic religious system of early Christians. Gnosticism held that matter is evil and spirit good, and that salvation comes from secret knowledge (gnosis)

Since 1922, the Swiss Saanen has been used for breeding in other countries. It has a good reputation for high milk production over a long lactation period.

The Toggenburg is a hardy, hornless breed, which originated in Switzerland, but is now used in many countries for crossbreeding. The familiar white markings on its head are usually reproduced in Toggenburg crossbreeds.

A Spanish breed, the black hornless Granada is kept for its milk. It is still popular in Spain, but has not spread further afield.

granted to initiates. Gnosticism declined after the 2nd century A.D.

Gnotobiotics, laboratory organism that is either free of all known contaminating organisms (bacteria, fungi, yeasts) or specifically contaminated with a known organism. Gnotobiotic animals are used in medical research.

Gnu, or wildebeest, antelope (genus *Connochaetes*) with a large buffalo-like head and shoulders, curved horns, and a horse-like body and tail. The brindled gnu (*C. taurinus*) lives in herds in South and East African grasslands. It weighs 500 lb (225 kg) and is 4 ft (135 cm) tall.

Goa (pop. 1,200,000), an Indian state on the country's west coast. Goa covers about 1,350 sq mi (3,500 sq km). The port of Panaji is the capital and largest city. Tourism and agriculture are the most important sources of income. Goa was held by the Portuguese from 1510 until 1961, when it was seized by India and incorporated into a union territory. Goa became a state in 1987.

Goanna *See:* Monitor.

Goat, member (genus *Capra*) of the cattle family and closely related to sheep. Goats have hollow horns, coarse hair, and 'beards.' They live in herds in mountainous areas, grazing on bushes and grass. They are valuable for their milk and their hair (mohair) and wool (cashmere).

Goatsucker, or nightjar, mostly night-flying bird of the family Caprimulgidae, which includes the nighthawk and whippoorwill. Goatsuckers are found in temperate and tropical regions. They are primarily brown and gray in color and fly with their mouths gaping open in order to catch insects.

Gobi, vast desert in central Asia, which extends to North China. It covers about 500,000 sq mi (1,295,000 sq km) in the Mongolian plateau and is between 3,000 to 5,000 ft (910 to 1,520 m) high, with fierce wind and sand storms. Its steppeland fringes are inhabited by Mongol herdsmen. There are valuable coal and oil deposits in the Gobi.

God, in religion, term for the 'supreme being.' In polytheistic systems, one god is generally regarded as the ruler of the others. The Hindu pantheon reflects this hierarchy by regarding Brahman as the supreme being, although other gods are worshiped as aspects of his being. True monotheism emerged in the religion of the Hebrews, whose one God, Yahweh, is a personal being with whom the Hebrews established a covenant. The Christian concept of God is based on the Hebrew tradition, expanded to include the doctrines of the divine nature of Jesus Christ and the Trinity of 3 persons in 1 God. Another monotheistic religion, Islam, worships Allah. The major religions of the Far East-Buddhism, Shintoism, Taoism, and Confucianism-are philosophical, moral, and contemplative, but they are not essentially monotheistic. The principal arguments developed in the West to prove the existence of God are the ontological, put forth by Anselm of Canterbury, that the idea of a perfect being necessitates the existence of that being; the cosmological, best stated by Thomas Aquinas, arguing there must be a First Cause; the teleological, that the order of the universe indicates an orderer; and the moral, enunciated by Immanuel Kant, based on humanity's inherently moral nature. Another school of thought holds that God is revealed directly through mystical experience.

Philosophers have often conceived of God as a transcendent and impersonal being that shows itself in the world and the universe but creates no personal relationship with people. The pantheists believe that God is the sum of the universe and that all things, including humanity, are part of God. Deists see God expressed in the rational pattern of the universe but withdrawn from the events of the world. Both the industrial and scientific revolutions have had far-reaching effects on the nature of belief in God. For many people, materialism and skepticism have replaced the earlier certainty of religion. Considerable numbers of people are agnostic (neither believing nor disbelieving in the existence of God), with a smaller group professing to be atheist. The old opposition of science and faith has lessened, as science has uncovered more mystery in the universe and religion has shown itself less dogmatic about the nature of the objective world.

Godard, Jean-Luc (1930-), French film director, a pioneer of the 'new wave' school with his film *Breathless* (1959). Godard's imagery and innovative camera techniques in films such as *My Life to Live* (1962) and *Weekend* (1967) influenced a whole generation of filmmakers.

Godavari, River in Central India; 901 mi (1450 km). Rises in the Western Ghats, flows through the Eastern Ghats and discharges into the Bay of Bengal near Rajahmundry in the form of a delta. With the exception of the Ganges, it is the most important holy river to the Hindus.

Goddard, Robert Hutchings (1882-1945), U.S. physicist, pioneer of rocketry. In 1926 he launched the first liquid-fuel rocket. He developed many of the basic ideas of modern rocketry; among over 200 patents was one for a multistage rocket.
See also: Physics; Rocket.

Godden, (Margaret) Rumer (1907-1998), British author whose novels, poems, and children's books are distinguished by their warm characterization and lyric style. Her novels include *Black Narcissus* (1939), *The River* (1946), *In This House of Brede* (1969), and *The Dark Horse* (1982).

Goddess *See:* Mythology.

Godetia, genus of flowering annuals named after the Swiss botanist Charles H. Godet. There are about 25 different kinds of godetias grown in North America. They belong to the family Onagraceae, characterized by flowers with 4 sepals, 4 petals, and 4 or 8 stamens. The farewell-to-spring (*G. Amoena*) grows 12 to 30 in (30 to 76 km) high and produces white, pink, or red flowers.

Godiva, Lady (c.1040-1080) noted for her legendary ride through Coventry, England, to persuade her husband Leofric, earl of Mercia, to reduce heavy taxes. She rode naked on a white horse.

Gods *See:* Mythology; Polytheism; Religion.

Godthåb (pop. 10,000; Greenlandic: *Nuuk*), capital city of Greenland, located on the southwestern shore of the island, on Davis Strait. The harbor is icefree in winter and fishing, canning, smoking, and drying fish are the main industries. Europeans first settled near Godthåb in the 11th century.
See also: Greenland.

Godwin, William (1756-1836), English political theorist and novelist. In his *Enquiry Concerning Political Justice* (1793) and in his novels *The Adventures of Caleb Williams* (1794), and *Fleetwood* (1805), Godwin rejected government as corrupting; he believed that humans are rational beings able to live without laws and institutions. Godwin influenced his son-in-law, poet P. B. Shelley.

Godwit, large wading bird with long, slightly upcurved bill, belonging to the snipe and sandpiper family. It is found worldwide on grassy plains, wet meadows, and prairie marshes. Many of its breeding places on the Canadian prairies have been plowed up.

Goebbels, (Paul) Joseph (1897-1945), Nazi propagandist. Appointed minister of propaganda by Hitler in 1933, Goebbels skillfully organized political campaigns and used the mass media (cinema, radio, newspapers) to promote Nazism throughout Germany until the end of World War II. He committed suicide with his family in Berlin in 1945.
See also: Nazism; World War II.

Goeduck *See:* Geoduck.

Goering, Hermann Wilhelm (1893-1946), German National Socialist politician, who became Reichs Marshal in 1940. He was the son of the Reichs Commissioner for German Southwest Africa. He was a war pilot during the First World War, became a test pilot for the Danish aircraft industry, and later became the leader of the SA (1922). Badly wounded at the Hitler putsch in Munich, he fled abroad and returned to Germany in 1928. He collaborated with Hitler, becoming Reichs Minister without portfolio and Reichs Commissioner for Aviation (1933). As Prussian Minister of Internal Affairs he founded the Gestapo and instituted concentration camps. In 1935 he became Commander-in-Chief of the Luftwaffe. Goering ordered the looting of many valuable works of art from occupied regions during the Second World War. He fell out of favor with Hitler because he wanted to negotiate with the Allied Forces following the Luftwaffe's lack of success. He was sentenced to death at Nurenberg, but was able to commit suicide by taking poison.

Goes, Hugo Van der *See:* Van der Goes, Hugo.

Goethals, George Washington (1858-1928), U.S. army engineer who completed construction of the Panama Canal, 1907-1914. Goethals overcame difficulties caused by the climate, disease, and the labor force.

He served as governor of the Canal Zone, 1914-1916.
See also: Panama Canal.

Goethe, Johann Wolfgang von (1749-1832), German poet, novelist, and playwright. His monumental work ranges from correspondence and poems to 14 volumes of scientific studies and is crowned by *Faust* (part I, 1808; part II, 1833), written in stages during 60 years, in which he synthesized his life and art in a poetic and philosophical statement of the search for complete experience and knowledge. Among his best-known novels are *The Sorrows of Young Werther* (1774) and *The Apprenticeship of Wilhelm Meister* (1795-1796).

Gogh, Vincent Van *See:* Van Gogh, Vincent.

Gogol, Nikolai Vasilyevich (1809-1852), Russian short story writer, novelist, and dramatist. His comic stories of Ukrainian peasant life and later bizarre tales set in St. Petersburg, such as 'The Overcoat' (1872), put him among the most original of Russian authors. Adverse reaction in Russia to his satirical drama *The Inspector-General* (1836) drove Gogol abroad, where he wrote his greatest work, the picaresque novel *Dead Souls* (1842).

Goiter, medical condition causing the front of the neck to swell, due to an enlargement of the thyroid gland. Goiters occur because the thyroid gland is too active (hyperthyroidism) or not active enough (hypothyroidism). When hyperthyroidism occurs, the thyroid gland produces too much thyroxine and the gland enlarges. Symptoms of this type of goiter include weight loss and nervousness. When hypothyroidism takes place, the pituitary gland secretes too much thyroid-stimulating hormone, causing swelling. Symptoms include physical and mental slowness and weight gain.

Golan *See:* Cities of refuge.

Golan, Menahem (Menahem Globus; 1929-), Israeli producer and film director, active in the U.S. as well. He made his debut in Israel in 1963 with the film *El Dorado* (director and producer). He started his own production company, 'Noah Films'. This company then became 'Golan-Globus', which he established together with his cousin Yoram Globus. The two of them bought a majority share in 'Cannon' in 1979, a film and theater company that rapidly expanded under their supervision, and that produced many low-budget movies with major stars. Business began declining at the end of the 1980s and he left the company in 1989. It was then sold to the Italian businessman Giancarlo Parretti. He began his own production company, '21st Century'. Films directed by Golan include *Lepke* (1970), *Kazablan* (1973), *Operation Thunderbolt* (1977), *The magician of Lublin* (1977), *Over the Brooklyn Bridge* (1984), *Delta Force* (1985), *Over the Top* (1987), *Hanna's War* (1988).

Golan Heights, strategic area, formerly part of Syria, between southern Lebanon and southwestern Syria. Israel occupied the

G

The northern part of the Jordan Rift with the Golan Heights, is a strategically important region for both Israel and Syria.

Golan Heights after the Arab-Israeli war of 1967, officially claiming it in 1981. Syria does not accept Israel's claim. Despite negotiations on Syrian sovereignty in the early 1990s no agreement was signed in the mid 1990s. The Golan Heights is 454 sq mi (1,176 sq km), overlooking the Sea of Galilee and the Jordan River.

Gold, chemical element, symbol Au; for physical constants see Periodic Table. Gold has been known and highly valued from earliest times. It is found free in nature and in combination with tellurium. It is recovered from its ores by cyaniding, amalgamating, and smelting. Gold is a soft, yellow, unreactive metal not attacked by common acids. Gold is used in coinage and is a standard for monetary systems in many countries. Gold and its compounds are used for jewelry, decoration, dental work, and plating.

Goldberg, Arthur Joseph (1908-1990), U.S. labor lawyer and public servant. He served as secretary of labor (1961-1962), associate justice of the Supreme Court (1962-

1965), and U.S. representative to the United Nations (1965-1968). Goldberg was instrumental in the 1955 merger of the American Federation of Labor and the Congress of Industrial Organizations (AFL-CIO).

Gold Coast *See:* Ghana.

Golden Age, in Greek and Roman mythology, era of perfect happiness, prosperity, and innocence that preceded recorded history. As described by the Latin poet Ovid, it knew no wars and laws were unnecessary; the earth bore fruits spontaneously and harmony prevailed.
See also: Mythology.

Golden Fleece, in Greek mythology, golden wool of a sacred winged ram. King Pelias sent his nephew Jason to retrieve the fleece from its guarded grove to determine whether Jason was worthy of the throne. Before succeeding, Jason had to sow the teeth of a dragon and fight the fierce men who grew from these seeds.
See also: Mythology.

Golden Gate Bridge, bridge spanning the entrance to San Francisco Bay, Calif., built in 1933-1937. Its 4,200 ft (1,280 m) central span, between 2,746 ft (227 m) towers, is the second longest in the world and carries 6 traffic lanes.

Golden Hind *See:* Drake, Sir Francis.

Golden retriever, gold-colored, thick-coated hunting dog, originally bred in Scotland around 1870. The good-natured, intelligent animal has been used as a guide dog for the blind and as a family companion. Heights average 23 in (58 cm) at the shoulder and weights range from 55 to 75 lb (25 to 34 kg).

Goldenrod, tall plant (genus *Solidago*) with masses of yellow or white flowers that bloom in the autumn. Growing wild in the eastern United States, goldenrod is the state flower of Kentucky and Nebraska.

Golden rule, precept stated by Jesus in the Sermon on the Mount: 'Treat others as you would like them to treat you' (Matt. 7.12). The rule existed earlier among Greeks and Jews in a negative form (that one should not treat others in a manner in which one would not wish to be treated oneself), and was also stated by the Chinese philosopher Confucius.

Goldenseal, or orange root, perennial herb (*Hydrastis canadensis*) of the buttercup family, found in the eastern United States and in Japan. Its yellow, knotted roots were once used medicinally.

Golden State *See:* California.

Goldfield, village in southwestern Nevada, seat of Esmeralda County. Goldfield flourished as a center of a gold-mining region after the discovery of gold nearby in 1903. Over $11 million worth of gold and other metals had been mined by 1910, but by 1918 extensive mining had almost exhausted gold deposits, and the population began to decline.
See also: Nevada.

Goldfinch, small, short-tailed bird (genus *Carduelis*) of the finch family, also called wild canary because of its musical song and the male's bright yellow color. North American goldfinches include the lesser goldfinch, Lawrence's goldfinch, and the American goldfinch. The European goldfinch was introduced to North America in the 1800s but is found only in Europe today. The American goldfinch is approximately 5 in (13 cm) long.

Goldfish (*Carassius auratus*), freshwater fish of the carp family. The goldfish is native to China and was domesticated more than 2,000 years ago. In its wild form it is olive in color and grows up to 16 in (40 cm) long; the domesticated goldfish may be as small as 1-4 in (2.5-10 cm) long and is often red, although some are bred for mottled colorings as well as elaborate fins.

Golding, William Gerald (1911-1993), English novelist. His powerful allegorical

The celestial goldfish is so named because its bulging, globular eyes are turned upward.
The veiltail has a short, heavy body and a long, sheer, double tail. The lionhead has rounded, blisterlike growths on its head that form a 'mane'.
The telescope black moor, a black goldfish, has large globular eyes that point forward.

celestial

lionhead

veiltail

common

telescope black moor

works explore the nature of humanity, and include *Lord of the Flies* (1954), *The Spire* (1964), and *Darkness Visible* (1979). He received Britain's Booker McConnell Prize in 1980 and the Nobel Prize for literature in 1983.

Goldman, Emma (1869-1940), Russian-born U.S. anarchist, she emigrated to the United States in 1886 and was imprisoned many times for her activities against militarism, for labor rights, and for advocating birth control. In 1919 she was deported to Russia along with Alexander Berkman, her copublisher of the paper *Mother Earth*. She opposed the repressive policies of the Bolshevik government and left Russia in 1921, for England and later Canada. Among her writings are *Anarchism and Other Essays* (1910) and her autobiography *Living My Life* (1931).
See also: Anarchism.

Goldoni, Carlo (1707-1793), Italian dramatist. His classical character comedy led to the decline in popularity of the rival commedia dell'arte. Goldoni directed the Comédie Italienne in Paris, 1762-1764. Among his 150 comic plays are *The Mistress of the Inn* (1753), *The Accomplished Maid* (1756), and *The Fan* (1763).

Gold Rush, influx of prospectors following the discovery of a new gold field. From 1848-1915, in the Americas, Australia, and South Africa, there were numerous gold rushes attracting thousands of prospectors: in California (1849), Australia (1851-1853), Canada and the Klondike (1897).

Goldsmith, Oliver (1730?-1774), Anglo-Irish author. His best-known works include the novel *The Vicar of Wakefield* (1766), the comedies *The Goodnatured Man* (1768) and *She Stoops to Conquer* (1773), and the pastoral poem *The Deserted Village* (1770). A member of the literary circle around Samuel Johnson, he achieved con-

siderable literary fame and widespread popularity in his day. His works attacked pedantry and sentimentalism and stressed simple virtues.

Gold standard, monetary system in which a standard currency unit equals a fixed weight of gold. Since World War II most countries no longer have an internal gold standard, but do use a limited international standard to convert their currencies into gold or U.S. dollars for international payments. In 1976 the International Monetary Fund created a system of controlled floating rates that diminished the importance of gold in international transactions. The U.S. went on the gold standard in 1900, but the Gold Reserve Act of 1934 prohibited the redemption of dollars into gold. And in 1970 the U.S. Treasury ended its requirement that Federal Reserve notes be backed 25% by gold deposits, in effect taking the U.S. completely off the gold standard.
See also: Money.

Goldwater, Barry Morris (1909-1998), U.S. conservative senator from Arizona (1953-1965, 1969-1987), and unsuccessful Republican presidential candidate against Lyndon B. Johnson in 1964. His writings include *The Conscience of a Conservative* (1960) and *Why Not Victory?* (1962).

Goldwyn, Samuel (Samuel Goldfish; 1882-1974), Polish-born U.S. film pioneer. He formed Goldwyn Pictures Corp. (1917), which later merged with L.B. Mayer's company (1924) to form Metro-Goldwyn-Mayer. The producer of more than 70 films, he won an Academy Award for *The Best Years of Our Lives* (1946).

Golf, game in which players hit a small, hard ball with special clubs on an outdoor course (links), attempting to use as few strokes as possible to deposit the ball into a cup (hole). Playing a hole, of which there are 18 on a standard course, involves driving the

ball from a raised peg (tee) across the fairway, which is flanked by obstacles to be avoided, such as sand traps and water, toward the green (a smooth area around the hole at a distance of 100-600 yd/91-541 m from the tee). Golf clubs include 3 or 4 woods, 9 or 10 irons, and a putter (used on the green). Written records of golf date from the 15th century in Scotland, and though the game may have been introduced to the United States in the 17th century, the first permanent U.S. golf club did not come into being until 1888. In 1916 the Professional Golfers' Association (PGA) championship began and to this day has been dominated by U.S. golfers such as Bobby Jones, Arnold Palmer, and Jack Nicklaus.

Golgotha *See:* Calvary.

Goliath, in the Bible, a Philistine giant, and a warrior who challenged the Israelites. He was killed by the young David, who struck him with a single stone from his sling (1 Sam.17.)
See also: Bible.

Goltzius, Hendrick (1558-1617), Dutch artist, engraver and painter. Extremely talented in a technical sense, inventive and versatile artist. His initially mannerist style was influenced by Carracci, among others, during a stay in Italy (1590-1591). Upon his return he made use mainly of the classicist language of shapes. Is regarded as one of the most important links between 16th-century mannerism and 17th-century realism in the Netherlands.

Gombrich, Ernst Hans Josef (1909-2001), British art historian of Austrian origin. Engaged himself in the psychology of observing art. He demonstrated in his book *Art and Illusion* (1960) that human observation uses diagrams. Knowledge of these diagrams enables the artist to create an illusion of reality on canvas. He has a very large oeuvre to his name.

G

A golfer's basic requirements are spiked shoes, a glove for his top hand, and a golf bag (1), containing woods (2), irons (3), a putter (4), tees (5), and balls (6). There are two sizes of balls in general use: the traditional British ball (min diameter 41.1 mm) and the larger American ball (min diameter 42.6 mm).

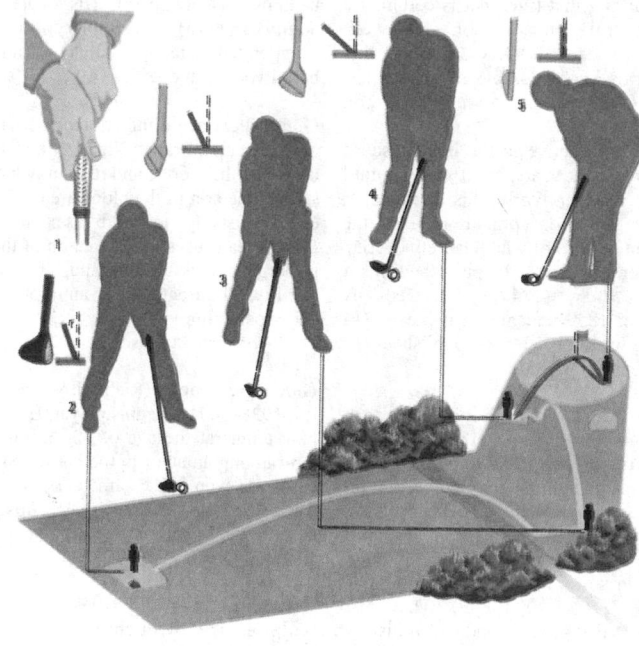

A hypothetical par-4 hole. Showing the use of various clubs, their angle of loft, and orthodox stance from which to execute the appropriate shot. Using the correct grip for the driver (1), the player drives off from the tee (2), down the fairway, clearing the natural hazard. Some 394 ft (120 m) from the hole, he plays a 5-iron approach shot (3), which lands in a bunker. He uses a sand wedge (4) to blast it out. The loft on this club means that there will be almost no run when the ball lands on the green. The player can putt (5) into the hole.

G

Gomorrah *See:* Sodom and Gomorrah.

Gompers, Samuel (1850-1924), English born U.S. labor leader. A member of the cigar makers' union, he helped found and became first president (1886-1924, except 1895) of the American Federation of Labor (AFL). Gompers fought for higher wages, shorter working hours, and more freedom. He opposed militant political unionism, and advocated organizing skilled workers on the basis of their trades, as opposed to industrial unionism, in which workers, skilled and unskilled, are organized by industry.

Gomulka, Wladyslaw (1905-1982), Polish communist leader. As first secretary of the Polish Communist Party (1956-1970), he encouraged social and economic freedoms for Poles while maintaining close ties with the USSR. He resigned following food price riots.

Goncharenko, Oleg Georgievitch (1931-1986), Russian skater. The first Russian skater to win the world championship speed skating, achieving a total number of points of 193,143 in the major four-event competition (Helsinki, 1953). Champion of the Soviet Union (1956, 1958), of Europe (1957-1958) and world champion (1953, 1956, 1958).
Member of the communist party of the Soviet Union as of 1953. Bearer of the Lenin order. Russian skaters have participated in the world championships and European championships since 1948, and in the Olympic Winter Games since 1956.

Goncharov, Ivan Aleksandrovich (1812-1891), Russian author, became famous for his novel *Oblomov* (1859), in which the main character, a country nobleman, becomes less and less capable of undertaking any type of activity and is reduced to a complete do-nothing. As a result he loses his beloved, his friends and his fortune. His condition can be regarded more than anything else as a cultural phenomenon of his environment during that time, but is certainly a more general phenomenon as well: Goncharov spoke of 'Oblomovchina', i.e. 'Oblomovitis' or 'Oblomovism', which has since become a commonly-used word in Russian.
Goncharov was active in the literary scene during his student years, but it was not until 1844 that he began writing his three major, somewhat autobiographical novels, the preparation periods of which largely overlap one another. The first to be published was *A Common Story* (1847), followed by *Oblomov* in 1859 and his third novel, *The Precipice*, in 1869. He also published *The Pallada Frigate* in 1855.

Goncourt brothers, Edmond Louis Antoine Huot de Goncourt (1822-1896) and **Jules Alfred Huot de Goncourt** (1830-1870), French authors who pioneered the naturalist school of fiction. Their novels explore aspects of French society, notably *Germinie Lacerteux* (1864), a study of working-class life, *Renée Mauperin* (1864), and *Mme Gervaisais* (1869). They also wrote perceptively on art and social history, publishing the famous *Journal des Goncourt*, depicting Parisian society, 1851-1895. The Goncourt Academy annually awards the prestigious Goncourt Prize for fiction.

Gondwanaland, presumed to be one of the original continents, located in the southern hemisphere, from which - after it broke into parts as a result of continental shifting - what is now South America, Africa, Madagascar, India, Arabia, Malaysia, Indonesia, Australia and Antarctica originated. The continent in the northern hemisphere that corresponded to Gondwanaland was Laurasia.
There is evidence of a bridge of land existing between South America, Antarctica, Madagascar, India and Australia after the disintegration of Gondwanaland (which began ca. 200 million years ago). The remains of a certain type of dinosaur, which lived after the continent split apart, have only been found in that area, and not in Africa.

Gong, disk-shaped percussion instrument, usually made of bronze, which produces sound by vibrating when struck with a special kind of hammer. Gongs are made in many different sizes; the larger the size, the deeper the pitch.

Gong Li (1965-), Chinese film actress. Her career was inextricably connected to that of director Zhang Yimou, who gave her the leading role in all of his films: *Hong gaoliang* (1987), *Ju Dou* (1989), *Dahong denglong gaogao guo* (Raise the Red Lantern; 1991), *Qiu Ju da guanshi* (The Story of Qiu Ju; 1992), *Huozhe* (Lifetimes; 1994) and *Shanghai Triad* (1995). She also acted in various films by Chen Kaige: *Bawang bieji* (Farewell to my Concubine; 1993), *Temptress Moon* (1996) and *Chinese Box* (1998).

Góngora y Argote, Luis de (1561-1627), Spanish poet. One of the great figures of Spain's Golden age, he originated an ornate style in his sonnets and ballads that came to be known as Gongorism. His greatest work, *Solitudes* (1613), is exemplary in its use of exaggerated metaphors, allusion, and Latin-based vocabulary.

Gonorrhea, acute infectious disease of the mucous membranes lining the urethra, cervix of the uterus, and rectum, which may spread bacteria in the bloodstream. The disease is usually spread by sexual contact. Gonorrhea causes inflammation of the genital organs and urethra and, if untreated, sterility. The treatment is antibiotics, especially penicillin
See also: Venereal disease.

Gonzales, Pancho (Richard Alonzo Gonzales; 1928-), U.S. tennis player. He began to play tennis at the age of 12, becoming the top-ranking amateur in the United States by 1948. He won 2 U.S. amateur singles titles and helped the U.S. team defeat Australia in the 1949 competition. He became a professional player in 1949.

González, Julio (1876-1942), a Spanish sculptor. His wrought-iron and welded sculptures influenced many of his contemporaries. González's works include the realistic, as in *Montserrat* (1937), and the surrealistic, as in *Angel* (1933). After studying art in his native Barcelona, González settled in Paris. He was influenced by Picasso, and in turn taught Picasso welding and soldering techniques for use in creating sculpture.

González Márquez, Felipe (1942-), prime minister of Spain (1982-1996) and head of Spain's first leftist government since the 1936 Civil War. González Márquez also holds the position of first secretary of Spain's Socialist party and is a lawyer. Under his leadership, Spain joined the European Common Market in 1986. In 1995 he was accused of involvement in death squads (GAL) that killed over 20 ETA supporters in the 1980s. At the general elections of 1996 he was defeated by José María Aznar. In 1997, González resigned his post as party leader.
See also: Spain.

Goober *See:* Peanut.

Goodall, Jane (1934-), English zoologist who gained recognition through her years of study and work with chimpanzees. She learned that chimpanzees' use of tools is second only to humans'. She also discovered that they eat pigs, small monkeys, and other medium-sized game, and that groups may actually war on each other. Her books include *My Friends, the Wild Chimpanzees* (1967), *In the Shadow of Man* (1971), *The Innocent Killers* (1971), and *The Chimpanzees of Gombe* (1986).
See also: Zoology.

Good Friday, in Holy Week, the Friday before Easter, the anniversary of the Crucifixion of Jesus Christ, observed in most Christian churches as a day of fasting and mourning. Its observance dates from the 2nd century.
See also: Holy Week.

Good Hope, Cape of *See:* Cape of Good Hope.

Goodman, Benny (Benjamin D. Goodman; 1909-1986), U.S. clarinetist and bandleader, known as the King of Swing. A big-band leader since the 1930s, he performed for radio, motion pictures, and records, and also led small ensembles with such talents as Gene Krupa and Lionel Hampton. In addition to jazz, his classical virtuosity inspired compositions for the clarinet by Béla Bartók (*Contrasts*, 1938) and concertos by Aaron Copland and Paul Hindemith.

Good Neighbor Policy, policy initiated by President Franklin D. Roosevelt and endorsed at the seventh Pan-American conference in Montevideo (1933). The policy stated that no American nation would interfere in the internal affairs of another. Exchange programs were set up for teachers and technical experts, and the United States agreed to help develop Latin American agriculture, business, education, and health facilities.
See also: Roosevelt, Franklin Delano.

G

The Canada goose (left), snow goose (middle) and the white-fronted goose (right).

Goodyear, Charles (1800-1860), U.S. inventor (in 1839) of vulcanized rubber (patented 1844). In his search to find a way to keep rubber from melting and sticking in hot weather, he bought the patents of N.M. Hayward, who had had some success treating rubber with sulfur. Vulcanization gives rubber its elasticity and strength.
See also: Rubber.

Goose, swimming bird (family Anatidae) related to the swan and duck. Technically, 'goose' refers to the female of the species, 'gander' to the males. Geese migrate in flocks (known as skeins) reportedly flying as high as 29,000 ft (8,838 m). The Canada, or wild, goose (*Branta canadensis*) is the best known in North America, and the domestic Toulouse, or gray, goose is a descendant of the European graylag. In medieval times the Barnacle goose of Europe was thought to arise from barnacles, and, as such, was counted as fish and could be eaten on Fridays.

Gooseberry, shrub (genus *Ribes*) bearing purple berries, originally found growing wild in southern Europe and North Africa. First cultivated in the 17th century, the berries are eaten fresh or used in pies, sauces, or preserves. Cultivation of the shrubs are banned by law in some states because they are host to blister rust disease.

Gopher, or pocket gopher, burrowing rodent of the family Geomyidae, native to North and Central America. The gopher is a solitary animal, from 5 to 12 in (13 to 30 cm) in length, with large claws and very long teeth. It has fur-lined outside cheek pouches for carrying food and nesting material.

Gorbachev, Mikhail Sergeyevich (1931-), Soviet political leader who succeeded Konstantin Chernenko as general secretary of the Communist party of the Soviet Union in 1984 and became President of the USSR (1990-1996). Gorbachev had worked his way up through the ranks of the Communist party in the Russian city of Stavropol in the 1950s and 1960s. In 1970 he was elected to the Supreme Soviet. In 1971 he was added to the Communist party's Central Committee. He moved to Moscow in 1978 and in 1980 became a full member of the party's Politburo, then the country's chief policy-making body. Soon after he became general secretary, Gorbachev launched a series of reforms in both domestic and international policy. His program of *perestroika* (restructuring) was aimed at altering the economic and social systems, loosening central state control. The reforms of *glasnost* (openness) eased the system of censorship, allowing considerable freedom of speech and of the press. The Communist party's formal monopoly on political activity was lifted, and a new political system, involving some free elections, was introduced. Internationally, Gorbachev withdrew Soviet troops from Afghanistan and proclaimed a policy of non-interference when Communist rule collapsed in Eastern Europe in 1989 and 1990. Gorbachev's cooperation was instrumental in the reunification of Germany, and for this and other aspects of his international policy, he was awarded the Nobel Peace Prize in 1990.
Major problems faced by Gorbachev included the continued crisis of the Soviet economy, the rise of ethnic conflicts and of demands for independence by various republics of the USSR, and the continuing power of the old Communist party bureaucracy, especially in the army and police. With the disintegration of the USSR Gorbachev was forced to resign in 1991. He was an unsuccessful presidential candidate in 1996. In 1999, he founded the Social-Democratic Party, of which he became leader in March 2000.
See also: Perestroika.

Gordian knot, in Greek mythology, an intricate knot by which King Gordius of Phrygia joined the yoke and pole of an oxcart. A prophecy holding that anyone undoing the knot would rule all Asia came true when Alexander the Great severed the knot with his sword.
See also: Mythology.

Gordimer, Nadine (1923-), a South African writer, winner of the 1991 Nobel Prize for literature. Her fiction is noted for careful construction, precise detail, and psychological insight. It usually deals with the effects of *apartheid* (a government policy of racial segregation from 1948 to 1991) and its aftermath on the lives of blacks and whites in South Africa. *A Guest of Honour* (1970), perhaps her best-known novel, differs in that it is set in a fictional, newly independent African nation. Gordimer was born in the Transvaal and spent most of her life in Johannesburg. Other works include: *My Son's Story* (1990), *Jump* (1991), *None to Accompany Me* (1994), and *The Pickup* (2001).

Gordon, Charles George (1833-1885), British soldier, known as 'Chinese Gordon.' He helped suppress the Taiping Rebellion (1863-1864) in China, and governed the Egyptian Sudan (1877-1880), where he established law, improved communications, and attempted to suppress the slave trade. In 1885 he was killed while defending Khartoum against the Mahdi's forces.

Gordon, Douglas (1966-), Scottish visual artist. His main theme is selective memory and memory. In the early 1990s he based his work on everyday texts that are transferred by various means of communication, and he undertook telephone and correspondence projects with which he exposed social conventions. Since the mid-1990s he works mainly with video, in which images from old films (thrillers and B-movies), old pop songs, old film material, are displayed on various screens and mirror-wise. The result is dream-like and mysterious.

Gordon setter, breed of hunting dog dating from 17th-century Scotland. Its superior sense of smell and retrieving ability make it an excellent hunting companion. The Gordon setter adapts well to families and has a natural guarding instinct. It weighs 55 to 75 lb (24 to 33 kg) and reaches 23 to 25 in (59 to 64 cm) at the shoulder. Its long coat is black and tan.

Gore, Albert Jr. (Al) (1948-), American politician and the 45th Vice President of the United States. At the beginning of his career he worked as a journalist. Gore, a moderate Democratic senator from Tennessee, was elected to the Vice Presidency in 1992 as the running mate of Bill Clinton. He was re-elected Vice President in 1996. Gore is interested in environmental issues, he published *Earth in the Balance. Ecology and the Human Spirit* (1992).

Gorgon, in Greek mythology, term for 3 hideous winged and snake-haired sisters-Stheno, Euryale, and Medusa-who turned anyone who looked at them to stone. Medusa, the youngest Gorgon and the only mortal one, was killed by Perseus.
See also: Mythology.

Gorilla, largest of the primates (*Gorilla gorilla*), native to equatorial western Africa. A quadruped that rises to 2 legs only when displaying, the male ranges from 5 to 6 ft (150 to 190 cm) in height and weighs c.450 lb (200 kg); his brow ridge is prominent and his canine teeth enormous. Females are about half the size of males. Gorillas are generally shaggy, brown or black in color. They are highly intelligent, mostly vegetarian, and usually shy and gentle, despite their great strength. The mountain gorilla of central Africa is an endangered subspecies.

Gorki *See:* Nizhny Novgorod.

Gorki, Maxim (Alexey Maximovich Pyeshkov; 1868-1936), Russian author. His pen name is the Russian word for *bitter*. Gorki's works, noted for their stark natural-

G

ism, include the play *The Lower Depths* (1902), the novel *Mother* (1906), and the autobiographical trilogy *Childhood* (1913), *In the World* (1916), and *My Universities* (1923). Gorki was exiled to the United States after the failure of the Russian Revolution of 1905. He returned to Russia in 1914. A personal friend of Lenin, he became head of the state publishing house after the 1917 revolution, until 1921, when he went abroad again. He returned in 1928 and became a supporter of the Stalin regime. Many consider him the founder of the literary style called socialist realism.

Gorky, Arshile (1904-1948), Armenian-born U.S. painter, pioneer of abstract expressionism. Influenced by surrealism, he began to create abstractions of organic forms (c.1940). He influenced the work of Jackson Pollock and Willem de Kooning.
See also: Abstract expressionism; Pollock, Jackson; De Kooning, Willem.

Gorno-Altay (pop. 200,000), autonomous republic in Russia on the Mongolian border; 35,767 sq mi (92,600 sq km). The capital city is Gorno-Altaysk. The republic borders on the Kazachstan steppes, the Siberian taiga, and the Mongolian semidessert, allowing a diversity of plants and wildlife to flourish. There are more than 7000 lakes. Industries are forestry, cattle breeding, gold, mercury, and brown coal mines. At least 35% of the population finds employment in agriculture. Two thirds of the population is Russian and one third is Altay (Altayans). The region became part of the Soviet Union in 1922.

Gorno-Badakhshan (pop. 167,000), autonomous region (oblast) in the republic Tadzhikistan; it includes the Pamir Mountains that border on Afghanistan and China; 24,604 sq mi (63,700 sq km). It is very remote, almost inaccessible in the winter. The capital is Chorog. The main industries are agriculture (wheat, fruit, and fodder crops), cattle and sheep breeding, also gold mining, mica, salt, and coal.

Goshawk *See:* Hawk.

Gospel, one of the 4 New Testament books-Matthew, Mark, Luke, and John-that tell the story of the life of Jesus, written to spread the gospel ('good news') of Christian salvation. The first 3, called the Synoptic Gospels, agree on the order of events.
See also: Bible; New Testament.

Gossaert, Jan (Called Mabuse; 1478/1488-1532) Southern Dutch painter. After travelling to Italy (1508-1509) he played an important part in propagating the ideas of the renaissance in his own country. He was the first Flemish painter to use mythological themes. In addition to many versions of the Madonna with Child, he painted a series of excellent portraits.

Göteborg (pop. 437,500), second largest city in Sweden and its most important coastal port. Its harbor is ice-free throughout the year. It has fisheries and shipyards, and is the largest shipbuilding site in Scandi-

navia. It was founded by Charles IX in 1604.
See also: Sweden.

Gothenburg *See:* Göteborg.

Gothic art and architecture, the Gothic style of art and architecture flourished in Europe, particularly in France, from the mid-12th century to the end of the 15th century. The style was first referred to as 'Gothic' (after the Goths, who invaded the Roman Empire in the A.D. 200s) by Renaissance artists and writers who sought to condemn it as barbaric. Gothic architecture developed from the style called Romanesque, combining the latter's barrel vault and the stone rib to produce its most characteristic feature, the rib vault. This was first perfected at the Abbey Church of St. Denis near Paris (1140). The rib vault made possible a lighter, almost skeletal building. The flying buttress, also characteristic, was first used at Notre Dame in Paris. During the 13th century, the style known as High Gothic was perfected, and cathedrals with higher vaults and more slender columns and walls were constructed, as at Chartres and Reims in France, Salisbury in England, and Cologne in Germany. In the 14th and 15th centuries Gothic works became more elaborate and ornate. Sculptural decoration was an essential part of Gothic architecture, as were stained glass windows, the most notable examples of which are at Chartres. The period is also noted for its manuscript illumination in missals, books of hours, Bibles, and psalters.

Gothic novel, genre of fiction whose terror-laden stories are usually set against a menacing, medieval background. Early examples are Horace Walpole's *Castle of Otranto* (1765) and Ann Radcliffe's *The Mysteries of Udolpho* (1794). Modern Gothic novels are often formulaic historical romances.

Goths, ancient Germanic peoples, split into Ostrogoths (East Goths) and Visigoths (West Goths) in the 3rd century. The Ostrogoths, subjects of the Huns until A.D. 453, went on to settle in Pannonia (modern Hungary) as allies of the Byzantine Empire, and then (after 493) in Italy, claiming lands when their ruler, Theodoric the Great, defeated the barbarian ruler Odoacer. Defeated in turn by Justinian I, their kingdom was crushed after an Ostrogothic revolt in 552. The Visigoths moved (376) into Roman territory, sacking Rome (410) and heading north to the Loire valley; they made Toulouse their capital before taking Vandal lands in Spain. At the peak of their power they were led by King Euric (r. 466-c.484). After losing lands north of the Pyrénées to the Franks, they were restricted to Spain, became Christians, and merged with the Spanish population. Defeat by the Moors in 711 ended the Visigothic kingdom.

Gottfried von Strassburg, medieval German poet (late 12th-early 13th century), famous for his unfinished Middle High German masterpiece *Tristan* (c.1210), an epic based on Celtic legend. It became the basis of Richard Wagner's opera *Tristan und Isolde* (1859).

Gottlieb, Adolph (1903-1974), U.S. artist, known for his oversized abstract expressionist landscapes, which feature bursts of color. He derived his early style from pictographs, arranging abstract symbols in grids.

Gottsched, Johann Christoph (1700-1766), German man of letters, who studied philosophy and literature and taught esthetics and poetics at Leipzig from 1725 onwards. He attempted to lay down rules and standards for literature based on rationalism and in doing so became the trailblazer for German classicism. He wrote the tragedy *Sterbender Cato* (1732) and published, amongst other books, *Versuch einer critischen Dichtkunst vor die Deutschen* (1730) and *Grundlegung einer Deutschen Sprachkunst* (1748).

Gottwald, Klement (1896-1953), Czechoslovakian politician who was active in the Socialist youth movement and who joined the Czechoslovakian Communist Party as soon as it was founded (1921). He quickly held a prominent place in the party; editor-in-chief of various party journals, member of the Central Committee (from 1925) and secretary-general (from 1929). Gottwald was a member of parliament from 1929 to 1938. After the Conference of Munich he fled to the Soviet Union, where he formed, among other organizations, a national front. He returned in May of 1945 as the vice premier of the Benes government. Gottwald became prime minister in 1946, in February of 1948 he led the Communists to power; in June of 1948 he succeeded Benes as president. His stalinistic regime was infamous, in particular because of the cleansing at the Slansky trial. Gottwald died suddenly after returning from Stalin's funeral.

Gould, Glenn (1932-1982), Canadian virtuoso pianist, famous for his performances of Bach, Beethoven, and Brahms. From the late 1960s he abandoned live performances, making records and documentary films.

Gounod, Charles François (1818-1893), French composer, best known for the operas

French composer (1818-93). Charles Gounod

G

Faust (1859) and *Romeo and Juliet* (1867), and the song 'Ave Maria,' based on Bach's first prelude. Additional works include 10 other operas, oratorios, masses, and cantatas.

Gourd, any of a variety of plants, chiefly vines, of the family Cucurbitaceae, producing fruit known as gourds that are used as food and utensils. The *Cucumis* genus includes melons (except watermelons), cucumbers, and gherkins (*C. anguria*); the *Cucurbita* genus represents winter squash (*C. maxima*) and summer squash and pumpkins (varieties of *C. pepo*). Durable-shelled gourds have been used as water carriers, ornaments, resonators of musical instruments, and utensils (ladles, dippers, bowls). The fruit of the loofah (*Luffa cylindrica*), fibrous in texture, is dried for use as a sponge.

Gout, recurrent acute arthritis of peripheral joints caused by excess uric acid in the blood and tissue fluids. It may be precipitated by minor injury, overindulgence in food or alcohol, surgery, fatigue, emotional stress, infection, or administration of penicillin, insulin, or mercuric diuretics. The symptoms and signs include severe pain in a single joint, swelling of overlying skin, and inflammation. Treatment medicines help to speed elimination of uric acid by the kidneys. *See also:* Arthritis.

Government, system of control and regulation of social activities by the state, also referring to the agency that exercises such control. Governments have the power of coercion to enforce law. They define crimes and administer punishment. To defend its existence and the integrity of its territory against both internal and external enemies, most governments maintain armed forces. In modern industrialized countries the economic and social functions of governments include providing public services (such as building roads, and supplying water and sanitation facilities), and supervising education. The issuance of currency is a government monopoly. In recent times, governments have become involved in the direct management of the economy, regulating commerce, labor relations, and international trade and credit. Governments have also undertaken responsibility for social security, unemployment insurance, old age pensions, and aid to dependent children.

Government of India Act (Also known as the Montagu-Chelmsford Reforms; 1919). Bill that slightly extended the right of the Indian population to vote (property and education remained the criteria for eligibility to vote). A dyarchic system was introduced at a provincial level: from then on the governor's cabinet consisted of elected and appointed ministers, in which public safety remained in the hands of an appointed minister.

Government regulation, government supervision of industry to protect the interests of individuals and society as a whole. Federal, state, and local agencies regulate, oversee, and control prices, health and safety measures, and quality of service.

Goya, Francisco (1746-1828), Spanish painter and graphic artist. Master of satire, his keen sense of observation and ability to depict reality graphically and with almost savage detail served him from his early works, designing cartoons for tapestries (1775-1779), to his later appointment (1799) as court painter to Charles III and Charles IV. However, illness, which left him deaf in 1793, marked a turning point in his work. A world that had previously been depicted with brilliant colors, suggesting charm and delight, became grim and grotesque. His disillusionment became apparent in works from this period, including the paintings *Maja Nude* and *Maja Clothed*; the frescoes for Madrid's Church of San Antonio de la Florida, and the etchings *Disasters of War*, suggested by Napoleon's invasions of Spain. Near the end of his life, Goya surrounded himself with his 'Black Paintings,' including *Witches' Sabbath* and *Satan Devouring His Children*. Goya's work was a major influence on Edouard Manet and the French impressionists.

Gracchus, family name of 2 Roman brothers, social reformers and political leaders, known together as the Gracchi. **Tiberius Sempronius Gracchus** (163?-133 B.C.), was elected to the popular tribune in 133. He proposed what became called the Sempronian Law to redistribute public land to landless citizens in order to restore the ruined middle class of small independent farmers. At the next election he renominated himself, and when the Senate ordered the election postponed, there was a riot in which Tiberius was killed. **Caius Sempronius Gracchus** (153?-121 B.C.), was elected a tribune in 123 and took over leadership of the reform movement, suggesting democratic government to replace aristocracy and proposing citizenship for all Latins. When the Senate moved to revoke his bills, fighting broke out and Caius was killed.

Grace, in Christian theology, favor shown by God toward sinful and needy people. Grace is at the heart of salvation and is necessary for faith and good works. The means of grace include holy scripture, the sacraments, prayer, and Christian fellowship.

Graces, in Greek mythology, goddesses of fertility, personifying charm and beauty. Also known as the Charites, they were daughters of Zeus and the nymph Eurynome. Their names were Aglaia (radiance), Euphrosyne (joyfulness), and Thalia (bloom). The Romans called them the Gratiae.

Grackle, songbird of the family Icteridae, including blackbirds, orioles, and bobolinks. The grackle, generally black-hued, feeds on a wide variety of foods, including grain, bananas, and nuts; it is also known to destroy the eggs and young of other birds.

Grade school *See:* Elementary school.

Graduate school *See:* Universities and colleges.

Graevenitz, Gerhard Von (1934-1983), German visual artist, a member of the *nouvelle tendence*. He created white structures,

Francisco de Goya's painting *The Third of May, 1808* (1814-15) memorializes the execution of Madrid citizens by Napoleon's troops of occupation. The intense drama and brutality of the act is depicted in glowing color and nocturnal light, apotheosizing the plight of these and all victims of political tyranny.

composed of systematically ordered, isomorphous elements such as dots, holes, and spheres. From 1962, he was engaged with kinetic art and light art. Among other things, he placed rotating, shining panels to reflect the light, creating irregular patterns of reflections.

Graf, Steffi (1969-), German tennis player, known for her powerful forehand. Ranked number one in the world (1987-1990), in 1988 Graf won the grand slam (consisting of the Australian Open, the French Open, Wimbledon, and the United States Open) and Olympic gold medal in women's singles. In 1989 Graf captured 3 out of the 4 grand slam events, losing only in the finals of the French Open. In 1990 she won the Australian Open, in 1991 and 1992 Wimbledon, in 1993 Roland Garros, the US Open, Wimbledon, and the Masters, in 1994 the Australian Open, in 1995 the French Open, Wimbledon, and the US Open, and in 1996 Roland Garros and Wimbledon. By 1998 she had won more prize money than any other sportswoman. In 1999 she ended her career.

G

Life-size sculpture of a horse rider in the Cathedral of Bamberg (13th century). A characteristic of the Gothic style is that the sculptures are more realistic than the ones from Roman times. People or animals were no longer portrayed as thickset or too long; they were more natural in their proportions, and for the first time since the ancient Romans, the body's natural form could be seen under the clothes.

The rear view of the Notre Dame in Paris. Because the thin walls could not take the pressure of the high nave, the construction was strengthened using characteristic flying buttresses and domes.

Stained glass windows in a chapel of the Cathedra of Reims (first half 13th century).

The worship of the three kings (1423), an altar piece by Gentile da Fabriano (1370-1427). The people, animals and plants have all been painted true to life. The exuberant wooden frame has the same ornamental features as Gothic architecture.

G

English architecture developed in a different manner than that on the continent. The perpendicular style focused on vertical lines that came together in complicated fanned arches.

G

Graffiti, words, names, and pictures painted on walls, for example, in the subway. It was elevated to mainstream art in the United States in the 1980s. Keith Haring's work is a well-known example of this art form.
See also: Haring, Keith.

Grafting, in horticulture, uniting of 2 closely related varieties of plants so that they grow as one. The stem or bud of the plant to be grafted (the scion) is attached to the stem or roots of the other (the stock or rootstock). The result is known as a hybrid. Grafting is used to increase productivity, to create seedless fruits, to breed disease- and pest-resistant stock, and to grow plants in unfamiliar environments by using stock compatible to that environment.

Graham, Billy (William Franklin Graham; 1918-), U.S. evangelist. Ordained a Southern Baptist minister (1939), he gained national prominence on the revivalist circuit (c.1949) and went on to establish an international reputation as a leader of mass religious rallies and an adviser and confidante of U.S. presidents.

Graham, Martha (1894-1891), U.S. dancer, choreographer, and teacher. A pupil of Ruth St. Denis, she made her debut in the Denishawn companies (1920) and formed her own troupe in 1929. A major influence and pioneer in modern dance, she choreographed such works as *Appalachian Spring* (1944), *Clytemnestra* (1958), and *The Archaic Hours* (1969). In 1976 she was awarded the U.S. Medal of Freedom.
See also: Ballet.

Grahame, Kenneth (1859-1931), British writer of children's stories *The Golden Age* (1895), *Dream Days* (1898), and the classic *The Wind in the Willows* (1908), featuring animals with appealingly human characteristics.

Grail, Holy *See:* Holy Grail.

Grain, in agriculture, the dry seedlike fruit of a cereal grass; also, the plant that bears these fruits, including wheat, rice, oats, millet, maize, and rye. The main dietary staple of both humans and domesticated animals, grain, whole and ground, is primarily a source of carbohydrates, though some protein, vitamins, and other nutrients are present. Half of the world's cropland grows grain (corn, wheat, and rice).

Grainger, Percy Aldridge (1882-1961), Australian-born composer and pianist, a naturalized American from 1914. Influenced by his friend Grieg, he collected and edited English folk music, basing short orchestral pieces upon it.

Grain sorghum (*Sorghum vulgare*), plant of the grass family (Gramineae) producing clusters of small starchy seeds. It is used widely for livestock feed; in Asia and Africa, it is ground into flour for making bread and cereal. The plant is native to Africa, but is grown widely in the United States today. It grows about 2 to 6 ft (61 to 183 cm) tall.

Grain weevil, or snout beetle, small destructive beetle of the weevil family that attacks and damages stored grain. The female bores into healthy grain seeds with her snout and lays eggs. Hatched grubs consume the inside of the seed and mature in about a month. This worldwide pest is controlled by spraying silos and grain bins before a new harvest.

Grammar, structures of a language and of its constituents; also, the science concerned with the study of those structures. The grammarian concentrates on *syntax*, the ways that words are put together to form sentences; *accidence*, or *morphology*, the ways that words are inflected (altered) to convey different senses, such as past or present tense or singular and plural; and *phonology*, the ways that sounds are used to convey meaning. Since sentences of widely different outward form may have the same meaning, many grammarians hold that there is a deep structure of language that can be resolved into a few basic elements whose combinations can be used to produce an infinite number of sentences. As a consequence, grammatical studies are probing at the very roots of the human psyche.
See also: Language.

Grammar school *See:* Elementary school.

Granada, name of a province of southeastern Spain and of the capital (pop. 246,000) of that province. The Moorish sovereignty of that name was overtaken by Ferdinand and Isabella's armies in 1492. In the 1800s it was divided into the 3 provinces of Granada, Málaga, and Almería. The province of Granada is 4,838 sq mi (12,530 sq km). It is rich in minerals and has fertile soil. The Alhambra, a Moorish fortress and palace, and the palace of Charles V, a Holy Roman emperor, are the city's major tourist attractions.

Granada (pop. 127,000), oldest city in Nicaragua, located on Lake Nicaragua. The city, founded in 1523, was raided by pirates throughout the 1600s. It was burned in 1856 by U.S. adventurer William Walker, and rebuilt shortly thereafter. The city has many ornate Spanish-style churches and fine mansions.

Granada, Kingdom of, medieval Arab Islamic kingdom in southern Spain. Founded 1238 by the Nasrid dynasty, with its capital in Granada, the kingdom was the center of Moorish culture, a leading world center of art, science, and literature, with an extremely tolerant policy toward non-Muslims. In the 15th century internal dissensions furthered the kingdom's ultimate conquest by the Spanish monarchs Ferdinand and Isabella, who took over in 1492 and drove the Muslims and Jews out of Spain.

Granados y Campiña, Enrique (1867-1916), a Spanish pianist and composer. In 1900 he established the Sociedad de Conciertos Clásicos in Madrid and in 1901 the Academia Granados in Barcelona. Such works as *Spanish Dances* (1892-1900) are filled with the rhythms characteristic of Spanish music. *Goyescas* (1911), a series of piano pieces based on the work of the Spanish painter Goya, is considered his masterpiece. His opera *Goyescas*, based on the piano pieces, was produced in 1916. Granados was the founder of Spanish school of romantic nationalism.

Gran Chaco, lowland plain in Paraguay, Argentina, and Bolivia. Occupying c. 250,000 sq mi (647,500 sq km), this extremely hot, sparsely populated region is prone to droughts and flooding. Among its resources are oil and quebracho (a source of tannin).

Grand Alliance, or League of Augsburg, name of 3 separate European alliances created to control the invasions of King Louis XIV of France. The first (1673-1679) included the Holy Roman Empire, Prussia, and several German states. The second alliance (1689-1697), between the Netherlands, England, Spain, and the Holy Roman Empire, fought against France in the

Harvesting the grain.

War of the League of Augsburg. The third alliance (1701-1714), made up of some German states, Prussia, Austria, England, and the Netherlands, fought France in the War of the Spanish Succession.
See also: Succession wars.

Grand Banks, underwater plateau off southeast Newfoundland, Canada, where the Labrador Current and Gulf Stream meet. Its shallow waters abound in cod, haddock, and halibut, making it one of the world's richest fishing grounds.

Grand Canyon, spectacular gorge cut by the Colorado River in northwest Arizona. It is more than 200 mi (320 km) long, 4-18 mi (6-29 km) wide, up to 1 mi (1.6 km) deep, and flanked by a plateau 5,000-9,000 ft (1,524-2,743 m) above sea level. The main canyon contains many smaller canyons, peaks, and mesas, and is walled by colorful layers of rock dating back more than 2 million years. Grand Canyon National Park attracts about 2 million visitors each year.

Grand Coulee Dam, 550 ft (168 m) high and 4,173 ft (1,272 m) long dam on the Columbia River in the state of Washington. Built 1933-1942, it is part of one of the world's largest hydroelectric generating plants.
See also: Columbia River.

Grand jury, group of citizens who decide whether there is enough evidence to charge an individual with a crime. A grand jury never tries a case; its job is only to inquire and accuse. Originally, during the time of Henry III of England (1216-1272), the grand jury not only inquired and accused, but also tried cases.

Grandma Moses *See:* Moses, Grandma.

Grand National, world's most prestigious steeplechase race held annually since 1839 at the Aintree race course in England. The difficult and dangerous 4.5 mi (7.2 km) course includes 30 jumps, mostly over thorn hedges. Horses must be at least 6 years old to enter.

Grand Old Party *See:* Republican Party.

Grand Ole Opry *See:* Country and western music.

Grand Prix *See:* Automobile racing.

Grand Rapids (pop. 189,000), city (inc. 1850), in western Michigan, on the Grand River; seat of Kent County. Famous for its furniture manufacturing, begun by Dutch settlers in the early 1800s, the city today supports many industries and is the market for the area's truck farming industry. Other products include gypsum and gravel. It is also the home of several colleges, and is a gateway to Michigan's recreation area.
See also: Michigan.

Grand unified theories (GUT's), theories that attempt to explain the physical universe by a unified concept of 3 of the 4 fundamental forces: the weak nuclear force, which

The Grand Canyon, in northwestern Arizona.

controls radioactive decay of atomic nuclei; electromagnetism, which secures the electrons to the nucleus; and the strong nuclear force, which ties the nucleus together. The fourth fundamental force, gravitation, has not yet been included in GUT's. It is not known if it is indeed possible to explain all events and phenomena of the universe in such a unified manner.

Grange, Red (1930-1991), U.S. football player. He was known as the Galloping Ghost after scoring 5 touchdowns for the University of Illinois in a game against the University of Michigan in 1924. Grange became a professional player in 1925 and joined the Chicago Bears. He retired in 1935 after scoring 1,058 points and in 1963 was inducted into the Pro Football Hall of Fame.

Granite, coarse-grained rock, composed chiefly of feldspar (orthoclase and microcline) and quartz. Generally believed to have solidified from a molten form (igneous), some granite is also believed to have been metamorphic (rock transformed by heat, pressure, or chemically active fluids). A hard, weather-resistant rock, usually pink or gray, granite is often used in building, paving, and monuments.

Grant, Cary (Archibald Leach; 1904-1986), English born U.S. actor. Honored in 1970 with an Academy Award for general excellence, his films include *Bringing Up Baby* (1938), *The Philadelphia Story* (1940), *To Catch a Thief* (1955), and *North By Northwest* (1959).

Grant, (Hiram) Ulysses Simpson (1822-1885), American general and 18th president of the United States (1869-1877). As Commander-in-Chief of the Northern States, he forced the Confederates to surrender. Because of his military successes in 1868 and 1872, he became the Republican candidate for the presidency. During his presidency the internal administration was augmented (for example, by the institution of the Justice Department), but his reputation was damaged by financial scandals.

Grape, shrub and its fruit, of the family

Vitaceae, native to tropical, subtropical, and temperate regions. One of the oldest of all cultivated fruits, grapes are eaten fresh or dried (raisins), and are used in wine making. There are 2 main types of grapes: European, from the wine grape of Europe and Asia, and American, native to North America or developed from crossbreeding with the European variety.

Grapefruit, evergreen tree (*Citrus paradisi*) of the rue family, and its citrus fruit, which weigh from 1-5 lb (0.45-2.27 kg). First discovered in the West Indies, the grapefruit is believed to be a mutation of the Asian pomelo (*C. maxima*).

Graph, diagram showing the relations between quantities.

Graphic arts, techniques of drawing and engraving words and pictures, including block printing, etching, lithography, silkscreening, and engraving. The capacity to reproduce identical books quickly came about in 1440 when Johannes Gutenberg invented movable print. Block printing and engraving were mastered in Europe at the end of the Middle Ages, and graphic arts were used for original artwork as well as to create reproductions. Graphic artists include Albrecht Dürer of Germany, and Francisco Goya and Pablo Picasso of Spain.

Graphite, also known as carbon plumbago or black lead, mineral that is the crystalline form of carbon. Graphite is a good conductor of electricity and is used to make electrodes. Its inertness makes it valuable for the construction of metallurgical crucibles. It is also used as a lubricant, a moderator in nuclear reactors, and, mixed with clay, becomes the 'lead' of pencils.

Graphology, the study of handwriting, particularly for information about the character of the writer.

Grass, any plant of the family Gramineae. This group of mostly annual and perennial herbs has great economic importance: as a food source (cereal grass: wheat, rice, corn, rye, barley, and oats; hay and pasture plants, e.g., bluegrass and sorghum; sugarcane); in construction and thatching (bamboo and reed species); as raw material for paper and

Wine is a fermented alcoholic beverage, made from the juice of the cultivated grape *Vitis vinifera*.

G

G

liquors. Grass-family plants, with their hollow or pithy jointed stems, are also instrumental in preventing erosion.

Grass, Günter Wilhelm (1927-), German novelist and playwright. His works, deeply affected by the post-World War II sense of national guilt, are usually centered around grotesque motifs and have strong moral content. His best-known works include the novels *The Tin Drum* (1959), the controversial play *The Plebeians Rehearse the Uprising* (1965), *Local Anaesthetic* (1969), *The Flounder* (1977), *The Call of the Toad* (1992), and *Crabwalk* (2002). In 1999 Grass won the Nobel Prize for literature.

Author Günter Grass (1927) took active part in the political life of the Federal Republic of Germany. Here, he is shown during the 1973 SPD-campaign for the re-election of Willy Brandt as federal chancellor. The button says: 'Bürger für Brandt' (citizens for Brandt).

Grasshopper, plant-eating, winged insect of the order Orthoptera, with powerful hind legs for jumping and springing to flight. Divided into 2 families, long-horned (e.g., katydid) and short-horned (e.g., locust), grasshoppers range from 0.5-4 in (1-10 cm) in length. The males sing by rubbing their hind legs against folded wings.

A grasshopper has large compound eyes, leathery forewings that protect its veined, membranous hindwings, and long, powerful hindlegs, used for jumping. Its coloration enables the grasshopper to blend into its habitat, mainly bushes and grass.

Grassland, land whose predominant vegetation consists of grasses and forage plants; excellent for cultivation. Savanna, or tropical grassland found in Africa and South America, has coarse grasses, occasional clumps of trees, and some shrubs; prairie has tall, deep-rooted grasses and is found in Middle and North America, Argentina, the Ukraine, South Africa, and Australia; steppes have short grasses and are found mainly in Central Asia.

Grave Creek Mound *See:* Mound Builders.

Graves, Morris Cole (1910-), U.S. painter. His interest in Eastern art and Native American mythology is seen in his delicate images of blind birds, pine trees, and waves.

Graves, Robert Ranke (1895-1985), English poet and novelist, best known for his novels set in imperial Rome: *I, Claudius* and *Claudius the God* (both, 1934). *Good-bye to All That* (1929) described his experiences in World War I, and *The Long Week-End*, the interwar period.

Graves' disease, a thyroid disorder with an excessive secretion of thyroid hormone (hyperthyroidism), usually accompanied by diffuse primary overgrowth of the entire thyroid gland (goiter), protrusion of the eyeballs with eyelid retraction (exophthalmos). The patient experiences fibrillation (rapid, irregular contractions of the heart muscle) and sometimes palpitations or rapid heartbeat (tachycardia). Due to a reduced functioning of the eye muscles, double or blurred vision sometimes occurs. Other symptoms of an overactive thyroid gland are nervousness, hyperexcitability, 'hot flushes', loss of libido and weight loss despite having a good appetite. Graves' disease occurs four times as often in women as in men. Treatment entails administration of drugs that slow down the overactive thyroid and iodine, if necessary, in combination with surgical removal of all or part of the thyroid gland.

Gravitation, one of the fundamental forces of nature, the force of attraction existing between all matter. It is much weaker than nuclear or electromagnetic forces and plays no part in the internal structure of matter. It plays a vital role in the behavior of the universe: The gravitational attraction of the sun keeps the planets in their orbits, and gravitation holds the matter in a star together.

Gravity, Center of, in physics, point within an object where gravitational forces appear to act, and where the mass can be considered concentrated. This point is the same as the object's center of mass. The movement of an object is determined by where force is exerted in relation to the center of gravity.
See also: Physics.

Gray, Thomas (1716-1771), English poet. His 'Elegy Written in a Country Churchyard' (1751) is one of the most popular English poems; among his other main works are the odes 'The Progress of Poesy' and 'The Bard' (both 1757).

Gray fox *See:* Fox.

Grayling, freshwater game fish (genus Thymallus) whose flesh is regarded as a delicacy. It is related to the trout but has a smaller mouth and a larger dorsal fin. The largest grayling weigh about 4 lb (2 kg). Graylings are found in only a few parts of the northern United States, but are abundant in the colder waters of Canada and northern Eurasia.

Robert Graves (1895-1985).

Graz (pop. 238,000), second largest city in Austria, capital of the province of Styria, located on the Mur River. The city was founded around the 12th century. Local industry produces iron and steel products, leather, paper, and textiles. Graz has a 15th-century cathedral, the Johanneum museum, and the Schlossberg castle.
See also: Austria.

Graziano, Rocky (1922-1990), American boxer. Graziano was born in a New York slum as Thomas Rocco Barbella, but renamed himself after his sister's boyfriend, to make a clean break with his past (minor offences, reformatory school). In 1946 he challenged the middleweight world champion Tony Zale and lost, but won the world title the following year. In 1948, he again lost the title to Tony Zale. His background and the toughness of these three fights made him incredibly popular. In 1956 Paul Newman played the leading role in *Somebody up There Likes Me*, a film about Graziano's life.

Greasewood, any of various spiny shrubs of the alkaline soils of southwestern deserts and semideserts, especially *Sarcobatus vermiculatus*. One shrub, *Larrea divaricata*, is also known as the creosote bush for the tarry odor of its leaves.

Great Barrier Reef, series of massive coral reefs off the northeast coast of Australia, extending for about 1,250 mi (2,000 km). The reef, which is the world's largest coral formation, can be safely crossed only at certain passages, the chief of which is Rains Inlet.

Great Basin, desert region in the western region of the United States between the Wasatch and Sierra Nevada mountains, in Nevada, Utah, and parts of adjacent states. A subdivision of the Basin and Range physiographic province, the Great Basin of Nevada contains Death Valley, Reno, Las Vegas, and Salt Lake City. Mineral mining and agriculture are the main industries.

Great Bear Lake, largest lake in Canada and fourth largest in North America. It has an area of 12,275 sq mi (31,792 sq km) and an elevation of 390 ft (119 m) above sea level. Its deepest point is 1,350 ft (411 m). It is located about 250 mi (402 km) east of the Rocky Mountains, and lies partly within the Arctic Circle. Pitchblende ore, which contains radium and uranium, is mined on the southeast shore of the lake.

Great Britain *See:* United Kingdom.

Great-circle route, route on the earth's surface based on the *great circle*, any circle that divides a sphere into equal halves. The great-circle route is always the shortest route between 2 points. It appears on a *gnomonic projection* map as a straight line; on flat maps it often appears as a longer curve. By the 1800s ship navigators set their compasses to follow lines called *rhumb* lines, which join selected points along the great-circle route. Airplanes follow the great-circle route by using a method called *inertial guidance*.

Great Dane, large, strong dog developed in Germany in the 1500s and originally used as a boarhound and a guard dog. It weighs from 120 to 175 lb (54 to 79 kg) and is from 30 to 34 in (76 to 86 cm) high at the shoulder. Great Danes have short, thick coats that may be tan, brown with black stripes, black, or blue to white with black patches.

Great Depression, period of world economic depression during the 1930s that was immediately precipitated by the disastrous stockmarket collapse on Wall Street on Black Friday, Oct. 29, 1929. This heralded a period of high unemployment, failing businesses and banks, and falling agricultural prices. Millions of workers were unemployed during the period. There were many causes of the depression: Easy credit had led to widespread stock speculation; the world had not completely recovered from World War I; U.S. economic policies under President Herbert Hoover had created domestic overproduction and less foreign trade. Full recovery of the economy occurred only with the beginnings of defense spending immediately prior to World War II. *See also:* United States of America.

Great Divide, or Continental Divide, mountain points in North America that separate the waters ultimately flowing into the Atlantic Ocean from those flowing ultimately into the Pacific. In the United States and Canada, the Great Divide runs through the Rocky Mountains.

Great Lakes, chain of 5 large freshwater lakes in North America, forming the largest lake group in the world and covering an area of 95,170 sq mi (246,490 sq km). From east to west the lakes are Ontario, Erie, Huron, Michigan, and Superior. They are connected by several channels. Once important for fur trade, the lake system is used for the transportation of iron ore, steel, petroleum, coal, grain, and heavy manufactured goods. Import Great Lakes cities include Milwaukee, Chicago, Detroit, Cleveland, Buffalo, and Toronto. In recent years, the lakes, particularly Lake Erie, have suffered from serious pollution.

Great Lakes-Saint Lawrence Seaway *See:* Saint Lawrence Seaway and Great Lakes Waterway.

Great laurel *See:* Rhododendron.

Great Leap Forward, plan for concentrated economic growth in China from 1958 to 1960. Inspired by Mao Zedong (1893-1976), the Great Leap Forward was a program devised by the Communist Party in an attempt to mobilize the population to eliminate China's economic backwardness. Industry and agriculture were reorganized into peoples' communes, centers for dwelling and producing that would also provide the ideological schooling of the masses. The experiment failed due to a combination of natural disaster (floods) and bad management. The industrial and agricultural productivity decreased, the Soviet Union recalled its advisers and broke contracts with China. The campaign was brought to a close in 1961. *See also:* Mao Zedong.

Great Plains, large plateau in the western region of central North America, extending for over 1,500 mi (2,400 km) from the Saskatchewan River in northwest Canada to the Rio Grande in Mexico and the Gulf coastal plain in the southern part of the United States. The plateau slopes gently downward from the Rockies in the west, extending about 400 mi (640 km) east. The natural vegetation is buffalo grass, and the area generally has hot summers and cold winters with an average annual rainfall of 20 in (50 cm). The plains are the 'granary of the world' owing to their vast wheat production; livestock is also important.

Great Purge *See:* Union of Soviet Socialist Republics.

Great Pyrenees, breed of sheepdog originating in the Pyrenees Mountains. The dog, 27 to 32 in (69 to 81 cm) in height and weighing 90 to 125 lb (41 to 57 kg), is strong and muscular with a bearlike head. Its thick coat is white, sometimes with tan or gray markings. Obedient, hardworking, and easily trained, the Great Pyrenees is used as a guard dog, guide dog, and rescuer of avalanche victims.

Great Rift Valley, large geological depression extending more than 3,000 mi (4,800 km) from southeast Africa to northern Syria. In Africa its west course is partly occupied by lakes Malawi (Nyassa), Tanganyika, Kivu, Edward, and Albert; its east course by Lake Turkana.

Great Salt Lake, shallow saline inland sea in the northwestern region of Utah, about 5 mi (8 km) northwest of Salt Lake City. Its size and depth vary yearly, but on average the lake is 72 mi (116 km) long and 30 mi (48 km) across at its widest point, with a maximum depth of 270 ft (82 m). It is the largest brine lake in North America. Industrial plants along the shore extract some 300,000 tons of salt from the lake every year, and plans are under way for tapping other mineral resources.

Great Salt Lake Desert, part of a flat low area in northwest Utah, about 140 mi (225 km) by 80 mi (130 km), bordering Great Salt Lake to the northeast. The explorer John Frémont discovered it in 1845. The Bonneville Salt Flats occupy its west central area, and are famous for auto speed testing.

Great Schism, 2 divisions in the Christian Church. The first was the breach between the Eastern and Western churches. Longstanding divergences in tradition, combined with political and theological disputes, came to a head in 1054 when Pope Leo IX sent legates to refuse the title of Ecumenical Patriarch to the patriarch of Constantinople and to demand acceptance of the *filioque* ('and from the Son') clause in the Nicene Creed. The patriarch refused and rejected the claim of papal supremacy. Reciprocal excommunications and anathemas followed. Later councils were unsuccessful in healing the breach. The second Great Schism was the division within the Roman Catholic Church (1378-1417) when there were 2 or 3 rival popes and antipopes, each with his nationalistic following. The Council of Constance ended the schism by electing Martin V sole pope.

Great Slave Lake, located in Canada's Northwest Territories, 250 mi (400 km) east of the Rocky Mountains. Fed mainly by the Slave River and marking the beginning of the Mackenzie River, the lake is one of America's largest and the deepest in North America-2,015 ft (615 m). It covers an area of 10,980 sq mi (28,438 sq km). The name was derived form the tribe called the Slave, who originally inhabited the area. Small settlements around the lake are supported by fishing, lumbering, and the mining and smelting of lead, zinc, and gold ores.

Great Society *See:* Johnson, Lyndon Baines.

Great Victoria Desert, large area of shifting sand dunes in southwestern Australia, south of Gibson Desert and north of the Nullarbor Plain. The desert, 250,000 sq mi (647,000 sq km) in area, was named by explorer Ernest Giles in 1875. An aboriginal reserve occupies much of the desert's eastern end. The area is tracked for the recovery of missiles from the weapons-testing range at Womera.

Great Wall of China, world's longest wall fortification, in northern China. It extends over 1,500 mi (2,400 km), roughly following

The 1,522 mi (2,450 km) long Chinese wall, the longest structure in the world, part of which dates from the Ch'in period (221-206 B.C.). This defensive construction, once intended as a means of guarding the northern border of the empire, was completed by a number of subsequent emperors.

G

the southern border of the Mongolian plain. Construction was begun in the Ch'in dynasty (third century B.C.) to defend China against invasion from the north and mostly completed during the Ming dynasty (1368-1644). Its average height is 25 ft (7.6 m); it is wide enough (about 12 ft/3.6 m) for people on horseback to ride along it.
See also: China.

Grebe, group of highly specialized aquatic birds of the family Podicipedidae, of which 6 species are found in North America. They are diving birds of lakes or coastal waters. The feet are not webbed but 'lobed' with flaps along the toes. Many of the grebes are brightly colored and bear tufts or crests. Courtship displays are often complex and spectacular. All grebes eat quantities of their own feathers, which collect around fishbones in the gut, allowing these indigestible remains to be formed into a pellet and evacuated.

For most of the year, great crested grebes are found on reed-fringed lakes and ponds throughout the Eastern hemisphere. In spring they pair up, perform elaborate courtship displays, raise their young and remain in family units until autumn. Each pair usually has one brood of three to four chicks. Nests are constructed in early April. By the end of the month, each nest has three or four eggs. Both male and female great crested grebes (*Podiceps cristatus*) carry the chicks on their backs for protection.

Greco, El (Domenikos Theotokopoulos; 1541-1614), Greek-born Spanish painter. First in Venice, where he was influenced by Tintoretto, and later in Toledo, Spain, he developed his distinctive style of painting characterized by dramatically elongated figures and contrasting colors. Among his most famous works are *The Burial of the Count of Orgaz* (1586), *The Portrait of Cardinal Niño de Guevara* (1600), and *View of Toledo* (1608).

Greco, José (1918-), world renowned dancer. In 1942, he joined with the dancer Argentinita to form a nightclub act. In 1949, Greco created his own company.

Greece

Capital:	Athens
Area:	50,949 sq mi
	(131,957 sq km)
Population:	10,645,000
Language:	(New) Greek
Government:	Republic
Independent:	1830
Head of gov.:	Prime minister
Per capita:	US$ 17,900
Monetary unit:	1 Drachma = 100 lepta

Greece, independent country in southeast Europe, occupying the southern part of the Balkan peninsula and many surrounding islands in the Ionian, Mediterranean, and Aegean seas. Greece is bordered by Albania, Macedonia and Bulgaria on the north, by Turkey and the Aegean Sea on the east, by the Ionian Sea on the west, and by the Mediterranean Sea on the south.
Land and climate. Almost 20% of its land area is accounted for by its islands, of which the largest is Crete. More than 160 other islands are inhabited, including Corfu, Lesbos, Milos, Rhodes, and Samos. The mainland is mountainous. The climate of Greece is typically Mediterranean along the

Boeotia is a province (nomos) in central Greece. It borders on Attica to the southeast, on the Gulf of Corinth to the south, on the province of Phocis to the west, on the province of Phtiotis to the north, and on the Gulf of Euboea to the east. It consists of two wide fertile plains, divided by a low mountain range on which Thebes is located. Boeotia is mainly agricultural, but tourism is gaining in importance. Levádhia is the administrative center of the province.

coasts, which have hot, dry summers and mild winters. Most rain falls in the winter months and is concentrated along the western shores.
Economy. The leading farm products are fruits and vegetables, wheat, cotton, tobacco, wine, and olive oil. Both sheep and goats are raised in large numbers. Recently, industry has outdistanced agriculture as the major source of income. Products include textiles, chemicals, and ships, with most manufacturing in or near Athens. Greece has traditionally had a prosperous shipping industry; in 1983 its merchant fleet ranked third in the world. In the past several decades tourism has become increasingly important to Greece's economy. In 1981 the country joined the European Economic Community.
History. In the 15th century, with the fall of the Byzantine Empire, Greece was conquered by Turkey and was part of the Ottoman Empire until the successful War of Independence (1821-1829). A constitutional monarchy was then established, but the country was marked by continual political instability and conflict between monarchists and republicans. During World War II Greece was occupied by German forces (1941-1944). A major civil war between 1944 and 1949 between monarchists and a left-wing coalition led by communists left nearly a million dead. U.S. intervention was a major factor in ensuring the victory of the monarchists. Continuing political instability during the 1950s and 1960s led to a military coup and the establishment of a dictatorship in Apr. 1967. The monarchy was abolished in July 1973, and a revolt Nov. of that year overthrew the dictatorship. In 1974 the Greek people voted for a constitutional republic rather than a restoration of the monarchy, and a new constitution was adopted in June 1975. Since then Greece has lived under democratic rule. In 1981 Greece joined the European Union. In the 1990s, relations with Turkey were tensed over some small islands in the Aegean Sea and over Cyprus. Discord also arose between Greece and the Republic of Macedonia concerning the republic's name. Greece asserted that use of the name Macedonia implied territorial claims on the region in Greece known by the same name. Greece refused to recognize the republic and imposed a trade embargo on that country. Agreements in 1995 led to Greek recognition of the republic and to the lifting of the embargo.
In 2004 the Olympic Games will be held in Athens.

Greece, Ancient, independent cities and states of classical times occupying the Balkan peninsula and the surrounding islands. The earliest major civilization in this area was the Minoan culture centered on the island of Crete (c.2200-1500 B.C.). In the next few centuries the Mycenaean civilization (named after the city of Mycenae on the mainland) flourished (1600-1200 B.C.). The period between 1200 and 750 B.C. is known as the Dark Ages of Greek history. Dorian invaders overwhelmed the culture of Mycenae, but the Greek iron age was introduced. In the 8th and 7th centuries B.C. the first Greek city-states emerged, along with a culture based on the Greek language.

Homer's epics date from this time. Trade with Egypt, Syria, and Phoenicia grew, and the city-states formed colonies throughout the Mediterranean area. From the 6th century, Athens and Sparta became the most powerful city-states. The 5th century B.C. began with a thwarted Persian invasion. The Persians were defeated on land at the Battles of Marathon (490 B.C.) and Plataea (479 B.C.) and at sea near Salamis. Athens emerged as the undisputed leader of Greece and led a number of Ionian cities in the formation of the Delian League, whose purpose was to protect commerce and resist further Persian invasions.

The latter half of the 5th century B.C., especially the reign of Pericles, was the Golden Age of Athens, a period of unparalleled cultural activity ranging from the building of the Parthenon to the ideas of Socrates. But resentment against Athenian power led eventually to Athens' defeat by Sparta in the Peloponnesian War (431-404 B.C.).

In the 4th century B.C. Athens' artistic and intellectual achievements continued to flourish. This was the century of Plato, Aristotle, the sculptor Praxiteles, and many others. In 338 B.C. Philip of Macedon became the ruler of Greece. Philip's son, Alexander the Great (356-323 B.C.), expanded Greek power into an empire that extended eastward to the Iudus River, and south to Egypt. In the period that followed his death, called the Hellenistic Age, Greek culture and civilization spread throughout the western world. Rome first became involved in Greek affairs in 220 B.C. and in 197 B.C. Greek opponents of Macedonia helped the Romans defeat the Hellenistic rulers. From 146 B.C., Greece fell under Roman domination and in 27 B.C. it became the Roman province of Achaea. From A.D. 395, when the Roman Empire was divided into a Western and an Eastern Empire, Greece was incorporated into the Byzantine Empire, which lasted until 1453. After the fall of Constantinople (1453), it became part of the Ottoman Empire.

The agora, the ancient marketplace in   Athens.

Greek, language of ancient and modern Greece, one of the oldest Indo-European languages. The ancient and modern tongues use the same alphabet (which the Greeks adopted from the Phoenicians in the 8th century B.C.), but differ greatly in grammar, vo-

A gold mask from Mycenae.

cabulary, and pronunciation. The earliest known records of ancient Greek date from around 1400 B.C. and use a form of writing known as Minoan linear script. Classical Greek is based on Athenian dialects spoken from the 6th to the 4th centuries B.C. During Hellenistic times a simplified Greek known as Koine became the common language of the civilized world. There are 2 forms of modern Greek: Koine for everyday use and an official state language that incorporates classical forms and words.

Greek Church *See:* Eastern Orthodox Church; Greece.

Greek fire, liquid mixture of unknown composition that took fire when wet, invented by a Syrian refugee in Constantinople in the 7th century A.D. and used by the Byzantine Empire and others for the next 800 years. Thrown in grenades or discharged from syringes, it wrought havoc in naval warfare until superseded by gunpowder. It appears to have been a petroleum-based mixture.

Greek games *See:* Olympic Games.

Greek gods *See:* Mythology.

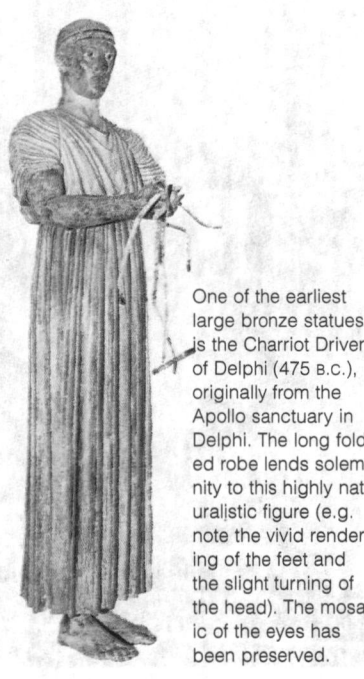

One of the earliest large bronze statues, is the Charriot Driver of Delphi (475 B.C.), originally from the Apollo sanctuary in Delphi. The long folded robe lends solemnity to this highly naturalistic figure (e.g. note the vivid rendering of the feet and the slight turning of the head). The mosaic of the eyes has been preserved.

Greek literature, earliest and most important literature known to the Western world. It is completely original and natural in that there were no earlier literary models that the Greeks could look to for guidance. The distinguishing characteristic of classical Greek literature is that it was oral, meant to be delivered by mouth and heard by the ears.

Early literature. Epic poetry, long narratives depicting heroic deeds of both gods and mortals, was the first important form of Greek literature. Homer, the greatest Greek poet, composed 2 epics, the *Iliad* and the *Odyssey*, in the 8th century B.C. The *Iliad* tells the story of the Trojan War. The *Odyssey* records the adventures of the Greek hero, Odysseus, upon his return home after the fall of Troy. Both emphasize the importance of honor and bravery. Hesiod, the first major poet to follow Homer, flourished during the 7th century B.C. Hesiod founded the didactic epic, which celebrated the hard work, thrift, and good judgment of the Greek peasant.

Lyric poetry, sung to the music of the lyre, evolved about 650 B.C. and dealt with human emotions. Sappho, a poet of the 6th century B.C., composed a special type of lyric poem called the melic poem, which was sung, not recited. The melic poems are characterized by highly emotional, non-didactic text. Sappho's love poetry is without parallel in Greek literature and is noted for its expression of passion and tragedy. Choral lyrics, sung by groups accompanied by music and dancing, were another form of lyric poetry. The victory odes of Pindar are choral masterpieces.

Elegiac poetry, which is related to lyric poetry, consisted of couplets that alternated a line of hexameter (6 feet) with a line of pentameter (5 feet).

The Golden Age. For a period of about 200 years, beginning in the late 500s B.C., Athens was the center of Greek culture. The height of this period, from 461 B.C. to 431 B.C., is often called the Golden Age. During this period, largely as a result of the emergence of democracy, literature flourished.

Drama in the form of tragedy became the most important literary form. Aeschylus, Sophocles, and Euripides are the 3 greatest tragic playwrights. Aeschylus's plays are noted for seriousness, majestic language, and complexity of thought. Those of Sophocles are noted for characterization, graceful language, and sense of proportion. Euripides, the 'philosopher of the stage,' explored human emotions and passions.

Comedy was also prominent in the 400s B.C. The plays of Aristophanes, a writer of bawdy and satiric comedy, reflected the sense of freedom, vitality, and spirit that pervaded Athens at the time.

Herodotus, called the 'father of history,' traveled throughout the civilized world in the mid-400s B.C., recording the manners and customs of nations and peoples. He and the other historians wrote in prose. Thucydides, in his account of the Peloponnesian War, attempted to explain the effects of politics on history.

Philosophical literature evolved about 450 B.C. with a group of philosophers called sophists. Scholars and teachers of theories of knowledge, they invented rhetoric, the art of

G

G

Doric temple for Pallas Athene, Greek Goddess of Wisdom, on the Acropolis in Athens. Built during the 5th century B.C.

Athena Pronaia, de Marmaria's shrine in Delphi. Part of a large religious center in honor of Apollo, which flourished in the period 590-450 B.C.

Roman copy of an Apollo statue by Praxiteles (middle of 4th century B.C.), one of the greatest artists from ancient times.

Mosaic floor decorated with images of stage masks. The Western stage as we know it developed during Ancient Grecian times.

G

The Gods of Greek mythology were ruthless in their punishments. Left on this bowl is Sisyphus, who had to carry a heavy rock up a hill. Every time he almost reached the top, the rock rolled back down. On the right Prometheus, who was chained to a rock in the Caucasus by Zeus, where an eagle gouged out his constantly re-growing liver every day.

Detail from the frieze of the Parthenon in Athens, 438-432 B.C.

The goddess Athene was born from the head of Zeus wearing full armor. The Greeks decided to honor her as the Goddess of Science and Art, and, in times of war, as the Goddess of Intelligence combined with Bravery. Detail of an Attic bowl (around 550 B.C.).

G

persuasive speaking. Literature was essentially oral and spoken in prose. The ideas of Socrates are preserved in the writing of his student, Plato.

The Hellenistic Age. During the reign of Alexander the Great in the 300s B.C., Greek ideas and culture spread throughout the civilized world to the East. The period following his death in 323 B.C. is called the Hellenistic Age. During this time, Athens gave way to Alexandria, Egypt, as the center of Greek civilization. Theocritus, an important poet of this period, introduced pastoral poetry, which expressed an appreciation for nature. Callimachus and others produced short, witty poems called epigrams. Apollonius of Rhodes continued to write the traditional long epic poetry.

The Greco-Roman Age. The period of the Roman conquest of Greece in 146 B.C. saw prose as the prominent literary form. Plutarch wrote biographies contrasting Greek and Roman leaders. Lucian of Samosata satirized the philosophers of his day. Epictetus founded the stoic school of philosophy, which stressed acceptance and endurance. Pausanias wrote an important history of ancient Greece in the A.D. 100s. Galen's medical writings appeared in this period. Ptolemy, an astronomer, mathematician, and geographer, produced scientific writings. Longus wrote *Daphnis and Chloë,* the forerunner of the novel, in this period. Plotinus founded the Neoplatonic school, the last great creation of ancient philosophy.

Medieval literature. From 395 until 1453 Greece was a part of the Byzantine Empire. Constantinople (Istanbul) was the center of Greek culture and literature. Christian religious poetry became the dominant form. Romanos the Melode, who composed long metrical hymns called *kontakia,* was the greatest Greek poet of the medieval period.

Modern Greek literature. In the 1800s Dionysios Solomos wrote his poems in demotic Greek, the language of the common people. Prior to World War I Greek prose was limited to short stories depicting provincial life. The period after the war saw the rise of the psychological and sociological novel. Greek poets achieved renown in this period. In 1963 George Seferis, a lyric poet, became the first Greek to win the Nobel Prize for literature. Odysseus Elytis, also a poet, was awarded the Nobel Prize for literature in 1979.

Greek mythology *See:* Mythology.

Greek Orthodox Church *See:* Eastern Orthodox Church.

Green, Julian (also Julien Green; 1900-1998), a French author of American parentage. His novels are similar in style to the novels of psychological realism of 19th century France. As in two of his best novels, *Moïra* (1950) and *Each to His Darkness* (1960), Green's protagonists usually are torn between sensual and spiritual desires. Green was born to American parents living in Paris and retained his American citizenship. He wrote in French, however, and lived in Paris most of his life. In 1971 he was elected to the French Academy, becoming its first member who was not a French citizen. Other works include *The Closed Garden* (1927), *Midnight* (1936), *The Other One* (1971), and *The Distant Lands* (1991).

Green almond *See:* Pistachio nut.

Greenaway, Kate (1846-1901), English children's book illustrator. She designed Christmas and Valentine's Day cards and drew magazine sketches. Her best-known works are *Under the Window* (1878), *The Language of Flowers* (1884), and *Marigold Garden* (1885).

Greenbrier, horse brier, or catbrier, any of a genus (*Smilax*) of common thorny vines of the lily family. Found primarily in the eastern United States, greenbriers spread rapidly and are considered weeds. They produce yellowish-green flowers and black or red berries.

Greene, Graham (1904-1991), British novelist, best known for *The Ministry of Fear* (1943), *Our Man in Havana* (1958), and the screenplay for *The Third Man* (1950). His more serious work is influenced by Roman Catholicism, expressing the need for faith and the possibility of personal salvation, as in *Brighton Rock* (1938), *The Power and the Glory* (1940), and *The Heart of the Matter* (1948).

Greenhouse, structure, built mainly of glass, for the cultivation and protection of young or delicate plants. It enables plants to be grown where the climate would normally be unsuitable, makes it possible to 'force' plants so they blossom or fruit out of season, and provides suitable conditions for the raising of young plants. Not all greenhouses are heated, but even unheated houses help protect plants from frost. Proper ventilation is vital to prevent the greenhouse from becoming too hot in summer and to reduce the risk of fungus diseases that flourish in such damp atmospheres. Shading may also be necessary to keep the temperature down.

Greenhouse effect, phenomenon whereby the earth's surface becomes hotter. Sunlight radiated at visible and near-ultraviolet wavelengths provides most of the earth's incoming energy. Some of it is absorbed, some reradiated. Although the atmosphere is transparent to incoming solar radiation, reradiated heat from the earth's surface is absorbed by atmospheric water vapor and carbon dioxide and again reradiated toward the surface. Over time, the process causes the surface temperature of the earth to rise. A relatively small increase in the amount of carbon dioxide in the atmosphere might have the effect of causing a long-term warming of the earth that could threaten life.

Greenland (officially Kalâtdlit Nunât), world's largest island that is not considered a continent, located mainly north of the Arctic circle, in the North Atlantic. Greenland is a province of Denmark with its own 16-member legislature.
Land. An ice cap covers four-fifths of the island and reaches a thickness of about 3 mi (4.8 km). Along the coasts mountain peaks penetrate the ice. At the edge of the ice cap

Even at the southernmost tip of Greenland, the mountain valleys are still covered by snow in summer. However, the coastal strip and the fjord water are free of ice, as is the case in the village of Igaliko, near Julianehab. This area has been inhabited since Greenland's earliest times, and the village is famous for its Viking ruins.

wide glaciers sometimes move toward the coast at speeds of up to 20 yd (18 m) per day and have carved deep fjords in the coast. When these glaciers reach the sea, large pieces break off to form icebergs.

The island is about 1,670 mi (2,688 km) long and 800 mi (1,287) across its widest part, but only two narrow coastal strips are habitable. Vegetation along the coasts is sparse and small but highly varied; there are about 400 species of flowering plants and several hundred types of mosses and lichens. Animals include muskoxen, reindeer, arctic hares, lemmings, blue and white arctic foxes, the white arctic wolf (almost extinct), and the polar bear. Birds include geese, gulls, sea eagles, owls, ptarmigan, buntings, and falcons. There are freshwater fish but not reptiles or amphibians.

Economy. Hunting and fishing are the two most important occupations. The world's main deposit of cryolite (used in making aluminum) is at Ivigtut. Iron, graphite, and lead are mined. The Royal Greenland Trading company handles all the island's im-port and export trade, with about 75% of exports going to Denmark. There is almost invariably an annual trade deficit, made up by the Danish government. When Denmark joined the Common Market in 1973, Greenland also became a member, but the island independently withdrew from the organization in 1982.

History. It is uncertain when Eskimo tribes first crossed to Greenland from northern Canada. The Vikings, led by Eric the Red, reached the island in 981. Eric the Red returned in 985 with a fleet of 14 ships to settle the Greenland shores. In about 1000 Lief Ericsson, his son, began to convert the population to Christianity, and Greenland was given its own bishop. The colonies were a republic until 1261, when they placed themselves under Norwegian sovereignty. In 1380 both Greenland and Norway fell under Danish rule. In 1953 Greenland gained control over its local affairs.

Green Mountain State *See:* Vermont.

Greenpeace, international organization of environmental activists, particularly protesting against nuclear and atomic testing and waste. The organization, founded by Canadians in 1969, uses nonviolent means to protest and block activities it considers environmentally harmful. On its way to the French testing grounds in Oceania in 1985, the Greenpeace ship *Rainbow Warrior* was attacked and sunk and one person killed. The French government admitted responsibility.

Green Revolution, recent agricultural trend that has greatly increased crop production in India, Pakistan, and Turkey. Based on new varieties of crops and dependent on pesticides and fertilizers, the Green Revolution's goals of feeding the world's increasing population have been thwarted by high prices and ecological problems.

Greensboro (pop. 184,000), second largest city in North Carolina, seat of Guilford County. It is a major industrial center, an insurance center and trading center for tobacco grown in the surrounding region. Noted for its textile manufacturing, it also has terra-cotta works, machine shops, and cigarette plants. Among its many educational institutions are Greensboro College, the North Carolina Agricultural and Technical College, and the University of North Carolina. Settled in 1749, it was chartered in 1808. The city is named for the Revolutionary War general Nathanael Greene, who commanded one of the last battles of the war, fought in the vicinity.

Greenspan, Alan (1926-), U.S. economist. Greenspan served as chairman of the Council of Economic Advisers from 1974 to 1978, under Presidents Richard Nixon and Gerald Ford. He was appointed chairman of the Board of Governors of the Federal Reserve System (FRS) by President Ronald Reagan in 1987. Greenspan is credited with helping banks remain solvent during the New York Stock Exchange crash on Oct. 19, 1987. Shortly after he took office in 1987, the stock market collapsed, but the effects were limited because Greenspan quickly relaxed monetary policies. In 1995, he was appointed chairman of the Federal Government for a third term. His influence on the American economy, and even, the world economy, is considered to be enormous. He manages to influence the stock market by merely giving a slight clue of a possible change of the rate of interest.

Greenwich Meridian, also called the prime meridian, the longitude line passing through the London country of Greenwich, labelled 0° longitude. Designated by an international conference in 1884 as the prime meridian, all other meridians of longitude are numbered east or west of it. The Greenwich Meridian is also the beginning of the earth's 24 time zones, each of which covers an area of 15° longitude.
See also: Longitude.

Greer, Germaine (1939-), Australian-born feminist author. In *The Female Eunuch* (1970), she charged that society tried to force women into passive, insipid feminine roles that they should reject. Greer received a doctorate from Cambridge University and taught at the University of Warwick (1967-1973). Other works include *Daddy, We Hardly Knew You* (1989), and *The Change: Women, Ageing and the Menopause* (1991).

Gregorian calendar, system of measuring years used by most of the world today. Developed by Pope Gregory XIII in 1582, it replaced the Julian calendar established by Julius Caesar in 46 B.C. The Julian calendar year, which was about 11 minutes longer than the solar year, had become 10 days ahead by A.D. 1580. Gregory dropped 10 days from October 1582 to bring the calendar year into conformity with the solar year. He also established leap year.

Gregory, name of 16 popes. **Saint Gregory I** (540-604), called Gregory the Great, was pope from 590 to 604. His papacy laid the foundation for the political and moral authority of the medieval papacy. He reorganized the vast papal estates scattered all over Italy, providing an economic foundation for the Church's power. In 596 he sent St. Augustine to Britain, beginning its conversion to Christianity. **Saint Gregory II** (669-731), pope from 715 to 731, held office at a time of increasing conflict between Rome and Byzantium, and eventually excommunicated Patriarch Anastasius of Byzantium. **Saint Gregory III** (d. 741), pope from 731 to 741, continued to be involved in conflicts with Byzantium, excommunicating Byzantine Emperor Leo III. **Saint Gregory VII** (Hildebrand; c.1025-1085), was pope from 1073 to 1085. One of the great medieval reform popes, he attacked corruption in the Church, and insisted on the celibacy of the clergy and on the sole right of Church to appoint bishops and abbots. These reforms threatened the power of the German monarchy, leading to disputes and war with Henry IV of Germany. In 1084 Henry seized Rome, forcing Gregory to flee. **Gregory IX** (Ugolino; c.1170-1241) was pope from 1227 to 1241. His papacy was marked by conflict with Holy Roman Emperor Frederick II, leading eventually to war in Italy between imperial and papal factions. **Gregory X** (Tedaldo Visconti; 1210-1276) pope from 1271 to 1276, instituted policies that regulated papal elections and prevented vacancies of long duration. **Gregory XI** (1329-1378) was pope from 1370 to 1378. Elected pope in Avignon, he managed to return the papal court to Rome in 1377. **Gregory XIII** (Ugo Buoncompagni; 1502-1585), pope from 1572 to 1585, promoted the Counter-Reformation through his pledge to execute the decrees of the Council of Trent. A patron of the Jesuits, he is remembered for the calendar reform he sponsored and for his lavish building program, which emptied the papal treasury. He celebrated the massacre of the Huguenots on St. Bartholomew's Day, 1572, with a *Te Deum*. **Gregory XVI** (1765-1846), pope from 1831 to 1846, strengthened the papacy, aligning it with Austria under Metternich, with whose help he suppressed a revolt in the Papal States.

Gregory, Lady (1859-1932), Irish dramatist and director, responsible for the production of Yeats's and Synge's plays at the famous Abbey Theatre in Dublin. Her plays include *Spreading the News* (1904), *The Rising of the Moon* (1907), and *The White Cockade* (1908). She wrote *Our Irish Theatre* (1913), on the Irish renaissance.

Grenada

Capital:	Saint George's
Area:	133 sq mi (345 sq km)
Population:	89,000
Language:	English
Government:	Parliamentary monarchy in the British Commonwealth
Independent:	1974
Head of gov.:	Prime minister
Per capita:	US$ 4,750
Monetary unit:	East Caribbean dollar = 100 cents

Grenada, island country in the West Indies, one of the smallest independent countries in the Western Hemisphere. Its area is 133 sq mi (345 sq km).
Land and climate. The island of Grenada is the southernmost of the Windward Islands, 90 mi (145 km) north of Trinidad. The state consists of the main island, which is mountainous, and the southern group of the Grenadine islands. The climate is semitropical.
People and economy. The population is descended from African slaves and European settlers. Exports include nutmeg, cocoa, mace, sugar, cotton, coconut, lime oil, and bananas. Tourism is becoming an important source of income.
History. Discovered by Christopher Columbus in 1498, Grenada was first colonized by the French but became British in 1762. It achieved internal self-government in 1967 and became fully independent within the British Commonwealth in 1974. After a bloodless coup in 1979 a left-wing government was installed. In the course of an army-supported coup in 1983, prime minister Maurice Bishop and several other leaders were slain. The United States then sent troops, aided by units from other Caribbean nations, to protect about 1,000 U.S. citizens on the island and to restore constitutional government. In 1997, Grenada and Cuba came to an agreement regarding technical

G

G

and economic cooperation. Grenada was blacklisted by the Financial Action Task Force along with other tax havens for not taking enough action against money laundering in 2001. The growth in tourism has generated its own problems, in the form of environmental threats.

Grenade, small explosive device used in warfare. It is activated by pulling a pin and throwing it toward a specific target. When grenades explode, they send deadly metal fragments flying or release lethal gas. Some grenades are used to illuminate darkened areas. Developed in the 1400s, they became standard infantry weapons in the 20th century.

This familiar type of hand grenade has been used by the U.S. Army for 50 years. It closely resembles the British no.36 grenade (`Hills bomb'). The thrower crooks his left forefinger through the ring (1), holding the grenade in his right hand. Pulling the right hand to the right, withdrawing the pin, the thrower then hurls in an over-arm action. The lever (4) will fly off, the sprung striker (3) will detonate the percussion cap (2), and the powder train (5) will fire the detonator (6), after a four-second delay. This will detonate the main charge (7), sending lethal fragments of the cast-iron case (8) into all directions.

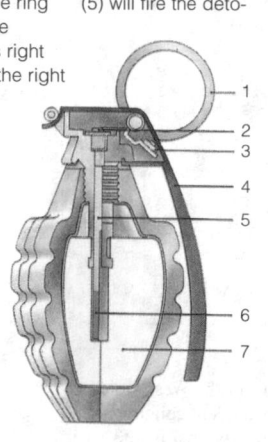

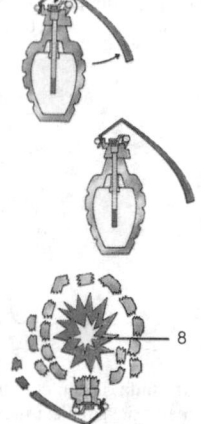

Grenadines, group of about 600 small islands, part of the Windward Islands in the West Indies, between Grenada and St. Vincent. The northern group and the north part of Carriacou (the largest island) belong to St. Vincent. The southern group belongs to Grenada.

Grendel *See:* Beowulf.

Grenoble (pop. 160,000), city in eastern France, located in a valley of the French Alps. A winter sports center, Grenoble hosted the 1968 Winter Olympics. The city is also a center for manufacturing and scientific research and is home to the University of Grenoble, founded in 1339. Grenoble was established by the Gauls c.400 B.C.
See also: France.

Grenville, Sir Richard (1542-1591), English naval hero. He commanded Raleigh's first expedition (1585) to colonize Roanoke Island, N.C. In a British attempt (1591) to intercept Spanish treasure ships off the Azores in his ship, *Revenge*, Grenville held an entire Spanish fleet in combat for 15 hours before he was mortally wounded and captured.

Gresham's Law, economic principle (attributed to Sir Thomas Gresham) that 'bad money drives out good.' This means that when coins of the same face value but of different market value circulate together, the coins of higher market value will disappear from circulation to be hoarded or used as an open-market commodity.

Gretna Green, village in Scotland. Located just across the border from England, for centuries it was a mecca for eloping couples seeking a quick marriage. Couples had only to state their desire to be married before witnesses. With revisions in marriage laws, the Gretna Green ceremonies became illegal in 1939.
See also: Scotland.

Gretzky, Wayne (1961-), Canadian-born National Hockey League (NHL) center. The first professional hockey player to score 2,000 regular season points in a career, he holds or shares nearly 50 records, including most goals (92) in a season (1981). He has led the NHL in scoring 9 times (1980-1987, 1988), won 9 Most Valuable Player awards (1980-1987, 1989), and while playing for the Edmonton Oilers led the team to 4 Stanley Cup championships (1984, 1985, 1987, 1988). In 1988 he was traded to the Los Angeles Kings. In 1999 Gretzky ended his career.

Grey, Charles, 2nd Earl Grey (1764-1835), English prime minister (1830-1834) responsible for the passage of the Reform Bill (1832), which extended the vote to the middle classes. As Whig leader of the House of Commons, he helped abolish the slave trade (1807).
See also: England.

Grey, Lady Jane (1537-1554), queen of England for 9 days in 1553. The Duke of Northumberland, her father-in-law and powerful advisor to the dying Edward VI, persuaded the king to name Jane heir to the throne. She reluctantly accepted the crown, but Mary Tudor, Edward's half sister, had the country's support, and was proclaimed queen by the lord mayor of London. Lady Jane and her husband were beheaded for treason.

Grey, Zane (1875-1939), U.S. author of sagas about the American West. His 54 novels, of which *Riders of the Purple Sage* (1912) is the most popular, have sold over 15 million copies.

Greyhound, breed of dog used widely in racing. First raised in Egypt 5,000 years ago, greyhounds were used for hunting in England and North America before being adapted for racing. Greyhounds weigh 60-70 lb (27-30 kg) and have long, slender bodies, powerful legs, and short coats.

Grieg, Edvard Hagerup (1843-1907), Norwegian composer who based much of his work on traditional national folk music. He wrote many songs and piano pieces. His best-known orchestral works are the *Piano Concerto* (1869), the *Peer Gynt* suites (1876), and the *Holberg Suite* (1885).

Griffin, mythological animal having the head and wings of an eagle and the body and hindquarters of a lion. The legend of the griffin probably originated with the ancient Hittites and was a popular subject for Assyrian and ancient Greek sculpture. In heraldry the griffin appears as a symbol of vigilance.

Griffith, Arthur (1872-1922), Irish nationalist who founded Sinn Féin, a major force in Ireland's struggle for independence from England. He led the Irish delegation in negotiating the treaty (1921) that established the Irish Free State. He was the first vice president of the Dáil Eireann, an assembly that declared Irish independence, and briefly succeeded de Valera as its president (1922).
See also: Sinn Féin.

David Griffith (1875-1948, left) owes much of his development as a filmmaker to his cameraman G.W. 'Billy' Bitzer (1874-1944). This photograph was taken during the shooting of *Birth of a Nation* (1915).

Griffith, D(avid) W(ark) (1875-1948), U.S. silent-film director and producer, often considered the father of modern cinema. His immensely popular *Birth of a Nation* (1915), later much criticized for its racist views, introduced major principles of film technique. Griffith also pioneered the film 'spectacular.' Among his other films are *Intolerance* (1916), *Way Down East* (1920), and *Orphans of the Storm* (1922).

Grillparzer, Franz (1791-1872), most important Austrian playwright, who was influenced by Calderón and Shakespeare and attempted to bridge baroque drama and German classicism. His later work excels due to his deep psychological insight. Examples of his work are: *Die Ahnfrau* (1817), *Melusina* (1833), *Der Traum ein Leben* (1840), *Libussa* (1872), and *Die Jüdin von Toledo* (1873).

Grimm brothers, **Jakob Ludwig** (1785-1863) and **Wilhelm Karl** (1786-1859), German folklorists and philologists who compiled a collection of popular fairy tales. They began the project in 1812 and wrote the final volume of 210 stories in 1857. Some of the best-known tales are 'Hansel and Gretel,' 'Snow White,' 'Sleeping Beauty,' 'Cinderella,' and 'Little Red Riding Hood.' Jakob also wrote *German Grammar*

(1819-1837), and the brothers collaborated on the *German Dictionary* which began in 1854 and was completed by others in 1960. *See also:* Grimm's fairy tales.

Grimmelshausen, Hans Jakob Christoffel von (1625?-1676), German novelist. His picaresque romance *Simplicissimus* (1669),set during the Thirty Years' War, ranks as the most important 17th-century German novel.

Grimm's fairy tales, stories by two brothers, Jakob (1785-1863) and Wilhelm (1786-1859) Grimm, who collected folk tales from friends and acquaintances in and around Kassel, 1807-1814. They saw the tales as an expression of the romantic spirit of the German people. They include 'Hansel and Gretel,' 'Little Red Riding Hood,' 'Snow White,' 'Rumpelstiltskin,' 'Sleeping Beauty,' 'Cinderella,' and 'Rapunzel.'
See also: Grimm brothers; Fairy tale.

Grinding and polishing, finishing of metal and other surfaces by the use of abrasive materials. In grinding, hard abrasives are used to wear down the metal surface appreciably. In polishing, much softer abrasives are used to smooth the surface, removing a negligible amount of metal.

Gris, Juan (José Victoriano González; 1887-1927), Spanish cubist painter. A follower of Picasso, he developed the style known as synthetic cubism, which he applied to still lifes in increasingly free compositions.

Grison, weasel-like animal (genus *Galictis*), also known as huron. There are 2 types of grisons-the greater grison, which has gray/brown fur and may reach a length of 27.5 in (70 cm), and the little grison, which has yellow/brown fur and is considerably smaller. All grisons have a white strip of fur across their forehead and down the sides of their neck and their diet includes snakes, mice, birds, and insects. Found in Central and South America, grisons are diurnal creatures who live in both forests and open country and make their dens under tree roots, rocks, or logs.

Grizzly bear (*Ursus arctos horribilis*), one of the largest of the North American brown bears. The name refers to the grizzled coat rather than to the beast's temper, but despite this the grizzly population has been killed off and the species is considered threatened in the United States. Though classed with the carnivore, the grizzly is largely vegetarian and rarely eats fish. An imposing, even terrifying animal, the grizzly plays a major role in the legends of the North American pioneers.

Grofé, Ferde (1892-1972), U.S. composer and pianist. His best-known works are the *Mississippi Suite* (1924), the *Grand Canyon Suite* (1931), and the orchestration of George Gershwin's *Rhapsody in Blue* (1924).

Gromyko, Andrei Andreyevich (1909-1989), Soviet politician and diplomat. In a

In 1852, the Grimm brothers, Jacob (1785-1863) and Wilhelm (1786-1859), cooperated at the start of the great *Deutsches Wörterbuch*. This dictionary was completed by others after the Grimm's deaths. The Grimm brothers became famous not only as linguists, but also for their large collection of folk tales. Portrait by Elisabeth Jerichau.

rapid rise after Stalin's purges, he became ambassador to the United States in World War II and UN representative of the USSR after the war. Named foreign minister in 1957, he held that post until 1985, during periods of cold war, disarmament talks, détente, and incidents of Soviet military interventions in several countries. He was a member of the Politburo, the governing body of the Communist party. He became president of the USSR in 1985.
See also: Union of Soviet Socialist Republics.

Gropius, Walter (1883-1969), German architect and teacher. He was founder of the Bauhaus school and originated the profoundly influential style, characterized by a marriage of form and function and the use of modern materials (especially glass). He fled Germany when the Nazis came to power, settling in the United States in 1937. His designs include the Bauhaus in Dessau (1926) and (in collaboration) the Pan Am Building in New York (1958).
See also: Bauhaus.

Grosbeak, name of various finches having a strong conical bill for cracking seeds. The male of the blue grosbeak of the southern United States (*Guiraca caerulea*) is dark blue all over and can be mistaken for the indigo bunting. The pine grosbeak (*Pinicola enucleator*), native to Canada, is mainly pink. The females are drab.

Gross Domestic Product, the gross domestic product (GDP) consists of the sum of the added value of the final goods and services produced by a nation's economy during a specific period of time (usually a year). At market prices the GDP consists of: the net domestic product against factor costs (wages and profits, leases, etc.); taxes that increase the cost price minus subsidies; and write-offs. The GDP is the international standard for a nation's productive power. The actual prosperity can differ due to revenues from

abroad or because the country is more involved in exporting than in importing goods. This usually goes hand in hand with net capital outflow or repatriation of profits. The GDP growth is usually related to the real GDP, i.e. at steady prices (or rather, corrected before inflation).

Gross national product (GNP), total value of goods and services produced by a national economy before any deduction has been made for depreciation (net national product). The annual growth of the GNP is often taken as an indicator of the state of a country's economy. *Real GNP*, which is adjusted for inflation, is of greatest significance.

Gros Ventre (French: 'big belly'), 2 Native American tribes, the Atsina and the Hidatsa, of the northern Great Plains. The Gros Ventre were named for their sign language, which consisted of hand signals in front of their stomachs. The Atsina, a branch of the Arapaho, live on Montana's Fort Belknap Reservation; the Hidatsa, relatives of the Crow, live on Fort Berthold Reservation in North Dakota.

Grosz, George (1893-1959), German-American satirical artist, a Dadaist. His powerful caricatures, especially those attacking corruption and militarism in post-World War I Germany, include *Fit for Active Service* (1918) and *The Face of the Ruling Class* (1919); *The Stickman* (c.1947) is American influenced.
See also: Dada.

Grotius, Hugo (1583-1645), Dutch jurist, considered the founder of international law. In 1619 he was condemned to life imprisonment for his political activity, but he escaped to Paris. There he wrote *On the Law of War and Peace* (1625), a study of all the laws of humanity with an emphasis on rules of conduct applying to states, nations, and individuals.
See also: International law.

A bust of Hugo Grotius (1583-1645).

Grotowski, Jerzy (1933-1999), Polish theater director and critic, leader of the experimental Laboratorium Theatre in Wrockaw (Breslau). After finishing drama school in Krakow, Grotowski continued his studies in Moscow and China. In 1959, together with a small group of actors, he formed the *Teatr 13 rzedów* (Theater with 13 Rows). In 1965,

G

G

this group, already well known abroad, was merged into the Laboratorium Theatre in Wrockaw. During this time the laboratory theatre's program was formulated by Grotowski in his book *Towards a Poor Theatre* (1968).

The actors' collective at the Laboratorium Theatre leads an austere life similar to that of a sect. The members submit themselves to a strict training program, which develops their physical and vocal acting technique. Grotowski makes use of the biomechanic method developed by the Russian director Vsevolod Mejerhold (1874-1942) for this technique. The actor has astounding control over his body and is completely submerged in his role. In this respect, Grotowski subscribes to the theories of Konstantin Stanislavski (1863-1938), the Russian director who developed this realistic acting style.

Ground effect machine *See:* Air cushion vehicle.

Ground hog *See:* Woodchuck.

Groundnut *See:* Peanut.

Ground pine *See:* Club moss.

Ground sloth (genus *Megatherium*), prehistoric member of the sloth family, about the size of an elephant. They originated in South America and migrated to North America during the Ice Age. Ground sloths were herbivores (plant eaters). They probably used their powerful hind legs and tails to stand and feed on high branches and leaves.

Ground squirrel, any of various small burrowing rodents (genus *Citellus*) of the squirrel family. North American species include the 13-striped ground squirrel, or spermophile, of the prairies, the rock squirrel of canyons and rocky slopes in the West, and the golden-mantled squirrel of woodlands. Chipmunks, prairie dogs, and woodchucks may also be considered ground squirrels.

Ground water, water accumulated beneath the earth's surface in the pores of rocks, spaces, cracks, etc. Most underground water originates as precipitation that sinks into soil and rocks. Permeable, water-bearing rocks are *aquifers*; rocks with pores small enough to inhibit the flow of water through them are *aquicludes*. Buildup of groundwater pressure beneath an aquiclude makes possible construction of an artesian well. The uppermost level of groundwater saturation is the water table.

Group dynamics, in sociology, study of the behavior and interactions of people as members of groups. It includes setting up specially constructed experimental groups, as well as the study of existing groups such as committees and military units. Some of the simpler studies have been carried out to try to determine the chain of command within a group and its influence on the group's performance.

Grouper, sea fish of the sea bass family with large mouth and sharp teeth, mainly of tropical seas. Groupers are as small as 1 in (2.5 cm) long; the Queensland grouper of the Great Barrier Reef grows up to 7 ft (2 m) and can be a danger to skindivers. The Nassau grouper of the coasts of the southeastern states is noted for its ability to change color.

Group therapy *See:* Psychotherapy.

Grouse, family (Tetraonidae) of chicken-like game birds usually brown, gray, or black in plumage, native to cool regions of the Northern Hemisphere. They are ground birds living on open moorland or heath, and are well camouflaged. Three species moult into a white or particolored winter plumage for camouflage in snow. Grouse feed largely on plant material-shoots, buds, and fruits-but will also eat insects. In many species males perform elaborate courtship displays at established display grounds, or 'leks.' Common North American species include the ruffed grouse (*Bonasa umbrellus*) and the spruce grouse (*Dendragapus canadensis*).

Growth, increase in the size of an organism, reflecting an increase in the number of its cells, an increase in its protoplasmic material, or both. Cell number and protoplasmic content do not always increase together. Cell division can occur without any increase in protoplasm, thus giving a larger number of smaller cells. Alternatively, protoplasm can be synthesized with no cell division so that the cells become larger. Any increase in the protoplasm requires the synthesis of cell components (such as nuclei, mitochondria, thousands of enzymes) and cell membrane. These, in turn, require the synthesis of macromolecules such as proteins, nucleic acids, and polysaccharides from amino acids, sugars, and fatty acids. These subunits must be synthesized from still simpler substances.

One of the major differences between plants and animals is that the final shape and size of an animal can be predicted within fine limits, whereas it is much more difficult to say just how tall a plant will be or how many branches it will have. Growth in plants is, however, better understood than animal growth.

Grub, wormlike larva of insects. The body is fat and soft and there are no legs. Since the grub is surrounded by food, in the case of certain flies and beetles, or is fed by adults, as with bees and wasps, there is no necessity for it to be able to move.

Grünewald, Matthias (c.1475-1528), German painter who, with his contemporary Albrecht Dürer, is considered one of the 2 great masters of the German Renaissance. His most characteristic theme is the crucifixion, a subject in which he combined beauty and delicacy of style with a savage and harrowing realism. His masterpiece is the altarpiece of St. Anthony's monastery at Isenheim, with subjects such as the *Resurrection* and the *Temptation of St. Anthony* (1513-1515).
See also: Renaissance.

Grunion (*Leuresthes tenuis*), small fish whose breeding habits have become a tourist attraction in California. For 3 or 4 nights in succession, when the tide is at its highest, the grunions leap from the waves onto the beach in thousands. Each female is accompanied by a male who fertilizes her eggs as she lays them in the sand. After spawning, the fish go back into the water. Two weeks later, when the tides are at their peak again, young grunions pop out of the eggs and are washed back into the sea.

Grunt, colorful marine fish (family Pomadasidae) found in warm waters. The pigfish (*Orthopristis chrysopterus*) is a grunt

In geology, groundwater is water — mainly from rain and melted snow— that has penetrated the earth's surface and completely filled zones of porous rocks and other voids. In certain regions, where beds of dense, nonporous limestone rock near the surface prevent penetration, rainwater may enter the ground along small cracks in the limestone. Chemical action of the water and the carbon dioxide from the air gradually dissolves the limestone, thus enlarging the cracks, to form wide surface grooves, or grikes (1), and large underground caves (2). If the limestone

(3) is lying on impermeable rock (4), the water will eventually emerge as a spring (5). Below the water table (6), or the top of the saturated rock layer (7), the groundwater moves downward under the influence of gravity (light-blue arrows). Additional rainwater (dark-blue arrows) may flow downward along the water table to a lower level and

seep into a perennial stream (8). Other groundwater may enter between two impermeable rock layers (9) in an inclined waterbearing rock zone, or aquifer (10). If an artesian well (11) is drilled into the aquifer at a lower level, the pressure of overlying water will be sufficient to raise some water above ground level (12).

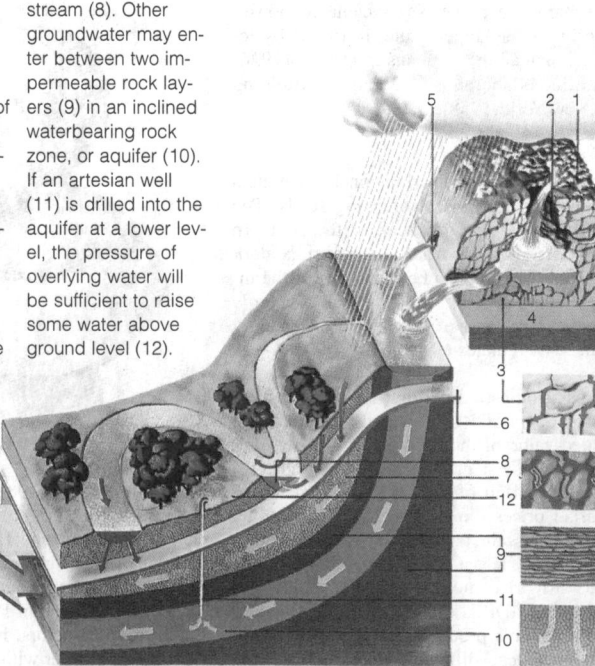

found along the Atlantic and Gulf coasts of the United States. Grunts are named for the sounds they make by grinding their teeth, which are in the throat. Many species are important food fish.

Guacharo *See:* Oilbird.

Guadalajara (pop. 1,650,000), second-largest city in Mexico and capital of the state of Jalisco. Located on a high plain in west-central Mexico, Guadalajara is an important manufacturing center known for glassware and pottery, textiles, soft drinks, beer, bottled water, construction materials, animal feed, and fertilizer.
See also: Mexico.

Guadalcanal, largest of the Solomon Islands, in the South Pacific. Volcanic and mountainous, it supports extensive coconut plantations that are the economic mainstay; copra and timber are the main exports. The island was the scene of a decisive battle of World War II in 1943, when it was recaptured by Allied troops from the Japanese.
See also: Solomon Islands.

Guadeloupe, overseas department of France in the eastern part of the Caribbean Sea, composed of Grande-Terre, Basse-Terre, and some smaller islands, covering a total area of 687 sq mi (1,779 sq km). Discovered by Columbus (1493) and a French settlement since 1635, it was captured by the British in the Seven Years' War and confirmed as French in 1815. The population, of mixed African and European ancestry, speaks a French patois. Bananas, coffee, cacao, and vanilla are produced.

Guam, largest and southernmost of the Mariana Islands, in the Pacific Ocean 6,000 mi (9,656 km) west of San Francisco. A U.S. territory since 1898 and an important U.S. naval and air base, Guam was captured by the Japanese in 1941, and was recaptured by the United States in 1944.
See also: Mariana Islands.

Guan, tropical Central and South American game bird of the family Cracidae, resembling small or medium-sized turkeys. Guans have dark feathers and eat mostly fruit.

Guanaco, wool-bearing member of the camel family, found on the mountains or

The guanaco, *L. guanacoe*, which is the only wild relative of the domestic llama and the alpaca, enjoys loitering in swiftly running streams.

plains of South America. Guanacos have long, thick, reddish brown hair above and white hair below, with a grayish head. They feed on grass and small plants and grow 3 1/2 to 4 ft (107-122 cm) high at the shoulder.

Guangdong (Kuang-tung; pop. 69,610,000), province in South China, bordering on the South China Sea, including the enclaves Macao and Hong Kong: 76,129 sq mi (197,100 sq km). Kuang-Tsu (Canton, pop. 3.6 million) is the capital and most important port. It is a mountainous region, with the exception of the fertile Xijiang delta, where the population is concentrated. Moist and subtropical climate, enabling the production of sugar beet, wheat, tobacco, lychees, bananas, fish, silk, and timber. Industry is concentrated in the main cities. Petroleum, manganese, iron ore, coal, and wolfram are mined here. Hong Kong fell to the British after the Opium War, but was turned over to the Chinese government in 1997.
The province also includes the cities Shenzen, Shantou, and Zhuhai, which were given the status of Special Economic Zone in 1980. This meant that they were free to experiment with different forms of business management and planning. The aim was to attract foreign investors and to increase trade with foreign businesses.

Guangxi Zhuang (Kwangsi-chung; pop. 44,000,000), autonomous region in South China, bordering on Vietnam; 91,155 sq mi (236,000 sq km). Capital city: Nanning. It lies mainly in the basin of Xijiang, lowlands where among other things rice, corn, sugar cane, and sweet potatoes are cultivated. The forestry in the north and fishing in the Bay of Tonkin are also of importance. Manganese and tin mines. In 1957, it became an autonomic region of the Zhuang, a Thai people and the largest ethnic minority in China.

Guangzhou (pop. 3,600,000), called Canton by Westerners, largest city in southern China and one of China's most important ports. Located at the head of the Pearl River, the city is linked to the interior by a network of

railroads, and its economy has been based on trade for centuries. Locally produced products include paper, sewing machines, cement, and textiles. Shipbuilding and sugar refining are other important industries, as are handicrafts. China's largest trade fair is held annually in Guangzhou, which is also known for being the birthplace of the Chinese Nationalist leader Sun Yat-sen and a center of the revolution of 1911.
See also: China.

Guantánamo (pop. 200,000), city in southeast Cuba, about 20 mi (30 km) inland from Guantánamo Bay, the location of a U.S. naval base established in 1903. Since the revolution of 1959, Cuba has refused to cash the $2,000 per year rental check the United States has sent and has pressed for the base's return to Cuba. Guantánamo is a sugar-refining center and also serves as a hub for processing cacao, coffee, and corn.
See also: Cuba.

Guar, tough legume (*Cyamopsis tetragonoloba*) of the pea family, often grown to enrich worn-out soil. The seeds and pods are used as fodder. Guar was brought to the United States from India in the early 1900s.

Guaraní, group of South American tribes, linked by language, who once lived in an area now included in Paraguay, Brazil, and Argentina. Conquered by Spain in the 16th century, their numbers have been reduced by disease. Their language, however, is now the second language of Paraguay.

Guardi, Francesco (1712-1793), an Italian painter considered a forerunner of Impressionism. Initially, he worked with his brother Gianantonio Guardi (1698-1760). When his brother died, Francesco developed into one of the most productive painters of townscapes. His paintings have luminous, cool colors and soft atmospheric effects. *View on the Cannaregio, Venice* and *Santa Maria Della Salute* are typical of his sparkling views of Venice. Guardi, born in Venice, was not highly regarded during his lifetime, and most of his paintings were sold

The landscape of the northern part of the southeastern province of Guangxi is characterized by cone-shaped mountains.

G

G

to tourists as souvenirs. His works won acceptance in the 1900s.

Guarneri, family of violin makers of Cremona, Italy. **Andrea Guarneri** (1626-1698), with Antonio Stradivari, an apprentice of Nicolò Amati, founded the dynasty. His sons **Pietro Giovanni Guarneri** (1655-1720?) and **Giuseppe Guarneri** (1666-1739?), and grandson **Pietro Guarneri** (1695-1762) continued the trade. The most renowned member of the family was the eccentric and experimental **Giuseppe Bartolomeo Guarneri** (1687-1745), known as 'Giuseppe del Jesu,' nephew of Andrea.

Guatemala

Capital:	Guatemala City
Area:	42,042 sq mi (108,889 sq km)
Population:	13,314,000
Language:	Spanish
Government:	Presidential republic
Independent:	1839
Head of gov.:	President
Per capita:	US$ 3,700
Monetary unit:	1 Guatemala quetzal = 100 centavos

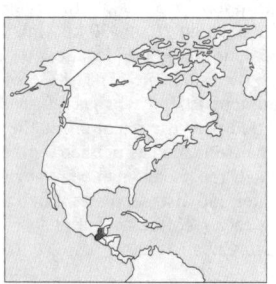

Guatemala (Republic of), northernmost republic of Central America, bordered by Mexico on the north and west, Belize and the Caribbean Sea on the east, Honduras and El Salvador on the southeast, and the Pacific Ocean on the southwest.
Land and climate. Guatemala is a mountainous country composed largely of volcanic highland. The eastern and western highlands are not very fertile. To the north is the Petén, a rain forest plateau with areas of savanna, covering a third of the country. The climate varies from the tropical Petén and coastal areas to the subtropical and temperate highlands.
People. The Native Americans (predominant Mayans) account for more than 60% of the population; most of the rest are a mixture of Spanish and Mayan. The official language is Spanish, but many Native American languages are also spoken. The main religion is Roman Catholicism.
Economy. Coffee accounts for almost half the nation's revenues. Cotton is also an important product, having superseded banana

Lake Atitlán with Toliman volcano. The lake can be found in the southern mountains of Guatemala, at a height of 5,125 ft (1,562 m). The cli- mate, the beautiful surroundings and the presence of Indian settlements, make the lake a powerful tourist attraction.

cultivation since the 1930s. Other exports are tobacco, vegetables, fruit, and beef. Manufacturing industries are mainly devoted to the processing of local produce. Although Guatemala joined the Central American Common Market in 1961, the United States remains its principal trading partner.
History. The Mayas ruled the area from about A.D. 300, but they were unable to offer much resistance to the invading Spaniards in 1524. Guatemala became independent in 1821 and subsequently was a member of the Central American Federation (1824-1839). The post-World War II governments, especially under Jacobo Arbenz Guzmán, had socialist tendencies. After a U.S.-supported military coup in 1954, Guatemala was plagued by political violence and coups. A civil war between the army and the Communist guerrillas began in 1961. In 1985 Marco Vinicio Cerezo Arévalo became the first civilian to be elected president of Guatemala in 15 years. In 1986, a new constitution went into effect. However, government corruption and human rights violations remained problems into the 1990s. In 1994 the government and the guerrillas signed an agreement concerning the strengthening of human rights and in 1996 they signed a peace treaty, which brought an end to the 35-year-old civil war. Economic problems were caused by a lengthy period of dryness and the collapsing coffee prices in 2001. Human rights are still being violated and kidnapping remains a serious problem: among the kidnap victims is the President of the Central Bank, in 2002.

Guatemala City (pop. 1,167,000), capital and largest city of Guatemala, in Central America. The city's population nearly doubled in the 1980s. The hub of the country's social, cultural, and political life, Guatemala City is also the chief manufacturing center, producing textiles, beverages, and processed foods. It was almost completely destroyed by an earthquake in 1917, and another earthquake killed thousands in 1976.
See also: Guatemala.

Guava, small tree (genus *Psidium*, especial-

ly *P. guajava*) with thick leaves and white flowers, cultivated for its red or yellow fruit. Native to Mexico, South America, and the West Indies, and now grown in Florida and California. The fruit, up to 4 in (10 cm) in diameter, is slightly acid and musky. It is used in jellies, pies, and drinks and is eaten raw.

Guayaquil (pop. 1,900,000), Ecuador's largest city, main port, and industrial center, located 40 mi (64 km) from the Pacific Ocean on the Guayas River. Founded by Spaniards in 1535, the city was liberated from Spain in 1821. Guayaquil manufactures textiles and has flour mills, sawmills, breweries, ironworks, and a cement plant. *See also:* Ecuador.

Guayule, desert shrub (*Parthenium argentatum*) of the composite family containing rubber that can be accessed only by crushing the top of the plant. Guayule is native to the Chihuahuan desert of Mexico and southwestern Texas. It grows to about 2 ft (60 cm) and has silver, spear-shaped leaves.

Guelphs and Ghibellines, opposing political and warring factions in 13th to 15th-century Italy. The Guelphs supported the pope, the Ghibellines the Holy Roman emperor. Both originated in 12th-century Germany, in opposition over territories of the Holy Roman Empire.
See also: Holy Roman Empire.

Guenon, any of approximately twenty species of monkeys of the family Cercopithecidae living in Africa south of the Sahara Desert. All have long tails and weigh from 3 to 15 lb (1.4 to 7 km). Almost all guenons live in trees in tropical rain forests, wooded plains, or swamps. Humans, leopards, and eagles are the guenon's chief enemies.

The moustached guenon, *Ceropithecus cephus*, is a tree-dwelling African monkey. Distinctive features include a blue nose, yellow whiskers, and a pale area resembling a moustache on its upper lip.

Guericke, Otto von (1602-1686), a German physicist. He is best known for his invention of the vacuum pump, which he devised about 1650. In 1687, he used the pump in a dramatic demonstration to show the effect of air pressure on a hollow globe containing a vacuum. Guericke fitted together two metal hemispheres to form the globe and evacuat-

G

ed the air from it. To each hemisphere he attached a team of eight horses. The teams were driven in opposite directions but failed to separate the hemispheres, which came apart only when Guericke allowed air to reenter the globe. In addition to the vacuum pump, he is also credited with inventing a device that continuously produced static electricity.

Guericke was born in Magdeburg. (The hemispheres of his demonstration became known as the Magdeburg Hemispheres.) He was elected to the city council in 1627, and from 1646 to 1681 served as one of the city's four burgomasters (mayors).

Guernsey *See:* Cattle.

Guernsey, second-largest of the Channel Islands at the west end of the English Channel, 30 mi (48 km) west of Normandy, France. The triangular-shaped island is approximately 24 sq mi (63 sq km) in area. The Guernsey cattle for which it is famous are found mostly in the south. Greenhouses in the north produce tomatoes, flowers, and grapes. Guernsey was home to French author Victor Hugo from 1855 to 1870; his house is now a museum. St. Peter Port is the capital and main town.

Guerrilla warfare, warfare waged by irregular forces in generally small-scale operations, often in enemy-held territory. The term (Spanish: 'little war') originally applied to the tactics of Spanish-Portuguese irregulars in the Napoleonic Wars. Traditionally, guerrilla warfare has been waged against larger and better-equipped conventional forces, as in the Viet Cong forces opposing the United States in Vietnam. It is often part of a wider strategy, as for example the activities of the resistance movements in Nazi-occupied Europe, which were part of overall Allied strategy. Guerrilla fighters must avoid open battle as much as possible, exploiting the mobility gained from lack of equipment and supply lines, and making use of popular support. They must rely on hit-and-run tactics, ambush, sabotage, and the psychological effects of unpredictable attack.

Recent years have seen the development of the 'urban guerrilla,' whose desire is not to expel an invader by a general insurrection but to so disorganize the fabric of society that a faction can seize power without relying on popular support. To this end, ambush, hijacking, and bombing, directed both at specific targets and at the populace at large, have become increasingly common. With the advent of the nuclear age, guerrilla warfare is perceived to have distinct advantages. It avoids large-scale confrontations that might lead to escalation, is less expensive for aggressors than all-out war, and can be easier to disclaim.

Guevara, Ché (Ernesto Guevara de la Serna; 1928-1967), Argentinean-born Cuban communist revolutionary and guerrilla leader who helped organize Fidel Castro's coup in 1959. After serving as president of the Cuban national bank and minister of industry, he went to Bolivia in 1966 to direct the guerrilla movement there. He was cap-

tured by the Bolivian army and executed. In 1997, his remains were taken to Cuba.

Guggenheim, name of a family of U.S. industrialists and philanthropists. **Meyer Guggenheim** (1828-1905) emigrated to Philadelphia from Switzerland in 1847 and set up a business importing Swiss lace. Aided by his 7 sons, he later established large smelting and refining plants. One son, **Daniel Guggenheim** (1856-1930), extended the concern internationally and set up an aeronautics research foundation. Another son, **Simon Guggenheim** (1867-1941), was a U.S. senator from Colorado and established a memorial foundation awarding fellowships to artists and scholars. The sixth son, **Solomon Robert Guggenheim** (1861-1949), founded the Guggenheim Museum in New York. **Marguerite (Peggy)** (1888-1979), a granddaughter of Meyer Guggenheim, was born Marguerite Guggenheim in New York City. She was the chief patron of the group of abstract expressionists known collectively as the New York School, which gained fame in the decade following World War II. She also amassed one of the world's foremost private collections of modern art, which she displayed in a museum occupying part of her residence in Venice, Italy.

Guggenheim Museum, major gallery of modern art, noted above all for its building, designed by Frank Lloyd Wright and completed in 1959, Wright's final work and his only one in New York City. The circular glass-domed structure houses major sculptures and paintings of the 19th and 20th centuries. The Solomon R. Guggenheim Foundation promotes art education and maintains the museum, established in 1939.

Guiana, region in northern South America that includes the states of French Guiana, Suriname, and Guyana. Guyana (formerly British Guiana) became independent in 1966; Suriname (formerly Dutch Guiana) became independent in 1975; French Guiana remains still an overseas department of France.

Guided missile, flying weapon that can alter its course during flight toward a target. It usually consists of a rocketlike body containing a rocket or jet engine and an explosive warhead. The length of a guided missile may range from 4 ft (1.2 m) to 60 ft (18 m). Its course may be controlled by instruments in the missile itself or by a crew operating ground controls. Guided missiles are commonly classified as surface-to-surface, surface-to-air, air-to-air, and air-to-surface. They can be fired from permanent or mobile launchers, from ships and submarines, and from airplanes. Though unguided rockets were first developed by the Chinese in the 13th century and used by the British in war during the 19th century, the first guided missiles used in combat were developed by Germany during World War II. Since then, the United States and the former USSR have been leading developers of guided missiles.

Guido d'Arezzo (or **Guido Aretino**) (955?-1050?), an Italian Benedictine monk who

was a music teacher and theorist. He is credited with inventing the four-line staff and using both the lines and the spaces to indicate pitch. Guido named the six tones of the scale used in his day *ut, re, mi, fa, sol, la*. When the seven-note scale was adopted *si* (later called *ti*) was added and *ut* was called *do*.

Guild, economic and social association of merchants or craftspeople in the same trade or craft to protect the interests of its members. Guilds flourished in Europe in the Middle Ages. Merchant guilds were often very powerful, controlling trade in a geographic area; the Hanseatic League controlled trade in much of northern Europe. The craft guilds (as of goldsmiths, weavers, or shoemakers) regulated wages, quality of production, and working conditions for apprentices. Wealthy guilds built extensive headquarters for themselves, some of which still stand. The guild system declined from the 16th century because of changing trade and work conditions.

Guillemot, seabird of the auk family (genera *Uria* and *Cepphus*). The black guillemot (*C. grylle*) is found on Atlantic coasts and the pigeon guillemot (*C. columba*) on Pacific coasts. Both are black with large white patches on the wings. In winter both become mainly white. Like other auks, guillemots swim underwater with their wings instead of paddling with their feet. They spend most of their time at sea, feeding on fish, and come to land only to breed. They nest on cliffs, usually laying a single egg in rocky clefts.

Guimarães Rosa, João (1908-1967), the most important prose writer of the third and latest phase of the Brazilian 'modernismo', the 'generation of 45'. His work brought about a radical change from Portuguese prose and is regarded as the greatest revolution in Brazilian literature this century.

Joao Guimaraes Rosa worked as a doctor in the interior of his native state. From 1934 onwards he was engaged in the diplomatic service in various countries. His first collection of stories *Sangrana*, written in 1937, was published in 1946 and was immediately recognized as a landmark in Brazilian literature. The publication of each of his books was always a national event, reaching a climax in the year 1956, when his collection of short stories *Corpo de Baile* and his only novel *Grande sertao: veredas* were published.

All the works of Guimaraes Rosa are situated in the sertao (the interior) of his native state Minas Gerais. His work is highly symbolic and continually refers to the transcendental, the magical, and the mystical in an attempt to arouse the indolent feeling for the miraculous again. His serao represents the world, where man searches for the 'third bank of the river', as the title of one of the main stories of his work reads.

To describe this theme, which is unusual for Brazilian literature, Guimaraes Rosa used highly personal language, composed of vocabulary and syntactic constructions of the sertanejo (sertoa dweller), from Old Portuguese, from other languages (of which he knew many), and from innumerable surprising neologisms and word combinations.

Guinea

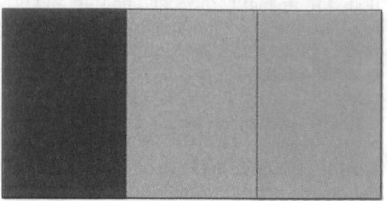

Capital:	Conakry
Area:	94,926 sq mi
	(245,857 sq km)
Population:	7,775,000
Language:	French
Government:	Presidential republic
Independent:	1958
Head of gov.:	Prime minister
Per capita:	US$ 1,970
Monetary unit:	1 Guinean franc
	= 100 centimes

Guinea (Republic), independent country in West Africa, bordered by Guinea-Bissau and Mali on the north, Mali and the Ivory Coast on the east, Liberia and Sierra Leone on the south, and the Atlantic Ocean on the west. The capital Conakry is located on Tombo Island.
Land and climate. Guinea is tropical and humid, with cooler conditions and greater temperature ranges in the inland highlands. The rainy season is from Apr. through Nov., and rainfall is exceptionally heavy along the coast. Vegetation includes the oil-palm of the coastal plain; the lianas, bamboos, and gum-producing trees of the forests; and the rare grasses and sedges of the Fouta Djallon, a mountainous region. Wildlife includes the lion, leopard, antelope, hippopotamus, buffalo, chimpanzee, and crocodile. Guinea also has parrots, egrets, pelicans, and many other varieties of birds.
People and economy. Agriculture is central

Conakry, Guinea's capital and leading seaport, is a rapidly expanding urban center. Although the French influence is still evident in the older part of the city, on Tombo Island, Conakry's industries and suburbs have spread to the mainland.

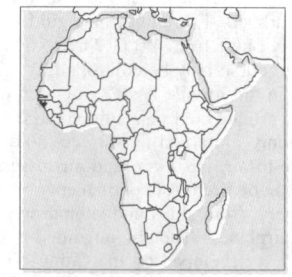

to the country's economy. Major exports are palm kernels, coffee, pineapple, bananas, aluminum, bauxite, iron ore, and diamonds. Islam is the main religion, and French is the official language.
History. Portuguese exploration in the 15th century led to a slave trade in which the British and French were major participants. France made most of the country a protectorate in 1849, and in 1895 Guinea became part of French West Africa. In 1958 Guinea, led by the nationalist revolutionary Sékou Touré, rejected membership in the French community and opted for full independence. Sékou Touré established a one-party state, which lasted until his death in 1984. Power was then seized by military officers. In the late 1980s and early 1990s a process of democratization began to develop slowly. The country became involved in the war between the army and the guerrillas from 2000. Hundreds of thousands of refugees came from Liberia and Sierra Leone to Guinea, increasing the strain on the economy of this potentially rich country.

Guinea, region with indistinct boundaries on Africa's west coast. Guinea is also part of the name of three separate countries in the area-Equatorial Guinea, Guinea-Bissau, and the Republic of Guinea. Equatorial Guinea was once a Spanish colony, Guinea-Bissau belonged to Portugal, and the Republic of Guinea was a French colony.

Guinea-Bissau

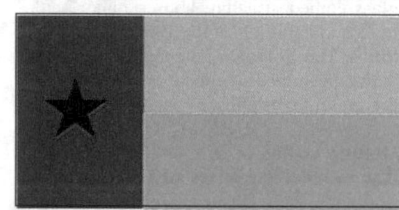

Capital:	Bissau
Area:	13,948 sq mi (36,125 sq km)
Population:	1,345,000
Language:	Portuguese
Government:	Presidential republic
Independent:	1974
Head of gov.:	Prime minister
Per capita:	US$ 900
Monetary unit:	1 CFA franc = 100 centimes

Guinea-Bissau (formerly Portuguese Guinea), republic in West Africa between Senegal to the north and the Republic of Guinea to the east and west, with various coastal islands and an offshore archipelago in the Atlantic. The mainland consists of coastal swamps, a heavily forested central plain, and savanna grazing land in the east.

The climate is hot and humid, with heavy rains from May to Oct. Africans form 98% of the population; most are engaged in agriculture, on which the economy is based. Seafood is an increasingly important export. Industry is limited but expanding. The largest town and main port is Bissau, the capital. Since 1993 the country has a multiparty system. Guinea-Bissau is considered to be one of the twenty poorest countries in the world. President Kumba Yala was elected in 2001.

Guinea fowl (*Numida meleagris*), bird that resembles a turkey and has been domesticated since Roman times. It is distinguished by a naked head and dark gray, spotted plumage. Wild guinea fowl live in Africa and Madagascar, moving about woods or grassland in flocks. They are eaten in some places, but run from danger, rather than fly, and attempts to raise them as game birds have, therefore, failed. They do fly up into trees to roost.

Guinea pig (*Cavia porcellus*), domestic pet related to the cavies, South American rodents. It has a plump body, no tail, and extremely short legs. Guinea pigs are generally 6-10 in (15-25 cm) long, and weigh 1-2 lb (450-900 g).

Guinness, Sir Alec (1914-2000), English stage and screen actor, remarkable for his versatility in both comic and serious roles. His films include *Kind Hearts and Coronets* (1949), *The Lady Killers* (1955), *The Bridge on the River Kwai* (1957), for which he won an Academy Award, *Lawrence of Arabia* (1962), *Star Wars* (1971), *A Passage to India* (1984), and *Mute Witness* (1994). He was awarded the European Film Prize in 1996.

Guitar, stringed musical instrument, related to the lute, played by plucking. Unlike the lute, it has a flat back and curve-waisted sides. The guitar evolved in Spain during the Middle Ages, apparently from Arabic instruments introduced by the Moors. The 5-string Spanish guitar evolved in the 1500s, becoming the Spanish national musical instrument. The modern guitar has 6 strings, generally made of metal or nylon. The guitar has become an important instrument in blues, jazz, and rock music.

Guiyang (Kwéi-yang; pop. 2,000,000), capital city of the Chinese province Guizhou. It is an important center of transport and industry. There are aluminium, iron, steel, machine, food, pharmaceutical, cement, textile, and chemical industries. Coal and bauxite mines are nearby. University (1958) and colleges for agriculture and medicine are situated here.
There is an airport (it was an American airbase in the Second World War, where supplies for the Chinese were delivered).

Guizhou (Kwéi-chow; pop. 35,000,000), province in Southeast China, between the Changjiang and Xijiang rivers: 67,980 sq mi (176,000 sq km). Capital city: Guiyang. The central part is an upland plain, where corn and wheat are cultivated. Tea, rice, and to-

G

bacco are grown in the deeply-eroded river valleys. There is forestry in the north. Subtropical climate in the south allows crops such as sugar cane and bananas. The region is famous for its horse breeding. Coal, manganese, mercury, bauxite, and copper mines. In the 1930s, during the Japanese occupation, industrial and administrative activities were transferred to this province. The completion of the railroad in the fifties was followed by fast industrialization. A quarter of the population are from ethnic minorities, including the Bouyei, Dong, Miao, Sui, and Yi. The first Chinese arrived during the Ming dynasty (1368-1644).

Guizot, François Pierre Guillaume (1787-1874), French statesman and historian. Under Louis Philippe he held various offices, notably the education and foreign ministries. He became premier in 1847 but resigned when the monarchy was overthrown in 1848. Thereafter he wrote history, most notably a history of the 17th-century English revolution.
See also: Louis Philippe.

Gujarat (pop. 41,310,000), federal state (since 1960) in the northwest of India, bordering the Arabian Sea. 75,714 sq mi (196,024 sq km). Capital city: Gandhinagar. Gujarat is one of the most industrialized states in India, producing, among other things, electronic apparatus, textile, (petrol) chemical and building materials. The larger part of the working population finds employment in agriculture, i.e. the cultivation of rice, peanuts, jowar (grain sorghum), tobacco, corn, and cotton, also cattle, goat, and sheep breeding. Fishing is also an important industry. Petroleum and natural gas. There are salt, manganese, limestone, and bauxite mines. Gujarati is the most important language next to Hindi. There are 24,000,000 Hindus and 2,250,000 Muslims. Important cities are Ahmadabad (capital of Gujarat between 1960 and 1970; pop. 3.3 million), Surat (pop. 1.5 million) and Bhavnagar (pop. 400,000).

Gujranwala (pop. 1.7 mln), Pakistan, one of the nation's largest cities. It lies in the Punjab region of northern Pakistan, near the Indian border. Gujranwala is the commercial center for a rich irrigated agricultural area, with trade in wheat, rice, and fruit. Manufactured goods include textiles, processed foods, and brass and copper wares. The city rose to prominence in the early 19th century under Ranjit Singh, the first great Sikh ruler, who was born there. A mausoleum contains the ashes of Ranjit and his father, Mahan. Gujranwala became a part of British India in the late 1840's and a part of independent Pakistan in 1947.

Gulf of California, 700-mi (1,100-km) arm of the Pacific Ocean separating Baja (Lower) California, Mexico, from the Mexican states of Sonora and Sinaloa to the east.
See also: Pacific Ocean.

Gulf of Mexico, arm of the Atlantic Ocean bounded by the southeastern United States, Mexico, and Cuba. It is linked to the Atlantic by the Strait of Florida and to the Caribbean by the Strait of Yucatan. Extensive petroleum deposits are worked offshore.
See also: Atlantic Ocean.

Gulf of Saint Lawrence, almost landlocked body of water, opening into the Atlantic Ocean in eastern Canada. Newfoundland borders the gulf on the east, Nova Scotia and New Brunswick on the south, and Quebec on the west. As the outlet for the Great Lakes and St. Lawrence River, the gulf is the gateway to trade for the interior of North America.

Gulf of Tonkin Resolution, resolution put before the U.S. Congress on Aug. 4, 1964, by President Lyndon B. Johnson, following attacks by North Vietnamese vessels on U.S. destroyers. The resolution gave the president power to take measures necessary to repel other attacks and prevent aggression. The resolution was later seen as the beginning of full-scale U.S. involvement in the Vietnam War and was attacked for giving excessive power to the president. In July 1970 the Senate voted to revoke its authorizations.
See also: Vietnam War.

Gulf Stream, warm ocean current flowing north, then northeast, off the east coast of the United States. Its weaker, more diffuse continuation is the east-flowing North Atlantic Drift, which is responsible for warming the climates of western Europe. The current, often taken to include the Caribbean Current, is fed by the North Equatorial Current, and can be viewed as the western part of the great clockwise water circulation pattern of the North Atlantic.

Gull, strong seabird forming the subfamily Larinae. The plumage is basically white with darker wings and back. Some species develop a dark hood in the breeding plumage. There are altogether some 40 species of gulls, and the group is widespread. Gulls are a very successful and adaptable group and many species have now become common inland as scavengers on refuse or on plowed land.

Gullit, Ruud (Real name: Ruud Dil; 1962-), Dutch association football player who made his debut as a professional player at sixteen. In 1987, he left to play for AC Milan for the recordbreaking sum of $8.5 million, where he had brilliant achievements together with Frank Rijkaard, Marco Van Basten, and others. In that same year, he was voted European Football Player of the Year. In 1995, he signed up with the London club, Chelsea, as player and manager and led it to victory in the FA Cup in 1997. At the start of 1998, he was fired by Chelsea, allegedly due to a breakdown in pay talks. During the 1998-1999 season, he was the trainer for Newcastle United. Gullit made his debut in the national Dutch eleven at 19 and played 66 international matches. He could cover various positions on the field and was a powerful player. In 1998, an autobiography was published, titled *My Autobiography*.

Gulliver's Travels, satire published in London in 1726 as *Travels into Several Remote Nations of the World*, under the name of Lemuel Gulliver, supposedly a ship's surgeon. The actual author was Jonathan Swift, who was satirizing both England and human foibles more generally.
See also: Swift, Jonathan.

Gum, sticky substance from plants that hardens when dry. *Gum arabic* is obtained from certain African acacia trees. It is used as an adhesive on envelopes and postage stamps. *Gum guaiacum*, from the lignum vitae tree, is used for treating gout and for detecting bloodstains, which cause it to change color. Chewing gum comes from the sap of the sapodilla tree.

Gum resin, vegetable substance obtained by making an incision in a plant and allowing the juice that flows out to solidify. Gum resins are often used in medicines and perfumes.

Gum tree, popular name for the eucalyptus tree.

Gun, weapon of destruction able to project a missile at a distant target. Heavy guns, such as cannons, mortars, and howitzers, are usually regarded as artillery, whereas lighter, portable guns such as pistols, rifles, revolvers, and machine guns are regarded as firearms.
See also: Revolver; Rifle.

Gun control, laws aimed at governing ownership of firearms. Advocates of tighter gun control argue that stricter laws would reduce violent crime.
See also: Gun.

Guncotton, form of cellulose nitrate resembling cotton, used in explosives and propellants. Guncotton is prepared by first treating cotton or wood fibers with a mixture of strong nitric and sulfuric acids. After this nitration process, the fibers are washed, ground, pressed, and dried. Extreme care is necessary in the handling and storing of guncotton, as it can be ignited by impact, friction, or excessive heat.

Gunpowder, or black powder, low explosive, the only one known in the West from the 13th century until the mid-19th century. It consists of about 75% potassium (or sodium) nitrate, 10% sulfur, and 15% charcoal; it is readily ignited and burns very rapidly. Gunpowder was used in fireworks in 10th-century China, as a propellant for firearms from the 14th century in Europe, and for blasting since the late 17th century. It is now used mainly as an igniter, in fuses and in fireworks.
See also: Explosive.

Gunpowder Plot, conspiracy of a group of English Roman Catholics to blow up King James I, his family, and Parliament on Nov. 5, 1605. Guy Fawkes was arrested while setting charges under the Houses of Parliament; the conspirators were executed. In England Guy Fawkes Day, Nov. 5, is celebrated with bonfires, fireworks, and the burning of effigies.
See also: Fawkes, Guy.

G

G

Guppy (*Poecilia reticulata*), small fish of northern South America and the Caribbean named for the Reverend Thomas Guppy, who discovered it in Trinidad in 1866. It is also called the rainbow fish, a more appropriate name, because the male is brilliantly colored. The females are usually drab and grow up to 2 in (5 cm) long-twice as big as the males. Guppies are popular aquarium fish. The young are born alive and have to take a gulp of air before they can swim properly. Guppies feed on algae and insect larvae. For this reason they have been released into ponds in many parts of the world to control mosquitoes.

Gupta dynasty, North Indian dynasty that ruled from A.D. 320 to 550, a period that produced some of the finest Indian art and literature. From a small area in the Ganges valley their power spread out to most of India, and under Chandragupta II (385-414) scholarship, law, and art reached new heights. The White Hun invasion (450) reduced the Gupta empire to a portion of Bengal.

Gurnard, common name for tropical fish of the family Dactylopteridae. The gurnard has large pectoral fins with lower fin rays that move separately like fingers. Gurnards seem best suited for life on sea bottoms.

The flying gurnard, *Dactylopterus volitans*, a bottom-dwelling fish found in tropical waters, uses its stiff-spined pelvic fins to slowly 'walk' along the ocean floor.

Gusmao, Xanana (José Alexandre Gusmao; 1946-), member of the East-Timorese resistance movement, reporter, poet and President (2002-). Gusmao worked for the Portuguese army in Dili on Timor. In 1981,

Gusmao Xanana

he became head of Fretilin, which fought for the independence of East-Timor. In 1992, Gusmao was arrested and sentenced to twenty years of imprisonment. During his captivity, he became the symbol for the resistance. President Habibie changed his imprisonment into house arrest in 1999. He was released in that same year, and he returned to East-Timor. After the outright violence following the referendum in which the population declared themselves in favor of independence, the UN temporarily governed the area. Gusmao won the 2002 presidential elections by a landslide; he received over 82% of the votes and became East Timor's first President.

See also: Timor; Habibie, Bacharuddin Jusuf.

Gustavus, name of 6 kings of Sweden. **Gustavus I Vasa** (1496?-1560) was founder of the modern Swedish nation. A Swedish noble, he led the successful revolt against the Danes (1520-1523) and was elected king. Instrumental in the establishment of Lutheranism and the growth of the economy, he took firm control of the country and established an hereditary monarchy. **Gustavus II Adolphus** (1594-1632) reigned from 1611. One of the great generals of modern times, he made Sweden a European power. When he came to the throne, Sweden was at war with Denmark, Russia, and Poland. He ended the Danish war (1613) and the Russian war (1617) victoriously. With his chancellor Count Oxenstierna he introduced wide internal reforms. He joined the Thirty Years' War in 1631, scoring the first Protestant victory at Breitenfeld (1631). He was killed in his victory at Lützen in 1632. **Gustavus III** (1746-1792) became king in 1771, at a time of factionalism and unrest. He regained much of the monarchy's lost power in 1772, and ruled well, introducing many liberal reforms. He was assassinated by a conspiracy of discontented nobles. **Gustavus IV** (1778-1837) reigned from 1792 to 1809. In 1805 he joined a coalition against Napoleon and lost Swedish Pomerania and territory in Germany; despite English help he lost Finland to Russia in 1808. He was then deposed and exiled. **Gustavus V** (1858-1950), a popular sovereign, reigned from 1906. **Gustavus VI Adolphus** (1882-1973) reigned from 1950. He was an able and popular monarch; in 1971 the monarchy was stripped of its powers, but this was deferred during his reign and did not take effect until 1975. He was also a noted archeologist.

Gutenberg, Johannes (c.1400-1468), German printer, usually considered the inventor of printing from separately cast metal types, used for movable type. By 1450 he had a press in Mainz, financed by Johann Fust (1400-c.1466). In 1455 he handed the press (and his invention) over to Fust in repayment of debts; by which time the Gutenberg (or Mazarin) Bible was at least well under way.

Guthrie, Woody (Woodrow Wilson Guthrie; 1912-1967), U.S. folksinger whose compositions and guitar style have shaped modern folk music. As a migrant worker in the 1930s, he developed the characteristic social and political themes of his protest songs, which influenced younger performers like Bob Dylan. His son, **Arlo Guthrie** (1947-) has followed in his father's path as a performer and songwriter.

Gutiérrez, José Angel (1944-), proponent of Mexican-American civil rights and founder of *La Raza Unida*, a political party that ran Mexican-American candidates for public office. In 1970, the year he founded the organization, Gutiérrez was elected president of the school board of Crystal City, Tex. Gutiérrez was elected a county judge in Texas in 1974.

GUT's *See:* Grand unified theories.

Guyana

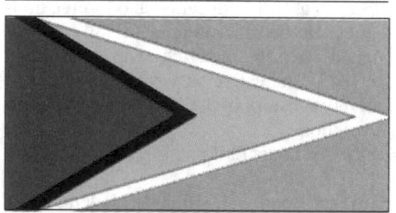

Capital:	Georgetown
Area:	83,000 sq mi
	(215,000 sq km)
Population:	839,000
Language:	English
Government:	Presidential republic
Independent:	1966
Head of gov.:	President, assisted by Prime minister
Per capita:	US$ 690
Monetary unit:	1 Guyana dollar = 100 cents

Guyana, republic on the northern coast of South America, largest of the three countries of the Guiana region. Guyana is bordered by the Atlantic Ocean on the north, Suriname on the east, Brazil on the south, and Venezuela and Brazil on the west. Most of the population lives along the coastal plain. The interior is hilly and heavily forested.

People. The main ethnic groups are East Indians (descendants of imported labor) and blacks; there are also about 40,000 Native Americans. Many of the professional classes are European or Chinese. English is the official language. The religions are Hinduism, Christianity, and Islam.

Economy. Sugarcane and rice are major crops. Important mineral reserves include bauxite (Guyana's chief export), diamonds, and gold. Hardwood is another important resource.

History. Guyana was colonized by the Dutch in the 1600s. Slaves were important to work sugar and tobacco plantations. The region became British in 1815 and was subsequently known as British Guiana. East Indian labor was imported in the 19th century. Guyana achieved self-rule in 1961 and full independence in 1966. The country has long-standing border disputes with Venezuela and Suriname. In 1979, over 900 members of Rev. Jim Jones's People's Temple cult committed mass suicide in the Guyana jungle. In the 1990s and 2000s, ethnic tensions between the two main population groups played an important part in politics. The U.S. aluminum company Alcoa withdrew from the bauxite extraction (Guyana's chief export) in 2001 which led to further strains on the local economy.

Gymnastics, sport and system of exercise designed to maintain and improve the physique. In ancient Greece, gymnastics-including track and field athletics and training for boxing and wrestling-were important in education. Competitive gymnastics are a series of exercises on set pieces of apparatus: parallel bars, horizontal bar, side and vaulting horses, beam, and asymmetric bars. The U.S. system, derived from the German, is designed to assist physical growth; the Swedish system aims at rectifying posture and weak muscles, and the Danish system seeks general fitness and endurance.

Gymnosperm, smaller of the 2 main classes of seed-bearing plants, the other being the angiosperm. Gymnosperms are characterized by having naked seeds usually formed on open scales produced in cones. All are perennial plants and most are evergreen. There are several orders, the main ones being the Cycadales, the cycads or sago palms; the Coniferales, including pine, larch, fir, and redwood; the Gingoales, the ginkgo; and the Gnetales, tropical shrubs and woody vines.

Gynecology, branch of medicine and surgery specializing in disorders of the female reproductive tract; often linked with obstetrics, which specializes in pregnancy and childbirth. Gynecology deals with contraception, abortion, sterilization, infertility, abnormalities of menstruation, and diseases of reproductive organs.
See also: Reproduction.

Györ (pop. 130,000; German: *Raab*), capital city of Györ-Sopron county, northwest Hungary. The city is a commercial and manufacturing center, producing machines and textiles. Györ was the site of a Stone Age settlement, a Celtic town, and a Roman camp. Lying on the trade route between Vienna and Budapest, it flourished in the Middle Ages. Industrialization began in the mid-19th century, and growth has been very rapid since the end of World War II.
See also: Hungary.

Gypsum, common soft white mineral, a hydrate of calcium sulfate ($CaSO_4 2H_2O$), used to make plaster. Alabaster, a variety of gypsum, is carved to make ornamental objects. Gypsum has been used as a fertilizer because of its calcium content. Hard well and spring water often contain gypsum.

The Russian gymnast   es at the Olympic
Olga Korbut (1955)   Games.
had varying success-

Gypsy, member of a nomadic people of Europe, Asia, and North America. Gypsies are believed to have originated in India; their language, Romany, is related to Sanskrit and Prakrit. They probably began their westward migration about A.D. 1000. By the 15th century they had penetrated the Balkans, Egypt, and North Africa. In the 16th century they were to be found throughout Europe. In World War II a half-million European gypsies were executed by the Nazis. There is a strong gypsy tradition of folklore, legend, and song, and this, combined with the independence of their lives, has inspired the romantic imagination of many musicians, artists, and writers.

Gypsy moth (*Porthetria dispar*), winged insect originating in Europe and later introduced to North America. In the New World, in the absence of natural enemies, it has become a serious pest; the caterpillars feed on the leaves of the deciduous trees, particularly fruit trees, and their occasional mass outbreaks can lead to complete defoliation.

Gyropilot, or automatic pilot, automatic device for keeping a ship or airplane on a given course using signals from a gyroscopic reference. The marine version operates a ship's rudder by displacement signals from the gyrocompass. In an airplane, the gyropilot consists of sensors that detect deviations in direction, pitch, and roll and pass signals via a computer to alter the controls as necessary.

Gyroscope, heavy spinning disk mounted so that its axis is free to adopt any orientation. The fact that a spinning top will stay upright as long as it is spinning fast enough demonstrates the property of gyroscopic inertia: the direction of the spin axis resists change. This means that a gyroscope mounted universally, in double gimbals, will maintain the same orientation in space however its support is turned, a property applied in many navigational devices.

H, eighth letter of the English alphabet, derived from the Semitic letter *cheth*, which represents a similar but more guttural sound. In Greek the *h* was dropped and remained only as a symbol for the long *e* vowel. It is

silent in many of the Roman languages and in English has a sound close to that of breathing. In many words that have a French origin, the *h* is silent (as in *honor*). This sound creates problems for foreigners learning English and for many native speakers.

Haakon VII (1872-1957), king of Norway from 1905. A Danish prince, he was elected constitutional monarch when Norway became independent of Sweden. During the German occupation of Norway (1940-1945), he led a government-in-exile in London. He was succeeded by his son, Olaf V.

Habakkuk, Book of, book of the Old Testament, eighth of the Minor Prophets. Though nothing is known of Habakkuk himself, the book probably dates from the late 7th century B.C. It consists of poems about God's using the Chaldaeans to punish Judah and includes promises of divine justice.
See also: Bible; Old Testament.

Habana, La *See:* Havana.

Habeas corpus, in common law, a writ ordering that a person held in custody or under arrest be brought before a court to determine whether the dentention is lawful. Habeas corpus (from the Latin 'you should have the body') originated in medieval England and became a major civil right with the 1679 Habeas Corpus Act. It was designed to make sure that arrested individuals received due process of law. Embodied in the U.S. Constitution, habeas corpus may not be suspended except in cases of rebellion or invasion. (President Lincoln suspended it in 1861 at the onset of the Civil War.)

Haber-Bosch process *See:* Haber process.

Haber process, main commercial method of manufacturing ammonia. The process was invented by Fritz Haber (1868-1934), a German chemist who received the Nobel Prize in chemistry for the discovery in 1918. It was developed on an industrial scale by Karl Bosch in 1913 and is also known as the Haber-Bosch process. The procedure involves the mixing of hydrogen and nitrogen at high temperatures and pressures.
See also: Ammonia.

Habibie, Bacharuddin Jusuf (1936-   ), Indonesian politician, friend and confidant of Suharto. Habibie was Minister of Research and Technology from 1978 to 1997. He was accused of overspending on expensive projects. Habibie became Vice President when Suharto was elected President for the 7th time in March 1998. In May 1998 Suharto was forced to resign due to fierce protests and riots. He assigned Habibie as his successor. He announced that parliamentary elections were to take place in 1999. Meanwhile, he would end nepotism. Freedom of press flourished. The corruption and nepotism of Suharto's government was expatiated upon. Furthermore, the army's outrageous behavior in East-Timor, Aceh and Irian Jaya was exposed. Habibie declared that Aceh was allowed to become autonomous. Almost 80% of the East-Timorese population voted for independence

H

H

in a referendum. He lost the Presidential elections of 1999 because he was held responsible for the loss of East Timor, his reputation was tarnished by bank scandals and the failing economy. The reformist Muslim leader Abdurrahman Wahid succeeded him. *See also:* Suharto; Timor; Aceh; Wahid, Abdurrahman.

Habit, learned stimulus-response sequence. The term is also used to apply to an automatic response to a specific situation, normally acquired through repetition.

Habitat, environment of an animal or plant. All living organisms can tolerate a certain amount of variation in their environment. Within the major divisions of habitat (sea water, fresh water, desert, swamp, etc.) there are minor factors, such as temperature, acidity, rainfall, and the presence of other organisms.
See also: Ecology.

Habsburg, House of, European family from which came rulers of Austria (1282-1918), the Holy Roman Empire (1438-1806), Spain (1516-1700), Germany, Hungary, Bohemia, and other countries. Count Rudolf IV, who was crowned King Rudolf I of Germany in 1273, founded the imperial line. Thereafter Habsburg (also spelled Hapsburg) power and hereditary lands grew until, under Charles V, they included most of Europe (excepting France, Scandinavia, Portugal, and England). After Charles, the Habsburgs were divided into Spanish and imperial lines. When the Spanish line died out, Charles V's granddaughter, Maria Theresa, gained the Austrian title. Her husband, Francis I (Duke of Lorraine), became Holy Roman Emperor (1745), and the Habsburg-Lorraine line ruled the Holy Roman Empire until its demise. The last Habsburg ruler, Charles I, emperor of Austria and king of Hungary, abdicated in 1918, after World War I.

See also: Austria-Hungary; Holy Roman Empire.

Hackberry, any of various trees (genus *Celtis*) of the elm family. The small, round fruit of many species are edible, and the wood is used for furniture; some varieties are grown ornamentally. The trees have smooth gray bark and pointed leaves that grow in two rows.

Hacker, computer hacker, someone who tries to break in to internet accessible computers and causes damage or benefits in some way. A hacker cracks password codes or skirts firewalls. It is a criminal offense to gain illicit access to an information system.
See also: Computer; Internet.

Hackmatack *See:* Larch.

Haddock, North Atlantic fish (*Melanogrammus aeglefinus*) resembling a cod, distinguished by its 3 dorsal fins and the dark patch just behind the gills, known as St. Peter's thumbmark, which the cod lacks. Haddock live in shoals and feed on worms, shellfish, and other bottom-living animals. They are caught in trawls along with cod, and are important commercially, being marketed salted or as smoked Finnan haddock.

Hades, in Greek mythology, the realm of the dead. The name originally referred to the

The haddock (*M. aeglefinus*) is an important North Atlantic food fish. In the market place, smoked haddock is also known as finnan haddie.

god of the underworld, Pluto, but it later came to refer to the underworld itself. It was pictured as guarded by Cerberus, a many-headed dog with a tail of snakes, and was separated from the land of the living by rivers. The most well-known river was the Styx, across which the dead were transported. The dead were met by 3 judges, who sent heroes to the Elysian fields, while the evil were sent to Tartarus.

Hadj *See:* Hajj.

Hadramawt (Hadrhamaut; pop. 831,000), region in South Yemen, on the Gulf of Aden, around the wadi of the same name; 57,937 sq mi (150,000 sq km). Capital: Al-Mukalla. Dry, bare plains are transected by fertile valleys with irrigated agricultural land: crops are dates, figs, cotton, millet, tobacco, and coffee. Coastal fishing and also the export of salt are important industries. The region was called Hazarmaveth in ancient times and a highly cultured society flourished; it was Turkish until 1913; from 1934 to 1967 it was dominated by the British first in the protectorate Aden and then in the South-Arabia Federation.

Hadrian, (Publius Aelius Hadrianus; 76-138 B.C.), Roman emperor from 117 to his death, successor of Trajan. He traveled the empire, reforming and restoring imperial rule. An effective administrator and soldier, he was a talented poet and an admirer of Greek civilization. He was responsible for the construction (c.122-126) of Hadrian's Wall in Britain. His plan to build a new city at Jerusalem sparked a Jewish revolt (132-135), which he repressed.
See also: Rome, Ancient.

Hadrian's Wall, ancient Roman fortification built by the emperor Hadrian (c.122-126) and lengthened about a hundred years later by the emperor Severus. It ran 74 mi (119 km) across the northern part of England and had a series of forts along its length. It represented the northern limit of the empire.

Hadron, name for two of the four basic classes of subatomic particles. These four classes, from lightest to heaviest, are: bosons, leptons, mesons, and baryons. Mesons and baryons are considered hadrons. Mesons are the particles that hold atomic nuclei together. Baryons are the largest class

When the rains arrive and the dry creeks fill with water, there is an influx of various species of animals and many flowers begin to bloom.
1. camel (*Camelus dromedarius*)
2. dingo (*Canis dingo*)
3. rabbit-eared bandicoot (*Macrotis lapotis*)
4. bushy-tailed rat (*Dasyuroides byrnei*)
5. fat-tailed marsupial mouse (*Smithopsis crassicaudata*)
6. budgerigar or parakeet (*Melopsittacus undulatus*)
7. naukeen or Australian kestrel (*Falco cenchroides*)
8. rainbow bee-eater (*Merops ornatus*)

9. frilled lizard (*Chlamydosaurus kingi*)
10. striped skink (*Lygosoma novaeguineae*)
11. eucalyptus tree (genus *Eucalyptus*)
12. paper daisy

(*Helipterum albicans*)
13. *Cleonie oxalidae*
14. sturt's desert pea (*Clianthus formosa*)

The Binnenhof, or Inner Court, one of The Hague's most famous medieval landmarks, serves as the seat of both houses of the Netherland's national legislature.

of particles; both protons and neutrons, which are the main particles of nuclei, are baryons. The reason that mesons and baryons are sometimes considered together as hadrons is that both are subject to the strong nuclear force (one of the four basic forces of nature; the others being gravitations, electromagnetisms, and the weak nuclear force). The other two classes of particles-bosons and leptons-are not subject to the strong nuclear force. Current theory assumes that all hadrons are composed of more basic particles, called quarks.
See also: Baryon; Meson; Quark.

Haeckel, Ernst von (1834-1919), German biologist best remembered for his vociferous support of Darwin's theory of evolution and for his own theory that ontogeny (the development of an individual organism) recapitulates phylogeny (its evolutionary stages), a theory now discredited.
See also: Biology; Darwin, Charles Robert.

Haefliger, Ernst (1919-), Swiss concert singer (tenor). Haefliger studied in Zurich with Julius Patzak and others and debuted in 1942. Although Haefliger, as a lyrical tenor, has taken part in a great many operatic productions (Berlin, Salzburg, Glyndebourne), he is best known as a concert singer, in particular as the evangelist in the *Johannes Passion* and for the *Matthäus Passion* by Bach, and *Das Lied von der Erde* by Mahler. From 1971, onwards Haefliger taught music at the *Musikhochschule* in Munich.

Hafiz (Shams ad-din Mohammed; c.1325-c.90 B.C.), Persian lyric poet and courtier at Shiraz, considered one of the greatest medieval Islamic poets. He used the traditional verse form ghazal (rhyming couplets), using it to express a sensuality and gaiety sharpened by the philosophical mysticism of sufism.

Hafnium, chemical element, symbol Hf; for physical constants see Periodic Table. Hafnium was discovered in 1923, by Dirk Coster and Georg von Hevesey, identified by means of X-ray spectroscopic analysis of zircon. It is found in most zirconium minerals. Zirconium and hafnium are 2 of the most difficult elements to separate. The element is prepared by reducing the tetrachlo-

ride with magnesium. Hafnium is a brilliant silver, ductile, corrosion- resistant metal. It is used in nuclear reactor control rods. The metal is pyrophoric in finely divided form and absorbs hydrogen at elevated temperatures. Hafnium carbide is the most refractory binary composition known, and hafnium nitride is the most refractory metal nitride. Hafnium is used in alloys and as a getter in gas-filled and incandescent lamps.

Hagar *See:* Ishmael.

Hagfish, any of a family (Myxinidae) of predatory marine fishes related to the lamprey. They resemble eels and have circular mouths ringed by tentacles. Their tongues have sharp teeth, and they feed on worms, crustaceans, and fish located by smell. Hagfish grow to just over 2 ft (61 cm) long and are found in seas around the world on soft mud in fairly deep water. If a hagfish is roughly handled, it secretes a large quantity of shiny mucus, for which it is sometimes called the slime eel.

Haggai, Book of, book of the Old Testament, 10th of the Old Testament Minor Prophets, dated 520-519 B.C. It consists of 4 oracles urging the Jews to rebuild the temple at Jerusalem and prophesying the glories of the messianic age.

Haggard, Sir Henry Rider (1856-1925), English author of romantic adventure novels with authentic African backgrounds. He is best known for *King Solomon's Mines* (1885) and *She* (1887).

Hagia Sophia, or Santa Sophia, massive cathedral raised in Constantinople (now Istanbul) by the Byzantine emperor Justinian I; completed in A.D. 537. Its name means 'Holy Wisdom' in Greek, and it was the greatest achievement of Byzantine architecture. Turned into a mosque after the Turkish conquest (1453), it is now a museum.

Hagihara, Yusuke (1897-1979), Japanese astronomer, director of the observatory in Tokyo from 1935 to 1957, and also professor. From 1957 to 1960, he was professor at Tohoku, from 1960 to 1964 he was president of Utsunomiya University. Among other things, Hagihara studied the mechanics

of the heavens, in particular, the stability of the solar system over very long periods of time.

Hague, The (Dutch: *'s Gravenhage* or *Den Haag*; pop. 442,000), seat of government of the Netherlands, capital of South Holland province, and headquarters of the International Court of Justice. Its Binnenhof palace houses the Dutch legislature. The city was the site of the Hague Conferences (1899, 1907) which were international meetings to discuss rules of war. The Hague has gained a reputation as the city for peace conferences. It is also an educational and cultural center.
See also: Netherlands.

Hague Peace Conferences, 2 conferences (1899, 1907) held at The Hague, the Netherlands, at Russia's request, to discuss belligerency rules and war conventions. The first conference established the International Permanent Court of Arbitration (the Hague Tribunal).
See also: Hague Tribunal; World War I.

Hague Tribunal, or International Permanent Court of Arbitration, court established by the first Hague Peace Conference (1899). It is now supported by 76 nations. The court supplies arbitrators to decide international disputes submitted to them. After World War I it was supplemented by the World Court and, later, the International Court of Justice.
See also: World War I.

Hahn, Otto (1879-1968), German chemist awarded the 1944 Nobel Prize for chemistry for his splitting of the uranium atom in 1939 and his discovery of the possibility of chain reactions.

Hahnemann, (Christian Friedrich) Samuel (1755-1843), German physician and founder of homeopathic medicine. He believed that diseases should be treated with small doses of drugs that produced symptoms in healthy persons similar to those caused by the disease to be treated.
See also: Homeopathy.

Haifa (pop. 575,300), port city in northern Israel, an important manufacturing and transportation center. The ancient city, dating from the 3rd century, was destroyed (1191) during the Third Crusade. Later re-

H

built, it became a major port in the late 19th century. It is the world headquarters of the Baha'i religion.
See also: Israel.

Haig, Douglas, 1st Earl (1861-1928), British commander in World War I, blamed for the misconduct of the Somme and Ypres campaigns (1916-17). Hampered by the hostility of British premier Lloyd George, Haig was denied effective command until 1918, when he displayed far greater generalship.

Haiku, traditional unrhymed Japanese poem of 3 lines of 5, 7, and 5 syllables. It evolved in the 17th century from a 31-syllable form. Haikus use images from nature to create a mood or feeling.

Hail, ice pellets that sometimes fall during thunderstorms. Hailstones usually consist of kernels of ice surrounded by distinct layers formed as moisture freezes around the kernel. As they are carried higher by winds, they collect further layers of ice. When they become too heavy to be supported, they fall. They are usually less than .5 in (1.3 cm) in diameter, but can reach diameters over an inch (2.5 cm) and can severely damage crops and buildings.

Haile Selassie (1891-1975), reigning name of Ras Tafari, emperor of Ethiopia (1930-1974). He led Ethiopia's resistance to the Italian Fascist invasion of the country in 1935-1936 and lived in exile until British forces restored him to his throne in 1941. His autocratic rule provoked opposition in

The rule of Haile Selassie (1891-1975), Emperor of Ethiopia, ended in July, 1974. In September, he was also compelled to of-ficially abdicate from the throne. He was subsequently kept under house arrest in one of his palaces.

later years, and he was deposed by his army in 1974 in the midst of a nationwide famine. He died in captivity.
See also: Ethiopia.

Hailwood, Stanley Michael Bailey (1940-1981; alias 'Mike the Bike'), English motorcycle road racer, became world champion nine times between 1961 and 1968 in the 250, 350, and 500 cc classes on Honda and MV Agusta. The Honda-Hailwood combination was virtually unbeatable in 1966: Hailwood rode a six-cylinder, 24-valve, 250 cc Honda (55 hp, 17,000 rpm. By 1968 he had won the Isle of Man TT races twelve times. In 1968 Hailwood switched to cars (the John Surtees team) and became the Formula 2 European champion. He stopped racing cars in 1974 after an accident on the Nürburgring, but won on the Isle of Man again on a 750 cc Ducati in 1978 and 1979. Once his active career was over he began campaigning for traffic safety, but died himself in a traffic accident.

Haiphong (pop. 1.6 million), city in northeast Vietnam, on the Red River delta near the Gulf of Tonkin. A major southeast Asian port, in the 19th century, Haiphong was the site of the main French naval base in Indochina. During the Vietnam War the city was heavily bombed by the United States (1965-1968, 1972). It has since been rebuilt as an industrial and shipping center.
See also: Vietnam; Vietnam War.

Hair, outgrowth of the skin in mammals, sometimes thickening to form wool or fur. Each hair consists of a shaft, most of which extends above the surface of the skin, and a root located in a tubular follicle below the skin surface. The lower end of the root is enlarged to form the bulb, the lower part of

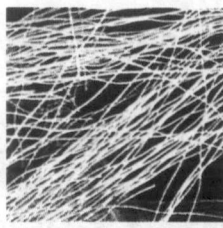

Enlargement of the hair of a common goat.

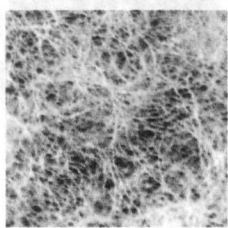

Enlargement of the hair of a sheep (wool).

Enlargement of the hair of a camel (yarn).

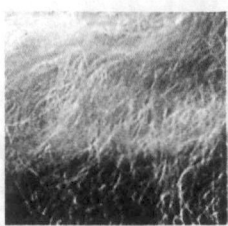

Enlargement of the hair of an angora rabbit.

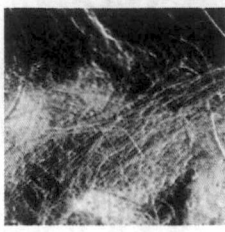

Enlargement of the hair of a kashmir goat.

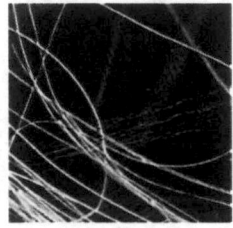

Enlargement of the hair of a horse.

which surrounds a cone-shaped projection of connective tissue, the papilla. The blood supply to the hair follicle comes through capillary networks that enter the papilla. The root of the hair forms a matrix of growing and dividing cells. As new cells are formed, the older cells are pushed upward and the hair 'grows.' The hairshaft in the upper part of the follicle and the exposed part of the shaft above the skin consists of dead, cornified cells. Cutting the exposed part of the shaft has no effect on the growth of the hair. Associated with the hair follicles are the sebaceous glands, which secrete an oily substance that lubricates the shaft of the hair.

Hairdressing, care and arranging of hair, including cutting, setting, styling, tinting, bleaching, straightening, waving, and other procedures. Professional salons usually offer manicuring, facial massage, make-up, eyebrow-shaping, and the making, cleaning, and styling of wigs and hairpieces. The styling and adornment of hair has often indicated social status, e.g. the Chinese braid, the elaborate Greek knot, and the fantastic creations of French aristocrats in the 18th century. Hair styles sometimes have religious significance, too, as shown by the shaved heads of Catholic nuns, monks, and Orthodox Jewish married women, or the long hair of Sikhs and Rastafarians. Earlier civilizations indicated mourning by unkempt hair strewn with ashes, and joy by annointing the hair with perfumes or unguents, as well as feathers, jewels, flowers, ribbons, or combs.
See also: Cosmetics.

Hair snake *See:* Horsehair worm.

Hairworm *See:* Horsehair worm.

Haiti

Capital:	Port-au-Prince
Area:	10,714 sq mi (27,750 sq km)
Population:	7,064,000
Language:	French, Creole
Government:	Presidential republic
Independent:	1804
Head of gov.:	Prime minister
Per capita:	US$ 1,700
Monetary unit:	1 Gourde = 100 centimes

Haiti, independent country occupying the western third of the island of Hispaniola in the Caribbean Sea. The Dominican Republic occupies the rest of the island.

Land and Climate. Haiti is mountainous, dominated by two peninsulas extending westward into the Windward Passage, which separates Hispaniola from Cuba. Between the peninsulas is the Gulf of Gonaïves, with Gonâve Island in the center. The coastline consists of beaches, coral reefs, mangrove swamps, and steep cliffs. Vegetation includes cedar, pine, and mahogany, as well as scrub forests.

People. The great majority of Haitians are descendants of African slaves. The official language is French, but most Haitians speak Creole, a mixture of French and African languages, with some English and Spanish words. The official religion is Roman Catholicism, but large numbers practice voodoo, a religion that mixes African beliefs with some elements of Catholicism.

Economy. Haiti is very densely populated and has one of the lowest per capita incomes in the Western Hemisphere. About 90% of the population is engaged in raising corn, rice, fruit, yams, and vegetables, or in fishing. The chief cash crop is coffee. Sisal fiber, sugarcane, cotton, and cocoa are also exported.

History. Officially a Spanish colony from the early 1500s, Hispaniola was settled by the French during the 1600s. Sugar plantations were created; and slaves were imported to work them. In 1697 Spain ceded Haiti to France. During the French Revolution, the ideas of liberty and equality spread to the colony and stimulated slave revolts. Under the leadership of Toussaint L'Ouverture, a freed slave, the slaves obtained their freedom in 1793. Proclaiming independence in 1801, Toussaint became governor-general of

Hispaniola but was defeated and captured by Napoleon. In 1803, a black army drove the French out, and independence was declared on January 1, 1804, making Haiti the second country of the Western Hemisphere to win its independence from a European colonizer. But stable rule was not established; and Haitian history has been marked by poverty and dictatorship. From 1915 to 1934 the country was occupied by U.S. marines.

In 1957 François ('Papa Doc') Duvalier became president and soon established an extremely repressive dictatorship, supported by a personal police force known as the *tontons macoutes*. In 1971 Duvalier died and was succeeded by his son, Jean-Claude ('Baby Doc.'), who fled the country during a mass rebellion in 1986. In 1991 Father Aristide was elected president in the first free election. Aristide was ousted by a military coup in 1991, but returned to Haiti in 1994 through the agency of the US. In 1995 Aristide's term expired and René Préval was elected to succeed him. Aristide was re-elected President in 2001. One year later, Haiti, the poorest country of the Americas, became a full member the Caribbean Community and Common Market (CARICOM).

Haitink, Bernard Johan Herman (1929-), Dutch orchestra conductor. Haitink studied the violin in Amsterdam and became a violinist with the Radio Philharmonic Orchestra. During this period, in 1954/1955, he followed a conductor's course with Ferdinand Leitner. In 1957 he became the first conductor of the Radio Philharmonic Orchestra in Hilversum. In 1961, he became, together with Eugen Jochum (and on his own from 1964), the first conductor of the *Concertgebouw Orchestra* in Amsterdam. From 1967 to 1979 he was also the first con-

When a rapidly growing rural population cannot find employment, and industrial development in the cities also stagnates, there is an ever-increasing urban proletariat, burdened by various forms of hidden unemployment, like this street hawking in Haiti.

ductor of the London Philharmonic Orchestra, from 1978 to 1988 he was artistic leader at Glyndebourne and from 1987, at the Royal Opera House Covent Garden (London). Haitink has international fame as a performer of Bruckner and Mahler and has recorded not only both their symphonic works, but also those of Brahms, Beethoven, Liszt, and Shostakovich.

In January of 1999, he was appointed honorary conductor of the *Royal Concertgebouw Orchestra*. In 2002, he became a conductor at the Sächsische Staatskapelle Dresden.

Hajj, or **Hadj**, pilgrimage to the Muslim world's holiest city, Mecca, in what is now Saudi Arabia. The goal of a hajj is the mosque whose court encloses the Kaaba, a cube-shaped building containing the sacred Black Stone. Muslims are required to make the pilgrimage to Mecca at least once in their lifetime, if at all possible.
See also: Mecca; Muslims.

Hake, any of various fish of the family Merlucciidae, related to the cod but with a different arrangement of fins. Hake live in deep water and have large mouths set with sharp teeth for catching other fish, such as herring. The teeth can hinge backward to allow large pieces of food to slip in easily. There are several kinds of hake, including the silver hake of the American Atlantic coast and the stockfish of South Africa. In some parts of the world, hake are extensively fished for food.

Häkkinen, Mika (1969-), Finnish racing driver, who made his debut in the GP of the US in 1991 in the Formula One race in a Lotus. Hakkinen started out in karting and made his way through the FF, Opel Lotus, and the Formula Three races to Formula One. He sometimes has a rather impetuous style, in particular at the start of a race. He was driving for McLaren when he won his first Grand Prix in October 1997 in Jerez (the European Grand Prix). The following year he became world champion by winning the last Grand Prix of the season (in Japan). Before that, he was the fastest in the Grand Prix of Spain, Monaco, Austria, Germany, and Luxembourg. He also won one Grand Prix in 1999.
He ended his racing career in 2001.

Hakluyt, Richard (1552?-1616), English geographer and promoter of exploration and colonization. He published many early accounts of the Americas and a major account of English voyaging and discoveries.

Halcyon days, period of tranquility. The phrase comes from the legend of the kingfisher, or halcyon, said to have incubated her eggs for 14 days on the ocean's surface, during which time the waves were perpetually calm.

Haldeman, H.R. *See:* Watergate.

Hale, George Ellery (1868-1938), U.S. astronomer who discovered the magnetic fields of sunspots and invented (c.1890) the spectroheliograph. His name is commemo-

H

H

rated by the Hale Observatories in California. He also founded the Palomar Observatory and founded and directed the Yerkes and Mt. Wilson observatories.
See also: Astronomy; Sunspot; Observatory.

Hale Observatories *See:* Mount Wilson Observatory; Palomar Observatory.

Halevi, Judah (1085?-1141?), Jewish rabbi, philosopher, and poet who lived and worked in Muslim Spain. His *Sefer ha-Kuzari* was his most important philosophical work.
See also: Philosophy.

Haley, Alex Palmer (1921-1992), U.S. author. His book *Roots* (1976) tells the story of his family, beginning in the mid-18th century with the capture of one of his African ancestors, who was taken to America as a slave. The book, which combines fiction with extensive research, was dramatized on U.S. television (1977) and earned Haley the Spingarn Medal and a citation from the Pulitzer Prize board. Haley's writing career began while he was serving in the U.S. Coast Guard (1939-59). He later became a journalist and collaborated with Malcolm X in the writing of *The Autobiography of Malcolm X* (1965).

Halffter, Jiménez Cristóbal (1930-   ), Spanish composer. Halffter studied in Madrid and was appointed as a teacher in 1960 and then in 1964 as the director of the Madrid Conservatory. He resigned both appointments in 1966 to be able to devote himself entirely to composing. Halffter's music was first influenced by M. De Falla, later by Stravinsky and Bartók, and finally by the Viennese school. Halffter also uses audiotapes *Espajos*, (1963) and electronic equipment *Líneas y puntos*, (1967). Other work includes *Requiem por la libertad imaginada* (1971), a cello concerto (1974), a violin concerto (1979) and *Missa Ducal* (1982).

Halley's comet on its return in 1910, photographed on May 12 and May 15, when the tail measured 30° and 40° respectively. The comet has been observed during all 27 appearances since the year 87 B.C. In 1986 viewing conditions were bad for observers in the northern hemisphere.

Half-life *See:* Radioactivity.

Halibut, any of various fish of the family Hippoglossidae. Halibuts are flatfish, living in cold water and having both eyes on one side of its body. The largest Atlantic halibuts (Hippoglossus hippoglossus) can reach lengths of 12 ft (3.6 m) and can weigh as much as 700 lb (317.5 kg), living as long as 40 years. They are important commercial fishes and are caught in North Atlantic and North Pacific waters by trawling or on long lines. Halibut liver oil was once an important source of vitamin A.

Halifax (321,000), capital of Nova Scotia and eastern Canada's chief winter (ice free) port. The industrial, cultural, and commercial center of the province, it stands on a rocky peninsula jutting into a harbor large enough to accommodate the world's biggest ships. The city was built as a British fortress in 1749, and repeated fortifications in succeeding years made it one of the best-defended cities outside Europe. It was a British army base until 1906, when it was handed over to the Canadian government. During World Wars I and II Halifax served as an important Allied naval base. The city is a manufacturing center for food products, candy, furniture, and electronic equipment. Exports are mainly fish and fish products, lumber, and foodstuffs.
See also: Nova Scotia.

Halite *See:* Salt.

Hall, James N. *See:* Nordhoff and Hall.

Hall effect, electrical effect produced when current flows through a magnetic field. Voltage occurs at right angles to the current. Its level is proportional to the intensity of the current and of the magnetic force.
See also: Electric current; Magnetism.

Haller, Albrecht von (1708-1777), Swiss biologist. Best known for his work on human anatomy and physiology, he is credited with being the founder of experimental anatomy. In physiology he investigated respiration, the blood circulation, the nervous system, and the irritability and sensibility of different types of body tissues.
See also: Anatomy; Physiology.

Halley, Edmund (1656-1742), English astronomer. In 1677 he made the first full observation of a transit of Mercury and in 1676-1679 prepared a major catalog of southern hemisphere stars. He encouraged Isaac Newton to write the *Principia*, whose publication he financed. In 1720 he succeeded John Flamsteed as astronomer royal. He is best known for his prediction that the comet of 1682 would return in 1758, based on Newton's calculations of the comet's elliptical orbit around the sun. When the prediction was born out, the comet was named after him.
See also: Astronomy.

Halley's Comet, first periodic comet to be identified (by Edmund Halley) and the brightest of all recurring comets. It has a period of about 76 years. Records exist for every appearance of the comet since 240 B.C., except that of 163 B.C. The comet's most recent reappearance was in 1986.
See also: Comet; Halley, Edmund.

Hall of Fame (formerly The Hall of Fame for Great Americans), memorial to Americans who have achieved great fame in various fields. It was founded in 1900 in a colonnade designed by Stanford White and has niches for about 150 busts. Elections of new members were suspended in 1977, but the monument is still open. It is on the campus of Bronx Community College, in New York City.

Halloween, festival held on Oct. 31, the eve of All Saints' Day, a holiday of the Roman Catholic and Anglican churches held to honor all the saints. The name comes from the medieval English 'All Hallows' Eve.' Originally a Celtic festival to mark the new year, welcome the spirits of the dead, and appease supernatural powers, Halloween was introduced to the United States by Scottish and Irish immigrants and is now a children's festival famous for 'trick-or-treat.'

Hallstatt culture, Celtic culture of Middle and Western Europe in the early iron age (800-450 B.C.), named after the town in Austria where, in 1846, more than 2500 prehistoric graves were exposed. In the Hallstatt culture, a caste of warrior-like nobles ruled a large population of poor farmers and herdsmen. The population lived in farmsteads and villages; the nobles lived in strongholds. Their wealth is evident from their royal graves: high burial mounds in which the dead were buried with weapons, chariots, and horses. There was trade in salt, tin, barnstone, various ores, animal hides, and slaves, in particular with the Greeks and Etruscans. The main areas of the culture lay in the Austrian Alps, Southern Germany and Burgundy. The Hallstatt culture merged into the La Tène culture in the 5th century B.C..

Hallucinogenic drug, consciousness-altering drug that causes hallucinations or illusions, usually visual, together with personality and behavior changes. LSD (lysergic acid diethylamide), mescaline (peyote), and psilocin and psilocybin (derived from certain mushrooms) are common hallucinogenic drugs. The type of hallucination is not predictable, and may be unpleasant. They have been used for centuries in many cultures in connection with religious rituals. Although they are not physically addictive, a high degree of tolerance to LSD and psilocybin develops rapidly, such that higher and higher doses are required to produce an effect. The long-term biological and psychological consequences are unknown.
See also: Drug; Drug abuse.

Halo, in meteorology, luminous ring sometimes observed around the sun or the moon, caused by refraction and reflection of light by ice crystals in the atmosphere of the earth. Such crystals are frequently contained in high clouds. The French philosopher and scientist René Descartes was the first to offer the correct explanation of the formation of a halo. In art, the circle of light often de-

picted around the head of a saint is also called a halo.
See also: Meteorology.

Halogen, any of the group of 5 elements consisting of fluorine, chlorine, bromine, iodine and astatine. These make up group VIIa of the Periodic Table and are highly reactive nonmetals. Apart from astatine, which is radioactive, the halogens are common elements and form many compounds with one another and with other elements. In their pure form, the halogens form molecules composed of 2 atoms.
See also: Element.

Halothane, chemical compound ($C_2HBrClF_3$) used as a general anesthetic. The clear, colorless liquid is inhaled as a vapor. Valued for being nonflammable and neither nauseating nor irritating, it has been in use since 1951.
See also: Anesthesia.

Hals, Frans (c.1580-1666), Dutch portrait painter. Many of his greatest works, such as the *Lady Governors of the Old Men's Home at Haarlem* (1664), are civic portraits. His later works have a somber serenity, but many portraits and genre scenes, such as *Banquet of the Officers of the St. George Militia* (1616) and the *Laughing Cavalier* (1642), are infused with a rich joviality. Five of his sons were also painters.

Halsey, William Frederick 'Bull', Jr. (1882-1959), U.S. admiral during World War II. After commanding a Pacific carrier division 1940-1942, he took command of the Pacific theater. As commander of the 3rd Fleet he helped destroy the Japanese fleet at Leyte Gulf in 1944. He resigned as fleet admiral in 1947.

Ham, cured thigh, buttock, or leg of a hog. The meat is usually cured with salt, and sometimes molasses or sugar. Some hams are impregnated with brine, either by injection or by soaking. The ham is then dried and smoked to prevent it from spoiling.

Hamadryas *See:* Baboon.

Hamburg (1,661,000), historic seaport, capital city of Hamburg state; largest city in western Germany, near the mouth of the Elbe River. Probably founded by Charlemagne, it was a dominant member of the Hanseatic League and has always been a flourishing commercial center. Hamburg was devastated in World War II, but has been rebuilt and now has shipyards and a wide range of industries.
It is a transport hub and a center of the country's fishing industry.
See also: Germany.

Hamilcar Barca (d. c.228 B.C.), Carthaginian general, father of Hannibal. He became commander of Sicily in 247 B.C., during the First Punic war. In 241 he returned to Carthage, quelled a mercenary revolt, and became a dictator. In 237 he led a successful occupation of Spain, but was later killed there.
See also: Carthage; Hannibal.

Hamilton (pop. 6,000), capital and principal port of Bermuda, situated on Main Island.

Hamilton (pop. 600,000), city in the province of Ontario, Canada, built on the plain between a landlocked harbor on Lake Ontario and the 250-ft (76-m) Niagara escarpment. Hamilton is heavily industrialized, being Canada's largest iron and steel producer. It is also a major Great Lakes port.
See also: Ontario.

Hamilton, Alexander (1775-1804), U.S. political leader. He was a strong supporter of the Constitution and was instrumental in getting it adopted. A founder of the Federalist Party, he advocated strong, centralized government and was co-author, with John Jay and James Madison of the *Federalist Papers* (1787-1788), considered classics of political theory. His advocacy of close ties with Britain and his opposition to the French Revolution brought him into conflict with Thomas Jefferson and the Democratic Republicans. In 1789 Hamilton became the first secretary of the treasury and in 1791 he created the Bank of the United States. Hamilton was killed in a duel.

Hamilton, Emma, Lady (1765-1815), celebrated English beauty who became the mistress of Lord Nelson and the subject of many portraits by leading artists. She was the wife of Sir William Hamilton, British envoy in Naples.

Hamilton, Richard (1922-), British visual artist, an important exponent of pop art. In the 1950s, he managed important exhibitions in London such as *This is Tomorrow* (1956). In his work he explored the influence that the avalanche of pictures that surround us in modern life, due to the rapid development of photographic and reproduction technology, has on our thoughts and ideas.
As well as collage he used photography, serigraphy, gouache and drawing techniques. After 1963 (press)photography even became the basis for his work.

Hamilton, Virginia (1936-), U.S. author of children's books. Her novel *M.C. Higgins* won the Newbery Medal and the National Book Award (1975). In addition to her fiction books concerned with the African-

American experience and her collections of black folk tales, Hamilton wrote biographies of notable African Americans for children, including *W. E. B. Du Bois* (1972) and *Paul Robeson* (1974).

Hamites, peoples inhabiting eastern Africa, especially Somalia and Ethiopia, and northern Africa, where they are known as Berbers. Strictly speaking, Hamitic is a linguistic classification rather than an ethnic one. Many believe that the Hamitic-speaking peoples originated on the Arabian peninsula, but this is not at all certain.

Hammarskjöld, Dag (1905-1961), Swedish politician, UN secretary general 1953-1961. He was instrumental in negotiations to bring about a truce in the Korean War and a settlement of the Suez crisis of 1956. In 1960 he directed the UN intervention in the Congo (now Zaire). His actions were condemned by the USSR, but he refused to resign. He was killed in an airplane crash in the Congo and was posthumously awarded the 1961 Nobel Peace Prize.
See also: United Nations.

Hammerstein, name of 2 U.S. theatrical producers. **Oscar Hammerstein** (1846-1919) a German-born tobacco magnate who emigrated to the United States and became an opera impresario, opening theaters in New York, London, and Philadelphia. **Oscar Hammerstein II** (1895-1960), his grandson, became famous as a lyricist and producer of musical comedies in partnership with composers Richard Rodgers, Jerome Kern, and others. Among his successes were *Oklahoma!* (1943), *Carousel* (1945), *South Pacific* (1949), *The King and I* (1951) and *The Sound of Music* (1959).

Hammer throw, Olympic sports event in which the athlete throws a 16-lb (7.26-kg) 'hammer' (actually a metal sphere with a handle), spinning in place to gain momentum before releasing it. The sport, which originated in the British Isles centuries ago, was standardized as a track and field event in 1875 and became part of the Olympic Games in 1900.

Hammett, (Samuel) Dashiell (1894-1961), U.S. writer and left-wing political activist.

Frans Hals's *Regentesses of the Old Men's Almshouse* (1664) shows the governing board of the institution where the artist spent his last years, producing such masterly portraits as this (Frans Hals Museum, Haarlem, the Netherlands).

H

H

He was known for his hard-boiled detective novels, and his character Sam Spade became one of the prototypes of the fictional U.S. detective. Hammett's best-known works are *The Maltese Falcon* (1930) and *The Thin Man* (1932).

Hammurabi, or Hammurapi, sixth king of the first dynasty of Babylonia (r. 1792-50 B.C.). He conquered and united Mesopotamia, establishing an empire that did not long survive him. He was responsible for the Code of Hammurabi, the fullest known collection of Babylonian laws. The best source of the code is a black stone column found at Susa, Iran, in 1901.
See also: Babylonia and Assyria.

Hampton, Lionel (1908-2002), U.S. jazz vibraphonist and bandleader. Originally a drummer with Louis Armstrong in 1928, he first recorded on vibraphone in 1930. He was a member of Benny Goodman's quartet 1936-40 and later became leader of his own band. He was known for his showmanship as well as his virtuoso technique.
See also: Jazz.

Hampton Court Conference, meeting held at Hampton Court Palace, England, in 1604 to consider Puritan demands for reform in the Church of England, especially of the episcopal system of Church government and the *Book of Common Prayer*. James I rejected most of these, but the conference endorsed the King James translation of the Bible.

Hampton Roads, natural harbor and port in southeast Virginia formed by the confluence of 3 rivers-the James, Nansemond, and Elizabeth-that flow into Chesapeake Bay. The Virginia cities of Newport News and Hampton face the channel on the north shore, Norfolk and Portsmouth on the south. The area is the headquarters of armed forces installations that make up the world's largest naval complex. Hampton was one of the earliest English settlements in the country, founded in 1610. During the Civil War Hampton Roads was the scene of the naval battle between the *Monitor* and the *Merrimack*, the first ironclad warships.

Hampton Roads, Battle of *See:* Monitor and Merrimack.

Hamster, any of various short-tailed rodents of Europe and Asia. Hamsters feed chiefly on cereals, but also on fruits, roots, and leaves. They carry food back to their nests in large cheek pouches. The most familiar species, the golden hamster (*Mesocricetus auratus*), makes an attractive pet. Both it and the common hamster (*Cricetus cricetus*) are nocturnal.

Hamsun, Knut (1859-1952), Norwegian novelist. In his youth he led a wandering life, which became the theme of many of his novels, such as *Hunger* (1890) and his masterpiece, *The Growth of the Soil* (1917). He was awarded the Nobel Prize for literature in 1920. His popularity declined as a result of his Nazi sympathies during World War II.

Handan (also Han-tan, pop. 2,900,000), city in China, in Hebei Province. Transportation and industrial center.

Handball, court game played by 2 to 4 people. There are 2 versions of the game: 1-wall handball and 4-wall handball. Players attempt to hit a hard rubber ball against 1 or more of the walls in such a fashion as to prevent opponents from returning it before it bounces twice on the floor. Handball may be one of the world's oldest games, dating back to ancient Egypt. The modern version was probably invented in the Basque country of northern Spain.

Handel, Georg Friedrich (1685-1759), German-born composer who settled in England in 1712, one of the greatest composers of the baroque period. After establishing himself as an opera composer in Germany and Italy, he turned to oratorio to suit British tastes. His most famous works in this genre are *Saul* (1739), *Israel in Egypt* (1739), *The Messiah* (1742), and *Belshazzar* (1745). The rest of his vast output includes 46 operas, almost 100 cantatas, many orchestral works, and 28 additional oratorios.

Handicap, physical or mental disability, congenital or acquired, that inhibits a person from participating in normal life. In recent years technology and changes in attitudes have greatly improved the lives of the disabled. Sophisticated rehabilitation techniques and other tools, often using computers, have allowed a wide range of vocational and recreational activity.

Handicraft, name given to the process of making objects by hand; also refers to the products of that process. Traditional handicrafts include basket-weaving, carpentry, carving, ceramics, embroidery, knitting, sewing, and leatherwork. The teaching of handicrafts has been widely included in school curricula and is also used in occupational therapy.

Handke, Peter (1942-), Austrian writer, who belongs to the group of avant-garde German-speaking writers and became well known by his play *Offending the Audience* (1966), that roughly, deals with the illusion of theater. In the play *Kaspar* (1968), he draws attention to the conditioning of man and the alienating power of language.
His work includes: *They Are Dying Out* (1973), *The Goalie's Anxiety at the Penalty Kick* (novel; 1972), *A Sorrow beyond Dreams* (novel, 1974; play, 1977) and *The Lefthanded Woman* (novel, 1976), *The Afternoon of a Writer* (novel, 1987), *Voyage to Sonorous Land, or the Art of Asking and the Hour We Knew Nothing of Each Other* (1989, play), and *On a Dark Night I Left My Silent House* (1999).
Handke won several literary prizes, including the Franz Kafka Prize.

Handwriting on the wall, incident in the Old Testament (Book of Daniel). The Aramaic words *mene, mene, tekel* mysteriously appeared written on the wall and only the Babylonian ruler Belshazzar could see them. The Hebrew prophet Daniel interpret-

ed them to mean that God intended to destroy Belshazzar and his kingdom, which fell to Cyrus of Persia that night. The phrase is now used to refer to any sign heralding disaster.

Handy, W(illiam) C(hristopher) (1873-1958), U.S. songwriter, bandleader, and jazz composer. He conducted his own band 1903-1921. In 1912 he published one of the first popular blues songs, 'Memphis Blues', and in 1914 wrote 'St. Louis Blues'. He became a music publisher in the late 1920s.

Han dynasty, dynasty that ruled China 202 B.C.-220 A.D. It was founded by Liu Bang after a period of oppressive centralized rule under the Ch'in dynasty. At the height of its expansion, the Han dynasty held power from Korea and Vietnam to Uzbekistan. It was during this period that Confucianism became the official ideology of the state and Buddhism was introduced in China.
See also: Liu Bang.

Terracotta statuette of a rider, from the late　Han period (around 200 A.D.).

Hanging Gardens of Babylon *See:* Seven Wonders of the Ancient World.

Hangzhou, or Hangchow (pop. 134 million), city of eastern China, capital of Zhejiang province. The city is a tourist center and manufactures chemical and electronic products, iron, steel, and motor vehicles. Historically it was a center of silk and tea production. The city was rebuilt after its destruction during the Taiping Rebellion (1850-1864). It was occupied by Japan (1937-1945).
See also: China.

Han Kao-tsu *See:* Liu Bang.

Hankou *See:* Wuhan.

Hannibal (247-183? B.C.), Carthaginian general who almost defeated Rome in the Second Punic War (218-201 B.C.). Son of Hamilcar Barca, he commanded Carthaginian forces in Spain. When the second war between Rome and Carthage broke out, he crossed the Pyranees with a seasoned force whose supplies were carried by elephants. In

H

an extraordinary feat of organization, he took his forces through the Alps in winter and invaded the Po River valley, defeating Roman forces under Scipio and winning great victories at Lake Trasimene in central Italy (217 B.C.) and at Cannae (216 B.C.). Rome detained him with harassing tactics while Roman armies reduced Carthaginian possessions in Spain, and Hannibal was recalled to defend Carthage itself. He was ultimately defeated at Zama (202 B.C.) by a Roman army commanded by Scipio Africanus Major. Driven into exile c.195 B.C., he joined Syrian operations against Rome. When the defeated Syrians promised to surrender him to Rome, he poisoned himself.
See also: Carthage; Punic Wars.

Hanoi (pop. 2,100,000), capital of North Vietnam (1954-1976) and of united Vietnam since 1976. Founded in the 7th century, it is an important shipping, industrial, and transport center on the Red River. The city suffered heavily from U.S. bombings during the Vietnam War.
See also: Vietnam War.

Hanover (pop. 525.000), or Hannover, region of northwest Germany. As Brunswick-Lüneburg it became an electorate of the Holy Roman Empire in 1692 (its elector, or ruler, helped elect the emperor). It began a period of association with England (1714-1837) when its elector became King George I of England. During this association Hanover was invaded twice: during the Seven Years War (1756-1763) and the French Revolutionary and Napoleonic Wars. Disputed by the French and Prussians, it was annexed by Prussia after the Seven Weeks' War (1866), remaining a part of Prussia until 1946, when it became part of the state of Lower Saxony, West Germany. Major cities of Hanover include Hanover and Göttingen.

Hanover (pop. 526,000), or Hannover, city on the Leine River in northwest Germany, capital of the state of Lower Saxony. A railway and manufacturing center, Hanover produces iron, steel, and machinery, and is known for its annual industrial fair. The city was chartered in 1241, and was the capital of the electorate of Hanover from 1692 and of the kingdom of Hanover 1815-1866. It has been rebuilt since its bombing during World War II.
See also: Germany.

Hanover, House of, reigning family of Hanover, in Germany, and of Great Britain (1714-1901). In 1658 the 1st Elector of Hanover married Sophia, granddaughter of James I, heir to the British throne by the Act of Settlement (1701). Her son became George I of Britain. By Salic law, his descendant, Victoria, could not become queen of Hanover, and from 1837, when she assumed the British crown, the thrones separated. On Edward VII's accession (1901) the family name became Saxe-Coburg (after Prince Albert), and in 1917 was changed to Windsor.

Hanseatic League, medieval confederation of North German towns and merchants organized to protect their trading interests in the Baltic Sea and throughout Europe. The league was created by the Hansas, companies having trading interests outside Germany. It arose informally in the late 12th century, and by the middle of the 14th century, more than 70 German cities had entered into mutual alliance treaties. In 1358 the league was formally declared. Its capital was Lübeck on Germany's northern coast. Assemblies were held there to decide on monopolies, trading rights, and other policy matters. Members of the league established commercial centers in many foreign towns, including Bergen (Norway), London, and Novgorod (Russia). The league's strength declined with the rise of nationalism in Europe, and it disappeared in the 17th century.

Hansen's disease *See:* Leprosy.

Hanson, Duane (1925-1996), American sculptor. Hanson was an exponent of hyperrealism in sculpture. He worked with live models, of which he made hollow plaster casts; these were filled with polyester and fiber glass, after which the limbs were joined together and painted in flesh color; finally he dressed the dolls and gave them the necessary accessories. His themes were often taken from political events (war, racial riots), but also from everyday life in America: housewives shopping, tourists, senior citizens, etc., by which he wanted to express the sadness of the 'American way of life'.

Hanson, Howard (1896-1981), U.S. conductor, teacher, and composer in the Romantic tradition. He won a Prix de Rome (1921) and was director of the Eastman School of Music, Rochester, N.Y. (1924-1964). Hanson's *Fourth Symphony* won a Pulitzer Prize in 1944.

Hanukkah, Jewish holiday commemorating the rededication of the Temple of Jerusalem in 164 B.C. after Judas Maccabeus's victory over the Hellenic king Antiochus IV. Known as the Festival of Lights, it is celebrated by the lighting of candles in an 8-branched candle holder called a menorah. The holiday lasts for 8 days, beginning on the 25th of Kislev the third month of the Jewish calendar (approximately Dec.).
See also: Judaism.

Hanyang *See:* Wuhan.

Hapsburg, House of *See:* Habsburg, House of.

Hara-kiri, or *seppuku*, ancient Japanese act of ceremonial suicide, in which a short sword was used to slash the abdomen from left to right, then upward. Used by warriors to escape capture by the enemy, obligatory hara-kiri was abolished in 1868.
See also: Samurai.

Harald V, King (1937-), King of Norway, successor to Olav V. Harald had already temporarily replaced King Olav after the latter's stroke in 1990. Harald is married to Queen Sonja. They have a son (Håkon, 1973) and a daughter (Martha Louise, 1971).

Harappa *See:* Indus Valley civilization.

Harare (formerly Salisbury; pop. 1,189,000), capital and largest city of the Republic of Zimbabwe. It was founded as Fort Salisbury in 1890 by the British South Africa Company and became the capital of the colony of Southern Rhodesia in 1923. It remained capital during the period of the colonial Federation of Rhodesia and Nyasaland (1953-1963), and under the white minority rule of the Ian Smith government (1964-1979). It became the capital of the independent country of Zimbabwe in 1980, changing its name to Harare in 1982. Harare is Zimbabwe's financial, commercial, and manufacturing center. Its industries include steel, chemicals, and textiles.
See also: Zimbabwe.

Harbin (pop. 4,7 million), city in northeast China on the Sungari River, capital of Heilongjiang province. Established by Russia as a railroad administration center (1895), Harbin once had a large European population. It was controlled by China and Japan jointly after the Russo-Japanese War (1904-1905) and was occupied by Japan 1932-1945. Still a major railway center, it is also an important port and a center for the Manchurian machinery, chemical, oil, and coal industries.
See also: China.

Hard edge, generic term for geometric abstract art after WW II. In the course of the 1960s, it came to mean in particular the tension that is created when two areas of color are placed exactly next to each other. The surfaces are smooth; the colors are usually spray painted, so that every illusion of depth is absent. Created by Kelly, Noland, and Stella, and others.

Hardening of the arteries *See:* Arteriosclerosis.

Harding, Warren Gamaliel (1865-1923), 29th president of the United States (1921-1923). Under Harding the U.S. refused to enter the League of Nations. In 1921 and 1921 the Washington Disarmament Conference took place. Harding's administration was marred by scandals such as the Teapot Dome scandal.

Hardness, measure of the resistance of a substance to being scratched by another substance. Resistance to scratching is measured on a scale named for Friedrich Mohs (1773-1839), who chose 10 minerals as reference points, ranging from talc (hardness 1) to diamond (10). A modified Mohs scale is now usually used, with 5 additional reference points. Resistance to indentation is also measured by other scales as well, such as the Brinell, Rockwell, and Vickers scales.

Hardy, Oliver *See:* Laurel and Hardy.

Hardy, Thomas (1840-1928), English novelist and poet. His first successful novel was

H

Far from the Madding Crowd (1874). Nine others, including *The Return of the Native* (1878) and *Tess of the d'Urbervilles* (1891), appeared over the next 20 years. *Jude the Obscure* (1895), partially autobiographical, so offended Victorian morality that Hardy abandoned novels but continued writing poetry. His epic verse drama *The Dynasts* (1903-1908) and his later lyric poetry are highly regarded. The 'last of the great Victorians,' Hardy influenced 20th-century English literature. His view of life was essentially tragic, his characters often seeming to be victims of malignant fate.

Hare, any of various species (genus *Lepus*) of herbivorous mammals of the rabbit family, including the jackrabbit. Adapted for swift jumping and characterized by long ears, powerful hindlegs and feet, and short tails, hares live entirely above ground in grasslands in Eurasia, Africa, and North America. Unlike rabbits, they move by jumping instead of running. Some species molt into a white coat in winter.

North American hare, genus *Lepus*.

Harebell *See:* Bluebell.

Hare Krishnas, popular name for members of a Hindu sect (the International Society for Krishna Consciousness), known for their orange robes, shaved heads, and public chanting of 'Hare Krishna' in praise of the Hindu god Krishna. The movement was founded in 1965 in New York City by A.C. Bhaktivedanta Swami Prabhupada and teaches devotion to Krishna as a way to enlightenment. *See also:* Hinduism.

Harelip *See:* Cleft palate.

Hargreaves, James (1720?-1778), British inventor of the spinning jenny (1764), a machine for spinning several threads at once. Public uproar over loss of jobs forced him to flee his native Blackburn for Nottingham (1768), where he patented the jenny (1770).

Hargrove, Roy (1969-), American jazz trumpeter. At the young age of seventeen he played at the North Sea Jazz Festival and soon after that signed several prestigious recording contracts. He is at his best in a relaxed atmosphere, evident from the record *Parker's Mood* (1995). Hargrove is classed as a new traditionalist, but at the end of the 1990s, he also played extensively with Latin American musicians.

Hari-kari *See:* Hara-kiri.

Haring, Keith (1958-1990), American artist. After finishing art school in New York, Haring threw himself into the New York subculture and attacked the walls of the subway with spray paint. His graffiti, mainly pictures of animal and human figures with black outlines, radiated enormous vitality and soon caught the eye of art dealers on the lookout for new talent. It was not long before his work was also exhibited in museums. He became extremely well known for his drawing in neon on Times Square in New York in 1982 and the painting he did on part of the Berlin wall in 1986. He certainly had commercial talent: T-shirts, posters, and badges with his designs are available everywhere.

Harkins, William Draper (1873-1951), U.S. chemist who predicted the existence of the neutron (1927) and theorized the possibility of nuclear fusion: the combination of 4 hydrogen atoms to become 1 helium atom with a minute extra mass converted into energy. He was the first to propose that this fusion process fueled stars.
See also: Fusion; Neutron.

Harlem Renaissance, period of cultural development among U.S. blacks, centered on Harlem, New York City, in the 1920s. In this period African-American literature changed from imitative works to penetrating analyses of black culture and novels of protest, displaying racial pride. Notable writers included Countee Cullen, Langston Hughes, Jean Toomer, and Zora Neale Hurston.

Harlequin snake *See:* Coral snake.

Harlow, Harry Frederick (1905-1981), U.S. psychologist who studied the effects in monkeys of deprivation of maternal love and other social contact. Harlow's conclusions were that social contact in childhood is necessary for adult sociability and that maternal attention in infancy is necessary for the development of adult maternal instincts.
See also: Psychology.

Harlow, Jean (1911-1937), platinum-blonde U.S. film actress who began her career as a sex symbol and developed into a gifted comedienne. Her films include *Hell's Angels* (1930), *Platinum Blonde* (1932), and *Dinner at Eight* (1933).

Harmonica, or mouth organ, musical instrument that contains a number of small metal reeds of graduated size enclosed in slots in a short narrow box. This is held to the lips and moved from side to side to obtain notes.

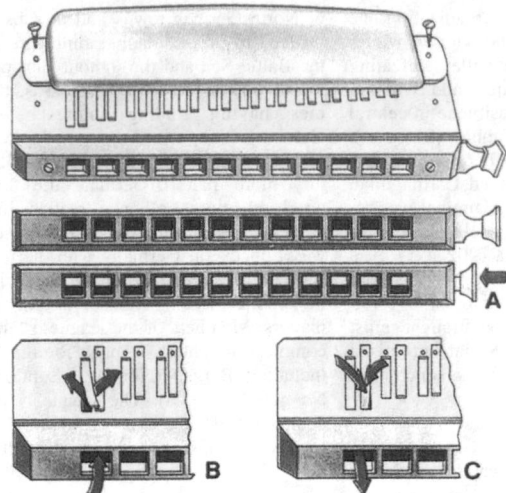

The chromatic harmonica is a simple reed organ, which contains two reed plates, placed one above the other, the bottom of which is brought into play by means of a slide (A). Each reed plate contains reeds that are positioned in a way that each hole operates two reeds, one being activated by blowing (B), the other by sucking (C).

Harmonic motion, vibrating or oscillating motion that repeats itself in equal time intervals, as in the motion of a swinging pendulum. This is known as simple harmonic motion (SHM). The central point about which oscillation takes place is called the *equilibrium point*, and the distance of the object from this point at a given time is called its *displacement*. Harmonic motion occurs only within certain limits. If either the pendulum or the spring is displaced too far, the motion will become irregular.

Harmonics, basic compounds of a musical tone, consisting of the various vibrations of sound that produce what sounds like a single tone. The string of a guitar, for instance, will vibrate along its whole length, but also in partial segments, making a blend of tones that gives the instrument its characteristic sound.
See also: Sound.

Harmonium, small reed organ with pedals for pumping air past the reeds. It was popular in the late 19th century as a family instrument, but has mostly been used in chapels as a substitute for a standard organ.

Harmony, in music, the simultaneous sounding of 2 or more tones or parts; also the relation and progression of chords and the rules governing their relationship. Traditional harmony is based on a 3-tone musical structure, with notes named for their position on the musical scale: the lowest tone is called the root, the middle tone is called the third (because it is the third tone above the root), and the next is called the fifth (5 tones above the root). Chords can be erected on any note of the traditional 8-note scale.

Harness racing, form of horse racing in which each horse draws a lightweight, two-wheeled cart (called a sulky) driven by a driver. Most harness races are run by pacers, horses who move two legs on the same side at the same time, producing a fast, rocking gait. Other races are for trotters, who move opposing pairs of legs together. Harness racing is generally run by standardbred horses on an oval dirt and clay track 1/2-1 mi (0.8-1.6 km) long. Harness racing originated in Asia Minor in ancient times and became popular in the United States and Europe in the 19th century.

Harnett, William Michael (1848-1892), Irish-born U.S. painter. Such still lifes as *After the Hunt* show his extremely realistic *trompe-l'oeil* (eye-deceiving) style.

Harnoncourt, Nicolaus (1929-), German-Austrian conductor, cello player and musicologist. From 1952 to 1969, he performed with the *Wiener Symphoniker*. Formed the *Concentus Musicus Wien* in 1953, with which he performed music from the renaissance and the baroque to great acclaim by attempting to approximate the original execution as closely as possible. Had great influence on performance. Many record productions, including Monteverdi and J.S.Bach. From the middle of the 1970's, he was a guest conductor at the Dutch *Royal Concertgebouw Orchestra*. Now his repertoire reaches as far as the 19th century. Publications: *Musik als Klangrrede: Wege zu einem neuen Musikverständnis* (1982), *Der musikalische Dialog* (1984). Together With Gustav Leonhardt, he received the Erasmus Prize in 1980.

Harold, name of two kings of England. **Harold I** (d. 1040), called Harefoot, ruled England 1035-1040. He was the illegitimate son of King Canute, Danish king and ruler of England, whose legitimate son Hardecanute succeeded Harold. Harold's reign was characterized by violent struggles with other royal claimants. **Harold II** (1022?-1066), last Anglo-Saxon king of England ruled in 1066. As Earl of Wessex (1053), he was one of the most powerful men in England. When King Edward the Confessor died in 1066, both Harold and Duke William of Normandy claimed the throne. The English nobility supported Harold's claim, and William invaded England. Harold was killed fighting William's forces in the Battle of Hastings. *See also:* England.

Harold, kings of Norway. **Harold I** or **Harold Fairhair** (c.860-c.940) was the first king of Norway. He succeeded his father, Halfdam the Black, as king of Vestfold (in southeast Norway) and then unified Norway by defeating contending local rulers. **Harold**

III or **Harold Hardrada** (1015-1066), ruled jointly with his nephew Magnus I (1046-1047), and singly after the death of Magnus (1047-1066). He founded the city of Oslo. He tried to extend his rule to Denmark and England, but was killed by the forces of Harold II of England during an invasion of England.
See also: Norway.

Harp, musical instrument consisting of a number of strings of different lengths stretched across a frame. The modern harp is over 5 ft (1.5 m) tall and rests on the ground, with the player seated next to it. It has 7 pedals to adjust the strings and alter the pitch of the notes and a range of nearly 7 octaves.

Harper, Frances Ellen Watkins (1825-1911), African-American writer and lecturer. Her collected *Poems* (1871), and other books (later published in such collections as *Poems on Miscellaneous Subjects*, 1954), deal with antislavery and other racial themes. She also wrote a novel, *Iola Leroy* (1893). Born in Baltimore of free parents, she began writing poetry in her teens, and in 1854 began delivering antislavery lectures in the United States and Canada. Later she spoke in support of women's suffrage and was active in the Woman's Christian Temperance Union.

Harpers Ferry (pop. 380), town in eastern West Virginia, USA, site of a federal armory established by George Washington. John Brown's dramatic raid on the arsenal there in 1859 was one of the events leading to the Civil War (1861-1865). Because of its strategic location, the town was the scene of many battles during this war.

Harpsichord, keyboard instrument in which the strings are plucked by quills rather than hit by felt hammers as in a piano. The harpsichord was very popular from the 14th to the 16th century, and much great music was written for it, notably by J.S. Bach, François Couperin, and Domenico Scarlatti. Its popularity declined with the development of the piano.

Harpy, in Greek mythology, birdlike monster with the head of a woman. Harpies were agents of divine punishment.
See also: Mythology.

Harpy eagle, large bird of prey (*Harpia harpyja*) of the hawk family, native to tropical forests of the Western Hemisphere. This large eagle weighs over 10 lbs (4.5 kg) and may have a wingspan of 7 ft (2 m). It has a black-crested gray head, black back, and white underside. It preys on monkeys, sloths, opossums, and porcupines. The harpy eagle is named for a flying predatory creature of Greek mythology.

Harrell, Tom (1946-), American jazz trumpeter, a modest, sophisticated soloist with a flawless technique. Did a great deal of studio work and played big band before making a name as a soloist. Has steadily partnered Phil Woods, the clarinet player, for years. He initiated and recorded the CD *Labyrinth* (1996) and others.

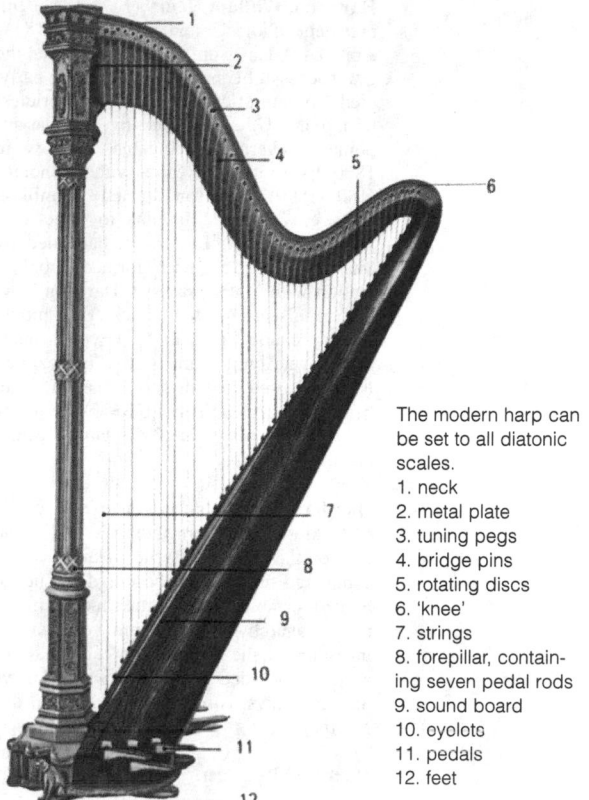

The modern harp can be set to all diatonic scales.
1. neck
2. metal plate
3. tuning pegs
4. bridge pins
5. rotating discs
6. 'knee'
7. strings
8. forepillar, containing seven pedal rods
9. sound board
10. eyelots
11. pedals
12. feet

Harrier, breed of dog developed for fox and hare hunting, possibly as long ago as A.D. 1,000 Harriers stand about 21 in. (50 cm) tall and weigh 35 to 55 lbs (16 to 25 kg). Compact and sturdy, with a keen sense of smell, they have been used in the U.S. for rabbit hunting since colonial times.

Harrington, James (1611-1677), English philosopher best known for his *Commonwealth of Oceana* (1656), a treatise on the ideal state ruler. His ideas prefigured doctrines of the American and French revolutions.

Harris, Frank (1856-1931), British author best known for his biographies of Shakespeare, Oscar Wilde, and G. B. Shaw. (1915-1927) and his 3-volume autobiography, *My Life and Loves* (1923-1927).

Harris, Roy (1898-1979), U.S. composer. He studied in Paris with Nadia Boulanger and later won fame as a teacher. The *Third Symphony* (1937) is perhaps his best-known work. His work is characterized by its energy and melodious tones.

Harrison, Benjamin (1833-1901), 23rd president of the United States (1889-1893). Under Harrison, U.S. expansionism took important strides forward. U.S. claims to Samoa were established, the first Pan-American Conference was held in Washington (1889). He also aided passage of the Sherman Antitrust Act, which declared illegal all trusts or monopolies that restrained trade.

Harrison, George *See:* Beatles.

H

H

Harrison, William Henry (1773-1841), 9th president of the United States (Mar. 1841-Apr. 1841). Harrison, a military hero and the first successful candidate of the Whig party, died 1 month after taking office-the briefest term of any U.S. chief executive. He was appointed governor of Indiana Territory in 1800. By a series of treaties with the Indians (1802-1809), Harrison opened 33 million acres of Ohio and Indiana to large-scale white settlement. But the Indians, led by Shawnee chief Tecumseh, formed a confederation with British support. Harrison however repulsed an Indian attack at the mouth of Tippecanoe Creek in 1811, which made him a national hero-'Old Tippecanoe.' Harrison used his image of 'new frontier hero' during presidential elections in 1840. It was the most colorful the United States had ever experienced.

Harsha, or Harshavardhana (A.D. 590?-647), king of northern India (606-647), patron of the arts, and writer. Harsha added conquered territory to the kingdoms he inherited, establishing a unified monarchy after the anarchy that had followed the Hun invasions of the 5th and 6th centuries. His writings included poetry and 3 well-known Sanskrit plays, *Nagananda*, *Ratnavali*, and *Priyadarsika*.

Hart *See:* Red deer.

Hart, Moss (1904-1961), U.S. dramatist and director. With George S. Kaufman he wrote *You Can't Take It with You* (1936) and *The Man Who Came to Dinner* (1939). He directed the Broadway hits *My Fair Lady* (1956) and *Camelot* (1960).

Hartebeest, large antelope (genus *Alcelaphus*) with a long and narrow head and lyre-shaped horns. Hartebeest used to live all over Africa and are still common in many places. Related to the gnu, they are very fast runners, perhaps second in speed only to the cheetah.

Hartley, Marsden (1877-1943), U.S. artist who experimented with cubism and abstraction and later returned to impressionistic but realistic depictions of natural scenes. He was best known for paintings of his native Maine.

Harun al-Rashid (ar-Rashid; 766-809), fifth Abbasid caliph of Baghdad (r. 786-809) whose empire extended from northern Africa to the Indus River in India. His rule marked the acme of Arab civilization and culture, with an unparalleled flourishing of science and the arts. He appears as a character in many of the stories of the *Arabian Nights*.

Harunobu (Suzuki Harunobu; 1725-1770), Japanese artist who perfected multi-colored printmaking. At a time when the Japanese were limited to black-ink prints with no more than 2 other colors, Harunobu refined a process of using wood blocks to print with as many as 10 colors. His subjects typically captured the calmness and intimacy of ordinary life.

Harvard University, oldest university in the United States, founded by the General Court of Massachusetts in 1636. Originally an educational institution for Puritan ministers, it evolved into a general university. Under the presidency of C.W. Eliot (1869-1910) Harvard developed into one of the world's great universities, with many graduate schools affiliated to it. It now has nearly 200 allied institutions, including libraries, laboratories, museums, and observatories. Harvard University derives its name from John Harvard, the first benefactor of the institution.

Harvestman *See:* Daddy longlegs.

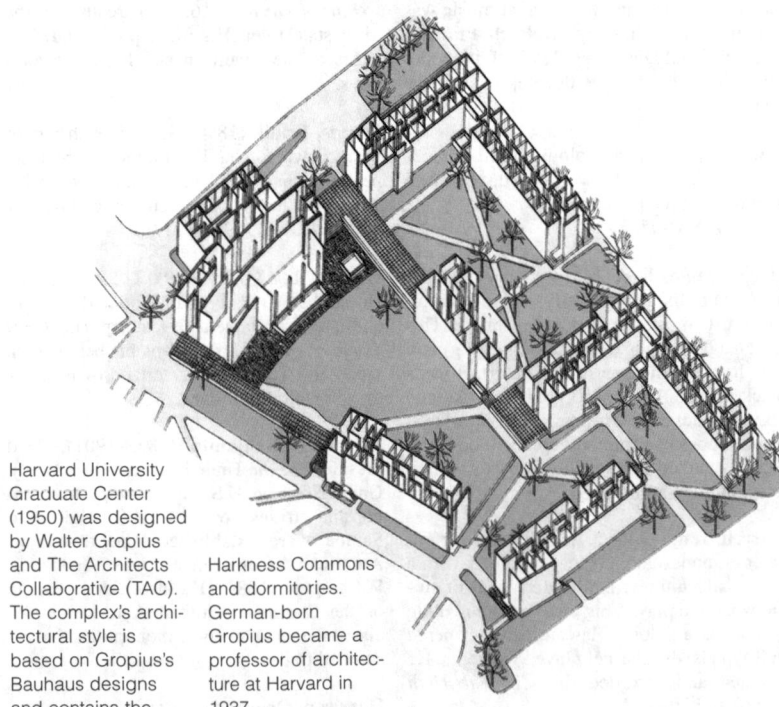

Harvard University Graduate Center (1950) was designed by Walter Gropius and The Architects Collaborative (TAC). The complex's architectural style is based on Gropius's Bauhaus designs and contains the Harkness Commons and dormitories. German-born Gropius became a professor of architecture at Harvard in 1937.

Harvest mite *See:* Chigger.

Harvest moon, popularly, the full moon that occurs nearest to the time of the autumnal equinox (around Sept. 23). The moon rises at about the same time for several nights and may be bright enough to help farmers in harvesting their crops. The effect is most pronounced in high latitudes, such as in Canada. In the southern hemisphere the harvest moon occurs around the time of the vernal equinox (around Mar. 21).

Harvey, William (1578-1657), British physician who pioneered modern medicine, discovering the circulation of blood. In *On the Movement of the Heart and Blood in Animals* (1628) he argued that the heart acts as a pump and that the blood circulates endlessly about the body; that there are valves in the heart and veins that cause blood to flow in one direction only; and that the necessary pressure comes from the lower left-hand side of the heart. His theories were not fully confirmed until the early 19th century. He also made important studies of the development of the embryo.
See also: Circulatory system; Heart.

Haryana (Sanskrit: Dwelling of God; pop. 16,464,000), federal state in North India (from 1966), made up of the Hindi-speaking parts of Punjab; 17,077 sq mi (44,212 sq km). The capital of Haryana and Punjab is Chandigarh, a separate union territory. The city Faridabad Complex is larger, with a population of 620,000. The south is a sandy lowland plain reaching up to the foothills of the Himalayas. There is little rainfall, but a large number of irrigation works: 60% of the land surface is irrigated. Temperatures in the summer reach 48° C. The population is mainly employed in agriculture, which produces rice, wheat, sugar cane, oilseed, cotton, potatoes, millet and corn. Much of the produce is for Delhi, situated nearby.
Haryana is historically important because the first Indian settlements dating back more than five thousand years ago are to be found here. The battle between the Kauravas and Pandavas, mentioned in the Mahabharata and dating back over 2000 years, and the battles of Panipat, which brought India under Mogul government in 1526, also took place here. The British took over in 1802 before they officially colonized India after the uprising of 1857.

Hashemite Dynasty, Arab royal family claiming descent from the grandfather of the prophet Muhammad, hereditary sharifs of Mecca from the 11th century until 1919. After World War I the Hashemites Faisal I and Abdullah Ibn Hussein became kings of Iraq and Jordan respectively; Abdullah's grandson Hussein is the present king of Jordan.

Hashimoto, Ryutaro (1937-), Japanese politician. Hashimoto held several political offices as well as ministerial posts for the Liberal Democratic Party (LDP). Subsequently, he became the LDP party President. In 1996, the Parliament elected him Prime Minister. He was the first postwar Prime Minister to visit the former colony Manchu.

In 1998, he was forced to step down after de LDP was trounced in the elections.

Hashish, drug produced from a resin obtained from the top and the flowers of the hemp plant (*Cannabis sativa*). It is a physically nonaddictive drug whose effects range from a feeling of euphoria to distortion of perception. Hashish comes from the same plant as marijuana (which is made from the dried leaves and stalks), but contains from 5 to 8 times as much Tetrahydrocannabinol (THC), the chemical responsible for the mind-altering effects. Hashish is mainly produced in the Middle East and India and has been in use for many centuries, although it is still illegal in many countries.
See also: Drug; Drug abuse.

Hasidism, Jewish pietistic movement, that can be divided into 3 distinct historical eras. During the 2nd and 3rd centuries B.C. the first Hasidim (Hasideans or Assideans) were devout members of the Jewish faith who resisted Greek influence. In Germany during the Middle Ages there developed a messianic Hasidim known as Hasidei Ashkenaz. In 18th-century Poland, Israel ben Eliezer (Ba'al Shem Tov), reacting against the studious formalism of rabbinical traditions established a movement grouped around *tzadikkim*, holy men, whose followers are *hasidism* ('pious ones'). Hasidism still flourishes in Israel and the United States.
See also: Ba'al Shem Tov.

Haskalah (Hebrew, 'enlightenment'), cultural movement that attempted to reform traditional Jewish customs. It was initiated during the late 18th century by some Jews who had experienced European lifestyle and wanted to modernize Jewish customs to fit more easily into mainstream society, after centuries of Jewish discrimination. Haskalah incorporated such ideas as having Jews wear a more contemporary dress instead of the traditional Jewish clothing and having Jews adopt the local language instead of speaking Yiddish. The movement also encouraged Jews to add nonreligious curriculum to schools and to begin careers in the liberal arts.

Haskil, Clara (1895-1960), Rumanian-Swiss pianist. Haskil studied in Vienna and Paris, where she won the first prize of the Conservatory (1910). Haskil played as a concert pianist together with the violinists Georges Enesco and Eugène Ysaye and the cello player Pablo Casals. In the 1950s, she formed a duet with the violinist Arthur Grumiaux. She owed her fame to her performances of Mozart, Beethoven, and Bach.

Hassan II (1929-1999), king of Morocco since 1961. He initiated a partial democratization in 1962, but retained nearly absolute power, despite an attempted coup in 1971. A protracted war (beginning in 1976) to gain control of Western Sahara, a former Spanish Sahara colony, has strained the Moroccan economy. Hassan II persued a pro-western policy.
See also: Morocco.

Hastings, Battle of, first decisive military encounter of the Norman conquest of England, fought between the troops of King Harold of England and Duke William of Normandy on Oct. 14, 1066. William crossed the English Channel while Harold was in northern England defeating a Norwegian invasion. Forced marches brought Harold south with an exhausted and depleted force. Harold's axmen were swept from a strong hilltop position, and Harold himself was killed in the battle. By 1070 most Anglo-Saxon nobles were dead or expropriated, and a new, French-speaking ruling class was imposed on England.
See also: Norman Conquest.

Hastings, Warren (1732-1818), first governor-general of British India (1774-1784). Starting as a clerk in 1750, he rose high in the British East India Company. Criticized in England as an aggressive and sometimes arbitrary governor, he was impeached (1787) on charges of extortion despite his earlier resignation. He was acquitted after a very long trial (1788-1795).

Hat, head covering, usually with a brim all around it, as distinct from a brimless cap or hood. In various countries and cultures hats symbolize social status or function, as well as being fashion items.

Hathor, or Athyr, in ancient Egyptian religion, goddess of the sky. She has been associated with both Horus, a sky god, and Re, the sun god. Her son, Ihy, was a god of music. Hathor was often pictured as a woman with a 2-horned headpiece that held a sun.
See also: Mythology.

Hatshepsut (d. 1481 B.C.), queen of Egypt, 18th dynasty. She ruled with her husband and half-brother Thutmose II (r. 1512-1504 B.C.), becoming regent to his son and then assuming the powers and titles of pharaoh. She presided over a period of prosperity, and built the great temple of Der el-Bahri near Thebes.

Hatta, Mohammed (1902-1980), Indonesian economist and politician. Hatta joined the movement for independence at an early stage. He was freed from Dutch imprisonment (1934-1942) by the Japanese and together with Sukarno proclaimed the Republic of Indonesia (August 1945). He became vice president (1948-1950) and prime minister. He represented the republicans at the round-table conference and signed the transfer of sovereignty (1949). His moderate attitude later brought him into conflict with Sukarno. In 1956, he resigned as vice premier.

Hauff, Wilhelm (1802-1827), German writer. Particularly renowned for his romantic narratives (*Phantasien im Bremer Ratskeller*, 1827) and fairytales (*Märchenalmanach*, 1826-1828). Also well known are *Das Wirtshaus im Spessart* and *Der kleine Muck*. *Lichtenstein* (1826) was one of the first German historical novels.

Hauptmann, Gerhart (1862-1946), German author and playwright who pioneered naturalism in the German theater. His first

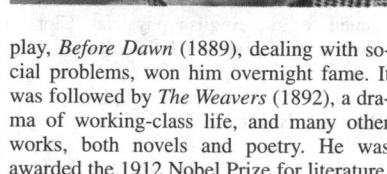

German playwright Gerhart Hauptmann.

play, *Before Dawn* (1889), dealing with social problems, won him overnight fame. It was followed by *The Weavers* (1892), a drama of working-class life, and many other works, both novels and poetry. He was awarded the 1912 Nobel Prize for literature.

Hausa, people of northwest Nigeria and neighboring Niger, numbering about 9 million, predominantly Muslim since the 14th century. Their language, also called Hausa, is widely spoken in West Africa, and they play a major role in Nigerian politics.

Haussmann, Georges Eugène Baron (Baron; 1809-1891), French civil servant, redesigned the city of Paris. With the aim of reorganizing the Parisian inner city and to make it easier to control, Haussmann was ordered to replace the medieval street layout with its narrow, winding alleys, with broad, straight boulevards and large squares (1853-1870). He also had bridges built and the water supply and sewage system were improved.

Havana (pop. 2,2 million), capital and largest city of Cuba, on the Gulf of Mexico. One of the largest cities in the West Indies, it was founded by the Spanish in 1515. It has an excellent harbor and is an industrial center. Oil and sugar refining, tobacco products, and rum distilleries are the main economic activities. The U.S. battleship *Maine* was sunk in Havana harbor and was the incident that ignited the Spanish-American War in 1898. The Cuban Revolution of 1959 deprived Havana of millions of dollars from U.S. tourists. In the early 1990s the government of Fidel Castro made some attempts to revive the previously important tourist industry.
See also: Cuba.

Havelange, Jean Marie Faustin Godefroid (1916-), Belgium sportsman and businessman. As a swimmer, he took part in the 1936 Olympics and as a water polo player in the Olympics in 1952. He worked himself up to become director of a bus company and an insurance company. In 1963, he became a member of the International Olympics Committee. At the start of 1974, he succeeded the legendary Stanley Rous as president of FIFA (world football association).

Havel, Václav (1936-), Czech playwright and political leader, elected president of Czechoslovakia in 1989. A resistence leader

H

H

under the Communist regime from the mid-1960s until 1989, he was repeatedly jailed, and his works (such as the play *The Memorandum*, 1965) were banned. Following the split of Czechoslovakia in December 1992, he became president of the Czech republic. He resigned as President in 2003.

Haversian canals, minute passages in the outer bone layers. The canals carry blood to the inner bone tissue through combined efforts of blood and lymph vessels, nerves, and connective tissues. The canals are surrounded by bone tissue; together they make up a compact bone structure called the *Haversian system*, or *osteon*. The structure is named for the English physician Clopton Havers, who first noted the canals in the 17th century.

Haw *See:* Hawthorn.

Hawaii (The Aloha State; pop. 1,187,000), one of the federal states of the United States of America, in the Pacific Ocean; 6,473 sq mi (16,759 sq km). Capital city: Honolulu (on Oahu). The most important islands are: Hawaii, Maui, Oahu, Kauai, Molokai, Lanai, Niihau, and Kahoolawe. They are of volcanic origin with volcanos that are still active (for example: Mauna Loa, 13,688 ft, 4,172 m). It has a tropical climate with heavy rainfall, in particular on the mountain sides. There are unique plants and wildlife due to the isolation of the islands. Forestry and agriculture (sugar cane and pineapples) for the American market. Plantation farming and the armed forces used to be the main sources of income; tourism and industry recently developed. The marine and airforce base was the target of a Japanese attack in December 1941 (Pearl Harbor), after which America declared war on the Axis powers. James Cook was the first West-European to set foot on the Islands of Hawaii (1788); he was killed here a year later. From 1819 onwards, the US expanded its influence gradually. Hawaii was an independent kingdom well into the 19th century, until Queen Liliukalani was deposed in 1893. In 1898, Hawaii was annexed and in 1959, it became the fiftieth state of the US. In 1974, G. Ariyoshi became the first governor of Japanese descent in the US; he was reelected in 78 and 82.

Hawaiian goose *See:* Nene.

Hawaiian honeycreeper, any of a family (Drepanididae) of small songbirds exclusive to Hawaii. There are 22 species. Honeycreepers have 3 types of bills, each suited to a different method of feeding. Honeycreepers with long, curved bills suck nectar from flowers, those with heavy bills crush seeds and insects, and those with strong, straight bills chisel tree bark. Many of the species are now extinct or endangered.

Hawk, any of various fast-flying hunting birds of the Accipitridae family. Hawks have rounded wings and live mainly in woodlands and forests. Some catch their prey by fast flight while others soar in circles overhead and then drop to catch their prey in their talons. Most hawks feed on rodents or small birds.

Hawke, Robert James Lee (Bob) (1929-), Australian politician. Hawke worked for the Australian trade unions from 1958 to 1980, in the period 1969 to 1980 as the chairman of the coordinating body of unions, ACTU. His actions as a negotiator during important trade talks gave him so much influence in Australian politics that he was nicknamed 'the second Prime Minister'. His activities as a member of the Labour Party led to his chairmanship of that party from 1973 to 1978. In 1983, he became party leader and after Labor's victory in the polls that same year he became Prime Minister. In 1991, Hawke came under pressure due to the economic crisis and division in the party; he resigned the same year. He withdrew from politics in 1992.

Hawkes, John (1926-1998), American writer, important postmodern experimental author with works such as *The Cannibal* (1949), *Lime Twig* (1961), *Second Skin* (1964), *Death, Sleep, and the Traveler* (1972), *The Passionate Artist* (1980) and *Virginie: Her Two Lives* (1982). *Humors of Blood and Skin* (1984) contains a selection of his work. His picaresque novel *Adventures in the Alaskan Skin Trade* was published in 1985. Later novels include *Innocence in Extremis* (1985), *Whistlejacket* (1988), and *Sweet William: A Memoir of Old Horse* (1993). *The Innocent Party* (1966) contains four short plays.

Hawking, Stephen William (1942-), British theoretical physicist and cosmologist who has applied general relativity and quantum mechanics to the theory of black holes in novel ways and produced results of great originality. In 1978 he received the Albert Einstein Award for his work. His book *A Brief History of Time* (1988) helped popularize current thinking on the development of the universe. He holds the post of Lucasian professor of mathematics, once held by Sir Isaac Newton. He has done all of this while suffering from Amyotrophic lateral sclerosis (Lou Gehrig's disease). *See also:* Black hole.

Hawkins, Coleman (1904-1969), U.S. tenor saxophonist. Hawkins's musical style, punctuated by full, energetic tones, forced people to recognize the tenor saxophone as an integral jazz instrument. His improvisational style was well liked internationally and influenced many musicians of the 1930s and 1940s.

Hawkins, Sir John (1532-1595), British admiral. He was a slave trader and ship captain who became treasurer of the navy and sponsored reforms in ship design and gunnery that contributed to victory over the Spanish Armada (1588), also commanding an English squadron during the battle.

Hawk moth, member of the Sphinx moth family. Hawk moths are distinguished by their large, powerful forms and their streamlined and hovering flight patterns. They suck nectar through a long proboscis, a feeding instrument which, in some species, extends as long as 13 in (32.5 cm). These moths are also known as hummingbird moths (because they can stop in front of flowers while sucking nectar) or as sphinx moths (because their resting position and profile resembles the Egyptian sphinx).

Hawks, Howard (1896-1977), U.S. film director who specialized in sharp dialogue and visual clarity. Hawks helped to create the film genre known as screwball comedy, in which the eccentric lifestyles of the rich were ridiculed. His movies include *Dawn Patrol* (1930), *Scarface* (1932), *20th Century* (1934), *The Big Sleep* (1946), and *Red River* (1948).

Hawthorn, any of several hundred species of shrubs and small trees (genus *Crataegus*) of the rose family. In the spring they are covered with fine white or pink blossoms that later turn red or develop into dark blue fruits (haws) resembling tiny apples. In Europe the hawthorn was the subject of many legends. Sprigs of hawthorn were thought to protect people against thunder or witches.

Hawthorne, Nathaniel (1804-1864), major U.S. novelist and short story writer whose novels *The Scarlet Letter* (1850) and *The House of the Seven Gables* (1851) are considered masterpieces of psychological portraiture, capturing the dark atmosphere of Puritan New England. His short stories-collected in *Twice-Told Tales* (1837, 1842) and *Mosses from an Old Manse* (1846)-did much to establish the genre in the United States. He also authored works for young people, *A Wonder Book* (1852) and *Tanglewood Tales* (1853).

Hayakawa, S(amuel) I(chiyé) (1906-1992), Canadian-born U.S. language expert, specializing in the study of semantics. He was also a U.S. senator. Hayakawa became president of San Francisco State College (now San Francisco State University) in 1969 amid numerous student protests and became famous for his firm stand against them. After retiring in 1973, Hayakawa, a Republican, represented California in the U.S. Senate from 1977 to 1983. His books include *Language in Thoughts and Action* (1941) and *Symbol, Status and Personality* (1963). *See also:* Semantics.

Hayden, Melissa (Mildred Herman; 1923-), Canadian-born U.S. ballet dancer, teacher, and director. Hayden was internationally renowned for her performances as a principal ballerina with the New York City Ballet from 1950 until 1973, during artistic director George Balanchine's regime.

Haydn, Franz Joseph (1732-1809), Austrian composer who established the accepted classical forms of the symphony, string quartet, and piano sonata. He was court musician to the Esterházy family from 1761 to 1790 and was a close friend of Mozart. His huge output includes 107 symphonies, hundreds of chamber works and violin and piano concertos, some 25 operatic works, several great masses (notably the *Nelson* mass), and various religious works, including two oratorios *The Creation* (1798) and *The Seasons* (1801).

Hayes, Rutherford Birchard (1822-1893), 19th president of the United States (1877-1881). Republican. Governor in Ohio 1869-1872 and 1876-1877. Hayes won office in a bitterly contested election in 1877: Samuel J. Tilden, Hayes's Democratic opponent, had won more popular votes than Hayes. However, the totals from 4 states were in dispute. To resolve the dispute, Congress appointed a special 15-member Electoral Commission. The Commission, dominated by Republicans, awarded the electoral votes, and the presidency, to Hayes.

Hayes began his term during a period of sectional and economic crisis. By the time he left office, economic prosperity had been restored and Reconstruction in the South brought to a close (1865-1877). These accomplishments carried a high price, however: For Southern blacks, the end of Reconstruction meant the loss of protection for newly won civil rights.

Hay fever, common allergy to the pollen of grasses and trees. Symptoms include rhinitis (runny nose) and conjunctivitis (itching eyes). Susceptibility is often associated with asthma, eczema, and aspirin sensitivity. Possible treatment includes avoiding the things to which the person is allergic, desensitizing injections, antihistamines (drugs that can reduce the severity of attacks), or steroid sprays in difficult cases.

Hay-Herrán Treaty, agreement (1903) between the United States and Colombia that would have given the United States rights to the Panama Canal Zone. When the Colombian congress refused to ratify, U.S. President Theodore Roosevelt gave aid to a revolutionary force, which declared Panama independent.

Hay-Pauncefote Treaties, agreements between the United States and Great Britain negotiated in 1899 and 1901, giving the United States the sole right to construct and control the proposed Panama Canal. The treaty derives its name from the two men who negotiated-U.S. Secretary of State John Hay and the British ambassador to the U.S. Lord Pauncefote. The first treaty was amended by Congress (1900) and then rejected by Britain. The second treaty gave the U.S. the right to control the canal and build fortifications.
See also: Panama Canal.

Hazardous wastes, chemicals and their byproducts that are dangerous to humans or pollute the environment. The Resource Conservation and Recovery Act of 1976 deems a material hazardous if it is poisonous, radioactive, or toxic; corrodes another material; explodes or ignites easily; reacts with water; or is unstable to heat. Industries, factories, laboratories, and hospitals are the biggest producers of hazardous wastes. The harmful effects include polluted groundwater, rivers, and lakes which could severely limit a city's drinking water and food supply. The Superfund Act, also known as the Comprehensive Environmental Response, Compensation, and Liability Act of 1980, helps fund ways to fix unsafe hazardous waste dumps.

Hazel, shrub or small tree (genus *Corylus*) that produces catkins early in the spring. The male catkins are yellow, dangling clusters, like 'lambs' tails.' Pollen from these fertilizes the small red-tipped female flowers, which then produce nuts with a thick green husk. Hazelnuts are edible and are particularly liked by squirrels. A related European tree, the filbert (*C. avellena*), is cultivated for its larger nuts.

Hazlitt, William (1778-1830), English literary critic and essayist. His observations of culture, politics, and English manners appeared in *Characters of Shakespeare's Plays* (1817) and *Lectures on the English Comic Writers* (1819). His wit and versatility are reflected in the miscellaneous essays of *Table Talk* (1821-22) and *The Spirit of the Age* (1825).

H-bomb *See:* Nuclear weapon.

HDTV (High Definition Television) An unclearly defined concept (as is hi-fi). Often understood to be the image enhancement based on 1250 video lines (we have 625 video lines now). There is still a long way to go before this is realized, though, since transmitters and cathode-ray tubes will have to be drastically adjusted. Others see HDTV as widescreen television based on the current 625 video lines, that is to say a screen with the proportions 16: 9 instead of the current 4: 3. This has already been realized, as has the possibility of stereo sound with CD quality.

Headache, common ailment and manifestation of many diseases and disorders involving the brain, eyes, nose, throat, teeth, and ears. Most headaches seem to arise from pressure upon or displacement of the blood vessels of the brain. The major covering of the brain (the dura mater) also registers pain. Other headaches derive from the vessels outside the skull, such as the scalp and neck muscles. Infrequent headaches can usually be related to acute causes, such as fatigue, fever, or the drinking of alcohol. The cause of chronic or recurrent headache is often difficult to diagnose.

Headhunter, one who cuts off the head of a defeated enemy to preserve it as a trophy or for religious reasons or in the belief that it strengthens one's own tribe while weakening the enemy. Many primitive tribes of Malaysia, Borneo, parts of Africa, Melanesia, and South America practiced headhunting.

Headphones, device that allows a person to hear sound reproductions in private. Headphones typically have 2 earphones connected by a band that fits over the head. They are often used when surrounding noise is overpowering or when the user needs freedom of hand movement. Headphones operate much like miniature speakers by transmitting electric sound waves from a central source to a private earphone.

Health, according to the World Health Organization, 'a state of complete physical,

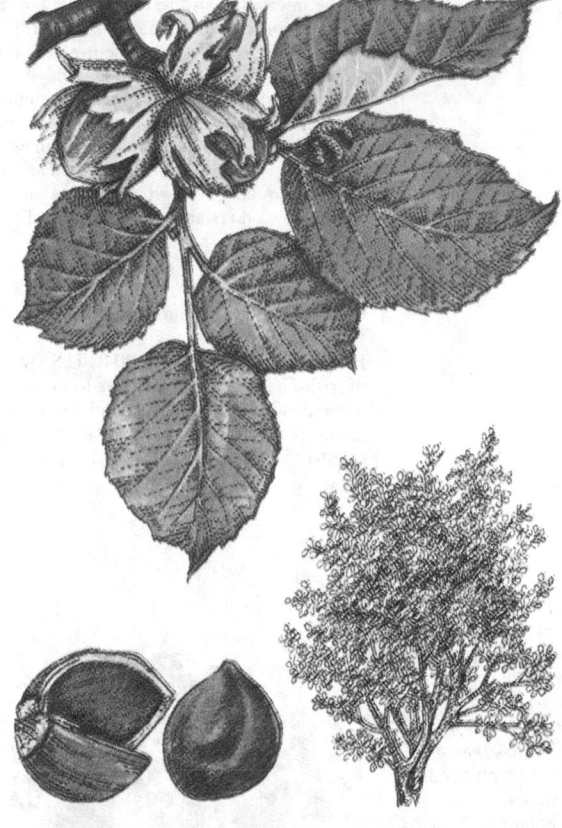

mental and social well-being and not merely the absence of disease or infirmity.'
The practices that help a person to maintain health -including proper nutrition, exercise, and cleanliness- are called hygiene.

Health, public *See:* Public health.

Health Insurance, National (NHI), program that provides health care for a country's citizens. Also known as socialized medicine, NHI began in Germany in the late 1800s and is found in all industrialized countries in the world except the United States.

Heaney, Seamus Justin (1939-), Irish poet. His most famous work is *Death of a Naturalist* (1966). After he had written *Field Work*, he was considered to be one of the greatest living English poets. Other works are *Eleven Poems* I>North (1975), *The Haw Lantern* (1987; Whitbread prize), *Seeing Things* (1991), *The Spirit Level* (1996), *Opened Ground: Poems 1966-96* (1998) and *Electric Light* (2001). He received the Nobel Prize in 1995 and his adaptation of the Old-English *Beowulf* was awarded the Whitbread Prize in 2000.
See also: Beowulf.

Hearing *See:* Ear.

Hearing aid, device to improve hearing by amplifying sound waves. The first hearing aid was a tube called the ear trumpet, a flared tube held up to the ear. The early electronic hearing aid consisted of a small battery-powered amplifier, housed with a mi-

Hazelnuts grow in the wild, but many cultivated varieties have been developed. They are grown especially in Kent, England, and Turkey. The trees do not fruit until they are about 6 years old, but will then continue to do so for as long as 50 years.

crophone in a small case. Signals picked up by the microphone were amplified, then fed via a flexible cord to a small earphone fitting over the ear. Transistors made it possible to reduce the size of hearing aids and to increase efficiency. Modern devices employ advanced microcircuitry and are small enough to be built into spectacle frames or hair slides. Some fit behind the ear and transmit sounds through the bones of the skull, while others are small enough to fit inside the ear.
See also: Ear.

Hearing loss *See:* Deafness.

Hearn, Lafcadio (1850-1904), U.S. writer of Irish-Greek origin. His move to Japan and naturalization as a Japanese citizen brought about his best work: *In Ghostly Japan* (1899), *Shadowings* (1900), *Kwaidan*

(1904), and *Japan: An Attempt at Interpretation* (1904).

Hearst, William Randolph (1863-1951), U.S. newspaper and magazine publisher. Hearst's business acumen emerged early in his career, and he quickly built a huge, powerful newspaper empire. Spending big sums to attract readers, he competed with other publishers by employing sensationalistic journalism, printing splashy headlines, and pioneering color comics. By 1937, Hearst owned 25 daily newspapers and such magazines as *Cosmopolitan*, *Good Housekeeping*, *House Beautiful*, and *Harper's Bazaar*. Politically ambitious, he represented New York in the U.S. House of Representatives (1903-07).

Heart, muscular organ whose purpose is to pump blood through the body. The human

heart is about the size of the closed fist, shaped like a blunt cone and is located in the chest cavity, slightly left of center. The heart is divided into right and left halves by a muscular partition. Each half is subdivided into two cavities, the upper (atrium) and the lower (ventricle). Blood from the veins of the body flows to the right atrium. From there it goes to the right ventricle, which pumps it to the lungs. From the lungs, the blood, now rich in oxygen, is carried back to the left atrium. It then flows into the left ventricle, from where it is pumped throughout the body. A series of valves between the right and left atria and ventricles and at the entrances to the main blood vessels prevent blood from backing up as it circulates. Diseases of the heart and blood vessels, are called cardiovascular diseases. In many countries, heart diseases are the number one cause of death. Three major kinds of heart

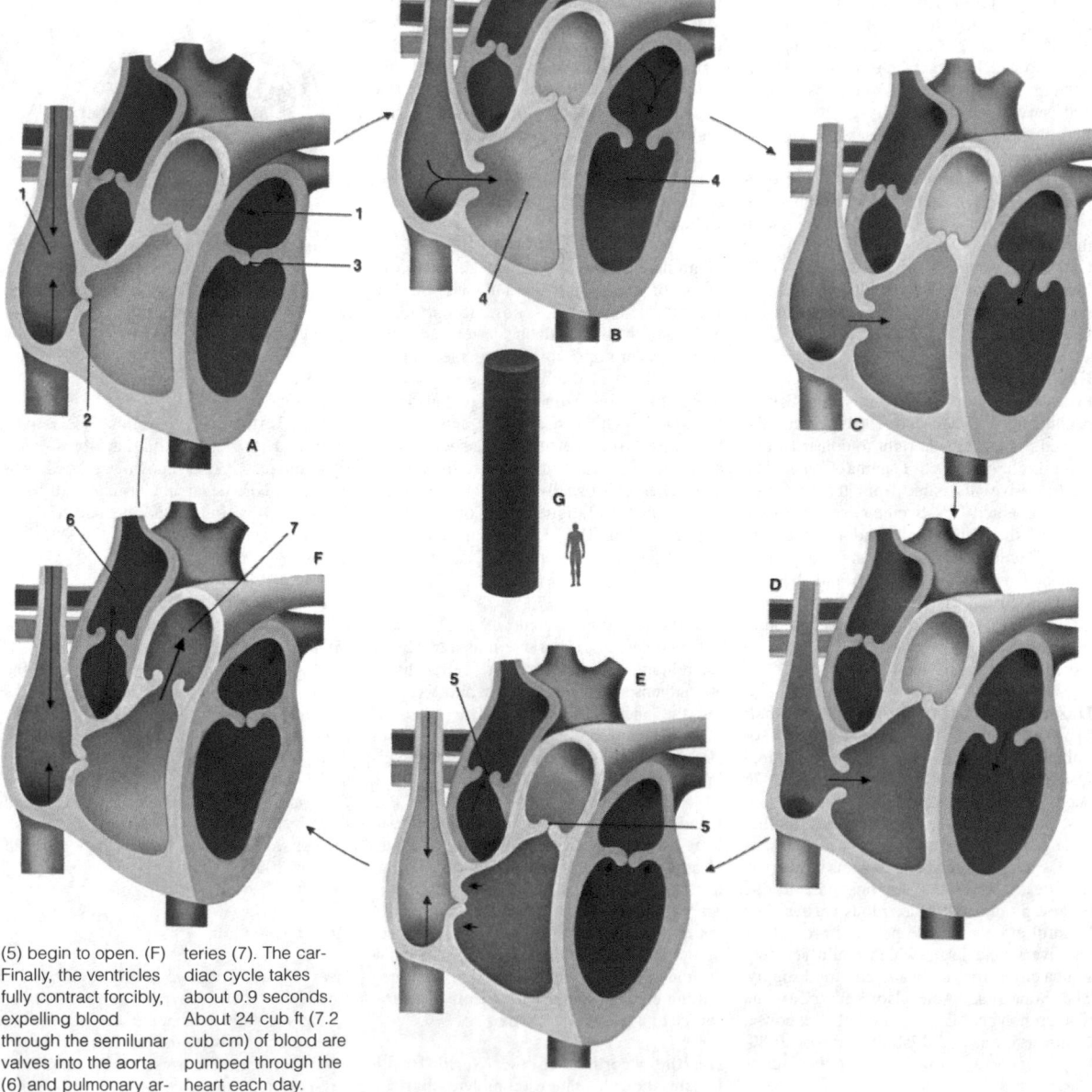

The cardiac cycle begins with a period of relaxation, or diastole, when blood fills the heart. It ends with a period of contraction, or systole, when blood is pumped from the heart. Throughout this cycle, the heart functions as two separate pumps: the right side of the heart accepts deoxygenated blood (blue) from the lungs and the rest of the body, and the left side fills with oxygenated blood (red). (A) During diastole, the atrial chambers (1) fill with blood, during which time the tricuspid (2) and mitral (3) valves are closed. (B) Pressure increases in the atria, and the atrioventricular valves push open, so that blood enters the ventricles (4). (C) The atria and the ventricles are now completely filled with blood. (D) Systole begins when the sinoatrial node of the right atrium fires impulses, thus stimulating the atria to contract and push all the blood into the ventricles. (E) Pressure in the ventricle, which is now engorged with blood, increases, and the atrioventricular valves are forced closed. The semilunar valves (5) begin to open. (F) Finally, the ventricles fully contract forcibly, expelling blood through the semilunar valves (6) and pulmonary arteries (7). The cardiac cycle takes about 0.9 seconds. About 24 cub ft (7.2 cub cm) of blood are pumped through the heart each day.

disease are hypertension, arteriosclerosis, and rheumatic fever.
See also: Circulatory system.

Heart murmur, abnormal sound heard on listening with a stethoscope to the chest over the heart. Normally there are 2 major heart sounds due to valve closure, separated by silence. Murmurs can arise in heart valve disease, with narrowing (stenosis) or leakage (incompetence). Holes between the heart's chambers, valve roughening, and high flow of blood also cause murmurs. Most murmurs are completely harmless.
See also: Heart.

Heat, internal energy of a body resulting from the motion of its atoms and molecules. The kinetic energy of these atoms and molecules is expressed as temperature. The quantity of heat energy may be measured in calories or BTUs (British Thermal Units).
See also: British thermal unit.

Heat capacity, quantity of heat required to increase the temperature of a system or substance 1° of temperature. It is expressed in calories per gram per degree Celsius or British thermal units per pound per degree Fahrenheit.
See also: Heat.

Heath, low woody plants (family Ericaceae) found on poor, acidic soil in parts of Asia and Europe and naturalized in North America. They may cover large areas of country, which are often called heaths. Other names for these plants are *ling* and *heather*. Scottish people have used the tough plants for bedding, thatching, and brooms. Sheep graze the fresh shoots and grouse eat the seeds, and a particularly fine honey is obtained from the bell-shaped flowers. Heaths are often grown in gardens, and white heath, or *bruyère*, of the Mediterranean is used to make briar pipes, manufactured from the roots.

Heath, Edward Richard George (1916-), British prime minister, 1970-1974. He was elected to parliament in 1950, and after holding Conservative Party positions, he became party leader in 1965. As prime minister, he brought Britain into the Common Market (now the European Community). He employed austerity measures to fight inflation and resorted to a 3-day work week to save fuel during a miners' strike. In 1975, a year after being turned out of office, he resigned as party leader. He was a member of the British House of Commons until 1983.
See also: United Kingdom.

Heath hen *See:* Prairie chicken.

Heating, process of providing heat and controlling the temperature in a particular environment. Human beings are warm-blood animals, most comfortable in an atmosphere between 70°F (21°C) and 78°F (26°C). Heating provides a way for people to function in very cold climates. Central heating systems provide consistent and monitored heat for a building or home and are regulated by a thermostat, a device that automatically measures and adjusts an area's temper-

ature. These systems are powered by electricity, gas, or oil and are common in the United States. Other countries often use fireplaces, room heaters, or wood-burning stoves.
See also: Heat.

Heat pipe, device that moves heat while keeping the temperature relatively constant. A heat pipe consists of a sealed metal tube with a porous lining that holds a boiling liquid. To transfer heat, one end is immersed in the heat source, and the liquid's temperature is gradually brought to boiling, which forces the vapor to move to the colder end of the pipe. The vapor then condenses and releases the heat. Heat pipes are extremely efficient because they can transfer large amounts of heat over long distances and keep the temperature constant without using an external power supply.

Heat pump, device that simultaneously transports heat and increases its temperature. To heat an area, the heat pump absorbs outside heat and brings it inside the area. A fluid called a *refrigerant* circulates through the heat pump, absorbs the outside heat, and travels first into a compressor that increases its temperature, and then into a heat exchanger to release its heat to room air. The refrigerant is then filtered through a valve that lowers its temperature and allows the process to begin again. The process can also be reversed to cool an area by absorbing inside heat and discharging it outside the area, as with a refrigerator.
See also: Air conditioning.

Heat rash *See:* Prickly heat.

Heatstroke *See:* Sunstroke.

Heaven, in many religions and cultures, the abode of God, gods or spirits, and the righteous after death. In the Old Testament God, who dwells in heaven, also transcends it. Not until late Judaism was heaven generally regarded as the abode of the righteous. In Christian thought heaven is the eternal home of true believers or the state of living in full union with Christ, which the perfected soul enters after death. In Islam heaven is viewed as a garden where faithful Muslims may see the face of God. In the Eastern religions of Buddhism and Hinduism heaven consists of many levels that must be achieved over many lifetimes until a soul attains the eternal state of nirvana.

Heaves, or broken wind, lung disease of horses, resulting in difficult expiration and a chronic cough. It can be caused by an allergic reaction to poor quality feed, inflammation of the lung airways by dust and mold, and viral or bacterial infections.

Heavy hydrogen *See:* Deuterium.

Heavy water, or deuterium oxide (D_2O), chemical compound that occurs as 0.014% of ordinary water, which it closely resembles. It is used as a moderator in nuclear reactors and as a source of deuterium and its compounds. It is toxic in high concentrations. Heavy water freezes at 38.8°F

(3.8°C) and boils at 214.5°F (101.4°C). Water containing tritium or heavy isotopes of oxygen (^{17}O and ^{18}O) is also called heavy water.
See also: Deuterium.

Hebbel, Christian Friedrich (1813-1863), a German dramatist known for his realistic tragedies. Hebbel was particularly successful in revealing the complex psychological motives of his characters, especially women. He also wrote comedies, lyric verse, and lively diaries. His first tragedy, *Judith* (1839), was introduced in Hamburg. *Maria Magdalena* (1944) follows the tradition of middle-class tragedy started by Gotthold Ephraim Lessing.
Hebbel was born in Holstein. His work attracted the attention of King Christian VIII of Denmark, who awarded him a grant to travel in France and Italy. In 1845 he settled in Vienna.
Other tragedies include: *Herodes und Marianne* (1849); *Agnes Bernauer* (1852); *Die Nibelungen*, a trilogy (1861).

Hebe, daughter of Zeus and Hera and in Greek mythology goddess of youth. She served youth-giving nectar to the gods and goddesses of Mount Olympus and was wife of Hercules.
See also: Mythology.

Hébert, Jacques René (1757-1794), French revolutionary. Through his newspaper *La Père Duchesne* he roused the extremist *sansculottes*. Falsely charged with conspiracy, he was executed in Mar. 1794.

Hebrew, Semitic language in which the Old Testament was written, and official language of the modern nation of Israel. The earliest extant Hebrew writings date from at least the 11th century B.C. Now a sacred tongue and a common written language for religious Jews, Hebrew died out as a spoken language by the 3rd century B.C. but was revived as the language of the modern Jewish nation, largely owing to Eliezer Ben Jehudah, who compiled a Hebrew dictionary in the 19th century. Hebrew is written from right to left.

Hebrews, Epistle to the, New Testament book of unknown authorship, traditionally ascribed to St. Paul. Addressed to Jewish converts to Christianity who were in danger of apostasy, it explains the fulfillment in Christ of the Old Testament.
See also: Bible; New Testament.

Hebrides, group of about 500 islands off the northwest coast of Scotland, fewer than 100 of them inhabited. The Outer Hebrides (Western Islands) include Harris, Lewis, North and South Uist, Benbecula, and Barra; Skye, Mull, and Iona lie among the Inner Hebrides. Apart from tourism, industries include fishing, farming, sheepraising, distilling, and tweed-making.

Hebron (pop. 75,000), city in Jordan, located near Jerusalem on the West Bank, one of the oldest cities in the world. Part of Palestine until 1950, the city has religious significance for Jews, Muslims, and

H

H

Christians alike. Hebron is a center of marketing, industry, and administration for the West Bank region. Israel occupied the city following the 1967 Arab-Israeli War.
See also: Jordan.

Hecate, in Greek mythology, goddess of ghosts and black magic. Originally represented as a beneficial goddess with the power to grant good fortune, she was later associated with evil and the underworld. According to myth, she haunted graveyards and crossroads, attended by hellhounds.
See also: Mythology.

Hecht, Ben (1894-1964), U.S. dramatist, screenwriter, and novelist. He collaborated with Charles MacArthur on the highly successful plays *The Front Page* (1928) and *Twentieth Century* (1932). He also worked on the screenplays for *Gunga Din* (1938), *Wuthering Heights* (1939), and *Notorious* (1946). His autobiography is *A Child of the Century* (1954).

Hector, in Greek mythology, hero prince of Troy, eldest son of the Trojan King Priam and Queen Hecuba and the husband of Andromache. In Homer's Iliad, Hector is the champion of the Trojans, killed in battle by the wrathful Achilles, who drags his body 3 times around the walls of Troy before Priam finally persuades him to give up the body to the Trojans. Hector is sometimes described as the son of Apollo.
See also: Mythology; Trojan War.

Hecuba, in Greek mythology, second wife of Priam, king of Troy and mother to Hector, Paris, and Polydorus. She was taken as a slave by Odysseus after the Trojan War. Upon discovering that King Polymestor of Thrace had murdered Polydorus, Hecuba blinded him and killed his two sons.
See also: Mythology.

Hedge apple *See:* Osage orange.

Hedgehog, small insectivore (genus *Erinaceus*) of Asia, Africa, and Europe covered with spines. Each spine is a modified hair about 1 in (2.5 cm) long. The Eurasian species is the common hedgehog, *E. europaeus*. Nocturnal mammals, they wander about searching the ground for worms, beetles, and slugs. Hedgehogs are able to roll up for protection against predators and become entirely enclosed by the spiny part of the skin.

Hedonism, philosophical doctrine that regards pleasure as the ultimate good. The view of the Cyrenaics and Aristippus (c.435-360 B.C.) was that the sentient pleasure of the moment was the only good, whereas Epicurus thought one's aim should be a life of lasting pleasure best attained by the guidance of reason. In the 19th century, utilitarianism, seeking 'the greatest good of the greatest number,' was a revival of hedonism. Hedonism has often been attacked, for instance by 18th-century English theologian Joseph Butler, who saw pleasure as a bonus when a desire is fulfilled, rather than as an end in itself.
See also: Philosophy.

Dialectic thought received a tremendous impetus from the work of German philosopher Georg Wilhelm Friedrich Hegel (1770-1831).

Hegel, Georg Wilhelm Friedrich (1770-1831), German philosopher of idealism. During his life he was famous for his professorial lectures at the University of Berlin, and he wrote on logic, ethics, history, religion and aesthetics. The main feature of Hegel's philosophy was the dialectical method by which an idea (*thesis*) was challenged by its opposite (*antithesis*), the two ultimately reconciled in a third idea (*synthesis*) that subsumed both. Hegel found this method both in the workings of the mind, as a logical procedure, and in the workings of the history of the world, which to Hegel was the process of the development and realization of the world spirit (*Weltgeist*). His chief works were *Phenomenology of the Mind* (1807) and *Philosophy of Right* (1821). Hegel had an immense influence on 19th- and 20th-century thought and history. Among his many important followers, Karl Marx developed the concept of dialectical materialism, explaining history without resorting to the fundamental idealism of Hegel.
See also: Idealism.

Hegira, also spelled hijra or hejira, flight of Muhammad from Mecca to Medina in A.D. 622, which is the year from which Muslims date their calendar.
See also: Muhammad; Muslims.

Heian period, period in Japanese history (794-1192), which was named after the capital city of that time, Heian. In 794, the Japanese emperor removed the residence from Nara to Heian-kyo, enabling him to free himself of the political influence of Buddhist priests. In the Heian period, the limited power of the emperor was undermined further by the Fujiwara clan and the growth of the shun, estates given by the emperor to Buddhist monasteries, princes, and

civil servants as payment for their services. This landownership was free of taxes and was governed by provincial governors. In the 11th century, half of Japan consisted of shun, which formed the economic base for the medieval feudal system in Japan. In the 9th century, the links with China were broken and the *the process of becoming Japanese* set in. The power of the Fujiwara was upset by the Taira clan. This noble family was in turn beaten by the Minamoto. This meant the end of the Heian period and the beginning of the Kamakura shogunate.

Heidegger, Martin (1889-1976), German philosopher. Influenced by Soren Kierkegaard and Edmund Husserl, he was concerned with the problem of how one's awareness of oneself is dependent on a sense of time and one's impending death. Heidegger rejected traditional metaphysics and criticized many aspects of modern technological and mass culture as a 'forgetfulness of being.' His major work, *Being and Time* (1927), has been fundamental in the development of existentialism, although Heidegger denied he was an existentialist.
See also: Philosophy.

Heidelberg (pop. 132,000), historic city in western Germany, in Baden-Wüttemberg on the Neckar River. Overlooking the city is the ruined castle of the former electors of the Palatinate. Heidelberg has the oldest German university (established 1386). The city is the European headquarters of the U.S. Army.
See also: Germany.

Heidelberg, University of, oldest university in Germany, established in 1386. Modeled on the University of Paris, Heidelberg became a center of Protestant education in the 1500s. Its focus shifted to the study of medievel literature and folklore in 1803. Today its faculties include theology, law, medicine, and philosophy.

Heidelberg man, prehistoric human thought to have lived over 300,000 years ago. Evidenced only by the discovery of a huge jaw found in 1907 near Heidelberg, Germany, Heidelberg man is a European example of *Homo erectus*. Scientists believe Heidelberg man lived by hunting and probably fashioned tools out of stone.
See also: Heidelberg; Prehistoric people.

Heiden, Eric (1959-), American speed skater, probably the best in skating history. Heiden became world champion in 1977 (sprinters, allround juniors, and seniors), 1978 (sprinter, allround, juniors, and seniors), 1979 (sprinters, allround seniors), 1980 (sprinters). He established many world records. During the Winter Olympics of 1980 (Lake Placid), Heiden won the 500, 1000, 1500, 5000, and 10,000 m races. After his career in skating, he was a professional cyclist for the Seven Eleven American team for a short period, after which he studied medicine and worked in television broadcasting.

Heidenstam, Carl Gustaf Verner Von (1859-1940), Swedish writer, who made his debit in 1888 with the neo romantic collection of poems *Vallfart och vandringsår*, (Pilgrimage and Wander Years) which contains many exotic themes and in which he sings the praises of his native country. He demonstrated strong national feeling in *Karolinerna* (The Charles Man) (1898); *Folkungaträdet* (The Tree of the Folkungs) (1905-1907) sketches the birth of medieval society. He received the Nobel Prize for Literature in 1916, in acknowledgement of his importance as a leading exponent of a new age in literature.

Heifetz, Jascha (1901-1987), Russian-born U.S. violinist. He was a child prodigy, giving concerts by 1911, and making his U.S. debut at Carnegie Hall in 1917. His virtuosity and technique were compared to those of Niccolò Paganini. He retired from the concert stage in 1972, but continued to teach at the University of Southern California in Los Angeles until shortly before his death.

Heimlich maneuver, emergency first-aid technique for choking victims whose breathing is blocked by food or a foreign element lodged in the airway. The person applying the technique places his or her arms around the standing victim and puts a fist above the navel; the person then grabs the fist with the other hand and presses in and up with short thrusts.

Heine, Heinrich (1797-1856), German romantic lyric poet and essayist. His best-known work, *Book of Songs* (1827), was influenced by German folk songs. His prose writings, such as *Travel Pictures* (1827-1831), although poignant, are often satirical. His poems have been set to music by composers including Robert Schumann, Franz Schubert, and Mendelssohn.

Heinlein, Robert Anson (1907-1988), U.S. author who specialized in science fiction for both adults and children. He attended the United States Naval Academy and served 5 years in the Navy. This provided Heinlein with a scientific/technological background which, combined with his interests in economics and history, give his novels unusual depth and complexity. Heinlein's *Stranger in a Strange Land* (1961) examines unconventional notions about religion, sex, and morality. His other works include *Tunnel in the Sky* (1955), *Starship Troopers* (1959), *The Moon Is a Harsh Mistress* (1966), and *I Will Fear No Evil* (1970).

Heisenberg, Werner Karl (1901-1976), German mathematical physicist generally regarded as the founder of quantum mechanics. His uncertainty principle (1927) overturned traditional physics. He received the Nobel Prize in physics in 1932.
See also: Quantum mechanics.

Heissenbüttel, Helmut (1921-1996), German poet and writer. He made his debut with the experimental collections of poems *Kombinationen* (1954) and *Topographien* (1956) and evolved into an avant-garde author. Between 1960-1967, he wrote six works that he called *Textbuch*. In these works he played with constantly changing

forms, worked with many quotations, and designed abstract poems of which the graphic design is the main subject. In the 1970s, he began a series of projects: *Eichendorffss Untergang. Projekt 3/1* (1978), *Wenn Adolf Hitler den Krieg nicht gewonnen hätte. Projekt 3/2* (1979), *Das Ende der Alternative. Projekt 3/3* (1980), in which collections of prose, the narrative genres such as fairytales, anecdotes, and short novel are parodied. These works were followed by a number of *Textbücher*. As a literary theoretician, Heissenbüttel became known for his essay *Über Literatur* (1966).

Heizer, Michael (1944-), American visual artist, an exponent of land art. Works on a monumental scale, preferably in the desert. Creates so-called negative sculptures, excavations in the soil in rectangular forms.

Hejira *See:* Hegira.

Hel, in Scandanavian and early German mythology, cruel, greedy goddess of the dead, ruler of the underworld (Niflheim), and daughter of the evil Loki. The underworld itself became known as Hel and, eventually, as a place of punishment like the hell of Christian belief.
See also: Mythology.

Helen of Troy, in Greek mythology, most beautiful of all women. Daughter of Zeus and Leda, she was wife of Menelaus, king of Sparta, from whom the Trojan prince Paris abducted her. The Greeks, seeking to return her to Menelaus, united in a 10-year siege of Troy, finally destroying the city. With the Greeks victorious, she returned to Sparta with Menelaus.
See also: Mythology; Trojan War.

Helgoland, or Heligoland, island in the North Sea. Strategically important to Germany during both world wars, it was the target of extensive Allied bombing during World War II. After the war, the British evacuated the population and destroyed the remaining military installations by setting off high explosives that altered the features of much of the island. Returned to West Germany in 1952, the island has been developed as a resort area.

Helicopter, exceptionally maneuverable aircraft able to take off and land vertically, hover, and fly in any horizontal direction without necessarily changing the alignment of the aircraft. Lift is provided by 1 or more rotors mounted above the craft and rotating horizontally about a vertical axis. Change in the speed of rotation or in the pitch (angle of attack) of all the blades at once alters the amount of lift; cyclic change in the pitch of each blade during its rotation alters the direction of thrust. Most helicopters have only a single lift rotor and thus have a tail-mounted vertical rotor to prevent the craft from spinning around; change in the speed of this rotor is used to change the craft's heading. Helicopter toys were known to the Chinese and in medieval Europe, but because of problems with stability, it was not until 1939, following the success of the autogiro (1923), that the first fully successful helicopter flight was achieved by Russian-born U.S. engineer Igor Ivanovich Sikorsky. Used in combat in Vietnam, the helicopter has become increasingly important in military use. It has given ground forces entree to areas hitherto inaccessible. Its firepower and maneuverability permit close air support of ground forces. Its extreme mobility allows evasive action and the potential to surprise the enemy. Its capacity to hover makes it a relatively stable weapons platform.

In civilian use, helicopters have proved valuable for city-to-airport and city-to-suburb

H

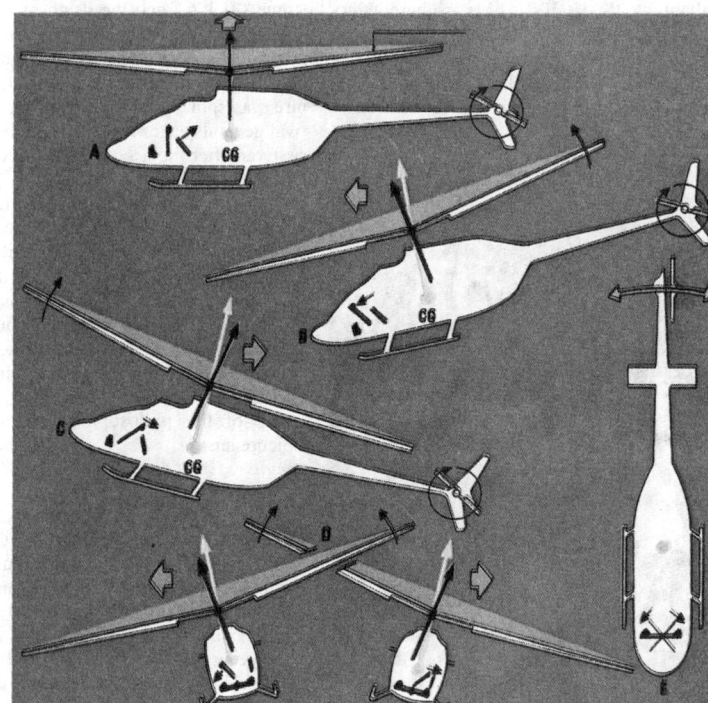

(A) The main rotor lifts along an axis in line with the centre of gravity (CG), while the tail rotor pushes sideways, in order to neutralize the drive torque. In forward flight (B), the main rotor is tilted, in order to give a forward thrust. To stop, or to fly backwards (C), the cyclic pitch lever is pulled back, changing the blade angles, so that the rotor will tilt backwards to give a backward thrust. A helicopter can roll sideways (D) by lateral cyclic movement. This would make it 'crab' sideways, but by operating the 'rudder pedals' (E), the tail will be swung round and the helicopter will change its course.

H

transportation and for monitoring traffic, spotting forest fires, patrolling pipelines, and performing rescue work.

Heliopolis (Greek, 'city of the sun'), ancient Egyptian city located at the apex of the Nile Delta, 6 mi (10 km) from Cairo. It was the center of worship of the sun god Ra until c. 2100 B.C.

Helios, in Greek mythology, god of the sun and son of the Titans Hyperion and Theia. Helios is often represented driving a 4-horse chariot that rises from the ocean in the east in the morning and descends into the western sea at night. In Hellenistic times he became identified with Apollo.
See also: Mythology.

Heliotrope, fragrant plant (genus *Heliotropium*) once popular in gardens. Its name, made up of the Greek words for *sun* and *turn*, points to the fact that it always turns its flowers and leaves to face the sun. The cultivated heliotropes come mainly from Peru and Ecuador, but there are a few North American species.

Helium, chemical element, symbol He; for physical constants see Periodic Table. Helium was discovered by Pierre J. Janssen during the solar eclipse of 1868, when he detected a new line in the spectrum of the sun's chromosphere. After hydrogen, it is the second most abundant element in the universe. It is important in the proton-proton reaction and the carbon cycle, which account for the energy of the sun and stars. In 1907 it was demonstrated that alpha particles are charged helium nuclei. Helium is obtained commercially from certain natural gas deposits with which it is associated. Helium is a monatomic, colorless, inert, lighter-than-air gas. It belongs to group VIIIA of the chemical elements, the inert gases. As a liquid it exists in 2 forms, He I and, below about 2.2 °K, He II. He II is a superconductor. Helium is used in airships and balloons, in synthetic breathing mixtures, for pressurizing liquid fuel rockets, and in lasers. Liquid helium is used in the production of low temperatures.

Hell, in several religions, abode of evil spirits and of the wicked after death, usually thought of as an underworld or abyss. In Christian theology, those damned by God are sent to hell for eternity. The New Testament describes hell as a place of corruption and unquenchable fire and brimstone. Muslims have a similar hell. Buddhists and Hindus may descend into one of many hells because of evil karma, but their souls may leave hell when the effects of the karma are removed.

Hellas, originally the name for a small region in Northern Greece. In the 8th century B.C., it became the name for Greece south of Macedonia. When the Greeks became aware of a common bond in language, traditions, and culture, they called themselves Hellenes and their land Hellas. It must be emphasized that Hellas implicates a cultural unity rather a geographical or political one. Nowadays Hellas is used to indicate the whole of Greece.

Hellebore, any of a genus *(Helleborus)* of perennial plants of the crowfoot family, found mainly in Europe and Asia. It has very thick roots and large flowers. The Christmas rose, or black hellebore (*H. niger*), blooms from late fall to early spring and has white and purple flowers, which contain a strong poison. The American white hellebore, or Indian poke (*Veratrum viride*), is a false hellebore, unrelated to the true hellebores. It can be found from Canada to Georgia and grows from 2 to 8 ft (0.6 to 2.4 m) high, with green flowers. Its roots are used as an insecticide.

Hellenistic Age, period in which Greco-Macedonian culture spread through the lands conquered by Alexander the Great. It is generally accepted to run from Alexander's death (323 B.C.) to the annexation of the last Hellenistic state, Egypt, by Rome (31 B.C.) and the death of Cleopatra VII, last of the Ptolemies (30 B.C.). After Alexander's death, and despite the temporary restraint imposed by Antipater, his empire was split by constant warring between rival generals eager for a share of the territory. Even after the accomplishment of the final divisions (Egypt, Syria and Mesopotamia, Macedonia, the Aetolian and Archaean Leagues in Greece, Rhodes, and Pergamum), Greek remained the international language and a commercial and cultural unity held sway. The age was marked by cosmopolitanism (sharply contrasting with the parochialism of the earlier Greek era), advances in the sciences, and naturalistic art. The Hellenistic age saw the emergence of the philosophies Stoicism and Epicureanism.
See also: Greece, Ancient.

Heller, Joseph (1923-1999), U.S. novelist and playwright best known for *Catch-22* (1961), a grotesquely humorous novel about a U.S. bombardier's 'deep-seated survival anxieties' during World War II. Other satiric works include the play *We Bombed in New Haven* (1967) and the novels *Good as Gold* (1979) and *God Knows* (1984).

Hellespont, ancient name for the Dardanelles, the strait separating Asia Minor from Europe, named for the legendary Helle, who drowned here while fleeing to Colchis with her brother Phrixus.
See also: Dardanelles.

Hellgrammite (*Corydalus cronutus*), large, brown, aquatic larva of the 4-winged dobsonfly. Hellgrammites live beneath rocks in North American streams and feed upon small water animals. When fully mature, they leave the water, cocoon for a 2-week period, and emerge as dobsonflies. Hellgrammites are widely used as fishing bait.

Hellman, Lillian (1905-1984), U.S. playwright, screenwriter, and autobiographer. A mordant social critic, she wrote plays, such as *The Children's Hour* (1934), *The Little Foxes* (1939), and *Watch on the Rhine* (1941), that studied the evil effects of ruthless ambition and exploitation in personal, social, and political situations. Her books of reminiscences, such as *An Unfinished Woman* (1969), for which she won a National Book Award, 1970) and *Scoundrel Time* (1976), are fascinating for their portraits of famous people and events.

Helmholtz, Hermann Ludwig Ferdinand von (1821-1894), German physiologist and physicist. In the course of his physiological studies he formulated the law of conservation of energy (1847). He was the first to measure the speed of nerve impulses, and he invented the ophthalmoscope (both 1850). He also made important contributions to the study of electricity, non-euclidean geometry, and musical acoustics.
See also: Ophthalmoscope.

Helmont, Jan Baptista van (1580-1644), Flemish chemist and physician, regarded as the father of biochemistry. He discovered that there were airlike substances distinct from air and first used the name 'gas' for them.
See also: Biochemistry.

Helms, Jesse Alexander (1921-), U.S. senator from North Carolina. Elected in 1973, he is known for his controversial bill denying a woman's right to seek an abortion during any time in her pregnancy. Other bills he has sponsored include those which support prayer in the public schools and prohibit school busing to achieve racial balance. In 1989-1990 he promoted a stipulation to appropriation bills for the National Endowment for the Arts prohibiting funding of 'obscene' art.

Héloïse *See:* Abelard, Peter.

Helsinki (Swedish: *Helsingfors*; pop. 540,000), capital of Finland, situated on a rocky peninsula of southern Finland, in the Gulf of Finland. Called 'white city of the north' because much of it is built of local white granite, it is Finland's chief industrial center and seaport. Its main industries are shipbuilding, foundries, textiles, and paper and machinery manufacture. Chief exports are timber, pulp, and metal goods. It was

Two or three months of the year, the port of Helsinki is frozen over, but icebreakers generally manage to keep it navigable. Helsinki has about 5 mi (7.5 km) of quays and a maximum harbor depth of 33 ft (10 m).

American author Ernest Hemingway (1899-1961), as photographed by Robert Capa (1913-1954). Capa attained world fame with his photographs of the Spanish Civil War, in which Hemingway worked as a war correspondent.

founded by Swedish king Gustavus Vasa in 1550 and established as the nation's capital in 1812.

Helsinki Accords, final act of the Conference on Security and Cooperation in Europe, which began in 1972, on Aug. 1, 1975, by the United States, Canada, the USSR and 35 European countries. Though nonbinding, it outlines a broad basis for peaceful relations in Europe, particularly between Western and Eastern (Soviet bloc) European nations, including the promise of 21 days notice of military maneuvers by more than 25,000 troops, respect for human rights, and recognition of existing European frontiers. Each side later accused the other of violating these accords. In Sept. 1983, nonetheless, 35 foreign ministers met in Madrid to mark the end of 3 years of negotiations on a document to augment the 1975 accords.

Helvetia *See:* Switzerland.

Helvetians, tribe that lived just east of the Roman province of Gaul, now northwestern Switzerland. When Switzerland was conquered by the Roman emperor Augustus, who ruled from 27 B.C. to A.D. 14, the Helvetians were forced to adopt the language and customs of Rome. The area as still sometimes called *Helvetia* by its residents.
See also: Rome, Ancient; Switzerland.

Hemangioma *See:* Birthmark.

Hematite, common mineral consisting largely of iron oxide. An important iron ore, it is also used for making paints and polishes. Hematite occurs as a gray-black to red-brown mineral in both sedimentary and metamorphic rocks. Hematite may form spectacular shapes. In Brazil it occurs as large flat plates 6 in (15 cm) or more across. In the Alps it is found in masses called iron roses, and in Cumberland, England, it occurs as kidney-shaped red-clack stones. In North America large deposits of hematite are found around Lake Superior and in the Appalachians.

Hemingway, Ernest (1899-1961), U.S. novelist and short-story writer. His terse prose style was widely emulated. His first major novel, *The Sun Also Rises* (1926), chronicled the postwar experiences of what his friend Gertrude Stein called the lost generation of World War I. *A Farewell to Arms* (1929) and *For Whom the Bell Tolls* (1940) were based on his own experiences in World War I and the Spanish Civil War, respectively, and added greatly to his reputation as a writer. *The Old Man and the Sea* (1952) won a 1953 Pulitzer Prize, and he won the Nobel Prize for literature the next year. Increasingly depressed and ill in later years, he committed suicide.

Hemisphere (from the Greek *hemisphairion*, 'half a sphere'), term referring to any half of the earth. The globe can be divided into 3 sets of hemispheres. The northern and southern hemispheres make up one set: everything north of the equator is in the northern hemisphere and everything south of the equator is part of the southern hemisphere. The eastern and western hemispheres form another set: the eastern hemisphere comprises Europe, Asia, Africa, and Australia, and the western hemisphere is made up of North and South America. The generally accepted boundary lines are 20' west and 160' east longitudes. The earth may also be separated into the land hemisphere (the half with the most land, centered close to London, England) and the sea hemisphere (the half made up mostly of water, centered near New Zealand).

Hemlock, or poison hemlock (*Conium macalatum*), poisonous herb of the parsley family found in Europe, Asia, and Africa. Hemlock was used in ancient Greece to put condemned prisoners, including Socrates, to death.

Hemlock, any of a genus (*Tsuga*) of evergreen trees belonging to the pine family. Found in the forests of North America and Asia, hemlock is used both ornamentally and for its lumber, bark, and pulp. Varieties of hemlock include Eastern hemlock (*T. canadensis*), Carolina hemlock (*T. caroliniana*), and Western hemlock (*T. heterophylla*). Poison hemlock is an herb unrelated to the pine family.

Hemoglobin (Hb), oxygen-carrying pigment found in the red blood cells of all vertebrates and some invertebrates. Produced in the bone marrow, hemoglobin carries oxygen from the lungs to the rest of the body.
See also: Blood.

Hemophilia, hereditary disease in which the blood clots very slowly, such that a minor cut or bruise can cause prolonged bleeding, and there is a tendency to bleed internally without any obvious cause. It affects only males, but is transmitted in the genes of females. The genetic defect is the inability to synthesize a protein-factor VIII-needed for normal clotting of the blood. The severity of the disease depends on how much factor VIII is produced by the body; in severe cases, where no factor VIII is made, internal bleeding can lead to massive hemorrhages and can erode the joints of the arms and legs. The disease can now be controlled by giving the hemophiliac transfusions or intravenous injections of factor VIII that has been collected from donated blood. A small percentage of hemophiliacs lack clotting factor IX; this type of hemophilia is known as Christmas disease.
See also: Blood.

Hemorrhoid, commonly called pile, varicose veins of the rectum or anus that may either be internal and bleed frequently, thus producing anemia, or become large and protrude from the anus, causing pain and discomfort. There is no known cause, although they are more common in pregnant women and in those with cirrhosis of the liver. The pain and discomfort can be relieved by the application of suppositories, and they can be treated by the injection of an irritant fluid that will cause scarring around the hemorrhoid and so obstruct it. Surgery can also be employed to close hemorrhoids off. All hemorrhoids should be treated by a doctor. They mimic the early signs of cancer of the rectum and colon, making a proper diagnosis vital.

Hemp (*Cannabis sativa*), tall herbaceous plant of the mulberry family native to Asia but now widely cultivated for fiber, oil, and a narcotic drug called cannabis, hashish, or marijuana. The fibers are used in the manufacture of rope. They are separated from the rest of the plant by a process called retting (soaking), during which bacteria and fungi rot away all but the fibers, which are then combed out. Hemp oil obtained from the seed is used in the manufacture of paints, varnishes, and soaps.

Henan (Honan; pop. 91,720,000) province in Eastern Central China; 64,504 sq mi (167,000 sq km). Capital: Zhengzhou. The most important river is the Huang He, which is used for irrigation. The south is mountainous, but there are fertile lowlands in the north and east, with the cultivation of cereals, cotton, soy beans rice, fruit, and tobacco. There are deposits of iron ore, coal, sulfur, and saltpeter. The industry (cotton and steel) is developing rapidly in the cities of Zhengzou, Kaifeng, and Luoyang.
It is one of the most populous regions of China. The city profited greatly from large-scale projects in the 1950s and 1960s aimed at avoiding floods. In 1975, when two dams burst, 230,000 people died in the floods and of the famine and epidemics that were the result of the flooding.

Henderson, Fletcher (1898-1952), jazz musician who first introduced the 'big band' sound. His band, which used written arrangements as well as improvised material, helped pave the way for the more formalized dance orchestras of the 1930s. Although never achieving the popular success critics felt he deserved, he played a part in bringing to public attention such famous musicians as Louis Armstrong, Benny Goodman, and Coleman Hawkins.

H

H

Hendrix, Jimi (1942-1970), U.S. rock music performer. An unconventional musician, he experimented with the electronic guitar, creating new sounds and expanding the guitar's capabilities. Hendrix's music was frequently loud and characterized by long, emotional solos and a powerful beat. After playing with various rhythm and blues musicians, he went to England in 1966 and formed a band called the Jimi Hendrix Experience, which enjoyed worldwide success with numerous world tours and concert performances. Hendrix died in London of a drug overdose.

Henequen, fiber made from the henequen plant. The leaves of the henequen, a plant that grows on the Yucatan peninsula in Mexico, consist of tough yellow fibers that are separated by machine and then dried to make twine and rope. Mexico is the only important producer of this fiber.

Heng Samrin (1934-), Cambodian politician. Heng joined the guerilla movement, Red Khmer in 1959. Within the movement, he belonged to the wing that mostly focused on Vietnam and believed in Scialist politics. He turned against Pol Pot's administration and fled to Vietnam after an unsuccessful coup. After the Vietnamese army banished Pol Pot in 1979, Heng became head of the government (chairman of the Revolutionary Peoples' Assembly). His government, supported by Vietnam, was not acknowledged by the West or by China - they supported the resistance movements, including that of Prince Sihanuk. Heng Samrin enhanced his position in 1981 by becoming leader of the Revolutionary People's Party of Kampuchea (at that time the only party in Cambodia). In 1990 a peace plan was drawn up with the co-operation of the UN. The Vietnamese troops withdrew and a multiparty system was instituted. In 1991, the highest authority fell into the hands of Sihanuk (chairman of the Highest National Assembly) and Heng Samrin lost his position as head of state.

Henna (*Lawsonia inermis*), small shrub from whose leaves an orange dye is extracted. The plant grows in Africa, southern Asia, and Australia. Its leaves are dried, then pounded and mixed with water to make a gumlike substance. This is applied to fabrics or to the skin and hair to dye it rust red. The use of henna as a cosmetic dates back to ancient Egypt, and its use is widespread in Asia and northern Africa, where many women paint intricate patterns on hands and feet, while men dye only the palms of the hands and the beard.

Henry VIII (1491-1547) was captured in a majestic pose by his court painter Hans Holbein the Younger (Museo Nazionale d'Arte Antica, Rome).

Hennepin, Louis (1640-1701?), Belgian Franciscan missionary and explorer. He went to Quebec (c.1675) as chaplain to La Salle and joined his 1679 expedition. Captured but well treated by Sioux, he was rescued in 1680. His exaggerated accounts of his travels were very popular.

Henry, Joseph (1797-1878), U.S. physicist best known for his electromagnetic studies. His discoveries include induction and self-induction, though in both cases Michael Faraday published findings first. He also de-vised a much improved electromagnet by insulating the wire rather than the core, invented one of the first electric motors, helped Robert Morse and Sir Charles Wheatstone devise their telegraphs, and found sunspots to be cooler than the surrounding photosphere.
See also: Electromagnetism.

Henry, O. (William Sidney Porter; 1862-1910), U.S. short-story writer noted for the 'surprise ending.' He began writing stories while imprisoned in Ohio for embezzlement, and was already popular when released. He moved to New York City in 1902 and wrote over 300 stories, collected in *The Four Million* (1906), *The Voice of the City* (1908), and many other books. His last years were marred by an unhappy marriage and financial difficulties.

Henry (England), name of 8 kings of England. **Henry I** (1068-1135), reigned 1100-1135. The son of William I, he seized the English throne on the death of his brother William II, while his other brother, Robert, was on a Crusade. **Henry II** (1133-1189), reigned 1154-89, was the grandson of Henry I. He founded the Plantagenet line. In 1152 he married Eleanor, Duchess of Aquitaine, thus acquiring vast lands in France. His policy of strengthening royal authority in England led to conflict with Thomas à Becket, the archbishop of Canterbury, who was murdered in 1170. **Henry III** (1207-1272), reigned 1216-1272, was a grandson of Henry II. His unpopular rule was marked by administrative and diplomatic incompetence and by the revolts of nobles who forced him to yield much power to them. **Henry IV** (1367-1413), was the first ruler of the House of Lancaster. He usurped the throne after forcing Richard II to abdicate. His reign was marked by struggles with Owen Glendower and Sir Henry Percy. **Henry V** (1387-1422), reigned 1413-1422, was the son of Henry IV. He defeated the French at Agincourt in 1415, married Catherine of Valois, and became successor to the French throne. **Henry VI** (1421-1471), reigned 1422-1461 and 1470-1471, became king as an infant. The country was ruled by 2 of his uncles, who led the English forces that were defeated by the French under Joan of Arc. Henry VI's rule was marked by factional struggles that led to the dynastic Wars of the Roses. He was deposed for 9 years and eventually murdered. **Henry VII** (1457-1509), reigned 1485-1509, was the first of the Tudor rulers, uniting the houses of York and Lancaster. He killed Richard III in the last battle of the Wars of the Roses. He restored order to England and Wales and promoted efficient administration. **Henry VIII** (1491-1547), reigned 1509-1547, was the son of Henry VII, and was one of the most powerful and formative rulers in British history. His religious policies and matrimonial problems led to clashes with the Pope and the Act of Supremacy (1534), in which Parliament renounced papal authority and established the Church of England with the king as supreme head. He replaced feudal authority with a central system of government and created the navy that later became the basis of British world pow-er. His matrimonial problems, which led to the conflict with the Catholic Church, arose from his search for a male heir. He was first married to Catherine of Aragon, whom he divorced for Anne Boleyn (mother of Elizabeth I). He had her beheaded, then married Jane Seymour (mother of Edward VI), who died in childbirth. His next wives were Anne of Cleves (divorced within a year), Catherine Howard (beheaded), and Catherine Parr, who survived him.
See also: England.

Henry (France), name of 4 kings of France. **Henry I** (c.1008-1060) reigned 1031-1060. His rule was disturbed by feudal conflicts organized by his mother and brother. One of his chief enemies was the future William I of England. **Henry II** (1519-1559) reigned 1547-1559. In 1533 he married Catherine de Medícis, but he was dominated by his mistress, Diane de Poitiers, and his military commander, Anne de Montmorency. A fanatic Catholic, he persecuted the Huguenots and continued the war against the Holy Roman Emperor and Spain. **Henry III** (1551-1589) reigned 1574-1589. He collaborated with his mother Catherine de Medícis in the Saint Bartholomew's Day massacre (1572). He was dominated by the Guise family, and his reign was unstable. He was assassinated by a Jacobin friar. **Henry IV** (1553-1610), who reigned 1589-1610, was king of Navarre 1572-1610, and the first French Bourbon king. A protestant leader of the Huguenots, he converted to Roman Catholicism in 1593, granting religious freedom with the Edict of Nantes (1598). He brought unity and economic stability to France but was assassinated by a Catholic extremist.
See also: France.

Sixteenth-century equestrian portrait of Henry IV (r. 1589-1610; Musée Condé, Chantilly).

Henry (Germany), name of 7 kings of Germany, 6 of whom were also Holy Roman emperors. **Henry I**, or Henry the Fowler (c. 876-936), reigned 919-936. He established Germany as a new kingdom. **Henry II** (973-

1024) reigned 1002-1024 and was emperor from 1014. By political astuteness he ensured secular and clerical support. He was canonized in 1146; his feast day is July 15th. **Henry III** (1017-1056) reigned 1039-1056 and was emperor 1046-1056. During his reign the Holy Roman Empire was probably at its greatest power and unity. He carried out important papal reforms. **Henry IV** (1050-1106) reigned 1056-1105 and was emperor 1084-1105. He deposed Pope Gregory VII, but Gregory excommunicated him, and Henry yielded to papal authority at Canossa in Italy in 1077. Gregory then supported a rival king of Germany, and Henry replaced him with the antipope Clement III. He captured Rome in 1084 and was crowned emperor. After 2 sons rebelled against him, he was forced to abdicate in favor of his son Henry V. **Henry V** (1081-1125) reigned 1105-1125, as emperor 1111-1125. He unified Germany and continued Henry IV's struggle against the papacy. **Henry VI** (1165-1197) reigned 1190-1197, as emperor from 1191. He was made king of Sicily in 1194. He died before being able to implement plans to invade the Holy Land. **Henry VII** (c.1275-1313) reigned 1308-1313, as emperor from 1312. He invaded Italy in 1310 in an abortive attempt to make it the base of imperial power.

Henry of Navarre *See:* Henry (France).

Henry the Navigator (1394-1460), Portuguese prince, third son of King John I of Portugal, whose active interest inaugurated Portuguese maritime exploration and expansion overseas. He sponsored the exploration and mapping of the west coast of Africa, and his expeditions discovered the Madeira and the Azore islands and rounded Cape Verde.
See also: Exploration.

Henson, Jim *See:* Muppets.

Henze, Hans Werner (1926-), German composer. He is known for his symphonies, concertos, and operas, which include *Elegie für junge Liebende* (1961), *Die englische Katze* (1980-1982), *Orpheus behind the wire* (1984), and *Das verratene Meer* (1990).

Hepatica, or liverwort, plant (genus *Hepatica*) of the buttercup family with 3-lobed leaves that derives its Latin and English names from its resemblance to the human liver. Medieval doctors used it as a cure for liver diseases. It is an almost stemless plant about 3 in (7.6 cm) high that grows in woodlands and produces brightly colored flowers in the spring. After the flowers have died, new leaves sprout and displace the old foliage that has persisted over the winter.

Hepatitis, inflammation of the liver, caused by a virus. The symptoms include fever, nausea, loss of appetite, and jaundice. At least two distinct forms of the disease are recognized. Hepatitis A (formerly called infectious, or epidemic, hepatitis) is spread by contaminated drinking water or food. In young children, the infections tend to be mild, but the clinical severity increases with the age of the patient. Hepatitis B (formerly called serum hepatitis) is usually transmitted by transfusions of infected blood or blood products. It is particularly common among intravenous drug users, who may use contaminated needles. The Hepatitis B virus has been detected in a variety of body secretions, including saliva, sperm, and vaginal fluid, and may be transmitted by some forms of sexual contact. Exposure to hepatitis B usually results in an acute self-limiting infection with mild symptoms. In adults, 5-15% of infections fail to resolve, and the affected individuals become persistent carriers of the virus, which is responsible for many cases of liver cancer. There is a vaccination against hepatitis B. In recent years, a third form of the disease, sometimes called hepatitis C, has been detected. Its cause is not known.
See also: Liver.

Hepburn, Katharine (1907-), U.S. stage and film actress. She has won 4 Academy Awards for best actress, for *Morning Glory* (1933), *Guess Who's Coming to Dinner* (1967), *The Lion in Winter* (1968), and *On Golden Pond* (1981).

Hephaestus, or Hephaistos, Greek god of fire. Blacksmith to the gods and the patron of metalworkers, he was responsible for such works as Achilles' armor and Zeus's throne. A powerful god, he was also lame. His marriage to Aphrodite represented the union of Art and Beauty.
See also: Mythology.

Hepplewhite, George (d. 1786), English furniture maker and designer, influenced by Robert Adam. His furniture is characterized by elegant, fine carved forms and painted or inlaid wood.

Heptarchy (from the Greek for 'rule of seven'), the 7 kingdoms of Anglo-Saxon Britain before the 9th-century Danish conquests. The kingdoms, founded by the Angles, Saxons, and Jutes, were Kent, Sussex, Wessex, Essex, Northumbria, East Anglia, and Mercia.

Hepworth, Dame Barbara (1903-1975), English sculptor. Her abstract work in stone and bronze, like that of Henry Moore, is concerned with surface textures and the contrast of space and mass.

Hera, in Greek mythology, queen of the Olympian gods and sister and wife of Zeus; the goddess of marriage and birth. A jealous and quarrelsome wife, she often persecuted those who rivaled her for Zeus's affections. She was the patroness of the cities of Argos, Sparta, and Mycenae and the island of Samos. Her sacred symbols were the cow and the peacock. Hera is often represented as a regal figure wearing a bridal dress, carrying a scepter or with a wreath on her brow. The Romans identified her with the goddess Juno. A supporter of the Greeks against the Trojans in Homer's *Iliad*, she was also the protector of heroes.
See also: Mythology.

Heracles *See:* Hercules.

Heraclitus (c.540-c.480 B.C.), Greek philosopher. His main theory was of universal impermanence ('You cannot step twice into the same river') and the interrelation of all things, especially opposites. He held that fire was the fundamental element of the universe.
See also: Philosophy.

Heraldry, system of devising designs or insignia displayed on shields or coats of arms to identify individuals, families, towns, universities, military regiments, or nations. Heralds of the Middle Ages announced tournaments and became expert in identifying

The bands of simple color, most commonly used on shields for the purpose of distinction, are known as ordinaries. They are often the only object on the shield.
1. chief; 2. fess; 3. bars; 4. bend sinister; 5. pale; 6. paly; 7. bend dexter; 8. bendy dexter; 9. chevron; 10. pile; 11. saltire; 12. cross.

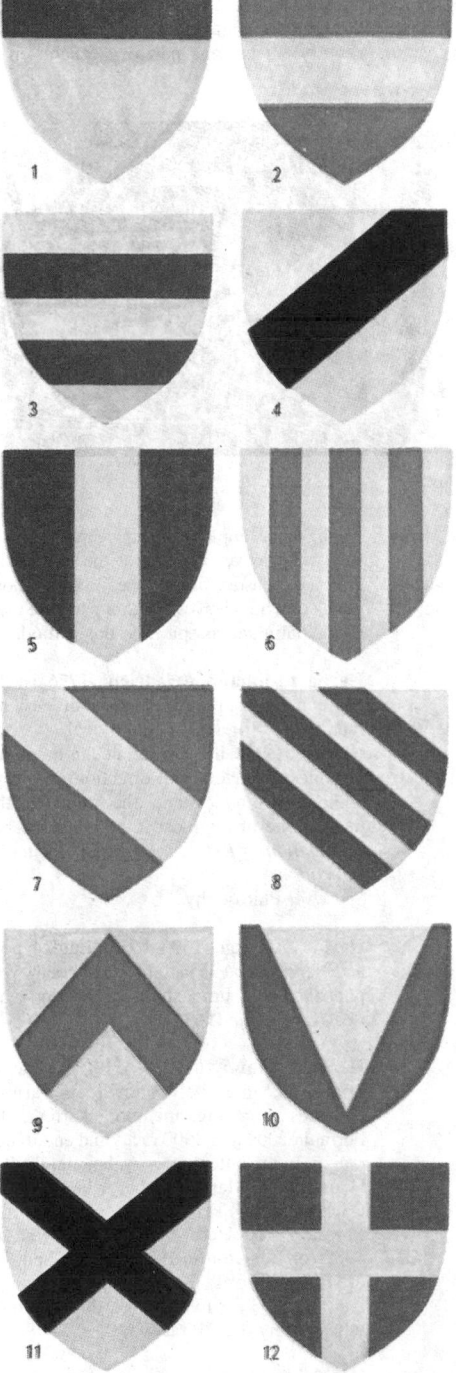

H

the armorial bearings of the participants. The origins of heraldry is uncertain but may have begun in 12th century Germany. Heraldry proliferated throughout Europe due to the popularity of tournaments which attracted Knights from many regions of Europe.

Herat (pop. 260,000), capital of the province of the same name in Northwest Afghanistan, along the Hari River. (province: 23,683 sq mi (61,315 sq km) pop. 808,000). Center of an area dominated by the cultivation of fruit, roses, and grapes. The manufacture of textiles and carpets takes place here. It is a walled city, conquered by Alexander the Great (4th century B.C.), destroyed by the Mongols (1222) and the center of culture under Timur Lenk (14th century). It became part of Afghanistan in 1863.

Hercules is the most important hero in Greek mythology. One of his famous twelve tasks, was to chain up the dog Cerberus. Picture on an amphore, around 510 B.C., from Vulci (Etruria), and made by the so-called Andocides painter (Louvre, Paris).

Herb, name applied to any plant with soft stems and leaves that die at the end of the growing season; more specifically, those plants of which leaves or other parts are used medicinally and as spices to flavor food.

Herbart, Johann Friedrich (1776-1841), German philosopher and educator best remembered for his pedagogical system, which stressed the interrelated importance of ethics (to give social direction) and psychology (to understand the mind of the pupil). One of his most important works is *Application of Psychology to the Science of Education*.
See also: Philosophy.

Herbert, George (1593-1633), English poet and clergyman. His metaphysical poetry was published posthumously in a collection entitled *The Temple* (1633).

Herbert, Johnny (1965-), English racing driver, became well known in various branches of racing, including karting, the Formula 2000 and 3000 races and endurance racing. In the latter category, he won the 24-Hours at Le Mans together with Bertrand Gachot and Volker Weidler in 1991 in a Mazda 787B. Herbert made his debut in 1989 for Benetton in Formula One and has driven for Tyrrell, Lotus, and others since then. In 1993, he reached fourth place three times during the GP races.

Herbicide, chemical compound used to kill plants. Selective herbicides kill only weeds.

Nonselective ones are used to clear land of plant life. Many of these chemicals are dangerous to human and animal life and must be used with great care. One of the more deadly herbicides in recent history was Agent Orange, a defoliant used by the U.S. during the Vietnam War. It is responsible for serious illnesses among veterans and their offspring.

Herbivores, dietary classification of the animal kingdom including all animals that feed exclusively on plant materials. Preyed on by many carnivorous animals, they form the lower links of food chains.

Hercegovina *See:* Bosnia and Hercegovina.

Herculaneum, ancient city at the foot of Mt. Vesuvius in Italy. Along with Pompeii, it was destroyed in A.D. 79 by the eruption of Vesuvius, which engulfed it in preservative volcanic mud. Rediscovered in 1709, it is still being excavated.
See also: Vesuvius, Mount.

Hercules, or Heracles, in Greek mythology, hero famed for his strength and courage. The son of Zeus and Alcmene, he was hated by Zeus's wife Hera, who caused him to go mad. While insane, he killed his own wife and children. He then tried to purify himself by performing 12 labors set for him by King Eurystheus. After his death he rose to Mount Olympus, the dwelling place of the gods and made his peace with Hera.
See also: Mythology.

Hercules, constellation located in the Northern Hemisphere. In the southernmost part of the constellation, a huge red star marks the head of Hercules. The northwest side of the constellation, 30,000 light-years away from earth, is barely visible without a telescope.

Hercules beetle, any of a genus (*Dynastes*) of large beetles belonging to the scarab family and found in North America. Males of the species have pincer-like horns that curve out from the head and upper body. Some male Hercules beetles may grow. to 5 or 6 inches (13 to 15 centimeters) in length.

Herder, Johann Gottfried von (1744-1803), German writer, critic, philosopher, and clergyman. A leader of the *Sturm und Drang (Storm and Stress)* movement in German literature, his ideas about poetry, art, language, religion, and history influenced many prominent theorists and writers. Opposed to German imitations of classic works, he translated folk songs as well as the plays of Shakespeare. These translations helped inspire the work of the German Romanticists who followed him, particularly Goethe.

Heredity, process by which characteristics are passed on to offspring. Inherited characteristics are passed on in units called genes. Genes are normally located on the chromosomes in the nuclei of cells. Each chromosome carries many genes that may be transmitted together and are said to be 'in coupling.' The genetic composition, or genome, of an individual is established at conception;

thereafter, a complex interaction of genes and environment (both internal and external) shapes his or her development.
See also: Genetics.

Herman, Woody (Woodrow Charles Herman; 1913-1987), U.S. musician and band-leader. He flourished during the 1930s and 1940s, but remained popular beyond the big band era because of his ability to adapt to changing styles in jazz. Herman played the clarinet and alto saxophone. His best known song was 'Woodchopper's Ball' (1939).
See also: Jazz.

Hermaphrodite, organism with both male and female reproduction organs. Usually, an individual functions in only 1 sexual role at a time, but in a few species, e.g., earthworms, each of a pair of partners fertilizes the other during copulation. Hermaphrodite plants are usually referred to as being bisexual.

Hermes, in Greek mythology, one of the 12 Olympian gods, son of Zeus, messenger of the gods, guard of roads and highways, and guide of souls to Hades. He was usually depicted wearing a hat with wings. The Romans identified him with Mercury.
See also: Mythology.

Hermes of Praxiteles, statue of Hermes, messenger of the gods in Greek mythology, created by the Athenian sculptor Praxiteles in 330 B.C. It portrays Hermes holding his infant brother Dionysus and offering him grapes. The original statue was lost, but a copy was made by the Greek sculptor Pasiteles c.100 B.C.

Hermitage, Russian art museum in St. Petersburg. Its famed collections, begun by Empress Catherine II in the 18th century, contain art treasures obtained worldwide, including masterpieces by Rembrandt, Picasso, and Matisse.

Hermit crab, crustacean with soft body that occupies the empty shells of sea snails. The hermit crab has a spiral-coiled abdomen, well-developed pincers, and two pairs of walking legs. It withdraws into the borrowed shell if attacked.

Herndon, William Henry (1818-1891), U.S lawyer and biographer (1889) of Abraham Lincoln, his friend and law partner from 1843. His portrayal of Lincoln is considered a valuable record of the president's life.

Hernia, protrusion of an internal organ through an opening in the wall surrounding it. Hernias may be congenital or caused by muscle weakness in the lower abdomen (inguinal hernia), diaphragm (hiatus hernia), or navel. Corrective surgery is sometimes necessary.

Hero and Leander, tragic lovers in Greek folklore. Hero was a virgin priestess of Aphrodite. Every night Leander would swim across the Hellespont, or Dardanelles, to meet her, guided by a light from her tower.

One night a storm blew out her lamp and Leander, unable to see his way across, drowned. The next morning, when Hero saw his body floating in the water, she drowned herself in sorrow.
See also: Mythology.

Herod, dynasty ruling in Palestine for nearly 150 years around the time of Jesus. The family fortune was founded in c. 65 B.C., but its best-known leader was **Herod the Great** (73-4 B.C.), who ruled Judaea from 37 B.C. His allies, who helped preserve his powers, included Marc Antony and Augustus. Although he was a skilled ruler, he was hated for his ruthlesness, ordering the massacre of the Innocents. His son **Herod Antipas** (21 B.C.-A.C. 39) ruled Galilee at the time of the crucifixion of Jesus and had John the Baptist executed.

Herodotus (484?-425? B.C.), Greek historian, often called 'the Father of History' for his writings about the causes of the Persian Wars fought between Greece and Persia (499-479 B.C.). Although his accuracy is often questioned, he was the first to treat human history in a narrative form. His work is characterized by warmth and a great diversity of information.

Heroin, highly addictive narcotic derivative of morphine. The symptoms of withdrawal may appear as early as 4 to 6 hours after the last dose of the drug; they generally peak within 36 to 72 hours. Heroin acts primarily on the central nervous system, and continued use can lead to addiction. In large doses heroin can be fatal. Treatment programs for physical and psychic dependancy involve counseling and the use of such drugs as methadone to reduce the trauma of withdrawal, and naltrexone to take away the craving for heroin.
Heroin was discovered during the search for a nonaddictive morphine substitute. It was first marketed in 1898 in Germany as a pain reliever. The drug was not carefully tested, and heroin's powerful addictive properties were not recognized until 1902. Because of its addictive nature, the manufacture, import, and use of heroin is banned in most countries. England and Canada have legalized the use of heroin for reducing pain in cancer patients who are terminally ill.
See also: Drug; Drug abuse.

Heron, long-billed, long-legged wading bird of the family Ardeidae. Herons are predators, with sharp bills that can kill frogs, fish, eels, and watervoles. The egret is in the same family.

Herpes, virus with various forms, causing painful blisters usually on the lips or genitals. The best known of several related herpes viruses is herpes simplex. It is the cause of the common cold sore (fever blister) that frequently appears on the lips. The herpes simplex infection is usually acquired before the age of 5. The virus then becomes dormant but causes recurrent blisters throughout the life of the infected person. In most instances, the sores heal within a week or two and are not serious. Herpes simplex II causes sores in, on, and around the genital

organs and urinary passageways. Genital herpes can cause miscarriage, especially in the early months of pregnancy, and can also damage the central nervous system of the fetus. A third strain of the virus is called herpes zoster, or varicella-zoster virus, the cause of chicken pox and shingles. While chicken pox is commonly a childhood disease, herpes zoster generally occurs in late-middle and old age.

Herrera, Tomás (1804-1854), Panamanian political leader. He led the 1840 movement to make Panama a free state, separate from Colombia. He served as president of Panama during its single year of independence. Herrera later became a high-ranking Colombian official and put down a rebellion in 1854.
See also: Panama.

Herrick, Robert (1591-1674), English lyric poet. Writing in the classical tradition of the Latin lyricists, he was also greatly influenced by the dramatist Ben Jonson. His poems are concerned with nature, youth, and love. His best-known line: 'Gather ye rosebuds while ye may.' Most of his work appeared in *Hesperides* (1648).

Herring, narrow-bodied blue and silver fish of the family Clupidae, common in the North Atlantic and the Pacific. Herring schools often contain millions of fish and are food for many other animals. They feed on plankton, minute sea organisms. Most of the herring eaten by people is preserved by salting or smoking.

Herriot, Edouard (1872-1957), French politician. As leader of the Radical Socialists Herriot was elected premier of France 3 times (1924-1925 and 1932). In 1942 he was imprisoned by the Germans for opposition to the Vichy government. He later became president of the National Assembly (1947-1954).
See also: France.

Herschel, family of British astronomers of German origin. **Sir Frederick William Herschel** (1738-1822) built reflecting telescopes, discovered Uranis (1781), showed the sun's motion on space (1783), discov-

ered the relative orbital motion of double stars (1793), and studied nebulae. His sister, **Caroline Lucretia Herschel** (1750-1848), discovered eight comets. His son **Sir John Frederick William Herschel** (1792-1871) published a catalog of nebulae and clusters, first used sodium thiosulfate as a photographic fixer, and studied polarized light.
See also: Astronomy.

Hersey, John Richard (1914-1993), U.S. author, Pulitzer Prize winner with his first novel, *A Bell for Adano* (1944). His experiences as a war correspondent gave him material for his books, which include *Hiroshima* (1946) and *The Wall* (1950).

Hertz, Gustav Ludwig (1887-1975), German physicist who shared with J. Franck the 1925 Nobel Prize for physics for their experiments showing the internal structure of the atom to be quantized. He developed a way to isolate isotopes (1932) that is in use today in uranium separation plants.
See also: Atom; Bohr, Niels Henrik David.

Hertz, Heinrich Rudolph (1857-1894), German physicist who first broadcast and received radio waves (1886). He showed that they could be reflected and refracted like light, and that they traveled at the same velocity. The hertz, a unit of frequency, is named after him.
See also: Physics; Radio.

Hertzog, James Barry Munnik (1866-1942), South African prime minister (1924-1939). Founder of the Nationalist party (1914), he worked for separate development

The herring, *Clupea harengus*. Found on both sides of the North Atlantic, it occurs in American waters northwards of Cape Cod, and in European waters from the Bay of Biscay to Norway, and off Greenland and Iceland. The size varies according to the available food, but averages between 10-12 in (25-30 cm). Fertile eggs (1) laid on the sea bed. Hatching time is between ten and fifty days, depending on the water temperature. Larva (2), after hatching measuring 0.2-0.3 in (5-8 mm). Advanced larval stage (3), living in stones and weed on the sea bed, 0.4-0.5 in (10-12 mm). Free-swimming stage (4), which shoals at different levels in the sea, 0.5-0.6 in (12-15 mm). A mature herring (5).

H

of Afrikaner culture and an independent republic of South Africa.

Herzen, Aleksander Ivanovich (1812-1870), Russian writer and early advocate of socialism. He was banished to the countryside in 1834 for subversive activities and left Russia for England permanently in 1847. His weekly journal *Kolokol* (1857-1862) was smuggled into Russia and influenced the revolutionary movement there. One of his more notable books is *My Past and Thoughts* (1855).

Herzl, Theodor (1860-1904), Austrian writer and founder of the political Zionist movement. Convinced by the anti-Semitism surrounding the Dreyfus Affair that Jewish assimilation was impossible, he proposed the establishment of a Jewish state and in 1897 organized the first Zionist World Congress.
See also: Zionism.

Hesiod (8th century B.C.), Greek epic poet. His major works are the didactic *Theogeny*, describing the gods and heroes of Greek mythology, and *Works and Days*, dealing with the everyday life of a farmer.

Hesperides, in Greek mythology, nymphs who guarded the golden apples, which were a wedding gift from Gaea, goddess of earth, to her children, Zeus and Hera, Hercules stole the apples as one of his 12 labors.

During the 1960s, German author Hermann Hesse (1877-1962) was rediscovered. In particular his novel *Steppenwolf* was very popular.

Hesperornis, any of a genus (*Hesperornis*) of extinct birds that lived in North America during the Cretaceous Period, 60 to 125 million years ago. One species, *H. regalis*, was nearly 6 ft (1.8 m) long. The hesperornis could not fly with its undeveloped wings, but was a good diver.

Hess, Myra (1890-1965), English pianist. Hess studied in London (one of the schools was the Royal College of Music) and made her debut in Queen's Hall with a performance of Beethoven's Fourth Piano Concerto. She became rapidly known after that and was one of most famous pianists of her generation. She devoted herself to the music of her fellow countrymen and was renowned as a performer of Bach and the Viennese classics.
During World War II, when London's con-

cert halls were closed, Hess established a series of morale-boosting lunchtime concerts in the National Gallery for which she was named Dame Commander in the Order of the British Empire by King George VI.

Hess, Rudolf (1894-1987), German Nazi leader, Hitler's deputy (1933-1939). In May 1941 he flew secretly to England in an attempt to convince Britain to withdraw from World War II. He was arrested and interned in Britain for the rest of the war. In 1946, at the Nuremberg Trials, he was condemned to life imprisonment for war crimes.
See also: Nazism.

Hesse, state in western Germany, located along the Rhine River in an important agricultural and mining region. Covering an area of 8,152 sq mi (21,113 sq km), the present boundaries of Hesse were formed after World War II from a combination of several other states and former Prussian provinces. The capital is Wiesbaden; other principal cities are Darmstadt, Frankfurt, and Kassel.
See also: Germany.

Hesse, Eva (1936-1970), American sculptress of German origin strongly influenced by minimal art. Her sculptures, which are often amorphic, are manufactured from materials such as textiles, rubber, and resin. The decaying process of materials became a more and more predominant theme.

Hesse, Hermann (1877-1962), German-born Swiss poet and novelist. The solitude, especially of artists, is a recurrent theme in his work. His novels include *Demian* (1919), *Siddhartha* (1922), *Steppenwolf* (1927), and *The Glass Bead Game* (1943). In 1946 he won the Nobel Prize in Literature.

Hessian fly, small, biting insect (*Mayetiola destructor*) so named because it was brought to North America from Europe in straw used for the horses of Hessian soldiers employed by the British during the American Revolution. The larvae of the Hessian fly burrow into wheat stems and destroy them.

Hessians, German mercenaries, mostly from Hesse-Kassel, sold into British military service by their government to fight against the colonials in the American Revolutionary War. After the war many settled in the United States and Canada.
See also: Revolutionary War in America.

Hestia, in Greek mythology, goddess of the hearth. She was also worshiped as protector of the home and the nation, as well as the guardian of fire. The oldest child of Cronus and Rhea, she helped her brother, Zeus, overthrow Cronus's rule over earth and was rewarded by Zeus with the largest portion of the people's material sacrifices. Her Roman counterpart was Vesta.
See also: Mythology.

Heterotropia *See:* Strabismus.

Hevesey, George Charles de (1885-1966), Hungarian chemist, awarded the 1943 Nobel Prize for chemistry for his work on radioac-

tive tracers. He was also the codiscoverer of the element hafnium.
See also: Hafnium; Chemistry.

Heydrich, Reinhard (1904-1942), German Nazi leader, head of the security police, chief deputy to Himmler, head of the SS and organizer of the extermination of European Jews. Known as 'the Hangman,' he was assassinated in 1942 by Czech resistance forces. In retaliation, the Nazis destroyed the town of Lidice, Czechoslovakia.
See also: Nazism.

Heyerdahl, Thor (1914-2002), Norwegian ethnologist and author best known for his expeditions to prove the feasibility of his theories of cultural diffusion. In 1947 he and his crew sailed the Pacific on rafts to demonstrate the possibility that the Polynesians may have originated in South America. His book *Kon-Tiki* was an account of the voyage. He also sailed across the Atlantic in rafts (*The Ra Expeditions*, 1969 and 1970) and did the same in the Persian Gulf, trying to show that the Sumerians could have reached Africa by sea (*Tigris*, 1977-1978).
See also: Ethnography.

Heyse, Paul Johann Ludwig von (1830-1914), German writer. Center of the traditionalist Munich circle, he was noted for his romantic short stories. He won the Nobel Prize for literature in 1910.

Heyward, DuBose (1885-1940), U.S. author, best known for his novel *Porgy* (1925), about the plight of Southern blacks, on which George Gershwin based his opera *Porgy and Bess*.

Heywood, Thomas (1574?-1651), English dramatist and actor. He wrote over 200 dramas, but only about 20 have survived. His best-known play is *A Woman Killed with Kindness* (1603).

Hezbollah, The Hezbollah, 'Party of God', Shiite movement and party in Lebanon. The Hezbollah has its strongholds in the southern districts of Beirut, Beka'a valley (Baalbek) and South Lebanon, traditionally poor and underdeveloped regions with a Shiite majority. The Hezbollah was formed in 1982 during the civil war by various militant groups that broke away from the more moderate, secular Amal movement, as well as a group of 1500 Iranian Revolutionary Guards (Pasdaran). The Hezbollah is an ally of Iran and aspires to an Islamic constitution. From 1983 onwards, the Hezbollah engaged in violent actions, which targeted the Israeli and Western presence in Lebanon. In 1983, more than 300 American marines and French soldiers were killed by Hezbollah bombings. After the civil war, the Hezbollah remained a prominent factor in Lebanon. In the 1990s the Hezbollah formed the greatest opposition to the Israeli occupation of South Lebanon. The Hezbollah continually fired Katusha missiles at the North Israel, to which Israel reacted with retaliatory actions. In 1996, the Hezbollah fired thousands of missiles at North Israel, causing Israel to undertake a large scale air and marine offensive, a campaign that was known as the

H

Grapes of Wrath. During the ceasefire of April 1996, Israel and the Hezbollah came to an agreement not to attack civilian targets. In 1997 and 1998 both parties regularly violated the agreement. In the nineties it was clear that the Hezbollah was divided into a radical branch that wanted war with the whole of Israel and a more moderate side that was focused on Lebanese society and politics and only challenged the Israeli occupation of Southern Lebanon.

Hezekiah (d. c.686 B.C.), Judean king (c.715-c.686 B.C.). He defied the Assyrian army under Sennacherib, which besieged Jerusalem (701 B.C.). With the prophets Micah and Isaiah as his advisers, Hezekiah removed idols from the Holy Temple and restored the temple's status as the focal point for Jewish religious worship.

Hibernation, protective mechanism whereby certain animals reduce their bodies' activity and sleep through winter. Animals prepare by storing extra fat several weeks before the onset of hibernation. When temperatures drop, the animal's pulse rate and breathing drop to a minimum.

Hibiscus, any of various herbs, shrubs, and trees (genus *Hibiscus*) of the mallow family, having large showy flowers. A single bloom can be over 6 in (15 cm) wide.

Hickok, Wild Bill (James Butler Hickok; 1837-1876), legendary U.S. frontier law officer. During the Civil War he was a Union scout and spy. As U.S. marshal at the lawless frontier towns of Hays and Abilene, Kans. (1869-1871), he won a reputation for marksmanship. He was murdered in South Dakota by Jack McCall.

Hickory, tree (genus *Carya*) of the walnut family. Commonly found in the eastern United States, the hickory produces edible nuts and strong wood used in industrial tool handles and golf clubs and is used to make top-grade charcoal for smoking meats. The tallest of the hickories, the pecan tree, produces America's second most popular edible nut.

Hicks, Edward (1780-1849), U.S. painter. A Quaker preacher, he is best known for over 50 versions of *The Peaceable Kingdom*, based on Isaiah's prophecy of peace among all creatures.

Hicks, John Richard (1904-1989), British economist. He was professor at the London School of Economics, at Cambridge, at Manchester, and Oxford. He became well known because of his work *Value and Capital*, which was regarded as one of the building blocks of modern economic thought. Hicks received the Nobel Prize for Economics in 1972 (together with Kenneth Arrow). In *Value and Capital*, he investigated micro economic thought in an abstract manner. Some economists found his ideas too abstract and lacking realistic value. In his works *Capital and Growth* (1965) and *Capital and Time* (1973), which were virtually ignored, he analyzed the possibilities of a theory that also allows for the factor of time.

Hidalgo y Costilla, Miguel (1753-1811), Mexican revolutionary priest, known as 'the father of Mexican independence.' He organized a rebellion against Spanish rule in 1810 and won initial victories with an army made up mainly of Indian peasants. The revolt was defeated in 1811, and Hidalgo was executed.

Hidatsa *See:* Gros Ventre.

Hideyoshi (Toyotomi Hideyoshi; 1536-1598), Japanese military leader and dictator (1585-1598). He served as a general in the army under the dictator Nobunga. As ruler of Japan, Hideyoshi brought order to the country following a civil war and formed alliances that enabled him to defeat all opposition to his rule. His attempts to conquer Korea were unsuccessful. He beautified his capital, Osaka, and made it a cultural center.

Hieroglyphics, writing system used in ancient Egypt and several other civilizations. It is based on pictures that represent objects, ideas, or sounds. Egyptian hieroglyphics were used from 3000 B.C. until about 500 B.C. They consisted of 604 symbols that could stand for words, sounds, or classifications. The French Egyptologist Jean François Champollion (1790-1832) was the first person in modern times to make real progress in deciphering hieroglyphics.

Hi-fi *See:* High fidelity.

High blood pressure *See:* Hypertension.

High fidelity, reproduction of an electronic signal or sound with a minimum of distortion, especially by phonographic equipment. High fidelity systems are sometimes called hi-fi systems.

High jump, track and field event. It requires jumping over a bar 6-8 ft (1.83-2.44 m) high and 12 ft (3.66 m) long. From a running start, jumpers must clear the bar and land in a cushioned pit on the other side. Two styles are used in high jumping, the 'straddle' (forward) and the 'Fosbury flop' (backward). Athletes are scored on their best jumps, but those who knock the bar down 3 consecutive times are disqualified.

Highlands *See:* Scotland.

High priest, in Jewish history, head of the Israelite priesthood, whose duties included supervising worship in the temple of Jerusalem and conducting services on the Day of Atonement. The office existed until the destruction of the temple by the Romans in A.D. 70.

High seas, in maritime law, the sea beyond territorial waters, usually 200 nautical mi (370 km) from the coasts of nations that border the oceans. Since the 19th century freedom of the seas has been recognized as a rule of international law, but recently the discovery of minerals under the sea and the importance of the airspace above it have made the concept crucial. Attempts by any state to extend its jurisdiction should be ratified by international agreement. The Law of the Sea Treaty (1982) received majority

Hieroglyphic symbols form part of this Egyptian 18th-dynasty royal snake frieze, from a funeral temple, painted during the reign of Queen Hatshepsut.

H

approval in the UN, largely because of Third World support, but the United States voted against it.

Highsmith, Mary Patricia (1921-1995), American writer. Patricia Highsmith wrote a number of suspense thrillers that belong to the best in this genre and in which the clever character analysis is particularly noticeable. The events are often improbable; the main theme is the inner reality, the confrontation between deception and truth. The best of her books include *Strangers on a Train* (1950, filmed by Hitchcock in 1951), *Deep Water* (1957), *This Sweet Sickness* (1960) and *The Cry of the Owl* (1962). Also famous are her books about the completely unscrupulous Tom Ripley, who continually slips through the net, as he does in *The Talented Mr. Ripley* (1955), *Ripley Under Ground* (1970) and *Ripley's Game* (1974).

Hijacking, the forcible seizure of an aircraft, ship, train, or motor vehicle in transit. The robbery of passengers or of a vehicle's goods without taking the vehicle itself is also known as hijacking. The crime of hijacking an ocean vessel is known as piracy. Airplane hijacking often is called air piracy or skyjacking; the hijacking of an automobile is commonly called carjacking. The term 'hijacking' came into use in the United States during the in the Prohibition era (1920-1933), when it referred to the theft by bootleggers of a rival's truckloads of liquor. Gradually the term took on a broader meaning. There was extensive hijacking of airplanes during the 1960's, sometimes as a means of blackmail or for the purpose of being transported to another country. Beginning in the 1970's, skyjacking became a tactic of international political terrorists. Carjacking, most commonly occurring at intersections, became a problem in the 1990's in some American cities.

Hijra *See:* Hegira.

Hiking, exercise in the form of endurance walking. It can range in duration from a few hours to a few days or weeks and can be done on woodland trails, riverbanks, lakeshores, mountains, or city streets. Hikes of more than 1 day involve camping out, and these hikers usually carry tents, sleeping bags, and backpacks with food supplies and changes of clothing.

Elegant, detailed portraits are typical of the art of the Elisabethan era. The one shown here, a miniature painted on parchment (approximately 1588) by Nicholas Hilliard, is one of the most well-known examples of this art form (Victoria and Albert Museum, London).

Hildebrandt, Johann Lukas Von (1668-1745), Austrian architect. Together with Fischer Von Erlach, he was the most prominent exponent of the Austrian baroque. He was the master builder for the emperor in Vienna (1701). He built the Schwarzenberg Palace in Vienna (1697-1740), Schloss Schönborn in Gollersdorf (1712-1717), and the Unteres and Oberes Belvedere (1714-1716, 1721-1723 in Vienna (his most important work).

Hill, Damon Graham Devereux (1960-), British racing driver who started out as a motorcycle racer. Hill first took part in Formula Ford, Formula Three and the F3000 before attempting Formula One in a Brabham-Judd in 1992. In 1994 he was second to Michael Schumacher in the final positioning of the Formula One race. In 1996 Hill won the Grand Prix of Argentina, San Marco, Canada, and France, bringing his total GP victories to 19. He is Graham Hill's son.

Hill, Graham (1929-1975), British racing driver, who followed a technical training and was in the Royal Navy for two years. After that he became a mechanic and drove in his first car race in 1954. He drove for Lotus twice (from 1950 to 1959 and from 1967 to 1969) and for BRM (British Racing Motor, from 1960 to 1966). His first GP victory was in 1962 at Zandvoort. In 1962 and 1968 Hill became the Formula One world champion. He also won the 500 miles at Indianapolis in 1966 and the 24-Hours at Le Mans in 1972. He won 14 Grand Prix. Hill was killed when his plane crashed in thick fog. His son Damon made his debut in 1995 in the Formula One race for Williams-Renault.

Hill, Octavia (1838-1912), English social reformer. She was instrumental in improving housing conditions for London's poor and in establishing and preserving the city's parks and playgrounds. Hill also served on the board of several charitable organizations, and her concern for the preservation of natural beauty and historic structures led to the formation of the National Trust.

Hillary, Sir Edmund Percival (1919-), New Zealand explorer and mountaineer. In 1953 he and Tenzing Norkay, a Sherpa from Nepal, were the first to reach the summit of Mt. Everest, the world's highest mountain. *See also:* Mount Everest.

Hillel (c.70 B.C.-10 A.D.), Jewish scholar born in Babylonia, one of the founders of rabbinic Judaism, and ethical leader of his generation. He was opposed by Shammai, another teacher. His 'Seven Rules' of exegesis laid the groundwork for a liberal interpretation of scriptural law. *See also:* Judaism.

Hilliard, Nicholas (1537-1619), English miniature painter. As court artist to Elizabeth I, his style was characterized by exquisite jewellike detailing and fine drawing.

Hilton, Conrad Nicholson (1887-1979), U.S. hotel chain founder. Beginning with his first hotels in New Mexico and Texas, Hilton expanded his holdings to most major U.S. and foreign cities and resort areas. By 1967 Hilton hotels were in 37 nations, and the international operation of the company became a subsidiary of Trans World Airlines (TWA).

Hilton, James (1900-1954), English novelist. His books include *Lost Horizon* (1933), *Good-bye, Mr. Chips* (1934), and *Random Harvest* (1941), which were made into films.

Himachal Pradesh (pop. 5,000,000), Indian federal state, bordering on Tibet; 21,504 sq mi (55,673 sq km). The capital is Simla with a population of 110,000 and founded by the British in 1819. It is 7,218 ft (2,200 m) above sea level. It is mountainous and forested. Apart from logging, there is agriculture, mainly the cultivation of fruit in the valleys, and salt mining.
After the fall of the Gupta Empire in the 6th century, the little country first had to pay tribute to the Mogul Empire before being occupied by the Moguls, the Gurkhas, and the Sikhs in succession.
It is the least urbanized of all the Indian states: only 9% of the population lives in towns. It has been part of India in this form since 1971. The spoken language is Pahari, a dialect of Hindi. 95% of the population is Hindu. The name means 'State of the Snowy Mountain'.

Himalayas, highest mountain system in the world, over 1,500 mi (2,410 km) long, extending from Pakistan through India, Tibet, Nepal, Sikkim, and Bhutan. The northern range is called the Trans-Himalayas. The southern range has three parallel zones: the Great Himalayas, including the 29,028-ft (8,848-m) Mt. Everest, the Lesser Himalayas, and the southernmost Outer Himalayas.

Himmler, Heinrich (1900-1945), German Nazi leader. A founder of the Nazi party, head of the SS from 1929 and of the Gestapo from 1936, he was responsible for the murder of millions in concentration camps. Named interior minister in 1943, he became the main leader of Germany's internal affairs. He was captured by the British army in 1945 and committed suicide. *See also:* Holocaust; Nazism.

Hinault, Bernard (1954-), French racing cyclist, who won many of the one-day classics as well as the great tours. He won the Tour de France in 1978, 1979, 1981, 1982, and 1985, the Spanish Tour in 1978 and 1983, and the Giro d'Italia in 1980, 1982, and 1985. Although Hinault was not a great climber, he won the mountain stage of the Tour. In particular, he was a strong time trial racer, whose victories include winning the Grand Prix des Nation five times. On the track, he won the chase in the French national championship in 1975 and 1976.

Hindemith, Paul (1895-1963), German-born U.S. composer and teacher. Denounced as a modernist because of his dissonant harmonies and counterpoint, he was banned by the Nazis in Germany and immigrated to the United States in 1937. He later returned to more tonal, neoclassical forms. Among his major works are the symphony (1934) and opera (1938) *Mathis the Painter, Symphonic Metamorphoses on Themes of Carl Maria von Weber* (1943), and *The Four Temperaments* (1944).

Hindenburg *See:* Airship.

Hindenburg, Paul von (1847-1934), German general, president of Germany (1925-1934). Together with Ludendorff he directed German military strategies in World War I. As president he was chiefly a figurehead. In 1933 he appointed Hitler chancellor. *See also:* World War I.

Hindenburg Line *See:* Siegfried Line.

Hindi, official language of India, a written form of Hindustani. It is written in Devanagari script, reading from left to right. Hindi belongs to the Indic group of the Indo-European family of languages.

Hinduism, chief religion of India, embracing many different sects and trends. In terms of numbers of adherents, it is the third largest of the world's religions, after Christianity and Islam. Hinduism is based on the Veda, sacred writings dating back some 3,000 years. The Veda comprised four types of writing: the Samhita, which in turn consists of 4 books of hymns, chants, and prayers-the Rig-Veda, the Sama-Veda, the Yajur-Veda, and the Atharva-Veda; the Brahmanas, which are prose; the Aranyakas, containing instructions for meditation; and the Upanishads, mystical works stating the Veda's doctrine of the soul.
Between 800 B.C. and 500 B.C. Hinduism began to change under the impact of two new, rival religions: Buddhism and Jainism. It absorbed many village and tribal gods into a

In Hinduism, the idea of reincarnation of the human soul is very important. Therefore, it is no surprise that a deity can also easily assume an earthly appearance. Here, we see representations of the fourth (left) and the tenth incarnations of Vishnu, in the Shree Cutch Satsang temple in Mombasa, Kenya.

pantheon dominated by Brahma (the creator), Vishnu (the preserver), and Shiva (the destroyer). In this period important social and philosophical changes occured: the caste system was established, and the learned Brahman, often a priest, became the supreme figure in society. The doctrine of reincarnation and the transmigration of the soul also became part of the creed. A further addition was the concept of *karma*, the idea that every individual is punished for wrongdoing and rewarded for righteousness, if not in the present life, then in a reincarnation. The aim of every Hindu should be to rise, through just living, higher and higher in the scale of existence with each reincarnation, finally attaining absorption into the personality of Brahma. Hinduism has various subcults, of which those of Shiva, Vishnu, Krishna, Shakti, and the Matris are the most important.

Hindu Kush, mountain range in Asia, stretching about 500 m (800 km) from northeast Afghanistan to north Pakistan. High-altitude passes cross the range. The highest peak is Tirich Mir (25,260 ft/ 7,699 m).

Hines, Earl 'Fatha' (1905-1983), U.S. jazz musician, pianist and composer. A member of Louis Armstrong's group, the Hot Five (late 1920s), he later formed a band of his own, featuring Charlie Parker and Dizzy Gillespie, which introduced bebop. Hines's powerful percussive style greatly influenced modern piano techniques.
See also: Jazz.

Hingis, Martina (1980-), Swiss tennis player, who first became known when she won, together with the Czech Helena Sukova, the women's doubles at Wimbledon in 1996. In October of that year, Hingis won her first ATP tournament in the singles. In January 1997, she won the Australian Open championships, making her, at sixteen, the youngest winner of a Grand Slam tournament. She won, together with Natasha Zvereva (White Russia), the women's doubles in Australia. She also won Wimbledon and the American Open Championships in 1997, and the Australian Open again in 1998 and 1999. During this last tournament, she also won, together with the Croatian Miryana Lucic, the women's doubles. Hingis reached first place in the world league on 31st March 1997. She lost this position at Wimbledon in 1999 to Lindsay Davenport, who won the title that year.

Hinton, S(usan) E(loise) (1948-), U.S. author of books for teenagers. Her novels are set in Tulsa, Okla., where Hinton was born and raised. Her characters, often teenagers themselves, reject authority and must cope with the problems of poverty, drug abuse, and violence on their own. Hinton's first and most widely recognized novel, *The Outsiders* (1967), written when she was 16, is noted for its action and harshly realistic characters. Her other works include *That Was Then, This Is Now* (1971), *Rumble Fish* (1975), and *Tex* (1979).

Hip, freely movable ball-and-socket joint formed by the cup-shaped hollow of the pelvic bone and the smooth, rounded head of the thighbone. The adult hipbone combines three bones that are separate in youth: the ilium, ischium, and pubis.

Hip Hop, African American underground culture, often used as a synonym for a form of musical expression: rap. Rap music is a variant of rhythm and blues, characterized by rhythmically recited text (rapping) and the large scale use of samples, digitally stored fragments of music by other people. Hip hop originated in the early 1970s in the slums of New York, and later Los Angeles. After the pioneering work of Grandmaster Caz & MC Kool Herc, Afrikaa Bambaataa, Grandmaster Flash, Melle Mel, Doug E. Fresh, and later Public Enemy, Run-D.M.C., the white Beastie Boys and others, it rapidly spread to all four corners of the world. The genre was then divided into various substreams such as gangster rap and G-funk, and merged into many other styles of music such as blues, jazz, reggae, dance, and metal.

Hipparchus (c.180 B.C.-125 B.C.), Greek scientist, pioneer of systematic astronomy. He compiled the first star catalog and ascribed magnitudes to stars. He also estimated the size of the moon and its distance from the earth, and was probably the first to discover the precession of the equinox.
See also: Equinox.

Hipparchus (6th century B.C.), Greek political figure. Son of Pisistratus, ruler of Athens in the mid-500s, Hipparchus shared power with his brother, Hippias, when their father died in 527. A patron of the arts, Hipparchus brought the poets Anacreon and Simonides to Athens. He got involved in a plot to overthrow his brother and was killed when the revolt was suppressed.
See also: Greece, Ancient.

Hippies, anti-establishment subculture in the 1960s, principally people under 25 who rejected conservative values and traditional authority. Opposed to the Vietnam War and known for loose sexual conventions, use of drugs, and long hair, hippies originated in the East Village in New York City and the Haight-Ashbury district in San Francisco.

Hippocampus *See:* Seahorse.

Hippocrates (c.460-c.377 B.C.), Greek physician often called the father of medicine. He was probably the author of the *Hippocratic Collection*, some 70 books on

H

The Greek physician Hippocrates (c. 460-c. 377 B.C.) is traditionally considered the founder of medicine. This painting is one of the 28 portraits of famous men, made around 1470 by Flemish painter Justus van Gent and Spanish painter Pedro Berruguete (1450-1504), for the Palazzo Ducale in the Italian city of Urbino. The assignment was commissioned by Renaissance monarch Federigo da Montefeltro.

H

all aspects of ancient medicine. The Hippocratic Oath, a statement of medical ethics and good practice, is still sworn to by graduates of many medical schools.
See also: Medicine.

Hippodrome, any open or closed structure for circuses or similar spectacles. Originally a Greek outdoor course for horse and chariot races, it was adopted by the Romans, who built numerous hippodromes. Shaped like the letter U, with tiers of open seats on 3 sides and closed across the fourth by an area for distinguished guests, such a stadium was frequently up to 400 ft (120 m) wide and 700 ft (210 m) long. The most famous hippodrome was the Circus Maximus at Rome, which could hold over 300,000 spectators.

Hippopotamus, one of the largest living terrestrial mammals (*Hippopotamus amphibius*), distantly related to the pig, widespread in Africa. Hippopotamuses generally are about 5 ft (1.6 m) tall and weigh about 5 tons (4,500 kg). They have massive bodies set on short legs, each with four toes with hoof-like nails. Their noses, eyes, and ears are on top of their heads, which allows them to spend most of the day submerged in rivers. At night they come on land to graze.

Hirayama, Kiyotsugo Rigakushi (1874-1943), Japanese astronomer, famous for his research on the paths of planets and planetoids. He discovered ten planetoid families, of which the members have similar paths. He theorized that these groups originated from a collision between two larger bodies.

Hirohito (1901-1989), emperor of Japan from 1926 until his death. After World War II the recognition of the emperor as a god was rescinded, and Hirohito became a 'symbol of the state and unity of the people,' without political or sovereign power. He was instrumental in persuading the government to accept unconditional surrender in World War II.
See also: Japan.

Hiroshige, Ando (1797-1858), Japanese painter and printmaker of the *ukiyo-e* (popular) school led by Hokusai. He is famous for his sets of woodblock color prints depicting atmospheric landscapes of snow, rain, mist, and moonlight. These inspired a number of

Columbus came to the island of Hispaniola on his second voyage to America in 1493 with 1200 men, in order to colonise it as the first territory in the New World. This fifteenth-century map of the island can be found in the Museo Amerigo in Madrid.

his contemporaries in the West, including Edouard Manet and James Whistler. Among his works is *53 Stages of the Tokaido Highway* (1833), a series of landscapes.

Hiroshima (pop. 1,1 million), industrial city on Honshu Island, Japan, located on a bay in the Inland Sea, capital of Hiroshima Prefecture. A thriving industrial and commercial center, it was chosen as the target for the U.S. atomic bomb attack of Aug. 6, 1945. There were at least 80,000 people killed, many more injured or made ill by radiation, and nine-tenths of the city was destroyed. It has been largely rebuilt since 1950 and is again an important industrial marketing center.
See also: Japan; World War II.

Hirst, Damien (1965-   ), British visual artist. He attended Goldsmith's College in London from 1986 to 1988. In particular he made sculptures and installations. He took part in the much talked- about exhibition 'Freeze', by young British artists in the Surrey Docks in London in 1988 with Gary Hume, Sarah Lucas, Georgina Starr, and others. Death, mortality, and a futureless existence are the central themes of his work, which often shocks people. For example, he used animals, decaying or dead, in glass containers filled with formaldihyde, or live fish in an aquarium. *Making Beautiful Drawings Machine* (1994) symbolizes the inner compulsion of the artist, who may never repeat himself.

Hispanic Americans, in the United States, those who have come from Spanish countries or their descendants. There are approximately 20 million Hispanic Americans, making up some 8% of the U.S. population, the second-largest minority in the country after African Americans. Thanks to both a high birth rate and continued immigration, Hispanic Americans are expected to become the largest minority in the United States in the 21st century.
Hispanic Americans are unified in certain important respects, principally the Spanish language and the Roman Catholic religion. Their diversity stems from differences of history and culture among their various countries of origin as well as the causes and circumstances leading to immigration to the United States.
The majority of Hispanic Americans, some 63%, are of Mexican descent. Puerto Ricans comprise 12% and Cubans 5% of the total. The remaining 20% come from Spain and countries of South and Central America, including Colombia, the Dominican Republic, Ecuador, Guatemala, El Salvador, and Nicaragua. Consequently, Hispanic Americans are referred to broadly as Latinos.

Hispaniola, second largest island in the West Indies, located west of Puerto Rico and east of Cuba. The island is shared between the Republic of Haiti (west) and the Dominican Republic (east).

Hiss, Alger (1904-1996), U.S. public official accused of spying for the USSR. Hiss was an adviser to the U.S. State Department on economic and political affairs. In 1948 he

was brought before the House Committee on Un-American Activities (HUAC), and in 1950 he was convicted of perjury. He served 4 years in prison. Maintaining his innocence, Hiss has devoted the rest of his life to clearing his name. Legal scholars are sharply divided on his guilt.

Histamine *See:* Allergy; Antihistamine.

Histology, scientific study of the structure of the tissues that make up organisms.

Histoplasmosis, infectious disease that is endemic in parts of Africa, South America, and the United States, caused by the fungus *Histoplasma capsulatum*. It is characterized by damage to the lungs and occasional anemia, with ulcerations of the mouth and the gastrointestinal tract, enlargement of the liver and spleen, disorder of the lymph glands, and necrosis (tissue death) of the adrenal glands. If not treated early with an antifungal agent, a severe attack can be fatal. It is particularly common in infants and older men.

History, study of the past through documents, reports, and other artifacts. The past can be inferred through many sources-chronicles, myths, buildings, monuments, business documents, newspapers, works of art, archeological objects. Earlier times for which no such sources exist are known as *prehistory*. History as a branch of knowledge is generally confined to the written records of human activities, which limits its scope to the invention of writing, about 5,000 years ago.
The oldest historical writings stem from China, where archeologists found historical records written before 1,000 B.C. In the older civilizations of Egypt and Mesopotamia historical records also appear soon after the introduction of writing. The conscious writing of history is generally considered to have begun in Greece about the 5th century B.C. with Herodotus's description of the wars between Greece and Persia. What made his work history was his conscious attempt to record events of importance and to set forth the motivations of the people involved. This causal approach to events of the past earned Herodotus the title 'Father of History,' although, unlike modern historians, he did not try to verify all his facts and mixed tradition, oral remembrances, and fable along with actual occurrences and customs. A more analytical method of writing about the past was developed by his successor, Thucydides, whose *History of the Peloponnesian War* is a grave, authentic account of the 27-year war between Athens and Sparta. A third great Greek historian, Xenophon, concentrated more on the purely narrative aspects of history. These types of historical writing, the compendious, the analytical, and the narrative, are still in evidence today. Roman historians include Livy (*History from the Founding of the City*), Tacitus (*Annals* and *Histories*), and Julius Caesar (*Commentaries*), although Caesar's work tends more towards reportage than pure history. During medieval times, Christian monks developed the idea of a *universal history*, which attempted to unite Christian his-

tory with the Greek and Roman records. Eusebius's *Ecclesiastical History* is an example, as is Saint Augustine's *City of God*, which presented, in addition, a philosophy of history. At the same time, annals of events called *chronicles* were compiled, mainly by members of the clergy. Bede's *Ecclesiastical History of the English Nation* was the great historical work of the Middle Ages. In more modern times, history developed into a serious discipline pursued by scholars. Edward Gibbon's *History of the Decline and Fall of the Roman Empire* (1776-1788) is an early example of dedicated and thorough scholarship. In the 1800s critical, objective history developed into an academic discipline, as exemplified by the works of the German historian Leopold von Ranke and his followers. This German school established canons of criticism and methods of historical analysis that are still in evidence today. The 20th century saw a broadening of the scope of history to include more than the concentration on political events that characterized history up until the 19th century. Today, events of the past are analyzed using tools from many disciplines, including economics, psychology, sociology, and anthropology. Our technological society also fostered an interest in the history of science and in the effect technology has on society. Today, all aspects of the life of peoples and societies form the proper concern of historians.

Hitchcock, Lambert (1795-1852), U.S. cabinetmaker who, in 1818, established a furniture factory at Barkhamsted, Conn. Hitchcock chairs, black with stenciled designs, combined simplicity with elegance. They are now collector's pieces.

Hitchcock, Sir Alfred Joseph (1899-1980), British film director known for his skillful suspense and macabre humor. He made over 50 films, among the best of which were *The Thirty-Nine Steps* (1935), *The Lady Vanishes* (1938), and, in Hollywood, *Rebecca* (1940),

After seventeen years of absence from London, Alfred Hitchcock shot another film there in 1972: *Frenzy*. Here he can be seen during shooting in Covent Garden, the well-known London vegetable market, where the key scenes of the film take place.

Spellbound (1945), *Notorious* (1946), *Rear Window* (1954), and *Psycho* (1960).

Hitler, Adolf (1889-1945), Austrian-born dictator of Germany, founder of the Nazi party. Drafted in World War I, he was wounded and awarded the Iron Cross. He blamed the German defeat in the war on Jews and Communists, and in 1920 helped to found the National Socialist (Nazi) Workers Party. In 1923, after an abortive coup against the Bavarian government (the 'beer hall putsch'), he served 9 months in prison. There he wrote *Mein Kampf* (My Struggle), an anti-Semitic, anti-Communist diatribe outlining his strategy for remaking Germany and becoming a conquering power throughout Europe. The Nazi party grew rapidly after the outbreak of economic depression in 1929, becoming the largest single party in the country. Although the Nazis never won a national election, their paramilitary street violence made them a powerful force. In 1933 Hitler was named chancellor, and in 1934 he secured his position by liquidating potential opponents within the party. The opposition was crushed, all other parties were outlawed, concentration camps were established, trade unions were eliminated or placed under state control, and anti-Semitism became state policy, enacted into law. In the meantime, a war economy was established. Hitler had the main responsibility for German war strategy, and despite a failed military coup against him in 1944, he remained in complete control of the German armed forces and insisted on fighting on in the face of defeat. He committed suicide in Apr. 1945 in his bunker in Berlin, as Soviet troops entered the city.
See also: Holocaust; Nazism; World War II.

Hittites, Indo-European people of the Middle East in the 2nd millennium B.C. Of unknown origin, they appear to have first settled in southern Turkey (c.1900 B.C.); they conquered central Turkey and became a dominant power. The downfall of the Hittite empire came about 1200 B.C. when it was overrun and fragmented by a vast migration of uncertain origin, called by the Egyptians 'peoples of the sea.'

HIV *See:* AIDS.

Hives, or urticaria, itchy skin condition characterized by the formation of welts with surrounding erythema (reddening) due to histamine release in the body's tissues. It is usually provoked by allergy to food, pollens, fungi, drugs, or parasites, but it may be symptomatic of infection, systemic disease, or emotional disorder. *Dermographism* is a condition in which slight skin pressure produces marked hives, like linear marks that appear after writing on the skin.

Hoad, Lew (1934-1994), Australian tennis player. Hoad was one of the members of the legendary Australian tennis generation of the 1950s. In 1956 he won the open championships in France, Australia, and Great Britain (Wimbledon). In the finals of the American Open of that year, he was narrowly beaten by his fellow countryman Ken Rosewall. Hoad was victorious at Wimble-

During breeding season the hoatzin (*O. hoatzin*) forms groups consisting of three to six birds that mate and share parental duties.

H

don again in 1957. As a member of the Australian team he won the Davis Cup for national teams five times. At the age of 22 he ended his career because of a back injury.

Hoatzin (*Opisthocomos hoatzin*), bird that lives in the flooded forests bordering the rivers of northern South America. The adult, which is slightly larger than a pigeon, has a long crest and blue cheeks. It can barely fly, its flight muscles being small to make way for a large crop in which it stores its meals of leaves and fruit. The chicks have 2 movable claws on each wing that help them clamber through foliage. When alarmed, they jump into the water, swimming and even diving easily, then clamber back up the tree when danger has passed.

Hoban, James (1762-1831), Irish-born U.S. architect. He designed and built the White House (1792-1801) and supervised construction of the Capitol and other buildings in Washington, D.C.

A basalt relief, showing King Katuwas and the Hittite hieroglyphs from Carchemish (approximately 9th century B.C.).

H

Hobart (pop. 184,000), capital of the island of Tasmania, south of the eastern tip of the Australian mainland. This port city, founded in 1804, was originally involved in Antarctic whaling. It took on its present name in 1881. Its industries include textiles, metal products, chemicals, and glass.
See also: Tasmania.

Ho Chi Minh (left) and Pham Van Dong, when he was North Vietnam's prime minister.

Hobbema, Meindert (1638-1709), Dutch landscape painter, taught by Jacob van Ruisdael. His atmospheric river scenes and his later forest and road landscapes, such as *The Avenue at Middelharnis* (1689), foreshadowed John Constable and others.

Hobbes, Thomas (1588-1679), English political philosopher who sought to apply rational principles to the study of human nature. In Hobbes's view, humans are materialistic and pessimistic, their actions motivated solely by self-interest, thus a state's stability can only be guaranteed by a sovereign authority, to which citizens relinquish their rights. *Leviathan* (1651), his most celebrated work, expresses these views. Hobbes saw matter in motion as the only reality; even consciousness and thought were but the outworkings of the motion of atoms in the brain. During and after his lifetime, Hobbes was known as a materialist and suspected of atheism, but in the 20th century his reputation as an able thinker has overshadowed his former notoriety.
See also: Philosophy.

Hobson, Laura Zametkin (1900-1986), U.S. author born in New York City, the setting for most of her novels. Her most famous work, *Gentleman's Agreement* (1947), deals with prejudice and religious intolerance. In *The Tenth Month* (1971) and *Consenting Adults* (1975), Hobson addressed the controversial issues of unwed motherhood and homosexuality, respectively. Her other works include *The Celebrity* (1951), *First Papers* (1964), and *Over and Above* (1979).

Hochhuth, Rolf (1931-), German playwright whose first controversial play, *The Deputy* (1963), attacked Pope Pius XII for his stand on the Jews in World War II, and whose second, *Soldiers* (1967), portrayed Winston Churchill as a murderer.

Ho Chi Minh (Nguyen Van Thanh; 1890-1969), president of North Vietnam (1954-1969). From 1911 to 1941 he lived in England, France, the USSR, and China. He helped found the French Communist Party and, later, founded the Vietnamese Communist Party. In 1941 he returned to Vietnam and organized an independence movement, the Viet Minh, that fought against the Japanese in World War II and then against the restored French colonial government. After the decisive Viet Minh victory over the French at Dien Bien Phu in 1954, Vietnam was temporarily divided at the 17th parallel, and Ho became president of North Vietnam. South Vietnam's refusal to hold national elections led to the Vietnam War, during which Ho and his military commander, Gen. Vo Nguyen Giap, proved resolute and tenacious war leaders. In failing health, Ho lived to see the Tet offensive of 1968 and the start of peace negotiations that led ultimately to North Vietnamese victory.
See also: Vietnam War.

Ho Chi Minh City (pop. 4,300,000), formerly Saigon, city in Vietnam, 60 mi (97 km) from the South China Sea, on Saigon River. An industrial center and river port with a trade in rice and textiles, the city was established as an Annamese settlement in the 17th century and was taken by the French in 1859. The city was capital of South Vietnam (1954-1975) and suffered considerable damage during the Vietnam War.
See also: Vietnam.

Höchstädt, Battle of *See:* Blenheim, Battle of.

Hockey, game played on ice in which 2 opposing teams of skaters, using curved sticks, try to shoot a flat, rubber disk called a puck, into the opposing goal, which is 4 ft (1.2 m) high and 6 ft (1.8 m) wide. Each goal scored is 1 point and the team with the most goals at the end of the game is the winner. The ice surface, or rink, is usually 200 ft (61 m) long and 98 ft (30 m) wide and is divided into three zones: offensive, defensive, and neutral. Each team has 6 players on the ice at once: 1 center, 2 wings, 2 defensemen, and 1 goaltender. Together, the center and wings are called forwards and they try to score goals for their team, while the defensemen work to prevent the opposing team from getting chances to score. The goaltender, or goalie, is the last line of defense and always plays directly in front of his team's goal, in an area called the crease. The goalie's only job is to prevent shots by the opposing team from entering the goal. Penalties of varying length are handed out by the referee to a player who breaks the rules, and the team must play with one less skater for the duration of their player's penalty. The most popular league is the National Hockey League (NHL) which consists of 21 teams from the United States and Canada. Hockey is played worldwide, with the Soviet Union historically dominating most Olympic and international competition.
Field hockey, a variation of ice hockey, is played outdoors and on foot. The 2 teams try to shoot a small ball into a slightly larger goal: 7 ft (2.13 m) high and 12 ft (3.66 m) wide. The field is 100 yards (91 m) long and 60 yards (55 m) wide and each team plays 11 players at once: 5 forwards, 3 halfbacks, 2 fullbacks, and a goaltender. Field hockey is an international sport and women's field hockey became an Olympic sport at the 1980 Summer Games.

Hockney, David (1937-), English artist whose emphases are on figurative work and brilliant color. His characteristic painting *A Bigger Splash* (1967) was also the title of a semi-autobiographical documentary film (1974).

Hodgkin, Alan Lloyd (1914-1994), English physiologist awarded (with A. F. Huxley and J. Eccles) the 1963 Nobel Prize for physiology or medicine for his work on the chemical basis of nerve impulse transmission.
See also: Physiology.

Hodgkin, Dorothy Mary Crowfoot (1910-1994), British chemist awarded the 1964 Nobel Prize for chemistry for determining the structure of vitamin B_{12}.
See also: Chemistry.

Hodgkin's disease, or lymphadenoma, form of cancer affecting the lymphatic system. It was named for Thomas Hodgkin, the English physician who first described the disease in 1832. It usually causes swelling of lymph glands in the neck, armpits, or the groin. The lymph glands manufacture lymphocytes, a type of white blood cell that fights the spread of infection. In Hodgkin's disease, these cells proliferate in a variety of abnormal forms, leaving the body with fewer normal lymphocytes to fight infection. As the disease progresses, the body becomes less able to combat infections, and damage to vital organs occurs.
See also: Lymphatic system.

Hoffa, James Riddle (1913-1975?), U.S. labor leader, president of the International Brotherhood of Teamsters from 1957. After an investigation (led by U.S. attorney general Robert F. Kennedy) into his underworld links, Hoffa was convicted in 1964 of tampering with a jury over a bribery charge and jailed from 1968 to 1971, when Richard M. Nixon commuted his sentence. In 1975 he disappeared mysteriously and is thought to have been murdered.
See also: Labor movement.

Hoffer, Eric (1902-1983), self-educated U.S. author and philosopher. A migratory worker and longshoreman until 1967, he won immediate acclaim with his first book, *The True Believer* (1951), a study of mass movements. *The Passionate State of Mind* (1955), a volume of maxims, followed.

Hoffman, Dustin (1937-), U.S. actor, known for his versatility in portraying different character types. Hoffman made his film debut in *The Tiger Makes Out* (1967) and became famous with his performance in *The Graduate* (1967). He was awarded the Academy Award for best actor for *Kramer vs. Kramer* (1979) and *Rain Man* (1988). His other films include *Midnight Cowboy* (1969), *All the President's Men* (1976), *Tootsie* (1982), *Rain Man* (1988), *Outbreak*

(1995), and *Sleepers* (1996). At the 1996 Venice Film Festival he was awarded a Golden Lion for his works.

Hoffmann, E(rnst) T(heodor) A(madeus) (1776-1822), German romantic author, composer, and critic. He is best remembered today for his fantastic short stories,which inspired E.A. Poe and others, and the opera *Tales of Hoffmann*, composed by J.L. Offenbach and based on 3 of his stories.

Hofmann, Hans (1880-1966), German-born U.S. artist and teacher, prominent in the abstract expressionism movement. His vigorous and colorful style, inspired by Wassily Kandinsky, is exemplified by *The Gate* (1959). In 1934 he opened the influential Hans Hofmann School of Fine Arts in New York City.

Hofmannsthal, Hugo von (1874-1929), Austrian neoromantic poet and dramatist. His early style was influenced by the German poet Stefan George (1868-1933) and the Pre-Raphaelites. His adaptation of Sophocles' *Elektra* (1903) was made into an opera by Richard Strauss in 1909, beginning a long collaboration, including *Der Rosenkavalier* (1911), *Ariadne auf Naxos* (1912), and *Die Frau ohne Schatten* (1919). His poems, plays such as *Jedermann* (Everyman, 1911), and opera librettos make him a major figure of Austrian literature.

Hugo von Hofmannsthal (1874-1929).

Hog, pig, or swine, domestic animal (family Suidae) bred for its flesh and fat. Hogs are descended from the wild boars (*Sus scrofa*) of Europe and Asia, which live in small herds in woodland. The weight of the male, or *boar*, can be up to 400 lb (181 kg), while the female, or *sow*, only weighs 300 lb (136 kg). The boar has tusks up to 1 ft (30 cm) long and can be dangerous. Hogs were probably among the earliest domesticated animals. They were allowed to run free in the woods, feeding on seeds such as acorns. Domestic hogs have retained the varied diet of their ancestors and will eat roots, fallen

E.T.A. Hoffmann (1776-1822).

fruit, and even meat. A sow produces litters of up to 12 piglets.

Hogan, Ben (1912-1997), U.S. professional golfer. His achievements include winning the PGA Championship (1946, 1948), U.S. Open (1948, 1950, 1951, 1953), Masters (1951, 1953) and British Open (1953).

Hogarth, William (1697-1764), British painter and engraver. He is best known for his 3 series of moralistic and satirical engravings, *The Harlot's Progress* (1732), *The Rake's Progress* (1735), and *Marriage à la Mode* (1745). His first success was as a portraitist, and some of his finest works, such as *Captain Thomas Coram* (1740) and *The Shrimp Girl* (1760), are in this field.

Hogg, Helen Sawyer (1905-1993), U.S.-born Canadian astronomer noted for her *Catalogue of Variable Stars in Globular Clusters* (1939). Her work involved measurement of the period of variable stars, which helps to determine their distance from earth.

Hognose *See:* Adder.

Hogweed *See:* Ragweed.

Hohenstaufen, medieval German dynasty of Swabian origin whose members ruled Germany and the Holy Roman Empire. The great Hohenstaufen emperors were Conrad III, Frederick I Barbarossa, Henry VI, Frederick II, and Conrad IV. Their concept of a strongly centralized empire brought them into continual conflict with the papacy and with the 2 powerful opposing groups, Guelphs and Ghibellines.

Hohenzollern, German ruling dynasty that first rose to prominence in the 12th century. In 1192 Frederick III of Zollern became the ruler of Nuremburg, and his descendants founded the Swabian and Franconian lines. From the latter were descended the electors of Brandenburg and the dukes and kings of Prussia, who ruled as emperors of Germany, 1871-1918.
See also: Germany.

Hokkaido (Also: Yezo, Jesso, Ezo; pop. 5.7 million), most northern and second largest island of Japan; 32,259 sq mi (83,518 sq km). Capital: Sapporo, most important harbor is Hakoate. The straits that divide it from the Russian island Sakhalin are called La Pérouse and are called Soya by the Japanese; the straits that divide it from the Russian Kurile Islands are called Nemero. The island is connected to Honshu Island by a railway tunnel, of which 14 mi (22 km) is under the Tsugaru-Kaikyo straits.
The climate is reasonably cold. The terrain is mountainous with a few live volcanos. The highest mountain, Ashidake (7,513 ft, 2,290 m), stands in the national park, Daisetsuzan.
The island yields 80% of the butter and cheese produce. The fish catch is important. Forestry and timber are of importance; agriculture (rice, cereals, and potatoes) is of lesser importance. Thirty percent of the national coal yield is produced here, and there are also deposits of iron, manganese, and sulfur. Industries are iron, steel, textile and paper.
It is the least populous of the large Japanese islands. The Ainu are an ethnic minority whose roots are still unknown. There is a Western influence in the architecture of the towns.

Hokusai, Katsushika (1760-1849), Japanese painter, printmaker, and book illustrator, greatest master of the Japanese *ukiyo-e* (popular) school. Interested in every aspect of life, Hokusai worked under a number of different names in a variety of styles, producing over 30,000 drawings of great imagination, compositional mastery, and technical excellence. The most famous collections are *36 Views of Fuji* (1823-1829) and *Mangwa, or Ten Thousand Sketches* (1814-1818), many of which were admired in Paris and London as well as in the Far East.

Holbein, name of 2 German painters, **Hans Holbein the Elder** (c.1465-1524) was a German Gothic painter of great distinction, best known for his many altarpieces and other church decorations, such as the Kaisheim altar (1502). His middle and later work may have been influenced by Grünewald. His son, **Hans Holbein the Younger** (1497?-1543), a religious painter and portraitist, lived in many European countries and later entered the service of Henry VIII of England, whose most famous portraits are by him.

Holberg, Ludvig (1864-1754), Norwegian-born Danish playwright and educator. A professor at the University of Copenhagen, he was a philosopher and historian as well as an author. His plays were mainly comedies influenced by earlier Roman works. The comedy *Erasmus Montaus* (1731), the satirical poem *Pedar Paars* (1719-1720), and *History of the Danish Kingdoms* (1732-1735) are among his best-known works.

Hölderlin, Johann Christian Friedrich (1770-1843), German lyric poet, noted for the grandeur of his images, derived from classical Greek themes. Among his best-known poems are *Bread and Wine, The Rhine,* and *The Death of Empedocles. Hyperion* is a semi-autobiographical prose novel.

H

Holding company, in finance, company that holds a majority or substantial minority of the stock in another company or companies in order to control policies. The constituent corporations of a holding company are called *subsidiaries*. By *pyramiding* such companies, that is, by creating additional companies to control the stock of holding companies lower in the pyramid, the firm at the apex can control assets many times greater than its own.
See also: Corporation.

Holiday, originally *holyday*, day commemorating an event, person, or religious occasion on which people set aside their normal work to rest, celebrate, or pray. Seasonal days of pagan origin are still celebrated at the summer solstice, the harvest, and the end of winter.

Holiday, Billie (Eleanora Fagan; 1915-1959), U.S. jazz singer. She started her career at 16, singing in Harlem cafés and night spots. Her highly individual style was soon recognized, and she sang with many famous bands and small groups in the 1930s and 1940s. In later years she suffered from heroin addiction.
See also: Jazz.

Holinshed's Chronicles, or *Chronicles of England, Scotland, and Ireland*, purported histories of the 3 countries, largely edited by Raphael Holinshed (d. c.1580). Colorful, imaginative, and inaccurate, they provided plots for many Elizabethan dramatists, including William Shakespeare.

Holistic medicine, approach to health and medical care based on the principle that the 'whole' person must be treated comprehensively, taking physical, psychological, and environmental factors into account. Treatments include herbs, acupuncture, relaxation therapy, yoga, meditation, vitamin therapy, and biofeedback (body self-monitoring technique). Traditional medicines and surgery are generally avoided.

Holland *See:* Netherlands.

Holland, John Philip (1840-1914), Irish-born U.S. inventor who built the first fully successful submarine, the *Holland*, launched in 1898 and bought by the U.S. Navy in 1900.
See also: Submarine.

Hollein, Hans (1934-), Austrian architect, who worked in Stockholm from 1955 to 1958, until 1960 in the US, and then in Vienna, where he joined *Gruppe 4*, a group engaged in architectural reform, inspired by the functionalism of the 1920's. Hollein designed, among other things, the Olivetti building in Amsterdam (1970), part of the Olympic Village in Munich (1972), and the municipal Museum Abteiberg in Mönchengladbach (1983), and published various essays on architecture.

Hollerith, Hermann (1860-1929), American statistician. He designed a code of punch marks that could be punched into cards with the aid of a cardpunch. The punch card was

One of the most famous detective-novel characters is Sherlock Holmes. This creation of Sir Arthur Conan Doyle (1859-1930) was so popular, that the Baker Street post-office had to reserve a special post-office box for the numerous letters that were addressed to the ingenious detective.

used for the first time during the American census (1890), after which the use increased enormously, but since then it has been made obsolete by other forms of information storage (electromagnetic, optic, etc.).

Holly, any of various species of evergreen trees and shrubs (genus *Ilex*) with glossy, spiny leaves and red or black fruits, usually called berries. The European holly (*I. acquifolium*), used at Christmas and in early pagan ritual, is very similar to the common American holly (*I. opaca*), but there are some species in the Americas that are not evergreen and not spiny. Yaupon (*I. vomitoria*), a holly of the southeastern states, has leaves containing large amounts of caffeine and was used by Native Americans to induce vomiting. The leaves of South American maté (*I. paraguayensis*) are dried and used to make maté tea.

Holly, Buddy (Charles Hardin Holly; 1936-1959), U.S. singer, guitarist, and composer, one of rock music's first major performers. Holly's style combined several components of country music with a powerful background rhythm. In 1957 his band, the Crickets, recorded the hit song, 'That'll Be the Day.' In the same year, Holly released a solo hit, 'Peggy Sue.' His career was cut short when he was killed in a plane crash outside of Mason City, Iowa.

Hollyhock (*Althaea rosea*), one of the tallest garden flowers. Its flowers grow on short stems along the tall, upright main stalk and open in succession from the bottom of the stem upwards. Cultivated from earliest times because it was thought to have healing properties, it has spread from its native China to the United States via Europe.

Hollywood (pop. 229,000), district of Los Angeles, Calif. Its name became synonymous with the U.S. film industry in the 1920s. Few films are made there, but it now produces a large percentage of U.S. television material.
See also: California.

Holmes, Oliver Wendell (1809-1894), U.S. author and physician. The father of jurist Oliver Wendell Holmes, Jr., he is best known for his light essays and poems, which appeared in the *Atlantic Monthly* from 1857, and in book form as *The Autocrat of the Breakfast-Table* (1858) and 3 sequels. He taught at Harvard, 1847-1882; his paper *The Contagiousness of Puerperal Fever* (1843) is considered the first major contribution to medicine by an American.

Holmes, Sherlock, fictional detective created by the English author Sir Arthur Conan Doyle. Holmes solves difficult crimes through observation and deduction. A complex character, he has knowledge of chemistry, literature, and the arts, and is an accomplished violinist. He is assisted by his close friend and partner, Dr. John Watson. Holmes first appeared in the novel *A Study in Scarlet* (1887).
See also: Doyle, Sir Arthur Conan.

Holmium, chemical element, symbol Ho; for physical constants see Periodic Table. Holmium was discovered spectroscopically in 1878 by M. Delafontaine and J.L. Soret. It occurs in gadolinite and other rare-earth minerals and is commercially obtained from monazite. Elemental holmium is prepared by reducing its anhydrous chloride with calcium metal. Holmium is a silvery, soft, reactive metal. It has interesting magnetic properties. Holmium belongs to the series of elements known as the rare-earth metals. Ion-exchange and solvent extraction techniques have led to much easier isolation of these elements. Holmium and its compounds are used in carbon-arc lighting applications, special types of glass, enamels, and refractory materials.

Holocaust, term applied to the systematic execution of 6 million European Jews by the German Nazi regime, 1933-1945. Adolf Hitler had exploited anti-Semitic feelings in his rise to power and later called for a 'final solution to the Jewish question.' Most Jews in countries overrun by the Nazis who did not emigrate in time were victims of the Holocaust, which effectively obliterated the Jewish secular and religious life that had flourished in Europe for centuries.
See also: Nazism; World War II.

Holography, technique for recording and reproducing 3-dimensional images by means of laser beams. The picture taken by the technique, the *hologram*, is a piece of photographic film that records not the scene itself but the unfocused pattern of light waves coming from the scene. A hologram is made by illuminating both the scene and the film with laser light, which has the important property of containing light of only 1 color (or wavelength). Light reflected from objects in the scene interferes with light from the direct, or *reference*, beam, producing a light-and-dark pattern of interference fringes. When light from a laser is passed through the developed hologram, the original pattern of light from the scene viewed is recreated in every respect. Thus the original scene will be visible in 3 dimensions, and the person viewing can look 'behind' it by moving his or her head sideways. The method was invented in the 1940s by D. Gabor, who received the Nobel Prize in physics in 1971 for his work.

Holst, Gustav Theodore (1874-1934), English composer. He is best known for *The Planets* (1914-1916), a massive symphonic suite, each piece representing a planet characterized in myth and astrology. Its popularity has overshadowed his other works, such as the opera *Savitri* (1908).

Holy Alliance, collective security agreement created at the Congress of Vienna in 1815 by Russia, Austria, and Prussia and later joined by most other European powers (excluding Britain, Turkey, and the Vatican). Its avowed aim was to promote mutual relations according to Christian principles. It had little importance in itself, except as a symbol of reaction; revolts in Spain and Naples in the 1820s were suppressed in its name.
See also: Vienna, Congress of.

Holy Bible *See:* Bible.

Holy Grail, legendary talisman, given various forms in various legends. In his *Conte del Graal* (c.1180) Chrétien de Troyes made it the chalice from which Christ drank at the Last Supper and that was used to catch his blood on the Cross. The knight Perceval, as in the poem by Wolfram von Eschenbach *Parzival* (1210), seeks the Grail to redeem himself and others. *Queste del Saint Graal* (1200) linked the Grail with the Arthurian legends and was the source of Thomas Malory's *Morte d'Arthur* (1470). The Grail legends have inspired such modern writers as T.H. White, T.S. Eliot, and Alfred Lord Tennyson, and also Richard Wagner's operas *Lohengrin* (1848) and *Parsifal* (1882).

Holy Land *See:* Palestine.

Holy Roman Empire, European empire centered in Germany that endured from medieval times until 1806. It was effectively established in A.D. 962 when the pope crowned Otto I, king of Germany, emperor of Rome. It derived its political claim to the Roman Empire based on Charlemagne's belief that his empire was the legitimate successor to ancient Rome. In theory, the Holy Roman emperor was God's temporal ruler of all christians. In reality, the political control was somewhat different. At its height, it included all the German principalities, Austria, Bohemia, Moravia, Switzerland, the Low Countries, eastern France, and northern and central Italy. Up until 1562 the emperor was crowned by the pope, thereafter the coronation was performed in Frankfurt. The Holy Roman Empire was in constant conflict with the pope and the Italian states over temporal and religious issues. It was seriously weakened by the Reformation which challenged the allegiance of German Protestant princes to the emperor. The Thirty Years War (1618-1648) almost totally destroyed the German people and the Holy Roman Empire. In fact, it never recovered from this conflict. France emerged as a central power from the war and its continued military successes, from the time of Louis XIV to Napoleon I, eradicated the political reality of the Holy Roman emperor. The official end came in 1806 when Francis II renounced the title, proclaiming himself Francis I, emperor of Austria.

Holy wars *See:* Crusades.

Holy Week, in the Christian church year, week preceding Easter, observed in most churches as a time of solemn devotion to the passion of Christ. From the 4th century the events of the week of the crucifixion have been liturgically reenacted, now especially on Palm Sunday, Maundy Thursday, Good Friday, Holy Saturday, and Easter Sunday.
See also: Christianity.

Home, Lord (1903-1995), British politician, prime minister (1963-1964). Early in his career he served as a Conservative party member in the House of Commons (1931-1945). He was also foreign secretary (1960-1963, 1970-1974).
See also: United Kingdom.

Home economics, in education, all the disciplines necessary to home maintenance: cooking, nutrition, sewing, the nature and use of textiles, household equipment, and budgeting. Originally it was not considered a scholastic subject, but today it is a common high school elective, and colleges offer degree courses in it. In the United Kingdom it is called domestic science.

Homelessness, term coined in the 1980s to describe the growing condition of mostly city-dwelling people who have no permanent place to live. In the United States, causes of homelessness range from untreated mental illness to joblessness among the poor and lack of low-income housing. The total number of homeless people in the U.S. is thought to be in the millions.

Homeopathy, system of treating disease by administering small doses of a drug that would cause a healthy person to have the symptoms of the disease under treatment. Homeopathy takes a holistic approach, claiming to treat the physical, emotional, and mental states of the patient at once. Homeopathy was introduced in the West by the German doctor Samuel Hahnemann (1755-1843), author of the controversial *Organon of the Art of Healing*.

See also: Hahnemann, (Christian Friedrich) Samuel.

Homeostasis, self-regulating mechanisms through which biological systems maintain a stable internal condition in the face of changes in the external environment. The French physiologist Claude Bernard (1813-1878) was the first to show that the internal environment of any living organism is maintained within certain limits. Homeostasis is generally achieved through on-off control and feedback control. Hormones often play a vital role in it.
See also: Bernard, Claude.

Homer (8th century B.C.?), Greek epic poet to whom are ascribed the *Iliad* and *Odyssey*, universally regarded as among the greatest works of western literature. Both poems deal with events related to the Trojan War. The *Iliad* is about a single episode of the war-the anger of the Greek warrior, Achilles, and its tragic results. The *Odyssey* tells of the adventures and quests of another Greek warrior, Odysseus, after the war. Historically, there has been much debate about whether the poems were really written by one author, but most scholars now believe that they were.
See also: Iliad; Odyssey.

This bust of Homer can be found in the Museo Nazionale at Naples. Homer is traditionally portrayed as a blind bard.

Homer, Winslow (1836-1910), U.S. painter who often worked in watercolor, best known for his landscapes and sea studies of New England and Florida, such as *Gulf Stream* (1899). Originally an illustrator, he recorded the Civil War for *Harper's Weekly*. His quasi-impressionist paintings revolutionized the style of U.S. painting in the 1880s and 1890s.

Home Rule, in the British Isles, a term used to refer to the movement to gain internal autonomy for Ireland under the British crown, 1870-1914. The term has also been used in reference to demands in Scotland and Wales for some measure of selfgovernment.
In the United States, the power of a local government unit, usually a city, to draft or change its own charter and to conduct its

H

H

own affairs. Under home rule, a municipality may handle local matters as long as its actions do not violate the state constitution or state laws. Most states allow cities to have some degree of home rule; some also provide limited home rule for counties. Municipal home rule may be permitted under the state constitution or be granted by legislation.

Homicide, killing of a human being by another. Criminal homicide is classified as either murder or manslaughter. Some homicides are determined to be excusable or justifiable, based on such circumstances as self-defense. Sentencing for homicide varies between U.S. states, some of which consider it a capital offense.
See also: Crime.

Homing pigeon, bird of the family Columbidae able to return to its loft from vast distances, selectively crossbred to combine speed and stamina. The racing of homing pigeons has been a popular sport since the 19th century. A well-trained bird may travel over 1,000 mi (1,600 km).

Homo erectus, early species of human being, having larger teeth and smaller brains than modern humans (*Homo sapiens*). They lived from about a million and a half years ago to 300,000 years ago. *Homo erectus* probably originated in Africa and later moved into Asia and Europe. Fossils of *Homo erectus* have been found in Indonesia (Java), China, and Kenya. *Homo erectus* made stone tools and used fire.
See also: Heidelberg man; Java man; Peking man.

Homogenization, process to delay the separation of fat in milk, an unstable emulsion containing fat globules that tend to coalesce. In homogenization the milk is heated to

about 140°F (60°C) and passed at pressure through small openings. The fatty clusters are broken up by shearing as they pass through the holes, by the action of pressure, and by impact with components of the homogenizer.

Homo habilis, oldest species of human being yet discovered, believed to have lived in Africa about 2 million years ago, probably the first known human to make stone tools. The brain of *Homo habilus* seems to have been about half the size of the modern human brain. Fossil discoveries in Kenya suggest that *Homo habilis*, like apes, spent a great deal of time in trees.
See also: Australopithecus; Homo erectus.

Homologue, in biology, structure or organ with the same evolutionary origin as an apparently different structure in another species. For example, there is little apparent similarity between a horse's leg and the flipper of a whale, but they have similar embryonic histories and are therefore homologues.
See also: Biology.

Homo sapiens, species of humans approximately 450,000 years old, with the oldest known fossil remains dating back about 375,000 years. Neanderthal man is the most well known example of *Homo sapiens* and lived in Africa, Asia, and Europe from 100,000 to 35,000 years ago. Modern human beings are classified as a subspecies of *Homo sapiens*, *Homo sapiens sapiens*.
See also: Neanderthal Man.

Homosexuality, sexual attraction to persons of one's own sex. Female homosexuality is called lesbianism. Many theories have tried to account for homosexuality as a deviation from the norm. Homosexuality was widely accepted in ancient Greece, and there have been prominent homosexuals throughout

history. However, legal persecution and public censure have forced homosexuals to live restricted and secret lives. In the 1980s the AIDS epidemic provided an excuse for a new rise in anti-homosexual attitudes.

Honan *See:* Henan.

Honduras

Capital:	Tegucigalpa
Area:	43,277 sq mi (112,088 sq km)
Population:	6,561,000
Language:	Spanish
Government:	Presidential republic
Independent:	1838
Head of gov.:	President
Per capita:	US$ 2,600
Monetary unit:	1 Lempira = 100 centavos

Honduras (Republic of), country in Central America bordered by the Caribbean Sea, Nicaragua, El Salvador and the Pacific Ocean, and Guatemala.
Land and people. Most of Honduras is mountainous, but there are swamps and forests in the east, along the Mosquito Coast. Enclosed within the mountain ranges are several basins that have become the major population centers. The official language is Spanish, and Roman Catholicism is the dominant religion.
Economy. U.S.-owned banana and coffee plantations dominate the economy, and the bulk of the population works on the land. Coffee replaced bananas as the main export in 1975; other exports are timber, meat, cotton, and tobacco. There is little industry, and transport facilities are poor.
History. From the 4th to the 7th centuries the ancient city of Copán was a center of the civilization of the Mayas, but when Columbus reached the Honduran coast on his 1502 voyage, the country was inhabited only by seminomadic tribes. A Spanish colony for almost 300 years, Honduras was generally governed from Guatemala. In 1821 it won independence from Spain and became part of the Mexican empire, along with 4 other Central American States. Subsequently the 5 states formed the United Provinces of Central America, of which the Honduran patriot Francisco Morazán was president until its dissolution in 1838. Since that time, Honduras has been an independ-

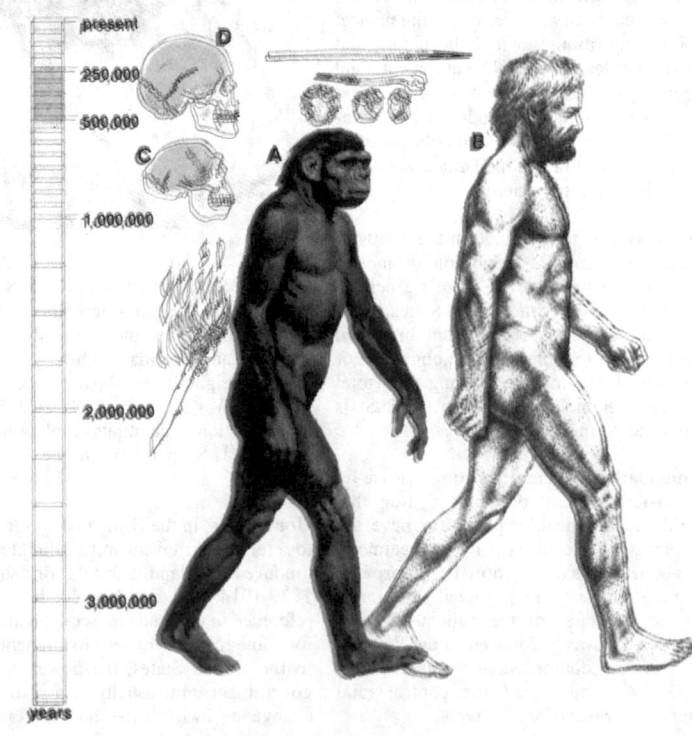

The remains of Peking man, *Homo erectus pekinensis*, were excavated at the site of Chou-k'ou-tien (1927-37). Peking man (A), who lived approximately 500,000 to 250,000 years ago, stood slightly more than 5 ft (1.5 m) tall (compare (B) modern *Homo sapiens*) and had a long, low skull with heavy brow ridges. Its cranial capacity (C) ranged from 52-79 cub in (850-1,300 cub cm). That of modern man (D) averages 79-82 cub in (1,300 tot 1,350 cub cm). *Homo erectus* used stone tools and was apparantly the first species to make use of fire.

ent republic. The idea of federation remained popular with many Central American leaders, but attempts by Honduras, El Salvador and Nicaragua in the 1840's and 1850's to form a new confederation failed. As an independant republic, Honduras has seen civil strife, revolt, and dictatorial rule. From 1855 to 1932, the country had 67 different heads of state. There were armed conflicts with neighbouring countries, usually over territorial claims, and military intervention by the United States (in 1907, 1912 and 1924-25). Boundary disputes were settled with Guatamala in 1933, Nicaragua in 1960, and El Salvador in 1980.

The military came to power in a bloodless coup in 1972. In 1980 a constitutional assembly was elected and a new constitution drafted. In 1981 civilian rule was restored when Roberto Suazo of the center-right Liberal party was elected president. The militairy, however, continued to play an important role. Although the Liberal party remained in power in the 1980's, and more democratic structures were imposed, rightist military officers generally dominated politics.

The 1980s also saw occasional border clashes with neighboring Nicaragua.

After a brief period under the National party in the early 1990's, Carlos Roberto Reina of the Liberal party was elected president in 1993. He pledged to reduce the militairy's role in civilian affairs. The 1990s however were also characterized by violations of human rights by the military. In 1997 Carlos Roberto Flores Facussé of the Liberal party was elected president. In 1998 Honduras was devastated by hurricane Mitch. Virulent crime waves take place in the cities, mainly conducted by youth gangs and death squads. President Ricardo Maduro, who was elected in 2002, is determined to put an end to the violence on the streets.

Honecker, Erich (1912-1994), leader of East Germany (1971-1989). He joined the Communist Party (1929) as a youth and was imprisoned by the Nazis (1935-1945). After World War II, he rose to the top of the political ranks in East German and Communist Party politics. He resigned in 1989, not long before the beginning of the process of German reunification. In 1992 he was tried for his involvement in the killings of people who had tried to escape from East Germany. Due to his poor health, the trial was discontinued.

Honegger, Arthur (1892-1955), Swiss-French composer, member of the French Les Six group, best known for his popular *Pacific 231* (1923) and his oratorio *King David* (1921-1923).

Honey, sweet substance made through enzyme action by bees from the nectar of flowers. As a sweetener, there is very little difference between honey and sucrose (table sugar), although the former does contain minimal quantities of vitamins, minerals, and amino acids. Honey is available in comb or syrup form. There are different types depending on what flowers the bees have fed on; some popular varieties are sage, clover, and wildflower.

Honey badger *See:* Ratel.

Honey bear *See:* Sloth bear.

Honey bee *See:* Bee.

Honeyeater, any of several birds of the family Maliphagidea, native to Australia, New Zealand, and the Pacific Islands. They feed on nectar and insects and some are pests in orchards because they eat flowers and fruit. Some species are very rare or extinct because they have been hunted and their forest homes cut down. The moho, which ranged as far as Hawaii, was prized for its yellow and black feathers, used by the Hawaiians for ceremonial cloaks. It is now extinct.

Honey locust, any of several trees (genus *Gleditsia*) of the pea family. Often used for its shade and ornamentation, the honey locust is commonly found in the eastern United States. It has large flat pods whose pulp cattle eat. Its wood is often used for railroad ties, fence posts, or fuel.

Honeysuckle, common name for shrubs and vines of the family Caprifoliaceae, found in the Northern Hemisphere. Their flowers contain a large amount of nectar, which makes them a favorite of insects, such as hawk moths. Many of them produce an attractive scent. The berries are popular with birds.

Hong Kong (pop. 7,300,000), former British Crown colony on the coast of southeast China, about 90 mi (145 km) from Canton, consisting of mainland territories and numerous offshore islands. Hong Kong island was ceded to the British after the Opium War in 1842. Mainland Hong Kong includes Kowloon, acquired in 1860, and the New Territories, leased to Britain for 99 years in 1898. In 1985 an agreement was reached between the United Kingdom and the People's Republic of China regarding the turnover of Hong Kong to Chinese sovereignty in 1997. Of the rocky land surface, 75% is unsuitable for building, and a mere 14% is urbanized, accommodating 90% of the population. Since the early 1900s refugees from China's political upheavals have swelled the colony's population. During Japanese wartime occupation (1941-1945) the trend was briefly reversed, but since then the population has increased rapidly. Hong Kong is a free trade area and one of the world's principal ports. It has much light industry, particularly textiles and electrical goods. The colony depends on China for most of its food and water. In 1997 Hong Kong was turned over to China. It was agreed upon that Hong Kong will maintain it's legal system and capitalistic economy for at least another 50 years. In 1998 a new airport came into use, situated in the sea.

Honiara (pop. 35,000), capital of the Solomon Islands, an independent state (and member of the British Commonwealth) in the southwest Pacific Ocean. Honiara is located on the island of Guadalcanal. It was the site of a World War II U.S. military base

and earlier of a Japanese military base. *See also:* Solomon Islands.

Honolulu (pop. 423,000), capital and chief seaport of Hawaii, seat of Honolulu County, located on the southeast coast of Oahu Island. Honolulu grew from a fishing village in 1820 to the capital of independent Hawaii (1845) and then the territorial capital when Hawaii was annexed by the U.S. (1898). It is important as a shipping center, for sugar and pineapple processing, and as the tourist hub of Hawaii.
See also: Hawaii.

Honorius I (d. 638), pope of the Roman Catholic Church, elected 625. An aristocrat from southern Italy, he oversaw missionary activities in Britain and negotiated a peace settlement with the German Lombard tribe. He apparently supported monotheletism, a theological trend that argued that Christ had a dual nature but a single will. This idea was declared heretical at the third Council of Constantinople (680).

Honorius III (d. 1227), pope of the Roman Catholic Church, elected 1216. He inaugurated campaigns for new Crusades in Spain and France and sanctioned new religious orders (the Dominicans, the Franciscans, and the Carmelites).

View from Victoria over Victoria Harbour, Stonecutters Island and Kowloon. Hong Kong is not only one of the largest ports in the world, but also one of the largest shipowning centers. According to the Hong Kong Shipowners Association, the total tonnage of its ships exceeds that of the entire British fleet by more than one half. About 80% of the ships carry the Liberian flag.

Honshu (Hondo; pop. 98,352,000), largest island of Japan, also known as 'the mainland': 89,239 sq mi (231,039 sq km). Capital: Tokyo. It is volcanic, wooded, and very mountainous, with fertile basins. The highest mountain is Mount Fuji at 12,389 ft (3,776 m). The eastern part has hot and moist summers, while the western part has cold winters with large amounts of snow. There is agriculture in the coastal regions.

H

H

The region between Kobe and Tokyo is heavily industrialized. It often experiences earthquakes and typhoons. It is connected to Kyushu and Hokkaido by tunnels under the sea and by bridge to Shikoku. The 2.4 mi (3.9 km) long bridge is to withstand earthquakes up to 8.5 on the Richter scale.

A village in the northern mountain region of Honshu, also called Tohoku. This region has a climate that is just inbetween that of the mild, subtropical southern and central parts of Honshu, and the colder island of Hokkaido.

Hood, Thomas (1799-1845), English humorist and editor, known for his *Comic Annuals* (1830-1839, 1842). He is also regarded as a poet of protest against industrial conditions, e.g. 'Song of the Shirt' (1843).

Hoof, enlarged, heavy toenail developed by many herbivorous animals. Since speed is a large herbivore's best defense against a predator, it is an advantage to be able to run on the tips of the toes, as this adds length to the stride. Hooves give stability to this tiptoe stance. Animals with hooves include horses, rhinoceroses, antelopes, goats, sheep, hogs, hippopotamuses, camels, and cattle.

Hoof-and-mouth disease *See:* Foot-and-mouth disease.

The hoopoe (*U. epops*) is related to the kingfisher. Portrayed in ancient Egyptian hieroglyphs, the bird is admired for its plumage. When threatened, the female sprays a foul-smelling liquid.

Hoogh, Pieter de (or **Hooch, Pieter de**) (1629-1683?), a Dutch painter of the 17th-century *genre* (everyday life) school. His interior and courtyard scenes of middle-class family life have intimacy and realism. Such works as *The Music Party* and *A Dutch Courtyard* show his use of light and shadow, warm colors, and sharp detail.
De Hooch was born in Rotterdam, and studied painting in Haarlem. About 1654 he settled in Delft. He knew Jan Vermeer and was influenced by him and Carel Fabritius, a pupil of Rembrandt. In 1667 de Hooch moved to Amsterdam. His style changed and many of his works are inferior to those of his Delft period.

Hooke, Robert (1635-1703), English experimental scientist and one of the greatest inventors of his age. Hooke entered his most creative period in 1662, when he became the Royal Society of London's first curator of experiments. He invented the compound microscope, the universal joint, the spiral spring for watches, and a type of telescope. His microscopic researches were published in the beautifully illustrated *Micrographia* (1665), a work that also introduced the term *cell* to biology. He is best remembered for Hooke's law (1678) that the deformation occurring in an elastic body under stress is proportional to the applied stress. He also theorized a precursor to Newton's law of universal gravitation.
See also: Microscope.

Hooker, Richard (1554-1600), English theologian whose 8-volume work *Of the Laws of Ecclesiastical Polity*, a landmark of Anglican theology, defended the Elizabethan religious settlement against both Roman Catholics and Puritans.
See also: Theology.

Hookworm, any of various intestinal parasites (order Strongiloidae) of humans and domesticated animal. The life cycle involves a free-living larval stage followed by direct infection of the host, with no intermediate host. The parasitic adults are blood feeders and attach themselves to vessels in the wall of the intestine. Each worm may cause the loss of up to 0.25 ml of blood a day.

Hoopoe (*Upupa epops*), large bird of Europe, Asia, and Africa, named for its call. Since recorded time hoopoes have been prized for their pink plumage, black and white barred wings, and large crest.

Hoosier State *See:* Indiana.

Hoover, Herbert Clark (1874-1964), 31st president of the United States (1929-1933). Republican. He served as Secretary of Commerce (1921-1928). He gave his name to the Hoover Moratorium (1931-1932), according to which the repayment of government debts was suspended for a year. This led to the Lausanne Conference (1932), following which Germany was relieved of its compensation.

Hoover, J(ohn) Edgar (1895-1972), director of the Federal Bureau of Investigation (FBI) from 1924 until his death. Hoover made the FBI an efficient apparatus to fight organized crime. After World War II, at Hoover's direction, the FBI began a crusade against 'subversives,' targeting leftist activists. By the 1960s and 1970s Hoover's conservative political views and the FBI's violation of the civil rights of its opponents made him the center of controversy. He published a number of books, including *Masters of Deceit* (1958) and *J. Edgar Hoover on Communism* (1969).
See also: Federal Bureau of Investigation.

Hoover Dam, formerly Boulder Dam (1933-1947), on the Colorado River between Nevada and Arizona. It is 736 ft (244 m) high and 1,244 ft (379 m) long. The dam impounds Lake Mead and has a hydroelectric capacity of 1.3 Mw. Built in 1931-1935, it began operating in 1936.

Hop, tall prickly perennial vine (*Homulus lupulus*) of the mulberry family whose dried female flowers, called hops, contain *lupullin*, a substance that gives beer its bitter flavor and is used as a preservative. Hops were first grown by the Greeks, who ate the young shoots. They were first used for flavoring beer by the Germans in the 8th century.

Hope, Bob (Leslie Townes Hope; 1903-), English-born U.S. comedian, born in Eltham, England. He emigrated to the United States as a child and began his career in vaudeville, becoming famous in the 1930s through radio and motion pictures, notably in the 'Road' series of movies with Bing Crosby. Since World War II he has made regular overseas tours to entertain U.S. troops and has specialized in topical political humor.

Hopewell *See:* Mound Builders.

Hopi, Pueblo Native American tribe of northeast Arizona. The Hopi have a complex society based on clans organized around matrilineal extended households. Since the 1820s there have been territorial conflicts between the Hopi and Navajo. In 1975 the federal government redrew territorial boundaries, making several thousand Navajo move. The Hopi are known for their elaborate religious ceremonies, which feature dancing and the kachina figure.

Hopkins, Gerard Manley (1844-1889), English poet and Jesuit priest. Hopkins's work was experimental, using natural speech and 'sprung rhythm' rather than syllable counts. Unappreciated in his lifetime, his poetry has had great influence in the 20th century. 'The Windhover' and 'God's Grandeur' are two of his major poems. His work was published posthumously in 1918.

Hopkins, Johns (1795-1873), U.S. financier and philanthropist. A Quaker, he made his fortune as a wholesale grocer. He bequeathed $7 million to endow Johns Hopkins University and Johns Hopkins Hospital in Baltimore.

Hopper, Edward (1882-1967), U.S. painter and engraver. First recognized for his etch-

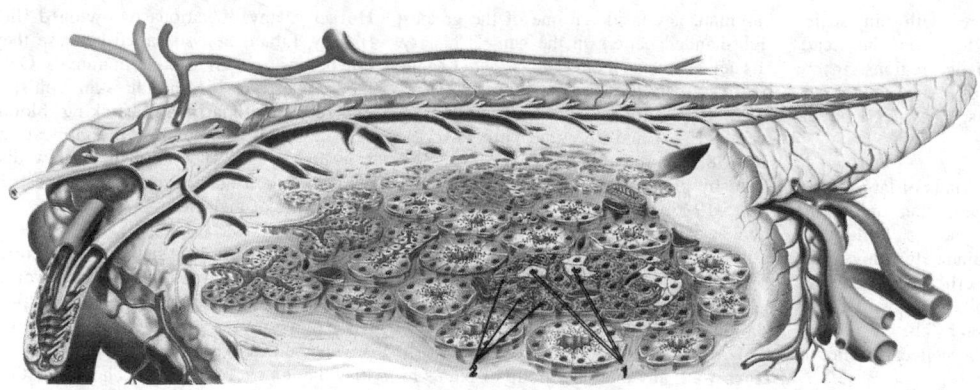

The pancreas is both an exocrine and an endocrine gland, secreting pancreatic juices into the duodenum, and secreting insulin and glucogon, two hormones concerned with carbohydrate metabolism. Here, we see two types of hormone-producing cells of the pancreas, alpha (1) and beta (2) cells from the islets of Langerhans. Alpha cells manufacture glucagon, which stimulates the conversion of amino acids into glucose in the liver (gluconeogenesis) and the breakdown of glycogen to glucose, raising the blood sugar level. Insulin, which is produced by the beta cells, promotes the uptake of glucose by muscle and fat cells, reducing the blood sugar level. Insulin stimulates glycogen, protein, and fat synthesis. Insufficient production results in diabetes mellitus. Also present are islet delta cells, which secrete somatostatin, a hormone that acts to inhibit excess glucagon or insulin secretion.

ings, he returned to painting late in life and became known for large, quiet urban studies of subtle composition, often reflecting loneliness and alienation.

Hopper, Grace Murray (1906-1992), U.S. computer scientist whose belief that computer languages should be more like everyday language led, in the 1950s, to the invention of COBOL (Common Business Oriented Language), a widely used computer language. After graduating from Vassar in 1928, Hopper went on to earn a Ph.D in mathematics from Yale. In 1943 Hopper joined the Navy, where she attained the rank of rear admiral.

Hoppner, John (1758-1810) English portraitist to the Prince of Wales (1789), elected to the Royal Academy (1795). His portraits include studies of Nelson, Wellington, and Sir Walter Scott.

Horace (Quintus Horatius Flaccus; 65-8 B.C.), Roman lyric poet and satirist. At first supported by a rich patron, Maecenas, he later became the favored poet of the emperor Augustus. Horace's surviving works include four books of *Odes*, two of *Satires*, two of *Epistles*, and his *Episodes*, These and the *Art of Poetry* have had deep influence on European literature.
See also: Rome, Ancient.

Horatius (Publius Horatius Cocles), legendary Roman hero. He and two companions are said to have held off an invading Etruscan army at the Sublician Bridge across the Tiber River. The Romans cut the bridge behind him, blocking the Etruscan advance, and Horatius escaped by swimming across the river.
See also: Rome, Ancient.

Horehound (*Marrubium vulgare*), aromatic plant in the mint family, with wrinkled leaves and clusters of small flowers found growing in waste places. It was once popular as a flavoring in candies and cough medicines.

Horizon, apparent line where the sky meets the land or sea. At sea, its distance varies in proportion to the square root of the height of the observer's eyes above sea level. The celestial horizon is the great circle on the celestial sphere at 90° from the zenith (the point immediately above the observer).

Hormone, chemical substance produced in living organisms by the endocrine system. Hormones act to regulate many biological processes, including growth, metabolism, digestion and reproduction. They are 'messengers,' usually acting at a distance from their site of origin. Hormones are carried from ductless glands through the bloodstream to their point of action.
See also: Endocrine system.

Hormuz, Strait of, 30-50 mi (48-80 km) wide waterway leading out of the Persian Gulf to the Gulf of Oman and the Indian Ocean. Most Middle East oil tankers pass through the strait, which is commanded by Qishm Island (Iran) and three other islands-Greater Tunb, Lesser Tunb, and Abu Musa currently held by Iran but claimed by the United Arab Emirates.

Horn, in music, brass wind instrument. Horns are derived from the animal horns used by primitive societies. Metal was found to produce a better tone, and horns became increasingly sophisticated and complex. Horns were introduced into orchestral music in the early 18th centrury. Valved horns (such as the trumpet) were developed in the 19th century.

Horn, bony extension, usually elongated and pointed, growing from the heads of some mammals, including cattle, sheep, and goats. The antlers of deer are not true horns. Both males and females may grow horns, which consist of a central core of bone-like material encased by a layer of the skin protein keratin. Animals use their horns for protection, either by fighting with them or by displaying them in a threatening manner.

Hornbill, any of various birds of the family Bucerotidae noted for their huge bills, which in some species bear an additional growth called a casque. Hornbills are found in most of Africa and southern Asia as far east as the Philippines. Most live in forests, but the large ground hornbill lives in open country. They feed mainly on fruit, but some hornbills eat insects or lizards. Their nesting habits are unusual. The eggs are laid in a hole in a tree trunk, and the female walls herself in with mud; while incubating the eggs, she is fed by the male through a slit in the mud wall.

Hornblende, dark green or black mineral of varied composition, usually including silicates of aluminum and other abundant elements. It forms vitreous glassy rocks. Often found in igneous and metamorphic rock, hornblende is a major constituent of the amphibole group of minerals.

Hornbook, children's primer used before printed books became cheap and widely available. Hornbooks consisted of printed sheets showing the alphabet and numerals; the sheets were pasted to a wooden, short-handled tablet and covered with a thin, transparent layer of horn for protection.

Horne, Lena (1917-), U.S. actress and blues singer. Horne began her career as a 16-year-old chorus dancer in New York City's Cotton Club and made her movie debut in *The Duke Is Tops* (1938). Horne gained widespread recognition for her singing in the movie *Stormy Weather* (1943) and went on to be a popular nightclub singer in Europe and the United States.

Horne, Marilyn (1934-), U.S. mezzo-soprano. A pupil of Lotte Lehmann, she is known for her mastery of bel canto roles in Bellini and Rossini operas. She made her Metropolitan Opera debut in 1970 as Adalgisa in Bellini's *Norma*.

Horned lizard, name for several species of lizards (genus *Phrynosoma*) native to North America, from Canada to Mexico. Because of their shape, they are often called horned

The great hornbill, *Buceros bicornis*, is more than 3 ft (1 m) long. It is found in the rain forests of India, Indochina, and Sumatra. Some people keep it as a pet, enjoying its amusing ability to catch food in the air and its habit of hopping about in a clownish manner.

H

toads. The body is covered with spiny scales that are particularly long on the head. Horned lizards live in dry regions, where they can bury themselves in the sand by rapid sidewise movements. They feed on insects, especially ants.

Hornet, any of several kinds of large social wasps (family Vespidae), that, unlike the more common yellow jackets, build their nests in trees or in human dwellings. The nest, enclosed in a paperlike shell, consists of a series of horizontal combs. Hornets make the papery material by chewing woody plant matters. Female hornets can inflict an extremely painful sting.

Horney, Karen (1885-1952), German-born U.S. psychoanalyst, founder of the American Institute of Psychoanalysis (1941). She stressed the importance of environmental and cultural factors in character development, rejecting many of the basic principles of Freud's psychoanalytic theory, especially his stress on the libido as the root of personality and behavior. Her best known work is *Neurosis and Human Growth* (1950).

Hornsby, Rogers (1896-1963), U.S. baseball player and manager. Hornsby, a second

The Shetland pony is one of the smallest horses, the Arabian is the oldest breed. The Shire, bred in England, is one of the largest horses and a powerful workhorse.

Shetland pony

Arabian

Shire

baseman, is considered one of the greatest right-handed batters in the game's history. His achievements include 7 National League batting titles (consecutively from 1920-1925, 1928), hitting .424-the single season record (1924), and a lifetime batting average of .358, second only to Ty Cobb's .367. Hornsby played for the St. Louis Cardinals (1915-1926, and 1933), New York Giants (1927), Boston Braves (1928), Chicago Cubs (1929-1932), and the St. Louis Browns (1933-1937). He went on to manage after his 1937 season and was inducted into the National Baseball Hall of Fame (1942).

Hornwort, any one of a group of plants related to liverworts and mosses and growing world-wide, but most commonly in warm, moist regions. A hornwort reproduces in a cycle known as the *alternation of generations*. It forms a gametophyte in the first stage of its life and a sporophyte in the second stage. The gametophyte is a small plant body called a *thallus*. The sporophyte is from 3/16-4 3/4 in (0.5-12 cm) high and resembles the horns of a cow.

Horowitz, Vladimir (1904-1989), Russian-born U.S. virtuoso pianist. After a brilliant debut in Kiev (1922), he toured the USSR and Europe (1924) and the United States (1928). He became a U.S. citizen in 1944.

Horse, hoofed, herbivorous mammal (genus *Equus*). This is the only living genus of the family Equidae; the donkey and the zebra are different species of the same genus. Wild horses occurred in prehistoric times over most of Eurasia. Today, the only surviving true wild horse is the Przewalski horse of Siberia, Mongolia, and western China. Domestic horses (*E. caballus*) can be grouped as ponies, heavy draft horses, lightweight draft, and riding horses; they originated from North African stock. Thoroughbreds are descended from Arabian stock. The fossil record of the horse family provides a classic example of evolution in action. The earliest animal that can be placed in the family was Eohippus, which was the size of a fox terrier and had 3 toes of equal size on each hindfoot and 4 toes on each forefoot. The development of the single-toed foot of modern horses was an adaptation to running on hard dry grassland. The changes in tooth pattern allowed the animal to eat abrasive grasses. The increase in size may be followed through a continuous series of intermediate stages to the present day. The various species of the genus *Equus* can often interbreed (e.g., horses and donkeys), but the offspring (e.g., mules) are generally sterile.

Horse brier *See:* Greenbrier.

Horse chestnut, popular name for various trees and shrubs (genus *Aesculus*) of the family Hippcastanaceae. In winter the twigs bear sticky buds that develop into conspicuous leaves and big flowers. In the fall large, shiny seeds similar to chestnuts are released from fleshy coats. The Ohio buckeye (*A. glabra*) is the state tree. Horse chestnut wood is light and strong and is used for boxes and coffins.

Horsefly, any of various two-winged flies (family Tabanidae), so called because they bite horses, as well as other mammals. Only the females bite, piercing the skin with specialized mouthparts and sucking blood. Female horseflies require a blood-meal before laying eggs. They transmit a few diseases, but their main significance as pests is in the sting of their bite.

Horsehair worm, hair snake, or hairworm, any of about 200 types of long, thin worms making up the phylum Nematomorpha. They may grow to 28 in (70 cm). The young are hatched from eggs and form cysts, which may be eaten by insects. The larva then leave the cysts and live in the insects as parasites. The worms leave the insects' bodies when they reach adulthood.

Horse latitudes, regions of calm, quiet winds situated on either side of the equator, between 30°N and S latitudes. In early colonial days, ships bound for the Americas were often becalmed in these latitudes. The horses died from lack of fresh water and were cast overboard. This gave the regions their name.
See also: Calms, Regions of.

Horse nettle *See:* Solanum.

Horsepower, unit of power used to indicate the rate at which work is done. In the 18th century inventor James Watt experimentally determined that a strong horse can lift up to 33,000 foot-pounds 1 foot per minute. This has become the definition of 1 horsepower. In electrical units 1 horsepower is equivalent to 746 watts; the heat equivalent is 2, 545 BTU (British thermal units) per hour.

Horse Racing, sport involving trials of speed between horses, watched by millions of people in many countries. Its interest as a spectator sport is largely based on the practice of on-and off-track betting. The oldest stake race is the English St. Leger, first run in 1776. In the United States, the most famous race is the Kentucky Derby, first run in 1875. Besides flat racing, there are steeplechasing and harness racing.

Horseradish, common name for a perennial herb (*Armoracia rusticana*), of the mustard family. Native to Eurasia, it is widely cultivated for its white, edible, pungent roots, which grow to a length of 12 in (30 cm) and are used to make a popular relish with a sharp flavor.

Horseshoe crab, or king crab, any of several marine arthropods of the order Xiphosura, 'living fossils' whose almost identical ancestors have been found in rocks 175 million years old. King crabs are not true crabs but are more closely related to spiders. If the dome-shaped shell is turned over it shows a horseshoe outline and a series of jointed legs. King crabs live near sheltered shores on the Atlantic coast of the United States and around the coast of Asia. In some places king crabs are fished for pig and chicken feed, and fertilizer. They are pests in clam beds.

Horseshoe Falls *See:* Niagara Falls.

Horseshoe pitching, game played on a court by 2 or more people, in which players attempt to throw horseshoes to encircle an iron stake. The court, usually out-of-doors, is 50 ft (15.2 m) long and 10 ft (3m) wide. The iron stakes, set at either end of the court, are 1 ft (0.3m) high. Scoring is based on a system of point values placed on how close a horseshoe is to a stake. Encircling the stake, called a *ringer*, is the highest point-scoring throw, with a value of 3. A horseshoe that is only touching the stake is called a *leaner* and has a value of 2. The game originated in Roman army camps c.100 A.D.

Horsetail, primitive plant (genus *Equisetum*) related to the fern that once dominated the plant world and was important in the formation of coal. One fossil horsetail was 100 ft (30 m) high, but living species are rarely more than 2 to 3 feet (0.6 to 0.9 m) high. Each horsetail plant lasts several years. It has an underground stem that sends up hollow vertical stems each year. Each vertical stem is jointed and at each joint there is a ring of small leaves. The plant is coated with gritty silica, thus it has been called scouring rush and has been used for cleaning pans. Some horsetails have 2 kinds of stems. The first bears a spore-producing organ at the tip. The spores are released and drift away to produce small sexual plants as in ferns. These stems then die down and are replaced by taller green stems that last all season.

Horta, Victor Baron (1861-1947), Belgian architect. Horta is regarded as one of the pioneers of art nouveau, the style that dominated the visual arts in Europe around 1900 and which he was the first to apply to architecture. It was characterized by playful interior layouts and design and sumptuous decorations, based on organic forms from the natural world. It is strongly abstract with flowing lines; it was applied, among other things, to the wrought iron banisters of staircases and to railings of balconies, in wall paintings and painted ceilings, and in stained glass windows. His masterpiece is the Hôtel Solvay in Brussels (1895-1900). Other well known works in Brussels include Hôtel Tassel (1892-1893) and his own house (1898-1900, now the Horta Museum). After the First World War he mostly constructed neo classical buildings, for example, the Palace de Belles Arts in Brussels (1922-1928).

Horthy de Nagybanya, Miklós (1868-1957), Hungarian admiral and politician who led the counter-revolutionary army that overthrew the Communist and socialist coalition under Béla Kun (1919). From 1920 he acted as regent. He joined the Axis powers in World War II, but after trying to make peace with the USSR in 1944, he was imprisoned in Germany. Freed by U.S. forces, he settled in Portugal (1949).
See also: Hungary.

Horticultural grafting, technique of propagating plants by attaching the stem or bud of one plant (the scion) to the stem or roots of

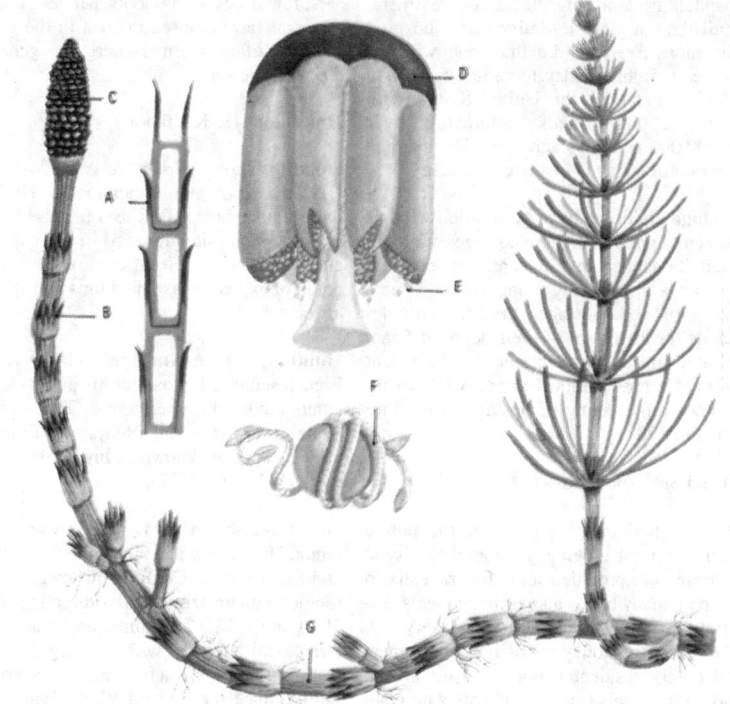

Horsetails are rushlike plants that grow along rivers, around lakes, and in swamps. They were most abundant (and even grew as large as trees) about 300 million years ago. One genus, *Equisetum*, survives today. The common, or field horsetail (also called Devil's gut), *E. arvense*, has a silica-rich, hollow stem (A, in longitudinal section). This stem is useful as a scouring material. The leaves (B) are reduced to scales. The cone reproductive structure (C) is a short axis bearing clusters of whorled sporangiophores (D), which have saclike sporangia that bear spores (E), which are attached to their inner surfaces. Changes in humidity cause elators (F), which are normally coiled around the spores, to uncoil and eject the sporangia. The rhizome (G), which is anchored in the soil by roots, can also produce a vegetative, sterile (coneless) shoot.

another (the stock, or rootstock). Only closely related species can be grafted. Roses and fruit trees are often grafted so that good flowering or fruiting varieties have the benefit of strong roots.

Horticulture, branch of agriculture concerned with producing fruits, flowers, and vegetables. It can be divided into *pomology* (growing fruit), *olericulture* (growing vegetables), and *floriculture* (growing shrubs and ornamental plants). About 3% of U.S. cropland is devoted to horticulture. It was originally practiced on a small scale, but crops such as the potato and tomato are now often grown in vast fields.

Horus, ancient Egyptian god. Originally a sky god, depicted as a falcon or as falcon-headed, he became thought of as the son of Isis and Osiris. He avenged his father's murder by defeating Set, the spirit of evil, and succeeded Osiris as king.
See also: Mythology.

Hosea, Book of, first of the Old Testament Minor Prophets. Its material originated in the prophecies of Hosea, delivered in Israel in the 8th century B.C. It compares God's abiding love for idolatrous Israel to Hosea's love for his prostitute wife, whom he divorced but remarried.
See also: Bible; Old Testament.

Hospice, facility for the care of terminally ill patients. Its professional staff seeks to provide alleviation of pain (rather than life-prolonging medical services), supportive psychological and spiritual counseling, and easy access for family and friends in a dignified and noninstitutional environment. The first hospice was opened in England in 1967 by Dr. Cecily Saunders. In the United States the cost of hospice care is now reimbursable under both Medicaid and Medicare.

Hospital, institution for the care of the sick or injured. Simple hospitals were first set up in Babylonian, Egyptian, Greek, and Roman communities, and in India hospitals had been established before A.D. 400. The early Christians did much to help the sick, and established the first charity hospitals, but medical knowledge was far from adequate, and death rates in hospitals were very high. Little had changed by the year 1123, when St. Bartholomew's Hospital was established in London. The majority of people admitted were either homeless or had little hope of recovery. Most physicians, apothecaries, and surgeons rendered their services at home or in an office rather than at a hospital. The first general hospital built in the United States was the Pennsylvania Hospital in Philadelphia, established in 1751. Others were built soon afterward, and medical technology improved rapidly during this period. but it was only when men like Joseph Lister obtained an understanding of the nature of infection and the importance of aseptic surgery that

H

H

hospitals became safe places for treatment. Until then, a patient admitted to a hospital was more likely to die than one who remained at home. Today there are more than 9,500 hospitals in the United States, with over 2,100,000 beds, admitting over 35,000,000 patients each year. The average duration of a stay is just over 1 week.

Hostage, traditionally, a person delivered as a token of good faith; now hostages are more often kidnapped and tortured by political dissidents demanding concessions. Iran's taking of U.S. hostages (1979), with demands for the return of their deposed Shah, resulted in a major crisis for President Jimmy Carter's administration. A UN treaty outlawing the taking of hostages went into effect in 1983.

Hostel *See:* Youth hostel.

Hotel, a building that provides the public with overnight lodging. Although the basic purpose is to provide rooms for travelers to sleep in, many hotels also provide meals, entertainment, and other personal services. There are 4 major types of hotel: commercial hotels, residential hotels, resort hotels, and motor hotels (motels). Hotels date from ancient times, and can be found in almost any country in the world.

Hot Line, direct White House-Kremlin emergency communications link, established in 1963. It aims to reduce the risk of war occurring by mistake or misunderstanding. Telegraphic and radio circuits run via London, Copenhagen, Stockholm, and Helsinki.

Hot springs, or thermal springs, natural discharges of heated water from within the earth. Most hot springs originate when water passes close to or through hot, igneous rock. They can form as streams, calm pools, gey-

sers, fumaroles, or mudpots. Modern energy concerns have aroused interest in the possible uses of geothermal energy to generate electrical power.

Hottentot *See:* Khoikhoi.

Houdini, Harry (Erich Weiss; 1874-1926), U.S. magician and escapologist. He was world famous for his escapes from seemingly impossible situations, as from a sealed chest underwater. He also pursued a campaign of exposing fake mediums and spiritualists.

Houdon, Jean-Antoine (1741-1828), French sculptor famous for his portraits. His sitters included Catherine the Great (1773), Voltaire (1781), and Benjamin Franklin (1791). The best known of his mythological works is *Diana* (1777).

Hou Hsiao-hsien (1947-), Taiwanese director. He was born on the Chinese mainland and fled from the Commmunist regime as a toddler with his family. After directing (from 1980 onwards) a few films, he attracted international attention with *The Time to Live and the Time to Die*, a fictional portrait of his family since the Second World War, composed of long, calm, and static shots. Hou's tender style makes him one of the most admired directors by film lovers at present and a leading figure during the boom of the Chinese cinema. The recent history of his country and the erosion of traditional values, in particular family life, under the influence of the economic boom are his predominant themes. Other films include *City of Sadness* (1989), *The Puppetmaster* (1994), *Good Men, Good Women* (1995) and *Farewell, South, Farewell* (1996).

Hound, group of dogs that hunt by sight or by following scent. Sight hounds chase quarry, overtake it, then kill or capture it.

They include the greyhound, Afghan hound, Saluki, and Irish wolfhound. Scent hounds, or tailing hounds, follow the scent of their quarry and flush it out. They include the beagle, bloodhound, bassett hound, and dachshund. In general, hounds are strong, alert, and loyal dogs.

Houphouët-Boigny, Félix (1905-1993), president of the Ivory Coast since it gained independence (1960) until his death in 1993. In 1946 he helped found the Rassemblement Democratique Africain (RDA), which paved the way for independence of the French West African colonies. He was a French minister of state from 1956 to 1957. *See also:* Ivory Coast.

Hour, one twenty-fourth of a day. In one hour the earth rotates through 15°. Therefore an event such as sunrise occurs one hour later for every 15° west on the earth's surface. Each hour contains 60 minutes and 3,600 seconds. In astronomy, degrees of longitude are not used for measuring star positions. Astronomers instead talk of *hours of right ascension*. Each hour of right ascension corresponds to 15° on the celestial sphere. The hour as a unit of timekeeping has been in use only since the invention of clocks.

Hourglass, ancient instrument to measure the passage of time. A quantity of fine, dry sand is contained in a bulb constricted at its center to a narrow neck. The device is turned so that all the sand is in the upper chamber. The time taken for the sand to trickle into the lower chamber depends on the amount of sand and on the diameter of the neck. Small hourglasses are used in the home as egg timers. *See also:* Time.

House, building in which one or a few families live. It may be built of wood, brick, or stone. It usually consists of several rooms,

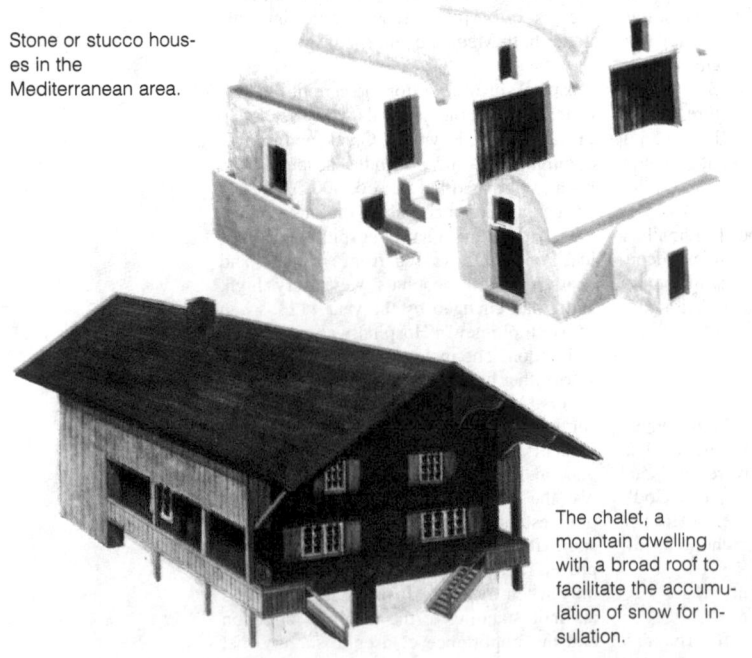

Stone or stucco houses in the Mediterranean area.

The chalet, a mountain dwelling with a broad roof to facilitate the accumulation of snow for insulation.

Trulli, circular dwellings of stone with stepped roofs, in Italy.

A masonry house in Provence, Southern France.

which are heated by a furnace and wired for electricity. Most modern houses also contain plumbing to supply water and carry away waste. They may vary in design, size, and in their number of rooms. The housing industry actually consists of a number of related professions and involves banks, real estate and insurance companies, architects, carpenters, plumbers, and electricians.

House of Commons, lower house of the British parliament. It consists of 635 members elected by simple majority in single-member constituencies. It is the assembly to which the government is ultimately responsible; it legitimizes legislation, votes money, and acts as a body in which complaints can be raised. Proceedings are regulated by the speaker, and a majority of members must assent before a bill becomes law.
See also: Parliament.

House of Lords, Upper house of the British parliament. In 1999 the House of Lords consisted of 1200 members, consisting of three groups: the nobility who inherit their titles ('hereditary peers', more than 600) the other lords ('life peers', 500) and the clergy ('Lords Spiritual', 26 bishops and archbishops).
Labour decided at the beginning of 1999 to end hereditary power. A Royal Committee is to decide what the construction of the new replacement house will be.
See also: Parliament.

House of Representatives, one of 2 chambers of the U.S. Congress, the legislative branch of the federal government. It consists of 435 members apportioned from each state according to population. Representatives serve 2-year terms. To be elected, they must be at least 25 years of age, a U.S. citizen for at least 7 years, and a resident of the state from which he or she is chosen. The House is presided over by the Speaker of the

House, who is elected by consensus of the majority party. He or she appoints joint committees and gives representatives permission to debate. Representatives serve on 4 committees: standing (permanent), select, conference, and joint. The committee system has the power to control proposed bills.
See also: Congress of the United States.

Housing, any building, or group of buildings, that provide shelter for people. In the United States people live in more than 80 million housing units, which may include single-family homes, condominiums, apartments, hotels, motels, motor homes (trailers), and shelters for the homeless. The production of housing has grown in complexity with the enlarging population and with the advent of city planning, transportation needs, commuter demands, community services, and the desire for safe dwellings.

Housman, A(lfred) E(dward) (1859-1936), English poet and classical scholar. His poetry, at its best intensely felt and always well crafted, is collected in *A Shropshire Lad* (1896), *Last Poems* (1922), and *More Poems* (1936).

Houston (pop. 1,700,000), city and seat of Harris County in southeastern Texas and a major U.S. seaport. It is situated about 25 mi (40 km) southwest of Galveston Bay on the Houston Ship Channel. Founded in 1836 and named for Sam Houston, it remained relatively unimportant until 1901 when oil was discovered in the area. It is now a prosperous industrial, manufacturing, and wholesale distribution center.
See also: Texas.

Houston, Sam(uel) (1793-1863), U.S. frontiersman and politician, leader in the struggle against Mexico to create an independent Texas. He commanded a force of fewer than 800 settlers in a decisive battle at San

Jacinto (1836) and went on to become the first president of the Republic of Texas (1836-1838). During a second term as president (1841-1844) he worked to bring Texas into the Union (1845). Houston served as U.S. senator (1846-1859) and was governor of Texas (1859-1861). He was deposed after refusing to support the Confederacy.
See also: Texas.

Sam Houston, a Texan general and statesman, was the first president (1836-38) of the Republic of Texas.

Hovercraft *See:* Air cushion vehicle.

Hovhaness, Alan (1911-), U.S. composer of Armenian descent, noted for his innovative use of Eastern musical materials. Among his best-known works are *Mysterious Mountain* (1955) and *Magnificat* (1957).

Howard, John (1726-1790), English public official and noted reformer. Serving as high sheriff of Bedfordshire, Howard had access to Bedford jail, where the conditions in which prisoners were kept appalled him. His subsequent efforts led to an act of Parliament (1774) to improve sanitation in prisons and abolish the systems of discharge fees. He visited prisons throughout Britain and Europe and published *The State of Prisons in England and Wales* (1777), a study that inspired further reform.

Howard, John Winston (1939-), Australian lawyer and politician. After studying law, Howard worked as a lawyer for several years. He has been a member of the federal parliament for the Liberal party since 1974. Between 1975 and 1983 he held various positions in the Liberal cabinets. From 1985 to 1989, he was the leader of the opposition. Howard became Prime Minister after the victory in the polls of the Liberal-National block over the Labor Party. He formed a coalition with the Liberal Party and the National Party, which continued during the elections in 1998. Howard's policy was classic economic. During the elections in 2001, his coalition won and he became Prime Minister for the third time.

Howard, Sidney (1891-1939), U.S. playwright whose work is noted for its realism. He won the 1925 Pulitzer Prize with *They Knew What They Wanted* (1924). Other well-

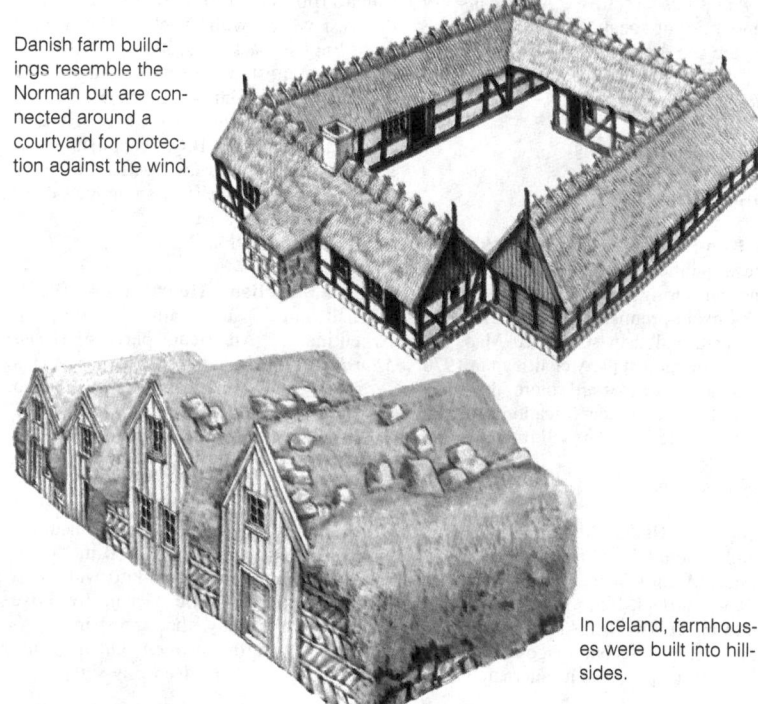

Danish farm buildings resemble the Norman but are connected around a courtyard for protection against the wind.

In Iceland, farmhouses were built into hillsides.

H

H

known plays include *Lucky Sam McCarver* (1925) and *The Silver Cord* (1926).

Howard University, private, coeducational institution in Washington, D.C., established in 1867 to educate newly freed slaves. The university includes 17 schools and colleges and 12 research centers and institutes and maintains the most extensive library collection of materials on African American life in the United States. Howard admits all students, but has a special responsibility, dating to its founding, to educate black students.

Howe, Elias (1819-1867), U.S. inventor of the first viable sewing machine (patented 1846). His early machines were sold in Britain, as in the United States there was at first no interest. Later Howe fought a protracted legal battle (1849-1854) to protect his patent rights from infringement in the United States.
See also: Sewing machine.

Howe, Gordie (1928-), record-setting U.S. ice hockey player. He played 26 seasons in the National Hockey League (NHL) with the Detroit Red Wings (1946-1971) and Hartford Whalers (1979-1980) and was named the league's most valuable player 6 times (1952, 1953, 1957, 1958, 1960, 1963). Howe holds career records for most games played (1,767), most goals scored (801) and was selected as an all-star 22 times. He played for the Houston Aeros (1973-1977) of the World Hockey Association (WHA) and was named its most valuable player (1974). Howe was inducted into the Hockey Hall of Fame in 1972.

Howe, Richard and William, name of 2 brothers who were British commanders in the American Revolutionary War. **Richard, Earl Howe** (1726-1799) commanded the British fleet in America (1776-1778) but is best known for his victory over the French off Ushant (1794) as commander of the Channel Fleet. **William, 5th Viscount Howe** (1729-1814) was a commander in the British army (1775-1778). He won 2 major

View of Huang He valley, between Hsin an and Lo yang, where the river leaves the mountains.

victories in 1777 at Brandywine and Germantown.
See also: Revolutionary War in America.

Howells, William Dean (1837-1920), U.S. author, critic, and chief editor of the *Atlantic Monthly* (1871-1881). He was a pioneer of U.S. social fiction. His finest and most famous novel is *The Rise of Silas Lapham* (1855). Among those influenced by his work were Stephen Crane and Theodore Dreiser.

Howler, monkey (genus *Alouatta*) named for its low, carrying call. Troops of howler monkeys set up a chorus of howls when they spot another troop near their territory. To produce this call they have a large bony box in the throat, which is a resonating chamber. Howlers are found in forests from southern Mexico to northern Argentina.

Hoxha, Enver (1908-1985), Albanian leader. He helped found the Albanian Communist party in 1941 and was the first premier of the new communist government (1944-1954). Continuing as party secretary after 1954, he remained a Stalinist and fell out with the USSR during the latter's de-Stalinization phase. Hoxha became allied with Communist China in the early 1960s. Later this friendship cooled when China moved toward closer ties with the West.
See also: Albania.

Hoyle, Edmond (1672-1769), English authority on card and board games, especially whist. He wrote *A Short Treatise on the Game of Whist* (1742), as well as treatises on other games, including chess and backgammon. The expression 'according to Hoyle,' meaning according to the rules, derives from his name.

Hrdlicka, Ales (1869-1943), Bohemian-born U.S. physical anthropologist. He expounded the generally accepted theory that the Amerinds (Native Americans or Eskimos) are of Asiatic origin. Among his works are *Old Americans* (1925) and *Alaska Diary 1926-1931* (1943).
See also: Anthropology.

Hsi Chiang *See:* Xi Jiang.

Hsun-tzu *See:* Xunzi.

Hua Kuo-Feng (Hua Guofeng; 1920-), Chinese political leader. Achieving swift promotion during the Cultural Revolution, he was made premier following Chou En-Lai's death and then succeeded Mao Tse-Tung as Communist party chairman in 1976. As China turned toward more pragmatic policies, Hua's close identification with Mao proved a handicap, and he fell from power in 1981.
See also: China.

Huang He, or Huang Ho, river in north-central and eastern China. The Huang He rises in Amne Machin Shan, Qinghai Province, and flows through Inner Mongolia, emptying into the Yellow Sea. At 2,903 mi (4,673 km), it is China's second longest river, but it is unused by ships due to its alternately swift

and shallow composition. Due to years of flooding, the river is also called 'China's Sorrow.'

Huang Ho *See:* Huang He.

Hubble, Edwin Powell (1889-1953), U.S. astronomer who first showed (1923) that certain nebulae are in fact galaxies outside the Milky Way. By examining the red shifts in their spectra, he showed that they are receding at rates proportional to their distances.
See also: Astronomy.

Hubble Space Telescope, orbiting reflecting telescope built to send data from space to astronomers on earth via radio waves. It was released into space on April 25, 1990 from the space shuttle *Discovery*. It orbits about 360 mi (580 km) above the earth's surface. With information sent to earth from the Hubble Telescope, astronomers hope to learn more about the cosmos, particularly 'dark matter,' areas in space that emit little or no light. Unfortunately, the telescope malfunctioned in space due to manufacturing flaws. In 1993 improvements were made, and as a result there has been a constant outpour of useful data. It is expected that the telescope will be able to function until 2005.
See also: Hubble, Edwin Powell; Telescope.

Huckleberry, shrub (genus *Gaylussacia*) related to the blueberry and cranberry that produces dark berry fruits. There are several species growing in the eastern United States, including the blue huckleberry (*G. frondosa*). The fruits are used to make jams and preserves.

Hudson, Henry (d. 1611), English navigator and explorer who gave his name to the Hudson River, Hudson Strait, and Hudson Bay. After voyages for the English Muscovy Company to find a northeast passage to China (1607 and 1608), Hudson turned to the west where, with Dutch and then once more English backing (1609 and 1610), he made his most successful voyages. He reached the river known as the Hudson in 1609 and the following year entered Hudson Strait and Hudson Bay, establishing an English claim to the area. After the bitter winter, he was set adrift by a mutinous crew and left to die.
See also: Exploration.

Hudson, William Henry (1841-1922), English author and naturalist, born in Argentina of American parents. *Green Mansions* (1904), his best-known novel, is set in the South American pampas. He also wrote studies of bird life and books on the English countryside, such as *A Shepherd's Life* (1910).

Hudson Bay, shallow, epicontinental sea in the northern part of Canada, named for Henry Hudson. Up to about 850 mi (1,370 km) long and 600 mi (970 km) wide, it is linked to the Atlantic Ocean by Foxe Channel. James Bay, the largest inlet, extends southward between Ontario and Quebec provinces. Hudson Bay shipping is

restricted because the bay freezes over in winter.
See also: Hudson, Henry.

Hudson River, U.S. river rising in the Adirondacks, flowing generally south for 315 mi (507 km) through New York, and emptying into the Atlantic at New York City. It was discovered in 1524, but only explored fully by Henry Hudson in 1609. It is an important commercial waterway, being navigable by ocean ships as far upstream as Albany. A canal system links it to the Great Lakes. A major program was begun in 1975 to prevent further pollution and make the river safe for fishing and swimming.
See also: Hudson, Henry.

Hudson River School, group of 19th-century U.S. landscape painters. The founders were Thomas Cole, Thomas Doughty, and Asher Durand, who were especially interested in the Hudson River Valley and New England. The school later included artists who took their inspiration from other parts of the United States.

Hudson's Bay Company, mercantile corporation established by the British in 1670 for trading in the Hudson Bay region. The original intention was also to colonize the area and seek a northwest passage, but the company's major activity was fur trading with the Native Americans. It played an important part during the next 2 centuries in opening up Canada. Although its vast lands were sold to the Dominion in 1870, it is still a major fur-trading company and one of Canada's chief business firms, with holdings in metal ores, oil, gas, and timber.

Hue (pop. 244,000), third largest city in Vietnam, located in central Vietnam, near the eastern coast. Founded in the 3rd century, Hue was capital of Vietnam during the rule of the Nguyen dynasty, beginning in the 16th century. The city was occupied by the French in 1883. It became a part of South Vietnam in 1954. Much of the city was destroyed during the Tet offensive in the Vietnam War, but it is under reconstruction.
See also: Vietnam.

Huerta, Victoriano (1854-1916), Mexican general and dictator (1913-1914). After first supporting President Porifiro Diaz and then Francisco Madero, he rebelled, proclaiming himself president in February 1913, and had Madero and his vice-president murdered. Revolution at home and U.S. hostility combined to force him into exile.
See also: Mexico.

Hugh Capet (c.938-996 A.D.), king of France (987-996), founder of the Capetian dynasty. The son of Hugh the Great, the duke of the Franks, he was elected king in the place of the legitimate Carolingian heir, Charles of Lower Lorraine.
See also: Capetians.

Hughes, Howard Robard (1905-1976), U.S. industrialist, aviator, and film producer. President of the Hughes Aircraft Company and of the Hughes Tool Company, he was a

billionaire who in his later years became an eccentric recluse. Years of litigation over his will followed his death.
See also: Aviation.

Hughes, (James) Langston (1902-67), African-American poet and writer. He is best known for adapting the rhythms of African-American music to his poetry. His works include the poetry collections *The Weary Blues* (1926), and *One-Way Ticket* (1949), and the prose *Not Without Laughter* (1930).

Hughes, Ted (1930-1998), English poet whose work is noted for its brutal, often violent animal imagery. Among his many collections are *The Hawk in the Rain* (1957), *Lupercal* (1960), *Crow* (1970), *Selected Poems: 1957-1967* (1972), *Moortown* (1980), *Wolfwatching* (1989), *New Selected Poems* (1995), and *Difficulties of a bridegroom* (1995). In 1984 Hughes was appointed *Poet Laureate*.

Hughes, Thomas (1822-1896), English jurist, reformer, and author of *Tom Brown's School Days* (1857) which, through its emphasis on Christian virtues and athletic ability, helped shape the popular image of the English public school.

Hugo, Victor Marie (1802-1885), French novelist, playwright, and poet. He is best known for his historical novel *The Hunchback of Notre Dame* (1831). Among his several important collections of verse are *Les Feuilles d'Automne* (1831) and *Les Châtiments* (1853). Hugo went into exile when Napoleon III became emperor (1851), and during this period produced his famous, socially committed novel *Les Misérables* (1862). He spent his last years in France, recognized as one of his country's greatest writers and republicans.

Huguenots, French Protestants, followers of John Calvin's teaching. The Huguenot movement originated in the 16th century as part of the Reformation and found support among all segments of French society, despite constant and severe persecution. Some respite was provided by Henry IV's Edict of Nantes (1598), but this was revoked in 1685, and many thousands of Huguenots were forced into exile in America and elsewhere.

During the first performance of Victor Hugo's play *Hernani* in 1830 in Paris, supporters and opponents of the play got so excited, that a veritable battle took place amongst members of the public (Bataille d'Hernani). The young romantics (recognizable by their red vests) were the victors.

Full civil and religious liberty was not granted to Huguenots until 1789.
See also: Calvin, John.

Huizinga, Johan (1872-1945), Dutch historian and writer, noted for his writings about the cultural history of the Middle Ages, which portrayed the spirit of the entire age. Huizinga's works include *The Waning of the Middle Ages* (1919), *In the Shadow of Tomorrow* (1935), and *Homo Ludens* (1938). During World War II, he was imprisoned by the Nazis and died shortly after his release.

Huizong, or Hui Tsung (1082-1135), last Chinese emperor of the northern Sung dynasty (r. 1101-1125). He founded the first imperial Chinese academy of painting. An accomplished painter himself, Huizong urged other artists to be 'true to color and form,' as his realistic paintings of birds and flowers show. He spent his final decade in captivity and died in exile in Manchuria, after being overthrown by the Tartars.
See also: China.

Hukbalahap, or Huks (full name: Hukbong

Friedrich Wilhelm, the Great Elector, receiving refugee Huguenots from France. A painting from 1885, by Hugo Vogel (1855-1934).

Magpapalayang Bayan, 'People's Liberation Army'), Communist guerilla movement that posed a serious threat to the Philippine government from 1945 to 1954. Growing out of the wartime resistance movement against Japanese occupation, the Huks were chiefly disaffected peasants. Eventually the Huks were largely won over by a program of land reforms and settlement schemes. Much of the credit for the rehabilitation of the Huks goes to Ramón Magsaysay, who, mainly on the strength of the achievement, was elected president of the Philippines in 1953.
See also: Philippines.

Hull, Bobby (Robert Marvin Hull; 1939-), Canadian ice hockey player. Thought to be the greatest left wing in the history of the sport, he ranks as the fifth highest goal scorer (610) in National Hockey League (NHL) history and was selected as an all-star 9 times. Hull was nicknamed the 'Golden Jet' because of his blond hair, his speed, and the power of his shots, which at times traveled at 110 mph (177 kph). In 1974-1975 Hull set a World Hockey Association (WHA) single season record by scoring 77 goals while playing for the Winnipeg Jets (1972-1978). He starred for the Chicago Black Hawks (1957-1972) and Hartford Whalers (1980) of the NHL. Hull retired in 1981, and in 1983 was inducted into the Hockey Hall of Fame.

Hull, Cordell (1871-1955), U.S. statesman, secretary of state (1933-1944) under F.D. Roosevelt. He was a congressman (1907-1921 and 1923-1930) and senator (1931-1933). As secretary of state he developed the 'Good Neighbor' policy in relations with South American states and helped maintain relations with the USSR in World War II. After the war he was a major force behind U.S. acceptance of the UN, for which he was awarded the 1945 Nobel Peace Prize.

Hulme, Keri (1947-), New Zealand writer of Maori origin, who won the Booker Prize in 1985 for her novel *The Bone People*. This was followed by *The Windeater* (1987), and *Bait* (1992).

Human being (*Homo sapiens*), extremely adaptable mammal with highly-developed brain and nervous system, and ability to speak. Related to monkeys and apes, human beings differ from them physically by having the ability to stand and walk upright and by having a larger and more fully developed brain. Humans also use language, a trait that significantly distinguishes them from every other animal. Most scientists believe that the first recognizably human-like beings appeared in what is now Africa some 2 million years ago. This prehistoric human, referred to as *Homo habilis*, later developed into *Homo erectus*, who lived throughout Africa, Asia, and Europe and probably learned how to make and use fire. *Homo erectus* also hunted and used tools. The physical form humans have today began to appear about 40,000 years ago. Generally, humans seem to have begun as hunters and gatherers of food and to have gradually developed agricultural and industrial societies.

Human body, complex organism consisting of some 50 trillion cells, organized into tissues, organs, and structures. The body can best be studied as a complex of systems.
(1) The skeletal system, the body's framework, consists of more than 200 bones tied together with strong yet elastic ligaments. It accounts for about 18% of the body's weight.
(2) The muscular system consists of more than 650 distinct muscles that, by pulling on bones and bending joints, cause the body to move. Also part of this system are the visceral muscles, which cause movement in internal organs. The muscular system accounts for about 40% of body weight.
(3) The skin covers the whole body, allowing the maintenance of a constant internal environment. The sweat glands play an important part in excretion. Nerve endings in the skin provide the sense of touch and warn the body of external danger. The skin serves as a barrier against destructive organisms and foreign bodies.
(4) The circulatory system, consisting of the heart and thousands of miles of blood vessels and lymphatics, carries blood to all parts of the body, supplying every cell with oxygen and food and carrying from it carbon dioxide, water, and other wastes. The blood also carries hormones (the body's chemical messengers), which attack invading microorganisms, and help repair wounds by clotting.
(5) The respiratory system-including the lungs and the respiratory passages-allows the interchange of oxygen and carbon dioxide with the blood.
(6) The digestive system takes in food and breaks it down into a usable form that can be absorbed into the bloodstream. Basically, it consists of a tube extending from mouth to anus, with various organs, such as the stomach and accessory glands (including liver and pancreas) attached.
(7) The main organs of the urinary system are the kidneys, which remove waste from the blood, and the bladder, which stores and then expels that waste in the form of urine.
(8) The reproductive system ensures the continuation of the species and the passing along of traits that may be necessary for survival.
(9) The nervous system consists of the central nervous system (CNS), comprising the brain and spinal cord, and the peripheral nervous system, the nerves that carry messages to and from the CNS.
(10) The endocrine system, consisting of the hormone-producing glands, responds to nervous commands or to other hormones and along with the nervous system, coordinates the activities of other organs and adjusts their functioning in relation to the external and internal environment.
(11) The body possesses a number of specialized senses, including sight, hearing, balance, and the visceral sensations such as hunger.

Humane society, organization whose purpose is to protect children and animals from mistreatment. Local humane societies in the United States fused in 1877 to become the American Humane Association.

Human Genome Project, public project by a consortium of twenty cooperating laboratories worldwide, officially started on October 1, 1990. Their goal was to map the complete genetic order of all human chromosomes (together called the genome). Genetics and molecular biologists were involved in the project. Two versions of the genetic code were published on February 12, 2001: one in *Nature*, the other one in *Science*. Celera, the company of the U.S. biologist Craig Venter published their code in *Science*, the Human Genome Project published theirs in *Nature*. Both versions of the human genetic map could not identify 10% of the genes.
Human DNA contains approximately 30,000 genes, far less than the estimated 100,000. Researchers use the identified genes of humans and nonhuman organisms to identify other genes. The major part of human DNA does not have any function. This is also known as junk-DNA (98.5%). Numerous genes can be found more than once. Individual humans share 99.9% of their genetic make-up. The relative genetic differences between the races are smaller on average than the difference between individuals. This huge similarity points towards the probability that the human race has been on the verge of becoming extinct: all humans are derived from a small group that managed to survive evolutionary crises. The cracking of the code of the human genome will probably have a major impact. Even though differences between individuals are relatively small, they will affect the way in which people react to medicine, nutrition and other environmental factors.
See also: DNA.

Humanism, originally, Renaissance revival of the study of classical (Latin, Greek, and Hebrew) literature following the scholasticism of the Middle Ages, more broadly, philosophy centered on humankind and human values, exalting human free will and superiority to the rest of nature. Renaissance thinkers such as Petrarch began a trend toward humanism that embraced such diverse figures as Boccaccio, Machiavelli, Thomas More, and Erasmus and that led to much subsequent secular thought and literature, as well as to the Reformation. Modern humanism tends to be nontheistic, emphasizing the need for people to work out their own solutions to life's problems, but has a strong ethic similar to that of Christianity. Both Roman Catholic and Protestant theologians have sought to show that Christian beliefs embody true humanism.
See also: Renaissance.

Human relations, study of group behavior and how the individual, as an inherently social being with personal needs, may achieve desired goals without losing, or causing others in the general population to lose, the basic rights of dignity, respect, and self-determination. Experts in the field of human relations must understand conflict, human needs, human nature, and how individuals and groups respond to one another.

Human Rights, Declaration of, United Nations document outlining the civil, eco-

nomic, political, and social rights and freedoms for all the people of the world. Adopted by the General Assembly on Dec. 10, 1948, it declares all people to be free and to have equal rights and dignity.
See also: United Nations.

Humber, River, river in Humberside county, England, flowing eastward into the North Sea. The river's length is about 40 mi (64 km); its width is 1-7 mi (1.6-11 km). Two important tributaries are the Ouse and Trent rivers. The cities of Hull and Grimsby lie on the Humber's banks. The Humber Bridge has the longest main span (4,626 ft/1,410 m) of any suspension bridge in the world.

Humboldt, Friedrich Heinrich Alexander, Baron von (1769-1859), German naturalist. With the botanist Aimé Jacques Alexandre Bonpland he traveled for 5 years through much of South America (1799-1804), collecting plant, animal, and rock specimens and making geomagnetic and meteorologic observations. Humboldt published their data in 30 volumes over the next 23 years. In his most important work, *Kosmos* (1845-1862), he sought to show a fundamental unity of all natural phenomena.

Humboldt Current *See:* Peru Current.

Hume, David (1711-1776), Scottish Enlightenment philosopher, economist, and historian. His *Treatise of Human Nature* (1739-1740) is one of the key works in the tradition of British empiricism, but it was his shorter *Enquiry Concerning Human Understanding* (1748) that prompted Immanuel Kant to his most radical labors. His influential *Dialogues Concerning Natural Religion* were published posthumously in 1779, long after their composition. In epistemology Hume argued that people had no logical reason to associate distinct impressions as cause and effect; if they did so, it was only on the basis of custom or psychological habit. His skepticism in this respect has always been controversial. In his own day, Hume's most popular work was his *History of England* (1754-1763).
See also: Philosophy.

Hume, Gary (1962-), British painter. He was at Goldsmith's College in London from 1986 to 1988. He took part in the much talked- about exhibition 'Freeze' by young British artists in the Surrey Docks in London in 1988, together with Damien Hirst, Sarah Lucas, Georgina Starr and others. Humes' paintings from 1988-89 are composed of glossily varnished panels that look like doors. He went on to paint pop stars and teddy bears. He also painted sugary patterns such as bunny rabbits and flowers, and sometimes paintings of old masters. These are often in the form of silhouettes and based on images from the media. Typical are the smooth foundation of hardboard, formica or aluminum and the use of ordinary house painters' varnish. The reflecting surface and the bright colors form hard contrasts. His work has been called neo pop. He does not aim to exalt mass culture, but to reflect it as it is.

Hume, John (1928-), Northern Irish Catholic politician, leader of the Social Democratic and Labour Party (SDLP) of Northern Ireland. In 1998, he received, together with David Trimble, the Nobel Prize for Peace for his contribution to the peace process in Northern Ireland. In his book *A New Ireland; Politics, Peace, and Reconciliation* he gives a personal view of the Northern Irish question and goes into the historical background. In 2001, he resigned as the leader of the SDLP due to health reasons.

Humidity, amount of water vapor in the air. *Absolute humidity* measures mass of water per unit volume of air. Saturation of the air, or *dew point*, occurs when the water vapor pressure reaches the vapor pressure of liquid water at the temperature concerned; this rises rapidly with temperature. *Relative humidity*, expressed as a percentage, is the amount of water in the air at any given time compared with the amount the air could hold at that temperature before becoming saturated. The physiologically tolerable humidity level falls rapidly as temperature rises, since humidity inhibits body cooling by impeding the evaporation of sweat.

Hummingbird, tiny nectar-feeding bird of the family Trochilidae. It takes its name from the noise of its rapid wingbeats-up to 70 a second in smaller species-as it hovers at flowers to feed. Hummingbirds are colorful, with a body size in most species 2 in (5 cm) or less. With their small size and fierce activity, hummingbirds must feed about once every 10-15 min. Highly adapted to flight, hummingbirds have short legs and little feet, used only for perching. They can hover in one place and are the only birds capable of flying backward.

Hummingbird moth *See:* Hawk moth.

Humor, according to the ancients, any of the 4 bodily elements: phlegm, blood, choler, and black bile, corresponding to the 4 natural elements: earth, air, fire, and water. In the well-adjusted person, the 4 humors are in balance. If one preponderates, the person is of unequal temper: If phlegm preponderates then the person is phlegmatic; if blood, the person is sanguine; if choler, the person is choleric; if black bile, the person is melancholic. The person not in 'good humor' behaves eccentrically, and is thus an

object of ridicule. The word 'humor' thus came to mean mocking laughter.

Humperdinck, Engelbert (1854-1921), German composer. He was much influenced by Richard Wagner, whom he assisted at the Bayreuth Festival. He wrote several operas; only *Hansel and Gretel* (1893) is widely performed today, although *The Royal Children* (1910) is revived from time to time.

Humphrey, Doris (1895-1958), U.S. modern dancer and choreographer. Influenced by Ruth St. Denis and Ted Shawn, she set up a school and company with Charles Weidman (1928) to develop her own expressive style, based upon her innovative theories of movement. Humphrey founded (with Martha Graham) the U.S. modern-dance form.

Humphrey, Hubert Horatio (1911-1978), U.S. political leader, vice president from 1965 to 1969. A Democrat, he was mayor of Minneapolis, then was elected senator from Minnesota in 1948. Identified with many liberal causes, as vice president under Lyndon Johnson he nonetheless supported U.S. Vietnam policy. Unsuccessful as the Democratic candidate for president (1968), he returned to the Senate (1970).

Humus, organic substance formed in soil when microorganisms, bacteria, and fungi decompose plant and animal material. Humus is soft, spongy, and dark brown. It affects the soil's structure, water retention, nutritional value to plants, and erosion resistance.

Hun, nomadic, probably Mongolian, race that invaded southeastern Europe during the 4th and 5th centuries. They crossed the Volga River in c.372 A.D. and attacked the Germanic Goth tribes. By 432 they had invaded the Eastern Empire. Under their great leader Attila, they threatened the Roman Empire, unsuccessfully invading Gaul in 451. In 452 their Italian invasion was halted at Lake Garda. After Attila's death in 453, the Hun empire gradually disintegrated.
See also: Attila.

Hunchback, or kyphosis, deformity of the spine causing bent posture with or without twisting (scoliosis) and abnormal bony prominences. Tuberculosis of the spine may cause sharp angulation, while congenital

Streamer-tailed hummingbird, *T. polytmus*, Jamaica, length 9 in (22.5 cm).

H

H

diseases, ankylosing spondylitis, vertebral collapse, and spinal tumors cause smooth kyphosis.

Hundertwasser, Friedensreich (Real name: Friedrich Stowasser; 1928-2000) Austrian painter, who underwent many influences. From 1953 onward he had a decorative abstract style, using a spiral as the predominant pattern. His work is very popular and not wholly without commercial content. He also designs 'alternative houses': with plenty of greenery, where straight lines are strictly forbidden. The 'Hundertwasser Haus' in Vienna (1983-1985) is well known.

Hundred Days, in French history, period between Napoleon's return to Paris from exile on Elba and the second Bourbon restoration (Mar. 20-June 28, 1815). During this time Napoleon attempted to reinstate himself as ruler of France on a more liberal basis. He was defeated at Waterloo, and Louis XVIII was restored to the French Throne. *See also:* Napoleon II.

Hundred Years War, sporadic series of wars fought mainly between England and France from 1337 to 1453. They originated in disputes over English possessions in France, and the claims of Edward III of England to the throne of France. In 1337 he invaded Gascony and won the battles of Sluis (1340), Crécy (1346), and Poitiers (1356), and seized Calais, gaining important concessions at the Treaty of Brétigny (1360). The French under Charles V retained much of their lost territory (1369-1375) and attacked the English coast. Henry V of England destroyed the resulting uneasy truce when he invaded France in 1415, in pursuit of a dream of establishing himself as monarch of Britain and France; he captured

During the Hundred Years War, cities were of great strategic importance. The citizens often had to sustain grave hardships, especially when they had chosen one side and were captured by the other. This fate struck Limoges, which was plundered and its inhabitants massacred by the English Black Prince (1330-1376), as a revenge for the city's support for the French king.

Harfleur and defeated a superior French force at Agincourt. At the Treaty of Troyes (1420) Henry V was recognized as heir to the French throne, and from 1422 his infant son, Henry VI, ruled the dual monarchy, with John, Duke of Bedford, as French regent. His able rule won French support, and only the resurgence led by Joan of Arc in 1429 halted English gains. Although the dauphin (French heir to the throne, son of Charles VI) was crowned Charles VII at Reims in 1429, the English position was not assailed until 1435, when Philip the Good of Burgundy recognized Charles VII as king of France. After 1444 the English were driven back until they held only Calais (until 1448) and the Channel Islands.

Hungarian, or Magyar, one of the Ungro-Finnic languages in the Uralic group. It is spoken mainly in Hungary, but also by groups in Czechoslovakia, Romania, and Yugoslavia. Its 6 dialects do not differ widely. Standard Hungarian is the speech of the Budapest area.

Hungarian pointer *See:* Vizsla.

Hungary

Capital:	Budapest
Area:	35,920 sq mi (93,033 sq km)
Population:	10,075,000
Language:	Hungarian, Magyar
Government:	Republic
Independent:	1918
Head of gov.:	Prime minister
Per capita:	US$ 12,000
Monetary unit:	1 Forint = 100 fillér

Hungary, country in east-central Europe, bordered by Slovakia, Ukraine, Romania, Yugoslavia, Croatia, Slovenia, and Austria. The capital is Budapest, where nearly 20% of the population lives.
Land. Hungary is basically a fertile plain, drained by the Danube River, which forms part of the border with Slovakia and then turns south through the country. The Dráva, which forms part of Hungary's border with Croatia, is the only other important river. Most of the country has black, very fertile soil. Lake Balaton, the largest lake in Europe (48 mi/77 km long), begins southwest of Budapest and extends southwest toward the

The puszta is a virtually treeless region in the Central Plain of Hungary. In the past, this region was used by nomads as a natural pasture for extensive cattle raising. At present, most of the puszta has been brought under cultivation.

Croatian border. The country is rich in game, including deer, fox, wild boar, and hare.
People. The official language is Hungarian. About two-thirds of the population is Roman Catholic, and one-third Calvinist.
Economy. Hungary was traditionally agricultural, but there has been significant industrialization since World War II. There are important electrical, chemical, food-processing and textile plants. Leading crops include corn, wheat, oats, rye, potatoes, sunflowers, and sugar beets. Apricots, grapes, paprika, and tobacco are also grown, and hogs, sheep, and cattle are raised.
History. The area that is now Hungary was conquered by the Magyars c.896 and Christianized in the 900s. A feudal system flourished until the Ottoman Turkish invasion defeated King Lewis II at Mohács (1526). Most of the country was divided between the Ottoman Empire and Austria, the west and north coming under Habsburg rule in 1687. A bid for independence led by Lajos Kossuth (1848) failed but led to the establishment of the Dual Monarchy (1867): the Austrian Emperor Francis Joseph I was crowned King of Hungary, and the Austro-Hungarian empire was born. That empire was destroyed in World War I, and an independent Hungarian state was proclaimed in 1918. A Communist revolution in 1919 was put down by Romanian intervention, and in 1920 Admiral Nicholas Horthy de Nagybanya, a right-wing dictator, came to power. Hungary was an ally of Nazi Germany during World War II. Occupied by the USSR (1945), it became a 'people's republic' in 1949. An uprising against the repressive regime was crushed by Soviet intervention (1956), and a puppet government under János Kádar was set up. Kádar introduced cultural and economic reforms in the 1960s that temporarily improved Hungarians' living standards, but his refusal to introduce further reforms during the economic decline of the 1970s led to his replacement in 1988. The Communist regime collapsed in 1989 during the general upheaval that swept Eastern Europe. Hungary held elections in 1990 and a coalition of parties, opposed to Communist rule, won a majority of seats. Elections in 1994 brought to

power the Socialist party, made up mainly of former Communists. In 1999 Hungary joined the NATO and has been formally invited to join the European Union in 2004. Nevertheless, it has yet to resolve a number of problems, such as the discrimination against the Roma minority, corruption and pollution.

Hunger, appetite (impulse, drive) for food, often referring also to the mass of uneasy sensations from the gut and particularly from hunger contractions in the stomach, which accompany the appetite; also used to describe sexual appetite.

Hunt, H(aroldson) L(afayette) (1889-1974), U.S. oil magnate. In the 1920s he invested in Arkansas oil fields. The Hunt Oil Company, founded in 1936, became one of the largest independent U.S. oil and natural gas corporations.

Hunt, James (1947-1993), English racing driver. James Hunt followed the usual course in motor sport: he began racing in Minis and reached Formula One through the Formula Ford, Formula Three, and Formula Two. He won his first Grand Prix in 1975 at Zandvoort in a Hesketh. The following year Hunt took over from Emerson Fittipaldi, who was leaving Mclaren and won the Formula One championship one point ahead of Nikki Lauda. After 1980, he was a TV commentator for the BBC on motor sport.

Hunt, (James Henry) Leigh (1784-1859), English critic, journalist, and poet. He was editor of the liberal *Examiner* (1808-1822) and other journals. Hunt was a friend of the leading literary figures of his day, notably Keats and Shelley, whose poetic careers he furthered; Lamb; Hazlitt; Byron; and eventually Carlyle. His most highly regarded works are *Lord Byron and Some of His Contemporaries* (1828), *Autobiography* (1850), and the short lyric poems 'Abou Ben Adhem' (1834) and 'Jenny Kissed Me' (1844).

Hunt, William Holman (1827-1910), English painter who helped found the Pre-Raphaelite movement. His work is noted for its brilliant color and accurate details. *The Light of the World* (1853) is his best-known painting.

Hunting, pursuit and killing of wild animals for subsistence, profit, or sport. In Western Europe hunting means the pursuit and capture of a wild animal with the aid of hounds. In the United States and elsewhere the term means the field sport of shooting large and small game.
Hunting was an important source of food, clothing, and sometimes shelter for primitive people. Cave paintings in France and Spain indicate that these people hunted wild horses, prehistoric cattle, reindeer, and mammoths, often with the bow and arrow. Hunting as a sport was practiced by the earliest known civilizations, such as those in Babylonia and Egypt. Hunts full of pageantry and splendor were popular with kings and princes, who often gained status according to the number of animals they had killed.
With the exception of the Native Americans of the Southwest, the Southeast, and adjoining regions, the North American tribes lived almost exclusively by hunting. With the arrival of European colonists, hunting became important for the fur trade. As white settlers occupied increasing amounts of land, however, the wild game gradually disappeared; thus, in most areas of the present-day United States, game animals, especially the larger ones, exist in relatively small numbers and sometimes are even brought into a region to provide quarry for hunters. Game is also limited in variety, with rabbits and deer probably the most plentiful overall.
Western and northern Canada and Alaska are exceptions to this general scarcity; wildlife of many sorts still abounds there. Regulatory measures and the vigilant efforts of conservationists help to save game animals threatened with extinction through indiscriminate hunting. Certain African countries, mostly in East and South Africa, have also made ambitious efforts to save their often unique wildlife by establishing and patrolling enormous animal sanctuaries where the camera is the only 'weapon' permitted.

Huntington's disease (Huntington's chorea), disease marked by progressive degeneration of the central nervous system. An inherited, ultimately fatal disease that breaks out in adulthood, its symptoms are involuntary, jerky body movements and mental disturbances. It was first identified in 1871 by the American neurologist Dr. George Huntington.

Huntsman's-cup *See:* Pitcher plant.

Hunza, district in northern Kashmir controlled by Pakistan. The largest city is Karimabad. Woolen cloth and handicrafts are leading industries. Burushaski is the spoken language, but there is no written language. Most of the people are Muslims.
See also: Pakistan.

Hurdling, track and field sport in which runners jump over obstacles called hurdles, which stand at specific heights and are set equal distances apart on the track. Runners adjust their stride and bring one leg over the hurdle at a time to clear hurdles without breaking stride. Hurdles may be knocked down, but disqualification occurs if done so by runner's hand.

Huron, league of 4 Native North American tribes, approximately 20,000 strong, who lived in South Ontario in the 1600s. Members of the Iroquoian language group, they were an agrarian society who were attacked and nearly destroyed by the Iroquois (1650). Small numbers of Hurons remain in Quebec and in Oklahoma.

Hurricane, tropical cyclone of great intensity. High-speed winds spiral in toward a low-pressure core of warm, calm air (the eye). Winds of over 185 mph (298 kmph) have been measured. The direction of spiral is clockwise in the southern hemisphere and counterclockwise in the northern hemi-

July 12   Hurricane   Stage X Cat. 3.5

sphere. Hurricanes form over water when there is an existing convergence of air near sea level. The air ascends, losing moisture as precipitation as it does so. If this happens rapidly enough, the upper air is warmed by the water's latent heat of vaporization. This reduces the surface pressure and thus accelerates air convergence. Since they require large quantities of moist warm air, hurricanes rarely penetrate far inland. Hurricanes of the North Pacific are often called typhoons.

Hurston, Zora Neale (1901-1960), U.S. author known for her literary interpretations of African-American folklore of the southern United States and the Caribbean. Her novels were *Jonah's Gourd Vine* (1934) and *Their Eyes Were Watching God* (1937). *Mules and Men* (1935) and *Tell My Horse* (1938) are collections of retold folktales.

Hus, Jan (1370-1415), Bohemian religious reformer and Czech national hero. Influenced by John Wycliffe, Hus attacked Church and papal abuses. He defended his ideas at the Council of Constance in 1414, where he was arrested, tried, and burned at the stake as a heretic. His followers, the Hussites, demanded many reforms in the Roman Catholic Church, with which they were involved in a series of wars in Bohemia in the 15th century.
See also: Bohemia.

Husák, Gustav (1913-1991), Czechoslovakian Communist leader. Taking a pro-Moscow line after 1968, he replaced Secretary Dubek as leader of the Communist Party in 1969 He served as president of Czechoslovakia from 1975 to 1989.
See also: Czechoslovakia.

Husein Ibn Ali (1854-1931), sharif of Mecca (1908-1916) and king of Hejaz (1916-1924). In 1916 he led the World War I Arab revolt against the Turks and proclaimed himself king of all Arabia. Assisted by T. E. Lawrence, he drove the Turks from Syria, northern Arabia, and Transjordan. In

A hurricane in its most distinctive stage. Photographs made by weather satellites, have added greatly to our knowledge of hurricanes and have enabled us to predict their course. However, this advance warning system is still far from perfect, as is being proved regularly by hurricanes that hit large areas of the world, leaving thousands of victims.

H

H

King Hussein I of Jordan (1935-1999).

1924 Ibn Saud forced him to abdicate, and he died in exile.

Husky *See:* Siberian husky.

Hussar, European soldier who was a member of light cavalry units used for scouting. The Hussar uniform included a high, cloth cap (busby), a loose cape (dolman), and a heavily braided jacket. Napoleon perfected the efficiency of these soldiers, who became known for their fighting abilities. Hussars were no longer used after World War I.

Hussein, Saddam (1937-), Arab nationalist leader, president and dictator of Iraq since 1979. As chair of the Revolutionary Command Council of the Arab Ba'ath Socialist Party, he established a regime marked by widespread repression, imprisonment, and fear. At the same time, the government made significant progress in industrialization. The Ba'ath took power in Iraq in 1963.
Hussein, though formally second in command, was the de facto ruler as early as 1969. In 1980, he launched an attack on Iran that led to the 8-year long Iran-Iraq war. Saddam repressed the national resistance of the Kurds and the Shiites in a bloody manner and with the aid of chemical weapons.
In 1990, the Iraq army invaded Kuwait. The pretext for the invasions was Iraq's territorial claim to Kuwait. Shortly after the invasion, the United States and a combined allied military force established a military presence in Saudi Arabia. After 6 months of UN diplomatic efforts at peace failed, the allied forces declared war on Iraq.
On Jan. 16, 1991 hostilities commenced and a ceasefire was announced on Feb. 21, 1991.
Following the Persian Gulf War, a trade boycott was imposed on Iraq and it's weapon industry was put under the surveillance of the UN. The UN weapon inspections were systematically thwarted and promises consistently broken, culminating in a bombing raid by the United States and Great Britain in Dec. 1998.
After the attacks in the USA on September 11, 2001, president Bush threatened war against Iraq, after which Saddam again allowed authorized weapon inspections in 2002. Saddam is believed to hide weapons

of mass destruction including biological ones.
See also: Iraq; Persian Gulf War.

Hussein ibn Talal (1935-1999), King of Jordan from 1953 to 1999. He guided his kingdom through the turbulent years of Arab nationalism and Palestinian resistance in the 1950s and 1960s. In 1970, he came into conflict with the PLO; he eliminated the guerrillas on Jordan territory at the expense of numerous Palestinian lives (Black September).
Hussein's support of Saddam Hussein during the Gulf War (1991) damaged healthy contacts between the Western world and Jordan. Afterwards, Hussein played an important role in the peace process between Israel and the Palestinians. In the 1990s, he liberalized domestic politics, and as a result, the Muslim fundamentalist opposition received a great deal of latitude. His fourth wife, Elizabeth Halaby, an American, whom he married in 1978, became Queen Noor. His son, Abdullah ll, succeeded him in 1999.
See also: Jordan; Palestine Liberation Organization; Hussein, Saddam.

Husserl, Edmund (1859-1938), Czech-born German philosopher who founded phenomenology. Professor at Göttingen and Freiburg universities, he was concerned with what constitutes acts of consciousness and how they relate to experience. He held that consciousness is 'intentional' in that it is always 'conscious of' an object. Husserl's investigations influenced Heidegger, Sartre, and other thinkers of 20th-century existentialism.
See also: Phenomenology.

Huston, name of 3 film personalities. **Walter Huston** (1884-1950), Canadian-born U.S. actor, is best known for his roles in the play *Dodsworth* (1936), the musical comedy *Knickerbocker Holiday* (1938), and the film *The Treasure of Sierra Madre* (1947) directed by his son
John Huston (1906-1987), Hollywood writer, then director, whose other films include *The Maltese Falcon* (1941), *The Asphalt Jungle* (1950), *The African Queen* (1951), *Moby Dick* (1956), *The Man who would be King* (1975), *Wise Blood* (1980), *Prizzi's Honor* (1985) and *The Dead* (1987).
John Huston's daughter **Anjelica Huston** (1951-) won the Academy Award for best supporting actress in *Prizzi's Honor* (1985).

Hutchins, Robert Maynard (1899-1977), U.S. educator, president (1929-1945) and chancellor (1945-1951) of the University of Chicago. He advocated the integration and synthesis of academic disciplines. In 1959 he founded the Center for the Study of Democratic Institutions as an ideal 'Community of Scholars.'
His books include *The Higher Learning in America* (1936) and *University of Utopia* (1953).

Hutterites, or Hutterlan Brethren, Protestant sect found primarily in South Dakota, and Canada. Like the Mennonites,

they believe in common ownership of goods and are pacifists.
The sect originated in 1533 as a branch of the Anabaptists and takes its name from Jacob Hutter, martyred in 1536.
See also: Anabaptism.

Hutton, James (1726-1797), Scottish geologist who proposed, in *Theory of the Earth* (1795), that the earth's natural features result from continual processes, occurring now at the same rate as they have in the past. These views were little regarded until Charles Lyell's work some decades later.

Huxley, British family of writers and scientists. **Thomas Henry Huxley** (1825-1895), biologist, is best known for his support of Darwin's theory of evolution, without which acceptance of the theory might have been long delayed. Most of his own contributions to paleontology and zoology (especially taxonomy), botany, geology, and anthropology were related to this. He also coined the word 'agnostic.'
His son **Leonard Huxley** (1860-1933), writer, wrote *The Life and Letters of Thomas Henry Huxley* (1900). Of his children, 3 earned fame.
Sir Julian Sorell Huxley (1887-1975) is best known as a biologist and ecologist. His early interests were in development and growth, genetics, and embryology. Later he made important studies of bird behavior, studied evolution, and wrote many popular scientific books.
Aldous Leonard Huxley (1894-1963) was one of the 20th century's foremost novelists. Important works include *Crome Yellow* (1921), *Antic Hay* (1923), and *Point Counter Point* (1928), characterized by their wit and attitude toward lofty pretensions, and the famous *Brave New World* (1932) and *Eyeless in Gaza* (1936). After experimenting with hallucinogenic drugs he became interested in mysticism. Later works include *The Devils of London* (1952), *the Doors of Perception* (1954), and *Island* (1962).
Andrew Fielding Huxley (1917-) shared the 1963 Nobel Prize for physiology or medicine with A.L. Hodgkin and Sir J. Eccles for his work with Hodgkin on the chemical basis of nerve impulse transmission.

Hu Yaobang (1915-1989), general secretary of the Chinese Communist Party (1981-1987). A friend and associate of Deng Xioping, he was removed as chairman of the party in January 1987 in the face of student demonstrations for freedom of expression.
See also: China.

Huygens, Christiaan (1629-1695), Dutch scientist. He formulated a wave theory of light, first applied the pendulum to the regulation of clocks, and discovered the surface markings of Mars and the rings of Saturn. In his optical studies he stated Huygens's Principle, that all points on a wave front may at any instant be considered sources of secondary waves that, taken together, represent the wave front at any later instant. Huygens' theory of light states that light is a disturbance traveling through some medium, such

as the ether. Thus light is due to wave motion in ether.
See also: Optics; Physics.

Hyacinth, plant (genus *Hyacinthus*, especially *H. orientalis*) of the lily family grown from a bulb that produces a head of beautifully colored and perfumed flowers. It originated in the Mediterranean region. Water hyacinths (*Eichhornia crassipes*) are unrelated plants. They float on water and have been introduced to many places where they become a nuisance by blocking waterways.

Hyaline membrane disease, or respiratory distress syndrome, lung condition that is a common cause of death in premature babies. The disease is characterized by underdeveloped lungs that lack pulmonary surfactant, a substance that prevents the collapse of air sacs after breathing has begun. Immature lungs produce a glassy membrane that covers open bronchioles. Breathing becomes strained and death frequently occcurs from lack of oxygen.

Hybrid, crossbred animal or plant; an offspring of 2 different breeds, genera, or varieties. A hybrid computer system is a system that uses both analog and digital equipment. Hybrids in data communications are circuits fabricated by interconnecting smaller circuits of different technologies mounted on a single substrate.

Hyderabad (pop. 1,7 million), third largest city in Pakistan, located on the Indus River in Sind province. It is an important transportation and trade center, with various chemical, engineering, and milling industries.
See also: Pakistan.

Hyderabad (pop. 3,146,000), capital of the Indian state of Andhra Pradesh and historically of the region also called Hyderabad. The metropolitan area is a trade and manufacturing center producing textiles, guns, and glass products.
See also: India.

Hyderabad, region on the Deccan plateau that was once a state of south central India. Historically, Hyderabad was the site of a Hindu civilization taken over by the Muslim Mogul Empire in the 17th century. It became part of India in 1948, after a plebescite rejected independence. In 1950 it was divided among the states of Andhra Pradesh, Maharashtra, and Karnataka. Crops include cotton, rice, and grain. Mineral deposits are also present in the area.
See also: India.

Hydra, in Greek mythology, serpent with many heads, also known as Lernaean Hydra or Hydra of Lerna. Whenever a head was cut off, 2 new ones replaced it. Hercules killed the Hydra, burning the necks after decapitating it.
See also: Mythology.

Hydra, genus of freshwater animal of the phylum Coelenterata, perhaps the most familiar of the class Hydrozoa. The hydra is found in ponds, lakes, and streams through-out the world. The body is an elongated 2-in (2.5-cm) column with a mouth at one end surrounded by tentacles. Normally attached by the other end to the substrate, hydras can move by 'looping' across a plane surface or by free-swimming. Hydras reproduce by asexual budding when food is abundant. When food is scarce, ovaries and testes develop on the column, and sexual reproduction gives rise to resistant, dormant embryos.

Hydrangea, genus of ornamental shrub of the saxifrage family originally from China and Japan, widely grown in pots and gardens. Its heads of small, flat-petaled flowers range from pale blue to pink, changing color in response to soil acidity.

Hydrate, any of various chemical compounds composed of water and some other substance. Common hydrates include blue vitriol ($CuSO_4 5H_2O$) and Glauber's salt ($Na_2CO_3 10H_2O$). As water evaporates, most hydrates change structure. Water that is retained by the hydrate is known as water of crystallization or hydration. Hydrates that have lost all water are called anhydrous.

Hydraulic brake *See:* Brake.

Hydraulic engine, or fluidic engine, machine that uses the motion or pressure of fluids (like oil, silicone, gas, and sometimes water) to produce power. These engines are used in jacks, hoists, hydraulic elevators, and some turbine generators.
See also: Hydraulics.

Hydraulics, branch of science concerned with the application of the properties of liquids (particularly water), at rest and in motion, to engineering problems. Since any machine or structure that uses, controls, or conserves a liquid makes use of the principles of hydraulics, the scope of this subject is very wide. It includes methods of water supply for consumption, irrigation, or navigation and the design of associated dams, canals, and pipes; hydroelectricity, the conversion of water power to electric energy using hydraulic turbines; the design and construction of ditches, culverts, and hydraulic jumps (a means of slowing down the flow of a stream by suddenly increasing its depth) for controlling and discharging flood water; and the treatment and disposal of industrial and human waste. Hydraulics applies the principles of hydrostatics and is hence a branch of fluid mechanics.

Hydrazine, chemical compound (H_2NNH_2), used in jet and rocket fuels, explosives, and corrosion inhibitors. Also known as hydronitrogen, it is a colorless liquid that absorbs water and alcohol. It has an acrid smell, burns in air, and is corrosive.

Hydriodic acid *See:* Hydrogen iodide.

Hydrobromic acid *See:* Hydrogen bromide.

Hydrocarbon, any organic compound of hydrogen and carbon. They are divided into two classes: *aliphatics*, in which the carbon atoms are arranged in chains, and *aromatics*, in which they are arranged in rings. The aliphatics are divided into various subgroups according to the way the carbon atoms are bonded together. Hydrocarbons occur in petroleum and natural gas. Commercial products include gasoline, kerosene, airplane fuel, lubricating oils, and paraffin.

Hydrochloric acid, chemical compound (HCL) with many industrial uses. A colorless, extremely corrosive liquid that fumes when exposed to air, it is used in metallurgy and food processing. It is produced naturally in the human stomach as a digestive aid, but stomach ulcers can form if it is present in excess.

Hydroelectric power *See:* Electric power; Water power.

Hydrofluoric acid, inorganic chemical compound (HF), also called hydrogen fluoride, formed when hydrofluoric gas is dissolved in water. It is used industrially in manufacturing aluminum, in etching glass, and as a catalyst for chemical reactions.

Hydrofoil, structure that, when moved rapidly through water, generates lift in exactly the same way and for the same reasons as does the airfoil. It is usually mounted beneath a vessel (also called a hydrofoil). Much of a conventional boat's power is spent in overcoming the drag (resistance) of the water; as a hydrofoil vessel builds up speed, it lifts out of the water until only a small portion of it (struts, hydrofoils, and propeller) is in contact with the water. Thus drag is reduced to a minimum. Hydrofoils can exceed 75 mph (121 kmph) as compared with conventional craft, whose maximum speeds rarely approach 50 mph (80 kmph).

Hydrogen, chemical element, symbol H; for physical constants see Periodic Table. Hydrogen was prepared for many years before it was recognized as a distinct substance by Henry Cavendish in 1766. It is the most abundant element in the universe, making up about three quarters of the mass of the universe. On earth hydrogen occurs chiefly in combination with oxygen in water. Hydrogen is prepared commercially by the

The French hydrangea (*H. macrophylla*) is admired for its large flower clusters.

H

H

On November 1, 1952, the Americans set off the first hydrogen bomb in the Pacific Ocean.

action of steam on heated carbon or iron. Hydrogen is a diatomic, colorless, explosively reactive gas, the lightest of all gases. Hydrogen gas is a mixture of 2 kinds of molecules, known as *ortho-* and *para*-hydrogen, which differ from one another by the spins of their electrons and nuclei. Hydrogen is used in nitrogen fixation, as rocket fuel, in reducing metallic ores, for welding, as heavy water in nuclear reactors, and as a neutron moderator. Liquid hydrogen is used in cryogenics.

Hydrogenation, chemical process that adds hydrogen to some other substance. The resulting reaction is used to change liquid oils into solid fats, powdered coal into crude oil, and nitrogen into ammonia.

Hydrogen bomb, or thermonuclear bomb, very powerful bomb whose explosive energy is produced by nuclear fusion of hydrogen isotopes, as of 2 deuterium atoms or of a deuterium and a tritium atom. The extremely high temperatures required to start the fusion reaction are produced by an atomic bomb. Lithium-6 deuteride (^{6}LiD) is the explosive; neutrons produced by deuterium fusion react with the ^{6}Li to produce tritium. The end products are the isotopes of helium, ^{3}He and ^{4}He. In warfare hydrogen bombs have the advantage of being far more powerful than atomic bombs, their power being measured in megatons (millions of tons) of TNT, capable of destroying a large city. In defensive and peaceful uses they can be modified so that the radioactivity produced is reduced. Hydrogen bombs were first developed in the United States (1949-1952) by Edward Teller and others, and have been tested by the USSR, Great Britain, China, and France.
See also: Fallout; Nuclear weapon.

Hydrogen bromide, chemical compound (HBr) that is a colorless, corrosive gas. If exposed to humid air it will fume; when combined with water it forms hydrobromic acid. The gas is used in various chemical reactions to make organic bromides and compounds, as a reducing agent, and as a catalyst.

Hydrogen fluoride *See:* Hydrofluoric acid.

Hydrogen iodide, chemical compound (HI) that is a colorless gas with a sharp odor. It fumes when exposed to humid air and combines easily with water to form hydriodic acid. It is used to make iodine salts, as a reducing agent, and for medical purposes in a diluted form.

Hydrogen peroxide (H_2O_2), unstable chemical compound that acts as an oxidizing agent that may cause poisoning. Hydrogen peroxide is marketed as an aqueous solution ranging from the common concentration of 3% as a topical antiseptic, 6% in hair preparations (bleaches, neutralizers, and so forth), to 30% for industrial and laboratory use and 90% for use in rocket propulsion. Decomposition of hydrogen peroxide may release large volumes of oxygen (10 times the volume for a 3% solution). Dropping a 3% solution on the eye, 3-5 times a day has been reported to be innocuous, but high-concentration hydrogen peroxide is generally feared as a cause of severe corneal damage. Ingestion of the commonly available household products (3-6%) should cause no problem other than possible mucous membrane and gastrointestinal irritation, while higher concentrations (such as 30%) are considered corrosive.
See also: Antiseptic.

Hydrogen sulfide, colorless, poisonous, flammable gas (H_2S) with an odor of rotting eggs. When combined with water it forms hydrosulfuric acid. The gas can be found around cesspools and in mines as a by-product of the decomposition of substances containing sulfur. The gas is also produced in laboratories for use as an analytical reagent.

Hydrology, branch of geophysics concerned with the hydrosphere (all the waters of the earth), with particular reference to water on and within the land. The science was born in the 17th century with the work of Pierre Perrault and Edmé Mariotte.
See also: Geophysics.

Hydrolysis, in chemistry, double decomposition effected by water, according to the general equation $XY + H_2O \rightarrow XOH + YH$. If XY is a salt of a weak acid or a weak base, the hydrolysis is reversible, and affects the pH of the solution. Reactive organic compounds such as acid chlorides and acid anhydrides are rapidly hydrolyzed by water alone, but other compounds require acids, bases, or enzymes as catalysts. Industrial hydrolysis processes include the alkaline saponification of oils and fats to glycerol and soap, and the acid hydrolysis of starch to glucose.

Hydrometer, device that measures the specific gravity of a liquid (its density relative to that of water). It is based on Archimedes' principle that states that a floating object is buoyed up by a force equal to the weight of the fluid it displaces. The instrument is a long thin glass bulb held upright by a weight at one end, allowed to float in the test liquid. The denser the liquid, the less the hydrometer sinks. The tube is calibrated in such a way that the specific gravity can be read off by comparing the level to which the bulb sinks with a scale along the side of the hydrometer. A form of hydrometer called an acidimeter is used in testing storage batteries by measuring the specific gravity, and therefore the strength, of the acid they contain.
See also: Density.

Hydrophobia *See:* Rabies.

Hydroplane, speedboat designed so that the hull rides above the surface of the water. When the boat accelerates rapidly and maintains speed, water pressure allows the flat or slightly curved bottom of the boat to skim the water.

Hydroponics, or soil-less culture, technique by which plants are grown without soil. All the minerals required for plant growth are provided by nutrient solutions in which the roots are immersed. The technique has been highly developed as a tool in botanical research, but commercial exploitation is limited primarily because of the difficulty of aerating the water and providing support for the plants. Gravel culture has overcome these problems to some extent and is used to grow some horticulture crops.

Hydrosphere, all the waters of the earth, in whatever form: solid, liquid, gaseous. It thus includes the water of the atmosphere, water on the earth's surface (e.g., oceans, rivers, ice sheets), and groundwater.

Hydrotherapy, external application of water for therapeutic purposes. The body or any of its parts may be immersed in water or water may be applied to the surface with or without the intermediary of absorbent materials. In partial baths, water may be applied by immersion, pouring, or compress to a small area of the body. For an eye wash, a hemispherical container filled to the brim with water is applied to the open eye, and as the head is tilted, the water bathes the corneal surface. The ear may be washed with a stream of water applied with a rubber bulb or syringe, usually to dislodge ear wax from the canal. The nasal passages may be bathed by sniffing water from the cupped hands, and the mouth may be washed by rinsing or irrigation.

Hydroxide, chemical compound containing the negatively charged hydroxyl ion (OH⁻), used in the manufacture of detergents and medicines. Most hydroxide compounds are water soluble and can be caustic to varying degrees. Household ammonia is a familiar example of a basic hydroxide. Hydroxides are inorganic compounds; organic compounds containing the hydroxyl ion are called alcohols.

Hyena, 3 species of carnivorous mammals, family Hyaenidae, native to Asia and Africa. They are distinctive in having the shoulders considerably higher than the hindquarters and having an unusual gait, moving both limbs on one side of the body together. All 3 species have massive heads with powerful jaws. Though reviled as scavengers and carrion feeders, hyenas are active and skillful predators in their own right, hunting in packs of up to 20.

Hygiene *See:* Health.

Hygrometer, device to measure humidity (the amount of water vapor the air holds). Usually, hygrometers measure relative humidity, the amount of moisture as a percentage of the saturation level at that temperature. In the hair hygrometer, which is of limited accuracy, the length of a hair (usually human) increases with increase in relative humidity. This length change is amplified by a lever and registered by a needle on a dial. The wet- and dry-bulb hygrometer (psychrometer) has 2 thermometers mounted side by side, the bulb of one covered by a damp cloth. Air is moved across the apparatus (e.g., by a fan) and evaporation of water from the cloth draws latent heat from the bulb. Comparison of the 2 temperatures, and the use of tables, gives the relative humidity. In the dewpoint hygrometer, a polished container is cooled until the dew point is reached, giving a measure of relative humidity. The electric hygrometer measures changes in the electrical resistance of a hygroscopic (water-absorbing) strip.
See also: Humidity.

Hyksos, Asian group who invaded Egypt in the 18th century B.C. and formed the 15th and 16th dynasties of Egypt. They introduced the Asian light horse and chariot, bronze weapons, and the compound bow.

Hymn, sacred song in praise of gods or heroes, found in almost all cultures, ancient and modern. Jewish psalms, sung in the temple worship, were adopted by the early Christian Church and supplemented by distinctively Christian hymns such as the canticles. There is a continuous English hymn, tradition from the 7th century that includes 16th-century carols such as 'Hark, the Herald Angels Sing.' Modern hymns were developed by Isaac Watts, John Wesley, and many others in the 1700s. There are over 400,000 hymns, ranging from Gregorian chants (plainsongs) to rousing gospel music.

Hyperactive child, excessively active child who cannot concentrate on any one task for more than a few minutes. Hyperacitivity is called hyperkinesis by physicians. Symptoms exhibited by a hyperactive child range from persistent yelling and moving about to disobedience and an inability to socialize. Once thought to be mentally deficient, hyperactive children are now known to be generally of average to above-average intelligence. New teaching methods and family counseling have become part of the treatment of the condition. Stimulants and tranquilizers may also be prescribed, though drug therapy has become less popular in recent years, because its long-term effects are unknown.

Hyperbola, in geometry, curve consisting of 2 separate branches opening out in opposite directions. The hyperbola is one of the conic sections, formed when a right circular cone is intersected by a plane. It may be expressed in analytic geometry by the equation $y = 1/x$.
See also: Geometry.

Hyperkinesis *See:* Hyperactive child.

Hyperopia *See:* Farsightedness.

Hyperrealism, movement in the visual arts, which flourished from 1965 to the early seventies of the 20th century. Typical are lifelike illustrations or portrayals of people or everyday situations. Reproduction occurs often with the aid of photographs or slides, which, after being enlarged, are painted over precisely. Well known works are those of R. Estes, C. Close, A. Colville, D. Van Golden, G. Richter, and D. Hanson. The last is renowned for deceptively life-like human figures.

Hypertension, abnormally high blood pressure. Blood pressure is the pressure that the heart and arteries apply in order to squeeze the blood around the body. In a normal person, when sitting or lying quietly, the blood pressure stays at a steady, or resting, level. In moments of exercise, excitement, anger, or anxiety, the level of blood pressure is raised by te release of adrenaline and other hormones to increase the blood flow to the brain and muscles. In the hypertensive individual, blood pressure remains high; although there may be no immediate symptoms, long-term effects can be serious or fatal, and may include damage to the heart and brain. Causes include diet, kidney disorders, stress, and hereditary factors. Hypertension is treated with diet and medication.
See also: Blood pressure.

Hyperventilation, abnormal, deep and rapid breathing, frequently caused by anxiety. The level of carbon dioxide in the blood decreases, which restricts arteries, lowers blood pressure, and may result in dizziness or fainting.

Hypnos, in Greek mythology, the god of sleep. His mother was the goddess of the night, and his twin brother was Thantos, or Death. Among his sons was Morpheus, the Greek god of dreams.
See also: Mythology.

Hypnosis, artificially induced mental state characterized by an individual's loss of critical powers and consequent openness to suggestion. It may be induced by an external agency or self-induced (autohypnosis). Hypnotism has been widely used in medicine (usually to induce analgesia) and especially in psychiatry and psychotherapy. Here, the particular value of hypnosis is that while in trance, the individual may be encouraged to recall deeply repressed memories that may be at the heart of an emotional conflict; once such causes have been elucidated, therapy may proceed. Hypnosis seems to be as old as human society. However, the first definite information comes from the late 18th century with the work of Franz Mesmer, who held that disease was the result of imbalance in a patient's 'animal magnetism,' and hence attempted to cure this by the use of magnets. Some of his patients were cured, presumably by suggestion; the term mesmerism is still used for hypnotism.

Hypochlorous acid, weak inorganic acid (HOCl) used in bleaches and disinfectants. It is formed when chlorine is combined with water. Used to disinfect public drinking water and swimming pools, hypochlorous acid is also a strong oxidant.

Hypochondria, or hypochondriasis, mental condition involving undue anxiety about real or supposed ailments, usually in the belief that these are incurable. The source of hypochondria was once thought to be the hypochondrium, that part of the abdomen containing the spleen and liver.
See also: Neurosis.

Hypoglycemia, abnormally low level of glucose in the blood. Symptoms are tremulousness, sweating, irritability and restlessness, feeling of extreme hunger, headache and nausea, chronic fatigue and weakness. With severe hypoglycemia, the person may lose consciousness. Another form of hypoglycemia occurs in people who have had a large amount of alcohol to drink, either without eating or along with very high quantities of sugar-containing mixes.

Hypothalamus, central part of the base of the brain, closely related to the pituitary gland. It contains vital centers for controlling the autonomic nervous system, body temperature, and water and food intake, and is the center for primitive physical and emotional behavior. It also produces hormones for regulating pituitary secretion and systemic hormones including vasopressin and oxytocin.
See also: Brain.

Hypothermia, subnormal temperature of the body. Initial symptoms are weakness, slurred speech, confusion, shivering, and clumsiness. If the condition progresses, the weakness is replaced by stiff muscles, the person feels unable to move, and drowsiness and sleepiness occur. The body is no longer able to conserve heat, and the body temperature falls rapidly. Eventually, if nothing is done to return the temperature to normal, breathing will cease and the heart will stop. Activities that involve a high risk of hypothermia are swimming or other water activities; mountain climbing, skiing, and other activities that couple cold, wetness, and wind with exertion and sweating; and being out in the cold weather without proper clothing to provide warmth and protection from wetness. Special precautions must be taken with the very young and the elderly, who are the principal victims of hypothermia.
Drunkenness, exhaustion, hunger, disease, and illness all put people at greater risk of hypothermia. It is critical to stop the process immediately. Remove all wet clothing (it retains the cold and wetness); if possible, rewarm the body with whatever is available (dry clothing, towels, blankets, jackets, sweaters, even paper), and in an emergency, use the warmth (body heat) of others; a

H

H

Rock hyraxes, *Heterohyrax*, live in large bands among rocks and feed on nearby vegetation. A hyrax young rides on its mother's back until it is two months old. The patch of colored hair on the animal's back covers a scent gland and bristles when it is angry or when mating.

warm (not hot) bath is helpful. The person should be seen by a doctor as soon as possible.

Hyrax, or cony, rabbit-sized mammal of Africa and South Asia, of the order Hyracoidea, closely related to the elephant. The hyrax resembles the guinea pig, with short legs, ears, and tail. Some species are tree-dwelling and others, called dassies, live among rocks. They feed on plants and fruits.

Hyssop, herb (*Hyssopus officinalis*) of the mint family. Once used as a household remedy for sore throat, hyssop is now used primarily as a seasoning for meats and vegetables. The oil from its evergreen leaves has been used in the manufacture of perfumes. Grown throughout southern Europe and in parts of the United States, the hyssop plant may reach 2 ft (61 cm) in height.

Hysterectomy, surgical removal of the womb, with or without the ovaries and fallopian tubes. It may be performed via either the abdomen or the vagina and is most often used for fibroid tumors (benign tumors of womb muscle), cancer of the cervix or body of the womb, endometriosis, or other diseases causing heavy menstruation. If the ovaries are preserved, hormone secretion remains intact, though menstrual periods cease and infertility is inevitable. Recent controversy has questioned the overuse of the procedure because of the negative effects on general health.

Hysteria, or conversion disorder, medical diagnostic term for illness characterized by physical complaints without physical cause. The word 'hysteria' derives from the ancient Greeks, who applied the term solely to diseases of women, which were explained as being due to malfunctioning of the uterus (hystera).

I, ninth letter of the English alphabet. It originated in the ancient Semitic alphabet, where

it may have derived from an early symbol for 'hand.' It later passed into the Greek alphabet and was called *iota*. The original letter was probably a consonant representing our *y* sound, but in most Greek and Latin, as well as in many modern European languages, its sound is that of the vowel in *meet*. In English it may be short, as in *fit*, or long, as in *fine*, or it may combine with other letters for a great variety of sounds. The dot over the lowercase *i* first appeared in the 11th century. In chemistry, *I* is the symbol for iodine.

Ialomita, 1. (pop. 304,000), district in Southeast Rumania; 1,718 sq mi (4,449 sq km). Capital: Slobozia. The industries are chemical, metal, textile, and food industry. There is agriculture (corn, barley, wheat, cotton, sunflowers, and rice). Sheep breeding.
2. River in the same region, a tributary of the Danube, 199 mi (320 km) long. Its source lies in the Transylvanian Alps.

Iasi (pop. 807,000), 1. District in Northeast Rumania; 2,112 sq mi (5,469 sq km). There is agriculture (wheat, oats, barley, corn, sugar beets, home produce.
2. (Formerly: Jassy) (pop. 343,000), capital of the district with the same name. It is the center of culture, education, and trade. The industries are metallurgic, pharmaceutical, furniture, textile, and food. There are monasteries (16th and 18th centuries)and old churches. The area is alluded to as early as in the 7th century.

IATA *See:* International Air Transport Association.

Ibadan (pop. 1.3 mln.), second largest city in Nigeria. Founded in the 1830s, Ibadan is located in the rich agricultural region of southwest Nigeria, and is a major commercial and industrial center. Ibadan's industries and products include brewing, producing canned goods, paint, plastics, furniture, and soap. Ibadan came under British protection

in 1893. It is the capital of Nigeria's Oyo state.
See also: Nigeria.

Ibáñez, Vicente Blasco *See:* Blasco Ibáñez, Vicente.

Iberian Peninsula, landmass in southwestern Europe, occupied by Spain and Portugal. It is mostly surrounded by the waters of the Mediterranean Sea (east) and the Atlantic Ocean (west) and separated from North Africa by the Strait of Gibraltar. The Pyrenees Mountains to the north form a natural barrier between the peninsula and the rest of Europe.

Ibert, Jacques (1890-1962), French composer of piano pieces, orchestral works, symphonic poems, and operas. Among his well-known works are a cantata, *Le Poète et la Fée* (1919), a ballet based on Oscar Wilde's *Ballad of Reading Gaol* (1922), the orchestral suites *Escales* (1922) and *Divertissement* (1930), and the light opera for radio *Barbe-bleue* (1943).

Ibex, 7 species of wild goats (genus *Capra*) of the Eastern Hemisphere that differ from true goats in their flattened foreheads and usually broad-fronted horns. Always found in mountainous areas, ibex live for most of the year in separate-sex herds, with the males forming harems only during the 7- to 10-day rut.

Ibis, heronlike wading bird (family Threskiornithidae) of moderate size, characterized by a long, thin, downward-curving bill. Ibises have a worldwide distribution in tropical, subtropical, and temperate regions, and are usually found near fresh water, feeding on small aquatic animals. Ibises are gregarious and frequently raucous. Species include the sacred ibis (*Threskiornis aethiopica*), honored in ancient Egypt, and the

The scarlet ibis (*Eudocimus rubra*) of tropical South America is about 24 in (60 cm) long. It nests in huge coastal colonies.

Norwegian playwright and poet Henrik Ibsen (1828-1906).

Eastern glossy ibis (*Plegadis Falcinellus falcinellus*), common in the United States.

Ibizan hound, rare dog breed from Ibiza, an island off the eastern coast of Spain. A modern relative of an ancient Egyptian hunting dog, it is similar to the greyhound, with a slender build, a long snout, upright ears, and a long neck. It has amber eyes and a pink nose, and its coat may be long or short and red, white, brown, or a mixture of colors. It stands up to 27 in (69 cm) high and weighs up to 50 lb (23 kg).

Ibn Batuta (1304?-1378?), greatest Arab traveler of the Middle Ages. He spent about 25 years traveling in Africa, Asia, and Europe. His notes (the *Rihlah*, or *Travels*) provide a priceless account of life before the rise of Europe.

Ibn Hawkal (Abu al-Kasim Mohammed ibn Ali; d. 977), Arabian merchant, explorer, and geographer. He explored North Africa, Spain, and Sicily. His geographical study *Book of Roads and Kingdoms* is famous.

Ibn Khaldun (1332-1406), Arab historian and sociologist. *Muqaddama*, the first volume of Ibn Khaldun's *Universal History*, contains the first attempt to interpret the patterns of history in the purely secular terms of geography, sociology, and allied subjects.
See also: Sociology.

Ibn Saud (1880-1953), creator of the kingdom of Saudi Arabia. Inheriting the leadership of the orthodox Wahabi movement, in 1900 he and a small band of followers captured the city of Riyadh, from which his family had been exiled, and by 1912 had conquered the Nejd from Turkey. During World War I the British favored his rival, King Husein ibn-Ali of Hejaz, in their campaign against the Turks, but in 1924-1925 ibn-Saud defeated Husein, combining Hejaz and the Nejd to form the kingdom of Saudi Arabia. He imposed order and religious orthodoxy. In the 1930s he awarded oil concessions to U.S. companies from which his family began to derive enormous wealth. Neutral in World War II, ibn-Saud took little part in the Arab-Israeli war of 1948.
See also: Saudi Arabia.

Ibn-Sina *See:* Avicenna.

Ibo *See:* Igbo.

Ibsen, Henrik (1828-1906), Norwegian playwright and poet. The pioneer of modern drama, his work developed from national Romanticism (*The Vikings at Helgoland*, 1858) to the realistic and effective presentation of contemporary social problems and moral dilemmas in such plays as *A Doll's House* (1879), *Ghosts* (1881), *The Wild Duck* (1884), and *Hedda Gabler* (1890). Very different, but as important to his philosophy, are his verse-dramas *Brand* (1866) and *Peer Gynt* (1867).

Ibuprofen, drug used for the relief of headaches, muscle aches, pain, and for the reduction of fever. Familiar trade names for ibuprofen include Advil, Motrin, and Nuprin. An anti-inflammatory agent and pain reliever, ibuprofen is also used to treat arthritis. Of a group of drugs called *propionic acid derivatives* developed in the 1960s and early 70s, ibuprofen is today the most widely used. Since 1984, ibuprofen has been available for sale without a prescription.
See also: Drug.

Icarus, in Greek mythology, son of Daedalus, with whom he was imprisoned in the labyrinth by King Minos of Crete. To escape Minos's wrath, they attached feathered wings to their shoulders with wax and flew away. Icarus, however, flew too high; the sun melted the wax, and he plunged into the sea and was drowned.
See also: Mythology.

ICBM *See:* Guided missile.

Ice, frozen water; colorless crystalline solid in which the strong, directional hydrogen bonding produces a structure with much space between the molecules. Thus ice is less dense than water and floats on it. The expansion of water on freezing may crack pipes and automobile radiators. Seawater freezes at about 28°F (-2°C). Ice has a very low coefficient of friction, and some fast-moving sports (ice hockey and ice skating) are played on it; slippery, icy roads are dangerous. Ice deposited on airplane wings reduces lift. Ice is used as a refrigerant and to cool some beverages.
See also: Water.

Ice age, any of several periods in geologic time when thick ice caps and glaciers covered large areas of the earth that now have temperate or warm climates. In 1837 Louis Agassiz, a Swiss-U.S. naturalist, was one of the first to argue that a great ice age in the past explained land features associated with glaciation hundreds of miles from permanent ice. Geologists later established that there have been several ice ages. Ice ages occurred in Australia, Canada, China, India, South Africa, and other places more than 700 million years ago, but little is known about them. Another great ice age affected the Southern Hemisphere during the early Permian period, which began c.275 million years ago. The ice ages about which most is known occurred in the Northern Hemisphere during the Pleistocene epoch in the past million years. There were 4 main glacial ages when the ice advanced: the Nebraskan (which began c.600,000 years ago), the Kansan (which began 476,000 years ago), the Illinoian (which began 230,000 years ago), and the Wisconsin (which began 115,000 years ago and ended c.10,000 years ago). The European names for these glacial ages are the Günz, Mindel, Riss, and Würm. These were separated by 3 interglacial ages during which the weather became warmer and the ice retreated. In North America the interglacials are named the Aftonian, the Yarmouth, and the Sangamon. Geologists do not know whether the close of the Wisconsin glacial age marked the end of the recent ice ages, or whether the present time is the fourth interglacial, preceding a fifth glacial age.

Iceberg, large floating mass of ice. In the Southern Hemisphere, the Antarctic ice sheet overflows its land support to form shelves of ice on the sea; huge pieces, as much as 150 mi (240 km) across, break off to form icebergs. In the Northern Hemisphere, icebergs are generally not over 175 yds (160 m) across. Most are 'calved' from some 20 glaciers on Greenland's west coast. Small icebergs (*growlers*) may calve from larger ones. Some 75% of the height and over 85% of the mass of an iceberg lies below water. Northern icebergs usually float for some months to the Grand Banks, off Newfoundland, there melting in a few days. They endanger shipping, the most famous tragedy being the sinking of the *Titanic* (1912). The International Ice Patrol now keeps a constant watch on the area.
See also: Ice.

Melting icebergs reveal typical features of coastal erosion: recent wave-cut notches (1), old notches that were cut when the iceberg was heavier and lower (2), water-runoff erosion (3), parent-glacier rock fragments (4), a water-eroded sea stack (5), and a wave-cut platform (6).

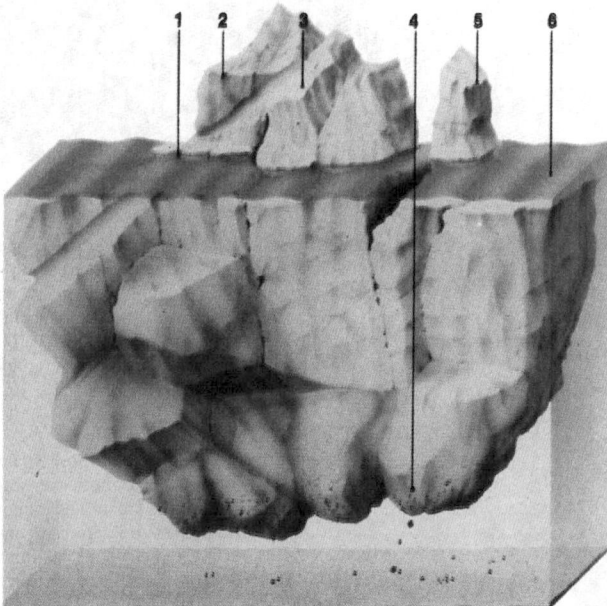

Icebreaker, vessel designed to break channels through ice for other ships, chiefly in harbors and rivers. They are of special importance in Canada, the former USSR, and Scandinavia. An icebreaker has a very strong reinforced hull and is equipped with high-powered engines that transmit power to the rugged propeller by electrical means. This enables the vessel to develop maximum power from a standing start. When breaking thin ice, the ship rams its way forward, sometimes assisted by turbulence created by a propeller at the bow. For breaking thick ice the vessel moves fast enough to ride up onto the ice, which then breaks under its weight. The shape of the hull makes icebreakers roll heavily in open water, but this also helps to break the ice. Special canting tanks containing water can also induce rolling and prevent the ship from getting trapped. The world's first atomic-powered icebreaker, the 16,000-ton (7,258 kg) *Lenin*, was launched by the USSR in 1957.

A Russian icebreaker.

Icecap, extensive perennial cover of ice and snow, covering huge sections of the earth's polar regions. The Antarctic icecap has an area of 5 million sq mi (13 million sq km) and an average thickness of 7,000 ft (2,100 m). The majority of Greenland is covered by an icecap.
See also: Ice.

Ice cream, frozen dairy food whose main ingredients are sugar, cream or butterfat, water, flavorings, and air. Ice cream has a high caloric value and a very high vitamin A content, as well as being protein- and calcium-rich. It is also a source of smaller quantitites of iron, phosphorus, riboflavin, and thiamin.

Water ices, which contain no milk products, have been known since ancient times in Europe and Asia. Ice cream probably reached the United States in the 17th century, and was first commercially manufactured by Jacob Fussel (1851). Today, the United States is the world's largest producer and consumer.

Ice hockey *See:* Hockey.

Iceland

Capital:	Reykjavík
Area:	39,769 sq mi
	(103,000 sq km)
Population:	279,000
Language:	Icelandic
Government:	Republic
Independent:	1944
Head of gov.:	Prime minister
Per capita:	US$ 24,800
Monetary unit:	1 Icelandic krona
	= 100 aurar

Iceland (Icelandic: *Island*), nation located on second-largest island of Europe, situated in the North Atlantic Ocean just south of the Arctic Circle, 200 mi (320 km) southeast of Greenland, 650 mi (1,050 km) west of Norway, and 500 mi (800 km) northwest of Scotland.
Land and climate. Iceland has more than 100 volcanic peaks with varying degrees of activity. Enormous ice explosions sometimes take place due to eruptions of volcanoes beneath ice fields, flooding large areas. Iceland's numerous hot springs and geysers are also of volcanic origin. Water from the springs is widely used for heating purposes.

Lava fields account for more than a tenth of Iceland's surface. There are also enormous glaciers. The coastline is highly irregular, indented with numerous fjords and navigable bays, including the large Faxa Bay on the southwest coast, where Reykjavík, the nation's capital, stands. A plateau at an altitude of 2,000 ft (610 m) covers a large portion of the interior of the country. There are numerous rivers, but none is navigable. There are also many lakes. Iceland's marine climate is modified by the warm North Atlantic Drift. The average winter temperature in Reykjavík, in the south, is 30°F (-1°C) and the average summer temperature is 52°F (11°C), but the north is much colder. Only about a quarter of Iceland's surface bears natural vegetation, often a thick moss carpet found in areas not covered with snow. Only in areas protected by a winter snow cover is vegetation more dense. The lowlands have large areas of grass and, in sheltered regions, even some trees, the most common being dwarf willows, birches, and mountain ash. Native animals include the Arctic fox and various birds, of which the eider duck is valued for its down. The reindeer and mink were imported to the island.
People. Except for some blending of Irish blood, most of the people of Iceland are directly descended from the Vikings or other Scandinavians. In the second half of the 19th century, due to the country's poor economic situation, about 25,000 emigrated, mainly to Canada. Three-quarters of the population is centered in urban areas along the coast, over one-third of the population living in Reykjavík, the cultural center, with its own university (founded 1911). The Icelandic language is of the Scandinavian group. It has undergone very few changes since the 12th and 13th centuries, an era in which the famous Icelandic sagas and prose narratives were written, so that this literature is still understandable to modern readers. Iceland was almost entirely free of illiteracy by the beginning of the 19th century. Education is compulsory and free from ages 7 to 15. The university of Reykjavik is one of the institutions for higher education. Christianity was established in Iceland about a thousand years ago. By far the most prominent church today is the Evangelical Lutheran Church.
Economy. Fishing (especially cod, haddock, and herring) and fish-processing are the

Thick layers of lava are characteristic of large parts of Iceland, a geologically young region, that is rich in volcanic phenomena.

mainstay industries and provide two-thirds of Iceland's exports. A long dispute with Great Britain over fishing rights in the waters off Iceland led to a series of 'cod wars.' In 1975 Iceland extended its 'economic' sea limits to 200 mi (322 km) and the next year broke diplomatic relations with Britain for 4 months. There is some small-scale agriculture and manufacturing. Iceland's vast resources of natural energy in its rivers, hot streams, and geysers, as well as its important volcanic mineral potential, are only beginning to be exploited for industrial and commercial purposes.

History. Discovered by the Norse c.A.D. 870, Iceland was under Norwegian rule from 1262 and then under the Danes from 1380. The tradition of democratic government dates from A.D. 930, when the Althing, the world's oldest parliament, was established. Iceland has been entirely self-governing since 1918, and it became a fully independent republic on June 17, 1944. In 1970, Iceland joined the European Free Trade Association. Iceland maintains very strict rules in the field of cattle breeding and fishing. In 1992, the country resigned from the International Whaling Commission (IWC), but 10 years later, re-joined to control whale catching.

Ice skating, winter sport in the United States, Canada, and the countries of northern Europe. Originally confined to natural settings and conditions, such as frozen lakes and rivers, the sport has been widely popularized by the introduction of artificial rinks. Competitive skating, which requires many years of intensive practice, consists of figure skating and speed skating. Figure skating is a highly technical and demanding form of body control. The skater must master a large number of school figures (including turns, brackets, rockers, and loops) based on a figure eight, and must develop striking routines of individual free skating (including jumps, spins, spirals, and free movements performed to music). In competition, school figures account for 60% of the skater's score and free skating for 40%. Speed skating takes place over distances from as little as 50 yd (46 m) to as much as 5 mi (8 km). In the United States, skaters generally race against each other directly whereas in European and Olympic events they race against the clock, 2 at a time. Good speed skaters can average 20 mph (32 kmph) or more. Ice skating dates back at least as far as the 8th century and attained its first national popularity in the Netherlands in the 15th century. Metal blades first appeared in the 16th century.

I Ching, or Book of Changes, ancient Chinese philosophical and literary classic dating to c.12th century B.C. Its set of symbols and texts are used for divination. The *I Ching* was a major influence on Confucianism and Taoism. There has been a revival of interest in the *I Ching* in recent years.
See also: Confucianism; Taoism.

Ichneumon wasp, parasitic wasp (family Ichneumonidae) equipped with a long egg-laying organ, the *ovipositor*, like a hypodermic needle. It lays its eggs in the larvae of other insects and when its own larvae hatch they feed on the tissues of host or hosts. The host, such as a caterpillar, continues to live with the ichneumon larva inside it until pupation. Then the parasite kills its host and pupates itself. Some species of ichneumon wasps can penetrate 2 in (5 cm) of wood with their ovipositors to lay eggs on the larvae of horntails (large sawflies that are pests in timber plantations). These ichneumon wasps have been specially introduced into plantations to keep down the numbers of horntails.

Ickx, Jacques-Bernard (Jackie) (1945-), Belgian racing driver, who achieved his first success in 1967 when he became the European Formula Two champion. Ickx excelled in various categories. For example, between 1966 and 1979 he raced in 116 Grand Prix races, of which he won eight. Both in 1969 and 1970 he was second in the final league of the Formula One world championship. Ickx also excelled in endurance races, winning the 24-Hours at Le Mans eight times and conquering the Canadian-American Canam title in 1979. In 1982 and 1983 he won the Porsche world championships for endurance races. He won the Paris-Dakar rally in 1983 (Mercedes Benz).

Icon (Greek, 'image'), religious image in the Eastern and Russian Orthodox churches. Icons play an important part in liturgy. The Virgin Mary and Jesus were traditional icon figures; by the 7th century icon worship was an officially encouraged cult in the Byzantine Christian Church.
See also: Eastern Orthodox Church.

Iconoclast (Greek *eikon*, 'image' + *klastes*, 'breaker'), person who practices iconoclasm, opposition to the religious use of images. Although religious pictures and statues

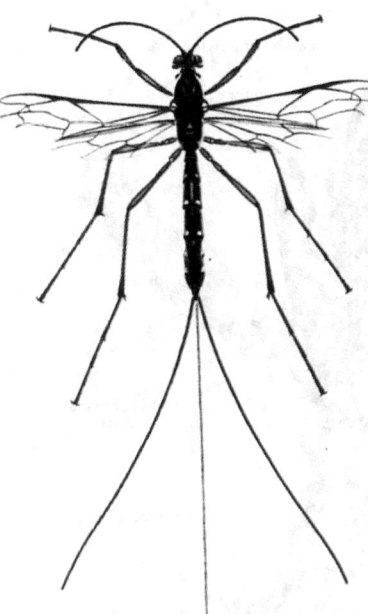

The ichneumon wasp or fly (*Rhyssa persuasoria*) from the British Isles. It parasitizes the wood wasp (Urocerus) whose larvae live in pine trees.

have long been an important part of Christian worship, iconoclasts claim they lead to idolatry. Historically, the use of images in religious worship has been in dispute. In A.D. 843 the Eastern Church reached a settlement that permitted pictures but not complete images or statues.

Id *See:* Psychoanalysis.

Idaho (Gem State; pop. 1,210,000), state in the Rocky Mountain region of the United States; bordered by Montana, Wyoming, Utah, Nevada, Oregon, Washington, and British Columbia.

Idaho is dominated by the Rockies. About 50 of the state's peaks are over 10,000 ft (3,000 m) high. The irrigated Snake River Plain is Idaho's major agricultural region. The high mountains have cool summers and severe winters, while the summers are hot on the Snake River Plain. Principal cities are Boise, Pocatello, and Idaho Falls.

Unlike many of the other western states, Idaho has vast water resources, and its dams provide hydroelectric power and water for irrigation. Idaho's chief agricultural products are cattle and dairy goods, and it is the leading producer of potatoes in the United States. Lumber and wood products are major manufactures of the heavily forested state, as are processed foods. The Sunshine Mine is the largest silver-producing mine in the country. Agriculture remains an important sector of Idaho's economy, although other industries, including tourism, continue to grow.

The area was inhabited by Native Americans more than 10,000 years ago. The first European Americans to explore the Idaho region were Meriwether Lewis and William Clark in 1805. At that time local tribes included the Nez Percé, Shoshone, Coeur d'Alene, and others. David Thompson, a British fur trader, set up Idaho's first trading post in 1809, and Mormons founded Franklin, Idaho's first permanent settlement, in 1860. That same year, gold was discovered, attracting scores of settlers. In 1863, the Idaho Territory was established. The U.S. Army defeated the Nez Percé Indians in 1877.

Idealism, any one of a variety of systems of philosophical thought that would make the ultimate reality of the universe expressible or intelligible only in terms of ideas rather than in terms of matter or space.
See also: Berkeley, George; Hegel, Georg Wilhelm Friedrich; Kant, Immanuel.

Ideology, set of beliefs based on related political, social, and economic assumptions. People who hold to a particular ideology often rely on its system of thought in forming decisions about the way they live or work. Ideologies may be religious, such as Catholicism, or artistic, such as Impressionism. Communism, socialism, democracy, fascism, and totalitarianism are different kinds of political ideologies. For example, until 1989 the government of West Germany adhered to a form of democracy, whereas the government of East Germany adhered to a form of communism: both democracy and communism are political ideologies.

I

Ides, 15th day of Mar. in the ancient Roman calendar and the day in 44 B.C. on which Julius Caesar was assassinated in the Roman senate. In the Roman calendar, the 15th of Mar., May, July, and Oct. and the 13th of the other months were called the ides.

Idolatry, in religion, worship of an image or statue representing a god or spirit. Overt forms of idolatry consist of explicit acts of reverence addressed to a person or object, such as dancing to the sun. Idols are generally found in animal or human form, and may be cared for as if they were alive. Christians, Jews, and Muslims consider the worship of images a sin, and the use of life-like images has been prohibited in Islamic and Jewish art since ancient times.
See also: Icon.

Idyl (Greek, 'little picture'), short poem that deals with rural scenery, beauty, and tranquility. Idyl is often used as a synonym for pastoral. The 10 famous idyls by the Greek Theocritus became the models for idyls written in later centuries. Selections from the Bible, such as the Song of Songs, are considered idyls. Many British poets of the 16th and 17th centuries wrote pastoral poems; John Milton's *Lycidas* is an example of one of the finest idyls from this time period.

Ièmochi (r. 1858-1866), Japanese shogun during whose reign the discussion whether or not to end the Japanese isolation reached a climax. In addition to this, the debate on the restoration of imperial rule became heated. In 1866, trade agreements were made with the US, England, France, and The Netherlands.

Ièsada (r. 1853-1858), Japanese shogun. During his reign, the debate on Japan's isolationist policy intensified. The American admiral, Perry, forced Japan to sign the Treaty of Kanagawa, after which Japan also reached agreements with other western countries. The Netherlands assisted the Japanese in building a navy.

Ife, town in the Oyo province in southwestern Nigeria. Ife is the oldest town of the Yoruba tribe. Beginning about A.D. 1000, Ife was an important center of black African culture. The Yoruba people created sculptures of terra cotta and bronze. Never having achieved great political or military power, Ife declined in the early 1800s. The current city of Ife is a major collecting point for cacao and cotton, palm oil and kernels, yams, cassava, maize, pumpkins, and kola nuts. Most of its inhabitants are town-dwelling farmers.
See also: Nigeria.

Igbo, or Ibo, large ethnic group in Nigeria. Although the origin of the Igbo people is not precisely known, recent archeological evidence suggests that the Igbo's artistic culture was supported by both agriculture and flourishing trade. Located near the Nigerian coast, the early Igbo civilization participated in the slave trade, which lasted from the 1400s to the 1800s. During the 1800s and 1900s Nigeria fell under British rule, and in 1967 the Igbo homeland, along with the entire Eastern Region of Nigeria, proclaimed itself the independent republic of Biafra.

Today, many Igbo occupy villages of dispersed homesteads in rain-forest country and are subsistence farmers.

Igloo, shelter or hunting ground dwelling for the Canadian Eskimos. Traditionally made of snow, sod, or stone, the best-known igloo was made of hard-packed snow cut into blocks from 2 to 3 ft (61 to 91 cm) long and 1 to 2 ft (30 to 61 cm) wide. After a first row of these blocks were laid down in a circle, the top surfaces of the blocks were shaved off in a sloping angle to form the first rung of a spiral. Additional blocks were added to draw it inward in a dome shape. One hole was left in the top for ventilation, and the igloo was kept warm mainly by a sealskin flap fit over the main entrance and seal oil lamps. Prefabricated houses have replaced igloos.
See also: Eskimo.

Ignatius Loyola, Saint *See:* Loyola, Saint Ignatius.

Ignatius of Antioch, Saint (d. C.A.D. 100), Christian bishop of Antioch, condemned to death in Trajan's reign. Ignatius wrote 7 letters (now precious early church documents) in which 'Catholic Church' was first used to denote Christians everywhere, and in which he tried to prove that Docetism, a doctrine that held that Jesus' bodily sufferings were only 'appearance,' was heresy.
See also: Christianity.

Igneous rock, one of the 3 main classes of rocks, that whose origin is the solidification of molten material, or detrital volcanic material. It crystallizes from lava at the earth's surface (extrusion) or from magma beneath (intrusion). There are 2 main classes: *Volcanic* rocks are extruded, typical examples being lava and pyroclastic rocks. *Plutonic* rocks are intruded into the rocks of the earth's crust at depth, a typical example being granite; those forming near to the surface are sometimes called hypabyssal rocks. Types of intrusions include batholiths, dikes, sills, and laccoliths. As plutonic rocks cool more slowly than volcanic, they have a coarser texture, more time being allowed for crystal formation.
See also: Basalt; Granite.

Ignition, system used to start an engine. In an internal combustion engine the ignition system sets fire to a mixture of fuel and air to generate power. Most automobiles use spark ignition systems, in which spark plugs create electric sparks to set fire to fuel. When a spark ignition system is turned on, an electric current flows from a battery to the ignition coil, where it is increased in voltage and then sent to a distributor. In the distributor, a rotor directs the current to the automobile's set of spark plugs. At this point, the spark plugs produce the electric sparks that ignite the fuel and air mixture to start the engine.
See also: Engine.

Iguana, family of lizards, the largest and most elaborately marked lizards of the New World. It includes insectivorous, carnivorous, and herbivorous species. Many species

The distributor distributes the high-voltage pulse of the ignition coil to the spark plugs. The rotating camshaft turns the distributor shaft and opens the contact-breaker points once every revolution. This induces a high-voltage pulse in the coil that is fed to the high-voltage terminal of the distributor and then to the rotor arm. Timing is such that the pulse occurs every time the rotor arm is in contact with a spark-plug terminal, producing a spark at each plug.

high-voltage terminal

spark-plug terminal

rotor arm

spark plug

contact breaker points

distributor shaft

cam shaft

are territorial. Iguanas characteristically show ornamental scales and a dorsal fringe, and bear tubercles on the head and body. Some species have an erectile throat fan. There are 2 major groups: ground iguanas and green iguanas; there is also 1 species of marine iguana. All species are hunted for food, although this is greatly depleting their numbers.

Ikebana ('living flowers'), Japanese form of flower arrangement. In Japan ikebana has been an art since the sixth century. All educated girls, and many boys, learn it. Nearly every home has a *tokonoma*, a nook with a flower arrangement. The arrangement is designed to simulate flowers growing in their natural surroundings. The container is usually low and unobtrusive in color; rocks, water, or soil give foothold for the cut flowers. Sometimes just bare twigs are used, simulating winter-barren trees. The basic Japanese design is triangular, representing Heaven, Man, and Earth. Various flowers and arrangements have symbolic meanings. Ikebana became a chief influence on western formal flower arrangement in the twentieth century.

Ikhnaton *See:* Akhenaton.

Ileitis, inflammation of the ileum, a section of the small intestine. Crohn's disease, also known as regional ileitis or regional enteritis, is the most frequently occurring form of ileitis and is characterized by sporadic attacks, which include abdominal cramps, fever, and diarrhea. These attacks are caused by a periodic swelling of the ileum, which prevents the passage of food and may eventually cause starvation. It is not known what causes ileitis, and there is no cure, although it can be treated with special diet, intravenous feeding, and surgery, which is successful 50% of the time.
See also: Intestine.

Iliad, ancient Greek epic poem of 24 books in hexameter verse, attributed to Homer; internal references suggest it was composed in the mid-8th century B.C. It describes a quarrel during the siege of Troy between the Greek warrior-hero Achilles and King Agamemnon, which results in Achilles' brutal slaying of Hector, the Trojan warrior-prince. A companion to the *Odyssey*, the *Iliad* is one of the world's greatest tragic works of literature.
See also: Homer.

Iliescu, Ion (1930-), Rumanian politician. He was elected a member of the Central Committee of the Rumanian Communist Party in 1968. After the bloody revolution of December 1989 and the disappearance of Ceausescu, Iliescu quickly became leader of the Democratic Front for National Rescue (FDSN), later renamed the Party of Social Democracy in Rumania. He won the presidential elections in 1990. After that he attempted to strengthen the bond with the West. Rumania was the first eastern European country to sign the Partnership for Peace with NATO in 1994. Iliescu lost the presidential elections in 1996 to the Christian Democrat Emil Constantinescu.

Illegal alien, person living in a country where he or she is not a citizen and without the government's consent. Illegal aliens are called undocumented workers because they have no immigration papers and therefore cannot legally be employed.

Illicium, sole genus of plant belonging to the family Illiciales, of the illiciales order. Comprised of 42 species, illicium is a group of trees and shrubs with evergreen leaves and bisexual flowers. The inner petals of the illicium flowers grade into stamens, or male, structures, while the female portion of the flower is usually located at its base and consists of 7 to 15 carpels (ovule-bearing structures). The name *illicium* means *allurement* in Latin, and probably alludes to the pleasant aroma of the illicium flower.

Illinois (Land of Lincoln, the Prairie State; pop. 11,900,000), state in the north central United States; bordered by Lake Michigan, Indiana, Kentucky, Missouri, Iowa, and Wisconsin.
Much of the north and central portions of the state are covered by dark prairie soils and loams, which are especially rich and productive. Illinois has a continental climate, with cold winters and hot summers. Chicago is the state's and region's leading city and is the third largest city in the nation. Other major cities include Springfield, Peoria, and Rockford.
A leading agricultural state, Illinois produces corn, hogs, cattle, and soybeans. Industry includes the manufacture of machinery, electrical and electronic equipment, processed foods, metal products, and chemicals. Illinois is a leading coal producer and also has significant oil resources.
A prehistoric Native American people, the mound builders, were the first known inhabitants of what is now Illinois. By the 17th century, the principal inhabitants of the region were the Illinois, a confederation of Algonquian-speaking tribes. The first Europeans known to have visited the region were Louis Jolliet and Jacques Marquette, in 1673. In 1763, at the end of the French and Indian War, Illinois was ceded to the British. After the American Revolution the region became part of the Northwest Territory of the United States. It was made a separate territory in 1809. With the defeat of the Sauk and Fox in the Black Hawk War of 1832, the last barrier to European American settlement of the state was removed. After the Civil War, industry made great progress as immigrants poured in on the newly completed railroads. Today Illinois continues to attract hundreds of new factories, and space age industries and atomic research facilities are thriving.

Illiteracy, inability to read and write at least simple messages. Illiteracy is therefore the absence of such ability. As civilization grows more complex, mathematical literacy also becomes an important factor, mathematics also being a kind of language.

Illumination, the decoration of a handwritten text with ornamental design, letters, and paintings, often using silver and gold leaf. Illumination flourished between the 5th and 16th centuries A.D. The art was highly developed in the Middle East, the Orient, and in Christian Europe, where monks and others skilled in calligraphy and painting often devoted their lifetimes to embellishing manuscripts of all kinds, particularly religious. Among the most celebrated manuscripts are the Irish *Book of Kells*, the Carolingian *Utrecht Psalter*, and the *Très riches heures* commissioned by Jean, duc de Berry, from the Limbourg brothers.

Illusion *See:* Optical illusion.

Illyria, ancient country in the northwestern part of the Balkan peninsula. It was settled in the 10th century B.C. by Illyrians, an Indo-European-speaking people who extended their influence from the Danube River to the Adriatic Sea in modern-day Yugoslavia and Albania. It became the Roman province of Illyricum (168 B.C.).

Ilmenite, heavy black metallic oxide mineral that is a source of titanium. Formed at high temperatures and containing 36.8% iron and 31.6% titanium, ilmenite is not widely used as iron ore because of difficulties in *smelting*, or separating the metallic constituents. The chemical formula for ilmenite is $FeTiO_3$.

ILO *See:* International Labor Organization.

Iloilo (pop. 310,000), major port of the Philippines located on the island of Panay, one of the Visayan Islands. It is also the main cultural location for the region.
See also: Philippines.

Imagists, group of poets writing in the early 20th century in the United States and England who rebelled against the artificiality and sentimentality of much 19th-century poetry. Free, idiomatic verse, unusual rhythms, and sharp, clear imagery were characteristics of their work, which was influenced by French symbolism. The movement embraced Ezra Pound, Hilda Doolittle (H.D.), Amy Lowell, D.H. Lawrence, and James Joyce.

Imago, psychoanalytic term for the unconscious, idealized representation of oneself or of an important figure from childhood, often a parent.
See also: Psychoanalysis.

Imam (Arabic, 'leader'), term used in Islam to denote a religious leader. In the Sunnite branch of Islam any devout Muslim may perform the services of imam in leading public worship. In the Shi'te branch the imam is a caliph, or ruler, and must be appointed by God in the line of descent from Muhammad. The term is also applied by some Muslims to any religious teacher or scholar.
See also: Islam.

Imamura, Shohei (1926-), Japanese director of critical films, which often depict the downside of Japanese society. His films include: *My Second Brother* (1959), *Pigs and Battleships* (1961), *The Insect Woman* (1963), *Vengeance is Mine* (1979),

I

Eiyanaika (1981), *The Ballad of Narayama* (1983; Golden Palm), *Blessing* (1987), *Unagi* (The Eel, 1997; Golden Palm), and *Warm Water Under a Red Bridge* (2001).

IMF *See:* International Monetary Fund.

Imhotep (fl.c.2980-2950 B.C.), Egyptian architect of the Step Pyramid at Saqqara. Chief minister, priest, and scribe to Pharaoh Zoser, Imhotep's fame spread and after his death he became a god of medicine. He is considered the first doctor known to history by name.

Immaculate Conception, Roman Catholic dogma, officially defined in 1854, that the Virgin Mary was conceived free from original sin, owing to a special act of redemptive grace. The feast of the Immaculate Conception is celebrated Dec. 8.
See also: Roman Catholic Church.

Immigration, movement of people into a country to establish a new permanent residence. People become immigrants primarily for economic, political, or religious reasons. The United States is a nation of immigrants. It has received more immigrants from more places than any other country-about 38 million from the 1820s to the 1930s-and is thus known as a 'melting pot' of the world's nations. South America received large numbers of immigrants before the 1930s. Since World War II an entirely new phase of immigration has taken place within Europe itself. West Indians, Asian Indians, and Pakistanis have settled in the United Kingdom, claiming their rights as members of the Commonwealth. Since 1962, the British government has introduced new laws reducing this trend. Western and northern Europe have admitted large numbers of immigrants from the less-developed parts of southern Europe. The European Community requires all its member countries to allow free movement of labor across their borders.

Immortelle (*Xeranthemum annuun*), any of several species of flower belonging to the composite family and related to the asters. The largest of what is known as everlasting flowers, the immortelle has flower heads composed of many small flowers, called florets. The yellow immortelle is characterized as an everlasting flower because it retains its natural form and color even after it has been dried.

Immunity, system of defense in animals protecting against foreign materials, specifically, infectious microorganisms, parasites, and their products. For many diseases, *humoral immunity*, exposure to the causative organism in disease itself or by vaccination, provides acquired resistance to that organism, making further infection with it unlikely or less severe. The antigen (foreign microorganism or other substance) provokes the formation of an antibody specific to that antigen. The antibody tends to neutralize viruses or to bind to antigens, encouraging destruction of bacteria by white blood cells. A number of diseases are due to the systemic effects of immune complexes (antibodies linked to antigens) that arise in the appropriate response to an infection or in serum sickness, and these especially affect the kidneys, skin, and joints. In *autoimmunity* antibodies are produced to antigens of the body's own tissues, for reasons that are not always clear; secondary tissue destruction may occur. The second major type of immunity, *cell-mediated immunity*, only occurs with certain types of infection (tuberculosis, histoplasmosis, and fungal diseases) and in certain probable autoimmune diseases. It is also important in the immunity of transplants. Lymphocytes, primed by infection or by the autoimmune or graft reaction, produce substances that affect both lymphocytes and the source of infection and result in a type of inflammation with much tissue damage. Investigation of the role of immunity and its disorders in the causation and manifestations of many diseases has led to the development of immunosuppressive drugs and other agents that are able to interfere with abnormal or destructive immune responses. Immune deficiency diseases have provided models for the separate parts of the immune system, and have led to methods of replacement of absent components of immunity. The epidemic of acquired immune deficiency syndrome (AIDS) has added some urgency to research. Passive immunity, the transfer of antibody-rich substances from an immune subject to a non-immune subject who is susceptible to disease, is important in infancy, where maternal antibodies protect the child until its own immune responses have matured. In certain diseases, such as tetanus and rabies, immune serum gives valuable immediate passive protection in non-immune subjects.

Immunization, process of becoming, or rendering a body, resistant to a particular disease. Immunization occurs naturally when disease antibodies develop through exposure or are passed from mother to fetus or nursing child, but the term generally refers to the medical procedure of administering vaccines or serums. *Vaccines* activate the production of antibodies by introduction into the bloodstream of germs, toxins, etc. (*active immunization*). *Serums* contain antibodies produced by another body (*passive immunization*) and provide only temporary immunity. The first method of immunization was Edward Jenner's smallpox vaccine (1796). Immunization should be performed in children for at least 5 dangerous diseases: whooping cough (pertussis), diphtheria, tetanus, poliomyelitis, and measles. Due to immunization, many serious diseases are now rare.
See also: Immunity.

Impala (*Aepyceros melampus*), one of the most abundant African antelopes. Impala are about 40 in (102 cm) high and red-brown in color. Males have long, black, lyre-shaped horns. Animals of the woodland edge, impala live in big herds in the dry season, breaking up into single-male harems in the wetter months for breeding. Impala herds of 10 associate with baboons for protection against predators.

Impeachment, formal accusation of a crime or other serious misconduct brought against a public official by a legislature. The term sometimes includes the trial by the legislature that follows. Impeachment began in England as a way of putting officials on trial who were derelict in their duties. Under U.S. constitutional procedure the House of Representatives has the power to impeach; the Senate tries the impeached officials. Grounds for impeachment are: 'Treason, Bribery or other High Crimes and Misdemeanors,' generally interpreted as being limited to demonstrably criminal acts in the United States. Conviction requires a two-thirds vote of all senators present and voting, providing there is a quorum, and entails automatic removal from office. The chief justice of the United States presides. In U.S. history Congress has impeached 11 officials and convicted 4. President Andrew Johnson was impeached but later acquitted in the Senate by one vote. In 1974, after the House Judiciary Committee recommended his impeachment, Richard M. Nixon resigned as president of the United States.

Imperialism, policy of one country or people, usually 'developed,' to extend its control or influence over other territories or peoples, usually 'underdeveloped.' There are many different kinds of imperialism-political, financial, economic, military, and cultural. The justification for imperialism has been that backward countries are advanced technologically, economically, and culturally by the influence of more developed nations. However, imperialist policies have also restricted individual and national freedoms and have often exploited undeveloped natural resources and native populations.

Impetigo, superficial skin infection, usually of the face, caused by streptococcus or staphylococcus. It starts with small vesicles that burst and leave a characteristic yellow

During the second half of the 19th century, mass emigration from Europe to the United States took place. The conditions under which many had to make the ocean crossing, indicate the financial circumstances of these emigrants. Here, you can see emigrants on their way to America, on board steamship Westernland (1890).

crust. It is easily spread by fingers from a single vesicle to affect several large areas and may be transmitted to other people. It is common in children and requires antibiotic cream or sometimes systemic penicillin.

Import *See:* Exports and imports.

Impressionism, dominant artistic movement in France from the mid-1860s to 1890, characterized by the use of brushstrokes of contrasting colors to convey the impression of objects by the light they reflect. The impressionist painters, who include Edouard Manet, Claude Monet, Camille Pissarro, and others, painted landscapes and scenes of leisure in contemporary Paris. They usually worked outdoors, recording the scenes before them spontaneously and directly. The term 'impressionist' was first used as a criticism of Monet's *Impression: Soleil levant* (1874). The artists organized 8 independent exhibitions for their pictures. The U.S. painters Mary Cassatt and Childe Hassam were influenced by the impressionists. The term 'impressionism' is also applied to other art forms, notably literature that uses symbolic imagery and music that expresses mood and feeling.

Inayat Khan, Hazrat (1881-1927), Indian musician, founder of the sufic movement. He was a member of an islamic mystic order and introduced sufism into the United States. In 1920 he moved to France. Wrote *The Sufi Message.*

Inca, Native American empire in the western region of South America which, at the time of the Spanish conquest, occupied what is now Peru, parts of Ecuador, Chile, Bolivia, and Argentina. It extended some 3,000 mi (4,800 km) from north to south, stretching back between 150 and 250 mi (240 and 400 km) from the narrow Pacific coastal plain into the high Andes. The name 'Inca' refers to the people of the empire and is also the title of the ruler. Communications

England, Germany, Russia, France and Japan (left to right) are busy dividing the Chinese cake, while a Chinese mandarin raises his hands in desperation. Caricature from *Le Petit Journal*, 1898.

Ballerina Posing for a Photograph (c. 1879), one of Edgar Dega's series of dancers, exemplifies the linearity and distinct form that distinguishes his work from that of other impressionists.

were maintained along brilliantly engineered and extensive roads, carried over the sheer Andean gorges by fiber cable suspension bridges. Trained relay runners carried messages 150 mi (240 km) a day and the army had quick access to trouble spots. Restive subject tribes were resettled near Cuzco, the capital. Detailed surveys of new conquests were recorded by *quipu*, a mnemonic device using knotted cords. Writing, like draft animals and wheeled transport, was unknown; so too was monetary currency. Taxation and tribute were levied in the form of labor services. In other respects the culture was highly advanced. At sites such as Machu Picchu, Inca architects raised some of the world's finest stone structures; precious metals from government-controlled mines were worked by skilled goldsmiths; bronze was also used; ceramic and textile design was outstanding. Agriculture was based on elaborate irrigation and hillside terracing. The Spanish domination of the Incas began with the arrival (1532) of Francisco Pizarro, who executed the Incan emperor and conquered their cities.

Incandescent lamp *See:* Electric light.

Inchon (pop. 2,400,000), Yellow River port city located in the northwestern part of South Korea. In ancient times Inchon relied mainly upon fishing, but after foreign nations forced Korea to open up to international trade in the 1880s, it developed into a major port. In 1950, during the Korean war, the U.S. made a surprise landing at Inchon, turning back the invading North Koreans. Located about 20 mi (32 km) from the capital city of Seoul, Inchon has been a major industrial center since the late 1960s. It produces chemicals, iron, steel, and textiles, in addition to thriving in the areas of fishing and shipping.
See also: Korean War.

Inchworm *See:* Measuring worm.

Vincent van Gogh's *Small House of Vincent at Arles* (1888) exemplifies the vigorous rhythm, brilliant color, and expressive power characteristic of his late work.

Incisor *See:* Teeth.

Income, payment, whether money (pecuniary, cash, or monetary income) or as goods and services (real income), received in return for goods and services. For most people cash income takes the form of a wage or salary, usually expressed as so much per week or month. Cash income is also derived from stock dividends and from rent paid for the use of property. Many people in developing countries depend largely on noncash incomes. Even in industrialized countries some people get at least a part of their income in the form of goods rather than cash, for example, farmers who use some of their own produce. Income is distinguished from assets. For example, say that a person spends $8,000 in the course of a year but earns only $6,000, drawing the remaining $2,000 from savings. That person's income is only $6,000. The remaining $2,000 has been spent by consuming assets. Equally, if a person borrows money or receives a gift of cash, such sums are not rated as part of income, since they do not stem from productive work or investment. People regularly spend more than their income, borrowing cash and buying on credit. Businesses, too, regularly look to borrowed funds to pay for their expansion. This presupposes that borrowed money can be repaid from future income.

Income tax, the major source of government revenue. As opposed to excise taxes levied on goods, it is a tax on the incomes of individuals, proportionate to their incomes, or on corporations. At first imposed only to meet extraordinary expenditures such as war financing, income tax became permanent in Britain in 1874. It is assessed on net income after allowances have been deducted for family dependents, contributions to charities, and certain other expenditures. Incomes below a certain level are entirely tax exempt; above this level the

I

rate rises progressively to about one-third of a person's earnings.
See also: Taxation.

Incubation, method of keeping microorganisms such as bacteria or viruses warm and in an appropriate medium to promote their growth (e.g., in identification of the organisms causing disease); also, period during which an organism is present in the body before causing disease. Infectious disease is contracted from a source of infective microorganisms. Once these have entered the body they divide and spread to different parts, and it may be some time before they cause symptoms due to local or systemic effects. This incubation period may be helpful in diagnosis and in determining length of quarantine periods.

Incubation
Incubation periods (in days)

Chicken pox	11-21
Common cold	1-2
Diphtheria	2-5
Dysentery (amebic)	2-28
(bacillary)	2-7
Encephalitis	4-21
German measles (rubella)	2-21
Glandular fever	5-15
Gonorrhea	1-8
Influenza	1-3
Malaria	7-14
Measles	10-15
Meningitis	2-10
Mumps	14-28
Paratyphoid fever	2-10
Poliomyelitis	3-21
Rabies	14-40
Scarlet fever	2-7
Smallpox	7-16
Syphilis	About 21
Tetanus	4-21
Tuberculosis	28-42
Typhoid fever	6-21
Typhus fever	About 12
Undulant fever	7-35
Whooping cough (pertussis)	7-21
Yellow fever	3-7

Indentured servant, person bound to labor for a stated period, usually 5 to 7 years. In the 17th and 18th centuries, people often agreed to indenture in return for passage to the American colonies. Others were enticed or kidnapped into indentured service. Convicts were sometimes sentenced and deported to indentured labor. With the use of slave labor, the practice of indenture disappeared.

Independence, Declaration of *See:* Declaration of Independence.

Independence, War for *See:* Revolutionary War in America.

Independence Day, or Fourth of July, the principal nonreligious holiday in the United States. It commemorates the signing of the Declaration of Independence (July 4, 1776).
See also: Declaration of Independence.

Index, reference list of the topics, subjects, or names in a printed work and where they may be found. There are 2 types of indexes: alphabetical, in which the entries are listed from A to Z, and analytical, in which subtopics are listed under major subject headings.

Index of Forbidden Books (*Index Librorum Prohibitorum*), official list of books banned by the Roman Catholic Church as being in doctrinal or moral error. A book could be removed from the index by expurgation of offending passages, and special permission could be given to read prohibited books. The index ceased publication in 1966.

India

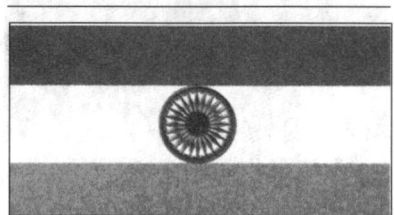

Capital:	New Delhi
Area:	1,269,219 sq mi
	(3,287,263 sq km)
Population:	1,045,845,000
Language:	Hindi
Government:	Federal republic
Independent:	1947
Head of gov.:	Prime minister
Per capita:	US$ 2,500
Monetary unit:	1 Indian rupee = 100 paisa

India, union of 29 states and 6 territories, the world's seventh-largest country, occupying most of the Indian subcontinent, the land mass of south central Asia that tapers southward from the Himalayan mountain system to Cape Comorin and Sri Lanka. India shares the subcontinent with Pakistan, Bangladesh, and the Himalayan states of Nepal, and Bhutan, with Sri Lanka off its coast. Only the People's Republic of China has a greater population than India.
Land and climate. The chief geographical regions of North India are the Thar Desert along the Pakistan border, the mountain valleys of Kashmir (disputed with Pakistan), the fertile plains of the Ganges and Brahmaputra rivers, and the Himalaya Mountains, which shield India from the cold winter winds of central Asia. The Deccan plateau, bordered by the western and eastern Ghats mountain ranges, occupies most of South India. The rich volcanic soil is used mainly for cotton growing, though there are also important mineral deposits. Most of the country has a tropical monsoon climate, temperatures reaching 120°F (48.8°C) in the hot season on the northern plains and, in the cool seasons, falling below freezing in the mountains. The monsoon rains are especially heavy on the western Ghats and in northeast India; some places average more than 426 in (1,082 cm) of rain a year.
People. The majority of the population lives in small villages, though the towns are growing fast. The chief cities are the seaports of Bombay, Calcutta, and Madras and the capital, New Delhi. The dominant religion is Hinduism. Islam, Christianity, Buddhism, Sikhism, and Jainism are also found. Education is free for ages 6-14.
Economy. Two-thirds of the labor force is engaged in agriculture. Rice, beans, peas, tea, sugarcane, jute, pepper, and timber are the main agricultural products. To increase the output, improvements are being sought in irrigation, land reclamation projects, and the introduction of improved strains of crops and fertilizers. About 45% of the industrial labor force works in the jute, cotton, and other textile mills. Mineral resources include oil, iron ore, coal, natural gas, copper, bauxite, and mica.
History. The Indus Valley civilization, in modern Pakistan, was the first great culture on the subcontinent. It succumbed in 1500 B.C. to Aryan peoples invading through the northwestern mountain passes; they brought the Sanskrit language and Hinduism to India. The Maurya Empire and Gupta dynasties represented high points of Buddhist and Hindu rule, but India was never united, and from the 10th century Muslim invaders added to the conflicts. In the 14th century the Delhi Muslim sultanate and the Hindu kingdom of Vijayanagar in the south were dominant. In the 1520s the Muslim empire of the Moguls was founded. Europeans also began to exert influence in the Indian subcontinent. In 1510 the Portuguese took Goa, and soon the Dutch, British, and French were vying for Indian trade. In the 18th century English and French interests contested for control of the moribund empire. Victory went to the British East India Company. After the Sepoy Rebellion (1857-1858), the British government took over rule of much of the country, and the remaining independent princes, both Muslim and Hindu, recognized British primacy. In 1885 the Indian National Congress Party was set up; under Mohandas Gandhi and Jawaharlal Nehru it led the movement for independence. Muhammad Ali Jinnah led the Muslim League, urging partition into India and Pakistan on religious grounds. Many thousands died in fierce communal riots following partition in 1947, the year in which India became independent. The constitution (1949) provided for a bicameral, democratically elected parliament and a cabinet government, with a prime minister and a president. Domestic politics has been concerned with the problem of food supply, the drive toward industrialization, the mitigation of the caste system, and, since the late 1960s, tension between the central and provincial governments. The dispute with Pakistan over Kashmir flared into war in 1965. A frontier war in 1962 also emphasized the strained relations between India and China. Sikkim became an Indian state in 1975, the

The major part of Indian agriculture is still making use of age-old methods.

same year Indira Gandhi, Nehru's daughter and successor as prime minister, was convicted of election irregularities. She declared the state of emergency, jailed her opponents, and began to rule by decree. Her party was defeated in the general election in 1977. The new government dismantled the state of emergency, but the coalition that had defeated Mrs. Gandhi began to disintegrate, and in 1980 she again became prime minister. In 1984, after attacks on Sikh separatists that left more than 1,000 Sikhs dead, she was assassinated by Sikhs in her bodyguard. Her son, Rajiv Gandhi, became her successor and prime minister (1984-1989). In 1991, he was murdered while campaigning for his re-election. After several governments ruled for very short periods in the mid-1990's, the Bharatiya Janata Party, a Hindu party, formed a coalition government in 1998. Several nuclear tests conducted by India and Pakistan in 1998 increased tensions between India and Pakistan. In 1999 the dispute between India and Pakistan over Kashmir flared up again. Relations with Pakistan deteriorated after a suicide squad attacked the Parliament in December 2001. Both countries started to test fire their long range missiles which led to a military buildup along the disputed Kahmir territory in 2002. Dr. Abdul Kalam was elected President in July 2002.

Indiana (Hoosier State; pop. 5,900,000), state of the north-central United States; bordered by Michigan and Lake Michigan, Ohio, Kentucky, and Illinois.
The Wabash River and its many tributaries drain about two-thirds of the state. Principal cities are Indianapolis, Fort Wayne, and Gary.
Steel and other metal production are Indiana's principal industries. Other industries produce transportation and electrical equipment and chemicals. About three-quarters of Indiana is covered by farmland. The state is a leading producer of corn, soy beans, and hogs. Bituminous coal is the state's most important mineral, and about two-thirds of the nation's limestone comes from Indiana.
Indiana's earliest known inhabitants were the prehistoric Mound Builders. The area was occupied mainly by the Miami tribe when French fur traders explored it in the 17th century. After the French and Indian Wars, the area passed to the British (1763) and, after the American Revolution, to the United States. The region became part of the Northwest Territory in 1787, and in 1800 the Indiana Territory was created. Native American resistance to European American settlement ended after the battles of Fallen Timbers (1794) and Tippecanoe (1811).

Indian, American *See:* Native Americans.

Indiana, Robert (real name: Robert Clark; 1928-   ), American visual artist, one of the most prominent exponents of American pop art. Letters and numbers are predominant themes in his work. The hard color contrasts and smooth treatment of the surfaces are typical of his work.

Indian Affairs, Bureau of, U.S. federal agency, part of the Department of the Interior, set up in 1824 to safeguard the welfare of Native Americans. It acts as trustee for tribal lands and funds, supervises the reservations, and provides welfare and educational facilities.

Indianapolis (pop. 747,000), capital and largest city of Indiana. The city is one of the largest in the world not situated on a navigable waterway. This deficiency made its growth slow from around 1819, when the first settlers arrived, until 1847, when the first railroad reached the town. Additional railroads and roads made it a leading transport terminus. The capital is the marketing and distribution center for much of Indiana's agriculture and industry. Its major industries include transportation equipment, chemicals, and electrical machinery. Others are livestock sales, printing and publishing, and telephones and hardware. Just outside the city is the famous Indianapolis Speedway, site of the yearly Memorial Day 500-mi (800-km) race.
See also: Indiana.

Indianapolis 500 *See:* Automobile racing.

Indian art and architecture, classical tradition dates from the fall of the Indus Valley civilization (1500 B.C.) and the establishment of the Indo-Aryan culture based on Hinduism. The naturalistic Aryan pantheon assimilated local deities and concepts to produce a complex system, celebrated in the sacred Hindu texts, the Vedas. Statues, paintings, and ornate temples symbolize and embody the gods and their attributes or powers. With the spread of Buddhism under Asoka (d.232 B.C.), the stupa, a round brick- or stone-faced earth mound, containing a relic or tomb and surrounded by a square stone railing, was the favored religious architectural form. Painting and sculpture, notably in the Ajanta caves and the art of Gandhara, portray episodes in the physical and spiritual life of the Buddha. The golden age of Indian culture came during the Gupta dynasty (A.D. 320-500). Resurgent Hinduism soon adapted the Buddhist styles in the classic porch, pillared hall, and cella of the Hindu temple, often surmounted by massive conical spires. In the 13th century southern India perfected the Dravidian pyramidal

Kaalbara fighting; a rock relief at Ellora (cave 29), India, from the end of the 6th, beginning of the 7th century.

I

temple and produced superb bronze sculptures, such as the famous dancing Siva. Indian Muslim art reached its peak under the Moguls.

Indian bean *See:* Catalpa.

Indian-Chinese War (1962-1963), border war between China and India. China did not acknowledge the borders laid down by the British in the colonial past. Border conflicts began in 1959 and after negotiations failed, China launched an attack on India in 1962. The Indian forces were devastated and Chinese troops marched deep into Indian territory. The Chinese withdrew after the ceasefire in 1963. Relations between India and China remained strained for a long time; diplomatic relations only returned to normal in 1976.

Indian Desert *See:* Thar Desert.

Indian fig *See:* Prickly pear.

Indian hemp *See:* Dogbane.

Indian mallow (*Abutilon theophrastii*), weed of the mallow family, a group of dicotyledonous flowering plants. The Indian mallow grows from under 1 ft (30 cm) to over 6 ft (1.8 m) tall, and has orange-yellow flowers. The Indian mallow was given its common name because it originally grew in India, but has also been called *velvet leaf* and *stump weed*, the latter because it was once used to stamp designs onto butter.

Indian Mutiny *See:* Sepoy Rebellion.

Indian Ocean, world's third largest ocean (28,350,000 sq mi/73,426,500 sq km), bounded by Antarctica to the south, Africa to the west, and Australia and Indonesia to the east. The Indian subcontinent divides the northern part of the ocean into 2 great arms, the Arabian Sea to the west and the Bay of Bengal to the east. Largest of its many islands are Madagascar and Sri Lanka.

Indian paintbrush, any of about 200 species (genus *Castilleja*) of wildflower in the figwort or snapdragon family of flowering plants. Also called *painted cup*, the Indian paintbrush gives forth tiny flowers that are mostly green, while its leaves are brightly colored-commonly red, pink, yellow, or lavender. A species (*C. linariaefolia*) of Indian paintbrush is the state flower of Wyoming.

Indian-Pakistan Wars, 1. (1948-1949), the First Indian-Pakistan war broke out due to a conflict about Kashmir. The Hindu prince of this mainly Islamic region wished to remain independent. When the Muslims, supported by Pakistan, turned to violence, the prince brought Kashmir under Indian rule. This started the war between Pakistan and India, which was ended through mediation by the United Nations. Kasmir was partitioned but remained a source of conflict between India and Pakistan.
2. (1965-1966), the Second Indian-Pakistan

war was again caused by disagreements about Kashmir. A ceasefire was signed after several weeks of fierce fighting in the Punjab and mediation by the Soviet Union. 3. (1971), the Third Indian-Pakistan war was caused by events in Bangladesh, at that time still a region of Pakistan. India gave military support to liberation organizations in Bangladesh who wanted to extricate the country from Pakistan. This started the war between India and Pakistan. India was victorious after two weeks; Bangladesh became independent in 1972.

Indian pipe (*Monotropa uniflora*), low, flowering plant of the family Ericaceae. Often mistaken for fungus, which actually serves as food for it, the indian pipe grows in moist woods in eastern Asia and North America. Its scaly stem grows 6 to 10 in (15 to 25 cm) tall. The Indian pipe got its name because it resembles a group of clay pipes.

Indian reservation, land set aside by the U.S. government for use by Native Americans. The first Indian reservation was established for a Delaware Indian tribe in the New Jersey colony in 1758. During the early and middle 19th century, as white settlers claimed more Indian land in the eastern U.S., the government established Indian reservations west of the Mississippi River. In 1823 the Bureau of Indian Affairs, an agency of the Department of the Interior, was formed to oversee affairs on these reservations. Since 1970, when President Nixon called for a new era of Indian self-determination, the tribes have had increased authority over all aspects of their welfare. There are now approximately 285 federal and state Indian reservations, covering 50 million acres in about 30 states.
See also: Native Americans.

Indian root *See:* Spikenard.

Indians *See:* Native Americans.

Indian tobacco *See:* Lobelia.

Indian turnip *See:* Jack-in-the-pulpit.

Indian wars, struggle in North America between the Native Americans and European colonizers from the earliest colonial times to the late 19th century. Despite peaceful trade under Powhatan, hostilities between Native Americans and the English settlers of Jamestown, Va., began in 1622, and by 1644 the native tribes had been crushed. In New England, war with the Pequot tribe (1636) resulted in their massacre. With the end of King Philip's War in 1678, Native American resistance in New England was broken. During the Revolutionary War trade regulations were introduced to protect Native Americans from exploitation. Trade and land companies continued to cheat them, however, provoking uprisings. In 1811 an alliance of southern and western tribes under the Shawnee chieftain Tecumseh was defeated at the Tippecanoe River; Tecumseh's death in 1813 ended tribal resistance in this area. The Seminole

in Florida, however, continued hostilities until 1816. In 1830 the Indian Removal Act, passed by President Andrew Jackson, authorized the transfer of southeastern tribes to land west of the Mississippi. Native American resistance was met by illegal force; Jackson even ignored a Supreme Court order upholding the land rights of the Cherokees. In 1855 the defeated Nez Percé tribes were given land in the northwestern states, but when gold was found in the area they were again forced to move. Chief Joseph led an unsuccessful revolt against this in 1877. The second half of the 19th century saw the final suppression of the Native Americans. The Navaho, holding the land between the Rio Grande and California, were defeated by Kit Carson in 1863 and transferred to northwestern Arizona. After the Civil War attempts were made to restrict the Apaches, though Cochise and others resisted; their last war chief, Geronimo, surrendered in 1886. In 1871 the government ceased to recognize tribes as independent nations. The Great Plains, home of the Sioux, Apache, and Cheyenne, were subdued in 1870-1890 by a combination of military force and the depletion of buffalo herds. The Native American victory at the battle of Little Bighorn only hastened their defeat. Crazy Horse surrendered in 1877, and there was a final massacre at Wounded Knee, S. Dak., in 1890.

Indies *See:* East Indies; West Indies.

Indigo bunting (*Passerina cyanea*), North American songbird of the family Emberizidae, which includes the bunting, finches, grosbeaks, and sparrows. The male bunting of this species has a deep indigo blue head and blackish wings and tail, while the female is brown with darker wings and lighter underparts. Helping farmers by feeding on insects and weed seeds, the indigo bunting ranges from Ontario and New Brunswick to as far south as the Gulf states.

Indium, chemical element, symbol In; for physical constants see Periodic Table. Indium was discovered spectroscopically by Ferdinand Reich and H.T. Richter (1863). The element is most frequently associated with zinc minerals, but is also found in iron, lead, and copper ores. It is prepared as a byproduct in the smelting of zinc. Indium is a silvery-white, soft, low-melting metal. Indium and its compounds are used in making dental alloys, bearing alloys, transistors, solar batteries, and other semiconductor devices.

Indochina, political term for peninsular Southeast Asia between China and India. It was formerly French Indochina, and is now divided into Vietnam, Laos, and Kampuchea (Cambodia). The area contains two densely peopled, rice-rich deltas (Red River in the North, Mekong River in the south), separated by the Annamite mountain chain. Thais, Laos, and Annamese (Vietnamese) settled Indochina from the north. From the second century A.D., many states and cultures affected by India and

China rose and fell there, including Funan, the Khmer Empire, Champa, and Annam. European penetration began in the 16th century. France concluded a treaty with Annam in 1787, annexed Cochin China in 1862, and by 1900 had welded separate states into the single political unit of French Indochina. World War II and militant nationalism destroyed France's authority and in 1949 Cambodia and Laos gained independence. The communist Vietminh drove the French out of Vietnam; the United States continued France's anticommunist role in the long Vietnam War, but by 1976 Indochina was effectively under communist control.

Indo-European languages, large family of language spoken throughout most of Europe and much of Asia, and descended from a hypothetical common ancestor, Proto-Indo-European, extant more than 5,000 years ago. There are 2 main branches: the Eastern, with 6 main groups, and Western, with 4. The Eastern branch includes the extinct Anatolian and Tocharian groups, as well as Albanian, Armenian, Balto-Slavic, and Indo-Iranian (with its important sub-group, the Indo-Aryan languages). The Western branch includes Celtic, Greek, Romance or Italic (Latin and the languages derived from it), and Teutonic or Germanic (one of which is English). Until the beginning of the 20th century it was thought that Sanskrit inscriptions represented the oldest written form of any of the family; however, both ancient Hittite and Linear B, which have since been deciphered, are older.

Indonesia

Capital:	Jakarta
Area:	741,101 sq mi
	(1,912,988 sq km)
Population:	231,328,000
Language:	Bahasa Indonesia
Government:	Presidential republic
Independent:	1949 (officially)
Head of gov.:	President
Per capita:	US$ 3,000
Monetary unit:	1 Indonesian rupiah
	= 100 sen

Indonesia, republic of southeast Asia occu-

pying most of the Malay archipelago, the world's largest archipelago, consisting of more than 13,000 islands and islets strung out along the equator from Sumatra facing the Indian Ocean in the west to New Guinea in the east. These were the Indies sought by Christopher Columbus and other explorers. The Moluccas, part of Indonesia, were the Spice Islands of the merchant venturers.

Land and climate. Extending for more than 3,000 mi (4,828 km) from west to east, Indonesia's islands range in size from small deserted reefs to large islands like Sumatra (182,860 sq mi/473,607 sq km), the world's sixth-largest island. About half of New Guinea, the world's second-largest island, and about three-quarters of Borneo, third-largest island, belong to Indonesia. More than 6,000 of Indonesia's islands are inhabited. Many of the islands have luxuriant tropical rain forests containing valuable hardwoods. Although some have areas of low-lying plain or swamp, most are mountainous. Java, Sumatra, and the Little Sunda group have a great line of volcanic peaks. The eruption in 1883 of Krakatoa, in the strait between Java and Sumatra, resulted in the loss of 30,000 lives. There are few large rivers. Rivers flowing into the comparatively shallow South China, Java, and Arafura seas build up deltas, often at a remarkably rapid rate. Coastal scenery ranges from coral reefs, sandy beaches, and mangrove forests to cliffs. Vegetation and wildlife are varied. Some islands, like Java and Borneo, have distinctly Asiatic types, while New Guinea has Australian types, both types being blended in the islands in between. The rain forests contain teak, ebony, and other hardwoods, giant creepers, and shade-loving plants. Along the coasts there are casuarina trees, coconut, and other palms and, where it is muddy, extensive mangrove forests. Wildlife includes elephants, tigers, rhinoceros, orangutans, and, in the eastern islands, pouched animals like the opossum, wallaby, and cuscus. There are many beautiful and brightly colored birds. Snakes and crocodiles abound, but Indonesia's most famous reptile is the Komodo dragon, the giant lizard of the small island of Komodo east of Sumatra. The main islands fall into 3 groups: (1) the Greater Sunda Islands: Java, Sumatra, Indonesian Borneo (Kalimantan), and Celebes (Sulawesi); (2) the Lesser Sunda Islands, including Bali, Flores, Lombok, Sumba, Sumbawa, and Indonesian Timor; (3) the Moluccas (Maluku), including Ambon, Aru Islands, Banda Islands, Buru, Ceram, Halmahera, and the Tanimbor Islands. Including West Irian (formerly Netherlands New Guinea), Indonesia has a total area of more than 735,765 sq mi (1,912,988 sq km). Its most important islands, in terms of population density and economic and cultural activity, are Java, Bali, and Sumatra. Indonesia has a hot, rainy, equatorial climate that is modified by monsoonal winds. From mid-June to Oct. the southeast monsoon brings dry air from Australia. From Nov. to Mar. a north or northeast monsoon blows from mainland Asia across the South China Sea, where it collects much moisture and brings heavy rains. Violent tropical thunderstorms occur almost daily.

People. Two-thirds of the population lives on Java, site of the capital and chief port, Jakarta. The population can be broadly divided into Malays and Papuans, with Chinese, Arabs, and others. Bahasa Indonesia is the official language, but over 250 other languages are spoken. Education is compulsory, and most Indonesians are literate. There are more than 50 universities and technological institutes.

Economy. Some 55% of the population is in farming, producing rice, coconuts, cassava, corn, peanuts, sweet potatoes, spices, and coffee, and raising cattle, goats, hogs, and chickens. The economy rests largely on agriculture, forestry, and fisheries, but mineral resources are being increasingly exploited. Coal, bauxite, copper, manganese, nickel, and precious metals are mined. Indonesia's most important products are oil, its chief export, and tin, of which it is one of the world's major producers. There is some light manufacturing, mostly centered on Java.

History. Hominids lived on Java 1 million years ago. Civilization grew under Indian influence after the 4th century A.D.; several kingdoms flourished from the 12th to 14th centuries. Islam spread swiftly in the 15th century. European impact began in 1511, when the Portuguese captured Malacca. But Portugal eventually kept only East Timor, losing control to the English and Dutch. The Dutch East India Company founded Batavia (Jakarta) in 1619 and dominated the so-called Dutch East Indies until the Netherlands assumed control in 1798. Britain occupied the islands (1811-1816) during the Napoleonic Wars, then returned them to the Dutch, who greatly expanded cash-crop exports during the 19th century. Nationalist movements emerged in the early 1900s, and after Indonesia's occupation by Japanese forces in World War II, Sukarno proclaimed Indonesia an independent republic. The Dutch were forced to grant independence in 1949. President Sukarno's dictatorial, anti-Western regime and extravagant spending damaged the economy. General Suharto deposed Sukarno in 1968. He suppressed left-wing groups, severed links with Communist China, and restored relations with the West, seeking to stabilize the economy. In 1975, after Portugal withdrew from East Timor, Indonesian troops in-

Rice terraces on the island of Bali mark the location of the small rural settlements of the mountainous interior.

vaded, and in 1976 the region was proclaimed a province of Indonesia, a move not recognized by the UN. Popular unrest, caused by economic crisis and a call for democratic reform, led to Suharto's resignation in 1998. He was succeeded by B.J. Habibie who had served as vice president. Large forest fires on Borneo and Sumatra caused heavy smoke production which endangered public health in Indonesia and Malaya (1997-1998). In 1998 and 1999 there were repeated violent clashes between various ethnic groups. In mid-1999 Habibie's government reached an agreement with Portugal for a referendum to be held on East Timor concerning its future as an autonomous province of Indonesia or an independant country. The majority chose for the latter. Meanwhile, moslimleader Abdurrahman Wahid was elected president, and the daughter of former president Sukarno, Megawati Sukarnoputri (democrat) vice president. The latter became President after Wahid was forced to resign due to corruption rumors in 2001. The provinces Aceh and Papua became autonomous, and East Timor became independent in May 2002. In December 2002, a bomb attack on a nightclub in Bali, presumably committed by Muslim terrorists, killed more than 180 people, mainly tourists from Australia and other countries. There is a possible connection with the al-Qaida network.

Indore (pop. 1,100,000), India, a city in west-central India, in Madhya Pradesh state. It is a commercial and industrial center, producing mainly textiles. Shortly after its founding early in the 18th century, Indore rose to prominence as the residence of the maharajas of Indore. A royal palace and a Jain temple are the city's leading attractions.

Induction, electric, name of the phenomenon whereby an electrically charged object charges another object without touching it. As distinct from electromagnetic induction, which is the force produced on an electrically charged particle by a changing magnetic field, electric induction is caused by the attraction that opposite electrical charges have

for each other (electrostatic attraction). In electric induction if a body is positively charged electrons in the uncharged body will be attracted to it; if the opposite end of the body is then grounded, electrons will flow into it to replace those drawn to the other end. Therefore, the body acquires a negative charge after the ground connection is broken. The Van de Graaff generator, used in nuclear physics experiments, utilizes electric induction.
See also: Van de Graaff generator.

Inductive method, logical process which starts from the particular and goes to the general. For example, a person may experience several rainy days while staying in a particular area and generalize that the area has a rainy climate; it is a method that leads to probabilities, not certainties. Francis Bacon proposed induction as the logic of scientific discovery, but the empirical sciences use both induction and deduction, which involves drawing particular conclusions by reasoning from general premises.
See also: Deductive method.

Indulgence, in the Roman Catholic Church, remission of the temporal punishment (on earth or in purgatory) that remains due for sin even after confession, absolution, and doing penance. In consideration of prayers and good works, the Church may grant plenary (full) or partial indulgences by administering the merits of Jesus and the saints. Sale of indulgences was denounced by the Protestant reformers, and the abuse was abolished by the Council of Trent.
See also: Trent, Council of.

Indurain, Miguel (1964-), Spanish racing cyclist, who, in 1995, was the first cyclist to win the Tour de France for the fifth time in succession. Indurain was a typical Tour cyclist: in 1990 he won the Paris-Nice race, in 1992 and 1993 he won the Giro d'Italia and also won several minor tours. In 1991 he came second on an electrically charged particle by a changing magnetic trials world championship, just behind Gianni Bugno. Indurain also excelled in time trials: for example, he won nearly all the time trials in

the major tours. He held the world record for two weeks in 1994, with 32,965 mi (53,040 km), before it was broken by Tony Romiger. In 1995, he became world champion in the time trials over 26 mi (42 km) and in 1996, he was Olympic champion in the road trials. Indurain ended his racing career in 1997.

Indus River, river rising in the Himalayas of western Tibet and flowing 1,800 mi (2,900 km) through Kashmir and Pakistan to its 75-mi-(121-km-)long delta on the North Arabian Sea. Cradle of the ancient Indus Valley civilization, it is now a source of hydroelectric power and irrigation.

Industrial arts, area of general education that includes automobile mechanics, electronics, graphic arts, industrial crafts, industrial drawing, metalworking, plastics, photography, and woodworking. Also known as *technology education*, industrial arts began as a curriculum area in the U.S. during the late 1800s. Until the 1970s most industrial arts programs enrolled only boys, but today most programs are coeducational. Industrial arts courses may focus on one skill in depth, or several skills in a broader way. Among the goals of industrial arts programs are to teach the use of tools and machines and to encourage creativity.

Industrial design, expression of the special relationship between the artist, the consumer, and the manufacturer in a developed, industrialized society. Its origins lie in the Industrial Revolution of the late 18th century, which began to link mass production with a powerful new form of distribution, the steam train, and with a growing consumer-oriented community. Its full expression is everywhere present-from the mass-produced automobile to the mass-produced ready-to-wear suit. Slowly but certainly, the craftsperson, whose products were based on an individual relationship with the consumer, has all but disappeared.

Industrialism *See:* Industrial Revolution.

Industrial pollution *See:* Environmental pollution.

Industrial relations, conduct of relations between organized labor and management and the relations between individual workers and their supervisors. Wage rates, work conditions, and productivity are among potential sources of conflict between the two sides. Unresolved conflicts can result in strikes and lockouts that cut output and profits and thus harm employees and employer alike.

Industrial Revolution, extensive mechanization of production processes in Europe set in motion by Great Britain in the second half of the 18th century. In the space of about 150 years (from around 1750-1900), the Industrial Revolution took agriculture's place in large parts of Europe as the most important way to earn a living. The revolution took place thanks to a surplus of agricultural workers, due to the agricultural revolution, the availability of raw materials,

The Rudolphs-Hütte (Hütte = blast furnace) of around 1850. This factory in Mährisch-Ostrau was set up at the beginning of Austria's rapid industrialization, and was owned by the Rothschild family.

A spinning mill from the beginning of the 20th century. The textile industry was one of the first to be mechanized, with more complex machines which simplified the work. Often times, employees did nothing more for twelve hours a day than carry out simple corrections, like tying broken threads together.

I

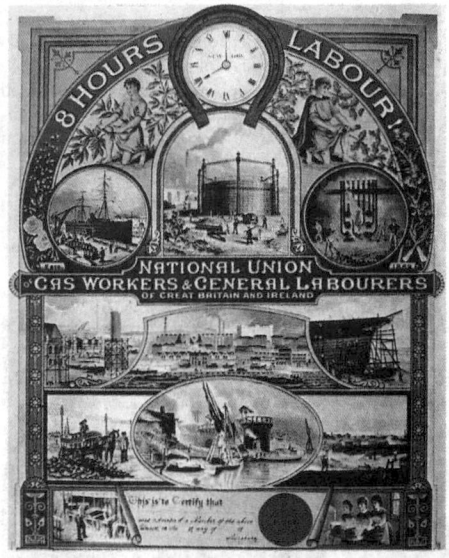

Membership card of the National Union of Gas Workers and General Laborers. This union was founded in 1889 in London after Beckton Gas Works fired a number of workers. The organization turned out to have an extremely big influence on the company: within a month, the normal working day of twelve hours had been changed to one of eight hours. After that, the union kept on growing and became an example for other similar organizations.

Proper working conditions were not as important as the demand for higher production and profit levels in most of the factories. Accidents happened all the time and the long working day was spent in dirty, damp rooms. This sentimental engraving from 1839 shows a –rather rose-colored- image.

The first continental railway was built between Brussels and Mechelen in 1835. The invention of the train helped the Industrial Revolution enormously: firstly, because products could be transported much more quickly by train, but also because the demand for iron (train tracks) and coal (for the steam engines) stimulated heavy industry.

A mechanical steam hammer in a factory, one of the many uses of steam that empowered the Industrial Revolution. The steam hammer could produce one hit a second, flattening red-hot steel plates that could not be handled before (manually).

I

good infrastructure (canals and roads), technical knowledge and an appreciation of entrepreneurship. The first phase (around 1750-1800) mainly took place in the cotton industry and the mines: thanks to technical innovations and the use of steam machines the production was immensely improved. This progress stimulated the second Industrial Revolution, which took place in the cities: the development of iron foundries, machine production and transport (railways). The Industrial Revolution intensively increased Europe's control over the world and was the beginning of an era of urbanization, economic expansion, population growth and scientific progress.

Strike Night (1893), by the Flemish artist E. Laermans. The Industrial Revolution resulted in the existence of large groups of factory workers, who all suffered the bad conditions of early industrialization. After a while they started to unite in (often socialist) unions and political parties that could protect them.

Indus Valley civilization, centered around the Indus River in India and Pakistan, the earliest known urban culture of the Indian subcontinent. Superimposed on earlier stone- and bronze-using cultures dating from 4000 B.C., the Indus Valley civilization, with its main cities Harappa and Mohenjo-Daro, lasted from 2500 to 1750 B.C. About 100 of its towns and villages, some with citadels, have been identified.
See also: Indus River.

Inert gas *See:* Noble gas.

Inertia, in physics, tendency of a body to persist in its state of rest or motion. The term is sometimes used in psychology to describe latency or resistance to change.
See also: Newton, Sir Isaac.

Inertial guidance, method by which a vehicle is guided without contact with a ground base. Used primarily to guide missiles, airplanes, and submarines, inertial guidance provides navigation information through use of an *inertial navigator*. This device consists of a *gyroscope*, which indicates direction, and an *accelerometer*, which measures changes in speed and direction. Then a computer processes this information to calculate the vehicle's position and guide it. The inertial guidance system is based upon the ancient navigational technique by which speed and direction were used to calculate a vehicle's direction.
See also: Navigation.

Inés de Castro (1320-1355), Inés de Castro,

a Spanish lady of great beauty, who came to Lisbon in the retinue of Princess Constança, when the latter married Prince Pedro, the son of King Alfonso IV of Portugal. Pedro and Inés immediately fell passionately in love. A marriage between the two was impossible, even after the death of Constança (1345) and despite the fact that several children had been born from their illicit affair, because the Portuguese feared that Inés would bring too much Spanish influence at court. After consulting his advisors, Alfonso IV had Inés beheaded on the 7th January 1355. Alfonso IV died in 1357; Pedro mounted the throne and had his father's advisors gruesomely killed. Inés' remains were taken to one of the two royal graves Pedro had had built for them in the church of Alcobaça. The historical adventures of Inés and Alfonso have become a theme in West-European literature.

Infant *See:* Baby.

Infantry, body of soldiers who fight on foot using light weaponry, such as rifles, machine guns, bazookas, mortars, and grenades. Despite the mechanization of warfare, infantry units still form the largest combat branch of most armies.
See also: Army.

A Frankish infantry soldier at the invasion of Gaul, 5th century AD, carried a battle-ax and a hide-covered roundshield.

Infection, state or condition in which the body or a part of it is invaded by a pathogenic (disease-causing) microorganism or virus that, under favorable conditions, multiplies and produces effects that are injurious. Localized infection is usually accompanied by inflammation, but inflammation may occur without infection.
The 5 classical symptoms of infection listed by early medical writers are: (1) *dolor*-pain; (2) *calor*-heat; (3) *rubor*-redness; (4) *tumor*-swelling; (5) *functio laesa*-disordered function.

Pain is especially prominent when the infection is confined within closed cavities and is in proportion to the virulence and extent of the infection. Redness and swelling are not evident when infection is within some rigid tissue or deep within some cavity; they are more apparent when superficial structures are involved. In fact, 'discoloration' would be a better term than 'redness,' for the color is more blue, or purple in advanced infections, while tuberculosis infections have long been called 'white swellings.' Heat may be evident on the surface, but there may be considerable elevation of body temperature even with small infections. 'Disordered function' depends upon the part affected as well as upon the virulence. With almost all acute infections, there is either an absolute or relative increase of polymorphonuclear leukocytes in the blood.

Infertility, inability or diminished ability to produce offspring. Infertility affects about 15% of couples in the United States and the United Kingdom. Male fertility depends on adequate production of sperm by the testicles, unobstructed transit of sperm through the seminal tract, and satisfactory depositing of it within the vagina. Causes of impaired spermatogenesis include certain environmental poisons, undescended testicles, injury- or infection-related testicular atrophy, drug effects, prolonged fever, and endocrine disorders. Obstruction of the seminal tract may result from congenital defects and from inflammation of the testicles, epididymis, vas deferens, and prostate gland, and seminal surgical division of both vasa deferens (vasectomy). Defective delivery of sperm into the vagina may result from surgery of the bladder neck, removal of the prostate gland, hypospadias, premature ejaculation, functional or organic impotence, or structural abnormalities of the female genital tract.
Female infertility first of all depends on the ability to develop ova (eggs) in the ovaries. These eggs must be able to leave the ovaries and travel into and down the fallopian tubes. For sperm to be able to reach them, the structure of the vagina, cervix, and the main body of the uterus must not impair them, and the mucus surrounding the cervix must be abundant, clear, and elastic. The fallopian tubes must be clear, from the uterus up to the place where the sperm meet the eggs. In addition, after conception has occurred, the lining (endometrium) of the uterus must be able to take the implantation of the fertilized egg; otherwise, there will be an early miscarriage. Infertility in women can result from disease, disturbance, or deformity of any of these structures or functions. The most common reason for infertility is hormonal imbalance that affects the woman's ability to produce viable eggs or the type of cervical mucus that she produces. The fallopian tubes can become blocked by scars due to inflammation. There also may be some abnormality of the vulva, cervix, or uterus.
See also: Reproduction.

Infinity (∞), quantity greater than any finite quantity. In modern mathematics infinity is viewed in 2 ways. In one, the word has a definite meaning; and with transfinite cardinal numbers, for example, it may have a plural-

ity of meanings. In the other, infinity is seen as a limit: to say that parallel lines intersect at infinity, for example, means merely that the point of intersection of 2 lines may be made to recede indefinitely by making the lines more and more nearly parallel. Similarly, in $f(x)=1/x$ it is meaningful to say that $f(x)$ tends to infinity as x tends to zero; again, the sequence $1,2,3,\ldots n$ tends to infinity because, however large n is chosen, there is an $(n+1)$ greater than it. In advanced set theory an infinite set is defined as one whose elements can be put in a one-to-one correspondence with those of a proper subset of the set (i.e., a subset that is not the whole set).
See also: Set theory.

Inflation (Diminishing worth of money), process of general price increases and the increase in the circulation of money. Many causes have been mentioned: economic growth (causing expenditure inflation: the demand outweighs the production capabilities), high government spending, etc. For example, government expenditure has the tendency to increase faster than the income. A wage and price spiral can occur with wage indexation, which is often applied: wages increase at the same rate as the prices. An increase in cost prices is often directly added to one's selling prices. This is particularly detrimental to people with fixed wages. Overdrafts become attractive because the debt steadily loses its value. Speculation is stimulated, in particular in real estate. Since the Second World War there has been, inflation, sometimes high, in all Western-oriented countries. The hyperinflation in Germany (1923) is infamous: within a few weeks the price of a tram ride, for example, increased to 1 million marks; wages were paid with baskets of paper money.
See also: Economics; Deflation.

Inflection, in grammar, changes in form that words undergo with each change in grammatical function. For example, the English verb *write* becomes *writes* in the third person singular of the present tense. *Write* has 3 additional forms: *wrote*, *written*, and *writing*. This set of inflections for a verb is called *conjugation*. The set of inflections for a noun or pronoun is called *declension*. For example, the English noun *dog* has 4 forms: *dog*, *dogs*, *dog's*, and *dogs'*.
See also: Grammar.

Inflorescence, arrangement of flowers on the stem of a plant. Tulips and anemones, among other plants, carry single flowers at the tops of their stems. Most plants, however, carry their flowers in clusters called *inflorescences*. This is especially true of those species whose individual flowers are small. The inflorescence is thought to be more attractive to pollinating insects than a single flower would be. The commonest type of inflorescence is the *raceme*, in which numerous flowers are borne on one or more sides of the main stem. The oldest flowers are always at the bottom. The individual flowers normally have short stalks. If they are stalkless the inflorescence is often called a *spike*. The foxglove is a typical raceme. In the *corymb* the individual flower stalks on the

lower part of the stem are longer than those higher up. The result is that all the flowers are brought to more or less the same level and make a conspicuous display. In the *umbel*, which looks similar to the corymb, the main stem stops growing after a while and all the flower stalks come from one point. The oldest flowers are on the outside. Umbels are characteristic of the carrot family. The *cyme* is an inflorescence in which the main stem produces only 1 or 2 side shoots before ending in a flower. Each of the side shoots then does the same. Where 2 branches are formed each time, there is a continued forking of the stem, with a flower in the center of each fork. There are several other kinds of inflorescence. The dandelion or daisy head, for example, is a very condensed inflorescence called a *capitulum*. Very often the flowering shoot will produce several branches, and each branch may then form a raceme, a corymb, or an umbel. Branched inflorescences of this kind are called *panicles*.

Influenza, specific acute respiratory disease caused by viruses and characterized by fever, head cold, cough, headache, malaise, and inflamed mucous membranes of the respiratory tract. It usually occurs as an epidemic in the winter. Hemorrhage, bronchitis, pneumonia, and sometimes death occur in severe cases. Acute epidemics occur about every 3 years. Persons at high risk of developing severe diseases are those with chronic lung disease, heart valve disease, or congestive heart failure; pregnant women in the third trimester; and elderly persons who are confined to bed. The antiviral drug amantadine has a beneficial effect on fever and respiratory symptoms if given early in uncomplicated influenza. It is of no benefit when the illness is complicated with pneumonia, but might improve recovery from a lung infection. The basic treatment otherwise is the relief of symptoms. Aspirin, paracetamol, and other drugs to lower the temperature and relieve pain are helpful. Vaccines that include the prevalent strains of influenza viruses have a 60% chance of reducing the incidence of infection for 1 to 2 years after vaccination. The immunity is less when the virus changes appreciably (antigenic drift) and when a major viral mutation occurs (antigenic shift). No significant protection is afforded unless the new strain is incorporated into the vaccine. Vaccination is especially important for the aged and for those with heart, lung, or other chronic diseases.

Information theory, or communication theory, mathematical discipline that aims to maximize the information that can be conveyed by communications systems and minimize the errors that arise in the course of transmission. The information content of a message is conventionally quantified in terms of bits (binary digits). Each bit represents a simple alternative: in terms of a message, a yes or no; in terms of the components in an electrical circuit, that a switch is open or closed. Mathematically the bit is usually represented as 0 or 1. Complex messages can be represented as a series of bit alternatives. Five bits of information only are needed to specify any letter of the alphabet, given an appropriate code. Thus able to quanti-

fy information, the theory employs statistical methods to analyze practical communications problems. The errors that arise in the transmission of signals, often termed *noise*, can be minimized by the incorporation of redundancy, wherein more bits of information than are strictly necessary to encode a message are transmitted so that if some are altered in transmission there is still enough information to allow the signal to be correctly interpreted. The handling of redundant information costs something in reduced speed of or capacity for transmission, but the reduction in message errors compensates for this loss. Information theoreticians often point to an analogy between the thermodynamic concept of entropy and the degree of misinformation in a signal.
See also: Mathematics.

Infrared rays, rays resembling light rays, but undetectable by the human eye. Also called *heat rays*, infrared rays are given off by objects in relation to their temperature. Emission of infrared rays increases as an object gets hotter. The British astronomer Sir William Herschel discovered infrared rays in 1800 by observing the effect of the heat they produced. The *sniperscope* is an instrument that perceives infrared rays from objects that are warmer than their surroundings. The military utilizes infrared radiation and the sniperscope in missile detection, guidance systems, and night-vision apparatus.
See also: Electromagnetic waves.

Inge, William (1913-1973), U.S. playwright. He was noted for psychological studies of life in small Midwestern towns, in such plays as *Come Back, Little Sheba* (1950), *Picnic* (1953), which won a Pulitzer Prize, *Bus Stop* (1955), and *A Loss of Roses* (1959).

Ingres, Jean Auguste Dominique (1780-1867), French neoclassical painter. He is known for his mastery of line and superb draftsmanship. *The Vow of Louis XII* (1824) won him acclaim as the foremost classicist of his time, but today he is better known for portraits and nude studies such as the *Odalisque* (1814). A disciple of Raphael, he was a determined opponent of the romantic movement and an inspiration to many later artists, including Edgar Degas, Pierre-Auguste Renoir, and Pablo Picasso.

Inheritance tax, assessment on property bequeathed by a deceased person to a specific legatee. It thus differs from an estate tax, levied on a deceased person's estate as a whole.
See also: Taxation.

Initiative, referendum, and recall, methods by which voters may directly intervene to influence government policy between elections. Initiative is a procedure whereby a new law is proposed in a petition, then submitted to a vote by the legislature or electorate or both. Laws so passed are generally not subject to veto. Referendum allows citizens a direct vote on proposed laws and policies. Recall provides for the removal of an elected official by calling a special election.

Injunction, formal written court order com-

I

I

manding or prohibiting any act. An injunction may be temporary, pending the outcome of a court action, or permanent, if the court's decision confirms the injunction's validity. Such writs are widely applied to prevent, for example, the misuse of property; the wrongful denial of, or cancellation of membership in, a union or other organization; the infringement of copyrights or patents; violent action in labor-management disputes; or the removal of a child from the care of a parent. Violation of an injunction is punishable as contempt of court.

Ink, liquid or paste used for writing or printing. Writing inks were used as early as c.2500 B.C. by Egyptians and Chinese, who created ink from natural materials such as berries, bark, linseed oil, and soot. Today, there are thousands of kinds of inks, used both in the printing industry and in ballpoint and fountain pens for writing. Most printing inks contain pigments, as opposed to dyes. Vehicles, which carry the pigment and help bind it to the paper, vary greatly in printing. Thick, sticky inks are used in the printing of books and magazines, and many contain *driers* to speed up the chemical reaction of oxidation and help the ink dry faster. Most writing ink consists of dyes and resins dissolved in a solvent, such as water and *glycol*, an alcohol.

Inkatha movement, originally a cultural organization of the Zulu population in the homeland Kwazulu (South Africa) In 1977 Inkatha leader Chief Mangosuthu Ghatsa Buthelezi broadened his organization to become an anti-apartheid movement for Blacks, Coloreds, and Asians. The movement chose to work together with the White minority. The influence of the Inkatha movement has grown since the early eighties of the 20th century. Important ideological differences with the ANC led to conflicts reaching a climax in 1990-1991, when bloody fighting broke out between the supporters of Inkatha, mostly Zulu's, and the supporters of the ANC. The Inkatha movement attempted to make itself known as a broadly based movement with many supporters to make decisions for the future of South Africa. The movement was discredited when it was discovered in 1991 that they had received (financial) aid from the apartheid regime.
In 1994 Buthelezi's Inkatha Freedom Party won 43 seats of the 400 in the first general elections for all citizens of South Africa, and Buthelezi became Minister of Internal Affairs in Nelson Mandela's government.

Inner Mongolia (Neimenggu Zizhiqu; pop. 23,000,000), autonomous Chinese dependency, bordering on Mongolia and Russia; 456,933 sq mi (1,183,000 sq km). Capital: Huhehaote (formerly Kweisu). It is a highland plain with steppes, where there is nomadic cattle herding. It has been an integral part of China since 1911.

Inness, George (1825-1894), U.S. landscape painter. His best-known works, such as *The Lackawanna Valley* (1855), show the influence of Jean-Baptiste Camille Corot and the Barbizon school. Another principal

work is *June* (1882). His later work, such as *The Home of the Heron* (1893), is less realistic and more atmospheric.

Innocence *See:* Bluet.

Innocent, name of 13 popes. **Saint Innocent I** (d.417) was pope from 401. He championed papal supremacy, but failed to prevent the sack of Rome by Alaric in 410. **Innocent II** (Gregorio Papareschi; d.1143) was pope from 1130. He convened the Second Lateral Council (1139). **Innocent III** (Giovanni Lotario de'Conti; 1161-1216) was pope from 1198. Under him the medieval papacy reached the summit of its power and influence. In an assertion of temporal power he forced King John of England to become his vassal and had Holy Roman Emperor Otto deposed in favor of Frederick II. He initiated the Fourth Crusade (1202) and supported the crusade against the Albigenses (1208). He presided over the Fourth Lateran Council (1215), the culmination of the entire medieval papacy. **Innocent IV** (Sinibaldo de'Fieschi; c.1190-1254), pope from 1243, clashed with Emperor Frederick II over the temporal power of the papacy, and was forced to flee to Lyons, France, until Frederick's death. He worked for the unification of the Christian churches. **Innocent VIII** (Giovanni Battista Cibo; 1432-1492), pope from 1484, was worldly and unscrupulous. He fomented the witchcraft hysteria and meddled in Italian politics. For a fee he kept the brother and rival of Sultan Bayazid II imprisoned. **Innocent XI** (Benedetto Odescalchi; 1611-1689) was

During the Spanish Inquisition, the solemn session that ended each inquiry, and at which the sentence was passed, was called the auto-da-fé. The accused were draped with cloths, upon which texts were printed. Here, two men are already at the stake, while others are receiving their last spiritual solace (Prado, Madrid).

pope from 1676. An opponent of quietism, he favored toleration of Protestantism, and over this and the issue of papal power clashed with Louis XIV of France. **Innocent XII** (Antonio Pignatelli; 1615-1700) was pope from 1691. A stern reformer, he abolished nepotism and was renowned for his piety and charity. **Innocent XIII** (Michelangelo Conti; 1655-1724) was pope from 1721. He bestowed Naples and Sicily on their de facto possessor, the Emperor Charles VI, and recognized the claims of James, the Old Pretender, to the British throne in the hope of a Catholic revival.

Innsbruck (pop. 118,000), capital of the Austrian Tyrol province, located on the Inn River, at an altitude of 1,880 ft (573 m) between steep Alpine ranges. Innsbruck became a prosperous town mainly because of its position near the Brenner Pass. Modern manufactures include textiles, chemicals, metal goods, and mosaics. There are many notable medieval castles in the city, including the 15th-century castle Fürstenburg. Innsbruck University was founded in the 17th century. The city is noted for the scenic beauty of its surroundings and is a popular tourist center in both winter and summer.
See also: Austria.

Inoculation, introduction of a germ, a poison produced by a germ, or serum into the body to set up the production of antibodies that will subsequently protect the individual from an attack of the disease, rendering the individual immune.
See also: Immunization.

Inoue, Yasushi (1907-1991), Japanese writer. Inoue wrote a large number of historical novels, which mostly concern the Japanese debt to China and Central Asia in cultural terms. In the 1970's, through the influence of his books, the Japanese became greatly interested in the Silk Route that had brought foreign influences to Japan. Some of his work has been translated into English, including *The Hunting Gun*, *Chronicle of My Mother*, *The Counterfeiter*, and *Roof Tiles of Tempyo*.

Input-output analysis, method of studying the relationship between various parts of the economy, developed by U.S. economist Wassily Leontif. It relies upon the use of complex numerical tables.
See also: Economics.

Inquest, formal legal inquiry to ascertain a fact. It is most commonly used to investigate death under circumstances where violence is suspected. The coroner, or in some cases a medical examiner, invites the jury to view the body. Then, depending on the evidence presented, the jury decides whether to order a post-mortem examination. It may recommend that a suspect be detained for trial. Inquests are also held to determine damages in cases where the defendant has not appeared in court. The institution is rooted in early English law.

Inquisition, medieval agency of the Roman Catholic Church to combat heresy, first made official in 1231 when Pope

Gregory IX appointed a commission of Dominicans to investigate heresy among the Albigen-sians of southern France. It aimed to save the heretic's soul, but a refusal to recant was punished by fines, penance, or imprisonment, and often by confiscation of land by the secular authorities. Later the penalty was death by burning. Torture, condemned by the former popes, was permitted in heresy trials by Innocent IV (d. 1254). The accused were not told the name of their accusers but could name their known enemies so that hostile testimony might be discounted. Often the Inquisition was subject to political manipulation. In 1524 it was reconstituted to counter Protestantism in Italy; its modern descendant is the Congregation of the Doctrine of the Faith.

The Spanish Inquisition, founded in 1478 by Ferdinand and Isabella, was a branch of government and was distinct from the papal institution. Its first commission was to investigate Jews and Muslims who had publicly embraced Christianity but secretly held to Judaism or Islam. Under the grand inquisitor Torquemada, it became an agency of official terror-even St. Ignatius Loyola was investigated. It was extended to Portugal and South America and not dissolved until 1820. In January 1998 the archives of the papal Inquisition until 1902, were made accessible to researchers.

See also: Torquemada, Tomás de.

Insect, member of the class Insecta, phylum Arthropoda, or invertebrate animals with jointed legs. There are about 750,000 known species of insects, and more are being discovered every year.

Anatomy. The body of an insect, like that of other arthropods, is covered by a hard, waterproof 'shell' that forms an external skeleton to which the muscles are attached. The head bears jaws and other structures for dealing with food. It also carries several sense organs, including the compound eyes made up of clusters of separate units. The antennae, or feelers, are organs of touch, smell, and occasionally of hearing. Sense organs are also found on other parts of the body: Grasshoppers and crickets have ears on the legs or thorax, and houseflies have tastebuds on their feet. The middle section, or thorax, bears the limbs. It consists of 3 parts, each of which carries a pair of jointed legs ending in hooks that allow the insect to hang on walls or ceilings. Two pairs of wings sprout from the back of the thorax. Some insects have no wings, and some have turned one pair into balancing organs. The abdomen is the largest section of the body and has no visible external organs except those concerned with reproduction and occasionally a pair of short sense organs, such as antennae called cerci (for example, in earwigs). Insects do not have a closed system of blood vessels. The heart simply pumps blood through the arteries to the extremities, where it washes around the organs and slowly drains back to the heart. Nor do insects have lungs. Air is carried into the body down minute tubes, called tracheae, which run from openings in the skin into each organ.

Life cycles. Most insects lay eggs, but some

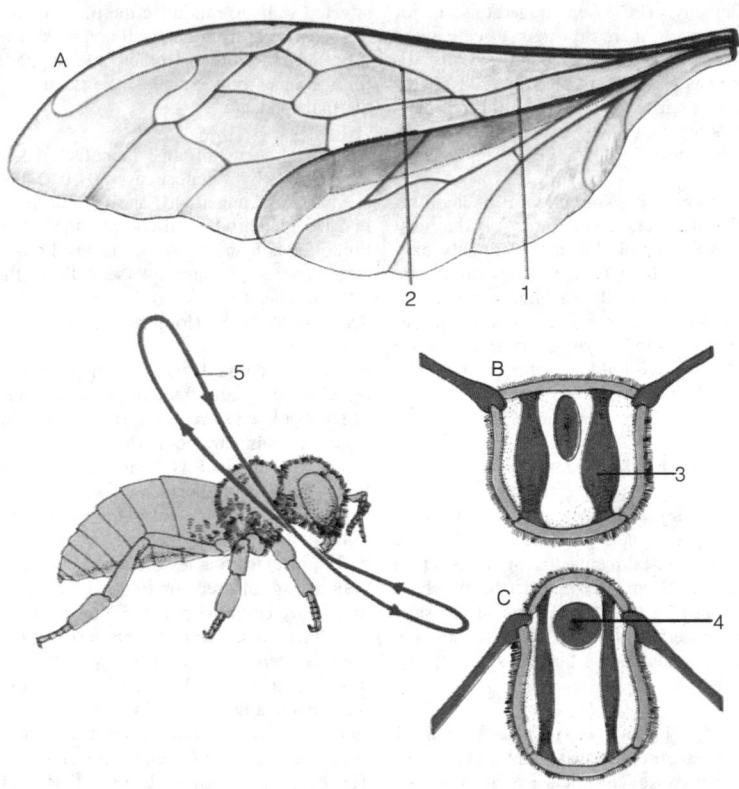

The wings (A) of flying insects such as the honey bee (*Apis mellifera*) are membranous outgrowths of the body wall, strengthened by longitudinal veins (1) and cross veins (2). The wings are moved indirectly by muscles that alter the shape of the thorax (cross sections). Elevation (B) of the wings is produced by contractions of the vertical muscles (3), contraction of the longitudinal muscles (4) produces a downward movement (C). During flight, complex wing movements follow a figure-8 path (5).

give birth to live young. The mother usually abandons her eggs, but the social insects, including bees and wasps, have elaborate systems of caring for their young. The eggs hatch into larvae, such as the maggots of flies, the caterpillars of butterflies and moths, and the nymphs of dragonflies. The development into an adult insect is accomplished in one of two ways. (1) *Incomplete metamorphosis*: In dragonflies, grasshoppers, and others, the newly hatched larva looks rather like the adult. It molts several times, shedding its skin each time and growing a little larger. Adult features such as wings become more apparent at each molt until, at the final molt, the adult insect crawls out of the old skin. (2) *Complete metamorphosis*: The larva is very different from the adult. After growing for some time, it changes into the adult in one drastic step. To do this it forms a pupa or chrysalis in which it can reorganize its structure. In this way a sausage-shaped caterpillar turns into a butterfly. A single insect is able to exploit 2 very different ways of life. Thus a caterpillar feeds on leaves and a butterfly drinks nectar.

Habitat. Insects vary in size from almost microscopic wasps to the huge extinct dragonflies with wingspans of over 2 ft (61 cm). They live in many different environments, boring into wood, burrowing underground, living in other animals, and swimming underwater. They are found in the hottest deserts, on the coasts of Antarctica, in hot springs, and in the saltiest lakes (such as Salt Lake, Utah); the petroleum fly lives in pools of crude petroleum oil in California. They may also exist in huge numbers. Locust swarms may contain 1 billion individuals, and springtails form dense carpets on the ground.

Insecticide, any substance toxic to insects and used to control them in situations where they cause economic damage or endanger the health of humans and their domestic animals. There are 3 main types: stomach insecticides, which are ingested by the insects with their food; contact insecticides, which penetrate the cuticle (exterior covering); and fumigant insecticides, which are inhaled. Stomach insecticides are often used to control chewing insects like caterpillars and sucking insects like aphids. They may be applied to a plant prior to attack and remain active in or on the plant for a considerable time. They must be used with considerable caution on food plants or animal forage. Examples include arsenic compounds, which remain on the leaf, and organic compounds, which are absorbed by the plant and transported to all its parts (systemic insecticides). Contact insecticides include the plant products nicotine, derris, and pyrethrum, which are quickly broken down, and synthetic compounds such as DDT (and other chlorinated hydrocarbons), organophosphates (malathion, parathion), and carbamates. Polychlorina-

ted biphenyls (PCBs) are added to some insecticides to increase their effectiveness and persistence. Highly persistent insecticides may be concentrated in food chains and exert harmful effects on other animals such as birds and fish.
See also: Insect.

I

Insectivore, order (Insectivora) of small insect-eating mammals, regarded as the most primitive group of placental mammals, having diverged little from the ancestral form. The skull is generally long and narrow, with a primitively large complement of unspecialized teeth in the jaw. Ears and eyes are small and often hidden in fur or skin. The group includes shrews, hedgehogs, and moles.

Insectivorous plant *See:* Carnivorous plant.

Installment plan, system of credit by which merchandise is paid for over a fixed period of time in installments known as deferred payments. Normally, part of the purchase price must be paid at the time of the sale. Goods generally bought using an installment plan are automobiles, farm machinery, and homes.

Instinct, in biology and psychology, behaviors in reaction to external stimuli that have not been consciously learned. It is in fact difficult to separate such inherited genetic behaviors from those stemming from learned and environmental factors, since higher animals placed from birth in artificial environments display some, but not all, instinctive reactions characteristic of their species. It has been further suggested that embryos may have some learning ability-that is, that some learning before birth is possible. Numbered among the instincts are the sex drive, aggression, territoriality, and the food urge, but much debate surrounds such classification. In psychology, 'instinct' (sometimes called 'drive') is studied particularly with regard to the frustration of or conflict between the existence of two fundamental instincts: the life instinct, akin to the libido, and its opposite, the death instinct.
See also: Biology; Psychology.

Insulation, inhibiting or limiting the conduction of electricity or heat through the use of specific materials. An electric current or voltage is contained by materials (insulators) that offer a high resistance to current flow, will withstand high voltages without breaking down, and will not deteriorate with age. The mechanical properties desired vary with the application: Cables require flexible coatings, such as polyvinyl chloride, while glass or porcelain is used for rigid mountings, such as the insulators used to support power cables. In thermal insulation, there is a reduction of transfer of heat from a hot area to a cold. Thermal insulation is used to keep something hot, to keep something cold, or maintain something at a roughly steady temperature. Heat is transferred through conduction, convection, and radiation. The vacuum bottle thus uses 3 techniques to reduce heat transfers: a vacuum between the walls to combat conduction and convection;

silvered walls to minimize the transmission of radiant heat from one wall and maximize its reflection from the other; and supports for the inner bottle made of cork, a poor thermal conductor.

Insulin, protein hormone manufactured in the pancreas by minute areas of tissue called the islets of Langerhans, and then secreted into the blood, where it controls the digestion of carbohydrates. A lack of insulin or a disturbance of its use by the cells is the cause of diabetes.
See also: Diabetes; Hormone.

Insurance, method of financial protection by which one party undertakes to indemnify another against certain forms of loss. An insurance company pools the payments for this service and invests them to earn further funds. Each insured person pays a relatively small amount, the premium, for a stated period of coverage. In return the company will, subject to an assessment of a claim, reimburse the insured for loss caused by an event covered in the policy. Forms of insurance have existed since the earliest civilizations. Modern insurance began with the medieval guilds, which sometimes insured members against trade losses. The specialized fields of fire and maritime insurance developed in the 17th and 18th centuries. The development of probability theory allowed the statistical likelihood of damage to be calculated, making insurance as a business possible.

Integrated circuit, combination of interconnected circuit elements and amplifying devices inseparately associated on or within a continuous layer of semiconductor material, called a substrate.

Integration, increasingly mutual relationship of cultural elements (standards, values, knowledge, attitudes, and artistic expressions) within a society, so that the culture is pervaded by one characteristic basic mentality. The term is also used to indicate the process in which immigrants and people in the region where the immigrants have settled both accept elements of each other's culture. It can then be called mutual assimilation.

Intelligence, mental ability, including learning ability, problem-solving ability, and the capacity for abstract thinking. There has been much debate as to whether intelligence is inherited or a product of the environment. The fact is that physical constitution may contain developmental potentialities, but the environment decides to what extent and in what ways these potentialities are realized. Heredity and environment interact to such a degree that a clear distinction between their contributions is often impossible.

Intelligence quotient (IQ), index of intelligence determined through a subject's answers to arbitrarily chosen questions. The IQ is merely a standard score that places an individual in reference to the scores of others within his or her age group. Mental age represents the age level corresponding to the

score reached on the test. Thus, if a child 10 years old gives a test score appropriate to that of the average 12year-old child, his or her mental age would be 12 and his or her IQ is 120. This method works reasonably well for younger children but has grave disadvantages when applied to older children or adults. In psychological literature, the following classification is found:

Above 140	'Near' genius or genius
120-140	Very superior intelligence
110-120	Superior intelligence
90-110	Average intelligence
80-90	Dull normal
70-80	Borderline deficiency
50-70	Educable mentally retarded
30-50	Trainable
20-30	Severely mentally retarded

See also: Binet, Alfred.

Intelligence service, institution of a national government that gathers information; particularly about clandestine activities of other countries or enemies, for the purpose of protecting national security. Such functions were once performed chiefly by foreign ambassadors. Under Elizabeth I, England was among the first Western countries to set up an elaborate intelligence service, privately financed by Sir Francis Walsingham. Joseph Fouché established an equally vital network for Napoleonic France. Britain's intelligence service reached its highest point during World War II, with the brilliant amateurs of MI-5. In the United States, military espionage first assumed great importance during the Civil War, in which it was employed extensively by both sides. During World War I the U.S. intelligence service was organized largely by the Office of Strategic Services (OSS). It was given its present form in 1947 with the creation of the Central Intelligence Agency (CIA). The CIA, which came under investigation and some censure in the late 1970s, coordinates the intelligence functions of all government departments and agencies. All the armed services have their own intelligence branches.

Intelligence test *See:* Intelligence quotient; Testing.

Inter-American conferences *See:* Pan-American conferences.

Intercontinental ballistic missile *See:* Guided missile.

Interest, money paid for the use of money loaned. It is generally expressed as a percentage of the principal (sum loaned) per period (usually per year or per month). In *simple interest*, interest is calculated on the basis of the sum loaned. In *compound interest*, interest is paid on the principal plus the accumulated interest, recalculated periodically. Actual payments for compound interest are thus higher (and more complex to calculate). *Discount interest* is subtracted from the principal before the money is given to the borrower.

Interference, in physics, mutual action of waves of any kind upon each other, by which their vibrations and effects are increased, diminished, or neutralized. In information science the term is used to denote the occurrence of unwanted signals that degrade the quality of wanted signals.
See also: Physics.

Interferometer, any instrument of measurement employing interference effects of waves. Interferometers are used for measuring the wavelengths of light, radio, sound, or other wave phenomena or the refractive index of gases. Some interferometers measure very small distances using radiation of known wavelength. In acoustics and radio astronomy, they are used for determining the direction of an energy source. In most interferometers the beam of incoming radiation is divided in two, led along paths of different but accurately adjustable lengths, and then recombined to give an interference pattern. Perhaps the best-known optical instrument is the Michelson interferometer devised in 1881. More accurate for wavelength measurements is the Fabry-Perot interferometer, in which the radiation is recombined after multiple partial reflections between parallel, lightly silvered glass plates.
See also: Interference.

Interferon, class of small soluble proteins produced and released by cells invaded by a virus, that inhibits viral multiplication. Interferon production may also be induced by certain bacteria and specifically sensi-

tized lymphocytes. There are indications that interferon may be useful in the treatment of certain types of cancer. A nasal spray containing interferon produced in the laboratory prevented between 78% and 84% of colds caused by rhinoviruses in families participating in 2 independent studies published in January 1986 in the *New England Journal of Medicine*.
See also: Cancer.

Interior decoration, design and arrangement of decorative elements in a home or public building. Until relatively recently, architectural and interior styles were almost inseparable and the names used to characterize each period applied both to the architecture of buildings and their interior decor.

Interleukin, generic term for a group of proteins, formed in white blood cells known as leucocytes, that activate the body's immune system. There are 3 types of interleukin: IL-1, IL-2, and IL-3. All 3 act in concert to remove or destroy any harmful bacteria or foreign substance that invades the body.
See also: Immunity.

Internal combustion engine, heat engine in which fuel is burned inside the engine itself. It contrasts with an external combustion engine (such as the steam engine), in which fuel is burned in a separate furnace. By far the most common type of internal-combustion engine is the gasoline engine, which propels

practically all automobiles. Another common type is the diesel engine used in trucks and many locomotives and ships. Both types work in a similar way, burning fuel inside closed cylinders to produce reciprocating (to and fro) motion of pistons. As machines, these engines are very inefficient. The gasoline engine can convert only about 20% of the heat energy released by burning fuel into useful work. The diesel engine is a little more efficient, being able to utilize some 30% of the energy released. Gas turbines and jet and rocket engines can also be classified as internal combustion engines, although they are of a rather different kind. They burn fuel continuously in a combustion chamber, generating hot gases that spin turbines or producing propulsive thrust by reaction.
See also: Engine.

Internal medicine, medical specialty that focuses on disorders of the internal body structures of adults. Through asking question and administering a thorough physical exam, a practitioner called an *internist* concentrates upon all the organ systems. He or she interprets all the information in order to make an evaluation and determine treatment.
See also: Medicine.

Internal revenue, the income a government takes in from its own sources, such as excise, sales, payroll, estate, income, and gift taxes. About 95% of the total U.S. revenue comes from its internal revenue, as opposed to outside revenue such as income from import and export duties. The U.S. government collects about $700 billion a year from the sum of its various types of internal revenue.
See also: Taxation.

International Air Transport Association (IATA), founded in 1919 in The Hague, the Netherlands, as International Air Traffic Organisation. The name was changed to International Air Transport Association in 1945. It is the world organization of airlines. Its purpose is to see to it that air traffic moves with the greatest speed, safety, and economy. Many governments have delegated to IATA the responsibility for negotiating agreements on international fares and rates. The association works closely with the

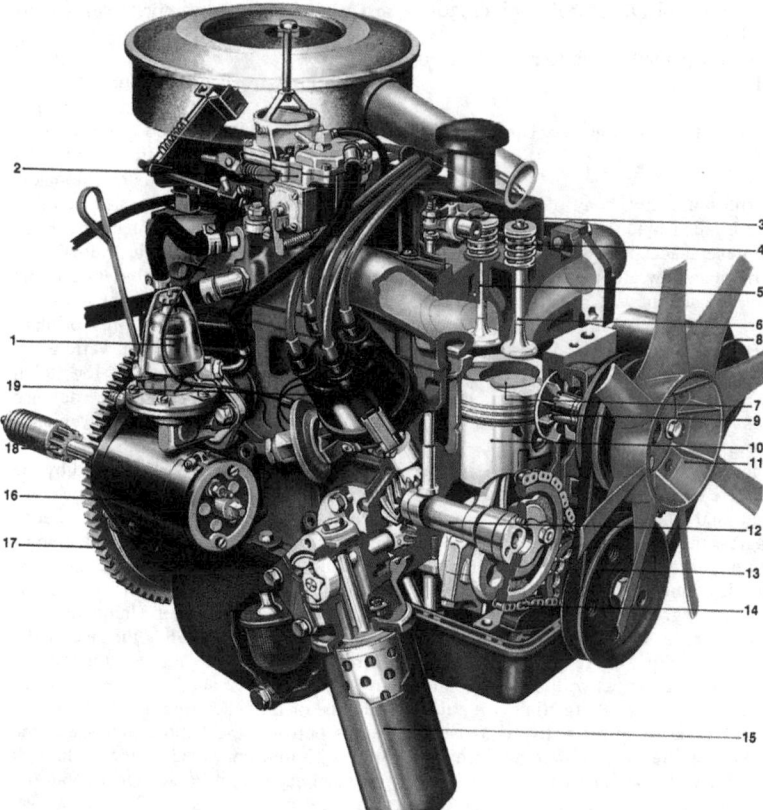

A four-cylinder overhead valve engine is used in most European and Japanese cars, as well as in some small American cars. Fuel, drawn from a gasoline tank by a fuel pump (1) is fed to a carburetor (2), where it is vaporized, mixed with air, and passed through an inlet valve (5) into a cylinder (10). The valve is kept closed by a spring (4), until it is opened by the action of a pushrod and a rocker arm (3), controlled by a camshaft (12). The camshaft also turns a distributor (19), which feeds electricity from a coil to spark plugs that ignite the fuel in each cylinder in sequence. The burning gases expand and force each piston (7) downward, rotating a crankshaft. A pulley (13) on the crankshaft drives a generator (8), a cooling fan (11), and a water pump (9) by means of a belt. The crankshaft also spins the camshaft via a timing chain (14) and drives an oil pump that circulates oil through a filter (15) and around moving engine parts. Exhaust gases are forced out of the exhaust valve (6) when the piston moves upward. The engine is started by an electric motor (16) that turns the flywheel (17), after engaging the gear (18).

I

International Civil Aviation Organization. IATA's headquarters are in Montreal, Canada.

International, The, common name of a number of socialist-communist revolutionary organizations. Three of these have had historical significance. The First International, officially the International Working Men's Association, was formed under the leadership of Karl Marx in London in 1864 with the aim of uniting workers of all nations to realize the ideals of the *Communist Manifesto*. Divisions grew between reformers and violent revolutionaries; these became increasingly bitter, culminating in the expulsion of the faction led by Mikhail Bakunin after a leadership struggle in 1872. The association broke up in 1876. The Second, commonly called the Socialist International, was founded in Paris in 1889 by a group of socialist parties that later made their headquarters in Brussels. The leading social democratic parties, including those of Germany and Russia, were represented. Among the representatives were Jean Jaurés, Ramsay MacDonald, Lenin, and Trotsky. The Second International influenced international labor affairs until World War I, when it broke up. The Third or Communist International, generally known as the Comintern, was founded by Lenin in 1919 in an attempt to win the leadership of world socialism; Zionview was its first president. Soviet-dominated from the outset, it aimed, in the 1920s, to foment world revolution. In the 1930s, under Stalin, it sought contacts with less extreme left-wing groups abroad, to assuage foreign hostility. Stalin dissolved it in 1943 as a wartime conciliatory gesture to the Allies.

International Bank for Reconstruction and Development *See:* World Bank.

International code *See:* Morse code.

International Court of Justice, highest judicial organ of the United Nations, founded in 1946 to provide a peaceful means of settling international disputes according to the principles of international law. Like its predecessor under the League of Nations, the World Court, it sits at The Hague, the Netherlands. In practice its authority is limited by frequent refusals of various states to accept its decisions.
See also: Hague, The; International law; United Nations.

International Criminal Police Organization *See:* Interpol.

International Criminal Tribunal for the former Yugoslavia, International tribunal established in The Hague since 1993. It is responsible for tracing and trying people who have been guilty of war crimes and other violations of the international humanitarian rights in former Yugoslavia since January 1, 1991. All UN -member states are obliged to cooperate in the execution of these actions. The tribunal compares itself to the international trials that were conducted against German and Japanese war crimi-

nals in respectively Nu-remberg and Tokyo after WW II.

International Date Line, imaginary line that runs down the middle of the Pacific Ocean and mostly follows the 180th meridian. Its purpose is to mark the spot on the earth's surface where each new calendar day begins. Clocks are set 1 hour earlier for every 15° ($^1/_{24}$ of the 360° circle) westward around the globe. A full circuit would move back the calendar as well as the clock. It has thus been necessary, particularly with the advent of rapid global communication and travel, to institute an arbitrary date line. When Tuesday is dawning just east of this line, Wednesday is dawning just west. Thus Japan is one of the first countries to reach the new day, while the United States is one of the last.

International Labor Organization (ILO) a specialized agency of the United Nations. Its purpose is to improve labor conditions and raise living standards throughout the world. ILO's experts train workers in underdeveloped lands and offer advice in various technical fields. The organization drafts conventions (agreements) and recommendations that together form the International Labor Code, which UN member countries commit themselves to observe. ILO delegates are drawn from government, employers, and labor.
ILO was established in 1919 as an autonomous institution associated with the League of Nations. In 1946 it became a United Nations agency. For its work in helping 'to create stable social conditions' and in this way contributing to world peace, the ILO was awarded the Nobel Prize for Peace for 1969.
ILO's headquarters are in Geneva, Switzerland.

International language *See:* Universal language.

International law, body of laws assumed to be binding among nations by virtue of their general acceptance. The beginnings of international law lay in attempts to humanize the conduct of war. The seminal work of Hugo Grotius, *On the Law of War and Peace* (1625), was one such; he also formulated several important principles, including a legal basis for the sovereignty of states. The works of Grotius and his successors were widely acclaimed but never officially accepted; however, legal principles were increasingly incorporated into international agreements such as the Congress of Vienna as well as into the constitution of the United Nations. International laws may arise through multilateral or bilateral agreements, as with the Geneva Convention, or simply by long-established custom, as with a large part of maritime law. In some cases, as with the war crimes rulings of the Nuremberg trials, they may be said to arise retrospectively. Because few nations are willing to relinquish any sovereignty, the law lacks a true legislative body and an effective executive to enforce it. The International Court of Justice is the international judicial body, and the UN in

the process of compiling an international legal code is the nearest thing to a legislature, but these bodies are limited by the willingness of states to accept their decisions. These difficulties have led some theorists to deny international law true legal status, but this is an extreme view. The need for international rules is widely recognized, as shown by the increasing tendency to anticipate problem areas such as space exploration and exploitation of seabed resources and to attempt to develop international rules to regulate them.

International Monetary Fund (IMF), a specialized agency associated with the United Nations. It is closely allied to the International Bank for Reconstruction and Development. The IMF seeks to promote international monetary cooperation, to help stabilize rates of exchange, and to assist in the removal of barriers imposed on international payments because of currency restrictions. A major long-term goal is to reform the international monetary system to make it more flexible and more equitable.
Member nations pay into the fund according to a quota system based on various economic criteria. They may then participate in the Special Drawing Rights (SDR's) program, which permits them to carry out exchange transactions among themselves with SDR's, or 'paper gold,' allocated by the IMF. Member nations may also borrow from the IMF to meet temporary deficits in their international payments.
The agency was created by the Bretton Woods Agreement of 1944 and was established in 1945. Each member country has a seat on the board of governors. Headquarters are in Washington, D.C.

International relations, relationships between nations, through politics, treaties, military confrontation or cooperation, economics, or culture. Peacetime contact is generally maintained through diplomacy; each nation maintains embassies in other countries it recognizes as nations. Even when states do not maintain mutual embassies, however, they may find it desirable to keep contacts open, often through the offices of a third nation. The other primary link is through membership in various international organizations, either for global politics (e.g., United Nations), defense (NATO), or simply mutual convenience (Universal Postal Union). From 1946 on international relations were dominated by the concept of the Cold War, in which the complications of world diplomacy were reduced to an oversimplified model of an ideological contest between 2 global antagonists, the communist and capitalist systems as personified by the Soviet Union and the United States. In the 1960s the rise of the Third World countries negated this simple division, though many of these countries took one or the other side. In the 1970s relations between the United States and the Soviet Union improved, largely through trade and nuclear limitation agreements and also because of the rise of China as a rival superpower. The endurance and value of the resulting detente, however, remained doubtful as the 1980s saw new-and continuing-areas of conflict between the superpowers. In 1990, the Charter of Paris for a New Europe was signed by the United States and the Soviet Union, effectively ending the Cold War.

International System of Units *See:* Metric system.

International trade, or world trade, exchange of goods and services between nations. Since the 18th century it has become a vital element in world prosperity, largely because it is thought more profitable for countries to specialize in producing goods in which such factors as natural resources, climatic conditions, availability of raw materials, and a skilled labor force or low labor costs give them a special advantage. This is known as the international division of labor. Some countries, such as Japan, rely largely on exports; U.S. exports amount to 15% of the world total, but are less vital to the country's economy. In prehistoric times the amber route carried trade between tribes thousands of miles apart. The ancient Greeks, Romans, and Phoenicians were active traders. Chinese merchants penetrated most of Asia, and Arabs operated trade routes on the Indian Ocean and in Africa. Most explorers before the 20th century sought to open trade routes. Early trade was largely in goods yielding high prices on small amounts because of the difficulty of transportation. Only with modern transport did international trade become economically vital. After World War II efforts were made to promote free trade throughout the world. In 1948 the United States and 23 other nations made an agreement within the framework of the United Nations known as the General Agreement on Tariffs and Trade (GATT). In 1962 Congress passed the Trade Expansion Act, enabling President J.F. Kennedy to lower or remove tariffs affecting the European Common Market countries. Subsequently, a series of tariff reductions have been negotiated under what is known as the 'Kennedy Round.' The Common Market had as its main aim free trade among its members, but it also created a system of common external tariffs in agriculture, a source of continual controversy. One of the biggest unsolved problems of international trade is the balance between industrialized countries and the developing countries of the Third World. Since the latter export mainly food and raw materials, which rise only slowly in price, and import manufactured goods, their expansion is much slower than that of rich countries.
See also: Trade.

Internet, Worldwide network of continually connected computer systems. The Internet arises from the need for fast communication means. This need was especially expressed by research institutes and universities. At first, the Internet was used by the (military) Arpanet. In the 1990s, more and more public bodies, companies and private individuals discovered the Internet. Contact with the Internet can be established through computer systems that are connected to each other

with fast, permanent lines, or via a (mobile) telephone connection or cable. Besides a computer, a modem and special software, this requires a provider, that maintains the connection with the Internet. It is possible to exchange E-mail, read about current affairs and other information and to participate in discussion groups that cover a great diversity of subjects on the net. The most popular and commercial part of the Internet is the World Wide Web.
See also: Computer; Electronic Mail.

Interpol, International Criminal Police Organization, a clearinghouse for police information that specializes in the detection of counterfeiting, smuggling, and trafficking in narcotics. Established in 1923, its headquarters are now in Paris.
See also: Police.

Intestine, in animals, alimentary canal extending from the pylorus of the stomach to the anus. The human intestine is approximately 24 ft (7 m) long and is divided into the small intestine and large intestine, or colon. The small intestine has a total length of approximately 10 ft (3 m). It begins with the duodenum, which receives the food mass from the stomach through the pylorus, bile from the liver and gall bladder, and pancreatic juice from the pancreas. It connects with the jejunum, which in turn joins the ileum, which is attached to the large intestine by the ileocecal, or colic, valve, controlling passage of food into the large intestine. The inner surface of the small intestine is folded to give a greater amount of surface-estimated to be 957 sq yd (800 sq m)-and it is entirely lined by minute fingerlike *villi*, through which the products of digestion are absorbed. There are 10-40 villi to each square mm of intestinal mucous membrane. The large intestine extends from the ileum to the anus, and consists of the cecum, colon, and rectum. The first portion of the colon, the ascending colon, extends from the cecum to the undersurface of the liver, where it becomes the transverse colon, which, in turn, at the splenic flexure, becomes the descending colon. This continues downward on the left side of the abdomen until it reaches the pelvic brim and curves like the letter *S* in front of the sacrum until it becomes the rectum. This S-shaped section is known as the sigmoid colon. The rectum passes downward to terminate in the lower opening of the tract, the anus, or anal opening.
See also: Digestive system.

Intifadah, The Palestinian uprising against Israeli domination in the Gaza Strip and the West Bank that broke out in December 1987. The uprising, which was mostly carried out by young people, also expressed dissatisfaction with the Israeli occupation. The Israeli government dealt forcefully with the mass demonstrations, which cost a thousand Palestinians their lives.The Intifadah exposed the political deadlock between Israelis and Palestinians and in this manner contributed to the realization of the Oslo Accords (1993-1995).
A second Intifadah broke out in 2000, after a visit by Ariel Sharon to the Temple Mount

had again brought tensions to head. A new development in this fight, which claimed hundreds of victims, was the action of Palestine suicide squads. Positions hardened on both sides leaving little hope of a peaceful resolution any time soon.

Intrauterine device *See:* Birth control.

Introvert, a nontechnical psychological term referring to someone whose thoughts are generally turned inward. The term originated with the 20th century Swiss psychiatrist Carl Jung, who also coined the term *extrovert*. meaning someone who tends to direct their thoughts and actions outward, and who is more naturally sociable. An introvert tends more toward shyness and a focus on the inner processes than he or she does toward extroverted behavior. Jung believed that a well-balanced person possesses qualities of both the introvert and extrovert.

Intrusive rock *See:* Igneous rock.

Inuit *See:* Eskimo.

Inverness (pop. 40,000), town in the Highland Region of northern Scotland which serves as the region's administrative and commercial center. Archeologists have shown evidence that people lived on the site of Inverness as early as 4000 B.C. It was the site of battle between British and Scottish forces before 1750. Lying on the River Ness in a lowland near Loch Ness and the Moray Firth, Inverness is overlooked by a castle built in the 19th century that now houses law courts and other offices. After World War II light industry was established; today the town's products include Scotch whisky and woolen textiles.
See also: Scotland.

Invertebrate, animal without a backbone. Invertebrates are a miscellaneous collection of groups from single-celled protozoa to highly specialized insects and spiders, although the term usually refers to multicellular organisms. Apart from the universal lack of an internal backbone of vertebrae, many of these groups have little in common.

Investment, in economics, productive employment of resources (capital) or the transformation of savings into active wealth (capital formation); more commonly, use of funds to obtain dividends, for example, from corporate stock or government bonds.
Investment, savings, and the economy. Modern industry's large demands for capital funds are met in large measure by employing the savings of innumerable individuals, scattered over vast areas. The complex structure of available savings and planned investment is achieved through an elaborate system of institutions and intermediaries, including stock markets, investment banks, industrial finance corporations, and commercial banks. Thanks to the work of the economist J.M. Keynes, it is now understood that the relation between investment and saving is a fundamental determinant of the level of national income. Investment is now one of the prime areas of concern for governments seeking to influence or control the progress

I

The French-Romanian dramatist Eugène Ionesco (1912-94).

of their economies. Many economists see capital formation (investment) as being one of the major problems faced by underdeveloped countries seeking to industrialize. U.S. economist W.W. Rostow has suggested that if a nation can reach and maintain a minimum investment rate of 10% of its national product, it will be launched into sustained economic growth.
Foreign investment. Foreign investment can take 2 forms: portfolio investment, which is simply the purchase of the stock of foreign corporations, and direct investment, the establishment or expansion of a corporation in a foreign country, where the corporation is under the investor's control.
See also: Economics.

Io, in Greek mythology, princess of Argos and mistress of the god Zeus. One myth maintains that Zeus changed Io into a cow in order to disguise her from his jealous wife, Hera. Another myth holds that Hera herself transformed Io into a heifer. Io was eventually driven to Egypt, and she has been identified with the Egyptian Isis.
See also: Mythology.

Iodine, a chemical element, symbol I; for physical constants see Periodic Table. Iodine was discovered 1811 by Bernard Courtois. It occurs as iodides in sea water, in brines, and in brackish waters from oil wells. It is obtained commercially from *caliche*, Chilean nitrate-bearing earth and from seaweed ash. Iodine is prepared by displacement of an iodine compound with chlorine. It is a shiny, bluish-black solid, which volatilizes at ordinary temperatures into an irritating, blue-violet gas. Iodine is the least reactive of the halogens. Lack of iodine in humans is the cause of goiter. Radioactive iodine has been used in treating the thyroid gland. Iodine and its compounds are used in organic chemistry, medicine, and photography.

Ion, atom or group of atoms that has become electrically charged by gain or loss of negatively charged electrons. In general, ions formed from metals are positive (cations), those from nonmetals negative (anions). Crystals of ionic compounds consist of negative and positive ions arranged alternately in the lattice and held together by electrical attraction. Many compounds undergo ionic dissociation in solution. Ions may be formed in gases by radiation or electrical discharge, and occur in the ionosphere. At very high temperatures gases form plasma, consisting of ions and free electrons.
See also: Atom; Electron.

The ionosphere, a region of the earth's atmosphere at an altitude of about 50 mi (80 km) to 248 mi (400 km), is composed of different layers of ions and electrons. Long-distance radio transmission on earth depends on them. Very short, or VHF radio waves pass through all the layers into outer space; successively longer waves are reflected to earth by different, lower layers. Because ionization of each layer results from the sun's radiation, the reflection characteristics of the layers vary with the time of day or night.

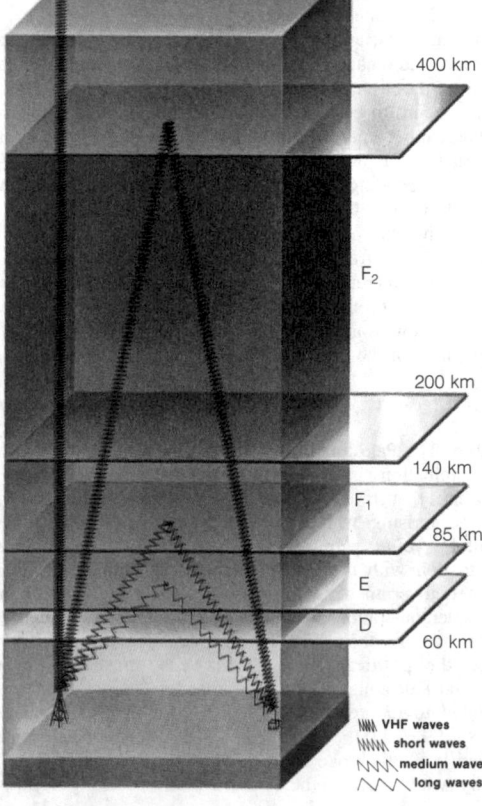

400 km

F_2

200 km

140 km

F_1

85 km

E

D

60 km

⋀⋀⋀ **VHF waves**
⋀⋀⋀⋀ **short waves**
⋀⋀⋀ **medium waves**
⋀⋀ **long waves**

Ionesco, Eugène (1912-1994), Romanian-born French playwright, a leading figure in the so-called theater of the absurd. Among his best-known works are *The Bald Soprano* (1950), *Rhinoceros* (1959), and *Exit the King* (1962).

Ionian Islands, group of islands off the southwest mainland of Greece, chief of which are Cephalonia, Cerigo, Corfu, Ithaca, Leukas, Paxos, and Zante. A Byzantine province in the 10th century, the islands passed through periods of Venetian, French, Russian, and British control before becoming part of Greece in 1864. Exports include wine, cotton, olives, and fish.
See also: Mediterranean Sea.

Ionians, ancient Greek people who colonized the west coast of Asia Minor that became known as Ionia (now in Turkey). They are said to have been driven from the mainland by invading Dorians. The Ionians made a major contribution to classical Greek poetry and philosophy.
See also: Greece, Ancient.

Ionian Sea, arm of the Mediterranean Sea, between southeast Italy and western Greece. It is connected to the Adriatic by the Strait of Otranto and to the Tyrrhenian Sea by the Strait of Messina.

Ionization detector *See:* Smoke detector.

Ion microscope, a magnifying instrument capable of magnifying up to 2 million times and with enough clarity to make individual atoms visible. Invented by the German physicist Erwin W. Muller, the ion microscope was used in 1951 to take the first picture of the arrangement of atoms on a metal's surface. The microscope works on the principle of electrical attraction and repulsion. Scientists use it, among other purposes, to study the physics and chemistry of surfaces and impurities in metals.
See also: Microscope.

Ionosphere, layer of the atmosphere extending from roughly 50 mi (80 km) to 250 or 300 mi (400 or 480 km) above the earth. It is composed of ions (atoms or molecules carrying an electric charge). The atmosphere is thin at that point, and radiation from the sun is able to ionize most of the particles of gas that are present. While the ionosphere is a permanent phenomenon, its structure varies according to season, latitude, and solar activity. The ionosphere is important in radio transmission. Longer-wave signals entering it from below are reflected back toward the earth, making it possible to receive such transmissions over long distances. Shorter waves, such as TV and FM waves, are not reflected by the ionosphere. The aurora borealis (northern lights) takes place in the ionosphere.
See also: Atmosphere.

Iowa (Hawkeye State; pop. 3,000,000), midwestern state in the north-central United States; bordered by Minnesota, Wisconsin and Illinois, Missouri, and Nebraska and South Dakota.
Great glaciers covered Iowa during the Ice Age, leveling hills and filling valleys with

rich soil. Northeast Iowa escaped most of the glaciers, and vertical cliffs rise as high as 400 ft from the river banks. All of Iowa's rivers drain into this great river system. Iowa's soil is probably the richest in the nation, and about one-fourth of all the finest U.S. agricultural land is found in Iowa. The state has a continental climate, marked by cold winters and hot summers. Principal cities are Des Moines, Cedar Rapids, and Davenport.

Iowa is a leading agricultural state. Corn is Iowa's leading crop; Iowa produces about one-fifth of all corn grown in the United States. Other major crops are soybeans, oats, and hay. Iowa raises more hogs than any other state, and ranks high in beef cattle, dairy cattle, and milk production. In manufacturing, food processing is Iowa's leading industry. Machinery production is second in importance. Iowa's chief mining product is limestone.

In prehistoric times, the area was home to Native Americans called the Mound Builders. When French explorers visited the region in 1673, it was home to Plains and Woodland tribes. The territory west of the Mississippi was ceded to Spain (1762-1800), but in 1803 France sold it to the United States under the Louisiana Purchase.

Iphigenia, in Greek mythology, daughter of Clytemnestra and Agamemnon and sister of Orestes. Iphigenia comes to a different fate in each of two versions of her role during the Trojan War. In one, she dies when her father Agamemnon sacrifices her to the goddess Artemis in exchange for Artemis favoring his fleet on its journey to Troy. In another version of the myth, Iphigenia does not die during the sacrifice, but is spared by Artemis and later becomes a priestess at Taurus. As this version goes, Iphigenia saves her brother, and the two flee to Greece.
See also: Mythology; Trojan War.

Ipoh (pop. 529,000), city in Malaysia, capital of the federal state Perak. Center of trade and transport for the tin mines, lime stone quarries, and rubber plantations in the area. It was founded in 1890 by the British, who recruited many laborers in China to work in the mines.

Iqbal, Sir Muhammad (1873-1938), Indian Muslim poet, philosopher, and politician. He was president of the Muslim League in 1930 and is considered one of the spiritual founders of Pakistan.
See also: Muslims.

IRA *See:* Irish Republican Army.

Iran

Capital:	Teheran
Area:	636,372 sq mi
	(1,648,196 sq km)
Population:	66,623,000
Language:	Farsi (Persian)
Government:	Islamic presidential republic
Independent:	1979 (republic)
Head of gov.:	President
Per capita:	less than US$ 6,400
Monetary unit:	1 Iranian rial = 100 dinars

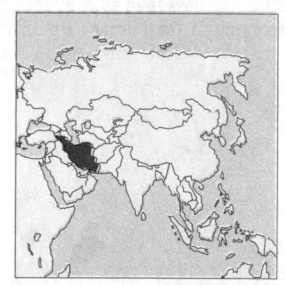

Iran, officially the Islamic Republic of Iran, country in southwest Asia, bordered by Turkmenistan, Azerbaijan, Armenia and the Caspian Sea in the north, Afghanistan and Pakistan in the east, Turkey and Iraq in the west, and the Persian Gulf and the Gulf of Oman in the south.

Land and climate. Most of the country is a high plateau lying between the Elburz and Zagros mountain ranges. An interior desert contains salt wastes. The climate is marked by hot summers and cold winters. About 11 percent of the land is forested. The country is also subject to numerous severe earthquakes, for example in 1990 which killed 40,000.

People. Persians comprise the largest ethnic group in Iran (more than 60% of the total). Other groups include Kurds, Azerbaijanis, Tatars, and Arabs. The official language is Persian (Farsi), an Indo-European language written in the Arabic script. The state religion is Islam. About 95% of the population are Muslims, the majority of them Shi'tes.

Economy. Iran is one of the world's major oil producers, and oil exports provide most of the country's foreign exchange, but nearly one-fourths of the work force is employed in agriculture and forestry. Natural resources other than oil include natural gas, coal, manganese, salt, and copper. Other manufacturing includes textiles, sugar refining, food processing, machine tools, and traditional handicrafts (most notably carpets).

History. Iran is an ancient country. The earliest village settlements of the Iranian plateau date back to c.4000 B.C., and by c.550 B.C. the Persian empire, founded by Cyrus the Great and centered in what is now Iran, was one of the world's major civilizations. In 331 B.C. the empire was overthrown by the Greeks under Alexander the Great, and later, c.250 B.C., Persia was invaded and occupied by armies from the kingdom of Parthia. In 224 A.D. the Persians regained control of their land under Ardashir, who founded the Sassanid dynasty, a state that lasted for about 400 years. In 641 the Sassanids fell to the Arab invasions, and the religion of Islam was introduced. Iran was invaded by the Turks (10th century), and by the forces of Genghis Khan (13th century) and Tammerlane (14th century). Order was restored by the Safavid dynasty (1501-1736). In the 18th century a decline began, leading to increased influence by European powers in Iran, although the country was never formally colonized. The discovery of oil in the early 1900s sharpened European interest, and the country was divided into British and Russian spheres of influence from 1907 until after World War I. In 1921, an army officer named Reza Khan seized power in a coup, and in 1925, as Reza Shah Pahlevi, he established the Pahlevi dynasty. In 1941 he abdicated in favor of his son, Mohammad Reza Shah Pahlevi, who became the new shah (king).
In the early 1950s the shah's power was

I

The Bachtiyares are one of the largest nomadic tribes in Iran. Many of them now live in permanent villages in their traditional region, the western part of the Zagros Mountains.

challenged by a new prime minister, Muhammad Mossadegh, who nationalized the oil industry. The shah fled, but recovered his throne in 1953, with support of Iranian military officers and the U.S. Central Intelligence Agency (CIA). The shah's regime became increasingly repressive, and popular support for it evaporated almost completely. In 1979 massive street demonstrations, though violently repressed, forced the shah to leave the country.

The Ayatollah Ruhollah Khomeini, a revered Islamic leader living in exile, returned to head the newly established Islamic Republic, a highly repressive regime based on the power of the mullahs, Muslim religious leaders who ultimately determine the way the country is run. In retaliation for U.S. support of the shah and an attempt to force the return of the shah to Iran, Iranians captured the U.S. embassy in Teheran, holding embassy workers hostage (1979). The shah died in exile (1980) and the hostages were eventually released (1981). The crisis was a major factor in Ronald Reagan's defeat of President Jimmy Carter in the 1980 election. Meanwhile, in Sept. 1980, Iraq invaded Iran, triggering an 8-year war that inflicted massive damage and high casualties on both countries. Khomeini died in 1989, and Ali Khamenei succeeded him as faqih, or guardian of the faith, the supreme religious leader and Rafsanjani became president. In 1997 the latter was succeeded by Mohammad Khatami, who tried to liberalize the economy. In 1998 and 1999 the persistent power struggle between Khatami and the conservatives resulted in a series of murders and disappearances. Khatami's supporters won the 2000 parliamentary elections, and he was re-elected President the following year. The U.S. President Bush called Iran part of the 'axis of evil', and warned against the supply of long-distance missiles by Iran and the construction of a nuclear reactor with Russia.

Iran-Contra affair, secret U.S. government effort in 1986 by the Reagan administration to gain the release of U.S. hostages in the Middle East by selling weapons and munitions to the Iranian government. The money raised from the sale was to be an illegal means of supporting the anti-government rebels (Contras) in Nicaragua. National Security Council members Admiral John Poindexter and Lt. Colonel Oliver North were implicated in the scandal by a Congressional committee in 1988 and were convicted on criminal charges in 1989 and 1990 trials, but North's convictions were set aside by the courts in 1990.
See also: North, Oliver Laurence.

Iran-Iraq War, war between Iran and Iraq (1980-1988). Iraq wanted to profit from the revolutionary turmoil in Iran and launched an invasion in order to gain complete control over the Shatt al-Arab, the waterway that flows from the merging Euphrates and Tigris to the Persian Gulf and which grants the Iraqi port of Basra access to the open sea. Iran managed to bring the invasion, which was initially successful, to a halt. In 1982 Iran had recaptured all of the land it had lost and occupied Iraqi border regions. Both

armies kept each other in balance and each attempted to destroy the other's oil industry, which led to attacks on neutral ships in the Persian Gulf, as a result of which the war threatened to become an international affair. The battle was very bloody, among other things due to the deployment of chemical weapons. Hundreds of thousands of people were killed and heavy bombings back and forth resulted in irreparable damage. The war ended in 1988 when the United Nations drew up a cease-fire, followed by peace negotiations in Geneva. After Iraq invaded Kuwait in August of 1990, the Iraqi government, which was internationally isolated, made major concessions to Iran.

Iraq

Capital:	Baghdad
Area:	169,235 sq mi
	(438,317 sq km)
Population:	24,000,000
Language:	Arabic
Government:	Presidential republic
Independent:	1932
Head of gov.:	President
Per capita:	less than US$ 2,500
Monetary unit:	1 Iraqi dinar = 20 dirham
	= 1,000 fils

Iraq, country in southwest Asia, bordered by Turkey in the north, Iran in the east, Kuwait and Saudi Arabia in the south, and Jordan and Syria in the west. Large cities are Baghdad, Basra and Mosul.
Land. Iraq is mountainous in the northeast, but much of the country is composed of low-lying grasslands between the Tigris and the Euphrates rivers. The lower plain includes the fertile delta where the 2 rivers meet, forming the Shatt al-Arab waterway, which flows into the Persian Gulf. The southwestern part of the country is desert.
People. Arabs comprise about 80% of the Iraqi population. Most of them are Shiite Muslims. The major non-Arab minority is the Kurds, about 20% of the population, who are mostly Sunni Muslims. The Kurds live mainly in the northern part of the country. They speak their own language, Kurdish. The official language of Iraq is Arabic.
Economy. Oil production, begun in 1928, dominates the Iraqi economy. The oil industry was nationalized in the early 1970s, and

A noria (a traditional water wheel), bringing up water from the Euphrates, which will be poured into irrigation ditches.

the income earned from oil was used to finance extensive efforts at industrialization. Agricultural products include dates, cotton, and grain.
History. Mesopotamia, the territory between the Tigris and Euphrates rivers, was the site of one of the world's first civilizations, dating back to c.3500 B.C. Sumeria, Assyria, and Babylonia were 3 of the ancient states of this region. In 539 B.C. it became part of the Persian empire, in turn conquered by the Greeks (under Alexander the Great) in 331 B.C. Subsequently the region was incorporated into the Roman, and later the Byzantine, empire. In 637 the Arabs swept into Mesopotamia, bringing the Arabic language and the religion of Islam with them. About a century and a half later, Baghdad became the capital of the Abbasid caliphate. As such, it was the center of the Arab world during its golden age (9th century). In 1258, Mongols from central Asia invaded Mesopotamia and sacked Baghdad. The country remained weak and impoverished for a long period. In 1534 Iraq was taken over by the Ottoman Empire, remaining under Turkish rule until the defeat of the Ottomans in World War I. In 1920 Iraq was made a British mandate by the League of Nations. A kingdom was established in 1921, under British control. In 1932 the League of Nations mandate was officially terminated, winning formal independence, though the British retained great influence. In 1958 the monarchy was overthrown in a military coup led by General Abdul Karim Qassim, a nationalist officer. In 1963 Qassim was overthrown by officers of the Baath Party. The Baathist regime established a repressive government ideologically based on pan-Arab nationalism and supported by an enormous military and police apparatus. The Baath Party took control of virtually all aspects of Iraqi society. The architect of that program was Saddam Hussein, who was the

power behind the scenes from 1968 onward and officially became president in 1979. The Saddam Hussein regime was marked by wars against the Kurdish minority in the north, the 8-year war against Iran, and the Persian Gulf War of 1991. After the Gulf War Iraq severely suffered under the UN embargo, a result of the country's refusal to allow the UN weapon inspections to be carried out properly. In 1998, Iraq repeatedly obstructed UN inspections. As a result, the United States and Great Britain carried out operation Desert Fox, which consisted of heavy bombing of the no-fly zones in the north and in the south. These zones were established to protect the Kurds and the Shiite Muslims. After the attacks on the Twin Towers in New York, U.S. pressure on Iraq increased. After a new UN resolution, Iraq allowed weapons inspectors, who had to report the possible presence of mass destruction weapons, to return in 2002. Saying the "danger is clear" that the Iraqi regime would provide terrorists with biological, chemical or nuclear weapons, on March 17th 2003, President Bush gave Saddam Hussein and his sons 48 hours to leave Iraq or face military action.
See also: Persian Gulf War.

Ireland

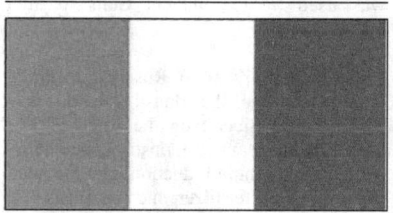

Capital:	Dublin
Area:	27,137 sq mi (70,283 sq km)
Population:	38836,000
Language:	Irish, English
Government:	Republic
Independent:	1922
Head of gov.:	Prime minister
Per capita:	US$ 27,300
Monetary unit:	1 Irish pound = 100 pence

Ireland (Gaelic: *Eire*), officially the Republic of Ireland, independent country in northwestern Europe, occupying five-sixths of the island of Ireland. The country is bounded on the west and south by the Atlantic Ocean and separated from Great Britain by the Irish Sea. A land boundary separates it from Northern Ireland (Ulster). Ireland is sometimes called *Erin*.
Land and climate. Ireland can be likened to a saucer, with a flat, central limestone plain, averaging 300 ft (90 m) above sea level, rimmed with low mountains along the coasts. On the eastern coast, north of Dublin, the plain stretches to the sea, and the eastern and southern coasts are generally regular. In contrast, the rugged Atlantic coast is broken by countless rocky inlets and islands, including Achill Island and the Aran Islands. The almost treeless central plain is studded with low ridges and innumerable lakes, around which are vast areas of peat bogs. The plain is drained into the Atlantic by the 250-mi (400-km) Shannon River, into the Irish Sea by the Boyne and Blackwater rivers, and into Dublin Bay by the Liffey. The largest lakes are the Ree and Derg on the Shannon, and the Mask, Corrib, and Conn in the northwest, but the most famous are the 3 Lakes of Killarney, in County Kerry. The chief mountain ranges are the Wicklow on the eastern coast south of Dublin, and the mountains of Kerry in the southwest. Ireland's climate is extremely moist. Strong southwest winds from the Atlantic bring heavy rainfall. The currents of the Gulf Stream warm the southwestern portion of the island, and temperatures generally vary only from an average of 40°F (4.4°C) in January to 60°F (15.5°C) in July. This damp, temperate climate produces the bright green grass of the 'Emerald Isle' and favors the dairy industry and livestock raising. It also supports the extensive marshlands and peat bogs. Heather and small shrubs cover the higher moorlands of the west. Many varieties of native grasses remain perpetually green. Fauna include a variety of birds and small mammals (hedgehogs, badgers, and foxes). Fishing is the chief occupation of the inhabitants of the western coastal villages and islands, where herring and mackerel are abundant.
People. The Mediterranean people who first reached Ireland c.6000 B.C. were assimilated by Celtic tribes that appeared in the 4th century B.C. Lesser immigrations of Scandinavians, Normans, and English were absorbed. About 20% of the population lives in Dublin and surrounding areas. Education is compulsory between ages 6 and 14.
Economy. The economy is based mainly on small mixed farms rearing cattle or engaged in dairying (especially in the south), with barley, wheat, oats, potatoes, turnips, and sugar beets as the chief arable crops. Ireland is relatively poor in minerals, but some coal is mined, along with recently discovered deposits of lead, zinc, copper, and silver. Peat from the bogs is a valuable fuel, used for home heating and electricity generation. Industries include food-processing, distilling, tobacco products, textiles, clothing, and engineering.
History. In the 4th century B.C. the Gaels evolved a Celtic civilization that in its full flowering, after St. Patrick introduced Christianity in the 5th century, produced superb works of art and sent religious and cultural missionaries to the rest of Europe. It was severely damaged by the Vikings in the 9th and 10th centuries. In 1166 the Anglo-Normans invaded Ireland, and thereafter the English tried continually to assert their authority over the native Irish and the settlers, who quickly became assimilated. The Act of Union (1801) ended parliamentary independence from England; nevertheless, despite the potato famine and Fenian violence, a measure of independence by constitutional means was slowly attained through agitation for Catholic Emancipation and the emergence of leaders like Daniel O'Connell and C.S. Parnell. One result was the cultural Celtic Renaissance of the 1890s. The inability of British governments to implement Home Rule led to the bitter Easter Rebellion (1916), and the armed struggle after World War I resulted in Britain's grant of dominion status to the Irish Free State (1921), but the civil war was continued on a terrorist basis by the Irish Republican Army (IRA) until 1923. Eamon de Valera, in power from 1932, broke with the British Crown and renamed the country Eire (1937). In 1949, as the Republic of Ireland, it left the British Commonwealth. After Ireland had joined the European Community (1973), the country experienced a fast economic growth. In a referendum in 1973, a provision of the constitution that made Roman Catholicism the official religion was repealed. In 1990 Mary Robinson was elected president; the first woman in Irish history to hold that office. A 1995 referendum overturned the country's constitutional ban on divorce. As part of the Anglo-Irish Agreement reached with Britain in 1985, Ireland participated in discussions over the future of Northern Ireland. In the mid-1990's Republican and Unionist groups from the North joined the negotiations after announcing cessation of their terrorist campaigns. In 1998 the parties signed an agreement establishing the Northern Ireland Assembly and ending direct rule from London. Irish voters rejected the Nice Treaty in 2001 (extension of the EU with East-European countries), but endorsed it in 2002. That same year, the euro replaced the Irish pound.

Irenaeus, Saint (A.D. 130?-202?), important theologian and leader during the 2nd century A.D. Born in Asia Minor, Irenaeus is thought to have served as a missionary to southern Gaul and as conciliator among the churches of Asia Minor that had been upset by heresy. A strong opponent of Gnosticism, a spiritual movement that took up pagan, Jewish, and Christian forms, Irenaeus attacked the movement in his preeminent work, *Against Heresies*. Irenaeus upheld the validity of the Old Testament, as well as of several writings that were destined to become part of the New Testament. He became the Bishop of Lugdunum, which is now Lyon, France, in about A.D. 177.

Irian Jaya (pop. 2 million), Indonesian province, part of the island New Guinea, west of 141° eastern longitude; 162,997 sq mi (422,000 sq km). Capital: Jayapura (formerly Hollandia, Sukarnopura; pop. 150,000). Economically speaking it is poorly developed: the industries are cottage industry (weaving, carpentry, and ironmongery), fishing and agriculture (including sago, corn, and rice). Three quarters of the island is covered in forest, mostly jungle. There is a large amount of rainfall, 216 in (5,500 mm) annually. The deposits of minerals (copper, petroleum, natural gas, gold, and uranium) have hardly been mined. Petroleum is exported. 80% of the population speaks a Papua or Melane-sian language; there are Chinese and Dutch minorities as well as the mainly Javanese population.

I

I

The Portuguese were the first Europeans to arrive, in 1511. The Dutch claimed the island in 1828 and annexed it in 1848. It was handed over to the UN by the Dutch in 1962, under great pressure from the Americans, and the UN handed over the government to Indonesia in 1963. In 1969, it became a part of Indonesia. The Indonesian government is carrying out a transmigration policy, so that the Javanese can settle on Irian Jaya. The Papua population feels that its culture is being contaminated. The guerilla movement, Organisasi Papua Merdeka (OPM), is resisting this development. The province was called Dutch New Guinea until 1963 and then Irian Barat (West Irian) until 1973. An estimate of thousands of people died in 1997 and 1998 due to continuing drought and food shortages caused by the drought. The drought was caused by the climatic phenomenon El Niño.

Iridium, a chemical element, symbol Ir; for physical constants see Periodic Table. Iridium was discovered by Smithson Tennant in 1803. It occurs in the presence of platinum and other metals in alluvial deposits. It is obtained as a byproduct of nickel smelting. Iridium is a silvery-white, hard, brittle, unreactive, metal. It is the most corrosion-resistant metal known. The metal is used in high-melting, hard, and unreactive alloys. Iridium and its compounds are used in crucibles, pen nibs, electrical contacts, and organic catalysts.

Iris, any of a genus (*Iris*) of perennial herbaceous plants with intricate and colorful flowers, found in temperate parts of Europe, Asia, Africa, and North America. The iris is a member of the family Iridaceae, which includes the crocus, freesia, and gladiolus. Irises grow from rhizomes (swollen underground stems) or from bulbs. Many varieties have been cultivated for their 3-part flowers, on which the *fleur-de-lis* (French: 'flower of the lily') of heraldry was based. The dried rhizome of certain irises is called *orrisroot*.

Iris, colored circular part of the eye made of muscle and fiber and surrounding the black pupil. Responsible for regulating the amount of light entering the eye, it separates the front and back chambers of the eyeballs and rests against the front of the crystalline lens. Its color is determined by the location of pigment bodies known as melanophores: if these are at the back of the iris, it appears blue or gray; if in the middle, it appears brown.

Irish *See:* Gaelic.

Irish literature, composite of folk tales, lyric and narrative poetry, novels, short stories and drama from ancient to present-day Ireland. Irish literature is notable for having been written in both Gaelic and English. During its Golden Age (c. 700-1,000), Gaelic lyric poetry and myths flourished. The Irish continued to write good poetry in Gaelic through the mid-1800's. During the 1800's a group of Irish writers, led by playwrights William Butler Yeats and Lady Gregory, created a singularly Irish literature

in English, and thereby an Irish literary revival. James Joyce, the author of the revolutionary *Ulysses* (1922), was a key figure in the development of modern Irish literature. Among other important modern authors are the playwright George Bernard Shaw and the fiction writer Frank O'Connor.

Irish moss, or carrageen (*Chondrus crispus* or *Gigartina mamillosa*), small red seaweed. It contains a large amount of gelatin and is used in jellies and puddings and as an ingredient in shampoos, cosmetics, and shoe polishes. Irish moss is harvested in Europe and Japan, and in Massachusetts.

Irish Republican Army (IRA), Irish nationalist organization opposed to British rule and committed to the unification of Northern Ireland and the Republic of Ireland. The IRA evolved from militant remnants of the Irish Volunteers, who planned and fought in the Easter Rebellion (1916). Refusing to accept the separation of Northern Ireland, it became a secret terrorist organization, connected with the Sinn Fein party. Loss of popular support because of its violence and pro-German activities in World War II, and strong repressive action by the government, reduced its role until the 1960s. In 1969 the IRA split into the antiterrorist 'officials' and the terrorist 'provisionals'. The provisionals then launched a campaign of bombings and assassinations in Northern Ireland and England, intended to maintain pressure on Great Britain. IRA terrorists were responsible for the murder of Lord Mountbatten in 1979. Imprisoned IRA gunmen resorted to hunger strikes, sometimes fatal, to gain attention for their cause in 1981 and 1985. In the 1980s and 1990s, the IRA did not restrict its terror to Northern Ireland and England. It also committed attacks on British institutions situated on the European mainland. A cease-fire, declared in 1997, made it possible for Sinn Féin, the political branch of the IRA, to take part in the peace talks between Great Britain, Ireland and the Northern Irish parties.
Negotiations resulted in April 1998 in a peace agreement, the Good Friday Agreement, and in 1999 in an independent Northern-Irish government in which Protestants and Catholics shared the power. However, as the IRA did not start decommissioning weapons soon enough, the British government postponed the Northern-Irish government several times in 2000, 2001 and 2002.
See also: Ireland; Sinn Féin; Northern Ireland.

Irish Sea, arm of the Atlantic, separating Ireland from the island of Great Britain. Connected to the Atlantic by the North Channel to the northwest and St. George's Channel to the south, it is about 130 mi (210 km) across.

Irish setter, sporting dog and popular pet. Bred originally in Ireland. The Irish setter has a coat of either solid red or red with white markings. In the U.S. and Canada the red coat is preferred for professional showing. Irish setters are between 25 and 27 in

(64 and 69 cm) high at the shoulder, and usually weigh 60 to 70 lb (27 to 32 kg). The Irish setter was developed in the 18th century as a hunting dog.

Irish terrier, dog that resembles a wire-haired fox terrier. About 18 in (46 cm) high and weighing about 27 lb (12.3 kg), the Irish terrier breed is though to be about 2,000 years old. Once used to bore into the dens of small animals, and to carry messages on battlefields during World War I and World War II, the Irish terrier today is mainly kept as a pet.

Irish water spaniel, dog breed from the early 1800's. Probably created by crossing a poodle and Irish setter, this spaniel has been called the clown of the dog family. A valuable hunting dog both on land and in the water, where it is an excellent duck retriever, the Irish water spaniel is 21 to 24 in (53 to 61 cm) high and weighs from 45 to 65 lb (20 to 29 kg).

Irish wolfhound, hound which is the tallest of all dog breeds. Standing at 32 to 34 in (81 to 86 cm) and weighing between 126 and 145 lbs (57 to 66 kg), the Irish wolfhound has a wiry coat and a gentle temperament. It was used by the ancient Celts to hunt wolves.

Irkutsk (pop. 694,000), Russia, the administrative center of the Irkutsk Oblast. It is in south-central Siberia on the Angara River west of Lake Baykal. Industries include oil refining, aluminum reduction, and the making of plastics, fertilizer, and chemicals. Irkutsk was founded as a Cossack fort in 1652. By the early 1700's it had become a center for trade between Russia and China, and a place of exile to which convicts from European Russia were banished. Development was stimulated by the arrival of the Trans-Siberian Railway in the 1890's and the completion of the Irkutsk dam in 1958.

Iron, a chemical element, symbol Fe; for physical constants see Periodic Table. Iron has been used since prehistoric times. It is the fourth most abundant element on earth. The earth's core is thought to be composed mainly of iron. It is found in nature as the minerals *hematite*, *magnetite*, *limonite*, *siderite*, and *taconite*. It is a major component of some meteorites. Iron is prepared by reduction of its oxides with carbon in a reverberatory furnace. Iron is a silvery-white, soft, malleable, ductile, magnetic, metal. The commercial metal appears in three forms: cast iron, wrought iron, and steel. Iron is used to produce many important alloys, particularly steels. Nickel, chromium (stainless), tungsten, molybdenum, manganese, and aluminum steels being the most widely used. Compounds of iron are used in inks, pigments, mordants, water purification, and medicine. It is essential to plant and animal life. Iron is the most important of all metals.

Iron Age, stage of humankind's material cultural development, following the Stone Age and the Bronze Age, during which iron was generally used for weapons and tools. Though used ornamentally as early as 4000 B.C. in Egypt and Mesopotamia, iron's difficulty of working precluded its general use until efficient techniques were developed in Armenia, 1500 B.C. By 500 B.C. the use of iron was dominant throughout the known world, and by 300 B.C. the Chinese were using cast iron. Some cultures, as those in America and Australia, are said not to have had an iron age.

Iron and Steel, materials essential to all modern industrialized economies. Iron is a common element throughout nature and is even an important component of our blood. This discussion focuses on iron as a useful metal. The highest natural concentrations of iron are found in meteors. A common element in the earth's crust, iron is combined in varying concentrations with oxygen, carbon, sulfur, and silicon. In its raw state it is iron ore. Steel does not occur in nature; it is man-made and requires refined iron for its manufacture. Steel is made by melting, purifying, and blending iron with other metals.

There are several kinds of iron ore; they are graded according to the percentage of iron they contain. The richest ores, hematite and magnetite, consist of about 70% iron. Other ores include limonite, pyrite, siderite, and taconite. Taconite is about 30% iron. When ore is found close to the earth's surface, it is gathered by open-pit mining. If it is necessary to reach an especially rich but deep seam of ore, shaft mining is used, but it is more expensive and more dangerous than open-pit mining. Though vast quantities of iron ore have been mined, including most of the top-grade ores, supplies are still abundant. The former USSR, Brazil, and Australia are major producers of iron ore. In the US, the Mesabi Range in Minnesota is a major source of ore.

Once it has been mined, the ore must be processed to separate the iron. The particular process used will depend upon the purity of the ore. The raw iron is then shaped into pellets; it is this iron that is further refined in furnaces, where it is mixed with various elements and melted to remove oxygen. The most common method for purifying iron is the blast furnace, so called because of the super heated air forced into the furnace through pipes located in its lower section. The blast of hot air melts the iron and burns off impurities. The purified molten iron is then poured into molds, where it hardens into pig iron. Pig iron can then be melted and combined with other elements to yield cast iron or wrought iron, but most pig iron is used to manufacture steel.

Huge furnaces are also used to make steel, but the processes are more varied and sophisticated. There are basically 4 kinds of steel. Carbon steel is the most common, with a carbon content of less than 1%. Stainless steel, with an ad mixture of chromium, is more resistant to corrosion. Tool steel is used to make special tools and is extremely hard. Finally, there is a wide variety of alloy steels whose composition may include aluminum, manganese, titanium, nickel, or vanadium.

Steel is made by further purifying or refining pig iron. The principal task in making steel

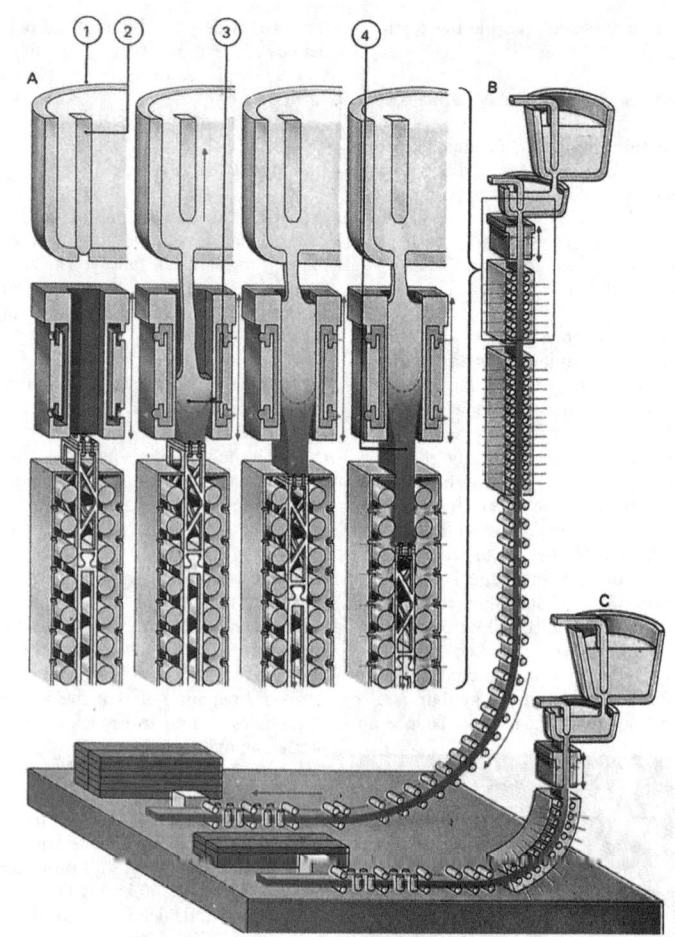

(A) In the continuous casting of steel rods and bars, molten steel from a reservoir (1), which is kept closed with a plug (2), is poured into a water-cooled copper mold (3). The plug at the bottom of the mold is withdrawn, bringing with it the partially solidified bar, which is cooled by water sprays as it is drawn between metal rolls (4). Earlier casting machines (B) required considerable headroom to accommodate their long, straight cooling sections. Newer machines (C) use short, curved cooling sections. After cooling, the bars are cut into whatever lengths are required.

is to reduce the carbon content of the iron to less than 2% and to blend the resultant metal with other metals or alloys to produce a steel of the appropriate hardness, tensile strength, lightness, malleability, or resistance to corrosion. Depending upon the application, the steel used may be fairly commonplace and inexpensive to produce or exotic and manufactured only for special purposes. Steel can be produced in huge open hearths, in electric furnaces, or in furnaces that use an oxygen process in which oxygen is blown into the furnace to purify the metal. Operating an open hearth furnace requires large amounts of fuel oil and causes considerable air pollution. As a result, the open hearth method has been largely replaced by the oxygen process or by cheaper and more efficient electric furnaces.

Molten steel is cast into various forms, one of the more common being ingots. Steel is then shaped or finished by means of rolling, forging, or extruding. Rolling literally presses or squeezes steel into sheets or strips. Forging requires that the steel be reheated and then hammered or pressed into the desired shape. Extrusion is a process whereby hot steel is forced through an opening that shapes it into forms like I-beams or rails.

Rolling, forging, and extruding are done in huge mills equipped with powerful machinery. Other common forms of finished steel include tubing and wire. At this point, the steel may be given its final form or it may be shipped to manufacturers who will use it in their own plants to produce everything from forks and spoons to automobiles, aircraft, machines, or appliances.

Iron, principally from meteorites, was used by our ancestors as early as 4000 B.C., but iron made from ore by means of systematic refinement dates to the Hittites about 1400 B.C. Over the centuries, various improvements were made in furnaces, but it was not until early modern times, about 1500 A.D., that large amounts of iron could be made for commercial purposes.

Small amounts of steel had been made from as early as 300 B.C., but even as late as 1740 steel could be made only in small quantities. The Englishman Henry Bessemer developed a process that revolutionized the making of steel by forcing hot air into the molten iron to purify it. After Bessemer's breakthrough in the mid-19th century, further developments in steel manufacture rapidly followed, giving birth to the steel industry and providing the material and

I

I

tools that have made possible the world as we know it.

Ironclad *See:* Monitor and Merrimack.

Iron Curtain, term for self-imposed isolation of the former USSR and its Eastern European satellite countries, a policy established after World War II. The term was popularized by Sir Winston Churchill in a speech at Fulton, Mo., on Mar. 5, 1946. *See also:* Cold War.

Iron Gate, a narrow gorge of the Danube River on the Romanian-Yugoslav border. It is about two miles (3 km) long. For centuries it was a serious obstacle to navigation. The first major improvement came in the late 1890's with the blasting of a channel (the Sip Canal) through boulder-strewed rapids in the river. In the early 1970's, the Iron Gate dam was completed at the lower end of the gorge. It was built jointly by Romania and Yugoslavia, and is one of Europe's largest producers of hydroelectric power. Its electrical output is evenly divided between the two countries. Locks on either side of the dam have further improved navigation. The dam is also used for flood control. A short distance up-

A dam in the Danube in the Iron Gate, on the Romanian-Serbian border. The water provides energy for the largest hydroelectric power station in Europe (capacity 1,400 mW). The project was carried out in cooperation with Yugoslavia.

stream from the dam is Lepenski Vir, the excavated site of Europe's oldest known settlement, which dates from about 6000 B.C. The gorge is noted for its scenic beauty.

Iron lung, tank covering the entire body except the head, in which air pressure is increased and decreased to provide artificial respiration. First developed in 1928 by Philip Drinker and Louis Shaw at Harvard's School of Public Health in Boston, the iron lung was widely used during the polio epidemics of the 1950s. Other types of respirators are employed today.

Iron ore *See:* Iron and Steel.

Iron pyrite *See:* Pyrite.

Ironwood, or hornbeam, name given to several plants with very hard wood, belonging to the birch family. The American hornbeam (*Carpinus caroliniana*), found in the northeastern United States, is an ironwood.

Irradiation, exposure to radiation such as ultraviolet rays, X rays, and gamma rays, or to beams of atomic particles such as neutrons. The body requires ultraviolet radiation to manufacture vitamin D. Ultraviolet irradiation is used in the food and pharmaceutical industry. Irradiation by X rays is used as a method of destroying cancerous tissue. Irradiation by gamma rays is used to sterilize insects and prevent them from reproducing and continually infesting grain and other foodstuffs. Gamma-ray irradiation may also kill bacteria in food and preserve it for long periods. Irradiation of elements with beams of particles in a nuclear reactor is a method of making radioisotopes. *See also:* Radiation.

Irrawaddy River, main waterway of Burma, formed by the confluence of the Mali and Nmai rivers. It flows south for about 1,350 mi (2,160 km) to empty into the Bay of Bengal. Its delta is one of the world's richest rice-growing areas.

Irrigation, artificial application of water to soil to promote plant growth. Irrigation is vital for agricultural land with inadequate rainfall. The practice dates back at least to the canals and reservoirs of ancient Egypt. There are 3 main irrigation techniques: *surface irrigation*, in which the soil surface is moistened or flooded by water flowing through furrows or tubes; *sprinkler irrigation*, in which water is sprayed on the land from above; and *subirrigation*, in which underground pipes supply water to roots. *See also:* Agriculture.

Irtys, river in West Siberia; 2,287 mi (3,680 km). Its source is in the Altay, it flows northwest, then to the north and into the Obbuzem, a branch of the Kara Sea. It is not easily accessible, being swampy and flowing through forested valleys. It has a shallow fall. The most important subsidiary is the Irtys: together they are 3,362 mi (5,410 km) long, making them the longest rivers in Asia. Fishing. Important route of transport for timber and grain, although it is frozen over from October to April. During the thaw, there are enormous floods.

Irvine, Eddy (1965-), Northern Irish racing driver, who originally drove in the British FF1600, in the British F3 series in 1983 en six years later in the F3000. Irvine reached Formula One in 1990, where he drove for Jordan. In 1994, he was suspended for three races for dangerous driving during the Brazilian Grand Prix.

Irving, John (1942-), U.S. author of the best-sellers *The World According to Garp* (1978) and *The Hotel New Hampshire* (1981). His writing stresses the passionate, comic, and grotesque aspects of life. Other works include *The Cider House Rules* (1985), *A Prayer for Owen Meany* (1989), *A Son of the Circus* (1994), *A Widow for One Year* (1998), and *The Fourth Hand* (2001).

Irving, Sir Henry (John Henry Brodribb; 1838-1905), greatest English actor-manager of his day. At the Lyceum Theater in London, from 1878 to 1902, he staged spectacular Shakespeare productions, often with Ellen Terry as his leading lady.

Irving, Washington (1783-1859), first U.S. writer to achieve international acclaim. Born in New York, he became a writer and publisher; he went to Europe in 1815 on business and remained there until 1832. His most famous stories, 'Rip Van Winkle' and 'The Legend of Sleepy Hollow,' appeared first in *The Sketch Book of Geoffrey Crayon* (1820). None of his later works approached the success of this collection. He served as U.S. minister to Spain 1842-1846, but spent the rest of his life in Tarrytown, N.Y., near the setting of many of his tales.

Isaac, in the Old Testament (Genesis), second of the Hebrew patriarchs. Son of Abraham and Sarah and half-brother of Ishmael, he was spared at the last moment from being sacrificed as proof of his father's faith. He married Rebecca and fathered Esau and Jacob.

Isabella, name of 2 queens of Spain. **Isabella I** (1451-1504) was queen of Castile from 1474 and of Aragon 1479-1481. Her marriage to Ferdinand II unified Christian Spain; royal power was strengthened and the Inquisition reestablished, Isabella supporting its call for the expulsion of Spanish Jews. She financed Columbus's expedition in 1492, and helped direct the conquest of Moorish Granada. **Isabella II** (1830-1904) was queen of Spain (1833-1868). Her succession was disputed by the Carlists, provoking civil war (1833-1839). Her personal rule proved arbitrary and ineffectual. She was deposed in 1868 and abdicated in 1870.

Isaiah, Hebrew prophet of the 8th century B.C. for whom the Old Testament Book of Isaiah was named; probably only the first 36 chapters represent his teachings, the remainder (often known as Deutero- and Trito-Isaiah) being additions by his followers. Isaiah condemned the decadence of the kingdom of Judah, foretelling coming disaster; he warned against trusting in foreign alliances rather than in God, and heralded the Messiah.

ISBN (ISBN), international coding system for publications that have been distributed by official publishers (excepting periodicals, which have their own code, the International Standard Serial Number = ISSN). It was brought into practice during the 1960's and is used by 90 % of publishers. It consists of 10 digits, of which the first two indicate the country (Great Britain and the US 00). Next follows the publisher's number, followed by a number that indicates the publishing capacity and finally the control number, which is calculated from the other numbers but can also be an X.

Iscariot, Judas *See:* Judas Iscariot.

ISDN (Integrated Services Digital Network), digital communication network that makes it possible to use a number of different connections (such as a (visual) telephone, a fax, and data) simultaneously on one terminal. There are two standard terminals on the ISDN: ISDN-2 (two communication channels of 64 kbit/s and a control channel of 16kbit/s) and ISDN-30 (30 communication channels of 64 kbit/s and a control channel of 64kbit/s).
The cable between the terminal and the exchange can be an ordinary telephone cables; fiberglass cable is often used between exchanges.

Ise (pop. 105,000), town on the Japanese island Honshu on the Ise Bay. Tea and oranges are produced in the surrounding area. The most important industrial sectors are the textile, paper, and tobacco industries; also electronic appliances and ship repairs. The town consists of two settlements that have merged, namely, Uji and Yamada.
The town houses a museum, a library, and the *Ise-jingu*, a temple in honor of the sun goddess Amaterasu. This temple is the most important holy place of Shintoism and is visited by thousands of pilgrims each year.

Isherwood, Christopher (1904-1986), English-born novelist and playwright who settled in the United States in 1939. His best-known novels are *Mr. Norris Changes Trains* (1935) and *Goodbye to Berlin* (1939), set in the decaying Germany of the 1930s. These were later adapted into a play, *I Am a Camera* by John Van Druten (1951), and into a film musical, *Cabaret*. Isherwood collaborated with W.H. Auden on 3 plays, the best known being *The Ascent of F.6* (1936).

Ishiguro, Kazuo (1954-), British writer of Japanese origin. He won three important literary prizes with his first three novels. In *A Pale View of Hills* (1982), a Japanese woman in England reflects on her difficult life in the 1950s in Nagasaki, then devastated by the war. *An Artist of the Floating World* (1986, Whitbread Book of the Year Award), depicts the hard fate in postwar Japan of an artist who painted strongly nationalistic propaganda art and who is, therefore no longer acceptable. In *The Remains of the Day* (1989, Booker Prize) he portrays the misplaced, self-sacrificing dedication of a butler in the 1930s, whose 'boss' gets involved in Nazism. Other works are *The Unconsoled* (1995) and *When We Were Orphans* (2000).

Ishmael (or **Ismael**), in the Old Testament, the son of Abraham by Hagar. Since Abraham had no children by his wife,

Sarah, she gave him her Egyptian maid, Hagar, as a concubine (Genesis 16:1-16). Later, Sarah did have a child - Isaac - and had Abraham send Hagar and Ishmael away. In the desert they almost died of thirst, but God caused a well to appear, and His angel foretold that Ishmael would found a nation. The Ishmaelites, his descendants, were a northern Arabian people. The Arabs, who consider him an ancestor, believe that it was Ishmael whom Abraham was ordered to sacrifice, and that Abraham and Ishmael built the Kaaba in Mecca. Hagar's search for water is part of the ritual in a Muslim pilgrimage.

Ishtar *See:* Astarte.

Isis, in ancient Egyptian mythology, nature goddess, sister and wife of Osiris, mother of Horus. The worship of Isis was associated with magic and mystery. The cult of Isis spread throughout the Mediterranean.

Islam (Arabic: 'submitting oneself to God'), one of the major world religions, the youngest of the 3 monotheistic religions developed in the Middle East. Most of the more than 600 million followers of Islam, or Muslims, live in the Arab countries of southwestern Asia, in northern and eastern Africa, Turkey, Iran, Afghanistan, Pakistan, the Malay Peninsula, and Indonesia. There are also large numbers in the Soviet Union, China, India, and the Philippines. Islam was founded by Muhammad, who was born c.570 A.D. in Mecca. In his travels as a merchant he came to know the Christian and Jewish religions. After a period of meditation, during which he said the archangel Gabriel spoke to him, Muhammad began preaching in Mecca. He denounced the worship of idols and proclaimed that there was only one God (*Allah*, in Arabic) and that he was God's messenger to carry the teaching to the pagans. He angered many of the people of Mecca, who forced him to flee to Medina c.622. There, he gathered followers and returned to Mecca in 630 to wage a *jihad* (holy war). Islam was finally accepted by the Meccans, who called Muhammad their prophet. In the 100 years after Muhammad's death (632), Arab armies swept across Asia as far as India and across North Africa and into Spain, building the great Muslim Empire, spreading their religion and culture. The holy book of Islam is the Koran (Qur'an), which sets forth the fundamental beliefs of Islam as revealed by God to Muhammad. These include the 5 basic duties of every Muslim and the rules that govern moral behavior and social life. Muhammad's teachings, called *Sunna*, are collected in the *Hadith* ('traditions'). Together, the Koran and the Sunna provide instructions governing all aspects of the personal and communal life of Muslims. A system of law, the *Shari'a*, has been developed on the basis of the Koran and the Sunna. At various times, the Shari'a has been the law of many Muslim countries. Public worship is held in buildings called mosques. At midday every Friday special services are held. Before entering a mosque, Muslims must ritually wash themselves in the courtyard. The

Interior of the early sixteenth-century mosque of Edirne (Adrianopole, Turkey).

mosques are usually elaborately decorated, but no representations of animal or human figures are permitted because of proscriptions against idolatry. When praying, 5 times during the day, Muslims face in the direction of their holy city, Mecca. Worship is led by a lay religious leader called an *imam*. Traditionally, Muslims are called to prayer by a *muezzin*, who chants from a rooftop or from a *minaret*, a tall tower attached to the mosque. The 2 main sects of Islam, Sunni and Shiah, originated in the 7th century as a result of disputes over the succession of *caliphs* or religious rulers. Sunnites form the majority, while the large Shi'te minority predominates in Iran and has given rise to other smaller sects.

Islamabad (pop. 293,000), city in northeast Pakistan, capital since its construction in the 1960s. This planned city replaced the former capital, Karachi.
See also: Pakistan.

Islamic art, art and architecture that grew out of the Islamic way of life. Because there was no strong tradition of Arab art, it adapted the Byzantine, Sassanian, and Coptic styles of Muslim-dominated lands. Arab influence added a sense of visual rhythm and an interest in astronomy and mathematics. Interpretations of the prophet Muhammad's sayings, however, forbade portrayals of people or animals either in religious art or elsewhere. In general, designs relied on abstract and mathematical forms, as well as the calligraphic rendering of Koranic texts; often every available piece

I

I

of a building is so decorated. Early examples of Islamic architecture are the Kaaba and the Dome of the Rock in Jerusalem. The dominant style of mosque, with a minaret tower, was introduced under the Umayyad dynasty. A characteristic feature of Islamic buildings is the arch, in horseshoe, trefoil, and zigzag forms. The greatest Muslim mausoleum is the Taj Mahal. The Moorish Alhambra in Granada, Spain, is the most famous palace in the Islamic style. In craftwork there is also a distinctive Islamic tradition; as well as its famous rugs and textiles, the Islamic world developed beautiful pottery, including luster-glazed ceramics and metalwork.
See also: Islam.

Islamic fundamentalism (Muslim fundamentalism), term that refers to groups and regimes that have an Islamic political base and strive for an Islamic state that is based on the Islamic legislation (*sharia*).
See also: Islam.

Island, land area entirely surrounded by water, but not so large that it ranks as a continent (such as Australia). The world's largest islands are Greenland (840,000 sq mi/2,175,600 sq km) and New Guinea (342,400 sq mi/886,820 sq km). Of the lesser islands, only Borneo, Madagascar, and Sumatra exceed 160,000 sq mi (414,400 sq km). Some islands were once part of the continents they adjoin (British Isles); others are built up by volcanic activity (Hawaii). Many Pacific islands are the work of coral polyps (marine animals).

Isle of Man *See:* Man, Isle of.

Isle of Wight *See:* Wight, Isle of.

Islets of Langerhans *See:* Pancreas.

Ismael *See:* Ishmael.

Isocrates (436-338 B.C.), Greek orator and pupil of Socrates who founded a celebrated school of rhetoric in Athens. His vision of a Greece united to invade Persia influenced Alexander the Great.

Isolationism, national policy of avoiding entanglement in foreign affairs, a recurrent phenomenon in U.S. history. In 1823 the Monroe Doctrine tried to exclude European powers from the Americas. The United States entered World War I reluctantly, stayed out of the League of Nations it helped create, and entered World War II only when attacked. Thereafter it joined the UN and international defense pacts (NATO, SEATO) and played an active role in international affairs. British policy was essentially isolationist in the period between the world wars.

Isomers, chemical compounds having identical chemical composition and molecular formula, but differing in the arrangement of atoms in their molecules, and having different properties. The 2 chief types are stereoisomers, which have the same structural formula, and structural isomers, which have different structural formulas.

Isoptera, order of insects that live in colonies and have a highly developed social organization. Insects in this category are called termites.

Isotope, atom of a chemical element which have the same number of protons in the nucleus, but a different numbers of neutrons, i.e., having the same atomic number but different mass. Isotopes of an element have identical chemical but varying physical properties. Most elements have several stable isotopes, being found in nature as mixtures. A few elements have natural radioactive isotopes (radioisotopes), which are unstable, and others of these can be made by exposing stable isotopes to radiation in a reactor.
See also: Element.

Isozaki, Arata (1931-), Japanese architect, started at Kenzo Tange, developed into postmodernism, which places form in a central position. In the Museum of Contemporary Art in Los Angeles (1986), he used geometric forms such as pyramids, cubes and a semi-cylinder, referring to the designs of the 18th-century French architect Ledoux. In Barcelona, he built the Palau Sant Jordi (1983-1991), a multi-purpose hall and gymnasium for the Olympics of 1992. The shape of the roof refers to the Montjuich, the mountain on which the building is situated. Characteristic of Isozaki's work is his meticulous use of materials.
See also: Tange, Kenzo.

Israel

Capital:	Jerusalem
Area:	7,992 sq mi (20,700 sq km)
Population:	6,030,000
Language:	Hebrew, Arabic
Government:	Republic
Independent:	1948
Head of gov.:	Prime minister
Per capita:	US$ 20,000
Monetary unit:	1 New shekel = 100 agorot

Israel, republic in southwest Asia, at the eastern end of the Mediterranean Sea.
Land. Israel is 7,992 sq mi (20,700 sq km). On the west is a long, straight coastline on the Mediterranean; to the south, a very short coastline gives it access to the Gulf of Aqaba of the Red Sea through the port of Elath. The 3 geographical regions are the mountainous Galilee region of the north, the western coastal plain, and the Negev desert in the south. To the east is an extensive depression, parts of which are the Huleh Valley, the Sea of Galilee, and the Jordan River. In the south the same geographical fault includes the Dead Sea and runs on to the Gulf of Aqaba, forming the southern border with Jordan. A short corridor extends from the coastal plain through the Judean hills to the city of Jerusalem. The narrow coastal plain (4-20 mi/6.4-32 km in width) is the most fertile part of the country. It is here that Israel's extensive orange groves are found. It also contains Tel Aviv-Jaffa, the country's most populous city. The northern Negev has fertile, wind-deposited soil but little rainfall; much of the southern Negev is dry, barren rock. Israel has seen extensive land reclamation and development undertaken by Jewish settlers in the 20th century. The former Huleh Lake in the north was drained to provide farmland. The Dead Sea, however, has remained much the same. Lands occupied by Israeli forces in 1967 during the Six-Day War included portions of Egypt (the entire Sinai Peninsula up to the banks of the Suez Canal, as well as the Gaza Strip, a mandated territory that had been administered by Egypt but was not formally a part of it), Jordan (the entire sector of that country west of the Jordan River), and Syria (the strategic Golan Heights, east of the Sea of Galilee).
People. The majority of Israel's citizens are Jews, and of these the greatest number are immigrants. The largest minority group (over 15% of the population) is of Arabs, for the most part in self-contained rural communities. Other minority groups include Druses, Circassians, and Samaritans. The official language is Hebrew, but because of the high percentage of immigrants, many Israelis remain more literate in languages other than Hebrew. The second most dominant language is Arabic, and many native-born Israeli Jews speak it. English is also widely spoken, along with French, German, and Yiddish. Elementary schooling is free and compulsory, and there are reduced fees and special grants for promising students in secondary schools. A large minority of pupils attend state-supported religious schools. Arab pupils generally attend their own schools. There are also schools run by Christian communities and missionary groups. Universities and institutions of higher learning include the Hebrew University in Jerusalem, Tel Aviv University, Bar Ilan University in Ramat Gan, the Technion in Haifa, and the Weizmann Institute of Science in Rehovot. The majority of Israel's population is urban, but its rural population is highly important. There are over 200 agrarian settlements known as *kibbutzim*, in which the members share all goods and receive no wages; all meals are eaten together, important decisions are made by a general meeting of all the members, and children are raised in special houses, away from their parents. Other agricultural settlements also practice cooperative or communal living to some degree,

High-rise apartment complexes ring the old city of Jerusalem, which Israel has declared its 'eternal city'.

Solomon (1020-922 B.C.), and then the breakaway state in the north founded by Jeroboam I in the territory of the 10 tribes. In 722 B.C. this was overrun by the Assyrians; the tribes were killed, enslaved, or scattered.

Israelites *See:* Jews.

Istanbul (pop. 8 million), city in northwest Turkey, lying on the Sea of Marmara and divided by the Bosporus (strait). Until 1930 its official name was Constantinople, of which Istanbul was originally a contraction. Built in A.D. 330 on the site of a former Greek town, Byzantium, it reached its cultural height under Justinian I in the 6th century. After years of decay it was taken by the Ottoman Turks in 1453, and was rebuilt as the Turkish capital, which it remained until 1923 when the capital was moved to Ankara. It is still the economic and cultural heart of Turkey, a port, transport hub, and manufacturing center.
See also: Turkey.

Isthmus, narrow strip of land connecting 2 large land masses. Examples are the Isthmus of Panama, linking North and South America, and the Isthmus of Suez, linking Africa and Asia.

Italian, one of the Romance languages, spoken in Italy and in parts of Switzerland, France, and Yugoslavia. It derives from colloquial Latin. The Tuscan dialect established in the late Middle Ages as a literary language by Dante, Petrarch, and Boccaccio became the foundation of modern Italian. Since the Renaissance, words from other Romance languages have been added. Many of the regional dialects of Italy are still spoken.

Italian literature, literature dated to Francis of Assissi's *Canticle of the Sun* (1226), written not in Latin but the vernacular. The love theme was expressed in Dante's *The Divine Comedy* (1321). Petrarch combined Christian living with classical ethics in *Il Canzoniere* (The Book of Songs) in the mid 1300s and Boccaccio's masterpiece, *The Decameron* (1349-1353), depicted characters of his time with humor. Machiavelli's *The Prince* appeared in 1513. Important works of the late Renaissance include Giorgio Vasari's *Lives of the Artists* (1550), Benvenuto Cellini's autobiography (1558-1562), and the pastoral dramas of Torquato Tasso (1544-1595) and Battista Guarini (1536-1612). The baroque period (1600s) gave rise to Marino's *Adonis*, Galileo's scientific prose and Camparella's *The City of the Sun*. The Age of Reason (1700s) was characterized by a less elaborate poetic style. Among the most significant works were the opera libretti (texts) by Pietro Metastasio (1698-1782) and plays of Carlo Goldoni (1707-1793), which drew heavily on the tradition of improvised comic theater called *commedia dell'arte*. Roman-ticism (1800s) celebrated sentiment over reason. A major figure was the poet, novelist, and playwright Alessandro Manzoni (1785-1873). A major movement in Italian literature and theater

such as common ownership of land or cooperative purchasing and marketing.
Economy. Land reclamation and irrigation have nearly tripled the cultivated area since 1955. Major crops include citrus fruit, grains, olives, melons, and grapes. Mineral resources include gypsum, natural gas, oil, and phosphates; potash, magnesium, and bromine come from the Dead Sea. Light industry is developing, and manufactures include chemicals, textiles, and paper. Tourism is a major industry. Because of heavy defense spending and reliance on imported oil, Israel suffers from severe payments deficits and one of the world's highest inflation rates.
History. In 1947 the UN voted to divide Palestine (then under British mandate) into Jewish and Arab states. After the subsequent British withdrawal, Palestine Arabs and Arab troops from neighboring countries immediately tried to eradicate Israel by force, but the Israelis defeated them, capturing almost all of Palestine. Arab refugees, settled in southern Lebanon, the West Bank, and Gaza Strip in UN-administered camps, are a continuing social and political problem. Refugee camps have proved a fruitful recruiting area and cover for Palestinian guerrilla groups. When Egypt nationalized the Suez Canal in 1956 and closed it to Israeli shipping, Israeli troops overran Gaza and Sinai, winning the right of passage from Elath to the Red Sea. In the Six-Day War (1967) Israel acquired large tracts of its neighbors' territories, including the West Bank and East Jerusalem; these it refused to return without a firm peace settlement. It lost some of these in the Yom Kippur War (1973). In 1978 Egypt and Israel reached the so-called Camp David accords, and Israel began returning the Sinai to Egypt. In 1978 and 1981

Israeli troops invaded south Lebanon in retaliation for Palestinian attacks in Israel, and Israeli bombers destroyed an alleged atomic bomb plant in Iraq in 1981. In 1982 Israeli forces invading Lebanon besieged Beirut; in time Palestinian guerrillas left the city and the Israelis partially withdrew from Lebanon. In 1985 Israeli forces left Lebanon except for a small strip of land in the south. Israel's continued occupation of the West Bank and Gaza remained a problem for Arabs and was a factor in making the country a target of Iraqi missiles in the War in the Persian Gulf (1991). In the early 1990s negotiations regarding the occupied territories improved, and the Jericho district on the West Bank and the Gaza Strip attained some form of autonomy in 1994. During the peace proces prime minister Rabin was killed (Nov. 1995). Execution of the Oslo agreements (1993 and 1995) was difficult under Rabin's successor Netan-yahu.
In October 1998 Netanyahu and Arafat reached an interim agreement. At the 1999 elections, Netanyahu was defeated by Ehud Barak. The second Intifada (Palestinian uprising) ended the peace process. At the elections of 2001, Sharon's Likud party defeated Barak's Labor Party. Due to Palestinian suicide attacks and Israeli reactions to these attacks, relations between Israel and the Palestine authorities deteriorated. Sharon wanted to exile Arafat. The expected U.S. attacks on Iraq increased the tension even more. At the beginning of 2003, there was only little hope for enduring peace in Israel.
See also: Palestine; Palestine Liberation Organization; Zionism.

Israel, Kingdom of, Hebrew kingdom, first as united under Saul, David, and

I

of the late 19th century was *verismo*, in which the harsh realities of the lives of the poor were portrayed. The futurism movement, typified by the writings of Filippo Tommaso Marinetti (1876-1944), employed language glorifying the violence of the machine age. Luigi Pirandello (1876-1936), who won the 1934 Nobel Prize for literature, wrote novels but was best known for such ironic and philosophical plays as *Six Characters in Search of an Author* (1921).

The post-World War II neorealists include Alberto Moravia (1907-1990) and Cesare Pavese (1908-1950). The novelist Italo Calvino (1923-1985) and the playwright Dario Fo (1926-) have achieved international fame. In 1975 the poet Eugenio Montale was awarded the Nobel Prize.

Italian Somaliland *See:* Somalia.

Italo-Ethiopian War (1935-1936), Fascist Italy's conquest of Ethiopia, launched from Italian-held Eritrea and Somalia. Refusing to accept the League of Nations proposals for settling border disputes, Benito Mussolini used planes, guns, and poison gas to overwhelm the ill-equipped Ethiopians, and to forge a new empire. Too weak to halt aggression, the League merely voted economic sanctions against Italy, which simply left the League.
See also: Mussolini, Benito.

Italy

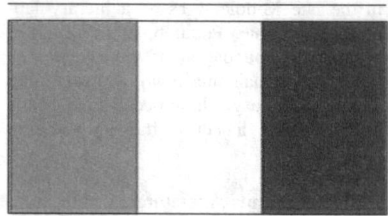

Capital:	Rome
Area:	116,324 sq mi
	(301,277 sq km)
Population:	57,716,000
Language:	Italian
Government:	Republic
Independent:	1946 (republic)
Head of gov.:	Prime minister
Per capita:	US$ 24,300
Monetary unit:	1 Lira = 100 centesimi

Italy, republic in southern Europe, mainly a long, narrow, boot-shaped peninsula that extends into the Mediterranean Sea. It is bounded on the north by France, Switzerland, Austria, and Slovenia; on the west by the Ligurian and Tyrrhenian seas; on the east by the Adriatic Sea; and to the south by the

The city of Palermo is the capital of Sicily, the largest island of the Mediterranean Sea. Such sights as this street vendor are commonly found throughout the city.

Ionian Sea. The islands of Sicily and Sardinia and numerous smaller islands are parts of its territory. Within its borders are 2 separate, sovereign states: the Republic of San Marino and the Vatican City.

Land and climate. A predominantly mountainous country, Italy is divided by a number of natural barriers into distinct regions. In the north is the great curve of the Alps, along which lie Italy's borders with its northern neighbors. In north-central and northeastern Italy are the lakes of Como, Maggiore, and Garda. The Apennine chain runs the length of the peninsula, extending in an easterly direction from Genoa to central Italy and then in a westerly direction into Calabria, the 'toe' of the Italian 'boot.' There are a number of crater lakes in these regions, and the volcanoes of Vesuvius near Naples, Etna in Sicily, and Stromboli in the Lipari Islands are still active. The mountains of Sicily are a continuation of the Apennines, and Sardinia is also mountainous. Italy's single large plain lies in the Po Valley, which crosses the country from west to east just below the Alps. There are narrow coastal plains on either side of the Apennines, and a low, relatively small plateau lies below the Gargano spur. These alluvial plains constitute Italy's most fertile soil. The mountainous areas are largely unproductive. The Po River is Italy's largest and most important river. The Tiber flows through Rome to the Tyrrhenian Sea, and the Arno passes through Florence and Pisa to empty into the Ligurian Sea. Both rivers rise in the Apennines. Most other rivers in Italy are seasonal, and their volume is greatly diminished during the summer. In the Alps, the Po Valley, and the high ranges of the Apennines, winters are cold and summers can be rainy and variable. The rest of the peninsula has a Mediterranean climate: hot, dry summers and mild, rainy winters. Southern Italy and Sicily are especially arid, and irrigation is essential for successful cultivation. Remnants of great forests are found in the Alps, where fir and pine trees grow,

and in the remote areas of the Apennines, where there are stands of chestnut, pine, oak, and beech trees. In central and southern Italy olive groves cover much of the land, while the southern regions also produce cacti, citrus trees, and palm trees. With the exception of bears, chamois, deer, and wolves in some remote mountain regions, Italy has few large mammals. Tuna, anchovies, and sardines are plentiful in offshore waters.

Rome contains imposing ruins of its past glory as capital of the western world and is of commercial and cultural importance. The cities of Milan, Turin, and Genoa in the north form the so-called industrial triangle, Milan leading in finance and commerce, Turin in heavy industry, and Genoa in international shipping. Italy's art cities-Venice, Verona, Bologna, Ravenna, Florence, and Siena-bear witness to the significance of Italian culture. Naples, the south's principal city and an international port, is a center for excursions to nearby Sorrento, the islands of Capri and Ischia, and the ruins of Pompeii and Herculaneum. Palermo, the capital of Sicily, has medieval relics of the Norman occupation.

People. Italy is a densely populated country (on average 192 inh./sq km). The highest concentrations are in the industrial cities of the north, the Po Valley, and the areas around Rome and Naples, more than half of the population being urban. Italian, which is derived from Latin, is the official language and is spoken by most citizens, along with a number of regional dialects. Roman Catholicism is the state religion and is taught in the public schools, but freedom of religion is guaranteed.

Economy. Foreign aid and founder membership in the European Common Market boosted postwar economy before the oil crises of the 1970s damaged it. Increased industrial output (steel, chemicals, automobiles, typewriters, machinery, textiles, and shoes) enriched the north, but a faltering agriculture kept the south poor. The main farm products are grapes, citrus fruits, olives, grains, vegetables, and cattle. Mineral resources are limited, but Italy has hydroelectric power, natural gas, and oil. There are also a few nuclear power stations. Tourism helps the trade balance.

History. The Romans, a Latin people of central Italy, held most of the peninsula by 200 B.C., absorbing the Etruscan civilization in the north and Greek colonies (dating from the 8th century B.C.) in the south. In the 5th-6th centuries A.D., barbarian tribes (Visigoths, Ostrogoths, and Lombards) overran Italy, forming Germanic kingdoms. These kingdoms were disputed by the Byzantine Empire, whose lands in Italy became the core of the Papal States. Italy was to remain divided for over 1,000 years, although nominally part of Charlemagne's empire from 774 and part of the Holy Roman Empire from 962. In the Middle Ages the south came under Norman rule. Powerful rival city-states emerged in the center and north, from the late Middle Ages under the Medici and other dynasties. Italy pioneered the Renaissance, but Spain (from the late 1400s) and Austria (from the early 1700s) controlled much of the land until the nationalistic Risorgimento culminated in unity and independence under King Victor Emmanuel II (1861). Italy gained Eritrea, Italian Somaliland, and Libya in Africa, and fought alongside the Allies in World War I. In 1922 the fascist dictator Benito Mussolini seized power, later conquering Ethiopia and siding with Nazi Germany in World War II. Defeated Italy emerged from the war as a republic shorn of its overseas colonies and firmly allied with the West. Since the beginning of the 1990s, Italy is trying to eliminate corruption and organized crime. Elections in 1994 ended nearly 50 years of Italian governments in which the Christian Democrats ruled or were part of a coalition government. The government formed after elections in 1996 included members of the Party of the Democratic Left (formerly known as the Communist party). It was the first government in nearly 50 years that included members of a leftist party. Silvio Berlusconi was able to form a center-right cabinet with his Forza Italia party in 2001 due to the discordance of the center-left parties. Berlusconi who had governed several months in 1994, was accused of a number of crimes, including corruption. Through legislation he tried to prevent legal prosecution.

Itami, Yuzo (1933-1997), Japanese movie director, who was originally an actor and who also played in a few western movies, such as *Lord Jim* (1965). As a director, he became famous with sharp satire about - for Japanese society - sensitive subjects. He had a large amount of success with his debut *Ososhiki* (1984), about funeral rituals, which was followed by *Tampopo* (1986), about a woman who tries to set up a café that sells noodle soup, which was his international breakthrough. *Mimbo no Onna* (1992), a satire about the 'yakuza', Japanese organized crime, got him into trouble with the underworld: he was attacked by gangsters and knifed. *Shizuka-na seikatsu* (1995) is the film of the novel of the same name by Nobel

Prize winner Kenzaburo Oë. Itami was seen as the most important Japanese film director after Akira Kurasawa.

Ito Hirobumi, Prince (1841-1909), a Japanese statesman who played a prominent role in modernizing Japan. As a young man he visited Europe and the United States, becoming a strong advocate of Westernization. Ito was four times premier of Japan during 1885-1901. He was the main author of the Japanese constitution, based primarily on the Prussian model, that was in force from 1889 to 1945. In 1895 Ito negotiated the treaty ending the Sino-Japanese War. He was made a marquis in 1895 and a prince in 1907. Ito strengthened Japan's control over Korea, adopted a policy of harsh treatment to keep the Koreans subjugated. He was assassinated by a Korean patriot.

Iturbide, Agustín de (1783-1824), Mexican revolutionary and emperor of Mexico (1822-1823). As a royalist officer, he united the revolutionaries with his Plan of Iguala (1821), which proclaimed Mexican independence. Exploiting political divisions, he became emperor of independent Mexico. But opposition to his capricious rule brought abdication, exile, and (on his return) execution.

Ivan, name of 6 Russian rulers. **Ivan I** (c.1304-1340) was grand prince of Moscow 1328-1340. **Ivan II** (1326-1359) was grand prince of Moscow 1353-1359. **Ivan III**, Ivan the Great (1440-1505), was grand duke of Moscow 1462-1505. He paved the way for a unified Russia by annexing land, repelling the Tatars, strengthening central authority over the Church and nobility, and revising the law code. **Ivan IV**, Ivan the Terrible (1530-1584), was grand prince from 1533 and the first tsar of Russia (1547-1584). He annexed Siberia, consolidated control of the Volga River, and established diplomatic and trading relations with Europe. He strengthened the law and administration, but was notoriously cruel. **Ivan V** (1666-1696) was co-tsar (with Peter I) 1682-1690. **Ivan VI** (1740-1764) was tsar 1740-1741.

Ivan V *See:* Peter I, the Great.

Ives, Charles Edward (1874-1954), U.S. composer. Ives was a major 20th-century innovator. His music (mostly pre-1915) incorporated popular songs and hymn tunes, and exploited dissonance, polytonality, and polymetric construction. Ignored by his contemporaries, he influenced later composers. His best known works include *Three Places in New England* (1908-1914) and *Piano Sonata No. 2 (Concord, Mass., 1840-1860)* (1909-1915). His *Symphony No. 3* (1904-1911) won a 1947 Pulitzer Prize.

Ivory, hard white dentine substance making up the tusks of elephants, walruses, and other tusked mammals. Ivory has been greatly prized as a material for carving decorative objects for centuries. The poaching of elephants for their tusks threatens their existence in Africa.

Ivory Coast

Capital:	Yamoussoukro
Area:	124,503 sq mi
	(322,462 sq km)
Population:	16,805,000
Language:	French
Government:	Presidential republic
Independent:	1960
Head of gov.:	Prime minister
Per capita:	US$ 1,550
Monetary unit:	1 CFA franc = 100 centimes

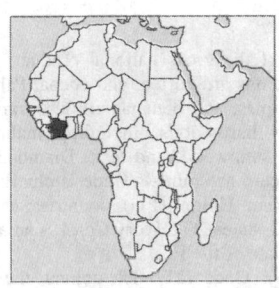

Ivory Coast, republic in West Africa.

Land and climate. The Ivory Coast occupies about 124,503 sq mi (322,462 sq km) on the northern coast of the Gulf of Guinea and is bordered on the east by Ghana, on the west by Liberia and Guinea, and on the north by Mali and Burkina Faso. Behind the sand spits, navigable lagoons, and surf beaches of the 315-mi (507-km) coastline, a dense rain forest extends northward over more than a third of the country. Beyond the forest the ground rises to a plateau, with grass and woodland savannas and isolated granitic masses. The northwest is mountainous. The Sassandra, Bandama, Comoé, Cavally, and other rivers flow southward to the Gulf of Guinea, but only short distances are navigable owing to the many rapids. The climate is hot. The rainy season lengthens and the amount of rain increases the farther one goes south. The extreme south has 2 distinct rainy seasons.

People. The population contains many ethnic and tribal groups, the most important being the Baoulé, Agnis-Ashantis, Kroumen, Mandé, Dan-Gouro, and Koua. Nearly a million Africans from Burkina Faso, Guinea, and Mali live in the Ivory Coast, and there are some 35,000 French, Lebanese, and others. Around 40% of the population lives in the towns, the largest of which is Abidjan, chief port, and university center. Over 60% of the population is animist; 25% (mainly in the north) is Muslim, and nearly 13% is Christian. Some 60 tribal languages are spoken, but French is used officially and in commerce and education. The republic devotes more than 25% of its annual budget to education.

Economy. The Ivory Coast was one of the most prosperous countries in West Africa. Farming, forestry, and fisheries provide

I

Pheasant-tailed jaçana (*Hydrophasianus chirurgus*). India to Java, Malaya and the Philippines. Height: approximately 10 in (25 cm).

most of the gross national product. Major cash crops are coffee, and cocoa. Palm oil, pineapples, and bananas are also exported, as are hardwoods, including mahogany, iroko, satinwood, and teak. Diamonds and petroleum are mined. Trade is chiefly with European Union (EU) countries and the United States. The Ivory Coast is an associated state of the EC.

History. Once a French colony, the Ivory Coast became autonomous within the French Community in 1958, but soon opted for full independence (1960). Close economic, cultural, and defense ties with France were retained. Its attitude has tended to be pro-Western, but so far as East-West relations were concerned its official line was neutrality. From 1960 until 1993 Félix Houphouet-Boigny dominated politics. The matter of his succession caused severe political and social unrest. In 1993 Houphouet-Boigny passed away and was succeeded by Henri Konan Bédié as president. After a Coup d' Etat in 1999, Bédié was toppled and replaced by Laurent Gbagbo as the President. Uprisings occurred between Gbagbo's Christian supporters and the supporters of opposition leader Ouattara, mainly Muslims. UNICEF focused attention on the large number of child soldiers in the country. French soldiers had to evacuate foreigners during the rioting of rebelling soldiers. Rebels captured the northern part of the country.

Ivory palm, or ivory nut palm (Phytelephas macrocarpa), slow-growing palm with a short trunk, native to South America. Plants are male or female. Female flowers form a cluster of seeds that ripen and fall to the ground. Hard and white, the seeds are easy to carve and are used for buttons, chess pieces, and small ornaments.

Ivy, hardy, evergreen plant (genus *Hedera*) of the family Araliaceae. The English ivy (*H. helix*) is a popular house plant, coming in a number of dwarf, climbing, and variegated varieties. Several other plants that have ivylike leaves are also called ivy, for example ground ivy (*Glectoma hederacea*) and Boston or grape ivy (*Parthenocissus tricuspidata*).

Iwo Jima, Japanese island in the western Pacific, scene of a fierce battle in World War II. Largest of the Volcano islands (about 8 sq mi/21 sq km), it was annexed by Japan in 1891 and captured by U.S. marines in Feb.-Mar. 1945 at the cost of over 21,000 U.S. casualties. U.S. administration ended in 1968.
See also: World War II.

Ixtacihuatl, or Iztaccihuatl (Aztec: 'white woman'), dormant volcano in central Mexico, about 35 mi (56 km) southeast of Mexico City. Its 3 snow-covered peaks resemble the head, breasts, and feet of a sleeping woman.

Izetbegovic, Alija (1925-), Bosnian politician, leader of the Party for Democratic Action, a secular nationalistic Bosnian Muslim party. In 1990, he was chosen to become head of state of Bosnia-Hercegovina, which declared itself independent in 1992. He dedicated himself to the preservation of Bosnia as a united state. In 1995, he co-signed the peace treaty in Dayton (U.S.), which was conducted in order to end the bloody war between the Bosnian Muslims, the Bosnian Serbs and the Bosnian Croats. After the elections of 1998, Izetbegovic, on behalf of the Bosnian Muslims, became a member of the Federal Presidium.

Izmir (Greek: Smyrna; pop. 2,1million), port city on the west coast of Turkey, at the head of the Gulf of Izmir, about 45 mi (72 km) from the Aegean Sea. Founded by Ionians in the 11th century B.C., the city came under Roman rule. In the 4th century A.D. it became part of the Byzantine Empire and, in 1424, of the Ottoman Empire. The Greeks occupied the city in 1919. The Treaty of Lausanne (1923) restored Izmir to Turkey, and an exchange of populations was made. The city is rich in antiquities, including the Agora, or ancient marketplace, and remains of aqueducts.
See also: Turkey.

J, tenth letter of the English alphabet. One of the last letters added to the alphabet, *j* is a variant of the letter *i*, from which it became formally distinguished only with the advent of printing. Before that time, *j* was simply an elongated *i*, and the 2 characters were used interchangeably. Thus, in Roman numerals, *j* sometimes replaced *i* to signify 1. It has the sound of *y* in Latin, German, and Scandinavian languages. In Spanish it has the sound of *h*.

Jabalpur (pop. 750,000), India, a city in Madhya Pradesh state. Jabalpur is in central India, on the Narmada River. Cotton mills, machine shops, and factories producing pottery and glassware are here.

Jabbar, Kareem Abdul- *See:* Abdul-Jabbar, Kareem.

Jabiru, any of various large birds of the stork family found from Mexico to Argentina. Jabirus are white with dark blue and red naked skin on the head and neck. Among the largest flying birds in the world, they may reach 55 in (125 cm) in length. They nest in palm trees.

Jaçana, any of several water birds of the jaçana family with long legs and toes that enable it to walk on water lilies and other floating plants. Jaçanas are brightly colored and are found in Africa, southern Asia, Australia, and in the Americas.

Jacaranda, any of various species of flowering tree (genus *Jacaranda*) native to South America and the West Indies and grown widely in Africa, the southern United States, and other warm places. The foliage is made up of fern-like fronds of small leaves; the blue or violet flowers grow in clusters.

Jackal, carnivorous mammal (genus *Canus*) closely related to dogs and wolves. The four species are distributed throughout Africa and South Asia. Though often considered primarily scavengers, jackals will also hunt and kill birds, hares, mice, and insects. Small packs may form temporarily, but they are usually solitary animals.

Jackdaw, small crow (*Carrus monedula*) of Europe, western Asia, and North Africa. It is renowned for its inquisitive and thievish nature and its ability to imitate speech.

Jack Frost, personification of winter, depicted in many children's stories as a rosy-cheeked imp. During the night he paints the world with frost, tracing delicate patterns on window panes and leaving icicles on trees. He probably originated in Scandinavian mythology.

Jack-in-the-pulpit, any of several plants of the arum family (genus *Arisaema*) that flower in spring before the leaves appear. The flower is really an elaborate, colored tubular structure called a spathe. It surrounds a stem, the spadix, on which many small flowers grow. The flowers are fertilized by flies, and by autumn the spathe falls away to reveal a cluster of bright red berries which are poisonous when eaten raw.

Jack rabbit, common name for hares of the genus *Lepus*. All seven species are found in central and western North America. Jackrabbits have large ears and longer hind legs than rabbits. Found in open, comparatively arid plains, they flourish in drought-stricken, overgrazed areas. They move by jumping rather than running.

Jackson, Andrew (1767-1845), 7th president of the United States (1829-1837). Jackson transformed the presidency with his rugged frontier virtues and devotion to 'the common man.' His 2 terms in office coincided with a great period of democratic reforms known as 'Jacksonian Democracy.'
Jackson's service in the War of 1812 made him a national hero. For his toughness, Jackson's men dubbed him 'Old Hickory.' In 1824, he ran for the presidency and won the most votes, but not a majority. The decision went to the House of Representatives, which elected John Quincy Adams. In 1828, Jackson won the presidency; John C. Calhoun became vice president.
To eliminate the closed political-caucus system and the rule of wealth and privilege, Jackson introduced a system of 'rotation in office.' The procedure, meant to shake up the bureaucracy and reward his friends, became known as 'the spoils system.'

Jackson, Helen Hunt (1831-1885), U.S. author who publicized the mistreatment of Native Americans. *A Century of Dishonor* (1881) condemned governmental malpractice; the novel *Ramona* (1884) described the plight of Native Americans in California's missions.

Jackson, Jesse Louis (1941-), U.S. clergyman and political leader. An associate of Martin Luther King, Jr. during the civil rights movement in the 1960s, Jackson later founded Operation Breadbasket (1966) and People United to Save Humanity (1971). He was the first African American to wage major, though unsuccessful, campaigns for the presidential nomination, running in Democratic primaries in 1984 and 1988. Since the 1988 elections, Jackson has continued his activities as an eloquent and effective speaker on vital national and foreign issues.

Jackson, Mahalia (1911-1972), African-American gospel singer whose powerful and expressive contralto voice gained her a worldwide reputation. She was active in the civil rights movement in the 1960s.

Jackson, Michael (1958-), U.S. rock singer, songwriter, and dancer. His album *Thriller* (1982) sold 40 million copies worldwide, making it the largest-selling record ever. Jackson's career began in 1966, when he was the lead singer of his family's band, The Jackson Five. He left the band in the mid-1970s, to pursue a solo career. His hits include *The Wiz* (film; 1978), *Off the Wall* (1980), *Bad* (1987), *Dangerous* (1994), *HIStory* (1995), and *Invincible* (2001).

Jackson, Shirley (1919-1965), U.S. author. Her best-known works, such as *The Haunting of Hill House* (1959) and the short story 'The Lottery' (1948), blend Gothic horror with psychological insight. Autobiographical works, such as *Raising Demons* (1957), are in a contrastingly humorous vein.

Jackson, Stonewall (Thomas Jonathan Jackson; 1824-1863), Confederate general in the American Civil War. He earned his nickname for his stand against the Union forces at the first battle of Bull Run (1861). At Chancellorsville he was fatally wounded by accidental fire from his own troops.
See also: Civil War, U.S.

Jackson, William Henry (1843-1942), U.S. photographer known for his documentation of the scenery of the West. His photos of Yellowstone for the U.S. Geological Survey led to its being named the first national park. After 1924, he worked as a painter.

Jack the Ripper, unknown murderer of at least seven prostitutes in London between Aug. 7 and Nov. 10, 1888. Each victim's throat was cut. Failure to solve the mystery led to the resignation of the head of Scotland Yard.

Jacob, in the Old Testament, son of Isaac and Rebecca, ancestor of the Israelites. He fled after tricking his older twin, Esau, out of his birthright. He settled in Mesopotamia, later returning to Canaan. After wrestling with an angel, he was given the name Israel. He had 2 wives, Leah and her younger sister, Rachel. (Gen. 25-50.)
See also: Bible; Old Testament.

Jacob, François (1920-), French biologist who shared with J.L. Monod and A.M. Lwoff the 1965 Nobel Prize for physiology or medicine for his work with them on regulatory gene action in bacteria.

Jacobean style, term applied to early English Renaissance architecture and furniture that flourished during the reign of James I. Decorative motifs from the late Perpendicular period were combined with crude classical details. In furniture of this period, strapwork, or forms carved in flat relief, was popular, along with Flemish-in-

In the 20th century, the spiritual, a religious song by former black slaves in North America, was no longer confined to the church. Great gospel singers, such as Mahalia Jackson (1911-1972), attracted huge crowds.

spired classical ornament. In furnishings, the style lasted into the late 17th century. Many examples of Jacobean style can be seen in the colleges of Oxford and Cambridge universities.
See also: Renaissance.

Jacobins, powerful political clubs during the French Revolution, named for the former Jacobin (Dominican) convent where the leaders met. Originally middle-class, they became increasingly radical advocates of terrorism. After they seized power in 1793, the extremists, led by Robespierre, instituted the Reign of Terror. In the Thermidor reaction the clubs were suppressed, to revive under the Directory and finally be put down by Napoleon.
See also: French Revolution; Robespierre, Maximilien Marie Isidore.

Jacobites, supporters of that branch of the House of Stuart exiled by the Glorious Revolution of 1688; a large number were Highland Scots. Jacobites sought to regain the English throne for James II and his descendants, notably James Edward Stuart (1688-1766), 'The Old Pretender,' and Charles Edward Stuart (1720-1788), 'Bonnie Prince Charlie.' After rebellions in 1715, 1719, and 1745, they were effectively crushed at the battle of Culloden Moor (1746).
See also: England; Stuart, House of.

Jacobs, Joseph (1854-1916), English scholar and writer of children's fairy tales. His works include *Aesop's Fables* (1889), *Celtic Fairy Tales* (1891), and *More Celtic Fairy Tales* (1894), which include 'Jack and the Beanstalk' and 'The Three Little Pigs.' He was also secretary (1882-1900) of the Russo-Jewish Committee (London), formed to improve the condition of Jews in Russia.

Jade, name for either of 2 tough, hard minerals with a compact interlocking structure, commonly green but sometimes white, mauve, or yellow. Jade is used as a gem stone to make carved jewelry and ornaments. Nephrite, the commoner form of jade, occurs in China, the former USSR, New Zealand, and the western United States. Jadeite, rarer and prized for its more intense color and translucence, is found chiefly in Burma, China, and Japan.

Jaeger, any of various large, fast-flying birds (genus *Stercoranius*) of the northern seas. Jaegers nest in the Arctic but migrate south along the coasts of the United States. They can be recognized by their slender, bent wings and their fan-shaped tails, with 2 long feathers in the center.

Jaffa, port on the coast of the Mediterranean Sea, just south of Tel Aviv, Israel, with which it was merged in 1949. Jaffa is one of the oldest cities in the world, dating back to ancient Egypt. Most of its mainly Arab population left in 1948.
See also: Israel.

Jaffna (pop. 130,000), city in north Sri Lanka, situated on a peninsular, capital of the district of the same name. It is a seaport and trading center for the fertile agricultural

J

J

region (coconuts, rice, tobacco, mangos, and curry), Fishing.

Tamils have dwelt there since 204 BC. The city was occupied by the Portuguese in 1617 and fell into Dutch hands in 1658; a fort and a church are reminders of this. Ethnic Dutch who live in Sri Lanka are called *burghers*. In 1795, while The Netherlands was occupied by the French, Jaffna was conquered by British expeditionary forces.

A large part of the population in this area consists of Hindu Tamils (18% of the national population) while the Singhalese (74% of the national population) are Buddhists. The LTTE (Tamil Tigers) are fighting for an independent state. The civil war between both groups has had devastating consequences; Jaffna in particular has been badly hit. There have been 30,000 fatalities since 1983 as a result of this war.

Jagger, Mick *See:* Rolling Stones.

Jaguar, large cat (*Panthera onca*) found in Mexico and Central and South America. The jaguar's coat bears black spots arranged in rosettes on a background varying from white to yellow. It lives in thick cover in forests or swamps. Though they are accomplished swimmers, jaguars hunt mostly on the ground or in trees. Adult males stand about 2.5 ft (76 cm) tall at the shoulder and weigh about 200 lb (90 kg).

Jaguarundi, long-tailed, short-legged cat (*Felis jaguarondi*) that resembles a large weasel. Its fur is rusty red or gray. The jaguarundi lives in brush and grassland from the southwestern United States to Argentina. It feeds on small animals and fruit.

Jahan, Shah *See:* Shah Jahan.

Jahangir (also known as Salim; 1569-1627), Grand Mogul of India (as of 1605), successor to Akbar. He managed to further expand the empire and was the first mogul to allow the British to establish themselves on the coasts of India. His wife, Nur Jahan, was very influential. Jahangir was a great admirer of art.

Jahn, Helmut (1940-), German-born U.S. architect whose work emphasizes steel, glass, and concrete, erected straight lines and overlapping planes, as exemplified in Kemper Arena (1974) and Bartle Convention Center (1976), both in Kansas City, Mo. In 1980 he shifted to a post-modern style combining modern and historical elements.
See also: Architecture.

Jai alai, or pelota, Spanish-Basque game similar to handball, from which it evolved in the 17th century. The ball, or *pelota*, is made of hard rubber covered with goatskin. Each player is equipped with a *cesta*, a narrow, basket-shaped racket of wicker, which is strapped to the player's wrist. The jai alai court, or *cancha*, is enclosed by three walls, the fourth side consisting of a wire screen that protects spectators. The players alternately throw the ball against the front wall, catching it in the cesta either on the fly or after one bounce on the floor. A player is awarded a point if he/she served, and their opponent is unable to return the ball off the front wall. The game is extremely popular in Cuba, Mexico, and Spain. It is usually associated with betting.

Jainism, philosophy and religion with about 2 million adherents, mainly in India. It was founded in about the 6th century B.C. as a protest against the ritualism of Hinduism. The last of its succession of 24 original saints, called Mahavira or Jina, seems to have been a historical figure. He taught the doctrine of *ahimsa*, or non-injury to all living animals. Jains do not believe in a creator God, but see the universe as divided into two independent eternal categories: 'life' and 'non-life'. They maintain that people can reach perfection only through ascetic, charitable, and monastic discipline.

Jaipur (pop. 1,900,000), India, the capital of Rajasthan state. It is in northern India 147 miles (237 km) southwest of New Delhi. Jaipur is a commercial and transportation center that trades in grain, wool, and cotton, and produces textiles, glass, and fine jewelry. Rajasthan University, a medical college, and a government art school and museum are here. Jaipur is one of the few Indian cities with wide streets and rectangular blocks. It was founded as a capital in 1727 by Maharaja Jai Sing II. His Hava Mahal (Palace of the Breeze) still stands.

Jakarta (pop. 9,300,000), capital and largest city of Indonesia, in northwestern Java. It is the country's commercial, transport, and industrial center, manufacturing automobiles, textiles, chemicals, and iron products, and processing lumber and food. Much of Indonesia's foreign trade passes through the port. The city grew out of the Dutch East India Company settlement of Batavia (1619). With independence in 1949 it was made the capital and renamed Djakarta, now officially spelled Jakarta.
See also: Indonesia.

Jakes, Milos (1922-), former president of Czechoslovakia (1987-1989). A politically active communist since 1945 who studied in Moscow, Jakes was appointed secretary-general of the communist party and president in 1987. The weakening of the communist party in 1989 and the growth of a reform movement led to his resignation that year.
See also: Czechoslovakia.

Jamaica

Capital:	Kingston
Area:	4,244 sq mi (10,991 sq km)
Population:	2,680,000
Language:	English
Government:	Parliamentary monarchy in the British Commonwealth
Independent:	1962
Head of gov.:	Prime minister
Per capita:	US$ 3,700
Monetary unit:	1 Jamaica dollar = 100 cents

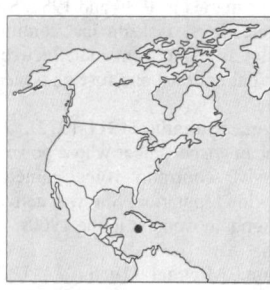

Jamaica, third-largest island in the West Indies, situated in the Caribbean Sea, 90 mi (145 km) south of Cuba and 100 mi (161 km) west of Haiti. The name Jamaica is derived from the Arawak Indian name *Xaymaca* (isle of woods and water).
Land and climate. Jamaica's surface is largely a limestone plateau, with a backbone of mountains and volcanic hills running east and west. In the east, Blue Mountain has an elevation of 7,402 ft (2,256 m), the highest point on the island. Sugar, bananas, allspice, coffee, ginger, and citrus fruits are grown on the warm mountain slopes. Rain forests in the north and northeast supply bamboo, mahogany, and ebony. Vegetation is generally richly tropical or subtropical, with over 3,000 species of flowering plants. Jamaica is

The jaguar (*P. onca*) the largest cat found in the Americas, looks like a leopard, but is more heavily built. The solitary animal establishes its own territory, and males and females disregard each other, except during mating season.

In 1494, Columbus discovered Jamaica and said that it was 'the most beautiful island ever seen by human eyes'.

generally rainy, with the heaviest falls occurring in May and Oct. Kingston, the capital, is fairly dry, with only 30 to 35 in (76 to 89 cm) per year. Hurricanes may occur between Aug. and Nov.

People. Most Jamaicans are of African descent. The others are East Indians, Chinese, and Europeans, mainly British. English is spoken throughout the island, and a local patois (a mixture of African and archaic English words) is also used. Most people are Protestants, either Anglican or Baptist. There are over 800 schools on the island, but people in remote rural areas are often illiterate. The principal campuses of the University of the West Indies are located in Jamaica. Over 30% of the people live in rural areas, but in recent years the population of the two major towns, Kingston and Montego Bay, has increased. The birthrate is high, and the density of population (564 persons per sq mi) creates serious problems.

Economy. Jamaica is predominantly agricultural. Sugar refining and the manufacture of molasses and rum are the principal industries. The island also has a thriving tourist industry. In 1942 deposits of bauxite were discovered, and today Jamaica is one of the world's chief suppliers of this aluminum ore. Gypsum is another important export commodity.

History. In 1494, Christopher Columbus discovered Jamaica, which was thinly settled by the Spaniards in 1509 and remained a Spanish colony until it was ceded to the British in 1670. By the 18th century the original inhabitants, the Arawak Indians, had been killed off by disease and the harsh treatment of their colonial rulers. From 1660 African slaves were imported to work in the lucrative sugar industry. Jamaica was particularly prosperous under Sir Henry Morgan, a buccaneer who served as lieutenant-governor from 1674 to 1683. By the 18th century the island was a leading slave trading center.

When slavery was abolished in 1834, the sugar industry declined. Thereafter unemployment, poverty, and overpopulation caused tension, and riots occurred, especially in the 19th and early 20th centuries. To improve conditions, crop diversification was encouraged, including the cultivation of bananas, and substantial governmental chan-

ges were made between 1930 and 1940. In 1962, after 3 centuries as a British colony, Jamaica became an independent nation within the Commonwealth of Nations. Political power in Jamaica has alternated between the conservative Jamaican Labour Party (JLP) in the 1960s and 1970s, and the Social-Democratic People's National Party (1970s, 1990s and nowadays). The country suffers heavily from increased crime, which is damaging tourism more and more.

James, name of 6 kings of Scotland. **James I** (1394-1437) technically became king in 1406, but he was held prisoner in England 1406-1424. After being ransomed by Scottish nobles, he returned to Scotland and suppressed a turbulent aristocracy; he was assassinated during an abortive aristocratic revolt. **James II** (1430-1460) reigned 1437-1460. His son, **James III** (1451-1488), reigned 1460-1488. His son, **James IV** (1473-1513), king from 1488 to his death, was the great Renaissance king of Scotland. He reformed law and administration, extended royal authority, built a powerful navy, and was a patron of the arts and sciences. He married Margaret, daughter of Henry VII of England. He was killed at the battle of Flodden Field during an attempted Scottish invasion of England. **James V** (1512-1542), his son, was king from 1513, but actually reigned 1528-1542, during the beginnings of the Reformation. He supported Catholicism for financial and political reasons. His daughter was Mary Queen of Scots. He died soon after his army was defeated by the English at Solway Moss. **James VI,** king of Scotland from 1567, became James I of England.
See also: Scotland.

James, name of 2 kings of England, Scotland, and Ireland, both belonging to the House of Stuart. **James I** (1566-1625), became king of Scotland in 1567, when his mother, Mary Queen of Scots, was forced to abdicate. Until 1583, when James turned 17, the country was ruled by regents. James supported Elizabeth I of England and in 1587 accepted the execution of his mother. In 1603 he succeeded Elizabeth, becoming king of England. His early popularity waned as he sought autocratic control over Parliament,

bolstered by his belief in the divine right of kings. He sponsored the translation of the Authorized Version of the Bible (1611), also known as the King James Version. His strict anti-Puritan views caused many Puritans to flee to America, where they founded Plymouth Colony (1620). **James II** (1633-1701), reigned 1685-1688. He was the second son of Charles I, successor of James I. During the English civil war he fled to France (1648). He returned to England in 1660, at the time of the Restoration. A Roman Catholic, James II acceded to the throne in 1685, after the death of Charles II. His autocratic methods and pro-Catholic appointments made him unpopular, and in 1688 James II was ousted by William of Orange, his Protestant son-in-law, in what became known as the Glorious Revolution. In 1689 James tried to restore his rule from his base, Ireland, but his forces were defeated in the battle of the Boyne (1690).
See also: England.

James, Epistle of, 20th book of the New Testament, traditionally attributed to St. James, the Less. One of the Catholic (general) Epistles, it is primarily a homily on Christian ethics.
See also: Bible; New Testament.

James, Henry (1843-1916), U.S.-born novelist and critic, brother of William James. He settled in London in 1876 and became a British citizen in 1915. A recurring theme in his work is the corruption of innocence, particularly as shown by the contrast between sophisticated, corrupt Europeans and brash, innocent Americans. James's most famous works, distinguished by subtle characterization and a precise, complex prose style, include *The Americans* (1877), *Daisy Miller* (1878), *The Portrait of a Lady* (1891), *The Turn of the Screw* (1898), and *The Golden Bowl* (1904).

Henry James (1843-1916), as painted in 1913 by John Singer Sargent (1856-1925). National Portrait Gallery, London.

James, Jesse (1847-1982), U.S. outlaw. A member of William Quantrill's raiders during the Civil War, he and his brother Frank led the James Gang, robbing banks and trains from Arkansas to Colorado and Texas, beginning in 1866. Living as an ordinary citizen in St. Joseph, Mo., he was murdered for a $5,000 reward by gang member Robert Ford.

J

J

James, P(hyllis) D(orothy) (1920-   ), English mystery writer. In her novel *Cover Her Face* (1962), she created the character of Adam Dalgliesh, Scotland Yard commander. He was also the hero of *Death of an Expert Witness* (1977) and *A Taste of Death* (1986). She also introduced Cordelia Gray, a London detective, in *An Unsuitable Job for a Woman* (1972) and *The Skull Beneath the Skin* (1982). In 1997 *A Certain Justice* was published.

James, Saint, Christian leader of the 1st century A.D., referred to as the brother of Jesus in the Galatian Epistles, though theologians have disputed any blood relationship between them. James is credited as the author of the Epistle of James in the New Testament, but true authorship is uncertain. His feast day is May 3.
See also: Apostles.

James, William (1842-1910), U.S. philosopher and psychologist, considered the originator of the doctrine of pragmatism; brother of novelist Henry James. His first major work was *Principles of Psychology* (1890). Turning his attention to questions of religion, in 1902 he published *The Varieties of Religious Experience*, which has remained his best-known work. James's pragmatism, which he called 'radical empiricism,' argued that the truth of any proposition rested on its outcome in experience, and not on any eternal principles.
See also: Pragmatism.

James Bay, inlet of the southern part of Hudson Bay, Canada. The bay was named for Captain Thomas James, who made extensive explorations of the area in 1631. Several early Hudson's Bay Company colonies were established there.

James the Greater, Saint, one of the twelve apostles of Jesus along with his brother, St. John. He was the first apostle to be martyred, and he is venerated widely in Spain, as Santiago.
See also: Apostles.

James the Less, Saint, one of the twelve apostles of Jesus. He is often associated with James the Younger and James, the 'brother' of Jesus, but they are probably three different people.
See also: Apostles.

Jammu and Kashmir *See:* Kashmir.

Janáček, Leo (1854-1928), Czech composer and collector of Moravian folk music, best known for his operas *Jenufa* (1904), *Katia Kabanova* (1921), and *The Makropulos Case* (1926). First professor of composition at the Prague Conservatory (1919), he wrote many songs, as well as chamber and choral works, in particular the *Glagolitic Mass* (1926).

Janissaries, elite Turkish infantry of the 14th-19th century, conscripted from prisoners of war and Christian children abducted and reared as fanatical Muslims. From 1600 Turks gradually infiltrated the highly privileged corps, which became increasingly corrupt. Unruly and rebellious, it was massacred by order of Sultan Mahmud II in 1826.
See also: Infantry.

Jan Mayen Island, Norwegian island northeast of Iceland; 144 sq mi (372 sq km). The island is unpopulated, excepting the staff of a NATO landing strip and several weather stations. Desolate and mountainous; the volcano Beerenberg (834.646 ft, 254.567 m) became active in 1970 after a long period of rest. The only plant life consists of moss and grass. It is a radio and weather station and is visited by seal hunters. It is named after the Dutch sailor Jan Jacobz. Mayen, who visited the island in 1614. In 1931, the Norwegians built a weather station here; it officially became Norwegian territory in 1929.

Jansen, Cornelius (1585-1638), Dutch Roman Catholic theologian. In 1636 he was appointed bishop of Ypres, Belgium. In *Augustinus* (published posthumously, 1640), Jansen argued for a return on the part of Christians to the positions of St. Augustine on grace, free will, predestination, and salvation. Though counter to church doctrine, these ideas attracted many Catholic followers in France and the Low Countries. Early 18th-century papal bulls discredited Jansenism, but in parts of the Netherlands Jansenists still have churches.
See also: Theology.

Jansky, Karl Guthe (1905-1950), U.S. radio engineer. While studying static interference for the Bell Telephone Laboratories (1931), he discovered radio waves from sources outside the earth. This led to the development of radio astronomy.

Janus, in Roman mythology, guardian of gateways and doors and god of beginnings.

A pagoda of the Horyuji temple (607).

The first hour of each day and first day of each month was holy to him. January is named for him, and many Roman doorways and arches bear his image: a double-faced head looking in 2 directions.
See also: Mythology.

Japan

Capital:	Tokyo
Area:	145,883 sq mi (377,835 sq km)
Population:	126,975,000
Language:	Japanese
Government:	Parliamentary monarchy
Independent:	1947 (constitutional monarchy)
Head of gov.:	Prime minister
Per capita:	US$ 27,200
Monetary unit:	1 Yen = 100 sen

Japan (Japanese: *Nippon*), country off the east coast of Asia, an archipelago of 4 principal islands (Hokkaido, Honshu, Kyushu, and Shikoku), 500 smaller islands, and 3,000 minor ones.
Land. The Japanese archipelago extends 1,300 mi (2,092 km) from northeast to southwest. Most of its area of 154,883 sq mi (377,835 sq km) is accounted for by the 4 main islands. More than 4/5 of Japan is mountainous; the highest peak is Mount Fuji (12,385 ft/3,775 m). More than 250 Japanese peaks are higher than 6,500 ft (1,981 m); there are about 50 active volcanoes. Most Japanese live in the 1/5 of the country that is relatively flat. There are many streams and rivers; among many inland lakes, Lake Biwa is the largest.
Japan is poor in certain resources, with almost no iron ore and with petroleum that meets less than 1/10 of its requirements. Luxuriant forests cover 2/3 of the country. Large mammals include deer, monkeys, bears, wild boars, and wolves; smaller mammals are badgers, ermines, foxes, hares, mink, otters, and squirrels. About 450 species of birds have been observed.
People. One of the world's most densely populated nations, Japan has more than 126 million people. Its population density of 817 people per sq mi creates economic, social, and pollution problems.
The Japanese are basically a Mongoloid people; centuries of isolation and inbreeding

have produced a homogenous racial stock. Japanese is the universal language, except among the 15,000 Ainus (a primitive people of Caucasian origin) and 707,000 foreigners (mostly Korean) living in the country. English is the main foreign language.

The 2 major religions are Shinto and Buddhism. Many Japanese observe practices of both, with a Shinto family shrine and a Buddhist family altar. Schools are crowded, but the literacy rate is 99%, Asia's highest. The higher education system includes 475 colleges and universities and 610 junior colleges.

Economy. Having moved from feudalism to capitalism in just over a century, Japan is one of the world's leading industrial nations. Products range from ships and automobiles to electronic equipment, cameras, and textiles. Imports include coal, petroleum, and industrial raw materials. Rice is the chief agricultural crop. Japan has extensive fisheries.

History. Artifacts dating from at least 4000 B.C. have been found in Japan. The first Japanese state was ruled by the Yamato clan, from whom the present imperial house is said to descend. Japan has been subject to cultural influences from China by way of Korea. Rice cultivation was introduced from China (c.250 B.C.) and Buddhism from Korea (c.A.D. 538). In the 7th century A.D., Chinese ideographic script was adapted to the Japanese language, and the administrative system of the T'ang Dynasty was adopted. Land became the property of the emperor, who distributed it, and clan chiefs became imperial officials.

In 1192 Minamoto Yoritomo seized power as shogun (military dictator). Successive shoguns ruled absolutely, with the emperors as figureheads. Power was based on a vassal class of warrior knights, or samurai. Feudal warfare (1033-1573) paved the way for powerful lords who were free of shogun rule.

In 1543, the Portuguese visited Japan, followed by other European traders and Christian missionaries. A policy of isolation (sakoku) closed Japan to all foreigners except a few Dutch and Chinese traders until 1853-1854, when U.S. Commodore Ma-

After two and a half centuries of almost complete isolation, Japan was 'opened up' in 1853 by American General Perry and his armoured ships.

tthew Perry negotiated a trade treaty. Similar treaties with Britain, France, the Nether-lands, and Russia followed. The shogunate collapsed in 1867. Under Emperor Meiji (1867-1912), Tokyo became the capital, and a program of westernization began.

Japan's victories in the Russo-Japanese War and Sino-Japanese Wars won her recognition as a world power, as did her support of the Allies in World War I. In the 1930s a militarist regime took power, built a large Asian colonial empire, and formed an alliance with Nazi Germany and Fascist Italy. Japan entered World War II with a surprise attack on Pearl Harbor (1941). The war brought economic ruin and nuclear devastation, and the Japanese surrendered in 1945. Since World War II, Japan has concentrated on economic development. In 1990 the Japanese real estate and stock markets crashed, leading to Japan's worst

The first wharf of the Mitsui Shipyards at Chiba, about 19 mi (30 km) east of Tokyo. Intensive research into cost-saving methods, has made Japanese shipyards highly competitive in tanker construction.

economic recession since World War II. An earthquake devastated the port city of Kobe in 1995. More than 6,000 were killed. A series of major banking and brokerage house failures in 1997 and 1998 increased Japan's economic problems. The Liberal Democratic Party (LDP) has governed the country, almost without exception. Koizumi became leader of the party in April 2001, and, as a result, Prime Minister. He tried to reform bureaucracy, but encountered fierce opposition by senior executives. At the end of 2002, he was the first Japanese leader to visit North Korea.

Japan, Sea of, arm of the Pacific Ocean between Japan and the eastern coast of Asia. It has an area of about 400,000 sq mi (1 million sq km) and is warmed by the Japan Current. Average depth is 4,500 ft (1,370 m), with some trenches descending to 12,000 ft (3,660 m).
See also: Pacific Ocean.

Japan clover *See:* Lespedeza.

Japan Current, or Kuroshio, warm strong ocean current running northeast along the southeastern Japanese coast. In summer, some of the current splits off, eventually reaching the Sea of Japan; most however, turns east past the Aleutians to form the North Pacific Current.

Japanese, language spoken by more than 100 million people, most of them in Japan. Japanese seems not to be related to any other language, although some linguists believe there may be a connection with Korean. Written Japanese originally used only adapted Chinese characters (*kanji*); in the 8th century phonetic characters (*kana*) were added.

Japanese beetle, metallic green beetle (*Popillia japonica*), related to the june beetle. In the United States, where it was accidentally introduced from Japan in 1917, it is an agricultural pest because none of its natural enemies was established. The larvae live underground and feed on plant roots.

Japanese chin, or Japanese spaniel, dog native to China. A favorite pet among Japanese royalty for centuries, the species was brought to the United States in the mid-1850s after Commodore Perry's expedition. The dogs have a soft white coat with uniform black or red patches around the face. They weigh about 5-9 lb (2-4 kg).

Japanese literature, one of the world's great literatures, consisting of works written in the Japanese language. Around the 6th century, largely through Korean influences, the Japanese came into contact with Chinese culture and civilization and adopted Chinese ideograms. By the early 8th century, the Japanese had begun to produce a native literature. The *Kojiki* (Record of Ancient Matters), the sacred book of Shinto, dates from 712 A.D. A work glorifying the imperial family and its divine descent, the *Kojiki* also recounts early folk tales, legends, myths, and songs. The *Nihonshoki* (The

J

J

Chronicles of Japan) are the earliest Japanese historical work; they date from 720 A.D. Toward the end of the 8th century, after 771 A.D., came the *Man'yoshu*, a remarkable compendium of 4,500 poems, a wide-ranging record of lyric expression in the native language.

The Heian period (794-1185) marked the end of Japan's absorption of the Chinese influence and the emergence of its own distinct literary character and genius. The Chinese ideograms were too complex for rapidly recording running throught or quick impressions, so the Japanese developed two distinct cursive scripts, the flowing *hiragana* and the angular *katakana*. The greatest work of the Heian period and one of the great works of world literature was composed in the *hiragana* script by a prominent woman of the Heian court, Lady Murasaki Shikibu. Her *Tale of Genji*, written in the early 11th century, is an elaborate tale of the love and intrigues of a certain Prince Genji. The work is not only a skillfully told story but is also rich in its portrayal of character and deeply colored by a Buddhist sensibility.

The Heian court and its aristocracy were replaced by a military government and, from 1185 to 1587, the samurai, or soldier, class became dominant. The change was reflected in literature. *The Tale of the Heike*, Japan's greatest historical fiction, was written in the early 1300s. *Tanka* continued to be composed, but poems called *renga* were also written. *Renga* consisted of chains of poems made by several poets, usually composed as they drank. But it was also during these centuries that two great literary forms were developed. The Noh drama, powerful in its solemnity and restraint, featured a masked actor, dance, chanting, and musical accompaniment. It was perfected by the actor and playwright Zeami Motokiyo. The *kyogen* was slapstick farces which accompanied Noh performances.

The reign of the samurai was marked by frequent instability and bloody warfare. Power was finally consolidated under a single clan which gave its name to an era, the Tokugawa (1603-1867). Under the Tokugawa, the written language was standardized. The kabuki theater developed with its brilliant costumes, melodramatic tales, and energetic acting style. And, in the early 1700s, the puppet theater, or *bunraku*, was brought to a high level of refinement.

Heian literature was dominated by an aristocratic sensibility; the literature of the Tokugawa era was patronized by the bourgeoisie. In the late 1600s, Ihara Saikaku (1642-1693) gave up a career as a poet to pursue a successful career writing fiction. His contemporary, Matsura Basho (1648-1694) developed the *haiku*, a poetic form of 17 syllables, which challenged and eventually supplanted the *tanka*. The Tokugawas pursued a policy of strict isolation for Japan. That policy ended with the arrival of Commodore Perry in 1858. In 1867, the samurai were replaced by the Emperor Meiji. Just as early Japan had studied China, Meiji Japan set out to study the West, and the impact of those studies opened new fields for Japan's literary talents. Prominent among the Meiji writers of the 1880s who learned western languages, studied western

literature, and took the first decisive steps toward mastering the new forms were Yamada Bimyo, Koyo Ozaki, Rohan Koda, Futabatei Shimei, and Tsubouchi Shoyo. Tsubouchi Shoyo was a Shakespeare scholar and urged Japanese writers to compose European-style novels. In response, Futabatei produced *Drifting Clouds* in 1889. In a remarkably short time, Japanese writers created outstanding works. Perhaps the greatest Japanese novelist was Natsume Soseki, who began his career with the now-famous *I Am a Cat* in 1905. Ryonosuke Akutagawa wrote brilliant stories and fables, including *Rashomon*. Shiga Naoya wrote *A Dark Night's Passing* in 1937. Japan's outstanding contemporary writers include Jun'ichiro Tanizaki, author of *The Makioka Sisters*; Jiro Osaragi; Osamu Dazai; Kobo Abe; Yasunari Kawabata, author of *Snow Country* and recipient of the Nobel Prize for literature in 1968; Yukio Mishima, author of *Confessions of a Mask*; and Oaka Shohei.

Virtually everyone in Japan can read. As a result, all branches of literature have benefited. Apart from numerous publications and periodicals, it has been observed that more works of the world's literature have been translated into Japanese than into any other single language.

Japanese print, fine art developed in 17th-century Japan. The artist drew a pattern onto a wood block and a carver cut the pattern, leaving only a portion of the surface raised. The design could be reproduced many times by applying ink to its surface and printing it on paper. Printmaking was originally done in black and white, but color techniques were introduced by the mid-1700s.

Japanese spaniel *See:* Japanese chin.

Jaques-Dalcroze, Émile (1865-1950), Swiss composer and music teacher, teacher at the conservatoire in Geneva (1892). He had an intense interest in rhythmical kinetics, which, in 1915, led to the founding of the *Institut Jaques-Dalcroze* in Geneva. The aim of the Dalcroze method is to turn rhythmical feeling into a physical experience, which has been a great influence on rhythmical gymnastics and artistic dance. In the French-speaking part of Switzerland many of Jaques-Dalcroze' songs have achieved the status of a national anthem.

Jarrell, Randall (1914-1965), U.S. poet and influential critic. His poetry is emotional and often pervaded with a sense of tragedy and alienation; best-known collections are *Selected Poems* (1955), *The Woman at the Washington Zoo* (1960), and *The Lost World* (1965). *Poetry and the Age* (1953) is the first of three collections of his criticism.

Jarry, Alfred (1873-1907), French writer. Jarry's work has influenced the dadaists and surrealists from the 1920's, who regarded Jarry as one of their own. The 'theater of the absurd' owes much to Jarry's pioneering work. His first book, published in 1894, was *Les minutes de sable mémorial*. Two years later he published *Ubu roi* 1896). In *Ubu roi* Jarry ridicules the self-satisfaction and greed

of the ordinary middle class man. The piece is also a parody of several well known plays. *Ubu roi* opened in the Théâtre de l'Oeuvre in Paris on 10th December 1890 and caused a commotion in the audience. It was taken off the bill after two performances. Jarry was not discouraged and continued to write about Ubu, as in *Ubu enchaîné* (1900). Jarry also wrote novels such as *Gestes et opinions du docteur Faustroll, pataphysician* (published after his death in 1911).

Jaruzelski, Wojciech (1923-), Polish general and politician, appointed both premier and Communist party leader in 1981 to resolve the crisis involving the independent trade union Solidarity. He arrested the Solidarity leaders and imposed martial law, but he was unable to remedy the country's economic difficulties. In 1985 he became president under a new system of government and resigned as premier. In Sept. 1990 he indicated his intention to step down in order that an election might take place. In 1996 he and eleven others had to appear in court for having violently crushed a workers' revolt in 1970, in which 44 people were killed.

Jasmine, or jessamine, vine or shrub (genus *Jasminum*) with yellow or white star-shaped flowers, noted for their fine scent. It is found throughout Europe, Asia, and Africa and has become naturalized in the United States. In the south of France, acres of jasmine are grown and their flowers plucked for the oil, which is used in perfumes.

Jason, Greek mythological hero. Jason laid claim to the kingdom of Iolkos, which his uncle, Pelias, had seized from Jason's father, Aeson. Pelias agreed to return the kingdom if Jason brought him the magical Golden Fleece, held by King Aeetes of Colchis. Jason assembled a force, the Argonauts, who set sail in the Argo to seek the fleece. After many adventures, they recovered the fleece, with the aid of Aeetes's daughter, Medea, who fell in love with Jason. She accompanied him back to Greece and became his queen. But when Jason tried to divorce Medea, she destroyed Creusa, his bride-to-be, as well as Creusa's father, and (in some versions of the story) her own children. The gods then caused Jason to wander aimlessly until his death.

See also: Argonauts; Mythology.

Jasper, opaque, compact, fine-grained variety of quartz used in jewelry and interior decoration. Its color varies from red, yellow, brown, and dark green to grayish blue.

Jaspers, Karl (1883-1969), German philosopher noted for his steadfast opposition to Nazism and his acute yet controversial analyses of German society. Early work in psychopathology led him into the Heidelberg University philosophical faculty in 1913. He there became one of Germany's foremost exponents of existentialism.

See also: Existentialism.

Jaundice, abnormal yellowing of skin and the whites of the eyes caused by excess bilirubin, normally removed by the liver and excreted as bile, in the blood. Jaundice occurs with liver damage (hepatitis, late stages of cirrhosis) and when the bile ducts leading from the liver to the duodenum are obstructed by gallstones or by cancerous tumors.

Java, island in southeastern Asia, part of the Republic of Indonesia, about 600 mi by 120 mi and bounded on the south and southwest by the Indian Ocean. Java accommodates nearly two-thirds of the population of Indonesia, together with the capital, Djakarta. Other important cities include Bandung, Surabaja, and Medan.

Java is traversed from east to west by a chain of volcanic mountains, the highest of which is Mt. Semeru (12,060 ft/3,676 m). The fertile tropical plain along the northern coast is drained by the Solo and Brantas rivers, and rainfall is heavy, for Java lies just south of the equator.

The Javanese are mainly farmers (many are smallholders), producing rubber, coffee, tea, sugar, cocoa, and cichona bark (from which quinine is derived) for export. Small-scale manufacture of consumer goods was encouraged by the former Dutch administration and has been further developed by the present Indonesian government. For centuries handicrafts have been important to the economy, and Java is noted for its artistic silverwork and batik textiles. By far the most important of Java's mineral resources, oil, is found in the northeastern part of the island and is well exploited. Other mineral deposits include gold, phosphate, and manganese.
See also: Indonesia.

Java man, early human species. Fossils found on the Indonesian island of Java in 1891 gave scientists evidence to date the species from 500,000 to 1 million years ago. Java man is an instance of *Homo erectus*, a stage of human development when humans began to stand erect. Examination of skulls show large jaws and teeth.
See also: Prehistoric people.

Javelin, spear made from lightweight metal or wood with a sharp pointed tip. Javelin throwing, a track and field competition, is an Olympic sport. After a running start, the competitor throws the javelin over the shoulder, releasing it in a high arc, in an attempt to gain the greatest distance on each throw.

Javelina *See:* Peccary.

Jawlensky, Alexej Georgewitsch (Von) (1864-1941), Russian painter who came into contact with Kadinsky in Munich in 1896 and later in Paris met Cézanne, Gauguin, and *Les fauves*, of whom Matisse in particular had great influence on him. He founded, together with Kadinsky, the *Neue Künstlervereinigung* in Munich in 1909 and took part in an exhibition of *Der blaue Reiter* in 1912, where his work stood out by his use of glowing colors and because it reminded one of Byzantine icons and Russian folk art. He had a preference for the human figure, the face in particular. Later his art developed into an abstract, spiritualized expressionism in dark colors with a tragi-religious atmosphere.

Crater landscape of the Bromo in Djawa Timor (East Java), a relatively dry region.

Jay, brightly colored, noisy bird of the crow family. Many jays bear crests. They are found in North and South America, Europe, and Asia. The blue jay (*Cyanocitta cristata*) lives in eastern North America, while the scrub jay (*Aphelocoma coerulescens*), Steller's jay (*C. stelleri*), and piñon (*Gymnorhinus cyanocephalus*) are found in the Rocky Mountains.

Jayavarman II (770-850), founder of the Khmer Empire in 802. He called it the Kambuja, *descendents of Kambu*. Kambu is the mythological patriarch of the Khmer.

Jayawardene, Junius Richard (1906-1996), Sri Lankan politician. Jayawardene was one of the founding members of the United National Party (UNP) in 1946 and held various ministerial positions during the following years. In 1973, he became chairman of the UNP and in 1977, after an electoral victory over Mrs. Bandaranaike's Sri Lanka Freedom Party, he became prime minister and successively president (1978-89). In this position he encountered the Tamil Tigers' struggle for their own state, which broke out in full intensity in 1983. His attempts to reach a compromise with the Tamils came to nothing. Jaywardene was one of the architects of the Colombo Plan and was known for his pro Western, anti Communist concepts and played an active part in the League of Nonaligned Nations.

Jazz, unique form of American music. A piece of jazz music begins with a melody and a harmonic scheme, on which the players improvise variations, typically using syncopated rhythms. The word 'jazz' may derive from a slang word describing a swaying kind of walk, or it may come from the French word *jaser*, to gossip.

The origins of jazz are found in the work songs, laments, and spirituals of the slaves of the U.S. South. With the abolition of slavery and the migration of thousands of black workers to southern towns and cities, especially New Orleans, these songs and spirituals were given a new impetus. As they were played by the street bands that accompanied weddings and funerals and by the smaller bands that played in the cafés of the Storyville district of New Orleans, such forms as the blues, ragtime, and the stomp were established.

The original New Orleans style started to change in the 1920s as blacks moved to the cities of the North. New styles emerged, such as the piano boogie woogie, and jazz began to find a wider audience, thanks to the radio and phonograph. In the 1930s and 1940s, big bands, composed mainly of white musicians, played a commercialized type of jazz called swing, which became the most popular dance music on both sides of the

The green jay (*Cyanocorax yncas*, order *Passeriformes*). Found in southern Texas, Central America. Length up to 11 in (28 cm).

J

J

During World War II, the jeep was the most widely used and versatile means of transport. The word 'jeep' is derived from General Purpose Vehicle. Its equipment included a rod mounted on the front to break wire traps set across roads (A), an M 1 rifle and ammunition holster (B), a hand-operated windshield wiper (C), a carbine rack (D), and antenna (E) and its mounting device (F), a Browning machine gun (G), its mounting device (H), and magazine (I), and all-weather hood (J), a radio transmitter-receiver (K), a spare fuel can (L), a spare wheel (M), survival tools—an axe and shovel—(N), and a capstan winch (O).

Atlantic. In the late 1940s a completely new jazz style, called bebop, appeared on the scene, pioneered by several brilliant black musicians. Bebop was the start of the modern jazz era. 'West Coast' and 'cool' jazz styles followed in the 1950s and 1960s. The latest jazz developments are almost totally removed in both form and spirit from the original New Orleans style.

One element in jazz that has not changed much is its instrumentation. The old New Orleans bands generally consisted of trumpet or cornet, trombone, clarinet, saxophone, piano, double-bass, and drums. The majority of jazz musicians still play one or another of these instruments.

Many jazz musicians figure in the history of 20th-century music. Joe 'King' Oliver, Edward 'Kid' Ory, Sidney Bechet, Ferdinand 'Jelly Roll' Morton, Louis Armstrong, Thomas 'Fats' Waller, and the first great white jazzman, Leon 'Bix' Beiderbecke, were among the early masters of jazz. Fletcher Henderson, Edward 'Duke' Ellington, and William 'Count' Basie led some of the great bands of the 1930s and 1940s, while Glenn Miller, Benny Goodman, and Woodrow 'Woody' Herman were among the band leaders of the swing era. Perhaps the most passionate jazz has come from the great blues singers, such as Bessie Smith and Billie Holiday. Modern jazz can be traced through the playing of musicians like Coleman Hawkins, Lester Young, Earl Hines, Charlie Parker, John 'Dizzy' Gillespie, Miles Davis, and John Coltrane. In the 1960s a new 'free form' jazz was developed by Ornette Coleman, Cecil Taylor, and others.

Jazz Age *See:* Roaring Twenties.

Jean Baptiste de la Salle, Saint (1651-1719), French Roman Catholic priest canonized in 1900. He founded the Order of the Christian Brothers, which brought religious instruction to the poor. In the 1680s he established the Institute of Brothers of the Christian School, and other schools were established by his order throughout Western Europe.

Jeanmaire, Renée Marcelle (Zizi) (1924-), French dancer, singer of *chansons* and film star, who studied with Boris Kniaseff. She made her debut in 1939 with the ballet of the Parisian Opera. She became famous after she danced the title role in *Carmen* (1949) with the *Balletes de Paris*. She played leading parts in American movies and appeared in Roland Petit's revues, marrying Petit in 1954. From 1969 till 1972 they managed The *Casino de Paris* together, until Roland Petit become director of the *Ballet de Marseille* and Renée Marcelle Jeanmaire danced as a guest in many ballet companies.

Jeanne d'Arc *See:* Joan of Arc, Saint.

Jeanneret-Gris, Charles Édouard *See:* Le Corbusier.

Jeep, 4-wheel-drive vehicle used for navigating rough terrain. Popular with the army, jeeps came into widespread use during World War II. The name evolved from the initials G.P., standing for 'general purpose' vehicle. They became the prototypes for civilian vehicles of the same name, which is now a registered trademark of the Chrysler Corporation.

Jeffers, Robinson (1887-1962), U.S. poet. His powerful poetry, its tone disillusioned, laments human fate and glorifies nature. *Tamar and Other Poems* (1924) is his best-known collection, but his chief success was an adaptation of Euripides' *Medea* (1946).

Jefferson, Joseph (1829-1905), U.S. actor best known for his portrayal of Rip van Winkle, a role he created in London in 1865 and played for the rest of his life.

Jefferson, Thomas (1743-1826), third president of the United States (1801-1809) and principal author of the Declaration of Independence. Jefferson was highly accomplished in many fields-politics, diplomacy, science, architecture, education, farming, and music, to name only a few.

A radical democrat, he believed men should be free to govern themselves, and opposed aristocracy of birth or wealth. His writings made him one of the leading political theorists in the colonies.

In 1776, Jefferson was named to a 5-man committee to prepare a declaration justifying independence; Jefferson wrote most of it. It is considered the most eloquent statement of his views on democracy and government. The Continental Congress adopted the declaration on July 4, 1776. Jefferson served as the U.S. minister to France (1785-1789) and as the first U.S. secretary of state (1789-1793). Two parties formed around Jefferson and Alexander Hamilton, secretary of the treasury. Jefferson's followers became known as Democratic-Republicans (or Republicans) and Hamilton's as Federalists. Jefferson believed in the rationality of man and saw the nation's future as an egalitarian, agricultural society of small landholders. He opposed the idea of strong, central government, believing that all governments should be kept from gaining too much power. Jefferson's greatest diplomatic coup was the Louisiana Purchase (1803), which doubled the size of the nation.

Jefferson's personal popularity carried him and running mate George Clinton to an overwhelming victory in the 1804 presidential election, but his second term was beset by foreign-affairs problems, particularly a conflict between Britain and France. Hoping to avoid war, Jefferson established an embargo forbidding the export of U.S. products and prohibiting U.S. ships from sailing to foreign ports. The embargo, however, hurt U.S. traders far more than it did Europe.

Jeffersonian democracy *See:* Jefferson, Thomas.

Jehoiakim, king of Judah (r.c.608-598 B.C.). Son of King Josiah, Jehoiakim was placed on the throne by Necho, the Egyptian pharaoh who defeated Josiah. Jehoiakim later switched his alliance from Necho to the Babylonian king, Nebuchadnezzar II, but then revolted against him. Jehoiakim died under mysterious circumstances during the Babylonian siege of Jerusalem.

Jehoshaphat, king of Judah (r.c.873-849 B.C.). An ally of King Ahab of Israel, Jehoshaphat was the first Judean king to make a treaty with Israel. He reigned during an era of relative peace and solidified his alliance with Israel by having his son, Jehoram, marry the daughter of King Ahab.

Jehovah, variant of the name of God in the Old Testament. The four Hebrew letters YH-WH, referring to God, were considered sacred and unpronounceable. In reading the Hebrew Bible, the word *Adonai* (Lord) was substituted. Medieval translators believed YHWH should be read 'Yahweh,' and the name 'Jehovah' was incorrectly derived from that.

Jehovah's Witnesses, international religious movement founded in 1872 by Charles Taze Russell in Pittsburgh, Pa. Their central doctrine is that the Second Coming of Christ is imminent. They avoid participation in secular government, which they see as diabolically inspired. Over a million members proselytize by house-to-house calls and through publications such as *The Watchtower* and *Awake*, issued by the Watchtower Bible and Tract Society.

Jehu, king of Israel (r. c.842-815 B.C.). An officer in the army of King Jehoram, Jehu was anointed king by a disciple of the prophet Elisha after Jehoram began promoting the worship of Baal. Jehu murdered Jehoram, Queen Jezebel (Jehoram's mother), King Ahaziah of Judah, and other members of the royal family. After ordering all the followers of Baal into their temple, Jehu's soldiers slaughtered them. Jehu restored traditional Jewish worship and began a dynasty that ruled for another century.
See also: Israel.

Jelinek, Elfriede (1946), Austrian writer whose novels are often regarded as 'women's literature', although she herself has a wider range of contemporary and social criticism in mind. *The Piano Teacher* (1983) sketches a complicated mother-daughter relationship. Jelinek has also written a great deal for the stage, film, radio, and TV, including *Clara S.* (1972), about the subjected life and suppressed creative power of Clara Schumann.

Jellicoe, Sir John (1859-1935), British admiral of the fleet (1919), commander of the British grand fleet at the battle of Jutland (1916). He was governor-general of New Zealand (1920-1924).
See also: Jutland, Battle of.

Jellyfish, familiar name for the free-swimming stage of various invertebrate animals of the phylum Cnidaria. They often have a pulsating jellylike bell and trailing tentacles. Many Cnidarian classes display an alternation of generations, where a single species may be represented by a polyp form, usually asexual, and a medusoid, sexually reproductive stage. These medusoid forms are frequently referred to as jellyfish. The true jellyfish all belong to the class Scyphozoa, where the medusa is the dominant phase and the polyp or hydroid is reduced or absent. Jellyfish are radially symmetrical. Rings of muscle around the margin of the bell contract to expel water and propel the jellyfish forward.

Jenghis Khan *See:* Genghis Khan.

Jenkins, Roy Harris (1920-2003), British political leader. Elected to the House of Commons in 1948 as a Labour Party member, he served as minister of aviation, chancellor of the exchequer, and twice held the post of home secretary. He was president of the Commission of the European Community (1977-1981). In the early 1980s he helped found the Social Democratic Party, a split from the Labour Party, and in 1982 he was elected to Parliament under the party's banner. He lost his seat in 1987.
See also: Parliament; United Kingdom.

Jenne, or Djenné, city in southern Mali. Founded c.1300 in a swampy lowland between the Niger and Bani rivers, Jenne became a trade hub between the West African coastal region and the lower Sahara. In 1468 it was conquered by the Songhai Empire, and in the mid-1600s it was a focal point for black Muslim culture and learning.
See also: Mali.

Jenner, Edward (1749-1823), English physician, pioneer of vaccination. He took note of the country saying that dairy-maids who had had cowpox would not contract smallpox, and this led him, in 1796, to inoculate a boy, James Phipps, with cowpox. When the procedure made the boy immune to smallpox, the modern science of immunology was born.
See also: Immunization; Vaccination.

Jenner, Sir William (1815-1898), Victorian-era British physician. Best known for his research on typhus and typhoid fever, Jenner was one of the first members of the medical profession to draw a distinction between them and prescribe appropriate treatment. Jenner was also a pioneer in the treatment of diptheria. He served as president of the Royal College of Physicians (1881-1888) and was the personal physician of Queen Victoria and other members of the royal family.
See also: Typhoid fever; Typhus.

Jensen, J. Hans (1906-73), German physicist who shared the Nobel Prize for physics (1963) with Maria Goeppert Mayer and Eugene Paul Wigner for research on the shell structure of atomic nuclei.

Jensen, Johannes Vilhelm (1873-1950), Danish writer, one of the great figures of Danish literature. He described his native region in the collection of novels *Himmerland Stories* (1898-1910). Jensen also gave voice to his theories on culture and history and Darwinian evolution theories, which finally resulted in a cycle of six novels *The Long Journey* (1908-1922), the evolutionary progress of the Gothic (Northern) race from before the ice ages until the discovery of

A jellyfish, family Medusae, propels itself through the ocean by shooting water from its gelatinous, bell-like body. The jellyfish stings and paralyzes prey that wanders into its curtain of tentacles.

J

America by Colombo. The myths and cultural/philosophical writings are the most important of his later works. In 1944, he won the Nobel Prize.

Jenson, Nicolas (1415?-1480), 15th-century French printer who designed several important typefaces still in common use today. He was sent by the king of France to Mainz, Germany, to learn book printing from Johannes Gutenberg. In 1470 Jenson devised a system of roman type that later evolved into other practical fonts.
See also: Printing.

Jerboa, any of various small desert-living rodent (family Dipodidac) with long tails and long hind legs. Jerboas have large eyes and ears, short front legs, and move by hopping. They are common in the deserts of North Africa and Asia, where they live in holes and emerge at night to feed on leaves and seeds.

Jeremiah, book of the Old Testament, 24th in the Authorized Version, second of the Major Prophets. It tells of the prophecies of Jeremiah, who called for moral reform, threatening the population with doom otherwise. He continued prophesying in Egypt after Jerusalem fell to Babylon.
See also: Bible; Old Testament.

Jericho (pop. 33,500), ancient village in Palestine, north of the Dead Sea. Excavations have suggested that Jericho may be the site of the oldest known human permanent settlement in the world. In the Bible, it was captured from the Canaanites by Joshua. It has periodically been destroyed and rebuilt. In 1967 it was occupied by Israel. After years of negotiations the Palestinians attained some form of autonomy over Jericho district in 1994.
See also: Palestine.

Jeroboam, 2 kings of ancient Israel. **Jeroboam I** (r. 922-909 B.C.) led the rebellion of the northern tribes of Judea after

J

King Solomon died, which resulted in Israel and Judah splitting into separate kingdoms. He restored Jewish shrines at Bethel and Dan, thus releasing the people from their obligation to make pilgrimages to the Holy Temple in Jerusalem, the capital of Judah. **Jeroboam II** (r. 785-745 B.C.) ruled during a time when Israel was a political and economic power, despite widespread corruption.
See also: Israel.

Jerome, Jerome Klapka (1859-1927), English humorist and playwright, who wrote the classic comic novel *Three Men in a Boat* (1889), a work cherished for its broad humor and sentimentality.

Jerome, Saint (Sophronius Eusebius Hieronymus; c. 340-420), biblical scholar, one of the first theologians to be called a Doctor of the Church. After being educated in classical studies, he fled to the desert as a hermit to devote himself to prayer. Subsequently papal secretary, he translated the Old Testament into Latin and wrote New Testament commentaries. His feast day is Sept. 30.
See also: Bible.

Saint Jerome (c. 340-420) was one of the most important fathers of the young Church, particularly because of his translation of the Old and New Testaments into Latin. Painting by Italian painter Antonella de Messina, about 1430-79. (National Gallery, London)

Jersey, largest and southernmost of the British Channel Islands. Its main industries are tourism and agriculture. It contains numerous remnants of prehistoric life and was known to the Romans as Caesarea.

Jersey Lily *See:* Langtry, Lillie.

Jerusalem (pop. 600,000), capital (since 1980) and largest city of Israel. It stands on a ridge west of the Dead Sea, 35 mi (56 km) from the Mediterranean. The city may date from the 4th millennium B.C. In c.1000 B.C. King David captured it from the Jebusites and made it his capital. The great Temple was built by David's son Solomon in 970 B.C. David's dynasty was ended in 586 B.C. by the invasion of King Nebuchadnezzar, who sacked the Temple and deported most of the Jews to Babylon. Cyrus II of Persia allowed the Jews to return and the Temple was rebuilt. Jerusalem was subsequently ruled by Syria, the Roman Empire, and the Byzantine Empire. It was taken over by the Muslims in 637 and has been part of the Muslim world ever since, except for a period of rule by the Crusaders (1099-1187). The 1947 UN resolution establishing the state of Israel made it an international city, but in the 1948 Arab-

Israeli conflict it was divided, the Old City being under Jordanian administration, the New City under Israeli rule. In the 1967 Arab-Israeli War, Israel took the Old City, and all of Jerusalem was placed under unified administration. There are traditional Armenian, Christian, Jewish, and Muslim quarters in the Old City, which is also the site of three of Jerusalem's holiest places: the Wailing Wall (Jewish); the Church of the Holy Sepulcher (Christian); and the Dome of the Rock (Muslim).
See also: Israel.

Jerusalem artichoke (*Helianthus tuberosus*), North American flowering plant closely related to wild sunflowers. It produces edible tubers that have a taste similar to artichokes, hence the name. They are also a source of fructose and alcohol. The plants can grow to 12 ft (3.7 m) in height. They bear yellow flowers.

Jespers, Oscar (1887-1971), Belgian sculptor. Jespers started out as an impressionist, but - after a short cubist period - developed an expressionist style. His forms are powerful and tense, very close and full; he preferred to work immediately in full scale. His most important works include: the War Monument in East Dunkirk and the monument for his friend the poet Paul Van Ostaijen in Antwerp.

Jessamine *See:* Gelsemium.

Jesuits, name given to members of the Society of Jesus, an order of Roman Catholic priests and brothers dedicated to foreign missions, education, and studies in the humanities and sciences. Jesuit life is regulated by the constitutions written by the founder of the Society, St. Ignatius of Loyala. Vows of poverty, chastity, and obedience to the pope are taken, and training may last up to 15 years. After its founding in 1534, the order undertook missions in Asia under St. Francis Xavier and participated in the Counter-Reformation in Europe. Their influence and power led to their expulsion from many countries, and in 1773 Pope Clement XIV dissolved the Society. It was restored, however, in 1814.
See also: Roman Catholic Church.

Jesus Christ (4? B.C.-A.D. 29?), central figure of the Christian religion. Jesus is be-

lieved by Christians to be the Son of God and the Lord and Savior of mankind. The name 'Jesus' is the Greek rendering of the Hebrew *Joshua* (Savior). The title 'Christ' comes from *Christos*, the Greek translation of the Hebrew *Messiah* (Anointed One).
The main source for information about the life and teachings of Jesus are the 4 Gospels-Matthew, Mark, Luke, and John-and the epistles of the New Testament. From the numerous details given there, it is possible to form a vivid picture of Jesus. These details are given with an intention expressly stated by John: 'These are written that you may believe that Jesus is the Christ, the Son of God, and that believing you may have life in his name' (John 20:31).
According to the Gospels, Jesus was born of the Virgin Mary, wife of Joseph, in Bethlehem, Judea. Their home was in Nazareth, Galilee. Little is known of his childhood except that, when he was 12, he went to the Temple in Jerusalem with Mary and Joseph. When Jesus was about 30 years old, his cousin John the Baptist began preaching repentance in the wilderness of Judea and baptizing penitents in the Jordan River. As Jesus was being baptized by John, a voice from heaven affirmed that Jesus was the Son of God (Mark 1:11). For some time after that Jesus traveled about the country, teaching and healing, mainly in Galilee but also in other parts of Palestine. He gathered 12 followers, or disciples, who helped spread the new ideas.
Jesus' interpretation of the Jewish law and his messianic claims alarmed the established religious authorities. On his last journey to Jerusalem for the Passover, Jesus entered the city in triumph. The authorities, threatened by his popularity, plotted against him. After the Last Supper, Jesus went to the Garden of Gethsemane to pray. One disciple, Judas Iscariot, betrayed him, and he was taken prisoner. Brought before members of the ecclesiastical court of the Jews, he was found guilty of blaspheming. He was then taken for sentencing to the Roman civil governor, Pontius Pilate, who charged him with treason against Rome and condemned him to death by crucifixion.
The resurrection of Jesus on the third day after his death and burial convinced the disciples that he was indeed the Son of God. They continued to spread Jesus' teachings, and hundreds of Jews and later Gentiles were converted to the new faith. Although

Jesus is shown preaching the Sermon on the Mount in this fresco by Fra Angelico. Jesus brought solace to a people accustomed to the tyrannies of foreign rule (Monastery of San Marco, Florence).

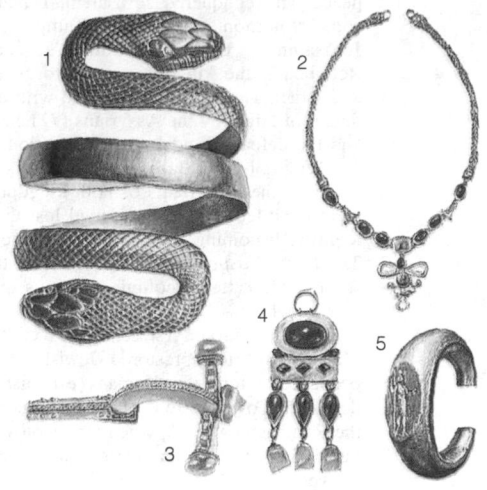

(A) A turbojet engine, (B) a turbofan en- gine, and (C) a turbo- prop engine.

---

the Christian Church eventually split into many parts, the accuracy of the Gospels and the divinity of Jesus are universally held Christian beliefs.
See also: Bible; Christianity; New Testament.

Jet, form of lignite coal valued for its gem-like properties. In its raw state it is hard and black and has a smooth surface. After polishing, it resembles black glass and is often used to make buttons, costume jewelry, and other decorative items.

Jet airplane *See:* Airplane; Aviation.

Jet engine *See:* Jet propulsion.

Jet lag *See:* Biological clock.

Jet propulsion, propulsion of a vehicle by reaction to the rapid expulsion of a gas backward. The reaction imparts an equal forward momentum to the vehicle. The chief use of jet propulsion is to power airplanes. The first jet engine was designed and built by Sir Frank Whittle (1937), but the first jet-engine aircraft to fly was German (Aug. 1939). Jet engines are internal-combustion engines. The turbojet is the commonest form. Air enters the inlet diffuser and is compressed in the air compressor. It then enters the combustion chamber, where the fuel is injected and ignited, and the hot, expanding exhaust gases pass through a turbine that drives the compressor and engine accessories. The gases are expelled through the jet nozzle to provide the thrust.
See also: National Aeronautics and Space Adminstration.

Jet stream, narrow bands of fast easterly-flowing winds, stronger in winter than in summer, found at altitudes of 7 to 8 mi (11-13 km). Speeds average about 40 mph (64 kmph) in summer and 80 mph (128 kmph) in winter, though more than 200 mph (320 kmph) has been recorded.

Jetty, man-made pier designed to aid in navigation. They are constructed primarily of wood, stone, concrete, or combinations of these materials. Breakwater jetties reduce the force of waves on a harbor or shoreline, while river jetties expedite the flow of silt through a delta. Jetties at the mouths of rivers such as the Mississippi and the Columbia funnel the water through narrow channels, thus forcing the currents to carry silt further out to sea.

Jewelry, ornaments worn by people to enhance their physical appearance, to display wealth, or to follow custom. Bracelets, rings, necklaces, and earrings are the most common types of jewelry. Made from precious metals such as gold and silver, colorful polished stones (gems), or other attractive natural materials, jewelry is an art form that has existed since earliest times. Ancient peoples wore jewelry made from such materials as feathers, shells, and teeth before they wore clothes. Jewelry found at the sites of early civilizations can yield clues to the technological development of ancient cultures.

Jewett, Sarah Orne (1849-1909), U.S. author. She wrote about late 19th century life in her native New England, often using seaports and rural towns of Maine as settings. Her best-known works are *Deephaven* (1877), *A Country Doctor* (1884), and *The Country of the Pointed Firs* (1896). She also wrote poetry and children's stories.

Jewfish (*Epinephelus itajara*), large game fish of the sea bass family. Jewfish and related species inhabit the eastern and western coastal waters of the United States and Latin America. The largest known species grows to 12 ft (3.75 m) and weighs up to 680 lb (310 kg).

Jewish feasts *See:* Judaism.

Jews, followers of Judaism, a group held together by a shared religion and a common

A selection of jewellery from the Roman Imperial period, 1st-3rd century A.D.
1 Gold snake bracelet
2 Necklace—gold
and mounted stones, with a pendant of sapphires, garnet and crystal
3 Fibula—crossbow type in gold
4 Earring—gold with
drop pendant, set with garnets
5 Ring—oval bezel, incised with standing figure

J

---

history and culture more than 3,000 years old.

Jewish history begins with the patriarchs: Abraham, his son Isaac, and his grandson Jacob (also named Israel). Abraham led his family from Mesopotamia to Canaan (Palestine). The children of Israel (Joseph and his brothers, the sons of Jacob) migrated to Egypt, where a pharaoh enslaved the Israelites until Moses led them out in the Exodus.

After 40 years of wandering, the Israelites reentered Canaan (c.1200 B.C.). They united in a monarchy under King Saul. His successor, David, brought prosperity and

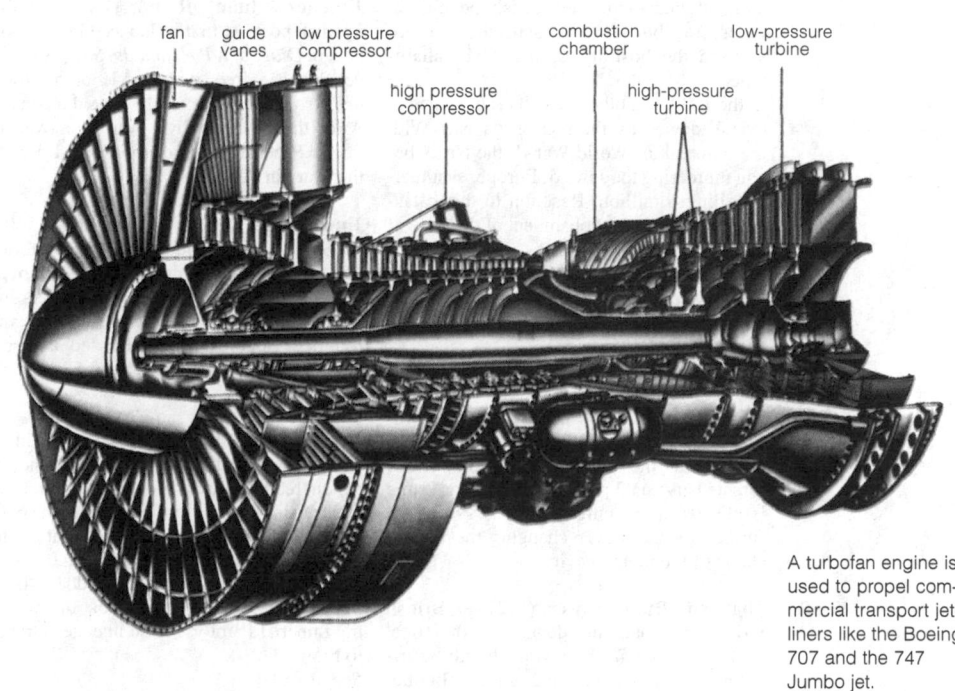

A turbofan engine is used to propel commercial transport jetliners like the Boeing 707 and the 747 Jumbo jet.

J

peace, and conquered Jerusalem. David's son, Solomon, built the Temple at Jerusalem. Under Solomon's son Rehoboam, the kingdom split into Judah and Israel. The monarchies ended with the defeat of Israel by the Assyrians (721 B.C.) and the defeat of Judah and destruction of the Temple by the Babylonians (587 B.C.). Many of the inhabitants of both kingdoms were deported; those from Israel lost their identity, becoming the 'Ten Lost Tribes.' The term *Diaspora* is used to refer to the settling of scattered colonies of Jews outside Israel.

During the 2nd and 1st centuries B.C., the Maccabees briefly restored Jewish independence before the Romans established domination over the Jews. They rose against the Romans in A.D. 66; when the revolt was put down 4 years later, Jerusalem was destroyed.

The rise of Christianity brought increasing harassment of the Jews. During the Middle Ages in many countries they were confined to ghettos and excluded from trades, professions, and ownership of land. At the time of the Crusades, a new wave of persecution began; one by one Western European nations expelled the Jews, until they were allowed to live only in parts of Germany and Italy. The Jews found refuge in the Ottoman Empire, in the New World, and in Eastern Europe, where they became increasingly trapped in a life of poverty and persecution in lands under Russian rule.

The Enlightenment and the advent of capitalism for a time benefitted the Jews economically and socially. Prejudice against them (anti-Semitism) continued, however, and gave rise in the late 19th century to renewed Zionism, the movement for reestablishing a Jewish state in Palestine that dated from the destruction of Jerusalem in A.D. 70. Meanwhile (1881-1914), one-third of Eastern European Jews (1 million people) emigrated; 90% settled in the United States. In 1917 the Balfour Declaration guaranteed 'a national home for the Jewish people' in Palestine, but Jewish settlement there aroused the hostility of the Arab inhabitants.

In the 1930s, all other Jewish problems were overshadowed by the rise of Nazism. With the outbreak of World War II, the Nazis began murdering the Jews of Europe, eventually killing 6 million. Reaction to this catastrophe led to the establishment of the state of Israel in 1948.

Today there are 15 million Jews worldwide. The Jews of Israel number more than 4 million, and some 6 million Jews live in the United States.
See also: Israel; Judaism.

Jew's-harp, or jaw's harp, musical instrument that produces a resonant sound. It is held up to the mouth, and a thin, metal tongue between 2 prongs of a circular frame is plucked, producing vibrations. Notes are formed by the player changing the size or shape of the mouth cavity.

Jhabvala, Ruth Prawer, (1927-), British writer, who made her debut with the novel *To Whom She Will*. She writes lightly satirical novels in which the cultural conflict be-

tween east and west is the main theme. She also writes screenplays for the Indian film industry. In 1983, the novel *In Search of Love and Beauty* was published, which is about the problems that Europeans face adapting to life in New York. Other prose works include *The Nature of Passion* (1956), *Esmond in India* (1958), *An Experience of India* (1971), *Heat and Dust* (1975), *The Nature of Passion* (1986), *Three Continents* (1987; short stories), *Poet and Dancer* (1993). She won an Oscar for her adaptation of *Howard's End* into a screenplay in 1993.

Jiang Qing, or Chiang Ch'ing (1914-1991), Chinese Communist leader; widow of Mao Zedong. She joined the Communist Party in 1933 and married Mao in 1939. During the 1960s she led the Cultural Revolution and was elected to the Politburo in 1969. Accused by Mao's successors of leading a coup attempt, she and 3 other radicals (the 'Gang of Four') were arrested and charged with treason. Jiang was condemned to death, but her sentence was commuted to life imprisonment in 1983.
See also: China; Gang of Four; Mao Zedong.

Jicama, yam bean, or Mexican turnip, vine belonging to the pea family, native to parts of Latin American and Asia. The Jicama plant is cultivated for its edible tubers.

Jidda, or Jiddah (pop. 2,000,000), city in western Saudi Arabia, situated on the Red Sea. Jidda has the country's largest airport and is the port of entry for millions of Muslims making pilgrimages to Mecca and Medina. Founded in the 7th century A.D., Jidda is a banking, oil refining, and manufacturing center.
See also: Saudi Arabia.

Jigger *See:* Chigger.

Jiménez, Juan Ramón (1881-1958), Spanish poet. At first influenced by symbolism, in *Diary of a Poet and the Sea* (1917) he developed a free, direct style of his own: *poesía desnuda* (Spanish 'naked poetry'). After the Spanish Civil War he moved to Puerto Rico. He received the Nobel Prize for literature in 1956.

Jiménez de Quesada, Gonzalo (1500?-1579?), Spanish conquistador who claimed the area around Colombia for Spain as New Granada. He settled there, doing much to improve the colonists' lot, and founded Bogotá (1538). He led a disastrous expedition in search of El Dorado (1569-1571).

Jimmu Tenno, mythical Japanese military and political leader. According to legend, he conquered large areas around the Inland Sea and became Japan's first emperor in the 600s B.C., but historians dispute the dates and question his existence. Jimmu Tenno is said to be a descendant of the sun goddess, leading to popular acceptance of the divinity of the Imperial Family, whose lineage is traced to him.
See also: Japan.

Jimsonweed, or thorn apple, low shrubby plant (*Datura stramonium*) with thick leaves and white trumpet-shaped flowers. All parts of the plant are poisonous. It is named for Jamestown, Virginia, where a party of English soldiers died after eating it as a vegetable.

Jinan (pop. 1,481,000), capital of the Chinese province of Shandong in the Huang He valley. Center of trade, industry, administration, culture, and education (university). Several temples from the Manchu dynasty (1636-1911). After the railroad was built to Zhengzhou (1904), and Peking (1912), the city saw enormous expansion.

Jinnah, Muhammad Ali (1876-1948), Indian Muslim lawyer and political leader, founder of Pakistan. At first a member of the Indian Congress Party, he resigned in 1921, charging it with Hindu bias. From 1934, as head of the Muslim League, he campaigned for Muslim rights in an independent state. In 1947 he became Pakistan's first head of state.
See also: Pakistan.

Jinrikisha, or ricksha, 2-wheeled passenger vehicle pulled manually. The runner, or *hiki*, runs between 2 long poles extending from the body of the carriage. Used as a public vehicle in China and Japan around the turn of the century, jinrikishas carried 1 or 2 people. Jinrikishas were later considered demeaning to humans and outlawed.

Jiulong *See:* Kowloon.

Jiva *See:* Jainism.

Jívaro, South American tribe inhabiting the lower Andes mountains in eastern Ecuador and Peru. Their principal activities are fishing, hunting, pottery-making, and weaving. A people once famous for ritual head-shrinking, they fiercely resisted Spanish encroachment.

Joachim, Joseph (1831-1907), a Hungarian violinist. He was known for his technical mastery and his interpretations of Beethoven's quartets and Bach's sonatas. Joachim began studying the violin at the age of five.
He was concertmaster at Weimar (1849-1854) and Hanover (1854-1866), and organized the Joachim Quartet in Berlin in 1869. Joachim taught violin and composed many virtuoso violin pieces, including *Hungarian Concerto* (1860).

Joan of Arc, Saint (1412?-1431), French heroine of the Hundred Years War. A peasant girl from Domremy, Lorraine, she heard 'voices' telling her to liberate France from the English. Given command of a small force by the Dauphin (later Charles VII), she inspired it to victory at Orléans in 1429. She stood beside the Dauphin when he was crowned Charles VII that year and joined him in his unsuccessful siege of Paris. Captured at Compiègne (1430), she was tried for heresy by an ecclesiastical court of French clerics who sympathized with the English, and burnt at the stake. The verdict

was posthumously reversed in 1456, and she was canonized in 1920.
See also: Hundred Years War.

Job, Book of, book of the Old Testament, 18th in the Authorized Version. Apparently based on a folk tale in dialogue form, it is about the problem of good and evil. God permits Satan to torment the virtuous Job with the loss of family, wealth, and health. Finding small comfort in wife and friends, Job is bitter, but remains faithful. He is restored to good fortune in old age.
See also: Bible; Old Testament.

Jobs, Steven Paul (1955-), U.S. computer designer and businessman, founder with Stephen Wozniak of Apple Computer, Inc. (1976). The company's success reshaped the personal computer industry. Managerial disputes caused Jobs to leave Apple in 1985. In 1988 he unveiled a computer system aimed at the college and university market, called NeXT.
See also: Computer.

Jodl, Alfred (1890-1946), German-Nazi officer, chief of operations in World War II. He signed the surrender at Rheims, May 7, 1945. Convicted of war crimes at the Nuremberg Trials, he was executed.
See also: Nazism.

Jodrell Bank Observatory, or Nuffield Radio Astronomy Laboratories, English space tracking station and research facility, located near Manchester. Housing one of the world's largest radio telescopes, Jodrell Bank tracked *Sputnik I*, the first satellite ever launched. It also transmitted the first photographs from a Soviet probe on the moon in 1966.
See also: Astronomy.

Joel, Book of, book of the Old Testament, 29th in the Authorized Version, second of the Minor Prophets. Messianic in nature, it forecasts the Day of the Lord in apocalyptic terms.
See also: Bible; Old Testament.

Joey *See:* Kangaroo.

Joffre, Joseph Jacques Césaire (1852-1931), commander-in-chief of the French army (1914-1916). He underestimated German power at the start of World War I, but he shared credit with Gen. J.S. Gallieni for the victory on the Marne. After the mismanagement of Verdun he resigned, but he was immediately made a marshal of France.

Joffrey, Robert (1930-1988), U.S. dancer and choreographer. His company, the Robert Joffrey Theater Dancers, was founded in 1954. By 1976, when it became the Joffrey Ballet, it was one of the most highly regarded of U.S. companies. The touring Joffrey II Company was formed in 1970 to develop young dancers.

Johanan Ben Zakkai (d. c.80), Jewish Pharisee who, after the destruction of the Temple by Rome in A.D. 70, founded the academy at Jabneh (Yibna), thus ensuring the survival of Judaism.
See also: Judaism.

The skyline of Johannesburg in South Africa, as seen over one of the immense slag heaps, left over from gold mining.

Johannesburg (pop. 2.2 mln.), city in northeastern South Africa. It is the hub of a prosperous mining region, with the world's largest gold field, the Witwatersand, nearby. First settled by prospectors in 1886, Johannesburg is South Africa's largest metropolitan area and a thriving cultural, commercial, and industrial center.
See also: South Africa.

Johanson, Donald Carl (1943-), U.S. anthropologist. His discovery of fossilized remains in Africa, estimated to be between 2.5 and 3 million years old, gave scientists evidence of some of the earliest origins of the human species. In 1974 Johanson uncovered the skeleton of what is believed to be the first humanlike creature to walk erect (classified as *Australopithecus afarensis*). In 1986 he found a skull and bones of an individual of the species *Homo habilis*, enabling scientists to piece together a link between humans and their ape-like predecessors.
See also: Anthropology; Prehistoric people.

John, name of 22 popes and 2 antipopes. **Saint John I** (d.526), pope (523-526), was sent to Constantinople by Theodoric, the Ostrogoth king, to win toleration for Arianism from the emperor; Theodoric imprisoned him when he failed. **John VII** (d.882), who reigned from 872 to 882, sought political power for the papacy. He attempted (and failed) to keep the Muslims out of Italy and was forced to pay tribute in order to spare Rome. He momentarily resolved a dispute with the Eastern Church by recognizing Photius as patriarch of Constantinople (879), after the death of his enemy, St. Ignatius. He crowned emperor Charles II (the Bald, in 875) and Charles III (the Fat, in 881). He was assassinated by members of his household. **John XXII** (1249-1334) was the second pope (1316-1334) at Avignon; he filled the college with French cardinals. A skillful administrator, he lost popularity when he persecuted the Franciscan Spirituals, observers of strict evangelical poverty. When he contested the election of Louis IV, the king attempted to have him declared a heretic; this prompted John to imprison Nicholas V, the antipope Louis had appointed. The name of **John**

XXIII was first taken by Baldassare Cossa (c.1370-1419), a Neapolitan antipope (1410-1415). As a cardinal, he supported the Council of Pisa (1409), which tried (unsuccessfully) to end the Great Schism between the popes of Rome and Avignon. Elected pope by the Council, he defended Rome against his rival, Gregory XII, and, pressured by Emperor Sigismund, convened the Council of Constance to attempt reconciliation again. He agreed to abdicate if his rivals would as well, but then reneged. The Council accepted Gregory's resignation and deposed the other two. The name **John XXIII** was next taken by Angelo Giuseppe Roncalli (1881-1963). Of peasant stock, he was elected pope in 1958 after serving as cardinal and patriarch of Venice since 1953. He made major changes in the church, promoting cooperation with other Christian churches and other religions. The encyclical *Mater et Magistra* (1961) advocated social reform in underdeveloped countries. In 1962 he convened the Second Vatican Council.

John (1167-1216), king of England, from 1199 to his death. The youngest son of Henry II, John succeeded his brother Richard I as king. John's refusal to accept a papal nominee as archbishop of Canterbury led to his excommunication in 1209. High military spending during his reign alienated the nobles, and in 1215 they forced John to sign the Magna Carta, confirming their feudal rights. John later repudiated it and waged a war against the barons, who summoned

The English King John (1167-1216), approving of the contents of the Magna Carta (1215) in the presence of his barons.

J

French support. John died while the issue was still in doubt.
See also: England.

John III Sobieski (1624-1696), late-17th-century king of Poland. Ascending to the throne in 1674 during a time of frequent wars and civil unrest, Sobieski united the Polish people against the incursions of their warlike neighbors and led a Christian army to victory over Turks outside the gates of Vienna in 1683. Following his victory, Sobieski formed a military alliance with the pope, the Holy Roman emperor, and Venice against the Muslims.

John, Elton (real name: Reginald Kenneth Dwight; 1947-), British pop star, pianist, and composer. Partly due to his text writer Bernie Taupin, he evolved into a very successful musician around 1970, with record sales that surpassed those of the Beatles. LPs included *Empty Sky* (1969), *Don't Shoot Me, I'm Only the Piano Player* (1972), *A Single Man* (1978), *Too Low for Zero* (1983), *Reg Strikes Back* (1988) and *The One* (1992). In 1997, Elton John wrote a special adaptation of his former hit song *A Candle in the Wind* for the occasion of Princess Diana's funeral. The single of the song broke the 55 year sales record of Bing Crosby's *I'm Dreaming of a White Christmas*. In just over a month, 35 million copies had been sold. In 1997, Elton John was knighted.

John, Epistles of, three New Testament epistles (23rd-25th) ascribed to St. John the Apostle. First John is a discourse about the 2 aspects of religion, practical and mythical. Second John warns against denials of the reality of Jesus's history. Third John protests an obstinate church leader's failure to receive missionaries.
See also: Bible; New Testament.

John, Gospel of *See:* Gospel.

John, Saint, one of the Twelve Disciples, (called the Evangelist, the Divine, and the Beloved Disciple), son of Zebedee and brother of St. James the Greater, thought to be the author of the fourth Gospel, 3 New Testament epistles and the Revelation.

John Bull, personification of the typical Englishman, created by John Arbuthnot (1667-1735) in a series of pamphlets (1712) satirizing Whig policy. The character was usually portrayed as a burly, good-natured farmer or tradesman.

John Chrysostom, Saint *See:* Chrysostom, Saint John.

John of Austria (1547-1578), Spanish military commander, illegitimate son of Emperor Charles V. Noted for his skill and gallantry, he commanded the Christian fleet and defeated Turks at Lepanto (1571) and conquered Tunis (1573). Governor general of the Spanish Netherlands (1576-1578), he fought the rebellion of William the Silent.

John of Damascus, Saint (c.675-c.749), orthodox Syrian theological writer and antagonist of iconoclasm. He resigned an inherit-

ed post under the Saracen caliph to become a monk.

John of Gaunt (1340-1399), duke of Lancaster, fourth son of Edward III of England. Through marriage to his cousin Blanche, he became the duke of Lancaster. (Their eldest son became King Henry IV.) A commander in France under his brother, Edward the Black Prince, during the Hundred Years War, he married again, in 1371. Through his second wife, Constance of Castile, he gained a claim to the kingship of Castile and Léon. He ruled England for his senile father when the Black Prince was taken ill and his nephew, Richard II, was too young to assume leadership. His economic policies made him unpopular in many quarters, as did his unsuccessful campaigns (1386-1388) to claim the Castilian throne. He remained influential during Richard II's reign, helping to effect peace between Richard and his barons. In 1396 he married Catherine Swynford, his third wife. They were ancestors of the Tudors.
See also: England; Tudor, House of.

John of Leiden (c.1509-1536), Dutch innkeeper who became leader of the Anabaptists in Münster and in 1534 set up a brutally corrupt theocracy, the Kingdom of Zion, with himself as 'king,' in which private ownership was abolished. In 1535 the bishop of Münster crushed the revolt; John was tortured and executed.

John of the Cross, Saint (1542-1591), Spanish poet and mystic, founder of a reformed Carmelite order. Influenced by St. Theresa of Avila, he is remembered for such treatises as *The Dark Night of the Soul.* Canonized in 1726, he was made a Doctor of the Church in 1926.

John Paul I (Albino Luciani; 1912-1978), pope (1978). A moderate traditionalist, patriarch of Venice when elected pope, he died of a heart attack 34 days after his election. His was the shortest papal reign in nearly 400 years.

John Paul II (Karol Wojtyla; 1920-), first non-Italian pope elected in 450 years (1978). A Pole who was archbishop of Krakow before becoming pope, John Paul II has maintained a theologically conservative position on such controversial issues as birth control, abortion, and liberation theology. He has been outspoken on world events, and has spent much of his time traveling to many countries around the world.In 2001 he paid a historic visit to Damascus: for the first time a pope entered a mosque.

Johns, Jasper (1930-), U.S. artist. A leading exponent of pop art, he used common objects in artistic contexts in such works as *Flag* (1958), and *Painted Bronze* (1960). Johns was influenced by Marcel Duchamp.

Johnson, Andrew (1808-1875), 17th president of the United States (1865-1869). American Republican politician, governor of Tennessee (1853-1857), then senator (1857-1862). Johnson stayed loyal to the Union, so after the withdrawal of Tennessee

he was appointed its military governor. In 1864, he was candidate for vice president under Lincoln, whom he succeeded as president after Lincoln's death (1865). Despite opposition from his own party, he aimed at reconciliation with the South. The Senate started the impeachment procedure against him, after he had dismissed his minister of war, Edwin Stanton, unlawfully. Although the necessary two-thirds majority of the votes was not quite reached in this procedure, Johnson's presidency was badly weakened and in 1869 he retired from federal politics.

Johnson, Benjamin Sinclair (Ben) (1962-), Canadian sprinter of Jamaican origin, who first became known in 1987 when he became world champion in the 100m sprint, beating Carl Lewis. Johnson's time of 9.83 meant a new world record. After the finals of the 100m. during the Olympic Games in Barcelona in 1988 came a shocking revelation. Johnson had won the 100m yet again in record time (9.79), but the doping test revealed that he had used stanozolol. After a two-year suspension, he was not able to reach the speeds of his earlier performances. In 1993, drug tests proved to be positive yet again and he was suspended for life.

Johnson, Charles Spurgeon (1893-1956), U.S. educator, sociologist, and first black president of Fisk University (1946-1956). He also helped reorganize the Japanese educational system after World War II and was U.S. delegate to UNESCO.

Johnson, Earvin *See:* Johnson, Magic.

Johnson, Eyvind Olof Verner (1900-1976), Swedish writer. He made his debut with a collection of short stories in 1924, but became well known for his autobiographical development novel *The Story of Olof* (1934-1937). His disgust at national socialism is clear from the novel *The Return of the Soldier* (1940) and the trilogy about a group of resistance fighters *The Story of Krilon* (1941-1943). After the Second World War, he published a number of autobiographical works and historical novels. In 1974, he won the Nobel Prize for literature together with his fellow countryman Harry Martinson.

Johnson, Jack (1878-1946), U.S. boxer, first African American to win the world heavyweight championship (1908). He fled the country (1912), jumping bail after his arrest on charges of violation of the Mann Act (a law prohibiting the transportation of women across state lines for immoral purposes). Johnson's outspokenness and refusal to submit to white supremacy made him highly controversial in the United States. He lost the title to Jess Willard in Havana in 1915, in a fight that he later claimed was fixed.

Johnson, John Harold (1918-), U.S. publisher of black-interest magazines such as *Negro Digest, Ebony*, and *Jet*. He founded the Johnson Publishing Co. in Chicago in 1942. Since 1962 he has also published books directed mainly to black readers.

Johnson, Lyndon Baines (1908-1973), 36th president of the United States (1963-1969). Johnson became chief executive upon the assassination of President John F. Kennedy, then was elected to a full term by an unprecedented majority.

After teaching high school for 2 years, he went to Washington, D.C., as the secretary to a new member of Congress from Texas. In 1934, Johnson married Claudia Alta 'Lady Bird' Taylor. In 1937, Johnson was elected to the U.S. House of Representatives. In 1948, he was elected to the Senate; in 1955, he became Senate majority leader. Johnson became one of the most powerful figures on Capitol Hill. One of his most notable achievements was the Senate's 1957 passage of the first major civil-rights bill since Reconstruction.

In 1960, Johnson ran for the Democratic presidential nomination, but John F. Kennedy won it. Johnson accepted the vice-presidential nomination. The Kennedy-Johnson ticket narrowly defeated Republican candidates Richard M. Nixon and Henry Cabot Lodge.

As vice president, Johnson held an office with relatively little power. That changed suddenly when President Kennedy was assassinated in Dallas, Tex. Johnson took the oath of office the same afternoon. Johnson promised to continue the Kennedy program, and Congress soon passed the Civil Rights Act of 1964 and a new tax law, both Kennedy measures. Johnson also proposed a 'War on Poverty' and persuaded Congress to appropriate almost $950 million for anti-poverty programs. In 1964, Johnson and running mate Hubert H. Humphrey won a landslide victory over Barry Goldwater and William Miller. Now president in his own right, Johnson formulated a wide-reaching program, called 'the Great Society,' for improving U.S. life. At first, Johnson enjoyed unrivaled popularity and wielded tremendous influence. But the overwhelming issue of Johnson's presidency was an unpopular and bloody war. Kennedy had sent the first U.S. troops to Vietnam, but under Johnson their advisory role became a combative one. Johnson gradually committed more troops; by mid-1966, 300,000 U.S. troops were in Vietnam and the fighting showed no signs of nearing an end, despite massive U.S. bombing of North Vietnam and heavy loss of life on both sides.

By 1966, the U.S. was deeply divided over the war. Racial unrest-including riots in the overcrowded slums of several large cities-further taxed an already strained administration. On Mar. 31, 1968, Johnson announced that he would not run for reelection.

Johnson, Magic (1959-), American basketball player who became famous as star player of the Los Angeles Lakers. He was given the honorary name 'Magic' for his inimitable technique. He won the title Most Valuable Player (MVP) 7 times. The American ' Dream Team' won the golden medal at the Olympics in Barcelona in 1992 partly due to his performance . Johnson was appointed goodwill UN -ambassador in April 1998.

Johnson, Michael (1967-), American ath-lete, who specialized in the 200 m and 400 m sprint. He won the world championship ti-tle for the 200 m in 1991 and for the 400m in 1993. Two years later, he was the first ath-lete to win both the 200 m and the 400 m. At the Olympic Games in Atlanta, he won the 200 m (in a world record time of 19.32) and the 400 m again. Four years later in Sydney, he prolonged his title on the 400 m. In 1997 and 1999 he renewed his 400 mworld cham-pionship -title. He ended his athletic career in 2001.

Johnson, Philip Cortelyon (1906-), U.S. architect and historian. Together with Henry-Russell Hitchcock, he wrote *The International Style* and became a major ex-ponent of the new architecture. His glass house (1949) at New Canaan, Conn., won him international recognition. It is clearly influenced by Miës van der Rohe, with whom he designed the Seagram Building, New York City (1958). Johnson's later work includes the New York State Theater at Lincoln Center (1964) and the American Telephone and Telegraph Headquarters Building (1978), in New York City.
See also: Architecture.

Johnson, Samuel (1709-1784), English au-thor, one of the major poets, critics, conver-sationalists, and lexicographers of his time. He wrote for various London magazines be-ginning in 1737, publishing the poem *London* (1738), which inaugurated his fame. From 1746 to 1755 he prepared his pioneering *Dictionary of the English Language* (1755). The moral romance *Rassalas* (1759) followed, and then the *Idler* essays (1758-1760). In 1763 he met James Boswell, his biographer, who record-ed much of Johnson's brilliant conversation. In 1764 he founded the Literary Club (with Joshua Reynolds), an elite circle centered around 'Doctor' Johnson, which included Burke, Garrick, Boswell, and Goldsmith. In 1765, he published his edition of Shakespeare, the model for those to follow. *Lives of the Poets* (1779-1781), a 10-volume work, was one of his last. Johnson's contri-butions were central in defining the period of English literature that came to be known as the Augustan Age.

Johnson, Uwe Klaus Dietrich (1934-1984), German writer. He was one of the most prominent novelists of postwar German literature. The main theme in al-most all his work is the division of Germany, in which he does not so much care for the politics as for the individual people who have to cope with a particular social system. In *Speculations about Jakob* (1959) Johnson sketches a portrait of Jakob Abs, who was killed in an accident, told from accounts by friends and acquaintances. This first novel is written in the form of a police interrogation. The author gives the statements of the peo-ple involved without any form of comment and does not attempt to find the 'truth'. He emphasizes that reality as described by the author is always a 'fictitious reality': every person experiences this in his own way (depending on his personality and therefore from a restricted point of view), so that there will always be different 'realities'.

Johnson also wrote, among other things, *The Third Book about Achim* (1961) and *Two Views* (1965).

Johnson, Walter (1887-1946), U.S. base-ball player. Nicknamed 'The Big Train,' Johnson was a right-handed pitcher famous for his fastball. His achievements include winning the second most games in major league history (416) and pitching the most career shutouts (110). He played for the Washington Senators (1907-1927) and was among the first group of players inducted in-to the National Baseball Hall of Fame (1936).

John the Baptist, Saint (d. c.A.D. 30), Jewish prophet, son of Zacharias and Elizabeth, who was a relative of Mary. John preached a mission of repentance in the Jordan Valley, predicting the imminent com-ing of the Messiah. He baptized his follow-ers and also baptized Jesus, whom he con-sidered the son of God.

John the Evangelist, Saint *See:* John, Saint.

John VI (1769-1826), early-19th-century king of Portugal. He became regent in 1792 when his mother, Maria I, was judged men-tally unfit to rule. He fled to Brazil in 1807 when an invasion by Napoleon was feared. In 1816, while still in Brazil, John became Portugal's king, but he didn't return until a revolution in his favor 5 years later. In 1822 his son, Pedro I, declared Brazil independ-ent.

Johor (formerly Johore; pop. 2.32 million), state in the south of the Malaysian mainland, situated between the Malacca Straits and the South China Sea; 7,333 sq mi (18,985 sq km). The capital is Johor Baharu (pop. 250,000). It is a flat jungle region with swamps along the coast. It is bordered in the north by a mountain range. Rubber, palm oil, pineapples, coconuts, timber, pepper, coffee, and bauxite are exported via Singapore Harbor, to which it is linked by a dam.
It was founded by Mahmud, Sultan of Malacca, after his flight from the Portuguese, in 1511. A long battle was fought for the supremacy of the Malacca Straits, both with the Dutch and with the state of Aceh (Atjeh), which is situated on North Sumatra. During the 17th and 18th centuries, the state fell into neglect, but when the British founded Singapore in 1819,

Jesus being baptized by John the Baptist in the River Jordan. Above the water is a dove, symbolizing the Holy Spirit, referring to the Biblical story of creation: 'God's Spirit moved upon the face of the waters' (Gen. 1:2). Baptistery, Florence.

J

J

they acknowledged its independence. Despite that, the sultan had to tolerate a British 'advisor' beside him from 1914 onwards.

Johor was only developed after 1919, when a railroad from Singapore to the north was finished. The state has more financial links with Singapore than with the rest of Malaysia. Half the population is ethnic Malayan, one third is Chinese and 6% is Indian. The local language was the foundation for the national Bahasa Malaysia language.

Joint, in anatomy, junction or union between two or more bones, especially one in which bones move. Generally speaking, three kinds of junctions can be distinguished. A fibrous junction consists of connective tissue; almost no movement is possible in this type of joint. A cartilaginous junction is composed of cartilage; here only moderate movement is possible. The synovial junction is the most familiar type of joint. Here the extremities of the facing bones are covered with a thin layer of smooth cartilage, separated from each other by synovial fluid. This kind of joint permits the greatest amount of movement. The type of movement possible depends on the type of joint. Some examples are the hinge (knee and elbow), the pivot (neck and skull connection), and the ball and socket (hip and shoulder).
See also: Bone.

Joint-stock company, forerunner of the modern corporation, a form of business association in which the working capital is obtained by selling shares of stock to individuals who may transfer them without the consent of the group. The shareholders are collectively responsible for the company's debts. The most famous early joint-stock companies were the British East India Company (1600), the Dutch East India Company (1602), and the Hudson's Bay Company (1670).
See also: East India Company.

Joint tenancy, ownership of real property by 2 or more persons, each having equal rights to its use during their lifetimes. To qualify, the partners must enter into possession at the same time and hold the title in common. If one tenant dies, the property falls in its entirety to the survivor(s).

Jojoba (*Simmondsia californica* or *S. chinensis*), desert plant of northern Mexico and the U.S. Southwest. Jojoba beans yield a high-quality oil similar to sperm whale oil, which has been banned in the United States since 1971. Processed as a substitute for whale oil, jojoba is used in shampoos, cosmetics, and industrial chemicals.

Joliot-Curie, Irène (1897-1956), French physicist, daughter of Pierre and Marie Curie. She and her husband, **Frédéric Joliot-Curie** (1900-1958), shared the 1935 Nobel Prize in chemistry for artificially producing radioactive materials by bombarding elements with alpha particles. In 1940 they turned their attention to the chain reaction in nuclear fission. Both helped organize the French atomic energy commission, but Frédéric was removed as first chairman in 1950 because of his leftist political views. Irène became chairwoman in 1951. Like her mother, Irène died from leukemia probably contracted as a result of prolonged exposure to radioactive materials.
See also: Nuclear energy; Radiation.

Jolson, Al (Asa Yoelson; c.1866-1950), Russian-born U.S. singer and actor. Star of the first full-length sound film, *The Jazz Singer* (1927), Jolson popularized such songs as 'Sonny-Boy,' 'Swanee,' and 'Mammy.'

Jonah, Book of, in the Old Testament, 32nd in the Authorized Version, 5th of the Minor Prophets. Unique in its entirely narrative form, it tells of the Hebrew prophet Jonah, who disobeyed God's command to travel to Nineveh to convert the city. Instead Jonah sailed away, and his crew threw him overboard during a storm brought on by his disobedience. Swallowed by a 'great fish,' Jonah was cast out of the fish's body three days later. He then returned to Nineveh to fulfill his mission.
See also: Bible; Old Testament.

Jones, Bobby (Robert Tyre Jones, Jr.; 1902-1971), U.S. golfer. Although he was an amateur, he won the U.S. Open four times (1923, 1926, 1929, 1930) and the British Open three times (1926, 1927, 1930). In 1926 he became the only golfer ever to win both those titles in the same year. He won a total of five U.S. Amateur tournaments (1924, 1925, 1927, 1928, 1930). In 1930 he won golf's grand slam, winning the amateur and open championships in both Britain and the United States. After his retirement, he and banker Clifford Roberts founded the Augusta National Golf Club in Georgia, establishing what is now called the Masters tournament.

Jones, Ernest (1879-1958), British physician and psychologist. A colleague of Sigmund Freud and author of a comprehensive 3-volume book on him, Jones introduced Freudian theories and principles to the United Kingdom, the United States, and Canada. His efforts led to the general acceptance of Freud by the medical and scientific communities. In 1911 Jones was one of the founders of the American Psychoanalytic Association, and 2 years later he helped establish its British counterpart.
See also: Freud, Sigmund; Psychoanalysis.

Jones, Inigo (1573-1652), English architect. After studying the works of Palladio in Italy, he designed sets and costumes for court masques and later became the king's surveyor of works (1615-1644). His masterpieces include the Queen's House at Greenwich, the banquet hall at Whitehall, and St. Paul's Cathedral in Covent Garden, London. His departure from the Jacobean style marked the beginning of England's Renaissance and Georgian periods, and he is considered one of the first great architects of England.
See also: Renaissance.

Jones, James (1921-1977), U.S. novelist. His first book, *From Here to Eternity* (1951), portrayed the degradation of army life on the eve of World War II. Other works include *Some Came Running* (1957), *The Pistol* (1959), and *The Thin Red Line* (1962).

Jones, James Earl (1931-), U.S. actor who achieved stardom for his portrayal of Jack Johnson in the stage productions of *The Great White Hope* (1968). He is also an acclaimed Shakespearian actor noted for his role in *Othello* (1963, 1982). Jones won a Tony Award for his performance in the Broadway production of *Fences* (1986). His distinctive voice was used as that of DarthVader, in the classic science fiction film series, *Star Wars*.

Jones, LeRoi *See:* Baraka, Imamu Amiri.

Jones, Marion (1975-), American athlete, who excels in sprinting. Disappointed about not being selected for the Olympic Games in 1992, she withdrew from athletics and took up basketball, in which she also excelled. In 1996 she turned to athletics again, and quickly reached the top. In Athens in 1997, she became world champion in the 100m sprint. She won gold medals in the 100 m and 200 m and the 4x400 m relay at the Olympics in Sydney . During the World Championship of 2001, she won a gold medal in the 200 m and on the 4x100 m relay.

Besides sprinting, she also excels in long jump, although this sport does not have her preference.

Jonson, Ben (1572-1637), English dramatist and lyric poet. His play *Every Man in His Humour* (1598) established his reputation. That was followed by *Every Man out of His Humour* (1599) and *The Poetaster* (1601), a satire. His best-known works were biting comic plays: *Volpone* (1606), *Epicoene* (1609), *The Alchemist* (1610), and *Bartholomew Fair* (1614). His poetry includes the collections *The Forrest* (1616), containing the song 'Drink to me only with thine eyes,' and *Underwoods* (1640).

Jooss, Kurt (1901-1979), German dancer, choreographer, teacher, and exponent of expressionism. He was the founder of the *Folkwangschule* in Essen (1927) was the master of the ballet for the Opera there (1930). In 1932, he founded the *Kurt Jooss-ballet*. He gained international fame for the antiwar ballet *The Green Table* (1932). As a teacher, he has had much influence. His ballet *The Green Table* is still in the repertoire of different companies such as the Joffrey Ballet (New York), where it is continually being practiced by Kurt Jooss' daughter, Anna Harkard, who does this with the help of Labanotation. A second ballet of his, still being performed, is *Big City*.

Joplin, Janis (1943-1970), American rock singer, who was all the rage in the late sixties of the 20th century with raw songs and sensational recitals. She recorded three LPs with her backing group 'Big Brother & The Holding Company', of which *Cheap Thrills* (1968) was the most successful. She died of a drug overdose. After her death a number of records were released with material that had not formerly been used, including *Pearl* (1971).

Joplin, Scott (1868-1917), African-American composer and pianist, the best known practitioner of the style called ragtime. His works include the 'Maple Leaf Rag' (1899) and the opera *Treemonisha* (1911).

Jordan, nonnavigable river beginning in north Israel and flowing about 200 mi (320 km) south through the Sea of Galilee and the Ghor Valley into the Dead Sea. The portion of the river between the Sea of Galilee and the Dead Sea forms the border between the Kingdom of Jordan and the West Bank, occupied by Israel since the 1967 war.

Jordan

Capital:	Amman
Area:	37,738 sq mi (97,740 sq km
Population:	4,312,000
Language:	Arabic
Government:	Parliamentary monarchy
Independent:	1946
Head of gov.:	Prime minister
Per capita:	US$ 1,650
Monetary unit:	1 Jordan dinar = 1,000 fils

Jordan, officially Hashemite Kingdom of Jordan, country in southwest Asia, bordered by Israel to the west, Syria to the north, Iraq to the northeast, and Saudi Arabia to the south and east.
Land and climate. The area east of the Jordan River, with 94% of the country's area, is mostly desert. West of this area is the Jordan Rift, which includes the Jordan River, the Dead Sea, and the Araba, a low, dry riverbed extending down to the Gulf of Aqaba. West of the Jordan River is the most fertile part of the country, the West Bank. It was incorporated into Jordan in 1950 but has been occupied by Israel since June 1967. In addition to the Old City of Jerusalem (annexed by Israel in 1967), the West Bank contains the cities of Nablus, Bethlehem, Hebron, Jericho, Jenin, Rama-llah, and Tulkarm.
People. The population is mainly Arab, and about half are Palestinians, most of whom live in the urban centers. Almost 95% of the

people are Sunni Muslims, the remainder Shi'te or Christians. The official language is Arabic.
Economy. Jordan's economy is largely agricultural, with wheat, barley, and fruits the principal crops. Most industry is limited to food processing and textiles, although there is some oil refining, and cement and fertilizer manufacturing. Phosphate is mined. The economy was greatly disrupted by the loss of the West Bank, and Jordan relies heavily on remittances and foreign aid, mostly from Saudi Arabia and the US.
History. The region that is now Jordan has been ruled by many different empires, including Alexander the Great's, the Roman, and the Byzantine. It was conquered by the Arabs in the 7th century and from then on was part of the various Arab dynasties, including the Umayyads and Abbasids. In 1516 the Ottoman Empire took control, and until the end of World War I Jordan was ruled by the Turks. After the war, it became part of the mandate of Palestine. The Hashemite family, driven out of Arabia by the Saudis, became the local rulers. In 1946 Jordan became an independent state, with the Emir Abdullah as king. In the 1948 war with Israel, the Jordanian army conquered the West Bank. In 1951 Abdullah, who had made a truce with Israel, was assassinated; his grandson, Hussein, was enthroned the following year. Jordan's subsequent involvement in the June 1967 Arab-Israeli War cost it the West Bank, which was occupied by Israel. In 1970 the growing power of the Palestinian guerrillas in Jordan led to a bitter civil war after which the Palestinian fighters were expelled from the country. In 1974, however, Hussein recognized the Palestine Liberation Organization as the sole legitimate representative of the Palestinian people, and in 1988 he renounced Jordan's claim to the West Bank. In 1994 Jordan and Israel signed a peace treaty. Hussein died in 1999 and was succeeded by his son Abdallah. The Muslim-fundamentalist opposition demanded a tougher stand against Israel concerning the Palestinian-Israeli conflict.

Jordan, Ernst Pascual (1902-), German physicist. He was a pioneer in the field of quantum mechanics, a method of analyzing atomic structures and particle motion. Along with Max Born and Werner Heisenberg, Jordan contributed to the development of the first mathematical formula for quantum mechanics in 1925.
See also: Quantum mechanics.

Jordan, Michael (1963-), U.S. basketball player, member of the 'Dream Team' which won the Olympic golden medal in 1984 en 1992. He was nicknamed ' Air' due to his fantastic jumping abilities. Jordan was top scorer 8 times and was awarded the MVP (Most Valuable Player) Prize 5 times: in 1988, 1991, 1992, 1996 and 1999. In 1999 he ended his basketball career, but he made his comeback in the NBA with the Washington Wizards in 2001.

Joseph, in the Bible, favored son of Jacob and Rachel. His brothers, jealous of his dreams and his coat of many colors, sold him into slavery. He was eventually taken to

Egypt, where he became an influential member of the house of Potiphar. He was later unjustly imprisoned, on the basis of accusations made by Potiphar's wife. Joseph won his release by interpreting the pharaoh's dreams, and the pharaoh made him governor of Egypt. While holding that post, he rescued his family from famine.

A desert patrol in Jordan. This task is mainly performed by Bedouin, who have their own elite corps within the Jordanian army.

Joseph, Chief (Hinmaton-Yalaktit; c.1840-1904), leader of the Nez Percé, a Native American tribe. He non-violently resisted the forced resettlement of his people under a treaty fraudulently obtained by the United States in 1863. In 1877, when fighting broke out, he led a 1,000-mi (1,609-km) mass flight from Oregon to Canada. The Nez Percé were defeated only 30 mi (48 km) from the border. Joseph lived out his life on Colville Reservation in Washington.

Joseph, Saint, in Christian tradition, husband of the Virgin Mary, a descendant of David. He is honored by Orthodox and Roman Catholics as the foster father of Jesus. His feast day is March 19.

Josephine (Marie Josèphe Rose Tascher de la Pagerie; 1763-1814), first wife of Napoleon Bonaparte; empress of France (1804-1809). At 17 she married Vicomte Alexandre de Beauharnais, who was executed by the revolutionary government in 1794. Two years later, she met and married Napoleon. Josephine's inability to bear children who could succeed Napoleon resulted in an amicable divorce in 1809. She remained in love with him for the rest of her life and asked to join him in exile on Elba. He refused, but she died before his refusal reached her.
See also: Napoleon I.

Josephus Flavius (c.A.D. 37-100), Jewish historian and soldier in the Jewish revolt against the Romans (A.D. 66). After the revolt, Josephus won the favor of the Roman general Vespasian. He took Roman citizenship and became governor of Galilee. His writings include *History of the Jewish War*, *Antiquities of the Jews*, and *Against Apion* (a defense of the Jews).

J

Joshua, book of the Old Testament, sixth in the Authorized Version. Joshua was the successor of Moses as leader of the Israelites. The book of Joshua describes his command of the Israelite armies in their campaign of conquest of Canaan and the division of the land among the Twelve Tribes of Israel. The Battle of Jericho was one of the major victories of the conquest.

Joshua tree *See:* Yucca.

Josiah, king of ancient Judah (r. 639-609 B.C.). His reign was marked by a revival of traditional Jewish worship. Josiah reinstated religious services in the Jerusalem Temple after destroying the idols his father, King Amon, had placed there. During restoration of the Temple, the laws of Moses were found and Josiah read them to the people. Josiah declared independence from the Assyrian Empire and was killed in battle with the Egyptian Pharaoh Necho II at Megiddo.

Jospin, Lionel (1937-), French politician. Jospin became a member of parliament for the Socialist Party (PS) in 1981. In 1988, he became minister of education. Jospin was the socialist candidate in the presidential elections in 1995, succeeding Mitterand. The Gaullist candidate Chirac was victorious after the second round of elections. After the victory of the left in the snap elections in 1997, Jospin became the new prime minister. After Jospin had not survived the first round of the presidential elections of 2002, he resigned as Prime Minister.

Joule, James Prescott (1818-1889), English physicist who determined the relationship between heat energy and mechanical energy and discovered the first law of thermodynamics, a version of the law of conservation of energy. The joule (a unit of work or energy) is named for him.
See also: Thermodynamics.

Journalism, preparation of information for communications media, including newspapers, magazines, radio, and television. Education to formalize journalism began in the late 19th century, and universities and colleges now offer degrees in journalism.

Jouvet, Louis (1887-1951), a prominent French actor and director. In 1909, he founded, together with a few friends, *Groupe d'action d'art*, which gave performances in small Parisian theatres. In 1913, Jouvet was engaged to perform with Jacques Copeau (1878-1949), who wanted to realize his ideas about the theater in his own theatre, the *Théâtre du Vieux-Colombier*. In 1922, Jouvet founded his own company, which used the Comédie des Champs-Elysées. He achieved great success with the production of Jules Romains' *Doctor Knock*, in which he also played the part of Dr. Knock, a role he played more than a thousand times. Jouvet's versatility was acknowledged when he was appointed a teacher at the *Conservatoire* in 1935. A year later he became one of the directors at the Comédie Française. Besides being an actor and a director, he was also a scene designer and he

developed his own lighting system. Furthermore, Jouvet was interested in the theory of acting, about which he wrote various treatises, such as *Réflexions du comédien* (1939). Jouvet also has a number of films to his name, including *Topaze* (1933), *Volpone* (1939), and *Goldsmith's Wharf* (1947).

Jove *See:* Jupiter.

Joyce, James (1882-1941), Irish novelist, considered by many the leading 20th-century master of the English language. Though Joyce left his homeland at age 20, returning only infrequently for brief visits, he nevertheless was greatly influenced by his Irish roots. *Dubliners*, short stories written in 1914, was published in London but suppressed in Ireland because of its topical references. During World War I he worked on the autobiographical novel *A Portrait of the Artist as a Young Man* (1916), following his protagonist as he comes to realize the grip Irish society has on him and his need for freedom from it. *Ulysses*, written 1914-21, follows Homer's *Odyssey* in themes and allusions. It recounts a particular day-June 16, 1904-in the life of three characters, the salesman Leopold Bloom, his wife, Molly, and Stephen Dedalus (the young man in *A Portrait*). Publication was delayed due to charges of obscenity, and *Ulysses* did not appear in the United States until 1933. In *Finnegans Wake* (1939) Joyce develops a complex exploration of dream consciousness. The meaning of the work has been vigorously debated since its publication. Other writings include three volumes of poetry-*Chamber Music* (1907), *Pomes Penyeach* (1927), and *Collected Poems* (1937)-and the play *Exiles* (1918).

Joyner-Kersee, Jacqueline (1962-), American athlete, who specialized in the heptathlon and in long jump. She became Olympic champion in 1988 and in 1992 in the heptathlon. During the world championships for athletics, she won gold in 1987 and 1993 in the heptathlon, which she repeated during the Goodwill Games in 1986, 1990, and 1994. As a long jumper she became world champion in 1987 and 1991, and became the Olympic champion in this sport in 1988. Her world record of 7.291 points in the heptathlon, which she made on the 17th July 1988, still stands.

J particle *See:* Psi particle.

Juana Inés de la Cruz (1651-1695), Mexican-Spanish poet and scholar. As a girl she left court to become a nun. Criticized for her 'unwomanly' studies, she defended women's education in a vigorous letter to her bishop (1691). Her lyric poems, especially the sonnets, are among the finest in Spanish. She died nursing epidemic victims in Mexico City.

Juan Carlos I (1938-), king of Spain since 1975. Groomed as Gen. Francisco Franco's successor, he was so named in 1969. In 1975, when Franco died, he became the first Spanish king since the deposition of his grandfather (1931). He proved to be an unexpectedly strong force for stability and

democracy and was instrumental in thwarting an attempted right-wing military coup in 1981.

Juan Fernández, 3 small, sparsely populated Chilean islands in the Pacific Ocean. Lying 400 mi (640 km) west of Chile, they were discovered by Spanish explorer Juan Fernandez c.1563. One of the islands, Róbinson Crusoe, is believed to be the site of the self-imposed exile of Alexander Selkirk, the inspiration for Daniel Defoe's *Robinson Crusoe*. The other islands are Alejandro Selkirk and Santa Clara.

Juárez (pop. 790,000), or Ciudad Juarez, city in Mexico, situated on the Rio Grande opposite El Paso, Tex. Juarez serves as a major port of entry from the United States. Founded by Spanish colonial soldiers in 1662, the city's original name was El Paso del Norte ('North Pass'). In 1888 it was renamed in honor of Mexican leader Benito Juarez. Today Juarez is an important cotton-processing center and popular tourist destination.
See also: Mexico.

Juárez, Benito Pablo (1806-1872), Mexican political leader and president (1857-1865, 1867-1872). He enacted major reforms within the military and the church to reduce their power and redistributed large portions of land to poor farmers (*peons*). In the mid-1850s, he overthrew the dictator, Santa Anna, and led the nation's liberal faction in the 'War of Reform.' Between 1864 and 1867 he fought the French and deposed their puppet emperor, Maximilian.

Judah, biblical figure of ancient Canaan. He was the ancestor of one of the 12 tribes of Israel that bears his name. As the fourth son of Jacob and Leah, Judah is credited with persuading his other brothers not to kill Joseph. During the great famine in Canaan, Judah, his brothers, Jacob, and their families settled in Egypt at Joseph's invitation. Judah's name was later given to the kingdom with Jerusalem as its center.

Judah Halevi *See:* Halevi, Judah.

Judah Maccabee (d.160-? B.C.), Jewish leader of the Hasmonean dynasty who, upon his father's death, took leadership of the revolt against the Syrian ruler Antiochus IV, who had initiated religious persecution of the Jews. Judah Maccabee's rededication of the temple of Jerusalem is commemorated by the Hanukkah.

Judaism, religion of the Jewish people, the oldest of the world's monotheistic faiths. The essence of Judaism is the belief in one God. At daily prayers and services Jews repeat the words of Deuteronomy 6:4: 'Hear O Israel: The Lord our God, the Lord is One.' In Jewish beliefs, Abraham, the Jewish patriarch, made a covenant with God that he and his descendants would carry the message of the one God. This covenant, the burden of special service to God, is Judaism's reason for being, and the relationship between God and the Chosen People is the subject of the Hebrew Bible, the foundation

J

The twelfth-century Altneu synagogue in Prague is one of the oldest synagogues in Europe. In the Ark of the Covenant the Torah scrolls are kept (14th century).

On the first night of the eight-day festival of Pesach, the Seder is celebrated, a ritual, commemorating the Jews' oppression in and their exodus from Egypt. Unleavened bread, a slaughtered Passover lamb and bitter herbs are eaten and wine is drunk. Very often, Jews have special dishes for Pesach, such as this earthenware seder dish from 1673, made by Isaac Cohen (Israel Museum, Jerusalem).

of Judaism. The Torah, the first part of the Bible (known as the Five Books of Moses, or the Pentateuch), contains the Ten Commandments and the ritual laws and ethical precepts that form the structure of the Jewish religion. In the centuries after the Bible was completed, its text was explained and adapted by a set of traditions and interpretations known as the Oral Law. When the Temple of Jerusalem and the hereditary priesthood were destroyed in A.D. 70, the Oral Law was recorded in a work known as the Mishnah, the discussion and interpretation of which forms a commentary called the Gemara. These two works together make up the Talmud, second only to the Bible in its authority. Differences over ritual observance are the chief characteristics of the groups within Judaism today. Reform Judaism began in the 19th century in answer to the challenge of rationalism. Reform Jews believe

that each generation has the right to adapt or discard traditions it finds no longer meaningful. Much of the Reform synagogue service in the United States is in English, and the compatibility of Judaism with modern secular values is emphasized. Orthodox Judaism accepts the totality of the Bible and the Oral Law as divine revelation and holds strictly to all dietary laws and codes of conduct. Religious services are conducted solely in Hebrew, men and women sitting in separate parts of the synagogue. The extremes of Reform and Orthodox Judaism have to some extent been bridged in the United States by the Conservative movement, which has attempted to combine the traditions of Orthodox observance with some of the freedom of choice and adaptability found in Reform Judaism.

Judas Iscariot, in the Bible, one of the Twelve Apostles, the one who betrayed Jesus. For 30 pieces of silver he identified Jesus to the soldiers at Gethsemane by a kiss of greeting. According to Matthew, he later repented and hanged himself.
See also: Apostles.

Judas Maccabaeus *See:* Judah Maccabee.

Judas tree *See:* Redbud.

Judd, Donald (1928-1994), American visual artist. Judd was one of the purest exponents of 'minimal art'; a movement in sculpting from the mid sixties of the 20th century onwards, which contemplated the existence of art as a reaction to abstract expressionism and the realistic themes of pop art. The language of form in sculpting was drastically reduced to a number of basic geometric forms: the cube, the square, the oblong, the circle, and the cylinder, in which the personal signature of the artist is completely reduced. Judd's work usually consists of modules: and is constructed from a number of identical forms. Color, material, and the use of space are determining factors. In 1986, he founded the Chinati Foundation in Marfa, Texas: a permanent exhibition of his own work and that of others.

Juddah *See:* Jidda.

Judea, ancient name for south Palestine. Originally known as Canaan, it was called Judea after the Hebrews returning from Exodus took possession of it. The name was derived from Judah, ancestral patriarch of one of the 12 tribes of Israel, and the term Jews is a shortened form of Judeans. King David was the first ruler of a united Judea, with Jerusalem as the capital. After the death of his son, King Solomon, Judea split into 2 kingdoms: Israel and Judah.

Jude, Epistle of, brief letter near the end of the New Testament. It warns against false teachers and the consequences of heresy within the church. Of unknown authorship, the 25-verse epistle is believed to have been written around A.D. 100.
See also: Bible; New Testament.

Jude, Saint, or Saint Judas, one of the Twelve Apostles, also called Lebbaeus or

Thaddaeus, possibly the author of the New Testament epistle of Jude, which warns against heresy. Jude is an anglicized form of Judas, to distinguish him from Judas Iscariot. His feast day is Oct. 28.
See also: Apostles.

Judges, Book of, in the Old Testament, 7th of the Authorized Version, the sequel to Joshua. It recounts the Hebrews' successive apostasies from God and their punishment by enemy oppression. The judges were mainly military leaders sent by God to deliver the people. The main judges are Barak, Deborah, Gideon, Abimelech, Jephthah, and Samson.
See also: Old Testament.

Judgment, legal decision made by a court. A judgment is legally binding upon the parties named in it and often involves restitution imposed on a guilty party by a judge or someone acting in a legal capacity. Once a judgment is handed down, it has the force of law behind it, and violations can be punished by the court. Judgments made in criminal cases can usually be appealed to a higher court, which can either overturn or uphold a lower court ruling.

Judith, book of the Apocrypha of the Authorized Version of the Bible, present in the Old Testament of the Western canon but not in the Hebrew Bible. It tells how a young Jewish widow, Judith, saves her city, Bethulia, by seducing and murdering the Assyrian general Holofernes.
See also: Bible.

Judo, form of unarmed combat, a Japanese sport developed by Jigoro Kano in 1882 using the principles of jujitsu. It combines the use of balance, timing, and force to use one's opponent's own strength against him. Colored belts, ranging from white for beginners to black for experts, denote proficiency grades.

Judson, Adoniram (1788-1850), U.S. missionary. His 30-year work in Burma resulted in the first translation of the Bible into Burmese (1834) and an English-Burmese dictionary (1849). Judson entered the ministry and helped organize a Congregationalist missionary society, which sent him to India in 1812. Disagreements with certain Congregationalist practices led him into the Baptist ministry. He helped the Baptists organize a similar missionary society, and in 1813 he was assigned to Burma.
See also: Baptists.

Juggernaut, or Jagannatha (Sanskrit, 'lord of the world'), Hindu temple and idol in Puri, India. The shrine was completed in the 12th century. Once a year, during the June-July Rathayatra festival, the huge Juggernaut and its brother and sister idols are placed on wheeled carts and rolled through the streets, requiring the work of hundreds of people to move them. The word *juggernaut* has come to mean a heavy, unstoppable force.

Juggling, art of keeping several objects in motion in the air simultaneously and catch-

J

ing them. Juggling was practiced by the Egyptians, Greeks, and Romans; the French equivalent was a medieval troubadour who juggled, sang, and danced. Juggling came into its own in circuses and music halls in the 19th century. The word juggling has also come to mean dishonest manipulation, especially of money.

Jugoslavia *See:* Yugoslavia.

Jugular vein, any of several veins on each side of the neck that return venous blood from the head. Their proximity to the surface makes them liable to trauma.
See also: Vein.

Jujitsu *See:* Judo.

Julian (A.D. 331-363), 4th-century Roman emperor, known as *The Apostate* (the traitor). He was the last ruler to oppose the spread of Christianity in the Roman Empire. The nephew of Constantine I, Julian rejected his Christian education and tried to promote worship of the Roman gods after becoming emperor in 361. He prevented Christians from teaching in Roman schools, but his death in battle against the Persians 2 years later ended the persecutions.

Juliana (1909-), queen of the Netherlands (1948-1980) following the abdication of her mother, Queen Wilhelmina. She abdicated (1980) in favor of her daughter Beatrix.
See also: Netherlands.

Julian calendar, system of time measurement widely used between 46 B.C. and 1582. It was named for Julius Caesar, who devised it. The Julian calendar was based on solar cycles. The year was divided into 12 alternating 30- and 31-day months, with Feb. (29 days) being the exception. The Julian year was 11 min. and 14 sec. longer than the annual solar cycle, resulting in a discrepancy of 10 days by 1582. Pope Gregory XIII corrected the problem, bringing his Gregorian calendar into synchronization with the solar year.
See also: Calendar.

Julius Caesar *See:* Caesar, (Gaius) Julius.

Julius II (1443-1513), pope (1503-1513). As Cardinal Giuliano della Rovere he went into exile (1492-1503) when his bitter enemy Borgia became pope Alexander VI. As pope, Julius commanded the armies that reconquered the Papal States; he then led the Holy League against France (1510). The fifth Lateran Council (1512), which he assembled, attacked corruption in the church. A patron of Raphael, Michelangelo, and Bramante, Julius II laid the foundation stone of St. Peter's Cathedral.

July Revolution, popular revolt in France in July 1830 against King Charles X. Middle-class opposition was aroused when the king's ultraroyalist minister, Jules Armand de Polignac, published the July Ordinances, which suspended freedom of the press, dissolved the chamber of deputies, and reduced the electorate by 75%. Rioting broke out, and though Charles repealed the Ordinances, he was forced to abdicate. His cousin the

The Swiss psychiatrist of analytical psychology Carl Jung dedicated ogy during the early his life to the founding 20th century.

duke of Orleans became King Louis Philippe.
See also: France.

Jumblatt, Kamal (1917-1977), born to a Lebanese family of Muslim feudal rulers. In a society that was dominated by Maronite rule, Jumblatt developed an ideology based on social equality. On these grounds he founded the Progressive Socialist Party in 1949, and in 1972, at the founding of the *Arabic Front in Support of the Palestinian Revolution*, he was elected general-secretary. This movement attempted to link the Palestinian resistance to the battle of oppressed opposition in various Arabic countries, which led to growing solidarity among the population, in Lebanon in particular. During the Lebanese civil war, which broke out in 1975, Jumblatt's progressive alliance opposed the Christian factions that received support from a 20,000-strong Syrian occupying force. After the war, Jumblatt was assassinated.

Jumna River, or Yamuna River, tributary of the Ganges, in Northern India. It begins in the Himalayas and is nearly 900 mi (1,400 km) long. Canals draining water from the Jumna irrigate about 12,000 sq mi (31,100 sq km) in central India. The cities of Delhi and New Delhi lie along the banks of the Jumna, and it flows close to Agra, site of the Taj Mahal. The Jumna joins the Ganges near Allahabad. Their confluence is considered sacred to Hindus.

Jumping *See:* Olympic Games; Track and field.

Jumping bean, seed of various Mexican shrubs, principally those of the genera *Sebastiania* and *Sapium* of the spurge family. The appearance of jumping is due to movement of the larva of the moth *Carpocapsa saltitans* contained inside.

Junco, any of several species of small North American finches (genus *Junco*), usually ashen in color but with conspicuous white lateral tail feathers. The slate-colored junco nests up to the treeline in Alaska, migrating south in winter. Some have crossed the Atlantic.

June bug, or June beetle, any of many large flying beetles (family Melolonthidae) that feed on the leaves of trees. The white larvae live underground, feeding on the roots of grasses and plants, causing considerable damage.

Jung, Carl Gustav (1875-1961), Swiss psychiatrist, founder of analytical psychology. Jung's work on mental complexes brought him into contact with Sigmund Freud in 1907, a relationship that lasted until 1912, when Freud broke with Jung upon the publication of Jung's *Psychology of the Unconscious*. In this book Jung argued that there were two components of the unconscious: repressed or forgotten information of an individual's life and collective information shared by all human beings or by those in particular cultural groups. In 1921 Jung expounded on introversion and extroversion in *Psychological Types*. Jung believed that harmony between the conscious and unconscious was the most important psychological goal for the individual.
See also: Psychoanalysis.

Jünger, Ernst (1895-1998), German prose writer. Junger is particularly important because of his novels, which have war as a theme and in which he comes to terms with his experiences in the First World War. After his father removed him from the French Foreign Legion in 1914, he volunteered for the army. He was wounded fourteen times and received the highest military honors. After WW I he studied philosophy and physics in Leipzig and Naples. During the Second World War, he was stationed in Paris as a soldier for a few years. Both the Communists and the National Socialists attempted to make use of him because of his writing on nationalism in the 1920's. He refused to speak out in preference of either. He developed an aristocratic attitude, emphasizing the intellect.
In *On the Marble Cliffs* (1939), he condemns every form of tyranny and oppression. He also published *Heliopolis* (1949), *Glass Bees* (1957), and *A Dangerous Encounter* (1985).

Jungfrau (German, 'maiden'), mountain in the Swiss Alps. The Jungfrau is 13,642 ft (4,158 m) high and presents a formidable challenge for mountain climbers. It is also the site of the highest railroad in Europe, constructed between 1896 and 1912. The railway ends at a level pass, 11,333 ft (3,454 m) high, between the Jungfrau and its neighboring peak.

Jungle fowl, any of several wild birds (genus *Gallus*), from which domestic fowls probably descended. Found in the forests of southeast Asia, the jungle fowl is becoming rarer as its habitat is destroyed.

Juniper, any of several species of evergreen trees or shrub (genus *Juniperus*) of the cypress family, found in northern temperate zones. The cones of the common juniper (*J. communis*) are fleshy, like berries, and are used to flavor gin. Some junipers are used for lumber and oil; those called cedars, e.g., the American eastern red (*J. virginiana*), supply insect-repellant closets and fence-posts. Its oil is used in perfume and medicine.

Junk, any of various Chinese sailing vessels, used in the Far East for thousands of years. Junks are wooden craft, up to 30 by 10 ft (9 by 3 m), with flat-bottoms, high sterns (rears) and square bows (fronts). They have tall, heavy masts, up to 5 in number, with sails made of cotton cloth or straw matting. They have deep rudders and little or no keel. Though some people live on junks, they are now mainly used for transporting goods on rivers and coastal waters.

Juno, in Roman mythology, queen of the gods. She was the sister and wife of Jupiter, king of the gods, and revered by Roman women as the goddess of marriage and childbirth. Representations of Juno adorned some of the most famous temples of the Roman Empire, and she played a prominent part in *The Aeneid*, Vergil's epic poem about the founding of Rome. Juno's Greek counterpart was Hera.

Jupiter, in astronomy, largest planet in the solar system (equatorial diameter of 89,400 mi/143,800 km), fifth planet from the Sun (average distance 483.6 million mi/778.3 million km). Jupiter is larger than all the other planets combined, with a mass 317.9 times that of Earth. Believed to have a solid core of rocky material, it is mostly gaseous with an atmosphere composed mostly of hydrogen and helium but including traces of ammonia and methane. Prominent cloud belts paralleling its equator are occasionally interrupted by stormlike turbulences, particularly the Great Red Spot, an elliptical area at least 300

yrs old and measuring 30,000 by 10,000 mi (48,000 by 16,000 km). Jupiter has 39 known moons of which the last 11 were discovered in 2002. Io, the satellite closest to Jupiter, exhibits volcanism, probably because of tidal action resulting from its close proximity to the planet. Jupiter, also has a ring system, much fainter than that of Saturn and invisible from Earth. In 1973, 1974, and 1979, U.S. space probes (*Pioneers 10* and *11* and *Voyagers 1* and *2*) collected data on the Jovian system. Another probe, the *Galileo* collected data on Jupiter (1995).
See also: Planet; Solar System.

Jupiter, in Roman mythology, king of the gods and supreme ruler over the entire universe. Patterned after Zeus, king of the Greek gods, Jupiter overthrew his father, Saturn, and married his sister, Juno. Jupiter's other brothers and sisters were Neptune, Pluto, Ceres, and Vesta. His children were Mars, Vulcan, Apollo, Bacchus, Mercury, Diana, Hercules, and the 9 Muses of the arts. Jupiter's temple on the Capitoline Hill in Rome was the focal point of Roman polytheistic worship.
See also: Mythology.

Jura Mountains, forested mountain range in western Europe, crossed by gorges, and fertile valleys, extending from the Rhone River to the Rhine River on the Swiss-German border. The highest peak in the Juras is Cret de la Neige (5,652 ft/1,723 m).

Jurassic, the middle period of the Mesozoic era, lasting from about 195 to 140 million years ago.

Jury, in common law, body of laypeople as-

sembled to study evidence and make judgments in legal proceedings. In England, the jury was probably an extension of the Norman practice of calling character witnesses, people who had personal knowledge of a dispute. Over time, the make-up of the jury changed: disinterested parties were presented with formally produced evidence.

Justinian Code, collection of early Roman civil laws, known as *Corpus Juris Civilis* (Latin, *Body of Civil Law*). Compiled by legal scholars at the behest of the Byzantine emperor Justinian I (r. A.D. 527-565), the code formed the basis of the legal systems of many Western nations for centuries afterward. Justinian had his scholars determine which Roman laws should remain in force, be modified, or be repealed. The code also proposed new laws. The 4 parts of the code are the *Institutes*, the *Digest*, the *Codex*, and the *Novels*.
See also: Law; Rome, Ancient.

Justinian I (483-565), Byzantine emperor (527-565), nephew of Justin I. His attempts to impose heavy taxation and religious orthodoxy on the diverse peoples and sects of the empire, especially the Monophysites (a Christian minority), led to the Nika riots (532), which were quelled by Empress Theodora, aided by Justinian's generals Belisarius and Narses. Among Justinian's accomplishments are the codification of Roman law (*Digests*) and such great churches as Hagia Sophia and San Vitale.
See also: Byzantine Empire.

Justin the Martyr, Saint (c.100-165), Christian theologian who opened the first school of Christian studies in Rome. He was

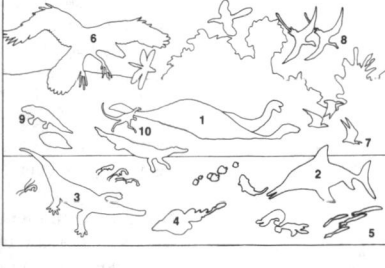

The reptiles of the Jurassic Period not only conquered the land, but they also evolved to fill the air and seas. Some dinosaurs that had adapted to terrestrial life, returned to the sea, including *Plesiosaurus* (1), a turtlelike creature with a long neck and flippers. *Ichthyosaurus* (2), a marine reptile existing in the Triassic Period, reached a length of up to 25 ft (7.5 m) and lived during the Jurassic Period. Crocodiles, such as *Steneosaurus* (3), first appeared at this time and have changed little in the following 140 million years. These sea creatures fed upon the newly developed banjo fish (4) and other fishes. Shrimps and small lobsters inhabited the Jurassic seas, along with belemnites (5), who are cousins of the modern squid. One of the most significant developments of the period is the appearance of the first bird, *Archaeopteryx* (6). Although already covered with feathers, the crow-sized creature retained its reptilian teeth, claws, and tail. Winged reptiles, such as *Pterodactylus* (7) and *Rhamphorhynchus* (8), had neither feathers nor scales, their wings consisted of a leathery skin, that was supported by a single extended digit. Two dinosaurs inhabiting the shoreline environment, were *Homeosaurus* (9) and the tiny *Compsognathus* (10), which attained a length of only 24 in (60 cm). Fossil remains of dinosaurs have been found in parts of every continent except Antarctica.

J

martyred under Marcus Aurelius. His *Apology* and *Dialogue* defended Christianity against charges of impiety and sedition.

Jute, annual plant (genus *Corchorus*) of the linden family, and its fiber. Cultivated in India and Bangladesh, stems of the *C. capsularis* and *C. olitorius* are cut and laid in water until the long fibers can be separated. The fibers are then dyed and spun and used for making burlap, insulation, and rope.

Jutes, Germanic people who originated in Scandinavia, probably in Jutland, the Danish peninsula. With the Angles and Saxons they invaded England in the 5th century, settling in the south and southeast. Their national identify was soon lost, although some cultural influence seems to have survived in Kent.

Jutland, Battle of, only major naval battle of World War I, fought between the British and German fleets off the coast of Jutland (Denmark) on May 31, 1916. Though greatly outnumbered the Germans performed masterfully and escaped in the fog. The British fleet under Admiral Jellicoe suffered heavy losses leading to controversy about Jellicoe's tactics.

Juvenal (Decimus Junius Juvenalis; A.D. 60?-140?), Roman poet. His 16 satires are scathing attacks on the corruption of social and political life in Rome. Many of his epigrammatic sayings ('A sound mind in a sound body') have passed into everyday use.

Juvenile court, court with special jurisdiction over young offenders (usually up to age 18). In many nations, special provisions are made in legal proceedings involving minors. Rehabilitation, rather than punishment, is normally emphasized, including removal from parental care if the home environment is thought to contribute to delinquency. In the interest of flexibility and informality, certain ordinary courtroom practices may be suspended in juvenile court.

Juvenile delinquency, term applied to violations of the law by those legally considered under the age of majority. The maximum age for juveniles varies from place to place. Most countries deal with young offenders in special juvenile courts. Many sociologists contend that criminal activities are only one expression of a disturbed life pattern, of which transiency, violence, poverty, and the failure of family relationships are also typical. The high rate of illegal activity in adolescence probably reflects the general disturbances common to this age group. Action taken by the juvenile courts is theoretically correctional rather than punitive.

K, 11th letter of the English alphabet, is derived from the Semitic *kaph*, representing the palm of the hand, and from the ancient Greek *kappa*. After C was given the K sound, the Romans stopped using K except as an abbreviation. K is sometimes used as an abbreviation for *knight*, as in K.C. (Knights of Columbus); for *kilo*, a prefix

The ushpizin prayer comes from the world of the Kabbalah. Ushpizin is an Aramaic corruption of the Latin hospes (= guest) and refers to the seven guests (Abraham, Isaac, Jacob, Moses, Aaron, Joseph and David), who visited the temporary tabernacle during the Feast of Tabernacles (Israel Museum, Jerusalem)

meaning 1,000; and in chess, for *king*. In chemistry K is the symbol for potassium.

K2, mountain peak in the Himalayas of northern Kashmir, near the China-India border, second highest in the world. Also known as Mount Godwin-Austen and Dapsang, K2 is 29,064 ft (8,859 m) high. It was first scaled in 1954 by an Italian team under the leadership of Ardito Desio. Henry Haversham Godwin Austen surveyed the mountain in 1856.

Kaaba, or Caaba, most sacred shrine of Islam, the chief goal of pilgrimage, in the courtyard of the Great Mosque at Mecca, Saudi Arabia. Pilgrims must circle this flat-roofed building 7 times, and then kiss the venerated object encased within-the Black Stone, said to have been given to Adam on his fall from paradise. The Kaaba is the center of the Muslim world, and it is in its direction that Muslims face in prayer.
See also: Black stone.

Kabalevsky, Dmitri (1904-87), Russian composer and critic. His works include symphonies, ballet, chamber music, and operas, such as *Colas Breugnon* (1938) and *The Taras Family* (1949).

Kabardino-Balkaria (Karbadinian Balkarian Republic; pop. 768,000), Russian federal state on the northern side of the Greater Caucasus; 4,828 sq mi (12,500 sq km). There is agriculture, cattle breeding, and very important mining (gold, chrome, nickel, wolfram, etc.). It became a republic in 1936.

Kabbalah, or Cabala (from the Hebrew

word for 'traditional lore'), mystical Jewish interpretation of the Torah and other holy writings. Based largely on doctrines of post-biblical sages, it entails the idea that every word and letter of the holy writings contains hidden meanings whose mystery must be uncovered through constant study. Under the guidance of Isaac Luria in the late 16th and early 17th century, Kabbalism became more messianic in orientation. Hasidism, a Jewish movement that began in the 18th century, adopted many Kabbalist beliefs.
See also: Judaism.

Kabila, Laurent Désiré (1939-2001), Congolese/Zairian rebel leader. In 1996, he led the armed resistance against dictator Mobutu. A year later, he deposed Mobutu and proclaimed himself President of the Democratic Republic Congo. Cruelties towards Hutu refugees led to international criticism of his regime (UN fact-finding committee). Resistance from his own supporters led to a civil war in which Uganda, Rwanda and Burundi were involved. In July 1999, a peace treaty was signed. Kabila was murdered by a bodyguard in 2001; he was succeeded by his more moderate son Joseph (b 1970).

Kabir (1440-1518) Indian spiritual teacher and enlightened one. He attempted to unite Islamic Sufism with (Bhakti) Hinduism. After conflict with the orthodox leaders of these two movements, he was driven from Benares and became a wandering preacher. His universal love for life is expressed in the collection of sermons *Bijak*. The most prominent of his followers today are Sikhs.

Kabuki, traditional Japanese popular theater that developed in the 17th century in contrast to the aristocratic Noh theater. A blending of dance, song, and mime, kabuki dramatizes both traditional stories and contemporary events in a stylized but exuberant fashion. It remains popular today and has influenced much Western theatrical thought.

Elaborate masklike makeup and intricately decorated costumes are integral parts of Kabuki, a form of Japanese drama that evolved during the late 17th century and that remains popular today.

Laurent Désiré Kabila (left)

Kabul (pop. 1,036,000), capital and largest city of Afghanistan. Strategically located in the Hindu Kush Mountains, Kabul has been a battleground for invading empires during much of its 3,000-year history. It became the capital of Afghanistan in 1773. It is now an economic and commercial center, as well as the site of Afghanistan's leading university. High-quality rugs and karakul sheepskins produced in Kabul are among Afghanistan's leading exports. The city has been the scene of heavy fighting at various times during the Afghan civil war; from 1979 to 1989 it was the headquarters of the Soviet occupying troops. In 1996 it was taken by the fundamentalist Taliban. Kabul was retaken by the Northern Alliance in 2001.
See also: Afghanistan.

Kádár, János (1912-89), Hungarian Communist leader. In the 1956 uprising, he left his position in Imre Nagy's cabinet to lead the Soviet-supported counter-government that crushed the revolt. He became premier (1956-58, 1961-65) and first secretary of the party (1956). His leadership brought a liberalization to all facets of Hungarian life.
See also: Hungary.

Kaddafi, Muammar Muhammad al- *See:* Qadhafi, Muammar Muhammad al-.

Kaesong (pop. 418,000), city in North Korea near the South Korean border, about 30 mi (48 km) northwest of Seoul. It is a key agricultural and industrial hub and the site of many historic cultural landmarks. Chosen as the first capital of a united Korean kingdom (Koryo) in the 10th century, Kaesong was the country's leading city until 1392, when the ruling dynasty fell and the capital was moved to Seoul. In 1951 it was the site of the first peace talks aimed at ending the Korean War.

Kafelnikov, Yevgeni (1974-), Russian tennis player, who was both a good singles and doubles player. He turned professional in 1992 and climbed the ATP league tables slowly but surely. Kafelnikov won the Open French Tennis Championships in 1996. In the doubles, he won the Grand Slam tournaments of France (1996 and 1997) and the US (1997). In 1999 he won the Open Australian

title and reached first place in the world league tables.

Kafir (*Sorghum vulgare*), type of grain of the grass family. Commonly grown on the North American plains and used as cattle feed, kafir was imported from Africa. The plants resemble cornstalks, attaining heights of 4 to 7 ft (1.2 to 2.1 m). Kafir is closely related to the sorghum grains of Africa and Asia.

Kafka, Franz (1883-1924), German writer. Kafka was born in Prague, of Jewish parents. Kafka created stories of conflicts for isolated, guilt-ridden protagonists-conflicts that could not be resolved or escaped, no matter their personal effort. His executor ignored instructions to destroy all his work, and subsequently published his novels, including *The Trial* (1925), *The Castle* (1926), and *America* (1927), and his short stories, including 'The Metamorphosis' (1915), 'A Country Doctor' (1919), and 'In the Penal Colony' (1920).

Kagame, Paul (1957-), Rwandan soldier, politician and President (2000-), belonging to the Tutsi community. His parents fled their home ground, which was dominated by Hutu's, and Kagame grew up in Uganda. He ended his studies in order to join the rebels of Museveni. He was an officer in Museveni's National Resistance Army (NRA), and he was head of the military information office for several years after the civil war, which was won by the NRA. In 1990, shortly after the invasion from Uganda by the Front Patriotique Rwandaise (FPR) and the death of the FPR commander-in-chief, Kagame took over the command from the FPR. After the victory in the Rwandan civil war in 1994, he became Vice President and Minister of Defense in a government of national unity, which was appointed by the FPR. In 1997, at the insistence of the donor countries, he started reducing the number of soldiers. In 2000, he became Rwanda's first Tutsi President.

Kagel, Mauricio Raúl (1931-), Argentinean-German composer, currently one of the most progressive. He went to West Germany in 1957 and since then, he has led the Institution for New Music and the Ensemble for New Music in Cologne. He has an intense interest in the borders of certain art forms, including forms of music theater. In *Sur scène* (1960) the actions of the dancers, mime artists, singers and instrumentalists, for example, have been included in the musical composition, right down to the smallest details. Other work includes *Match* (1964), *Staatstheater* (1967-70), *Chorbuch* (1978), *Aus Deutschland* (1977-80), and the *Sankt-Bach-Passion* (1981-85).

Kahn, Herman (1922-1983), American information theorist. He worked as a military analyst and senior physicist for the Rand Corporation (1948-61). On government orders, he studied the possibility of a Third World War with atomic weapons. This led to the founding of the Hudson Institute, of which he became the director (1961). Kahn was a controversial futurologist. His work

includes *On Thermonuclear War* (1960), *Thinking about the Unthinkable* (1962), and *The Year 2000* (1967).

Kahn, Louis Isadore (1901-74), U.S. architect, noted for his work on housing projects like Carver Court (1944), Coatesville, Pa., and university buildings. His work also included the planning of the Kimbell Art Museum (Fort Worth, Tex.), and the Yale University Art Gallery. Kahn held a professorship at the University of Pennsylvania from 1957 until his death.
See also: Architecture.

Kahnweiler, Daniel Henry (1884-1979), French art dealer and publisher, who originally came from Germany. He stimulated many avant-garde artists, such as Derain, Braque, Gris, and Picasso.

Kaifu, Toshiki (1931-), Japanese politician. Kaifu quickly climbed the ranks in the Liberal Democratic Party (LDP). Before becoming prime minister in 1989, he had been minister of education twice. Kaifu made good use of a few political scandals to strengthen his position within the LDP. He did this further in 1990, when the LDP won 57% of the seats that were eligible for election. Kaifu linked his appointment for a second term of office to the introduction of a new franchise law, which would end the 'money politics'. The faction of elders within the LDP stopped the introduction of this new bill and in this way, they removed power from the younger generation, to which Kaifu belonged. Kaifu withdrew from the race for the post of prime minister, and was succeeded by Kiichi Miyazawa in 1991.

Kala-azar, dumdum fever, or visceral leishmaniasis, severe infectious disease found chiefly in Asia and caused by a protozoa (*Leishmania donovani*) and transmitted by the bite of sand flies. Symptoms include fever, anemia, leukopenia, and enlargement of the spleen and liver.

Kalahari Desert, arid plain in southwest Africa, lying mainly in Botswana but extending into Namibia and South Africa. The region, 100,000 sq mi (260,000 sq km) in area, has low annual rainfall (5-20 in/13-51 cm), seasonal pasture for sheep, and a wide variety of game. It is inhabited principally by the nomadic San (Bushmen) and Khoikhoi.

Kale, edible green vegetable (*Brassica oleracea*) of the mustard family. Valued as a source of vitamins A, B-complex, and C, kale's curled leaves are usually boiled or steamed before eating. Plants may attain heights of 24 to 30 in (61 to 76 cm), while dwarf varieties range from 12 to 15 in (30 to 38 cm).

Kaleidoscope, optical device that produces colorful patterns and designs. It consists of a tube with mirrors and pieces of colored beads and glass that is held to the eye and rotated to form symmetrical color patterns. Patented in 1817, the kaleidoscope is used by designers to formulate carpet and wallpaper patterns.

K

Banjarmasin is the largest city of Kalimantan Tengarra (Southeast Borneo). It lies 25 mi (40 km) from the Java Sea, in a marshy region at the mouth of the Martapura River. Most of its inhabitants are either living in houses with pile foundation, or in boats.

K

Kalimantan, the three-quarters of the island of Borneo that belongs to Indonesia; 208,435 sq mi (539,640 sq km). The capital city is Banjarmasin (pop. 480,000). It is mountainous and mostly covered with tropical rain forests; along the coast, there are lowlands with mangrove forests. It is scarcely populated; the government's transmigration programs have brought approximately one million Javanese to the island. There is agriculture, forestry and cattle breeding. Petroleum, gold, diamonds, bauxite, iron ore, antimony, and lead are mined here. Pontianak is an export harbor. If the deforestation continues at the present rate there will be no more jungle on Kalimantan in 2010. There was a seafaring nation here as early as the 5th century to which Sanskrit inscriptions give witness. It fell under Dutch authority in the 19th century. It was occupied by the Japanese during WW II, then by the Dutch again. In 1950, it became a part of the Indonesian Republic.
The Dayaks are the native population; there are also many Islamic Malayans and Chinese traders.

Kaliningrad (pop. 419,000), port city in western Russia, on the mouth of the Pregolya River, which flows into the Baltic Sea. Formerly called Königsberg, Kaliningrad was founded in 1255 as part of East Prussia. In 1945 it was absorbed by the Soviet Union and renamed Kaliningrad. Today it is a naval base for the Baltic Fleet. Fishing, machine building, and shipbuilding are the main industries.
See also: Union of Soviet Socialist Republics.

Kálmán, Imre (Emmerich) (1882-1953) Hungarian composer. He studied in Budapest, then went to Vienna in 1908 and became one of the great composers of Viennese operetta. His successes include *Die Czardasfürstin* (1915), *Die Bajadere* (1921), *Gräfin Maritza* (1924), *Die Zirkusprinzessin* (1926), and *Das Veilchen von Montmartre* (1930).

Kalmar Union, treaty whereby Denmark, Norway, and Sweden were united under Margaret of Denmark and her heirs. It was signed at the Swedish port of Kalmar (1397), which became the Union's political center. The Union endured until 1523.

Kalmia *See:* Mountain laurel.

Kalmukkia (pop. 322,000), Russian federal state, northwest of the Caspian Sea; 29,316 sq mi (75,900 km). The capital is Elista. The region consists mainly of steppes, semi deserts and deserts. Irrigation for agricultural purposes is only possible in the hilly eastern part. The main agricultural activity is cattle breeding, of which the products are meat, leather, and dairy products. The industry is based on the processing of these.
The population, originally from Mongolia, trailed west during the 16th and 17th centuries. During the reign of Catherine II, a large part returned, to Dzungaria. The ASSR (autonomous republic within the Russian Federation), which was founded in 1935, was dissolved and the population banned as a punishment for collaborating with the Germans (1943). Since 1993, the republic has been governed by the young millionaire Kirsan Ilyumshinov (who is also chairman of the World Chess League FIDE).

Kama, a major tributary of the Volga River in Russia. From its source in the hills west of Perm it flows generally southward 1,260 miles (2,028 km) to the Volga. Much of its length is navigable about six months a year. Several dams on the Kama provide electrical power to Perm and other nearby industrial cities.

Kama Sutra, an Indian guide to the art of lovemaking, written in Sanskrit and presumed to be from the 4th century. It is comparable to Ovid's *The Art of Love*. The author of this work, which is also well known outside India, is Mallanga Vatayayana.

Kamchatka Peninsula, peninsula in northeastern Russia, extending 750 mi (1,210 km) south from the Asian mainland to separate the Sea of Okhotsk from the Bering Sea and Pacific Ocean. It is largely tundra and pine forest, with 2 volcanic ranges. Geographic features include Siberia's highest peak, Kluychevskaya Sopka (15,584 ft/4,750 m), and 22 active volcanoes, along with geysers and hot springs. Main occupations include lumbering, fur-trapping, and fishing. The

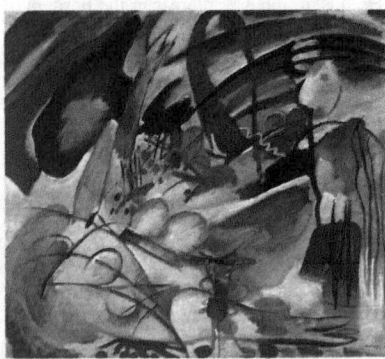

Russian-born Wassily Kandinsky (1866-1944) is considered as one of the princi-pal founders of abstract art. He painted this *Improvisation 33 for Orient* in 1913.

peninsula's main city is Petropavlovsk-Kamchatski.
See also: Union of Soviet Socialist Republics.

Kamehameha I (1738?-1819), Hawaiian king from 1790. This benevolent despot, who conquered and ruled all the Hawaiian islands (1810), encouraged foreign contact and trading.

Kamenev, Lev Borisovich (1883-1936), Russian Bolshevik leader, active in the Russian Revolution and member of the first politburo of the Communist party. After Lenin's death (1924) he joined Stalin and Zinoviev to defeat Trotsky's bid for power. However, Stalin ousted Kamenev and Zinoviev in 1925 and they joined Trotsky's opposition movement. In 1936, Stalin had both Kamenev and Zinoviev arrested and executed for treason.
See also: Bolsheviks; Russian Revolution.

Kamikaze (Japanese, 'divine wind'), Japanese force of suicide pilots in World War II. Inspired by the ancient samurai code of patriotic self-sacrifice, they deliberately crashed bomb-bearing planes onto Allied ships and installations. They inflicted particularly heavy damage at Okinawa.
See also: World War II.

Kampala (pop. 800,000), capital and largest city of Uganda, on Lake Victoria in east Africa. When Uganda became self-governing in 1962, Kampala superseded Entebbe as the capital. The city was originally constructed on six adjacent hills. Uganda's agricultural and commercial markets are concentrated in Kampala.
See also: Uganda.

Kampuchea *See:* Cambodia.

Kandahar (or **Qandahar**) (pop. 330,000), Afghanistan, the capital of Kandahar province and the second largest city in the nation. It lies in a semiarid region of southern Afghanistan, about 280 miles (450 km) southwest of Kabul, the national capital.
Kandahar is primarily a market center for the surrounding agricultural area, where sheep are raised and grain, fruit, and cotton are produced. Food processing and textile making are the city's chief industries. Kandahar is served by an international airport and paved roads to Kabul and Herat. In the center of the city is the domed mausoleum of Ahmad Shah, the founder of independent Afghanistan.
Kandahar is an old city, dating back perhaps to the 4th century B.C. It has been ruled by many conquerors and has frequently been sacked. The present city was begun by Ahmad Shah, and it served as his capital from 1747 until 1773. The British occupied the city twice (1839-42 and 1879-81) during the Anglo-Afghan wars.

Kandinsky, Wassily (1866-1944), Russian painter and theorist, widely regarded as one of the originators of abstract art. Influenced by fauvism in postimpressionist Paris, his early work aimed at pure aesthetic expression by using bursts of color in nonrepresentational paintings. He was a founder, along with Paul Klee, of the Blaue Reiter art movement in Munich (1911; named for his own painting, *Le cavalier bleu*, 'The Blue Rider'). He studied the psychology of color and its effects in *Concerning the Spiritual in Art* (1912) and expressed his viewpoint on art and color in *The Art of Spiritual Harmony* (1914). Geometric compositions came into play in his paintings of the 1920s, at which time he also joined the faculty of the Bauhaus design school in Weimar (1922-33).

Kanem, African empire that lasted from 700 A.D. through the 1800s. It included parts of modern Cameroon, Chad, Libya, Niger, Nigeria, and the Sudan. Kanem declined in the late 1800s when trade routes shifted away from it.

Kangaroo, herbivorous, marsupial mammal of the family Macropodidae, with large hind feet, strong hind legs, and a tail used for balancing, native to Australia and nearby islands. Like other marsupial females, female kangaroos have a pouch in which they carry and suckle their young. The red kangaroo (*Megaleia rufa*) of the Australian plains may reach 7 ft (2.1 m) in height and over 200 lb (90 kg) in weight. Its top speed is about 40 miles (64 km) an hour, with each hop extending as much as 18 ft (5.5 m). Other members of the kangaroo family, classified as genus *Macropus*, include wallabies and tree kangaroos.

Kangaroo apple *See:* Solanum.

Kangaroo court, unofficial and illegal gathering of unauthorized persons for the purpose of passing sentence upon a wrong-doer. Such sentences have been imposed in many countries by citizens' groups, such as vigilante societies in the United States and the illegal Irish Republican Army. The name was first used c.1853 to refer to the 'instant justice' meted out by frontier judges in the United States who 'hopped' like kangaroos from place to place on their legal circuits.

Kangaroo rat, pouched, burrowing, nocturnal rodent (genus *Dipodomys*) similar to the gerbil. It has long hind legs, a long tail, and moves by jumping. Kangaroo rats live in arid regions of the southwestern United States.

Kanishka (d.A.D. 160?), greatest king of the Kushan Empire, which included what is now Pakistan, Afghanistan, and northern India. A patron of Buddhism, Kanishka built a monument in his capital, Peshawar, to house relics of Buddha. He established the Gandharan school of art, which blended eastern and western influences in sculpture. *See also:* Kushan Empire.

Kano Jigoro (1860-1938), Japanese sportsman and teacher, founder of modern judo. Jigoro studied various forms of unarmed self-defense in ancient Japanese educational centers. He opened his own school in 1882, the *kodokan*, where judo was taught and other self-defense sports were practiced.

The red kangaroo (*Megaleia rufa*, order *Marsupalia*), height 7 ft (2 m), occasionally indulges in fighting. He uses his forelegs to grasp the opponent, and the hind legs to inflict wounds. The tail is sometimes used as an additional support.

Kanpur (pop. 2,300,000), city in the state of Uttar Pradesh, north central India, on the Ganges River. An industrial center manufacturing silk, cotton, wool, and leather goods, Kanpur first became an economic power in 1801, when it was ceded to the British East India Company. During the Sepoy Rebellion of 1857 the entire British garrison of the city was wiped out.

Kansas (Sunflower State; pop. 2,500,000), state in the US, bordered by Oklahoma, Missouri, Nebraska and Colorado. Capital city: Topeka. It is one of the four largest cattle-producing states; also arable farming (wheat, corn, sorghum, other cereals, and soy beans), service industries and various other industries (agricultural machinery, aviation, machinery, chemicals, petrochemical and printing). Petroleum, natural gas, coal, salt and sand are mined.

The Spanish crossed the region between 1541 and 1601, and French fur traders were active here between 1682 and 1739. In 1803, the US bought Kansas from France; until 1854 only soldiers, missionaries, traders and Native Americans were allowed into the area. The Kansas constitution was only sufficiently acceptable for it be be a member of the Union in 1861. The Indian Wars lasted until 1878. The east is densely populated.

Kansas City (pop. 1,500,000), name of 2 adjacent cities at the junction of the Missouri and Kansas rivers, one in northeast Kansas (inc. 1859) and one in northwest Missouri (inc. 1850). This area, as eastern terminus of the Santa Fe trail (1850), served as the starting point for many Western expeditions and gave rise to several settlements in the early 19th century. The building of the railroads increased the importance of Kansas City. Today the cities serve as an industrial, cultural, transportation, and commercial center, with extensive stockyards, grain elevators, mills, and refineries.

Leading products include automobiles, farm machinery, and printed materials. Sights include the Nelson Gallery-Atkins Museum (Missouri), a Shawnee mission (1839), and an agricultural museum (Kansas). *See also:* Kansas; Missouri.

Kant, Immanuel (1724-1804), German philosopher, founder of critical philosophy. Though originally influenced by the rationalism of Leibniz, Kant was awakened from his 'dogmatic slumber' by the work of skeptic David Hume and thus led to greatness as a metaphysician. In *Critique of Pure Reason* (1781), Kant proposed that objective reality (the phenomenal world) can be known only because the mind imposes its own structure (time and space) on it. Things beyond experience (noumena) cannot be known, though we may presume to know them. The questions of the existence of God, immortality, freedom-all metaphysical questions-cannot be answered by scientific means, and thus cannot be proved or disproved. But, according to Kant in *Critique of Practical Reason* (1788), their existence must be presumed for the sake of morality. Kant's absolute moral law states, 'Act as if the maxim from which you act were to become through your will a universal law.' In *Critique of Judgment* (1790), beauty and purpose form the bridge between the sensible and the intelligible worlds that he sharply divided in his first 2 *Critiques*. Kant's influence is extensive, particularly in Germany. G.W.F. Hegel, F.W.J. von Schelling, and J.G. Fichte, influenced by Kant, developed German idealism; Ernst Cassirer of the physical sciences and Heinrich Rickert of the historical and cultural sciences applied neo-Kantian insights to their studies. Kant influenced the theology of F.D.E. Schleiermacher, the pragmatism of U.S. philosophers William James and John Dewey, and Gestalt psychology. *See also:* Metaphysics; Philosophy.

This portrait of Kant, painted in 1931 by Kuhnt, after a 1791 miniature by G. Doeppler, can be found in the Staatliches Kantgymnasium in Berlin.

Kantor, MacKinlay (1904-77), U.S. screenwriter and author. A newspaper writer (1921-31), Kantor also wrote screenplays and several books, including *Long*

K

K

Remember (1936), *The Voice of Bugle Ann* (1935), *Arouse and Beware* (1936), *Happy Land* (1943), and *Andersonville* (1955).

Kaohsiung (pop. 1,500,000) Taiwan, the second largest city of Nationalist China. It is on the southwest coast about 180 miles (290 km) from Taipei, the capital. Kaohsiung is the leading seaport of southern Taiwan and a manufacturing center. One of the island's two international airports, a naval base, a technological institute, and a medical college are in or near Kaohsiung. Kaohsiung was settled early in the 17th century and was opened as a Chinese treaty port in 1863. After Japan gained control of the island in the Sino-Japanese War of 1894-95, Kaohsiung was developed as a center for processing and exporting agricultural products. Japanese control of the city ended in 1945. Rapid growth and industrial development occurred after 1950.

Kaolin, or china clay, soft, white clay composed chiefly of the mineral kaolinite, mined in England, France, former Czechoslovakia, China, and the southern United States. It is used for filling and coating paper, filling rubber and paints, making pottery and porcelain, and in medicine, to treat diarrhea.

Kapitsa, Pyotr (1894-1984), Russian physicist best known for his work in low-temperature physics (cryogenics). During the 1920s and early 1930s he worked at Cavendish Laboratory in Cambridge, England. After returning to the USSR (1934) he directed the Institute for Physical Problems. He was an outspoken advocate of freedom of thought and scientific exchange and was awarded the 1978 Nobel Prize for physics.
See also: Physics.

Kapok (*Ceiba pentandra*), tropical tree; also, the water-repellent fiber of its seeds. Kapok is used as a stuffing for life jackets, mattresses, pillows, and cold-weather clothing, and as insulation against heat and sound. Oil from its seeds is used in the manufacture of soap. Kapok trees are found in India, Indonesia, Africa, and other tropical regions.

Kaprow, Allan (1927-), American visual artist, promotor of junk art. Kaprow is also a composer of electronic music. In 1959 he organized the first happening (a creative and artistic event of the 1960s and 1970s) in New York.

Karachi (pop. 10,000,000), former capital (1947-59) of Pakistan, and the country's largest city, major port, and industrial center. It stands on the Arabian Sea near the Indus River delta in Sind province, of which it is the capital. Among its manufactures are automobiles, steel, petroleum products, and textiles. Karachi began to develop as a trading center in the early 18th century. In 1843 the British took over and made it a military outpost, a major seaport, and the seat of the Sind government. Upon independence, Karachi became the capital of the new nation, until the new city of Islamabad was made capital in 1960. The tomb of Pakistan's founder, Muhammad Ali Jinnah, rests there.
See also: Pakistan.

Karadzic, Radovan, Bosnian-Serb politician. Karadzic, originally a psychiatrist, was one of the founders of the Serb Democratic Party (SDS; 1990). He led the Bosnian Serbs in Bosnia-Herzegovina against the Bosnian Croats and the Bosnian Muslims. In attempt to have the Bosnian Serbs join Serbia, he became dependent on Serb support and that of President Milosevic. Karadzic is suspected of having given the orders for ethnic cleansing and war crimes. For these reasons, he is wanted by the international war crimes tribunal on Yugoslavia.

Karaganda (Qaraghandy; pop. 613,000), city in Kazakhstan. It is a mining town with industries for building materials, iron, steel and food.
It was founded in 1856 for copper mining and was rapidly developed during the 1930's. During WW II it was occupied by the Germans. It was a place of exile for dissidents during the Communist regime.

Karajan, Herbert von (1908-89), Austrian conductor. He directed the Berlin State Opera (1938-45), the Vienna State Opera (1956-64), and the Berlin Philharmonic Orchestra (1955-89).

Karakalpakstan (pop. 2,000,000), federal republic in Uzbekistan, near the Aral Sea; 63,962 sq mi (165,600 sq km). The capital is Nukus. There is agriculture in the valley of the Amu Darya (cotton, among other things). Fishing takes place in the Aral Sea. It became a republic in 1932.

Karakoram (or Karakorum), a mountain range in central Asia. With the Himalayas, the Kunlun Shan, and other ranges, it is part of the great mountain system extending from the Pamirs to Indochina. The Karakoram Range lies north of the western Himalayas and stretches for 300 miles (480 km) along or near the China-Kashmir border. Some of the world's highest peaks are here; K2 reaches 28,250 feet (8,611 m) and is second only to Mount Everest in height. Karakoram Pass, at 18,290 feet (5,575 m), was long part of an important trade route between central and southern Asia.

Karakorum, ancient capital of Genghis Khan's empire. Its ruins, discovered in 1889, stand in what is now the Mongolian People's Republic, on the Orhon River. Established c.1220, it fell into decay by the 16th century. Marco Polo visited Karakorum c.1275.
See also: Genghis Khan.

Karakul, any of several species of sheep of Central Asia, bred primarily for their fur-bearing skin. The pelts of the Karakul are called Persian lamb, broadtail, and caracul. The wool of the lamb is lustrous, smooth, and often black. A mature Karakul's fleece is thick and rough in texture and may have a range of colors including white, brown, gray, and yellow.

Kara Kum, desert region in Turkmenistan, in central Asia, covering about 135,000 sq mi (330,000 sq km) in area. The Kara Kum canal, extending from the Amu Darya River through two oases to the city of Ashkhabad, enables parts of the desert to be irrigated and used for grazing sheep, goats, and camels.

Karamanlis, Constantine *See:* Caramanlis, Constantine.

Karaoke, Japanese expression for 'orchestra without a voice', or 'empty orchestra'. In and outside Japan it is a much-loved social event. An audiotape or videotape is played - with well-known hits but without the vocals. Instead, one or more persons sing along into one or two microphones and have the opportunity of being 'a star'. If it is karaoke with a videotape, the words of the song appear on the television screen so one can sing along. The performance can be recorded on a tape recorder.

Kara Sea, branch of the Arctic Ocean about 300 miles (480 km) long and 200 miles (320 km) wide off the north central coast of Siberia. The sea is bounded on the east by the Yamal Peninsula and on the west by the Novaya Zemlya Islands.
See also: Arctic Ocean.

Karate (Japanese: 'empty hand'), unarmed combat and sport, originating in the Orient. Hands, knees, elbows, and feet are all used to deliver blows against vulnerable pressure points on the body of the attacker.

Karbala, city in South Iraq. Karbala is one of the holy sites of Shiite Islam. A battle took place here between the Omayad army and the rebel army under the command of the Imam Hussein, the son of Ali ibn Abu Talib and the grandson of Mohammed, in 680 on the day of Ashura. Hussein died a martyr's death here and his beheaded body was buried here. The head of Hussein was taken to Damascus and is kept there in the great Omayaden mosque. His mausoleum in Karbala, which is called Mashad al-Hussein, became an important center of pilgrimage particularly for the Shiite Muslims. Sunni Muslims also revere Hussein. Karbala evolved into an important theological Shia center. The city has extensive burial grounds, because many Shiites wish to be buried in the vicinity of Imam Hussein.

Karelia, self-governing republic in northwestern Russia. Its capital city is Petrozavodsk. Bordering Finland, it has an area of about 70,000 sq mi (181,000 sq km), with vast pine forests and more than 2,000 lakes. Lumbering, forest industries, iron working, and fishing are the major sources of employment.
See also: Union of Soviet Socialist Republics.

Karen, Mongoloid tribal people in Burma and West Thailand. In Burma under British rule, the position of the Karen improved a great deal and they gained a large amount of autonomy. The Karen National Union (KNU) is currently one of the most important opposition movements struggling against the Burmese government forces. The Karen in Thailand are mainly farmers (rice) with a matriarchal lineage systems. Their language, which can be divided into three groups, belongs to the Sino-Tibetan language group.

Karimov, Islam Abduganiyevich (1938-), Uzbekian politician. From 1966 onwards, Karimov worked at the Economic Planning Bureau in the Soviet Union and in 1986, he became regional leader of the Communist Party. In 1989, he became a member of the Uzbekian Communist Party, and in 1990 a member of the Polit Bureau. In reality, it meant that he was the president of Uzbekistan. In 1991, the former Communists united as the People's Democratic Party, but little changed: the democratic and Islamic opposition was supressed and strict censureship was introduced. Under Karimov's leadership a few careful reforms were made (price liberalization and privatization). In 1995, Karimov's term of office was extended to the year 2000 by referendum.
At the presidential elections of 2000, Karimov was re-elected for his last 5 year term. In 2002, however, he held a referendum that prolonged his presidency to 7 years (2007).

Karlfeldt, Erik Axel (1864-1931), Swedish poet. He studied in Uppsala and was a librarian from 1900 to 1912. Afterwards, he became the secretary of the Swedish Academy, of which he had been a member since 1904. In 1918, he was presented with the Nobel Prize for Literature, which he refused. This was awarded to him posthumously in 1931 for his complete works. Karlfeldt is the poet of his native region Dalecarlia, which he personified in the figure of Fridolin. He expresses the dark mysticism of nature as well as an idealization of country life. Karlfeldt's poems and verses consist of artfully crafted rhyming. His collections of poems include *Songs of the Wilderness and of Love* (1895), *Fridolin's Song* (1898), *Fridolin's Pleasure Garden* (1901), *Flora and Pomona* (1906), *Flora and Bellona* (1918), and *The Horn of Autumn* (1927).

Karl-Marx-Stadt, nowadays Chemnitz (pop. 273,000), industrial city in eastern Germany and chief center of the Karl-Marx-Stadt district, situated on the Chemnitz River. Famous since medieval times for its textiles, Karl-Marx-Stadt now also produces machinery, machine tools, chemicals, and optical instruments. The city was chartered in 1143, destroyed during the Thirty Years War, and severely damaged in World War II. It was renamed Karl-Marx-Stadt in 1953. In 1990 the name was reverted back to Chemnitz.
See also: Germany.

Karloff, Boris (William Henry Pratt; 1887-1969), English-born U.S. actor renowned for his parts in horror films. His most famous roles were as the monster in *Frankenstein* (1931) and *The Bride of Frankenstein* (1935).

Karlovy Vary (pop. 58,000), resort and spa in western Bohemia, Czech Republic, famed for its mineral springs. The most celebrated of its 17 functioning springs is the Vridlo. Glassware, china, and pottery are the main industrial products.
See also: Czech Republic.

Karma, Sanskrit term denoting the inevitable effects of a person's physical and mental actions on his or her destiny in successive lives, central to Buddhist and Hindu thought.
See also: Sikhism.

Karmal, Babrak (1929-1996), Afghan politician. Karmal was a member of the banned communist People's Democratic Party of Afghanistan (PDPA) since its founding in 1965 and within this party he became one of the leaders of the Parcham faction, which leaned towards the Soviet Union. After the April revolution in 1978, which brought the PDPA to power, he became vice premier, but was forced to resign from this position when the Parcham faction was defeated by the rival Khalk wing of the party. After the Soviet invasion of December 1979, he was helped into power as the head of state and the leader of the party. He was unable to break the Islamic resistance or even to reconcile the Parcham and Khalk factions. In 1986, he was replaced by Najibullah.

Karnak, village east of Luxor, on the Nile in central Egypt, part of ancient Thebes. It is the site of the Great Temple of Amon, perhaps the finest example of ancient Egyptian religious architecture.
See also: Egypt.

Karnak, Temple of *See:* Thutmose III.

Karnataka Wars, war between the French and the British over the coast of Karnataka (Southwest India) in the 18th century. In this region, Madras and other places were governed by Clive, who was British; the French governor Dupleix ruled Pondichéry. The main provocation was the situation in Europe in the Austrian Succession Wars (1740-1748). During the seven-year war (1756-1763), the French were driven from Karnataka.

Karpov, Anatoly (1951-), a Russian chess prodigy who became the Soviet champion in his early 1920's. He was awarded the world chess championship in 1975, after reigning champion Bobby Fischer of the United States had repeatedly refused to defend his title. In 1981 Karpov defeated his principal challenger, Viktor Korchnoi, for the second time. In 1985 he lost his title to Gary Kasparov in a second match for the world title. Karpov's most recent attempt to regain his championship ended unsuccessfully when he was beaten again by Gary Kasparov in a 24-game match in Dec. 1990. In 1993 and 1996 Karpov became world champion in the FIDE version.
See also: Chess.

Karsavina, Tamara Platonovna (1885-1978), Russo-British ballerina. She made her debut in 1902 at the Marinsky Theater in St. Petersburg, where she (until 1917) danced the leading roles of the classic repertoire. From 1909 onwards, she was also engaged in Diaghilev's *Ballets Russes*, where she excelled in the ballets of Folkine. From 1930 to 1955 she was the vice president of the Royal Academy of Dancing in London and was active up until late in life as a consultant for ballet companies and solo dancers. She published, among other things, *Theatre Street* (1930,1931 and 1961) and *Ballet Technique* (1956). Karsavina is regarded as one of the greatest dancers of all times.

Kart racing, sport that features single-seated, rear-engine racing cars. Referred to as go-karts, these automobiles can reach speeds of 140 mph (225 kmph) In most national competitions, drivers must be 16 years or older, but competitions for children ages 8 and 9 are quite popular. Very popular in Europe, kart racing was invented in 1956 in the United States.

Karzai, Hamid (1957-), Afghan politician and President (2002-), descending from the powerful Popolzai-clan. Karzai was in Pakistan during the occupation of Afghanistan by Soviet troops. He was an advisor to the Mujaheddin and a diplomat. In the early days of the Taleban, in the beginning of the 1990s, he supported the movement hoping that it would be able to put an end the violence. In 1992, after the departure of the Soviet troops, he became Secretary of State. He resigned from the government after a short period of time, due to the many mutual disputes and the continuous violence

Hamid Karzai (green jacket)

K

K

between the various clans. After the Taleban had consolidated its grip on Afghanistan in 1996, he was forced to flee. He left for Pakistan, where he organized the opposition against the Taleban. They reacted by shooting Karzai's father, leader of the Popolzai-clan. Karzai became the new Popolzai-leader and laid the foundation for his position as an Afghan leader. A few days after the attacks of September 11, 2001, he started raising weapons, money and communication means, with the intention of mobilizing a tribal militia that was to bring down the Taleban government. In October, after the American bombardments had started, he crossed the border to Afghanistan. In December 2001, he was sworn in as the leader of the (new) interim government. In 2002, he was elected President of the transitional government.

Kasavubu, Joseph (1917?-69), African politician, first president (1960-65) of the Republic of the Congo (now Zaïre). He ousted Premier Patrice Lumumba but was himself supplanted (1965) by Gen. Joseph Mobutu.
See also: Congo (Zaïre).

Kashmir, disputed territory in southern Asia, administered since 1972 as the Indian state of Jammu and Kashmir (capital: Srinagar; 54,000 sq mi/139,000 sq km) and the Pakistani Azad Kasmir (capital: Muzafarabad; 32,000 sq mi/82,900 sq km), bordering China. This beautiful region, which includes sections of the Himalayan and Karakorum mountain ranges, centers around the Vale of Kashmir, the agricultural area where rice and wheat are grown, fed by the Jhelum River. After years of rule by Hindus and Buddhists, Islam took hold in the late 14th century, and Kashmir became part of the Mogul empire (1586). In the mid-19th century the British restored Hindu rule. Since India's partition (1947) the territory has been the source of a dispute between India and Pakistan, with some interference from China (1959-63). Current boundaries were established in 1972. In 1996 the Indian

Kathmandu's Pashupatinah Temple, a Hindu holy place.

government sent troops to fight armed movements such as the Hizbul-Mujahedeen and the Harkat-al-Ansar. In the same year, elections for a representative for the federal parliament took place. The elections caused turmoil when the Islamic parties called for a boycot of the elections whereas the government sometimes tried to force people to vote.
See also: India; Pakistan.

Kasparov, Gary (1963-), Russian chess prodigy who at 22 became the sport's youngest world champion by beating Anatoly Karpov (1985). He has successfully defended his title, most recently by beating Anatoly Karpov in a 24-game match that ended on Dec. 31, 1990. In 1993, he was one of the founders of the Professional Chess Association (PCA), which organized its own world championship. In 1995 Kasparov prolonged his world title in the PCA version. In 1996 he defeated Deep Blue, the IBM chess computer. The next year, however, Deep Blue won.

Katanga (between 1971 and 1997: Shaba; pop. 4.8 million), province in the southeast of Congo (Zaire); 191,952 sq mi (496,965 sq km). The capital is Lubumbashi. There are many gorges and mountain ranges running from north to south. Economically, it is a very important region; it is a rich mining area with copper, gold, coal, iron, cobalt, cadmium, silver, radium, uranium and manganese; the industry is based on this. There is agriculture (tobacco, cotton, and coffee), cattle breeding and fishing. The Lubas (Baluba) inhabit this area. Their ancestors have come here since the colonial era from other parts of the country to work in the mines. From 1960 to 1963, Katanga tried, unsuccessfully, to become independent of the Congo.

Katayev, Valentin Petrovich (1897-1987), Russian novelist, poet, and playwright. Among his best-known works are the novels *The Embezzlers* (1926) and *Lonely White Sail* (1936), and the farce *Squaring the Circle* (1928).

Kathmandu (pop. 420,000), capital of Nepal, 4,500 ft (1,370 m) above sea level in a Himalayan valley in central Nepal. The city lies on an ancient route from India to Tibet and China and is a vital commercial and administrative center. Important sites include temples, the royal palace, and Sanskrit libraries.
See also: Nepal.

Katowice (pop. 360,000) Poland, the capital of Katowice province. The city lies about 160 miles (257 km) southwest of Warsaw in Upper Silesia, a major industrial and coalmining region. Katowice's main industries include the manufacture of machinery, chemicals, and fertilizers, and the processing of zinc and lead, which are mined in the region. The city is also a major railway junction. Educational institutions her include the University of Silesia and the Medical Academy of Silesia. Katowice was founded in the late 16th century. It came under Prussian control in 1742 and was incorporat-

ed into the German Empire in 1871. The city transferred from Germany to Poland after World War I. From 1953 to 1956 Katowice was called Stalinogród.

Katsukawa Shunei (1762-1819), Japanese painter, Shunyo's pupil. He was famous for his dramatic prints of actors and sumo (Japanese wrestling), which was a popular sport during the Tokugawa dynasty and a much-loved theme for artists.

Katydid, name for several large, green, winged insects of the long-horned grasshopper family (Tettigoniidae), native to the Western Hemisphere. Katydids, which range in length from 1.25 to 5 in. (3 to 12.5 cm), are tree-dwelling and nocturnal. Males produce a song, which sounds like 'Katy did, Katy didn't,' by rubbing together specialized parts of their wings.

Katyn forest, site in the former USSR of a massacre of some 4,250 Polish officers in World War II. The mass grave was reported in 1943 by the Germans, who accused the Soviets, who in turn accused the Germans. Stalin refused a Red Cross inquiry, and the Polish government-in-exile in London took this as an admission of Soviet guilt. A U.S. congressional investigation in 1952 charged the Soviets with responsibility. In 1990 the Soviet government admitted responsibility for the massacre.
See also: World War II.

Kauffmann, Angelica (1741-1807), Swiss painter. Her works often depict mythological and historical events from ancient Greece and Rome. Initially a portrait painter in Italy, she traveled to England and in 1768 became a founding member of London's Royal Academy of Arts. Kauffmann returned to Italy in 1781. She is known for her wall paintings decorating English residences designed by Robert Adam. Other works include *Religion* and *La Pensierosa*.

Kaufman, George S. (1889-1961), U.S. playwright and stage director. His collaborations (over 40 plays and musicals), often noted for their satire, included *Beggar on Horseback* (1924, with Marc Connelly), *Of Thee I Sing* (1932, with Morrie Ryskind and George Gershwin; Pulitzer Prize), *Dinner at Eight* (1932, with Edna Ferber), and some of his most successful, written with Moss Hart, *You Can't Take It with You* (1936, Pulitzer Prize) and *The Man Who Came to Dinner* (1939).

Kaunas (pop. 429,000), former capital city of Lithuania. Founded in 1030, it is Lithuania's second largest city and produces one-quarter of its manufactured goods, which include machine tools, paper, radio, and textiles. A cultural center as well, Kaunas has several museums and many buildings dating from the 15th century.
See also: Lithuania.

Kaunda, Kenneth David (1924-), African political leader, president of Zambia (1964-91). From 1953 he worked for African rule in Northern Rhodesia, which was then a British dependency, suffering exile and im-

prisonment. Released in 1960, he headed the new United National Independence Party, and became Zambia's first president upon independence (1964). In December 1997, Kaunda was arrested on suspicion of involvement in the attempted coup in October. In 1998 he was acquitted and left politics.
See also: Zambia.

Kava, shrub (genus *Piper*) native to the Pacific Islands and Australia, closely related to the pepper plant. Kava may reach a height of 5 ft (1.5 m), and has round leaves and yellowish-cream flowers. Juice taken from the root of the shrub is used to produce a nonalcoholic intoxicant called kava or kavakava.

Kawabata, Yasunari (1899-1972), Japanese novelist. He is noted for his impressionistic, lyrical style and a preoccupation with loneliness and death. One of his best-known works is *Snow Country* (1947). He was awarded the 1968 Nobel Prize for literature, the first Japanese to win the prize.

Kawara, On (1933-), Japanese visual artist, representative of conceptual art. He is famous for time/place documentations, which are consistently carried out (*I'm Still Alive Series*) and gain shape because of the texts. His art has a strongly existential character.

Kawasaki disease, disease believed by many doctors to be caused by a virus, affecting children, primarily boys of Asian ancestry from middle- and upper-class backgrounds. Its symptoms include high fever, sore throat, redness of the eyes, and sore, bleeding lips. It can result in inflammation and scarring of the artery walls. Palliative treatment with aspirin and gamma globulin reduces the risk of heart damage.

Kaye, Danny (1913-87), American comedian and entertainer whose films, television shows, and personal appearances made him an international personality. He first gained attention in 1940 in the Broadway musical *Lady in the Dark*. Among his more important films were *The Secret Life of Walter Mitty* (1947), and *The Inspector General* (1949). He was an ambassador-at-large for Unicef.

Kayseri (pop. 421,000), city in Turkey, in Central Anatolia at the foot of the extinct volcano Erciyas (Argaeus), it is the capital of the province of the same name; (province 6,387 sq mi (16,537 sq km, pop. 871,000) It is a center of trade and industry with textile, meat processing, and aviation industries. In the 11th century, the city was conquered by Selyukan Turks and by Ottoman Turks in 1515. Kayseri has very ancient minarets, mosques, and forts. In the vicinity, lie the ruins of Caesarea Mazaca, which was the center of Cappadocia.

Kaysone Phomvihane (1920-1992), Laotian politician. Kaysone studied law in Hanoi, where he became influenced by the North Vietnamese leader Ho Chi Minh. During the struggle against French domination of Laos, he joined the communist resist-

ance movement Pathet Lao, of which he became general-secretary after the French had left. After the communist rise to power in 1975, he was both party leader and prime minister. He dominated the politics of Laos until his death as party leader and president from August 1991.

Kazakhstan

Capital:	Astana
Area:	1,049,150 sq mi
	(2,717,300 sq km)
Population:	16,472,000
Language:	Kazakh
Government:	Presidential republic
Independent:	1991
Head of gov.:	Prime minister
Per capita:	US$ 5,900
Monetary unit:	1 Tenge = 100 tyin

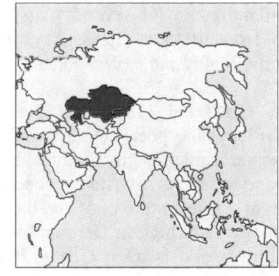

Kazakhstan (Republic of), independent country in central Asia, bordered on the west and the north by Russia, on the east by China, on the south by Kyrgyzstan, Uzbekistan, and Turkmenistan, and on the west by the Caspian Sea. The capital is Astana (since 1998; Astana was formerly called Akmola).
Land and people. Two thirds of the country is (semi) arid. The Caspian Sea is a great salt lake (92 ft/28 meters below sea level). Kazakhstan has a continental climate, with considerable differences between different areas. The population is 43% Kazakh and 37% Russian and Ukrainian. One half of the population are Christians, the other half are Muslims. The official language is Kazakh.
Economy. A producer of wheat, cotton, sheep, and cattle, Kazakhstan is also rich in minerals. Amongst other things, it possesses huge oil and gas supplies.
History. Formerly one of the 15 constituent republics of the USSR (Soviet Union), Kazakhstan became independent in 1991. After independence the differences between the north, where most Russians live, and the south became more pronounced. Kazakhstan is a member of the Commonwealth of Independent States and has close ties with Russia. In 1993 Kazakhstan signed the international nuclear nonproliferation treaty and agreed to dismantle or remove all nuclear weapons from the country by the year 2000. In 1998 two

border disputes were settled, one with Russia, the other with China. President Nursultan Nazarbayev has been feudally governing the country since 1990, for example by placing some members of the opposition under house arrest. The pope visited the country in 2001. In that same year, the first pipeline for the transport of oil to the Russian Black Sea was opened.
See also: Union of Soviet Socialist Republics.

Kazan (pop. 1,107,000), capital of the Tatar Autonomous Republic in eastern European Russia. Founded in 1401, it is the cultural center for the Tatars. It was conquered by Ivan the Terrible in 1552. A major port on the Volga River, it is an industrial center.
See also: Union of Soviet Socialist Republics.

Kazan, Elia (1909-), Turkish-born U.S. film and stage director. He is best known for realistic films on social issues, such as *On the Waterfront* (1954). Other films include *A Streetcar Named Desire* (1951) and *Viva Zapata!* (1952). He also wrote and directed *The Arrangement* (1967) and *The Assassins* (1972).

Kazantzakis, Nikos (1883-1957), Greek writer and statesman. He served as minister of public welfare (1919-27) and minister of state (1945-46). Among his best-known works are the novels *The Greek Passion* (1938) and *Zorba the Greek* (1946) and his epic poem *The Odyssey: A Modern Sequel* (1938).
See also: Greece.

Kea (*Nestor notabilis*), New Zealand parrot with an immensely powerful bill. Keas live in flocks and feed mainly on insects, leaves, buds, nectar, and berries; in winter they occasionally attack living sheep.

Kean, Edmund (1787-1833), English actor. Popular both in England and the United States, he was known for his roles in Shakespearean tragedy, notably Othello, to which he introduced a dynamic naturalistic style, and Shylock in *The Merchant of Venice*.

Keaton, Buster (Joseph Francis Keaton; 1895-1966), U.S. silent-film comedian and director. In such films as *The Navigator*

A scene from the classic silent movie *The General* (1927). Buster Keaton, who was nicknamed 'the great stone face', wrote, produced, directed and starred in it.

K

(1924) and *The General* (1927), masterpieces of comic inventiveness, he created the character of a deadpan innocent in conflict with malevolent machinery. Keaton designed and performed his own elaborate and often dangerous film stunts.

Keats, John (1795-1821), English Romantic poet. He gave up medicine in 1816 to devote himself to poetry. The epic 'Hyperion,' the ballad 'La Belle Dame sans Merci,' and 'The Eve of St. Agnes' were written about 1817. In May 1819 he wrote 4 great odes-'To a Nightingale,' 'On a Grecian Urn,' 'On Melancholy,' and 'On Indolence.' 'Lamia' and 'To Autumn,' effectively his last works, followed that summer. In 1820 he developed tuberculosis and died in Rome at age 25.

Kedah (pop. 1.3 million), state in Northwest Malaysia, on the Malacca Straits; 3,640 sq mi (9,426 sq km). The capital is Aloh Star. Kedah is an important producer of rice, also of rubber, tin, wolfram, and iron. Tourism is encouraged. The population is mostly Malaysian. The ruling family was already in power as far back as the Hindu period (7th century). From 1511 to 1909, it was under Thai control, then under British rule.

Keeshond, or Dutch barge dog, national dog of the Netherlands, related to the Samoyed and chow chow. The keeshond has a foxlike face with a long, thick, black-tipped gray coat. Fully grown, it stands 17-18 in (43-46 cm) and weighs 35-40 lb (16-18 kg). The Keeshond makes an excellent guard and companion.

The keeshond has long been the national dog of Holland, where it is used as a watchdog.

Keitel, Wilhelm (1882-1946), German field marshal, head of the armed forces high command during World War II. On May 8, 1945, he ratified Germany's unconditional surrender in Berlin. He was convicted at Nuremberg of violations of international law and executed.
See also: World War II.

Kekkonen, Urho Kaleva (1900-86), president of Finland, 1956-81. Head of the Agrarian Party, he held cabinet posts and was prime minister 1950-56. He resigned the presidency in 1981 because of poor health and was succeeded in 1982 by Mauno Koivisto.
See also: Finland.

Kekulé von Stradonitz, Friedrich August (1829-96), German chemist regarded as the father of modern organic chemistry. At the same time as Archibald Scott Couper (1831-82) he recognized the quadrivalency of carbon and its ability to form long chains. With his later inference of the molecular structure of benzene as a ring, structural organic chemistry was born.
See also: Chemistry; Organic chemistry.

Kelantan (pop. 1.2 million), state in Malaysia, bordering on Thailand; 5,771 sq mi (14,943 sq km). The capital is Kota Bahru. There are rubber plantations and the cultivation of coconut palms, oil palms, and tabacco. Iron, tin, and manganese are mined. There is shipbuilding and a timber industry in the vicinity of the capital, which will probably be greatly stimulated by the building of the East-West Highway. The population consists of Malaysians. Kelantan has been strongly influenced by Javanese culture. The region was colonized by the Javanese in the 14th century. It was a sultanate from the 15th century onwards. Kelantan belonged to Thailand between 1780 and 1909 and was then British until the Japanese invasion in 1942. After belonging to Thailand again for several years, it was British from 1945 to 1948. After this, it joined the Malaysian Federation.

Keller, Gottfried (1819-1890), a Swiss German-language poet, novelist, and short-story writer. Keller originally trained to be a landscape artist. As a writer, he became an important representative of realism. His lyric poems rank high in German literature. his major work is *Der Grüne Heinrich* (*Green Henry*, first version 1854; second version, 1879-80), an autobiographical novel. Keller was born in Zurich. He studied at Heidelberg University, and at various times lived in Munich, Berlin, and Zurich.

Keller, Helen Adams (1880-1968), U.S. author and lecturer. Blind and deaf from age 1 1/2, she was taught by Anne Sullivan from 1887, learned to read, write, and speak, and graduated from Radcliffe College with honors in 1904. Her books include *The Story of My Life* (1902) and *Helen Keller's Journal* (1938).

Kellogg, Frank Billings (1896-1937), U.S. diplomat, senator (1917-23), ambassador to Great Britain (1924-25), and U.S. secretary of state (1925-29). His most important achievement was the Kellogg-Briand Peace Pact (1928). He was awarded the Nobel Prize for peace and became a judge of the Permanent Court of International Justice (1930-35).
See also: Kellogg-Briand Peace Pact.

Kellogg, Will Keith (1860-1951), U.S. industrialist and philanthropist. He made his fortune through the breakfast cereal industry he established in 1906 at Battle Creek, Mich., originally to manufacture the cornflakes developed as a health food by his physician-brother.

Kellogg-Briand Peace Pact, or Pact of Paris, agreement signed on Aug. 27, 1928, by 15 nations (eventually ratified by 64) renouncing 'war as an instrument of national policy.' Conceived by Aristide Briand of France and U.S. Secretary of State F.B. Kellogg, it lacked enforcement powers and proved ineffectual.

Kelly, Ellsworth (1923-), American visual artist; he is considered to be a member of the 'postpainterly abstraction' and 'hard edge' movements. His work is strictly geometrical and color has an independent function. He works with shaped canvas.

Kelly, Gene (1912-96), U.S. actor, dancer, and director, known for his spontaneous, athletic dancing routines. Kelly made his Broadway debut in *Leave It to Me* (1938), gained recognition for his role in *Pal Joey* (1940), and made his first film appearance in *For Me and My Gal* (1942). He helped choreograph many of his musicals, including *Cover Girl* (1944), *Anchors Aweigh* (1945), *On the Town* (1949), and *Singin' in the Rain* (1952).

Kelly, George Edward (1887-1974), U.S. playwright. Kelly achieved success with his satiric renderings in *The Torch Bearers* (1922), *The Show-Off* (1924), and *Craig's Wife* (1925), for which he received the Pulitzer Prize (1926).

Kelly, Grace (1929-82), U.S. motion picture actress and, later, Princess of Monaco. Kelly first appeared in the film *Fourteen Hours* (1951) and her first starring role was opposite Gary Cooper in *High Noon* (1952). She won an Academy Award for her role in *The Country Girl* (1954) and appeared in several other films, including *Dial M for Murder* (1954), *To Catch a Thief* (1955), and *High Society* (1956). Kelly married Prince Rainier III of Monaco in 1956. She died in an automobile crash near Monaco.

Keloid, scar tissue raised above the skin surface at the site of a wound. Keloids result from an overproduction of fibrous tissue in the skin. They can be surgically removed but frequently reappear. Keloids are found most frequently in people of African descent.

Kelp, name for various large brown seaweeds of orders Laminariales and Fucales. Edible kelps are rich in iodine, calcium, potassium, and the trace minerals. Dehydrated kelp tablets, powder, and granules are used as a mineral supplement and as a salt substitute.

Kelvin, William Thomson, Lord (1824-1907), British physicist. He formulated the second law of thermodynamics and introduced the Kelvin, or absolute temperature, scale. His work on electromagnetism gave rise to the theory of the electromagnetic field, and his papers influenced J. Clerk Maxwell's work on the electromagnetic theory of light. His work on telegraphic signaling played an essential part in the successful laying of the first Atlantic cable.
See also: Galvanometer; Thermodynamics.

Kelvin scale *See:* Absolute zero; Kelvin, William Thomson, Lord; Metric system; Temperature.

K

Kemal Atatürk *See:* Atatürk, Kemal.

Kempis, Thomas à *See:* Thomas à Kempis.

Keneally, Thomas (1935-   ), Australian writer, known for his powerful and turbulent novels, which often take place in a particular historical period. His works include *The Chant of Jimmie Blacksmith* (1972), *Schindler's List* (1982), *Jacko: the Great Intruder* (1993), *A River Town* (1995), *Homebush Boy* (1995), and *The Great Shame* (1999).

Kennan, George Frost (1904-   ), U.S. diplomat, one of the main authors of the U.S. postwar policy of 'containment' of Russian expansionism. He served as ambassador to the USSR (1952) and Yugoslavia (1961-63). His books include *Russia Leaves the War* (1956) and *Memoirs, 1925-1950* (1967), both Pulitzer Prize winners.

Kennedy, U.S. family prominent in government, politics, and business. **Joseph Patrick Kennedy** (1888-1969) chaired the Securities and Exchange Commission (1934-35) and the U.S. Maritime Commission (1936-37) and served as U.S. ambassador to Great Britain (1937-40). The oldest son of Joseph Patrick and Rose Kennedy, **Joseph P. Kennedy, Jr.** (1915-44), a U.S. Navy pilot, was killed in World War II. **John Fitzgerald Kennedy** (1917-63) was elected 35th president of the United States in 1960. **Robert Francis Kennedy** (1925-68) was appointed U.S. attorney general in 1961 and elected U.S. senator from New York in 1965. A fourth son, **Edward Moore Kennedy** (1932-   ), has been a U.S. senator from Massachusetts since 1962. The 5 Kennedy daughters are Rosemary, Kathleen, Eunice, Patricia, and Jean.
See also: Kennedy, Edward Moore; Kennedy, John Fitzgerald; Kennedy, Robert Francis; Smithsonian Institution.

Kennedy, Edward Moore (1932-   ), U.S. political leader, U.S. senator from Massachusetts since 1962. Like his brothers John and Robert, 'Ted' Kennedy became a national leader of the Democratic party and an articulate advocate of liberal causes. His career suffered (1969) when a woman companion drowned after he drove his car off a bridge on Chappaquiddick Island, near Martha's Vineyard, Mass. He unsuccessfully challenged Carter for the 1980 presidential nomination.

Kennedy, John Fitzgerald (1917-63), 35th president of the United States (1961-1963). Kennedy was the youngest person and the first Roman Catholic ever elected to the post. Kennedy was killed in Dallas, Tex., after 1,037 days in office.
Kennedy graduated *cum laude* from Harvard University in 1940. While serving in the Navy (1941-45), he was honored for his heroism. At age 29, Kennedy was elected to the U.S. House of Representatives (1947-53). In 1953, he married socialite Jacqueline Lee Bouvier. In 1952, Kennedy was elected to the U.S. Senate. While convalescing from 2 spinal operations, he wrote *Profiles in Courage*, which won a Pulitzer Prize.

In 1960, he and running mate Lyndon B. Johnson narrowly defeated Republicans Richard M. Nixon and Henry Cabot Lodge. His White House was known for its elegant receptions for artists and intellectuals and for the restoration of the White House supervised by Mrs. Kennedy. Kennedy's program was largely unsuccessful in Congress. However, he did obtain the first major minimum-wage increase in a generation and passage of an urban-renewal and housing program. He also called for a bold new space program, promoted foreign aid and freer trade, launched a new program of cooperation for economic and social development in Latin America, and created the Peace Corps to aid underdeveloped areas of the world.
In 1961 Kennedy sent military advisers and equipment to Vietnam; allowed a U.S.-backed invasion of Cuba at the Bay of Pigs, which failed; and called up U.S. army reserves after East Germany erected the Berlin Wall. In Oct. 1962 the Cuban Missile Crisis took the United States to the brink of nuclear war with the Soviet Union.
Kennedy was fatally shot as he rode in an open car through Dallas, Tex., on Nov. 22, 1963. The presumed assassin, Lee Harvey Oswald, was shot to death 2 days later. Despite an investigation by a special commission headed by Chief Justice Earl Warren, the circumstances of the assassination remain a source of controversy.

Kennedy, Robert Francis (1925-68), U.S. attorney general (1961-64) and U.S. senator from New York (1965-68). He was chief counsel to the Senate subcommittee investigating labor union racketeering in the late 1950s, and elder brother John's senatorial campaign manager in 1962. As attorney general in President John F. Kennedy's cabinet, Robert Kennedy supervised enforcement of civil rights legislation in the South. After his brother's death he led the liberal wing of the Democratic party. In a controversial move after Eugene McCarthy's strong showing in the New Hampshire primary of 1968, Kennedy entered the race for his party's presidential nomination. On the evening of his victory in the California primary, June 5, 1968, he was shot and killed in Los Angeles by Sirhan Sirhan.

Kennedy, Ted *See:* Kennedy, Edward Moore.

Kennedy Center for the Performing Arts, part of the Smithsonian Institution, Washington, D.C., designed by U.S. architect Edward Durell Stone as a national memorial to the late president. The center, which opened 1971, houses 3 main theaters: the Eisenhower Theater, which seats 1,000 persons and offers dramatic productions; the Opera House, which seats 2,200 and presents opera, ballet, and musical comedies; and the Concert Hall, which seats 2,750 and features concert music.

Kenny, Elizabeth (1886-1952), Australian nurse. She is best known for developing the treatment of infantile paralysis combining hot, moist applications with exercise. She coauthored *The Kenny Concept of Infantile Paralysis and Its Treatment* (1942) and *And They Shall Walk* (1943).

Kent, William (1684-1748) English architect, who designed in the style of Christopher Wren. He is regarded as one of the creators of free landscape gardening (as opposed to the French garden). This evolved into the typical English gardening style.

Kenton, Stan (1912-79), U.S. bandleader, pianist, and composer. Kenton experimented with the size and concept of his bands and sometimes combined Afro-Cuban music, modern jazz, and classical music. He introduced a brass instrument called the mellophonium, with a range between the trumpet and the trombone. His compositions include 'Artistry in Rhythm' and 'Eager Beaver.' He helped establish the careers of jazz greats Lee Konitz and Art Pepper on alto saxophone, trumpeter Maynard Ferguson, drummer Shelly Manne, and trombonist Kai Winding.

Kentucky (Bluegrass State; pop. 4,000,000), state in the south central United States; bordered by Illinois, Indiana, Ohio, West Virginia, Virginia, Tennessee, and Missouri.
Kentucky can be divided into 3 distinct topographical regions: the Gulf Coastal Plain, the Interior Low Plateau, and the Appalachian Plateau. Kentucky lies in the drainage basin of the Mississippi River and the Ohio, which forms the state's northern boundary. Important rivers include the Tennessee, Cumberland, Green, Kentucky, and Licking rivers. Principal cities are Louisville and Lexington. The capital is Frankfort.
Service industries account for more than half of Kentucky's gross state product (GSP)-the total value of all the goods and services a state produces in a year. Manufacturing, however, is Kentucky's major economic activity. Leading manufactured products are transportation equipment, chemicals, electrical equipment, and machinery. Kentucky's agricultural income is led by livestock and livestock products, including beef cattle, milk, hogs, eggs, and broilers (chickens). The state is famous for its thoroughbred horses-and the annual Kentucky Derby horse race. Important crop products include tobacco, soybeans, corn, and wheat. Kentucky leads the U.S. in coal production. Other important mining products include natural gas, petroleum, and limestone.
In the late 1760s, Daniel Boone opened settlement by blazing the Wilderness Trail through the Appalachians' Cumberland Gap. Originally part of Virginia, Kentucky gained statehood in 1792, becoming the first state west of the Appalachians.

Kentucky Derby, annual thoroughbred horse race for 3-year-olds run over a course of 1 1/4 mi (2 km) at Churchill Downs, Louisville, Ky. The Derby was founded in 1875 by Col. M. Lewis Clark, and is currently attended by more than 120,000 fans each year, and is the most popular horse race in the United States. The Preakness and the Belmont Stakes are the other 2 races which comprise the Triple Crown of horse racing.

Kenya

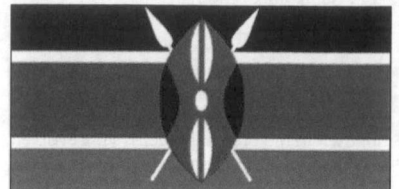

Capital:	Nairobi
Area:	224,022 sq mi
	(580,367 sq km)
Population:	31,139,000
Language:	Swahili
Government:	Presidential republic
Independent:	1963
Head of gov.:	President
Per capita:	US$ 1,000
Monetary unit:	1 Kenya shilling = 100 cents

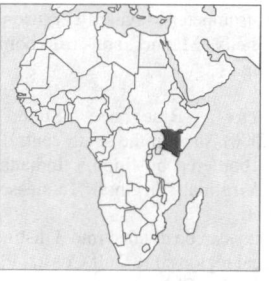

Kenya, independent republic of East Africa. Since achieving independence from Britain in 1963, Kenya has been one of the most prosperous and politically stable new African states for a long time. Economic and social progress has been made more difficult by the rapid growth of population.

Land and climate. Kenya has an area of 224,960 sq mi (582,646 sq km). Its northern neighbors are the Sudan and Ethiopia, with Somalia in the northeast. On the west, Kenya is bordered by Uganda; on the south,

Lake Nakuru, a shallow saline lake located in the Great Rift Valley of East Africa, is a noted refuge for such species of waterfowl as the flamingo, which nests there in huge flocks. Lake Nakuru National Park is one of Kenya's many preserves.

by Tanzania. Straddling the equator, the country has a varied landscape, with 4 main regions: the coastal strip bordering the Indian Ocean; the vast, dry plains of the Nyika; the highlands; and the western plateau.

The coastal strip is narrow and fertile, with scattered rain forest, mangrove swamps, and coconut palms. The plains extend from northern Kenya over more than half of the country, and are about 150 mi (240 km) wide in the south, where they are crossed by Kenya's 2 chief rivers, the Tana and the Athi. They are mostly scrubland pasture, but the Tana Valley and the Taita Hills are cultivated.

The highlands, where most Kenyans live, are mainly in the southwest, and are cut from north to south by the Great Rift Valley, of which Lake Rudolf (in the north) is part. They are mostly 5,000-8,000 ft (1,525-2,440 m) above sea level, but volcanic action has raised such lofty cones as Mount Kenya (17,058 ft/5,200 m), Kenya's highest mountain, and Mount Elgon (14,178 ft/4,321 m). With rich volcanic soils, moderate temperatures, and ample rainfall, the highlands provide most of Kenya's farm crops.

Beyond the Great Rift Valley and the highlands, the western plateau (sometimes called the Nyanza Plateau) stretches to Lake Victoria. At an average altitude of 4,000 ft (1,220 m), this well-watered plateau has good farmlands, forests, and grasslands. Kenya is famous for its big game, including elephants, hippos, giraffes, and antelopes. There are many national parks and game reserves, the largest and best known being the Tsavo National Park (8,034 sq mi/20,809 sq km) in southeast Kenya. Every year many visitors come from abroad to go on safari.

People. Nearly 98% of the population is African, comprising more than 40 ethnic groups, chief among which are the Kikuyu. There are also Indian, Arab, and European (primarily British) communities. Most Kenyans live in the southwest, mainly in the highlands where Nairobi, the capital and largest city, is situated.

Economy. Agriculture is the major occupation, with coffee, tea, timber, fruit, and vegetables the main exports. Chief industries center around food processing, textiles, footwear, and clothing. There is also a large livestock industry. Kenya has few natural resources, and its reliance upon imported oil places a strain on the economy. Hydroelectric and geothermal power sources are being developed. Tourism is also important.

History. Until 1887 the coast was under Arab control. The British then opened the interior with imported Indian labor and encouraged European settlement. In 1944 the first African nationalist party was set up, and Jomo Kenyatta became its leader in 1947. Discontent led to the formation of the Mau Mau terrorist organization. Pacified by reforms, Kenya gained independence in 1963, becoming a republic in 1964 under Kenyatta's presidency. Kenyatta died in 1978 and was succeeded by his vice president Daniel Arap Moi. Falling prices for the country's two principal exports, coffee and tea, caused a depression during the first years of Moi's rule, but the economy revived

in the mid-1980's when world prices for these commodities rose. Moi was reelected president in 1992 in the first multiparty election in 26 years. Mwai Kibaki, who won the December 2002 elections by a landslide victory, replaced him. Earlier that year, al-Qaida claimed responsibility for an attack on an Israeli-owned hotel in Mombassa. Kenya is considered to be one of the world's most corrupted countries, but will possibly be eligible for IMF support again.

Kenyatta, Jomo (1893?-1978), Kenya's first president (1964-78). His early political career was concerned with rights of his Kikuyu people. In 1953 he was imprisoned by the British on charges of leading the Mau Mau, a terrorist Kikuyu group. His release came in 1961 following pressure from African nationalists; he negotiated Kenya's independence in 1963.
See also: Kenya.

Keogh plan *See:* Pension.

Kepler, Johannes (1571-1630), German mathematician and astronomer. Kepler advanced Copernicus's heliocentric model of the solar system in showing that the planets followed elliptical paths. His 3 laws describing the revolution of the planets around the sun, presented in *Astronomia nova* (1609) and *Harmonice mundi* (1619), guided Isaac Newton to the formulation of his theory of gravitation.
See also: Copernicus, Nicolaus; Newton, Sir Isaac.

Kerala (pop. 30,000,000), Indian federal state on the Arabian Sea; 15,011 sq mi (38,863 sq km). The capital city is Trivandrum. It is mountainous in the east; the coastal area has many deltas with rice paddies and coconut plantations. Sugar cane, coffee, tea, rice, tapioca, cardamom, oil seed, rubber, and black pepper are cultivated here. There is cattle breeding (buffaloes, sheep, and goats) and fishing. The industries are chemical, ceramic, textile and glass industry. Mica and lime stone are mined.

The region traded with the ancient Greeks and Romans more than two thousand years ago. There are Syrian Christian and Jewish communities. In the 8th century, Arab traders introduced Islam and in 1498, the Portuguese Vasco da Gama landed at Calicut (now called Kozhikoden). Large Islamic and Christian minority groups still live here, in harmony with the Hindu majority.
After the British and the French founded a trading post in Calicut in the second half of the 17th century, the British seized the city and the surrounding area. It has been a federal state since 1956.

Keratin, any of various fibrous proteins concentrated in the outermost layer of the skin of vertebrates and acting as a constituent of hair, nails, claws, and horns.

Kérékou, Mathieu Ahmed (1933-   ), Beninese soldier and President (1996-   ). He received military training in France and served in the French army. In 1961, he returned to Benin (formerly Dahomey). In

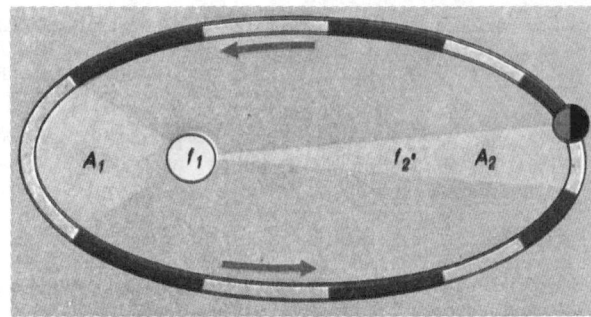

Johannes Kepler was the first to describe the planetary orbits as ellipses with the sun at one of the two focal points (f_1 and f_2). Although a planet's speed varies, the line joining the sun and a planet sweeps out equal areas (A_1 and A_2) in equal time periods, represented by the colored section of the orbit.

K

1972, as substitute Chief of staff of the army, he was in charge of a successful coup against President Justin Ahomadegbe, who had succeeded Hubert Maga shortly before. In spite of many attempted coups, Kérékou succeeded in remaining in power as President until 1991. In 1974, he converted Dahomey into a Marxist-Leninist state and nationalized companies and banks, and, one year later, he changed the name into République Populaire du Bénin. In 1979, he replaced the military government with a civil government, appointing himself President. Under his leadership, Benin attempted to develop relationships with the western world, but the government did not succeed in improving the economic situation of the country. In 1989, under great internal pressure, he carried out political reformations. They led to elections in 1991, which were won by Nicéphore Soglo. In 1996, Kérékou succeeded Soglo as President after an election triumph. In 1998, he became Prime Minister as well.

Kerensky, Alexander Feodorovich (1881-1970), Russian revolutionary, head of the provisional government that followed the Russian Revolution from July to Oct. 1917. Overthrown in the Bolshevik Revolution (Nov. 1917), he fled to Western Europe and in 1940 escaped to the United States. His books include *The Prelude to Bolshevism* (1919), *The Catastrophe* (1927), and *The Kerensky Memoirs* (1966).
See also: Russian Revolution.

Kerguelen Islands *See:* French Southern and Antarctic Territories.

Kern, Jerome (1885-1945), U.S. composer. His most famous musical is *Show Boat* (1927), which includes the song 'Ol' Man River.' Among his classic songs are 'Smoke Gets in Your Eyes' and 'The Song Is You.'

Kerosene, colorless, thin oil, a mixture of hydrocarbons, used mainly as a fuel for jet engines, and also for heating and lighting and as a solvent and paint thinner. Although it can be derived from oil, coal, and tar, most kerosene is produced from distilled petroleum.

Kerouac, Jack (Jean-Louis Lebris de Kerouac; 1922-69), U.S. novelist and poet. His best-known book is *On the Road* (1957), describing his life of freedom from conventional middle-class values. He was a leading figure of the Beat Generation.

Kerry blue terrier, breed of dog produced by the union of the Irish terrier and the Dandie Dinmont. Named for County Kerry in Ireland, where it was originally bred in the 1700s to herd sheep and cows, the Kerry blue has a thin, elongated body, stands about 18-19 inches tall (46-49 cm), and weighs 33-38 pounds (15-17 kg).

Kesselring, Albert (1885-1960), German field marshal of World War II. He became commander in chief in Italy (1943) and in the West (1945). He was convicted of war crimes (1947) and sentenced to life imprisonment, but he was released in 1952.

Kestrel, name given in the Old World to various small falcons. The European kestrel (*Falco tinnunculus*) is closely related to the American sparrow hawk.

Kettering, Charles Franklin (1876-1958), U.S. inventor of the first electric cash register and the electric self-starter. He made significant contributions to automobile technology.

Kettledrum *See:* Drum.

Jack Kerouac (1922-1969) was one of the most important representatives of the Beat Generation, a group of American authors who opposed the established values of the 1950s consumer's society.

Kettle hole, depression or cavity in solid rock formed by a block of glacial ice. The size may vary from 15 ft (5 m) to 8 mi (13 km) in diameter with depths of up to 140 ft (45 m).

Key, musical term denoting the arrangement of notes in a certain kind of scale. On the piano keyboard there are 12 notes, black and white, between each octave, each of which can be the starting point for 2 scales, one in the major mode and one in the minor mode. Thus if a piece of music is written for a major scale starting on the note C, then the key of the piece will be C major. If the piece is written for the minor scale starting on the note G, then the key will be G minor. Major scales all have one particular sequence of pitch intervals between the notes, while all the minor scales have a different sequence of pitch intervals. To maintain the same sequence of pitch intervals for all the major and minor scales, adjustments to the pitch of individual notes need to be made from scale to scale. Notes will either need to be raised by half a tone (sharpened) or lowered by half a tone (flattened). The number of sharpened or flattened notes required for any key is called the *key signature* and is always written at the start of a piece. Each major key has a corresponding minor key in terms of a shared key signature. For example, a sharpened F is the key signature for both the key of G major and E minor; a flattened B indicates either the key of F major or D minor; and so on through the 24 major and minor keys.

Keyboard instrument *See:* Celesta; Clavichord; Harpsichord; Organ; Piano.

Keynes, John Maynard (1883-1946), British economist at Cambridge University, a pioneer in the development of modern economics. He resigned in protest as treasury representative at the Versailles Peace Conference after World War I, stating his objections to the possible outcome of the treaty in *The Economic Consequences of the Peace* (1919). His chief work, *The General Theory of Employment, Interest, and Money* (1936), formed the basis of Keynesian economics, showing how government intervention could be used to maintain high levels of economic activity.
See also: Economics.

KGB, Committee for State Security, government organization in the former USSR functioning as a secret police force. The KGB is one of the state bodies exercising control over Soviet oppositionists. Its intelligence network keeps track of political and military activities abroad as well. Given its present name in 1953, the KGB is the successor to the earlier state security groups, the Cheka and the NKVD.

Khabarovsk (pop. 785,000), capital of the *kraj* of the same name in Russia, on the Amur. Largest industrial center in Siberia, favorably located on the Amur and the Trans-Siberian Railroad. Petroleum refineries, iron manufacturing industry and steel industry, machine factories, motor vehicles, grain processing, and tanneries. Primarily

forestry and mining industry (among others, gold, iron and coal) in the kraj (965,623 sq mi, 2,500,000 sq km).
The city was established as a fort in 1858 and quickly developed following the construction of the railroad in 1905.

Khachaturian, Aram Ilich (1903-78), Soviet-Armenian composer. His music was influenced by the folk music of Armenia and the Orient. He is famous for the *Violin Concerto* (1940), the 'Saber Dance' in his ballet *Gayané* (1942), and the orchestral suite *Masquerade* (1944).

Khachaturian, Aram Ilyich (1903-1978) Armenian-Russian composer. Became vice-chairman of the committee of the Soviet-Russian composers' organization in 1939. He became a teacher of composition at the Moscow Conservatory in 1951; as of 1957, he was the secretary of the composers' organization. Khachaturian draws from Armenian folk music in his work and his preference for dance is virtually always audible. He became known for his piano concert (1937), violin concert (1940), and his ballets *Gajaneh* (1942) and *Spartacus* (1956). He also composed symphonies, choir music, film, stage, and chamber music.

Khakasia (pop. 585,000), federal republic in Russia, on the upper course of the Yenisey, in the south of West-Siberia; 23,909 sq mi (61,900 sq km). Capital: Abakan.
Very mountainous, with sheep breeding, mining (gold, coal, various metals) and forestry. The republic's main export products include aluminum, tungsten, and molybdenum. Russia's largest hydroelectric power station, located near Sayanogorsk.
The original inhabitants, the Khakasians, accounted for more than two-thirds of the population at the beginning of the 20th century. The Khakasians consist of five Turkish-speaking groups with varied ethnic backgrounds. They now make up approx. 10%; approx. 80% of the population is Russian.
During the time of the Soviet Union, Khakasia became an independent province in the Krasnoyarsk kraj in 1930; it has been a federal republic in the Russian Federation since 1991.

Khalid ibn Abd al-Aziz Al Saud (1913-82), king of Saudi Arabia (1975-82). Appointed crown prince in 1965, Khalid acceded to the throne in 1975 on the death of his brother Faisal. His regime showed some restraint on oil prices and otherwise took cautious positions on Middle East issues.

Khamenei, Seyed Ali (1940-), Iranian religious leader and politician. From 1960 onwards, he was active in the Council of Militant Clergy. After the revolution of 1979, he became an authocrat politician. He was President from 1981 to 1989. After the death of the Ayatollah Khomeiny, he appointed Rafsanjani as President and he himself became a religious leader. The conservative Khomeiny shared political power with the pragmatist Rafsanjani until 1997, which led to conflicts on the policies that should be pursued. These conflicts contin-

ued under the leadership of Rafsanjani's successor Khatami, who was known as a moderate-minded politician.

Kharkiv (pop. 1,600,000), capital of the Ukrainian province of the same name.
Kharkiv lies in the eastern part of the Ukraine, along the northern border of the basin of the Donets, the largest tributary found to the right of the Don. Rich coal and iron deposits can be found in the direct vicinity.
Despite the fact that Kharkiv is a center of industry, the townscape conveys a green and open impression and has an ample number of parks and gardens.
A few historical buildings survived WW II, including the 17th century Pokrovski Cathedral. Modern buildings of interest include the University building and the Industry building.
The metal and machine industries account for a large part of Kharkiv's industry. Two-thirds of the working population is employed in these fields. The main products include tractors, trains, turbines, tools, bicycles, electrical appliances, precision instruments, and finally, any and all possible devices for the mining industry (elevators, pumps, drills, etcetera). In addition to the metal industry, light industry is represented in the form of food factories, construction materials,, and a graphic industry. The industrial products are distributed throughout the entire Federation of Russia and exported abroad as well.
Because of its central location between the Ukrainian grain region, the Donets basin, and the area surrounding Moscow, Kharkiv has become an important center of transportation, where 8 major railways, numerous highways, and 20 airlines meet.
Besides many scientific and cultural institutions (including the Ukrainian Academy of Sciences), the city has over twenty institutions for higher education; the University of Kharkiv (established in 1804), many colleges of technology and a conservatory, There are a few hundred high schools and technical training schools.
The city has a few hundred public libraries, six theatres (opera and ballet, Ukrainian drama, Russian drama, music, puppet theater and a youth theater), a circus, a planetarium, two museums (history and art) and a large television center.
There are many beautiful forests, rivers, and lakes in the vicinity of Kharkiv that fulfil an important recreational function.
The origin of the city of Kharkiv lies in the 17th century (presumably 1655). It was initially a Cossack garrison, but soon became an important trade center thanks to its favorable location between the heart of Russia (Moscow) and the Sea of Azov (adjacent to the Black Sea).
Kharkiv developed into an industrial city after 1850, when rich deposits of coal and iron ore were discovered in the Donets basin to the south of the city and an iron and steel industry developed. Following the Russian Revolution of 1917, Kharkiv became the capital of the Ukrainian Soviet Republic, and remained so until 1934, when Kiev was chosen as the new capital.
The population increased from 200,000 in

1917 to approx. 800,000 in 1934. Half of the population consists of Ukrainians, Russians account for 40%, and the remainder is made up of, among others, Poles and people from the Caucasus.
The city was seized by the Germans during World War II, at which time all of the factories and a large part of the houses were destroyed. To a certain extent, this proved advantageous for the industry sector, as it could be thoroughly modernized during the reconstruction following the war.

Kharkov (pop. 1,536,000), city in Ukraine, at the confluence of the Kharkov, Lopan, and Udy rivers. Founded in the 18th century, Kharkov is now the fifth largest city in the Soviet Union and was the capital of the Ukraine until 1934, when it was superseded by Kiev. An industrialized city, Kharkov produces metals, chemicals, and heavy machinery.
See also: Ukraine.

Khartoum (pop. 925,000), capital of Sudan. It is a cotton trading center linked by rail and river to Egypt and Port Sudan, and headquarters for the Bank for African Development, linking North and South Africa economically. The city was founded in 1821 as an Egyptian army camp. British General Gordon was killed here in 1885 defending the city against the Muslim religious leader known as the Mahdi.

Khatami, Seyyed Mohammad (1943-), Iranian politician, who was elected president in 1997. He became minister of culture in 1982 and in this position gave the press and artists a remarkable amount of freedom. Khatami was displaced by the conservative faction and was appointed, in succession, director of the National Library and advisor to President Rafsanjani. In his role as president, Khatami advocates in particular the protection of civil rights and social justice. In 2001, he was re-elected with a large majority.

Khayyam, Omar *See:* Omar Khayyam.

Khazars, Turkic people whose empire in southern Russia and the Caucasus controlled trade between the Slavs, Byzantium, and the Far East from 550 until the Byzantines and Russians overwhelmed it (969-1030). The king and nobility adopted Judaism in about 740.

Khmer *See:* Cambodia.

Khmer empire, ancient Southeast Asian empire dating from the 6th century, occupying much of modern Laos, Thailand, and Vietnam. Its Angkor period (889-1434) produced beautiful architecture and sculpture. After the empire fell to the Thais in 1434, the court moved to Phnom Penh.

Khmer Rouge *See:* Cambodia.

Khoikhoi, or Hottentot, member of a southern African group similar to the San. Members of the group call themselves 'Khoikhoi'; 'Hottentot' is now considered an insulting name. Small in stature, they have brown skin, prominent cheekbones, broad noses, and coarse hair. They were nomadic herders and farmers, but this way of life largely disappeared as a result of conflicts with other tribes and the Dutch settlers. Remaining members of the group live in Namibia.

Khomeini, Ruhollah (Ruhollah Moussavi; 1900?-89), spiritual and political leader of Iran, 1979-89. Khomeini received the title *Ayatollah* (Persian, 'reflection' or 'sign') for achieving the highest status that can be bestowed upon a Shi'te Muslim. He was forced into exile in 1963 because of his opposition to the rule of the shah (king), Muhammad Reza Pahlevi. In exile in Turkey, Iraq, and France, he emerged as the leader of the anti-shah forces, which overthrew the Pahlevi regime. He returned to Iran in Jan. 1979 to become absolute leader of his new Islamic republic. He held U.S. hostages (1979-81) and waged war with Iraq (1980-88).
See also: Iran.

Khorana, Har Gobind (1922-), Indian-American biochemist. He studied protein synthesis and the making of co-enzyme A; he synthesized all codons of the DNA (for which he received the Nobel Prize for Chemistry in 1968). He was the first to synthesize a whole gene and to build this into a bacterium.

Khorasan (pop. 6.86 million), province in Northeast Iran; 121,026 sq mi (313,337 sq km). The capital is Mashhad (Meshed), with a population of three million, making it one of the largest cities in Iran. The northeast is mountainous; in the west lies the salt desert. Coal and salt are mined. There is caravan trade and a little industry. It was conquered by Muslims in the 7th century. The conquest by the Mongolian leader Ghengis Khan at the beginning of the 13th century meant the end of the Islamic culture. It became Persian again in the 16th century.

Khorus I (Anushirwan the Righteous; governed from 531-579), most famous Persian king of the Sassanids dynasty. He reformed the government (four satrapies), made Mazdaism the official religion, reorganized the armed forces, improved irrigation and the infrastructure, and promoted arts and science (among others, the introduction of chess). He waged war against, among others, Rome (540-562) and the Byzantines (576-578).

Khorus II (Khusru Parviz; governed from 589-628), last great ruler of the Persian dynasty of the Sassanids. The Persian Empire reached its largest size under his rule. He was driven away by Bahram (590-591), but regained power with the help of the Byzantines. He besieged Byzantium with the help of the Avars (626), but was defeated by the Roman emperor Heraclius a year later.

Khrushchev, Nikita Sergeyevich (1894-1971), Soviet premier, 1958-64. As a loyal Stalinist during the great purges of the 1930s he managed the Communist Party in the Ukraine. During World War II he was a po-litical adviser in the army, defending Stalingrad. When Josef Stalin died in Mar. 1953, Khrushchev became a member of the Soviet Union's 'collective leadership,' taking over as first secretary of the Central Committee. His famous 'secret speech' of 1956, attacking Stalin, inaugurated the policy of 'de-Stalinization,' and by 1958 Khrushchev had made himself both premier and party head. During his rule Khrushchev traveled extensively, addressing the UN General Assembly in New York in 1959 on disarmament, and meeting with President Kennedy in Vienna in 1961. His main setback in foreign policy came in 1962, when the United States forced him to withdraw Soviet missiles secretly installed in Cuba. This crisis, his rift with the People's Republic of China, and repeated crop failures led to his removal from power.
See also: Union of Soviet Socialist Republics.

Khuang Aphaiwong (1902-1968), Thai politician, four times prime minister of Thailand. Khuang was involved in a coup in 1932 that ended the reign of King Prajadhipok. During the Second World War, he was a minister in the Pibul Songh Kram government, whom he succeeded as prime minister in 1944. After the war, he founded the Democratic Party, the first real Thai opposition party. He was prime minister another three times (of a civilian government) before he was deposed by Pibul.

Khufu, or Cheops (fl. c.2680 B.C.), Egyptian pharaoh of the 4th dynasty. He built the greatest pyramid at Gizeh, near Cairo; it is known as one of the Seven Wonders of the Ancient World.

Khyber Pass, mountain pass on the Pakistan-Afghanistan border, about 3,500 ft (1,070 m) high and 28 mi (45 km) long. For centuries it was the main western land entry to India. Now a modern highway and a 34-tunnel railroad are on this site.

Kiarostami, Abbas (1940-), Iranian movie director. He produces films mostly for the Institute for the Intellectual Development of Children and Young Adults, better known by the Persian acronym *Kanun*. He is considered by many film producers (Godard, Kurasawa) to be the best director of this period.
Kiarostami made his debut in 1969 with the short movie *Nan va kucheh* (Bread and Alley) about a little boy who defies an enormous dog. Kiarostami became best known for his trilogy, which was filmed in the mountainous northern region of Iran, *Khanah-ye dust kojast?* (Where is my Friend's House; 1987) *Va zendegi edameh darad* (And Life Goes On; 1992), and *Zir-e derakhtan-e zeytun* (Through the Olive Trees; 1994). He won the Golden Palm in Cannes in 1997 for *Ta m'e guilass* (Taste of Cherry).

Kibbutz, type of collective farm in Israel established in the early 20th century. Land held by the Jewish National Fund is rented to the kibbutz inexpensively. Nearly all property on the kibbutz is collectively owned. All work, economic, and municipal activities are done communally. Kibbutzim provide food, accommodations, nurseries, and elementary education.

Kidd, William (1645?-1701), British pirate. Employed in 1695 by the British to privateer against French ships in King William's War, he later plundered the British in the Indian Ocean and was hanged in London for murder and piracy.
See also: Pirate.

Kidnapping, the forcible abduction of a human being, whether or not for ransom. A famous early example was the kidnapping of Richard I of England for a huge ransom, on his way home from the crusades in 1192. In the 17th century the term referred to the practice of abducting children for labor on U.S. plantations. The first major U.S. kidnapping case occurred in 1874, but after 1920, with the growth of gangsters kidnappings increased at an alarming rate. The abduction and murder of the infant son of Charles A. Lindbergh in 1932 so aroused the public that legislation making kidnapping a federal crime, in some cases punishable by death, was passed in 1932 and 1934. Thereafter, kidnappings for ransom in the United States declined sharply. In modern times revolutionary groups have kidnapped ambassadors, consuls, businesspersons, and politicians, sometimes for ransom, sometimes to force the release of political detainees.

Kidney, one of a pair of organs of the urinary system, located in the back part of the abdomen, on each side of the vertebral column; the left lies slightly higher than the right. A high concentration of blood vessels gives the kidney a dark, reddish-brown color, and each is bean-shaped and slightly tilted. In adults, the kidney is about 4 in (10 cm) long and 2.5 in (6.5 cm) wide. At least one kidney must function for life to be maintained.
Through the activity of millions of nephrons, filtering units that are the organ's basic functional components, the kidneys perform a number of tasks: the removal from the blood of nitrogenous waste, mostly in the form of urea (a main constituent of the urine that the kidneys form); the maintenance of the body's electrolyte balance; the maintenance of the body's water balance; the regulation of the body's acid-base balance. In addition, the kidneys release a number of chemical substances (acting as hormones) into the blood.
Urine is formed in the kidneys as an aqueous solution (95% water) containing metabolic waste products, foreign substances, and water-soluble constituents of the body. The quantity of urine produced by the kidneys depends on the balance of water and other essential substances in the body.
Among the most common kidney diseases are pyelonephritis, or kidney infection, and a type of inflammation called glomerulonephritis (formerly Bright's disease). If a person loses or suffers damage to both kidneys, he or she may be kept alive by a dialysis machine. The machine is attached to an artery in the patient's arm; blood flows

K

K

The kidneys filter out waste products from the blood and maintain the salt and water balance of the body. A kidney has an outer cortex (1) and an inner medulla (2), which is divided into 10 to 15 segments, known as pyramids (3). A renal artery (4) carries blood to the kidneys, and a renal vein (5) carries purified blood back into the general system. The nephron, which is the basic unit of a kidney, includes a glomerulus (6) that filters waste products from the blood. The waste products form a con-

centrated fluid (7) that passes through a descending tubule (8) to the loop of Henle (9) and into an ascending tubule (10). These tubules are surrounded by blood vessels that absorb and recycle water and salts from the fluid. A collecting tubule (11) carries the product, urine, from the nephron to the renal pelvis (12), which connects to a ureter (13).

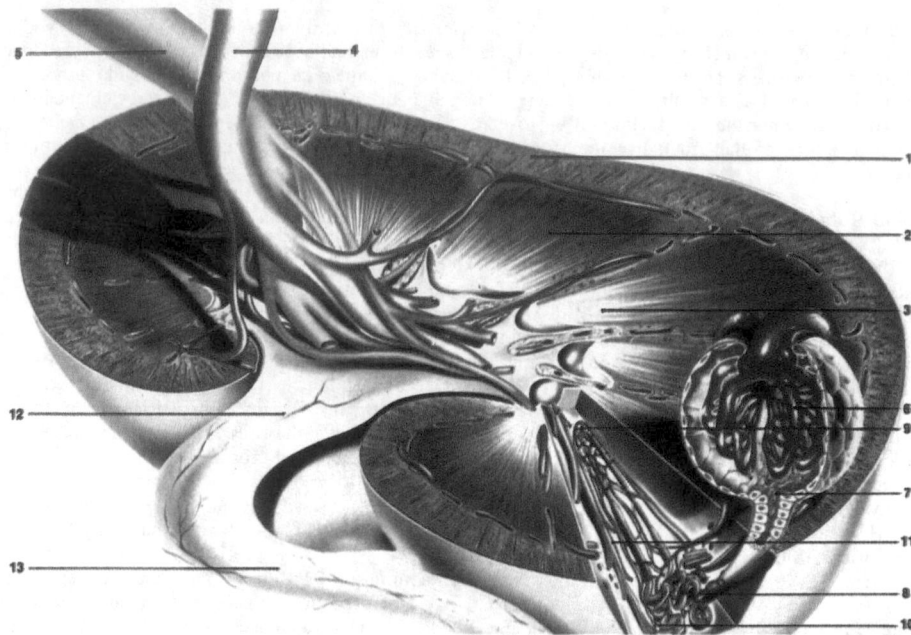

Not only is Kiev surrounded by a green belt, the inside of the city is also full of parks and tree-lined avenues.

through one tube into the machine, which removes wastes, and then flows back into the patient through a second tube. The patient must undergo this procedure for several hours, three days a week.

Kidney stone, hard mineral deposit that forms in the kidney as a result of excessive concentrations of mineral salts in the urine. If the stone is not passed through the urine or dissolved by natural or medical means, it can seriously disrupt regular kidney function.

Kidney transplant *See:* Tissue transplant.

Kiefer, Anselm (1945-), German artist. He derives his themes from German history and myths, sagas, and legends from Northern European culture. The dramatic effect of his work is partially achieved by the complex manner in which different materials (straw, sand, paint, paper, and lead) are applied to

the canvas and processed (by means of burning, scratching, and sticking).

Kiel (pop. 250,000), city in northwest Germany, on the Baltic Sea at the eastern end of the Kiel Canal. An important shipping and industrial center, it was Germany's chief naval base, 1871-1945. Kiel was founded in 1242 and joined the Hanseatic League in 1284.
See also: Germany.

Kiel Canal, German canal extending 61 mi (98 km) from the mouth of the Elbe River to Holtenau near Kiel. It opened in 1895 to facilitate movement of the German fleet between the North and Baltic seas. Because of its military and commercial value, it was internationalized after World War I until Hitler denied its status in 1936.

Kienholz, Edward (1927-1994), American artist, who gained acclaim with his realistic 'environments'. One of the best known of those is *The Beanery* (1965; Stedelijk Museum, Amsterdam), a simulated cafe, with puppets made from synthetic resin at the bar, with clocks instead of faces. The unexpected products of Kienholz's fantasy also intensify reality in a gruesome, sometimes humorous manner in a number of other environments, *Roxy's* (1961), a brothel, *The State Hospital* (1966), a scene from a hospital, *Back Seat Dodge '38* (1966), a couple making love in the back seat of a car, *Portable War Memorial* (1968), and *Five Car Stud* (1972), about racial discrimination. He began collaborating with his wife, Nancy Reddin Kienholz, in 1973.

Kierkegaard, Søren Aabye (1813-55), Danish religious philosopher, precursor of existentialism. Opposing G.W.F. Hegel, he emphasized that one has a free will and can pass from the aesthetic (or material) to the ethical point of view and finally, through 'a leap of faith,' to the religious. Ignored in the 19th century, he has influenced 20th-century Protestant theology and modern literature

and psychology. His main works are *Either/Or* (1843), *Fear and Trembling* (1843), and *Philosophical Fragments* (1844). *See also:* Existentialism.

Kiev (pop. 2,600,000), capital and largest city of Ukraine, on the Dnieper River. Founded before the 9th century, it was the seat of the Russian Orthodox Church from 988. More than 40% of Kiev was destroyed in World War II, but after extensive reconstruction it is now an industrial, communications, and cultural center.
See also: Ukraine.

Kigali (pop. 235,000), capital and largest city of Rwanda. Established by German colonists in 1907, Kigali is now an administrative and commercial center. In 1994 life in the capital was brutally disturbed by the genocide that followed the death of president Habyarimana.
See also: Rwanda.

Kikutake Kiyonori (1928-), Japanese architect, a member of the 'metabolism' school, which was founded in the 1960s and which Kenzo Tange also joined. This group wanted to create a dynamic, modern type of urban architecture, composed of flexible parts. In 1959, Kikutake published a plan for a future city, to be situated on a concrete island in a bay near Tokyo, and offering room to half a million people. This Ocean City was to consist of two concentric circles: an inner circle, in which the citizens would live, and an outer circle, where production was to take place; the two circles were to be joined by administrative buildings. The town hall of Miyakonoja (1960) is an example of Kikutake's work.

Kikuyu, agricultural Bantu-speaking tribe, one of the largest groups (about 2 million) in Kenya, living north of Nairobi. Racial and tribal tensions led to the formation of the Mau Mau, a secret terrorist Kikuyu group involved in a nationalist uprising against European colonists in the late 1940s and 1950s.

Kilauea, world's largest active volcano, located on the southeastern part of Hawaii island. It is about 8 mi (13 km) in circumference and 3,646 ft (1,111 m) deep, with a lake of molten lava 740 ft (230 m) below its rim.

Kilimanjaro, extinct volcano and Africa's highest mountain, in northeastern Tanzania, near the Kenyan border. Its highest, snow-capped peaks are Kibo (19,340 ft/5,895 m) and Mawenzi (17,564 ft/5,354 m).

Killanin, lord Michael (b. Michael Morris, 1914-1999), Lord of an aristocratic Irish family, who received a true British education at Eton, Cambridge and also studied in Paris. He rowed and boxed, and was a keen horseman. After having finished his studies he started working as a war correspondent in China and during the Second World War, after which he went into business, working for multinationals such as Shell and BP. In addition, he wrote books and produced films starring Grace Kelly, John Wayne, and others.
He is best known for his work for the International Olympic Committee. In 1950 he became chairman of the Irish Olympic Committee, two years later he was the Irish representative at the IOC, in 1968 he was appointed vice chairman of the committee, and in the period 1972-80 he succeeded Avery Brundage as the sixth Chairman of the IOC. His chairmanship commenced during the Munich Olympics, where he was confronted with the Palestinian attempt on lives of the Israeli athletes. He also organized the Summer Olympics twice, both of which were overshadowed by boycotts: in 1976 in Montreal, 30 African countries remained absent, and in 1980 the Russian invasion of Afghanistan led a number of Western countries to avoid the Moscow Olympics. After having resigned his position at the IOC he made an unsuccessful attempt to reconcile the American President Carter and the Russian Breshnev. He also wrote *My Olympic Years* (1983).

Killarney (pop. 8,000), town district in southwestern Ireland, County Kerry. Though it has some light industry, Killarney is primarily a tourist center, the main attraction being the surrounding countryside, especially the Lakes of Killarney.
See also: Ireland.

Killdeer (*Charadrius* or *Oxyechus vociferus*), shorebird, named for its noisy call. Marked with bold black and white rings on head and breast, killdeer breed from Canada to Chile, spending the winter in large flocks. They feed on insects and other small animals and kill harmful ticks and boll weevils.

Killer whale (*Orcinus orca*), small, toothed, carnivorous whale of the dolphin family, but lacking a beak. Voracious predators, killer whales eat dolphins, porpoises, seals, and fish. They may hunt in small groups or form packs of 40 or more, driving their prey into shallow water where escape is impossible. Their average length is about 20 ft (6 m), and they are found worldwide.

Killy, Jean-Claude (1943-), French skier, who won six world titles and three Olympic gold medals in the downhill, slalom and giant slalom events between 1966 and 1968; in addition, he also won the Alpine World Cup twice. Killy, who was famous for his spectacular downhill descents, turned professional after the 1968 Winter Olympics.

Kiln, oven or furnace usually designed for 'firing' earthy materials to make bricks, pottery, or quicklime. Limestone for quicklime is often roasted in a *shaft kiln*, being heated by hot gases flowing upward as it falls through the shaft. Clay and limestone, used to make cement, are usually burned in a *rotary kiln*, a long tube (up to 610 ft/186 m) that rotates slowly. The materials are heated as they shift gradually along it. Bricks and pottery, stacked on small cars, may be fired continuously in a *tunnelkiln*. The clay is prewarmed and hardened as it approaches the center firing zone and gradually cools as it leaves. Clayware is also fired in batches in *periodic kilns*. Ware is stacked, heated, and allowed to cool before repeating the process. *See also:* Pottery and porcelain.

Kimberley (pop. 150,000), city in Cape Province, South Africa, about 540 mi (870 km) northeast of Capetown, famed for having some of the world's largest diamond mines. The city was named for the Earl of Kimberly, colonial secretary at the time the area was settled by Britons.

Kim Dae Yung (1924-), South Korean President (1997-2003), who made name in the final days of the liberation, when he was active with a people's committee. He later joined the Democratic Party, opposing Syngman Rhee's regime. In 1971, he was nominated by the opposition to run for president. Park Chung Hee won the elections and became president. But Kim Dae Yung got 36% of the votes. He was kidnapped from his hotel room in Tokyo by Korean intelligence agents in 1973. Intense political pressure from both Japan and the United States saved his life. He remained confined to his house until Park was murdered in 1979. During the regime of Chun Doo Hwan, Kim Dae Yung was charged with being responsible for the Kwangju uprising in 1980, and was sentenced to death. That sentenced was transmuted into a life sentence owing to intense international pressure. In 1982, Kim Dae Jung went into exile in the United States, only to return to South Korea in 1985. On returning, he was once again confined to his house. He regained his political rights after democratization in 1987; in the same year, he again ran for president unsuccessfully. This happened for the third time in 1992, after which he withdrew from politics. However, he returned again to run for president in 1997, this time winning a convincing victory. Dae Yung's presidential policy is characterized by increasing economic liberalization, as required by the IMF, and by reconciliation with North Korea. In 2003, he was succeeded by Roh Moo Hyun.

Kim Il Sung (1912-1994), North Korean political leader, premier 1948-72, president (1972-94). Trained in Moscow, he returned to Korea as head of a provisional Soviet-supported government in 1946. His invasion of South Korea precipitated the Korean War, and only Communist Chinese intervention saved his regime. He then launched a vast industrial and military buildup.

Kim Yong Il (1942-), North Korean statesman. Kim Yong Il was born in a Soviet camp in Khabarovsk, where his father had retreated with his guerrilla group. In 1964 he joined the Central Committee of the Korean Labor Party in Pyongyang. In 1973 he became the secretary of the Central Committee of the Korean Labor Party, and in 1974 a member of the Politburo. In 1980 he was officially appointed as his father's future successor. Kim Yong Il's name of the 'beloved father' dates from this time.
In 1991, he was appointed commander-in-chief of the North Korean armed forces. After his father died in 1994, he took over the control of the country, but did not have himself appointed Secretary-General of the reigning Korean Labor Party until 1997. In 1998, Kim Yong Il was reelected as chairman of the National Defense Committee of the High People's Council, the North Korean parliament. That position is defined as the highest public office by North Korea's new constitution. At the same time, he arranged for his father to be granted the title of 'eternal president' posthumously.

Kim Young Sam (1927-), South Korean politician and statesman. Kim is one of the leading figures in the Liberal Democratic Party, DLP. During the late 1980s, he was politically isolated. His opposition to Park Chung Hee's rule caused him to be arrested several times. In 1987, he was a cofounder of the Democratic Party of the Reunification. In 1990 he became the chairman of the DLP, the ruling party, and in 1993 he succeeded Roh Tae Woo as president of South Korea. Political reform followed almost immediately. Kim included former dissidents in his cabinet, replaced the army command, and tackled corruption. This brought him great popularity. Although his party, the New Korea Party (NKP) lost eleven seats at the elections in 1996, and therefore its absolute majority in parliament, it gained the support of a number of independent members, and so remained in power. Kim Young Sam took no part in the 1997 presidential election; in 1998 he was succeeded by Kim Dae Jung, the leader of the opposition.

Kindergarten, school for children aged 4-6, conceived by German educator F.W.A. Froebel in 1837. The school aims to develop a child's self-expression and sociability through games, play, and creative activities. One of the first American kindergartens was opened in 1860 by E. Peabody.
See also: Froebel, Friedrich Wilhelm August.

Kinesics, systematic study of nonverbal communication through body motions. Developed by Ray L. Birdwhistell, an American anthropologist, kinesics examines gestures such as winking, or eyebrow raising, as well as involuntary reactions like

K

blushing, in an effort to interpret the feelings and messages being relayed through such gestures.

Kinetic Art, school in the visual arts which focuses on movement in art. This movement arose in the 1950s and 1960s. Kinetic artworks can be roughly divided into movable and moving pieces; the movable works are set in motion by random factors, such as the wind or an action by the viewer, whereas the moving works are powered by a motor or by natural forces. Although movement was already being studied as a central theme in art at the beginning of this century, the 1950s saw the start of extensive experimentation. Numerous groups concentrated on kinetic art, as did individual artists, including Calder, Pan, and Tinguely.

King, Billie Jean (Billie Jean Moffitt; 1943-), U.S. tennis player. She was a prominent figure in the international game, whose efforts have done much to improve the status of women in tennis. Kings achievements include winning the U.S. Open 4 times (1967, 71, 72, 74), Wimbledon 6 times (1966, 67, 68, 72, 73, 75), and the Australian Open and French Open once (1968, 1972).

The western kingbird (right; *T. verticalis*), and the eastern kingbird (left; *T.tyrannis*), are named for their domineering behavior.

King, Coretta Scott (1927-), U.S. civil rights leader, widow of Martin Luther King, Jr. As president of the Martin Luther King, Jr. Center for Social Change, she continues the legacy of her late husband's work. She is the author of *My Life with Martin Luther King, Jr.* (1989).
See also: Civil Rights; King, Martin Luther, Jr.

King, Ernest Joseph (1878-1956), U.S. admiral, commander of the U.S. fleet and naval operations chief in World War II. His recognition of the importance of the air war and the superiority of aircraft carriers to battleships led to Japan's naval defeat.
See also: World War II.

King, Martin Luther, Jr. (1929-1968), black U.S. clergyman and civil rights leader, recipient of the 1964 Nobel Peace Prize for his work for racial equality in the United States. King organized the boycott of the Montgomery, Ala., transit company in 1955 to force desegregation of the buses. Under

his leadership in the late 1950s and 1960s, civil disobedience and nonviolent tactics, like the Washington March of 250,000 people in 1963, brought about the Civil Rights Act of 1965. Black militants challenged his methods in 1965, but in 1966 he extended his campaign to slum conditions in the northern cities of the United States, and in 1968 he set up the Poor People's Campaign. He was less successful in this effort because the Vietnam War distracted national attention from civil rights and urban issues. He was assassinated in Memphis, Tenn. In 1983 Congress designated the third Monday in January a national holiday to commemorate his birthday.

King Arthur *See:* Arthur, King.

King, Stephen (1947-), U.S. novelist and short-story writer. His best-selling occult thrillers about families threatened by malevolent supernatural forces include *Carrie* (1974), *The Shining* (1976), *Cujo* (1981), and *Misery* (1987). Other works include *Gerald's Game* (1992), *Insomnia* (1994), *Wizard and Glass* (1997), *Bag of Bones* (1998), and *Dreamcatcher* (2001).

King, William Lyon Mackenzie (1874-1950), Canadian statesman, Liberal prime minister (1921-30, 1935-48). He established Canada's right to act independently of Great Britain in international affairs, introduced old age pensions (Canada's first national social security scheme), and directed the Canadian war effort in World War II.
See also: Canada.

Kingbird, aggressive North American flycatcher (genus *Tyrannus*), usually with gray head and a black stripe through the eye. It feeds on insects and defends its nest vigorously, even attacking humans.

King crab *See:* Horseshoe crab.

Kingdom, in biology, large group of organisms that share basic characteristics. Biologists recognize 5 kingdoms of organisms: Monera, Protista, Fungi, Plantae, and Animalia.
See also: Classification.

Kingfish, any of several large food and game fishes, including the mackerel and drum, especially of the genus *Menticirrhus*. Kingfish live in the warm waters of the Atlantic and Pacific coasts.

Kingfisher, family (Alcedinidae) of brightly colored, strong-beaked birds of rivers, lakes, and streams worldwide. The bird perches until prey is sighted, then dives arrowlike into the water to take the fish.

King George VI Falls, collection of waterfalls and rapids descending some 1,600 feet (488 meters), situated in northwestern Cape Province, South Africa. The falls, on the Utishi river, are the major attraction of the Aughrabies National Park.

Kinghead *See:* Ragweed.

King James Version *See:* Bible.

Kinglet, tiny, olive-green songbird (genus *Regulus*) living in the temperate woodlands of the Northern Hemisphere. It feeds on small insects with its thin, pointed bill.

Kingmaker *See:* Warwick, Earl of.

Kings, Books of, in the Old Testament, called First and Second Kings in the Authorized Version, and Third and Fourth Kings in the Greek versions and the Western canon. They cover Israelite history from the reign of Solomon through the period of the 2 kingdoms of Israel and Judah to the destruction of Judah by the Babylonians.
See also: Old Testament.

Kingsley, Charles (1819-75), English writer and clergyman and an advocate of social reform. His early novel *Alton Locke* (1850) is a sympathetic study of working-class life. He also wrote historical novels, notably *Westward Ho!* (1855) and the children's fantasy *The Water Babies* (1863).

Kingsnake, nonpoisonous snake (genus *Lampropeltis*) of the central and southern United States. Kingsnakes grow up to 6 ft (2 m) long and are often brightly colored. They feed on rodents, birds, and snakes, even rattlesnakes, since kingsnakes are immune to venom.

Kingston (pop. 584,000), capital and largest city of Jamaica, in the Caribbean Sea. Famed for its botanical gardens, Kingston is the economic hub of the island nation. Industries include oil refining, food processing, and tourism. The city was founded in 1693 and superseded Port Royal as capital in 1872.
See also: Jamaica.

King William's War *See:* French and Indian Wars.

Kinkajou (*Potos flavus*), relative of the raccoon that can hang by its tail. It grows up to 3 ft (1 m) long and has short legs and a very long tail covered in soft fur. The kinkajou lives in tropical forests from southern Mexico to Brazil. It moves cautiously through the branches using its tail as an anchor. Although kinkajous are members of the Carnivora (flesh eaters), they eat mainly fruit and a few insects.

Kinnock, Neil Gordon (1942-), British politician, elected youngest Labour Party leader in 1983 at the age of 41. Known for his left-wing views and fervent public speaking skills, Kinnock has strived to promote unity between the party's left-wing and moderate factions in the area of policy. In 1993 he was succeeded by John Smith. Kinnock became a member of the European Commission in 1994.

Kinsey, Alfred Charles (1894-1956), U.S. biologist best known for his statistical studies of human sexual behavior, published as *Sexual Behavior in the Human Male* (1948) and *Sexual Behavior in the Human Female* (1953).
See also: Biology; Sex.

K

Kinshasa (pop. 4,400,000), capital and largest city of Zaïre. It was founded in 1881 by the British explorer Henry M. Stanley, who named it Leopoldville after King Leopold II of Belgium. Its name was changed to Kinshasa in 1966, after Zaïre became independent.
See also: Congo (Zaïre).

Kiowa, Native American tribe of the North American plains. A nomadic people, they were followers of sun dance and ghost dance cults. A Kiowan uprising was put down by the U.S. army in 1874. They were settled in Oklahoma, and presently number about 2,000.

Kipling, Rudyard (1865-1936), Indian-born English writer. Among his works are short stories about Anglo-Indian life, such as *Plain Tales from the Hills* (1888); poems, including 'Mandalay' and 'Gunga Din'; and children's books, including *The Jungle Book* (1894), *Kim* (1901). He won the Nobel Prize for literature in 1907.

Kippenberger, Martin (1953-1997), German artist, the enfant terrible of the German art scene, a true provocateur. His paintings, collages, and installations are characterized by a sharp sense of humor and an unconventional approach to the subjects. He drew inspiration from contemporary city life, and applied a wide range of styles, containing elements of neo expressionism, pop art, and dadaism. He often gave his works provocative titles. For example, *Ich Kann beim Besten Willen kein Hakenkreuz Entdecken* effectively challenges the viewer to find a swastika in the painting. He also parodied the works of colleagues such as Buren, Polke, and Toroni.

Kirchhoff, Gustav Robert (1824-87), German physicist best known for his work on electrical conduction, showing that current passes through a conductor at the speed of light, and deriving Kirchhoff's Laws. With Robert Bunsen he discovered the elements cesium and rubidium and pioneered spectrum analysis, which he applied to the solar spectrum, identifying several elements and explaining the Fraunhofer lines.
See also: Physics.

Kirchhoff's Laws, two laws governing electric circuits involving Ohm's law conductors and sources of electromotive force, stated by Kirchhoff. They assert that the sums of outgoing and incoming currents at any junction in the circuit must be equal and that the sum of the current-resistance products around any closed path must equal the total electromotive force in it.
See also: Kirchhoff, Gustav Robert.

Kirchner, Ernst Ludwig (1880-1938), German expressionist graphic artist and painter, cofounder of the Brücke (bridge) movement (1905-13). He is noted for his powerful, savagely expressive woodcuts and, in his painting, for his vigorous, distorted use of color and form. When his work was condemned by the Nazis as degenerate, Kirchner committed suicide.

Kiribati

Capital:	Bairiki
Area:	277 sq mi (811 sq km)
Population:	96,000
Language:	I-Kiribati, English
Government:	Presidential republic
Independent:	1979
Head of gov.:	President
Per capita:	US$ 840
Monetary unit:	1 Australian dollar = 100 cents

Kiribati, independent island republic in the central Pacific, consists of 3 groups of coral atolls and 33 islands astride the equator. The land area is 324 sq mi (811 sq km), spread across 2,400 mi (3,860 km) of ocean. The population of 75,000 is mostly Micronesian. The capital, Bairiki, is on Tarawa, where over 30% of the total population lives. Fishing constitutes the mainstay of the subsistence economy, supplemented by the cultivation of taro and fruits. Formerly part of the British protectorate called British Gilbert and Ellice Islands (since 1892), Kiribati was granted independence in 1979. Kiribati was the first inhabited place to greet the new millennium in 2001. The past few years, Australia approached the country to take up unwanted asylum seekers.

Kirijenko, Sergej (1962-), Russian politician, who became director of the NORSI oil company in 1996 and went on to earn his spurs at the Ministry for Energy. In April 1998, he was nominated as prime minister by President Boris Jeltsin. Initially, the Russian parliament rejected his candidacy twice, owing to his youth and lack of experience. President Jeltsin subsequently threatened to disband the Duma, after which they finally agreed. Kirijenko was fired within months.

Kiritimati Atoll, or Christmas Island, one of the largest coral islands in the Pacific, covering 140 sq mi (360 sq km) and with a coastline of 80 mi (130 km). It is 1,300 mi (2,100 km) south of Honolulu. On Christmas Day, 1777, British explorer James Cook became the first European to reach the island. It was used for nuclear testing by both Britain and the United States. In 1979 it became part of the nation of Kiribati.

Kirkpatrick, Jeane Jordan (1926-), U.S. ambassador to the United Nations (1981-85). A professor of political science at Georgetown University, she was a charter member of the conservative Coalition for a Democratic Majority, advocating a tougher U.S. foreign policy. After leaving her UN post she joined the Republican Party and was appointed by President Ronald Reagan to serve on the National Commission on Space and the Foreign Intelligence Advisory Board.

Kirlian photography, or electromagnetic discharge imaging (EDI), technique of recording an image on photographic film by applying a high-frequency electric field to it and recording the resulting pattern of luminescence. The electromagnetic field causes electrons and positive ions in the gas surrounding an object to accelerate and frees them from the object's surface. When the electrons and ions recombine, the objects photographed appear surrounded by light. The process is named after Soviet scientists Semyon and Valentina Kirlian, who systematized it c.1940.
See also: Photography.

Kirov Ballet, Soviet ballet company, the descendent of the imperial ballet that was founded in 1735 in St. Petersburg. The current name originates from 1935, and is taken from Sergej Mironovich Kirov, a communist leader. It is one of the world's key ballet companies, and has had a number of famous choreographers, such as Fokine and Perrot Petipa, and dancers, such as Marie Taglioni and Olga Preobrajenska, on its payroll. After the fall of communism, the company changed its name to Ballet of the Marinsky Theater in St. Petersburg. It has been led by Oleg Vinogradov since 1972.

Kirstein, Lincoln (1907-96), U.S. ballet promoter who persuaded George Balanchine to come to the United States and helped him organize the School of American Ballet in New York (1934) and the New York City Ballet (1948). Kirstein also wrote several books on ballet.
See also: Ballet.

Kissinger, Henry Alfred (1923-), German-born U.S. adviser on foreign affairs. Professor at Harvard when his book *Nuclear Weapons and Foreign Policy* (1957) brought him international recognition, Kissinger served as special assistant for national security affairs (1969-75) and secretary of state (1973-77) under presidents Nixon and Ford. He was instrumental in initiating the Strategic Arms Limitation (SALT) Talks on disarmament (1969), in ending U.S. involvement in Vietnam, and in opening U.S. policies toward China.

Kitaj, Ronald B. (1932-), American visual artist, who moved to London in 1958. He is one of the most important proponents of British pop art. His sources of inspiration include politics, philosophy, literature, and art history.

Kitakyushu (pop. 2,500,000), Japan, a city and seaport in Fukuoka prefecture, northern

K

Kyushu. It lies on the coast of the Korean Strait near Shimonoseki Strait, which leads to the Inland Sea. Kitakyushu is a center of Japan's heavy industry and one of the world's leading iron- and steel-producing cities. It was formed in 1963 by combining the cites of Kokura, Moji, Tobata, Wakamatsu, and Yahata.

Kitasato, Shibasaburo (1852-1931), Japanese bacteriologist. He discovered with Emil von Behring that graded injections of toxins could be used for diphtheria immunization (1890). He also discovered (1894) the infectious agent of bubonic plague (which he described simultaneously with A.E.J. Yersin). *See also:* Bacteriology.

Kitchener, Horatio Herbert (1850-1916), British field marshal, secretary of state for war in World War I. In the Sudan in 1898, he defeated the Mahdis at Omdurman and retook Khartoum. He was commander in chief in the Boer War, 1900-2, and in India, to 1909. His appeals during World War I raised thousands of army volunteers. He drowned when a ship taking him to Russia hit a mine and sank. *See also:* Boer War; World War I.

Kite, any of various predatory birds of the hawk family (Accipitridae) with long, pointed wings and a forked tail. Kites live near water in tropical zones, preying on reptiles, frogs, and insects.

Kite, aircraft consisting of a light frame covered with thin fabric (e.g., paper) and flown in the wind by aerodynamic lift at the end of a long string. Originating in the ancient Far East, kite flying has long been a popular sport, and has been used for meteorological observations.

Kittikachorn, Thanom (1911-), Thai general and politician. Together with Thanarat, Kittikachorn overthrew Pibul's regime (1957), after which he became deputy prime minister (1957- 58), prime minister (1958), deputy prime minister (1958-63), prime minister (1963-73), and minister for foreign affairs and defense (1973). His policies were authoritarian and pro Western. The country's economy deteriorated during that period, and in 1973, after a series of serious student

The flightless landbirds of the southern continents are known as ratites, because of their raft-like breast bone, which lacks a keel. The keel on the breast bone of flying birds is for the attachment of the large wing muscles.

riots caused by the extremely high price of rice and other factors, he was forced to resign. He went into exile in Singapore, and since his return in 1976 has lived as a Buddhist monk.

Kittiwake, small gull (genus *Rissa*) that nests on narrow cliff ledges around the coasts of the North Atlantic, the North Pacific, and on the islands of the Arctic Ocean. Named for its noisy call, the kittiwake feeds on fish, mollusks, and plankton and flies far out to sea.

Kitty Hawk *See:* Wright brothers.

Kiwi, 3 species of flightless New Zealand birds (genus *Apteryx*), about 18 in (46 cm) high, lacking a tail, with gray-brown, hairlike feathers concealing their wings. The long slender bill probes into soil at night for worms, insects, and berries.

Kiwi fruit, or Chinese gooseberry (*Actinidia chinensis*), fruit originating in China and named for the kiwi bird of New Zealand (where it was first established as a commercial crop). Green-fleshed, with a thin, fuzzy, brown skin, it is similar in size and shape to an egg. It has a pungent flavor and is rich in vitamin C. The fruit is also found in France, the United States, Italy, Spain, and Japan.

Klaipeda, or Memel (pop. 208,000), city in western Lithuania, on the Baltic Sea. Named Memelburg by Teutonic Knights who conquered a fort here in 1252, it was renamed after the Memel Territory became part of Lithuania in 1923. It is an ice-free seaport and trade center specializing in fishing, food processing, shipping, shipbuilding, and textile production. *See also:* Lithuania.

Klaus, Václav (1941-), Czech politician. At the end of 1989, Klaus became a member of the Burgerforum, the main opposition movement in the Czech Republic. In 1991, he founded the Civic Democratic Party (Obcanska Demokratická Strana - ODS), which supported economic reforms. After the parliamentary elections of 1992, he formed a coalition government with the Christian-Democrats and the Civic Alliance. He carried out drastic economic reforms. He succeeded in suppressing inflation, realizing economic growth and, at the same time, keeping the unemployment rate under control. His success seemed complete when the Czech Republic, as the first communist country, became a member of the Organization for Economic Cooperation and Development in 1995. However, in the following two years, the Czech Republic suffered a disappointing economic growth and an increasing deficit in the balance of payments. Nevertheless, the ODS won the elections of 1996, although the government coalition did lose its absolute majority. With the same partners, Klaus formed a minority government, which the social democrats tolerated and which later obtained a small majority due to the support of a few independent members of parliament. As a result of financial problems within the ODS, Klaus resigned in 1997.

Klaveren, Lambertus (Bep) (1907-1992), Dutch boxer, who delighted The Netherlands in 1928 by winning the gold featherweight medal at the Amsterdam Olympics. Three years later, he became European lightweight champion, and in 1938 he won the same title for middleweights. As a professional boxer, Van Klaveren traveled all over the world, and enjoyed particular success in the United States, where he was nicknamed the Dutch Windmill, and in Australia. At the age of almost forty, he beat 27-year-old Luc van Dam to win the Dutch title. His aggressive, pugnacious boxing style made Van Klaveren highly popular.

Klee, Paul (1879-1940), Swiss painter, graphic artist, and art theorist. From 1906, he exhibited with the German expressionist Blaue Reiter (Blue Rider) group. He taught at the Bauhaus 1920-31, publishing a textbook on painting (*Pedagogical Sketchbooks*, trans. 1944). Sensitive line, color, and texture are combined in Klee's paintings with wit and fantasy: *Landscape with Blue Birds* (1919), *Jorg* (1924), and *Diana* (1931).

Kleiber, Erich (1890-1956), Austrian-Argentinean director. Kleiber directed operas at various theaters between 1912 and 1922. In the period 1922-35, he headed the Berlin National Opera, directed, among others, Alban Bergs Wozzeck's world premiere in 1926. In 1934, he resigned in protest against the Nazi's cultural policy and emigrated to Argentina. Kleiber accepted a post at the Teatro Colón in Buenos Aires in 1936, but returned to Europe in 1949, where he appeared on various occasions as a guest director until his death. Kleiber was a great director, and was famous for his renderings of Mozart, Beethoven, and Strauss. He was also an active composer. He directed and performed not only classical music, but also a great deal of contemporary works.

Klein, Lawrence Robert (1920-), U.S. economist. A professor at the Wharton School of the University of Pennsylvania from 1958, he was an adviser to President Jimmy Carter (1976-81) and winner of the 1980 Nobel Prize in economic science. *See also:* Economics.

Klein, Naomi (1970-), Canadian journalist and activist. In *No Logo: Taking Aim at the Brand Bullies* (2000), she takes a stand against the supposed violence of commercials and marketing and the dictatorship of logos and brand names. She accuses multinationals of exploitation and pollution and detests consumerism, moral decay, mass culture and the dependence on sponsors. Klein became the figurehead of antiglobalists. In 2002, her work *Fences And Windows. Dispatches From the Front Lines of the Globalization Debate* was published.

Kleist, Heinrich von (1777-1811), German dramatist and writer of novellas, known for his power and psychological insight. His works include the plays *Penthesilea* (1808) and *Prince Friedrich von Homburg* (1821) and the novels *Michael Kohlhaas* (1808) and *The Marquise of O* (1810-11).

Klemperer, Otto (1885-1973), German conductor. As director of the Kroll Opera House, Berlin (1927-33) he introduced many modern works and new interpretations of classics. After a period of crippling illness he revived his career in 1947, notably as an interpreter of Beethoven and Mahler.

Klerk, Frederik Willem de (1936-), South African politician. Before starting on his political career, De Klerk worked as a lawyer. In 1972, he was elected to parliament for the National Party. He held various cabinet posts between 1978 and 1989 (minister for social affairs, internal affairs, and education), and in 1989, after Botha's resignation, he became president of South Africa. Under his regime, the last apartheid laws were revoked, and the ANC was legalized. In 1993, De Klerk was awarded the Nobel Peace Prize, together with the leader of the ANC, Mandela. After the ANC won the elections in 1994 (the National Party gained 20% of the votes), De Klerk was appointed vice president, a position which he shared with the ANC's Thabo Mbeki. In May 1996, De Klerk's National Party withdrew from the national unity government. The majority of the party found the newly adopted constitution unacceptable. De Klerk left politics in 1997. In 1999 he published his autobiography *The Last Trek*.

Klezmer, Jewish party and funeral music, the roots of which lie in 19th century eastern Europe. Klezmer has also enjoyed a great deal of popularity outside the Jewish community since the 1970s. Some confusion exists as to the meaning of the word 'klezmer'. Originally, its everyday meaning came close to 'bum' or 'third-rate musician'. Since the 1970s, it has been used for the musical idiom. In general, klezmer is regarded as a mixture of Jewish and western music that originated chiefly in the United States. During the final decades of the nineteenth century, a great number of Jews fled the pogroms of eastern Europe and Russia. Many of them ended up in North America. Their number included many musicians and cantors (precentors in the synagogue) - one of the few professions which had been open to Jews for centuries - who continued working with music in their new surroundings. In this manner, folk music from eastern Europe was combined with the popular sounds of the United States, including Dixie and musicals. The clarinet replaced the violin, which had been the leading instrument for a long time. The first great Jewish clarinet players included the emigrants Dave Tarras (born Dovid Tarraschuk, 1897-1989) and Naftule Brandwein. Their pupil Max Epstein (1912) started performing with his Epstein Brothers Orchestra, which also included his brothers Willie (trumpet) and Julius (rhythm section). In New York in the 1980s a new mixture appeared: klezmer with influences of modern jazz and improvised music. The resulting sound is known simply as 'new Jewish music'. An important figure in this scene is the alto saxophone player and composer John Zorn (1954).

Klimt, Gustav (1862-1918), Austrian painter and designer, a leader of the Vienna Secession (1897), noted for his lavishly ornamented, mosaic-patterned style. His interior designs, as for the Palais Stoclet, Brussels, and in Vienna, influenced Jugendstil (German 'art nouveau').

Kline, Franz (1910-62), U.S. abstract expressionist painter. His huge, stark, black-and-white compositions influenced the 'calligraphic' style of the 1950s New York school. Later, Kline reintroduced color into his works.

Klinger, Max (1857-1920), German painter, graphic artist and sculptor. He is best known for the allegorical nature of his graphic work, which makes him one of the most important proponents of symbolism in Germany. His work shows influences of Arnold Böcklin. The allegorical and fantastical element shows most clearly in his graphic work, which is at times reminiscent of Goya's sketches. His series of prints *On Death I Opus XI* (1882-89) and *On Death II Opus XIII* (1885-98), both of which deal with the theme of the Dance of Death (Kunsthalle, Bremen), are well known. His sculptures are reminiscent of those of Rodin, and include busts of Beethoven, Nietzsche (1902) and others.

Klondike, subarctic region in the west central Yukon Territory, northwest Canada, site of the gold rush of 1896. By 1900 $22 million was being panned annually from a tributary of the Klondike River, but the creeks were mined out in about 10 years. *See also:* Yukon Territory.

Klopstock, Friedrich Gottlieb (1724-1803), a German epic, lyric, and dramatic poet. His major work is *Der Messias (The Messiah)*, an epic poem modeled on Milton's *Paradise Lost*. The first three cantos appeared in 1748, and the remaining 17 at intervals during the next 25 years. The epic is written in classical hexameter and marked by religious fervor. Some of his poems collected in *Odes* (1771) are written in classical meter, others in a form approximating free verse.

Klopstock studied theology at the universities of Jena and Leipzig. From 1751 until 1771 he lived in Copenhagen, where the king of Denmark provided him with a pension while he worked on *Der Messias*. Most of his time after he returned to Germany was spent near Hamburg.

His other books include: *Geistliche Lieder* (2 volumes; 1757, 1769) and *Die Gelehrtenrepublik (The Scholar's Republic*, 1744), a prose work.

Knee, front of the leg where the femur (thighbone) and tibia (shinbone) meet, and the joint itself, covered by the patella, or kneecap. Because the bony surfaces do not match exactly, the knee joint is one of the body's weakest joints. Its strength lies in the

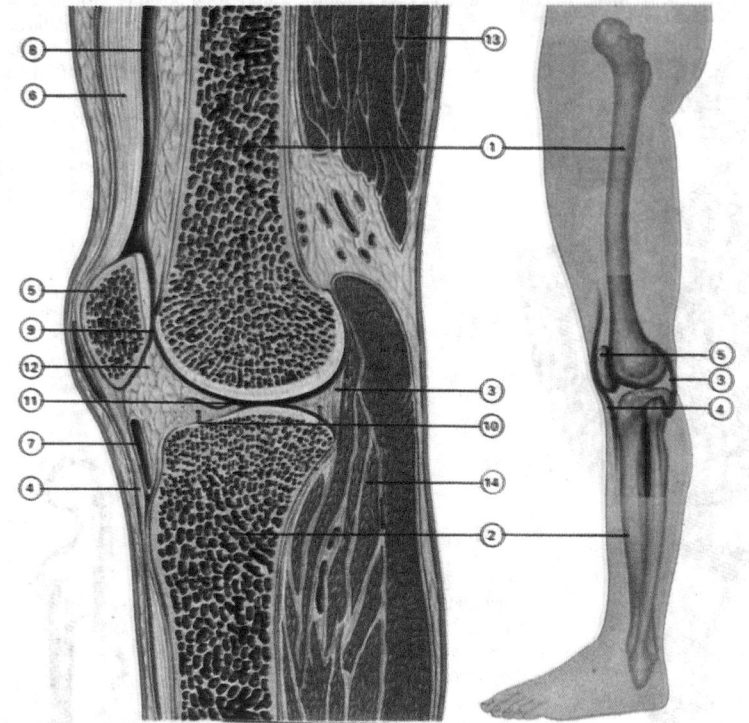

The knee is the largest and most complicated joint in the human body. The femur (1) and tibia (2) are joined at the back and sides by the capsular ligament (3), which is continuous with the periosteum, or outer membrane of the bones. In front, the patellar ligament (4) and tendon of the quadriceps muscle (6) are attached to the patella (5), or knee cap. The bursae (7 and 8) and articular cavity (11), which are filled with synovial, or lubricating fluid and protected by fat cells (12), increase the mobility of the joint, as does the cartilate (9), which covers the articulating surfaces of the bones. The menisci (10) and ligaments give stability to the knee. The biceps muscle (13) controls flexion and lateral rotation of the knee; the gastrocnemius muscle (14) controls ankle flexion.

K

number, size, and arrangement of the ligaments, and the powerful muscles and fibrous membranes that pass over the joint and enable it to withstand the leverage of the 2 longest bones in the body.
See also: Joint.

Knife, hand-held cutting instrument used as a tool and a weapon since early history. Made from stone, bone, metal, wood, and plastic, knives are broadly categorized as fixed-blade or folding, also known as pocket knives.

Knight, Eric (1897-1943), English-American author best known for his children's novel *Lassie Come Home* (1940). Other works include the novels *The Flying Yorkshireman* (1937), *This Above All* (1941), and the short-story collection *Sam Small Flies Again* (1942). He was killed in an airplane crash while on a World War II mission.

Knighthood, Orders of, religious, honorary, or other fraternal society. Knights of the Middle Ages, vowing loyalty to their king, formed orders to defend his lands. During the crusades religious orders of knights fought the Muslims for the Holy Lands. The most famous of the religious orders were the Knights of St. John, the Knights Templars, and the Teutonic Knights. In Great Britain honorary orders of knights include the Order of the Garter (1349), the Order of the Thistle (1687), the Order of the Bath (1725), the Order of St. Michael and St. George (1818), the Royal Victorian Order (1896), and the Order of the British Empire (1917). Other European orders are the Seraphim of Sweden (1748), the Golden Fleece of Spain and Austria (1429), the Danish Order of the Elephant (1462), St. Andrew of Russia (1698), the Black Eagle of Prussia (1701), the Legion of Honor of France (1802), the Order of St. Olaf in Norway (1847). In the United States, the Knights of Columbus are a fraternal order of Roman Catholic men.

Knights and knighthood, part of the feudal system of the Middle Ages in Europe. Knights were mounted and armed sworn defenders of a feudal superior, generally having previously served as page and squire. Chivalry was the code of honor practiced by knights. They were known by their clothing, armor, and participation in tournaments in which they fought each other. The legend of King Arthur is the most famous literary account of knighthood.
See also: Feudalism.

Knights Grand Cross of the Bath *See:* Bath, Order of the.

Knights Hospitallers *See:* Knights of Saint John.

Knights of Saint John (officially, Order of the Hospital of St. John of Jerusalem; also known as Hospitallers, Knights of Rhodes, or of Malta), religious order founded by papal charter (1113) to tend sick pilgrims in the Holy Land. It became a military order as well in 1140, and after the fall of Jerusalem was based successively on Cyprus (1291), Rhodes (1309), and Malta (1530) to provide a defense against Muslim seapower. Expelled from Malta by Napoleon in 1798, the Knights have been established at Rome since 1834.
See also: Knighthood, Orders of.

The illustration is based upon the effigy of Sir Edmund de Thorpe, who fought under Henry V and was killed in Normandy in 1418. The quarterly 'arms' of De Thorpe and Baynard are shown beside him, with the detail of an eagle clasp from his left shoulder, and a detail of his centre belt buckle.

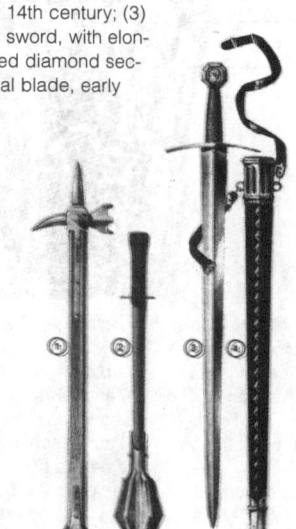

The Medieval knight's weapons: (1) war hammer, early 15th century; (2) mace, late 14th century; (3) war sword, with elongated diamond sectional blade, early 15th century; and (4) decorated velvet-covered sword scabbard.

Knights of the Bath *See:* Bath, Order of the.

Knights of the Round Table *See:* Arthur, King; Round Table.

Knights Templars, Christian military order founded in 1118, with its headquarters on the site of Solomon's Temple in Jerusalem, to protect pilgrims. It provided elite troops for the kingdom of Jerusalem. Its immense riches from endowments and banking excited the greed of Philip IV of France, who (1307-14) confiscated its property and forced the pope to suppress the order.

Knitting, production of fabric by using needles to interlock yarn or thread in a series of connected loops, using basic knit and purl stitches. It was practiced in North Africa in the 3rd century B.C. and was taken to Europe by Arab traders.

Knitting machine, manufacturing device for knitting fabrics ranging from delicate lace to rugs, invented by the Englishman William Lee in 1589. The 2 main types of machines are weft, which produces fabric that stretches elastically, and warp, with lengthwise stitches that produce a flat, less elastic fabric.
See also: Knitting.

Knopf, Alfred A. (1892-1984), U.S. publisher. He founded Alfred A. Knopf, Inc. (1915), a prestigious publishing house with many Nobel Prize-winning authors. Random House acquired the company in 1960, but the imprint remains.

Knossos, ancient city on the north coast of Crete, the center of Minoan civilization. Excavations by Sir Arthur Evans revealed settlements dating from before 3000 B.C.. The great palace of Knossos comprises more than 5 acres (2 hectares) of halls, ceremonial rooms, and staircases, with magnificent fresco decorations, advanced sanitation, and every luxury. Fire destroyed it c.1400 B.C.
See also: Crete.

Knotgrass, knotweed, or doorweed (*Polygonum aviculare*), plant of the buckwheat family, found in Canada and the northern United States. It is short and thick with bluish green leaves and pinkish green flowers.

Knots, hitches, and splices, methods to tie or fasten ropes. A knot is a fastening of cord or ropes. A hitch is used to tie a rope to a ring, spar, post, or other object. A splice joins 2 rope ends permanently. Sailors, explorers, mountain climbers, and builders make wide use of knots. The Gordian knot of Greek mythology, which reputedly could not be untied except by a person predestined to do so, is used as a metaphor for any unsolvable problem.

Knox, John (1514?-72), Scottish Protestant Reformation leader. A Catholic priest, Knox converted to Protestantism and fled in 1554 from the Roman Catholic regime of English queen Mary I to Geneva, where he became a follower of John Calvin. He returned to Scotland in 1559 ardently preaching

Protestantism. When it became the state religion (1560) Knox gained great political influence, opposing Mary Queen of Scots. His writings include his unfinished *History of the Reformation in Scotland* (pub. 1644), *First Blast of the Trumpet Against the Monstrous Regiment of Women* (1556-58), and the *Book of Common Order*.
See also: Reformation.

Koala, or koala bear (*Phascolarctos cinereus*), pouched tree-dwelling mammal of eastern Australia. Koalas have thick, gray fur, a black nose, and no tail, and are 2-2$^1/_2$ ft (60-75 cm) long. They eat only eucalyptus leaves. Koalas are marsupials, bearing and nursing their young in a pouch, although unlike must marsupials, they do have a true placenta. The koala has been considered an endangered species.

Kobayashi, Masaki (1916-1996), Japanese movie director, who established his reputation on the scene with *Ningen no joken* (*The Human Condition*; 1959-61), his great trilogy about the Japanese occupation of Manchuria. This was followed by *Seppuku* (*Hara-Kiri*; 1962), *Joi-uchi* (*Samurai Rebellion*; 1967), which brought him recognition as the master of the samurai movie, *Kaidan* (1964), which films a number of supernatural Japanese tales, *Tokyo Saiban* (The Tokyo War Tribunal; 1983), about the Japanese aggression in Asia, and others. A recurring theme in his work is the conflict that arises when a changing society causes traditional behavior to clash with ideas of human dignity.

Kobe (pop. 1,420,000), city located on the southern coast of the island of Honshu, Japan. This major seaport is a hub for export and import as well as industry and shipbuilding. It is also considered to be a cultural center, with many places of worship and centers of learning. Modern Kobe is largely the result of rebuilding after the heavy bombings of World War II. In 1995 the city was struck by an earthquake that destroyed thousands of houses and buildings and caused the death of more than 5,000 people.
See also: Japan.

Koblenz, or Coblenz (pop. 111,000), city in west-central Germany, located on the Rhine River in the state of Rhineland-Palatinate. It serves as an administrative, industrial, trade, and cultural center for Germany. One of the oldest German settlements, it was founded in 9 B.C. as a Roman fortress. A popular landmark is the Ehrenbreitstein Castle, a fortress built around the 11th century, destroyed by the French in 1801, and restored by 1832.
See also: Germany.

Koch, Robert (1843-1910), German bacteriologist. He was awarded the 1905 Nobel Prize for physiology or medicine for developing a test for tuberculosis. His innovative methods of obtaining pure cultures are still used. He discovered the bacilli responsible for anthrax (1876), tuberculosis (1882), and cholera (1883).
See also: Bacteriology.

Kocher, Emil Theodor (1841-1917), Swiss surgeon. He won the 1909 Nobel Prize for medicine for his research of the physiology, pathology, and surgery of the thyroid gland. In 1878 he performed the first operation for the removal of an enlarged thyroid gland.

Kodály, Zoltán (1882-1967), Hungarian composer and, with Béla Bartók, an ardent researcher of Hungarian folk music. Folk influences are evident in such works as the cantata *Psalmus Hungaricus* (1923), the opera *Háry János* (1926), and the orchestral 'Peacock' Variations (1938-9).

Koestler, Arthur (1905-83), Hungarian-born British writer. His novel *Darkness at Noon* (1941), based on his own experiences in a Spanish death cell, analyzed the psychology of victims of Stalin's 1930s purges. Many later works on philosophical and scientific subjects include *The Sleepwalkers* (1964), *The Case of the Midwife Toad* (1971), and *The Thirteenth Tribe* (1978).

Koffka, Kurt (1886-1941), German-born U.S. psychologist who, with Wolfgang Köhler and Max Wertheimer, was responsible for the development of Gestalt psychology.
See also: Gestalt psychology; Köhler, Wolfgang; Wertheimer, Max.

Koh-i-noor (Persian for 'mountain of light'; originally 186 carats, now 106) is said to have been stolen from an Indian rajah in 1304. The British East India Company obtained it in the 19th century and gave it to Queen Victoria. The diamond has been among the British crown jewels since the 1850s. It is on display in the Tower of London.

Kohl, Helmut (1930-   ), West German politician and former Chancellor (1982-1998). In 1973, he was called to the chair of the Christian Democratic Union (CDU). He was leader of the opposition in the Bundestag from 1976 to 1982, after which he became Chancellor and leader of a coalition with the CDU, the CSU and the liberal FDP. He played an important role in European politics and guided the reunification of former East and West Germany (1990). He was re-elected in 1994, but was defeated by the Social-Democrat Gerhard Schröder in 1998. He withdrew as party chairman and turned his back on active politics. At the end of 1999, Kohl became discredited due to a large bribery scandal, after which he resigned his post as Honorary Chairman of the party in 2000.

Köhler, Wolfgang (1887-1967), German-born U.S. psychologist, a founder of Gestalt psychology. He studied problem-solving among chimpanzees.
See also: Gestalt psychology; Koffka, Kurt; Wertheimer, Max; Gestalt psychology.

Kohn, Walter (1923-   ), Austrian chemist. He was awarded the 1998 Nobel Prize for Chemistry for his contribution to the development of the density-functional method in quantum chemistry.

Kohout, Pavel (1926-   ), Czech playwright, poet and prose writer, who fled to Austria in 1978. He was very active during the Prague Spring of 1968, which led to his writings being banned from publication. He also signed Charta 77. His works include dramatizations of Verne, Hasek and Capek. In 1977 he was awarded the Austrian national prize for European literature. Kohout's writings include *From the Diary of a Counterrevolutionary* (1969), *Roulette* (1975, drama), *The Hangwoman* (1978).

Koizumi, Gunji (1885-1965), Japanese judoka and founder of European judo. In 1918 he opened the first European judo school in London, the Budokwai, which had close ties with Kano Djigoro's Kodokan in Tokyo. In his teachings, Koizumi - who held the eighth Dan - particularly stressed the mental development related to judo. He was also a calligrapher and a great authority on Oriental art.

Kojong (ruled 1864-1907), Korean king from the Yi dynasty. His father, Hung-son, who ruled as regent for him until 1873, was very hostile toward foreign influences, particularly Christian ones. Christians were persecuted systematically, leading several western countries to send military expeditions to Korea. In 1876 Japan succeeded in forcing Korea open. Following the Sino-Japanese War (1894-95) for the peninsula and the Russian-Japanese War (1904-05), Japan gained increasingly more influence in Korea. Three years after Kojong's abdication Korea was annexed by Japan.

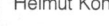

Helmut Kohl

K

The Vienna opera house, painted by Oskar Kokoschka (1886-1980).

Kokoschka, Oskar (1886-1980), Austrian expressionist painter and writer. He is known for psychologically acute portraits such as *The Tempest* (1914) and forlyric land- and townscapes including *Jerusalem* and *View of the Thames* (1925-26).

Kola, tropical tree (genus *Cola*, especially *C. nitida*) that yields fruit containing caffeine-producing seeds. In its native West Africa, the seeds are chewed to combat feelings of tiredness and are also exported for use in beverages (colas) and medicine.

Kollwitz, Käthe (1867-1945), German artist known for her lithographs, woodcuts, and sculpture. Opposed to social injustice, she often depicted human misery and tragedy using the theme of mother and child. Among her well-known works are *War* (1923), a series of 7 wood-block prints, and the sculptures *The Mother* and *The Father* (1931-32), a war memorial.

Köln *See:* Cologne.

Kolyma, river in eastern Siberia, 1,616 mi (2,600 km) in length. Its source lies in the Cersky mountains, and its delta on the East Siberian Sea. It is navigable for a distance of over a thousand miles, and is frozen for eight months each year. The Kolyma basin contains gold and lignite. The river is notorious for the infamous penal camps.

Komodo dragon (*Varanus komodoensis*), largest of living lizards, reaching a length of 10 ft (3 m). It lives on Komodo and a few other Indonesian islands.

Komondor, all-white Hungarian sheep dog. These dogs weigh approximately 90 lb (40 kg), and are about 31 in (76 cm) tall. Komondors were brought to Hungary in the late 9th century by Magyar invaders.

Kongo, kingdom of central Africa from the 15th to the 18th century, covering an area now in Angola and Zaïre, south of the Congo River. The king or *Mani-Kongo* ruled from the capital of Mbanza over a hierarchy of provincial and village governments, exercising political and religious authority without military force. The Kongolese traded in ivory, copper, and slaves. The Portuguese, who first explored the area in 1482, began converting the Kongolese to Christianity, but soon also became active in enslaving them. Portuguese slave trade seriously weakened the hierarchy of the kingdom, and Portugal took control by invading the Kongo in 1665, killing the king. By the early 18th century the kingdom was destroyed.

Konoye, Prince (Fumimaro Konoye; 1891-1945), Japanese premier (1937-39, 1940-41). A moderate, he appeased the military extremists and so furthered expansionism. His suicide prevented his trial as a war criminal after World War II.
See also: Japan; World War II.

Konrád, György (1933-   ), Hungarian writer, sociologist and political dissident. A descendent of a wealthy Jewish family which was decimated by the nazis, he studied literature, sociology and psychology in Budapest. *The visitor* (1970), his first novel, tells the gripping tale of a child protector. The novel criticized 'the system' to such an extent that he was instantly labeled 'suspicious' by the authorities. *The Accomplice* (1980), a semi-autobiographical novel, relates the horrifying experiences of Jewish intellectuals during the nazi regime, Stalinism and during the popular uprising of 1956. This book could only be published abroad, as could *The Garden Party* (1987). The novel *Melinda and Dragoman* followed in 1991.

Kon-Tiki *See:* Heyerdahl, Thor.

Konya (pop. 513,000), Turkey, a city in the south-central part of the country. Konya lies on a fertile plain of the Anatolian plateau. It manufactures carpets, cotton, and silk goods, and leather goods. In ancient times Konya, known as Iconium, was a large and wealthy city. Saint Paul visited the city as a missionary. The Seljuk Turks conquered Konya during 1072-74 and made it their capital soon after. In 1472 the city became part of the Ottoman Empire.

Kookaburra, or laughing jackass (*Dacelo novaguineae*), crow-sized bird, an Australian kingfisher, named for its gurgling, laughing call.

Koolhaas, Rem (1944-), Dutch architect. In 1978 he published, in collaboration with Madelon Vriesendorp, *Delirious New York*, an illustrated analysis of Manhattan. In 1976 he founded the Office for Metropolitan Architecture (OMA) in London, together with Vriesendorp, Elia and Zoe Zenghelis. He settled in Rotterdam in 1980, and later moved to Lille and Paris. He formulated a new, dynamic attitude toward metropolitan architecture, and introduced modern decorative elements such as slopes, flowing roofs and materials with contrasting colors, which have often been imitated.

Koons, Jeff (1955-   ), American visual artist. Starting in 1979, he exhibited new utensils in brightly illuminated showcases. In the mid-1980s he won acclaim with his brightly colored, grotesque objects made from porcelain, wood, steel and glass which copy and magnify the banalities of mass culture. The challenging, exuberant nature of his art, in which the line between kitsch and art becomes blurred, and his sharp media and marketing strategy have made Koons a controversial figure.

Koppel, Ted (Edward James Koppel; 1940-   ), U.S. news reporter, host of the popular T.V. news program *Nightline*. A Vietnam war correspondent, Koppel was made chief diplomatic correspondent for ABC News in 1971. He became famous for his coverage of the Iran hostage crisis in 1979 and has won many journalistic awards.

Koran, sacred scripture of the religion of Islam and the supreme authority of the Islamic tradition. To Muslims the book is not only divinely inspired but enshrines the actual words of God, as made known by the angel Gabriel to Muhammad in the 7th century A.D. After his death in 632 these sayings were collected in the Koran, and a standard text was formulated about 652. Basically the Koran is a collection of laws, moral teachings, and stories written in highly charged, poetic Arabic, much of it rhymed. About 80,000 words long, it is made up of 114 *suras*, or chapters, arranged according to length from the longest to the shortest-except for the first, 'The Opening,' which is a brief prayer, the equivalent of the Lord's Prayer in Christianity.

Just as the word *Islam* means 'surrender' to the will of God, so the Koran passionately demands this same spiritual surrender. The Koran, it teaches, is the revelation of God, known in Arabic as *Allah*, who is compassionate and merciful. It was given to Muhammad, last and greatest of the prophets, but Adam, Noah, Abraham, Moses, and Jesus are also counted among the prophets. However, the requirement in the Koran that the faithful should make at least one pilgrimage to Mecca probably reflects earlier Arab religions, and the complete subordination of women in the Koran is also in the Arabic tradition.

The Koran sets forth many rules governing moral behavior and social life. Alcoholic drinks and gambling are forbidden. The Koran is far more than a religious scripture. Because, as the first book written in Arabic, it formed a point of unity for all Arabs and for the diverse peoples they conquered, it is in a sense the foundation of Islamic civilization, as well as the molder and preserver of the Arabic language. As it is forbidden to recite the Koran in any language other than Arabic, the language was perpetuated in its purest form, with no corruption from the languages of the many peoples who were converted to Islam. The Koran today is the inspiration and guide for millions of Muslims.
See also: Islam.

Korchnoi, Viktor (1931-   ), Soviet chess grandmaster. He became champion of the Soviet Union four times (in 1960, 1962, 1965 and 1970), and was placed for the candidates' championship (1962, 1968, 1971, 1974 and 1977). In 1968 and 1974 he was runner up, beaten by Spasski and Karpov, respectively, but after having defeated Petrosyan, Polugayevski and Spasski in 1977 he challenged world champion

United Nations troops in the city of Seoul during a counteroffensive to regain the city, which had fallen to the North Koreans on June 28, 1950.

K

Karpov. He managed to turn a 5-2 disadvantage into 5-5, but nevertheless lost 5-6. Korchnoi's great asset is his active defense, and he is a true master of the counterstrike. In 1976, after having participated in the Amsterdam IBM tournament, he decided not to return to the Soviet Union, causing quite a degree of excitement. He occupied the second place behind Anatoli Karpov on the world ranking for a long time.

Korea *See:* North Korea; South Korea.

Korean War (1950-1953), conflict between forces of the UN (primarily the United States and South Korea) and forces of North Korea and (later) communist China. In 1945 Korea was divided along latitude 38°N, Russia occupying lands north of this line, and the United States those south of it. The war began when North Korea launched a surprise invasion against South Korea and UN forces were sent to assist South Korea under Gen. Douglas MacArthur. By Nov. 1950 Chinese troops had joined North Korean forces and the fighting was situated over the 38th parallel. MacArthur was replaced in April 1951 by Gen. Matthew B. Ridgway. Two years of negotiations achieved an armistice signed at Panmunjom on July 27, 1953.
See also: United Nations.

Kornberg, Arthur (1918-   ), U.S. biochemist awarded with Severo Ochoa the 1959 Nobel Prize for physiology or medicine for discovering an enzyme (DNA polymerase) that could produce from a mixture of nucleotides exact replicas of DNA molecules. He thus extended Ochoa's related work.
See also: Biochemistry.

Korsakoff's syndrome, amnesic state in which, because of an inability to record new memory traces, a person can carry out complex tasks learned before his or her illness but cannot learn the simplest new skills. The syndrome is often transient and has a good prognosis in head injury. In alcoholism (where the syndrome, sometimes called alcoholic dementia, is caused by a lack of thiamine, a B vitamin that is destroyed by alcohol) and in other conditions where destruction is irreversible, the prognosis is poor and prolonged institutional care may be required.

Korzeniowski, Józef *See:* Conrad, Joseph.

Košice (German: *Kaschau*; Hungarian: *Kassa*; pop. 196,000), city in Slovakia, on the Hornad River. Since the end of World War II it has been the chief industrial city of the region of Slovakia, with large steelworks as well as chemical, food-processing, and textile plants. The old center city was established by Hungary in 1241; its St. Elizabeth cathedral was built in the 14th century. The region became part of the newly established Czechoslovakia in 1918. It was controlled by Hungary and Germany during World War II, but returned to Czechoslovak control in 1945. Since 1993 it is controlled by the Slovak Republic.
See also: Czechoslovakia.

Kosinski, Jerzy (1933-91), Polish-born U.S. writer best known for his semi-autobiographical novel *The Painted Bird* (1965). Its vivid, often shockingly brutal imagery deals with 'daily life among the violations of the spirit and body of human beings.' Among his other works are *Steps* (1968), for which he won a National Book Award, and *Being There* (1971).

Kosovo (Pop. 1,950,000), region in Yugoslavia (Serbia); 4,205 sq mi (10,887 sq km). Its capital is Pristina. Its main produce includes grain, vegetables, tobacco, forestry products and cattle. Minerals include lead, coal, lignite (silver and gold). In 1991, 90% of the population consisted of ethnic Albanians, the other 10% being either Serb or Montenegran. The region has a great historical significance for the Serbs: in 1389, Kosovo Polje was the site of a great battle against the Turks, the Battle of the Field of Blackbirds. The Ottoman victory was followed by a long period of Serbian uprisings. The Turks were not driven out until 1912. After a brief period of Albanian independence, Kosovo was divided between Serbia and Montenegro in 1918 by the great powers, at the urging of Russia.
After World War II, Kosovo became an autonomous region within Tito's Yugoslavia. The year 1988 saw great civil unrest, as the Albanians wished to join Albania. Slodoban Milosevic, the populist-nationalist leader of the Serbs, deprived the region of its autonomy in 1989.
In 1998 the ethnic struggle reached such extremes that the Albanians fled Kosovo en masse in fear of Serb violence. In 1999, when negotiations proved fruitless, NATO commenced air strikes on Serbian military targets near Pristina and Belgrade, with the intention of forcing the Serbs to cease their aggressive actions against the Albanians. In response, the Serbs started a large-scale ethnic purge in Kosovo.
Only when Milosevic accepted the peace plans of the G8 in June, did NATO end it's actions and Kosovo was placed under international supervision. The return of the Albanese refugees was accompanied by aggression towards the Serbs. The United Nations peace keeping force KFOR was assigned to bring peace and stability to the territory. Ibrahim Rugova, who had been leader of the opposition against the Serbian government for many years, was elected President in 2002.

Koss, Johann Olav (1969-   ), Norwegian skater. He achieved fame in 1990 when he won the world title for all-rounders. The following year he won both the European title and the world title for all-rounders, and became world champion once again in 1994. Although he had only won the 1500 meters at the 1992 Winter Olympics, he reigned supreme at the 1994 Winter Olympics, winning gold on the 1500 meters, the 5000 meters, and the 10,000 meters. He also set a new world record for each of those distances, recording times of 1.51.29, 6.34.96 and 13.30.55, respectively. In 1994, Koss left competitive skating in order to study medicine.

Kossuth, Lajos (1802-94), Hungarian patriot and statesman who campaigned against Austrian rule and led the Hungarian revolution of 1848-49. A minister in the government set up in 1848, he engineered Hungary's declaration of independence as a republic the following year and became president. Austria, with the aid of Russian troops, forced a surrender, and Kossuth fled. He was received as a hero in the United States and England, where he lived for many years, and he died in Italy.
See also: Hungary.

Polish-American writer Jerzy Kosinski, known for his stark, surrealistic style.

Lajos Kossuth (1802-1894), a 19th-century Hungarian national hero.

Kostunica, Vojislav (1944-   ) Yugoslavian politician and Serbian nationalist. He was one of the founders of the Democratic Party (DS). Part of this party splintered off under his leadership after the collapse of Yugoslavia in 1992. The splinter group con-

K

tinued as the Democratic Party of Serbia (DSS). He was nominated for the presidential elections of 2000 by the Democratic Opposition of Serbia (DOS; a coalition of 18 small political parties), in order to compete with President Milosevic. When it became clear that Kostunica was going to win the elections, Milosevic attempted to manipulate the outcome and demanded a second round. However, these attempts failed and Kostunica was inaugurated as President of Yugoslavia in 2000. Two years later, the DSS broke with the government coalition DOS. The break was a result of the struggle for power between the supporters of Kostunica and those of the Serbian Prime Minister Zoran Djindjic. In 2002, Kostunica ran for the Serbian Presidential elections.

Kosuth, Joseph (1945-), American artist, representative of the analytical school of conceptual art. He belonged to 'Art & Language' from 1969-76. *One and three chairs* (1965), consisting of the combination of a real chair, a photograph of that chair and the dictionary definition of the word 'chair', is regarded as a key work in that school of art. In Kosuth's opinion, works of art should be tautological: they should not refer to themes outside art, but should describe only themselves. One of his early neon pieces, dating back from the mid-1960s, consists of the phrase *five words in red neon*. In the 1980s, his work included philosophical writings on walls.

Kosygin, Aleksei Nikolaevich (1904-80), Soviet premier, 1964-80. In 1939 he was appointed to the central committee of the Communist party; in 1960 he became first deputy to Nikita Khrushchev, whom he succeeded. Sharing leadership with Leonid Brezhnev, Kosygin concentrated on modernizing industry and agriculture.
See also: Union of Soviet Socialist Republics.

Koufax, Sandy (1935-), U.S. baseball player. Koufax is considered one of the best left-handed pitchers of all time. His achievements include winning 3 Cy Young awards (1963, 65, 66), the Most Valuable Player (MVP) award (1963), striking-out 382 batters in one season (1965), and pitching 4 no-hit games. Koufax pitched with the Brooklyn and (later) Los Angeles Dodgers (1955-66). In 1972 he was inducted into the National Hall of Fame.

Koumiss *See:* Kumiss.

Kounellis, Jannis (1936-), Greek artist who, around 1958-59, began making letter paintings and later number paintings. After 1967 the nature of his works changed; he started to include elements of nature, such as coal, fire, living creatures and plants, in his compositions. This work was related to the arte povera. In the 1970s a clear cultural-historical background began to appear in his works: relics from the past determined the appearance of his work.

Kouprey, also known as the Indonesian forest ox, rare wild cattle found in southeastern Asia. Six ft (1.8 m) tall at the shoulder,

kouprey have small ears and a long tail, with the males (bulls) having large horns and blackish-brown hides. Females (cows) and calves are gray.

Koussevitzky, Serge (1874-1951), Russian-born U.S. conductor. He left the USSR for England in 1920 and settled in the United States, where he became conductor of the Boston Symphony Orchestra (1924-49). In 1940 he established the Berkshire Music Center at Stockbridge, Mass. He is remembered as a champion of contemporary composers.

Kowloon, Juilong, or Chiulung (pop. 2,100,000), peninsula across Kowloon Bay from the island of Hong Kong, near Guangzhou (Canton), southern China, but part of the British Crown Colony of Hong Kong since 1860. Only 4 sq mi (10 sq km), it is one of the most densely populated areas in the world. It is an important transportation and commercial link between the People's Republic of China and the West. As part of British Hong Kong it was reverted to Chinese control in 1997.
See also: Hong Kong.

Koxinga (Cheng Ch'ang-kung, Zheng Chenggong; 1626-1664), Chinese Ming loyalist and pirate, who after the fall of the Ming dynasty (1368-1644) led the resistance against the new Manchu dynasty (Ch'ing dynasty, 1644-1911). After Nanying was taken, Cheng and his father fled to the Fukien province in the south. There they organized the resistance around the Ming pretender, the 'Prince of T'ang', who granted Cheng the title Kuo-sing-yè ('Lord of the Imperial Family Name'). After his father had withdrawn and he suffered a defeat at the hands of the Ch'ing, Koxinga gathered a fleet and crossed to the island of Formosa (Taiwan), managing to wrestle it from the Dutch. After establishing a Chinese style of government, he died the following year. In the 20th century he became a national hero for all Chinese; in Taiwan he is still revered as a god.

Kozhikode (Calicut; pop. 457,000), city in the Indian federal state Kerala, by the Arabian Sea. Port from which coffee, coconut, tea, ginger, pepper and other spices are exported. Processing of cotton, coffee, wood and production of soap. This is where Portugal's Vasco da Gama landed in 1498. Between 1513 and 1525 the Portuguese produced *calicot* textile there. During the second half of the seventeenth century the British and the French established trading posts in Calicut, and the British took possession of the city and the surrounding area at the end of the eighteenth century. The city still boasts large Muslim and Christian minorities, who maintain peaceful relationships with the Hindu majority.

Kozyrev, Andrei (1951-), Russian politician. For a long time, Kozyrev worked in the Soviet Union at the state institute for international relations and at the Ministry of Foreign Affairs (1974-86). Between 1986 and 1990 he headed the International Organizations Department of the Ministry of

Foreign Affairs. During President Jeltsin's regime he was appointed Minister for Foreign Affairs of the Russian Federation (1991). Kozyrev was greatly criticized for his pro-Western attitude. He resigned his position in January 1996, choosing to hold the seat in Parliament he had won in the Murmansk district during the elections in December 1995.

Krajicek, Richard (1971-), Dutch tennis player, the first Dutchman to win a Grand Slam title: he defeated the American Malivai Washington in three sets during the men's final at Wimbledon in 1996. Before that, he had reached the semi-finals and quarterfinals of various international tournaments, and won nine ATP tournaments. Krajicek has mastered all aspects of the game, but is best known for his service, which is among the hardest of the international top.
Krajicek has announced that he wishes to end his tennis career after the US Open in 2003.

Krakatoa, volcanic island in the Sunda Strait, Indonesia. The eruption of Aug. 1883, one of the most violent ever known, caused a tidal wave killing 36,000 people in neighboring Java and Sumatra, and threw debris as far as Madagascar.

Kraków, or Cracow (pop. 741,000), city in south-central Poland, on the Vistula River. By the 8th century the city was a major trading center on routes between Europe and Asia. It was the capital of Poland from the late Middle Ages until Warsaw was made capital in 1596. Dating from that period are the Jagiellonian University (founded 1364), the 14th-century cathedral and market square, and the 16th-century royal castle. From the 18th century it was at times under Austrian, Prussian, and Russian rule, but it has once again been part of Poland since 1920. It is now a manufacturing center for iron and steel, chemicals, textiles, and other products.
See also: Poland.

Kramer, Jack (John Albert Kramer; 1921-), U.S. tennis player, Wimbledon singles (1947) and doubles (1946-47) champion. He won the U.S. singles (1946-47), doubles (1940-41, 43, 47) and mixed doubles (1941) titles. In 1942, Kramer won 10 straight singles tournaments and in 1946 and 1947 was a member of the United States Davis Cup team that defeated Australia in the finals. An active promoter and organizer of professional tennis tours, Kramer was elected to the National Lawn Tennis Hall of Fame in 1968.

Krasnodar (pop. 756,000), Russia, a city on the Kuban River near the Caucasus Mountains. Krasnodar is primarily a manufacturing city, producing foods, textiles, machinery, and petroleum products. It is also a railway hub. Kuban State University and several technical institutes are here. Krasnodar was founded in the 1790s as a frontier Cossack settlement and was originally named Yekaterinodar, in honor of Empress Catherine the Great. In 1920 it was renamed. Growth came mainly in the late

19th century and the 20th century, mostly under the Soviet Union.

Krasnoyarsk (pop. 930,000), Russia, a port in central Siberia. It is a major transportation and industrial center. Machine-building, metalworking, and food processing are important industries. Located here are polytechnic, agricultural, and forestry insitutes. Nearby on the Yenisey is Krasnoyarsk Dam, one of the world's most powerful hydroelectric stations. The city was founded in 1628 as a Cossack fortress.

Krauze, Zygmunt (1938-), Polish composer and pianist, won the Gaudeamus prize for interpreters of contemporary music in 1966. Performs regularly with his own contemporary music ensembles. His works include *Dyptyk* (1967), *Voices* (1968/72), *Folk Music* (for orchestra; 1972), *Fête galante et pastorale* (for orchestra; 1975), *Piano Concerto* (1976), *Violin Concerto* (1980), *Tableau Vivant* (1982), *Terra incognita* (1994), and *La terra* (1995).

Kravchuk, Leonid (1934-), Ukrainian politician. Kravchuk was appointed head of the Department of Ideology of the Ukrainian Communist Party in 1989, and in 1990 became president of the Highest Soviet of Ukraine. After the disintegration of the Soviet Union he became president of the republic. Under his strict regime the republic tried to escape from the grasp of Moscow. During the presidential elections of 1994 Kravchuk was defeated by Leonid Kuchma.

Krebs, Sir Hans Adolf (1900-81), German-born British biochemist awarded (with F.A. Lipmann) the 1953 Nobel Prize for physiology or medicine for his discovery of the citric acid cycle, or Krebs cycle, the principle means by which living organisms produce energy.
See also: Biochemistry.

Kreisler, Fritz (1875-1962), Austrian-U.S. violinist. He was an extremely popular performer, known for his elegance of style. A collector of manuscripts of violin music, he published violin pieces of his own composition which he at first attributed to various baroque and classical composers. He composed the operettas *Apple Blossom* and *Sissy* as well as numerous violin pieces, including *Liebesfreud*, *Liebesleid*, and *Caprice*. His arrangements of compositions by earlier composers became part of the standard repertoire.

Kremer, Gidon (1947-), Soviet Russian violin player, who was taught by Oistrach and won various competitions, including the Queen Elisabeth International Music Competition (1967) and the Tchaikovsky Competition (1970). Kremer is an extremely gifted violinist, one of the greatest of his generation. His repertoire covers both classical and contemporary music.

Kremlin, fortified portion of medieval Russian cities, originally a place of refuge to nearby inhabitants; especially, the Kremlin in Moscow, now the political and adminis-

trative center of the Russian Federation. The greater part of the Moscow Kremlin dates from the 15th and 16th centuries. Peter the Great transferred the capital to St. Petersburg (1712), but in 1918 the Russian regime returned the government to Moscow and the Kremlin. A leading tourist attraction, the Kremlin contains 3 cathedrals, a bell tower, and the throne and banqueting hall of the czars.
See also: Moscow.

Krill, small marine animal (genus *Euphausia*) resembling shrimp. There are over 90 species, ranging from 3/8 in (1 cm) to nearly 6 in (15 cm). Krill live in the open sea at depths of more than 6,600 ft (2,000 m). Most species have special organs (photophores) that make them visible in the dark. At night they swim in swarms of thousands to the surface to feed on microorganisms. Krill are an important food source for birds, seals, and whales, especially blue and finback whales. Rich in vitamin A, krill have been considered as a possible human food source.

Krishna (Kistna), river in southern India, 802 mi (1290 km) in length. Its source lies in the Western Ghats, Karnataka, and is a sacred place for Hindus. The river flows eastward and reaches the Bay of Bengal at False Divi Point, the northernmost point of the Coromandel coast. During the rain season it causes heavy flooding. The water contains a great deal of mud, and the delta is optimally suited for growing rice.

Krishna *See:* Vishnu; Bhagavad-Gita.

Krishnamurti, Jiddu (1895-1986), Indian philosopher. He was educated according to Western ideas in his youth, and was made head of the 'Order of the star in the East' by the British theosophist Annie Besant in 1912. Besant believed the young Hindu to be a new 'world teacher'. Krishnamurti traveled to Europe many times. In 1929 he disbanded the order. He founded schools of philosophy in the United States, Britain and India.

Kris Kringle *See:* Santa Claus.

Kristiansen, Ingrid (1956-), Norwegian athlete, successful on both medium and long distances. In 1984 she ran her first world record: the 5,000 meters in 14 minutes and 58.89 seconds. The following year she won the London marathon, recording the fastest time ever by a woman: 2 hours, 21 minutes and 6 seconds. She also became second in the 1985 world cross-country championship,

and in the same year set a world record for the 10,000 meters (30.59.42). In 1986 she recorded two more world records: 5,000 meters in 14.37.33, and 10,000 meters in 30.13.74. In 1987 she became world champion in the 15,000 meters, which she repeated the following year. In 1988 she also gained the world cross-country title.

Krivoj Rog *See:* Kryvyy Rih.

Kronstadt (pop. 40,000), city and fortress in Russia, on the island of Kotlin in the Gulf of Finland. It is a naval port where machines and ships are built. It was founded in 1703 by Peter the Great as Kronslot, in order to defend the approach to St. Petersburg. It is well-known for the mutinies which took place there, i.e. in 1825, 1905, 1906, 1917 and 1921. Early March 1921 was the beginning of the Kronshtadt rebellion, when the garrison was inspired by the Mensheviks to mutiny. Its objective was a 'third' revolution with freedom of speech was its goal. The Bolsheviks suppressed the mutiny, under the leadership of M.N. Tukhachevski (1893-1937). Lenin, who was alarmed by the dissension in the country, announced the New Economic Policy (NEP).

Kruger, Paulus (1825-1904), South African Boer leader. He opposed the annexation (1877) of the Transvaal by the British and the Boer rebellion of 1880. He was elected president of the new self-governing Transvaal Republic (1883). During the second Boer War (1899-1902) he went to Europe and sought vainly for support for the Boers.
See also: Boer War.

Krupa, Gene (1909-73), U.S. jazz musician, member of the Benny Goodman Orchestra (1935-38). The first famous drum soloist, Krupa was known for his frenzied performing style and exceptional drum technique. From 1938 to 1951 he played with his own successful band and continued to perform and tour with a quartet throughout the 1950s and 60s.

Krupp, family of German armaments makers. The firm was founded in Essen (1811) by **Friedrich Krupp** (1787-1826) with a small steel casting factory, and under his son, **Alfred Krupp** (1812-87), became the largest cast steel enterprise in the world, playing a key role in the Franco-Prussian War, World War I, and World War II. After World War II, **Alfred Krupp von Bohlen und Halbach** (1907-67), head of the firm from 1943, was imprisoned (1948-51) for war crimes. The company, now a public cor-

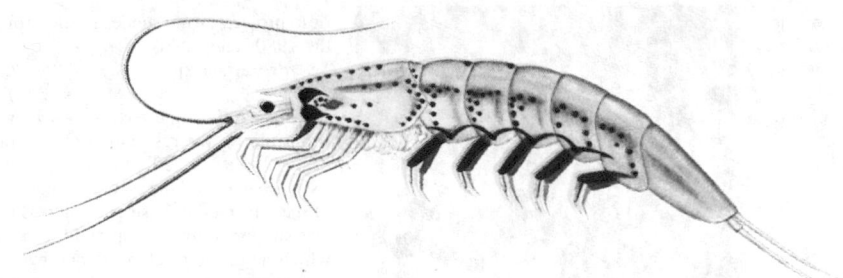

Krill, *Euphausia similis*, is mostly found in the subantarctic ocean, where it is food for whales. The largest recorded specimen is 1.3 in (33 mm) long.

K

Kublai Khan, founder of the Mongol dynasty in China, receives the Venetian travelers Nicoló, Marco, and Maffeo Polo at his court in Peking.

K

poration, concentrates on heavy industrial equipment. In 1992, Krupp merged with Hoesch and in 1997 with Thyssen.

Krupskaya, Nadezhda Konstantinovna (1869-1939), Russian revolutionary and educational theorist. She married Vladimir Ilyich Lenin (1898) while both were exiled in Siberia, thereafter sharing his life in Europe and after his return (1917) to Russia. An opponent of Stalin, she lost her considerable influence in the Communist party after Lenin's death.
See also: Russian Revolution; Lenin, V.I..

Krypton, gaseous element, symbol Kr; for physical constants see Periodic Table. Krypton was discovered by William Ramsay and M.W. Travers in 1898. It is a colorless, odorless, and chemically inert gas. Krypton is used in certain flash lamps for high-speed photography and some types of electric bulbs.

Kryvyy Rih (Krivoy Rog; pop. 715,000), city in Ukraine, lying on the Ingulets. It boasts blast furnaces, where a great deal of steel is produced, factories where mining installations are constructed, and a chemical industry. The surrounding area is rich in iron, which has been mined there since 1881.

Kuala Lumpur (pop. 1,200,000), capital and largest city of Malaysia. It lies at the confluence of the Ketang and Gombak rivers in Peninsular Malaysia, about 20 miles (30 km) from the Strait of Malacca. Kuala Lumpur is Malaysia's chief manufacturing, transportation, and financial center. The city is noted for its wide variety of buildings, which include Moorish-style mosques, British colonial structures, Buddhist pagodas, and modern office buildings. One of Kuala Lumpur's major landmarks is a Moorish-style clocktower. Another landmark is the Petrona Twin Towers building. At 1,483 feet (452 m), it is the tallest building in the world. Museums in the city include the National Art Gallery and the National Museum (history and archeology). The University of Malaya, the nation's largest university, is in the city. Kuala Lumpur was founded as a mining camp. The city owed much of its rapid growth to the local abundance of tin and rubber. In 1896 it became the capital of the Federated Malay States and in 1963, the capital of Malaysia. Large-scale construc-

tion projects were undertaken throughout the 1980s and 1990s.
See also: Malaysia.

Kuang-wu ti, Chinese emperor who was responsible for the restoration of the Han dynasty (206 B.C. - 220 A.D.), after popular uprisings had ended the 'socialist' interregnum of the reformer and usurper Wang Mang. He was supported by the imperial Liu family, to which he himself belonged, and by wealthy landowners. He spent the first ten years of his reign crushing rebellions, driving back the nomads in the north and achieving military expansion in the south; he also tried to establish a strong, centralized state. He did not fully succeed with the latter objective, as he remained dependent on the powerful families that had supported him. In 27 A.D. he transferred his capital from the war-torn Ch'ang-an to Lo-yang, further to the east, giving rise to the term 'eastern' Han dynasty (25-220 A.D.).

Kublai Khan (1216-94), Mongol emperor from 1259, founder of the Yüan dynasty of China and grandson of Genghis Khan. He defeated the Chinese Sung dynasty in 1279. Under his rule China flourished both economically and culturally; his new capital Cambuluc, described by Marco Polo, became the nucleus of modern Peking.
See also: Mongol Empire.

Kubrick, Stanley (1928-99), U.S. film director and writer noted for the strong social commentary of his work. His most famous films include the controversial *Dr. Strangelove* (1964), which treated the accidental triggering of nuclear war as a bitter joke; *2001: A Space Odyssey* (1968), his own story of humanity's distant past and future, which won an Academy Award for special effects; and *A Clockwork Orange* (1971), a terrifying look at criminal rehabilitation. *Paths of Glory* (1958) was Kubrick's first feature-length film, and *Lolita* (1962) his treatment of Vladimir Nabokov's novel of obsession. More recent movies include *The Shining* (1980) and *Full Metal Jacket* (1987). Kubrick died months before the premiere of his film *Eyes Wide Shut* (1999).

Kuching (pop. 148,000), capital of Sarawak, a Malaysian state on the island of Borneo. Archeologists confirm it to have been an ancient trading center. The modern city was founded by the British in 1841. Located on the Sarawak River 18 mi (29 km) inland from the South China Sea, it is a major livestock trading and fishing center. It exports rubber, pepper, and timber. Kuching is home to a modern airport and the Sarawak Museum, which is set in scenic gardens and exhibits collections representing the history and archeology of Borneo.
See also: Sarawak.

Kudo Tetsumi (1935-   ), Japanese visual artist who received his training at the Tokyo Fine Arts Academy (1954-58). In 1962 he started working in Paris. He is one of those artists whom Western society does not understand. He uses ghostly and cadaverous impressions to express himself as a prosecutor of the violence in modern-day civiliza-

tion. Kudo Tetsumi has made environments and organized happenings with the phallus as their central theme, followed by cocoons and snakeskins. He also make assemblages of caged objects, or objects set on couches (his *Your Portrait* series). He also makes use of electronic elements and all kinds of modern, alienating equipment. His *Monument of Metamorphosis* (1969) is gigantic, an immense relief carved into the rock face of Mount Nokogiri, overlooking the bay of Tokyo.

Kudu, large antelope (*Tragelaphus strepsiceros*) with long spiral horns. It feeds mainly on leaves. The coat is fawn or gray with white spots and stripes. The greater kudu lives in Africa, south of the Sahara, in scrub or dry bush country. The lesser kudu lives in the northeastern corner of Africa.

Kudzu, long semi-woody vine (*Pueraria thunbergiana*) belonging to the pea family. Kudzu is common to the southeastern United States, where it was introduced in the 1800s from Asia. It can grow to 60 ft (18 m) and has broad leaves. The pealike purple flowers have a yellow patch on the upper petal and smell like grapes. Kudzu has been used as a decorative porch vine, as food for livestock, and as ground cover to prevent soil erosion, but it grows so quickly out of control that it is most often treated as a weed. A fine white flour can be made from the peeled and washed roots.

Kuhn, Richard (1900-1967), Austrian chemist. He was awarded the 1938 Nobel Prize for chemistry, but the Nazi government prevented him from accepting the award until after World War II. Noted for his research into vitamins and carotenoids (yellow to red coloring found in plants and animals), he isolated vitamins B_2 (riboflavin) and B_6.
See also: Chemistry.

Kuibyshev *See:* Samara.

Kuiper, Gerard Peter (1905-1973), Dutch-born U.S. astronomer who discovered carbon dioxide in the atmosphere of Mars (1948) and satellites of Uranus and Neptune (1948-49). He directed the Ranger space program (early 1960s), which provided close-up photographs of the moon essential in the landing site selection for the moon landings (1969).
See also: Astronomy.

Kukenaan Falls *See:* Cuquenán Falls.

Ku Klux Klan, secret organization originally begun (1866) by ex-Confederates in the U.S. South to conduct a campaign of terror against newly enfranchised blacks. Its members disguised themselves in hoods and white sheets and used whippings and lynchings to terrorize their victims. Although the first Klan was officially disbanded in 1869, many members remained active throughout reconstruction and beyond. The second Klan, organized in 1915, extended its hostilities to Jews, Catholics, pacifists, and the foreign born. In the 1920s it had 5 million members and its political power extended to the North. Officially disbanded in 1944, the

K

Klan revived in response to civil rights activism of the 1960s and was involved in violent racial confrontations in the early 1980s. *See also:* Racism.

Kukrit Pramoj (1911-1995), Thai politician. Kukrit Pramoj came from an aristocratic family and studied political and economic science in Oxford. He held a seat in the Thai parliament between 1946 and 1950 and then founded a newspaper, Siam Rath, in which he criticized the military regimes sharply, making him a people's hero. The army relinquished its power after the popular uprising of 1973, and Kukrit founded the Social Action Party. He became Prime Minister of a coalition government after the 1975 elections. This government fell after a year, however, and six months later another military coup took place. Kukrit's unremitting criticism of the military authorities made him the conscience of Thailand.

Kukui (*Aleurites moluccana*), tree of the spurge family, Hawaii's state tree. Commonly found on mountain slopes, it has light green leaves and may grow as tall as 60 ft (18 m). Its branches spread out and grow long, making it a popular shade tree. The oil produced from these trees is used for fuel and in the manufacture of varnish.

Kumiss, koumis, kumys, or koumyss, alcoholic milk beverage of Asian origin. Primarily a product of the former USSR, it is traditionally made from mare's or camel's milk. This thick, sour, effervescent drink was at one time used for treating tuberculosis in sanitoriums.

Kumquat, dwarf evergreen (genus *Fortunella*) belonging to the ruè family, grown for its citrus fruits, which resemble small oranges. The kumquat tree measures from 10 to 15 ft (3 to 5 m); it is grown in China, Japan, and in warm regions of the United States such as Florida and California. The fruits are eaten whole or in preserves.

Kundera, Milan (1929-), a Czech author. Kundera typically focuses on his character's struggles to develop emotionally in a repressive society. His works are distinguished by eroticism, ironic humor, and philosophical asides. he gained international acclaim with the novel *The Unbearable Lightness of Being* (1984), in which two pairs of lovers attempt to find meaning (heaviness) in a world filled with meaninglessness (lightness). Kundera emigrated to France in 1975. Other novels include: *The Joke* (1967), *Life is Elsewhere* (1973), The Book of Laughter and Forgetting (1980), and *Immortality* (1990).

K'ung Hsiang-Hsi (Kong Xiangxi, a.k.a. H.H. K'ung; 1881-1967), Chinese businessman and banker who played an important role in Nationalist China, i.e. before 1949. After having studied economics in the United States he befriended Sun Yat-sen, the revolutionary leader, on his return to China. Sun Yat-sen, like himself, was married to one of the daughters of the Sung family. After Sun's death in 1925, he supported Chiang Kai-shek and even arranged the marriage of this ambitious young man with yet another of the Sung daughters. He held the office of Minister of Finance in the period 1933-44, and was responsible for revising the country's monetary system. He was president of the republic in 1938-39. His wealth, great business interests and his intimate connection with the Sungs and the Chiangs made him a controversial politician. He fled to the United States in 1948.

Kunming (K'un-ming; pop. 1,800,000), city in China, built at 6,200 ft (1,890 m) above sea level, on the northern shore of the Dianchi lake. Capital of the Yunnan province. It is a transport hub with iron and steel, machine, chemical, cement, textile and optical industries. The surrounding area yields iron, copper, lead, zinc and coal; it also has a hydroelectric power plant and facilities for processing agricultural products. In addition, it is a cultural and educational center with a university and a medical college. The city became Chinese during the 13th century, and has a monastery that dates back to that period. It was opened for foreign trade in 1908. Its name then was Yunnan; the city received its current name five years later. During WW II it was an important supply center, and acted as an airforce base for the Americans and as the headquarters of the Chinese army. Industrialization began in the 1940s, when chemical complexes and iron and steelworks were built.

Kuomintang *See:* Chiang Kai-shek.

Kupka, Frantisek (1871-1957), a Czech painter. He experimented with Fauvism and Cubism and was among the first artists to create totally abstract paintings. Such works as *Disks of Newton* and *Amorpha, Fugue in Two Colors* are marked by areas of contrasting colors that convey the illusion of movement. Kupka was born in Opocno, Bohemia. He studied art in Prague and Vienna and settled in Paris about 1895.

Kurchatovium *See:* Element 104.

Kurds, people of Kurdistan in western Asia. Traditionally nomadic, most Kurds today are settled farmers and are Muslims. Kurds have struggled vigorously against various rulers for an independent Kurdistan; in the 1970s Kurds fought Iraqi troops unsuccessfully for self-government. With the defeat of Iraq in the Persian Gulf War (1991), the Kurds once again took up arms against Iraqi authority. The Kurds, lacking adequate military equipment, were supressed, but then were subject to massacres staged by the Iraqi military. Fearing annihilation, the Kurds fled their homes for the borders of Turkey and Iran. This mass migration caused incredible suffering and thousands of deaths and forced the U.S. government to establish refugee camps in the north of Iraq. *See also:* PKK.

Kureishi, Hanif (1954-), British playwright and writer of movies and novels. Having a Pakistani father and an English mother, he is inspired by contemporary social problems such as racial and class prejudice and sexual freedom. His first works were performed in small theaters. In 1981 and in 1985 and 1986, he gained practical experience as the Writer-in-Residence of the Royal Court Theater, where *Borderline* was produced in 1981, a play about the conflicts within London's Asian community and about the question of whether one could 'Anglify' or not. He wrote two movie scripts: *My Beautiful Launderette* (1986) and *Sammy and Rosie Get Laid* (1987). In 1991 he made his debut as a movie director with *London Kills Me*, which he also produced in novel form. His first novel was the semi-autobiographical *The Buddha of Suburbia* (1990; winner of the Whitbread Prize). In 1995, *The Black Album* appeared, followed by *Love in a Blue Time* (1997), *Intimacy* (1998), *Midnight All Day* (short stories; 1999), and *Gabriel's Gift* (2002).

Kuril Islands, chain of 56 volcanic islands, stretching from the Kamchatka Peninsula of Siberia to Hokkaido Island, Japan. Sparsely inhabited, the islands are the subject of a territorial dispute, held by Russia since the Soviet occupation during World War II but claimed by Japan.

Kurosawa, Akira (1910-98), Japanese film director. Renowned for cinematography, his films include *Rashomon* (1950), *Seven Sumurai* (1954), and *Ran* (1985), an interpretation of *King Lear*. He often adapts foreign classics, blending Eastern and Western styles.

Frantisek Kupka produced in 1912 one of the earliest abstract paintings, *Fugue in Red and Blue* (National Gallery, Prague).

Kuroshio *See:* Japan Current.

Kursk (pop. 439,000), Russian city on the river Seym, capital of the region with the same name. Center of a rich agricultural area with various industries. The detection of geomagnetic disturbances in the area lead to the discovery of rich iron ore reserves (1920; Kursk magnetic disturbance). The Battle of Kursk (1943), the last great German panzer offensive on the Eastern front, ended with huge German losses.

Kurtág, György (1926-), Romanian-Hungarian composer and pianist, a Hungarian national since 1948. He studied at the Budapest Music Academy from 1946-55, where he was appointed teacher of piano and chamber music in 1967. His development as a composer was greatly influenced by his time spent studying in Paris in 1957-58, where he was taught by Messiaen and Milhaud. In 1959 Kurtág began composing

K

in his own style, which is as concise as it is dramatic. After his international breakthrough in the 1980s, he also began writing compositions for larger ensembles, rather than his normally just small settings. His works include *String Quartet* (Op. 1; 1959); *Hommage à András Mihály* (Op. 13; 1977-78); *Omaggio a Luigi Nono* (Op. 16; 1979); *Kafka-Fragmente für Sopran und Violine* (Op. 24; 1985-87); and *Stèle* (Op. 31 for orchestra; 1994).

Kush, ancient kingdom located along the Nile River in what is now Sudan. Lasting from about 2000 B.C. to A.D. 350, Kush was an important center of trade and learning. Exports included cattle and gold. It was also an important slave trading center. The people of Kush developed their own spoken language, writing system, architectural styles, and religion. Exact details of the kingdom's decline and end remain unknown.

Kushan Empire, dynasty of northern India, Afghanistan, and central Asia, from A.D. 50 to the 3rd century. Emperors of the dynasty opened important trades routes between China and India and between India and Rome. Along these trade routes both goods and ideas were exchanged. The dynasty's greatest ruler and an important proponent of Buddhism, its chief religion, was Kanishka, who lived in the 1st century A.D. During his reign Buddhism probably first reached China, and influential artistic concepts from Greece and Rome were incorporated into Indian religious art.
See also: Kanishka.

Kusunoki Masashige (1294-1336), Japanese war hero and strategist, whose loyalty to the emperor made him a legend in Japanese history. Emperor Go-Daigo lost much territory in his campaign against the Hodjo shogunate until Kusunoki achieved a

Modern architecture in Kuwait.

number of military successes and general Ashikaga Takauji defected to his side. The Hodjo shogunate fell when Kamakura was recaptured. Early in 1336 Kusunoki repelled an attack from Ashikaga Takauji, a powerful lord, who later returned with a strong army. Kusunoki recommended retreating, but the emperor commanded Kusunoki to take lead an attack. After a courageous but futile struggle, Kusunoki committed hara-kiri.

Kuvasz, breed of powerful, sturdily built dog. Bred in Hungary, it was popular in the Middle Ages as a guard dog of the nobility. Used now as a shepherd and guard dog, the typical kuvasz has a pure white, mostly short-haired coat, stands 26 in (66 cm), and weighs about 70 lbs (32 kg).

Kuwait

Capital:	Kuwait
Area:	6,880 sq mi (17,818 sq km)
Population:	2,112,000
Language:	Arabic
Government:	Monarchy (emirate)
Independent:	1961
Head of gov.:	Sjeikh
Per capita:	more than US$ 15,100
Monetary unit:	1 Kuwaiti dinar = 10 dirham = 1,000 fils

Kuwait, small independent Arab state on the northwest coast of the Persian Gulf, bordered by Iraq (northwest) and Saudi Arabia (south). Though mostly desert, it has been a major oil-producing country and possesses more than 10% of the world's estimated oil reserves. Its independence was jeopardized in Aug. 1990, when Iraq, on the pretext of settling a border dispute but also interested in obtaining control of Kuwaiti oil, invaded the country and announced its annexation. The ensuing Persian Gulf War (begun in Jan. 1991) pitted the United States and its allies, with the sanction of UN resolutions calling for the restoration of Kuwait's independent status, in a military action against Iraq to roll back the invasion.
Economy. Kuwait's traditional economy was based on the export of wool and hides and pearl fishing. With the discovery (1937) and exploitation (1946) of its huge oil reserves, the enormous wealth generated by the petroleum industry allowed the government to es-

tablish a widespread social welfare system that made Kuwait one of the world's wealthier nations on the basis of per capita income. In the 1960s the government also embarked on an ambitious modernization and diversification program. Until the Iraqi invasion, the capital, also called Kuwait, was a thoroughly modern city. The ruler, called *emir*, appointed the prime minister. More than half the population was madeup of non-Kuwaiti citizens, who held a majority of the jobs, as many native Kuwaitis lacked adequate education and training. The government had put special effort into training Kuwaitis to help them take more control of their economy.
History. In the early 18th century Arabs settled on the southern shore of Kuwait Bay and elected the head of the Al-Sabah family to be their ruler, establishing a dynasty unbroken to the present. Even as part of the Ottoman Empire, Kuwait retained its independent government under the Al-Sabahs. It was a British protectorate from 1899 until 1961, when it became independent. In 1967 Kuwait sided with Egypt in its war against Israel, as it did again in 1973. Also in that year, Kuwait, a member of the Organization of Petroleum Exporting Countries (OPEC), joined with other Arab oil-exporting countries in halting oil shipments to countries that supported Israel. In 1976 the emir dissolved the National Assembly. A new assembly was elected in 1981 but dissolved by the emir in 1986. During the Iran-Iraq War (1980-88) Iran began attacking Kuwaiti oil tankers because Kuwait had sided with Iraq and was aiding that country with financial and other support. In 1987 Kuwait requested help from the Soviet Union and the United States to protect its shipping. The Soviet Union leased some ships to Kuwait that carried the Soviet flag, which prevented Iran from attacking them. The U.S. Navy provided armed escorts for Kuwaiti-flagged ships in the Persian Gulf.
Soon after a cease-fire in 1988 ended Iran-Iraq hostilities, Iraq turned on its former ally and demanded settlement of a dispute involving an oil field along their mutual border and some small islands in the Persian Gulf. In Aug. 1990 Iraq sent troops into the lightly defended country and proclaimed it part of Iraq. Saudi Arabia and other Gulf states, fearful that a powerful Iraq might continue its agression against them, asked the United States and the United Nations to condemn the action and restore Kuwait to its independence. A large multinational force, overwhelmingly composed of the U.S. military, rushed to Saudi Arabia to protect it against aggression. In Jan. 1991 this force commenced hostilities against Iraq and its troops in Kuwait with the aim of restoring the pre-invasion status of Kuwait. However, as many Kuwaitis fled the country and as Kuwait itself suffered so much damage from the occupation and the allied efforts to dislodge it, expectations are that restoring Kuwait to its former condition will be a long process. After the attacks on September 11, 2001, Kuwait was the only Gulf State to promise full cooperation in the war against the al-Qaida-network. The Kuwaiti women's movement was defeated when the National Assembly rejected a decree giving women full political rights.

Kuwait (pop. 45,000), capital and the most important city in the country of Kuwait and founded in the 18th century by a tribal confederation of Arabic people. It is the chief economic center with an excellent harbor on the Persian Gulf. The port was established in the 18th century and was a shipbuilding center. The city is highly modernized because of the wealth generated by the petroleum industry which has developed since the end of World War II. In Aug. of 1990, the military forces of Iraq invaded the nation of Kuwait and occupied the city. This event precipitated the Persian Gulf War.
See also: Persian Gulf War.

Kuybyshev *See:* Samara.

Kwakiutl, Native American tribe of Wakashan linguistic stock, native to Vancouver Island and coastal British Columbia, Canada. Skilled in fishing and crafts, they had a strictly hierarchical society in which the potlatch ceremony played a significant part.

Kwangju (Gwangju; pop. 1.3 mln), city in the southwestern part of South Korea, capital of the South Cholla province. It has been a center for trade, transport and government since the first century A.D.; its industries include rice-hulling works, textile and automobile plants, and breweries. The most recent wave of industrialization came after the railroad to Seoul was made to pass through the city, in 1914. A university was built in 1946. The surrounding area boasts many historic buildings and ancient temples.

Kwashiorkor, severe condition of protein deficiency common in children of some areas of the Third World. It causes excess body fluid, distended abdomen, skin and hair changes, loss of appetite, apathy, diarrhea, liver disturbance, stunted growth, and sometimes, death. Its name derives from the Ghanaian for 'deposed one,' from its occurrence in children who are removed from breastfeeding too soon.

Kyanite, or cyanite, blue or white aluminum silicate mineral found in metamorphic rocks, occurring as long crystal blades. Because it is heat resistant, kyanite is used in spark plugs and as lining for ovens used in the manufacture of glass. Some kyanite is used for jewelry. It is found in the United States, India, Italy and the former USSR.

Kyd, Thomas (1558-94), English dramatist whose *The Spanish Tragedy* (c.1586) was a prototype of the Elizabethan and Jacobean revenge tragedy. The work is partly modeled on Seneca but is more lurid and more psychologically acute. Kyd may have written a version of the Hamlet story.

Kylián, Jiri (1947-), Czech dancer and choreographer. He became director of art of the Nederlands Dans Theater in The Hague in 1975. Under his leadership this group has grown into a world-class ballet. His productions include *Symphony in D* (1976, music by Haydn), which mocks classical dance, *Sinfonietta* (1978, music by Janacek), his master piece, *Stamping Ground* (1983, music by Carlos Cháves), *Silent Cries* (1986, music by Debussy), *l'Histoire du Soldat* (1986, music by Stravinsky), *Sweet Dreams* (1990, music by Anton Webern), *Arcimboldo* (1995), *One of a Kind* (1998), and *Claude Pascale* (2002).

Kyoto (pop. 1,700,000), capital of Kyoto prefecture, Honshu Island, Japan, about 25 mi (40 km) northeast of Osaka. The national capital from its foundation A.D. 794 until supplanted by Tokyo in 1868, Kyoto is rich in architectural relics and art treasures. Still a cultural and religious center, it also has leading educational establishments and large-scale mixed industry with manufactures that include electrical equipment, cameras, chemicals, silk, and porcelain.
See also: Japan.

Kyoto protocol, Name for the agreement on global warming, negotiated at the UN climate conference in Kyoto, Japan on December 11, 1997. The Kyoto conference followed a climate convention in Rio de Janeiro in 1992. During this conference, each party promised to commit itself to reducing the so-called greenhouse effect. These effects accelerate the gradual increase of the global temperature. In Kyoto, these promises were converted into measurable agreements. One of the agreements was that industrialized countries would reduce the production of pollutants by an average of 5.2% in 2012 compared to output in 1990. The EU promised an 8% reduction, the U.S. a 7% reduction and Japan 6%. The developing countries did not have to meet any obligations. At the UN climate conference in Bonn, Germany in July 2001, the details were set out in the Kyoto Protocol. Concessions had to be made to include as many countries as possible. There were no sanctions: for example, control on meeting the terms of the treaty remained unclear and countries were allowed to redeem their reduction with (cheaper) energy-saving projects elsewhere and the extension of forests. The U.S. refused to sign the protocol.
See also: Greenhouse effect; Environmental pollution.

Kyrgystan

Capital:	Bishkek
Area:	76,600 sq mi (198,500 sq km)
Population:	4,576,000
Language:	Russian, Kirghiz
Government:	Presidential republic
Independent:	1991
Head of gov.:	Prime minister
Per capita:	US$ 550
Monetary unit:	1 Som = 100 tyin

Kyrgystan, or Kirghyzstan, republic in central Asia, bordered by on the north by Kazakhstan, on the east by China, on the south by Tajikistan, and on the west by Uzbekistan. Its capital is Bishkek.
Land and climate. The country is almost entirely mountainous, it is part of the Tien Shan mountains (highest peak 24,406 feet/7440 m). The rivers are important for irrigation and for generating electricity. The climate varies from subtropical to alpine in the high mountains.
People. About 60% of the population are Kirgyz, a Muslim people speaking a Turkic language; other inhabitants include Russians and Uzbeks. Official languages are Kyrgyz and Russian. Besides Islam, one can find Christianity and Buddhism.
Economy. The wool from its sheep is an important product, and the region also has de-

K

An artist's impression of a Kwakiutl village scene. A hunting party visits an allied village in their painted and carved canoe. The Indian standing in the canoe, holds an offering of fish in one hand, and a harpoon in the other. On the shore, we can see two women wearing cedar bark-cloth: one weaving baskets, and the other collecting the shellfish abalone. Fish are dried in the open air. Decorations at the fronts of the wooden houses are totem poles.

K

posits of coal and natural gas. When after 1991 the economic ties with Russia disappeared, this had a disastrous effect on the Kyrgyz economy

History. Formerly one of the 15 constituent republics of the USSR (Soviet Union), the country became independent in 1991. After independence the political and economic policies of the government have been aimed at reforming the old communist structures. The country is a member of the Commonwealth of Independent States en made radical reforms during the last years. In 1994, Kyrgyzstan joined Uzbekistan's and Kazakhstan's free trade zone. In 1996, Kyrgyzstan, Russia, Kazakhstan, and Byelorussia signed an agreement concerning closer economic cooperation. The country made the airport available to the American air force. Kyrgystan has to import oil from neighboring countries but possesses enough drinkable water in return, which is needed by these countries.

Kyushu (pop. 15 million), southernmost of Japan's four great islands, with a surface area of 16,275 sq mi (42,137 sq km). Its capital city is Nagasaki. Its center is covered by volcanic mountain chains; agricultural area along the Chikugo and the coastal flatlands. Forestry, fishing and silk farming. The Fukuoka coal basin has mines that produce approximately half of the country's coal. The cities boast heavy and light industry. The island in connected with Honshu by the tunnel under the Kamon Strait; the Bungo Strait separates Kyushu from the island of Shikoku. The south coast is marked with deep and narrow inlets, the west coast by shallow and wide inlets. The largest city is Fukuoka, Nagasaki and Kagoshima are the island's principal cities. The first Western settlements date from the seventeenth century, and can be found on the west coast and on Deshima, where the Dutch had a trading post between 1641 and 1859.

Kyzyl Kum, or Kizil Kum, sandy desert of Central Asia, lying southeast of the Aral Sea and covering about 88,000 sq mi (228,000 sq km) of southern Kazakhstan and northern Uzbekistan between the Syr Darya and Amu Darya rivers. Some parts have been irrigated for crop growing (cotton, rice, and wheat), and the area has significant deposits of gold.

L, the 12th letter of the English alphabet. It is derived from the Semitic *lamedh* (perhaps itself based on an Egyptian hieroglyphic), representing an oxgoad, and from the Greek *lambda*. In Roman numerals, L is 50. The British symbol for the pound sterling (£) is another form of the letter, derived from the Latin *libra*, originally a pound in weight.

Laban, Rudolf von (born Rudolf Laban de Varaljas; 1879-1958), Hungarian dancer, choreographer and dance pedagogue, founder of the 'free' or 'modern' style of dancing. He ended his dancing career in 1907 and founded a dancing school in Munich and an institute for choreography in Würzburg in 1911. He was ballet master at the Berlin State Opera between 1930 and 1934. In 1936 he choreographed the great stadium show at the Berlin Summer Olympics. He moved to Great Britain in 1938 and began teaching at the Art of Movement Centre in Weybridge. He developed a style of dancing based on stimulating expressiveness and inventiveness, including a manner of writing for that system-the 'labanotation'. Von Laban made a great contribution to expressionist dance.

Labor *See:* Birth.

Labor *See:* Labor movement.

Labor Day, official holiday in the United States and Canada since 1894, held on the first Monday in Sept. to honor the workers. In socialist countries, labor is honored on May Day (May 1).

Labor force, that part of the population above a certain age, that is involved in the labor process, including the labor reserves, i.e. unemployed persons, persons seeking employment and persons temporarily excluded from the labor process. Labor force and labor reserve are commonly expressed as a percentage of the total population, broken down to age groups and gender.

Labor movement, laborers' organization which came into being around the end of the eighteenth century. Western Europe, in particular Great Britain, is the birthplace of the labor movement, as it was there that the Industrial Revolution first took place in the eighteenth and nineteenth centuries. The labor movement was originally suppressed, and laborers expressed their dissatisfaction spontaneously by rioting and destroying factory machines. The abolishment of the Combination Acts in England in 1824 gave rise to the trade union movement. The second half of the nineteenth century, with the industrialization now spread to mainland Europe, saw the labor movement-ideologically supported by the Marxist movement-become more internationally focused. After the First Communist International failed in 1876, the labor movement developed mainly on a national basis, collaborating with socialist parties. The national parties gave rise to a new international collaboration of workers in 1889, the Second Communist International. This too failed, when the various socialist parties remained loyal to their countries and governments during the First World War. International and revolutionary aspirations were kept alive by the Komintern, or Third Communist International, which was founded in the Soviet Union, and the various organizations which derived from it. Elsewhere, the labor movement integrated with social democracy.

Labor union *See:* Unions, labor.

Labour Party, English political party founded in 1900 by trade unions and socialist groups-the Independent Labour Party (1893) and the Fabian Society-with James Keir Hardie as its first leader. It gained nationwide support after World War I, first coming to power under Ramsay MacDonald in 1924. His second administration (1929-1931) ended in coalition with the Conservatives, division within the party, and electoral defeat. The first effective socialist program was implemented by the Labour government of Clement Attlee (1945-1951), instituting the National Health Service and nationalizing the Bank of England and major industries. Attlee was followed as leader by Hugh Gaitskell, who was succeeded at his death (1963) by Harold Wilson. Prime minister in 4 Labour governments (1964-1970, 1974-1976), he was succeeded by James Callaghan. Callaghan yielded leadership in 1979 to Michael Foot, a member of the party's left wing. As Labour became deeply embroiled in factionalism, several leaders resigned to form the new Social Democratic Party in 1981. After the party's decisive loss in the June 1983 general election, Neil Kinnock replaced Foot as leader. At the 1997 general elections, Labour achieved the highest gain in seats ever. Tony Blair became the new prime minister.

Labrador, large peninsula in northeast Canada. It is a land of long, severe winters with temperatures falling to -40°F (-40°C), and short, hot summers, during which temperatures rise to 80°F (27°C). Its population is about 97% white and 3% Inuit (Eskimos), Naskapi, and Montagnais. Labrador is rich in iron ore, timber, and cod fish. Its hydroelectric plant, which began operation in 1971 on the Churchill River at Churchill Falls, is one of the largest in the Western Hemisphere, with a capacity of $5^1/_4$ million kilowatts of electricity.
See also: Canada.

Labrador retriever, breed of sporting dog originating in Newfoundland, Canada and further developed in England. A strongly built dog standing 21-24 in (93-100 cm) and weighing 60-75 lb (27-34 km), the Labrador has a stable temperament, a keen sense of smell, and an innate love of water. Distinctive features are its short, thick, water-resistant coat (usually black, but sometimes yellow or dark red-brown) and its thick-based 'otter tail.' The Labrador is used in hunting to retrieve waterfowl and other small game.

The Labrador retriever is an accomplished swimmer, used to retrieve and to flush out game birds.

Labrador tea, 6 species of small evergreen shrubs (genus *Ledum*; especially, *L. groenlandicium*) containing in their aromatic leaves tannin and a mild narcotic that is the active ingredient in the tea and beer brewed from the leaves. These plants are found in swampy areas of subarctic North America, Greenland, and northern Europe.

Laburnum, genus of small trees belonging to the pea family (Fabaceae or Leguminosae), characterized by glossy green leaves, yellow blossoms, and fine-grained, hard wood. A poison called cytisine is present in their roots, seeds, and other parts. The common laburnum (*L. anagyroides*) is native to Asia and is also called golden chain, bean tree, and bean trefoil.

Labyrinth, complex of buildings or hedges with many passages and dead ends, designed to baffle strangers trying to find the way in or out; a maze. The most famous labyrinth of antiquity, according to Greek legend, was built in Crete by Daedalus to house the Minotaur. Other famous labyrinths were in Lemnia and in Italy. The maze at Hampton Court Palace, England, is an example of a garden labyrinth.

Lac, sticky residue secreted by a species of scale insect (*Laccifer lacca*) and used to produce shellac and lac dye. The secretion, called stick lac in its natural state, is harvested by gathering the twigs in which the insect resides.

Laccadive Islands (or Cannanore Islands; population 52,000), a group of small coral islands and many reefs in the Arabian Sea, some 150 to 250 miles (240 to 400 km) west of the southwestern coast of India. Together with Minicoy Island, to the south, and the Amindivi Islands, to the north, they make up a union territory of India named Lakshadweep. Most of the islanders are Muslims and live by fishing and coconut farming.
The Portuguese explorer Vasco da Gama discovered the Laccadives in 1498. They were under British rule from 1792 to 1947.

Lace, fine openwork decorative fabric made by braiding, looping, knotting, or twisting thread, usually linen or cotton, sometimes silver and gold. Before 19th-century mechanization, it was handmade by needlepoint or with bobbins. Lace was developed in 16th-century Italy and Flanders.

Lacewing, insect of the order Neuroptera, named for its double pair of delicate, lacy wings. The two most common families are the green or golden-eyed lacewings (Hemerobiidae) and the smaller brown lacewings (Chrysopidae). These insects are also called stinkflies because of the strong odor they emit to repel predators. Larvae, often called aphid lions, use their large jaws to suck fluids from aphids and other insects.

The giant lacewings, such as *Osmylus fulvicephalus*, are the largest types of lacewing, with wingspans up to 75 mm (nearly 3 in).

Laclos, Pierre Ambroise François Choderlos de (1741-1803), French novelist. He chose a military career, but the monotonous garrison duty led him to begin writing in his free time. This resulted in *Les liaisons dangereuses* (Dangerous Liaisons; 1782), his world-famous epistolary novel, which tells the moralizing tale of a count with the character of a Don Juan who is ruined, and with him three women, by his desire for conquests. The novel's success displeased army officials, after which Laclos published no more writings. He rose to the rank of brigadier (1800) and fell during Napoleon's Italian campaign.

Lacoste, René (1904-1996), French tennis player. With Jean Borotra, Jacques Brugnon and Henri Cochet he won the Davis Cup for France in 1927 and 1928. Lacoste also won the French Open championships in 1925, 1927 and 1929, the US Open in 1926 and 1927, and Wimbledon in 1925 and 1928. After having left competitive tennis, he successfully produced and sold sports goods. The Lacoste brand name, with the green crocodile logo, has become famous over the whole world.

Lacquer, solution used as a coating for wood, metal, paper, clothing, or porcelain to provide a lustrous, protective finish. Lacquers can be made from either natural (tree sap, resins, lac, cellulose) or synthetic compounds.

Lacrimal gland *See:* Tears.

Lacroix, Christian (1950-), French designer of *haute-couture* fashion. In 1987 the Council of Fashion Designers of America voted him best foreign designer. He is best known for his 'bubble' dress.

Lacrosse, team game derived by French settlers from the Native American game of baggataway, now the national game of Canada. It is played with a stick called a crosse having a net at one end. The crosse is used to catch, throw, and carry a hard rubber ball, with the aim of sending it into the opposing goal. In men's lacrosse, played in Canada, the United States, and the United Kingdom, each team has 10 members. Women's lacrosse is usually played with 12 to a side.

Lactic acid ($C_3H_6O_3$), organic acid that is the end product of the metabolism of sugar, the formation of which causes milk to sour. Lactic acid is produced in muscles after their cells have broken down glycogen for energy; it is this accumulation of lactic acid that causes muscle fatigue. Blood levels of lactic acid are also elevated in persons with lactic acidosis, diabetes, anemia, leukemia, and other abnormal conditions.
See also: Scheele, Carl Wilhelm.

Laden, Osama bin *See:* Osama bin Laden.

Ladybug, lady beetle, or ladybird, small, almost round beetle of the family Coccinellidae. Ladybugs are named for their association with the Virgin Mary. Their shiny wing-cases are brightly colored (red, yellow, or black) and usually have patterns of spots (black with a red or yellow case, or

red or yellow with a black case). They hibernate in groups under bark or in caves and rock crevices. They emerge in the spring to lay their eggs, and both adults and larvae feed on aphids and scale insects, thus playing an important role in controlling these insect pests. A few species eat plants, and the Mexican bean beetle is a pest of beans, alfalfa, clover, and other crops.

Lady's-slipper, moccasin flower, or squirrel's shoes, any of various species of the orchid family that bear a single flower on each stem. The lower petal is shaped like a slipper, and the sepals look like a bow securing it. Lady's-slippers are found in damp woodlands and bogs in North America, Europe, and Asia. They are fertilized by queen bumblebees, which are heavy enough to force their way in through a slit in the 'slipper.'

Lady's-thumb *See:* Smartweed.

Laënnec, René Théophile Hyacinthe (1781-1826), French surgeon, physician, and inventor of the stethoscope. Laënnec specialized in heart and lung pathology and is considered the founder of chest medicine. He described his research in *A Treatise on Mediate Auscultation* (1819).
See also: Stethoscope.

La Fayette, Marie Madeleine Pioche de la Vergne (1634-1693), French writer. She is especially noted for *The Princess of Clèves* (1678), whose sensitivity and psychological realism make it the first great French novel. She also wrote *The Princess of Montponsier* (1622) and *Zayde* (1670).

Lafayette, Marquis de (1757-1834), French soldier and statesman who fought in the American Revolution and worked for French-American alliance. He came to America in 1777, joined George Washington's staff as major general, and fought in the campaigns of 1777-1778 and at Yorktown (1781). On a visit to France (1779) he persuaded Louis XVI to send troops and a fleet to aid the colonists. In the French Revolution he supported the bourgeoisie, helped set up the National Assembly, drafted the Declaration of the Rights of Man, and commanded the National Guard, but he fell from power after ordering his troops (July 1791) to fire on the populace. In 1824 he revisited the United States, hailed as a hero. He was a leader of the July Revolution (1830) in France.
See also: French Revolution; Revolutionary War in America.

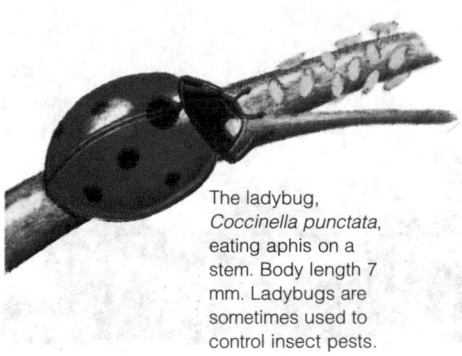

The ladybug, *Coccinella punctata*, eating aphis on a stem. Body length 7 mm. Ladybugs are sometimes used to control insect pests.

L

One of La Fontaine's most well-known fables is about a fox, who cunningly tricks a raven out of a choice piece of cheese. The theme is used here, very appropriately, on a cheese wrapper.

L

La Fontaine, Jean de (1621-1695), French writer. He is remembered especially for his *Fables* (1668-1694), moral tales drawn from Aesop and Asian sources that he used to comment satirically on contemporary society, and for his humorous, bawdy *Tales and Novels in Verse* (1664-1666).
See also: Canada.

Lagerkvist, Pär Fabian (1891-1974), Swedish poet, novelist, and dramatist, winner of the 1951 Nobel Prize for literature. He was much disturbed by World War I and later also protested against fascism. His works, which include the novels *The Hangman* (1933) and *Barabbas* (1950), and the play *Man Without a Soul* (1936), explore the problem of good and evil in humanity.

Lagerlöf, Selma (1858-1940), Swedish novelist, the first woman to win a Nobel Prize for literature (1909). Her works, rooted in legend and the folklore of her native Värmland, include *The Story of Gösta Berling, The Wonderful Adventure of Nils* (1906, a children's classic), and a trilogy, *The Ring of the Lowenskolds* (1931).

Lagos (pop. 1,400,000), former capital and chief port of Nigeria, on the Gulf of Guinea (West Africa). The city occupies Lagos, Victoria, and Iddo islands, between the Bight of Benin and Lagos Lagoon, and also part of the mainland, where its main deepwater harbor and the terminal of the Lagos-Kano-Nguru railroad are located at Apapa. Lagos has been a trade center since the 15th century. It now handles most of Nigeria's seaborne exports, mainly palm products, peanuts, cocoa, tin, hides, and skins. Manufactures include textiles, furniture, and metal products. Its university (1962) specializes in law, medicine, and business administration.
See also: Nigeria.

Lagrange, Joseph Louis (1736-1813), French mathematician and astronomer who made important contributions to calculus and differential equations and was influential in adopting the decimal system in metrics. He worked also on celestial mechanics, in particular explaining the moon's libration (swinging movement). His most important work is the *Mécanique analytique*.
See also: Number theory.

La Guardia, Fiorello Henry (1882-1947), U.S. statesman and mayor of New York City. As a Republican member of Congress (1917-1919, 1923-1933) he supported liberalizing and prolabor measures, including the Norris-La Guardia Act forbidding the use of injunctions in labor disputes. As mayor (1933-1945) he instituted major reforms in New York and fought corruption.

Lahore (pop. 5,200,000), city in eastern Pakistan, capital of the province of Punjab, lying on the Ravi River. Lahore is Pakistan's second largest city and is a center for education, steel production, film-making, and textile manufacturing. The city served as a capital for the Mogul and Sikh empires before being taken over by the British in 1849.
See also: Pakistan.

Laissez faire (French, 'leave alone'), doctrine that opposes state intervention in economic affairs. First enunciated by the French physiocrats in the 18th century as a reaction against mercantilism, the idea was taken up by Scottish economist Adam Smith and became a cornerstone of classical economics.
See also: Smith, Adam.

Lake Agassiz, ancient North American lake that covered much of what is now the Canadian province of Manitoba and parts of other provinces and the United States. It was formed by melting glaciers during the last ice age. Lake Agassiz was the largest of the glacial lakes, reaching its maximum size (approximately 135,000 sq mi/350,000 sq km) between 7900 and 7500 B.C. The continued runoff from the glaciers caused the lake to drain into the Hudson Bay, except for the deeper areas that became smaller lakes such as Manitoba, Winnipeg, and Winnipegosis.

Lake Albano, crater lake inside an extinct volcano in west-central Italy, southeast of Rome in the Albani hills. Lake Albano served as a vacation spot for ancient Romans and is still a site for resorts, including Castel Gandolfo, the papal summer residence.

Lake Albert, or Lake Mobutu Sese Sekolake, lake in east central Africa between Zaire and Uganda, linked to Lake Edward to the south by the Semliki River. It was named (1864) for England's Prince Albert, husband of Queen Victoria. The lake is approximately 100 mi (160 km) in length and 20 mi (32 km) in width, covering about 2,059 sq mi (5,333 sq km). It is a water source for the Nile River.

Lake Baikal, world's deepest lake (maximum depth 5,315 ft/1,620 m), located in southeastern Siberia, USSR. It is about 395 mi (636 km) long and 49 mi (79 km) wide, covering an area of about 12,200 sq mi (31,500 sq km). It contains about 20% of the world's unfrozen fresh water (more than any other lake).

Lake Chad, largest lake in west central Africa, fourth largest on the African continent. Lake Chad lies within the boundaries of 4 African nations: Chad (containing the major portion of the lake), Cameroon, Nigeria, and Niger. Its shallow basin, approximately 22 ft (7 m) at the deepest, allows easy overflow into surrounding areas. The size of the lake fluctuates depending on the season, the volume of water received from inflowing rivers, and the rate of evaporation.

Lake Champlain, long, narrow lake forming much of the border between New York State and Vermont, with its northern tip extending into the Canadian province of Quebec. Named after the first European to see it, French explorer Samuel de Champlain, it is 107 mi (172 km) long, 1-14 mi (1.6-22 km) wide, and up to 400 ft (122 m) deep. Lake Champlain was the site of many naval battles during the Revolutionary War and the War of 1812.

Lake Como (Italian: *Lago di Como*), lake in the northern Italian province of Lombardy, at the foot of the Alps, 25 miles (40 km) north of Milan. Lake Como is a popular tourist attraction, famed for the beauty of its setting and the elegant villas lining its shores.

Lake District, scenic region in northwestern England, about 30 mi (50 km) wide. It contains the highest mountain in England (Scafell Pike, 3,210 ft/978 m) and 15 lakes, including Windermere, Ullswater, and Derwentwater. William Wordsworth, Samuel Coleridge, and Robert Southey are among the writers and artists who lived here in the early 19th century.

Lake dwelling, shelter built on stilts or piles in the waters of a lake. Stone Age and Bronze Age lake dwellings can be found in parts of Europe, and in some parts of the world they are still built. Crannogs, strongholds built on artificial islands, were built in Ireland, Scotland, and England from the Late Stone Age until the Middle Ages.

Lake Edward, lake in the Rift valley of East Africa, on the border between Uganda and Zaire. Explorer Henry M. Stanley named it in 1889 for Albert Edward, Prince of Wales (later King Edward VII). Lake Edward, approximately 40 mi (64 km) long, 32 mi (51 km) wide, and 830 sq mi (2,150 sq km) in area, is a water source for the Nile. The Semliki River connects it to Lake Albert to the north.

Loweswater, one of the smaller lakes in the Lake District.

L

Lake Erie, one of the 5 Great Lakes, fourth on the border between the United States and Canada. Lake Erie is 240 mi (386 km) long, 38-57 mi (61-92 km) wide, and has an area of about 10,000 sq mi (26,000 sq km). It is the southernmost of the Great Lakes and is a link in the St. Lawrence Seaway.
See also: Great Lakes.

Lake Garda, largest lake in Italy, about 143 sq mi (370 sq km). Its southern end is about 65 mi (105 km) east of Milan. Its scenery has made it a popular resort area.

Lake Geneva, crescent-shaped lake, one of Europe's largest, between southwestern Switzerland and France. With an area of about 224 sq mi (581 sq km), Lake Geneva is known for the clear, blue water of its western end and its lakeshore resorts.

Lake Huron, one of the 5 Great Lakes, 206 mi (332 km) long and 183 mi (295 km) wide, with an area of about 23,000 sq mi (60,000 sq km). Lake Huron is bordered by the Canadian province of Ontario on the north, east, and southeast, and by Michigan on the west and southwest. It is part of the St. Lawrence Seaway and is heavily used by maritime commercial traffic.
See also: Great Lakes.

Lake Ilmen (Ozero Il'men), lake in Russia, 99 mi (160 km) south of St. Petersburg. The surface area of the lake varies with the seasons (up to 386 sq mi; 1000 sq km). It is fed by the Pola, the Msta, the Lovat and others. The water flows out through the Wolchow into Lake Ladoga. Fishing is the main economic activity. Excavations on the shores have unearthed prehistoric settlements.

Lake Ladoga, lake in northwest Russia, about 40 mi (64 km) northeast of Leningrad. At 6,835 sq mi (17,703 sq km), Lake Ladoga is the largest in Europe. It forms part of a canal system connecting the Baltic and White Seas.

Lakeland terrier, dog originally bred in northern England's Lake District to hunt foxes and protect sheep. The average lakeland has a narrow body, stands 14.5 in (37 cm) at the shoulder and weighs 17 lbs (7.7 kg). It has a wiry coat, a bearded chin, and an upright, docked tail.

Lake Lugano, lake on the border between Switzerland and Italy. It is located east of Lake Maggiore at the southern foot of the Alps. It is connected to Lake Maggiore by the Tresa River. It is 20 m (32km) in length and 2 m (3 km) wide.

Lake Maggiore, lake lying mostly in Italy, but extending into the Swiss Alps. Its area is 82 sq mi (212 sq km), making it Italy's largest lake. The western and eastern shores are home to lakeside resorts and small villages.

Lake Maracaibo, lake in northwestern Venezuela, in the oil-producing region. Connected to the Carribean Sea by a dredged channel, Lake Maracaibo has an area of 5,217 sq mi (13,512 sq km), making

it South America's largest lake. The southern shore produces agricultural products, notably sugarcane, coconuts, cacao, and coffee.

Lake Michigan, largest freshwater lake lying entirely within the United States, and the third largest of the 5 Great Lakes. It is 307 mi (494 km) long, 118 mi (190 km) at its widest point, and up to 923 ft (281 m) deep. Its borders are Wisconsin and Illinois on the west, Michigan on the east and north, and Indiana on the southeast. It is connected to the Great Lakes St. Lawrence Seaway that goes east to the Atlantic Ocean and south to the Gulf of Mexico via the Mississippi River, serving international commerce.
See also: Great Lakes.

Lake Neagh *See:* Lough Neagh.

Lake of Lucerne (German: *Vierwaldstätter See*), major lake in Switzerland, between the Rigi and Pilatus mountains. It is around 24 mi (39 km) long and up to 2 mi (3 km) wide and has the appearance of an imperfect cross. Adventures of the legendary William Tell took place along Lake Uri's shores.
See also: Tell, William.

Lake Okeechobee (Seminole, 'big water'), largest freshwater lake in the southern part of the United States, located in central Florida just north of the Everglades. The lake is 35 mi (56 km) long, about 680 sq mi (1,760 sq km) in area, and up to 15 ft (4.6 m) deep. In 1937 a 155-mi (249-km) cross-state waterway was completed to control seasonal flooding. Canals were constructed as outlets to the Atlantic Ocean and Gulf of Mexico, and to supply needed water to communities along Florida's eastern coastline.

Lake Onega, second largest lake in Europe (3,753 sq mi/9,720 sq km), located in the northwestern part of the former USSR. It is an important transportation connection between the Baltic and White seas. The lake has productive fisheries along its coast.

Lake Ontario, one of the 5 Great Lakes, located in New York State and Ontario, Canada. It is fed mainly by the Niagara River, and flows into the Atlantic Ocean through the St. Lawrence River, making it an important part in transportation of goods through the St. Lawrence Seaway system. It is about 193 mi (311 km) long and 53 mi (85 km) wide, with depths ranging from 500 to 802 ft (152 to 244 m). Its low elevation above sea level (245 ft/75 m) and great offshore depths keep it from freezing during the winter. It tempers the surrounding climate, producing cool summer days along the eastern shore and allowing fruit crops to produce successfully on the southern shore.
See also: Great Lakes.

Lake Peipus, or Chudskoe, lake in the former USSR between Estonia and Russia. It has depths up to 50 ft (15 m) and an area of 1,400 sq mi (3,626 sq km), and is frozen about 6 months out of the year. During World War II, when the Germans surrounded Leningrad and cut off all supply routes, Russian volunteers used small trucks to

transport food across the thick ice to feed more than 3 million starving people.

Lake Placid, small lake in the northeastern Adirondack Mountains, New York, about 3 mi (5.6 km) long and 1 mi (2.4 km) wide. Its beauty attracts visitors for boating, swimming, hiking, ice skating, and skiing. It was the site of the 1980 Winter Olympics. Just south of Lake Placid lies the grave of abolitionist John Brown.

Lake Poets, name given to the English poets William Wordsworth, Samuel Taylor Coleridge, and Robert Southey, who lived in the Lake District for a time. The critic Francis Lord Jeffrey was first to characterize them as constituting the 'Lake school of poetry,' although the 3 friends do not form a group stylistically.
See also: Coleridge, Samuel Taylor; Wordsworth, William.

Lake Pontchartrain, lagoon-like lake in southern Louisiana, connected to the Mississippi River through the Inner Harbor Navigation Canal. Its briny water provides abundant game fish for the numerous small resorts along its shores. It is 40 mi (64 km) long and 25 mi (40 km) wide. It is crossed by the Lake Pontchartrain Causeway, the world's longest bridge (29.2 mi/47 km).

Lakes of Killarney, 3 scenic lakes lying southwest of the town of Killarney in County Kerry, Ireland. The lakes-Lough Leane ('Lower Lake'), Muckross Lake, and Middle Lake-have a combined area of nearly 10 sq mi (17 km). They form part of Killarney National Park, a popular tourist attraction.

Lake Superior, largest freshwater lake in the world, largest of the 5 Great Lakes, located along the United States-Canadian border, with Michigan and Wisconsin on the south, Minnesota on the west, and Ontario on the north. It is 350 mi (563 km) long, 160 mi (257 km) wide, and up to 1,333 ft (406 m) deep. An important waterway for shipping, it connects to the Atlantic Ocean through the St. Lawrence Seaway, and to the Gulf of Mexico through the Great Lakes and the Mississippi River.
See also: Great Lakes.

Lake Tahoe, deep glacial lake on the California-Nevada border. It is 22 mi (35 km) long, 12 mi (19 km) wide, and up to 1,640 ft (500 m) deep. Its waters flow into the Truckee River and on to Pyramid Lake. It is a popular tourist resort offering fishing, boating, waterskiing, and hunting.

Lake Tana, major water source for the Blue Nile River, located in northwestern Ethiopia. Its blue color comes from the lake's silt-free water. It is 47 mi (76 km) long and 44 mi (71 km) wide, and lies 6,000 ft (1,800 m) above sea level.

Lake Tanganyika, longest freshwater lake in the world (420 mi/680 km), located in the Great Rift valley between Tanzania and Zaire in east central Africa. The lake has depths to 4,708 ft (1,435 m).

L

Lake Titicaca, on the border of Bolivia and Peru, covers an area of 3,221 sq mi (8,340 sq km) and is the highest navigable lake in the world. The surface is over 12,500 ft (3,800 m) above sea level, and in some places, the lake is 919 ft (280 m) deep.

Charles Lamb (1775-1834) painted by his fellow essayist William Hazlitt (1778-1830).

Lake Tiberias *See:* Galilee, Sea of.

Lake Titicaca, highest lake in South America, located in the Andes Mountains between Peru and Bolivia. Its altitude of 12,507 ft (3,812 m) makes it the highest lake in the world to provide large boat transportation. It is 110 mi (180 km) long and 45 mi (72 km) wide, with depths up to 919 ft (280 m). There are 41 islands of varying size throughout the lake. Over 25 rivers empty into the lake, but only the Desaguadero River acts as drainage. The shores have been home to Native American settlements for centuries.

Lake trout *See:* Trout.

Lake Victoria, largest freshwater lake in Africa, located in Tanzania, Uganda, and Kenya; major water source for the Nile River. The lake is 210 mi (337 km) long and 150 mi (241 km) at its widest point. The Owen Falls Dam, constructed on the Nile River to generate hydroelectric power (1954), raised the level of the lake about 3 ft (1 m) to a depth of 270 ft (82 m). Numerous islands rise from the lake, Ukerewe being the largest and most populated. There are several million people living within a 50-mi (80-km) radius of Lake Victoria, making it the most heavily populated area in Africa.

Lake Volta, one of the largest human-made reservoirs in the world, in Ghana, West Africa. Created by the construction of the Akosombo Dam across the Volta River (1965), it is 250 mi (400 km) long and covers 3,275 sq mi (8,482 sq km). Water from the lake is used to produce electric power.

Lake Winnipeg, located in Manitoba, Canada, it is one of the largest lakes in Canada. The lake is 258 mi (416 km) long and ranges from 20 to 60 miles (32 to 97 km) in width. The fisheries on the lake are the most important in Manitoba.

Lake Xochimilco, 5 shallow 'floating garden' lakes in Mexico City, Mexico, made by building mud dikes in the original lake and seeding them with flowers and vegetables. The gardens thus created are a tourist attraction.

Lalo, Édouard (1823-1892), French composer. Many of his works were influenced by Spanish music, including *Symphonie Espagnole* (1875) for violin and orchestra, first performed by Spanish virtuoso violinist Pablo Sarasate. Other famous works are the ballet *Namouna* (1882) and the opera *Le Roi d'Ys* (1888).

Lamaism, popular term for Tibetan Mahayana Buddhism, which evolved from Indian Buddhism starting in the 7th century A.D. This religion combined intellectual discipline with the ritual of tantric yoga and shamanism. The spiritual and political head of the hierarchy of monks or *lamas* is the Dalai Lama (Tibetan, 'oceanic teacher'). He is chosen as a young boy and considered to be the reincarnation of previous lamas and of Avalokitesvara, a *bodhisattva* (spiritually enlightened being who remains on earth to help others achieve enlightenment). The intensely religious society remained unchanged until the Communist Chinese invasion of Tibet (1959), which forced the Dalai Lama into exile.
See also: Buddhism.

Lamarck, Jean Baptiste de Monet, chevalier de (1744-1829), French biologist whose pioneering work in taxonomy (especially that of the invertebrates) led him to formulate an early theory of evolution. Where Darwin was to propose natural selection as a mechanism for evolutionary change, Lamarck theorized that organisms could develop new organs in response to their need for them and that these acquired characteristics could be inherited. His theory is known as Lamarckism.
See also: Biology; Evolution.

Lamartine, Alphonse Marie Louis de (1790-1869), French poet and politician, briefly head of government after the 1848 revolution. His collection *Poetic Meditations* (1820) was a landmark of French Romantic literature and contains the famous poem 'The Lake'; lyric evocations of love and nature are underlaid by gentle melancholy and religious feeling. *Harmonies* (1830) and *Jocelyn* (1836) were other poetic works.

Lamb, Charles (1775-1834), English essayist and critic who often wrote under the name 'Elia.' With his sister Mary Ann Lamb he wrote *Tales from Shakespeare* (1807) for children. His *Essays of Elia* (1823, 1833) contain insightful and humorous personal comments on many subjects. He helped revive interest in Elizabethan drama with *Specimens of English Dramatic Poets* (1808).

Lambaréné (pop. 24,000), town in Gabon on the Ogooué River where in 1913 Albert Schweitzer founded a hospital for people suffering from tropical diseases.

Lamb's-quarters, pigweed, or goosefoot (*Chenopodium album*), annual herbaceous plant related to spinach, sugar beets, and chard. The plants, native to Europe, Asia, and North America, grow from 1 to 10 ft (30 cm to 3 m) and have diamond-shaped leaves and groups of small greenish flowers.

Lamentations, book of the Old Testament, traditionally ascribed to the prophet Jeremiah, though this is disputed by modern scholars. It consists of a series of 5 poems (the first 4 are acrostics) lamenting the fall of Jerusalem at the hands of the Babylonians (586 B.C.).
See also: Bible.

Lammergeier, bird belonging to the Old World vulture family and native to the mountain regions of Europe, Asia, and Africa. One of the largest of the vultures, it has a wingspread of 9 to 10 ft (2.7 to 3 m). It is recognized by its dark wings with white streaks, its orange neck and breast, and by the black feathers underneath its bill. It subsists on the flesh of dead animals but is also known to kill live ones.

Lamp, implement that produces light and usually heat using one of 3 methods: combustion of fats or oils, combustion of gases, or electricity. Fat lamps burn fat, oil, paraffin, or grease utilizing a simple wick that pulls the fuel up to the flame. These were the first lamps, dating from prehistoric times, when they were made of hollowed rocks with grass wicks. Gas lamps, dating from 1792, produce light when air mixes with such gases as natural gas, butane, or acetylene. Electric lamps, developed about 1879, utilize electrical energy by directing it through a glass bulb containing inert gas that charges a tungsten filament.

Lampedusa, Giuseppe Tomasi di (1896-1957), Italian writer. The descendant of an aristocratic Sicilian family, he spent his childhood in Sicily and then moved to England, France and Latvia. He fought in both the First and the Second World Wars. He achieved international fame with *Il gattopardo* (The Leopard), a novel which he wrote during his final years and which was published posthumously in 1958. Visconti filmed the novel in 1962.

Lamprey, primitive fish of the Petromyzontidae family, one of the 2 remaining groups of jawless fish (Agnatha), found both in freshwater and in the sea. Its body is eel-like, and its round, sucking mouth has horny teeth with which it rasps away at its prey. Many species are parasitic when adult, feeding on the flesh of living fishes. The blind, wormlike, filter-feeding larva is totally unlike the adult.

Lanai *See:* Hawaii.

Lancaster, English royal family. **Edmund Crouchback** (1245-1296), second son of Henry III, was first earl of Lancaster (1267); his son **Thomas** (d. 1322) led baronial opposition to Edward II. **John of Gaunt** (1340-1399) became duke of Lancaster by marriage in 1362, and his son and grandson became Henry IV (1399) and Henry V (1413). The Lancastrians were deposed by the house of York during the Wars of the Roses (1455-1485), which began during the reign of Henry VI, but the heir to Lancaster claims, Henry Tudor, reestablished the line (as the house of Tudor) in 1485, becoming Henry VII.
See also: England.

Lancelet *See:* Amphioxus.

Lancelot, Sir, legendary medieval knight. The son of the king of Brittany, he was taken as an infant to the undersea castle of the Lady of the Lake, who brought him to the court of King Arthur after he had attained manhood. As a Knight of the Round Table, he achieved great fame and fortune, however his passionate involvement with King Arthur's wife, Queen Guenevere, led to scandal and Lancelot's ultimate ruin. During his life he involved himself in the search for the Holy Grail, but his moral flaw prevented him from finding it. The Holy Grail was, however, found by Galahad, Lancelot's illegitimate son-the product of Lancelot's youthful affair with a British Princess. Lancelot was the hero of various medieval romances. He was also a central figure in a series of poems by Alfred Lord Tennyson called *Idylls of the King*.
See also: Arthur, King; Round Table.

Lan-chou *See:* Lanzhou.

Land art, art form which takes the countryside and natural materials readily available as its starting point. A land art project may bring nature into the work, but it may also drastically alter the natural reality. It has been used by artists from various different parts of the world since 1965, and is often recorded with the aid of photographs and video cameras. Artists such as C. Andre Christo, J. Dibbets, M. Heizer, R. Long and W. de Maria have experimented with this art form.

Landowska, Wanda (1877-1959), Polish harpsichord virtuoso, largely responsible for the revival of the harpsichord. Living in

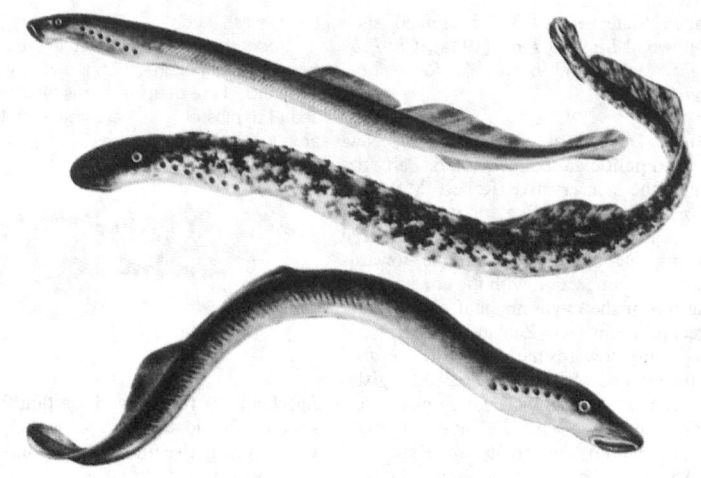

The sea lamprey (top, *Petromyzon marinus*) can reach a length of about one metre. With its sucking snout, that is filled with considerably more teeth than that of the river lamprey, it sometimes attaches itself to a whale. The river lamprey (center, *Lampetra fluviatilis*) is a protected species that may attain a length of about 12 in (30 cm). It attacks smaller types of fish, and sometimes bottom-dwelling animals or carrion. The brook lamprey (bottom, *Lampetra planeri*) is also a protected species that can become about 6 in (15 cm) long. It never parasitizes other fish.
In its adult state, the brook lamprey stops feeding, and it will die after spawning.

Paris (1900-1940), she founded the Ecole de Musique Ancienne. In the United States after 1940, she was famous as a performer, teacher, and authority on early music.

Land reform, governmental redistribution of land ownership, the purpose of which is to lessen the personal wealth, power, and political influence accorded those with large land holdings. Land reform is usually utilized at times of social or political unrest to more fairly distribute land, particularly farmlands, to those with little or no land of their own. The recipients of land are often given technical training, favorable financing, and low tax rates.

Landsbergis, Vytautas (1932-   ), Lithuanian politician who in 1988 was elected chairman of Sajudis, the nationalist popular front. In 1990 Sajudis won an overwhelming victory in the elections for the Supreme Soviet, after which Parliament proclaimed the country's independence. Landsbergis, a non-communist, was elected president. Economic problems detracted from Sajudis' popularity in 1992. The government resigned, and the subsequent elections were won by the former communists. In 1993 Landsbergis became chairman of the Fatherland Union, which he himself had founded, and in 1996 he became chairman of the Lithuanian Parliament. He lost the 1997 presidential elections.

Land's End, England's westernmost point of land, located in Cornwall. Land's End, a turf-covered headland of granite cliffs 60-100 ft (18-30 m) high, juts into the English Channel, near the Atlantic Ocean, and is surrounded by rocky shores and hazardous reefs.

Landsteiner, Karl (1868-1943), Austrian-born U.S. pathologist. He was awarded the 1930 Nobel Prize for physiology or medicine for discovering the major blood groups and developing the ABO system of blood typing. He also contributed to the identification of the Rh factor.
See also: Blood type; Rh factor.

Lanfranc (d. 1089), archbishop of Canterbury (1070-1089). He appointed reforming Norman bishops, enforced clerical celibacy, and strengthened the monasteries. As a scholar he helped shape the doctrine of Transubstantiation, writing *Concerning the Body and Blood of the Lord* (c. 1059).
See also: Church of England.

Lang, Andrew (1844-1912), Scottish writer and scholar. He explored folklore in *Custom and Myth* (1884) and *Myth, Literature, and Religion* (1887), and published translations of Homer, fairy tale collections, poetry, and historical works.

Lang, Fritz (1890-1976), Austrian-U.S. film director. He first established himself as a leading director of expressionist silent films, including *Metropolis* (1926), a bleak futuristic drama. In *M* (1931), a sound film about a child murderer, Lang explored the psychology of evil. After emigrating to the

Scene from the film *Metropolis* (1928), by Austrian-American film-director Fritz Lang (1890-1976). This film is set in a mechanized society, in the year 2000. Mankind is divided into classes: a small group that lives in prosperity above the ground, and the great masses that are oppressed and forced to perform heavy and boring work underground. The climax of the film is the eventual revolt of the subhumans.

L

United States in 1933, he created such Hollywood films as *Fury* (1936), *Clash by Night* (1952), and *Beyond a Reasonable Doubt* (1956).

Lange, David Russell (1942-), New Zealand politician. Lange's Labor Party defeated the conservative Robert Muldoon, who had been in office for nine years in 1984. As Prime Minister, he was admired for his uncompromising attitude towards France (in connection with the attack on the flagship of the environmental organization Greenpeace in New Zealand in 1985) and his position towards the U.S., which refused to take notice of the New Zealand legislation concerning the nuclear-free public territory. He was one of the most important people behind the Treaty of Rarotonga (1985), which declared the entire southern area of the Pacific Ocean a nuclear-free zone. Lange resigned in 1989. Geoffrey Palmer became the new leader of the Labor Party.

Lange, Dorothea (1895-1965), U.S. documentary photographer. Her powerful, stark pictures of Depression victims, migrant workers, and the rural poor greatly influenced photo-journalistic technique. In 1939 she published *An American Exodus*.

Langland, William (1332-1400), presumed poet of *The Vision of Piers Plowman*, a religious allegory representing a dream-vision of the Christian life and a satire, one of the finest examples of Middle English alliterative verse.

Langley, Samuel Pierpont (1834-1906), U.S. astronomer, physicist, and meteorologist. He invented the bolometer, which measures radiant energy (1878), and an early heavier-than-air flying machine. His most important work was in the investigation of the sun's role in bringing about meteorological phenomena.
See also: Bolometer.

Langmuir, Irving (1881-1957), U.S. physical chemist awarded the 1932 Nobel Prize

Lantern fish, such as *Myctophum punctatum*, are common inhabitants of the deep sea at depths of around 2,000 metres. They are rarely more than 6 in (15 cm) long, and have light organs (yellow) that are concentrated on the lower part of their bodies.

for chemistry for his work on thin films on solid and liquid surfaces (particularly oil on water), giving rise to the new science of surface chemistry.

Langost (member of the *Palinuridae* family, of the order of the decapods), long-tailed lobsters with very long antennae, no pincers, and extremities which are not designed for swimming. Many kinds are popular delicacies, including the scampi (*Palinurus vulgaris*), which inhabits rocky shorelines along the Atlantic Ocean and the Mediterranean Sea, weighs up to 17.5 lb. (7.9 kg), lives mainly on mussels and snails, and is nocturnal.

Langton, Stephen (c. 1155-1228), English cardinal and theologian whose appointment as archbishop of Canterbury (1207) led to a quarrel between Pope Innocent III and King John. Langton led opposition to the king, and his is the first signature on the Magna Carta.
See also: Magna Carta.

Langtry, Lillie (Emily Charlotte Le Breton; 1853-1929), English actress. Known, because of her birthplace (Jersey, Channel Islands), as the Jersey Lily. In 1881 she made a sensation by being the first society woman to go on the stage, making her debut at the Haymarket Theatre, London, in *She Stoops to Conquer*.

Language (from Latin *lingua*, 'tongue'), means by which humans express themselves vocally and communicate with others. A language subset is part of a language that can be used independently of the rest of the language. Language translation is the process of changing information from one language to another.

Langur, any of various brightly colored, long-tailed monkeys (family Colobidae) of India and Southeast Asia. Langurs have patches of colored skin, crests of hair on the head, bushy eyebrows, and a chin tuft, and some have long, upturned noses, as in the proboscis monkey. Langurs live in troops in forests, where they eat leaves. The entellus, or Hanuman langur, is sacred in India.

Lanier, Sidney (1842-1881), U.S. poet and musician. A Southerner who fought in the Civil War (recalled in his novel *Tiger-Lilies*, 1867), he practiced law, and became a professional flutist, writing a study of the interrelation of music and poetry, *The Science of*

English Verse (1880). He also published *Poems* (1877).

Lanternfish, deep-sea fish (family Myctophidae) that has numerous light organs along the sides of its body and on its head. Lanternfish are found in both the Atlantic and Pacific oceans. The particular pattern of light identifies sex and species. Lanternfish come to the surface at night to feed on small animals.

Lanthanide *See:* Rare earth.

Lanthanum, chemical element, symbol La; for physical constants see Periodic Table. Lanthanum was discovered by Carl Mosander in 1839. It occurs in the minerals *cerite*, *bastnasite*, and *monazite* which is the principal source of the element. The metal is prepared by reducing the anhydrous fluoride with calcium. Lanthanum is silvery-white, malleable, ductile, and soft enough to be cut with a knife. Ion-exchange and solvent extraction techniques have led to much easier isolation of the so-called 'rare-earth' elements. Lanthanum and its compounds are used in carbon lighting applications, special glasses, hydrogen sponge alloys, and misch metal.

Lanza, Mario (real name Alfred Cocozza; 1921-1959), American singer (tenor) of Italian descent. Lanza initially developed his vocal talent on his own, but later followed lessons at the New England Conservatory in Boston. He achieved international acclaim for his work in musical movies such as *The Great Caruso* (1951). He was a celebrated belcanto singer.

Lanzhou, or Lanchow (pop. 1,800,000), capital city of Gansu Province in northwestern China, on the Huang He River. An industrial and transportation hub, the city produces chemicals and petroleum products and is the center of China's nuclear energy industry.
See also: China.

Laocoön, in Greek mythology, priest of Apollo who warned the Trojan people not to accept the gift of the wooden horse from the Greeks, with whom they had been at war for 10 years. When Laocoön was killed while worshipping, the Trojans took this as a sign of the gods' displeasure with him and brought the horse into Troy. The horse was filled with Greek soldiers, who seized the city.
See also: Mythology; Trojan War.

L

The sacred langur of the forests of Southeast Asia, *Presbytis entellus*, measures about 3 ft (1 m including tail) in length.

L

Laos

Capital:	Vientiane
Area:	91,400 sq mi
	(236,800 sq km)
Population:	5,777,000
Language:	Lao
Government:	People's republic
Independent:	1953
Head of gov.:	Prime minister
Per capita:	US$ 1,630
Monetary unit:	1 Kip = 100 at

Laos, officially Lao People's Democratic Republic, Southeast Asian country formerly part of French Indochina. It is bordered by China to the north, Vietnam to the east, Cambodia to the south and Thailand and Myanmar to the west. It is a small country (650 mi/1,046 km-long and in places barely 50 mi/81 km-wide).

Land and climate. Laos is dominated by mountain chains and plateaus, cut by deep, narrow valleys, covered by forests interspersed with patches of grassland. The Mekong, the river that creates the important Mekong Basin, forms the border with Myanmar and most of Thailand.

Laos has a tropical monsoon climate, with near-drought from Nov. to Apr. and a wet season from May to Oct.

People. The people of Laos include various ethnic groups, the largest being the Lao, who total over half of the population. Their language, Lao, is the official language. Most practice Hinayana (Theravada) Buddhism. The rest of the population consists of the Kha-original inhabitants of Laos-and mountain tribes, which include the Mons, Thai, Meos and Hos. The education system is poorly developed. There is one university, at Vientiane, the University of Sisavang Vong. Smaller urban areas include Luang Prabang (the royal capital), Pakse and Savannakhet.

Economy. Laos is one of the poorest countries in the world. The people of Laos are mostly primitive farmers who mainly grow rice. Some coffee, corn, hemp, cotton and opium poppies-although illegal-are grown, and the Mekong River and its many tributaries provide fish for local consumption as well as the major means of transportation. The forests provide good teak and bamboo,

charcoal, benzoin (used in perfumes) and stick lac (for shellac). Rich iron ore deposits are known to exist, but only the tin ore is exploited commercially. Industry is on a very limited scale. There are no railways and few reliable roads. There is an international airport at Vientiane.

History. Part of the Khmer empire, the territory was settled from the 10th to 13th centuries by Thai Lao. By the 17th century a powerful Lao kingdom had emerged; but in the early 1700s it split into the principalities of Luang Prabang, Vientiane, and Champasak. In 1893 France made Laos a protectorate. After World War II national insurgency of various factions (including the Communist Pathet Lao with Vietnamese support) won the country independence within the French Union in 1949; it remained in the French Union until 1954. In 1959 renewed civil war between the neutralist premier Souvanna Phouma and right- and left-wing rivals brought intervention from the great powers. A coalition government was formed in 1973. In Dec. 1975 the king abdicated, and the country became a Communist republic under the Pathet Lao, strongly influenced by Vietnam. In 1990 a small guerrilla resistance force took action against the communist government, but the effect was minimal. In 1997 Laos signed a trade agreement with the United States and was admitted to the ASEAN. Since 1999, the economy has been suffering from the Asian crisis and domestic instability. As a result, Laos received support from both the IMF and the UN World Food Program (WFP). At the 2002 parliamentary elections, all seats but one were won by the governing Lao People's Revolutionary Party (LPRP).

Lao Tzu, or Lao Tze (Old Master or Master Lao), legendary Chinese philosopher of the 6th century B.C., said to be the founder of Taoism. According to Taoist legend, Lao Tzu was named Li Erh and had the courtesy name Lao Tzu. Tao, or the Way (of Nature), emphasizes simplicity, naturalness, and spontaneity in life. He was keeper of the royal archives. In his old age he is reported to have met the young Confucius. He is said to have written the sacred book, the *Tao-te-ching* (The Way and Its Virtue), at the request of a border guard after having left the court, because of political disturbances, to live a solitary life in the mountains. Many scholars, however, believe that this book was written several centuries after its time. Tao-te-ching teaches that those who want to live the good life must follow Tao.
See also: Taoism.

Laparoscopy, form of medical examination in which the abdominal organs are examined with the aid of a special instrument, a laparoscope. This is inserted into the abdominal cavity through a small incision in the upper abdomen, after a quantity of gas has been pumped into the cavity to create more space. Small operations can also be performed in this manner, for example the sterilization of a woman. This type of examination or operation takes place while the patient is under an anesthetic.

La Paz (pop. 1,200,000), largest city and ad-

ministrative capital of Bolivia (the legal capital being Sucre). Founded in 1548 by the conquistadors, it is located in the La Paz river valley in western Bolivia. At some 12,000 ft (3,700 m) above sea level, it is the world's highest capital. Local products include cement, glass, textiles, and consumer goods. Lake Titicaca, South America's largest freshwater lake, is a popular tourist attraction of the region.
See also: Bolivia.

Lapis lazuli, a stone of a rich azure blue, often flecked with golden iron pyrites. It is a silicate, a type of rock consisting of silicon, oxygen, and one or more metals. The stone is used to make mosaics, vases, jewelry, and other ornamental articles. Lapis lazuli is about half as hard as the diamond. It was formerly used to make the pigment *ultramarine*. The stone is found in Asia, Chile, and California. It occurs mainly in crystalline limestone.

Laplace, Pierre Simon de, Marquis de Laplace (1749-1827), a French astronomer and mathematician. Laplace explored almost every branch of the physical sciences. For his *Celestial Mechanics* (5 volumes, 1799-1825), he is called 'the Newton of France.' In this work Laplace showed that the movements of the solar system were in conformi-

The women of the Meo (with red head-covering) and the Yao meet at the market, near Luang Prabang in North Laos. Both the Meo and the Yao are Sino-Tibetan-speaking peoples, originating from Yuunan (South China).

The French mathematician and astronomer Pierre de Laplace (1749-1827).

L

ty with Newton's theory of gravitation. He convinced his age that the solar system was a stable self-regulating machine. He proposed the theory that the solar system developed from condensed gases.

Working with Lavoisier, Laplace conducted experiments on specific heat and the heat of combustion. In mathematics Laplace contributed to the theory of probability. He discovered a differential equation highly useful in physics.

While Laplace was a student at the University of Caen, his genius was so evident that he was appointed professor of mathematics at the École Militaire when only 18 years old. Although Laplace was an ardent republican during the French Revolution, Napoleon made him a count and senator. When Napoleon was exiled Laplace changed his politics and was made a marquis in 1817 by Louis XVIII.

Lapland, region in the extreme north of Europe, the homeland of the Lapps (or Finns, as they are called in Norway). Lying primarily within the Arctic Circle, it embraces northern parts of Norway, Sweden, and Finland, and the Kola Peninsula of the former USSR, with an area of 150,000 sq mi (388,000 sq km). It has tundra vegetation, with some forest vegetation in the south. Its wildlife, especially the economically important reindeer, were severely hurt by radioactive contamination from the 1986 Chernobyl nuclear disaster.

Lapps *See:* Lapland.

The skylark (*Alauda arvensis*, order *Passeriformes*, family Alaudidae), is found throughout temperate Eurasia and in northern Africa. It has a length of up to 7 in (18 cm).

Lapwing, or peewit (*Vanellus vanellus*), shore bird found in Western Europe and the British Isles. The lapwing, named because of its slow, ungainly wingbeat, has an iridescent green-black back, blue-black throat, white belly, and long, wispy, black crest.

Larceny, in law, the unlawful removal of the property of another person without the owner's consent and with intent to steal. Grand larceny, a felony, is generally the theft of valuable property, while petty larceny, usually a misdemeanor, involves less valuable goods. Embezzlement, robbery, and fraud are generally considered larceny.
See also: Crime.

Larch, pine (genus *Larix*) that is unusual in being deciduous rather than evergreen, shedding its needles in winter, becoming completely bare. The several kinds of larch flourish in the Northern Hemisphere as far north as the Arctic Circle. The European larch is a source of turpentine, and several larches, including the tamarack (*L. laricina*), yield a timber that lasts well in water and is used for piers.

Lardner, Ring (1885-1933), U.S. sports journalist and short-story analyst. Stories like 'You Know Me, Al' (1916), satirize vulgarity and greed in U.S. life. Short-story volumes include *What of It?* (1925) and *Round Up* (1929). With G.S. Kaufman, he wrote the play *June Moon* (1929).

Lares and penates, in Roman mythology, household guardian gods. The lares were godly ancestor figures; the penates were guardians of the storeroom.
See also: Mythology.

Larionov, Michael (real name Mikhail Fyodorovich; 1881-1964), Russian painter who moved to France in 1938; married the painter Nathalie Gontcharova. He was initially influenced by French impressionism and neo-impressionism. He founded the Rayonist movement, which formed an influence in the development of abstract art in Russia (Malevich, Tatlin). In 1913, he published his *Rayonist and Futuristic Manifesto*, describing his theories on color, lines, movement and relations between forms. In collaboration with his wife he designed stages and costumes for Diaghilev's ballet.

Lark, any of a family (*Alaudidae*) of small terrestrial songbirds of Europe, Asia, North America, and Africa. The birds are streaked brown or gray, and feed on insects and seeds, walking or running at great speed along the ground. Larks are known for their beautiful songs, usually delivered on the wing.

Larkin, Philip Arthur (1922-1985), English poet, a friend of Kingsley Amis and John Wain. Together with Thom Gunn and Ted Hughes, he is regarded as one of the most important poets of his generation. His oeuvre, which is not very extensive, consists of the collections *The North Ship* (1945), *The Less Deceived* (1955), *The Whitsun Weddings* (1964) and *High Windows* (1974). His poem *Church Going* is seen as the credo of himself and his colleagues, who were reacting against the complexity of Dylan Thomas, Auden and Spender. Larkin is a typically English poet, subtle and reticent, with a tendency towards a defeatist agnosticism, as can be seen in *The Building*, *Ambulances* and *Days* and other works. He also wrote two novels, *Jill* (1946) and *A Girl in Winter* (1947).

Larkspur, any of a genus (*Delphinium*) of flowering plants of the buttercup family, growing mostly in the temperate zones of the Northern Hemisphere. The loosely clustered flowers, which grow on spikes ranging from 1 to 7 ft (30 cm to 2.1 m), have 5 sepa-

ls, one of which forms a spur. Larkspurs may be white, blue, or pink.

La Rochefoucauld, François, Duc de (1613-1680), French writer. He is known for his *Memoirs* (1662) of the Fronde, and his *Maxims* (1665), a collection of more than 500 moral reflections and epigrams, generally paradoxical, often pessimistic, usually acute.

La Rochelle (pop. 76,000), French city on the Atlantic coast, capital of the Charente Maritime department. The city, chartered in the 12th century, is a yachting and fishing center. During the persecution of the Huguenots (French Protestants) by the Roman Catholics in the 16th century, La Rochelle was among the 100 communities established by the Edict of Nantes as a haven for Protestants. In 1627 the city was forced to return control to the French government.
See also: France.

Larrocha, Alicia de (real name Alicia de Larrocha y de la Calle; 1923-), Spanish pianist. De Larrocha was already performing in public at the age of five; she made her debut with orchestra in 1934 in Madrid. She studied piano with Frank Marshall and theory with Ricardo Lamote and in 1940 embarked upon a professional career, albeit initially limited due to the war. A successful concert tour of the United States in 1947 heralded her definite international breakthrough. De Larrocha, who accepted a position as principal of the Academia Marshall in Barcelona in 1959, is mainly famous for her impassioned interpretations of the Spanish masters from the period between 1850 and 1950.

Larva, metamorphic stage of development in some animals in which the young are noticeably different in feature and behavior from their parents. Larvae most often occur in the metamorphoses of insects and aquatic animals. The length of the larval phase varies according to species. Examples of larvae are the tadpoles of frogs and toads and the caterpillars of butterflies and moths.

Larynx, specialized organ of the respiratory tract used in voice production. It lies above the trachea in the neck, forming the Adam's apple, and consists of several cartilage components linked by small muscles. Two folds, or vocal cords, lie above the trachea and can be pulled across the airway so as to regulate and intermittently occlude air flow. It is the movement and vibration of these that produce voice.

La Salle, Jean *See:* Jean Baptiste de la Salle, Saint.

Las Campanas Observatory *See:* Mount Wilson Observatory.

Las Casas, Bartolomé de (1474-1566), Spanish missionary in Central America. He exposed the forced labor of the Indians, persuaded Madrid to enact the New Laws for Indian Welfare (1542), and in his *History of the Indies* recorded data valuable to modern anthropology.

Lascaux Grotto, prehistoric cave in France near Montignac in the Vezère chalk range of the Dordogne. It was discovered in 1940, and contains very well-preserved carvings and paintings in red, russet and black, chiefly of animals such as horses, deer, giant bulls and bison; probably dates back to the late Magdalenian period (ca. 15,000-10,000 B.C.). In order to protect the paintings against moisture (breath exhalation), the cave has been closed to the public since 1963. An exact copy of the cave, Lascaux II, can be visited.

Laser, device that produces an intense beam of light with a precisely defined wavelength. The name is an acronym for 'light amplification by stimulated emission of radiation.' The light produced by conventional sources travels in all directions. With lasers, the source atoms radiate in step with each other and in the same direction, producing coherent light. Laser beams spread very little as they travel and thus provide high-capacity communication links. They can be focused into small spots and have been used for cutting and welding-notably for refixing detached retinas in the human eye. Lasers also find application in distance measurement by interference methods, in spectroscopy, and in holography.

Laski, Harold Joseph (1893-1950), English political theorist and economist, active in the Fabian Society and the Labour Party. A lecturer at the London School of Economics (1920-1950), his books include *Democracy in Crisis* (1933), *Liberty in the Modern State* (1948), and *The American Democracy* (1948).
See also: Fabian Society; Labour Party.

Las Palmas (pop. 356,000), Canary Islands, the largest city on the islands and the capital of the Spanish province of Las Palmas. It is situated on Grand Canary Island, about 780 miles (1,255 km) southwest of mainland Spain. Las Palmas has food processing industries, but is primarily a port and a tourist center. Vacationers, mainly Europeans, are attracted by the mild climate, sandy beaches, and fine hotels.
Spaniards founded Las Palmas in 1478, and it became a major base for expeditions en route to America, including Columbus's first voyage in 1492.

Lassalle, Ferdinand (1825-1864), a German socialist and labor leader. He was influenced by Karl Marx, but dit not accept Marx's idea that a revolution of the working class was necessary. Instead, Lassalle favored a form of state socialism in which workers would gain political control democratically. To help accomplish this, in 1863 he organized the General Association of German Workers, the first socialist party in Germany and the forerunner of the German Social Democratic party. Lassalle's party pressed for universal suffrage and the establishment of cooperative associations for workers.
Lassalle was born in Breslau and attended the universities of Breslau and Berlin. He was killed in a duel.

Lassnig, Maria (1919-), Austrian painter who worked in Paris and New York. In 1968 she began drawing cartoons in addition to paintings, drawings and watercolors. The central theme in her art is the experience of one's own body, both internally and in relation to the outside world. After a period of informal paintings in the 1950s, she began painting her own bodily contours in various positions as well as parts of those contours (the 'Body awareness' paintings). In the early 1960s she combined these with e.g. machines and animals, and increased the size of her art, using expressive red and green lines. In the late 1960s her work became more realistic, and she combined the self-portraits with animals, the dominant colors being emerald green and pale yellow. The 1980s saw her paintings become more narrative and filled with violet colors. Her influence on the younger generation of Austrian painters was considerable.

Lasso, Orlando di (1532-1594), Flemish Renaissance singer, choirmaster, and composer of a wide range of more than 2,000 sacred and secular works. Orlando di Lasso is the Italian version of his Flemish name, Roland de Lassus.

Last Supper, the final passover meal held by Jesus and his disciples in Jerusalem before his crucifixion. In it he distributed bread and wine to them, instituting the Christian sacrament of Holy Communion. Leonardo da Vinci's well-known fresco of the Last Supper is in Milan.
See also: Jesus Christ; Passover.

Las Vegas (pop. 478,000), city in southwestern Nevada, seat of Clark County. It is renowned for 'The Strip,' with its casinos (state-legalized gambling), luxury hotels, bars, and nightclubs. The city is also a mining and cattle-farming center. There are artesian springs nearby. It is one of the fastest growing cities in the United States.
See also: Nevada.

Latakia, or Al-Ladhiqiyah (pop. 284,000), principal seaport city in western Syria, on the Mediterranean Sea, about 110 mi (177 km) north of Beirut. Latakia dates to antiquity, when it was the Phoenician city Ramitha. Exports include tobacco, cotton, bitumen, asphalt, and coffee.
See also: Syria.

Lateran, district of southeastern Rome, given to the church by Emperor Constantine I in 311. The Lateran palace-the papal residence until 1309-was demolished and replaced in the 16th century. The basilica of St. John Lateran is the cathedral church of the pope as bishop of Rome.

Lateran Treaty, concordat between the papacy and the government of Italy, signed

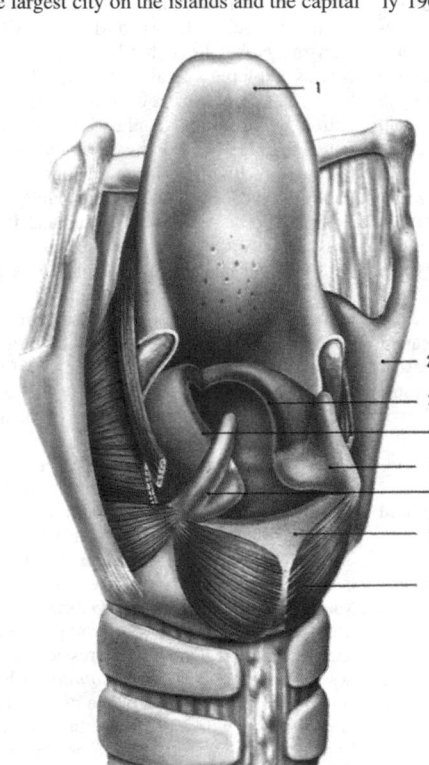

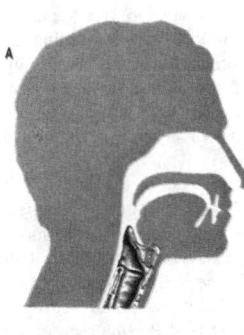

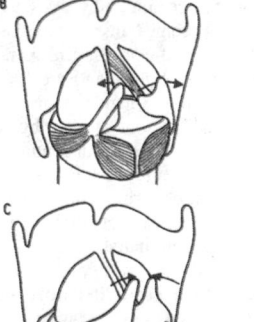

The larynx is a specialized organ of the respiratory tract, used in voice production. It lies above the trachea (A) in the neck, forming the Adam's apple, and consists of several cartilage components linked by small muscles (6). Two folds, or vocal cords (3), lie above the trachea, inbetween cartilage components (2, 4 and 5). They can be pulled across the airway, in order to regulate and intermittently occlude the air flow. It is the movement and vibration of the vocal cords that produce voice. When swallowing, the tongue (1) is down, thus closing the trachea. In normal breathing (B), the vocal cords are kept apart, in speaking or singing (C), they are tightened and close to one another.

L

L

1929 in the Lateran palace and confirmed by the 1948 Italian constitution. It established Roman Catholicism as Italy's state religion and Vatican City as an independent sovereign state.

Latex, milky substance extracted from various plants and trees that serves as the source of natural rubber. Synthetic latex has been used since the 1940s to make paints and coatings. Its properties are hardness, flexibility, toughness, adhesion, color retention, and resistance to chemicals. *See also:* Rubber.

Latimer, Hugh (c.1490-1555), English Protestant martyr and Reformation leader. He defended Henry VIII's divorce from Catherine of Aragon, and was made bishop of Worcester in 1535. With Nicholas Ridley, he was burned at the stake as a heretic by order of the Roman Catholic Queen Mary I.

Latin, Indo-European language of the Italic group, language of ancient Rome, and ancestor of the Romance languages. Originating in Latium (about 8th century B.C.), Latin spread with Roman conquests throughout the empire, differentiating into vulgar Latin and classical (literary) Latin. It is a logical and highly inflected language that has furnished scientific and legal terminology and is still used in the Roman Catholic Church. It was the international language of scholarship and diplomacy until the 18th century. About half of all English words are Latin in origin.

Latin America, 33 independent countries and 13 other political entities in Central and South America where Romance languages are spoken: Spanish in most of Latin America; Portuguese in Brazil; and French in Haiti. Sometimes the term includes Guyana, Suriname, and French Guiana in South America, and, less often, also all the Caribbean islands.
People. The population growth of almost 2% per year is one of the highest in the world. The population lives by the Pacific or Atlantic oceans, rivers, or in highland farm

In 1519, Hernando Cortèz (1485-1547) conquered Mexico. This picture (Mexico, 1519) shows the meeting between a Spaniard (left) and a representative of Montezuma II (1466-1520), the ruler of the Aztecs.

A relief showing the meeting in Guayaquil between the two heroes of the Latin- American independence wars: San Martin and Bolivar.

areas. The people are of European, African, Indian, and mixed ancestry. After World War II, large numbers of people moved from rural to urban areas in search of employment, and most large cities suffer from overcrowding, pollution, homelessness, inadequate medical services, and high unemployment. The literacy rate varies from less than 50% (Haiti) to more than 90% (Argentina).
Economy. Historically, Latin America economies depended on one export commodity-oil, copper, tin, coffee, bananas, livestock, fish-to earn foreign currency. In several countries there have been efforts at diversification, but economic development is hampered by poor transport, political instability, and burdensome effects of foreign aid. Although about half of the people work on the land, agriculture is mostly primitive and inefficient. Important changes in recent decades include the emergence of Brazil as a leading industrial power, and use of oil revenues in Mexico and Venezuela to finance economic growth. Argentina, Brazil, Mexico and other nations borrowed huge sums from the International Monetary Fund and from private banks, leading to a near-crisis in the 1980s when they were unable to repay their debts.
History. Before the arrival of Columbus in 1492, several highly developed civilizations flourished in the region, most notably the Mayans, Aztecs and Incas. During the conquest the indigenous populations were decimated by war and European diseases. Spanish and Portuguese colonial rule lasted about three hundred years, and by 1825 most of the colonies, inspired by the leadership of Bolivar and San Martin, gained their independence. Power and wealth, however, remained in the hands of tiny minorities, and political life was marked by corruption and instability. In the 20th century, several countries have enjoyed long peaceful periods of constitutional rule while others have experienced military dictatorships, revolution, and violent factional strife.

Latin-American literature, literature of the Spanish-speaking countries of the Western Hemisphere. It also includes Brazil, where the native language is Portuguese, not Spanish. The literary period began with the

explorations in the 1400s and lasted some 300 years. The earliest literature was written by soldiers and missionaries describing new lands and civilizations. Hernando Cortés, the conqueror, wrote his *Five Letters* (1519-1526) for King Charles I of Spain, outlining his campaign in great detail. Many works deal with the period of conquest. Bartolomé de las Casas wrote of the brutal treatment of the Indians by the Europeans in *The Devastation of the Indians: A Brief Account* (1552). *La Araucana* (1569-1589) by Alonso de Ercilla y Zúñiga is considered the greatest poem of the time and heralded the bravery of the Chilean Indians in resisting the Spanish invaders.
The ornate baroque style arose in the latter 1600s. The Mexican nun, Sor Juana Ines de la Cruz, wrote plays, satire, philosophical works and poetry in the baroque style.
In the early 1800s, Romanticism, stressing individualism, nationalism and artistic freedom spread to Latin America. Nomadic cowboys called Gauchos became a literary topic. The best example of this is the epic poem *Martin Fierro* (1872-1879) by José Hernandez of Argentina. The Romantic period gave rise to the novel. Jorge Issacs of Columbia wrote a sentimental love story *Maria* (1867) that remains popular today. The 'noble savage' theme was popular among the romantics who felt that the Indians were superior to the corrupt Europeans. Realist writers, seeking to capture external reality in an objective way, emerged in the 2nd half of the 19th century. The modern period lasted from 1888 to 1910 and Nicaraguan poet Rubén Darió gave it its form. His books of poems *Azul* (1888) marked the beginning of the period. Jose Martí of Cuba was a celebrated journalist, essayist and poet of this period.
In the 20th century women poets emerged with work dealing with love and the role of women in society. Gabriela Mistral of Chile won the Nobel Prize for literature (1945). Novels explored social and political problems. The Mexican revolution (1910) inspired Mariano Azuela's novel *The Underdogs* (1916). Poets experimented with form and technique. Vincente Huidobro and Pablo Neruda of Chile, César Vallejo of Peru, Mario de Andrade of Brazil and Jorge Luis Borges of Argentina created poetry with unusual imagery. In the mid 1940s the 'new novel,' combining authentic subject matter with various themes and experiments, appeared. *The President* (1946) by Miguel Angel Asturias of Guatemala and *The Edge of the Storm* (1947) by Augustín Yáñez of Mexico are well known examples of the new novel.
Since the 1950s Latin American novelists have enjoyed international renown. The best known authors of this period are Carlos Fuentes of Mexico; Alejo Carpentier of Cuba, who coined the term 'magical realism;' Julio Cortázar of Argentina; Mario Vargas Llosa of Peru; and Gabrial García Márquez of Colombia, who brought the use of realism to its greatest expression in his novel *One Hundred Years of Solitude* (1967), considered by many one of the most important literary works of the 20th century. Márquez was awarded the Nobel Prize for literature in 1982.

Latinina, Larissa (1934-), Russian gymnast who took part in the Olympic Games three times (1956, 1960, 1964) and also took part in various world championship tournaments and European championship tournaments, winning-either individually or as part of a team-24 gold medals, 15 silver medals and 5 bronze medals. Her grace in performing the various exercises (combined exercises, beam, horse, asymmetric bars) and her perfectionism gained gymnastics a great deal of popularity.

Latin literature, all literary works of ancient Romans, written in Latin. Latin literature, beginning as a derivation of Greek literature, and evolving over several literary eras, came to express the nature, politics, and history of the people, and developed into a highly distinctive standard for all written language. Although early Latin literature (240 B.C.) contained translations of the Greek classics, poetry, and drama, much of it has been preserved in the form of comedies. The comedies of Plautus and Terence were based on Greek themes with creative variations. Cato the Elder (f. 160 B.C.) produced the most impressive prose of the early period. He also wrote the first history of Rome in Latin. The early period ended with a new kind of poetry by Gaius Lucilius. The *Satires* of Juvenal are also of this era. The apex, or Golden Age, occurred around the 1st century B.C. Cicero was the most accomplished writer of this period. His literary works are a treasure chest of information about life in Rome. His works on education, philosophy, and oratory have endured throughout the ages as classics. In this period, Julius Caesar wrote his works on the Gallic and Civil Wars. The lyric poetry of Catullus appeared at this time. The reign of the emperor Augustus (27 B.C. to A.D. 14) saw the creation of Vergil's *Aeneid* and *Georgics*. The work of Horace and Ovid also appeared in this era. After the death of Augustus, Roman writers demonstrated new styles. The works of Seneca, Lucan, and Petronius' *Satyricon* are of this era. The *Satyricon* is considered the first Latin novel. Other notable writers are the historian Tacitus and Pliny the Younger. The foundations of Christian Latin literature were laid during the 4th and 5th centuries by church fathers like Augustine, Jerome, and Ambrose.

Latitude, distance from the equator, measured in degrees, of any point on the surface of the earth. The equator is considered 0° latitude; the north pole is 90°N, the south pole 90°S. Lines of latitude run parallel to one another.
See also: Equator; Longitude.

Latium, historic region of Italy, 'the cradle of the Roman people,' extending from the Tiber River to the Alban Hills. It is now part of the western region of Lazio, and includes the provinces of Rome, Frosinone, Latina, Rieti, and Viterbo.

La Tour, Georges Dumesnil de (1593?-1652), a French painter noted for his religious and genre (everyday life) paintings. Simplicity of form, uncluttered back-

grounds, and muted but luminous color give his works great expressive power. Most of his paintings are night scenes in which he uses the light from a single candle or torch to cast dark shadows and create strong contrasts. *Saint Sebastian Mourned by Saint Irene* and *Repentant Magdalen* are notable examples. His daylight pictures, such as *The Hurdy-Gurdy Player* and *The Cheat*, are realistic in nature and reveal his skillful handling of color.
Very little is known of La Tour's life. He was born in the province of Lorraine and spent most of his life there. Although he was highly successful in his time, his works were forgotten until the 20th century. He is now considered one of the major 17th-century French painters. Some of the paintings attributed to him may be forgeries.

Latter-day Saints, The Church of Jesus Christ of *See:* Mormons.

Latvia

Capital:	Riga
Area:	24,938 sq mi (64,589 sq km)
Population:	2,364,000
Language:	Latvian
Government:	Republic
Independent:	1991
Head of gov.:	Prime minister
Per capita:	US$ 7,800
Monetary unit:	1 Lat = 100 santims

Latvia (Republic of), independent country, bordering on the Baltic Sea (west), between Estonia (north), Russia (east), Belarus (South east) and Lithuania (south).
Land and climate. It is a lowland country, covering some 24,938 sq mi (64,589 sq km), with a moderate continental climate.
People. Nearly a third of the people are Russians, but the majority are Latvians, an ancient Baltic people. Minorities include Belarussians, Ukrainians, Lithuanians, and Poles. The official language is Latvian. Over 90% of the population are Christians.
Economy. While cattle and dairy farming, fishing, and lumbering are of considerable importance, highly developed industries also exist and include shipbuilding, engineering, and the manufacture of steel, textiles, cement, and fertilizers. The country hardly has any natural resources.

History. Christianized by the German Livonian Knights in the 13th century, Latvia was ruled by Poles, Swedes, and, from the 18th century, Russians. From 1920 to 1940 (when it was reabsorbed into the USSR (Soviet Union)), it enjoyed a precarious independence. Beginning in the late 1980s, Latvia, together with Lithuania and Estonia, was involved in a sometimes violent struggle for economic self-determination, religious freedom, and autonomy from the central Soviet government. With the collapse of communism in the USSR in 1991 Latvia formally attained independence. After independence Latvia pursued Western political and economic policies, and its relationship with Russia deteriorated.
Vaira Vike-Freiberga became President in 1999 and, consequently, the first female Head of State in Eastern Europe. Latvia was invited to join the NATO in 2002 and the EU in 2004.
See also: Union of Soviet Socialist Republics.

Lauda, Niki (Andreas Nikolaus Lauda; 1949-), Austrian racing driver, Formula One world champion for Ferrari in 1975 and 1977, and for McLaren/TAG in 1984. Lauda was almost killed in a crash on the Nürburgring on 1 August 1976 when his car caught fire, but six weeks later, wearing a bandage around his head, he won the Italian Grand Prix. He won 25 of the 171 Grand Prix races he entered. After leaving professional racing he founded an airline company, Lauda Air.
From 2001 till 2003 he was leader of the Formula One Jaguar team.

Laudanum *See:* Opium.

Laud, William (1573-1645), archbishop of Canterbury from 1633 and a chief advisor of Charles I. He enforced High Church beliefs and ritual, and his persecution of English Puritans and Scottish Presbyterians provoked parliamentary impeachment (1640). He was executed for treason.
See also: Church of England.

Laue, Max Theodor Felix von (1879-1960), German physicist awarded the 1914 Nobel Prize for physics for his discovery of X-ray diffraction in crystals.
See also: Physics; X ray.

Laughing gas *See:* Nitrous oxide.

Laughlin, Robert B. (1950-), American physicist. In 1998 he was awarded the Nobel Prize for Physics, together with D. Tsui and H. Störmer, for their discovery of and explanation for the Fractional Quantum Hall Effect (FQHE). Störmer and Tsui had already discovered this phenomenon in 1982, but it was another ten years before Laughlin's explanation in terms of quasiparticles was accepted and proved.

Laughton, Charles (1899-1962), English-born actor, a U.S. citizen from 1950. Films include the award-winning *The Private Life of Henry VIII* (1933), *The Hunchback of Notre Dame* (1939), and *Advise and Consent* (1962). He directed *Night of the Hunter* (1955).

L

Oliver Hardy (left) and Stan Laurel in *The Flying Deuces* (1939).

Laureate *See:* Poet laureate.

Laurel, family (Lauraceae) of evergreen trees and shrubs that grow in the tropics and subtropics. The flowers are inconspicuous and last for only a short time before forming a berry. The classical, or bay, laurel (*Laurus nobilis*), which produces the bay leaf used popularly as a seasoning, is a native of the Mediterranean. It was sacred to Apollo, and its shiny leaves were woven into garlands by the Greeks and Romans. Other laurels include avocado, camphor, cinnamon, and sassafras.

Laurel and Hardy, famous comedy team of Hollywood films. The English-born **Stan Laurel** (Arthur Stanley Jefferson; 1890-1965) and the U.S.-born **Oliver Hardy** (1892-1957), thin man and fat man, simpleton and pompous heavy, made over 200 films between 1927 and 1945. Their style, shaped by Laurel, ranged from slapstick to slow-paced comedy of situation and audi-

ence anticipation. In the early 1990s several original films were released on videotape.

Laurencin, Marie (1885-1956), French painter and printmaker, designer of textiles, clothing, and stage decorations for the Ballet Russe and the Comédie Française. Her personal style was characterized by simplified images, usually of women, and pastel colors. Works include *The Assembly* (1910) and *In the Park* (1924).

Laurentian Plateau *See:* Canadian Shield.

Lausanne (pop. 262,000), city in western Switzerland, on the north shore of Lake Geneva. An ancient Celtic, then Roman, settlement, it was a bishopric from A.D. 590 until 1536, when it was defeated by Bern, which established Protestantism. The Bernese retained power until 1798, and in 1803 Lausanne became the capital of the new Vaud canton. It is a cultural, industrial, and tourist center. The Flon and Louve rivers flow through the city. Historic features include the Cathedral of Notre-Dame (consecrated 1275) and the tower of the former Bishop's Palace, now a history museum. *See also:* Switzerland.

Lava, molten rock rising to the earth's surface through volcanoes and other fissures, or the same after solidification. Originating as magma deep below the surface, most lavas are basaltic (subsilicic) and flow freely for considerable distances. Lavas of intermediate silica content are called andesite. Silica-rich lavas, such as rhyolite, are much stiffer. *See also:* Volcano.

Laval, Pierre (1883-1945), French politician who collaborated with the Germans in World War II. A socialist and pacifist, he served as premier (1931-1932, 1935-1936). Believing that Nazi victory was inevitable, he allowed himself to be installed as a Nazi puppet premier (1942-1944). He surrendered to the Allies (1945) and was executed for treason.

Lavender (*Lavandula vera*), shrub of the mint family, cultivated for its aromatic flowers that, along with the leaves, are used for medicinal purposes. Lavender is normally used in the form of an oil derived from the flowers and distilled with water. It is used for flatulence, migraine, headache, fainting, and dizziness. It also has some antiseptic properties and is useful against putrefactive bacteria in the intestines.

Laveran, Charles Louis Alphonse (1845-1922), French army physician. He won the Nobel Prize in medicine (1907) for his research on protozoa in the generation of tropical diseases. As a surgeon in Algeria (1880), he discovered the malarial parasite and demonstrated its spread by mosquito. He joined the Pasteur Institute in Paris in 1894. *See also:* Malaria.

Laver, Rod (Rodney George Laver; 1938-), Australian tennis player. He was the first person to win the grand slam (consisting of the Australian Open, the French Open, Wimbledon, and the United States Open)

twice (1962, 1969). He also played on 4 winning Davis Cup teams and captured 4 Wimbledon titles (1961, 1962, 1968, 1969).

Lavoisier, Antoine Laurent (1743-1794), French scientist, foremost in the establishment of modern chemistry. He showed that when substances burned, they combined with a component in the air (1772). In 1779 he named this substance *oxygen* (from Greek *oxys*, 'acid'), believing it was a component of all acids. He discredited the phlogiston theory of combustion, proposed a new chemical nomenclature (1787), and published the epoch-making *Elementary Treatise of Chemistry* (1789). In the years before his death on the guillotine, he also investigated the chemistry of respiration, demonstrating its analogy with combustion. *See also:* Chemistry.

Law, body of rules governing the relationships between the members of a community and between the individual and the state. In England, the British Commonwealth, and the United States, the law is based upon statute law, or laws enacted by legislative bodies such as Congress, and upon common law, the body of law created by custom and adherence to rules derived from previous judgments. The other main system, civil law, derives from the laws of ancient Rome and relies not on precedent but on a code of rules established and modified only by statute. This is the dominant system in most of Europe and in many other countries of the world.
All major bodies of law break down into 2 divisions, public law and private law. Public law governs matters that concern the state. Private law governs the relationship between individuals (including corporate bodies such as companies).
The first legal system of which we have any detailed knowledge is that of the Babylonian king Hammurabi in 1700 B.C., whose complex code linked crime with punishment and regulated the conduct of everyday affairs. Like the Hebrew Mosaic Law, it treated law as a divine ordinance. The ancient Greeks were probably the first to regard law as made by man for his own benefit. Roman law was based on the Laws of the Twelve Tables, compiled 451-450 B.C. The Romans developed a complex equity system when these principles became outdated; the Byzantine emperor Justinian I produced the last definitive code in an attempt to clear up resulting difficulties. Much medieval law was based on Church law, although an independent system arose quite early in England. This grew into the common law and spread outwards with the growth of the British Empire. Napoleon revised Roman law as the basis for his Code Napoléon, the model for most subsequent civil law codes. U.S. law grew out of the common law, but has been much modified by the federal system.

Law, Clara (Law Chuck-Yu, 1957-), Hong Kong movie director who played a leading role in the emerging Hong Kong cinema. She studied English literature and attended the British National Film and Television School, where she directed her first full-length movie, *They Say the Moon is Fuller*

The Napoleonic Code Crowned by Time (1833) celebrates the first modern codification of civil law, enacted (1804) by the French emperor as the Code Napoléon. This code became the basis for civil law throughout Europe and parts of the Americas.

Here (1985). She worked on soap series and television documentaries, and directed six full-length movies. The last three of those movies increasingly gained international acclaim: *Farewell, China* (1990), *Qiuyue* (Autumn Moon; 1992), *You seng* (Temptation of a Monk; 1993), *Floating Life* (1997), and *The Goddess of 1967* (2001).

Law enforcement, method used by the various levels of government to regulate social conduct. Laws, the rules by which society recognizes obedience, are enforced by agencies given public authority to impose penalties or sanctions when they are broken. These agencies are usually a combination of a police force and the courts. In the United States most municipal police forces operate independently of state influence, and city police chiefs are traditionally appointed, while sheriffs, who enforce county laws, are elected to office. The Federal Bureau of Investigation (FBI) maintains an enforcement branch and assists local authorities in federal cases. The International Court of Justice, an agency of the UN with 15 international judges, sits at The Hague, Netherlands, and hears disputes between countries.

Lawn tennis *See:* Tennis.

Lawrence, D.H. (David Herbert Lawrence; 1885-1930), English author. He combined a vivid prose style with a solid background of ideas and intense human insight. From a working-class background (reflected in *Sons and Lovers*, 1913), he believed that the Industrial Revolution had resulted in dehumanization. Stressing the supremacy of instinct and emotion over reason in human relationships, he advocated absolute sexual candor; his novel *Lady Chatterley's Lover* (1928) was notorious for this to the exclusion of its other themes. His other novels include *The Rainbow* (1915) and *Women in Love* (1920).

Lawrence, Ernest Orlando (1901-1958), U.S. physicist awarded the 1939 Nobel Prize for physics for his invention of the cyclotron and his studies of atomic structure and transmutation.

Lawrence, T(homas) E(dward) (1888-1935), called Lawrence of Arabia, English scholar, writer, and soldier, legendary guerrilla fighter with the Arabs against the Turks in World War I. As a British intelligence officer he joined Prince Faisal I in a successful guerrilla campaign against Turkish rail supply lines and was with the Arab forces that captured Damascus in 1918. In *The Seven Pillars of Wisdom* (1918) he described his wartime experiences and his personal philosophy. He joined the Royal Air Force and Royal Tank Corps under assumed names (1923-1925, 1925-1935).

Lawrence of Arabia *See:* Lawrence, T(homas) E(dward).

Lawrencium, chemical element, symbol Lr; for physical constants see Periodic Table. Lawrencium was discovered by Albert Ghiorso and co-workers in Mar. 1961. It was incorrectly identified as Lawrencium-257, later changed to Lawrencium-258. It was prepared by bombarding a mixed-isotope californium target with boron-10 or boron-11. It has also been prepared by bombarding americium-243 with oxygen-18 ions. It is a metallic element and a member of the actinide series. Lawrencium-261 has a 40 minute half-life. That is the longest of the ten isotopes of the element now known. Lawrencium is the last member of the actinide transition series.

Lawson, Eddie (1958-), American motor racer; made his debut in Europe in 1981 in the 250 cc class on the Hockenheim ring for Kawasaki. In that year and in the next, Lawson won the American Superbike championship. In 1984 he became world champion in the 500 cc class for Yamaha, and repeated that performance for the same team in 1986 and 1988. In 1989 he won the world championship in the 500 cc class for Honda.

Laxative, drug or food taken to promote bowel action and to treat constipation. Laxatives may act as irritants (cascara, senna, phenolphthalein, castor oil), softeners (mineral oil), or bulk agents (bran, methylcellulose, magnesium sulphate). Laxative abuse may cause gastrointestinal tract disorders, potassium deficiency, and lung disease.

Laxness, Halldór Kiljan (real name Halldór Gudjónsson; 1902-1998), Icelandic writer. He studied theology and liberal arts and intended to become a priest, but left the Church in 1928 in favor of left-wing socialism. He wrote a number of broad epic novels, which are remarkable for their detailed descriptions of surroundings and clever psychological analyses. They include *Salka-Valka* (1931-1932), *Free men* (1934-1935), *Olafur Kárason* (in four parts, 1937-1940), a cycle telling the story of the Icelandic popular poet Magnus Magnússon (1873-1916), and *Iceland's Clock* (1943-1946), a historical trilogy. In 1955 Laxness was awarded the Nobel Prize for Literature.

Lazarus, in the New Testament, brother of Mary and Martha of Bethany, who was re-

Lawrence of Arabia in British uniform and Arab costume. Lawrence, who spoke several Arabic dialects fluently, helped the Arabs, with British aid, in their fight for independence against the Turks (1916-19), using spectacular desert guerrilla tactics (1962).

stored to life by Jesus 4 days after his death (John 11:1-44; 12:1-5); also in the New Testament, beggar at the rich man's gate in a parable (Luke 16:19-25).
See also: New Testament.

Lazarus, Emma (1849-1887), U.S. poet best known for the sonnet, 'The New Colossus,' engraved at the base of the Statue of Liberty. Much of her work is based on Jewish culture, such as the poems *Songs of a Semite* (1882).

Lead, chemical element, symbol Pb; for physical constants see Periodic Table. Lead was known and used by the ancients. It is sometimes found native and occurs in the minerals *anglesite*, *cerussite*, *mimetite*, and *pyromorphite*. It is obtained by roasting its most common ore, *galena*, a sulfide, to its oxide and reducing with carbon in a blast furnace. Lead is a silvery, soft, heavy, metal. It is a poor conductor of heat and electricity. The metal has long been used in the lead-chamber process for the production of sulfuric acid. In the decay of uranium, thorium and actinium, a different stable isotope of lead is the end product. Lead and its compounds are used in storage batteries, X-ray shielding, cable sheathing, insecticides, detonators, solders, shot, and type metal.

Lead monoxide *See:* Litharge.

Lead pencil *See:* Graphite.

Lead poisoning, cumulative chronic disease caused by excessive lead levels in tissues and blood. Lead may be absorbed in industrial settings, through air pollution due to lead-containing fuels, or, in children, through eating old paint. Brain disturbance, with coma or convulsions, peripheral neuritis, anemia, and abdominal colic are important effects. Chelating agents are used in treatment, but preventive measures are essential.
See also: Lead.

Leadwort *See:* Plumbago.

Leaf, green outgrowth from the stems of higher plants; the main site of photosynthesis. The form of leaves varies from species to species, but the basic features are similar. Each leaf consists of a flat blade or *lamina* attached to the main stem by a leaf stalk or *petiole*. Leaflike stipules may be found at the base of the petiole. The green coloration is produced by chlorophyll, located in the *chloroplasts*. Most leaves are covered by a waterproof covering or *cuticle*. Gaseous exchange takes place through small openings called *stomata*, through which water vapor also passes. The blade of the leaf is strengthened by veins that contain the vascular tissue responsible for conducting water and the substances essential for metabolism through the plant. Leaves may be adapted to catch insects or to reduce water loss. *Bracts*, leaves produced immediately below the flowers, may be highly colored and thus mistaken for flowers (as in the poinsettia).

Leafhopper, about 70 genera and over 700 species of slender, sucking insects of the

L

Stick and leaf insects belong to the insect order *Phasmida*. They are large sluggish insects that are remarkable for their close protective resemblance to the foliage or twigs of the vegetation on which they live and feed.
A. leaf insect (*Phyllium crunifolium*)

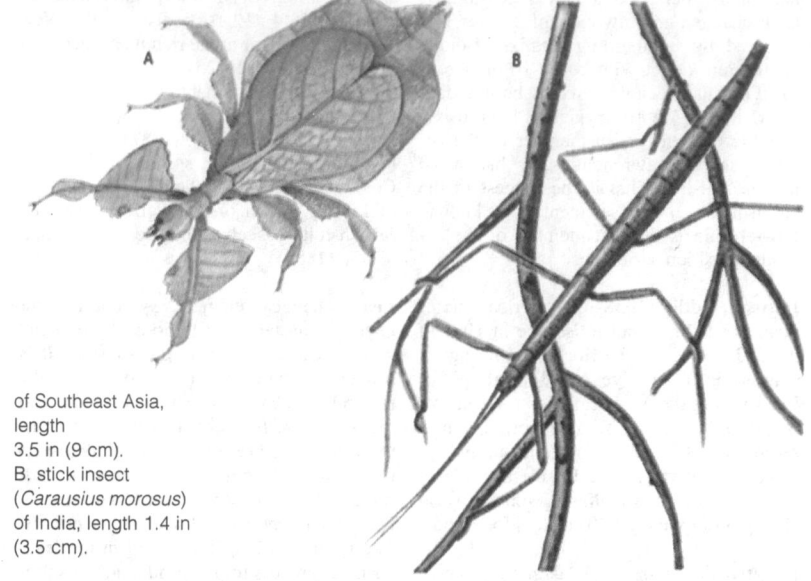

of Southeast Asia, length 3.5 in (9 cm).
B. stick insect (*Carausius morosus*) of India, length 1.4 in (3.5 cm).

family Cicadellidae. Leafhoppers may be brilliantly colored, green, or brown, and are 1/20-1/2 in (1.3-12.7 mm) long. They occur worldwide and on almost any type of plant, particularly fruits, grains, sugar beets, and roses. Leafhoppers carry fungus and bacterial diseases and in large numbers may cause severe crop damage.

Leaf insect, any of about 25 species of herbivorous, tropical, usually nocturnal insects of the family Phylliidae, whose green, ribbed, and veined wings and flat shape make them appear leaflike. Leaf insects are 3-4 in (8-10 cm) long and have irregularly shaped bodies.

Leaf miner, name for many species of insect, including flies, moths, wasps, caterpillars, beetles, and weevils, whose larvae infest and feed within leaves. Leaf miners burrow into leaves and other plant parts and leave blotches or tunnels.

Leaf-monkey *See:* Colobus; Langur.

League of Nations (1920-1946), the first major international association of countries, set up after World War I. The charter, or covenant, was incorporated into the Treaty of Versailles by the War's victors, among them France, Great Britain, Italy, Japan, and the United States. The United States failed to ratify the treaty and join the League. Though the League grew during the 1920s, it was never effective in settling major disputes (e.g., Italy's invasion of Corfu in 1923, Japan's invasion of Manchuria in 1931, Italy's invasion of Ethiopia in 1935). After World War II proved it a failure, the League was dissolved (1946), but its successor, the United Nations, used it as a model.
See also: United Nations; Versailles, Treaty of.

Leakey, family name of English archeologists and anthropologists. **Louis Seymour Bazett Leakey** (1903-1972) is best known for his findings of hominoid fossils and artifacts, especially in the region of Olduvai Gorge, Tanzania, and for his (sometimes

controversial) views on their significance. His wife, **Mary Leakey** (1913-1996), collaborated with him. Their son **Richard Leakey** continued their work.
See also: Anthropology; Archeology.

Leander *See:* Hero and Leander.

Leaning Tower of Pisa, white marble bell tower, or campanile, in Pisa, Italy. Building was started in 1174, reputedly by Bonanno Pisano, but the foundations were unsound and the 184.5-ft (56-m) tower had already begun to lean by the time of its completion in the 14th century. It now tilts more than 17 ft (5 m) from the perpendicular.

Lear, Edward (1812-1888), English artist and writer, best known for his limericks and nonsense rhymes, such as 'The Owl and the Pussy-Cat' (1871). His landscapes and illustrated journals are highly regarded.

Learning, the process by which behavior is modified through experience and practice. All animals are capable of learning. Humans far surpass all these in the ability to learn, especially in the ability to acquire a language. Psychologists do not agree about how learning takes place, but certain principles seem clear.
Classical conditioning. The simplest type of learning is the formation of *conditioned reflexes* in this process, an individual learns to associate 2 events, or stimuli, and to respond in the same way to both. During early life, much behavior is learned in this way. A wide range of behavior patterns are conditioned and always occur when the right stimuli are presented.
Instrumental conditioning. Much behavior is learned as a result of random acts that *elicit,* or draw forth, a response. Satisfying *drives,* such as hunger and thirst, are important in this kind of learning. If a particular act reduces the drive, that act will more likely be repeated next time the drive seeks satisfaction. Positive reinforcement-reduction of a drive by a satisfying reward-is usually more effective than negative reinforcement; thus a child who wins approval for performing a task well is more likely to be successful than a child whose 'reward' is simply the avoidance of punishment for performing the task badly. Instrumental conditioning is particularly important in the development of acceptable social behavior during the early years of life.
Problem solving and insight learning. There are 2 ways to solve a problem: firstly, by *trial and error* and secondly, by reasoning out a solution, using *insight.* Learning by trial and error is encouraged by presenting the problem a number of times and only rewarding the correct solution. Insight learning involves thinking about the problem and grasping the solution without any trial and error.
Human learning. Many psychologists agree that the upper and lower limits of a person's ability to learn are determined by inherited factors. But related factors such as personality, social background, early childhood experiences and level of motivation make it difficult to predict how well a person will perform. A given amount of time is more ef-

A cutaway drawing of Olduvai Gorge, in northern Tanzania, indicating the four major geological beds and the levels at which fossil hominids have been found. The earliest level in Bed I dates from about 2 million years ago. Remains of modern humans, Homo sapiens, occur in Bed IV. The beds, formed from the sediments of a Lower Pleistocene lake, were exposed by an earthquake during the Upper Pleistocene.

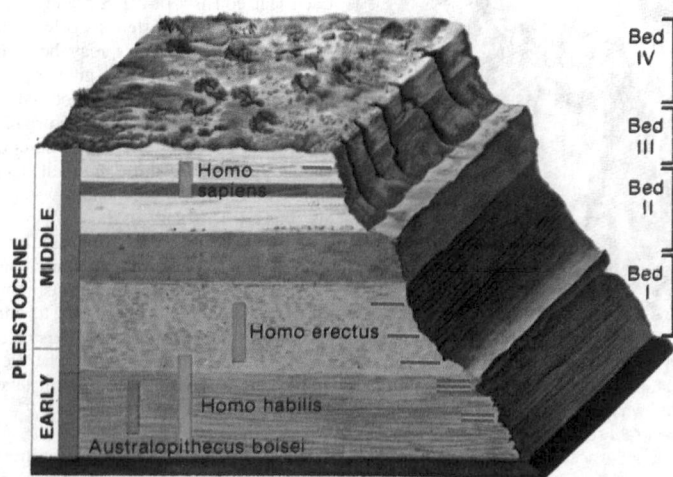

■ Mainly stone-axe industries
■ Pebble tool industries
— Living sites

fective if distributed over several short sessions. Practice is more efficient if directed toward part of a learning task at a time. Trying to learn 2 similar pieces of information at the same time often leads to confusion between the 2. Actually performing a practical task is better than watching others do it. Activities such as writing down notes will lead to faster learning than just reading about or listening to the facts. Mastering one subject will make it easier to learn a closely related subject. It is easier to remember something if there is a period of inactivity, especially sleep, between learning and attempts to remember.

An especially important aid to learning is knowledge of performances as one is actually progressing with a learning task. This is one advantage of teaching machines, which only move on to a new problem after the student has correctly solved the previous one.

Learning disabilities, conditions or factors that hinder one's comprehension or impairs one's ability to use standard educational tools and methods. An inability to perform in the school environment at the same level as one's peers can be the result of an inherited condition causing mental retardation, a developmental defect, a physical handicap such as impaired hearing or vision or muscle incoordination, an allergy causing hyperactivity, or even a reaction to medications taken to control hyperactivity. Learning problems are first identified through tests that measure reading, writing, and arithmetic performance correlated to age, experience, and family background. One common learning disability is *dyslexia*, the mental reversing of printed letters and inability thus to comprehend the meaning of written text. Its cause can lie in the brain, the eyes, or another part of the body. Writing disabilities frequently come from a lack of coordination between the brain and the muscles. A mathematics disability seems to reflect problems of memory and can exist with or without a reading problem.
See also: Dyslexia; Hyperactive child.

Leather, animal hide or skin preserved by tanning. After the hair, fat, and flesh have been removed from the hides, they are soaked in enzymes for softening, then pickled in acid. The tanned leather is lubricated with oil and resins, and often dyed.

Cedars in the
Lebanon Mountains.

Lebanon

Capital:	Beirut
Area:	4,015 sq mi (10,452 sq km)
Population:	3,678,000
Language:	Arabic
Government:	Republic
Independent:	1943
Head of gov.:	Prime minister
Per capita:	US$ 5,200
Monetary unit:	1 Lebanese pound = 100 piastres

Lebanon, small republic of about 4,3 million people in southwest Asia, on the Mediterranean, bordered by Syria on the north and east and Israel on the south. Modern Lebanon is the only Arab State with a large Christian community. Since the Civil War and subsequent conflicts (beginning in the 1970s), the strong financial and trade industries have weakened as well as other sectors of the Lebanese economy.

Land and climate. Geographically the country can be divided into 4 regions, all more or less parallel to the sea: a flat coastal strip along the Mediterranean, the Lebanon mountain range, the narrow Bekaa (Biqa) Valley, only 10 mi wide and the Anti-Lebanon Mountains of the eastern border. The Bekaa Valley, lying between the 2 major mountain ranges, is the country's most fertile area, though the coastal strip is also entirely fertile. Lebanon is fortunate in having more rainfall and a more moderate climate than most of the neighboring countries. In the past the country was famed for the cedars of Lebanon, which probably covered large tracts of its mountain ranges. Today only a few small cedar groves remain. The capital, Beirut, is a seaport of relatively recent origin. Other important cities are Tripoli (Tarabulus), the ancient Tyre and Sidon along the coast, and Zahle in the interior.
People. The people of Lebanon are of mixed ancestry, but mostly Arab. About 40% are Christians. An Armenian community also exists. Most of the remainder are Shi't Muslims, with a smaller group of the Sunni Muslims. The small Druze sect has played a significant part in Lebanese history, especially as a political and military force in the recent conflicts.

History. Lebanon is the site of ancient Phoenicia. Although engulfed by successive invaders-Greek, Roman, Arab and Turkish-it preserved some degree of autonomy. Lebanon's inaccessible mountains were an early refuge for persecuted religious groups, especially Christians. Freed from Turkish rule after World War I, the country passed into French hands, becoming effectively independent in 1943. Civil war erupted in 1975 between the conservative Christian Phalangists and leftist Muslim and Palestinian militias, including the Palestine Liberation Organization (PLO). In 1982 after years of skirmishes with the PLO in southern Lebanon, Israel invaded Lebanon, occupying Beirut and eventually forcing many PLO guerrillas to leave the country. A multinational peace-keeping force, including U.S. marines, arrived (1982) in Beirut, but withdrew within 1 year. The withdrawal was due, in part, to a terrorist attack on U.S. and French compounds which killed 24 U.S. Marines (Oct. 23, 1983). By 1985 Israeli troops also withdrew from all but southern Lebanon. Since 1985 various attempts at ceasefires and political settlements have been made by Syria and other countries involved in the conflict. In 1996 the violence in South Lebanon escalated when Hezbollah fired missiles at North Israel. In return, Israel bombarded Beirut and South Lebanon. The violence caused new streams of refugees. Israel withdrew its troops from Southern Lebanon in 2000, but they were immediately replaced by Hezbollah units. The UN Interim Force in Lebanon (UNIFIL) has been present since 1978.

Lebed, Aleksandr Ivanovich (1950-2002), Russian soldier and politician. Lebed served as a battalion commander in Afghanistan in 1981-1982. During the coup d'etat against President Gorbachev in 1991, Lebed was initially put into action to rescue the parliament building in Moscow, which had been occupied, but instead he quickly joined forces with those opposing the coup. He commanded the 14th army from 1992-1995 in Transdnester (Moldavia). He succeeded in ending the civil war there. In 1996 President Yeltsin appointed him secretary of the Security Council. While he held this position, Lebed concluded a peace treaty with the Chechens, who were rebelling. Lebed was elected governor of the Siberian provoke Krasnoyarsk in May 1998.

Le Brun, Charles (1619-1690), a French painter. As principal painter to Louis XIV and director of the royal tapestry and furniture works, he dominated French art for 20 years. Le Brun studied in Paris and Rome. In 1648 he helped found the Academy of Painting and Sculpture, and in 1683 he became its director. Le Brun designed the Apollo Gallery of the Louvre and painted five of its ceiling panels. During 1679-1684 he decorated the Hall of Mirrors in Versailles Palace. His series of paintings on Alexander the Great is in the Louvre.

Le Carré, John (David John Moore Cornwell; 1931-), English author of novels of international espionage, including *The Spy Who Came in from the Cold* (1963),

L

Tinker, Tailor, Soldier, Spy (1974), *The Little Drummer Girl* (1983), *The Russia House* (1989), *The Secret Pilgrim* (1991), *The Night Manager* (1993), *Our Game* (1995), *The Tailor of Panama* (1996), and *Single and Single* (1999).

Lecithin *See:* Soybean.

L

Le Clézio, Jean-Marie Gustave (1940-), French writer whose work is dominated by a mystical ecstasy (extase matérielle) and by thoughts of death. Both motives are presented in a prose style which is mainly characterized by its detailed descriptions. Le Clézio's own personal manner of treating language is sometimes referred to as 'écriture sismographique' (seismographic writing), for its attention to detail. His writing career began with *Le procès-verbal* (1963), which received the Prix Renaudot. Other works include *La fièvre* (1965), *Le désert* (1980), *La quarantaine* (1995), *La fête chantée* (1997), *Angoli Mala* (1999), *Le hasard* (1999), and *Coeur brûlée et autres romances* (2000).

Le Corbusier (Charles-Édouard Jeanneret; 1887-1965), Swiss-born, French-trained architect, a founder of the international style. His austere, rectangular designs of the 1920s and 1930s reflect his view of a house as a 'machine to live in.' Later influential designs (featuring reinforced concrete) include apartments at Marseilles, a chapel at Ronchamp, and buildings in Chandigarh, India.
See also: Architecture.

LED (Light-emitting Diode), a solidstate electronic device using semiconducting materials to give off light when an electric current is applied. The LED has several advantages over other types of light sources. Because it has no delicate parts such as filaments or glass tubes, the LED is not affected by shock or vibration, and thus has a longer useful life than most other types of lights. Like the transistor, the LED is usually made in small sizes and has a very low power consumption. Because of its compatibility with other solid-state devices, the LED is often used to form any numeral from 0 to 9 when lit in the proper combination. Assembled in groups, these LED displays are used in electronic calculators, in electronic wristwatches and stopwatches, and in many types of scientific and industrial instruments.

Lederberg, Joshua (1925-), U.S. geneticist awarded (with G.W. Beadle and E.L. Tatum) the 1958 Nobel Prize in physiology or medicine for his work on bacterial genetics. He showed that sexual recombination occurs in bacteria. Later he established that genetic information could be carried by bacterial viruses.
See also: Genetics.

Lederman, Leon Max (1922-), U.S. physicist who was part of a team that won the 1988 Nobel Prize. Together with colleagues Melvin Schwartz and Jack Steinberger, he discovered a new subatomic particle (neutrino) and developed a way of synthesizing neutrinos in the laboratory. Lederman served on the faculty of Columbia University and was an adviser to the Atomic Energy Commission.
See also: Neutrino.

The organic forms of the chapel of Notre Dame du Haut (1950-54), Ronchamp, France, exemplify Le Corbusier's sculptural treatment of industrial materials and his post-World War II "anti-rational" architecture. The chapel, a pilgrimage site, is designed for interior and exterior use, featuring a pulpit both inside and out. Irregularly shaped and positioned windows provide illumination.

Le Duc Tho (real name Phan Hinh Khai; 1912-1990), North-Vietnamese politician and diplomat. He was one of the founders of the Communist Party of Indochina in 1930, and was one of the first to support Ho Chiminh in the struggle for independence. For a long time, Le Duc Tho occupied one of the highest positions in the Politburo. In 1968 he was appointed adviser to the North-Vietnamese delegation in Paris. He was less closely involved in the secret negotiations between Kissinger and Xuan Thuy, but in 1971 he stepped into the spotlight once again. The secret negotiations with Kissinger reached a decisive stage towards the end of 1972, when he accepted a truce with South Vietnam without demanding that President Thieu resign. After the Vietnam treaty was signed (January 1973), Le Duc Tho continued to play an important role in the negotiations surrounding the final details of the truce. In 1973 he and Kissinger were awarded the Nobel Peace Prize, which he refused.

Lee, Ang (1954-), Taiwanese-American movie director. In New York, he made a co-production between the United States and Taiwan in 1992, *The Wedding Banquet*. In this movie, a young Chinese homosexual tries to hide his lifestyle from his conservative relatives when they visit him. He subsequently went to Taiwan to make another bittersweet movie about family relationships, *Eat Man, Drink Woman* (1994). He was next to direct the movie version of Jane Austen's *Sense and Sensibility* (1995), which enjoyed great success and for which lead actress Emma Thompson won an Oscar for her adaptation for cinema.
In 2000, he produced and directed *Crouching Tiger, Hidden Dragon*, which was awarded the Oscar for Best Foreign Film.

Lee, Bruce (real name Bruce Lee Hsaio Loong; 1940-1973), American actor, who became famous mainly for his great martial art skills in movies made in Hong Kong, e.g. *The Big Boss* (1971), *Fist of Fury* (1972), *Way of the Dragon* (1972), and *Enter the Dragon* (1973).

Lee, Charles (1731-1782), American major general in the Revolutionary War. He refused orders from George Washington (1776), planned betrayal while in British captivity (1776-1778), and retreated at the Battle of Monmouth (1778), robbing Washington of a victory. He was court-martialed and dismissed (1780).
See also: Revolutionary War in America.

Lee, Chung-Dao (1926-), Chinese-American physicist, who held a position as professor at Columbia University in New York from 1956 to 1960. He was awarded the Nobel Prize for Physics in 1957 (together with Chen Ning Yang) for the theory that no parity is retained in weak interaction. His work focuses on nuclear physics, theory of fields and statistical mechanics.

Lee, Harper (1926-), U.S. author whose only novel, *To Kill A Mockingbird* (1960), won the Pulitzer Prize for fiction. The novel vividly depicts the racism and prejudice of a small southern town by focusing on the sensitive perceptions of the story's narrator, Finch's young daughter.

Lee, Robert Edward (1807-1870), U.S. general and commander of the Confederate Army in the Civil War.

When in 1861 civil war appeared imminent, President Abraham Lincoln offered Lee the post of field commander of the Union forces. Although opposed to slavery and secession, Lee declined out of loyalty to his native state. He accepted a post in the Confederate Army and was given command of the Army of Northern Virginia in June 1862.

After the Confederate victory at the second Battle of Bull Run, Lee invaded Maryland but was halted at Antietam, one of the bloodiest battles of the war, and withdrew to Virginia. Lee again invaded the North and met the Union forces at Gettysburg, Pa. (July 1863).

Lee's mastery of maneuver, his skills in communication, and his ability to inspire devotion in his men had delayed but could not prevent the Union victory.
See also: Civil War, U.S.

Leech, annelid (segmented) worm (class Hirudinea) with a prominent attachment sucker at the posterior end and another sucker around the mouth. Leeches are hermaphroditic. Freshwater or semiterrestrial animals, they feed by sucking the blood or other body fluids of mammals, small invertebrates, worms, insect larvae, or snails.

Leechee *See:* Litchi.

Leeds (pop. 727,000), city in western Yorkshire, northern England. A weaving town in the Middle Ages, it remains a major center for textiles and clothing, particularly woolens. Other industries include electronics, machinery, chemicals, aircraft, vehicles, and food products. On the River Aire, Leeds has canal links to both coasts, and the Yorkshire coal fields lie nearby. It is the site of Leeds University as well as the 12th-century Kirstall Abbey ruins and Temple Newsom, once a mansion of the Knights Templar.
See also: England.

Leek (*Allium porrum*), relative of the onion, originating in the Middle East. This biennial plant is now cultivated throughout Europe and is the national plant of Wales.

Lee Kuan Yew (1923-), Singaporean politician and statesman. He founded the socialistic People's Action Party (PAP) and became Prime Minister in 1959. Membership of the Malaya Federation was a failure and full independence for Singapore was the result. Under his guidance, Singapore became one of the most important trade and industrial centers of Asia, with a relatively high income per head of the population and high-level social services. He resigned in 1990.
See also: Singapore.

Lee Teng-hui (1923-), Taiwanese politician and President (1988-). Lee, who was mayor of Taipei from 1978 to 1981, became

Vice President in 1984. In 1988, he succeeded the deceased President Chiang Ching-kuo. He was re-elected for another six years in 1990. Lee has focused his policies on advanced democratization and more détentes between China and Taiwan. However, in the build-up to the elections of 1996, a serious crisis arose. China carried out military exercises off the Taiwanese shore and threatened with an armed intervention if Lee would aim for independence of the island. As a consequence of this Chinese display of power and a number of other factors, Lee won re-election by a large majority in 1997.
See also: Taiwan.

Leeuwenhoek, Anton van (1632-1723), Dutch microscopist who made important observations of capillaries, red blood corpuscles, and sperm. He is best known for being the first to observe bacteria and protozoa (1674-1676), which he called 'very little animalcules'.
See also: Microscope.

Leeward Islands, chain of about 15 islands and many islets in the West Indies, northernmost group of the Lesser Antilles. They include Antigua, Anguilla, Montserrat, and the British Virgin Islands (British colonies); St. Kitts-Nevis (a former British colony, independent since 1983); St. Eustatius, Saba, and St. Martin (Dutch); Guadeloupe and dependencies (French); and the U.S. Virgin Islands.

Lefkosía (formerly Nicosía; pop. 207,000), city in north-central Cyprus, capital of the island nation. An ancient agricultural trade center, it is now a center for the manufacture of textiles and other goods and for governmental and commercial business. Ancient artifacts from previous colonists are housed in its museums.
See also: Cyprus.

Léger, Fernand (1881-1955), French painter. A cubist, he used strong colors and geometrical shapes and introduced industrial images like cogwheels and pistons. His preoccupation with the machine age may be seen in paintings like *The City* (1919). He designed a mural for the United Nations General Assembly auditorium in New York City (1952).

Legion, principal unit of the Roman army, having between 3,000 and 6,000 infantry with attached cavalry. By the 1st century B.C. the cohort, composed of 6 companies, was the tactical unit. There were 10 cohorts to a legion. The leader of a legion was a legate or a consul. Soldiers of the Roman Empire were recruited to a legion for a term of 20 to 25 years.

Legion, Foreign *See:* Foreign Legion.

Legionnaires' disease, severe lung infection. Legionnaires' disease appeared in 1976 when 182 delegates attending an annual convention of the American Legion in Philadelphia contracted a severe respiratory infection. Of 147 of those hospitalized, 90% developed pneumonia and 29 died. All had stayed in, or visited, the same hotel during the 4-day convention. Five months later, the

Anton van Leeuwenhoek (1632-1723) was a brilliant researcher, who studied an enormous amount of different materials under his self-built microscope: blood, milk, sweat, the deposit on teeth, and ditch water. He discovered the sperm cells in male sperm and believed that they contained a complete embryo. This view was opposed by others.

It was not until the early 19th century that it was first propounded that a sperm cell would have to fuse with an egg cell, before an embryo could be developed.

organism responsible, a small Gram-negative, non-acid-fast bacillus, was isolated from the lung tissues of 4 fatal cases, and was subsequently named *Legionella pneumophila*. It is now clear that the organism is a significant respiratory pathogen, in both the United States and Western Europe.

After an incubation period of 2 to 10 days, the illness begins with symptoms of malaise, headache, and muscular aches and pains, succeeded in a few hours by high fever and shivering. A dry cough, or a cough producing small amounts of bloodstained sputum, begins on the second or third day, with pleurisy (inflammation of the pleura, the membrane covering the lungs) a common occurrence. Watery diarrhea with abdominal distention, occurring in around 50% of the sufferers, may precede the onset of fever. The antibiotic erythromycin is the most effective treatment for the disease.

Legislature, representative assembly empowered to enact, revise, or repeal the laws or statutes of a community. The earliest modern legislatures were the British Parliament and the French States-General, which were forerunners of the contemporary bicameral system of upper and lower houses. In the United States the 2 chambers are the Senate and the House of Representatives, which together are called the Congress. In most bicameral systems both chambers must approve a bill before it becomes law. Under a parliamentary system, like Britain's or Canada's, the prime minister, who heads the government, remains in power only as long as his or her party retains a majority in the main legislative chamber. Under the U.S. system, the president's stay in office is independent of the majority party in the legislature.

Legrand, Michel (1932-), French composer, chiefly famous for his soundtracks for *Lola* (1961), *Les parapluies de Cherbourg* (1964), *The Three Musketeers* (1974) and

L

L

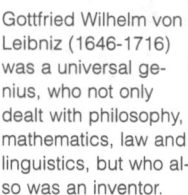

Gottfried Wilhelm von Leibniz (1646-1716) was a universal genius, who not only dealt with philosophy, mathematics, law and linguistics, but who also was an inventor.

Gable and Lombard (1976). He won an Oscar for the theme tune for Demy and Godard's *Vivre sa vie* (1962). He also composed 'The Windmill of Your Mind' from *The Thomas Crown Affair* (1968), *Summer of '42* (1971) and *Yentl* (1983).

Legume, any of nearly 17,000 species of plant of the pulse or pea family (Leguminosae) including peas, beans, lentils, soybeans, and peanuts, fodder plants such as clover, alfalfa, and cowpeas, and hardwoods such as ebony, locust, mahogany, and rosewood. Legumes are widely distributed and variable in growth. The species are distinguished by their flowers, usually bilaterally symmetrical blooms, and by their fruits, seed pods with 2 splitting sides.

Lehár, Franz (1870-1948), Hungarian composer of Viennese-style light opera. His works include the melodious operetta *The Merry Widow* (1905).

Le Havre (pop. 193,000), French seaport on the English Channel and the Seine River. It is a transatlantic trade center that manufactures and imports ships, automobiles, electronics, petroleum products, steel, chemicals, sugar, flour, and beer. A fishing village before 1516, when Francis I began the harbor construction, Le Havre lost 80% of its buildings in World War II. The city was subsequently rebuilt, and the harbor was renovated and expanded in the 1970s.
See also: France.

Lehmann, Lotte (1888-1976), German-born U.S. soprano. She sang with the Vienna State Opera (1914-1938) and in the United States at the Metropolitan (1934-1945). Famous for her portrayal of the Marschallin in *Der Rosenkavalier*, she created roles in other Richard Strauss operas and was a skilled interpreter of lieder.

Lehmbruck, Wilhelm (1881-1919), German sculptor noted for his images of pathos and heroism of spirit. Influenced by Rodin, Brancusi, and Maillol, he depicted his human subjects as ascetic, angular figures, such as *Standing Woman* (1910) and *Kneeling Woman* (1911).

Lehn, Jean-Marie (1939-), French chemist and university professor who was part of a team that won the 1987 Nobel Prize for chemistry. Along with Americans Donald James Cram and Charles John Pedersen, Lehn created an artificial molecule that transmits signals to the human brain.
See also: Chemistry.

Leibniz, Gottfried Wilhelm von (1646-1716), German philosopher, historian, jurist, geologist, and mathematician, codiscoverer of the calculus, and author of the theory of monads. His discovery of the calculus was independent of, though later than, that of Sir Isaac Newton; it is the Leibnizian form that predominates today. He devised a calculating machine and a symbolic mathematical logic. His concept of the universe as a 'preestablished harmony,' his analysis of the problem of evil, his epistemology, logic, and philosophy of nature place him in the foremost rank of philosophers and helped mold the German Enlightenment. His writings include *New Essays on Human Understanding* (1704), *Theodicy* (1710), and *Monadology* (1714).
See also: Calculus.

Leicester (pop. 295,00), important historic and industrial city in central England known for hosiery, shoes and machinery products. It is the site of the University of Leicester, Jewry Wall (built by the Romans in the A.D. 100s), landmark churches and a castle that dates back to the 1100s.
See also: England.

Leicester, Robert Dudley, Earl of (1532-1588), favorite of Elizabeth I of England. Although his political and military performances were poor and his reputation was marred by suspicions of treason, wife-murder and bigamy, he wielded great power and was made a privy councillor (1558) and army commander.

Leiden, or Leyden (pop. 118,000), city in western Netherlands, center for science and light industry, particularly printing and textiles. It is the seat of Leiden University (est. 1575), the oldest in the Netherlands and important for Protestant theology and scientific research. Leiden is noted for its museums, laboratories, and botanical gardens. It was Rembrandt's birthplace and home to some of the English Pilgrims from 1609 until they sailed for the New World in 1620.
See also: Netherlands.

Leipzig (pop. 481,000), city in eastern Germany, former capital of Leipzig district. A major cultural, commercial, and manufacturing center, it has fine medieval and renaissance architecture. Composers J.S. Bach, Felix Mendelssohn, and Robert Schumann were active in the city.
See also: Germany.

Leiris, Michel (1901-1990), French writer and ethnologist. Leiris made his debut in 1925 with *Simulacre*, a collection of surrealist poetry. In 1934 he published *l'Afrique fantôme*, an account of an ethnographer in which he bares his own soul. This process of self-analysis, which characterizes his subsequent works, reaches its zenith in *La règle du jeu*, an autobiography in four volumes, *Biffures* (1948), *Fourbis* (1955), *Fibrilles* (1966) and *Frêle bruit* (1976). In these volumes he describes his own development with the aid of fantastic plays on words and allusions. *Le ruban au cou d'Olympia* (1981) continues the story.

Le Mans (pop. 149,000), city in northwestern France on the Sarthe and Huisne rivers, dating from pre-Roman times. A diocese from the 3rd century, Le Mans was invaded by the English in the Hundred Years War (1337-1453) and was the site of important battles in the French Revolution (1793). It is a marketing and industrial center, and is best known for its 24-hour annual sports car competition on 8 mi (13 km) of winding road.
See also: France.

Lemming, arctic rodent, about 3-6 in (7-15 cm) in length, closely related to the vole. Genera include *Lemmus* and *Dicrostonyx*. Like many small mammals of simple ecological systems, lemmings show periodic fluctuations in numbers. These 3- to 4-year fluctuations result in spectacular mass migrations in search of food. One species, *L. lemmus*, is particularly noted for migrations that lead many members to accidental drowning in the ocean.

Lemon (*Citrus limon*), small evergreen tree that produces sour yellow fruits that are rich in vitamin C. The fruits also contain an oil that is used in cooking and the manufacture of perfume. The United States and Italy are chief producers of lemon fruit.

Lemond, Greg (1961-), American cyclist. Lemond became World Junior Road Race Champion in 1978 and he became the first American World Pro Road Race Champion in 1983. He won the Tour de France in 1986, 1989 and 1990. In 1989, he won the World Pro Road Race Championship for the second time. He focused more on the Tour de France than on the Classics during his career. Lemond's importance has been due to the attention he paid to the materials used in this field of sport. For example: he introduced the triathlon handlebars for time trial bicycles, which had already been used by American triathletes.

Lemur, family of cat-sized primates found only on Madagascar and small islands nearby, related to primitive ancestors of the whole primate group of monkeys and apes. They are nocturnal and strictly arboreal, feeding on insects, fruit, and even small mammals. The family Lemuridae includes 2 subfamilies: the Cheirogaleinae, or mouse lemurs, and the Lemurinae, true lemurs.

Lena River, one of the world's longest rivers and the longest in Russia. Its length is about 2,650 miles (4,265 km). The Lena's source is in the Baykal Range near Lake Baykal, in south-central Siberia. The river flows generally northeast and then north, emptying into the Laptev Sea of the Arctic Ocean. It reaches a width of 81/2 miles (14 km) in some places; its delta is 150 miles (240 km) wide. The Lena has some 1,000 tributaries and drains an area of 936,000 square miles (1,506,000 sq km). Its most important tributaries are the Aldan and the Vilyui.

The Lena is navigable almost from source to mouth, but is frozen in the north except in summer. The region through which it flows is sparsely populated. Yakutsk is the only important town on the Lena. Mining of gold, coal, and iron ore is the chief occupation in the basin.

Lendl, Ivan (1960-), Czechoslovakian-born U.S. tennis player. Known for his power and consistency, Lendl held the number one ranking from 1985 to 1987. His achievements include victories at the United States Open (1985, 1986, 1987), the French Open (1984, 1986, 1987) and the Australian Open (1989, 1990).

Lend-lease, program by which the United States sent aid to the Allies in World War II, during and after neutrality. President Franklin D. Roosevelt initiated the program in 1941 to help countries 'resisting aggression.' Total aid exceeded $50 billion and not only bolstered Allied defense but developed the U.S. war industries and helped mobilize public opinion.
See also: World War II.

Lenglen, Suzanne (1899-1938), French tennis player who dominated women's tennis for years with her powerful and aggressive style. She reigned as the French singles, ladies doubles and mixed doubles champion in 1920-1923, 1925 and 1926. At the 1920 Summer Olympics in Antwerp she won two gold medals and a silver medal. In 1926 she started playing professionally for Cash and Carry Pyle; she later founded a tennis school in Paris.

Lenin, V.I. (1870-1924), Russian revolutionary, founder of the Bolshevik (later Communist) Party, leader of the Bolshevik Revolution of 1917, and founder of the Soviet state. Born Vladimir Ilyich Ulyanov, Lenin became a revolutionary after his older brother was executed (1887) on charges of plotting to assassinate the tsar. By then a follower of the ideas of Karl Marx, Lenin was arrested and exiled to Siberia in 1895. In 1900 he and his wife, Nadezhda Krupskaya, went into exile in western Europe. In 1902 he published his famous pamphlet *What is to*

Lenin on the balcony of the building of the Moscow Soviet, October 16, 1919.

Be Done? arguing that only a highly disciplined party of revolutionaries could cause the overthrow of the tsar. In 1903 the Russian Social Democratic Workers Party, meeting in London, split over this and related issues. Lenin's supporters became known as the Bolsheviks (from the Russian word for 'majority'); his opponents were called Mensheviks (from 'minority'). Lenin and his fellow Marxists returned briefly to Russia during the unsuccessful revolution of 1905. In 1907 he went into exile again. When the tsar was overthrown by the Feb. 1917 revolution, in the midst of World War I, Lenin returned to Russia. Reacting against the rush of Socialist parties in Europe to support their own governments in World War I, he issued a call for the formation of a new revolutionary international organization. In Oct. 1917 the Bolshevik Party, under the leadership of Lenin and Leon Trotsky, seized power in Russia at the head of a popular insurrection, and Lenin became the head of the new, Soviet state. The revolutionary organization he had called for came into being as well, as the Communist International.Lenin led the revolutionary state for its first 6 years, a period that saw the civil war and the nationalization of industry. With the end of the civil war in 1921 he turned to a more liberal economic approach, known as the New Economic Policy. This allowed some development of private enterprises, especially in the countryside. At the same time, however, his government banned all opposition parties. Considerable

state resources were devoted to the Communist International and to attempts to foster other revolutions in other countries, especially in Europe. In the late months of 1923 Lenin began warning about the rising bureaucratization of the state and about the growing ambition of Stalin. In Jan. 1924, however, before any of those warnings would be acted on, he died from a series of strokes. Lenin had a greater influence on communism than anyone else except Karl Marx. In fact, after his death the theory of communism came to be called Marxist-Leninism. His major contribution to the political doctrine was his concept of the revolutionary party, and he was the first to implement that concept successfully. In that sense he was one of history's greatest revolutionaries and one of the most influential political leaders of the 20th century.

Leningrad (pop. 5,0 million), second largest city and chief port of the RF, on the Gulf of Finland, and former Russian capital (as St. Petersburg, 1712-1914, and Petrograd, 1914-1924). It was founded in 1703 by Tsar Peter I (Peter the Great). Linked by its port with western Europe, it rapidly became a cultural and commercial center. Industrial expansion during the 19th century was followed by a temporary decline during World War I and the Russian Revolution. The city was renamed for V.I. Lenin in 1924. Leningrad endured great destruction and loss of life in the German siege

The ring-tailed lemur of the montane regions of Madagascar, *Lemur catta*, measures about 4.10 ft (1.25 m, including the tail) in length.

(1941-1944) during World War II. Today industries include heavy machinery manufacturing, shipbuilding, chemicals, and textiles. The city is home to the University of Leningrad, one of Russia's largest universities; the Hermitage, a world-renowned museum, and the Conservatory of Music, whose graduates include the composers Sergei Prokofiev and Peter Ilich Tchaikovsky. Leningrad has figured in the writings of Russian authors A. Pushkin and F. Dostoevsky. In 1990 the name was reverted back to St. Petersburg.
See also: Union of Soviet Socialist Republics.

A group of statues in front of the Great Palace in Petrodvorets, formerly known as Peterhof. This is a suburb to the west of Leningrad, that sprang up around the palace, which was completed in 1721 for Tzar Peter I the Great (1672-1725). In World War II, the palace was badly damaged, but it has been restored to its former splendour.

Lennon, John (1940-1980), rock musician, a founding member of the Beatles. Along

with Paul McCartney he wrote most of the Beatles' music, including 'Help' (1965), 'Strawberry fields' (1966) and 'A Day in the Life' (1967). As a social critic he wrote 'Give Peace a Chance' (1969) and 'Imagine' (1971). Lennon married Yoko Ono in 1969 and continued to compose and sing after the Beatles disbanded (1970). He was shot to death on Dec. 8, 1980 by Mark David Chapman.
See also: Beatles.

Lenoir, Jean Joseph Étienne (1822-1900), French inventor. He built the first practical internal combustion engine for use in industrial machinery and one of the first gas-powered automobiles (1862). He also invented a railroad brake (1855) and a motorboat (1886).
See also: Internal combustion engine.

Le Nôtre, André (1613-1700), French landscape architect. Under Louis XIV, his strictly geometrical creations, including the gardens of Versailles and the Tuileries, featured splendid vistas and radiating paths.
See also: Architecture.

Lens, transparent substance, usually glass, having 2 opposite surfaces, either both curved or one curved and one straight, used for refraction, (changing the direction of light rays). Lenses are used in eyeglasses to correct errors of vision, in cameras to focus images on film, and in microscopes and telescopes to magnify images. The term is also used for the part of the eye that focuses light rays on the retina.

Lent (from Old English *lencten*, 'spring'), period of 40 days dedicated by Christians to penitential prayer and fasting as a preparation for Easter. In the West it begins on Ash Wednesday.

See also: Christianity; Easter.

Lentil (*Lens culinaris*), leguminous plant grown in warm parts of the Old World. It was one of the first cultivated crops. The seeds, which are rich in proteins, are cooked as porridge or soup. The mess of potage for which Esau sold his birthright (Genesis 25-28) was made from lentils.

Lenya, Lotte (1900-1981), Austrian-born U.S. singer and actress. She performed on the stage in Berlin (1920-1933), notably in *The Three-Penny Opera* (1928), composed by her husband, Kurt Weill, in collaboration with Brecht. She sang and acted in several Weill works, including *Mahogonny* and *Cabaret*, in the United States after 1933.

Leo, name of 13 popes. **Saint Leo I** (c. 400-461), an Italian, r. 440-461. Called 'the Great,' he suppressed heresy and established his authority in both the West and East. He persuaded the barbarian leaders Attila (in 452) and Genseric (in 455) not to destroy Rome. **Saint Leo III** (d. 816), a Roman, r. 795-816. He crowned Charlemagne 'Emperor of the Romans' in Rome on Christmas Day, 800, thus allying church and state. **Saint Leo IX** (Bruno of Egisheim; 1002-1054),a German, r. 1049-1054. He fought against simony (the selling of church offices) and vigorously enjoined clerical celibacy. The Great Schism between the Western and Eastern churches began in his reign. **Leo X** (Giovanni de Medici; 1475-1521), a Florentine, r. 1513-1521. He made Rome a center of the arts and literature and raised money for rebuilding St. Peter's by the sale of indulgences-a practice attacked by Martin Luther at the start of the Reformation. **Leo XIII** (Gioacchino Pecci; 1810-1903), an Italian, r. 1878-1903. He worked to reconcile Roman Catholicism

with science and liberalism and generally applied Christian principles to the religious and social questions of his time. His *Rerum Novarum* (1891), an encyclical (letter to the Roman Catholic Church) on the condition of the working classes, strengthened Roman Catholicism's links with the working-class movement and helped counter anticlericalism at home and abroad.

León, medieval kingdom of northwestern Spain, including the provinces of León, Salamanca, and Zamora. Forged in the 10th century by the rulers of Austria, the kingdom spearheaded the Christian reconquest of Spain from the Moors. It was permanently joined to Castile in 1230.

Leonard, Sugar Ray (Ray Charles Leonard; 1956-), U.S. boxer. He was the Olympic gold medalist in the light welterweight class (Summer Games, 1976), and won the World Boxing Council (WBC) welterweight title (1979) and World Boxing Association (WBA) junior middleweight title (1981). After suffering a detached retina Leonard retired (1982) but staged a comeback, capturing the WBC middleweight title (1987) and WBC super middleweight and light heavyweight titles (1988). He retired again in 1991 and staged an unsuccessful comeback in 1997.

Leonardo da Vinci *See:* Da Vinci, Leonardo.

Leoncavallo, Ruggiero (1858-1919), Italian opera composer. *I Pagliacci* (The Clowns, 1892), a classic *verismo* (realistic) opera, is the only one of his works that is still widely known.
See also: Opera.

Leonidas I (d.480 B.C.), king of Sparta. Leonidas, with 300 Spartans and about 1,000 other Greeks, died heroically defending the pass of Thermopylae against the huge invading Persian army of Xerxes.
See also: Sparta; Thermopylae.

Leopard (*Panthera pardus*), big cat similar to the jaguar, with a yellow coat marked with black rosettes, or with black fur (the panther). Found in a variety of habitats across Africa and Asia, it is agile and relies when hunting on its power to spring quickly. The leopard is known for its habit of dragging its kill up into a tree out of the reach of jackals and hyenas. The kill may weigh more than the leopard itself.

Leopard cat *See:* Ocelot.

Leopardi, Giacomo (1798-1837), Italian poet and philosopher, foremost writer of his time. Acutely unhappy, he expressed himself most fully in his brilliant, supple, lyric poetry: *Songs* (1836). *Moral Essays* (1827) reveals his bleak philosophy.
See also: Philosophy.

Leopold I (1790-1865), reigned from 1831 to 1865. He was elected the first king of independent Belgium after its separation from Holland. Leopold was the fourth son of a German duke, Francis of Saxe-Coburg-

Lenses consist of pieces of glass, bounded by a spherical surface on one or both sides.
A. Convex lens: parallel rays are converged to a focal point (F) by a convex (positive) lens.
B. Concave lens: parallel rays are diverged by a concave (negative) lens, so as to appear to originate at a negative focal point (F).
Lenses are used to correct defects in vision. For normal vision, an image must be formed on the retina. In long sight (1), the image is focused behind the retina. A convex lens (2) will converge the light, thus projecting the image on the retina. In short sight (3), the image is formed in front of the retina. A concave lens (4) can correct this.

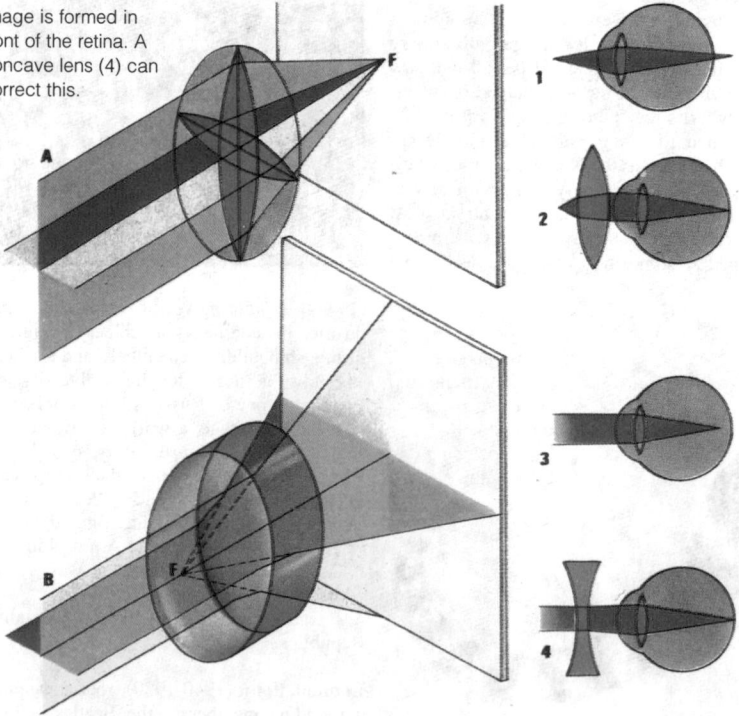

The leopard, *P. pardus*, is rarely seen, even by its prospective victims, because of its silent, wary habits. The black panther (left) is actually a leopard with black coat pigmentation.

Saalfeld. He was an uncle of Queen Victoria, and was closely related to many other members of European royal families. His first wife was a daughter of George IV of England. She died in 1817, and in 1832 he married Princess Louise, daughter of Louis Phillipe of France. Leopold served in the Russian army during the Napoleonic Wars and lived in England, 1817-1830. A shrewd diplomat, Leopold won the support of all the great powers by promising that Belgium would remain 'perpetually neutral'.

Leopold II (1835-1909), reigned from 1865 to 1909. He was the son of Leopold I. During the Franco-Prussian War, 1870-1871, Leopold preserved Belgium's neutrality despite pressure by both warring nations. With the help of the explorer Henry M. Stanley, Leopold in 1885 gained personal sovereignty over the Congo (now Zaire) and amassed a fortune. World criticism of the brutal exploitation of natives by Leopold's agents caused him to turn the region over to the Belgian government in 1908.

Leopold III (1901-1983), reigned during 1934-1944 and 1950-1951. He was the son of Albert I and the grandnephew of Leopold II. In World War II Leopold surrendered Belgium to the Germans (May, 1940) after 18 days of fighting. Although the military situation was hopeless, he was severely criticized for this action, which was against the wishes of the Belgian cabinet. During the war Leopold chose to remain in Belgium rather than go into exile, although he was interned by the Germans and did not actively reign. He was taken to Germany as a prisoner in 1944. After the war he was exiled by the Belgian parliament and lived in Switzerland until 1950, when a plebiscite approved this return to the throne. Leopold's return caused rioting in many parts of Belgium, leading him to abdicate in favor of his son, Baoudouin.

Léopoldville *See:* Kinshasa.

Le Pen, Jean-Marie (1928-), French politician. Le Pen, a lawyer, has been the leader of the ultra right-wing Front National (FN) since 1972. In the 1980s this controversial political party, with its extremely nationalist policy, gained increasing support among the French population, becoming one of the largest parties. Le Pen also won a seat in the European Parliament in 1984. In the first round of the 1995 presidential elections he won 15% of the votes, although in the end Chirac was elected president.
In 2002, he ended second in the first round of the presidential elections. In the second round Le Pen was defeated by the current president Chirac, who had an overwhelming victory by gaining over 82% of the votes.

Lepidoptera *See:* Butterfly; Moth.

Leprosy, or Hansen's disease, chronic infectious disease caused by *Mycobacterium leprae* and chiefly found in tropical zones. It leads to skin nodules with loss of pigmentation, mucous membrane lesions in nose and pharynx, and neuritis with nerve thickening, loss of pain sensation, and patchy weakness, often involving face and hand muscles. The type of disease caused depends on the number of bacteria encountered and basic resistance to the disease. Treatment is with sulfones.

Lepton, one of the 4 classes of elementary particles (the others are bosons, measons, and baryons). Leptons are larger than the massless bosons, but smaller than mesons and baryons. There are a total of 12 particles in the lepton class, of which the electron is probably the most familiar. These 12 come in pairs, one of each pair being positively charged, the other being negatively charged. (The positron is the positively charged mate of the electron, which is negative.)
See also: Particle physics.

Lermontov, Mikhail Yurievich (1814-1841), a Russian poet and novelist. Lermontov, influenced by Pushkin and Byron, was a leading Russian Romanticist. His writing reflects his life as a tormented outsider and portrays brooding idealists struggling against fate. He became famous with the poem ''The Death of a Poet' (1837), which criticized the government and resulted in his exile for a year in the Caucasus. The poems 'Demon' (1829), 'Angel' (1831), and 'The Novice' (1840) exemplify his Romantic style. His novel *A Hero of Our Time* (1840) influenced Russian literature by using psychological rather than chronological plot development. Lermontov was born in Moscow. He died in a duel.

Lerner, Alan Jay (1918-1986), U.S. lyricist and dramatist. Along with the composer Frederick Loewe, he created such musical comedies as *My Fair Lady*, *Brigadoon*, *Paint Your Wagon*, and *Camelot*. Lerner and Loewe won an Academy Award for the title song in *Gigi*. Lerner himself won Academy Awards for the screenplays of *Gigi* and *An American in Paris*.

Le Sage, Alain René (1668-1747), French novelist and dramatist. His picaresque masterpiece *Gil Blas* (1715-1735), a witty satirical account of French society, influenced the development of the realistic novel in France. He also wrote the comedy *Turcaret* (1709).

Lesbos, Greek island in the Aegean Sea, near Turkey. Also known as Mitilini, it spans about 630 square miles (1,630 sq km) and produces olives, wheat, wine, grapes, and tobacco. A cultured center of ancient Greece, Lesbos was the home of Sappho, Aristotle, and Epicurus.
See also: Greece.

Lesch-Nyhan syndrome, hereditary metabolic disorder, affecting the central nervous system. First described in 1964 by William Nyhan and Michael Lesch, it is caused by a defective enzyme hypoxanthine-quinine-phosphoribasyl-transferase, which is normally very active in brain cells. It is characterized by mental retardation, aggressive behavior and a tendency to inflict self injury. The syndrome is transmitted by a recessive sex-linked gene and primarily affects males. There is no cure or effective treatment.

Lesotho

Capital:	Maseru
Area:	11,720 sq mi (30,355 sq km)
Population:	2,208,000
Language:	Sesotho, English
Government:	Constitutional monarchy
Independent:	1966
Head of gov.:	Prime minister
Per capita:	US$ 2,450
Monetary unit:	1 Loti = 100 lisente

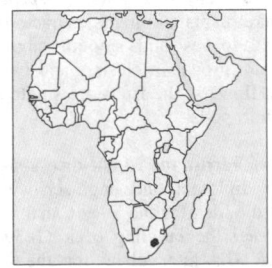

L

85% of Lesotho consists of pasture-land, which is used for extensive cattle breeding. Wool and mohair (from the angora-goat) are important export products.

L

Playwright Gotthold Ephraim Lessing (1729-1781), painted by Swiss painter Anton Graff (1736-1813). Lessing was a representative of the German Enlightenment, a forerunner of the Sturm und Drang period.

Lesotho (formerly Basutoland), landlocked kingdom surrounded by, and economically dependent on, the Republic of South Africa.
Land and climate. Part of the great plateau of South Africa, Lesotho lies mainly between 8,000 ft (2,439 m) and 11,000 ft (3,353 m). In the east and the north is the Drakensberg mountain range. The chief rivers are the Orange River and its tributaries. Annual rainfall averages less than 30 in (76 cm), and temperatures vary seasonally from 93°F (34°C) to 30°F (-1°C). Sparsely forested, Lesotho is mainly dry grassland.
People and economy. The Sotho, who comprise 99% of the population, are chiefly rural. Education is mainly in the hands of missionaries. The literacy rate is about 80%, and around 90% of the people are Christians. An agricultural country, Lesotho is heavily dependent on livestock and food crops such as wheat and maize. Poor farming techniques have resulted in a shortage of good land. Although Lesotho was opposed to apartheid, it depended heavily upon South Africa for trade and employment.
History. The nation was established c.1829 by Chief Moshoeshoe I, who secured British protection from Boer encroachment. As Basutoland, it was under British rule from 1884, gaining independence in 1966. The first king was Moshoeshoe II. A military junta seized power in 1986 and deposed the king in 1990. His eldest son succeeded to the throne as Letsie III. In 1995 Letsie abdicated and Moshoeshoe was reinstated as king. He died in an automobile accident in 1996 and was succeeded by Letsie.
The Lesotho Congress for Democracy (LCD) won the 1998 elections. Bethuel Pakalitha Mosoli became Prime Minister. The following elections in 2002 were also won by the LCD.

Lespedeza, any of a genus (*Lespedeza*) of shrublike plants and herbs characterized by 3-parted leaves and smooth edges. The plants are grown in clusters and have pea-shaped flowers; the fruits are single seeded with short pods.

Lesseps, Ferdinand Marie de (1805-1895), French diplomat and engineer who conceived the idea for the Suez Canal. Lesseps supervised the building of it (1859-1869) himself. His later plans for the Panama Canal ended in bankruptcy (1888) and a conviction for misappropriation of monies. *See also:* Suez Canal.

Lessing, Doris (1919-), British novelist, raised in Southern Rhodesia (now Zimbabwe), who has dealt perceptively with the struggles of intellectual women for political, sexual, and artistic integrity. Her major works include *The Golden Notebook* (1962), *The Four-Gated City* (1969, part of the *Children of Violence* series), *The Sirian Experiments* (1981), and *The Fifth Child* (1988). *Under My Skin* (1994) was part one of her autobiography. Part two, *Walking in the Shade*, was published in 1997. Other works are *Ben, in the World* (2000), and *The Sweetest Dream* (2001).

Lessing, Gotthold Ephraim (1729-1781), German playwright, critic, and philosopher. He rejected French classicism and pioneered German bourgeois tragedy with *Miss Sara Sampson* (1755). He also wrote the influential comedy *Minna von Barnhelm* (1763), the prose tragedy *Emilia Galotti* (1772), and the dramatic poem *Nathan the Wise* (1779). His treatise *Laokoön* (1766) critically contrasted the natures of poetry and painting.

Lethe (Greek, 'forgetfulness'), in Greek mythology, river in Hades. When the souls of the dead drank from Lethe, they forgot their lives on earth.

Lettuce, popular garden plant (genus *Lactuca*) of the composite family. Cultivated for salad since ancient times, lettuce is harvested before its flower stem shoots up to bear its small yellow flowers. There are 3 main types: leaf lettuce has a loose crown of leaves; head lettuce has compact leaves; romaine (or Cos), with elongated leaves, is the most resistant to heat.

Leucippus (c.400 B.C.), Greek philosopher who developed the theory of atomism (from Greek *atomos*, 'uncuttable'). He was the first to state that matter consists of small, constantly moving particles, or atoms. Although little is known about Leucippus's life, *The Great World System* and *On The Mind* are believed to have been written by him.

Leukemia, common name for any of various cancerous diseases of the blood or bone marrow, characterized by malignant proliferation of white blood cells. It may be divided into acute and chronic forms. In acute forms, progression is rapid, with patients suffering anemia, bruising, and infection. Chronic forms may have milder systemic symptoms, including susceptibility to infection and enlarged lymph nodes. Chemotherapy and antibiotics have greatly improved survival prospects.
See also: Cancer.

Le Vau, Louis (also: Levau or Leveau; 1612-1670), French baroque architect. He designed e.g. Vaux-le-Vicomte castle near Fontainebleau (1655-1661); worked on the Louvre and the Tuileries. He played a key role in the construction of the Versailles palace (from 1661) and designed, among other things, its *Escalier des ambassadeurs* (1669).

Lever, simplest type of machine, consisting of a rigid beam supported at a stationary point (the fulcrum) so that a force applied to one point of the beam can shift a load at another point. There are 3 classes of lever: those with the fulcrum between the effort and the load; those with the load between the fulcrum and the effort; and those with the effort between the fulcrum and the load.

Levi, Primo (1919-1987), Italian-Jewish prose writer, essayist and poet. In 1943 he joined the resistance against German occupation, although his group was arrested fairly quickly. In 1944 he was deported to Auschwitz, where his labors included that of a chemist (his actual profession). He wrote of his experiences in a number of works, including *Se questo è un uomo* (If This Is a Man; 1947), *La tregua* (The Truce; 1963), and *Il sistema periodico* (The Periodical Table; 1975), in which he describes the profession of chemist, and puts chemistry in both a metaphorical role and a structuring role in relation to the narration. Levi also published poetry (e.g. *Ad ora incerta* [1984]) and stories which can be regarded as fantasy (e.g. *Storie naturali*, [The Sixth Day and Other Tales; 1966]). In 1987 he committed suicide.

Levi-Montalcini, Rita (1909-), U.S. scientist, shared the Nobel Prize for physiology or medicine (1986) with Stanley Cohen for their discovery (1952-53) of a natural substance that stimulates the growth of nerve cells.

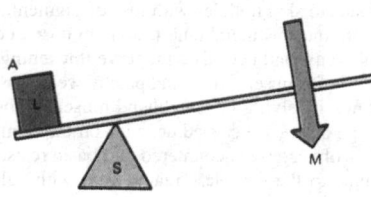

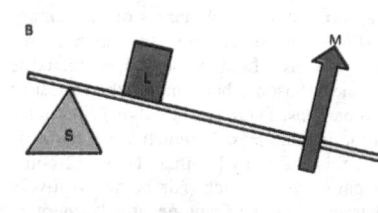

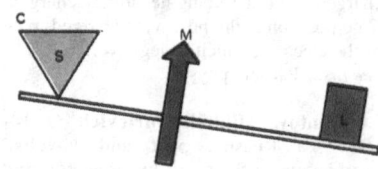

Levers may be divided into three classes, depending on the application of the effort, in relation to the fulcrum and the load. A. The effort (M) is applied opposite to the fulcrum (S) and the load (L). B. The load (L) is between the fulcrum (S) and the applied effort (M). C. The effort (M) is applied between the load (L) and the fulcrum (S).

Levine, James (1943-), U.S. pianist and conductor. In 1964-1970 he was an apprentice conductor of the Cleveland Symphony Orchestra under George Szell and then assistant conductor. In 1972 he became principal conductor at the Metropolitan Opera, where he was appointed music director in 1975 and artistic director in 1983. In 2001, he was appointed Chief Conductor of the Boston Symphony Orchestra. His 5-year contract takes effect in 2004.

Lévi-Strauss, Claude (1908-1990), Belgian-born French anthropologist, best known as the founder of structuralism, an analytical method whereby different cultural patterns are compared so as to examine the way they order the elements of their environment into systems. His writings include *Structural Anthropology* (1958), *The Savage Mind* (1962), and *The View from Afar* (1985).

Levites, in ancient Israel, tribe descended from Levi, son of Jacob. As priestly auxiliaries, they were assigned responsibility for the care of the Ark and the Sanctuary; in Jerusalem they had hereditary duties at the Temple.

Leviticus, book of the Old Testament, third of the 5 books of the Pentateuch, traditionally ascribed to Moses. It is a collection of liturgical and ceremonial laws.

Lewis, C(live) S(taples) (1898-1963), British author, literary scholar, and defender of Christianity. Of more than 40 books his best-known is *The Screwtape Letters* (1942), a diabolical view of humanity. *The Allegory of Love* (1936), his major critical work, studies love in medieval literature. He also wrote a science-fiction trilogy and the *Narnia* fantasies.

Lewis, Frederick Carlton (Carl) (1961-), American athlete. During the Athletic World Championships in 1983, he won gold medals in the 100 m, the long jump and the 4x100 m relay. In 1991, he won the long jump and the 100 m again. At the Olympics in Los Angeles (1984), he won gold in the 100 m, the 200 m, the 4x100 m relay and the long jump. In Seoul (1988), he won the long jump and the 100 m and in Barcelona (1992) and Atlanta (1996), he again won the long jump. At the end of 1999, the International Amateur Athletics Federation declared Lewis Best Male Athlete of the 20th century.

Lewis, Jerry (Joseph Levitch; 1926-), American actor and director. From 1946 to 1956, he featured in many comedies, such as *At War with the Army* (1950), *Sailor Beware* (1951), *Living it Up* (1954) and *Artists and Models* (1955). *The Nutty Professor* (1963) is considered to be his best film. In Scorcese's *King of Comedy* (1983), he made a successful comeback. In 1998, he received a Life Achievement Award for his comedies.

Lewis and Clark expedition, first overland expedition to the northwest Pacific coast (1804-1806), under the command of Meriwether Lewis (1774-1809) and William Clark (1770-1838), with Sacagawea, the Native American wife of an expedition member, acting as interpreter and guide. Setting out from St. Louis, the expedition explored the Louisiana Purchase and crossed the Rockies, reaching the Pacific Ocean at the mouth of the Columbia River. It caught the popular imagination and played a major part in establishing the view that it was the 'Manifest Destiny' of the U.S. to expand to the Pacific Ocean.
See also: Clark, William.

Lewis, Sinclair (1885-1951), U.S. novelist, best known for 5 novels presenting a devastatingly critical view of life in the Middle West. *Main Street* (1920) was his first major success. *Babbitt* (1922), a portrait of a provincial small businessman, is perhaps his best-known book. He refused a Pulitzer Prize for *Arrowsmith* (1925), a satirical look at the medical profession. *Elmer Gantry* (1927) and *Dodsworth* (1929) followed. In 1930 he became the first American to win the Nobel Prize in literature.

Lewis, Wyndham (1882-1957), controversial English painter, critic, and writer, the founder of the vorticism movement, which simplified forms into machinelike angularity. He is best known for his savage satirical novel, *The Apes of God* (1930).

LeWitt, Sol (1928-), American visual artist, of the minimal school of art. His sculptures are characterized by simple, geometric shapes and open compositions, symbolizing the relationship between space and mass. His drawings, which are sometimes regarded as conceptual, consist of square patterns made up from combinations of horizontal, vertical and diagonal lines. He later also created monumental murals in lined patterns, which he made in collaboration with others.

Lexington, Battle of *See:* Revolutionary War in America.

Leyden *See:* Leiden.

Leyden, Lucas van (1494?-1533), a Dutch painter and engraver. One of the master engravers of the 16th century, he was known for his detailed, sensitive drawings and skillful technique. He studied in his native Leiden with his father, Huig Jacobsz (an engraver), and with Cornelis Engelbrechtsen. Lucas was a child prodigy, producing the notable copperplate *Ecce Homo* while still in his early teens. While visiting Antwerp in 1521, he met Albrecht Dürer and was influenced by him.

Leyden jar, simplest and earliest form of capacitor, a device for storing electric charge, developed at the University of Leiden, Holland, in the 18th century. It consists of a glass jar coated inside and out with metal foil, and a conducting rod that passes through the jar's insulated stopper to connect with the inner foil. The jar is usually charged from an electrostatic generator. The device is now little used outside the classroom.

Leyte (pop. 1.69 mln), island in the Phi-

The Potala Palace (early 17th century) in Lhasa was built against the Red Hill. The building impresses by the way in which the differences in level have been exploited.

lippines, with a surface area of 2,786 sq mi (7,213 sq km). The capital is Tacloban. The island is mountainous, and products include sugarcane, rice, hemp and coconut palm trees. Fishing. There are facilities for refining manganese. In 1521 the Portuguese explorer Magellan was the first European to land here. The island was invaded by American forces in October 1944, and two Japanese interceptor fleets were destroyed in the Battle of Leyte Gulf.

Lezama Lima, José (1912-1976), Cuban poet and novelist. He was co-founder of the periodical *Orígenes* (1944-1957), the mouthpiece for a group of experimental Roman Catholic poets. Collections of his poems include *Muerte de narciso* (1937)and *Dador* (1960). His poems are not easily accessible as the poet uses very personal associations and images. His essays include *La expresión americana* (1957), and *Las eras imaginarias* (1971). He also wrote a novel, *Paradiso* (1966); fragments of a second novel, *Fronesis*, were published, e.g. in *Narrativa cubana de la revolución* (collected by J.M. Caballero Bonald; 1969).

Lhasa (pop. 116,000), capital and largest city of the Tibet Autonomous Region of China. Once known as the Forbidden City, Lhasa was the center of Tibetan Buddhism until the Chinese invasion of 1951. The Potala, former palace of the Dalai Lama, head of Tibetan Buddhism and now in exile, is in the city.
See also: Tibet.

Lhasa apso, small dog, 10 in (25 cm) high, that originated in Tibet as a watchdog. The Lhasa apso is covered with long hair that falls over its face, and its thick tail curls over its back.

Liana, any climbing vine with roots in the ground, most often found in tropical forests. Lianas wind around trees or other plants for support. Kudzu, grapevines, and ivy are lianas.

Libel, false and malicious statement in permanent form, such as in writing or on film,

L

tending to injure the reputation of a living person, or blacken the memory of the dead. The truth of the statement creates a valid defense in an action for libel.

Liberalism, political philosophy that stresses individual liberty and equality of opportunity. Classical liberalism developed in Europe in the 18th century as part of a rationalist critique of traditional institutions and a distrust of state power. Since the 1930s, modern liberalism has advocated state intervention in the economy but is still concerned with social issues such as civil rights and equality of opportunity.

Liberal Party, British political party, powerful from about 1832 to 1922. Originating in the Whig party, the Liberals were backed by the industrial owners and were associated with such policies as free trade, laissez-faire economics, and religious liberty, while initially opposing most social legislation. The Liberal party enjoyed its golden age under the prime ministers Gladstone, Asquith, and Lloyd George. In the 1920s it was supplanted by the Labour party as the chief opposition to the Conservative party, and by the 1930s it became a relatively small third party attracting about 10% of the vote nationally. In 1981 the party formed an alliance with the new Social Democratic party, but its strength has not substantially increased.

Liberia

Capital:	Monrovia
Area:	37,743 sq mi
	(111,370 sq km)
Population:	3,288,000
Language:	English
Government:	Presidential republic
Independent:	1847
Head of gov.:	President
Per capita:	less than US$ 1,100
Monetary unit:	1 Liberian dollar = 100 cents

Liberia, independent republic on the west coast of Africa, with a land area of 43,000 sq miles (97,754 sq km). It has a coastline of over 300 mi (483 km) on the Atlantic Ocean. Liberia is the oldest republic in Africa. It originated from the efforts of American phi-

Workers' cottages on the Firestone Rubber plantation. Rubber is the chief agricultural product of Liberia.

lanthropists who in 1822 organized the first settlement of freed American black slaves near the place where the capital, Monrovia, now stands. In 1847 Liberia became an independent republic modeled on the United States.

Land and climate. The terrain varies from a sandy coastal plain cut by lagoons to densely forested mountains in the north. The central part consists mainly of plateau, a rolling plain broken by many hills that are encircled by swamps. Edged in places by steep escarpments above the coastal plain, the plateau ranges in height from 600 ft (183 m) to 1,500 ft (457 m) above sea level. The Nimba Mountains in the northeast rise to 4,528 ft (1,380 m). Several rivers flow from the mountains and plateau into the Atlantic, the most important being the St. Paul, with Monrovia at its mouth.

Liberia is hot and humid, with an average temperature of 80°F (26°C). The rainy season lasts from Apr. to Oct., when the region receives about 150 in (381 cm) of rain, and inland areas about 100 in (254 cm). The *harmattan*, a hot, dry wind from the Sahara, often blows during the dry season. About half the land is covered by dense tropical rain forests. Wildlife includes chimpanzees, monkeys, zebras, antelopes, the rare pygmy hippopotamus, and birds and reptiles. Among Liberia's mineral resources are rich deposits of iron ore, some gold, and diamonds.

People. Over 90% of the people are indigenous Africans belonging to more than 26 tribal groups. The leading citizens are the descendants of freed American slaves, known as Americo-Liberians. There are some Lebanese traders, and Europeans who manage the industries. Most of the tribal peoples are subsistence farmers. The Mandingos practice Islam, but most other tribal groups are christians or animists. The Americo-Liberians, who dominate the government, education, and the professions, are mainly Christians and live in the urban coastal areas.

Although English is the official language, most of the people speak one of many African languages or dialects. The education system includes public, mission, and tribal schools, but about 60% of the population is illiterate. Liberia has one university. There are few urban areas, except along the coast. The capital, largest city, and chief port is

Monrovia. Eight smaller ports include Marshall, Robertsport, Buchanan, Greenville, and Harper.

Economy. The Liberian economy is underdeveloped. Its main industries are rubber plantations, established in the 1920s, and the mining of iron ore, dating from the 1950s; both have been run and maintained by U.S. firms. Liberia also exports several crops, including coffee, sugarcane, bananas, and cocoa. Foreign exchange is earned by registering foreign ships under lax rules (almost 2000 ships, mainly oil tankers).

History. The first repatriated slaves arrived from the United States in 1822 under the sponsorship of the American Colonization Society. The settlement was named Monrovia in honor of U.S. President James Monroe. In 1847 the settlers declared their independence. Liberia gradually extended its territory by signing treaties with local chiefs, or by buying or claiming land. Inequities in the wealth and political power have caused antagonisms between Americo-Liberians and Indigenous Africans, and resulted in the outbreak of a civil war in 1989. The war, in which about 150,000 people were killed, ended when a peace agreement was signed in Ajuba (1996).

Charles Taylor, an American Liberian, has been harshly governing the country since 1997. The UN Security Council imposed a weapon embargo in 2001, because Taylor had been trading weapons for diamonds from Sierra Leone. The instability of the country poses a threat to neighboring countries.

Li Bo, Li Po, or Li Bai (A.D. 701-762), considered one of China's foremost poets. He is admired for his descriptions of nature and for his poems on ethics and morality.

Library, collection of books, manuscripts, films, musical recordings, and other materials arranged in convenient order for use but not for sale. The earliest libraries were kept by the ancient peoples of Mesopotamia; inscribed clay tablets have been found going back to about 3500 B.C. The first public library in Greece was established in 330 B.C. The most famous library of the ancient world was begun at Alexandria, in Egypt, by Ptolemy I Soter (305-283 B.C.). The Roman Empire acquired many libraries through their conquests of Greece, Asia Minor, and Syria (1st-2nd century B.C.). During the Middle Ages the Church kept the library tradition alive in Europe. The Renaissance saw the formation of many new libraries, such as the Vatican Library (1447), the oldest public library in Europe. The growth of libraries was further stimulated by the invention of printing in the 15th century. The Bodleian Library, Oxford, England, dates from 1602. It was the 18th century that saw the formation of many of the great national libraries: the British Museum Library (1753), Italy's National Central Library at Florence (1741), and Russia's Saltykov-Shchedrin Library in Saint Petersburg. In the 20th century the public library system has been extended and consolidated and has at its disposal such technological innovations as microfilm, photocopier, and computer data banks.

Library of Congress, U.S. national library located east of the Capitol in Washington, D.C. Originally established by Congress in 1800, it now contains more than 80 million items-including books, pamphlets, maps, photographs, and the like-making it one of the world's largest research libraries. The library's catalog, the National Union Catalog, lists books in libraries all over the United States and Canada.
See also: Library.

Libreville (pop. 366,000), the capital of Gabon. It is situated at the mouth of the Gabon River on the Gulf of Guinea on the west-central coast of Africa. Wood and cacao are shipped from here. Libreville was founded in 1849.

Libya

Capital:	Tripoli
Area:	685,524 sq mi
	(1,775,500 sq km)
Population:	5,369,000
Language:	Arabic
Government:	Islamic-socialist people's
	republic
Independent:	1951
Head of gov.:	President
Per capita:	US$ 7,600
Monetary unit:	1 Libyan dinar
	= 1,000 dirham

Libya, independent Arab republic in North Africa, consisting of 10 administrative divisions that occupy an area of 685,524 sq mi (1,775,500 sq km). Less than 10% of Libya's land is fertile, most of the remainder being part of the Sahara Desert. The exploitation of oil resources (discovered in the late 1950s) provides the wealth that is transforming Libya from a poor peasant nation into an educated and affluent one.
Land and climate. Most of Libya is covered by the shifting sands of the Sahara,though the fertile strip along the Mediterranean coast, with an average rainfall of 10 in (15 cm) and mild winters, supports some cultivation. Even on the coast the rainfall fails about 2 years in every 10. Inland extreme desert conditions exist, and many areas do not see rain for several years at a time. The range of temperature is very wide, from over 120°F (48°C) in summer, to frost level in winter. Suffocating dry desert winds, the *quibli*, bring quantities of dust that destroy much vegetation in the interior.
Most of the country's inhabitants live within 75 mi (120 km) of the Mediterranean coast. In this belt enough rain falls to grow citrus fruit, barley, wheat, dates, olives, and almonds. Further inland is a grazing area in which only scrub or tough esparto grasses can grow.
In the central part of the Sahara region, there are massifs as high as 2,000 ft (610 m) but no real mountains exist in the country other than the low Tibesti Mountains on the southern border, with altitudes of 4,000 ft (1,220 m) or more. The highest point in Libya is Bette Peak in the south, at 7,500 ft (2,286 m).
Economy. Though the economy depends on the export of crude oil, which accounts for more than 95% of export revenue, agriculture employs 15% of the labor force. In the coastal area barley, wheat, millet, oranges, olives, almonds, and groundnuts are grown. Dates are plentiful in the desert oases, and nomads raise livestock. Libya consumes much of its own agricultural produce and is a net importer of foodstuffs. Petrochemicals have been added to the traditional textile and leather industries.
History. Because of Libya's strategic position on the Mediterranean coast, it has been occupied by many foreign powers-the ancient Greeks, Egyptians, Romans, Arabs, and Ottoman Turks controlled the country successively. In 1912 Italy annexed Libya, although it was not able to end Libyan armed opposition until 1932. In World War II Libya was an Axis military base and the scene of desert fighting between the Axis powers and the British. In 1951 the United Nations declared Libya an independent sovereign state under the rule of King Idris I. He was overthrown in 1969 by a military coup led by Colonel Muammar al-Qaddafi, who proclaimed Libya a republic; it is now in effect an Islamic military dictatorship. In 1973 Qaddafi launched a 'cultural revolution,' including nationalization of key industries. A prominent follower of pan-Arabism, he has attempted to unite Libya with Egypt (1973), Tunisia (1974), and Syria (1980), and has intervened militarily in Chad (1980-1994). Qaddafi is a fervent opponent of Israel. The United States launched an air strike on Tripoli (1986) and shot down 2 Libyan fighters (1989) in retaliation of alleged Libyan backing of terrorist activities. In 1998, negotiations began regarding the trial in The Hague of two Libyans who were suspected of the 1988 bombing of Pan American Flight 103 over Lockerbie, Scotland. In 1999 Libya finally agreed to hand over the two suspects for trial in the Netherlands and UN sanctions (since 1992) were lifted. One of the suspects was found guilty by The Scottish Court in 2001. After the appeal had been denied, Libya declared it was willing to pay compensation to families of victims of the Lockerbie bombing. Libya has been elected chairman of the UN Human Rights Commission in 2003, despite opposition from the United States.

Lichee *See:* Litchi.

High-grade Libyan petroleum extracted from well sites in the nation's interior is conveyed through pipelines to the Mediterranean coast for shipment to refineries in Western Europe and the United States. Libyan petroleum is particularly valuated for its low sulfur content.

Lichen, name given to plants that consist of algae living in association with fungi. The fungi gets food from the algae and absorbs the water that is used by the algae to make its own food in the process called photosynthesis. This relationship is a form of symbiosis. Lichens generally live on the bark of trees, rotting wood, rocks, or soil.

Lichtenstein, Roy (1923-1997), U.S. painter prominent in the Pop Art movement of the early 1960s. He depicted comic strip frames and used commercial art techniques, such as Benday dots, in his work.

Licorice, European herb (*Glycyrrhiza glabra*) with blue flowers and lemon yellow roots that contain a juice used as a flavoring. Licorice has long been used to treat sore throats and is often added to medicines to mask disagreeable tastes. It is also widely used to flavor candy.

Lidice (pop. 500), village in the northwestern Czech Republic. In 1942 the Nazis completely demolished the village, killing the men and deporting the women and children, in retaliation for the assassination of Reinhard Heydrich, Nazi governor of Bohemia, by the Czech Resistance. A new village has been built near the site, which is now a national monument.
See also: World War II; Czechoslovakia.

Lidocaine, drug used as a local or block anesthetic, which bars pain in specific areas of the body. It can be administered by injection or used topically, directly on the skin.

Lie, Trygve (1896-1968), Norwegian political leader, first secretary-general of the United Nations, 1946-53. He incurred

L

Soviet hostility because of his support of UN action in Korea. After leaving office, he returned to Norway, serving in ministerial posts.

Liebknecht, Karl (1871-1919), son of Wilhelm Liebknecht, was a lawyer and leader of the left wing of the Socialist party. He was elected to the Reichstag in 1929. Liebknecht withdrew from the Socialist party because of its support of Germany's involvement in World War I. He organized the Spartacus Union, which developed into the German Communist party. Liebknecht was imprisoned during 1916-1918 for organizing an antiwar demonstration in Berlin. In January 1919, he and Rosa Luxemburg led an uprising in an attempt to set up a Communist governement in Berlin. The insurrection failed, and both leaders were killed by government troops after their arrest.

Liebknecht, Wilhelm (1826-1900), took part in the Revolution of 1848. After the revolution failed in 1849, he went to England, where he became a follower of Karl Marx. Liebknecht returned to Germany in 1862 and became a journalist. In 1869 with August Bebel he formed a socialist party, which in 1875 united with another socialist group to become the Social Democratic Party (SPD). He spent two years in prison because of his opposition to the Franco-Prussian War. From 1874 until his death he was a Social Democratic member of the Reichstag (the German parliament).

Liechtenstein

Capital:	Vaduz
Area:	62 sq mi (160 sq km)
Population:	32,800
Language:	German
Government:	Parliamentary monarchy
Independent:	1719
Head of gov.:	Prime minister
Per capita:	US$ 23,000
Monetary unit:	Swiss franc = 100 rappen

Liechtenstein, European principality in the Alps, between Switzerland and Austria. With a total area of 62 sq mi (160 sq km), Liechtenstein is one of the world's smallest countries. Because of low taxes and bank se-

The capital Vaduz and the castle of   Francis Joseph II.

crecy, it is the nominal headquarters of thousands of international corporations, and Vaduz is a thriving tourist center. Roman Catholicism is the state religion; German is the official language. Liechtenstein was a principality of the Holy Roman Empire from 1719. It was incorporated into the German Confederation in 1815 and became independent in 1866. Until 1919 it was closely associated with Austria, but since then its interests abroad have been represented by Switzerland, and much of its economy is owned by the Swiss. In 1990, Liechtenstein became a member of the UN and, one year later, the country joined the European Free Trade Association (EFTA). In 2001 Liechtenstein was listed by the Organization for Co-operation and Development (OECD) as one of the seven countries that do not comply with the demands of financial transparence and of providing financial information.

Liège (pop. 184,000), city and cultural center on the Meuse River in eastern, French-speaking Belgium. Liège is an industrial city noted for its production of glassware and armaments

Lifar, Sergei Mihailovitch (1905-1986), French dancer and choreographer of Russian origin. Made his debut at the Ballets Russes (1923). From 1929 until 1958, with some interruptions, he was a dancer and ballet master at the Paris Opera. He was greatly influential on the development of ballet in France. Created a very personal, predominantly aesthetic neoclassical dancing style. Made about 60 choreographies.

Life, despite the lack of any generally accepted definition of life, physiologists regard as living any system capable of eating, metabolizing, excreting, breathing, moving, growing, and reproducing, and able to respond to external stimuli. Metabolically, life is a property of any object surrounded by a definite boundary and capable of exchang-

ing materials with its surroundings. Biochemically, life subsists in cellular systems containing both nucleic acids and proteins. For the geneticist, life belongs to systems able to perform complex transformations of organic molecules and to construct from raw materials copies of themselves capable of evolution by natural selection. As to the origin of life, many believe it was created by God. Scientists believe in the formation of organic substances in the atmosphere over 2 billion years ago; they joined water to form a 'nutrient broth' that evolved into life.

Life expectancy, number of years a person in a particular population group is expected to live, based on actuarial calculations. A statistical quantity, it is not meant to be a prediction applied to individuals.

Ligament, band of strong fibrous tissue connecting bones at a joint or serving to hold body organs in place.
See also: Human body.

Ligeti, György Sándor (1923-), Austrian composer of Hungarian descent, important representative of Contemporary music. He became famous with a style of composing in which instrumental voices are merged completely, typified by Ligeti as inaudible or micropolyphony. This leads to an apparently static sound pattern with continuous blending timbres. After 1970 he left this technique and went from inaudible to audible polyphony, in which melodic and rhythmic structures are more clearly distinguished. His actual breakthrough as a composer started in 1960 with the first performance of his orchestral piece *Apparitions* (1958-1959). Other works include: *Atmosphères* (1961), *Nouvelles aventures* (1962-1965), *Requiem* (1963-1965), *Lux aeterna* (1966), *Continuum* (1968), *San Francisco polyphonie* (1973-1974), *Nonsense Madrigals* (1988-1993).

Light, the portion of electromagnetic radiation that the human eye can see. To be seen, light must have a wavelength between 400 and 750 nanometers, a range known as the visible spectrum. The eye recognizes light of different wavelengths as being of different colors, the shorter wavelengths forming the blue end of the visible spectrum, the longer the red. The term *light* is also applied to radiations of wavelengths just outside the visible spectrum: those of energies greater than that of visible light are called ultraviolet light, and those of lower energies are called infrared. For many years the nature of light aroused controversy among physicists. Although Christiaan Huygens had demonstrated that reflection and refraction could be explained in terms of waves (1690), Isaac Newton preferred to think of light as composed of material corpuscles, or particles (1704). Thomas Young's interference experiments reestablished the wave hypothesis (1801) and A. J. Fresnel gave it a rigorous mathematical basis (1814-1815). At the beginning of the 20th century, the nature of light was again debated as Max Planck and Albert Einstein proposed explanations of blackbody radiation (1900) and the photoelectric effect (1905) respectively, both of

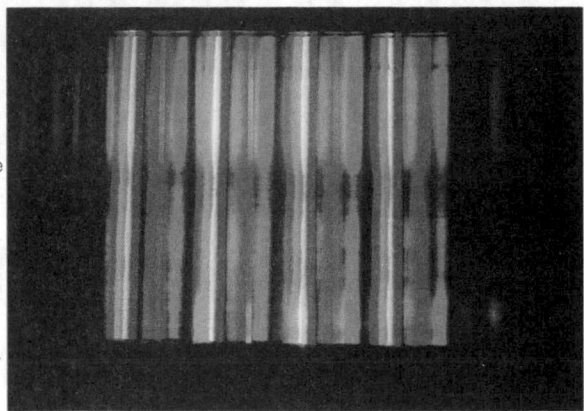

An interference pattern, formed by white light. The exposure is made through a diffraction grating: a piece of glass onto which countless fine scratches have been made. This grating was held before four lighted slits, arranged in a row. The light, on reaching the grating, will bend in all directions, and – through interference – four coloured interference patterns will come about.

which assumed that light comes in discrete quanta (bundles) of energy.

Light, invisible *See:* Infrared rays; Ultraviolet rays.

Light art, artistic style in which artificial light is consciously used as a means of expression. Light art received a strong impulse around 1950, mainly owing to the research of Frank Malina and Nicolas Schöffer. The following categories can be discerned within light art: an object which is dependent on an outside source of light, an object with a built-in source of light, light environment, and light spectacle. Light art also often involves sound and movement.

Light bulb *See:* Edison, Thomas Alva; Electric light.

Lighthouse, tower with a light at its head, erected on or near a coast or on a rock in the sea, as a warning to ships. One of the earliest lighthouses was on the Pharos peninsula in 3rd-century B.C. Alexandria, considered one of the 7 wonders of the world. In modern lighthouses, the lantern usually consists of a massive electric light with an elaborate optical system producing intense beams.

Light meter, device that measures the intensity of light. Some light meters contain photo cells made up of the chemicals cadmium sulfide or gallium arsenide, while others utilize cells of selenium. Both are used in specialized professions such as astronomy and photography.

Lightning, discharge of atmospheric electricity resulting in a flash of light in the sky. Flashes range from a few miles to about 100 mi (170 km) in length and typically have an energy of about 300 kWh and an electromotive force of 100 MV. Lightning results from a buildup of opposed electric charges, usually in clouds. The electrical nature of lightning was proved in 1752 by Benjamin Franklin.

Lightning bug *See:* Firefly.

Lignum vitae, either of 2 species (*Guaiacum officinale* and *G. sanctum*) of flowering evergreen tree of the West Indies, Mexico, and Florida. Its extremely heavy wood is used for ship construction, furni-

ture, and mallets. The wood also contains a resin used in some drugs.

Ligurian Sea, portion of the Mediterranean Sea enclosed by the Italian regions of Liguria and Tuscany in the north and east and the French island of Corsica in the south.
See also: Mediterranean Sea.

Lilac, shrub or small tree (genus *Syringa*) whose pyramids of small, sweet-scented flowers cap heart-shaped leaves. Lilacs originated in Asia and eastern Europe and are now widely grown as ornamentals.

Liliuokalani, Lydia Kamekeha (1838-1917), last queen of Hawaii, who reigned 1891-1893. She succeeded her brother, King Kalakaua. When she tried to assert her royal powers, American sugar planters living in Hawaii fomented a revolt in which she lost her throne. She wrote the well-known farewell song 'Aloha Oe.'

Lille (pop. 175,000), city in northern France. Best-known for its textile industry, Lille also produces automobiles, electronic equipment, and petrochemicals. Lille was founded c. 1030 by the Flemish, who gave the city to France in 1312.
See also: France.

Lilongwe (pop. 396,000), capital, since 1975, of Malawi in southeast Africa. Located on the Lilongwe River, the city is the center of a rich agricultural region. Lilongwe, settled in 1902, became a city in 1966.
See also: Malawi.

Lily, common name for plants of the family Liliaceae, which have prominent flowers and grasslike leaves. True lilies have 3 showy sepals and petals and 6 stamens, and generally grow from bulbs. The best known varieties are the Madonna lily (*Lilium candidum*) and white-trumpet lily (*L. Longiflorum*), which flower in the spring and are seen at Easter. Many wild lilies flower only once in several years.

Lily of the valley, any of several species of woodland plants (genus *Convallaria*) widely grown in gardens and indoor pots. It produces white, bell-shaped flowers that hang from a long stalk and show up against a

The interior structure of Eddystone Lighthouse, which rises 40.4 metres above the English channel. This famous warning beacon, situated 22.5 km off the Plymouth coast, was constructed in 1882, on the site of two earlier lighthouses.

1. watertank
2. entrance
3. energy supply
4. storage room
5. hoisting hook
6. storage room
7. living room
8. bedroom
9. storage room
10. service room
11. light source with optical system

L

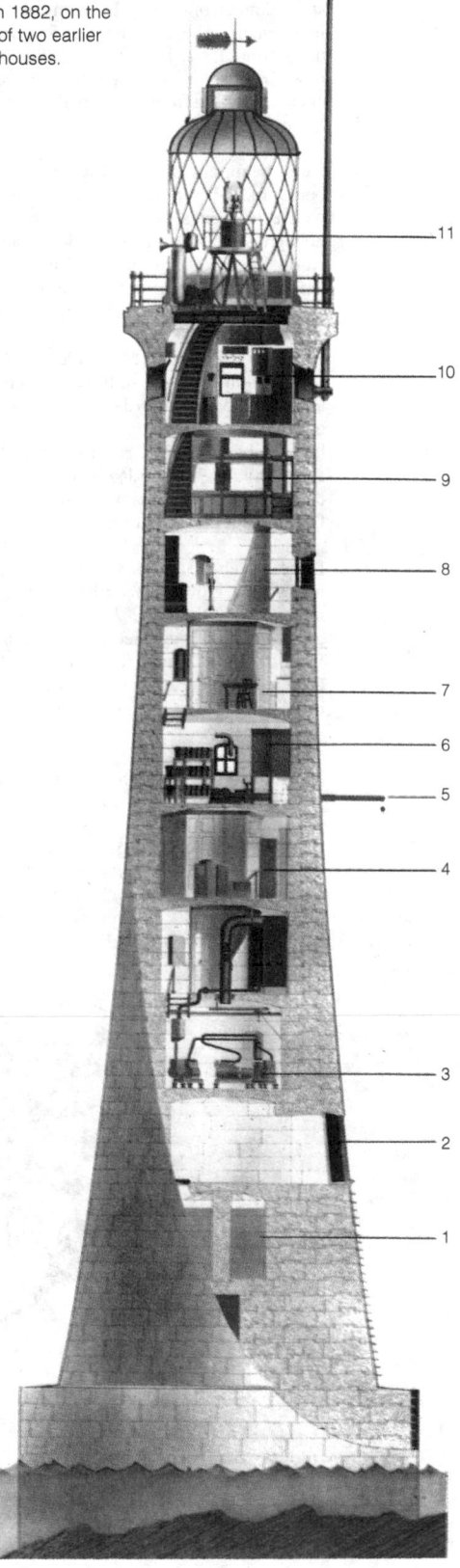

L

backdrop of 2 broad, overlapping leaves. The flowers are sweet-scented and are used in perfume. They produce large red berries.

Lima (pop. 7,700,000), capital and largest city of Peru, about 8 mi (13 km) inland from the Pacific port of Callao. Founded in 1535, Lima was the chief residence of the Spanish viceroys. Earthquakes in 1687 and 1746 destroyed much of the city, but many old buildings remain. The University of San Marcos dates from 1551. Rapidly expanding, Lima now has many industries, including textiles, chemicals, oil refining, and food processing. *See also:* Peru.

Lima bean, any of several highly nutritious beans of the pea family, rich in protein. Native to tropical America, lima beans are now grown in warm climates throughout the world. The beans grow in 2- to 3-in (5- to 7.6-cm)-long pods on a bush, or on a vine that can be trained to grow on trellises or poles.

Limbourg, Pol de (d.1416), Flemish manuscript illuminator, one of three brothers who after 1404 worked for the Burgundian duke of Berry. Their renowned devotional book of hours, the *Très Riches Heures* (c.1415) shows courtly life and landscape in brilliant detail and dazzling color; it profoundly influenced Flemish painting.

Lime, shrublike citrus tree (*Citrus aurantifolia*) that grows a green fruit smaller and more acidic than the lemon. Limes are grown around the Mediterranean, in the West Indies, Central America, and India. Rich in vitamin C, they were once important in preventing scurvy among sailors on long sea voyages.

Lime, quicklime, or calcium oxide, a caustic industrial chemical (CaO). It is most often made by heating limestone until carbon dioxide is released. Lime's uses include purifying sugar, neutralizing acidic soil and sewage, and making porcelain and glass.

Limerick, humorous verse form consisting of 5 lines, named for the Irish city of Limerick but of unknown origin. Limericks were popularized by the English poet Edward Lear (1812-1888). An example:
There was a young lady named Bright
Whose speed was far faster than light
She went out one day
in a relative way
And returned on the previous night.

Limestone, sedimentary rock consisting mainly of calcium carbonate. Some limestones, such as chalk, are soft, but others are hard enough to be used in building. Limestone may be formed inorganically by the evaporation of seawater or freshwater containing calcium carbonate, or organically from the compressed shells of mollusks or skeletons of coral on sea beds.

Lime tree *See:* Linden.

Limon, José (1908-1972), Mexican-U.S. dancer and choreographer. In the 1930s he danced with the Humphrey-Weidman company. He formed his own company in 1946, choreographing *Moor's Pavane* (1949), *The Visitation* (1952), and *A Choreographic Offering* (1963).

Limonite, or brown hematite, mineral formed by the decomposition of other minerals that contain iron, found in France, Cuba, and Canada. It is used as an iron ore and as a source of ocher, a yellow iron ore used as a pigment.

Limpet, mollusk, related to the pond snail, with a conical instead of a spiral shell and a muscular foot that can cling to rocks. Limpets can trap water under their shells to survive even when exposed by the ebbing tide. They can grow as long as 4 in (10 cm), but are usually smaller.

Limpopo River, or Crocodile River, river dividing South Africa from Botswana and Zimbabwe. The Limpopo, which empties into the Indian Ocean, is about 1,000 mi (1,600 km) long.

Lincoln, Abraham (1809-1865), 16th president of the United States (1861-1865). Lincoln led the North during the Civil War, the nation's greatest crisis. He was determined to restore the Union at any cost-and prevailed. Besides his preservation of the Union and the Emancipation Proclamation, Lincoln is remembered for his eloquent oratory, particularly his Gettysburg Address and inaugural speeches.

Lincoln was born in a log cabin on the frontier in Kentucky, to a poor carpenter and his wife. Lincoln had less than a year of formal schooling, but taught himself to read. In 1837, he was admitted to the bar and moved to Springfield, Ill., to practice law. Soon after moving there, he met Mary Todd, whom he married in 1842.

Lincoln, a successful lawyer, was more interested in politics. He lost his first election in 1832, but in 1834 won a seat in the state legislature, where he served 4 2-year terms. He rose quickly within the Whig party, becoming Whig floor leader in the Illinois house by age 28. In 1847, he was elected to the U.S. House of Representatives, where he served only 1 term, because his opposition to the Mexican War made him unpopular with his constituents. He returned to his Springfield law practice in 1849. A national debate over slavery brought Lincoln back into politics-he gave speeches attacking slavery as a 'great moral wrong'. Before Lincoln even took office, 7 Southern states had seceded. The great question was no longer slavery or freedom in the territories, but the preservation of the Union itself. Lincoln was inaugurated on Mar. 4, 1861; on Apr. 12, 1861, the Civil War broke out when the South attacked Fort Sumter in Charleston, S.C. Affairs began badly for Lincoln: 5 more states seceded and the North lost the war's earliest battles. Lincoln issued the Emancipation Proclamation on Sept. 22, 1862. It freed all slaves in states or parts of states in rebellion against the Union as of Jan. 1, 1863.

The tide of the war slowly turned in 1863, with important Northern victories. Lincoln was gloomy about his prospects of reelection in Nov. 1864, but he and running mate Andrew Johnson did win. Soon after Lincoln's second inauguration, the war ended with Gen. Robert E. Lee's surrender on Apr. 9, 1865.

Five days later, Lincoln and his wife went to Ford's Theatre for a performance of *Our American Cousin*. During the third act, John Wilkes Booth crept into the presidential box and shot Lincoln. Lincoln died the next morning. Booth, who had fled, was eventually found and shot while trying to escape.

Limestone is slowly dissolved by water, containing carbon dioxide. Calcium carbonate is converted into water-soluble calcium bicarbonate. The removal of the latter by runoff surface water, forms deeply grooved cracks, or grikes (1). In areas where water collects, the cracks enlarge, to form funnel-shaped holes, known as sink holes, or swallow holes (2). These holes may eventually enlarge by a continued solution of the limestone beneath them, and create deep shafts, or chasms (3). Sometimes, the roofs of long underground chasms or caves collapse and produce steep-sided ravines, or dry valleys (4). If limestone rock rests on impermeable rock (5), water flowing from swallow holes through underground joints and caves will surface again as springs (6) or streams (7). The evaporation of water, dripping from the roofs and sides of caves or chasms leaves deposits of calcium carbonate. These deposits accumulate and build up from the floors of caves as stalagmites (8), or grow downward from the roofs to form stalactites (9).)

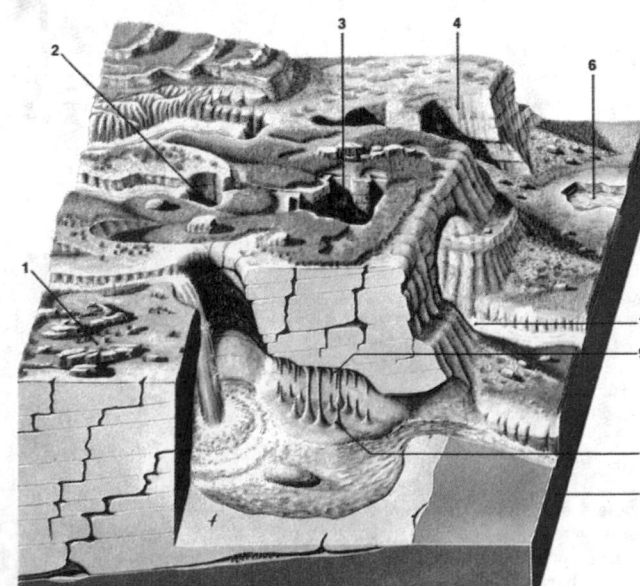

L

See also: Civil War, U.S.; Emancipation Proclamation

Lincoln Center for the Performing Arts, in New York City, complex of buildings (constructed 1959-1972) designed by leading modern architects including Eero Saarinen and Philip Johnson, to accommodate a number of vital performing arts institutions, which today include the Metropolitan Opera, New York Philharmonic Orchestra, the New York City Opera, and the Chamber Music Society of Lincoln Center. Also at Lincoln Center is a branch of the New York Public Library devoted to the performing arts; a prominent school of music, dance, and theater, the Juilliard School; and other institutions devoted to film and jazz.

Lincoln Memorial, marble monument to Abraham Lincoln in Washington, D.C., dedicated in 1922. Its 36 Doric columns represent the states of the Union when Lincoln was president. The great hall contains a huge statue of Lincoln by Daniel Chester French and 2 murals by Jules Guerin.

Lind, Jenny (1820-1887), Swedish soprano who had brilliant success in opera, concert singing, and oratorio. In 1850-1852 she toured the United States under the management of the promoter P.T. Barnum.

Lindbergh, Charles Augustus (1902-1974), U.S. aviator who made the first solo, nonstop flight across the Atlantic, in 33 1/2 hours, on May 21, 1927, in *The Spirit of St. Louis*. The flight made him a popular hero. The kidnapping and murder of his son in 1932 led to a federal law on kidnapping, popularly known as the Lindbergh Act. Lindbergh and his wife, the writer Anne Spencer Morrow Lindbergh, moved to England in 1936. Criticized for his pro-German, isolationist stance in 1938-1941, Lindbergh resigned his commission in the air reserves, but he later flew 50 combat missions in the Pacific during World War II. He won a Pulitzer Prize for his autobiography, *The Spirit of Saint Louis* (1953).

Linden, any of a family (Tiliaceae) of shade trees native to temperate regions. Lindens are also known as lime trees, bee trees, and basswoods. There are 35 species. The most common North American species is the American linden (*Tilia americana*), which can reach 120 ft (37 m).

Lindgren, Astrid Anna Emilia (1907-2002), Swedish writer of highly imaginative children's books. Despite the often fairytale-like events, the stories show a great awareness of reality, hiding much tragedy behind the often innocent humor. Created famous characters such as Pippi Longstocking, Bill Bergson, Karlsson Who Lives On The Roof, Rasmus, Ronja Robber's Daughter, etc. Her fairytale novel *Mio, My Son* (1954) is also well-known.

Lindsay, Vachel (1879-1931), U.S. poet of rhythmic, ballad-like verse designed to be read out loud. Among the best known are 'The Congo' (1914) and 'Abraham Lincoln

The Lincoln Memorial, a neo-classic building with impressive pillars, symbolizes the greatness of this president in the eyes of his countrymen.

Walks at Midnight' (1914). *Collected Poems* was published in 1938.

Linear accelerator, device that produces beams of electrons, protons, and other charged particles and directs them against various atomic targets in order to study the structure of atomic nuclei. Linear accelerators vary in the way in which they speed up particles to produce the beams, which move in straight paths. (Other particle accelerators produce circular paths of particles.) Usually the acceleration is accomplished by means of electromagnetic waves.
See also: Particle accelerator.

Linear electric motor, automatic device used to move vehicles without wheels. The motor consists of a row of electromagnets that are turned off and on in succession, producing a wave of magnetism that propels the vehicle. In the linear induction motor the electromagnets are located in the vehicle and face a strip of nonmagnetic metal called a reaction rail. The magnetism induces an electric current in the reaction rail, which in turn produces a second magnetic field that pushes against the first, thereby moving the vehicle. In the *linear synchronous motor* an electromagnet is mounted beneath the vehicle's track. It reacts with magnets on the vehicle itself to propel the vehicle.

Line Islands, string of 11 coral islands in the west and southwest Pacific Ocean. Also known as the Equatorial Islands, they total 222 sq mi (576 sq km) in area and are politically divided. Some of the Northern Line Islands are part of the British crown colony, while others are under U.S. jurisdiction. The Central and Southern Line Islands are part of Gilbert and Ellice Islands, a British crown colony.

Line of Demarcation, line decreed by Pope Alexander VI in 1494 to divide Spanish and Portuguese colonial possessions on a world scale. Running from north to south about 350 mi (563 km) west of the Azores and Cape Verde islands, the Line of Demarcation granted Spanish rights to all land west of the line and Portuguese rights to all land east of

it. The line was moved farther west under the 1592 Treaty of Saragossa, thus allowing Portugal to claim what is now eastern Brazil and Spain to claim the Philippine Islands.

Lingonberry, small fruit of an evergreen shrub (*Vaccinium vitisidaea*), related to the cranberry. A member of the heather family, the lingonberry grows wild in northern North America. The berry is shiny and bright red. As the raw berry is bitter, it is usually cooked into jellies and sauces.

Linguistics, scientific study of language in all its aspects. This includes, first, the physical and biological factors that are involved in speech. Secondly, it embraces the study of the structure of language, which includes its range of sounds (phonology), its grammatical structure (morphology and syntax), and the relation of words to what they mean (semantics). In comparative linguistics, the aim is to study the relationship between various languages, especially in terms of comparative grammar. At its most general, comparative linguistics leads to a search for those features common to all languages, which is really the philosophical problem of finding a universal grammar. Finally, linguistics considers how language is related to human activity in general, what its function is in the active life of a society, and its importance as a medium for handing down a cultural tradition.
See also: Language.

Linn *See:* Linden.

Linnaeus, Carolus (Karl von Linné; 1707-1778), Swedish botanist and physician, founder of taxonomy, the scientific classification of plants and animals. He presented his system of classification in 2 major works, *Systema Naturae* (1735) and *Genera plantarum* (1737). Although many of his particular classifications have been modified, the overall system is still in use.
See also: Botany.

Carolus Linnaeus (1707-1778) is known under several names. He was born as Karl von Linné, and he still used this name in Sweden, even after he had latinized his name. The signature under this 1739 oil painting by J.H. Scheffel, is therefore Karl Linnaeus.

Linnet, small, seed-eating bird (*Carduelis cannabina*) of the finch family, characterized by light tan and brown feathers with darker patches on the back and shoulders.

L

The crown and breast of the male linnet change to crimson in the spring and summer. In the fall and winter linnets flock together in open country regions, some migrating to warmer areas.

Linotype, mechanical typesetting machine that revolutionized printing and made possible the publication of low-priced books and newspapers. Invented by Ottmar Merganthaler in 1884, the machine, operated by a typewriter keyboard, assembles brass matrices of type into a line and casts the line as a single metal slug. Various photographic and lithographic printing techniques have virtually replaced the linotype machine.
See also: Printing; Mergenthaler, Ottmar.

Lin Piao (1908-1971), Chinese communist general and politician. A leader in the Long March (1934-1935), he was crucial in the final defeat of Chiang Kai-shek by his capture of Manchuria in 1948. Minister of defense from 1959, he was a leader of the Cultural Revolution (1965-1969). In 1969 he was designated the successsor of Mao Zedong. He died mysteriously in an air crash.

Linton, Ralph (1893-1953), U.S. anthropologist best known for his studies in cultural anthropology in Africa, the Americas, and the South Pacific. His works include *The Study of Man* (1936) and *The Tree of Culture* (1955).

Lion, largest member of the cat family (*Panthera leo*), now found only in Africa, Asia, and zoos. Lions once lived in Europe, India, and the Middle East, but the expanding human population has eliminated lions from these regions. Lions live in family groups called prides. There may be as many as 30 lions in one pride, and they usually spend their time playing, resting, sleeping (a lion can sleep almost 20 hrs a day), eating, and hunting. The pride tends to live together like a family for many years, but males are forced to leave at two or three years of age. A hungry lion may travel as much as 20 miles in one day in search of food. The male lion may reach 9 ft (2.7 m) and weigh as much as 400 lb (180 kg). The female can weigh up to 300 lb (140 kg) and can achieve

a length of 8 ft (2.4 m). Because lions do not have exceptional speed, they must rely on the element of surprise for the hunt. They are fond of hunting at night. Most hunting is done by the lioness, and the prey is usually a large animal.

Lipatti, Dinu (actual name Constatin Lipatti; 1917-1950), Romanian pianist and composer. Lipatti studied in Bucharest and from 1934-1939 in Paris (with Nadia Boulanger, Charles Münch and Cortot). His brilliant career as a concert pianist ended prematurely with an early death. From 1944 on he held a masterclass in Geneva. Lipatti excelled in the classical repertoire, especially Bach, Mozart, Chopin and Ravel. His few compositions include orchestral, chamber and piano music.

Lipchitz, Jacques (1891-1973), Lithuanian-born French sculptor whose early works consisted of spaces and volumes in a cubist style. Beginning in 1925 he produced a series called 'transparents', which, as in the *Harpist* (1928), emphasized contour. His later work was more romantic and metaphorical.

Li Peng (1929-), Chinese politician, orphan. raised by former Prime Minister Zhou Enlai. In 1981, he became Vice Minister of Power Industry, after which he rapidly moved up the hierarchic ladder; in 1983 he became Vice Prime Minister and in 1987, Prime Minister. He revealed himself as an advocate of hard-line politics and he was involved in the violent suppression of the student protest on the Square of Heavenly Peace in 1989. In 1998, he was elected chairman of the National People's Congress. *See also:* Zhou Enlai.

Lipid, any of a group of organic compounds found in plants, animals, and micro-organisms that are insoluble in water but dissolve in fat solvents such as ether, chloroform, and alcohol. Lipids are classified into fatty-acids, phospholipids, waxes, steroids, terpenes, and other types, according to their products on hydrolysis.

Li Po *See:* Li Bo.

Lippi, name of 2 Italian Renaissance painters in Florence. **Fra Filippo Lippi** (c.1406-1469) was influenced by Masaccio, Donatello, and by Flemish painting. His frescoes in the Cathedral of Prato are his most important works. **Filippino Lippi** (c.1457-1504), his son, influenced by Botticelli, painted the brilliantly detailed *Adoration of the Magi* (1496).

Lippmann, Walter (1889-1974), influential U.S. political columnist and foreign affairs analyst. His column, 'Today and Tomorrow,' first appeared in the *New York Herald Tribune* (1931-1962), then the *Washington Post* (1962-1967); it won two Pulitzer prizes (1958, 1962).
Books include *Public Opinion* (1922) and *The Good Society* (1937).

Lisbon (pop. 1,900,000), capital and largest city of Portugal, on the Tagus River estuary near the Atlantic Ocean. Its harbor handles the bulk of the country's foreign trade. A Roman settlement from c.200 B.C. Lisbon was conquered by the Moors in 716. It was reconquered in 1147 and became the capital c.1260. In the 16th century it was the center of Portugal's colonial empire. Much of the city was rebuilt after a disastrous earthquake in 1755. Current industries include steel, petroleum refining, textiles, chemicals, paper, and metal products.
See also: Portugal.

Lissitzki, El (proper name Eliezer; 1890-1941), Russian painter and graphic artist, one of the founders of constructivism. He gave shape to the relation between construction and space (which he calls 'proun': the first characters of the Russian words for founding new forms in art) in many paintings, drawings and lithos. His dynamic designs, in which diagonals dominate and three-dimensional effects were achieved by using perspective, form an important contribution to Modern art.

Lister, Sir Joseph (1827-1912), English surgeon who pioneered antiseptic surgery. Pasteur had shown that microscopic organisms (bacteria) are responsible for infection, but his sterilization techniques were unsuitable for surgical use.
Through experimentation Lister succeeded in using carbolic acid as a sterilization agent. This greatly reduced post-operative fatalities caused by infection.

Liszt, Franz (1811-1886), Hungarian composer and virtuoso pianist who revolutionized keyboard technique. Director of music in Weimar, Germany, 1843-1861, he later moved to Rome and took minor holy orders in 1865. His music includes 13 symphonic poems (a form he invented), symphonies such as *Faust* (1854), the Sonata in B Minor for piano (1853), *Transcendental Studies* for piano (1852); and 20 Hungarian rhapsodies. His daughter, Cosima, married Richard Wagner.

Litchi, or lichee, evergreen Chinese tree (*Litchi chinensis*) grown in warm climates, a member of the soapberry family. Prized for its juicy fruit, the litchi has been cultivated

The lion (*Panthera leo*) usually hunts in groups, one lion driving the prey toward the other lions lying in wait. The adult male (back) often takes no active role in the hunt, but nevertheless, he will claim his portion of the kill. Lions live in groups, called prides, each including several males, several females, and cubs. Common throughout central Africa, lions are in danger of extinction in India.

in southern China for over 2,000 years. The round fruit ranges from 1/2 to 1 1/2 in (1.3 to 3.8 cm) in diameter and has a rough, brittle skin and white flesh with a single large brown seed inside. Rich in vitamin C, the fruit is eaten fresh or canned in a syrup. When dried, it is called litchi nut.

Literature for children, a special branch of creative writing that is geared to young readers, ranging from the preschool age to the teenage years. The literature consists of almost every genre used in adult literature: novels, plays, biographies, poetry, collections of folk tales, and informative works on the arts, science, and social affairs. These works for children are written expressly at their level, and they are designed and illustrated to capture the imagination of young readers. Some books that were written for adults have taken on the status of children's literature because of their popularity with young people. Among these are the collection of folk tales assembled by the brothers Grimm (*Grimm's Fairy Tales*), Mark Twain's *Tom Sawyer* (and to a lesser extent *Huckleberry Finn*), Daniel Defoe's *Robinson Crusoe*, and Jonathan Swift's *Gulliver's Travels*. Also, many adult works have been adapted for children in different versions, for example, the ever-popuar story of King Arthur and his knights, from Thomas Malory's *Morte D'Arthur*. Adults, of course, have told stories to children from time immemorial. It must be remembered that before the invention of printing in Europe (around the mid-1500s), there was little literacy in the general population. The ability to read was confined largely to the clergy and the nobility. Moreover, books were copied out laboriously by hand and were much prized by the few who could afford them or use them. Children's literature, under those circumstances, was, like the literature of the general public, based on an oral tradition, which consisted for the most part of myths, fables, ballads, and poems. Some early books for children were produced, but they were primarily instructional in nature. Saint Aldhelm, Bishop of Sherborne, is thought to have written the first such text for children in English some-

Fragment of the original handwritten version of *Alice in Wonderland*, written and illustrated between July 1862 and February 1863 by Lewis Carroll (pseudonym of the English mathematician Charles Lutwidge Dodgson, 1832-1898).

time during the A.D. 600s. It was written in catechism style, that is question and answer, and that format for children's instructional and devotional texts remained popular for the next 1,000 years. The first recognized classic of children's literature appeared in France in 1697, a book of eight tales collected by Charles Perrault entitled *Stories and Tales of Times Past with Morals; or, Tales of Mother Goose*. In England, in 1744, John Newbury published *A Little Pretty Pocket-Book*, one of the first children's books designed primarily to amuse rather than to educate. Newbury was also one of the first important publishers of children's books.

During the 1800s, publishing and writing for children became a distinct branch of literature. Also at that time, illustration developed as a major feature of books for children, as exemplified by John Tenniel's illustrations for *Alice in Wonderland* and *Through the Looking Glass*. It was the 20th century that saw an explosive growth in children's books. The picture book, a book where illustrations carry the story and interest as much as the text, developed in the 20th century. Beatrix Potter's *The Tale of Peter Rabbit* (1901) is the first of this genre. Books are now available for almost every stage of childhood, covering almost every possible subject. Fantasy and adventure are always popular, but children's books today deal with social problems (race, drugs, sex) as well as with history and biography. Children's books are now available in all formats and price ranges, and they are very much a part of growing up in the modern world.

Litharge, poisonous compound (PbO) of lead and oxygen, also called lead monoxide. Litharge is a yellow or reddish-yellow solid produced by heating lead or lead compounds in air. It is used in storage batteries and in making lead glass, rubber, and pottery glazes.

Lithium, chemical element, symbol Li; for physical constants see Periodic Table. Lithium was discovered by Johann August Arfvedson in 1817. It is found in nearly all igneous rocks. *Spodumene* (lithium aluminum silicate) is an important mineral of lithium. Lithium is recovered commercially from brines. The metal is produced by the electrolysis of its fused chloride. Lithium is a silvery-white, reactive metal, the first of the alkali metal group. It is the lightest of all metals and has the highest specific heat of any solid element. Lithium and its compounds are used in lithium-hardened bearing metals, batteries, heat transfer applications, special glasses and ceramics, and in medicine for manic-depressive illness.

Lithography, form of printing used in both fine art and in commercial printing, invented by Aloys Senefelder in Germany c.1798. The technique consists of making a drawing in reverse on the surface of a stone, usually limestone, with an ink containing grease. When the grease has penetrated the stone, the drawing is washed off with water. The grease resists the water, but will accept ink, which is spread over the moist stone. The stone is then used to print the drawing. In the United States, lithographic artists include A.B. Davies, George Bellows, and Currier & Ives.
See also: Printing; Senefelder, Alois.

Lithography, an art form and a printing process. Lithography means 'stone writing', and in the original process prints were made directly from designs drawn on slabs of stone. Many changes, however, have been made in the process. Stone slabs have been largely supplanted by metal sheets. Photography, as well as drawing, is used to make the designs to be printed. Most commercial lithography is done by an indirect process called offset printing. In this process the printing press first transfers the design to a rubber blanket, and then to the material to be printed. The principle of lithography is based on the fact that oil and water do not

Anonymous caricature of Franz Liszt (1811-1886), entitled *Chromatic Gallop by the devil of harmony*, April 18, 1843.

L

mix. The material to be printed is marked on printing surface with a greasy substance. Water is then applied to the printing surface. The water is repelled by the grease but adheres to the ungreased areas. Next, ink is applied. The ink will stick to the grease but not to the wet areas. The ink is then transferred to paper, either directly or (in offset) indirectly. Lithography was invented in Germany in 1796 by Aloys Senefelder.

Lithuania

Capital:	Vilnius
Area:	25,212 sq mi (65,300 sq km)
Population:	3,601,000
Language:	Lithuanian
Government:	Republic
Independent:	1991
Head of gov.:	Prime minister
Per capita:	US$ 7,600
Monetary unit:	1 Litas = 100 centas

Lithuania (Republic of), independent country bordering on the Baltic Sea, surrounded by Poland (south), Russia (exclave Kaliningrad), Belarus (east), and Latvia (north).
Land and climate. The country exists of a low-lying plain, with numerous rivers and lakes. The east has a continental climate, the west has a more moderate climate.
People. Roman Catholicism is the traditional religion. Lithuanian, a member of the Baltic branch of the Indo-European family, is the main language. About 80% of the population is Lithuanian; Russians and Poles are the largest minorities.
Economy. Although timber and agricultural products remain important, Lithuania is now mostly urban. As such, shipbuilding, and the manufacture of machinery and building materials have taken over as the most important industries. The chief cities and industrial centers are Vilnius (the capital), Kaunas, and Klaipeda, the main port.
History. Fourteenth-century Lithuania, which included Belarus and parts of the Ukraine and Russia, was central Europe's most powerful state. In 1386 Lithuania and Poland were united under Grand Duke Jagiello. In 1795 the partition of Poland brought Lithuania under Russian rule. In 1918 independence was declared, and Lithuania, like the other Baltic republics, be-

came a separate state, although Poland occupied Vilnius from 1920 to 1939. In 1940 the Soviet Union invaded Lithuania and the other Baltic republics, and after World War II all 3 were incorporated in the Soviet Union. Nationalist sentiment grew in the late 1980s, and in 1990 the Lithuanian republican government declared independence from the USSR, a declaration not recognized by the Moscow government until 1991. After independence, Lithuania sought affiliation with western countries and organizations, which resulted in an invitation to join the NATO and the EU in 2004.
See also: Union of Soviet Socialist Republics.

Little Bighorn, Battle of, battle in southeastern Montana, near the Little Bighorn River, June 25-26, 1876, in which Colonel George A. Custer was killed and his troops annihilated by Sioux and Cheyennes led by chiefs Sitting Bull and Crazy Horse.

Little Dipper *See:* Big and Little Dippers.

Little Rock (pop. 176,000), state capital and principal commercial center of Arkansas, on the Arkansas River. Little Rock, originally a river crossing, became the capital of the Arkansas territory in 1821. During the Civil War it was a Confederate stronghold but was captured by the Union forces in 1863. Today it produces metal products, cottonseed, cotton fabrics, furniture, hardwood products, electronic equipment, and processed meats. In 1957 Little Rock became a center of the civil rights struggle when federal troops were mobilized to enforce the desegregation of Central High School.
See also: Arkansas.

Liu Bang (248?-195 B.C.), Chinese emperor who founded the western Han dynasty,

which ruled from 202 B.C. to A.D. 220 Liu Bang (r.202-195 B.C.) is known for furthering unification by establishing regional kingdoms presided over by a central government. Although he defeated Mongolian tribes that invaded China and eliminated certain harsh laws, Liu Bang is historically considered a cruel emperor. He began his career as one of the generals who led revolutionary forces against the Ch'in dynasty in 207-206 B.C.
See also: Han dynasty.

Liu Pang *See:* Liu Bang.

Liu Shao-Ch'i (1893-1969), Chinese communist leader who succeeded Mao Tse-Tung as chair of the Chinese People's Republic (1959-1968). In 1968 he was publicly denounced for embracing capitalism and dismissed. In 1980 he was posthumously exonerated by Deng Xiaoping.
See also: China.

Live oak, any of several species of North American evergreen trees (genus *Quercus*) of the beech family. The American oak, *Q. virginiana*, flourishes along the southeastern coast of the United States and is also found in Cuba. It can reach a height of about 50 ft (15 m), and many of its limbs fan out horizontally to form a dense web. Its leaves are dark green and shiny above, whitish and furry below. The live oak is both a timber tree and a popular ornamental tree.

Liver, in anatomy, the largest glandular organ in the human body, lying on the right of the abdomen beneath the diaphragm. It consists of 4 lobes made up of between 50,000 and 100,000 lobules. The metabolic cells of the lobules perform the work of the liver, which includes several functions. The liver aids in digestion by converting nutrients in the blood into a form suitable for storage

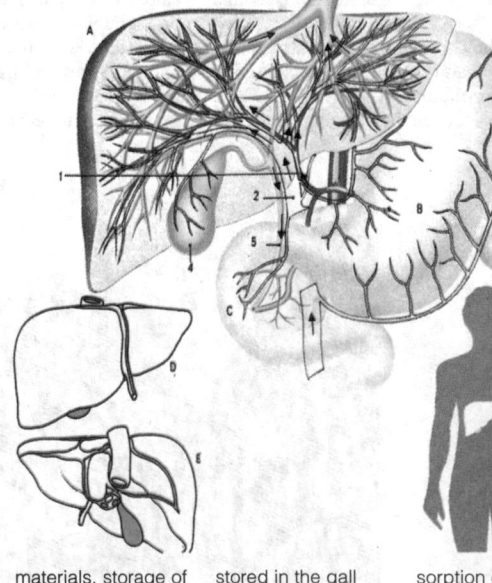

The liver (A) is situated below the diaphragm, on the right side of the body, next to the stomach (B) and above the duodenum (C). It performs more chemical functions than any other organ in the body. It receives oxygenated blood via the hepatic artery (1), and blood from the intestines carrying digested food materials, via the portal vein (2). Blood will seep through the liver and enter into the venous system via the hepatic vein (3). Liver functions include synthesis, storage, metabolism and interconversion of fats, amino acids and carbohydrates, detoxification of harmful materials, storage of various minerals and vitamins, and the production of energy-rich ATP-molecules and bile juice. Bile is stored in the gall bladder (4), to be later released into the duodenum via the bile duct (5). Bile is important for the absorption of fats in the intestine. Front and rear views (D en E) of the liver show the position of the gall bladder in the body.

L

called glycogen and by producing bile, which breaks down fats. The liver also purifies the blood by converting harmful substances into products that may be excreted in urine or bile. Diseases of the liver include cirrhosis and hepatitis.
See also: Human body.

Liverleaf *See:* Hepatica.

Liverpool (pop. 461,000), industrial city in northwestern England, one of its major ports, on the Mersey River, 3 mi (5 km) from the Irish Sea. The borough was chartered in 1207. In the 18th century it was a major slave-trading port. Food processing and chemicals are now important local industries.
See also: England.

Liverwort, primitive plant that lives in moist places. With the mosses, liverworts bridge the gap between the water-dwelling algae and the land-dwelling ferns and flowering plants.

Livestock, general term for animals raised to be sources of meat, milk, wool, leather, or labor. Cattle, hogs, poultry, sheep, and horses are all considered livestock. In some parts of the world donkeys, goats, mules, and rabbits are also livestock.

Livingstone, David *See:* Stanley and Livingstone.

Livy (Titus Livius; c.59 B.C.-A.D. 17), Roman historian. Of his 142-volume *History of Rome*, 35 books survive, with fragments and an outline of the rest. It traces the city from its founding in 753 B.C. to the end of the reign of Nero Drusus in 9 B.C. Although Livy is not always accurate, he is admired for his style and for his effort to view the development of the empire historically.

Li Yuan (A.D. 566-636), first emperor (618-627) and founder of the Tang dynasty (618-907), one of the greatest periods in China's history. His son, Li Shimin, forced him from power.
See also: Tang dynasty.

Lizard, any of many reptiles of the order Squamata, which also includes snakes. Lizards usually possess well-developed limbs, though these are reduced or absent in some species. Lizards typically eat insects, though some will take eggs or small mammals. Unlike snakes, lizards have ear openings and movable eyelids. The smallest are less than 3 in (7.6 cm); the largest is the Komodo dragon of Indonesia, which can be 10 ft (3 m) long.

Ljubljana (300,000), the capital and largest city of Slovenia. It is near the Sava River and the Julian Alps in the extreme northwestern part of the country. The city is a prosperous manufacturing, educational, and transportation center. Ljubljana was founded as Emona by the Romans in 34 B.C. The Austrian Hapsburgs ruled the city form 1278 to 1918, when Ljubljana became a part of the Kingdom of Serbs, Croats, and Slovenes (later known as Yugoslavia). During World War II the city was occupied by the Italians and Germans. In 1992, when Slovenia became independent, Ljubljana became the national capital.

Llama, domesticated South American hoofed mammal of the camel family. Resembling a large, long-necked sheep, it has thick fleece that may be used for wool and is the principal beast of burden of Native Americans from Peru to Chile, thriving at altitudes of 7,500-13,000 ft (2,280-4,000 m).

Lloyd, Harold Clayton (1894-1971), U.S. comedian of the silent screen, famous as the disaster-prone naive young man in glasses and straw hat. Among his best-known films are *Safety Last* (1923), *The Kid Brother* (1927), and *Feet First* (1930).

Lloyd George, David (1863-1945), Welsh political leader, British prime minister 1916-1922. Elected a Liberal Member of Parliament in 1890, he served the same Welsh constituency until his death. As chancellor of the exchequer (1908-1915) under Prime Minister Herbert Asquith he led in initiating British welfare legislation. In World War I Lloyd George became, successively, minister of munitions, minister of war, and finally prime minister of a coalition government. He was one of the architects of the Treaty of Versailles, which ended the war. His coalition fell in 1922, when the Conservatives withdrew from it. In the 1930s he led the remains of the Liberal Party and opposed policies of appeasement toward Nazi Germany.

Lloyd Webber, Andrew (1948-), popular British composer whose first success was the musical *Jesus Christ Superstar* (1971). His other musicals include *Evita* (1978), a fictional account of the life of Eva Peron; *Cats* (1981), based on the poems of T.S. Eliot; and *The Phantom of the Opera* (1986), based on Gaston Leroux's novel. He was knighted in 1992.

Loadstone, hard black mineral (Fe_3O_4) with magnetic properties, also called lodestone and magnetite. It is found in the form of rocks, crystals, and sand in Siberia, South Africa, and parts of Italy and the United States. Loadstone was used as a precursor to

The llama (*L. peruana*), a relative of the camel, can carry loads of up to 45 kg for 16-32 km a day over rugged slopes at high altitudes. Besides being a means of transportation in parts of South America, the llama also furnishes wool that is being used for clothing and blankets.

the compass, when ancient Europeans discovered that if an oblong piece of it was suspended from a string, it would point north and south.
See also: Magnetism.

Lobbying, attempting to influence legislators' votes by an agent of a particular political pressure group. The word derives from the practice of agents talking with legislators in the lobby of the legislature. The system is controlled by the Federal Regulation of Lobbying Act of 1946.

Lobelia, any of several species of annual or biannual plants (genus *Lobelia*) found in pastures, meadows, and cultivated fields. Its clusters of flowers are used for medicinal purposes because of its antispasmodic, diuretic, emetic, and expectorant properties.

Lobster, large marine crustacean with 5 pairs of jointed legs, the first bearing enormous claws. True lobsters (genus *Homarus*) live in shallow water and feed on carrion, small crabs, and worms. The 2 large claws differ in structure and function, one being adapted for crushing, the other for fine pick-

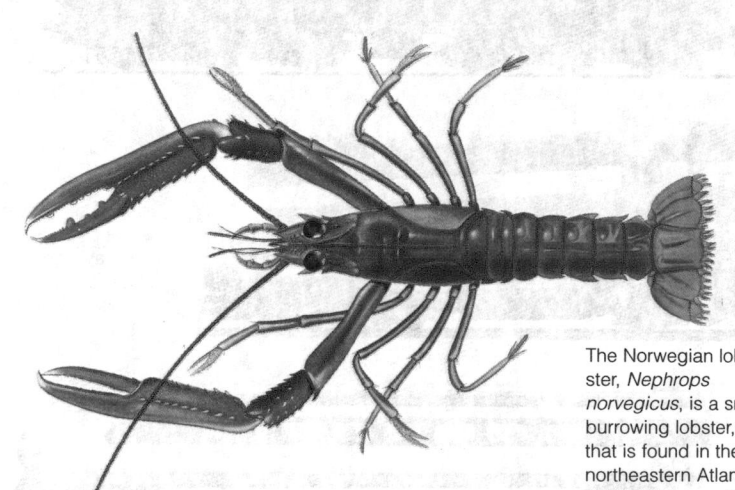

The Norwegian lobster, *Nephrops norvegicus*, is a small burrowing lobster, that is found in the northeastern Atlantic, especially along the west coast of Norway. Eaten as scampi, this lobster may become up to 7.9 in (20 cm) long (excluding its antennae).

L

ing or scraping. The dark blue pigment of the living lobster is a complex compound that turns red when exposed to intense heat.

Lobworm, also called lugworm or lugbait, seaworm (class Polychaeta) much used as bait for deep-sea fishing. Lobworms live along the Atlantic coasts of North America and Europe and near the Mediterranean Sea.

Local government, embraces a wide variety of governmental units, such as cities, counties, townships, and school districts. The average citizen comes into contact with local government quite often because it provides a variety of functions and services important in his daily life. These include garbage collection, police protection, education, firefighting, traffic regulation, street and road lighting, water supply and sewage control, public health and medical services, the recording of births, deaths, and marriages, and many others.

Locarno Treaties, pacts drawn up in Locarno, Switzerland, in 1925 providing for the demilitarization of the Rhineland and specifying the borders of Belgium, France,

Germany, Poland, and Czechoslovakia. The participants included those 5 countries plus Britain and Italy. The 'spirit of Locarno,' supposedly heralding peace, died in 1936 when Hitler denounced the pacts and moved troops into the Rhineland.

Loch Lomond, largest lake in Scotland, located in the highlands about 20 mi (32 km) north of the city of Glasgow. It is 23 mi (37 km) long and 5 mi (8 km) wide at its widest point. Loch Lomond is the subject of a familiar Scottish folk song, and Scottish clans in ancient times used its shores as a gathering place.

Loch Ness, one of the largest and deepest lakes in Scotland. It is in northcentral Scotland in the Great Glen (Glen Mor). The lake is about 25 miles (40 km) long (southwest-northeast) and about one mile (1.6 km) wide. Loch Ness is part of the Caledonian Canal system joining the North Sea with the Atlantic Ocean. Since the early 1930's there have been periodic, but unverified, reports of a giant monster living in the lake. Some scientists believe the sightings actually may be of large sturgeon, which are present in the lake. (An often-published photograph sup-

posedly showing the monster was revealed in 1994 to be a hoax.)

Lock, device that fastens shut and prevents the opening of doors, windows, lids, and other objects. Types of lock include key, combination, chain, and electronic. Most common door locks have a bolt that fits into a metal plate in the door frame. The first key-operated lock, invented in Egypt c.2000 B.C., was a large wooden bolt fastened to the outside of a gate and stabilized by pegs inserted through it; a key raised the pins to free the bolt.

Locke, John (1632-1704), English philosopher, founder of empiricism, whose writings helped initiate the European Enlightenment. His *Essay Concerning Human Understanding* (1690) opposed the view that there were innate ideas; he held instead that the human mind was like a blank slate on which knowledge is inscribed by experience. His *Second Treatise of Civil Government* (1690) established him as Britain's leading philosopher of politics. In it he argued that all people had the right to 'life, health, liberty, and possessions.' He proposed a 'social contract' to guarantee these rights. Locke also held that revolution was justified and even necessary in some circumstances, and he upheld both religious toleration and government by checks and balances, as later adopted in the U.S. Constitution. A believer in progress and the scientific method, Locke was one of the most influential thinkers of the modern era.

Lockjaw *See:* Tetanus.

Locomotive, power unit used to haul railroad trains. The earliest railroad locomotives, invented in England in the early 19th century, used steam engines, which remained popular until the mid-20th century. Although electric locomotives have been in service in the United States since 1895, the high capital cost of converting tracks to electric transmission has prevented their widespread adoption. Since the 1950s, most U.S. locomotives have been built with diesel engines. Elsewhere in the world, particularly in Europe, much greater use is made of electric traction, the locomotives usually collecting power from overhead cables via a pantograph. Although some gas-turbine locomotives are in service in the United States, this and other novel power sources have not made much headway.

Locomotor ataxia *See:* Ataxia.

Locoweed, any of several leguminous plants of the genera *Astragalus* and *Oxytropis* native to dry regions of the west and southwestern United States. The plants are poisonous, causing livestock to become stuporous and to stagger, a disease commonly known as locoism.

Locust, in zoology, name for about 50 species of tropical grasshoppers that have a swarming stage in their life cycle. Locusts breed in huge numbers where conditions are suitable, then fly in swarms when they reach maturity. The swarms may contain as many

In 1938, the London and North Eastern Railway's Pacific 'Mallard', designed by Sir Nigel Gresley, broke the world speed record for a steam locomotive by reaching a speed of 125.5 mph (202 km/h).

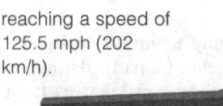

The Santa Fé Class 2900 is a good example of a large American fast freight locomotive.

The French National Railway's Class CC 7100 electric locomotive broke the world rail speed record in March 1955, by reaching a speed of 205.7 mph (331 km/h).

Great Northern's diesel engine, built by General Motors, is a typical large American general-purpose diesel locomotive.

The New Tokaido Line, a high-speed electric line, runs between Tokyo and Osaka, Japan.

as 100 billion insects and can cause agricultural disaster when they land and devour crops.

Locust, in botany, deciduous tree or shrub (genus *Robinia*) with large thorns. Locusts have flowers like those of sweet peas and compound leaves made up of double rows of leaflets. They grow rapidly, and their roots send up suckers, making them effective for holding shifting ground. The timber does not shrink or swell and is used to make wooden pins and railroad ties.

Lodestone *See:* Loadstone.

Lódz (pop. 818,000), city in central Poland, the country's second largest. Chartered in 1423, the city was taken over by Prussia in 1793 and by Russia in 1815. Only in 1919 did it revert to Poland. German troops occupied and severely damaged Lódz during World War II; it has since been rebuilt. Today it is Poland's leading textile manufacturing city, as well as the center of its motion picture industry.
See also: Poland.

Loeb, Jacques (1859-1924), German-born U.S. biologist best known for his work on parthenogenesis, especially his induction of artificial parthenogenesis in the eggs of sea urchins and frogs. Parthenogenesis is the process by which an unfertilized egg develops into an embryo.

Loesser, Frank (1910-1969), U.S. composer of music and lyrics. He won the Academy Award for his song 'Baby It's Cold Outside' (1949) and shared the Pulitzer Prize with Abe Burrows for the musical comedy *How to Succeed in Business Without Even Trying* (1962).

Löffler, Friedrich (1852-1915), German bacteriologist who co-discovered the diphtheria bacillus in 1884. Löffler found a way to cultivate the bacillus and perfected a staining method by which it could be carefully observed under a microscope. His demonstration that some animals are immune to diphtheria influenced Emil von Behring in the development of a diphtheria antitoxin. Löffler is also credited, along with Paul Frosch, for discovering that foot-and-mouth disease is viral and for developing a serum against it.

Lofting, Hugh (1886-1947), English-born U.S. author and illustrator of the famous *Dr. Dolittle* stories, begun in letters to his children during World War I. *The Voyages of Dr. Dolittle*, the second in the series, won him the Newbery medal in 1923.

Log, in nautical measurement, device used to measure a ship's speed. It consists of a piece of board in the form of a quadrant of a circle, balanced so as to float upright. When thrown from the ship, it drags on the line to which it is attached, causing it to unwind at a rate corresponding to the ship's velocity.

Loganberry, hybrid bramble produced from the dewberry and the raspberry. It is named for Judge Logan, who developed it in 1881.

Logarithm, power to which a fixed number, called the base, must be raised to produce a given number. The base is usually 10 or *e*. For example: $2^3 = 8$; 3 is the logarithm of 8 to the base 2.
See also: Napier, John.

Logic, the science of dealing with formal principles of reasoning and thought. Aristotelian, or classical, logic is characterized by a concern for the structure and elements of argument based on the belief that thought, language, and reality are interrelated. Classical logic's influence on Western Civilization has been enormous and enduring. In the 19th and 20th centuries symbolic logic has achieved preeminence. It is rooted in mathematical theory (Set Theory) and has been instrumental in the evolution of modern mathematics.

Loire River, longest river in France, rising in the Cévennes Mountains of central France and flowing north and west through the Massif Central about 650 mi (1,050 km) to the Atlantic. The Loire Valley is famous for its opulent chateaux.

Loki, in Norse mythology, the god who personified trouble and deceit. Although some myths show Loki to be helpful to the gods, he is generally portrayed as evil. He is most infamous for his role in the killing of Balder, the son of the chief god Odin.

Lollards, name given to the 14th-century followers of the English religious reformer John Wycliffe (c.1328-84). Wandering preachers, the Lollards taught that ministers should be poor and that Christians should interpret the Bible themselves. They held that the Bible, and not an organized church, should be the supreme authority. Although repressed during the early 15th century, Lollard beliefs were linked with radical social unrest and remained as underground influences on later movements.

Lombards, Germanic people who moved from northwestern Germany toward Italy in the fourth century. In 568 they crossed the Alps and conquered most of northern Italy, dividing it into dukedoms until 584, when they united into a kingdom against the threat of Frankish invasion. The kingdom reached its height under Liutprand in the 8th century, but was soon overrun by the Franks under Charlemagne in the 770s.

Lombardy, region of northern Italy, once part of the kingdom of the Lombards, for whom it is named. Italy's main industrial and commercial region, it also has efficient and prosperous agriculture. Its capital, Milan, is a major transport and commercial center.

Lombok (pop. 2.5 million), Indonesian island in the province Nusa Tenggara Barrat. One of the Lesser Sunda Islands, south of the Balinese sea; 2099 sq mi (5435 sq km). The capital city is Mataram, the most important harbor is Ampenam. Partly volcanic mountain country (Rindjani, 12,225 ft, 3726 m). In the central plain coffee, sugar, rice, tobacco, corn and cotton are cultivated.

Low tide in the Thames near Chiswick in East London.

Some industry (processing of precious metals and iron). The flora and fauna are more Australian than Balinese or Southeast Asian. After a long period of Balinese government the island came under direct Dutch rule in 1894; since 1950 it is part of the Republic of Indonesia.

Lomé (pop. 650,000), capital, largest city, and chief seaport of Togo. It is on the Gulf of Guinea, 110 miles (177 km) east of Accra, Ghana, and 160 miles (257 km) west of Lagos, Nigeria. The city has an airport and rail connections to the interior. Coffee, cocao, palm nuts, cotton, and peanuts are exported. Lomé was founded by Germans in the late 19th century.

London (pop. 331,000), manufacturing and commercial city on the Thames River in southeast Ontario, Canada. Settled by British colonists on Iroquois land in 1826, London was destroyed by fire in 1845, but soon rebuilt. Today it is the home of more than 300 manufacturing plants, producing goods such as beverages, foods, diesel vehicles, chemical and electrical products, and telephone equipment.
See also: Ontario.

London (pop. 7,600,000), capital of Great Britain. Divided into 33 boroughs, Greater London covers over 650 sq mi (1,684 sq km) along both banks of the Thames River in southeast England. The national center of government, trade, commerce, shipping, finance, and industry, it is also one of the cultural centers of the world.
The Port of London handles over 33% of British trade. London is also an important industrial region in its own right, with various manufacturing industries. Many of the most important financial and business institutions, such as the Bank of England, the Stock Exchange, and Lloyd's of London, as well as many banking and shipping concerns, are concentrated in the single square mile (2.6 km) known as the City. The ancient nucleus of London, the City has its own Lord Mayor. To the west of the City are the Law Courts, the Inns of Court, and the governmental area in Westminster centered on the House of Commons and House of Lords. London is a historic city with many beautiful buildings; the Tower of London, Westminster Abbey, and Buckingham Palace are major tourist attractions. Home of

L

universities, colleges, and some of the world's greatest museums and libraries, it also has a flourishing night life. London's art galleries, concert halls, theaters, and opera houses are world-famous. Distant areas of London are linked by the complex and highly efficient subway system known as the Underground.
See also: United Kingdom.

London, Jack (John Griffith London; 1876-1916), U.S. author of novels and short stories, many set during the Yukon Gold Rush and treating the struggles of men and animals to survive. His works include *The Call of the Wild* (1903), *The Sea Wolf* (1904), *White Fang* (1906), and *Burning Daylight* (1910). He also wrote an autobiographical novel *Martin Eden* (1909), and a political novel, *The Iron Heel* (1907), dramatizing his socialist beliefs and predicting the rise of fascism. Alcoholism and financial problems led him to commit suicide at the age of 40.

The first stone-built bridge was London Bridge. Its construction was started in 1176, under the supervision of Peter of Colechurch, and was completed in 1209. It was the only bridge in London until 1749, when Westminster Bridge was completed.

London Bridge, historical succession of bridges over the Thames River in London, England. The first bridge, dating from the 10th century, was wooden. In 1176-1209 it was replaced by a stone bridge with many buildings along it, including a chapel and defensive towers. Rebuilt many times, it was demolished and replaced in 1831 by a granite bridge, called New London Bridge. That structure was dismantled in 1968 and moved to Lake Havasu City, Ariz. as a tourist attraction. A new concrete bridge over the Thames replaced it.

Londonderry (pop. 99,000), seaport in northwest Northern Ireland, on the Foyle River. It was known as Derry until 1613 and is still called that by Irish nationalists. It has a traditional shirtmaking industry and some light manufacturing industries. Since 1968 it has been a center of violent conflict between Protestants and Roman Catholics.
See also: Ireland.

Lone Star State *See:* Texas.

Long, Richard (1945), British expressive artist, representative of land art. He goes on hikes and bicycle rides through landscapes which he finds interesting, making sculptures on the road of material he finds on the spot. He also makes sculptures indoors using natural materials. Also presents landscape pictures as a form of sculpture.

Longbow *See:* Archery.

Longfellow, Henry Wadsworth (1807-1882), U.S. poet, one of the most popular poets of his generation. A contemporary of Hawthorne at Bowdoin College, he became a professor of modern languages there (1829-1835) and at Harvard (1836-1854). His principal works were the narrative poems *Evangeline* (1847), *The Song of Hiawatha* (1855), and *The Courtship of Miles Standish* (1858), and *Paul Revere's Ride* (1861). Famous individual poems include 'The Wreck of the Hesperus' and 'Excelsior.'

Longinus (fl. 1st cent. ?A.D.), Greek writer to whom the ancient Greek essay on literary criticism *On the Sublime* has been attributed. The treatise discusses 'loftiness of style' in literature. It quotes the Greek orator Demosthenes and the Roman orator Cicero to make comparative points about literary style, and it is the source of the text of Sappho's second ode.

Longitude, measure of the distance, in angular degrees, of any point on the earth's surface east or west of the prime meridian, which is 0° longitude. The prime meridian is the imaginary great circle line, running from pole to pole, that runs through the city of Greenwich, England. Meridians of longitude and parallels of latitude form a grid that can be used to locate the position of any point on the earth's surface.
See also: Latitude; Prime meridian.

Long March, the 6,000 mi (9,656 km) march (1934-35) of the Chinese communists, from Jiangxi in the Southeast to Shaanxi in the extreme Northwest, which saved the movement from extermination by the Nationalist (Kuomintang) forces of Chiang Kai-shek. Led by Mao Zedong, the Red Army of some 100,000 trekked over 18 mountain ranges and 24 rivers under constant air and land attack by Kuomintang troops and local warlords. The march, which lasted for one year, took the lives of almost one-half of its participants.
See also: China; Mao Zedong.

Long Parliament, English legislative assembly that met between 1640 and 1660. Convened by Charles I, it tried to check his power. The conflict between the crown and Parliament culminated in the Civil War (1642-1645), during which Parliament remained in session. In 1648 it was 'purged' of accused supporters of the king, and in 1649 those who were left, known as the Rump Parliament, had Charles beheaded for treason. In 1653 Parliament was suspended under the Protectorate led by Oliver Cromwell. It was briefly reconvened in 1660 prior to the Restoration.
See also: Parliament.

Lon Nol (1913-1985), Cambodian general and head of state (1970-1975). In 1970 he led a coup to depose Prince Norodom Sihanouk. Although Lon Nol declared Cambodia as a republic he ruled as a dictator, cooperating with the U.S. invasion in the spring of 1970. Overthrown by Khmer

Rouge guerillas in 1975 after a bloody civil war, Lon Nol fled to Hawaii, where he settled.
See also: Cambodia.

Loon, waterbird (family *Gaviidae*) of northern countries, known in England as the diver. These birds have webbed feet set well back on their bodies and are very ungainly on land. They are best known for their eerie, wailing calls. They make their nests on the edges of ponds, and the chicks sometimes ride on their parents' backs. They catch fish by diving, sometimes below 200 ft (61 m).

Loos, Adolf (1870-1933), Austrian architect. Contacts with the school of Chicago during a stay in the United States (1893-1896) were greatly significant. He rejected Jugendstil and propagated a functional architecture without ornaments. Built among other things the Café Museum in Vienna (1899), Villa Karma near Montreux (1904-1906) and the Tristan-Tzara house in Paris for the Dadaists (1926). His publications include *Ornament and Crime* (1908).

Loosestrife, popular name of any of several species of primulaceous plants (genus *Lysimachia*) with leafy stems and yellow-white flowers.

Lopez, Jennifer (1970-), American pop singer and film actress of Puerto Rican origin. Lopez started her career in musicals, after which she obtained a few minor roles in films and television series. Her breakthrough came when she played the leading parts in box-office hits such as *Money Train* (1995), *Selena* (1997), *Out of Sight* (1998) and *Enough* (2002). Her career in music experienced similar success. The mix of Latin pop and R&B on albums such as *On The 6* (1999) and *J.Lo* (2000), made her a major Latino star.

López de Santa Anna, Antonio *See:* Santa Anna, Antonio López de.

López Portillo, José (1920-), president of Mexico (1976-1982), during a period of rapid economic growth, especially in the energy field. He was notably assertive in his relationship with the United States.
See also: Mexico.

Lop-Nor, salt lakes in China in the east of the Tarim basin. Initially considered to be one lake. Surface area and location keep changing as a result of the varying water supply of the Tarim. Uninhabited area, used for nuclear testing.

Loquat, subtropical evergreen tree (*Eriobotrya japonica*) of the rose family that bears an egg-shaped orange or yellow fruit. Loquats grow from 18 to 25 ft (5.5 to 7.6 m) tall and have fleshy, tough-skinned, many-seeded fruits borne in loose clusters. Most widely found in Japan, the loquat was introduced to the United States in 1784. Its fruit has a pleasant tart flavor and can be eaten raw, cooked, or in the form of jelly.

Lorca, Federico García *See:* García Lorca, Federico.

Lord's Prayer, or Our Father, chief Christian prayer, taught by Christ to his disciples (Mat. 6.9-13; Luke 11.2-4) and prominent in all Christian worship. Addressed to God the Father, it contains seven petitions, the first three for God's glory, the last four from bodily and spiritual needs. The closing doxology, used by most Protestants ('For thine is the kingdom' etc.), was added to the Roman Catholic version after the Second Vatican Council (1962-1965). *See also:* Christianity.

Lorelei, an imposing cliff, 433 feet (132 m) high, rising above the right (east) bank of the Rhine River near the town of St. Goar, Germany. The cliff is a landmark on the scenic river between Koblenz and Bingen. Here the river flows over a ledge of rocks and is broken into dangerous rapids and whirlpools. Many ships have been lost here. The Lorelei is famous for its echo. There is an old legend about a river nymph, the Lorelei, who lived here. It was said that when ships passed, the Lorelei would sit on the cliff singing and combing her gold hair so that she might distract the sailors and lead them to their doom on the rocks.
Heinrich Heine, a German poet, wrote 'The Lorelei' (1823), a popular ballad, which was set to music by Franz Schubert, Robert Schumann, and other composers. Alfredo Catalani told the story in grand opera (1890).

Lorentz, Hendrik Antoon (1853-1928), Dutch physicist awarded with Pieter Zeeman the 1902 Nobel Prize for physics for his prediction of the Zeeman effect (the effects of magnetism on light). Lorentz also introduced the idea of 'local time,' that is, that the rate of time's passage differed from place to place. Incorporating this idea with George Francis Fitzgerald's proposal that a moving body decreases in direction of motion (the Fitzgerald contraction), he derived the Lorentz transformation, a mathematical statement that describes the changes in length, time, and mass of a moving body. His work, with Fitzgerald's, laid the foundations for Albert Einstein's theory of relativity. *See also:* Zeeman effect.

From 1877 to 1912, Hendrik.Antoon Lorentz (1853-1928) was a professor of theoretical physics at Leiden University.

Lorenz, Konrad Zacharias (1903-1989), Austrian zoologist, founder of ethology, the study of animal behavior. He is best known for his studies of bird behavior and of human and animal aggression. His books include *King Solomon's Ring* (1952) and *On Aggression* (1966). He shared the 1973 Nobel Prize for physiology or medicine with Karl von Frisch and Nikolaas Tinbergen. *See also:* Ethology.

Lorenzetti, Ambrogio (mentioned between 1319 and 1347), painter from Siena, brother of Pietro. Famous for his monumental frescos *Allegories and Effects of Good and Bad Government in the Town and in the Country* (1337-1340; Palazzo Pubblico, Siena), which reflect daily life in a remarkably realistic way.

Lorenzetti, Pietro (d. 1348?), Italian painter form Siena, brother of Ambrogio Lorenzetti. His work, among whose influences are Simone Martini, is characterized by an increasing plasticity and expressiveness and a pursuit of three-dimensional effects. Works include frescos in the church of S. Francesco in Assisi: *Passion of Christ* (ca. 1330) and *Birth of Mary* (Siena, Cathedral Museum).

Lorenzini, Carlo *See:* Collodi, Carlo.

Lorenzo the Magnificent *See:* Medici.

Loris, any of several species of primates related to the lemurs. They have large eyes, no tail, spindly legs, and hands adapted for grasping twigs. Native to the forests of southern Asia, they move slowly but deliberately along the lower branches of trees and bushes at night in search of fruit, leaves, and small animals such as insects and nesting birds.

Lorrain, Claude *See:* Claude Lorrain.

Lorraine *See:* Alsace-Lorraine.

Los Alamos, town in New Mexico, 25 mi (40 km) northwest of Santa Fe. It was selected as the site for a scientific laboratory where the world's first atomic and hydrogen bombs were developed (1942). Government research continued at this location until 1962. The University of California currently operates The Los Alamos Scientific Laboratory. The laboratory has been designated as a national landmark. *See also:* Manhattan Project; New Mexico.

Los Angeles (pop. 3,500,000), city in southern California, second-largest in the United States, a sprawling city of some 464 sq mi (1,201 sq km), the center of a metropolitan area with a population of over 8 million. Los Angeles is the third-largest industrial center in the United States, producing among other things aircraft, electrical equipment, canned fish, and refined oils. It is also a major center of the motion-picture and television industries, and a distribution and commercial center for the nearby mining regions, oilfields, and rich farm areas. Its port, San Pedro, handles more tonnage than any other U.S. Pacific port, and accommodates a large

Automobile facilities form the most striking element of Los Angeles. In the background you can see part of the Central Business District.

L

fishing fleet. The city has several museums and 4 universities. The geographical setting and the large concentration of automobiles and industry have created a serious problem of smog and air pollution, the worst in the United States. Founded by the Spanish in 1781, Los Angeles was taken from Mexico in 1846. It was linked with the transcontinental railroad system in the 1870s and

The loris (*Nycticebus pygmaeus*) is a slow nocturnal animal that lives in the tropical forests of Southeast Asia.

1880s. Oil was discovered in the region in the 1890s, leading to rapid population growth. *See also:* California.

Lot, in the Old Testament, son of Abraham's brother Haran. He lived in the city of Sodom. Warned that both Sodom and Gomorrah were to be destroyed because of their wickedness, he fled with his wife and 2 daughters. Told not to look back, his wife disobeyed and was turned into a pillar of salt (Gen. 11-14:19).

Lotus, any of several kinds of water lilies. The sacred lotus of India figures in paintings of Buddha. It grows in marshes from Egypt to China, its leaves and pink flowers growing on stalks that rise about 3 ft (1 m) from the water. Related to the Indian lotus is the American lotus or duck acorn. Both are edible. The Egyptian lotus is a water lily with floating leaves 2 ft (6 m) across and large white flowers. In ancient times it was cultivated for its fruit.

Lotus-eaters, legendary inhabitants of the north coast of Africa mentioned in Homer's *Odyssey*. They lived on the fruit and flowers of the lotus tree, which drugged them into happy forgetfulness. Tennyson wrote a poem titled after them.

Louganis, Gregory Efhimios (1960-   ), U.S. diver. He won gold medals in the Olympic Games (1984, 1988) for springboard and platform diving.

Lou Gehrig's disease *See:* Amyotrophic lateral sclerosis.

Lough Neagh, lake in Antrim, Northern Ireland. At about 18 mi (29 km) long and 11 mi (18 km) wide, Lough Neagh is the largest lake in the British Isles. Among the wild fowl found on or near the lake is the rare whooper swan. Plentiful in eel, salmon, and trout, the lake is a popular fishing site.

Louis, name of 18 kings of France. **Louis I** (778-840), Holy Roman Emperor 814-840, known as the Pious. The third son of Charlemagne, he divided the empire among his sons, thereby contributing to its fragmentation but laying the foundations of the state of France. **Louis II** (846-879), reigned 877-879. **Louis III** (c.863-882), reigned 879-882. As king of northern France he defeated Norman invaders. **Louis IV** (c.921-954), reigned 936-954. He was called Transmarinus because of his childhood exile in England. **Louis V** (c.966-987), reigned 986-987. The last Carolingian ruler of France, he was known as the Sluggard. **Louis VI** (1081-1137), reigned 1108-1137. He subdued the robber barons around Paris, granted privileges to the towns, and aided the Church. He engaged in war against Henry I of England (1104-1113 and 1116-1120). **Louis VII** (1120-1180), reigned 1137-1180. He joined the Second Crusade (1147-1149) in defiance of a papal interdict. From 1157 onward, Louis was at war with Henry II of England, who had married Louis' former wife, Eleanor of Aquitaine. **Louis VIII** (1187-1226), reigned 1223-1226. Nicknamed the Lion, he was a great soldier

Louis IX the Holy of France (1214-1270) is the prototype of a medieval feudal monarch. This miniature shows this very religious king, who also took part in one of the Crusades, saying his prayers during his travels (Bibliothèque Nationale, Paris).

and was at first successful in his attempts to aid the barons rebelling against King John of England. **Louis IX, Saint** (1214-1270), reigned 1226-1270. He repelled an invasion by Henry III of England (1242) and led the Seventh Crusade (1248), but was defeated and captured in Egypt and had to be ransomed. In 1270 he led another crusade, but died of plague after reaching North Africa. A just ruler, he was regarded as an ideal Christian king. **Louis X** (1289-1316), reigned 1314-1316, a period in which the nobility reasserted their strength. **Louis XI** (1423-1483), reigned 1461-1483. A cruel and unscrupulous king, he plotted against his father for the throne but unified most of France. **Louis XII** (1462-1515), reigned 1498-1515. Nicknamed Father of the People, he was a popular ruler who inaugurated reforms in finance and justice and was ambitious for territorial gains. **Louis XIII** (1601-1643), reigned 1610-1643. A weak king, he was greatly influenced by the chief minister, Cardinal Richelieu. **Louis XIV** (1638-1715), reigned 1643-1715, known as Louis the Great and the Sun King. The archetypal absolute monarch, he built the great palace at Versailles. 'The state is myself,' he is said to have declared. His able ministers, Mazarin and Colbert, strengthened France with their financial reforms. But Louis squandered money in such escapades as the War of Devolution (1667-1668) and the War of the Spanish Succession (1701-1714), which broke the military power of France. **Louis XV** (1710-1774), reigned 1715-1774), nicknamed the 'Well-Beloved.' He was influenced by Cardinal Fleury until the cardinal's death in 1743. A weak king dependent on mistresses (especially Madame de Pompadour), his involvement in foreign wars created enormous debts. **Louis XVI** (1754-1793), reigned 1774-1792. Although he accepted the advice of his ministers on the need for social and political reform, Louis was not strong enough to overcome the opposition of his court and his queen, Marie Antoinette. This led to the outbreak of the French Revolution in 1789, with the formation of the National Assembly and the storming of the Bastille. In 1791 Louis attempted to escape but was brought back to Paris and guillotined. **Louis XVII** (1785-1795), son of Louis XVI, king in name only. He was imprisoned in 1793 and was reported dead in 1795. **Louis XVIII** (1755-1824), brother of Louis XVI. He escaped from France in 1791 For more than 20 years he remained in exile, but after the final defeat of Napoleon in the Battle of Waterloo (1815), he became firmly established, proclaiming a liberal constitution. On his death the reactionary Ultraroyalists gained control under Charles X.

Louis, Joe (Joseph Louis Barrow; 1914-1981), U.S. boxer. Louis won the heavyweight title in 1937, held it longer than anyone in boxing history (1937-1949), and fought 25 successful title defenses. He retired in 1949 having lost only once, to Max Schmeling (1936), a defeat he later avenged, knocking Schmeling out in a rematch (1938). In 1950 he tried to return to the ring, but quit after losing to Ezzard Charles and Rocky Marciano.

Louis XIV and his entourage, hunting near Chateau Chambord. A painting by Pierre Denis Martin, 1663-1742.

Louisiana (Pelican State; pop. 4,352,000), state in the south-central United States; bordered by Arkansas to the north, Mississippi to the east, the Gulf of Mexico to the south, and Texas to the west.

The Mississippi is Louisiana's most important river. Its rich delta covers about one-third of the state's land area. Other major rivers include the Red, Sabine, Pearl, Ouachita, Atchafalaya, and Calcasieu rivers. The largest of the state's numerous lakes is Lake Pontchartrain, which lies north of New Orleans. Principal cities are New Orleans, Baton Rouge (capital), and Shreveport.

Service industries account for about two-thirds of the total value of all the goods and services Louisiana produces in a year. A leading producer of petroleum and natural gas, Louisiana is second (after Texas) in mineral production. Soybeans are the leading farm product. Other major crops include rice, sweet potatoes, cotton, sugarcane, and corn. Livestock produced are beef and dairy cattle, chickens, eggs, and hogs.

Spanish explorers were the first Europeans in the area-already home to about 12,000 Indians-in the 1500s. The region was claimed by France in 1682; parts were later transferred from France to Spain and back again. The U.S. acquired it in the Louisiana Purchase (1803). Louisiana became the 18th state in 1812. The discovery of large deposits of oil (1901) and natural gas (1916) attracted many new industries to Louisiana, but farmers suffered hard times in the 1920s and 1930s. World War II revived the state's industries.

Louisiana Purchase, territory purchased by the United States from France in Apr. 1803. It stretched from the Mississippi River on the east into the Rockies on the west, north almost to the Canadian border and south to the Gulf of Mexico, some 828,000 sq mi (2,144,520 sq km) in all. Its acquisition more than doubled the area of what was then the United States. The price was $15 mil-

Louisiana's many swamp areas, such as this swamp near the Mississippi border, are excellent hunting and fishing grounds.

lion. In 1800 Napoleon persuaded the Spanish to return what had been the French province of Louisiana. President Thomas Jefferson instructed Robert R. Livingston and James Monroe to purchase New Orleans and other strategic parts of Louisiana from France. To the surprise of the U.S. delegation, Napoleon, who was expecting war with England, offered to sell the entire territory to the United States, and the envoys quickly accepted the offer.

Louis Napoleon *See:* Napoleon III.

Louis Philippe (1773-1850), king of France, 1830-1848. Exiled from France in 1793, he traveled in Europe and the United States until 1815. He was accepted as a compromise candidate for the crown in 1830. As king he refused to extend the voting franchise, and the revolution of Feb. 1848 led to his abdication. The monarchy was abolished and Louis Philippe fled to England, where he died.

Louisville (pop. 256,000), largest city in Kentucky, on the Ohio River, whose falls provide hydroelectric power for the city. A major river port, transportation hub, and commercial, manufacturing, and cultural center, Louisville produces tobacco products, whiskey, and gin, as well as plumbing equipment, motor vehicles, and baseball bats. Among the several institutions of higher learning is the University of Louisville (1798). Incorporated in 1828, Louisville was named for King Louis XVI of France in recognition of his help during the American Revolutionary War.
See also: Kentucky.

Lourdes (pop. 17,000), town in southwestern France and site of Roman Catholic pilgrimage. The Virgin Mary is said to have appeared to St. Bernadette, then a 14-year-old peasant girl, in Lourdes in 1858. Lourdes is visited by some 1 million pilgrims annually.

Louse, any of several wingless parasitic insects of 2 orders, *Mallophaga* (bird lice or biting lice) and *Phthiraptera* (mammalian or sucking lice). With flattened bodies and broad, clearly segmented abdomens, lice are well adapted to moving between hair or feathers, and are usually host-specific. Bird lice feed by chewing on feather fragments or dead skin, occasionally biting through the skin for blood. Mammalian lice feed purely on blood obtained with needlelike sucking mouthparts. The human lice spread several diseases.

Louvre, historic palace in Paris, mostly built during the reign of Louis XIV, now one of the world's largest and most famous art museums. Its treasures include paintings by Rembrandt, Rubens, Titian, and Leonardo da Vinci, whose *Mona Lisa* is there. Other masterpieces in its collection are the painting *Arrangement in Gray and Black*, known as 'Whistler's Mother,' and the Greek statues, the *Venus of Milo* and *Victory of Samothrace* ('Winged Victory').

Lovebird, any of various small gray or green parrots known for their close pairbond and the frequency with which they preen their mate, particularly genus *Agapornis* of Africa.

Lovelace, Richard (1618-1657?), English Royalist soldier and Cavalier poet. His poems, in 2 volumes, were published in 1649 and 1660.

Lovell, James Arthur, Jr. (1928-), U.S. astronaut who commanded Apollo 13, the spacecraft scheduled to land on the moon in 1970. The safety of this flight was endangered when an oxygen tank aboard Apollo 13 exploded. The others were forced to cancel the mission and pilot the spacecraft to a premature landing in the Pacific Ocean. Lovell's first space flight was the 14-day earth orbit of Gemini 7 in 1965. Gemini 7 joined in space with Gemini 6 to achieve the

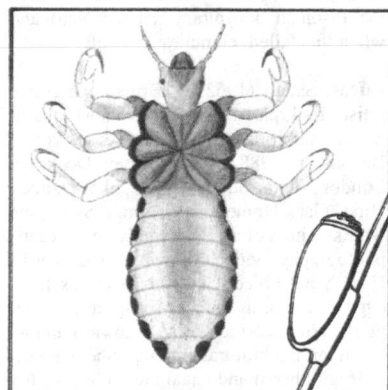

Biting and sucking lice belong to the insect order *Phthiraptera*. They are small, wingless insects, that live as external parasites on birds and mammals. On the left, a body louse (*Pediculus humanus*), length 0.2 in (4 mm). Lower right a louse egg, attached to a human hair.

first successful space rendezvous. Lovell was also on the crew of Gemini 12 and Apollo 8, which was the first manned craft to orbit the moon.

Lovell, Sir Bernard (1913-), British radio astronomer. As director of the Jodrell Bank (now Nuffield Radio Astronomy Laboratories) he was instrumental in constructing one of the world's largest steerable radio telescopes (1957).
See also: Astronomy; Jodrell Bank Observatory.

Lowell, Amy (1874-1925), U.S. critic and poet of the imagist school. Her collections of verse include *Sword Blades and Poppy Seed* (1914), *Men, Women and Ghosts* (1916), and the Pulitzer Prize-winning *What's o'Clock?* (1925).

Lowell, James Russell (1819-1891), U.S. poet, editor, essayist, and diplomat. His poetry includes the didactic *Vision of Sir Launfal* (1848) and the satirical *The Bigelow Papers* (1848 and 1867). He was professor of modern languages at Harvard (1855-1876) and U.S. minister to England (1877-1885); his speeches were published in *Democracy and Other Addresses* (1887).

Lowell, Percival (1855-1916), U.S. astronomer. He predicted the existence of Pluto (confirmed 1930). He also believed that the 'canals' of Mars were an irrigation system built by an intelligent race.
See also: Astronomy; Pluto.

Lowell, Robert (1917-1977), U.S. poet and playwright. His collections include the autobiographical *Life Studies* (1959), and the Pulitzer Prize-winning *Lord Weary's Castle* (1946) and *The Dolphin* (1973). His free adaptations of Greek tragedy and European poets brought him acclaim as a translator.

Lowry, Malcolm (1909-1957), English novelist. His greatest work, *Under the Volcano* (1947), was concerned in part with alcoholism, which eventually proved fatal to the author. A reworking of his first novel, *Ultramarine* (1933), and two volumes of short stories were published posthumously.

Loyola, Saint Ignatius (1491-1556), Spanish founder of the Society of Jesus (Jesuits), a Roman Catholic order. A Basque nobleman and soldier, Loyola converted to

In 1540, Pope Paul III approved of the order that was established by Ignatius of Loyola (1491-1556). This painting by an anonymous artist can be found in the Gesu Church, where Ignatius was buried.

L

L

religious life in 1521. His major work, *Spiritual Exercises*, was begun 1522-1523. He later went to Paris with St. Francis Xavier to form the new order (1534). Loyola was its first general (1541-1556). His feast day is July 31.
See also: Jesuits.

LPG *See:* Butane and propane.

LSD, or lysergic acid diethylamide, hallucinogenic drug that induces a state of excitation of the central nervous system and overactivity of the autonomic nervous system, manifested as changes in mood (usually euphoric, sometimes depressive) and perception. LSD was invented in 1938 by 2 Swiss chemists, Arthur Stoll and Albert Hofmann. No evidence of physical dependence can be detected when the drug is abruptly withdrawn. A high degree of tolerance develops and disappears rapidly. The chief danger to the individual is the psychological effect and impairment of judgment, which can lead to dangerous decisionmaking or accidents. Responses to LSD depend on several factors, including the individual's expectations, the setting, and his or her ability to cope with perceptual distortions. Untoward reactions to LSD apparently have become rare, but adverse reactions appear as anxiety attacks, extreme apprehensiveness, or panic states. Most often these reactions quickly subside with appropriate management in a secure setting. However, some individuals remain disturbed and may even show a persistent psychotic state. It is unclear whether the drug use has precipitated or uncovered a pre-existing psychotic potential or whether this can occur in previously stable individuals.
Some persons, especially those who are chronic or repeated users, may experience drug effects after they have discontinued use of the drug. Referred to as 'flashbacks,' these episodes most commonly consist of visual distortions, but can include distorted perceptions of time, space, or selfimage. Such episodes may be precipitated by the use of marijuana, alcohol, or barbiturates or by stress or fatigue, or they may occur without apparent reason. The mechanisms that produce flashbacks are not known, but they tend to subside over a period of 6 months to 1 year.
See also: Drug; Drug abuse.

Luanda (pop. 2,200,000), capital and largest city of Angola. Located on the west coast of Africa, Luanda is a manufacturing center and port. Its industries include saw and textile mills, cement, printing, and food processing plants. Luanda was founded in 1576 by Portuguese settlers who built fortresses, churches, and public buildings patterned after European styles of architecture. After Angola gained independence from Portugal in 1975, most of the Portuguese left.

Luba, African ethnic group comprised of Bantu-speaking tribes. Living predominantly in the grasslands of central and southeastern Zaire, the Luba are composed of tribes linked by similar cultures and related languages. The 3 major Luba subdivisions-the Luba-Shankaji of Shaba, the Luba-Bambo of Kasai, and the Luba-Hemba of northern Shaba and southern Kivu-are connected by history, language, and culture to other peoples of the Congo basin. Traditionally, they live in thatched-roof huts along single-street villages. During the twentieth century many Luba-Kasai moved to urban areas.

Lübeck (pop. 220,000), city in Schleswig-Holstein, northern Germany, on the Trave River near its mouth at the Baltic Sea. Lübeck has been an important trading center since its founding in 1143. Today it is also a center of ship-building and machine manufacturing. It is also known for its candy products, especially the almond and sugar candy known as marzipan.
See also: Germany.

Lubitsch, Ernst (1892-1947), German film director, noted for the sophisticated comedies he made after his emigration to Hollywood in 1923. Among his films are *Forbidden Paradise* (1924), *Ninotchka* (1939), and *Heaven Can Wait* (1943).

Lubumbashi (pop. 795,000), Zaire, a city and the capital of Shaba province. It lies near the Zambian border, about 970 miles (1,560 km) southeast of Kinshasa, the national capital. Lubumbashi is the commercial and industrial center for a rich mining region producing copper, zinc, and cobalt, and has large smelting, metal fabricating, and food processing industries. Railways link the city with Zambia, Angola, and the Congo River system. It is also served by an international airport. Lubumbashi was founded in 1910 as a mining camp called Elisabethville and grew with the copper industry. From 1960 until 1963 it was the capital of the secessionist state of Katanga. The name was changed in 1966.

Lucan (Marcus Annaeus Lucanus; A.D. 39-65), Roman poet, nephew of Seneca, best known for his *Bellum civile*, an epic literary work on the clash between Julius Caesar and Pompey. A protégé of Nero, he eventually aroused the latter's jealousy. Lucan joined the Pisonian conspiracy against Nero and when this failed, committed suicide.

Lucas, Sarah (1962-), British expressive artist. Took part in one of the most talked-about exhibitions called 'Freeze' by young Britons in 1988 in the Surrey Docks in London, with others artists like Damien Hirst, Gary Hume and Georgina Starr. She works with collage, assembly, wax casts, photography, video, drawings and words. Uses banal objects and food such as fruit, eggs and fish, as well as self-portraits. Her work shows a critical attitude toward human behavior and cultural patterns. She expresses it with harsh and banal humor and with a certain aggression. She exposes i.e. female stereotypes.

Lucerne (pop. 60,000), city in central Switzerland, on the banks of the Reuss River and western shore of Lake Lucerne, capital of Lucerne canton. The city is considered one of the most picturesque in Switzerland, the old town on the bank of the Reuss containing many historic structures, including houses dating back to medieval times. Lucerne is a major European tourist center, with casinos, beaches, horse-racing and jumping competitions, and a traditional pre-Lenten carnival.
See also: Switzerland.

Lucian (A.D. 125-190), Syrian-Greek satirist. Among his best-known works are *Dialogues of the Gods*, a parody of mythology; *Dialogues of the Dead*, a biting satire on human vanities; and *True History*, a lampoon of fantastic travelers' tales, which influenced Rabelais and Jonathan Swift.

Lucifer, the devil. In the Bible, the reference to Lucifer is applied to the King of Babylon, but was misunderstood to mean the fallen angel. Lucifer thus came to be another name for Satan.

Lucinschi, Petru (1940-), Moldavian politician. Soviet President Gorbachev brought him to Moscow in 1990, where he became a member of the politburo. After the Soviet Union collapsed in 1991, Lucinschi went back to Moldavia. During his candidacy for the presidency in 1996 he opposed the current President Mircea Snegur, who supported a course oriented toward Romania and Europe. In contrast, chairman of parliament Lucinschi pleaded for closer connections with Russia and other members of the CIS, and announced less drastic economic reforms than those Snegur advocated. At the end of 1996 he beat Snegur in the presidential elections, succeeding him as president in early 1997.

Lucknow (pop. 2,200,000), capital of the state of Uttar Pradesh in northcentral India. Founded as a Muslim fort in the 13th century, Lucknow was incorporated into the British empire in 1856. Indian soldiers seized the city during the Sepoy Rebellion in 1857, but it was reclaimed by Britain the following year. Today Lucknow combines modern offices and industries with an old commercial district of silversmith and handicraft shops.
See also: India.

Lucretia, According to a Roman legend, the wife of Lucius Tarquinius Collatinus. She was conquered and raped by Sextus Tarquinius and thereupon committed suicide in public. This made her into the symbol of virtuousness and as such she was sung about by poets like Petrarch, Dante and Shakespeare. From the 16th century onwards the story was dramatized by e.g. Thomas Heywood (*The Rape of Lucrece*, 1608), Johann Elias Schlegel (*Lucretia*, 1740) and André Obey (*Le viol de Lucrèce*, 1932), which was also the basis for Benjamin Britten's opera *The Rape of Lucretia*. In the visual arts her conquest as well as her suicide have been recorded by painters like Botticelli, Rubens, Dürer and Rembrandt.

Lucretius (c.99-c.55 B.C.), Roman poet and philosopher. He was the author of *De rerum natura* ('On the nature of things') and the last classical exponent of atomism, a belief

that everything is made up of atoms controlled by the laws of nature. Considered antireligious in his time, many of his theories were later validated.
See also: Philosophy.

Lüda (Lüta; pop. 2,700,000), China, a municipality on the southern coast of the Liaodong peninsula in Liaoning province, Manchuria. It includes the cities of Dalian (formerly Dairen), Manchuria's chief commercial port; and Lüshun (formerly Port Arthur), an important naval base. Lüda is also a major industrial center. Industries include shipbuilding, oil refining, food processing, and the manufacturing of railway cars and locomotives, steel, chemicals, and machine tools. Several technical schools and a medical college are here. Lüshun and Dalian have been port cities for hundreds of years. Japan held the cities briefly at the close of the Sino-Japanese War in 1895. They came under Russian authority in 1898, byt were lost to Japan in 1905, after the Russo-Japanese War. Japan maintained control until defeated in World War II. Russia and Japan did much to develop the ports, railways, and industries of the area. After World War II China and the Soviet Union shared control until 1955, when China regained sole possession of the cities. The municipality was created soon thereafter.

Ludendorff, Erich (1865-1937), German general who with von Hindenburg did much to defeat the invading Russian armies in World War I. He was responsible for German military strategy 1917-1918 and for the request of an armistice in 1918. After the war he took part in Hitler's abortive coup in Munich in 1923.
See also: World War I.

Ludhiana (pop. 1,200,000), city in India, marketplace in the northwestern state of Punjab. Grain trade, steel and silk industries, machine factories, agricultural university (1962). Founded by a Lodi sovereign (1480) and conquered at the beginning of the 19th century by the Sikhs, who had to give up Ludhiana to Great Britain after the 1845-1846 Sikh war. Industrialized after 1947.

Ludwig, Christa (1928-), Austrian singer (mezzo-soprano). Ludwig was educated by her mother and became, after engagements in Frankfurt am Main (1946-1952), Darmstadt (1952-1954) and Hannover (1954-1955), one of the greatest singers of the Viennese State Opera. She sang many star roles (including Bayreuth, Salzburg and Luzern) and often performed as a concert singer (including Mahler's *Das Lied von der Erde* and Bach's *Christmas Oratorio*). She is also famous as a singer of *lieder*, especially those by Schubert and Mahler. In 1994, she siad goodbye to the concert platform.

Luftwaffe, title of the German air force. Formed in 1935 under Hitler, it was commanded by Herman Goering during World War II.

Luge, winter sport competition where one or two persons ride a sled feet first down an ice covered track. The sled is about 4 ft (1.2 m) long, 18 in (46 cm wide and 8 in (20 cm) high and is steered by shifting weight, pulling straps attached to the runners and using the feet.

Luisetti, Hank (1916-), U.S. basketball player. His revolutionary one-handed push shot increased the scoring and tempo of the game. As a Stanford University student, Luisetti broke the national college four-year scoring record, with 1,596 points. In 1938 he became the first player to score 50 points in a single game, against Duquesne University.

Luke, Saint (fl. 1st century A.D.), traditional author of the third Gospel and the Acts of the Apostles. A Gentile and a physician, he was influenced by his friend, St. Paul, whom he accompanied on missionary journeys. His feast day is Oct. 18.
See also: Bible.

Lully, Jean-Baptiste (1632-1687), Italian-born French composer. A favorite with Louis XIV, he conducted the court orchestra and wrote numerous court ballets. He wrote stage music for Molière, and his operas, particularly *Alceste* (1674), *Amadis* (1684), and *Armide* (1686), founded a French operatic tradition.

Jean-Baptiste Lully (1632-1687) played a very important role in the development of the opera.

L

Lumber, cut wood, especially when prepared for use. There are two kinds of lumber: hardwood and softwood. Softwood comes from trees called conifers, or evergreens, such as pines and firs. Hardwood comes from deciduous trees such as oak, maple, birch, aspen, and cottonwood. Lumbering,

 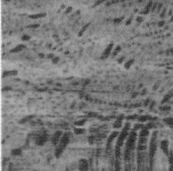  

The largest quantities of teak (*Tectona grandis*) come from India, Burma and Indonesia. Durability, strength and ease of working, make it one of the most popular timbers.

The European Beech (*Fagus sylvatica*) is used in large quantities by the furniture industry and in the manufacturing of plywood. It is a strong timber, straight grained, even and close in texture.

Originally from North America, the Douglas fir (*Pseudotsuga menziesii*) is now grown in vast quantities in European forests. Because long lengths of clear timber can be obtained from this tree, it is often used in heavy construction work and joinery.

The American mahogany (*Swietenia macrophylla*) is a native of Central and South America. It grows best in damp situations. The timber has a natural lustre and is used for furniture and in the shipbuilding industry, especially for interior fittings.

L

the extraction of timber from the forest, is a major industry in the United States. In world timber production, the former USSR is first, then the United States, Japan, and Canada.

Lumen *See:* Candela.

Lumière brothers, Auguste (1862-1954) and **Louis Jean** (1864-1948), French inventors noted for their 'Cinématographe,' a motion-picture camera/projector. The brothers are credited with producing the first movie, whose title in English is *Lunch Break at the Lumiere Factory*. Although the Cinématographe was patented in 1895, the brothers did not regard it as important as some of their improvements in color photography.

Luminescence, nonthermal (heatless) emission (particularly light) caused by electron movement from more energetic states to less energetic states. Including fluorescence and phosphorescence, types of luminescence are named for the mode of excitation. In chemiluminescence the energy source is a chemical reaction, while bioluminescence occurs in biochemical reactions.
See also: Bioluminescence; Fluorescence; Phosphorescence.

Lumpfish, common name for various fishes of the Cyclopteridae family, that inhabit cold, northern ocean waters. They have short, thick-set bodies with scaleless skin. Lumpfish have strong sucking discs on their underside, which they use to hold themselves to the sea bottom.

Luna, in Roman mythology, goddess of the

moon, who drives across the night sky in a chariot. According to the myth, when Luna leaves the sky to visit her lover, the mortal shepherd Endymion, the night is moonless. *See also:* Mythology.

Lunar eclipse *See:* Eclipse.

Lunda, indigenous people of Zaire, Angola, and Zambia. The Lunda people, who speak a Bantu language, had a powerful kingdom in the early 1600s, encompassing large parts of present-day Zaire, Angola, and Zambia. Although most Lunda still live in small country villages where they farm and fish for a living, many have migrated to urban areas since the 1960s.

Lundy, Benjamin (1789-1839), U.S. abolitionist. An activist whose efforts paved the way for the national antislavery movement, Lundy organized the Abolitionist Union Humane Society in Ohio in 1815. As an editor, he published *The Genius of Universal Emancipation* and the *National Enquirer*. Lundy traveled widely in search of places where free blacks could settle. In his effort to prevent slavery from expanding, Lundy worked closely with John Quincy Adams, when Adams was a congressman.
See also: Abolitionism.

Lung, major organs in the respiratory system of mammals, birds, reptiles, and most adult amphibians. These elastic organs pick up oxygen from the air and release carbon dioxide back out. The body requires oxygen to burn food for energy; carbon dioxide is a waste product. In humans, air passes

through the *pharynx* and *larynx* to the *airways*, the tubes leading to the lungs. One of these tubes, the *bronchi*, branches off within the lungs, leading to the many *alveolar sacs* that make up the *respiratory units*. The exchange of gases takes place within the *pulmonary capillaries* of this part of the lungs. Lungs help clean the blood of impurities. By exhaling air that makes vocal chords vibrate, they help to effect the sound of speech.
See also: Human body; Respiration.

Lungfish, name for various fishes of Africa, Australia, and South America that can breathe through lungs. The African (family Protopteridae) and South American (family Lepidosirenidae) lungfishes are eellike, with slender fins. They can survive dry conditions by burrowing into mud and forming a cocoon. The Australian lungfish (family Ceratodontidae) has a broad body covered with large scales and cannot survive drying out. In 1997 DNA research indicated that the lungfish is the predecessor of the amphibian.

Lungwort (*Pulmonaria officinalis*), perennial plant that grows in shady areas. Its flowering herb is used medicinally for lung disorders.

Luoyang (Lo-yang; pop. 1,250,000), city in the Chinese province of Henan on the Luo river. Machine, textile, cement and chemical industries. Is seen as the cradle of Chinese culture and Chinese Buddhism. Cave temples (Caves of Longmen) in the area. Many treasures from ancient times. Capital city of China from 770 to 256 B.C., from 25 to 220 A.D. and during the Chinese-Japanese War

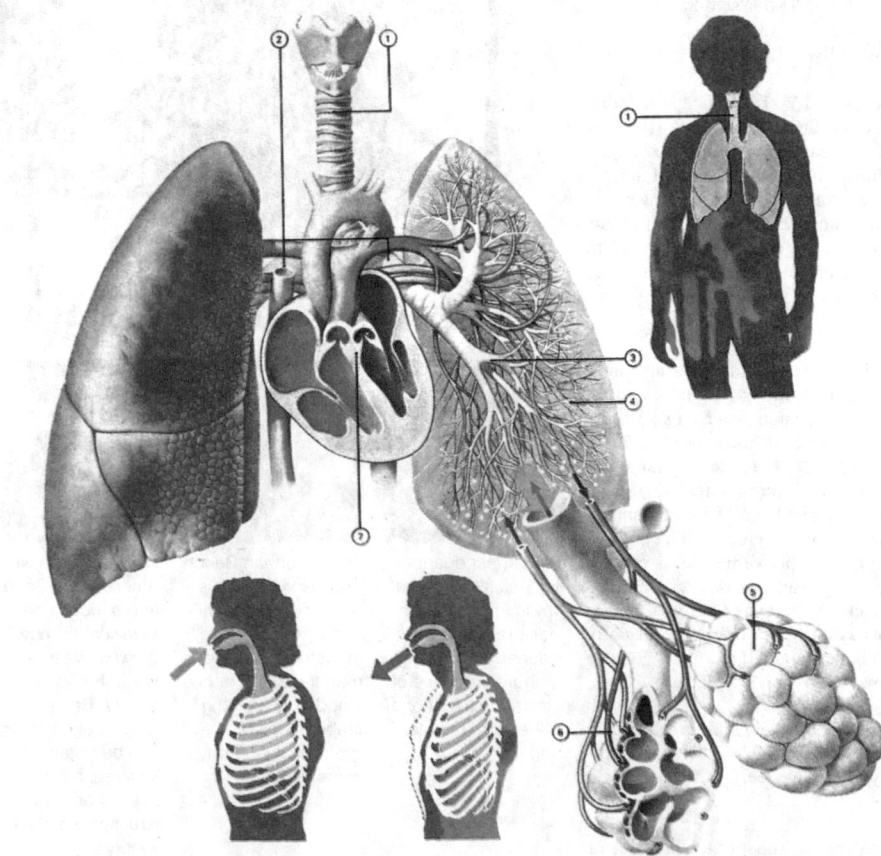

In the – under normal circumstances – automatic process of 'breathing in', fresh, oxygen-rich air is drawn into the lungs, where an exchange of O_2 and CO_2 takes place. After one or two seconds, this is followed by 'breathing out', when oxygen-depleted air is being expelled from the lungs. Blood circulating through the lungs, will transports O_2 to, and CO_2 from the cells in the body. Breathing in involves an expansion of the rib cage and a lowering of the diaphragm. Air is drawn in through the mouth and the nose, down the trachea (1) and the bronchi (2), into the expanded lungs. Inside the lungs, the bronchioles (3) are divided into a million or more tubules (4), ending in minute air sacs, the alveoli (5), surrounded by a network of capillaries (6). The heart (7) will pump oxygen-depleted blood through the lungs, where rapid diffusion of gases will take place, across a thin membrane between the alveoli and their surrounding capillaries. Fresh and oxygenated blood then returns to the heart. Breathing out follows, involving a passive relaxation and raising of the diaphragm, and a sagging of the rib cage. Then, the cycle repeats itself.

(1932-1945). Between 1644 and 1912 the city was called Honan(fu).

Lupercalia, ancient Roman religious festival celebrated on Feb. 15, to enhance fertility for people, animals, and land. The most noted of the activities of the celebration involved naked young men called *luperci* circling the walls of the Palentine Hill in Rome and thrashing women with whips made from the skins of sacrificed animals. It was believed that the women struck by the whips would be rendered fertile.

Lüpertz, Markus (1941-), German painter, precursor of the new Expressionism. After the Dythyrambe series, in which the same motive gets repeated, a period follows in which he paints emotionally charged motives such as uniform caps and canons. Afterwards, in the mid 1970s, he worked with style quotations within one work, a method which enables him to be abstract and figurative at the same time. He works using large formats. Since 1981 he also does sculptures.

Lupine, plant (genus *Lupus*) found wild in North America and around the Mediterranean. Lupines range from 2 in (5 cm) to 10 ft (3 m) in height. The flowers are pealike and cluster around a tall stem.

Lupus, disease in which the immune system produces antibodies that attack healthy tissue. In Systemic lupus erythematosus (SLE) patients develop antibodies to their own cell structures, ultimately causing the failure of many organs, especially the heart and the kidneys.

Lurçat, Jean (1892-1966), French painter, designer and important renewer of tapestry art in France. Lurçat was influenced by Cubism and made small paintings which he called 'poèmes de poche'. After WW I he undertook journeys to Spain, North Africa, Greece and Asia Minor, where he gained inspiration for his tapestries. Within a few years he trained himself thoroughly in the making of cardboard art. Upon discovering the renowned medieval Apocalypse tapestry of Angers, Lurçat was surprised to find that the masterpiece only had about 20 ranges of coloring. In 25 years he drew more than 100 cardboards and became world-famous. Well-known works are: *Le Chant du Monde* (1957-1964; Musée St-Jean, Angers), a 0.193 sq mi (500 sq m) tapestry *Les Quatre Saisons* (1939), and *Liberté*, on a poem by Paul Eluard (1943; Musée National d'Art Moderne, Paris).

Lurie, Alison (1936-), American novelist, gives a critical view of American society from the world of experience of children growing up. Her most famous novel is *The War Between the Tates* (1974).

Lusaka (pop. 1,0 million), capital and largest city of Zambia, in the south-central part of the country. Founded as a European trading post (1905), it was the capital of British-ruled Northern Rhodesia from 1935 until Zambian independence (1964). Intersecting road and railway lines make Lusaka a transportation center, with highways leding to Tanzania, Malawi, and Zimbabwe. The city is also a commercial and government center as well as home to the University of Zambia.
See also: Zambia.

Lusitania, British passenger ship torpedoed and sunk by a German submarine during World War I, on May 7, 1915. A total of 1,198 people were killed, 128 of them U.S. citizens. The Germans claimed that ammunition was being transported on the ship. The incident aroused popular sentiment in the United States for joining the Allied side in the war.
See also: World War I.

Lute, plucked string instrument with a pear-shaped body and a fretted neck, related to the guitar. It was most popular in Europe between 1400 and 1700. Instruments of the lute type date at least from 2000 B.C. in Mesopotamia. The direct ancestor of the European lute of the Renaissance was an Arabian instrument, from which it gets its name (Arabic: *al-oud*, the wood); the Middle Eastern lute is still called an oud.

Lutetium, chemical element, symbol Lu; for physical constants see Periodic Table. Lutetium (formerly spelled 'lutecium') was discovered by Georges Urbain in 1907, by separating the ytterbia then known into neoytterbia and lutetia, rare-earth oxides. It occurs in all minerals contaning yttrium, and in *monazite*, which is the source. Lutetium is prepared by reducing the anhydrous chloride or fluoride with an alkali or alkaline earth metal. Lutetium is a silvery-white, soft, reactive metal. It is the second rarest of the rare earth metals. Ion-exchange and solvent extraction techniques have led to much easier isolation of the so-called 'rare-earth' elements. Lutetium and its compounds are as catalysts in organic chemistry reactions.

Luther, Martin (1483-1546), German Reformation leader and founder of Lutheranism. Following a religious experience he became an Augustinian friar, was ordained in 1507, and visited Rome (1510), where he was shocked by the worldliness of the papal court. While professor of Scripture at the Univ. of Wittenberg (from 1512), he wrestled with the problem of personal salvation, concluding that it comes from the unmerited grace of God, available through faith alone. When Johann Tetzel toured Saxony (1517) selling papal indulgences, Luther denounced the practice in his historic 95 theses, for which he was fiercely at-

The British Lusitania, one of the first liners powered by steam turbines, shared speed records for transatlantic crossings with its sister ship, the Mauretania. In 1915, the vessel was sunk by a German submarine, which led to U.S. entry into World War I.

tacked. In 1520 he published *To the Christian Nobility of the German Nation*. It denied the pope's final authority to determine the interpretation of Scripture, declaring instead the priesthood of all believers, and it rejected papal claims to political authority, arguing for national churches governed by secular rulers. Luther denied the special spiritual authority of priests and advocated clerical marriage. In Dec. 1520 he publicly burned a papal bull of condemnation and a copy of the canon law; he was excommunicated in 1521. Summoned by Emperor Charles V to renounce his heresies at the Diet of Worms (1521), he refused. He was outlawed but, protected by Frederick III of Saxony, he retired to the Wartburg castle. There he translated the New Testament into German in 6 months and began work on the Old. His hymns have been translated into many languages, and he wrote 2 catechisms (1529), the basis of Lutheranism.
See also: Protestantism; Reformation.

Lutherans, supporters of the Protestant church founded by Martin Luther (1483-1546), German leader of the Reformation. Luther, a scholar and priest, believed that faith rather than Catholic ritual would save people from sin and enable them to receive the grace of God. The largest Protestant sect in the world today, Lutheranism is the state church in the Scandinavian countries and is strong in Germany. In the 18th century German immigrants founded Lutheran churches in the mid-Atlantic American colonies, and the Evangelical Lutheran Church is now the fourth largest Christian sect in the United States.
See also: Christianity; Luther, Martin.

Luthuli, Albert John (1898-1967), Zulu chief and political leader in South Africa. As head of the African National Congress (ANC), he won the 1960 Nobel Peace Prize for his efforts to end apartheid in South Africa through non-violent passive resistance. In that same year, the ANC was banned and Luthuli's activities were severely restricted by the South African government.

Lutoslawski, Witold (1913-1994), a Polish composer. He became known especially for his colorful orchestral works that blend tra-

L

L

ditional music with elements of aleatory and twelve-tone music. Among his works are *Funeral Music* (1958), *Venetian Games* (1961), *Concerto for Cello and Orchestra* (1970), *Partita* (for violin, piano, and orchestra, 1985), and *Symphony No. 4* (1993). Lutoslawski was born in Warsaw and studied at the conservatory there. In the 1950's he helped found Warsaw Autumn, and annual festival of contemporary music. He also taught composition and appeared as a conductor of his own works.

Luxembourg

Capital:	Luxembourg
Area:	999 sq mi (2,586 sq km)
Population:	449,000
Language:	Letzebuergic, French, German
Government:	Parliamentary monarchy
Independent:	1867
Head of gov.:	Prime minister
Per capita:	US$ 43,400
Monetary unit:	1 Luxembourgian franc = 100 centimes

Luxembourg (pop 449,000) small independent duchy in Europe, bordered by Germany, France, and Belgium, and without access to the sea. Under their hereditary ruler, the Grand Duke, the bilingual Luxembourgers (just over one-third of a million) show a strong sense of national pride. The majority live in compact village communities. Luxembourg is one of the Low Countries and a member of the European Union.

Land. Only 55 mi (89 km) long and 35 mi (56 km) wide, Luxembourg is divided into several topographical areas. The Oesling, or E'sleck, in the north is part of the rugged highland of the Ardennes, with large forests but poor soil. The Bon Pays, or Gutland (Good Country), in the south is a low, hilly, fertile area of intensive farming; it is also the site of the capital. The southwest region is rich in iron ore. The largest industrial center here is Esch-sur-Alzette. The area to the southeast, where the Moselle River marks the German border, is fertile and widely cultivated.

People. The native dialect, a low German with French and Dutch components, is referred to as Letzeburgesch. French and

German are also widely spoken. The prevailing religion is Roman Catholic, and there are small numbers of Protestants and Jews. Education is compulsory between the ages of 6 and 15. There are several technical and professional colleges. The capital is the site of the International University of Comparative Science, founded in 1958.

Economy. The iron and steel industry, centered in the southwest, provides a large proportion of Luxembourg's gross income. Banking is also an important cornerstone of the economy. There is no coal, but fuel for the steel works is imported, and they in turn provide electricity for much of the country. Slate and limestone are the only other mineral resources. Agriculture provides 3% of the national income and employs 3% of the labor force. The fertile Gutland provides potatoes, rye, barley, oats, and wheat. Frisian cattle are kept. Near the German border the equally fertile Moselle region produces fruits and white wine.

History. Founded by Count Siegfried of Ardennes in 963, Luxembourg grew in size during the reigns of his successors. It was converted from a county into a duchy by Emperor Charles IV in 1354. After a long period of foreign rule, Luxembourg was granted independence at the London Conference of 1867. The Treaty of London also declared Luxembourg's neutrality and it was demilitarized. In 1945 Luxembourg became a charter member of the United Nations. Three years later it entered into a customs union with Belgium and the Netherlands, referred to as Benelux. Luxembourg was a charter member of the European Community, now the European Union (EU). The EU pressures the country to put an end to bank secrecy: banks will charge interest on secret foreign credits and transfer this money to the relevant countries anonymously.

Luxembourg (pop. 77,000), capital and largest city of the country of Luxembourg, located on a plateau above the Alzette and Petrusse rivers. It is an international financial center. Luxembourg grew up around a castle built by Siegfried, count of Ardennes, in A.D. 963. A picturesque city, its points of interest include the Grand Ducal Palace (16th century) and the Cathedral of Notre Dame (early 17th century).
See also: Luxembourg.

Luxemburg, Rosa (1871-1919), Polish-born German Marxist revolutionary. She was cofounder with Karl Liebknecht of the Spartacus Party, Germany's first Communist party, and editor of their journal, *Red Flag*. She was killed by soldiers during an uprising in Berlin.
See also: Marxism.

Luzern *See:* Lucerne.

Luzon (pop. 30.8 million), largest and northernmost island of the Philippines; 40,828 sq mi (105,704 sq km). The capital city is Quezon City. Mountainous areas (Pulog, 10,341 ft, 3151 m) with scattered volcanoes; inland flat and fertile. Agriculture (rice, corn, sugarcane, tobacco, coffee, mango, coconut trees and bananas), fishing and forestry. Varied industry (e.g. leather and food products). Extraction of gold, iron, manganese, copper and chrome. In WW II Manila was one of the country's first cities bombed by the Japanese; Quezon City was conquered immediately. The north (Bataan) resisted the Japanese for some time.

Lvov (pop. 802,000), city in Ukraine, near the Polish border. A major center for industry, culture, and transportation, Lvov was founded c.1256 and became a commercial center on the trade route between Vienna and Kiev, the Ukrainian capital. The region around the city was ruled by Poland, Turkey, and Sweden between the 13th and the 18th century. In 1772 Austria took control of the city and changed its name to Lemberg, making it the capital of the region called Galicia. Poland again ruled the city from the end of World War I until 1939. Lvov is known for its university, founded in 1611.
See also: Ukraine.

Lyceum, gymnasium in ancient Athens where male youth received physical and intellectual training. In 335 B.C. Aristotle established his famous Lyceum outside the walls of the city. The school was named in honor of the god Apollo Lykeios. In the U.S. during the 19th century there was a lyceum movement which attempted to improve education.
See also: Greece, Ancient.

Lychee *See:* Litchi.

The historic city of Luxembourg is a center of trade, industry, and transportation.

Lycopodium *See:* Club moss.

Lycurgus, ancient Greek political leader, possibly legendary, credited as founder of the legal institutions of the city-state of Sparta. Tradition says that during the 7th century B.C. Lycurgus instituted a new system of military discipline and training. Ancient historians cite him as a member of one of Sparta's royal families.
See also: Sparta.

Lydia, ancient kingdom of western Asia Minor, of legendary wealth. The Lydians invented metal coins in the 7th century B.C. Sardis was the capital and cultural center of this growing empire until the defeat of Croesus (546 B.C.) by Cyrus of Persia.

Lye, strong alkali used in soap-making and cleaning. Originally the name was given to potassium carbonate (K_2CO_3), which was obtained by soaking wood ash in water. It now most often refers to sodium hydroxide (NaOH) solution.

Lyell, Sir Charles (1797-1875), British geologist. He promoted James Hutton's theory of uniformitarianism and Charles Darwin's theory of evolution in his *Principles of Geology* (1830-33).
See also: Geology.

Lyly, John (c.1554-1606), English author best known for his *Euphues* (*The Anatomy of Wit*, 1578; *Euphues and His England*, 1580), a two-part prose romance in a highly artificial and suggestive style. Lyly also wrote elegant comedies on classical themes, influencing other Elizabethan playwrights.

Lyme disease, infection caused by the bacterium *Borrelia burgdorferi* and transmitted by ticks. It is accompanied by fever and a red, ring-shaped skin rash surrounding the tick bite. The disease is treated with antibiotics. Left untreated, it can lead to nervous disorders and arthritis. The disease derives its name from the town of Lyme, Conn. where a high incidence of the disease occurred in the 1970s.

Lymphatic system, network of vessels and nodes that carry tissue fluid, or lymph, from the tissues to the veins of the circulatory system. Lymph is a transparent fluid that carries oxygen and nutrients to cells and carries away waste products. Ingested fats are digested and absorbed into the bloodstream with the help of lymphatic vessels. The body fights infections through lymphocyte and macrophage cells found in lymph nodes in the armpits, groin, neck, and other parts of the body. Most lymph passes directly into capillaries, but some is carried back to the blood by the lymphatic system; whose main ducts feed into the circulatory system near the collarbone.

Lynx, any of various ferocious cats with a short tail, long legs, and tufted ears, found in northern regions of North America, Europe, and Asia. They are hunted for their fur and because they kill domestic animals. Species include the North American, or Canadian,

lynx (*Lynx canadensis*), and the common lynx of Europe and Asia (*L. lynx*).

Lyon (pop. 422,000), city in southeastern France. Capital of the Rhône department in the Rhône-Alpes region, it is the third largest city in France. During Roman times, Christianity was introduced to the Gauls from Lyons. Since the 16th century, Lyons has been known for its textiles, and today it

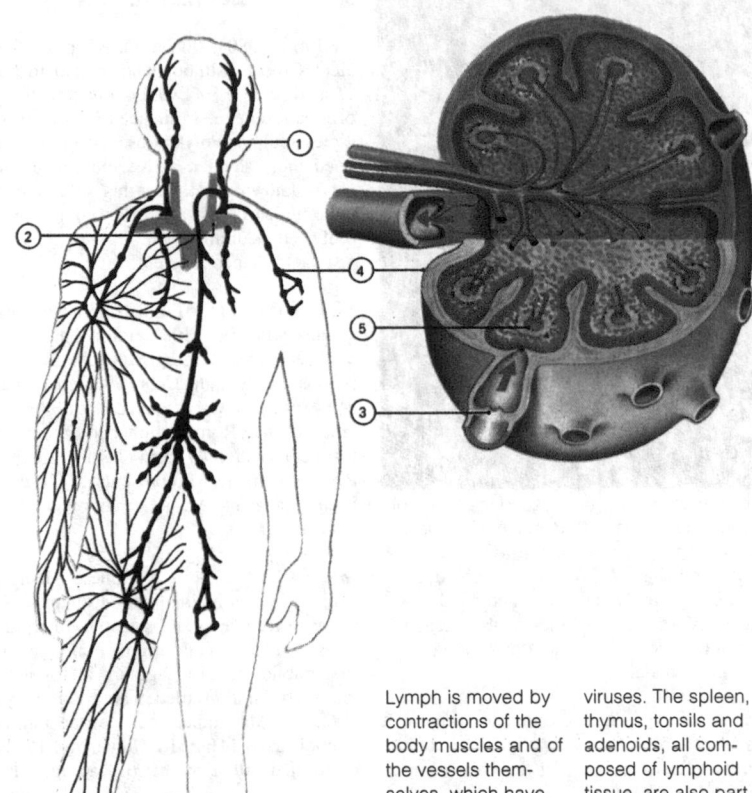

Lymph, or lymphatic fluid, which transports nutrients to tissues and collects tissue wastes, is carried by the lymphatic system, a network of interconnecting vessels (1). The pressure of the blood, circulating through the capillaries, forces lymph out and into the tissue spaces. This fluid is collected by the lymphatic vessels and eventually returned to the bloodstream through ducts, which empty into large veins near the collarbones (2). Lymph is moved by contractions of the body muscles and of the vessels themselves, which have valves (3) in order to prevent backflow. Lymph nodes (4), which are distributed throughout the system, remove wastes and other particles and contain large concentrations of white blood cells (5), which attack invaders such as bacteria and viruses. The spleen, thymus, tonsils and adenoids, all composed of lymphoid tissue, are also part of the immune system.

Spanish lynx (*Lynx pardina*), found in the forests of Southern Europe, distinguished by its prominent spots. Grows to a length of 3 ft (1 m).

L

L

The oldest part of Lyon includes the medieval St. Jean Cathedral (in the foreground) and the quarters around Place Bellecour between the rivers.

Beyond the group of trees on the square, is the Tour de Charité and the Hôtel des Postes, behind that is La Guillotière quarter.

is a leading producer of silks and rayons. It is also known for being the center of the French Resistance during the Nazi occupation (1940-1944).
See also: France.

Lyre, musical stringed instrument. In ancient Greece the lyre, with 3 to 12 strings, was a symbol for the God Apollo. The English term *lyric* comes from the Greek use of the lyre to accompany songs and poems. The strings were plucked either with the fingers or with a pick. They were strung vertically from a sound box to a crossbar held in place by 2 outer vertical arms.

Lyrebird, either of 2 species of Australian birds (genus *Menura*) of the family menuridae. The male has very long tail feathers he displays, shaped like a lyre, during courtship. Similar in appearance to chickens, lyrebirds nest on the ground and do not fly.

Lysander (?-395 B.C.), naval commander of Sparta. During the Peloponnesian War he led the Spartan forces to victory against Athens in the decisive battle of Aegospotami (405 B.C.). He died in battle during the Corinthian war.
See also: Sparta.

Lysergic acid diethylamide *See:* LSD.

Lysias (459?-380 B.C.), ancient Greek orator and speech writer. Although as many as 35 speeches attributed to Lysias have survived, he is best known for a simple though passionate attack on a ruling tyrant of Athens entitled 'Against Eratosthenes.' A citizen of

Athens, he escaped after his arrest by the Thirty Tyrants, Spartan rulers installed at the end of the Peloponnesian War. When democracy was restored in Athens, Lysias returned and again wrote speeches on a professional basis.
See also: Greece, Ancient.

Lysippus (380s?-306 B.C.), sculptor of ancient Greece. Although he is said to have created some 1,500 works, no authenticated originals remain. Influenced by the earlier Greek sculptor Polykleitos, Lysippus developed more slender, active looking figures. He is known mostly for his sculptures of male athletes, cast and often copied in his preferred medium, metal.
See also: Greece, Ancient.

M, 13th letter of the English alphabet, corresponds with the 13th Semitic letter *mem*, represented by a zigzag, wavelike form that scholars relate to the Hebrew *mayim* (water). M is *mu* in the Greek alphabet and the 12th letter of the Roman alphabet. Its present form comes directly from classical Latin. In Roman numerals M represents 1,000. In the French language M. is the abbreviation for *monsieur* (Mr.).

Ma, Yo-Yo (1955-), a Chinese-American cellist. He won international acclaim for his virtuoso technique and sensitive interpretations. Ma was a child prodigy and gave his first public recital at age six in his native Paris. The family settled in New York City in 1962, and Ma studied music at the Juilliard School and at Harvard University. He has performed with a number of leading orchestras, including the New York Philharmonic, Chicago Symphony, and Vienna Philharmonic.

Maazel, Lorin (1930-), U.S. conductor. A musical child prodigy born in France, he first conducted an orchestra in the United States at the World's Fair in New York (1939). He has gone on to become musical director of famous orchestras worldwide, including the Pittsburgh Symphony since 1986, the Cleveland Orchestra (1972-1982), and the Vienna State Opera (1982-1988). In 2002, he succeeded Kurt Masur as Chief Conductor of the New York Philharmonic Orchestra.

Macadam, road-building system devised by the Scots engineer John Loudon McAdam (1756-1836). The soil beneath the road, rather than foundations, bears the weight, the road being waterproof and well-drained to keep this soil dry. For modern highways a first layer of larger rocks is laid, then smaller rocks and gravel; the whole is bound with (usually) asphalt or tar.
See also: McAdam, John Loudon.

Macadamia nut, edible seed from the macadamia tree (*Macadamia terrifolia*), a member of the *protea* family. Native to Australia, the nut of this tropical evergreen is an important Hawaiian crop today. Roasted, the round white nuts-also known as bush nuts, among other names-may be eaten by themselves or incorporated into baked or cooked foods.

Macao

Capital:	Macao
Area:	6.5 sq mi (17 sq km)
Population:	461,000
Language:	Portuguese, Chinese
Government:	Chinese overseas territory under Portuguese rule (until 1999)
Dependent:	on Portugal until 1999; thereafter on China
Head of gov.:	Governor
Per capita:	more than US$ 9,636
Monetary unit:	1 Pataca = 100 avos

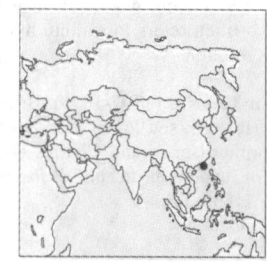

Macao, or Macau, former Portuguese overseas province in southeastern China, on the western side of the Pearl River Estuary, at the head of which is Canton. Lying just within the tropics, Macao is 6.5 sq mi (17 sq km) in area. The territory came into Portuguese possession in 1557 and was granted broad autonomy in 1976. In December 1999 Macao reverted to China. The territory comprises a narrow peninsula projecting from the mainland province of Kwangtung, as well as the adjacent islands of Taipa and Colôane. Macao is a popular gambling center and important commercial port. Fishing and some textile manufacturing are significant economic activities.

Macaque, several species (genus *Macaca*) of the Old World monkey family. They are found in North Africa, Japan, India, and Malaysia. A reddish face and rump are features seen in all macaques. The Barbary ape is tailless, while the bonnet macaque and toque monkey of southern India and Ceylon have tails longer than their bodies. The Japanese macaque has brown fur but a short tail. The rhesus monkey of India is used in medical research.

MacArthur, Douglas (1880-1964), U.S. general and hero of World War II. He commanded the 42nd (Rainbow) Division in World War I and was superintendent of West Point (1919-1922). In 1930 he became chief of staff of the U.S. Army, the youngest man ever to hold the post, and was promoted to general. He retired from the army in 1937, but was recalled in 1941 as commander of U.S. Army forces in the Far East. In 1942 he became Allied commander of the Southwest Pacific Allied forces, and in 1944 general of

the army. MacArthur received the Medal of Honor for his defense of the Philippines. Signatory of the Japanese surrender, he led the reconstruction of Japan, as Allied supreme commander from 1945. When the Korean War broke out (1950) he was selected commander of the UN forces sent to aid South Korea. His unwillingness to obey President Harry S. Truman's orders to restrict the war to Korea rather than extend it to China led to his dismissal the following year. Some Republicans tried unsuccessfully to nominate MacArthur for the presidency in 1944, 1948, and 1952. His memoirs, *Reminiscences*, were published in 1964.
See also: Korean War; World War II.

Macau *See:* Macao.

Macaulay, Thomas Babington (1800-1859), historian and essayist. Babington was elected to Parliament in 1830, became a brilliant speaker, and served on the Supreme Council governing India before undertaking his *History of England from the Accession of James II* (5 vol, 1849-1861). The clarity and readability of this work made it a success. Like the *History*, his *Essays* display great range and brilliance, together with supreme confidence of judgment. While continuing as a leading orator in Parliament and holding several government jobs, Babington also wrote *Lays of Ancient Rome* (1842), a popular collection of poems.

Macaw, any of several colorful, long-tailed parrots of the genus *Ara*. Macaws have powerful beaks, which they use for cracking open nuts, and their faces are bare of feathers. The largest parrots, macaws measure 12-39 in (30-100 cm) long and eat nuts, seeds and fruit. Easily tamed, they live in screeching flocks in forested areas of tropical America and Mexico.

Macbeth (d. 1057), king of Scotland, formerly chief of the province of Moray. Macbeth seized the throne of Scotland after killing King Duncan I in battle (1040). He upheld his wife's royal descent as his basis for claiming the crown. In 1057 Malcolm III, son of Duncan I, killed Macbeth at Lumphanan. Shakespeare's tragedy *Macbeth* is partially based on Holinshed's *Chronicles* of these events.
See also: Scotland; Shakespeare, William.

Maccabee, Judah *See:* Judah Maccabee.

Maccabees, Books of, 2 books of the Old Testament Apocrypha that tell the story of the Maccabees, or Hasmoneans, Jewish rulers of the 2nd and 1st centuries B.C. who fought for the independence of Judea from Syria. First Maccabees, a prime historical source, was written c.100? B.C. Second Maccabees is a devotional work of low historical value, written before A.D. 70. Two other books, Third and Fourth Maccabees, are among the Pseudepigrapha.
See also: Old Testament.

MacDiarmid, Hugh (Christopher Murray Grieve; 1892-1978), Scottish poet. Founder of the Scottish Nationalist Party, he gave fresh impetus to Scottish literature. He is best known for the long rhapsodic poem *A Drunk Man Looks at the Thistle* (1926).

MacDonald, James Ramsay (1866-1937), English statesman who led Britain's first Labour Party government. He was prime minister of the first and second labour governments (1924 and 1929-1935). He headed a national coalition government of Labour, Conservative and Liberal Party members (1931-1935) that attempted unsuccessfully to deal with England's depressed economic conditions. He was replaced as prime minister in 1935.
See also: Labour Party.

Macdonald, Sir John Alexander (1815-91), Canadian statesman, first prime minister of the Dominion of Canada. Elected to the Ontario legislature in 1844, he became prime minister in 1857 as head of a Conservative coalition that was joined (1864) by George Brown and others. He led subsequent negotiations that resulted (1867) in the confederation of Canada, for which he was knighted by Queen Victoria. The Pacific Scandal (1873), involving corruption charges in completing the Canadian Pacific Railway, caused his government's resignation. However, Macdonald served as prime minister again from 1878 until his death.
See also: Canada.

MacDowell, Edward Alexander (1861-1908), U.S. composer and pianist. He is remembered for his lyrical piano works, such as the collection *Woodland Sketches* (1896). He headed the newly formed music department at Columbia University in New York City (1896-1904). His widow founded the MacDowell Colony in Peterborough, N.H., a retreat for creative artists.

Macedonia (sometimes called Macedon) an ancient kingdom in the Balkan Peninsula at the northwest corner of the Aegan Sea. It occupied an area that today is part of Greece, Bulgaria, and the Republic of Macedonia. The region is generally mountainous; in several areas peaks rise to more than 6,500 feet (1,980 m) above sea level. Fertile lowlands occur at the head of the Gulf of Therma, into which flow the Axiós (Vardar) and Aliákmon rivers.

Prehistoric inhabitants of Macedonia were among Europe's earliest farmers. The region was settled shortly after 2000 B.C. by an Indo-European people akin to the Greeks. The Macedonians were rough and warlike, but their kings admired Greek culture and tried to make Pella, their capital, a second Athens. Philip II, who became king in 359 B.C., created an army that was the best the world had yet seen. By conquest, threat, and treaty Philip made himself master of the entire Greek peninsula by 338 B.C. His son, Alexander the Great (reigned 336-323 B.C.), continued the program of expansion. At Alexander's death, Macedonia ruled an area reaching to India. Alexander's empire was divided among several of his generals, who established Hellenistic (Greek) culture throughout the Middle East. In 276 B.C. Macedonia came under the rule of the Antigonids, whose kingdom included Greece.

Macedonia sided with Carthage in the

The blue-and-yellow macaw, A. ararauna, a brightly plumaged bird of Central and South American rain forests, is a favorite pet and zoo bird. It has a powerful bill and feeds on fruit and nuts.

Second Punic War and fought against Rome's allies in Greece, 215-205 B.C., until a peace was negotiated. In a second war with Rome, 200-197 B.C., Macedonia was forced to give up Greece. In 171-168 B.C. Macedonia took up arms against Rome once more and was overwhelmingly defeated. A final campaign against Rome in 149-148 B.C. ended with Macedonia becoming a Roman province.

Macedonia was part of the Eastern Roman (later Byzantine) Empire, which was created in 395 A.D. The interior was raided repeatedly by Huns, Slavs, and Avars. Thessalonica (modern Thessaloniki) on the coast grew into an important port. By the late 800's the Bulgars were established in the interior, and by 1200 they held the northern part of the region. In 1204 knights of the Fourth Crusade seized the rest of Macedonia and named it the Kingdom of Thessalonica. The kingdom was conquered by Epirus in 1222, by Bulgaria in 1230, and by the Byzantines of Nicaea in 1246. Except for the region of Thessalonica, all of Macedonia was then gradually absorbed by Serbia. Between 1354 and 1430 the entire region fell to the Ottoman Turks.

At the end of the Balkan Wars (1912-1913),

M

Macedonia was partitioned among Greece, Serbia, and Bulgaria. The region that went to Serbia became part of Yugoslavia; it seceded in 1991 and became the Republic of Macedonia.
See also: Alexander the Great; Greece, Ancient; Yugoslavia.

Macedonia, Republic of

Capital:	Skopje
Area:	9,928 sq mi (25,713 sq km)
Population:	2,055,000
Language:	Macedonian
Government:	Republic
Independent:	1991
Head of gov.:	Prime minister
Per capita:	US$ 4,400
Monetary unit:	1 Denar = 100 deni

Macedonia, Republic of, Former Yugoslav Republic of Macedonia (FYROM), until 1991 a federal republic of the Yugoslav Federation, in the South-east of Europe. In the north it borders on Servia (Yugoslavia), in the east on Bulgaria, in the south on Greece, and in the west on Albania.
Land and climate. Macedonia is very mountainous. It is struck by earthquakes on a reg-

A cloister dedicated to John the Baptist in the Greek part of Macedonia.

ular basis. The climate is largely continental. Approximately 30% of the country is covered with forests.
People. Apart from Macedonians (67%), Albanians are the largest minority (23%). The orthodox Church has the most followers. The official language is Macedonian.
Economy. Macedonia is, when it comes to agriculture, just about selfsufficient. The machinery is out of date. Next to the metallurgic industry, the chemical industry and the textile industry are important. The country has several natural resources, such as coal, chrome, and nickel.
History. Macedonia as a region is mountainous, extending from the northwestern Aegean coast into the central Balkan peninsula. Divided among Greece, Yugoslavia, and Bulgaria, it covers 25,636 sq mi (66,397 sq km). Ethnically mixed, Macedonia is inhabited mainly by Slavs in the north and Greeks in the south. The region is primarily agricultural, with tobacco, grains and cotton the chief crops. One of the great powers of the ancient world under Alexander the Great, Macedonia was later ruled by Romans, Byzantines, Bulgars, and Serbs. From 1389 to 1912 it was part of the Ottoman Empire. With the collapse of Yugoslavia in 1991 Yugoslavian Macedonia became an independent country. Macedonia's independance however, was not recognized internationally, mainly because Greece opposed the use of the name Macedonia, which Greek leaders thought implied territorial claims to the region in northern Greece known by the same name. In 1993 Macedonia was admitted to the United Nations as 'the Former Yugoslav Republic of Macedonia' (F.Y.R. Macedonia). Relations with Greece worsened, however, and Greece imposed a trade embargo on Macedonia in 1994. Tensions subsided somewhat in 1995 and the embargo was lifted. Meanwhile, in 1993 the UN sent peacekeeping troops to Macedonia to help prevent fighting between various South Slav groups, which was occurring in other former Yugoslav republics, from spreading to Macedonia. In 1998 Ljubco Georgijevski

of the rightist VMRO-DPMNE party was elected premier.
In 1999, the Kosovo crisis led to an exodus of Albanian Kosovans to Macedonia. Two years later, their presence in Macedonia nearly caused a civil war, but a peace treaty, the Ohrid-agreement, was signed in 2001. The NATO operation Essential Harvest supervised the weapons-collection. An amendment of the law provided greater constitutional rights for the ethnic minorities.

MacGregor, Robert *See:* Rob Roy.

Machado de Assis, Joaquim Maria (1839-1908), Brazilian writer. Worked from 1873 in several government departments, from 1897 onwards was president of the Brazilian Academy of Arts. Published a vast body of works (poetry, plays, literary reviews, many short stories), but became especially famous for his psychological novels. His work is typified by a penetrating character analysis and an exceptionally melancholy style which especially criticizes human vanity. Other works include *Dom Casmurro* (1900) and *Aires Memorial* (1908).

Mach, Ernst (1838-1916), Austrian physicist and philosopher. His name is commemorated in the Mach number, used as a measure of the speed of bodies in terms of the speed of sound. His greatest influence was in philosophy; he rejected from science all concepts that could not be validated by experience. This approach helped inform the logical positivism of the Vienna Circle-a prominent group of intellectuals in Vienna at that time.
See also: Philosophy; Physics.

Machaut, Guillaume de (1300-1377), French poet and composer. He was a leading figure in the 14th-century Ars Nova ('new art') school of music, which developed many new forms. His *Mass for Four Voices* was the first complete polyphonic setting by a single composer.

Mâche, François-Bernard (1935-   ), French composer, active member of the Groupe de Recherches Musicales between 1958 and 1963. Mâche wrote many electroacoustic works, assimilating old languages from Africa and the sound of exotic instruments. Works include *La peau du silence* (1962), *Rituel d'oubli* (1969), *Korwar* (1972), *Temes nevinbür* (1973), *Kassandra* (1977), Uncas (1986), Cassiopée (1989) and l'Estuaire du temps (1993)..

Machiavelli, Niccolò (1469-1527), Florentine politician and political theorist. He served the Republic of Florence, and was its emissary on several occasions. When the Medici family returned to power in 1512, Machiavelli was imprisoned and tortured on suspicion of plotting against Medici rule; on his release less than a year later he devoted himself principally to writing. Despite his belief in political morality and his undoubted love of liberty, as revealed in his *Discourses* (1531), his master-work *The Prince* (1532; written 1513) describes the amoral and unscrupulous political calculation by which an 'ideal' prince maintains his

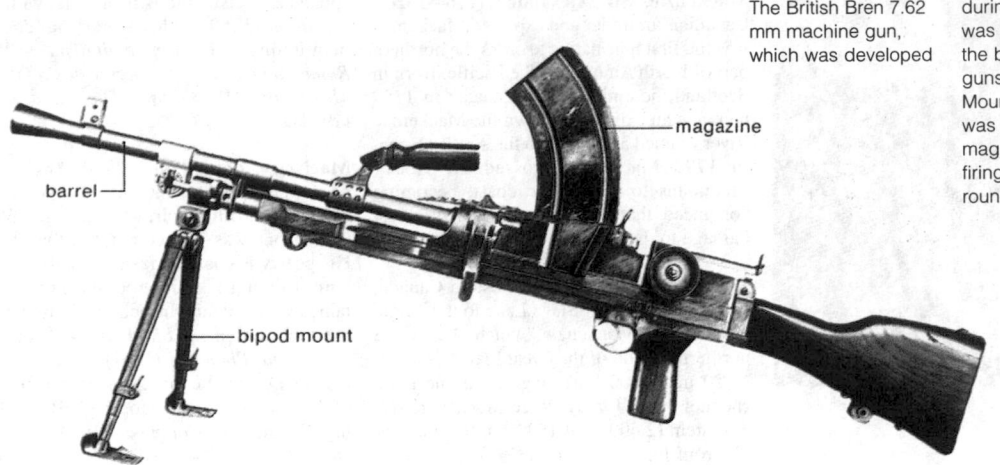

The British Bren 7.62 mm machine gun, which was developed during the mid-1930s, was considered one of the best light machine guns of World War II. Mounted on a bipod, it was gas operated and magazine fed, with a firing rate of 500 rounds per minute.

M

power. Machiavelli also wrote *History of Florence* (1532). The expression 'Machiavellian' denotes devious political manipulations.

Machine Age *See:* Industrial Revolution.

Machine gun, military small arm capable of rapid fire. After the invention of the percussion cap by Joshua Shaw, the reliability of firing was greatly increased. In 1862, Richard Jordan Gatling invented a single-barreled machine gun with a rotary chamber, it was used in the Civil War. Gatling's multi-barreled gun was capable of firing up to 3,000 rounds a minute.
The first fully automatic machine gun was a single-barreled water-cooled weapon patented by Hiram Steven Maxim in 1885. In World War I, the machine gun was responsi-

ble for over 80% of all casualties. In 1957, the U.S. Air Force introduced the Vulcan gun, capable of firing up to 7,000 rounds per minute.

Machine tool, nonportable, power-driven tool used industrially for working metal components to tolerances far finer than those obtainable manually. The fundamental processes used are cutting and grinding, individual machines being designed for boring, broaching, drilling, milling, planing, and sawing. Essentially a machine tool consists of a jig to hold both the cutting tool and the workpiece and a mechanism to allow these to be moved relative to each other in a controlled fashion. A typical example is the lathe. Auxiliary functions facilitate the cooling and lubrication of the tool and workpiece while work is in

progress using a cutting fluid. The rate at which any piece can be worked depends on the material being worked and the composition of the cutting point. High-speed steel, tungsten carbide, and corundum are favored materials for cutting edges. Modern industry would be inconceivable without machine tools. It was only when these began to be developed in the late 18th century that it became possible to manufacture interchangeable parts and thus initiate mass production.

Mach number *See:* Mach, Ernst.

Machu Picchu, ancient (16th-century) Inca fortress city in Peru, about 50 mi (80 km) northwest of Cusco. An impressive ruin dramatically situated on a high ridge of the Andes, the pre-Columbian city is 5 sq mi (13

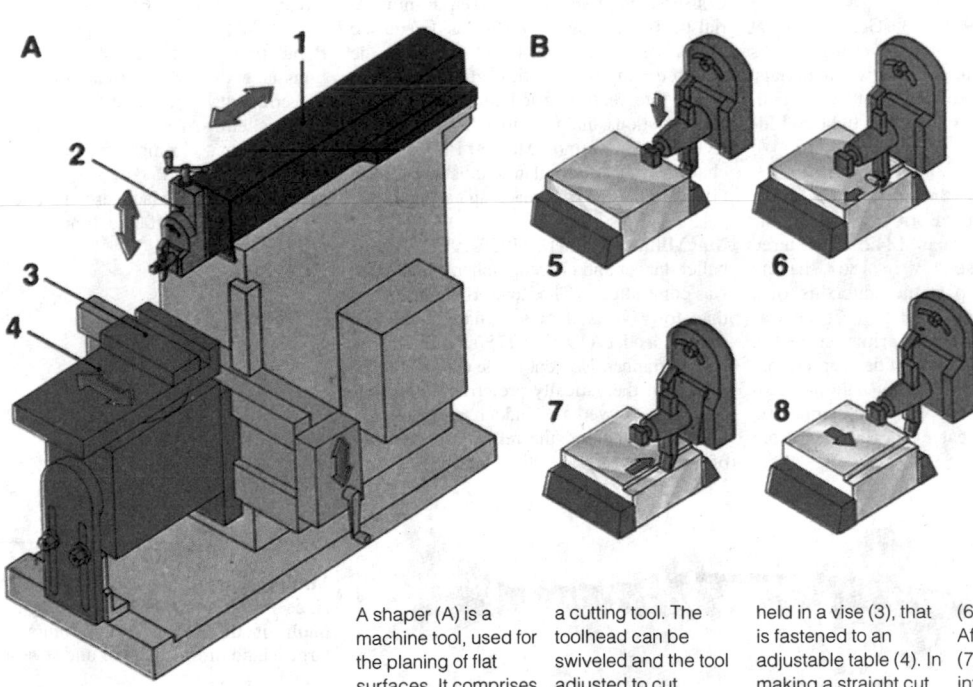

A shaper (A) is a machine tool, used for the planing of flat surfaces. It comprises of a reciprocating ram (1), which carries a toolhead (2) that holds a cutting tool. The toolhead can be swiveled and the tool adjusted to cut horizontally, vertically, or at any angle. The work is usually held in a vise (3), that is fastened to an adjustable table (4). In making a straight cut (B), the tool is lowered to the proper level (5) and moved forward (6) to peel off a chip. After the return stroke (7), the work is moved into position (8) for the next cutting stroke.

M

Machu Picchu, an Inca fortress in Peru.

sq km) of terraced stonework connected by 3,000 steps. Probably the last Inca stronghold after the Spanish Conquest (begun 1532), it was discovered almost intact in 1911 by the U.S. explorer Bingham.
See also: Peru.

Macintosh, Charles (1766-1843), British chemist and inventor. Trained as a chemist, he developed a method (1823) by which fabrics were treated with chemicals to create a waterproof garment. One raincoat, popularly referred to as a macintosh, is named after him.
See also: Chemistry.

Mack, Connie (Cornelius McGillicuddy; 1862-1956), U.S. baseball manager and owner. Known for his work and dedication to baseball, Mack helped establish the American League. As owner and manager of the Philadelphia Athletics (1901-1950), he led his team to victory in 5 World Series. He was inducted into the National Baseball Hall of Fame in 1937.

Mack, Heinz (1931-), German visual artist, co-founder of Zero (1958). Works with transparent and reflective materials, with which he makes objects that are considered to belong to the art of light and kinetic art.

Mackenzie, Alexander (1822-1892), Canadian politician. Born in Scotland, he emigrated to Canada in 1842. He entered the legislative assembly in 1861, having worked his way up to the editorship of a Liberal paper. From 1873 to 1878 he was Canada's first Liberal prime minister. Serving during a worldwide depression, Mackenzie confronted many national economic difficulties. He promoted democratic government and greater independence from Great Britain.

Mackenzie, Sir Alexander (1764-1820), Canadian fur trader and explorer. Mackenzie was the first non-native to cross the northern part of North America to the Pacific. Born in Scotland, he emigrated to Canada; in 1789 he made an expedition down the Mackenzie River (named after him) to the Arctic Ocean. In 1793 Mackenzie crossed the Rocky Mountains to the Pacific coast, becoming convinced that searching for a Northwest Passage to the Orient would be futile.

Mackenzie River, in northwestern Canada, flowing from Great Slave Lake to the Arctic Ocean. The Mackenzie, which drains the northern portion of the Great Plains, is about 1,120 mi (1,800 km) long and is the main channel of the Finlay-Peace-Mackenzie river system (2,600 mi/4,180 km). It is navigable from June to Oct. only.
See also: Mackenzie, Sir Alexander.

Mackerel, commercially important food fish of the family Scombridae. Mackerel have small scales, deeply forked tails, and rows of finlets on the rear part of their streamlined bodies. Known as fast swimmers, the species includes the tuna (the largest, up to .75 ton/680 kg), albacore, and bonito.

MacLeish, Archibald (1892-1982), U.S. poet and playwright. His works include *Conquistador* (1932), a long narrative on the conquest of Mexico; the lyrical verse of *Collected Poems 1917-1952* and *J.B.* (1958), a verse drama based on the story of Job, all of which won Pulitzer prizes. Cultural adviser to Franklin D. Roosevelt, he was librarian of Congress (1939-1944) and undersecretary of state (1944-1945).

Macmillan, Harold (1894-1986), British politician. Entering Parliament as a Conservative in 1924, he served in ministerial posts throughout World War II and the 1950s. As prime minister (1957-1963), he restored Anglo-U.S. ties after the Suez Canal intervention, tried to improve East-West relations, and tried to gain Britain's entry into the Common Market. He served as chairman of Macmillan publishing house (1963-1974) and was made an earl in 1984.

MacMillan, Kenneth (1929-1992), British ballet dancer and choreographer. MacMillan was committed to The Royal Ballet for more than forty years, first as a dancer, then as artistic leader (1970-1977) and finally as choreographer. He kept to the classical technique but thematically preferred ballet dramas that showed the hidden passions and frustrations behind the refined conventions of a civilized society, thus introducing out-

spoken eroticism into British ballet with *The invitation* (1960). Other works that deserve mentioning are: *Somnambulism* (1953), *Romeo and Juliet* (1965), *Anastasia* (1967), *Mayerling* (1978) and *The Judas Tree* (1992).

MacNeice, Louis (1907-1963), Anglo-Irish poet, play and prose writer. MacNeice was befriended with Stephen Spender and W.H. Auden but was less committed than them. His poetry is characterized by intellect, brilliant technique and a consistently maintained ambivalence in opinions. His poems are published in e.g. *Blind Fireworks* (1929), *Plant and Phantom* (1941), and *Solstices* (1961). During the forties he wrote a number of dramatic radio plays for the BBC, including *Christopher Columbus* (1944) and *The Dark Tower* (1947). His prose contains *I Crossed the Minch* (1938) and *Letters from Iceland* (1937; with Auden).

Macramé, art form based on knotting techniques. This art, originally an activity of 13th century Arab sailors before its popularity in Europe, was revived in the 1960s. Garment accessories, wall hangings, and other practical or decorative items are created through arrangements of knots in various patterns.
See also: Knots, hitches, and splices.

Madagascar

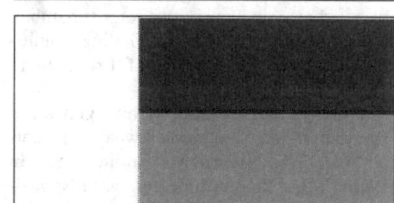

Capital:	Antananarivo
Area:	226,658 sq mi
	(587,041 sq km)
Population:	16,473,000
Language:	Madagascan, French
Government:	Republic
Independent:	1960
Head of gov.:	Prime minister
Per capita:	US$ 870
Monetary unit:	1 Madagascan franc (FMG)
	= 100 centimes

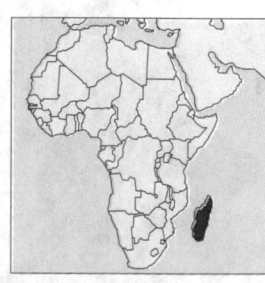

Madagascar, formerly Malagasy Republic, since 1975 the Republic of Madagascar, republic in the Indian Ocean comprising the large island of Madagascar and several small islands.
Land and climate. Separated from the southeast African mainland by the Mozambique Channel, Madagascar is the

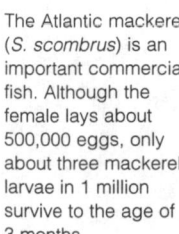

The Atlantic mackerel (*S. scombrus*) is an important commercial fish. Although the female lays about 500,000 eggs, only about three mackerel larvae in 1 million survive to the age of 3 months.

world's fourth largest island. It has rugged central highlands and fertile low-lying coastal plains. The highlands have several extinct volcanoes and mountain groups which rise to over 9,000 ft/2,743 m. In the highlands the climate is pleasantly cool, but it occasionally becomes cold. The coastal plains tend to be hot and humid, with luxuriant vegetation.

People. The people of Madagascar can be broadly divided into two groups. The Merinas, of Indonesian and Polynesian descent, live mainly in the highlands. The majority of people living in the coastal regions are of black African descent. The principal languages are French and Malagasy, an Indonesian language. Over 80% of the people live in rural areas. About 40% of the population is Christian, 5% is Muslim, and the remainder observe various traditional beliefs. The capital is Antananarivo (Tananarive).

Economy. The island is predominantly farming and stock-raising country. Coffee, cloves, and vanilla are principal foreign exchange earners. Meat and prawns are also exported. Chromite, graphite, mica, and phosphates are important minerals. Oil and gas deposits have been discovered. Growing industries include food processing, oil refining, vehicle assembly, and textile manufacture.

History. The first peoples to settle Madagascar were black Africans and Indonesians some 2,000 years ago. Western Europeans did not reach the island until the 16th century. A native kingdom, the Merina kingdom, gained hegemony over the island in alliance with Europeans. At the same time, the Portuguese, English, and French

In the dry southern and western parts of Madagascar, extensive cattle breeding is the most important means of existence. In addition to zebus, in recent years, goats and sheep have also been bred.

strove with one another for dominance. Finally, the French invaded and annexed the island in 1885, but had to fight until 1905 to overcome a determined Merina kingdom. In 1947, a revolt against French rule was crushed, but in 1958 the island gained self government as the Malagasy Republic and became fully independent in 1960. 1972 marked the beginning of a period of political and economic unrest and in 1975 a Marxist military took power. In 1977, national elections were held to create a legislature. Didier Ratsiraka, who had ruled as Madagascar's military leader since 1975, won the first presidential election (1982); under his leadership, the government has loosened its re-

strictions on the economy and introduced democratic reforms in the 1990s. In 1997 he again won the presidential elections. Opposition candidate Ravalomanana won the unconstitutional presidential elections of 2001. He promised to apply himself to fight poverty.

Madder, tropical and subtropical trees, shrubs, and herbs of the family Rubiaceae, native to northern South America. The family yields economically important crops, e.g., coffee and quinine, and ornamentals, e.g., the gardenia, madder, and bedstraw (used for mattress filling because of its pleasing odor). Also called turkey red, the true madder (*rubia tinctorum*) of southern Europe was used to create brilliant red dye pigments, now produced artificially.

Madeira Islands, archipelago, 308 sq mi (789 sq km), owned by Portugal, in the Atlantic Ocean about 350 mi (560 km) west of Morocco. Madeira, the largest island and site of the capital, Funchal, is a year-round resort; Porto Santo is also inhabited. The Desertas and Selvagens are uninhabited islands. Known to the Romans and rediscovered under Henry the Navigator in the 15th century, the islands produce sugarcane and Madeira wine.

Madeira River, largest tributary of the Amazon River. Flowing northeastward, this important South American waterway runs along the Brazil-Bolivia border and continues for approximately 2,000 miles (3,200 km)-some of which are still uncharted or explored. The river is navigable by boat for the first 700 miles (1,126 km), then a railroad follows the riverbank for more than 200 miles (320 km) of rapids. The river opens into the Amazon east of the city of Manaus, Brazil.

Maderna, Bruno (1920-1973), Italian composer and conductor, a dominating figure in music life in the second half of the 20th century. He was a great expert on Renaissance music, especially that of Monteverdi, and mastered a large repertoire as a conductor. His compositions combine Italian melodiousness with serial techniques and make economic use of the aleatory. The particularly high productivity of Maderna's last years culminated with the opera *Satyricon* (1973) and *Hyperion* (theater work; 1960-1969).

Madero, Francisco Indalecio (1873-1913), president of Mexico (1911-1913). A democratic idealist, he opposed Porfirio Díaz in the 1910 election and was imprisoned. He escaped to Tex. and there declared a revolution; joined by Pancho Villa and Emiliano Zapata, he deposed Díaz in 1911 and was elected president. His administration was marred by his ineptitude and division and corruption among his followers. In the face of widespread revolt he was deposed and murdered by Gen. Victoriano Huerta in 1913.
See also: Mexico.

Madhya Pradesh (pop. 66,181,000), largest state of India, exists in its current form since 1956; 171,280 sq mi (443,446 sq km).

Capital city: Bhopal. Paramount agricultural (rice, wheat, cotton, oilseeds). The summers are dry and hot, winters dry and cold. Only 16% of the surface suitable for agriculture is irrigated. Most of the precipitation occurs in the Southeast and between June and September. Steel factory at Bhilai; additional cement, machine, cotton, paper, sugar and textile industries. Other domestic industries (spinning, weaving, woodworking, pottery-making). Extraction of manganese, bauxite, coal and iron. Eighty percent of the population lives in the country and 85% speaks Hindi. More than a million people live in Bhopal and Indore, 700,000 in Jabalpur and Gwalior.

Madison, James (1751-1836), 4th president of the United States (1809-1817). Madison, called 'the father of the Constitution,' was more succesfull as a penetrating political thinker who guided the deliberations of the Constitutional Convention than as a president. He drafted the Virginia Plan (also called the Randolph Plan), which was developed into the Constitution. Madison wrote many of the pro-Constitution papers known as *The Federalist*. During the Constitution's ratification process, many state conventions called for it to be amended to protect individual rights. Madison, elected to the House of Representatives in 1789, helped draft what became the Bill of Rights, the first 10 amendments to the Constitution. During Madison's presidency the U.S. was at war with Britain (1812-1814).

As president, Madison faced the same foreign-relations problem he had as secretary of state: the continuing war between France and Britain. mpressment of U.S. sailors, seizure of goods, and blockades had serious damaged U.S. shipping. Tensions arose until Congress declared war on Britain in June 1812.

The War of 1812 went badly for the U.S. Madison's popularity fell. With peace, however, Madison regained his popularity. After leaving the presidency in 1817, Madison retired to Montpelier, his Virginia plantation. In 1826, he became rector (president) of the University of Virginia. He died at Montpelier in 1836.

Madonna (Madonna Louise Ciccone; 1958-), U.S. rock and roll performer. Madonna's early training was as a dancer studying ballet, modern, and jazz dancing. In the 1970s

Francisco Madero, a Mexican revolutionary, organized the political uprisings that led to the collapse of Porfirio Díaz's autocratic regime.

M

she performed with the Pearl Lange and Alvin Ailey dance companies. After joining a series of club bands as an instrumentalist, she set out to become a singer. The success of her singing career began when her songs became dance club favorites. She rose to superstar status with her songs and trend-setting fashions. Some of her well-known hits are 'Like a Virgin', 'Material Girl', and 'Crazy For You'. Madonna has also starred in various films: *Desperately seeking Susan* (1985), *Dick Tracy* (1990), *Snake Eyes* (1994), *Evita*, (1997).

Madonna and Child, among the most important art subjects of Christian religion. The Virgin Mary and child Jesus were first accepted as symbols of Christian faith following the Council of Ephesus in A.D. 431.

The emperor Asoka (3rd century B.C.) was a great propagandist for Buddhism, and also did great work for Buddhist architecture. Some stupas are still standing in Sanchi, Madhya Pradesh. The large stupa from the first century B.C. is the most well-known·one.

The earliest Madonna and Child paintings were found in early Christian catacombs; styles developed and transformed through the Byzantine and Renaissance periods. There are 5 general styles of treatment of Madonna paintings: portrait, the Madonna enthroned, in glory (hovering in the sky with halo and attendants), in pastoral scenes, and in a home environment. Raphael's *Sistine Madonna* (1515) hangs in the Dresden Gallery in Germany. Other painters who depicted the Madonna and Child include Luca Della Robbia, Giovanni Bellini, Leonardo da Vinci, Michelangelo, Fra Filippo Lippi, Andrea del Sarto, and Titian.
See also: Christianity.

Madras (pop. 6,100,000), large coastal city in southeastern India. Capital city of the state of Tamil on the Bay of Bengal, Madras once served as a British outpost (17th century) and center for trade. Today it serves as one of India's important ports and commercial centers. Hindu and Christian landmarks as well as the Univ. of Madras and the British Fort St. George may be found alongside modern industry and transportation.
See also: India.

Madrid (pop. 4,100,000), city, capital of Spain and of Madrid province, on the Manzanares River in New Castile. A 10th-century Moorish fortress captured by Castile in 1083, it was made the capital by

Philip II (1561) and expanded by the Bourbons in the 16th century. Now Spain's administrative,financial, and transportation center, it has a wide range of industries. A cultural center, its landmarks include the Prado art museum, the royal palace, and the university city.
See also: Spain.

Madrid Hurtado, Miguel de la *See:* De la Madrid Hurtado, Miguel.

Madrigal, poetic part song for 2 or more voices singing separate melodies. Originating in 14th-century Italy, it reached the height of its popularity in the 16th century, through the works of Monteverdi and Gesualdo. *The Triumphes of Oriana* (1601) is a famous collection of English madrigals by 21 composers.

Madroña, shrub or tree (*Arbutus menziesii*) in the heath family. Commonly found on the west coast of the United States and Canada, this species also called laurelwood, grows to about 75 ft (23 m), has cinnamon-colored peeling bark, thick evergreen leaves, tall white flowers, and red berrylike fruit. The tree is used for decorative purposes.

Madyapahit kingdom, Old Hindu realm, founded in 1923 by the sovereign Raden Widyaya in the area which contains current Indonesia. The prime of Madyapahit was in the 14th century, also called the golden age of Indonesia. It owes its wealth to the traditional rice culture and the active overseas trade. Two factors caused the realm's downfall: the arrival of Islam in the 15th century and of the Portuguese in the 16th century. Madyapahit still appeals to people's imaginations because it is seen as Indonesia's first attempt at unification.

Maecenas, Gaius (70?-8 B.C.), Roman statesman famous as the patron of Horace, Vergil, and Propertius. Friend, adviser, and agent of the emperor Augustus, he was criticized by Seneca for his extravagance. His name came to symbolize patronage.
See also: Rome, Ancient.

Madrid's Plaza de España, an elaborately designed public square, is at the junction of three of the city's busiest avenues.

Maekawa, Koenio (1905-1986), Japanese architect, of great influence on contemporary Japanese architecture. Introduced an expressive concrete architecture. Designer of the Japanese pavilion at the 1958 Expo in Brussels. His works include university buildings in Tokyo (1961).

Maenads, in Greek and Roman mythology, female devotees of Dionysus or Bacchus. Also called *bacchantes*, they were known for their ecstatic frenzies.
See also: Mythology.

Maeterlinck, Maurice (1862-1949), prolific Belgian poet and playwright influenced by French symbolists. His works include the tragedy *Pelléas et Mélisande* (1892), set as an opera by his friend Debussy, *Manna Vanna* (1902), and the dramatic fable *The Blue Bird* (1909). He was awarded the Nobel Prize for literature in 1911.

Maffei, Paolo *See:* Maffei galaxies.

Maffei galaxies, 2 galaxies near the Milky Way, discovered behind cosmic dust clouds through the use of a special infrared-sensitive telescope and photographic system by Italian astronomer Paolo Maffei (1968). Maffei I is an elliptical galaxy of about 100 billion stars, located approximately 3,000,000 light-years away. Maffei II is a spiral galaxy of about 10 billion stars, located approximately 9,000,000 light-years away.
See also: Galaxy.

Mafia, name given in the 19th century to Sicilian secret criminal societies who sought justice outside of the established legal system and dominated the peasantry through terrorism (e.g., the vendetta). Despite repression by successive governments, including Mussolini, in the late 19th and early 20th centuries, the Mafia survived. *Mafiosi* emigrated to the United States organized in 'families,' and prospered in bootlegging, gambling, narcotics, labor unions, and some legitimate business.

Magdalene *See:* Mary Magdalene.

Magdeburg (pop. 241,000), Germany, a city in Saxony-Anhalt state. It is on the Elbe River, about 80 miles (130 km) west-southwest of Berlin. The city is a river port and a railway and industrial center. Magdeburg was a Saxon trading post by 805 A.D. It became a leading member of the Naseatic League in the 1200's. The city was burned in 1631, during the Thirty Years' War.
A famous physics demonstration involving two metal hemispheres (the 'Magdeburg Hemispheres') was performed here in 1687. The city was severely bombed during World War II, and was taken by United States forces in 1945. From 1949 until 1990 Magdeburg was part of East Germany.

Magellan, Ferdinand (c.1480-1521), Portuguese navigator who commanded the first expedition to sail around the world. Magellan received Spanish backing (from Charles I) for his proposed voyage in search of a western route to the Spice

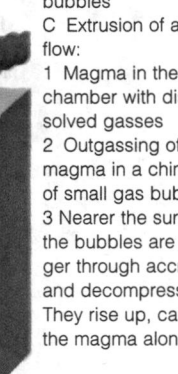

Islands (East Indies), then believed to be only a few hundred miles beyond America. He set sail with 5 ships in 1519, explored the Río de la Plata, sailed south to Patagonia, discovered the straits now named for him, then sailed northwest across the Pacific. Near starvation, the expedition reached Guam and the Philippines in 1521; Magellan was killed 10 days later in a skirmish with natives. Only one ship, the *Victoria*, returned to Spain.

Magellan, Strait of, north of Cape Horn, separating mainland South America from Tierra del Fuego; about 330 mi (530 km) long and 2.5-15 mi (4-24 km) wide. An important route before the Panama Canal, the straits were discovered by Ferdinand Magellan in 1520.
See also: Cape Horn.

Magellanic Clouds, 2 irregular galaxies nearest the Milky Way, visible in the far southern sky. The Large Magellanic Cloud (Nubecula Major), about 15,000 light-years in diameter, is located mostly in the constellation Dorado; the Small Magellanic Cloud (Nubecula Minor) is about 10,000 light-years across and is almost entirely in the

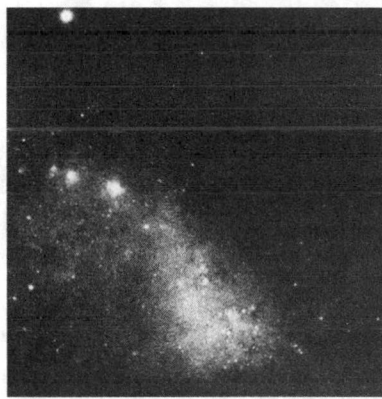

The Small Magellanic Cloud is known mainly for its many variable stars of the Cepheid type, which led to the determination of the well-known period - light power relation.

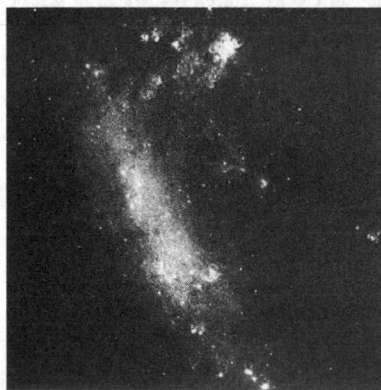

The Large Magellanic Cloud is a small constellation of stars, at a distance of about 170,000 light-years from the earth. It is thus sometimes called a satellite system of the Milky Way constellation. Above you can see the 30 Doradus cloud, which is clearly recognizable as a clear spot.

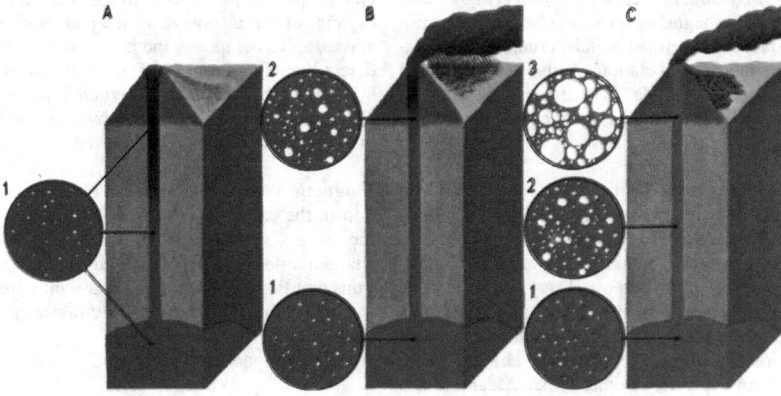

When the magma starts to rise, its pressure drops, forcing dissolved gases out of the melt. This decreases the overall density and speeds up the upwards motion. The bubbles will congregate and expand, with further pressure drop, and carry the melt along. The process is the same as the uncorking of a bottle of champagne: a sudden pressure drop, the formation and ascension of bubbles, and the spilling out.
A Before the eruption:
1 Gas dissolved in magma
B The eruption starts: internal pressure of outgassing, and the rise of magma force the plug out
1 Magma in the chamber with dissolved gasses in ascending column
2 Outgassing and formation of small gas bubbles
C Extrusion of a lava flow:
1 Magma in the chamber with dissolved gasses
2 Outgassing of magma in a chimney of small gas bubbles
3 Nearer the surface, the bubbles are bigger through accretion and decompression. They rise up, carrying the magma along.

constellation Tucana. Both are about 200,000 light-years from the earth.
See also: Galaxy.

Maggot, the soft-bodied larva of a winged insect, e.g., a fly. It has no legs and lies in its food, which may be plants, meat, or decaying matter.

Maghreb (or **Maghrib**) an Arabic name for western North Africa, meaning 'place where the sun sets'. It usually refers to Tunisia, Algeria, and Morocco. The people of the Maghreb are predominantly Arab and are of the Islamic faith.
The original inhabitants of the Maghreb were mainly Berbers. Muslim states developed in the region during the seventh century. The area was colonized by France in the 19th century. The French withdrew from the Maghreb during the 1950's and 1960's.

Magi, hereditary members of the priestly class of the ancient Persian Empire. Revered for their wisdom and their ability to interpret dreams and omens, the Magi were also the acknowledged priests of the ancient Persian religion Zoroastrianism, which advocated worship of a single supreme deity. According to one tradition, the Magi kept watch for a great star that was to signal the arrival of a savior. This helps to explain the connection between the Magi and the three wise men who, according to the New Testament, were led by a star to Bethlehem, where they honored the infant Jesus with gifts.
See also: Persia, Ancient; Zoroastrianism.

Magic, prescientific belief that an individual, by use of a ritual or spoken formula, may achieve superhuman powers. Should the magic fail to work, it is assumed to be due to deviations from the correct formula. In his classic work *The Golden Bow* (1890) Sir James George Frazer classified magic under 2 main heads: imitative and conta-

gious. In *imitative magic* the magician acts upon or produces a likeness of the desired object: Rainmakers may light fires, the smoke of which resembles rain clouds; voodoo practitioners stick pins in wax models of their intended victims. In *contagious magic* it is assumed that 2 objects once close together remain related even after separation: the magician may act upon hair clippings in an attempt to injure the person from whose body they came. Magic is crucial to many primitive societies, most tribes having at least an equivalent to a medicine man, who is believed to be able to provide them with extra defense against hostile tribes or evil spirits.

Maginot Line, massive French fortifications system, built 1930-1934 between the Swiss and Belgian borders. Named for war minister (1929-1932) André Maginot, it linked underground fortresses and was considered impregnable. However, it was easily flanked by the German mobile advance in World War II.

Magma, molten material formed in the upper mantle, or crust, of the earth, composed of a mixture of various complex silicates in which are dissolved various gaseous materials, including water. On cooling, magma forms igneous rocks, though any gaseous constituents are usually lost during the solidification. Magma extruded to the surface forms lava. The term is loosely applied to other fluid substances in the earth's crust.

Magna Carta, or *Magna Charta* (Latin, 'great charter'), major British constitutional charter forced on King John I by a baronial alliance at Runnymede (1215). A reaction to John's heavy taxation and his exclusion of the barons from government, the charter was designed to prevent royal restriction of baronial privilege and feudal rights and to safeguard church and municipal customs. Altered forms of the decree were issued on

M

John's death in 1216 and again in 1217 and 1225. Now generally recognized as a reactionary measure to guarantee feudal rights, it has, in the past, been interpreted to suggest and defend such civil rights as habeas corpus and jury trial. It paved the way for constitutional monarchy by implicitly recognizing that a king may be bound by laws enforceable by his subjects.

Magnesia, chemical compound (MgO), also called magnesium oxide. Used in the manufacture of refined metals, crucibles, and materials for insulation, it also has medicinal purposes. Made from magnesia chloride, magnesia is a white, powdery substance that has no taste.

Magnesium, chemical element, symbol Mg; for physical constants see Periodic Table. Compounds of magnesium have been known and used for hundreds of years. It was discovered by Humphry Davy in 1808. The eighth most abundant element in the earth's crust, it is extracted commercially by the electrolysis of fused magnesium chloride taken from sea water or other brines. Magnesium is a light, silvery-white, hard, reactive, metal. It plays an essential role in both plant and animal life. Magnesium and its compounds are used in light metal alloys, incendiary devices, flash bulbs, flares, and in medicine.

Magnetic compass *See:* Compass.

Magnetic equator, also called the *aclinic line*, imaginary line around the earth where the magnetic pull of the 2 poles is equal. In theory, the earth is a magnet with poles that are magnetized in the north (Bathurst Island, Canada) and south (Wilkes Land, Antarcti-

ca). A metal object placed on the magnetic equator, near the geographic equator, will not be inclined north or south.

Magnetic pole *See:* North Pole; South Pole.

Magnetic resonance imaging (MRI), technique which produces images of tissues inside the body and allows physicians to identify abnormal tissue without surgery. MRI enables physicians to see through bones and organs using a powerful magnet, radio waves, and a computer, and has been used to detect tumors, diseases of the circulatory system, birth defects, and certain injuries. The examination is supervised by a radiologist though no radiation is involved.

Magnetic storm, temporary, violent agitation in the earth's magnetic field caused by the *solar wind*-a stream of positively charged atoms and negatively charged electrons that flow from the sun. Solar winds are caused by the energy created during bursts of solar activity.
See also: Magnetism; Solar wind.

Magnetism, name for a force that occurs naturally in certain substances and can be transferred to or induced in others. The basic properties of magnetism are its complementary forces of attraction and repulsion and its capacity to align itself on a roughly north-south axis. These properties occur naturally in magnetite and, in the form of the lodestone, were observed and exploited to some degree in ancient times. The force of magnetism is dipolar, on a north-south axis, corresponding approximately to the north and south magnetic poles of the earth. In a magnet, unlike poles attract; like poles repel.

And if it is divided, the parts of a magnet will also be dipolar. It was early discovered that magnetism not only attracts iron, but can be transferred to iron. Metals which can be readily magnetized are called ferromagnetic and, besides iron and steel, include nickel and cobalt. A magnet, then, is anything that has the properties of magnetism. Magnetism also exhibits a field. The shape of a magnetic field and its lines of force can be seen by sprinkling iron filings over a sheet of paper placed on top of a magnet. In the 19th century, scientists made discoveries about the relationship between magnetism and electricity. It was found that the forces between magnetic dipoles are identical to those between electrical dipoles and that electric currents generate a magnetic field. Further research revealed that it is possible to generate an electric current in a conductor by changing the magnetic fields around it, a phenomenon known as electromagnetism. This interrelation between electrical charge and magnetic force is present in matter on the atomic level as well. And the earth itself has a magnetic field which scientists hypothesize is generated and maintained by large electric currents caused by movement in the planet's liquid core.

Magneto, small electric generator that produces pulses of electricity. Magnetos are used as an ignition source in airplane piston engines and motorcycle engines, among other things. In mining, magnetos are used to fire explosives. The magneto works on the principle of electromagnetic induction. It consists of a permanent magnet and a soft iron core wound with wire. The core is rotated between the poles of the magnet, generating a low-voltage alternating current in the coil windings. This low voltage may be transformed to a higher voltage by induction in a second set of coil windings.
See also: Electric generator.

Magnetohydrodynamics (MHD), method of generating electricity by passing a high-velocity stream of plasma (gas at very high temperature) across a magnetic field. As the stream moves through the magnetic field, it has an electric current generated in it. The principle is the same as that of the electric generator, except that in magnetohydrodynamics the plasma stream rather than a coil of wire acts as the conductor. If electrodes are inserted into the plasma, a current will flow in an external circuit between them. In this way heat can be almost directly converted into electrical energy. But magnetohydrodynamics is still in the development stage, and a full-scale MHD plant has yet to be built. In practice the plasma would be heated by burning fuel or by a nuclear reactor to a temperature of 2,000°C-3,000°C (3,632°F-5,432°C). At these temperatures the gas is ionized (has electrons stripped from its atoms) and becomes conducting. Strong magnetic fields are required, and these may be provided by superconducting magnets. So far a few kilowatts of power have been generated by MHD for only a few seconds, and improvements in high-temperature technology will be needed before substantial progress can be made. MHD plants could in theory be smaller than conventional power

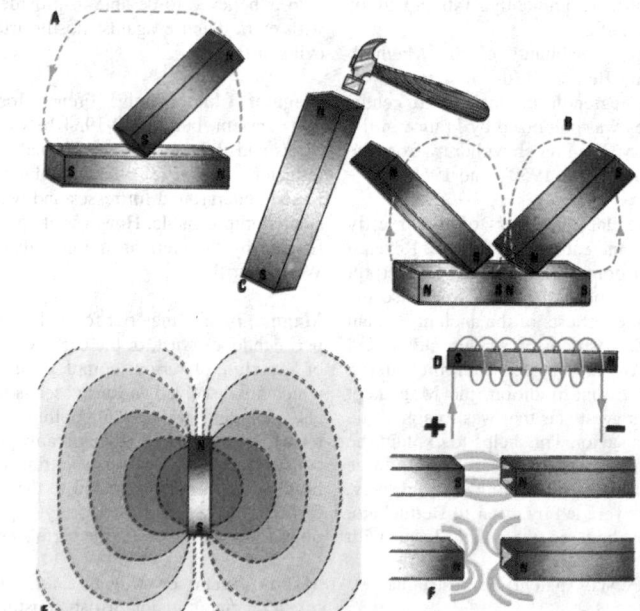

A magnet can be made by a number of methods, depending on the metal to be magnetized and the permanency required. A simple method is the single touch method (A). The specimen to be magnetized, is repeatedly stroked in one directon. The end that was last touched, has an opposite polarity to the stroking pole. The divided-touch method (B) uses two stroking magnets.
A magnet can also be made by hammering the metal bar in the earth's field (C). In the northern hemisphere, the lower end of the specimen is found to have a north polarity, and in the southern hemisphere a south polarity. The best and the quickest method, is to place the specimen inside a current-carrying coil (D). The lines of the magnetic field run from north to south poles (E). Like poles will repel each other, and unlike poles will attract (F).

stations and achieve a much greater efficiency because of the elimination of moving parts.
See also: Electric generator; Magnetism.

Magnetometer, instrument that surveys the strength of a magnetic field and registers its results through electronic voltage. Magnetometers are used by biomedical technicians to measure the magnetic field of certain body organs, such as the brain. They are used in industry, especially by those working with superconductors, and by prospectors attempting to detect ore or petroleum beneath the ground.
See also: Magnetism.

Magnitogorsk (pop. 443,000), Russia, a city on the Ural River in the Ural Mountains, 880 miles (1,420 km) east of Moscow. The city is the site of an iron and steel plant and also produces chemicals and heavy machinery. Nosov Institute of Ore Mining and Metallurgy is here. Magnitogorsk was founded in 1929.

Magnitude, measure of a celestial object's brightness. The foundations of the system were laid by Hipparchus (120 B.C.), who divided stars into 6 categories of relative brightness, as seen from the earth (apparent magnitude). On a logarithmic scale, the difference of 1 magnitude of brightness between objects is determined by a factor of 2,512 (the 5th root of 100). The sun's magnitude is 26.8; bright stars, about +1. *Absolute magnitude* (measure of intrinsic brightness) is defined as the apparent magnitude if located at a distance of 10 parsecs.
See also: Astronomy; Hipparchus.

Magnolia, any of the evergreen or deciduous trees or shrubs (genus *Magnolia*) from the family Magnoliaceae, often with showy flowers, found chiefly in temperate zones. Principally an Asiatic genus, native American magnolia species include the southern magnolia, or the bull bay (*M. grandiflora*), the cucumber tree (*M. acuminata*), the umbrella tree (*M. tripetala*), and the tulip tree, or yellow poplar (*Liriodendron tulipifera*), whose soft, yellowish wood is valued for furniture and cabinetwork.

Magnolia State *See:* Mississippi.

Magpie, long-tailed bird of the crow and jay family (especially genus *Pica*). The North American *black-billed magpie* (*Pica pica*) has black feathers and white wings and abdomen. These scavengers, collectors of bright objects, often learn to imitate words in captivity.

Magritte, René (1898-1967), Belgian surrealist painter. His style, influenced by Chirico, often combined realism with irony, as in fantasy painting such as *The False Mirror* (1928), *The Red Model* (1935), and *The Empire of Lights* (1950).
See also: Surrealism.

Maguey, plant in the agave family. The Mexican plant, which grows up to 9 ft (3 m) long and 1 ft (30 cm) wide, has long green stalks with green flowers. The pulque agave (*Agave atrovirens*) is used to make beverages, both pulque and tequila. In Indonesia and the Philippines, the maguey is referred to commonly as cantala, and fibers from the plant, which may grow to 30-60 ft (75-150 cm) long, are used to produce twine.

Magyars, dominant people of Hungary and their language (from the Finno-Ugric language group). A nomadic warrior people, originally from the Urals, they were forced into present-day Romania by the Turkish Pechenegs and then into Hungary in the 9th century. They went on to conquer Moravia, advancing into Germany until stopped by Otto I in 955. They adopted Christianity in the 11th century.

Mahabharata, Sanskrit epic poem ascribed to the sage Vyasa, comprising some 110,000 32-syllable couplets, probably written before 500 B.C. though with many later passages in 18 books. It concerns the lengthy feud between 2 related tribes, the Pandavas and the Kauravas, and has as its central episode the Bhagavad-Gita, the religious classic of Hinduism.
See also: Hinduism.

Mahan, Alfred Thayer (1840-1914), U.S. naval officer and historian. His works on the historical significance of sea power, classics in their field, stimulated worldwide naval expansion. They include *The Influence of Sea Power upon History, 1660-1783* (1890) and *The Influence of Sea Power upon the French Revolution and Empire, 1793-1812* (1892).

Mahathir bin Mohammad, Datuk Seri (1925-), prime minister of Malaysia since 1981. Trained in medicine, he has made his career in politics. Mahathir served as deputy prime minister (1976-1981) before succeeding Prime Minister Hussein bin Onn. A Malay nationalist, he was elected president of his party, the United Malays National Organization, in 1981. At the 1995 parliamentary elections his party won 80% of the votes.
See also: Malaysia.

Mahatma *See:* Gandhi, Mohandas Karamchand.

Mahayana *See:* Buddhism.

Mahdi (Arabic, 'the guided one'), the prophet or savior who Muslims believe will bring peace and justice to the world. A notable claimant was Ubaydullah (r. 909-934), founder of the Egyptian Fatimid dynasty. Another was Muhammad Ahmad (1843?-1885), who raised a revolt against Egyptian rule in the Sudan and fought the British (1883-1885).
See also: Muslims.

Mahfouz, Naguib (or Mahfuz, Nagib; 1911-), Egyptian novelist, playwright, and screenwriter. Among his works, which focus on urban life, are *Midaq Alley* (tr. 1975), *Miramar* (tr. 1978), and the short story collection *God's World* (tr. 1973). He won the 1988 Nobel Prize for literature. His books have been banned in many Arab countries for his expression of support of the 1979 Egypt-Israel peace treaty and other controversial views.

Mahican, Native American group of tribes of the Eastern Woodlands. These Native Americans lived along the Hudson River in longhouses and spoke an Algonquian language. They were active in the 17th-century fur trade along with their rivals, the Mohawks. Today surviving Mahicans live on Stockbridge Reservation in Wisconsin, named after the western Massachusetts town to which they were driven in the 17th century. Both Mahicans and Mohegans, a tribe of the Mahican group, are often referred to as Mohicans, after the fictional tribe in James Fenimore Cooper's *The Last of the Mohicans*.
See also: Mohegan.

Mah-jongg, game of Chinese origin played with a set of 136 standard domino-like tiles and several additional tiles, usually by 4 players. It is a collecting game where tiles are drawn and discarded until 1 player has a winning hand.

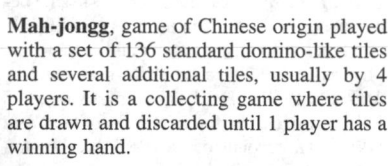
Black-billed magpie (*Pica pica*, order *Passiformes*, family Corvidae). Found in Eurasia, Northwest Africa and western North America. Length up to 18 in (45 cm).

M

Mahler, Gustav (1860-1911), Austrian composer and conductor. He completed 9 symphonies and a number of song cycles, most notably *Songs of a Wayfarer* (1883-1885) and *Kindertotenlieder* (*Songs on the Death of Children*; 1901-1904). The symphonies are a culmination of 19th-century romanticism, but their startling harmonic and orchestral effects link them with early 20th-century works. Mahler was director of the Imperial Opera in Vienna (1897-1907).

Mahmud I (Ottoman Empire) (1696-1754), Sultan of the Ottoman Empire from 1730 to 1754. Mahmud I came to power by suppressing the Patrona Khalil rebellion, thus forcing his predecessor, Ahmet III - whose decadence was the center of the rebellion - to resign. In military matters Mahmud I was successful by bringing about the treaty of Belgrade in 1739, thereby establishing peace between Russia and Austria, and by bringing the war with Persia, which had been ongoing since 1731, to a favorable end in 1746. Mahmud's interest for literature and music was greater than that for political affairs. He founded a large number of buildings in Istanbul, among which libraries and mosques can be counted. His austerity made Mahmud I a beloved sovereign.

Mahogany, chiefly tropical trees and shrubs, family Meliaceae, whose scented, termite-resistant hardwood is used extensively for furniture. The American genus *Swietenia* and the African genus *Khaya* are the principal sources of mahogany.

Mahomet *See:* Muhammad.

Mahratta, or Maratha, central Indian Hindu warrior people. Their empire was founded by Sivaji in 1674; it dominated India for about 150 years, following the Mogul empire, but the British broke its power in 1818.

Maidenhair tree *See:* Ginkgo.

Mailer, Norman (1923-), U.S. novelist and journalist. After the great success of his first novel, *The Naked and the Dead* (1948), he became a critic of the American way of life. He combines journalism, fiction, and autobiography, as in his collection *Advertisements for Myself* (1959). He has been awarded 2 Pulitzer Prizes, one for *the Armies of the Night* (1968), an account of the 1967 Washington peace march, and the other for *The Executioner's Song* (1979). Other works include *Though Guys don't Dance* (1984), and *Oswald's Tale: an American Mystery* (1995).

Maillol, Aristide (1861-1944), French sculptor. His chief subject was the female nude, which he sculpted in monumental, static forms that represent a revival of classical ideals.

Aristide Maillol's (1861-1944) bronze statue of Pomona, the Roman goddess of tree fruits (Tuileries, Paris).

Maimonides, Moses (Solomon ben Maimon; 1135-1204), medieval rabbi, physician, and Jewish philosopher. Born in Muslim Spain, his family was driven to Egypt under persecution, where Maimonides became renowned as court physician to Saladin. Two of his major works were the *Mishneh Torah* (*Strong Hand*; 1180), a codification of Jewish doctrine, and *Guide to the Perplexed* (1190), in which he attempted to interpret Jewish tradition in Aristotelian terms. His work influenced many Jewish and Christian thinkers.
See also: Philosophy.

Maine (Pine Tree State; pop. 1,242,000), state in the Northeast of the U.S. (New England), bordering on Canada, the Atlantic Ocean and the state of New Hampshire; 33,278 sq mi (86,156 sq km). Capital city: Augusta; important port: Portland. Hilly in the west, flat coastal strip. Agriculture (e.g. potatoes, apples), cattle breeding, forestry and fishing. Paper, food, textile, wood, electronics and leather goods industries. Tourism is also important.
In 1622 the first permanent settlement of Europeans (mainly Britons) was established. Before that, the area was populated by about 20 different Indian nations which were converted to Roman Catholicism by French missionaries. Two of these nations remain nowadays. In 1691 the area became part of Massachusetts; since 1820 it is a member of the Union as an independent state. After WW II economic problems arose in the country as well as in cities, but in the 1980s and 1990s the economy developed successfully, just as in other states of New England.

Mainstreaming *See:* Special education.

Maintenon, Marquise de (1635-1719), second wife of Louis XIV of France. After the death of her first husband (1660), she became governess to the sons of Louis and his mistress, Mme de Montespan. She replaced the latter in Louis' affections and, on the death of the queen, was married to him though she did not share his title and estate.

Mainz (pop. 185,000), city in west-central Germany. As the capital of the state of Rhineland-Palatinate state, it is located on a junction of two German rivers, the Rhine and the Main. Originally a Roman camp (1st century B.C.), it became an important religious and printing center in medieval times and a fortress for the German Empire (1873-1918). The city is known as home to historic buildings, a center for German Rhine wines, and manufacturing (e.g., motor vehicles and chemicals).

Maitland, Frederic William (1850-1906), English jurist and legal historian. He was particularly concerned with early English law and founded the Selden Society (1887). Notable among his works is *The History of English Law before the Time of Edward I* (1895), written with Sir Frederick Pollock.

Maize *See:* Corn.

Major *See:* Rank, military.

Major, John (1943-), former British Prime

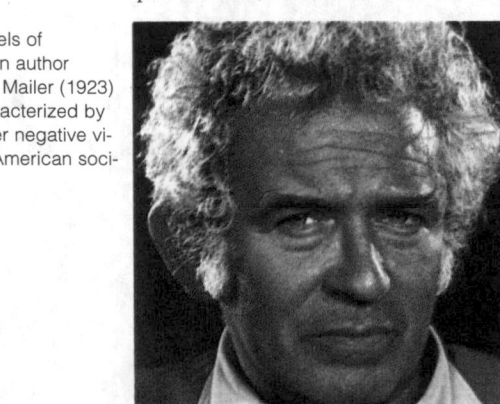

The novels of American author Norman Mailer (1923) are characterized by his rather negative vision of American society.

The picturesque village of Boothbay Harbor is situated on a peninsula in southern Maine between the Sheepscott and Damariscotta rivers.

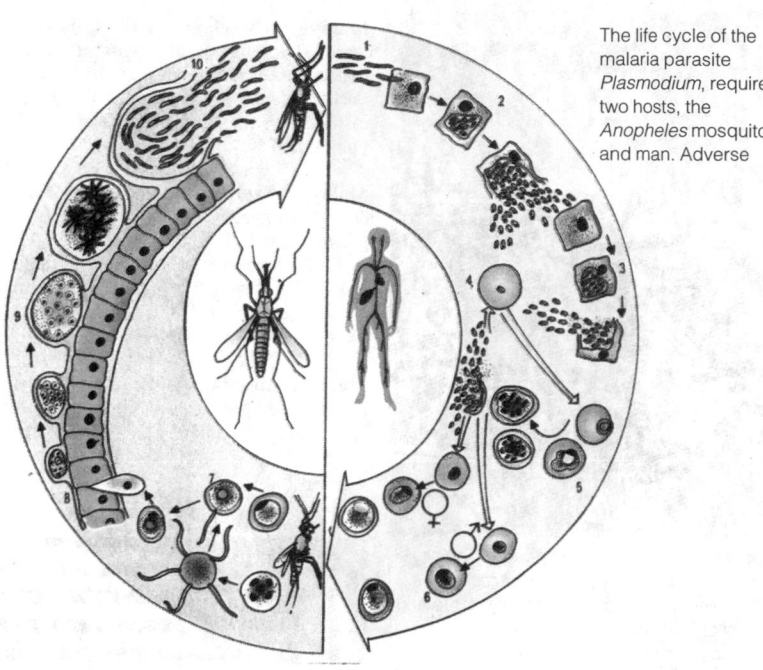

The life cycle of the malaria parasite *Plasmodium*, requires two hosts, the *Anopheles* mosquito and man. Adverse effects of such an infection only appear in man. When biting a person, an infected mosquito will inject thousands of *Plasmodium* organisms into the bloodstream (1). These will penetrate the liver cells, then multiply and cause cell rupture (2). Some of the released organisms may then reinfect the liver cells (3), others will progress to infect red blood cells (4) and (5). Male and female parasites shortly appear in the red blood cells (6). At this stage, when another mosquito will bite, it will get infected blood (7). In the red blood cells fertilisation takes place, and the `embryo' will penetrate the wall of the stomach (8). Within the cyst that is formed there (9), thousands of organisms will develop. When this cyst ruptures, the organisms are released (10). They will travel to the salivary glands, and from there, they may be injected into another human host (1).

Minister from the Conservative Party who succeeded Margaret Thatcher in 1990. Prior to becoming Prime Minister, Major was a member of Parliament, Foreign Secretary, and Chancellor of the Exchequer. Major left school at the age of 16 and never attended college. He entered the banking industry at the age of 22 before entering politics. He was the youngest British prime minister in the 20th century. Following the defeat of the Conservative Party at the 1997 elections, Major resigned as party leader.
See also: United Kingdom.

Majorca, or *Mallorca*, largest of the Balearic Islands of Spain, in the west Mediterranean. Majorca is a major tourist center with many resorts, including its capital, Palma.

Major leagues *See:* Baseball.

Makarios III (Michael Christodoulos Mouskos; 1913-1977), archbishop of the Cypriot Orthodox Church from 1950, and president of independent Cyprus (1960-1977). During British rule he led the movement for *enosis* (union with Greece). As president after independence, he worked to reduce conflict between the island's Greek and Turkish population. He survived 4 assassination attempts and fled temporarily during the political disturbances of 1974.

Maki, Fumihiko (1928-), Japanese architect, educated in Japan and the U.S. (Harvard); momentarily teaches in both countries. In 1964 he received the highest decoration for architecture in Japan. His writings include *Metabolism* (1960) and *Movement Systems in the City* (1965). He designed the Steinberg Hall of Washington University (1960) and the Auditoriums of Nagoya (1961) and Chiba Universities (1965) in Japan. His work shows great imaginative powers.

Mako shark *See:* Shark.

Malabo (pop. 31,000), capital city of Equatorial Guinea. Founded by the British (1827) as Clarencetown, it was later named Santa Isabel by the Spanish (1844) until the independence of Equatorial Guinea (1973). Located on the island of Bioko in the Gulf of Guinea, the city is important in import-export trade.

Malacca, Strait of, important sea passage that links the South China Sea and Indian Ocean. Singapore is the chief port located on this 500 mi (800 km) strait, which flows between Sumatra and the Malay Peninsula. The width of the channel varies from 30 to 200 mi (50 to 320 km).

Malachi, Book of, Old Testament book, 39th and last in Authorized Version, 12th of the Minor Prophets. Written anonymously c. 5th century B.C., it prophesies judgment for insincerity and negligence at the coming of the Messiah.
See also: Old Testament.

Malachite, $CU_2CO_3(OH)_2$, green, translucent mineral containing crystals of hydrated copper carbonate. It is widely distributed, usually occurring near copper deposits, in the United States, the former USSR, Chile, Zaïre, Zimbabwe and Australia. It is used as a source of copper, an ornamental stone, and, when ground, as a pigment.

Malagasy Republic *See:* Madagascar.

Malamud, Bernard (1914-1986), U.S. novelist and short story writer. He won a National Book Award for his stories in *The Magic Barrel* (1958) and the Pulitzer Prize for his novel *The Fixer* (1966). Malamud's work deals mainly with Jewish life and traditions in the United States. The heroes of his books are often humble, solitary individuals, though *Dubin's Lives* (1979) marked a departure in subject matter.

Malamute *See:* Alaskan malamute.

Malang (pop. 695,000), city on the Brantas river in the Indonesian province of Java Timor, 49 mi (80 km) south of Surabaya, situated on a plateau surrounded by volcanoes. Trade center for the area, where sugarcane, rice, coffee, tea, corn, peanuts, cassava and cinchona (for quinine) are cultivated. Encampment of land and air forces. University (1963). Before independence Malang was an important Dutch garrison town, and the capital city of the Malang residence.

Malaria, infectious parasitic disease causing fever, violent chills, enlargement of the spleen, and occasionally jaundice and anemia. Bouts often reoccur and can be acute or chronic. Widespread in tropical and subtropical areas, malaria is due to infection with the *Plasmodium* parasite carried by the *Anopheles* mosquitoes from the blood of infected persons. Derivatives of quinine are used both in prevention and treatment of the disease.

Malawi

Capital:	Lilongwe
Area:	45,747 sq mi (118,484 sq km)
Population:	10,702,000
Language:	English, Chichewa
Government:	Presidential republic
Independent:	1964
Head of gov.:	President
Per capita:	US$ 660
Monetary unit:	1 Kwacha = 100 tambala

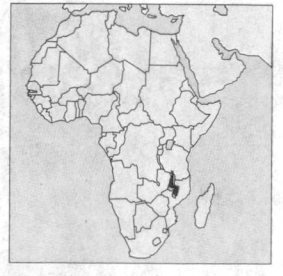

M

Malawi, republic of east Africa lying west and south of Lake Malawi, and bordered by Tanzania to the north, Mozambique to the east and south, and Zambia to the west.

Land and climate. Malawi has a area of about 45,747 sq mi (118,484 sq km), controls much of lakes Malawi and Chiuta, and includes Malambe, Chilwa, and several other large lakes. The lakes are part of the great Rift Valley, which crosses the region from north to south and includes the Shire River valley. Bordering highlands and plateaus average 3,500 ft (1,067 m) in height, and the Shire highlands in the south and southeast rise to 9,843 ft (3,000 m) at Mlanje Peak. The valleys are hot; the highland climate is moderate.

People. The people of Malawi are almost entirely Bantu-speaking black Africans. About 75% of the people are Christians with the balance professing Islam or practicing native religions. English and Chichewa are the country's official languages, though other African languages are spoken. The largest city is Blantyre, the capital is Lilongwe.

Economy. Malawi's economy is agricultural. Tea and tobacco are grown in the highlands; cotton in the lowlands. Other crops include peanuts, corn, rice, and sugar. There is some light industry at Blantyre and Lilongwe. The Shire River is harnessed for hydroelectricity at Nkula Falls. The country's mineral resources remain mostly undeveloped.

History. Seat of a powerful black African kingdom between the 15th and 18th centuries, Malawi was later prey to the slave trade. In 1859 the British missionary Dr. David Livingstone visited Malawi. An attempt by the Portuguese to seize the south was defeated leading to the establishment of a British protectorate in 1890. Shortly thereafter the area became known as Nyasaland. In 1953 the country entered the Federation of Rhodesia and Nyasaland, but

George Town on Penang Island, a few kilometres off the east coast of the Malay Peninsula, in the late 17th century developed into Malacca's most important trading centre. At the beginning of the 19th century, however, it lost its position to Singapore. The city experienced new prosperity by the end of the 19th century, when the continent was opened up and the development of agriculture and mining caused the immigration of many thousands of Chinese and Indians.

the association with white dominated Rhodesia was an uneasy one and lasted only until 1963. In 1964, Nyasaland became the independent state of Malawi. On July 6, 1966 it was proclaimed a republic under the presidency of Dr. Hastings K. Banda. Under Dr. Banda Malawi has pursued a controversial foreign policy of openly maintaining relations with South Africa. After years of one party rule, Banda held a referendum in 1993 om his rule under pressure of the West, which halted foreign aid. Banda lost when people voted for multiparty democracy. In 1994 elections, Banda was voted out of office. He was succeeded by Bakili Muluzi.

Malay Archipelago (East Indies), the world's largest group of islands, off the coast of southeastern Asia, between the Indian and Pacific Oceans. It includes the 3,000 islands of Indonesia, the 7,000 islands of the Philippines, and New Guinea.

Malayo-Polynesian languages, or Austroenesian languages, family of some 500 languages found throughout the Central and South Pacific, especially in Malaysia and the Indonesian islands. There are 2 main groups: Oceanic to the east and Indonesian to the west.

Malay Peninsula, southernmost peninsula in Asia, comprising western Malaysia and southern Thailand. It is one of the world's richest producers of rubber and tin.

Malaysia

Capital:	Kuala Lumpur
Area:	127,584 sq mi (329,758 sq km)
Population:	2,662,000
Language:	Bahasa Malaysia (Malay)
Government:	Federal constitutional monarchy
Independent:	1963
Head of gov.:	Prime minister
Per capita:	US$ 9,000
Monetary unit:	1 Ringgit = 100 sen

Malaysia, Federation of Malaysia, independent federation in Southeast Asia, comprising West Malaysia on the Malay Peninsula and East Malaysia, formed by Sabah and Sarawak, on the island of Borneo.

Land and climate. East Malaysia is separated from the Malay Peninsula for a distance of about 400 mi (644 km) by the South China Sea. West Malaysia is bordered by Thailand to the north, Singapore to the south, the South China Sea to the east, and the Strait of Malacca and the Andaman Sea to the west. East Malaysia is bordered on the south and west by Indonesia, on the north by the South China and Sulu Seas and by Brunei, and on the east by the Celebes Sea. West Malaysia is mainly mountainous with narrow coastal plains and lush equatorial forests. Sarawak and Sabah also have mountainous interiors and large areas of rain forest.

People. The majority of Malaysians live on

One of the numerous traditional villages in Malawi. The villages (mudzi) are usually small, since their size is limited by shortage of water and arable land. In the last few years, many traditional houses have been replaced by brick buildings with corrugated roofing.

the peninsula and most are Malays or Chinese with sizable minorities of Indians and Pakistanis. Malay is the official language, but many Malaysians also speak other languages including Chinese, English, and Tamil. Islam is the official religion. The capital is Kuala Lumpur.

Economy. Malaysia is rich in natural resources, but the economy is largely agricultural. Rice is the chief food crop, but bananas, yams, cocoa, pepper, tea, and tobacco are also grown. In addition, the forests yield valuable timber, palm oil, and coconuts. The industrial sector produces petroleum, iron ore, bauxite, coal, and gold. The country's principal exports are petroleum, rubber, tin, palm oil, and timber.

History. In the 9th century Malaysia was the seat of the Buddhist Srivajava Empire. Beginning in the 14th century the population was converted to Islam. The Portuguese took Malacca in 1511, but were ousted by the Dutch in 1641. The British formed a trading base of the East India Company in Penang in 1786, and in 1826 united Penang, Singapore, and Malacca into the Straits Settlement. Between 1888 and 1909 the British established many protectorates in Malaya and Borneo. In 1946, after the defeat and the departure of the Japanese army after WW ll (1942-1945), the British government united Penang, Malakka and 9 Malayan States to the Malayan Union. Singapore, Sarawak and Northern-Borneo became crown colonies. This union became independent within the British Commonwealth in 1957. In 1963 the Malayan Union with Singapore, Sarawak, and Sabah formed the Federation of Malaysia. Indonesia waged guerilla warfare against the Federation from 1963 to 1965, after which Singapore seceded and became an independent republic. Parliament was suspended for 22 months in 1969 after riots had broken out between Malays and Chinese in West Malaysia. Racial and religious problems again occurred among Malays, Chinese, and Hindus in the late 1970s and early 80s. In the 1980s and 90s the export-oriented economy flourished. At the end of the 1990s the country suffered from terrible forest fires. Economically, the country suffered severely from the Asia crisis in 1997 and, after 2000, from the falling world market. Prime Minister Mahathir bin Mohammad, who has been governing since 1981, announced he would resign in 2003.

Malcolm X (Malcolm Little; 1925-1965), U.S. black militant leader. He was also known as El-Hajj Malik El-Shabazz. While in prison for burglary (1946-1952), he was converted to the Black Muslim faith and upon release became a Muslim minister and leader of the black separatist movement. In 1964 he split with another leader, Elijah Muhammad, to form the Organization of Afro-American Unity, speaking for black nationalism but allowing racial brotherhood. He was assassinated at an OAAU meeting in New York City in 1965, purportedly by Black Muslims. The *Autobiography of Malcolm X* (1964) is a classic concerning the black power movement of the 1960s.
See also: Black Power.

Maldives

Capital:	Malé
Area:	115 sq mi (298 sq km)
Population:	320,000
Language:	Divehi (Maldivian)
Government:	Presidential republic
Independent:	1965
Head of gov.:	President
Per capita:	US$ 3,870
Monetary unit:	1 Rufiyaa = 100 laari

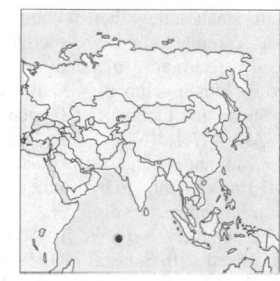

Maldives, officially Republic of Maldives, formerly *Maldive Islands*, republic, a series of coral atolls (115 sq mi/298 sq km) in the northern Indian Ocean, about 420 mi (675 km) southwest of Sri Lanka. They comprise some 1,200 islands, of which about 200 are inhabited. The official religion is Islam and the language, Dhivehi. Malé, the capital, is on the largest island. The chief industries are fishing, coconut products, shipping, and tourism. Grains are grown on a limited scale, but most food staples are imported. Originally settled by southern Asians, the introduction of Islam in the 12th century and the arrival of the Portuguese in the 16th century strongly influenced the history of the islands. They became a British protectorate (1887-1965) with internal self-government before finally achieving independence as a

Malcolm X (1925-1965).

sultanate in 1965. When the ad-Din dynasty, which had ruled since the 14th century, ended in 1968, a republic was declared. Britain closed its air force base on Gan in 1976. In 1988 a group of 80 Tamil Tigers attempted a coup but were unsuccessful. In 1997 the country adopted a new constitution. President, since 1978, is Maumoon Abdul Gayyoom.

Male *See:* Reproduction.

Malé (pop. 63,000), port and capital city of the Republic of Maldives, or Maldive Islands, in the Indian Ocean. Located on the island of the same name in this South Pacific atoll, Malé's main products are fish and tropical fruits and vegetables. Islam is the religion of its people, and Muslim mosques make Malé an important tourist site.

Malemute *See:* Alaskan malamute.

Malenkov, Georgi Maximilianovich (1902-1988), Soviet premier 1953-1955, after Stalin's death. Beginning as an aide to Stalin, followed by entrance to the politburo and deputy premiership (1946), Malenkov as prime minister curbed the power of the secret police and promoted reconciliation in his foreign policy. He was replaced by Bulganin in 1955, expelled from the Presidium in 1957, and from the party in 1961.

Malevich, Kasimir (1878-1935), Russian painter, a pioneer of abstract art. In 1913 he began painting works based on geometric shapes and published a manifesto to propagate suprematism. Among his works is *White on White* (1918).

Kasimir Malevich's (1878-1935) *Eight Red Rectangles* (before 1915, Municipal Museum, Amsterdam).

Malherbe, André (1956-), Belgian motocross racer, became world champion for the first time in 1980 (on a Honda), as well as in 1981 and 1984.

Malherbe, François de (1555-1628), French poet; court poet to Henry IV and Louis XIII. A critic of the classical style of the Pléiade poets, he emphasized the importance of French classic language and of precision in expression. His best-known poem is *Cosolation à Monsieur du Périer* (c.1590).

M

M

Mali

Capital:	Bamako
Area:	478,841 sq mi
	(1,240,192 sq km)
Population:	11,340,000
Language:	French
Government:	Presidential republic
Independent:	1960
Head of gov.:	Prime minister
Per capita:	US$ 840
Monetary unit:	1 CFA franc = 100 centimes

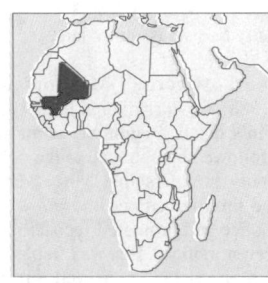

Mali, officially Republic of Mali, West Africa's largest country (478,764 sq mi/1,240,000 sq km), Mali is bordered by Senegal, Guinea, and Mauritania (west), Niger (east and southeast), Algeria (north), and Burkina Faso and Ivory Coast (south). *Land and economy.* The land in the south, fed by the Niger and Senegal rivers, supports the chief cash crops of peanuts and cotton and subsistence crops of rice, millet, maize, and sorghum. Exports include fish from the Niger and livestock. Extensive mineral re-

sources are largely untapped, though some salt, gold, and phosphates are mined. Industries include textiles, food processing, and cotton ginning. Land in the north, is primarily arid, supporting minimum grazing (cattle, goats, sheep).
People. The population comprises over 10 ethnic groups, who speak the official language, French, and several indigenous tongues. The Moors and the Tuaregs live in the north. About 90% are Muslims; the rest are animists.
History. The early 14th century saw the zenith of the powerful medieval empire of Mali, one of the world's chief gold suppliers. Its cities of Timbuktu and Djenné were major cultural and trade centers. The Songhai empire of Gao was prominent in the late 15th century before a Moroccan army destroyed its power (1590) and the region divided into small states. French conquest of Mali was complete by 1898, though they had faced a resurgence of Islam and were opposed by Muslim emperors. Mali became French Sudan and then part of French West Africa. After World War I, the Sudanese Union, a militant political force of the new nationalist movement, led by Modibo Keita, gained momentum, resulting in the autonomous Sudanese Republic in 1958. The republic joined with Senegal in 1959 to become the Mali Federation, a union that ended in 1960 as the Republic of Mali became fully independent and broke with the French Community. The one-party, socialist state, led by President Keita, left the French bloc (1962) but returned in 1967, due to financial difficulties. Keita was overthrown by the military (1968), displaced by Lt. Moussa Traoré as head of the military regime. In the 1970s a severe drought damaged Mali's agrarian economy and contributed to the deaths of nearly 100,000 people. A new constitution calling for civilian rule was implemented in 1979, reelecting Traoré as president. Traoré's rule lasted 25 years and ended

with a coup in 1991. The new leaders announced a transitional period as a stepping stone to democracy. In 1997 Swiss banks reimbursed money which had been embezzled by Traoré. Traoré was sentenced to death in 1999, but this was commuted to life-imprisonment. General Amadou Toumani Touré won the presidential elections of 2002. He promised education and jobs. France promised to cancel 40% of the debts owed by Mali.

Mali Empire, one of the great Sudanese empires of West Africa. Founded in the 13th century, it reached its height under Mansa Musa, who reigned 1312-1337. He and his successors were devout Muslims, and the towns of Mali and Timbuktu became centers both of the caravan trade and of Islamic culture. The empire declined in the 15th century, mainly because of expansion of the Songhai empire of Gao.
See also: Mansa Musa.

Malinke *See:* Mandingo.

Malinowski, Bronislaw (1884-1942), Polish-born English anthropologist, founder of social anthropology. In his theory of 'functionalism,' all the mores, customs, and beliefs of a society perform a vital function that must be taken into account in the study of that culture. His research included the cultures of Trobriand Island, Africa, and the Americas. Writings include *Crime and Custom in Savage Society* (1926), *Sex and Repression in Savage Society* (1926), and *Magic, Science and Religion* (1948).
See also: Anthropology.

Mallard, wild duck of the family Anatidae. The dull brown feathers of the female are in sharp contrast to the iridescent green head and purple chest feathers of the courting male. These ducks, which grow to 28 in (71 cm), migrate from northern marshes in summer to warmer southern wetlands in winter. They are abundant in North America, Europe, and Asia.

Mallarmé, Stéphane (1842-1898), French poet, forefather of the symbolists. He held that poetry should suggest or evoke the transcendental, not describe in literal terms. Although the language of his poems is obscure and nontraditional, he had considerable influence on French poetry. His works include *Herodias* (1869), *The Afternoon of a Faun* (1876), which inspired Debussy, and *A Throw of the Dice Will Never Eliminate Chance* (1897).

Mallorca *See:* Majorca.

Mallow, shrub and herb of the family Malvaceae, usually with showy flowers and disk-shaped fruits. True mallows (genus *Malva*) of the Old World, false mallows (genus *Malvastrum*), and rose, or swamp, mallows (genus *Hibiscus*) of North America comprise the family. The perennial hollyhock (*Althea rosea*), from China, is the most popular ornamental; the pods of the mallow okra, or gumbo, are used as a vegetable; and the most economically important member is cotton. The marsh mallow of Europe is used

Mali is predominantly a low and flat country. In some places, however, the monotony is broken by very steep rocky walls (falaises), which constitute the transition from rather low sandstone plateaus to lower areas.

The mallow family (Malvaceae) are recognised by the long stamen tubes of their flowers, which run up the style, bringing the anthers near to the five knobs of the stimga. The petals are shades of pink, orange and red. The capsular fruit keeps its seeds arranged in a ring, or torus.
A. flower of a split-petalled hibiscus, *Hibiscus schizometalus,* Southeast Asia
B. flower of a marsh mallow, *Althaea officinalis,* Europe
C. fruit of a hollyhock, *Althaea rosea.*

medicinally and was once used to make marshmallow.

Malnutrition, shortage of vital nutrients. Malnutrition may be partial or total and may be the result of poor eating habits, as often occurs among the aged, or due to the unavailability or lack of food caused by disasters such as famine, drought, or war. Malnutrition may also be symptomatic of a gastrointestinal disorder, a malfunctioning of one of the body's major organs, or it may even be associated with diarrhea. Malnutrition affecting all parts of the diet is called marasmus. In marasmus, the body breaks down its own tissues to meet the needs of metabolism. The result is extreme wasting and, in children, extreme growth retardation. A shortage of the body's essential proteins is a variety of malnutrition known as kwashiorkor and shortages of essential vitamins manifest themselves as pellagra, beriberi, or scurvy.

Malnutrition is especially dangerous in pregnant women and in children. In children it can lead to growth disorders, both physical and mental, and reduce their resistance to disease. Though malnutrition is most readily associated with poor and underdeveloped countries in which its manifestations can be severe and are often fatal, it also occurs in rich and developed countries as the result of poverty or diets lacking in essential nutrients.

Malocclusion *See:* Orthodontics.

Malory, Sir Thomas (?-1471), English author who wrote *La Morte d'Arthur.* With romances (adventure stories) a favorite genre of his time, Sir Thomas Malory was the first to write, in English, the popular and legendary tales of King Arthur and his Knights of the Round Table. Believed to be completed in 1470, a first edition was printed by the first English printer, William Caxton (1485).

Malot, Hector (1830-1907), French writer of a large number of romantic-realist novels, of which *Sans famille* (1878) gave him lasting fame.

Malpighi, Marcello (1628-1694), Italian physician and botanist who made significant advances in the understanding of human anatomy. His mastery of the microscope enabled him to perform important research on animal tissues. He discovered that lungs are made up of small air sacs, called alveoli and that the veins connect to the arteries. He was the first person to describe red blood cells. Other significant contributions were made in the study of insect and plant anatomy. Malpighi was also a professor of medicine at the University of Bologna and served as the personal physician to Pope Innocent XII.
See also: Botany; Anatomy.

Malraux, André (1901-1976), French author and political activist. His social novels, such as *Man's Fate* (1933) and *Man's Hope* (1937), describe political struggles both factually and poetically. In real life, Malraux became involved in many political struggles, including the Chinese civil war, the Spanish civil war, and the French resistance against the Nazis in World War II. He was France's first secretary of cultural affairs (1958-1968), under Charles De Gaulle.

Malt, product made from any cereal grain by steeping it in water, allowing it to germinate, and then drying it. This activates dormant enzymes, such as diastase, that convert the kernel starch to maltose (malt sugar). Malt is used as a source of enzymes and flavoring.

M

Malta

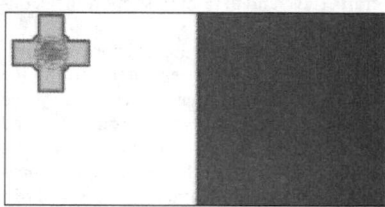

Capital:	La Valletta
Area:	122 sq mi (316 sq km)
Population:	396,500
Language:	Maltese, English
Government:	Republic
Independent:	1964
Head of gov.:	Prime minister
Per capita:	less than US$ 15.000
Monetary unit:	1 Maltese lira (pound) = 100 cents = 1,000 mils

Malta, officially Republic of Malta, republic in the Mediterranean Sea south of Sicily, made up of the islands of Malta, Gozo, Comino, and some uninhabited islets, for a total area of 122 sq mi (316 sq km).

British Navy ships, leaving the port of Malta. The navel and airforce bases on the island were closed to the West, and Malta strove to join the group of non-aligned nations.

M

Land. The islands are chiefly layers of limestone, with a thin topsoil, and reach their greatest height (827 ft/252 m) near Dingli, on Malta. Their fertile slopes and valleys are intensively cultivated, usually under irrigation.

People. The state religion is Roman Catholicism, and the official languages are English and Maltese, a Semitic language; Italian is widely spoken.

Economy. Malta has almost no mineral wealth or valuable natural resources and must import most of what it needs. Agriculture, tourism, shipbuilding, and light industry, as well as traditional handicrafts (lave and ceramic), support the economy.

History. Malta is rich in prehistoric remains, but the first known inhabitants were the Phoenicians, who were succeeded by the Greeks, Carthaginians, Romans, and Saracens. Saint Paul was shipwrecked on Malta about A.D. 60. In 1530, after occupation by the Arabs, Normans, and Spaniards, Malta was granted to the Knights Hospitalers (later Knights of Malta), who defeated the Turks in the Great Siege (1565) and built Valletta. They were ousted by Napoleon I (1798), and 2 years later Malta passed to the British. Malta's courage under siege and intensive Axis bombardment during World War II was recognized by the award of the George Cross to the entire population. The country became independent within the Commonwealth in 1964. Under the terms of independence, Great Britain was allowed to continue to maintain a base on the island and to station troops there. In 1972 Malta negociated a new agreement with Great Britain; under it, British troops and the base would remain for seven years. At the expiration of the agreement in 1979, British forces were withdrawn, the base closed, and Malta declared itself a neutral nation.

Malta has been invited to join the European Union in 2004. Eddie Fenech Adami's governing Nationalist Party advocates this, whereas the socialistic Malta Labour Party does not. The Maltese population will vote by a referendum in 2003.

Malta fever *See:* Brucellosis.

Maltese, breed of toy dog. This breed probably descends from lap dogs popular 2,000 years ago with women of Greek and Roman nobility. Standing no taller than about 5 in (12.7 cm) and weighing no more than about 7 lb (1.4 kg), the long white hairs of this dog part down the middle and, sometimes, grow to floor length.

Malthus, Thomas Robert (1766-1834), English economist, sociologist, and pioneer in the study of the population problem. In *An Essay on the Principal of Population* (1798; rev. ed. 1803), he asserted that any attempt to improve the human social condition was doomed to failure since food production would never grow as rapidly as population, a condition checked only by famine, disease, war, and moral restraint. His doctrine, adapted by neo-Malthusians, has influenced such economists as David Ricardo.
See also: Population.

Maltose, malt sugar; a disaccharide sugar produced by the action of diastase on starch and yielding glucose with the enzyme maltase.

Maluku (Moluccas; pop. 2,141,000), Indonesian province consisting of a group of islands between Sulawesi, Irian Jaya, Timor and the Philippines; 28,778 sq mi (74,505 sq km). Capital city: Ambon. The largest island is Halmahera. Partly volcanic, partly consisting of coral islands. Population largely of Malay origin; many ethnic groups and different languages. Fertile islands. Largely agricultural with copra, cloves, nutmeg apples and other spices as most important products. Other exports include fish, coffee, tobacco, resin, rattan and ebony.

Europeans (Portuguese, Spaniards, English, Dutchmen) started arriving in the 16th century and founded fortresses (e.g. at Ambon). Discovered in 1512 by the Portuguese and conquered after a heavy battle around 1605 by Jan Pieterz. Coen for the Dutch East India Company. This was the beginning of the Dutch presence in the Far East, which was prompted by the desire to gain control of the spice trade.

Military base during the Japanese occupation (1942-1945). In 1946 part of the state of East Indonesia and after the transfer of sovereignty part of the Republic of Indonesia, against which a guerilla war was fought by the Republic of South Moluccas (RSM), which was proclaimed in 1950. Taken over by Indonesia in 1949.

The group of islands is also called the Spice islands.

Mamba, any of 4 or 5 species of snakes in the cobra family. Found in sub-Saharan Africa, these aggressive, thin, whip-like snakes can inflict a fatal, poisonous bite to man. Hoodless, unlike the familiar image of a cobra, the green mamba grows to about 9 ft (2.7 m) and the black mamba grows to about 14 ft (4.3 m).

Mamelukes, group of ruling warriors in Egypt. First brought to Egypt as slaves (10th century), many members of this warrior caste eventually rose to power (1250-1517). After 1517, when Ottoman rule of Egypt was established, the Mamelukes became influential whenever the ruling Turks' power waned. The Mamelukes headed an unsuccessful attack against Napoleon I in Egypt (1798), and were massacred by the Turks shortly afterwards.

Mamet, David (1947-), U.S. playwright. Among his successful works, which compare the American dream with the corruption of modern society, are *American Buffalo* (1977, New York Drama Critics Circle Award), *Glengarry Glen Ross* (1984, Pulitzer Prize and New York Drama Critics Circle Award), and *Speed-the-Plow* (1988). He also wrote screenplays for such movies as *The Verdict* (1982), *The Postman Always Rings Twice* (1984), and *The Untouchables* (1987). He wrote and directed *Things change* (1989), *Homicide* (1991), and *State and Main* (2001).

Other works include *The Cabin* (1992; autobiography) and *The Village* (1994; novel).

Mammal, warm-blooded animal best distinguished by the possession of milk glands for feeding its young. Hair is a feature of mammals, although some, like the whales, have little or none. All mammals, except monotremes like the platypus, bear their young alive. Other shared characteristics are a lower jaw formed from 1 bone, 3 small bones in the middle ear, a neck of 7 vertebrae (even in giraffes), a diaphragm that forms a partition under the ribs, and a 4-chambered heart.

Mammals evolved from reptiles, but due to gaps in the fossil record, various stages in their development from reptiles are as yet undetermined. It is probable that the different groups of mammals arose independently from several kinds of intermediate mammal-like reptiles, so that there was no single ancestral mammal. The first mammals are believed to have been small and lived at the same time as the giant dinosaurs.

Mammals have evolved into many forms, and constitute some 3,200 species alive today. Mammals are divided into 3 main groups. The monotremes are the most primitive mammals and include the platypus of Australia. They lay eggs and feed their babies milk secreted from pores in the skin and not from milk glands with nipples. Marsupials are the pouched animals, including the kangaroo, opossum, wallaby, and Tasmanian devil. The young are born in an undeveloped state and complete their development in a pouch. Marsupials are found only in Australia and parts of America. Placental mammals, including humans, are the largest and most successful group. The young are born in varying states of development, from the relatively helpless human offspring to those like horses that are able to run within a few hours after their birth or, in the case of whales and dolphins, are able to swim as soon as they are born.

Mammary glands, special glands present in mammals, situated ventrally in pairs, modified in females to produce and secrete milk to nourish offspring. The milk, secreted by cells lining the small compartments, or lobules, that make up each gland, then travels from the lobules along ducts to the nipple, where it is emptied. Mammary glands, which develop in female humans at the onset of adolescence, remain undeveloped in male mammals.

Mammoth, any of several extinct, prehis-

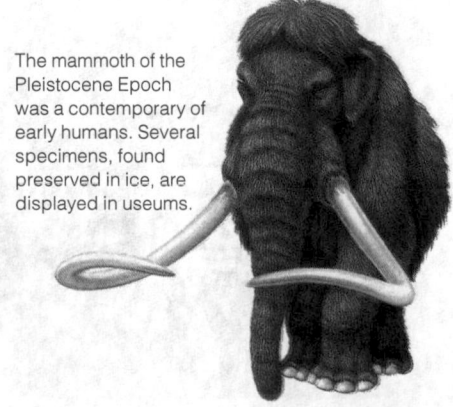

The mammoth of the Pleistocene Epoch was a contemporary of early humans. Several specimens, found preserved in ice, are displayed in useums.

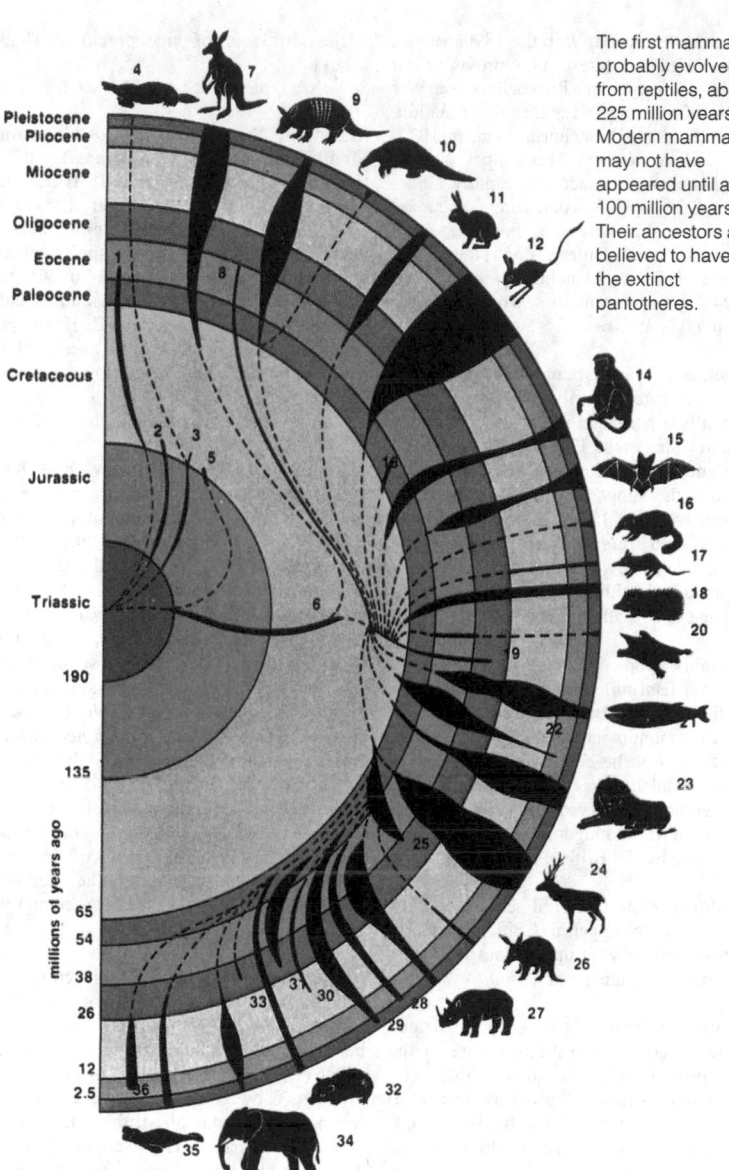

The first mammals probably evolved from reptiles, about 225 million years ago. Modern mammals may not have appeared until about 100 million years ago. Their ancestors are believed to have been the extinct pantotheres.

1. *Multituberculata*
2. *Triconodonta* (extinct)
3. *Docodonta* (extinct)
4. *Monotremata*
5. *Symmetrodonta* (extinct)
6. *Pantotheria* (extinct)
7. *Marsupiala*
8. *Taenoiodontia* (extinct)
9. *Edentata*
10. *Pholidota*
11. *Lagomorpha*
12. *Rodentia*
13. *Tillodontia* (extinct)
14. *Primates*
15. *Chiroptera*
16. *Scandentia*
17. *Macroscelidia*
18. *Lipotyphla*
19. *Proteutheria*
20. *Dermoptera*
21. *Cetacea*
22. *Creodonta* (extinct)
23. *Carnivora*
24. *Artiodactyla*
25. *Condylartha* (extinct)
26. *Tubulidentata*
27. *Perissodactyla*
28. *Litopterna* (extinct)
29. *Notoungulata*
30. *Astrapotheria* (extinct)
31. *Amblypoda* (extinct)
32. *Hyracoidea*
33. *Embrithopoda* (extinct)
34. *Proboscidea*
35. *Sirenia*
36. *Demostylia* (extinct)

M

toric elephants (genus *Mammuthus*) found in North America and Eurasia. Distinguishable from today's elephants by their shaggy coats, long, upward-curving tusks, and complex molar teeth, the species included the imperial mammoth of North America, 13.5 ft (4.1 m) high at the shoulder.

Mammoth Cave, limestone cavern about 85 mi (137 km) southwest of Louisville, Ky., containing a series of vast subterranean chambers. It includes lakes, rivers, stalactites, stalagmites, and formations of gypsum crystals. The mummified body of a pre-Columbian man has been found there. It is part of Mammoth Cave National Park.

Man *See:* Human being.

Managua (pop. 1,2 million), capital city of Nicaragua, located on the southern shore of Lake Managua. Made capital in 1855 to end a feud between León and Granada, it has been rebuilt on numerous occasions after destruction by earthquakes (1931, 1972) and fires (1931, 1936).
See also: Nicaragua.

Man, Isle of, island, 227 sq mi (588 sq km) in the Irish Sea off the northwestern coast of Great Britain; the capital is Douglas. It became the base for Irish missionaries after St. Patrick, and at one time was a Norwegian dependency sold to Scotland (1266). A dependency of the British Crown since 1765, it has its own legislature (Court of Tynwald) and representative assembly (House of Keys). Tourism is the main industry. The Manx language is now virtually extinct.

Manakin, bird in the family Pipridae. Found in Central and South America, these small birds are known for the male courtship rituals. In specially selected dancing grounds called leks, the males create unusual sounds and movements in competitions as the females look on. Both sexes are greenish in color, although the males have splashes of color. These birds grow to no more than 5 in (13 cm) and are believed to live approximately 20 years.

Manama (pop. 137,000), also known as al-Manamah, capital city of Bahrain. Located in the Persian Gulf, this major port for the island nation of Bahrain lies on an important trade and shipping route. Since the discovery of oil (1932), Manama has become a center for finance and commerce, with a new harbor fully equipped to dock and repair large oceangoing vessels.
See also: Bahrain.

Manassas, Battles of *See:* Bull Run, Battles of.

Manatee, large, aquatic, herbivorous mammal of tropical and subtropical Atlantic coasts and large rivers. They and the dugongs are the only living sea cows (order Sirenia). They have powerful, flat, rounded tails that provide propulsion. The forelimbs are small and hindlimbs completely absent. Manatees may be 12 ft (3.6 m) long and weigh 600 lb (270 kg).

Manaus (pop. 1,100,000), Brazil, one of the nation's major cities and the capital of Amazonas state. It is in northwestern Brazil on the Rio Negro near its junction with the Amazon River. Manaus manufactures diverse products, mostly consumer goods, and is a major river port, shipping products of the Amazon Basin. Though roughly 1,000 miles (1,600 km) from the sea, Manaus is accessible to oceangoing ships. Paved roads reached the city in the 1970's; one leads southward to the Trans-Amazon Highway. There is also an international airport. Located in Manaus are the University of Manaus and the Amazon Theater.
Manaus was founded in the 1660's but remained small and relatively unimportant until late in the 19th century, when a rubber boom brought several decades of great prosperity. Decline of the rubber industry in the early 20th century caused the city to languish, especially after the 1920's. Rapid growth began again in the 1970's with the development of the Amazon Basin.

Manchester (pop. 435,000), city in northwest England, on the Irwell, Irk, and Medlock rivers. Located about 35 mi (56 km) off England's western coast, it is connected to the Irish Sea by the Mersey River and a canal and serves as a major inland port. The city is also a center for trade and finance and is an important industrial area, the

M

products of which include computers, chemicals, clothing, and industrial machinery. The city began as a village established around A.D. 700 on the site of what had been a Roman fort. By the 19th century, it had become an important industrial center and one of the world's major producers of cotton textiles.
See also: England.

Manchester School, group of English businessmen and members of Parliament (1820-1860), mostly from Manchester, who advocated worldwide free trade. They were led by John Bright and Richard Cobden, who formed the Anti-Corn-Law League in 1838 and brought about the repeal of the corn laws in 1846.

Manchester terrier, popular breed of dog. They were bred into existence in the 1800s in Manchester, England, when black and tan terriers were mated with swift whippets to compete in rat-killing matches. They are black with tan markings on their faces and chests and weigh 12-22 lb (5.4-10 kg). A toy variety weighs 5-12 lb (2.3-5.4 kg).

The toy Manchester terrier (foreground) and the standard Manchester terrier (background).

Manchineel, or poison guava tree (*Hippomane mancinella*), native to tropical regions of the United States. A member of the spurge family, manchineels grow from 10 to 50 ft (3 to 15 m) high and produce yellowish green fruit that look like crab apples. The fruit and sap are extremely poisonous and were used by ancient Carib tribes as poison for their arrows.

Manchuria, region of northeastern China comprising Heilongjiang, Jilin, and Liaoning provinces and part of the Inner Mongolian Autonomous Region; c.600,000 sq mi (1,554,000 sq km). Manchuria is bordered by the Russia, North Korea, and Mongolia. It is an important agricultural and industrial area. Historically, Manchuria was the home of the Manchus. Chinese settlement in the area increased steadily after 1900. It was a barren steppe until Western exploitation of its vast mineral resources be-

gan in the 19th century. In the 1890s Russia had declared an interest in the province; but Russia's defeat in the Russo-Japanese War (1904-1905) brought Japanese domination, first of Southern Manchuria, then, in 1932, of the whole country. The puppet state of Manchukuo was created and rapidly industrialized. In 1945 Russian forces occupied the area, dismantling the industries upon their withdrawal. Bitterly contested in the Chinese civil war, Manchuria was captured in 1948 by the communists, who redrew the provincial boundaries.

Manchus, a Manchurian people descended from the Jurchen tribe of the Tungus. Originally a nomadic, pastoral people, they came to China in the 12th century, only to be driven out by the Mongols. They eventually settled in the Sungari Valley and went on to conquer China in 1644, forming the Ch'ing dynasty and reigning until 1912. The Manchus have now been racially and culturally absorbed with the Chinese, and their language is virtually extinct.

Mandalay (pop. 685,000), city in central Myanmar (Burma), on the Irrawaddy River. It is the center of Burmese Buddhism, with numerous monuments, including the Arakan pagoda, and is the country's transportation center. Mandalay was founded in the mid-19th century and served (1860-1885) as the last capital of the kingdom of Burma before annexation by the British.

Mandarin, important civil servant or military official in imperial China. Mandarin Chinese, formerly an upper-class language, is the official language of China.

Mandela, Nelson (1918-), South African political leader and a major figure in the black protest movement against the racial segregation policies (known as apartheid) of the white-dominated South African government. Son of a tribal chief of the Transkei territory, he became a lawyer in 1942 and joined the African National Congress (ANC) in 1944. He gained prominence as a leader of the black protest movement in the 1950s. In 1960 he was arrested and charged with treason but was acquitted. Arrested again in 1962, he was later convicted of sabotage and conspiracy and sentenced to life imprisonment. In jail he became an international symbol of black defiance of the apartheid system. In 1990 Mandela was released from prison and assumed leadership of the ANC, pledging to work for a peaceful end to the hated apartheid regime. In early 1991, President F.W. de Klerk of South Africa called for the end of the racial segregation laws that were the underpinning of apartheid, and Mandela's goal of a race-free state seemed possible. Despite the opposition of conservative white South Africans, apartheid was abolished and the transition to a democratic government started. The ANC won the majority in parliament in the first democratic elections held in 1994, and Mandela became South Africa's first black president. In 1997, he appointed Thabo Mbeki to be his successor as president of the ANC. In 1999, he retired as president of South

Africa, in favor of vice president Thabo Mbeki.
See also: Apartheid; South Africa.

Mandela, Winnie (Winifred Nomzamo Madikileza; 1936?-), anti-apartheid activist in the Republic of South Africa, wife of Nelson Mandela until their divorce in 1996. During her husband's imprisonment (1962-1990) she frequently spoke on his behalf and led the campaign to win her husband's freedom. Winnie Mandela held several high posts in the ANC. Her popularity has declined since 1988 as a result of her supposed involvement in various crimes.
See also: Apartheid; Mandela, Nelson.

Mandelstam, Osip Emilievich (1891-1938?), Russian poet. At first a member of the neoclassicist Acmeist school, he was arrested in 1934 and exiled until 1937. Rearrested in 1938, he reportedly died soon afterwards in a Siberian prison. His works include *Stone* (1913) and *Tristia* (1922). After his death his widow, **Nadezhda Mandelstam** (1899-1981), spent many years collecting his verse and smuggling it to the West. Her memoirs, *Hope Against Hope* (1970) and *Hope Abandoned* (1972), were powerful indictments of Stalinism.

Mandeville, Bernard (c.1670-1733), Dutch-born English philosopher and satirist. Best known as the author of a work in verse, *The Fable of the Bees* (1714), he attempted to establish that every virtue is based on self-interest.

Mandingo, West African ethnic group, descendants of the founders of the Mali Empire, (fl.1240-1500). Most Mandingos belong to the Malinke group and practice tribal religions and customs in small rural villages. They are chiefly farmers and cattle ranchers and about one-fifth of them have converted to Islam. Their language, which has many different dialects, belongs to the Mande language group.

Mandolin, instrument of the lute family. It has a pear-shaped body, fretted neck, and 4 or 5 pairs of strings that are plucked with a plectrum. Composers who have used the mandolin in their works include Mozart and Beethoven, but it is best known as a popular Neapolitan instrument.

Mandrake, herbaceous perennial plant (*Mandragora officinarum*) of the nightshade family, with purplish or white flowers, a thin stalk, and a forked root resembling the human form. A native of the Himalayas and the Mediterranean, its poisonous root has been used to produce vomiting and bowel movements and as a painkiller. In North America, the mayapple is called mandrake.

Mandrill, colorful monkey (*Mandrillus sphinx*) of central West Africa. Mandrills are jungle dwellers that move about on the ground and through trees and they feed on fruits and insects. They resemble baboons and may weigh up to 90 lb (40 kg). The males are brightly colored with blue, purple,

M

Mandrill (*Mandrillus sphinx*), equatorial West Africa, length 3 ft (1 m).

yellow, and red faces and rumps and can protect groups of up to 150 against predators.

Manen, Hans van (1932-), Dutch dancer and choreographer. He danced with ballets such as the Dutch Opera Ballet (1953-1957) and the Ballets de Paris of Roland Petit (1957-1959). In 1960, he joined the Nederlands Dans Theater, first as a dancer, and later as artistic leader and choreographer. In 1973, he was appointed choreographer of the Dutch National Ballet. His ballets developed from anecdotally narrative to more and more abstract and contained classical as wel as modern elements. He was awarded the Erasmus Prize in 2000.

Manet, Edouard (1832-1883), French painter. Influenced by Goya and Velázquez, his work, in broad, flat areas of color, introduced a new pictorial language, and was often severely criticized by the art establishment, who considered his subject matter and technique heresy. His paintings *Olympia*, a nude courtesan, and *Luncheon on the Grass*, a nude woman and a partially dressed woman lunching in the woods with 2 clothed men (both 1863 Louvre), were thought scandalously bold. He strongly influenced the impressionists, though he did not employ their techniques and refused to exhibit with them. Another major work is *The Fife Player* (1866).

Manga, Comics originating in Japan. In the 1990s, the comics and animated movies (*anime*) that arose from the comics, reached their full potential. Both genres had been very popular for years in Japan, before they appeared on the western market. Manga is easy to recognize: for its style (large eyes, colorful fantasy scenery) and for the rapid montage and storyline: ordinary characters become involved in a futuristic nightmare or a violent fairytale world.

Manganese, chemical element, symbol Mn; for physical constants see Periodic Table. Manganese was discovered by J.G. Gahn in 1774. It is a steel-gray, hard, brittle, reactive, metal. The element forms many important alloys with steel, as well as with aluminum,

ferromagnetic alloys, antimony, and copper. It is an essential trace element in humans and animals. Manganese and its compounds are used in dry cell batteries, paint dryers, as an oxidizing agent, and in medicine.

Mange, disease of the skin that affects domestic and farm animals. Small parasites (mites) burrow into the skin and cause inflammation. The skin is usually covered with sores, and the animal's hair falls out. There are a number of different mites that can cause mange, and the exact symptoms and severity of the disease depend on the species of mite involved. Inadequate nutrition is also an important factor. Mange is treated by pesticides and by ensuring that the animal receives a nutritious diet.

Mango, tropical evergreen tree (*Mangifera indica*) of the sumac family, and its fruit, originally from eastern Asia. The trees, which can grow to 90 ft (27 m), produce a rich yellowish-red juicy fruit with a hard pit, a staple in the tropics.

Mangosteen (*Garcinia mangostana*), tropical tree of the garcinia family, native to Southeast Asia; also, the fruit of that tree. The tree grows about 30 ft (9 m) tall, bearing large, stiff leaves and large white or pink flowers. The fruit, about 2 in (6 cm) in diameter, has a thick red-brown rind and white flesh tasting something like pineapple, peach, and tangerine.

Although the mangosteen is considered to be one of the most delicious tropical fruits, it is rarely grown on a large scale. The berry-like fruits contain segments of pulp, and into each segment are embedded several seeds.

Mangrove, evergreen tree (genus *Rhizophora*) native to tropical and subtropical coasts, estuaries, and swamps. The trunk of the mangrove produces aerial roots, which support the tree and form a mass of tangled vegetation. Its fruit, a cone-shaped berry, contains a single seed that germinates within the fruit and produces a long root that imbeds the seedling within the mud when the fruit falls. The mangrove's bark is rich in tannin.

Manhattan, one of the 5 boroughs of New York City, consisting mainly of Manhattan

Island, bounded by the East River, the Harlem River, the Hudson River, and New York Bay. Peter Minuit originally bought the island from a Native American tribe, the Manhattan, for $24 worth of beads and cloth in 1626 and called it New Amsterdam. The commercial and financial center of New York City, Manhattan is linked to the other boroughs by numerous bridges, tunnels, and ferries. Its many land marks and tourist attractions include the Empire State Building, World Trade Center, Central Park, Lincoln Center, the United Nations headquarters, and Rockefeller Center. Wall Street, the financial capital of the world for much of the 20th century, is located in downtown Manhattan. Inaddition, Manhattan is a center of the arts. Museums such as the Metropolitan Museum of Art, the Museum of Natural History, the Museum of Modern Art, and the Guggenheim Museum house some of the world's most prized and renowned exhibits. A variety of clubs, especially in the Greenwich Village area, offer many forms of music, and the Broadway area, located in the heart of Manhattan, is considered one of the premier theater districts in the world.

Manhattan Project, wartime project begun in 1942 to develop nuclear weapons. A team headed by Enrico Fermi initiated the 1st self-sustaining nuclear chain reaction. In order to obtain the necessary amounts of the required isotopes, uranium-235 and plutonium-239, centers were established in Tennessee and Washington. Actual design and construction of the atomic bombs was carried out at Los Alamos, N.M., by a group headed by J. Robert Oppenheimer. On July 16, 1945, the first atomic bomb was detonated near Alamogordo, N.M. The following month a uranium bomb was dropped on Hiroshima (Aug. 6) and a plutonium bomb on Nagasaki (Aug. 9).

Mani *See:* Manichaeism.

Mania *See:* Mental illness.

Manic-depressive disorder, or bipolar disorder, mental illness characterized either as mania (excitement, irrational judgment, increase in activity) or depression (lethargy, feelings of worthlessness, guilt), and, in some cases, alternating between mania and depression. Treatment involves the drug

The coast of the island of Trinidad has a typical mangrove vegetation. The various types of plants have their roots in the air, in order to breathe.

M

lithium, to control mood swings, and anti-depressants.

Manichaeism, or Manichaeanism, religion founded by Mani (C.A.D. 216-76), a Persian sage who claimed to be the Paraclete (intercessor) promised by Christ. Mani borrowed ideas from religions such as Buddhism, Christianity, Gnosticism, and Zoroastrianism; he preached dualism (between good and evil), the continuing life of the soul, and the hope of salvation. The Magians, who opposed him and his teachings, brought about his crucifixion. St. Augustine was a Manichee in his youth. The religion survived until the 6th century in the West and until the 13th century in the East. *See also:* Religion.

Manila (pop. 1,600,000), city (founded 1571) on Manila Bay, capital of the Philippines (before 1948 and after 1976). It is the commercial, industrial, and cultural center, developed by Spanish missionaries and then taken by the United States (1898) in the Spanish-American War, and chief port of the islands. Manila was occupied by the Japanese (1942-1945), nearly destroyed in the Allied attack, and almost completely rebuilt after the war. Buildings of interest include the Church of San Agustin (1606) and the Philippine Cultural Center complex. Industries include textiles, chemicals, and automobiles.

Manila hemp *See:* Abacá.

Manioc *See:* Cassava.

Manitoba, sixth largest province in Canada. Manitoba is bordered by Ontario and Hudson Bay on the east, Saskatchewan on the west, Minnesota and North Dakota to the south, and the Northwest Territories to the north. The capital is Winnipeg.
The province has an area of 251,000 sq mi/650,090 sq km including 39,225 sq mi/101,593 sq km of inland waterways. There are some 100,000 lakes in the province, most notably Lake Winnipeg, thirteenth largest lake in the world, as well as numerous rivers draining into Hudson Bay. About 60% of Manitoba is forested.
Manufacturing is Manitoba's largest indus-

Thomas Mann (1875-1955), a leading German writer of the early 20th century.

try, including processed foods and beverages, metal products, clothing, furniture, chemicals, and oil refining. Nickel, zinc, copper, and tantalite are mined. Agriculture, formerly the mainstay of the province's economy, is still one of its chief industries. The first European settlers to arrive in Manitoba were fur traders of the Hudson's Bay Company in 1670. French and English fur traders competed in the area until their rivalry was settled in the French and Indian War of 1763. As a result, France ceded its Canadian lands to Britain. The Dominion of Canada acquired the rights to land in Manitoba from the Hudson's Bay Company in 1869 and Manitoba became a province in 1870.

Mann, Heinrich (1871-1950), German writer and essayist. Younger brother of Thomas Mann. He developed into a sharp critic of his time, first the period under the reign of Wilhelm II and the ensuing war hysteria, later National Socialism. In 1933 he left Germany and settled in France, moving in 1940 to the U.S., where he established himself. Famous novels: *Im Schlaraffenland* (In the Land of Cockaigne, 1900), *Professor Unrat* (Small Town Tyrant, 1905; filmed in 1930 as *Der blaue Engel*), *Der Untertan* (The Patrioteer, 1918; filmed in 1950), *Henri Quatre* (2 volumes; 1935, 1938).

Mann, Thomas (1875-1955), German writer, winner of the 1929 Nobel Prize for literature. He left Germany (1933), settled in the United States (1938), and became a U.S. citizen (1944). His works include *Buddenbrooks* (1901), his first novel, which brought him fame; *Death in Venice* (1912), addressing Mann's recurring themes of the relationship between art and neurosis and the challenge to the values of an artist in a bourgeois society; and *The Magic Mountain* (1924), his major work. He denounced fascism in *The Order of the Day* (1942), a political writing. His later works include *Doctor Faustus* (1947) and *Confessions of Felix Krull* (1954).

Mannerheim, Carl Gustaf Emil von (1867-1951), Finnish soldier and president (1944-1946). He successfully led the Finnish nationalists against the Russo-Finnish communists in 1918. He also led the Finish forces in the Russo-Finnish War (1939-1940), holding the *Mannerheim Line* of defense, which he planned, on the Karelian Isthmus until 1940, when the Soviets broke through.
See also: Finland.

Mannerism, artistic and architectural style (c.1520-1600) developed in Bologna, Florence, and Rome as a reaction to the classical principles of the Renaissance. Exaggeration of form, and strained and unbalanced proportions, such as those in the Uffizi Palace and Laurentian Library in Florence (planned by Vasari and Michelangelo respectively) were the trademarks of the Mannerists. Other Mannerist artists were Parmigiano, Pontormo, Tintoretto, and El Greco; sculptors were Cellini, Bologna, and Goujon of France. They confused scale and spatial relationships, used harsh lighting,

The Madonna with the Long Neck (1534) by Parmigianino reflects the remarkable elongation, arbitrary scale, and fluid movement characteristic of Mannerism (Uffizi, Florence).

Lake Winnipeg, the third largest lake situated entirely in Canada, occupies a large portion of south central Manitoba. This shallow body of water is important for its commercial fisheries.

and depicted bizarre forms. The end of the 16th century the Baroque replaced Mannerism.

Manners and customs *See:* Custom; Etiquette.

Mannheim (pop. 1,600,000), city in southwestern Germany, one of Europe's major inland ports. Founded in the early 1600s, it is situated near the junction of the Rhine and Neckar rivers in the heart of a major industrial region. It has also been a center for art, music, and drama since the 1700s and is the site of a major university containing striking examples of Baroque architecture. Heavily damaged in World War II, Mannheim was extensively rebuilt. Cultural sights include the National Theatre and several art museums. *See also:* Germany.

Man-of-war bird *See:* Frigatebird.

Manometer, instrument for measuring the pressure of gases and vapors, especially those too low to be measured by a pressure gauge. A *sphygmomanometer* is used by doctors to measure blood pressure in the arteries. *See also:* Barometer.

Manorialism, socio-economic system of Europe in the early Middle Ages. It was a decentralized form of government that replaced the central authority of the Roman Empire and continued until the revival of commerce in the towns and cities in the later Middle Ages. Centering around a powerful lord who owned a large estate (manor), manorialism depended on peasants to work the land for the lord and themselves in exchange for protection and their homes. *See also:* Middle Ages.

Man Ray *See:* Ray, Man.

Manrique, Jorge (ca. 1440-1479), Spanish poet and soldier. His uncle was the poet Gómez Manrique (ca. 1412-ca. 1490), whose influence is felt in lyrical poetry. His most famous work, the elegy *Coplas por la muerte de su padre*, typifies the transition from the Middle Ages to the Renaissance. He also wrote love poetry. In 1479 Manrique was killed at the siege of the Garci-Muñoz castle. A translation by the American poet Henry Wadsworth Longfellow (1807-1882) was published in 1833.

Mansa Musa (?-1337?), ruler of the Mali Empire (1312-1337?). During his reign, Mali was the most powerful empire of West Africa, and the cities of Gao and Timbuktu became centers of learning, justice, trade, and culture. As a Muslim, Mansa Musa made a flamboyant pilgrimage to Mecca in 1324, bringing back scholars to help educate his people and architects to design the mosques of his cities. *See also:* Mali Empire.

Mansart (or **Mansard**) the name of two French architects.
(Nicolas) François Mansart (1598-1666), was born in Paris. Little is known of his life. His buildings, such as the Church of the Val de Grâce in Paris, are noted for their classical refinement. The château at Maisons-Laffitte, near Paris, was one of the first buildings in the Louis XIV style. The mansard roof is named after him.
Jules Hardouin-Mansart (1646-1708), grandnephew of François Mansart, was court architect to Louis XIV. He expanded the Palace of Versailles, adding the north and south wings and the Hall of Mirrors. The

dome of the Invalides in Paris, which now contains Napoleon's tomb, is considered his most important work. Hardouin-Mansart also designed the Place Vendôme and Place des Victoires in Paris, and many country homes.

Mansell, Nigel (1954-), British racecar driver, made his debut in the formula 1 in 1980. Although Mansell achieved several GP victories over the years, it took a long time before he definitely belonged to the top. In 1992 he was supreme in the Williams-Renault: during that year he won nine Grand Prix races and was already certain of the world title (his first) with still five races to go. He won a total of 30 Grand Prix races. In 1993 Mansell switched to the American Indy Car Races.

The short stories of Katherine Mansfield, born in New Zealand (1888-1923), contributed greatly to the development and appreciation of this genre. Portrait by Anne Estele Rice (National Art Gallery, Wellington, New Zealand).

Mansfield, Katherine (Kathleen Beauchamp; 1888-1923), New Zealand-born English writer. Known foremost as a master of the short story, collections include *Bliss* (1920), *The Garden Party* (1922), and *Something Childish* (1924).

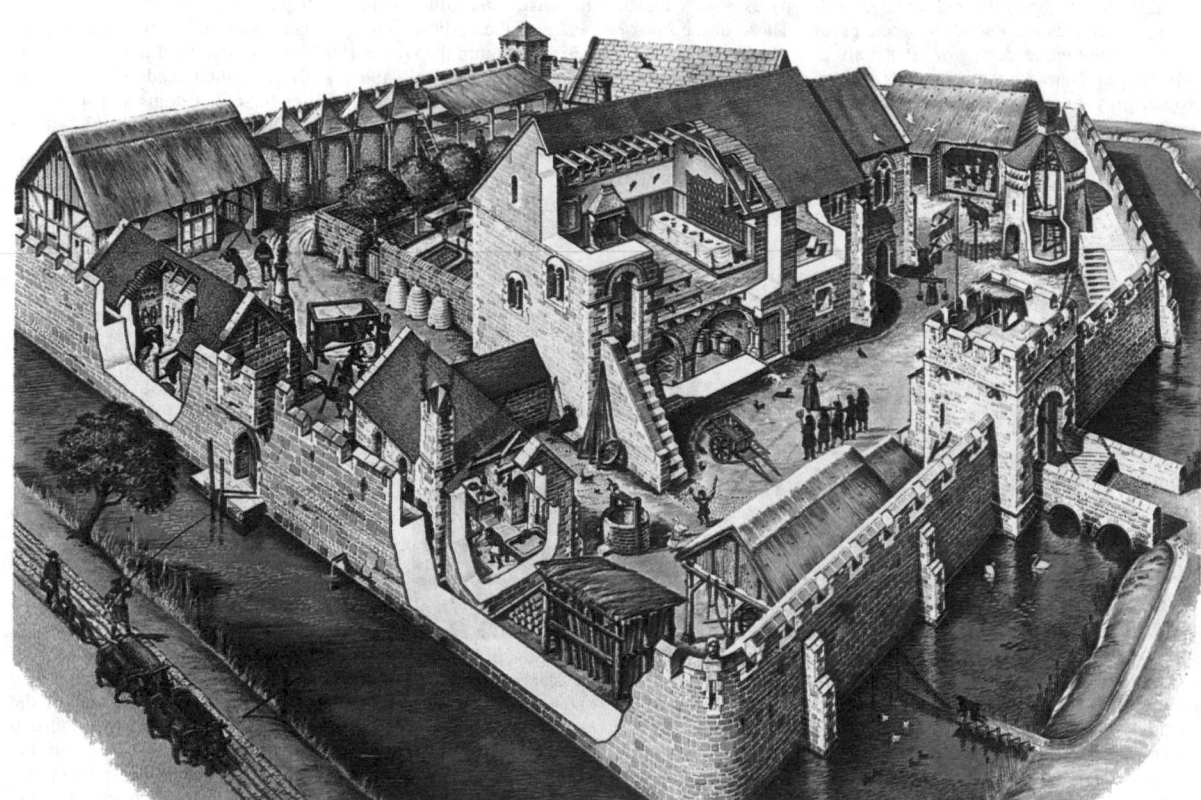

This kind of fortified manor house was built during the reign of King Henry II (r. 1154-1189), who forbade his nobles to build their own castles without his special permission. This manor house retains some of the features of a castle, especially in its moat and the enclosing turret wall.

M

Manslaughter, unlawful but unpremeditated killing of another human being. In general 2 kinds of manslaughter are defined: *voluntary*, where injury is intended, as in a killing arising out of a quarrel; and *involuntary*, where there is no such intent, such as death caused by reckless driving.
See also: Crime.

Manta ray *See:* Ray.

Mantegna, Andrea (1431-1506), Italian painter and engraver. He was a member of the Paduan school, acclaimed for his mastery of anatomy and illusionistic perspective, and was attracted to the antique, as evidenced in his collection of Greek and Roman works. Among his most famous works are the altarpiece at St. Luke's (Milan), the bridal chamber of the Gonzaga palace (Mantua), where the illusion of sky on the ceiling was widely copied during the Baroque period; and the cartoons of the *Triumph of Caesar* (1495). Also known for his copper-plate engravings and drawings, Mantegna was influential in the development of printing. His initial letters for *Geography*, by Strabo, recaptured the Roman art of inscription.

Mantid, or praying mantis, large predatory insect of the Mantidae family (or order Mantodea). Most species are native to tropical and subtropical climates, although some, including varieties that have been introduced in North America, are found in temperate zones. The nickname 'praying mantis' is suggested by the posture of its front legs and by its gentle swaying movement. Mantids measure 2-5 in (5-13 cm) and tend to resemble the green or brown twigs on which they perch, camouflaging them from both predators and insect or other prey. Females are known for their practice of eating males during or after mating. Mantids are harmless to humans and are sometimes useful in consuming insect pests.

Mantle, Mickey (1931-   ), U.S. baseball player. Primarily an outfielder, he played for the New York Yankees (1951-1968), hitting 536 home runs, 18 of them during World Series play. A switch-hitter (both right- and left-handed), he led the American League in 1956 with an average of .353 and 52 home runs and was voted the league's most valuable player 3 times (1956, 1957, 1962). Mantle was inducted into the National Hall of Fame in 1974.

Mantra, in Hinduism and Buddhism, sacred utterance believed to possess supernatural power. The constant repetition of a mantra is used to concentrate the mind on an object of meditation, e.g., the syllable *om*, said to evoke the entire Veda.

Manu, in Hindu mythology, the lawgiver. Compiled into the *Manu Smriti* (*Code of Manu*) between 200 B.C. and A.D. 200, these laws delineated the classes (castes) in Hindu society and formed the basis for the life plan of all Hindus in 4 stages. It also set forth the goals they are expected to attain during those 4 stages.

Manuscript, document or work written by hand as distinguished from those typewritten or printed (although the typescript of a book is often called the author's manuscript).
The oldest manuscripts are on papyrus, made from the papyrus plant, the writing material of ancient Egypt and also used in ancient Greece and Rome until superseded by parchment. The earliest surviving papyrus manuscript dates from about 3500 B.C. The Egyptians first wrote with brushes, using ink made from lampblack and water; later they used reed pens. They pasted their papyrus sheets together to make long rolls. Those of the *Book of the Dead*, the earliest known illustrated manuscript, are more than 100 ft (30.5 m) long. Wax tablets were also extensively used for manuscript writing in the ancient world.

Parchment, or vellum-made from the skins of sheep and other animals and more durable than papyrus-was first used in Pergamum in the 2nd century B.C., but did not come into general use in Europe until about A.D. 300. Some types (palimpsests) could be washed or scraped and used again or even a third time (double palimpsests). The illumination (ornamentation and illustration) of manuscripts was developed by the medieval monastic schools of Europe.
In the Far East paper (invented by the Chinese about A.D. 100), silk, bamboo, and palm leaves were used as writing materials. Paper did not reach Europe until the 11th century and did not begin to supplant parchment until the 1400s. Even after the development of printing, parchment was used for legal and other special documents.

Manzanita, ornamental shrub (*Arctostaphylos tomentosa*), of the heath family. Native to the Pacific Coast of the United States and Canada, manzanita is an evergreen that reaches heights of 20 ft (6 m). It produces pink or white bell-shaped flowers and bright red berries and is cultivated for its decorative value.

Manzoni, Alessandro (1785-1873), Italian novelist and poet. He was a leading figure in the romantic movement, and his novel *The Betrothed* (1825-1826) influenced Italian prose writers. Among his poems is the well-received *Fifth of May* (1821), on Napoleon's death. His own death inspired Verdi's *Requiem* (1874).

Maori, original inhabitants of New Zealand. Of Polynesian origin, they settled New Zealand between 800 and 1350 and were hunters and farmers. They lived in small villages of communal homes and each village shared a common ancestry. In the 1860s they fought the English colonists and lost most of their lands. Today many still practice the old customs and speak the Maori tongue, a language related to Tahitian and Hawaiian.

Mao Tse-tung *See:* Mao Zedong.

Mao Zedong (1893-1976), founder of the People's Republic of China. Born to an educated peasant in Hunan province, he joined the newly founded Shanghai Communist Party in 1921, and in 1927 led the Autumn Harvest uprising, which was crushed by the local Kuomintang militia, Mao fled to the mountains, where he built up the Red Army and established rural soviets. Surrounded by Kuomintang forces in 1934, the army was forced to embark on the famous Long March from Jiangxi to Yan'an in Shoanxi province. The appalling rigors of the march united the communists behind Mao, and he was elected chairman. In 1937 an uneasy alliance was made with the Kuomintang under Chiang Kai-Shek against the Japanese; after World War II Mao's forces expelled the Kuomintang to Taiwan. Mao then became chairman of the new People's Republic. In 1958 he turned his attentions to industrial growth, with his program the Great Leap Forward. Its failure spurred his replacement as chairman of the

At the fortieth anniversary of the Soviet Union, the relations between Moscow and Peking were still warm enough for Mao Zedong to visit Moscow. He was the guest of honour at a Remembrance Parade in 1957, where he appeared together with members of the Soviet leadership. From left to right: President Voroshilov, Defence Minister Malinovsky, party leader Khrushchev, Mao Zedong, Prime Minister Bulganin and party-theoretician Suslov.

party, but he retained party leadership. He later (1966-1969) attacked the chairman, Liu Shao-Sh'i, by organizing the Cultural Revolution, which created widespread agitation and led to a consolidation of Mao's power in the 1970s. Mao steered China ideologically away from the USSR and his teachings came to have great influence in the Third World. He appeared to favor a decree of détente with the West, especially Europe, and in 1972 met with President Nixon, signaling closer relations with the United States.
See also: Great Leap Forward.

Map, representation on a flat surface of part or all of the earth's surface, or of another spherical body, showing each point and feature on a predetermined reduced scale and in accordance with a definite projection. Globes provide the most accurate representation of the earth, with regard to area, scale, shape, and direction. Any flat map will create some distortion. The making and study of maps is called cartography. Of the many different kinds of maps, those for general reference include physical maps (relief and natural features) and political maps (national borders, administrative divisions, cities, and towns). Thematic maps include economic maps, (industrial centers, transportation routes and so on); demographic maps (distribution of the population); geological maps (classifying and dating the surface rocks); meteorological maps (information about climatic zones, rainfall, air pressures, and temperatures); historical maps and the road maps for tourists. There are also celestial and stellar maps showing the planets, stars, and constellations. Maps used for sea and aerial navigation are called charts.

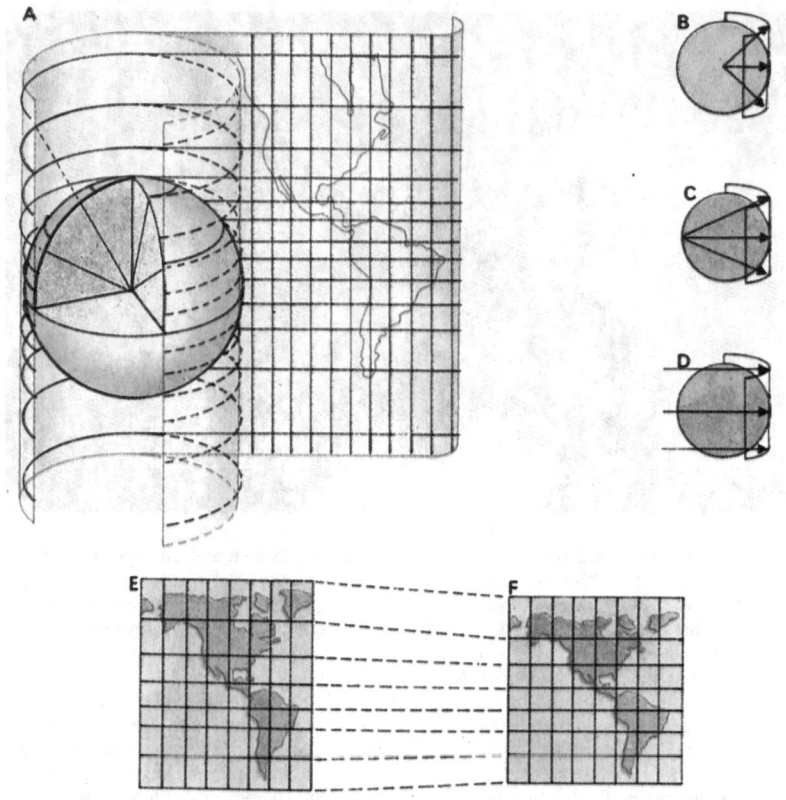

When making a flat map of the world, one should take into account the earth's curvature. The various techniques for representing this curvature involve the projection of the globe's parallels and meridians onto a cone, a cylinder (A), or a plane. In a cylindrical projection (B), the transferred lines are drawn from the perspective of a fixed point, set at the center of the sphere in a gnomonic projection (C), and at infinity in an orthographic projection (D). A Mercator projection (E) renders compass bearings as straight lines, making this map especially useful for navigation. Its gross distortion of the polar regions is partially corrected by Miller's projection (F).

Maple, common name for the deciduous trees and shrubs of the genus *Acer*, found throughout the Northern Hemisphere. Maples, which are characterized by their winged seeds, are noted for the breathtaking colors they produce in the fall. The North American sugar maple (*A. saccharum*) and the black maple (*A. nigrum*) are 2 of the species that provide the close-grained hardwood used for furniture making; they are also tapped to produce maple syrup. Two other members of the genus are the swamp, or red, maple (*A. rubrum*) and the box elder (*A. negundo*) tapped to produce maple syrup.

Maputo (pop. 1,006,000), capital (1907) and largest city of Mozambique. Founded around 1780 by Portuguese colonists, it was called Lourenço Marques until 1976, the year after Mozambique gained independence. Maputo is located on the Indian Ocean and is a popular beach resort. It also serves as a rail terminal for several of southern Africa's landlocked nations who ship their goods through Maputo's harbor.

Marabou, large stork (*Leptoptilos crumeniferous*) with a heavy bill, naked head and neck, and a pink, fleshy pouch dangling from its neck. Marabous, found in many parts of Africa, are scavengers and feed on refuse and carrion.

Maracaibo (pop. 1,7 million), city in northwestern Venezuela. Located on the shore of Lake Maracaibo, it is the capital of the state of Zulia and the hub of the nation's petroleum industry. Maracaibo was founded by the Spanish in 1571 and experienced a population boom after the discovery of oil in the lake in 1912. It is also a major coffee and seafood exporting port.

Maradona, Diego Armando (1960-), Argentine soccer player, played dozens of times in the national team as an attacking midfielder. He played for Argentinos Juniors, then for Boca Juniors and in 1982 went to FC Barcelona. From 1984 until 1992 he played for FC Napoli. With this club he won several championships, the cup and the UEFA cup (1989). The left-legged Maradona was a brilliant soccer player, and as a captain he was largely influential in winning the world championships for Argentina in 1986 (3-2 victory against the Federal Republic of Germany in the finals). In 1986 he became (besides Pelé) the second soccer player to be declared world sportsman of the year.

Marajó, Brazilian island in the mouth of the Amazon River. With an area of 15,500 sq mi (40,000 sq km), Marajó lies between the Amazon to the north, the Rio Pará to the south, and the Atlantic Ocean to the east. The island is flooded by river overflow 6 months of the year, and cattle and water buffalo graze the grasslands left by the flooding during the dry season.

Marat, Jean Paul (1743-1793), French Revolutionary politician. A doctor and journalist, he founded the journal *L'Ami du peuple* at the onset of the Revolution. His vociferous attacks on those in power led to outlaw status and flight to England (1790, 1791). He continued to publish in secret and was elected to the National Convention in 1792, a leader of the radical faction. Chief instigator of the September Massacre (1792) in which over 1,200 died, he was an active supporter of the Jacobins and their Reign of Terror. Marat was murdered in his bath by Charlotte Corday.
See also: French Revolution.

Marathon, village and plain northeast of Athens, Greece, site of an Athenian victory (490 B.C.) over the Persians. The runner Pheidippides carried a report of the victory to Athens, after which he collapsed and died. The modern Olympic Games (1896) standardized the marathon race at 26 mi, 385 yd (42.2 km) in 1908. Boston and New York City each hold annual marathons, attracting thousands of runners.
See also: Greece.

Marble, rock form of limestone consisting of crystals of calcite or dolomite. Marble is formed when limestone is *metamorphosed* (changed by great heat and pressure) so that

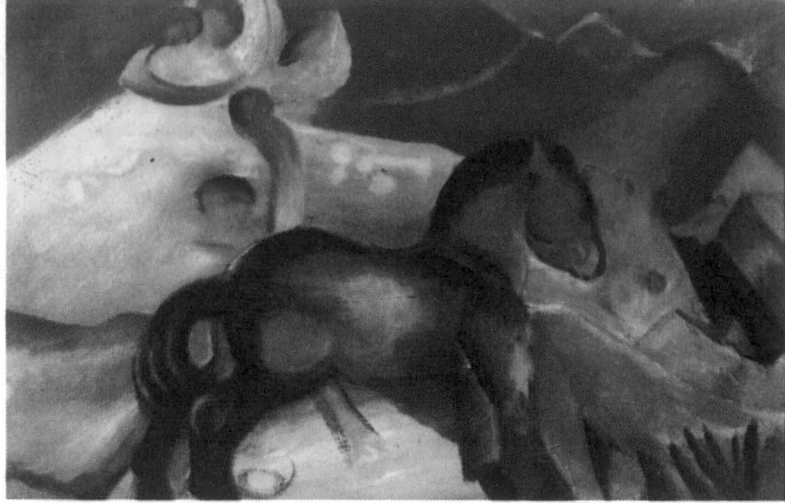

Animals are the main motif in the work of Franz Marc (1880-1916), a member of the German group of painters Der Blaue Reiter. This painting, *The Little Blue Horse* (1912), can be found in the Saarlandmuseum in Saarbrücken.

M

the rock is recrystallized and hardened. Pure marble, which is snow-white in color, has been prized by sculptors and architects since ancient times. Some of the finest marble comes from the Carrara quarries in Italy, and in the United States, from Vermont. Marble often contains impurities, which affect is color. Exposed to acid fumes and water, marble will corrode.

Marble bones *See:* Osteosclerosis.

Marc, Franz (1880-1916), German expressionist painter, with Wassily Kandinsky a cofounder of Der Blaue Reiter group. His work is characterized by vigorous lines and a vivid, symbolic use of color.

Marceau, Marcel (1923-), French mime. Marceau studied drama in Paris and rose to fame with a brief mime role in the film *Les Enfants du Paradis* (1944). His best-known characterization is the white-faced clown Bip. He became world famous with stage appearances in the 1950s.

Marcel, Gabriel (1889-1973), 20th-century French philosopher. A Christian existentialist, Marcel stressed the value of understanding life through human experience. His best-

Guglielmo Marconi (1874-1937).

known books include *Metaphysical Journals* (1927), *Being and Having* (1935), *Homo Viator* (1945), *Man Against Society* (1951), and *Presence and Immortality* (1959).
See also: Existentialism.

Marciano, Rocky (Rocco Marchegiano; 1923-1969), U.S. boxer, considered to be one of the most powerful punchers of all time. Marciano won the heavyweight championship by knocking out Jersey Joe Walcott in the 13th round (1952), and successfully defended his title until his retirement in 1956. He is the only major prizefighter to have remained undefeated throughout his professional career, fighting 49 bouts in 9 years, winning 43 by knockout. He was killed in a plane crash.

Marcion (d. A.D. 160), founder of a heretical Christian sect. He joined the church in Rome c.140 but was excommunicated in 144. Influenced by gnosticism, he taught that there were 2 rival Gods: one, the tyrannical creator and lawgiver of the Old Testament; the other, the unknown God of love and mercy who sent Jesus to purchase salvation from the creator God. Marcion rejected almost the complete bible. This forced the orthodox church to fix its canon of Scripture. Marcionism spread widely but by the end of the 3rd century had mostly been absorbed by Manichaeism.
See also: Christianity.

Marconi, Guglielmo (1874-1937), Italian physicist, awarded (with K.F. Braun) the 1909 Nobel Prize in physics for his work in devising a wireless telegraph. By 1895 he could transmit and receive signals at distances of about 1.2 mi (2 km). On Dec. 12, 1901, in St. John's, Newfoundland, he successfully received the first transatlantic radio communication.
See also: Telegraph.

Marco Polo *See:* Polo, Marco.

Marcos, Ferdinand Edralin (1917-1989), president of the Philippines (1965-1986). In 1972 Marcos declared martial law in the country and in 1973, under a new constitution, he assumed near-dictatorial authority. Although he lifted martial law in 1981, he

retained certain broad martial-law powers. Anti-Marcos forces attracted worldwide attention in Aug. 1983 when returning opposition leader Benigno Aquino was murdered at the Manila airport while in government custody. In Feb. 1986 Marcos was reelected president in an election marked by demonstrations and charges of fraud. His main opponent, Corazon Aquino, the widow of Benigno, refused to recognize the results of the election. After continued popular demonstrations against the government, Marcos and his wife, Imelda, left the country on Feb. 25th to settle in Hawaii. Corazon Aquino replaced him as president. Both Marcos and his wife were indicted by the U.S. government on charges that they embezzled from the Philippine treasury to purchase assets for themselves in the United States. Marcos proved too ill to stand trial and charges against him were dropped; he died in Hawaii. Court actions against Imelda continued into 1991 and ultimately resulted in her acquittal.
See also: Philippines.

Marcus Aurelius (Marcus Aurelius Antoninus; 121-180), Roman emperor and philosopher. Adopted at 17 by his uncle Antoninus Pius, he succeeded him as emperor in 161, after a distinguished career in public service. During this time he wrote *Meditations*, his spiritual philosophy and a classic work of stoicism. His reign was marred by plague, rebellion, barbarian attacks along the Rhine and Danube, and his own persecution of Christians, considered at that time to be the chief enemies of the empire. His government was otherwise noted for social reform, justice, and generosity.
See also: Rome, Ancient.

A bust in gold of emperor-philosopher Marcus Aurelius (reigned from 161-180), a confirmed Stoic, who took his responsibilities very seriously (Musée d'Archéologie, Lausanne).

Marcuse, Herbert (1898-1979), German-born U.S. political philosopher who combined Freudianism and Marxism in his social criticism. According to Marcuse, modern society is automatically repressive and requires violent revolution as the first step

toward a Utopian society. He became a cult figure of the New Left in the United States in the 1960s. His works include *Eros and Civilization* (1954) and *One Dimensional Man* (1964).
See also: Philosophy; Utopia.

Mardi Gras (French, 'fat Tuesday'), festivities prior to and on Shrove Tuesday, the last day of carnival before the start of Lent. Celebrated as a holiday in various Catholic countries, it was introduced into the United States by French settlers and is most notably observed in New Orleans.
See also: Shrove Tuesday.

Marduk, highest god of ancient Babylon. Called 'lord of the gods of heaven and earth,' Marduk rose to power by conquering Tiamat, the monster of chaos. Some of Babylon's most elaborate temples were built to worship Marduk, and, as the conquering armies of the empire overran most of the Middle East, worship of Marduk spread to those lands.
See also: Babylon.

Mari (Tall Hariri), city from ancient times in Mid-Mesopotamia on the upper course of the Euphrates, now the Tall Hariri hill of ruins. Royal city and trade center from the 3rd millennium B.C. onwards. Excavations (since 1933) include exposure of the palace of Zimrilim (ca. 1770 B.C.): about 3000 rooms, a throne room with frescos, temples and a palace archive (on about 20,000 clay tablets).

Maria, Walter de (1935-   ), American expressive artist, practitioner of land art and conceptual art. His works include the vertical earth kilometer, a brass bar with a diameter of 1.9685 in (5 cm) of which one kilometer (0.622 mi) had to disappear into the earth.

Mariana Islands, group of islands (184 sq mi/476.6 sq km) in the West Pacific, east of the Philippines. Discovered by Magellan in 1521 and owned by Spain until surrendered to the United States, in 1898, they were named the Ladrones (Thieves) Islands until renamed in 1668 by Jesuit missionaries. They were briefly under Japanese occupation (1941-1944) and became part of the United Nations Trust Territory of the Pacific Islands in 1947. In 1978 the northern islands became the Northern Mariana Islands and a commonwealth of the United States. The majority of the population lives on the largest and southernmost island, Guam, an outlying U.S. territory. The group's economy rests on subsistence agriculture, copra export, and government and military installations.

Mariana Trench, world's deepest discovered submarine trench 210 mi (338 km) southwest of Guam. More than 1,500 mi (2,414 km) long, it averages over 40 mi (64 km) in width and has a maximum known depth of 36,201 ft (1,034 m).

Maria Theresa (1717-1780), archduchess of Austria, queen of Hungary and Bohemia (1740-1780), and wife of Holy Roman Emperor Francis I. As a result of the Pragmatic Sanction of 1713, she acquired the Habsburg lands upon the death of her father, Emperor Charles VI (1740); the War of the Austrian Succession, in which she lost Silesia to Prussia but gained the election of her husband, Francis of Lorraine, as emperor, was immediately launched against her. She later allied with France in the Seven Years War against Prussia but was defeated. A capable ruler, she introduced administrative, agrarian, and fiscal reforms and maintained a strong army. After 1765 she shared her powers with son Joseph II, one of 16 children, including Marie Antoinette of France and Emperor Leopold II.

Marie Antoinette (1755-1793), queen of France from 1774. Daughter of Maria Theresa and the Emperor Francis I, she married the Dauphin in 1770 to strengthen ties between Austria and France and became queen on his accession as Louis XVI. The unpopular, unconsummated (for 7 years) marriage and youthful extravagances made her many enemies, as did her involvement in several scandals. When the French Revolution broke out she advised the attempted escape of the royal family, which ended with its capture at Varennes. She began her own negotiations, independent of her husband, first with comte de Mirabeau, later with Antoine Barnave, and even asked for Austrian intervention in France, to no avail. Imprisoned with Louis, her son, Louis XVIII, taken from her, she was guillotined 9 months after the king, in Oct. 1793.
See also: French Revolution; Louis.

Marie Louise (1791-1847), empress of France (1810-1815). Eldest daughter of Francis II of Austria, she married Napoleon after he divorced Josephine (1810) and was the mother of Napoleon II. After Napoleon's exile she became duchess of Parma.

Marigold, annual plant (genus *Tagetes*) with fragrant orange or yellow flowers, native to Central and South America. Two common species, native to Guatemala and Mexico, are the African marigold (*T. erecta*) and the French marigold (*T. patula*).

The African marigold (*T. erecta*), an annual herb, is actually planted in a vegetable garden. Marigolds ward off such pests as parasitic worms and rabbits.

Marihuana *See:* Marijuana.

Marijuana, or marihuana, nonaddictive drug derived from the hemp plant (*Cannabis sativa*). It is usually smoked, but can also be sniffed or taken as food. It is mainly used for the mild euphoria it produces; other symptoms include loss of muscular coordination, increased heart beat, drowsiness, and hallucination. The most potent form of the drug is hashish. Marijuana's use, the subject of much medical and social debate, is widespread throughout the world.

Marin, John (1870-1953), U.S. painter and print maker best known for his expressionistic watercolors of Manhattan and the Maine coast. Among his works are *Singer Building* (1921) and *Maine Islands* (1922).

Marine biology, study of the flora and fauna of the sea, from the smallest plankton to massive whales. It includes the study of the complex interrelationship between different marine organisms and between the organisms and their environment. Through experiments with marine organisms, marine biologists can increase our knowledge of human reproduction and development and the nervous system. Scientists have also discovered substances in certain marine animals, such as sponges and seaweeds, that may be used in treating cancer, infections, and pneumonia. These substances might possibly be used as commercial drugs in the future.

Marini, Marino (1901-1980), an Italian sculptor. He became known for his series of horses and horsemen, simple nude figures, and portrait busts. The surfaces of his dynamic figures often have rough textured finishes. *Cavalier, Horse and Rider,* and *Pomona I* are typical works. Marini was born in Pistoia, Italy, and studied in Florence. After traveling in Europe he settled in Milan, where he taught sculpture at the Brera Academy, 1940-1969.

Marionette *See:* Puppet.

Mariposa lily, or sego lily (genus *Calochortus*), tuliplike member of the lily family. Taking its name from the Spanish word for butterfly, mariposa lilies bloom in spring in the sandy soil of Western United States. They are perennials, growing from bulbs, and range in color from white or purple to yellow or orange. There are about 60 species, 40 of which are native to the U.S.

Maris, Roger (1934-1985), U.S. baseball player. In 1961, Maris made sports history by hitting 61 home runs, breaking Babe Ruth's single season home run mark of 60 set in 1927. Because Maris hit his home runs during a 162-game schedule and Ruth his during a 154-game schedule, both totals are considered records. Maris was also named the American league's most valuable player twice (1960, 1961). He played outfield for the Cleveland Indians (1957-1958), Kansas City Athletics (1958-1959), New York Yankees (1960-1966), and St. Louis Cardinals (1967-1968).

Marisol (Marisol Escobar; 1930-   ),

M

M

Venezuelan-born U.S. sculptor who satirizes and caricatures human society by creating Pop Art-type figures, usually from wood and clay. Reminiscent of South American folk art, her sculptures are stark representations, with many of the details drawn on them.

Maritain, Jacques (1882-1973), leading French neo-Thomist philosopher. He turned to the study of Thomism, the system of philosophy developed by St. Thomas, after his conversion to Catholicism in 1906. He was professor of modern philosophy at the Catholic Institute, Paris (1914-1939) and French ambassador to the Vatican (1945-1948).
See also: Philosophy.

Maritime law, body of law, based on custom, court decisions, and statutes, seeking to regulate all aspects of shipping and ocean commerce, such as insurance, salvage, and contracts for carriage of goods by sea. It is international to the extent that firm general principles exist, but these have no legal force except as they are incorporated by individual countries into their own legal systems; they are often modified in the process. Many derive from decisions of medieval maritime courts. In the United States, maritime law is administered by the federal district courts.

Marius, Gaius (157-86 B.C.), Roman general and politician. After successes on the battlefield, he was elected consul 7 times between 107 and 86 B.C.
See also: Rome, Ancient.

Marivaux, Pierre (1688-1763), French playwright and novelist, best known for his witty comedies. Sparkling dialogue is still termed *marivaudage*. Among his works are the comedy *The Game of Love and Chance* (1730) and the novel *The Successful Peasant* (1735-1736).

Marjoram, perennial herb of the mint family, native to the Mediterranean region and Asia. It is cultivated in the United States for flavoring foods and for use in toilet soaps. Sweet marjoram is *Marjorana hortensis*. Common marjoram (*Origanum vulgare*) is also called oregano.

Mark Antony *See:* Antony, Marc.

Mark, Saint, or John Mark (fl. 1st century A.D.), Christian evangelist and traditional author of the second Gospel, which derived information from St.Peter in Rome. Mark accompanied Barnabas (his cousin) and Paul on their missionary journeys. His feast day is Apr. 25.
See also: Christianity.

Marketing, refers to all activities concerned with the flow of goods and services from the producer to the consumer. It includes the various physical movements of the product including the pricing, wholesaling, transporting, and retailing of the product. It also involves packaging, design, and advertising. Marketing may be said to include everything that has to do with *how* a product is sold. In earlier times, when economic activities were

simpler, people concentrated on the actual manufacture of the product. The business of taking it to a market and selling it was relatively simple. Today, with a huge range of products to choose from (often almost indistinguishable from each other) marketing is an important operation. Most companies employ a team of people, working under a marketing director, to plan the marketing of a product. They have to decide, on the basis of market surveys, just what the consumer wants. Then they design and package the product to match the requirements of the consumer. Marketing decisions involve a whole complex of considerations: what country and climate, for example, the product will be sold in; which social groupings among the population will buy it; how it will be distributed-through supermarkets, department stores, or mail order; and whether, and how, it should be advertised.
Marketing plays a vital role in ensuring prosperity since, it is argued, consumers are given what they want at a convenient location and packaged in the most efficient way possible. On the other hand,however, there is the objection that too much money is spent on marketing and that it is sometimes more concerned with persuading people that they need a certain product, rather than finding out what they want.

Market research, process of gathering and analyzing information for marketing decision making. It dates back to the early 20th century in the United States before spreading to Europe and Japan. Business employs market research to identify customers (markets) for its products, to analyze their needs (through such techniques as polls and surveys), and to suggest strategies to develop interest among those customers for their products.

Markova, Dame Alicia (1910-), leading English ballerina. She was a member of Sergei Diaghilev's Ballets Russes (1925-1929) and became a prima ballerina with London's Vic-Wells Ballet in 1932. She founded her own company with Anton Dolin in 1935. This grew into the London Festival Ballet, which they headed from 1944-1952. She also directed the Metropolitan Opera Ballet (1963-1969) and taught at the University of Cincinnati (1969-1974).

Marlborough, Duke of (John Churchill; 1650-1722), English soldier and politician, one of the country's greatest generals. He helped suppress the Duke of Monmouth's rebellion (1685) for James II, but in 1688 transferred his allegiance to William of Orange, who made him an earl and a member of the Privy Council. His wife, Sarah Churchill, was the closest friend and attendant of Princess (later Queen) Anne; together they had great influence with the queen. After Anne's accession in 1702 Marlborough commanded English, Dutch, and German forces in the war of the Spanish Succession. In 1704 he won a great victory over the French at Blenheim. Further victories followed at Ramillies (1706), Oudenarde (1708), and Malplaquet (1709). His wife fell from favor with the queen in 1711, and Marlborough was dismissed; in

1714, however, he was restored to favor by George I.
See also: United Kingdom.

Marlin, gamefish related to the sailfish and the swordfish, found in warm oceans. The marlin is armed with a long spike extending from its upper jaw. Most marlins weigh 50-400 lb (23-180 kg), although the blue marlin (genus *Makira*) can reach 1,000 lb (454 kg).

Marlowe, Christopher (1564-1593), English poet and dramatist, a major influence on William Shakespeare. He developed the use of dramatic blank verse. His best-known plays are *Tamburlaine the Great* (c. 1587); *Dr. Faustus* (c. 1588), in which he developed a new concept of tragedy, that of a heroic character doomed to failure because of his ambition and power; and *Edward II* (c.1593). He also wrote the unfinished long poem *Hero and Leander* (1598) and the lyric 'The Pastoral Shepherd to His Love.'

Marmara, Sea of, sea between the Asian and European sections of Turkey. It is connected to the Black Sea on the northeast by the Bosporus and to the Aegean Sea on the southwest by the Dardanelles. The sea covers 4,300 sq mi (11,100 sq km) and is a key waterway for the passage of ships between the Mediterranean and the southern ports of the former USSR.

Marmoset, the world's smallest monkey, usually growing to less than 1 ft (30 cm) long. It is a member of the family Callitrichidae. Some marmosets have striking ear tufts. The pygmy marmoset (*Cebuella pygmaea*) is 5.5 to 6.25 in (14-16 cm). Marmosets live in the forests of South America, feeding on insects, leaves, and fruit.

Cotton-top marmoset   North Colombia.
(*Saguinus oedipus*).   Length: 24 in (60 cm).
Tropical forests of

Marmot, large round squirrel (genus *Marmota*) found in much of the Northern Hemisphere. Marmots dig burrows, where they hibernate in winter, and live in colonies. Most live in hill country, although the woodchuck, or groundhog (*M. monox*), prefers open areas. Marmots grow from 1-2 ft (30-61 cm) long.

Marne, Battles of the, two World War I battles fought in the Marne River area of France. In the first (Sept. 1914), the German advance on Paris was halted by an Allied offensive. The second (July 1918) countered the last German offensive.
See also: World War I.

Marne River, chief tributary of the Seine River, France, rising on the Langres Plateau of eastern France and flowing through 310 mi (500 km) of rich farmland before joining the Seine southeast of Paris. Several key battles fought there during World War I saved Paris from being overrun by the German army.

Marquand, J(ohn) P(hillips) (1893-1960), U.S. novelist best known for his detective stories centered on the Japanese agent Mr. Moto and for his gentle satires of New England society, such as *The Late George Apley* (1937), for which he won a Pulitzer Prize, and *Point of No Return* (1949).

Marquesas Islands, 2 clusters of mountainous and volcanic islands in the South Pacific, about 900 mi (1,400 km) northeast of Tahiti. The islands are governed by France since 1842. Their total area is about 492 sq mi (1,274 sq km). The largest islands are Hiva Oa and Nuku Hiva. The population is made up mainly of Polynesians. The islands are fertile, producing breadfruit, coffee, vanilla, and copra (dried coconut meat) for export.

Marrakech, or Marrakesh (pop. 745,500), city of southwestern Morocco, near the Atlas Mtns. Founded in 1062, Marrakech was the capital of the Berber Empire and a center of commerce and culture in the 15th century. It was captured by the French in 1912. Marrakech is a popular tourist attraction for its fine examples of Islamic architecture and its outdoor markets (*souks*). It is also a food-processing and leather manufacturing center.
See also: Morocco.

Marriage, union between man and woman for the purpose of cohabitation and usually also for raising children. The modern trend is towards monogamy, union between one man and one woman only. Many societies still permit polygamy, but it is increasingly rare. Forms of group and communal marriage have been tried from time to time, though with little success or social acceptance.
Marriage is in some senses a contract, often involving property and in some societies a dowry. In U.S. law marriage creates special ownership rights in marital property. It is still also a religious matter in many countries; marriage is a minor sacrament of the Roman Catholic Church.
Most societies limit marriage in certain ways. It is forbidden in most countries between partners who have too close a blood relationship, although the degree permissible varies widely among countries, religions, and U.S. states. In U.S. common law a purported marriage involving bigamy is void; other conditions, such as non-consummation, render marriage void or voidable, generally through the courts. A marriage is also void if not carried out in the prescribed legal form, although in some states common law marriage may arise after long cohabitation without any formality. Most societies have some provision for divorce. Marriages in the U.S. are performed either by a civil authority or by a religious ceremony with civil authorization; the ceremonies of most denominations are so authorized in most states. In general, a marriage valid in one state is recognized in the others. Some states require banns to be posted.

Marriner, Neville (1924-), English violinist and conductor. Marriner was a student at the Royal College of Music in London and the Paris Conservatoire. He became a teacher as well as a member of several chamber music societies and founded the Jacobean Ensemble in 1952 together with Thurston Dart. As second violinist of the London Symphony Orchestra he established the Academy of St. Martin-in-the-Fields in 1959, a chamber orchestra which under Marriner's direction quickly acquired world fame and makes many concert tours and recordings.

Marryat, Frederick (1792-1848), English author. An officer in the British Navy who spent 24 years at sea, Marryat's books all had maritime adventure themes. His best-known works are *Frank Mildmay* (1829), *The King's Own* (1830), and *Mr. Midshipman Easy* (1836).

Mars, the fourth planet from the Sun, with a mean solar distance of 141.6 million mi (227.9 million km) and a mean diameter of 4,223 mi (6,796 km). Mars takes about 687 earth-days to orbit the Sun. The planet's temperature ranges from -191° to 81°F (-124° to 27°C), and its tenuous atmosphere consists mainly of carbon dioxide. The distinctive Martian polar caps are composed of frozen carbon dioxide and water ice.
Telescopically, Mars appears as an ocher-red disk marked by extensive dark areas; these latter have in the past been erroneously termed *maria* (seas). Several observers in the past reported sighting networks of straight lines on the Martian surface-the famous canals-but observations with large telescopes and the photographs sent back by the United States' Mariner (1965, 1969, 1971) and Viking (1976) space probes showed these to be an optical illusion. Mars actually has a cratered surface marked with canyons, ancient volcanoes, and jumbled terrains. No probe has yet found evidence that life ever existed on the planet. Mars has 2 satellites (moons), Phobos and Deimos. In 1996 scientists of NASA, Lockheed Martin, and universities in Montreal, Georgia, and Stanford announced they had found fossil traces on a meteorite from Mars. These traces could be the result of early biological activity on Mars. Although this discovery was not seen as evidence of life on Mars, it led to other meteorites from Mars being studied more closely.
See also: Planet; Solar System.

Mars, in Roman mythology, the god of war. He was originally the god of agriculture, but later was identified with Ares, the Greek god of war. Second in importance only to his father, Jupiter, Mars had several children by Venus and was also regarded as the father of Romulus, legendary founder of Rome. His altar on the Campus Martius was the scene of festivals in Mar. (his month) and Oct.
See also: Mythology.

Marsalis, Branford (1960-), American jazz musician. Plays tenor and soprano saxophone. Extremely versatile soloist and band leader; worked with Art Blakey in the 1980s as well as with pop star Sting. He made the charts with the CD *Music Evolution* (1997) of his hip-hop project *Buckshot Lefonque*. Brother of trumpet player Wynton Marsalis.

Marsalis, Wynton (1962-), American trumpet player. Son of jazz pianist Ellis Marsalis. Made his debut in 1979 with Art Blakey. Since 1982 he leads his own groups and plays jazz as well as Classical music. In 1997 he was the first jazz musician to win a Pulitzer prize for his jazz oratorio *Blood on the Fields* (1994). His brother, Branford Marsalis (1960), also leads his own jazz and funk bands.

Marseille (pop. 807,700), second largest city in France, located in the southeastern part of the country. It serves as France's chief seaport and is a major industrial center. The oldest city in France, was settled by the Greeks c.600 B.C. and annexed by Rome in 49 B.C. The city's expansion began with the conquest of Algeria and the opening of the Suez Canal in the 19th century. Marseille's port handles about one third of French maritime trade.

Marsh, flat wetland area characterized by grassy plant growth. Distinguished from swamps where trees grow, marshes often occur in coastal regions where tidal flows add salt water to fresh water, usually at the mouths of rivers (estuarine marshes). Freshwater marshes occur in low-lying inland areas and both types of marshes are home to a wide variety of fish and wildlife.

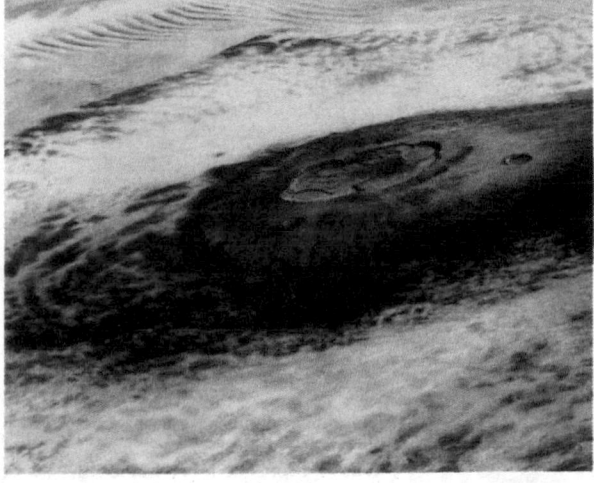
The extinct Martian volcano Olympus Mons is nearly three times as high as Mount Everst.

M

Marshall, Alfred (1842-1924), English economist, professor of political economy at Cambridge (1885-1908). His *Principles of Economics* (1890) systematized economic thought up to that time and was the standard text for many years. Through his work on cost, and value, and distribution Marshall developed a concept of marginal utility.

Marshall, Frank James (1877-1944), American chess master. From 1906-1936 he was U.S. champion and took part in more than 60 tournaments. His largest triumph was his victory in the Cambridge Springs tournament in 1904, which he won unbeaten against Lasker and Janowski. Other successes include Scheveningen (1905) and Nuremberg (1906). Marshall devoted himself to chess in his country; he founded Marshall's Chess Divan in New York (1915), which became a meeting point for all the prominent chess players. Marshall's Gambit is still a popular weapon among many chess players.

Marshall, George Catlett (1880-1959), U.S. general and politician. As chief of staff (1939-1945) he influenced Allied strategy in World War II. As secretary of state (1947-1949) under President Harry S. Truman, he introduced the European Recovery Program, or Marshall Plan, for which he was awarded the 1953 Nobel Peace Prize. As U.S. secretary of defense (1950-1951), he was active in the creation of the North Atlantic Treaty Organization (NATO).
See also: Marshall Plan; North Atlantic Treaty Organization.

Marshall Islands

Capital:	Dalap-Uliga-Darrit
Area:	70 sq mi (181 sq km)
Population:	73,600
Language:	English
Government:	Republic
Independent:	1990
Head of gov.:	Prime minister
Per capita:	US$ 1.600
Monetary unit:	1 US dollar = 100 cents

Marshall Islands, 2 curving chains, each about 650 mi (1,050 km) in length, of altogether 34 coral atolls and islands in the west central Pacific: the eastern *Radak* (Sunrise) chain and the western *Ralik* (Sunset) chain. Their total land area is 70 sq mi (180 sq km). The main atolls are Majuro, Amo, Ailinglaplap, Jaluit, and Kwajalein. The islands are named for a British sea captain, John Marshall, who discovered them in 1788. Germany occupied the Marshalls in 1886 and later bought them from Spain. They were seized by Japan in 1914, taken by United States forces in 1944, and included in the Trust Territory of the Pacific Islands in 1947. The Marshalls were given self-government in 1979. A compact of free association with the United States was signed in 1983 and became effective in 1986, when the Marshalls were withdrawn form the trust territory. After World War II the United States used the Eniwetok and Bikini atolls as atomic testing grounds. The island's population is predominantly Micronesian. Breadfruit is the main crop, and copra (dried coconut meat) is the chief export.
In 2001 the government submitted a claim to the U.S. government of $563 million, based on the damage done by nuclear testing. Radioactivity is still a risk to the population.

Marshall Plan, or European Recovery Program, program designed to help Europe's economic recovery after World War II, named for its originator, U.S. Secretary of State George C. Marshall. From 1948 to 1948 to 1952, material and financial aid amounting to almost $13 billion dollars was sent by the United States to the 17 European countries who formed the Organization for European Economic Cooperation (OEEC). The plan was administered by the Economic Cooperation Administration (ECA).
See also: World War II.

Marsh gas *See:* Methane.

Marsh hawk *See:* Northern harrier.

Marsh mallow (*Althaea officinalis*), herb found mainly in Europe, although it is now grown in the United States. The marsh mallow grows from 2 to 4 ft (61 to 120 cm) and has large leaves covered by soft hair.

Marsh marigold *See:* Cowslip.

Marston, John (1576-1634), English playwright best known for his comedy *The Malcontents* (1604). His *Antonio's Revenge* (1600) is one of the first examples of English tragedy.

Marsupial, any of an order (Marsupialia) of pouched mammals found mainly in Australia, Tasmania, and New Guinea. With few exceptions, marsupials do not develop placenta. They give birth to undeveloped young that attach themselves to the mother's teats inside a pouch on her abdomen, where they continue their development. Members of the order include the kangaroo, koala, and wombat.

Martel, Charles *See:* Charles Martel.

Marten, any of several large mammals (genus *Martes*) of the weasel family with valuable fur. The home of the marten is the pine forests of North America, Europe, and Asia. In Europe martens are also called sables. Their prey is mainly squirrels. American species include the American marten and the larger fisher or pekan.

Martha's Vineyard, island off the coast of southeast Massachusetts. About 100 sq mi (260 sq km) in area, it is separated from Cape Cod by Vineyard Sound. Named by Barthelomew Gosnold (1602), it was settled in 1632. A major whaling center in the 18th and 19th centuries, it is now a popular summer resort.

Martí, José Julian (1853-1895), Cuban poet and hero of the independence movement. While in exile in the United States (1881-1895) he founded the Cuban Revolutionary Party. His best known poems appear in *Ismaelillo* (1882), *Versos sencilles* (1891), and *Versos libres* (1913). A leader of the 1895 Cuban rebellion against Spanish rule, Martí was killed at the battle of Dos Rios.

Martial (Marcus Valerius Martialis; c.A.D. 40-104), Spanish-born Latin poet. He lived in Rome 64-98 and was favored by emperors Titus and Domitian. Martial wrote 15 books of epigrams famous for their wit and their unusual poetic meter.
See also: Epigram.

Martial law, temporary superimposition of military on domestic civil government, usually in wartime or other national emergency.

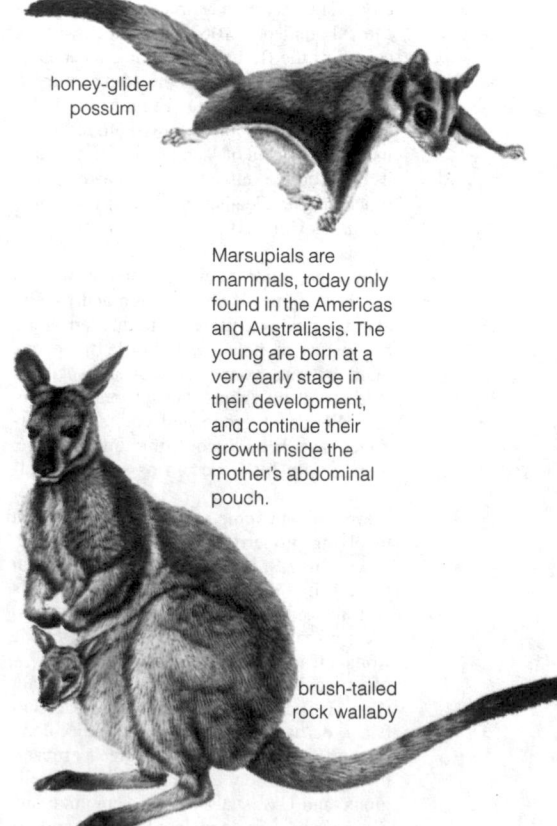

honey-glider possum

Marsupials are mammals, today only found in the Americas and Australiasis. The young are born at a very early stage in their development, and continue their growth inside the mother's abdominal pouch.

brush-tailed rock wallaby

The army takes over executive and judicial functions, and civil rights such as habeas corpus may be suspended. When an invading army assumes control of a country, it is said to act not under martial law but as a military government.

Martin, any of several birds of the swallow family. The best-known member of the species is the purple martin (*Progne subis*), valued throughout the Southern United States for its consumption of large quantities of mosquitoes and other insect pests. They are native to most of the United States and the lower portions of Canada and often flock together in large numbers, consuming swarms of winged insects in flight.

Martin, Dean (Dino Crocetti; 1917-1995), American singer and actor. Made comedies with Jerry Lewis (1926-), played secret agent Matt Helm and had his own successful TV shows. Films include *The Stooge* (1953), *Sergeants Three* (1962), *The Silencers* (1966), *Airport* (1969), *Mr. Ricco* (1975).

Martin, Frank (1890-1974), Swiss/Dutch composer. Studied in Geneva, where he founded the Société de musique de chambre in 1962; taught at the Institute Jacques-Dalcroze from 1928-1938. In 1946 he established himself in the Netherlands; from 1950-1957 still taught at the Conservatory in Cologne. After being influenced by the French late Romantic period, Martin opted during the 1930s for a twelve-tone system in combination with traditional harmonic fundamentals. He wrote a versatile body of

koala

numbat

works, the most famous being the oratorio *Le vin herbé* (1938-1941) and *Petite symphonie concertante* (1945). His oeuvre also includes operas, orchestral pieces, concertos, choral compositions, chamber music and songs.

Martin du Gard, Roger (1881-1958), French novelist known for his objective but somber exploration of human relationships and the large backgrounds in which he sets them. In *Jean Barois* (1913) it is the Dreyfus Affair; in *The Thibaults* (1922-1940), an 8-part novel cycle, it is World War I. In 1937 he won the Nobel Prize for literature.

Martineau, Harriet (1802-1876), British writer and social reformer. A writer of fiction as well as nonfiction on many topics, she is best known for her works on economics and social reform, particularly her *Illustrations of Political Economy* (1832-1834) and *Illustrations of Taxation* (1834), written for the layperson, and *Society in America* (1837), presenting her antislavery views.

Martinique, island in the Windward group in the east Caribbean, an overseas department of France since 1946. A volcanic island discovered by Columbus c.1502, Martinique was colonized by France as a sugar-growing center after 1635. Slave labor was used until 1848, and much of the present population is of African descent. The economy still rests on sugar, as well as rum, fruit, and tourism. The island is rugged and mountainous but very fertile. Its main town is Fort-de-France.

Martin of Tours, Saint (c.316-397), bishop of Tours. Son of a pagan, he served in the Roman army but after a vision of Christ sought a religious life. Bishop of Tours from c.371, he encouraged monasticism and opposed execution of heretics.
See also: Tours.

Martins, Peter (1946-), Danish dancer. He danced with the Royal Danish Ballet 1964-67, then joined the New York City Ballet, where he became a leading male dancer in such works by George Balanchine as *Violin Concerto* and *Duo Concertant* (both 1972). In 1983, following Balanchine's death, he became ballet master-in-chief (with Jerome Robbins).
See also: Ballet.

Martinson, Harry Edmund (1904-1978), Swedish writer and poet. Made his debut with symbolic nature lyrical poetry, after which he wrote many travel journals, novels, cultural criticism and autobiographical works. His works excel in the use of fresh, innovative language and is dominated by a skeptical attitude against technical progress and its use. A highlight is the cycle of epic poems *Aniara* (1956), about a spaceship headed for disaster. In 1974 he received the Nobel prize for literature, together with his fellow countryman Eyvind Johnson.

Martin V (Oddone Colonna; 1368-1431), 15th-century Roman Catholic pope. Elected to the papacy in 1417 at the Council of Constance, his accession ended the Great Schism in the church. Martin worked for reforms within the church structure and hierarchy and arranged agreements (concordats) with the most powerful nations of Europe. He also called several councils aimed at receiving input for the continued unity and betterment of the church.

Marvell, Andrew (1621-1678), English metaphysical poet. Assistant to John Milton from 1657, Marvell was also a member of Parliament from 1659. A Puritan, he was known as a wit and satirist, but is best remembered today for his lyric poetry, including such works as 'To His Coy Mistress' and 'The Garden.'

Marx, Karl (1818-1883), German philosopher and social and economic theorist, founder of modern socialism. Born in Prussia of Jewish parents, Marx studied philosophy in Bonn and Berlin. When the Cologne newspaper he edited the *Rheinische Zeitung*, was suppressed (1843), he moved with his wife Jenny von Westphalen to Paris, where he met Friedrich Engels in 1844, and later to London, where he spent most of his life in great poverty.
In 1848 Marx and Engels published the *Communist Manifesto*, which established the theoretical basis for a socialist movement based on class struggle and sociological analysis rather than moral appeals to natural rights. Marx and Engels later co-founded (1864) International Workingmen's Association, the first international revolutionary organization. Marx wrote prolifically on questions of philosophy, history, and politics, but his greatest work was *Capital*, his analysis of the system of capitalism. Only the first volume was published in his lifetime (1867). After his death, Engels completed the second (1885) and third (1894) volumes. Building on his criticism of the theories of Adam Smith and David Ricardo, Marx developed the theory of surplus-value to explain the exploitation of workers under capitalism. He predicted that the working class, or proletariat, would grow in numbers and power and would eventually overthrow capitalism, and establish socialism. The economic and political analysis of capitalism was integrated into a broader theory called historical materialism, which analyzed human history in terms of a sequence of kinds of society based on different forms of ownership of the means of production. Marx's influence has been widespread, and he is universally regarded as one of the major thinkers of the 19th century.
See also: Communism; Marxism.

Marx brothers, U.S. comedy team whose main members were Groucho (Julius; 1890-1977), Harpo (Arthur; 1888-1964), and Chico (Leonard; 1886-1961). Gummo (Milton; 1897-1961) left the team after their vaudeville days, and Zeppo (Herbert; 1901-1979) left in 1934. The Marx brothers made about a dozen movies (1933-1946). Their anarchic humor made hits of such memorable movies as *Duck Soup* (1933) and *A Night at the Opera* (1935).

M

M

Marxism, foundation philosophy of modern communism, originating in the work of Karl Marx and Friedrich Engels. Three of its basic concepts are that productive labor is the fundamental attribute of human nature; that the structure of any society is determined by its economic means of production; and that societies evolve by a series of crises caused by internal contradictions, analyzable by dialectical materialism.

Marx held that 19th-century industrial capitalism, the latest stage of the historical process, had arisen from feudalism by class struggle between the aristocracy and the rising bourgeois capitalist class. Dialectical materialism predicted conflict between these capitalists and the working class, or proletariat, on which the new industrialism depended. The triumphant dictatorship of the proletariat, an idea further developed by Lenin, would give way to a classless, stateless communist society where all would be equal, contributing according to their abilities and receiving according to their needs. A key concept of Marxist economics is the labor theory of value, that value is created by labor and profit is surplus value creamed off by the capitalist. The fact that the capitalist owns the means of production makes this exploitation possible. It also means that the worker cannot own the product of his labor and thus suffers alienation from part of his own humanity and the social system. Marx believed capitalism would be swept away by the last of a catastrophic series of crises.

Among numerous later Marxist theorists are Karl Kautsky and Rosa Luxemburg. In *The Accumulation of Capital* (1913), Luxemburg argued that capitalism was able to adapt and survive by exploitation of its colonial empires. In the USSR Stalin proclaimed Marxist-Leninism an active philosophy of society in forced evolutionary conflict. In China Mao Zedong adapted Marxism to an agricultural peasant situation. Yugoslavia's Tito gave Marxism a nationalist bias, still more marked in the thinking of Fidel Castro of Cuba. Some western economists, sociologists, and historians have been widely influenced by Marxism.
See also: Marx, Karl.

Mary, in the Bible, the mother of Jesus, also called the Blessed Virgin. The chief events of her life related in the Gospels are her betrothal to Joseph; the annunciation of Jesus's birth; her visit to her cousin Elizabeth, mother of John the Baptist; the birth of Jesus; and her witnessing his crucifixion. In the Roman Catholic Church Mary is accorded a special degree of veneration superior to that given to other saints, and is regarded as mediatrix of all graces and coredemptress. Roman Catholic doctrine holds she was born free from sin, remained always a virgin, and was assumed bodily into heaven.
See also: Bible; Jesus Christ.

Mary, name of 2 English queens. **Mary I** (1516-1558), daughter of Henry VIII and Catherine of Aragon, succeeded Edward VI in 1553. She strove to restore Roman Catholicism in England. Some 300 Protestants were burnt as heretics-a persecution unparalleled in England, which earned her the name 'Bloody Mary.' Her unpopular alliance with and marriage to Philip II of Spain (1554) led to war with France and the loss of Calais (1558). **Mary II** (1662-1694) was the Protestant daughter of James II and the wife (1677) of her cousin William of Orange, the Protestant ruler of the Netherlands. She helped found the College of William and Mary in Virginia in 1693. In the Glorious Revolution of 1688, William's forces attacked England, causing James to flee. Mary II was proclaimed joint sovereign with William in 1689.
See also: England.

Mary, Queen of Scots (1542-1587), queen of Scotland (1542-1567), daughter of James V and Mary of Guise. Brought up in France, she married (1558) the Dauphin, King Francis II (died 1560). Returning to Scotland (1561), she married (1565) Lord Darnley. In 1566 he murdered her counselor, David Rizzio; later Darnley himself was murdered, supposedly by the Earl of Bothwell, whom Mary married. Public outrage and Presbyterian opposition forced her abdication, and in 1568 she fled to England. Mary, heir presumptive of Elizabeth I and a Roman Catholic, soon became the natural focus of plots against the English throne. Parliament demanded her death; only in 1587, after Anthony Babington's plot, did Elizabeth reluctantly agree. Mary's trial and execution at Fotheringay castle inspired Schiller's tragedy *Maria Stuart*.
See also: Scotland; United Kingdom.

A painting of Mary Stuart (1542-1587), 'Queen of Scots', after François Clouet.

Mary, Virgin *See:* Mary.

Maryland (Free State; Old Line State; pop. 5,094,000), state in the East of the U.S. on the Atlantic Ocean, bordered by Pennsylvania, Delaware, Virginia and West Virginia; 12,412 sq mi (32,135 sq km). Capital city: Annapolis. The largest city is the port of Baltimore. The state encloses the District of Columbia with Washington D.C.
The economy is dependent on services and governmental activities (e.g. space research). Varied industry: electrical appliances, chemical products and food. Tourism and trade are also important. Agricultural products: grains, vegetables, fruit, tobacco; cattle breeding (mainly chicken) and forestry.
Founded by Lord Baltimore in 1634 by order of Charles I of England as a refuge for Roman Catholics. The state was called after the wife of Charles I, Henrietta Maria. In 1788 Maryland was one of the thirteen states that founded the Union. The large economic activity surrounding both World Wars led to a sound growth, especially in the larger cities. After WW II Maryland became a popular place of residence for employees of the federal government in Washington.

Mary Magdalene, in the New Testament, the woman of Magdala from whom Jesus cast out 7 demons (Luke 8:2). She became his devoted follower and may have been present at his death and burial. Mary was the first person to see the risen Jesus.
See also: New Testament.

Masaccio (Tommaso Guidi; 1401-1428), Florentine painter of the Renaissance, one of the great innovators of Western art. Possibly a pupil of Masolino, Masaccio produced paintings that inspired such painters as Michelangelo and Raphael. Through austere composition and inspired use of light Masaccio created expressive monumental paintings and frescoes, notably in the Brancacci Chapel of Santa Maria del Carmine in Florence. Other works include the *Trinity* fresco in Santa Maria Novella and the *Virgin with St. Anne* in the Uffizi Palace, both in Florence.
See also: Renaissance.

Masada, mountaintop rock fortress near the southeastern coast of the Dead Sea, Israel. The castle-palace complex, built (37-31 B.C.) largely by Herod the Great, was seized from Roman occupation by Jewish Zealots in A.D. 66. A 2-year seige, 72-73, was needed to recover it, but the Zealots committed suicide rather than surrender. The site has been excavated (1963-1965) and restored.

Masai, people of eastern Africa who speak the Masai language of the Sudanic group. The nomadic pastoral Masai of Kenya, the largest Masai tribe, practice polygamy and organize their society on a system of male age sets, graded from junior warrior up to tribal elder. They subsist almost entirely by herding.

Masaryk, name of 2 Czechoslovakian politicians. **Thomas Garrigue Masaryk** (1850-1937), was chief founder and first president of Czechoslovakia (1918-1935). Professor of philosophy at the Univ. of Prague from 1882, he was a fervent nationalist. During World War I he lobbied Western statesmen for Czech independence. His son **Jan Garrigue Masaryk** (1886-1948) was foreign minister of the Czech government-in-exile in London in World War II, broadcasting to his German-occu-

M

pied country. He continued as foreign minister in the restored government (1945). Soon after the Communist coup (1948) he was said to have committed suicide.

Mascagni, Pietro (1863-1945), Italian opera composer of the *verismo* (realist) school, known for the one-act *Cavalleria Rusticana* (Rustic Chivalry, 1890). In 1929 he became musical director of La Scala, Milan. Although he composed 15 operas, among them *L'Amico Fritz* (1891), Mascagni did not repeat his initial success.
See also: Opera.

Masefield, John (1878-1967), English poet, novelist, and playwright. As a youth he served on a windjammer ship, and love of the sea pervades his poems. He won fame with such long narrative poems as *The Everlasting Mercy* (1911), *Dauber* (1913), and *Raynard the Fox* (1919). In 1930 he became poet laureate.

Maser, in technology, acronym for Microwave Amplification by Stimulated Emission of Radiation, a device capable of amplifying or generating radio frequency radiation. Maser amplifiers are used in satellite communication ground stations to amplify the extremely weak signals received from communication satellites.
See also: Laser.

Maserati, Ernesto (1898-1975), Italian manufacturer of sports cars. He initially raced in cars which were built by himself, later he became occupied with designing high-quality vehicles. During the 1930s the Maseratis were supreme in a number of races. Maserati sold his financial interest already before World War II, but remained committed to the factory as a designer. Since 1997 Fiat and Ferrari each own half of the Maserati stock.

Masereel, Frans (1889-1972), Belgian painter, artist, sculptor and graphic artist. Contributed to the renewal of Flemish woodcutting. Stylistically his work belongs to expressionism; it is often socially involved, pacifistic and satirical.

Maseru (pop. 110,400), capital of Lesotho, a landlocked independent state in southern Africa. Standing near Lesotho's northwestern border with the Orange Free State (South Africa), the town is linked by a short railroad with the Bioemfontein-Natal line in South Africa. Maseru has a public library, hospital, and technical training school.
See also: Lesotho.

Mashhad (or Meshed; pop. 2,000,000), Iran, the capital of Khorasan province. It lies near the Turkman and Afghan borders and is the trade and transportation center for a productive agricultural valley. Food processing and the making of handicrafts, including fine carpets, are important industries. Ferdowsi University is here. Mashhad is a Shiite holy city with shrines visited by several million Muslim pilgrims each year. Mashhad is an ancient settlement that grew mainly after becoming a pilgrimage center in the ninth century A.D.

Maslow, Abraham Harold (1908-1970), U.S. psychologist, the major figure in the humanistic school of psychology. Rejecting behaviorism and psychoanalysis, he saw human beings as creative entities striving for self-actualization. His books include *Motivation and Personality* (1954), *Toward a Psychology of Being* (1962), and *The Psychology of Science* (1966).
See also: Psychology.

Mason and Dixon's Line, Mason-Dixon Line, traditional dividing line between the northern and southern states of the United States. Surveyed by Charles Mason and Jeremiah Dixon in 1767, the line formed the east-west boundary between Pennsylvania and Maryland and the north-south boundary between Maryland and Delaware. In 1779 the east-west line was extended to form the boundary between Virginia and Pennsylvania.

Masonry, or freemasonry, common name for the practices of the order of Free and Accepted Masons, one of the world's largest and oldest fraternal organizations. Members participate in elaborate, secret rituals and are dedicated to the promotion of brotherhood and morality. Membership, of which there are several grades, is restricted to men; allegiance to some form of religious belief is required. Modern Masonry emerged with the Grand Lodge of England, founded in 1717, although masons trace their ancestry to the craft associations or 'lodges' of medieval stone masons. There are associated organizations for women, boys, and girls. The worldwide membership is more than 6 million.

Masqat *See:* Muscat.

Masque, or mask, dramatic entertainment popular in the early-17th-century English court. It concentrated on spectacle rather than plot. Members of the aristocracy often took part with the actors, and masks were generally worn (hence the name). Ben Jonson was the most famous masque writer, and Inigo Jones designed many of the lavish sets.

Mass, term for the celebration of Holy Communion in the Roman Catholic Church and in Anglo-Catholic churches. Roman Catholics believe that the bread (host) and the wine become Christ's body and blood, which are offered as a sacrifice to God. The text consists of the 'ordinary,' spoken or sung at every celebration, and the 'proper,' sections which change according to the day or occasion-for example, the requiem mass has its own proper. In High Mass, celebrated with priest, deacon, and choir, the text is sung to plainsong with choral responses. Medieval choral settings of the mass were the first great masterpieces of Western music, remaining a major musical form into the 20th century. Low Mass, said by a single priest, is the basic Roman Catholic service. In 1965 the Vatican sanctioned the use of vernacular languages in place of Latin.

Mass, in physics, measure of the linear inertia of a body, i.e., of the extent to which it re-

sists acceleration when a force is applied to it. Alternatively, mass can be thought of as a measure of the amount of matter in a body. This view seems validated when one remembers that bodies of equal inertial mass have identical weights in a given gravitational field. The exact equivalence of inertial mass and gravitational mass is only a theoretical assumption, albeit one strongly supported by experimental evidence. According to Einstein's theory of relativity, the mass of a body is increased if it gains energy, according to the equation $E=mc^2$, where m is the change in mass due to the energy change E, and c is the electromagnetic constant. It is an important property of nature that in an isolated system mass-energy is conserved. The international standard of mass is the international prototype kilogram.
See also: Inertia.

Massachusetts (Bay State; Old Colony; pop. 6,118,000), state in the northeast of the U.S., on the Atlantic Ocean, in New England; 10,559 sq mi (27,337 sq km). Capital city: Boston, also industrial center. Agriculture, cattle breeding and fishing. Important industries are those which make high-grade products, especially the computer industry. During the 1980s and 1990s an important center of information technology grew around Harvard University (in Cambridge; oldest university of America [1636] and one of the most prestigious) and the Massachusetts Institute of Technology (MIT, also in Cambridge).
In 1524 Giovanni da Verrazano sailed along the coast. Before the arrival of English immigrants six Indian nations lived in the area, among which the Massachuset. In 1620 the first settlement of the Pilgrim Fathers was founded. During the 18th century the state was a center of resistance against English rule (Boston Tea Party). Massachusetts was one of the thirteen states which formed the U.S. in 1783. Very prosperous area, but the state also has problems such as environmental pollution and racial conflicts.

Massenet, Jules (1842-1912), French composer. Best known for his operas *Manon* (1884), *Werther* (1892), and *Thaïs* (1894), he frequently used spoken (accompanied) dialogue in the place of recitative.

Massine, Léonide (1896-1979), Russian-born U.S. ballet dancer and choreographer. He worked with Diaghilev as principal dancer and choreographer (1914-1921, 1925-1928), and directed the Ballet Russe de Monte Carlo 1932-1942. His works include *Parade* (1917) and *Jeux d' Enfants* (1943).

Massinger, Philip (1583-1640), English dramatist known for satirical comedies. Among his works are *A New Way to Pay Old Debts* (1621), *The City Madam* (1632), and the romantic tragedy *The Duke of Milan* (1621). He often collaborated with others, such as John Fletcher. A moralist, he criticized the frivolity in society.

Mass media *See:* Advertising.

Mass number *See:* Atom.

M

Masson, André (1896-1987), French painter and graphic artist. Influenced by surrealism, he developed a style of drawing ('automatic drawing') intended to be spontaneous and without a specific subject.

Massoud, Ahmed Shah (1953-2001), Afghan guerrilla leader, of Taijik heritage. From 1975, he participated in the battle against the dictator of that time, Daoed, and after that, against the communistic government. Being the most prominent military commander of the de Jamiaat-i Islami (Islamic Union), he was very successful. For years, he controlled the strategic valley of Pansjir. Massoud became Secretary for Defense after the assumption of power by the Mujahedin and 'strong man' behind President Rabbani's regime. He fought with the rival Hezb-i-Islami and was expelled from Kabul by the Taleban in 1996. He became the popular leader of the Northern Afghanistan resistance to the Taleban until his assasination in 2001 just months before the overthrow of the Taleban-regime.
See also: Afghanistan.

Mass production, production of large numbers of identical objects, usually by use of mechanization. The root of mass production is the assembly line, essentially a conveyer belt that transports the product so that each worker may perform a single function on it (e.g., add a component). The advantages of mass production are cheapness and speed; the disadvantages are lack of job satisfaction for the workers and resultant sociological problems.
See also: Assembly line; Machine tool.

Mass spectroscopy, spectroscopic technique in which electric and magnetic fields are used to deflect moving charged particles according to their mass; employed for chemical analysis, separation, isotope determination, or finding impurities. The apparatus for obtaining a mass spectrum (i.e., a number of 'lines' of distinct charge-to-mass ratio obtained from the beam of charged particles) is known as a mass spectrometer or mass spectrograph, depending on whether the lines are detected electrically or on a photographic plate. In essence, it consists of an ion source, a vacuum chamber, a deflecting field, and a collector. By altering the accelerating voltage and deflecting field, particles of a given mass can be focused to pass together through the collecting slit.
See also: Spectrometer.

Masters, Edgar Lee (1869-1950), U.S. poet, novelist, biographer, and playwright whose best-known work is *Spoon River Anthology* (1915), which reveals the life of a small town as seen through the epitaphs of its inhabitants. He also wrote critical biographies of Abraham Lincoln and Mark Twain.

Masters, William H. (1915-), and Virginia E. Johnson (1925-), U.S. sex researchers whose book *Human Sexual Response* (1966) was the first complete study of the physiology and anatomy of sexual activity.

Mastodon, any of a genus (*Mammut*) of the extinct mammals resembling elephants. Different from mammoths and elephants because of their molar teeth, they sometimes had 4 tusks (2 on the lower jaw, 2 on the upper jaw). Forest dwellers, mastodons lived in Africa during the Oligocene epoch.
See also: Mammoth.

Mata Hari (Margaretha Geertruida Zelle; 1866-1917), Dutch-born dancer and spy for Germany in World War I. She belonged to the German secret service in Paris. The mistress of many French officials, she allegedly passed on military secrets to the Germans, for which she was tried and executed.
See also: World War I.

Maté, also known as yerba maté or Paraguay tea, evergreen tree of the holly family. Its leaves are dried to make a tea containing caffeine that is widely drunk in South America.

Materialism, in philosophy, any view asserting the primacy of physical matter in explaining the nature of the world. The earliest materialists were the classical atomists, e.g., Democritus and Leucippus. Modern science has revived materialism, argued as a prerequisite for scientific thought, particularly in psychology.
See also: Democritus; Leucippus; Marx, Karl.

Mathematics, field of thought concerned with relationships involving concepts of quantity, space, and symbolism. Over the past several centuries mathematics developed to include *axiomatic-deductive reasoning*. This aspect of mathematics is credited to the classical Greeks and is traced back to Euclid, who formalized it in 300 B.C. with his work *Elements*. Axiomatic-deductive systems are based on elementary ideas assumed self-evident (*axioms*) and formal rules governing the mathematical system. Consequences (*theorems*) can then be deduced systematically and logically from axioms. All mathematical systems have this quality. Familiar examples include algebra, where relationships between known and unknown quantities are represented symbolically; arithmetic, the science of quantity and space concerned with numbers and rules for manipulating them such as addition or multiplication; calculus, dealing with relationships involving rates of change; and geometry, concerned with spatial relationships. Mathematics is pursued to solve practical problems as well as to enhance its logical and often abstract nature. Consequently it is often categorized as *applied* and *pure*. The applied mathematician uses or develops mathematics as a tool, solving problems or relationships in other fields. Physicists and engineers often apply calculus to questions of motion, economists apply concepts of linear algebra to determine cost effective solutions, and statistics and probability are frequently used by psychologists. The scholar of pure mathematics investigates logical relationships of abstract quantities or objects. Questions of the completeness and consistency within given mathematical constructs are addressed in pure mathematics.
Major contributions in the development of western mathematics came from Egypt (3000-1600 B.C.), Babylonia (1700-300 B.C.), Greece (600-200 B.C.), and the Hindu and Arab world (600 B.C.-A.D. 1450). Major achievements before modern times have also occurred in China, Japan, and Incan and Aztec empires.

Mathewson, Christy (Christopher Mathewson; 1880-1925), U.S. baseball player. Mathewson, a right-handed pitcher for the New York Giants (1900-1916) and Cincinnati Reds (1916) is considered one of the best pitchers of all time and is credited with developing the screwball. His achievements include being the first pitcher of the 1900's to win 30 games or more for 3 consecutive seasons (1903-1905), 373 career wins, and winning 20 games or more for 12 consecutive seasons (1901-1914). Mathewson was among the first group of players inducted into the National Baseball Hall of Fame (1936). A victim of poison gas in World War I, he died of tuberculosis.

Matisse, Henri (1869-1954), French painter, sculptor, and lithographer. He is regarded, with Picasso, as one of the 2 most important artists of the 20th century. He was a

Henri Matisse's (1869-1954) *Flowering Ivy* (1941, Mrs. Albert D. Lasker collection, New York).

M

Matthew writing his Gospel, from the Évangiles de la Sainte Chapelle (ascribed to the master of the Registrum Gregorii, a school for miniatures at Trier), from approximately 1000 (Bibliothèque Nationale, Paris).

leader of the fauves and was noted for his brilliant, expressive use of color in such paintings as *The Green Line* (1905) and *Landscape at Callioure* (1905). Earlier he had explored impressionism, as in his painting *The Dinner Table* (1897). In his last years he created abstract compositions out of handpainted cut paper, a technique he called 'drawing with scissors'.
From 1948 to 1951 he designed and decorated the Dominican chapel at Vence, France.

Mato Grosso, 1. (pop. 2.2 million), state in Southwestern Brazil; 340,286 sq mi (881,001 sq km). Capital city: Cuiabá. In the north tropical rain forest; south of the central plateau savannas and swamp forest (near Paraguay). Forestry, cattle breeding and agriculture (corn, rice, sugarcane, beans and tobacco). Extraction of gold.
2. (pop. 1,928,000), Mato Grosso do Sul, state south of Mato Grosso (split since 1979) 135,399 sq mi (350,548 sq km). Capital city: Campo Grande.

Matriarchy, Society in which women as a group are in power. During the 19th century evolutionists like Johann J. Bachofen (1815-1887) stated that matriarchal societies preceded patriarchal societies in prehistoric times. This theory is not supported by cultural anthropology anymore. It is even questionable whether real matriarchies ever existed.

Matta (Echaurren), Roberto Sebastian Antonio (Roberto Sebastian Antonio; 1911-2002), Chilean-French painter; studied architecture with Le Corbusier in Paris, where he joined the surrealists in the 1930s. From 1939-1948 he stayed in the U.S. (influenced by Ernst and Duchamp). His mainly large paintings have epic features with imaginative shapes and demonic figures, and are full of references to contemporary problems.

Matter, material substance existing in space and time. All matter has inertia, measured quantitatively by its mass and weight, exerting its gravitational pull on other such bodies. There are 3 common states of matter: solid, liquid and gas; scientists consider plasma a fourth. Atoms and molecules make up ordinary matter.

Matterhorn, 14,691-ft (4,478-m) high mountain in the Alps on the Swiss-Italian frontier. It was first climbed by Edward Whymper in 1865.

Matthew, Saint, one of the twelve apostles, traditionally the author of the first gospel. His gospel, the fullest of the 4 gospels, was probably written for Jewish Christians. By its many Old Testament quotes it shows Jesus as the promised Messiah. His feast day is Sept. 12.
See also: Apostles.

Mattingly, Don (Donald Arthur Mattingly; 1961-), U.S. baseball player. As first baseman for the New York Yankees, American League (AL), he distinguished himself as a batter and fielder. He was named AL Most Valuable Player in 1985, and batted over .300 for 6 consecutive seasons (1984-1989). In 1991 Mattingly became the tenth captain in New York Yankees history.

Mauger, Ivan Gerald (1939-), New Zealand motorcycle racer, won the speedway world championships five times (1968-1970, 1972, 1977, 1979) as well as the European championships three times (1966, 1970, 1971). Drove in the English competition for e.g. Wimbledon, Newcastle and the Manchester Belle-Vue team. Mauger is an all-round racer and excels in grass and sand track races (in the last discipline he also won three world titles).

Maugham, W(illiam) Somerset (1874-1965), British author. A playwright, short story writer, and novelist, his writing frequently was characterized by irony and cynicism. Maugham's novels include the autobiographical *Of Human Bondage* (1915), *The Moon and Sixpence* (1919), and the satirical *Cakes and Ale* (1930).

Maui *See:* Hawaii.

Mauldin, Bill (1921-), U.S. cartoonist. His cartoons of World War II GIs, Willie and Joe, published in the armed forces newspaper *Stars and Stripes*, became the national embodiment of the American infantrymen. He won the Pulitzer Prize for cartooning in 1945 and 1959. *Up Front* (1945) and *Brass Ring* (1971) are 2 of his books of cartoons.
See also: Cartoon.

Mau Mau, terrorist organization in Kenya (chiefly the Kikuyu tribe) whose main aim was to expel the British. Organized as a secret society, the Mau Mau ran a campaign of murder and sabotage (1952-1960); after 1956 the British put an end to most of the bloodshed.

Mauna Kea, dormant volcano in Hawaii. At 13,796 ft (4,205 m) high, Mauna Kea ('white mountain') is the world's highest island mountain. At the top of its snow-covered summit are several astronomical observatories and large telescopes.

Mauna Loa, active volcano in the Hawaii Volcanoes National Park. The world's largest volcano, it erupts every 3.5 years. It is 13,680 ft (4,170 m) high. Kilauea volcano is on its southeastern side.

Maundy Thursday, the Thursday before Easter, commemorating Jesus's washing of his disciples' feet and institution of Holy Communion at the Last Supper.
See also: Holy Week.

Maupassant, Guy de *See:* De Maupassant, Guy.

Mauriac, François (1885-1970), French author. A nonconformist Catholic, his novels concern man's vulnerability to sin and evil. Winner of the 1952 Nobel Prize for literature, his works include *The Desert of Love* (1925), *Thérèse Desqueyroux* (1927), and *The Knot of Vipers* (1932).

Maurice of Nassau (1567-1625), Prince of Orange from 1618, Dutch statesman, and military leader. A son of William the Silent, he conducted a successful war against Spanish rule and was an architect of the emerging Dutch republic. He was virtual ruler of the Netherlands, executing his former ally Johan van Oldenbarneveldt in 1619 and establishing the supremacy of the house of Orange.
See also: Netherlands.

Mauritania

Capital:	Nouakchott
Area:	398,000 sq mi
	(1,030,700 sq km)
Population:	2,829,000
Language:	Arabic, French
Government:	Presidential republic
Independent:	1960
Head of gov.:	Prime minister
Per capita:	US$ 1.800
Monetary unit:	1 Ouguiya = 5 khoum

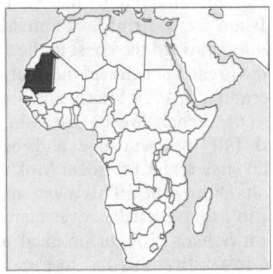

Mauritania, Islamic Republic of, former French colony in western Africa. Mauritania

Nomadic stock-breeding in Mauritania (until recently, at least two-thirds of the population were nomads) has suffered greatly from the drought that struck the Sahel in the early 1970s.

M

is some 398,000 sq mi (1,030,700 sq km) in area and is bordered by Morocco, Western Sahara and Algeria to the north, Mali and Senegal to the south, Mali to the east, and the Atlantic Ocean to the west.

Land and climate. Mauritania is principally a dry, rocky plateau averaging 500 ft (152 m) above sea level, a southern extension of the Sahara. There is a fertile grain growing district along the Senegal River in the south and cattle raising grasslands in the southeast. The climate is hot throughout the country, but rainfall varies considerably from less than 4 in (10 cm) annually in the north to about 24 in (61 cm) annually toward the south.

People. Some 80% of the population are Berbers or Moors and the remaining 20% are black Africans. About 50% of the people live in towns. The Berbers and Moors live a nomadic life principally in the north and the black Africans live in rural villages in the south. The capital is Nouakchott. The official languages are French and Arabic. Islam is the official religion.

Economy. There are large deposits of iron ore, gypsum, and copper, which account for about 80% of all exports. Fish and fish products are also important export products. Farmers in the south raise millet, sorghum, rice, and other cereals and vegetables while nomads raise sheep, goats, cattle, and camels. Recent droughts have dealt a serious blow to livestock.

History. In the 11th century, the Ghanaian Empire, to which most of Mauritania then belonged, was invaded by nomadic Berbers of the Almoravid group. In the 13th century South Mauritania fell to the Mali Empire and Islam was firmly established. The Portuguese probed the coast in the 15th century; the French penetrated the interior in the 19th century. In 1920 Mauritania became the colony of French West Africa. In 1960 it gained full independence and became a Muslim state under President Mokhtar Ould Daddah. During the 1970s a war against the Polisario Front guerrillas over claims to the Western Sahara brought political and economic instability, this led to a coup d'état and the ousting of Daddah. Mauritania relinquished its claim to the territory in 1979. In 1984, Lt. Col. Maaouya Ould Sid Ahmed Taya became Head of State. In the 1991 Gulf

War, Mauritania supported Iraq. As a result, relations with the U.S., France, and the Gulf states deteriorated and economic support of Mauritania was reduced or even terminated. In 1993 France and the Gulf states resumed their economic aid.

Mauritius

Capital:	Port Louis
Area:	788 sq mi (2,040 sq km)
Population:	1,200,000
Language:	English
Government:	Republic
Independent:	1968
Head of gov.:	Prime minister
Per capita:	US$ 10,800
Monetary unit:	1 Mauritian rupee = 100 cents

Mauritius, island republic 500 mi (805 km) east of Madagascar in the Indian Ocean, comprising the islands of Mauritius, Rodrigues, and associated archipelagos.

Land and climate. The main island, Mauritius, is surrounded by coral reefs. The island is principally a plateau and approximately 788 sq mi (2,040 sq km) in area. The climate is warm and humid with a cyclone season from Dec. to Mar.

People. More than 60% of the population consists of Indians, about 30% are Creole, a mixture of French and black African, and the remainder are principally Europeans, African, and Chinese. Religions reflect the diversity of the people and include the Hindu religion, Christianity, and Islam. The official language is English and the capital is Port Louis.

Economy. Sugar was the single most important export until the 1980s when it was surpassed by textile products. Tea and tobacco are also cash crops and tourism contributes to the economy as well. But with more than 1,000,000 inhabitants, overpopulation and unemployment are persistent problems for Mauritius.

History. Formerly uninhabited, Mauritius was settled by the Portuguese in the early 1500s but soon abandoned. After a period of Dutch occupation in the 17th century, the French settled the island in 1715, founded the sugar industry, and imported slaves from Africa to work the plantations. The British took Mauritius in 1810, during the

Napoleonic Wars and when they abolished slavery in the colonies in 1831, the planters resorted to indentured laborers from India. The British first initiated moves toward representative government for the colony in the late 19th century. In 1968 Mauritius became an independent nation within the British Commonwealth. In 1992 the country became a republic with Cassam Uteem as the first elected president. In 1995 Navin Ramgoolam was elected premier. Anerood Jugnauth, leader of the Socialist Militant Party, defeated him at the 2000 elections.

Maurois, André (Émile Herzog; 1885-1967), 20th-century French author. A soldier in World War I, his earliest works were novels about his war experiences, including *The Silence of Colonel Bramble* (1918) and *Les Discours du Docteur O'Grady* (1921). Maurois is known for his biographies of authors Percy Bysshe Shelley, Lord Byron, George Sand, Victor Hugo, and Alexandre Dumas and politicians George Washington, Benjamin Disraeli, and Chateaubriand. His *Memoirs: 1885-1967* was published posthumously in 1970.

Maurya Empire, Indian imperial dynasty, 325-183 B.C., founded by Chandragupta Maurya. Its capital was near modern Patna. Chandragupta Maurya's grandson Asoka (d. 232) brought almost the whole subcontinent under one rule and made Buddhism the state religion. Under Mauryan art, there was a flowering of the Indian Buddhist culture. *See also:* Asoka; Chandragupta, Maurya.

Mausoleum, a tomb, especially one that is large or elaborate. The name is derived from the marble tomb built for the Carian ruler Mausolus at Halicarnassus, Asia Minor (now Bodrum, Turkey). Begun before Mausolus' death in 353 B.C. construction of the Mausoleum was continued by his wife, Artemisia, but was not completed until after her death. It ranked as one of the Seven Wonders of the Ancient World.

The Mausoleum's height has been calculated at about 140 feet (43 m). Its massive rectangular base was surmounted by a colonnade of 36 Ionic columns. Above was a pyramid-shaped roof. At the apex were colossal figures of Mausolus and Artemisia in a four-horse chariot. In the 19th century, excavations were made at the site of Halicarnassus. Fragments of three friezes and other sculpture, including a statue of Mausolus, were taken to the British Museum.

Among other famous mausoleums are Hadrian's Tomb in Rome (now the Castel Sant' Angelo, a museum); Lenin's Tomb, Red Square, Moscow; the Taj Mahal, Agra, India; and Grant's Tomb, Riverside Drive, New York City.

Mauthausen, city near Linz, Austria; pop. 4400. In the concentrationcamp at Mauthausen (1938-1945) at least 120.000 prisoners from 20 different countries were murdered.

Maverick, Samuel Augustus (1803-1870), Texas politician and cattle rancher. He was a member of the convention that founded the

Republic of Texas (1836) and served as a member of the Texas Congress and its first state legislature. Owner of a large cattle ranch, Maverick did not brand his herd, and neighbors called his strays, 'mavericks'. The word came to mean all unmarked cattle. Today the term applies largely to politicians who have no distinct affiliations or party loyalties.

Maxim, U.S. family of inventors. **Sir Hiram Stevens Maxim** (1840-1916), invented (1854) the automatic, rapid-firing gun (Maxim machine gun) and tested a steam-powered aircraft (it successfully lifted off the ground). **Hudson Maxim** (1853-1927), Sir Hiram's brother, invented an explosive more powerful than dynamite, a smokeless powder, and a torpedo propellant. **Hiram Percy Maxim** (1869-1936), Sir Hiram's son, invented the gun silencer, designed an electric automobile, and helped develop mufflers for automobiles and jet engines.
See also: Explosive; Machine gun.

Maximilian, name of 2 Habsburg Holy Roman emperors. **Maximilian I** (1459-1519) reigned from 1493. He married, first, Mary of Burgundy (1477) and then Bianca, daughter of the Duke of Milan (1494). He arranged other family marriages that brought the Habsburgs much of Burgundy, the Netherlands, Hungary, Bohemia, and Spain. Maximilian I reorganized imperial administration and set up a supreme court of justice. However, he had to recognize Switzerland's independence (1499), and failed to hold Milan. His finances were severely strained by continual warfare in support of his ambitions. **Maximilian II** (1527-1576), emperor from 1564, was also king of Bohemia from 1549 and of Hungary from 1563. He was the son and successor of Ferdinand I. A humanist, he adopted a policy of religious toleration. Maximilian II arranged a truce with Turkey, according to which he would pay tribute to the sultan for his part of Hungary.
See also: Holy Roman Empire.

Maximilian I (1459-1519), who became Holy Roman Emperor in 1493.

Maximilian (1832-1867), emperor of Mexico from 1864 until his death. An Austrian archduke, he was given the throne by the French emperor Napoleon III, who hoped to extend his empire. Maximilian believed that the Mexicans would welcome him and attempted to rule liberally and benevolently, but found French troops essential against popular support for President Benito Juárez. After the troops withdrew (1866-1867), Maximilian was defeated by Juárez's forces and executed.

Maxwell, James Clerk (1831-1879), Scottish theoretical physicist. His most important work was in electricity, magnetism, and his kinetic theory of gases. He also studied color vision, elasticity, optics, Saturn's rings, and thermodynamics. *Maxwell's equations*, 4 linked differential equations, extend the work of Michael Faraday and others and completely define the classical theory of the electromagnetic field. Maxwell's most famous work was *Treatise on Electricity and Magnetism* (1873). Its main concepts are considered to be the basis for Albert Einstein's theory of relativity and the quantum theory.
See also: Electromagnetic waves.

Maxwell's rule, law stating that every part of an electric circuit is acted upon by a force tending to move it in such a direction as to enclose the maximum amount of magnetic flux.

May, Karl (1842-1912), German writer. May is especially well-known for his still popular Indian novels with the legendary main characters Old Shatterhand and Winnetou. These novels are among the most sold books in the world and have been translated into many languages. Some famous novels by Karl May are: *Im fernen Westen* (1880), *Der Bärenjäger* (1891), *Durch die Wüste* (In the Desert, 1892), *Winnetou* (3 volumes, 1893-1910), and *Der Schatz im Silbersee*, (The Treasure in the Silver Lake, 1894). The city of Bamberg has had a Karl May museum since 1862.

Mayakovski, Vladimir Vladimirovitch (1893-1930), Russian poet and playwright. Went to the academy for expressive art in Moscow in 1910; in 1912 he was one of the signers of the 'Futuristic manifesto', which forced him to leave the academy. He became one of the greatest Russian renewers of poetry, placing his art at the service of Communism after 1917. He played an important role in the literary organization 'Leftwing Art Front', which consisted mainly of radical futurists. Committed suicide in 1930 while in a depressive state of mind. His poetry includes *Man* (1917), *1.500.000* (1920); theatrical productions: *Mystery-bouffe* (1918), *The Bedbug* (1928), and *The Bathhouse* (1929), which exposed the bureaucracy of the Soviet Union.

May apple, or mayapple (*Podophyllum peltatum*), woodland plant native to eastern North America. Also known as mandrake, it produces white flowers between Apr. and June and edible yellow berries often used in jellies. A member of the barberry family,

may apple roots are used to manufacture types of herbal medicines.

Mayas, Middle American Indian confederation of Central America, covering the Yucatán peninsula, East Chiapas state in modern Mexico, most of Guatemala, and the western parts of El Salvador and Honduras. Its civilization was at its height A.D. 300-900. A farming people of the rain forests, the Mayas grew corn, cassava, cotton, beans, and sweet potatoes and kept bees for wax and honey. They had a hierarchy of priest-nobles under a hereditary chief. The Mayans developed an involved hieroglyphic form of writing, still undeciphered, and a knowledge of mathematics, astronomy, and chronology superior to that in contemporaneous Europe. The priests devised 2 calendars: a 365-day civil year and a sacred year of 260 days. Mayan art comprises fine sculpture, both in the round and in relief; painted frescoes and manuscripts; ceramics, and magnificent architecture, including the lofty stone pyramid topped by a temple. By 900 their main centers, such as Palenque, Peidras, and Copán, had been abandoned to the jungle for reasons unknown. A 'postclassical' tradition, under Toltec influence, sprang up in new centers, notably Chichén Itzá, but in the early 1500s the entire region came under Spanish rule.

May beetle *See:* June bug.

May Day, spring festival on May 1. Traces of its pagan origins survive in the decorated maypoles and May queens of England. Declared a socialist labor festival by the Second International in 1889, it is celebrated, particularly in communist countries, by parades and demonstrations.

Mayer, Julius Robert von (1814-1878), German physician and physicist who contributed (1842) to the formulation of the law of conservation of energy.
See also: Heat; Joule, James Prescott.

Russian futurist writer Vladimir Vladimirovitch Mayakovski (1893-1930) at a book fair in the Soviet Union, in 1929.

M

Mayflower, ship that carried the Pilgrims to America in 1620. It left Plymouth, England, on Sept. 21 and reached Provincetown, Mass., on Nov. 21. The Pilgrims settled what is now Plymouth, Mass., after signing the Mayflower Compact. The *Mayflower* a 2-

M

decker ship, probably 90 ft (27 m) long and about 180 tons (163 metric tons), has not survived, but an English-built replica, *Mayflower II*, sailed the Atlantic in 1957. It is now at Plymouth, Mass.

Mayfly, common insect (order Ephemeroptera) of ponds and rivers. The larvae live in the water and emerge to molt as subadults. The subadults immediately molt again into full adults. The adults have 3 fine 'tails' (as have the larvae), large transparent forewings, small or no hindwings, and weak legs. The mouthparts are also weak; adult mayflies do not feed during their short life, which may last no longer than an afternoon.

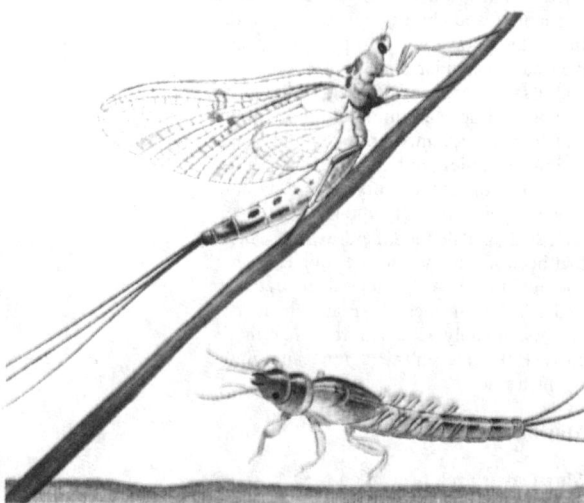

Mayflies, belonging to the insect order *Ephemeroptera*, have triangular shaped wings, held vertically over their backs when they are at rest. The immature form, or nymph, is aquatic. (*top*) The adult mayfly, *Ephemara danica*, of Europe, body length 0.47 in (12 mm); (*bottom*) Stream-living or underwater nymph.

Mayo Clinic, one of the world's largest medical centers. It was founded in 1889 at Rochester, Minn., as a voluntary association of physicians. It grew from an emergency hospital set up by Dr. William W. Mayo (1861-1939) to help cyclone victims. The Clinic treats about 175,000 patients a year and is financed by the Mayo Foundation.

Mays, Willie (1931-), U.S. baseball player. An outfielder for the New York (later, San Francisco) Giants (1951-1972), he hit 660 home runs in his career (third on the all time list) and was named the National League's most valuable player twice (1954, 1965). He was inducted into the National Baseball Hall of Fame in 1979.

Ma Yuan (c.1160-1225), Chinese Southern Sung period artist, who created some of China's greatest landscape paintings in ink. A contemporary of the painter Xia Gui (also spelled Hsia Kuei), Ma Yuan was noted for his spare and dramatically asymmetrical compositions. His romantic landsape style influenced the Japanese ink painters Shbun (early 15th century) and Sessh, and the ear-

View of Mbabane, the capital of Swaziland. There are still a number of the traditional round huts to be found in this otherwise fairly modern town.

ly masters of the Kan school during the Muromachi period (1338-1573).

Mayuzumi, Toshiro (1929-1997), Japanese composer. Mayuzumi, whose teachers included Tony Aubin in Paris, became the organizer of the group Ars Nova Japonica in 1957. In his work, in which he occasionally used serial and aleatory techniques, the electronic and concrete materials became more important from 1955 onwards. His most well-known works include *Nihon Sanka* (1972), a hymn about Japan for mixed choir and orchestra, and the opera *Kinkakuji* (1976), based on a work by Japanese writer Yukio Mishima.

Mazarin, Jules Cardinal (1602-1661), Italian-born French politician and cardinal. Born Giulio Mazarini, he strengthened the French monarchy and by successful diplomacy increased France's influence abroad. After the deaths of Cardinal Richelieu (1642) and Louis XIII (1643), he became the trusted chief minister of the regent, Anne of Austria, and educator of her son, the future Louis XIV. His policy of centralized power and his imposition of taxes provoked the revolts known as the Fronde of the Parlement (1648-1653), which he eventually crushed decisively. In foreign policy he gained favorable terms in the treaties that ended the Thirty Years War (1648) and the war with Spain (1659). He was patron of the arts.

Maze *See:* Labyrinth.

Mazepa, Ivan (1640?-1709), Cossack chief who vainly aided Charles XII of Sweden against Peter the Great, hoping to win independence for his native Ukraine. Byron's *Mazeppa* immortalizes a youthful incident in which he is said to have been tied to a wild horse by a jealous Polish nobleman.

Mazzini, Giuseppe (1805-1872), Italian patriot and a leading propagandist of the secret society, the Risorgimento, the nationalist involvement that achieved Italian unification. Exiled in 1831, he formed the Young Italy societies, and from France, Switzerland, and England promoted his ideal of a united, democratic Italy. In 1849 he became a leader of the short-lived republic of Rome, but was soon in exile again, continuing his revolutionary propaganda and organizing abortive uprisings. The actual unification of Italy, in which he took little part, fell short of his popular republican ideals.

Mbabane (pop. 52,000), town, administrative capital of Swaziland. Founded as a mining camp in a mountainous region of the former British colony, Mbabane is the center of a prosperous tin mining and agricultural region. Most of the city's residents are Swazi, a Bantu-speaking people of southern Africa, but English is also widely spoken there.

Mbeki, Thabo Mvuyelwa (1942-), South African politician, former resistance leader and President (1999-). Mbeki became a member of the African National Congress's youth department at the age of 14. Shortly afterwards he became youth leader. In 1962, the ANC asked Mbeki to leave South Africa and he found political asylum in Tanzania. He became a member of the ANC administration in 1975. After the ANC was legalized (in 1990), he was ANC's negotiator with the De-Klerk-government. In 1994, he became the first Vice President of Mandela's government. After the ANC won the 1999 elections, he became President. He shocked the entire world when he played down the causes and effects of AIDS. He did not allow AIDS medication until 2002.
See also: African National Congress; Mandela, Nelson.

Mboya, Tom (1930-1969), Kenyan political leader. General secretary of the Kenya Federation of Labor (1953-1963) and a member of the colonial legislative assembly (1957), he played a key role in securing Kenya's independence. Economics minister from 1964, he was established as a likely successor to Jomo Kenyatta. His assassination (1969) led to rioting and political tension.

McAdam, John Loudon (1756-1836), British engineer and surveyor. He developed a method of paving roads using layers of crushed stone, that revolutionized road building throughout the world. Macadamized roads built in the early 1800s lasted until the 20th century and were the forerunners of many highways still in use today.

McCarthy, Joseph Raymond (1908-1957), U.S. Republican senator from Wisconsin (1947-1957). The 'McCarthy era' was born in the early 1950s as a result of his sensational investigations into alleged communist subversion of U.S. life. These investigations were first made (1950) in federal departments, then in the army and among prominent civilians. *McCarthyism* became a word

A photograph of Joe McCarthy from 1950, at the beginning of his tempestuous career.

for charges made without proof and accompanied by publicity. After the Army focused national publicity on his activities during the McCarthy hearings (1954), McCarthy was formally censured by fellow senators, and his influence steadily diminished.

McCarthy, Mary (1912-1989), U.S. writer, best known for her satirical novel *The Group* (1963), about the lives of a generation of Vassar graduates. Her nonfiction works include *Memories of a Catholic Girlhood* (1957), *Vietnam* (1967), and a body of outstanding literary criticism.

McCarthyism, political movement named after Republican Senator Joseph R. McCarthy of Wisconsin that investigated suspected Communist activities in the United States in the early 1950s. Fearing a Communist takeover of the U.S. government, McCarthy conducted public investigations of suspected officials (and civilians). None of his suspicions were substantiated. He was 'condemned' by the Senate in 1954, after having ruined many lives and careers. In contemporary terminology, McCarthyism denotes accusations of disloyalty to the United States or subversive activities based on insufficient evidence.

McCartney, (James) Paul (1942-   ), English singer, guitarist, and songwriter, member of the Beatles (1959-1970). Most of the Beatles' songs were sung and written by McCartney and John Lennon. McCartney's contributions were predominantly ballads, including 'Yesterday' (1965), 'Hey Jude' (1969), and 'Let It Be' (1970). McCartney and his wife, Linda Eastman McCartney (1942-1998), subsequently formed and performed with the rock band Wings (1971-1981), recording such albums as *Band on the Run* (1973). His more recent solo albums include *Tug of War* (1982), *Flaming Pie* (1996), and *Driving Rain* (2001). In 1997 McCartney received a knighthood.
See also: Beatles.

McClintock, Barbara (1902-1992), U.S. geneticist. She won the 1983 Nobel Prize in physiology or medicine for her discovery in the 1940s of the mobility within the chromosome of genetic elements that had been believed to be stationary. McClintock found that certain genetic material is transferred unpredictably from generation to generation, and offered a means of understanding cell differentiation. Her work, considered a great contribution to DNA research, led to greater understanding of some human and animal diseases.
See also: Genetics.

McCloskey, John Cardinal (1810-1885), U.S. Roman Catholic prelate. He became archbishop of New York (1864) and was created the first U.S. cardinal (1875). He was responsible for the completion of St. Patrick's Cathedral in New York City.

McClure, Sir Robert John Le Mesurier (1807-1873), English arctic explorer and naval officer. On a search (1850-1853) in the Arctic Archipelago for Sir John Franklin, he discovered McClure Strait and became the first to prove the existence of the Northwest Passage.
See also: Northwest Passage.

McCollum, Elmer Verner (1879-1967), U.S. biochemist and professor. While teaching at the Univ. of Wisconsin, he pioneered the study of nutrition and was responsible for assigning letters of the alphabet to the individual vitamins (1915). He also studied the role of other minerals in the diet and the effects of Vitamin D. His published works include *The Newer Knowledge of Nutrition* (1918) and *Foods, Nutrition and Health* (1933).
See also: Biochemistry; Vitamin.

McCormack, John (1884-1945), Irish-American tenor. He began his operatic career in London, first appearing in the U.S. in 1909. He gained his greatest popularity as a concert singer.
See also: Opera.

McCormick, Cyrus Hall (1809-1884), U.S. inventor and industrialist. He invented (1831) an early mechanical reaper (patented 1934) that contained innovations used commonly in harvesting machines. The first models appeared under license from 1841 onward.
See also: Reaper.

McCrae, John (1872-1918), Canadian physician and poet of World War I, famous for his poem 'In Flanders Fields,' which was written under fire. It was first published in the magazine *Punch* in Dec. 1915.

McCullers, Carson (1917-1967), U.S. writer. She is best known for her novels portraying small-town life in the South, and particularly for her lonely, isolated characters, as in *The Heart Is a Lonely Hunter* (1940) and *Member of the Wedding* (1946; adapted by McCullers as a play, 1950). Her *Collected Stories* were published posthumously (1987).

McEnroe, John (1959-), U.S. tennis player. Known for his powerful serve and speed, he won 4 U.S. Open singles titles (1979-1981, 1984) and 3 Wimbledon singles titles (1981, 1983-1984).

McEwan, Ian (1948-), British writer who, after receiving his university degree, caused furor with two collections of stories: *First Love, Last Rites* (1975) and *In Between the Sheets* (1977). The frankness about sexual matters and other bodily functions, about perversion and obsessions, fascinated many readers and shocked others.
Other works include *The Cement Garden* (1978), *The Comfort of Strangers* (1981; filmed by Paul Schrader in 1990), *Amsterdam* (1998), and *Atonement* (2001). McEwan also wrote TV and movie scripts.

McGraw, John Joseph (1873-1934), U.S. professional baseball player and manager. A star third baseman for the American League's Baltimore Orioles, he became manager of the team in 1901. He then managed the New York Giants (1902-1932), who won 10 league championships and 3 World Series.

McGuffey, William Holmes (1800-1873), U.S. educator and clergyman. His series of 6 *Eclectic Readers* (1836-1857) sold an estimated 122 million copies. Almost universally used in elementary schools in the Midwest and South, they had an immense influence on public education. McGuffey was also president of Ohio Univ. (1839-1845).

McKinley, William (1843-1901), 25th president of the United States (1897-1901). Republican and protectionist. In his administration's early years, McKinley had to cope with the nation's economic problems. By 1898, however, the depression that had lasted for five years was ending. As the severe economic and social problems of the 1880s and 1890s subsided, U.S. attention turned outward and foreign-affairs problems took center stage. Spanish outrages during a Cuban insurrection that had begun in 1895 aroused indignation in the U.S. war hysteria grew after the battleship U.S.S. *Maine* was blown up in Havana's harbor on Feb. 15,

M

U.S. tennis star John McEnroe.

M

Margaret Mead (1901-1978), the well-known American cultural anthropologist.

1898. McKinley hoped to avoid war, but eventually yielded to public opinion and that of many Congress members and other high officials by asking Congress to authorize U.S. intervention in Cuba. On Apr. 24, two days after Congress authorized a U.S. blockade of Spanish ports, Spain declared war on the U.S.

The Spanish-American War, which lasted only 113 days, brought the U.S. into the arena of international politics and made it an imperial power. During the war, the U.S. annexed Hawaii; the following year, the U.S. demanded equal trade opportunities with China.

The war had brought on a period of booming prosperity, helping McKinley and running mate Theodore Roosevelt, who promised 'a full dinner bucket' for four more years, to win the 1900 election. McKinley was shot by anarchist Leon Czolgosz in Buffalo.

McKuen, Rod (1933-   ), U.S. poet and songwriter. His poetry collections include *Lonesome Cities* (1968) and *In Someone's Shadow* (1969). He has performed and recorded many of his own songs, and has also written film scores.

McLuhan, Marshall (1911-1980), Canadian professor of humanities and mass communications specialist. He is best known for his influential *Understanding Media* (1964). It contains the famous phrase, 'the medium is the message'-that is, the content of communication is determined by its means, with the implication that modern mass communications technology is creating a 'global village' and transforming our way of thinking and perceiving.
See also: Communication.

M'Clure, Sir Robert John Le Mesurier *See:* McClure, Sir Robert John Le Mesurier.

McNamara, Robert Strange (1916-   ), secretary of defense under presidents Kennedy and Johnson (1961-1968), who played an important part in the shaping of U.S. defense policy, including Vietnam War policy. Before this he had been president of the Ford Motor Company, and in 1968 he became president of the World Bank, serving until

1981. In his book *In Retrospect. The Tragedy and Lessons of Vietnam* (1995), he admits that America has made mistakes concerning the war in Vietnam.

McPherson, Aimee Semple (1890-1944), U.S. evangelist, famed for her flamboyant preaching. She worked as a missionary in China, then returned to the United States to become an itinerant preacher and faith-healer. She opened the Angelus Temple (1923) and founded the International Church of Foursquare Gospel (1927), both in Los Angeles. She was involved in numerous legal actions, including a sensational one for fraud, of which she was acquitted.

Mead, Margaret (1901-1978), U.S. cultural anthropologist known for *Coming of Age in Samoa* (1928), *Growing Up in New Guinea* (1930), *the Mountain Arapesh* (3 vols., 1938-1949), and *Male and Female* (1949), among other works. Her autobiography, *Blackberry Winter*, appeared in 1972. She was adjunct professor of anthropology at Columbia Univ. after 1954, and was associated with New York's American Museum of Natural History from 1926 until her death.
See also: Anthropology.

Meadowlark, common North American field bird of the family Icteridae, with a distinctive black V on its yellow underside. It is a relative of the blackbird and oriole. Also called a meadow starling, the meadowlark eats insects rather than grain and builds its nest on the ground. The eastern meadowlark, known for its whistling song, lives in moister areas than the western meadowlark.

The eastern meadowlark.

Meany, George (1894-1980), U.S. labor leader, president (1955-1979) of the American Federation of Labor and Congress of Industrial Organizations (AFL-CIO). He was president of the New York State Federation of Labor (1934) and secretary-treasurer (1939) and president (1952) of the AFL.
See also: Labor movement.

Measles, common infectious disease usually seen in children and caused by a virus. It involves a characteristic sequence of fever, headache, and malaise, followed by conjunctivitis and rhinitis, and the development of a typical rash, with blotchy erythema (redness) affecting the skin of the face, trunk, and limbs. Complications can include

pneumonia and encephalitis. Vaccination confers temporary immunity; one attack confers lifelong immunity.

Measuring worm, also known as inchworm or looper, hairless caterpillar, moth larvae found on every continent. Measuring worms move by extending their front end and holding on with their legs, then bringing up the rest of the body in a loop so that the rear end practically meets the front end. They move in this way because they have only 2 or 3 (rather than the usual 5) pairs of leglike structures on the back part of their bodies. Many measuring worms are difficult to detect when not moving, as they often resemble twigs and rest in twiglike positions.

Meat packing, industry that involves the butchering and processing of meat-producing animals for human consumption. Meat packing companies purchase large herds of cattle, sheep, and hogs from ranchers and farmers or from terminal markets. In the packing plants, the animals are slaughtered and cut up into their edible sections (dressed). The meat is treated to preserve freshness, frozen to keep it from being spoiled by bacteria, and shipped to consumer markets.

Mecca (Arabic: *Makka*; pop. 689,000), is the chief city of the Hejaz region of Saudi Arabia. It is the birthplace of the prophet Muhammad, the founder of Islam, and the most holy city of Islam. Only Muslims may enter the city. The courtyard of the great Haram mosque encloses the sacred shrine, the Kaaba, which Muslims face when they pray; nearby is the holy Zem-Zem well. Pilgrimage to Mecca, 'haji,' is a duty of all Muslims able to perform it; each year over a million pilgrims arrive. The economy of Mecca depends on the pilgrims.
See also: Islam; Saudi Arabia.

Mechanical engineering *See:* Engineering.

Mechanics, branch of applied mathematics that deals with the effects of forces on solids, liquids, and gases at rest or in motion. Dynamics studies the way in which forces produce motion; statics addresses the forces acting on a motionless body; kinematics deals with relationships among distance, time, velocity, and acceleration. Solid mechanics examines the motions of rigid bodies and deformable solid bodies and the causative forces. Continuum mechanics addresses deformable bodies, such as gases, liquids, and deformable solids.
See also: Aerodynamics; Hydraulics.

Mecklenburg, German state, renamed Mecklenburg-Western Pomerania upon Germany's reunification (1990). Primarily a farming region along Germany's Baltic coastal plain, Mecklenburg was ruled by powerful German princes and kings throughout the Middle Ages. It was divided many times into separate states, following wars during the 17th through the 19th centuries, and powerful landowners (Junkers) controlled vast estates from the mid-18th century through the end of World War II. Captured by the Communist army in 1945,

Mecklenburg was an East German state until 1952, when it was divided into 3 districts; Rostock, Schwerin and Neubrandenburg. In 1990, with the exception of Kreise Prenzlau, Templin and Perleberg, it was reunified as one German state.
See also: Germany.

Medal *See:* Decorations, medals, and orders.

Medan (pop. 1,942,000), Indonesia, a city on the island of Sumatra, and the capital of North Sumatra province. Railways lead to the oil fields of Sumatra's northeastern coast and to the port of Belawan. Rubber and tobacco are exported. The University of North Sumatra is here.

Medawar, Sir Peter Brian (1915-1987), Brazilian-born British zoologist who shared with Sir Macfarlane Burnet the 1960 Nobel Prize for physiology or medicine for their work on immunological tolerance. Inspired by Burnet's ideas, Medawar showed that if fetal mice were injected with cells from eventual donors, skin grafts made onto them later from those donors would 'take,' thus showing the possibility of acquired tolerance and hence, ultimately, organ transplants.
See also: Zoology.

Medea, in Greek mythology, sorceress and princess of Colchis. Through her magical powers she helped Jason obtain the Golden Fleece in Colchis where she was the daughter of King Aites. Returning with Jason to the Greek city of Iolkos where he claimed the throne, Medea conspired to kill King Pelias who had seized the throne from Jason's father. When Jason tried to divorce her, Medea had his bride-to-be killed and after plotting to kill the oldest son of the king of Athens, she was banished.
See also: Mythology.

Medellín (pop. 3,000,000), city in west-central Colombia. Medellín is the capital of Antioquia department and the hub of a rich mining and agricultural region. It was founded in 1675 near several gold mines and later became a textile, manufacturing, and coffee-processing center. Medellín also houses 3 universities and is a major educational center.

Medfly *See:* Mediterranean fruit fly.

Media, homeland of a nomadic people, the Medes, it was located in what is now northern Iran. Its history has been traced back to 836 B.C., when the Assyrians, under King Shalmaneser III, invaded Media in the first of many invasions. The Medes reached their peak under Cyaxares, who reigned from 625 to 585 B.C. His son, Astyages, the last Median king, was defeated by Cyrus the Great of Persia about 550 B.C. Media became a part of the Persian Empire.

Media, the plural form of 'medium.' The term is used to apply to communication systems, such as books, newspapers, radio, and television.
See also: Newspaper; Radio; Television.

Medici, Italian family of bankers, princes, and patrons of the arts who controlled Florence almost continually from the 1420s to 1737 and provided cardinals, popes (Leo X, Clement VII, and Leo XI), and 2 queens of France. The foundations of the family's power were laid by **Giovanni di Bicci de'Medici** (1360-1429), who achieved wealth through banking and commerce. His elder son, **Cosimo de'Medici** (1389-1464), was effectively ruler of Florence from 1434 and was voted 'Father of the Country' after his death. He founded the great Laurentian Library and patronized artists including Donatello and Lorenzo Ghiberti. His grandson **Lorenzo** (1449-1492), called 'the Magnificent,' was Italy's most brilliant Renaissance prince. Himself a fine poet, he patronized Sandro Botticelli, Domenico Ghirlandaio, the young Michelangelo, and many other artists. Lorenzo helped make Florence a powerful and beautiful Italian state, and took over the state government. His son **Pietro** (1471-1503) was expelled from Florence (1494) by a popular rising led by Girolamo Savonarola. The family was restored in 1512; Pietro's son **Lorenzo** (1492-1519) ruled from 1513 under the guidance of his uncle **Giovanni** (1475-1521), who was Pope Leo X and a bountiful patron of the arts in Rome. The ruthless **Cosimo I** (1519-1574) doubled Florentine territory and power and was made grand duke of Tuscany in 1569. **Catherine de Médicis** (1519-1589) was the wife of Henry II and mother of 3 French kings. She virtually ruled France from 1559. **Marie de Médicis** (1573-1642), the wife of Henry IV, reigned after his death (1610) until her son, Louis XIII, became king. The later Medicis were less distinguished; the line died out with Gian Gastone (1671-1737).
See also: Catherine de' Medici; Clement VII; Leo.

Medicine, the art and science of treating disease. Within the last 150 years medicine has become dominated by scientific principles. Prior to this, healing was mainly a matter of tradition and magic. The Greeks introduced anatomy and physiology and provided the Hippocratic oath, in use today. In the 17th century, William Harvey researched blood circulation and the heart; in the 18th century, Edward Jenner introduced vaccination; in the 19th century, Louis Pasteur proposed the germ theory and anesthesia made advances in surgery possible. Medicine in the 20th century uses new diagnostic techniques (x-rays, CAT scans, MRIs), organ transplants, a better understanding of nutrition and immunity, and new drugs, especially antibiotics.

Medicine, patent *See:* Patent medicine.

Medieval period *See:* Middle Ages.

Medina (pop. 600,000), holy Muslim city and place of pilgrimage in Hejaz, Saudi Arabia, 210 mi (338 km) north of Mecca. The prophet Muhammad came to Medina after his *hegira* (flight) from Mecca (A.D. 622), and the chief mosque contains his tomb. A walled city, Medina stands in a fertile oasis noted for its dates, grains, and vegetables.
See also: Muslims; Saudi Arabia.

Mediterranean fruit fly, or Medfly (*Ceratitis capitata*), pest of fruit in Africa, Australia, and the United States, attacking, in particular, peaches, apricots, and citrus fruits. The larvae destroy the fruits, and whole harvests may be lost. The maggots are capable of prodigious leaps of about 4 in (10 cm) high and over distances of 8 in (20 cm).

Mediterranean Sea, intercontinental sea between Europe, Asia, and Africa (over 965,000 sq mi-2,500,000 sq km). It opens into the Atlantic Ocean in the west through the Strait of Gibraltar, and into the Black Sea through the Dardanelles and Bosporus. The Suez Canal provides the Mediterranean Sea's link with the Red Sea and on to the Indian Ocean. Peninsular Italy, Sicily, Malta, and Pantelleria and Tunisia's Cape Bon mark the dividing narrows between the eastern and western basins. The many islands of the western basin include Sicily, Sardinia, Elba, Corsica and the Balearics. Crete, Cyprus, Rhodes, and the numerous Aegean islands are included in the eastern basin. Geologically the Mediterranean Sea is a relic of a sea that separated Eurasia from Africa about 200 million years ago, and was partially uplifted to form the Alps, South Europe, and the Atlas Mountains. The name (Latin, 'middle [of the] land'), reflects the sea's central position and importance in the ancient world. Limited access from the

This plant from a sixth-century manuscript, based upon the works of Dioscorides (1st century AD), can be clearly recognized by present-day biologists as the scarlet pimpernel (*Anagallis arvensis arvensis*), despite the fact that the little flowers are drawn as four-parted, instead of five-parted.

M

M

A picturesque view of the blue Mediterranean Sea near Monaco. Since the beginning of the 1970s, however, industrial wastes and mass tourism have begun to threaten nature in this country.

Atlantic Ocean and confined entries to both the Black and Red seas have given the Mediterranean Sea great strategic importance throughout history.

Medusa, in Greek mythology one of three equally hideous-looking sisters (Gorgons). She and her sisters, Stheno and Euryale, had snakes growing from their heads in place of hair and fangs for teeth. Anyone looking directly at them turned to stone but Perseus slew Medusa by looking at a reflection of her as he cut off her head. Later he gave the head to Athena.
See also: Mythology.

Medusa *See:* Jellyfish.

Medvedev, Roy Aleksandrovitch (1925-), Soviet-Russian historian and dissident writer. Between 1962 and 1968 he wrote the *K sudu istorii* (Let History Judge: the Origins and Consequences of Stalinism), an analysis of Stalinism unofficially published in the SU. In 1970 he argued in an open letter to Brezhnev together with Sakharov and Turchin for reformation and democratization of the political system. In the SU his work was only circulated in samizdat form (underground). Publications in the West include *The October Revolution* (1979), *On Stalin and Stalinism* (1979), and *All Stalin's Men, China and Superpowers* (1986).

Meerkat, or suricate (*Suricata suricatta*), small, insect-eating mammal of the family Herpestidae, native to dry regions of southern Africa. The meerkat's slim body and long tail measure about 20 in (51 cm) long, and it weighs about 2 lb (900 gm). It has silvery brown fur with dark markings. Its sturdy hind legs allow it to stand upright to search for predatory birds. Meerkats live in burrows in colonies of up to 30 animals. The name 'meerkat' is also sometimes applied to various mongooses.

Meerut conspiracy, alleged conspiracy of Indian communist union leaders against the state. The lengthy trial (1929-1933) was an attempt by the government to break the influence of the Communists on the Indian workers, but thanks to this trial the Communists' esteem and popularity increased.

Megalith, a monument made of huge, roughly hewn stone slabs erected by Stone Age or Bronze Age people. An individual stone slab that is part of a monument is also called a megalith. Megalithic monuments are found in many parts of the world, but the largest number are found in western Europe. A single, tall stone in an upright position is known as a *menhir*. A row of menhirs is called an *alignment*, or *avenue*. A circle of menhirs is sometimes called a *stone circle*, or *cromlech*. Standing stones capped by a flat stone form a *dolmen*. Many ancient *barrows* (burial chambers) are dolmens covered with earth.
Wiltshire, in southern England, contains many megalithic structures, the most notable of which is Stonehenge, near Salisbury. A 281/2 acre (11.5-hectare) site at Avebury has several stone circles and alignments of menhirs. Stones arranged to form a giant cross with a center circle stand at Callanish, on Lewis Island of the Outer Hebrides. At Carnac, on the Brittany coast of France, are long alignments of more than 2,000 menhirs. Ireland and Corsica also have notable megalithic remains.

Megawati Sukarnoputri (1947-   ), Indonesian politician and President (2001-). In 1987, Megawati obtained a seat in Parliament on behalf of the Partai Demokrasi Indonesia (PDI). In 1993, she was elected Chairwoman of the PDI, one of the two legal 'opposition parties' in Indonesia. She enjoyed increasing popularity amongst the Indonesian population, which resulted in her being a potential political competitor of President Suharto. In 1996, the ruling authorities deposed her as leader of the PDI and replaced her with Suryadi, leader of the pro-Suharto fraction within the PDI. This led to the worst riots in Jakarta in twenty years, during which many people were injured. That same year, Suharto was forced to resign and Vice President Habibie took over control. Megawati was re-elected as Chairwoman of the PDI in 1998. In the 1999 elections, Abdurrahman Wahid, leader of the National Awakening Party (Partai Kebangkitan Bangsa - PKB), was elected President and Megawati was appointed Vice President. In 2001, Wahid was deposed by the People's Congress and Megawati succeeded him as President.
See also: Suharto; Habibie, Bacharuddin Jusuf; Indonesia.

Mehmed II (Ottoman Empire) (also spelled Mohammed, Muhammad, Mehemet, Mehmet, and Mahomet; 1430?-1481) 'the conqueror', ruled 1451-1481. In 1453 he captured Constantinople, ending the Byzan-tine Empire after more than 1,000 years of existence. Mohammed made the conquered city his capital. He brought most of the Balkans under his rule by conquering Serbia, Bosnia, and Albania. Mehmet was a generous patron of scholarship and the arts.

Mehmed III (Ottoman Empire) (1566-1603; reigned 1595-1603) Sultan of the Ottoman Empire, succeeded his father Murad III. He was a sovereign with little power, whose politics were completely controlled by his mother. He was succeeded by Ahmed I.

Megawati Sukarnoputri

Mehmed IV (Ottoman Empire) (1642-1693; reigned 1648-1687) Sultan of the Ottoman Empire, successor of Ibrahim I. His siege of Vienna (1683) failed. He was deposed by the Janissaries and succeeded by Solyman II.

Mehmed V (Ottoman Empire) (1844-1918; reigned 1909-1918) Sultan of the Ottoman Empire, successor of Abdul Hamid II, who was deposed by the Young Turks. He was succeeded by Mehmed VI.

Mehmed VI (Ottoman Empire) (1861-1926), ruled 1918-1922. He succeeded his brother Mehmed V, and was the last Ottoman emperor. He cooperated with the Allies in imposing the harsh treaty of Sèvres (1920) on the defeated Turks. A nationalist movement under Mustafa Kemal (later called Kemal Atatürk) gained control in 1922 and Mehmed VI was deposed. He died in exile.

Mehta, Zubin (1936-), Indian-born U.S. conductor who studied at the Vienna Academy of Music and later became musical director of the Montreal Symphony (1961-1967), Los Angeles Philharmonic (1962-1978), and New York Philharmonic (1978-1991).

Meiji (1852-1912), emperor of Japan (1867-1912); his given name was Mutsuhito. The long isolation of Japan under the shoguns ended in 1868 with the restoration of imperial power. Meiji guided the transformation of Japan from a feudal empire into a modern industrial nation with a central administration. The court was moved from Kyoto to Tokyo.

Meiji restoration, Name for the period (1868-1912) starting with the capitulation of the troops of the shogun, when emperor Matsuhito began to reign, until his death. Matsuhito used the name 'meiji' (enlightened rule) as a title. In reality he had little power and was used to legitimize the reformations that were implemented at ministerial offices by a number of samurai (military). By merging all the militias into the imperial army and imitating Western culture in every respect, they succeeded in making the country into a world power and protecting it from European imperialism. During this period Japan defeated China (1894-1895) and Russia (1904-1905), thereby conquering the

Ryukyu Islands, Korea, Manchuria and South Sakhalin and obtaining Formosa and the Pescadores Islands.

Mein Kampf (German, 'My Struggle'), Adolf Hitler's book detailing his life and beliefs, published in 2 volumes (1925, 1927; English trans., 1933, 1939). The book, which advocates Germany's conquest of the world and expresses Hitler's views on the superiority of the German 'master race' and the inferiority and evil of Jews, became the Nazi manifesto.
See also: Hitler, Adolf; Nazism.

Meir, Golda (1898-1978), Israeli leader, prime minister of Israel (1969-1974). Born Golda Mabovitch in Kiev, USSR, she was raised in the United States and emigrated to Palestine in 1921. She was a prominent figure in the establishment of the State of Israel (1948). Elected to the Knesset (parliament) in 1949, Meir became foreign minister in 1956; in 1966 she was elected general secretary of the dominant Mapai party, later the Israel Labor Party (1968). In 1969 she succeeded Levi Eshkol as premier and formed a broad coalition government. During her time in office the Israelis fought off a 1973 Syrian-Egyptian surprise attack (the Yom Kippur War). In 1974 she resigned because of criticism of her lack of preparedness for that war.
See also: Israel.

Meitner, Lise (1878-1968), Austrian physicist who worked with Otto Hahn to discover protactinium (1917). Following the experiments of German physical chemists Hahn and Fritz Strassmann in bombarding uranium with neutrons, Meitner and her nephew, Otto Robert Frish (1904-), correctly interpreted the results as showing nuclear fission and predicted the chain reaction. This work contributed to the development of the atomic bomb and other uses of nuclear energy. Lise Meitner was the first woman to receive the Fermi-award (1965).
See also: Nuclear energy; Physics.

Mekong River, one of the chief rivers of the southeastern region of Asia, rising in the Tibetan highlands. It flows 2,600 mi (4,180 km) southward through the Yunnan province of China and Laos, along the Thailand border, and through Cambodia to its wide fertile delta in southern Vietnam, on the South China Sea. The lower 340 mi (547 km) can

accommodate medium-sized vessels. Phnom-Penh is an important port. The Mekong River's lower valley produces much of the world's rice.

Melaka (pop. 88,100), Malaysian port city. Located on the strategic Strait of Malacca, Melaka (formerly Malacca) is the capital of the state of the same name. In the 15th century, it was one of the most important ports in Southeast Asia and was captured by Portugal (1511), the Netherlands (1641), and Great Britain (1795). Melaka remained in British hands until Malaysia was granted independence (1957) as the Federation of Malaya.
See also: Malaysia.

Melanchthon, Philipp (1497-1560), German scholar and humanist, second to Luther in initiating and leading the Protestant Reformation in Germany. His *Loci communes rerum theologicarum* (1521), a systematic statement of Lutheran beliefs, was the first great Protestant work on religious doctrine; and his *Augsburg Confession* (1530) was one of the principal statements of faith in the Lutheran Church.
See also: Reformation.

Melanesia *See:* Pacific Islands.

Melanin *See:* Skin.

Melbourne (pop. 3.2 million), second-largest city in Australia and capital of Victoria, on the Yarra River. Founded by settlers in 1835 and named (1837) in honor of the British prime minister Lord Melbourne, the city is now one of the nation's chief ports; it ranks with Sydney as a major industrial center. Manufactures include textiles, leather goods, ships, automobiles, and aircraft; oil refineries also have been built. Melbourne was the seat of the Australian federal government (1901-1927).
See also: Australia.

Melodrama, originally a term used to refer to a passage in opera spoken over an orchestral accompaniment but more usually used to describe the sentimental drama of the 19th century in which characters were either good or bad. Melodramas were often based on romantic novels or bloodthirsty crimes. Thrills and narrow escapes played an important part in the plot.

Melon, fruit of *Cucumis melo*, a plant of the gourd family that grows wild in Africa and Asia. It is now widely cultivated in the United States, where the climate is hot and dry. The 2 main kinds of melon are the *watermelon* and the *muskmelon*, which includes *honeydews*, *casabas*, and *Persian melons*. The *cantaloupe* spoils rapidly, whereas the others will last for months, becoming softer as they ripen. The *tsamma melon*, a watermelon, supplies vital water to the Bush people of the Kalahari Desert. The round melons can grow to 1 ft (30 cm) across and vary in color.

Melos *See:* Mílos.

Meltdown *See:* Nuclear reactor.

During the Meiji period, Japan experienced modernization at a fast pace. In 1872, Meiji inaugurated the first Japanese railway, from Tokyo to Yokohama.

M

M

Melville, Herman (1819-1891), U.S. writer. His reputation rests mainly on the masterpiece *Moby-Dick* (1851), and the short novel *Billy Budd, Foretopman*, published posthumously (1924). Melville's whaling and other voyages provided material for several of his earlier, popular books. *Typee* (1846), his first, was based on his adventures and capture by cannibals after jumping ship in the Marquesas islands. *Moby-Dick*, a deeply symbolic work, combines allegory with adventure. Too profound and complex for its audience, this great novel was not successful; subsequent books did not recapture Melville's former popularity. Only in the 1930s did his talent receive full recognition.

Melville Island, Canadian island in the Arctic Ocean. Covering an area of 16,369 sq mi (42,396 sq km), Melville Island is one of the Parry Islands, discovered in 1819 by the British explorer Sir William Parry. The straits and seas surrounding the island are frozen most of the year; herds of musk-oxen inhabit the island, which is without human habitation.

Memel *See:* Klaipeda.

Memling, Hans (1430-1494), Flemish painter famous for his portraits and religious works, including the paneled *Shrine of St. Ursula* (1489). The German-born Memling (or Memlinc) worked in Bruges, Belgium, and was probably a pupil of Rogier van der Weyden.

The devotional paintings of Hans Memling, exemplified by this diptych panel (1487) of the Virgin and Child, are characterized by meticulous attention to realistic detail, subtle lightning, and balanced and unified composition (Musée Memling, Bruges, Belgium).

Memorial Day, or Decoration Day, U.S. holiday honoring the dead of all wars, observed on the last Mon. in May. Memorial Day originated in the South after the Civil War when the graves of both Confederate and Union soldiers were decorated.

Memphis, capital of the Old Kingdom of ancient Egypt until c.2200 B.C. Probably founded (c.3100 B.C.) by Menes, the first king of a united Upper and Lower Egypt, the city stood on the West bank of the Nile, about 15 mi (24 km) south of modern Cairo. Excavations have revealed the temple of Ptah, god of the city, and the 2 massive statues of Ramses II; cemeteries and pyramids also remain.

Memphis (pop. 650,000), largest city and chief river port of Tennessee, seat of Shelby County, on the high east banks bluffs of the Mississippi River below the mouth of the Wolf River. It was founded in 1819 and incorporated in 1826. Memphis is a leading market for cotton, hardwood lumber and livestock, as well as meat packing center and a transportation hub. Its manufactures include cottonseed products, textiles, farm machinery, paper, and drugs. It has foundries and rice mills. The city, noted for its fine churches, also has many educational institutions, including the medical divisions of the University of Tennessee. Memphis is the site of Beale Street, made famous by the composer W.C. Handy, and of Elvis Presley's estate, Graceland, a popular tourist attraction.
See also: Tennessee.

Menander (342-c.291 B.C.), leading Greek writer of New comedy. Of over 100 plays, only *Dyscolos* (The Grouch) survives complete; adaptations of his other plays, by the Roman playwrights Plautus and Terence, influenced 17th-century comedy. His plots are based on love affairs, and he is noted for his elegant style and debt characterization.

Menchú, Rigoberta (1959-   ), Indian (Quiché) human rights activist from Guatemala who received the Nobel prize for Peace in 1992 for her efforts to defend the native people of her country. She also coordinated protests in San Marcos against the festivities surrounding the commemoration of the arrival of Columbus in America. In 1981 she was forced to flee to Mexico because of military violence which had killed her parents and brother.
The American anthropologist David Stoll researched Menchú's past. In 1998 he published a book in which he proves that important facts from Menchú's 1983 autobiography are made up. The Nobel prize committee did not consider this a reason to take back the Nobel prize.

Mencius (Mengke; 370-290 B.C.), Chinese philosopher. A follower of Confucius, he was influential in the development of Confucianism. He held that humanity is naturally good and that the principles of true moral conduct are inborn. He was a champion of the ordinary people and exhorted rulers to treat their subjects well.
See also: Confucianism.

Mencken, H(enry) L(ouis) (1880-1956), U.S. journalist and author, caustic critic of U.S. society and literature. He wrote for the *Baltimore Sun* and founded and edited the *American Mercury* (1924). His collected essays appeared in *Prejudices* (6 vols., 1919-27). Among other works, he also wrote an authoritative study, *The American Language* (1919).

Mendel, Gregor Johann (1822-1884), Austrian botanist and Augustinian monk who laid the foundations of the science of genetics. His results with experiments on dwarf pea plants provided a mechanism justifying Charles Darwin's theory of evolution by natural selection; however, contemporary lack of interest and his unsuccessful experiments with the hawkweeds discouraged him from carrying this work further. Only in 1900, when scientists found his published results, was the importance of his work realized.
See also: Genetics; Heredity.

Mendeleev, Dmitri Ivanovich (1834-1907), Russian chemist who formulated (1869) the Periodic Law, stating that the properties of elements vary periodically with increasing atomic weight. This work enabled him to draw up the Periodic Table.
See also: Chemistry; Periodic table.

Mendelevium, chemical element, symbol Md; for physical constants see Periodic Table. An artificial radioactive element, mendelevium was discovered by Albert Ghiorso and his co-workers in 1955. Einsteinium-253 was bombarded with helium ions in the 60-inch cyclotron in Berke-ley. Mendelevium-256, having a half-life of 76 minutes, was produced. That is the longest-lived isotope of the element known. It is a metallic element and a member of the actinide series. Fourteen radioactive isotopes of mendelevium have been produced.

Mendel's laws *See:* Genetics; Mendel, Gregor Johann.

Mendelsohn, Erich (1887-1953), a German-born architect who supported functional design. The sweeping curves of the Einstein Tower, an observatory in Potsdam, are typical of much of his work. Mendelsohn designed stores and factories in his Munich office before he fled Nazi Germany in 1933. He worked in England and Palestine, and in 1941 settled in the United States. He became a citizen in 1946.

Mendelssohn, Felix (1809-1847), German Romantic composer. He wrote his concert overture to *A Midsummer Night's Dream* at age 17. Other works include his *Hebrides Overture* (also known as 'Fingal's Cave,' 1830-1832), *Scotch* (1842) and *Italian* (1833) symphonies, a violin concerto, chamber music, and the oratorio *Elijah*. He was also a celebrated conductor, notably of the Leipzig Gewandhaus orchestra, and he revived interest in the music of Johann Sebastian Bach.

Mendelssohn, Moses (1729-1786), German-Jewish philosopher and scholar, a lead-

ing figure of the Enlightenment in Prussia, and a promoter of Jewish assimilation into German culture. He wrote *Phädon* (1767) and *Jerusalem* (1783).
See also: Age of Reason; Philosophy.

Menem, Carlos Saúl (1935-), Argentinean politician, President of Argentina from 1989 to 1999. Menem made a career for himself within the Peronistic Party. After the military coup in 1976, he was arrested, placed under house arrest and not released until 1982. During his presidency, he expanded his power by becoming leader of the Peronists as well. Menem pursued pragmatic policies, fighting against inflation and the intensifying of the relations with the U.S. and Western Europe. In 2001, he was arrested for alleged arms smuggling, but was released later that year due to insufficient evidence.

Mengelberg, Josef Willem (1871-1951), Dutch conductor. Mengelberg became a conductor in 1892 in Luzern (Germany). In 1895 he succeeded Willem Kes as leader of the Concertgebouw Orchestra in the Netherlands, a function he held for almost 50 years. Mengelberg also conducted the 'Museumkonzerte' in Frankfurt am Main (1907-1920), the National Symphony Orchestra in New York (1921-1929) and since 1898 the Amsterdam Toonkunst Choir. Under Mengelberg's command the Concertgebouw Orchestra became one of the best and most renowned orchestras in the world, presenting numerous new works and making many international tours.
Mengelberg was a fervent advocate of R. Strauss, who dedicated *Ein Heldenleben* (1899) to Mengelberg and the Concertgebouw Orchestra, and Mahler, whose work Mengelberg introduced and performed in full in 1920. His attitude in World War II led to a conducting ban in 1945 and he died a lonely man in Switzerland.

Mengele, Josef (1911-1979?), Nazi war criminal. A doctor who conducted often inhuman medical experiments on inmates of Auschwitz, a Nazi concentration camp. Mengele is believed responsible for 400,000 deaths there. Captured by the Allies at the end of World War II, he was inadvertently released and fled to South America. Charged with war crimes by West Germany (1959), Mengele eluded capture for 20 years before dying in Brazil. Remains believed to be his were unearthed in a Brazilian cemetery in 1985.
See also: Auschwitz; Nazism.

Mengistu Haile Mariam (1937-), Ethiopian military man and politician. In 1974 Mengistu overturned the imperial rule of Haile Selassie. Initially he was the chairman of the Dergue (provisional military governing council), later secretary general of the Ethiopian Labor Party (Communist), which he founded. In 1977 Mengistu became head of state as well as head of government (1977-1987). He pursued a Marxist-Leninist policy and leaned mainly toward the Soviet Union. The resistance against the government army (by the Ethiopian People's Revolutionary Democratic Front and the Eritrean People's Liberation Front) became a considerable offensive in 1991. Mengistu had to flee to Zimbabwe. In 1994 a trial began against the fled Mengistu. He was accused of genocide and crimes against humanity. He was also held responsible for the murder of Emperor Haile Selassie in 1975, and for the murders of 1853 other functionaries whose names were retrieved.

Mengs, Anton Raphael (1728-1779), German painter, influential neoclassicist artist. Influenced in Rome (1741-1744) by, among others, Raphael and Correggio, befriended with Winckelmann. Court painter of August III of Saxony (1746) and of Charles III of Spain (1761). In his ceiling paintings, like *Parnassus* in the Villa Albani (1761; Rome), he broke with the illusionism of the Baroque. Especially valued for his portraits.

Menhaden, marine fish (*Brevoortia tyrannus*) of the herring family. Inhabiting the Atlantic coastal waters from Nova Scotia to Brazil, menhaden measure 12-18 in (30-46 cm) and weigh up to 1 lb (0.5 kg). They are edible but are most often processed for their oil or as livestock feed and fertilizer.

Meningitis (cerebrospinal meningitis), inflammation of the menninges caused by bacteria or viruses. Bacterial meningitis is of abrupt onset, with headache, vomiting, fever, neck stiffness, and sensitivity to light. Early and appropriate antibiotic treatment is essential as permanent damage may occur, especially in children. Viral meningitis is a milder illness with similar signs; only symptomatic measures are required. Tuberculous meningitis is an insidious chronic type that responds slowly to antituberculous drugs. Some fungi, unusual bacteria and syphilis may also cause varieties of meningitis. Diagnosis is made through an examination of the cerebrospinal fluid via a spinal tap.

Mennonites, Protestant sect originating among the Anabaptists of Zurich, Switzerland. They became particularly influential in the Netherlands, and are named for the Dutch reformer Menno Simons. They base their faith solely on the Bible, believe in separation of Church and State, pacifism, and baptism only for adults who renounce sin. They are known for the strict simplicity of their life and worship. The Amish Church is a well-known, conservative division of the Mennonites in the United States.
See also: Anabaptism.

Menotti, Gian Carlo (1911-), Italian-born U.S. composer of operas and founder (1958) of the Festival of Two Worlds at Spoleto, Italy. His works include *The Medium* (1946) and the television opera *Amahl and the Night Visitors* (1951). *The Consul* (1950) and *The Saint of Bleecker Street* (1954) won Pulitzer prizes for music. Other works include *The last Savage* (1963), *Arrival* (1973), *St. Teresa* (1982) and *Goya* (1986).

Mensheviks, name for the position of the minority group in the Russian Social Democratic Workers' Party-opposition to the Bolsheviks, the majority group led by Vladimir Ilyich Lenin. Unlike Lenin, the Menshevik theoretician Georgi Plekhanov favored mass membership and believed a spell of bourgeois rule must precede communism. Led by L. Martov (Yuly Osiporich Tsederbaum), the Mensheviks emerged in 1903, backed Aleksandr Feodorovich Kerensky's short-lived government (1917), and opposed the Bolshevik seizure of power. By 1921 they had been eliminated.
See also: Bolsheviks; Russian Revolution.

Menstruation, in women of reproductive age, specifically the monthly loss of blood (period), representing shedding of womb endometrium; in general, the whole monthly cycle of hormonal, structural, and functional changes, punctuated by menstrual blood loss. After each period, the endometrium (womb-lining) starts to proliferate and thicken under the influence of gonadotrophins

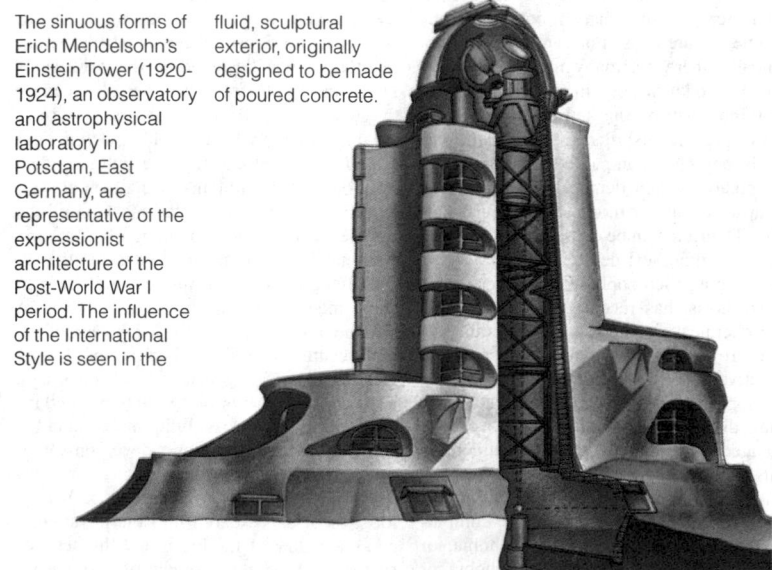

The sinuous forms of Erich Mendelsohn's Einstein Tower (1920-1924), an observatory and astrophysical laboratory in Potsdam, East Germany, are representative of the expressionist architecture of the Post-World War I period. The influence of the International Style is seen in the fluid, sculptural exterior, originally designed to be made of poured concrete.

M

M

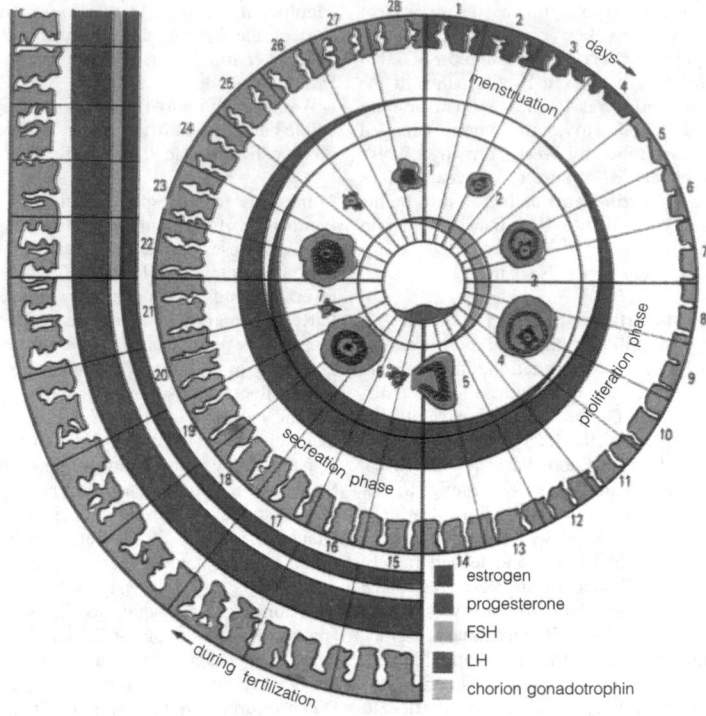

menstruation

days

proliferation phase

secreation phase

during fertilization

- estrogen
- progesterone
- FSH
- LH
- chorion gonadotrophin

The changes that occur during the menstrual cycle, are controlled by the balance of the follicle stimulating hormone (FSH) and the luteinizing hormone (LH), which are secreted by the pituitary. The diagram shows the changing levels of FSH and LH, and of oestrogen and progesterone induction from the ovarian follicle. The levels of these hormones are linked with certain changes in the structure of the uterine wall and the development of the follicle.
A complete cycle takes 28 days. A sharp increase in LH in the middle of the cycle will cause ovulation. When fertilization does not take place, the already formed corpus luteum will degenerate around the 26th day, as the hormone levels of the pituitary fall. The consequent withdrawal of oestrogen and progesterone, will cause the menstrual flow: the sloughing off of the already thickened part of the uterine wall. This will then proliferate again under the influence of oestrogen from a new follicle. If fertilization and egg implantation do take place, the placenta will produce chorionic gonadotrophin — possibly as early as day 21 — which allows the corpus luteum to continue to produce oestrogen and progesterone, until the placenta takes over this task

(follicle-stimulating hormone) and estrogens. In midcycle an egg is released from an ovarian follicle (ovulation). The endometrium is prepared for implantation of a fertilized egg. If the egg is not fertilized, pregnancy does not ensue; then blood-vessel changes that occur lead to the shedding of the endometrium and some blood, sometimes with pain or colic. The cycle then restarts. Cyclic patterns are established at puberty (menarche) and end in middle life (age 45-60) at the menopause, the 'change of life.' Disorders of menstruation include heavy, irregular, or missed periods; bleeding between periods or after the menopause; and excessively painful periods. These disorders are studied in gynecology.
See also: Reproduction.

Mental age See: Intelligence quotient.

Mental illness, any of several diseases of the mind manifesting itself as disordered thoughts or feelings, or behavior which is apparently irrational or which deviates from socially and culturally accepted norms. The modern concept of mental illness rests on 3 foundations. The oldest of these consists of norms of feeling, development, and behavior defined by society and prevailing in a culture at a particular time. One example of an important area bearing on an individual's mental health that is strongly defined by custom and belief is sexuality. Our definition of mental illness also proceeds from rationalism, the idea that a healthy mind is predominantly a logical mind. And we rely upon science, particularly neurophysiology and neurochemistry, for research into the organic causes of mental illness. Though it is widely accepted that many, if not most, mental illnesses are caused or can be treated organically, there are many mental disorders that have no known organic cause but whose symptoms may be masked or alleviated by drugs. Organic disorders include delirium, which may be accompanied by illusions or hallucinations, and dementia, characterized by lapses of one or more of the mental faculties. Delirium can be caused by alcoholism or certain illnesses; dementia often accompanies aging. Schizophrenia, a severe form of psychosis, has recently been associated with chemical imbalances in the brain and there are indications it may be hereditary. Affective disorders, including mania, depression, and manic-depression, are profound disturbances of mood which can be managed to some degree with antidepressants or tranquilizers.
Other forms of mental illness include a variety of anxieties such as obsessive-compulsive behavior or phobias (agoraphobia, or fear of public places, and claustrophobia, or fear of closed places, are examples). There are also dissociative disorders in which a person may suffer a change or loss of identity. These can manifest as one of several kinds of amnesia or as multiple personality disorder, in which a person has more than 1 personality with now one, then the other, being dominant. The underlying causes of these conditions are as yet unknown.
There are also certain kinds of mental illness unique to a particular age group. Children, for example, may be hyperactive or they may be afflicted with autism, a disorder in which the child appears remote, expressionless, and unresponsive. Alzheimer's, a disease of the brain cells that leads to impairment of the mental faculties, attacks people in their 40s and older.
The principal health professionals concerned with diagnosing and treating the mentally ill are psychiatrists and psychologists. Psychiatrists are medical doctors; psychologists are usually Ph.D.s in psychology. Treatment for the mentally ill may include drug therapy, various forms of psychotherapy, or periods of institutionalization. In many cases, a combination of therapies is used. For some patients, psychoanalysis is found useful, while others respond best to behavior modification. In extreme cases, electroshock treatments and even psychosurgery may be necessary, though both are highly controversial forms of treatment which now raise fundamental moral, ethical, and legal questions.
For the most part, society's treatment of the mentally ill has not been a bright page in human history. Mental disorders have been seen as curses and the work of malevolent spirits and the mentally ill, as often as not, were shunned, tormented, or persecuted. Among the Greeks, Hippocrates made a major advance in the 5th century B.C. by offering a rational explanation for mental illness as being due to imbalances in certain bodily fluids. But it would be another 2,000 years before humane and rational treatment of the mentally ill became the accepted standard. It was in the 1700s that Philippe Pinel, a French doctor, and the British merchant William Tuke, introduced modern reforms into mental institutions. Their innovations were taken up by Benjamin Rush in America, and reform of the country's mental institutions was hastened by the writings of Dorothea Dix. Reform was also advanced by the work of Clifford W. Beers, a former mental patient, whose book, A Mind That Found Itself, helped improve public understanding of the problems of the mentally ill. In 1909, he founded the National Committee for Mental Hygiene, which later became the National Association for Mental Health.
Simultaneously with institutional reform came medical advances and new forms of treatment and therapy. Toward the end of the 19th century, Emil Kraepelin and Eugen Bleuler classified most mental disorders. Early in the 20th century, Sigmund Freud introduced his psychoanalytic method and his ideas on the structure and development of the mind. Research into various forms of psychotherapy, the development of behaviorist theories, research into the physiology and chemistry of the brain and the nervous system, and the development of psychotrop-

ic drugs, have all had a significant effect upon the care and treatment of the mentally ill. But they are still, in many ways, feared, ignored, or discriminated against, and problems of care, treatment, and integration of the mentally ill into society are as urgent as the need for continued medical research.

Mental retardation, low intellectual capacity, arising not from mental illness but from impairment of the normal development of the brain and nervous system. Causes include genetic defect (as in Down's syndrome); infection of the embryo or fetus (hydrocephalus or inherited metabolic defects), injury at birth, including cerebral hemorrhage and fetal anoxia (lack of oxygen), and disease in infancy (for example, encephalitis). Retardation is initially recognized by slowness to develop normal patterns of social and learning behavior; it is confirmed through intelligence measurements. Although mental retardation cannot be cured, it is most important that affected children receive adequate social contact and education, for their development is generally retarded, not arrested. Special schooling may help them achieve a degree of learning and social competence. Proper prenatal, perinatal, and postnatal care may help prevent some cases of mental retardation.

Menuhin, Yehudi (1916-1999), U.S. violinist and conductor. He made his concert debut in San Francisco at age 7, played for Allied forces in World War II, and later performed to raise cash for war victims. He has revived forgotten masterpieces, promoted interest in Eastern music, and toured internationally with the Menuhin Festival Orchestra. In 1963 he opened the Yehudi Menuhin School of Music for musically gifted children in Suffolk, England.

Menzel, Adolph Friedrich Erdmann von (1815-1905), a German painter en illustrator. He was known for his historical paintings and realistic *genre* (everyday life) scenes. The 400 drawings illustrating Kugler's *History of Frederick the Great* (1841) are characteristic of his style. In many of his later paintings, such as *The Artist's Sister*, Menzel used impressionist techniques. Menzel was largely self-taught.

Mephistopheles, in medieval legend, the devil to whom Faust sold his soul. He is primarily a literary creation and appears in the famous plays by Christopher Marlowe and Johann Goethe.
See also: Devil.

Mercantilism, economic system prevailing in 16th- to 18th-century western Europe that reflected the increased importance of the merchant. Mercantilism was based on the concepts that a country's wealth was founded on its supply of gold and silver, and that in a world of limited resources one nation could prosper only at the expense of another. Mercantilists favored tariffs in order to secure a favorable international trade balance and thereby maintain reserves of previous metals. Their protectionism was succeeded by the free trade arguments of the French physiocrats and later the policy of

laissez faire. Today, mercantilism sometimes refers to policies that protect domestic businesses from foreign competition.
See also: Colonialism.

Mercator, Gerardus (Gerhard Kremer; 1512-1594), geographer and cartographer best known for his world map. With this map Mercator introduced a new map projection, or method of transferring features of the earth's surface onto a flat sheet of paper. On a map using the so-called Mercator projection, the lines of latitude, which are equidistant on a globe, are drawn with increasing separation as their distance from the equator increases. While this exaggerates the sizes of areas as they move away from the equator, it preserves their shapes. Mercator's method is still in use today by navigators.
See also: Geography.

Merchandising *See:* Marketing.

Merchant marine, commercial shipping operations of a maritime nation and the personnel who operate the ships. Privately-owned cargo ships make up the largest percentage of most nations' fleets, but state-owned vessels are operated in some countries, particularly those of the Communist bloc. Gross tonnage, the total cargo capacity of all ships of a nation's registry, is the figure used to measure a merchant marine's size.

Mercouri, Melina (proper name Melina Mersouris; 1923-1994), Greek actress and politician. Melina Mercouri gained international fame with her portrayal of the prostitute from Piraeus in the movie *Never on Sunday* (1960), directed by her second husband Jules Dassin. In antipathy for the colonels' regime that came into power in Greece in 1967, she went into voluntary exile and carried on a campaign in many countries against the regime, which ruled until 1974. In 1974 she was actively involved in the establishment of PASOK, the new socialist party of Papandreou, and in 1977 was elected to parliament. As minister of culture (1981-1989 and since 1993) she became well-known for her unflagging attempts to get the 'Elgin marbles' from London back to Greece. Movies include *Stella* (1955), *Topkapi* (1964), *Family Life* (1974), and *Once Is Not Enough* (1975).

Mercury (element), chemical element, symbol Hg; for physical constants see Periodic Table. Mercury was known to the ancient Chinese and Hindus. It is a silvery-white, heavy, liquid metal. Compared with other metals, it is a poor conductor of heat and a fair conductor of electricity. Mercury is the only common metal that is liquid at ordinary temperatures. It easily forms alloys with many other metals. Both the element and most of its compounds are poisonous. Mercury and its compounds are used in electrolytic cells, dentistry, thermometers, barometers, diffusion pumps, electrical switches, mercury-vapor lamps, paint, batteries, explosive detonators, and in medicine.

Mercury (mythology), in Roman mythology, god of commerce and wealth; associated with Hermes in Greek mythology. Known as

the messenger of the gods, he delivered his messages with great speed because he wore winged sandals. Mercury was the son of Jupiter, and Maia, a goddess. He was depicted as both crafty and deceptive.

Mercury (planet), in astronomy, planet closest to the sun, with a mean solar distance of 36 million mi (57.9 million km). Its eccentric elliptical orbit brings it within 28.5 million mi (46 million km) of the sun at perihelion (point nearest to the sun) and takes it 43.5 million mi (70 million km) from the sun at aphelion (point farthest from the sun). Its diameter is 3,031 mi (4,878 km), and its mass about 0.054 that of the earth. Mercury revolves around the sun in just under 88 days-faster than any other planet-and rotates on its axis in about 59 days. Albert Einstein's successful prediction that Mercury's orbit would advance by 43 in (109 cm) per century is usually regarded as a confirmation of the general theory of relativity. Night surface temperature on this dry and airless planet is believed to be about -315°F (-°193C), midday equatorial temperature over 648°F (342°C). No plant life is believed to exist. Mercury also has no known

Detailed photographs such as this one, made by *Mariner 10*, show that Mercury closely resembles the moon. The left side of this photograph shows part of the circular area, that was called 'Caloris' or 'Hot Plain', because it lies near the point facing the sun during the perihelion of Mercury, and is consequently exposed to tremendous heat. The ring-shaped structure has a maximum diameter of 807 mi (1,300 km), and is bordered by mountains of up to 1,2 mi (2 km) high. It is the largest plane on Mercury.

M

M

satellites. The U.S. *Mariner* space probe revealed (1974-1975) that Mercury has a moonlike, heavily cratered surface and a slight magnetic field.
See also: Planet; Solar System.

Mercury program *See:* Space exploration.

Meredith, George (1828-1909), English novelist and poet. His novels include the tragicomic *The Ordeal of Richard Feverel* (1859), *The Egoist* (1879), and *Diana of the Crossways* (1885). The sonnet sequence *Modern Love* (1862) grew out of the breakdown of his marriage. His writing offers piercing character and social analyses.

Merganser, fish-eating duck of the family Anatidae, found in many parts of the world. It is also called the sawbill because of its long serrated bill. Both sexes have a large head crest-the male dark, and the female brown. Mergansers nest in tree holes. They include the American, red-breasted, and hooded mergansers, all of which can be found in North America.

Mergenthaler, Ottmar (1854-1899), German-American inventor of the Linotype machine, an automatic typesetting device. Patented in 1884 and produced in 1886, the Linotype made the printing process more efficient and cost-effective, thus producing widespread changes in publishing.
See also: Linotype.

Merian, Maria Sibylla (1647-1717), German-Dutch painter and graphic artist. Studied and made watercolor paintings of plants, insects and fruit in places like the jungles of Surinam (1699-1702). These representations belong, in an artistic as well as scientific sense, to the most interesting examples of nature painting. A large part of her work was engraved, colored and published under her command, including *Metamorphosis insectorum Surinamensium* (1705, reprinted 1719).

Mérida (pop. 560,000), founded in 1542, now the largest city on the Yucatan Peninsula in Mexico. Mérida is surrounded by farmland and is located near the the ancient Mayan sites of Chichén Itzá and Uxmal. The city contains a magnificent cathedral and examples of early Spanish architecture.

Mérimée, Prosper (1803-1870), French author, historian, archeologist, and linguist. He is best known for his novelettes (long short stories such as 'Mateo Falcone' (1829), 'Colomba' (1840), and the romance 'Carmen' (1845), which was the source of Georges Bizet's opera. Mérimée also wrote essays and translations in the 1850s intended to interest the French in Russia and its literature.

Merlin *See:* Round Table.

Merovingian, dynasty of Frankish kings (A.D. 428-751) who governed Gaul. They were named for the 5th-century king Merovech; his grandson Clovis I first united much of France. The kingdom was later partitioned, but enlarged and reunited (A.D. 613) under Clotaire II. The Merovingians governed through the remnants of the old Roman administration and established Catholic Christianity. After Dagobert I in the 7th century, the kings became known as *rois-fainéants* (do-nothings), and power passed to the mayors of the palace, nominally high officials. The last of these, Pepin the Short, deposed the last Merovingian, Childeric III, and founded the Carolingian dynasty.
See also: Carolingian; Gaul.

Merrill, Robert (1919-), internationally acclaimed New York-born baritone opera singer. Known for his powerful voice and technical proficiency, he has performed extensively worldwide, notably with the Metropolitan Opera and on Broadway. Among his famous roles are Renato in Verdi's *Un Ballo in Maschera*, Amonasro in *Aïda*, and Escomillo in Bizet's *Carmen*. He wrote an autobiograhy, *Once More from the Beginning* (1965), and a novel, *The Divas* (1978).

Merrimack *See:* Monitor and Merrimack.

Mersey, River, major trade waterway rising in the Pennine Hills of northwest England and entering the Irish Sea. About 70 mi (110 km) long, the river has underwater tunnels for railroads and automotive traffic. Its many docks and basins, serving the cities of Liverpool and Birkenhead, have contributed to the development of Birkenhead as an important market for cattle. A canal connects the river to the city of Manchester.

Merton, Robert King (1910-), U.S. sociologist. His seminal work on the sociology of science produced *Science, Technology and Society in Seventeenth Century England* (1938), expressing the view that English Puritanism helped lead to the modern scientific age. He wrote an analysis of the function of deviant behavior in society (*Social Theory and Social Structure*, 1949), and was instrumental in developing quantitative (statistical) research methods in sociology.
See also: Sociology.

Merton, Thomas (1915-1968), U.S. religious writer of poetry, meditative works and an autobiography, *The Seven Storey Mountain* (1948). A convert to Roman Catholicism, he became a Trappist monk (1941) and was later ordained a priest. The French-born Merton also wrote *The Waters of Siloe* (1949) and *The Sign of Jonas* (1953) about the Trappist life.

Merv, ruined city in the former Turkmen Soviet Socialist Republic, situated near the modern city of Mary. Since ancient times an oasis in the desert, Merv was once a prosperous city and center of Islamic learning. Destroyed by the Mongols in 1221, it was rebuilt in the 15th century and occupied by the Russians in 1884. Farming is its main occupation.
See also: Turkmenistan.

Merz, Mario (1925-), Italian expressive artist, one of the most important representatives of the arte povera. Worked with natural materials such as wax, wood and stone, which he combined in a striking way with other materials like neon, metal and glass. His works include igloos of various materials such as wire-netting covered with clay and neon lights mounted in bins filled with wax. In 1981 he went back to painting: the various elements from earlier works were incorporated into colorful, figurative images (often of animals).

Mesa (Spanish, 'table'), used in the western and southwestern United States for a steep-sided, flat-topped hill or isolated tableland, such as Mesa Encantada (Enchanted Mesa) in New Mexico and Mesa Verde (Green Mesa) in Colorado. Often red or yellow, mesas were long ago part of much larger plateaus of softer rock that were gradually worn down. The mesas escaped erosion because they were capped by hard rock layers protecting the softer strata below.

Mescaline, nonaddictive hallucinogen derived from the Mexican peyote cactus (*Lophophora williamsii*). Because peyote is bitter-tasting and causes a burning sensation and itching of mucous membranes, the 'buttons' are brewed with tea or chewed while drinking beverages. Pure mescaline is more potent than peyote powder, which may be mixed with gelatine or injected intravenously in decoctions. About 10 minutes to 3 hours after taking mescaline, and lasting about 12 hours, one experiences nausea, dizziness, sweating, headache, palpitations, heat or chilliness, and cramps in chest, neck, or abdomen. Effects include multicolored visions; hypersensitivity to sound; disturbed senses of touch, taste, smell, space, and time; and a distorted concept of one's own body. Euphoria and glee are followed by anxiety (sometimes depression and hostility), loss of concentration and control over speech and action, and possibly general but temporary schizophrenic psychosis.
See also: Drug; Drug abuse.

Meshed (pop. 1,900,000), capital city of Khorsn province, northeastern Iran. Meshed, center of the northern wool trade, is also a religious center, visited by over 100,000 pilgrims annually. It contains the tombs of the caliph Hrn ar-Rashd (A.D. 809) and his son-in-law, religious leader Alar-Rid.
See also: Iran.

Mesmer, Franz, or **Friedrich Anton** (1734-1815), Austrian physician who theorized (1775) that a person may transmit universal forces to others through 'animal magnetism.' Controversy over his unusual techniques and theories, involving the beneficial effects of a magnet upon an occult force within the subject, forced Mesmer to flee Austria (1778) for Paris. Interest in mesmerism led the British surgeon James Braid, the French neurologist Jean Charcot, and the Viennese psychologist Sigmund Freud to develop the ancient practice of hypnotism for the study of psychology.
See also: Hypnosis.

Mesolithic Period *See:* Stone Age.

Meson, subatomic particle of a family called hadrons, which act via a strong nuclear force that holds together an atomic nucleus. Mesons are unstable particles that decay; they carry a positive, negative, or neutral electric charge. They consist of a quark and an antiquark. Mesons include pions (or pi-mesons), upsilon particles, k-mesons (or kaons), and psi particles (or J particles). British physicist Cecil Powell discovered the meson (1947) in cosmic radiation.
See also: Hadron; Quark.

Mesopotamia (Greek, 'between the rivers'), ancient region between the Tigris and Euphrates rivers in southwestern Asia. Called 'the cradle of civilizations' Mesopotamia mainly lies in Iraq, between the Armenian and Kurdish Mountains in the north and the Persian Gulf in the south. The north is mainly grassy, rolling plateau; the south is a sandy plain leading to marshes. Since ancient times the rivers have been used to irrigate the area; however, the ancient systems degenerated under Mongol invasion and Ottoman rule and were not replaced until the 20th century. Neolithic farming peoples settled Mesopotamia by 6000 B.C. By 3000 B.C. the Sumerians, who created the first system of writing (cuneiform), had developed a civilization of independent city-states in the south. From c.3000-625 B.C. Mesopotamia was dominated successively by Sumer, Akkad, the Sumerian dynasty of Ur, the empires of Babylonia and Assyria, and Chaldea. In 539 B.C. the Persian Empire absorbed Mesopotamia; in 331 B.C. it was conquered by Alexander the Great. It subsequently came under Roman, Byzantine, and Arab rule. The Abbasid caliphs made Baghdad their capital in 762, but prosperity collapsed with the Mongol invasion of 1289. After Ottoman rule (1638-1918), Mesopotamia was largely incorporated into Iraq. Today it is generally barren, but contains rich oil fields.

A votive relief of Ur-Nanshe and his family (2500 B.C.). Votive reliefs like these always have a hole in the center, of which the significance is not completely known yet. It is assumed that religious emblems or oblations were inserted into it (Louvre, Paris).

Mesosphere, layer of the atmosphere immediately above the stratosphere, marked by a temperature maximum (about 10°C/50 °F) between altitudes of about 30 mi-50 mi (58-80 km).
See also: Atmosphere.

Mesozoic Era *See:* Dinosaur; Reptile.

Mesquite, or screw bean, tough shrub or tree (genus *Prosopis*) that grows in the stony deserts of the southwestern United States and similar regions. The roots may penetrate as much as 70 ft (21 m) into the ground. It bears spines and small olive-colored leaflets. A member of the pea family, mesquite has seeds that develop into edible pods that can be used to make bread and a fermented beverage. The pods, wood, and gum from the stem have commercial value as food, fuel, and lumber.

Reconstructed drawing of the Tower of Babel (Babylon, 605-563 B.C.), also known as Marduk's ziggurat. Reconstructed from descriptions in ancient texts, as a likely example of a square double-ramped type of ziggurat.

Messenia, region in the southern peninsula of Greece and seat of the ancient Mycenaean civilization. Under Spartan domination for hundreds of years, the Messenians were finally freed in the 4th century B.C. by Theben leader Epaminondas. Messenia is noted for its Frankish and Turkish castles, and for its rich farmland.
See also: Mycenae.

Messiaen, Olivier (1908-1992), French composer, organist, teacher, and theorist. Much of his music, such as *The Ascension* (1935), was influenced by Roman Catholic mysticism. Others are based on Oriental music, such as the *Turangalila* symphony (1949), or on birdsong, such as the *Catalog of Birds* (1959). Other works include *Chronochromie* (1960), *Sept Haïkaï* (1963), *Couleurs de la Cité céleste* (1964), *Et exspecto Resurrectionem Mortuorum* (1964), *La Transfiguration de Notre Seigneur Jésus-Christ* (1965-1969), *Des Canyons aux Étoiles* (1974), *Saint Francois d'Assise* (1975-1983) and *La Ville d'en-Haut* (1987). He influenced many modern composers, among them Pierre Boulez of France and Karlheinz Stockhausen of Germany.

Messiah (Hebrew, 'anointed one'), according to Israelite prophets, especially Isaiah, the ruler whom God would send to restore Israel and begin a glorious age of peace and

Upright statue of Gudea, ruler of Lagash (2150 B.C.). Statues of Gudea can be recognized by their striking, turban-like hairdo (Louvre, Paris).

righteousness. He would be a descendant of King David. Christians recognize Jesus of Nazareth as the Messiah (or Christ); his role as 'suffering servant' was alien to Jewish hopes of a political deliverer. The concept of a forthcoming divine redeemer is common to many religions.
See also: Religion.

Messier, Charles (1730-1817), French astronomer and compiler of an extensive catalog of celestial sources of light that are not stars. Among these are galaxies, nebulae, and star clusters. In attempting to distinguish between nebulae and comets, he discovered 21 comets and predicted the return of Halley's Comet in 1758-59.
See also: Astronomy.

Messina (pop. 233,000), city on Sicily's

M

northeast coast, on the Strait of Messina. First mentioned in history as an ancient Sicilian colony (c.730 B.C.) it was occupied by the Greeks in the 700s B.C. and became a flourishing Greek colony. Throughout history it has been fought over and survived many rulers. Earthquakes in 1783 and 1908 almost destroyed Messina, which also sustained great damage during World War II. A gateway to Sicily, its principal exports are fruits, wine, olive oil, chemicals, pharmaceuticals, and medicinal products.
See also: Sicily.

Metabolism, sum total of all chemical reactions that occur in a living organism. It can be subdivided into *anabolism*, which describes reactions that build up more complex substances from smaller ones, and *catabolism*, which describes reactions that break down complex substances into simpler ones. Anabolic reactions require energy, while catabolic reactions liberate energy.
Metabolic reactions are set off by enzymes in a highly integrated and finely controlled manner so that there is no overproduction or underutilization of the energy required to maintain life. All this energy is ultimately derived from sunlight by the photosynthesis in plants, and most organisms use the products of photosynthesis either directly or indirectly.

Metal, element that has high specific gravity; high opacity and reflectivity to light (giving a characteristic luster when polished); ability to be hammered into thin sheets and drawn into wires (i.e., is malleable and ductile); and is a good conductor of heat and electricity, its electrical conductivity decreasing with temperature. Roughly 75% of the chemical elements are metals, but not all of them possess all the typical metallic properties. Most are found as ores and in the pure state are crystalline solids

combination with nonmetallic elements). *Hydrometallurgy* uses chemical reactions in aqueous solutions to extract metal from ore. *Electrometallurgy* uses electricity for firing a furnace or electrolytically reducing a metallic compound to a metal. *Pyrometallurgy* covers roasting, smelting, and other high temperature chemical reactions.

Metamorphic rock, one of the 3 main classes of rocks of the earth's crust-the class that has undergone change owing to heat, pressure, or chemical action. In plate tectonic theory the collision of lithospheric plates leads to widespread *regional metamorphism*. Igneous intrusion leads to changes in the rocks close to the borders or contacts of the cooling magma, and these changes, largely due to the application of heat, constitute *contact (thermal) metamorphism*. Common metamorphic rock types include marble, quartzite, slate, schist, and gneiss. Some occurrences of granite are also thought to be of metamorphic origin.
See also: Rock.

Metamorphosis, in zoology, changes undergone from larvae to a mature adult stage. The term, meaning 'transformation,' is generally used only for insects and amphibians, although other animals also have distinct larval and adult stages. Metamorphosis of insects may be *complete*, occurring in abrupt steps, or *incomplete*, a gradual process. Butterflies and moths have complete metamorphosis, changing from caterpillar to adult via one intermediate stage, the pupa. Grasshoppers and cockroaches mature gradually in a series of molts (the young are called *nymphs*) until they develop into adults. Metamorphosis of amphibians is generally from a water-dwelling, gill-breathing larva, such as a tadpole, into a less aquatic air-breathing adult, such as a frog.
See also: Zoology.

Metaphysics, branch of philosophy that addresses the fundamentals of existence or reality, such as the existence and nature of God, immortality of the soul, meaning of evil, the problem of freedom and determinism, and relationship of mind and body. Metaphysical systems have included Aristotelian scholasticism and the 17th-century rationalistic systems of Descartes, Spinoza, and Leibniz. Metaphysical thinking was criticized in the 18th century by Immanuel Kant, who claimed that traditional metaphysics, while raising morally necessary questions, sought to go beyond the limits of human knowledge. In the 20th century, the concerns of metaphysics were rejected as being meaningless by the logical positivists.
See also: Philosophy.

Metaxas, Ionannis (1871-1941), Greek general and from 1936 ultraroyalist premier and dictator of Greece. He made important social and economic reforms. He tried to maintain Greek neutrality in World War II, but after successfully resisting the Italian invasion in 1940 joined the Allied powers.
See also: Greece.

Metazoan, in zoology, multicellular animal, member of the group Metazoa, distinguished from single-celled protozoans. With increase in the number of cells comes differentiation of function of cells, tissues, and organs. Many zoologists divide the Metazoa group into sponges (Parazoa) and all other multi-celled animals (Eumetazoa).

Metchnikoff, Élie (1845-1916), Russian biologist who shared with Paul Ehrlich the 1908 Nobel Prize for physiology or medicine for his discovery of phagocytes (in humans, called leukocytes) and their role in defending the body from, for example, bacteria.
See also: Biology.

Grashoppers undergo a simple metamorphosis (A): the young insects, or nymphs, usually already resemble the adults, the wings develop with each molt. Butterflies undergo a complete metamorphosis (B): the young, or larvae, enter a quiescent stage (pupa) before becoming adults.

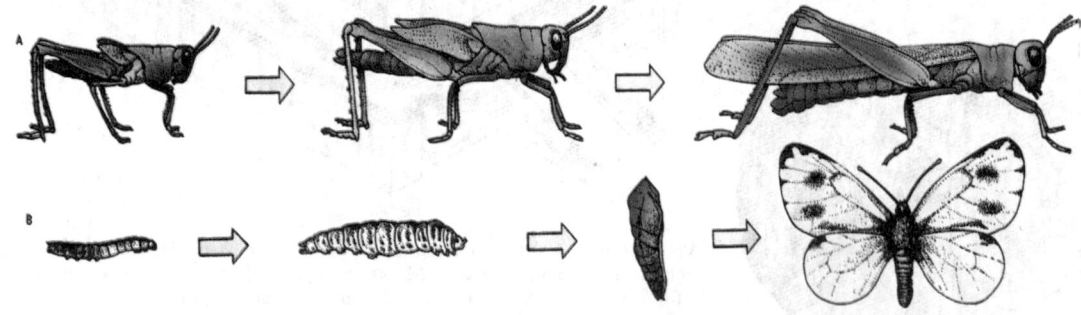

(mercury, liquid at room temperature, being a notable exception), their atoms readily losing electrons to become positive ions. Alloys are easily formed because of the nonspecific nondirectional nature of the metallic bond.

Metallurgy, the science and technology of extracting metals from ores, the methods of refining, purifying, and preparing them for use, and the study of the structure and physical properties of metals and alloys. A few unreactive metals such as silver and gold are found native (uncombined), but most metals occur naturally as minerals (i.e., in chemical

Metaphysical poets, early 17th-century English lyric poets whose style relied on the metaphysical conceit, an elaborate metaphorical image. Most famous among them is John Donne; others include Andrew Marvell, George Herbert, Richard Crashaw, Henry Vaughan, and Thomas Carew. The Metaphysical poets (a term first used by Samuel Johnson in 1744) extended the range of lyric poetry by writing about death, decay, immortality, and faith. They declined in popularity after about 1660, but their complex intellectual content and rich exploration of feeling was a major influence on 20th-century poetry.

Meteor, small speck of material from space, about the size of a grain of sand. Meteors become visible as they burn up in the earth's atmosphere. Friction with the air causes them to glow and vaporize, resembling a swift streak of light (*shooting star* or *falling star*). When the earth crosses the orbit of a comet, whole swarms of meteors, called *meteor showers*, can be seen burning up in the atmosphere.
A *meteorite* is a meteor that reaches the earth's surface before completely burning up in the atmosphere. An estimated 1,000 tons of meteoric material lands on the earth each day

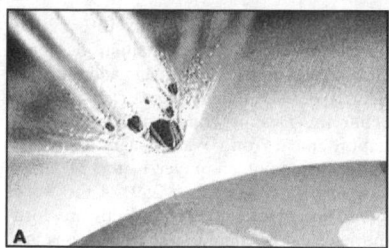

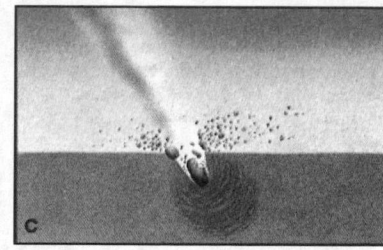

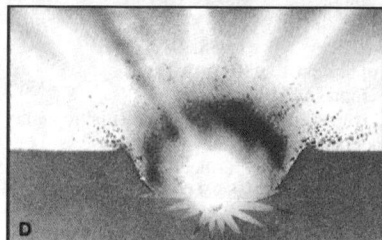

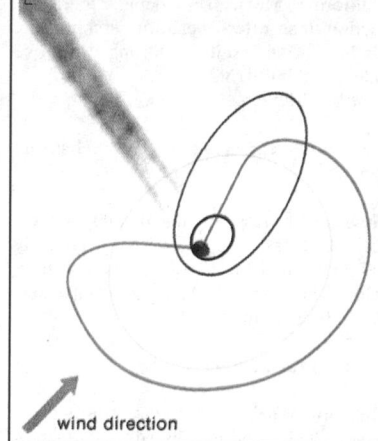

wind direction

The formation of the Meteor Crater took place more than 25,000 years ago. A meteorite, approaching at a high velocity (A), sent shock waves through the plateau upon impact (B). As the meteorite burrowed deeper (C), these shock waves culminated in an explosion (D) that carved out the crater. The entire formational process took only a few seconds. Distribution of meteorite fragments into the crater followed an asymmetrical pattern (E), possibly due to the prevailing winds (see arrow). These fragments include heavy boulders that are damaged by heat (black area); spheroids, formed by condensation of metallic vapors (red); small heat-altered fragments (yellow); and unaltered fragments (blue).

M

Meteorology, study of the atmosphere and its phenomena, weather, and climate. Based on atmospheric physics, meteorology is mainly applied in weather forecasting and control. The rain gauge and wind vane were known in ancient times. The other basic instruments-anemometer, barometer, hygrometer, and thermometer-were invented by 1790; however, simultaneous observations over a wide area were impracticable until the development of the telegraph. Since World War I, observations of the upper atmosphere have been made using airplanes, balloons, and radiosonde, and since World War II, using radar, rockets, and artificial satellites. Observed phenomena include clouds, precipitation and humidity, wind and air pressure, air temperature, storms, cyclones, air masses, and fronts.
See also: Atmosphere.

Meter, basic unit of length in the metric system. One meter is equal to 39.37 in. and to 1.1 yd.
See also: Metric system.

Methadone, synthetic narcotic used extensively to treat heroin addicts. Methadone causes less severe and dangerous withdrawal symptoms than other narcotic drugs, although it is also addictive. It is also used as an analgesic, particularly in terminally ill patients, and sometimes in very small doses as a cough suppressant.

Methamphetamine, generic name of a powerful drug that is a derivate of and similar to amphetamine. Also known as 'speed,' methamphetamine enables a user to work and talk for long periods. Legally obtainable only with a doctor's prescription, methamphetamine can be hazardous if misused. Withdrawal symptoms may occur when use is stopped.
See also: Amphetamine.

Methane (CH_4), colorless, odorless gas; the simplest alkane. It is produced by decomposing organic matter in sewage and in marshes (hence the name *marsh gas*), and is the 'firedamp' of coal mines. Nontoxic but highly flammable, methane when mixed with air, oxygen, or chlorine is explosive. It is the chief constituent of natural gas, occurs in coal gas and water gas, and is produced in petroleum refining. Methane is used as a fuel, for making carbon-black, and for chemical synthesis.

Methanol (CH_3OH), also called methyl alcohol or wood alcohol, type of alcohol with many industrial uses. Methanol is clear, colorless, flammable, and poisonous. Ways of lowering its manufacturing costs and enlarging its use as an alternate fuel are being sought.

Methodists, doctrine and polity of Protestant churches that originated in the 18th-century evangelical revival led by John and Charles Wesley. The name Methodist was first used in 1729 for members of the 'Holy Club' of Oxford University, led by the Wesleys, who lived 'by rule and method.' Influenced by the Moravian Church, Methodism began as an evangelical movement in 1738 when the Wesleys and George Whitefield began preaching. Banned from most Anglican pulpits, they preached in the open air and drew vast crowds. After Wesley's death in 1791, Methodist societies formally separated from the Church of England and became the Wesleyan Methodist Church. The American Methodist movement was established after 1771 by Francis Asbury and Thomas Coke. Methodist polity in Britain is in effect Presbyterian; in the United States it is Episcopal. Methodism traditionally stresses conversion, holiness, and social welfare.
See also: Protestantism; Wesley.

Methuselah, oldest person in the Bible. According to the Bible (Gen. 5.25-27) he lived to the age of 969. He was the grandfather of Noah. The term 'old as Methuselah' is a popular expression denoting an old person.
See also: Bible.

Methyl alcohol *See:* Methanol.

Methylbenzene *See:* Toluene.

Metre *See:* Meter; Metric system.

Metric system, decimal system of measurement, first adopted in France during the Revolution (1790s), called the Système International d'Unités, or SI. This simple system is used to measure length and distance, surface, volume and capacity, weight and mass, time, and temperature. The modern version of the metric system currently in use worldwide includes 7 base units: meter (length or distance), kilogram (mass), second (time), ampère (electricity),degrees (temperature, Celsius or Kelvin), candela (light), and mole (chemical substance).

Metropolitan Museum of Art, largest and most comprehensive art museum in the United States, founded in 1870 in New York City. Its collections include art, pottery, jewelry, and sculpture from ancient Egypt, Greece, Rome, Babylonia, and Assyria; Eastern paintings, sculptures, and artifacts; American art, sculpture, and period rooms; African art; and modern art, photography, and industrial design. The Uris Center hosts educational activities. Medieval art is housed in the Cloisters, located in Fort Tryon Park. It features parts of European medieval buildings, outdoor gardens, and medieval art, such as tapestries, ivories, and stained glass.

Metternich (Clemens Wenzel Nepomuk Lothar von Metternich; 1773-1859), Austrian diplomat. After a diplomatic career in Saxony, Prussia, and France he became Austrian foreign minister (1809-1848). He gradually dissociated Austria from France and organized an alliance of Austria, Russia, and Prussia against Napoleon. However, at the Congress of Vienna (1814-1815) he reestablished a system of power whereby Russia and Prussia were balanced by the combined power of Austria, France, and England. Appointed state chancellor in 1821, his authority declined after 1826, and he was overthrown in 1848. The period 1815-1848 is often called the Age of Metternich.
See also: Austria; Vienna, Congress of.

Metz (pop. 124,000), city in northeastern France on the Moselle River, a center for iron and coal mining. Of pre-Roman origin, it became a bishopric and capital of the Frankish kingdom of Austrasia. France annexed it in 1552, and Germany held it from 1871 to 1918.
See also: France.

Meuse River, rises in the Langres Plateau, France, and flows north for about 580 mi

M

(933 km) across Belgium and the Netherlands, where it is named *Maas*, into the North Sea. It is an important thoroughfare and line of defense for France and Belgium.

Mexicali (pop. 603,000), city in Mexico founded in 1903. Mexicali is the capital and second largest city of the Mexican state of Baja California Norte. The name is a combination of the words 'Mexico' and 'California.' Mexicali is a popular tourist attraction that offers beautiful architecture, handicrafts, and exciting sporting events like rodeos and bullfights.
See also: Mexico.

Mexican Americans *See:* Hispanic Americans.

Mexican hairless, dog that derives its name because it has no coat of hair. It typically weighs about 12 lb (5 kg) and is pinkish in color. The dog was brought to the New World from China.

Mexican turnip *See:* Jicama.

Mexican War (1846-1848), conflict between Mexico and the United States that resulted in the defeat of Mexico and America's acquisition of territory that became California, Nevada, Utah, most of New Mexico and Arizona, and parts of Colorado and Wyoming. The war took place against a background of expansionist sentiment (Manifest Destiny) in the United States, which held that it was destined to become a continental power and the dominant nation of the Western Hemisphere.

The war deeply divided the American people, not least because some feared an extension of slavery into the new territories. The Compromise of 1850 made California a free state but allowed the people of the other territories to decide whether they should be slave or free states. Bitter disputes followed, 12 years later contributing to the chain of events that led to the American Civil War.

An example of Churrigueresque style: the San Cayetano (also called 'la Valenciane') in Guanajuato, Mexico, 18th century.

Mexico

Capital:	Mexico City
Area:	761,530 sq mi
	(1,958,201 sq km)
Population:	103,400,000
Language:	Spanish
Government:	Federal presidential republic
Independent:	1821
Head of gov.:	President
Per capita:	US$ 9.000
Monetary unit:	1 Peso = 100 centavos

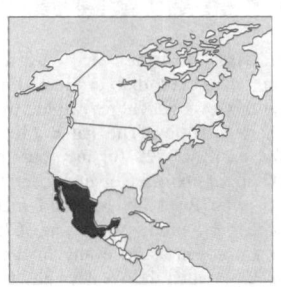

Mexico, the United Mexican States, a federal republic occupying the southernmost portion of the North American continent. Mexico is bounded by the United States to the north, Guatemala and Belize to the south, the Caribbean Sea and the Gulf of Mexico on the east, and the Pacific Ocean on the west.

Land and climate. Mexico is nearly 1,200 mi/1,930 km long with an area of 761,530 sq mi/1,972,544 sq km. Two mountain ranges run most of the length of the country from northwest to southeast, the Sierra Madre Occidental along the Pacific coast and the Sierra Madre Oriental along the Atlantic coast. Between the two ranges lies the great central plateau rising 3,000 to 4,000 ft/914 to 1219 m in the north to 8,000 ft/2,438 m in the south. Mexico City, the capital, is situated near the southern end of the plateau at an elevation of about 7,400 ft/2,256 m.

Mexico is a land of dramatic contrasts. Its mountain ranges include the extinct volcanoes Popocatépetl (17,888 ft/5,452 m), Ixtacihuatl (17,343 ft/5,286 m), and Orizaba (18,406 ft/5,610 m). Its high plateau gives way to semi-tropical coastal regions. To the northwest lies Baja California, mountainous desert, and to the southeast the low limestone plateau of the Yucatan which includes tropical forests in the south. As a result, Mexico's climate varies considerably from the mountains to the desert, from the temperate plateau to the tropical lowlands. In all, less than 15% of the land surface is cultivable and most of it is on the central plateau.

People. The majority of Mexicans are mestizos, a mixture of native Americans and Spanish, but nearly one-tenth of the population remains pure native American and many of Mexico's native Americans speak only

their native languages. About 10% of the population is of pure Spanish descent. Spanish is the official language and the people are overwhelmingly Roman Catholic.

Economy. Despite considerable industrialization since World War II, agriculture remains the major employer in the Mexican economy with more than 25% of the work force. The chief subsistence crops are corn and beans. The main commercial crops are wheat, corn, beans, cotton, coffee, sugarcane, sisal, and citrus fruits. The country also has valuable forests and fisheries which contribute to its economy. Mexico is rich in minerals and exports silver, zinc, lead, manganese, and sulfur. Abundant reserves of iron ore and uranium await development. Huge petroleum reserves, perhaps the second largest in the world, were discovered in the mid 1970s. Major industries include iron and steel, textiles, chemicals, electric goods, ceramics, paper, footwear, and processed foods. Mexico is plagued by inflation, government debt, and, until 2002, by a severe drop in world oil prices. Its economic problems are compounded by unemployment and illiteracy.

History. Prehistoric remains indicate that Mexico was inhabited as early as 10,000 B.C. Between A.D. 300 and 800, four classical native American civilizations developed in Mexico including the Maya of the Yucatán Peninsula. By the 15th century the Aztecs established the last Indian civilization in Mexico with its capital at Tenochtitlán, the site of present day Mexico City. It was this empire, under Montezuma, which was conquered by the Spanish under Hernán Cortés in 1521 thereby ushering the Spanish dominion. The Spanish consolidated their rule, exploiting the labor and mineral wealth of the colony they named New Spain. The colony was governed by a line of 62 viceroys appointed by the Spanish throne until independence in 1821. At the same time, the Roman Catholic church pursued a thorough policy of converting the Indians to Christianity and acquired considerable power. In September 1810, Father Miguel Hidalgo raised a rebellion against Spain which was subsequently crushed. Another priest, José María Morelos, took up the struggle in 1813, but he too was defeated. Finally, backed by conservative elements seeking independence from a more liberal Spain, the country achieved independence in 1821 under Augustín de Iturbide. Emperor Augustín I was deposed in 1823 by Antonio Lopes de Santa Anna who dominated the turbulent politics of the new federal republic until 1855. During that period, Mexico waged a costly war with the U.S., the Mexican-American War (1846-1848), which led to the loss of Texas and Mexico's considerable northwest territories in the U.S.

In 1855 Benito Pablo Juarez overthrew Santa Anna and introduced a more liberal constitution. Civil war between liberals and conservatives followed. In the ensuing turmoil, the French invaded and Napoleon III installed Maximilian of Austria as emperor in 1864. He was overthrown and executed in 1867. From 1876 to 1911 Mexico was governed by Gen. Porfirio Díaz, who brought a measure of stability and economic growth

The Plaza de las tres Culturas (Square of Three Cultures) contains the remainders of an Aztec pyramid, a sixteenth-century Franciscan church, the Santiago de Tlaltelolco, and high-rise apartment buildings built by the government.

M

to the country. But his oligarchic regime generated deep and widespread resentment. Pancho Villa, Emiliano Zapata, and Francisco Madero raised rebellions which led to the downfall of Díaz in 1911. In 1917 Venustiano Carranza established control and promulgated a new liberal constitution. President Alvaro Obregon (1920-1924) began a program of land redistribution and education and carried on a struggle with the Roman Catholic church which was not settled until 1929 when the church was granted autonomy in religious matters only. In 1929 Plutarco Elías Calles established the Institutional Revolutionary Party (PRI) which has effectively governed Mexico until the 1990's. President Lázaro Cárdenas continued educational reform and nationalized some industries. Since World War II, Mexico has been politically relatively moderate and stable, concentrating primarily on economic development. Despite progress, significant signs of strain and resistance were apparent under the presidencies of Luis Echeverria and his successor José Lopez Portillo. Mexico's economy suffered in the 1970s, due in part to the worldwide oil glut. Miguel de la Madrid Hurtado was elected president in 1982, promising new programs to deal with Mexico's grave economic problems, such as the crushing foreign debt and high unemployment. De la Madrid's programs failed, and Carlos Salinas de Gortari succeeded him in 1988. Under De Gortari's leadership, Mexico's economy has enjoyed a substantial revival, helped by new foreign investment and the turning over of government-run industries to the private sector. In the mid-1990's, two rebel groups began uprisings in southern Mexico; the Zapatista National Liberation Army (EZLN) demanded social reforms to help Indians in the state of Chiapas, and the Popular Revolutionary Army sought to overthrow the government and replace it with a Marxist regime. Also in the 1990's, an economic crisis developed as a result of the government's devaluation of the peso. In 1996, the government instituted major political and electoral reforms to lessen the dominance of the PRI over other political parties. At the 1997 elections, the PRI lost its absolute majority for the first time. Vicente Fox Quesada's opposition party Alliance for Change won the 2000 elections. He wanted to meet the demands of the EZLN, who pressed their argument by a march on the capital city in which 150,000 people took part. The final legislation was unacceptable according to the EZLN. A large number of classified security files were released in 2002. The files revealed that hundreds of political activists had been tortured and killed by security troops in the 1960s and 1970s. Fox stated that his government would not be afraid to prosecute.

Mexico City (pop. 9,800,000), capital and largest city of Mexico. Located at an altitude of about 7,400 ft (2,256 m) and at the southern end of Mexico's central plateau, it is surrounded by the mountain ranges of Ixtacihuatl and Popocatepétl. The climate is cool and dry, but the city has often been damaged by local floods. Mexico City is on the site of the old Aztec capital of Tenochtitlán, founded in 1325. Cortés captured the city in 1521, and for the next 300 years it was the seat of the viceroyalty of New Spain; consequently it possesses some of the finest Spanish colonial architecture. The city was hit by a severe earthquake in 1985 and suffers greatly from air pollution. *See also:* Mexico.

Meyer, Julius Lothar (1830-1895), German scientist who developed the periodic chart of the elements which organizes the elements according to atomic weight and property. He also demonstrated the relationship between atomic weights and the properties of elements. *See also:* Chemistry; Periodic table.

Meyerbeer, Giacomo (1791-1864), German composer. His romantic and spectacular operas, with librettos by A.E. Scribe, set the vogue for French opera. Most famous are his *Robert le Diable* (1831), *Les Huguenots* (1836), and *L'Africaine* (1865). Meyerbeer's music influenced that of Richard Wagner.

Meyerhold, Vsevolod Emilevic (real name Karl Theodor Kasimir Meyerhold; 1874-1940), Russian playwright of German descent, pioneering play reformer. Opposed the realistic views of Stanislavsky, experimented since 1902 with symbolic-abstract theater. After 1917 he joined constructivism and in 1924 began his own theater. He performed grotesque anti-illusionist theater based on his own methods of biomechanics which express human relationships through body eloquence. This caused clashes with socialist realism and he was arrested in 1939, after the theater had already been closed in 1938.

Miami (city) (pop. 2,100,000), city in southeast Florida, at the mouth of the Miami River on Biscayne Bay. Its near-tropical climate, fine hotels, beaches, and recreational facilities make it a world-famous resort center. Miami was chartered in 1896, when Henry Flagler brought the railroad to Biscayne Bay. Now an agricultural processing and shipping center, Miami is also a center for aircraft and ship rebuilding and textiles.

Mica, group of minerals that split into thin, flat sheets of aluminum, silicon, and oxygen. Varieties of mica include muscovite, biotite, phlogopite, and lepidolite. Mica can be found in glistening rocks such as igneous and metamorphic. In its sheet, scrap, or ground form, it has a wide variety of industrial uses. Most scrap mica is produced in the United States.

Micah, Book of, sixth of the Old Testament Minor Prophets. These prophets were oracles of the Judean prophet Micah, who flourished in the late 8th century B.C. (Chapters 4 through 7 are believed to have been written later.) Ethical in tenor, the book prophesies judgment for sin and redemption by the Messiah. *See also:* Old Testament.

Michaelmas daisy *See:* Aster.

Michaux, Henri (1899-1984), Belgian (French-speaking) writer (e.g. travel stories), also known as a painter and artist. Prose and poetry are united in his work. His poetic prose, of a bizarre nature, is for him a way to get to a higher degree of knowledge about himself as well as the world surrounding him, which he sees as hostile. Examples of his earlier work are *Equado* (1929) and *Un barbare en Asie* (A Barbarian in Asia) (1932), *Qui je fus* (Who I Was) (1927), *Apparitions* (1946), *l'Espace du dedans* (The Space Within) (1944). In the early 1960s Michaux was intensely involved with

The highway connection between Miami, on the mainland, and Miami Beach, located 2.5 mi (4 km) from the coast (via Belle Island and Venetian Island). Miami Beach 10 mi (16 km) long, 0.9 to 3 mi (1.5 to 5 km wide), one of America's most famous recreation areas, is connected to the mainland by four highways.

M

drugs like mescaline in an attempt to gain new knowledge about his own inner self. He wrote down his experiences in a number of texts, collected in volumes like *l'Infini turbulent* (1957) and *Connaissance par les gouffres* (1961). The collection *Passages* was published in 1963.

Michel, Hartmut (1948-), German biochemist. Michel, Johann Deisenhofer, and Robert Huber shared the 1988 Nobel Prize for chemistry for their study of the structure of protein molecules involved in photosynthesis. Michel crystallized the proteins in 1982, enabling Deisenhofer and Huber to analyze them.
See also: Biochemistry; Photosynthesis.

Michelangelo (Michelangelo Buonarroti; 1475-1564), Italian sculptor, painter, architect, and poet. As a child he was apprenticed to the Florentine painter Ghirlandaio; in adolescence he was a protégé of Lorenzo de Medici. He went to Rome in 1496, where his marble *Pietà* in Saint Peter's (1498-1499) established him as the foremost living sculptor. In Florence Michelangelo sculpted the magnificent *David* (1501-1504). In 1505 he returned to Rome to work on a sepulchral monument tomb for Pope Julius II. There he painted the ceiling of the Sistine Chapel (1508-1512), one of the most influential works in the history of art. After living in Florence (1515-1534) and building the Medici Chapel and Laurentian Library for the Medici family and assisting as engineer in the defense of Florence, Michelangelo moved permanently to Rome. He painted the *Last Judgment* in the Sistine Chapel (1536-1541) and was chief architect of Saint Peter's Basilica (1546-1564). His architectural designs were influential throughout Italy and in France and England.
See also: Renaissance.

Michener, James Albert (1907-1997), U.S. author. His Pulitzer Prize-winning *Tales of the South Pacific* (1947), based on his U.S. Navy experiences in World War II, inspired the famous musical *South Pacific* (1949) by Rodgers and Hammerstein. He also wrote such ambitious, historically based novels as *Hawaii* (1959), *The Source* (1965), *Centennial* (1974), *Chesapeake* (1978), *The Covenant* (1980), *Poland* (1983), *Texas* (1985), and *Caribbean* (1989). *A Century of Sonnets* (poems) was published in 1997.

Michigan (Wolverine State, Great Lake State; pop. 9,774,000), state in the U.S., bordered by Lake Superior, Lake Michigan, Lake Huron, Ontario (Canada), Lake Erie, Ohio and Indiana; 58,550 sq mi (151,586 sq km). Capital city: Lansing. The largest city is Detroit. The state is divided in two by the Strait of Mackinac. Largely at a low altitude. Agriculture (corn, wheat, sugar beets), cattle breeding (dairy and meat) and forestry. National center of the car industry, e.g. in Detroit; space travel industry. Other industries: cement, chemical, food and pharmaceutical. Extraction of iron ore and mineral oil.
Originally inhabited by Indians; during the 17th century French colonists and fur

traders arrived first, being chased away by the British in the 18th century. The name is derived from Lake Michigan, which was called the big water by the Indians. In 1837 Michigan became a member of the Union. The advantageous location of Detroit and the presence of a relatively highly educated working population resulted in the development of this city into an industrial center, especially in the automobile industry, particularly in the beginning of the 20th century. In the 1980s this industry came to a deadlock and the state went into an economic recession. The services sector should bring relief.

Michigan, Lake, third largest of the Great Lakes, in North America. It is the largest freshwater lake wholly within the United States, with an area of 22,178 sq mi (57,441 sq km). Important ports on the lake include Milwaukee, Wis., Chicago, Ill., and Gary, Ind. In the north, Lake Michigan empties into Lake Huron by the Straits of Mackinac. It is part of the navigable Great Lakes-Saint Lawrence Seaway; a series of connections link it to the Mississippi River and the Gulf of Mexico.
See also: Great Lakes.

Microbe, see: Microbiology.

Microbiology (formerly called bacteriology), study of microorganisms, including bacteria, viruses, fungi, protozoans, yeasts, and algae. Microbiology includes anatomy, physiology, genetics, taxonomy, and ecology, along with branches of medicine, veterinary sciences, and plant pathology, since many microorganisms are disease causing by nature. Microbiologists also play an important role in the food industry, particularly in baking and brewing. In the pharmaceutical industry, they supervise the production of antibiotics.
See also: Bacteriology.

Microcomputer, complete small computer system, consisting of hardware and software, whose main processing parts are made of semiconductor integrated circuits. The various applications include video games, traffic control systems, scientific instruments, credit card verification and cash machines, blood analyzers, pinball machines, microwave ovens, flow meters, sewing machines, pollution monitors, and control units for hundreds of other devices.
See also: Computer.

Microelectronics, branch of technology and electronics that deals with the production of miniature electronic devices that use minimal electric power. Approaches include forming integrated circuits, thin-film techniques, and solid logic modules.

Microfiche *See:* Microfilm.

Microfilm, photographic film used for recording and storing graphic information in a reduced size. Microfilm comes in rolls, often called microform, and rectangular sheets called microfiche. It is used extensively in government offices, libraries, banks, and businesses.

Micronesia

Capital:	Pohnpei
Area:	270 sq mi (700 sq km)
Population:	136,000
Language:	English
Government:	Federal republic
Independent:	1990
Head of gov.:	President
Per capita:	US$ 2,000
Monetary unit:	1 U.S. dollar = 100 cents

Micronesia (Federated States of), Island state of 670 islands and atols in the western Pacific Ocean. Part of the UN Trust Territory of the Pacific Islands since 1947. Internal self-government was granted in 1979. In 1982 the Federated States of Micronesia became independent and signed a compact of free association with the United States. Despite its independence, foreign policy and defense are administered by the US government. The US use a number of islands as a military base.
A new compact of free association was signed at the end of 2002.

Microorganism *See:* Microbiology.

Microphone, instrument (invented c.1880) for transmitting or intensifying sounds, by means of electricity that converts sound waves into electrical waves. It is used in radio and television broadcasting and the film and recording industries. Types of microphones include carbon, crystal and ceramic, moving coil, ribbon, and capacitor.

Microprocessor, integrated circuit that performs the functions of a large computer on a tiny 'chip' of silicon. Unlike a computer, which can be programmed to solve many different problems, a microprocessor is designed for a specific task. Microprocessors are called very large-scale integrated circuits because they may contain more than 100,000 transistors. First produced in 1971, microprocessors today can perform about 66 million functions per second. Microprocessors are used in a variety of 'smart' devices, including appliances used at home, businesses, and industrial plants.
See also: Computer; Integrated circuit.

Microscope, instrument for producing en-

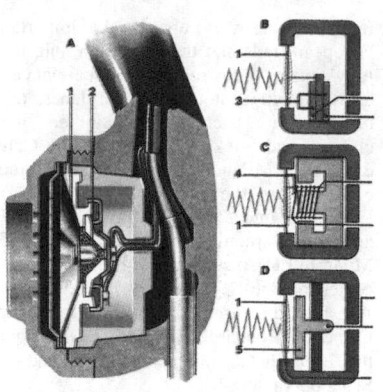

A microphone consists of a diaphragm (1), which vibrates in response to sound waves, and an attached transducer, which converts the vibrations into a corresponding variable current. The varying current may be obtained by a change in: (A) electrical resistance of carbon granules (2); (B) voltage induces by deformation of a piezoelectric crystal (3); (C) voltage induces in a coil (4) moving in a magnetic field; and (D) capacitance between diaphragm and fixed plate (5).

M

larged images of small objects. In the compound microscope a magnified, inverted image of an object resting on the 'stage' (a platform) is produced by the objective lens, or lens system. This image is viewed through the eyepiece (or ocular) lens, which acts as a simple microscope, giving a greatly magnified image. Generally the object is viewed by transmitted light, illumination being controlled by mirror, diaphragm, and 'substage condenser' lenses. Near-transparent objects are often stained to make them visible; phase-contrast microscopy, in which a 'phase plate' produces a diffraction effect, is an alternative to staining. Objects too small to be seen directly can be made visible in dark-field illumination, in which an opaque disk prevents direct illumination; the object is viewed in the light diffracted from the remaining oblique illumination. Although theoretically the magnifying power of the optical microscope is unlimited, magnifications greater than about 2,000 offer no improvement in resolving power for light of visible wavelengths. The shorter wavelength of ultraviolet light allows better resolution and hence higher useful magnification. For yet finer resolution, physicists use electron beams and electromagnetic focusing. The field-ion microscope, which offers the greatest magnifications is quite dissimilar from the optical microscope. The compound microscope was invented in the early 17th century.
See also: Leeuwenhoek, Anton van.

Microwave, electromagnetic wave in the superhigh frequency radio spectrum (890 to 300,000 megacycles per sec). Microwaves are electromagnetic radiations of wavelength between .03937 in (1 mm) and 1 ft (30 cm). Microwaves first received attention through the use of radar in World War II (1939-1945); today they are used in radar, telecommunications, and spectroscopy and for cooking (microwave ovens).
See also: Radio; Television; Ultrahigh frequency waves.

Midas, in Greek mythology, king of Phrygia who was given the power by the god Dionysus to turn whatever he touched into gold. At first a cause for celebration, this power soon became a curse when even Midas' food turned to gold. With the aid of Dionysus, Midas was able to reverse his powers by bathing himself in the Pactolus River.
See also: Mythology.

Middle Ages (A.D. 400-1500), also known as the medieval period, era in western European history between the fall of the Roman Empire and the beginnings of modern European civilization. By the year 400 A.D., Germanic tribes, called barbarians by the Romans, began to invade the territories of Rome. By this time, the Roman Empire had lost much of its power and could not prevent the invasions. Tribes such as the Visigoths, Angles, Jutes, Saxons, Franks, and Ostrogoths divided the huge Roman Empire into different kingdoms. Because of the primitive legal and economic structures of these tribes, much of the Roman legacy in law, trade, and education was destroyed or lost for centuries. It is for this reason that the term 'Dark Ages' is sometimes incorrectly applied to this era. The laws that once provided safety and security to Roman citizens gave way to tribal allegiances and superstitions. The great network of roads built by Rome to maintain trade and communication were destroyed by the barbarians. In the absence of a trade economy, money was no longer necessary. Farming became the economic mainstay of Europe. By the 9th century, most of western Europe was organized into large estates called manors. The manors were owned by a handful of wealthy landowners, but the actual work was accomplished by peasants. The increased power of the manor diminished the need for towns and the need for a merchant class. Consequently, the Middle Ages is characterized by a diminishment in urban life and the loss of culture. Education and cultural institutions were almost totally destroyed during this period. Knowledge of Greece and Rome was lost, and the Latin language was unknown to most, and the disciplines of literature, painting, and architecture were forgotten. The sole civilizing force during the Middle Ages was the Christian Church, which saved western Europe from intellectual and cultural oblivion. By the 11th and 12th centuries some powerful lords had succeeded in establishing stable governments that provided peace and security. This, in turn, stimulated thought and economic activities-merchants and towns reappeared, trade routes were established, technological advances occurred, and people ventured far beyond the borders of the manor. This era also experienced remarkable artistic and intellectual achievements such as the cathedral of Notre Dame, the writings of St. Thomas Aquinas, the introduction of the works of Aristotle, and the establishment of universities. Between the 14th and 16th centuries, the Middle Ages slowly yielded to a more modern Europe characterized by the advances of the Renaissance.

Middle East, region, mostly in southwestern Asia but extending into southeastern Europe and northeastern Africa. Today the term usually includes Bahrain, Cyprus, Egypt, Iran, Iraq, Israel, Jordan, Kuwait,

Apart from the metal industry, the textile industry was the only medieval branch of more than local significance. Well-known centres were northern Italy and Flanders. In some towns the laborers were engaged in cottage industry.

The compound microscope is a magnifying precision instrument that utilises two converging lens systems: an objective (the system nearest to the specimen that is to be magnified), and an eyepiece (the system nearest to the eye). The objective forms a magnified image of the specimen, which is further magnified by the eyepiece.
1 Objective: field lens
2 Eyepiece: eye lens
3 Specimen
4 Eyepiece: objective
5 The microscope effectively increases the angle: light from the specimen enters the eye, the virtual image appears to lie in this plane
6 Mirror

M

Arabs in a supermarket in Abu Dhabi. The clash between the traditional values of the Arab society and modern influences, is a growing cause of concern among Saudi Arabian leaders in particular, who anxiously watch how more liberal views rapidly gain ground in neighbouring states (e.g. Bahrain).

Lebanon, Libya, Saudi Arabia and the other countries of the Arabian peninsula, and Sudan. Politically, other countries of predominantly Islamic culture, such as Algeria, Morocco, and Tunisia, are sometimes included. The site of early civilization (including that of Sumer and Egypt, 3500-3100 B.C.), the Middle East was also the birthplace of Judaism, Christianity, and Islam. It has been the seat of many great empires, including the Ottoman Empire, which began in the 14th century and survived until 1923. The Tigris-Euphrates and the Nile are the Middle East's 2 major river systems; agriculture has been its most important economic activity. Today, the Middle East has assumed geopolitical importance as the world's primary oil-producing region; it is also the focus of international tensions and strife.

Middleton, Thomas (1580-1627), English dramatist. He wrote lively, naturalistic comedies, the Lord Mayor of London's pageants and various masques, and 2 tragedies concerning human corruption: *The Changeling* (1621) and *Women Beware Women* (1657). *A Game at Chesse* (1624) was his satire on political marriages with Spain, suppressed under James I.

Midge, large group (about 2,000 species) of tiny flies belonging to the Chironomidae family. Although related to biting midges and resembling mosquitos, midges do not bite. They often appear in swarms around streams and ponds. Their larvae, found in water, mud, tree bark, or manure, provide food for certain varieties of insects and fish.

Midget, human dwarf having normal body proportions, mental capacity, and sexual development. This type of dwarfism is caused by a deficiency of pituitary growth hormone. *See also:* Dwarf.

Midway Island, group of islands (2 sq mi/5.2 sq km) northwest of Honolulu. Annexed by the United States in 1867 and used as a naval base, the island was the site of the Battle of Midway, the first important U.S. naval victory of World War II. *See also:* World War II.

Mies van der Rohe, Ludwig (1886-1969),

German-born U.S. architect, famous for functional but elegant buildings in the International Style, constructed of brick, steel, and glass. His work includes the Illinois Institute of Technology campus (1939) in Chicago, and the Seagram Building (1958, with Philip Johnson) in New York. Although he had no formal training, he was a director of the Bauhaus school and one of the leading architects. *See also:* Architecture; Bauhaus.

Mifune, Kiuzo (1883-1965), Japanese judoka, was appointed as a teacher in 1923 at the Kodokan in Tokyo, after he had won an impressive series of victories at a young age. He achieved a high level of perfection in judo and at the time of his death he was the only judoka in the world to possess the tenth dan.

Mifune, Toshiro (1920-1997), Japanese actor. Mifune became famous with his roles in the movies of Akira Kurosawa; between 1948 and 1965 he played in sixteen them, of which especially *Rashomon* (1950) and *Seven Samurai* (1954) made a great impression in the West as well. He became the personification of the samurai, which he played with great psychological profundity. In 1965, after *Red Beard*, he broke off the cooperation with Kurosawa, began his own production company and cashed in on his success by playing in Western films as well, such as Boorman's *Hell in the Pacific* (1969) and Spielberg's *1941* (1979). In addition to Kurosawa's movies he also played in films by other big Japanese directors, such as *The life of Oharu* (1952) by Mizoguchi and *Rebellion* by Kobayashi, and in countless other Japanese movies which never reached the West.

Mignonette, decorative garden plant belonging to the Resedaceae family. Found in North America and Europe, it has bushy leaves and tall spikes on which appear small, fragrant, yellowish-white or flowers with reddish pollen sacs.

Mikan, George (1924-), U.S. basketball player. Known for his strength and accurate hook shot, he was named the Associated Press' Player of the Half Century. Standing at 6-ft 10-in (208-cm), Mikan became the first center known for scoring (11,764 career points). He played in the National Basketball Association (NBA) for the Minneapolis Lakers (1946-1955), and led them to 5 championships (1949, 1950, 1952-1954). In 1967, he was named commissioner of the newly founded American Basketball Association. Mikan was inducted into the Basketball Hall of Fame in 1960.

Mikulic, Branko (1928-), premier of former Yugoslavia (1986-1988). He joined the League of Communists in 1943 and was a member of the Central Committee Presidium (1984-1986). Mikulic was appointed as premier, but he and his entire cabinet resigned in 1988 over disputes with the Yugoslav parliament regarding economic planning.

Milan (pop. 1,359,000), city in northern

Italy, capital of Lombardy. An important European trade and transportation hub, it is Italy's major industrial and commercial center, producing automobiles, airplanes, textiles, chemicals, electrical equipment, machinery, and books. Founded by the Celts c.400 B.C., Milan was a major late Roman city; it was the principal city state of Lombardy under the Visconti (1277-1447) and Sforza families. Spanish from 1535, Milan fell to Austria in 1714 and became a center of the 19th-century Risorgimento. Artistic treasures include the Milan Cathedral, Leonardo da Vinci's *Last Supper*, the Brera palace and art gallery, and La Scala opera house.

Milan Decree, order issued by Napoleon I of France in December, 1807. Hoping to bring about a complete economic blockade of Britain, the decree stated that even neutral ships were subject to capture. Although its effect was felt by the neutral nations-including the United States-the decree could not be enforced due to the superior naval strength of the British. *See also:* Continental System; Napoleon I.

Mildew, general name for superficial growth of many types of fungi often found on plants and material derived from plants. Powdery mildews, numbering about 50, are caused by fungi belonging to the Ascomycetes order Erysiphales; the powdery effect is due to the masses of spores. Downy mildews are caused by Phycomycetes. Both types of disease can be controlled by the use of fungicides.

Milhaud, Darius (1892-1974), French composer, one of the Parisian group called Les Six, noted for his polytonality (the simultaneous use of different keys). His vast output includes the jazz-influenced ballet *Creation of the World* (1923), *Saudades do Brasil* (1921), and various operas, among them *Christophe Colombe* (1930).

Military service, compulsory *See:* Draft, military.

Milk, liquid secreted by the mammary glands of female mammals. It contains water, protein, fat, sugar, vitamins A, C, and D, and some B vitamins, as well as inorganic salts and minerals (calcium and phosphorus). In any species, milk serves as a complete food for the young of that species until weaning. Milk for human use is commercially produced by cows and water buffalo (especially in India); goat's milk is also commonly used in some areas, particularly the Middle East. An extremely perishable liquid, milk must be cooled to a temperature of not more than 10°C (50°F) within two hours of milking and maintained at that temperature until delivery.

Milk snake, small kingsnake (*Lampropeltis triangulum*), found in North America, from the northeastern United States to Mexico. About 4 ft (1.2 m) long, milk snakes are bright red, black, and yellow when young and gray and brown when adult.

Milkweed, any of various perennial plants

(genus *Asclepias*) that secrete latex. They are common in fields and waste areas of North America. Milkweed is poisonous in large quantities especially for children.

Milky Way, spiral galaxy with a radius of about 50,000 light-years, containing some 100 billion stars. The Milky Way is shaped like a flat disk about 10,000 light-years thick in most places, about 30,000 light-years at the center. It is a modest-sized galaxy. Our solar system is in one of its spiral arms, just over 30,000 light-years from the galactic center. The galaxy rotates about a roughly spherical nucleus, the sun circling the galactic center once every 230 million years or so. The Milky Way is surrounded by a spheroidal halo some 165,000 light-years in diameter composed of gas, dust, occasional stars, and globular clusters. The name of the galaxy is derived from its appearance as a hazy, milklike band of stars in the night sky. Irregular dark patches are caused by intervening clouds of gas dust.
See also: Galaxy; Solar System.

Mill, name of British literary family famed for their work in history, philosophy, economics, and psychology. **James Mill** (1773-1836) gained recognition with his book *A History of British India* but whose great contribution came through his work as the disciple of Jeremy Bentham, the father of utilitarianism. Mill was instrumental in explaining the fundamental tenets of the utilitarian doctrine. He also wrote a work on psychology, *Analysis of the Phenomena of the Human Mind* (1829), the first textbook of English economics, *Elements of Political Economy* (1821); and a work on moral philosophy, *Fragment on Mackintosh* (1835). His other accomplishments include being a Presbyterian minister, journalist, and head of the East India Company (1830-1836). **John Stuart Mill** (1806-1873), son of James Mill, is considered one of the most important thinkers of the 19th century. Mill was the head of the utilitarian movement and worked actively to promote the rights of workers and women. His most important work, *System of Logic* (1834), is a seminal work. Other works include *Principles of Political Economy* (1848), the famous *On Liberty* (1859), *The Subjection of Women* (1869), and *Autobiography* (1873). Mill followed in his father's footsteps and became head of the East India Company but then went on to become a member of Parliament in 1865.
See also: Economics; Philosophy; Psychology.

Millais, Sir John Everett (1829-1896), English painter, a founder of the Pre-Raphaelite 'brotherhood' (1848). The realism of his *Christ in the Carpenter's Shop* (1850) caused a scandal. Later works such as *The Blind Girl* (1856) and *Bubbles* (1886) were more sentimental.

Millay, Edna St. Vincent (1892-1950), U.S. poet. Her reputation was established with *A Few Figs from Thistles* (1920). *The Harp Weaver* (1922) won a Pulitzer Prize. Other works include *Wine from These Grapes* (1934) and the verse drama *Aria da Capo* (1920).

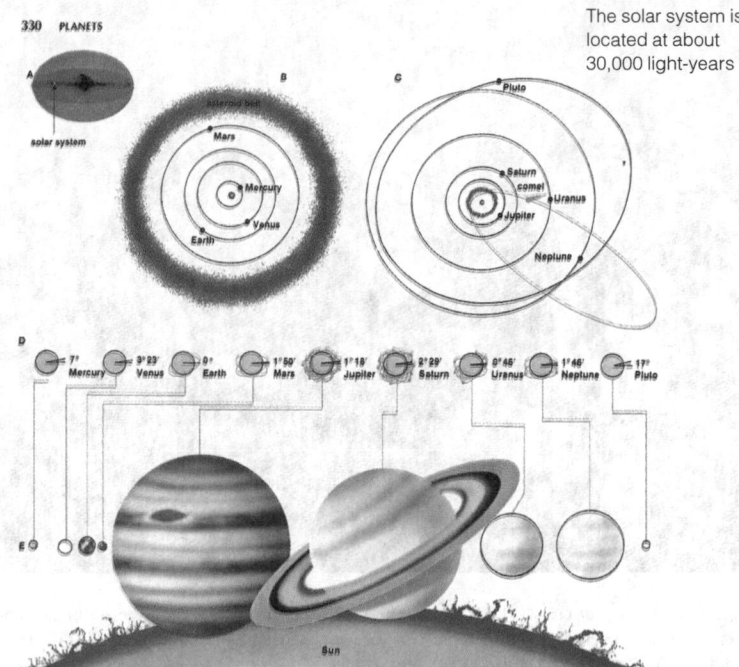

330 PLANETS

The solar system is located at about 30,000 light-years from the center of our galaxy (A). Its nine planets follow nearly circular, but definitely elliptical, orbits around the sun. The four inner planets (B) are earth-like in composition, and are surrounded by an asteroid belt, a zone of debris. Of the five outer planets (C), Pluto's orbit is the most eccentric and actually crosses Neptune's orbit. The path of a comet is much more elliptical than that of a planet. The orbital planes of the planets (D) are inclined no more than 17 degrees to the ecliptic, or earth's path around the sun. The planetary sizes (E) are shown in comparison with a segment of the sun.

Miller, Arthur (1915-), U.S. playwright. He has explored individual and social morality in plays like *Death of a Salesman* (1949; Pulitzer Prize); *The Crucible* (1953), about the witch trials in Salem, Mass.; *A View from the Bridge* (1955; Pulitzer Prize); the partly autobiographical *After the Fall* (1964); and the screenplay *The Misfits* (1961). His autobiography, *Time Bends*, was published in 1987.

American Arthur Miller (1915) became especially famous as a dramatist. His play *Death of a Salesman* (1949) was very successful.

Miller, Glenn (1904-1944), U.S. trombonist and bandleader of the big band 'swing' era of the late 1930s and early 1940s. His blend of instrumental colors, the 'Glenn Miller sound,' had great success. Among his most popular recordings were *In the Mood*, *Moonlight Serenade*, and *Chattanooga Choo-Choo*. He died in a plane crash in Europe during World War II.

Miller, Henry (1891-1980), U.S. writer, noted for his candid treatment of sex and his espousal of the 'natural man.' *Tropic of Cancer* (1934) and *Tropic of Capricorn* (1939) were banned as obscene in the United States until 1961. Other books include the trilogy *The Rosy Crucifixion* (1949-1960). He was a major influence on the Beat Generation of writers.

Millerites *See:* Adventists.

Millet, common name for several varieties of cereal that grow on poor soil and ripen rapidly in hot sun. These characteristics have made it a popular crop in hot, dry countries, particularly in Africa and Asia. The grains can be stored for a long time and are richer in protein than rice, though the yield is small. Fermented millet grain is used to make beer in some countries, e.g. South Africa. In western countries millet is generally grown as cattle feed and for cage-birds. The tall elephant grass of Africa is a millet.

American author Henry Miller (1891-1980) has had many conflicts with censorship, because the subject sexuality has a central place in his works. His book *Sexus*, a volume of the trilogy *The Rosy Crucifixion*, was published only in England, in 1969.

M

M

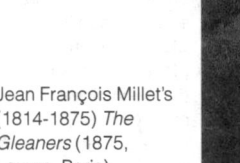

Jean François Millet's (1814-1875) *The Gleaners* (1875, Louvre, Paris).

Millet, Jean François (1814-1875), French painter. His peasant subjects, for example *The Gleaners* (1857) and *The Angelus* (1859), are naturalistic, though romanticized in style.
See also: Barbizon school.

Millî Görüc, Turkish religious-political movement. This broad societal movement developed during the 1970s in Turkey. It pursues the organization of a society on the basis of Islamic legislation. The political party, the Refah, which is associated with Millî Görüc, is one of the largest parties in Turkey. The Millî Görüc is involved in the Turkish migrant communities in Europe and its headquarters are situated in Cologne. The movement aims at the preservation and reinforcement of Islamic identity in a non-Islamic environment and focuses mainly on young persons. After the separation of the radical side in 1983, the movement - especially the branch for the young - opened up for dissident Muslims. However, the relation with Turkish organizations which keep close connections with the Turkish government remained tense and the older supporters have anti-Western feelings.

Millikan, Robert Andrews (1868-1953), U.S. physicist. He was awarded the 1923 Nobel Prize for physics for determining the electron's charge and for his work on the photoelectric effect. He also studied and named cosmic rays.
See also: Photoelectric effect.

Milliliter, in the metric system, unit of capacity equal to one-thousandth (.001) of a liter.
See also: Metric system.

Millimeter *See:* Metric system.

Millimicrosecond *See:* Metric system.

Millipede, segmented arthropod having two pairs of legs on each body segment (unlike centipedes, which have only one pair of legs per segment). Millipedes live in damp soil, rotting vegetation, or under stones. They eat mainly decaying vegetation. Some roll into a ball when molested, while others squirt a spray of poison that can burn the skin. Some tropical millipedes grow to several inches in length, and a few are brightly colored. One species, living among the sequoias of California, is luminous.

Mills, C(harles) Wright (1916-1962), U.S. sociologist and critic of U.S. capitalism and militarism whose work was influential with radical social scientists of the 1970s. His books include *White Collar* (1951), *The Power Elite* (1956), and *The Sociological Imagination* (1959), which argues that sociologists should not be passive observers but agents of social change.
See also: Sociology.

Milne, A(lan) A(lexander) (1882-1956), English writer and dramatist. His fame rests

on stories and poems he wrote for his son Christopher Robin: *Winnie-the-Pooh* (1926), *The House at Pooh Corner* (1928), *When We Were Very Young* (1924), and *Now We Are Six* (1927).

Milo *See:* Sorghum.

Mílos, or Milo, one of the Greek Cyclades islands in the Aegean Sea. The seat of ancient Athenian civilization, it is known as the place where the celebrated statue of Venus de Milo was discovered in 1820. Tourism is important to the economy of the island. Other industries include olive and tobacco production.
See also: Greece.

Milosevic, Slobodan (1941-   ), Yugoslavian/Serbian politician and President (1989-2000). In 1986, he became leader of the Serbian Communist Party and, in 1989, President of Serbia. He pursued a nationalistic policy. In 1990, he became leader of the Serbian Socialist Party. He opposed the independence of Slovenia and Croatia (in 1991). He strived for the annexation of the areas in Croatia and Bosnia and Hercegovina (Great Serbia), the majority of its population being Serbs. In July 1997, he became President of the Federal Republic Yugoslavia. His regime led to the intensification of the ethnic battle in Kosovo, followed by air attacks committed by the NATO. In June 1999, he was forced to capitulate. After Milosevic refused to acknowledge his electoral defeat in October 2000, he was deposed during a revolt. In April 2001, he was arrested and handed over to the International Criminal Tribunal for the former Yugoslavia in The Hague, the Netherlands, which indicted him on a charge of war crimes, crimes against humanity in Croatia and Kosovo and genocide in the Bosnian war. The trial started in 2002.

Milosz, Czeslaw,

Milstein, Nathan (1904-1992), a Russian-American violinist. His virtuoso technique and discerning interpretations brought him wide acclaim. Milstein studied in his native Odessa and with Leopold Auer in St. Petersburg. He left Russia in 1925 and toured Europe and South America as a concert soloist. He made his United States debut in 1929. He became an American citizen in 1942.

Miltiades (c.540?-488? B.C.), Athenian general who defeated the invading Persians at the battle of Marathon (490 B.C.). Earlier, he had served the Persian king Darius I against the Scythians.
See also: Greece, Ancient; Marathon.

Milton, John (1608-1674), English poet. His blank-verse epic *Paradise Lost* (1667), detailing Lucifer's revolt against God and the fall of Adam and Eve in the Garden of Eden, is one of the masterpieces of English literature. His major early works are the ode 'On the Morning of Christ's Nativity' (1629), 'L'Allegro' (1630), 'Il Penseroso' (c. 1631), *Comus* (c. 1632), and 'Lycidas' (1638). A supporter of the anti-monarchists

Slobodan Milosevic (right)) at the International Criminal Tribunal for the former Yugoslavia

during the English Civil War, he wrote many political pamphlets and a defense of freedom of the press, *Areopagitica* (1644). He retired after the Restoration (1660), and though totally blind, dictated his final great works: *Paradise Lost*, *Paradise Regained* (1671), and *Samson Agonistes* (1671).

Milwaukee (pop. 594,000), largest city in Wisconsin, seat of Milwaukee County, in the southeast region of the state. An industrial center and leading Great Lakes port (on Lake Michigan), Milwaukee was incorporated in 1848. Notable landmarks include the Greek Orthodox Annunciation Church, designed by Frank Lloyd Wright; the War Memorial Center, housing the Milwaukee Art Center, designed by Eero Saarinen; the Performing Arts Center (1969); and the Civic Center downtown. The city has many spacious parks. Its educational institutions include the University of Wisconsin at Milwaukee, Marquette University, and 16 other universities and colleges.
See also: Wisconsin.

Mimosa, any of several tropical American plants (genus *Mimosa*) of the pulse family, with pink flowers and small leaves. One variety is called the sensitive plant (*M. pudica*), because its leaves fold together when touched, though after a few minutes they return to the normal position.

Minahasa (pop. 500,000), area in the northern part of the Indonesian island Sulawesi; 1,815 sq mi (4,700 sq km). Agriculture (rice, coffee, corn, copra, tobacco, spices and fruit); export of agricultural products through the port of Manado. Population of Manado (Menado) is 230,000, many of which are Chinese. During the colonial period the Manado residence was important. University (1961). Extraction of gold, copper, tin, sulphur, salt, diamond and other precious stones. The level of education is relatively high because of the intensive involvement of the Dutch mission, and more than 80% of the inhabitants of Minahasa are Christian.

Minas Gerais (Port.: general mines; pop. 16.7 million), state in the southeast of Brazil; 226,796 sq mi (587,175 sq km). Capital city: Belo Horizonte. Densely populated and heavily industrialized area. Influences Brazil strongly in the economic and social areas. Agriculture with a large variety of products. Cattle breeding and forestry in the northern savanna area. Extraction of e.g. gold, iron ore, diamond, bauxite, uranium, manganese and chrome. Tropical climate. The first Portuguese gold diggers arrived in the 16th century. The state played an important role in the conspiracy against the Portuguese in 1789.

Mindanao (pop. 14.5 million), southern, second largest island of the Philippines; 38,358 sq mi (99,311 sq km). Capital city is Davao. Central part is forested and mountainous (the volcano Apo's height is 9,692 ft (2,954 m). Inhabitants live mainly along the coast and in river valleys. On the fertile soil rice, corn, hemp, rubber, coconut trees and pineapples are cultivated and partially exported. Cattle breeding is of great economic importance. Fishing. Extraction on a limited scale of coal, gold, iron, silver, bauxite, copper and chrome. The Islamic Moro National Liberation Front (MNLF) fought for years for the independence on Mindanao. In 1996 an agreement was reached between the MNLF and the Philippine government, which anticipated further autonomy of the island. However, a second movement, the Moro Islamic Liberation Front (MILF), continued the struggle for an independent fundamentalist Islamic state.

Mindszenty, József (1892-1975), Hungarian Roman Catholic cardinal who was sentenced (1949) to life imprisonment for his opposition to communism. Released in the uprising of 1956, he took refuge in the U.S. legation in Budapest. He refused to leave until the charges against him were rescinded. In 1971, after an agreement between the Vatican and the Hungarian government, Mindszenty left for Rome.

Mineral, in biology, inorganic element vital to human health. Minerals are usually obtained from food. The essential ones are calcium, chlorine, cobalt, copper fluorine, iodine, iron, magnesium, manganese, phosphorus, potassium, sodium, sulphur, and zinc. Other minerals, known as trace elements, are present in the body in minute quantities and are presumed to be necessary for health: aluminum, boron, bromine, chromium, molybdenum nickel, silicon, and silver.

Mineral, in geology, naturally occurring inorganic substance with a particular chemical composition and definite physical properties. The rocks of the earth's crust are composed of minerals, which are generally classified in order of increasing complexity: elements, sulfides, oxides, halides, carbonates, nitrates, sulfates, phosphates, and silicates

Minerva, in Roman mythology, daughter of Jupiter. She was modeled on the Greek goddess Athena. Worshiped for her skill in handicrafts as well as for her artistic and intellectual gifts, Minerva came to symbolize military prowess and was often depicted wearing a helmet and suit of armor.
See also: Mythology.

Ming dynasty, imperial family that ruled China from 1368-1644. Following years of Mongolian rule, this period was characterized by a return to civil service and an emphasis on scholarship, the arts, and architecture. Achievements included the building of the imperial palace in Beijing's Forbidden City and the creation of exquisite porcelain vases.
See also: China.

Miniature (Lat.: miniare = paint red) 1. Image of a manuscript. Images of clarification or decoration of texts were already found on papyrus rolls from the third millennium B.C.; they were also found in the art of Byzantium, Persia, India, and in Arab and American cultures (Mayas, Aztecs). However, this art of illumination is most well-known for the many beautiful manuscripts that were produced in medieval Europe before the invention of typography. The illumination focused on the first letter (initial) of a part of a text, the blank margin around the text and the actual images: the miniatures. The subjects are very diverse, despite the attachment to text and tradition: worldly and religious scenes, landscapes, star signs and seasons, etc. The design ranges from simple pen drawings to large-scaled compositions in many hues. Well-known examples: 'Book of Durrow' and 'Book of Kells' (both 8th century; Trinity College, Dublin), 'Utrechts Psalterium' (ca. 840; University library, Utrecht) and 'Très riches heures de Jean, duc de Berry' (1413-1416; Musée Condé, Chantilly). Well-known miniature makers: Jean le Tavernier, the brothers Van Limburg and Simon Bening.
2. Very small painting, mostly a portrait, which was made in France since the 15th century and which also became popular in England and the Netherlands. At the end of the 16th century it often had the shape of a round or oval medallion and was frequently worn as a piece of jewelry.

Miniature schnauzer, dog breed developed in Germany in the 19th century. Standing at 12 to 14 inches (30 to 36 centimeters) and possessing a variety of colorations, it is characterized by wiry hair that bristles out in its spiky eyebrows and beard. It is considered to be intelligent, energetic, affectionate, and a good watchdog and mouser.

Minimalism, art movement initiated in the 1960s that stressed pure color and geometry. In both painting and sculpture-generally executed with great precision-it rejected emotionalism, striving for an 'exclusive, negative, absolute, and timeless' quality. Minimalism comprises, among styles and techniques, color-field painting, hard-edge painting, pop art, the shaped canvas, serial imagery, and primary structures.

Mining, extraction of minerals and ores from the earth. There are various types of

A writing monk on a miniature from a fourteenth-century manuscript (Bibliothèque Nationale, Paris). On the table are his writing materials, including a knife, that was used to erase mistakes.

M

M

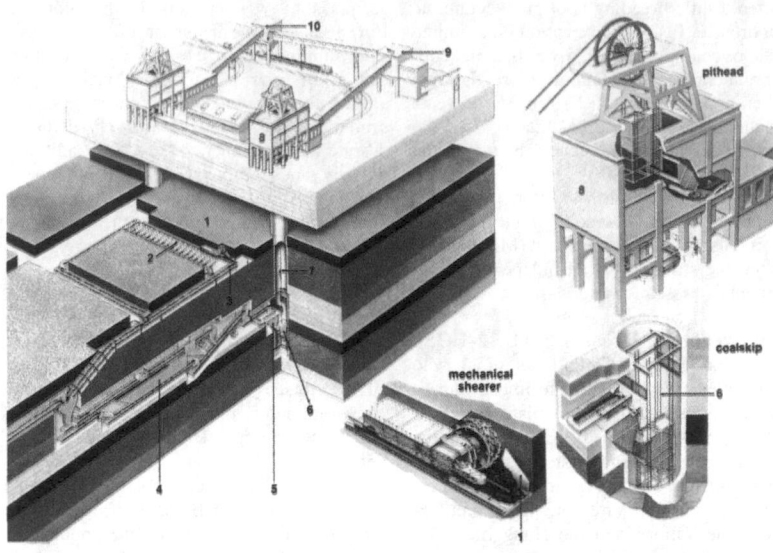

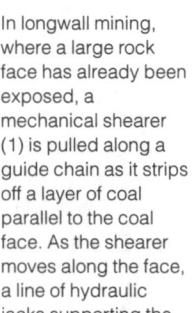

In longwall mining, where a large rock face has already been exposed, a mechanical shearer (1) is pulled along a guide chain as it strips off a layer of coal parallel to the coal face. As the shearer moves along the face, a line of hydraulic jacks supporting the roof (2) automatically keeps pace with it. The broken coal is guided by a scoop onto a conveyor belt (3), which moves it into a storage bunker (4). The bunker delivers a constant stream of coal to a measuring hopper (5), which feeds it into a coal skip (6). The skip is then lifted up a concrete shaft (7) to a pithead (8) of the surface. Here, the coal is dropped from the skip onto a conveyor and moved first to a washing and grading plant (9) and finally to the train-loading tower (10), a giant hopper that feeds coal into the gondolas of a waiting freight train.

mines. The open pit mine is used when the desired minerals lie near the surface. It usually consists of a series of terraces that are worked back in parallel so that the mineral is always within reach of the excavating machines. In strip mining a surface layer is peeled off to reach a usually thin mineral seam (often coal). When minerals lie far below the surface, various deep mining techniques must be used. Access to the mineral-bearing strata is obtained through a vertical shaft or sloping incline dug from the surface or through a horizontal adit driven into the side of a mountain. Underground mines require ventilation and lighting, facilities for pumping out any groundwater or toxic gases, and some means (railroad or conveyor) for carrying the ore and waste to the surface. Several serious occupational diseases (e.g., pneumoconiosis, or 'black lung') are associated with mining and extractive metallurgy, particularly where high dust levels and toxic substances are involved.

Mink, semiaquatic carnivore (genus *Mustela*) of the weasel family, extensively farmed for its fur. There are two species: *M. lutreola*, of European distribution, and *M. vision*, originating in North America but now widely distributed throughout Europe. Feeding on small fish, eggs, young birds, and small mammals, minks are avid hunters, often killing more than they can eat.

Minneapolis (pop. 373,000), largest city of Minnesota and seat of Hennepin County, on the upper Mississippi River, contiguous to its twin city, St. Paul. Minneapolis is a manufacturing, trading, and financial center noted for its many large flour mills and grain elevators. Its products include farm machinery, electronic equipment, linseed oil, paint, precision instruments, and furniture. Site of the University of Minnesota, the city also has an institute of art, a symphony orchestra, and a repertory theater.
See also: Minnesota.

Minnesinger, minstrel-poet of medieval Germany. Minnesingers composed and sang songs of courtly love (*minne*). Heirs to the Provençal troubadours, they flourished from c.1150 to c.1350.

Minnesota (Gopher State, Land of 10,000 Lakes, North Star State; pop. 4,686,000), state in the U.S., bordered by Canada, Lake Superior, Wisconsin, Iowa, South Dakota and North Dakota; 84,435 sq mi (218,601 sq

This reconstructed Minoan jug, from the first palace at Phaestos, is from around 1800 B.C. (Heraklion Museum).

km). Capital city: St. Paul. Largely prairie landscape with many lakes and rivers (including the Mississippi). The largest part of the land has been cultivated.

The rivers supply power for the hydroelectric power station. Industry: food and production of electrical appliances, office supplies, computers and plastic articles. Agriculture (e.g. wheat, corn), cattle breeding (meat and dairy) and forestry. Extraction of iron ore and manganese ore. Tourism. Originally the whole state was Indian territory; colonized from the 17th century onwards by the French. Minnesota is a member of the Union since 1858.

Minnow, common name for many small freshwater fishes found throughout the world except for South America and Australia. The original minnow is a 3-in (7.6-cm) European fish, but the name has also been extended to its relatives, which include carp, cutlips, shiners, roach, and tench. Minnows feed on insects and crustaceans and are important in the food chain, since larger fish feed on them. The largest American minnow is the squawfish, or Pacific pike, which may grow to several feet. Minnows have long pharyngeal teeth around their gills. They lay their eggs in gravel or in special nests.

Minoan civilization, Bronze Age culture that flourished on the island of Crete during the 3rd and 2nd millenniums B.C. The first great Aegean civilization-with cities, palaces, a highly developed art and architecture, writing, extensive trade, and complex religious beliefs-Minoan culture reached its high point c.2200-1500 B.C. The city of Cnossus on the north coast of Crete was its center, from which the Minoan fleet carried goods to Egypt, Syria, Phoenicia, Asia Minor, Sicily, and Greece. By c.1000 B.C. Minoan civilization had declined, and its remains were incorporated by Greece. The word 'Minoan' comes from the legendary King Minos, who was said to have ruled in Cnossus.
See also: Crete; Greece, Ancient.

Minorca, or Menorca, one of the Balearic Islands off the eastern coast of Spain. The second largest of the islands, it was seized several times by France and by England, who eventually ceded it to Spain in 1802. Minorca is known for its farm crops, light manufacturing, lobster fishing, and beaches. Tourism is also important.

Minor leagues *See:* Baseball.

Minos, in Greek mythology, wealthy king of Crete who commanded the artisan Daedalus to construct a labyrinthine prison for a beast called the Minotaur, to whom the young people of Athens were regularly sacrificed. One of these, Theseus, succeeded in killing the Minotaur and running away with Minos' daughter Ariadne. Minos was married to Pasiphaë; his other children included Androgeous, Glaucus, and Phaedra.
See also: Mythology.

Minot, George (1885-1950), U.S. physician who developed a cure for the once-fatal

blood disease called pernicious anemia. He found that feeding patients a diet consisting largely of raw liver normalized their red blood count. He was awarded the Nobel Prize for medicine (1934, with G.H. Whipple and W.P. Murphy). Minot wrote numerous articles on blood disorders and dietary deficiency.
See also: Anemia.

Minsk (pop. 1,700,000), capital city of the Byelorussia, located on the Svisloch River. After suffering extensive damage during World War II, the city was revitalized by the creation of factories and new housing. Among the goods produced in Minsk are trucks, machine parts, tools, and radios. The city is also noted for its academic and cultural institutions.
See also: Belarus.

Minstrel, wandering professional entertainers who flourished in medieval Europe. Known variously as *troubadours* or *jongleurs* in France, *bards* in Ireland, *skalds* in Scandinavia, and *minnesingers* in Germany, they were generally singers but also used storytelling and mime. Because they wandered from town to town, they spread local news and helped to preserve oral traditions. They began to die out in the 15th century, largely due to the appearance of the printing press.

Minstrel show, form of entertainment popular in the United States from about 1840 to 1900. White performers blackened their faces in imitation of African Americans and alternated jokes with African American songs, many of which thus became well-known American folk songs. Minstrel shows reinforced negative stereotypes of blacks that lasted for decades after the shows had ceased to exist.

Mint, in botany, family of square-stemmed plants with white, blue, purple, or red flowers in the form of a lipped tube. Many are aromatic. Familiar examples are lavender, sage, oswego tea, marjoram, and thyme. The true mints (genus *Mentha*) include spearmint (*M. spicata*) and peppermint (*M. piperita*).

Minto, Earl of (1845-1914), British governor general of Canada (1898-1904) and viceroy of India (1905-1910). As governor general, he was criticized by French-speaking Canadians for sending Canadian troops to South Africa during the Boer War. As viceroy, he angered Indian nationalists by instituting reforms that resulted in the intensification of divisions between Hindus and Muslims.

Mintz, Shlomo (1957-), Israeli violinist of Russian descent. Studied at the Juilliard School of Music and is one of the most talented violinists of our time. Combines immense virtuosity with a great expressiveness.

Minuet (French: menu pas = small step) French national dance in three-four time, introduced as a court dance by Louis IV. It is an elegant dance for a couple, which spread fast from France over to Europe. Was integrated into the instrumental suite and added as part of the symphony (between the slow middle movement and the fast final movement) by the Mannheim School. In this form the minuet was followed by a second, contrasting minuet, after which the first one was repeated. This second minuet was generally called trio. Beethoven replaced the minuet with the faster scherzo.

Miocene, last epoch but one of the Tertiary period, which lasted from 25 to 10 million years ago.

By the Miocene Epoch, climates had moderated and grassland habitats became extensive. Herds of mammals roamed the savannalike plains of North America. Many animal remains have been found in deposits from the Lower Miocene, from about 20 million years ago. *Parahippus* (1) was the first horse with high-crowned teeth, an adaptation to grazing. Although it had three toes on each foot, the side toes were reduced and it walked mainly on its middle toes. *Stenomylus* (2) was a small, graceful, long necked camel. *Dinohyus* (3) was a giant piglike animal about 11 ft (3.2 m) long. *Diceratherium* (4), a small, three-toed rhinoceros, possessed a pair of short horns on the end of its nose. *Moropus* (5), a relative of the horse, measured about 9 ft (2.7 m) in length and had claws, rather than hooves. Numerous corkscrew-shaped burrows (6) were presumably inhabited by a form of rodent that has been named *Daemonelix*.

Mir (Ru: village community) Traditional farmer community in Russia, based on communal ownership of land and communal obligations such as tax and statute labor. The land was periodically redivided as needed. The mir originated around the year 1000 and was abolished in 1906.

Mira, variable star about 270 light-years away from the earth. The German astronomer Fabricius first observed the brightening and dimming of the star in 1596; later, variations in diameter and temperature were also noted. The diameter of Mira can be imagined as equal to that of the sun and all nearby planets, extending to a point somewhere beyond Mars. It is visible to the naked eye for about half the year; otherwise it can be seen through a telescope.
See also: Star.

Mirabeau, Comte de (1749-1791), French revolutionary leader. A powerful orator, he became an early leader of the moderate wing of revolutionary forces, representing the third estate (the commoners) in the States-General (the French parliament). He worked secretly to establish a constitutional monarchy but was mistrusted by both revolutionaries and royalists. He was elected president of the National Assembly in 1791 but died a few months later.

See also: French Revolution; Jacobins.

Miracle play *See:* Mystery play.

Mirage, optical illusion in the atmosphere in which the refraction of light passing through air layers of different densities causes nonexistent images to be seen. Distant objects may appear to be reflected in water, as light rays traveling initially toward the ground have been bent upward by layers of hot air close to the surface. In some mirages objects seem to float in the air. This commonly occurs over cold surfaces such as ice or a cold sea, where warmer air overlies cooler air and bends light rays downward.

Miranda, Francisco de (1750-1816), Venezuelan patriot who fought for the forces of freedom on 3 continents. While an officer in the army of Spain he served in the American Revolution, receiving the British surrender at Pensacola, Fla. He later joined the French revolutionary forces, fighting in several major battles. When in 1810 patriots in Venezuela formed a provisional government, he returned home, where he and Simón Bolivar proclaimed the first South American republic, in Caracas on July 5, 1811. Captured by royalists, he died in prison in Spain.
See also: Venezuela.

Miró, Joan (1893-1983), Spanish painter. A pioneer of surrealism, Miró produced freely drawn works characterized by bright colors and clusters of abstract symbolic forms. His work includes murals and large ceramic decorations for UNESCO in Paris.

Mir (space station), Permanently manned Russian space station, brought into an orbit around the Earth on 19 February 1986. Through the years the Mir has been expanded with several modules for astronomic and material research.

M

In 1997 Mir got into trouble: a collision with a supply ship caused massive damage; one crew member was under strain; due to a human error there was no electricity on board for several days. In February 1999 an attempt was made to light cities and areas on Earth at night with the help of a mirror which was fixed onto a space ship. It failed because the mirror and spaceship burned in the atmosphere.

Misdemeanor, crime that is not as serious as a felony. In general, offenses punishable only by a fine or short imprisonment in county jails are misdemeanors. These may include traffic violations, assault and battery, and theft of small amounts of money. Convictions that carry punishment by imprisonment in state penitentiaries are felonies.
See also: Crime.

Mishima, Yukio (Kimitake Hiraoka; 1925-1970), Japanese author. His writing is obsessed with the conflict between traditional and post-World War II Japan. He formed a private army devoted to ancient martial arts and committed hara-kiri. His work includes the novels *The Temple of the Golden Pavilion* (1956), *Sun and Steel* (1970), *Sea of Fertility* (4 vols., 1970), and *Patriotism* (1966), on ritual suicide, and modern Kabuki and Noh plays.

Missile, guided *See:* Guided missile.

Missionary, individual sent to a foreign territory or country to educate others in particular religious tradition. While their goal is religious conversion, missionaries also work to provide agricultural information, social services, and literacy skills. The Christian church, with the greatest number of missionaries, sponsors activities in Asia, Latin America, Africa, and the Pacific islands.

An example of ecumenical co-operation: a Baptist nurse and a Roman Catholic priest working together for the poor in Karachi.

Mississippi (Magnolia State; pop. 2,731,000), state in the South of the U.S., bordered by Alabama, Tennessee, Arkansas, Louisiana and the Gulf of Mexico; 47,709 sq mi (123,516 sq km). Capital city: Jackson. The climate is warm and humid. It is a flat, low-lying state; the highest point is just 807 ft (246 m) above sea level.
Agricultural state (cotton); also cattle breeding and forestry. The cotton sector's former leading role has been taken over nowadays by cattle breeding (70% of companies in contrast to 10% of cotton companies). Industry (wood products, chemical industry) along the coast. Extraction of oil and natural gas.
The first European visitors spoke of their admiration for the way the Indians (especially the Choctaw) had found an ecological balance with their natural environment. In 1540 the Spaniard Hernando de Soto explored the area; he did not find valuable minerals, thus abandoning the idea of exploitation. Around 1682 the establishment of French Canadians started; the area became part of the French colony Louisiana. Later it fell under British rule; in 1817 Mississippi became a member of the Union. For a long time it was an area of fierce racial contrasts (e.g. the Ku Klux Klan), which among other things was very disadvantageous for the economy.

Mississippian *See:* Mound Builders.

Mississippi River, chief river of the North American continent and the longest river in the United States, flowing about 2,350 mi (3,780 km) south from Lake Itasca in northwestern Minnesota to its enormous delta at the Gulf of Mexico, below New Orleans. Called the 'father of waters' by Native Americans, the Mississippi drains an area of about 1.25 million sq mi (3,237,500 sq km). With the Missouri and Ohio rivers (its chief tributaries), it forms the world's third longest river system, after the Nile and the Amazon. It receives more than 250 tributaries in all. The Mississippi is noted for sudden changes of course, its length varying by 40-50 mi (64-80 km) per year. The river's average discharge is 1.64 million cu ft (46,412 cu m) per sec, but in high water season this soars to some 2.3 million cu ft (65,090 cu m) per sec. Flooding is a serious problem, but dikes and levees contain its periodic massive overflows. The river is a major transportation artery of the United States and was of fundamental importance in the development of the North American continent.

Missouri (Show Me State; pop. 5,402,000), state in the U.S. Midwest, bordered by Arkansas, Tennessee, Kentucky, Illinois, Iowa, Nebraska, Kansas and Oklahoma; 69,724 sq mi (180,516 sq km). Capital city: Jefferson City. Diverse landscape. Cold winters and warm, humid summers. The state lies in the 'Tornado Alley', an area which regularly experiences tornadoes.
There is trade, agriculture and tourism as well but the state is mainly industrial: primarily food, chemical, machine, aviation and graphic industries. Manufacture of vehicles and electrical appliances. Industry in Saint Louis and Kansas City. Extraction of

lead, limestone, coal and iron ore.
The state was named after the Missouri, one of the Indian nations that lived in the area before the arrival of Europeans. The first French settlement was founded around 1735. The first colonists concentrated on hunting, trade and lead mining. Missouri is a member of the Union since 1821. The area flourished during the great migration to the west, when it served as a supply station. The most important point of controversy during the 19th century was the abolition of slavery. The 20th century was a period of industrialization and urbanization. Many villages became depopulated; smaller cities near large centers grew significantly after WW II, especially because the white middle class left the larger cities. Centers of employment situated in the old town centers are easy to reach thanks to improved freeways.

Missouri River, second-longest river in the United States (about 2,500 mi/4,023 km) and chief tributary of the Mississippi, with which it forms the world's third-largest river system. Rising in southeastern Montana in the Rocky Mountains, the Missouri river flows north and then east through Montana; it then crosses North Dakota, and continues generally southeast until emptying into the Mississippi north of St. Louis. Its main tributaries include the Cheyenne, Kansas, Osage, Platte, Yellowstone, James, and Milk rivers. The Missouri was explored by Joliet and Marquette in 1673 and by the Lewis and Clark expedition in 1804-1805. Like the Mississippi, it is subject to serious flooding, which is under control since three decades.

Mistletoe, any of many species of evergreen parasitic plants of the family Loranthaceae with small, inconspicuous flowers. In Europe the common mistletoe (*Viscum album*) grows on apples, poplar, willow, linden, and hawthorns, while common U.S. mistletoes (*Phoradendron flavescens*, for example) occur on most deciduous trees and some conifers. Mistletoes derive some of their nutrients from the host plants, but they also produce some by photosynthesis. Their seeds are spread by fruit-eating birds.

Mistral, Frédéric (1830-1914), French poet. He won the 1904 Nobel Prize for literature and for his work as leader of a movement to restore the former glories of the Provençal language and culture. Among his works are the epic poems *Mirèio* (1859), *Calendau* (1867), *Nerto* (1884), and *Lou Pouémo dúo Rose* (1897).

Mistral, Gabriela (Lucila Godoy Alcayaga; 1889-1957), Chilean poet, educator, and diplomat awarded the Nobel Prize for literature in 1945. Her simple, lyrical poems express sympathy with nature and mankind. Her works include *Desolation* (1922) and *Tenderness* (1924).

Mitanni, kingdom that flourished in northern Mesopotamia (now southeastern Turkey) from about 1500 B.C. A warfaring people renowned for their skills with horses and chariots, the early Mitannians fought the Egyptians for control of Syria, but the threat of a common enemy-the Hittites-caused these empires to form an alliance. Ultimately, the kingdom of Mitanni was captured in 1350 B.C. and became part of the Assyrian Empire.

Mitchell, Margaret (1900-1949), U.S. writer. Her best-selling and only novel *Gone With the Wind* (1936) won the 1937 Pulitzer Prize and was made into a successful film (1939).

Mitchell, Maria (1818-1889), U.S. astronomer who discovered a comet in 1847. She was the first woman to be elected to the American Academy of Arts and Sciences (1848) and was professor of astronomy at Vassar College (1865-1888).
See also: Astronomy.

Mite, tiny arachnid, a relative of the spider with a rounded body and four pairs of legs. Mites feed by sucking the juices of plants and animals. Some are pests and may carry diseases, e.g. scrub typhus. Others cause itching and scabs when they get under the skin. Chiggers are the larvae of one form of mite.

Mithra, ancient Indo-Iranian sun-god, one of the ethical lords, or gods, of Zoroastrianism. He was the chief Persian deity during the 5th century B.C., and his cult spread over most of Asia Minor reaching Rome, according to Plutarch, in 68 B.C.. Mithraism was especially popular among the Roman legions. Roman Mithraism, which competed with early Christianity for converts, thought that the forces of good and evil waged a struggle in the world. It made ethical demands on its followers and offered them the hope of immortality. It declined after A.D. 200 and was officially suppressed in the 4th century.
See also: Zoroastrianism.

Mithridates VI (132 B.C.-63 B.C.), king of ancient Pontus, on the Black Sea, who fought three wars against the Roman state. In the first (88-84 B.C.), he overran Asia Minor but was subsequently forced to make peace. He won the second war (83-81 B.C.) but lost the third (74-63 B.C.). Pompey drove him into exile in the Crimea, where he had himself killed by a mercenary.
See also: Pontus.

Mitterrand, François Maurice (1916-1996), French politician, president of the republic from 1981-1995. A cabinet minister in 11 governments during the Fourth Republic (1946-1958), he opposed De Gaulle's establishment of the Fifth Republic in 1958. A socialist and candidate of the non-Communist left, he first ran for the presidency in 1965, but was defeated by De Gaulle. He became head of the Socialist Party in 1971 and ran unsuccessfully for the presidency a second time in 1974, losing to Valéry Giscard d'Estaing. He finally won in 1981. His party also won a majority in the National Assembly and initiated a program of mild nationalization and social reform. In the late 1980s his government became increasingly moderate.
See also: France.

Mix, Tom (1880-1940), U.S. film actor and

Harvest mite (*Trombicula autumnalis*, class Arachnida, order *Acarina*), length about 0.04 in (1 mm).

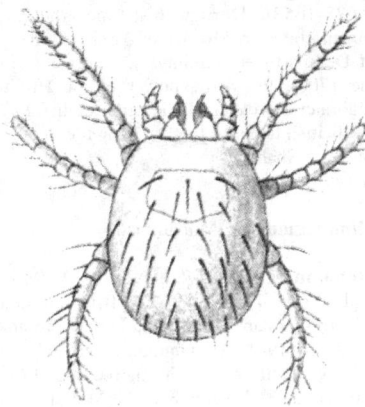

director whose popular westerns featured spectacular photography and daring horseriding. He starred in the silent films *Desert Love* (1920) and *Riders of the Purple Sage* (1925) and in numerous films of the 1930s.

Mizoram (pop. 690,000), state (since 1987) in Northeast India, until 1972 part of Assam; 8,142 sq mi (21,081 sq km). Capital city: Aizawl (pop. 154,000). Annexed by the British around 1895. Formed to suppress the war of independence (1966-1986) of the Mizo National Front. The official languages are English and Mizo, which is written in Roman characters.
Very learned population of which 80 percent is Christian as a result of the intensive missionary work during the 19th century. The society is largely tribal and centralized in villages.
Their means of living consists for three quarters of agriculture, on terraces as well as with *shifting cultivation*. Also cattle breeding and fishing. Industry is restricted to traditional industry, mainly as a result of the bad opening up of the area.
The name means 'land of the highlanders'. The Mizo hills can be up to 6,562 ft (2,000 m) high and the capital city is at a 4,003 ft (1,220 m) altitude.

Mladic, Ratko (1943-), Serbian soldier, was trained in the Yugoslavian People's Army. In 1992, he was appointed highest military authority of the Bosnian-Serbian army. In 1995, he was leader of the offensive in East Bosnia, when the Muslim enclave Srebrenica fell into the hands of the Serbs on July 11. The subsequent massacre amongst Muslims cost the lives of approximately 7,500 men. In 1995, Mladic was charged by the International Criminal Court for the Former Yugoslavia, due to, among other things, his leading role in the genocide in Srebrenica and war crimes in Bosnia and Hercegovina. Mladic has repeatedly managed to avoid arrest.

Moabite stone, ancient, black-basalt stone containing writing in Hebrew-Phoenician characters. Probably inscribed about 865 B.C., the stone stands 3 ft, 8 in (112 cm) high

and 2 ft, 3 in (68 cm) wide. Its inscription narrates the deeds of Mesha, king of the Moabites, in his wars against Israel and against the Edomites.

Mobile, a type of sculpture in which the various parts move. Mobiles are usually constructed of wire and a group of objects or shapes. The structure must be perfectly balanced so that it will move at the slightest touch or breeze. Mobiles may either be hung from a support, such as a ceiling, or balanced on a pedestal. The first mobiles were constructed by Alexander Calder, a United States sculptor, in the 1930's.
The main artistic feature of mobiles is movement. How a mobile moves through space, and the changing patterns it forms, are more important than the various objects of which it is constructed. By nature, mobiles are abstract or semiabstract. Mobiles may be simple, but more often they are highly complex. In complex versions, each element tends to have a different pattern of movement. With proper lighting, the shadows cast by the mobile add to its effect and beauty.
Mobiles can be easily constructed at home using three types of materials - strong wire, such as that used for coat hangers; string or thread; and objects to be suspended. The wire gives the mobile width, so that all the objects do not hang down from one point. The strings are used to suspend the objects from the wire. Household articles, such as corks, bottle tops, spools, and buttons, make suitable objects for mobiles. Cardboard cutouts are also used to create a wider variety of shapes. A hanging mobile is suspended while being constructed to ensure proper balance.

Möbius, August Ferdinand (1790-1868), German mathematician and astronomer who developed the field of topology, which derived from his work in geometry. Topology studies the qualities of a geometric form that do not change when subject to twisting, bending, and stretching.
See also: Topology.

Mobutu Sese Seko (1930-1997), president of the Republic of Zaïre (formerly the Belgian Congo) from 1966-1997. He took power in a coup and in 1967 established a dictatorial regime with himself as president. In 1997 he was ousted by Laurent Kabila and went into exile.

Moccasin flower *See:* Lady's-slipper.

Moccasin snake *See:* Water moccasin.

Mockingbird, any of several species of birds of the family Mimidae native to the Americas, with long tails, short rounded wings and well-developed legs. They feed on insects and fruit. The name is derived from their ability to mimic the calls of other birds.

Mock orange, or syringa, small garden bush belonging to the saxifrage family and known for its clusters of tiny, light-colored, often-fragrant flowers. Various hybrids are grown in the United States and Mexico.

M

M

Model Parliament, English parliament set up in 1295 by King Edward I. The Model Parliament's wide representation (clergy, earls, barons, two knights from each county, and two burgesses from each borough) was symbolic of Parliament's developing representational role, although the principles of membership were by no means strictly observed through much of the 14th century.
See also: Parliament.

Modiano, Patrick Jean (1945-), French novelist. Modiano made his debut in 1969 with *La place de l'étoile*. He received the Prix du roman de l'Académie Française for *Les boulevards de ceinture* (1972) and the Prix Goncourt (1978) for *Rue des boutiques obscures*. His novels often take place during the occupation period with a first-person narrator who is searching for his identity. Later novels take place about 20 years after the occupation, but the theme is the same. Other work includes *Paris tendresse* (1990), *Dora Bruder* (1997) and *La petite bijou* (2001).

Modigliani, Amedeo (1884-1920), Italian painter and sculptor best known for his nudes and portraits, works characterized by elegant elongated forms. He was influenced by African sculpture and by Constantin Brancusi.

Amadeo Modigliani (1884-1920): *Nude.*

Mogadishu, or Mogadiscio (pop. 1,000,000), capital and major port city of the Somali Democratic Republic, located on the Indian Ocean. Long under Arab rule, it was made the colonial capital of Italian Somaliland in 1905. When Somalia gained its independence in 1960, Mogadishu remained as its capital. Both Arabic and Italian influences are evident in the city, which was heavily damaged during the civil war in the early 1990s.

Mogul Empire, Muslim empire in northern India (1526-1857), founded by Babur, who invaded India from Afghanistan. His son Humayun was defeated by the Afghan Sher Shah Sur, but Mogul power was restored by Akbar (1556-1605), who established centralized government throughout Afghanistan and northern and central India. The Mogul 'golden age' was in the reign of Shah Jehan (1628-1658). During this time, the Taj Mahal, the Pearl Mosque of Agra, and many of Delhi's finest buildings were erected. In the 1700s, the rising power of the Hindu Mahratetas weakened the empire. In 1857 the British deposed the last Mogul emperor, Bahadur Shah II.
See also: Akbar.

Mohammad *See:* Muhammad.

Mohammad Reza Pahlavi (1919-1980), shah of Iran (1941-1979). The British forced his pro-German father, Reza Pahlavi, to abdicate in 1941. Mohammad Reza Pahlavi left the country briefly during the rule of the left-wing Nationalist Muhammad Mossadegh (1953), but returned with CIA-backing to consolidate his power. He instituted certain western social reforms, but exercised a dictatorship bolstered by a pervasive secret police, the Savak. An Islamic revolution forced him into exile in 1979. He died in exile in Egypt.

Mohawks, Native American tribe, of what is now New York State, one of the five tribes of the Iroquois League, which had a highly developed culture that flourished through the 17th and 18th century.

Mohegan, North American Indian tribe of the Eastern Woodlands. Mohegans formed a branch of the Mahican group, which occupied southwestern Connecticut in the 17th and 18th centuries. In the 1600s, the Mohegan chief, Uncas, and the settlers formed an alliance against hostile native groups. In the 1700s, however, many Mohegans were driven from the land, had died of disease, or were converted to Christianity. A few remaining descendants still live on a Connecticut reservation. Both Mohegans and Mahicans are sometimes called Mohicans, after the fictional tribe in James Fenimore Cooper's *The Last of the Mohicans*.
See also: Mahican.

Mohenyo-Daro (Mohenyo-Daro) City of ruins in the Indus valley in the province Sind in South Pakistan, from the Indus civilization (2300-1700 B.C.) The orderly rectangular street plan and an excellent sewer system is striking. Houses as well as a citadel and granaries have been preserved.

Mohican *See:* Mahican; Mohegan.

Moholy-Nagy, László (1895-1946), Hungarian painter, designer, and member of the German Constructivist school. He was professor at the Bauhaus, 1923-1928. He founded the Institute of Design at the Illinois Institute of Technology in Chicago in 1939 and was an important influence on U.S. industrial design.

Mohorovicic discontinuity, or Moho, seismic boundary of the earth originally regarded as separating the crust and mantle, evidenced by rapid increase in the velocity of seismic waves.

Moi, Daniel Torotich Arap (1924-), Kenyan politician and President (1978-2002). In 1948, Moi obtained a seat in the Legislative Council of the British colony Kenya. He was leader of the movement for electoral suffrage, which produced results in 1957. He became one of the first eight African people to be elected as a member of the Legislative Council. Moi became the leader of the Kenya African Democratic Union (KADU) and represented this party in Parliament, where he eventually accepted a coalition with the Kenya African National Union (KANU). In 1967, he was appointed Vice President of Kenya. He became the most important advisor and substitute of Jomo Kenyatta, whom he succeeded as President in 1978. Moi is considered to be a pragmatist, who strives for reconciliation between minority groups and the influential Kikuyu. In 1988, he was re-elected President for the third time. In the beginning of the 1990s, economic regression, corruption and violence led to increasing protests against his regime. Moi reacted with political repression, thereby cutting out political opponents, censoring the media and continually closing down universities. Partly due to international pressure, Moi finally agreed to a multi-party system winnig elections in 1992 and 1997. However in the national elections of December 2002 the National Rainbow coalition (NARC) won two thirds of the parliamentary seats, dislodging the Kenya African Union (KANU) from power for the first time since independence in 1963. A new president, 71 year old Mwai Kibaki was elected.

Moisture *See:* Humidity; Weather.

Mojave Desert, barren area of mountains and desert valley in southeastern California. It includes Death Valley in the north and the Joshua Tree National Monument in the south.

Bold geometric abstraction *Construction VII* (1922), by the abstract artist László Moholy-Nagy (1895-1946), who worked outside his country Hungary and was a teacher at the Bauhaus (Van Abbe Museum, Eindhoven).

Molar *See:* Teeth.

Mold, general name for a number of filamentous fungi that produce powdery or fluffy growths on fabrics, foods, and decaying plant or animal remains. Best known is the blue bread mold caused by penicillium, from which the antibiotic penicillin was first discovered.
See also: Fungi.

Moldova

Capital:	Chisinao
Area:	13,010 sq mi (33,700 sq km)
Population:	4,435,000
Language:	Moldavian
Government:	Presidential republic
Independent:	1991
Head of gov.:	Prime minister
Per capita:	US$ 2,550
Monetary unit:	1 Leu = 100 bani

Moldova, Republic in Eastern Europe, between Romania in the south and the Ukraine in the north.
Land and climate. Moldova lies between the Prut River and the Dnestr River. Almost everywhere in Moldova, the land consists of fertile black soil. The climate is continental, in the south it is slightly more moderate. In the deciduous forests wolves can still be found.
People. Moldavians constitute 65% of the population; Ukranians and Russians are important minorities. The official language is Moldavian. The most important churches are the Romanian-orthodox Church and the Russian-orthodox Church.
Economy. Agriculture is important to the country's economy. After the disintegration of the Soviet Union, the viniculture and the defense industry broke down. After 1994 the economy improved.
History. Moldavia was a region in eastern Romania, divided by the Prut River from the Moldavian Soviet Socialist Republic (MSSR), part of the Soviet Union. Moldavia belonged to Romania from 1918 to 1940, when a portion of it was annexed by the Soviets as the MSSR, with Kishinev as its capital. After the collapse of communism in the USSR in 1991, the MSSR became an independent republic, named Moldova. Soon after, fighting broke out in the region east of

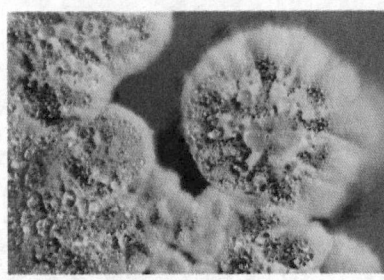

the Dniester River (Trans-dniester) between Moldovan government forces and ethnic Russians living there, who were seeking independence. The Russian 14th Army, stationed in the region since before the collapse of the Soviet Union, came to the aid of the ethnic Russians. A cease-fire went into effect in July, 1992. In an accord signed by Moldova and Russia in 1994, Russia agreed to withdraw the 14th Army and Moldova agreed to seek a peaceful resolution to the conflict with the ethnic Russians. The OSCE (Organization for Security and Co- operation in Europe) extended the deadline for withdrawal of the Russian troops from Trans-dniester from the end of 2002 to 2003.
See also: Romania; Union of Soviet Socialist Republics.

Mole, any of various small burrowing insect-eating mammals of the family Talpidae native to the Northern Hemisphere. Moles have spade-shaped front feet and long, mobile muzzles. Their eyes are small and often covered with fur, and they have no external ears, though their sense of hearing is acute.

Mole, in chemistry, a quantity of particles equal to Avogadro's number, or 6.02252×10^{23}. One mole of a given compound is that number of molecules of the compound. The gram-atomic weight of an element is the weight, in grams, of a mole of that element. The gram-molecular weight of a compound is the weight in grams of a mole of molecules of that compound.
See also: Chemistry.

Mole, in dermatology, pigmented spot or nevus in the skin, consisting of a localized group of special cells containing melanin. Dramatic change in a mole, such as an increase in size, change of color, or bleeding, may indicate that the mole has developed into a cancerous tumor called a melanoma, which can spread to other parts of the body.

Green mold (*Penicillium notatum*) is an important source of the antibiotic drug penicillin, a substance that destroys many species of infectious bacteria. The closely related *P. chryso-* *genum*, another common mold, is also used to produce penicillin.

Molecular biology, study of the structure and function of the molecules that make up living organisms. This includes the study of proteins, enzymes, carbohydrates, fats, and nucleic acids, and their interactions in the life processes.
See also: Biology.

Molecular weight, sum of the atomic weights of all the atoms in a molecule, expressed in atomic mass units.

Molecule, smallest particle of a chemical compound that retains all the chemical properties of that compound. Molecules are made up of atoms joined to one another by chemical bonds. The composition of a molecule is represented by its molecular formula. Molecules range in size from two atoms to macromolecules (chiefly proteins and polymers), which may be composed of 10,000 or more atoms.

Molière (1622-1673), French playwright of high comedy and farce, also known for his skills as an actor and director. He was born Jean Baptiste Poquelin. Granted patronage by Louis XIV and given his own theater, Molière wrote satiric plays with controversial themes that often offended religious groups. Among these were *The School for Wives* (1662), *The Imposter* (1664), and *The Misanthrope* (1666).

Molina, Scott (1960-), American triathlete, won his first triathlon in 1982. Later Molina won several more competitions, including the Ironman of Hawaii in 1988, which at the time was the unofficial full-distance world championship.

M

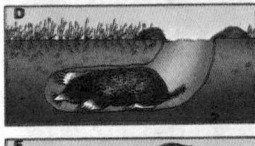
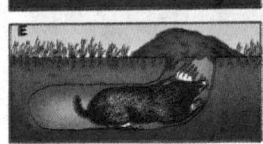

The common European mole, *Talpa europaea*, has strong front feet that are armed with claws for the digging of burrows. During the summer months, moles use a breast-stroke action to dig shallow surface runs, in search of insects and worms. In winter, they dig out a system of deeper burrows, expelling the soil, making the familiar molehills.
A. beginning of a burrow
B. a horizontal section through a surface run
C. a vertical section through a surface run
D. digging action in a deep burrow
E. a mole turns round and pushes loose soil to the surface
F. a deep burrow system

M

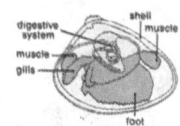

Bivalve mollusks, or pelecypods, include the mussel (A), cockle (B), scallop (C), and razor shell (D). All bivalves have two shells hinged by powerful adductor muscles, a digestive system, gills and a foot.

Mollusk, any of many soft-bodied invertebrate animals (phyllum Mollusca), typically having a shell into which the body can withdraw. Mollusks constitute the second largest phylum of invertebrates. They include slugs and snails, limpets, winkles, clams, mussels, and oysters, as well as octopuses and squids. Mollusks have adapted to niches in the sea, in fresh water, and on land. Major groups of mollusks include bivalves, cephalopods, chitons, and gastropods.

Molnár, Ferenc (1878-1952), Hungarian author and playwright. His play *Liliom* (1909) was adapted as the musical *Carousel* (1945). He also wrote novels and short stories. He lived in the United States from 1940.

Moloch, or Molech, Canaanite god of fire, to whom children were sacrificed, identified in the Old Testament as a god of the Ammonites. His worship, introduced by King Ahaz, was condemned by the prophets, and his sanctuary at Tophet near Jerusalem later became known as Gehenna.

Molokai *See:* Hawaii.

Molotov, Vyacheslav Mikhailovich (1890-1986), Soviet diplomat and politician. Born Vyacheslav Mikhailovich Skriabin he became a Bolshevik in 1906. After the Russian Revolution of 1917 he quickly rose to power in the ruling Communist Party. He was Soviet Premier (1930-1941) under Joseph Stalin. As foreign minister (1939-1949 and 1953-1956) he negotiated the 1939 nonaggression pact with Germany and played an important role in the USSR's wartime and postwar relations with the West. Expelled from the party central committee in 1957 for opposing Nikita Khrushchev, he held only minor posts. In 1964 he was expelled from the party itself, but he was reinstated in 1984.
See also: Union of Soviet Socialist Republics.

Molting, shedding of the skin, fur, or feathers by an animal. It may be a seasonal occurrence, as a periodic renewal of fur or plumage in mammals and birds, or it may be associated with growth, as in insects or crustaceans. In birds and mammals the molt is primarily to renew worn fur or feathers so that pelage or plumage is kept in good condition for waterproofing, insulation, or flight. It also may serve to shed breeding plumage or to change between summer and winter coats. In invertebrates the rigid external skeleton must be shed and replaced to allow growth within. In larval insects the final molts are involved in the metamorphosis to adult form.

Moltke, Helmuth Karl Bernhard von (1801-1891), Prussian and, later, German chief of staff (1858-88). A strategist of genius, he won victories against Denmark (1864), Austria (1866), and France (1870), greatly furthering German unification.

Molybdenum, chemical element, symbol Mo; for physical constants see Periodic Table. Molybdenum was discovered by Karl Scheele in 1778. It occurs in nature in the minerals wulfenite and powellite and is obtained principally from molybdenite, a sulfide. Molybdenum is a silvery-white, hard, ductile, unreactive, metal. It is a valuable alloying agent for steels and for nickel-based, heat-resistant, and corrosion-resistant alloys. Molybdenum and its compounds are used in nuclear energy applications, missile and aircraft parts, ultra-high-strength steels, high-temperature lubricants, and as catalysts.

Mombasa (pop. 540,000), large port city in Kenya, on the Indian Ocean, an international center of shipping and industry. It contains an airport, state buildings, an oil refinery, and tourist facilities. Its major industries include cement, food processing, and glass. First settled by the Persians and Arabs in the 8th century, Kenya was later ruled variously by Portugal, Oman, and Great Britain until it was declared independent in 1963.

Mommsen, Theodor Christian Matthias (1817-1903), a German historian and classical scholar. His *History of Rome* (3 volumes, 1854-1856) was long popular in English translation. He was awarded the Nobel Prize for literature in 1902.
Mommsen was born in Schleswig, and received a Ph.D. degree from the University of Kiel in 1842. From 1844 to 1847 he was in France and Italy, collating manuscripts and inscriptions for the Berlin Academy. He was appointed professor of law at Leipzig University in 1848, but was dismissed two years later because of his liberal political views. As a Liberal member of the Prussian parliament, 1873-1882, Mommsen opposed Bismarck's policies. He taught Roman law at the universities of Zurich and Breslau, and was professor of ancient history at the University of Berlin, 1858-1903.

Monaco

Capital:	Monaco
Area:	0.7 sq mi (1.9 sq km)
Population:	32,000
Language:	French
Government:	Parliamentary monarchy
Independent:	1489
Head of gov.:	Prime minister
Per capita:	more than US$ 27,000
Monetary unit:	1 French franc = 100 centimes

Monaco, independent principality on the Mediterranean near the French-Italian border, about 370 acres (150 hectares) in area. It is a tourist center, with a yachting harbor and a world-famous casino. The reigning constitutional monarch, Prince Rainier III, succeeded to the throne in 1949 and married the U.S. film actress Grace Kelly in 1956. In 1962, after a crisis with France over Monaco's tax-free status, Rainier proclaimed a new constitution, guaranteeing fundamental rights, giving the vote to women, and abolishing the death penalty. The government consists of three councilors, headed by a minister of state who must be French. There is an 18-member National Council, elected for five-year terms by universal suffrage, which shares legislative powers with the Prince. In 1993 the country joined the United Nations. 1997 commemorated the fact that in 1297 the Genoese Grimaldi became Monaco's sovereign. The EU and, especially, France pressured Monaco to put an end to the lax tax policy in 2001.

Mona Lisa *See:* Da Vinci, Leonardo.

Monarchy, form of government in which sovereignty is vested in one person, usually for life. The office may be elective but is usually hereditary. A monarch who has unlimited power is an *absolute monarch*; one whose power is limited by custom or constitution is a *constitutional monarch*. In modern parliamentary democracies a monarch is usually a nonparty political figure and a symbol of national unity

Monasticism, religious way of life, usually communal and celibate, generally involving withdrawal from worldly concerns. People who join a monastic order are secluded from society; men (called monks) live in *monasteries* and women (called nuns) in *convents*. Monasticism exists in various religions, including Buddhism, Islam, and Christianity (also Greek Orthodox church). In Christianity, monasticism is mostly a phenomenon of Catholicism. Monastic orders include Franciscans, Carmelites, and Dominicans.

The monastery conception of the Christian world already existed in the early centuries of the Church. Particularly in the East, a number of recluses or hermits led a sober life in the desert. When eventually they started to live together, a community was formed and living rules were drawn up. This miniature from a Byzantine manuscript shows monks from the 10th or 11th century, settling in caves in Cappadocia (Turkey, Bibliothèque Nationale, Paris).

Monazite, yellow to brown mineral containing phosphates of the rare earth elements cerium, lanthanum, and neodymium. It also contains yttrium and thorium. Found mainly in India, Brazil, and Australia, monazite is the prime source of thorium, a nuclear fuel. The rare earths, important for the manufacture of glass are also extracted from monazite

Mondale, Walter (1928-), 41st U.S. vice president (1977-1981), under Jimmy Carter. As a Democratic senator from Minnesota (1964-1977) he was known as a liberal and populist reformer. Carter and Mondale ran again in 1980 but lost to Ronald Reagan and George Bush. Mondale was the Democratic nominee for president in 1984. His running mate, Geraldine Ferraro, was the first woman to be chosen for the vice presidency by a major U.S. party. Mondale and Ferraro lost to Reagan and Bush. In 1993, Mondale became ambassador to Japan.

Mondrian, Piet (Pieter Cornelis Mondriaan; 1872-1944), Dutch painter and theorist, a founder of the Stijl movement. At first a symbolist, he was later influenced by cubism and evolved a distinctive abstract style relating primary colors, black, white, and gray in gridlike arrangements.

Monera, group of primitive one-celled organisms that have no nucleus. Scientists place monera in the Monera kingdom or in the plant or protist kingdom. Bacteria and blue-green algae comprise the group's single division. Monera, found throughout the world, live in soil (parasitic species live in organisms) and are able to survive the extreme temperatures of hot springs and frozen tundra.

Monet, Claude (1840-1926), French painter, leading exponent of impressionism, a term coined after his picture *Impression, Sunrise* (1872). He painted his landscapes outside, in natural light, applying paint in a multitude of variously colored strokes and swatches, thus conveying the appearance of a subject in a particular light, in a particular season, and at a particular time of day. His last pictures of water lilies are virtually abstract patterns of color.

Monetarism, theoretical position in economics, chiefly associated with the work of Milton Friedman of the University of Chicago. This contemporary theory is based on the 19th-century 'quantity-of-money' theory, which directly related changes in price levels to changes in the amount of money in circulation. Monetarism, which stands generally in opposition to Keynesianism, advocates curing inflation and depression not by fiscal measures but rather by control of the nation's money supply-for instance, by varying the interest rate charged by the Federal Reserve System and expanding or limiting the sale of treasury bills.
See also: Economics.

Money, in an economic system, anything accepted as a medium of exchange, measure of value, or means of payment. In primitive societies, barter, or direct physical exchange, was commonly used. The precise origin of money is unknown. It evolved gradually out of the needs of commerce and trade. Many objects have at one time or another been used as money: shells, nuts, wampum, beads, and stones. Gradually, metal was adopted because of its easy handling, durability, divisibility, and-especially with gold or silver-for its own value. The oldest coinage dates back to 700 B.C., when coins of gold and silver alloys were made in Lydia (Asia Minor). Paper money was known in China as early as the 7th century A.D., but it did not develop in Europe until the 17th century. The stability and value of paper currency is usually guaranteed by governments or banks (those invested with legal authority to issue currency) with some bullion holdings. The monetary system of the United States during most of the 19th century was based on bimetallism, which meant that both gold and silver were legal money. With the passing of the Gold Standard Act of 1900, the dollar was defined only in terms of gold. The Gold Reserve Act of 1934 reduced this dependence on gold, and in 1971 the nation went off the gold standard altogether. The nation's money supply is controlled by the Federal Reserve System, a central banking system created in 1913. Most currency in circulation today consists of Federal Reserve notes.

Mongol Empire, empire founded in the early 13th century by Genghis Khan (1167?-1227). Superb horseriders and archers, the Mongols of Central Asia were united into a well-disciplined, highly mobile army that conquered northern China by 1215 and then swept west through the Middle East and southern Russia, establishing a vast empire with its capital at Karakorum, in Mongolia.

A miniature from a fifteenth-century Arabic manuscript, showing an extraordinarily regal and civilised Genghis Khan (1155-1227), entering a mosque in Buchara (east of the Caspian Sea). In reality, the behaviour of the greatest conqueror in history had little to do with religious tolerance.

After Genghis Khan's death, the Mongol invasions were continued under his son Ogotai. During 1237-1240 the Mongol general Batu Khan, a grandson of Genghis Khan, crossed the Volga, crushed the Bulgars and Kumans, and invaded Poland and Hungary. Baghdad, seat of the Abbasid caliphate, was sacked in 1258. The Mongol troops had a reputation for great ferocity, in particular when attacking and destroying cities.
By about 1260 the Empire was organized into four Khanates, centered in Persia, southern Russia, Turkestan, and China. Kublai Khan's rule in China (1260-1294) saw the foundation of the Yüan Dynasty. The Mongol tradition of conquest was revived by Tamerlane in the 14th century and by Babur (founder of the Mogul Empire) in the 16th century.
See also: Genghis Khan; Kublai Khan.

Mongolia

Capital:	Ulaanbaatar (Ulan Bator)
Area:	604,800 sq mi
	(1,565,000 sq km)
Population:	2,694,000
Language:	Mongolian (Chalcha)
Government:	Republic
Independent:	1921
Head of gov.:	Prime minister
Per capita:	US$ 1,770
Monetary unit:	1 Tögrög = 100 möngö

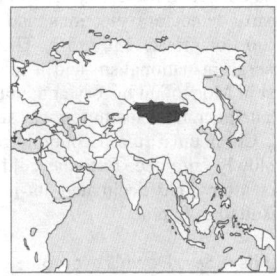

Mongolia, area in east central Asia divided into Outer Mongolia, or the Republic of Mongolia, and Inner Mongolia, or the Inner Mongolia Autonomous Region of China. Mongolia as a whole is bordered by Russia to the north and by China to the south, east, and west.
Land and climate. The land is largely a steppe plateau with an average elevation of 3,000 ft/914 m. The Hentiyn, Sayan, and other mountain ranges hem the area to the north and northeast and the Altai Mountains mark the end of the plateau to the southwest. Much of the southeast is part of the Gobi Desert which straddles a large part of Outer and Inner Mongolia. The climate is harsh with great extremes of heat and cold. The capital is Ulan Bator.
People. Although both Inner and Outer Mongolia were communist, many

A nomadic woman from Mongolia.

M

Mongolians continued to practice Tibetan Buddhism (Lamaism). Mongolian is the official language.

Economy. The economy is based upon livestock farming, the principal livelihood of a traditionally nomadic people. There is also some agriculture. Coal, iron ore, gold, and other minerals are mined. Industry is limited to felts, furniture, and other consumer goods. The chief exports are livestock, wool, hides, meat, and ores.

History. Formerly the heartland of the Mongol Empire founded by Genghis Khan in the 13th century, Mongolia became a province of China in 1691. Mongolia declared its independence in 1911, but was reoccupied by China in 1919. With support from the Soviet Union, Outer Mongolia declared its independence again in 1921. In 1924 it became the Mongolian People's Republic, the world's second communist state although China did not recognize Mongolia's independence until 1946. In 1990 liberalizing trends in the Communist world affected Mongolia. Opposition groups forced a change in leadership, the holding of multiparty democratic elections, and the introduction of private enterprise. There was an upsurge of nationalism and a revival of interest in Mongolian history and culture. In 1992 a democratic constitution was adopted, ending Communist rule. Economic reforms were slowly enforced. Extreme cold in the winters after 2000 decimated its livestock and resulted in famine.

Mongolism *See:* Down's syndrome.

Mongoose, small carnivorous mammal with a reputation for killing snakes and stealing eggs. There are about 48 species occupying a variety of habitats around the Mediterranean, in Africa, and in southern Asia. Most are diurnal, feeding on lizards, snakes, eggs, and other small mammals. Mongooses generally resemble weasels.

The banded mongoose (*Mungos mungo*), East and Central Africa, length 21 to 29 in (53 to 74 cm).

Monitor, any of a family of mostly tropical lizards of the Eastern Hemisphere that includes the world's largest, the 10-ft (3-m) Komodo dragon, of Indonesia.

Monitor and Merrimack, pioneer ironclad warships that fought the world's first battle between iron-armored vessels, at Hampton Roads, Va., on Mar. 9, 1862, during the U.S. Civil War. The *Merrimack* was a scuttled Union steam frigate, salvaged by the Confederates and renamed the *Virginia.* The Union's *Monitor* was equipped with a revolving gun turret. Neither vessel was victorious in the engagement.

Monk, Thelonious (1917-1982), U.S. composer, pianist, bandleader, and one of the innovators of modern jazz in the 1940s. His compositions 'Round Midnight,' '52nd Street Theme,' 'Epistrophy,' and 'Straight No Chaser' are jazz standards.

Monkey, any of several primates, suborder Anthropoidea. There are two superfamilies of monkeys, New World and Old World. Though there is little uniformity in the group, monkeys have flattened faces, the Old and New World families being distinguished by nose shape. Monkeys are normally restricted to tropical or subtropical areas of the world. Old World forms include langurs, colubuses, macaques, guenons, mangabeys, and baboons. Monkeys of the New World include sakis, uakaris, howlers, douroucoulis, squirrel monkeys, and capuchins.

Monkey bread *See:* Baobab.

Monkey flower, name of large group of herbs and shrubs (genus *Mimulus*) in the figwort family. Found mostly on the western coast of North America in wet areas, these plants grow to a height of 6 to 36 in (15 to 91 cm). The spots on their petals give the impression of a monkey.

Monmouth, Duke of (1649-1685), illegitimate son of King Charles II of England. When he did not inherit his father's throne, he invaded England (1685) with his own army and demanded that his father's successor, James II, relinquish the crown to him. Monmouth's army lost the battle that ensued. He was captured and executed.

Monnet, Jean (1888-1979), French economist and politician, known as the architect of a united Western Europe. His Monnet Plan (1947) helped France's economic recovery after World War II. He served as first president of the European Coal and Steel Community (ECSC), and helped organize the Common Market (European Community).
See also: European Community.

Mononucleosis, also called infectious mononucleosis or glandular fever, infectious disease commonly affecting adolescents and young adults. Symptoms include severe sore throat, headache, fever, and enlargement of the lymph nodes and spleen. It is believed to be caused by a herpes virus. Severe cases may require steroids, and convalescence

may be lengthy.
See also: Herpes; Epstein-Barr (EB) virus.

Monopoly, economic term describing significant control or ownership of a product or service (and thereby its price) because of command of the product's supply, legal privilege, or concerted action. There are different kinds of monopoly. Patents and copyrights are legal monopolies granted by a government to individuals or companies. A nationalized industry or service, such as the U.S. Postal Service, has a monopoly. A franchise granted by government to a public company to run a public utility (such as an electrical company) creates a monopoly. Trading and industrial monopolies have the power to decide upon supply and price of goods. Sometimes labor unions act as monopolies in the supply of workers' services. In the case of national monopolies it is considered that they can provide mass-produced goods or services at a lower price, or more efficiently, than could be provided in a competitive situation; in practice this is not always true. Business or manufacturing monopolies may often discourage competitors from entering the field of competition. There is legislation designed to control monopolies that conspire to restrain price or trade.

Monotheism, belief in one God, contrasted with polytheism, pantheism, or atheism. Classical monotheism is held by Judaism, Christianity, and Islam; some other religions, such as early Zoroastrianism and later Greek religion, are monotheistic to a lesser degree. In the theories of Sir Edward B. Tylor, religions have evolved from animism through polytheism and henotheism (the worship of one god, ignoring others in practice) to monotheism. There is, however, evidence for residual monotheism (the 'High God') in primitive religions.
See also: Religion.

Monroe, James (1758-1831), fifth president of the United States (1817-1825). Democrat. Envoy in Paris (1794-1796; 1802-1803) and London (1803-1806) and from 1811 until 1817 Secretary of State under Madison, from 1814 to 1815 Secretary of Defense as well. In 1816 he was elected president, and reelected in 1820. He formulated the Monroe Doctrine, a statement of principles about the independent foreign policy of the U.S. In this statement to Congress (1823), composed by his Secretary of State J.Q. Adams, he warned European powers not to interfere with matters which took place on the American continent; America would do the same in Europe.

Monroe, Marilyn (Norma Jean Baker; 1926-1962), U.S. movie star who became world famous as a sex symbol. A comic actress of considerable talent, she acted in such films as *Gentlemen Prefer Blondes* (1953), *The Seven-Year Itch* (1955), *Bus Stop* (1956), and *Some Like It Hot* (1959).

Monroe Doctrine, declaration of U.S. policy toward the newly independent states of Latin America, issued by President James Monroe on Dec. 2, 1823. It stated that the United States would not tolerate any

European interference with the former colonies of the Americas, which were 'henceforth not to be considered as subjects for further colonization by any European powers.' President Theodore Roosevelt's corollary to the doctrine (1904) asserted that the United States had the right to intervene to prevent any interference in the affairs of the hemisphere by outside governments and to ensure that acceptable governments were maintained there. This became known as the 'big stick' policy and was invoked often by Presidents Taft and Wilson to justify armed U.S. intervention in the Caribbean.

Monrovia (pop. 470,000), capital city of Liberia, in West Africa, on Bushrod Island. Situated on the Atlantic coast at the mouth of the Saint Paul River, it is the administrative, commercial, cultural, and educational center of Liberia. Monrovia's modern harbor is the main source of its revenue. Monrovia, named for the U.S. president James Monroe, was founded in 1822 by the American Colonization Society as a place where freed U.S. slaves could live.
See also: Liberia.

Monsoon, wind system in which the prevailing wind direction reverses in the course of the seasons, occurring where large temperature (hence pressure) differences arise between oceans and large land masses. Best known is that of Southeast Asia. In summer, moist winds, with associated hurricanes, blow from the Indian Ocean into the low-pressure region of northwestern India caused by intense heating of the land. In winter, cold, dry winds sweep south from the high-pressure region of southern Siberia.

Montaigne, Michel Eyquem de (1533-1592), French writer, generally regarded as the originator of the personal essay. The first two books of his *Essays* (1580), written in an informal style, display insatiable intellectual curiosity tempered by skepticism. A third book of essays, which appeared in 1588, includes his last reflections. The essays deal with a range of subjects, most revolving around the nature of human life and the requirements of knowledge and happiness.

Montale, Eugenio (1896-1981), Italian poet and literary critic. Recipient of the 1975 Nobel Prize for literature, his books of poetry include *Cuttlefish Bones* (1925), *The Occasions* (1939), *Satura* (1971), and *Notebook of Four Years* (1977). In his writings, Montale expressed the complexity of modern life and the difficulty of achieving happiness. Montale also wrote short stories and essays, and translated English writings by Emily Dickinson, T.S. Eliot, and William Shakespeare into Italian.

Montana (Treasure State; pop. 879,000), state in the U.S., bordered by Canada, Idaho, Wyoming, North and South Dakota; 147,102 sq mi (380,848 sq km). Capital city: Helena. Is situated partly in the Rocky Mountains and partly in the Great Plains. Montana is one of the most thinly populated states of America. Most of the inhabitants descend from immigrants from Great

Britain, Ireland, the Netherlands, Germany, France and the Scandinavian countries. Agriculture (grain, sugar beets, hay, potatoes, alfalfa), forestry and cattle breeding (mainly sheep). Extraction of e.g. copper, petroleum, phosphate and natural gas. Industry is based on mining, forestry and agriculture, and is the second economic activity after agriculture.
The various Indian nations, among which the Crow, Cheyenne and Blackfoot, lived mainly from hunting and the collection of food. The members of the Lewis and Clark expedition (1804) were probably the first Europeans in the area; during the 19th century a gold rush took place. After several big battles (e.g. at Little Bighorn) between Native Americans and white Americans, Montana became a member of the Union in 1889.

Monte Carlo (pop. 13,000), town in Monaco, on the Mediterranean coast. An international resort with a gambling casino, a yacht harbor, and an annual automobile rally, it is the home (and tax haven) of many international firms.
See also: Monaco.

Monte Cristo, small Italian island. Located in the Tyrrhenian Sea between Italy and Corsica, this mountainous island has an area of 6 sq mi (16 sq km) and rises to 2,116 ft (645 m) above sea level. Ruins of a 13th-century Benedictine monastery abandoned in 1553 after pirates destroyed it still stand there. Alexandre Dumas made the island fa-

The 16th-century French author Michel Eyquem de Montaigne developed the literary genre of the personal essay, establishing its importance in Western literature. His *Essays*, which record his observations on diverse subjects as friendship, education, and government, are valuable historical records of an individual's reaction to the immediate environment. Montaigne's skepticism is reflected in his famous motto, 'Que sais-je?' ('What do I know?'). His portrait was painted by an unknown 16th-century artist (Musée Condé, Chantilly).

mous in his novel *The Count of Monte Cristo* (1844).
See also: Italy.

Montenegro, smallest of the two constituent republics of the Federal Republic of Yugoslavia. Its capital is Podgorica. Its former capital, Cetinje, was absorbed into Serbia after World War I. The area is mountainous with heavy forests. Mining, agriculture, and the raising of livestock are its chief occupations.
See also: Yugoslavia, Federal Republic of.

The Montenegro town of Kotor, at the end of the Bay of Kotor. The bay, which is connected to the Adriatic Sea, has been a favourite haven for ships since antiquity, because of the shelter provided by the surrounding mountains.

Monterrey (pop. 3,100,000), Mexico, one of the nation's principal cities and the capital of Nuevo Leon state. It is in northeastern Mexico near the Sierra Madre Oriental range at an elevation of about 1,750 ft (530 m). Monterrey is a major industrial and financial center, second only to Mexico City in these respects. Steel, textiles, glass, and beer are among the chief products. Nearby is one of the leading citrus-producing areas in Mexico. Monterrey is an important highway and railway junction and has an international airport. Educational institutions include the state university and a technological institute. Monterrey was founded in 1596 and remained small for nearly three centuries. In 1846, during the Mexican War, it was occupied by United States troops. Rapid growth began in the 1880's with the construction of railways to Monterrey.

Montesquieu (Charles de Secondat; 1689-1755), French political philosopher. He inherited the title Baron de la Brède et de Montesquieu. His theory that governmental powers should be separated into legislative, executive, and judicial bodies to safeguard personal liberty was developed in his most important work, *The Spirit of Laws* (1748). His ideas influenced the framers of the U.S. Constitution. Montesquieu's *Persian Letters* (1721), which satirized contemporary French sociopolitical institutions, won him early fame.

Montessori, Maria (1870-1952), Italian psychiatrist and educator. The first woman to gain a medical degree in Italy (1894), she developed a system of preschool teaching, the Montessori Method, which is designed to encourage individual initiative. Children of three to six are given a wide range of materials and equipment that enables them to learn by themselves or with minimal adult intervention. There are more than 600 schools in the United States using this method.
See also: Psychiatry.

M

M

Monteux, Pierre (1875-1964), a French-born conductor. As conductor of the Ballet Russe, 1911-1916, he led the first performances of Stravinsky's *Petrouchka* and *Le Sacre du Printemps*, Reval's *Daphnis et Chloé*, and other works. Monteux was born in Paris and attended the conservatory there. From 1919 to 1924 he conducted the Boston Symphony Orchestra. He founded the Paris Symphony in 1929 and was its conductor until 1938. After conducting the San Francisco Symphony, 1936-1952, he made many guest appearances and in 1961 became conductor of the London Symphony. He became a United States citizen in 1942.

Monteverdi, Claudio (1567-1643), Italian composer. His innovative operas were the predecessors of modern opera, in which aria, recitative, and orchestral accompaniment enhances dramatic characterization. *Orfeo* (1607) is considered the first modern opera. His other compositions include many madrigals, *Vespers* (1610), much other sacred music, and the operas *The Return of Ulysses to His Country* (1641) and *The Coronation of Poppaea* (1642).
See also: Opera.

Claudio Monteverdi (1567-1643), as painted by Domenico Fetti (1588-1623).

Montevideo (pop. 3,2 million), capital and largest city of Uruguay, located in the south on the Rio de la Plata. It is the country's industrial, cultural, and transportation center, as well as a seaport and popular resort. Founded in 1724, it became the capital in 1828.

Montezuma, or Moctezuma, name of two Aztec rulers of Mexico before the Spanish conquest. Montezuma I (1390-1469) was a successful military leader who ruled from 1440. His descendant, Montezuma II (1466?-1520), was the last Aztec emperor (c.1502-1520). When the Spanish conquistadors arrived, Montezuma failed to resist them because he believed Cortés to be the god Quetzalcoatl. When Montezuma was taken hostage, the Aztecs rebelled against the Spanish, and Montezuma was killed in the struggle.
See also: Aztecs.

Montfort, Simon de (1208?-1265), Anglo-French leader who mounted a revolt against King Henry III. The Baron's War, led by de Montfort, followed Henry's annulment (1261) of the Provisions of Oxford which he had been forced to sign in 1258. The war was ended with the capture of the king (1264). The parliament of 1265, summoned by Montfort and including representatives from every shire, town, and borough, was a landmark in English history. In subsequent fighting Montfort was killed at the Battle of Evesham.

Montgolfier, Joseph Michel (1740-1810) and **Jacques Étienne** (1745-1799), French brothers noted for their invention of the first manned aircraft, the first practical hot-air balloon, which they flew in 1783. That same year Jacques Montgolfier assisted Jacques Charles in the launching of the first gas (hydrogen) balloon.
See also: Balloon.

Montgomery (pop. 221,000), capital of Alabama. Lying in the cotton-belt, it is a major Southern agricultural market center. Its other industries include manufacturing of furniture, glass, machinery, paper, and textiles. Named after Brigadier General Richard Montgomery, a Revolutionary War hero, Montgomery played a key role in the Civil War, and is often referred to as the 'Cradle of the Confederacy.' In 1861, the Confederate States of America were established there, Montgomery was made the first Confederate capital, and Jefferson Davis was inaugurated as president of the Confederacy in its capital. More recently, Montgomery was a focus in the Civil Rights Movement. Dr. Martin Luther King, Jr. led demonstrations there to promote equal treatment for all people. In 1956, Montgomery was one of the first Southern cities to ban racial segregation on buses.

Montgomery, Bernard Law (1887-1976), British field marshal who defeated the Germans by Gen. Rommel at El Alamein (1942), thus driving the Germans out of northern Africa. Montgomery later commanded the British forces in the invasion of Normandy (1944). After the war he served as supreme commander of NATO (1951-1958). *See also:* North Atlantic Treaty Organization.

Montherlant, Henri Millon de (1896-1972) French writer. Montherlant is considered to be one of the most important postwar playwrights in France. His plays are of a very psychological nature and have a traditional structure. He is also a well-known novelist and essayist. He made his debut with novels set against the background of World War I: *Le relève du matin* (1920); *Le songe* (1922). He shows his preference for manliness-sturdiness in the novels *Les Olympiques* (1924) and *Les bestiaires* (1926), about sports and bullfights respectively; he showed his aversion to femininity in the novel *Les célibataires* (1935) and the four-volume series *Les jeunes filles* (1936-1939). His successful play *La reine morte* (1942; about Inés de Castro) led to other plays such as *Demain il fera jour* (1949), *Le cardinal d'Espagne* (1960) and *La guerre civile* (1965). Impending blindness made him take his life in 1972.

Monti, Eugenio (1928-), Italian bobsledder, became world champion eleven times between 1957 and 1968 (eight times in the two-man sled, thrice in the four-man sled). Although he had already participated in the 1956 and 1964 Olympic Games (silver and bronze, respectively), he only won the Olympic gold (two and four-man sled) in 1968. Subsequently he became coach of the Italian team. Typical of Monti were his starting techniques, steermanship and sportsmanship.

Monticello, 640-acre (260-hectare) estate planned by Thomas Jefferson in Virginia, just outside Charlottesville. Construction of the neoclassical mansion atop a small mountain began in 1770; Jefferson moved in before it was completed and lived there for 56 years. His tomb is nearby. The house was declared a national shrine in 1926 and is open to the public.

Montreal (officially Montréal; pop.

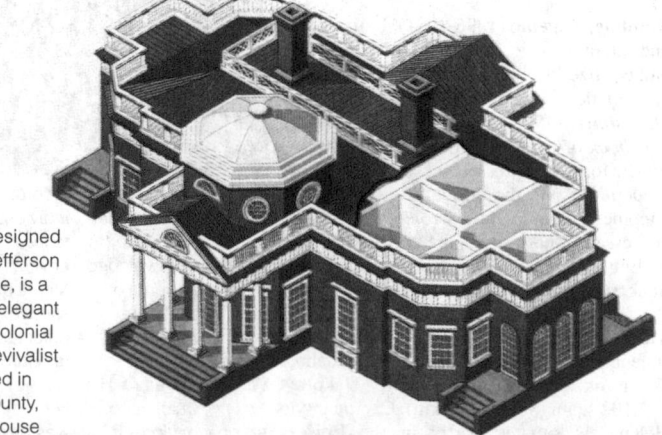

Monticello, designed by Thomas Jefferson for his own use, is a graceful and elegant synthesis of colonial and classic revivalist styles. Located in Albemarle County, Virginia, the house was constructed in two stages, in 1770-82 and 1793-1809. Its interior of 35 rooms features irregular shapes, and such innovations as a bed that was placed between the dressing room and the study, and two narrow staircases, whose width of 24 in (61 cm) minimizes their intrusion on the dwelling space.

1,018,000), city in southern Quebec, Canada, located on the island of Montréal at the confluence of the St. Lawrence and Ottawa rivers. A major inland port on the St. Lawrence Seaway, Montreal is Canada's largest city. It is named for 764-ft (233-m) Mount Royal, which rises in the city's center. A French mission was built on the site in 1642, which soon become an important fur-trading center. Ceded to Britain in 1763, the city has retained much of its French character. In the 19th century Montreal grew into an important transportation and industrial center, aided by its many natural resources and an abundance of hydroelectric power. It is the site of McGill University and the University of Montréal.

Mont Saint Michel, rocky isle off the northwestern French coast. A tourist attraction, it contains a small town and a Benedictine abbey founded in 708. The abbey's church is renowned for its Gothic architecture.

Montserrat, Leeward Island in the West Indies, situated southeast of Puerto Rico. It was discovered and named in 1493 by Christopher Columbus, and colonized by the British in 1632; they took possession of it in 1783. Montserrat contains 3 mountain groups within an area of 38 sq mi (98 sq km). A British dependency, Montserrat has been self-governing since 1960. Plymouth is its capital. Its chief crops include cotton, limes, and vegetables. In 1997 the Soufrière Hills volcano erupted after having been dormant for four centuries. As a result, the largest part of the island became uninhabitable.

Monty Python, Group of British actors who made a series of comedy programs between 1969 and 1974 called *Monty Python's Flying Circus*. The most important members were John Cleese, Graham Chapman, Michael Palin, Terry Jones, Eric Idle and Terry Gilliam. Their work became classical thanks to their sketches' confrontational subjects and typical English humor, combined with their great qualities as scriptwriters and actors. Monty Python also made five movies, including *Monty Python and the Holy Grail* (1974), *Monty Python's Life of Brian* (1979) and *Monty Python's The Meaning of Life* (1983).

Monzon, Carlos (1942-1995), Argentinian boxer. Monzon was very popular in Argentina as much for his sporting achievements as for his flamboyant way of life. As a professional middleweight boxer he built up an impressive record: out of 89 fights he won 61 on knock out and lost only three. He successfully defended his world title, conquered in 1970, on fourteen occasions. He ended his boxing career in 1977.

Moody, Helen Wills *See:* Wills, Helen Newington.

Moon, natural satellite of the earth. The moon is 2,160 mi (3,476 km) in diameter, or about one-fourth the size of the earth, and has a smaller mass than the earth. It would take 82 moons to tip the scales against the earth. The moon is about 239,000 mi (384,623 km) from earth.

The moon takes just under a calendar month, or 27.322 days, to orbit the earth. In fact, the word 'month' is derived from the word 'moon.' As it orbits the earth, it also rotates on its axis. The result is that the moon always presents the same side toward the earth.

In the course of its orbit, the moon is seen to go through phases. It reflects sunlight and its phases are the result of the progressive increase and decrease of the portions of its surface reflecting sunlight as it orbits the earth. The new moon occurs when the moon's reflecting surface is turned away from the sun and is completely in shadow. The full moon occurs when the whole of the moon's reflecting surface is illuminated by the sun.

With the naked eye, the moon appears to be divided unevenly into bright and dark areas. Through a telescope astronomers are able to identify the bright regions as upland areas and the dark regions as lowlands, plains, or depressions. The plains are called 'maria,' from the Latin for 'seas,' because they were once thought to be expanses of water. It is not certain whether there are bodies of water on the moon, although in 1972 Apollo 17 did discover possible traces of water. Neither is there a lunar atmosphere. Without an insulating atmosphere the daytime temperature of the lunar surface reaches 200°F (93°C), and at night it falls to -250°F (-157°C).

The 'seas' of the moon are lowland areas that appear to have been flooded with volcanic lava. Scientists reason that the lava has obliterated many craters. But for more than a century, scientists argued about the origin of the moon's many craters. One theory was that the moon's features were the result of explosive impacts by giant meteors. Opponents of that view argued that some form of volcanic action had built up the craters. Closeup photographs by orbiting space probes have provided evidence of both processes. On July 20, 1969, the United States succeeded in landing the first man on the moon. In March of 1998, measurements made by the space probe Lunar Prospector indicated that ice caps might be present on the moon.

See also: Solar System.

Moon, Sun Myung (1920-   ), Korean-American leader of a sect, founder of the Unification Church (Unified Family, 1954). Raised in a Presbyterian family, he had a vision at the age of 16 in which Jesus called on him to perform his uncompleted task. He wrote *Divine Principle* (1957). Is considered by some of his followers as the messiah. Made frequent propaganda trips in the West. In 1973 he settled in Irvington (N.Y.).

Moonflower, flowering climbing plant (*Ipomaea bona-nox* or *Calonyction aculeatum*) in the morning glory family. The vine can grow to a height of 10 ft (3 m). It bears large, heart-shaped leaves and large, white, funnel-shaped flowers that bloom at night. The flowers have a delicate fragrance and can grow to be from 3 to 6 in (8 to 15 cm) across.

Moore, Douglas Stuart (1893-1969), U.S. composer and teacher. Most of his major works deal with American themes and peo-

ple. In 1951 he won the Pulitzer Prize for music for *Giants in the Earth*, an opera about the difficulties faced by Norwegian farmers in the Dakotas in the 1800s. His other operas include *The Devil and Daniel Webster* (1939), set in New England, and *The Ballad of Baby Doe* (1956), set in Colorado. He also wrote orchestral pieces, such as *Pageant of P.T. Barnum* (1924) and *Moby Dick* (1928). He taught music at Columbia University. His book *From Madrigal to Modern Music* (1942), is a study of musical styles.

Moore, George Augustus (1852-1933), Irish writer. Influenced by the realism and naturalism of Honoré de Balzac and Émile Zola, he stirred English literary society with his realistic novels *Esther Waters* (1894) and *Héloise and Abélard* (1921). He contributed greatly to the Irish renaissance revival and to the success of the Abbey Theatre.

Moore, Gerald (1899-1987), English pianist. Moore studied in Toronto and started his career as a church and movie house pianist, but owes his reputation to his work as accompanist to the great singers of his time. He traveled around the world with soloists of international fame such as Kathleen Ferrier, Elisabeth Schwarzkopf, Victoria de los Angeles and Dietrich Fischer-Dieskau. Writings include *The Unashamed Accompanist* (1943) and *Singer and Accompanist* (1953). In 1967 he ended his career, having worked as a professional pianist for 50 years. After his retirement he remained active exclusively as a recording artist.

Moore, Henry (1898-1986), English sculptor. His inspiration came from natural forms, such as stones, roots, and bones, and was often expressed in curving abstract shapes perforated with large holes. His work, with repeated themes, such as mother and child, is monumental. It includes *Family Group* (1949) and *Reclining Figure* (1965).

Moore, Marianne (1887-1972), U.S. poet, winner of the 1952 Pulitzer Prize for her

M

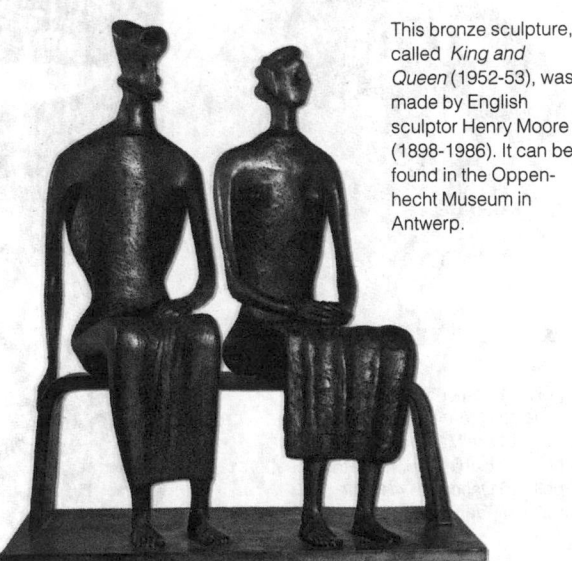

This bronze sculpture, called *King and Queen* (1952-53), was made by English sculptor Henry Moore (1898-1986). It can be found in the Oppenhecht Museum in Antwerp.

M

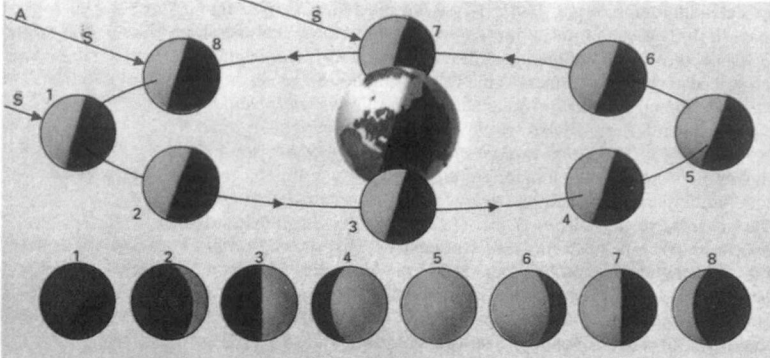

A. As the moon rotates around the earth, it goes through phases. At each phase, the amount of sunlight reflected by the moon towards the earth changes. In position 1, when the moon is between the sun and earth, it is called a new moon, in position 5, it is a full moon, in positions 3 and 7 it is a half moon, and in positions 4 and 6 it is a gibbous moon.
B. The moon rotates on its axis once every 27 1/3 days. Since it rotates around the earth at the same rate, the same moon face always faces towards earth.
C. From point 1 to point 2, the moon makes one complete revolution. To an observer on earth, however, the moon has not made a complete revolution until it reaches point 3, since the earth is itself orbiting around the sun.

The crater Erastosthenes on the moon, photographed by Apollo 12

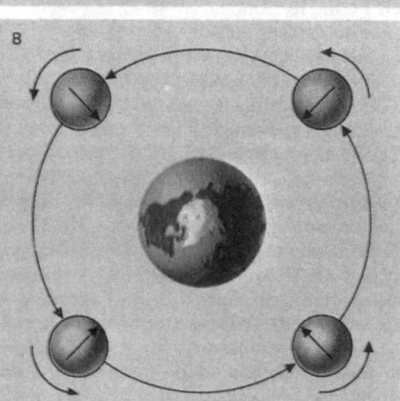

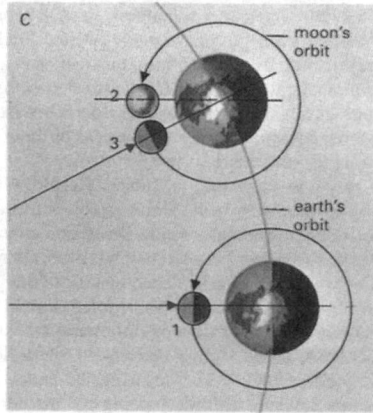

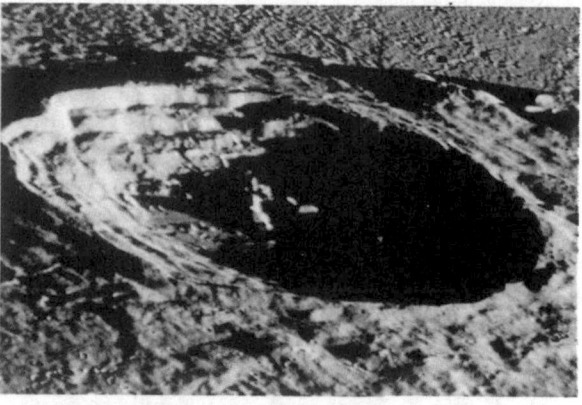

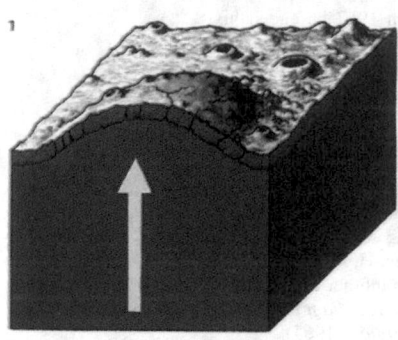

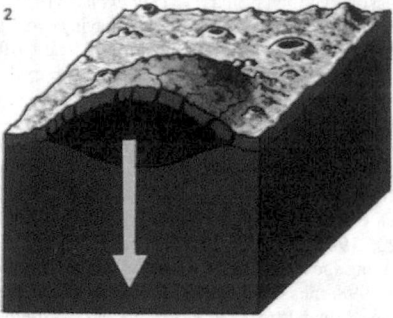

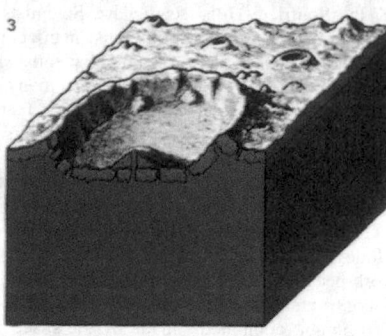

The volcanic theory states the following: Domes formed on the hot lunar crust by such processes as magmatic convection (1). On cooling, the material under these domes descended, leaving a void (2). The surface layer then collapsed, forming a walled plain or crater (3). Central volcanic peaks can also form, as magma penetrates through fissures in the collapsed dome.

Apollo

Apollo 11 Sea of Tranquility 7/20/69
Apollo 12 Ocean of Storms 11/19/69
Apollo 14 Fra Mauro Region 2/05/71
Apollo 15 Hadley-Aponine Region 7/30/71
Apollo 16 Descartes 4/16/72
Apollo 17 Taurus-Lithrow 12/72

The lunar rover of the Apollo 15 mission, used to carry the astronauts over 17 mi (27 km) of lunar terrain

M

Collected Poems. She edited *Dial* magazine (1925-1929) and translated La Fontaine's *Fables* (1954).

Moor hen *See:* Gallinule.

Moorish art *See:* Islamic art.

Moors, North African nomadic people who adopted Islam and became ethnically fused with the Arabs during the expansion of Islam in the 7th century. The Moors went on to conquer much of Spain and Portugal in the early 8th century, crossing into France, where they were stopped by the army of Charles Martel in 732. Their rule in Spain, centered in the cities of Córdoba and Granada, saw an unparalled development of philosophy, the sciences, and architecture. The Moors lost much of their land in Spain by the late 13th century. They were finally driven from the Iberian peninsula (along with the Jews) by Christian forces under King Ferdinand and Queen Isabella in 1492.

Moose, large, long-legged mammal (genus *Alces*) of the deer family, native to cold climates. The species *A. alces,* found in Europe, is called an elk. The males have large, palmate antlers, as wide as 7 ft (2 m) across. Often living near water, the moose feeds on aquatic plants and bushes and mature trees.

Mora, Juan Rafael (1814-1860), president of Costa Rica (1849-1859). His accomplishments included creating a public school system, building public buildings, establishing the first Costa Rican national bank, and promoting the coffee industry. Considered a hero for his defense of Central America in 1956 and 1957 against William Walker of the United States, he was nevertheless ousted by rebels in 1859 and executed during a revolution in 1860.
See also: Costa Rica.

Morality play, form of drama popular at the end of the Middle Ages, from about the 14th to the 16th century. It was intended to instruct its audience on the eternal struggle between good and evil for human souls. The characters were personifications of virtues and vices. The most noted English example is *Everyman* (from the late 15th century), which is still sometimes performed. Morality plays grew out of earlier religious pageants and were an important step in the secularization of drama.

Morandi, Giorgio (1890-1964), Italian painter, aquarellist and etcher. For a short period he was part of the metaphysical movement (1918-1920). Except for some landscapes, he only painted still-lives with carefully arranged objects like bottles, bowls and boxes. The effect of isolation was created by a sober reproduction of faint colors and classical means such as the use of light and composition.

Morava River, a major river of Serbia; 550 km. It flows 152 miles (245 km) northward from the union of its two branches in central Serbia, and meets the Danube river about 25 miles (40 km) east of Belgrade.

Morava River, a tributary of the Danube River draining the Moravia region of the Czech Republic. It flows 227 miles (365 km) southward from the Sudeten Mountains near the Polish border and at its southern end forms part of the border with Austria.

Moravia, eastern region of the Czech Republic, bounded on the west by the Bohemian highlands and on the east by the Carpathian Mountains. Historically the homeland of the Moravian Empire, from 1029 Moravia was a province of Bohemia. In 1526 it passed under Hapsburg rule, and was part of Austria-Hungary until 1918. Its border areas were annexed by Germany after the Munich Conference of 1938. Germany held all Moravia from 1939 until late in World War II. Moravia became part of the Czech Republic when Czechoslovakia split into two nations in 1993. Moravia is a fertile and now highly industrialized region. Brno, the largest city, is noted for textile manufacturing.
See also: Czech Republic.

Moravia, Alberto, the pen name of Alberto Pincherle (1907-1990), an Italian author. He is noted for his skill as a storyteller and his accurate portrayal of contemporary Italy. His first novel, *Time of Indifference* (1932), won critical acclaim for exposing the superficiality and decadence of the bourgeoisie. *The Women of Rome* (1949) and *Two Women* (1958) focus on the lives of workingclass Italians.
Moravia was born in Rome. He was bedridden with osteomyelitis (tuberculosis of the bone) for most of his childhood. He did not receive much formal education but read extensively on his own. Moravia worked as a foreign correspondent for several Italian newspapers, 1930-1939. He later worked as a film critic and magazine editor. His other works include; *The Empty Canvas* (1961), *Time of Desecration* (1980), *1934* (1983), *The Voyeur* (1987), *Command and I will obey you* (1969), *Bought and sold* (1973), *Beatrice Cenci* (1965) en *The God Kurt* (1968).

Moravian Church, Protestant church, also known as the *Unitas Fratrum* (Unity of Brethren), formed in 1457 by Bohemian followers of Jan Hus. They believed in simple worship and strict Christian living, with the Bible as their rule of faith. They broke with Rome in 1467. During the Thirty Years' War (1618-1648), they were persecuted almost to extinction, but they revived in Silesia and in 1732 began the missionary work for which they are still known.
See also: Hus, Jan; Protestantism.

Moray *See:* Eel.

Mordvinia (pop. 960,000) Republic of the Russian Federation, situated in the center of European Russia: 10,119 sq mi (26,200 sq km) capital Saransk. Approximately one third of its population consists of Mordvinians; the remaining inhabitants are ethnic Russians.
Cultivation of grain, vegetables and potatoes, and cattle breeding. Roughly half of the national income comes from machine building and metallurgic industry. The production of building materials is also well de-

veloped, especially sand, clay, and cement (Mordovtsement, largest cement factory in Europe). Also processing of petroleum and chemical industry (Rezinotechnika, largest oil processing company of Russia).
The area became part of Russia in 1552 after the collapse of the Mongolian Empire of the Golden Horde. Despite the absence of an intense national awareness the area became an autonomous SSR (Socialistic Soviet Republic) in 1934. In late 1991, when the Soviet Union collapsed, Mordvinia became a republic of the Russian Federation.

More, Saint Thomas (1478-1535), English statesman, writer, and saint who was executed for his refusal to take the oath of supremacy recognizing Henry VIII as head of the English church. A man of brilliance, subtlety, and wit, he was much favored by the king. When Cardinal Wolsey fell in 1529, More was made lord chancellor. Probably because of Henry's determination to divorce Catherine of Aragon in defiance of the pope, More resigned only 3 years later. Considered dangerously influential even in silence and retirement, More was condemned for high treason. His best-known work is *Utopia,* a description of an ideal society based on reason. Long recognized as a martyr by the Catholic church, More was canonized in 1935.
See also: Utopia.

Morgagni, Giovanni Battista (1682-1771), anatomist, the first person to make the study of diseases a science. An anatomy professor at the University of Padua, Morgagni believed that the key to diagnosing and treating diseases lay in knowledge of the body and how it functions. He studied hundreds of corpses to find the causes of their deaths. His findings are recorded in *On the Seats and Causes of Diseases* (1761).
See also: Anatomy; Pathology.

Morgan, U.S. banking family famous for its immense financial power and its philanthropic activities. The banking house of J.S. Morgan & Co. was founded by **Junius Spencer Morgan** (1813-1890) and developed into a vast financial and industrial empire (J.P. Morgan & Co.) under his son, **John Pierpont Morgan** (1837-1913).

Morgan, Sir Henry (1635-1688), English adventurer and leader of the West Indies buccaneers. The destruction of Panama City (1671), his most daring exploit, took place

Italian novelist Alberto Moravia (1907-1990) is famous, both in his home country and abroad.

Saint Thomas More (1478-1535) was a brilliant lawyer and author of the classic *Utopia.* He was renowned for his penetrating wit and profound conviction.

M

after the signing of a treaty between England and Spain. Recalled under arrest, he was subsequently pardoned, knighted (1673), and made lieutenant governor of Jamaica (1680-1682).

Morgan, Thomas Hunt (1866-1945), U.S. biologist who, through his experiments with the fruit fly *Drosophila*, established the relation between genes and chromosomes and thus the mechanism of heredity. For his work he received the 1933 Nobel Prize for physiology or medicine. His books include *The Physical Basis of Heredity* (1919), *Evolution and Genetics* (1925), and *Embryology and Genetics* (1934). *See also:* Genetics; Heredity.

Morgenthau, Henry, Jr. (1891-1967), U.S. secretary of the treasury (1934-1945). During World War II he raised billions of dollars through the sale of government bonds. In 1945 he helped establish the World Bank and the International Monetary Fund, organizations to help countries develop self-sufficiency and economic prosperity.

Mori, Mariko (1967-), Japanese visual artist. She takes photographs of herself dressed as a futuristic comic character, who has created her own timeless reality. She presents herself as art, as a star, someone who could have originated from both the fashion as well as the music business. After being used in her performance, her costumes are welded into large Plexiglass coverings, not to be opened for at least 25 years. Mori's later works are increasingly striking: the photographs developed into layered pictures that appear to move, after that videos accompanied by penetrating music, and finally a 3D-movie.

Mörike, Eduard (1804-1875), German lyric poet. His poetry, first collected in the volume *Gedichte* (1838), is small in quantity but varied in theme and technique. He also wrote a novel *Maler Nolten* (1832) and some short stories.

Morisot, Berthe (1841-1895), French impressionist painter. Her paintings, which often included family members, were noted for the originality of their design and their exquisite color. Morisot was a prominent figure in the Parisian art world, and was good friends with Degas, Renoir, and Eduard Manet, whose brother she married.

Morley, Thomas (1557?-1603?), English composer noted for his madrigals. A pupil of William Byrd and organist of St. Paul's Cathedral, he also wrote *A Plaine and Easie Introduction to Practicall Musicke* (1597), an invaluable source of information on Elizabethan musical practice.

Mormon cricket, insect (*Anabrus simplex*) belonging to the family of grasshoppers and katydids. Found in the Great Plains and Western United States, Mormon crickets grow to a length of approximately 2 in (5 cm) and can be black, green, or brown. Although they have small wings, they cannot fly. In 1848 Mormons in Utah almost lost all their crops to a swarm of these in-

sects. Miraculously, a flock of seagulls appeared in time and ate the crickets. Farmers today use poisons and baits to destroy them.

Mormons, members of The Church of Jesus Christ of Latter-Day Saints, founded in 1830 by Joseph Smith. Mormons accept Smith as having miraculously found and translated a divinely inspired record of the early history and religion of America, the *Book of Mormon*. With Smith's own writings and the Bible, this forms the Mormon scriptures. The Mormons' attempts to settle in Ohio and Missouri met with recurrent persecution, culminating in the murder of Smith in 1844. In 1847 Brigham Young led the Mormons west to Salt Lake City (still the location of their chief temple). In 1850 Congress granted them the Territory of Utah, with Young as governor. Hostility to the flourishing agricultural community that developed focused on the Mormon sanction of polygamy and came to a climax with the 'Utah War' (1857-1858). In 1890 the Mormons abolished polygamy, and Utah was admitted to the Union in 1896. The Mormons have a president and counselors; their membership is about 3 million. *See also:* Utah; Young, Brigham.

Morning-glory, common name for herbs, shrubs, and small trees of the family *Convolvulaceae*. Predominantly climbing plants, morning-glories are found in warm climates. Their fast-growing vines bear colorful, funnel-shaped flowers (some of which only open in the morning) and can grow to heights of 10-20 ft (3-6 m). The sweet potato, bindweed, moonflower, and garden morning glory are some plants belonging to this family.

Morning star *See:* Evening star.

Morocco

Capital:	Rabat
Area:	177,117 sq mi (458,730 sq km)
Population:	31,168,000
Language:	Arabic
Government:	Parliamentary monarchy
Independent:	1956
Head of gov.:	Prime minister
Per capita:	US$ 3,700
Monetary unit:	1 Moroccan dirham = 100 centimes

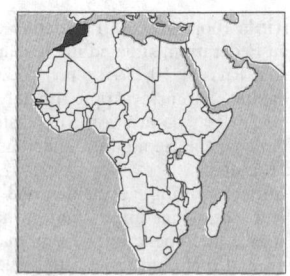

Morocco, kingdom in northwest Africa bordered by the Mediterranean Sea on the north, the Atlantic Ocean to the west, Algeria to the east and Western Sahara to the south.

Land and climate. Morocco occupies an area of c.177,117 sq mi (458,730 sq km). In the north and east of the coastal plain, the ridges of the Rif Mountains form an arc from Ceuta to Melilla, 2 ports under Spanish suzerainty. South of the Rif, the Atlas Mountains extend southwestward across central Morocco. And southeast of the Atlas Mountains is the Sahara Desert and the as yet undefined section of the border with Algeria. The climate of the fertile coastal plain is Mediterranean, with hot dry summers and mild winters. The climate of the interior plains and mountainous regions is harsh. Morocco's capital is Rabat, and its cities include Casablanca, Marrakesh, and Fez.

People. Moroccans are mostly of Arab descent, but about one-third of the people are Berbers, and there are Jewish, French, Spanish and Tuareg communities. Less than one-third of the people live in the cities and towns. The official language is Arabic.

Economy. Morocco's economy rests primarily on mining and agriculture. Farming accounts for about 10% of the gross domestic product and wheat, barley, corn, beans, dates, citrus, and other fruits are grown. Coal, manganese, iron ore, lead, cobalt, zinc, silver, and some are produced, but the principal source of export revenue is phosphate. Morocco leads the world in production of this important mineral. Tourism and handicrafts also contribute to the economy.

History. Once ruled by Carthage and then Rome, Morocco was later invaded by the Vandals (429 A.D.). The Arabs conquered in 683 A.D. and Moroccan Berbers helped them in their subsequent conquest of Spain. In the 11th century, Morocco was part of the great Almoravid empire. A haven for pirates in the 18th century, Morocco was coveted by France, Spain, and Germany, and they struggled for dominance throughout the 19th century. In the Algeciras Conference of 1906, the great powers pledged Moroccan independence but ceded special rights to France, enabling that country to establish a protectorate in 1912, part of which was ceded to Spain. The Moroccans resisted and effective French and Spanish control was not complete until 1930. Resistance continued after World War II and Morocco was granted its independence in 1956, though Ceuta, Melilla, and a few small islands remain under Spanish control. King Muhammed V governed from 1957 to 1961 and was succeeded by his son Hassan II. He reigned as absolute monarch, but his rule was constantly threatened by attempted coups and assassinations. In 1970, a new constitution was adopted and, in 1972, amended to further limit Hassan's powers. Morocco, though not one of the hard-line Arab states, supported Syria in the 1973 Arab-Israeli War. Since the discovery of oil in the Middle Atlas Mountains, Hassan has pressed Morocco's claims to the western Sahara. The Polisario Front has resisted those claims, and with Algerian aid and backing has waged a guerrilla war against the king's forces. A cease-

The 'suq' (market) of the wool dyers in Marrakech. This traditional trade is more than a remnant from earlier times; its products are still being exported.

M

fire between Morocco and the Polisario Front was declared in 1991. The cease-fire called for a United Nations-supervised referendum to determine the future of the region, but the referendum was repeatedly postponed. Hassan II died in 1999 and was succeeded by his son Muhammad VI.
Morocco wants to join the EU, but in 2003 the EU-countries were less than enthusiastic. One of the reasons being the large number of illegal immigrants that yearly try to cross the Street of Gibraltar.

Moronobu, Hishikawa (1618-1694), Japanese illustrator. Moronobu was known for his book illustrations and picture books. Moronobu practised *ukiyo-e* (pictures of the passing, floating world). Ukiyo-e prints mirror ordinary people and daily life in a realistic way. Moronobu was one of the first artists to develop the woodblock print as an art form. Although ukiyo prints were not considered fine art by the Japanese, they had a profound influence on Western art.

Morpheus, in Greek mythology, one of the many offspring of Hypnos (Somnus), god of sleep. Morpheus and 2 brothers are gods of dreams; while he is responsible for the appearance of humans in dreams, his brothers Phobetor (Ikelos) and Phantasus produce forms of animals and inanimate objects.
See also: Mythology.

Morphine, addictive opium derivative used as a narcotic painkiller. It suppresses anxiety and produces euphoria. Morphine also weakens mental and physical powers and reduces sex and hunger urges. It depresses respiration and the cough reflex, induces sleep, and may cause vomiting and constipation. Medically it is valuable in the treatment of heart failure and as a premedication for anesthetics.
See also: Drug; Drug abuse.

Morphy, Paul Charles (1837-1884), American chess master of extraordinary intelligence. Won the first American chess congress in 1857, beating the strong German theoretician Louis Paulsen (1828-1901). In 1858 he came to Europe and played several twosomes in London and Paris, beating the best European players. His most important match was against Anderssen in Paris (1858-1859). This match lasted eight days and Morphy won 8-3 (+7, -2= 2). His motto-develop first, then attack-ousted romantic chess, which put the offensive above all. Upon his return to the United States he was welcomed as a hero, but soon afterwards withdrew completely from the world of chess and died an embittered and introvert eccentric.

Morris, William (1834-1896), English artist, poet, and designer. One of the Pre-Raphaelites, he sought to counteract the effects of industrialization by a return to the aesthetic standards and craftsmanship of the Middle Ages. In 1861 he set up Morris and Co. to design and make wallpaper, furniture, carpets, and stained glass. Influenced by John Ruskin, he formed the Socialist League (1884). His founding of the Kelmscott Press (1890) had a primary impact on typographical and book design.

Morrison, Toni (Chloe Anthony Wofford; 1931-), U.S. novelist. She is known for imaginative, poetic, emotional portrayals of individuals in relation to society and the African American experience in such novels as *Song of Solomon* (1977), *Tar Baby* (1981), the best-seller *Beloved* (1987, Pulitzer Prize), *Paradise* (1998) and *The Big Box* (2000).

Morse, Samuel Finley Breese (1791-1872), U.S. inventor of an electric telegraph and portrait painter. Morse spent 12 years developing the range and capabilities of his system; he was granted a U.S. patent for his telegraph in 1840. His famous message-'What hath God wrought!'-was the first sent on his Washington-Baltimore line on May 24, 1844. For this he used Morse code, which he devised in 1838.
See also: Telegraph.

Morse code, telegraphic signal system devised (1838) by Samuel Morse for use in transmitting messages. Letters, numbers, and punctuation are represented by combinations of dots (brief taps of the transmitting key) and dashes (3 times the length of dots).

Moscow (Russian: *Moskva*; pop. 9,300,000), capital of the Russian Federation and capital of the former USSR, on both banks of the Moskva River. It is Russia's largest city, and its political, cultural, commercial, industrial, and communications center. Some leading industries are chemicals, textiles, wood products, and a wide range of heavy machinery, including aircraft and automobiles. Moscow became the capital of all Russia under Ivan IV in the 16th century. Superseded by St. Petersburg (now Leningrad) in 1713, it regained its former status in 1918, following the Russian Revolution. At the city's heart is the Kremlin, location of government headquarters and a palace housing architectural relics of tsarist Russia. Red Square, the site of parades and celebrations, along with the Lenin Mausoleum and St. Basil's Cathedral, is nearby. Among outstanding cultural and educational institutions are the Bolshoi Theater, the Moscow Art Theater, the Maly Theater, Moscow University, the Academy of Sciences, the Tchaikovsky Conservatory, and the Lenin State Library.

Moscow Art Theater, influential Russian repertory theater famed for its ensemble acting and its introduction of new techniques in stage realism. Founded in 1897 by Konstantin Stanislavski and Vladimir Nemirovich-Danchenko, it introduced plays by Chekhov, Dostoyevsky, Gorky, and Tolstoy.
See also: Stanislavski, Konstantin.

Moselle, or **Mosel River**, tributary of the Rhine River, about 339 mi (545 km) long, arising in northeastern France; it flows into Germany, where it empties into the Rhine at Koblenz. Along its French banks lie power stations and iron and steel plants. In the German Moseltal, the renowned Moselle wines are produced.

Moses (c.13th century B.C.), Hebrew lawgiver and prophet who led the Israelites out of Egypt. According to the Bible, the infant Moses was found and raised by the pharaoh's daughter. After killing an Egyptian, he fled to the desert. Speaking from a burning bush, God ordered Moses to return and demand the Israelites' freedom

Moses receives from God the essence of the Law or Torah, on Mount Sinai. Moses' hands are covered, with regard to the holiness of the Law, and the people of Israel, standing near the tents, are looking on in awe (from the twelfth-century manuscript *Kosmos Indicopleustes*, St. Catharine Monastery, Sinai).

M

under threat of ten plagues. At last, Moses led them out of Egypt (the 'exodus'); the Red Sea miraculously parted to let them cross to safety. On Mt. Sinai Moses received the Ten Commandments. After years of ruling the wandering Israelites in the wilderness, Moses died within sight of the promised land. Traditionally he was the author of the first five books of the Bible, the Torah.
See also: Bible.

Moses, Edwin Corley (1955-), U.S. track and field athlete in hurdling events. He won the 1976 and 1984 Olympic gold medals for the 400-m (438-yd) hurdle, and held the world record in that event from 1983. In 1990 he became eligible to represent the United States in international bobsled competitions.

Moses, Grandma (Anna Mary Robertson Moses; 1860-1961), U.S. artist of the primitive style. Self-taught, she began painting at age 76 and won wide popularity with her lively, unpretentious pictures of rural life in upstate New York.

Moses, Phoebe Ann *See:* Oakley, Annie.

Mosque, Muslim place of worship. The name derives from the Arabic *masjid,* meaning 'a place for prostration' (in prayer). Mosques are typically built with one or more *minarets* (towers); a courtyard with fountains or wells for ceremonial washing; an area where the faithful assemble for prayers led by the *imam* (priest); a *mihrab* (niche) indicating the *qiblah* (direction) of Mecca; a *mimbar* (pulpit) and sometimes, facing it, a *maqsurah* (enclosed area for important persons). Some mosques include a *madrasah* (religious school).
See also: Islam.

A common sight at a mosque, in Konya (formerly: Iconium), Turkey. It is forbidden to wear shoes inside.

Mosquitia *See:* Mosquito Coast.

Mosquito, any of 35 genera of small insects belonging to the fly order Diptera of the family *Culicidae.* Mosquitoes have long legs and 2 wings capable of beating about 1,000 times a second. Males survive on plant juices; females feed on the blood of mammals. They are able to pierce skin with needlelike parts in their proboscises. Certain species transmit diseases such as malaria, yellow fever, and encephalitis.

Mosquito Coast, coastal landstrip in Nicaragua and Honduras, along the Caribbean Sea. It begins at the San Juan River on the eastern coast of Nicaragua and continues to the Aguan River on the northeastern coast of Honduras, it is about 40 mi (65 km) wide and 200 mi (320 km) long and is named after the indigenous Mosquito tribe.

Mosquito hawk *See:* Nighthawk.

Moss, primitive plants related to the liverworts. The mosses and liverworts together make up the phylum bryophyta. Of the 2 groups, the mosses are the more advanced because they have a vertical stem with simple leaves and roots. From the tip of the leaf-covered stem springs a tall stalk bearing a capsule containing the spores. Mosses display alternation of generations, with both sexual and asexual stages in their life cycles. Mosses are dependent on water for their life and reproduction. They are found in damp woods, crevices, bogs, and a few live underwater in ponds. They play an important part in preventing erosion and in the formation of soil. The peat mosses, are of considerable economic importance. They are extremely absorbent, taking up over 100 times their weight of water, and have been used in surgical dressings. Their rotted remains collect in bogs to form peat, which is used in many parts of the world as fuel and in garden cultivation.

Mossad, Mossad le-Modiin ule-Tafkidim Meyuhadim (Institute for Intelligence and Special Assignments); Israeli foreign intelligence service. The Mossad was founded in 1951 and is known as one of the best-organized intelligence services in the world. The organization achieved fame especially for the execution of some very daring and successful actions, like the kidnapping of Adolf Eichmann from Argentina in 1960.

Mossadeq, Mohammad Hedayat (1880-1967) Iranian politician. As a prime minister (1951-1953) he nationalized the Anglo-Iranian Oil Co., causing an economic crisis. He lost the struggle for power with the Shah (1953), was jailed until 1956 and placed under house arrest after his release.

Mössbauer, Rudolf Ludwig (1929-), German physicist. In 1961 he shared the Nobel Prize for physics for his discovery (1957) of the Mössbauer effect, a method of producing gamma rays. Among other applications, Mössbauer's work led to the verification of Albert Einstein's theory of relativity. Mössbauer taught physics briefly at the California Institute of Technology (1961) before returning to Munich to teach at its Technical University.
See also: Gamma rays.

Mossbunker *See:* Menhaden.

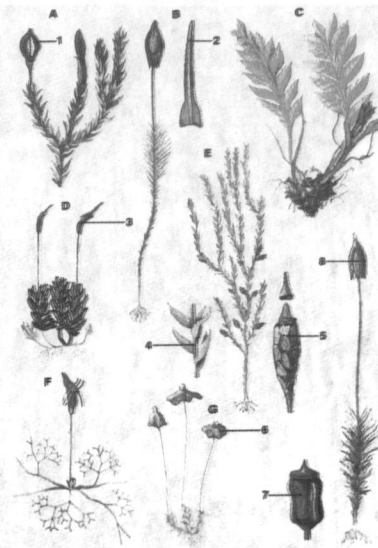

Andreaea rupestris (A) is a reddish brown moss that sheds spores through four slitlike valves in the capsule (1). The Australian species *Dawsonia polytrichoides* (B) has thin, pointed leaves (2). *Schistostega pennata* (C) is a luminous European moss. *Atrichum undulatum* (D) has a long, pointed cap (3) on the capsule. *Fontinalis antipyretica* (E), an aquatic moss with boat-shaped leaves (4) and elongated capsules (5), is among the largest species; *Ephemeropsis tjibodensis* (F) is among the smallest. *Splacnum luteum* (G) has a yellow umbrella-shaped apophysis (6). The four-sided capsule (7) of *Polytrichum commune* (H) is protected by a long brown cap (8).

Mostar (pop. 63,400), city in Bosnia-Herzegovina on the Neretva river. Commercial center for the agricultural area (wine, fruit, tobacco). Tobacco and textile industries. In the early 1990s the city was the scene of fights between Croatians and Muslims in which the 16th century bridge over the Neretva river (built on Roman foundations) was destroyed. In 1994 the city was placed under the administration of the European Union and divided between the two ethnic groups. Still, this did not put a stop to the violence.

Mosul (pop. 730,000) capital of Mosul province, Iraq. It is on the Tigris River 220 miles (354 km) north-northwest of Baghdad, and is the railway, road, and trade center of northern Iraq. Nearby are rich oil fields. Mosul produces textiles, leather, cigarettes, and cement. *Muslin* was named after the city, once famous for its cotton textiles. Across the Tigris are the ruins of ancient Nineveh. The people of Mosul are mainly Arabs; those of the surrounding country are mainly Kurds. Several Christian sects are concentrated in the area. Mosul became the chief city of northern Mesopotamia in the eighth century. In 1925 the area was made part of Iraq, which had been carved from the Ottoman Empire after World War I.

Moth, insect that, together with the butterfly, makes up the order *Lepidoptera*. Most moths have intricately patterned, dull-colored wings to camouflage them. When a moth larva, or caterpillar, hatches out from its egg, it eats the leaf, plant, or fabric on which it was laid. Caterpillars cause extensive damage to trees, crops, and clothes. As caterpillars grow, they shed their skin. In the final stage of growth, when it is known as a pupa, the caterpillar changes into an adult moth. Most moths sleep during the day and come out at night. They are drawn by the radiation around bright lights. There are about 120,000 known species of moths, ranging from minute wingless forms to giants several inches across.

Mother Carey's chicken *See:* Petrel.

Mother Goose, fictitious character who wrote many collections of fairy tales and nursery rhymes. The name seems to have been first associated with Charles Perrault's French *Tales of Mother Goose* (1697). Others say the American *Mother Goose Melodies* (1719) was the origin.

Mother of Canada *See:* Saint Lawrence River.

Mother Teresa *See:* Teresa, Mother.

Motherwell, Robert (1915-1991), U.S. painter and theoretician, a leading exponent of abstract expressionism. His work is characterized by restrained colors and large, indefinite shapes. His best-known series is *Elegies to the Spanish Republic* (1975).

Mo-ti (Micius, Mo-tsuh: 4th century B.C.) Chinese philosopher, foremost opponent of Confucius and his formalistic ethics. Mo-ti pledged for simplicity and universal love. Mo-tse, a book that appeared later, contains the pronouncements attributed to Mo-ti.

Motion, Andrew (1952-), British author, chairman of the arts committee of the British Art Council and professor of creative writing at the University of East Anglia. His collection of poems include *The Pleasure Steamers* (1978), and *The Price of Everything* (1993). He also wrote the novels *The Pale Companion* (1989) and *Famous for the Creatures* (1991), and biographies of Keats and Philip Larkin. For this last work he was awarded the Whitbread Award for Biography in 1994. In May 1999 he was appointed Poet Laureate (court poet) of Great Britain, succeeding Ted Hughes.

Motion, perpetual *See:* Perpetual motion machine.

Motion pictures, the art of interpreting reality and presenting entertainment or information by projecting a series of connected photographs in rapid succession onto a screen. The illusion of motion pictures rests upon the eye's tendency to retain an image for a fraction of a second after that image has been withdrawn. If a series of pictures is prepared showing, in gradual progression, the different phases of an action and the pictures are then viewed in rapid succession, the eye tends to connect the pictures, result-

ing in the illusion of a moving image. In fact, a movie is a series of still photographs printed on a long strip of celluloid. The strip is run through a projector which, by means of a shutter, shows each picture, or frame, for a split second. Modern movies run at a speed of 24 frames per second; silent films ran at 16 frames a second. Thomas A. Edison and his assistant, W.K.L. Dickson, made the first significant step toward the development of a motion picture camera by exploiting this principle. Dickson, using the new celluloid film developed by another American inventor, George Eastman, contrived a method of moving the film through the camera using sprocket wheels. By 1894, Edison had perfected the Kinetoscope, in which a viewer could see minute-long scenes from vaudeville acts and boxing matches. European inventors, adapting the Kinetoscope, devised a means of projecting pictures onto a screen for public showings, and projectors were developed almost simultaneously by Robert Paul in London and the Lumière brothers in Paris. Nickelodeons were replaced by movie theaters, and soon moving pictures were shown in many of the world's major cities.

Following the work of early pioneers, like the French magician Georges Méliès and the U.S. director Edwin S. Porter, D. W. Griffith brought the art of movie-making to its first maturity. In films such *The Birth of a Nation* (1915) and *Intolerance* (1916), he refined the elements of film language to create a highly effective narrative technique and style. He made conscious use of selective editing, closeups, and carefully considered camera positioning and movement. At about the same time, Mack Sennett produced superb silent comedies starring comedians like Charlie Chaplin, Buster Keaton, and Harold Lloyd. The studio star system developed.

Relying upon an ever more sophisticated technology and the cooperation of large groups of skilled and semiskilled professionals, the new art form also became a new industry. Until 1912, the U.S. movie industry was dominated by the Motion Picture Patents Company. But as movies attracted rapidly growing audiences, production companies learned they could ensure profits through distributing movies to chains of theaters they had bought or built. Theater owners, for their part, banded together and formed their own studios. Until World War

On location for *The Big Chill* (1983), director Lawrence Kasdan checks the camera viewfinder. Mounted on a movable platform, the camera can be positioned high enough to get a long shot of the scene.

A scene from the classic silent movie *The General* (1926). Buster Keaton, who was nicknamed 'the great stone face', wrote, produced, directed and starred in it.

I, the movies were international, but after the war the United States dominated the industry. By 1920, the combination of the star system, distribution monopolies at home, and large markets abroad made Hollywood the world's film capital and the center of a multimillion-dollar industry. Its great stars included Clara Bow, Lon Chaney, Charlie Chaplin, Greta Garbo, Lillian Gish, Tom Mix, Gloria Swanson, and Rudolph Valentino. Westerns and slapstick comedies were the most popular movies.

Europe did less movie-making in this era, but its work was influential. German directors like F. W. Murnau and G. W. Pabst introduced original and highly expressive techniques into film-making, which were studied and adapted by Hollywood. And in Russia, after the revolution, Sergei M. Eisenstein perfected his montage technique in *Battleship Potemkin* (1925).

In the meantime, technicians were advancing the new art form. An American, Lee De Forest, devised a method for recording sound onto the margin of the film alongside the frames. The innovation was demonstrated in 1923, but it was not until 1927, with the release of *The Jazz Singer* featuring two songs sung by Al Jolson, that 'talkies' revolutionized the movies. Overnight, silent films were abandoned. Studios embraced talking pictures and, a few years later, the technological breakthrough of color films. Joining the ever-popular dramas, costume epics, and screwball or romantic comedies, the new genres of musical and gangster films dominated the movies in the 1930s and 1940s. Joining Garbo and a few other silent stars who made the transition, a new generation arose, among them Fred Astaire, Humphrey Bogart, James Cagney, Claudette Colbert, Bette Davis, Marlene Dietrich, Judy Garland, Cary Grant, Katharine Hepburn, Edward G. Robinson, and Spencer Tracy; the innovative new directors included George Cukor, Howard Hawks, Alfred Hitchcock, Preston Sturges, William Wyler, and actor Orson Welles.

The end of World War II and the advent of television brought a period of ferment to the movie industry. Hollywood studios turned to making TV films and shooting their movies throughout the United States and abroad.

M

The studio system's virtual monopoly on the international film scene gave way to foreign influences. The Italians and French broke new ground under directors like Michelangelo Antonioni, Federico Fellini, Roberto Rossellini, Luchino Visconti, Jean-Luc Godard, and François Truffaut, as did the Japanese with Akira Kurosawa and Yasujiro Ozu. Meanwhile, technology continued to redefine the industry and its markets, most recently with the production of videocassettes for home viewing and the construction of multitheater complexes. The result is an industry and art form that continue to be as dynamic as they were in their formative years.

Motmot, indigenous forest-bird family of South America. Motmots are beautiful birds with feathers of blue, black, green, and orange. Motmots possess an unusual tail configuration caused by the loss of feathers which creates paddlelike shapes at the end of the tail.

Motor *See:* Electric motor; Engine; Rocket.

Motor car *See:* Automobile.

Motorcycle, motorized bicycle developed in 1885 by Gottlieb Daimler. The engine of a motorcycle may be either 2-stroke or 4-stroke and is usually air cooled. Chain drive is almost universal. In lightweight machines ignition is often achieved by means of a magneto inside the flywheel. Motorcycles were first widely used by dispatch riders in World War I. Between the wars the motorcycle industry was dominated by simple, heavy British designs. After World War II Italy developed the motor scooter, designed for convenience and economy, with 150cc 2-stroke engines. In the 1960s the Japanese introduced a series of highly sophisticated, lightweight machines that are now used all over the world.

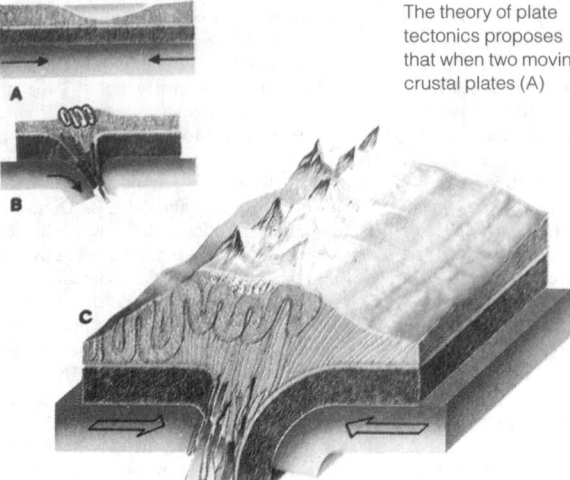

The theory of plate tectonics proposes that when two moving crustal plates (A) converge, one of the plates will slide under the other (B), and will be consumed by the molten mantle. The thick overlying buoyant continental and oceanic sedimentary layers, however, are scraped off and crumpled as the plate descends. Continued plate movement and compression (C) in the upper crust produces huge folded mountains.

Mound bird, any of 12 species of birds in the megapode family. Found from Australia westward to the Nicobar Islands, this bird is also known as mound builder or incubator bird because of the mound in which it incubates its eggs. The male uses his large feet to heap plant matter into a mound, which may take up to 11 months to build; the female lays her eggs in it, and then covers them with more matter. As the materials in the mound decay, they release heat. That and the heat of the sun keep the mound warm, and the eggs hatch in 6-7 weeks. Mound birds use the same mound year after year, adding to it each time. A mound can become as large as 14 ft (4 m) high and 70 ft (21 m) across.

Mound Builders, in archeology, early native North Americans who built large mounds, primarily in valleys of the Mississippi and Ohio rivers and the Great Lakes region. Mound Builders were active from approximately 5000 B.C. to 600 B.C. Their mounds served as burial places,

fortresses, or as platforms for temples or official residences. Built entirely by human labor, thousands of mounds remain, ranging in size from 1 to 100 acres (0.4 to 40 hectares). Their shapes vary from geometric patterns to those resembling animals.

Mount Aetna *See:* Mount Etna.

Mountain, land mass elevated substantially above its surroundings. Most mountains occur in ranges, chains, or zones. The earth's crust is made up of various moving fragments; hence, land masses are in constant motion. Thus the Andes have formed where the Nazca oceanic plate is being forced under the South American continental plate, and the Himalayas have arisen at the meeting of 2 continental plates.
Mountains are classified as volcanic, block, or folded. Volcanic mountains occur when lava and other debris build up a dome around the vent of a volcano. Block mountains occur where land has been uplifted between

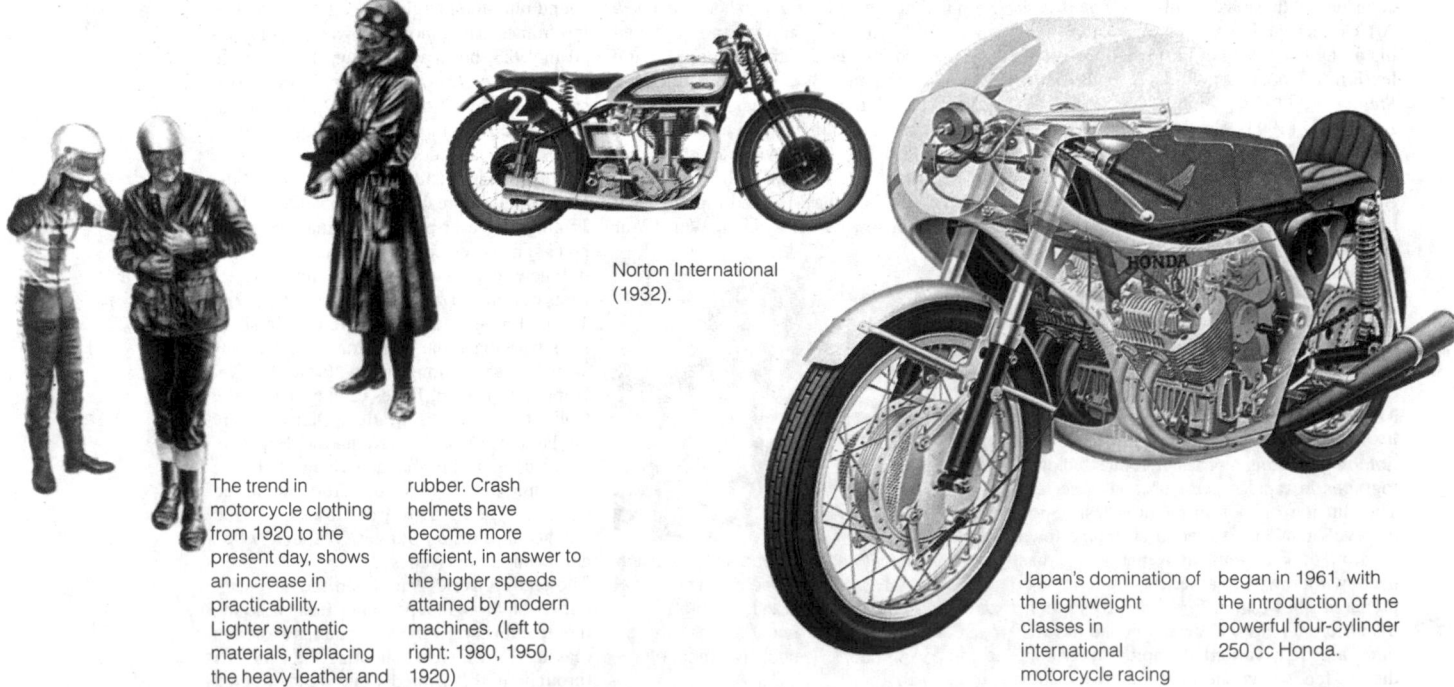

Norton International (1932).

The trend in motorcycle clothing from 1920 to the present day, shows an increase in practicability. Lighter synthetic materials, replacing the heavy leather and rubber. Crash helmets have become more efficient, in answer to the higher speeds attained by modern machines. (left to right: 1980, 1950, 1920)

Japan's domination of the lightweight classes in international motorcycle racing began in 1961, with the introduction of the powerful four-cylinder 250 cc Honda.

earthquake faults. Folded mountains occur through deformations of the earth's crust; when vast quantities of sediments accumulate, their weight causes deformation. Erosion eventually reduces all mountains to plains.

Mountain ash, name for various trees and shrubs of genus *Sorbus*, rose family, native particularly to high elevations in the Northern Hemisphere. The leaves are compound, with leaflets opposite each other on the leaf stem. The white clustered flowers develop into clusters of orange or red berry-like fruit. The mountain ash provides food for wildlife, shade, and wood for implements. The American mountain ash (*S. americana*) grows in eastern Canada and the United States.

Mountain beaver, or sewellel (*Aplodontia rufa*), nocturnal, burrowing rodent of western North America. Perhaps the oldest rodent species on earth still in existence, the mountain beaver has lived in North America at least 60 million years. Unrelated to the beaver, it looks like a vole, with a stout body about 1 ft (30 cm) long, short legs, and very short tail. Colonies of mountain beavers live in burrow systems dug in stream banks.

Mountaineering, climbing of hills, cliffs, or mountains for exploration or sport. There are two types of climbing: *free climbing*, in which the climber ascends by using protrusions and cracks in the rocks as holds; and *artificial climbing*, where ladders and slings are used as aids in climbing difficult places having no natural holds. Mountaineers usually climb in a team, roped together for safety. Depending on circumstances, they will use climbing boots, ropes, pitons (steel pegs), small hammers, carabiners (rings to hold rope), and insulating clothing; in addition, for snow climbing, sunglasses, crampons (spikes attached to boots), and ice axes; and on large mountains, concentrated food, signaling devices, medical supplies, camping and cooking equipment, and oxygen masks. Two of the most famous and challenging objectives for mountaineers have been Mount Blanc in the Alps, first scaled in 1786, and Mount Everest in the Himalayas, first conquered in 1953 by Sir Edmund Hillary and his Sherpa guide Tenzing Norkay.

Mountain goat *See:* Chamois; Ibex; Rocky Mountain goat.

Mountain laurel (*Kalmia latifolia*), evergreen shrub or tree in the heath family. Native to eastern North America, it grows on mountains. A shrub can reach a height of 5 to 10 ft (1.5 to 3 m); a tree can grow to be 33 ft (10 m) tall. Mountain laurels have pink or white clustered flowers and dark, long, oval leaves with pointed ends.

Mountain lion, also known as catamount, cougar, panther, or puma, member of the cat family that inhabited the United States and Canada prior to settlement. The mountain lion can be found in Mexico, Central America, and South America. It has a tawny-colored coat and stands about 5 ft (1.5 m)

long. The mountain lion is a hunter that feeds on elk and deer.

Mountain nestor *See:* Kea.

Mountain sheep *See:* Bighorn.

Mountbatten, Louis (Francis Albert Victor Nicholas, 1st Earl Mountbatten of Burma; 1900-1979), English admiral and politician. In World War II he was supreme allied commander in Southeast Asia and liberated Burma from the Japanese. After the war he was the last British viceroy of India (1947), and led the negotiations for India's and Pakistan's independence. He later served as first sea lord, admiral of the fleet, and chief of the defense staff (1959-1965). He was killed by Irish Republican Army terrorists.

Mounted Police *See:* Royal Canadian Mounted Police.

Mount Elbrus, highest mountain peak in Europe. Located in the Caucasus Mountains in the south of Russia, it is 18,481 ft (5,633 m) high and covers an area of 55 sq mi (140 sq km). Covered by approximately 22 glaciers, it is a major tourist and mountain climbing center.

Mount Etna, active volcano on the eastern coast of Sicily. Its height is about 11,000 ft (3,352 m) and its base is approximately 100 mi (160 km) in circumference. It has erupted over 250 times since its first recorded eruption in 700 B.C., some of which have been extremely destructive to nearby inhabitants.

Mount Everest, highest mountain on earth. Located in the Himalayas, in Tibet and Nepal, it rises to a height of about 29,000 ft (8,839 m). Reaching its top has been the goal of many climbing expeditions. The first to succeed were Sir Edmund Hillary and Tenzing Norkay in 1953. Several other expeditions have since been successful. According to the Sherpa tribes of the area, Mt. Everest is the abode of the Abominable Snowman, or Yeti.
See also: Hillary, Sir Edmund Percival.

Mount Fuji, highest mountain in Japan. Situated on Honshu, an island west of Tokyo, it is 12,388 (3,776 m) high. Its slopes create almost a perfect cone. The Japanese revere Mount Fuji as a sacred place; thousands climb to its top yearly. Fuji contains an inactive volcano.

Mount Kilimanjaro *See:* Kilimanjaro.

Mount McKinley, highest mountain in North America, part of Denali National Park. Located in south-central Alaska near the center of the Alaska Range, it has 2 peaks: South Peak, rising 20,320 ft (6,194 m), and North Peak, 19,470 ft (5,934 m). *Denali*, meaning 'High One,' is the Native American name for the mountain; McKinley was the name given in honor of William McKinley, U.S. president (1897-1901). In the early 1900s, several attempts were made to reach the mountain's summit. The first successful ascent was made in 1913, by

Hudson Stuck, Harry P. Karstens, and 2 companions.

Mount Olympus, highest mountain in Greece. It rises 9,570 ft (2,917 m) at the east end of a 25-mi (50-km) range along the Thessaly-Macedonia border. The summit is snowcapped most of the year. The ancient Greeks believed Olympus to be the home of Zeus and most other gods.

Mount Palomar Observatory *See:* Palomar Observatory.

Mount Parnassus *See:* Parnassus.

Mount Royal *See:* Montreal.

Mount Rushmore National Memorial, memorial, carved into the northeast side of Mt. Rushmore, of the heads of U.S. Presidents George Washington, Thomas Jefferson, Theodore Roosevelt, and Abraham Lincoln. Located in the Black Hills of South Dakota, it was designed by the sculptor Gutzon Borglum. He and his son supervised execution of the project, which took 6.5 years of actual work to complete, and used dynamite and drills to sculpt the granite. The heads, each about 60 ft (18 m) high, are the largest sculptures in the world and can be easily seen from many miles away.

Mount Saint Helens, active volcano in the Cascade Range of the southwest region of Washington. Long considered dormant, the volcano became seismically active in Mar. 1980 and erupted for the first time in 120 years on May 18, 1980. Preceded by two magnitude-5 earthquakes, the eruption was the first in the 48 coterminous states since Mt. Lassen erupted in 1915. More than 60 people were killed; there were widespread floods and mudslides. Surrounding forests were scorched or devastated, and much of Washington, Oregon, Idaho, and Montana was blanketed with volcanic ash.

Mount Sinai *See:* Sinai.

Mount Vernon, restored Georgian home of George Washington (1747-1799) on the Potomac River in Virginia, south of Washington, D.C. The tomb of Washington and his wife, Martha, is nearby.
See also: Washington, George.

Mount Vesuvius, only active volcano on mainland Europe, in southern Italy near Naples. Its height (about 4,000 ft/6,440 km) varies with each eruption. Capped by a plume of smoke, it is a famous landmark. Its lower slopes are extremely fertile. In A.D. 79 it destroyed the cities of Pompeii and Herculaneum. Recent eruptions occurred in 1906, 1929, and 1944.
See also: Pompeii.

Mount Wilson Observatory, astronomical observatory located on Mount Wilson 5,710 ft (1,740 m) above sea level, near Los Angeles, California. The observatory's many powerful telescopes, including both solar and reflecting telescopes, have facilitated the work of such astronomers as Edwin

M

M

P. Hubble, who discovered the expansion of the universe. Founded in 1904 by the astronomer George Hale to study the solar surface, it was operated by the Carnegie Institute and the California Institute of Technology until 1989, when administrative control was assumed by the Mount Wilson Institute.
See also: Astronomy.

Mourning dove (*Zenaida macroura*), bird belonging to the pigeon and dove family. Native to North America, it measures about 12 in (30 cm) long and has a long, tapered tail. It is predominantly grayish brown, with pink and violet marks on its neck and a white border on its tail. Its name is derived from the seemingly mournful calling sound it makes. In the winter, mourning doves migrate south to warmer climates.

Mouse, term applied loosely to many small rodents. The house mouse (*Mus musculus*), found worldwide, is gray-brown with large ears, a pointed nose, and a naked tail. It is about 6 in (15 cm) long and weighs under 1 oz (28 grams). The house mouse eats almost everything, nesting in paper. The field mouse is an important herbivore, and in turn important as prey for many birds and mammals.

The house mouse, *Mus musculus*, is probably the world's most well-known species.

Europe's common dormouse, *Muscardinus avellanarius*, is noted for its hibernation.

Africa's striped field mouse, *Rhabdomys pumilio*, is sometimes found in large groups.

Leaf-eared mice, *Phyllotis*, of South America, are named for their wide, thin ears.

Mousorgski, Modest *See:* Mussorgsky, Modest.

Mouth, opening through which humans and animals take food. This cavity contains the jawbone, the teeth and gums, the palate, and the tongue. Food passes through the mouth into the digestive tract. The mouth's tongue is also essential for speaking.

Movie *See:* Motion pictures.

Mozambique

Capital:	Maputo
Area:	303,075 sq mi
	(799,380 sq km)
Population:	19,608,000
Language:	Portuguese
Government:	Republic
Independent:	1975
Head of gov.:	Prime Minister
Per capita:	US$ 900
Monetary unit:	1 Metical = 100 centavos

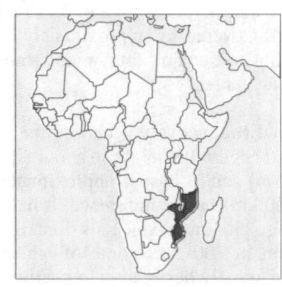

Mozambique, country in southeast Africa, bordered on the north by Tanzania, on the northwest by Malawi and Zambia, on the west by Zimbabwe and South Africa, on the southwest by South Africa and Swaziland, and on the east by the Indian Ocean.
Land and climate. Mozambique has an area of 303,075 sq mi (784,964 sq km), mostly fertile low-lying plateau and coastal plain. Of the country's many rivers emptying into the Indian Ocean, the most important, and a source of hydroelectric power, is the Zambezi, some 820 mi (1,320 km) of which flows in Mozambique. The highest peak is Monte Binga (7,992 ft/2,436 m). The climate is predominantly humid; the interior uplands are cooler.
People. The Mozambique people are mainly Bantu-speaking black Africans. More than half practice native religions but there are sizable numbers of Muslims and Christians as well. Portuguese is the official language.
Economy. Mozambique's economy depends principally on agriculture, forestry, and fishing. Principal exports are cashews, seafood, and cotton. Mineral wealth remains underdeveloped and a limited industry engages in food processing and cement and fertilizer manufacturing.
History. The Portuguese explorer Vasco da Gama visited the Mozambique coast in 1498, and the first Portuguese settlement was established in 1505. During the next 2 centuries, colonists exploited the native populace for cheap plantation labor and carried on a lucrative slave trade. From the mid- to

late-19th century, Portugal expanded its control and private businesses, like the Mozambique Company, were allowed to rule and exploit large areas. After World War II, Mozambique's territory was increased by the addition of land formerly part of German East Africa. Confronted, as in Angola, with active guerrilla movements for independence, dominated by the Mozambique Liberation Front (Frelimo), the Portuguese maintained strict control over the native population. After a military coup in Portugal, a decade of warfare in Mozambique ended in 1974 with an agreement for joint Portuguese-Frelimo rule. On June 25, 1975, Mozambique became the 45th African state to achieve full independence. The establishment of a black African, Marxist regime was followed by nationalization and the flight of most Europeans from the country. The country was also troubled by persistent guerrilla resistance by a rightwing organization, Renamo. Mozambique's fledgling government supported Zimbabwe nationalists during the war in Rhodesia. In 1980, Mozambique began establishing diplomatic and trading ties with the West and began moderating socialist parties to allow free enterprise. In 1990 Mozambique adopted a new constitution, and in 1992 the Mozambique Liberation Front (Frelimo) and the Mozambique National Resistance (Renamo) agreed to a limited ceasefire after 15 years of fighting. The first multiparty elections in Mozambique were held in 1994. The Frelimo party gained a slim majority over the Renamo party in the assembly.
In 2000 and 2001, Mozambique suffered the worst floods in its history, while in 2002 a severe drought hit the country. This led to severe economic problems. The IMF and the World Bank granted the country HIPC-status, marking the country as heavily indebted.

Beira, a port city in central Mozambique, is the capital and principal port of the country. In recent years, refugees fleeing drought and civil war have swelled the city's population.

Mozart, Wolfgang Amadeus (1756-1791), Austrian composer whose brief career produced some of the world's greatest music. A child prodigy of the harpsichord, violin, and organ at the age of 4, he was concertmaster to the archbishop of Salzburg (1771-1781). In 1781 he moved to Vienna, where he became Court Composer to Joseph II in 1787. He became a close friend of Haydn and set Lorenzo Da Ponte's opera librettos *The Marriage of Figaro* (1786) and *Don Giovanni* (1787) to music. In 1788 he wrote

Tea with the Prince de Conti. At the center, child prodigy Wolfgang Amadeus Mozart (1756-1791) at the grand piano. Painting from 1766, by Michel Ollivier (1712-1784).

3 of his greatest symphonies (numbers 39 to 41). Mozart composed over 600 works, including 50 symphonies, over 20 operas, nearly 30 piano concertos, 27 string quartets, and about 40 violin sonatas. In all these genres his work shows great expressive beauty and technical mastery.

MS *See:* Multiple sclerosis.

Mswati III (Prince Makhosetive; 1968-), king of Swaziland since 1986, son of King Sobhuza II, whom he succeeded to become the world's youngest head of state. He named himself for 19th-century king Mswati (Mswazi), who unified the nation of the Ngwane (who subsequently became known as the Swazi).
See also: Swaziland.

Mubarak, Hosni (1928-), president of Egypt since 1981. A graduate of Egypt's military academy, he was trained as a bomber pilot and rose in rank to air force chief of staff (1969) and air force commander (1972). He launched the surprise air attack in the 1973 war with Israel. Chosen by President Anwar Sadat to be Egypt's vice president in 1975, Mubarak became president, by public referendum, after Sadat was assassinated. In 1995, an attempt on his life was made.

Mucha, Alfons Maria (Alphonse) (1860-1939), Czech painter, designer and graphic artist. Representative of Jugendstil. Designed jewelry, sceneries, costumes and posters for Sarah Bernhardt. While in America (1904-1911) he dedicated himself to painting (portraits, symbolic themes).

Muckraker, term coined in 1906 by President Theodore Roosevelt to journalists specializing in sensational exposés of corrupt businesses and political procedures. The muckrakers included Lincoln Steffens, who wrote about political corruption, Ida Tarbell, who exposed the exploitative practices of an enormous oil company, and Upton Sinclair, who uncovered deplorable conditions in the Chicago meat-packing industry.
See also: Sinclair, Upton; Steffens, Lincoln.

Mucoviscidosis *See:* Cystic fibrosis.

Mud hen *See:* Coot.

Mudpuppy, or water dog (*Necturus maculosus*), salamander growing up to 2 ft (0.6 m) that lives in many North American rivers and streams. It retains its gills even when adult. Mud puppies get their name because they are reputed to emit barking sounds; however, they possess no voice organs of any kind

Mugabe, Robert Gabriel (1924-), Zimbabwean politician and President (1987-). In 1961, he and Joshua Nkomo founded the Zimbabwe African People's Union (ZAPU). In 1963, the party rifted and Mugabe founded the Zimbabwe African National Union (ZANU). He became Prime Minister after the independence in 1980. He adopted a conciliatory attitude towards his former opponents. He became President in 1987. Due to great poverty in his country decreased in the 1990s. He lost much international respect as a result of his negative remarks on homosexuality and his refusal to extradite the Ethiopian former dictator Mengistu. Prior to the presidential elections of 2002, he oppressed the opposition increasingly harshly and passed restrictive laws, which led to international criticism. He won the elections, after which Zimbabwe was suspended from membership of the British Commonwealth for a year.
See also: Zimbabwe.

Mughal Empire *See:* Mogul Empire.

Mugwump, term for independent voter or political fence straddler.

Muhammad (570?-632), prophet founder of Islam. Born in Mecca into the ruling Qureish tribe, Muhammad spent his early years as a merchant. At the age of 40 he had a vision of the archangel Gabriel bidding him go forth and preach. His teachings are recorded in the Koran, which Muslims believe is the word of God. Muhammad proclaimed himself the messenger of the one true god, Allah. At first he made few converts, among them his wife (Khadija), his daughter (Fatima), and her husband (Ali). The Meccan rulers persecuted Muhammad's followers. In 622, he escaped to Yathrib, a nearby city, thereafter called Medinat al-Rasul (City of the Prophet), or Medina, for short. The Muslim calendar dates years from this event, known as the *Hegira* (departure). In Medina, Muhammad formed an Islamic community based on religious faith rather than tribal or family loyalties. He rapidly won converts and his influence grew. In 630, after several years of warfare with Mecca and his victories in the battles of Badr (624) and Uhud (625), he captured Mecca with little bloodshed, making it both the political and religious capital of Islam. By the time of his death, Muhammad had unified the entire Arabian peninsula and the worldwide expansion of Islam had begun. Within a century, the Islamic empire extended from the Iberian peninsula in the west to the borders of India in the east.
See also: Islam.

Muhammad, Elijah (Elijah Poole; 1897-1975), U.S. Black Muslim leader. In 1931 he met Wali 'Prophet' Farad, founder of the first Temple of Islam in Detroit, Mich. Elijah became a prominent disciple, and on Farad's disappearance (1934) he became leader of the movement.
See also: Black Muslims.

Muhammad Ali *See:* Ali, Muhammad.

Muhammadan art *See:* Islamic art.

Muhammad II (1430?-1481), sultan and ruler of the Ottoman Empire (Turkey). He founded the Ottoman Empire when he captured Constantinople (1453), which he made his capital. He also conquered other territo-

ries in southeast Europe and around the Black Sea. As a ruler, he restructured his government and had government officials trained. He also founded colleges and set up charities, in the interest of his people's welfare.
See also: Ottoman Empire.

Robert Mugabe during his inauguration in 2002

Muhammad Reza Pahlavi *See:* Mohammad Reza Pahlavi.

Muir, John (1838-1914), Scottish-born U.S. naturalist and writer, an advocate of forest conservation. He described his walking journeys in the northwestern part of the United States and Alaska in many influential articles and books. Yosemite and Sequoia national parks and Muir Woods National Monument in California were established as a result of his efforts.

Mujibur Rahman, Sheikh (1920-1975), Bengal politician, fought for the independence of East Pakistan (the 'Bengali Tiger'). Mujibur Rahman gained an electoral victory with his Awami League in 1970 and declared an independent Bangladesh. During the civil war which followed immediately he was kept imprisoned. After the independence of Bangladesh he became the country's first prime minister (1972-1975). In later years he became alienated from his people and declared a state of emergency (1974) after riots and the League became the only political party in the country (National Party). In 1975 he became president and was killed during a coup d'état.

Mukden *See:* Shenyang.

M

M

Mulberry, medium-sized deciduous or evergreen tree (family Moraceae) that carries edible fruits, such as berries, figs, and breadfruit. The red mulberry grows in the eastern states and the Mexican mulberry in the southwest. The black mulberry is grown in Asia for its fruit. The leaves of the white mulberry of the Far East form the food of the silkworm.

Mule, infertile offspring of a male donkey and a mare (female horse). Mules have the shape and size of a horse and the long ears and small hooves of a donkey. They are favored for their endurance and surefootedness as draft or pack animals.

Mule deer, medium-sized deer (*Odocoileus hemionus*), of the western United States, closely related to the Virginia, or white-tailed, deer. The two are distinguished by the shape of the antlers and by the Virginia deer's habit of carrying its white tail up when running. Both live in open country and have increased as forests have been cut down. They are the main prey of deer hunters, and in many places their numbers have to be regulated to prevent crop damage.

Mullein, large herbal plants (genus *Verbascum*) of the figwort family. Found in northern regions with mild climates, there are 300 species. The common mullein, which grows to a height of 2 to 7 ft (0.6 to 2 m), has a single stem with large, thick, velvety leaves on the bottom and yellow flowers that grow in clusters, in the form of a spike at the top of the plant. When touched, the mullein's leaves and stem inflame the skin. Its leaves were once used to create a medicinal tea.

Müller, Heiner (1929-1995), German playwright. Originally Müller wrote, together with his wife, Inge Schwenkner, Marxist plays like *Die Korrektur* (1957) and *Der Lohndrücker* (1958), in which the problems of socialist development were analyzed in a Brechtian way. From the mid 1960s onwards Müller occupied himself with the adaptation and Marxist actualization of the Classic authors, from which plays such as *Philoktet/Herakles 5* (1966), *MacBeth* (1971) and *Die Hamlet-maschine* (Hamlet Machine) (1977) originated.

Müller repeatedly clashed with the East German government because of his critical writings. After the premiere of the play *Die Umsiedlerin* (1961), which was banned from the theaters, he was barred from the Writers' Union. In 1986, however, he was rehabilitated with the award of the East German State Prize for literature. *Germania 3 Gespenster am toten Mann* (Germania) was published posthumously in 1996.

Muller, Hermann Joseph (1890-1967), U.S. geneticist awarded the 1946 Nobel Prize for physiology or medicine for his work showing that X-rays greatly accelerate mutation processes.
See also: Genetics.

Müller, Karl Alexander (1797-1840), German philologist and archeologist. He wrote extensively on the ancient Macedonians, Etruscans, and Greeks. His books include *Handbuch der Archaeologie der Kunst* (Handbook on the Archaeology of Art, 1830) and *A History of the Literature of Ancient Greece* (1840).
See also: Archeology.

Müller, Paul Hermann (1899-1965), Swiss chemist. His discovery of DDT (dichlorodiphenyltrichloroethane) as an insecticide won him the 1948 Nobel Prize for medicine or physiology. The subsequent use of DDT led to increased food production in the world and to a decrease in diseases spread by insects. However, its widespread, long-term use eventually led to a buildup of DDT in the environment that threatened animal life and disrupted ecological food chains. As a result, several countries, including the United States, have banned its use.
See also: DDT.

Mullet, any of several species of fish of either the mullet or goatfish families. Fish in the mullet family (also known as gray mullets) have large scales and silvery, stocky bodies that can reach a length of 1 to 3 ft (30 to 90 cm). Their mouths are small and their teeth weak. Living on a mainly vegetarian diet, they inhabit shallow coastal waters in tropical and temperate regions throughout the world. They are fished commercially for their tasty flavor. The common or striped mullet (*Mugil cephalus*) is the best-known species of this family. Mullets in the goatfish family also live in warm waters.

Mulliken, Robert Sanderson (1896-1986), U.S. chemist and physicist awarded the 1966 Nobel Prize for chemistry for his work on the nature of chemical bonding and hence on the electronic structure of molecules.
See also: Chemistry; Molecule.

Multiple sclerosis, degenerative disease of the brain and spinal cord in which myelin sheath around nerve fibers is destroyed. Its cause is unknown, although slow viruses, abnormal allergy to viruses, and abnormalities of fats are suspected. It particularly affects young adults. Episodic symptoms are blurring of vision, double vision, vertigo, paralysis, muscular weakness, and bladder disturbance. Symptoms can disappear and recur over a remission of many years. Steroids, certain dietary foods, and drugs acting on muscles and bladder spasticity can help. The course of the disease is extremely variable, some subjects having only a few mild attacks, others progressing rapidly to permanent disability and dependency.

Mumford, Lewis (1895-1990), U.S. social critic and historian concerned with the relationship between people and environment, especially in urban planning. His books include *The Culture of Cities* (1938), *The Condition of Man* (1944), and *The City in History* (1961).

Mummy, corpse preserved, particularly by embalming. The earliest known Egyptian attempts to preserve bodies were c.2600 B.C., It is believed that the body was being prepared for a reunion with the soul. Natural mummification was seen in bodies buried in Danish peat bogs from 300 B.C. to A.D.300.

Mumps, common viral infection causing swelling of the parotid salivary gland. It can also cause problems in swallowing and fever. Usually occurs in children ages 5 through 15 but can occur in adults. For adults, the condition is more severe and can cause swelling of the testes and sterility. It is highly contagious.

Munakata Shiko (1903-1975), Japanese engraver. One of the greatest contemporary Japanese engravers, whose wood and copper engravings are characterized by a directly appealing, realistic naive style related to primitive art. According to himself, he found inspiration in a universally creative principle, which make the words 'expanded' and 'unlimited' particularly apply to his art. The museum of primitive art in Tokyo keeps a large collection of his art. The Willard Gallery in New York owns his *God and the Rain* (1955), from a series on the twelve months.

Munch, Edvard (1863-1944), Norwegian painter and printmaker. His work foreshadowed expressionism and was influential in the development of modern art. His powerful, often anguished pictures, for example, *The Shriek* (1893), *The Kiss* (1895), and *Anxiety* (1896) show his obsession with the themes of love, death, and loneliness.

Munchausen, Baron von, the hero of a collection of tall tales called *Baron Munchausen's Narrative of His Marvellous Travels and Campaigns in Russia*. Authorship has been credited to Rudolph Erich Raspe (1737-1794), curator of the Kassel university museum, who fled to England after being accused of stealing. His book was published there in an English edition in 1785. The stories were attributed by their author to a real person, Baron Karl Friedrich Hieronymus von Münchhausen (1720-1797), a German cavalry officer who had served the Russians in a war against the

Thanks to special embalming methods, the bodies of the Egyptian pharaohs and other highly placed persons, have sometimes remained almost completely intact. This is the mummy of King Ramses II (r.1290-1237 B.C.).

Turks; supposedly, the baron had told them to his friends.

A typical tale is that of the Baron being lost in a blizzard. Tying his horse to what he thought was a post, he fell asleep on the snow. When he awoke the morning, he found himself lying on the bare ground. A south wind had melted the deep snow. Looking up, he saw his horse hanging from the church steeple to which it had been tied. The Baron drew his pistol and with a well-aimed shot cut the halter strap. The horse slid to the ground unhurt, and the traveler went on his way.

On another occasion, the Baron played a tune on a horn during a cold spell, but he notes froze before they reached the outside air. When the horn was placed by a fire, the notes melted en sounded forth.

Munich, or München (pop. 1,240,000), capital of Bavaria, southwestern Germany, on the Isar River about 30 mi (48 km) north of the Alps. A cultural center with a cathedral and palace, it is also heavily industrialized (beer, textiles, publishing), and is Germany's third-largest city. Founded in 1158 by Duke Henry the Lion, it was ruled (1255-1918) by the Wittelsbach family (dukes and kings of Bavaria). Munich was the birthplace and headquarters of Nazism and the site of the Munich Agreement in 1938.
See also: Germany.

Munich Agreement, pact signed Sept. 30, 1938, prior to World War II, forcing Czechoslovakia to surrender its Sudetenland to Nazi Germany. The Sudetenland in western Czechoslovakia contained much of the nation's industry and about 700,000 Czechs. The agreement, which allowed an immediate German takeover, was signed by Hitler, Neville Chamberlain (Britain), Edouard Daladier (France), and Benito Mussolini (Italy). Neither the Czechs nor their Soviet allies were consulted. In Mar. 1939 Hitler occupied the rest of Czechoslovakia.
See also: World War II.

Municipal government *See:* City government.

Munro, Alice (1931-), a Canadian author. Her detail-rich writings reveal the profound and complex feelings hidden in ordinary people's lives. *Dance of the Happy Shades* (1968), deals with the values and attitudes of people in a small town. Her novel *Lives of Girls and Women* (1971) focuses on a young girl faced with social pressures and expectations that lead her to examine the relationships in her life. Munro's themes include the difficulty of successful communication and the balancing of love and personal freedom. Other short-story collections include: *Something I've Been Meaning to Tell You* (1974), *The Moons of Jupiter* (1982), *Friend of My Youth* (1990), *Open Secrets* (1994), and *Hateship, Friendship, Courtship, Loveship, Marriage* (2001).

Munro, Hector Hugh (1870-1916), British writer who wrote under the pen name Saki, known for his inventive, satirical, and often fantastic short stories. Among his published works are stories collected in *Reginald*

(1904) and *Beasts and Super-Beasts* (1914) and a novel, *The Unbearable Bassington* (1912).

Muppets, puppet family created by the master puppeteer Jim Henson in 1955. Henson was strongly influenced by the diversity of the European puppet theater. The first network television appearance of the Muppets occurred on 'The Steve Allen Show' in 1956. The Muppets continued to grow in popularity through the early 1960s but it was their appearance on the Children's Television Workshop production of 'Sesame Street' that brought them global recognition. The likes of Kermit the Frog, Big Bird, Bert and Ernie, Oscar the Grouch, and Cookie Monster, among many others, provided entertainment and education. In 1976, a new group of Muppets characters that included Kermit began starring in 'The Muppet Show,' which received a total of 3 Emmy awards during its 5-year run and became the most popular TV show in the world. Another Henson creation, 'Fraggle Rock,' recently became the first U.S. television series to be broadcast in the USSR. Other Henson creations are the 'Muppet Babies' cartoon show, winner of 7 Emmy awards, *The Great Muppet Caper*, *The Dark Crystal*, *The Muppets Take Manhattan*, and 'The Storyteller.' Henson's philanthropic work included the creation of the Henson Foundation and a close affiliation with the United Nations which issued a Kermit the Frog stamp in 1991. He also supported environmental causes. On May 16, 1990, Jim Henson died of a sudden illness.

Murad I (Ottoman Empire) (Murad; ca. 1326-1389), Sultan of the Ottoman Empire (1360-1389), successor to Orhan I. He conquered Macedonia and Thracia and was succeeded by Bayezid I.

Murad II (Ottoman Empire) (Murad; 1404-1451), Sultan of the Ottoman Empire (1421-1451), successor to Mehmed I. He conquered Saloniki in 1430 and was succeeded by Mehmed II.

Murad III (Ottoman Empire) (Murad; 1546-1595), Sultan of the Ottoman empire (1574-1595), successor to Selim II. He was succeeded by Mehmed III.

Murad IV (Ottoman Empire) (Murad; 1612-1640), Sultan of the Ottoman Empire (1623-1640), successor to Mustapha I. He conquered Baghdad from the Persians and was succeeded by Ibrahim.

Murad V (Ottoman Empire) (Murad; 1840-1904), Sultan of the Ottoman Empire, son of Abdul Mejid. He ascended to the throne in 1876 after a coup d'état which was led by Midhat Pasha.

Murano (pop. 6700), district of Venice. Situated on an island in the lagoon of Venice. Center of the glass industry since 1292. Situated on the island because of potential fire hazard. Basilica of Santa Maria (12th-13th century), houses in Renaissance style, museum of glass.

Murasaki, Shikibu, or Lady Murasaki

(978-1026?), pseudonym of Japanese court figure and author of *The Tale of Genji*, one of the first great works of fiction written in Japanese.

Murat, Joachim (1767-1815), French marshal under Napoleon Bonaparte and king of Naples (1808-1815). Murat gained his reputation as a brilliant cavalry leader in the Italian and Egyptian campaigns (1796-1799), and contributed to French successes in the Napoleonic Wars. He married Napoleon's sister, Caroline. As king of Naples he fostered the beginnings of Italian nationalism. Although he joined the Allies in 1814, he supported Napoleon during the Hundred Days and was executed after an attempt to recapture Naples.
See also: Napoleon I.

Murdoch, Iris (1919-1999), Irish-born British novelist. Her novels, such as *A Fairly Honourable Defeat* (1970), *The Sea, the Sea* (1978), *Nuns and Soldiers* (1980), *The Good Apprentice* (1986), *The Book and the Brotherhood* (1988), and *Jackson's Dilemma* (1995), display wit and a gift for analyzing human relations.

Muriatic acid *See:* Hydrochloric acid.

Murillo, Bartolomé Estéban (1617-1682), baroque painter, Spain's most famous in his time, known as the Raphael of Seville. He produced religious narrative scenes expressing deep piety and gentleness, works of realism, and fine portraits. Among his many paintings are the *Vision of St. Anthony* (1656), *The Ragged Boy* (c.1670), and the *Two Trinities* (known as the *Holy Family*) (1678).
See also: Baroque.

Murmansk (pop. 472,000), city in northwestern Russia, lying on the Kola Gulf of the Barents Sea, within the Arctic Circle. An important ice-free port since 1916, it served as an Allied supply base during World War II. It is a shipping and fishing center, with lumber and shipbuilding industries, and is connected by rail with Leningrad.
See also: Union of Soviet Socialist Republics.

Muromachi period (Also: Ashikaga period) Period of Japanese history (1338-1573) in which the country was plagued by civil wars. The Muromachi period began when general Ashikaga Takauji (1305-1358) committed treason against the emperor and founded his own shogunate (dominion) in Muromachi. The battle between shogun and emperor lasted until 1392 and enabled the daimios (lords) to expand their territory. In 1543 Japan came into contact with Portuguese traders, after which the missionaries arrived. Christianity was initially successful in Japan. The country also adopted other Western elements (clocks, firearms, tobacco, glasses). The Ashikaga shogunate was overthrown by Oda Nobunaga (1534-1582). Toyotomi Hideyoshi (1536-1598) restored unity in Japan and in 1600 Tokugawa Ieyasu (1542-1616) came into power. This was the beginning of the Tokugawa period.

Murphy, Audie (1924-1971), U.S. soldier

M

and actor. The many medals he received for his gallantry in action during World War II (1939-1945) made him the most highly decorated hero of the war. *The Red Badge of Courage* (1951) and *To Hell and Back* (1955) were two of his most successful films. He died in a plane crash.
See also: World War II.

Murray River, Australia's chief river, an important source of irrigation and hydroelectricity. Rising in the mountains of New South Wales, it flows for 1,609 mi (2,589 km), passing through Hume reservoir and Lake Victoria and on to Encounter Bay and the Indian Ocean.

Murre, seabirds (genus *Uria*) in the auk family. They inhabit cliffs on the coasts of the North Atlantic and North Pacific oceans. Murres, approximately 16 in (41 cm) long, are brownish black, with white breasts. In their breeding season, they nest in large numbers, the female in each pair laying one egg on the bare rock.

Muscat, or Maskat (pop. 622,000), capital of Oman. A major port and commercial center, it lies on the Gulf of Oman in southeast Arabia. The city has existed since ancient times. Two Portuguese forts testify to Portugal's occupation of Muscat (1508-1648). In 1741 it became Oman's capital. Muscat and its modern suburbs are known as the Capital Area.
See also: Oman.

Muscle, contractile tissue that produces movement in the body. We consciously control striated muscle at will through the central nervous system, such as when we walk or run. We cannot, however, control the smooth muscle lining most organs, such as organs in the digestive system.

Muscular dystrophy, group of inherited diseases in which muscle fibers are abnormal and become wasted. Duchenne dystrophy occurs only in boys, beginning with swelling of calf muscles before age 3. Death often occurs by age 30. A similar disease, Becker dystrophy, can affect females. There are many variants, largely due to structural or biochemical abnormalities in muscle fibers. A waddling gait and exaggerated curvature of the lower spine are typical. If pneumonia and respiratory failure or heart muscle are affected, early death may result.

Muses, in Greek mythology, 9 patron goddesses of the arts, worshiped especially near Mt. Helicon. Daughters of Zeus and the titan Mnemosyne (Memory), they were attendants to Apollo, god of poetry. The chief muse was Calliope (epic poetry); the others were Clio (history), Euterpe (lyric poetry), Thalia (comedy, pastoral poetry), Melpomene (tragedy), Terpsichore (choral dancing), Erato (love poetry), Polyhymnia (sacred song), and Urania (astronomy).
See also: Mythology.

Museum of Modern Art, one of the world's pre-eminent museums of modern art, New York City. Founded in 1929, it is privately supported and has a collection of more than 100,000 objects, including paintings, sculptures, drawings, architecture and design, decorative arts, crafts, industrial design, prints, and illustrated books. Its holdings of film and photography are especially notable. The museum also has programs of loan exhibitions and publications.

Museveni, Yoweri Kaguta (1944-), president of Uganda since 1986. His Front for National Salvation helped overthrow dictator Idi Amin (1979). After a prolonged struggle he overthrew President Milton Obote by force (1985); when his National Resistance Army seized the capital of Kampala, ousting the ruling military council, Museveni was installed as president. Museveni maintains good relations with Europe and the West and has helped stabilize the country, but has been accused of human rights violations. In 1996, he won the first presidential elections since the independence. He was re-elected in 2001. His government experiences armed opposition in the northern and western areas of the country, where three resistance movements are operating.

Musharraf, Parvez (1943-), Pakistani military leader and President (2001-). Musharraf moved with his family to the new Muslim state Pakistan after India became independent. He joined the army in 1961 and gradually climbed the ranks. In 1998, Prime Minister Sharif appointed him Chief of the Land Forces and six months later, he became Chief of Army Staff.
He supported the Pakistani invasion of the Indian-held territory of Kashmir (1999). Angered by Sharif's decision to withdraw from Kashmir, he seized power after learning that he had been dismissed as Chief of Army Staff. Sharif was arrested and Musharraf was subsequently sworn in as Prime Minister of Pakistan. He suspended the constitution, dissolved parliament, established a National Security Council, and attempted to ease the increasing tension in connection with India. In 2001, he declared himself President. A large majority voted in favor of the prolongation of his presidency for another five years in a referendum held in 2002.

Mushroom, popular name given to an umbrella-shaped gill fungi. Edible mushrooms have 5% protein and are mostly water. Poisonous, or inedible, mushrooms are called toadstools. The common field mushroom (*Agaricus campestris*) is the wild species most frequently eaten; *bisporus* is the cultivated mushroom. Some mushrooms are parasites of wood, plantation trees, and garden plants.

Musial, Stan(ley) (1920-), U.S. baseball player. An outfielder and first baseman for the St. Louis Cardinals (1941-1963), he is

These illustrations show front and rear views of the human male's external skeletal muscles. There are other layers of muscle beneath these. The skeletal, or voluntary muscular system, which constitutes about 40 percent of the human body weight, is responsible for the body's movement and support. The 700 or more muscles pull the bones — in the same way forces act on levers — to produce motion. Limb muscles often work in opposing groups. For example, contraction of biceps brachii causes a flexion of the arm at the elbow joint, while contraction of triceps brachii produces extension of the arm. The cerebral cortex of the brain controls and coordinates voluntary muscular activity.

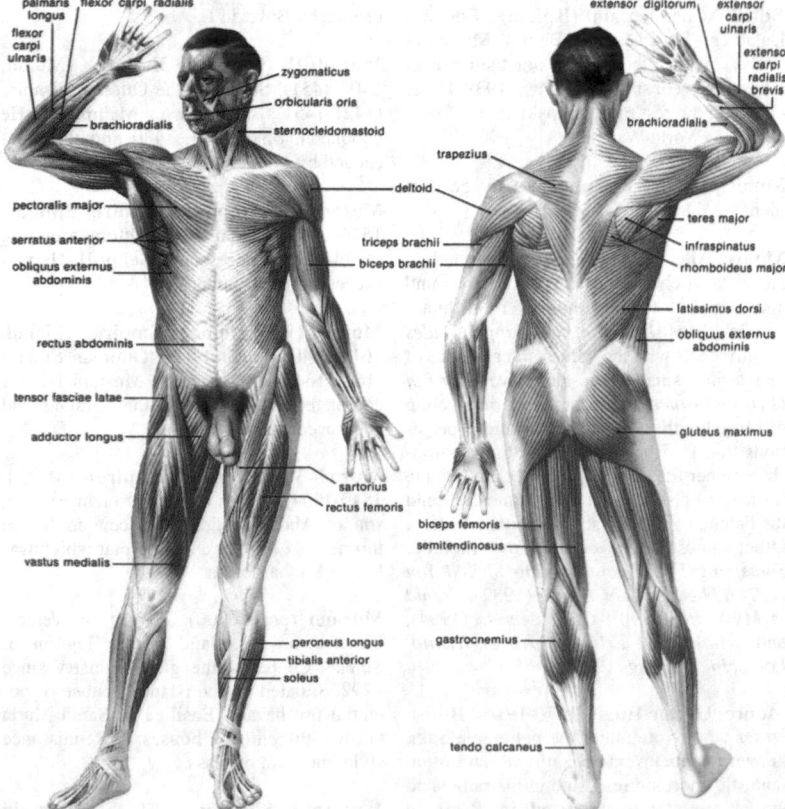

acclaimed as one of baseball's great hitters. 'Stan the Man' was named the National League's most valuable player 3 times (1943, 1946, 1948), had a lifetime batting average of .331, hit 475 career home runs, and held the National League record for career hits (3,630) until 1981, when it was topped by Pete Rose. He was inducted into the National Baseball Hall of Fame in 1969.

Music, sound organized and arranged as a means of expression and for sensual and intellectual pleasure. Of the major arts, music may be the most ancient, because the urge to sing and dance in response to feelings of anger, joy, or sorrow springs from the body itself.

Music may also be described as sound shaped by time. Its 2 most important elements are rhythm and melody, rhythm being organized in terms of intervals of time and beats to the bar, and melody in terms of notes whose pitch is determined by frequency, or the number of sound vibrations per second. These basic characteristics of music can be considered universal, but musical expressions and traditions are quite distinct and diverse. Oriental music, for instance, does not rely upon harmony, a late but significant development in Western music. And although any music can be arranged according to scale and notated, the development of musical notation was gradual and is a relatively recent phenomenon.

Western music evidently originated in the Middle East, was developed by the Greeks, and, in the form of Byzantine ecclesiastical music, was embraced by the early church. Such music was originally limited to plainsong, a form of chant unadorned by any kind of harmony or accompaniment sung by church or monastery choirs. During the 9th and 10th centuries, choirs began to be divided into sections, each with a different melody line. This gave rise to polyphonic music, the so-called *ars antiqua*, which reached its height in the motet in the 13th century. Following this was the *ars nova*, the new art, a style of musical composition that departed from the excessive formalism and complexity of the *ars antiqua* and achieved its finest expression in the madrigal of the 14th and 15th centuries. This period also saw the rise and spread of the first comprehensive system of musical notation.

Though the church dominated ancient and medieval music, alongside the ecclesiastical was a lively secular tradition closely related to sung poetry and represented in the works of minstrels, troubadours, and minnesingers. As in the other arts, the secular would become independent and eventually supplant the ecclesiastical, beginning with the Renaissance.

From c.1400 to 1600, great changes in music occurred. It turned to nonecclesiastical themes. New instruments were developed, played by groups of musicians-the nuclei for the modern orchestra. In the work of Claudio Monteverdi, early opera developed. Other composers of the period were Josquin Desprez and Orlando di Lasso in Flanders, Andrea and Giovanni Gabrieli in Venice, and Thomas Morley and John Dowland in England.

The Baroque period was born with

Pierluigida Palestrina (c.1526) and culminated in the works of Johann Sebastian Bach (d.1750). The era saw major improvements in instruments, particularly the violin and cello, inspiring composers like Antonio Vivaldi and Arcangelo Corelli. François Couperin and Domenico Scarlatti exploited the newer keyboard instruments. A new harmonic structure of scales and keys familiar today was finally established, and the music of the period achieved a formal complexity, balance, and richness, above all in the work of Bach, which to many remains the highest achievement of Western music.

The late 18th century saw a new age in music, the classical period, pioneered and perfected in the work of Franz Josef Haydn and Wolfgang Amadeus Mozart. The period was marked by the growth and completion of several musical forms-the sonata, symphony, concerto, *opera buffa*-and by works that, as the result of greater mastery and skill with instruments, were musically richer and contained, particularly in Mozart's, an expressiveness that opened new possibilities for music.

Ludwig van Beethoven seized that opportunity and, in the spirit of the times, revolutionized the concept and the practice of the art of music. In his work and influence, Beethoven, in effect, gave a charter of liberties to individual expression that inspired the Romantic movement and, by extension, modern music as well. Franz Schubert, Robert Schumann, Frédéric Chopin, Franz Liszt, Felix Mendelssohn, and Hector Berlioz, Anton Bruckner, Gustav Mahler, and Jan Sibelius completed the Romantic period in music, each with a signal style and distinct sensibility, and each the heir of Beethoven.

As *ars antiqua* gave rise to the rebellion and innovations of *ars nova*, so the classical and Romantic traditions, particularly in the wake of World War I, gave rise to 20th-century modernism in music. It is heard in the neoclassicism of Paul Hindemith and Igor Stravinsky and the more radical atonalism of Arnold Schönberg, which offered an entirely new set of rules for music and gave rise, in turn, to serial and 12-tone music. Influenced by music of non-Western cultures as well as the innovations of jazz and modern technology, often disturbing and unsettling in the way it deliberately explores the untried and the unconventional, serious modern music defies the kind of clear-cut and comfortable categories that make traditional music seem more comprehensible and familiar.

Musical, a stage entertainment that contains tuneful songs, elaborate dance routines, and spoken dialogue, all presented at a swift pace. A musical in which the plot is a mere device for tying the songs together is generally called a *revue*. One with a dramatic, well-constructed story is a *musical play*. Between these two lies the *musical comedy*. There is no distinct dividing line between a musical comedy and musical play on the one hand and an operetta on the other. However, an operetta usually is more formal in structure and generally requires singers trained in the operatic tradition.

Many popular songs come from musicals,

remaining favorites long after the musical itself is forgotten. Among popular standards are Irving Berlin's 'Easter Parade' from *As Thousands Cheer* (1933), Harold Arlen's 'Stormy Weather' from a 1933 revue written for the Cotton Club in Harlem, Cole Porter's 'Begin the Beguine' from *Jubilee* (1935), and Kurt Weill's 'September Song' from *Knickerbocker Holiday* (1938).

Musicals originated in the United States, developing out of burlesque, minstrel shows, operetta, and variety shows. Many scholars consider *The Black Crook* (1866), a melodrama adapted for a troupe of ballet dancers, the first musical. The term *musical comedy* was first used in the 1890's. *A Trip to Chinatown* (1890), with the song 'The Bowery!', and *The Wizard of Oz* (1903) were among the first successes. In the early 1900's George M. Cohan dominated the musical stage with fast-moving, exuberant musicals, such as *Little Johnny Jones* (1904) and *George Washington, Jr.* (1906).

At the same time, the revue was developing. The revue featured risqué humor, satirical skits, pretty chorus girls in spectacular costumes, and specialty acts. Irving Berlin, Cole Porter, Victor Herbert, and George Gershwin were among composers writing songs for the annual *Ziegfield Follies* and *George White Scandals*. The revue reached its height of popularity shortly after World War I. Popular musical comedies of the era included *No, No, Nanette* (1925), by Vincent Youmans, and *A Connecticut Yankee* (1927), by Richard Rodgers and Lorenz Hart. Jerome Kern's *Show Boat* (1927) was a forerunner of the musical play.

The Great Depression of the 1930's brought more contemporary and American themes to musical comedy. Fanciful, often improbable, plots were discarded for more literate, well-constructed stories. Gershwin's *Of Thee I Sing* (1931), for example, dealt with politics and elections. *Pal Joey* (1940), by Rodgers and Hart, had lifelike characters. Serious dance was introduced into musical comedy in the 1930's. George Balanchine did the choreography for 'Slaughter on Tenth Avenue' in *On Your Toes* (1936).

Use of better stories and of ballet led to development of the musical play, in which spoken dialogue, dances, plot, and music are carefully integrated. Beginning with *Oklahoma!* (1943), by Rodgers and Oscar Hammerstein, it became the leading type of musical show presented on Broadway. Many plots are adapted from existing stories and plays. Cole Porter's *Kiss Me Kate* (1948) was based on Shakespeare's *The Taming of the Shrew*, and Alan Jay Lerner and Frederick Loewe's *My Fair Lady* (1956) was adapted from George Bernard Shaw's *Pygmalion*. Leonard Bernstein's *West Side Story* (1957) was inspired by Shakespeare's *Romeo and Juliet*.

Among the successful musicals made into motion pictures are Jule Styne's *Funny Girl* (stage production, 1964), Jerry Bock's *Fiddler on the Roof* (1964), Jerry Herman's *Hello, Dolly!* (1964), and John Kander's *Cabaret* (1966). *Hair* (1967), by James Rado, Gerome Ragni, and Galt MacDermot, introduced rock music to the American musical theater.

In the last decades of the 20th century the

M

musical in all its forms continued to be a favorite form of entertainment. There were revivals of classic musicals as well as a variety of imaginative new productions. Successful rock musicals included *Godspell* (1971), by Stephen Schwartz, and *Grease* (1972), by Jim Jacobs and Warren Casey. *The Wiz* (1975), by Charlie Smalls, *Ain't Misbehavin'* (1978), set to the music of Fats Waller, and *The Tap Dance Kid* (1983), by Henry Krieger and Robert Lorick, were among the musicals that featured black American performers and music. Other musicals, such as *Annie* (1977), by Charles Strouse and Martin Charnin, and *Doonesbury* (1983), by Gary Trudeau and Elizabeth Swados, were based on comic strips.

Dance dominated such musicals as Marvin Hamlisch's and Michael Bennett's *A Chorus Line* (1975), Gower Champion's *42nd Street* (1980), and Tommy Tune's *The Will Rogers Follies* (1991). Other hit musicals included Andrew Lloyd Webber's *Cats* (1981); *Sophisticated Ladies* (1981), based on the music of Duke Ellington; Stephen Sondheim's *Sunday in the Park with George* (1984); and *The Phantom of the Opera* (1986), by Lloyd Webber, Charles Hart, and Richard Stilgoe.

Musil, Robert (1880-1942), Austrian writer. He is known for *The Man Without Qualities* (3 vols., 1930-1942), an encyclopedic novel about the ills of prewar Austria. Posthumous collections include *Tonka and Other Stories* (1965) and *Three Short Stories* (1970).

Musk deer (*Moschus moshiferus*), a deer of the family Cervidae. The musk deer stands about 20-24 in (50.8-60.9 cm) at the shoulder, slightly higher at the rump. It has a coarse, gray-brown coat. The male has long upper canine teeth resembling tusks, no antlers, and a musk gland on its abdomen. The deer marks its territory with the musk; people use musk to scent perfumes and soaps. Unlike most deer, musk deer are solitary. They live in the mountains of Asia.

Benito Mussolini, Italy's fascist leader, enjoyed great popularity during the twenties and thirties.

Muskellunge (*Esox masquinongy*), the largest fish of the pike family. Most muskellunges are 2 1/2-4 ft (6.4-10.2 cm) in length and 5-36 lb (2.3-16 kg) in weight. Its slender body may be brown, gray, green, or silver with dark bars or spots on the side. A distinctive feature of the muskellunge is the absence of scales on its lower head. The muskellunge is solitary and carnivorous. It is found in southern Canada and northern United States. A strong fighter, the muskellunge is sought for sport and food.

Musket, shoulder firearm developed in Spain in the 16th century and used into the 19th century. A musket could be 5.5-7 ft (1.7-2.1 m) long and weigh 20-40 lb (9-18.1 kg). It was loaded from the muzzle with a single ball, or a ball plus small lead shot, and fired by igniting a powder charge. Unlike the rifle, the musket had a smooth bore; this made it an inaccurate weapon against targets beyond 100 yd (91 m). The matchlock, earliest musket, was succeeded by the flintlock, caplock, and wheel lock.

Musk hog *See:* Peccary.

Muskmelon, edible fruit of certain plants (*Cucumis melo*) belonging to the gourd family. Cantaloupes, Persian melons, casabas, and honeydew melons are subspecies of muskmelon. The plants are annual, grow along the ground, and produce hairy, heart-shaped leaves and 5-lobed yellow flowers. The fruit varies: the skin may be smooth, ridged, or latticed, and the flesh white, pale green, or orange. Muskmelons grow best in a hot, dry climate. They are believed to have originated in western Asia.

Musk ox (*Ovibos moschatus*), shaggy-furred, hoofed animal of Arctic America, related to sheep and goats. With a pronounced hump over the shoulders and a musky odor, these highly aggressive animals live in herds of up to 100. When threatened, adults circle the calves, with horns facing outward.

Muskrat, or musquash, aquatic rodent of North America, *Ondrata ziethica*, up to 2 ft (6 m) long. It lives in fresh water or salt marshes, feeding mainly on water plants. The feet are broad; the hindfeet webbed; and the fur is thick and waterproof.

Muslims, practitioners of the religion of Islam as preached by the prophet Muhammad in the 600s. Muslim is an Arabic word meaning one who submits to God. Muslims form the majority of the population of the Middle East, North Africa, Bangladesh, Indonesia, Malaysia, and Pakistan. The Koran, believed to be the revelations of God (Allah) to Muhammad, is the book to which Muslims are devoted. A dispute, dating back to the first centuries of the Muslim era, caused a fundamental division of Muslims into the Sunni and Shi'te sects.
See also: Islam.

Mussel, two-shelled mollusk that lives in masses on most rocky shores and is exposed at low tide. It feeds on minute particles sifted from the sea and is anchored to the rock

by the byssus, a series of strong, silky threads.

Musset, (Louis-Charles) Alfred de (1810-1857), French romantic poet and playwright. After an affair with George Sand, he wrote *Les Nuits* (1835-1837), some of the finest love poetry in French, and the autobiographical novel *Confession of a Child of the Century* (1836). His witty plays, including *Lorenzaccio* (1834), are often produced today.

Mussolini, Benito (1883-1945), founder of fascism, dictator of Italy (1924-1943). Editor of the Socialist party paper (1912-1914), Mussolini split with the Socialists when he advocated Italy's entry in World War I. In 1919 he formed a fascist group in Milan; in 1921 he was elected to parliament and founded the National fascist party. In 1922 he led the fascist march on Rome and was made premier. His dictatorship ended parliamentry go vernment in 1928. As *Duce* leader he signed the Lateran Treaty, creating Vatican City, in 1929. He conquered Ethiopia (1935-1936) and annexed Albania in 1939. Joining Hitler in 1940, he declared war on the Allies but suffered great military failures in North Africa and Greece. Mussolini was imprisoned by the king (1943), only to be made a puppet ruler in northern Italy by the Germans. He was shot by partisans after the German defeat.
See also: Fascism; World War II; Italy.

Mussorgsky, Modest (1839-1881), Russian composer, one of the first to develop a style around characteristically Russian idioms. His *Boris Gudonov* (1874) is one of the finest Russian operas. Other major works include *Night on Bald Mountain* (1860-1866), the piano suite *Pictures at an Exhibition* (1874), later orchestrated by Maurice Ravel; and the song cycle *Songs and Dances of Death* (1875-1877).

Mustafa Kemal Pasha *See:* Atatürk, Kemal.

Mustard, any of several herbs (genus *Brassica*) of the Cruciferae family. The Cruciferae include food plants (e.g., many cabbage varieties, watercress, turnip, radish, and horseradish) and such condiment plants as the white mustard (*B. alba*) and black mustard (*B. nigra*), native to the Mediterranean region. They are cultivated for their seeds, which are ground and used as a condiment, or used as medicine.

Mustard gas *See:* Chemical and biological warfare.

Muster, Thomas (1967-), Austrian tennis player, one of the world's leading clay court players during the 1990s. He won 40 international tournaments, including the Open French Championships over Roland Garros and the Open Italian Championships. In 1995 Muster remained unbeaten on the clay court for 40 games, which puts him third behind Guillermo Villas (53 games in 1977) and Björn Borg (44 games in 1979). Muster is known for his heavy training sessions and his aggressive, powerful style of playing in which he strains himself to the limit.

Mutawakkil (822-861), Caliph from the dynasty of Abbasids, which ruled the Arabic world from 750 until 1258 from Iraq. Mutawakkil was very orthodox, especially in the religious sense. Christians and Jews were required to wear special attire, while the caliph ordered churches and synagogues in Baghdad to be demolished. His ban on pilgrimages to the grave of the popular Islamic martyr Hussein in Kerbela, which was destroyed by his order, was very radical. In the military area the battle against the Byzantine armies eventually took a turn for the better, and a number of rebellions in the border regions was suppressed. Mutawakkil was murdered by followers of his son al-Muntasir.

Mutsuhito (1852-1912), emperor of Japan (1867-1912); his regal title was *Meiji* ('enlightened rule'). The long isolation of Japan under the shoguns ended in 1867 with the restoration of imperial power. Mutsuhito guided the transformation of Japan from a feudal empire into a modern nation. He established industries, promoted education, gave farmers titles to their land, and modernized the armed forces. Japan's defeat of China (1895) and Russia (1905) and its alliance with England (1902) helped to establish the nation as a great power.

Mutual fund, investment company that pools its shareholders' funds and invests them in a broad range of stocks and shares. A shareholder receives dividends for his or her shares in the fund, rather than for individual company shares. Mutual funds are popular among small investors because of the low risk involved (due to the variety of stocks invested in by the mutual fund) and the expert management provided.

Myanmar

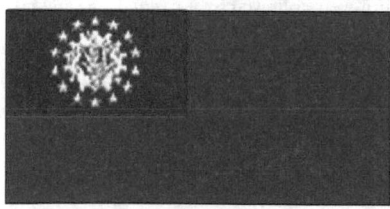

Capital:	Yangon (Rangoon)
Area:	261,228 sq mi
	(676,577 sq km)
Population:	42,238,000
Language:	Burmese
Government:	Republic
Independent:	1948
Head of gov.:	Chairman of the State Peace
	and Development Council
Per capita:	less than US$ 3,250
Monetary unit:	1 Myanmar kyat = 100 pyas

Myanmar, republic in Southeast Asia, formerly called Burma, bordered by India, Bangladesh, and the Bay of Bengal on the west, by China on the north and northeast, by Laos and Thailand on the east, and by the Andaman Sea on the south.
Climate. Myanmar's climate is typical of the tropical monsoon regions of southeast Asia and India. The rainy season lasts from June to October, and rainfall averages 200 in (508 cm) annually.
People. The people are predominantly (about 70%) Burmans, but there are minorities of Karens, Shans, Chins, Kachins, Indians, Chinese, and Bangladeshis. More than 85% are adherents of Theravada Buddhism. Although more than 100 different languages are spoken, the official language is Burmese.
Economy. The majority of Myanmar's work force is engaged in agriculture and forestry. The forests are sources of teak and rubber. There are also rich mineral deposits of oil, silver, tungsten, tin, zinc, and lead. Myanmar is famous for its rubies, sapphires, and rich deposits of jade, but agriculture remains the mainstay of the country's economy.
History. Myanmar was settled in the 9th century by peoples who established a kingdom that reached its height under the Buddhist King Anawrahta in the 11th century. The kingdom and its capital fell to Kublai Khan in 1287, and the area was not reunited until the 16th century. After a series of wars (1826-1885), Britain annexed Burma to its Indian empire. It was granted separate dominion status in 1937. The Japanese occupied the country during World War II, and it was not until after the war, with the foundation of the Union of Burma in 1948, that the country became independent. The first prime minister, U Nu, was overthrown by Gen. Ne Win in 1958. In 1960 U Nu returned to power but was again overthrown by Ne Win in 1962. In 1973 a new constitution made Burma a one-party socialist republic. In 1981 Ne Win resigned the presidency but retained control of the Burma Socialist Program Party. Pro-democracy demonstrations were crushed by the military late in 1988. In elections for a National Assembly in May 1990 the National League for Democracy won 80% of the vote, but the military arrested the League's leaders and the country remained under military rule. The economy deteriorated in the late 1990s. Opposition leader and Nobel Prize winner (1991) Aung San Suu Kyi continued her fight for the restoration of democracy. In 1997 Myanmar joined the ASEAN (the Association of South-East Asian Nations).

Myasthenia gravis, disease of the junctions between the peripheral nerves and the muscles, probably due to abnormal immunity and characterized by muscle fatigue. It commonly affects eye muscles, leading to drooping lids and double vision, but it may involve limb muscles. Weakness of the muscles of respiration, swallowing, and coughing may lead to respiratory failure and aspiration or bacterial pneumonia. Speech is nasal, regurgitation into the nose may occur, and the face is weak, lending a characteristic snarl to the mouth. It is associated with disorders of thymus and thyroid glands. Treatment is with cholinesterase inhibitors; steroids and thymus removal may control the causative immune mechanism.

Mycenae, city of Bronze Age Greece. It was founded c. 2000 B.C. by an Indo-European Greek-speaking people on the southern peninsula. Mycenaean culture benefitted from contact with the Minoans on Crete. By 1600 B.C. Mycenae had risen to cultural, political, and commercial prominence in the Mediterranean world. Between 1400 and 1200 B.C. it was at its height. In 1100 B.C. Mycenae was invaded by the Dorians. Mycenae remained unknown to the modern world until Heinrich Schliemann began excavations at the site and discovered 5 royal tombs (1876).

A gold death mask, found in the Mycenaean royal tombs, dating from 1600-1500 B.C. (National Museum, Athens).

See also: Greece, Ancient.

My Lai, hamlet in South Vietnam where nearly 350 Vietnamese civilians were massacred by U.S. soldiers in 1968. Subsequent revelations led to army and congressional investigations. Lt. William Calley, in immediate command during the incident, was convicted of killing 22 persons and imprisoned for 3 years. Two generals were censured for failing to conduct an adequate investigation. *See also:* Vietnam War.

Myna, several birds of the starling family, native to Indian and Asian forests but dispersed to the Pacific tropics. These noisy birds adapt well to living near people and livestock. The hill or talking myna (*Gracula religiosa*) is kept as a pet and can be trained to mimic the human voice. About 12-15 in (30-38 cm), this glossy black bird has yellow feet, wattles, and beak.

Myocarditis, inflammation of the heart muscle (myocardium). It may be due to a variety of diseases, certain chemicals or drugs, or injury-for instance, electric shock or excessive X-ray treatment.

Myoelectricity *See:* Artificial limb.

Myopia, commonly called nearsightedness, inability to clearly see objects at a distance. The image is focused in front of the retina rather than on it, due to an overly strong refractive power of the eye or an eyeball that is too long. Eyeglasses with concave lenses compensate for myopia.

Myrdal, Gunnar (1898-1987), Swedish

M

economist who wrote a classic work on race relations, *An American Dilemma* (1944), an influential study of Third World economic development, *Asian Drama* (1968), and *Challenge of World Poverty* (1970). He won the 1974 Nobel Prize for economics.

Myrtle, common name for the Myrtaceae family of trees and shrubs. Myrtles are native to temperate Asia and tropical America and Australia. They include the clove, eucalyptus, guava, and pimento. Myrtles are valued for their aromatic oils, timber, spices, and fruit. The common or classical myrtle (*Myrtus communis*) grows in the Mediterranean region. The ancient Greeks associated the glossy evergreen with Aphrodite and awarded Olympic athletes wreaths of myrtle.

Mysore (pop. 607,000) city in Karnataka state, India. Mysore lies about 85 miles (135 km) south-southwest of Bangalore, the state capital. The city is a major center for the production of incense and sandalwood oil. Formerly a royal capital, Mysore has several impressive palaces. Among the city's other attractions are a zoo and an art museum. The University of Mysore (founded in 1916) is here. The Dasara, a colorful Hindu festival, takes place in the city each fall. The site of Mysore was inhabited before the third century, B.C. The city was the capital of several dynastic states from the early 17th to the mid-20th century.

Mysteries, secret religious cults of ancient Greece and Rome; their rites were revealed only to initiated persons. The mysteries involved purification rites, dance, drama, and the display of sacred objects such as an ear of corn. The Orphic mysteries were also important.

Mystery play, medieval religious drama based on biblical themes, chiefly those concerning the Nativity, the Passion, and the Resurrection. The form is closely related to that of the miracle play, which is generally based on nonbiblical material, for example, the saints' lives. The distinction between the 2 forms is not clear-cut, and some authorities refer to both as miracle plays. Mystery plays, which are liturgical in origin, can be ambitious in scale, treating the whole of spiritual history from the Creation to Judgment Day in vast cycles. Examples are the English York and Wakefield cycles, the French cycle *Miracle of Notre Dame*, and the Oberammergau Passion of Bavaria.

Mysticism, experience of a transcendental union in this life with God, the divine, through meditation and other disciplines. Cleansing away of physical desires, purification of will, and enlightenment of mind are the stages along the path to unification. Mystics suggest either that God is indwelling and can be reached by delving within, or dwells outside the soul and is reached by the soul's rise in successive stages. Mysticism, which has broad association in English to include the occult and magic, is found in Greek Neoplatonism, Christianity, Judaism, Hinduism, Buddhism, Islam, and Taoism.

A Greek amphora from the 5th century B.C., made by Milo. The Gods are fighting the giants of prehistoric times. At the top, the supreme god Zeus, with the goddess Nike (victory) on a chariot, at the bottom Hercules with his lionskin and bow, and the goddess Pallas Athena with her Gorgon shield (Louvre, Paris).

Mythology, stories or explanations of the origin and meaning of the world and the universe and their relation to a particular culture or civilization. Mythological stories differ from folk tales and legends in that they tend to be integrated in the religious doctrine of a particular culture and are considered sacred and factual. Mythological stories also contain supernatural and divine elements. Folk tales and legends, on the other hand, are more lighthearted, entertaining, and fictive. Though mythological stories are characteristic of the pre-scientific world many aspects and beliefs of the modern world perpetuate the mythic tradition. The most well-known myths in western civilization are those of ancient Greece. The historic sources for our knowledge of this mythology are the *Theogeny* by Hesiod and the *Illiad* and the *Odyssey* by Homer. All three works date from the 8th century B.C. Other significant mythologic systems are Teutonic, or Norse, mythology of Scandinavia and Germany. The sources for this mythology are the *Eddas* (1200s B.C.).The source for the Hindu mythology of Asia and India are the *Vedas* (1200 to 600 B.C.) The basis of Irish Celtic mythology are three cycles of stories-the mythological cycle, the Ulster cycle, and the Fenian cycle. Other significant mythological systems are those of Africa, Native America, and the Pacific Islands.

Many theories have been developed by scholars about how and why myths began. Some of the more significant theories are those of Euhemerus, the Greek scholar (3rd century B.C.) who believed that myths are based on historical fact; Friedrich Max Muller, a German scholar (late 1800s) who held that mythic heroes were representations of nature; Sir Edward Burnett Tylor, an English anthropologist (1800s) who stated that myths were an attempt to explain the unexplainable events in dreams; Bronislaw Malinowski, a British anthropologist (early 1900s), who held a more psychologic perspective; and Sir James George Frazer, a Scottish anthropologist (early 1900s), who concluded that myths reflect the cyclical nature of life-birth, growth, decay, and rebirth.

Frazer is the author of *The Golden Bough*, one of the most famous works in the study of mythology. Among modern psychologists, the work of Sigmund Freud and Carl Jung are significant in their interpretation of myths. In more recent times, the work of Joseph Campbell in the area of comparative mythology has also made a contribution to human knowledge.

N, 14th letter of the English alphabet, corresponds with the 14th Semitic letter *nun*, denoting a fish. After it was adopted by the Greeks from the Phoenicians, *nun* became *nu*. Its present form is that used by the Romans. When written with a tilde (common in Spanish words), *n* is pronounced as if it were followed by a *y* (*cañon* = canyon). As an abbreviation, *n* represents noun, neuter, name, and north. In mathematics it may stand for any number. It is the chemical symbol of nitrogen.

Nabis, Les (Hebrew: prophets), group of late 19th century artists. Sérusier, Denis, Bonnard and Vuillard belonged to the core of the group. They regarded themselves as prophets of a new art in which religion and mysticism played an important role. Gauguin's theories formed the basis for their usually symbolistic work. They made use of non-blended colors and left out any details or outlines. Unlike the impressionists, their point of departure was not visible reality: instead, they wanted to express their inner feelings in the shape of color and form. Their group slowly fell apart after 1899.

Nabokov, Vladimir (1899-1977), Russian-born U.S. novelist and critic. Born in St. Petersburg, he came to the United States in 1940 and taught at Cornell (1948-1959). Noted for his originality and satiric wit, he published poetry, essays, short stories, and novels in Russian and in English. His first novel in English was *The Real Life of Sebastian Knight* (1938); he became famous after the U.S. publication of *Lolita* (1958), the story of a middle-aged man's passion for a young girl. Other works include *Pnin*

(1957), *Pale Fire* (1962), *Ada* (1969), and an English translation of *Eugene Onegin* (1964).

Nadir, in astronomy, point on the celestial sphere directly opposite the zenith, that is, directly below an observer.
See also: Zenith.

Nadir Shah (1688-1747), shah of Iran (1736-1747), often called the Napoleon of Iran. He created an Iranian empire reaching from the Indus River to the Caucasus Mountains by ruthless military conquest, including the capture of the Delhi (and its famous Koh-i-noor diamond and peacock throne).

Nadjaf (pop. 310,000), city in the south of Iraq. Nadjaf is one of the holy places of Shiite Islam. The city was built on the place where, assumedly, the imam Ali ibn Abu Talib was buried. The martyrdom of Ali plays a less important role within Shiite Islam than that of his son Hussein. Nadjaf developed as place of pilgrimage and a Shiite theological center. Because of the fact that many worshippers wanted to be buried near imam Ali, Nadjaf-like other holy places-has widespread burial grounds.

NAFTA, abbreviation of North American Free Trade Agreement. Agreement between Canada, the U.S. and Mexico over the formation of a free trade area. The agreement was signed on 12 August 1992 in Washington and became effective on 1 January 1994. By signing the treaty the three countries agreed to dispel all mutual trade barriers within the next 15 years. Expansion of NAFTA was not ruled out and there have been negotiations with Chile, Costa Rica and Guatemala.

Nagana *See:* Tsetse fly.

Nagasaki (pop. 450,000), city on western Kyushu Island, Japan, capital of Nagasaki prefecture. A major port on the China Sea, it has been a foreign trading center since 1571. In World War II about 75,000 residents were killed or wounded and much of the city was destroyed when the United States dropped the second atomic bomb (Aug. 9, 1945). Today shipbuilding is the city's major industry.

Nagorno-Karabach (pop. 193,000), area in Azerbaijan; 1,699 sq mi, (4,400 sq km). Capital is Stepanakert. Mostly agricultural, e.g. silk industry. The industry is based on agriculture (processing). Cattle breeding. Its population is mainly Armenian.
Christian Armenians enjoyed, formally speaking, an autonomous status within Azerbaijan (pop. largely Muslim), but felt oppressed and wanted to become part of Armenia. In 1988 fights broke out between groups of Armenians and Azeri government troops. The conflict escalated and resulted in a war between Azerbaijan and Armenia. In 1994 both parties declared a cease fire. Approximately 15,000 people were killed during the struggle; one million inhabitants fled the area.

Nagoya (pop. 3,0 million), capital of Aichi

prefecture, Japan, on the island of Honshu. It is a major port and a manufacturing center for textiles, steel, and ceramics. In 1610, the feudal lord Ieyasu Tokugawa built a magnificent castle at Nagoya.

Nagpur (pop. 1,624,000), city in Maharashtra state, India. It is on the Deccan Plateau in central India. Nagpur is a commercial, industrial, and transportation center. The city is noted for its trade in oranges. Products manufactured here include textiles, iron, and brassware. The University of Nagpur is the city's leading educational institution. Nagpur was founded early in the 18th century and soon became the military stronghold of one of the states that made up the Maratha Confederacy. The city was annexed by the British in 1853. In 1861 Nagpur was made the capital of the Central Provinces, formed by the British. It remained the capital when the Central Provinces became Madhya Pradesh state in 1950. In 1956 Nagpur became a part of Maharashtra state.

Nagy, Imre (1895?-1958), Hungarian communist leader and premier (1953-1955). His criticism of Soviet influence led to his removal from office, but during the Oct. 1956 revolution he became premier again briefly. After Soviet troops crushed the uprising, Nagy was tried and executed in secret.

Nahum, Book of, seventh of the Old Testament Minor Prophets, the oracles of the prophet Nahum. It foretells the fall of Nineveh (612 B.C.).
See also: Bible.

Naiad *See:* Nymph.

Nail, metal shaft, pointed at one end and usually with a head at the other, that can be hammered into pieces of material, usually wood, to fasten them together.

Nail, thin, horny plate growing on the ends of the fingers and toes of humans and other primates. Dead nail cells are pushed outward by dividing cells in the root. Nails are made of a sulfur-containing protein material called keratin.

Naipaul, V(idiadhar) S(urajprasad) (1932-), Indian writer, born in Trinidad, who has lived in England since 1950. A critic and essayist, Naipaul has been especially praised for his novels of life in the Third World, including *A House for Mr. Biswas* (1961), *Guerrilas* (1975), *A Bend in the River* (1979), *A Way in the World* (1993), *Beyond Belief* (1998), *Letters Between a Father and a Son* (1999), and *Half a Life* (2001). In 2001, he was awarded the Nobel Prize for Literature.

Nair, Mira (1957-), Indian film director and scriptwriter. Nair won the Golden Lion at the Film festival of Venice with her low budget film *Monsoon Wedding* (2001). She was the first Indian and the first woman to win this award. Her films focus on people who live on the edges of society. Her works include *Salaam Bombay!* (1988), *Mississippi Masala* (1991), *The Perez*

Family (1995) and *Kama Sutra: A Tale of Love* (1996).

Nairobi (pop. 2,0 million), capital of Kenya. A modern city on the east African plateau, it is Kenya's administrative, commercial, manufacturing, and transportation center. The city encompasses Nairobi National Park, a wildlife reserve. The city was founded in 1899, became a British colonial capital (1905) and railroad center, and then the capital of independent Kenya (1963).

Naismith, James (1861-1939), inventor of basketball. He developed the game (1891) while a physical education teacher at the YMCA in Springfield, Mass. The first game was played indoors with a soccer ball and 2 peach baskets.
See also: Basketball.

Najd (Nejd, Nedzjed, Nadjd), highland of the Arab peninsula in Saudi Arabia, between Mekka and Ar-Riyad; 641,174 sq mi (1,660,000 sq km). Height: 3,937 ft (1,200 m). Dry climate; agriculture (dates, grains) to be found in a chain of oases which runs from north to south. Surrounded by deserts and the Al Hijaz mountains. Tribal land of the Wahabites, whose leader Abdul Aziz Ibn Saoud conquered Ar-Riyad in 1901, thus laying the foundation for the state of Saudi Arabia.

Najdorf, Miguel (1910-1997), Polish-Argentinian chess master. Najdorf took part in the 1939 Chess Olympiad in Buenos Aires and decided to stay in Argentina afterwards. Initially a businessman, but as his successes increased he decided to make chess his profession. Between 1935 and 1939 he played for Poland during international chess tournaments, after 1939 he represented Argentina. Najdorf remained one of the strongest chess players until well into the 1950s; he was successful on several candidates' tournaments and won various tournaments with strong opponents in e.g. Prague (1946), Venice (1948), Amsterdam (1950), Havana (1962) and Mar del Plata (1959, 1961 and 1965). The Najdorf system, which he created, has become one of the most popular defence systems.

Najiabullah, Mohammad (1948-1996), political leader of Afghanistan (1986-1993). He was the leader of the People's Democratic Party. With his election to the presidency of the legislative Revolutionary Council (1987) he officially assumed presidency of the nation. His government has consistently been opposed by Muslim factions.

Nakasone, Yasuhiro (1917-), Japanese politician. As a member of the Liberal Democratic Party (LDP), Nakasone had fulfilled several ministerial posts and was elected prime minister in 1982. After his reelection in 1984 he succeeded in 1986 in implementing an amendment to LDP statutes which enabled him to extend his term of office for another 12 months, until November 1987. In 1989 Nakasone left the LDP after a turbulent period of scandals and a major electoral defeat for the party; Nakasone re-

N

mained an independent member of parliament.

Namaliu, Rabbie (1947-), prime minister of the south Pacific nation of Papua New Guinea (1988-1992). He became head of the Pangu Pati Party shortly before the party was voted into power.

Namibia

Capital:	Windhoek
Area:	318,261 sq mi
	(824,292 sq km)
Population:	1,821,000
Language:	English
Government:	Republic
Independent:	1990
Head of gov.:	Prime minister
Per capita:	US$ 4,500
Monetary unit:	1 South African rand
	100 cents

Namibia, Republic of, in southern Africa, an area covering about 318,261 sq mi (824,292 sq km), bordered by Angola, Zambia, Botswana, South Africa, and the Atlantic Ocean.
Land and climate. From the Namib Desert, which stretches north-south on the Atlantic coast, the land rises to a plateau averaging 3,500 ft (1,067 m) above sea level covered by rough grass and scrub. The Kalahari, a desert region, lies to the east. The climate is hot and dry. In the north are the Kunene and Okavango rivers, and in the south, the Kwando and Zambezi rivers. The Orange River runs along the southern border. The Etosha Game Park protects elephants, cheetahs, antelope, giraffes, zebras, lions, and rhinoceros.
People. The population of more than 1,529,000 is 86% black, overwhelmingly Bantu, and 7% white. Ovambos (the largest ethnic group), Bushmen, and Kavango live to the north in Ovamboland. The Hereros, Nama, and Damara live in the south plateau, chiefly around Windhoek, home to most of the country's Europeans. About 30% of the population live in urban areas. The Tswana people live in the east. The Rehoboths, or coloreds, of African and European ancestry, are another important group. Except for the Bushman, these groups mostly farm, raise cattle, or work in mines. In addition to native African languages, Afrikaans, English, and German are spoken. The few black Namibians who go beyond high school may attend the University of Namibia.
Economy. Minerals account for most exports, led by diamonds and uranium. Livestock has dominated agriculture, which has been weakened by numerous droughts since the 1970s. Fishing remains important. Railroads connect cities in Namibia and South Africa, and Windhoek has an international airport.
History. The original peoples of Namibia were the Damara and the San; other Africans moved there over the centuries. The territory was annexed as a protectorate in 1884 by Germany, who named it South-West Africa. In 1920 the League of Nations mandated it to South Africa, which refused to place it under UN trusteeship after World War II. An independence move was launched in 1966 by the South-West Africa People's Organization (SWAPO), a Marxist guerilla group. Renaming the country Namibia in 1968, the UN declared (1970) South Africa's occupation of it was illegal, a move backed by the International Court of Justice (1971), pointing to South Africa's practice of apartheid. Through referendums and mediation from 1977, the UN continued to seek the country's freedom in spite of opposition from South Africa and factions of Namibian white voters and black opposition parties. Since Mar. 21, 1990, Namibia has been an independent nation with black majority rule. In 1991, Namibia and South Africa established a temporary joint administration over the Walvis Bay enclave and in 1994 South Africa ceded Walvis Bay to Namibia.
President Sam Nujoma, who has been President since 1990, has announced he will stand for a fourth period in 2004. In 2001, he made the battle against AIDS/HIV a national priority.

Namphy, Henri (1933-), military ruler of Haiti 1986-1988. After Jean Claude Duvalier stepped down as ruler of Haiti, a military-civilian council took power, with Lt. Gen. Namphy, then armed forces chief of staff, as its head. Namphy repeatedly promised free elections and the protection of civil rights. Amidst widespread violence and general strikes, repressive measures continued and the elections did not take place until Jan. 1988. The newly elected president, Leslie Mandigat, was ousted by Namphy in June, but Namphy was arrested and exiled in Sept. 1988.

Nanchang (Nan-ch'ang; pop. 1,400,000), city in China, capital of the Jiangxi province on the Ganjiang river. Trade in local products. Aircraft construction, textile, rubber, food, chemical industries and agricultural engineering. Traffic junction, center of education. Airport. The walled city center dates from the second century B.C. Formerly a naval center. Old name Hung-chou. In 1927 the Communists founded a Soviet Republic here for a short period. Industrialized after 1949.

Nan-ching *See:* Nanjing.

Nancy (pop. 102,000), capital of Meurthe-et-Moselle *département* in the Lorraine region of northeastern France, on the Meurthe River. Once an industrial center, Nancy now serves as a financial and administrative center. The city's central plan and civic buildings exemplify 18th-century French architecture.

Nanjing, or Nanking (pop. 3,000,000), industrial and manufacturing city on the Yangtze River in east-central China. Originally the only capital of China, it is now the southern capital, Beijing being its northern counterpart. Oceangoing ships dock at the city's wharves and facilitate transportation of products which include steel, coal, petroleum, tea, grain, and vegetables. The Chinese Communists, the nation's ruling force since 1949, are responsible for greater industrial development. A 3-mi (5-km) bridge crosses the Yangtze at Nanjing.

The bridge over the Yangtze River in the centre of Nanjing, was built between 1961 and 1968. The lower level is used for trains, pedestrians and cars use the upper level.

Mining is one of the few branches of modern industry in Namibia. Foreigners and white Namibians own the enterprises, but without the (cheap) labour of the black Namibians they can not function.

Nanking *See:* China; Nanjing.

Nansen, Fridtjof (1861-1930), Norwegian explorer, scientist, and humanitarian. He is best known for his explorations of the Arctic. His attempts at reaching the North Pole by drifting on ice across the polar basin in a crush-resistant ship yielded information on oceanography and meteorology. He was awarded the 1922 Nobel Peace Prize for his work as the League of Nations' high commissioner for refugees.

Nantes (pop. 252,000), port city in western France near the Loire River, capital of the Loire-Atlantique department. It is linked to the Atlantic Ocean through the port of St.-Nazaire and a ship canal. Shipbuilding and transporting food products and farm equipment provide revenue. King Henry IV signed the Edict of Nantes (1598) in the city's 10th-century castle, providing restricted religious freedom for Protestants.

Nantes, Edict of, proclamation of religious toleration for French Protestants (Huguenots) issued in the city of Nantes by Henry IV in 1598. Protestants were granted civil rights and freedom of worship. In 1685 Catholic pressure led Louis XIV to revoke the edict.
See also: Huguenots.

Napalm, mixture of gasoline and thickeners, used in flame throwers and incendiary bombs. It burns relatively slowly, and sticks to its target. Developed in World War II, it was used extensively in the Vietnam War.

Naphtha, volatile inflammable hydrocarbon liquid (distilled from substances that yield carbon). It is used as a solvent, cleaning fluid, or fuel.

Napier, John (1550-1617), Scottish mathematician, the inventor of logarithms. He also developed the decimal point in writing numbers. His *Rabdologiae* (1617) deals with abbreviating mathematical calculations.
See also: Logarithm.

Naples (pop. 1,200,000), third-largest city in Italy, capital of the region of Campania, on the Bay of Naples, 120 mi (193 km) southeast of Rome. Founded by the Greeks (600 B.C.), it was part of the kingdom of Sicily and later capital of the Kingdom of Naples. The historic city has a 13th-century cathedral and university and medieval castles and palaces. Nearby are the ruins of the Roman city of Pompeii. Naples is the financial and intellectual center of southern Italy.

Naples, Bay of, bay of the Tyrrhenian Sea (arm of the Mediterranean west of Italy), southwest of Naples. It is 20 mi (32 km) wide from Cape Miseno to Point Campanella and penetrates the land 10 mi (16 km). Along its shoreline are the ancient Roman ruins of Pompeii and Herculaneum.

Naples, Kingdom of, region once comprised of all Italy south of the Papal States, including Sicily. It emerged after the conquests by the Norman Robert Guiscard in the 11th century; his nephew, Roger II, took the title King of Sicily and Apulia (1130). Naples was ruled in turn by the Hohenstaufens, the Angevins, the Aragonese, and the Spanish. The Austrians conquered the kingdom in 1707, but it was taken by the Spanish Bourbon kings in 1738. Napoleon I annexed the kingdom to his empire and made his brother, Joseph, king (1806), followed by his brother-in-law, Joachim Murat. In 1815, after Napoleon's defeat, the Bourbon Ferdinand IV was restored; he reunited Naples and Sicily as the Kingdom of the Two Sicilies. Bourbon rule collapsed before the advance of the revolutionary forces of Garibaldi (1860). When Victor Emmanuel was confirmed by the Italian parliament as king of all Italy (1861), Naples became a part of the new Italian state, ending 700 years as an independent kingdom.

Napoleon I (1769-1821), general and emperor of France (1804-1814). Napoleon Bonaparte was born in Corsica, went to military schools in France, and became a lieutenant in the artillery (1785). He associated with Jacobins on the outbreak of the French Revolution, drove the British from Toulon (1793), and dispersed a royalist rebellion in Paris (Oct. 1795). He defeated the Austro-Sardinian armies in Italy (1796-1797) and signed the treaty of Campo Formio, extending French territory. He then campaigned in Egypt and the Middle East, threatening Great Britain's position in India. Although he won land battles, the French fleet was destroyed in the Battle of the Nile in 1798. Returning to Paris Napoleon engineered the coup d'état of Nov. 9, 1799, establishing a Consulate with himself as first consul and dictator. He reorganized the government and established the Bank of France and the Code Napoléon, still the basis of French law.
The Treaty of Lunéville (1801) made peace with Austria; the Treaty of Amiens (1802) made peace with Britain. Napoleon became first consul for life (1802) and crowned himself emperor (1804). In the Napoleonic Wars he won victories over the European alliance at Austerlitz (1805), Jena (1806) and Friedland (1807), dissolving the Holy Roman Empire (1806), and becoming ruler of almost the whole continent. After Jena he inaugurated the Continental System whereby he hoped to keep European ports closed to British trade, but the battle of Trafalgar (1805) established the dominance of Britain at sea.
In 1809 Napoleon divorced Joséphine de Beauharnais and married Marie Louise, who bore him an heir, Napoleon II. The Peninsular War revealed growing French weakness, and in 1812 Napoleon began his disastrous campaign against Russia. A new alliance of European nations defeated the French at Leipzig (1813); in 1814, after France was invaded, Napoleon abdicated and was exiled to the island of Elba. In March 1815 he escaped, returned to France, and ruled for the Hundred Days, which ended in French defeat at Waterloo (1815). Napoleon was then exiled to Saint Helena, where he died in 1821.
See also: Napoleonic Wars.

Napoleonic Code *See:* Code Napoléon.

Napoleonic Wars (1803-1815), fought by France after Napoleon I became emperor. After the Treaty of Amiens (1802), which had ended the French Revolutionary Wars (1792-1802), Britain declared war on France (1803), maintaining that Napoleon was not keeping the treaty. Napoleon planned to invade Britain, but the British fleet proved too strong for him, especially after the Battle of Trafalgar (1805). The British, Swedes, Austrians, and Russians formed an alliance (July 1805); Napoleon defeated the Austrians and Russians at Austerlitz (Dec. 1805), the Prussians at Jena (1806), and the Russians at Friedland (1807); the Peace of Tilsit (1807) left him nearly master of Europe. Meanwhile, Britain had secured supremacy of the seas at Trafalgar. The Continental System begun after Jena was Napoleon's attempt to blockade British trade; on the pretext of enforcing it he invaded Portugal (1807) and Spain (1808). During the defeat of his armies by the British in the Peninsular War (1808-1814), he signed the Peace of Schönbrunn (1809) with the defeated Austrians. In 1812 Napoleon invaded Russia with an army of some 500,000. He barely won the Battle of Borodino (1812) and marched unchallenged to Moscow, but his troops suffered from lack of supplies and the cold weather. Their retreat from Moscow and Russia was horrifying; only about 30,000 of Napoleon's soldiers returned. The French, by now drained of manpower and supplies, were decisively beaten at Leipzig (1813). Paris fell, and on

The pompous reception of First Consul Napoleon Bonaparte in Antwerp (1803), as painted by M.I. van Bree (National Maritime Museum, in the Steen, in Antwerp). The French occupation, which lasted twenty years, was in many respects rather favourable for the southern Netherlands.

An English caricature of Napoleon's attack on Russia, floundering in the icy cold. The Russian bear is about to deal with Napoleon (begging for mercy) with a razor, while he is trampling the French armies with his gigantic paws (British Museum, London).

N

April 11, 1814, Napoleon abdicated. The victorious allies signed the Treaty of Paris with the Bourbons. After Napoleon's escape from Elba and return (the Hundred Days) and his defeat at Waterloo (1815), the second Treaty of Paris was signed (1815).

Napoleon II (1811-1832), son of Napoleon I and Marie Louise, proclaimed king of Rome at birth. After his father's abdication (1814), he lived in Austria as Duke of Reichstadt. He died of tuberculosis.

Napoleon III (Louis Napoleon Bonaparte; 1808-1873), emperor of the French (1852-1870); son of Louis Bonaparte (king of Holland), nephew of Napoleon I. He attempted several coups against King Louis Philippe, was jailed, but escaped to England (1846). After the 1848 revolution, he was elected president of France. He then dissolved the legislature and made himself emperor (1852). His regime promoted domestic prosperity, but by the 1860s opposition had grown. Among his military efforts were the Crimean War (1854-1856), in which France was a victor, and an intervention in Mexico (1861-1867), in which he failed to maintain Maximilian as emperor of Mexico. In 1870 his ill-judged war with Prussia ended in defeat, capture, and the collapse of his empire; he died in exile in England.

Narayan, R(asipuram) K(rishnaswamy) (1906-2001), Indian novelist writing in English who created the fictitious town of Malgudi in a series of novels that dealt with the ironies of daily life in contemporary India. These include *The Bachelor of Arts* (1937), *The Financial Expert* (1952), *The Vendor of Sweets* (1967), *The Painter of Signs* (1977), *A Tiger for Malgudi* (1983), *The World of Nagaraj* (1990), and *The Grandmother's Tale and Other Stories* (1993). *My Days* (1974) is his autobiography.

Narcissus, fragrant yellow, white, or pink perennial flower (genus *Narcissus*) of the amaryllis family, named after the youth Narcissus of Greek mythology. Its large, brown, poisonous bulbs are planted in the fall and bloom each spring. The yellow daffodil and jonquil are varieties of narcissus.

Narcissus, in Greek mythology, name of a self-centered, handsome youth loved by many, including the nymph Echo. Having rejected all, he was denounced by the gods and sentenced to reflect upon his own image near a small pool. He gradually deteriorated until just a flower, the narcissus, remained. Echo, too, wasted away, leaving only her voice in the forest.

Narcolepsy, chronic disease marked by uncontrollable attacks of deep sleep of brief duration. The cause of the disease is unknown, although it may be hereditary. There is no cure.
See also: Cataplexy.

Narcotic, drug that induces sleep; specifically, the analgesics (painkilling drugs) opium, codeine, morphine, and heroin. These affect the higher brain centers, numbing the senses, lessening pain, causing mild euphoria and sleep (narcosis). They may act as hallucinogenic drugs and are addictive.
See also: Drug abuse.

Nard *See:* Spikenard.

Narwhal (*Monodon monoceros*), tusked whale native to the Arctic. The body of the narwhal is about 18 ft (2.5 m) long. It is a toothless whale except for the single spiral tusk, present only in males, on the left-hand side of the jaw, up to 8 ft (2.5 cm) long. The function of the tusk is unknown. The narwhal is hunted for the ivory of its tusk and for oil.

NASA *See:* National Aeronautics and Space Administration.

Nash, Charles William (1864-1948), U.S. automobile manufacturer. He influenced the industry as head of Buick Motors (1910-1912) and General Motors (1912-1916), and as founder and head of Nash Motors, from which he retired in 1932. In 1954 Nash Motors and Hudson Motors became American Motors.

Nash, John (1752-1835), British architect; was inspired not only by the Classics, but also by Gothic and Oriental art. From 1812 onwards he designed in London, e.g. Regent's Park, Regent Street (1813-1820), the Haymarket Theatre (1821), Trafalgar Square and part of the Strand. Renovated Buckingham Palace in London (from 1821 onwards) and the Royal Pavilion in Brighton (1815).

Nash, Ogden (1902-1971), U.S. humorous poet. His witty, sometimes satirical style was punctuated by puns, asides, and unconventional rhymes. He published 20 volumes of verse, including *Hard Lines* (1931), *The Private Dining Room* (1953), and *Bed Riddance* (1970).

Nashville (pop. 511,000), capital city of Tennessee, on the Cumberland River. The last major battle of the Civil War was fought nearby (Dec. 1864). Nashville is a commercial, industrial, and agricultural city, and a religious, educational, and publishing center. It is the center of the country music recording industry, and its 'Opryland' is a major entertainment complex.

Nassau (pop. 170,000), capital city of the Bahama Islands, a port on the northeastern New Providence Island. Long a pirate haunt, it is now a world-famous tourist resort.

Nasser, Gamal Abdel (1918-1970), Egyptian president (1956-1970) and Arab leader. He led the military coup d'état overthrowing King Farouk (1952), and named himself prime minister (1954). He ended British military presence in Egypt (1954) and nationalized the Suez Canal (1956), precipitating a brief war with Britain, France, and Israel. Elected president of Egypt unopposed (1956), he was also president of the short-lived United Arab Republic (1958-1961). His 'Arab socialism' policy brought new land ownership laws and agricultural policies, more schools, and the building of the Aswan Dam. He resigned after the disastrous 1967 Arab-Israeli War but resumed office by popular demand.

Nasturtium, annual plant (*Tropaeolum majus* and *T. minus*) native to mountainous areas of the American tropics and cultivated in gardens for its red, orange, and yellow flowers. Nasturtiums may be used medicinally for respiratory congestion. Their leaves and flowers are used in salad.

Natal, former province of South Africa, on the Indian Ocean. It is 33,578 sq mi (86,967 sq km) in area, with its capital at Pietermaritzburg. It produces sugar, fruit, cereals, and coal and manufactures fertilizers and textiles, mainly near Durban, the chief city. Natal was a British colony (1856-1910). In 1994 Natal was consolidated with Kwazulu, the former homeland of the Zulu population.

National Aeronautics and Space Administration (NASA), U.S. government agency responsible for nonmilitary space exploration and related research. Founded by President Eisenhower (1958), it has numerous research stations, laboratories, and space flight launching centers, including the Kennedy Space center at Cape Canaveral, Fla., the Johnson Space Center at Houston, Tex., and the Jet Propulsion Laboratory in Pasadena, Calif.
See also: Space exploration; Observatory; Telescope; Radio telescope.

National anthem, official song of a nation, played on state or ceremonial occasions, intended as an expression of unity and loyalty to the country's ideals. One of the best-known national anthems is France's *La Marseillaise*, composed during the French Revolution of 1792. The text of the American anthem, *The Star-Spangled Banner*, was written in 1814 by Francis Scott Key, set to a popular English tune.

National debt, amount of money owed by a government, borrowed to pay expenses not covered by taxes. National debts are incurred to pay for wars, public construction programs, recessions, etc. To obtain money, governments sell bonds or short-term certificates to banks, other organizations, and individuals. Some governments in crisis have defaulted on their debt or devalued the currency.

National Football League (NFL) *See:* Football, American.

National Geographic Society, nonprofit scientific and educational organization, established in Washington, D.C. (1888) 'for the increase and diffusion of geographic knowledge.' It publishes *National Geographic* magazine, books, maps, and school bulletins, and sponsors expedition and research projects.

National income, total of labor and property earnings from the current production of goods and services by the nation's economy. It is the sum of employee compensation, proprietor's income, rental income, corporate profits, and net interests. The gross national product is the total national output of goods and services valued at market prices.

Nationalism, political and social attitude of people who share a common culture, language, and territory as well as common aims, and thus feel a deep-seated loyalty to their group. Nationalism had its roots in the rise of strong centralized monarchies, in the economic doctrine of mercantilism, and the growth of a substantial middle class.

Nationalist China *See:* Taiwan.

Nationality, in law, recognized citizenship of a particular country. Two basic principles for deciding nationality are acknowledged by most countries: the right of blood, based on the nationality of a parent, and the right of place of birth.
See also: Citizenship.

Nationalization, governmental control and ownership of an industry. It is often practiced by socialist or communist governments, which believe that a nationalized industry can provide goods and services to the citizenry more efficiently and equitably than private businesses can. Underdeveloped countries have also nationalized industries to remove them from foreign control. Industries commonly nationalized include transportation, electric and gas utilities, and telephone services.
See also: Socialism.

National Motto, United States, 'In God We Trust.' This phrase, printed on coins since 1864, probably came from the fourth stanza of 'The Star-Spangled Banner': 'And this be our motto: "In God is our trust."' Congress made it the official U.S. motto in 1956.
See also: E pluribus unum.

National Museum of American History, bureau of the Smithsonian Institution in Washington, D.C., that houses more than 17 million artifacts relating to the social, cultural, political, and technological development of the United States. Alexander Graham Bell's first telephone and George Washington's Revolutionary War field headquarters are among many displays.

Nation of Islam *See:* Black Muslims.

Native Americans, preferred term to designate aboriginal peoples who inhabited the Americas before the arrival of the Europeans. It is generally believed that the ancestors of these first Americans migrated from Asia 26,000 years ago across a land bridge (now the Bering Strait) between Siberia and Alaska. A less popular theory suggests that the Native Americans evolved on the American continent. It is certain that by 6000 B.C. they were distributed widely throughout North and South America.
Central and South American tribes. The major Native American groups in Central and northern South America at the beginning of the European conquest (16th century) included the Caribs, Arawaks, Aztecs, Mayas, and Incas. The Maya civilization had

reached its zenith some 700 years before, but the Inca and Aztec were at their peak. The cultures were overthrown and millions were killed by warfare and disease during the 16th-century Spanish conquest. The Spanish government proclaimed the Native Americans to be subjects and not slaves, but the settler community treated them as chattels and subjected them to forced labor. The situation was little better in Portuguese Brazil, though Jesuit-run plantations treated the indigenous population humanely. Where they were able to, Native Americans withdrew physically and psychologically from European culture. South American independence in the 19th century did little to improve their status. Atrocities committed against them by robber barons in the early 20th century brought a degree of government protection. In Mexico Native American influence in the 1910-1917 revolution, the restitution of certain Native American property rights, and some integration between Native Americans and European cultures greatly improved the status of Native Americans. In South America progress continues to be fitful, however, for cultural more than racial reasons. There is still a good deal of exploitation and maltreatment of remote tribes, often by government officials; they are still sometimes brutally driven off their lands or simply massacred.
North American tribes. By the time of the European incursion, there appeared to have been about 900,000 Native Americans north of the Rio Grande. European weapons, diseases, and destruction of natural resources took their toll, however, and the Native American population declined rapidly. Comprising hundreds of peoples and nations, with as many languages, Native Americans can be divided into 6 broad culture areas (the Eskimos are treated separately). (1) Early inhabitants of the Eastern Woodlands region in the eastern part of the United States were the mound builders of the Mississippi Valley. Later tribes in the area belonged to the great Algonquian and Iroquoian linguistic families, which included Cherokee, Chickasaw, Choctaw, and Creek. In the southeast the Seminole were the dominant tribe, living largely by farming. (2) The vast Plains area lay between the Mississippi River and the Rocky Mountains. It was uninhabited until the 1600s, when the introduction of horses and guns by settlers made it possible for tribes to live as nomadic buffalo hunters. These included the Apache, Cheyenne, Sioux, Comanche, Blackfoot, and Arapaho. The Plains tribes maintained a long resistance to white encroachment with skill and courage. (3) The original inhabitants of the Southwest included a group called the basketmakers (A.D. 100-700), who may have been the ancestors of the Pueblos. The peace-loving Pueblo peoples depended on agriculture for food, while their neighbors, tribes of the Apache and Navaho, relied on hunting and marauding. (4) The Plateau region included most of what is now California and the Great Basin between the Rocky Mountains and the Sierra Nevada Rangers. Most tribes lived simply by gathering. Their culture was not sophisticated, and there was little warfare. (5) The tribes of the Northwest Coast, notably the Haida,

An illustration of Cheyenne Indians on horseback, made with coloured beads on a leather waistcoat, around 1900.

Kwakiutl, and Nootka, lived along the Pacific coast from southern Alaska to northern California. The area was rich in food, principally fish, freeing the tribes to develop an elaborate and sophisticated culture. Art, particularly carving, was complex and developed; it still flourishes today. The northern tribes retain much of their culture. (6) The peoples of the sparse North, or Subarctic, region from Newfoundland to Alaska belonged to the Athabascan language group in the west and the Algonquian group around Hudson Bay. Warfare played a small part in their seminomadic life styles; too much energy was required in the search for food.
Religion. Most Native American religion reveals a deeply felt communion with nature and a belief in a divine power. Individuals and kin groups of many tribes had spiritual ties with particular totems and animals. Shamans performed sacred rituals and treated the sick. The 1800s saw the tragic rise and fall of another Native American religion, the millenarian Ghost Dance.
North American Native Americans and European Americans. The paternalistic attitudes of the first English colonists did not stop their encroachment on Native American lands, leading to the Indian Wars. Native Americans were caught up in British and French rivalry in the French and Indian Wars. With the Northwest Ordinance (1787), the newly independent United States, in need of Native American support, proclaimed a policy of peaceful coexistence, yet with new expansion hostilities increased. The Indian Removal Act of 1830 was followed from 1850 by campaigns against Plains tribes, which ended in the massacre of Native Americans at Wounded Knee, S. Dak., in 1890. In 1871 Congress ceased to recognize the tribal nations' independent rights; the Dawes Act (1887), by breaking up tribal land into individual grants, deprived the Native Americans of around 86 million acres (35 million hectares), more than half their territory. Reform began with the Indian Reorganization Act of 1934, aimed at increasing Native American autonomy and improving their economic position; it restored some lands. Other reforms followed, but poverty, poor education, and un-

N

The ancient Incan city of Machu Picchu was discovered in 1911 by Hiram Bingham.

Aztec drawing of an encounter between a Spanish man (left) and a messenger of Montezuma II, leader of the Aztecs

Toltec statue of the rain god chac-mool, located near the Warrior Temple in Chichen Itza.

Chimú tapestry

Pre-Columbian gold earring

European painting depicting a battle between two groups of Native Americans. The group on the right is supported by the Europeans (note the gun).

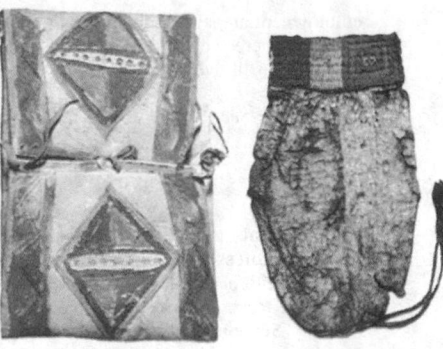

N

Typical utensils of the Sioux: On the left is a parfleche, a rawhide bag used to carry food; on the right is a water pouch.

Left: Hopi Native Americans performing the Snake Dance, a prayer for rain

A village of Kitwancool (British Columbia) with totem poles

Left: Arapaho women perform the Ghost Dance (1893).

George Catlin's Buffalo Chase

N

employment are still problems on the reservations, where the majority of U.S. Native Americans still live.

Native bear *See:* Koala.

NATO *See:* North Atlantic Treaty Organization.

Natorp, Paul (1854-1924), German philosopher, professor in Marburg (1885). Together with his master H. Cohen the most important representative of the Neokantian Marburg School. Works include *Die Philosophie, ihr Problem und ihre Probleme* (1911), *Platos Ideelehre* (1903); contributed to pedagogy with *Sozialpädagogik* (1899) and *Pestalozzi* (1909).

Natural gas *See:* Gas.

Natural gas liquids (NGL), chemical compounds in liquid form obtained from natural gas. The main NGL compounds are ethane, butane, pentane, hexane, and heptane. Natural gas liquids (NGL) are light hydrocarbons. The 2 methods of producing NGL are condensation and absorption.
See also: Butane and propane; Gas.

Naturalism, aesthetic movement attempting to apply the scientific view of the natural world (particularly that of Darwin) to the arts. According to naturalism, there is nothing real beyond nature; humans are thus prisoners of their environment and heredity. This movement, inspired by Émile Zola's argument for a scientific approach to literature in *The Experimental Novel* (1880), influenced such writers Guy de Maupassant (France), Stephen Crane and Theodore Dreiser (U.S.), Henrik Ibsen (Norway), August Strindberg (Sweden), and Maxim Gorki (Russia). The naturalist influence is also evident in the work of French painter Gustave Courbet. More recent naturalists are U.S. playwrights Arthur Miller and Tennessee Williams.

The peppered moth, *Biston betularia* (A), of Britain and western Europe, lives on lichen-covered trees, where its light color supplies for effective camouflage. In industrial areas, where trees have become blackened by soot, however, darkened (B) or black (C) forms have largely replaced the light forms. Natural selection operates through increased mortality among the forms that are most easily observed by predators.

Naturalization, process whereby a resident alien obtains citizenship of a country. Usually, naturalization takes place when a person has lived in a country for a certain period of time.
See also: Citizenship; Immigration.

Natural law, body of law supposed to be innate, discoverable by natural human reason, and common to all people. Under this philosophy, human or positive law, though changeable and culturally dependent, must-if truly just-be derived from the principles of natural law. The concept was rooted in Greek philosophy and Roman law. Particularly in the Christian philosophy of Thomas Aquinas, natural law-the sense of right and wrong implanted in humans by God-is contrasted with revealed law. It lay behind Hugo Grotius's ideas on international law (17th century). It was used as a basis for ethics, morality, and even for protests against tyranny by Spinoza, Leibniz, Locke, Rousseau, and many others, but with the development of scientific philosophies in the 19th century, natural law largely lost its influence.
See also: Aquinas, Saint Thomas.

Natural resources, earth's products or features that support life or are used to make food, fuel, and raw materials. Natural resources include air, water, and sunshine; biological resources like plants and animals; and mineral resources like oil and coal.

Natural selection, mechanism central to Charles Darwin's theory of evolution (1830s). According to Darwin, evolution occurs when an organism is confronted by a changing environment. Organisms able to adapt to this change survive and are thus 'naturally selected,' passing their useful traits on to offspring. Darwin saw this process as analogous to the artificial selection practiced by animal breeders.
See also: Darwin, Charles Robert; Wallace, Alfred Russel.

Nauman, Bruce (1941-), American artist. Initially a painter. Became known for his three-dimensional work, which is very diverse and belongs to the arte povera, conceptual art and land art. He makes use of various materials and techniques like rubber, plaster, wax, concrete, video, film, light and sound. His work shows mostly autobiographical aspects and often constitutes a visual comment on art in general. A frequent user of neon since the 1980s.

Nauru

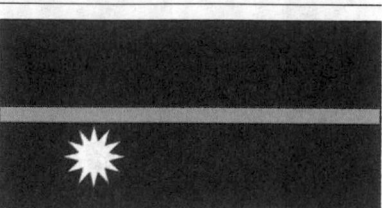

Capital:	Yaren
Area:	8.2 sq mi (21.2 sq km)
Population:	12,300
Language:	Nauruan, English
Government:	Republic
Independent:	1968
Head of gov.:	President
Per capita:	US$ 5,000
Monetary unit:	1 Australian dollar = 100 cents

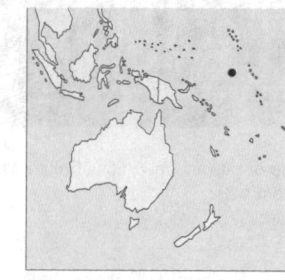

Nauru, officially the Republic of Nauru, independent island republic in the western Pacific Ocean. The island is 40 mi (64 km) south of the equator and about 8 sq mi (20 sq km) in area. Revenues come primarily from the export of phosphate rock. Discovered in 1798 and annexed by Germany in 1888, it was captured by Australia in World War I and administered as a trust territory until independence was granted in 1968. Since Naura is running out of phosphates (presumably in 2003), it is looking for alternative sources of income.

Nausea, feeling of discomfort in the stomach, with a distaste for food and a tendency to vomit. Nausea is a typical symptom of seasickness, the original meaning of the word.
See also: Vomiting.

Nautilus, or chambered nautilus, genus of shellfish native to the South Pacific and Indian oceans, having a spiral shell divided into chambers. As the nautilus grows it adds on new and larger chambers, sealing off the old ones and living in the new ones. The nautilus breathes by means of gills and uses tentacles to catch the animals on which it feeds. It is a member of the class of cephalopods (which includes squid and octopi), mollusks with a tubular siphon and a circle of tentacles around the head.

Nautilus, U.S.S., first nuclear-powered submarine, launched Jan. 1955. It was named for one of the first successful submarines (1800-1801), invented by Robert Fulton. Capable of submerged speed of over 20 knots, the *Nautilus* made the first transpolar voyage beneath the North Pole on Aug. 3, 1958. It measured 323 ft (98 m) in length and had a crew of over 100.

Navajo, Native American tribe, thought to have migrated from the north to settle in Arizona and New Mexico c.A.D. 1000. They learned agriculture, weaving, and sand painting from the Pueblo. After the Spanish introduced sheep in the 1600s, they became shepherds. Raiders of Spanish settlements in the southwest, they were subdued (1864) by Kit Carson and held at Fort Sumner, N.M., until their resettlement on a reservation (1868), now over 16 million acres in Arizona, New Mexico, and Utah.

Navarre, Basque province in northern Spain. Formerly an independent Basque kingdom, it was strategic in international politics as a buffer state between Spain and France because it controlled a principal Pyrenees mountain pass, Roncesvalles, on the border. Most of Navarre was conquered in 1515 by Ferdinand V; it sank to provincial status in 1841. Bordering the province, in France, is Lower Navarre. It remained independent until 1589, when Navarre's ruler became Henry IV of France as well. Today that district is part of the French department of Pyrénées-Atlantiques.

Navel *See:* Umbilical cord.

Navigation, science of finding the position and directing a marine, air, or space vessel from one place to another. Ocean navigators were dependent on landmarks and observations of the heavenly bodies until the invention of the compass around the 12th century gave them an independent means of determining direction. Latitude has been found using the astrolabe, cross-staff, and quadrant since the Middle Ages, and longitude has been determined with the chronometer and the sextant since the 18th century. Radio signals and satellites are now used.

Navigation acts, laws regulating navigation at sea or in port or restricting commercial shipping in the national interest-more specifically, regulations promulgated (from 1650) by the British during the American colonial period to try to ensure that benefits of commerce would accrue to England (and to a lesser extent, the colonies) rather than to England's enemies. After 1763 strict enforcement of the acts caused friction between England and the American colonies and was a major factor leading to the outbreak of the Revolutionary War.
See also: Revolutionary War in America.

Navratilova, Martina (1956-), Czechoslovakian-born U.S. tennis player. Known for

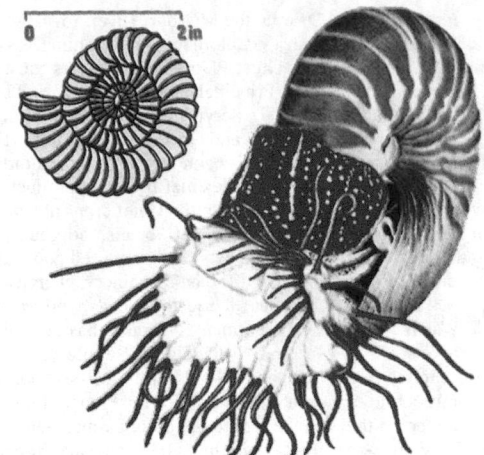

The deep-sea nautilus, found in tropical waters, is one of the three surviving species of hard-shelled cephaloped molluscs which numbered 2,500 species, until their extinction 100 million years ago. Related to squids and octopi, the nautilus has an advanced nervous system, a 36-chambered shell, and it feeds by catching prey with its contractible tentacles. Also shown here, is the fossil shell of an ammonite mollusc, an early relative of Nautilus, sized 2 in (5 cm) approximately.

N

her aggressive and powerful play, in singles competition she won a record 9 Wimbledons (1978, 1979, 1982-1987, 1990), 4 U.S. Opens (1983, 1984, 1986, 1987), 3 Australian Opens (1981, 1983, 1985) and 2 French Opens (1982, 1984). Navratilova defected in 1975 and became a U.S. citizen in 1981. Navratilova ended her professional tennis career in 1994, but returned in the 90's. In 2003 she won the mixed double of the Australian Open.

Navy, seaborne armed force maintained for national defense or attack. In ancient times, Greek and Roman ships ruled the Mediterranean. In Scandinavia the Vikings ravaged the coasts of Europe from c.A.D. 800 for over 200 years. By the later 16th century most western European nations had acquired naval forces. Spain emerged as the leading naval power, but after its Armada was defeated by the English in 1588, England had mastery of the seas. England's naval supremacy was challenged by Holland and France, but the Battle of Trafalgar in 1805 restored it for another 100 years. The submarine and the aircraft carrier have replaced armored battleships. In the post-World War II period, Britain was overshadowed as a leading naval power by the United States and the former USSR.

Nazareth (pop. 59,000), historic town in northern Israel, lower Galilee, where Jesus lived as a youth. A place of Christian pilgrimage, the town has many shrines and churches.

Nazism, or National Socialism, the creed of the National Socialist German Workers' Party (Nazi Party) led by Adolf Hitler from 1921 to 1945. The Nazi movement began (1918-19) when Germany was humiliated and impoverished by defeat in World War I and by the severe terms of the Treaty of Versailles. From a membership of around 100,000 in 1928, the party increased in strength to 920,000 in 1932. The ideas behind the program were rooted in nationalism, racism (especially anti-Semitism), authoritarianism, and militarism, expressed by Hitler in *Mein Kampf* (My Struggle, 1923). Recovery of the German nation was to be accomplished by rearmament, territorial ex-

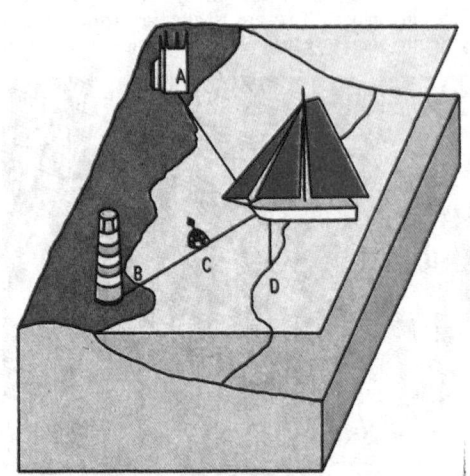

A map plot of azimuth lines from a vessel to a tower (A) and a lighthouse (B) or buoy (C) indicates the ship's position at the point where the lines intersect. If depth charts are available, a depth sounding (D) will also indicate positions.

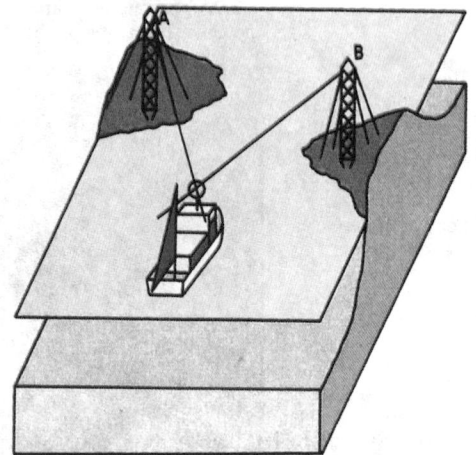

Radio Direction Finding (RDF) is a method of establishing a ship's position, by plotting on a chart the directions of radio aerials.
A Radio aerial 1
B Radio aerial 2.

N

pansion to acquire *lebensraum* ('living space') for the Teutonic master race, and the restoration of self-respect under a unified military regime. With the aid of the secret police (Gestapo), Hitler's Nazi dictatorship exterminated millions of Jews, gypsies, slavs, and other minorities, in concentration camps in the 1940s. Hitler's Nazi program of expansionism temporarily improved the German economic position, but led to World War II, resulting in the defeat of Germany and its allies and the end of the Nazi Party.
See also: Hitler, Adolf; World War II.

N'Djamena (pop. 700,000), capital and largest city of the North African republic of Chad, on the Chari and Logone rivers in the southwestern part of the country. It was named Fort-Lamy in 1900 by the French, who founded it and ruled Chad until 1960, and renamed N'Djamena in 1973. It is the export and trade center for Chad's livestock and agricultural products.

Neanderthal Man (*Homo sapiens neandertalensis*), prehistoric man, belongs to the *Homo sapiens* from the Middle Pleistocene 150,000-35,000 B.C.. Remains from the Neanderthal Man were discovered in the Neandertal in Germany. The Neanderthal Man, with his heavy eyebrows and receding forehead, appears to have the been the last stage in the development of a type of man who was especially adjusted to cold climate. In Western Europe he lived in caves and in Eastern Europe usually in open-air settlements.
In 1997 a theory was put forward on grounds of DNA research, claiming that the Neanderthal Man was a split-off from human evolution and could therefore not be the ancestor of modern man. It was supposedly displaced by *H. sapiens sapiens*, the predecessor of modern man.
See also: Homo sapiens.

Nearsightedness *See:* Myopia.

Nebraska (Cornhusker State; pop. 1,657,000), state in central United States in the Great Plains region; bordered by South Dakota, the Missouri River, Iowa, Missouri, Kansas, Colorado, and Wyoming.
The Great Plains region covers most of the state. Principal cities are Omaha and Lincoln (capital). Service industries-wholesale trade, finance, and insurance-are important to Nebraska's economy, as is agriculture. Beef cattle are the chief livestock product; others are hogs and milk. Chief crops are corn, hay, soybeans, wheat, beans, sorghum, sugar beets, and oats. Manufactured goods include processed foods, machinery, chemicals, primary and fabricated metals, and transportation equipment. Nebraska has few minerals. In 1682, the French explorer La Salle claimed all lands in the Mississippi Valley-including Nebraska-for France. France ceded the area to Spain for a time, then sold it to the U.S. in the 1803 Louisiana Purchase. In 1867 Nebraska joined the Union.

Nebuchadnezzar, name of three kings of Babylonia. **Nebuchadnezzar I** (ruled 1124-1103 B.C.) conquered Elam and extended Babylonian rule over most of ancient Mesopotamia. **Nebuchadnezzar II** (605-562 B.C.) waged military campaigns to consolidate the Neo-Babylonian or Chaldean Empire, crushing the kingdom of Judah, destroying Jerusalem (586 B.C.), and taking captive Jews to Babylon. His conquest of the Jews is described in the Old Testament book of Daniel. **Nebuchadnezzar III** (6th century B.C.) usurped the throne from Darius I for 10 weeks before he was killed.
See also: Babylon.

Nebula, enormous interstellar cloud of gas and dust, often luminous. *Diffuse nebulae* can measure 100 light-years in diameter. *Bright nebulae*, such as the Orion Nebula, appear to shine due to nearby bright stars, whose light they either reflect (reflection nebula) or absorb and re-emit (emission nebula). *Dark nebulae*, such as the Horsehead Nebula, are distant from stars, and hence appear as dark patches in the sky obscuring the light from stars beyond them. *Planetary nebulae* are cast off by stars that have exploded. They are usually symmetrical, forming an expanding shell around the central

A photograph of the Crab Nebula, taken with the 5.5 yards (5 m) Hale telescope at Mount Pelomer. The threadlike filaments are the remnants of the gaseous envelope that was once ejected by the central star. The diffuse light of the nebula is due to electrons, moving almost at the velocity of light, in the nebula's magnetic field. The lower of the two stars close to the middle of the nebula, is the star that exploded in the year 1054. This star is pulsating in both the radio range and the optical range with a period of 1/30 second.

star, often still visible within. The Ring Nebula is an outstanding example.
See also: Solar System.

Nebular hypothesis, theory accounting for the origin of the solar system, developed by Immanuel Kant and given scientific form by P.S. Laplace in the late 1700s. It suggested that a rotating nebula had formed gaseous rings that condensed into the planets and moons, the nebula's nucleus forming the sun.
See also: Solar System.

Necker, Jacques (1732-1804), Swiss-born French banker; finance minister under Louis XVI. In 1777 he tried to raise money to support French involvement in the American Revolution. Later, before the States-General, he proposed sweeping public reforms. His dismissal (1789) led to the storming of the Bastille. Once more he was recalled to office, but he resigned in 1790.
See also: France.

Necrosis, death of a diseased cell, tissue, or organ while still in contact with living cells.

Nectar, sweet substance secreted from the nectaries, or glands, in plant blossoms, stems, and leaves, and from which honeybees make honey. In Greek mythology, the drink of the gods was nectar, which, along with ambrosia-food of the gods-gave them youth and immortality.

Nectarine, (*Prunus persica*), tree in the rose family whose fruit is a smooth-skinned peach. The nectarine and peach trees are very closely related, and both peach and nectarine fruit may grow on either variety of tree.

Needle, long, slender tool used to sew, embroider, crochet, and knit. Needles are generally pointed at one end to allow them to pass easily through material. Most varieties have 'eyes,' holes near one end through

The Hortus cave, near Montpellier in southern France, was used as a summer shelter about 40,000 years ago by a prehistoric human population, known as the Neanderthal people. The reconstruction shows a hunter sharpening a wooden spear. Behind him is a young man, making fire with the help of an elder, and a woman scraping hides. The Mousterian tool kit in the foreground includes points, scrapers, and backed blades.

which the thread is passed so as to be pulled through the material, but crocheting and knitting needles are eyeless. Different sizes and shapes of needles are designed for various uses-upholstery, garment creation or repair, decoration, and surgery. A complex manufacturing process produces the steel needle. Predating the modern steel needle were prehistoric bone or horn needles and medieval iron needles.

Needlepoint, canvas work, or tapestry, form of embroidery. Designs for needlepoint are outlined on a box grid of the work surface or *canvas*. A blunt needle and soft yarn are used to create decorative patterns using such stitches as the cross stitch, tent stitch, knotted stitch, and bargello or Florentine stitch. Used to create pictures or patterns for upholstery or clothing garments, needlepoint is classified as *petit point, gros point,* and *quick point*, according to the size of the boxes (and thus the stitches) on the canvas.

Nefertiti, or Nefretete (fl. c.1372-1350 B.C.), queen of ancient Egypt, wife of Ikhnaton (reigned c.1370-1350 B.C.), and aunt of Tutankhamen. Nefertiti and Ikhnaton promoted monotheism, and their rule was a time of great social and cultural change.

Negev, or Negeb, triangular region of hills, plateaus, and desert in southern Israel, extending south from Beersheba to Elath on the Gulf of Aqaba. It covers around 5,000 sq mi (13,000 sq km), or more than half of Israel. Irrigation has made many areas fertile. It is rich in mineral and natural gas resources.

Negligence, in law, inadvertent failure to act with the degree of care a situation demands. The degree may be determined by a contractual obligation or what the law defines as the standard of conduct of a 'reasonable' person. Conduct of an accident victim that contributed to an accident is contributory negligence and may prevent or reduce compensation. Negligence is usually a civil offense but may lead to a criminal charge, such as manslaughter.

Negotiable instrument, paper document that represents money. Money orders, checks, and traveler's checks as well as promissory notes, certificates of deposit, and bills of exchange are kinds of negotiable instruments. These documents are endorsed, or signed to indicate to whom or what the money value of the document is to be credited. Negotiable instruments, which must fulfil certain requirements for legal transfer, are regulated by the Uniform Commercial Code in all but one state in the United States-Louisiana.

Negroes *See:* African Americans.

Nehemiah (fl. 5th century B.C.), Jewish leader of the return from the Babylonian Captivity. In the Old Testament book of Nehemiah (written with the Book of Ezra by the author of Chronicles), he rebuilt Jerusalem's walls and enforced moral and religious reforms.
See also: Bible.

Nehru, Jawaharlal (1889-1964), first prime minister of independent India (1947-1964). An English-educated lawyer, he embraced the cause of India's freedom after the British massacre of Indian nationalists at Amritsar (1919), becoming president of the Indian National Congress (1929). He spent most of 1930-1936 in prison for his part in civil disobedience campaigns. During World War II he and Gandhi united in their opposition to aiding Britain unless India was freed. Released in 1945 after 3 year's imprisonment, Nehru began negotiations with Britain that culminated, in 1947, in the establishment of independent India. Nehru's daughter Indira Gandhi was prime minister of India (1966-1977 and 1980-1984); his grandson became prime minister in 1984.
See also: India.

Nelson, Horatio (1758-1805), British naval hero who defeated the French and Spanish fleets at the Battle of Trafalgar (1805). His destruction of the French fleet off Aboukir (1798) brought him fame. The scandal of his liaison with Emma, Lady Hamilton, was dispelled by his defeat of the Danes at Copenhagen (1801). The victory at Trafalgar cost Nelson his life, but ensured British naval supremacy for 100 years.
See also: Trafalgar, Battle of.

Neman River (Lithuanian: *Nemunas*; Polish: *Niemen*), river in the former Soviet Union. Approximately 582 mi (937 km) long, the Neman River flows westward from the republic of Byelorussia, then northward through the republic of Lithuania, to empty into Kurland Gulf of the Baltic Sea. Although the river freezes for up to 5 months each year, it is used as a transportation route for timber. The river also supports a dam for a hydroelectric plant.

Nematoda, class of worms known as roundworms. Separate entities within this class are referred to as *nematodes*. Ranging from microscopic size to over 3 ft (1 m) long, these worms live in soil, water, or in plants or animals as parasites. Hookworms, pinworms, and trichinae are all parasitic nematodes that may live in humans or animals.

Nematomorpha *See:* Horsehair worm.

Nemean Games, athletic and musical competition of ancient Greece held every other year at the shrine of Zeus in Nemea, on the Peloponnisos. These games, recorded as early as 597 B.C., along with the Olympic, Isthmian, and Pythian games, made up the national festivals of the ancient Greeks.

Nemerov, Howard (1920-1991), U.S. poet, novelist, and critic noted for his satiric power. His *Collected Poems* (1977) won a National Book Award and a Pulitzer Prize in 1978. Among his novels are *The Melodramatists* (1949) and *The Homecoming Game* (1957).

Nemertinea *See:* Ribbon worm.

Nemesis, in Greek mythology, goddess of just retribution, avenger of evil. She was the agent of punishment for violations of sacred law. More generally, the word 'nemesis' now means any formidable opponent.

Nemtsov, Boris (1959-), Russian politician, vice-premier from 1997-1998. Former physician and governor of Nizjni Novgorod with a reputation of decisiveness and reformatory persuasion. When commencing his duties for the Supreme Soviet he immediately activated an ambitious project of economic reforms. Campaigned against the war in Chechnya. Nemtsov was taken on by President Yeltsin to modernize social policies and to reform the state monopolies in the mining industry. When Yeltsin called back former premier Tchernomyrdin to the Kremlin during the 1998 crisis, Nemtsov resigned.

Nene, or Hawaiian goose (*Nesochen sandvicensis*), bird that lives among the lava in the hills of Hawaii. Through hunting and the ravages of pigs and dogs, it nearly became extinct. By 1950 only 34 survived, 17 in captivity. These were sent to England, where a small population was built up; some were taken back to Hawaii in 1962.

Neodymium, chemical element, symbol Nd; for physical constants see Periodic Table. Neodymium was discovered by C.F. Auer von Welsbach in 1885 after he separated didymia into earths (oxides) called praseodymia and neodymia. Neodymium is a silvery, soft, reactive metal, belonging to the series of elements known as the rare-earth metals. It occurs in the minerals monazite and bastnasite, the 2 principal sources of the rare-earth elements, and is prepared by reducing the anhydrous chloride with calcium. Neodymium is present to the extent of 18% in misch metal. Ion-exchange and solvent extraction techniques have led to much easier isolation of the rare-earth elements. Neodymium and its compounds are used in laser materials, carbon lighting applications, special glasses and enamels, and refractory materials.

Neofascism, post-war ideology based on the fascism of National Socialism. Fascism went down with the collapse of Mussolini's Italy and Nazi Germany in the Second World War. After the war, surviving fascists and National Socialists got organized in various groups and parties. Later on, younger people formed fascist movements as well. For many years the Italian *Movimento Sociale Italiano* (MSI) was the only significant neofascist movement.
See also: Fascism.

Neolithic Period *See:* Stone Age.

Neo-Malthusianism *See:* Malthus, Thomas Robert.

Neon, chemical element, symbol Ne; for physical constants see Periodic Table. Discovered by William Ramsay and Morris W. Travers in 1898, it occurs in the atmosphere to the extent of 1 part in 65,000. It is obtained by liquefaction of liquid air and separated from other gases by fractional distillation. Neon is an inert gas, but is said to form a compound with fluorine. It belongs

N

to the so-called noble gas group of elements. In a vacuum discharge tube, neon glows reddish-orange and is the most intense of all the rare gases at ordinary voltages and currents. The largest use of neon is in neon advertising signs. It is also used in gas lasers, voltage indicators, lightning arrestors, wave meter tubes, and TV tubes. Liquid neon is an economical cryogenic refrigerant.

Neoplatonism, school of philosophical thought, founded by the Greek philosopher Plotinus, influenced by the late writings of Plato. This mystical belief, popular from the 3rd through the 6th centuries, was based on the concept of *emanation*-a process by which an essential sense of things permeates different levels of existence. A diagram of these levels would show the *One*, that incomprehensible thing beyond being, as uppermost, emanating through to the *Logos* or intellect, where ideas reign, then to the *World Soul*, where the intellect and the material world are linked, and finally to the lowest level, the *Material*, the level from which humanity begins. Philosophers ranging from St. Augustine (3rd-4th century) to St. Thomas Aquinas before his conversion to Christianity (13th century) to G.W.F. Hegel (19th century) were influenced by neoplatonism.
See also: Plato; Plotinus.

Nepal

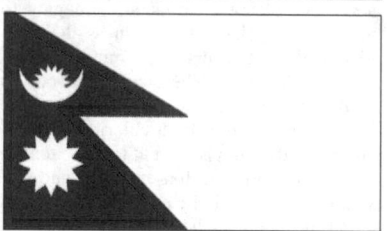

Capital:	Kathmandu
Area:	56,827 sq mi
	(147,181 sq km)
Population:	25,874,000
Language:	Nepali
Government:	Parliamentary monarchy
Independent:	1769
Head of gov.:	Prime minister
Per capita:	US$ 1,400
Monetary unit:	1 Nepalese rupee
	= 100 paisa

Nepal, kingdom of southern Asia, bordered by India, and China (Tibet).
Land and climate. Nepal has an area of 56,827 sq mi (147,181 sq km). It is an elongated country on the southern flanks of the towering Himalayas, extending some 500 mi (805 km) westward from its borders with

India to the Sarda River, a tributary of the Ganges.

Along its borders with India and Tibet are some of the world's loftiest peaks, including Mt. Everest (29,028 ft/8,848 m), the world's highest. The Bheri, Sun Kosi, and other rivers flow through wild gorges between the mountain spurs, forming a series of fertile, longitudinal valleys called *duns*. South of the Dundwa, Sumesar, and Churia Ghati hills (2,000-3,500 ft/610-912 m), are the swampy jungle-plains, called Terai, and the border with India.

Icy-cold temperatures in the high Himalayas sometimes fall to -40°F (1°C). The peaks are always snow-capped. In central Nepal, temperatures average 50°F (10°C) in January and 78°F (25°C) in July. The main rainy season is June through October, the yearly average being about 60 in (152 cm).

People. The population is of mixed Mongolian (Tibeto-Burmans) and Indo-Aryan origin. Its main ethnic groups are the Newars, the Bhotias (who include the Sherpas, well-known mountain guides), and the Gurkhas (noted soldiers). Hinduism, the dominant religion, has long coexisted with Buddhism. About 90% of the people are farmers who live in villages. Although educational programs were begun in the 1950s, only 41.7% are literate (2002). The official language is Nepali.

Economy. In this predominantly agricultural country, crops include rice, wheat, corn, oilseeds, potatoes, jute, tobacco, opium, and cotton. Livestock is important. The Terai forests provide wood, and medicinal herbs are exported from the Himalayan slopes. Nepal has little industry and only a few paved roads. There are several airports, including an international facility at Kathmandu. Tourism is important to the economy.

History. Nepal, the world's only Hindu kingdom, lay isolated from the world until recently. In 1768 Ghurkhas took command of the Nepal Valley, still the home of most Nepalese, but expansion into Tibet was checked by the Chinese. In the south the Nepalese fought the British (1814-1816) and were defeated only after a hard struggle, but remained independent. From 1846 the Rana family reigned as a military oligarchy until 1951, when the present Shah family took control, establishing a constitutional monarchy. Polygamy, child marriage, and the caste system were abolished. In 1962 the *panchayat* system of government was established, in which various political leaders, including the king, serve as prime minister. In response to pro-democracy protests, political parties were legalized in 1990, and the first multiparty elections were held in 1991. In 2001, in a drunken rage, the crown prince killed the complete royal family before committing suicide. The new king, Gvanendra Bir Bikram Shah Dev, declared martial law the following year, due to continuing attacks of the Maostic guerrilla movement. Since 1995, this movement has been fighting for the abolition of the monarchy and the establishment of a people's republic.

Nephrite *See:* Jade.

Nephritis, general term for several diseases, especially glomerulonephritis, involving inflammation of the kidneys caused by infection or degenerative changes in the renal vessels. Acute or chronic renal failure or nephrotic syndrome may result. The treatment is chemicals, drugs, or steroids.

Neptune, in Roman mythology, god of the sea, son of Saturn and Ops. Seafaring Romans prayed to Neptune for safe voyages and returns. He came to be identified with the Greek god Poseidon.
See also: Mythology.

Neptune, fourth-largest planet in the solar system and the eighth from the sun, with a mean distance of 2.7941 billion mi (4.4966 billion km). Its diameter is about 30,760 mi (49,500 km), and it has 2 known moons. Its atmosphere contains hydrogen, helium, methane, and ammonia. Neptune was first discovered in 1846 by Johann Galle using computations by Urbain Leverrier based on the irregularities of Uranus's orbit. Neptune circles the sun once for every 164.8 earth years, and its day (one rotation on its axis) is 15.8 hours.
See also: Planet; Solar System.

Neptunium, chemical element, symbol Np; for physical constants see Periodic Table. Discovered by Edwin M. McMillan and P.H. Abelson in 1940, it was produced by bombarding uranium with neutrons in a cyclotron. Neptunium was the first synthetically produced transuranium element of the actinide series to be discovered. It is produced in nuclear reactors as a by-product of plutonium production. Neptunium is a silvery, radioactive metal. Neptunium-237 has a long half-life (2.14 million years) and is used in neutron detection instruments.

Nereus, in Greek mythology, sea god and father of the sea nymphs known as nereids. He was Homer's 'Old Man of the Sea,' who had the ability to foretell the future and change his shape. Heracles, a Greek hero, obtained directions to the Hesperides as he successfully held Nereus, who changed into numerous shapes during the struggle. Nereus is also known for his prophecy about the Trojan War.
See also: Mythology.

Neri, Saint Phillip (1515-1595), mystical leader and founder of the Congregation of the Oratorians during the Counter-Reformation in Italy. He was ordained in 1551. A room above his church, called an *oratory,* held large audiences for religious conferences and recreation. His congregation is named after this room, as is the musical genre known as oratorio. A spiritual rather than political leader of the church, he claimed to have experienced unusual religious moments, including miracles that are ascribed to him.
See also: Counter-Reformation.

Nernst, Walther Hermann (1864-1941), German physical chemist awarded the 1920 Nobel Prize in chemistry for his discovery of the third law of thermodynamics, dealing with matter at temperatures approaching absolute zero.
See also: Thermodynamics.

Nero (Nero Claudius Caesar, originally Lucius Domitius Ahenobarbus; A.D. 37-68), Roman emperor. He was the adoptive son of the emperor Claudius, whom he succeeded in A.D. 54. Nero had Claudius's son Britannicus murdered in A.D. 55. In A.D. 59 he killed his mother Agrippina, and in A.D. 62 his wife Octavia, Claudius's daughter. Nero rebuilt Rome after the fire in A.D. 64. He accused the Christians of starting it, and the first Roman persecution followed. His cruelty, instability, and imposition of heavy taxes led to a revolt. Deserted by the Praetorian Guard, Nero committed suicide.
See also: Rome, Ancient.

Neruda, Pablo (Neftalí Ricardo Reyes Basualto; 1904-73), Chilean poet, diplomat, and communist leader. He won the 1971 Nobel Prize for literature. His verse collections, written in the surrealist vein, include *Twenty Love Poems and One Song of Despair* (1924), the highly regarded *Canto General* (1950), and *A New Decade: 1958-1967* (tr. 1969).

Nerval, Gérard de (Gérard Labrunie; 1808-1855), French romantic writer who anticipated the symbolist and surrealist movements in French literature. His works include a collection of sonnets, *Les Chimères* (1854); some short stories, *Les Filles de Feu* (1854); and his autobiography, *Aurélia* (1854-1855).

Nerve *See:* Nervous system.

Nerve gas *See:* Chemical and biological warfare.

Nervi, Pier Luigi (1891-1979), Italian civil engineer and architect. In the 1940s he invented *ferrocemento,* a form of reinforced concrete. Notable among his bold and imaginative designs are the Turin exposition hall, the railway station in Naples, and the Olympic buildings in Rome. He also collaborated on the UNESCO headquarters in Paris.
See also: Architecture.

Nervous system, network of specialized tissue that coordinates and controls the various activites of the body, both voluntary and involuntary. The nervous system can be

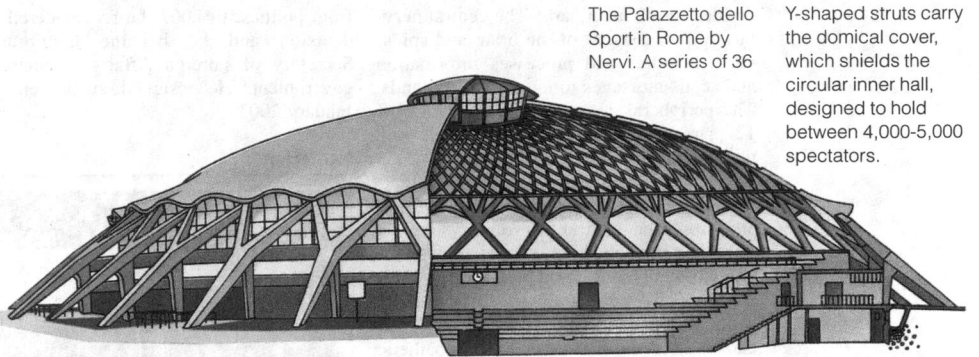

The Palazzetto dello Sport in Rome by Nervi. A series of 36 Y-shaped struts carry the domical cover, which shields the circular inner hall, designed to hold between 4,000-5,000 spectators.

N

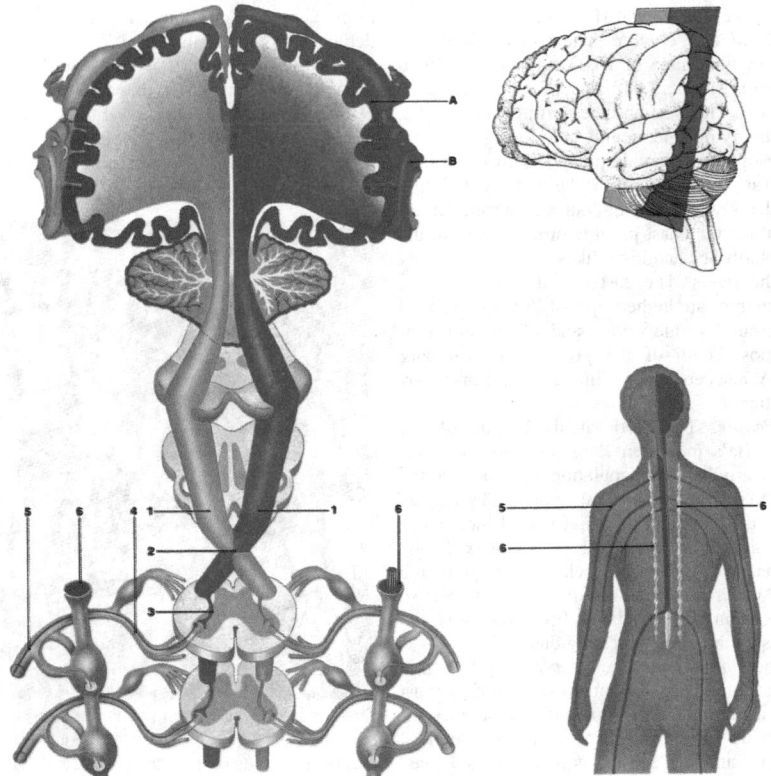

The motor nervous system controls the voluntary activity of the skeletal muscles. Integrated messages from the motor centers in the spinal cord, brainstem, cerebellum, and cerebral cortex coordinate posture and movement. Many nerve cells that transmit impulses to muscles are located in motor areas near the surface of the cerebral cortex (A), especially in the area known as the motor cortex. The body parts shown on the motor 'homunculus' (B) are controlled by neurons at those locations on the cortex. The size of each body part is proportional to the amount of cortical area serving it. Nerve fibers from the cortex collect and descend through the spinal cord in corticospinal, or pyramidal, tracts. Because the two lateral corticospinal tracts (1), which contain 75% to 90% of the fibers, cross (2) in the medulla, each cerebral hemispere mainly controls muscles on the other side of the body. The corticospinal tracts, each of which may contain more than a million fibers (3) at each level of the spinal cord. These fibers relay impulses to roots (4) of spinal nerves (5), which carry the messages directly to skeletal muscle fibers. The two sympathetic trunks shown (6) belong to the autonomic nervous system, which controls the involuntary actions of smooth and cardiac muscle and regulates the activity of glands.

N

divided into 2 main parts. The central nervous system consists of the brain and spinal cord. It stores and processes information and sends messages to muscles and glands. The peripheral nervous system consists of 12 pairs of cranial nerves located in and near the medulla oblongata at the rear of the brain and 31 pairs of spinal nerves originating in the spinal cord. It carries messages to and from the central nervous system. A third system, the autonomic nervous system, normally considered part of the peripheral nervous system, controls involuntary actions such as heartbeat and digestion. It can be divided into 2 parts: the sympathetic system, which speeds up the heartbeat and prepares the body for 'fight-or-flight,' and the parasympathetic system, which slows down the heartbeat and controls the body's vegetative functions. The balance between the 2 systems is regulated by the central nervous system. The nervous system transmits messages by means of highly specialized nerve cells, called neurons. Tubelike extensions called axons and dendrites branch out from the neuron cell body. Axons, which vary greatly in length and speed of conduction, carry messages. An axon from one neuron may transmit impulses to as many as 1,000 other neurons. Dendrites receive impulses from axons. Adjacent neurons communicate through specialized contact points, called synapses. Messages are also carried from axon to dendrite by chemical messengers known as neurotransmitters across the synaptic gap. The elaborate circuitry involved in synaptic contact is responsible for much of behavior, from simple reflex reactions such as the 'knee-jerk response' to complex thought-communication patterns.

Nestor *See:* Messenia.

Nestorians, members of the heretical Christian sect named for Nestorius (patriarch of Constantinople, 428-431). The sect was condemned by the Council of Ephesus (431) for rejecting the title 'Mother of God' for the Virgin Mary, and teaching the existence of 2 persons-divine and human-in Jesus. The modern Nestorian (Assyrian) Church has about 100,000 members.

Netanyahu, Benjamin (1949-   ), Israeli diplomat and politician. He studied in the United States and after a business career became a permanent representative of Israel at the United Nations (1984-1988) and vice-secretary at the Ministry of Foreign Affairs (1988-1991). He became the leader of the right-wing Likud party. After his brother was killed when taking part in the liberation of Israeli hostages in 1976, Netanyahu proved to be a determined enemy of terrorism. As opposition leader he was against granting major concessions to the Palestinians and sharply criticized the government for the persisting acts of terror by Hamas and the Islamic Jihad. During the 1996 elections he defeated Shimon Peres, then prime minister. During Netanyahu's period in office the progress in peace negotiations that had been made under Shamir and Peres was nullified. In 1999 Netanyahu lost the elections and decided to withdraw from politics. In 2002, he reconsidered his decision and he became temporarily Secretary of Foreign Affairs in Sharon's government. He resigned at the end of January 2003.

Netherlands

Capital:	Amsterdam
Area:	16,033 sq mi (41,526 sq km)
Population:	16,068,000
Language:	Dutch
Government:	Constitutional monarchy
Independent:	1648 (1814 constitutional monarchy)
Head of gov.:	Prime minister
Per capita:	US$ 25,800
Monetary unit:	1 guilder = 100 cents

Netherlands, constitutional monarchy of western Europe bordering the North Sea, Germany, and Belgium. It is popularly but inaccurately called Holland.
Land and climate. The country is a flat, low-lying area of 16,033 sq mi (41,526 sq km). Most (13,042 sq mi/33,779 sq km) is land. The west and the north consist of flat, low-lying land, mainly below sea level (lowest point: Alexanderpolder, -6,2m). The land was reclaimed from the sea by building dikes and pumping out the water. Dunes along the coast provide protection from the North Sea and high dikes are situated along the rivers. The east and the south of the country are higher; up to 105 m on the sand grounds of the Veluwe and 322 m in the outmost south of the province of Limburg (Vaalseberg). The climate is mild and maritime.
People. The Netherlands is one of the world's most densely populated countries. Nearly half the population lives close to the three largest cities-Amsterdam, The Hague, and Rotterdam, the chief port. There are 11 universities, including the famous public ones at Leiden, Utrecht, Groningen, and Amsterdam. Dutch is the official language. Roman Catholicism, Protestantism and Islam are the major religions.
Economy. There are reserves of oil, natural gas, and coal, but most raw materials must be imported for industries; major ones include oil-refining, iron and steel, textiles, machinery, electrical equipment, and plastics. Dairy produce, the basis of The Netherlands' intensive agriculture, sustains a large food-processing industry. International financial services and petroleum interests, the diamond industry, and tourism contribute significantly, as does fishing and the advanced transportation system, which includes the natural waterways and canals that crisscross the country. Rotterdam, at the Rhine's mouth, handles more cargo than any other ocean port in the world. The Netherlands is a member of the European Union.
History. After the Romans left the Low Countries in the 5th century, Frankish tribes dominated. Dukes of Burgundy in the later Middle Ages began unifying the regions small principalities, which included Holland, Brabant, and Flanders. Through intermarriage, the Spanish King Phillip II was sovereign until the growing popularity of Calvinism in the late 16th century caused the Dutch to expel the Catholic Spanish, except in the south. Naval and economic eminence made the 17th century a golden age for the independent Dutch republic, then Europe's leading commercial nation. Philosopher Baruch Spinoza and the natural scientist Anton van Leeuwenhoek flourished, as did painters Rembrandt van Rijn and Jan Vermeer (the late-19th-century Dutch painter Vincent van Gogh would equal their fame eventually). Wars and treaties with other European nations brought political confusion and economic decline after 1715. Napoleonic control (1795-1813) and revolutionary ferment ended with the issuance of a constitution (1814) providing a monarchy to rule the United Kingdom of The Netherlands, formed by the Congress of Vienna (1815). The kingdom ended (1830) when the Catholic people of the south seceded, founding modern-day Belgium. But The Netherlands remained a constitutional monarchy and is today a parliamentary democracy. Neutral in World War I but occupied by the Nazis in World War II, The Netherlands afterward became one of NATO's original members. In 1949 the Dutch recognized the independence of Indonesia, their colony since the 17th centu-

The cheese market of Alkmaar in the Netherlands, has little economic significance today. It is being maintained chiefly as a tourist attraction.

ry, and in 1963 transferred to it another colony, West New Guinea. The Netherlands Antilles-2 groups of Caribbean islands-are still under Dutch control.

From 1994 to 2002, the country was governed by a center-left coalition. It was the first time since World War ll that the Christian Democrats were not part of the government. However, at the 2002 and 2003 elections, they won a lot of seats (43 seats in 2002 and 44 in 2003 of the 150 seats in total) and they became part of the coalition again.

Netherlands Antilles

Capital:	Willemstad
Area:	308 sq mi (798 sq km)
Population:	202,000
Language:	Dutch
Government:	Semi-autonomous overseas territory of the Netherlands
Independent:	1954 (semi-autonomy)
Head of gov.:	Prime minister
Per capita:	more than US$ 9,635
Monetary unit:	1 Antillean guilder = 100 cents

Netherlands Antilles, also called the Dutch Antilles or Dutch West Indies, 2 groups of islands in the Caribbean Sea, collectively an autonomous part of the Netherlands since 1954. The southern group-the Leewards-includes Curaçao (location of the capital, Willemstad), Aruba, and Bonaire. They lie off the coast of Venezuela. The northern

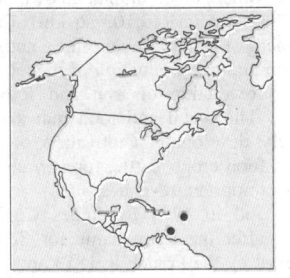

This photograph shows how sand is being pumped up, in order to form the long dike sections of Southwest Flevoland (IJsselmeer).

group-the Windwards-includes Saba, St. Eustacius, and St. Martin, which are east of Puerto Rico. The processing of Venezuelan oil accounts for the majority of export earnings. There is also tourism and offshore banking. Aruba was constitutionally separated from the other islands in 1986. The islands are still financially dependent on the Netherlands. In 1995 St. Martin was devastated by hurricane Luís. In 2001 U.S. government personnel came to assist narcotic checks. The laundering of money will also be curbed.
See also: Netherlands.

Netsuke, originally an elegant belt button, part of the Japanese way of dressing. Initially made of wood and used to carry small objects. Developed in the 18th century into an ornamental pendent, usually made out of ivory or metal, with a mere decorative function. Because of its beautiful lacquerwork and many folkloristic and mythological portrayals, it enjoys the increasing appreciation of art lovers.

Nettle, common name for a family of plants (Urticaceae) including shrubs and trees, many species of whose leaves bear brittle hollow hairs that can penetrate the skin. The hairs contain fomic acid, a toxic substance that causes irritation and sometimes blistering. Nevertheless, cattle eat stinging nettles, and in parts of Europe young nettles are cooked and eaten.

Nettle tree *See:* Hackberry.

Netzahualcóyotl (pop. 2,500,000), city in south-central Mexico, east of Mexico City. Founded as a suburb (1900), then incorporated as a city (1963), it has rapidly grown to become the second most populous city in the country.
See also: Mexico.

Neuralgia, severe pain along the course of a nerve, often coming in sharp bursts and normally lasting for a short time. Nerves commonly affected include the digital nerves of toes and facial nerves. Neuralgia may be caused by inflammation or trauma.
See also: Nervous system.

Neuritis, inflammation of a peripheral nerve. More generally, any disorder of the peripheral nervous system that interferes with sensation, muscle control, or both may be considered neuritis. Symptoms include numbness, tingling, weakness, and in extreme cases, paralysis. Neuritis often occurs in patients with rheumatoid arthritis, and various genetic disorders.
See also: Nervous system.

Neurofibromatosis, hereditary disorder that produces pigmented spots and tumors of the skin, tumors of peripheral, optic, and acoustic nerves, and subcutaneous bony deformities. Deep tumors are treated by surgical removal or radiation. The underlying cellular disorder is unknown, and no general treatment is available.

Neurology, branch of medicine concerned with diseases of the brain, spinal cord, and peripheral nervous system, including multiple sclerosis, epilepsy, migraine (headache), stroke, Parkinson's disease, neuritis, encephalitis, meningitis, brain tumors, muscular dystrophy, and myasthenia gravis.
See also: Nervous system.

Neuron *See:* Nervous system.

Neuropathology, study of the intrinsic causes of disorders of the nervous system.
See also: Nervous system.

Neurosis, mild mental disorder involving any of a number of varied symptoms, including phobias, anxiety, psychosomatic illnesses, and compulsive behavior. Neurosis is commonly distinguished from psychosis in that psychosis entails a loss of touch with reality, whereas neurosis does not.
See also: Mental illness.

Neurotransmitters *See:* Nervous system.

Neutra, Richard Joseph (1892-1970), Austrian-born U.S. architect who brought the International style of architecture to the United States. The Tremaine House (1947) in Santa Barbara, Calif., demonstrates his skill in relating a building to its setting.

Neutral countries, countries that are not members of the great militairy alliances. They first came together in Belgrade (1961) on the initiative of Nasser, Nehru and Tito, then leaders of Egypt, India and Jugoslavia, respectively. They strive for peaceful coexistence, independence in foreign politics and banishment of colonialism in all its forms. They tried to counteract a further break-up of the world in power blocks. They regard the antithesis between East and West as less important than the contrast between rich and poor. When the Cold War ended, the organization lost sigificance and was devaluated.

Neutrality, status of a country that elects not to participate in a war between other countries. Under international law the boundaries and territorial waters of a neutral state must be respected.

Neutralization, in chemistry, reaction in which the hydrogen ion of an acid and the

N

hydroxyl ion of a base unite to form water and a salt.
See also: Acid; Base.

Neutrino, elementary particle with no electrical charge emitted during the decay of other particles. The existence of the neutrino was first postulated by Wolfgang Pauli in 1930 to account for the conservation of energy in the beta decay process, but the particle was not actually detected until 1956. There are distinct types of neutrinos associated with the electron and the muon. All 3 are part of the class of elementary particles known as leptons. Each type of neutrino has a corresponding particle, called an antineutrino, which differs from its neutrino only in a quality known as spin. Neutrinos are stable particles, being created or destroyed only in interactions involving the weak nuclear force, one of the 4 fundamental forces of nature. In 1998, Japanese and American researchers were able to demonstrate that neutrinos do have mass, a fact which had been unknown previously.
See also: Lepton.

Neutron, electrically uncharged elementary particle with a mass slightly greater than that of the proton. All elements except hydrogen contain neutrons in their nuclei, along with protons. Free neutrons (those not bound within a nucleus) or excess neutrons in the nucleus of heavy elements are subject to a process called beta decay. In this process the neutron decays in a proton, an electron, and an antineutrino. The neutron is a member of the baryon class of elementary particles. It was discovered by James Chadwick in 1932. Its antiparticle, the antineutron, was discovered in 1956.
See also: Chadwick, Sir James; Quark.

Neutron bomb, variant form of the hydrogen bomb in which an atomic-bomb trigger is surrounded by non-fissionable material, the result being a much smaller blast than in a hydrogen bomb, along with a rain of neutrons that would leave non-living structures relatively intact while killing living things. Although theoretically feasible, no neutron bomb has ever been tested.
See also: Nuclear weapon.

Neutron star, hypothetical extremely small star, of large mass but very great density. It is believed that when certain stars explode as supernovas their cores collapse and form either a neutron star or a *collapsar* (black hole). Neutron stars are thought to be made up of elementary particles and neutrons created from the compressed protons and electrons of the original supernova core, emitting powerful X-rays and reaching extremely high temperatures in the first few months of their existence. They may be more than 72,000 times smaller in diameter than the sun but with the same mass. In 1938 scientists predicted the existence of neutron stars, and in 1967 astronomers in Great Britain located *pulsars*-objects in space that emit radio waves, believed to be rotating neutron stars.
See also: Pulsar.

Nevada (Silver State, Sagebrush State, Battle Born State; pop. 1,677,000), state in western United States in the Rocky Mountain region; bordered by Oregon, Idaho, Utah, Arizona, and California.
Most of Nevada lies in the Great Basin, a vast desert area. Principal cities are Las Vegas and Reno. The capital is Carson City. Tourism-to the states's canyons, lakes, ski resorts as well as to its casinos and nightclubs-is Nevada's main source of income. Mining and manufacturing are also important. The most valuable mineral products are gold, diatomite, petroleum, and silver. Agriculture accounts for only a small part of the economy. Livestock ranching is the main source of agricultural income. Chief crops are hay, alfalfa, barley, potatoes, and wheat. In 1776, the first Europeans-Spanish explorers-came to the area. In 1848, after the Mexican War, the U.S. acquired the area from Mexico. In the 1950s and 1960s, Nevada became a center for testing and research in atomic and nuclear energy.

Nevelson, Louise (1900-1988), Russian-born U.S. sculptor famous for her intricate wood constructions, both freestanding and wall-hung, that suggest vast ranges of box-like shelves with found objects placed on them.

Nevis *See:* Saint Kitts and Nevis.

Nevsky, Alexander (1220-1263), Russian national hero. His military victories over the Swedes at the Neva River (1240) and over the Teutonic Livonian knights on the ice of Lake Peipus (1242) made him pre-eminent among Russian princes. He later became grand duke of Kiev and Novgorod (1252).

Newark (pop. 275,000), largest city of New Jersey and the seat of Essex County. Eight miles (13 km) west of Manhattan, Newark is a major transportation, commercial, and industrial center. The port was opened during World War I and became one of the nation's major shipbuilding centers. Industries now include chemicals, alcoholic beverages, automobile parts, electrical equipment, foodstuffs, and paints. Since the 1930s, however, Newark's economic and population growth rates have declined because of urban poverty and decay. Newark is the site of several universities, including Newark Campus of Rutgers University. The huge waterfront development of Port Newark is run by the Port Authority of New York and New Jersey, as is Newark Airport, one of New York City's three major air terminals.
See also: New Jersey.

New Britain (pop. 312,000) island in the Bismarck Archipelago east of the island of New Guinea, and part of the nation of Papua New Guinea since 1975. It is approximately 300 mi (480 km) long and 50 mi (80 km) wide, with a center portion containing active volcanic mountains. Previously it was controlled by Germany (1884-1914), Australia (1914-1942), and Japan (1942-1945). William Dampier, an English navigator, was the first European to reach the island (1700). The people of New Britain, mostly Melanesians, farm and fish.

New Brunswick (pop. 724,000), province in the Southeast of Canada which borders on the United States and the Gulf of St. Lawrence; 28,366 sq mi (73,440 sq km). Capital: Fredericton. Low-lying with foothills from the Appalachian Mountains; deeply indented coast.
Extraction of coal, natural gas, plaster, lead, zinc and copper. Traditionally, most income came from the exploitation of minerals and forests, but in the 1990s industry (dairy, meat and paper industry) and the provision of services has become more important.
Visited in 1534 by the French sailor Jaques Cartier, but not penetrated into until a century later; France handed it over to England with the Treaty of Utrecht (1713). The province has been Canadian since 1867. The city has universities which date back to 1785, 1840 and 1864.
For 64% of the population English is the mother tongue, 33% speaks French. There is a community of 10,000 Native Americans. The province was named after the British royal house of Brunswick-Lünenburg, the House of Hanover.
See also: Canada.

New Caledonia (pop. 202,000), French overseas territory in the South Pacific. Includes: New Caledonia (Grande Terre), the Loyauté Islands, Isle de Pins, the Bélep archipelago, the Chesterfield Islands and several other small uninhabited archipelagos; 7,378 sq mi (19,103 sq km). Capital: Nouméa. Primary economic activities: tourism and the production of nickel. There is also extraction of iron and ferromanganese. The metal and food industries are strongly developing. Cultivation of copra, coffee, food crops, cattle, forestry and fishing are important revenues.
Discovered in 1774 by James Cook and named after the Latin name for Scotland. Annexed by the French in 1853 and French overseas territory since 1946. 43% of the population is native (Kanakans), 37% is European (most of them of French origin, called Caldoches). The remaining part of the population is Vietnamese, Polynesian and Indonesian. Since the early 1980s part of the population struggles for independence from France. Occasionally this struggle becomes violent. In July 1998 the French parliament agreed to grant New Caledonia limited autonomy.

Newcastle (pop. 429,000), city in New South Wales, southeastern Australia, on the Pacific Ocean, at the mouth of Hunter River. Coal, steel, and other industrial products are produced and transported through this port city. Newcastle was founded as a European convict settlement in 1804 and recognized as a city in 1885.
See also: Australia.

Newcastle upon Tyne (pop. 284,000), city in northern England, on the North Sea and the river Tyne. It is a center for industry, known mainly because of its coal mines, which have been active since the 18th century. It is also a center for education. An ancient Roman community, the city received its current name from the 'new castle' built

there by William the Conqueror (1080).
See also: England.

Newcomb, Simon (1835-1909), U.S. astronomer. He computed new planetary tables whose data were so accurate that they were used for more than 50 years. He was director of the *American Nautical Almanac* (1877-1897) and taught at Johns Hopkins University (1884-1894).
See also: Astronomy.

Newcomen, Thomas (1663-1729), British inventor of the first practical steam engine, c.1711. His device, employed mainly to pump water from mines, used steam pressure to raise the piston and, after condensation of the steam, atmospheric pressure to force it down again: it was thus called an atmospheric steam engine.
See also: Steam engine.

New Deal, program adopted by President Franklin D. Roosevelt to alleviate the effects of the Great Depression. During its initial phase, the New Deal was centered on programs designed to stimulate economic activity, reduce unemployment, and introduce regulations to control business practices that threatened to deepen the depression. Measures were also taken to control the Stock Exchange. Though the term 'New Deal' fell out of use, much of its legislation has remained, and it altered the direction of social legislation, increasing government intervention into the economy and changing the U.S. public's attitude to the role of the federal government.

New Delhi (pop. 7,207,000), capital of India, on the Jumna River, in the north-central part of the country. It was built by the British in 1912-1929 to the south of Delhi, replacing Calcutta as the capital. Designed as a spacious city by the architect Sir Edwin Lutyens, New Delhi is noted for its official buildings, large shops, and industrial quarters.
See also: India.

New Economic Policy (NEP), plan adopted (1921-1928) by the USSR to deal with the effects of the previous civil war years. The NEP made concessions to private enterprise in industry, trade, and agriculture and allowed peasants to sell produce profitably. By 1927 the NEP had successfully restored the prewar national income level.

New England, Dominion of, separate colonial government within the colonies established in 1686 by King James II, controlling Connecticut, Massachusetts, New Hampshire, New Jersey, New York, Plymouth, and Rhode Island. Used to further English control of the American colonies, this government was resented by colonists and abolished with the overthrow of King James II (1688).

Newfoundland (pop. 568,000), province in Canada, consisting of an island bearing the same name and the coast of Labrador; 156,709 sq mi (405,720 sq km). Capital: St. John's (pop. 100,000), easternmost city of Canada. Rocky, with a deeply indented coast

and many islands; densely wooded; relatively poor province where the exploitation of minerals is the most important source of income. The extraction of iron (90%), lead, copper, zinc, uranium, gold, silver, petroleum and natural gas are important. Hydroelectric power station. The island of Newfoundland was discovered in 1497 by John Cabot. 98% of the population speaks English as its native tongue. 5,000 Indians and 4,000 Inuits live in the area. Initially the term Newfoundland was used to indicate the entire area of Atlantic North America.
See also: Canada.

Newfoundland dog, breed of large, heavy dog known for its strength, patience, and intelligence. It weighs up to 150 lb (68 kg) and stands as high as 28 in (71 cm) at the shoulder. Its webbed feet and thick oily black or black-and-white coat aids it in performing water rescues. The breed is most likely a cross between the Great Pyrenees dog of the Basque region of Europe and dogs native to Newfoundland.

New France, North American territories held by France from the 16th century to 1763. These included what is now Quebec. France lost these territories to Britain in a series of colonial wars.

Newgate Prison, prison in London, England. Begun as a jail above the West Gate to London in the early 15th century, it continued to house hardened criminals along with debtors and minor offenders until its demolition (1902). The public often complained of the unsanitary and unfair conditions of this jail. Early in the 19th century, prison reform allowed debtors to await trial in separate facilities.

New Granada, 16th-century Spanish colony in northwestern South America that included present-day Colombia, Panama, Ecuador, and Venezuela. Named by Gonzalo Jiménez de Quesada in 1537, it was attached to the viceroyalty of Peru until 1717, when it became a viceroyalty itself until independence in 1819.

New Guinea, world's second largest island, in the southwestern Pacific, just south of the equator and separated from northern Australia by the Torres Strait and the Arafura and Coral Seas. The island has an area of 319,713 sq mi (828,057 sq km), being about 1,500 mi (2,410 km) long and 400 mi (640 km) wide. The interior is mountainous, the coastal lowlands densely forested. Djaja Peak is the highest mountain, at 16,503 ft (5,030 m). The western part of New Guinea is a province of Indonesia, Irian Jaya. Papua New Guinea, the eastern part, is self-governing since 1973. Melanesians and Papuans are the two largest population groups. In remote mountain areas there are tribes that still practice headhunting. New Guinea was explored by Portuguese in the 16th century and named for Guinea, then a Portuguese colony in West Africa. It was later colonized by the Dutch, Germans, and British. The German sector was taken over by Australia after World War I. The island was bitterly con-

tested by the Japanese and the Allies during World War II.

New Hampshire (Granite State; pop. 1,173,000), state in New England, the northeastern region of the United States; bordered by Canada, Maine, the Atlantic Ocean, Massachusetts, and Vermont. The state's major cities line the Merrimack River, the power source for New Hampshire's early factories and cotton mills. Principal cities are Manchester, Nashua, and Concord (capital). Wholesale and retail trade and other service industries have supplanted manufacturing as New Hampshire's major source of income; however, manufacturing remains important to the state's economy. Major manufactured goods are machinery, electrical and electronic equipment, wood and paper products, fabricated metal products, plastics, and leather products.
The first white settlement was established by England in 1623. In 1641, New Hampshire was made part of Massachusetts, but again became a separate colony-one of the original 13-in 1680.

New Haven (pop. 130,000), third largest city in Connecticut, a river port leading to Long Island Sound, and the seat of Yale University. New Haven is noted as a cultural center and is important for its varied industrial products. It was founded in 1638 by Puritans from Boston led by John Davenport and Theophilus Eaton.
See also: Connecticut.

New Hebrides Islands, *See:* Vanuatu.

Ne Win, U (Shu Maung; 1911-2002), Burmese general, political leader, and president (1974-1981). After serving as prime minister, he assumed power in 1962 in an army coup and attempted to establish a form of socialist republic in Burma. After resigning the presidency, he remained head of the ruling party until 1988.

New Ireland, island in the Bismarck Archipelago north of New Britain, part of the nation of Papua New Guinea since 1975. It is a narrow and rugged volcanic island, approximately 230 mi (370 km) long. The first European to reach and name the island was Philip Carteret. Germany

Lake Winnipesaukee, whose Indian name means 'smile of the great spirit', is the largest lake in New Hampshire. It is located in a major summer resort area in the central part of the state.

N

N

claimed the island (1884) until, at the end of World War I, Australia took over its control. Except for the Japanese occupation (1942-1945), Australia administered the island until the independence of Papua New Guinea (1975).

New Jersey (Garden State; pop. 7,879,000), state in the Middle Atlantic region of eastern United States; bordered by New York, the Atlantic Ocean, Delaware, and Pennsylvania. Two great rivers, the Delaware and the Hudson, flow along New Jersey's borders. The Delaware Water Gap, formed by the Delaware River as it cuts through the Kittatinny Mountains, is one of the most scenic areas in the East. Many beaches and seaside resorts, including Atlantic City and Asbury Park, line the Atlantic coast. Principal cities are Newark, Jersey City, and Paterson. The capital is Trenton. It is the most densely populated state in the United States.

New Jersey is a leading industrial state. Its chief industrial products are chemicals, processed foods, electronic and electrical equipment, nonelectrical machinery, printed materials, and fabricated metal products. Service industries, including tourism, account for a large share of the state's income. The first European settlers were Dutch and Swedish traders who arrived in the 1630s. England won control of the area in 1664. New Jersey, one of the original 13 colonies, became a prosperous farming area. The site of some of the American Revolution's major battles, New Jersey became the nation's third state in 1787. Through the 1800s, New

Jersey's importance as an industrial and transportation center grew.

Newly Industrializing Countries (NIC's), countries which have evolved from developing countries to industrialized nations since the 1970s. After decolonization they initially kept themselves occupied with industrial production for the internal market, but succeeded, with the help of foreign (Western) investments, to tap export markets. Factors that, in varying combinations, contributed to the growth were e.g. low wages at home, social and political stability, a large internal market, the raise in oil prices and an international surplus of capital. The industrialization concerns not only the production of footwear, clothing and wood, but also branches of industry like shipbuilding, electronics and car manufacturing. Examples of Newly Industrializing Countries are Singapore, Taiwan, Hong Kong, South Korea, Brazil, Mexico, Malaysia and the Philippines.

Newman, Barnett (1905-1970), U.S. painter. He was a member of the abstract expressionist school of painting based in New York City after World War II. Newman's large canvases often consisted of a simple, stark vertical image presented on a large field of color. His work influenced the color field movement of the 1960s as well as the minimalist artists.
See also: Abstract expressionism.

Newman, John Henry Cardinal (1801-1890), English religious thinker, writer, and founder of the Oxford Movement. Ordained by the Church of England (1824), he became an Oxford Movement leader, calling for an emphasis on traditional belief that was akin to Catholicism. He converted to Catholicism (1845) and later became a cardinal (1879). Outspoken and often controversial both as an Anglican and as a Catholic, his beliefs were expressed in influential writings-his Oxford Movement tracts (*Tracts for the Times*, begun in 1833) and his Catholic autobiography *Apologia pro vita sua* (1864).
See also: Oxford Movement.

Newman, Paul (1925-   ), U.S. film and stage actor, director. Newman first appeared on Broadway in *Picnic* (1953), and on film in *The Silver Chalice* (1955). He appeared in Tennessee Williams's *Sweet Bird of Youth* both on the Broadway stage (1959) and in the film version (1962). He has starred in many films, including *The Hustler* (1961), *Butch Cassidy and the Sundance Kid* (1969), *The Sting* (1973), *The Color of Money* (1986; Academy Award), *Nobody's Fool* (1994), and *Message in a Bottle* (1999). He also directed *Rachel, Rachel* (1968), *The Effect of Gamma Rays on Man-*

Each year, Mardi Gras (French for 'Fat Tuesday') in New Orleans, a festival that was introduced into America by French colonists in 1766 is celebrated. It attracts visitors from all over the United States. Already weeks before this day, members of carnival troupes will pass through the streets in parades.

in-the-Moon Marigolds (1972), *Harry and Son* (1984), and *The Road to Perdition* (2002).

New mathematics, educational curricula developed in the 1950s and 1960s, emphasizing knowledge of mathematical concepts and principles over the mastery of mathematical computation. This educational movement, inspired by technological leaps, left many educators and parents confused. While some have acclaimed new math curricula, others have doubted its merits.

New Mexico (Land of Enchantment; pop. 1,730,000), state in the Southwest of the United States, Bordering on Mexico, Arizona, Colorado, Oklahoma, Texas and Utah; 121,639 sq mi (314,925 sq km). Capital: Santa Fe. Despite a fast-growing population after WW II, New Mexico is one of the least populated states of the U.S. Almost 40% of the population is of Mexican or Spanish descent. Next to English, Spanish is a frequently used language. Approximately 10% of the population is Native American, like the Navaho, Pueblo, Mescalero Apache and Zuni. In the center of the state are the Rocky Mountains; the eastern area consists of highland prairies and the western part is desert-like.
There is cattle breeding and some agriculture and horticulture. Extraction of oil, natural gas, uranium, copper, zinc, potash and manganese. Graphic, food, chemical and wood industries. Booming tourism.
It is likely that the area was already populated by Indian tribes some 10,000 years ago. New Mexico became part of the U.S. after the Mexican-American war (1848). In 1912 the state became a full member of the Union. The world's first atom bomb was detonated at Alamogordo (1945). The defense industry, the discovery of oil and the warm, dry climate were responsible for the rapid population growth after WW II.

New Netherland, Dutch colonial territory extending roughly from what is now Albany, N.Y., to Manhattan Island, and including parts of New Jersey, Connecticut, and Delaware. It was granted in 1621 by the government of Holland to the Dutch West India Company. In 1626 the company purchased Manhattan Island from Native Americans and named it New Amsterdam. In 1664 the British seized New Amsterdam, changing its name to New York.

New Orleans (pop. 477,000), city in Louisiana, between the Mississippi River and Lake Pontchartrain, 107 mi (172 km) from the river's mouth. Called the Crescent City because of its placement on a bend in the river, New Orleans is one of the world's great ports and the business and financial capital of the South. Excellent transport facilities serve the port, and the city is surrounded by oil and natural gas deposits. It is also a center of the aerospace, shipbuilding, oil and chemical industries, and has many manufacturing and processing plants. The city is famed for its French Quarter (Vieux Carré) and the Mardi Gras Carnival. It is also known as the birthplace of jazz. Its varied population includes French-speaking Cre-

oles, who are descended from early French and Spanish settlers. The Creole cookery of New Orleans is world famous.
See also: Louisiana.

New Orleans, Battle of *See:* Jackson, Andrew.

New South Wales, oldest state of Australia, lying in southeastern Australia between the Great Dividing Range and the Pacific Ocean. Because of its mild climate, good harbors, sandy beaches, and fertile land, it is the most populous state in Australia. Agriculture, mining (coal, silver, zinc), and manufacturing are the major components of the economy. Sydney, its capital and coastal city, contains the majority of the population, made up of people of British and other European descent, native Aborigines, and Asian immigrants. James Cook, an English navigator, was the first European to reach New South Wales (1770). With a group of English convicts, Captain Arthur Phillip established the first English settlement (1788).
See also: Australia.

Newspaper, daily or weekly publication of current domestic and foreign news. In 59 B.C., Julius Caesar ordered the daily publication of a newsheet, the *Acta diurna*. Johann Guttenberg's invention of movable type in the mid-15th century was an important step in the development of newspapers. *The London Gazette* (1665) was the first paper issued regularly in newspaper format. The first American paper was the *Boston Newsletter* (1704). James Gordon Bennett, Horace Greeley, and Adolph Ochs publishing daily penny papers, such as the *New York Sun* (1833), the *New York Herald* (1835), and the *New York Times* (1851). With the end of the Civil War, newspapers became increasingly sensational. In the late 19th and early 20th centuries Joseph Pulitzer and William Randolph Hearst were czars of vast newspaper empires and important forces in international politics. Technological advances in the 1970s, such as photocomposition and satellites, have changed the industry.

New Sweden, Swedish colony on the Delaware River extending from the present site of Trenton, N.J., to the mouth of the river. Founded by the New Sweden Company in 1638 under the leadership of Peter Minuit, it was taken over by the Dutch, led by Peter Stuyvesant, in 1655.

Newt, any of various small salamanders found in many areas of the Northern Hemisphere. The adults feed on small animals and spend much of their time on land, but they return to water to breed. The male deposits a bag containing the sperm cells that is picked up by the female. She lays her eggs one at a time, wrapping each in the leaf of a water plant. The eggs hatch into larvae that have external gills. By the fall, they emerge onto land as efts, with lungs and rough skins.

New Testament, part of the Bible that is distinctively Christian. It consists of 27 books recording the life and teachings of Jesus Christ and the beginnings of Christianity. The books were written in the popular form of Greek spoken in Palestine since the time of Alexander the Great. They include the 4 Gospels (Matthew, Mark, Luke, and John), the Acts of the Apostles, the Epistles (early evangelical letters), the Book of Revelation, and various others. The earliest fragments of the New Testament date from the early 2nd century. The present canon, used by all major Christian churches, was not decided on until 367, when other early Christian writings were excluded from the compilation.

New Thought, school of religious and philosophical thought originated in the mid-19th century United States and emphasizing the power of the mind to solve problems and heal the body. New Thought was developed mainly by Phineas Quimby (1802-1866), who was influenced by New England transcendentalists such as Ralph Waldo Emerson. It influenced the later Christian Science movement, begun by Mary Baker Eddy.
See also: Bible.

Newton, Sir Isaac (1642-1727), English natural philosopher and mathematician, the discoverer of the calculus and author of the theory of universal gravitation. Professor of mathematics at Cambridge University (1669-1701), he wrote *Mathematical Principles of Natural Philosophy* (*Principia*; 1687), covering dynamics, fluid mechanics, and tides. His theory of light was developed in *Optics* (1704). He built the first reflecting telescope (1668). He is best known for his work in gravitation.
See also: Calculus; Gravitation.

Newton's rings, optical phenomenon of *interference* created when light waves travel through a convex piece of glass placed on top of a flat piece of glass. The light reflected from each piece interferes with that reflected from the other, creating patterns of rings. Strong sunlight produces rings in every color of the spectrum. Light of a single color produces rings of that same color. The phenomenon was studied by 17th-century English scientist Sir Isaac Newton.
See also: Newton, Sir Isaac.

New Year's Day, first day of the new calendar year, celebrated since ancient times by many peoples, including Babylonians, Assyrians, Persians, Egyptians, Jews, Greeks, Romans, and Chinese. Rites were usually held on the days of the vernal or autumnal equinox or the winter or summer solstice, when there was feasting and an exchange of gifts. The Julian calendar decreed Jan. 14 as New Year's Day, but when the Gregorian calendar was ordained in the 16th century, the date was changed to Jan. 1. The Jewish New Year (Rosh Hashanah) is in late Sept. or early Oct., at the time of the autumnal equinox. The Chinese base their New Year date on the waning and waxing of the moon, usually between the middle of Jan. and the middle of Feb. Christmas Day is now more observed as a festive holiday in many countries, but New Year's Day remains the major occasion in France, Scotland, and Italy.

New York (Empire State; pop. 18,137,000), state in the Northeast of the United States; New York is situated between the Atlantic Ocean and Lake Ontario and borders on Canada, Vermont, Massachusetts, Connecticut, New Jersey and Pennsylvania. Capital: Albany.
Economically speaking New York, with the city of New York as the country's financial center, is one of the most important states. Industry includes almost all trade branches. Dairy, horticulture and fruit farming. Exploitation of sand, gravel, zinc, salt, petroleum and natural gas.
First settlement in 1609 by the Dutch. New York was one of the first thirteen states of the U.S.; many of the battles of the Civil War were fought here.

New York City (pop. 7.380.000), city in the southeastern region of New York state. It is divided into 5 boroughs: Manhattan, the Bronx, Brooklyn, Queens, and Richmond (on Staten Island). The long, narrow island of Manhattan, upon which New York's complex network of bridges and tunnels converges, is the city's economic and cultural heart. New York is the nation's largest port and a world leader in trade and finance. It is also a manufacturing (notably garments), communications (broadcasting, advertising, and publishing), and performing arts center. In 1626, Dutch settlers of New Netherland purchased Manhattan from the resident Native Americans and it became New Amsterdam. Population doubled in the wave of immigration between 1880 and 1900.
Manhattan's skyscrapers form the basis of the most famous skyline of the U.S.A. Buildings of the 18th and 19th century are also present in between the skyscrapers, such as the city hall Gracie Mansion (1801), Italian and Chinese districts: Little Italy and Chinatown. Several large parks, such as Central Park. Cultural and educational centers, such as City University of New York and St. John's University. An entertainment center (Fun City; Big Apple), among which Broadway and Greenwich Village. Museums, such as the Metropolitan Museum of Art and the Guggenheim Museum. The Statue of Liberty has become an international symbol of the city. In 2001, the towers of the World Trade Center in Manhattan collapsed after the attacks on September 11, 2001.

New York World's Fair, 2 fairs in New York City that presented art, culture, science, and technology exhibits. The first fair (1939 and 1940), based on the theme 'Building the World of Tomorrow,' introduced the public to such new products as television. The second fair (1964-1965), based on the theme 'Peace Through Understanding,' introduced computers and communications satellites. Each fair developed symbolic monuments: An obelisk called the Tryon and a sphere called the Perisphere were erected in 1939 and a steel globe called the Unisphere was erected in 1964.

N

N

New Zealand

Capital:	Wellington
Area:	103,883 sq mi (270,534 sq km)
Population:	3,908,000
Language:	English
Government:	Parliamentary monarchy in the British Commonwealth
Independent:	1947
Head of gov.:	Prime minister
Per capita:	US$ 19,500
Monetary unit:	1 New Zealand dollar = 100 cents

New Zealand, sovereign state within the British Commonwealth situated in the southwest Pacific Ocean. It is administered by a governor general (representing the British sovereign), a prime minister, and a House of Representatives.

Land and climate. Lying some 1,200 mi (1,931 km) east of Australia across the Tasman Sea, New Zealand comprises 2 main islands (North, South); Stewart Island; the Chatham Islands, about 400 mi (644 km) east of the South Island; and various minor islands. The total area is 103,883 sq mi (269,057 sq km). The main islands stretch about 1,000 mi (1,609 km) from north to south. They exhibit scenic contrasts ranging from sandy subtropical beaches and smok-

A glacial landscape in Fjordland National Park, in the southwest of South Island, New Zealand.

ing volcanoes to lush pastures, majestic forests, placid lakes, glaciers, and snow-capped Alpine peaks.

The North Island (44,281 sq mi/114,688 sq km) is mostly hilly or mountainous. Remarkable thermal springs have been tapped for geothermal power; most of the native Maoris (Polynesians) live in this region. Active volcanoes, such as Mt. Egmont (8,260 ft/2,518 m), are found in Tongariro National Park. The island also has New Zealand's largest lake, Taupo (234 sq mi/629 sq km), and longest, most important river, the Waikato (220 mi/354 km).

The South Island (58,093 sq mi/150,460 sq km), separated from the North Island by Cook Strait, is long and narrow. New Zealand's highest peak, Mt. Cook (12,349 ft/3,764 m) lies in its massive mountain backbone, the Southern Alps. The southwest coast is famed for its fjords. Near Milford Sound are the Sutherland Falls (1,904 ft/580 m), one of the world's highest waterfalls.

Stewart Island (670 sq mi/1,735 sq km) is separated from the South Island by Foveaux Strait. The island is rugged and hilly. The minor islands, except Raoul in the Kermadec group, are uninhabited.

Overall, the climate is pleasant and moderate, without extremes of heat or cold in the lowlands, and rainfall is sufficient.

People. In New Zealand's population, 10% are Maoris and 87% are descended from British settlers. They live and work together as a peaceful, integrated people. Over 80% of the population reside in urban areas, notably Auckland (the leading port, on North Island), Christchurch, and Wellington. The major cities have state university branches; the literacy rate is 99%.

Economy. With only 2% of the land arable, sheep- and cattle-raising are the main sources of income. Principal exports are frozen meat (mainly lamb), wool, and dairy products. Tourism provides income, and privately run industry includes fishing, food processing, textiles, and machinery; mining and forestry are state-owned.

History. The chief Maori migrations were from 1200 to 1400. Abel Janszoon Tasman, a Dutch navigator, was the first European to sight the islands (1642). Although the Maoris would not let him ashore, the islands were named after the province of Zeeland in The Netherlands. The English navigator Captain James Cook claimed the country in 1769, and the first missionaries arrived in 1815. Systematic colonization was begun by the New Zealand Company in 1840, when the Treaty of Waitangi acknowledged British sovereignty. Despite harsh land disputes with the Maoris (1845-1870), the country was given a constitution providing for self-government in 1853. Social welfare programs began in the 1890s, and in 1907 Britain made New Zealand a dominion. New Zealanders fought with the Allies in both World Wars and in Vietnam; the country joined the South East Asia Treaty Organization (SEATO) in 1954. Nuclear weapons and nuclear-powered ships have been banned from its ports since 1985. In 1997 the government and the Maoris of the South Island came to an agreement regarding restoration of their rights. New Zealand's relationship with France deterio-

rated following France's attack of the Greenpeace vessel Rainbow Warrior (1985), but was normalized in 1997.

Ney, Michel (1769-1815), French Napoleonic marshal and military hero. His rearguard defense during Napoleon's retreat from Moscow (1812) was the most notable achievement of a brilliant career. After helping persuade Napoleon to abdicate in 1814, Ney was made a noble by the Bourbon Louis XVIII. When Napoleon returned from exile, however, Ney supported him, fighting at the battle of Waterloo. When Napoleon was defeated, Ney was condemned for treason by the house of peers and was executed.
See also: Napoleon I.

NF *See:* Neurofibromatosis.

Ngo Dinh Diem (1901-1963), Vietnamese politician and first president of the Republic of Vietnam (South Vietnam). Born of a royal Roman Catholic Vietnamese family, he fled into exile after arrest by Ho Chi Minh and the Communist forces (1945). With the division of Vietnam into north and south (1954) he returned and was appointed prime minister and later elected to the presidency (1955). Known for his dictatorial rule and cruelty-especially toward Buddhist monks accused of communist Viet Cong sympathy-his popularity waned. He and his brother and sister-in-law (Ngo Dinh Nhu and Madame Nhu) were assassinated when his regime fell in a coup d'état.
See also: Vietnam.

Ngor, Haing (1940-1996), Cambodian-American actor. Haing Ngor, who was shot outside his apartment in Los Angeles (supposedly during a robbery), received an Oscar in 1984 for his role as the Cambodian photographer and journalist Dith Pran in the film *The Killing Fields*. Ngor was himself a victim of the reign of terror by the Khmer Rouge and spent four years in a 're-education camp'. After the award he decided to help relieve the fate of his countrymen and have the officers of the Khmer Rouge tried before an international tribunal. He was co-founder of *Enfants d'Angkor* (*Children of Angkor*) and Aides aux Personnes Déplacées (*Help for Displaced Persons*).

Nguyen, Thi Binh (1927), Vietnamese stateswoman. Nguyen joined the Vietnamese independence movement very early on and was kept prisoner by the French from 1951-1954. She was spokeswoman for the National Liberation Front for South Vietnam during the four-party peace talks in Paris in 1968. As minister of foreign affairs for the Temporary Revolutionary Government of South Vietnam (from 1969 onwards) she played again an important role during peace negotiations; in 1973 she signed the Vietnam Treaty for her party.

Nguyen Van Linh (1915-1998), secretary-general of the Vietnamese Communist Party, 1986-1990. Nguyen had been active in government 1975-1982, but for several years was in political disgrace, and did not reappear in the party organization until 1985.
See also: Vietnam.

Nguyen Van Thieu (1923-2001), Vietnamese politician and president (1967-1975) of the Republic of Vietnam (South Vietnam). Ori-ginally a supporter of Ngo Dinh Diem, first president of the Republic of Vietnam, he took part in the 1963 coup d'é-tat that deposed Diem. Elected to the presidency, he ruled with U.S. support. Two years after the withdrawal of U.S. troops from Vietnam (1973), he resigned his office to promote peace talks between the South and North. Shortly thereafter, in April 1975, Saigon and the rest of South Vietnam fell to the North Vietnamese, and Thieu went into exile in Taiwan and Great Britain. *See also:* Vietnam.

Nha Trang (pop. 220,000), seaport in south-eastern Vietnam, capital of the Phu Khanh province, at the Song Cai estuary. History dates back to the third century. Various Buddhist sanctuaries. French territory until 1862. Due to its sandy beaches a popular vacation spot during the French period. During the Vietnam War an American airforce base was situated here. The port was modernized in the 1970s.

Niacin *See:* Vitamin.

Niagara Falls, large waterfall in the Niagara River along the border between western New York state and Ontario, Canada. A world-famous spectacle and an important source of hydroelectric power, the falls are divided by Goat Island into the American Falls (1,060 ft/323 m wide and 167 ft/51 m high) and the Canadian, or Horseshoe Falls (2,600 ft/792 m wide and 158 ft/48 m high). The Niagara Gorge, below the falls, is about 7 mi (11 km) long and is noted for its Whirlpool Rapids and Whirlpool. Some 2,200 cu ft (6,005 cu m) of water pass over the falls every second.

Niamey (pop. 400,000), capital and largest city of Niger, located on the Niger River in the southwestern part of the country. It serves as Niger's center for the export of peanuts and other agricultural products. Colonized by the French in the late 1800s, it became the capital in 1926. *See also:* Niger.

Nibelungenlied ('Song of the Nibelungs'), German epic dating from the early 1200s, partly based on Scandinavian myths. It tells the story of Siegfried, who wins the treasure of the Nibelungen dwarfs and is given Kriemhild in marriage as a reward for helping Kriemhild's brother Gunther win Brunhild by trickery. In revenge Brunhild has Siegfried killed by Hagen, who hides the treasure in the Rhine. Kriemhild's subsequent vow to avenge Siegfried ends in a holocaust. The story inspired Richard Wagner's operatic tetralogy, *The Ring of the Nibelungs*.

Nicaragua

Capital:	Managua
Area:	46,430 sq mi (120,245 sq km)
Population:	5,024,000
Language:	Spanish
Government:	Presidential republic
Independent:	1838
Head of gov.:	President
Per capita:	US$ 2.500
Monetary unit:	1 Nicaragua new córdoba oro = 100 centavos

N

Nicaragua, largest of the Central American republics.

Land and climate. Nicaragua covers an area of 46,430 sq mi (120,254 sq km). The country is bounded on the north by Honduras, on the south by Costa Rica, has a Caribbean coastline (the Mosquito Coast) of about 300 mi (483 km) and a 200-mi (322-km) Pacific coastline. A narrow volcanic belt runs southwest across the country from Honduras to Costa Rica, between the Pacific and two lakes: Lake Nicaragua, Central America's largest at 3,089 sq mi (8,006 sq km), and its connecting Lake Managua (386 sq mi/1,000 sq km), both containing small active volcanos. The country's population and productive wealth are concentrated in this region. Earthquakes, like the one that devastated Managua in 1972, are not uncommon.

North of the region are wedge-shaped, forested highlands. Eastward, these fall away to broad lowlands extending to the coast, where Nicaragua's chief rivers-the Coco, Rio Grande, Escondido, and San Juan-empty into the Caribbean.

The climate of the coastal lowlands is mainly hot and humid, with temperatures averaging 80°F (25°C). The rainy season, May through December, brings plentiful rainfall, especially in the eastern lowlands and slopes of the central highlands.

People. The population is predominantly mestizo (mixed Spanish-Indian descent). Minorities include those of Spanish or African descent, and native Indians. About 80% of the people, poor farmers mostly, live in the Pacific region. Spanish is the official language. Most Nicaraguans are Roman Catholics. Before 1980 the literacy rate was less than 50%, but government-built schools and literacy programs raised it to 68% by 1995. The National University is centered in

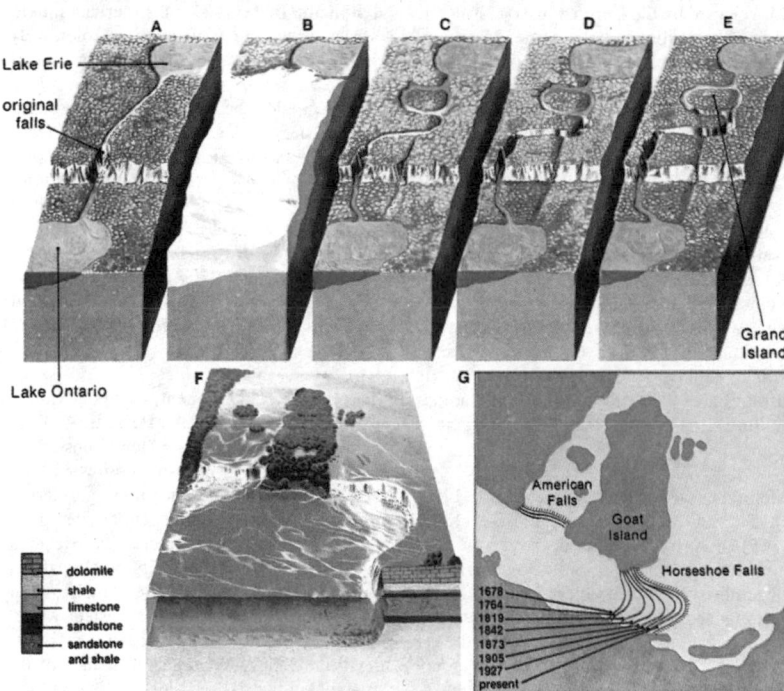

Niagara Falls lies along the course of the Niagara River, which flows north from Lake Erie to Lake Ontario. (A) Experts believe that the original falls began south of the present-day falls, forming Saint David's Gorge, about 14,000 years ago. (B) This gorge became glaciated about 1,000 years later. Once the ice retreated (C), another 2,000 years later, the river ran along a new course beside Saint Davids' Gorge. The power of the water gradually eroded the river bed to the present-day position of the falls (D). In the future (E), the falls will divide at Grand Island and ultimately reach Lake Erie. (F) The top layer of rock beneath the river is highly resistant Lockport dolomite. The deeper layers of shale, limestone, and sandstone, however, are easily eroded from underneath the dolomite, which then breaks off in large pieces. (G) The retreat of the falls from 1768 to 1927 is illustrated here.

Shantytowns grew up in the heart of downtown Managua, the capital of Nicaragua, after the city was almost totally destroyed by an earthquake in 1972.

N

León and Managua, which also has the Jesuit Central University.

Economy. Only 10% of the land is cultivated, but agriculture is the mainstay of the economy, along with forestry, fisheries, and mining (gold, silver, copper, tungsten). Main exports are coffee, cotton, and sugar.

History. The Nicarao Indians, who probably gave the country its name, were conquered by Spanish conquistador Gil González de vila in 1522; various other Indians had inhabited it previously. Francisco Fernández de Córdoba, after whom Nicaragua's currency is named, founded Léon and Granada (1524). From 1570, the country was ruled as part of Guatemala. Nicaragua won independence from Spain in 1821, but was annexed by Mexico, then became part of the Central American Federation (1825-1838). Independent thereafter, the country experienced internal power struggles and conflicts with British and U.S. military and commercial interests. After asking the United States for aid in 1912, it was occupied by U.S. Marines almost continuously until 1933. From 1937, it was ruled dictatorially by the Somoza family until 1979, when Marxist Sandinista guerrillas forced President Anastasio Somoza-Debayle into exile. A socialist Government of National Reconstruction, led by Daniel Ortega, was installed. Domestic reforms helped the Nicaraguan people, but military actions caused turmoil internally (against opposing contra forces), with its neighbors, and in the U.S. government (the Iran-Contra arms scandal). In 1990, elections replaced the Sandinistas with a new, pro-U.S. government led by Violetta Chamorro. Chamorro was succeeded by Arnoldo Alemán Lacayo in 1997. In 1998 hurricane Mitch devastated the country; thousands lost their lives and the country's infrastructure was severely damaged. Ortega lost the 2001 presidential elections to the conservative candidate Enrique Bolaños. Bolaños needed the help of the United States and the IMF to restore the economy. The coffee prices on the world market had dropped and, consequently, shortages increased on world commodity markets.

Nice (pop. 346,000), city in southeastern France, on the Mediterranean Sea, capital of the Alpes-Maritimes department. Originally a Greek settlement (from the 5th century B.C.), it is now a favorite vacation spot for tourists visiting the French Riviera. In addition to tourism, the city is known for the

manufacture of olive oil and electronic products.

Nicene Councils, first and 17th Ecumenical Councils, held in Nice (modern Iznik, Turkey). The first Nicene Council, called in 325 by the Byzantine Emperor Constantine, condemned Arianism and drew up the Nicene Creed. The second Nicene Council (787) ruled in favor of the restoration of images in churches.

Nicholas, name of 5 popes, especially Nicholas I, Nicholas II, and Nicholas V. **Saint Nicholas I**, or Nicholas the Great (c.825-867), a Roman, was pope from 858 to 867. A strong pontiff, he supported St. Ignatius, Patriarch of Constantinople, after the Byzantine emperor Michael III deposed Ignatius in favor of Photius, and he excommunicated Photius (863). After Nicholas's death Photius counterdeposed the pope (867), an act that culminated in the Photian Schism, a split between the Eastern and Western churches. **Nicholas II** (Gerhard; 1010?-1061), who was French-born, was pope from 1059 to 1061. His papacy is famous for the Lateran synod of 1059, which eliminated the Roman nobility's influence on papal elections. The 7 cardinal bishops were given the power to choose a candidate that the rest of the cardinals would have to approve. The other clergy and the people would be presented with their new pope, and the emperor would be sent notice. This edict was rejected by the German bishops in 1061, ending their alliance with Rome. The council also passed church laws enforcing celibacy, prohibiting the selling of clerical offices, and preventing secular persons from investing members of the clergy with the symbols of their office. **Nicholas V** (Tommaso Parentucelli; 1397-1455), an Italian, was pope from 1447 to 1455; he was the first Renaissance pope. He sought to reestablish Rome's importance in the Christian world. Toward that end, he patronized famous humanists and literary scholars and founded what would became the Vatican Library, an important collection of ancient Greek, Roman, and early Christian manuscripts. He also initiated the restoration of many famous buildings in Rome, including St. Peter's Church.

Nicholas, tsars of Russia. **Nicholas I** (1796-1855), tsar of the Russian empire (1825-1855), notorious for his despotic rule. His first action as ruler was to crush the Decembrist Revolt. A determined absolutist, he opposed all liberal political reforms, while expanding Russian territory at the expense of Turkey. He also suppressed an uprising in Poland (1830-1831) and aided the Austrian state in crushing the 1849 revolution in Hungary. He died during the Crimean War. **Nicholas II** (1868-1918), who ruled 1894-1917, helped bring about the Russian Revolution through his inflexibility and misgovernment. His wife, the empress Alexandra, filled the court with irresponsible favorites, of whom the monk Rasputin was the most influential. The repression of political oppositionists and of non-Russian nationalists was intensified. Russian defeats in the Russo-Japanese War (1904-1905) led

to a popular uprising, and Nicholas granted limited civil rights and called the first representative parliament, or Duma (1905). The military defeats of World War I led to the Feb. 1917 revolution and his abdication, in March. He was executed by the Bolsheviks during the civil war that followed the Oct. 1917 revolution. He and most members of his family were buried in the family grave in St. Petersburg in 1998.

Nicholas, Saint, 4th-century patron saint of children, scholars, merchants, and sailors, traditionally identified with a bishop of Myra in Asia Minor. In many European countries he is said to visit children and give them gifts on his feast day (Dec. 6). The custom was brought to America by the Dutch, whose Sinterklaas became the Santa Claus of Christmas.

Nicholas of Cusa (1401-1464), German theologian and philosopher. He became a cardinal in 1440. Nicholas is better known for his interest in astronomy-he held that the earth rotates on its axis, that space is infinite, and that the sun is a star-and for his neo-Platonist writings on the limits of reason.

Nicholson, Ben (1894-1982), British abstract sculptor and painter of landscapes and still lifes. His reliefs, like *White Relief* (1939), are composed in an elegant, pure, linear style.

Nicholson, Jack (1937-), American movie actor. After having played various roles in B-movies, he achieved fame with his role in *Easy Rider* (1969). From then on, he demonstrated to be a first-rate acting talent in many movies such as *Five Easy Pieces* (1970), *Chinatown* (1974), *One Flew Over the Cuckoo's Nest* (1975), *The Shining* (1980), *The Postman Always Rings Twice* (1981), *The Witches of Eastwick* (1987), *Batman* (1989), *Hoffa* (1992), *As Good as it Gets* (1997), *The Pledge* (2001), and *About Schmidt* (2002). Nicholson also directed movies like *Drive, He Said* (1971) and *The Two Jakes* (1990).

Nickel, chemical element, symbol Ni; for physical constants see Periodic Table. Nickel was discovered by Alex Cronstedt in 1751. It is found in most meteorites and occurs in the minerals niccolite, garnierite, millerite, pyrrhotite, and pentlandite, from which it is extracted commercially. Nickel is prepared by concentrating its ores by flotation and roasting to the oxide, which is then reduced with carbon. Nickel is a steel-white, hard, ferromagnetic, corrosion-resistant metal. It strongly resembles iron and cobalt. Most nickel is used to prepare alloys, among them German silver, Monel metal, nichrome, and nickel bronze. Nickel and its compounds are suspected carcinogens. Nickel and its compounds are used in stainless steels, coinage metal, batteries, magnets, and catalysts.

Nickel silver, or German silver, silver-colored alloy of copper, nickel, and zinc, first produced in Germany. It is harder than silver, and although it tarnishes easily and has a duller appearance, it can easily be polished. Nickel silver dinnerware is silver-plated, although the silver plating wears off.

Nicklaus, Jack (1940-), U.S. golfer. Before turning professional (1962) he won the United States Amateur tournament 2 times (1959, 1961). His professional victories include the British Open (1966, 1970, 1978), U.S. Open (1962, 1967, 1972, 1980), Masters tournament (1963, 1965, 1966, 1972, 1975, 1986), and the Professional Golfers' Association (PGA) tournament (1963, 1971, 1973, 1975, 1980). Nicklaus became the first golfer to be a repeat winner of all 4 of these major professional tournaments.

Nicolson, Sir Harold (1886-1968), British writer and diplomat, born in Iran. After diplomatic service (1909-1929), he was a member of Parliament (1935-1945). He published many reviews and biographies of Verlaine, Byron, Tennyson, Swinburne, and King George V.

Nicosía *See:* Lefkosía.

Nicotine, poisonous alkaloid ($C_{10}H_{14}N_2$) found in all parts of the tobacco plant, but especially in the leaves. When pure, it is a colorless oily fluid with little odor, but a sharp, burning taste. On exposure to air it becomes deep brown, with the characteristic tobacco-like smell.
See also: Smoking; Tobacco.

Nictitating membrane, mucous membrane that acts like a third eyelid in many vertebrates. This thin transparent or semitransparent membrane, located under the outer eyelid of birds and reptiles, pulls down over the animal's eyeball.

Niebuhr, name of 2 U.S. brothers, leading Protestant theologians. **Reinhold Niebuhr** (1892-1971) was an active socialist in the early 1930s. After World War II he turned back to traditional Protestant values, relating them to modern society in his 'conservative realism.' His *Nature and Destiny of Man* (2 vols., 1941-1943) greatly influenced American theology. **Helmut Richard Niebuhr** (1894-1962) Niebuhr taught at Yale Divinity School (1931-1962) and wrote on ethics and the history of Christian thought in such books as *The Kingdom of God in America* (1937) and *Radical Monotheism and Western Culture* (1960).
See also: Theology.

Nielsen, Carl August (1865-1931), Danish composer. His 6 symphonies are notable for their original harmonic structure. He also wrote chamber music, operas, and concertos for flute, clarinet, and violin.

Niemann, Gunda (1966-), German skater, born as Gunda Kleemann, who won her first European all-round title in 1989 and again in 1990. In 1991 she won the double for the first time, winning the European and World Championships in the same year. In 1993 she won the all-round European Championships. In 1995 and 1996 Niemann won again the double and also became world champion on the 3-km race. In 1997 she lost

her European title. Later that year Niemann did succeed in becoming the all-round world champion. In 1998 and 1999 she won this title again and also won the 3 and 5-km race. During the 1992 Winter Olympics Niemann won gold medals on the 3 and 5-km races, silver on the 1500 m. In 1994 she won silver on the 3 km and bronze on the 1500 m. In 1998 she won a gold medal on the 3 km.

Niemeyer Soares Filho, Oscar (1907-), Brazilian architect whose outstanding work in Brazil culminated in that country's capital city, Brasília (1956-1960). His most characteristic style uses curved, sculptural, reinforced concrete. In 1996 he was awarded a Golden Lion for his contributions to 20th century architecture.
See also: Brasília.

Niemöller, Martin (1892-1984), German Lutheran pastor who opposed the Nazis and Adolf Hitler. He was confined in concentration camps (1938-1945). He organized the 'Declaration of Guilt' (1945), in which German churches admitted their failure to resist the Nazis. He was president (1961-1968) of the World Council of Churches.

Nièpce, Joseph Nièpce (1765-1833), French physicist and inventor who produced the first successful permanent photograph (1826). The image, recorded in asphalt on a pewter plate, required an 8-hr exposure in a camera obscura. In 1829 Niepce went into partnership with Louis Daguerre, who later perfected his process, which became widely known as daguerrotype.

Nietzsche, Friedrich (1844-1900), German philosopher. In *Thus Spoke Zarathustra* (1833-1892) he introduced the concept of the 'superman,' who would transcend what he considered the slavish morality of Christianity and whose motivating force would be a 'will to power,' directed toward creativity, that would set him off from lesser human beings. Nietzsche's ideas, further elaborated in *Beyond Good and Evil* (1886), have been much misrepresented, particularly

Friedrich Nietzsche (1844-1900), critic of the values of Western civilization and a brilliant stylist. Portrait by Norwegian Edvard Munch (1863-1944), to been seen in the Thielske Galleries, Stockholm.

by the Nazis, who misappropriated the concept of the superman to justify their own concepts of Aryan racial superiority.
See also: Philosophy.

Niger

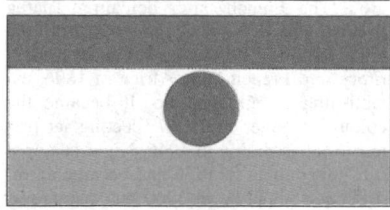

Capital:	Niamey
Area:	489,189 sq mi
	(1,267,000 sq km)
Population:	10,640,000
Language:	French
Government:	Presidential republic
Independent:	1960
Head of gov.:	Prime minister
Per capita:	US$ 820
Monetary unit:	1 CFA franc = 100 centimes

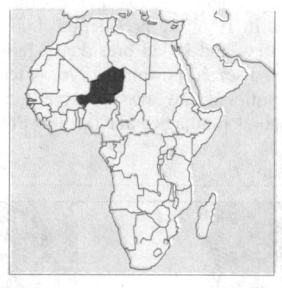

Niger, largest republic (in area) in the interior of northern Africa.
Land and climate. Niger is bordered on the north by Algeria and Libya, on the east by Chad, on the south and southwest by Nigeria, Benin, and Burkina Faso, and on the west by Mali. A landlocked desert country, with an area of 489,189 sq mi (1,267,000 sq km). The north is typically Saharan, the northeast virtually uninhabitable. Agadez, in central Niger south of the Aïr Massif (5,905 ft/1,800 m), has an annual rainfall of only 7 in (18 cm), all of it coming in an 8-week period. Temperatures there in May exceed 100°F (37°C). Conditions are better in the south, where rainfall averages 22 in (55.88 cm), and in the southwest, which profits from the seasonal flooding of the Niger River. Most Nigerians live in this region, between Lake Chad and Niamey.
People. Half the population are Hausa peoples; the rest are the Djerma-Songhai and Beriberi-Manga, mainly farmers in the south, and the nomadic Fulani, Tuareg, and others in the north. French is the official language; Hausa and Djerma are also spoken. The literacy rate is less than 25% (1999). Animism is practiced but Sunni Moslem is the predominant religion.
Economy. Though one of the world's poorest countries, Niger is rich in mineral potential. Principal exports are uranium (third producer in the world), livestock, and vegetables. Chief food crops are peanuts, cotton, millet, cassava, sorghum, vegetables, and rice.
History. Niger was once part of ancient and

N

N

medieval African empires, such as Mali and Songhai. In the 9th century, a Bornu kingdom was founded near Lake Chad by Berbers from North Africa, who were converted to Islam in the 11th century. In the late 18th century, Europeans explored the region. The French, after defeating Tuareg fighters who had invaded the area from the north a century before, incorporated the territory into French West Africa in 1896, establishing a military rule. It became the colony of Niger in 1921. Electing its first territorial assembly in 1946, Niger acquired self-government in 1956 and became an independent republic in 1960 but maintained close economic and military ties with France. Its first president, Diori Hamani, ruled until 1974, when he was ousted by a military coup. Drought and famine wreaked disaster 1973-1975, with half the population reportedly starving, but this eased. In 1989, the drafting of a new constitution provided for a new National Assembly and the installation of a civilian government. In 1996 president Ousmane was overthrown by a military junta, which suspended the constitution. In 1999 the presidential body-guard overthrew and killed president Mainassara, who had seized power in 1996. After a new constitutional law was accepted in 1999, Mamadou Tandja became the new President.

Nigeria

Capital:	Abuya
Area:	356,669 sq mi (923,768 sq km)
Population:	129,935,000
Language:	English
Government:	Federal presidential republic
Independent:	1963
Head of gov.:	President
Per capita:	US$ 840
Monetary unit:	1 Nigerian naira = 100 kobo

Nigeria, federal republic in West Africa.
Land and climate. Nigeria has an area of 356,667 sq mi (923,768 sq km). It is bordered on the north by Niger, on the east by Chad and Cameroon, on the west by Benin, and on the south by the Gulf of Guinea. Its 500-mi (800-km) coastline has sandbars, swamps, mangrove forests, lagoons, and the mouths of several navigable rivers, predominantly the delta of the country's most

The Emir of Kano (Nigeria) and his household in a New Year's procession.

important river, the Niger. Beyond the coast and rain forests are savannas. North of the Niger River and its tributary, the Benue, the grass-covered Jos plateau falls away to the sandy high plains of Hausaland. Another watershed lies to the southwest, where the Yoruba highlands, covered with tall grass and hardwood forests, form the divide between northward-flowing rivers and those draining south to the gulf. Other highlands run along Nigeria's border with Cameroon, where Vogel Peak (6,700 ft/2,040 m) is the highest. In the far north, central highlands merge with the Sahara along the Niger border. Annual rainfall in this entirely tropical country, hot the year round, ranges from more than 150 in (381 cm) on the central coast to only 25 in (64 cm) in the northeast.
People. Nigeria is one of the most populous country on the African continent. Of the 250 ethnic groups that comprise two-thirds of the population, there are 3 major peoples: some 35.7 million Hausa-Fulani live in the Muslim north, and about 44 million Ibo and Yoruba live in the Christian south and east. With 31% of the land arable, more than half the Nigerians are farmers and herders. The country is one of Africa's most urbanized, with Lagos and Ibadan having more than 1 million inhabitants. English is the official language; Hausa, Yoruba, and Ibo are also spoken.
Economy. Oil is the leading export. Its revenues have fueled massive, mostly private development. Other leading exports are cocoa, palm kernels and palm oil, peanuts, soybeans, rubber, cotton, and bananas. Manufacturing includes oil refining, vehicle assembly, food processing, textiles, building materials, and furniture. In the south there are extensive fisheries.
History. The Nok, an advanced Iron Age culture (800 B.C.-A.D. 200), is the earliest known in Nigeria. From about A.D. 1000, small city-states arose. The sacred Yoruba city of Ife in the southwest developed its great culture during the 12th century, and during the 14th century Islam become predominant in the north, where several cities were trans-Saharan trade centers. In the south, the ancient city-state of Benin was a flourishing center when the Portuguese

(1483) and the British (1553) arrived and began the trade in Nigerian slaves for Europe and the Americas. By the mid-19th century, palm products replaced slaves as the leading export, and Lagos, the chief port, was ceded to Britain (1861), which made it an outpost to fight the slave trade, and then a colony (1886). Soon the entire country was under control of the British, who made it a protectorate (1914). After World War II, responding to militant nationalists, the British increased self-government, and Nigerians from the 3 major ethnic groups took over by democratic means when the country became a federation of regions (1954), an independent country in 1960 and then a republic (1963). However, rival ethnic military factions battling for control tore Nigeria apart. Thousands of Ibos were massacred or fled their homeland, Biafra. When the military government reorganized Nigeria into ethnic states (1967), Biafra seceded. The ensuing civil war ended (1970) with Nigeria's unity preserved, but at the cost of perhaps 1 million Ibo dead from starvation. With a new constitution (1976), Nigeria returned to a democratically elected civilian government (1979), but it was ousted in a military coup (1983). Promises to restore the civilian government were not kept. Elections were held in 1992, but the military leadership under Sani Abacha (1943-1998) remained in power. In 1998 general Abdusalam Abubakar succeeded Sani Abacha. The 1999 elections were won by Olusegun Obasanjo, who had been head of state from 1976-1979.
In 2001, four states adopted Islamic law in the face of the opposition of the Christian minority. Islamic law was imposed in 12 northern states, which led to violent clashes between Muslims and Christians, causing hundreds of deaths.

Niger River, third-longest river of Africa. Along with its eastern branch, the Benue, it drains an area of more than 1 million sq mi (2.59 million sq km) in west Africa. Rising in southwestern Guinea, it flows 2,600 mi (4,180 km), curving northeast, east, and then southeast into Nigeria, eventually running south to the Gulf of Guinea, where it forms a delta.

Common nighthawk (*Chordeiles minor*, order *Apodiformes*, family *Apodidae*). Found in temperate North America. Length up to 9 in (23 cm).

N

Nighthawk, bullbat, or mosquito hawk (*Chordeiles minor*), nocturnal, insect-eating bird in the goatsucker family (Caprimulgidae), not a true hawk. It measures approximately 10 in (25 cm) long, with white wing bars and a white throat patch on a mottled brown, black, and white body. Nighthawks reside in South America during the winter and the United States and Canada for the rest of the year.

Nightingale, bird (*Luscinia megarhynchos*) of the thrush family, renowned for the male's beautiful song. A small brown bird feeding on insects and other invertebrates, it lives in deciduous woodlands throughout most of Europe.

Nightingale, Florence (1820-1910), English founder of modern nursing, known as the 'Lady with the Lamp' because she worked night and day during the Crimean War (1854), establishing sanitary methods and discipline in 2 huge army hospitals. In 1860 she set up a nurses' training school in London. She was the first woman to be awarded the British Order of Merit (1907).
See also: Crimean War; Nursing.

Nightshade, common name for a number of plants (family Solanaceae) with small but distinctive tubular or flared flowers. Some nightshades (e.g., deadly nightshade and Jimson weed) produce rounded fruits that may contain poisons, but many are edible crops, e.g., tomato, potato, red pepper, and eggplant.

Nihilism, doctrine that denies all values, questions all authority, and advocates the destruction of all social and economic institutions. The movement, romantic in origin and anarchist in outlook, arose in 19th-century Russia. Its most noted exponent was Prince Piotr Kropotkin.

Nijinsky, Vaslav (1890-1950), Russian ballet dancer. His career began in St. Petersburg in 1907. His outstanding technique and magnetic stage presence contributed greatly to the impact of Russian ballet in the West when Sergei Diaghilev brought a company to Paris in 1909. With Diaghilev's encouragement, Nijinsky devised original choreography, based on Greek vase paintings, for Claude Debussy's *Afternoon of a Faun*. Mental illness ended his career in 1919.
See also: Ballet.

Nikolais, Alwin (1910-1993), U.S. dancer and choreographer. He formed his own dance company, now known as the Alwin Nikolais Dance Theatre, in 1949. Nikolais not only choreographs his works, but designs the pieces' other elements, such as the costumes and scenery, and composes the music. Among his works are *Kaleidoscope* (1956), *Imago* (1963), and *Cent Dom* (1980).
See also: Ballet.

Nile River, longest river in the world, flowing generally north about 4,145 mi (6,671 km) from east-central Africa through the Sudan and Egypt to the Mediterranean. Its remote headstream is the Luvironza River in Burundi above Victoria Nyanza (Lake Victoria), where the White Nile originates. The Blue Nile rises above Lake Tana in northwestern Ethiopia and joins the White Nile at Khartoum, Sudan, to form the Nile proper. North of Cairo, Egypt, the Nile fans out into a delta 115 mi (185 km) wide, with principal outlets at Rosetta near Alexandria and Damietta near Port Said. Silt deposited by the Nile's annual overflow brought agricultural prosperity throughout Egypt's history. The river has been harnessed, notably at the Aswan High Dam in Upper Egypt, to supply hydroelectricity as well as constant irrigation. The Nile is navigable the year round from its mouth to Aswan, and in full spate it is generally navigable as far south as Uganda.

Nilsson, Birgit (1918-), Swedish soprano, widely regarded as the greatest Wagnerian soprano of her time. She is famed as Brünnhilde in *Der Ring des Nibelungen* but is also known for her roles in Giacomo Puccini's *Turandot* and Richard Strauss' *Elektra*.

Nimitz, Chester William (1885-1966), U.S. admiral who commanded naval operations in the Pacific after the United States entered World War II. Credited with originating the strategy of 'island hopping,' he had an outstandingly successful command. On Sept. 2, 1945, the Japanese surrender was signed aboard his flagship, the U.S.S. *Missouri*.
See also: World War II.

Nimrod, in the Bible (Genesis), grandson of Noah and son of Ham, a hunter and founder of the city Nineveh. Living many years after the great flood, Nimrod constructed great cities and became a legendary hunter. Nineveh was located in present-day Iraq.
See also: Bible.

Nin, Anaïs (1903-1977), French-born U.S. author whose novels and stories depict the inner worlds of women in surrealistic and psychoanalytic fashion. Her novels include *The House of Incest* (1936) and *Collages* (1964). She is best known for *The Diaries of Anaïs Nin* (7 vols., 1966-1980), which span the years 1931-1974 and include portraits of such contemporaries as Lawrence Durrell, Henry Miller, William Carlos Williams, and Marguerite Young.

Nineveh, ancient capital of Assyria, on the Tigris River, opposite modern Mosul, Iraq. Invaluable remains survive from its period of greatness under Sennacherib and Assurbanipal, in the 7th century B.C. Its destruction by Babylonian, Medean, and Scythian invaders in 612 B.C. ended the Assyrian Empire.

Ningbo, or Ning-po (pop. 553,000), formerly Ninghsien, port city on the Yung River in northern Zhejiang province, eastern China. In 1843 Ningbo became one of 5 Chinese ports open to foreign trade. Although nearby Shanghai is now the more prominent center of international trade, Ningbo remains a major commercial and manufacturing center for the region. Textiles, food processing, shipbuilding, and machine production are among its chief industries.
See also: China.

Ning-po *See:* Ningbo.

Niobe, in Greek mythology, daughter of Tantalus and wife of Amphion, and a figure of eternal sorrow. Queen Niobe, who had 12 children, claimed that her child-bearing powers were greater than those of the goddess Leto, who had only 2 children. Leto punished Niobe for this boast by having all of her children slain. The gods, pitying the grieving queen, turned her into a weeping rock, which, according to tradition, is on Mt. Sipylon in Turkey.

Niobium, chemical element, symbol Nb; for physical constants see Periodic Table. Niobium was discovered by Charles Hatchett in 1801. It occurs associated with tantalum in the minerals pyrochlore, and euxenite. It is obtained commercially from columbite-tantalite, a mixed oxide with tantalum and iron and manganese. The element is prepared by the high-temperature reaction of niobium oxide with niobium carbide in a vacuum. Niobium is a shiny, soft, white, ductile metal. Ferroniobium is used in arc-welding rods and stainless steels. Niobium is used in high temperature alloys and nuclear applications. Niobium is also known as columbium.

Nipkow, Paul Gottlieb (1860-1940), German engineer. In 1884 he designed the Nipkow disc, which was used for the transfer of scanning lines and the reconstruction of images; it was later used for the first experimental TV systems.

Nippon *See:* Japan.

N

Nirvana, Sanskrit term used in Buddhism, Jainism, and Hinduism to denote the highest state of existence, reached when all bodily desires have been quelled and the self is free to dissolve into the ocean of peace, or God. It means literally *extinguished*, denoting freedom from ego. Nirvana is the final escape from the cycle of rebirth.
See also: Buddhism.

Nisei (Japanese, 'second generation'), those born of immigrant Japanese parents in the United States. After the Japanese attack on Pearl Harbor (1941), some 110,000 Americans of Japanese ancestry were forcibly evacuated from their homes on the West Coast and placed in detention centers, in most cases until World War II had ended.

Nitrate, chemical compound, generally sodium ($NaNO_3$) or potassium nitrate (KNO_3), formed in the soil by bacteria. Plants use nitrates to make protein. Nitrates are used in making explosives, fireworks, heart medicine, and photographic film, and are added to the soil as fertilizers to replace depleted nitrogen.

Nitrate of silver *See:* Silver nitrate.

Nitre *See:* Saltpeter.

Nitric acid, corrosive, colorless liquid (HNO_3) with powerful oxidizing properties, used in the manufacture of medicine, dyes, explosives, and metal products.

Nitrite, salt or esther of nitrous acid. Certain nitrites cause dilation of small blood vessels and thus help to lower blood pressure. Examples are amyl nitrite, sodium nitrite, nitroprusside, and nitroglycerin.

Nitrocellulose *See:* Guncotton.

Nitrogen, chemical element, symbol N; for physical constants see Periodic Table. Nitrogen was discovered by Daniel Rutherford in 1772. It is present in air to the extent of 78% and is commercially obtained by the liquefaction and fractional distillation of air. Nitrogen is a colorless, odorless, and chemically inert gas. When heated, however, it combines directly with magnesium, lithium, or calcium. The largest use of elemental nitrogen is in the Haber process, where nitrogen is heated under pressure to form ammonia. In the Ostwald process it is oxidized to nitric acid. Millions of tons of elemental nitrogen are produced in the United States each year. Nitrogen is used as an inert atmosphere for the production of electronic components and in the annealing of steel. In liquid form it is used as a refrigerant. Nitrogen compounds are used in the manufacture of fertilizers, explosives, and pharmaceuticals.

Nitrogen cycle, cycle of chemical changes that keep nitrogen flowing through the biosphere, in air and soil. Nitrogen is a fundamental part of living protoplasm. In order to be absorbed by living things, however, it has to be combined into hydrogen and oxygen compounds that plants can use. This process, called nitrogen fixation, is carried on by bacteria in the soil that produce ammonia and nitrates. Plants then absorb these from the soil and use them to make protein. When animals eat plants, they convert the plant protein into animal protein. Meanwhile, some of the nitrates present in soils seeps into groundwater and rivers, and the remainder undergoes denitrification, a process that breaks nitrates down into nitrogen and nitrous oxide, which is then released into the atmosphere, soil, and water. When remains of dead animals and wastes decay, nitrogen is put back into the soil in the form of ammonia, which bacteria oxidize to nitrites and then to nitrates, thus beginning the cycle again.

Nitroglycerin, unstable, oily compound ($C_3H_5N_3O_9$) that explodes when exposed to heat or shock. It is used to make dynamite, which is basically nitroglycerin mixed with an absorbing material to make it less easily exploded. Nitroglycerin also causes the dilation of blood vessels and is therefore used in the treatment of angina pectoris.
See also: Dynamite; Glycerol.

Nitrous oxide, colorless, odorless gas (N_2O) first prepared by British chemist Joseph Priestley in 1772. Used by dentists as an anesthetic, it is also called laughing gas because it produces a euphoric effect when inhaled.

Niven, (James) David (Graham) (1910-1983), British movie actor, was the popular personification of the phlegmatic British gentlemen in both society comedies as in adventure movies. Movies include *Thank You Jeeves* (1936), *Raffles* (1940), *A Matter of Life and Death* (1946), *Around the World in Eighty Days* (1956), *The Pink Panther* (1964), *Casino Royale* (1967), *Murder by Death* (1976), *Escape to Athena* (1979), *Trail of the Pink Panther* (1982) and *Curse of the Pink Panther* (1983).

Nixon, Richard Milhous (1913-1994), 37th president of the United States (1969-1974), who became the only president to resign from office. In 1974, facing impeachment in the wake of the Watergate scandal, Nixon surrendered the presidency. Although Nixon's presidency ended in disgrace, he effected important breakthroughs in U.S.-Soviet and U.S.-Chinese relations. In addition, in 1973, Nixon signed the ceasefire agreement that ended U.S. participation in the Vietnam War.
He became well known nationally as a member of the House Committee on Un-American Activities. From 1953 to 1961, he served as vice president under President Dwight D. Eisenhower. In 1960, Nixon lost the election to Democrat John F. Kennedy. In 1968, Nixon won the elections. He inherited a nation troubled by serious social and economic problems. Many Americans were opposed to the Vietnam War and held protests and rallies demanding an end to the U.S. role in the fighting. In 1969, Nixon, who had pledged to seek an end to the war, began a program of gradually withdrawing U.S. troops from Vietnam. U.S. military action in Vietnam did not end until 1973, however. In 1972, President Nixon visited China and the USSR and met with the leaders of both countries. He was the first U.S. president to do so. The historic meetings improved troubled relations between the United States and the 2 Communist nations.
On June 17, 1972, burglars carrying wire-

The nitrogen cycle involves the conversion of nitrogen gas in the air (N_2), into nitrates in the soil, by nitrogen-fixing bacteria (1). Plants will take up the nitrates (2) and use the nitrogen to produce tissues. Herbivorous animals feed on the plants (3), and when the animals and the plants die, their bodies will be decayed by bacteria and fungi (4), and ammonium compounds (NH_4^+) will be released into the soil. These are then converted into nitrites (NC_2^-) and then nitrates (NC_3^-) by nitrifying bacteria, thus making nitrogen available to the plants once more (5). Ammonium compounds, nitrates and nitrites are also converted back to nitrogen gas by denitrifying bacteria (6), thus completing the cycle.

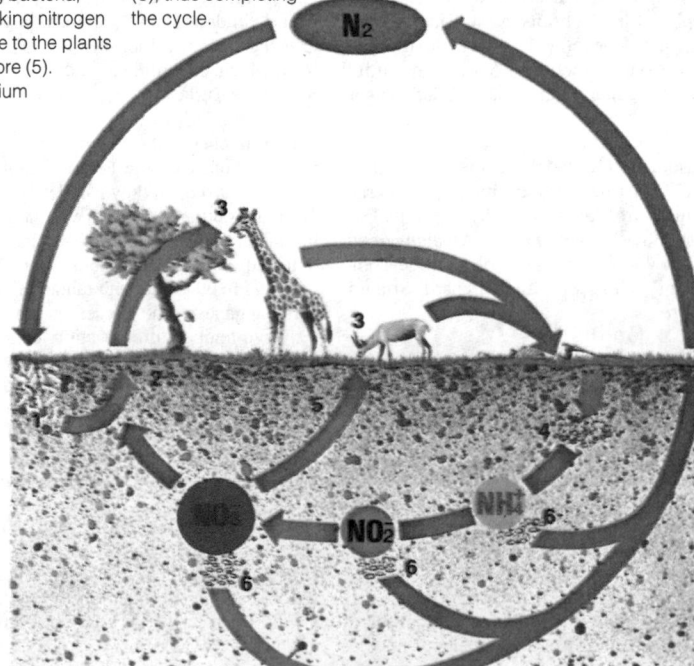

tapping equipment had broken into the Democratic national party headquarters in the Watergate buildings in Washington, D.C. Although the burglars were members of Nixon's 1972 reelection committee, Nixon denied any White House involvement in the crime. Later investigations revealed, however, that top White House aides had been involved both in planning the break-in and trying to hide evidence concerning it. Ultimately, tapes of White House conversations would prove that Nixon himself had authorized the cover-up. Nixon resigned from office on Aug. 9th, 1974.

Nizhny Novgorod (formerly Gorki or Gorky; pop. 1,443,000), city in the eastern European port of the Soviet Union, situated at the confluence of the Oka and Volga rivers. Its diverse industries include automobiles, airplanes, locomotives, machinery, and chemicals, as well as the refining of petroleum and natural gas. The city was named Gorki from 1932-90, in honor of the writer Maxim Gorki, who was born there.

Nkrumah, Kwame (1901-1972), African political leader who led his country, Ghana, to independence. A champion of pan-Africanism, he became the first prime minister of independent Ghana (formerly a British colony called the Gold Coast) in 1957. In 1960 he assumed dictatorial powers as president and in 1966 his government was overthrown by a military coup.
See also: Ghana.

Noah, in the Bible (Genesis 6-10), man who built the ark, at God's direction, that saved human and animal life from the great flood. His sons were Shem, Ham, and Japheth. Shem became the father of the Semitic people, including Jews and Arabs. Ham was the father of the Hamitic people. Japheth was the father of the people of Asia Minor and Europe.
See also: Bible.

Nobel, Alfred Bernhard (1833-1896), Swedish chemist and inventor of dynamite and other explosives. About 1863 he set up a factory to manufacture liquid nitroglycerin, but the factory exploded in an accident killing his younger brother. Nobel then set out to find safe handling methods for the substance. In 1867 he developed dynamite, a combination of nitroglycerin and inert, stabilizing filler. Later he invented gelignite (1876) and ballistite (1888). A lifelong pacifist, Nobel wished his explosives to be used solely for peaceful purposes and was embittered by their military use. He left most of his fortune to the Nobel Foundation, which has used the money to reward Nobel Prize winners since 1901.
See also: Dynamite.

Nobelium, chemical element, symbol No; for physical constants see Periodic Table. Nobelium was discovered by Albert Ghiorso and his coworkers at the Lawrence Radiation Laboratory in Berkeley, Calif., in 1958. A target of curium isotopes was bombarded with carbon-12 ions in a heavy-ion linear accelerator (HILAC) to produce nobelium-254. It is a metallic element and a member of the

actinide series. Eleven radioactive isotopes of nobelium are now known. Nobelium-259, an alpha-emitter with a half-life of 58 minutes, is the most stable.

Nobel Prizes, annual awards given to individuals or institutions judged to confer 'the greatest benefit on mankind' in each of 6 fields: physics, chemistry, physiology or medicine, literature, peace, and economics. Prizes for the first 5 categories have been given since 1901; the economics prize was first awarded in 1969. The winner of the peace prize is decided by a committee of the Norwegian parliament; the other winners are determined by the corresponding bodies in Sweden: the Royal Academy of Sciences, the Caroline Medico-Chirurigal Institute, and the Academy of Literature. Winners receive a gold medal and a cash payment, now consisting of several hundred thousand dollars. The prize money comes from the foundation set up by Alfred Nobel.
See also: Nobel, Alfred Bernhard.

Here, you see the document that accompanied the Nobel Prize for Chemistry, that was presented to J.H. van 't Hoff (1852-1911), in 1901.

Nobile, Umberto (1885-1978), an Italian aviator, engineer, and explorer. He was a pioneer in the development of lighter-than-air craft and one of the first men to fly over the North Pole.
In 1926 Nobile designed the dirigible *Norge* and took part in its flight over the North Pole, on an expedition led by Roald Amundsen. While in command of a 1928 expedition, Nobile landed his airship *Italia* at the Pole. The dirigible was wrecked on the return trip, resulting in the death of several of the crew and the loss of Amundsen on a rescue mission. A board of inquiry, generally believed to have been stacked against him by Fascist enemies in the Italian air force, held him partly responsible for the wreck. Protesting the findings, Nobile resigned his commission in the air force and spent years attempting to vindicate himself.
Nobile was an aviation consultant in the

Soviet Union in the early 1920's and taught aeronautical engineering in the United States, 1936-1942. He returned to Italy in 1943. After World War II, he won vindication and was reinstated as a general in the air force. He wrote several books on the flight of the *Italia*.

Nobility, class of people considered to have social prominence. The titles that often accompany high social position, such as *duke*, *count*, or *baron*, may be inherited or granted by monarchs. Great Britain's noble class is called the *peerage*. The U.S. Constitution prohibits government-awarded titles. France, Russia, and Germany no longer recognize titles of nobility.

Noble gas, or inert gas, any of the elements in Group 0 of the Periodic Table, comprising helium, neon, argon, krypton, xenon, and radon. These are colorless, odorless gases whose outermost electrons are complete, making them chemically unreactive. Helium has 2 electrons in its outer shell; all the others have 8.
See also: Periodic table.

Nogi, Maresuke (1849-1912), Japanese general who fought in conflicts such as the Chinese-Japanese War (1894-1895). During the Russian-Japanese War (1904-1905) he was in command of the 3rd Army, with which he conquered the city of Port Arthur from the Russians after a prolonged siege, inflicting a decisive blow on them at Mukden. After the death of Emperor Mutsohito (1912), he and his wife committed hara-kiri. Nogi is a national hero in Japan.

Noguchi, Isamu (1904-1988), U.S. abstract sculptor whose works, especially those created for specific architectural settings (such as the UNESCO building in Paris), won him international recognition. He was a student of Constantin Brancusi.

Noh, or No, classical drama of Japan, developed under court patronage in the 14th century. Typically, a Noh play dramatizes the spiritual life of its central character. The play is short but moves slowly in a highly ritualized style. The performers are all male and use traditional wooden masks. Noh gave rise to the more popular Kabuki theater.

Nok, civilization that existed in West Africa from c.500 B.C. to A.D. 200. Its artifacts were found in the village of Nok, Nigeria, in the valley between the Niger and Benue rivers.

Noland, Kenneth (1924-), U.S. painter whose work features bands of color. With Morris Louis he developed a technique of employing thinned paints for staining and became one of the best-known color field painters.

Nolde, Emil (Emil Hansen; 1867-1956), German expressionist engraver and painter, notably of landscapes and figures, whose bold, visionary, and highly emotional style is typified in *The Prophet* (1912), *Life of Maria Aegyptiaca* (1912), and *Marsh Landscape* (1916).

N

Nomad, member of a population group that moves from place to place for subsistence. The nomadic way of life, though fast declining, is still found among some herders, such as the Arab Bedouins, and hunters, such as some groups of Australian aborigines. Some peoples, like the Lapps of northern Scandinavia, are semi-nomadic, residing in one place during the warmer months and moving to another during the winter.

N

The cattle-breeding Tuareg people of northwest Africa, live a typically nomadic life.

Nonaggression pact, agreement between nations to reconcile differences without the use of force. After World War I, many nations signed nonaggression pacts, most of which were violated during World War II. The pacts became obsolete in 1945, when the United Nations became the forum for peaceful solutions to international conflicts. However, the UN has not resolved whether only military attacks are acts of aggression or if such acts include hostile economic policies and seditious propaganda as well.

Nonaligned nation *See:* Third World.

Nonconformists, in religion, those who will not conform to the doctrine or practice of an established church. Notable were Protestant dissenters from the Church of England, mainly Puritans, who were expelled by the Act of Uniformity (1662). They now include Baptists, Congregationalists, Methodists, Presbyterians, and Quakers.

Nono, Luigi (1924-1990), Italian composer. Studied at the Benedetto Marcello school of music in Venice from 1941 to 1945. He continued his music studies with Bruno Maderna and Hermann Scherchen. From 1950 onwards he attended the Ferienkurse in Darmstadt, where he established his name as one of the leaders of post-war music. Electronic music plays an important role in many of Nono's compositions, as does the vocal element, especially the high-range vocals. Being a confirmed Communist, his work shows a strong social and political involvement. His works include: *Polifonica-monodia-ritmica* (1951), *Il Canto Sospeso* (1955-1956), *Intolleranza* (1960), *La fabbrica illuminata* (1964), *Per Bastiana Tai-Yang Cheng* (1967), *... sofferte onde serene...* (1976), *Frabmente - Stille, an Diotima* (1980, *Promoteo: Tragedia dell'ascolto* (1981-1985).

Non-proliferation Treaty (NPT), treaty against the spread of nuclear arms and nuclear arms technology, signed 1 July 1968. In 1994, 163 nations were affiliated to the treaty. Among the non-affiliated countries are Israel, India, Pakistan, Argentina and Brazil. The NPT, which was prolonged for an indefinite period of time on 12 May 1995, establishes that the nuclear powers are not allowed to put nuclear arms or technology at the disposal of non-affiliated countries, who in turn are not allowed to possess nuclear weapons. Nuclear energy used in a peaceful manner is allowed. The NPT divides the world into five nations that are allowed to possess nuclear weapons (China, France, Great Britain, the Russian Federation and the United States), and the remaining nations who are not permitted to possess nuclear weapons. Those countries who are allowed possession of nuclear technology for peaceful means declare in the treaty that they will not put this technology at the disposal of the 'have-nots'. In order to continue the NPT, the five nuclear powers, under pressure of a number of developing countries, made a non-binding statement in which they declared, among other things, to reduce their nuclear arsenal and to arrange for a speedy agreement concerning a global ban on nuclear tests. The so-called threshold countries-India, Israel and Pakistan (countries that are in the possession of nuclear weapons or who are able to fabricate these weapons on short notice and who have never signed the treaty)-have been called upon to join the NPT after all.
The International Organization for Nuclear Energy (IONE) is responsible for inspection on the compliance of the treaty. The organization also enforces inspections at nuclear civil installations. The supply of nuclear material depends on whether the receiving country and the organization can come to a Safe Guards Agreement. Inspection of the observance has proven not to be airtight. Iraq, who has signed the treaty and is therefore subject to inspections, was still able to set up and carry out a nuclear program, as became apparent in 1991 when the Gulf War came to an end.

Nonviolent resistance *See:* King, Martin Luther, Jr.; Gandhi, Mohandas Karamchand.

Nopal *See:* Prickly pear.

Nordenskjöld, Nils Adolf Erik (1832-1901), Finnish-born Swedish geologist, cartographer, and explorer of Spitsbergen and of Greenland, where he studied inland ice. He was the first to navigate the Northeast Passage (1878-1879).
See also: Northeast Passage.

Nordhoff and Hall, U.S. writing team.

Charles Bernard Nordhoff (1887-1947) and **James Norman Hall** (1887-1951) are best known for a trilogy of novels (*Mutiny on the Bounty*, 1932; *Men Against the Sea*, 1934; *Pitcairn's Island*, 1934) based on the 1789 mutiny against British naval officer William Bligh, who was infamous for his cruelty.

Norfolk Island, Australian territory in the South Pacific, between New Caledonia and New Zealand. Tourism is the small island's chief industry. The first European on the island was James Cook (1774). It was used as a penal colony, 1788-1814 and 1825-1856. Descendants of the HMS *Bounty* mutineers relocated there from Pitcairn Island in 1856.

Norfolk terrier, breed of hunting dog developed in Great Britain. One of the smallest terriers, it is distinguishable from the Norwich terrier only by its forward-bending ears. These affectionate, hardy, and active dogs usually weigh 10-12 lbs (4.5-5.4 kg), stand 10 in (25 cm) tall, and have short legs and a wiry coat.

Noriega, Manuel (1938-), Panamanian general, leader of Panama 1985-1988. He commanded the National Defense Forces to unseat civilian president Nicolas Ardito Barletta (1985). His 1987 indictment in the United States for violations of racketeering and drug laws was controversial; he had been operating with close ties with the U.S. Central Intelligence Agency (CIA) supplying them with information on the drug trade and other intelligence. The United States offered to drop charges if Noriega stepped down, but he refused (1988). He eluded capture during the 1989 invasion of Panama, but finally surrendered to the United States and was arraigned on charges of cocaine trafficking. In 1992 he was sentenced to 40 years imprisonment by the federal court of Miami. A year later, the Panamese court sentenced him to 20 years imprisonment because of the murder of opposition leader Spadafora in 1985.
See also: Panama.

Norman, Jessey (1945-), United States operatic and concert soprano. The wide range and flexibility of her voice and a commanding stage presence brought her international acclaim. Aida, Ariadne in *Ariadne auf Naxos*, and Cassandra and Dido in *Les Troyens* are among her varied roles. Norman studied piano as a child. After graduating from Howard University she continued her music studies at the Peabody Conservatory and the University of Michigan. In 1969 she made her operatic debut at the Deutsche Oper in West Berlin. She made her debut with the Metropolitan Opera in 1983.

Norman architecture, medieval style characterized by massive scale, 6-part vaulted ceilings, and rounded arches. Structures in this style were built in Norman-conquered lands (northern France, England, southern Italy, Sicily), 1066-1154. La Trinité church in France and Ely Cathedral in England are examples.

Norman Conquest, era of English history following the Battle of Hastings (1066), when William, Duke of Normandy, defeated and killed England's Saxon king, Harold. William claimed the English throne and quickly crushed resistance. By 1070 most Anglo-Saxon nobles had been either killed or subjugated, their land distributed to Normans in return for their agreement to supply the king with mounted soldiers. After the conquest French became the language of the royal court and had a major and lasting influence on English.
See also: Hastings, Battle of; William I.

Normandy, region of northwestern France facing the English Channel, noted for dairy products, fruit, brandy, wheat, and flax. Le Havre, Dieppe, and Cherbourg are the main ports; Rouen and Caen are historic cathedral and university cities. In World War II it was the site of the D-Day landing on June 6, 1944.
See also: France.

Normandy, Duke of *See:* William I.

Normandy invasion *See:* World War II.

Normans, inhabitants of Normandy, a region and former province of northwestern France, along the English Channel. The name is derived from 'Norsemen'. In 911 Rollo, leader of Viking raider-settlers, was recognized as duke of the area by King Charles III of France. They adopted Christianity in the 10th century. In the 11th their duke, William, initiated the Norman Conquest of England. Normans were also active in the Crusades, in the reconquest of Spain, and in southern Italy and Sicily.

Norns, in Scandinavian mythology, 3 sisters who represent past (Urd or Wyrd), present (Verdandi), and future (Skuld). Like the Greek Fates, they spin and cut the thread of life. According to earlier beliefs, there was a lesser Norn that controlled the fate of each individual.

Norodom Sihanouk (1922-), leader of Cambodia (1941-1970, 1975-1976, 1993-). Originally installed as king, he abdicated and became premier (1955) while his father ruled. On his father's death he again became head of state (1960). During the French war in Indochina and the Vietnam War he tried to keep Cambodia neutral. He was forcibly overthrown by right-wing military leader Lon Nol (1970). Fleeing to China, he formed a government in exile, and was returned to power when Lon Nol was deposed by the left-wing guerrilla forces known as the Khmer Rouge (1975). He resigned from power April 1976. During the 1980s he remained involved in resistance to the Vietnam-backed government, leading the rebel coalition. In 1991 Sihanouk returned from exile and became head of the rebellion coalition and government. He won the 1993 elections and was then crowned king again.
See also: Cambodia.

Norris, Frank (Benjamin Franklin Norris; 1870-1902), U.S. novelist and newspaper columnist. His best-known novels are *McTeague* (1899), a naturalist account of life in San Francisco slums, and his 2 exposés of the railroad and wheat industries, *The Octopus* (1901) and *The Pit* (1903). These were part of an uncompleted trilogy entitled *The Epic of Wheat*.

Norsemen *See:* Vikings.

Norse mythology *See:* Mythology.

North America, third-largest continent, situated in the Western Hemisphere and bounded on the north by the Arctic Ocean, on the south by South America, on the west by the Pacific Ocean and Bering Sea, and on the east by the Atlantic Ocean. Besides the area covered by Canada and the United States, it includes Mexico and Central America, the islands of the Caribbean Sea, and Greenland.
Land and climate. North America, roughly triangular in shape, covers about 9,400,000 sq mi (24,346,000 sq km) with a coastline of about 190,000 mi (300,000 km). Hudson Bay in the north and the Gulf of Mexico in the south break into the triangle. The continent contains several regions of coastal and mountain ranges, and interior plains. The Great Divide formed by the crest of the Rocky Mountains creates 2 great groups of rivers. One group, including the Colorado, Columbia, Fraser, and Yukon rivers, flows west into the Pacific; the other, which includes the Mackenzie, St. Lawrence, Rio Grande, Missouri, and Mississippi rivers, drains into the Atlantic Ocean or the Gulf of Mexico.
North America's climate ranges from polar in the north to tropical in the south. Climatic differences account for a wide variety of vegetation on the continent, ranging from arctic tundra in Greenland, northern Canada, and much of Alaska, to desert scrub in the Mojave, Sonora, and other deserts of the southwestern United States and Mexico, to tropical rain forests in the lowlands of Central America. Coniferous forests cover much of Canada, the northern Pacific ranges, and the southeastern United States. In the Appalachians, mixed forests predominate, while deciduous forests are characteristic of the coastal plain and the eastern part of the Interior Plain. Grassland covers vast areas of the rest of it, including the Great Plains.
People. With a total population of about 276,000,000, North America ranks third among all the continents. The most heavily populated regions lie in the eastern United States, southeastern Canada, along the Pacific coasts of both these countries, and in Central America. Indians were North America's first inhabitants; today the largest concentration of Native Americans and mestizos (mixed Indian and Spanish ancestry) is found in mainland Central America. Africans and mulattos (mixed black and white descent), whose ancestors were brought from Africa as slaves, constitute a large proportion of the population of the Caribbean islands. In the United States, about 10% of the population are of African-American descent. Caucasians of European descent form the great majority of North Americans.
Early history. It is thought that about 25,000 years ago peoples from Mongolia moved out of Asia across a natural land bridge that then linked the Asian and North American continents, where the Bering Strait is today. These people are believed to be the ancestors of all Native North American groups. It is known that Eric the Red, a Norseman, reached Greenland from Iceland in about A.D. 980, and Leif Ericsson reputedly landed in Nova Scotia about 1000. The first permanent contacts made by Europeans came in the 15th century, when Christopher Columbus landed on Hispaniola (1492) in the Bahamas, and John and Sebastian Cabot explored the coast of Newfoundland (1497).

North, Oliver Laurence (1943-), U.S. Marine lieutenant colonel, involved in the Iran-contra affair of the 1980s. A National Security Council aide under President Ronald Reagan, he was involved in illegal clandestine operations to divert funds raised by arms sales to Iran to aid the right-wing contra rebels seeking to oust the left-wing government of Nicaragua. He was finally convicted of criminal charges (1989). In 1990 he succeeded in having one of his 3 convictions overturned, and requested appeal of the remaining charges.
See also: Iran-Contra affair.

North Atlantic Treaty Organization (NATO), military defense organization of nations established in 1949 by Belgium, Canada, Denmark, France, Great Britain, Iceland, Italy, Luxembourg, the Netherlands, Norway, Portugal, and the United States. Greece and Turkey joined in 1951, West Germany in 1955, Spain in 1982, and Poland, the Czech Republic and Hungary in 1999. Its purpose originally was to protect Western Europe against attack particularly by the Soviet Union and its East European satellites. The falling of the totalitarian regimes in many Eastern European countries and the Soviet policy of glasnost has greatly reduced the military threat to NATO.
Since 1992, NATO has been cooperating in peace-operations under the mandate of The Organization for Security and Co-operation in Europe (OSCE) or the UN. After the attacks of September 11, 2001 in the U.S., the NATO invoked article 5 of the NATO constitution which claims that an attack on one member is an attack on all.

North Carolina (Tar Heel State, Old North State; pop. 7,425,000), state in the U.S., bor-

N

Mount Mitchell, the highest peak east of the Mississippi River, rises to a height of 6,683 ft (2,037 m) in the Black Mountains of western North Carolina.

N

dering on Tennessee, Georgia, South Carolina, the Atlantic Ocean and Virginia. Capital: Raleigh. Flat landscape in the coastal area, rising in the West into the Appalachian Mountains. Subtropical climate.

North Carolina is traditionally an agricultural state (tobacco, corn, grain, fruit); cattle and poultry; forestry. Also textile, tobacco, chemical and electrotechnical industries. Exploitation of mica, phosphate, stone, sand and gravel. Largest producer of brick, textile, cigarettes and furniture in the U.S. Colonized in the 16th century by the English. Was one of the first 13 states of the U.S.

Northcliffe, Viscount (1865-1922), publisher who created modern British journalism. On a base of popular journals, starting with the weekly *Answers to Correspondents* (1888), he built the world's biggest newspaper empire. He founded or bought the London *Evening News*, *Daily Mail*, *Sunday Dispatch*, *Daily Mirror*, *Observer*, and *Times*.

North Dakota (Flickertail State, Peace Garden State, Sioux State; pop. 641,000), midwestern state in north-central United States; bordered by Canada, the Red River (with Minnesota on the other side), South Dakota, and Montana.

North America's geographic center is in North Dakota, near Rugby. North Dakota's major rivers are the Missouri River and the Red River, and their tributaries. Devils Lake is the largest natural lake. Forests cover about one percent of the state. Principal cities are Fargo, Bismarck (capital), and Grand Forks.

Agriculture and mining are the mainstays of North Dakota's economy. Wheat is the most important crop. Beef cattle are the main livestock product. Chief mining products are petroleum, natural gas, lignite coal, sand and gravel, and clay. Chief manufactured products are processed foods, farm equipment, and printed materials. Tourism also contributes to the economy.

Until they gained statehood in 1889, North Dakota shared much of its history with South Dakota. A number of Indian tribes-including the Lakota (or Dakota) Sioux, Mandan, Assiniboine, and Cheyenne-lived in the area before the first Europeans, French explorers, arrived about 1738. The area had already been claimed for France by explorer La Salle in 1682. France ceded it to Spain, 1762-1800, then sold it to the United States under the 1803 Louisiana Purchase. North Dakota became the 39th state in 1889.

Northeast Passage, sea route linking the Atlantic and Pacific oceans. It passes north of the Eurasian mainland along the Arctic coast of Norway and the Russian Federation. Adolf Nordenskjöld, the Swedish explorer, was the first to sail its length (1878-1879), although its exploration dates from the 16th century. Area explorers included William Barents, Henry Hudson, James Cook, and Vitus Bering.
See also: Nordenskjöld, Nils Adolf Erik.

Northern harrier, or marsh hawk (*Circus cyaneus*), North American bird of prey. It belongs to the Old World vulture family, Accipitridae. Males are pale gray with a wingspan up to 45 in (114 cm) and a body 19 in (48 cm) long. Females are streaked brown; their bodies are slightly longer than the males'. Both have a white patch above the tail. They feed on snakes and fowl.

Northern Ireland (Ulster, pop. 1,663,000), northern part of the island of Ireland; 5,466 sq mi (14,153 sq km). Capital: Belfast. Mountainous; central Lough Neagh is lowest point. Cattle, agriculture; highly industrialized. Exploitation of basalt, lignite, gold ore, chalk, sand and gravel. High unemployment. Booming tourist industry. Remained part of the United Kingdom after Ireland's independence in 1921. The Catholic minority (35%), which is also less well-off than the Protestant majority, wishes to join the Republic of Ireland.

Ulster was occupied by Scottish and English colonists in 1603. They were, in contrast to the Irish, Protestant and royalist. They battled against the Irish struggle for independence in the 19th and 20th centuries. During the Government of Ireland Act in 1920, Ulster and the Irish Free State were both allowed their own governments. The British rule over Ulster and the neglected position of the Catholic minority (35%) in Northern Ireland were the cause of riots in the 1920s and again an Irish civil war in the 1960s. During this civil war the situation became so tense that the English government decided to make an end to the autonomous position of Northern Ireland in 1972 by sending in troops to restore peace. The IRA tried to end the British hegemony over Northern Ireland with various terrorist actions. In 1996 negotiations began between the North Irish parties and the Irish and British governments. This resulted in April 1998 in a peace treaty (Good Friday Agreement) in which the reinstatement of the Northern Irish Parliament, a closer cooperation between Ulster and the Irish Republic, and autonomy for Northern Ireland were the major points. The Unionist David Trimble was voted prime minister. However, the disarming of the IRA remained a serious obstacle in the peace process and stood in the way of a protestant and catholic government formation. Finally, an agreement was reached. Sinn Féin, the political branch of the IRA, was able to take part in the government under the condition that the IRA would give up its arms. At the end of 1999, the new government took office under the leadership of David Timble, which was suspended multiple times by the British government because the IRA did not proceed to disarm. It wasn't until 2001 that the IRA started to give up its arms, under pressure from Sinn Féin. A year later it suspended disarmament claiming Great Britain was not living up to the Good Friday agreement, therefore the Northern Ireland government was suspended once more.
See also: United Kingdom.

Northern lights *See:* Aurora.

Northern Mariana Islands (pop. 77,000), group of volcanic islands situated on the Mariana reef in the Pacific, 1,553 mi (2,500 km) east of the Philippines; 181 sq mi (471 sq km). With the exception of Guam, the islands form part of the Trust Territory of the Pacific Islands (U.S.) since 1947. Agricultural (sugar, coffee, coconuts). Main island is Saipan; capital Susupe; airport. Discovered by Magellan in 1521; Christianized by the Spaniards, sold to Germany in 1899.

Guam is part of the U.S. since 1898; conquered by the Japanese on 12 October 1941 and recaptured from 21 July to 10 August 1944 (1,400 Americans and 10,000 Japanese killed). The other islands were occupied by Japan during WW I, Japanese mandate since 1921. Tinian (24 July 1944) and Saipan (15 June to 9 July 1944) conquered by the U.S. (3,100 Americans and 27,000 Japanese killed). Since 1976 a Commonwealth in free association with the U.S.; since 1986 the inhabitants are American citizens without voting rights during the presidential elections. Economically the islands are dependent on the financial support of the U.S.

Northern pike *See:* Pike.

Northern Rhodesia *See:* Zambia.

Northern Territory, north-central region of Australia. Controlled first by New South Wales and then South Australia, it was granted self-government in 1978. Nearly a quarter of the territory is reservation land, home of the Aborigines, Australia's native people. Darwin, on the coast, is the capital and largest city. Numerous cattle and sheep ranches are in the dry interior. Mining, tourism, and pearling are important industries.
See also: Australia.

North Island *See:* New Zealand.

North Korea

Capital:	Pyongyang
Area:	46,540 sq mi (122,762 sq km)
Population:	22,893,000
Language:	Korean
Government:	People's republic
Independent:	1948
Head of gov.:	Prime minister
Per capita:	US$ 1.000
Monetary unit:	1 North Korean won = 100 chon

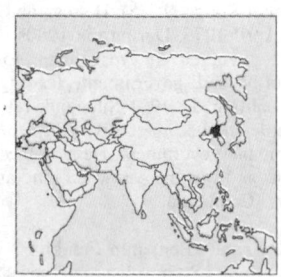

Small lumbering, mining, and manufacturing villages in North Korea's northern provinces have been developed to exploit the region's rich natural resources.

North Korea, isolated Republic in Eastern Asia. 22,893,000 people populate an area of 46,540 sq mi (120,540 sq km). Bordered to the north by Russia and by South Korea to the southeast. The Korea Bay and the Sea of Japan are on either side of the country.
Land and climate The northern part of the Korean peninsula is mainly mountainous and woody. The highest point is the Baitou Shan (or Paektu, 2744 m, a dormant Vulcan with a Crater Lake on top of it). Not far away from there, the Tuman and the Yaly, who border with China, rise. Flat and are deforested areas are situated along the west coast and the south coast. The coutry has a cold, continental climate with long, icy winters.
People Being one of the last communistic countries of the world, the authoritarian governed country is internationally isolated. The centrally planned economy is based on self-reliance, but the country is unable to produce enough food for its own population on the scanty fields. Malnutrition is widespread.
History The half-legendary founder of the kingdom of Choson was Kija, who led a group of exiles from China to Korea in 1122 B.C. But there were other kingdoms on the peninsula, and Korea was not united until the 7th century A.D. Most of its early civilization was destroyed by the Mongol invasions (1231-1292), but with the establishment of the Yi dynasty (1392) Korea entered a golden age that lasted until 1592, when Japan invaded the peninsula.
Although the invaders were finally driven out, the Koreans never fully recovered from the years of bloody fighting. For 300 years Korea, known as the Hermit Kingdom, cut itself off from the world. In the late 1800s, Japan and the U.S. began trading with Korea. In 1910 Japan annexed Korea. After 35 years of Japanese exploitation, Korea was liberated in 1945 by Russia in the North and by the U.S. in the South. Despite UN intervention, no agreement was reached on a united Korea. The North became a rigidly controlled Communist state under leader Kim II Sung. Free elections held in the South, under UN supervision, produced a republic under Syngman Rhee.
On June 25, 1950, the Communists of the North invaded South Korea, thus beginning the Korean War. The heavy fighting was eventually stopped by an armistice between the UN forces and the Communists, and by the establishment of the demilitarized zone (1953). Since then the uneasy peace has often been disturbed.
After the armistice (1953), Kim Il Sung aims at both political and economical independence. Kim eliminated all resistance against his communist dictatorship. He established a leadership dependent on the cult of personality. Since 1990, North and South Korea have sought for a dialogue aimed at unification. The results of the maladministration and serious floods forced the country to accept international help to fight the famine in the 1990s. Kim Yong Il succeeded his father after his death in 1994. He welcomed the South Korean President Kim Dae Yung in 2000, an important step to diplomatic thaw.
In 2002 the U.S. President George W. Bush said North Korea was part of an 'axis of evil' in 2002. The country agreed to freeze the nuclear program in return for free fuel and 2 nuclear reactors. However, North Korea reactivated its program at the end of 2002 and in 2003, the country withdrew from the Nuclear Non-Proliferation Treaty (NPT).
See also: South Korea; Korean War; Kim Il Sung; Kim Yong Il; Kim Dae Yung.

North magnetic pole *See:* North Pole.

Northmen *See:* Vikings.

North Pacific Current, ocean current fed by the Japan Current, heading east from the region of Japan to the U.S. West Coast, where it becomes the Alaska Current and California Current.

North Pole, northernmost point of the earth's axis, located at lat. 90°N, long. 0°, some 466 mi (750 km) north of Greenland. The North Pole is a geographical designation that does not coincide with the North Magnetic Pole. The Pole lies roughly in the center of the Arctic Ocean, which is permanently covered with ice. The pole was first reached by Robert E. Peary in 1909.
See also: Peary, Robert Edwin.

Northrop, John Howard (1891-1987), U.S. biochemist who received the 1946 Nobel Prize for chemistry, with James B. Somner and Wendell M. Stanley, for the crystallization of several pure enzymes (proteins that assist the body's chemical reactions). Professor of bacteriology at the University of California at Berkeley during the 1950s, he was a member of the Rockefeller Institute for Medical Research (now Rockefeller University), 1925-1987. *Crystalline Enzy-mes* (1939), written with M. Kunitz and R. M. Herriot, is his most important book.
See also: Enzyme.

North Sea, arm of the Atlantic Ocean lying between Great Britain, Scandinavia, and northwest Europe. Rich in fish, gas, and oil, the sea covers 222,125 sq mi (575,304 sq km), and has an average depth of 300 ft (91 m), falling to 2,400 ft (732 m) off Norway. Major gas and oil deposits have been found off the Dutch, Norwegian, and Scottish coasts.

North Star, also called Polaris, Cepheid variable star (Alpha Ursae Minoris) nearest the north celestial pole. Also known as the Polestar, it has been used in navigation for centuries.
See also: Star.

Northumbria, Anglo-Saxon kingdom of the 7th-10th centuries, extending from the Mersey and Humber rivers in the south to the Firth of Forth in the north. It became the cultural center of England due to the civilizing work of monks. After Danes overran the kingdom, the north remnant became subject to Wessex.

North Vietnam *See:* Vietnam.

Northwest Passage, inland water routes along the north coast of North America linking the Atlantic and Pacific Oceans. John Cabot explored the coast around Newfoundland in 1497, thinking it was China; Henry Hudson sailed to Hudson Bay and beyond (1609-1611); William Baffin and Robert Bylot sailed up Davis Strait an found a passage between Baffin Island and Greenland (1616). Explorations opened up important new lands, but not until Robert McClure's expedition of 1850-1854 was the existence of a passage weaving among the Arctic islands proved. The first complete journey was made when Roald Amundsen sailed west from Baffin Bay through Lancaster Sound (1903-1906). The first west-to-east journey was accoplished by a ship of the Royal Canadian Mounted Police, *St. Roch*, in 1942.

Northwest Territories, Canadian territories consisting of the districts of Mackenzie, Keewatin and Franklin; 1,323,441 sq mi (3,426,390 sq km). Capital: Yellowknife. Thousands of so-called *arctic islands*, some of which are situated 497 mi (800 km) from the North Pole, are part of the Northwest Territories. The climate runs from arctic to sub-arctic; many lakes and forests. The area is sparsely populated; almost a quarter of the entire population is formed by Inuit and

N

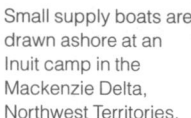

N

Small supply boats are drawn ashore at an Inuit camp in the Mackenzie Delta, Northwest Territories.

Native Americans. Since WW II mining (petroleum, natural gas, gold, silver, uranium, iron, copper and lead) is a more importance source of income than the fur trade; also fish processing industry and oil refinery, hunting and fishing.

Originally the territories were in the possession of the Hudson's Bay Company, which sold its rights to Canada in 1869. Since 1912 the territories exist in their present form. In 1999 this form will be adjusted according to new agreements with the native population; over 20% of the area will become a separate Inuit region under the name of Nunavut. *See also:* Canada.

North Yemen *See:* Yemen.

Norway

Capital:	Oslo
Area:	125,050 sq mi
	(323,878 sq km)
Population:	4,525,000
Language:	Norwegian
Government:	Parliamentary monarchy
Independent:	1905
Head of gov.:	Prime minister
Per capita:	US$ 30,800
Monetary unit:	1 Norwegian krone
	= 100 ore

Norway, kingdom of northern Europe, occupying the smaller western portion of the Scandinavian peninsula. It is sometimes called the 'Land of the Midnight Sun' since about one-third of it lies north of the Arctic Circle, where from mid-May into July there is continuous daylight; conversely, for part of the winter only twilight occurs at midday.

Land and climate. Norway covers 125,050 sq mi (323,878 sq km). It is bordered by Russia, Finland, and the Barents Sea in the north, Sweden in the east, the Skagerrak arm of the North Sea in the south, and the Atlantic Ocean in the west. Thousands of islands dot the coast, and the Norwegian territory also includes the Svalbard island group 300 mi (483 km) north of the mainland in the Arctic Ocean; also Jan Mayen, 500 mi (805 km) northeast, and Bouvet Island, Queen Maud Land, and Peter I Island in Antarctica. The extremely fragmented and indented coastline is perhaps Norway's most spectacular feature. Glaciers of the past dug deep valleys as they moved down mountains to the sea. When it flooded these depressions, it created the long indentions called fjords or fiords, which are usually ice-free in winter. Mountains cover almost the entire length of Norway, over half the country. The highest peak (and of Scandinavia) is Galdhpiggen (8,097 ft/2,468 km); west of it lies the largest icecap in mainland Europe, the Jostedalsbreen. Most of Norway's rivers are short and swift, used for logging and dams but with rapids preventing navigation. The longest is the Glomma, flowing 400 mi (644 km) into the Skagerrak. Of the many glacier-formed lakes, the largest is Mjösa (140 sq mi/363 sq km), north of Oslo. Despite its Arctic proximity, Norway has a relatively mild climate because of its maritime situation and the prevailing on-shore winds, which bring heavy rainfalls. Summers are cool, winters usually below freezing, although temperatures inland and in the mountains are much colder.

People. Scandinavians comprise most of the population, although there are some Lapps and Finns in the north. Most Norwegians live in urban areas. The largest cities are Oslo and Bergen, in the heavily populated south, and Trondheim in the north. There are 2 official Norwegian languages, Nynorsk and Bokmål, although Lapps speak Ugro-Finnic. The state religion is Evangelical Lutheran.

Economy. Abundant hydroelectric power supports industrialization, giving the Norwegians one of the world's highest living standards. Petroleum output from oil and mineral deposits under the continental shelf provides revenue. Rich coal deposits are mined in Spitsbergen, largest of the Svalbard islands. Although less than 3% of Norway's land is arable, grains, potatoes and fruits are grown. Sheep and other livestock are raised. Whaling and fishing, particularly of cod, mackerel, and herring, is a leading industry, as is lumbering, although only 25% of the land is forested. Since World War II, the thriving economy has been developed through restricting imports and promoting industrialization. The chief industries are pulp and paper manufactures, fish canning, electrochemicals, electrometellurgicals, oil and gas refining, and shipbuilding; Norway has one of the world's largest merchant fleets.

History. For 2 centuries after A.D. 800, Vikings from Norway, the Norsemen, raided and occupied European coastal towns, notably Normandy, as well as islands off Scotland and Canada, and parts of England, Iceland, and Ireland. Later, civil wars preoccupied the country, though it enjoyed prosperity too, before it was united with Denmark (1397-1814), then Sweden. In 1905 Norway became a constitutional monarchy under

The north coast of Europe is very much indented. There are many fjords, especially along the coast of Norway. Fjords are inlets of the sea between steep mountain slopes, formed by glacial erosion and the subsequent submergence of trough-shaped valleys, as the result of a rise in sea level.

Haakon VII, a Danish prince. Mass emigrations to the United States, arctic explorations, and the socialized government's social welfare legislation have predominated since. Germany occupied Norway throughout World War II. It is a member of NATO and the European Free Trade Association but, in a 1972 referendum, rejected membership in the Common Market. The country has continued to debate since then whether to join the European Union, and the debate took a sharp turn in 1990 when the Progress Party came out in favor of membership. However, in a popular referendum held in 1994 and in 2001 a small majority of the electorate voted against membership.

Norwegian, language of Norway, developed from the Norse and influenced by union with Denmark (1397-1814). There are 2 official versions: *Nynorsk* or *Landsmäl*, based on native dialects, and *Bokmäl* or *Riksmäl*, a Dano-Norwegian used by city dwellers, writers, and the press. Differences between them are diminishing.

Norwegian elkhound, breed of dog originally used by Norwegian hunters and shepherds in the 4000s B.C. At about 50 lb (23 kg) with a thick gray coat, it is a high-spirited dog known for its ability to smell prey from as far away as 3 mi (5 km). It was used to hunt elk, mountain lion, lynx, and game birds.

Norwich terrier, hunting dog first bred in England around 1880. Characterized as rugged, alert, energetic, and affectionate, it has a stocky build, a thick wiry coat, and stands about 10 in (25 cm) high at the shoulder. It is often used in England in fox hunting and in the United States to hunt rabbits and other small animals.

Nose, organ of breathing and smell, located in the middle of the face. The nose consists of bone and cartilage extension with 2 external openings, or nostrils. These pass into the nasal cavities, which are separated from each other by a septum and contain turbinates that increase the mucous membrane surface and direct the air flow. The chemoreceptors for smell lie mainly in the roof of the nasal cavities, but fine nerve fibers throughout the nose contribute both to tactile sensation and smell.

Nostradamus (Michel de Nostredame; 1503-1566), French astrologer, famed for his prophecies published in verse, *Centuries* (1555). He was court physician to Charles IX, and his prediction of Henry II's death 4 years ahead made his name, though his prophecies were generally vague.
See also: Astrology.

Notary public, state-appointed official who certifies the authenticity of documents and takes oaths. Birth certificates, marriage licenses, and property deeds require notarizing, to avoid the possibility of forging. A notary affixes a seal to a document when he or she is certain that the person who signed it is known to him or her and that the signature is genuine. In most states anyone can become a notary with proof of good character, legal age, and residence in the area in which he or she wishes to be appointed.

Notation, in music, method of writing down notes to be read for study or performance. The method was formalized between the 10th and 18th centuries into a system, now in general use, of stave notation. This consists of five horizontal lines, or staves, as the framework on which any of 8 notes can be written: A, B, C, D, E, F, G (in ascending or descending order of pitch), then to A again an octave higher or lower, and so forth. Each note's placement on or between the lines depends on its pitch: if low, in the bass clef of staves; if higher, in the treble clef. A middle, or alto, clef is sometimes used.
The key in which the music is to be performed is indicated by symbols for sharps and flats on the staves next to the clef sign at the beginning of the score. Sometimes such a symbol is placed against a single note on a line to indicate that its pitch is to be momentarily sharped or flatted. The length the notes are to be held, relative to each other, is shown by the form they are notated in. Commonly, there are 7 ways the notes can be formed, from the longest held to the shortest. The beat of the music is shown by dividing the staves with vertical lines into bars and marking at the outset how many beats there are to each bar. This establishes rhythm. Other notations are the *tonic sol-fa*, in which notes are related to each other, not to the established pitch of the written stave; and *tablature*, in which a diagram indicates where to place the fingers on various instruments to obtain notes. For electronic music, new signs are being devised.

Note, or promissory note, written record in which an individual agrees to pay a designated sum of money to a specified individual. Like bank checks, notes are negotiable and can be transferred from one holder to another.

Notre Dame, Cathedral of, cathedral church of Paris, on the Île de la Cité in the Seine River. Begun in 1163, it was consecrated in 1183. The nave was completed in 1196. In 1230 flying buttresses were added and the nave was rebuilt. Chapels were later added, and the cathedral was not complete until 1313. It is one of the finest examples of early Gothic architecture, especially for the rose window of the west facade and the sculptured portals. Some restoration was necessary after the French Revolution.

Nottingham (pop. 283,000), city in England, administrative seat of Nottinghamshire. Located on the River Trent, Nottingham is a transportation center and industrial city known for its manufacture of tobacco, pharmaceuticals, hose, lace, and bicycles. The city is noted for its medieval architecture and for its proximity to Sherwood Forest, the legendary home of Robin Hood.

Nouakchott (pop. 600,000), the capital of Mauritania and an important port city on the Altantic coast of West Africa. Once a small fishing village, it became the capital when Mauritania won independence from France in 1957. Severe droughts in rural areas have driven large numbers of people into the city, contributing to serious problems of overcrowding. Its industries include handicrafts, chemical products, and soft drinks.
See also: Mauritania.

Nouveau réalisme (New Realism), group of artists formed in 1960 in France and named by Pierre Restany, who wanted to analyze the identity of everyday objects of modern society by placing them outside their daily

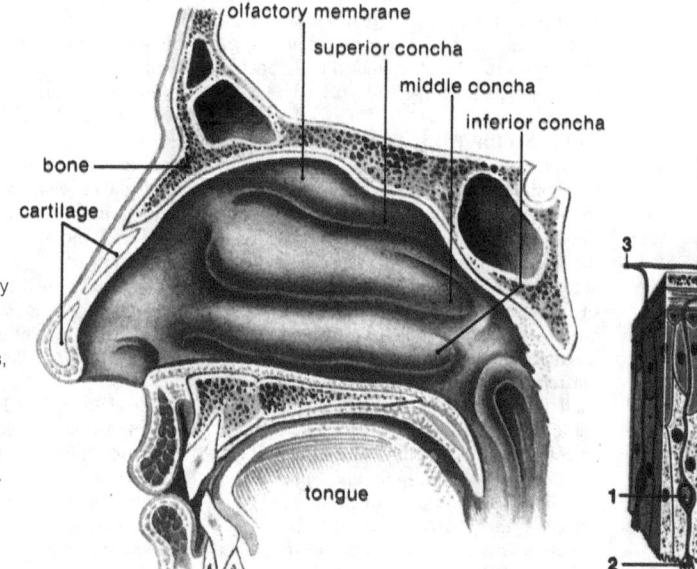

The nose is divided by the septum into two cavities, each containing three folds, called conchae, and lined with a mucous membrane. Air taken in through the nostrils is filtered by the cilia - small hairs in the mucous membrane - moistened by the mucus, and warmed by the blood vessels of the superior conchae. The olfactory membrane (detail), which is located in the mucous membrane of the superior conchae and the adjacent part of the septum, contains olfactory cells (1), which are nerve cells that are sensitive to odours. Airborne chemicals interact with the ciliated endings (2) of these cells, then nerve impulses are carried by the olfactory nerve (3) to the brain.

N

surroundings. The result is a certain form of alienation. This is how the movement distinguishes itself from the pop art movement, which uses mostly everyday objects that are reproduced.

Artists belonging to the nouveau réalisme include Arman, Yves Klein, Martial Raysse, Daniel Spoerri and Jean Tinguely, and later also César, Christo and Niki de Saint-Phalle.

Nouvelle Tendance (New Tendency), umbrella name for various European artists' alignments from the 1960s which came about as a response to abstract expressionism. For their non-emotional art they made use of elementary visual means in which the artist's personal trademark was eliminated as much as possible. The artist's work was dependent on outside influences such as light, time and space, therefore approaching kinetic art, the art of light and the environment. The contribution of science and technique to Nouvelle Tendance was significant. Groups such as Zero are also regarded as belonging to the Nouvelle Tendance movement. The same can also be said for artists like Alviani, Manzoni, Soto and Takis.

Nova, relatively small, very hot variable star that suddenly (usually within a few days) increases up to thousands of times in brightness. It is thought that the increase in brightness is caused by violent explosions that eject some of the star's mass, which escapes the star's gravitational field. The decline to the previous luminosity generally takes months or years. Recurrent novas are stars that flare in this way at irregular periods of a few decades. Dwarf novas are subdwarf stars that go nova every few weeks or months.
See also: Binary star; Supernova.

Novalis (Friedrich Leopold von Hardenberg; 1772-1801), German poet. His works, notably *Heinrich von Offerdingen* (1802), influenced later European exponents of Romanticism. He attempted to unite poetry, philosophy, and science allegorically.

Nova Scotia (pop. 923,000), Canadian province on the Atlantic Ocean, including the homonymous peninsula; 21,432 sq mi (55,490 sq km). The capital is Halifax. Nova Scotia is a watery area which forms part of the Appalachian Mountains. The services sector is the largest of the economy, but also of importance are industry (iron, steel, chemical, food and paper), fishing (crustaceans, scrod and herring), mining (coal, plaster, tin, copper, lead, salt, asphalt, clay, sand and gravel) and agriculture (especially cattle and poultry farming).
In 1605 part of French Acadie, later British. In 1755 the French-speaking population was deported by the British colonial government to what is now the U.S.; the American poet Longfellow wrote about this in his poem *Evangeline* (1847). This is why Nova Scotia is also called *Land of Evangeline*. During the formation of Canada (1867) Nova Scotia was one of the first provinces. The name is Latin for New Scotland; in the 1620s the area was named by Scottish colonists.

Novaya Zemlya, group of 2 large islands and several smaller ones in the Russian Federation, in the Arctic Ocean between the Barents Sea on the west and the Kara Sea on the east. Total area is 36,000 sq mi (93,600 sq km). The 2 large islands are separated by a narrow strait, the Matochkin Shar. Used as a Soviet nuclear testing site, the islands have a small native population that fishes and hunts in the southern tundra areas.

Novel, work of prose fiction longer than the short story and novella. Although there were precursors in ancient Greece and Rome and in medieval Japan, the novel arose primarily in late medieval and early Renaissance Europe. The term come from the Italian *novella*, a literary form typified by Giovanni Boccaccio's *Decameron*. François Rabelais' *Gargantua* and *Pantagruel* (1532-1552) and Miguel Cervantes' *Don Quixote* (1605-1615) are prototypes of the European novel. In English literature the form was established in the 18th century by authors such as Daniel Defoe, Samuel Richardson, and Henry Fielding. In the 19th century the novel became the dominant form of literature in Europe and the Americas. Major authors included Jane Austen and Charles Dickens (England), Victor Hugo, Gustave Flaubert, Emile Zola, and Honoré de Balzac (France), Leo Tolstoy, Fyodor Dostoevski, and Ivan Turgenev (Russia), and Nathaniel Hawthorne, Herman Melville, and Mark Twain (United States). All these novelists told stories of individual characters faced with social and psychological problems that had a universality that went beyond the particular setting. In the 20th century, novelists began experimenting with more varied forms of language, dialogue, and structure. Another development that has enriched the novel in the 20th century was the spread of the form to non-European cultures, such as China, Africa, and the Arab world. Since 1980, the Nobel Prize for literature has been won by novelists from Colombia (Gabriel García Márquez), Nigeria (Wole Soyinka), and Egypt (Naguib Mahfouz).

Noverre, Jean-Georges (1727-1810), French dancer and choreographer. Founder of the ballet d'action (narrative ballet). Pleaded for the abolishment of wigs, hoop skirts and masques (which prevent facial expression) and aimed for total coherence between dance, music, scenery and costumes. Published his revolutionary ideas in *Letters on Dancing and Ballet* (1760).

Novgorod (pop. 240,000), city in the northwestern Russian Federation, capital of Novgorod Oblast. Located on the Volkhov River, it long formed a trade link between the Baltic and the Orient and was the capital of the Russian state in 862. Although later superseded as the capital by Kiev, in 1136 it again became the capital of a north Russian state. During the Middle Ages Novgorod was a cultural and a commercial center carrying on trade with the Hanseatic League. Its importance declined after 1703, when the city of St. Petersburg was founded. Many of Novgorod's medieval buildings were dam-

aged during the German occupation (1941-1944) in World War II, but some remain.
See also: Russian Federation.

Novi Sad (pop. 186,000), city in the Federal Republic of Yugoslavia, transportation center and capital of the autonomous region of Vojvodina, in the Serbian republic. Located on the Danube River and the Belgrade-Budapest railway line, Novi Sad has many cultural institutions serving an ethnically diverse population including Hungarians, Serbs, Croats, and Romanians. Its industries include food processing, textiles, milling, and electrical equipment.
See also: Yugoslavia.

Novocaine *See:* Procaine.

Novokuznetsk (pop. 600,000) Russia, a city on the Tom River in southern Siberia, about 1,850 mi (2,980 km) east-southeast of Moscow. Novokuznetsk is the chief industrial city in the coal-rich Kuznetsk Basin and has one of Russia's largest iron and steel works. There are also large engineering, chemical, ferro-alloy, and aluminum plants. The city was founded in 1617 as Kuznetsk. It was a small settlement until 1929, when work began nearby on a giant iron and steel plant. During 1932-1961 the city was known as Stalinsk.

Novosibirsk (pop. 1,400,000), city in southern Siberia, Russian Federation, on the Ob River and the Trans-Siberian railway line. Founded in the late 19th century as a camp for railway workers, Novosibirsk developed into a river, rail, and air transport center during World War II. Its industries include textiles, heavy machinery, metals, and chemicals. Novosibirsk is the also the site of an important Soviet scientific research center.
See also: Russian Federation.

Novotna, Jana (1968-   ), Czech tennis player who won various ATP tournaments after her debut in 1986. She reached the finals of a Grand Slam tournament three times (1991 Australia, 1993 and 1997 Wimbledon), but did not win her first title until 1998, when she beat French Nathalie Tauziat in the Wimbledon final. In the same year Novotna also won the title in the women's doubles at Wimbledon with her partner Martina Hingis. Novotna has a top-ten ranking since 1991, with a second place in 1997 as best result.

Novotny, Antonín (1904-1975), president of Czechoslovakia (1957-68) and communist leader. As a Stalinist and supporter of Moscow, Novotny fell from power after years of economic stagnation and political unrest. He was succeeded by a liberal regime led by Alexander Dubek and others.
See also: Czechoslovakia.

Noyes, Alfred (1880-1958), English poet, a traditionalist known for his popular, vigorous, rhythmic ballads, such as 'The Highwayman,' and patriotic, blank-verse epics, such as *Drake* (1908), about the Elizabethans, and *The Torch Bearers* (1922-1930), a trilogy praising scientific progress. His *Collected Poems* were published in 1950.

Nu, U (1907-1995), Burmese political leader, prime minister (1948-1956, 1957-1958, and 1960-1962). A founder of the Anti-Fascist People's League after World War II, he was the first prime minister of independent Burma. Twice ousted by army coups, he left Burma in 1969 but continued to support minority rebel groups against the government until 1973. He returned from exile in 1980.

Nubia, ancient region of northeastern Africa, now mostly in the Sudan, along both banks of the Nile River from Khartoum in the south to Aswan (Egypt) in the north. In the 8th and 7th centuries B.C. Egypt was ruled by a Nubian dynasty that was ousted when the Assyrians took over c.667 B.C. In the 3rd century A.D. the Nobatae, a black tribe, settled in Nubia and founded a kingdom that lasted for centuries. It was Christianized in the 6th century and disintegrated under Muslim pressure in the late 14th century.

Nuclear bomb *See:* Nuclear weapon.

Nuclear energy, energy released through the fission or fusion of atomic nuclei. In fission, the nucleus of a heavy atom absorbs an extra neutron, which causes it to become unstable and split apart into 2 lighter nuclei plus other subatomic particles, including other neutrons. Fission can occur only in a few of the heaviest, least stable nuclei. The energy released by a fission reaction consists mainly of the transformation of nuclear forces (the forces holding the nucleus together) into heat. Fusion is the opposite process: here the lightest nuclei (usually isotopes of hydrogen) are squeezed together under conditions of extreme heat and pressure until they merge, forming a new nucleus whose mass is very slightly smaller than the total masses of the nuclei that were fused. The extra mass is converted into energy (mostly heat) according to Einstein's formula $E=mc^2$, where E is energy, m is mass, and c is the speed of light. Since c^2 is a very large number, the energy yielded by this reaction is large even when the mass, m, is very small. Fission reactions were first observed in 1938. When the nucleus of Uranium-235 is bombarded with neutrons, it splits apart, releasing an average of 2.5 free neutrons. If these released neutrons collide with other nuclei of U-235, a chain reaction ensues. If this reaction is uncontrolled, the result is an atomic explosion like the one caused by the atomic bombs dropped on the Japanese cities of Hiroshima and Nagasaki in 1945. This is what happens in a nuclear reactor. Fusion, unlike fission, requires very high temperatures. In a hydrogen bomb, these temperature are brought about by a fission explosion, which triggers uncontrolled fusion reactions in the hydrogen that is packed around the fission bomb. So far, attempts to create controlled fusion reactions are only at the research stage. One line of experimentation has been to use magnetic fields to contain hydrogen fuel in the form of a plasma, a fully ionized gas containing equal numbers of positive and negative ions. Another has been to bombard pellets of frozen deuterium (a hydrogen isotope) with high-powered laser beams. The successful control of fusion would be an epoch-making achievement in providing energy. Unlike fissionable fuel and fossil fuels like oil, hydrogen is virtually limitless, and fusion produces far fewer radioactive by-products than fission. This means that fusion reactors, if they are possible, would produce much less radioactive waste than today's fission reactors do.

Nuclear fission *See:* Fission; Nuclear energy.

Nuclear force *See:* Grand unified theories.

Nuclear magnetic resonance (NMR) *See:* Magnetic resonance imaging.

Nuclear medicine, branch of medicine that uses radioisotopes in diagnostic and treatment procedures.

Nuclear physics, study of the physical properties, structure, and laws of the atomic nucleus and subatomic particles. Its primary area of concern is the nature of matter and the behavior of elementary particles. The subject has grown rapidly with the technical exploitation of nuclear energy. *See also:* Atom; Particle physics; Radio-activity.

Nuclear power *See:* Nuclear energy.

Nuclear reactor, device containing sufficient fissionable material to produce a controlled chain reaction of neutrons able to split other nuclei. Many types of reactors ex-

N

The pressurized water reactor at the Ko-Ri power station, near Pusan in South Korea, is typical of nuclear reactors that are most commonly used throughout the world for producing electricity. Water under high pressure serves both for regulation of the fissioning process, and for extraction of the heat from the hot core. The heat is then utilized to produce high pressure steam, driving conventional turbines and electric generators.

Among the many components of this plant are: a seawater inlet tunnel (1), a cooling water pump house (2), a cooling water supply to the turbine house (3), a cold-water discharge (4) and a discharge house (5), an auxiliary-building ventilation (6), a waste-drum storage area (7), a steam generator (8), a water pressurizer (9), a refueling gantry (10), a reactor coolant pump (11), a fuel-handling crane (12), a spent-fuel drum (13), a fuel-loading and unloading bay (14), a new fuel-storage area (15), a decontamination pit (16), a reactor vessel (17), a drum-loading area (18), a spent-fuel storage rack (19), a main control room (20), a condenser (21), transformers (22), and an electricity-distribution center (23).

N

ist; all produce neutrons, gamma rays, radioactive fission products, and heat. A fission reactor consists of a fuel, a moderator, and a cooling system. The fragments produced by fission of a heavy nucleus have a large amount of energy, and the heat they produce may be used for carrying out a variety of high-temperature processes or for heating a working fluid (such as steam) to operate a turbine and produce electricity. Nuclear reactors are also used to power ships and submarines. The 1979 accident at Pennsylvania's Three Mile Island reactor-involving a partial fuelcore meltdown and the release of radioactive gases into the atmosphere-brought the issue of nuclear safety to the public. Concern for safety increased with the 1986 explosion and fire at a nuclear power plant at Chernobyl in the former USSR.

Nuclear submarine *See:* Submarine.

Nuclear weapon, powerful explosive weapon whose power derives from nuclear energy. There are 2 main types of such weapons: fission bombs and fusion, or thermonuclear, bombs. The bombs dropped by the United States on the Japanese cities Hiroshima and Nagasaki in 1945, during World War II, were fission bombs. Fusion bombs (also called hydrogen bombs, or H-bombs) were

developed in the early 1950s and have never been used in warfare. Various countries today have fission bombs, but only 5 countries-the United States, the former Soviet Union, Britain, France, and China-have produced and tested fusion bombs.
See also: Nuclear energy.

Nuclear winter, term referring to the global environmental catastrophe that might occur as a result of dramatic changes in the earth's atmosphere caused by nuclear war. The theory holds that the dust and debris hurled into the sky by nuclear bombs would remain in the air for years, blocking a large percentage of the sun's light and resulting in freezing temperatures throughout the world. Nearly all crops would die, food chains would be interrupted, and many species of plant and animal life would become extinct. Agriculture as we know it would no longer be possible.
See also: Nuclear weapon.

Nucleic acid, the vital chemical constituents of living things; a class of complex threadlike molecules comprising 2 main types: DNA (deoxyribonucleic acid) and RNA (ribonucleic acid). DNA is found almost exclusively in the nucleus of the living cell, where it forms the chief material of the chromosomes. The DNA molecule's ability to du-

plicate itself (replicate) makes cell reproduction possible; by directing protein synthesis, DNA controls heredity. RNA performs several important tasks connected with protein synthesis, and is found throughout the cell.

Nucleus, in biology, the central part of a cell, containing the genetic material; also, a group of nerve cells or mass of gray matter in the central nervous system. In physics, the central core of an atom, positively charged, containing the vast majority of the atom's mass.
See also: Biology; Cell.

Nuer, people living in southern Sudan on both banks of the Nile River. The raising of cattle for sacrifice is central to their way of life. Because of seasonal flooding, the Nuer spend part of each year on higher ground, where they grow crops such as millet and peanuts.

Nullification, form of invalidity of legal acts in which the legal act does not lead to the desired legal effect. Legal nullification of legal acts can take place automatically or be invoked. When the latter occurs, it is said to be reversible. Legal acts can automatically become nullified when e.g. they are in defiance with public decency or public order, or in some cases when legal demands have not been carried out. As a consequence of this, the legal objective is not reached. Legal acts can be reversible when, for instance, they have been performed under the absence of consensus ad idem.

Numbers, Book of, book of the Old Testament, fourth of the 5 books of the Pentateuch (or Torah), describing the 40-year wanderings of the Israelites through the desert after their exodus from Egypt and before their arrival in Palestine.
See also: Bible; Old Testament.

Number theory, branch of mathematics that deals with the integers (or whole numbers), which include zero and the negative whole numbers. One of the important concepts of number theory is that of the prime numbers, those numbers greater than 1 divisible only by 1 and themselves. For instance, 2, 3, 5, and 7 are prime numbers, whereas 9 is not, since it is divisible by 3. One of the best-known theorems of number theory, called *the fundamental theory of arithmetic,* states that every positive integer can be expressed as the product of prime numbers that are unique. For example, the number 15 can be expressed as 3 x 5 and by no other product of primes (except for 5 x 3, which is regarded as the same thing). This theorem is attributed to the ancient Greek mathematician Euclid, who may be considered the founder of number theory.

Numeration systems, or number systems, method of arranging and representing numbers. The most familiar and widely used system today is the decimal system. Based on innovations of Hindu mathematicians of the 4th and 3rd centuries B.C., and introduced to Europe by the Arabs, it uses 10 numerals or digits, 0 through 9, which stand for different values according to whether

In each type of organism, the cell nucleus contains a number of chromosomes (A), each of which (B) consists of a threadlike complex of DNA and protein (1), coiled into a tightly packed structure. Each DNA molecule (C) consists of a backbone of two chains — composed of the sugar deoxyribose (2) and phosphate molecules (3) — linked by purine-pyrimidine base pairs. DNA has four bases: thymine (magenta) always pairs with adenine (green), and cytosine (yellow) with guanine (purple). The order of the bases in each chain forms the genetic code. The entire DNA molecule twists to form a double helix.

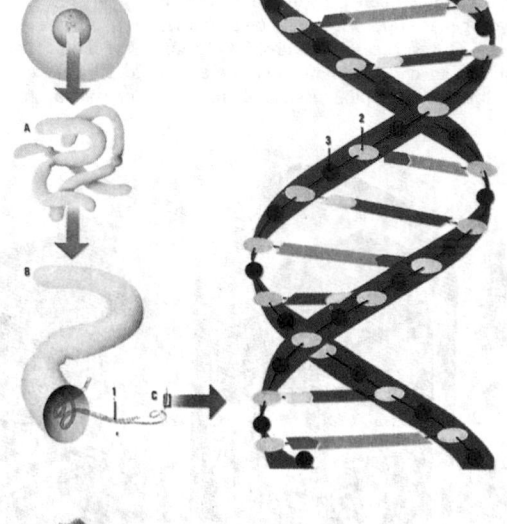

When a DNA molecule (A) replicates, the two strands (1, 2) uncoil and the base pairs separate. Free bases in the cell nucleus then form bonds with corresponding bases of the DNA strands; that is: cytosine bonds with guanine and adenine with thymine. Sugar and phosphate molecules attach to these new bases and form the new backbones (3, 4) of two new double-stranded DNA molecules (B, C). Each original strand thus serves as a template for the formation of a complementary new strand, a process known as semiconservative replication. DNA replication occurs in cells during the period inbetween cell divisions.

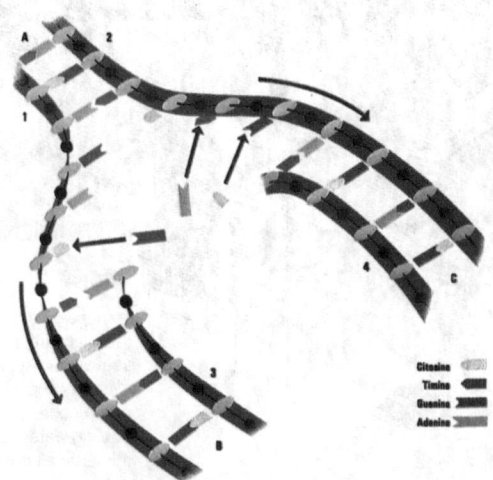

they represent 1s, 10s, 100s, or other powers of 10. For this reason the decimal system is also called 'numbers to the base 10.' Originally, numerals 1-9 were combined with words to accomplish this. The number 263 might be read as '2 hundreds, 6 tens, and 3 ones.' With the Hindu invention of the zero C.A.D. 600, a more efficient method became possible. Here the position of the digit determines its value. In the number 200, 2 zeros are needed to hold the positions of the tens and ones, so that the digit 2 can be correctly interpreted as 2 hundreds. This system, disseminated by Arab mathematicians, reached Europe in the 12th century. The decimal system was later extended to include a representation of fractions. Positions of digits representing fractions are separated by those representing integers (whole numbers) by a decimal point. Thus, while values to the left of the decimal point represent 10^0 (ones), 10^1 (tens), 10^2 (hundreds), and so on, values to the right of the decimal point represent 10^{-1} (1/10 or tenths), 10^{-2} (1/100 or hundredths), 10^{-3} (1/1,000 or thousandths), and so on. Numeration systems can be based on numbers other than 10 while applying the same principle of positional value. The binary system or base 2, for example, uses only 2 digits, 0 and 1; positional values are based on powers of 2. For instance: in the binary system 1011 means $(1 \times 2^0) + (1 \times 2^1) + (0 \times 2^2) + (1 \times 2^3) = 1 + 2 + 0 + 8 = 11$. Invented by the German mathematician Gottfried Wilhelm Leibniz (1646-1716), the binary system became important in the development of computers, because 'on' and 'off' switches or electrical circuits could be used to represent 0 and 1. The hexadecimal system, base 16, uses 16 digits (commonly, 0-9 and A-F), with place values equal to powers of 16. It is also of importance in computers. The number system of the ancient Babylonians, which had a base 60, survives in the division of the hour into 60 minutes, each divided into 60 seconds. It is also reflected in the degrees, minutes, and seconds in which angles may be measured.

Numerology, use of numbers to predict future events or provide insight into personality. Numerology translates the letters in particular names and dates into numbers, each of which is claimed to have certain unique properties. There is no evidence whatever that numerology has the slightest validity.

Numidia, ancient region of northern Africa, generally corresponding to present-day Algeria. The Numidian chieftain Massinisa helped the Romans defeat the Carthaginians in the Second and Third Punic wars in the 3rd and 2nd centuries B.C. Julius Ceasar later turned Numidia into a Roman province.

Numismatics *See:* Coin collecting.

Nummulite, single-celled sea organism from the Eocene and Oligocene periods. Nummulite fossils are abundant in rocks from this period, such as the limestone that was used to build the pyramids of Egypt. Nummulites belong to the camarind family.

N

Nun, woman member of a religious order, who devotes her life to religious service. In Roman Catholic canon law, a nun takes solemn vows of poverty, chastity, and obedience; some orders are devoted to prayer and contemplation.

Nuremberg (pop. 500,000), historic city of Bavaria, southwestern Germany, on the Pegnitz River. Founded in the 11th century, it became a cultural and trading center in the Middle Ages and was the first city to accept the Reformation. Hitler staged annual rallies here in the 1930s and proclaimed anti-Jewish laws in 1934. Now a major manufacturing city, it was the scene of war crimes trials following World War II.
See also: Germany.

Nuremberg Trials, series of war crimes trials held in Nuremberg, Germany (1945-1949) by the victors of World War II: the United States, USSR, Great Britain, and France. The accused, including Joachim von Ribbentrop, Hermann Goering, and Rudolf Hess, were tried for crimes against peace, war crimes, and crimes against humanity. In total more than 200 Germans were tried in 13 separate trials from October 1945 until 1949.
See also: International law; War crime; World War II.

Nureyev, Rudolf (1938-1993), Russian ballet dancer who sought asylum in the West when touring with the Kirov Ballet in 1961. As a guest artist of the Royal Ballet, London, Nureyev was famous as a leading classical and modern dancer and for his partnership with Margot Fonteyn. He also staged several ballets. He was director of the Paris Opéra from 1983 onwards.
See also: Ballet.

Nurmi, Paavo Johannes (1897-1973), Finnish athlete, won medals on three Olympic tournaments. In 1920 he won the 10 km and the 10 km cross country (both individually and with his team). In 1924 he won the 1500 m, 5 km, 3 km relay race and the 10 km cross country (again both individ-

ually and with his team). During the 1928 Olympics he won the 10 km. Nurmi also achieved twenty world records on various distances. Because of his status he carried the Olympic flame into the stadium in Helsinki in 1952.

Nursery rhyme, short, rhymed poem or tale intended to amuse children. The term nursery rhyme was first used in *Blackwood's Edinburgh Magazine* in 1824. There are 8 types of popular nursery rhymes: lullabies, singing game rhymes, nonsense rhymes, rhyming riddles, counting-out rhymes, tongue twisters, verse stories, and cumulative rhymes. The majority of nursery rhymes were created after 1600 and for many years, nursery rhymes were passed from generation to generation orally. *Mother Goose's Melody* (1781) was one of the first published compilations of nursery rhymes. Other collections include *The Nursery Rhymes of England* (1842) and *The Oxford Dictionary of Nursery Rhymes* (1951).

Nursery school, preschool care and early education for children from about 3 to 5 years old. Nursery schools developed from 19th-century infant care programs for factory women's children, launched by Robert Owen (1771-1858) in Great Britain and copied in Europe as the Industrial Revolution spread. Johann Pestalozzi (1746-1827), Friedrich Froebel (1782-1852), and Maria Montessori (1870-1952) pioneered preschool methods of nursery education. Nursery schools today have developed programs in which the young learn by experience and through play to understand others, the world around them, and themselves.

Nursing, care of the sick, injured, or handicapped. Until the 19th century nursing was administered by religious bodies such as the Sisters of Charity (founded in 1634). In 1860 Florence Nightingale opened a school in London to establish nursing as a career. Today training includes classroom and hospital experience. Specialized nursing also exists, for example, coronary care and nursing of the mentally handicapped.

N

Nursing home, institution in which patients are nursed who do not need the specialist care of a hospital, but who cannot be taken care of at home (chronically sick patients, terminal patients and people who need rehabilitation). Less expensive than a hospital (mostly because, contrary to hospitals, which employ nurses, nursing homes employ orderlies) and better adapted to the specific needs of people who suffer from a protracted illness.

Nut, the edible kernel of a dry fruit, such as the walnut or chestnut, enclosed in a hard shell. Nuts are rich in minerals and some vitamins, abundant in carbohydrates and fats. Peanuts, in spite of their name, are legumes.

All four major nuts shown here are classified as true nuts. Most edible chestnuts (A) grow on large deciduous trees native to Europe. Usually found in small clusters enclosed in a prickly bur, chestnuts have a thin brown shell and a sweet kernel.

Brazil nuts (B) grow on large evergreen trees found in South America, primarily in Brazil near the Amazon river. This round, woody fruit contains 18-30 seeds, or nuts. The threesided nuts have a tough outer shell, a papery inner covering, and white kernels.

Most commercial hazelnuts, or filberts (C), come from deciduous trees or shrubs grown in parts of Turkey, Italy, Spain, and the northwestern United States. The nuts grow in clusters of 1-8, each in a separate husk. Hazelnuts have smooth shells that are thin and hard and kernels that are rich in oil.

Walnuts (D) are found on tall deciduous trees native to North and South America and parts of Europe and Asia. The nuts grow in small clusters, each in a thick woody or pulpy husk. The sweet kernels are enclosed in a hard shell.

Nutcracker, any of several birds of the crow family. Found in the mountainous pine regions of North America and Eurasia, nutcrackers feed mainly on nuts, seeds, and pine cones.

Nuthatch, any of various small birds of the family Sittidae, found in temperate climates worldwide. The name derives from the birds' ability to open nuts by wedging them into the bark of trees. Known to be tame and sociable, they will look for food in places inhabited by humans.

Nutmeg, evergreen tree (*Myristica fragrans*) grown in the tropics for the sweet, tangy spices it produces. The spice called nutmeg comes from the tree's seed kernels; another spice, mace, comes from the fiber that covers each kernel.

Nutmeg State *See:* Connecticut.

Nutria, large South American water rodent (*Myocastor coypus*), also found in the Mississippi Delta, raised commercially in Europe and North America for its reddish-brown fur, which resembles that of the beaver or muskrat. Because it feeds on water plants, it is considered a threat to the ecology. It is also known to destroy certain crops.

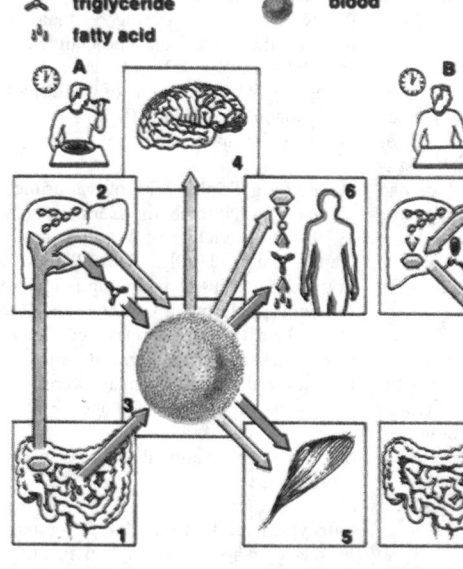

The body produces energy by burning fuel in its cells. Food is converted into fuel during the digestive process, and is stored in the form of carbohydrate or fats, to be used when needed. The body's primary fuel is the sugar glucose, which is stored in solid form as glycogen, and in liquid form as glycerol. Surplus sugar, combined with fatty acids forms triglyceride, a fat compound that may be broken down into small combustible molecules, called ketones. Fuel production (A) begins in the small intestine (1), which absorbs glucose and fatty acids from digested food. Glucose is processed in the liver (2), which stores one portion and passes the rest on to the bloodstream, partly in triglyceride form. Once in the bloodstream (3), the fuel is carried to all body tissues, including the organs (4) and the muscles (5). The fuel that is not immediately required for energy is deposited in adipose tissue (6). During periods of fasting (B), these stored fuels will be retrieved and sent to the liver, where they will be broken down into easily burned ketone and glucose molecules. Thus, the muscles and organs continue to receive fuel supplies through the bloodstream, even when the digestive system is dormant.

Nutrition, process by which living organisms take in and utilize nutrients, the substances required for growth and for the maintenance of life. Essential nutrients are those that cannot be produced within living cells and must be derived from food. Unlike plants, which can synthesize their nutritional requirements from exposure to sunlight, soil, and air, animals depend largely on the eating of plants or other animals. A broad array of essential nutrients are required by the human body. These include protein, carbohydrates, fats, vitamins, and minerals. Deficiencies in any of these can result in stunted growth or in a variety of illnesses involving malfunctions of organs or systems.

Nuvolari, Tazio Giorgio (1892-1953), Italian racecar driver who started out as a motorbike racer. Nuvolari claimed victories for several brands of cars. He won various Grand Prix races for Bugatti and Maserati. With Alfa Romeo he won in 1930 and 1933 the Mille Miglia (Thousand Miles), and in 1936 won the Vanderbilt cup in the U.S. In 1938 Ferdinand Porsche persuaded him to drive for Auto-Union, with which he also won several races. During his thirty-year career he was flagged down as victor in seventy races.

Nyasaland *See:* Malawi.

Nyerere, Julius Kambarage (1921-1999), founder and first president (1964-1985) of the East African state of Tanzania. He led Tanganyika to independence (1961) and united it with Zanzibar. He believed in a one-party socialist democracy and helped overthrow Ugandan dictator Idi Amin. He was succeeded in 1985 by Hassan Mwinyi, former President of Zanzibar, a semiautonomous island off the Tanzanian coast.
See also: Tanzania.

Nylon, heat-resistant, strong, elastic, synthetic material introduced in 1938. Nylon is made into fibers or cast and molded into bearing, gears, zippers, etc.

Nymph, in Greek mythology, female divinity normally considered the guardian of an object or place occurring in nature. Nymphs were depicted as beautiful young women and were named according to the geographic features with which they were associated. Naiads, for example, watched over brooks, rivers, and other bodies of fresh water; nereids were identified with the sea, dryads with trees, and oreads with mountains.

Nystagmus, rhythmic rolling of the eyes that occurs normally when the head rotates. The eyes attempt to focus on a fixed spot, then rapidly move back. Abnormal nystagmus may be caused by nervous system disorders.

Nzinga a Nkuwa (d. 1506), ruler of the Congolese people of west-central Africa. Following the arrival of the Portuguese in 1482, he promoted trade with Europe. Although considered by his people to be divine, he converted to Christianity and was baptized in 1491.

O, 15th letter and 4th vowel of the English alphabet. It was the only Semitic letter (*ayin*) adopted by the Greeks, who called it *omicron*. It passed into the Roman alphabet as the 14th letter and was also used in medieval roman numbering to indicate 11. In chemistry, O is the symbol of the element oxygen.

Oahe Dam, in South Dakota, one of the world's largest embankment dams. Completed in 1960 by the U.S. Army, it has a volume of 92 million cu yd (70 million cu m). Facilities include seven 150-ft (46-m) high generators that together can produce 595,000 kw of electricity.

Oahu *See:* Hawaii.

Oak, tree that grows in moderate climates and subtropics. There are more than 600 species of oak found in the Northern Hemisphere. Seeds of the oak are called acorns. Oak wood is used in construction and for flooring and furniture. The bark is used for medicinal purposes.

Oakland (pop. 395,000), city on the east side of San Francisco Bay in northern California. The port handles over 5 million tons of cargo a year. Much of the farm produce of California's Central Valley passes through Oakland; it is also a major industri-

al city for shipbuilding, food processing, and oil refining.
See also: California.

Oakley, Annie (Phoebe Anne Oakley Mozee; 1860-1926), U.S. entertainer. Known as 'Little Sure Shot,' she was a sharpshooter star of Buffalo Bill's Wild West Show.

Oakum, loose fibers of hemp or flax, used to make the seams of wooden ships watertight-a process called caulking. Oakum may be made from tow, a byproduct in the manufacture of linen. The best oakum is made from ships' ropes, picked apart and tarred.

Oarfish, or ribbonfish (*Regalecus glesne*), eellike fish with a flattened body 20 ft (6 m) or more long, 1 ft (1/3 m) deep and only 2 in (5 cm) across. Oarfish are found in all warm and temperate seas.

OAS *See:* Organization of American States.

Oasis, area in a desert where there is sufficient water for plants to grow. Oases vary in size, from small ponds to vast regions covering thousands of square miles. The Nile Valley, the home of most of Egypt's people, is a large oasis flanked by barren desert. Many oases occur in areas bordering mountain ranges because the rain that falls on the mountains often seeps through porous rock layers under the desert. Oases may also occur around springs where the porous rock comes to the surface, or the water may be tapped through wells. Artificial oases are found in many deserts.

Oates, Joyce Carol (1938-), prolific U.S. novelist, short-story writer, poet, playwright, and critic whose work often deals with insanity, violence, and other nightmarish aspects of society. Among her many books are the novels *A Garden of Earthly Delights* (1967), *Them* (1969; National Book Award, 1970), *Bellefleur* (1980), *Solstice* (1985), *Because It Is Bitter, and Because It Is My Heart* (1990), *Black Water* (1992), *Foxfire* (1993), *Man Crazy* (1997), and *The Collector of Hearts* (1999).

Oates, Titus (1649-1705), English conspirator who in 1678 claimed to have discovered a Roman Catholic plot (called the Popish Plot) against Charles II. No such plot existed, but his story set off a wave of persecution in which some 35 innocent persons were executed. Exposed and imprisoned in 1695, he was freed and pensioned (1689) after the Glorious Revolution.

Oath, pledge used to guarantee the honesty of an individual's statements. In legal situations, a witness can commit the crime of perjury for giving false testimony under oath. Although the oath originally had religious significance, it is used today primarily, but not exclusively, for judicial procedures. Other types of oaths include oaths of office and military oaths.

Oats, cereal plants (genus *Avena*) cultivated in cool, damp climates in the Northern

Hemisphere. Rich in starch and protein, the grain is used mainly as a livestock feed; less than 5% is processed for human consumption.

Oaxaca, southern Mexican state bordering the Gulf of Tehuantepec, founded by Aztecs c.1500. Oaxaca de Juárez is the capital. Covering 36,821 sq mi (95,366 sq km), it is mountainous with deep, fertile valleys; farming is the most important activity. Mineral resources include gold and silver. The population is predominantly Indian.
See also: Mexico.

Obadiah, Book of, shortest book of the Old Testament, 4th book of the Minor Prophets. Probably written in the 6th century B.C., its 21 verses foretell the triumph of Israel over its rival Edom.
See also: Bible; Old Testament.

Obelisk, 4-sided pillar tapering to a pyramidal top. Pairs of these, often as tall as 105 ft (32 m), were erected in front of ancient Egyptian temples, carved with hieroglyphs for decorative, religious, and commemorative purposes. Cleopatra's Needles in London and New York City, dating from c.1500 B.C. in Egypt, are notable examples.
See also: Cleopatra's needles.

Oberammergau (pop. 5,400), village in Germany's Bavarian Alps, famous for its Passion Play. Every 10 years inhabitants of the village reenact the suffering, death, and resurrection of Christ, in fulfillment of a vow made by the villagers during a plague in 1633.
See also: Germany.

Oboe, soprano wind instrument consisting of a double-reed mouthpiece at the end of a conically bored tube. It is controlled by keys and finger holes. Developed in 17th-century France, the oboe is essentially an orchestral instrument.
See also: English horn.

Obote, Apollo Milton (1924-), president of Uganda (1966-1971, 1980-1985). The first prime minister of independent Uganda (1962), Obote made himself president under a new, centralizing constitution (1966). In 1971 he was overthrown by Idi Amin. After Amin's overthrow in 1979, Obote was reelected president.
See also: Uganda.

Obregón, Alvaro (1880-1928), president of Mexico (1920-1924). He joined Carranza in overthrowing President Huberta in 1914, served in Carranza's government, but led the revolt against him in 1920. As president, Obregón promoted economic and educational reforms. Four years after leaving office he was elected again, but was assassinated by a religious fanatic before taking office.
See also: Mexico.

Ob River, fourth longest river in the world, located in Siberia, Russia. With about 19,000 m (30,600 km) of navigable waters, the Ob river and its tributaries offer a major route for the transportation and shipping of goods to western Russia and other parts of

O

the world. Major ports are found at Novosibirsk and Barnaul.

Obscenity and pornography, terms referring to material believed to be publicly offensive. Although the terms are used interchangeably, obscenity refers to morally indecent language or behavior, while pornography refers to sexually explicit printed or pictorial material. U.S. antiobscenity laws attempt to inhibit the sale, presentation, or expression of obscenity and pornography, but heated controversy over the legal definitions of these terms makes it difficult to enforce the laws. Many nations have antiobscenity laws while others, such as Denmark in the late 1960s, dropped legal barriers against adult pornography.

Observatory, in astronomy, a scientific site at which systematic observations of the sky are made. The first observatories were set up by ancient civilizations to regulate the calendar and predict eclipses and the rising of the sun and the moon. The sextant, quadrant, and astrolabe were devices for sighting positions of stars and planets. The invention of the telescope in the early 17th century revolutionized observational astronomy. Contemporary observatories contain optical or radio telescopes housed in rotating domes. Satellite telescopes allow X-ray observation.
See also: Telescope.

The observatory on the Pic du Midi de Bigorre 9,423 ft (2,872 m) in the Hautes Pyrenees, southeast of Lourdes. The rugged ranges in the background attest to the relative youth of the mountains.

Obsidian, igneous rock, also called volcanic glass. It is formed from molten lava. Obsidian is composed of the same chemicals as granite, but it solidifies so quickly that there is no time for crystals to form, so it becomes smooth and glasslike. Obsidian is generally black in color, but it can be brown or red. It can be shattered into sharp-edged pieces. The Native Americans of the western United States used such fragments for arrowheads and spear points.

Obstetrics, the care of women during pregnancy and childbirth, a branch of medicine and surgery linked with gynecology. Control of risk factors for both mother and baby-anemia, toxemia, high blood pressure, diabetes, venereal disease, frequent miscarriage-have greatly contributed to the reduction of maternal and fetal deaths.
See also: Birth; Pregnancy.

Obuchi, Keizo (1937-), Japanese liberal politician. Keizo Obuchi has been an active member of the LDP, the Liberal Democratic Party. He was minister of foreign affairs in the last Hashimoto government. In July 1998 he was elected prime minister by the Japanese House of Commons. He succeeded Ryutaro Hashimoto, who was forced to resign earlier that year after losing the elections for the House of Lords.

Öcalan, Abdullah (1949-), Kurdish PKK leader from Turkey. Öcalan founded the Kurdish Labor Party (PKK) in 1978. The PKK fought for an independent Kurdish State, to be situated in the border areas of Turkey, Iran, Iraq and Syria. The violent guerrilla battle the PKK has fought against the Turkish army since 1984 has caused numerous victims. At the beginning of the 1990s, Öcalan fled to Syria, from where he remained the leader of the PKK. Turkey threatened with an armed intervention if Syria would not extradite Öcalan in 1998. Consequently, he fled to Moscow, Italy and the Greek embassy in Kenya. He was kidnapped by Turkey and brought to Ankara for trial. After a lengthy trial, he was sentenced to death. The news of his arrest led to great indignation under Kurdish communities in the western world. In 2000, the Turkish government parties decided not to carry out the death penalty, for fear of not being allowed to join the European Union. In 2002, Öcalan's death penalty was officially replaced by a life sentence.
See also: PKK.

O'Casey, Sean (1880-1964), Irish playwright whose sardonic dramas depict the effects of poverty and war. His early plays, such as *Juno and the Paycock* (1924) and *The Plough and the Stars* (1926), are the most highly regarded. His later works, such as *The Silver Tassie* (1929), were written in self-imposed exile due to hostility from Irish nationalists who objected to his unglamorous portrayal of the independence movement.

Occam, William of *See:* William of Ockham.

Occultism, wide range of practices and theories based on belief in the supernatural; among them witchcraft, mind reading, astrology, divination, and telepathy. Definitions of occultism have changed over the years; certain occult practices are now considered to have a scientific base. Although occultism is generally repudiated by the scientific community, there has been much renewed popular interest in occult beliefs and practices.
See also: Parapsychology; Spiritualism.

Occupational therapy, rehabilitative medicine concerned with practical measures to overcome disability due to disease. It includes work and/or play activities under a therapist's guidance.

Ocean, combined area of interconnected water that covers about 71% of the earth's surface. The salt waters of the earth are divided into 4 main oceans: the Pacific, Atlantic, Indian, and Arctic. Scientists are interested in the food and mineral resources of the oceans. Marine biologists concentrate on the study of the food chain, the distribution of plankton, fish, and aquatic mammals, and the effects of pollution on marine life.

Ocean Drilling Program, geological research program established (1984) by the United States and other nations to determine the composition of the earth beneath the ocean floor. Drilling expeditions provide information on the evolution of life forms, the creation of the earth's land masses, shifts in the earth's climate, and the location of fossil fuels. Cylindrical cores of sediment and hard rock beneath the ocean floor are removed through a drill pipe and studied. The Ocean Drilling Program is operated by Texas A & M Univ. in College Station, Tex.

Oceania, vast section of the Pacific Ocean, stretching roughly from Hawaii to New Zealand and from New Guinea to Easter Island, divided into 3 broad cultural areas: Melanesia, Micronesia, and Polynesia. The area has about 25,000 small islands ranging from large masses of ancient rock to minute coral atolls and the vegetation varies from lush jungles to scanty palm trees. The native islanders live mainly by fishing and farming.
See also: Pacific Islands.

Ocelot, medium-sized wildcat marked with black spots, rings, and stripes, of forests from the southwestern United States to Paraguay. Although their fur is valuable, the ocelot is abundant. They feed on small animals.

Ochoa, Severo (1905-1993), Spanish-born U.S. biochemist who shared with Arthur K. Kornberg the 1959 Nobel Prize for physiology or medicine for first synthesizing a nucleic acid (RNA).
See also: Biochemistry; Nucleic acid.

Ockham, William of *See:* William of Ockham.

Ockham's Razor *See:* William of Ockham.

O'Connell, Daniel (1775-1847), Irish statesman, called the Liberator, who led the fight for Catholic emancipation. He founded the Catholic Association (1823) and after his election to Parliament (1828) refused to take his seat until public opinion precipitated the Catholic Emancipation Act (passed in 1829). He contested the 1801 act uniting Ireland with Britain.
See also: Ireland.

O'Connor, Flannery (1925-1964), U.S. fiction writer noted for her brilliant style and grotesque, tragicomic vision of life in the South. Her work includes the novel *Wise Blood* (1952) and the short-story collections *A Good Man Is Hard to Find* (1955) and *Everything That Rises Must Converge* (1965).

O'Connor, Frank (1903-1966), Irish short-story writer whose works are admired for their oral quality and portrayals of Irish life. His collections include *Guests of the Nation* (1931), *Bones of Contention and Other Stories* (1936), and *A Set of Variations* (1969). O'Connor also published poetry, criticism, and translations of old Irish literature from the Gaelic.

O'Connor, John Joseph Cardinal (1920-), cardinal of the Roman Catholic Church. The former archbishop of New York City, he was named cardinal (1985) by Pope John Paul II. In 1983, he worked with other bishops to draft a letter, approved by the National Conference of Catholic Bishops, denouncing the nuclear arms buildup. He was an auxiliary bishop (1979) of the Military Ordinariate, serving members of the U.S. armed forces.

Ocotillo, or coach whip, tall, slender plant of U.S. southwestern deserts that grows new leaves after each rain. When dry, the stems are burnt as candlewood.

OCR, Optical Character Recognition, optical graphical recognition. Special software that registers and identifies scanned pictures or signs. For this, a form of pattern recognition is needed which deduces letters and layout from the pixels of the screen so these can be edited with a word processor.

Octane, colorless, liquid, highly flammable hydrocarbon, commonly used in gasoline. Since the 18 octane compounds vary in their molecular structure, they have different physical properties.
Octane number is the designation given to gasoline based on the amount of isooctane present. Fuels with a lower octane number have a larger amount of normal heptane and

are prone to engine 'knock,' which decreases the power of the engine.
See also: Hydrocarbon.

Octane number, measure of a liquid fuel's ability to resist premature ignition (knocking) and to burn evenly in an internal combustion engine. Gasolines with higher octane numbers produce less knocking than those with lower octane numbers. Desirable octane numbers range from 90-100.
See also: Gasoline.

Octave, in music, the interval between two pitches, one of which having twice the frequency of the other. In the diatonic scale these are the first and the eighth tones. Because of its unique consonance, the octave gives an aural impression of a single tone duplicated.

Octavia (65?-9 B.C.), wife of Marc Antony and sister of Emperor Augustus of Rome. Her marriage ended hostilities between her husband and brother, but war recommenced when Antony left her for the Egyptian queen Cleopatra in 37 B.C.
See also: Rome, Ancient.

Octavian *See:* Augustus.

October Revolution (November Revolution according to Western chronology), coup d'état in Russia in October 1917 during which the Temporary Government, which had come to power during the February Revolution of the same year, was overthrown by the Bolshevists. The government appeared to be insufficiently inclined to live up to the expectations of agricultural and social reforms that were created during the February Revolution. Also, the government was not likely to put an end to the war against Germany. Lenin (1870-1924), who had returned from exile, set himself up as leader of the Bolshevists and demanded that the government step down. On 25 October 1917 the Bolshevists came into power, after which a new government, predominantly Bolshevist, came to power under the leadership of Lenin.

Octopus, marine mollusk (genus *Octopus*)

The celebration of the 50th anniversary of the Soviet October Revolution, Moscow, 1967.

with 8 tentaclelike arms that surround the mouth; a cephalopod. Behind the beaked head is a saclike body containing the internal organs. Octopods can change color for camouflage and eject a black pigment which forms a smokescreen to foil predators.

Odd Fellows, Independent Order of, secret organization promoting good will and brotherhood and committed to helping its members in time of need, hardship, or sorrow. Created in England in the early 1700s, in 1819 it spread to the United States, where it now claims more than 1 million members. Its logo of 3 links, skull and crossbones, and a single eye represents friendship, love, and truth, our limited state of being, and an omnipotent God. Rebekah lodges of Odd Fellows are mostly women.

Ode, stately lyric poem usually expressing praise. It is often addressed to the person, object, or concept (such as Joy or Autumn) being celebrated. It originated in the ancient Greek choral songs. Pindar used a three-part structure in his odes; strophe, antistrophe (both in the same meter), and epode (in a different meter). Horace's odes were in stanzaic form. English poets of the 19th century, such as John Keats and Percy Shelley, wrote odes with irregular structures.

Oder-Neisse border, border between Germany and Poland, named after the two homonymous rivers. The Soviet Union donated a large territory to Poland, which previously had belonged to Germany, as compensation for the loss of pre-war Polish territory in the East which had been annexed by the Soviet Union, thus making the Oder and the Neisse Poland's western border. The oth-

The ocelot, *Leopardus pardalis*, is a proficient swimmer and climber.

O

er Allies protested against this during the conference in Potsdam (1945), to no avail. A definite arrangement would not be made until a peace agreement was reached between Germany and Poland. In 1950 the border was acknowledged by the German Democratic Republic, and the Federal Republic of Germany did the same in 1970. After the German reunification in 1990 both Germanys and Poland signed-as a result of the Two-plus-Four Treaty-a treaty in which the Oder-Neisse border and the rights of the German minority in Poland were established.

Oder River, European water route forming a large part of the border between Poland and Germany, economically essential and mostly navigable on its 551-mi (886-km) length. Originating in the Oder Mountains of Czech Republic, it joins the Neisse River near western Poland and drains into the Baltic Sea through the Stettin Lagoon. Along the river are major cities in Poland, Germany, and Czech Republic.

Odessa (pop. 1,100,000), city and port in Ukraine, on the Black Sea. It is a major transportation, industrial, commercial, and cultural center. During World War II about 280,00 residents of Odessa, mostly Jews, were massacred.
See also: Ukraine.

Odets, Clifford (1906-1963), U.S. playwright and screenwriter noted for social-protest dramas about ordinary people in the Depression. A leading figure in the Group Theatre in New York City, his works include *Waiting for Lefty* (1935), *Awake and Sing!* (1935), and *Golden Boy* (1937).

Odin, in Germanic mythology, the chief god, also known as Woden (whose name gave us Wednesday). God of war, poetry, wisdom, learning, and magic, he had a single all-seeing eye. He made the world from the body of the giant Ymir, man from an ash tree, and woman from an elm.
See also: Mythology.

Odoacer (435-493), German chief who overthrew the last of the West Roman emperors in 476 and was proclaimed king of Italy. The East Roman Emperor Zeno sent Theodoric the Great to depose him. After a long war, Theodoric killed Odoacer.

Odometer *See:* Speedometer.

Odysseus *See:* Homer; Odyssey; Ulysses.

Odyssey, ancient Greek epic poem ascribed to Homer, one of the masterpieces of world literature. Its 24 books relate the adventures of Odysseus and his companions following the Trojan War. Eventually, Odysseus reaches his home in Ithaca and is reunited with his wife, Penelope.
See also: Homer.

Oë, Kenzaburo (1935-), Japanese author who was awarded the Nobel Prize for literature in 1994. During World War II Oë lived as a small child through the bombing of Hiroshima and the American occupation.

Jaques Offenbach, a 19th-century French composer whose comic operettas achieved immense succes, created the genre that dominated the musical theatre of his day.

These events can be found back in his work. The influences of Sartre, Norman Mailer and Henry Miller can also be seen. Initially Oë was part of a group of young, left-wing intellectuals in Japan. His best-known works include: *Hiroshima Notes* (1963), *A Personal Matter* (1964) and *The Silent Cry* (1967).

Oedipus, in Greek legend, king of Thebes who was fated to kill his father, King Laius, and marry his mother, Jocasta. When he discovered what he had done, he blinded himself. His story and that of his daughter, Antigone, inspired tragedies by Sophocles: *Oedipus Rex* and *Oedipus at Colonus*.
See also: Mythology.

Oedipus complex, sexual obsession by a son for his mother accompanied by resentment and aggression toward his father. It is named after the mythological Greek hero Oedipus who killed his father and married his mother.

Oersted, Hans Christian (1777-1851), Danish physicist. His discovery (1820) that a magnetized needle can be deflected by an electric current passing through a wire gave birth to the science of electromagnetism. The unit of magnetic field strength, the oersted, is named after him.
See also: Electromagnetism.

Oerter, Al (1936-), American discus thrower. Oerter is the only athlete to have won a gold medal in the same discipline during four consecutive Olympic tournaments: in 1956 in Melbourne, 1960 in Rome, 1964 in Tokyo and 1968 in Mexico. Beside his Olympic titles he also won several international tournaments and championships with a strong field of competitors.

O'Faolain, Sean (1900-1991), Irish short-story writer, novelist, and biographer. Among his works, which often give an un-

flattering yet sympathetic view of everyday Irish life, are *Midsummer Night Madness and Other Stories* (1932), the novel *A Nest of Simple Folk* (1933), *The Great O'Neill: A Biography of Hugh O'Neill* (1942), and his autobiography, *Vive Moi!* (1964).

Offenbach, Jacques (1819-1880), French composer. He wrote over 100 operettas including *Orpheus in the Underworld* (1858), containing some famous can-can music, and *La Belle Hélène* (1864). His masterpiece is considered to be the opera *Tales of Hoffmann* (1881).

Offset, printing process whereby ink is transferred from a chemically treated printing plate, used so that only the printing or design will receive the ink, onto a rubber-covered cylinder, to paper. Offsetting is an improvement over other printing methods in its ability to print on numerous uneven surfaces and textures, such as rough paper, tin, or celluloid. Offset has been used successfully with color printing and rare book reproductions.
See also: Printing.

O'Flaherty, Liam (1897-1984), Irish novelist known for his realistic stories of ordinary people in trouble, such as *The Black Soul* (1924), *The Informer* (1925), and *The Assassin* (1928).

Ogaden *See:* Ethiopia.

Ogino-Knaus, method of, arithmetic method to decide during which days of the menstrual cycle sexual continence is necessary in order to prevent pregnancy. Named after the Japanese gynecologist Kinsakou Ogino (1882-1974) and the Austrian gynecologist Hermann Knaus (1892-1970). Can be applied only after the woman has accurately kept up the dates of her menstruation for at least a year. In general, when having a regular cycle, abstinence is effective between the 10th and the 17th day from the beginning of the last menstruation.

Oglala *See:* Red Cloud; Sioux.

O'Hara, John (1905-1970), U.S. journalist and fiction writer known principally for his vigorous accounts of urban and suburban life in the United States. His novels include *Appointment in Samarra* (1934), *Butterfield 8* (1935), and *A Rage to Live* (1949).

O. Henry *See:* Henry, O..

Ohia, mountain apple tree with evergreen leaves found in many tropical climates, of the family Myrtaceae. Its hard wood is used to produce furniture and railroad ties.

O'Higgins, political family in South America. **Ambrosio O'Higgins** (1720-1801), born in Ireland and educated in Spain, was governor of Chile (1789-1796) and viceroy of Peru (1796). **Bernardo O'Higgins** (1778-1842), his son, liberated Chile from Spanish rule and became its dictator (1817). His reforms aroused such opposition that he was exiled to Peru in 1823.

Ohio (Buckeye State; pop. 10,887,000), midwestern state in the northern United States; bordered by Michigan, Pennsylvania, West Virginia, Kentucky, and Indiana.
Excellent ports on Lake Erie, together with the Ohio River and two major canals, have made Ohio a major transportation hub of the Midwest. Forests cover about one-fourth of the state. Principal cities are Cleveland, Columbus (capital), and Cincinnati.
Manufacturing is by far the most important economic activity in Ohio, which is one of the nation's leading industrial states. Chief manufactured products are transportation equipment, machinery, primary and fabricated metal products, household appliances, chemicals, processed foods, and rubber products. Wholesale and retail trade is the chief service industry.
Prehistoric Native Americans called Mound Builders were the area's first-known inhabitants. French explorer La Salle was probably the first European to explore the area, about 1670. France claimed the entire Ohio Valley, as did England. The conflicting claims led to the French and Indian wars (1754-1763), after which France ceded the area to England. Ohio became the 17th state in 1803.

Ohio River, main eastern tributary of the Mississippi River. The Ohio is formed at Pittsburgh, Pa., by the junction of the Allegheny and Monongahela rivers. It flows generally southwest for c.980 mi (1,557 km) and is navigable throughout.

Ohira, Masayoshi (1910-1980), Japanese prime minister (1978-1980). First elected to parliament as a member of the Liberal Democratic Party (1952), he held numerous ministerial posts before becoming party leader and prime minister. He was unable to hold together antagonistic factions of his party and died ten days before new parliamentary elections.

Ohm, Georg Simon (1787-1854), Bavarian-born German physicist who formulated Ohm's Law, from his studies of electric current. He also contributed to acoustics, recognizing the ability of the human ear to resolve mixed sound into its component pure tones.

Ohm's law, law stating that the electric potential difference across a conductor is proportional to the current flowing through it, the constant of proportionality being known as the resistance of the conductor. It holds well for most materials and objects, including solutions.
See also: Electric current.

Ohsawa, George (real name Sakurazawa Nyoiti; 1893-1966), Japanese physician, founder of macrobiotics. Introduced them in the West in the 1930s during a stay in France. Later returned to Japan and founded a training institution for macrobiotics (1952) and started propagating his teachings in other parts of the world.

Oil, any substance that is insoluble in water, soluble in ether, and greasy to the touch. Mineral oils include gasoline and other fuel oils, heating oils, and lubricants. Fixed vegetable oils change when they absorb oxygen

(linseed, tung, and olive oil). Volatile vegetable oils usually have a distinct odor and flavor (peppermint, turpentine).

Oilbird, or guacharo (*Steatornis caripensis*), night-flying bird that lives in caves in northern South America and on Trinidad. It finds its way by echo-location, a batlike sonar device in its ears that emits audible, echoing clicks. It is called the oilbird because Native Americans used the fat of its chicks as cooking oil.

Oilcloth, fabric treated with oil or thick paint to become waterproof. Designs printed on it produce attractive tablecloths and shelf lining. It originated in China c.7th century, was made in England in the 1500s, and in the United States after 1809.

Oil refinery *See:* Petroleum.

Oil shale, fine-grained, dark-colored sedimentary rock from which oil suitable for refining can be extracted. The rock contains an organic substance called kerogen, which may be distilled to yield oil. Significant deposits occur in Wyoming, Colorado, and adjacent states.

Oil well *See:* Petroleum.

Oistrakh, David (1906-1974), Russian violinist. His brilliant technique and strong emotional interpretation (especially of the romantic composers) brought him worldwide acclaim. Sergey Prokofiev and Dmitry Shostakovich wrote works for him. His son, **Igor** (1931-), is also a violinist and conductor of world renown.

Ojibwa, or Chippewa, large Algonquian-speaking tribes of Native Americans. Small bands of hunter-gatherers lived in woodland areas around Lakes Superior and Huron, and to the west. They fought with the Sioux, but had little contact with white settlers. Longfellow's *The Song of Hiawatha* was based on Ojibwa mythology. Today some 60,000 Ojibwas live on U.S. and Canadian reservations.

Ojos del Salado ('Salty Eyes'), mountain in the Andes range in northwest Argentina,

22,572 ft (6,880 m) high. The year-round snow on its 4 well-defined peaks gives it its name.

Okapi, a large, split-hooved mammal related to the giraffe. Okapis live in the forests of the upper basin of the Congo River in Africa, where they were discovered by Europeans in 1901. They stand up to five feet (1.5 m) tall at the shoulder, and have much shorter necks and legs than giraffes. The males have two blunt, five-inch (13-cm) horns covered with skin and hair, similar to those of giraffes. Males and females have large, broad ears. In size and structure, okapis resemble fossil predecessors of giraffes.
The coat of an okapi is purplish-brown on the back, black striped horizontally with white on the upper leg, and white on the lower leg. The okapi has a short tail ending in a tuft of black hair, and buff-colored markings on its head. Okapis are ruminants (cud chewers) and eat the leaves and twigs of forest trees. They live singly or in small family groups.
The okapi is *Okapia johnstoni*. It belongs to the giraffe family, Giraffidae.

Oka River, a river in western Russia. It is 940 miles (1,513 km) long. From its source in the Central Russian Uplands, the river flows generally northward to Nizhniy Novgorod, where it joins the Volga River.

O'Keeffe, Georgia (1887-1986), U.S. painter noted for her delicate, abstract designs incorporating symbolic motifs drawn from nature such as *Cow's Skull, Red, White, and Blue* (1931). She is also known for sexually symbolic flower paintings such as *Black Iris* (1926). Her paintings were first exhibited in 1916 by photographer Alfred Stieglitz. She was greatly influenced by the geography of the American southwest and was an early settler of the artistic community in Taos, New Mexico.

Okefenokee Swamp, warm, boggy, unsettled region in southeastern Georgia and somewhat into northeastern Florida, covering 700 sq mi (1,800 sq km). A recreation wetland for people, 460 sq mi (1,200 sq km) are designated a wildlife area. Protected are alligators, 50 kinds of fish, countless varia-

The okapi (*O. johnstoni*), a shy, reclusive animal dwelling in the dense jungles of the Upper Congo basin in Africa, is similar in appearance to the short-necked giraffe of the late Tertiary Period.

O

O

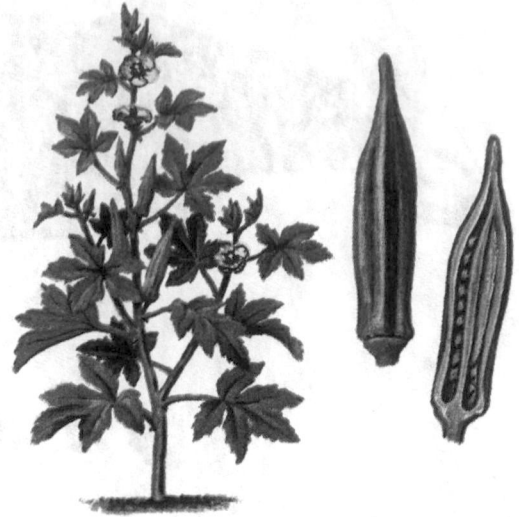

Okra (*A. esculentus*) is a vegetable originally from Africa or Asia. It bears hibiscuslike flowers and large, star-shaped leaves. The pod, harvested when young and tender, is a basic ingredient in gumbo.

tions of birds and animals, and lush vegetation on many small islands.

Okhotsk, Sea of, branch of the northern Pacific Ocean, 1,000 mi (1,600 km) long and 600 mi (970 km) wide, along Russia's eastern border and used as a travel and trade route to former Soviet ports. It joins the Sea of Japan by way of the Tatar and La Pérouse Straits. Travel is inhibited when severe storms occur between November and April, and ice and fog cover the sea.
See also: Pacific Ocean.

Okinawa, largest (454 sq mi/1,176 sq km) of the Ryukyu Islands in the West Pacific, part of Okinawa prefecture, Japan. Naha is the capital. Mountainous and jungle-covered in the south, hilly in the north, it is fertile-sugarcane, sweet potatoes, and rice are grown, and there are good fisheries. Captured by the United States during World War II, Okinawa was formally returned to Japan in 1972.

Oklahoma (Sooner State; pop. 3,317,000), state in the southwestern United States; bordered by Colorado, Kansas, Missouri, Arkansas, Texas, and New Mexico.
Oklahoma's topography varies immensely. There are broad, flat plains in the west, rolling hills in the center, and mountain ranges in the east. All of Oklahoma's large rivers-the 2 greatest being the Red and the Arkansas-are part of the Mississippi River system. There are about 300 small lakes. Forests cover about one-fifth of the state. Principal cities are Oklahoma City (capital) and Tulsa.
Wholesale and retail trade, mining, and manufacturing lead Oklahoma's economy. Chief mining products are natural gas, petroleum, coal, crushed stone, gypsum, iodine, and sand and gravel. Chief manufactured goods are nonelectrical machinery, fabricated metal products, and rubber and plastic products.
Oklahoma was among the lands that La Salle claimed for France in 1682. France ceded it to Spain, 1762-1800, then sold it to the U.S. under the 1803 Louisiana Purchase. Oklahoma became the 46th state in 1907.

Oklahoma City (pop. 506,000), capital of Oklahoma, on the North Canadian River. It was founded on April 22, 1889, when that portion of Indian territory was first opened for white settlement. For the landrush some 10,000 people set up tents in the region that day. Incorporated in 1890, it became the state capital in 1910. Oil was discovered in 1928, and the city's large reserves of crude oil and natural gas have made it a major petroleum production area. Industries include farming, ranching, building materials, aircraft production, and electronic and communications equipment.
See also: Oklahoma.

Okra, or Gumbo, hibiscus plant cultivated in West Africa, India, and the southeastern United States for its fruits, which are pickled or cooked. They contain watery solutions of vegetable gum used to thicken and flavor broths. The seeds yield an oil and are used as a coffee substitute.

Okri, Ben (1959-), Nigerian author who attracted attention at a very young age with two semi-autobiographical novels about city life in his home country: *Flowers and Shadows* (1980), and *The Landscapes Within* (1982). In the narrative volume *Incidents at the Shrine* (1986) his vision seems to have broadened, especially in a political sense. The Nigerian civil war is discussed in one of the stories. For his ambitious mixture of fantasy and realism and poverty and corruption in Lagos, *The Famished Road*, he was awarded the 1991 Booker Prize. Afterwards he wrote *Songs of Enchantment* (1993), *Astonishing the Gods* (1995), *Infinite Riches* (1998), and the epical poem *Mental Fight* (1999).

Olav V (1903-1991), king of Norway (1957-1991). After Germany took Norway (1940) in World War II, he was active in the resistance and in 1944 took command of the Norwegian forces.
See also: Norway.

Old Bailey, main criminal court in London, England, on Old Bailey Street (a bailey was an area between the inner and outer city walls in medieval times). Trials heard in Old Bailey include that of the judges responsible for the death of King Charles I, Germany's World War II radio broadcaster William Joyce, and Oscar Wilde's on morality.
See also: Newgate Prison.

Old Catholics, group of churches that seceded from the Roman Catholic church. Some in Germany, Austria, and Switzerland would not accept the dogmas of papal infallibility and jurisdiction defined by the First Vatican Council (1870). Later, several smaller Slavic churches separated. Virtually high Anglican in doctrine and practice, Old Catholics have been in fellowship with the Church of England since 1932.

Oldenbarneveldt, Johan van (1547-1619), Dutch statesman. As advocate of Holland (from 1586), he supported self-government for the burgher towns of the United Provinces, recently liberated from Spain, and encouraged commerce during the early years of the Dutch East India Company.
He came into conflict with Maurice of Nassau and the nobles over the role of the States-General and in the Calvinist-Remonstrants controversy. Ol-denbarneveldt was arrested on unfounded treason charges and executed.

Oldenburg, Claes (1929-), Swedish-born U.S. pop artist best known for his soft constructions (sculptures) that satirize America. His hamburgers, ice cream cones, telephones, and bathroom fixtures are usually larger than normal size. His works include *Giant Saw, Hard Version* and *Lipstick*.

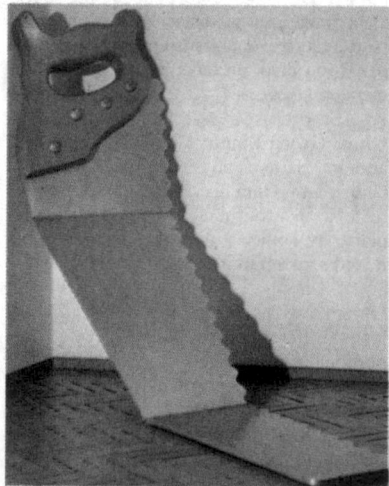

Giant *Saw* (1970)
by Claes Oldenburg.

Old English *See:* English language; English literature.

Old English sheepdog, working dog that resembles an unshorn sheep. The breed, developed in 19th-century England, has long, abundant, coarse hair and is used to herd sheep and cattle and as a family guard dog. Its colors are gray or blue, with or without white, and as a full adult it weighs 55-65 lbs (24.9-29.5 kg).

Old Faithful *See:* Yellowstone National Park.

Old Testament, or the Hebrew Bible, the first part of the Christian Bible, describing God's covenant with Israel. The Old Testament is traditionally divided into 3 parts: the Law, the Prophets, and the Writings. Christianity regards the Old Testament as an inspired record of God's dealings with his people in preparation for the coming of Christ.
See also: Bible.

Olduvai Gorge *See:* Leakey.

Old World, refers to the Eastern Hemisphere, which includes Europe, Asia, Africa, and Australia. Botanists and zoologists often categorize plants and animals into Old World and New World (Western Hemisphere) terminology.
See also: Hemisphere.

Oleander (*Nerium oleander*), poisonous, evergreen ornamental shrub with roselike flowers. It grows as tall as 30 ft (9 m) high.

Oligocene, third epoch of the Tertiary, c.40-25 million years ago.

Olive, evergreen tree (*Olea europaea*) growing in Mediterranean climates and one of the world's oldest cultivated crops. Its unripe fruits are pickled, treated with lye solution to remove the bitter taste, and stored in brine. When left to ripen they turn black and are pressed for their oil.

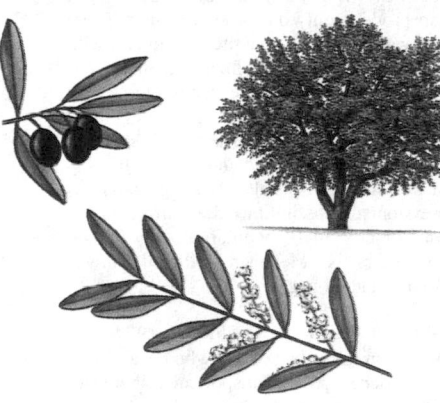

The olive tree (*O. europaea*) is an evergreen grown primarily in the Mediterranean region. It is cultivated for its fruit, the source of olive oil, and for its wood, which is exceptionally hard and fine grained.

Olive oil, clear edible substance obtained from the fruit of the olive tree. The fruit is pulped, then the pulp is pressed and the oil is expressed. The best quality, virgin olive oil, comes from the first pressing of fruits picked just after ripening.

Olivier, Laurence (1907-1989), English actor, producer, and director. Immensely versatile and brilliant in classical as well as modern stage roles, such as John Osborne's *The Entertainer* (1957), he also acted in such films as *Wuthering Heights* (1939) and *Hamlet* (1948; Academy Award). He was director of Britain's National Theatre (1962-1972).

Olivine, group of minerals or chemical compounds made from silicon, oxygen, magnesium, and iron, found in igneous rocks (those formed from a molten state), schists, and gray, pink, or white marble. A hard substance, olivine can withstand temperatures of more than 2,700°F (1,500°C) before igniting. It is used in making bricks and glass. Colors vary from clear green to brown; the gemstone peridot is deep, yellowish-green olivine.
See also: Peridot.

Olmec, people of the southeastern coastal lowlands of ancient Mexico (c.500 B.C.-A.D. 1150). Skilled in artistic stone work, they produced huge sculptured basalt heads, beautiful jewelry, fine jade, white ware, and mosaics. They knew how to record time and write in hieroglyphics. Their culture influenced that of the Zapotec and Toltec.

Olmsted, Frederick Law (1822-1903), U.S. landscape architect and writer. With Calvert Vaux he planned Central Park in New York City. He himself designed parks in Philadelphia, Brooklyn, Montreal, and Chicago. In the 1850s he was well known for his perceptive books on the South.

Olson, Charles (1910-1970), U.S. critic and poet whose persuasive ideas challenged writers to reexamine their poetic style, structure, and phrasing, to intensify and further project its meaning. His essay *Projective Verse* (1950) describes his complex and distinctive mode of writing. *The Maximus Poems* (1960, 1968), a series of 38 poems, was his major work. He also wrote about the Mayan Indians, U.S. history, and Herman Melville.

Olympia, ancient sanctuary near the confluence of the Alpheus and Cladeus rivers in southwest Greece. The great temple of Zeus, one of the 7 wonders of the world, contained his gold and ivory statue by Phidias. To the north was the temple of Hera (600 B.C.). In the excavation of Olympia in the late 19th century, archeologists found the important statues of the *Nike* (Victory) of Paeonius and the *Hermes* of Praxiteles.
See also: Greece, Ancient; Olympic Games.

Olympiad, ancient Greek method of figuring a 4-year calendar time period. The Olympiad was set in conjunction with the first full moon after the longest day of the year and fell between consecutive Olympic Games. After 304 Olympiads, this way of telling time ceased (c.A.D. 440).
See also: Greece, Ancient.

Olympians *See:* Hera; Zeus.

Olympias (375?-316 B.C.), powerful, influential wife of Philip II of Macedonia, whom she had killed to secure the throne for her son, Alexander the Great. Upon his death in 323 B.C., she tried to ensure the dominion for her grandson, Alexander IV, but failed and was executed when Cassander came to power.
See also: Alexander the Great; Philip II.

Olympic Games, oldest and most famous international sporting contest. Traditionally for amateurs, it is held once every 4 years. The Olympics probably developed from the ancient Greek custom of holding athletic contests in honor of a god or a dead hero. A list of male champions exists from 776 B.C. The Olympics continued through the Roman period in Greece. Gradually, however, they lost their popular esteem, largely through the growth of cheating. In A.D. 394 they were abolished by decree of the Emperor Theodosius.
In 1894 a French nobleman, Pierre de Coubertin, called a meeting in Paris that led to the first modern Olympic Games, held in Athens in 1896. Thirteen nations sent a total of 285 men, and the Games were effectively revived. Since then the Olympics have been held in different cities once every 4 years, with the exception of the war years 1916, 1940, and 1944. Women first competed in 1912. In 1924 the Winter Olympics were instituted at Chamonix, France.
There are more than 30 Summer Olympics sports, including swimming, basketball, soccer, gymnastics, boxing, weightlifting, yachting, cycling, and equestrian events. Skiing, ice-skating, and ice hockey are among the 15 Winter Game sports. A competitor must be a citizen of the country he or she represents. No more than 3 entries from any country are permitted in each event (4 in the winter games). Only 1 team per country is allowed in team sports.

O

Pierre de Coubertin proposed a revival of the Olympic Games in 1894.

Oman

Capital:	Muscat
Area:	82,030 sq mi (212,457 sq km)
Population:	2,713,000
Language:	Arabic
Government:	Absolute monarchy (sultanate)
Independent:	1951
Head of gov.:	Sultan
Per capita:	US$ 8.200
Monetary unit:	1 Oman riyal = 1,000 baiza

O

Oman (formerly Muscat and Oman), independent sultanate on the southeast coast of the Arabian peninsula. One area of the country, a peninsula separated from the rest of Oman by the United Arab Emirates, juts into the strategic Straits of Hormuz. Oman's area is 120,000 sq mi (300,000 sq km). Its population is 2,265,000. Much of Oman is barren, with little rainfall and temperatures reaching 130°F (54°C). Dates are grown on the Batinah coastal plain, northwest of Muscat (the capital), and Dhofar province is noted for sugarcane and cattle. Grains and fruits are grown around Jebel Akhdar. Oil was discovered in 1964, and over 100 million barrels are produced yearly. Closely associated with Britain since 1798, Oman has a population that is mostly Arab but includes blacks, Indians, and Pakistanis. In 1970 the reformist Sultan Qabus bin Said ousted his father and has become a prominent moderate in Middle Eastern affairs.

In 1991, Saudi Arabia and Oman signed an agreement concerning the border between the two countries. A year later, a similar agreement was signed by Yemen and Oman. In 1999, Oman and neighboring United Arab Emirates (UAE) signed a similar border agreement.

Broad beans (*Vicia faba*) are grown around Nazwa, a small settlement south of al-Jabal al-Akhdar. The stems and leaves are used for forage. In the background, you can see datepalms. Dates are Oman's principal export product (after petroleum).

Omar Khayyam (1048-1131), Persian poet, astronomer, and mathematician. His epic poem *Rubaiyat*, dealing with nature and love, is known in the West through its translation (1859) by Edward FitzGerald.
See also: Rubaiyat.

Omayads, Arab dynasty and caliphate (661-750), founded by Muawiya, a prominent member of the Omayad family from Mecca, who refused to accept the authority of the fourth caliph, Ali ibn Abu Talib, because the latter refrained from taking action against the murderers of the third caliph, Uthman. When Muawiya came to power, the center of the Islam Empire shifted from Medina to Damascus. After caliph Abd al-Malik, who reigned from 685-705, had put down a rebellion led by the Shiites in 692, the Omayads extended their empire as far as Spain and the Indus Valley, which formed the bridgehead to India. By then the Islam Empire had become bigger than ever. A Persian rebellion in 746, which was supported by the Shiites, caused the collapse of the Omayad Empire. They were succeeded by the Abbasid dynasty. A branch of the Omayads ruled over the emirate of Cordoba in Spain until 1031.

Ombudsman, official appointed to investigate complaints by citizens against government officials or agencies. The office originated in Sweden in 1809 and since 1955 has been adopted by Denmark, New Zealand, the Netherlands, and Britain. Since 1995 there is an ombudsman for the European Community.

Omdurman (pop. 526,000), largest city in Sudan, on the White Nile, established in 1885 by Muhammad Ahmed, who is entombed here. It is a religious site for Sudan's Muslims and the region's commercial market. Many business people live here and work across the river in Khartoum, Sudan's capital.
See also: Sudan.

Ommatidium *See:* Compound eye.

Omnibus bill, legislation that includes many nonrelated bills lumped into 1 cumbersome package. Inadequate bills, those in dispute, and those of lesser importance are grouped together in hopes of being passed under the guise of propriety.

Omsk (pop. 1,300,000), industrial city in Siberia, Russian Federation, about 1,360 m (2,190 km) east of Moscow. Commercial development began when the Trans-Siberian Railroad reached Omsk in 1894. Industrial growth spurted during World War II when factories were moved out of war zones to the comparative safety of Siberia. Today Omsk has oil refineries and grain mills and manufactures railroad equipment and farm machinery used nearby.
See also: Russian Federation.

Onager (*Equus hemionus*), wild relative to the donkey found in Asia. It was domesticated long ago and is possibly an endangered species. Colored different shades of brown with a white stomach and a black stripe down its back, it has a short mane and reaches 4 ft (1.2 m) at the shoulder.

Onassis, Aristotle Socrates (1906-1975), Greek shipping magnate since the early 1930s. With relatives Stavros Livanos and Stavros Niarchos he developed the world's most powerful shipping partnership. He held citizenships in Greece and Argentina. In 1968 he married Jacqueline Bouvier Kennedy, widow of President John F. Kennedy.

Oñate, Juan de (c.1549-1628), Spanish explorer of the American southwest. He colonized what is now New Mexico from 1598. He led expeditions to the Wichita area of present-day Kansas (1601) and to the Colorado River and Gulf of California (1605).

Oncology, branch of medicine concerned with the diagnosis and treatment of cancer, and research into its causes.
See also: Cancer.

Ondaatje, Michael (1943-), Canadian poet and novelist. Ondaatje was born in Sri Lanka and moved first to England in 1954 and then to Canada in 1962. He made his debut in 1967 with a collection of poems, *The Dainty Monsters* followed by e.g. *The Man with 7 Toes* (1969), *Rat Jelly* (1973), *Elimination Dance* (1976), *Secular Love* (1984), and *The Cinnamon Peeler* (1992; collection). His first novel, *Coming Through Slaughter* (1976), is about the life of New Orleans trumpet player Buddy Bolden (1868-1931). Ondaatje also wrote *Running in the Family* (1982), *The English Patient* (1992; filmed 1997), for which he won the 1992 Booker Prize, and *Anil's Ghost* (2000).

Ondes Martenot, one of the first electrical instruments, built in 1928 by the French radio technician Maurice Martenot (1898-1980). Martenot called his machine Ondes musicales. It is a monodic instrument, i.e. it can produce only one tone at a time. There are two ways of playing the instrument: with the right hand one can either play the seven-octave keyboard, or one can move a ring along a seven-octave string, producing large glissandi while dynamics and timbre can be made with the left hand and the feet by way of switches and pedals. Because of its expressionistic possibilities, the instrument became increasingly popular among French composers like Messiaen, Milhaud, Varèse, Boulez and Honegger.

O'Neal, Shaquille Rashuan (1972-), American basketball player who became one of the richest American sportsmen thanks to his performance in the American professional basketball league. The 2.14 meter-high O'Neal plays for the Orlando Magic. His strongest point is his rebound. He was part of the illustrious Dream Team II, named after Dream Team I, which won the gold medal during the 1992 Olympic Games.

O'Neill, Eugene Gladstone (1888-1952), U.S. playwright, winner of the 1936 Nobel Prize for literature and several Pulitzer Prizes. He started to write plays during a convalescence from tuberculosis and was initially involved in off-Broadway efforts to introduce seriousness into American theater. Whether expressionistic (*The Emperor Jones*, 1920), naturalistic (*Anna Christie*, 1921), symbolist (*The Hairy Ape*, 1922), or updated Greek tragedy (*Mourning Becomes Electra*, 1931), his plays were ambitious in scope and relentlessly tragic (except for the comedy *Ah, Wilderness!*, 1933). His work included the masterpieces *The Iceman Cometh* (1946) and *Long Day's Journey into Night* (1956).

The celebrated American playwright Eugene O'Neill (1888-1952).

Onetti, Juan Carlos (1909-1994), Uruguayan writer. His work, largely situated in the fictional town of Santa María, is marked by strong pessimistic tendencies and an alienating atmosphere. Decay, powerlessness, hopelessness, desperation and sexual frustration are important themes. In 1980 Onetti was awarded the Premio Cervantes for his entire oeuvre. He also wrote *A Brief Life* (1950), *The Shipyard* (1961), *Let the Wind Speak* (1979) and *Cuando ya No Importe* (1993).

Onion (*Allium cepa*), biennial or perennial plant of either the amaryllis or the lily family. Onions have a bulb that is edible, as are the leaves. There are many varieties: the red onion, the yellow onion, the white onion, and the larger Bermuda and Spanish onions. Other onions include the garlic, the shallot, the leek, and the chive.

Ontario (pop. 11,000,000), Canadian province since 1867, bordering on the Hudson Bay, Quebec, the Great Lakes and Manitoba; 412,738 sq mi (1,068,580 sq km). Capital: Toronto. Ontario is a very watery area and has a continental climate. It is the industrial heart of Canada with e.g. car, chemical, food and wood processing industries. Exploitation of nickel, copper, iron, gold, silver, platinum, cobalt, lead and zinc. There are also supplies of gypsum, uranium, sulfur and petroleum and natural gas. Agriculture can be found in the fertile south, especially cattle, grains, potatoes, fruit, tobacco and vegetables. In 1611 the Frenchman Etienne Brûlé was the first European to set foot in Ontario. Between 1671, the year in which the British founded their first settlement in the region, and 1763, when the Treaty of Paris was signed, there was an often bloody rivalry between the French and the British. In the late 18th century many American immigrants, known as Loyalists, came to Ontario because of the War of Independence. In the early 19th century streams of immigrants came from England, Scotland and Ireland. One of the first oil drillings took place here in 1858 in Oil Springs, Lambton County. At the beginning of the 20th century large groups of Southern European immigrants arrived in Ontario, followed later by immigrants from other parts of Europe and the Commonwealth countries.
Five percent of the population is French-speaking and the Native American population is 115,000. The largest city and most significant port of Ontario is Toronto, with a population of 4 million.

Onyx, hard form of quartz made up of extremely small crystals. Onyx can be recognized by its regular and straight parallel bands of white, black, or brown. The regular banding of onyx distinguishes it from agate, a virtually identical mineral. Black-and-white onyx is a popular material for cameos. Sardonyx, which is commonly used as a gemstone, is a red-brown variety of onyx with white or black bands.

Oostende *See:* Ostend.

Ooze, any mud deposit, but especially that found on the ocean floor, often made up primarily of the remains of plankton (microscopic sea plants and animals that float on the surface of the water).

Opal, cryptocrystalline variety of porous hydrated silica, deposited from aqueous solution in all kinds of rocks, and also formed by replacement of other minerals. Opals are variously colored; the best gem varieties are translucent, with milky or pearly opalescence and iridescence.

Oparin, Alexander Ivanovich (1894-1880), Russian biochemist whose hypothesis on the origin of life became rationale for others' research. Presuming that earth's original atmosphere contained no nitrogen or oxygen but instead consisted of ammonia, hydrogen, methane, and water in a gaseous state, he theorized that life formed spontaneously in this type of atmosphere and developed as we know it today. He wrote about his theory in *Origin of Life* (1936).
See also: Biochemistry.

Op Art, non-figurative stream in modern visual art, which tries to create by means of optic effects an illusion of movement through changes in shape and/or color. Contrary to kinetic art, the object does not actually move, but the illusion of movement is created. Members of the op art movement are J. Albers, Z. Kemeny, F. Morellet, B. Riley and V. Vasarely.

Victor Vasarely's *Cheyt-G* creates a surface of diamond shapes and shades of color that appears to advance and recede. A master of complex optical techniques, Vasarely was a key figure in the development of Op Art (Collection of the artist).

OPEC *See:* Organization of Petroleum Exporting Countries.

Open-Door Policy, policy of equal commercial rights for all nations involved in an area. The term emerged in the late 19th century when the United States sought trade with China on a basis of equality with other nations, which had divided China into spheres of influence. The Open-Door Policy ended with World War II.

Open housing, enforcement of equal rights provided by fair-housing laws. These prohibit discrimination, in selling homes or renting property, against minorities, the handicapped, or for reasons of religious preferences or national origins.

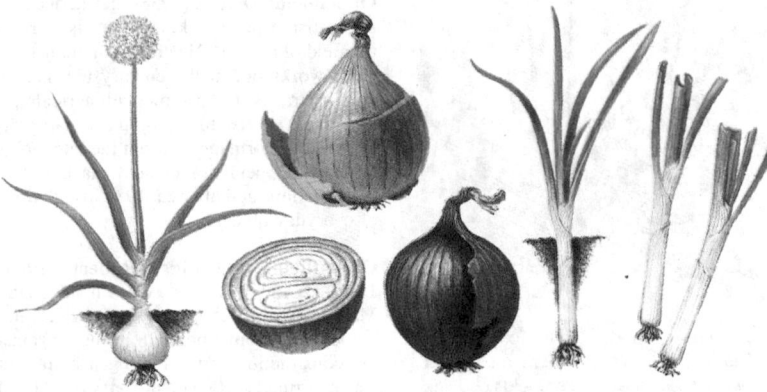

The onion is cultivated for its bulb. Mature bulb onions (center) develop a skin of dried leaves. When cut, the flesh is roughly circular and is separated by membranes. Scallions (right) are either bunch onions or young bulb onions harvested before the bulbs mature. Both the bulb and leaves are eaten.

O

O

Open shop, business that does not restrict its employees to labor union members. It is the opposite of a closed shop, where only union members may be employed.

Opera, staged dramatic form in which the text is wholly or partly sung to an instrumental or orchestral accompaniment. It originated in 17th-century Italy, in an attempt to recreate Greek drama. Much early opera was a mere excuse for spectacle, but works by Claudio Monteverdi, Jean Baptiste Lully, and Henry Purcell advanced the art. Dramatic standards declined in the 18th century, despite fine works by George Frederic Handel. Christoph Willibald von Gluck sought to unify plot, music, and staging into a dramatic whole, while Wolfgang Amadeus Mozart introduced greater depth of feeling into the music and realism of character on stage. The form was further enriched by the Romantics: Ludwig van Beethoven and Karl Maria von Weber in Germany and Hector Berlioz and Georges Bizet in France. The great Italians Vincenzo Bellini, Gaetano Donizetti, and Gioacchino Rossini developed the stylized bel canto form to which Giuseppe Verdi, in his later operas, gave depth and naturalism, a trend carried further in the works and theories of Richard Wagner, who sought to add a philosophical basis to Gluck's synthesis by creating *Gesamtkunstwerk*, the total work of art. Wagner influenced such later composers as Richard Strauss and Claude Debussy. The Italian verismo (naturalistic) school produced smaller-scale, often sensational works: Giacomo Puccini mastered both this and a more epic, fantastic style. Among eminent 20th-century opera composers are Leos Janácek, Alban Berg, and Benjamin Britten.

Operetta, light, amusing, semi-operatic form using spoken conversation and tuneful songs. Most plots deal with human folly, foolishness or romance, remind the listeners of conscience and good behavior, and have happy endings. Some familiar operettas are *Die Fledermaus*, by Johann Strauss, Jr., *The Merry Widow*, by Franz Lehár, *H.M.S. Pinafore*, by Gilbert and Sullivan, and *Naughty Marietta*, by Victor Herbert.

Ophthalmia, disease of the eye tissue, extremely serious and usually occurring from a wound, poison, or contamination, although it can also be acquired through birth. Sympathetic ophthalmia results when the unaffected eye responds to the affected one, causing disease in both eyes.
See also: Blindness.

Ophthalmology, branch of medicine and surgery concerned with diagnosing and treating diseases of the eye.
See also: Eye.

Ophthalmoscope, instrument for examining the retina and structures of the inner eye. A powerful light and lens system allows the retina and eye blood vessels to be seen at high magnification.

Opiates, 1. Substances like opium, morphine and heroin which have a pain-reducing and calming effect. These substances bind themselves to special receptors in the brain. These receptors can be found there because the body itself also produces opiates, i.e. endorphins. Opiates quickly create a feeling of tolerance and dependence.
2. Other substances that bind themselves to the opiate receptors but which lack the pain-reducing effects are also considered to be opiates. These substances block the effects of the first group of opiates. An example of such a substance is naloxone.
See also: Drug.

Opinion poll *See:* Public opinion.

Opium, narcotic extract derived from the immature fruits of the opium poppy, native to Greece and Asia Minor. The milky juice is refined to a powder that has a sharp, bitter taste. Drugs derived from opium include heroin, morphine, laudanum, and codeine. Because these drugs can cause severe physical and psychologic dependencies, their use outside the pharmaceutical industry is strictly controlled in the West. The period necessary for physical dependency to occur varies with the type of drug and the amount and frequency of dose. With drugs of the morphine type, harm is often experienced indirectly, through preoccupation with drug-taking, personal neglect, malnutrition, and infection. These effects may lead to disruption of personal and family relationships, economic loss, and crime. When opiates use is stopped, withdrawal symptoms may occur,

The green seed pods of *Papaver somniferum* are the source of a milky juice: crude opium, a mixture of about twenty alkaloids. This juice is the only source of the pain killer morphine, but also yields codeine, a milder pain killer, and heroin, which is no longer used medicinally.

often within a few hours after the last dose and reaching a peak within the next 24-48 hours. The most severe symptoms generally disappear within 10 days. The time of onset, peak intensity, and duration of the withdrawal symptoms vary with the type of drug and degree of dependence. Withdrawal symptoms include alterations in behavior, excitation of the nervous system, and feelings of depression and anxiety. Physical disturbances, such as weight loss, abdominal cramps, nausea, and body aches, are also common.
See also: Drug; Narcotic.

Opium War (1839-1842), fought in China by the British, the first in a series aimed at opening ports and gaining tariff concessions. The pretext was the burying of 20,000 chests of opium by the Chinese. China had banned the opium trade in 1799, but with the aid of corrupt Chinese officials British merchants still made enormous profits from it. British troops occupied Hong Kong in 1841, and the fall of Chinkiang (Zhen-jiang) in 1842 threatened Peking (Beijing) itself. The Treaty of Nanking (Nanjing) ceded Hong Kong to Britain and granted British merchants full rights of residence in the ports of Amoy (Xiamen), Canton (Guangzhou), Foochow (Fuzhou), Ningpo, and Shanghai; Britain was also to receive over $50 million war indemnity. The United States gained trade facilities by the 1844 Treaty of Wanghai. Further hostilities, in which French joined British troops (1856), led to more concessions, notably in the Treaties of Tientsin (1858) to which Britain, France, Russia, and the United States were parties, which legalized the opium trade, and when Kowloon was ceded to Britain and part of Manchuria to Russia (1860).

Opossum, primitive arboreal marsupial of the Americas. Opossums are carnivorous and usually have a prehensile tail, which coils around to grasp. The pouch is developed only in some species, but all have an uneven number of teats, as many as 17 in the Virginian opossum. In size, opossums vary from mouselike to the size of a domestic cat.

Oppenheim, Dennis (1938-), American visual artist, especially known for his work in the field of land art. He creates monumental-scale works out in the countryside, i.e. by making tracks in the snow with agricultural machines. He also took part in body-art projects and performances. From the late 1970s onwards Oppenheim created machine-like constructions and after ca. 1985 installations of everyday objects.

Oppenheimer, J(ulius) Robert (1904-1967), U.S. physicist who headed the Manhattan Project (1942-1945) which developed the atomic bomb. He fought against the construction of the hydrogen bomb but was overruled by President Harry S. Truman in 1949. His main aim was the peaceful use of nuclear power, but because of his left-wing friendships, he was unable to pursue his researches in this direction after being labeled a security risk in 1954. He also

worked out much of the theory of black holes in the universe.
See also: Manhattan Project.

Opposition, in astronomy, placement whereby 2 heavenly bodies are aligned with a third in a somewhat straight line. The planet Venus is in opposition when Earth lines up between Venus and the Sun.

Optical disc, thin, flat, circular plastic plate covered with a reflective substance that receives coded information from a laser beam to record sound, data, or pictures. The beam marks the disc, which can be stored or decoded by a weaker laser upon playback. Some optical discs have only prerecorded material, which cannot be erased. Optical discs have a greater storage capacity and wear longer than magnetic discs.
See also: Videodisc; Compact disc (CD).

Optical fiber *See:* Fiber optics.

Optical illusion, visual distortion of reality. To an observer standing at the corner of a street and looking down the row of houses on the street, the closest house will appear to be the biggest, while the house at the end will seem the smallest. Since the houses are all roughly the same size, the perception that the closer ones are large and the further ones are small is an optical illusion. This differs from an illusion, where a person sees an object but it isn't really there.

Optic nerve *See:* Eye.

Optics, branch of physical science that deals with vision and light: its properties and phenomena, its origin and effects, and its role as a medium of sight.

Optometry, measurement and examination of the visual powers; the art and practice of testing the eyes by means of instruments or appliances for defects of vision in order to correct them with eyeglasses.

Oracle, in ancient times, the answer by a god or goddess to a human questioner, or the shrine at which the answer was given, usually through a priest or priestess (also called oracles). There were oracles in Egypt and Rome, but the greatest were in Greece: at Dodona, with Zeus's oracle, and at Delphi, where Apollo spoke through a priestess, the Pythia. Answers, often to important political questions, were obtained directly or derived from dreams, from signs (such as the rustling of leaves in a sacred tree), and from divination by lot.
See also: Mythology.

Oraibi *See:* Hopi.

Oral contraceptive *See:* Birth control.

Oral surgery *See:* Periodontitis.

Oran (pop. 890,000), Algerian port city about 225 mi (362 km) west of Algiers on the Mediterranean Sea. Settled by the Moors in the 10th century, it fell successively to the Spanish (1509 and 1732) and the Turks (1708 and 1791). In the aftermath of an

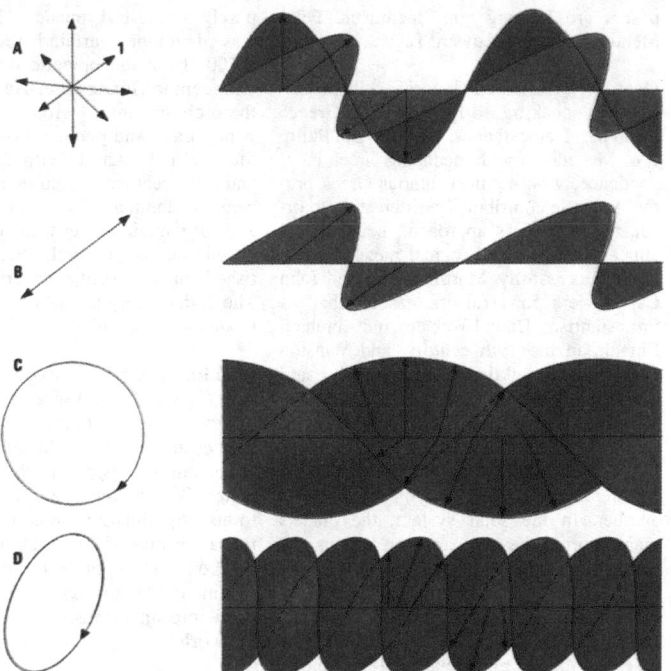

Light can be described as an electromagnetic wave, with electric and magnetic fields oscillating about the direction of the wave. As the electric vector appears to be responsible for polarisation, it can, for all practical purposes, be considered as a light vector. The electric vectors of unpolarized light (A) viewed head-on at any instant in time (1) vary continually in magnitude and direction. In polarized light, the variation of the electric vector is completely predictable. In linearly polarized light (B), it will lie in a plane. The electric vector of polarized light may also follow a path, whose projection at right angles to the direction of propogation, is a circle (C) or an elipse (D).

earthquake, it became French (1831), who controlled it during World War II, when it was a U.S. base of operations.
See also: Algeria.

Orange, tree (genus *Citrus*) of the rue family; also, the fruit of the tree. Oranges, which have been cultivated since ancient times, probably originated in tropical regions of Asia. The sweet, or China, orange (*C. sinensis*) and the mandarin orange (*C. reticulata*), the main species in cultivation, are used as dessert fruit and for making orange drinks. The Seville, or sour, orange (*C. aurantium*) is mainly used to make marmalades. The chief orange-growing states are Florida, California, Arizona, and Texas.

Orange Free State, province in the Republic of South Africa, with Bloemfontein as its capital. The region was settled c.1836 by the Boers, South Africans of Dutch descent, who named it in 1854 and remained there, despite strife with native Africans, until defeated in war by the British (1899-1902). Under British rule, the state became part of the Union of South Africa. The majority of the state's people are black Africans, yet the majority of farms, land, and mines are owned by whites.
See also: South Africa.

Orange hawkweed *See:* Devil's paintbrush.

Orangemen, or Loyal Orange Institution, Protestant (chiefly Ulster) society that since the first (1795) lodge has identified with the Protestant ascendancy in Ireland and, more

recently, union with Britain. The name is from William of Orange (William III of England, who succeeded the Catholic king James II in 1690).
See also: Protestantism

Orange River, South African river with dams along its course (1,300 mi/2,090 km) to generate hydroelectric power, plus canals and tunnels that control flooding and bring irrigation water to 750,000 acres (300,000 hectares). It originates in Lesotho's mountains and flows into the Atlantic Ocean but is not navigable because of shallow water and numerous sandbars.

Orange root *See:* Goldenseal.

Orangutan, large, red, anthropoid ape (*Pongo pygmaeus*), native to the rain forests of Sumatra and Borneo. They are truly arboreal apes-walking quadrupedally along branches, or bipedally, with the arms holding on above. Occasionally the orangutans progress by swinging by their arms for short distances. They can move along the ground but rarely descend from the trees. They are vegetarians, feeding mainly on leaves, buds, and fruit.

Oratorio, musical composition for vocal soloists, chorus, and orchestra, usually with a religious subject. The form evolved from medieval sacred drama. Early oratorio composers include Alessandro Scarlatti, Johann Sebastian Bach, and George Frideric Handel, whose *Messiah* is probably the most famous oratorio. Among later oratorio composers are Ludwig von Beethoven, Felix Mendelssohn, and Edward Elgar.

Oratory, also called rhetoric, skill in persuasive speaking, originating in Greece c.460 B.C. Demosthenes, who charged Philip II of Macedonia with menacing Greek independence, was the most famous Greek orator. Aristotle contributed written style to organize a speaker's approach, incorporating ethical, pathetic, and logical means to persuade successfully. Martin Luther and John Calvin were powerful orators on behalf of Protestantism. Daniel Webster and Abraham Lincoln in the 19th century, and Winston Churchill, Franklin D. Roosevelt, and Martin Luther King in the 20th were most effective U.S. orators.

Orbit, path followed by 1 celestial body revolving under the influence of gravity about another. In the solar system, the planets mainly orbit the sun, and the moons the planets, in elliptical paths. The point in the planetary, asteroidal, or cometary orbit closest to the sun is called its perihelion; the farthest point is termed the aphelion. In the case of a moon or artificial satellite orbiting a planet or other moon, the corresponding terms are perigee and apogee. Celestial objects of similar masses, particularly double stars, may orbit each other.

Orcagna (1308-1368), painter, sculptor, and architect of Florence, Italy, leading artist in the Byzantine Gothic style. His work includes the Strozzi Chapel altarpiece in Santa Maria Novella and the Or San Michele tabernacle, and the facade of Orvieto Cathedral.

Orchestra, instrumental group of more than a few players. The modern orchestra dates from the birth of opera, c.1600. The first great operatic composer, Claudio Monte-verdi, wrote for orchestra, and for some time opera and orchestra music were closely linked. As the violin family replaced viols, composers like Antonio Vivaldi, Johann Sebastian Bach, and George Frideric Handel began to write purely orchestral music. The symphony was developed around the same time (1700) from the operatic overture. In the 18th century Franz Josef Haydn organized the orchestra into 4 groups: string, woodwind, brass, and percussion-a basic pattern that has not altered. With the great 18th- and 19th-century composers, the orchestra came to dominate the musical scene. New and more numerous instruments were introduced, permanent orchestras were established, and the art of conducting developed. The 20th century has seen a move to return to smaller ensembles.

Orchid, plant of the large family Orchidaceae (15,000-30,000 species) that produces colorful and elaborate flowers. Some species are native to cold and temperate regions, but most occur in tropical, damp climates. Orchid flowers are specially adapted to insect pollination, some requiring a particular species of insect. Orchids are of little economic importance except as curious ornamental plants; cultivation has developed into an extensive hobby throughout the world.

Orczy, Baroness Emmuska (1865-1847), Hungarian author best known for the French Revolution adventure novel *The Scarlet Pimpernel* (1905). Her 2 sequels to it did not achieve the acclaim of the original. She also wrote numerous short detective stories.

Order in Council, statement or instruction from the British crown rule usually set forth in times of emergency or great national threat and without initial Parliamentary consent. Orders in Council were issued during World Wars I and II, and when immediate, prudent economic regulations have been needed.
See also: Continental System; Privy Council.

Ordinance, rule, decree, or command usually prepared locally to maintain order and control in cities, towns, or settlements where constitutions or laws of command have not yet been prepared.

Ordovician, second period of the Paleozoic Era, c.500-440 million years ago, immediately following the Cambrian.

Ore, aggregate of minerals and rocks from which minerals (usually metals) can be extracted. An ore has 3 parts: the country rock in which the deposit is found; the gangue, the unwanted rocks and minerals of the deposit; and the desired mineral itself. Mining techniques depend greatly on the form and position of the deposit.

Oregano *See:* Marjoram.

Oregon (Beaver State; pop. 3,2 million), Pacific Coast state in the northwestern United States; bordered by Washington, Idaho, Nevada, California, and the Pacific Ocean.
The Columbia River and its tributary, the Willamette, are Oregon's major rivers. There are many waterfalls along the Columbia River Gorge. Oregon's volcano-formed Crater Lake is the deepest body of water in the U.S. Forests cover nearly half of the state. Principal cities are Portland and Eugene. The capital is Salem.
Manufacturing is Oregon's leading economic activity. Chief manufactured goods are lumber and wood products, processed foods, scientific instruments, machinery, paper products, printed materials, primary metals, and fabricated metal products. Wholesale and retail trade is also important.
In the early 1800s, U.S. and British fur traders competed in the region; in 1843, thousands of American settlers began arriving via the Oregon Trail. Oregon became the 33rd state in 1859.

Oregon grape, wild, flowering, low-growing evergreen plant producing small blue edible berries in the fall, of the family Berberidaceae (genus *Mahonia*). Also known as the Oregon hollygrape, it is neither a holly nor a grape. Found also in Washington and British Columbia, it is Oregon's state flower.

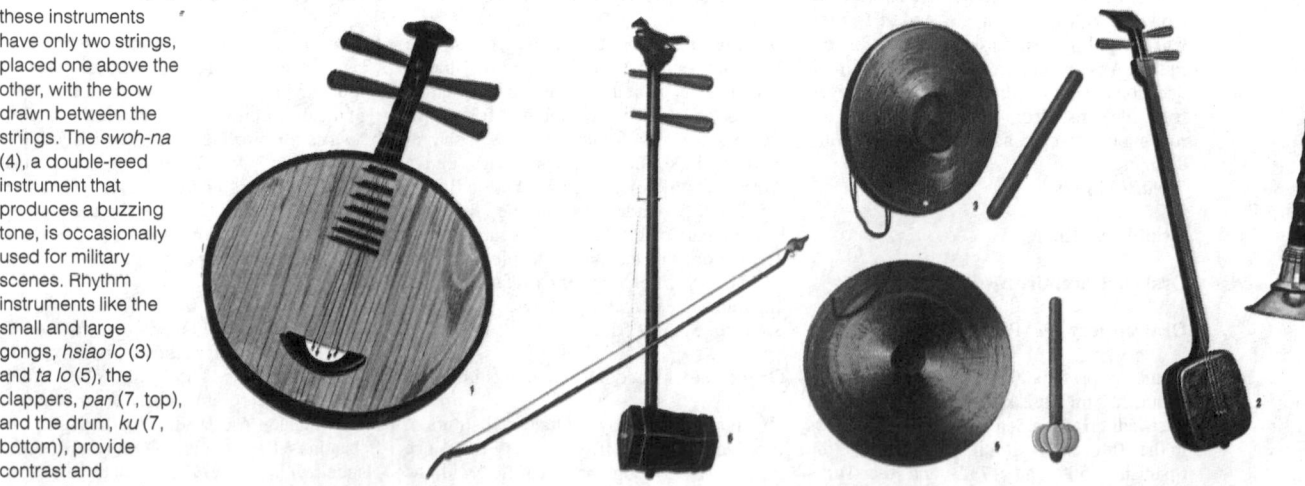

Instruments such as these are used in the traditional Chinese musical theater, a major form of musical expression for the Chinese, with specific contributions to both music and drama. The flat lute (*yuĕh-ch'in*, 1), and the unfretted long lute (*san hsien*, 2), are used with other stringed instruments for melodic expression. Fiddles, such as the *hu-ch'in* (6) and the *erh-hu* (8) lead the melody. Unlike western violins, these instruments have only two strings, placed one above the other, with the bow drawn between the strings. The *swoh-na* (4), a double-reed instrument that produces a buzzing tone, is occasionally used for military scenes. Rhythm instruments like the small and large gongs, *hsiao lo* (3) and *ta lo* (5), the clappers, *pan* (7, top), and the drum, *ku* (7, bottom), provide contrast and expression.

Oregon Trail, pioneer wagon route between Independence, Mo., on the Missouri River, and the Columbia River region of the Pacific Northwest. The 2,000-mi (3,200-km) trail was most popular in the 1840s, before the beginning of the California gold rush. In that decade at least 10,000 pioneers made the arduous trek from northeast Kansas along the Platte River in Nebraska, to Fort Laramie, Wyo. From there they crossed the Rocky Mountains at South Pass and proceeded through Snake River country to Fort Vancouver. The journey was recounted in Francis Parkman's classic, *The Oregon Trail* (1849).
See also: Westward movement.

Orellana, Francisco de (c.1511-1546), Spanish soldier and explorer of the Amazon River. On an expedition with Pizarro east of Quito, Ecuador, Orellana and a group of soldiers left to search for provisions but never returned. Instead, they continued to the Atlantic Ocean, floating down the river later named the Amazon, after his comparison of tribal women he had seen there to those in Greek myths. On a subsequent expedition to the Amazon, his boat capsized and he drowned.

Orenburg (pop. 575,000), Russia, a city and the administrative center for Orenburg Oblast. It is on the Ural River, about 750 miles (1,200 km) southeast of Moscow. Products include leather, silk, and machinery. There are flour mills and meat-packing plants here. Orenburg was founded in 1735. The city was called Chkalov from 1938 to 1958.

Orestes, in Greek mythology, son of Agamemnon and Clytemnestra. Orestes killed his mother and her lover, Aegisthus, after they murdered Agamemnon. Thereafter, the Furies, goddesses of vengeance, harassed Orestes. Fleeing to Athens, he was purified and found innocent of the killings by a jury.
See also: Mythology.

Orff, Carl (1895-1982), German composer and music teacher. His works are marked by short melodic motifs and strong rhythms from a large and varied percussion section. His best-known work is the oratorio *Carmina Burana*.

Organ, musical instrument in which air is blown into pipes of different shape and size to produce a range of notes. Organ pipes are of 2 kinds: flue pipes that work like a flute or recorder, and reed pipes that operate on the same principle as a clarinet or oboe. Although organs existed in ancient times, the major developments in organ building took place between the 14th and the 18th centuries. Composers like Jan Pieter Sweelinck and Dietrich Buxtehude paved the way for Johann Sebastian Bach, the greatest of all composers for the organ. Bach and George Frideric Handel wrote for the baroque organ, a relatively small instrument. In the 19th century many great organs were built, precursors of the huge electric-powered instruments built in the 1920s and 1930s in cinemas and theaters. The modern Hammond organ produces its sound electronically. Small electronic organs are now frequently used by popular musical groups.

Organic chemistry, branch of chemistry comprising the study of hydrocarbons, or carbon compounds containing hydrogen. (Simple carbon compounds such as carbon dioxide are usually considered inorganic.) Because of carbon's ability to form linked chains of atoms of any length and complexity, there are far more organic compounds than inorganic. Organic compounds form the basic stuff of living tissue. Organic chemistry is also of fundamental importance in the textile, petrochemical, and pharmaceutical industries.
See also: Chemistry.

Organization for Economic Cooperation and Development (OECD), international governmental body representing 29 countries, created in 1961 to develop trade and support and assist in each other's growth and economic welfare. An administrative body, the Council, having representatives from each country, governs OECD. Its headquarters are in Paris, France.

Organization of African Unity (OAU), association of independent African states (excluding South Africa) that aims to promote unity among its members and improve economic and cultural relations in Africa. It has been opposed to the government of South Africa and endorses majority rule for the country. Founded in 1963, the OAU has a permanent secretariat in Addis Ababa, Ethiopia, and has had great influence at the United Nations.
In 2002, 53 African States signed up to the newly formed African Union, thereby ending the OAU.

Organization of American States (OAS), association of republics of the Americas that aims to settle disputes peacefully, to create a collective security system, and to coordinate the work of other intra-American bodies. The OAS was founded in Bogotá, Colombia,

O

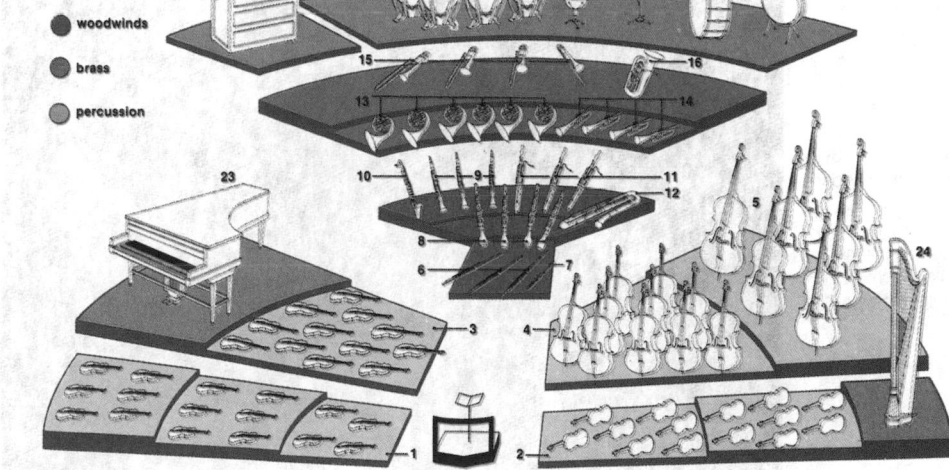

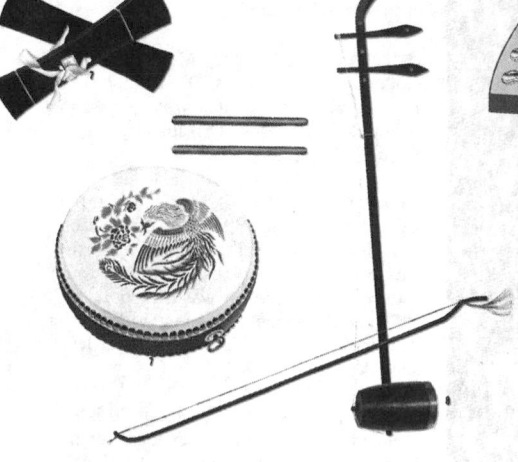

The instruments of a modern symphony orchestra are generally grouped by category in order to concentrate and blend the sounds of a given tone color. The strings, which include first (1) and second (2) violins, violas (3), cellos (4), and double basses (5), form the backbone of the orchestra. Their vibrant tones range from the sweetness of the violin to the deep resonance of the double bass. The woodwinds include the flute (6), piccolo (7), oboe (8), clarinet (9), bass clarinet (10), bassoon (11), and contrabassoon (12). Their tone quality is mellow, encompassing both the plaintive oboe and the clear, soft-spoken flute. Brass instruments, including French horns (13), trumpets (14), trombones (15), and tuba (16), contribute briliance and clarity. The percussion instruments, which stress rhythm and provide emphasis, include the timpani (17); kettle (18), snare (19), and bass (20) drums; the celesta (21), a keyboard chime; and the gong (22). The piano (23) and harp (24) are standard solo instruments.

in 1948 and has a permanent secretariat, the Pan American Union. Its activities have included support for the U.S. blockade of Cuba in 1962 and mediation between Britain and Guatemala in 1972. In 1998 there were 35 members.

O

Organization of Petroleum Exporting Countries (OPEC), group of 12 oil-producing countries that attempts to control oil prices in world sales. Organized in 1960, its members are Algeria, Gabon, Indonesia, Iran, Iraq, Kuwait, Libya, Nigeria, Qatar, Saudi Arabia, United Arab Emirates, and Venezuela. OPEC's 4 administrative sections, each with its own responsibilities, work toward the common goals of oil pricing and supplying world demands.

Organ transplant *See:* Tissue transplant.

Oriental exclusion acts, edicts either limiting or halting immigration of Asians into the United States. Initially, Chinese laborers were welcomed and protected by the Burlingame Treaty (1868), but when the U.S. economy slipped the Chinese were blamed, and the Chinese Exclusion Act of 1882 was passed. Japanese immigration met the same fate when the Immigration Act of 1924 prohibited all Asian immigration. The Immigration and Nationality Act of 1952 gave Asians the same rights as other immigrants, but the U.S. quota system did not end until 1965.

Origami, Japanese form of art made by folding various-sized squares of paper into birds, flowers, fish, and abstract shapes. Pleated ceremonial decorations attached to presents are a form of origami called *noshi*.

The decorative folding of paper is not exclusively Japanese; it has thrived in Spain and South America, and in Germany as a teaching tool for commercial design.

Origen (Origines Adamantius; A.D. 185?-A.D. 254?), one of the foremost radical theologians of the early Christian Church. Born in Alexandria, Egypt, Origen tried to reconcile Greek philosophy with Christian theology in works like *De Principalis* (On First Principles) and *Contra Celsum* (Against Celsus), a defense of Christianity.Charles R.; Evolution.

Orinoco River, tributary of Venezuela, about 1,700 mi (2,736 km) long. Mostly navigable, it rises in the Parima highlands of southeastern Venezuela and eventually flows into the Atlantic Ocean through a 7,000-sq-mi (18,130-sq-km) delta.
See also: Venezuela.

Oriole, name of several members of the blackbird family. Most species live in tropical America, where both sexes are brightly colored; in temperate regions the females are olive drab or brown. The Baltimore oriole, now called the Northern Oriole, is black and brilliant orange. Orioles build their nests of woven grass, and some build hanging nests or large communal nests occupied by several families.

Orion (the hunter), star constellation resembling the shape of a man, named from Greek mythology. Three bright aligned stars make up Orion's belt and a group of fainter stars depict his sword. The yellow-red star Betelgeuse identifies the left shoulder, and the star Rigel his right foot. Innumerable

The Baltimore oriole, the state bird of Maryland, is a subspecies of the northern oriole (*I. galbula*). It prefers woodland habitats.

faint stars and luminous masses of gas and dust complete Orion's figure.

Orion, in Greek mythology, giant hunter killed by the goddess Artemis, who then turned him into a constellation.
See also: Mythology.

Orissa (pop. 31,660,000), federal state in the east of India, on the Gulf of Bengal; 60,141 sq mi (155,707 sq km). Capital: Bhubaneswar. Foothills of the East-Ghats; there are no good natural ports. The coastal area is very fertile. Rice, sugarcane, cattle, legumes, cotton and tobacco. There are metal, textile, cement, paper and glass industries and sugar refining. Exploitation of chromium, graphite, quartz, iron, manganese, coal, limestone, bauxite and dolomite. There is also a small-scale textile industry. Remains of the ancient Hindu civilisation. In 1592 the district was annexed by the Mogul Empire and in 1803 it became British territory. From 1912-1936 Orissa and Bihar were one province. Until 1947 the state's capital was Cuttack.

Orissa (Arabian: al-Asi), a 354 mi (570 km) long river which runs through Lebanon, Syria and Turkey. Originates in Lebanon and flows into the Mediterranean near Antakya. The estuary of the Orontes is very fertile. The river is unnavigable, but important for irrigation. In ancient times it was of strategic importance and made up the northern border of the Egyptian Empire.

Orizaba, or Citlaltépetl, Mexico's highest mountain, elevation 18,701 ft (5,700 m). The snow-covered extinct volcano is about 30 mi (48 km) west of Orizaba city.
See also: Mexico.

Orizaba (pop. 118,000), Mexican resort city located in a scenic valley between Veracruz and Mexico City. Settled by the Spanish in the 1500s to protect essential travel routes between the 2 cities, it was incorporated in 1774 and developed into an agricultural and industrial site. In 1973, an earthquake devastated the area.

Orkney Islands, group of about 70 islands north of Scotland, of which they are part. Their total area is 376 sq mi (974 sq km) but

The Orion Nebula is a huge cloud of gas and dust, illuminated by four hot stars (the Trapezium) near its center. Its turbulent image is created by the alternation of dark and luminous clouds. Because of these clouds, part of the Nebula is completely invisible to the naked eye.

fewer than half are inhabited. The climate is mild and the soil fertile. Farming is the chief activity (grains, sheep, cattle, poultry), and there is some fishing.

Orlando (pop. 1,500,000), resort city and retirement center in central Florida, with a year-round temperate climate for its fast-growing population. Nearby Walt Disney World, Epcot Center, Disney-MGM Studios, aerospace industries, and a large citrus crop provide employment.
See also: Florida.

Orlando, Vittorio Emanuele (1860-1952), Italian statesman and prime minister (1917-1919). He led the Italian delegation at the Paris Peace Conference of 1919-1920, but left the conference because of opposition from U.S. President Wilson regarding territorial compensation for Italy. Orlando retired from politics with the advent of Fascism but returned after the fall of Mussolini.
See also: Italy.

Orléans, family name of 2 branches of the French royal line. The house of Valois-Orléans was founded by **Louis, duke of Orléans** (1372-1407), whose grandson ascended the throne (1498) as **Louis XII**. The house of Bourbon-Orléans was founded by **Philippe, duke of Orléans** (1640-1701), brother of King Louis XIV. His son, **Philippe** (1674-1723), was regent of France (1715-1723). **Louis Philippe** (1773-1850) was the sole member of the house to become king (1830-1848).
See also: France.

Orléans (pop. 250,000), city in the Loire Valley, northwest France. Among the ancient buildings still standing are remnants from the time of Julius Caesar's occupation. When the English attacked it in 1429 during the Hundred Years War, Joan of Arc led French soldiers to victory. Industries include flower production, candies, liqueurs, automobiles, and farm machinery.
See also: France.

Ormandy, Eugene (Eugene Ormandy Blau; 1899-1985), Hungarian-born U.S. symphony conductor, music director of the Philadelphia Orchestra 1938-1980. Ormandy originally came to the United States (1921) as a violinist, but began to conduct, becoming conductor of the Minneapolis Symphony Orchestra in 1931. During his tenure with the Philadelphia Orchestra he established its lush sound, particularly that of its string sections, and became a leading interpreter of Romantic music.

Ornithischian *See:* Dinosaur.

Ornithosis *See:* Psittacosis.

Orozco, José Clemente (1883-1949), Mexican painter. He exploited the fresco technique in his large-scale murals, which express strong social convictions. His most famous works include the fresco *Prometheus* (1930), *Mankind's Struggle* (1930), and the mural *Epic Culture in the New World* (1932-1934).

Orpheus, in Greek mythology, renowned musician of Thrace. Son of the muse Calliope, he could tame wild beasts with his lyre playing. After the death of his wife, Eurydice, Orpheus sought her in Hades. He was allowed to lead her back to earth providing he did not look at her, but he could not resist the temptation, and Eurydice vanished forever. He was regarded as the founder of the Orphic mystery cult, which saw both good and evil in human nature, and followed a strict ethical and moral code.
See also: Mythology.

Orr, Bobby (1948-), Canadian-born, U.S. hockey player. Known for his leadership and scoring, he played in the National Hockey League (NHL) for the Boston Bruins (1967-1976), where he was chosen the NHL's most valuable player 3 times (1970, 1971, 1972) and was named the most outstanding defensemen 8 consecutive times (1968-1975). He finished his career with the Chicago Black Hawks (1976-1979) after suffering serious knee injuries. Orr was inducted into the Hockey Hall of Fame in 1979.

Orrisroot, root body of 3 species of irises, which produce an oil with the fragrance of violets. In powdered form, the substance was once used extensively in perfumes but high costs now limit it to expensive brands. It is also an ingredient in medicine.

Orsted-Pedersen, Niels-Henning (1946-), Danish jazz musician. One of Europe's most sought-after, all-round virtuosos on the acoustic bass. Has worked professionally since age fourteen and accompanied various American musicians like Chet Baker, Oscar Peterson and Dexter Gordon, as well as formed his own bands. Was sometimes criticized for his inclination to show off his technique. He can, however, be also very lyrical, as in e.g. *Those Who Were* (1996) and *This Is All I Ask* (1997).

Ortega, Daniel (1945-), revolutionary leader of the Sandinista National Liberation Front in Nicaragua (1984-1990). In 1979 Ortega removed A. Somoza-Debayle from power and took control of the government. He improved education and welfare services but controlled the press, and limited civil rights. The contras opposed Ortega's government and engaged in guerrilla warfare until a 1988 cease-fire. The United States cut back trade with Ortega, claiming he formed a Communist government. Lack of U.S. trade, the contra war, and ongoing welfare services presented overwhelming adverse conditions for Ortega, who was defeated by Violeta Chamorro in a general election in 1990. Ortega was reelected as secretary-general of the FSLN in 1994. In 1996 he lost the presidential elections.
See also: Nicaragua.

Ortega y Gasset, José (1883-1955), Spanish philosopher whose best-known work, *The Revolt of the Masses* (1929), attributes Western decadence to the revolt of 'mass man' against an intellectual elite. His philosophy attempts to reconcile reason with individual lives and needs.
See also: Existentialism.

Orthodontics, in dentistry, correction or prevention of the arrangement or number of teeth in people and animals. Procedures include tooth extractions and using metal or plastic braces and wires to adjust unaligned teeth, a problem which usually occurs during childhood as the teeth develop. These abnormalities in teeth position are called malocclusions.
See also: Dentistry.

Orthopedics, specialty within surgery dealing with bone and soft-tissue disease, damage, and deformity. Its name derives from 17th-century treatments designed to produce 'straight children.' Treatment of congenital deformity, fractures and tumors of bone, osteomyelitis, arthritis, and joint dislocation are commonly treated by orthopedic professionals. Methods range from the use of splints, physiotherapy, and manipulation, to surgical correction of deformity, the fixing of fractures, and the refashioning or replacement of joints. Suture and transposition of tendons, muscles, and nerves are also performed.

Orwell, George (Eric Arthur Blair; 1903-1950), English writer, famous principally for *Animal Farm* (1945), a satire on communist revolution, and *Nineteen Eighty-Four* (1949), which depicts a dehumanizing totalitarian society. Orwell was also a critic and essayist. Other works include the semi-autobiographical *Road to Wigan Pier* (1937) and *Homage to Catalonia* (1938), an account of his experiences in the Spanish Civil War.

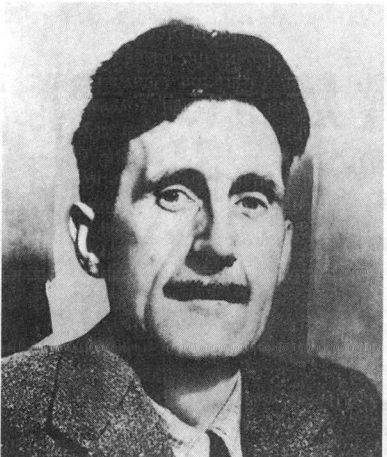
George Orwell (1903-1950).

Oryx, genus of African antelopes with a white or fawn coat and long curving horns. All 5 species have been reduced by hunting.

Osage orange (*Maclura pomifera*), tree originally found only in Texas, Oklahoma, and Arkansas. Its large green fruit is known as a hedge apple, and its elastic timber is used for making archery bows.

Osaka (pop. 2,600,000), Japan's third-largest city, an industrial and commercial center, on Honshu Island at the mouth of the Yodo River on Osaka Bay. Lack of land (it covers only 80 sq mi/206 sq km) has forced a rapidly increasing population into apart-

O

O

ments or to the suburbs, and shopping centers underground. It has centuries-old cultural and religious monuments and several universities and museums. Steel, chemicals, and textiles are leading products. A great port, it is connected by the world's fastest railway system to Tokyo and Asia's busiest airport.
See also: Japan.

Osama bin Laden (1957-), Saudi multi-millionaire and guerrilla leader. Osama supported the Afghan resistance movement in his struggle against the Soviet occupation. He founded his first military training camps when the end of the war was near. This was the beginning of the extremist organization Al-Qaida ('the base'). In 1989, Soviet troops withdrew from Afghanistan and Bin Laden returned to Saudi Arabia. During the Persian Gulf War (1991) Saudi Arabia was a U.S. ally. Bin Laden was a fierce critic of the royal Saudi family, which allowed the presence of American troops in the vicinity of sacred Muslim cities such as Mecca and Medina. He was expelled from Saudi Arabia in 1991 and fled to Sudan. Many of the former Afghan warriors joined him. In Sudan he founded several companies and military training camps. He returned to Afghanistan in 1996, where he was able to hide under Taliban protection. Since his alleged connection with the bombings of the American embassies in Kenya and Tanzania and the 11 September, 2001, attacks on New York and Washington, he has become America's most wanted criminal. Bin Laden disappeared during the attack of the United States on the Taliban administration in Afghanistan.
See also: Al-Qaida; Taliban; September 11, 2001.

Osama bin Laden

Osborne, John (1929-1994), English dramatist whose *Look Back in Anger* (1956) made him the first Angry Young Man of the 1950s and established a new and vigorous realism in the British theater. His later plays include *The Entertainer* (1957), *Luther* (1961), and *Inadmissible Evidence* (1964).

Oscar *See:* Academy Awards.

OSCE (Organization for Security and Co-operation in Europe), by changing the name CVSE (Conference on Security and Cooperation in Europe) on 1 January 1995

into OSCE, the transformation was completed after a succession of periodic meetings (CVSE process) in which the détente between East and West and the end of the Cold war came to a conclusion into an international organization for conflict prevention and crisis management. The first step towards institutionalization of the CVSE was taken with the Paris Charter of 1990. It was decided then to establish a Council of Ministers which would meet at least once a year, and a Committee of Higher Officials which would back up and coordinate the activities of the Council. Also established were a Secretariat under the leadership of a secretary-general, a Conflict Prevention Center and a Bureau for Free Elections (later renamed Bureau for Democratic Institutions and Human Rights). At a next meeting in Helsinki in 1992 the chairmanship was strengthened by establishing a troika. Also established was the position of High Commissioner concerning National Minorities. It was decided to change the name of the organization into CVSE during a summit in Budapest on 5 December 1994. The organization has arbitrated in e.g. the Chechnya conflict.
In August 1997 the following countries were members of the organization: all European nations (with the exception of Andorra), Canada and the United States, and all republics of the former Soviet Union.

Oscilloscope, device using a cathode ray tube to produce line graphs of rapidly varying electrical signals. Since nearly every physical effect can be converted into an electrical signal, the oscilloscope is widely used. Typically, the signal controls the vertical deflection of the beam while the horizontal deflection increases steadily, producing a graph of the signal as a function of time.
See also: Cathode ray.

Oshima, Nagisa (1932-), Japanese movie director. Incorporated into his work his criticism of traditional values of Japanese society in e.g. *Koshikei* (Death by Hanging; 1968), *Shinjuku Dorobu Nikku* (Diary of a Shinjuku Thief; 1969) and *Gishiki* (The Ceremony; 1971). His movies *Ai No Corrida* (Empire of the Senses; 1976) and *Ai No Borei* (Empire of Passion; 1978) caused great commotion because of the eroticism and violence they showed. After these movies Oshima directed *Merry Christmas, Mr. Lawrence* (1982), *Max mon Amour, Max my Love* (1986), and *Gohatto* (2001).

The monumental town hall of Oslo, which was completed in 1950. The interior contains murals by E. Munch and in the right tower there is a carillon.

Osier, tough, pliable twigs or branches from the willow family, used for weaving baskets or furniture. The common osier (*Salix viminalis*) and the purple osier (*Salix purpurea*), which originated in Europe and Asia, thrive in the United States beside streams and ponds.

Osijek (Germ. Esseg; Hung. Eszék; pop. 107,000), city in Croatia, on the Drava river. Ancient town with a fortress. It is also a river port. There is production of textile, soap and agricultural machines. To the north of the city there is a large state farm. Osijek has a university since 1975. In 1991 Osijek was heavily damaged during the struggle between the Croatian and Yugoslav armies.

Osiris, ancient Egyptian god, brother and husband of Isis, and father of Horus. He was killed by his evil brother Set but restored to life by Isis. His cult was important in dynastic Egypt and later became popular in the Roman Empire. A benefactor of mankind, Osiris was a ruler of the underworld and also a life-giving power, symbolizing the creative forces of nature.
See also: Mythology.

Öskemen (Ust-Kamenogorsk; pop. 330,000), city in Kazakhstan, on the Irtys river. Öskemen is a regional center for the surrounding mining area. There are also electrotechnics, machinery and chemical industries. Manufacturing of non-ferrometals. Exploitation of lead, zinc, copper, magnesium and titanium in the area. There is a hydroelectric power station. Is also a railroad junction and has various colleges. In 1720 the city was founded as a military post; it carries its present name since Kazakhstan gained its independence in 1991.

Oslo (pop. 732,000), capital, largest city and chief seaport of Norway. Founded c.1050, it was rebuilt after the great fire of 1624. Known as Christiania or Kristiania from 1625 to 1925, today Oslo is Norway's chief commercial and industrial center, producing chemicals, paper, textiles, and wood products. The hub of Norways's railroad system, Oslo is also serviced by an international airport located just outside the city. Home to Norway's oldest university, the city also features many fine museums, including the Norwegian Folk Museum and the Viking Ships Museum (which displays Viking ships that date back to the 10th century).
See also: Norway.

Oslo Agreements, two agreements between the Palestinian Liberation Organization (PLO) and Israel, reached under the mediation of the Norwegian government. The preliminary talks were held in secret in e.g. Oslo. In Oslo 1 (1993), Israel and the PLO acknowledged each other's right of existence and came to agreements over Palestinian self-rule in the Gaza strip and the city of Jericho. In Oslo 2 (1995) the two parties came to further agreements: withdrawal of the Israeli army from Hebron and other parts of the West Bank, and presidential elections as well as elections for the Palestinian Council. Both agreements included time schedules for the negotiations of the status of eastern Jerusalem and the transferred territories.

Osmium, chemical element, symbol Os; for physical constants see Periodic Table. Osmium was discovered by Smithson Tennant in 1804. It occurs native associated with platinum and in the mineral iridosmine. The element is obtained commercially as a byproduct of nickel-bearing ores. Osmium, a bluish-white, lustrous, dense, hard and brittle metal, is a member of the platinum group of metals, and has the highest melting point of the group. Osmium forms a volatile oxide that is highly toxic. Powdered osmium metal, like palladium, adsorbs large amounts of hydrogen. The primary use of osmium is to harden other platinum metals. It is used in machine bearings, pen points, and as catalyst. Osmium tetroxide is used as an organic reagent to convert olefins to glycols.

Osmosis, diffusion of a solvent through a semipermeable membrane that separates 2 solutions of different concentration. The movement is from the more dilute to the more concentrated solution, because of the thermodynamic tendency to equalize the concentrations. The liquid flow may be opposed by applying pressure to the more concentrated solution; the pressure required to reduce the flow to zero from a pure solvent to a given solution is known as the osmotic pressure of the solution.

Osprey, large fish-eating bird of prey (*Pandion haliaetus*), found worldwide, except in South America. Also known as the fish hawk, the osprey occupies marine and freshwater areas, cruising above the water and plunging to take the fish in its talons.

Ostade, Adriaen van (1610-1685), was known for his genre paintings of peasants and villagers. Many works, such as *Taste*, are vivid portrayals of tavern scenes. Ostade probably studied with Frans Hals. His later works show the influence of Rembrandts.

Ostend (pop. 68,000), port city in northwest Belgium on the North Sea. Its worth as a port has caused it to be attacked by the Dutch, French, Spanish, Germans, British, and Allied Forces over the centuries. Since Belgium's independence in 1803, the city has developed into a significant import-export link with a Channel link to England. Products include tobacco, soap, fish, and oyster cultivation.

Osteomyelitis, bacterial infection of bone, usually caused by staphylococcus, streptococcus, or salmonella carried to the bone by the blood or through open fractures. It commonly affects children, causing fever and local pain. If untreated or partially treated, it may become chronic.

Osteopathic medicine, method of therapy that concentrates on manipulation of bones and muscles, developed in 1874 by Andrew Taylor Still. The musculoskeletal system is focused upon to treat the whole person rather than an isolated region. Osteopathic physicians are fully qualified to use surgery and all medications as part of their medical care. In the United States, there are 15 osteopathic colleges, 180 osteopathic hospitals, and over 28,000 osteopathic-practicing physicians.

Osteoporosis, loss of bone mass and density. It occurs mainly among older people, especially postmenopausal women. Osteoporosis increases the risk of bone fractures in all parts of the body, can cause a weakening of the jaw and loss of teeth, and contributes to collapse of the spine. Preventive measures include exercise, calcium supplements, and, for older women, estrogen treatments.

Osteosclerosis, abnormal hardening or thickening of the bone, causing brittleness and an inclination to fracture. Called osteopetrosis in children, the disease becomes increasingly serious as growing bone density crowds the bone marrow and limits space for red blood cell production, resulting in extreme anemia.

Ostrava (pop. 327,000), industrial city in northeastern Moravia, Czech Republic, about 170 mi (274 km) east of Prague. Industries include coal mining, oil refineries, and chemical factories. Manufactured goods include clothing, building supplies, and food products.
See also: Moravia.

Ostrich, *Struthio camelus*, Africa, 8.2 ft (2.5 m) tall.

Ostrich (*Struthio camelus*), the largest living bird, at one time found throughout Africa and southwest Asia but now common only in east Africa. Flightless birds, well adapted to a terrestrial life, they have long powerful legs, with two toes on each foot, an adaptation for running over dry grassland.

Ostrogoths (East Goths), branch of the Goths, a Germanic people who originally occupied the lands to the north of the Black Sea. The accession of their king Theodoric the Great (A.D. 471) heralded an alliance with Zeno, emperor of the East Roman Empire. On Zeno's orders, Theodoric invaded Italy in 488, overthrew Odoacer (493), and ruled from Ravenna. The Byzantine generals, Belisarius and Narses destroyed Ostrogothic rule in the 530s; the final

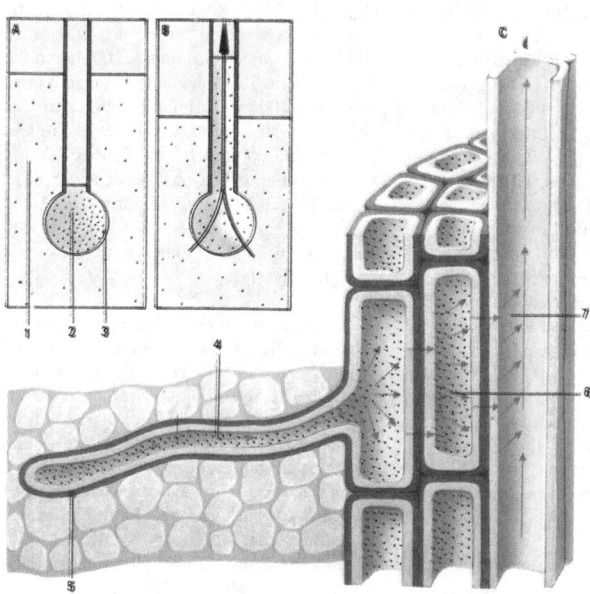

(A) If water (1) is separated from a concentrated solution (2) by a semi-permeable membrane (3), the water will pass into this solution by a process that is called osmosis. (B) Eventually, the column of water will exert a pressure which prevents more water from entering. (C) Here, we can see a section of a plant root that shows how plants absorb water by osmosis. The water from inbetween the soil particles is drawn through the wall of the root hair (5), a semi-permeable membrane, into the higher concentrated cytoplasm inside (4) (the red dots indicate the concentration of the solution). The cytoplasm of the cell (6) is now more concentrated than that of the solution inside, which causes water to be drawn into the cell by osmosis. The process will be continued until the water reaches the water conducting tubes (7).

O

Ostrogothic revolt under Totila was swiftly crushed by Narses in 552.

Ostrovsky, Aleksander (1823-1886), Russian dramatist whose plays, usually about merchants and minor officials, are marked by powerful characterization and strong drama. His masterpiece is *The Storm* (1860), a domestic tragedy.

Ostwald, Wilhelm (1853-1932), German physical chemist regarded as a father of physical chemistry, awarded the 1909 Nobel Prize for chemistry for his work on catalysis. He also developed the Ostwald process for manufacturing nitric acid.
See also: Chemistry; Catalysis.

Oswald, Lee Harvey (1939-1963), the alleged assassin of President John F. Kennedy in Dallas, Tex., on Nov. 22, 1963. A former marine, he had lived in the USSR (1959-1962). He was shot dead by Jack Ruby while under arrest. The Warren Report (1964) on the investigation of Kennedy's assassination declared Oswald the sole assassin.

Otis, Elisha Graves (1811-1861), U.S. inventor of the safety elevator (1852), first installed for passenger use in 1857.

O'Toole, Peter (1932-), Irish actor who became an internationally renowned movie star after his lead in *Lawrence of Arabia* (1962). He also starred in movies such as *Lord Jim* (196), *What's New, Pussycat?* (1965), *The Night of the Generals* (1967), *Man of La Mancha* (1972), *Rosebud* (1974), *Caligula* (1977), *The Stunt Man* (1980), *Supergirl* (1984), *The Last Emperor* (1986) and *Wings of Fame* (1990).

Otoscope, instrument for examining the internal parts of the ear.

Ottawa (pop. 1,030,000), capital city of Canada, located at the junction of the Ottawa and Rideau rivers, near the southeastern tip of the province of Ontario. Across the Ottawa River is the twin city of Hull, Quebec. In 1968 the city of Ottawa was combined with a number of communities to form a regional government area called Ottawa-Carleton. Ottawa is principally concerned with the business of government. Its most striking feature is the group of Parliament buildings in Victorian Gothic style on a bluff (Parliament Hill) overlooking the Ottawa River. The city has numerous educational and cultural institutions. The National Arts Center (1969) contains a theater and an opera house-concert hall. Over a third of the metropolitan area's residents are French Canadians. Ottawa developed in the early 19th century when the Rideau Canal was built by Colonel John By, and was known as Bytown until it was incorporated (1854) as the city of Ottawa. In 1858 Queen Victoria selected the city as the capital of the United Provinces of Canada, and on confederation (1867) it became the national capital.
See also: Canada.

Otter, aquatic or semiaquatic carnivore of the weasel family. The body is lithe and muscular, built for vigorous swimming and

The elite army corp of the Ottoman Empire consisted of Janissaries, who were initially recruited Christian children who were seized from their parents for this purpose and given a strict Muslim training. This print shows three Janissaries in their original uniforms (c. 1618).

covered with thick fur. The paws are generally webbed. The nostrils and eyes may be shut when swimming underwater. Unlike most other wild animals, otters remain playful as adults.

Otter hound, working dog, dating to 14th-century England, used for hunting otters. Its webbed paws and coarse oily skin enable it to swim in chilly waters. It is 24-27 in (61-69 cm) high and weighs 65-100 lbs (29-45 kg). Colors range from dappled blue to light brown to black and tan.

Ottey, Merlene (1960-), Jamaican athlete, specialized in short distances. She was one of the fastest sprinters of her time, but never succeeded in winning a gold medal on the Olympics. During the 1980 Olympics she won a bronze medal on the 4 x 100 m. In 1984 she became third on the 200 m and the 4 x 100 m; in 1992 she ended up again third on the 4 x 100 m. During the 1996 Olympics Ottey won silver medals on the 100 m and the 200 m and bronze on the 4 x 100 m. Besides winning various silver and bronze medals, Ottey did win gold during the World championships in 1991 (4 x 100 m) and 1993 (200 m). Ottey is known for her supple and gracious style.

Otto, name of 4 Holy Roman Emperors. **Otto I the Great** (912-973) was founder and first emperor of the Holy Roman Empire from 962. King of Saxony from 936, he invaded Italy and declared himself king of the Lombards (951). He subdued the Poles and Bohemians and routed the Magyars of Hungary (955). Otto was crowned emperor in Rome for helping Pope John XII against an Italian king, Berengar II. **Otto II** (955-983) succeeded his father as emperor (973-983). He crushed the rebellion of Henry, duke of Bavaria, defeated the Danes (974),

but failed to extend his empire in Italy and was badly defeated by the Saracens in southern Italy (982). **Otto III** (980-1002) succeeded his father as emperor (996-1002), after a regency. He planned to make Rome the capital of a vast theocratic empire. **Otto IV** (c.1174?-1218), emperor (1209-1215), was excommunicated by Pope Innocent II for attempting to master parts of Italy (1210) and later deposed.
See also: Holy Roman Empire.

Otto I (1815-1867), Austrian-born king of Greece (1833-1862). He was unpopular for many reasons, among them his attempts to discard the constitution, his use of German advisers, the loss of the chief port of Piraeus to France and Britain during the Crimean War, and failure to free Greek prisoners in Turkish-held Crete, Thessaly, and Macedonia. He was deposed by a military revolt.
See also: Greece.

Ottoman Empire, vast empire of the Ottoman Turks that at its height, during the reign of Sultan Suleyman I, stretched from the far shore of the Black Sea and the Persian Gulf in the east to Budapest in the north and Algiers in the west. The Ottoman Turks, led by Osman I, entered Asia Minor in the late 1200s and, expanding rapidly, made Bursa their capital in 1326. They crossed to the Balkan Peninsula (1345), and in 1453 Constantinople fell to Muhammad II. The empire continued to expand in the 16th century under Selim I, the Terrible (1512-1520), and reached its zenith under Suleyman I. However, Suleyman failed to capture Vienna (1529) and was driven back to Malta (1565). Directly after his death, the Ottoman fleet was annihilated at the naval battle of Lepanto (1571). During the 1700s and 1800s the decaying empire fought against Russia, and Greece won its independence. The reformist Young Turk movement led the empire into World War I on the German side, with disastrous results. The nationalists, led by Kemal Atatürk, deposed and exiled the last sultan, Muhammad, and proclaimed the Turkish republic in 1922.

Ouagadougou (pop. 500,000), capital of Burkina Faso, land of the Mossi people in western Africa. The city has many mosques, a museum, and a university. An airport and a railroad provide transportation to the Ivory Coast. Manufactured goods include textiles, building materials, and food processing.
See also: Burkina Faso.

Oubangui River *See:* Ubangi River.

Ouida (Maria Louise de la Ramée; 1839-1908), English novelist. Among her works are *Under Two Flags* (1867), *A Dog of Flanders* (1872), and *Moths* (1880).

Oursler, Tony (1957-), American visual artist who makes videos, performances, sculpture and paintings. He has experimented with deviating forms of video projection ('psychometriscapes'). During the 1990s he combined video with sculptural installations. Best known are his works with puppets which have no bodies and whose heads are made up of pillows, on whom faces are projected with the help of a video projector. A recorded monologue can be heard with it. From 1994 onwards Oursler has projected moving figures on synthetic fibers which hang from the ceiling (*The Cloud Pieces*). Oursler also works with sounds. He addresses personal feelings and puts question marks on the achievements of modern technology.

Outboard motor, high-speed boat motor having 1 to 8 cylinders. Attached outside the stern, it operates an underwater propeller that drives the boat forward. Usually gasoline-powered, it can also use electric power operating off of rechargeable storage batteries.

Ouzel *See:* Dipper.

Ovambo (Ambo), largest community in Namibia. Lives on agriculture as well as cattle breeding; also hunting, fishing and gathering. They speak a Bantu language and have a matrilineal kinship system.

Ovary, female reproductive organ. In humans it contains the follicles in which the eggs (*ova*) develop.
See also: Reproduction.

Ovenbird (*Seiurus aurocapillus*), member of the wood warbler family, a 6-in (15-cm) long bird whose grassy rounded nest, with a side opening built on the ground, resembles an adobe oven. Sometimes referred to as the teacher bird because its repeated call sounds like the word 'teacher,' it is dull green with a white flecked breast and a rust crown.

Overture, independent instrumental musical work, often serving as a prelude to a major musical presentation and including portions of that production's music. In developing the form for French opera, Jean Baptiste Lully wrote the first standardized overture c.1660, and Wolfgang Amadeus Mozart used it as a single movement in the 1700s. Familiar concert overtures, not part of another work, are Tchaikovsky's *1812* and Johannes Brahms's *Academic Festival*.

Ovid (Publius Ovidius Naso; 43 B.C.-A.D. 18), Latin poet. Popular in his time, he was exiled by the Emperor Augustus to the Black Sea in A.D. 8 and died there; his *Sorrows* and *Letters from Pontus* are pleas for his return. He was a master of erotic poetry, as in his *Amores* and *The Art of Love*, but his *Metamorphoses*, a collection of myths linked by the common theme of change, is considered to be his finest work.

Oviparous animal, one hatched from a fertilized egg that matured after being expelled from its parent's body. Most birds, fish, reptiles, and some mammals are oviparous.

Ovulation *See:* Reproduction.

Owen, 2 industrialists and social reformers. **Robert Owen** (1771-1858) was a socialist and pioneer of the cooperative movement. He introduced better conditions in his cotton mills in Scotland and was active in the trade union movement in Britain. In the United States Owen set up short-lived 'villages of cooperation,' such as that at New Harmony, Ind. **Robert Dale Owen** (1801-1877), his son, campaigned in the U.S. for birth control, women's property rights, state public schools, and slave emancipation. He was a member of Congress from Indiana (1843-1847).

Owen, Wilfred (1893-1918), English poet, deeply influenced by Siegfried Sassoon, who wrote movingly of the savagery and human sacrifice in World War I. Owen was killed in action a week before the end of World War I. Nine of his poems form the text of Benjamin Britten's *War Requiem* (1962).

Owens, Jesse (1913-1980), U.S. African-American athlete. He once broke 3 world records at a single college meet (1935). At the 1936 Berlin Olympics Owens won 4 gold medals (100-meter, 200-meter, 4 x 400 relay, and long jump) breaking olympic records in both the 200-meter and long jump competitions. Owens' record-setting achievements proved to be an embarrassment to German dictator Adolf Hitler, who had hoped to use the Games to prove his theory of Aryan German supremacy.

Owl, nocturnal bird of prey of the family Tytonidae or the family Strigidae. Owls have large eyes, directed forward, and all have pronounced facial disks of feathers. Some species develop ear tufts, and most have extremely sensitive hearing. Many species hunt primarily on auditory cues. Their eyes are also extremely powerful: some 35-100 times more sensitive than our own. All owls are soft-feathered, and their flight is almost silent.

Ox, term zoologically applied to many members of the family Bovidae; also, in common usage, a castrated bull used for draft purposes or for its meat.

Oxalic acid $(COOH)_2 \cdot 2H_2O$, colorless, poisonous, organic acid. Found in many vegetables and in the rumex and oxalis plants, it is also produced by the body. The synthetic type is used to process textiles, as a paint-stripper, and in laundries to remove stains.

Oxalis, group of about 850 kinds of plants of the wood-sorrel family, occurring mostly in South Africa and South America. Most grow from bulbs producing thick tubers bearing both white and pastel-colored flowers and clover-shaped leaves.

Oxbow lake, shallow U-shaped or serpentine lake, formed from a riverbed when the river has changed to a straighter course. The deposits of earth left by the new course help separate the lake from the river. Oxbow lakes are common along the lower Mississippi River.

Oxenstierna, Axel Gustaffson (1583-1654), Swedish politician. As chancellor (1612-1654) he served under King Gustavus Adolphus (Gustavus II, r. 1611-1632), Queen Christina (1632-1654), and Charles X (1654), also acting as head of the regency (1632-1644) until Queen Christina came of age. A close friend and adviser of Gustavus II, he was chief administrator during the military conflicts with Denmark and Russia and the Thirty Years War (1618-1648). He also wrote the 1634 constitution, which strengthened Sweden's central government.
See also: Sweden.

Oxford (pop. 109,000), city of south-central

O

Short-eared owl *Asio flammens*, found worldwide. Length up to 16 in (40 cm).

Crested Owl (*Lophostrix cristata*, order *Strigiformes*). Found in South Mexico and the Amazon region. Length up to 17 in (42 cm).

O

England, the seat of Oxford University. The city existed in the early 900s. The university began to form in the early 1100s. Standing on the Thames River (known locally as the Isis) where it is joined by the Cherwell, Oxford is rich in historic buildings, including the many colleges, the Ashmolean Museum, the Bodleian Library, the cathedral, and the Norman castle. The city is the county seat of Oxfordshire.
See also: England.

Oxford Movement, religious movement begun in 1833 in Oxford that aimed to revitalize the Church of England by reintroducing traditional Catholic practices and doctrines. Its leaders, John Keble, J. H. Newman, and, later, Edward Pusey, wrote a series of *Tracts for the Times* (1833-1841) and became known as the Tractarians. Despite violent controversy, the movement has had great influence in the Anglican Church.
See also: Church of England.

Oxford University, English university in Oxford comprising nearly 50 affiliated but autonomous colleges and halls, a great center of learning since its foundation in the 12th century. The oldest men's college is University (1249), and the oldest women's is Lady Margaret Hall (1879). The major university library is the Bodleian.

Oxidation, any process that increases the proportion of oxygen or acid-forming element or radical in a compound.
See also: Reduction; Rust.

Oxide, chemical compound of oxygen and another element or, in the case of organic oxides, an organic compound. The formation of an oxide, called oxidation, occurs rapidly, in burning, or slowly, as in rusting. Metallic oxides such as quicklime or calcium oxide (CaO) react with water to form alkalis and with acids to form salts. Nonmetallic oxides such as sodium trioxide (SO_3) react with water to form acids and with bases to form salts. Sulfur dioxide and nitrogen oxides are common air pollutants that combine with water to form acid rain. Industrial uses of oxides include the production of acids and the manufacture of glass.

Oxyacetylene *See:* Acetylene.

Oxygen, chemical element, symbol O; for physical constants see Periodic Table. Oxygen was discovered by Joseph Priestley in 1772. It is present in air to the extent of 21% and is commercially obtained from the air by liquefaction and fractional distillation. The element makes up 49.2%, by weight, of the earth's crust and is the most abundant element. Oxygen is a colorless, odorless, reactive gas, capable of combining with most other elements. Ozone, a poisonous allotrope of oxygen, is formed by the action of ultraviolet light, or an electrical discharge on oxygen. The greatest use of the gas is in the oxygen enrichment of steel blast furnaces. Large quantities of oxygen are used in the synthesis of ammonia, methanol, and ethylene oxide, as well as for oxy-acetylene welding, and as rocket propellent. Oxygen

consumption in the United States is 20 million short tons per year.

Oxygen tent, enclosed space, often made of plastic, in which a patient is nursed in an atmosphere enriched with oxygen. It is mainly used for small children with acute respiratory diseases and for adults when the use of a face mask is impractical.
See also: Anoxia.

Oyster, bivalve mollusk of shallow coastal waters. While other bivalves are able to move by means of a muscular 'foot,' oysters have lost this foot, and the animal lives cemented to a hard substrate of rocks or shells. Like all bivalves, oysters feed by removing suspended organic particles from a current of water drawn into the shell. Edible oysters are extensively fished and cultivated worldwide. The pearl oyster is a tropical species.

Oystercatcher, any of a family (Haematopodidae) of shorebirds found in most parts of the world. The oystercatcher is distinguished by a flat, long, sharp orange-red bill, used to open the shells of the mollusks on which it feeds. It measures 16-20 in (40-50 cm) long and is black or white and black.

Oyster plant *See:* Salsify.

Oz, Amos (1939-), Israeli writer. Was one of the founders of the Peace Now organization in 1977, a progressive political movement which was especially popular in the 1980s. His work is inspired by Israel's turbulent history. He paints an often critical and pessimistic picture of Israeli society. His best known novels include *Where the Jackals Howl and Other Stories* (1965), *My Michael* (1968), *Touch the Water, Touch the Wind* (1973), *Perfect Peace* (1982), *Black Box* (1987), *The Third Condition* (1991) and *The Silence of Heaven* (1993).

Özal, Turgut (1927-1993), Turkish politician. Özal held several influential positions in Turkey as well as abroad before becoming prime minister after the military coup of 1980. He became the architect of a program of economic reforms. He and his Motherland Party, which he himself founded, won the majority of votes during 1983 parliamentary elections. When his party suffered a crushing defeat at the local elections of 1989, Özal had the Turkish parliament elect him as president. This enabled him to continue his influence on Turkish politics. His policy was characterized by striving towards a free-market economy which was strongly oriented toward the West. After the fall of the Soviet Union, Özal also strengthened ties with the Turkish-speaking former Soviet republics. He had to face criticism for his nepotism and the fact that human rights in his country were not held in high regard.

Ozalid process, trademarked photocopying process using Ozalid paper, which is chemically treated to receive an impression made by ultraviolet rays, and then developed by the Ozalid machine.

Ozark Mountains, plateau of rugged beauty in southern Missouri, northern Arkansas,

and northeastern Oklahoma. The heavily forested hills and mountains of the Ozark region are thinly populated. Farming and mining (lead, limestone) are the region's major economic activities. Tourists are attracted by the scenery and clear air.

Ozawa, Seiji (1935-), Japanese conductor, best known for his fiery interpretations of Romantic and modern French composers. He served as director of the San Francisco Symphony Orchestra (1970-6) and of the Boston Symphony Orchestra and the Berkshire Music Festival from 1973.

Ozone, O_3, triatomic oxygen; a blue gas with a pungent odor. It is a very powerful oxidizing agent and decomposes rapidly above 212°F (100°C). The upper atmosphere contains a layer of ozone, formed when ultraviolet radiation acts on oxygen, that protects the earth from the sun's ultraviolet rays. Ozone, made by subjecting oxygen to a high-voltage electric discharge, is used for killing germs, bleaching, removing unpleasant odors from food, and sterilizing water.

Ozu, Yasujiro (1903-1963), Japanese movie director who made 53 motion pictures between 1927 and 1962, which together form a consistent oeuvre. As one of the greatest stylists in the history of cinema, Ozu stayed clear of complicated camera movements, zooms and editing tricks. In his static movies the camera always remains at eye level of a Japanese person sitting on the ground, approximately one meter above the floor. There are fixed themes in his movies: family life between tradition and modernization, often depicted by a single and elderly father who, because he needs nursing, prevents one of his daughters from getting married. His best known movies are *Tokyo Monogatari* (Tokyo Story; 1953), *Akibiyori* (Late Autumn; 1960) and *Samma no Aji* (An Autumn Afternoon; 1962).

P, 16th letter of the English alphabet, corresponding with the letter *pe* of the Semitic alphabet, which was represented by a diamond-shaped symbol based on the Egyptian hieroglyph for 'mouth.' The Greeks adopted the letter as *pi*, and it took its modern form in Latin. As an abbreviation it represents phosphorus in chemistry, pence and peso in currency, and piano (Italian for 'softly') in music.

Paca, any of a genus (*Cuniculus*) of large, nocturnal, plant-eating rodents of the tropical forests of North and South America. Pacas measure up to 30 in (75 cm) in length and weigh as much as 22 lb (10 kg). They are hunted as food by humans, and their hides are used for leather.

Pacemaker, small mass of cells in the right atrium of the heart that gives rise to the electrical impulses that initiate contractions of the heart; also called sinoatrial (S-A) nodes. Under abnormal circumstances, other cardiac tissues may assume the pacemaker role. The artificial pacemaker is a battery-powered device that controls the beating of the heart by a series of rhythmic electrical discharges. If the electrodes that deliver the discharges to the heart are placed on the outside of the chest, it is called an external pacemaker. If they are placed within the chest wall, it is called an internal pacemaker. *See also:* Heart.

Pacific Islands, also Oceania, consisting of the 20,000 to 30,000 islands scattered over thousands of square miles of the Pacific Ocean. The outer limits of Oceania, known as the Pacific Rim, are defined by the archipelagos of Indonesia, the Philippines, and Japan on the Asian side, and by the Aleutians, Galapagos, and other island groups close to the northern and southern continents on the American side. The southern limit is Australia. Within the Rim is a vast area of ocean with numerous islands, but divided into three distinct regions: Melanesia, Micronesia, and Polynesia.

Land and climate. Melanesia consists of New Guinea, the Solomon Islands, New Caledonia, Vanuata, and Fiji. Micronesia, consisting of some 2,000 islands, is situated north of Melanesia. Its principal islands include Guam, the Caroline Islands, the Mariana Islands, the Marshall Islands, the Gilbert Islands, and Nauru. Polynesia is the largest division of Oceania. It extends some 5,000 mi (8,047 km) north to south from midway to New Zealand and some 4,000 mi (6,437 km) east to west from Easter Island to New Zealand and includes the Hawaiian Islands, Samoa, the Marquesas, and the Society Islands.

The Pacific islands are of two types, high islands or low islands. High islands are distinguished by hills and mountains, some of them snow covered. New Britain, New Caledonia, New Guinea, and New Zealand are all high islands. Low islands, the type most frequent in Polynesia, are coral islands. Many are atolls, coral reef surrounding a lagoon. They are low-lying islands and some of the lesser ones are only a few feet above sea level. Typical low islands are the Gilbert Islands, the Marshall Islands, Phoenix, Tuamotu, and the Tuvalu groups.

The prevailing climate throughout the Pacific Islands is tropical and it is warm the year round. On high islands, it is cool in the mountains, and the lowlands are often dense with tropical rain forest. Throughout the region, rainfall varies. Most islands have a wet and dry season, and typhoons are frequent.

People. The three divisions of Oceania are ethnically as well as geographically distinct. It is believed that the peoples who originally settled the islands were from southeast Asia. Over the long period of dispersion throughout the islands, different cultures developed, but all of them centered on village life. Kinship bonds have been and remain important and the community was traditionally led by a chief. People's diets were principally fish and native plants. There are some 26,500,000 people living in the islands, many of them still in traditional villages. Throughout the islands some 1,200 native languages are spoken. Of non-native languages, English is the most common in the region, but Japanese, French, and Pidgin English are also used. Christianity is the dominant religion, but in many areas the system of native beliefs remains quite strong, particularly in New Guinea, the Solomon Islands, and Vanuatu. Cannibalism is still practiced among certain of the natives in New Guinea.

Economy. Hawaii, New Zealand, and Nauru have modern economies and most of their people are wage earners. But on the other islands, most people live in traditional and self-sufficient economies and earn little or no money, though recently, more and more islanders have begun moving to towns to join the money economy. Beyond those of Hawaii and New Zealand, there are few towns or cities, principally Port Moresby in Papua New Guinea, Apia in Western Samoa, Nouméa in New Caledonia, Papeete in French Polynesia, and Sura in Fiji. The islands are, in general, not suitable for farming and have few minerals for export. Among the exceptions are New Caledonia, whose nickel, chromium, and iron ore are mined, Nauru which exports phosphates, and New Guinea. Bougainville, New Guinea, is the site of one of the world's largest copper mines. Otherwise, agriculture is the main industry and copra, dried coconut meat, the main export. Some coffee, sugar, cocoa, and bananas are grown, too. Tourism is also a source of income, but has met with resistance from people concerned about its adverse effects upon native cultures and the environment.

History. The first European to visit the islands was Ferdinand Magellan in 1521. The Dutchman, Abel Janszoon Tasman, discovered New Zealand in 1642 and the Englishman, James Cook, explored the region in the 18th century. The missionaries followed the explorers and the islands were opened for exploitation which, at the time, included the slave trade. In the 19th century the United States competed with France, Germany, and Spain for dominance in the region. Australia and New Zealand became independent in the early 20th century, and, following World War I and Germany's defeat, Japan took control of its Pacific possessions and became a presence in the region. In World War II Japan made a bid for dominion in the region; its defeat led to major changes. In the decades since the 1960s a number of individual islands and island groups have become independent. Others have joined in what is called free association, an arrangement in which an island is internally self-governing but leaves external affairs to a larger stronger partner such as New Zealand or the United States. After World War II, islands taken from Japan were placed by the United Nations under U.S. administration as the Trust Territory of the Pacific Islands. Since the war, islands within the Trust Territory have become independent within a free-association arrangement wherein the United States retains control over foreign affairs and guarantees the islands' security.

Pacific Islands, Trust Territory of the, trust territory of the UN administered by the United States (1946-1981). There are about 2,180 islands in all (only 96 inhabited) scattered over about 3 million sq mi (7.77 million sq km) of the Pacific Ocean within the area known as Micronesia. The formerly German islands were mandated to Japan in 1922 and, after U.S. occupation in World War II, to the United States. Among constituent territories, the Marianas gained separate status as the Northern Marianas and became a U.S. commonwealth (1978); the Marshall Islands became self-governing (1979); the islands of Truk, Yap, Ponape, and Kosrae became the Federated States of Micronesia (1978); and Palau became self-governing as the Republic of Belau (1981).

Pacific Ocean, world's largest and deepest ocean, extending from the Arctic to the Antarctic oceans and from the Americas to Asia, covering an area of about 70 million sq mi (181.3 million sq km), or one-third of the earth's total surface. The average depth of the Pacific is 14,000 ft (4,267 m); the deepest point is 36,198 ft (11,033 m) in the Challenger Deep, in the Marianas Trench, southwest of Guam. Plateaus, ridges, trenches, and sea mountains make for many variations in depth. Japan, the Philippines, New Zealand, and thousands of islands lie on the connected series of ridges running from the Bering Straits southwest to the South China Sea. Despite its name, the ocean is not generally calm. In the tropical and subtropical zones an average of more than 130 cyclones occur per year.

Pacifism, belief that violence is never justified and hence that peaceful means should always be employed to settle disputes. A pacifist may refuse not only to use force but also to abet its use, as by refusing to help produce weapons of war. Pacifists who refuse to serve in the armed forces are called

The paca (*C. paca*), which may be recognized by the rows of white spots on its coat, is a delicacy to South American Indians, who hunt it for its meat.

P

P

conscientious objectors. Supporters of nuclear disarmament or opponents of specific wars are not necessarily pacifists.
See also: Gandhi, Mohandas Karamchand; King, Martin Luther, Jr.

Pacino, Al (1940-), American actor who received his training in the Actors' Studio. Pacino was very successful on stage, but gained international fame with movies like *The Godfather* (1972), *Serpico* (1974), *The Godfather Part II* (1974), *Bobby Deerfield* (1977), *Cruising* (1980), *Scarface* (1983), *Sea of Love* (1989), *The Godfather Part III* (1990), *Frankie and Johnny* (1991), *Carlito's Way* (1993), *Scent of a Woman* (1993; Academy Award and Golden Globe), *Heat* (1995), *The Insider* (1999) and *Insomnia* (2002). Pacino won a Golden Lion for his entire oeuvre in 1994. He also directed the documentary *Looking for Richard* (1996), which deals with various opinions about Shakespeare's play *Richard III*.

Pack rat *See:* Wood rat.

Padang (pop. 631,000) City in Indonesia, the main port on Sumatra's western coast, bordering the Indian Ocean. It is 285 miles (459 km) west-southwest of Singapore. Roads and a railway cross the coastal mountains here, and airlines serves the city. Padang grew from a Dutch trading post established about 1680. It exports coal, coffee, tea, copra, rubber, spices, and tobacco.

Paddlefish, any of various freshwater relatives of the sturgeon, resembling a shark with a long, paddlelike snout. A Mississippi River paddlefish, also known as the spoonbill sturgeon, grows to 6 ft (1.8 m) in length, and another, the swordbill sturgeon of the Yangtze River in China, may grow to twice that size. Paddlefish are sometimes eaten, and their large black eggs make caviar.

The Mississippi paddlefish (*P. spathula*) is a survivor of a group of fishes that dates back more than 100 million years.

Paderewski, Ignace Jan (1860-1941), Polish concert pianist, composer, and politician. An internationally acclaimed interpreter of Frédéric Chopin, Franz Liszt, Anton Rubinstein, and Robert Schumann, he frequently toured the United States, where he sometimes gave concerts to raise funds for Polish causes. He was the first prime minister of the Polish republic (1919) and led the Polish government in exile (1940-1941). He died in the United States.
See also: Poland.

Padua (pop. 214,000), oldest city in northern Italy, on the Bacchiglione River, 22 mi (35 km) southwest of Venice. Padua is a

renowned renaissance center noted for its architecture and art treasures, including works by Giotto, Donatello, and Fra Filippo Lippi. *See also:* Italy.

Paestum, ancient city (fl. 6th century B.C.) situated south of Salerno, southern Italy. Founded by Greek colonists as Posidonia (c.600 B.C.), it became a Roman colony and was renamed in 273 B.C. Over a period of several centuries the silting up of the surrounding River Sele made the vicinity unhealthy, and it was abandoned after being sacked by Saracens in 871. Two 6th-century B.C. Doric temples and one from the 5th century survive; excavations have also revealed a Temple and an amphitheater.

Paéz, José Antonio (1790-1873), Venezuelan soldier and President (1831-1846, 1861-1863). He assisted Bolívar in the Spanish defeats at Carabobo (1821) and Puerto Cabello (1823). He led the successful Venezuelan independence movement (1829) and ruled Venezuela (as president or the power behind other presidents) from 1831 to 1846, and, after a period of exile, from 1861 to 1863, before being exiled again.

Paganini, Niccolò (1782-1840), Italian virtuoso violinist. By his use of adventurous techniques, such as diverse tuning of strings and the exploitation of harmonics, he extended the range of the instrument. His best-known compositions are his 24 *Caprices.*

Page *See:* Knights and knighthood.

Page, Geraldine (1924-1987), U.S. stage, film, and television actress. She made her New York City stage debut in *Seven Mirrors* (1945). Page starred opposite Paul Newman in Tennessee Williams's *Sweet Bird of Youth* both on stage (1959) and on film (1962). Nominated for an Academy Award many times, she won for her role in *The Trip to Bountiful* (1986).

Pagnol, Marcel (1895-1974), French playwright, screenwriter, director, producer, and critic. He wrote the screenplays *Marius* (1930) and *Topaze* (1932), both adapted from his own plays. *Marius* was the first in his Provençal trilogy, which also included *Fanny* and *César.*

Pago Pago *See:* American Samoa.

Pahang (pop. 1,037,000), federal state of Malaysia on the South Chinese Sea; 13,891 sq mi (35,965 sq km). The capital Kuantan is

the most important port on the West Malayan east coast. The area is largely covered with tropical rain forests. Rubber, gold, iron and are exploited. There are also large supplies of iron ore and off-shore petroleum and natural gas. Production of rice, palm oil and rubber. The area was first named in a Chinese chronicle from 1225. The region is sparsely populated with native mountain peoples, Chinese and Malayans.

Pahlavi, Mohammad Reza *See:* Mohammad Reza Pahlavi.

Pahlavi, Reza Shah *See:* Reza Shah Pahlavi.

Paige, Satchel (Leroy Robert Paige; 1906-1982), U.S. baseball pitcher. Barred as an African-American from the major leagues for most of his career, Paige played with the Negro Leagues. He pitched dozens of no-hitters and was considered one of the greatest pitchers in the game by major league players who faced him in exhibition games. Paige was the first African-American pitcher in the American League, playing with the Cleveland Indians (1948-1951) and the St. Louis Browns (1951-1953). He was inducted into the National Baseball Hall of Fame in 1971.

Pai Jang (1920-), one of the most popular movie actresses from 1930-1950's China. She is also known as an elocutionist. As a member of various cultural missions she made several trips abroad and was, among other things, vice-chair of the Chinese Union for Movie Personnel. She achieved her greatest fame with *The Tears of the Yangtze*, a 4-hour production from 1947. The movie shows the up and downs of the Chinese people in wartime against the background of corrupt government rule.

Paik, Nam June (1932-), Korean graphic artist, pioneer of video art. Originally a composer, strongly influenced by his teacher John Cage. Paik was part of the Fluxus group. He made connections between music, modern technology and the audience, as in *Symphony for 20 Rooms* (1961), in which the audience changed places, and *Exposition of Music* (1963), in which the audience itself played the instruments. Experimented intensively with television and video (*Moon is the Oldest TV*, 1976) and also with laser, satellite links and computers. Since the 1970s he has been making sizeable video installations with many monitors.

Paine, Thomas (1737-1809), English-born writer and radical, a leading figure of the American Revolution. His highly influential pamphlet *Common Sense* (1776) urged the American colonies to declare independence. His pamphlet series *The Crisis* (1776-1783) inspired the Continental Army. After returning to England, he wrote *The Rights of Man* (1791-1792), a defense of the French Revolution and of republicanism. Forced to flee to France, he was elected to the National Convention and was later imprisoned (1793-1794) during the Reign of Terror. His controversially deistic *The Age of Reason* (1794-1795) alienated much of his U.S. support. He returned there in 1802 and died in obscurity.

Paint, fluid applied to a surface in thin layers, forming a colored, solid coating for decoration, representation, or protection. Paint consists of a pigment dispersed in a 'vehicle' or binder that adheres to the substrate and forms the solid film, and usually a solvent or thinner to control the consistency. Many specialized paints have been developed, for example to resist heat or corrosion. After applying a primer, the paint is brushed, rolled, or sprayed on; dip coating and electrostatic attraction are recently developed methods of application.

Painted-tongue, or salpiglossis, flowering garden annual (*Salpiglossis sinuata*) of the nightshade family. Its flowers, similar to those of the related petunia, are trumpet-shaped and range from white to yellow, orange, pink, red, or purple.

Painter's colic, or lead colic, symptom of lead poisoning characterized by severe abdominal pain. It is so called because lead may be absorbed into the body by skin contact with paints or by the breathing of vapors from paints.
See also: Lead poisoning.

Painting, depiction by means of line and color of a subject, rendered representationally or abstractly, on a 2-dimensional surface. The art of painting dates from more than 20,000 years ago, with cave paintings of animals and hunters, to ancient Egyptian tomb paintings, Cretan celebratory paintings on buildings, and the painted pottery of the Greeks. The Romans were the first to paint lifelike figures in perspective with depth, shade, and shadow. Asian painting includes the religious paintings of India, a means of communicating with the gods; Chinese painting, related to calligraphy, expressing a deep love of nature; and Islamic painting, primarily the elegant calligraphy and illustrations of books. Medieval painting (300s-1300s) centered on Christianity as its source of inspiration and was expressed in paintings lacking perspective and using symbols to tell stories.
Italian painting, 1300-1600. Giotto's fresco works broke away from Byzantine art with his realistic depiction of people and their

This 18th-dynasty *Fowling Scene* in the tomb of Menena at Thebes reveals the ancient Egyptian stylistic trait of depicting the human body with a combination of frontal and profile views.

P

emotions. His monumental, sculptural style was generally followed in 14th-century Florence. In Siena, the decorative linear style of Duccio and Simone Martini prevailed. The Florentine discovery of linear perspective was first employed by Masaccio, and the tradition was continued by Fra Angelico, Piero Della Francesca, and Botticelli. Western painting reached an apogee in the High Renaissance works of Leonardo da Vinci, Raphael, and Michelangelo. Mannerism, developed by Giulio Romano and Andrea del Sarto, influenced the arresting style of El Greco. From the mid-15th century a distinct Venetian school emerged, notable for its use of color. The most influential Venetian artists were Titian, Tintoretto, and Veronese.
Painting outside Italy, 1400-1600. Flemish art was finely detailed, as in the work of Jan Van Eyck who, with his brother Hubert, created innovative oil paintings. A more emotional style was developed by Rogier Van der Weyden, while Hieronymus Bosch and Pieter Bruegel developed grotesque fantasy pictures. In the late 15th century, German art became influential with Albrecht Dürer's woodcuts and engravings, Mathias Grünewald's Isenheim Altar piece, and Hans Holbein's portraits.
Painting, 1600-1850. The prominent artists of the baroque period were the Italian painter Caravaggio; the brilliant and imaginative Flemish painter Peter Paul Rubens; the Spaniard Diego Velázquez; the classical French painters Nicolas Poussin and Claude Lorrain; Dutchman Rembrandt van Rijn; and the Dutch painters Jan Steen and Jan Vermeer, who specialized in genre scenes. The rococo style was characterized by elegant, sensuous, often frivolous works by painters like Antoine Watteau and François Boucher. English portraiture was developed

by Sir Joshua Reynolds and Thomas Gainsborough, influencing the first important American artists, John Singleton Copley and Benjamin West. The Spanish rococo painter, Francisco Goya, depicted the savagery of the Napoleonic Wars. The first half of the 19th century in France was dominated by the classicism of Jean Auguste Dominique Ingres and the romanticism of Eugène Delacroix.
Painting since 1850. Gustave Courbet rendered large-scale pictures of ordinary life and Édouard Manet influenced impressionism. Claude Monet and Pierre Auguste Renoir pioneered painting outdoors and experimented with the effects of light. The postimpressionists Paul Gauguin and Vincent Van Gogh, through their novel use of paint and simplified forms, greatly influenced expressionism and fauvism. Paul Cézanne's work was crucial to the development of cubism, largely invented by Pablo Picasso and Georges Braque. Wassily Kandinsky and Casimir

Fra Angelico's *Annunciation* (1438-45) is characterized by calm spirituality and simplicity, a purity of line and color, and the use of a strict linear perspective (Convento di San Marco, Florence).

In his wedding portrait of the Arnolfinis (1434) Jan van Eyck gave new emphasis to depicting accurate detail and he created a complex symbolism for the work (National Gallery, London).

Portrait of the French art-dealer Daniel Henry Kahnweiler (1911), by Pablo Picasso (1881-1973). To be seen in the Art Institute, Chicago.

P

Malevich developed forms of abstract art. Surrealism used imagery taken from dreams, such as in the works of Salvador Dali and Max Ernst. In the 1960s pop art was developed by Jasper Johns, Robert Rauschenberg, and Andy Warhol. A resurgence of interest in various aspects of realism occurred in the 1970s and 1980s.

Paisley (pop. 84,000), industrial city in western Scotland near Glasgow, on the White Cart River. A medieval village that grew up around an abbey, Paisley became a center for linen weaving in the 18th century. In the 19th-century it was known for its manufacture of paisley shawls. Its industries now include engineering, shipbuilding, and food processing.

Pakistan

Capital:	Islamabad
Area:	307,374 sq mi (796,095 sq km)
Population:	147,663,000
Language:	Urdu, English
Government:	Federal islamic republic
Independent:	1947 (federal republic)
Head of gov.:	Prime minister
Per capita:	US$ 2,100
Monetary unit:	1 Pakistani rupee = 100 paisa

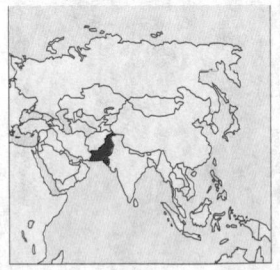

Pakistan, Islamic Republic of Pakistan, nation state on the Indian subcontinent. Pakistan covers about 307,374 sq mi (796,095 sq km) and is bordered on the west by Iran, on the northwest by Afghanistan, on the northeast by China, on the southeast by India, and on the south by the Arabian Sea. *Land and climate.* Pakistan is dominated by the mountains of the Hindu Kush in the north, but there are fertile valleys in the northwest. The west is arid, but there is arable land in the east, drained by the Indus River.

People. Most of the people of Pakistan are Punjabis, but other groups include the Pathans and the Baluchi. The people are overwhelmingly Muslim and the official languages are Urdu and English. The capital is Islamabad. Most Pakistanis live in small villages.

Economy. Pakistan's is primarily an agricultural economy. Wheat is the main subsistence crop, and fruit and livestock are important in the north. Pakistan has diverse mineral resources. Low-grade coal and iron ore, chromite, gypsum, and limestone are being mined. Deposits of natural gas and oil are potentially large. Pakistan exports wool and cotton textiles and leather goods and has a growing industrial base.

History. Present-day Pakistan was once at the center of the ancient Indus Valley civilization. It was subsequently invaded by Aryans, Persians, Greeks, and Arabs and became part of the Mughal Empire in the eighteenth century. Dominated for a time by the Sikhs, the area came under British control as part of its Indian empire. The modern state was formed with the partition of India in 1947 into India and Muslim East and West Pakistan under Muhammad Ali Jinnah and his Muslim League. The partition was accompanied by terrific bloodshed and, almost immediately, the new states of Pakistan and India fought bitterly over Kashmir. Separated by 1,000 miles of Indian territory, tensions grew between Bengali East and Punjabi West Pakistan. In 1958 Gen. Muhammad Ayub Khan seized power and instituted a reform program. He was replaced in 1969 by Gen. Ayub Mohammad Yahya Khan. In 1969, East Pakistan took its first formal steps toward self-government and in 1971 declared its independence. In the ensuing civil war, Indian troops took the side of East Pakistan, now Bangladesh, and West Pakistan was defeated in the fighting. Pakistan formally recognized Bangladesh in 1974, but the loss was a considerable blow to Pakistan's economy and prestige. After the war, separatist violence broke out in the

Karachi, Pakistan's largest city and principal seaport, is situated along the Arabian Sea on the Indus River delta. Karachi was the capital of Sind during the British colonial era and served as national capital from 1947, when Pakistan became independent, to 1959.

western province. Zulfikar Ali Bhutto succeeded Yahya Khan, and was re elected in 1977. But opposition to his government was intense, the vote was declared fraudulent, and in the ensuing disorder Bhutto was overthrown and Gen. Mohammad Zia ul-Haq took control of the government. Bhutto was subsequently tried for treason and other charges and executed in 1979. After postponing elections and constitutional reform, Gen. Zia formally ended military rule in January 1986, but no formal elections were held. Following his death in a plane crash, Gen. Zia was succeeded by Benazir Bhutto, Ali Bhutto's daughter, who was elected Prime Minister in 1988. In August 1990, Bhutto's government was dismissed by President Ghulam Ishaq Khan, amidst charges of corruption and abuse of power. The subsequent government collapsed in 1993 and Bhutto returned to power. In 1996 she was again dismissed and in 1999 sentenced to five years imprisonment. In 1997 Nawaz Sharif of the Pakistan Muslim League was elected Prime Minister. Like India, Pakistan carried out nuclear tests in 1998. As a result, tensions between the two countries increased. In 1999, the army, led by General Musharraf, seized power. In 2002, both India and Pakistan tested missiles bearing ballistic warheads, but a conflict was prevented. Tension still persists however er over claims of both Pakistan and India to the disputed Kashmir territory.

Pakubuwono, name of twelve monarchs of

Parched lands of the northern Indus valley near Rawalpindi, Pakistan, are cultivated to produce wheat, cotton, and other crops. Although the region has an arid climate, the development of extensive irrigation systems has greatly increased its productivity.

Mataram and Surakarta in mid-Java. The first was Pageran Poeger, who-under the name of Susuhunan Pakubuwono-was recognized (after granting several concessions) by the Dutch East India Company as the ruler of Mataram until 1719. His grandson Pakubuwono II (governed 1727-1749) lost most of his land to the Dutch East India Company after the Chinese revolt of the 1740s. In 1746 he moved his court from Fartasura to Surakarta. During the rule of Pakubuwono III (1749-1788; real name Sunan Swarga) Mataram was divided into Surakarta, which he ruled, and the sultanate Yogyakarta, which was ruled by Hamengkubuwono I (1755-1792). The title Susuhunan Pakubuwono remained reserved for the rulers of Surakarta. Pakubuwono X (governed 1893-1939) carried through financial and agricultural reforms. The last was Pakubuwono XII, installed in 1944, whose land was merged into the independent republic of Indonesia.

Palate, bodily structure dividing the mouth from the nose and bounded by the upper gums and teeth; it is made of bone and covered by mucous membrane. At the back of the palate is a soft mobile connective-tissue that can close off the nasopharynx during swallowing and speech.
See also: Mouth.

Palatinate, 2 regions of Germany: the Lower, or Rhine, Palatinate is on the Rhine River bordering France and the Saar; the Upper Palatinate is in northeastern Bavaria.

Palau Islands

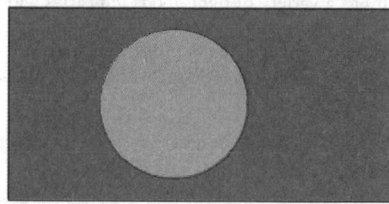

Capital:	Koror
Area:	196 sq mi (508 sq km)
Population:	19,400
Language:	English, Micronesian languages
Government:	Presidential republic
Independent:	1994
Head of gov.:	President
Per capita:	US$ 9,000
Monetary unit:	1 US dollar = 100 cents

Palau Islands, = Palau (UN) = Belau (synonym). Independent group of coral and volcanic islands in the western Pacific Ocean. Of the nearly 200 islands totaling 196 sq mi

(508 sq km) in area, only 8 are inhabited. Babelthaup is the largest; Koror is the capital. The small population lives on subsistence farming and fishing. Tourism is of great economic importance. The islands were under Spanish control for several hundred years before being sold to Germany (1899). Japan seized them during World War I, and the United States took them over during World War II. A UN trust territory 1947-1987, they became self-governing in 1981 and remained under U.S. administration until 1994 when they became independent. Paulau relies on financial aid from the U.S., who are responsible for defense and maintain several military bases on the islands.

Palawan (pop. 528,000), island belonging to the Philippines, between the Sulu Sea and the South China Sea; 4,551 sq mi (11,785 sq km). Capital: Puerto Princesa. Mountainous (up to 6,562 ft, 2,000 m) and many earthquakes. The island's economy is not very developed. Forestry, rubber plantations, cultivation of rice, sugarcane, coconut palm and cattle, fishing and winning of chromium and mercury.

Palembang (pop. 1.4 mln.) City on Sumatra, Indonesia, and capital of South Sumatra Province. It lies 269 miles (420 km) northwest of Jakarta, and is on the Musi River. Though 55 miles (88 km) inland, Palembang handles seagoing traffic. Its refineries and docks serve rich oilfields. Its port handles petroleum products, timber products, rubber, coffee, and spices. Palembang was once the capital of a vast Buddhist empire called Sri Vijaya that was at its peak in the eighth century.

Paleocene, first epoch of the Tertiary period, c.65-55 million years ago.

Paleogeography, science of the construction from geologic, paleontologic, and other evidence of maps of the earth's surface at specific times in the past. Paleogeography has been of considerable importance in studies of continental drift.

Paleography, the study of handwritten material from the ancient and medieval times. It deals with writing on papyrus, parchment, paper, and other perishable materials, as opposed to epigraphy, which deals with writing on metal or stone. Paleographers study handwriting to interpret and date events and to trace the evolution of the written alphabet.

Paleolithic Period *See:* Stone Age.

Paleontology, study of fossils. The principal branches of study are paleobotany and paleozoology, dealing with plants and animals respectively. These studies are essential in charting the history of the evolution of life and in tracking continental drift.
See also: Fossil.

Paleozoic, earliest era of the Phanerozoic Eon, comprising the Lower Paleozoic (570-400 million years ago), containing the Cambrian, Ordovician, and Silurian periods; and the Upper Paleozoic (400-225 million years ago), containing the Devonian, Carboniferous (Mississippian and Pennsylvanian), and Permian periods.

Palermo (pop. 734,000), capital, largest city, and major port of Sicily, Italy, on the northwestern coast. Shipbuilding, textiles, and chemicals are leading industries. Palermo was founded by Phoenicians between the 8th and 6th centuries B.C. The city was ruled by Byzantines (535-831), Arabs (831-1072), and Normans (1072-1194), and its notable medieval architecture exhibits features of all these cultures.
See also: Sicily.

Palestine, the biblical Holy Land, named for the Philistines and also called Canaan. Its boundaries, often imprecise, have varied widely. Palestine now usually refers to the region bounded by the Mediterranean on the west, the Jordan River and the Dead Sea on the east, Mt. Hermon on the Syria-Lebanon border to the north, and the Sinai Peninsula in the south. It includes almost all of modern Israel and extends, as well, into present-day Jordan and Egypt.
There were Paleolithic and Mesolithic cultures in Palestine, and Neolithic Jericho emerged by about 7000 B.C. Semitic peoples arrived about 3000 B.C. and founded a Bronze Age civilization.
About 1000 B.C., after warring against Canaanites and Philistines, the Jews succeeded in establishing a kingdom that later split into Israel to the north and Judah to the south. In the eighth century B.C. the Assyrians overran Israel and in the sixth century B.C., Judah was conquered by the Babylonians. Palestine later fell to Alexander the Great, the Ptolemies of Egypt, and the Seleucids of Syria. An independent Jewish state arose again briefly in the second century B.C., but the region was then incorporated into the Roman empire.
In the fourth century A.D., control passed to the Byzantines and the conquest of Palestine by the Arabs, beginning in A.D. 630, marked the beginning of 1300 years of Muslim rule,

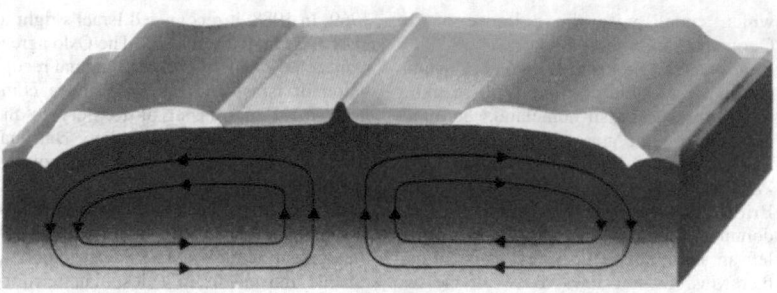

Hot lava from the earth's interior rises through rifts in ocean ridge systems, thus creating new seafloor crust. The new crust forms and spreads on both sides of a ridge, pushing back older crust into the mantle along ocean trenches.

P

which ended with the collapse of the Ottoman empire in 1918.

In response to Zionism, Jews had been emigrating to Palestine since the 1850s. Seeking to establish a Jewish homeland, the immigrants met with increasing resistance and hostility from Muslim Palestinians.

With its Balfour Declaration in 1917, the British government, which had become dominant in the region after World War I, left an ambiguous legacy that satisfied neither Muslims nor Jews. Between the two world wars, Jewish immigration increased as did political tensions between Jews and Muslims.

Following World War II and the Nazi-organized mass murders of European Jews, there was a mass exodus to Palestine. In 1948, the Jews accepted a U.N. recommendation to divide Palestine into Jewish and Arab states, but the Arabs rejected partition. The British left the region and, since the founding of Israel, Palestine has been the focal point of a struggle between the State of Israel and its Arab neighbors and inhabitants, a struggle that has resulted in chronic warfare and terrorism.

As a result of an agreement between Israel and the PLO (1993), limited authority was given to the Gaza Strip and Jericho.

The Palestinian parliament on March 10th 2003, approved the new position of prime minister as part of reforms sought by the United States, Europe and Israel to curb Yasser Arafat's near absolute powers.

President Bush has said that the Palestinians have to choose new leaders as a precondition for statehood.

Mahmoud Abbas is Mr. Arafat's appointee for prime minister.

See: Palestinian National Authority.

Palestine Liberation Organization, (PLO) an organization of various Palestinian groups that wants to establish an independent state in the former mandate area Palestine. Founded by the Arab League in 1964. Yasser Arafat has led the PLO since

The works of author Flavius Josephus (37-100) contain important information on the history of Palestine. The most well-known are his *History of the Jews* in 20 volumes, and *The Jewish Wars* in 7 volumes, whence this miniature, from the end of the 15th century.

1969. In 1988, it recognized Israel's right to exist and abjured terrorism. The Oslo agreements (1993 and 1995) stated mutual recognition of Israel and the PLO and a commencement of transfer of territory to the Palestinians. The Palestinian National Authority (PNA) took over internal government of the Gaza strip and parts of the West Bank and Arafat became President (1996). Escalating violence, problems with Israel, the opposition of HAMAS (most important Islamic movement in Palestinian territory that opposes the Oslo peace process) and corruption within the Palestinian self-government produced major problems for the PLO.

See also: Arafat, Yasir.

Palestinian National Authority, authority over the Gaza strip and the West Bank, that, in accordance with the Oslo agreement, was handed over by Israel to the Palestinian National Authority (1994). The areas cover 5879<\!p>km^2 on the West Bank and 363<\!p>km^2 on the Gaza strip, and have a population of 3,100,000 inhabitants. The capital is East-Jerusalem and the national currency is the Shekel. An elected Parliament of 88 members (Palestinian Council) and an elected President form the government. Yasir Arafat became the first President to be elected in 1996. After the Oslo agreements, however, the peace process quickly stagnated. Israel repeatedly delayed withdrawal from the West Bank and continued founding settlements, while Arafat's PNA failed to contain the Muslim fundamentalist movement HAMAS. In 2000, the second Intifadah broke out and the violence escalated: Palestinians continued their terrorist and suicide attacks and Israel retaliated by almost destroying the infrastructure of the Palestinian territories. In 2003 a solution did not seem at hand.

See also: Arafat, Yasir; Intifadah; Sharon, Ariel.

Palestrina, Giovanni Pierluigi da (c.1525-1594), Italian Renaissance composer of unaccompanied choral church music. He wrote over 100 masses and is perhaps best known for his *Missa Papae Marcelli*. He was organist and choirmaster in several Roman churches.

See also: Renaissance.

Palladio, Andrea (Andrea di Pietro; 1508-1580), Italian architect, creator of the immensely influential Paladian style. His designs for villas, palaces, and churches stressed harmonic proportions and classical symmetry. Palladio's *The Four Books of Architecture* (1570) helped to spread his style throughout Europe.

Palladium, chemical element, symbol Pd; for physical constants see Periodic Table. Palladium was discovered by William H. Wollaston in 1803. It occurs native associated with platinum, gold, and silver and also as a selenide. Commercially, it is obtained as a byproduct in the production of platinum, nickel, and copper. It is prepared in sponge form by the thermal decomposition of palladium dichlorodiamine. Palladium is a steel-white, malleable, soft, ductile metal. It is a

member of the platinum group of metals and is the least dense, lowest melting, and most readily fused. Palladium metal resists oxidation. It absorbs up to 900 times its volume of hydrogen at ordinary temperatures. Hydrogen gas is purified by diffusing it through heated palladium. Palladium is used in the finely divided state as a catalyst for hydrogenation and dehydrogention reactions. Palladium is used in jewelry, dentistry, surgical instruments, electrical contacts, and high temperature solders. It is the least expensive of the platinum metals.

Pallas *See:* Athena.

Palm, any of over 3,000 species of trees, shrubs, and vines of the family Palmae, native mainly to tropical and subtropical regions. Palms are characterized by an unbranched stem bearing a cluster of feather-like (pinnate) or fanlike (palmate) leaves at its crown. Flowers are greenish, borne in spikes, and the fruits are covered with a leathery, fibrous, outer layer. Palm products are of great economic importance: the coconut and date palms produce staple crops; wax is obtained from the carnauba palm; the African oil palm and the coconut palm yield oil used in food, soap, toiletries, and industrial processes. Fibers yielded include rattan and raffia.

Palma de Mallorca (pop. 320,000) Spain, chief city of the Balearic Islands and the capital of Baleares Province. It is on the island of Mallorca, 165 miles (265 km) east of Valencia. Palma, a seaport, is a railway, road, and airline center, and attracht tourists. It has a variety of light-goods industries and is the chief trading center of the island. A Gothic cathedral begun in 1229 and the 14th century Castle of Bellver overlook the Bay of Palma.

Palmer, Arnold (1929-), U.S. golfer. Palmer's playing style and charismatic personality helped make golf a popular spectator sport. Palmer won the U.S. Open (1960), the British Open (1961, 1962), and was the first to win the Masters tournament 4 times (1958, 1960, 1962, 1964).

Palmerston, Viscount (1784-1865), British politician remembered for his successful and often aggressive foreign policy. As foreign secretary (1830-1834, 1835-1841, 1846-1851), he was instrumental in securing Belgian independence and maintaining peace in Europe during the revolutions of 1848. As prime minister (1855-1858, 1859-1865), he led Britain to victory in the Crimean War, maintained neutrality in the American Civil War, and aided the unification of Italy.

See also: United Kingdom.

Palmetto, any of a genus (*Sabal*) of fan-leaved, usually small, palm trees, common to the southeastern United States and the West Indies. The name refers especially to the cabbage palm (*S. palmetto*).

Palmistry, practice (over 4,000 years old) of reading the markings on a person's palm for the purpose of predicting the future.

The various lines on the palm are held to indicate the individual's character and destiny.

Palm oil, substance obtained from the fruit and seed kernel of the African oil palm (genus *Elaeis*). It is used in candles, cosmetics, margarine, lubricants, and soaps.

Palm Sunday, Sunday before Easter and the first day of Holy Week, commemorating Jesus's triumphal entry into Jerusalem, when palm leaves were spread in his path. Palm leaves are blessed and carried in procession.
See also: Holy Week.

Palmyra, ancient city in central Syria. Prominent as a trading center, Palmyra prospered under Roman rule and reached its height (A.D. 30) as an independent state under Queen Zenobia. In 273 it was largely destroyed by the Romans under Aurelian; more than a century later it was sacked by Tamerlane. Imposing ruins remain.

Palmyra palm, tall, fan-leaved tree (*Borassus flabellifer*) of tropical Asia. Its trunk, which may grow to 70 ft (21 m), supplies lumber. The large leaves, which ancient Hindus used as paper, provide thatching. The fiber of the palmyra is used to make rope, and the fruit, seeds, and shoots are edible.

Palomar Observatory, astronomical observatory on Palomar Mt. 5,660 ft (1,725 m) above sea level, northeast of San Diego, in southern California. Its Hale telescope, with its 200-in (500-cm) reflector, is capable of photographing objects several billion light years away. At the time of its construction (1948), the telescope was the world's largest. The observatory's Schmidt telescopes have photographed all of the northern and half of the southern sky. The Palomar Observatory, the Mount Wilson Observatory, and the Las Campanas Observatory were jointly administered and known collectively as the Hale Observatories until 1980, when

The Roman ruins of Palmyra, the oasis town that, according to tradition, was founded by king Solomon. Under the Romans, Palmyra became one of the most important cities in the Eastern Roman Empire (3rd century A.D.). The ruins are near the village of Tadmor or Tadmur ('city of palms'), the biblical name for Palmyra.

the California Institute of Technology assumed separate control of the Palomar Observatory.
See also: Astronomy.

Paloverde, any of a genus (*Cercidium*) of small trees of the pea family native to the southwestern United States and other hot, dry regions of the Americas. A yellow-flowering tree that loses its small leaves in the spring, it gets its name (Spanish, 'green tree') from its smooth green bark. The beanlike seeds were an important food for Native Americans.

Palpitation *See:* Tachycardia.

Palsson, Thorsteinn (1947-), Icelandic politician, prime minister since 1987. He was director of the Employer's Federation (1979-1983), head of the Independence Party (1983-1987), and minister of finance (1985-1987).
See also: Iceland.

Palsy, paralysis, especially a progressive form culminating late in life, characterized by tremors of the limbs and muscular weakness and rigidity.
See also: Paralysis.

Pamirs, mountainous region of central Asia, predominantly in Tajikistan, but extending into Afghanistan, China, and Kashmir. The mountains form a hub from which radiate the Hindu Kush, Karakorum, Kunlun, and Tien Shan ranges. Communism Peak (24,590 ft/7,495 m) and Lenin Peak (23,508 ft/7,165 m) are the highest.
See also: Hindu Kush.

Pampa, term for several plains of South America, specifically for the great grass plain of central and northern Argentina. The Pampa covers some 250,000 sq mi (647,500 sq km) and is the economic heart of Argentina, where its livestock and much of its crops are raised. Pampas grass, with its mass of plumed flowers, is often grown as an ornamental.

Pan, in Greek mythology, god of fertility, usually portrayed as a man with the legs, ears, and horns of a goat. All of his myths deal with his many love affairs. Worship of Pan began in Arcadia in southern Greece.
See also: Mythology.

Panama

Capital:	Panama City
Area:	29,762 sq mi (77,082 sq km)
Population:	2,882,000
Language:	Spanish
Government:	Presidential republic
Independent:	1903
Head of gov.:	President
Per capita:	US$ 5,900
Monetary unit:	1 Balboa = 100 centésimos

Panama, small Central American republic situated on the Isthmus of Panama, which is a narrow strip of land forming the connecting link between Central and South America that also separates the Atlantic and Pacific Oceans. Panama is bisected by the Panama Canal, which cuts through the low hills of the country's central area. The canal is the most important feature of Panama, and it has played a major role in the creation of the country and in its subsequent development.
Land and climate. There are highlands in the west and east, wooded hills in the center, and lowland shelves along the Atlantic and Pacific coasts. The climate is tropical, with little variation from season to season.
People. Mestizos and mulattos (people of mixed racial ancestry) make up about 70% of the population; the rest is mostly composed of unmixed Indian, white, or black ancestry. Panama is a Spanish-speaking, predominantly Roman Catholic country. Nearly one-third of the population lives in the capital Panama City and Colón.
Economy. Agriculture employs a lot of people. The Panama Canal is one of the major factors in the country's economy, providing about 10% of national income. It also provides many jobs. Exports-bananas, shrimp, sugar, and petroleum products-lag far behind imports, and Panama suffers from a huge trade deficit. International banking (offshore banking, insurance) and the industry provide more jobs than the Panama Canal.
History. Indians were the first inhabitants of what is now Panama, but little is known

P

P

Panama City, the capital and largest city of Panama, lies on the Pacific coast at the terminus of the Panama Canal. Founded in 1672 as a port of the Spanish Empire, the city is today a center of trade of the canal and the neighboring port of Balboa.

about them. Spain took control of the region during the early 1500s and established settlements there. In 1513 Vasco Núñez de Balboa crossed the isthmus and became the first European to see the eastern shore of the Pacific. Panama became a springboard for Spanish conquests in the Americas and a route for transshipping Peruvian gold to Spain, but it lost importance in the 18th century after buccaneer attacks forced treasure ships from Peru to sail around South America. In 1819, Colombia broke away from Spanish rule, and in 1821 Panama freed itself from Spain and became part of Colombia. Relations between the two nations, however, were always strained. The California gold rush of 1848 caused many people from the eastern part of the United States to travel to Panama, cross the isthmus, and continue their sea journey on to California, and the idea of a canal across the isthmus took on new significance. In 1903, the United States tried to negotiate a deal with Colombia whereby it would build the canal, but Colombia refused. Panama, with encouragement from the United States, revolted from Colombia, became an independent nation, and agreed to the United States' plan. The completion of the canal in 1914 brought some prosperity to Panama, but also

A freighter en route from the Pacific to the Atlantic Ocean enters the Pedro Miguel Locks of the Panama Canal. The canal, which was opened to commercial navigation in 1914, is under full Panamanian control since December 1999.

led to discontent with the United States' control of the canal and of the Panama Canal Zone. Those in favor of Panamanian control of the canal rioted in 1959, 1962, and 1964. General Omar Torrijos Herrera seized control of Panama in 1968 and backed the movement to return the canal to Panama. In 1977, Panama and the United States signed a treaty that transferred control of the Canal Zone to Panama in 1979 and provided for full transfer of the canal to Panama in 1999. In 1983, General Manuel Antonio Noriega became head of the army and Panama's most powerful figure. In 1988, grand juries in the United States indicted him for narcotics smuggling and racketeering. The Panamanian president dismissed him, but the military forced the president from office. In 1989, Panama held an election in which Noriega was apparently defeated. The government, under Noriega, declared the election invalid and refused to let the winning candidate, Guillermo Endara, take office. The United States intervened by imposing economic sanctions on Panama. When these failed to change the government, President Bush in 1989 ordered a United States expeditionary force to Panama to oust Noriega and restore the duly elected president. Noriega was captured and brought to the United States to stand trial. Panama's economy, however, remained in a weakened condition. With the return of a civilian government the political situation stabilized. In 1999, Panama took full control over the Panama Canal. The canal was broadened in several places. Mireya Moscoso became the country's first female President that year. In 2001, she instigated an investigation into the crimes against humanity, committed during Noriega's military regime in the 1980s.

Panama Canal, artificial waterway crossing the Isthmus of Panama, linking the Atlantic and Pacific oceans. The canal is 51 mi (82 km) long; traverses 2 natural lakes, one of which is 85 ft (26 m) above sea level; and has 6 locks. It was built by U.S. military engineers in 1904-1914, after U.S. troops helped Panama secede from Colombia. The United States was granted rights in perpetuity to a zone 10 mi (16 km) wide across the isthmus. After World War II there was U.S.-Panamanian friction over canal sovereignty, and in 1977 U.S. and Panamanian representatives signed a new treaty ceding administration of the canal to Panama in 1979 and full control in 1999, with guarantees of its neutral operation.
See also: Clayton-Bulwer Treaty; Hay-Pauncefote Treaties.

Panama Canal Zone, strip of land (553 sq mi/1,432 sq km) extending 5 mi (8 km) on either side of the Panama Canal. The Canal zone was controlled by the United States until Oct. 1979, when Panama took control after U.S.-Panamanian treaties were ratified by the U.S. Senate (1978).

Panama City (pop. 667,000), capital of Panama, on the Gulf of Panama, at the Pacific entrance to the canal. Mainly a modern industrial city, it owes its growth to the building of the canal. The city was founded in 1672, after the original Panama, founded

by Pedrarias the Cruel (1519) 4 mi (6.4 km) distant, had been sacked by Sir Henry Morgan (1671). The city also served as port for the shipment of Andean gold during Spanish colonial days.
See also: Panama.

Panamarenko (real name Henri van Herreweghe; 1940-), Belgian graphic artist. In the mid 1960s engaged in the organization of happenings. Initially made objects in the character of New Realism and assemblages. Soon his technical interest surfaced and he integrated mechanical elements into his work. Became well-known for his designs of gliders, flying machines and racing cars that appeal to the imagination and which function 'in principle' for Panamarenko, and therefore do not need to be tested.

Pan, Marta (1923-), Hungarian-French sculptor. Her work is abstract; made of wood, metal, or (white) synthetic material in flowing forms.

Pan-American conferences, or Inter-American conferences, meetings of representatives of independent nations of the Western Hemisphere to discuss political, legal, military, economic, and social issues. The first such conference, organized largely through the efforts of Simón Bolívar, was held in Panama City in 1826. Further meetings were held throughout the 19th century. A conference in 1889 established the International Union of American Republics, later called the Pan American Union. Conferences organized by F.D. Roosevelt (1938-1947) dealt with economic and defense issues. The Organization of American States (OAS), formed in 1948, added anti-communism to the agenda.
See also: Bolívar, Simón; Organization of American States.

Pan American Games, quadrennial amateur sports contest between nations of the Americas. The event is based on the Olympic Games and includes many of the same events. Proposed at the 1940 Pan-American Congress, the games were postponed due to World War II and were first held in 1951.

Pan American Highway, road system linking Latin American countries with each other and with the U.S. interstate highway system. The Pan-American link was conceived at the Fifth International Conference of American States (1923).

Pan American Union, organization of independent states of North and South America founded in 1910. Its stated purpose was to foster economic, political, and social cooperation among member nations. When the Organization of American States (OAS) was founded in 1948, the Pan American Union became its central office. In 1970 the Union was renamed the General Secretariat of the OAS.
See also: Organization of American States.

Pancasila (also Panca Sila), literally: five pillars. These are the principles included in the preamble of the constitution on which the unified Indonesian state is based. The pancasila are: nationalism, belief in one God, social justice, popular sovereignty and humanity.

Panchen lama, Tibetan spiritual leader. The Panchen Lama is Tibet's second religious leader. He is designated as the reincarnation of his deceased predecessor. After the failed revolt of 1959 the Panchen Lama - unlike the Dalai Lama, the highest spiritual leader - remained in Tibet. He recognized Chinese sovereignty but criticized Chinese interference with Tibetan religion. In 1964 he called for independence and support for the Dalai Lama. After years of house arrest in Beijing he was rehabilitated and tried to exert his influence on the authorities in favor of the Tibetan people.

Pancreas, glandular organ that secretes enzymes and hormones essential to the digestive process. Located beneath the stomach, the pancreas is connected to the small intestine at the duodenum. Powerful digestive-system enzymes (trypsin, lipase, amylase) are produced and secreted to aid in the digestion of proteins, fats, and carbohydrates, respectively. Insulin and glucagon, hormones secreted by the islets of Langerhans, small cell groups in the pancreas, have important roles in glucose and fat metabolism and regulate blood-sugar levels.
See also: Diabetes; Insulin.

Pancreatin, mixture of enzymes from the pancreatic juice, a secretion of the pancreas that helps the body to digest starch, fats, and proteins.
See also: Pancreas.

Panda, either of 2 Asian mammals anatomically similar to raccoons and each having an unusual sixth digit on each hand. This digit has evolved to thumblike size and flexibility in the giant panda of central China (*Ailuropoda melanoleuca*), remaining vestigial in the red, or lesser, panda (*Ailurus fulgens*), found in the Himalayas and the mountains of western China and northern Burma. Though they have evolved from carnivores, both pandas are vegetarians. The giant panda, resembling a bear, with its predominantly white body, black ears, limbs, and eye patches, weighs from 200-300 lb (90-140 kg).

Pandit, Vijaya Lakshmi (1900-1990), Indian diplomat and political leader. The sister of Jawaharlal Nehru, Pandit was active in the struggle for India's independence and helped implement a postwar policy of nonalignment. She was ambassador to the Soviet Union (1947-1949) and the United States and Mexico (1949-1951), and the first woman to serve as president of the UN General Assembly (1953-1954). She was high commissioner to Great Britain while serving also as ambassador to Ireland (1954-1961), and to Spain (1958-1961). She was governor of Maharashtra (1962-1967) and a member of India's Parliament (1952-1954 and 1964-1969). In 1977 Pandit retired from the Congress Party.
See also: India.

Pandora, in Greek mythology, first woman on earth. Created by Hephaestus on the orders of Zeus, she was given a box that she was ordered never to open. Unable to contain her curiosity, she disobeyed, thus releasing all the evils that plague humanity. The only thing that had not escaped when she closed the lid was hope.
See also: Mythology.

Pangolin, any of a group of mammals found in Asia and Africa whose bodies are covered by hard, overlapping scales. Only their undersides are soft and hairy. Many pangolins (genus *Manis* or related genera of the order Pholidota) climb trees, and some can hang by their tails. They have strong claws for tearing open the nests of termites and ants, and long tongues for drawing them into their mouths.
See also: Anteater.

Pan Jixun (1521-1595), most important hydraulic engineer of the Ming dynasty (1368-1636). Was appointed four times to try to control the Yellow River (Huang). He opposed, with varying success, the representatives of the traditional method, who wanted to reduce the power of the stream by means of branches; his motto was: 'build banks to check the water and use the current to carry down the silt'. In addition to this he propagated the construction of a sort of summer and winter banks system. He wrote a number of hydraulic engineering works, the most important of which were republished in 1936.

Pankhurst, English family of women's rights activists. In 1903, **Emmeline Goulden Pankhurst** (1858-1928), a suffragist, and her daughters, **Christabel Pankhurst** (1880-1958) and **Sylvia Pankhurst** (1882-1960), founded the Woman's Social and Political Union, a base for their increasingly militant actions to further women's rights. Emmeline was repeatedly imprisoned (1912-1913) and conducted several hunger strikes (1908-

The small-scaled tree pangolin (*M. tricuspis*), a scaly mammal of Africa, hangs upside-down from a tree branch by its strong, flexible tail.

P

1914). She died a month before British women gained full voting equality with men and was revered nationally for her work during the war and to extend suffrage.
See also: Women's movement.

Panmunjom, village in the demilitarized zone between North and South Korea, where the truce to end the Korean War was negotiated (1951-1953) and signed (July 27, 1953). The joint security area was partitioned in 1976 by North Korea and the UN command after the killing of 2 U.S. soldiers by the North Koreans.
See also: Korean War.

Pansy, cultivated plant (*Viola tricolor hort-*

The giant panda (*A. melanoleuca*), a zoo favorite, is a bearlike animal that is possibly related to the raccoon. This extremely rare animal, which inhabits snowy regions of central China, has been designated a national treasure by the People's Republic of China.

P

ensis) bred from the European violet. It has variously colored flowers with 5 broad, velvety petals and is a popular garden plant.

Pantheon, historically, temple dedicated to the worship of all the gods. In modern times it refers to a structure in which a nation's heroes are buried or honored. The Pantheon of Rome, a domed, circular temple, was built in 27 B.C. Later destroyed, it was rebuilt C.A.D. 120 by Hadrian. It became a Christian church in 609.

Panther, common name for the black leopard, found in Asia and Africa. The North American puma, also known as the cougar or mountain lion, is sometimes referred to as a panther.
See also: Leopard.

The panther (*L. pardus*) is rarely seen, even by its prospective victims, because of its silent, wary habits. The black panther (left) is actually a leopard with black coat pigmentation.

Pantomime, drama performed entirely through facial expression, movement, and gesture, without speech. Popular in Roman times, it was developed in Italy by the commedia dell'arte in the 16th century, which created the popular Harlequin and Columbine characters. Popular 20th-century pantomimists include Marcel Marceau and Charlie Chaplin.

Pantothenic acid *See:* Vitamin.

Pan-Turkish Movement, movement that aims to unite all Turkish people in one state. At its prime during World War I when it was propagated by the Young Turks. However, the Pan-Turkish movement never had much effect or influence. The founder of modern Turkey, Mustafa Kemal Pasha (1881-1938), opposed Pan-Turkish sentiments.

Pao, Sir Yue-Kong (1918-1991), Hong-Kong shipping tycoon. Pao fled to Hong-Kong in 1949, shortly before the Communists came into power in China. There he bought his first ship in the mid 1950s and in a few decades became by far the biggest ship owner in the world, with a merchant fleet six times bigger that that of the well-known Greek ship-owner Onassis. In 1978 Pao was created a peer.

Papadopoulos, George (1919-1999), Greek army officer, prime minister (1967-1973) and president (June-Nov. 1973) of Greece

under a military junta. Overthrown by a military coup in 1974, he and others were tried and found guilty of crimes against the state. His death sentence was commuted to life imprisonment.
See also: Greece.

Papal States, lands in Italy under the rule of the popes from 754 to 1870. The states date from the donation of conquered Lombard lands to the papacy by the Frankish King Pepin the Short. Augmented by later gifts and conquests, the states stretched from coast to coast across central Italy by the early 13th century. Napoleon I conquered the Papal States in 1796, but they were restored to the pope in 1815. King Victor Emmanuel II annexed the Papal States during the Risorgimento, Rome itself coming under Italian rule in 1870. The papacy did not officially accept the loss of its lands until the Lateran Treaty (1929) created an independent Vatican City.

Papandreou, 2 premiers of Greece. **George Papandreou** (1888-1968) was premier from 1964-1965. His removal by King Constantine II led to the military coup of 1967 and to the abolition of the monarchy in 1973. His son, **Andreas Papandreou** (1919-1996) was premier of Greece from 1981 to 1989. Imprisoned and then exiled under the military dictatorship (1967-1974), he founded in exile the socialist party known as Pasok (for Panhellenic Socialist Movement). As premier, he instituted numerous reforms.
See also: Greece.

Papaw *See:* Papaya; Pawpaw.

Papaya, small, tropical, American fruit tree (*Carica papaya*), widely cultivated for its yellow, oblong, edible fruit of the same name. The juice of the stem, leaves, and unripe fruit contains the protein-digesting enzyme papain. The papaya is sometimes called a papaw.

Papeete *See:* Tahiti.

Papen, Franz von (1879-1969), German diplomat and politician. Lacking support as chancellor (1932), he resigned and helped engineer the appointment of Hitler. He was Hitler's vice-chancellor (1933-1934) and as German minister to Austria (1934-1938) paved the way for German annexation of Austria. Acquitted of war crimes by the Nuremberg tribunal (1946), he was convicted by a German 'denazification court' (1947), but its sentence was rescinded.

Paper, flat sheet, usually made of plant fibers, used for writing and printing, probably invented in China C.A.D. 105, using bark and hemp. Cotton rags and cloth-still used for special high-grade papers-were the raw materials most often used until generally replaced by wood-pulp processes developed in the mid-19th century. In chemical pulping, wood chips are cooked under pressure in a solution (soda, sulfate, or sulfite) that dissolves all but the cellulose. The pulp is then bleached, washed, and refined, the fibers being crushed, frayed, and cut by mechanical beaters. This increases their surface area and bonding power. At this stage various substances are added: fillers (mainly clay and chalk) to make the paper opaque, sizes (rosin and alum) for resistance to water, and dyes and pigments as necessary. The pulp is fed to the paper machine, where it flows onto a moving belt or cylindrical drum of fine wire mesh, and most of the water is drained off by gravity and suction. The newly formed continuous sheet is pressed between rollers, dried by evaporation, and subjected to calendaring. Some paper is coated to give a special surface.

Paper nautilus *See:* Argonaut.

Paperwork, paper designed and used for decorative purposes, including wallpaper and gift wrapping. Although now mostly machine-made, such paper has often been made and decorated by hand. Decorative book endpapers were traditionally used to line the insides of book covers. Origami is the Japanese art of folding paper to represent objects.

Papier-mâché, molding material made of pulped paper mixed with flour paste, glue, or

In the aqueous stage, the formation and drainage of the paper slurry takes place. For this purpose, the slurry track is passed over a rotating straining cloth, made of bronze thread or a synthetic material, so that the major part of the water can run off. Here, the paper also obtains the characteristics that are important for its processing later on, such as the direction of the fibres, and the roughness of the bottom and top surfaces.

Until 1800, all paper was handmade. This Japanese painting from 1820 illustrates the process (from right to left). A fibrous pulp was made from linen rags, by pounding them in a mortar. This pulp was mixed with water and then scooped up in a rectangular copper sieve. After the water had been drained off, the paper was hung to dry.

resin. It is usually molded while wet, but in some industrial processes is pressure-molded. The technique of making papier-mâché decorative objects began in the Orient and reached Europe in the 18th century.

Papillon, originally, dwarf spaniel, breed of small dog with a long, silky coat and butterfly-shaped ears. Papillons stand up to 11 in (28 cm) tall and weigh up to 11 lb (5 kg). The breed was developed in 16th century Spain and later became popular among the French nobility.

Papua New Guinea

Capital:	Port Moresby
Area:	178,704 sq mi
	(462,840 sq km)
Population:	5,172,000
Language:	English
Government:	Parliamentary monarchy in the British Commonwealth
Independent:	1975
Head of gov.:	Prime minister
Per capita:	US$ 2,400
Monetary unit:	1 Kina = 100 toea

Papua New Guinea, since 1975, independent nation in the Pacific located just north of Australia.
Land and climate. The eastern half of New Guinea Island comprises five-sixths of the nation's territory, which also includes the islands of Bougainville, Buka, and the Bismarck archipelago to the northeast and smaller islands to the southeast. Papua New Guinea is a mountainous, densely forested region with a monsoon climate and a rich variety of plant and animal life. The capital is Port Moresby.
People. The population consists of several distinct ethnic and cultural groups, including Stone Age peoples who inhabit the remote interior. A wide variety of native languages are spoken and Pidgin English is used as a common tongue. The majority of the population is Christian, some of whom also adhere to traditional animistic beliefs.
Economy. Plantation farming has replaced traditional subsistence agriculture in some areas. Exports include timber and coconut products, rubber, cocoa, tea, and coffee. Copper and gold are mined.There are reserves of petroleum and natural gas.
History. The northern region of present day Papua New Guinea was part of German New Guinea from 1884 to 1914, when it was seized by Australia and became the Trust Territory of New Guinea. The southern region was British New Guinea from 1884 to 1905, then, as the Territory of Papua, it was under Australian rule. The two regions were merged administratively in 1949 as the Territory of Papua and New Guinea and administered by Australia. It was renamed Papua New Guinea in 1971, became self governing in 1973, and independent in 1975. A treaty with Indonesia in 1979 ended efforts by Papuan nationalists in neighboring Irian Jaya to unite with Papua New Guinea. In 1988, an independence movement on the island of Bougainville led to an open rebellion. Despite several cease-fires and rounds of negotiations, fighting has continued throughout the 1990s. In 1997 and 1998 the country suffered from starvation and floods. The copper rich island of Bougainville was granted a certain degree of autonomy in 2000. It aspires to unite with the ethnically similar Solomon Islands.

Papyrus, stout, reedlike plant (*Cyperus papyrus*) of the sedge family widely used in ancient Egypt. Sails, baskets, sandals, and clothing were made from the stem, as was a material for writing on (a predecessor of paper). The pith was eaten, and the roots were used as fuel.
See also: Paper.

Parable, short tale or anecdote designed to make a moral point or to present a spiritual truth, using everyday language and homely imagery. The literature of the ancient Greeks and the Old Testament abound in parables. In the New Testament Jesus conveys much of his most profound teaching in the form of parables. Some of these are the stories of the house built on rock and sand (Matthew 7.24-27), the pearl of great price (Matthew 13.45-46), the talents (Matthew 25.14-29), the sower and the seed (Mark 4.3-8; 14-20), the mote and the beam (Luke 6.41-42), the Good Samaritan (Luke 10.29-37), and the prodigal son (Luke 15.11-32).

Parabola, geometrical curve, similar in shape to the path followed by a projectile when it is fired into the air. A parabola is a conic section, obtained by the intersection of a right circular cone and a plane. If a parabola is rotated about its axis, it traces out a three-dimensional parabolic surface. When a light source is placed at the focus of a mirror with this shape, all the light rays are reflected parallel to the axis. A reflecting telescope uses the principle in reverse, collecting parallel rays of light from space and concentrating them at the focus.

Paracel Islands (Chinese: Xisha Qundao; Vietnamese: Quan Dao Hoang Sa), group of

ca. 130 coral islands and reefs in the South China Sea. None of the islands is inhabited on a permanent basis, except by tortoises and sea birds. The islands are being claimed by China, Taiwan and Vietnam. In 1974, after the discovery of petroleum at the bottom of the South China Sea, Chinese forces occupied the islands, which have in fact been under Chinese rule ever since.

Paracelsus, Philippus Aureolus (1493?-1541), Swiss alchemist and physician who channeled the arts of alchemy into the preparation of medical remedies. Born Theophrastus Bombastus von Hohenheim, he adopted the name Paracelsus, boasting that he was superior to the renowned first-century Roman medical writer Celsus.
See also: Alchemy.

Parachute, collapsible, umbrellalike device used to retard movement through the air. It

Port Moresby, the capital of Papua New Guinea, is named for Capt. John Moresby, who explored the area in 1873. The city has become Papua New Guinea's most important commercial center partly because of its proximity to Australia.

P

was invented in the late 18th century by French aeronaut Jacques Garnerin for descent from a balloon. When opened-either manually, by pulling a ripcord, or automatically, by a line attached to the aircraft-the canopy traps a large air mass, which produces the desired drag force. The canopy consists of numerous strong panels of canvas, silk, and nylon and has a series of cords connecting to a harness worn by the user. Parachutes are used for safe descent from airplanes, for dropping cargo from airplanes, and as braking devices for returning space vehicles, rockets, and airplanes. Sport parachuting, or skydiving, is a popular sport.

Paraguay

Capital:	Asunción
Area:	157,048 sq mi
	(406,752 sq km)
Population:	5,884,000
Language:	Spanish
Government:	Presidential republic
Independent:	1811
Head of gov.:	President
Per capita:	US$ 4,600
Monetary unit:	1 Paraguayan guaraní =
	100 céntimos

Paraguay, landlocked country in South America. Paraguay has an area of 157,047 sq mi (406,752 sq km) and is bordered by Bolivia on the northwest, Brazil on the northeast, and Argentina to the south and southeast.
Land and climate. The Paraguay River, flowing north-south, divides the country into two sharply contrasting regions: the eastern region, sometimes called Paraguay Proper, and the western Chaco region. The Chaco is largely flat, scrub country and is thinly populated. Though some of it is suitable for raising cattle, much of it is arid. The far richer eastern region is divided into two contrasting areas by a clifflike ridge running northward from the Paranà River near Encarnación. West of the ridge, where most of the people live, is rolling hill country that falls away to low-lying areas along the Paraguay River. East of the ridge is the Paraná Plateau, about 2,000 ft (610 m) above sea level and covered by dense tropical forest. The country has a subtropical climate, very like that of Florida, with hot wet

In Paraguay, thirty-two million hectares (80% of the land) belong to over 2,000 feudal cattle-farming families. Between them, they own about seven million head of cattle. Food production for the population is neglected. In the 1970s, for example, imports and smuggling had to be used to provide over two-thirds of the grain that was needed.

summers and warm and drier winters. Thunderstorms are frequent in summer. The capital of the country is Asunción.
People. The majority of the people are mestizo, a mixture of the Spanish and the native Guaraní people. Many people speak Guaraní, but Spanish is the official language and Roman Catholicism the official religion.
Economy. More than 50% of the work force is employed on the land, and over one-third of the gross national product comes from agriculture. Cotton, tobacco, coffee, timber, tannin, and oils are the chief exports. Some processing of agricultural products constitutes the country's main industry.
History. Originally inhabited by the Guaranís, by the 1550s the region had become Spain's power base in southeastern South America. Jesuit influence in the 17th century contributed significantly to the merging of Guaraní and Spanish cultures. From 1776 to 1811 Paraguay was part of the Spanish vice-royalty of La Plata. It became independent in 1811 after a relatively peaceful revolt. Following José Gaspar Rodriguez Francia, and Carlos Antonio López, the dictator Francisco Solano López led the country in the disastrous War of the Triple Alliance against Brazil, Uruguay, and Argentina from 1865 to 1870. Paraguay was laid waste and more than half the population died. Clashes with Bolivia over a border dispute led to the Chaco War (1932-1935). Political turmoil was followed by the relatively stable regime of Pres. Higinio Morinigó from 1940 to 1948. Civil War followed the overthrow of Morinigo and in 1954 Gen. Alfredo Stroessner seized power and governed ruthlessly until he too was overthrown in 1989 and government of the country was returned to civilians. A new constitution was adopted in 1992. In 1993 the country elected its first democratically elected civilian President, Juan Carlos Wasmosy Monti, of the Colorado Party. However, the country remained unstable, particularly because of the widening gap between rich and poor. The Presidential elections of 1999 were won by Luiz Gonzalez Macchi. In 2002, a state of emergency was proclaimed after violent public protests

against President Macchi, who had been accused of corruption.

Paraguay River, chief tributary of the Paraná River, in South America. It rises in the Mato Grosso region of western Brazil and flows about 1,300 mi (2,090 km) southward to join the Paraná near Corrientes. Part of the Río de la Plata system, its chief branches, the Pilcomayo and the Bermejo, enter from the west. It is mostly navigable; Asunción, Paraguay, is its chief port.

Parakeet, popular name for any of various small parrots, usually with green plumage and a long tail, popular as a cage bird and native to the Indo-Malayan region. The best known of the true parakeets is the budgerigar (*Melopsittacus undulatus*), also called the zebra, shell, or grass parakeet.

Parakramabahoe I (ca. 1123-1186; reigned 1153-1186) Ceylonese king from the Sinhala dynasty, originally one of the four kings of Ceylon. He succeeded in conquering the entire island, reformed Buddhism and granted freedom of religion to the Hindu population.

Parakramabahu II (ruled 1236-1270), Ceylonese king of the Dambadeniya dynasty. During his rule the Dambadeniyas acquired great power. The Kalinga kings, of

Parakeets include the budgerigar (*M. undulatus*, right) and the crimson rosella (*P. elegans*, left), both native to Australia.

South Indian descent, were driven off the island and an invasion from Malaysia could be resisted.

Parallax, change in the apparent position of an object due to a change in the position of the observer. Parallax in nearby objects may be observed by closing each eye in turn so that a more distant object appears to move relative to a closer one. The brain normally assembles the 2 images to produce a stereoscopic effect. If the length and direction of the line between the 2 points of apparent observation is known, parallax may be used to calculate the distance of an object. In astronomy, the parallax of a star is defined as half the greatest parallactic displacement when the star is viewed from earth at intervals of 6 months.

Paralysis, temporary or permanent loss of muscle power or control. It may consist of the inability to move a limb or part of a limb or individual muscles. Paralysis may be due to brain damage (e.g., from strokes or tumors), diseases of or damage to the spinal cord (poliomyelitis), nerve roots (slipped disk), peripheral nervous system (neuritis), or muscles (muscular dystrophy).
See also: Palsy.

Paramaribo (pop. 195,000), capital and chief port of Suriname, on the Suriname River, 17 mi (27 km) inland from the Caribbean Sea. Settled by British from Barbados in the 1630s, Paramaribo was taken over by the Dutch in 1815. Canals from that time give today's city a Dutch character. Paramaribo is an export center for bauxite, sugar, shrimp, rice, rum, molasses, and coffee.
See also: Suriname.

Paramecium, single-cell, microscopic animal (genus *Paramecium*) in the phylum Protozoa. The most complex of one-celled organisms, paramecium live in fresh water and propel themselves by the coordinated beating of minute, hairlike projections called cilia. Paramecium feed on bacteria and algae and reproduce by splitting in 2.
See also: Protozoan.

Paramedic, person who assists medical personnel. Paramedics perform routine medical procedures (X-rays, injections, blood pressure) that allow physicians to treat more critically ill patients. Emergency Medical Technician-Paramedics perform emergency procedures for car crash and heart attack victims and for illnesses of sudden occurrence. They usually travel in ambulances equipped with the appropriate medical equipment for such events and communicate with police and hospital by radio. Paramedic services were introduced by the 1960s.

Paraná (pop. 211,000), river port in northeastern Argentina, capital of Entre Ríos province, on the Paraná River. The city is primarily a shipping center for agricultural products, but also manufactures cement and glass. Founded in 1730, it was capital of Argentina, 1853-1862.
See also: Argentina.

Paraná River, southeastern South American river, formed by the confluence of the Rio Grande and the Paranaíba rivers in southeastern Brazil. A commercial artery, it flows some 2,000 mi (3,200 km) south-southwest to meet the Uruguay River in Argentina (at the head of the Río de la Plata estuary) The Paraguay River is its major tributary.

Pará nut *See:* Brazil nut.

Parapsychology, scientific evaluation of ESP (extrasensory perception) and phenomena concerned with life after death, reincarnation, etc., particularly claims to communication with souls of the dead (spiritism, or, incorrectly, spiritualism). Tests of the former have generally been inconclusive; of the latter, almost exclusively negative. But in both cases many believers hold that such phenomena cannot be subjected to laboratory evaluation. Because of the disparity among various accounts of the spirit world, parapsychology is generally treated with skepticism.
See also: Extrasensory perception; Psychical research.

Parasite, organism that is physiologically dependent on another organism, the host, from which it obtains nutrition and to which it gives nothing in return. Most parasites cannot survive if separated from their host, whom they may or may not harm. Besides the viruses (a wholly parasitic group), parasites include bacteria, flatworms, and various invertebrates.

Parathyroid gland, any of 4 small endocrine bodies behind the thyroid that regulate calcium and phosphorus metabolism. Parathyroid hormone, produced when the concentration of calcium ions in the blood is low, takes calcium from the bone and increases absorption of calcium in the intestines and kidneys. The hormone also decreases the phosphate ion concentration. An imbalance in parathormone levels leads to calcium deficiency (low levels) or bone degeneration (high levels).
See also: Gland.

Parchment, skin of sheep, goats, or calves, which is cleaned, stretched, and rubbed with pumice or chalk to make a material that can be written on, used to make drumheads, or bookbinding. Invented in the 2nd century B.C. as a substitute for papyrus, parchment was widely used until superseded by paper in the 15th century. Vellum is fine-quality parchment.
See also: Paper.

Pardon, official act of forgiveness extended to a convicted person, generally by a country's chief executive. A pardon is usually given because innocence is discovered after a conviction, but it may be used because the law was too harsh.

To a terrestrial observer a nearby star appears to shift its position among farther, relatively fixed background stars as the earth orbits the sun (1). The apparent motion, or parallax, is defined as the angle P at which the star subtends the radius of the earth's orbit. A star (2) located in the plane of the earth's orbit, or ecliptic, appears to oscillate in a straight line (3). A star that lies at a pole (4) of the ecliptic moves in a nearly circular path (5).

Experimental parapsychological research is carried out with modern equipment and under strict conditions. In this experiment, the examiner and the subject have absolutely no contact with each other (they are seated in different rooms), and thus cannot influence one another by means of — unvoluntary — movements, gestures, etc. When there is a flash of light, the person has to guess which of the five figures the examiner recorded. The answer is recorded on the subject's own machine. This system is known as the Zener cards, after the American Karl Edward Zener (1903-1964). The sequence of the figures is usually determined randomly before the experiment.

P

Paré, Ambroise (1517?-1590), French surgeon whose many achievements (e.g., using ligatures of arteries in place of cauterization, introducing the use of artificial limbs) earned him regard as a pioneer of modern surgery.

Parent, biological or social father or mother. Biological parents are those from whose egg and sperm cells the individual was produced. The genetic make-up of the parents is passed on to the offspring, resulting in various combinations of inherited physical and mental traits. Social parents, who may or may not be biological parents, are those who care for the child.

Pareto, Vilfredo (1848-1923), Italian economist and sociologist. He followed Léon Walras in applying mathematics to economic theory. His theories on governing elites, developed in *Mind and Society* (1916), influenced Benito Mussolini's fascists. *See also:* Economics.

Paria (untouchable), lowest group in the Indian caste system. The untouchables originate from groups that, according to Hindu standards, traditionally had unclean work or had a sinful life. Although legal measures have been taken to improve their situation, the untouchables can still be found in the lowest social positions.

Paris, in Greek mythology, son of Priam (king of Troy) and Hecuba. Left alone to die on Mt. Ida because his mother dreamed that she had given birth to the destroyer of Troy, the infant Paris was rescued and raised by shepherds. Years later the gods ordered Paris to judge a beauty contest between Hera, Athena, and Aphrodite. Hera promised him greatness and Athena victory in war, but he awarded the prize, the golden apple of discord, to Aphrodite, who promised to give him the most beautiful of women-Helen, wife of the Spartan king, Menelaus. Paris's abduction of Helen led to the Trojan War, in which Paris was killed. *See also:* Mythology.

Paris, Pact of *See:* Kellogg-Briand Peace Pact.

Paris, Treaty of, name given to several treaties concluded at or near Paris, France. The **Treaty of Paris, 1763**, along with the Treaty of Hubertusburg, ended the Seven Years War, including the French and Indian Wars in America. France lost its military rights in India (and thus any chance of ousting the British) and its American possessions. Britain gained Canada, Florida, and parts of Louisiana, and Spain regained Cuba and the Philippines. Freed from the French threat, American colonists stepped up the struggle for independence, which was finally confirmed by the **Treaty of Paris, 1783**, ending the Revolutionary War. U.S. boundaries were agreed upon as Canada in the north, the Mississippi in the west, and Florida (regained by Spain) in the south, and the United States won fishing rights off Newfoundland. The **Treaty of Paris, 1814**, attempted to end the Napoleonic Wars after Napoleon Bonaparte's first abdication. France under the restored Bourbon monarchy was allowed to retain its 1782 boundaries and most of its colonies. The **Treaty of Paris, 1815**, signed after Napoleon's final defeat at Waterloo, dealt with France more harshly. French boundaries were reduced to those of 1790, and France had to pay reparations and support an army of occupation for up to 5 years. The **Treaty of Paris, 1856**, ending the Crimean War, was signed by Russia, Britain, France, Turkey, and Sardinia. Designed largely to protect Turkey from Russia, it guaranteed Turkish independence, declared the Black Sea neutral, opened Danube navigation to all nations, and established Moldavia and Walachia (later Romania) as independent states under Turkish suzerainty. The **Treaty of Paris,**

When the Communards were forced to relinquish Paris, during the last week of the Commune (May 21-28, 1871), they tried to slow down the army's advance by setting fire to a number of buildings. A number of other buildings were set fire to by the army. But the persistent legend arose that it was the wives of the Communards, armed with cans of oil (in French 'pétrole', whence their name pétroleuses), who had set fire to the entire city.

1898, ended the Spanish-American War and effectively ended the Spanish empire. Cuba became independent, and the United States gained Puerto Rico, Guam, and the Philippines. After World War I the treaties of Neuilly, Saint-Germain, Sèvres, Trianon, and Versailles were concluded at the Paris Peace Conference. Treaties were also signed in Paris after World War II.

Paris, University of, France's renowned institution of higher learning. Growing out of the medieval cathedral schools of Notre Dame, it has granted master's degrees since 1170. The Sorbonne (founded 1253) became its single most famous college. Reconstituted during the Napoleonic era as a modern university, it was reorganized again in 1970 into 13 autonomous units.

Paris (city) (pop. 2,200,000), capital and largest city of France, in the north-central part of the country. World-famous for its beauty, historic importance, and social, intellectual, and cultural life, Paris is a major transportation center and France's chief industrial hub. In the city itself, tourism, fashion, and service industries predominate. Heavier industry (chiefly automobile manufacturing) is based farther out in the metropolitan area. The city, made up of 20 *arrondissements* (boroughs), is divided by the Seine River, which flows 110 mi (177 km) northwest to the English Channel; 30 city bridges span the river. Its left (southern) bank is home to government offices and much of the intellectual community. Landmarks here include the Sorbonne, the Panthéon, the Luxembourg Palace, and the well-known Latin Quarter. The right bank,

View of Paris in the direction of the Eiffel Tower, from the Arc de Triomphe de l'Etoile, built by Napoleon. The intersection of seven traffic arteries, the Place de l'Étoile, now the Place Charles de Gaulle, is the most important traffic junction in the city center.

with its fashionable streets and shops, is the site of the Louvre, the Arc de Triomphe, Sacré Coeur, and Place de la Concorde. In the middle of the Seine, on the Île de la Cité, is the Cathedral of Notre Dame de Paris and the Palais de Justice. The island was inhabited by Gauls when Caesar set up a colony at this important crossroads in 52 B.C. In the early 6th century, the Frankish King Clovis I made Paris his capital. It became a national capital in 987 when Huge Capet, count of Paris, became king of France. The city flourished during medieval times as a center of commerce and scholasticism, but suffered greatly during the Hundred Years War. Following the French Revolution (1789) much of Paris was rebuilt, most characteristically during Napoleon III's reign (1852-1870), when Georges Haussmann constructed the parks, wide avenues, and tree-lined boulevards. Growth was interrupted (1870-1871) by the Franco-Prussian War and the conflict over the Paris Commune. German occupation during World War II (1940-1944) inflicted little damage.
See also: France.

Parity, in economics, equivalence in the values of currencies or the price of goods over a period of time. If the exchange rate between the currencies of 2 countries is such that the purchasing power of the 2 currencies is equivalent, then they are said to be in parity.
See also: Economics.

Parity, in physics, symmetry between an event and its reflection in a mirror. Physicists say that parity is conserved when an event and its mirror image both satisfy identical laws of nature. In 1956, 2 Chinese physicists, Tsung Dao Lee and Chen Ning Yang conducted experiments which showed that parity is not conserved in a type of nuclear event called a weak interaction. Their work and other experiments demonstrated that conservation of parity is not a universal law of nature.
See also: Physics.

Park, David (1911-1960), U.S. painter and art teacher. Park painted human figures in a representational style. He was head of the art department at Windsor School, Boston (1936-1941) and later taught at the California School of Fine Arts, San Francisco, and the University of California.

Park, Mungo (1771-1806), Scottish explorer of West Africa. He made 2 exploratory journeys along the Gambia, upper Senegal, and Niger rivers (1795-1797 and 1805-1806), the former described in *Travels in the Interior of Africa* (1799). He drowned at Bussa during an attack by hostile Africans.

Park Chung Hee (1917-1979), President of South Korea (1963-1979). Leader of the 1961 military coup, he was later elected President 3 times. Increasingly more dictatorial, in 1972 he assumed almost unlimited power, and was a strong ally of the United States. He was assassinated by Kim Jae Kyn, director of the Korean C.I.A.

Parker, Charlie (Charles Christopher Parker, Jr.; 1920-1955), U.S. jazz musician and composer, known as Bird or Yardbird. An alto saxophonist, he and Dizzy Gillespie were the originators and leaders of the bop movement, an innovative and influential revolution in jazz.
See also: Jazz.

Parker, Dorothy (1893-1967), U.S. writer and critic. She wrote short stories, satirical verse, and newspaper columns, and was a celebrated conversationalist. Her tone is poignant, ironic, and sometimes cruelly witty and cynical. Her story collections include *Laments for the Living* (1930), *After Such Pleasures* (1933), and *Here Lies* (1939); her verse collections include *Enough Rope* (1926) and *Sunset Guns* (1939).

Parkinson's disease, or Parkinsonism, degenerative brain disorder, usually appearing after age 40, characterized by trembling lips and hands, shuffling gait, and muscular rigidity. Causes are often unknown, although in some cases the disorder is a result of carbon monoxide poisoning, influenza, encephalitis, or drugs. Because the disorder is often accompanied by depression, it is hard to measure its effects on mental capacity, which may often be impaired. Named after the English surgeon James Parkinson, who first described it in 1817, the disease is treated with the drugs L-Dopa (and carbidopa for side effects) and amantadine.

Parkinson's law, principle that in any bureaucracy 'work expands so as to fill the time available for its completion.' This humorous formulation of bureaucratic practices first appeared in C. Northcote Parkinson's *Parkinson's Law and Other Studies in Administration* (1957).

Parkman, Francis (1823-1893), U.S. historian of the frontier and of the Anglo-French struggle for North America. Despite a severe nervous affliction, his commitment to his research and writing made him a leading historian. Among his works are *The Oregon Trail* (1849), an enormously popular account of a journey made in 1846; *History of the Conspiracy of Pontiac* (2 vols.; 1851); and his chief work, *France and England in North America* (7 vols.; 1865-1892). He was also an expert horticulturalist.

Parlement, French high court of justice in Paris that operated from the Middle Ages until 1789. It had some political influence through its power of questioning the king's edicts. Membership became a hereditary privilege. There were also 12 provincial parlements. Deemed reactionary and exclusive, they were swept away in the French Revolution.

Parliament, legislative body of Great Britain, technically comprising of the monarch (sovereign in name only), the House of Lords (a relatively powerless body composed of nobles and Anglican prelates), and the 635-member House of Commons, chosen by elections. The term Parliament usually refers to the Commons, the sovereign power of the nation. They elect the prime minister and the nonpartisan speaker who

U.S. writer and critic Dorothy Parker (1893-1967).

P

presides over them. The executive head of government also comes from the Commons, and government ministers are selected from either house. The major parties of Parliament today are Labour, Conservative, Liberal Democratic, and Social Democratic. Elections must be held every 5 years, although they may be called more frequently by the prime minister. If the party in power loses its parliamentary majority on a major issue, Parliament is dissolved and new elections held. The beginnings of Parliament go back to medieval times. The Curia Regis (great council), an executive and judicial body gathered from the nobility and the church to aid the monarch, evolved into the House of Lords. Knights and burgesses were summoned to give their approval to royal acts in the 13th century. In the 17th century Parliament won legislative power over taxation and expenditures and then ultimate sovereignty as a result of the Glorious Revolution (1688). The Industrial Revolution brought demands for suffrage from the new classes it created; universal suffrage for men and women was won in the 20th century.

Parliamentary procedure (parliamentary law, parliamentary practice, rules of order), rules that govern the functioning of legislative bodies and other institutions-such as clubs, political parties, or corporations-that hold meetings that resemble those of legislatures. The most popular book on parliamentary procedure is Robert's Rules of Order, originally compiled in 1876 and frequently revised since then. In the English-speaking world, parliamentary procedure is ultimately derived from the traditions of the British Parliament.

King Edward I of England, flanked by the rulers of Scotland and Wales, conducts a session of Parliament in this medieval miniature. Although the composition of his Parliament varied greatly, Edward I helped to institutionalize the calling of knights and burgesses to Parliament.

P

Parma (pop. 167,000), city in the Emilia-Romagna region of northern Italy, capital of Parma province, on the Parma River. The city is an important junction on the Milan-Bologna rail and road route. The surrounding area is primarily agricultural and is known for the production of Parmesan cheese. Other local products include machinery and pharmaceuticals. Parma was founded by the Romans in 183 B.C.
See also: Italy.

Parmenides (b. c.515 B.C.), Greek pre-Socratic philosopher, founder of the Eleatic school. His philosophy, anchored on the proposition 'What is *is*,' denied the reality of multiplicity and change, claiming that they were illusions of the senses.
See also: Pre-Socratic philosophy.

Parmigianino, Il (also Il Parmeggianino, real name Girolamo Francesco Maria Mazzola [Mazzuoli]; 1503-1540), Italian painter, influenced by Raphael. Important representative of mannerism. Painted numerous frescos in churches in Bologna and Parma. Well-known for his portraits with long, slender figures in a clear coloring.

Parnassus, or Parnassós, mountain 8,060 ft (2,430 m) high, in central Greece, north of Delphi and the Gulf of Corinth. In ancient times Parnassas was considered sacred to

Parrots, macaws and lovebirds belong to the order *Psittaciformes*, the members of which are brightly plumaged, mainly tropical and Southern hemisphere birds. They have large heads, short necks, down-curved upper bills, and grasping feet with two toes in front and two behind. Most members of the order feed on fruit and nuts. Lories and lorikeets, however, feed on nectar, and in winter, the kea will eat animal food, scavenging or killing small prey.

Dionysus and Apollo and celebrated as the home of the Muses.

Parnell, Charles Stewart (1846-1891), Irish nationalist, leader of the Irish Home Rule movement. A member of the British Parliament from 1875, he obstructed parliamentary business, demanding attention to Irish land reform, and his supporters' agitation persuaded William Gladstone to adopt a home rule policy. His political career was ruined in 1889 when he was named correspondent in a divorce case.
See also: Ireland.

Parole, system of releasing a convict from prison before the end of a sentence. Generally, parole is granted for good behavior in prison, if the parole board considers a prisoner psychologically and socially ready to readjust to the outside world. A parolee usually must observe certain standards of conduct, stay within certain areas, and report regularly to a parole officer.

Parotid gland *See:* Saliva.

Parotitis *See:* Mumps.

Parrot, popular name for about 320 species (family Psittacidae) of brightly colored birds distributed throughout the tropics. Parrots have large heads, short necks, heavy, hooked bills, and strong feet for climbing and grasping. Popular as cage birds (especially those that learn to mimic speech), some species are parakeets, cockatoos, and macaws. Parrots range in size from the pygmy (3.5 in/8.7 cm) of the South Pacific to the Amazon parrot (40 in/100 cm) of South America.

Parrot fever *See:* Psittacosis.

Parry, Sir William Edward (1790-1855), British Arctic explorer. Parry led British naval expeditions in search of the Northwest Passage (1819, 1821, 1824); his *Voyage for the Discovery of a Northwest Passage* (1821) describes these experiences. In *Narrative of an Attempt to Reach the North Pole in Boats* (1828) he recounted his 1827 journey by ship and then by boats equipped with steel runners (to permit travel on ice), finally coming to within 500 mi (800 km) of the pole, 82°45' north latitude, a record not broken until 1876.
See also: Melville Island.

Parsec, unit of distance in astronomy, equivalent to 3.26 light-years. Nearby stars show a slight shift in position (a parallax) when observed from opposite sides of the earth's orbit. A star with a parallax of one second of arc (1/3,600 of a degree) is said to be one parsec away. Proxima Centauri, the nearest star, is somewhat less than 1 1/3 parsecs away.
See also: Astronomy.

Parsis, or Parsees, religious group centered in Bombay and northwest India, followers of Zoroastrianism. Numbering about 120,000 today, their ancestors came from Persia in the 8th century to escape Muslim persecution. The Parsis, many of whom are traders,

are among the wealthiest and best educated groups in India. They revere aspects of nature, especially fire, as manifestations of Ahura Mazdah (the divinity).
See also: Zoroastrianism.

Parsley, biennial or perennial herb (*Petroselinum crispum*) of the carrot family, native to southern Europe. Its leaves are used as seasoning and garnish, the plants and seeds for medicinal purposes.

Parsnip, carrotlike plant (*Pastinaca sativa*) native to Europe, grown for its edible, sweet-flavored, yellowish-white root.

Parsons, Talcott (1902-1979), U.S. sociologist. A professor at Harvard University (1927-1974), he advocated a structural-functional theory, a framework for classifying the characteristics of a stable social system. Works include *The Structure of Social Action* (1937), *The Social System* (1951), and *Politics and Social Structure* (1969).
See also: Sociology.

Pärt, Arvo (1935-), Estonian composer. Studied at the academy of music of Tallinn. Was initially influenced by Prokofiev and Shostakovich, but from 1964 onwards he increasingly used serial techniques, and later also collages and old polyphonic and harmonic techniques with elements from Gregorian chant and minimalism. Pärt established himself in Western Europe in 1981. His work includes three symphonies (1964, 1966, 1971), several major choral compositions, a Concerto for violin, cello and chamber orchestra (1980), *Fratres* (1980), a St. John's Passion (1981-1982), *Te Deum* (1985), *Miserere* (1989), *Beatus Petronius* (1990), *Litany* (1994) and *Pokajaanen* (1998).

Partch, Harry (1901-1974), U.S. composer who devised a special notation for his microtonal music, based on an octave divided into 43 intervals instead of the traditional 12. His works received slight public attention as they could only be performed on instruments of his own devising.

Parthenogenesis, procreation through unfertilized female reproductive cells. Can be found in plants (e.g. the dandelion), in many invertebrate animals (e.g. insects, shellfish, echinoderms and round-worms), and some vertebrate animals (e.g. chickens, turkeys and lizards). Depending on whether the egg-cell has or hasn't yet undergone a reduction division, diploid (2n) or haploid (n) individuals (respectively) develop from the egg-cell. In e.g. plant-louses and stick-insects the offspring is diploid, thus identical to their mother. Only now and then, after reduction division of the egg-cell, haploid, male individuals appear. In contrast, with e.g. bees only haploid, male offspring (drones) comes into being through parthenogenesis.
There are experimental possibilities to develop unfertilized egg-cells with the help of physical and/or chemical means for many species of animals and plants.

Parthenon (Greek, 'the virgin's place'), temple to Athena, on the Acropolis. It was

built of marble (447-432 B.C.) by the architects Ictinus and Callicrates; Phidias supervised the sculptures. The temple featured 46 Doric columns surrounding a main hall, behind which rested an inner chamber (the Parthenon proper). The main hall was divided by a Doric colonnade into a broad nave and side aisles. Sculptures of Athena's birth and her contest with Poseidon were depicted on the east and west pediments. Of the sculptures on the interior frieze, most of the originals still exist, though some (the Elgin Marbles) are in the British Museum in London. The temple became a Christian church (6th century) and later a mosque (with added minaret). It was well preserved until 1687, when a Venetian bombardment caused the explosion of gunpowder stored within it. Today the temple ruins are threatened by industrial pollution.
See also: Acropolis.

Parthia, ancient country of Asia, southeast of the Caspian Sea. The Parthian empire was established in 250 B.C., following a revolt, led by Arsace, against the Syrian empire. The Parthian empire reached its zenith under Mithradates I (171-138 B.C.) and II (123-188 B.C.). The Parthians conquered Persia and nearby lands, and their mounted archers successfully withstood Roman attacks until 38 B.C. In A.D. 226 the territory that had been under Parthian rule was taken over by Ardashir I, the founder of the Sassanid dynasty of Persia.

Particle accelerator, research tools used to accelerate electrically charged subatomic particles to high velocities. Physicists can focus the resulting particle beams to interact with othr particles or to break up atomic nuclei, in order to learn more about the fundamental nature of matter. Accelerators use electromagnetic fields to accelerate the particles in a straight line or in a circular or spiral path. The devices are rated according to the kinetic energy they impart, which is measured in electron volts (eV).
The first accelerator, designed by John Douglas Cockcroft and Ernest Thomas Walton in 1932, accelerated protons to energies of 700 keV.
The first *linear accelerator*, or *linac*, was built in 1928 by R. Widerøe. The largest linear accelerator still in operation, 2 mi long (3.2-km), at Stanford University, can accelerate electrons to energies of 20 GeV.
The first *circular accelerator, the cyclotron,* was built by E.O. Lawrence in 1931. The particles were accelerated twice in each revolution, spiraling outward and eventually shot out toward a target; however the relativistic gain in mass tended to throw them out of phase with the acceleration pulses. The solution was the *synchrocyclotron,* or *frequency modulated cyclotron,* which varies the acceleration frequencies to keep them in phase with the particles. The largest synchrocyclotron today achieves energies of more than 700 MeV.
As still higher energies continued to be sought, the *synchrotron* was developed, guiding the particles around a ring of magnets through a thin evacuated tube. The largest now operating, at the Fermi National Accelerator Laboratory in Batavia, Ill.,

achieves energies in excess of 500 GeV. The latest accelerators are *colliding-beam machines*, in which positive and negative particles circle in opposite directions. The resulting head-on collisions yield much higher effective energies than collisions with stationary targets.

Particle physics, study of subatomic particles (those particles that are smaller than atoms), including protons, neutrons, electrons, and a wide variety of much more unstable particles. Physicists now classify subatomic particles into 4 general classes. The smallest of these are the bosons, which have no mass. They include the photon, which is a packet of energy, and 8 types of gluons. The next class, the leptons, has 12 particles: the electron, which carries a negative electromagnetic charge, the positron, which is identical but carries a positive charge, 2 muons (of opposite charge), and a neutrino associated with each of these 3 pairs. The third class of particles is the mesons, which are larger in mass than the leptons. They are nuclear particles that serve to hold the nuclei of atoms together. The most massive of the 4 classes is the baryons, which include the proton, the neutron, and heavier particles called hyperons. Mesons and baryons, unlike the other 2 classes, are governed by the strong nuclear force, which is one of the 4 fundamental forces of nature (the others being gravity, electromagnetism, and the weak nuclear force). For this reason, these 2 classes of particles are sometimes grouped together under the term hadrons. Many particle physicists today subscribe to a theory first put forward in 1964 by Murray Gell-Mann and George Zweig stating that all the hedrons are ultimately composed of still more elementary particles called quarks. Particle physics studies all these various particles and the relationships and interactions among them.
See also: Atom; Boson; Lepton; Quark.

Partnership for Peace, (PfP, Partnership for Peace), initiative that was first set out at a NATO meeting in 1994. All members of the Euro-Atlantic Partnership Council (EAPC) and all participating members of the Organization for Safety and Cooperation in Europe were asked to become
'Partners for Peace'. The partnership aims to develop the armed forces of the participating countries. This will enable them to improve co-operation with the NATO. It also promotes transparency in national defense planning and military budgeting and the democratic control of national armed forces. The PfP is distinctive because the cooperation is bilateral and the degree of cooperation differs from country to country. The participating countries regard partnership as a preamble to NATO membership. In 2002, 26 countries signed the PfP Framework Document.
See also: North Atlantic Treaty Organization.

Partridge, any of several game birds distributed through Europe, Asia, and Africa. Best known is the gray, or common, partridge (*Perdix perdix*) of Europe, with a chestnut horseshoe on its breast. The true partridge belongs to the pheasant family; the name is also applied to the bobwhite, or

quail, in the northern and western parts of the United States.

Pascal, Blaise (1623-1662), French scientist and religious philosopher. A mathematical prodigy, discoverer of the properties of the cycloid, and founder of the modern theory of probability, his work also contributed to the formulation of differential calculus. In physics he pioneered hydrodynamics and fluid mechanics, discovering Pascal's Law, the basis of hydraulics. His religious thought, influenced by Jansenism and by a religious experience (1654) that led him to enter the convent of Port-Royal, emphasizes 'the reasons of the heart' over those of logic and intellect. It is expressed in his *Provincial Letters* (1656) and his posthumously published *Pensées* (1670).

The most well-known seventeenth-century apologist, Blaise Pascal, wrote a sketch of an apology in his posthumously edited *Pensées.*

Pascal's law, in fluid mechanics, states that the pressure applied to an enclosed body of fluid is transmitted equally in all directions with unchanged intensity. The application of Pascal's law may be seen in hydraulic presses, jacks, and elevators.
See also: Pascal, Blaise; Pressure.

Paschal II, or Pascal II (d.1118), pope, 1099-1118. During his reign he was involved in the investiture controversy, a power struggle to determine whether kings or popes had the right to appoint ecclesiastical authorities. The Holy Roman Emperor Henry V invaded Italy and kidnapped Paschal to force him to renounce the papal right of investiture. Paschal later repudiated the renunciation.

Pasmore, Victor (1908-1998), British painter and sculptor. Painted in neo-impressionistic style from 1936 until 1947, landscapes among other things. After 1947 his work became completely abstract, especially through his contact with Ben Nicholson. From 1950 onwards Pasmore also included concrete elements in his work, such as wood and Plexiglas, giving his work more relief. Also made three-dimensional constructions of wood, plastic, metal and glass. Aimed towards an integration of architecture, sculpture and painting.

Pasqueflower, common name for spring-flowering anemones of the buttercup family. The North American pasqueflower (*Anemone patens*) is abundant in the prairies, and

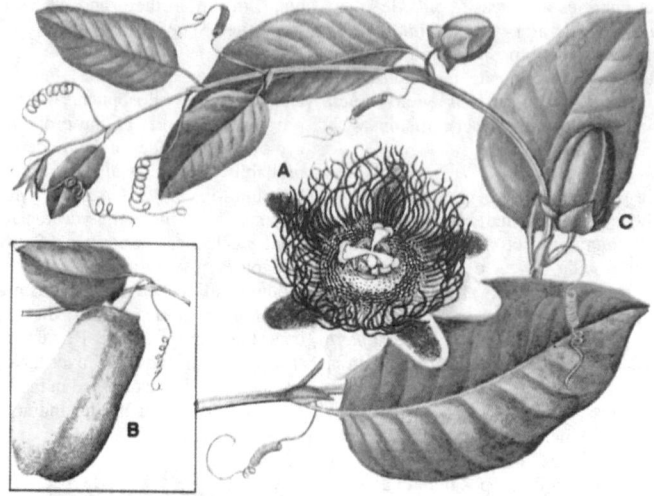

The passionflower (*P. quadrangularis*), a climbing vine of tropical America, produces fragrant, intricately formed flowers (A), which are symbolically linked with the passion of Jesus Christ. The egg-shaped, juicy fruit (B) matures from large buds (C).

P

the European pasqueflower (*A. pulsatilla*) grows in chalky pastures.

Passenger pigeon, extinct bird (*Ectopistes migratorius*) of the pigeon family, extremely common until the 19th century throughout most of North America. Highly gregarious and social birds that migrated in huge flocks, passenger pigeons fed on invertebrates, fruits, and grain, often doing extensive damage to crops. Hunted both as pests and for food, they became extinct.

Passionflower, any of a group of tropical climbing plants (genus *Passiflora*) grown for the juice of their berries and for their ornate flowers. The name is derived from the religious symbolism attributed to the flowers: the 3 stigmatas are considered to represent the Holy Trinity, while the hairy corona recalls the crown of thorns. The 5 petals and sepals represent the 10 Apostles present at the Crucifixion.

Passion play, dramatic presentation of Jesus's suffering, death, and resurrection. It was one of the popular medieval mystery plays that were performed by amateurs at religious festivals. The most famous passion play still performed is that at Oberammergau, Germany, staged every ten years since 1633.

Passover, or Pesach, major Jewish festival held for 8 days from the 14th to the 22nd of the month of Nisan (March/April). It celebrates the Israelite's escape (led by Moses) from Egypt. At the *seder* feasts on the evenings of the first 2 days, special dishes symbolize the hardships of the escape, and the story of the exodus is read from the Haggadah.
See also: Judaism.

Pasternak, Boris (1890-1960), Russian novelist, poet, and translator. His poetry *Over the Barriers* (1916) and *My Sister, Life* (1922) brought him his first successes. During the Stalinist repression of the 1930s, he stopped publishing his own work and turned to translating the works of Shakespeare and Goethe. *Doctor Zhivago*, his epic novel of 20th-century Russian histo-

ry, was denied publication in the USSR but was published in Italy (1957) to worldwide acclaim. Awarded the Nobel Prize in literature (1958), Pasternak was forced to decline it as a result of Soviet pressure. *Doctor Zhivago* was finally published in the USSR in the late 1980s, under Mikhail Gorbachev's policy of glasnost.

Pasteur, Louis (1822-1895), French microbiologist and chemist. He conducted important studies on fermentation and bacteria (which resulted in his theory that living germs spread disease). He disproved the theory of spontaneous generation and popularized the sterilization of medical equipment, which saved many lives. He discovered anthrax and rabies vaccines and developed pasteurization (the use of heat to kill germs), a process of great economic import. The Pasteur Institute (Paris) was founded in 1888 as a teaching and research center on contagious and virulent diseases.
See also: Bacteria; Fermentation.

Pasteurization, process for partially sterilizing milk, originally developed by Louis Pasteur for improving the storage qualities of wine and beer. The milk was held at 145°F (63°C) for 30 min in a vat, but today is usually held at 162°-185°F (72°-85°C) for 16 sec. Disease-producing bacteria, particu-

A ceramic platter (1673) used for the seder, celebrated at the beginning of Passover, commemorates aspects of Jewish history and tradition.

larly those causing tuberculosis, are thus destroyed with a minimum effect on the flavor of the product. Since the process destroys a majority of the harmless bacteria that sour milk, the milk's keeping properties are also improved.
See also: Pasteur, Louis.

Pastoral, literature idealizing simple shepherd life, free of the corruption of the city. Typical forms are the verse elegy, prose romance, and drama. Originating with Theocritus in the 3rd century B.C., the form was used by many ancient authors, including Vergil in his *Bucolics* (eclogues). In England, after a Renaissance revival, it was used by William Shakespeare (in *As You Like It*), Sir Philip Sidney (in *Arcadia*), and John Milton (in *Comus*).

Patagonia, dry plateau of about 300,000 sq mi (777,000 sq km) in southern Argentina, between the Andes Mountains and the Atlantic Ocean. Sheep-raising is the main activity of the few inhabitants. There are oil, iron ore, and coal deposits, as well as other untapped mineral resources.

Patchen, Kenneth (1911-1972), U.S. poet, novelist, and painter who often illustrated his own work. *The Collected Poems of Kenneth Patchen* appeared in 1969. His novels include *The Memoirs of a Shy Pornographer* (1945).

Patel, Vallabhbhai Jhaveri (1875-1950), Indian statesman, studied law in England. After his return to India he joined Gandhi's movement and was called 'Sardar' (leader) by the farmers because of his leadership qualities. In 1931 he became president of the Congress and played a big role in the independence talks with Great Britain. After India became independent in 1947, Patel was appointed vice-premier and minister of internal affairs in the first Nehru cabinet.

Patent, in law, governmental grant of the exclusive right to make, use, or sell an invention or grant others that right. The term derives from the medieval 'letters patent'-public letters by which a sovereign conferred monopolistic control of certain goods on a subject.

Patent medicine, or proprietary medicine, over-the-counter drugs that can be sold without prescription. Patent medicines include aspirin, acetaminophen, ibuprofen, mouthwash, antiseptics, and laxatives. The term 'patent' is outdated, referring to a time when the formulas for such products were kept secret. 'Proprietary' trade names of many preparations are registered, but some (like Aspirin) pass into common usage.

Pathans *See:* Pushtuns.

Pathet Lao, communist guerilla organization in Laos. After Laos became completely independent from French colonial rule in 1954, a civil war broke out between monarchists, pro-American army officers and the Pathet Lao. The civil war, which took place at the same time as the conflict between North and South Vietnam, worked out favorably for the communists. In 1973 the Pathet Lao formed a government together with the monarchists. After the fall of South Vietnam in 1975 the Pathet Lao took complete power and the country became very much influenced by Vietnam.

Pathology, study of the causes of diseases and of the changes they produce in the body. Techniques include X-rays and biopsies (removal and microscopic examination of tissue, fluid, or cells).
See also: Disease.

Pa Tjin (Ba Jin; org. Li Féi-kan; 1904-), one of the most read Chinese authors. Reached the height of his popularity in the 1930s and 1940s. Pa Tjin came into contact with radical ideas at a Western-oriented school in Czengtu. He was especially impressed by the work of Bakunin and Kropotkin. A stay in France (1927-1929) was followed by a period of great literary activity (1930-1950) during which he wrote a series of anarchistic-oriented essays and social novels in which he especially opposed the traditional family system. After 1949 he repudiated his anarchistic past and held several positions in cultural organizations of the People's Republic. He fell in disfavor during the Cultural Revolution, but was later rehabilitated.

Patmos, northernmost of the Dodecanese Islands of Greece, in the southeast Aegean Sea, near Turkey. Patmos is a barren volcanic island 13 sq mi (34 sq km) in area. Grapes, citrus fruits, olives, and cereals are grown, but the economy is dependent mainly on tourism and sponge fishing. Its 11th-century monastery contains an important library. The island was settled in ancient times by the Dorians and Ionians, and was used as a place of exile by the Romans. It was while in exile on Patmos that the apostle John is said to have written the Fourth Gospel and the Book of Revelation of the New Testament. Patmos was controlled by Turkey (1537-1912) and Italy (1912-1947) before it returned to Greek rule.

Patna (pop. 1,4 million), India, the capital of Bihar state. It is on the Ganges River in northeastern India, 290 miles (467 km) northwest of Calcutta. Patna is a commercial center for a rice-growing area. Handicrafts and processed foods are produced. Patna University, Bihar College of Engineering, Pasteur Insitute, and the Hindi Institute are here. Buried beneath Patna is the ancient city of Pataliputra, capital of the Magadha kingdom in the sixth century B.C. Patna was made capital of Bihar state in the 16th century, and again in 1912.

Paton, Alan Stewart (1903-1988), South African writer. His novel *Cry, the Beloved Country* (1948), drawing on his experience as principal of a reform school for Africans, describes apartheid. In 1953 he became president of the Liberal Party, which was banned in 1968.

Patrese, Riccardo (1954-), Italian racing driver, made his debut in 1977 in the Formula 1. He proved to be a fast and spec-

tacular driver, who was lucky more than once. Until 1985 he took part in 112 Grand Prix, winning two.

Patriarch, Old Testament title for the head of a family or tribe, especially the Israelite fathers, Abraham, Isaac, Jacob, and Jacob's sons. The title was adopted by the early Christian bishops of Constantinople, Rome, Alexandria, Jerusalem, and Antioch, and now extends to certain other sees, especially of the Eastern Orthodox churches. It implies jurisdiction over other bishops.
See also: Eastern Orthodox Church.

Patricians (Latin, 'of the fathers'), in ancient Rome, members of the aristocratic class. In the early Republic the heads of the chief families dominated political power in the Senate. The plebeians fought for equality (500-300 B.C.), until the term 'patrician' eventually became an honorary title.
See also: Rome, Ancient.

Patrick, Saint (c.385-461), Christian missionary, patron saint of Ireland. Controversy surrounds his identity, dates, and works. In the popular version he was born in Roman Britain, was captured by pagan Irish, and was enslaved for 6 years. After escaping to Gaul and studying there, he returned (432) to convert Ireland, winning spectacular success in Ulster. He founded an archiepiscopal see in Armagh (444 or 445). Author of the autobiographical *Confessions*, he died in a Christianized Ireland. His feast day is March 17.

Patterson, family of U.S. newspaper publishers and editors. **Joseph Medill Patterson** (1879-1946) was coeditor and copublisher of the *Chicago Tribune* (with Robert McCormick). He was cofounder, coeditor, and publisher of the *New York Daily News*, the largest-circulation tabloid in the United States. His sister, **Eleanor Medill Patterson** (1884-1948), published the merged *Washington Times-Herald* (1939-1948). His daughter, **Alicia Patterson** (1906-1963), founded (with her husband, Harry F. Guggenheim), published, and edited *Newsday*, which she developed into one of the largest suburban dailies in the United States.

Patterson, Floyd (1935-), American boxer, won the Golden Gloves at age sixteen and again the next year. In 1952 he also became Olympic boxing champion in the middleweight category. In the same year Patterson became a professional boxer and in 1956 won the world title in the heavyweight category. After he was beaten by Ingemar Johansson in 1959, Patterson was the first boxer to regain this title (1960). In 1962 he lost his world title to Sonny Liston.

Patton, George Smith, Jr. (1885-1945), U.S. general whose ruthlessness and tactical brilliance as a tank commander in World War II won him the nickname Old Blood and Guts. He was highly successful in North Africa and led the Third Army's liberation of France (1944) and thrust into Germany (1945).

Saint Patrick, a British bishop who had escaped from slavery in Ireland as a youth, returned to convert the heathen Irish to Christianity (National Museum of Ireland, Dublin).

P

Patzak, Julius (1898-1974), Austrian singer (lyrical tenor). Patzak initially studied composition in Vienna and worked as a conductor until 1926. In 1928 he joined the State Opera in Munich, where he stayed until 1945. After that he worked at the Vienna State Opera until 1959. He retired in 1965. Patzak was in great demand as a singer and sang for many years in venues like the Salzburg Festival. He also enjoyed a good reputation as a concert singer, excelling in Mahler's *Das Lied von der Erde* and as the Evangelist in Bach's *St. Matthew's Passion*.

Paul (1901-1964), king of Greece 1947-1964, successor to his brother, George II. He was succeeded by his son, Constantine II.
See also: Greece.

Paul, name of 6 Italian popes. **Paul III** (Alessandro Farnese; 1468-1549), pope (1534-1549), encouraged the first major reforms of the Catholic Reformation, recognized the Jesuit order, and convened the Council of Trent (1545). **Paul IV** (Giovanni Caraffa; 1476-1559), reigned (1555-1559), increased the powers of the Inquisition, enforced segregation of the Jews in Rome, and introduced strict censorship. His fanatical nepotism created widespread hostility. **Paul V** (Camillo Borghese; 1552-1621), pope (1605-1621), clashed with the Venetian Republic over papal jurisdiction; a member of the Borghese family, he too was notorious for nepotism. **Paul VI** (Giovanni Montini; 1897-1978), pope (1963-1978), continued the modernizing reforms of his predecessor, John XXIII, including vernacularization of the liturgy, relaxing of rules regarding fasting and abstinence, and reversal of some restrictions on intermarriage. He also reaffirmed the church's ban on contraception. The first pope to travel outside Italy in more than 150 years, Paul made a pilgrimage to the Holy Land (1964), followed by trips to India, the United States, Africa, and Southeast Asia. He also helped to forge limited doctrinal agreements with Lutherans and Anglicans. Though criticized by both

P

liberals and traditionalists, Paul was widely respected for his spirituality, intellect, and compassion.

Paul, Alice (1885-1977), U.S. leader of the women's movement for equal rights. A founder of the National Woman's Party (1917) and the World Woman's Party (1938), she was active in the struggle for passage of the 19th Amendment to the U.S. Constitution, giving women the right to vote. After it was ratified (1920), she worked for the Equal Rights Amendment, first submitted to Congress in 1923.

Paul, Jean (1763-1825), German author. His satirically humourous novels such as *Hesperus* (1795) and *Titan* (1803) made him important in the German Romantic movement. Rambling in structure and rich in imagery, they sometimes make difficult reading because of Paul's fondess for coining words or using odd ones. Paul also wrote verse and philosophical works. An advocate of freedom, he supported the French Revolution and a free press.

Paul, Saint (d.A.D.64? or 67?), apostle to the Gentiles. The son of a Roman citizen, Paul was a zealous Jew who was active in the persecution of Christians until a vision of Christ seen on the road to Damascus made him a fervent convert to the new faith. After being baptized, Paul began preaching. He went on extensive missionary journeys (A.D.47-59) to Cyprus, Asia Minor, and Greece. Returning to Jerusalem, he was violently attacked by the Jews and imprisoned for 2 years. Claiming his Roman citizen's right, he was transferred (A.D. 60) to Rome, where he was imprisoned again. His final fate is uncertain. His tomb and shrine are in Rome at St. Paul's Without the Walls. His life is recorded in the Acts of the Apostles and the Pauline Epistles. The epistles attributed to Paul are Romans, Corinthians, Galatians, Philippians, Colossians, First Thessalonians, and Philemons; also generally accepted to

The apostle Paul was the most important preacher in the early days of the Church (mosaic in Ravenna).

be his work are Ephesians and Second Thessalonians.
See also: New Testament.

Pauli, Wolfgang (1900-1958), Austrian-born U.S. physicist awarded the 1945 Nobel Prize in physics for his discovery of the exclusion principle, which stated that no 2 electrons in any atom could be in the same quantum state. He also postulated the existence of the neutrino before it was actually observed.
See also: Neutrino.

Pauling, Linus Carl (1901-1994), U.S. chemist and pacifist, awarded the 1954 Nobel Prize in chemistry for his work on chemical bonding and the 1962 Nobel Peace Prize for his support of the campaign for nuclear disarmament. Other contributions include his work in molecular biology, his support in advancing the use of chemotherapy for mental diseases, and the use of Vitamin C in the treatment of the common cold.
See also: Quantum mechanics.

Pautow (Baotau, Baotou; pop. 3,000,000), city in China in Inner Mongolia, on the Huang He river. Processing of agricultural produce (sugarcane, cotton) from the surrounding area; iron, steel, machine, chemical and cement industries. Industrialization developed when the city was part of the Meng-chiang province (1937-1945) which was dominated by Japan.

Pavarotti, Luciano (1935-), Italian tenor. A leading singer internationally since his Italian debut (1961) as Rodolfo in *La Bohème*, he has performed regularly at New York City's Metropolitan Opera (N.Y.C.) since his 1968 debut there. He is noted for his interpretations of the works of Puccini, Verdi, Donizetti, and Bellini. He is considered to be one of the greatest tenors of all times and is often compared with Caruso, Domingo, and Carreras.

Pavese, Cesare (1908-1950), Italian writer, started his career as a translator. His translation of Moby Dick has become a classic. By also introducing Contemporary American writers into Italy Pavese made an important contribution to the renewal of Italian literature. The central themes in his work are: the failure of interpersonal relationships, loneliness and alienation. Works include: *The House on the Hill* (1949), *The Moon and the Bonfire* (1950) and his posthumously published diary from 1935-1950 *Il Mestiere di Vivere*(1954), a revealing document about this writer who was tortured by melancholy, fears and obsessions.

Pavlova, Anna (1881-1931), Russian ballerina, considered the greatest of her time. After her debut (1899) in St. Petersburg, she danced with Diaghilev's Ballets Russes before forming her own company. She was famed for her interpretations of *The Dying Swan*, choreographed for her by Michel Fokine, and of the title role in *Giselle*.
See also: Ballet.

Pavlov, Ivan Petrovich (1849-1936), Russian physiologist and experimental psycholo-

gist. For his studies of the physiology of the digestive system of dogs, he received the 1904 Nobel Prize in physiology or medicine. Continued experiments with dogs, this time involving the stimulation of gastric secretions, led to his discovery of the conditioned reflex (physiological reaction to environ-

Ivan P. Pavlov (right) (1849-1936) in his laboratory.

mental stimuli), which in turn influenced the development of behaviorism. His major work was *Conditioned Reflexes* (1926).
See also: Physiology; Psychology.

Pawnee, Native American tribe of Caddoan linguistic stock who inhabited river valleys of what is now Nebraska and Kansas (16th-19th centuries). They had an elaborate religion, including a supreme being, and for a time performed human sacrifice to their god of vegetation. They lived by farming and buffalo hunting. By 1876 they had ceded all their land to the U.S. government and were settled on a reservation in Oklahoma.

Pawpaw, or papaw, tree (*Asimina triloba*) of the custard-apple family, whose fruits have a creamy edible pulp. Most pawpaws are grown in tropical countries, but the North American pawpaw thrives along streams in many parts of the eastern United States.

Anna Pavlova, a Russian dancer, was one of the most gifted and highly acclaimed ballerinas of the 20th century.

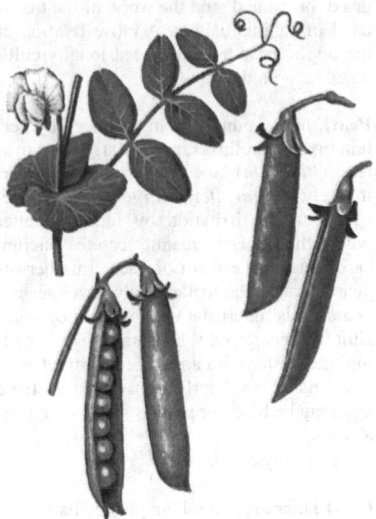

The garden pea (*P. sativum*) has been cultivated for centuries for its edible green seeds, which grow in pods. Gregor Mendel conducted experiments with pea plants that led to the science of genetics.

Payne, John Howard (1791-1852), U.S. playwright and actor. He wrote his first play, *Julia, or, The Wanderer*, at age 14. Payne lived in London and Paris 1813-1832, during which time he adapted many French plays and collaborated with Washington Irving. After his return to the United States (1832), he was an advocate for Native American rights. He also served as U.S. consul in Tunisia (1842-1845, 1851-1852). Payne's most important works include *Brutus, or, The Fall of Tarquin* (1818) and *Clari, or, The Maid of Milan* (1823), for which he wrote the words to the song 'Home, Sweet Home.'

Payton, Walter (1954-   ), U.S. football player. Known for his powerful running and ability to break tackles, he holds the National Football League (NFL) record for yards rushed in a single game with 275 (1977) and career rushing yards (16,726). Payton played for the Chicago Bears (1975-1987) of the NFL, and led them to a Super Bowl victory (1985).

Paz, Octavio (1914-1998), Mexican poet and essayist who received the 1990 Nobel Prize for literature. His writings are known for their synthesis of many influences, including Aztec and Mexican culture, French surrealism, and Tantric and Buddhist thought. Paz traveled to Spain as a left-wing activist in the Spanish Civil War (1930s) and then to Paris (1940s). He lived in the United States during the 1940s, returning in the 1970s to teach in universities. He also traveled to India and Japan (1952) and became Mexican ambassador to India (1962-1968). His writings include the poetry collections *Liberty Under Oath* (1960) and *The Collected Poems of Octavio Paz, 1957-1987* (1987) and the essay collections *The Labyrinth of Solitude* (1950) and *One Earth, Four or Five Worlds* (1985).

PCB *See:* Polychlorinated biphenyl.

Pea, herbaceous annual leguminous plant of the pulse family cultivated mainly for its edible seeds. Peas have white or purple flowers and a many-seeded fruit pod, or legume, which is high in protein. The garden pea (*Pisum sativum*) is native to Middle Asia and is now widely cultivated in North America, Europe, and Asia. The field pea (var. *arvense*) provides split peas. The sweet pea and chick-pea are of different genera.

Peace, condition that exists when nations or other groups are not fighting; the treaty that ends a war; harmony; tranquility.

Peace Corps, agency of the U.S. government established to help raise living standards in developing countries and to promote international friendship and understanding. Peace Corps projects, ranging from farm assistance to nursing instruction, are established at the request of the host country. Its volunteers normally serve for 2 years. The program was initiated by President John F. Kennedy in 1961 and transferred to ACTION, the agency coordinating federal volunteer programs in 1971.

Peace Enforcement, (also: peace operation), military operation carried out by the United Nations (UN) or a regional peace organization, consisting of UN members. There are three different peace operations: peace keeping, peace enforcement and preventive deployment. Peace keeping aims at conflict control with the consent of disputing parties. A UN peace authority separates the parties and supervises the compliance with the armistice. An example of a peace keeping operation can be found in Cyprus. When the disputing parties cannot reach an agreement, peace enforcement takes place (for example in Bosnia and Hercegovina). Peace enforcing instruments can be non-military (enforcing an embargo) or military (an armed intervention). Preventive deployment is used to deter violence in a zone of potential conflict where tension is rising among parties. A peace operation is put into action when the UN Security Council decides it is time to send soldiers and after it has formulated the tasks and authorities of the UN peace authority in a resolution.
See also: United Nations; Peace.

Peace River, largest branch of the Mackenzie River, in northwestern Alberta and eastern British Columbia, Canada. The river, formed at Williston Lake from the Finlay and Parsnip rivers, crosses the Rocky Mountains north and east and joins the Slave River at Lake Athabasca. It is about 1,000 mi (1,600 km) long. It was explored in 1792-1793 by Sir Alexander Mackenzie.

Peach, tree (*Prunus persica*) of the rose family; also, its fuzzy-skinned fruit. Native to China, it is now cultivated in warmer regions throughout the world (notably in California). There are several thousand varieties, divided into freestone or clingstone types according to the ease with which the flesh comes away from the pit. The nectarine is a smooth-skinned variety of peach.

Peach moth (*Grapholitha molesta*), small brown moth whose larvae are major fruit tree pests. Each year the adult deposits eggs on the leaves of peach and other fruit trees. The larvae feed on new twigs and on fruit. Growers attempt to control the peach moth with natural predators (parasitic wasps and flies) and with chemical sprays such as malathion.

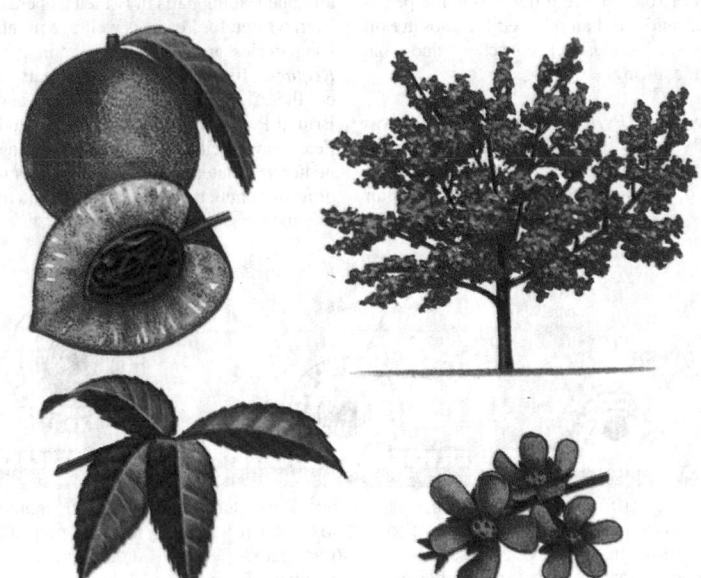

The peach tree (*P. persica*) is grown as an ornamental because of its beautiful flowers and in orchards for its fruit. The peach is second in popularity to the apple as a temperate-climate dessert fruit.

P

P

Peach State *See:* Georgia.

Peacock, or peafowl, large ground bird of the pheasant family, native to east Asia; there are 2 genera, *Pavo* and *Afropavo*. The common peacock male (*P. cristatus*) has a train of up to 150 colorful tail feathers, which he displays to the peahen during courtship.

Peacock, Thomas Love (1785-1866), English novelist and poet, a satirist of contemporary intellectual trends. He was a close friend of Percy Bysshe Shelley and an able administrator in the East India Company. His best poetry is contained in his novels, which he described as comic romances. They include *Headlong Hall* (1816), *Nightmare Abbey* (1818), and *Crotchet Castle* (1831).

Peale, 19th century American family of painters, of which the most important members were: Charles Willson Peale (1741-1827), studied with Benjamin West in London and was one of the best-known portrait painters of his time, e.g. of George Washington (Metropolitan Museum of Art, New York). Founded the first museum in the US (the Peale Gallery in Philadelphia; 1784); James Peale (1749-1831), Charles Willson's brother and educated by him, was a well-known miniaturist. The children and grandchildren of both brothers were also painters.

Peale, Norman Vincent (1898-1893), U.S. clergyman. He is well known through his popular writings, particularly *The Power of Positive Thinking* (1952), and his radio and television broadcasts. Since 1932 he has been pastor of the Marble Collegiate Reformed Church, New York City.

Peanut, also known as goober or groundnut (*Arachis hypogaea*), low, bushy, leguminous plant cultivated in tropical and subtropical regions. The 'nut,' the most popular in the United States, is a protein-rich fruit containing 1-3 seeds, and is produced when the yellow flowers grow down into the ground to mature after pollination. Peanuts are eaten fresh or roasted, are ground to make peanut butter, and yield an oil used for cooking oil, margarine, industrial purposes, and soap manufacturing.

Pear, tree (*Pyrus communis*) of the rose family; also, the oval-shaped, soft-fleshed fruit produced by the tree. Bartlett, Bosc, Anjou, and Seckel are among the fruit's hundreds of varieties. Pears are eaten fresh, dried, or canned, and the wood of the tree is used in cabinetmaking. A close relation of the apple, pear trees are occasionally cultivated as ornamentals.

Pearl, hard, rounded gem produced by certain bivalve mollusks, particularly pearl oysters (*Pinctada*) and the freshwater pearl mussel (*Margaritifera margaritifera*). In response to an irritation by foreign matter within the shell, the mantle secretes calcium carbonate in the form of nacre (mother-of-pearl) around the irritant body. Over several years, this encrustation forms the pearl. Cultured pearls may be obtained by 'seeding' the oyster with an artificial irritant such as a small bead. Pearls are variable in shape and may be black or pink as well as the usual white.
See also: Oyster.

Pearl Harbor, natural landlocked harbor on Oahu island, Hawaii. Of great strategic importance, it is best known as the target of the Japanese surprise bombing of the U.S. Pacific fleet on Dec. 7, 1941. Damaged or sunk were 19 ships; 188 planes were destroyed on the ground at Wheeler Field. The raid caused more than 2,200 casualties with negligible losses to the Japanese and brought the United States into World War II. Today it is a national historic landmark.
See also: Hawaii; World War II.

Pears, Peter Neville Luard (1910-1986), British singer (tenor). Pears initially worked as an organist (from 1928), studied from 1933 to 1934 at the Royal College of Music in London and started his singing career in 1935 in the BBC Choir. From 1936 to 1939 he was a member of the New English Singers, in 1943 he joined Sadler's Wells Opera Company and in 1946 the English Opera Group. He made his debut as an opera singer in *The Tales of Hoffman*. After that he sang many opera parts, like that of the duke in *Rigoletto*, Tamino in *The Magic Flute* and Ferrando in *Cosi fan Tutte*. From 1938 onwards he formed a duo with Benjamin Britten (piano) which became world-famous and went on numerous concert tours. Nearly all male leading parts in Britten's operas have been written for Pears, as well as a number of song cycles and the tenor part in the *War Requiem*. Together with Britten, Pears founded the Aldeburgh Festival (1948) and the Britten-Pears School for advanced students. Pears gave recitals of Old English songs together with lutenist Julian Bream. His renditions of Schubert are also famous, and underline the versatility of this great artist.

Pearson, Karl (1857-1936), English mathematician best known for his pioneering work on statistics (e.g., devising the chi-square test), *The Grammar of Science* (1892), and his contributions to the philosophy of mathematics. He was also an early worker in the field of eugenics.
See also: Statistics.

Pearson, Lester Bowles (1897-1972), Canadian diplomat, prime minister (1963-68), and winner of the 1957 Nobel Peace Prize for his mediation in the Suez crisis (1956). In 1928 he joined the Department of External Affairs, becoming the first secretary, and in 1945 he was appointed ambassador to the United States. As secretary of state (1948-1957) he made notable contributions in the creation of the UN and NATO. In 1958 he became the Liberal leader. After resigning as prime minister, he headed the World Bank commission, which produced the Pearson Report on developing countries.
See also: Canada.

Peary, Robert Edwin (1856-1920), U.S. Arctic explorer who discovered the North Pole. He entered the U.S. Navy in 1881 and first journeyed to the interior of Greenland in 1886. On leaves of absence from the Navy he led a series of exploratory expeditions to Greenland that culminated in his reaching the North Pole on Apr. 6, 1909. Peary's books, including *The North Pole* (1910) and *Secrets of Polar Travel* (1917), give an account of his extraordinary stamina and courage. In recent years his claim of reaching the North Pole has been challenged by some scholars.
See also: North Pole.

Peasants' War, popular revolt (1524-1526) that began in southwestern Germany and spread to many parts of Germany and Austria. The social turmoil created by the Reformation and the decay of Feudalism seems to have been at the root of the discontent. The movement collapsed when Martin Luther denounced the uprising and supported its ruthless suppression.

Peat, partially decayed plant material found in layers, usually in marshy areas. It is composed mainly of the peat mosses sphagnum and hypnum, but also of sedges, tress, etc. Under the right geological conditions, peat forms coal. It is used as a mulch and burned for domestic heating.

Peat moss, moss (genus *Sphagnum*) that grows and accumulates on the surface of freshwater marshes in Canada, northern Europe, and Siberia. Peat moss grows up to 20 in (50 cm) high, forming a spongy mat without true roots. Its ability to absorb and hold water makes it commercially useful as a mulch (soil covering to prevent drying). It is also used as a growth medium for mushrooms and orchids and as a packing material.

Pecan, nut-bearing tree (*Carya illinoensis*) of the walnut family native to North America, a member of the genus that also includes the hickory. It has furrowed bark and groups of long, thin leaflets. The tree, which

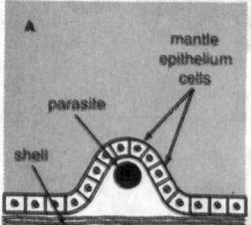

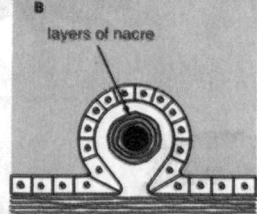

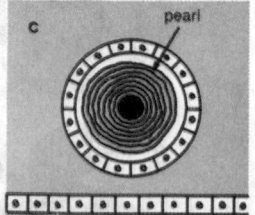

A pearl begins to form when foreign matter (A) enters the mantle, or tissue, under a pearl oyster's shell. Epithelium cells on the tissue surface secrete successive layers (B) of lustrous calcium carbonate (nacre) and conchiolin (a cementing material) to form a pearl (C) around the intruder.

grows up to 180 ft (55 m) high, takes 10 years to become a prolific nut-bearer. Nuts are harvested from both wild and orchard pecan trees. The tree is also valued for its wood, which is used for flooring and furniture.

Peccary, pig-like mammal of the southwestern United States and northern South America, inhabiting bushy thickets or forests. There are two species within the family Tayassuidae, the collared peccary (*Pecari tajacu*) and white-lipped peccary (*Tayassu pecari*). Both are long-legged, with thick bristly hair and an erectile mane along the back.

Peck, (Eldred) Gregory (1916-), American actor working in the movies since 1943, usually playing a decent, reliable middle-class American. Films include *Spellbound* (1945), *Duel in the Sun* (1946), *Roman Holiday* (1953), *The man in the Gray Flannel Suit* (1956), *To Kill a Mockingbird* (1963), *I Walk the Line* (1970), *MacArthur* (1977), *The Boys from Brazil* (1978), *The Sea Wolves* (1980), *Old Gringo* (1988).

Pecos River, originates in New Mexico's Sangre de Cristo mountains and flows southeast more than 800 mi (1,300 km) through New Mexico and Texas. The longest tributary of the Rio Grande, it is controlled by several dams of the Carlsbad Reclamation Project and drains nearly 35,000 sq mi (91,000 sq km).

Pectin, substance found in many fruits, especially apples. Pectin is available in tablet form as a digestive aid.

Pederson, Charles John (1904-1989), U.S. chemist. Pederson, Donald J. Cram, and Jean-Marie Lehn won the 1987 Nobel Prize for chemistry for their discovery of simple molecular structures that mimic the behavior of the complex molecules produced by living cells. Pederson was a researcher in the laboratories of du Pont, 1927-1969.
See also: Chemistry.

Pediatrics, branch of medicine concerned with the care of children. This care starts with the newborn, especially with premature, babies for whom intensive care is required. An important aspect is the recognition and treatment of congenital diseases or disease acquired during development of the embryo or fetus. Pediatricians also deal with infectious disease, growth or development disorders, mental retardation, diabetes, asthma, and epilepsy.

Pedro, two emperors of Brazil. **Pedro I** (1798-1834) was the son of John VI of Portugal, who fled with his family to Brazil when Napoleon Bonaparte invaded his homeland in 1807. On his father's return to Portugal in 1821, Pedro remained in Brazil, declared Brazilian independence (1822), and was crowned emperor. His subsequent mismanagement led to his abdication (1831). He was succeeded by his son **Pedro II** (1825-1891), declared of age in 1840, who gave Brazil over half a century of stable government. But his liberal policies, espe-

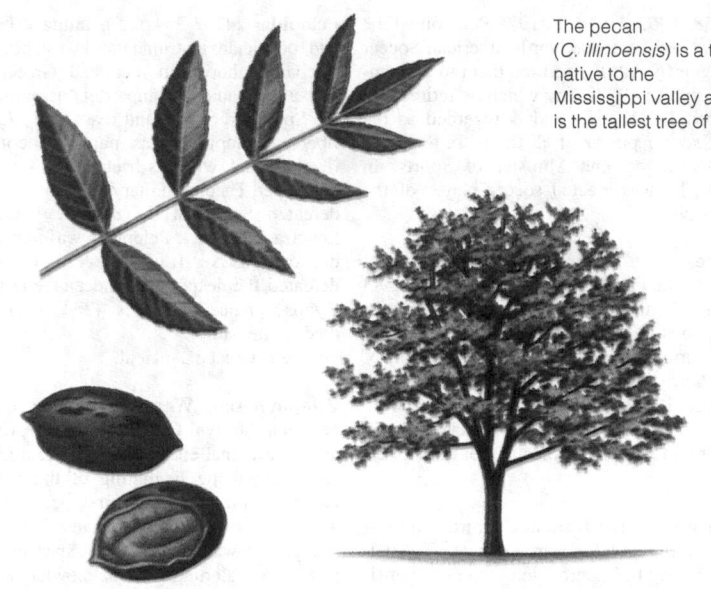

The pecan (*C. illinoensis*) is a tree native to the Mississippi valley and is the tallest tree of the *hickory* genus. The pecan's thin-shelled nut is prized for its rich, sweet taste.

cially his attempt to abolish slavery, alienated the Brazilian landowning classes. They organized a bloodless coup in 1889 and made Brazil a republic.
See also: Brazil.

Peel, Sir Robert (1788-1850), English statesman. As home secretary in the 1820s Peel set up the British police force (thereafter called Bobbies) and sponsored the Catholic Emancipation Act (1829). Though he opposed the Reform Bill (1832), became more progressive, and after a brief term (1834-1835) as prime minister, he organized the new Conservative Party out of the old Tory Party, aided by young politicians like Benjamin Disraeli and William Gladstone. His second term in office (1841-1846) saw the introduction of an income tax, banking controls, and Irish land reforms, and the further removal of discriminatory laws against Roman Catholics. The repeal of the Corn Laws (1846) led to an era of free trade but caused a party split that led to his resignation.
See also: Conservative Party; United Kingdom.

Peeper *See:* Tree frog.

Peewit *See:* Lapwing.

Pegasus, in Greek mythology, the winged horse, represented by a large constellation of stars whose most famous feature is the Great Square, picked out by four bright stars, one at each corner, appearing high in the sky during fall in the Northern Hemisphere. Springing from the blood of the beheaded Medusa, Pegasus caused the fountain of Muses to flow and was associated with poetry. The hero Bellerophon rode Pegasus but was thrown to his death when he tried to reach heaven.
See also: Mythology.

Pegmatite *See:* Beryl; Feldspar.

Pei, I.M. (1917-), Chinese-born U.S. architect of public buildings and urban complexes, e.g., the Mile High Center in Denver,

Place Ville Marie in Montreal, the John Hancock Tower in Boston, and the National Gallery's East Wing in Washington, D.C. Most are noted for their simplicity and environmental harmony. In the early 1990s his pyramid-shaped addition of the Louvre (Paris) was completed.

Peiping *See:* Beijing.

Peirce, Charles Sanders (1839-1914), U.S. philosopher, a pioneer of pragmatism. He is also known for his work on the logic of relations, theory of signs, and other contributions in logic and the philosophy of science. He wrote no comprehensive work but published numerous articles in philosophical journals, some of which were collected posthumously in *Chance, Love and Logic* (1925).
See also: Pragmatism.

Peking *See:* Beijing.

Pekingese, toy dog of Chinese origin with a flat, wrinkled face, protruding eyes, and bowed legs. The Pekingese has a long, thick coat of any color with longer hair around the neck and on the tail. It is 6-9 in (15-23 cm) at the shoulder and weighs 6-10 lbs (2.7-4.5 kg). Sacred to Chinese nobility from the 8th century, the breed reached Europe in the 1860s.

Peking man (*Sinanthropus pekinensis*), prehistoric upright human of the species *Homo erectus* whose first fossil remains were discovered near Beijing, China (1929). Intermediate between Java man (*Pithecanthropus erectus*) and Neanderthal man, Peking man lived between 500,000 and 250,000 years ago, had less brain development than modern humans, and reached about 5 ft (1.5 m) in height. Peking man used fire and developed stone tools.
See also: Prehistoric people.

Pelé (Edson Arantes do Nascimento; 1940-), Brazilian soccer player. He was known for his precise passing and shooting and led the Brazilian national team to 3 World Cup titles

(1958, 1962, 1970). In 1975 Pelé joined the N.Y. Cosmos of the North American Soccer League (N.A.S.L.) and led them to a championship in 1977, after which he retired. He scored 1,281 goals and is regarded as the best soccer player of all times. In the early 1990s he became Minister of Sports. In 2000, he was elected soccer player of the century.

Pelée, active volcano in Martinique, an island in the French West Indies. Rising 4,583 ft (1,397 m) above sea level, it had minor eruptions in 1702 and 1851. In 1902 a major eruption occurred, destroying the port of St. Pierre and killing approximately 38,000 people. Between 1929 and 1932 there were several milder eruptions. A volcano observatory on top of the volcano monitors its activity.

Pelican, large aquatic bird (genus *Pelecanus*) found in warm climates. The pelican's long bill is provided with an expansible pouch attached to the lower mandible, used not for storage, but simply as a catching apparatus, a scoop-net. Pelicans are social birds, breeding in large colonies. Most species also fish in groups, swimming together, herding the fish in horseshoe formation. All are fine fliers.

Brown Pelican (*P. occidentalis*). Southern North America, Central and South America. Length: 49 in (125 cm).

Pelican flower (*Aristolochia grandiflora*), woody flowering vine of the birthwort family Aristolochiaceae. The Pelican flower grows wild, has heart-shaped leaves, and the yellow-green blossoms may grow as wide as 18 in (46 cm) across.

Pellagra, vitamin deficiency disease (due to lack of niacin), often found in maize- or millet-dependent populations. A dermatitis, initially resembling sunburn but followed by thickening, scaling, and pigmentation, is characteristic; internal epithelium is affected (sore tongue, diarrhea). Confusion, delirium, hallucination, and ultimately dementia may ensue.

Pelopidas (410?-364 B.C.), military leader and politician instrumental in establishing Theban authority in mainland Greece. In 379 B.C. he and 6 compatriots assassinated the Spartan dictators and reasserted Theban liberty. Pelopidas was named boeotarch (leader), and, with his friend Epaminondas, developed Theban military supremacy. They defeated Sparta at the decisive battle of Leuctra (371 B.C.). Pelopidas was ambassador to Artaxerxes II of Persia (367 B.C.) and defeated the despot Alexander of Pherae at Cynoscephalae, Thessaly (364 B.C.), but died in the battle.
See also: Greece, Ancient.

Peloponnesian War (431-404 B.C.), war between the rival Greek city-states, Athens and Sparta, that ended Athenian dominance and marked the beginning of the end of Greek civilization. The first phase (431-421) was inconclusive because Athenian sea power was matched by Spartan land power. A stalemate was acknowledged by the Peace of Nicias, named for the third Athenian leader in the war, following Pericles and Cleon. His leadership was then challenged by Alcibiades, who initiated the second and decisive phase of the conflict (418-404). In an attack on Syracuse in 413, the Athenians suffered a major defeat. The Spartans, with Persian aid, built up a powerful fleet under the leadership of Lysander, who blockaded Athens and forced the final surrender.
See also: Athens; Greece, Ancient; Sparta.

Peloponnesus, peninsula forming the southern part of the Greek mainland, linked with the north by the Isthmus of Corinth. It is mostly mountainous, but its fertile lowlands provide wheat, tobacco, and fruit crops. Its largest city and port is Patras. In ancient times it was the center of the Mycenaean civilization and later was dominated by Sparta in the southeast.
See also: Greece.

Pelvis, lowest part of the trunk, bounded by the pelvic bones and in continuity with the abdomen. The principal contents are the bladder and lower gastro-intestinal tract (rectum) and reproductive organs, particularly in females the uterus, ovaries, fallopian tubes, and vagina. The pelvic floor is a powerful muscular layer that supports the pelvic and abdominal contents and is important in urinary and fetal continence. The pelvic bones articulate with the legs at the hip joints.
See also: Human body.

Pemmican, concentrated food, used by Native Americans on journeys, consisting of buffalo meat, venison, or fish, dried and ground to paste, then mixed with fat and dried fruit and packed in hide bags. Hunters and expeditions still use a beef, suet, and raisin version of pemmican.

Penal colony, overseas settlement in which convicts were isolated from society. The forced labor that was part of their punishment was often used for colonial development. All colonial powers had penal colonies, as had Russia in Siberia. Britain

transported large numbers of convicts to the American colonies and to Australia.

Penck, A.R (real name Ralf Winkler; 1939-), German painter. Forerunner of the New Expressionism. His work is conspicuous for its express primitivism and balances on the border of figuration and abstraction. His symbols refer to complex processes or theories.

PEN Club, an international literary society, founded in London on 5 October 1921, with the aim of uniting all writers to stimulate peace and friendship. The P stands for poets and playwrights, the E for essayists and editors, and the N for novelists. The first chairman was John Galsworthy, who induced Anatole France to found a PEN Club in Paris so the idea could be introduced in the continent. In 1923 the first International PEN Congress took place in London. During the fifth congress (Brussels, 1927) the Charter was passed which states among other things that literature should be freely exchanged between peoples, that censure is fundamentally wrong and that PEN members are committed to improve international relations and to ban race, class and cultural hatreds. The PEN Club comprises about eighty centers and over eight thousand members.

Penderecki, Krzysztof (1933-), Polish composer. His innovative works used such unorthodox sounds as sawing and typing, scraping instruments, and hissing singers and include *Threnody for the Victims of Hiroshima* (1960), *St. Luke Passion* (1965), and *Credo* (1997-1998).

Pendulum, rigid body mounted on a fixed horizontal axis that is free to rotate under the influence of gravity. Many types of pendulum exist, the most common consisting of a large weight (the bob) supported at the end of a light string or bar. An idealized simple pendulum, with a string of negligible weight and length, l, the weight of its bob concentrated at a point, and a small swing amplitude, executes simple harmonic motion. The time, T, for a complete swing (to and fro) is given by Huygens' formula $T=2\pi\sqrt{l/g}$, depending only on the string length and the local value of the gravitational acceleration, g. Actual physical or compound pendulums approximate this behavior if they have a small angle of swing. They are used for measuring absolute values of g or its variation with geographical position and as control elements in clocks (Huygens, 1673).
See also: Foucault, Jean Bernard Leon; Galileo Galilei.

Penelope, in Greek mythology, wife of Odysseus and symbol of faithfulness and domestic virtue. In Homer's *Odyssey*, Penelope is besieged by suitors during her husband's long absence. Wishing to remain faithful to Odysseus, she refuses to remarry until she can weave her father-in-law's shroud, but she unravels her work each night. Eventually Odysseus returns, and they are reunited.
See also: Mythology.

P'eng Chen (Peng Zhen; 1899-1997), Chinese politician, held key positions in the party committee of the Chinese Communist Party and the highest organs of the national government until the Cultural Revolution (1966). P'eng came into contact with radical views at an early age and joined the CCP in 1926. During the Chinese-Japanese war he led the Central Party school in Jen-an, the provisional 'capital' of the Chinese communists; he was one of the main party ideologists. After 1949 he made a career for himself in the party as well as the government and had an increasing influence on foreign policy. From 1951 onwards he was mayor of Beijing. In 1966 he was one of the first top officials to be attacked and 'cleansed' by the Red Guards. He was relieved of his duties and banished to the countryside. In 1978 he was allowed to join the Central Committee of the CCP; in 1982 he became chairman of the People's Congress. He remained influential after his retirement in 1988.

P'eng-hu *See:* Pescadores.

P'eng P'ai (1896-1929), Chinese communist leader, one of the first to propagate an agricultural revolution. P'eng played a pivotal role in the political mobilization of the farmers in the Haifeng region. In 1927 this activity led to the proclamation of the 'Hai-loefeng-soviet', which was chaired by P'eng. After several months, however, this soviet was destroyed by nationalist troops. P'eng fled to Shanghai, but was betrayed and was executed by order of the authorities (1929). Since then he has been one of the most important martyrs of Chinese communism.

Penguin, the most highly specialized of all aquatic birds, with 17 species in the order Sphenisciformes, restricted to the southern hemisphere. Completely flightless, the wings are reduced to flippers for 'flying' through the water. Ungainly on land, penguins only leave the water to breed. The nest is usually a skimpy affair, emperor and king penguins brood their single eggs on their feet, covering them with only a flap of skin. Most species nest in colonies, some with as many as 500,000 members. Penguins are long-lived birds: the yellow-eyed penguin may live for 20 years or more.

Penicillin, substance produced by a class of fungi that interferes with cell wall production by bacteria and was one of the first, and remains among the most useful, antibiotics. The property was noted by A. Fleming in 1928, and production of penicillin for medical use was started by E.B. Chain and H.W. Florey in 1940. Staphylococcus, streptococcus, and the bacteria causing the venereal diseases of gonorrhea and syphilis are among the bacteria sensitive to natural penicillin, while bacilli negative to Gram's stain, which cause urinary tract infection, septicemia, etc., are destroyed by semisynthetic penicillins like ampicillin, oxacillin, and methicillin.
See also: Antibiotic; Fleming, Sir Alexander.

Peninsular War (1808-1814), part of the Napoleonic Wars, in which the French, fighting against the British, Portuguese, and

Spanish, were driven out of the Iberian Peninsula. To increase his security in Europe, Napoleon sent General Andoche Junot to occupy Portugal (1807), and in 1808 dispatched Joachim Murat to occupy his ally, Spain. The Spanish and the Portuguese soon rebelled, and, with the aid of the British under Arthur Wellesley (later duke of Wellington), the French were driven out of Portugal (1809). In the long struggle that followed, the British, aided by Portuguese and Spanish guerrillas, gradually gained the upper hand, despite many reverses. By 1813 the French forces in Spain had been defeated, and Wellesley invaded southern France. The war ended on Napoleon's abdication.
See also: Napoleonic Wars.

Peninsula State *See:* Florida.

Penis, male reproductive organ for introducing sperm and semen into the female vagina and uterus; its urethra also carries urine from the bladder. The penis is made of connective tissues and specialized blood vessels which become engorged with blood in sexual arousal and which cause the penis to become stiff and erect; this facilitates the intromission of semen in sexual intercourse. A protective fold, the foreskin, covers the top and is often removed for religious or medical reasons in circumcision.
The penis has a fixed root situated in the urogenital triangle of the perineum and a free shaft. At the root of the corpora cavernosa diverge to be attached to the boney structure of the pelvis. The corpus spongiosum expands to form the bulb of the penis. The skin of the shaft of the penis forms a fold, the prepuce, which projects from a sulcus to cover the glans. The skin of the penis is thin, distensible, devoid of fat, and closely attached to the underlying fascia. On one end it is continuous with the skin of the abdominal wall, and the scrotum and peritoneum.
See also: Reproduction.

Penn, William (1644-1718), English Quaker, advocate of religious tolerance, and founder of Pennsylvania. He wrote numer-

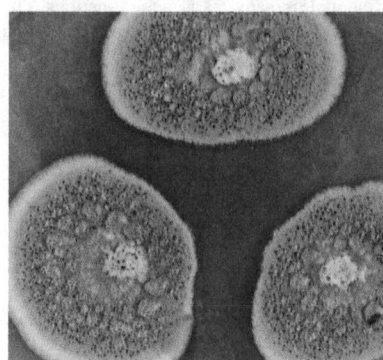

Penicillium chrysogenum is a penicillin-producing brush fungus. The penicillin is excreted by the fungus, in order to prevent the development of bacteria and other fungi in its vicinity. The material is now frequently being used in medicine and it is, together with *P. notatum*, cultivated in large quantities.

A breeding colony of the king penguin (*Aptenodytes patagonia*) in the south of Georgia. Within the colony, each pair of parents has its own small territory. Breeding together in large numbers renders the penguins with protection from the cold, as well as greater safety for their brown young.

ous tracts on Quaker beliefs and was several times imprisoned for his nonconformity. In 1681, he and 11 others bought the rights to eastern New Jersey, and he received a vast province on the west bank of Delaware River in settlement of a debt owed by Charles II to Penn's father. Thousands of European Quakers emigrated there in search of religious and political freedom. In 1682 Penn visited the colony and witnessed the fulfillment of his plans for the city of Philadelphia. He returned in 1699 to revise the constitution.
See also: Quakers.

Pennsylvania (Keystone State; pop. 12,0 million), state in the Middle Atlantic region of eastern United States; bordered by Lake Erie, New York, New Jersey, Delaware, Maryland, West Virginia, West Virginia, and Ohio. Pennsylvania's major rivers are the Allegheny, Ohio, Monongahela, Susquehanna, Schuylkill, and Delaware. Forests cover about three-fifths of the state. Pennsylvania's climate is humid, with warm summers and cold winters. Principal cities are Philadelphia, Pittsburgh, and Erie. The capital is Harrisburg.
Manufacturing is the mainstay of Pennsylvania's economy. Chief manufactured products are processed foods, chemicals, machinery, electrical equipment, fabricated metal products, and primary metals (mainly steel). Chief livestock produce are milk and beef cattle; chief crops are corn and hay. Chief mining products are coal, natural gas, and limestone. Tourism and other service industries also are important. In recent years, Pennsylvania has moved toward newer technologies and service industries.
Algonquin and Iroquois Indians were living in the area when English explorer Henry Hudson arrived in 1609. Swedes built the first permanent European settlement in 1643, near present-day Philadelphia. The Dutch took control of the area in 1655, but lost it to the British in 1664. In 1681, it was granted to William Penn, an English Quaker. Pennsylvania became one of Britain's 13 American colonies. The Declaration of

William Penn (1644-1718).

P

Independence and the Constitution were signed in Philadelphia, which was the nation's capital from 1790 to 1800.

Pennyroyal (*Mentha pulegium*), any of 4 species of low-growing herb of the mint family Labiatae native to Europe, Asia, and North America. Pennyroyal has purple flowers on prostrate stems. The oval leaves are cultivated for their oil, used in medicine, perfume, and insect repellents.

Penology *See:* Criminology.

Penone, Giuseppe (1947-), Italian visual artist, from 1969 onwards deals with the manipulation of growth and the relation between man and nature. He artificially stunted the growth of trees and influenced the form of e.g. potatoes in the soil by inserting objects. In *Alberi* (1969) he cut away trees' annual rings to lay bare the growth process. The physical contact of the body with the material became visible in the imprint of his fingers in the clay of terracotta vases and in the photographic magnifications of his skin. The mythical image of man made of clay, water and air plays a role here. In the 1990s he made sculptures of branches that change into transparent crystal.

Pension, regular payment received after retirement from employment because of age or disability, from the government under Social Security programs, or from private employers, or both. Pensions were originally allowances made by royalty, nobility, or wealthy individuals to those who served them well, or to artists and writers. The establishment of pension plans for all employees of businesses and other organizations did not begin until the late 19th century.
See also: Social security.

Penstemon *See:* Beardtongue.

Pentagon, The, five-sided building in Arlington, Va., that houses the U.S. Department of Defense, built in 1941-1943. The largest office building in the world, it consists of five concentric pentagons covering a total area of 34 acres.

Pentagon Papers, 2.5-million-word, top-secret history of U.S. involvement in Indochina from 1945 to 1968, compiled by order of Secretary of Defense Robert S. McNamara, and leaked by Daniel Ellsberg, a former government researcher, to the *New York Times*. A court order secured by the Justice Department barring publication was overturned by the U.S. Supreme Court in June 1971. Later attempts to prosecute Ellsberg were thrown out of court because evidence against him was obtained by wiretaps and other illegal means (May 1973).

Pentateuch (Greek, 'five books'), the first five books of the Old Testament: Genesis, Exodus, Leviticus, Numbers, and Deuteronomy. They were traditionally assigned to Moses, but are now regarded as a compilation of four or more documents dating from the 9th to the 5th centuries B.C. and distinguished by style and theological bias.
See also: Old Testament.

The peony (*P. officinalis*) has spectacular flowers. Its seeds once were used in herbal teas to ward off nightmares.

Pentathlon, track and field competition that consists of 5 events. The ancient Greek contest included jumping, racing, wrestling, discus, and javelin. The modern pentathlon, part of the Summer Olympic Games since 1924, consists of horseback riding, shooting, fencing, swimming, and cross-country running.

Pentecost (Greek, '50th'), Jewish and Christian festivals. The Jewish Pentecost, called Shavuot, celebrated on the 50th day after Passover, is a harvest feast. The Christian Pentecost (Whitsunday in England), the 50th day inclusively after Easter, commemorates the descent of the Holy Spirit upon the Apostles, marking the birth of the Christian Church.

Pentecostalism, Protestant fundamentalist and revivalist movement that emphasizes holiness and spiritual power as initiated by an experience ('baptism in the Spirit') in which the recipient 'speaks in tongues.' The Pentecostal churches base their distinctive doctrines and practice of charismata on New Testament teachings and accounts of the bestowal of the Holy Spirit. Pentecostalism began c.1906 and spread rapidly; it is now influential in many major denominations. The largest Pentecostal churches in the United States are the Assemblies of God and the United Pentecostal Church.
See also: Protestantism.

Pentothal *See:* Thiopental.

Penzias, Arno Allan (1933-), German-born U.S. physicist who shared (with Robert Wilson) the 1978 Nobel Prize in physics for discovering cosmic microwave radiation emanating from outside of the galaxy, providing evidence for the big bang theory of the origins of the universe.

Peonage, form of coercive servitude by which a laborer (*peon*) works off debts-often inescapable and life-long-to a creditor-master. In Spanish America, where it was most prevalent, and in the southern states of the United States (in a modified form as share-cropping), peonage did not end until the 20th century.

Peony, cultivated member of the buttercup family (genus *Paeonia*) with large showy blossoms. Most peonies are herbaceous plants that sprout new stems each year, but the tree peony (*P. suffricosa*) has a woody trunk that grows to 5 ft (1.5 m).

Pepin the Short (c.714-768), first Carolinian king of the Franks, who succeeded on the deposition (751) of Childeric, the last of the Merovingian kings. He was the younger son of Charles Martel and father of Charlemagne. In return for papal recognition he helped to establish the temporal power of the papacy.
See also: Carolingian; Charlemagne.

Pepper (*Capsicum frutescens*), woody plant of the family Solanaceae; also, its edible fruit. Commercial garden, or bell, peppers are grown in warm regions of the United States. Red peppers are widely distributed and have been cultivated since pre-Incan times. They include the mild peppers grown and dried for paprika and pungent Chili peppers. Garden peppers are also marketed as unripe green peppers.

Pepper, pungent spice obtained from the black pepper (*Piper nigrum*) plant, a woody climbing vine of the family Piperaceae native to Java. The unripened berries of the plant are dried and ground to make the black pepper common in every household; white pepper is made from the ripened berries of the same plant.

The pepper (*P. nigrum*), native to Java, is a climbing vine that bears fruit on stalks. The dried fruit is a highly valued spice.

Peppermint (*Mentha piperita*), wild herb of the family Labiatae whose leaves contain an oil widely used for flavoring. Menthol, derivative, is used in medicines.

Peppertree (*Schinus molle* and *S. terebinthifolius*), tropical ornamental tree of the cashew family Anacardiaceae. It bears yellow-white flowers in clusters and red berries that are used medicinally. The long thin leaves store a volatile oil. The peppertree grows to about 50 ft (15 m).

Pepsin, enzyme secreted by glands in the walls of the stomach to break down and digest protein.
See also: Enzyme.

P

Peptide, compound containing from 2 to as many as 50 amino acids linked through the amino group of one acid and the carboxyl group of the other. The linkage is termed a peptide bond. Peptides containing 2 amino acids are called dipeptides; with 3, tripeptides, and so on; those with many amino acids are polypeptides.

Pepys, Samuel (1633-1703), English diarist. Although he was a successful reforming naval administrator and president of the Royal Society (1684-1685), it is his talent in recording contemporary affairs and the events in his own private life for which he is famed today. His diary, written in cipher (1660-1669) was not decoded and published until 1825.

Pequot, Native Americans of the Algonquian language group who lived in southern New England. Their murder of a colonial trader by whom they had been mistreated led to the Pequot War (1637), the first major European massacre of Native Americans in North America, in which almost the entire tribe was slaughtered or enslaved. The Pequot were resettled (1655) on a Connecticut reservation.

Perahia, Murray (1947-), American pianist and conductor. Perahia (of Sephardic-Jewish descent) studied piano, composition and conducting at the Mannes College in New York. After his graduation (1966) he studied with the Polish maestro Mieczyslaw Horszowski for a considerable period. He made his piano debut in Carnegie Hall in 1968, but his international breakthrough came in 1972, when he won first prize in the Leeds Piano Competition. He has received many awards since. His recordings of the complete piano concertos of Mozart, which he plays and conducts, have become renowned. Perahia is reputed to be the only pianist never to have made a mistake: his precision is fabulous.

Perak (Mal.: tin; pop. 1,880,000), Malaysian state on the Thai border; 8,112 sq mi (21,004 sq km). Capital: Ipoh. Largest quantities of tin in the country, with mines in the Kinta valley (silver and gold). Agriculture includes rice, oil palms, pineapple, timber and rubber tree cultivation; also fishing. Naval base. Investments in industry and tourism due to falling tin profits. After the Portuguese had taken the kingdom of Malakka in 1511, the Chinese, the Dutch and the British also became interested in Perak. In 1826 the British gained control of the coastal areas and in 1874 they appointed a resident. The Perak war (1874-1876) followed some measures the first resident had proclaimed; after that, residents cooperated more with local leaders. In 1896 Perak joined the Federation of Malaysian States, a British protectorate.

Percentage, literally by the hundred, numerical computation indicating the ratio of a given number to a total number when the total number is compared to 100, shown by the symbol %. One hundred percent of something is all of it; 1 percent of something is one hundredth part of it. To find what per-

The diary of British writer and administrator Samuel Pepys (1633-1703), which, for security reasons, was written in secret code, gives a lively account of life in his time. This portrait, painted by John Hayls in 1666, can be seen at the National Portrait Gallery in London.

centage a number is of another, divide the number being compared by the number it is compared to, and multiply the quotient by 100. Percentages are commonly used to express interest rates, scientific data, statistics, market and production figures, and taxes.
See also: Fraction.

Perception, recognition or identification of something. External perception relies on the senses, internal perception, on the consciousness. Some psychologists hold that perception need not be conscious; in particular, subliminal perception involves reaction of the unconscious to external stimuli and its subsequent influencing of the conscious.
See also: Senses.

Perch, freshwater fish of the family Percidae, often having colorful striped bodies. They live in slow-flowing rivers and lakes and feed on other fish. The smallest perch is little more than 1 in (2.5 cm) long. The largest are the walleyes or pike perch which are fished commercially on the Great Lakes. Yellow perch is particularly tasty. It breeds so prolifically that it may sometimes crowd out other fish and even outrun the supply of food.

Percussion instrument, musical instrument from which sound is produced by striking. These are divided into 2 main classes: idiophones, (e.g., bells, castanets, cymbals) and gongs, whose wood or metal substance vibrates to produce sound, and membranophones, chiefly drums and tambourines, in which sound is produced by vibrating a stretched skin. Although the celesta, triangle, xylophone, and glockenspiel can be classed as percussion instruments, the term commonly denotes those instruments used for rhythmic effect.

Percy, Walker (1916-1990), American novelist. Percy studied medicine and made his debut in 1961 met *The Moviegoer* (awarded the National Book Award). *The Last*

Gentleman (1966), *Love in the Ruins* (1971), *Lancelot* (1976), *The Second Coming* (1980) and *The Thanatos Syndrome* (1987) followed. His novels are set in the South of the United States and have higher middle class protagonists who are somewhat alienated from the world. Roman Catholicism also plays an important role. Characteristic is the way in which the modern-world conflict between spiritual depreciation and the old Roman Catholic world view is expressed in a detached yet poetic style. Percy was one of the most important exponents of the literature of the Southern states of the U.S. since William Faulkner.

Perec, Georges (1936-1982), French writer. Lost both his parents during WW II and, with them, access to their language and traditions. Main theme in his work is the search for his own identity. His first novel, *Les choses* (1965), was awarded the Prix Renaudot. His language is often playful; in *La disparition* (A Void; 1969) the letter e is not used, while in *Les revenentes* (1972) the e is the only vowel used. A highlight in his body of work is *La vie mode d'emploi* (Life: a User's Manual; 1978), for which he was awarded the Prix Médicis and in 1996 the literary critics' Mekka award. Other novels include *W ou le souvenir d'enfance* (W or the Remembrance of Childhood; 1975), *Je me souviens* (1977), *Epithalames* (1981).

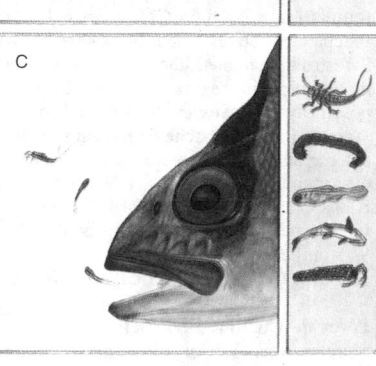

The diet of the European Perch (*P. fluviatilis*) changes with age. A young perch feeds mostly on small invertebrates, while young adults eat fish (including young perch). When adults become very large, they become isolated from the shoal and they revert to a diet of invertebrates and dead fish.
A. Perch fry
B. Adult, shoal-living perch
C. Old, solitary perch

Peregrine falcon *See:* Falcon.

Perelman, S.J. (1904-1979), U.S. humorous writer noted for his collaboration as screenwriter on several Marx Brothers' films, humorous books like *The Rising Gorge* (1961), and many articles that appeared in *The New Yorker.*

Perennial, any plant that continues to grow for more than two years. Trees and shrubs are perennials whose woody stems thicken with age. The herbaceous perennials, such as the peony and daffodil, have stems that die down each winter and regrow in the spring from underground perennating organs, such as tubers and bulbs.

Peres, Shimon (1923-), Israeli politician. Emmigrated to Palestine in 1934. He has held several political and ministerial offices since 1969. He became Minister of Foreign Affairs in Rabin's cabinet in 1992, holding a key position in the negotiations with the PLO that led to a peace agreement on the Palestinian authority in the occupied areas. In 1994, Peres, Rabin and PLO leader Arafat were awarded the Nobel Peace Prize. Peres was also important to the ongoing agreement, known as Oslo 2 (1995). He became Prime Minister after Rabin's assassination (1995-1996). In 1999, he became Minister for Regional Cooperation and in 2001 Minister of Foreign Affairs.
See also: Israel; Rabin, Yitzhak; Arafat, Yasir; Palestine Liberation Organization.

Perestroika (Russian: restructuring), name of the reform policy pursued by president and party leader Mikhail Gorbachev (1931-) from 1985 onwards in the Soviet Union. Perestroika is aimed at reforming the rigid and impenetrable Soviet society, in which the Communist party had always played a dominant role, into a new society. Perestroika was introduced to solve problems (especially economic stagnation and technological disadvantage) that could not be solved in the old situation. Perestroika led to the initially hesitant adoption of principles of Western market economy, free speech and-to a increasingly larger extent-free elections. Economically, Perestroika initially led to a deterioration of the situation. While the old planned economy was collapsing, the market economy was not yet functioning. Another unintended effect of Perestroika was the growing nationalism in several republics of the Soviet Union. This ultimately led to the disintegration of the Soviet Union in December 1991 and the foundation of the Commonwealth of Independent States (CIS). In Eastern Europe Perestroika enabled the dismantlement of the Communist regimes that had been imposed by the Soviet Union and of the Warsaw Pact. Gorbachev's radical policy of détente also paved the way for far-reaching disarmament agreements (INF, CSE and START) and led at the end of 1990 to the official proclamation of the end of the Cold War in the Paris charter.
See also: Gorbachev, Mikhail Sergeyevich.

Pérez de Cuéllar, Javier (1920-), former secretary general of the United Nations (1982-1991), succeeded by Boutros Boutros Ghali. As a Peruvian diplomat, he represented Peru as ambassador to the USSR (1969-1971) and to the United Nations (1971-1975). Since 1992 director of the Republican National Bank in New York. He became Prime Minister of Peru in 2001.
See also: United Nations.

Pérez Galdós, Benito (1843-1920), Spanish novelist who avowed his liberal beliefs in various newspapers and magazines and actively took part in political life. He gained national fame and in 1897 he was admitted into the Spanish Academy. Pérez Galdós made his debut with *La fontana de oro* (1870), a novel set during the government of Ferdinand VII (1814-1833). In the same period Galdós wrote the novels *La sombra* (1870), *El audaz* (1871), *Doña Perfecta* (1876), the first novel set in his own time, *Gloria* (1877), *La familia de León Roch* (Leon Roch; 1878) and *Marianela* (1878). In these novels Galdós denounced over and over the disastrous effects of religious fanaticism; he also dealt with the contrast between the old, dogmatic and superstitious Spain and the new liberal and revolutionary Spain. In 1873 Galdós started working on the novel cycle *Episodios nacionales*. This gigantic work comprises 46 volumes and deals with Spanish history between 1805 (the battle of Trafalgar) and 1874 (the restoration after the First Spanish Republic). The novel *Fortunata y Jacinta* (1887) is considered his masterpiece.

Performance, 1) Form of art originated in 1965, in which the artist performs planned actions with the help of video, air, music, etc. The audience does not participate. Performances are often recorded on video or photos.
2) In linguistics, performance is used to indicate language achievements as opposed to competence, i.e. pure linguistic skills. Especially in young children performance is not a pure reflection of competence, because factors like a limited short term memory cause mistakes that cannot be blamed on an inadequate linguistic competence.

Perfume, blend of substances made from plant oils and synthetic materials that produce a pleasant odor. Perfumes were used in ancient times as incense in religious rites, in medicines, and later for adornment. Today they are utilized in cosmetics, toilet waters, detergents, soaps, and polishes. A main source of perfumes is the essential oils extracted from parts of plants, e.g., the flowers of the rose, the leaves of lavender, cinnamon from bark, and pine from wood. The development of synthetic perfumes began in the 19th century. There are now a number of synthetic chemicals with flowerlike fragrances.

Pergamum, ancient capital of Mysia in Asia Minor, now western Turkey. An independent kingdom from 282 B.C. and a sovereign monarchy from 262 B.C., Pergamum was Hellenistic in culture and orientation. It sided with Rome under the Attalid kings (263-133 B.C.) and received large holdings in Asia Minor as a reward. Pergamum achieved its peak as a center of art and learning during the rule of Eumenes II (197-159 B.C.). Its public buildings, particularly its library, were among the greatest in the Greek world. Eumenes's successor, Attalus II, doubted his heirs' ability to maintain Pergaman liberty and at his death (133 B.C.), he willed the kingdom to Rome. Pergamum was famed for the manufacture of textiles, parchment, perfumes, tiles, and bricks. It was a seat of early Christianity.

Pergolesi, Giovanni Battista (1710-1736), Italian opera composer famed for his comic intermezzo *The Maid as Mistress* (1733). He also composed serious opera and religious music, such as the *Mass in F* (1734) and *Stabat Mater* (1736).
See also: Opera.

Pericles (c.495-429 B.C.), Athenian general and statesman. A strong critic of the conservative and aristocratic council, he obtained (461) the ostracism of Cimon and became supreme leader of the Athenian democracy. The years 462-454 saw the furthering of that democracy, with salaried state offices and supremacy of the assembly. Pericles's expansionist foreign policy led to a defeat of Persia (449), truce with Sparta (445), and the transformation of the Delian League into an Athenian empire. The peace of 445-431 was the height of Athenian culture under his rule. The Parthenon and Propylaea were both built at Pericles's request. One of the instigators of the Peloponnesian War, he was deposed but re-elected in 429; his death in a plague soon after may have lost Athens the war.
See also: Athens; Peloponnesian War.

Under Pericles, leader of the city-state of Athens , the system of direct democracy (meaning direct — and not representative — government by the people) briefly flourished. After Pericles' leadership, the Athenian Empire began its rapid decline. This marble bust of the great Greek politician is probably a Roman copy of an original Greek bronze bust from the 5th century B.C., ascribed to Kresilas. It can be seen at the Vatican Museum in Rome.

Peridot, transparent green olivine of gemstone quality. Deposits of the mineral occur on Saint John's Island in the Red Sea, Burma, and the southwest United States. Most peridots used in jewelry are faceted.

Perigee *See:* Orbit.

Periodic table, table of the elements listed in order of increasing atomic number, arranged in rows and columns to illustrate periodic similarities and trends in physical and chemical properties. In 1869 Dmitri Mendeleev published the first fairly complete periodic table, which was later revised by Henry Moseley. The numbers and arrangement of the electrons in the atom are responsible for the periodicity of properties; hence the atomic number is the basis of ordering. Each row, or period, of the table contains elements that have the same number of electron shells. The number of electrons in these shells equals the element's atomic number; these numbers increase from left to right within each period. The elements are arranged in vertical columns, or groups, containing elements of similar atomic structure and properties, with regular gradation of properties down each group. The longer groups, with members in the first three (short) periods, are known as the main group; they are usually numbered IA to VIIA, and 0 for the noble or inert gases. The remaining groups, the transition elements, are numbered IIIB to VIII, IB, and IIB. The elements in group IA are called The alkali metals; in group IIA, the alkaline-earth metals; and in group VIIA, the halogens.
See also: Mendeleev, Dmitri Ivanovich.

Periodontitis, or *pyorrhea alveolaris*, disease of the gums and bones surrounding the teeth. Caused by inadequate hygiene or nutrition, periodontitis is symptomized by inflamed, bleeding, or receding gums and loose teeth. It may be treated by plaque removal or oral surgery.
See also: Dentistry.

Peripatetic philosophy, method of teaching philosophy attributed to the ancient Greek philosopher Aristotle. The word *peripatetic* is derived from the Greek term for walking. This refers to Aristotle's practice of strolling with his students under the portico of his school in Athens, the Lyceum, as he gave his lectures.
See also: Aristotle.

Peritonitis, inflammation of the peritoneum (abdominal lining), usually caused by bacterial infection or chemical irritation of peritoneum when internal organs become diseased (as with appendicitis) or when gastrointestinal tract contents escape (as with a perforated peptic ulcer). Characteristic pain, sometimes with shock, fever, and temporary cessation of bowel activity, is common. Urgent treatment of the cause is required, often with surgery; antibiotics may also be needed.

Periwinkle, any of a genus (*Littorina*) of edible snails found in northern Europe and on the Atlantic coast of the United States. The periwinkle has a thick, spiral shell that

During the Permian Period, the Appalachian Mountains began to rise, and the climates became cooler and more diverse. The North American landscape contained regions of red desert sand, swamps of black and gray mud, and restricted sea areas. In fact, many regions of North America and western Europe still have red sediment deposits (red beds), characteristic of Permian geology. Many traces of these environments can be found in the Lower Permian deposits of central Texas. Lower Permian plants include *Sigillaria* (1), a treelike relative of the club mosses;

Medullosa (2), a seed fern; and several forms of *Calamites* (3, 4) and other horsetail genera (5). The reptiles include the plant-eating *Edaphosaurus* (6) and the carnivorous *Dimetrodon* (7), both pelycosaurs, which measured up to 11 ft (3.5 m) in length. The amphibians include the reptilelike *Seymouria* (8), about 24 in (60 cm) long; the fish-eating *Eryops* (9), with a barrel-shaped body that could reach 7 ft (2.1 m) in length; and the mud-dwelling *Diplocaulus* (10), whose thick skull was shaped like an arrowhead.

ranges in color from grayish-brown to black. It feeds on algae and seaweed.

Perjury, willful false statement made under oath during judicial or administrative proceedings. As a criminal offense perjury is usually a felony punishable by imprisonment or a substantial fine. Subornation to perjury, the act of getting someone else to lie under oath, is also punishable as a crime.
See also: Felony.

Perkins, Anthony (1932-1992), American actor. Perkins became known for his roles as a lanky, nervous, neurotic young man, of which the role of Norman Bates in *Psycho* (1960) become the most famous. He played the same role in *Psycho II* (1983) and *Psycho III* (1986). The latter he also directed. His other films include *Fear Strikes Out* (1957), *Aimez-vous Brahms?* (1961), *Le procès* (1963), *Catch 22* (1970), *Crimes of Passion* (1984) en *Edge of Sanity* (1988). He was also a successful stage actor.

Perlis (pop. 184,000), Malaysian state on the Thai border and the Andaman Sea; 307 sq mi (795 sq km). Capital: Kangar. Cultivation of rice and, more recently, sugarcane and mangos. Also cement production, tin winning and fishing. The area is connected by rail with Thailand via Padang Besar; a new port is being built in Kuala Perlis. Thanks to this Perlis will profit from the 'growth triangle', the cooperation with Thailand and Northern Sumatra. Until 1821 part of the Kedah state. In 1841 Thailand made the area into a sultanate. In 1909 it came under British protection, but was annexed by Thailand from 1943 until 1945. In 1948 it joined the Federation of Malaysia, the precursor of the present Malaysian state.

Perlman, Itzhak (1945-), U.S.-Israeli violinist. Although partly crippled by polio in childhood, he quickly became an accomplished musician, performing publicly from the age of 10. He made his professional New York debut in 1963 and won the Leventritt Competition in 1964. Known for his tone and technical excellence, and supported professionally by violinist Isaac Stern, he has become one of the world's leading violin soloists. His many recordings include works of the standard repertoire as well as Scott Joplin rags. He has also premiered many new works, including concertos by Earl Kim and Robert Starer.

Perm (pop. 1,094,000) City in Russia, on the Kama River near the Ural Mountains, about 700 miles (1,130 km) east of Moscow. Perm is within the Urals industrial region and is an important manufacturing and transportation center. The city has a state university, a symphony orchestra, and an opera and ballet company. Perm was settled in the 16th century and became a regional administrative center. During and after World War II, industrialization and population growth were rapid. Perm was called Molotov between 1940 and 1957.

Permafrost, permanently frozen ground, typical of the treeless plains of Siberia, though common throughout polar regions.

Permalloy, alloy that may be temporarily magnetized by electric current. Developed by G.W. Elmen, an engineer for Western Electric Company (1916), permalloy is an important component in transformers. It is made of nickel and iron.

Permian, last period of the Paleozoic era, stretching between c.280 and 230 million years ago.

Permutations and combinations, mathematical term for ways of counting out, ar-

P

P

ranging, and choosing objects in a group. A permutation is simply a way in which the elements of a set can be ordered. For instance, a set of 3 objects-say the numbers 1, 2, and 3-can be arranged in 6 different ways: 123, 132, 231, 213, 312, and 321. Each of these is a permutation. A combination is a choice of a certain number of elements from a larger set, without regard to the order of the elements. For instance, given the same set-1, 2, and 3-we may be asked to pick 2 out of the 3 numbers. Here there are 3 possibilities: 1 and 2, 1 and 3, 2 and 3. In other words, there are 3 different ways of picking 2 elements out of a set of 3 elements. Each different way is a combination. The techniques of permutations and combinations are of central importance in problems of probability and statistics.

Perón, Eva Duarte de (1919-1952), popularly known as Evita, second wife of Argentina's President Juan Perón. A powerful presence in the politics of Argentina, she ran the ministry of labor in her husband's first government (beginning in 1946). She attempted to run for the vice presidency (1951), but leading Argentine military officers blocked her bid for that position. Her background was humble-she was an actress from a poor family. She died of cancer in 1952.
See also: Argentina.

Perón, Juan Domingo (1895-1974), president of Argentina (1946-1955, 1973-1974) as head of an army clique, he helped overthrow Ramón Castillo in 1943. He won union loyalty as secretary of labor. Elected president (after police intervention), he began with his second wife Eva (1919-1952) a program of industrialization and social reforms. Church and army opposition to corruption and repression forced him into exile. Peronist influence survived, however; he returned in 1973 and was reelected president. He served until his death and was succeeded by his third wife, Isabel.
See also: Argentina.

Perpetual motion machine, concept of a machine that would work continuously without external interference, or at least with 100% efficiency. Perpetual motion machines of the first kind do work without energy being supplied, they are disallowed by the first law of thermodynamics. Those of the second kind take heat from a reservoir (such as the ocean) and convert it wholly into work, although energy is conserved, they are disallowed by the second law of thermodynamics. Those of the third kind do no work merely continuing in motion forever; they are not achievable, because some energy is always dissipated-as heat by friction, for example. However, electric current flowing in a superconducting ring continues undiminished indefinitely and is in a sense a perpetual motion machine of the third kind.
See also: Thermodynamics.

Perrault, name of two French brothers. **Claude Perrault** (1613-1688), architect, scientist, and physician, is remembered for his buildings, notably the colonnade of the Louvre (1667-1670), and the Paris

Observatory (1667-1672), and for his translation of the works of Vitruvius (1673). **Charles Perrault** (1628-1703), poet, fairytale writer, and belle lettrist, is best known for his *Comtes de ma mére l'Oye* (Tales of Mother Goose; 1697), which includes 'Little Red Riding Hood,' 'Cinderella,' 'Puss in Boots.'
See also: Mother Goose.

Perret, Auguste (1874-1954), French architect known for his use of reinforced concrete in housing projects (Paris, 1903), in the Théâtre des Champs Élysées (1913), and in the church of Notre-Dame, Le Raincy (1922-1923).
See also: Architecture.

Perrot, Joseph (Jules) (1810-1882), French dancer and choreographer, trained by Auguste Vestris. Made his debut with the Paris Opéra (1830). One of the greatest dancers of his time. Initially partner of Marie Taglioni. Later danced with Carlotta Grisi, for whom he created, together with Jean Coralli, the ballet *Giselle* (premiere 1841, m. Adolphe Adam).

Perry, name of two U.S. brothers who became distinguished naval officers. **Oliver Hazard Perry** (1785-1819), became a hero of the War of 1812. After assembling a fleet of nine ships at Erie, Pa., he defeated six British warships on Sep. 10, 1813, off Put-in-Bay, Ohio, the Battle of Lake Erie. He announced his victory in the famous message, 'We have met the enemy and they are ours.' **Matthew Calbraith Perry** (1794-1858) was instrumental in opening Japan to the U.S. and world trade. He commanded the first U.S. steam warship, the *Fulton II* (1838) and led U.S. naval forces suppressing the slave trade; he also fought in the Mexican War. In 1853 Commodore Perry took four vessels into Tokyo Bay and remained there until a Japanese envoy agreed to receive President Millard Fillmore's request for a diplomatic and trade treaty. He returned in Feb. 1854 to conclude the treaty, which was a turning point in U.S.-Japanese relations.

Perry, Frederick John (1909-1995), British tennis and table tennis player. Perry first made his mark by becoming table tennis world champion (Budapest 1928). As a tennis player he made his debut on Wimbledon in 1929, and won the tournament in 1934, 1935 and 1936. In addition he won many other tournaments, such as the U.S. Open (1933, 1934, 1936), the Australian Open (1934) and the French Open (1935). In 1936 he became a professional. As a player he was notable for his timing and powerful forehand. After his active career he became a reporter and set up his own line of clothing, of which the sports shirt became best-known.

Perse, Saint-John (1887-1975), French poet and diplomat whose real name was Alexis Saint-Léger. Under his real name, he was the secretary-general of the ministry of foreign affairs (1933-1940). When the Nazis occupied France, he went into exile in the United States. Under his pseudonym he authored

many books of lyrical poetry, including the long poem *Anabasis* (1924). Other works written in his exile include *Exile* (1942) and *Seamarks* (1957). He returned to France in 1959 and won the 1960 Nobel Prize for literature.

Persephone, in Greek and Roman mythology, goddess of the underworld; the Romans called her Proserpina. The daughter of Demeter (Ceres in Roman mythology) and Zeus (Jupiter), Persephone was kidnapped by Hades (Pluto) and taken to the underworld. Demeter refused to allow anything on earth to grow until Persephone was returned; Zeus then worked out a compromise where Persephone would stay with Hades for half the year and with Demeter the other half. The Greeks and Romans used this myth to explain the seasons: when Persephone was with Hades, nothing grows (autumn and winter), and when she was with Demeter, crops flourish (spring and summer).
See also: Mythology.

Persepolis, ancient ceremonial capital of the Achaemenian kings of Persia, lying 30 mi (48 km) northeast of Shiraz, southwestern Iran. It flourished under Darius I (d. 486 B.C.) and his successors but was later destroyed by Alexander the Great in 330. In 1971 the 2,500th anniversary of the Iranian monarchy was celebrated among the ruins of the city.
See also: Persia, Ancient.

Perseus, in Greek mythology, son of Zeus and Danaë, a mortal. His grandfather, King Acrisius, set him adrift at sea with his mother after learning from an oracle that his grandson would one day kill him; King Polydectus rescued them. Perseus beheaded Medusa, the Gorgon, and saved Andromeda from being sacrificed to a sea monster. Perseus later accidentally killed his grandfather, realizing the oracle's prediction.

Perseus, in astronomy, constellation containing the variable star Algol. The Perseid meteors appear to radiate from the constellation during the first two weeks of Aug. Perseus is high in the sky during the Northern Hemisphere fall and winter.

Pershing, John Joseph (1860-1948), U.S. general. After distinguished service in the Indian Wars (1886, 1890-1891), the Spanish-American War (1898), and the Philippines (1899-1903), he was promoted to brigadier general (1906). He led a punitive expedition to Mexico against U.S. Villa (1916) and a year later became commander of the World War I Expeditionary Force in Europe. In 1919 he became general of the armies, and he was chief of staff from 1921 until his 1924 retirement.
See also: Army, U.S.

Persia *See:* Iran; Persia, Ancient.

Persia, Ancient, ancient high plateau of Iran, home of several great civilizations. In 2nd millennium B.C. the literate civilization of Elam developed in the southwest of the plateau, with its capital at Susa. It was end-

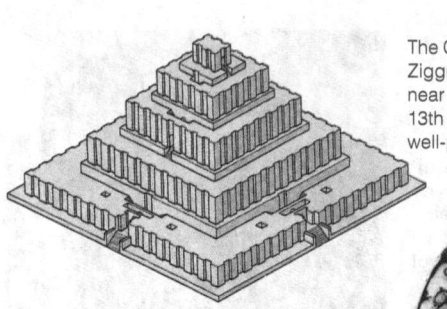

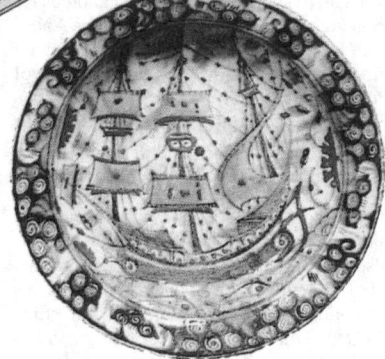

The Choga-Zambil Ziggurat at Elam, near Susa, Persia, 13th century B.C. A well-preserved ziggurat of five tiers, with an elaborate system of inner chambers and stairways.

A sixteenth-century polychrome with a ship (Musée des Beaux-Arts, Rouen).

A fifteenth-century fragment from a manuscript of the *Shah-nama* (Book of the Kings) by Firdausi (died in 1020). The miniature shows that polo was already played back then.

P

ed in 639 B.C. by the invasion of Ashurban-ipal of Assyria. Assyrian downfall followed in 612 after the sacking of Nineveh by the Babylonians and the Medes. The area of Parsumash to the south of the Medes was ruled by the Achaemenians. Cyrus the Great expanded the Achaemenid empire, and at his death (529) he controlled the Middle East from the Mediterranean to the Indus River. Under Darius I (522-486) a road system linked the great empire and a canal linked the Nile and Red Sea. Flourishing trade, commerce, and public works continued under Xerxes I (586-465). Xerxes' murder by his son was followed by intrigues and rebellions that weakened the Achaemenians. In 330 the empire was conquered by the Parthians. The empire of Parthia (3rd century B.C. to 3rd century A.D.) halted the nomads in the northeast and the Romans in the west, defeating Crassus in 53 B.C. and later Mark Antony. In C.A.D. 224, a successful revolt by Ardashir, ruler of the Fars (the southern Persian homeland), established the vigorous Sassanian empire. Arts, architecture, and religion (Zoroastrianism) revived, the wars with Rome continued, and in 260, Shapur, the son of Ardashir, captured the Emperor Valerian. After constant struggles with the Byzantines, the Sassanian empire was overwhelmed by the Arabs and converted to Islam in 651.

Persian, or Farsi, principal language of Iran, widely spoken in Afghanistan. It is an Indo-European language. Modern Persian emerged after the Arab conquest in the 7th century. It has many borrowed Arabic words and a modified Arabic alphabet.

Persian Gulf, or Arabian Gulf, arm of the Arabian Sea between Iran and Arabia. About 550 mi (855 km) long and 120 mi (193 km) wide, the gulf is entered from the Gulf of Oman by the Straits of Hormuz. The bordering regions of Iran, Kuwait, Saudi Arabia, Bahrain, Qatar, and the United Arab Emirates contain more than half the world's oil and natural gas resources. The effects of the Persian Gulf War (1991) caused serious environmental damage to gulf waters because of enormous oil spills.

Persian Gulf War (Second Gulf War; 1990-1991), international conflict, which started as a result of the Iraqi occupation of Kuwait on August 2, 1990. In November 1990, the Security Council of the UN gave permission to apply all necessary means if Iraq had not withdrawn from Kuwait on January 15, 1991. After the ultimatum had expired, a coalition of over 30 western and Arab countries fought against the Iraqi armies who were defeated in Operation Desert Storm. On February 28, 1991, an armistice was agreed and Kuwait was liberated. There were approximately 15,000 Iraqi casualties and several hundred on the side of the allied forces.
See also: Iraq; Kuwait.

Persian lamb *See:* Karakul.

Persian wars (500-449 B.C.), wars between Greek states and the Persian Empire. Athenian support of the revolt of Greek states within the empire precipitated three Persian offensives in Greece. The 2nd Persian expeditionary force was forced back by the Athenians at the Battle of Marathon (490). The 3rd expedition is famous for the resistance at Thermopylae, at which 300 Spartans fought to the death, holding off the overwhelming Persian force. By 449 B.C. Greek strength had secured Europe from further Persian invasions.

Persimmon, any of several trees (genus *Diospyros*) of the ebony family. These trees are grown especially for their fruit of the same name. The kaki persimmon (*D. kaki*), produced for commercial purposes, is native to Asia, while the common persimmon (*D. virginiana*) is native to the United States. When ripe, persimmon fruit is sweet, with a wrinkled or brown-streaked reddish-orange skin.

Personality, in psychology, characteristics and ways of behavior that define the uniqueness of an individual. Most studies conclude that the formation of personality is a complex process, influenced by a variety of factors both inherent and learned.

Perspective, method of producing the appearance of three dimensions on a flat surface. Linear perspective, developed during the Renaissance, exploits the fact that the size of an object seems to shrink to a point as its distance increases. Lines in a picture would, if extended, meet a vanishing point which is always on the horizon line, one the level of the observer's eye. Depending on the view, there may be more than one vanishing point in a picture. Aerial perspective, depends on the fact that the atmosphere disperses the light from distant objects. An artist paints features fainter and bluer to convey the impression of distance.

Perspiration, watery fluid secreted by the skin as a means of reducing body temperature. Sweating is common in hot climates, after exercise, and in the resolution of fever; the evaporation of sweat allows the skin and thus the body to be cooled. Humid atmosphere and high secretion rates delay evaporation, leaving perspiration on the surface. Excessive fluid loss, and of salt in cystic fibrosis, may lead to sunstroke. Most sweating is regulated by the hypothalamus and autonomic nervous system, but there is also a system of sweat glands, especially on the palms, that secretes at times of stress. Hyperhidrosis is a condition of abnormally profuse sweating.
See also: Skin; Temperature, body.

Perth (pop. 1,300,000), capital of Western Australia, a western state with a coast on the Indian Ocean. Located on the Swan River, Perth is a port that supports industry (especially mining) as well as business, educa-

The Japanese kaki persimmon (*D. kaki*) grows up to 40 ft (12 m) tall and has yellowish white flowers.

P

tion, and recreation. A goldrush in the 1890s encouraged its development and growth. It was founded by James Sterling, an officer in the British Navy (1829).
See also: Australia.

Pertussis *See:* Whooping cough.

Peru

Capital:	Lima
Area:	496,225 sq mi
	(1,285,216 sq km)
Population:	24,288,000
Language:	Spanish, Quechua
Government:	Presidential republic
Independent:	1827
Head of gov.:	Prime minister
Per capita:	US$ 2,420
Monetary unit:	1 Nuevo sol = 100 céntimos

Peru, third largest country in South America. With an area of 496,225 sq mi (1,285,216 sq km), Peru is bordered on the north by Ecuador and Colombia; on the east by Brazil and Bolivia; on the south by Chile; and on the west by the Pacific Ocean.
Land and climate. The 1,400 mi (2,253 km) long coastal strip, a central mountain region,

and the eastern Amazonian plains are the country's main regions. The coastal zone is mainly desert, but the sands are very fertile when irrigated and the region supports agriculture and contains about 35% of the population. Most of Peru's important cities are also located on the coast. The mountainous region consists of parallel ranges of the Andes with intervening deep valleys and mountain bases. Among the lofty peaks in this part of Peru is Huascarán (22,205 ft/6,768 m). Straddling the border with Bolivia is also Lake Titicaca at 12,500 ft (3,810 m) above sea level, the highest navigable body of water in the world. Although conditions are harsh and the soil mostly poor, more than half of Peru's people live in the region. It is also susceptible to earthquakes and on May 31, 1970, a devastating quake took the lives of some 50,000 Peruvians and left some 800,000 homeless. The lush eastern slopes of the Andes with their heavy rainfall give way to the dense tropical forests of the eastern plains draining into the Amazon River. The climate of the coastal area is dominated by the Humboldt Current that comes northward from the Antarctic Ocean. In the mountains, the western slopes are generally dry while the northern and eastern areas have heavy rainfall from October to April. The climate of the eastern plains is tropical. The capital of Peru is Lima.
People. The people are about 50% Native American, 32% mestizo (a mixture of Spanish and Native American), and 12% Spanish. The majority of the mestizos and Spanish are Roman Catholic. The official languages are Spanish and Quechua.
Economy. Cotton, sugarcane, and coffee are grown for export. Fishing is a major industry and processed fish meal is the country's chief

Grass vegetation dominates the plateaus of Peru, which are about 13,124 ft (4,000 m) above sea-level. Men and women work very

small parcels of land and they tend llamas, sheep and sometimes cattle. The lakes in the background are used for fishing.

Girls from Cuzco in southern Peru, the region of origin of the mighty Inca empire, that was conquered by Pizarro (1471-1541).

export. Copper, iron, silver, phosphates, and other minerals are mined and exported; some are also processed and refined in Peru.
History. The Inca empire, the last of several great indigenous cultures, was conquered by the Spanish conquistador Francisco Pizarro beginning in 1532. Spanish rule, based in Lima, continued until the revolution led by Simon Bolívar and José de San Martín from 1820 to 1824. After independence, power continued to be concentrated in the hands of a small number of wealthy landowners. Attempts to redress inequalities or retrench privilege have dominated Peru's politics since its independence and throughout the twentieth century, leading to unstable regimes and military coups. In 1968 Gen. Juan Velasco Alvarado instituted a program of social reform, suspended the constitution, and seized U.S. owned companies. Gen. Alvarado was overthrown by military coup in 1975 under the leadership of Francisco Morales Bermudez. The country returned to constitutional rule in 1980 and on July 28, 1985, Alan Garcia Perez was elected president in a democratic election. He was succeeded by Alberto Fujimori in 1990. In 1996-1997 the guerrilla movement Túpac Amaru occupied the Japanese embassy

On the islands off the coast of Peru, bird excrement can accumulate to a height of 98 ft (30 m). For decades, Peru has been the world's largest supplier of

guano — natural manure — which paid for the construction of the country's railway system in the 1880s. When artificial manure came into use, exports decreased

and guano is now used mainly by Peru's own farmers. In the foreground, you can see some young rock pelicans (*Sula variegata*, 'piquero' in Spanish).

Indian women near Cuzco, the old Inca capital. Their hats are typical of this

particular group, but the blankets worn as coats, are common throughout the region.

where they held hostages. After several months the hijack was ended by the military. In 1998 the 160 year old border dispute with Ecuador was ended when the two countries signed a peace treaty. President Fujimori resigned in 2000. His resignation was followed by the exposure of several political and financial scandals. He fled to Japan the subsequent year. Alejandro Toledo won the presidential elections of 2001, becoming the first President of Indian heritage. He said he was determined to dedicate every minute of his life and all his governmental powers to initiating a head-on war on poverty. The guerrilla movements Shining Path and Tupac Amaru oppose him.

Peru Current, or Humboldt Current, cold ocean current originating in the South Pacific and flowing north along the coasts of north Chile and Peru, whose climates it moderates, before turning west to join the South Equatorial Current.
See also: Humboldt, Friedrich Heinrich Alexander, Baron von.

Perugino (Pietro Vannucci; 1446-1523), Italian Renaissance painter, teacher of Raphael. His frescoes in the Vatican's Sistine Chapel, including *Christ Giving the Keys to St. Peter* (1481), established his fame. He worked much in Florence and later in his native Umbria.
See also: Renaissance.

Perutz, Max Ferdinand (1914-), Austrian-born English biochemist who shared with J.C. Kendrew the 1962 Nobel Prize for chemistry for their research into the structure of hemoglobin and other globular proteins.
See also: Biochemistry; Hemoglobin.

Pescadores, group of about 64 small islands c. 50 sq mi (130 sq km) of land area belonging to Taiwan, in the Formosa strait. The chief occupations are fishing and farming.

Peshawar (pop. 1,0 million), Pakistan, the capital of North-West Frontier Province. It lies in a mountainous area about 700 miles (1,130 km) northeast of Karachi and 30 miles (48 km) east of the famed Khyber Pass. Because of its strategic location near the pass, Peshawar has long been an important trade center and a military post. The city produces fine handicrafts, has modern light manufacturing industries, and is served by several highways, a railway, and an airport. Located here are the University of Peshawar and the Peshawar Museum, which has an unrivaled collection of Buddhas and other religious sculptures. Peshawar is an ancient city, dating back centuries before Christ. Successive invasions, mainly by way of the Khyber Pass, brought many and varied rulers, including Buddhist, Scythian, Hindu, Pathan, Turk, Mogul, Sikh, and British. British rule began in 1848 and ended in 1947, when Pakistan gained independence.

Pessary, ring-shaped object which is fitted into the vagina and supports a subsiding vagina and/or uterus. The diaphragm, which is used as a contraceptive, has a cap of rubber attached to the ring (in this case a flexible one), which stops sperm cells. After specialist instruction the woman is able to put it around the cervix, from about two hours before sexual intercourse; six hours afterwards it can be removed again. Is only reliable when combined with spermicides.

Pessoa, Fernando António Nogueira (1888-1935), Portuguese poet. He started his career as a critic and an essayist, before he understood his poetic being: the splitting of himself into four poets. This not only makes him - in the extreme form in which it happened - a unique individual in world literature, but also one of the most complex.
Pessoa was born in Lisbon. In his youth he lived in Durban, South Africa, where he learned English and even won a prize with a literary essay in English. In 1905 he returned to Lisbon. In 1912, after a few failures in his studies as well as in business, he published a number of literary essays in *A Aguia*, the organ of the 'Renascença Portuguesa', the literary revival in the beginning of the 20th century. Pessoa launched post-symbolic movements such as the 'paulismo', the 'interseccionismo' and the more futuristic 'sensacionismo' - movements that were embraced by other poets but dismissed by Pessoa himself. His life changed completely on 8 March 1914, when in some kind of ecstasy his first alter ego appeared, and he wrote over thirty poems in one go under the name and person of Alberto Caeiro. Shortly after this the other 'heteronyms' followed: Alvaro de Campos and Ricardo Reis. While a pseudonym is another name for the self, a heteronym is a name for another 'self'. Pessoa gave all these names their own biography, philosophy, style and opinions to express his split personality. The collected works of Pessoa were published in eight volumes between 1942 and 1956.

Pestalozzi, Johann Heinrich (1746-1827), Swiss educator. At his school at Yverdon he stressed the importance of the individual and based his methods on the child's direct experience, rather than on mechanical learning. *How Gertrude Teaches Her Children*

Johann Heinrich
Pestalozzi (1746-1827).

(1801) was his most influential work.
See also: Education.

Pesticide, substance used to kill plants or animals responsible for economic damage to crops or ornamental plants or that prejudice the well-being of humans and domestic or conserved wild animals. Pesticides are subdivided into insecticides (which kill insects), miticides (which kill mites), herbicides (which kill plants), fungicides (which kill fungi), and rodenticides (which kill rats and mice). A major question with all pesticides is the possibility of unfortunate environmental side effects.

Pétain, Henri Phillippe (1856-1951), French World War I hero who became chief of state in the collaborationist Vichy regime (1940). Famous for his defense of Verdun (1916), he was made chief-of-staff (1917), and subsequently held important military offices. In 1934 he served briefly as war minister. Recalled from his post as ambassador to Spain in June 1940, he became premier and negotiated an armistice with the Nazis. As head of the Vichy government, he aided the Nazis, and in 1945 was convicted of treason and sentenced to life imprisonment.
See also: Vichy; World War II.

Peter, Epistles of, 2 New Testament letters, traditionally attributed to St. Peter. The first is written to encourage persecuted Christians in Asia Minor; the second closely parallels the Epistle of Jude and refers to the Second Coming. Authorship is doubtful, particularly of the second, which some scholars date c.A.D. 150 and which was admitted late to the canon.
See also: New Testament.

Peter, Saint (Simon Peter; d. c.A.D. 64), leader of the 12 Apostles, regarded by Roman Catholics as the first pope. A Galilean fisherman when Jesus called him to be a disciple, he was a dominating but impulsive figure, and he denied Jesus after his arrest. He played a leading role in the early Church, especially in Jerusalem, as related in the Acts of the Apostles. By tradition, he died a martyr at Rome and is buried beneath St. Peter's church in Rome.
See also: Apostles.

Peter I (1844-1921), king of Serbia. A Serbian prince, he spent years in exile, and joined the anti-Turkish Herzegovinian revolt in 1875. He became an honorary senator of Montenegro in 1883 and was elected king of Serbia in 1903.
See also: Serbia.

Peter I, the Great (1672-1725), became joint tsar in 1682 and sole tsar in 1696. He traveled in western Europe (1697-1698), learning techniques of war and industry and recruiting experts to bring back to Russia. He warred against Turkey to gain access to the Mediterranean, and his Northern War with Sweden (1700-1721) led to Russian domination of the Baltic Sea. He established his new capital of St. Petersburg on the Baltic as a symbol of his policy of westernization. Domestically he introduced sweeping military, administrative, and other re-

Czar Peter the Great
(1672-1725).

P

A caricature on the politics of Peter the Great, which was directed towards a 'westernization' of Russian society. As a part of this process, he urged Russian noblemen to shave off their long beards and to adopt Western dress.

forms. A man of enormous size, strength, and energy, Peter was also savage in the exercise of power, and although he modernized, reformed, and strengthened Russia, it was at great human cost.

Peter II (1923-1970), king of Yugoslavia. On the death of his father Alexander I, his cousin governed as regent (1934-1941). Peter fled to London after the Nazi invasion (1941) and set up an exile government. In 1945 Yugoslavia became a republic, and Peter a pretender.
See also: Yugoslavia.

Petersburg, Siege of *See:* Civil War, U.S..

Peterson, Oscar Emmanuel (1925-), Canadian jazz pianist. In the 1950s he often played on the JATP concerts that were organized by Norman Granz. He usually performs as a soloist or with his own trio, which through the years has included musicians like Joe Pass, Ray Brown, Barney Kessel, Herb Ellis and Niels Henning Orsted Pederson. Also an outstanding accompanist.
Petipa, Marius (1819-1910), French dancer and choreographer who created the modern classical ballet. An outstanding dancer and mime, he joined the Russian ballet at St. Petersburg in 1847, becoming chief choreographer in 1869. There, he created over 60 full-length ballets, including *The Nutcracker*, *Swan Lake*, and *The Sleeping Beauty*.
See also: Ballet.

Petit, Roland (1924-), French dancer and choreographer. A founder (1945) and premier danseur of Les Ballets des Champs-Elysées, in 1948 he formed Les Ballets de Paris. He choreographed *Carmen* (1949), *La Croqueuse de diamants* (1950), and many other ballets for stage and film. From 1972-1998 he directed the Ballet National de Marseille-Roland Petit.
See also: Ballet.

Petitgrain oil, oil manufactured from parts of the bitter orange tree, produced abundantly in Paraguay, South America. It is used in

the making of perfume. The highly-valued petitgrain bigrade is produced from another variety of bitter orange tree in the Mediterranean countries of Europe.

Petition of Right, document presented to Charles I of England by Parliament (1628) in protest against his arbitrary fiscal methods. It asserted four principles: no taxation without parliamentary consent, no imprisonment of subjects without due legal cause, no billeting of soldiers in private houses without payment, and no declaring of martial law in peacetime. Accepted (although later disregarded) by the king, it represents a landmark in English constitutional history.
See also: United Kingdom.

PETN, common designation for the explosive pentaerythritol tetranitrate, an organic compound essential to the detonation system of certain explosive devices. Introduced after World War I, it is more powerful than TNT. It also serves as a medication for certain heart disorders.
See also: Explosive.

Petoskey stone, fossilized coral and state stone of Michigan, found outside the town of Petoskey. Valued by mineral collectors, Petoskey stones reveal a 6-sided shape with a pattern of lines radiating from the center. The column-shaped formation of this coral is the result of the actions of natural forces on deposited limestone over 350 million years.

Petra, ancient city in south-western Jordan. Famous for its tombs and temples cut into sandstone cliffs, it was the capital of the Nabataeans, prospered under the Romans, but lost its trade to Palmyra. Its decline continued under Muslim rule. Its ruins were discovered by Burckhardt in 1812.

Petrarch (Francesco Petracco; 1304-1374), Italian poet and early humanist. Supported by influential patrons, he spent his life in study, travel, and writing. He wrote poetry, epistles, and other prose works in Latin, but also much in the vernacular Italian, of which he is one of the earliest masters. He himself rated his Latin works highest, but his fame now rests on the Italian *Canzoniere*, mostly sonnets inspired by his love for the enigmatic Laura, who died of plague in 1348.

A petrochemical cracking installation. The big tower in the middle is the cracking tower.

Wilson's petrel (*Oceanites oceanicus*). Antarctic, Atlantic, South Pacific and Indian Oceans. Wing span: 16 in (40 cm).

Petrel, name for seabirds of the tubenosedbird order Procellariformes, particularly the typical petrels and shearwaters of the families Procellariidae and Hydrobatidae. All have webbed feet and hooked bills, with nostrils opening through horny tubes on the upper mandible. They swim and fly expertly, feeding far from the shore on fish, squid, and offal. Normally they go ashore only to breed.

Petrie, Sir William Matthew Flinders (1853-1942), English archeologist and Egyptologist. As a result of his system of sequence dating, a relative chronology could thus be established between sites and dates attributed to the superimposed layers of a site. In 1894 he founded the British School of Archaeology in Egypt.
See also: Archeology.

Petrified forest, stone-covered trunks of coniferous trees. The trunks were buried in mud, sand, or volcanic ash and mixed with running water, which carried dissolved minerals. The result is stone that shows the detail of the original wood. Many logs are rainbow colored as a result of oxidation. The most famous such forest is in Petrified Forest National Park in eastern Arizona.
See also: Fossil.

Petrochemical, any chemical made from petroleum or natural gas; includes organic chemicals, plus the inorganic substances carbon black, sulfur, ammonia, and hydrogen peroxide. Polymers, detergents, solvents, and nitrogen fertilizers are major products.

Petrograd *See:* Leningrad.

Petrol *See:* Gasoline.

Petroleum, naturally occurring mixture of hydrocarbons, usually liquid 'crude oil,' but sometimes taken to include natural gas. Petroleum is believed to be formed from organic debris, chiefly of plankton and simple

plants, which was rapidly buried in fine-grained sediment under marine conditions unfavorable to oxidation. After some biodegradation, increasing temperature and pressure caused cracking, and oil was produced. As the source rock was compacted, oil and water were forced out and slowly migrated to porous reservoir rocks, chiefly sandstone or limestone. Finally, secondary migration occurred within the reservoir as the oil coagulated to form a pool, generally capped by impervious strata and often associated with natural gas. Some oil seeped to the earth's surface; this was used by the early Mesopotamian civilizations. The first oil well was drilled in western Pennsylvania in 1859. The industry now supplies about half the world's energy, as well as the raw materials for petrochemicals. The chief world oil-producing regions are the Persian Gulf, the US, the former USSR, northern and western Africa, and Venezuela. After the removal of salt and water, the petroleum is refined by fractional distillation, producing the fractions natural gas, gasoline, naphtha, kerosene, diesel oil, fuel oil, lubricating oil, and asphalt. Undesirable compounds may be removed by solvent extraction, treatment with sulfuric acid, etc., and less valuable components converted into more valuable ones by cracking, reforming, alkylation, and polymerization.

Petroleum coke, byproduct of the process of refining crude oil. Petroleum coke is used in the production of flashlight batteries, drycells, and the synthetic graphite required for nuclear reactors. It is also used in the manufacture of certain abrasives, heat resistant materials, and chemicals.

Petronius Arbiter, Gaius (d.A.D. 66), Roman satirist. He became Nero's 'arbiter of taste,' but fell from favor and committed suicide. 'Trimalchio's Dinner' is the best known fragment of his *Satyricon*, a sensual, amoral, often obscene, and satirical romance, considered the first Roman novel.

Petrosian, Tigran Vartanovitch (1929-1984), Soviet Russian chess player, became an international master in 1950 and a Grandmaster in 1952. In 1962 he won the candidates' tournament on Curaçao and the next year he beat world champion Botvinnik. Petrosian won the game against contender Spassky, but lost the title to him in 1969. Petrosian was champion of the Soviet Union in 1959, 1961 and 1969. He had a very positional style, which led to many ties.

Petunia, group of popular herbs (genus *Petunia*) from South America. They belong to the nightshade family, but the flowers differ from the basic pattern of the family. Each plant bears a succession of white to red or blue funnel-shaped blooms; these are pollinated by hawkmoths and hummingbirds. In the U.S. it is grown for its beautiful flower.

Pevsner, Antoine (1886-1962), Russian-born sculptor who studied in Paris (1911-1913) and settled there from 1922. In 1920 he launched constructivism with his brother Naum Gabo in Moscow. Light and space play important roles in his sculptures.

Pewter, class of alloys consisting chiefly of tin, now hardened with copper and antimony, and usually containing lead, which increases malleability. Today lead is now omitted because it can be toxic. Pewter has been used in the west since Roman times for bowls, drinking vessels, and candlesticks.

Peyote *See:* Mescaline.

pH, measure of hydrogen gas in a solution. a pH of 7, which is neutral (neither acid nor alkaline), means there are 100 nanoequivalents of hydrogen ions per liter of blood. The human body functions best when the blood pH is 7.40, that is, when it contains about 40 nanoequivalents of hydrogen ions per liter. Therefore, the blood is normally very slightly alkaline. When the pH goes below 7.38, normal body functions are disrupted and the pathological, possibly fatal conditions of acidemia (acidosis) exists. Should hydrogen ions be lost from the body (or neutralized) and the blood pH rise above 7.44, alkalemia (alkalosis) occurs. Either condition reflects an acid-base balance disturbance. Breathing out carbon dioxide (which is acid) helps keep the pH properly balanced. The pH is measured in blood, urine, spinal fluid, lung fluid, semen, and many other body secretions.

Phaëton, or Phaëthon, in Greek mythology, mortal son of the sun god Helios and the sea goddess Clymene. Helios granted him his wish to drive the chariot of the sun, but he was unable to control it. He first flew it too high, freezing the earth and creating the scar in the sky known as the Milky Way, and then too low, burning and nearly destroying the earth. Zeus was forced to kill him with a thunderbolt to protect the earth.
See also: Mythology.

Phalanx, ancient Greek infantry formation, consisting of rows of eight men, each heavily armed with an overlapping shield and

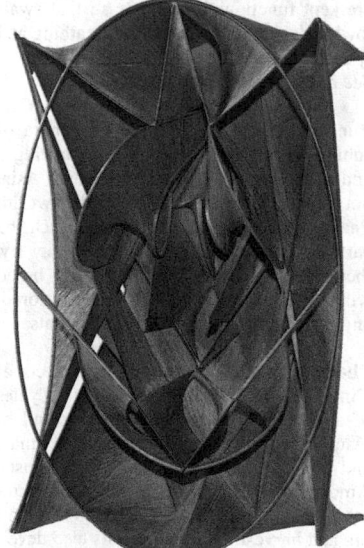

Antoine Pevsner's *Oval fresco* (1945), an abstract assemblage of bronze and oxidized tin, is typical of his constructivist works.

long pike. Philip II of Macedon developed a phalanx of 16 men, which his son Alexander the Great used in defeating the Persians. After defeat by Rome in 168 B.C. the phalanx became outmoded.
See also: Greece, Ancient; Infantry.

Phalarope, any of various small seabirds of the family Phalaropodidae. They fly to the Southern Hemisphere in winter but breed in Arctic regions during the summer. The females court and establish territory. Their eggs are incubated by the smaller, less colorful males, who are also the nest builders. The birds resemble sandpipers and are up to 10 in (25 cm) long.

Pham Hung (1912-1988), Vietnamese politician. Pham Hung became a member of the Indo-Chinese Communist Party in 1930, the year it was founded. He played an important role during the struggle for independence against the French and was imprisoned for fifteen years. During the war in Vietnam he eventually became the leader of the southern communists. Pham Hung was responsible for internal safety as minister of the interior (1980-1987) in the government of the reunified Vietnam. He became prime minister in 1987. During the nine months of his prime ministership Pham Hung proved to be, to some extent, a supporter of economic reforms.

Pham Van Dong (1906-2000), Vietnamese prime minister (1955-1987), joined the liberation movement of Ho Chi Minh as early as the 1920s. From 1929 until 1936 he was imprisoned by the French. In 1941 Pham was co-founder of the Vietminh. He was vice-premier (1949-1955) and minister of

A considerable part of Lybian oil is pumped through pipelines, from the area south of the Gulf of Sidra to the coast, from where it is transported mainly to Western Europe.

Wilson's phalarope (*S. tricolor*) is an uncommon shorebird that inhabits inland pools rather than coastal waters. The female (foreground) is somewhat larger and more colorful than the male.

P

P

The flamboyant ring-necked pheasant (*P. colchicus*) is commonly seen in fields and brush throughout the northern United States, where it feeds on seeds, berries, and grains. The female, camouflaged by protective dull coloration, often lays its eggs directly on the ground.

foreign affairs (1954-1961) in the Democratic Republic of Vietnam, which was proclaimed in 1945. In 1954 he represented the Republic at the Geneva Convention. From 1951 onward Pham was a member of the Politburo of the Communist Party. In 1955 he became prime minister of North Vietnam and in 1976 prime minister of the Socialist Republic of Vietnam (the reunified Vietnam).
Only after he resigned from this position in 1987, did the regime become less rigid and, as a result, Vietnam started having commercial foreign relations.

Pharaoh, Hebrew form of the title of the kings of ancient Egypt. The term (actually *per'O*: great house) described his palace and, by association, the king. The Egyptians believed the pharaoh to be the personification of the gods Horus and, later, Amon.

Pharaoh hound, breed of hunting dog originating in ancient Egypt. It is built for speed, standing 21-25 in (53-64 cm) at the shoulder and weighing 35-50 lb (16-23 kg). It has a short, tan, glossy coat, with white markings on the toes, chest, tail, and face, and distinctive amber eyes. It is pictured in Egyptian paintings dating to 2300 B.C.

Pharisees, member of an ancient Jewish sect devoted to strict observance of the holy law and strongly opposed to pagan practices absorbed by Judaism and to the Sadducees. Their moral fervor and initially progressive nature made them an important political force. Tradition has made them synonymous with hypocrisy and self-righteousness, but Jesus only attacked the debasement of their ideals.

Pharmacology, study of drugs, their chemistry, mode of action, routes of absorption, excretion, metabolism, drug interactions, toxicity and side effects. The dispensing of drugs is called pharmacy.
See also: Drug.

Pharmacopoeia, text describing all available drugs and pharmacological preparations. It includes the properties and formulation, routes and doses of administration, mode of action, metabolism, and excretion, known interactions, contraindications and precautions, and toxicity and side effects of drugs. The first pharmacopoeia appeared in

the 16th centruy in Germany (The Nuremberg pharmacopoeia). In the United States the first *United States Pharmacopoeia* (USP) was published in 1820. In 1888 the *National Formulary* was created. The two publications merged in 1980 and continue to be published.
See also: Drug.

Pharmacy, preparation or dispensing of drugs and pharmacological substances used in medicine; also, the place where this is practiced. Most drugs are now formulated by drug companies, and the pharmacist only measures them out and instructs the patient in their use. The first U.S. pharmacy school was established in Philadelphia, Pa., in 1821.

Pharos of Alexandria *See:* Seven Wonders of the Ancient World.

Pharyngeal tonsils *See:* Adenoids.

Pharynx, part of the digestive system, back of the throat where the mouth (oropharynx) and nose (nasopharynx) pass back into the esophagus. It contains specialized muscle for swallowing. The food and air channels are kept functionally separate so that swallowing does not interfere with breathing and speech.
See also: Digestive system.

Pheasant, game bird of the 16 genera of subfamily Phasianidae, including partridges and the peacock. They originated in Asia, but are now found all over the world. Pheasants are ground birds that scratch the earth for seeds and insects. When they fly, they rise almost vertically on short, broad wings. Males are usually brightly colored, and many species are kept as ornaments.

Phenology, science studying the effects of climate on biological phenomenon. Cycles of animal migration or hibernation and of plant flowering are dependent on climate and are therefore studied by phenologists. Among other results, phenology helps farmers correctly time procedures such as planting and harvesting. Phenologists also develop phenological maps that chart global phenological events.
See also: Biology; Climate.

Phenolphthalein, white or yellowish white

chemical compound ($C_{20}H_{14}O_4$) used medicinally as a laxative and as an indicator of alkalies and acids. (Its solution is bright red in alkalies and colorless in acid.) The German chemist Adolf von Baeyer discovered the compound (1871).

Phenomenology, modern school of philosophy based largely on a method developed by Edmund Husserl. Unlike the naturalist, who describes objects without subjectivity, the phenomenologist attempts to describe the 'invariant essences' of objects as objects 'intended' by consciousness. The first step is 'phenomenological reduction,' a suspension of all preconceptions about experience.
See also: Husserl, Edmund.

Phenylketonuria (PKU), inborn error of metabolism, characterized by a virtual absence of phenylalanine hydroxylase activity and an elevation of plasma phenylalanine, that frequently results in mental retardation. Early and well-maintained treatment, which consists in limiting the phenylalanine intake of the child so that the essential amino acid requirement is met but not exceeded, makes normal development possible and prevents involvement of the central nervous system. Treatment must be intiated during the first days of life to prevent mental retardation. Some clinicians believe that treatment must be continued for life; others think that it can be terminated when myelinization of the brain is virtually complete, at about five years of age.

Pheromone, chemical substance secreted by animals and serving to stimulate behavioral responses by other individuals of the same species. Some pheromones are alarm siganls or mark territory, but many are sex attractants, especially among insects.

Phi Beta Kappa, most prestigious U.S. honor society for college and university students in the liberal arts and sciences. Members are generally elected in their third or fourth year on the basis of academic achievements. The fraternity was founded at William and Mary College, Va., in 1776.

Phidias, or Pheidias (500-432 B.C.), perhaps the greatest Greek sculptor, whose work showed the human form idealized and with great nobility. None of his work survives; his reputation rests on contemporary accounts, Roman copies, and on the Parthenon statues made under his direction. Under Pericles he had artistic control over the Acropolis.
See also: Parthenon.

Philadelphia, name of several ancient Greek cities. One, founded in the 2nd century B.C., was in Amman, now the capital of Jordan. It was renamed Philadelphia in the 3rd century B.C. by Ptolemy II, one of the successors of Alexander the Great. The name is Greek for 'brotherly love.'

Philadelphia (pop. 1,500,000), historic city in the southeastern region of Pennsylvania, the fourth largest in the United States. It is a key shipping port, with important metal, machinery, clothing, petroleum, chemical, and food industries and has long been a center

for publishing, education, and the arts. It was one of the first planned cities. Its founder, William Penn, created his colony in 1682 as a 'holy experiment' in which all sects could find freedom. Philadelphia (Greek, 'brotherly love') attracted immigrants and brought commerce that made it the largest and wealthiest of New World cities. The city was U.S. capital, 1790-1800. Today the city has the world's largest freshwater port, linked with the Atlantic by the Delaware River.
See also: Pennsylvania.

Philanthropy, acts of charity meant to improve the welfare of people. Philanthropy has been a part of many cultures, from the ancient Hebrews (who introduced a tax to help the poor) to the Greeks, Egyptians, Muslims, and Europeans of the Middle Ages. In the United State, philanthropy is often carried out through charitable foundations established by wealthy families.

Philemon, Epistle to, New Testament letter written C.A.D. 61 by St. Paul to Philemon, a Colossian Christian, asking him to forgive his runaway slave Onesimus, who had become a Christian and who carried the letter.
See also: New Testament.

Philip, name of six kings of France. **Philip I** (1052-1108) reigned from 1060. He enlarged his small territories and prevented the union of England and Normandy. His practice of simony and his disputed second marriage led him into conflict with the papacy. **Philip II**, or Philip Augustus (1165-1223), reigned from 1180 and established France as a European power. He joined the Crusades, only to quarrel with Richard the Lion Heart and seize his French territories. By 1204 he had added Normandy, Maine, Anjou, Touraine, and Brittany to his domain, in which he set up new towns and a system of royal bailiffs. **Philip III**, or Philip the Bold (1245-1285), reigned from 1270 and secured Auvergne, Poitou and Toulouse for France. **Philip IV**, or Philip the Fair (1268-1314), reigned from 1285 and added Navarre and Champagne to the kingdom, but his attempts to overrun Flanders led to his defeat at Courtrai in 1302. He seized Pope Boniface VIII in a quarrel about taxation of clergy, obtained the election of Clement V, a puppet pope residing at Avignon, and seized the land of the crusading order of the Knights Templar. **Philip V**, or Philip the Tall (1294-1322), reigned from 1317, having invoked the Salic Law of male succession, and carried out reforms to strengthen royal power. The succession in 1328 of **Philip VI** (1293-1350) through the Salic Law was disputed and led to the Hundred Years War against England.

Philip, name of five kings of Spain. **Philip I**, or Philip the Handsome (1478-1506), was archduke of Austria, duke of Burgundy, and inheritor of the Netherlands. He became first Habsburg king of Castile in 1506, ruling jointly with his wife Joanna. **Philip II** (1527-1598), crowned in 1556, united the Iberian peninsula and ruled an empire that included Milan, Naples, Sicily, the Netherlands, and vast tracts of the New World. Though son of the Holy Roman

This thirteenth-century miniature shows French King Philip VI of Valois (1293-1350) and his vassals during a lawsuit against Count Robert III of Artois (1287-1342).

Emperor Charles V, he never became emperor. A fanatical Catholic, he married Mary I of England, supported the Inquisition, and tried in vain to crush the Protestant Netherlands. He was recognized king (Philip I) of Portugal in 1580 but lost naval supremacy to England after the defeat of the Armada (1588). His son **Philip III** (1578-1621), crowned in 1598, made peace with England and the Netherlands but was frustrated in Italy by the Thirty Years' War. **Philip IV** (1605-1655), crowned in 1621, son of Philip III and the last Habsburg king of Spain, was the patron of Diego de Velázquez. He attempted unsuccessfully to dominate Europe by fighting France, Germany, and Holland in the Thirty Years' War, and lost Portugal in the process (1640). **Philip V** (1683-1746), crowned in 1700, founder of the Bourbon line, restored influence, but his accession led to the war of the Spanish Succession. By the Treaty of Utrecht (1713) his title was recognized, though he ceded possessions in Italy and the Netherlands to Austria.

Philip, Prince (1921-), consort of Queen Elizabeth II of England. The son of Prince

Philip II (1527-1598), king of Spain.

Andrew of Greece and Princess Alice of Battenberg, he renounced his Greek title, became a British subject, and married Elizabeth in 1947. He was created duke of Edinburgh in 1947 and prince in 1957.
See also: United Kingdom.

Philip, Saint, one of the Twelve Apostles. Born in Bethsaida, he was martyred at Hierapolis in Phrygia, according to legend.
See also: Apostles.

Philip II (382-386 B.C.), king of Macedonia from 359 and father of Alexander the Great. His powerfully reorganized army conquered northern Greece, acquiring the gold mines of Thrace and advancing south as far as Thermopylae, the key to central Greece. He defeated Athens and Thebes at Chaeronea (338) and became ruler of all Greece. His reign marked the end of the independent, warring city-states.
See also: Greece, Ancient.

Philip II (382-386 B.C.) of Macedonia.

Philippi, ancient city of Macedonia, in present-day Greece, named for Philip II of Macedon. It was there Brutus and Cassius were defeated (42 B.C.) by Mark Antony and Octavian, and where St. Paul first preached the gospel in Europe.

Philippians, Epistle to the, New Testament letter written by St. Paul from prison in Rome (A.D. 62) to the Christians at Philippi, whom he himself had converted. He encourages them affectionately and quotes an early hymn on Christ's humility.
See also: New Testament.

Philippines

Capital:	Manila
Area:	115,830 sq mi
	(300,000 sq km)
Population:	84,526,000
Language:	Pilipino, English
Government:	Presidential republic
Independent:	1946
Head of gov.:	President
Per capita:	US$ 4,000
Monetary unit:	1 Philippine peso =
	100 centavos

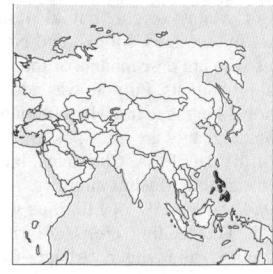

Philippines, archipelago and republic in the southwest Pacific Ocean.

P

Manila, located on the western coast of Luzon, on Manila Bay, is the capital, largest city, and main port of the Philippines. The city is bisected by the Pasig River. Founded in 1571, Manila was devastated during World War II but has since been rebuilt.

Land and climate. The Philippines consists of more than 7,000 islands with a total area of 115,830 sq mi (300,000 sq km). A far-flung archipelago, the Philippines is bounded by the South China Sea to the west, the Celebes Sea to the south, the Philippine Sea to the east and, in the north, the Bashi Channel separates the Philippines from Taiwan. The islands range in size from tiny rocks and islets to Luzon, the largest of them, with an area of 41,845 sq mi (108,378 sq km). Only 2,870 of the islands are named, about 730 are inhabited, and 11 account for most of the total land area and most of the population. The landscape of the Philippines is characterized by coastal mangroves, fertile plains, luxuriant tropical jungles, rugged mountains, and active volcanoes and hot springs. The area is prone to earthquakes. Each island has its own distinct features. Luzon is mountainous, but has fertile plains and rolling hills. Among its many fine harbors is Manila Bay, site of the nation's capital, Manila. Mindanao, the archipelago's second largest island with an area of 36,381 sq mi (94,227 sq km) is even more mountainous, but also has the Cotabato Valley, an important agricultural area. The Philippines has a consistently hot and humid monsoon climate and is exposed to destructive Pacific typhoons.
People. The Philippine people are predominantly of Malay origin, but also include Chinese, Indonesians, Moros, and Negritos, pygmies who are descendants of the island's original inhabitants. Pilipino was adopted as the national language in 1946, but many other native languages are also spoken. The majority of the people are Christians, but there is also a sizeable Muslim minority.
Economy. About 45% of Filipinos work on the land. The leading crops are rice, coconut, corn, and sugar. Abaca (Manila hemp) and timber are important exports. The islands are rich in mineral resources, in particular lead, nickel, zinc, copper, and cobalt. Metro Manila is the main industrial center and manufacturing includes wood products, textiles, aluminum, electronic parts and tobacco.
History. The islands were first visited by Europeans on Magellan's expedition of 1521, and were later named in honor of the future Philip II of Spain. By the 1570s Spanish rule was secure and lasted until the end of the Spanish-American War in 1898, after which the Philippines were ceded to the United States. A revolutionary nationalist movement under the leadership of Emilio Aquinaldo helped the United States defeat Spain. The issue of independence loomed large in U.S. relations with the Philippines until the establishment, in 1935, of the internally self-governing Commonwealth of the Philippines, with Manuel Quezon as president. Occupied by the Japanese during World War II, the country was made an independent republic in 1946, with Manuel Roxas and later Ramon Magsaysay as presidents. Communist revolutionary movements have been active since 1949. The powers of the presidency were greatly increased in 1972 with the imposition of martial law (until 1981) under President Ferdinand Marcos. The murder of Benigno Aquino (1983) and charges of fraud in the presidential elections of February 7, 1986, led to the ouster of Ferdinand Marcos. Corazon Aquino, wife of Benigno Aquino, claimed victory in the elections and accused Marcos forces of manipulating election returns. Weeks of political turmoil ensued. Finally the army took the side of Mrs. Aquino and Ferdinand Marcos and his wife, Imelda, fled the country. Under Aquino, a new constitution was ratified in 1987. Based on a three year phased-out withdrawal agreement, the U.S. navy closed it's Subic Bay base on September 30, 1992. Under Fidel Ramos, who was elected president in May 1992, political stability led to economic growth. Liberalized economic policies, deregulation, and privatization produced consumer confidence and attracted substantial foreign investment. In 1996, Ramos signed a peace agreement with the Moro National Liberation Front. In 1998 Joseph Estrada, a former movie actor, was elected president. In 2000 he was accused of corruption, favoritism and misadministration. Vice-president Gloria Macapagal Arroyo succeeded him in 2001.

Philip the Evangelist, also called Philip the Deacon, early Christian preacher chosen by the apostles to work in the church of Jerusalem. He is said to have preached in Judea and Samaria and later became bishop of Tralles, in Asia Minor.

Philistines, non-Semitic people who lived in Palestine from the 12th century B.C. They were hostile to the Israelites and for a time held considerable power. The term *philistine* may nowadays denote an uncultured person.

Philodendron, genus of South American evergreen plants frequently grown as greenhouse and house plants. Many are vigorous climbers and produce attractive foliage, but they rarely flower in cultivation. The most popular climbing species are *Philodendron oxycardium* (heart-leaf philodendron), *P. sodiroi* (silver-leafed), and *P. pandurae-* *forme* (fiddle leaf, or horsehead), while *P. bipinnatifidum* and *P. selloum* are self-heading cut-leaved types, closely resembling monstera except for their nonclimbing habit. Propagation is by shoot cuttings or air layering.

Philo Judaeas (c.20 B.C.-C.A.D. 50), Egyptian-born Jewish philosopher, 'the Jewish Plato.' His attempt to fuse Greek philosophical thought with Jewish biblical religion had a profound influence on both Christian and Jewish theology.
See also: Philosophy; Theology.

Philology (Greek), study of the language and literature of a specific people or language group. A long time ago, philology focused solely on the two classic languages, Greek and Latin; other languages came later (e.g. Germanic, Slavic philology). In the 20th century the emphasis shifted to studying texts and other language documents of a literary or cultural significance in relation to the culture in which they came about. Philology was the onset for the studies of comparative linguistics and historical linguistics. Important aspects include textual criticism (restoring old texts to their original state) and dialectology, the study of dialects.

Philosophe, member of the 18th-century French school of thinkers, scientists, and belles lettrists who believed that the methodology of science should be applied to contemporary social, economic, and political problems. Inspired by René Descartes and the school of Skepticism, they included Montesquieu, Voltaire, Denis Diderot, and Jean-Jacques Rousseau.

A seventeenth-century edition of the works of René Descartes (1596-1650), carries this engraving of the famous French philosopher opposite the title page. The artist is unknown.

Philosophy, study of the nature of being and thinking, and more specifically of the human experience. Traditionally, philosophers have focused on four main areas: (1) logic, or the study of the formal structure of truthful arguments; (2) metaphysics, or the study of the nature of 'being' or ultimate reality; (3) epistemology, or the theory of knowledge;

(4) ethics, or moral and political philosophy. The earliest known attempts to raise distinctively philosophical questions go back to the 7th century B.C., when the pre-Socratic Greek philosophers were active. Their intellectual heirs were Socrates, Plato, and Aristotole. Later ancient philosophies included epicureanism, stoicism, and neo-Platonism. Foremost among medieval philosphers in the West were St. Augustine and St. Thomas Aquinas. Modern philosophy, identified by the parallel development of rationalism and empiricism, began with René Descartes and culminated in the philosophy of Immanuel Kant. The idealism of G.F.W. Hegel and the positivism of August Compte were major forces in 19th-century philosophy, forming a basis for the philosophy of dialectical materialism espoused by Karl Marx. The philosophical orientations of most 20th-century philosophers have their roots in Marxism, Kantianism, logical positivism, pragmatism, phenomenology, or existentialism. Although at one time areas such as the natural sciences, psychology, sociology, logic, and mathematics were all considered to be within the domain of the philosophers, today's philosophers tend to concentrate on more specialized areas of inquiry, such as the philosophy of logic, the philosophy of science, and the philosophy of religion.

Phlebitis, inflammation of the veins, usually causing a blood clot, or thrombosis (thrombophlebitis), and obstruction to blood flow. Pain, swelling, and redness over the vein are typical, with the vein's becoming a thick, tender cord. Occasionally, phlebitis indicates systemic disease (for instance, cancer). Treatment includes anticoagulant medication.
See also: Embolism.

Phlogiston, elementary substance (without color, weight, taste, or odor) postulated by G.E. Stahl and Johann Becher to be lost from matter when it is burned. The phlogiston concept provided 18th-century chemistry with its unifying principle. The phlogiston theory of combustion found general acceptance until displaced by its inverse, Antoine Lavoisier's oxygen theory.

Phlox, genus of plants of North America and eastern Siberia that are grown in gardens around the world. The plants are either low-growing or upright and bear masses of tubular flowers that open to a flat whorl of petals.

Phnom Penh (pop. 1,000,000), capital and river port of Cambodia, on the Tônlé Sap River, where it joins the Mekong. It is the country's administrative, commercial, communications and cultural center. Founded in the 14th century, it was first made Khmer capital in the 1430s. Phnom Penh was the focus of a massive civil war campaign in 1970-75 in which almost the entire population was evacuated and put to forced labor. In 1979 the city was conquered by a Vietnamese invasion.
See also: Cambodia.

Phobia, inordinate and overwhelming fear of certain events, situations, and objects.

Some common fears include fear of heights (acrophobia), small spaces (claustrophobia), water (hydrophobia), foreigners (xenophobia), spiders (arachnophobia), and open spaces (agoraphobia). Phobias can severely restrict an individual's daily life and prevent the execution of daily routines. Phobias are considered a psychological disorder and treatment usually requires psychoanalysis or behavior therapy.
See also: Neurosis.

Phoebe, any of several small birds (genus *Sayornis*) in the flycatcher family. The eastern phoebe *(S. phoebe)*, with its pale yellow breast and dull green back, is prevalent in the northeastern United States. The say's phoebe *(S. saya)*, slightly larger with light tan undersides, lives in the western United States. The black phoebe *(S. nigricans)*, a dark-backed bird with a white underside, ranges southward from the southwestern United States through the continent of South America.

Phoenicia, ancient territory corresponding roughly to the coastal region of modern Lebanon, inhabited by the Phoenicians (originally called Canaanites) from 3000 B.C. It included the city-states of Sidon and Tyre. Being on the trade route between Asia Minor, Mesopotamia, and Egypt, Phoenicia became an important center of commerce. By 1200 B.C. with the decline of Egyptian dominance, Phoenicians led the Mediterranean world in trading and seafaring. They colonized many Mediterranean areas that later became independent states, such as Carthage and Utica. From the 9th century B.C. Phoenicia was intermittently dominated by Assyria, and in 538 came under Persian rule. By the time Alexander the Great conquered Tyre (332) Phoenician civilization had largely been eclipsed. The Greeks were the inheritors of their outstanding cultural legacy-most notably their alphabetic script, from which the modern Western alphabet is descended.

Phoenix (pop. 2,0 million), largest city in and capital of Arizona and the seat of Maricopa County. Phoenix lies in the Salt River Valley in south-central Arizona, in the heart of an irrigated area that contains the state's most productive cropland. Industries include the processing and shipping of the

Buddhist monks burn incense for peace in the city of Phnom Penh.

Gold masks from Byblos, Phoenicia from approximately 1000 B.C. Their exact ritual significance is unknown.

P

cotton, vegetables, fruit, hides, and other products of the nearby farms, metal processing, and the manufacture of electronic equipment, aircraft parts, and air conditioners. Tourism is also important.
See also: Arizona.

Phoenix, symbol of rebirth. Originally a mythical bird of ancient Egypt, it was sacred to the sun god Ra and worshipped at Helipolis. There was said to be only one phoenix in the universe at any one time; large as an eagle, brilliantly plumed, it lived 500 or more years, then made a pyre of aromatic boughs, consumed itself in the fire and rose reborn from its own ashes.
See also: Mythology.

Phonetics, systematic examination of the sounds made in speech, concerned with the classification of these sounds, the physical and physiological aspects of their production and transmission, and their reception and interpretation by the listener. Phonology, the study of phonetic patterns in languages, is of importance in comparative linguistics.

Phonograph, or record player, instrument for reproducing sound recorded mechanically as modulations in a spiral groove. It was invented by Thomas Edison (1877), whose first machine had a revolving grooved cylinder covered with tinfoil. Sound waves caused a diaphragm to vibrate, and a stylus on the diaphragm made indentations in the foil. These could then be made to vibrate another stylus attached to a reproducing diaphragm. Wax disks and cylinders soon replaced tinfoil, then when metal master disks could be made by etching or electroplating, copies were mass-produced in rubber, wax, or plastic. The main parts of a phonograph are the turntable, to rotate the disk at constant angular velocity; the stylus, which tracks the

P

groove and vibrates with its modulations; the pickup, or transducer, which converts these movements piezoelectrically or electromagnetically into electrical signals; the amplifier; and the loudspeaker.
See also: Edison, Thomas Alva.

Phosphate, derivative of phosphoric acid, either a phosphate ester or a salt containing phosphate ions. Of many phosphate minerals, the most important is apatite, which is treated with sulfuric acid or phosphoric acid to get superphosphate, the major phosphate fertilizer. Phosphates are used in making glass, soaps, and detergents.

Phosphor, substance emitting light (or other electromagnetic radiation) on nonthermal stimulation. Important phosphors include those used in television picture tubes (where stimulation is by electrons) and those coated on the inside wall of fluorescent lamp tubes to convert ultraviolet radiation into visible light.

Phosphorescence, light produced by certain substances after the absorption of certain forms of energy, especially radiant energy. The light is produced when the electrons of the substance, excited by the radiation, drop back to lower energy levels. Phosphorescence is similar to fluorescence except that fluorescence occurs *while* the substance is subject to radiation, whereas phosphorescence continues even after the radiation has stopped. Natural forms of phosphorescence occur in gems and minerals. Some insects, such as fireflies, exhibit it too. Scientists use phosphorescent substances to track and examine body systems with X-rays. Manufacturers use phosphorescence in clock faces, computer monitors, and other products.
See also: Fluorescence; Luminescence.

Phosphoric acid, also called orthophos-phoric acid, syrupy acid (H_3PO_4) produced from phosphate rock or, in purer form, from white phosphorus. This acid has various applications in the manufacture of fertilizers, flavored syrups, dental adhesives, detergents, water softeners, and anti-corrosive coatings for metals.

Phosphorus, chemical element, symbol P; for physical constants see Periodic Table. Phosphorus was discovered by Hennig Brand in 1669. The element is found in nature as phosphate rock containing *apatite*, an impure tri-calcium phosphate. It is prepared by heating tri-calcium phosphate with carbon in an electric furnace, with the vapor being collected under water. Phosphorus, a nonmetallic element, exists in three or more allotropic forms, white, red, and black. It catches fire spontaneously in air and must be kept under water. It may cause severe burns to the flesh and must be handled with forceps. It is an essential component of animal tissue and bone. Phosphorus and its compounds are used in fertilizers, fine china, safety matches, pesticides, incendiary weapons, cleaning agents, and water softeners.

Phosphorus cycle, the cycling and recycling of phosphorus in the living world, or biosphere. Phosphates (the natural occurring salt-form of phosphorus) are absorbed by plant life and later released into the atmosphere and the sea. In time, decayed matter containing phosphates returns to the soil. In this way phosphorus, a substance necessary for life, works its way through the living matter of the earth.
See also: Phosphorus.

Photochemistry, branch of physical chemistry dealing with chemical reactions that produce light or are initiated by (visible or ultraviolet) light. Important examples include photosynthesis, photography, and bleaching by sunlight.

Photocomposition, also called phototype-setting, system by which words are arranged for printing on photographic film or paper. In the past typesetters hand placed and arranged metal dies with letters on them for the printing of newspapers, magazines, and books. Today this job is done quickly and efficiently through a keyboard connected to a photographic device, both of which are controlled by a computer. Computers allow instantaneous changes of typeface, or font. The computer can also automatically reposition an entire body of type whenever a change is made.
See also: Printing; Type.

Photoconductive cell *See:* Electric eye.

Photocopying, duplication of printed images or words through a process involving photographic techniques. The most popular of these techniques, *Xerography* (1938), is a dry process in which light-sensitive material is charged with static electricity to produce an image when a toner (powdered ink) adheres to heated paper and recreates the original image. Older processes depended on liquid developers, such as photostats and blueprints. Libraries and other document storage facilities use microfilming to make miniature copies, up to 1/100th the original size.

Photoelectric cell *See:* Electric eye.

Photoelectric effect (properly photoemissive effect), the emission of electrons from a surface when struck by electromagnetic radiation, such as light. In 1905 Albert Einstein laid one of the twin foundations of quantum theory by explaining photoemission in terms of the action of individual photons, which are quanta of light. The effect is used in phototubes (electron tubes having a photoemissive cathode), often employed as 'electric eye' switches.

Photoengraving and photolithography, processes by which plates or cylinders containing matter for printing are created. Techniques of photographing and etching (acid engraving) replicate illustrations and drawings to be printed in the photoengraving process. In this method line engravings reproduce lines and halftone engravings reproduce continuous ranges of tone. Photography is used to transfer printed matter to the printing plate. The body of text to be printed is then treated with water that will accept the oily ink from the rollers, while the unprinted portions of the plate are treated with an oil that accepts only water from the rollers.
See also: Engraving; Lithography; Printing.

Photogrammetry, method for making measurements for maps or surveys through photographs. Cameras-often mounted on aircraft or space vehicles-take 2 or more shots of the same area from different angles. Land masses as well as the moon are subjects for photogrammetry. A stereoplotter corrects errors in measurements due to photographic distortions. Photogrammetry was developed by a French colonel, Amie Laussedat (1859).
See also: Map; Surveying.

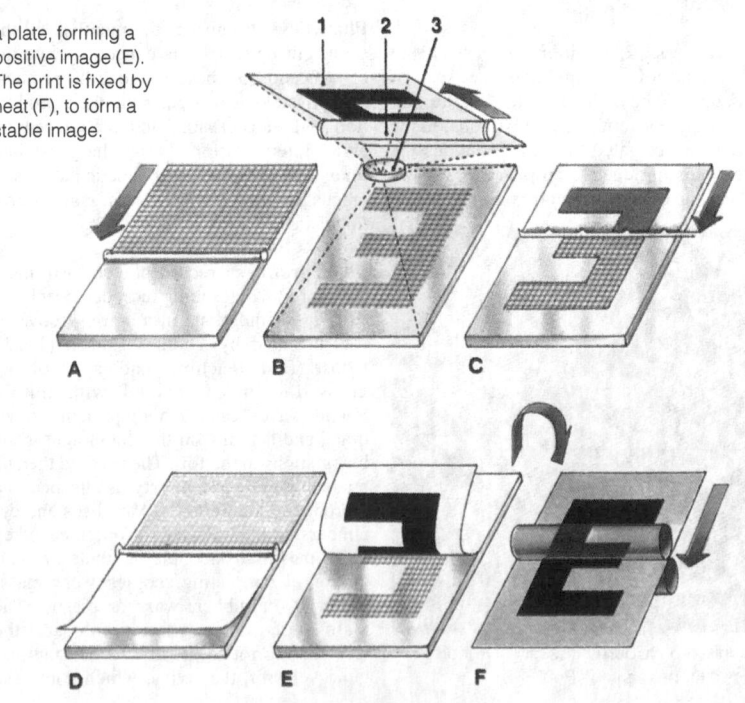

The Xerox copying process uses a metal plate, coated with a material that only conducts electricity after exposure to light. In (A) the surface of the plate is positively charged by a moving grid. The original (1) is strongly illuminated by a light (2), and projected through a lens (3) onto the coated plate, which dissipates the positive in the areas that have been exposed to light (B).
A negatively charged toning powder is dusted over the plate (C), and a sheet of paper is placed over it (D). This paper receives a positive charge, thus attracting the toner powder from a plate, forming a positive image (E). The print is fixed by heat (F), to form a stable image.

Photography, a very broad description of photography is: the registration of optical images. Classic photography used chemical processes, usually based on the principal of silver links going black when exposed to visible light and other radiation.

The first useable method was developed by L.J.M. Daguerre and J.N. Nièpce around 1840, but it was far too complicated for general use. Another problem was that the images were one-off, because they had not developed a way to create a non-perishable negative. Producing several prints was made possible with the development of gelatine emulsion, but it was the invention of the film roll in 1870 and the introduction of the 35-millimetre camera and color film in the 30s of the 20th century that turned photography into a popular mass medium.

Besides the usual negative-positive method, other methods have been developed, such as the positive method (slides) and the ready-at-once method, used by Polaroid, for example. These last few decennia, digital photography has been becoming increasingly popular. In digital photography, the image is not recorded chemically, but electronically. The quality – especially the resolution – often is not as good as in chemical photography, but it is not necessary to go through the whole process of developing and printing. Another pro is that the digital images can be modified on the computer straightaway, and sent on using electronic means, such as (satellite) telephones or the Internet.

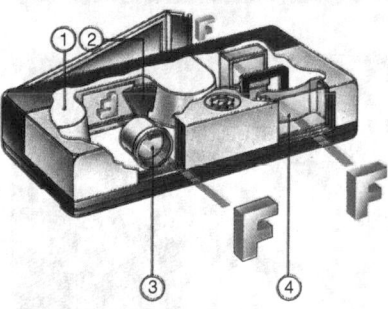

The Instamatic 100 is a slim camera with a plastic lens and a moulded polystyrene body. It uses 16 mm film, giving a picture size of 17x13 mm and is cassette-loaded.
1 Cassette
2 Shutter
3 Lens
4 Viewfinder

Photometry, science of the measurement of light, particularly as it affects illumination engineering. The brightness experienced when light strikes the human eye depends not only on the power but also on the wavelength of the light. In SI (international system) units, the photometric base quantity is luminous intensity, which measures the intensity of light radiated from a small source. The base unit of luminous intensity is the candela (cd). The illuminance falling on a surface (formerly known as its illumination) is measured in luxes (lx). Up to the 1970s scientists were not in agreement about the concepts and terminology to be used in photometry, so many alternative units-apostilbs, blondels, foot-candles, and lamberts-are still encountered.

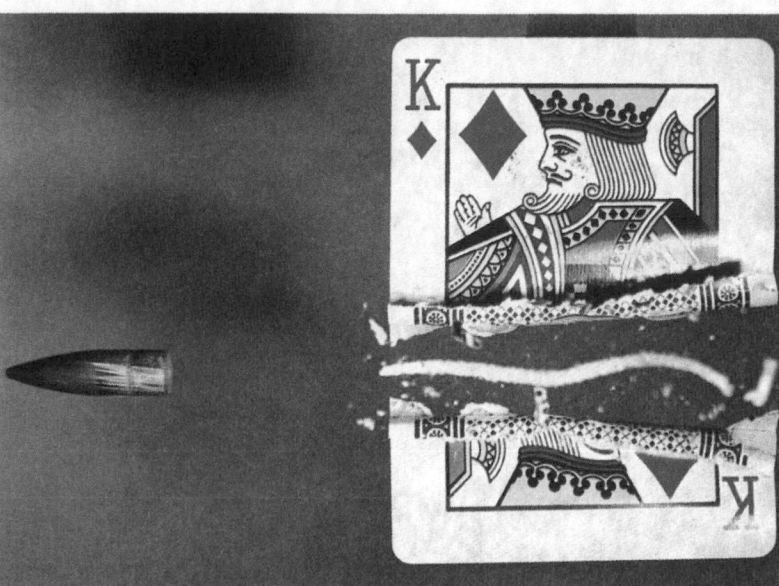

High-speed and microphotography can capture events and details invisible for the human eye. The flight of a bullet was caught by a camera equipped with a high-speed shutter and a strobelight attachment in an exposure lasting one-millionth of a second.

P

Photon, quantum of electromagnetic energy, often thought of as the particle associated with light or other electromagnetic radiation. Its energy is given by hv, where h is the Planck constant and v the frequency of the radiation.
See also: Light; Quantum mechanics; Radiation.

Photosynthesis, process by which green plants convert the energy of sunlight into chemical energy that is stored as carbohydrate. The process can be written as:
$$6CO_2+6H_2O \rightarrow C_6H_{12}O_6+6O_2 \ (\rightarrow = light)$$
In the 'light reaction,' chlorophyll (the key chemical in the whole process) is activated by absorbing a quantum of light, initiating a sequence of reactions in which the energy-rich compounds (ATP) adenosine triphosphate and the reduced form of triphosphopyriden nucleotide (TPNH) are made, water being decomposed to give free oxygen in the process. In the second stage, the 'dark reaction,' the ATP and TPNH provide the energy for the assimilation of carbon dioxide gas, yielding a variety of sugars from which other sugars and carbohydrates, including starch, can be built up.

Phrenology, theory that the various faculties of the mind occupy distinct and separate areas in the brain cortex and that the predominance of certain faculties can be predicted from modifications of the parts of the skull overlying the areas where these faculties are located. Phrenologists studied the shape and detailed contours of the skull as indicators of personality, intelligence, and individual characteristics. The method, developed by F.J. Gall and promoted in the United Kingdom and United States by George Combe (1788-1858), had many 19th century followers and led to the more enlightened treatment of the mentally ill.

Phrygia, ancient region and sometime kingdom (8th-6th centuries B.C.) in present-day central Turkey. Its early kings included Midas and Gordius. Excavation shows the Phrygians to have been highly cultured. The

The thin blade of a leaf consists of several layers of cells, each performing special functions. The upper and lower surfaces consist of a layer of protective epidermal cells (1), coated with waterproof cutin and pierced by stomata (2), through which gases can enter and escape. The palisade layer (3) below the upper epidermis, contains long cylindrical cells packed with chloroplasts, in which photosynthesis takes place. Between the palisade layer and the lower epidermis, is the spongy mesophyll (4), where the starchy products of photosynthesis are temporarily stored.

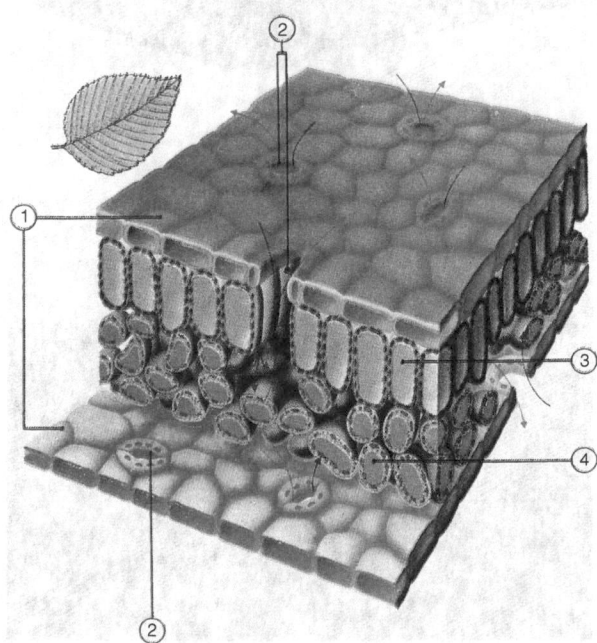

P

Digital rendering of a beach photo. Modern technology has had a large impact on the work of photographers. Besides the traditional dark room, they are now using advanced computers that can modify analog as well as digital photos. This rendering gives the impression of an impressionist painting (left), but less in-your-face effects can also be achieved.

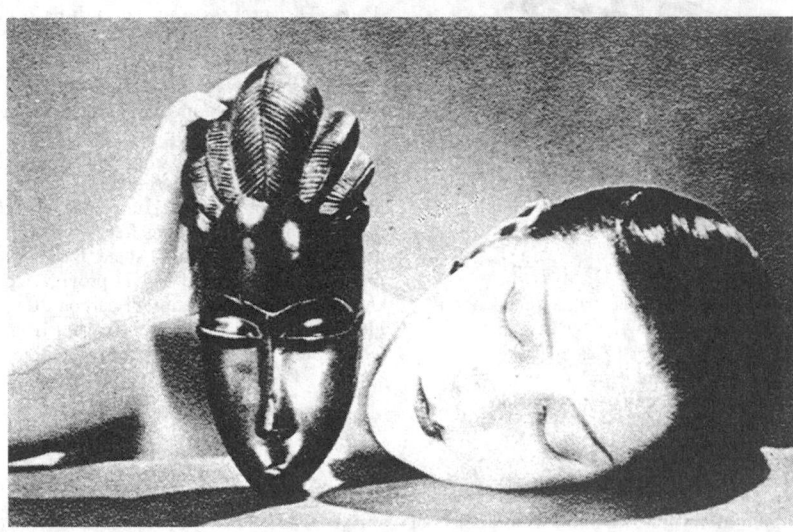

A camera from 1839 like the one used by Louis Daguerre (1787-1851). Focusing was done by pushing the rear chamber, that was equipped with a special glass plate, in or out.

Portrait of Kiki de Montparnasse with mask from 1926, taken by the American photographer Man Ray (1890-1976). She introduced the use of photos by artists: sometimes for inspiration or as a reference for paintings or sculptures, but most of the time simply as an artistic impression.

Finish photograph of a sprinting match (World Championships, Rome 1988). The focus is narrowed to the finish line using a special lens. While the camera remains open, the film keeps going at a speed of one hundredth second a recording. The special effect of this photo is achieved by actually sticking finish photos of the different athletes after each other. The cameras have a direct connection to a computer and the times – 9.83 seconds for the winner Ben Johnson – automatically appear on the photo's negative.

P

The interior of a modern mirror reflex camera with auto-focus. You can see the lens elements (1), the mirror (2), the prism (3) and the lithium battery (4), that provides the energy. A rotating display on the back of the camera provides all the information concerning the settings of the diaphragm and the shutter time.

A digital camera. Unlike an analog camera, that produces the image on a light-sensitive emulsion, a digital camera forms the image using a CCD (charged coupled device). The basis of a CCD is a photoelectrical sensitive plate consisting of a large amount of small, electrical, independent cells, so-called pixels. What really happens is that the light is turned into electricity, which generates an image. Digital cameras can be plugged into computers so the images can be saved, modified and archived. This technology enables photojournalists to send their work around the world in a second.

P

Phrygian worship of Cybele was taken over by the Greeks.

Phyfe, Duncan (c.1768-1854), Scottish-born U.S. cabinetmaker, designer of the most distinctive U.S. neoclassical furniture. He based his work on European styles such as the Sheraton and the Empire style.

Phylloxera, louse resembling an aphid that is a serious pest in vineyards. In North America, where phylloxera originated, the native grapes are resistant to it, but when it was imported into Europe in the middle of the 19th century this insect nearly caused disaster in some of the most famous wine-making regions. The problem was solved by grafting plants onto American grape rootstocks.

Phylum *See:* Classification.

Physical chemistry, branch of chemistry in which the theories and methods of physics are applied to chemical systems. Its main divisions are the study of molecular structure, colloids, crystals, electrochemistry, chemical equilibrium, gas laws, chemical kinetics, molecular weight determination, photochemistry, solution, spectroscopy, and chemical thermodynamics.

Physical education, instruction designed to further the health, growth, and athletic capacity of the body. It may include gymnastics, sports, and Asian techniques like yoga. Culturally important in ancient China and ancient Greece, physical education later had a primarily military application until the 19th century, when it began to be incorporated into school programs in Europe and the United States.

Physical therapy, or physiotherapy, system of physical treatment for disease or disability. Techniques include active and passive muscle movement, electrical stimulation, balancing exercises, heat, ultraviolet, or shortwave radiation; and manual vibration of the chest wall with postural drainage. Rehabilitation after fracture, surgery, or stroke or other neurological disease, training unimpaired muscles to compensate for those whose function has been lost, and the treating of lung infections such as pneumonia and bronchitis are among the aims.

Physics, science that deals with the interaction of matter and energy. Physics attempts to explain the nature of the physical world from the movements of planets to the smallest sub-atomic particles. Physics is important because many of the conclusions drawn from scientific study are applied to medicine and technology. Physics is usually divided into 2 large categories-classic physics and modern physics. Classic physics is primarily concerned with matter, motion, and energy. It can be subdivided into other areas of investigation which include mechanics, thermodynamics, acoustics, optics, and electromagnetism. The outstanding contributions to classical physics are found in the works of Archimedes, Copernicus, Galileo, Kepler, Descartes, Huygens, and Newton. Modern physics is primarily concerned with the structure of the physical world and contains a number of different disciplines including, atomic, nuclear, particle, solid state, and fluid physics. The major contributions to modern physics can be found in the works of Max Planck, Niels Bohr, and Albert Einstein, Enrico Ferni, Theodore H. Maiman, Murray Gell-Mann, George Zweig, Burton Richter, Samuel C.C. Ting, and Carl Rubbia.

Physiocrat, member of 18th century French school of economists founded by François Quesnay, who held that agriculture, rather than industry or commerce, was the basis of a nation's prosperity, and that land alone should be subject to tax. The physiocrats' belief in a natural economic law, which merely required non-interference to be successful, is reflected in their famous formula *laissez faire* (let it be). The physiocrats influenced Adam Smith.
See also: Economics.

Physiology, study of function in living organisms. Based on knowledge of anatomy, physiology seeks to demonstrate the manner in which organs perform their tasks and in which the body is organized and maintained in a state of homeostasis. Normal responses to stress are studied. Branches deal with respiration, blood circulation, the nervous system, the digestive system, the kidneys, the fluid and electrolyte balance, the endocrine glands, and metabolism.

Physiotherapy *See:* Physical therapy.

Pi, in mathematics, name of the symbol π, which denotes the ratio of the circumference of a circle to its diameter (3.1416).

Piaf, Edith (Edith Giovanna Gassion; 1915-1963), French cabaret and music-hall singer. She began singing for a living at 15 and won international fame with stirringly interpreted songs like *Milord* and *Je ne regrette rien*.

Piaget, Jean (1896-1980), Swiss psychologist whose theories of the mental development of children, though now often criticized, have been of paramount importance. He held that children develop intellectually in clear stages and that the ability to reason logically is absent from the early stages. His many books include *The Psychology of the Child* (1969), and *Biology and Knowledge* (1971).
See also: Psychology.

Piano, or pianoforte, musical stringed keyboard instrument. Depression of the keys causes the strings to be struck with felt-tipped hammers; these hammers rebound immediately after striking, so the strings go on sounding their notes until the keys are released, at which point the strings' vibrations are stopped with dampers. Bartolomeo Cristofori made the first piano in 1709, and by 1800 it had overtaken the harpsichord and the clavichord, whose plucked strings offered less volume and expressiveness, in popularity. Today the two basic types of piano are the upright piano, with vertical strings, and the grand piano, with horizontal strings, which has a range of seven octaves. Composers noted for their writing for the piano include Bach, Mozart, Beethoven, Chopin, Liszt, and Rachmaninov.

The evolution of the piano over the last 250 years. The fundamental principle – a mechanism of hammers, thrown by the keys at strings of different lengths – has remained unchanged. 1. Italian Cristofori piano of about 1720, the ancestor of all modern pianos. Its shape is that of a harpsichord. 2. Modern grand piano, immensely powerful, with a massive iron frame and the strings 'overstrung' (with the bass strings overlapping the treble strings and at an angle to them). 3. Square piano, shaped like a clavichord and a popular domestic instrument around 1800. 4. The nineteenth-century 'giraffe' piano, in effect a vertical grand piano, designed to save floor space. 5. Modern upright, overstrung piano, with the strings taking up the lower half of the instrument.

In *Guernica* (1937), Picasso fused elements of the surrealism and symbolism seen in his earlier work. This painting, 11.5 x 25.67 ft (3.5 x 7.8 m), a disturbing vision of destruction, was inspired by the April 1937 bombing of a town in northern Spain (Prado, Madrid).

Piatigorsky, Gregor (1903-1976), Russian-born U.S. cellist. He made his debut as a concert cellist in the United States in 1929 and became a U.S. citizen in 1942. Together with the violinist Jascha Heifetz and violist William Primrose, he was esteemed for his performance of chamber music.

Picabia, Francis Martínez de (1879-1953), French painter, graphic artist and writer. Initially influenced by impressionism, later by cubism. One of the founders of the Dada movement in the U.S. In Paris he joined the surrealists. After that he made figurative paintings, but after WW II returned to abstract paintings.

Picasso, Pablo (Pablo Ruiz y Picasso; 1881-1973), Spanish-born French painter, sculptor, graphic artist, and ceramist, considered by many the greatest artist of the 20th century. A precocious painter, after his melancholy 'blue period' and his lyrical 'rose period' (1901-1906), he was influenced by African and primitive art, as shown in *Les Demoiselles d'Avignon* (1907). Together, he and Georges Braque created cubism (1907-1914), its principles seen already in *Demoiselles*. His friends at this time included the poet and critic Apollinaire, the ballet impresario Serge Diaghilev (for whom he made stage designs), and the expatriate author Gertrude Stein, who acted as a patron for modernist artists. In 1921 he painted both the cubist *Three Musicians* and the classical *Three Women at the Fountain*. In the 1930s he adopted the style of surrealism, using it to horrify in the large antiwar canvas *Guernica* (1937). His later work employed both cubist and surrealist forms and could be beautiful, tender, or grotesque. His output was enormous, and near the end of his life he produced a brilliant series of etchings.

Piccalilli, relish made from chopped and pickled vegetables (green pepper, onion, cucumber, among others) and spices (mustard seed, celery seed, etc.).

Piccard, name of Swiss scientists who were twin brothers. **Auguste** (1884-1962), a physicist, set a world ballooning altitude record (1931), and an ocean-depth record (1953) in the bathyscaphe, which he designed. **Jean Felix** (1884-1963), a chemist, measured cosmic radiation during a 57,000-ft (17,374-m) balloon ascent (1934).
See also: Bathyscaph.

Piccolo, small woodwind instrument resembling a flute. Measuring 12 in (30 cm), the piccolo plays an octave higher than the concert flute. Developed in the late 1700s in Europe, it is used in concert bands, military bands, and orchestras.

Pickerel, carnivorous freshwater fish, smaller relative of the pike (family Esocidae), also with a snout like duck's bill. The grass's, or redfin, pickerel, found from Nova Scotia to Texas, grows up to 2 ft (0.6 m), and the chain pickerel, of the eastern United States grows to 14 in (36 cm).

Pickford, Mary (Gladys Smith; 1893-1979), Canadian-born U.S. movie actress. Her roles in films like *Daddy Long Legs*, under D. W. Griffith, won her the title 'America's Sweetheart'. In 1919 she and her husband, Douglas Fairbanks, helped found United Artists.
See also: Fairbanks, Douglas, Sr..

Pickle, food preserved in vinegar or brine to prevent the development of putrefying bacteria. Spices are usually added for flavor. Cucumbers, onions, beets, tomatoes, and cauliflowers make popular pickles. Pigs' feet and corned beef are also sometimes pickled.

Picric acid, also known as trinitrophenol, toxic, explosive, crystalline acid ($C_6H_3N_3O_7$) with industrial applications. Originally an explosive, it is now more commonly used in textile dyes, electric batteries, burn ointments, and the manufacture of glass. Peter Woulfe, a British chemist, first isolated this acid solid in 1771.

Pictography, writing by means of pictures, particularly ancient methods of using actual pictures as symbols. Many alphabetic symbols have been simplified from such pictures. over the course of time. For instance, our letter *A*, which developed from the Greek *alpha* and the Hebrew *aleph*, was adapted from a pictograph showing the horns of an ox.

The Baptism of Christ (c. 1450), by Piero della Francesca, demonstrates the artist's ability to use the newly discovered laws of perspective (National Gallery, London).

Picts, ancient inhabitants of Scotland whose forebears probably came from the European continent c.1000 B.C. By the 8th century A.D. their kingdom extended from Fife to Caithness. In 843 they united with the kingdom of the Scots (Dalriada) and were assimilated into the Scottish nation.
See also: Scotland.

Pidgin, language of simplified grammar and vocabulary, most often based on a western European language, with some vocabulary from or based on another or several other languages. Pidgins originate as a means of communication (e.g., for trading purposes) between peoples with different mother tongues.

Piedmont, region in northwestern Italy, including both mountainous terrain-the Alps and the Appenines-and the upper Po River valley, a rich farm area. Turin, the capital city, is a leading industrial center, the home of Fiat. The Savoy family was powerful in the region beginning in the 11th century. France ruled the region from 1798 to 1814 and had a lasting influence on local cultures. Piedmont was a center of Italian nationalism during the 19th century and played a leading role in the Risorgimento, the movement for Italian unification. Turin became the first capital of the united kingdom of Italy in 1861.
See also: Italy.

Pieplant *See:* Rhubarb.

Pierce, Franklin (1804-1869), 14th president of the United States (1853-1857). Pierce was a pliable and vacillating chief executive. He formed a Cabinet of inharmonious sectional spokesmen rather than a politically coherent team. Subservient to warring party managers, Pierce was conciliatory, bland, and yielding to all sides.
Partly to divert attention from domestic problems, he promised an expansionist foreign policy. However, plans to annex Hawaii and to acquire Cuba from Spain failed. Pierce encouraged development of the West. In 1853, his administration acquired the Gadsden Purchase-with its right-of-way for a southern route to the Pacific-from Mexico. The Kansas-Nebraska Act of 1854, repealed the Missouri Compromise (which had prohibited slavery in the region), leaving the question of allowing slavery in the territories to be decided by the settlers. It upset the careful balance between North and South, and wrecked Pierce's administration.

Piero della Francesca (c.1420-1492), Italian painter, one of the greatest Renais-

P

sance artists. His concern for the harmonious relationship of figures to their setting was expressed through simple, elegant forms, clear colors and tones, atmospheric light, and perspective, as seen in his fresco *Legend of the True Cross* (1452-1459) in Arezzo.
See also: Renaissance.

Pietà, in the visual arts, a depiction of the Virgin Mary holding the dead body of Jesus on her lap. For example, that of Michelangelo in St. Peter's (Rome).

Pietermaritzburg, also called Maritzburg (pop. 126,000), capital of Kwazulu Natal Province in northeastern South Africa. The city was founded by Boers (Dutch settlers in South Africa) after a Zulu defeat (1839). It is known for manufacturing, higher education, and its parks and gardens.
See also: South Africa.

The North American pika (*O. princeps*) lives on or near rocky slopes in the mountainous regions of California, New Mexico, and Utah. Also called the whistling hare, this highly vocal animal calls other pikas with whistles and short barks.

Piezoelectricity, reversible relationship between mechanical stress and electrostatic potential exhibited by certain crystals with no center of symmetry, discovered in 1880. When pressure is applied to a piezoelectric crystal, such as quartz, positive and negative electric charges appear on opposite crystal faces. Replacing the pressure by tension changes the sign of the charges.If an electric potential is applied across the crystal, its length changes. A piezoelectric crystal placed in an alternating electric circuit will alternately expand and contract. Resonance occurs in the circuit when its frequency matches the natural vibration frequency of the crystal. This way of coupling electrical and mechanical effects is used in microphones, phonograph pickups, and ultrasonic generators.
See also: Quartz.

Pigeon, name for family (Columbidae) of some 255 species of birds, with worldwide distribution. The typical pigeon is pastel gray, pink, or brown with contrasting patches of brighter colors. The body is compact, the neck short, and the head and bill fairly small. Most species are gregarious, and many are seen in very large flocks. The food may be stored in a distensible crop. The name *dove* is synonymous with *pigeon*.

Pigeon guillemot *See:* Guillemot.

Pigfish *See:* Grunt.

Pig iron *See:* Iron and Steel.

Pigment, coloring substance. Pigments dif-

fer from dyes, which dissolve in a medium and stain the upper layers of a surface. Pigments are finely ground insoluble substances that are suspended in a medium and form a colored layer on top of the surface to which they are applied. Paints consist of pigments suspended in liquids, such as resins. Many of the pigments used in paints consist of oxides of various metals. The colors of animals and plants are caused by pigments in their skins or outer tissues. Human skin and hair contains malanin, and plants contain the green pigment chlorophyll.
See also: Color.

Pigmy *See:* Pygmy.

Pigweed, any of several weeds of the Amaranth family. This weed is easy to grow because of its strong roots. It rises to 3 ft (91 cm) in height and displays large coarse leaves and heads of small green hair-covered flowers.

Pika, group of small mammals (family Ochstonidae) related to the hares and rabbits, also known as mousehares, whistling hares, and rock conies. They look like rabbits but have short ears and lack tails. Two species live in the Rocky Mountain regions, and the rest live in mountainous parts of Asia. Pikas are known for their piping calls and for 'making hay': rather than hibernate, they survive the winter by feeding on grass and herbs that they cut, dry in the sun, and store under a rock or log.

Pike, carnivorous freshwater fish (family Esocidae) with ducklike snout and sharp teeth. The northern pike, or jackfish (*Esoxlucius*), lies in the rivers and lakes of the Northern Hemisphere. It grows up to 4.5 ft (1.4 m) long and a weight of 53 lb (24 kg). Northern pike are green with yellow spots, a color scheme that harmonizes with the weeds in which they lurk, ready to shoot out and snap up another fish, a duck, or even a muskrat. Other pikes are the muskellunge and pickerel.

Pilate, Pontius, Roman procurator of Judea (A.D. 26-36) who ordered the crucifixion of Christ, afterward washing his hands to declaim responsibility. Hated by the Jews, he was recalled to Rome after his behavior provoked a riot that had to be put down by troops.
See also: Jesus Christ; Rome, Ancient.

Piles *See:* Hemorrhoid.

Pilgrimage *See:* Hajj; Lourdes.

Pilgrims, English settlers who first landed in New England in 1620 in the location now known as Plymouth, Mass. Fearing religious persecution in England, these Pilgrims first fled to Holland but could not tolerate the cultural differences. With the support of English merchants, they set sail in the *Mayflower* on September 1620. Upon their arrival they established the Plymouth colony. The origin of the word 'Pilgrim' to designate these settlers is not certain, but it is often attributed to William Bradford, a governor of Plymouth Colony, who referred to the settlers as 'Pilgrims.'
See also: Colonial period, American.

Pillsbury, Harry Nelson (1872-1906), chess master who was virtually unknown when he won the famous tournament in Hastings and beat (161/2 out of 21) all the well-known chess players of that time, like Tchigorin, Lasker, Tarrasch and Steinitz. Pillsbury played many famous and brilliant games, but he never equaled his first success. His best result was the first place he shared with Tarrasch in Vienna in 1898 (271/2 out of 38), but he lost the following twosome with 21/2-11/2. In 1902 he played in Hannover blind against 21 opponents (some of them masters) and in Moscow against 22 opponents, which was a world record for many years. A debilitating venereal disease affected his performance in his last years and was the cause of his untimely death.

Pilotfish (*Naucrates ductor*), fish (family Carangidae) once believed to guide sharks and even ships. Pilot fish grow to 2 ft (0.6 m) and are patterned with conspicuous bands. When young, they shelter under jellyfish or pieces of floating seaweed and driftwood. As adults, they swim very close to sharks, whales, sailing ships, or manta rays. It is thought that they feed on scraps from the shark's meals, but this does not explain why they follow ships or whales.

Pilotweed *See:* Compass plant.

Pilot whale, also called blackfish, any of several species of smalltoothed whales (genus *Globicephala*) of the dolphin family. Pilot whales are named after those members that lead the large schools-sometimes in the hundreds or thousands-in which they travel. They can detect obstacles in the water through a fatty organ called the melon. Black with white on the underside, pilot whales can weigh up to 2.5 tons (2.3 m tons) and are about 20 ft (6 m) in length. They live mainly in warmer oceans.

The northern pike (*Esoxlucius*) is a popular sports fish that has larger range of distribution than any other freshwater game fish.

Pilsen *See:* Plzen.

Pilsudski, Józef (1867-1935), Polish general and politician. Imprisoned several times for his nationalism, he led a private army against Russia in World War I and directed the Russo-Polish War. He was president of the new Polish republic (1918-1922). After a coup d'état in 1926 he became virtual dictator.
See also: Poland.

Piltdown man (*Eoanthropus dawsoni*), fraudulent human ancestor whose 'remains' were found (1908-1915) under Piltdown Common, Sussex, United Kingdom. These consisted of a skull with an apelike jaw but a large, human cranium and teeth worn down unlike those of any extant ape, surrounded by fossil animals that indicated an early Pleistocene date. In 1953 the fraud was exposed: The skull was human but relatively recent; the even more recent jaw was that of an orangutan; the teeth had been filed down by hand; and the fossil animals were not of British origin. The remains had been artificially stained to increase confusion. The hoax has been attributed to Sir Arthur Conan Doyle, among others.

Pimento, tree (*Pimenta officinalis*) of the myrtle family whose small berry-like fruit is used to make the spice allspice. The pimento is native to the Caribbean island of Jamaica. It grows 20-40 ft (6-12 m) tall; the small black fruits appear on the slender top branches. When dried, these fruit become allspice. This tree should not be confused with the red pepper commonly called pimento or pimiento.

Pimpernel (*Pimpinella magna*), perennial plant that grows along the edges of woods and in many meadows; the rootstock is used for medicinal purposes, in treating sore throats, colds, bronchitis, and inflammation of the larynx.

Pinang (Penang, George Town; pop. 328,000), capital of the West Malaysian state of the same name (state 399 sq mi, 1033 sq km pop. 1,200,000). Industrial and commercial center. Shipbuilding, iron foundry, and processing of agricultural products. Export of tin, rubber and copra. University. Founded in 1786 by the British East India Company as the first British colony in what is now Malaysia. Snake temple and Pagoda of the 10,000 Buddha's. Botanic garden.

Pinching bug *See:* Stag beetle.

Pindar (518-438 B.C.), ancient Greek lyric poet, inventor of the Pindaric ode, a poetic form in which complex rhythms in a series of stanzas hailed the victors in national athletic contests such as the Olympics. His odes were actually sung by a choir. The Pindaric ode influenced later English poetic forms developed by poets such as John Dryden and Thomas Gray.

Pine, common name for the evergreen conifer trees of the family Pinaceae. Pines have needlelike leaves and reproduce

through wind-dispersed seeds contained in pine cones. These trees are found in many places in the Northern Hemisphere. They are commercially valuable for their timber (used in the making of furniture, cabinetry, and paper pulp) and their resin (used in the making of paint, soap, and turpentine). Some western pines, such as the *Pinus Ponderosa*, grow as tall as 130 ft (40 m). Some pine cones, such as those of the Sugar pine, can be as long as 30 in (76 cm). One species, the Bristlecone pine, live over 4,000 years. Existing bristlecones are some of the oldest living things on earth.

Pineal gland, pea-sized glandlike structure situated over the brain stem that appears to be a vestigial remnant of a functioning endocrine gland in other animals. It has no known function in humans, although Réné Descartes thought it to be the seat of the soul. It has a role in pigmentation in some species; calcium deposition in the pineal makes it a useful marker of midline in skull X-rays.

Pineapple, short-stemmed plant (*Ananas comosus*) with pointed, spiny leaves. At the tip there is a dense head of flowers that form a single compound fruit, the sweet, juicy pineapple Columbus found in the West Indies. Pineapples were transported from mainland South America to European colonies in Africa and Asia. The British developed new varieties in greenhouses. Hawaii's pineapples, now 75% of the world's crop, came from England via Australia.

Pinero, Sir Arthur Wing (1855-1934), British playwright known both for his farces and for his plays based on social realism. *Dandy Dick* (1887) is an example of the former, while *The Second Mrs. Tanqueray* is an instance of the latter.

Pine siskin, North American bird (*Spinus pinus*) of the finch family, measuring about 5 in (13 cm) in length. It summers in northern regions and winters as far south as Mexico. Yellow wing and tail markings stand out from the gray to brown colored bird when it is in flight.

Pink, common name for various flowering plants in the family Caryophyllaceae. These flowers bloom from white to pink to purple. They are appreciated for their scent. Among them are the carnation (*Dianthus caryophyllus*), the common pink (*D. plumarius*), and sweet William (*D. barbatus*).

Pink bollworm, small, dark-brown moth (*Pectinophora gossypiella*) of the gelechiid moth family. The larvae dig into cotton plants, on which they feed, destroying the plants. The adult develops within a cocoon inside or near the cotton plant. Introduced into the Americas at the beginning of the 20th century, the pink bollworm has caused serious problems for farmers.

Pink-eye *See:* Conjunctivitis.

Pinocchio, name of a speaking wooden puppet, protagonist of the children's book *Le avventure di Pinocchio. Storia di un burattino* (The Adventures of Pinocchio; 1877) by Carlo Collodi (1826-1890).
See also: Collodi, Carlo.

Pinochet Ugarte, Augusto (1915-), president of Chile (1973-1988). A right-wing general, he led a bloody coup overthrowing Marxist president Salvador Allende (1973). His authoritarian regime was affirmed by a plebiscite in 1980, but he was ousted (1988) because of his government's economic incompetence despite increasingly repressive measures. Pinochet was commander-in-chief until March 1998, when he became senator for life. In October 1998 he was arrested in a British hospital and accused of genocide, torture, and terrorism. Due to health problems he was not extradited, but was able to return to Chile in 2000, where he also had to stand trial. After an Appeals Court ruled that he was mentally unfit to stand trial, the process was suspended indefinitely.
See also: Chile.

Pinochle, card game played with a 48-card deck containing 2 each of the cards 9, 10, jack, queen, king, and ace in each of the 4 suits. In the most popular version of the

P

The pineapple plant (*A. comosus*), grows up to 4 ft (1.2 m) tall and has bladelike leaves. Flowers form on a stalk and fuse to form the fleshly center of the fruit (detail).

P

game, 3 players engage in a series of bids before playing the hand. Other versions of the game-developed in the United States in the 19th century-depend upon different methods of gaining points.

Piñon, small, low-growing nut pines (genus *Pinus*) of the southwestern United States and northern Mexico. The 4 main species are noted for the edible seeds-called pine nuts-found in their cones.

Pinta *See:* Columbus, Christopher.

Pintail, duck (*Anas acuta*) of the family Anatidae. Living in fresh waters throughout the Northern Hemisphere, it is so named because of its long, pointed tail. It has a brown head and neck, and a white breast that continues into a white line on each side of the neck. The rest of the plumage on the male is predominantly gray, whereas that of the female is brown.

Pinter, Harold (1930-), English dramatist and stage director. His 'comedies of menace' have intricate and oblique human relationships, ambiguous and deceptively casual dialogue, and a fine balance of humor and tension. Notable are *The Caretaker* (1960), *The Homecoming* (1965), and *No Man's Land* (1974). His successful screenplays include *The Servant* (1963) and *The French Lieutenant's Woman* (1981) and *The Trial* (1989).

Pinworm, parasitic nematode worm (family Oxyuridae) that infests the intestines of vertebrates. An infestation by *Enterobius vermicularis* in humans is characterized by perianal itching. The pinworm is the most common parasite infecting children in temperate climates. The parasitic relationship is seldom harmful, and treatment is usually not indicated. However, pyrantel pamoate will eradicate pinworms in about 90% of cases.

Pinyin (sometimes (py)), abbreviation of the Chinese term Hanyu pinyin fang'an, i.e. 'Draft for the transcription (in Roman print) of Chinese script'. Since January 1 1979 this transcription system is used in all foreign publications of the People's Republic of China. Many Western countries have now adopted the system. It was developed in the 1950s from the so-called Latinxua system, a Latinization of Chinese, which was the product of the cooperation of Chinese and Russian linguists in the late 1920s. Since 1958 pinyin has been the official transcription system of the People's Republic of China. The introduction of pinyin should be understood within the context of attempts to generalize the Beijing pronunciation and to arrive at a complete switchover to a phonetic alphabet.

Pinzón, family of 3 Spanish brothers, navigators who took part with Columbus in discovering America. **Martín Alonso** (1440?-1493) commanded the *Pinta*; he left Columbus after reaching Cuba and unsuccessfully tried to reach Spain first. **Francisco Martín** (c.1441-1493?) served under his brother on the Pinta. **Vicente Yáñez** (c.1460-1524?) commanded the *Niña*

and stayed with Columbus; he went on to discover Brazil (1500) and to explore the coasts of Central and northern South America.

Pion *See:* Meson.

Pioneer life in America, way of life characteristic of the people who first settled the western reaches of the continental United States. Pioneer life in America has two aspects. It is the story of migration and settlement. It is also an important part of American identity, and an important part of the development of the country's values and customs.

In one sense, the pioneering life was characteristic of America from the beginning. The country's original settlers faced the same challenges, risks, and opportunities the pioneers later faced. But there are at least two important differences. America's original settlers were colonists and, to one degree or another, most came to America seeking refuge from Europe. By contrast, the pioneers were driven by the desire to own their own land.

Pioneer life developed in two great migrations between 1760 and 1850. The first lasted from the late 1700s to the early 1800s and took in areas of what are now the states of Kentucky, Tennessee, Ohio, and Illinois. The second migration, which continued into the 1850s, settled California, the Northwest, the Southwest and, eventually, the Great Plains. These migrations coincided with and were often triggered by political events like the Louisiana Purchase, the Mexican-American War, and the acquisition of Oregon, and by the Gold Rush of 1848. Settlement was also encouraged by generous federal land grant programs.

The usual patterns of these migrations began with the trailblazing of frontiersmen, fur trappers, or explorers. They were followed by the first wave of settlers, principally small farmers, who cleared the land. These settlers would often move on to virgin land and their places were taken by a second wave of settlers who established more permanent communities and, eventually, towns. The process was completed when towns

The earliest pipelines were probably those used in China during ancient times. They were made of hollow bamboo and used to transport water. To prevent leakage, the bamboo pipe was wrapped with a waxed cloth.

were connected by roads, the post, and, above all, by the railroads.

The second great migration was undertaken by wagon trains. A wagon train heading west would start in the spring in time to pass the Rocky Mountains before winter set in. Several known trails were followed, among them the Oregon Trail across the Great Plains, the South Pass across the Rockies to California, the Santa Fe Trail to the Southwest, and the Old Spanish Trail to Los Angeles. It was a difficult and dangerous journey. Indians were a constant threat, especially as settlers began to clear and farm the Great Plains. Both migrations were marked by frequent bloody episodes between settlers and Native Americans and by warfare that eventually decimated the latter. Blacks also participated in the settlement of the west. Slavery was forbidden in the Northwest Territory and freed or escaped slaves had an opportunity to begin new lives in those frontier regions.

The pioneers lived a rough, dangerous, and demanding life. There were no doctors and medical care had to be improvised. A serious illness or injury often meant death and epidemics were devastating. Pioneers built their own homes (often helping one another in the hard work), grew and hunted their own food, made their own yarn and cloth, bullets, candles, medicines, shoes, and other necessities. Their way of life fostered values of independence and self-reliance that were reinforced by religion and a strong sense of community. The struggles, hardships, and experiences of the first settlers continued to influence the later community.

Pipal *See:* Bo tree.

Pipe, musical instrument consisting of a tube of wood or metal, that produces sounds when air is blown through it. Holes along the pipe's length are covered and uncovered by fingers to produce a variety of notes. The length of the pipe, as well as whether it is stopped or open at one end, also affects the sounds it creates. The pipe was one of the first musical instruments. Other wind instruments-such as the flute, oboe, clarinet, trumpet, and pipe organ-developed from it.

Pipe, hollow stem connected to a small bowl used for smoking tobacco. Tobacco is placed in the bowl and ignited, and its smoke is drawn into the mouth through the stem. Pipes have been used in many cultures for thousands of years. They are often named for the material used to create the bowl; a corncob pipe, for instance, has a bowl made of a corncob. Other kinds of pipes include meerschaum (a clay-like material), briarwood, and porcelain.

Pipe and pipeline, tube for conveying fluids-liquids, gases, or slurries. Pipes vary in diameter considerably, according to the flow rate required and the pressure gradient. Materials used include steel, cast iron, other metals, reinforced concrete, fired clay, plastic, bitumenized-fiber cylinders, and wood. They are often coated inside and out with bitumen or concrete to prevent corrosion. Concrete, plastic, and steel pipes can now be made and laid in 1 continuous process, but

The water pipit (*A. spinoletta*) is a bird commonly found on shores and in fields. Like wagtails of the same family (Motacillidae), pipits walk rather than hop, flicking their tail.

most pipes still need to be joined by means of welding, screw joints, clamped flange joints, couplings, or bell-and-spigot joints caulked with lead or cement. Pipelines, consisting of long lengths of pipe with valves and pumps at regular intervals (about 60 mi/98 km for oil pipelines), are used chiefly for transporting water, sewage, chemicals, foodstuffs, crude oils, and natural gas.

Pipefish, eellike fish with tubular mouth of the family Syngnathidae. They live in tropical seas and estuaries, feeding on minute plankton. The U.S. species can change color to match their backgrounds and swim vertically so that they look like waving weeds. Like the related sea horses, the male carries the eggs and babies.

Pipit, small songbird (family Motacillidae) of open country that looks and sings rather like a lark. Pipits nest under clumps of vegetation. They are found all over the world, including the subantarctic island of South Georgia. The water pipet and Sprague's pipit are the only North American species.

Piquet, Nelson (Nelson Souto Major; (1952-), Brazilian racing driver, adopted his mother's name after a quarrel with his father about his career. He made his debut in 1978 in an Ensign in the Formula 1 during the Grand Prix of West Germany. Piquet won his first world title in 1981 in the Formula One in a Brabham. He became world champion again in 1983 in a car of the same make. In 1987 he won his third world title, this time in a Williams-Honda.

Piraeus (pop. 196,000), city in Greece. It is the port for Athens and the largest Greek port, handling most of Greece's importing and exporting. The port is very modern, and is linked by railway and highway to Athens. Piraeus is also a manufacturing center, producing cloth, leather-goods, soaps, metals, and alcohol. Athenians created a port in Piræus in the 5th century B.C. The arrangement of streets in modern Piræus is based on a city plan developed in 460 B.C. Romans destroyed Piræus in 86 B.C. Piræus' harbors remained unused until A.D. 1834, when the Greeks rebuilt it. It has been an important port ever since. Artifacts from early Greek and Roman times are on display in the Archeological Museum in Piræus.
See also: Greece.

Pirandello, Luigi (1867-1936), Italian dramatist and author, winner of the 1934 Nobel Prize for literature. He is noted for his grimly humorous treatment of psychological themes and of the reality of art compared with 'real' life, as in his best-known play, *Six Characters in Search of an Author* (1921).

Piranesi, Giovanni Battista (1720-1778), Italian etcher, draftsperson, and architect, known for his prints of old and contemporary Roman buildings, *Views of Rome* (begun 1748), and for a series of fantastic *Imaginary Prisons* (c.1745). They are notable for their grandeur and lighting contrasts.

Piranha, or caribe, small, extremely ferocious, shoaling freshwater fish (family Characidae) of South America. The jaws are short but powerful, armed with sharp cutting teeth. They quickly strip the flesh from other fish and mammals and have been known to attack humans.

Pirate, person who robs ships at sea. Pirates were active in the sea routes of trading ships. They also attacked and plundered coastal villages. Although piracy still occurs in such waters as the South China Sea and the Gulf of Thailand, it no longer occurs on the scale it once did. In Roman times, pirates along the Eastern Mediterranean Sea robbed ships from importing goods into Rome. From the 1500s through the 1700s, pirates from the Barbary Coast of northern Africa roamed the Mediterranean to plunder European ships. During that same period, English, Dutch, and French pirates sailed the Caribbean to rob Spanish ships carrying goods from the Spanish-controlled West Indies islands and South America. During the 1700 and 1800s pirates attacked ships carrying cargo between North America and Europe. By the mid-1800s, the navies of various countries successfully rid the sea of pirate ships.

Pisa (pop. 100,000), historic city in the northwestern region of central Italy, on the Arno River in Tuscany. Galilei Galileo was born at Pisa. The city is famous for its marble campanile (the Leaning Tower) and rich in architecture and art.
See also: Leaning Tower of Pisa.

Pisa, Council of (1409), uncanonical Roman Catholic Ecumenical Council of 500 prelates and delegates from throughout Europe that met to try to heal the Great Schism. It deposed the rival popes of Rome and Avignon and elected a 3rd pope, Alexander V. This, however, merely created 3 separate parties.

Pisa, Leaning Tower of *See:* Leaning Tower of Pisa.

Pisanello (real name Antonio (di Puccio) Pisano; 1395-1455), Italian painter, artist and medallist. Important master of international Gothic. Together with Gentile da Fabriano he worked on the frescos in the Palazzo Ducale in Venice (1415-1422) and in the S. Giovanni in Laterano in Rome (1431-1432). Was held in high regard as a medallist. Made many portrait medallions of prominent people.

Pisano, Andrea (real name Andrea di Ser Ugolino da Pontedera; ca. 1290-1348/49), Italian sculptor and architect, initially a goldsmith. Involved with the construction of the cathedral and the bell tower in Florence. Designed one of the bronze doors of the baptistery (completed 1336) and a series of marble relief carvings on the bell tower (1337).

Pisano, Giovanni (di Niccolò) (1250?-1314?), Italian sculptor and architect. Pisano studied with his father, Nicola Pisano. The pulpit in Pisa Cathedral and the Madonna in the Arena Chapel, Padua, are among his

The west facade of the Cathedral of S. Maggiori, Pisa. Construction of the Cathedral, which was designed by Buscheto, started in 1063, was interrupted in 1095, and resumed again in 1099. The west facade (1200) is attributed to Mastro Rainaldo.

Luigi Pirandello (1867-1936) was one of the leading twentieth-century Italian playwrights, although it was not until later in his life that he was recognized as such.

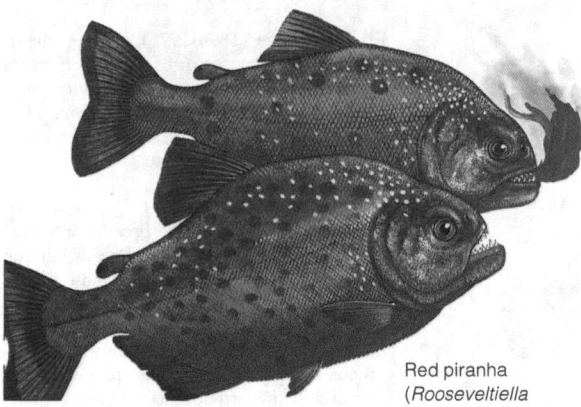

Red piranha (*Rooseveltiella nattereri*, order *Cypriniformes*), maximum length 13 in (33 cm), found in South America, abundant in the Amazon Basin, the Orinoco River and the Parana Basin.

Members of this family are generally known as Characins, with paranhas noted as Saw-bellied characins. This terminology relates to the serrated belly and keel.

P

P

main works. As an architect, Giovanni Pisano did much work on the Siena Cathedral.

Pisano, Nicola (1210?-1278), Italian sculptor. Inspired by ancient Roman sculpture, he worked in a classical style that anticipates the Renaissance movement. The reliefs he created for the six-sided baptistry in Pisa showing events in Christ's life was his first masterpiece. Other important works include the eight-sided pulpit for the Cathedral of Siena and the fountain at Perugia. His son, Giovanni, helped him design and execute some of his works. Pisano lived in Pisa.
See also: Relief.

Piscator, Erwin (1893-1966), German stage director whose innovations had a great influence on the theater. Made his debut as an actor in 1914, tried in vain to propagate his left-pacifistic ideas in his own Proletarisches Theater in Berlin (1920-1921). From 1924 until 1927 he was a director at the Berliner Volksbühne and there he introduced the use of projections and film. From 1927 until 1931 he led his own Piscator Bühne, worked in Moscow until 1936, and after that in Paris. Stayed in the U.S. from 1939 until 1951, where he set up the Dramatic Workshop. From 1962 onwards worked with the Berlin Freie Volksbühne, where he directed e.g. *The Representative* (1963).

Pisemski, Aleksei Feofilaktovitch (1821-1881), Russian novelist and playwright. Wrote in the tradition of Russian realism of the 1850s and 1860s. During his college years he came in contact with English, French and German literature. Especially the theories of George Sand about the freedom of feelings and the emancipation of women have had an influence on his work. His first novella, *Boyartchina* (1846), was banned by the censors and was not published until 1858. His best-known novel is *One Thousand Souls* (1858), other work includes *The Simpleton* (1850). Pisemski's later work was severely criticized, also because he reacted more and more venomously against idealists, nihilists, socialists and radicals.

Pisistratus, or Peisistratus (600-527 B.C.), tyrant of Athens, whose benign rule and fostering of commerce and the arts made Athens the foremost city in Greece. In 560 B.C. he seized power in a popular coup d'état. Aristocrats, having returned from exile, ousted him in 552, but in 541 he established

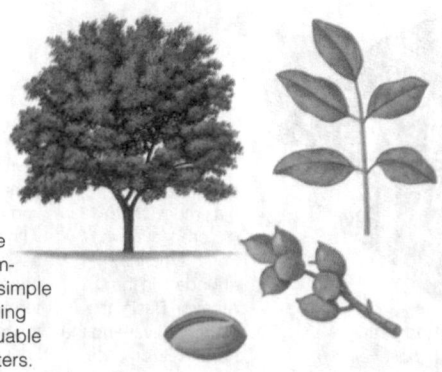

The pistachio tree (*P. vera*) is a warm-climate tree with simple leaves on spreading branches. Its valuable nuts grow in clusters.

Nicola Pisano (1210?-1278) designed the hexagonal pulpit of the baptisterium of Pisa Cathedral (1259). The balustrade consists of marble reliefs, representing the birth of Christ, the worship of the three kings, the dedication in the temple, the crucifixion (which is clearly visible here) and the Last Judgement.

himself firmly. He enforced Solon's laws, promoted public works, and was succeeded by his sons.

Pissarro, Camille (1830-1903), French impressionist painter. Influenced by the Barbizon School at first, he was, with Cézanne, Monet, and Renoir, a founder of impressionism. His works, especially landscapes and street scenes, are noted for their freshness, vividness, and luminous color.

Pistachio nut (*Pistacia vera*), seed of the pistachio tree in the cashew family. Pistachio trees grow in western Asia, the Mediterranean, and southwestern U.S. The nut, which is about 1 in (2.5 cm) long, consists of a hard shell, smooth husk, and an edible green kernel. The kernel, which has a mild flavor, can be eaten whole. When ground, kernels are used to flavor foods; when pressed, they produce a cooking oil.

Piston, Walter (1894-1976), U.S. neoclassical composer, professor of music at Harvard (1926-60). His austere but dynamic music incorporates complex rhythms and harmonics in traditional forms. His *Symphony No. 7* (1961) won a Pulitzer Prize.
See also: Counterpoint.

Pit bull, any of several breeds or cross-breeds of dogs having a mixture of bulldog and terrier. The American pit bull terrier, bull terrier, bulldog, and Staffordshire bull terrier are breeds of pit bulls. They have strong muscular bodies, and are very courageous fighters. When trained properly, they are excellent guard dogs as well as obedient,

affectionate companion dogs. However, pit bulls can become dangerous when their owners abuse them or train them to be aggressive. Then they become capable of attacking and even killing other dogs, as well as people. This has led some communities to enact laws regulating pit bulls to ensure that the dogs will not threaten public safety.

Pitcairn Island, British colony (2 sq mi/4 sq km) in the Pacific Ocean midway between New Zealand and Panama, famous as the uninhabited island settled by *Bounty* mutineers and Tahitian women (1790). Its present English-speaking islanders are descended from them.

Pitch, frequency of the vibrations constituting a sound. The frequency associated with tones of the musical scale has varied over the years. The present international standard sets Concert A (A above middle C) at 440 cycles per sec.
See also: Music.

Pitchblende, or uraninite, brown, black, or greenish radioactive mineral, the most important source of uranium, radium, and polonium. The composition varies between UO_2 and $UO_{2.6}$; thorium, radium, polonium, lead, and helium are also present. Principal deposits are in Zaire and Czechoslovakia, at Great Bear Lake in Canada, and in the U.S. Mountain States.

Pitcher plant, name given to several insect-eating plants of 3 different families (North American, Old World, and Australian) in which the leaves form a pot-shaped trap for insects. Unwary insects make their way into the pitcher and are drowned in the water that collects there. Among the pitcher plant's many local names are huntsman's-cup and sidesaddle flower.

Pitt, name of 2 English statesmen. **William, 1st Earl of Chatham** (1708-1778), known as Pitt the Elder and a noted orator, was war minister during the Seven Years' War (1756-1763). Through defeating the French, by 1761 he had gained imperial supremacy for Britain in Europe, Canada, and India, and

William Pitt 1st Earl of Chatham (1708-1778).

made the British navy a formidable force. Out of office after 1768, he opposed taxing American colonists and defended their rights, but was against granting them independence. His second son, **William** (1759-1806), known as **Pitt the Younger**, at 24 became Britain's youngest prime minister. He dominated British politics until his death. From 1784, supported by a weakened George III, Pitt's ministry strengthened national finances and the government's power in India, but agitation by radicals at home forced him to suppress some civil rights (1794) and shelve parliamentary reforms. Continental wars waged, and lost (1793-1805), by coalitions of Britain's allies against Napoleon I required Pitt's financial support, which he raised through higher taxes. To quell continuing Irish rebellions, Pitt proposed a parliamentary union with England and Catholic Emancipation (1798), but King George refused it.
See also: United Kingdom.

Pitti Palace, palace in Florence, Italy. Currently, it is an art museum housing an extensive collection of Renaissance art. It was originally built for the wealthy merchant Luca Pitti and later became the home of several Italian kings. The structure was begun in 1458, and major expansions were added subsequently. As the largest palace in Florence, it is impressive for its size and for the beautiful gardens (Boboli Gardens) located behind it.

Pittsburgh (pop. 367,000), steel-producing city in southwestern Pennsylvania, seat of Allegheny County, and the state's 2nd-largest city. Settled in 1758 as Fort Pitt and incorporated as a city in 1816, it now occupies over 55 sq mi (142 sq km) around its business center, the Golden Triangle, where the Allegheny and Monongahela rivers meet to form the Ohio. The city's economic wealth is based on steel mills, coke from Allegheny coal, pig iron, glass, and various manufactured products. The University of Pittsburgh and the Carnegie Institute are among its educational institutions.
See also: Pennsylvania.

Pituitary gland, major endocrine gland, situated just below the brain, under the control of the adjacent hypothalamus and in its turn controlling other endocrine glands. The posterior pituitary is a direct extension of certain cells in the hypothalamus and secretes vasopressin and oxytocin into the bloodstream. The anterior pituitary develops separately and consists of several cell types that secrete different hormones, including growth hormone, follicle-stimulating hormone, luteinizing hormone, prolactin, thyrotrophic hormone (which stimulates thyroid gland), and adrenocorticotrophic hormone (ACTH). Feedback from organs occurs at both the hypothalamic and pituitary levels. Pituitary tumors or loss of blood supply may cause loss of function; however, some tumors may be functional and produce syndromes like gigantism or acromegaly (due to growth hormone imbalance).
See also: Human body; Hypothalamus.

Pit viper, predominantly New World venomous snake (family Crotalidae). Pit vipers have a pit on each side of the head, each containing a temperature-sensitive organ that can detect the minute changes in temperature caused by the presence of other animals, enabling the snake to detect and strike at its prey. Pit vipers have fangs that fold back when not in use. Most species give birth to live young. Pit vipers include the copperhead, water moccasin, fer-de-lance, and rattlesnake.

Pius, name of 12 popes. Saint **Pius V** (Michele Ghislieri; 1504-1572), an Italian, was elected in 1566. With some severity he restored a degree of discipline and morality to the papacy in the face of the Protestant challenge and organized the Spanish-Venetian expedition that defeated the Turks at Lepanto in 1571. **Pius VII** (Gregorio Luigi Barnaba Chiaramonti; 1740-1823), an Italian, was elected in 1800. Under an 1801 concordat French troops were withdrawn, but the Papal States were later annexed by Napoleon I, whom Pius had consecrated emperor in 1804. **Pius IX** (Giovanni Maria Mastai-Ferretti; 1792-1878), an Italian, began the longest papal reign, in 1846, with liberal reforms but became an extreme reactionary in both politics and dogma after the revolution of 1848. The Immaculate Conception became an article of dogma (1854), and papal infallibility was proclaimed in 1870 by the 1st Vatican Council. In 1871 the new kingdom of Italy passed the Law of Guaranties, defining relations between the state and the papacy, but Pius refused to accept the position. **Saint Pius X** (Giuseppe Melchiorre Sarto; 1835-1914), an Italian, was elected in 1903. He condemned modernism in the church. **Pius XI** (Ambrogio Damiano Achille Ratti; 1857-1939), an Italian, was elected in 1922. He concluded the Lateran Treaty (1929) with the Italian state and issued encyclicals condemning communism, fascism, and racism. **Pius XII** (Eugenio Pacelli; 1876-1958), a Roman, was elected in 1939. He was an active diplomat in a difficult period and undertook a considerable amount of humanitarian work during World War II, although he was criticized for refusing to condemn Nazi policy toward the Jews. His encyclical *Mediator Dei* led to changes in the Masses.

Pizarro, Francisco (c.1474-1541), Spanish conquistador who destroyed the Inca empire in the course of his conquest of Peru. He was with Vasco de Balboa when he discovered the Pacific Ocean (1513). In 1524 and 1526-1527, Pizarro attempted, with Diego de Almagro and Fernando de Luque, to conquer Peru. In 1531, with royal assent, he began a new campaign and found Peru in an unsettled state under the Inca emperor Atahualpa. At Cajamarca in the Andes, Pizarro's small band, at first pretending friendship, kidnapped Atahualpa and massacred his unarmed followers. Pizarro, a vicious and greedy man, forced the emperor to pay a massive ransom, then executed him. Turning on Almagro, Pizarro cheated him and eventually had him killed; Almagro's followers assassinated Pizarro.
See also: Conquistadors.

Like all pit vipers, the eastern diamondback rattlesnake (*Crotalus adamanteus*) has a deep sensory pit between its nostril and eye, which detects warm-blooded animals up to 20 in (50 cm) away.

PKK, Turkish-Kurdish Labor Party. The PKK, led by Abdullah Öcalan, is a guerilla movement in the mountainous southeast of Turkey. The movement strives for an autonomous Kurdish state since 1984. About 7% of the Turkish population is Kurdish. The PKK also has many supporters in the West, who to a large extent provide the funding of the PKK. Terrorist activities (aimed at Turkish goals) of the PKK in Europe caused the party to be banned in Germany and France. In 1992 a conflict arose between the PKK (which also operates from bases in Northern Iraq) and the Iraqi-Kurdish parties about the trade between Turkey and the Kurdish area. This caused the Iraqi Kurds to start an armed operation together with the Turkish army against PKK bases in Northern Iraq. In 1995 the PKK proclaimed a unilateral truce. The Turkish army ignored the truce and started a big spring offensive in 1996. Refuges and arms depots of the PKK in the southeast of Turkey and northern Iraq were attacked and hundreds of Kurds died. In subsequent years the war dragged on. In 2002, the PKK changed its name to Congress of Freedom and Democracy in Kurdistan (Kadek) and declared that the organization would from now on only use legal resources to attain a solution for the Kurdish problem. However, the Turkish government still considered the PKK to be a terrorist organization.
See also: Kurds.

PKU *See:* Phenylketonuria.

Placebo, tablet, syrup, or other form of seeming medication that is inactive, prescribed in lieu of active preparations. Placebos are prescribed for psychological purposes and are used as controls in experimental studies of drug effectiveness.

Placenta, specialized structure derived from the uterus lining and part of the embryo after implantation. It separates and yet ensures a close and extensive contact between the maternal (uterine) and fetal (umbilical) blood circulations. This allows nutrients and oxygen to pass from the mother to the fetus, and waste products to pass in the reverse direction. Gonadotropins produced by the placenta prepare the maternal body for delivery and the breasts for lactation. The placenta is delivered after the child at birth (the afterbirth) by separation of the blood-vessel layers.
See also: Reproduction.

P

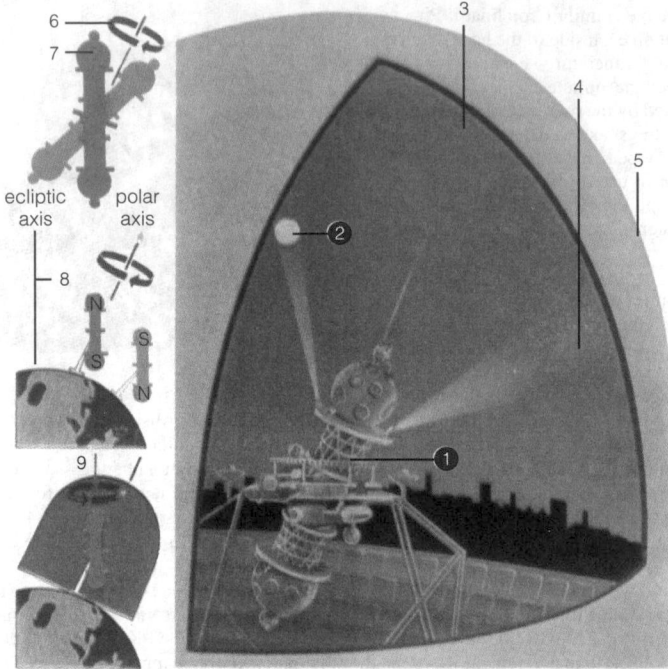

ecliptic axis   polar axis

A planetarium is an instrument (1) designed to protect images of celestial objects (2,3,4) on a large domed ceiling (5). A star's daily motion (6) about the celestial pole can be depicted for any latitude by tilting the projector (7) about a horizontal axis. A view of the night sky as seen from the polar regions (8) is obtained by turning the planetarium to a

vertical position. One project for (N) depicts the stars visible at the North Pole; the

opposite project for (S) shows those seen at the South Pole. Changes

(9) in the polar star (arrow) resulting from precession of the Earths axis are

duplicated by moving the planetarium about a specifically designed axis.

Max Planck (1858-1947).

Plagiarism, the act of copying another's work (ideas, writings, or other creative work) and presenting it as one's own. As it is in essence stealing, plagiarism is unethical. Copyright laws make plagiarism a punishable crime in many countries. However, the borrowing of ideas or thoughts and expressing them in one's own words is not considered plagiarism.
See also: Copyright.

Plain, expanse of nearly level land, usually surrounded by higher land forms. About half of the world's land area is made up of plains, and they are found on ocean and sea floors as well. On land, there are three major kinds of plains: coastal, inland, and flood. Coastal plains stretch along seacoasts and often slope from sealevel to higher land. Inland plains are found in the interior of continents. Flood plains occur along rivers and are formed by materials (silt, sand, mud) deposited when the rivers overflow during floods. Depending on the climate, plains can be very fertile areas conducive to farming. A large percentage of the world's population lives on plains because they are food-producing, easy to build on, and to travel across.

Planarian, type of flatworm (turbellarian) having a flat, long body and broad head. Planarians are found in fresh or salt water, as well as in moist earth. Depending on the species, they are white, gray, brown, or black, and range in size from $1/4$ in to $1 1/2$ in (7 mm to 35 mm) long. Some planarians living in tropical soil may grow as long as 2 ft (60 cm). Planarians are meat eating, and feed on small animals and dead bodies of larger animals. They can reproduce by laying eggs

or by dividing their bodies into parts, each part then becoming a complete body.

Planck, Max Karl Ernst Ludwig (1858-1947), German physicist whose quantum theory, with Albert Einstein's theory of relativity, ushered physics into the modern era. Initially influenced by Rudolf Clausius, he made fundamental researches in thermodynamics before turning to investigate blackbody radiation. To describe the electromagnetic radiation emitted from a blackbody, he evolved the Planck radiation formula, which implied that energy, like matter, can exist only as quanta (discrete amounts).Planck himself was unconvinced of this, even after Einstein had applied the theory to the photoelectric effect and Bohr in his model of the

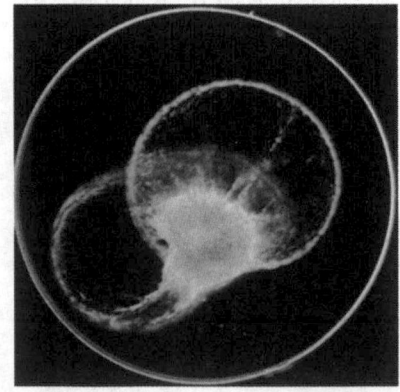

Unicellular Dinoflagellates (class *Dinophyceae*) are the most important constituent of vegetable plankton.

The saltwater species are often capable of luminescence, like this *Noctiluca* from the Caribbean Sea.

atom, but Planck received the 1918 Nobel Prize for physics for his achievement.
See also: Quantum mechanics; Radiation.

Plane, in mathematics, surface having only length and breadth, any 2 points of which can be joined by a straight line composed entirely of points also in the plane. A plane may be determined by 2 intersecting or parallel lines, by a line and a point that does not lie on the line, or by 3 points that do not lie in a straight line. The intersection of 2 planes is a straight line; the intersection of a plane and a line in a different plane is a point. An infinite number of planes may pass through a single point or line. A plane is parallel to another plane if all perpendiculars drawn between them are of equal length.

Planet, in the solar system, 1 of the 9 major celestial bodies (Mercury, Venus, Earth, Mars, Jupiter, Saturn, Uranus, Neptune, and Pluto) orbiting the sun; by extension, a similar body circling any other star. In 1963 it was discovered that Barnard's Star has at least 1 companion about 1.5 times the size of Jupiter, and in 1983 scientists detected possible evidence of an evolving planetary system around the star Vega.
See also: Solar System.

Planetarium, optical device representing the relative positions and motions of celestial objects on the interior of a hemispherical dome. Of great assistance to students of astronomy and celestial navigation, planetariums also attract large public audiences. The 1st modern planetarium, built in 1923 by the firm of Carl Zeiss, is still in use at the Deutsches Museum, Munich, Germany.

Planetoid *See:* Asteroid.

Plane tree *See:* Sycamore.

Plankton, microscopic marine animals and plants. They drift under the influence of ocean currents and are vitally important links in the marine food chain. A major part of plankton comprises minute plants (phytoplankton), mainly algae but including dinoflagellates and diatoms. Phytoplankton may be so numerous as to color the water and cause it to have a 'bloom.' They are eaten by various animals (called zooplankton) that are in turn an important food for large animals, such as whales, and countless fishes. Phytoplankton is confined to the upper layers of the sea, where light can reach, but zooplankton has been found at great depths.

Plant, living organism belonging to the plant kingdom (Planta). Green plants are unique in being able to synthesize their own organic molecules from carbon dioxide and water, using light-energy, by the process known as photosynthesis. Mineral nutrients are absorbed from the environment. Plants are the primary source of food for all other living organisms.
The possession of chlorophyll, the green photosynthetic pigment, is probably the most important distinction between plants and animals. Plants are generally stationary and have no nervous system, and the cell wall generally contains large amounts of cel-

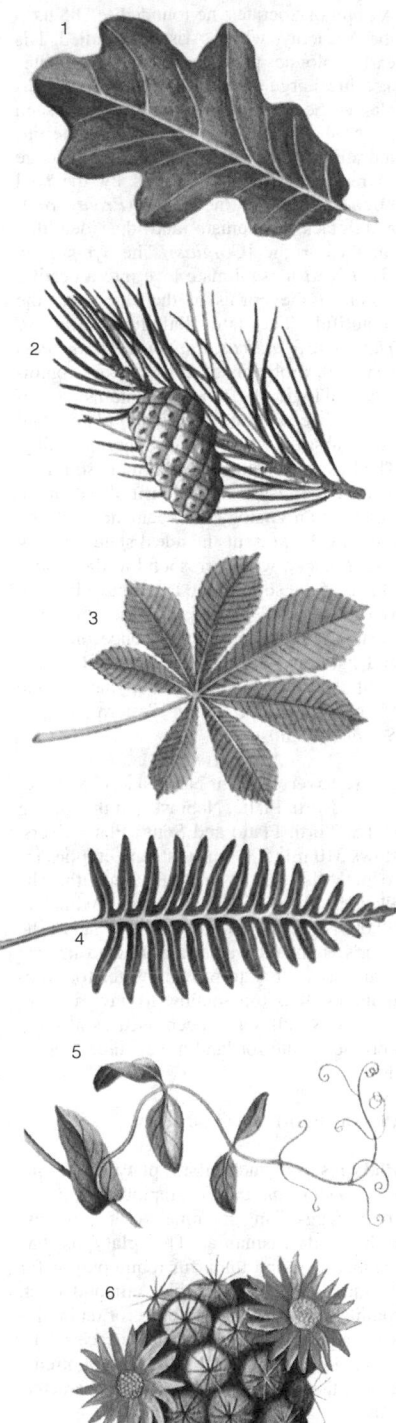

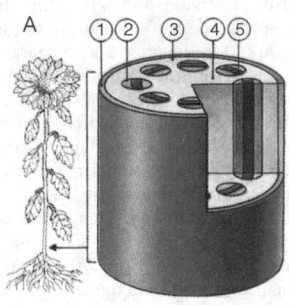

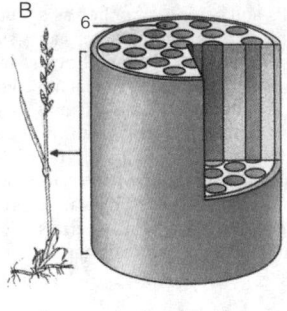

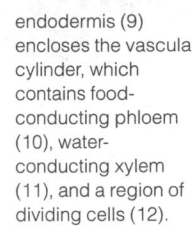

P

The stem of a dicotyledonous plant, such as the sunflower *Helianthus*, is surrounded by epidermis (1), and has bundles of vascular tissue (2), arranged in a circle, dividing the stem into an outer cortex (3) and inner pith (4). Each bundle has a layer of actively dividing cambium (5), which produces more vascular tissue when the stem thickens. A typical monocot, such as grass (B), has its vascular bundles (6) scattered throughout the stem. No distinction exists between pith and cortex, and the vascular bundles, which lack a cambial layer, are closed to further growth. A cross section of an angiosperm root (C) reveals the distinct tissue layers. The epidermis (7) absorbs water and minerals through root hairs. Cells of the cortex (8) store starch and other substances. A thin endodermis (9) encloses the vascular cylinder, which contains food-conducting phloem (10), water-conducting xylem (11), and a region of dividing cells (12).

lulose. Some insectivorous plants obtain their food by trapping insects.

The higher plants (gymnosperms and angiosperms) are much the same in their basic anatomy and morphology. In a typical angiosperm, 4 main regions can be recognized: root, stem, leaf, and flower. Each region has one or more basic functions.

Plants cells are not all alike, and each one is adapted to do a certain job, but all are derived from a basic pattern. This basic plant cell tends to be rectangular and has a tough wall of cellulose, which gives it its shape. The cell membrane is inside the wall. Inside the membrane is the protoplasm, which contains the nucleus and chloroplasts and many other microscopic structures. In the center of the protoplasm there is a large sap-filled vacuole that maintains the cell's shape and plays an important part in the working of the whole plant.

Both sexual and asexual reproduction are widespread throughout the plant kingdom. Many plants are capable of both forms, and in some cases the life cycle of the plant may involve the two different forms.

Plantagenet, name given to the branch of the Angevin dynasty descended from Geoffrey Plantagenet that ruled England from 1154 to 1485. From Henry II until the deposition of Richard II in 1399 the succession was direct. Thereafter, the crown passed to other branches of the family until the defeat of the Yorkist Plantagenet, Richard III, at the hands of Henry Tudor (Henry VII), who had remote Plantagenet connections. *See also:* United Kingdom.

Plantain, group of herbs in the family *Plantaginaceae*. Growing close to the ground, they have spikes growing out of a circular cluster of leaves. Many plantains are weeds and are undesired by gardeners. Some plantain plants, however, are grown for their medicinal value. Plantain is also the name of a tropical plant related to the banana. Hard and full of starch, this plantain is eaten cooked and is a major food in some tropical regions.

Leaves vary widely in form. The broad leaf of the English oak, *Quercus robur* (1), and the needles of the Scots pine, *Pinus sylvestris* (2), are simple leaves, with a single leaf blade. The horse chestnut, *Aesculus hippocastanum* (3), bears palmately compound leaves, with leaflets radiating from one point. The leaf of *Polypodium* (4), a fern, has segments arranged pinnately along a main stalk. The garden pea, *Pisum sativum* (5), has leaflets modified as coiling tendrils. The leaves of *Mammillaria* (6) and other cacti are modified into spines.

Plantain lily *See:* Day lily.

Plantation, large farm on which a crop is planted, tended, and harvested by workers who live there. Plantations are most often in tropical or semitropical regions. Crops raised on plantations include cotton, tobacco, coffee, cocoa, tea, rubber, sugar-cane and tropical fruits. Most plantations specialize in one product. Many plantations developed by Europeans who colonized regions throughout the world, including America, were once worked by slaves and by servants who were indebted to the plantation owner. After slavery was abolished, plantations hired laborers who were paid very little or else received a share of the crop for their work. In modern times, the development of agricultural techniques has led many plantations to use more farm machinery and fewer workers.

Planting *See:* Agriculture.

Plant louse *See:* Aphid.

Plasma, in physics, almost completely ionized gas containing equal numbers of free electrons and positive ions. Stars and interstellar gas consist of plasma. Unlike un-ionized gas, plasma conducts electricity and is affected magnetically. Plasma may be a 4th state of matter (besides gases, liquids, and solids). Because the temperature of a plasma is theoretically high enough to support a controlled nuclear fusion reaction, plasmas are being widely studied as a means to contain such a reaction to create energy. Plasmas are formed by heating low-pressure gases until the atoms have sufficient energy to ionize each other. Unless the plasma can be successfully contained by electric or magnetic fields, rapid cooling and recombination occur. *See also:* Physics.

Plasma, in biology, fluid portion of the blood, including fibrinogen; distinguished from serum, from which fibrinogen has been separated. *See also:* Blood.

P

Plaster, mixture of water, sand, and lime used to coat walls and ceilings. Applied as a wet paste, it hardens as it dries. Plaster can be applied to various bases, such as brick, stone, or thin strips of wood or metal that are laid out parallel. It creates an airtight and durable finished surface. Several coats of plaster are usually necessary to build up the surface to the desired thickness. Materials such as hair or fiber can be added to plaster to make it stronger. Other kinds of materials can be added to make it fire resistant or sound absorbing.

Plastic, material that can be molded (at least in production) into desired shapes. A few natural plastics are known, e.g., bitumen, resins, and rubber, but almost all are synthetic, made mainly from petrochemicals. They have a vast range of useful properties, including hardness, elasticity, transparency, toughness, low density, insulating ability, inertness, and corrosion resistance. Plastics are high polymers with carbon skeletons, each molecule being made up of thousands or even millions of atoms. Thermoplastics soften or melt reversibly on heating; they include celluloid or other cellulose plastics, Lucite, nylon, polyethylene, styrene polymers, vinyl polymers, polyformaldehyde, and polycarbonates. Thermosetting plastics, although moldable when produced as simple polymers, are converted by heat and pressure, and sometimes by an admixed hardener, to a cross-linked, infusible form. These include Bakelite and other phenol resins, epoxy resins, polyesters, silicones, ureaformaldehyde and melamineformaldehyde resins, and some polyurethanes.

Plastic explosive, puttylike, flexible explosive. Because it can be molded into any shape and is weather resistant, it can be placed and hidden easily and is difficult to detect. Developed by the U.S. Army during World War II, it has since become a powerful weapon often used by political terrorists. *See also:* Explosive.

Plastic surgery, branch of surgery devoted to reconstruction or repair of deformity, surgical defect, or the results of injury. Using

The influence of the Greek philosopher Plato (427-347 B.C.) cannot be exaggerated. According to British-American philosopher A.N. Whitehead (1861-1947), the history of Western philosophy solely consists of a series of footnotes to Plato's work. Here, we see a marble copy (3rd century A.D.) of a 4th century B.C. bust (Louvre, Paris).

bone, cartilage, tendon, and skin from other parts of the body, or artificial substitutes, the surgeon can restore function and appearance in many cases. In skin grafting, the most common procedure, a piece of skin is cut, usually from the thigh, and stitched to the damaged area. Bone and cartilage (usually from the ribs or hips), or sometimes plastic, are used in cosmetic remodeling and facial reconstruction after injury. Congenital defects such as harelip and cleft palate can be treated in infancy. 'Face lifting,' the cosmetic removal of excess fat and tightening of the skin, is a delicate and often unsuccessful operation, carrying the added risk of infection. *See also:* Skin grafting.

Plateau, high plain. A plateau is formed by the erosion of lands bordering it, a build-up of recurrent lava flows, or the earth's upward movements. Heights of plateaus vary. Lower altitude plateaus, such as some in Australia and the U.S., can be valuable to people because they are often excellent grazing lands for livestock. High altitude plateaus, such as those in the Himalayas, have climates not suitable for human habitation. *See also:* Plain.

Plate tectonics *See:* Tectonics; Volcano.

Platform tennis, game resembling tennis in which players use paddles to hit a sponge rubber ball back and forth over a net. It is played on an outdoor elevated court 44 ft (13 m) long and 20 ft (6 m) wide surrounded by a wire fence 12 ft (3.7 m) high. Usually two pairs of players play against each other. In platform tennis, a player has one serve per point, and may return balls that have bounced off the fence. Created in 1928, platform tennis was devised so that it could be played in the winter. The court allows for the easy removal of snow.

Plath, Sylvia (1932-1963), U.S. poet whose taut, melodic, highly imagistic works explore the nature of womanhood and her fixation with death. *Ariel* (1965), published after Plath's suicide, won her international acclaim as a major U.S. 'confessional' poet. Her other works include *The Bell Jar* (1963), a semiautobiographical novel about a young woman's emotional breakdown, and *Complete Poems* (1981), edited by her husband, Ted Hughes.

Platinum, chemical element, symbol Pt; for physical constants see Periodic Table. Platinum was discovered by Julius Scaliger in 1557. It is a metallic element occurring native, and as the mineral sperrylite, an important source of the element. Platinum is a silver-white, malleable, ductile metal. The element does not oxidize in air at any temperature, but reacts with halogens, cyanides, sulfur, and caustic alkalis. The metal absorbs large volumes of hydrogen at ordinary temperatures. It is used in resistance wires for constructing high-temperature electric furnaces. In the finely divided state the metal is used as a catalyst. Platinum and its compounds are used in plating, jewelry, wire, corrosion-resistant apparatus, magnetic alloys, electrical contacts, and dentistry.

Plato, Greek philosopher (c.427-347 B.C.).

A pupil of Socrates, he founded (c.385 B.C.) the Academy, where Aristotle studied. His early dialogues present a portrait of Socrates as critical arguer, but in the great middle dialogues he develops his own doctrines-such as the theory of Forms (*Republic*), the immortality of the soul (*Phaedo*), knowledge as recollection of the Forms by the soul (*Meno*), virtue as knowledge (*Protagoras*)-and attacks hedonism and the idea that 'might is right' (*Gorgias*). The *Symposium* and *Phaedrus* sublimate love into a beatific vision of the Forms of the Good and the Beautiful. The late dialogues (*Sophist, Theaetetus, Politicus, Philebus, Parmenides*) deal with problems of epistemology, ontology, and logic; the *Timaeus* contains cosmological speculation. In the *Republic* Plato posits abstract Forms as the supreme reality. The highest function of the human soul is to achieve the vision of the Form of the Good. Drawing an analogy between the soul and the state, he presents his ideal state ruled by philosophers, who correspond to the rational part of the soul. In the late *Laws* Plato develops in detail his ideas of the state. His idealist philosophy, his insistence on order and harmony, his moral fervor and asceticism, and his literary genius have made Plato a dominant figure in Western thought. *See also:* Philosophy.

Platte River, river in Nebraska, U.S. It begins at North Platte, Nebraska, at the joining of the North Platte and South Platte rivers, flows 310 mi (500 km) east, and empties into the Missouri River at Plattsmouth. The Platte and its tributaries drain approximately 90,000 sq mi (233,000 sq km) of land. The river's abundant waters are used to irrigate farms, as well as to provide water for communities. It is too shallow to navigate, but the river's valley has been used as a transportation route for land travel since pioneer days.

Platyhelminth *See:* Flatworm.

Platypus, or duck-billed platypus (*Ornithorhynchus anatinus*), amphibious monotreme (egg-laying mammal) found in Australia and Tasmania. The platypus has webbed feet and thick fur (equipping it for an aquatic life); a short, thick tail, and a flat, toothless, bill-like mouth used for taking insects and crustaceans off the surface of the water. Like echidnas, the other monotreme group, they retain many reptilian characteristics.

Plautus (c.254-184 B.C.), Roman writer of comedies, 21 of which have survived. He based them on Greek New Comedy, especially Menander, but adapted them to Roman tastes and situations, and added his own brand of lively, bawdy humor. Popular in his time, he influenced William Shakespeare, Ben Jonson, and Molière, among others.

Play, in animals, a distinctive type of behavior of both adults and juveniles, of unknown function and involving the incomplete, ritualized expression of normal adult behavior patterns. Play occurs particularly in carnivores, primates, and certain birds.

P

The duck-billed platypus or duck mole (*O. anatinus*) uses its broad, flat tail to steer itself while swimming in freshwater rivers.

Plea bargaining, agreement between the accused and the prosecutor under which the accused agrees to plead guilty to a lesser offense in order to receive a lighter sentence from the judge. Plea bargaining has been accepted by judges, prosecutors, and lawyers as necessary though undesirable, saving time and speeding up the work of overcrowded courts, but denying the accused a fair trial and not requiring the prosecutor to prove the accused's guilt beyond a reasonable doubt.

Plebeians, nonaristocratic classes in ancient Rome. In their continual rivalries with the ruling patrician aristocracy, they created their own assemblies and officers, and gained full political and civil rights by c.300 B.C.
See also: Rome, Ancient.

Plebiscite, in Roman history, law enacted by the plebeian *comitia*, or assembly of tribes. In modern times a plebiscite is a direct vote of a whole body of citizens on a specific issue.

Plecoptera, or stonefly, order of insects that lays eggs in water. When the young hatch, they live along the rocky edges of ponds, lakes, and streams. Although adults have wings, they are poor fliers and so tend to live on rocks near the water. Larvae and adults constitute a large percentage of the diet of freshwater fish.

Pleiades, in astronomy, a cluster of stars in the constellation Taurus. With a telescope, several hundred stars are visible in the cluster. However, only six stars can be easily seen with the unaided eye. On a very clear night, several more can sometimes be seen. Alcyone is the brightest star in the Pleiades. Bright *nebulae* (clouds of gas and dust) surround several of the stars in the cluster. The stars are about 400 light-years away.

Pleistocene Epoch (diluvium) also known as the Great Ice Age, an earlier epoch of the Quaternary Period, stretching from between c.2 million and 3 million through 10,000 years ago.
See also: Ice age.

Plekhanov, Georgi Valentinovich (1857-1918), Russian Marxist thinker. Always opposed to political terror, he at first supported V. I. Lenin, but after 1903 he espoused Menshevik views and, during World War I,

supported military defense of Russia. After the successful Bolshevik-led revolution, he retired from public life.
See also: Marxism; Russian.

Plesiosaur, huge, prehistoric marine reptile now extinct. It lived approximately 200 million years ago in what is currently Europe and North America. It resembled a large whale with paddlelike limbs.

Pleura, thin connective membrane that covers the inside of the thorax (chest cavity) and the lungs in mammals.

Pleurisy, inflammation of the pleura, the thin membrane covering the outer lung surface and the inner chest wall. It causes a characteristic chest pain, which is often worsened by deep breathing and coughing. It may be caused by infection (e.g., pneumonia, tuberculosis) or by tumors and inflammatory diseases.

Plexiglas, trademarked name of a type of plastic. Made from acrylic it is very clear and does not break easily. Because of its transparency and durability, Plexiglas is widely used instead of glass in such things as aircraft windows, picture frames, eyeglasses, appliances, and light fixtures.
See also: Plastic.

Plexus, network of stringlike structures, such as of nerves or blood vessels. A plexus can consist of interweaving fibers, such as the nerve fibers in a nerve plexus. In a blood carrying plexus, veins or arteries intertwine,

opening into each other in many different places.
See also: Solar plexus.

Plimsoll mark, line or series of lines on the side of a seagoing ship indicating the safe loading limit. Samuel Plimsoll (1824-1898) first secured the compulsory marking of British ships in 1876.

Pliny, name of 2 Roman authors. **Gaius Plinius Secundus**, or **Pliny the Elder** (C.A.D. 23-A.D. 79), is known for his *Natural History*, a vast compendium of ancient sciences, which though of little scientific merit was popular throughout antiquity and the Middle Ages. He died attempting to help the citizens of Pompeii in the eruption of Vesuvius. **Gaius Plinius Caecilius Secundus**, or **Pliny the Younger** (A.D. 61?-c.113), a nephew of Pliny the Elder, was a lawyer, politician, and administrator, primarily known for his elegant *Letters*.
See also: Rome, Ancient.

Pliocene, final period of the Tertiary, immediately preceding the Quaternary, c. 5-1.8 million years ago.

PLO *See:* Palestine Liberation Organization.

Ploiesti (pop. 259,000), large city in southeastern Romania, center of the Romanian oil industry. One of the world's first oil refineries started operations there in 1856. Besides refining and storing oil, Ploiesti produces oil-mining equipment as well as chemicals derived from petroleum. Other industries include textile manufacturing and food processing.

Plotinus (205?-270?), Greek philosopher, founder of Neoplatonism. Born in Egypt, he moved to Greece to study philosophy. His learning led him to develop Neoplatonism and to found a school where he taught that philosophy. Based on the philosophy of Plato and other Greek philosophers, as well as on Indian philosophy, Neoplatonism is the belief that the material world is an unimportant illusion, and that reality is spiritual and can only be experienced by those whose souls are pure. After 244, Plotinus moved to Rome to continue his teachings there. His beliefs were popular with many Romans, and he inspired early Christians, particularly

The Pleiads, in the Taurus constellation, are the brightest of a young and open cluster of stars. This photo shows that the brightest stars in it are surrounded by nebulae. It is possible that these reflection nebulae are the remains of the nebulae from which the star accumulation was originally formed. The light of the nebulae is strongly polarized, which indicates that it is reflected from very small particles.

P

St. Augustine. *The Enneads* is a collection of some of his lectures.
See also: Neoplatonism.

Plovdiv (pop. 379,000), second-largest city in Bulgaria, situated on the Maritsa River. Plovdiv is a major industrial, agricultural, and marketing center and is the site of a biannual international trade exhibition. Its products include textiles, metals, leather, and dairy products. Founded by the Thracians before the 4th century B.C., it was held successively from the 4th century B.C. to the 8th century A.D. by Macedonia and by the Roman Empire. Around 1360 it was captured by the Turks; in 1877 it became part of the Russian empire. It became annexed to Bulgaria in 1885.
See also: Bulgaria.

Plover, common name for various small or medium-sized wading birds of the family Charadriidae, which includes the lapwings and the true plovers. Most plovers have an olive or brown back, with lighter underparts. Typically they have a dark band across the belly and a white band on a black head. Plovers feed on insects or crustacea in mud and sand.

Plow, implement for tilling the soil: breaking up the surface crust for sowing and turning under stubble and manure. Essentially it is a horizontal blade (the share) that cuts the furrow and a projecting moldboard to turn the soil over. Plows have been used since the Bronze Age. Roman plows had an iron-shod share with a beam to draw it. Wheels were used in Saxon plows, and developments after 1600 led eventually to the steel plow of the U.S. engineer John Deere (1837), disk plows with revolving concave disks instead of shares and moldboards, and tractor-drawn plows that make multiple furrows.
See also: Deere, John.

The 17th-century plow is still made of wood except for a few vital iron parts.

Plum, common name for many species of trees (genus *Prunus*) of the rose family that produce soft-fleshed fruits enclosing a single pit. The European plum (*P. domestica*) has been cultivated for 2,000 years. Wild species of North American plum include the American plum and the Canada plum. Wild species have been crossed with the European plum to make hardy varieties. Prunes are plums that have been preserved by drying.

Plumbago, any of several plants and shrubs belonging to the leadwort family, grown mostly in warm climates. The plumbago's clusters of white, blue, or purple flowers make it an attractive garden plant. It has shiny, dark-green, oval leaves.

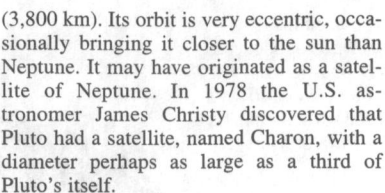

The European plum (*P. domestica*) has been cultivated since ancient times for its beautiful flowers and sweet, juicy fruit. Some varieties are eaten fresh; others are dried as prunes.

Plumbing, system of pipes and fixtures through which water and drainage flow into and out of a building. Water travels through large underground pipes called *mains*. These connect with smaller pipes called service lines which bring the water into buildings. A network of pipes distributes the water to fixtures and appliances, providing cold water. One pipe carries water to a hot-water heater, which is connected to pipes that distribute the heated water to fixtures and appliances. The water in pipes is constantly kept under pressure, so that when the faucets or valves are opened, the water will flow out. Drainage pipes carry used water and wastes from sinks, toilets, and appliances, such as washing machines, from a building to a sewer or septic tank. Because they may carry solid materials, drainage pipes are larger than water pipes.

Plutarch (c.A.D. 46–c.A.D. 120), Greek philosopher and biographer. His *Parallel Lives* of famous Greeks and Romans, paired for comparison, exemplifies the private virtues or vices of great men; it has had great influence on European literature, notably on William Shakespeare (in *Julius Caesar*, *Antony and Cleopatra*, and *Timon of Athens*).
See also: Greece, Ancient; Philosophy.

Pluto, in astronomy, ninth planet of the solar system, orbiting the sun at a mean distance of 3.67 billion mi (5.9 billion km) once every 248.4 years. Pluto was discovered in 1930 following observations of perturbations in Neptune's orbit. Little is known of Pluto's composition, atmosphere, or mass. Its diameter is estimated to be between 1,500 mi (2,400 km) and 2,400 mi

(3,800 km). Its orbit is very eccentric, occasionally bringing it closer to the sun than Neptune. It may have originated as a satellite of Neptune. In 1978 the U.S. astronomer James Christy discovered that Pluto had a satellite, named Charon, with a diameter perhaps as large as a third of Pluto's itself.
See also: Planet; Solar System.

Pluto, in Greek and Roman mythology, ruler of the underworld and god of the dead. The Greeks also called him *Hades*; the Romans also called him *Dis Pater* and *Orcus*. He was originally a Greek god. The Romans incorporated him and the myths about him into their religion during the 7th century B.C.
See also: Mythology.

Plutonium, chemical element, symbol Pu; for physical constants see Periodic Table. Discovered by Glenn Seaborg and co-workers in 1940. It was produced by bombarding uranium with deuterons in a cyclotron. It exists in trace quantities in nature in uranium ores. It is produced in large quantities in nuclear reactors from uranium-238. Plutonium is prepared by the reduction of its trifluoride with alkaline-earth metals. It is a silvery, radioactive, toxic metal, a member of the actinide series. Plutonium is used as an explosive in nuclear weapons and as nuclear reactor fuel. Plutonium-238 is used as a thermoelectric generator and heat source. In handling plutonium and its compounds, care must be taken to ensure that a critical mass is not formed, especially in liquid solution. Plutonium is the most important of the transuranium elements.

Plymouth (pop. 258,000), city in Devon county, southwest England, on Plymouth sound, from which the *Mayflower* sailed in 1620. It was also the home port of Sir Walter Raleigh's and Sir Francis Drake's expeditions to the Americas and was the launching point of the British fleet in its attack on the Spanish Armada in 1588. It is now an important maritime center and naval base.
See also: England.

Plywood, strong, light wood composite made of alternate layers of veneer glued together with their grain at right angles. Thick plywood may have a central core of sawn lumber. It is made of an odd number of layers and is termed 3-ply, 5-ply, etc., depending on the number of layers. Strong and almost free of warping and splitting, plywood is used for construction of all kinds.

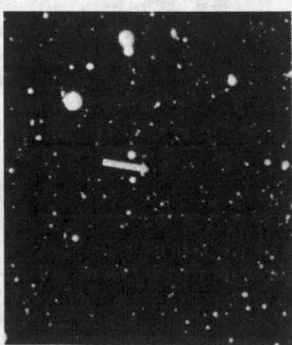

On Feb. 18, 1930, Clyde W. Tombaugh discovered Pluto while comparing photographic plates taken on Jan. 23 (left) and Jan. 29 (right), 1930, at the Lowell Observatory in Arizona. Pluto is seen as a dot of light (arroes) moving slowly in relation to the star field.

P

Plzen (pop. 175,000), city in Bohemia, a western region of Czech Republic. Situated at the junction of the Radbuzza and Me rivers. Plzen is a leading industrial, economic, and cultural center. Skoda Works, a factory noted for its production of military aircraft, automobiles, machinery, and locomotives, operates there. Its other products include paper products, chemicals, and metal hardwares. Pilsner, a world-renowned beer, has been brewed there since the Middle Ages. Founded before the 10th century, Plzen was a Roman Catholic stronghold during the religious wars of the 15th century. Its town square dates back to medieval times. *See also:* Bohemia.

Pneumoconiosis *See:* Black lung.

Pneumonia, inflammation and consolidation of lung tissue (giving it a solid consistency). It is usually caused by bacteria (pneumococcus, staphylococcus, Gram's stain negative bacilli); it results rarely from pure virus infection (influenza, measles); other varieties occur if food, secretions, or chemicals are aspirated or inhaled. In response to inflammation, lung tissue fills with exudate and pus, which may center on the bronchi (bronchopneumonia) or be restricted to a single lobe (lobar pneumonia). Cough, with yellow or green sputum (sometimes containing blood), fever, malaise, and breathlessness are common. The involvement of the pleural surfaces causes pleurisy. Antibiotics and physiotherapy are essential in treatment for the bacterial forms, which are generally the more severe.

Pneumothorax, condition in which air is present in the pleural space between the lungs and the chest wall. This may result from trauma, rupture of lung bullae in emphysema or in asthma, tuberculosis, pneumoconiosis, cancer, etc. Drainage of the air through a tube inserted in the chest wall allows reexpansion of the lungs.

Pnom Penh *See:* Phnom Penh.

Pocahontas (1595-1617), Native American who strove to improve relations between Native Americans and English settlers in Jamestown, Va. The daughter of chief Powhatan, she is credited with saving the colonist John Smith's life just as her father was about to execute him. When fighting broke out between Native Americans and colonists, she was captured by the English. During her captivity, she fell in love with John Rolfe. She became a Christian and married him in 1614. In 1616, she accompanied Rolfe to England, where she was favorably received. She died of smallpox the following year and was buried in England.

Podgorica (Ribnica, formerly Titograd; pop. 118,000), capital of the Yugoslavian Republic of Montenegro on the Moraca. Fast growing industry. Airport. Came into being in the Middle Ages; was successively named Ribnica and Podgorica. Later the city was named after Tito. In 1992 it was changed again into Podgorica.

Podgorny, Nikolai Viktorovich (1903-1983), Soviet political leader. After rising through the Communist Party ranks in the Ukraine, he was named to the party secretariat of the Soviet Union (1963). After Nikita Khrushchev's fall, he became (1965) chairman of the Presidium of the Supreme Soviet, or head of state, holding that post until his demotion to deputy of the Supreme Soviet (1977).
See also: Union of Soviet Socialist Republics.

Podiatry, science of disorders and diseases of the feet. Podiatrists treat nails, corns, calluses, bunions, and toe deformities and may prescribe orthopedics and perform minor surgery.

Poe, Edgar Allan (1809-1849), U.S. short-story writer, poet, and critic, famous for his tales of mystery and the macabre, such as *The Murders in the Rue Morgue* (1841) and *The Purloined Letter* (1844), prototypes of the detective story, and *The Fall of the House of Usher* (1839). His poems, including *The Raven* (1845) and *Annabel Lee* (1849), are musical and striking in imagery. Poe discussed beauty and form in art in *The Philosophy of Composition* (1846), which influenced Charles Baudelaire and the French Symbolists.

Poet laureate, royal appointment held by a British poet who writes poems for state occasions. The title is now largely honorific. John Dryden first had the title in 1668, but the custom started when Ben Jonson received a royal pension in 1616. In the U.S., the poet laureates have been appointed by the Library of Congress. Robert Penn Warren was the first (1986), Richard Wilbur (1987), Howard Nemerov (1988), Mark Strand (1990), and Joseph Brodsky (1991), who is the first foreign-born poet to be named laureate.

Poetry, meaningful arrangement of words into an imaginative or emotional discourse, with a strong rhythmic pattern. The language, seeking to evoke image and idea, uses imagery and metaphor. Rhyme or alliteration may also be important elements. The length of poems varies from brief lyric poems to long narrative poems or epic poems, with the length and scope of the novel. The kind of forms and devices used (for example, alliteration, assonance, onomatopoeia) depends on the tone and intentions of the poet. Since the sense of poetry is intimately tied to its sound, it is extremely difficult to translate. In most cultures poetry, linked by its rhythmic elements to music and dance, develops before prose literature; the poetic form aids memory in oral transmission. Eventually poetry is written down; a 'higher' form then develops-poetry carefully crafted for the printed page and intensely involved reader. Even such written poetry, however, must remain to some extent 'musical'.

Pogrom (from Russian for 'devastation' or 'riot'), term for the officially condoned mob attacks on Jewish communities in Russia between 1881 and 1921. More generally, it is used to describe any massacre of a defenseless minority, particularly Jews, such as those organized by the Nazis. The pogroms were a major factor in the large-scale emigration of European Jews to the United States.
See also: Jews.

Pohnpei, island in the western Pacific Ocean. The largest of the eastern Caroline Islands, Pohnpei has an area of approximately 129 sq mi (334 sq km). Many tropical crops are raised there, including yams, bananas, taros, and breadfruit. It has been controlled successively by Spain, Germany, Japan, and the United States. Pohnpei and the other Caroline Islands currently make up the self-governing Federated States of Micronesia.

Poincaré, Jules Henri (1854-1912), French mathematician, cosmologist, and scientific philosopher, best known for his many contributions to pure and applied mathematics and celestial mechanics.
See also: Cosmology; Mathematics.

Poincaré, Raymond (1860-1934), French politician, three times premier (1912-1913, 1922-1924, 1926-1929) and president (1913-1920). A strongly nationalist conservative, he ordered the French occupation of the Ruhr (1923). His financial policies succeeded in stabilizing the currency (1928).
See also: France.

Poinciana, any of various tropical flowering trees in the pea family. The poinciana has large red or orange flowers that grow in clusters. Each flower has 5 petals and ranges in size from 3 to 4 in (8 to 10 cm) across. The royal poinciana (*Delonix regia*), which grows in southern Florida, has flaming red flowers and delicate leaves made up of small leaflets. Royal poinciana trees can grow to a height of 40 ft (12 m).

Poinsettia, name for a variety of spurges (genus *Euphorbia*) with colorful, attractive bracts (whorled leaves that enclose the small flower). A popular indoor ornamental plant with red, yellow, or white bracts, *E. pulcherrima*, native to Mexico and Central America, grows up to 10 ft (3 m) high in the wild. Propagation is by shoot tip cuttings taken in the spring.

Edgar Allan Poe (1809-1849), famous writer of detective stories and thrillers, was also an important poet and critic.

P

Pointer, large hunting dog. It uses its keen sense of smell to hunt game birds. When the pointer detects a bird, it stands absolutely still and points its nose towards the bird to show the hunter where it is. A pointer has a short white coat with black, yellow, orange, or reddish-brown marks. Its shoulder height ranges from 23 to 28 in (58 to 71 cm), and it weighs from 45 to 75 lb (20 to 34 kg).

Pointillism, painting technique in which tiny paint dots of color are juxtaposed on a canvas to build up the form. This method was developed by the post-impressionist painters Georges Seurat and Paul Signac to achieve more luminosity and greater control of tone.

Poison, substance that causes illness or death when it is eaten or absorbed into the body. There are many different kinds of poisons. Some are found in nature. For example, some plants contain poison. Caution should always be taken before eating wild foods, such as mushrooms or berries. Some animals eject poison when they bite, such as rattlesnakes, wasps, and scorpions. In the home, various products contain poisonous chemicals, such as cleaning fluids and insect sprays. Such products should always be used according to instruction and should be kept away from children. Medicines taken in large doses can become poisonous. Gases such as carbon monoxide are deadly when inhaled in large amounts. Drugs called *antidotes* can be taken to reverse the harmful effects of some poisons.
See also: Toxin.

Poison gas *See:* Chemical and biological warfare.

Poison ivy, vine that grows plentifully in the United States and southern Canada. Its leaves appear red in early spring, turn shiny green later in spring, and red or orange in autumn. It contains a poisonous oil that is extremely irritating to the skin, causing blisters and red, itching spots.

Poison oak, vine similar to poison ivy and poison sumac. It contains an irritant, urushiol, which causes skin eruptions and watery blisters.

Poisonous plant, any plant that produces harmful effects to people or animals. The harmful effects of a poisonous plant range from minor irritation to death, depending on the plant. Some plants are poisonous when eaten, such as poisonous mushrooms, and others when merely touched, such as poison ivy. Some plants have parts that are safe to eat and other parts that are poisonous. Potatoes, for example, have poisonous leaves. It is not possible to make general statements about the appearance, taste, and smell of poisonous plants. The poison from some plants is used to create medicines, which are prescribed in controlled doses. For example, the leaves of the foxglove, a tall plant with bell-shaped flowers, is used to create digitalis, a medicine used to stimulate the heart.

Poison sumac *See:* Sumac.

Poitier, Sidney (1927-), U.S. film and stage actor. He was the first African American actor to become accepted as a star in films made for largely white audiences. Many of these films (e.g., *The Blackboard Jungle*, 1955; *In the Heat of the Night*, 1967) deal specifically with racial issues. Poitier directed and starred in *A Patch of Blue* (1965), played Porgy in *Porgy and Bess* (1959), and won an Academy Award for his role in *Lilies of the Field* (1963). Other films are *Little Nikita* (1988), *Sneakers* (1992), *The Jackal* (1997) and *True Crime* (1999). He received an Honorary Academy Award for his outstanding career in film in 2002 .

Poitiers, Battle of, English victory in the Hundred Years' War, fought in 1356, near Poitiers in west-central France. The English, led by Edward the Black Prince, were outnumbered four to one by their French opponents but won a brilliant victory over John II and Philip the Bold.
See also: Edward the Black Prince; Hundred Years War.

Poker, card game whose earliest forms date back to 520 in Europe, developing into bet-and-bluff games like **brag** in England, **pochen** ('bluff') in Germany, and **poque** in France. The French brought **poque** to America (1800), where it was developed and reexported to Europe as poker (1870). It is now one of the world's top 3 card games. There are many variations, but basically 5 or 7 cards are dealt, and each player tries to make up a winning combination, on which he or she bets and bluffs in a contest of skill and nerves against the unknown combinations ('hands') of his opponents. The winner either has the best hand or has bluffed all opponents into 'folding' (dropping out of the game).

Pokeweed (*Phytolacca americana*), tall, herbal plant belonging to the pokeweed family. Native to North America, it is also known as *poke*, *pigeonberry*, *pokeberry*, *pokeroot*, and *inkberry*. Pokeweed has small white flowers and berries that ripen to a deep red-black color. Its stem is red and grows to a height of 4 to 10 ft (1.2 to 3 m). The root, stem, leaves, and seeds of the pokeweed are poisonous, but its young shoots can be eaten if properly prepared.

Poker hands in ascending order of value: one pair (1), two pairs (2), three of a kind (3), straight (4), flush (5), full house (6), four of a kind (7), straight flush (8), and royal flush (9).

Poland

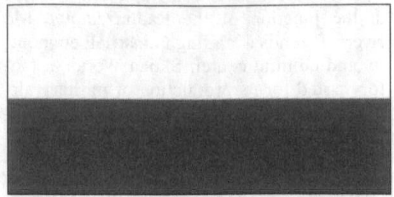

Capital:	Warsaw
Area:	120,727 sq mi
	(312,683 sq km)
Population:	38,625,000
Language:	Polish
Government:	Republic
Independent:	1918
Head of gov.:	Prime minister
Per capita:	US$ 8,800
Monetary unit:	1 Zloty = 100 groszy

Poland, Republic, former communist state in central Europe.
Land and climate. Poland is situated on the Baltic Sea and borders Russia, Lithuania, Belarus, Ukraine, Slovakia, Czech Republic and Germany. The land is generally low, with about 90% of it less than 1,000 ft/305 m above sea level, but in the south are the peaks of the Sudeten and Carpathian mountains, forming a natural border with Czech Republic. Poland's climate is moderate, with cool summers and cold winters.
People. World War II saw the destruction of Poland's ethnic minorities; the country is now almost entirely Polish. The official language is Polish and the people are overwhelmingly Roman Catholic.
Economy. Until World War II, Poland was an agricultural country; since then it has been rapidly industrialized. The former communist regime attempted to impose collectivized farms, but was effectively resisted by the peasantry. The chief agricultural products are wheat, rye, barley, oats, potatoes, and sugar beets. Poland's industries produce coal, zinc, steel, petroleum, and sulfur. Its manufactures include machinery, textiles, cement, and chemicals with a sizeable shipbuilding industry at Gdansk. The country's principal exports have been coal, textiles, metal products, and processed meat. With the end of communist control of the economy, Poland faces the massive task of shifting to privately owned enterprises and must simultaneously cope with sudden and acute shortages of essential goods, a weak currency, and a critical need for investment capital.
History. Poland's recorded history dates back to the 10th century when local Slavic tribes first united. Later, Germans settled in Poland, particularly on the Baltic coast. From the 14th through the 16th centuries

The High Tatra, the highest mountain group on Poland's southern border.

Poland was governed by the Jagiello dynasty and flourished in its most sustained period of freedom and independence. But the country was invaded by both Swedes and Russians in the 17th century, and then divided among Austria, Prussia, and Russia in 1772, 1793, and again in 1795. In 1919 the Treaty of Versailles established a new Poland that survived barely twenty years before it was invaded by Nazi Germany in 1939. The USSR occupied the eastern part of the country until 1941 when Germany invaded the USSR and took control of all of Poland. As a result of the German invasions and occupation, the population was decimated by massacres, starvation, and imprisonment in death camps like Auschwitz. After the last Germans were expelled early in 1945, a provisional government was set up under Soviet auspices. The communists dominated the 1947 elections, gained control of the government and, in 1952, declared the country a people's republic modeled on Soviet lines. With the death of Stalin, opposition to Soviet control led to widespread rioting in 1956, and Wladys-law Gomulka became leader of the anti-Soviet revolt. But by the early 1960s, Gomulka was following Russian policies. In 1970 Edward Gierek replaced Gomulka, instituted many reforms, and sought to control inflation. In the late 1970s, a new wave of unrest swept the country, stimulated primarily by the higher food prices. Polish workers formed the independent trade union Solidarnosé (Solidarity) in 1980, headed by Lech Walesa, and sought a greater measure of worker control in industry. Gierek fell from power that same year and Gen. Wojciech Jaruzelski took the reins of government. In 1981 Gen. Jaruzelski imposed martial law, arrested Solidarity's leaders, and banned the trade union in 1982. Within a year of the ban, martial law gradually came to an end. By 1984, martial law had ended and by 1986 the imprisoned members of Solidarity had been released. As a result of the liberalization of domestic politics within the Soviet Union and its decision to relinquish much of its former empire, Poland found itself free to chart its own course. In 1989, the ban on Solidarity was lifted and free elections were held. Lech Walesa, was elected president in 1990. After the elections in 1995, Walesa was succeeded by Aleksander Kwasniewski. Poland joined the NATO in 1999.

In December 2002, Poland was formally invited to join the EU in 2004. A referendum will be organized in 2003 to decide on membership.

Polanski, Roman (1933-), Polish film director, naturalized French. As a Jewish child in the ghetto he survived the horrors of World War II; acted and started to direct in the late 1950s. His first big movie, *Knife in the Water* (1962), received immediate praise. His films are partly absurdist-humorous, partly suspenseful and macabre; his oeuvre includes *Repulsion* (1965), *Rosemary's Baby* (1968), *Macbeth* (1971), *Chinatown* (1974), *Tess* (1979), *Pirates* 1986), *Frantic* (1988), *Bitter Moon* (1992), *Death and the Maiden* (1995), *The Ninth Gate* (1999) and *The Pianist* (2002; Acadamy Award in 2003). Autobiography: *Roman* (1984).

Polanyi, John Charles (1929-), Canadian chemist. He shared the 1986 Nobel Prize for chemistry with U.S. collaborators Yuan T. Lee and Dudley Herschbach for his work in chemiluminescence, the faint infrared light emitted by molecules as they recombine. He is the son of noted chemist Michael Polanyi. *See also:* Chemistry.

Polar bear, large (up to 1,650 lb/750 kg), white-furred, arctic bear (*Thalarctos maritimus*). It can swim strongly and is also agile on land. It hunts seals, whale calves, fish, and, on land, arctic foxes and even lemmings.

Polaris *See:* North Star.

Polarized light, light that exhibits unmixed properties (a particular vibration) in a given direction at a right angle to the line of propagation.

Polecat, small carnivore of the weasel family (*Mustela putorius*), found throughout northern and central Europe. It feeds at night on birds, small mammals, frogs, other animals, and eggs. In the United States the name is sometimes given to the skunk, a close relative.

Polestar *See:* North Star.

Pole vault, sporting event in which an athlete jumps over a crossbar using a pole to push him- or herself off the ground. The crossbar is supported by 2 uprights and is set at a specified height. The pole is usually made of fiberglass and is from 12 to 16 1/2 ft (3.7 to 5 m) long. The vaulter grips one end of the pole, runs at top speed, and plants the other end of the pole into the take-off box. The pole bends and catapults the vaulter upwards towards the crossbar as it straightens again. The vaulter pulls his or her body up into a handstand position at the top of the pole, swings his or her feet over the crossbar, pushes the pole away, travels across the bar, and drops down. The vaulter lands onto a soft area called a pit. The vaulter has been successful when he or she has cleared the crossbar without dislodging it.

Polgar, Zsuzsa (1969-), Hungarian chess player, at the age of four she became junior champion of Budapest. She won several tournaments with strong competition and became world champion in 1996 by beating the then world champion Xie Jun with 81/2-41/2.

Police, civil body charged with maintaining public order and protecting persons and property from unlawful acts. Most modern forces are descended from the Metropolitan Police established in London by Sir Robert Peel in 1829. Police powers are in most countries strictly circumscribed by law and constitution. *See also:* Peel, Sir Robert.

Polio *See:* Poliomyelitis.

Poliomyelitis, or infantile paralysis, viral disease causing muscle paralysis as a result of direct damage to motor nerve cells in the spinal cord. Current polio vaccine (Sabin vaccine) is a live strain taken by mouth that induces immunity. Poliomyelitis vaccination, originally developed by Jonas Salk (using a killed-virus vaccine), has been one of the 20th century's chief successes in preventive medicine. *See also:* Sabin, Albert Bruce; Salk, Jonas Edward.

Polisario, liberation movement in the former Spanish Sahara, now called the Western Sahara, founded in 1976 when Spain divided its colonial property between Morocco and Mauritania. Polisario, which strives for an independent state in the Western Sahara, opposes this division and as a reaction proclaimed the Saharan Arabic Democratic Republic (SADR). In 1979, after three years

P

The Polish government did only have a weak hold on the agrarian sector. For a long time, 80% of agricultural land was in private hands. However, with the establishment of co-operatives, the first steps on the path to agricultural collectivization were taken.

P

of war, Mauritania recognized the SADR. Since then Polisario has been waging war with Morocco, with the support of Algeria and Libya. The SADR has been recognized by a large number of countries.

Polish, West Slavic language, the official and literary language of Poland. Modern literary Polish, dating from the 16th century, was originally based on dialects in the vicinity of Porzna.

Polish Corridor, strip of Polish land about 25-65 mi (40-105 km) wide and 90 mi (145 km) long. Formerly German, it was granted to Poland in 1919 to give it access to the Baltic Sea. The predominantly German port of Danzig (now Gdansk) adjoining the corridor was declared a free city. The separation of East Prussia from the rest of Germany by the corridor precipitated the German invasion of Poland (1939).
See also: World War II.

Polishing *See:* Grinding and polishing.

Polish Succession War *See:* Succession wars.

Politburo (Political bureau of the Central Committee of the communist party), most important decision-making organ in the former Soviet Union (where this organ was called Presidium between 1952 and 1962) and in the communist countries of Eastern Europe. Founded in 1917. Formally the members and the candidate members were appointed by the Central Committee, in reality members were appointed by co-option. The important position of the Politburos ended in 1989-1990 in the Soviet Union and Eastern Europe, even before the communist one-party state was abolished in many countries.

Political convention, gathering at which political parties nominate their candidates for president and vice president of the United States. The two major parties in the United States are the Democrats and the Republicans. Each party holds a political convention every four years, in the summer before a national election. The delegates represent each state in the United States, as well as Washington, D.C., and U.S. territories such as Puerto Rico and the Virgin Islands. Delegates draw up a platform, which is a description of the party's goals and positions on current issues of importance. They then nominate presidential and vice presidential candidates who will run in the national election using that platform.

Political party, long-term organized grouping whose members have a number of opinions in common about the desirable organization of society and try to gain and exercise political power in order to realize these ideas. They differ considerably from the politically-active groupings that used to control the political scene before the rise of representative democracies. After a start as organizations through which growing numbers of citizens could be involved in government, parties have grown into the traditional form of political participation, into an 'intermediary structure' between citizens and political decision-making organs.

Political science, study of government and political institutions and processes. It was initiated by Plato's *Republic* and Aristotle's *Politics*, and well-known political theories have included those of Niccolò Machiavelli, Jean Bodin, Thomas Hobbes, John Locke, Montesquieu, Jeremy Bentham, Jean-Jacques Rousseau, and Karl Marx. Traditionally, the study was primarily concerned with the nature of the state, sovereignty, and government. Today greater emphasis is placed on the human associations, the behavior of interest groups, and the decision-making processes. Past theories cannot provide for the complexity of modern society; a standard view today regards society as a set of interacting interdependent systems.

Poliziano, Angelo (real name Angelo Ambrogini; 1454-1494), Tuscan writer and humanist scholar. His literary body of work stands out for the completely natural way in which this author used motifs from classical antiquity in his poems. The ruler of Florence, art connoisseur and maecenas Lorenzo de Medici (1449-1492, also known as 'Il Magnifico') accepted him in his court in 1473. In 1480 Poliziano was appointed professor of Greek and Latin in Florence. The poems Poliziano wrote in Italian and Latin all date from the period between 1470 and 1480. Well-known are the elegies *In violas* and *In morte di Albiera degli Albizzi*, melancholy poems with the transitoriness of female beauty as their theme. The same motif can be found in Poliziano's masterpiece, the *Stanze per la giostra* (1478, uncompleted). He wrote the play *Orfeo* (1480) in three days and it is the oldest known play about a non-biblical subject, constructed according to the scheme of the 'sacra rappresentazione', the religious drama. The prose that Poliziano wrote in colloquial language, the Tuscan dialect, includes his letters to various members of the Medici family. After 1480 Poliziano only wrote scientific prose. Poliziano compiled the accounts of the discussions during his lectures at the university of Florence under the title *Miscellanea* (1489).

Polk, James Knox (1795-1849), 11th president of the United States (1845-1849). Democratic politician and jurist, member of the House of Representatives (1825-1839), subsequently governor of Tennessee (1839-1841). As a compromise candidate for the Democrats he was unexpectedly voted president in 1844. During his presidency the U.S. acquired Oregon, California and, because of the Mexican War (1846-1848), Texas and New Mexico. He did not stand for reelection.

Polke, Sigmar (1941-), German visual artist. In 1963 he developed together with Konrad Lueg and Gerhard Richter a way of painting they called 'capitalist realism', which was aimed at revealing the mechanisms of consumer society. In 1964 Polke started to make screen paintings, usually enlargements of coarse-grained magazine and newspaper photographs, mass media that interpret and manipulate reality. Shortly afterwards he made fabric paintings, named after the canvas it was made of e.g. lining fabric and curtain material. Later his paintings were made of patterns and existing images that were put on top of one another, like reproductions of paintings and prints, that were painted on with a thin paint. Polke is a major influence on younger artists.

Poll *See:* Public opinion.

Pollack *See:* Pollock.

Pollaiuolo, Antonio Del (1429?-1498), Italian painter, sculptor, and goldsmith. His knowledge of the human anatomy and his mastery in portraying figures in action inspired Renaissance artists such as Michelangelo and Leonardo da Vinci. He used Hercules as the subject of some of his most famous works; including several paintings and a bronze piece. He created the bronze tombs of Popes Sixtus IV and Innocent VIII in Rome.

Pollen, fine yellow powder produced in the male part of flowers and in the male cone of conifers (cone-bearing plants). The male organs of flowers are called *stamens*; the female parts are called *pistils*. Pollination is the transference of pollen from the plant's

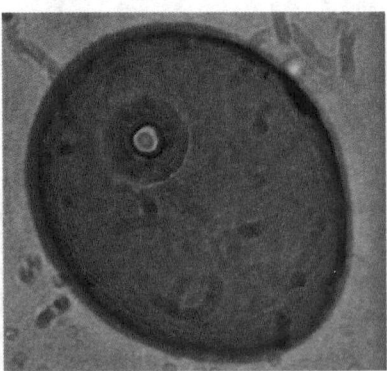

Pollen grains of all grasses, including wheat (*Triticum aestivum*) have a distinct pore, or aperture, in the outer layer, or exine, of the wall. Wheat pollen is nearly spherical and measures about 50 microns (2/1,000 in) across.

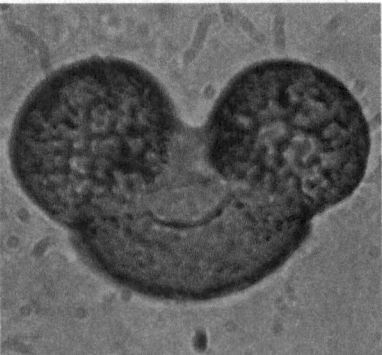

Protruding air sacs characterize the pollen grains of the pines, genus *Pinus*, and certain other gymnosperms. It has been estimated that a single pine tree may produce several billion pollen grains in 1 year.

stamen to its pistil. In conifers, pollination occurs when pollen is transferred from the male pollen cone to the female seed cone. Pollen can be transferred by the wind or by birds or insects who come into contact with the flowers. The pollen clings to them and is transferred as they move from flower to flower. After a plant is pollinated, it becomes fertile and begins seed production.

Pollination, in plants, the transfer of pollen from the male stamen of a flower to the female pistil of the same or another flower for fertilization. Wind-pollinated plants, such as grasses, produce inconspicuous flowers with large, feathery stamens and stigmas and usually large quantities of pollen. Insect- or bird-pollinated flowers have large, conspicuous, and colorful flowers, produce nectar, and have small stigmas.

Pollini, Maurizio (1942-), Italian pianist, made his debut at age 9. Pollini studied with Carlo Vidusso at the Academy of Music in Milan (until 1959). He also studied with Michelangeli. First prize at the Ettore Pozzoli Competition in Seregno (1959). Also first prize at the Chopin Competition in Warsaw (1960), after which an international career followed. Pollini is considered one of the greatest pianists of this age, excelling in Romantic (Chopin and Beethoven) and Contemporary music (e.g. Boulez, Nono, Schönberg, Stockhausen).

Pollinosis *See:* Hay fever.

Polliwog *See:* Tadpole.

Pollock (*Pollachius virens*), fish belonging to the codfish family. A valuable food fish, it is found in the northern Atlantic Ocean. It grows to a length of 2 to 3 1/2 ft (61 to 107 cm) and has a protruding lower jaw. Pollocks move in schools and feed on smaller fish.

Pollock, Jackson (1912-1956), U.S. painter, leader of abstract expressionism. Influenced by surrealism, he developed 'action painting': dripping paint on canvas placed flat on the floor, and forming marks in it with sticks, trowels, and knives. His work, such as *Number 32* (1950) and *Blue Poles* (1953), comprises intricate networks of lines. *See also:* Abstract expressionism.

Poll tax, tax collected from every adult in a community. All people pay the same amount, no matter what their incomes or what properties they own. This kind of taxation is controversial because many feel that it places an unfair burden on the poor and that a fairer way would be to tax according to how much a person owns. *See also:* Taxation.

Pollution *See:* Environmental pollution.

Pollux *See:* Castor and Pollux.

Polo, game played on horseback (polo ponies), with a ball and mallets. It is played between two teams of four on a field 300 yd (271 m) long and 200 yd (183 m) wide, with a goal at each end. The object is to score points by striking the 3-3.5 in (7.6-8.9 cm) diameter ball into the goal with the mallet, which is 48-54 in (122-137 cm) long. The game originated in Persia and spread through Turkey, Tibet, India, China, and Japan. It was revived in 19th-century India and learned by British army officers, who introduced it into England in 1869 and into the United States in 1876.

Polo, Marco (1254?-1324?), Venetian explorer famous for his overland journey to China (1271-1295). Reaching China in 1275, he served as an envoy of the ruler, Kublai Khan. He was appointed governor of Yangchow for 3 years and assisted in the capture of the city of Sainfu. He returned home to Venice (1295) laden with a treasure in precious stones. Commanding a galley against the Genoese at the battle of Curzola (1298), he was captured. In prison he wrote an account of his travels that later inspired explorers like Christopher Columbus to search for a sea passage to the East.

Polonium, chemical element, symbol Po; for physical constants see Periodic Table. Discovered by Marie Curie in 1898. Polonium was the first element to be discovered by virtue of its radioactivity. It occurs in pitchblende and other uranium minerals in minute amounts. The element is a decay product of radium and is also called Radium F. It is produced artificially by irradiating bismuth-210 with neutrons in a high-flux nuclear reactor. Polonium is a low-melting metalloid. It resembles tellurium and bismuth. Several compounds have been synthesized, including a polonide. Polonium-210 is a powerful _-emitter and is dangerous to handle even in small amounts. It is alloyed with beryllium as a neutron source. Polonium is used in devices for removing dust particles and static electricity. It is one of the most toxic substances known.

Pol Pot (real name Saloth Sar; also Brother Number One; 1928-1998), Cambodian guerilla leader and politician. Pol Pot started in 1963 with the illegal Communist Party of Cambodia (CPC, called the Khmer Rouge), a guerilla against prince Sihanouk, who was overthrown in a coup d'état in 1970. In 1976 Pol Pot became prime minister in the government of Democratic Cambodia. He was responsible for the radical policy of the Cambodian communists, which cost about two million Cambodians their life. After the fall of the government of the Khmer Rouge in 1979, he resumed the guerilla. He was found guilty of genocide and sentenced to death by default. Later he resigned as political (1979) and military (1985) leader of the Khmer Rouge. In 1997 video footage was shown of a lawsuit brought against Pol Pot by the Khmer Rouge, in which he was sentenced to life imprisonment. It turned out to be a show trial, meant to convince the outside world of the good intentions of the Khmer Rouge. *See also:* Cambodia.

Polyandry *See:* Polygamy.

Polychlorinated biphenyl (PCB), any of several compounds formed by substituting hydrogen (H) atoms in biphenyl ($C_6H_5C_6H_5$)

On his way back from Asia, Marco Polo visited India. Here, he is inspecting the pepper harvest. This plate appeared in the thirteenth-century *Book of Wonders* about his journeys.

with chlorine (Cl) atoms. PCBs were once widely used in the manufacture of many products, including lubricants, paints, and adhesives. However, scientific studies have concluded that PCBs are a poisonous threat to the environment, killing wildlife and creating health problems for people. Their use has been banned in the United States.

Polyclitus, name of 2 Greek sculptors. **Polyclitus the Elder** (5th century B.C.) was renowned for bronze statues of athletes, of which numerous marble copies survive. His most famous works, a colossal statue of Hera, now lost, and the *Doryphorus* (Spear Bearer), became the models for ideal proportion. **Polyclitus the Younger** (4th century B.C.) was known primarily as an architect but also produced figures of athletes.

Polyester, any of several strong, light synthetic products made from chemical substances derived from petroleum. Polyesters are manufactured in 3 forms: textiles, plastics, and films. Products made from polyester have great strength and durability. Polyester textiles are colorfast and wrinkle-resistant and are widely used in the creation of clothing and home furnishings. Polyester plastics are used to manufacture such products as bottles, household fixtures and appliances, boats, and automobile parts. Polyester films are used to create Mylar, insulation wires, sealing tapes, computer tapes, and other items.

Polyethylene *See:* Plastic.

Polygamy, marriage in which a man has more than one wife at one time (polygyny), or a woman has more than one husband (polyandry). It is still practiced in parts of Asia and Africa; both the Muslim and Hindu religions permit polygyny. It was once also a custom of U.S. Mormons but is now forbidden by them.

Polygon, closed plane figure bounded by three or more straight lines, such as triangles (3 sides), pentagons (5 sides), and dodecagons (12 sides). Convex polygons have interior angles that are all either acute or obtuse; in concave polygons one or more of these angles is reflex. A polygon with equal angles and sides equal in length is called a regular polygon. A *spherical polygon* is a closed figure on the surface of a sphere bounded by arcs of great circles.

P

Polyhedron, three-dimensional figure bounded by 4 or more polygon sides. There are only 5 types of convex polyhedron that can be regular (i.e., have faces that are equal regular polygons, each face being at equal angles to those adjacent to it); the tetrahedron, the octahedron, and the isocahedron, with 4, 8, and 20 faces, respectively, each face being an equilateral triangle; the hexahedron, with 6 square faces; and the dodecahedron, with 12 pentagonal faces. Regular polyhedrons may be circumscribed about or inscribed in a sphere.

Polymer, substance composed of very large molecules (macromolecules) built up by repeated linking of small molecules (monomers). Natural polymers include proteins, nucleic acids, polysaccharides, resins, rubber, and many minerals. The ability to make synthetic polymers (e.g., plastics and synthetic fibers) lies at the heart of modern technology. Polymerization, which requires that each monomer have two or more functional groups capable of linkage, takes place by condensation, with elimination of small molecules, or by simple addition. Catalysis is usually required, or the use of an initiator to start a chain reaction of free radicals. If more than one kind of monomer is used, the result is a copolymer with the units arranged at random in the chain.

Polymerization, chemical process in which many small molecules, called monomers, are joined together to produce a large molecule, called a polymer. The monomers combined can be all of one kind or of many different kinds. The characteristic of the polymer is determined by what monomers are combined. Some polymers, such as starch and rubber, are found in nature; others, like plastic and paint, are synthetically produced.

Polymorphism, in zoology, the existence of more than two forms or types of individual within the same species of animal. An example is seen in some social insects, such as ants and bees, in which many different types of worker are structurally adapted for different tasks within the colony.
See also: Zoology.

Polynesia *See:* Pacific Islands.

Polyphony (Greek, 'many sounds'), music made up of several independent melodic lines linked harmonically through counterpoint.

Polytheism, belief in many gods, as opposed to monotheism or dualism; characteristic of most religions, notably Hinduism and Greek and Roman religion. It may arise from the personification of forces worshiped at a more primitive level in animism. One god may dominate the others (e.g., Zeus); sometimes a supreme being is recognized, transcending the gods.
See also: Religion.

Pomegranate, family of tropical shrubs and small trees native to Asia and India and cultivated in the United States. Pomegranates in the wild are shrublike; when cultivated, they grow as trees and can reach a height of 15 to 20 ft (4.6 to 6 m). A pomegranate is valued for its golden red fruit. The fruit is the size of a large apple and has a tough rind. Inside are many small seeds, each of which is enclosed by fleshy pulp. The pulp has a pleasant flavor and is eaten fresh or used to create syrup for drinks.

Pomerania, region in north-central Europe, south of the Baltic Sea. The greater part of Pomerania lies in Poland; the rest lies in Germany. Pomerania is mostly made up of fertile lowlands. Agriculture is the main occupation. Industries in the area include the manufacture of metals, ships, and paper. Pomerania was first settled as early as A.D. 100 by Germanic tribes. It has been occupied and governed by Slavs, Germans, Prussians, and Swedes. After World War II, it was divided between Germany and Poland.

Pomeranian, small dog, weighing from 3 to 7 lbs (1.4 to 3.2 kg) and standing approximately 6 in (15.3 cm) tall at the shoulder. The Pomeranian has long, fluffy hair on its body and a furry collar around its neck. Its face has sharp, foxlike features. Related to large dogs of the Arctic, the pomeranian became a popular 'toy dog' pet in the late 1800s.

Pomo, Hozan-speaking tribe living in North California, noted for their intricate basket making. A wealthy tribe with many natural resources, they used shells as currency.

Pompadour, Marquise de (1721-1764), mistress of King Louis XV of France from 1745. She was a patroness of the arts and had much influence on the political and artistic life of France.

Pompano, any of several saltwater fishes belonging to the jack family. Found in warm waters throughout the world, the pompano is valuable as a delicious food fish. Pompanos vary in size, shape, and color, depending on the species. The size range is 1 ft to 3 ft (46 cm to 114 cm); the weight range is from 3 lbs to 50 lbs (1.4 kg to 23 kg). Some of the species found along the Atlantic coast include the common pompano, the great pompano, and the palometa.

Pompeii, ancient Roman city in southern Italy, buried by an eruption of Mt. Vesuvius (A.D. 79). It was rediscovered in 1748. Excavations have revealed a town preserved much as it was on the day of its destruction, even to several bodies. The site has yielded invaluable information on Roman urban life and beautiful examples of Roman art.
See also: Rome, Ancient.

Pompey the Great (106-48 B.C.), Roman general and political leader. He started his career in 83 B.C. when he helped Lucius Sulla win a war against Gaius Marius. A few years later, he was sent to Spain to end a rebellion by Marius' supporters. In 72 B.C. he suppressed the slave revolt led by Spartacus. He was elected a Roman consul in 70 B.C. In 67 B.C. he was given the task of ridding the Mediterranean Sea of pirates. The next year he fought and defeated Mithridates VI of Pontus, conquering Palestine, Syria, and parts of Asia Minor. When the senate disapproved of some of his actions, Pompey united with Julius Caesar, a senate opponent. In 60 B.C., Pompey, Caesar, and Marcus Crassus formed the First Triumvirate (a triumvirate is a trio who head a government together), which ruled for several years. However, Pompey became competitive for Caesar's power and consequently broke with him. Pompey went over to senate's side and became a consul again in 52 B.C. In 49 B.C., Caesar defied the senate and initiated military action that resulted in civil war. Pompey was defeated at Pharsala. He fled to Egypt and was captured and executed there by the Roman-controlled Egyptian government.
See also: Caesar, (Gaius) Julius.

Pompidou, Georges Jean Raymond (1911-1974), president of France from 1969 to 1974. He was a literature professor before he began his political career in 1944 as an aide to Charles De Gaulle. De Gaulle was at that time a general and head of a temporary government. Pompidou's subsequent political career consisted of various posts in connection with De Gaulle. De Gaulle was elected president in 1958. When he resigned his presidency, Pompidou was elected to take his place. As president, Pompidou strove to better France's economy.
See also: France.

Ponape *See:* Pohnpei.

Ponce de León, Juan (c.1460-1521), Spanish discoverer of Florida. He sailed with Christopher Columbus in 1493, and in 1508 he conquered Puerto Rico and became its governor. Leading an expedition, possibly to find the mythical Fountain of Youth, he discovered and named Florida in 1513, but when he attempted to colonize it in 1521, he was driven off and mortally wounded by Indians.
See also: Florida.

Marquise de Pompadour (1721-1764), mistress of Louis XV (1710-1764), who has had great influence on his policy. This portrait of her was made by Maurice Quentin de la Tour (1704-1788).

Poncelet, Jean Victor (1788-1867), French mathematician, professor in Metz (1825-1835). As an officer of Napoleon he was a prisoner of war in Russia for some time. Pioneer in the field of projective geometry (*Traité des propriétés projectives des figures*, 1822).

Ponchielli, Amilcare (1834-1886), Italian opera composer. His best-known works are *I Promessi Sposi* (1856) and *La Gioconda* (1876), with its famous ballet, *Dance of the Hours.*
See also: Opera.

Pond, still body of water smaller than a lake. Ponds can be natural or artificial. Ponds are located in many different kinds of terrain, form arctic to tropical regions. Their location, depth, soil, and water level and quality determine the kind of plant and animal life found in them.
See also: Marsh; Swamp.

Pondicherry (pop. 401,000; conurbation) Capital of the union territory of the same name in Southeast India (territory 190 sq mi, 492 sq km; pop. 808,000). French colony in 1674, developed as trade center. Presently textile industry. Disputed by the French, the Dutch and the British. In 1954 it became part of India. Presently tourist center. Archbishop's seat (Roman Catholic). Airport.

Pond lily *See:* Water lily.

Pondweed, name for freshwater plants (genus *Potamogeton*) that sometimes clog streams and ponds. Their leaves may lie flat on the surface of the water or be completely submerged. The sago pondweed has branching stems and hairlike leaves. Like all pondweeds, its flowers open above the water. Its fruits are an important food for migrating ducks.

Ponomarev, Boris Nikolaevich (1905-), prominent official in Soviet Communist Party. He first became prominent in 1956 when he was voted into the party's Central Committee. In 1961, he became a secretary of the Central Committee. Ponomarev has also been a member of the Soviet Union's parliament since 1958.
See also: Union of Soviet Socialist Republics.

Ponta Delgada (pop. 22,000), city on Saõ Miguel Island, the largest of the Portuguese Azores islands. Its harbor is the main port of the Azores, exporting tropical fruits, vegetables, tea, and other products from the area. Other important industries in Ponta Delgada include sugar refining and liquor distilling. Its beautiful setting and favorable climate also makes it an active tourist resort.

Pontianak (pop. 398,000), city in Indonesia on the island of Borneo, at the junction of the Landak and the northern arm of the Kapuas, capital of the province of Kalimantan Barat. Important port with export of copra, rubber, timber and palm oil. Archbishop's seat, university (1963). Airport.

Founded around 1770 by a pirate, who brought the city to prosperity. Subsequently capital of sultanate. In 1778 a Dutch trading post was founded here. During the Japanese occupation (1942-1945) thousands of inhabitants were killed. From 1947 to 1950 capital of the state West Borneo. Many inhabitants are ethnic Chinese.

Pontifex, high priest of ancient Rome, one of the 16 members of the Pontifical College presiding over the state religion. The highest religious authority was the *pontifex maximus* (supreme pontiff); this title was adopted by the emperors and later by the popes.
See also: Rome, Ancient.

Pontiff *See:* Pope.

Pontine Marshes, swamp region in Italy. Located in central Italy, it covers an area of about 175,000 acres (70,820 hectares). The hills and mountains around this area prevent its water from being drained into the sea, creating an unhealthy environment. For centuries, it was the cause of malaria epidemics. Attempts to drain the area by digging waterways date back to as early as 312 B.C. In 1926, Benito Mussolini initiated a project that successfully drained the marshes. The reclaimed land has become a fertile agricultural area with several cities.

Pontoon bridge, bridge held up by pontoons (flat-bottomed boats), sealed metal tubes, or other floating objects. Because it can be built relatively quickly and is made up of materials that are transportable, it is especially convenient for military purposes. An army can set it up when invading or defending a territory to transport troops and equipment across a river when no bridge exists, or when the enemy has destroyed a once-existing bridge. A pontoon bridge was used as early as 480 B.C. by the Persian army. More recently, pontoon bridges were important to U.S. troops in Europe during World War II, where many bridges had been annihilated. Because a pontoon bridge blocks navigation, it is not a viable permanent structure. However, several long-span permanent concrete pontoon bridges exist. Washington has three, and Tasmania and Istanbul have one each.

Pontoppidan, Henrik (1857-1943), Danish writer and engineer, most important writer

of Danish naturalism. In his social-realist novels he described the hard life in the countryside, e.g. in *Det forjaettede land* (The Promised Land; 1891-1895). *Lykke-Per* (Lucky Peter; 1898-1904) dealt with the problem of liberation from upbringing and parental environment. In 1917 he shared the Nobel Prize for literature with K.A. Gjellerup.

Pontormo, Il (real name Iacopo Carrucci; 1494-1557), Florentine painter and artist, pupil of e.g. Leonardo da Vinci. Made an important contribution to the development of mannerism. Characteristic are the expressive strength and the curious color and light effects. One of the greatest artists of his time.

Pontus, ancient kingdom in northeastern Asia Minor by the Black Sea. Dating from the 4th century B.C., it reached its height under Mithridates VI, who was, however, defeated by the Roman general Pompey in 65 B.C. Pontus was annexed by the Roman Empire in 9 B.C. after it had challenged Roman power.
See also: Mithridates VI.

Pony *See:* Horse.

Pony express, famous relay mail service between St. Joseph, Mo., and Sacramento, Calif. (Apr. 1860 to Oct. 1861). It used horses, not ponies, with riders chosen for their small size. The route covered 1,966 mi (3,164 km), with stations at 10-15 mi- (16-24 km-) intervals. The goal of 10-day delivery was often met. The pony express was superseded by the transcontinental telegraph.

Poodle, breed of intelligent dogs. Poodles have curly hair that can be trimmed in various styles. Their coats are of one solid color, and can be white, black, gray, brown, orange, or blue. There are three varieties of poodles. The *toy poodle* has a shoulder height of up to 10 in (25.4 cm) and weighs up to 6 lbs (2.7 kg). The *miniature poodle* has a shoulder height of 10 to 15 in (25 to 38.1 cm) and weighs 14 to 16 lbs (6.4 to 7.3 kg). The *standard poodle* has a shoulder height of over 15 in (38.1 cm) and weighs 40 to 60 lbs (18.1 to 27 kg). Poodles originated in Germany and were once used to retrieve game. However, they are no longer hunting dogs.

The poodle is among the most intelligent of all dogs. The standard (left), was originally used as a waterfowl retriever. The poodle clip was developed to increase its effectiveness as a water dog. The miniature (center), bred from the standard, was used to produce the still smaller toy (right).

Pool *See:* Billiards.

Poona (or Pune; pop. 3,1 mln.) A city in Maharashtra State. It is on the Mula and Mutha Rivers, 80 miles (129 km) southeast of Bombay. Poona is a commercial, manufacturing, and transport center for an agricultural area. Among the attractions here are the Botanical Gardens and several museums, including one devoted to Indian art. Poona University is here. Poona was under Marathas in the 17th century, and became capital of the Maratha empire in the 18th century. It fell to the British in 1817.

Poorwill *See:* Whippoorwill.

Pop art, modern art movement dating from the mid-1950s, based on images of advertising, commercial illustration, and mass-produced objects. Developed in England and the United States, it included the artists Richard Hamilton, David Hockney, Andy Warhol, and Robert Rauschenberg, among others.

Maybe (1965) by Roy Lichtenstein, one of the foremost exponents of pop art (Wallraf-Richartz Museum, Cologne).

Popcorn (*Zea mays everta*), type of corn that opens and puffs open when it is heated. It belongs to the family Gramineae. A popular snack, it is a good source of fiber and does not contain many calories. A popcorn kernel contains moist starch. When the kernel is heated, the moisture turns into steam that creates pressure and causes the kernel to burst and the starch to puff out. Native to America, popcorn was cultivated by Native Americans for thousands of years before they introduced it to settlers.

Pope, head of the Roman Catholic church and head of state of Vatican City. The pope is the bishop of Rome, successor in a long line that Roman Catholics believe began with St. Peter, the first bishop of Rome. Basing their authority upon Peter and, ultimately, upon the words of Jesus of Nazareth, the popes, as early as Clement I (c. 92-101), claimed paramount authority over all Christians and primacy over all other bishops. In succeeding centuries, the popes would maintain and extend their claim to absolute spiritual authority and eventually, to political authority as well. But over the centuries, the content and extent of papal authority, power, and prestige, spiritual and political, has varied considerably and was contested almost from the outset. The early church had been governed loosely and informally as a community of believers and bishops who were the equals of each other. The memory of that tradition persisted in Eastern Orthodoxy and when the capital of the Roman empire was moved east to Constantinople in the fourth century, the ground was laid for a contest between east and west for supreme authority over Christendom. That contest, begun in the fourth century, culminated in 1054 during the papacy of Leo IX in a complete schism, or break, between the Roman Catholic and Eastern Orthodox churches. The pope eventually faced two greater challenges to his claims in the Protestant Reformation of the 16th century and the rise of nationalism beginning in the Renaissance. The one effectively put an end to the pope's hitherto unchallenged spiritual authority among Western Christians and the other put an end to his once considerable political power. At the height of political power under Pope Innocent III (1198-1216) the popes claimed to have the power to elevate and depose monarchs as well as bishops and cardinals and the Holy See included considerable territories and drew upon revenues from throughout Europe. The rise of nationalism and the loss of church property and income eventually reduced the pope's domain. The Papal States, founded in 756 and at one time quite extensive, were all part of Italy by 1870, and what was left to the pope, Vatican City, was eventually created an independent state by the Lateran Treaty of 1929. While the modern papacy is vastly reduced politically, the popes continue to enjoy and exercise considerable political influence and prestige. As a head of state, the pope sends ambassadors, or *nuncios*, throughout the world to represent the position and policies of the papacy on a wide range of issues affecting Roman Catholics.

The history of the papacy is a story of popes who were great administrators, visionaries, saints, jurists, and politicians. Among them, too, were diplomats and scholars, discerning patrons of arts and letters, sensualists, weaklings, and scoundrels. The fall of Rome and the subsequent power vacuum ushered in a centuries' long period of lawlessness in the West known as the Dark Ages. For most of that period, the popes took a leading role in the struggle to restore order and civilized life to the West. Pope Gregory I, the Great (590-604) defended Italy from barbarian attack and imposed a measure of enduring order upon the chaos. In the 9th and 10th centuries, the pope's influence declined but was restored by a powerful reform movement. Pope Gregory VII (1073-1085) established the pope's authority over clerics and kings and ushered in the greatest years of papal power and prestige. Decline set in with the capture of Pope Boniface VIII by troops of the French King Philip IV in 1303. The pope had become just one more of the many players in the ruthless game of politics. From 1309 to 1377 the popes resided in Avignon, France, and the result was the Great Schism in the western church that lasted from 1378 to 1417, a period in which rival popes claimed to be Peter's true heir and successor. The period raised fundamental questions about the papacy and church governance. In the centuries that followed the popes rapidly lost ground to the Reformation and nationalism. Wealth and power had corrupted the ecclesiastical bureaucracy and hierarchy and many popes, among them Borgias and Medicis, led lives that scandalized pious Christians, particularly those who lived outside of Italy. But among these Renaissance popes were outstanding men, like Pope Sixtus IV (1471-1484), a patron of arts and letters, and Pope Julius II (1503-1513), patron of Raphael and Michelangelo. But the popes were not to recover lost ground. Despite the internal reforms and the work of the Counter-Reformation, through the 1700s and 1800s the popes were clearly taking a rear guard action, supporting politically conservative forces, and widely perceived as reactionary. Ideologically, the popes retrenched. They claimed infallibility in matters of faith and morals and there have since, for the most part, appeared departures from orthodoxy and the influences of modern thought.

The pope is elected for life. Upon his death, a conclave, or gathering, of cardinals is called to convene within 20 days. Voting is usually by ballot and for a man to be declared pope he must win a 2/3 majority plus one vote. A woman may not be pope. After a man is elected and accepts, a coronation ceremony is held. The current pope, John Paul II, was elected in 1978. He is the first non-Italian pope since Adrian VI (1522-1523). John Paul II is Polish; Pope Adrian II was Dutch. The pope receives an annual salary and, in the course of discharging his many duties and responsibilities, leads a busy, demanding, and relatively spartan life absorbed in administrative, theological, ceremonial, and political matters bearing on the lives of Roman Catholics throughout the world.

See also: Roman Catholic Church.

Pope, Alexander (1688-1744), the greatest English poet and satirist of the Augustan Age. He was 4 ft 6 in (1.4 m) tall and partly crippled by tuberculosis. He first set out his literary ideals in his *Essay on Criticism* (1711), written in rhymed (heroic) couplets. His best-known works are the mock epic *The Rape of the Lock* (1712), his translations of the *Iliad* (1720) and the *Odyssey* (1726), *The Dunciad* (1728, 1743), a satirical attack on literary critics, and his essays on moral philosophy, *An Essay on Man* (1733-1734) and *Moral Essays* (1731-1735).

Poplar, name of group of trees belonging to the willow family. Poplars are found in Europe, Asia, and North America. They grow quickly and produce a soft, light wood used in the manufacture of crates and boxes. Depending on the species, they may be heart-shaped, triangular, or diamond-shaped. The name of some poplars are: balsam poplar, white poplar, white or silver poplar, and Carolina poplar.

Pople, John A. (1925-), British chemist. In 1998 won the Nobel prize for chemistry for his contribution to the development of arithmetic methods in quantum chemistry. His work includes *Approximate Molecular Orbital Theory* and *High-Resolution Nuclear Magnetic Resonance*.

Pop Music, songs and dance music designed to please a wide audience. In popular music the melodies and rhythms are easily identified and are repeated many times. The words (lyrics) are often simple, sentimental, and easy to remember. Most of the songs are written by composer and lyricist in collaboration. A song that has a deep-rooted acceptance and remains popular for many years, is called a *standard*. The invention of rock and roll (around 1955) is generally seen as the startingpoint of pop music. During the 1960's folk music gained popularity and the bossa nova, a combination of jazz and Brazilian rhythms, was introduced. Songs supporting the civil rights and antiwar movements were written and performed by Bob Dylan, Joan Baez, and others. Soul music, a type of rhythm-and-blues, led to a revival of the blues. Rock, many forms, continued to dominate the pop scene in the 1970's. Disco, a style played primarily for dancing, flourished. Reggae, music that combines traditional Jamaican styles with elements of rock and soul music, became popular. In the last decades of the century there was a renewed interest in the big-band sound; country music, jazz, and rock continued to attract wide audiences; and rap music became popular. (In rap, rhymed lyrics are rapidly recited over heavily percussive music.)

Popocatépetl, volcanic mountain in Mexico. Its name is the Aztec word for 'smoking mountain.' With an altitude of 17,887 ft (5,452 m), it is one of the highest mountains in North America, and the second-highest mountain in Mexico. Its peak is always snow-covered. 'Popo,' as it is sometimes called, has not had a major eruption since 1702. It does occasionally emit smoke clouds and sulfur gas, and, less frequently, ashes and stones.

Popper, Sir Karl Raimund (1902-1994), Austrian-born English philosopher, best known for his theory of falsification in the philosophy of science. Popper contends that scientific theories are never more than provisionally adopted and remain acceptable only as long as scientists are devising new experiments to test (falsify) them. He attacks the doctrine of historicism (presuming to understand phenomena entirely through their development) in *The Open Society and Its Enemies* (1945) and *The Poverty of Historicism* (1957).
See also: Philosophy.

Poppy, name for annual or herbaceous perennial plants of the genus *Papaver* and related genera. There are about 100 species, which are mostly native to temperate and subtropical areas in Eurasia and northern Africa. The flower bud is enclosed by two thick, green sepals that drop off to allow the thin petals to unfold. The seeds are enclosed in a capsule. The sap of the unripe capsules of the opium poppy (*P. somniferum*) yield opium; its seeds (poppyseed) are not narcotic.

Popular music, term used to describe several kinds of music that are not classical. Classical music includes symphonies, operas, and ballet works performed by an orchestra. Popular music includes rock and roll, country and folk music, jazz, and other styles and blendings of styles. It is called 'popular' because it is usually appreciated by a large number of the general public.

Population, number of or term for all the inhabitants of a designated territory. For the world as a whole, population doubled between 1930 and 1975, from 2 to 4 billion, and increased to 4.7 billion by mid-1983, and to 6 billion in 1999. The sharpest increases have been in developing nations, which are least able to provide food, education, and jobs for all. Averting world famine depends on the few countries able to export food. Many nations now have population-control programs, but the control of infectious diseases and increases in the food supply because of modern growing techniques have combined to encourage population growth. In some societies, however, fertility rates have declined somewhat, and an increase in abortions, approaching the number of live births in a few countries, has helped defuse the population bomb, though not without great controversy.

Populism, under the name of populism a large variety of ideological and political movements are grouped, all of which call upon the wisdom of the people, which they consider superior, and glamorize the national character. It is closely connected with nation building and often functions as a developmental ideology, as in a decolonization process. Populism can be found in e.g. Peronism (Argentina) and Poujadism (France). Populism is generally at the expense of minorities.

Poquelin, Jean Baptiste *See:* Molière.

Porcelain, a kind of white earthenware. It is hard, fine, and translucent. Porcelain is made from a mixture of kaolin (a pure white clay) and petuntse (a hard mineral). After the mixture is shaped, it is fired at an extremely high temperature that causes the petuntse to melt into glass that is fused to the kaolin which retains the shape. Porcelain is used to create such items as tableware, vases, and figurines. It is most often decorated with painted designs. Because it was first developed by the Chinese (7th century), it is sometimes referred to as china. Europe, Japan, and the United States produce most of the world's porcelain.

Porcupine, name for large, spiny vegetarian rodents of two distinct families: Erithizontidae, confined to the Americas, and Hystricidae, to the tropics of the Old World. Old World forms, including about a dozen species in Africa and South Asia, are among the largest rodents, and the entire body is covered with spines. The American porcupines have an equal armory of spines, but when relaxed, these are concealed in a thick underfur.

Porcupinefish, slow-moving tropical fish that can blow up its body when alarmed. It takes in water through the mouth to swell its body into a sphere; at the same time, sharp spines are raised, making it very difficult to handle. Porcupinefish feed on shellfish and coral. Pacific Islanders used to make the skins into helmets.

Pore, minute opening of a gland in skin. Skin has many small glands that produce perspiration and oil. Pores serve as an outlet for the perspiration and oil. When pores are blocked up, skin becomes inflamed, resulting in a skin rash or acne.

Porgy, deep-bodied fish (family Sparidae) with powerful teeth. Porgies are found in shallow tropical and temperate seas. The largest is the 100-lb (45-kg) South African mussel-cracker. On the Atlantic coast of America there are the northern porgy, the sheepshead, and the pinfish.

Porifera *See:* Sponge.

Po River, longest river in Italy. Beginning in the Cottian Alps, it flows east for 405 mi (652 km) and drains into a huge delta in the Adriatic Sea. Most rivers in northern Italy empty into it, as do the Garda, Como, Maggiore, Lecco, and Iseo lakes. The Po carries a tremendous amount of water and has created many devastating floods. Efforts were made as early as 300 B.C. to control the river by building embankments. Several large Italian cities are situated on the Po,

David Bowie, an English singer and composer, gained recognition in the early 1970s with his science-fiction songs, extravagant costumes, and flamboyant performances. Bowie's work has explored a number of musical styles, including folk, glitter rock, disco, and –with avant-garde musician Brian Eno– art rock.

P

The porcupinefish (*Diodon holacanthus*), a feeder on small mollusk, is seen in normal and inflated form. The eyes of the fish move independently of one another.

P

such as Cremona and Turin. From the mouth of the Po to Turin, the river is deep and wide enough for the navigation of freight ships transporting cargo. On the upper section of the river are several electric power plants.

Pork, pig flesh used for food. Pork may be eaten cooked. It may also be cured with salt and then smoked or dried. Smoking and drying cured pork prevents the meat from spoiling, and gives it an added flavor. Ham and bacon are cured pork. Pork may contain small worms that, when consumed, create a disease called trichinosis. Fresh pork should always be thoroughly cooked until the meat becomes gray-this kills any worms that may be in it.

Pornography, term applied to materials, including books, pictures, magazines, and films, with obscene or offensive content designed to cause sexual excitement. The term is derived from the Greek *pornographos* ('writing of harlots') and most often refers to sexual material, though it is now sometimes applied to other forms of offensive material, such as that which portrays gratuitous violence. In the United States each state has laws concerning the publication and distribution of obscene material; these are backed up by extensive international agreements designed to inhibit the import and export of pornography.

Porphyry (A.D. 233-304), ancient Greek philosopher, author of *Introduction to the Categories*, a book which discussed how the qualities of things could be put into categories and groups. He studied in Athens before moving to Rome, where he became a member of the Neoplatonic group led by Plotinus.
See also: Neoplatonism.

Porpoise, small toothed whale (family Phocaenidae), distinguished from dolphins in being smaller and having a rounded head with no projecting beaklike mouth. They feed mainly on shoaling fishes. The name is sometimes loosely applied in the United States to the various species of dolphin.

Porsche, Ferdinand *See:* Volkswagen.

Port, sweet wine, usually red, fortified with brandy. It comes from grapes grown in the Douro Valley, Portugal, and is shipped from Oporto, whence its name.

Port Arthur (Chinese: Lüshun; Japanese: Ryo-jun) Strategically situated port city at the Liaodong peninsula, naval base, and part of the city Lüda. It was named for W. Arthur, commander of the British war vessel Algerine, who was the first to sail into the bay in 1857. In 1904 Japan attacked the Russian fleet here, which resulted in the Russo-Japanese War (1904-1905). The port was conquered by the Japanese in 1905. From 1945-1955 it was Russian-Chinese and from 1955 Chinese.

Port-au-Prince (pop. 846,000), capital, largest city, and leading port of Haiti. It stands on a sheltered bay facing the Caribbean Sea. In spite of local industries,

including textile, flour, and sugar milling, some imposing buildings, and a modern airport, the city is one of the Western Hemisphere's poorest capitals. French colonists founded Port-au-Prince in 1749.

Portcullis *See:* Castle.

Port Elizabeth (pop. 652,000), city in South Africa. Situated on a bay of the Indian Ocean, it was founded in 1799. The modern city was laid out in 1820 by Sir Rufane Donkin, who named it for his wife, Lady Elizabeth. Port Elizabeth is a major seaport and manufacturing center with important rubber and automobile industries.

Porter, Cole (1893-1964), U.S. popular song composer. After World War I he achieved great success as a writer of sophisticated songs and musical comedies, providing both the words and music. His prolific output includes *Anything Goes* (1934), *Kiss Me Kate* (1948), *Can-Can* (1953), the film score for *High Society* (1956), and many classic songs.

Porter, Katherine Anne (1890-1980), U.S. short-story writer and novelist who won the 1966 Pulitzer Prize for her *Collected Short Stories* (1965). Her collections of short stories include *Flowering Judas* (1930) and *Pale Horse, Pale Rider* (1939). *Ship of Fools* (1962) is her only novel.

Porter, William Sydney *See:* Henry, O..

Portisch, Lajos (1937-), Hungarian chess player, became Grandmaster in 1961. He became national champion many times and was a very successful tournament player with a solid yet by no means passive style. Portisch reached the candidates' matches five times, but every time was defeated in the quarterfinals: in 1965 by Tal, in 1968 by Larsen, in 1974 by Petrosian, in 1977 by Spasski, in 1980 by Robert Hübner and in 1989 by Jan Timman.

Portland (pop. 504,000), largest city in Oregon, a leading West Coast port. It stands in northwestern Oregon on the Willamette River near its junction with the Columbia River, c. 60 mi (97 km) due east of the Pacific Ocean. Ocean-going ships reach Portland by river, enabling it to handle more dry cargo than any other Pacific port. Lumber, fruit, and wheat are the main exports. Important educational institutions include the University of Oregon's schools of medicine and dentistry, Portland State College, and the Roman Catholic University of Portland. The city's rose gardens are nationally famous.
See also: Oregon.

Portland cement *See:* Cement.

Port Louis (pop. 180,000), capital and largest city of the island nation of Mauritius. Located on a sheltered harbor of the Indian Ocean on the northwestern shore of the country's main island, Port Louis is a key agricultural and industrial export center. It was founded by the French in 1735 and named for King Louis XV.

Port Moresby (pop. 312,000), capital and largest city of Papua New Guinea. It lies on a harbor of the Coral Sea in the southeastern part of the country and was founded in 1873 by the British explorer Capt. John Moresby. During World War II (1939-1945) Port Moresby served as an Allied military operations center for the South Pacific.

Porto, or Oporto (pop. 336,000), second largest city in Portugal. Situated on the Douro River near its mouth at the Atlantic Ocean, Porto was founded during the Roman Empire and several of its medieval landmarks, including a cathedral, survive today. Porto is the major commercial and industrial hub of northern Portugal and is famous for its port wines. Fishing and food processing also contribute greatly to the city's economic base.

Pôrto Alegre (pop. 3,4 million), city in southeastern Brazil. It is located on the Guaíba River near the Atlantic Ocean and is the capital of the state of Rio Grande do Sul. Pôrto Alegre is a key shipping and commercial port, as well as an important cultural and educational center.

Portobelo (pop. 550), village in Panama. Named by Columbus in 1502 and founded as a Caribbean shipping port, Portobelo was often the starting point for Spanish treasure ships bound for Spain from its New World colonies. Repeated attacks by English pirates in the 17th and 18th centuries destroyed much of the town and its importance declined after the opening of the Panama Railroad in the 1850s.

Port-of-Spain (pop. 60,000), capital and largest city of Trinidad and Tobago. Situated on the northwest coast of the island of Trinidad, Port-of-Spain was founded by the Spanish around 1560 and was briefly the capital of the Federation of the West Indies (1958-1962), a group of British-owned Caribbean islands. It is a major agricultural export center for the nation and the southern Caribbean region.

Porto-Novo (pop. 178,000), capital and second largest city of Benin. Lying on the Gulf of Guinea, it was founded and named by the Portuguese in the 17th century and became a hub for the West African slave trade. Captured by the French in 1883, Porto-Novo was made the capital of the colony of Dahomey and remained the capital when independence was granted in 1960. It is a major port and rail terminal for the rest of the nation.

Port Said (pop. 470,000), port city in Egypt. Located on the Mediterranean Sea at the northern terminus of the Suez Canal, Port Said was founded in 1859 as a camp for workers building the canal. Because of its key location, it is a major commercial center for ships using the canal and the site of a free trade zone established by the Egyptian government to encourage commerce.
See also: Egypt.

Portsmouth (pop. 189,000), major port and naval center in southern England. Situated

on the English Channel, Portsmouth was founded in the 1100s and became a key shipbuilding city in the 16th century. Shipbuilding and naval activity provide the city with much of its economic base and its busy harbor handles much of the country's import and export trade. Historic sites there include the 12th century cathedral, the birthplace of Charles Dickens, and Lord Nelson's flagship, *Victory*.
See also: England.

Port Sudan (pop. 360,000), chief port city of Sudan. It is on the Red Sea and was built between 1905 and 1909 to replace an earlier Arab port that became choked off by coral reefs. With modern harbor facilities, Port Sudan handles most of the nation's overseas trade and is the fourth largest city in Sudan.
See also: Sudan.

Portugal

Capital:	Lisbon
Area:	35,672 sq mi (92,389 sq km)
Population:	9,930,000
Language:	Portuguese
Government:	Republic
Independent:	1143 (1910 republic)
Head of gov.:	Prime minister
Per capita:	US$ 10,160
Monetary unit:	1 Escudo = 100 centavos

Portugal, republic on the Iberian peninsula in the extreme southwest of continental Europe.
Land and climate. Excluding the Azores and Madeira, Portugal covers an area of 34,340 sq mi/88,941 sq km and is bordered by Spain to the east and north and by the Atlantic Ocean to the west and south. Portugal lies at the point where the western ridge of the high Spanish plateau slopes downward towards the Atlantic Ocean. Most of the highest land lies in the northeast gradually giving way to undulating hills and low fertile plains. Three large rivers, all rising in Spain, cross the country: the Douro, the Tagus, and the Guadiana. Coastal Portugal has a mild climate; the interior has colder winters and is often subject to drought. The capital is Lisbon.
People. The Portuguese people are a mixture of the original inhabitants of the land and successive waves of invaders. The Portu-

guese language is closely related to Spanish and almost everyone in Portugal is Roman Catholic.
Economy. Portugal is one of Europe's poorer countries. Most of the people live in villages and small towns and agriculture is an important occupation. Most farms are small and poor. Portuguese raise livestock, olives, grapes, citrus fruits, and almonds and produce wine and olive oil. Portugal is a major producer of cork. Fishing is important, the chief catches being sardines and tuna. Industries include food processing, textiles, metals, mining, and hydroelectricity.
History. Over the centuries, the area that is now Portugal was invaded by Celts, Greeks, and Romans and later by Visigoths, Berbers, and Moors. The Moors arrived in 711 and remained until 1249. Their influence upon Portuguese culture has been deep. Portugal became an independent Christian kingdom in 1143 under Alfonso I and over the next century the country was completely reconquered from the Moors. In 1385, John I founded the Aviz dynasty and by the second half of the 16th century, Portugal was at the pinnacle of its power with an empire that included much of South America, Africa, and South and Southeast Asia. Philip II of Spain seized Portugal in 1580 and the Spanish ruled until a successful revolt established the ruling house of Braganza in 1640. By then, Portugal had lost most of her former power and influence. During the Napoleonic Wars, Portugal was invaded by both the French and the Spanish. By 1825 Brazil had become an independent empire. A Portuguese republic was declared in 1910 and after a military coup in 1926 Antonio de Oliveira Salazar rose to power and became virtual dictator until he was succeeded by Marcello Caetano in 1968. A coup in 1974 ushered in a government that brought democratic reforms. Subsequently, Portugal shed virtually all of its overseas territories. Guinea-Bissau became independent in 1974, followed by Angola, the Cape Verde Islands, Mozambique, and São Tomé and Príncipe in 1975. In 1976 Portuguese Timor became part of Indonesia and Macao has been reverted to China in 1999. In the process, Portugal has also recovered a measure of political stability. In 1987 the government, headed by Premier Anibal Cavaco Silvas, was democratically elected. The 1995 elections were won by the Socialists. António Guterres became Prime Minister. The 2002 elections were won by the Social Democratic party. José Manuel Durão became the new Prime Minister.

In small fishing villages like Nazaré, in the centre of Portugal on the Atlantic Ocean, very small boats are still used. Here, the fish is carried ashore.

Portuguese, official language of Portugal and Brazil. It is one of the Romance Languages and developed from the Latin spoken in Roman Iberia. Brazilian Portuguese has absorbed words and phrases from the languages of the Native American and African slave populations.

Portuguese Guinea *See:* Guinea-Bissau.

Portuguese man-of-war (*Physalia physalis*), colorful jellyfish of the order Siphonophora. It consists of an assemblage of four kinds of polyps, the most obvious of which is a gas-filled bladder about 1 ft (30.5 cm) long, which carries a high crest and is colored blue or purple. Below this float are supported other polyps, including the long, stinging tentacles used for catching prey. The sting can be painful to humans.

Portuguese water dog, web-footed dog capable of swimming great distances. Portuguese fishermen trained and used the dogs to retrieve fish and nets from the water and they have also been used to carry messages between ships. Males range from 20 to 23 in (51 to 59 cm) tall and weigh between 42 and 60 lb (19-27 kg), while females are smaller.

Portulaca, flower of the purslane family. Producing colorful blossoms that open only in full sunlight, portulacas are cultivated in gardens and several species are used as potted plants. The petals are most commonly red, yellow, pink, white, or purple and the plant may grow from 1 to 1.5 ft (30-46 cm) tall.

Poseidon, in Greek mythology, god of the sea. The son of Cronus and Rhea and brother of Zeus, Poseidon was also the god of horses, earthquakes, and sea storms. He was

In the mountains of northern Portugal terraces are carved into the slopes to provide additional arable land. The small fields and hilly terrain make mechanized agriculture difficult. In recent years Portugal has had to import food and fodder.

P

P

often pictured with a long white beard driving a chariot and wielding a trident with which he stirred up the earth or sea when venting his wrath. His Roman counterpart was Neptune.

Positivism, philosophical theory of knowledge associated with the 19th-century French philosopher Auguste Comte. It holds that the observable, or 'positive,' data of sense experience constitute the sole basis for assertions about matters of fact; only the truths of logic and mathematics are additionally admitted. The speculative claims of theology and metaphysics, regarded as the primitive antecedents of 'positive' thought, are discounted.
See also: Comte, Auguste.

Positron emission tomography (PET), technique used to study brain activity. A person undergoing a PET scan is injected with a glucose solution containing low-level radioactive particles that produce positrons, electrically charged particles that help produce gamma rays. The person places his or her head inside a ring containing sensors that measure gamma ray signals from the brain, and these signals are translated by colors onto a screen. Scientists reading the screen can interpret the colors in a way that measures brain activity.
See also: Brain.

Possum, tree-dwelling mammal of the family *Phalangeridae*, native to Australia and New Guinea. There are about 40 species of possums, ranging in weight from 1/2 oz (14 grams) to 11 lb (5 kg). They are nocturnal animals, foraging through forests and garbage cans for their food. As with other marsupials, the babies are born prematurely and are nurtured in the mothers' pouches. Their practice of lying absolutely still when frightened gives rise to the term 'playing possum.'

Post, Emily Price (1872-1960), U.S. writer, accepted authority on correct social behavior because of her book *Etiquette* (1922).

Postal Union, Universal (UPU), United Nations agency governing the international flow of mail. Begun in 1874 with 22 nations attending the first International Postal

A commemorative stamp dated 1847 bears the portrait of Benjamin Franklin, the first postmaster general of the United States.

Congress in Berne, Switzerland, the UPU became a UN agency in 1947. Today it includes all 170 member nations. The UPU sets policies and uniform procedures for the exchange of mail and parcels between countries and establishes reasonable postal rates. It also provides technical assistance and advice to its members and strives toward the improvement of all services under its supervision.

Post, Wiley (1899-1935), U.S. aviator. In 1933 he was the first person to fly solo around the world, a feat he accomplished in a little over a week (July 15-22). During this flight, which covered 15,596 mi (25,099 km), Post proved the effectiveness of an automatic pilot system that enabled the plane to stay aloft while he rested. On Aug. 15, 1935 he was killed in a plane crash near Point Barrow, Alaska.

Postimpressionism, term coined by critic Roger Fry to describe the work of certain painters (1880-1890) whose styles, though dissimilar, flowed from, and were a reaction to, impressionism. Paul Cézanne, Paul Gauguin, Georges Seurat, and Vincent Van Gogh are considered the principal postimpressionists.

Post-modernism, movement in the arts that combines apparently arbitrary, and often decorative elements. Post-modernists prefer a plural definition of art: expressions of art co-exist on all social levels and all over the world. They consider the world to be an ensemble of signs, which only have meaning within certain cultural codes. Post-modernists try to expose and deconstruct these codes to show processes in current society. The movement evolved in the late 1970s and played an important role in the design of the 1980s. In the meantime, this movement has also surfaced in architecture and literature.

Post mortem *See:* Autopsy.

Postpainterly Abstraction, form of abstract art that started in 1955. The spontaneous

emotional releases and material expression of abstract expressionism are rejected. This is replaced with art in which form and composition are reduced and color dominates. Apart from hard edge and colorfield painting, this movement also includes the beginnings of minimal art and systematic art. Exponents are: Kenneth Noland, Ellsworth Kelly, Morris Louis, Barnett Newman and Frank Stella.

Pot *See:* Marijuana.

Potash, potassium-based salts used in fertilizers. Most potash comes from the mineral sylvite and is often found in underground salt beds or in salt lakes. Potassium chloride (KCI) is the most important type of potash but another type, potassium carbonate (K_2CO_3), can be manufactured by running water through wood ashes and boiling the solution in large iron pots.

Potassium, chemical element, symbol K; for physical constants see Periodic Table. Potassium was discovered by Sir Humphrey Davy in 1807. It was the first metal isolated by electrolysis. It is found mainly as *sylvite* (potassium chloride) but occurs in many other minerals. It is obtained commercially by electrolysis of the hydroxide. Potassium is a silvery-white, soft, reactive metal of the alkali metal group. It catches fire spontaneously in water and oxidizes rapidly in air and must be stored in a dry oxygen-free liquid such as mineral oil. It is essential to plant growth and is found in most soils. Potassium and its compounds are used in fertilizers, photography, organic synthesis, and heat transfer media.

Potassium nitrate *See:* Saltpeter.

Potato (*Solanum tuberosum*), herbaceous plant of the nightshade family, with an edible, fleshy, tuberous, underground stem. It originated in the South American Andes. The tubers became a popular European foodstuff in the 18th century, the Irish in particular becoming dependent on the high-carbohydrate crop.

The white potato (*S. tuberosum*) is a herbaceous plant with stems that grow up to 3 ft (1 m) long, odd-pinnate compound leaves, and clusters of white to purple flowers. The edible portion of the plant is a tuber – the enlarged end of a stolon, or underground stem – with tan to purple skin.

Potato beetle (*Lema trilineata*), destructive insect of the leaf beetle family. The larvae feed on the leaves and stems of potato plants, causing extensive damage and diseases that harm proper potato tuber growth. The most common type is the Colorado potato beetle (*Leptinotarsa decemlineata*), which measures 1/2 in (13 mm) long and is yellow with black stripes on its wing covers.

Potato famine, in 19th-century Ireland, famine caused by potato blight. In 1845 and 1846 potato crops failed; in the subsequent famine nearly a million people died, and over a million emigrated, particularly to the United States. Ireland's population fell from about 8.5 million in 1845 to 6.55 million in 1851. *See also:* Ireland.

Potemkin, Grigori Aleksandrovich (1729-1791), Russian soldier and favorite of Catherine the Great. For the last 20 years of his life, he was the most powerful man in Russia. He enlarged the Russian army and navy, and annexed (1783) and administered the Crimea.

Potential, electric, work done against electric fields in bringing a unit charge to a given point from some arbitrary reference point (usually earthed), measured in volts (i.e., joules per coulomb). Charges tend to flow from points at one potential to those at a lower potential; potential difference, or voltage, thus plays the role of a driving force for electric current. In inductive circuits, the work done in bringing up the charge depends on the route taken, and potential ceases to be a useful concept.

Potentiometer, device used to obtain a precise measure of the electromotive force (emf), or voltage, of an electrical cell. It employs a special circuit incorporating a variable resistor (rheostat) and a galvanometer. Using a standard cell of known emf, the rheostat is adjusted until no current flows in the circuit, as indicated by the galvanometer. The cell of unknown emf is then placed in the circuit instead of the standard cell, and the rheostat is adjusted again so that no current flows. The difference in the 2 settings of the rheostat indicates the emf of the unknown cell. The potentiometer can be used to calibrate electrical instruments and as a variable resistor. The volume control in a radio is a type of potentiometer.

Potlatch, in many tribal cultures, especially among the Native Americans of the Northwest Coast, an elaborate ceremonial feast at which the host distributes or destroys his own wealth to gain status or office in his tribe. Wealthier guests are expected in turn to match or exceed this in future potlatches. Although banned for a while in Canada, the potlatch is still an important tribal institution.

Potok, Chaim (1929-2002), American author. The main issue in his novels is the confrontation of Jewish standards and values with modern society. His work includes *The Chosen* (1967), *My Name is Asher Lev* (1972), *The Book of Lights* (1981), *Davita's Harp* (1990), and *I Am the Clay* (1992).

Potomac River, U.S. river flowing through Washington, D.C. Formed by the confluence of the 110-mi (177-km) long northern branch and the 140-mi (125-km) long southern branch, it flows 287 mi (462 km) into Chesapeake Bay. Navigation for large ships is prevented above Washington, D.C., by the Great Falls. The river is noted for its scenic attraction.

Potsdam (pop. 140,000), city in eastern Germany, near Berlin. In the 18th century it was chosen by Frederick II as his principal residence and became a center and symbol of Prussian militarism. Noted for its royal palaces, it is now also an industrial city. It was the site of the 1945 Potsdam Confer-ence.

Potsdam Conference (July 17 to Aug. 2, 1945), a summit meeting at Potsdam, Germany, between Premier Joseph Stalin, President Harry S. Truman, and in succession, Prime Ministers Winston Churchill and Winston Attlee. They agreed that a four-power Allied Control Council would rule defeated Germany, disarming it and fostering democratic government; Poland would gain part of East Germany; the German economy would be decentralized; Germans in Hungary, Poland, and Czechoslovakia would be repatriated. The conference also discussed reparations payments and issued an ultimatum to Japan. Almost all the agreements were breached as the Cold War hardened. *See also:* World War II.

Potter, Beatrix (1866-1943), English author and illustrator of children's books. Her works, illustrated by herself, have become classics, including *The Tale of Peter Rabbit* (1902), *The Tailor of Gloucester* (1903), *Benjamin Bunny* (1904), *Mrs. Tiggy-Winkle* (1905), *Jemima Puddle-Duck* (1908), and *Pigling Bland* (1913).

Potter, Dennis (Christopher George; 1935-1994), British writer who became known for his TV-dramas that broke fresh ground as far as form and content were concerned. His first TV-plays were broadcast in 1965; especially *Stand Up, Nigel Barton* and *Vote for Nigel Barton* made an impression. Other work includes *Son of Man* (1969), *Brimstone and Treacle*, (written in the mid 1970s for the BBC, not broadcast until 1987, although filmed earlier), *The Singing Detective* (1986), in which hospital scenes are alternated with daydreams inspired by Hollywood movies, *Pennies from Heaven* (1978), released as a Hollywood movie in 1982 and also published as a novel. Later serials such as *Ticket to Ride* (1986) and *Blackeyes* (1987) were also similarly published.

Pottery and porcelain, ceramic articles, especially vessels, made of clay (generally kaolin) and hardened by firing. In the manufacture of pottery the clay is made plastic by blending with water. The article is then shaped-traditionally by hand, by building up layers of strips (coiled pottery), by 'throwing' on the potter's wheel, or by molding, industrially by high-pressure molding or by a rotating template. The clay is fired in a kiln, slowly at first, then at higher temperatures to oxidize and consolidate it. The glaze (if desired) is then applied by spraying or dipping and the article is refired.

Potto (genus *Perodicticus*), various slow-moving African primates related to the lorises. The potto has large, staring eyes, thick, woolly fur, and a short tail; spines from the neck bones protrude through the skin. It leads a solitary life, emerging at dusk to search for fruit, insects, lizards, or birds' nests.

Poulenc, Francis (1899-1963), French composer, member of the post-World War II group of composers called *Les Six*. His music is light in texture, although serious. His best-known works include *Mouvements perpetuels* for piano (1918), the ballet *Les Biches* (1924), and the opera *Dialogue des Carmélites* (1957). He was also a notable songwriter.

Poultry farming, rearing of all types of domesticated farm fowls for eggs and flesh. Chickens are the most popular bird, followed by turkeys, ducks, geese, and other

The English class chickens include the Australorp (A), Cornish (B), Dorking (C), and Sussex (H). The Leghorn (D) is an important Mediterranean breed. The American class chickens include the New Hampshire (E), Plymouth Rock (F), and Rhode Island Red (G).

P

P

types. Nearly all economically valuable fowls live in controlled environments, with artificial lighting and heating and small pens for individuals or groups. Chickens are hatched in incubators, reared in brooders and transferred to laying or fattening quarters. An annual output of 200-250 eggs per bird is essential for good profits.

Pound, Ezra Loomis (1885-1972), U.S. poet, critic, and translator. A gifted linguist, he went to Europe in 1908 and soon won recognition. His most important works are *Homage to Sextus Propertius* (1918), *Hugh Selwyn Mauberley* (1920), and the epic *Cantos* (1925-1960). He championed the imagist and vorticist movements, and influenced T.S. Eliot, Robert Frost, and W.B. Yeats, among others. He supported Benito Mussolini, and after broadcasting pro-Fascist propaganda during World War II, he was indicted for treason by the United States; he was found unfit to plead and confined to a mental institution until 1958.

Pound, Roscoe (1870-1964), U.S. jurist and educator who championed flexibility in the law and efficiency in court administration. Professor of law at Harvard (1910-1937), he advocated a 'sociological jurisprudence' that would adapt the law to changing social and economic conditions.

Poussin, Nicolas (1594-1665), greatest 17th-century French Baroque painter. He worked mostly in Rome and based his style on Raphael and antiquities. He was first painter to Louis XII. His classical and religious subjects, such as *Shepherds of Arcadia* (1629), *The Rape of the Sabine Women* (1635), and *The Seven Sacraments* (1644-1648) are rich in color, austere in handling, dramatic, and evocative in mood. He influenced Jacques-Louis David, Paul Cézanne, and Pablo Picasso.

Poverty, shortage of income or resources necessary for a minimum standard of living in a particular society. In the United States,

Edison's first direct-current generator was displayed at the Paris World Exhibition in 1881. A year later Edison set up a commercial electric generating station in New York City. He used a generator of this type to provide power for the first electric streetlights.

where a poor minority exists in the midst of an affluent society, a major element in poverty is the feeling of psychological deprivation. In the poor countries of Asia, Africa, and Latin America, where the poor constitute a majority of the people, poverty consists more of physical deprivation, but even in the third world the economic expectations of the poor have been substantially raised by exposure to the mass media.

Powder metallurgy, process of reducing metals into powder. The process is used to make metal alloys by mixing them as powder and heating them to bind the powders together. They are then pressed into the desired shape or form. Metals can be broken down into powders by crushing them or by submittting them to intense heat. They can also be reduced through electrolysis or by atomization of the metal in molten form.

Powell, Anthony Dymoke (1905-2000), English novelist, best known for his contemporary comedy of manners *A Dance to the Music of Time*, a 12-volume series of novels starting with *A Question of Upbringing* (1951) and ending with *Hearing Secret Harmonies* (1976). In 1986 he added another novel *The Fisher King* to the series.

Powell, Colin, (1937-), American General and politician. Powell joined the army and was wounded in Vietnam (1962-1963). He has been working as a military advisor to several Presidents at the Pentagon in Washington since 1972. In 1987, President Reagan appointed him Security Advisor and in 1989-1993, President Bush Sr. made Powell Chairman of the joint chiefs-of-staff, the first African-American officer to receive this highest military position in the U.S. In 1989 he opposed the military action against the Panamanian dictator, Noriega and won world wide respect for his astute handling of Operation Desert Storm (1990-1991) against Iraq after the invasion of Kuwait. After the Gulf War, he gained considerable reputation and respect. Great Britain awarded him a honory knighthood in 1993. At that time he retired from the army and wrote his best-selling autobiography, *My American Journey* (1995) from which Powell emerged as a popular national and international figure.
During the electoral campaigns of 1996, both political parties tried to win Powell to a leadership role in their party. In 1996 he announced he was not interested in running for President. President George W. Bushew appointed him Secretary of State at the end of 2000. After the attacks of September 11, 2001, Powell and Bush were the driving forces behind the diplomatic offensive to gain international support for military actions, followed by Operation Enduring Freedom in Afghanistan.
See also: Persian Gulf War; Bush, George W.; September 11, 2001.

Powell, John Wesley (1834-1902), U.S. geologist and ethnologist best known for his geological and topographical surveys and for his anthropological studies of Native Americans. He helped establish and headed the U.S. Geological Survey (1881-1894).
See also: Geology.

Power, in physics, the time rate at which work is done. The amount of power that is put forth determines the amount of work that can be done per unit time. Power can be calculated with the following formula:

$$P = \frac{W}{t}$$

In this formula, P stands for power, W for work, and t for time. Work is measured by multiplying the force times the distance. The formula for power is then written:

$$P = \frac{Fd}{t}$$

In this formula, F stands for force and d stands for distance.
The basic unit of power in the English system of measurement is *foot-pounds per second*. When a force of 1 pound moves an object 1 foot, 1 foot-pound of work is done. In the metric system, the customary unit of power is the watt. A watt is the power needed to do 1 joule of work per second.

Power, in the social sciences, the ability to exercise control over others. Power is most often exerted by individuals, groups, or nations through superior physical strength, social position, or intellect. Greater resources or attributes usually give a person or entity power to impose penalties on those who fail to

Colin Powell

yield to their demands. Fear of the imposition of those penalties is what most often keeps weaker individuals or nations from rebelling against those holding power over them.

Power, in mathematics, the total of a number multiplied by itself a given number of times. It was developed as a shortcut to having to write the same number multiplied by itself many times, for example, 5 to the fourth power means that the number 5 is multiplied by 5 four times. It is written as a cardinal number with a superior number to the upper right of it ($5^4=625$). In the example, 5 is called the base and 4 is the exponent.
See also: Mathematics.

Powers, Hiram (1805-1873), U.S. sculptor. He worked in Florence, Italy, from 1837. His work includes the neoclassical *Greek Slave* (1843) and busts of eminent Americans, including Andrew Jackson, Thomas Jefferson, and Benjamin Franklin.

Poznan (pop. 590,000), city in Poland. Located on the Warta River in the west-central part of the country, it was founded in the 9th century A.D. It became part of Poland in 1919 when the national boundaries were realigned following World War I. In 1956 labor riots against communist government policies there led to major reforms for the Polish people. Today, Poznan is an important industrial and educational center.

PR *See:* Public relations.

Pradmoedya Ananta Toer (1925-   ), Indonesian writer, son of a teacher, who from 1945 onwards took part in the struggle against the Dutch and started to publish in the 1950s. As a critical observer of the developments in his country he was imprisoned from 1965 until 1979 for being a communist sympathizer. Since 1979 he has been living in Djakarta with limited freedom of movement. Internationally he became known for the four-volume *Karya Buru* (Buru Quartet) which he conceived during his imprisonment. It deals with the metamorphosis of a Javan boy into a self-confident Indonesian (*This Earth of Mankind*, 1981; *Child of all Nations*, 1983; *Footsteps*, 1986; and *Glass House*, 1988). In Indonesia these books are banned. Other titles include: *The Girl from the Coast* (1991), *The Mute's Soliloquy: A Memoir* (1999), *It's Not An All Night Fair* (2001), and *The Girl From the Coast* (2002).

Prado *See:* Madrid.

Praetor, in ancient Rome (from 366 B.C.), a magistrate elected annually to administer justice, 2nd in rank to the consul. By 197 B.C. there were six praetors; four were responsible for provincial administration.

Praetorian Guard, elite household troops of the Roman emperors, consisting of 9 (later 10) cohorts of 1,000 foot soldiers with higher rank and pay than ordinary troops. Instituted by Augustus in 2 B.C., they assumed enough power to overthrow emperors. Constantine disbanded them in 312.

Pragmatic sanction, edict by a ruler pronouncing on an important matter of state, such as the succession. The most famous was issued by the Holy Roman Emperor Charles VI in 1713 (published 1718), declaring that his eldest daughter, Maria Theresa, would inherit the Austrian throne in the absence of a male heir. This resulted in the War of the Austrian Succession (1740-1748).

Pragmatism, philosophical method whose criterion of truth is relative to events and not, as in traditional philosophy, absolute and independent of human experience. A theory is pragmatically true if it 'works'-if it has an intended or predicted effect. All human undertakings are viewed as attempts to solve problems in the world of action; if theories are not trial solutions capable of being tested, they are pointless. The philosophy of pragmatism was developed in reaction to late 19th-century idealism, mainly by the U.S. philosophers C.S. Peirce, W. James, and John Dewey.
See also: Dewey, John; James, William; Peirce, Charles Sanders.

This old Jewish graveyard, the oldest in Europe, evokes the time when Prague still had a large Jewish community.

Prague, or Praha (pop. 1,205,000), capital and largest city of the Czech Republic, on the Vlatava River. One of Europe's great historic cities, it became prominent under Emperor Charles IV, who founded the university in central Europe (1348). The Hapsburgs ruled Prague for nearly 300 years, beginning in 1526, until Czechoslovakia's independence after World War I. Prague was invaded by the Nazis in 1939 and by Warsaw Pact countries in 1968. The city has great cultural, commercial, and industrial importance and is the center of the country's manufacturing industries.
See also: Czech Republic.

Prairie, rolling grassland that once covered much of interior North America. There are three types of prairie: tall-grass, midgrass (or mixed-grass), and shortgrass, which is found in the driest areas. Typical prairie animals are the coyotes, badgers, prairie dogs, and jackrabbits and the now largely vanished bison and wolf.

Prairie chicken, name for two species of grouse (genus *Tympanuchus*) that were once common in the eastern half of North America. Plowing of the prairies and cutting down of the woodlands have destroyed their homes. The males have airsacs on their throats for making booming calls. The airsacs are orange in the greater prairie chicken and violet in the lesser prairie chicken. The heath hen, which was a race of the greater prairie chicken, has been extinct since 1932.

Prairie dog, ground squirrel of the genus *Cynomys*. Social animals of the open plains of North America, they live in large colonies in connected burrows. They are short-tailed, marmot-like creatures, active by day, feeding, grooming, or sunbathing near their burrows. They frequently raise themselves on their hindlegs to watch for danger. A sharp

whistle, given as warning, sends the colony dashing into the burrows.

Prairie Provinces, popular name for the Canadian provinces of Manitoba, Saskatchewan, and Alberta.

Prairie wolf *See:* Coyote.

Prambanan, village in Mid-Java, renowned for its nearby complex of Hindu temples, built in the 9th and 10th century. The Lara Jonggrang, also called the Tjandi Prambanan (Temple of Prambanan), is the largest temple dedicated to Shiva in Indonesia. There are also temples dedicated to Vishnu and Brahma. They contain reliefs that represent the Hindu epic poem Ramayana.

Praseodymium, chemical element, symbol Pr; for physical constants see Periodic Table. Praseodymium was discovered by C.A. von Welsbach in 1885 after he separated didymia into earths (oxides) called praseodymia and neodymia. The element occurs in the minerals monazite and bastnasite, the two principal sources of the rare-earth elements. It is prepared by reducing the anhydrous chloride with calcium. Praseodymium is a silvery, soft, reactive metal, belonging to the series of elements known as the rare-earth metals. Ion-exchange and solvent extraction techniques have led to much easier isolation of the so-called rare-earth elements. Praseodymium and its compounds are used in carbon lighting applications, special glasses and enamels, and refractory materials.

Prawn *See:* Shrimp.

Praxiteles (active c.370-330 B.C.), greatest Greek sculptor of his time. Of his major works, which introduced a new delicacy, grace, and sinuosity of line, only the marble statue *Hermes with the Infant Dionysus* sur-

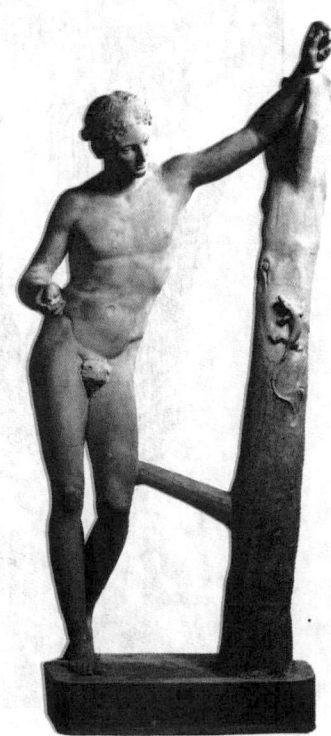

The Apollo Sauroktonos (Apollo killing a lizard) is a Roman marble copy of a statue by the fourth-century sculptor Praxiteles. Many Greek statues are only known thanks to their Roman copies.

P

P

vives. There are Roman copies of his *Aphrodite of Cnidus* and *Apollo Sauroctonus.*

Prayer book, collection of commonly used prayers in Judeo-Christian religious services. They contain statements of doctrine, ordinances, and explanations of the sacraments, in addition to prayers. The Church of England developed its *Book of Common Prayer* in 1549 and other Christian faiths have devised similar concepts. Prayer books are also widely used in Jewish temple (synagogue) services and ceremonies.

Pré, Jacqueline du (1945-1987), British cellist. Jacqueline du Pré was a child prodigy, she started to play the cello at the age of 4 and began her studies at the London Violoncello School at the age of 6. She studied with William Pleeth, Tortelier and Rostropovich. Du Pré made a glorious debut at age 16 in London (Wigmore Hall); she played on a Stradivarius cello made in 1672 - an anonymous gift. Even before she was twenty she was considered a leading performer of the main cello concertos. In 1965 she went on a tour of the U.S. with the BBC Symphony Orchestra. In 1967 she married Daniel Barenboim, with whom she gave recitals. After the first signs of multiple sclerosis, at age 28, she had to end her career. She did keep teaching until her death.

Precambrian, whole of geological time

from the formation of the planet Earth to the start of the Phanerozoic (the eon characterized by the appearance of abundant fossils in rock strata), thus lasting from about 4.55 billion to 570 million years ago. It is essentially equivalent to the Cryptozoic eon.

Precipitation, in meteorology, all water particles that fall from clouds to the ground, including rain and drizzle, snow, sleet, and hail. Precipitation is important in the hydrologic cycle (the circulation of water between the surface of the earth and the atmosphere).

Pre-Columbian art, art of what is now Latin America prior to Columbus' discovery of the Americas (1492). The two main cultural areas were the central Andes (southern Colombia, Ecuador, Peru, Bolivia, northwestern Argentina and northern Chile) and Meso-America (Mexico and Central America). In both areas artistic development took place after 3000 B.C. Monochrome-decorated pottery, female figurines, and elaborately designed textiles have been discovered in Ecuador and Peru dating from 3000-2500 B.C. The great Andean classical period noted for textiles, ceramics, gold and silver work, jewelry, and stone masonry took place in 1000 B.C.-A.D. 800, prior to the Inca kingdom. The great city buildings at Cuzco, Machu Picchu, and Tiahuanaco are striking achievements. The Meso-Americans excelled in the graphic and plastic arts. From about

A golden pre-Colombian breastplate from Campohermosa in Colombia, in the 'Calina' style. A vast collection of artifacts produced in this style, can be seen in the Museo de Oro (oro = gold) in Bogota.

A.D. 1000 the illuminated codex writings of the Mayas, Mixtecs, and Aztecs recorded mythological stories. Their temples, as at Chichén Itzá, are decorated with elaborately carved stone sculptures and reliefs, with wall frescoes inside. The Olmecs made small jade carvings and colossal stone heads. In Colombia the Chibcha Indians were skilled in ceramics, textiles, and jewelry.

Predestination, in theology, doctrine that through God's decree the souls of certain persons (the elect) are destined to be saved. Premised on God's omniscience and omnipotence and buttressed by the doctrines of God's providence and grace, predestination was taught especially by St. Paul and was elaborated by St. Augustine in opposition to Pelagianism (which denied Original Sin and asserted that people are free to do good or evil). Calvinism taught additionally the predestination of the nonelect to damnation, denying individual free will and regarding saving grace as irresistible and wholly gratuitous. Jansenism was a similar Roman Catholic movement. Islam likewise teaches absolute predestination.
See also: Religion; Theology.

Pregnancy, time between conception and birth. In the human female this takes about 39 weeks, or 9 months. The first symptom of pregnancy is usually a missed menstrual period (though this in itself is not proof) followed perhaps by 'morning sickness,' which can continue for some weeks. Tenderness of the breasts and darkening of the nipples usually occur, and frequent urination is common.
As the fetus develops, swelling of the abdomen can first of all be felt and then seen. Inside the womb the fetus develops rapidly, and is well formed by 3 1/2 months. After the 28th week, the child is capable of surviving outside the womb, but infant mortality is higher in premature babies than in those carried to full term.
See also: Reproduction.

Prehistoric animal, animal that became extinct before human beings began to produce written records. Our knowledge of these animals is therefore derived almost completely from fossils. Although scientists believe life on earth began over 3 billion years ago, few

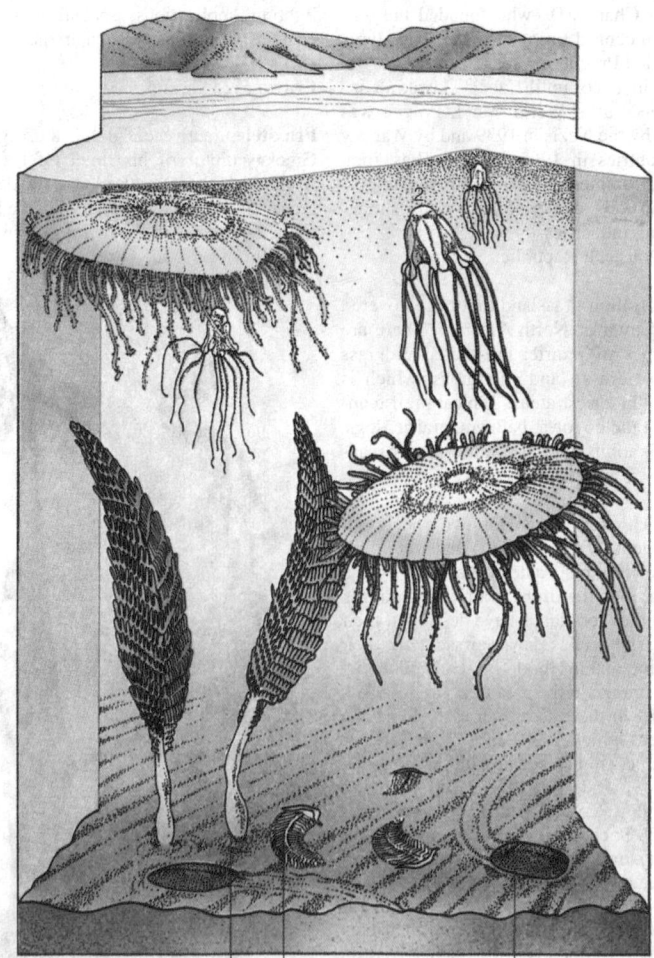

The Precambrian fossils, found at Ediacara in South Australia, indicate a shallow water, sandy marine environment, populated by soft-bodied animals, like worms, jellyfish and sea-pens.
1 *Eoporpita*: drifting jellyfish with chondrophore-type float, similar to the modern Porpita.
2 *Kimberella*: actively swimming jellyfish, similar to the modern sea-wasp.
3 *Arborea*: a sea-pen, sessile organism.
4 *Spriggina*: annelid worm with a well-defined head and a segmented body.
5 *Dickinsonia*: a disk-shaped animal of uncertain affinities, probably an annelid, but sometimes classed as a jellyfish.

fossils have been found that are more than 600 million years old. The earliest are all invertebrates, or animals without skeletal backbones. These include ammonites, snails, clams, worms, and animals resembling jellyfish. The most common prehistoric invertebrate seems to have been the trilobite-a kind of flat shellfish with jointed legs. The first fishes appeared about 480 million years ago. They had no jaws and were covered with heavy, bony armor. Fishes as we know them did not appear until about 130 million years later. Some of these had fleshy fins that probably evolved into legs. The first amphibians appeared about 400 million years ago.

An extensive fossil record indicates that the first land vertebrates-the reptiles-evolved about 290 million years ago. They were bigger and more powerful than the amphibians, and were able to hatch their eggs on land. Reptiles dominated the earth for about 100 million years. Dinosaurs are perhaps the best known of the prehistoric animals. Although some grew to enormous size and were very powerful, they all became extinct, although the reason why remains a subject of controversy. Among the dinosaurs was the carnivorous Tyrannosaurus rex, the 85-ton Brachiosaurus, the 87-foot-long Diplodocus, the horned Triceratops, and the armored vegetarian Stegosaurus. Flying reptiles began to appear during the Jurassic period. One of these-the Archaeopteryx-is believed to be the earliest ancestor of modern birds. Placental mammals, or animals who carry their young within their bodies, have been on earth for about 65 million years. Later, when mammals came to dominate the land, larger variants of modern-day mammals existed. Megatherium was a 20-foot-long mammoth that resembled a large, hairy elephant. Some of these prehistoric mammoths have been found deep-frozen in the icy soil of Siberia.

Prehistoric people, general term for a variety of species of human ancestors. Humans and apes, who share common ancestors, began to diverge in their evolutionary development about 14 million years ago. The first certain ancestor of modern humans is *Australopithecus afarensis*, discovered in 1978, a species that flourished in Ethiopia and Tanzania 3.8-2.5 million years ago. Adult individuals walked upright and had a brain size of about 400 cc. They inhabited grasslands and ate a wide variety of food, including some meat. There were other species within the genus *Australopithecus*, but they are believed to have left no descendants. *Homo habilus*, the earliest true human being, dates back about 2 million years. They used primitive tools, hunted in groups, and had a brain capacity of 500 to 750 cc. *Homo erectus*, whose earliest remains date back about 1.5 million years, had a brain size of 800 cc, which increased to 1,300 cc over the next million years. *Homo erectus* lived originally in Africa and used fire and the ax. This species evolved into an early form of *Homo sapiens* some 400,000 years ago. These ancestors of ours cooked meat, wore clothes, made wooden tools, and built huts. It is unknown whether the Neanderthal, who flourished about 75,000 to 35,000 years

ago, was within the human line of descent or represented a competitor exterminated by the expansion of modern humans. There is much evidence that *Homo sapiens sapiens*,modern humans, first appeared about 40,000 years ago. Cro-Magnon, an example of this modern species, used a variety of tools, domesticated animals and plants, and created cave paintings.

Prejudice, opinions and attitudes formed by individuals or groups about other individuals or groups, usually without ample sustaining evidence. Most forms of prejudice are unfavorable or even hostile, based on fears or preconceived notions against a religious, ethnic, or national group. Extreme forms have resulted in persecution or acts of violence by one group of people against another. Prejudice can be overcome or eliminated through openmindedness, understanding, education, and interaction with groups or individuals targeted for discrimination.

Premadasa, Ranasinghe (1924-1993), Sri Lankan politician. Since 1960 Premadasa was in the parliament for the United National Party (UNP). In 1978 he became prime minister, and president at the beginning of 1989. Having grown up in the slums himself, he always spoke up for the poor: he launched public housing programs, granted loans and donations, and set up textile factories in the countryside to stimulate employment. He was, however, unable to end the civil war, in which the separatist Tamil Tigers resisted the central government. He did convince the Indian government to withdraw its intervention troops, which had been in Sri Lanka since 1987. He was killed by a Tamil Tiger.

Premature birth, birth of a baby before the 40th week of pregnancy. A birth before the 28th week of pregnancy, when the fetus is not viable, is a miscarriage.
See also: Birth.

Prem Tinsulanonda (1920-), Thai military and statesman. Prem was successively deputy minister of home affairs (1977), commander-in-chief of the army (1978) and minister of defense (1979). In 1980 he succeeded prime minister Kriangsak Chomanan. As a military man known for his integrity and ties with the royal family, Prem turned out to be the perfect man to negotiate between army and civilian politicians. After the parliamentary elections of 1983 and 1986 he became prime minister again. His governments achieved great economic successes. In 1988 he was succeeded by Chatichai Choonhavan.

Presbyterianism, form of Christian church government based on bodies of clergy and lay presbyters. Midway between episcopacy and congregationalism, it was espoused at the time of the Reformation by the reformed churches, which viewed it as a rediscovery of the apostolic practice of church government. There is a hierarchy of church courts. The lowest is the kirk-session, composed of the minister and elders elected by the local congregation. This is followed by the presbytery, including representative ministers

and elders from a given area, the synod, composed of members chosen from several presbyteries, and the general assembly, the supreme body, consisting of ministers and elders from all the presbyteries. (Various names are used for these courts.) Presbyterian doctrine is biblical Calvinism.

Prescott, William Hickling (1796-1859), U.S. historian. Despite the handicap of near blindness, he became an authority on Spain and the Spanish conquest of America. His *History of the Reign of Ferdinand and Isabella the Catholic* (1837), *History of the Conquest of Mexico* (1843), and *History of the Conquest of Peru* (1847) became classics, admired for their narrative skill as well as their historical rigor.

Presidential Medal of Freedom *See:* Decorations, medals, and orders.

President of the United States, elected official, head of the executive branch of the U.S. government. The office of president derives its authority from the U.S. Constitution.

The president's basic roles and duties include being the country's chief executive in charge of enforcing federal law, commander in chief of the armed forces responsible for the country's defense, the formulator of foreign policy, lawmaker, head of a political party, a popularly elected leader, and head of state.

In most cases, presidents have been nominated by one of the major political parties and have won the presidency in contested elections. A person can also become president by succeeding to the presidency from the vice presidency. And, in the event no candidate in an election receives a majority of electoral votes, the president is elected by a vote of the House of Representatives. To be eligible for president, one must be a natural-born citizen, at least 35 years of age, and living in the United States 14 years. In the event the office is vacant between elections, succession to the presidency is to the vice president, followed by the Speaker of the House. Presidents serve for a term of 4 years and, since the 22nd Amendment in 1961, no one can serve more than two terms. Presidents may also be removed from office. The process requires first that a president be impeached, that is, charged with some offense or offenses. The president is then tried by the Senate, the chief justice of the Supreme Court presides, and the outcome is determined by vote. A two-thirds majority is required for conviction.

Presley, Elvis (1935-1977), U.S. singer, first major rock star, and present-day cult hero. From 1956 to the mid-1960s, Presley's versions of rhythm-and-blues songs ('Hound Dog') and ballads ('Love Me Tender') were instant hits, as were his 33 films. His Memphis, Tenn., home, Graceland, became a shrine for his many fans.

Pre-Socratic philosophy, general term applied to the thought of the early Greek philosophers (c.600-400 B.C.) who lived before Socrates. Their writings survive mostly in obscure fragments, but their fame and im-

Elvis Presley, an American recording artist and film actor, is seen as one of the figures most responsible for the emergence of rock 'n' roll music during the 1950s.

P

portance lie in their being the first to attempt rational explanations of the universe. Some of the major pre-Socratics were Anaximander, Anaxagoras, Heraclitus, Parmenides, and Pythagoras.
See also: Philosophy.

Press *See:* Journalism; Newspaper; Printing.

Pressburg *See:* Bratislava.

Pressure, force acting on a surface per unit of area. All liquids and gasses exert pressure on any body immersed in them and on the walls of their containers, if any. According to the kinetic theory of matter, the pressure in a closed container of gas arises from the bombardment of the container walls by gas molecules: it is proportional to the temperature and inversely proportional to the volume of the gas.
See also: Physics.

Prester John, legendary Christian priest-king. A purported letter from 'Presbyter John,' probably of Western authorship, reached the papal court in 1165. It described a great Christian utopia in the 'three Indies,' identified in later legend as Ethiopia.

Pretoria (pop. 1,200,000), administrative capital of South Africa. It is also the capital of the province Pretoria-Witwatersrand-Vereeniging. Founded by the Boers in 1855, the city was named for Andries Pretorius, who defeated the Zulus in 1838. It became the administrative capital of the Union of South Africa when it was formed in 1910 and is a major manufacturing and cultural center.
See also: South Africa.

Pretorius, Andries Wilhelmus Jacobus (1799-1853), commandant of the Boers and Great Trek leader. His defeat of the Zulus at Blood River (1838) led to the founding of the Republic of Natal. He led the 1848 trek into the Transvaal.

Pretzel, popular snack biscuit. Pretzels are made from twisted dough that is usually glazed, salted, and baked until hardened, but some varieties are large and soft. They are believed to have originated in southern Europe where monks gave them to children as a reward for learning their prayers, and the name comes from a Latin word meaning 'small reward.' Its popularity spread to the United States in the 1860s and is a favorite snack food today.

Prévert, Jacques (1900-1977), French writer. His popular poems, sometimes satirical, sometimes melancholy, include *Paroles* (1946). Among his screenplays is that for Marcel Carné's *Les Enfants du Paradis* (1944).

Previn, André (1929-), German-born U.S. musician. Originally an adapter of stage musicals for the screen, he won Academy Awards for his arrangements in the films *Kiss Me Kate* (1953) and *Gigi* (1958). As a jazz pianist he made several successful recordings and is also a classical composer and pianist. Principally a symphony conductor since 1960, he has led seasons of the Houston Symphony, the London Symphony, and the Pittsburgh Symphony, recording widely as well.

Prévost d'Exiles, Antoine François, or Abbé Prévost (1697-1763), French writer, priest, and adventurer. *Manon Lescaut* (1731), a love story, is the masterpiece among his novels. It is the basis of operas by Jules Massenet and Giacomo Puccini.

Pribilof Islands, group of 4 small islands of volcanic origin in the Bering Sea, about 300 mi (483 km) southwest of Alaska. St. Paul and St. George are the largest. Every spring some 80% of the world's fur seals visit the islands to breed. Since 1911 the seal herds have been protected, and the United States, which acquired the islands in 1867, regulates the harvesting of seals.

Price, Leontyne (1927-), U.S. soprano. Her first success was as Bess in Gershwin's *Porgy and Bess* (1952-1954). She made debuts in televised operas (1955), at the San Francisco Opera (1957), and at the New York Metropolitan Opera (1961), winning international fame for her performances in works by Verdi and Puccini. She retired from opera in 1985 but continues as a recitalist.
See also: Opera.

Prickly ash, shrub or tree (*Zanthoxylum americanum*) growing in damp soils. The bark and fruit are used for medicinal purposes in the treatment of rheumatism and such stomach problems as flatulence and poor digestion.

Prickly heat, or heat rash, uncomfortable itching sensation caused by excessive sweating in hot weather.

Prickly pear, any of a genus (*Opuntia*) of branching cactus with flat stems and yellow flowers. It is found in most of the southern United States and grows farther north (into New England) than other cacti. Prickly pears are grown in many places as hedges. Introduced to Australia, they spread so rapidly as to become a pest, but were brought under control by introducing a moth whose caterpillars burrowed into the stems.

Priest, in most religions, a cultic officer who communicates the sacred to the followers; a spiritual leader expert in ritual and generally the offerer of sacraments.

Priestley, J(ohn) B(oynton) (1894-1984), English writer and critic. Besides many plays, he wrote popular novels such as *The Good Companions* (1929) and *Angel Pavement* (1930), and criticism, of which his major work is *Literature and Western Man* (1960).

Priestley, Joseph (1733-1804), British theologian and chemist. Encouraged and supported by Benjamin Franklin, he wrote *The History and Present State of Electricity* (1767). His most important discovery was oxygen (1774; named later by Lavoisier), whose properties he investigated. He later discovered many other gases-ammonia, carbon monoxide, hydrogen sulfide-and found that green plants require sunlight and give off oxygen. Priestley's theological writings and activity led some English Presbyterians into Unitarianism, and he is regarded as a principal architect of the Unitarian church. He was also an opponent of the slave trade and a supporter of the French Revolution.
See also: Oxygen; Unitarianism.

Primary color *See:* Color.

Primary election, an election in which supporters of a political party elect candidates to run in a subsequent general election.

Primate, member of an order of mammals including humans, anthropoid apes, monkeys, tarsiers, pottos, galagos, and lemurs. Compared with most mammal groups, primates are anatomically less specialized; the brain, however, is larger and more developed.

Prime meridian, meridian that indicates zero degree longitude. Meridians are imaginary lines drawn on the earth's surface from the North to the South Pole. The prime

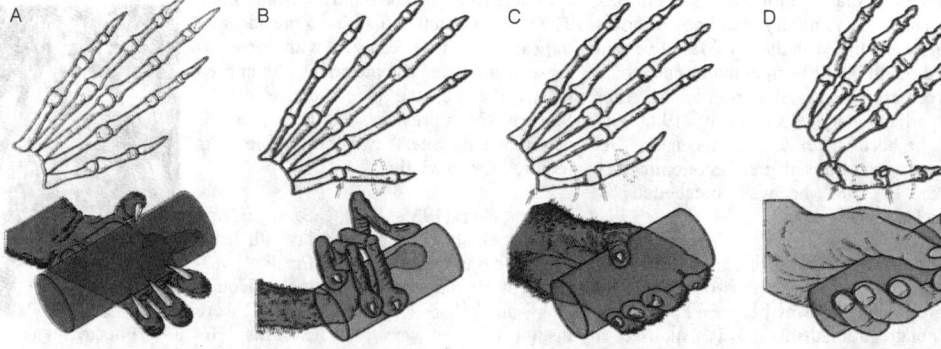

A. Primate hands show an evolutionary trend toward increased opposability of the tumb. The tree shrew has clawed digits and nonopposable thumbs — unable to rotate in their sockets — that provide minimal grasping ability. B. The tarsier, a leaping primate, has disks on the fingertips that help it cling to tree trunks. C. Hands of the macaque, an Old World monkey, can lift objects between the thumb and fingers. D. In humans, whose thumbs are set at a wider angle from the hands, manipulative ability is even more precise.

P

meridian passes through Greenwich, England. All other longitudes are identified in degrees by their distance from the prime meridian.
See also: Longitude.

Prime minister, or premier, head of the government in a parliamentary system. The prime minister appoints and directs his or her own cabinet, which is the source of all major legislation, and also has the power to make and dismiss ministers and to call an election before the full term of a government. The office developed in 18th-century England under Robert Walpole. Most parliamentary democracies distinguish between the head of state (a monarch or president) and the prime minister, who is head of the government.

Primo de Rivera, Miguel (1870-1930), Spanish general and politician. Supported by King Alfonso XIII, he overthrew the government in 1923 and became dictator. Popular discontent, economic failure, and loss of army support forced him to resign in 1930. His son, **José Antonio Primo de Rivera**, founded the Falanga (a Fascist political party) and was executed by Loyalists (republicans) in 1936.

Primogeniture, law by which the eldest son inherits all the lands of a family. It originated in medieval Europe as a reward for the son who gave military service to his king. Never widely established in the United States, primogeniture is still customary in England.

Primrose, perennial plant (*Primula officinalis*) growing in dry meadows, lightly wooded areas, and along forest edges; the flowers, herb, and rootstock are used for medicinal purposes.

Prince Albert (pop. 40,000), city in central Saskatchewan. Situated on the North Saskatchewan River, it was founded in 1866 and named for Queen Victoria's prince consort. It is an important lumbering and manufacturing center and due to its location near the entrance to Prince Albert National Park, it is a major tourist center as well.
See also: Saskatchewan.

Prince consort, husband of a reigning queen. A prince consort is not given the title of king in European countries where the sovereign's daughter may inherit the throne and he has no place in the royal succession under ordinary circumstance. These rules apply in the monarchies of Denmark, the Netherlands, and the United Kingdom.

Prince Edward Island (pop. 137,000), atlantic province of Canada; 2,186 sq mi (5,660 sq km). Capital: Charlottetown. Most densely populated province of Canada. Mixed economy with agriculture, industry and provision of services. After 1970 development of agriculture (potatoes, grain, vegetables, fruit and cattle) and tourism. Fishing. Industry is based on the processing of agricultural products. Timber industry. University.
Before the arrival of the first Europeans (Ja-

cques Cartier in 1534), summer residence of the Micmac Indians. The Conference of Charlottetown (1864) was the beginning of the Canadian Confederation, although the island itself only joined the confederation six years later. There are remains of British and French forts and there is a reconstructed Indian village.
95% of the population speaks English as its only mother tongue and 4% French. One percent of the population is American Indian.
After the Treaty of Paris (1763) the island became British territory and it was renamed St. John's Island instead of Ile-St-Jean; in 1799 it was named after Edward Augustus, son of King George III and commander-in-chief of the British troops in North America.
See also: Canada.

Princeton University, private university in Princeton, N.J. Chartered as the College of New Jersey in 1746, it was renamed in 1896, when it became a university. A leading U.S. educational institution, it includes world-famous graduate schools of public and international affairs, architecture, and scientific research. It has admitted women since 1969.

Príncipe Island *See:* São Tomé and Príncipe.

Printing, reproduction of words and pictures in ink on paper or other suitable media. Despite the advent of information retrieval systems, the storage and dissemination of knowledge are still based primarily on the printed word. Modern printing began with the work of Johann Gutenberg, who invented movable type and type metal in the 15th century. Individual characters could be used several times. The process was little changed for 400 years, until the invention of machines that could cast type as it was required.

Letterpress and lithography are today the two most used printing techniques. Letterpress uses raised type that is a mirror image of the printed impression. The type is inked and the paper pressed to it. Lithography depends on the mutual repulsion of water and oil or grease. In fine art a design is drawn with a grease crayon on the surface of a flat, porous stone, which is then wetted. Water is repelled by the greasy areas; but ink is repelled by the damp and adheres to the greasy areas. Modern mechanized processes use the same principle. Commonest is photo-offset, where the copy to be printed is photographed and the image transferred to a plate such that the part to be printed is oleophilic (oil-loving), the rest hydrophilic (water-loving). Gravure is another major printing technique. The plate is covered with a pattern of recessed cells in which the ink is held, greater depth of cell increasing printing intensity. Little-used for books, it is used extensively in packaging.

Prion, microscopic particle that produces a fatal disease in goats and sheep. Prions are linked to scrapie, a disorder that attacks and destroys the central nervous systems of the grazing animals, but scientists do not fully understand how the disease is caused. It is believed that prions contain an excess of protein that disrupts normal cell activity in infected animals and might possibly affect humans as well.

Prism, in geometry, a solid figure having 2 equal polygonal faces (the bases) lying in parallel planes and several others (the lateral faces) that are parallelograms. Prismatic pieces of transparent materials are much used in optical instruments. In spectroscopes and devices for producing monochromatic lights, prisms are used to produce dispersion

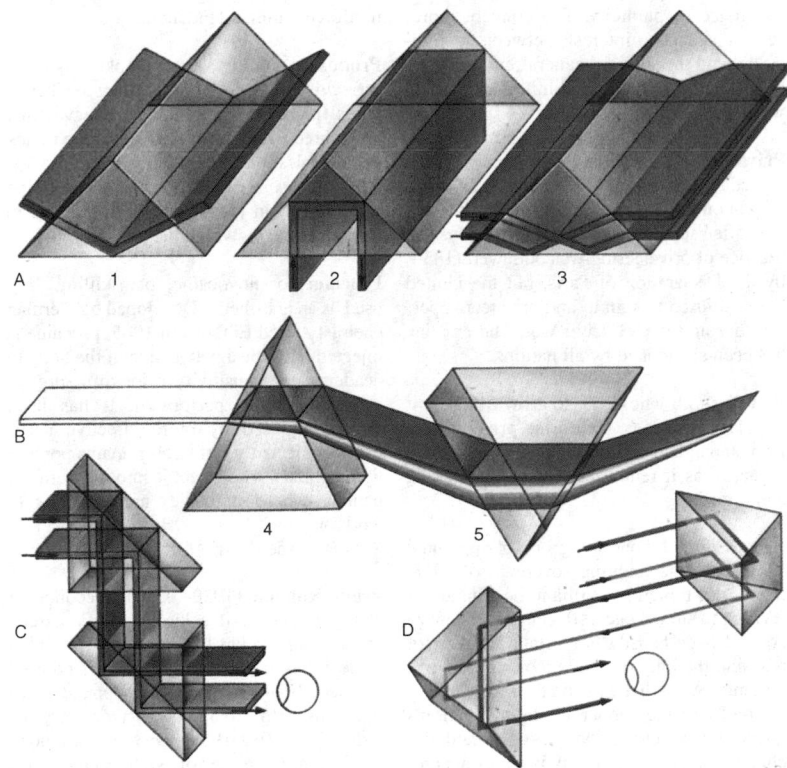

(A) Light entering a right-angle total reflecting prism (1) is bent toward the normal, then reflected internally at an angle equal to the angle of incidence, and then bent away from the normal as it emerges. The direction of light entering perpendicular to the hypotenuse face (2) is reversed; the direction of light travelling parallel to that face (3) is unchanged. (B) White light dispersed into colors by a triangular prism (4) can be recombined by an inverted prism of slightly greater angle (5). Prisms are used in periscopes (C) and in binoculars (D), where they reverse the initially inverted image.

P

effects, just as Newton first used a triangular prism to reveal that sunlight could be split up into a spectrum of colors. In binoculars and single-lens reflex cameras, inflecting prisms (employing total internal reflection) are used in preference to ordinary mirrors. The Nicol prism is used to produce polarized light.

Prison, institution for confining people convicted of breaking a law. By the early 20th century imprisonment had replaced corporal punishment, capital punishment, and exile as the chief method of dealing with criminals. The purpose of prisons is threefold: to punish the wrongdoer; to protect society; and to act as a deterrent. Overpopulation is a serious problem in modern prisons.

Prisoner of war, combatant who has been captured by or has surrendered to an enemy state. The Hague Convention of 1907 and the Geneva Conventions of 1919 and 1949 established rules in international law for the protection of such prisoners, notably that they should not be maltreated nor required to give any information other than their name, rank, and serial number, and that they should be repatriated upon the cessation of hostilities.
See also: Geneva Conventions.

Pritchett, V(ictor) S(awdon) (1900-1997), English novelist, short-story writer, and literary critic. Many of his works are based on his travels in Spain. They include *Marching Spain* (nonfiction, 1928), *The Spanish Temper* (nonfiction, 1954), and *Clare Drummer* (novel, 1929). *A Cab at the Door* (1968), and *Midnight Oil* (1971) are autobiographical.

Privacy, Right of, customary right of a citizen to have a private life free of 'undue' interference or publicity. The concept represents a balance of interests between the individual and the state. In general, privacy may be interfered with only in limited, prescribed ways.

Privateer, armed vessel that was privately owned but commissioned by a government to prey upon enemy ships in wartime. Privateers thus often supplemented a nation's navy. The practice of privateering was outlawed (1856) by the Declaration of Paris, but the United States refused to sign it, and privateers operated during the U.S. Civil War. The practice has been abandoned by all nations.

Privet, shrub whose dense growth makes it popular for hedges. California privet comes from Japan and is suitable for use in colder climates, as it retains its leaves in freezing conditions.

Privy Council, honorary group of appointed advisers to the reigning sovereign of Great Britain. Instituted by William the Conqueror (William I) in the late 11th century, the privy council once had the important function of advising the king on matters of national importance. As parliament and the prime minister replaced the monarchy in the nation's governing structure, the privy council declined in importance. Today it serves a large-

ly ceremonial function, overseeing matters of commerce, scientific research, and the arts.

Probability, branch of mathematics that deals with the likelihood that an event will occur. Most commonly, the number of possible outcomes is counted, and the probability of any particular outcome is expressed as a fraction between 0 and 1. For instance, in rolling 2 dice there are 36 possible outcomes. Only one of these is that a 12 will turn up (a 6 on each die). The chance of rolling a 12 is therefore 1/36. On the other hand, there are 6 possible ways of rolling a 7: 1-6, 6-1, 5-2, 2-5, 3-4, 4-3. The chance of rolling a 7 is therefore 1/6. As more complicated theories and problems arise, more sophisticated techniques arise, such as permutations and combinations. Probability theory has contributed vital understanding in many fields of physics, including statistical mechanics. Its importance in science has risen dramatically in recent decades. Statistics, a related field, is the application of probability theory to data collected from research samples.
See also: Mathematics.

Probate, legal process of proving that a will is valid. Before a will can take effect, it must be shown that it is genuine, that it was the deceased's last will, that he or she signed it voluntarily and was of sound mind. Probate requires all possible heirs of the testator's property to be notified before a special hearing is held in a probate court, where objections can be lodged.
See also: Will.

Probation, alternative to prison, whereby convicted offenders are placed under the supervision of a probation officer, on condition that they maintain good behavior. The aim is to encourage reform, particularly for the young, when a spell in prison might simply reinforce criminal tendencies.

Proboscis monkey, large monkey (*Nasalis larvatus*) native to Borneo. They are herbivores (plant eaters), feeding on leaves that they shred easily with well-developed back teeth. Males may weigh up to 52 lb (24 kg) and females about half that. They stand about 21-30 in (53-76 cm) tall and live in trees near rivers, which they swim easily.

Procaine, or novocaine, pain-killing drug used as an anesthetic. Developed by German chemist Alfred Einhorn in 1905, procaine is injected into a designated area of the body to deaden nerve sensitivity prior to a surgical procedure being performed. It has been largely replaced by more effective nerve blocks in recent years but it remains popular with dentists, who inject it into the gums of patients whose teeth they are preparing to work on.
See also: Anesthesia.

Prodi, Romano (1939-), Italian economist and politician. After his scholarly career, specializing in industrial economy, Prodi became minister of industry in an Andreotti cabinet (1978-1979). He was president of the Instituto per la Riconstruzione Industriale (1982-1989; 1993-1996), a powerful conglomerate of state enterprises.

Initially a Christian Democrat, Prodi was pushed forward as a party leader of the center left L'Ulivo, the Olive tree, in 1995. After this alliance won the elections in April 1996, Prodi was appointed prime minister. He was popular because there were no scandals in his past. In 1999 he was elected chairman of the European Committee.

Profit, amount of money a company or individual engaged in business makes after all costs have been subtracted. Profit is the chief motivation for the establishment of all businesses in a free enterprise economic system and the goal of all employers and individuals seeking monetary gain. Profits can be increased by keeping production costs, including labor, as low as possible and employers are constantly seeking means of generating greater profits than others engaged in competing businesses and industries.

Profit sharing, incentive developed by businesses and employers to give workers a share of the extra money a company makes. It was devised to instill workers with greater company loyalty and motivate them toward higher productivity. Profit sharing provides workers with a source of income above their regular wages and may be disbursed in the form of direct cash payments, shares of company stock, or deferred payments made in lieu of pension plans.

Progeria, or Hutchinson-Gilford syndrome, rare disease that causes premature aging in children and early death. Sir Jonathan Hutchinson researched the disease in 1886 and there is no cure or treatment for it. Symptoms begin appearing by the second year of life; they include hair loss, wrinkled skin, stunted growth, and other signs of aging normally associated with older persons. Half of all progeria deaths occur by age 13 and the oldest known victim lived only to 27.

Progesterone, female sex hormone that causes changes in the womb lining necessary for the implantation of a fertilized egg.
See also: Hormone; Reproduction.

Programmed learning, teaching method whereby matter to be learned is arranged in a coherent sequence of small, clear steps (programmed), enabling the student to instruct, test, and, if necessary, correct him or herself at each step. The learning program is usually embodied in a book or booklet or adapted for use in conjunction with a teaching machine. The linear program, based on the work of psychologist B.F. Skinner, obliges the student to compare his or her own response at each step with the correct response. The intrinsic (or branching) program offers a limited choice of responses at each step. The correct response is immediately reinforced; an incorrect response obliges the student to follow a corrective subprogram leading back to the point at which the error occurred.

Progression, in mathematics, a sequence of numbers (terms) that have a direct relationship to one another. The most common types are arithmetic, which involves addition; geometic, which involves multiplication;

and harmonic, which involves fractions. Each successive term in a progression is added by or multiplied by the same number all the way through the sequence. An arithmetic progression that begins with 2, 4, and 6 will continue with 8, 10, and all successive numbers that are 2 larger than the preceding number. The same principle applies to all other types of progressions.
See also: Mathematics.

Progressive education, reform movement that grew from the idea that schooling should cater to the emotional as well as the intellectual development of the child and that the basis of learning should be the child's natural and individual curiosity, rather than an enforced discipline.
See also: Education.

Prohibition, restriction or prevention of the manufacture and sale of alcoholic drinks. It refers in particular to the period from 1919 to 1933, when (by means of the 18th Amendment to the Constitution) there was a federal prohibition law in the United States. In spite of the intensive economic and group pressures that had brought it about, it soon became apparent that the law was too unpopular and too expensive to enforce. A notorious era of gangsterism followed, with a vast illegal liquor business (the activities involved were known as bootlegging) under the control of men such as Al Capone. Prohibition was repealed (1933) by the 21st Amendment. A few U.S. states maintained local prohibition laws as late as 1966.
See also: Capone, Al.

Projector, machine that passes light through film to show pictures on a screen. Lenses magnify the images on the film, showing them larger than they appear on the film itself. Projectors consist of several types-slide projectors that show still photos, movie projectors that show continuously moving film, and overhead projectors such as those used in planetariums that show images in all directions above the viewers.

Prokhorov, Aleksandr Mikhailovich (1916-), Soviet physicist awarded, with N.G. Basov and C.H. Townes, the 1964 Nobel Prize for physics for work with Basov leading to development of the maser.
See also: Maser.

Prokofiev, Sergei Sergeyevich (1891-1953), Russian composer who created a fierce, dynamic, unemotive style that later became somewhat softer and more eclectic. His works include seven symphonies, the operas *The Love for Three Oranges* (1921) and *War and Peace* (1943); *Peter and the Wolf* (1936), for narrator and orchestra; *Romeo and Juliet* (1936), a ballet; concertos for piano, violin, and cello; film scores; and chamber music.

Proletariat, name given to industrial employees as a social and economic class. In Marxist theory, the proletariat is exploited by and must inevitably overthrow the bourgeois class, made up of employers and property owners.
See also: Marxism.

Prometheus, in Greek mythology, one of the Titans and a brother of Atlas. He was sometimes said to have created humankind out of earth and water and to have stolen fire from the gods for the benefit of mankind. Zeus punished Prometheus by having him bound to a rock, whereupon his liver was devoured by an eagle.
See also: Mythology.

Promethium, chemical element, symbol Pm; for physical constants see Periodic Table. Branner, in 1902, predicted the existence of an element between neodymium and samarium. This element, promethium, was discovered by J.A. Marinsky, Lawrence E. Glendenin, and Charles D. Coryell in 1945 by fission of uranium and neutron bombardment of neodymium with neutrons. This was the first chemical identification by use of ion-exchange chromatography. Promethium is not found in the earth's crust but is obtained from nuclear reactors as a fission byproduct. Promethium-145, the most stable isotope, has a half-life longer than 17.7 years. Promethium, a metallic element, has been prepared by the reduction of the fluoride with lithium metal. It is a member of the rare-earth series of metals. Promethium isotopes are used in thickness gauges, self-luminous compounds, nuclear-powered batteries, portable X-ray sources, and auxiliary power sources.

Pronghorn, resembling an antelope (*Antilocapra americana*) the only horned animal that sheds its horn sheath and the only one with branched horns as distinct from antlers. They live in groups in arid grasslands and semi-desert of western North America, feeding on weeds and browse plants. Conservation efforts have restored numbers from an estimated 30,000 in 1924 to a present 400,000.

Proofreading, reading and correcting of printed matter prior to publication. It is done by skilled proofreaders using universally understood marks and symbols on the copy itself to indicate what corrections need to be made on the final draft. Newspapers, magazines, and printing shops employ proofreaders to check over all copy before it is published, in an effort to eliminate or minimize errors that might appear in print. Book publishing companies also use proofreaders, who mark up authors' original manuscripts as well as typeset copy (galley proofs) before they appear in book form.

Propaganda, selected information, whether true or false, designed to persuade people to adopt a particular belief, attitude, or course of action. During the 20th century all the major political ideologies have employed propaganda and made use of modern media to reach a mass audience. It plays an important role in modern warfare, and during World War II separate offices and ministries were established to promote morale and subvert the enemy. The Nazi Ministry of Propaganda, headed by Joseph Goebbels, was one of the most active. In the business world, professional propagandists-communicators in public relations and advertising-are increasingly in demand.

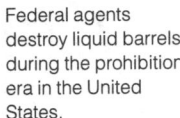

Propane *See:* Butane and propane.

Propeller, mechanical device designed to impart forward motion, usually to a ship or airplane, operating on the screw principle. It generally consists of two or more inclined blades radiating from a hub, and the amount of thrust it produces is proportional to the product of the mass and the fluid it acts on and the rate at which it accelerates the fluid. The inclination, or pitch, of the propeller blades determines the theoretical distance moved forward with each revolution. A variable-pitch propeller can be adjusted while in motion, to maximize its efficiency under different operating conditions; it may also be possible to reverse the propeller's pitch, or to feather it-i.e., minimize its resistance when not rotating. John Fitch developed the first marine screw propeller in 1796; John Ericsson perfected the first bladed propeller in 1837.

Propertius, Sextus (50?-16 B.C.), Roman elegiac poet, whose poems center on his love affair with his mistress Cynthia. Though often obscure, he is vivid and imaginative.

Property, social concept and legal term indicating the ownership of, or the right to enjoy, something of value; it may also be an interest in something owned by another. Under some systems such as feudalism or communism, ownership of some or all kinds of property is vested not in the individual, but in the state or its head. The U.S. Constitution establishes the individual's right to property.

Federal agents destroy liquid barrels during the prohibition era in the United States.

The pronghorn (*A. americana*), a mammal related to deer and antelope, once lived in vast numbers on the North American plains.

P

Common law distinguishes between real property (land and generally nontransportable goods, such as houses and trees) and personal property) (all other kinds). Financial rights, such as copyrights or patent holdings, are personal.

Property tax, money collected by state and local governments from owners of property. It is levied upon land, homes, buildings, and in some cases on farm equipment, based on a fixed percentage of the property's estimated (assessed) valuation. Monies collected from property taxes are usually used to pay for government services such as road repair, schools, and police and fire protection.
See also: Taxation.

Prophet, in the Old Testament of the Bible, a man who by special revelation proclaimed the word of God by oracles and symbolic actions; originally a seer or ecstatic. Often a scourge of the establishment, prophets were religious and social reformers who called for righteousness and faithfulness to God and pronounced judgment on the ungodly. In the early Christian Church prophecy was a recognized charisma, but soon died out except in Montanism, a heretical sect. It was revived among Anabaptists, Quakers, Mormons, and Pentecostals. In Islam Muhammad is the last and greatest prophet. Oracular prophets are found in many religions.
See also: Old Testament.

Prophylaxis, general term for the prevention of diseases. This is most often done through preventative treatments given prior to a person's contracting a disease. Vaccinations are a form of prophylaxis that build up immunities within the human body against certain types of disorders. Pasteurization of milk and milk products is another form of prophylaxis, as is proper sanitation on a community-wide scale.

Proportion, in mathematics, equality of two ratios. The numbers a, b, c, and d are said to be in proportion if $a/b = c/d$. The expression may also be written as $a:b::c:d$. The term *proportion* is useful in describing the relationship between quantities whose ratio is constant-for example, the ratio between the radius and circumference of a circle. If there are two circles with circumferences $c1$, $c2$ and radii $r1$ and $r2$ then $c1 = 2\pi r$, and $c2 = 2\pi r2$. This can be written $c1/r1 = 2\pi = c2/r2$. The figures $c1$, $r1$, $c2$ and $r2$ are in proportion, and we say that the circumference of a circle is proportional to its radius.
See also: Mathematics.

Proportional representation, system of electing members to a legislature in which political parties or groups contesting the election are awarded a number of seats in the legislature more or less proportional to the number of votes they get. For instance, if 3 parties are running for seats in a 300-member legislature, and one party gets half the vote while the others roughly split the remaining half equally, the largest party would be allotted about 150 seats, the 2 others about 75 each. There are various ways of organizing such elections and of calculating the results. The system is generally used in places where there are more than 2 significant-sized parties. Supporters of proportional representation argue that it is the most democratic system, since it most accurately reflects the political desires of the population. Opponents argue that it can give unreasonable power to small groups, which can sometimes gain decisive leverage in a divided multiparty assembly.

Prospecting, process of searching for minerals worth exploiting economically. The simplest technique is direct observation of the local surface features characteristically associated with specific mineral deposits. This is often done by prospectors on the ground, but aerial photography is increasingly employed. Other techniques include examining the seismic waves caused by explosions (which supply information about the structures through which they have passed); testing local magnetic fields to detect magnetic metals or the metallic gangues associated with nonmagnetic minerals; and, especially for metallic sulfides, testing electrical conductivity.

Prost, Alain (1955-), French racing driver, became European cart champion in 1973 and made his debut in the Formula 1 (McLaren) a year after his European title in the Formula 3 (1979). From 1981 onwards Prost won several Grand Prix races every year for Renault. In 1984 he returned to McLaren, with which make he became world champion in 1985, 1986 and 1989. Back with Renault, Prost became world champion for the fourth time in 1993 (Williams-Renault). After he had ended his racing career, he started his own Formula One team, which went bankrupt in 2002.

Prostaglandin, variety of naturally occuring aliphatic acids with various biological activities including increased vascular permeability, smooth muscle contraction, bronchial constriction, and alteration in the pain threshold. Seminal fluid contains lipid-soluble substances that stimulate smooth muscle, and it has been suggested that the active principle should be called prostaglandin. Although prostaglandins are present in highest concentration in seminal fluid, they have been found in numerous other tissues, such as the kidney, iris, pancreas, lung, and brain.

Prostate gland, male reproductive gland that surrounds the urethra at the base of the urinary bladder and that secretes prostatic fluid. This organ is formed of fibrous muscular and glandular tissue. It is described as having the shape of a chestnut and as being an inverted pyramid whose base is applied to the neck of the bladder. The normal gland usually measures about 1 in (2.54 cm) from front to back, 1 1/4 in (3.18 cm) from above downward and nearly 2 in (5 cm) from side to side. The connective tissue around the gland is condensed to form a fibrous capsule. There is a groove between the neck of the bladder and the base of the prostate that contains a venous plexus.
The prostate is traversed from top to bottom by the urethra. The glandulary tissue consists of secretory acini. After middle age, acini may contain concretions of secretion and desquamated cells.
The glands of the median lobe and mucosal glands constitute the glands of the inner zone, in which penile enlargement usually starts. Cancer of the prostate usually starts in the outer zone which consists of the main prostatic gland.
See also: Reproduction.

Prosthetic, mechanical or electrical device inserted into or onto the body to replace or supplement the function of a missing, defective, or diseased organ. Artificial limbs were among the first prosthetics, but metal or plastic joint replacements and bone fixations are now also available. Replacement teeth are also prosthetics. The valves of the heart may be replaced with mechanical devices, and electrical pacemakers can be implanted to stimulate the heart muscle at a set rate.

Prostitution, practice of exchanging sexual favors for material profit, usually money. Prostitution is as old as civilization and has flourished throughout history, especially in urban centers, which generate demand and provide conditions of relative anonymity. Although there is some male prostitution, the term usually refers to the practice as performed by women.

Protactinium, chemical element, symbol Pa; for physical constants see Periodic Table. Discovered in 1917 by 2 teams of scientists working independently; Otto Hahn and Lise Meitner of Germany and Frederick Soddy and John Cranston of Great Britain. It is found in the mineral *pitchblende* in minute quantities. Protactinium is a lustrous, radioactive metal, and a member of the actinide series. The element was initially prepared by decomposing its iodide in a vacuum with an electrically heated filament. The longest lived is an alpha emitter with a half-life of 32,500 years. It is a dangerous and toxic material.

Protagoras (c.490-421 B.C.), Greek Sophist, remembered for the maxim 'Man is the measure of all things.' A respected figure in Athens, where he spent most of life, he taught rhetoric and the proper conduct of life ('virtue'), and was appointed lawmaker to the Athenian colony of Thurii in 444 B.C. Little is known of his teaching, but he is thought to have been a relativist concerning knowledge and a skeptic about the gods, although he upheld conventional morality.
See also: Sophist.

Protective coloration, adaptation of coloration by animals, often providing a means of defense against predators. Except where selection favors bright coloration for breeding or territorial display, most higher animals are colored in such a way that they blend in with their background: by pure coloration, by disruption of outline with bold lines or patches, or by a combination of the two. The most highly developed camouflage is found in ground-nesting birds, or insects. Associated with this coloration must be special behavior patterns enabling the animal to seek out the correct background for its camouflage and to 'freeze' against it. Certain animals can change their body texture and coloration to match different backgrounds: octopuses, chameleons, and some flatfishes. An alternative strategy adopted by some animals, particularly insects, is the use of shock-coloration: when approached by a predator, these insects flick open plain wings to expose bright colors, often in the form of staring 'eyes,' to scare the predator.

Protectorate, country that is nominally independent but surrenders part of its sovereignty, such as control over foreign policy, in return for protection by a stronger state. The degree of control and dependency varies.

Protein, high-molecular-weight compound that yields amino acid through hydrolysis. Although hundreds of different amino acids are possible, only 20 are found in appreciable quantities in proteins, and these are all alpha-amino acids. Proteins are found throughout all living organisms. Muscle, the major structural material in animals, is mainly protein; the 20% of blood that is not water is mainly protein. Enzymes may contain other components, but basically they, too, are protein. Approximately 700 proteins are known; of these, 200-300 have been studied and over 150 obtained in crystalline form. Some are very stable, while others are so delicate that even exposure to air will destroy their capability as enzymes. The best food sources for proteins are meat, fish, eggs, milk, and cheese. These foods provide all the essential aminoacids and are known as complete proteins. Vegetables and nuts do provide proteins but are not complete proteins. The absence of protein in the diet can diminish growth and reduce energy levels.

Protestant ethic, set of values that esteems hard work, thrift, duty, efficiency, and self-discipline. The Protestant ethic follows from the beliefs, identified with Calvinism, that a person's time and talents are gifts from God and that prosperity is a sign of piety and salvation. The concept of a protestant ethic was formalized by the German sociologist Max Weber in his essay, 'The Protestant Ethic and the Spirit of Capitalism' (1904-1905). He attributed the economic success of Protestant groups to Protestant values.
See also: Weber, Max.

Protestantism, principles of the Reformation. The name derives from the *Protestatio* of the minority reforming delegates at the Diet of Speyer (1529). Protestantism is characterized by subordinating tradition to the Bible as the basis for doctrine and practice, and stresses justification by faith, biblical preaching, and a high personal morality. In reaction to Roman Catholicism it rejects papal claims, the mass, and the worship of saints. The main original branches were Lutheranism, Calvinism, Anglicanism, and Zwinglianism, with small Anabaptist sects. Exercise of the right of privacy judgment in interpreting Scripture led to fragmentation, a trend reversed in recent decades by the Ecumenical Movement. Later Protestant churches include the Congregational

churches, Baptists, Quakers, Methodists, the Moravian Church, and the Pentecostal churches.
See also: Reformation.

Protista, members of a proposed group of organisms having characteristics of both the plant and the animal kingdoms. The classification usually includes single-celled organisms that have a distinct nucleus and organelles (structures that perform specific functions): protozoans, diatoms, bacteria, and some algae. Some scientists consider multicelled fungi and seaweeds as protista. The classification was proposed by the German zoologist Ernst H. Haeckel (1866).

Proton, elementary particle having a positive charge equivalent to the negative charge of the electron but possessing a mass approximately 1,837 times as great. A member of the baryon class of elementary particles, the proton was discovered in 1919 by Ernest Rutherford. The proton is, in effect, the nucleus of the hydrogen atom. Every atomic nucleus contains at least one proton.
See also: Atom.

Protoplasm, basic substance of which all living things are made up. Mostly water, protoplasm also contains proteins, fats, and inorganic salts. It is present in all cells, usually differentiated into the nucleus and the cytoplasm. The latter is generally a transparent viscous fluid containing a number of specialized structures; it is the medium in which the main chemical reactions of the cell take place. The nucleus contains the cell's genetic material.

Protozoan, single-celled organism belonging to the phylum Protozoa. Protozoans fall into 4 classes: flagellates, sarcodines, sporozoans, and ciliates. Most are aquatic, living in fresh or salt water. Some live in plants or animals and cause serious diseases. A few protozoans contain chlorophyll and make their own food, but the majority must ingest their food. They reproduce in many ways, including undergoing fission (cell division) or budding. Protozoans tend to be solitary; a few cluster in colonies.

Protractor, semicircular device used to measure or to construct angles. The curve is usually marked in degrees, (0-180), or sometimes in mils (0-3,200). A plane protractor is used to measure angles within a plane. A spherical protractor is used in navigation and astronomy to measure spherical angles.
See also: Angle.

Proudhon, Pierre Joseph (1809-1865), French social thinker. He first gained notoriety with his book *What is Property?* (1840). He advocated a society in which property would be distributed among free individuals who cooperated spontaneously outside a framework of state authority-a philosophy he called *mutualism*. In 1847 he clashed with Karl Marx, thus starting a struggle between libertarian and authoritarian views on socialism which continued long after his death.

Proust, Joseph Louis (1754-1826), French chemist who established the law of definite proportions, or Proust's law.
See also: Chemistry.

Proust, Marcel (1871-1922), French novelist whose seven-part work *Remembrance of Things Past* is one of the greatest novels of the 20th century. It was written during the period 1907-1919, after Proust, who suffered continually from asthma, had retired from Parisian high society and become virtually a recluse. A semiautobiographical exploration of time, memory, and consciousness, with an underlying theme of the transcendency of art over the futility of one's best efforts, it broke new ground in the art of the novel and was enormously influential.

Provençal, or langue d'oc, Romance language developed from the Latin spoken in southern France, principally Provence. During the Middle Ages, Provençal produced a notable literature that reached its highest point with the courtly love poetry of the troubadours.

Provence, region and former province of France, embracing the lower Rhone River (including the Camargue) and the French

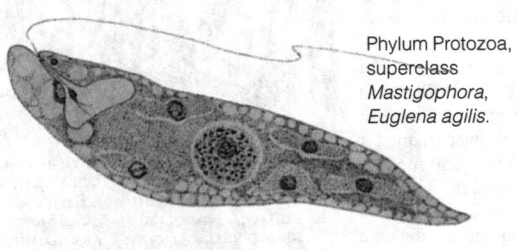

Phylum Protozoa, superclass *Mastigophora*, *Euglena agilis*.

Mastigophorans move by means of flagella. Euglena is a plant-like Phytomastigopho containing photosynthetic pigment.

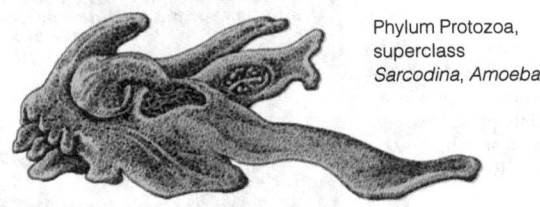

Phylum Protozoa, superclass *Sarcodina*, *Amoeba*

proteus. Sarcodine protozoans produce outflowing extensions of their cell, used to capture food and, in types like the amoeba, for locomotion.

A village in the Provence Alps. Due to the relief, farming is usually still done in the traditional manner on laboriously constructed terraces.

Riviera. The chief cities are Nice, Marseilles, Toulon, Avignon, Arles, and Aix-en-Provence (the historic capital). It is a sunny and picturesque region, famous for historical associations and its fruit, vineyards, and olives. It was the first transalpine Roman province (hence the name), and later it became an independent kingdom (879-933), finally passing to the French kings in 1486.
See also: France.

Proverbs, Book of, book of the Bible's Old Testament; an example of the 'wisdom literature' popular in post-exilic Judaism. Its eight sections, attributed in their headings to various authors, including Solomon, consist of numerous pithy proverbs and mostly unconnected moral maxims, probably dating between the 9th and 2nd centuries B.C.
See also: Old Testament.

Providence (pop. 161,000), capital of Rhode Island, on the Providence River at the head of Narragansett Bay. The second-largest city in New England (after Boston), Providence is an important industrial, commercial, and education center. Its major industries include jewelry, silverware, textiles, machinery, and metal products.
Providence is among the oldest cities in the United States, founded by Roger Williams in 1636 after his expulsion from the Plymouth Colony. Williams and his followers named it for 'God's merciful providence' and made it a haven for religious dissenters. The city maintains a number of historic old homes and public buildings, many of which date from colonial times.
See also: Rhode Island.

Province, region governed or administered by a country, empire, or diocese. Some nations are formed by a union of provinces, while others are divided into provinces, e.g., Canada. To the Romans, a province was a conquered land ruled from Rome as a self-contained unit.

Provincetown *See:* Cape Cod; Mayflower.

Prud'hon, Pierre Paul (1758-1823), French painter. His best-known works are the portrait of the Empress Josephine (1805) and *Crime Pursued by Vengeance and Justice* (1808). His painting, influenced by Correggio, is soft and sensual in character.

Prune, dried plum. Certain plum varieties, especially French prune plums, are suited for prune production. The ripe fruit is dried in a dehydrator for 14-24 hours, dipped in a lye solution, and allowed to cure for at least 2 weeks.

Pruning, the cutting away of a plant's branches, shoots, buds, or roots. Pruning is done to shape a plant, increase air and light circulation among the branches, increase fruit and flower quality, remove dead, diseased, injured, or hazardous parts, retard water loss after transplanting, or renew growth. A gardener prunes certain plants according to the season and makes the cut at a prescribed place and angle.

Prussia, state in north central Europe that became the foundation of the modern state of Germany. At the height of its strength it stretched from west of the Rhine to Poland and Russia. The Baltic territory later known as East Prussia was Germanized by the Teutonic Knights in the 1200s and later became the duchy of Prussia. In 1618 it came under the rule of the Electors of nearby Brandenburg, the Hohenzollerns; and Frederick I declared himself king of Prussia in 1701. Under his successors, particularly Frederick the Great, the Prussian state expanded to become the strongest military power in northern Europe. In 1862 Bismarck became premier, and as a result of a planned series of wars and skillful diplomacy conducted under his direction, King William I of Prussia was declared Emperor of Germany in 1871. Prussia was the largest and most powerful of the states of the united Germany until 1934, when by a decree of Hitler the separate German states ceased to exist as political entities. After World War II former Prussian territory was divided among East Germany, Poland, and the USSR.
See also: Germany.

Prussian blue, category of deep-blue pigments containing ferrocyanide. It is used to color paint, enamel, lacquer, printing ink, and carbon paper. Some Prussian blue is prepared from sodium ferrocyanide that has been oxidized in the presence of sodium chlorate, sodium chromate, or other reagent. Others are made by oxidizing a mixture of ferrous sulfate and potassium ferrocyanide. Prussian blue was first made in 1704.

Prussic acid (HCN), also called hydrocyanic acid, a colorless, highly toxic, aqueous solution of hydrogen cyanide. The acid is flammable and evaporates readily. It is used in the manufacture of plastics, fumigants, and dyes. Prussic acid was first derived from the pigment Prussian blue.

Przewalski's horse, or Eastern wild horse, last remaining race of true wild horses. Of the three subspecies of *Equus przewalskii,* two-the steppe tarpan and forest tarpan-were exterminated by the middle of the 19th century. Only Przewalski's horse remained, undiscovered until 1881. Ancestors of domestic horses, they are about the size of a pony, yellow or red-brown, and with an erect mane. It is probable that they, too, are now extinct in the wild. Today it is an endangered species with less than 200 animals living in zoos and fewer than 50 living in the wild.

Psalms, Book of, collection of 150 songs in the Old Testament, used as the hymn book of Judaism since the return from exile and prominent in Christian liturgy. Metrical psalms are sung in the Reformed churches. Many psalms are traditionally ascribed to David; modern scholars date them between the 10th and 2nd centuries B.C. Their fine poetry embodies a rich variety of religious experience, both national and individual.
See also: Old Testament.

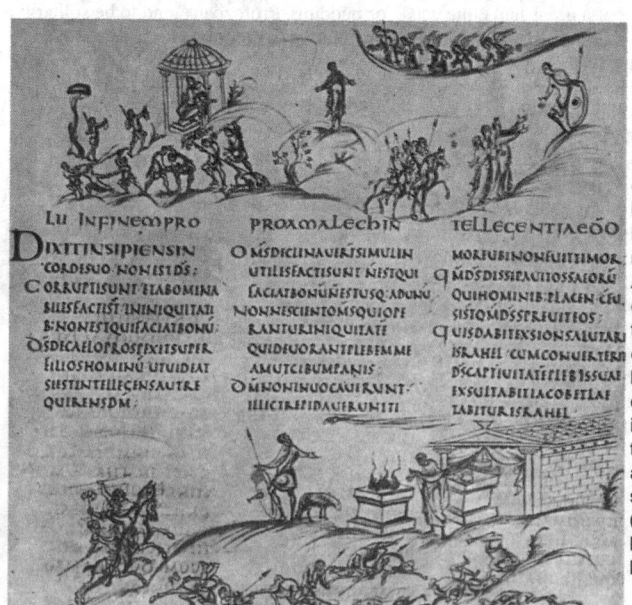

Psalm 52 (according to modern numeration, number 53) in the *Utrecht Psalter* (9th century). The heading is written in red ink, the remainder in black. A captivating line drawing illustrates the text: 'God looks down from the heavens on the children of man, to investigate whether there is a wise one among them, seeking God' (Verse 3, Rijksuniversiteit Library, Utrecht).

Psi particle, subatomic particle consisting of a charmed quark and an anticharmed quark bonded by their opposite electric charges and a strong nuclear force, or strong interaction. The psi particle itself has no electric charge. The psi particle, also called a J particle, was discovered in 1974 by two separate teams of U.S. physicists.
See also: Quark.

Psittacosis, infectious atypical form of pneumonia caused by *Chlamydia psittaci* and transmitted by certain birds. Human infection usually occurs by inhaling dust from feathers or excreta of infected birds; it may also be transmitted to humans by a bite from an infected bird or, rarely, by cough droplets of infected bird or, rarely, by cough droplets of infected persons. The onset may be insidious or abrupt, with fever, chills, general malaise, and anorexia. The temperature gradually rises and a cough develops, initially dry but at times becoming mucopurulent. During the second week pneumonia and frank consolidation may occur with secondary purulent lung infection. Convalescence is gradual and may be prolonged, especially in severe cases. Tetracycline is an effective treatment.
See also: Pneumonia.

Psoriasis, skin condition characterized by patches of red, thickened, and scaling skin. It often affects the elbows, knees, and scalp but may be found anywhere. Several forms are recognized, and the manifestations may vary over time in each individual. Coal tar preparations are valuable in treatment, but steroid creams and cytotoxic chemotherapy may be needed. There is also an associated arthritis.

Psychedelics *See:* Hallucinogenic drug.

Psychiatry, field of medicine concerned with the study and treatment of mental disorders, including neurosis and psychosis. Its major branches are psychotherapy, the application of psychological techniques to the treatment of mental illness where a physiological origin is either unknown or does not exist; and medical therapy, where attack is made either on the organic source of the disease or on its physical or behavioral symptoms.
See also: Mental illness.

Psychical research, field of study concerned with the evaluation of phenomena having to do with so-called extrasensory perception. So far, no scientific evidence for such phenomena has been found.
See also: Extrasensory perception; Parapsychology.

Psychoanalysis, system of psychology having as its base the theories of Sigmund Freud; also the psychotherapeutic technique based on that system. The distinct forms of psychoanalysis developed by Carl Jung and Alfred Adler are more correctly termed *analytical psychology* and *individual psychology*, respectively. Freud's initial interest was in the origins of neuroses. On developing the technique of free association to replace that of hypnosis in this therapy, he observed that

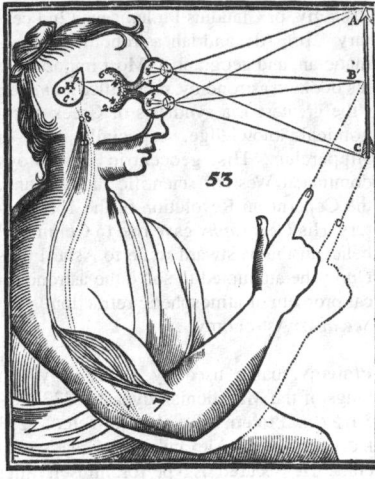

A woodcut diagram by René Descartes illustrates his theory that sensory impressions are converted into motor impulses through the agency of the pineal gland in the brain. Descartes believed that the pineal gland was the human soul, without which the body would be simply a machine.

certain patients could in some cases associate freely only with difficulty. He decided that this was due to repression, where memories of certain experiences being held back from the conscious mind, and noted that the most sensitive areas were in connection with sexual experiences. He thus developed the concept of the unconscious (later to be called the *id*) and suggested (for a while) that anxiety was the result of repression of the libido. He also defined *resistance* by the conscious mind to acceptance of ideas and impulses from the unconscious, and *transference*, the idea that relationships with other people or objects in the past affect the individual's relationships with other people or objects in the present.
See also: Freud, Sigmund; Psychology.

Psychological warfare, various propaganda methods directed at a nation's enemy. The objective is to demoralize the enemy's people, break their will, and discredit their leaders. Civilians, soldiers, and prisoners of war may be subjected to psychological warfare.
See also: Propaganda.

Psychology, originally the branch of philosophy dealing with the mind, then the science of mind, and now, considered in its more general context, the science of behavior, whether human or animal, and of human thought processes. Psychology is closely connected with medicine, psychiatry, and sociology. There are a number of closely interrelated branches of human psychology. *Experimental psychology* embraces all psychological investigations undertaken by the psychologist. The experiments may center on the individual or on a group, in which latter case statistics will play a large part in the research. *Social psychologists* use statistical and other methods to investigate the effect of the group on the behavior of the individual. In *applied psychology*, the discoveries and theories of psychology are put to practical

use, as in industrial psychology. *Comparative psychology* deals with the different behavioral organizations of animals, including humans. *Physiological psychology* attempts to understand the neurology and physiology of behavior. *Clinical psychologists* diagnose and treat mental disorders, principally using psychological tests, psychotherapy, and behavior therapy. They also do research on psychological factors affecting mental illness.

Psychosis, any mental disorder that, whether neurological or purely psychological in origin, renders an individual incapable of distinguishing reality from fantasy. Symptoms may include delusions and hallucinations, severe mood swings, dissociation, etc. If the loss of mental capacity is progressive, the illness is termed a deteriorative psychosis. Today, the term is less often used in psychiatric diagnosis.
See also: Mental illness; Schizophrenia.

Psychosomatic medicine, that aspect of medical treatment that considers the emotional and mental component of physical illness. Emotional and mental disturbances undermine a person's physical health. They can also make a person feel sick when there is no physical cause. Disorders linked with emotional disturbances include asthma, headache, ulcers, hypertension, neurodermatoses (chronic skin disorders), sexual dysfunction, gastrointestinal upsets, and rheumatoid arthritis, among others. A patient whose complaint is determined to be psychosomatic may be treated by a physician, psychiatrist (or other therapist), or both.

Psychotherapy, application of the theories and discoveries of psychology to the treatment of mental illness, particularly in the form of some sort of relationship between the therapist and the patient. Psychoanalysis, the technique pioneered by Sigmund Freud, was the first form of psychotherapy. Since then many others have been developed, including behavior therapy and Gestalt therapy. Most approaches to psychotherapy involve some type of support, confrontation, or interpretation. Any approach may be applied in a group setting of 5 to 12 people. Group therapy enables a therapist to serve more people, and members of a group can learn from and provide support for one another.
See also: Behavior therapy; Gestalt psychology; Psychology.

Psyllium, herb belonging to the plantain family, Plantagnaceae. *Plantango psyllium* and *P. ovata* are common species. An annual, the plant may grow 20 in (51 cm) high. It has narrow leaves, $1-2^{1}/_{2}$ in (2.5-6.4 cm) long, and tiny flowers along spikes. Psyllium is cultivated in southern Europe and India for the medicinal, especially laxative, properties of its seeds.

Ptarmigan, any of several birds of the grouse family that can be identified by their white wings and underparts. The willow ptarmigan and rock ptarmigan live in Arctic regions, while the white-tailed ptarmigan is

P

found above the treeline of the Rocky Mountains. Ptarmigans turn white in winter. They have feathered toes that act as snowshoes, and they can burrow under snow for food.

Pteranodon *See:* Pterosaur.

Pteridophyte, class of plants that produce spores and have roots, stems, and leaves. Having vascular tissue places pteridophytes in the division, or phylum, Tracheophyta. Among other plants, the class includes ferns, horsetails, club mosses, and numerous species known from fossils. The pteridophyte's life cycle is one of alternating generations and asexual (with spores) and sexual (with egg and sperm) reproduction. Spores released from spore cases develop into a plant unlike the parent. This second form develops male and female reproductive organs. These produce eggs and sperm that unite to begin the first form of the plant. Pteridophytes that lived millions of years ago are the source of today's coal.

Pterosaur, member of a group of flying reptiles that lived 195-65 million years ago, during the Mesozoic era. The compact body had a pointed head with powerful, toothed jaws. Skin between the hindlimb and the forelimb's 4th finger served as a wing. The other 3 fingers were clawed and free for clutching. The slender hindlimbs seem to have been adapted for suspending the animal. Scientists believe that the pterosaur, besides gliding and soaring, flapped its wings. There are 2 known groups of pterosaurs: the earlier rhamphourhynchoids, the size of a sparrow; and the various sized pterodactyls. The *Pteranodon*, a pterodactyl descendant, had a wingspan estimated at up to 51 ft (15.5 m), making it the largest flying reptile.

Pterodactylus is a genus of flying reptiles, or pterosaurs, that existed during the latter part of the Mesozoic Era. These pterosaurs had heads nearly as long as their bodies, which ranged from sparrow to hawk size. Fossil remains of *Pterodactylus* have been found in East Africa and Europe.

Ptolemy, or Claudius Ptolemaeus (2nd century A.D.), Alexandrian astronomer, mathematician, and geographer. Most important is his book on astronomy, now called *Almagest* ('the greatest'), a synthesis of Greek astronomical knowledge, especially that of Hipparchus. His geocentric cosmology dominated Western scientific thought until the Copernican Revolution of the 16th century. His *Geography* gave rise to Columbus' belief in the westward route to Asia. In his *Optics* he attempted to solve the astronomical problem of atmospheric refraction.
See also: Astronomy.

Ptolemy, name used by all 15 Egyptian kings of the Macedonian dynasty (323 B.C.-30 B.C.). **Ptolemy I Soter** (367 B.C.- 283 B.C.) was one of Alexander the Great's generals. He secured Egypt for himself after Alexander's death and defended it in a series of wars against Alexander's other generals. He founded the library of Alexandria, which became a center of Hellenistic culture. **Ptolemy II Philadelphus** (308 B.C.-246 B.C.) succeeded in 285. Under him Alexandria reached its height; he completed the Pharos lighthouse and appointed Callimachus librarian. **Ptolemy III Euergetes** (c.280-221 B.C.) Succeeded in 246. He extended the empire to include most of Asia Minor, the eastern Mediterranean, and the Aegean islands. After 221 the Ptolemaic empire entered a long period of decline, gradually losing its overseas possessions. **Ptolemy XV Cesarion** ('son of Caesar'; 47-30 B.C.) ruled from 44 B.C. jointly with his mother, Cleopatra VII. On their defeat at the battle of Actium (31 B.C.), Egypt became a Roman province.

Ptomaine poisoning, type of food poisoning caused by spoiled foods.

Puberty *See:* Adolescence.

Public domain, ownership of a property or resource by the people. Processes, plans, and creative works not protected by patent or copyright are said to be in the public domain.

Public health, organization and practice of preventative medicine within a community. Many threats to health are beyond individual control: Disease, epidemics, pollution of the air, and purity of water can only be effectively regulated by laws and health authorities. Among the strictest controls are those on sewage and waste disposal. Most advanced countries have pure-food laws controlling food purity, freshness, and additives. The work of individual countries in the public-health field is coordinated by the World Health Organization. Some countries have complete public-health services that provide free or low-cost medical treatment of all kinds.

Public opinion, opinions held by many people on issues of local, national, or worldwide importance. Public opinion is shaped by factual information and individuals' values and emotions. It is circulated and further influenced by conversation, fora, the media, schools, public figures, and special interest groups, such as political parties, labor unions, religious organizations, and businesses. Public opinion polls survey the range of public opinion within a group. In a democratic society, government and private institutions are responsive to public opinion and divergent public opinion is permitted.

Public opinion poll, technique for measuring the range of opinions held by the general public or by specifically limited groups of people. It developed during the 1920s. Opinion polls rely on certain statistical laws that show that small, carefully chosen samples of any group can accurately represent the range of opinions of the whole group, or population. The population in question, known as the 'universe,' may be a general one (all voters in a country) or a limited one (all car workers in a city). Accuracy depends on the care with which the sample is constructed and on the size of the sample.

Public relations (PR), general term for fostering goodwill for a person, corporation, institution, or product without actually paying for advertisements. Practitioners of PR supply information to the media in the hope that the media will not bother to make any changes in what they want to have said. PR people suggest improvements in behavior, grooming, packaging, etc., to a client or employer. The term *public relations* is thought to have been used first by Ivy L. Lee, who styled himself an 'adviser' on 'public relations' as early as 1919.

Public utility, business that performs a service for the public and is subject to government regulation. Companies that supply electricity, water, and natural gas and provide sewage treatment, waste disposal, telephone service, and transportation are examples of public utilities. In Canada and Europe, the state owns the public utilities. In the United States, most public utilities are privately owned; some are owned by municipalities

Ancestors of the Pueblo Indians built hundreds of pueblos throughout the Four Corners region–where Arizona, Colorado, New Mexico, and Utah meet–in the period 900-1300 A.D. Among the most spectacular are the Cliff Palace ruins at Mesa Verde National Park in Colorado.

and counties. Government regulation assures that the public utility, a monopoly, charges a reasonable fee and supplies adequate and safe service to all who apply for it.

Publishing, preparation, manufacture, and distribution of printed materials. In Europe, publishing became distinct from printing and bookselling soon after the introduction of printing (15th century). By the 1800s, book publishing was an important industry. Today, large publishers are often owned by conglomerates. Many publishers specialize as to subject matter; type of book: trade, text, or reference; and means of distribution. Trade books (fiction and nonfiction) are sold to readers through stores; textbooks reach students through school purchases; reference books are sold to libraries and individuals. Some books are sold by subscription or through book clubs. In a publishing house, the steps needed to bring a manuscript to book form are carried out by separate departments: editorial, production, promotion, and distribution.
See also: Printing.

Puccini, Giacomo (1858-1924), Italian opera composer. His first international success, *Manon Lescaut* (1893), was followed by *La Bohème* (1896), *Tosca* (1900), *Madama Butterfly* (1904), and *Turandot* (uncompleted at Puccini's death, produced 1926). A lyric style and strong orchestration are characteristic of his operas, which have great dramatic and emotional power. Puccini's works are among the most popular in the operatic repertoire.
See also: Opera.

Pudding stone, kind of conglomerate rock. It consists of pebbles and gravel embedded in a fine-grained, loosely cementing matrix. The term is chiefly British.

Puebla (pop. 20500,000), capital of Puebla, Mexico. The city, one of Mexico's largest, was founded in 1531. It is known for its architecture, much of which is decorated with colored tiles. Puebla's products include pottery, glass, tiles, cotton textiles, fruits, and vegetables.
See also: Mexico.

Puebla, state of Mexico, in central Mexico, near Mexico City. It produces agricultural products and textiles. Three of Mexico's highest mountains, Orizaba (Citlatltépetl), Popocatépetl, and Ixtacihuatl, are within Puebla. Its capital is the city of Puebla.
See also: Mexico.

Pueblo, several Native American tribes living in southwestern United States (Arizona and New Mexico) in permanent villages (*pueblos*). They have the oldest and most developed pre-Columbian civilization north of Mexico.
The various tribes, which include the Hopi and Zuñi, are descended from the basket makers and cliff dwellers. Pueblo Indians are noted for their handiworks; their social system and religious practices remain largely intact today.

Puerto Rico

Capital:	San Juan
Area:	3,515 sq mi (9,104 sq km)
Population:	3,857,000
Language:	English, Spanish
Government:	Self-governing commonwealth associated with the United States
Independent:	dependent
Head of gov.:	Governor
Per capita:	US$ 6,610
Monetary unit:	1 U.S. dollar = 100 cents

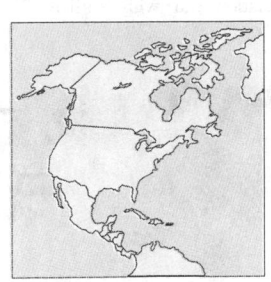

Puerto Rico, officially the Commonwealth of Puerto Rico, island in the Caribbean Sea.
Land and climate. Puerto Rico is the smallest and easternmost island of the Greater Antilles, the other members of which are Cuba, Jamaica, and Hispaniola.

A number of offshore islands, including Vieques, Cule-bra, and Mona, also belong to Puerto Rico, bringing the commonwealth's total area to about 3,515 sq mi (9,104 sq km). The capital city is San Juan. The official language is Spanish, but English is also spoken.
People. The people of Puerto Rico are a mixture of Spanish and African. Some two-thirds of the population lives in the cities of San Juan, Ponce, and Mayagüez. Most Puerto Ricans are Roman Catholic.
Economy. Puerto Rico's was formerly a single-crop economy based upon sugar, but it now depends largely upon the manufacturing of metals, chemicals, textiles, and sugar products. Coffee, tobacco, oil refining, and tourism are also important.
History. Puerto Rico was discovered in 1493 by Christopher Columbus. In 1508, Juan Ponce de Leòn founded a colony. The island was ceded to the United States in 1898 following the Spanish American War. In 1917, the Puerto Ricans received U.S. citizenship. In 1952, Puerto Rico became a commonwealth in free association with the United States. Under the arrangement, Puerto Ricans remain U.S. citizens, though they cannot vote in U.S. elections and are not obligated to pay U.S. taxes. Following World War II and Operation Bootstrap, a program for strengthening the island's economy, Puerto Rico experienced increased investment that spurred economic growth and diversification. However, high unemployment coupled with a high birth rate have led large numbers of Puerto Ricans to emigrate to the United States. The island's relationship to the United States remains a political issue. Mainstream political parties are divided between those favoring statehood and those favoring the commonwealth arrangement. A nationalist minority outside the mainstream seeks independence.
Since 1992, Pedro Rosselló has been governor. His main goal is to maintain the commonwealth arrangement with the U.S.

Puff adder *See:* Adder.

Puffball, fungus of the family Lycoperdaceae. Puffballs produce a roundish fruiting body (basidiocarp) that contains spores. Before maturity, the basidiocarp is firm and edible. The dry, mature puffball often has cracks from which the powdery spores issue.

Fort San Gerónimo, on one of the two islets of Old San Juan in San Juan Bay, was built in 1771. Originally called Puerto Rico ('rich port'), San Juan is the capital and largest city, as well as the manufacturing, trade, and tourist center, of Puerto Rico.

P

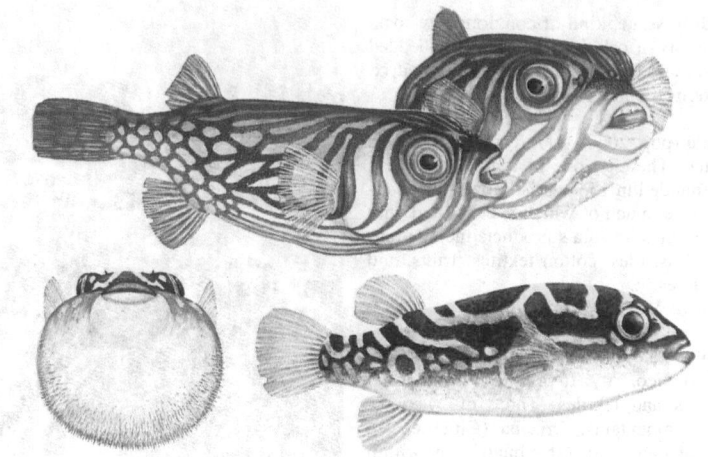

Reticulated puffers (*Arothron reticularis*, found in sand and shingle reaches of the Pacific (above). Fish, displaying semi-inflation under attack (above right). *Tetraodon palembangensis*, (below), a purely freshwater species, sex distinction is unknown (as is the case with most puffers). Fully inflated specimen (left below).

Puffer, or globe fish, fish that blows up its body like a balloon. It is found in warm and temperate seas, and some grow to 3 ft (0.91 m) long. The bodies of some puffers contain a deadly poison, tetradontoxin. In Japan they are a delicacy, but a cook has to have a license to prepare puffers, for it is necessary to remove the poison parts.

Puffin, any of several stubby seabirds of the auk family. Black or black-and-white, they are characterized by their large, laterally compressed bills, which become further enlarged and brightly patterned at the beginning of the breeding season. Puffins live in colonies on sea cliffs, nesting in burrows.

Pug, breed of toy dog. It has a squarish build, wrinkled face, short muzzle, and curled tail. Adults stand 10-11 in (2.5-2.8 cm) and weigh 13-18 lb (6-8 kg). The pug probably originated in China.

Pugachev, Emelian Ivanovich (1742-1775), Cossack leader of the great Urals peasant revolt (1773-1774). Claiming to be Peter III, murdered husband of Catherine II of Russia, he declared serfdom abolished and led an army of serfs and Cossacks that seized several cities and killed thousands before he was captured, sent to Moscow in an iron cage, and executed.
See also: Cossacks.

Pugin, Augustus Welby Northmore (1812-1852), English architect and architecture theoretician. One of the most important fig-

ures of the English Gothic revival. He built mainly Neo-Gothic churches; he stated that real Christian art could only be expressed in the Gothic style. In his book *Contrasts* (1836) he compared the architectural styles of his time, which he thought were absurd, with the greatest architectural achievements of the Catholic church in the late Middle Ages, which he described as an utopian ideal. He continued to write about this in *The True Principles of Pointed or Christian Architecture* (1841) and *An Apology for the Revival of Christian Architecture* (1843). Pugin's designs for church interiors were richly decorated, but because the church lacked money the realizations were usually much more sober. Only in the Houses of Parliament (London) was he able to completely utilize his talent for decoration. The interior of the House of Lords is the most pure example of Pugin's style. Pugin also made the furniture of Windsor Castle (ca. 1827). His numerous churches can be found all over England. Best-known are St. Giles in Cheadle, Staffordshire (1842-1846), St.-Barnabas cathedral in Nottingham (1842-1844) and St. Augustine's in Ramsgate, Kent (1847-1851).

Pulitzer, Joseph (1847-1911), Hungarian-born U.S. publisher who created the Pulitzer Prizes. In 1883 he bought the New York *World* and raised the circulation tenfold in seven years by aggressive reporting (the term *yellow journalism* was coined to describe its style). In the 1890s Pulitzer was involved in a circulation war with William Randolph

Hearst's New York *Journal*. He regularly ran liberal crusades. He also endowed the school of journalism at Columbia University.

Pulitzer Prizes, awards for achievement in U.S. journalism and letters, given every May since 1917 through a foundation created by the estate of Joseph Pulitzer and administered by Columbia University. There are eight cash awards for journalism ($1,000 each), five for literature ($500 each), and four traveling scholarships. An award for music was added in 1943.
See also: Pulitzer, Joseph.

Pulley, grooved wheel mounted on a block with a cord or belt passing over it. A pulley is a simple machine applying the equilibrium of torque to obtain a mechanical advantage. Thus the block and tackle is a combination of ropes and pulleys used for hoisting heavy weights. A belt and pulley combination can transmit motion from one part of a machine to another. Variable speed can be obtained from a single-speed driving shaft by the use of stepped or cone-shaped pulleys with diameters that give the correct speed ratios and belt tensions. To help prevent excessive belt wear and slipping, the rim surface of a pulley is adapted to the material of the belt used.

Pullman, George Mortimer (1831-1897), U.S. industrialist and inventor of the first modern railroad sleeping car, the Pullman (patented 1864). In 1880 he built a model company town, Pullman, Ill. (now part of Chicago), later site of the Pullman Strike.
See also: Railroad.

Pulsar, short for *pulsating radio star*, a celestial radio source emitting brief, extremely regular pulses of electromagnetic radiation. Each pulse lasts a few hundredths of a second, and the period between pulses is of the order of one second or less. The pulse frequency varies from pulsar to pulsar. The first pulsar was discovered in 1967 by Anthony Hewish and S.J. Bell. The fastest pulsar yet observed has a period of 0.033 sec, emitting pulses of the same frequency in the X-ray and visible regions of the spectrum. It is likely that there are some 10,000 pulsars in the Milky Way, though fewer than 100 have as yet been discovered. It is believed that pulsars are the neutron star remnants of supernovas, rapidly spinning and radiating through loss of rotational energy.
See also: Astronomy.

Pulse, throb in the artery walls due to the beating of the heart. The walls expand when the heart contracts and contract when the heart relaxes. This creates a wave of pressure that can be felt externally. The pulse is usually counted on the thumb side of the wrist, but it may be taken over any artery that can be felt. A doctor takes the pulse to determine if the heart is beating normally.
See also: Artery; Heart.

Puma, cougar, panther, or mountain lion (*Felis concolor*), the most widespread of the big cats of the Americas, occupying an amazing variety of habitats. Powerful cats, resembling a slender and sinuous lioness

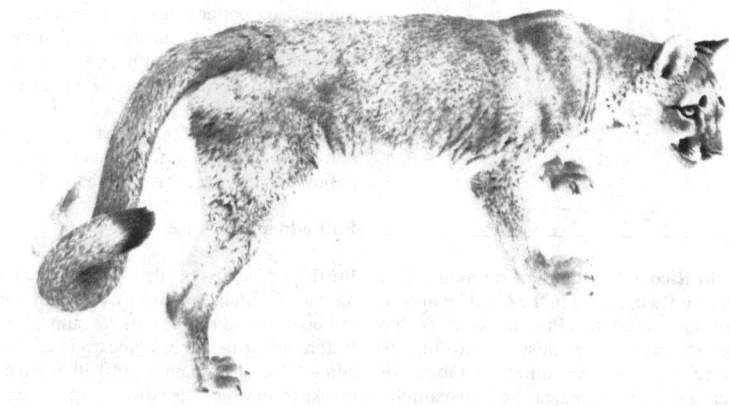

The solitary puma (*F. concolor*), a large North American cat, has been hunted by farmers and ranchers, because it sometimes attacks livestock.

with a small head, they lead solitary lives, preying on various species of deer. The lifespan of a puma in the wild is about 18 years. A puma can cover up to 20 ft (6.1 m) in a bound and will regularly travel up to 50 mi (80.5 km) when hunting.

Pumice, porous, frothy, volcanic glass formed by the sudden release of vapors as lava cools under low pressure. It is used as an abrasive, an aggregate, and a railroad ballast.

Pump, device for taking in and forcing out a fluid, thus giving it kinetic or potential energy. The heart is a pump for circulating blood around the body.

The steam engine was developed to power pumps for pumping out mines. Piston pumps-the simplest of which is the syringe-are reciprocating *volume displacement pumps*, as are diaphragm pumps, with a pulsating diaphragm instead of the piston. One-way inlet and outlet valves are fitted in the cylinder. Rotary volume displacement pumps have rotating gear wheels or wheels with lobes or vanes. *Kinetic pumps*, or fans, work by imparting momentum to the fluid by means of rotating curved vanes in a housing: Centrifugal pumps expel the fluid radially outward; and propeller pumps, axially forward. Air compressors use the turbine principle. *Air pumps* use compressed air to raise liquids from the bottom of wells, displacing one fluid with another. If the fluid must not come into direct contact with the pump, as in a nuclear reactor, *electromagnetic pumps* are used. An electric current and a magnetic field at right angles induce the conducting fluid to flow at right angles to both; or the principle of the linear induction motor may be used. To achieve a very high vacuum, the *diffusion pump* is used, in which atoms of condensing mercury vapor entrain the remaining gas molecules.

Pumpkin, plant (genus *Cucurbita*) of the gourd family. The genus includes winter squashes (*C. maxima* or *C. moschata*) and summer squashes, but the term *pumpkin* usually refers to the round, orange-skinned fruit of the vine *C. pepo*. The pumpkin's stringy pulp is used as food and pie filling. The seeds, which fill the pumpkin's cavity, are also eaten. At Halloween, pumpkins are carved into jack-o'-lanterns. The pumpkin probably originated in North America.

Punch and Judy, leading characters in a children's handpuppet show of the same name. Punch, descended from Pulcinella (Punchinello) of the Commedia Dell'Arte, is a hooknosed, hunchbacked, wife-beating rogue who usually ends on the gallows or in a crocodile's mouth. He is accompanied by his shrewish wife, Judy (originally called Joan), and their dog, Toby. The Devil, Baby, Hangman, Policeman, and Doctor may also appear.

Punic Wars, 3 conflicts between Carthage and Rome. Rome emerged from the Punic Wars as the dominant Mediterranean power. The **First Punic War** (264-241 B.C.) involved a local dispute over the control of the Strait of Messina, between Sicily and Italy. Carthage, led by Hamilcar Barca, and the

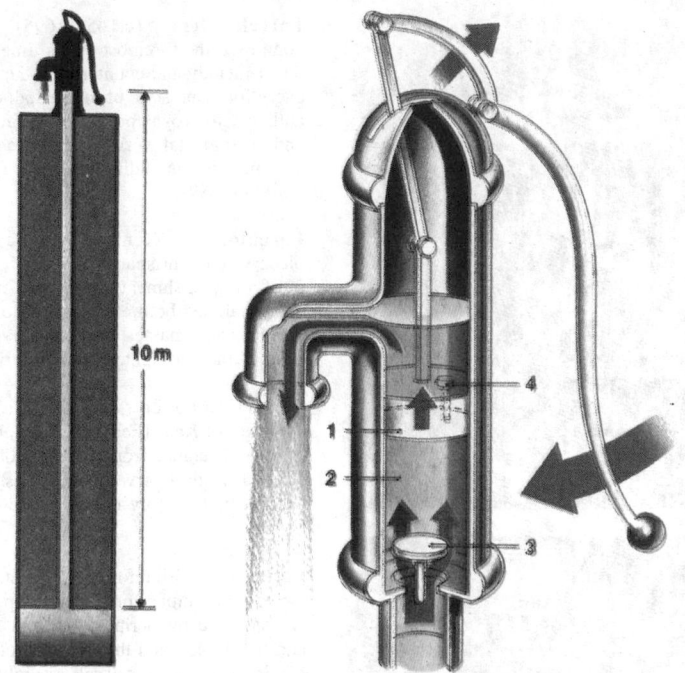

10 m

Sicilian town Syracuse fought well on land but yielded to Rome's greater sea power. During the **Second Punic War** (218-201 B.C.), Hannibal, the Carthagenian general, crossed the Alps into Italy. The Romans struggled to contain him and finally defeated him (202 B.C.) in Africa. Rome gained Carthage's Spanish provinces. The **Third Punic War** (149-146 B.C.) resulted from Carthage's alleged violation of the 201 B.C. treaty. Rome blockaded Carthage and sacked the city.
See also: Carthage; Hannibal; Rome, Ancient.

Punishment *See:* Capital punishment.

Punjab (Sanskrit, 'five rivers'), large wheat-growing region in the northwest of the Indian subcontinent, on the upper Indus River plain. Formerly the British Indian province of Punjab, it was divided in 1947 into what became known as Punjab (Pakistan) and Punjab (India). In 1966 Punjab (India) was divided into two further provinces, Punjab and Haryana.
See also: India.

Punta Arenas (pop. 132,000), city in Chile on the Peninsula de Brunswick on the Strait of Magellan, capital of the province of Magallanes. Southernmost city in the world. Center for an area with extraction of oil, forestry, fishing and sheep breeding; the port exports wool, petroleum, natural gas and meat (free port). Varied industries. Tourism. Airport. Airforce base and naval port. Founded in 1849 to support the Chilean claims to the Strait of Magellan. At the beginning of the 20th century it was called Magallanes for eleven years and it developed due to the discovery of gold and oil in the area. Important supply port until the Panama canal was opened. Bishop's seat.

Pupa, immature stage in the development of those insects whose larval form is complete-

ly different in structure from the adult form and in which complete metamorphosis occurs. The pupa normally is a resting place in which the larval structure is reorganized to form the adult. Everything but the nervous system changes, and feeding and locomotion are suspended.

Pupfish, about 30 species of fish (genus *Cyprinodon*) belonging to the killifish family. Pupfish live in the southwestern United States and Mexico, in springs and streams. A few species can tolerate water temperatures of 108°F. (42°C) and thrive in hot springs. Some pupfish are endangered or extinct. Efforts are being made to protect the remaining species.

Pupil *See:* Eye.

Puppet, figure of a person or animal manipulated in dramatic presentations. There are hand (or glove) and finger puppets; jointed marionettes string-controlled from above; and rod puppets, often used in shadow plays.

A piston pump. On the downward stroke, the piston (1) will be moved upwards, thus producing a vacuum in the cylinder (2). Water is then being forced into the cylinder by atmospheric pressure on the surface of the water outside the pump. Theoretically, the atmospheric pressure can sustain a 33 ft (10 m) head, however, the actual suction head (A) will be about 23 ft (7 m). Water is being discharged on every downward stroke. On every upward stroke, valve number 3 will close, and valve number 4 will open, to allow the piston to move down through the trapped water.

P

A puppet, based upon a character from the original Indian Mahabharata epic, used in the Javanese form of galanty show, the wayang.

P

English puppet dolls, Punch and Judy.

Nineteenth-century Sicilian puppets (Puppet Theatre, Munich).

Puppetry, with which ventriloquism is associated, is an ancient entertainment, popular in many countries.

Puranas (Sanskr.: ancient), Hindu scriptures, following the Vedas and the heroic poems (epics) in sacredness. Probably composed between 300 and 1200 A.D. from old stories about kings, wise men and gods (esp. Vishnu and Shiva). There are eighteen important Puranas, eighteen less important and many related texts.

Purcell, Edward Mills (1912-1997), U.S. physicist who shared the 1952 Nobel Prize for physics for his discovery of nuclear magnetic resonance (NMR) in solids.

Vladimir Putin

Purcell, Henry (c.1659-1695), English composer, the foremost of his time. A master of melody and counterpoint, he wrote in every form and style of the period: odes and anthems for royal occasions, many choral and instrumental works, and music for plays and masques, including his opera *Dido and Aeneas* (1689).

Purgatory, in Roman Catholicism, the place where Christians after death undergo purifying punishment and expiate unforgiven venial sins before admission to heaven. Indulgences, masses, and prayers for the dead are held to lighten their suffering.

Purim (Feast of Lots), Jewish festival of the 14th day of Adar (Feb.-Mar.), a celebration of the deliverance from massacre of Persian Jews through intervention by Esther and Mordecai. The story is told in the Book of Esther.

Puritans, English reforming Protestants who aimed for a simpler form of worship expressly warranted by Scripture, devout personal and family life, and the abolition of clerical hierarchy. They stressed self-discipline, work as a vocation, and the Christianizing of all spheres of life. Most were strict Calvinists. The term was first used in the 1560s for those dissatisfied with the compromise of the Elizabethan settlement of the Church of England; under James I, after their unsuccessful pleas for reform at the Hampton Court Conference (1604), some separated from the Church of England. Archbishop Laud set about systematic repression of Puritanism, causing some to emigrate to the colonies. The English Civil War-known also as the Puritan Revolution-led to the establishment of Presbyterianism, but under Oliver Cromwell Puritan dominance was weakened by internal strife. Most Puritans were forced to leave the Church after the Restoration (1660), becoming Nonconformists. Many New England settlers were Puritans, and their influence on the colonies was profound, especially their concern for education and church democracy.
See also: Protestantism.

Purple Heart *See:* Decorations, medals, and orders.

Purus River, third-longest river in South America and a major tributary of the Amazon River. It rises in the Andes in Peru and meanders 1,956 mi (3,148 km) in a northeasterly direction into Brazil.

Pusan (pop. 4,1 million), second-largest city in South Korea, in the southeast. Having an excellent natural harbor, it is a major port and a center for commerce, shipbuilding, and the fishing industry. It is also a manufacturing and transportation center. Visitors come to its religious and historic landmarks, beaches, and hot springs. During the Korean War, it was South Korea's capital and a landing site for men and arms.

Pushkin, Alexander (1799-1837), poet, widely recognized as the founder of modern Russian literature. A sympathizer of the Decembrist Revolt, he spent his adult life in

exile or under police surveillance. His poetic range included the political, humorous, erotic, lyrical, epic, and verse tales or novels like *Russlan and Ludmilla* (1820), *The Prisoner of the Caucasus* (1822), and his masterpiece *Eugene Onegin* (1833). Other works are the great drama *Boris Godunov* (1831) and such prose works as 'The Queen of Spades' (1834) and *The Captain's Daughter* (1836).

Alexander Sergeyevich Pushkin (1799-1837), as painted in 1827 by O.A. Kiprensky (1782-1836).

Pushtuns, ethnic group comprising about one half the population of Afghanistan and one fifth the population of Pakistan. They are also called Pathans, Pashtuns, Pakhtuns, and Pukhtuns. Their language, called Pashto, Pushtu, or Pukhtu, is related to Persian. Most Pushtuns live as farmers or nomadic herders and follow Islam. The group is divided into about 40 tribes. Each consists of groups of extended families and is governed by a democratic council. Ancestors of the Pushtuns can be traced to 4000 B.C. During the Soviet invasion of Afghanistan (1979-1989), guerrilla bands of Pushtuns resisted the Soviets.

Pussy willow, small tree (*Salix discolor*) particular to North America and characterized by a silky, often drooping flower cluster called a catkin, produced in the early spring.

Putin, Vladimir (1952-), Russian politician and President (2000-). Putin started his career in the KGB (the Russian secret security service). As an intelligence officer he was stationed mainly in East-Germany (1975-1990). Following the collapse of the Soviet Union in 1991, he retired from the KGB and became deputy mayor of St. Petersburg. In 1996, Putin left for Moscow. Due to the experience he had acquired in the KGB, he rapidly worked his way up and became the chief of Department of Economic Safety of the FSB, the successor of the KGB, in 1998. In 1999, President Yeltsin appointed him Prime Minister. Yeltsin voluntarily resigned from office on December 31 of that same year. Initially, Putin became acting President, but at the presidential elections of March 2000, he was officially elected President of Russia. He started reforming policies, prioritizing reduction the civil service, legislative and fiscal reform and reducing bureaucracy.
See also: KGB.

Pu Yi (1906-1967), as Hsuan T'ung, the last emperor (1908-1912) of China. The Japanese installed him as Emperor K'ang Te of the puppet state Manchukuo (1934-1945). He was captured by the Soviets and returned to China (1950), where he was imprisoned until 1959.

PVC *See:* Vinyl.

Pygmalion, in Greek mythology, king of Cyprus who carved a statue of a beautiful woman and then fell in love with it. The goddess Aphrodite brought the statue (named Galatea) to life as an answer to Pygmalion's prayer for a wife just like her, and they were married. The Pygmalion theme has been used by many authors, particularly George Bernard Shaw in his play *Pygmalion* (1913).

Pygmy, term used to denote those people whose adult males are on average less than 5 ft (1.52 m) tall. Some Kalahari desert Bushmen are of pygmy size, but the most notable pygmies are the Mbuti, or Bambuti, of the Ituri Forest, Zaïre, who, through their different blood type, skin color, thick lips, and scant body hair but thick head hair, are regarded as distinct from the surrounding peoples and were probably the original inhabitants of the region. A Stone Age people, they are nomadic hunters, living in groups of 50 to 100. Asian pygmies are generally termed *Negritos*. Peoples rather larger than pygmies are described as pygmoid.

Pylos (modern Greek Pilos, formerly Navarino), ancient port in the southwestern Peloponnese, Greece, site of a Mycenaean palace of the 13th century B.C., associated with king Nestor. In the modern Greek War of Independence, it was the site of the Battle of Navarino (1827).
See also: Greece.

Pym, John (1584-1643), English statesman. A Puritan, he led parliamentary opposition to Charles I and organized the impeachment of the Duke of Buckingham (1626). Dominating the Short and Long Parliaments, he narrowly escaped arrest by the king in 1642 and then arranged an alliance with the Covenanters in 1643.

Pynchon, Thomas (1937-), U.S. novelist whose works, influenced by James Joyce and Vladimir Nabokov, are noted for their ingenious wordplay and complexity. His novels include *V* (1963), *The Crying of Lot 49* (1966), *Gravity's Rainbow* (1973), a National Book Award winner, *Vineland* (1990), and *Mason & Dixie* (1997).

Pyongyang (pop. 2,8 million), capital and largest city of North Korea. It lies on the Taedong River in an important coal-mining area and is a major industrial center producing iron, steel, machinery, and textiles. An ancient settlement, it was the capital of the Choson kingdom in the 3rd century B.C. The city was severely damaged during the Korean War.

Pyorrhea *See:* Periodontitis.

Pyramid, polyhedron whose base is a polygon and whose sides are triangles having a common vertex. A pyramid whose base is triangular is termed a tetrahedron (or triangular pyramid); one whose base is a regular polygon is termed regular; one with a square base, square; one with a rectangular base, rectangular.

Pyramids, structures built by the Egyptians and other ancient peoples as royal tombs or temples; they are composed of square bases and 4 triangular faces that meet at a common point, the apex. The Egyptian pyramids, erected around 4,500 years ago, are the largest and most notable. The first pyramid dates back to the Old Kingdom and was built by the architect Imhotep for King Zoser c.2650 B.C. The largest pyramid was constructed for King Khufu (reigned c.2589-c.2566 B.C.), also known as Cheops. It is 13 acres (5.3 hectares) in area and 482 ft (147 m) high. It is considered one of the Seven Wonders of the Ancient World. Pyramidal structures were also constructed by the native peoples of Central and South America. The Mayan pyramids were characterized by level tops that were probably used as pulpits.

Pyrethrum, any of a group of flowers (genus *Chrysanthemum*) that produce insect powder. Similar in appearance to the daisy, pyrethrums have stems measuring up to 1 ft (30 cm). The insecticide is developed from the powdered or dried flowers and is considered one of the least harmful to humans and animals. Kenya is the world's chief exporter of pyrethrum.

Pyridoxine *See:* Vitamin.

Pyrite, or iron pyrites (FeS_2, iron (ll) disulfide), hard, yellow, common sulfide known as fool's gold for its resemblance to gold. Of worldwide occurrence, it is an ore of sulfur that crystallizes in the isometric system, usually as cubes. It alters to goethite and limonite.

Pyromania, recurring impulse to set fire to objects or buildings.

Pyrometry, process of measuring exceedingly high temperatures through the use of a pyrometer, an instrument that can function in heat far hotter than that tolerated by ordinary thermometers. Most pyrometers measure temperature by detecting the rise in electrical resistance in a metal, by the increase in the intensity of light, or by similar electrical or radiation techniques.

Pyroxene, general term for a group of crystalline silicate minerals containing iron, calcium, and magnesium, prevalent in igneous, metamorphic, and lunar rocks. The color of pyroxenes ranges from black and brown to colorless.

Pyrrho of Elis (360-270 B.C.), Greek philosopher, the founder of skepticism. He taught that because nothing can be known with certainty, suspension of judgment and imperturbability of mind are the true wisdom and source of happiness.
See also: Skepticism.

Pyrrhus (c.318-272 B.C.), king at the age of 12 of Epirus, northwestern Greece, he served with Demetrius I of Macedonia in Asia Minor, was helped by Ptolemy I of Egypt to regain his throne, and later won and lost Macedonia. His costly victory over the Romans at Asculum (279), gave rise to the term *Pyrrhic victory*. Further campaigns in Macedonia and Sparta failed. He was killed in Argos.
See also: Greece, Ancient.

Pythagoras (c.582-507 B.C.), Greek philosopher who founded the Pythagorean school. Attributed to the school are: the proof of the Pythagorean theorem (the suggestion that the earth travels around the sun, the sun in turn around a central fire); observation of the ratios between the lengths of vibrating strings that sound in mutual harmony, and ascription of such ratios to the distances of the planets, which sounded the 'harmony of the spheres'; and the proposi

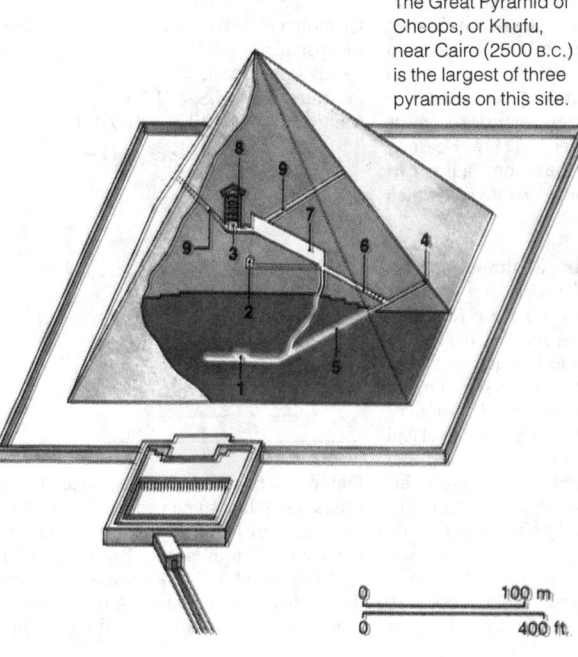

The Great Pyramid of Cheops, or Khufu, near Cairo (2500 B.C.) is the largest of three pyramids on this site.

It was originally 479 ft (146 m) high and 755 ft (230 m) square. The four sides, facing the cardinal points, are almost equilateral triangles, making an angle of 51 degrees with the ground. Due to several changes of plan during construction, there are three separate internal chambers. The original, subterranean chamber (1) and the so-called Queen's Chamber (2), are projects that were abandoned in favour of the King's Chamber (3), which contains Khufu's granite

sarcophagus. The entrance (4), 55 ft (16.8 m) above ground level, leads to a corridor (5), descending to the original chamber. An ascending corridor (6) was added, and the Queen's Chamber constructed, this corridor later extended into the Grand Gallery (7), leading to the King's Chamber. This chamber was covered with five tiers of stone beams, topped by a vault (8). Two shafts (9) from the King's Chamber to the pyramid exterior may have provided ventilation or allowed free passage of the dead king's spirit.

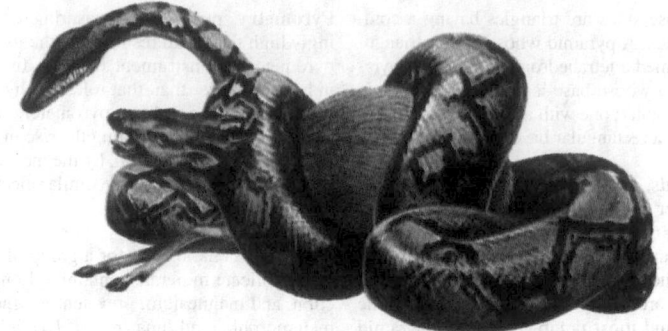

The Asiatic reticulated python (*P. reticulatus*) wraps around its prey and then constricts its body so that the animal cannot breathe. The python's specialized jaw hinge allows it to swallow large prey.

P

tion that all phenomena can be reduced to numerical relations. The Pythagoreans were also noted for their concept of the soul, the life of moderation, and their interest in medicine. They exerted great influence on Plato and ancient philosophy generally.
See also: Philosophy.

Pythagorean theorem, statement that, for any right-angled triangle, the square of the hypotenuse is equal to the sum of the squares of the other two sides. The earliest known formal statement of the theorem is in the *Elements* of Euclid, but the basis of it was known long before this time.
See also: Geometry.

Pythias *See:* Damon and Pythias.

Python, Old World equivalent of the New World boa, a snake bearing small spurs as the vestiges of hindlimbs. These two groups are clearly the closest relatives of the ancestral snake type. Like boas, pythons are non-venomous constrictors. They are found from Africa to Australia in a wide variety of habitats. All have bold color patterns in browns and yellows. The largest species, the reticulate python of Asia, reaches 33 ft (10.1 m). Pythons feed on small mammals, birds, reptiles, and frogs; the larger African species also feed on small antelopes.

Q, 17th letter of the alphabet, can be traced back to the letter *koph* in the Semitic alphabet and *koppa* in ancient Greek, on through the Etruscan alphabet, taking its modern form in Latin, usually followed by *u*. As an abbreviation, a capital *Q* is used for 'Quebec' and for 'queen' in titles such as Q.C. (Queen's Counsel). A lower-case *q* may stand for 'quart,' 'question,' and is part of *q.v.* for the Latin phrase *quod vide* (which see), meaning 'refer to.'

Qadhafi, Muammar Muhammad al- (1942-), Libyan leader. One of a group of army officers who deposed King Idris I in 1969, he became chairman of the ruling Revolutionary Command Council and commander-in-chief of the armed forces. One of the world's most controversial heads of state, he has been vehemently anti-Israel and supported several insurgent and terrorist groups around the world. In response to his support of terrorists, in 1986 U.S. planes attacked Tripoli, destroying a military camp.
See also: Libya.

Qandahar, or Kandahar (pop. 600,000), city in southern Afghanistan, second largest

Afghan city, and major international trade center. Industries include farming and fruit processing and exportation.
See also: Afghanistan.

Qassemlu, Abdel Rahman (1930/31-1989), Kurdish politician from Iranian Kurdistan. After a failed revolt against the central government at the end of World War II he went to Europe. There he came in contact with Marxism and later tried to organize Kurdish revolts from Prague. In 1973 he was elected leader of the Democratic Party Kurdistan of Iran. He distanced himself from Marxism and moved to Paris, where he taught Kurdish at the Sorbonne. After the fall of the shah he returned to Kurdish Iran, led a failed revolt against the Islamic rulers in 1980 and fled to Europe again. He was murdered by unidentified individuals.

Qatar

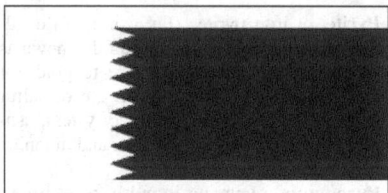

Capital:	Doha
Area:	4,378 sq mi (11,337 sq km)
Population:	793,000
Language:	Arabic
Government:	Absolute monarchy (emirate)
Independent:	1971
Head of gov.:	Sheikh
Per capita:	U.S. $21,200
Monetary unit:	1 Rihal = 100 dirham

Qatar, oil-rich emirate in Arabia. It comprises a low limestone peninsula, about 120 mi (193 km) long, that juts north into the Persian Gulf from eastern Saudi Arabia. Its 4,416 sq mi (11,437 sq km) consist of barren desert that receives under 4 in (10 cm) of rainfall a year. The only natural vegetation is

scrub. Oil accounts for the majority of exports and government income. Most of Qatar's workers are employed in the oil fields; others are goat and camel herders, fishers, or pearl divers. The merchants and industrial workers live in Doha, the capital, in eastern Qatar. Industry has expanded since 1939, when an oil strike led to the growth of the Dukhan oil field in western Qatar, one of the richest in the Middle East. In 1971 Qatar ceased to be a British protectorate and became a fully independent member of the UN. In 1991 Qatar participated in the Persian Gulf War, in which Iraq was defeated by a coalition of Middle Eastern and Western powers. In 1995 Sjeik Khalifa bin Hamad al-Thani was dethroned by his son Hamad bin Khalifa al-Thani.
The Qatari satellite television station Al Jazeera became one of the most important broadcasting stations in the Middle East.

Qin dynasty, also Ch'in dynasty, era of totalitarian Chinese rule dating from 221 B.C.-206 B.C. Under the rule of Shi Huangdi, the Chinese regions and regional chiefs were unified into one central empire. The dynasty is noted for advancing national unity and for the building of China's Great Wall.
See also: Great Wall of China; Shi Huangdi.

Qingdao (also Ch'ing-tao; pop. 3,4 million), China, a city and major naval and commercial seaport in Shandong province. It is on Jiaozhou bay, an inlet of the Yellow Sea, about 340 miles (547 km) southeast of Beijing. Qingdao's fine beaches make it a popular resort. The city is also a center of heavy industry. Manufactured goods include steel, machinery, and chemicals. Qingdao was only a fishing village when the Germans occupied it in 1898 and began building a modern city and port. The city was under German control until 1914, when it was occupied by the Japanese. Qingdao returned to Chinese control in 1922 but was again occupied by the Japanese during 1938-1945.

Qinghai (Ch'ing Hai, pop. 4,6 million), province in the Tibetan Highlands in the west of China, 278,486 sq mi (721,000 sq km). Practically the entire population lives in its far east. The only city of some size is the capital Xining (pop. 650,000). Borders on two autonomous areas, Tibet (Xizang) and Xinjiang (Xinjiang-Uygur). Agrarian area; agriculture, nomadic cattle breeding and forestry. Rich in minerals, e.g. petroleum, coal, iron ore, bauxite and gold; salt and phosphate are obtained from the salt lakes. Qinghai was assimilated into China at the beginning of the eighteenth century and is its most thinly populated province (6 inhabitants per sq km). Only one third of the population is of Chinese origin; the rest are Tibetans, Mongols, Hui Moslems and Kazakhs. Since minerals were found in the 1950s and the railroad from Xining to the east was finished, the area has become more economically developed.

Qiqihar (or Ch'i-ch'i-ha-erh; pop. 1,600,000), China, a city in Heilongjiang province, Manchuria. It lies on the Nen Jiang plain, east of the Da Hinggan Ling (Great Khingan

Range). Qiqihar is an industrial city. Products include machinery, textiles, and pharmaceuticals. The city is also a trading and processing center for the surrounding agricultural area. Qiqihar was founded by the Manchus in 1691.

Quadhafi, Muammar Muhammad al-
See: Qadhafi, Muammar Muhammad al-.

Quadrilateral, in geometry, plane 4-sided polygon. Quadrilaterals with 2 pairs of sides parallel are called parallelograms; with one pair of sides parallel, trapezoids; with no 2 sides parallel, trapeziums (the word *trapezium* is often used as a synonym of *trapezoid*). Parallelograms whose sides are all of equal length are termed rhombuses. Each side of a parallelogram is equal in length to the side parallel to it, and each interior angle is equal to the interior angle diametrically opposite it. A parallelogram whose interior angles are each 90° is a rectangle; a special case of this is the square, all of whose sides are equal. The sum of the interior angles of a quadrilateral is always 360°.

Quadruple Alliance, alliance of 4 countries. Historically, the most famous are (1) alliance among Britain, France, Austria, and the Netherlands (1718) to prevent Spain from changing the terms of the Peace of Utrecht (Spain later joined the alliance), (2) alliance among Britain, Austria, Russia, and Prussia (signed 1814, renewed 1815) to defeat Napoleon and, after his defeat and first abdication, to ensure that France abided by the terms of the 1815 Treaty of Paris, and (3) alliance among Britain, France, Portugal, and Spain (1834), supporting Queen Isabella II of Spain.

Quail, name for 2 distinct groups of game birds of the pheasant family. About 45 species of quail exist. Small ground birds of open country, quail are found on every continent except Antarctica. They feed on insects, grain, and shoots and rarely fly, even when disturbed. Quail live in groups called coveys in the fall and winter. The tiny painted quail was carried by Chinese mandarins to warm the hands.

Quaker-ladies *See:* Bluet.

Quakers, or Society of Friends, church known for its pacifism, humanitarianism, and emphasis on inner quiet. Founded in 17th-century England by George Fox, it was persecuted for its rejection of organized churches and any dogmatic creed. Many Quakers emigrated to America, where in spite of early persecution they were prominent among the colonizers. In 1681 William Penn established his 'Holy Experiment' in Pennsylvania; from that point the church's main growth took place in America. The early Quakers adopted a distinctive, simple style of dress and speech; simplicity of manner is still a characteristic Quaker Trait. They have no formal creed and no clergy, putting their trust in the 'inner light' of God's guidance. Their meetings for worship, held in 'meeting houses,' follow a traditional pattern of beginning in silence, with no set service and no single speaker. The Quakers

have exercised a moral influence disproportionate to their numbers through practicing what they believe, particularly pacifism. In the United States they were prominent abolitionists and have been among the pioneers of social reform.
See also: Penn, William.

Quantum electrodynamics, or QED, concept in theoretical physics. It concerns the motions and relationships between charged electrical particles including electrons, positrons, and photons and their interaction with electrical and magnetic fields. QED allows highly accurate predictions of changes in the properties of these particles. Physicists Richard P. Faynman and Julian S. Schwinger of the United States and Sin-itiro Tomonaga of Japan contributed in the 1940s to the development of QED.
See also: Feynman, Richard Phillips.

Quantum mechanics, fundamental theory of small-scale physical phenomena (such as the motions of electrons within atoms). This theory was developed during the 1920s, when it became clear that the existing laws of classical mechanics and electromagnetic theory were not successfully applicable to such systems. French physicist Louis De Broglie suggested (1924) that particles have a wavelike nature, with a wavelength h/p (h being the Planck constant, and p the particle momentum). This wavelike nature is significant only for particles on the molecular scale or smaller. These ideas were developed by Erwin Schrödinger and others into the branch of quantum mechanics known as wave mechanics. Werner Heisenberg of

Germany worked along parallel lines with a theory incorporating only observable quantities, such as energy, using matrix algebra techniques. His uncertainty principle (that a subatomic particle's momentum and position cannot both be accurately known) is fundamental to quantum mechanics, as is Wolfgang Pauli's exclusion principle (that each electron in an atom is in a quantum state shared by no other electron in that atom). Paul Dirac incorporated relativistic ideas into quantum mechanics.
See also: Atom; Physics.

Quantum theory *See:* Quantum mechanics.

Quarantine, period during which a person or animal must be kept under observation in isolation from the community after having been in contact with an infectious disease. The duration of quarantine depends on the disease(s) concerned and their maximum length of incubation. The term derives from the period of 40 days that ships had to wait before their crews could disembark at medieval European ports, due to fear of their carrying plague.
See also: Epidemic.

Quark, particle believed by physicists to be the basic subunit of neutrons and protons. The quark theory was first proposed by 2 American physicists, Murray Gell-Mann and George Zweig in 1964. The theory holds that neutrons and protons consist of even simpler particles called quarks. Scientific studies have indicated evidence of quarks since 1971.
See also: Gluon; Hadron.

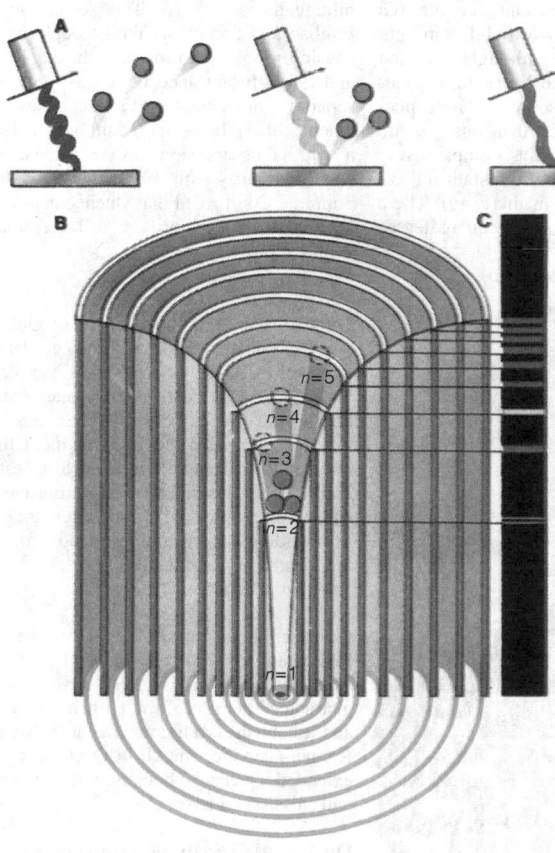

Quantum mechanics According to the quantum theory, light is emitted and absorbed by matter in quanta, or discrete amounts of energy that are related to the frequency of the light. In the photoelectric effect (A), electrons are ejected when light quanta fall on certain metals. More electrons are expelled as the light intensity increases because the number of quanta increase, but the electron velocities depend only on the light's frequency and decrease from a high value for violet light to a lower value for red light. When the electrons in an excited atom (B) drop from an orbit of high energy to one of lower energy, they emit light and produce the bright lines in the element's spectrum (C).

Q

Quarrying, excavation, from open-pit mines, of dimension stone (cut stone) or crushed stone to be used for building projects or ornamentation. The 3 major methods of quarrying are the plug and feather method, by which rock is loosened by applied pressure; the use of explosives; and channeling with special machinery.

Quartering Act *See:* Revolutionary War in America.

Quartz, rhombohedral form of silica, usually forming hexagonal prisms, colorless when pure. A common mineral (SiO_2), it is the chief constituent of sand, sandstone, quartzite, and flint and an essential constituent of high-silica igneous rocks, such as granite, rhyolite, and pegmatite. It also occurs as the gems chalcedony, agate, jasper, and onyx. Quartz is piezoelectric and is used to make oscillators for clocks, radio, and radar and to make windows for optical instruments. Crude quartz is used to make glass, glazes, and abrasives, and as a flux.

Quartzite, hard metamorphic rock composed of and cemented by recrystallized quartz grains. The fracturing of quartzite takes place through the grains, rather than between them, due to the extreme strength of the bonding.

Quasar, or quasi-stellar object, a starlike celestial object whose spectrum seen telescopically shows an abnormally large red shift. Quasars may be extremely distant objects-perhaps the inexplicably bright cores of galaxies near the limits of the known universe-receding from Earth at high velocities (which would account for the red shift). Quasars also show variability in light and radio emission. (Although the first quasars were discovered by radio astronomy, not all are radio sources. These phenomena might indicate that quasars are comparatively small objects comparatively close to us (large and more distant objects being unlikely to vary in this way). There are about 200 quasars in each square degree of the sky.
See also: Astronomy; Red shift.

The 59 ft (18 m) wide wooden Dufferin Terrace of Chateau Frontenac in Quebec is day and night a popular promenade. It is famous for its superb view of the Saint Lawrence and the region across the river, and for its 'European' atmosphere.

Quasimodo, Salvatore (1901-1968), Italian poet and translator of poetry awarded the 1959 Nobel Prize for literature. During and after World War II he turned (originally because of his opposition to fascism) from a complex, introverted, 'hermetic' style to social protest and examination of the plight of the individual, as in *Day after Day* (1947). His first poems were collected in *Waters and Lands* (1930).

Quaternary Period, period in geologic time, of the Cenozoic era whose beginning is marked by the advent of humans. It has lasted about 4 million years, up to and including the present.

Quebec (pop. 7,4 million), province in Canada, 524,059 sq mi (1,356,790 sq km). Capital: Québec. Extraction of copper, iron ore, zinc gold, titanium, sand and gravel. Hydroelectric power stations provide about 40% of Canadian water-powered electricity. Quebec was a French colony in Canada, where Frenchman Samuel de Champlain founded the first settlement in 1608. In the time of Louis XIV the number of French settlements increased significantly. When France came into conflict with England, Quebec was one of the areas that was fiercely fought over. In 1759, during the Seven Years' War (1756-1763), the English assumed power in Quebec. In 1774 England proclaimed the Quebec Act, which gave some autonomy to the French in the area. At the end of the nineteenth century an increasingly stronger French nationalism emerged, followed in 1900 by a movement that demanded autonomy for the French-speaking area. The result was the introduction of full bilingualism in 1910. The separation of English and French-speaking people keeps causing problems to this day. In the 1970s and 1980s, for instance, there was a growing separatist movement of Francophones (Le Québec libre). In a referendum held in 1995 a proposal of secession was voted down by a small majority. In 1998 the Canadian Supreme Court ruled that Quebec could only secede if a majority of all Canadians would approve.
See also: Canada.

Quebec (pop. 170,000), capital of Quebec province, situated on the St. Lawrence River. Founded in 1608 by Samuel de Champlain, it is Canada's oldest city. Despite British dominance since 1759, Quebec has remained essentially French, and more than 90% of its citizens claim French ancestry. Today it is a leading manufacturing center and transatlantic port. Industries include shipbuilding, paper milling, food processing, machinery, and textiles.
See also: Quebec.

Quebec Act, passed by the British Parliament in 1774, one of the Intolerable Acts that led to the American Revolution. It guaranteed the use of the French civil code and established religious freedom for the Roman Catholic Church in Quebec. It also extended Quebec's boundary to the Ohio and Mississippi rivers.

Quebec, University of, also Université du Québec, largest Canadian university, founded 1969. The university has 6 campuses, in Chicoutimi, Hull, Montreal, Rimouski, Rouyn, and Trois-Riviéres. All instruction is in French.

Quebec Conference (1864), conference in the city of Quebec that laid the foundations of the Canadian Confederation. Representatives from the British provinces in North America produced a series of 72 resolutions outlining a centralized federal union. This union was desirable in that it promoted better defense and economic growth, and eased friction between French- and English-speaking groups. The Quebec Conference became the basis of the British North America Act (1867), which created the Dominion of Canada.

Quebec separatist movement, various French-Canadian political factions in Quebec, Canada, which demand that French be the sole language of Quebec and that Quebec separate from Canadian rule and become an independent nation. The movement, begun in the early 1960s as the Quiet Revolution, and furthered by legislator René Lévesque and his Parti Québécois, stemmed from anger with British-centered policies, and governmental discrimination against French-speaking peoples. Despite the terrorist tactics of some groups, the separatist movement is growing in popularity. Nevertheless a popular referendum held in 1995 indicated that a majority of the electorate was against separation from Canada.

Quebracho, South American hardwood tree (genus *Schinopsis*) of the cashew family, with a high content of tannin, an extract used to tan leather. The quebracho grows mainly in Paraguay and Argentina. *Quebracho* means *ox-breaker* in Spanish.

Quechua, also Kechua or Quichua, linguistic family belonging to natives of South America. They were once part of the Inca Empire and now live mostly as peasants in the Andean highlands from Colombia to North Chile. Quechua is also the name of the family to which the official language of the Incas belonged; some 28 languages of the family are still spoken.

Queen, female monarch or the wife of a king, with all the powers allowed by the country that she rules. A queen regnant rules in her own right, by virtue of her birth; a consort is the wife of a king; and a dowager queen is the widow of a king.
See also: Monarchy.

Queen, Ellery, pen-name and fictional hero of American detective writers Frederic Dannay (1905-1982) and Manfred B. Lee (1905-1972). Their successful *The Roman Hat Mystery* (1929) was followed by over 100 other novels characterized by complexity of plot. *Ellery Queen's Mystery Magazine* was founded in 1941.

Queen Anne's lace *See:* Wild carrot.

Queen Anne's War *See:* French and Indian Wars.

Queens, largest and second most populous of the 5 boroughs that make up the city of New York. Queens is located at the western end of Long Island and is linked to Manhattan by an intricate network of tunnels and bridges crossing the East River. A largely middle-class area of small homes, Queens includes such residential neighborhoods as Forest Hills, Flushing, and Kew Gardens, as well as the industrial and commercial centers of Long Island City and Astoria, directly opposite Manhattan. In the southern part of the borough are a racecourse (Aqueduct), several beaches, and the John F. Kennedy International Airport. Flushing Meadow was the site of the 1939-1940 and 1964-1965 World's Fairs. Queens was founded by the Dutch in 1635, became part of the British province of New York in 1683, and became part of New York City in 1898.
See also: New York City.

Queensberry rules, basic rules of modern boxing, drawn up in 1865 under the auspices of John Sholto Douglas, 8th Marquess of Queensberry, supplanting London prize-ring rules. Innovations included the use of padded gloves instead of bare fists, a 10-sec count to determine a knockout, and the division of the bout into rounds with intermissions.
See also: Boxing.

Queensland, second largest Australian state, in the northeastern region of Australia, covering 667,000 sq mi (1,727,530 sq km). Tropical and eucalyptus forests in the rugged east contrast with pasture and desert on the vast western plain. It produces sheep, nearly half of Australia's cattle, and such crops as sugarcane, wheat, cotton, and fruit. It has valuable oil and mineral deposits. Founded as a penal colony (1824-1843), Queensland became a state of the Commonwealth in 1901.
See also: Australia.

Quemoy, or Chin-men, island group on the Formosa Strait off southeastern China. The islands have a combined area of about 58 sq mi (150 sq km), with 2 large islands and 12 islets. The Quemoy Islands remained a Chinese Nationalist garrison after the communist takeover in 1949.

Queneau, Raymond Auguste (1903-1976), French writer, studied philosophy and from 1924 to 1929 was part of the surrealist movement. Queneau employed all possibilities of language with great virtuosity: plays on words, phonetic spellings, argot, etc. Interesting in this respect is *Exercices in Style* (1947), in which one event is narrated in 99 different ways. His novel *Zazie in the Metro* (1959) became world-famous. It was filmed in 1960 by Louis Malle. Of his many poems *Si tu t'imagines...* (1952) became best-known, partly due to the rendition of Juliette Gréco.

Querétaro, state in central Mexico, on the Mexican Plateau, 6,119 ft (1,865 m) above sea level. Querétaro covers about 4,420 sq mi (11,450 sq km) of land, which includes mountainous areas, plains, and fertile val-

leys. Industries include farming and the mining of opals, silver, iron and copper. The Mexican constitution was drafted there (1916-1917).
See also: Mexico.

Quesnay, François (1694-1774), French economist and a leader of the physiocrats. Although trained in medicine (he was physician to Louis XV), his fame rests on his essays in political economy, which first began to appear in 1756 in Denis Diderot's *Encyclopédie*, and on his *Economic Table* (1758), which influenced Adam Smith.
See also: Physiocrat.

Quetzal (*Pharomacrus mocinno*), bird in the trogon family. Compared to the cream-colored females, the resplendent quetzal males display long tails-up to 3 ft (91 cm)-and brilliant feathers colored green on their backs, gold on their heads, with deep red on their undersides. The national bird of Guatemala, the quetzal lives in countries of Central and South America as well as in Mexico.

Quetzalcóatl (Nahuatl, 'plumed serpent'), ancient Mexican god identified with the morning and evening star. He is said to have ruled the pre-Aztec Toltec empire and to have invented books and the calendar. He represented the forces of good and light; whether he was an historical leader or merely mythological is not certain. The Aztec leader Montezuma II welcomed Hernándo Cortés, believing him to be descended from the god.
See also: Mythology.

Quevedo Villega, Francisco de (1580-1645), Spanish satirist, poet, and prose writer. Master of the *conseptismo* style of terse and arresting intellectual conceits, he is best known for *the Life of a Swindler* (1626), a parody of the picaresque novel, and *Visions* (1627), a bitter, fantastic view of Spanish society.

Quezon City (pop. 1.9 million), Philippine city on Luzon Island, near Manila. Once the capital of the Philippine Islands (1948-1976), Quezon City is primarily a residential area. It is the seat of Ateneo de Manila University and the University of the Philippines.
See also: Philippines.

Quezon y Molina, Manuel Luis (1878-1944), Filipino statesman who played a leading role in the Philippine independence movement before becoming the first president of the Philippine Commonwealth (1935). His presidency, continued in exile after Japanese invasion, was marked by efforts to improve conditions for the poor.
See also: Philippines.

Quicksand, sand saturated with water to form a sand-water suspension possessing the characteristics of a liquid. Quicksands may form at rivermouths or on sandflats; they are dangerous because they appear identical to adjacent sand. In fact, the density of the suspension is less than that of the human body, so a person who does not struggle may escape being engulfed.

The quetzal, *P. mocino*, a Central American bird of great beauty, is the national bird of Guatemala. Aztecs and Mayans regarded it as sacred, and they plucked tail plumes from living male birds for ceremonial purposes.

Quicksilver *See:* Mercury (element).

Quilt, bedcover made from 2 layers of cloth with an inner padding of insulating material. The layers are sewn together with plain or decorative stitching. The top cover of most quilts is made of brightly colored or patterned fabric pieces cut in geometric or fanciful shapes. Some quilts, particularly older ones, are considered folk art.

Quinine, alkaloid derived from cinchona bark from South America, long used in treating a variety of ailments (now rarely used). It was preeminent in early treatment of malaria until the 1930s, when atabrine was introduced. Quinine is also a mild analgesic and may prevent cramps and suppress heart rhythm disorders. Its side-effects include vomiting, deafness, vertigo, and vision disturbance.
See also: Cinchona; Malaria.

Quinn, Anthony Rudolph Oaxaca (1915-2001), American actor of Mexican descent. Powerful character, usually playing exotic and adventurous roles. Films include *Parole* (1936), *Viva Zapata* (1952; Oscar), *La strada* (1954), *Lust for Life* (1956), *The Black Orchid* (1958), *The Guns of Navarone* (1961), *Lawrence of Arabia* (1962), *Zorba the Greek* (1964), *Lost Command* (1966), *The Shoes of the Fisher Man* (1968), *The Don is Dead* (1973), *The Greek Tycoon* (1978), *The Passage* (1979), *Omar Mukhtar - Lion of the Desert* (1981), *Treasure Island* (1987), and *Somebody to Love* (1994).

Quinsy, acute complication of tonsillitis in which abscess formation causes spasm of the adjacent jaw muscles, fever, and severe pain. Incision and drainage of the pus produce rapid relief; antibiotics are helpful; and the tonsils may be removed when the infection diminishes.
See also: Tonsillitis.

Quintana Roo, state in southeastern Mexico on the Yucatán Peninsula, whose capital is Chetumal. The state, covering an area of about 19,387 sq mi (50,212 sq km), is a flat plain covered by dense jungle, with a hot and humid climate. Population is sparse. Quintana Roo became a Mexican territory in 1902 and a state in 1974.
See also: Mexico.

Quintilian (Marcus Fabius Quintilianus; A.D. 35?-95?), Roman rhetoric teacher, whose fa

Q

mous 12-volume *Institutio Oratoria*, covering rhetorical techniques, educational theory, literary criticism, and morality, deeply influenced Renaissance culture.

Quirinal Hill, one of the famous 7 hills of Rome. The hill was named for Quirinus, a mythological deity, and was the habitation of the Sabines. Many temples, gardens, and a public bath were built there.
See also: Sabines.

Quirinus, in Roman mythology, god responsible for the well-being and prosperity of the community. Believed by some to be either Mars in a different bodily form, or the divine incarnation of Romulus, Quirinus lost importance after about 200 B.C.
See also: Mythology.

Quisling, Vidkun Abraham Lauritz (1887-1945), Norwegian fascist leader who assisted the German invasion of Norway (1940) during World War II and was afterward appointed premier of Norway's puppet government (1942-1945) by Adolf Hitler. He was executed for treason. His name has come to mean 'traitor.' He had formed his own political party, the National Union, in 1936, and contacted German Nazi leaders.
See also: World War II.

Quito (pop. 1,4 million), capital and second largest city of Ecuador and oldest capital in South America. It is located just south of the equator at the foot of the Pichincha volcano, at an altitude of 9,350 ft (2,850 m). Seized from the Incas by a Spanish conquistador in 1534, it is famous for its Spanish colonial architecture.
See also: Ecuador.

Quixote, Don *See:* Don Quixote.

Qumran, village on the northwestern shore of the Dead Sea, on the West Bank of Jordan, near the caves where the Dead Sea Scrolls were found (1947). Built by Essenes (130-110 B.C.), it was destroyed by an earthquake (31 B.C.), rebuilt, and destroyed again by the Romans (A.D. 68).

Quoits, game similar to horseshoes in which 2 players alternately attempt to toss a ring (quoit) around a stake (hob or mott). The quoit is metal and has 1 rounded and 1 flat surface and weighs at least 3 lb (1.5kg). The distance between the hobs is 54 ft (16 m). Points are scored by circling or touching the hob. A game is 21 points.

Quorum, minimum number of members who must be present before an organization can legally transact business. This number, or proportion, varies with the constitution or by-laws of the organization concerned; legislative bodies usually cannot pass laws unless a majority of their members is present (but all are not necessarily voting).

Qur'an *See:* Koran.

R, 18th letter of the English alphabet, corresponding to the Semitic letter *resh*, meaning 'head,' and represented by a sign based on an ancient Egyptian picture symbol for a human head. R is *rho* in the Greek alphabet and the 17th letter of the Roman alphabet. The present form of the capital R comes from classical Latin, the small r from Carolingian script.

Ra *See:* Re.

Rabat (pop. 1.5 million), capital city of Morocco, in the north, on the Atlantic Ocean. Dating from the Phoenician civilization, the city was founded in the 12th century and presently is a governmental center. Industries include textile, brick, and cement production.
See also: Morocco.

Rabbi (Hebrew, 'my master' or 'my teacher'), leader of a Jewish religious congregation with the role of spiritual leader, scholar, teacher, and interpreter of Jewish law. The term originated in Palestine, meaning merely religious teacher, after the return from exile and destruction of the hereditary priesthood (1st century A.D.).
See also: Judaism.

Rabbit, herbivorous lagomorph (gnawing) mammal (family Leporidae), usually with long ears and a white scut for a tail. Best known is the European rabbit (*Oryctolagus cuniculus*), which lives in discrete social groups in colonial burrows. Territory is de-

fended by all members of the group, and within the group there is distinct dominance ranking. It attains maturity at three months and can breed every month thereafter.

Rabbit fever *See:* Tularemia.

Rabelais, François (1492?-1553), French monk, doctor, and humanist author. With his *Gargantua and Pantagruel* (five books, 1532-1562), an exuberant mixture of popular anecdote, bawdiness, and erudition, Rabelais created a comic masterpiece that is also an important social vehicle for exploring the important issues of society: education, law, philosophy, and religion. It is considered one of the great masterpieces of world literature.
See also: Humanism.

Rabi, Isidor Isaac (1898-1988), U.S. physicist whose discovery of new ways of measuring the magnetic properties of atoms and molecules paved the way for the development of the maser and the atomic clock. His work earned him the 1944 Nobel Prize in physics.
See also: Maser; Physics.

Rabies, or hydrophobia, acute infectious disease of mammals, characterized by irritation of the central nervous system, followed by paralysis and death. The cause is a virus often present in the saliva of rabid animals. These animals transmit the infection by biting animals or humans. In humans, the incubation period varies from 10 days to over a year. The disease commonly begins with a short period of mental depression, restlessness, malaise, and fever. Restlessness increases to uncontrollable excitement, with excessive salivation and painful spasms of the laryngeal and pharyngeal muscles. As a result, the person cannot drink (hence hydrophobia: fear of water). Rabies rarely occurs in humans if proper treatment (vaccination) is carried out immediately after exposure.
See also: Pasteur, Louis.

Rabin, Yitzhak (1922-1995), late prime minister of Israel (1974-1977, 1992-1995) and Israeli military leader. Rabin, after distinguished service in and after World War II, commanded Israel's defense forces from 1964-1967, including the Six-Day War. He served as ambassador to the United States (1968-1973), as minister of labor (1974), and as minister of defense (1984-1990). During his second office as premier he successfully negotiated with the PLO on peace measures in the occupied territories. For their efforts Arafat, Peres, and Rabin won the Nobel Peace Prize in 1994. Rabin was killed in 1995 by an extreme right-wing Israeli.
See also: Israel.

Rabinowitz, Soloman *See:* Sholem Aleichem.

Raccoon, stout, bearlike, nocturnal mammal (genus *Procyon*), with a distinctive black mask and five to eight black bands on the bushy tail. Raccoons are found in North and South America. They live in trees, alone or in small family groups, descending at night to forage for crayfish, frogs, and fish in shallow pools.

Cottontail rabbits are named for their white tails, which resemble balls of cotton. The eastern cottontail rabbit (*S. floridanus*) has the widest distribution, ranging from southern Canada to the northern tip of South America. All domestic rabbits are descended from the Old World rabbit (*O. cuniculus*).

Raceme, type of flower cluster characterized by multiple flowers with separate short stems ranging along a common stalk (or peduncle). Racemous flowers multiply along the main stalk as it grows.

Racer, any of several species (family Colubridae) of swift North American snakes. Racers are broad-headed, varied in color, and measure from 3 1/2 ft (107 cm) to 6 ft (1.8 m) in length.

Races, human, subdivisions of the species *homo sapiens*. The concept of race provides distinctions that are useful in the scientific study of the human species, its dissemination and adaptation to various environments and conditions throughout the world. It can also provide useful clues and insights for historians and cultural anthropologists into a people's development. Like Darwin's theory of evolution, the concept of race has a history outside of science, in social and political thought and mass psychology. Racism is any ideology which assigns superiority to one group of people and inherent inferiority to others on the basis of certain physical characteristics. Both the scientific concept of race and the ideology of racism have histories.

In the West, by late medieval and modern times, all human beings were considered divisible into people of white, black, or yellow skin. A fundamental distinction was observed among humans based upon a leading physical characteristic. By the 19th century, this elementary classification was filled in with more study and research and the three basic races were held to be Caucasoid, Negroid, and Mongoloid. These distinctions were based upon observed physical differences characteristic of each group or race, including skin color, hair, stature, body proportions, skull shape, and facial features. Advances in science have significantly changed the content of the term *race*. It was discovered that the groupings are more than three and the traits that distinguish peoples are more mutable, or changeable, and more subtle than was formerly known. For example, the study of blood types has revealed not only significant differences among Europeans, Asians, and Africans, but within the group that was classified Negroid, there are significant differences among Australian Aborigines, Micronesians, and Negritos of the Philippines.

Most anthropologists now understand races as geographical and local groups and identify nine instead of three. The nine in the current classification are African, American Indian, Asian, Australian, European, Indian, Melanesian, Micronesian, and Polynesian. The geographical groups are defined by major blood types and genetic groups whereas local races are defined by more restricted gene pools. Examples of local races in Europe are the Basques and Lapps.

Human races develop as a result of evolution and in response to the environment. In addition to the obvious inherited differences, such as melanin or inner eyefolds, modern science has discovered the importance of blood types. In some races, certain blood types are dominant, and certain races are susceptible to particular blood disorders.

Africans, for instance, may succumb to sickle cell anemia. But scientists have determined that the same trait in the blood responsible for the anemia also makes Africans relatively immune to malaria, suggesting an inherited trait formed by natural selection and conditioned by a specific environment. Human races are understood as less static and more in flux not only as the result of natural selection, gene mutation, and changes in which genes dominate in a group's gene pool, but also as the result of war, migrations, and intermarriage. Rather than providing any evidence for the notion of superior and inferior groups, scientific study indicates the basis for physical differences among humans and studies the remarkably wide and varied adaptations of a single highly successful species.

Ideologies of race, though they claim to be scientific, are not, but they remain potent. Though not unique to the West, ideologies of race have claimed scientific authority in the West beginning with the theories of Joseph Arthur Gobineau in the 19th century and later with Huston Stewart Chamberlain, the anti-Semitism of Nazis, and theories of the inherent racial inferiority of blacks. At bottom, all these theories of race advance the same propositions: that certain peoples are inherently superior and certain others inherently inferior, and that these qualities of superiority or inferiority are inherited, characteristic of an entire group and each of its individual members, and readily identifiable by certain physical traits. Growing and flourishing side by side with advances in modern science and claiming to be grounded in science, theories of race persist in spite of the fact that there is no scientific basis for their claims.
See also: Racism.

Rachel, in the Old Testament, daughter of Laban, wife of Jacob, and mother of Joseph and Benjamin. Rachel was one of the four Jewish matriarchs.
See also: Bible; Old Testament.

Rachmaninoff, Sergei Vassilievich (1873-1943), Russian composer and virtuoso pianist. After a successful career in Russia he left in 1917, settling in Switzerland (until 1935) and then the United States. His extensive output of piano music, symphonies, songs, and choral music incudes such popular works as *Prelude in C Sharp Minor* (1892) and *Second Piano Concerto* (1901).

Racial segregation *See:* Segregation.

Racine, Jean (1639-1699), French tragic dramatist. After a Jansenist education at Port Royal schools, he surpassed his rival Pierre Corneille with seven tragedies, from *Andromaque* (1667) and *Britannicus* (1669) to *Phèdre* (1677), possibly his masterpiece. His greatness lies in the beauty of his verse, expressing both powerful and subtle emotions, and the creation of tragic suspense in a classically restrained form. Racine's work are the epitome of French classical theater.

Racing, contest of speed in both individual and team competition, popular throughout history. The ancient Greek Olympics (700s B.C.) featured only a foot race. The

marathon, a race of 26 mi 385 yds (42.2 km), is a test of both speed and endurance. Among the many types of races, which can involve machine operation or animals, are swimming, skiing, walking, roller skating, motorboat racing, and dog racing.
See also: Automobile racing; Track and field; Horse Racing.

Racism, belief that some races are inherently superior to others. Racism in the early 19th century was an offshoot of nationalism, placing emphasis on the differences among cultures. Also, the study of human types revealed some physical differences among the races. Despite the theories of Carolus Linnaeus and J.F. Blumenbach, that environment rather than heredity molded intellectual development, many associated culture with race, assuming white superiority. Guided by thinkers like Joseph Arthur Gobineau (1816-1882), the concept of 'tribal nationalism' began to appear. It was used to justify imperialism, the imposition of colonial status on less technologically accomplished peoples, and finally the concept of the 'master race' fostered by the Nazis. Horror at the mass exterminations before and during World War II, together with greater understanding through the social sciences, such as anthropology, discredited racism.
See also: Prejudice; Races, human; Segregation.

Rack, implement of torture made of a wooden structure with rollers at two ends. The rollers were wound, pulling the attached legs and arms of a victim from their joint sockets.

Rackham, Arthur (1867-1939), English artist best known for his fanciful, delicately colored illustrations for children's books, such as *Grimm's Fairy Tales* (1900), *Peter Pan* (1906), and *A Wonder Book* (1922).

Racquetball, fast-paced indoor court game played by 1-4 players with 18-in (45.7-cm) racquets and a hollow rubber ball. Played on a 4-sided handball court, racquetball basically follows the same rules as 4-wall handball.
See also: Handball.

Radar (*radio detection and ranging*), system that detects long-range objects and determines their positions by measuring the time taken for radio waves to travel to the objects, be reflected, and return. Radar is used for navigation, air control, fire control, storm detection, in radar astronomy, and for catching speeding drivers. It developed out of experiments in the 1920s that were measuring the distance to the ionosphere by radio pulses. R.A. Watson-Watt showed that the technique could be applied to detecting aircraft, and from 1935 Britain installed a series of radar stations that were a major factor in winning the Battle of Britain in World War II. From 1940 the United Kingdom and the United States collaborated to develop radar. *Continuous-wave radar* transmits continuously and detects the signals received by their instantaneously different frequency. *Pulsed radar* has a highly directional antenna, alternately a transmitter or a receiver. As a transmitter, it scans the area sys-

R

R

Some anthropologists have subdivided the human species into population groups, largely on the basis of their geographic region. These groups may include the (1) Northwest European; (2) Northeast European; (3) Alpine; (4) Mediterranean; (5) Hindu; (6) Turkic; (7) Tibetan; (8) North Chinese; (9) Mongoloid; (10) Eskimo; (11) Southeast Asiatic; (12) Ainu of northern Japan; (13) Lapp of northern Scandinavia; (14) North American Indian; (15) Central American Indian; (16) South American Indian; (17) Fuegian of southern South America; (18) East African; (19) Sudanese; (20) Forest African; (21) Bantu; (22) San (Bushman) and Khoikoi (Hottentot); (23) African Pygmy; (24) Dravidian of southern India; (25) Pacific Negrito; (26) Melanesian Papuan; (27) Murrayian Australian; (28) Carpenterian Australian; (29) Micronesian; (30) Polynesian; (31) Neo-Hawaiian; (32) Ladino of Central and South America; (33) American Black; and (34) Cape Coloured of South Africa. Various classification schemes based upon arbitrarily selected visible traits have distinguished from 3 to more than 200 geographical 'races'. The minimal biological significance of such visible traits, as well as problems of classification and definition, have however, led a growing number of scientists to question the value of human racial categories.

Radar was first developed for military use and became prominent during the Second World War. Its use and efficiency have improved so greatly, that nowadays it is an almost indispensable tool in warfare, as well as in many civilian applications, such as meteorology, naviga- tion, air traffic control and surveillance.
(A) German radar equipment, put into service in 1942
(B) ship with missile tracking radars
(C) a radar, protected against adverse weather conditions by a rigid ray dome
(D) a surveillance radar of the ballistic missile early warning system

tematically or tracks an object, emitting pulses, typically 400 per second. As a receiver, the antenna amplifies and converts echo pulses to a video signal that is displayed on a cathode-ray tube. The time-lag between transmission and reception is represented by the position of the pulse on the screen. Various display modes are used: commonest is the plan-position indicator (PPI), showing horizontal position in polar coordinates.

Radcliffe, Ann (1764-1823), English novelist remembered for her Gothic novels, notably *The Mysteries of Udolpho* (1794) and *The Italian* (1797).

Radcliffe-Brown, A(lfred) R(eginald) (1881-1955), British anthropologist and author of studies of kinship and social organization. His *Andaman Islanders* (1922; rev. 1948) was a pioneering work.
See also: Anthropology.

Radcliffe College, private liberal arts college affiliated with Harvard University, in Cambridge, Mass. Established in 1879 for women undergraduate students, Radcliffe maintains its own board of trustees while sharing faculty and facilities with Harvard.

Radhakrishnan, Sarvepalli (1888-1975), an Indian philosopher and statesman. He was the foremost interpreter to the Western world of Hindu religion and philosophy. He held that the contemplative intuition of the East was as important a means of discovering truth as the rationalism of the West. Radhakrishnan graduated from Madras Christian College in 1909. He taught at Calcutta University and other institutions, including Oxford. He was knighted in 1931. Radhakrishnan was India's ambassador to the Soviet Union, 1949-1952, and then served as vice president of India, 1952-1962, and president, 1962-1967.

Radian, in geometry, metric unit for measuring angles, used to simplify calculations. The radian measure of an angle is the ratio a/r; a being the length of the arc intercepted by the given angle; and r being the radius of the circle. An angle of approx. 57.3 (or 360° divided by 2 pi) = 1 radian.
See also: Angles.

Radiant energy *See:* Star; Sun.

Radiation, emission and propagation of energy through space or through a material medium in the form of waves. The term may be extended to include streams of subatomic particles-alpha-rays or beta-rays-and cosmic rays. In the case of electromagnetic radiation (light), energy is transmitted in bundles (photons). Acoustic radiation is made up of sound waves.
See also: Radioactivity.

Radiation belt *See:* Van Allen belts.

Radiation detector *See:* Geiger counter.

Radiation sickness, malaise, nausea, loss of appetite, and vomiting occurring several hours after exposure to ionizing radiation in large doses. This occurs as an industrial or a war hazard or more commonly following radiation therapy for cancer, lymphoma, or leukemia. Large doses of radiation may cause bone marrow depression, or gastrointestinal disturbance. Skin erythema and ulceration, lung fibrosis, nephritis, and premature arteriosclerosis may follow radiation, and there is a risk of malignancy.
See also: Fallout.

Radiator, device in which steam or hot water circulates and gives off heat. Through a process called convection, hot air expands and rises as surrounding cooler air is drawn in. This constant circulation of air can take place within the radiator tubing in convector radiators; radiators also heat air via direct radiation. Radiators are found in homes, offices and stores, as well as in automobiles and other engine-powered vehicles.

Radical, atom or group of atoms having an unpaired electron. Most radicals combine with other atoms to form compounds or ions, although free radicals, those remaining unbound to others, may exist briefly.
See also: Atom.

Radicalism, political philosophy whose purpose is to root out economic, political, and social injustices. Radicals may support different causes in different societies at different times. An English radical reform movement in the 18th to 19th centuries called Radicalism or Utilitarianism supported suffrage and greater democracy. In the 20th century, prodemocracy movements in Communist countries and procommunist movements under noncommunist governments are referred to as groups based on radicalism. Official radical political parties exist in some countries, but not the United States.

Radio, communication of information between distant points using electromagnetic radiation (radio waves). Radio waves are often described in terms of their frequency, which is measured in hertz (Hz) and found by dividing the velocity of the waves by their wavelength. Radio communications systems link transmitting stations with receiving stations. In a transmitting station a piezoelectric oscillator generates a steady radio-frequency (RF) 'carrier' wave, which is amplified and 'modulated' with a signal carrying the information to be communicated. The simplest method of modulation is to pulse (switch on and off) the carrier with a signal in, for example, Morse code. Speech and music enter the modulator as an audiofrequency (AF) signal from tape or a microphone, and can also interact with the carrier. The modulated RF signal is then amplified to a high power and radiated from an antenna. At the receiving station, another antenna picks up a minute fraction of the energy radiated from the transmitter, together with some background noise. This RF signal

R

is amplified, and the original audio signal is recovered (demodulation, or detection). In point-to-point radio communications most stations can both transmit and receive messages, but in radio broadcasting a central transmitter broadcasts program sequences to a multitude of individual receivers. Because there are potentially so many users of radio communications, use of the RF portion of the electromagnetic spectrum is strictly controlled to prevent unwanted interference between signals having adjacent carrier frequencies. The International Telecommunication Union (ITU) and national agencies like the U.S. Federal Communications Commission (FCC) divide the RF spectrum into banks that they allocate to the various users.

Radio, amateur, hobby practiced throughout the world by enthusiasts ('hams') who communicate with one another on shortwave radio, by voice 'phone,' or by using international Morse code. In the United States, the various grades of license may be obtained by passing tests of progressively greater difficulty. Citizens' Band (CB) radio, a more informal kind of 'ham' radio, became popular in the United States in the late 1970s, with a vast network of amateur radio operators.

Radioactive fallout *See:* Fallout.

Radioactivity, spontaneous disintegration of unstable atomic nuclei, accompanied by the emission of alpha particles (weakly penetrating helium nuclei), beta rays (more penetrating streams of electrons), or gamma rays (electromagnetic radiation capable of penetrating up to 4 in/100 mm of lead). In 1896, Antoine Becquerel noticed the spontaneous emission of energy from uranium compounds (particularly pitchblende). The intensity of the effect depended on the amount of uranium present, suggesting that it involved individual atoms. The Curies discovered further radioactive substances such as thorium and radium; about 40 natural radioactive substances are now known. Their rates of decay are unaffected by chemical changes, pressure, temperature, or electromagnetic fields, and each nuclide (nucleus of a particular isotope) has a characteristic decay constant, or half-life (amount of time for half of a substance to decay). Rutherford

and F. Soddy suggested in 1902 that a radioactive nuclide decays to a further radioactive nuclide, a series of transformations that ends with the formation of a stable 'daughter' nucleus. A large number of induced radioactive nuclides have been formed by nuclear reactions taking place in accelerators or nuclear reactors.
See also: Radiation.

Radiocarbon, or Carbon 14, naturally occurring radioactive isotope of carbon. With an atomic weight of 14, it is heavier than ordinary carbon, which has an atomic weight of 12. Radiocarbon is produced when cosmic rays disturb nitrogen atoms in the upper atmosphere, causing them to gain a neutron and lose a proton. Radiocarbon, found in 1.1% of CO_2 (carbon dioxide) molecules, is absorbed by plants in CO_2 gas and passed on to animals and humans. Radiocarbon dating, developed in the 1940s by U.S. chemist Willard F. Libby, can calculate the age of organic matter to about 50,000 years, by comparing its remaining amount of radiocarbon to that in a contemporary radiocarbon sample. Radiocarbon breaks down by releasing particles over a period measured by the half-life (the time it takes half the isotope to decay)-5,700 years. Counting radiocarbon involves burning a portion of it to release the CO_2 gas; today a particle accelerator and a magnetic field are used to separate out the carbon 14 atoms. Artificially produced radiocarbon is used medically as a 'tracer' to study biological functions. The artificial isotope was first produced (1939) in the United States by chemists Martin D. Kamen and S. Ruben.

Radiochemistry, use of radioisotopes in chemistry, especially in studies involving chemical analysis. Tracer techniques, in which a particular atom in a molecule is 'labeled' by replacement with a radioisotope, are used to study reaction rates and mechanisms.

Radio Free Europe/Radio Liberty (RFE/RL), radio broadcasting networks based in Munich, Germany. It was originated in 1950 to broadcast political, social, and cultural information to people in Communist nations of Central Europe. Privately owned and run, it is supported by the U.S. government.

The radio-telescope at Green Bank (U.S.), with its 295 ft (90 m) mirror, is one of the largest movable radio telescopes in the world. The instrument is only adjustable in height. The rotation of the earth ensures permanent scanning: one small region of the sky after the other. Thus, the individual radio sources are only observable for a short time. On the other hand, this type of telescope costs considerably less than a movable telescope.

Radiogeology, branch of geology in which scientists measure radioactive elements in rocks, fossils, and other geological specimens to determine their age. The measurement that enables this determination is called half-life-the time it takes one-half of the atoms of a radioactive isotope to decompose and form a different isotope. Radioactivity, found in all living things, is caused by uranium and thorium and their decay products: radioactive potassium, samarium and rubidium, and raciocarbon.

Radioisotope *See:* Isotope; Radioactivity; Radiochemistry.

Radiology, in medicine, diagnosis and treatment through the use of radioactivity, gamma rays, and X-rays.

Radiosonde, meteorological instrument package attached to a small balloon capable of reaching the earth's upper atmosphere. The instruments measure the temperature, pressure, and humidity of the atmosphere at various altitudes, the data being relayed back to earth via a radio transmitter.

Radio telescope, basic instrument of radio astronomy. The receiving part of the equipment consists of a large dish that operates on the same principle as the parabolic mirror of a reflecting telescope. The signals that it receives are amplified and examined. It is possible to build radio telescopes far larger than any possible dish by using several connected dishes; this is known as an array.
See also: Jansky, Karl Guthe; Lovell, Sir Bernard.

Radio waves *See:* Electromagnetic waves; Radio.

Radish, herb (*Raphanus sativus*), relative of mustard whose edible root looks like a small white to red turnip and has a burning flavor. A native of Europe, it was introduced as a garden plant but has become a weed. Radishes are eaten raw but the related *horse-*

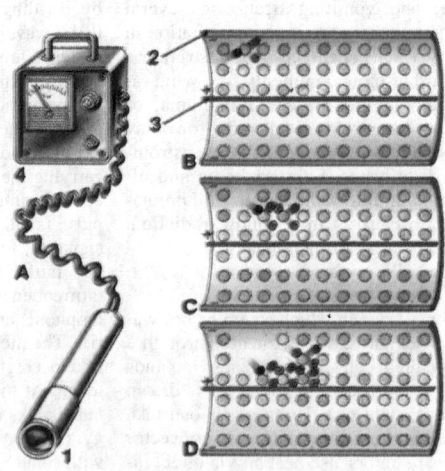

A Geiger Müller counter detects radioactive particles with a tube (A) containing a negatively charged cylinder (1), neon gas (grey dots), and a positively charged wire (2). A particle (3, black) entering the tube, knocks out a (negative) electron (blue) from a neon atom and forms a positive ion (red). (C) These collide with other atoms. (D) Electrons collect on the wire. A meter (4) records them as a pulse of current.

radish, not a true radish, is ground up and served as a condiment.

Radium, chemical element, symbol Ra; for physical constants see Periodic Table. Radium was discovered by Pierre and Marie Curie in 1898. It occurs in the minerals carnotite, uraninite, and pitchblende. Radium is produced by electrolysis of its chloride. Radium is a brilliant, white, radioactive, reactive metal. It is decomposed by water and turns black in air. It is a member of the alkaline-earth metals. Its salts color a flame carmine red. Radium is radioactive and emits alpha, beta, and gamma rays. The curie (Ci), a unit of radioactivity, is defined as the amount of radioactivity that has the same disintegration rate as 1 g of radium-226 (3.7×10^{10} disintegrations/second). Radium and its compounds are used in medicine, neutron sources, and self-luminous paints. Radium is a source of the element radon.

Radon, chemical element, symbol Rn; for physical constants see Periodic Table. Radon was discovered by Friedrich E. Dorn in 1900. Radon is present in the air to the extent of one part in 10^{21} and occurs in some spring waters, such as those at Hot Springs, Ark. Radon is a colorless, odorless, and chemically inert gas. It is a radioactive byproduct of the alpha-decay of radium, thorium, and actinium and is a member of the noble, or inert, gases. It is the heaviest known gas. It has been reported that fluorine reacts with radon to form radon fluoride. Radon is a radiation hazard, and remedial action is recommended for homes where the activity is greater than 4 picocuries/liter.

Raeburn, Sir Henry (1756-1823), Scottish painter. He was a lesser known portraitist than his famous English contemporary, Sir Joshua Reynolds. He painted directly on canvas with strong brush strokes and without the assistance of preliminary sketch marks. These portraits, mostly of well-to-do Scots, also were painted so that light and color produced dramatic effects.

Raffia, Asian palm (*Raphia ruffia*) whose long, tough leaf fibers are used for making baskets and tying up plants.

Raffles, Sir Stamford (1781-1826), British colonial administrator who refounded the ruined city of Singapore (1819). He persuaded the British government to seize Java, which he governed from 1811 to 1815. His career was marked by his liberalism, especially in his opposition to slavery.
See also: Singapore.

Rafflesia, genus of parasitic Indonesian plants with the largest flower in the world, up to 1 yd (0.9 m) across. The flower lacks petals but bears broad fleshy sepals. It smells of decaying meat, which attracts flies to pollinate it. It is named for Sir Thomas Raffles, the founder of Singapore.

Rafsanjani, Ali Akbar Hashemi (1934-), Iranian politician. Rafsanjani, who was arrested several times during the rule of the shah, was one of the confidants of ayatollah

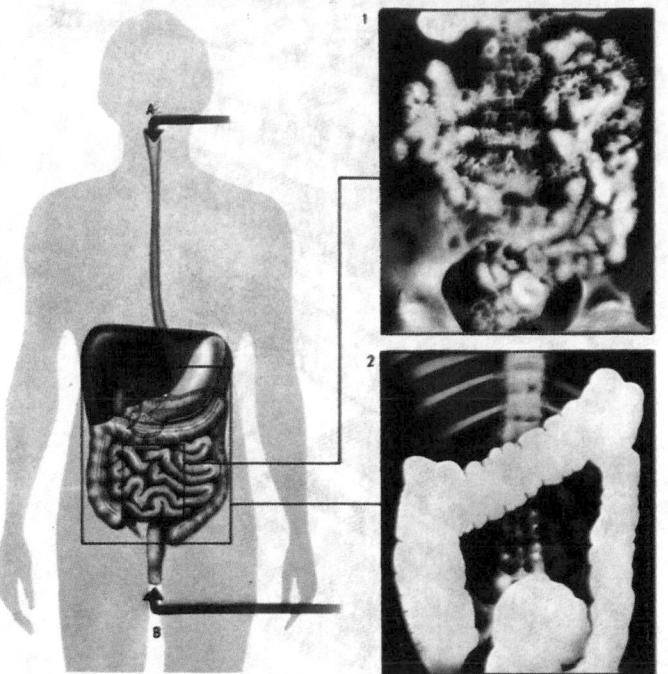

X-rays are a form of radiated energy—like light rays and sound waves are—but they have very short wave lengths and they are able to penetrate soft body tissues. Internal organs such as the digestive system and kidneys, can be made opaque to X-rays, by filling them with radiopaque fluids. Thus, they will appear as white areas on X-ray-sensitive film. In order to make an X-ray picture of the organs of the digestive tract, barium sulphate is either swallowed (A) or introduced into the rectum (barium enema) (B). This thick, paste-like fluid is radio-paque, completely harmless and cannot be absorbed by the intestines. Because the progress of this 'meal' through the tract can be easily traced, ulcers and structural defects in the organs can be detected. Here, we see X-rays of the small intestine (1) and the large intestine (2).

Khomeini. He was one of the leading characters within the Islamic Republican Party (founded after the revolution of 1979) and became chairman of the parliament in 1980. After Khomeini's death (1989) Rafsanjani was elected president as well as prime minister of Iran by a large majority; in 1993 he was reelected. The policies of Rafsanjani were aimed at the liberalization of the domestic economy and the improvement of relations with the West. He met with much opposition from radical spiritual leaders, who wanted to keep the country pure of Western influences. Because of this, Rafsanjani's position of power was undermined. In 1997 he was succeeded by Muhammad Khatami.

Raft, simple platform, usually square or rectangular, that floats on water. One of the earliest forms of water travel, rafts originally were made from logs, reeds, or animals skins tied with vines. Today they are often constructed from synthetic materials that are inflated for buoyancy. Rafts travel on water currents, often aided by the use of poles, paddles or sails; they have been used as a means to cross wide rivers, such as the Mississippi. Adventurers, including Thor Heyerdahl of Norway (1947) and William Willis of the United States (1963-1964) have successfully crossed oceans on simple rafts.

Rafting, water recreation that gained popularity in the 1960s. On inflatable rafts, usually 12-16 ft (3.7-5 m) long, people travel the rapid currents, or white water, of rivers. A 6-person crew guides the raft with paddles as the passengers enjoy the ride and scenery. The Colorado River, where it cuts through the Grand Canyon, is among the most popular rafting sites in the United States.

Ragtime, style of piano playing in which the left hand provides harmony and a firm beat, while the right hand plays the melody, usually syncopated. Famous exponents of the style, which was the immediate predecessor of jazz, are Scott Joplin and Jelly Roll Morton.
See also: Jazz.

Ragweed, or hogweed, composite weedy herb (genus *Ambrosia*) with inconspicuous flower heads. The giant ragweed, or buffaloweed, grows up to 18 ft (5.5 m) high. Ragweed pollen is an important cause of hay fever. Some ragweeds have tiny seeds, others have spiny burs that catch in hair and clothing.

Rahman, Mujibur (1920-1975), Bengali politician, champion of the independence of East Pakistan (the 'Bengal Tiger'). Mujibur Rahman won the elections with his Awami Liga (1970) and proclaimed an independent Bangladesh. He was imprisoned during the ensuing civil war. After independence he became the first prime minister of Bangladesh (1972-1975). Later he alienated himself from the people, proclaimed a state of emergency following riots (1974), and made the Liga into the only party allowed (National Party). He also became president (1975). He was killed during a coup d'état.

Rail, family of marsh birds, including gallinules, coots or mud hens, and rails proper. Protected by their camouflage coloring, rails eat seeds, grasses, worms, and insects. These extremely slender birds are often classified by their long or cone-shaped short bills. They lay their eggs in nests built on the ground or among grass in or near a marsh. Types of rails, found throughout the

Freight cars with varying functions are used by railroads around the world. Here, we see a flatcar (A), bearing storage containers used by Coras Lompair Eireann of Ireland; a car carrier (B) of French National Railways; a tank car (C) used by Austrian Federal Railway to haul liquid gas; box cars of Canadian Pacific (D) and Western Pacific (E) railways; a coal hopper car (F) of New Zealand Railways; an open gondola car (G) of Penn Central Railway; a grain hopper car (H) of South Australian Railway; a flatcar (I) of Finnish State Railway; a refrigerated car (J) of Italian State Railway; a cement car (K) used by British Rail; and a hopper car (L) of Indian Railways.

R

Modern hump yards, or switchyards, are automated and computerized for sorting and coupling freight trains. The yardmaster, in the tower, guides each car to the proper siding, by way of remote control.

world, include the water rail, land rail (corncrake), king rail, black rail, yellow rail, Virginia rail, sora rail, and clapper rail.

Railroad, land transportation system in which cars with flanged steel wheels run on tracks of two parallel steel rails. Railroads are economical in their use of energy because the rolling friction of wheel on rail is very low; however, costs of maintenance are high, so high traffic volume is needed. Costs, rising competition and overmanning led to the closure of many minor lines in the United States and Europe. Maintenance, sig-

naling, and many other functions are now highly automated.

Railroads developed out of the small mining tracks or tramways built in the United Kingdom and Europe from the mid-16th century. They used gravity or horse power, and the cars generally ran on flanged rails or plateways. The first public freight railroad was the Surrey Iron Railway (1801). The modern era of mechanized traction began with Richard Trevithick's steam locomotive *New Castle* (1804). The first public railroad to use locomotives and to carry passengers was the English Stockton and Darlington Railway (1825). The boom began when the Liverpool and Manchester Railway opened in 1830 using George Stephenson's *Rocket*, a much superior and more reliable locomotive. In the 1880s track gauges were standardized at 4 ft 8 1/2 in (1.435 m), allowing various lines to use one another's rails. After ever-increasing development in the 2nd half of the 19th century, railroads began to decline in the 1920s because of competition from other forms of transportation, such as air travel, trucking, and passenger cars. The sharp increases in oil prices in the early 1970s appeared to give railroads a new lease on life; however, railroads were limited mostly to commuter lines, rather than to hauling freight. In the United States the national Amtrak system survived with the aid of federal subsidies.

Railroad, electric *See:* Electric railroad.

Railroad, model, hobby in which a minia-

ture railroad system is developed. The model railroader, who often uses kits with to-scale (size proportionate to the original) parts, assembles and then operates the cars, tracks, signals, bridges, and other railroad equipment. Miniature towns accompanied by scenery are also developed. Carpentry, electrical skills, and imagination are involved in building and operating a model railroad. Demand for manufactured model railroad products in the United States arose after model railroads were exhibited at the Century of Progress Exposition in Chicago (1933-1934). The National Model Railroad Association was formed (1935) to create standards for model railroad materials.

Raimondi, Ruggero (1941-), Italian opera singer (bass). Raimondi studied in Milan and Rome on the recommendation of conductor Francesco Molinari Pradelli, and made his debut in 1964 in Spoleto. Shortly afterwards he was engaged by the Teatro La Fenice in Venice, after which he sang in La Scala for the first time in 1968. He also sang in New York, Paris and Berlin and is considered to be one of the leading contemporary singers.

Rain, water drops falling through the atmosphere, the liquid form of precipitation. Raindrops range in size up to 0.16 in (4 mm) in diameter; if they are smaller than 0.02 in (0.5 mm), the rain is called *drizzle*. The quantity of rainfall is measured by a *rain gauge*, an open-top vessel that collects the rain, calibrated in inches or millimeters and so giving a reading independent of the area on which the rain falls. Light rain is less than 0.1 in (2.5 mm) hr, moderate rain up to 0.3 in (7.6 mm) hr, and heavy rain more than 0.3 in/hr. Rain may result from the melting of falling snow or hail, but it is commonly formed by direct condensation. When a parcel of warm air rises, it expands, almost without loss of heat; thus its relative humidity rises until reaching saturation, water vapor begins to condense as droplets, forming clouds. These droplets coalesce into raindrops chiefly through turbulence and nucleation by ice particles (and also cloud seeding). Moist air may be lifted by convection, producing *convective rainfall*; by forced ascent of air as it crosses a mountain range, producing *orographic rainfall*; and by the force within cyclones, producing *cyclonic rainfall*.

Rainbow, arch of concentric spectrally-colored rings seen in the sky by an observer looking at rain, mist, or spray with his or her back to the sun. The colors are produced by sunlight's being refracted and internally reflected by spherical droplets of water. The primary rainbow, with red on the outside and violet inside, results from one total internal reflection. Sometimes a dimmer secondary rainbow with reversed colors is seen, arising from a second total internal reflection.

Rain forest *See:* Tropical rain forest.

Rain gauge, instrument that measures accumulated rainfall in a specific location during a particular period. The open vessel is calibrated to measure linear units. These devices vary in type: some collect the water in an inner tube marked with measurements, some empty and simultaneously record the amount of collected rainwater, some collect and weigh falling rain. Computer analysis is used to calculate the amount of rainfall.

Rainier III (Rainier Louis Henri Maxence Bertrand de Grimaldi; 1923-), prince of Monaco since 1949. He married the U.S. actress Grace Kelly (1929-1982) in 1956. *See also:* Monaco.

Rainmaking, method by which cloud precipitation is increased. Modern techniques of cloud seeding create conditions within clouds in which crystals, or water drops, become heavy and large enough to fall to earth as rain. Generators or airplanes inject the bottoms of clouds with substances called seeding agents-such as ammonium nitrate and urea, silver iodide crystals, or dry ice-to begin this crystalmaking process. Rainmaking can increase an area's water supply or reduce the intensity of an approach storm.

Rain tree, or monkeypod tree (*Pithecellobium saman*), shade tree found in tropical climates of the Americas. This short tree has branches that may span 100 ft (30 m) or more. Monkeys often eat its black seed pods. The rain tree has pink to white flowers, as well as a transparent fluid-rainlike in appearance-that drips from its branches.

Raisin, dried grape. Ripe grapes that are 20% sugar by weight are picked and then laid out in the sun to dry for 10-14 days on brown paper. Machines help stem, grade, rinse, and package the raisins. Raisins are mainly produced in California, Australia, Greece, Iran, and Turkey. A delicacy since ancient times, raisins are noted for their natural sugar content and various vitamins and minerals. Requiring no preservatives, they are eaten as is or used in cooking or baking. Thompson Seedless grapes are most commonly used; other types are Muscat of Alexandria, Black Corinth, and Sultana.

Raja, or Rajah (from Sanskrit *rjan*, 'king'),

Indian or Malay prince (extended to other men of rank during British rule). Higher-ranking princes were called *maharajas* (or *maharajahs*). A *raja's* wife is a *rani*.

Rajasthan (pop. 44,005,000), Indian state, bordering on Pakistan; 132,190 sq mi (342,239 sq km). Population consists of a large number of ethnic groupings. Capital: Jaipur. The southeast is the most fertile. Mainly agrarian: millet, rice, corn, cotton and largest wool producer in the country; irrigation agriculture is developing. Largest producer of lead and zinc ore, gypsum and silver. Extraction of gem stones. Industry is concentrated around the major cities and comprises agricultural industry, manufacturing of machines, chemical products, textile, cement and glass. Many Buddhist, Jainist and Mughal ruins worth seeing. Many Muslim and Hindu festivals. Important literary tradition. Three-quarters of the population is Hindu.

Rajneesh Chandra Mohan (Bhagwan Shree Rajneesh; 1931-1990), Indian spiritual leader, originating from Jainism. Lectured philosophy in several places. In 1974 he founded a center in Poona, where, as a guru, he initiated many people from the West as followers (sannyasin). Teachers applied a great number of Eastern religious techniques, mixed with psychotherapeutic ideas. Founded the Rajneeshpuram commune in Oregon (U.S.) in 1981. Was arrested in 1985 for breaking immigration laws and in connection with financial scandals. Went to India and discontinued the movement.

Rajputs (Sanskrit, 'kings' sons'), military and landowning caste mostly of the Rajasthan (now Rajputana) region, India. Their origins date back nearly 1,500 years. Although their influence in northern and central India has waxed and waned and at times has been considerable, since India's independence (1947) it has steadily declined.

Rake, tool with large teeth that gathers hay or leaves. As part of a tractor system, mod-

ern rakes gather large amounts of cut hay and place them in piles called windrows. Hand rakes with long handles are used to collect smaller amounts of material, usually lawn leaves. Rakes may also be used to break up top soil.

Rákóczy, Francis II (1676-1735), prince of Transylvania who led a Hungarian rising against the Habsburg Empire. Initially successful, he was elected prince (1704), but after several crushing defeats he left the country (1711) and died in exile in Turkey. *See also:* Transylvania.

Raleigh, or **Ralegh, Sir Walter** (1554?-1618), English adventurer and poet, a favorite of Queen Elizabeth I. His efforts to organize colonization of the New World resulted in the tragedy of the Lost Colony of Roanoke Island, Va. In 1589 he left court and consolidated his friendship with Sir Edmund Spenser, whose *Faerie Queene* was written partly under Raleigh's patronage. Returning, he distinguished himself in raids at Cadiz (1596) and the Azores (1597). James I imprisoned him for treason in the Tower of London (1603-1616), where he wrote poetry and his uncompleted *History of the World*. After two years' freedom, during which he made an unsuccessful expedition to the Orinoco River, he was executed in England under the original treason charge.

Ram *See:* Battering ram; Sheep.

Ramadan, the ninth month of the Islamic lunar calendar. Muslims believe that it was at this time when Allah (God) revealed the first part of the Koran to Mohammed. During Ramadan Muslims perform an act of worship known as *sawm,* a fast during daylight hours. (Food and drink can be consumed after sunset en before sunrise.) *Id al-Fitr* (Feast of the Fast Breaking) marks the end of Ramadan and typically is celebrated by attending religious services, visiting family and friends, and eating special foods.

Ramakrishna Paramahansa (1836-1886), Indian saint whose teachings, now carried all over the world by the Ramakrishna Mission (founded in Calcutta in 1897), emphasize the unity of all religions and place equal value on social service, worship, and meditation.

Raman, Sir Chandrasekhara Venkata (1888-1970), Indian physicist awarded the 1930 Nobel Prize in physics for his discovery of the *Raman effect*: When molecules are exposed to a beam of infrared radiation, light scattered by the molecules contains frequencies that differ from that of the beam by amounts characteristic of the molecules. This is the basis for Raman spectroscopy. *See also:* Physics.

Ramapithecus, prehistoric ape. Its remains were discovered in Pakistan (1932) by the U.S. anthropologist George E. Lewis. Named after a mythological Indian prince, Ramapithecus lived approximately 8 to 14 million years ago. Its remains have also been found in China, Kenya, Greece, and Hun-

A rainbow is created when rays of sunlight are bent by atmospheric water particles, acting as prisms. Each color within the ray of white light is refracted at a different angle, forming successively wider bands of color (A). Together, these bands produce a full spectrum (B). The spectra from many raindrops together combine to form a circular pattern, the rainbow (C). Only a short segment of the circle is visible to an earthbound observer. The position of this arc in the sky varies with the viewer's position, but its angular size is always the same (D). A cross section (E) shows that all bands of a given color refract in the same direction, relative to the source of light, the sun.

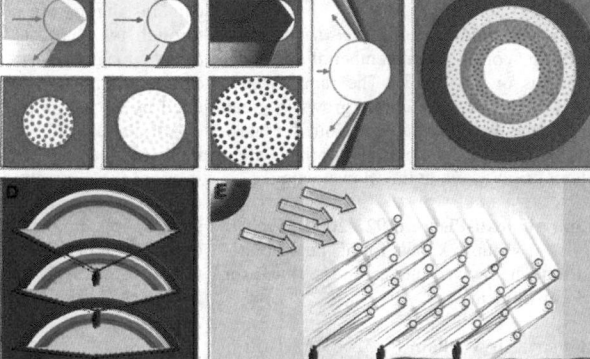

R

gary. In the late 1970s, scientists came to believe that Ramapithecus is most likely related to the orangutan rather than being a hominid, of the human family.
See also: Prehistoric people.

Rama Rao, Nandamuri Tarak (1923-1996), Indian movie star and politician. Rama Rao was one of India's biggest movie idols. He made over three hundred movies and was mainly beloved for his portrayal of Indian gods. In 1982 he became a politician. As leader of the Telugu Desam Party (TDP) he was prime minister of the state of Andhra Pradesh from 1983 until 1989. In 1994 he came into power again after a major electoral victory, but after nine months was deposed as prime minister of the state by his son-in-law, Chandrababu Naidu, during an coup d'état within his family. The funeral of the charismatic Rama Rao was attended by tens of thousands of people. Indian prime minister P.V. Narasimha Rao called him 'a champion of the people'.

Ramayana, major Hindu epic poem, composed in Sanskrit in about the 3rd century B.C., concerning the war waged by the legendary hero Rama against Ravana, the demon-king of Lanka. Helped by Hanuman, king of the monkeys, Rama eventually rescues his wife, Sita, abducted by Ravana, and slays the demon, enabling the righteous once more to live in peace.

Rambert, Marie (real name Miriam Ramberg; 1888 - 1982), Polish-British dancer and ballet pedagogue. Studied medicine in Paris. Was inspired to dance by Isadora Duncan. After being with the Ballets Russes she opened a ballet school in London (1920). Performed with her own company, 'Marie Rambert Dancers' (1926), which was called Ballet Rambert from 1931 onwards. Many well-known choreographers have been trained by her, including Frederick Ashton and Antony Tudor.

Ram (computer) (Random Access Memory), randomly accessible computer memory in which data can be filed and retrieved at any moment. This is only for temporary storage. The files are lost when the power is turned off.

Rameau, Jean Philippe (1683-1764), French composer and one of the founders of modern harmonic theory. He achieved recognition with his *Treatise on Harmony* (1722) and composed some 30 operas, among them *Hippolyte et Aricie* (1733) and *Castor et Pollux* (1737).

Rameses II *See:* Ramses II.

Ramie (*Boehmeria nivea*), perennial plant of the nettle family, grown for its fiber. Native to Asia, it is now also grown in Florida. Stalks grow from 3-7 ft (1-2 m) high and produce large leaves. When the plants are mature, the fiber is stripped from the stalks, washed to remove impurities, and dried. Ramie is one of the oldest sources of fiber and is ideal for the manufacture of canvas, ropes, and nets because its strength increases when it is wet.

Ramos, Fidel (1928-), Filipino soldier and politician; president from 1992 to 1998. Ramos, who received his military education in the U.S., rose quickly through the army ranks and was named chief of staff in 1986. He was a supporter of President Aquino, and was seen during her period of government as her chosen follower. Although a large part of the ruling LDP (Power of the Democratic Filipinos) did not back him, Ramos still won the elections in 1992. He made it clear that he intended to continue Aquino's policies (democratization, privatization), but when he tried to implement the intended liberalization of the economy he came up against much resistance from the Congress. His program to actively limit the birth rate was strongly condemned by the Roman Catholic Church and its members (1994). The position of Ramos was strengthened by the results of the parliamentary elections in May 1995, which resulted in a victory for the coalition between the Lakas/NUCD party he set up in 1992 and the LDP. Joseph Estrada succeeded him after the presidential elections of 1998.

Ramos, Graciliano (1892-1953), Brazilian writer. Only began to publish later on in life; some of his books are among the most important works in Brazilian literature. They are particularly noted for their sharp observation of the environment, psychological insight, and a sober yet effective style. In 1937 he moved to Rio de Janeiro, where he died on 20 March 1953. He wrote *Sao Bernardo* (1934), *Anguish* (1936), *Barren Lives* (1938), and *Childhood* (1945). Another impressive work about his prison experiences was published posthumously *Memórias do cárcere* (1953).

Ramos Horta, José (1949-), East Timorese fighter for an independent East Timor, which was annexed by Indonesia in 1975, and where resistance to the occupation has been bloodily beaten down ever since. Ramos Horta, who fled the country just before the Indonesian invasion, became the most important spokesperson of the resistance in exile. In 1996 he received the Nobel Prize for peace together with Bishop Carlos Ximenes Belo for their support to the East Timorese population in their struggle against systematic oppression by Indonesia. Unlike Belo, Ramos Horta does not preclude the use of violence to achieve his aims. He returned to East-Timor at the end of 1999. At a referendum in August that same year, a majority of the voters voted for independence.

Ramp, or wild leek (*Allium tricoccum*), wild plant considered a member of either the amaryllis or lily family. The ramp, which smells and tastes like onion, grows in great abundance in the Midwest United States. The leaves appear in early spring, after which green-to-white tiny flowers appear.

Rampal, Jean-Pierre (1922-2000), French flutist. A virtuoso known for his pure luxuriant tone, he revived interest in the flute as a solo instrument.

Ramsay, Sir William (1852-1916), British chemist awarded the 1904 Nobel Prize in chemistry for his discovery of helium, codiscovery (with Lord Rayleigh) of argon, and codiscovery (with Morris Travers) of krypton, neon, and xenon.
See also: Chemistry; Helium.

Ramses II (c.1304-1237 B.C.), called 'the Great,' Egyptian pharaoh, 4th king of the 19th dynasty, who built hundreds of temples and monuments, probably including Abu Simbel and the columned hall at Karnak. He campaigned against the Hittites, and celebrated a battle at Kadesh (1300 B.C.) on many of his monuments, but was eventually obliged to make peace (c.1283). His long reign marked a high point in Egyptian prosperity. He may have been the Pharaoh who allowed the Hebrews to leave Egypt, as told in Exodus in the Bible.

Ranching, breeding and raising usually of cattle or sheep on large tracts of land; in California also the name for farms smaller than 10 acres. Ranches, called stations in Australia, exist throughout the world. Land boundaries for U.S. ranches in the West were established in the mid 1800s. Cowboys (sometimes cowhands or cowpunchers), brand young animals with the farm insignia, oversee grazing cattle, and round up and lead animals in a cattle drive to market. Sheep ranchers harvest sheered wool from sheep as well as manage the herds. Today, in addition to horses, ranchers use trucks, jeeps, and sometimes helicopters to increase production.

Rand, Ayn (1905-1982), U.S. writer. Her 'objectivist' philosophy-individualistic, egoistic, and capitalist in inspiration-is at the core of such novels as *The Fountainhead* (1943) and *Atlas Shrugged* (1957). She also wrote nonfiction, including *For the New Intellectual* (1961) and *Capitalism, the Unknown Ideal* (1966).

Range, or stove, appliance that creates heat for cooking and area warming. U.S. cast iron ranges were first produced in the mid-1600s; Europeans developed ranges in the 15th century, while the Chinese invented them in the 8th century. Modern ranges provide individual cooking units on top, and one or more ovens within. They are fueled by gas or electricity; some ovens use microwaves.

Range finder, instrument used to ascertain the distance of an object from the observer. In *coincidence* range finders, used in many cameras, light from a distant object passes through two separate apertures, forming a double image that can be viewed through the eyepiece; a mirror in one aperture can be rotated by a knob until both images coincide exactly, and a calibrated scale on the knob indicates the distance of the object. In the *stereoscopic* range finder, which has mainly military uses, adjustment is made until a stereoscopic image produced by a special optical system coincides with the image of a reference mark; the range may then be read from a calibrated scale.
See also: Radar.

Rangoon *See:* Yangon.

Ranjit Singh (1780-1839), ruler of India who united many Sikhs in a great kingdom. As head of the Sikhs, a religious group of India that lives mainly in the northwest state of Punjab, he began his rule upon his father's death (1792). He conquered neighboring Indian states and overthrew Afghan control, gaining the title 'Lion of the Punjab.' Through treaties signed with British colonists, Ranjit kept the peace in India, although his efforts to unite all Sikhs were curtailed.
See also: India; Sikhism.

Rank, military, designation of position in the military service. Often called grade when associated with salary level and lower-level personnel, rank also refers to an officer's authority. In the U.S. titles for rank include the President as commander in chief, commissioned officers, and noncommissioned officers, which include warrant officers and enlisted personnel.

Rank, Otto (1884-1939), Austrian psychoanalyst and pupil of Sigmund Freud, best known for his suggestion that the trauma of birth is the basis of later anxiety neurosis and for applying psychoanalysis to artistic creativity.
See also: Psychoanalysis.

Ranke, Leopold von (1795-1886), German historian, one of the founders of modern historical research methodology. Professor of history at Berlin (1834-1871), Ranke insisted on objectivity and the importance of original documents.

Ransom, John Crowe (1888-1974), U.S. poet and proponent of the New Criticism, which emphasized textual, rather than social or moral, analysis. Professor of poetry at Kenyon College, Ohio (1937-1958), he founded and edited the *Kenyon Review* (1939-1959). His poetry includes *Chills and Fever* (1924).

Rape, crime of forced sexual intercourse without the consent of the subject, who may be male or female. Statutory rape refers to sexual intercourse with someone who is under the legal age of consent, is mentally defective, or does not comprehend the physical or other consequences of the act. In most societies of the world, rape is considered a serious crime. Rape crisis centers offer counseling for rape victims and encourage them to report the crime to the police. Some psychologists hold that rape is an antisocial act that is only peripherally sexual.
See also: Crime.

Rape, flowering plant in the mustard family. Rape is used for animal feed; its seed is used in the production of a cooking oil. This deep green plant, originally from Europe, has jagged leaves and clusters of tiny yellow flowers. The plant may grow up to 3 ft (91 cm) tall and may be an annual or biennial.

Raphael (Raffaello Santi or Sanzio; 1483-1520), Italian High Renaissance painter and architect. He was early influenced by Perugino, as in *Marriage of the Virgin* (1504). In Florence (1504-1508) he studied the work of Michelangelo and Leonardo da Vinci, being influenced especially by the latter, and painted his famous Madonnas. From 1508 he decorated the Vatican rooms for Julius II; the library frescoes, masterly portrayals of symbolic themes, use Raphael's new knowledge of classical art. His Sistine Chapel tapestries (1515-1516) and his sympathetic portraits were much imitated. Chief architect of the Vatican (from 1514), he worked at rebuilding Saint Peter's Basilica.
See also: Renaissance.

Rapid Deployment Force, special U.S. military unit trained to act quickly upon command. Called the RDF, the force was founded in 1980 particularly to protect U.S. interests in oil-rich regions of the Middle East. Headquartered in Tampa, Fla., the RDF has ships and personnel stationed on the Diego Garcia Island in the Indian Ocean. The island location helps this force move swiftly when necessary to areas around the globe.

Rare earth, name for the elements scandium and yttrium and the lanthanide series, Group IIIB of the Periodic Table, occurring throughout nature as monazite and other ores. They are separated by chromatography and ion-exchange resins. Rare earths are used in alloys, including misch metal, and their compounds (mixed or separately) are used as abrasives, for making glasses and ceramics, as 'getters,' as catalysts in the petroleum industry, and to make phosphors, lasers, and microwave devices.
See also: Berzelius, Jöns Jakob, Baron.

Ra's al Khaymah (pop. 305,000), one of the United Arab Emirates, on the Persian Gulf; 657 sq mi (1,700 sq km). Capital of the same name. Extensive agriculture: vegetables, dates, tobacco, fruit. Oil was only found in 1983. Signed treaty with Great Britain in 1820. After the British left in 1971 it lost the Tunb islands in the Gulf to Iran.

Rasmussen, Knud Johan Victor (1879-1933), Danish explorer and ethnologist. From Thule, Greenland, he undertook many expeditions to study Eskimo culture, including the longest dog-sled journey known, from Greenland to Alaska (1923-1924), described in his *Across Arctic America* (1927).
See also: Eskimo; Ethnography.

Raspberry, fruit-bearing bushes (genus *Rubus*), including some 200 species. European cultivated red-fruited varieties are derived from *B. idaeus*, while North American varieties, including a number that are black-fruited, are derived from three species.

Rasputin, Grigori Yefimovich (1872-1916), Russian mystic (the 'mad monk') who gained influence over the Tsarina Alexandra Fyodorovna after supposedly curing her son's hemophilia in 1905. The scandal of his debaucheries, as well as his interference in political affairs, contributed to the undermining of the imperial government in World War I. He was assassinated by a group of ultraconservatives.

Ras Tafari *See:* Rastafarians; Haile Selassie.

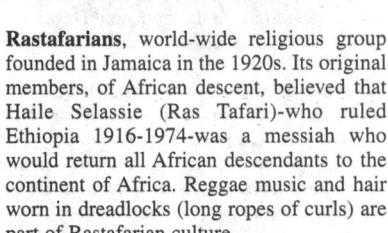

Bushy-tailed cloud rat (*Crateromys schadenbergi*, order *Rodentia*). Body length up to 14 in (36 cm), tail length up to 16 in (40 cm). Found in the Philippine Islands.

Rastafarians, world-wide religious group founded in Jamaica in the 1920s. Its original members, of African descent, believed that Haile Selassie (Ras Tafari)-who ruled Ethiopia 1916-1974-was a messiah who would return all African descendants to the continent of Africa. Reggae music and hair worn in dreadlocks (long ropes of curls) are part of Rastafarian culture.
See also: Haile Selassie.

Rat, name for numerous species of rodents belonging to many different families, largely Muridae and Cricetidae. The brown (*Rattus norvegicus*) and black (*R. rattus*) rats are familiar farmyard and warehouse pests. A strong exploratory urge and an ability to feed on almost anything make them persistent pests; in addition, they transmit a number of serious diseases, such as typhus and plague. Rats native to the New World include wood rats or pack rats, cotton rats, and the rice rats.

Ratchet, toothed wheel that operates with a catch, or *pawl*, so as to rotate in only one direction. Typically, the toothed ratchet wheel is rotated by a handle. The pawl is curved and pivoted so that it rests on or presses against the wheel teeth. When the wheel rotates in the permitted direction, the teeth can move beneath the pawl. As soon as the rotation ceases, the pawl engages one of the wheel teeth and prevents any motion backward. A release mechanism is usually incorporated to disengage the pawl when required. The escapement in clocks and watches is an example of a ratchet.

Ratel, or honey badger, carnivorous nocturnal African mammal (genus *Mellivora*) with

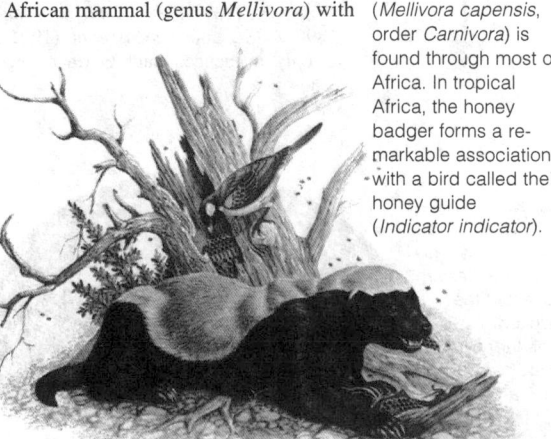

Honey badger or ratel (*Mellivora capensis*, order *Carnivora*) is found through most of Africa. In tropical Africa, the honey badger forms a remarkable association with a bird called the honey guide (*Indicator indicator*).

R

distinctive grayish back and black underparts. It has powerful legs and strong claws and eats almost anything, even pythons. Its fondness for honey has led to a close association with the honeyguide, a bird that directs it to bees' nests.

Rate of exchange *See:* Exchange rate.

Rationalism, philosophical doctrine that reality has a logical structure accessible to deductive reasoning and proof. Against empiricism, it holds that reason unsupported by sense experience is a source of knowledge not merely of concepts (as in mathematics and logic) but of the real world. Major rationalists in modern philosophy include Descartes, Spinoza, Leibniz, and Hegel. *See also:* Age of Reason.

Rationing, method by which distribution of food and other important products are controlled. Governments usually impose rationing policies in times of large demand and short supply, such as war or severe inflation. Rationing was used in the United States, among other countries, during World War II. Coupons or a point system are allocated to families to obtain rationed products. Rationed products bought outside of the rationing system are considered black market products.

Rattan, stems from any of 200 species of climbing palm of the genus *Calamus*, family Palmaceae. The stems are strong and pliant and are used to make furniture, baskets, canes, rope, and umbrellas. Rattan palms are native to the East Indies and Africa, and some are edible or have medicinal or veterinary uses. The stems may grow to 500 ft (150 m).

Rattlesnake, any of two genera (*Crotalus* and *Sistrurus*) of pit vipers of the Americas, referring to a rattle, composed of successive pieces of sloughed-off dead skin, at the end of the tail. Rattlers have moveable fangs that fold up into the roof of the mouth when not in use and are shed and replaced every three weeks. They are extremely venomous snakes, with the diamondback rattler being the largest and most dangerous.

Ratzel, Friedrich (1844-1904), German geographer. With works such as *Anthropogeography* (1882-1891), *Political Geography* (1897), *The History of Mankind* (1896-1898), and *Lebensraum* (1901), he strongly influenced later German geopolitics. *See also:* Geopolitics.

The timber, or prairie, or banded rattlesnake, *Crotalus horridus*, is found from the eastern coast of the United States (as far north as New Hampshire) to Kansas and Oklahoma.

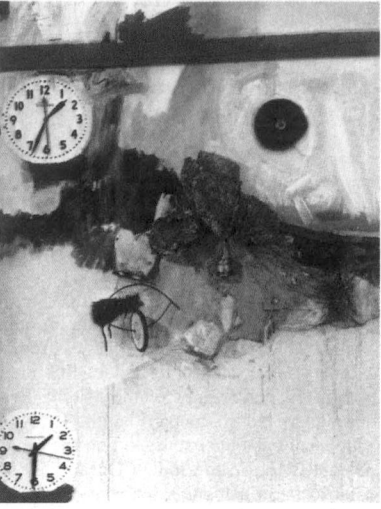

Robert Rauschenberg's *Reserve* (1961, National Gallery of Art, Washington), a so-called 'combine painting'.

Rauschenberg, Robert (1925-   ), U.S. artist, an initiator of the pop art of the 1960s. His 'combines' (collages) use brushwork along with objects from everyday life, such as pop bottles and news photos.

Rauwolfia serpentina *See:* Reserpine.

Ravel, Maurice (1875-1937), French composer, known for his adventurous harmonic style and the combination of delicacy and power in such orchestral works as *Rhapsodie Espagnole* (1908) and *Bolero* (1928), and the ballets *Daphnis and Chloé* (1912) and *La Valse* (1920). *Gaspard de la Nuit* (1908) is among his many masterpieces for the piano, his favorite instrument.

Raven, largest member of the crow family, with a wedge-shaped tail. The common raven (*Corvus corax*) is found in the United States and in the Old World, where it appears in many European legends as a prophet of doom. Ravens eat many things but are particularly fond of carrion.

Ravenna (pop. 136,000), city in northeastern region of Italy, famous for its superb mosaics, notably in the 5th-century mausoleum of Galla Placidia and 6th-century churches (notably San Vitale and Sant'Apollinare Nuovo). Emperor Honorius made Ravenna his capital; it was seized by Odoacer in 476 and was later seat of the Byzantine exarch. It was given to the Pope in the 8th century by the Carolingean King Pepin the Short. Papal control was lost and not regained until the 16th century. Modern Ravenna, an agricultural and manufacturing center, has a port and petrochemical plants. *See also:* Italy.

Rawalpindi (pop. 1,29 million), Pakistan, a city in Punjab province, about 180 miles (290 km) northwest of Lahore and 7 miles (11 km) southwest of Islamabad, the national capital. Rawalpindi is the commercial center for a productive agricultural region and has chemical, textile, and metalworking industries. An engineering complex at nearby Taxila produces machinery, foundry products, and electrical equipment. Strategically located on the main route to Kashmir, Rawalpindi has been an important military post since 1850. It was the nation's capital from 1959 until 1967.

Rawlinson, Sir Henry Creswicke (1810-1895), British soldier and archeologist who deciphered the cuneiform inscriptions of King Darius I of Persia. *See also:* Archeology.

Ray, any of a group of more than 400 species of flat-bodied marine fish (order Rajiformes) with a boneless skeleton made from a tough, elastic substance called cartilage. Rays resemble sharks in having gill slits, but under the pectoral fins. Most rays live on the sea floor and feed on smaller species. Rays eggs are fertilized and hatched inside the female. The largest rays are the mantas, which may grow to 22 ft (7 m) wide and weigh up to 3,000 lbs (1,360 kg).

Ray, John (1627-1705), English naturalist, who, with Francis Willughby (1635-1672), made important contributions to taxonomy, especially in *A General History of Plants* (1686-1704).

Ray, Man (1890-1976), U.S. abstract artist and photographer, a founder of the Dada movement. He recreated several 'lost' photographic techniques and produced surrealist films. *See also:* Dada.

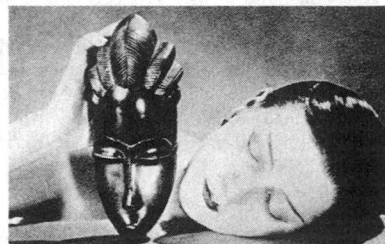

A portrait of Kiki de Montparnasse holding a mask (1926) by Man Ray (1890-1976). The similarities and contrasts between the dead mask and the living face make a fascinating photograph.

Ray, Satyajit (1921-1992), Indian film director. *Pather Panchali* (1954) was his acclaimed debut. His many other films include *Aparajito* (1956), *The Music Room* (1958), and *The World of Apu* (1959). He received an Oscar for his works.

Rayleigh, John William Strutt, 3rd Baron (1842-1919), English physicist awarded the 1904 Nobel Prize in physics for his measurements of the density of the atmosphere and its component gases, work that led to his isolation (with William Ramsay) of argon. *See also:* Atmosphere; Physics.

Rayon, synthetic cottonlike fiber with a sheen. Patented in 1884 by the French inventor, Hilaire Chardonnet, it was named rayon in 1924. Rayon is produced from cellulose fiber of wood pulp or cotton. Chemicals reduce the cellulose to a thick liquid, which is forced under pressure into a metal spinneret and emerges as filaments. The filaments are twisted into silky yarn or cut and spun. Spun rayon can be treated to simulate wool, linen, or cotton. The 3 main processes for making rayon are viscose, cuprammonium, and acetate.

Razor, sharp-edged instrument used to shave hair from the skin. Razors in crude forms, such as clam shells and flints, have been used since prehistoric times. They evolved into the 3 basic types in use today. Straight-edged razors (blades 3-4 in (8-10 cm) long encased in a safety handle) and safety razors (hoe-shaped with shorter blades and protected cutting surface) manually remove hair from a lathered surface. Electric razors, powered by motors, move a series of small, sharp blades over unlathered skin. Many electric razors are 'cordless,' able to operate on batteries.

RCMP *See:* Royal Canadian Mounted Police.

RDX, or Research Department Explosive ($C_3H_6O_6N_6$), powerful explosive used in bombs. Discovered by Hans Henning in Germany (1899), RDX was used extensively by the air forces of both sides in World War II. Known also as hexogen and cyclonite, it is a white, insoluble, crystalline solid. RDX is produced by the action of nitric acid on a product of formaldehyde and ammonia. Its chief nonmilitary use is in blasting caps, detonators, and fuses. RDX can also be mixed with trinitrotoluene (TNT) to form a more powerful explosive known as Composition B.
See also: Explosive.

Re, or Ra, in Egyptian mythology, the sun god. Worshipped as the creator of the entire earth, Re evolved into the chief deity of ancient Egypt. Many myths and legends came to be associated with Re; early pharaohs claimed to be descended from him. Re has appeared in Egyptian hieroglyphics as the sun, lion, cat, or bird, and is symbolized by a pyramid.
See also: Mythology.

Reaction, chemical *See:* Chemical reaction.

Reactor, nuclear *See:* Nuclear reactor.

Reading, process of assimilating language in the written form. Initial language development in children is largely as speech and has a primarily auditory or phonetic component; the recognition of written letters, words, and sentences represents a transition from the auditory to the visual mode. In reading, vision is linked with the system controlling eye movement, so that the page is scanned in an orderly fashion. Reading is represented in essentially the same areas of the brain as are concerned with speech, and disorders of the two often occur together. In dyslexia, pattern recognition is impaired, and a defect of reading and language development results.

Reagan, Ronald Wilson (1911-), American actor and politician, 40th president of the United States (1981-1989). Reagan began as a radio sports commentator (1932-1937) and played nice, friendly roles in 53 films between 1937 and 1966. He acted in many TV productions, and was chairman of the professional association for actors (1947-1952; 1959). In 1967 he became Republican governor of California (until 1974); in this period he built a reputation as a capable administrator. Reagan set his sights on the presidency as early as 1966 and nearly managed to beat Ford for the nomination in 1976. As the undisputed Republican candidate in 1980, he achieved a large victory over the incumbent President Carter. His extensive cutbacks on government expenditure ('the best government is the least government'), favorable tax measures for the wealthy, rearmament, and a more polarized policy with regard to the Soviet Union gave him increased popularity at home. This tendency was strengthened when he was hit by a bullet in an assassination attempt by the right-wing extremist J. W. Hinkley on 13 March 1981. In 1984 he was reelected, and in 1988 succeeded by fellow Republican George Bush. Reagan retired to his ranch in California.

Real estate, term used to describe land and that which is attached to it, including buildings, trees, and underground resources, such as minerals or water. Real estate is generally sold by plots of ground (parcels), which are surveyed, sized, and registered with the particular governing agency for that area. Real estate properties for sale can be listed with agencies and sold by brokers or realtors, but often the owners of the property sell it themselves.
See also: Property.

Realism, in art and literature, the faithful imitation of real life; more specifically, the artistic movement which started in France c.1850 in reaction to the idealized representations of romanticism and neoclassicism, with a social dimension derived from scientific progress and the revolutions of 1848. In France the leading painters were Jean-Baptiste Corot, Gustave Courbet, Honoré Daumier, Jean François Millet, and its main literary expression was in the novels of Honoré de Balzac, Gustave Flaubert, and Emile Zola. In the United States, Thomas Eakins, Winslow Homer, and members of the Ashcan School were realistic painters, and Stephen Crane, Theodore Dreiser, William Dean Howells, Henry James, and Frank Norris led the literary movement.

Reaper, machine for harvesting grain. The U.S. inventor Cyrus Hall McCormick's horse-drawn reaping machine (1831) consisted simply of a long knife, or cutter bar, a platform, and a rotating reel to bend the grain back against the knife and knock it onto the platform. The modern reaper, or self-binder, cuts the standing grain, binds it into sheaves with twine, and then ejects the sheaves onto the ground. Reapers are seldom used today for cutting grain, however; the harvesting of grain is done mostly with combine harvesters, machines that combine reaping and threshing.
See also: McCormick, Cyrus Hall.

Reasoning *See:* Logic.

Rebecca *See:* Isaac.

Recall *See:* Initiative, referendum, and recall.

Receiver, in law, person, bank, or trust company appointed by a court and paid a fee to take charge of a company or a person's assets, most frequently in cases of bankruptcy. The receiver maintains existing assets in good order, since creditors will ultimately have a claim on them and may also carry on the business, collecting money that is due, paying out salaries, and dealing with suppliers.
See also: Bankruptcy.

Recession, extended period of economic decline. During recessions, business activities such as buying, selling, and overall productivity decline, causing increases in unemployment and unpredictable fluctuations in stock markets. Until the 1970s, recessions caused prices to fall, but since then they have continued to increase despite several recessions. A sudden shortage of vital goods, such as oil and petroleum-based products, often triggers recessions and accompanying rising prices, which result in decreased consumer spending. A pattern is formed in which manufacturers decrease production to keep pace with reduced demands for their goods, and fewer workers are needed to produce those goods. Recessions are often worldwide; an extended period of recession could develop into a depression. Short-term recessions are called economic slumps.
See also: Business cycle; Depression.

Recife (pop. 1,350,000), capital of Pernambuco, state in northeastern Brazil. Located at the mouths of the Capibaribe and Berberibe

Gustave Gourbet's *The Artist's Studio* (1855), subtitled *A True Allegory Concerning Seven Years of My Artistic Life*, portrays the artist at work amid an inattentive assembly of undistinguished figures (left). A nude model replaces the traditional Muse, who may represent unadorned Nature or Truth. Courbet's emphasis on the familiar so offended accepted aesthtic precepts that he was forbidden to display his work at the Paris Exhibition of 1855 (Louvre, Paris).

R

R

rivers on the Atlantic Ocean, the city was settled by the Portuguese in 1535. The British held it briefly (1595), as did the Dutch (1630-1654). In 1710 Recife became a Brazilian town, and in 1823 a city. Part of Recife is on an island; because of many intersecting waterways, is often called the Brazilian Venice. Manufactured goods include textiles, ceramics, synthetic rubber, paper and leather products, and agricultural goods. Its port exports large quantities of bananas, sugar, coffee, and cotton. Recife is an educational center with 4 universities. *See also:* Brazil.

Reciprocal trade agreement, mutual tariff reduction pact enacted between 2 or more nations. Such agreements began in response to the trend toward protectionism that prevailed throughout most of the 19th century, in which steadily increasing tariffs on imported goods hampered international trade. Bilateral trade agreements were worked out in the early 20th century, when 2 nations consented to lower import duties on certain goods they exchanged. Such pacts were later expanded to include other nations. The United States passed the first Reciprocal Trade Agreements Act in 1934; in 1947, 23 countries ratified the General Agreement on Tariffs and Trade (GATT), which reduced tariffs on specified goods by rates believed to be beneficial to all the signatory nations. Today, reciprocal trade agreements are universal, although worldwide economic conditions are continually requiring changes in the nature of these agreements. Industrially developed nations have been encouraging developing countries through modified trade agreements. *See also:* Tariff.

Reclamation, Bureau of, agency of the Department of the Interior created to administer the Reclamation Act of 1902 for reclaiming arid land by irrigation in the 16 western states. Its responsibilities were later progressively expanded.

Reconquista, the reconquest of Spain from the Moors (Muslims), who conquered practically the whole Iberian peninsula between

The fall of Granada in 1492, meant the official end of the Reconquista (the recapture of Spain from the Moors). This renaissance wooden altarpiece by Felipe Vigarné (1498-1543) shows the entrance of *los reyes catholicos* (the catholic kings) Ferdinand and Isabella.

711 and 718. The Reconquista came out of a desire for expansion and a keenness to spread Christianity, and began in 1030 with the reconquest of a large part of Spain. Towards 1180 a second offensive was launched with the aim of driving the Moors completely out of Spain. The Reconquista was finally completed in 1492 when the last bastion of Islam, in Granada, fell into the hands of the Catholics. All Muslims and Jews were driven from Christian areas and Spain became a Catholic country with a Catholic king, a condition still reflected in the official title of the Spanish monarch.

Recorder, wind instrument related to the flute but held vertically, with a mouthpiece that channels the airstream and without keys. Relatively easy to play, soft and sweet in tone, it was most popular about 1600-1700 and is again popular today. There are soprano, alto, and (with some keys) tenor and bass recorders.

Recording industry, group of businesses that produce and sell sound recordings. The industry records primarily popular forms of music, as well as verbal communication such as speeches and seminars. The industry began with Thomas Edison's invention of the phonograph (1877), which pushed a sound-sensitive needle along the grooves of a cylinder to reproduce sound. The cylinder was replaced by flat disc-the phonograph record-in the early 1900s; this evolved into today's compact disc, which plays recorded sounds by means of a laser beam. Invention of magnetic recording tape in the 1940s enabled the development of cassette tapes. Most recordings today are done in studios.

Record player *See:* Phonograph.

Recreation, leisure activities that people enjoy. Recreation has become an important aspect of modern life that often relieves stress; many businesses and hospitals provide various forms of recreation for their workers and patients. These activities can be passive ones, such as reading or watching television or movies, or participatory forms ranging from hobbies and games to strenuous amateur sports. Donation of time by volunteers to help others is another form of recreation. Commercial recreation includes watching sporting, cultural, and other entertainment events, or active forms, such as tourism or visiting theme parks. State, national, and local agencies set aside scenic or historic lands for public recreational use, usually financed through taxes and user fees.

Recreational vehicle (RV), temporary living quarters on wheels, used for traveling or camping. Five basic types of RVs are in use today. Motor homes contain an engine and living quarters, which have conveniences such as running water and facilities for cooking, heating, and food-storage. This type includes vans adapted for overnight use. Travel trailers are not motorized and must be pulled by another vehicle, as must campers (camping trailers), which are smaller than these trailers. They have collapsible sides that can fold out to provide extra sleeping or storage space. Truck campers are

adapted to fit over the bed and cab of a pickup truck. Pickup covers enclose only the bed of a pickup truck.

Rectangle, 4-sided plane figure with sides that meet at 4 right-angles. Rectangles are classified as special cases of parallelograms, in that the opposite sides are parallel and of equal length, but all 4 sides are not necessarily equal. When they are equal, rectangles are called squares. The word is derived from the Latin *rectus angulus*, meaning *straight angles*.

Rectum *See:* Colon; Intestine.

Recycling, recovery and use of waste material. Paper, aluminum cans, and glass are the most commonly recycled materials and can be used to make insulation, new cans and glass containers, and material for road construction. As concern over the earth's environment increases, recycling has emerged as an effective method for cutting down on pollution and conserving important natural resources. It has also become an increasingly vital source of material for modern industry.

Red Baron *See:* War aces.

Redbreast *See:* Robin.

Redbud, flowering tree (genus *Cercis*) of the pea family, native to North America, southern Europe, and Asia. Redbuds display their pink blossoms in early spring before their heart-shaped leaves unfold. The flowers ripen into seed pods that wild game feed on. The reddish-brown trees grow as high as 40 feet (12 m) and thrive on fertile, sandy soil. Redbuds are sometimes called Judas trees because, according to legend, Judas Iscariot hanged himself from a redbud tree after betraying Jesus.

Red cedar *See:* Juniper.

Red Cloud (1822-1909), chief of the Oglala Sioux and leader of the Native American struggle against the opening of the Bozeman Trail. The trail was closed in 1868 following the Fetterman Massacre (1866).

Red Cross, international agency for the relief of victims of war or disaster. Its two aims are to alleviate suffering and to maintain a rigid neutrality so that it may cross national borders to reach those otherwise unaidable. An international committee founded by J.H. Dunant and four others from Geneva secured 12 nations' signatures to the first of the Geneva Conventions (1864) for the care of the wounded. Aid was given to both sides in the Danish-Prussian War the same year. During World Wars I and II the Red Cross helped prisoners of war, inspecting camps and sending food and clothing parcels; it investigated about 5 million missing persons and distributed $200 million in relief supplies to civilians. The International Red Cross won the Nobel Prize in 1917 and 1944. It works through the International Committee (1880), made up of 25 Swiss citizens. Over 100 national Red Cross societies (Red Crescent in Muslim countries) carry

out peacetime relief and public health work.
See also: Dunant, Jean Henri.

Red deer (*Cervus elaphus*), member of the deer family, native to Europe, Asia, and North Africa. They are named for the color of their coat, which is reddish-brown in summer, fading to grayish-brown in winter. The American elk is classified as a subspecies of red deer. Male red deer are called harts, standing 3.5-4.5 ft (1.-1.4 m) tall, weighing 250-350 lb (113-159 kg), and sporting multibranched antlers, which are shed each year. Female red deer, called hinds, are smaller than harts and do not have antlers.

Redding, Otis (1941-1967), American soul singer, generally considered to be one of the greatest talents responsible for creating the genre; he died far too young. First album, *These Arms of Mine* (1964), managed in subsequent years to win a large public, both black and white, with sensitive soul ballads, including *That's How Strong My Love Is* and *Pain in My Heart* (both later performed by the Rolling Stones). In 1967 America's 'singer of the year' Died the same year in an airplane accident. The posthumously released *The Dock of the Bay* soon became a worldwide hit.

Red drum *See:* Redfish.

Redfield, Robert (1897-1958), U.S. cultural anthropologist best known for his comparative studies of cultures, and for his active support of racial integration.
See also: Anthropology.

Redfish, name for several types of popular gamefish found off the Atlantic coasts of North America. Known as red drum, channel bass, California sheepshead, red (sockcyc) salmon, or by other names, the most popular types of redfish are found in the Gulf of Mexico and adjoining waterways. The gulf species are marked by a distinctive red spot near the base of the tail; they grow to 5 ft (1.5 m) long and usually weigh up to 40 lb (18 kg). Widespread restaurant demand for redfish in the late 1980s resulted in such large commercial catches that federal restrictions were imposed to protect the species.

Redford, Robert (1937-), U.S. actor and director, winner of the Academy Award for best director (1980) for *Ordinary People*. He made his film debut in *War Hunt* (1962), and his best-known roles include *Butch Cassidy and the Sundance Kid* (1969), *The Sting* (1973), *Out of Africa* (1985), and *Havana* (1990). Other films he directed include *The Milagro Beanfield War* (1988), *A River Runs Through It* (1993), *Quiz Show* (1994), *The Horse Whisperer* (1998), and *The Last Castle* (2002). He received an Honorary Academy Award for his outstanding performance as an actor, director, producer and founder of the Sundance Film Festival in 2002.

Red fox *See:* Fox.

Redgrave, Sir Michael (1908-1985), English actor. An accomplished Shakespearean performer, Redgrave was a noted stage director and appeared in many contemporary plays and more than 50 movies, including *The Lady Vanishes* (1938), *Dead of Night* (1946), *The Importance of Being Earnest* (1952), and *The Loneliness of the Long Distance Runner* (1962). Redgrave was knighted by Queen Elizabeth II in 1959. He was married to Rachel Kempson, a popular stage actress; their daughters, Vanessa and Lynn, became famous actresses in their own right.

Red gum *See:* Sweet gum.

Redmond, John Edward (1856-1918), Irish politician. He succeeded Charles Stewart Parnell as Irish nationalist leader in the British parliament and secured the passage of the 1914 Home Rule bill. After the repression of the 1916 Easter Rising, he lost power to the revolutionary Sinn Fein movement.
See also: Ireland; United Kingdom.

Redon, Odilon (1840-1916), French painter and engraver associated with the Symbolists. His oil paintings, usually of flowers and full of color and light, contrasted with bizarre lithographs such as *The Cyclops* (1898).

Red pepper *See:* Capsicum.

Redpoll, small bird (*Acanthis flammea*) of the finch family. Redpolls are commonly found in northern North America and migrate as far south as California and the Carolinas. Both males and females have reddish crowns; the male also has a rosy-pink breast. Adult redpolls feed on plant buds and insects. They build their nests in bushes and small trees and line them with feathers. Usually 5-7 blue speckled eggs are laid at a time.

Red River, river that rises in northern Texas and flows southeast to join the Mississippi River between Natchez and Baton Rouge, forming most of the Oklahoma-Texas boundary. Named for its red sediment, it drains about 90,000 sq mi (233,100 sq km) and is 1,222 mi (1,967 km) long.

Red River of the North, river formed at Wahpeton, N. Dak., by the junction of the Bois de Sioux and Otter Trail rivers. About 540 mi (866 km) long, it flows north as the North Dakota-Minnesota boundary and enters Manitoba, Canada, emptying into Lake Winnipeg. It drains some 43,500 sq mi (112,665 sq km) of rich wheatlands.

Red Sea, sea separating the Arabian Peninsula from the northeastern region of Africa. It extends some 1,300 mi (2,090 km) from the Bab al-Mandab strait by the Gulf of Aden in the south to the gulfs of Suez (with the Suez Canal) and Aqaba in the North. It is up to 250 mi (402 km) wide and up to 7,800 ft (2,377 m) deep.

Red shift, increase in wavelength of the light from an object (toward the red end of the visible spectrum), usually caused by its

The Cyclops (1898, Rijksmuseum Kröller-Müller, Otterloo) by painter Odilon Redon (1840-1916) shows a vague dreamworld, full of potential threat.

R

rapid recession. The spectra of distant galaxies show marked red shifts; this is usually, though far from always, interpreted as implying that they are rapidly receding from us.
See also: Quasar.

Red snapper *See:* Snapper.

Red Square *See:* Moscow.

Redstart, bird (*Setophaga ruticilla*) of the wood warbler family. Adult males have black plumage with brilliant orange-red or salmon-red streaks; females and young birds are brown and dull yellow. They are found throughout most of North America and in winter migrate to the Caribbean region and northern South America. Eggs, usually laid in groups of 4 or 5, are creamy white with reddish-brown markings. Redstarts' diets consist mostly of insects.

Red tape, expression used to describe inaction or delay caused by official or bureaucratic inefficiency, inflexibility, or complexity, so called for the red string once used by lawyers to bind legal documents. Scottish author Thomas Carlyle (1795-1881) made the term popular.

Red tide, natural phenomenon caused by a sudden increase of microscopic reddish organisms on the surface of a body of water. Under optimum conditions, one celled organisms called dinoflagellates multiply by the millions and float on rivers, lakes, oceans, and arms of the oceans. Most red tides are harmless, but some types kill large fish and marine life by poisoning the water or using up the available oxygen supply. Why the dinoflagellate population suddenly proliferates is not completely understood, but scientists theorize that a combination of factors such as temperature, amount of sunlight, water currents, and availability of nutrients create ideal conditions for spawning. Some sea creatures feed off large numbers of the dinoflagellate colonies or eat the food the colonies thrive on, thus decreasing or ending the red tide.

R

(A) The tendon jerk is the simplest reflex pathway, involving only a receptor (sensory, afferent) neurone (blue) and an effector (motor, efferent) neurone (red). It traverses only one synapse in the spinal cord, while all other reflexes are polysynaptic.
When the patellar tendon (1) is tapped sharply, the quadriceps muscle (2) will stretch, and receptors (muscle spindles, 3) are being activated. Messages are transmitted along the sensory neurones (blue), whose cell bodies (4) lie in the dorsal root ganglion.
(B) In the spinal cord

(5), motor neurones (red, 6) are activated and the messages are transmitted back to the motor endplates (7) in the same muscle, to cause its contraction. The arc crosses only one segment of the spinal cord. The knee jerk is completely automatic and independent of higher centres of the brain. It appears to have little functional significance, but is used clinically to indicate whether the muscle cord segment and relevant nerves are intact and working normally.

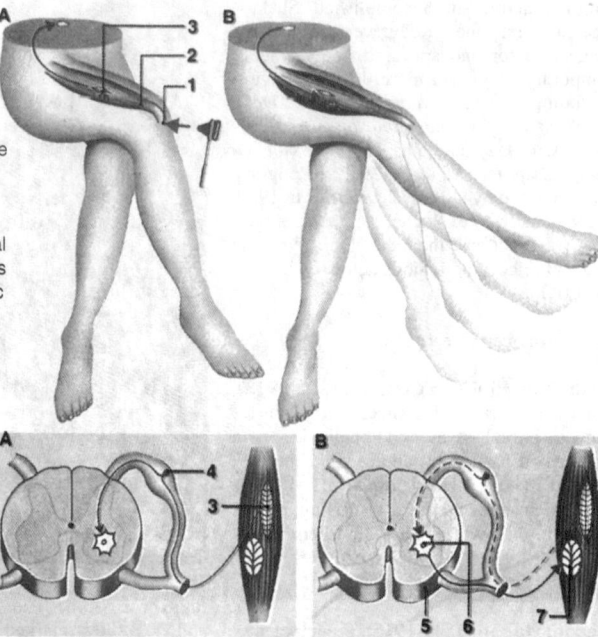

Reduction, in chemistry, any process that increases the proportion of hydrogen or base-forming elements or radicals in a compound. Reduction is also the gaining of electrons by an atom, an ion, or an element, thereby reducing the positive valence of that which gained the electron.
See also: Oxidation.

Red-winged blackbird *See:* Blackbird.

Redwood (*Sequoia sempervirens*), world's tallest living tree. Growing primarily in a narrow, mountainous strip along the Pacific Ocean from northern California into southern Oregon, redwoods thrive in the region's cool, foggy climate. They are closely related to the giant sequoias that grow further inland along the western slopes of the Sierra Nevadas. Coast redwoods average 200-275 ft (61-84 m) high; the tallest measured tree in the world is a redwood standing 368 ft (112 m) along Redwood Creek in Humboldt County, Calif. Redwood trunks average 8-12 ft (2.4-3.7 m) in diameter, and the wood, resistant to decay and insects, is valued by the lumbering industry for its durability. Redwoods are also among the world's oldest living things, some trees being an estimated 3,500 years old.

Reed, name for cosmopolitan grasses of wet ground and shallow water. They have feathery flowers, give shelter to many birds, and are used in thatching. They grow from a tangled mass of rhizomes that are hard to uproot.

Reed, John (1887-1920), U.S. journalist and radical, author of the eyewitness *Ten Days That Shook the World* (1919), which recounts the Russian October Revolution. Reed was instrumental in the creation of the Communist Labor Party in the United States. Reed is buried in front of the Kremlin in Moscow.
See also: Russian Revolution.

Reed, Walter (1851-1902), U.S. Army pa-

thologist and bacteriologist who demonstrated (1900) the role of the mosquito *Aëdes aegypti* as a carrier of yellow fever, so enabling the disease to be controlled.
See also: Pathology; Yellow fever.

Reef *See:* Atoll; Coral.

Reference book *See:* Almanac; Dictionary; Encyclopedia.

Referendum *See:* Initiative, referendum, and recall.

Refining *See:* Metallurgy; Petroleum; Sugar cane.

Reflection, bouncing back of energy waves (e.g., light radiation, sound or water waves) from a surface. If the surface is smooth, 'regular' reflection takes place, the incident and reflected wave paths lying in the same plane as, and at opposed equal angles to, the normal (a line perpendicular to the surface) at the point of reflection. Rough surfaces reflect waves irregularly, so an optically rough surface appears matt or dull, whereas an optically smooth surface looks shiny. Reflected sound waves are known as echoes.

Reflex action, automatic response of the human body to stimuli. If a part of the body such as the hand touches a hot object, it pulls away involuntarily, without conscious decision. Reflex action is caused by sensitive nerve endings transmitting messages to the brain which, in turn, sends a message about corrective action to the body part receiving the stimuli. Reflex action involves 4 stages-reception, conduction, transmission, and response-all occurring in a fraction of a second. Often the action is taken before pain is felt. Some types of reflex action can become 'conditioned reflexes,' in which association or anticipation, rather than actual stimulus, causes a certain reaction in the body.
See also: Nervous system.

Reformation, religious and political upheaval in western Europe in the 16th century. Primarily an attempt to reform the doctrines of the Roman Catholic church, it led to the establishment of Protestantism. Anticlericalism spread after the movements led by John Wycliffe and the Lollards in 14th-century England and by John Hus in Bohemia in the 15th century. At the same time the papacy had lost prestige due to its 70-year exile, the Babylonian Captivity at Avignon, and the 50-year Great Schism. Renaissance thought, particularly humanism, stimulated liberal views, spread by the invention of printing. Many, like Martin Luther, criticized the low moral standards of Rome and the sale of indulgences. Luther also challenged papal authority and the accepted Roman Catholic doctrines, such as transubstantiation and celibacy, and argued strongly for justification by faith. Luther's ideas spread in Germany after the Diet of Worms (1521) and after the Peasants' War, when Luther won the support of many German princes and of Denmark and Sweden. The protest made by the Lutheran princes at the Diet of Speyer (1529) provided the term *Protestant*. The Swiss divine Huldreich Zwingli won a large following in Switzerland and southwestern Germany. He carried out radical religious reforms in Zürich, abolishing the mass. After his death (1531), John Calvin led the Swiss reform movement and set up a reformed church in Geneva. Calvin's *Institutes of the Christian Religion* (1536) had great influence, notably in Scotland, where Calvinism was led by John Knox. In France Calvin's religious followers, the Huguenots, were involved in the complex political struggles leading to the Wars of Religion (1562-1598). The Protestant movement in the Low Countries was linked with the national revolt that freed the Dutch from Roman Catholic Spain. The English Reformation was initiated by Henry VIII, who denied papal authority, dissolved and seized the wealth of the monasteries, and made the Church of England autonomous. Henry remained in doctrine a Catholic, but the influence of reformers such as Nicholas Ridley and Hugh Latimer established Protestantism under Edward VI, when Thomas Cranmer issued a new prayer book (1549). There was a Roman Catholic reaction under Mary I, but in 1558 Elizabeth I established moderate Protestantism as the basis of the English Church. The religious position of Europe as a whole, however, was not settled for another century.
See also: Luther, Martin; Protestantism.

Reform bills, 3 acts of Parliament passed in Britain during the 19th century to extend the right to vote. The first (1832) abolished rotten boroughs (localities that sent members to Parliament long after their populations had disappeared) and enfranchised industrial cities, such as Birmingham and Manchester, and the propertied middle class. The second bill (1867) gave the vote to urban dwellers, and the third (1884) extended it to agricultural workers.

Reformed churches, Protestant churches arising from the Reformation that adhere to Calvinism doctrinally and to Presbyterian-

R

A Calvinist community: The Temple of Lyon, called Paradise. This anonymous painting (1564) provides some insight into Calvinist services in the early days of Calvinism. The relative simplicity is striking, as are the central place of the pulpit (with an hourglass, to limit the vicar's eloquence), the separation between men and women, and the more ornate benches for people of rank. Children and dogs were admitted in those days (Bibliothéque publique et universitaire, Geneva).

ism in church polity and are thus distinct from the Lutheran churches and the Church of England. They grew up especially in Switzerland, Germany, France, Holland, Scotland, Hungary, and what is now Czechoslovakia. Each had its own simple formal liturgy, and all acknowledged the Reformed Confessions. There are several Reformed Churches in the United States, the largest being the Christian Reformed Church. *See also:* Calvinism; Presbyterianism; Reformation.

Refraction, deviation of a ray of light passing through one transparent medium to another of different density, as for instance an object that is half in and half out of water. *See also:* Light.

Refractory, nonmetallic materials that can withstand high temperatures without losing their hardness. Refractory substances include magnesite, dolomite, silica, alumina, chromite, and zirconia. Firebrick or fire clay is a common refractory, using aluminum silicates and other substances to retain their original properties. Refractories are used industrially in kilns, furnaces, and crucibles, where they line or insulate the walls of these high-heat chambers or containers. Refractories are also required in nuclear power plants, where high levels of radioactivity are capable of generating intense heat.

Refrigeration, removal of heat from an enclosure in order to lower its temperature. It is used for freezing water or food, for food preservation, for air conditioning, and for low-temperature chemical processes and cryogenics studies and applications. Modern refrigerators are insulated cabinets containing a compressor, which forces a refrigerant

gas, such as ammonia or freon, to pass through a condenser; losing heat through condensation, the refrigerant gas goes through refrigeration coils, where it vaporizes, removing heat from the coils, and returns as a gas to the compressor for another cycle. In another system compression is accomplished by absorbing the refrigerant in a secondary fluid, such as salt water, and pumping the solution through a heat exchanger to a generator, where it is heated to drive off the refrigerant at high pressure. Other cycles, similar in principle, using steam or air, are also used.

Refugee, or displaced person, person fleeing a native country to avoid a threat or restriction.

Regelation, melting of ice under pressure and refreezing when the pressure is removed. When compressed, ice changes into water; when temperature conditions are at or below 32°F (0°C), it freezes again when the pressure is taken off. A large rock on frozen water gradually sinks as the pressure melts the ice directly below it, but as the rock sinks the water refreezes around it. Glaciers undergo a slow process of regelation, melting and refreezing as they move along, in some cases pushing ice fields high up the slopes of mountains.

Regency style, English architectural and decorative style popular during the regency and reign of George IV (1811-1830). It was characterized by neoclassical elegance, refinement, and the use of Egyptian and Oriental forms. John Nash was the foremost architect of the period. The term also refers to the elaborate decorative style of the French Régence (1715-1723).

Regeneration, in biology, regrowing of a lost or damaged part of an organism. In plants this includes the production, for instance of dormant buds and adventitious organs. All animals possess some power to regenerate, but its extent varies from that in sponges, in which all the cells in a piece of the body, almost completely separated, will come together to build up new but smaller sponges, to that in the higher animals, in which regeneration is limited to the healing of wounds. *See also:* Biology.

Regent, in monarchies, person designated to rule when the rightful ruler is absent, ill, mentally incapable of ruling, or a minor. A regent may be a single member of the nation's royal family or a council of several persons in line for the succession to the crown. Throughout the history of England and other European monarchies, regents often directed the affairs of state when a child of a deposed or deceased king succeeded to the throne; other regents ruled when the rightful monarch was in exile or judged to be mentally unstable. Prior to passage of the Regency Act in England (1937), no specific guidelines existed governing the selection of a regent, and past regents were acknowledged by common consensus. In the United States, members of governing bodies of schools, higher learning facilities, and other

institutions are often called regents. *See also:* Monarchy.

Reger, Max (1873-1916), a German composer and conductor. He admired the works of Bach and Brahms and in his music combined elaborate contrapuntal forms with lyrical melodies and complex chromatic harmony. Reger wrote chamber music; choral and orchestral works; piano, organ, and violin pieces; and more than 300 songs. *Variations and Fugue on a Theme by Mozart*, *Serenade for Orchestra*, and *Variations and Fugue on an Original Theme* are typical works. Reger was director of the Leipzig Conservatory form 1907 until his death.

Reggae, popular Jamaican musical style that combines U.S. rock and soul music with calypso and other Latin American rhythms. The 1973 film *The Harder They Come* introduced reggae to the United States, where performers such as Bob Marley (1945-1981) won huge audiences.

Regiment, military term for what was once the largest infantry and armored division unit in an army. Regiments today, largely administrative units not assigned to combat duty, have been replaced by more mobile units called brigades. A regiment generally has groups of battalions and squadrons under its aegis, assigned to other units called divisions. The earliest units to be called regiments were French cavalry soldiers in 1558; regiments initially recruited, equipped, and trained troops for combat. In the early United States and 19th-century Europe, each regiment usually contained 10 smaller units or companies; in the 20th century companies were phased out as war became more mechanized. *See also:* Army.

Regina (pop. 196,000), capital and largest city of the Canadian province of Sas-

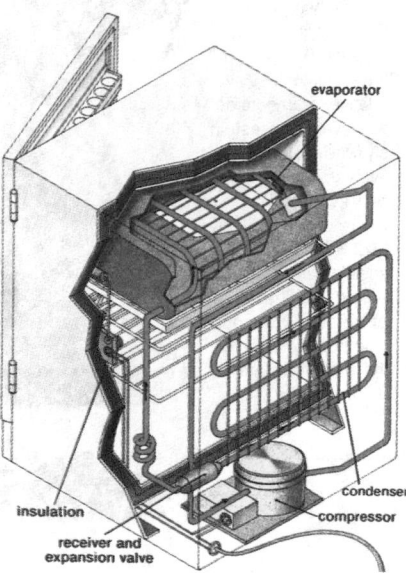

The refrigeration cycle alternately evaporates and condenses a refrigerant, such as Freon-12. A liquid refrigerant that is stored under high pressure in the receiver, is released through an expansion valve into the evaporator coils inside the refrigerator. With the pressure reduced, the refrigerant evaporates and absorbs heat from the interior. A compressor circulates the vaporized refrigerant to the exterior condenser coils, where it is condensed again by pressure. Heat from the inside of the refrigerator is lost to the environment. The cooled liquid then returns to the receiver.

R

katchewan. The city, on the Trans-Canada Highway, lies in the plains of southcentral Saskatchewan, about 100 mi (161 km) from the U.S. border. Founded in 1883 as the new capital of the Northwest Territories, it became the capital of the new province of Saskatchewan in 1905. The community originally bore the picturesque name Pile O'Bones, but was renamed Regina in honor of Queen Victoria. Major industries include steel and steel products, agricultural machinery, meat packing, and oil refining. The city is also the headquarters of the Saskatchewan Wheat Pool.
See also: Saskatchewan.

Regulators, movement in the western part of North Carolina (1764-1771) that resisted extortion and oppression by colonial officials. After failing to effect reforms, they rose in revolt but were defeated at Allemance Creek (1771), and 6 leaders were hanged for treason.

Regulus, Marcus Atilius (d. c.249 B.C.), roman general captured in the first Punic War (255 B.C.). He was sent to Rome to deliver Carthage's peace terms, under parole to return if they were rejected. He nevertheless urged their rejection, returned, and was apparently tortured to death.
See also: Punic Wars.

Reich, German term used to designate an empire. Derived from the Old High German word *rihhi*, meaning realm, the term came into widespread use during Adolf Hitler's proclamation of a Third Reich (1933-1945). The First Reich was considered to be the Holy Roman Empire (9th century-1806). The Second Reich was the German empire built by Chancellor Otto von Bismarck and Kaisers Wilhelm I and Wilhelm II (1871-1919).
See also: Germany.

Reich, Stephen (Steve) (1936-), American composer, studied at the Juilliard School of Music in New York, and then with Berio and Milhaud. By experimenting with tape recorders he created the technique of phase deferment and gradual deferment. From 1965 onwards he turned these techniques into an instrumental style called minimal music. His works include *It's Gonna Rain* (1965), *Drumming* (1971), *Music for 18 Musicians* (1976), *Octet* (1979), *Tehillim* (1981), *Desert Music* (1984), *Different Trains* (1988), *The Cave* (1993), and *Proverbs* (1996). He published *Writings about Music* (1974).

Reich, Wilhelm (1897-1957), Austrian psychoanalyst who broke with Sigmund Freud over the function of sexual repression, which Reich saw as the root of neurosis. He held the controversial theory that there exists a primal life-giving force called orgone energy. His design and sale of 'orgone boxes' for personal therapeutic use led to his imprisonment for violating the Food and Drug Act.
See also: Psychoanalysis.

Reichstag, imperial parliament of the Holy Roman Empire and, from 1871 to 1945, Germany's lower legislative house (the upper house was called the Reichsrat). The ruling body of the Weimar Republic, the Reichstag lacked real power under the Nazi regime.
See also: Holy Roman Empire; Weimar Republic.

Reichswehr, German term meaning 'army of the state.' Set up by the German republic after World War I, it had 300,000 troops until the Treaty of Versailles reduced it to 100,000. During the Wiemar Republic (1919-1933), the Reichswehr developed into a training program that enabled its ranks to swell and its combat efficiency to increase after Adolf Hitler came to power. In World War II, the Reichswehr made up the core of Hitler's army, which overran most of Europe.

Reid, Whitelaw (1837-1912), U.S. journalist, ambassador to Britain (1905-1912).

Editor of the *New York Tribune*, (1872-1912) he was the Republican vice-presidential candidate in 1892.

Reign of Terror, period (1793-1794) during the French Revolution when fanatical Jacobin reformers, including Maximilien Robespierre, Georges Jacques Danton, and Jacques René Hébert, seized control from the Girondists. They guillotined over 2,600 'counterrevolutionaries' (including Danton and Hebert, eventually) in Paris and sanctioned 'Terrors' elsewhere, notably in Nantes. The Terror ended with the guillotining of Robespierre himself in 1794.
See also: French Revolution.

Reims, or Rheims (pop. 185,000), city in northern France, about 100 mi (161 km) east of Paris on the Besle River. Dating from Roman times, it is famed for its Gothic cathedral (built 1211-1430). All but two French kings were crowned in Reims (1179-1825). Center of champagne and woolen production, it also produces chemicals, machinery, and paper.

Reincarnation, or transmigration of the soul, belief that the soul survives death and is reborn in the body of another person or living thing. It is an important concept in Buddhism, Hinduism, Jainism, Sibhism. In India, reincarnation is related to the law of karma, which dictates that a person's actions in life determine the type of body the soul will enter during reincarnation.
See also: Karma.

Reindeer, deer (genus *Rangifer*) widely distributed in arctic and subarctic regions of Europe, Asia, and North America, closely related to the caribou. Reindeer stand about 3-4 ft (90-120 cm) tall and can weigh up to 400 lb (180 kg). The Lapps of northern Scandinavia have used reindeer for food, clothing, and transportation for centuries.

Reindeer moss (*Cladonia rangiferina*), type of lichen commonly found in the Arctic. It is a principal food source for reindeer, moose, caribou, and musk oxen; in northern Scandinavia people have used it to make bread and alcohol. A short, multibranched plant that covers vast areas sufficient to feed large herds of grazing mammals, it grows more rapidly during the spring and fall months, aided by cool temperatures and high levels of humidity.

Reinforcement *See:* Learning.

Reinhardt, Max (Max Goldmann; 1873-1943), Austrian theatrical director famous for his vast and spectacular productions-especially of *Oedipus Rex* and *Faust*-and for his elaborate and atmospheric use of stage machinery and management of crowds.

Relapsing fever, bacteria-transmitted ailment that may recur several times in the same person. Usually occurring in the tropics, relapsing fever is caused by spirochetes carried by lice and ticks, which thrive on unsanitary living conditions. Symptoms of the disease include fever, chills, headaches, muscular pain, and sometimes vomiting. An

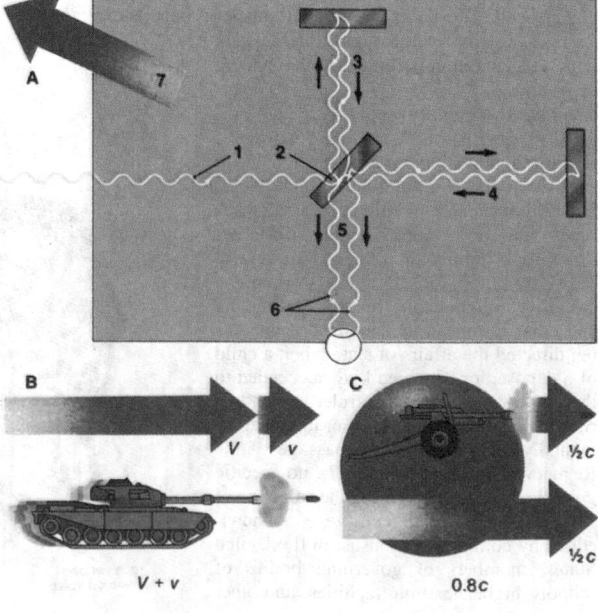

(A) The Michelson-Morley experiment was designed to detect the ether medium that was once thought to carry light waves. A light beam (1), split by a mirror (2), followed separate light paths (3 and 4) and recombined (5), forming interference bands (6). If ether were present, light should take longer to make the round trip in the direction (7) of earth's motion, than at right angles to it. No time difference was observed, indicating no presence of ether.
(B) Newton's laws of motion predict that a shell that is fired with a velocity (v) from a tank that is moving at a speed (V), should have a velocity V+v relative to an outside observer. (C) Einstein showed that the relative velocity should be $v+V : 1+vV/c^2$, where c is the velocity of light. Thus, if a shell is fired a 0.5c on a planet that is orbiting at 0.5c, an outside observer will see the shell moving at 0.8c.

infected person may be violently ill for several days or a week, return to good health, but if not treated properly have a relapse-as many as 10-12 times. The body's natural defenses may successfully combat the disease for a time, but infected spirochetes still in the body may reinvade the bloodstream, causing relapses when the body's defenses weaken. Penicillin and other antibiotics combined with extensive bed rest is effective treatment.

Relativity, theory of the nature of space, time, and matter. Albert Einstein's special theory of relativity (1905) is based on the premise that different observers moving at a constant speed with respect to each other find the laws of physics to be identical, and, in particular, find the speed of light waves to be the same (the principle of relativity). Among its consequences are (1) that events occurring simultaneously according to one observer may happen at different times according to an observer moving relative to the first (although the order of two causally related events is never reversed), (2) that a moving object is shortened in the direction of its motion, (3) that time runs more slowly for a moving object, (4) that the velocity of a projectile emitted from a moving body is less than the sum of the relative ejection velocity and the velocity of the body, (5) that a body has a greater mass when moving than when at rest, and (6) that no massive body can travel as fast as, or faster than, the speed of light. These effects are too small to be noticed at normal velocities; they have nevertheless found ample experimental verification and are common considerations in many physical calculations. The relationship between the position and time of a given event according to different observers is known (for H.A. Lorentz) as the Lorentz transformation. In this, time mixes on a similar footing with the three spatial dimensions, and it is in this sense that time has been called the fourth dimension. The greater mass of a moving body implies a relationship between kinetic energy and mass; Einstein made the bold additional hypothesis that *all* energy is equivalent to mass, according to the famous equation $E = mc^2$. The conversion of mass to energy is now the basis of nuclear reactors and is indeed the source of the energy of the sun itself.
Einstein's general theory (1916) is of importance chiefly to cosmologists. It asserts the equivalence of the effects of acceleration and gravitational fields and that gravitational fields cause space to become 'curved,' so that light no longer travels in straight lines, while the wavelength of light falls as the light falls through a gravitational field. The direct verification of these last two predictions, among others, has helped deeply to entrench the theory of relativity in the language of physics.
See also: Einstein, Albert.

Relief, form of sculpture in which the elements of the design, whether figures or ornament, project from their background. In *high relief* the elements stand out prominently and may even be undercut; in *low*, or *bas*, *relief* they hardly emerge from the plane of the background.

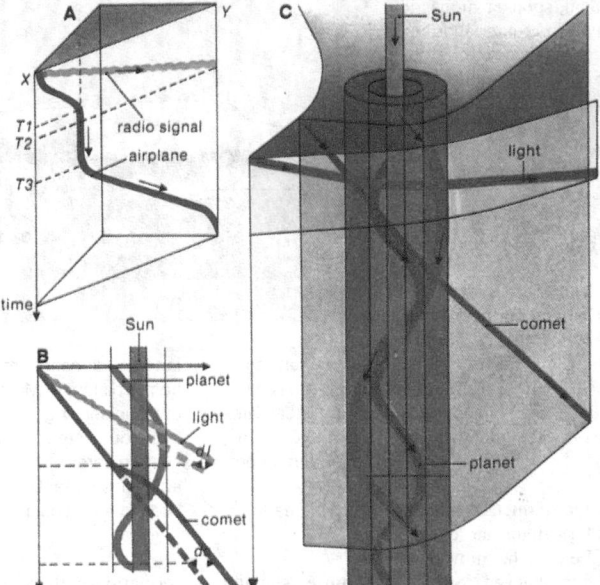

The concept of space-time requires time as a fourth dimension, in order to specify location—because relative motion affects both space and time. An object's path in space-time is called a world line, and a graph of a world line uses two space coordinates and time as a third. (A) In an airplane's flight from X to Y, the slope of its world line increases as its speed decreases, becoming vertical when the plane makes a fueling stop (times T1 to T3). A radio signal starting from X arrives at Y at time T2. In relativity theory, acceleration of an object as it passes near a massive body, is viewed as a local distortion in space-time. (B) A comet passing the sun is deflected (dc) in space-time, as is a ray of licht (dl); a planet, slower, oscillates between extreme positions. (C) Space-time around the sun is distorted differently for objects moving at different speeds, but each object, in its own version of space, appears to travel in a path of constant velocity.

R

Relief *See:* Welfare.

Religion, system of belief to which a social group is committed, in which there is a supernatural object of awe, worship, and service. It generally provides a system of ethics and a worldview that supply a stable context within which each person can relate to others and to the world and can understand his or her own significance. Religions are found in all societies and are generally dominant (modern secularism being an exception).Some form of religion seems to fulfill a basic human need. Some features are common to most religions: the recognition of a sacred realm from which supernatural forces operate, a mediating priesthood, the use of ritual to establish a right relationship with the holy (though ritual used to manipulate the supernatural becomes magic), and a sense of group community. Some religions have no deity as such, but are natural philosophies (e.g., Buddhism, Confucianism, and Taoism).

Religion, Wars of, French civil wars (1562-1598) caused partly by conflict between Roman Catholics and Protestant Huguenots, and partly by rivalry between the French kings and such great nobles as the dukes of Guise. The worst event was the St. Bartholomew's Day Massacre (1572). The Edict of Nantes (1598) established religious freedom and concluded the wars.
See also: France.

Religious education, program of instruction in the doctrines, beliefs and practices of a given religion. This is done primarily through church-related schools or programs or religious organizations. Large sanctioned faiths, such as Roman Catholic, Protestantism and Judaism, have extensive, well-organized programs of religious education with well-qualified teachers. Smaller churches and religious sects may offer informal systems of teaching their beliefs, often in members' homes. Religious education usually uses books (primarily the Bible), visuals, and oral transmissions of doctrine. Persons planning to teach religious education must often undergo a formal program of study.

Religious festivals *See:* Holiday.

Religious life, lifestyle voluntarily chosen by persons to enhance their own spirituality. People who adopt this way of life for becoming holy and for being of the greatest service to others include monks, nuns, brothers, sisters, priests, and ministers. A religious life may be followed and practiced by individuals on their own, or within the organized framework of an established practice or religious order. Roman Catholic religious followers take vows of poverty and chastity and may belong to a religious order to practice their beliefs in a public place, such as a church. Other religions, such as

Jews reading a part from the Torah in the synagogue. Phylacteries (tefillim) can be seen on the forehead and the left hand of the man with the glasses. All the men are wrapped in prayer shawls (tallit). According to Jewish custom, the men cover their heads when in a synagogue and reading the Torah. The man who reads from the scroll, is using a pointer (yad) to avoid defilement of the holy text (Portuguese Israelite Synagogue, Amsterdam).

R

Hinduism and Buddhism, sponsor monastic orders, although many Hindu and Buddhist holy men and women practice a religious life as individuals. Some Protestant faiths have established orders, but most Protestant ministers, as do Islamic and Jewish religious leaders, impart the knowledge acquired during their religious lives to their congregations.

Religious Society of Friends *See:* Quakers.

Remarque, Erich Maria (1898-1970), German-born novelist famous for his powerful antiwar novel *All Quiet on the Western Front* (1929), describing the horror of the trenches in World War I. In 1932 Remarque emigrated to Switzerland, later becoming a U.S. citizen. Other works include *Arch of Triumph* (1946).

Rembrandt (Rembrandt Harmenszoon van Rijn; 1606-1669), Dutch painter and etcher. Born and trained in Leiden, he moved to Amsterdam in 1631 and achieved recognition with a group portrait, *The Anatomy Lesson* (1632). Adapting the styles of Caravaggio, Hals, and Rubens, his painting became, during 1632-1642, Baroque in style, as in *Saskia as Flora* (1634), *Blinding of Samson* (1636), and *The Night Watch* (1642). The years 1643-1656 were notable for his magnificent drawings and etchings, predominantly of New Testament themes, such as *The Three Crosses* (1653-1661). From the mid-1650s his painting was more solemn and spiritual in mood and richer in color, as shown in portraits (*Jan Six*, 1654, *The Syndics of the Amsterdam Cloth Hall*, 1662), a series of moving self-portraits, and religious paintings like *David and Saul* (c.1658).

Remington, Frederic (1861-1909), U.S. painter, sculptor and writer chiefly known for his portrayals of the Old West, where he traveled extensively. His paintings, usually of Native Americans, cowboys, and horses, skillfully convey violent action and are notable for authenticity of detail.

Remora, warmwater fish (family Echeneidae) that feeds off other marine animals. A remora uses an oval disc at the top of its head as a suction cup to attach itself to a host animal-usually a shark, whale, sea turtle, or other large marine animal-and is carried along with them as they swim. Ranging 7 in (17 cm) to 3.5 ft (110 cm) in length, remoras enjoy a symbiotic relationship with the animals they attach themselves to, eating leftover scraps of food not eaten by the hosts while removing parasites from the hosts. Some remoras cling to the hulls of ships and boats.

Remote control, control of a system from a distance. It can range from a television set to a guided missile or satellite, over a few feet or thousands of miles. Types of remote control include radio, infrared, ultrasonic, laser, electrical, human voice, and mechanical. Radio-controlled motorboats used by the German Navy in World War I (1914-1918) were the first machines operated by remote control. Today some robots are run by remote control.

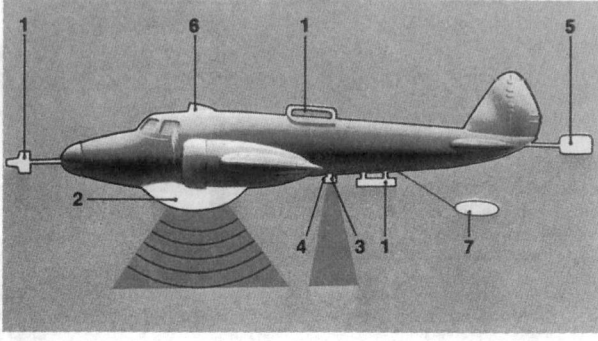

Remote-sensing equipment is often carried in satellites and in aircraft, to gather and record information about the earth's surface and atmosphere from a distance. Most of these sensing techniques are shown in the diagram. The actual instruments used in a particular survey depend upon the information desired. A search for new oil fields, for example, would require identification of particular geological features and would therefore utilize sound waves, radar, photography, television, and magnetic techniques. 1. electromagnetic system 2. microwave radar system 3. photographic optical system 4. television system 5. system for measuring gamma radiation 6. system for sampling air 7. system for measuring the magnetic field

Remote sensing, information-gathering process that operates independently of physical contact with the object being studied. Modern technology has developed complex forms of remote sensing through the use of electronic sensors that pick up and transmit visual images. Television is a form of remote sensing, and TV cameras are used in spacecraft to receive and translate visual data about Earth or the celestial body being studied. Satellites convey meteorologic conditions of the atmosphere or geologic conditions of the earth's surface or underground resources. Radar and sonar use sound to detect physical objects. Some sensors detect infrared (heat) rays sent out by the earth; the information is translated by computer into color images that scientists can interpret.

REM sleep *See:* Sleep.

Remus *See:* Romulus and Remus.

Renaissance (French, 'rebirth' or 'revival'), transitional period between the Middle Ages and modern times (1350-1650). The term was first applied by the Swiss historian Jakob Burckhardt in 1860. The Renaissance saw the Reformation challenge the unity and supremacy of the Roman Catholic Church, along with the rise of humanism, the growth of large nation-states with powerful kings, far-ranging voyages of exploration, and a new emphasis on the importance of the individual.

The origins of the Renaissance are disputed, but its first flowering occurred in Italy. In the world of learning a new interest in secular Latin literature can be detected in early 14th century, and by the middle of the century Petrarch and Giovanni Boccaccio were searching for old texts and self-consciously cultivating a prose style modeled on Cicero. They inaugurated an age of research and discovery in which the humanists ransacked the monastic libraries of Europe for old manuscripts, and scholars like Desiderius Erasmus set new standards in learning and critical scholarship. Greek was also studied, particularly after the fall of Constantinople (1453) drove many Greek scholars to the West. The invention of printing (1440) and the discovery of the New World (1492) by Columbus gave further impetus to the search for knowledge.

The Renaissance marked the end of feudalism and the rise of national governments, for example, in Spain under Ferdinand II of Aragon, in France under Francis I, in England under Henry VIII and Elizabeth. In Italy, however, independent city states engaged in fierce rivalry, providing Niccolò Machiavelli with his notorious 'ideal' of a Renaissance prince. Prosperous trading provided money for the arts, and princes like Cosimo de'Medici eagerly patronized artists, musicians, and scholars. Renaissance painting and sculpture flourished in Florence and Rome with the works of Sandro Botticelli, Leonardo da Vinci, Michelangelo, and Raphael. Literary revivals occurred in England, France, and Spain; William Shakespeare and Edmund Spenser were prominent in Renaissance English literature, and some of the finest French writing came from François Rabelais and Pierre de Ronsard. In science the findings of the astronomers Nicolaus Copernicus and Galileo Galilei were the basis of modern astronomy and marked a turning point in scientific and philosophical thought.

René of Anjou (1409-1480), duke of Anjou and Provence. He inherited a claim to the kingdom of Naples (1435) but was defeated by Alfonso V of Aragon in 1442. His daughter, Margaret of Anjou, married Henry VI of England. René's court at Angers in France was a brilliant cultural center.

Reni, Guido (1575-1642), Italian Baroque painter. He developed an elegant classical style, using light tones, for religious and mythological themes, such as *Aurora* (1613) and *Baptism of Christ* (1623).
See also: Baroque.

Reno (pop. 184,000), second-largest city in Nevada and a major resort and gambling center. Situated on the Truckee River, 14 mi (22.5 km) from the California state line, the city was founded in 1868 and incorporated in 1879. Legalized gambling in Nevada

Renaissance religious reform without the approval of the pope was a dangerous activity. A painting depicting the burning of the Dominican monk Girolamo Savonarola and two of his followers in the Piazza della Signoria in Florence on May 23, 1498.

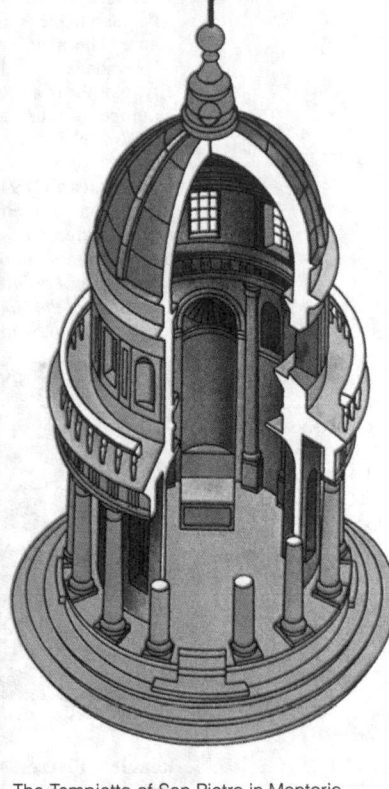

R

A perspective study by the greatest intellect of the Renaissance Leonardo Da Vinci

The Tempietto of San Pietro in Montorio, Rome, designed by Donato Bramante. This chapel was built to commemorate the site of St. Peter's crucifixion. With its emphasis on architectural volume, not space, it marks the beginnings of High Renaissance in Rome.

One of the most important thinkers of the Renaissance, the Christian humanist Desiderius Erasmus. Portrait of Erasmus painted by his friend Hans Holbein the Younger

Great patron of Renaissance scholars, the Florentine grand duke Cosimo de' Medici, depicted in a bronze bust by Benvenuto Cellini (1450)

The Villa Rotunda (16th century) in Vicenza, Italy, designed by Andrea Palladio (1508-80). The columns and triangular keystones of this building were influenced by the architecture of the ancient Greeks, a major inspiration for Renaissance architects.

R

brings thousands of tourists to Reno every year, and liberal Nevada laws on divorce have also made Reno a well-known divorce center. The main campus of the University of Nevada is located on hills overlooking the city. Not far from Reno are Lake Tahoe and a number of other noted recreation areas. *See also:* Nevada.

Renoir, Jean (1894-1979), French film director, son of Pierre Auguste Renoir. His motion pictures are characterized by a sensitive feeling for atmosphere and a strong pictorial sense. *La Grande Illusion* (1937) and *The Rules of the Game* (1939) are two of his most important works.

Scene from *La grande illusion* (1937) by Jean Renoir (1894-1979) with (in the middle) Jean Gabin (1904-1976) and (on the right) Pierre Fresnay (1897-1975) in the main roles. The film is about an attempt to escape by French prisoners-of-war in World War I.

Renoir, Pierre Auguste (1841-1919), French Impressionist painter. He started painting-with Claude Monet, Camille Pissarro, and Alfred Sisley-scenes of Parisian life, such as *La Grenouillère* (1869) and *The Swing* (1876), using vibrant luminous colors. Later he became mostly interested in figure painting, usually large female nudes set in rich landscapes. One of his best-known works is *Luncheon of the Boating Party* (1881).

Rent, in law, the price a tenant pays for the use of another's property. In economics, rent means any income or yield from something capable of producing wealth. In general usage, the term covers the monetary return from anything from real estate to cars and computers.

Reparations, term applied since World War I to monetary compensation demanded by victorious nations for material losses suffered in war. In 1919 Germany was required to pay enormous reparations to the Allies (although the United States subsequently waived all claim). After World War II, reparations were exacted from Germany and Japan.

Repetitive Strain Injury *See:* RSI.

Repin, Ilya Yefimovich (1844-1930), Russian painter. His realistic paintings often expressed criticism of the Russian social order during the late 19th century.

Representative government *See:* Democracy; Republic.

Representatives, House of *See:* House of Representatives.

Repression *See:* Psychoanalysis.

Reprieve, in criminal law, the postponement of a sentence that has been imposed by the courts. The term is usually used to refer to a stay of execution when the death sentence is involved and is often granted to allow the investigation of new evidence in a case.

Reproduction, process by which an organism produces offspring. In asexual reproduction parts of an organism split off to form new individuals; the process is found in some animals but is more common in plants: e.g., the fission of single-celled plants; the budding of yeasts; the fragmentation of filamentous algae; spore production in bacteria, algae, and fungi; and the production of vegetative organs in flowering plants (bulbs, rhizomes, and tubers). In sexual reproduction, special (haploid) cells containing half the normal number of chromosomes, called gametes, are produced: in animals, sperm by males in the testes and ova by females in the ovary; in plants, pollen by males in the stamens and ovules by females in the ovary. The joining of gametes (fertilization, or conception) produces a (diploid) cell with the normal number of chromosomes, the zygote, which grows to produce an individual with genes inherited from both parents. Fertilization may take place inside the female (internal fertilization) or outside (external fertilization). Internal fertilization demands that sperm be introduced into the female-insemination by copulation- and is advantageous because the young spend the most vulnerable early stages of their life histories protected inside the mother.

Reproductive system *See:* Reproduction.

Reptile, cold blooded vertebrate with dry, scaly skin. Reptiles can be found in a wide variety of habitats, including the sea and points north of the Arctic Circle, but most live in the tropics. There are no reptiles in Antarctica. There are about 6,000 species of reptiles. They range in size from 2 in (5 cm) to 30 ft (9 m). They breathe through lungs and are cold blooded, meaning that their body temperatures vary with external conditions making it necessary for reptiles to seek conditions favorable to their metabolisms. Most reptiles lay eggs. Certain snakes and lizards retain the eggs in their bodies until the young hatch, and they are born live. The major species of reptiles are lizards and snakes, turtles, crocodilians, and tuatoras. The last are related to the now-extinct dinosaurs and live on islands off the coast of New Zealand. Lizards and snakes account for some 3,000 species, among them certain venomous types. The turtles comprise some 250 species and some are among the longest lived of all animals. Crocodilians include alligators, caymans, crocodiles, and gavials, about 20 species altogether. Most reptiles live by eating other animals and are descendants of the dinosaurs, or giant reptiles.

Reptiles, Age of *See:* Dinosaur; Prehistoric animal.

Republic (from Latin *res publica*, 'thing of the people'), form of government in which the head of state is not a monarch (and today is usually a president). Popularly, the idea of a republic includes the notion of elected representation and democratic control by the people, although many present-day governments that do not meet this requirement call themselves republics.
See also: Democracy.

Republican Party, one of the two major political parties of the United States. It is sometimes called the G.O.P., which stands for Grand Old Party, a nickname dating from the 19th century. It was founded in 1854 by dissidents of the Whig, Democratic, and Free Soil parties to unify the growing anti-slavery forces. Its first national nominating convention was held in 1856; J.C. Frémont

In fertilizing the egg cell, a sperm cell dissolves the outer surface of the egg. Then it travels towards the egg's nucleus, and fuses with it.
A. unfertilized egg: as the sperm fuses with the egg, acrosome at the tip of the sperm head will release enzymes (yellow), which will aid penetration of the head.
B. fertilized egg: after the sperm head has entered, a fertilization membrane will rise over the egg's surface. The sperm nucleus then migrates towards the egg nucleus, their nuclear membranes break down, and the chromosomes will line up, as a prelude to the first division.

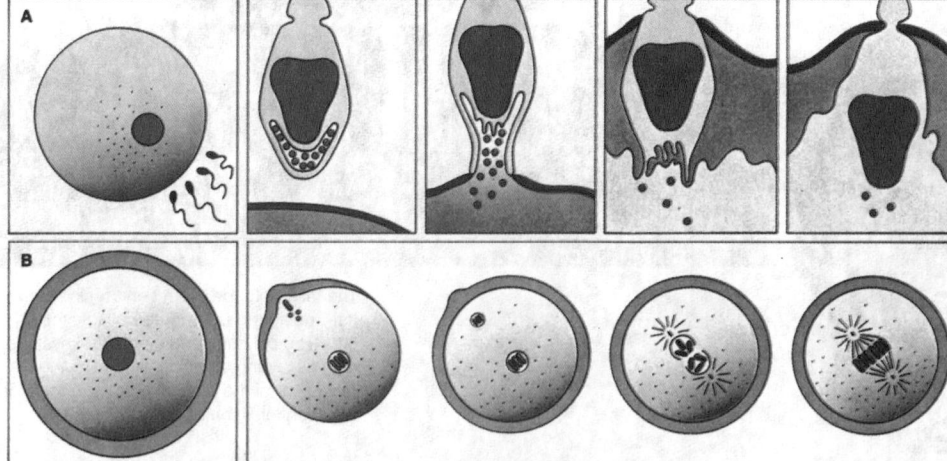

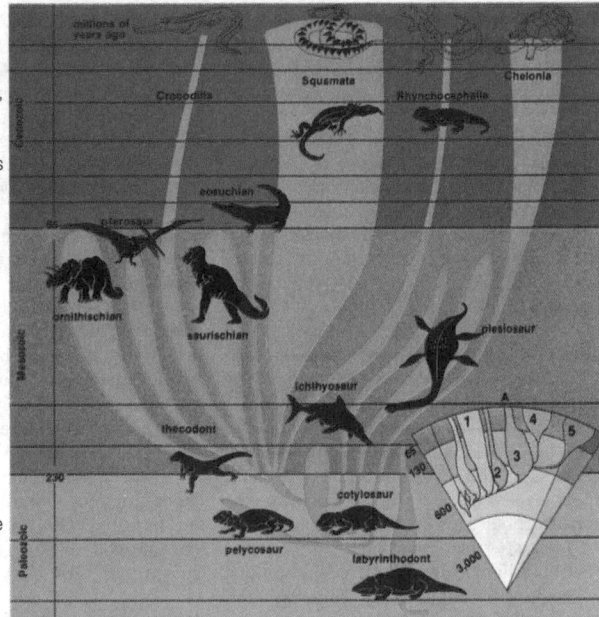

The evolutionary tree of reptiles. The living orders are: *Chelonia* (turtles and tortoises), *Squamata* (lizards and snakes), *Crocodilia* (crocodiles and alligators), and *Rhynchocephalia* (tuatara). Unlike amphibians, reptiles have evolved a type of egg that could be laid on land, thus avoiding the highly vulnerable 'tadpole' stage. The earliest ancestors of the reptiles were the cotylosaurs, also known as 'stem reptiles', which emerged in the Carboniferous period (the age of the great coal swamps). The Mesozoic was the great Age of the Reptiles, in which flourished forms as dinosaurs, ichtyosaurs, and pterosaurs, at the end of which a great number of species became extinct, an event that may have been evoked by climatic changes. (A) shows the relationship between reptiles and vertebrates on the time scale (millions of years ago): (1) fishes, (2) amphibians, (3) reptiles, (4) birds, and (5) mammals.

was adopted as presidential candidate. Campaigning for the abolition of slavery and of polygamy in the territories, he captured 11 states. Abraham Lincoln became the first Republican president, and in spite of the unpopularity of the post-Civil War Reconstruction policies and the secession of the Liberal Republican Party in 1872, the Republicans remained dominant in U.S. politics, winning 14 out of 18 presidential elections between 1860 and 1932. In an era of scandal, the Republicans consolidated a 'probusiness' and 'conservative' reputation with the nomination and election of William McKinley in 1896. His successor, Theodore Roosevelt, adopted a progressive stance; he defected to the Bull Moose Party in 1912. In 1932 the Democrats swept to power, not to be dislodged until the election of the Republican Dwight D. Eisenhower in 1952. His successors, John F. Kennedy and Lyndon Johnson, were Democrats, but Richard Nixon's landslide victory in 1972 marked a zenith of party strength. The Watergate scandal shattered this, contributing to the defeat of Gerald Ford in the 1976 elections. The Republicans rallied again in 1980 to elect Ronald Reagan president and to capture control of the Senate. In 1988 the Republican George Bush was elected president. Bush was succeeded by the Democrat Bill Clinton in 1993, who had to face a Republican majority in the Congres and Senate from 1994.

Research, use of appropriate methods to discover new knowledge, develop new applications of existing knowledge, or explore relationships between ideas or events. Scientific discoveries, technological achievements, and scholarly publications are the fruits of research. Research always involves three basic steps; the formulation of a problem, the collection and analysis of relevant information, and an attempt to discover a solution or otherwise resolve the problem based on evidence.

Reserpine ($C_{33}H_{40}N_2O_9$), tranquilizing drug used to treat mild forms of hypertension (high blood pressure). Extracted from the roots of the Rauwolfia serpentina plant of India and Southeast Asia, reserpine was isolated in 1952. It came into Western medical usage to calm mental patients in 1953. For centuries, the powdered whole root had been used in India to treat the mentally ill. Since the 1960s, more effective drugs have superseded it, but low doses of reserpine are still used to relieve minor cases of hypertension.

Reservation *See:* Indian reservation; Native Americans.

Reservoir, body of water or receptacle used for storing large supplies of water. Reservoirs are most often manmade lakes, caused by damming up rivers and streams or dredging a basin into a flat stretch of land; water towers and holding tanks atop buildings are also reservoirs. Whether manmade or natural lakes, reservoirs usually supply drinking water to cities and towns, and are used to irrigate, supply power, or control flooding. Water is drawn from reservoirs through pipes (aqueducts) and in some cases is pumped hundreds of miles away.

Reshevsky, Samuel (1911-1992), Polish/American chess grandmaster. Reshevsky became famous as a chess prodigy, but it was not until 1932 that he regularly began to play in tournaments. He was champion of the U.S. several times, for the first time in 1936, and for the last time in 1969. He achieved many tournament victories and came joint second in the candidates' tournament in Zurich (1953, won by Smyslov). In 1967 he qualified once again for the candidates' tournament, but was beaten by Korchnoi 51/2-21/2 in Amsterdam.

Resin, high-molecular-weight substance characterized by its gummy or tacky consistency at certain temperatures. Naturally occurring resins include congo copal and bitumen (found as fossils), shellac (from insects), and rosin (from pine trees). Natural Resins have for the most part been replaced by synthetic resins.
See also: Resin, synthetic.

Resin, synthetic, industrial chemical compound made up of many simple molecules linked together to form large, complex molecules. Most plastics and polymers are a form of synthetic resin. Complicated chemical processes are used to convert petroleum, coal, water, air, and wood into more complex chemicals, such as alcohol, phenol, ammonia, and formaldehyde; these, in turn, are combined to form synthetic resins. The first totally synthetic resin was Bakelite, which was produced by L.H. Baekeland in 1910 from phenol and formaldehyde. The work in the 1920s of H. Staudinger on the polymeric nature of natural rubber and styrene resin, which laid the theoretical basis for polymer science, was a major factor in stimulating the extremely rapid development of a wide range of synthetic plastics and resins. Resins have a wide variety of uses in manufactured goods for which durability and flexibility are required, and are also used in paints, adhesives and coatings for cloth, metal, and paper.
See also: Plastic.

Resnais, Alain (1922-), French film director. Became famous after WW II for a number of documentaries, including *Van Gogh* (1948), *Guernica* (1950) and *Nuit et Brouillard* (1955). His first film, influenced by the nouvelle vague, *Hiroshima, Mon Amour* (1959), established his name for good. Contacts with the Nouveau Roman and actor Alain Robbe-Grillet led to *L'année dernière à Marienbad* (1961), a perfect synthesis of dream and reality. Nostalgia and oblivion dominate his films, which include *Muriel ou le temps d'un retour* (1963), *Je t'aime, je t'aime* (1968), *Stavisky* (1974), *Providence* (1977), *Mon oncle d'Amérique* (1980), *La vie est un roman* (1983), *Melo* (1986), and *Smoking/No smoking* (1994; won 4 Césars in 1994).

Resorcinol ($C_6H_4[OH]_2$), compound used to manufacture resins, dyes, medical products, and other chemical compounds. A phenol, it is produced by fusing benzenedisulfonic acid with sodium hydroxide (caustic soda). A key agent in commercial skin-treatment products, resorcinol is often added to external skin-treatment lotions and ointments and is an effective antibacterial, antifungal treatment. Dermatologists use it to treat acne and eczema. Resorcinol is also used to make eosin, a dye used in red ink, and is useful in photographic developers.

R

R

Resources, natural *See:* Natural resources.

Respighi, Ottorino (1879-1936), Italian composer, director (1924-1926) of the Accademia di Santa Cecilia in Rome. He is best-known for tone poems, such as *The Fountains of Rome* (1917) and *The Pines of Rome* (1924).

Respiration, term applied to several activities and processes involving the exchange of gases with the environment, occurring in all animals and plants. Breathing movements, if any, and the exchange of oxygen and carbon dioxide, may be called external respiration, while energy-releasing processes at the cellular level are termed 'internal respiration,' or tissue respiration. Air, which contains about 20% oxygen, is drawn into the lungs (inspiration) via the nose or mouth, the pharynx, trachea, and bronchi. Expiration is usually a passive process of relaxation of the chest wall and diaphragms allowing the release of the air, which is depleted of oxygen and enriched with carbon dioxide. Exchange of gases with the blood circulating in the pulmonary capillaries occurs by diffusion across the lung alveoli. Disorders of respiration include lung disease (e.g., emphysema, pneumonia and pneumoconiosis), muscle and nerve disease (e.g., brain-stem stroke, poliomyelitis, myasthenia gravis, and muscular dystrophy, skeletal deformity, asphyxias, and disorders secondary to metabolic and heart disease. Tissue respiration involves the combination of oxygen with glucose or other nutrients to form high-energy compounds. This reaction also produces carbon dioxide and water.

Respirator, machine that aids the respiratory process in human beings, especially in extreme circumstances when a patient has difficulty breathing normally or if breathing stops altogether. Some respirators administer oxygen directly to the patient. Hospitals, mobile medical units, and other treatment facilities constantly monitor respirators to ensure proper breathing in patients hooked up to them. Portable respirators, attended by qualified personnel, may be used in a patient's home or room in an extended-care facility (nursing home). Positive-pressure respirators force or assist the flow of air into the lungs. Negative-pressure types, such as the 'iron lung,' create a vacuum that causes the chest to expand, thus inhaling air.

Respiratory distress syndrome *See:* Hyaline membrane disease.

Respiratory system *See:* Respiration.

Restaurant, food-and-drink facility that serves the public. Table-service restaurants seat patrons; they have a meal brought to them or can serve themselves at a buffet (cafeteria). Ethnic restaurants are table-service facilities that specialize in the food of a particular country or ethnic group. Other unusual (gourmet) food is sold in more highly specialized restaurants. Fast-service restaurants are characterized by large-scale production of food items, inexpensive prices, and quick service. Some provide tables but no table service for their customers. Food is ordered and paid for at a counter.

Restoration, name given to the return of Charles II as king of England in 1660, after the fall of the protectorate. Coinciding with a national mood of reaction against the Puritans, the Restoration was widely popular. The Restoration period (1660 to the fall of James II, in 1688) was one of irreverent wit, licentiousness, and scientific and literary achievement. Politically, it was a period of uneasy relations between king and parliament, culminating in the Glorious Revolution (1688-1689).
See also: Glorious Revolution.

Resurrection, act of God believed to restore life in perfected form to the dead. Many faiths believe resurrection-in physical or spiritual form-will come in the final days of the earth's existence when all people will stand as equals before God and be judged for their deeds in life. In Christianity, the Resurrection refers specifically to the return of Jesus after his crucifixion and the belief that his triumph over death was a spiritual redemption for all humanity. Those who follow his beliefs and practices in their own lives expect to be similarly resurrected and redeemed after their deaths. Easter is a Christian celebration of Jesus's resurrection, said to have occurred 2 days after his death on Good Friday.
See also: Religion.

Resurrection plant, one of several species of plants that curl up when dry but turn green when exposed to water. The rose of Jericho (*Anastatica hierochuntica*), a member of the mustard family, grows from seeds and, when dry, loses its leaves and curls up into a ball. The wind carries the balls, thus scattering the seeds. Another plant, also called the rose of Jericho (*Selaginella lepidophylla*), a member of the selaginella family, is most commonly found in the arid regions of the Middle East and North Africa. It reproduces by microscopic spores.

Resuscitator *See:* Respirator.

Retailing, selling of merchandise or services to the public. When a business sells at retail prices, that means it buys its goods or services from a supplier, usually a wholesaler, or directly from the factory. The business then sells the goods to consumers at a higher price designed to make a profit for the business. Specialty stores sell particular types of product and accessories, such as shoes, clothes, jewelry, or books. Department stores offer a wide variety of items in separate areas (departments) of the store. Discount stores sell their inventory at prices below normal retail prices. Supermarkets sell food and other household products. Chain stores are those under the same name or ownership in 2 or more locations. Nonstore retailing involves selling goods by mail order, telephone, vending machines, and door-to-door methods.

Retainer, in law, agreement between an attorney and client for legal representation. A retainer can be a formal or special type, in which the lawyer agrees to represent a client on a particular case, or it can be a special retainer, in which the lawyer agrees to act on behalf of the client when necessary. A retaining fee paid by a client to an attorney is also called a retainer. Once a retainer, either general or special, is agreed to, the attorney has a legal obligation to represent the client to the best of his or her abilities. The attorney cannot act on behalf of the opposing party or parties in a legal action.

Retardation *See:* Mental retardation.

Retina *See:* Eye.

Retriever, breed of sporting dog trained to search out and bring back small game shot by hunters. Easily trainable, retrievers are excellent swimmers with water-resistant coats and a highly developed sense of smell. The popular golden retriever and the Labrador retriever can also be trained as guide dogs for blind persons and the hearing-impaired. Other recognized breeds are the Chesapeake Bay, curly-coated, and flat-coated retrievers.

Reunion, volcanic island covering 970 sq mi (2,512 sq km) in the West Indian Ocean. Discovered in the early 1500s by the Portuguese, Reunion has been a French possession since 1642 and an overseas department of France since 1946. The islanders, mostly of mixed descent, are nearly all Roman Catholic and speak a Creole patois. Its products include sugar, rum, corn, and vanilla. The capital is Saint-Denis. A 36-member elected council governs the city.

Reuter, Baron de (Paul Julius von Reuter; 1816-1899), German-born founder of Reuters, the worldwide news agency. He pioneered the use of the newly invented telegraph to transmit news between major European cities and, later, to other continents via underseas cables. In 1849 he set up a carrier pigeon service between Aachen, Germany, and Brussels, Belgium. In 1851 he moved to London, where he opened a telegraph office near the Stock Exchange and reported on European financial news, expanding to other types of news events. Several major daily newspapers subscribed to his supplying service, and over the years he expanded it throughout Europe and the world.

Reuters, one of the largest international news agencies, based in Britain, that distributes information to local agencies, newspapers, television, and radio to more than 150 countries. Founded by Baron de Reuter in Germany in 1849, it moved to London in 1851. Reuters expanded its coverage from financial to general news in 1858. Today it is a trust owned mainly by the British press.
See also: Reuter, Baron de.

Revelation, Book of, or Apocalypse, the last book of the New Testament. Traditionally ascribed to St. John the Apostle, it was probably written by another John, and dated c.96. It is addressed to people being persecuted. After 7 letters to the Asia Minor churches, it contains a series of apocalyptic visions in Old Testament imagery, giving a Christian philosophy of world history.
See also: New Testament.

Revenue, internal *See:* Internal revenue.

Revivalism, in religion, emphasis on personal experience and salvation of the soul. This form of worship is often characterized by emotionally charged gospel preaching that is extemporaneous and requires audience participation. Revivalism began in Europe in the 1700s and spread quickly to North America in a series of 'Great Awakenings.' Prayer meetings, outdoor services, often called camp meetings, and tent meetings, or chautauquas, were practiced widely in the 1800s and early 1900s, much less so today. Itinerant preachers would travel from town to town with their entourages, set up tents, and exhort congregations to receive eternal salvation for their souls. Today, revivalism is practiced primarily by organized, denominational churches, principally Baptist and Methodist, many of whom broadcast their congregations' services to at-home audiences as well.

Revolution, fundamental change in the form or nature of a government or societal way of life. A revolution can be a violent one that completely changes a form of government, such as the Russian Revolution (1917). It can also be nonviolent yet have a profound effect on the lives of people, such as the Industrial Revolution or other great changes brought on by technological innovations. Political revolutions usually occur when an outspoken leader or faction is able to capitalize on widespread dissatisfaction with an existing ruler or governing system. Some political revolutions have been nonviolent, with popular opposition forcing a decisive change, while other revolutions have resulted in large numbers of casualties and extensive property damage.

Revolutionary War in America, this term is used to describe the struggle in which the North American colonists fought for their

Berlin, 1848: on the barricades for the revolution. In each revolution, there is a period in which the masses (the people) revolt. In this case, the net result was poor. In Prussia, like in most other European countries, the revolution was soon crushed.

independence against the English fatherland. The struggle resulted in the creation of the United States of America. The revolution came about due to the growing dissatisfaction amongst the colonists about their relationship with England. The most contentious issue was the raising of import duties. Apart from the concrete objections to British rule, the American resistance was influenced by the liberation theories of Enlightenment and Puritanism. The conflict with England was fought out in the American War of Independence (1775-1783), which ended with the Treaty of Versailles and American independence.

Revolution of 1848, series of unsuccessful revolutionary uprisings in France, Italy, the Austrian Empire, and Germany in 1848. Each was relatively spontaneous and self-contained, but all had a number of common causes: the successful example of the French

Revolution of 1789, economic unrest due to bad harvests and unemployment, and a growing frustration, fired by nationalist fervor, about the repressive policies of conservative politicians like Prince von Metternich and François Guizot. In 1848, a major uprising in Paris overthrew King Louis Philippe and Guizot, but it was suppressed and the Third Republic proclaimed. In Italy, during the Risorgimento, short-lived republics were proclaimed, and there was agitation to secure independence from Austria, which was itself shaken by revolutions in Vienna, Prague, and Hungary. The demand for a representative government led to an all-German Diet in Frankfurt that failed in its efforts to unite Germany. In England there was working-class agitation (Chartism), and other European countries were also affected.

Revolver, pistol with semiautomatic action made possible by the incorporation of a revolving cylinder carrying several bullets. In 1835 Samuel Colt patented the first practical revolver. The modern revolver is based on the Colt design and is used by police and other armed forces throughout the world. *See also:* Colt, Samuel.

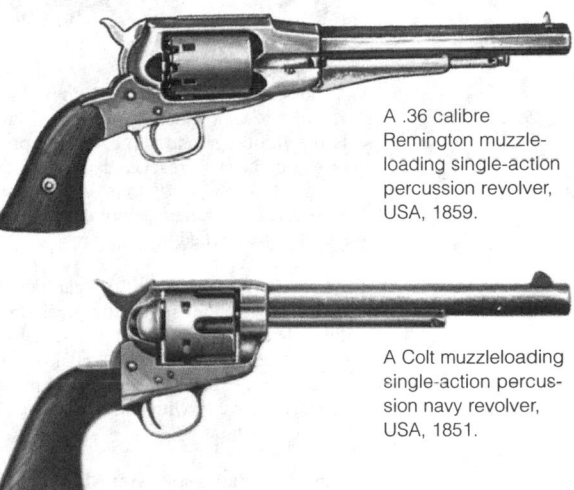

A .36 calibre Remington muzzle-loading single-action percussion revolver, USA, 1859.

A Colt muzzleloading single-action percussion navy revolver, USA, 1851.

Rexroth, Kenneth (1905-1982), U.S. poet. In the 1940s and 1950s he developed a style that broke with traditional forms of poetry and became the forerunner of what is now considered the 'Beat generation' of San Francisco poets and writers. His best-known works are *In What Hour* (1940), *The Dragon and the Unicorn* (1952), and *In Defense of the Earth* (1956). *The Collected Shorter Poems* (1967) and *The Collected Longer Poems* (1968) further enhanced Rexroth's literary reputation, as did a collection of his essays, *The World Outside the Window* (1987). He was also a gifted painter and translator of Chinese, Latin, and Greek poetry.

Reye's syndrome, rare disease that attacks the liver and central nervous system of children age 4-15. Of unknown cause, it is contracted by most victims following a viral illness, such as chicken pox or the flu. Aspirin use may be associated with the syndrome. Symptoms include vomiting and may progress into convulsions, disorientation,

Three examples of military dress from the American Revolution. Left: the infantry man from Washington's Continental Army had far better equipment than his counterparts in colonial militia units. Center: camouflage dress of a colonial rifleman, which was by no means a standard uniform, proved its worth in battles that were contested over forested terrain. Right: the grenadier of the Second Foot Guard, an elite force within Britain's colonial army, was among the finest combat soldiers of his time.

R

Common rhea, *Rhea americana*, South America, 5 ft (1.5 m) tall.

R

and possible brain damage and comas. Treatment is with glucose and other nutrients or with drugs and surgery when pressure within the skull reaches dangerous levels. About 3-5% of victims die. Named (1963) after Australian pathologist R.D.K. Reye, who researched it.

Reykjavik (pop. 110,000), capital of Iceland and its chief port, commercial and industrial center, and home of its cod-fishing fleet. Settled in A.D. 877, Reykjavik means 'smoking bay,' from the nearby hot springs that provide the city with central heating.
See also: Iceland.

Reymont, Wladyslaw Stanislaw (1868-1925), Polish writer, began as a naturalist. His masterpiece *Chlopi* (The Peasants; 1904-1909) is an epic description of rural life in the style of neo-romantic Young Poland. Received the Nobel Prize for literature in 1924.

Reynard the Fox, leading character in a popular medieval series of fables. Appearing first in the area between the Flanders and Germany in the 10th century, the tales, with their cunning but sympathetic hero and biting satire, became popular in France, Germany, and the Low Countries.

Reynaud, Paul (1878-1966), French statesman. After holding a number of cabinet posts (from 1930), he became premier (1940). An opponent of the Nazis, he spent World War II in prison. Afterward he held several posts and helped draft the constitution of the Fifth Republic (1958).
See also: France.

Reynolds, Sir Joshua (1723-1792), perhaps the most famous English portrait painter. Ambitious and popular, he became first president of the Royal Academy of Arts (1768). He held that great art is based on the styles of earlier masters and espoused the 'Grand Style.' He painted nearly all his notable contemporaries, including his friend Samuel Johnson (1772). His works also include William Robertsen (1772) and Sarah Siddons as the Tragic Muse (1784). He also published influential essays on art education called *Discourses* (1769-1790). Reynolds was influenced by the paintings of Anton Van Dyck, Tintoretto, Titian, Paolo Veronese, and Peter Paul Rubens.

Reza Shah Pahlavi (1877-1944), shah of Iran (1925-1941). An army officer, he led a coup in 1921, becoming prime minister and later (1925) founder of the Pahlavi dynasty. He made important military, administrative, and economic reforms, but the Allies forced him to resign in World War II for refusing to allow them to use Iran as a supply route.
See also: Iran.

Rhea, large flightless South American bird of the order Rheaformes. Closely resembling the ostrich, the rhea is smaller, with larger wings, more head and neck feathers, and 3 rather than 2 toes on each foot. Rheas generally stand 5 ft (1.5 m) tall and weigh up to 55 lb (25 kg). They are plains-dwellers in the temperate region south of the equator, usually flocking together in groups of 5-30. Often found grazing with cattle, they feed on leaves, roots, and insects. The male rhea digs a hole in the ground for a nest, where several females may lay as many as 30 eggs; the male sits on the eggs until they hatch.

Rhea, in Greek mythology, wife and sister of Cronus (ruler of the Titans), daughter of Gaea (the earth) and Uranus (the sky). She became queen of the gods after Cronus defeated Uranus. She had 6 children: Zeus, Poseidon, Pluto, Hestia, Hera, and Demeter. She later helped Zeus overthrow Cronus.
See also: Mythology.

Rhee, Syngman (1875-1965), president of South Korea. A leader in the movement to win Korean independence from Japan, he was in exile in Honolulu from 1910 to 1945, serving as president of the Korean Provisional Government for 20 years. Returning to Korea after World War II, he became the first president of the Republic of Korea (South Korea) in 1948. He resigned from office in 1960 because of corruption and mismanagement by some of his appointees. He wrote *Spirit of Independence* (1904) during his imprisonment (1897-1904) for heading demonstrations for independence.

Rhenium, chemical element, symbol Re; for physical constants see Periodic Table. Rhenium was discovered by Walter Noddack, Ida Tacke, and Otto Berg in 1925. It occurs in the minerals columbite, wolframite, gadolinite, and molybdenite. It is prepared by the high-temperature reduction of ammonium with hydrogen. Rhenium is a silver-white, ductile, high-melting, dense metal. It is resistant to wear and electrical corrosion. Rhenium and its compounds are used in alloys for electrical contacts and filaments, electron tube and semiconductor applications, high-temperature thermocouples, and poison-resistant catalysts. Dmitri Mendeleev predicted this element, which he called *dwi-manganese*.

Rheostat, variable resistor used to control the current drawn by an electric motor to dim lighting. It may consist of resistive wire wound in a helix, with a sliding contact varying the effective length, or of a series of fixed resistors connected between a row of button contacts. For heavy loads, electrodes dipped in solutions can be used, the resistance being controlled by the immersion depth and separation of the electrodes.

Rhesus monkey (*Maccaca mulatta*), monkey found in southern and southeastern Asia. Its use in medical and behavioral research led to the discovery of the Rh factor, a substance found in human red blood cells. Rhesus monkeys measure 18-25 in (48-64 cm) and weigh from 9-22 lb (4-10 kg) with a tail of 7-12 in (18-30 cm). They live in deserts, farm areas, forests, mountains and swamps. They eat birds, fruit, insects, leaves, roots, and farm crops.

Rhetoric *See:* Oratory.

Rheumatic fever, feverish illness, following infection with *streptococcus* and leading to systemic disease. It occurs mainly in children age 5-15. Symptoms include skin rash, subcutaneous nodules, and a migrating arthritis. Involvement of the heart (rheumatic heart disease) may lead to palpitations, chest pain, cardiac failure, myocarditis, inflammation of the pericardium, and permanent heart damage. Treatment includes bed rest, aspirin, and steroids. Penicillin treatment of this noncontagious disease may prevent recurrence.

Rheumatism, term popularly applied to pain affecting muscles, tendons, joints, bones, or nerves, in such widely varied disorders as rheumatoid arthritis, degenerative joint disease, spondylitis, bursitis, fibrositis, myositis, neuritis, lumbago, sciatica, and gout.

Rh factor, protein substance appearing on the surface of red blood cells of most people (85% or more), capable of inducing an immune response. It was first detected in a rhesus monkey in 1940 by Karl Landsteiner and Alexander Weiner.
See also: Landsteiner, Karl.

Rhineland, region of Germany along the Rhine River and its tributaries. From the Roman Empire through World War II, the Rhineland was strategically important; whoever controlled the river often exercised power over Western Europe. During the Middle Ages, Rhineland cities were political and religious centers of the Holy Roman Empire and, later, for the breakaway Protestant churches. For protection against raiding armies, heavily fortified castles-now tourist attractions-were built on hills overlooking the Rhine. In the Napoleonic Wars, the Franco-Prussian War, and both world wars, the Rhineland was a key battleground.

Rich mineral deposits there, especially iron and coal, led to Germany's development as a world power in the late 19th and early 20th centuries. The Rhineland is still a key industrial region, and has some the world's most productive vineyards.
See also: Germany.

Rhine River, longest river in western Europe, rising in Switzerland and flowing 820 mi (1,320 km) through Germany and the Netherlands into the North Sea near Rotterdam. It is of great historical and commercial significance, being navigable by seagoing ships up to Cologne and by large barges as far as Basel. Canals link it to the Rhône, Marne, Ems, Weser, Elbe, Oder, and Danube rivers. Some of its finest scenery is along the gorge between Bingen and Bonn, with terraced vineyards, ruined castles, and famous landmarks like the Lorelei rock.

Rhinitis, most frequent of the acute upper respiratory infections, characterized by edema, swelling and widening of the blood vessels of the mucous membrane of the nose, nasal discharge, and obstruction. It can result from infections, allergic reactions, hay fever, and unknown stimuli.
See also: Cold, common.

Rhinoceros, any of 5 species of heavy land mammals (family *Rhinocerotidae*) characterized by one or two nasal 'horn' or 'horns,' formed of a mass of compacted hairs. They are bulky animals with poor vision and thick, hairless skin, often falling in heavy, loose folds. They live in transitional habitats between open grassland and high forest, grazing or browsing at night on bushes or shrubs. All 5 species- the white rhinoceros (*Ceratotherium simum*), the black (*Diceros bicornus*), the Indian (*Rhinoceros unicornis*), the Sumatran (*Dicerorhinus sumatrensis*), and the Javan (*R. sondaicus*)-have been hunted for their horns to the verge of extinction.

Rhizoid *See:* Moss.

Rhizome, or rootstock, swollen horizontal underground stem of certain plants, such as ginger. The rhizome acts as an organ of perennation (ability to live over from season to season), and vegetative propagation lasts for several years. New shoots appear each spring near the scale leaves. If split, the rhizome lives on as numerous individuals.

Rhode Island (Little Rhody, Ocean State; pop. 1,000,000), smallest State of the U.S., in New England, bordering on Connecticut, Massachusetts, and the Atlantic Ocean; 1,213 sq mi (3,140 sq km). High population density. Capital, Providence. Low-lying, flat area. The state has a humid, continental climate: July average temperature 22°C, January -2°C; annual rainfall of 1000 mm. Cattle and poultry farming; arable farming and market gardening. Industry is the most important economic activity. Metal, textile, and jewelry industries. Manufacture of silverware, jewelry. Some fishing and mining. Present high growth in services sector. First colonized in 1636 by pioneers driven out of Massachusetts because of their religious beliefs. The state suffered much during the

Indian revolt (1675-1676, King Phillip's War). Rhode Island was one of the original 13 states that formed the U.S. in 1783.

Rhodes, or Ródhos, Greek island covering 540 sq mi (1,399 sq km), off the southwest coast of Turkey. The capital city is also called Rhodes. The island's exports include wine, fruit, and olive oil; tourism is its main industry. Rhodes was a prosperous city-state in the 3rd century B.C. At the harbor stood the Colossus of Rhodes, a statue that was one of the Seven Wonders of the ancient world.

Rhodes, Cecil John (1853-1902), English politician and business magnate who first opened up Rhodesia to European settlement. Having made a fortune in diamond mining, he founded the De Beers Mining Company in 1888 at Kimberly in South Africa. After helping bring about the British annexation of Bechuanaland (1884), he also obtained the territory to the north, later called Rhodesia (now Zimbabwe) in his honor, which he managed until 1890. Prime minister of the Cape Colony from 1890, he was forced to resign because of complicity in the Jameson raid (1896) into the Transvaal. Much of his £6 million fortune went to found the Rhodes scholarships.
See also: Rhodes Scholarship.

Rhodesia *See:* Zimbabwe.

Rhodesia and Nyasaland, Federation of, British federation in central Africa created in 1953 that included Southern Rhodesia, Northern Rhodesia, and Nyasaland. In 1963 Great Britain agreed to break up the federation and give the colonies their independence, largely as a result of widespread opposition by the black majority to the white-dominated government. The new nations of Malawi, Zambia, and Zimbabwe were later formed.
See also: Malawi; Zambia.

Rhodesian ridgeback, also called African lion hound, hunting dog that originated in

The Rhine in the Netherlands, near Pannerden, with Doorneburg castle in the foreground.

southern Africa. Hunters value its ability to find and hold off lions; it is also known as a good watchdog and companion. Ridgebacks are named for the ridge of hair that grows on their backs in the opposite direction from the rest of the coat, which is yellowish to reddishbrown. They have the drooping ears typical of most hounds, stand 24-27 in (61-69 cm) high, and weigh 65-75 lb (30-34 kg).

Rhodes Scholarship, award instituted (1902) at Oxford University by the bequest of Cecil John Rhodes, English politician and business magnate, for students from the Commonwealth, the United States, and Germany. The scholarship, awarded for 2 and sometimes 3 years, provides the student's university tuition and fees as well as living allowance. Elections are based on general grounds as well as on academic ability.

Rhodium, chemical element, symbol Rh; for physical constants see Periodic Table. Rhodium was discovered by William H. Wollaston in 1803. It occurs in the minerals sperrylite, iridosmine, and in some copper-nickel sulfide ores. Rhodium is a silver-white, high-melting, unreactive metal, a member of the platinum family of elements. It is one of the few substances that is not attacked by fluorine. The metal is used to

The African white rhino (*Cerato therium simum*, order *Perissodactyla*), and the yellow-billed oxpecker (*Buphagus africanus*, order *Passeriformes*), have a symbiotic relationship. The oxpecker, a type of African starling, feeds by pulling ticks from the rhino's hide and sipping blood that oozes from the tick wounds. The rhino benefits from the removal of extoparasites.

harden platinum and palladium. Plated or evaporated coatings of the element have high reflectance and are used in optical instruments. Rhodium and its compounds are used in thermocouples, crucibles, electrodes, and electrical contacts and as catalysts.

Rhododendron, genus of mostly evergreen shrubs (family Ericaceae) found mainly in forests of the arctic and north temperate zones. They bear leathery dark-green leaves and, in late spring, masses of fragrant blossom. North American species include the great rhododendron, also known as great laurel or rosebay (*R. maximum*), and the mountain rosebay (*R. catawbiense*).

Rhombus, parallelogram in which the sides are of equal length but usually not at right angles to each other. Its area can be computed by using the formula $A = bh$, where b is the base and h is the height.

Rhône River, important European river, 507 mi (816 km) long, rising in Switzerland and flowing through Lake Geneva and then southwest and south through France into the Mediterranean Sea. With its tributaries, particularly the Isère and the Saône, it has a large flow of water, which has been harnessed in major hydroelectric schemes. Navigable in part, it is linked by canal to the Camargue region.

Rhubarb, name for plants (genus *Rheum*) of the buckwheat family. First cultivated in China for its purgative medicinal rootstock, it is also used for food. The pink, fleshy leafstalks, or petioles, sprout from underground rhizomes and bear large green leaves that can be poisonous.

Rib, in humans, one of the 24 long, flat, curved bones forming the wall of the chest. *See also:* Human body.

Ribbentrop, Joachim von (1893-1946), German Nazi leader, ambassador to the United Kingdom (1936-1938) and foreign minister (1938-1945). He helped to negoti-

ate the Rome-Berlin Axis (1936) and the Russo-German nonaggression pact (1939) and to plan the invasion of Poland, but he wielded little influence in World War II. He was hanged for war crimes.
See also: Nazism; World War II.

Ribbon worm, any of a group of elongated marine worms (phylum Nemertina), ranging in size from less than 1 in (2.5 cm) to 90 ft (27 m) long. Most live in the open sea, but some live in fresh water or on land. They all have a long proboscis, sometimes spiked and poisonous, that can be thrown out with great accuracy to capture worms and other small animals.

Ribera, Jusepe de (c.1590-1652), Spanish painter who lived after 1618 in Naples. His work, influenced by Caravaggio, combines naturalism and mysticism, as in the *Martyrdom of St. Sebastian* (1630) and *The Penitent Magdalen* (c.1640).

Riboflavin *See:* Vitamin.

Ricardo, David (1772-1823), English economist, founder, with Adam Smith, of the classical school. He made a fortune as a stockbroker and then devoted his time to economics and politics, becoming a member of Parliament (1819-1823). His main work, *Principles of Political Economy and Taxation* (1817), pioneered the use of theoretical models in analyzing the distribution of wealth.
See also: Economics.

Ricci, Matteo (1552-1610), Italian Jesuit missionary. He entered China in 1583, learned Chinese, and eventually won acceptance. He introduced Western mathematics, astronomy, and geography to the Chinese, and sent the first detailed reports of China to the West.
See also: Jesuits.

Rice (*Oryza sativa*), grain-yielding annual plant of the grass family (*Graminae*). It is grown chiefly in southern and eastern Asia, where it is the staple food of hundreds of

millions of people. Rice needs hot, moist conditions to grow, which historically made it highly dependent on monsoon rainfall. Improved irrigation, fertilizers, pesticides, and the development of improved varieties have enormously increased the yield. Machinery for planting and harvesting rice is used in the United States and parts of South America, but in Asia rice farming uses hand labor. Rice has a reasonable nutrient value, but when brown rice is 'polished' (to make white rice), much of its vitamin B_1 content is lost.

Rice, Condoleezza (1954-), first woman to occupy the post of National Security Advisor of the U.S. President. She obtained her degree in Political Science at the University of Denver. Rice specialized in the former Soviet Union, learned to speak Russian and received her doctorate in 1981. She taught at Stanford (1981-1989), held several offices in Washington and published two books and numerous articles. President George Bush appointed her member of the National Security Council concerning the former Soviet Union and Eastern Europe in 1989. As a top advisor, she was directly involved in the American-Russian high-profile meetings. In 1991, she returned to Stanford, but she remained an active foreign policy expert. She was appointed National Security Advisor to President George W. Bush in 2001. Initially, she and Secretary of State, Colin Powel, had reservations about foreign interventions, but after the attacks of September 11, 2001, she became an advocate of military actions in Afghanistan, and against Saddam Hussein.
See also: Bush, George W.; Powell, Colin.

Rice, Elmer (1892-1967), U.S. dramatist. His plays on social themes include *The Adding Machine* (1923), an expressionist fantasy; *Street Scene* (1929), a Pulitzer Prize-winning portrait of life in a tenement; and the romantic comedy *Dream Girl* (1945).

Rice, Grantland (1880-1954), U.S. journalist known as the first famous sportswriter.

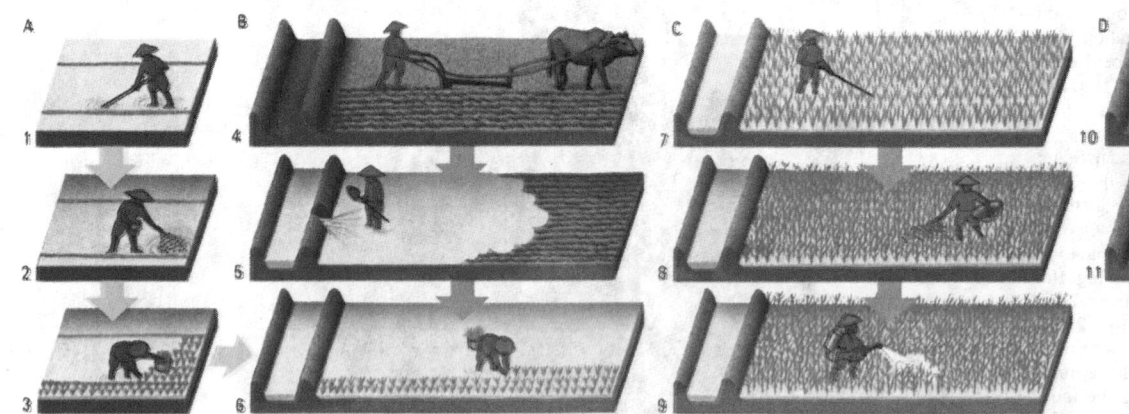

A paddyfield is ploughed up and irrigated. Seedlings, which have been raised in nursery plots, are transplanted into the field. The growing crop is tended until ready for harvest, when the rice grains are threshed from the straw.

A. (1) Nursery preparation,
B. (4) Ploughing,
(5) Irrigation,
(2) sowing seed,
(3) pulling seedlings.
(6) transplanting.
C. (7) Weeding,
(8) spreading fertiliser,
(9) spraying.
D. (10) Harvesting,
(11) drying,
(12) threshing.

R

Rice covered sporting events in the 1920s and 1930s and also produced poetry and his autobiography, *The Tumult and the Shouting* (1954).

Ricebird *See:* Bobolink.

Rice weevil *See:* Grain weevil.

Rich, Adrienne (1929-), U.S. feminist poet whose primary themes are women's issues and sexuality and the problem of human communication. Her works include *Diving into the Wreck* (1973), *Of Woman Born* (1976), *The Dream of a Common Language* (1978), *Time's Power: Poems 1985-1988, An Atlas of the difficult World* (1991), *Collected early Poems* (1993), and several volumes of selected prose.

Richard, name of three kings of England. **Richard I** (1157-1199), called Coeur de Lion (Lion-Hearted), was the third son of Henry II, whom he succeeded in 1189. He spent all but six months of his reign out of England, mainly on the Third Crusade. After taking Cyprus and Acre in 1191 and recapturing Jaffa in 1192, he was captured while returning to England and handed over to Holy Roman Emperor Henry VI, who held him for ransom until 1194. After a brief spell in England, he spent the rest of his life fighting against Philip II in France. **Richard II** (1367-1400), son of Edward the Black Prince, succeeded his grandfather Edward III in 1377. In his minority the country was governed by a group of nobles dominated by his uncle John of Gaunt. Richard quarreled with them but only began to assert himself after 1397; he executed his uncle the Duke of Gloucester and banished Henry Bolingbroke, Gaunt's son, and confiscated his estates. Bolingbroke returned in 1399 to depose Richard and imprison him in Pontefract castle, where he died. Bolingbroke succeeded as Henry IV. **Richard III** (1452-1485), third son of Richard Plantagenet, Duke of York, and the younger brother of Edward IV, usurped the throne in 1483. The traditional picture of him as a hunchbacked and cruel ruler who murdered his nephews in the Tower has little historical backing. He instituted many reforms and encouraged trade but had little hope of defeating his many enemies gathering in France under Henry Tudor (later Henry VII). They defeated and killed Richard at Bosworth Field, ending the War of the Roses.
See also: England; United Kingdom.

Richard, Maurice (1921-), Canadian-born hockey player. Known for his fast skating and blistering shots, 'The Rocket' was the first National Hockey League (NHL) player to score 50 goals in a 50-game season. Richard, named the NHL's most value player in 1947, played right wing for the Montreal Canadiens (1942-1960) and led them to 8 Stanley Cup championships (1944, 1946, 1953, 1956-1960). He was inducted into the Hockey Hall of Fame in 1961.

Richards, Dickinson Woodruff (1895-1973), U.S. physiologist awarded, with A.F.

Cournand and Werner Forssmann, the 1956 Nobel Prize in physiology or medicine for his work with Cournand using Forssmann's catheter technique to probe the heart, pulmonary artery, and lungs.
See also: Physiology.

Richards, Ivor Armstrong (1893-1979), English literary critic. He developed with C. K. Ogden the concept of Basic English, a primary vocabulary of 850 words. His books include *The Meaning of Meaning* (with Ogden, 1923) and *Principles of Literary Criticism* (1924).

Richardson, Henry Hobson (1838-1886), U.S. architect who pioneered an American Romanesque style. Among his important buildings are the Trinity Church in Boston and the Marshall Field Wholesale Store in Chicago.
See also: Architecture.

Richardson, Samuel (1689-1761), English novelist, best known for his novels in epistolary form, especially *Pamela; or, Virtue Rewarded* (1740-1741), the story of a servant girl's moral triumph over her lecherous master, and *Clarissa Harlowe* (1747-1748), his tragic masterpiece, also on the theme of seduction. *The History of Sir Charles Grandison* (1753-1754) portrays a virtuous hero, in contrast to the amoral hero of Henry Fielding's *Tom Jones*.

Richard Lion-Hearted *See:* Richard.

Richelieu, Cardinal (Armand Jean du Plessis, Duc de Richelieu; 1585-1642), French cardinal, statesman, and chief minister to Louis XIII for 18 years. By a mixture of diplomacy and ruthlessness he helped make France the leading power in Europe, with a monarchy secure against internal revolt. He destroyed Huguenot power by 1628, foiled an attempt by the king's mother, Marie de Médicis, to oust him in 1630, and suppressed the plots of the Duc de Montmorency in 1632 and of Cinq-Mars in 1642, at the same time reducing the power of the nobles. In foreign policy he opposed the Habsburgs, intervening against them in the Thirty Years' War. Richelieu strengthened the navy, encouraged colonial development, and patronized the arts (founding the Académie Française).
See also: France.

Richler, Mordecai (1931-2001), Canadian writer. His novels, especially *The Apprenticeship of Duddy Kravitz* (1959) and *Cocksure* (1968), are noted for their wry wit and biting satire.

Richter, Conrad (1890-1968), U.S. writer of fiction and nonfiction known for his novels about life on the American frontier. In 1961 he won the National Book Award for his novel *The Waters of Kronos*. He is best known for his trilogy, *The Awakening Land (1940-50)*, the story of a pioneer family living in Ohio; the third novel, *The Town*, won the 1950 Pulitzer Prize for literature.

Richter, Gerhard (1932-), German artist, born in the GDR, since 1961 professor in

Düsseldorf. His work consists of painting photographs, where he deliberately produces an unclear image in order to express the uncertainty of reality. Developed with Sigmar Polke and Konrad Lueg a method of painting in 1963 they called 'capitalist realism', whose aim was to depict the mechanics of consumption-oriented society. They became recognized as ironic commentators of their day, and of art in particular, and continually changed their style at will.

Richter, Hans (1843-1916), German conductor who presented the first performance of Wagner's *Ring* cycle at Bayreuth in 1876. A Brahms specialist also, he conducted in England for many years.

Richter, Johann Paul Friedrich (1763-1825), German humorous and sentimental novelist, who wrote as Jean Paul. He achieved popularity with such works as *The Invisible Lodge* (1793), *The Life of Quintus Fixlein* (1796), and *Titan* (1800-1803).

Richter scale, scale devised by C.F. Richter (1900-1985), used to measure the magnitudes of earthquakes in terms of the amplitude and frequency of the surface waves. The largest recorded earthquakes are about 8.5. A great earthquake of magnitude 8 occurs only once every 5-10 years. An increase of one unit corresponds to a tenfold increase in the size of an earthquake.
See also: Earthquake; Seismograph.

Manfred Richthofen (1892-1918), a World War I German fighter pilot, became known as the Red Baron.

Richthofen, Manfred von (1892-1918), German aviator, nicknamed the Red Baron. Known for the daring and chivalry with which he led his squadron in World War I, he shot down about 80 opponents before being killed in action.
See also: World War I.

Rickets, deficiency disease of infancy due to lack of vitamin D, characterized by poor nutrition and changes in the bones (bowleggedness, knock-knees, etc.). There is slight fever and sweating along with general symptoms.

Rickettsia, name for organisms partway between bacteria and viruses. Often borne by ticks or lice, they are responsible for a number of diseases, including typhus, scrub typhus, and Rocky Mountain spotted fever.

Rickover, Hyman George (1900-1986), Russian-born U.S. admiral who brought nuclear power to the U.S. Navy. Head of the navy's electrical division in World War II, he moved to the Atomic Energy Commission (AEC) in 1947 and developed the first nuclear-powered submarine, the *Nautilus* (1954). He attained the rank of full admiral at the age of 73 and retired in 1982.

Ricksha *See:* Jinrikisha.

Ridgway, Matthew Bunker (1895-1985), U.S. military leader. During World War II he led the first full-scale U.S. airborne attack in the invasion of Sicily (1943) and took part in the invasion of France (1944). He became commander of the United Nations forces in Korea (1951), supreme commander of NATO Allied Forces in Europe (1952-1953), and U.S. army chief of staff (1953-1955).
See also: Korean War; World War II.

Ridley, Nicholas (c.1500-1555), English Protestant martyr. Under Thomas Cranmer's patronage he became a chaplain to Henry VIII and bishop of Rochester (1547) and London (1550). He helped compile the Book of Common Prayer. On the accession of the Roman Catholic Mary I (1553) he was imprisoned and burned at Oxford, with Hugh Latimer, for heresy.
See also: Book of Common Prayer; Protestantism.

Riemann, Georg Friedrich Bernhard (1826-1866), German mathematician, whose best-known contribution is the initiation of studies of non-Euclidean geometry. Elliptic geometry is often referred to as Riemannian geometry.
See also: Geometry.

Riemenschneider, Tilman (c.1460-1531), German Gothic sculptor in wood and stone. He worked in Würzburg, where many of his works survive, and carved the marble tomb of Emperor Henry II and his wife in Bamberg Cathedral (1499-1513).

Rienzi, Cola di (1313-1354), Italian popular leader. With papal support, he became 'Tribune' of a popular republic in Rome (1347), but his plans for restoring the Roman Empire led to his overthrow.

Rietveld, Gerrit Thomas (1888-1964), Dutch architect and furniture designer. Very influential in 20th-century Dutch architec-

The Ecemenic Center (1959) in Rotterdam, by Gerrit Rietveld.

ture. Arrived at new spatial proportions. Represented 'De Stijl' ('The Style'): primary colors and rigid design. He later became an advocate of the functional architecture of The New Practicality. In 1928 he was joint founder of the Congrès International d'Architecture Moderne (CIAM). As a furniture designer he showed a preference for chairs throughout his whole career: in 1918 he designed his famous redblue chair. He set up his own architect's practice in Utrecht in 1919, where he worked from 1921 onwards together with furniture designer and interior architect Truus Schröder-Schräder, for whom he also designed the famous Schröder House in Utrecht in 1924.

Rifle, strictly, any firearm with a 'rifled' bore-i.e., with shallow helical grooves cut inside the barrel. These grooves, by causing the bullet to spin, steady it and increase its accuracy, velocity, and range. The term 'rifle' is more narrowly applied to the longbarreled hand weapon fired from the shoulder. Rifles are generally classified by caliber or decimal fractions or by mode of action.

Rift Valley *See:* Great Rift Valley.

Riga (pop. 916,000), capital of Latvia. Located near the Gulf of Riga at the mouth of the Daugava River, it is an important center of shipping and industry as well as the hub of Latvian cultural and political activity. The city, founded in 1201 and variously under the control of Poland, Sweden, and Russia, was incorporated into the USSR in 1940. In 1991 independent Latvian rule was restored.
See also: Latvia.

Rigel, one of the brightest stars in the galaxy. Located in the constellation Orion, it is about 50 times as large as the sun, with a diameter of about 40 million mi (64 million km). Its distance from the earth is about 900 light-years.
See also: Orion; Star.

Rigging *See:* Sailing.

Right of privacy *See:* Privacy, Right of.

Right of search, international law under which nations at war are allowed to search the vessels of neutral nations for contraband. Ships may also be searched during times of peace. Regulations regarding a ship's distance from the coast depend on the nature of the particular search. During Prohibition, some nations consented to extend the number of miles. This practice is still in effect.
See also: Contraband.

Right of way *See:* Easement.

Rights, Bill of *See:* Bill of rights.

Rights of Man, Declaration of the *See:* Declaration of the Rights of Man and the Citizen.

Right whale *See:* Whale.

Right wing, conservative faction within a

political group or party. The term derives from the custom-first used in revolutionary France-of seating nobility on the right side of the king. This convention is still used by some organizations.
See also: Conservatism.

Rigveda, Old Indian *Vedasamhita*, a collection of 1028 hymns (suktas), songs praising the gods, cosmogonic hymns; the oldest Indo-European document.

Rihm, Wolfgang (1952-), German composer, above all known for his Third Symphony and the chamber opera *Jakob Lenz* (1978). Leading composer of the young German generation, exponents of neo-expressionism. His works include *Doppelgesang* for viola, cello and orchestra (1980), Viola Concerto (1981), *Die Hamletmaschine* (1986), musical theatre after Heiner Müller, *Die Eroberung von Mexico* (1987-1989), *Klangbeschreibung I-II* (1982-1987), *Chiffre I-VII* (1982-1988), *Three Symphonies* (1969, 1975, 1976), and *Séraphin* (1994).

Rijeka (pop. 168,000), Croatia, a city in the northwest part of the country, on the Kvarner Gulf of the Adriatic Sea. Behind the city rises a coastal range of the Dinaric Alps, peaking at about 5,000 feet (1,500 m). Rijeka is a major seaport and an industrial city with shipbuilding, petroleum refining, and other manufacturing. The University of Rijeka, an ancient Roman gate, a 13th-century cathedral, and several museums are here. Nearby are several seaside resorts, most notably Opatija.
Rijeka has been a part of the Roman, Byzantine, French, and Austrian empires. The city was Hungary's chief seaport from 1779 until World War I. After World War I possession of Rijeka was disputed by Italy and Yugoslavia. In 1919 Gabriele D' Annunzio with a small company of Italian troops seized the city and proclaimed it an independent state. D' Annunzio was ousted after 15 months, and in 1924 Rijeka was taken over by Italy and named Fiume. Susak, an eastern suburb now included in Rijeka, became part of Yugoslavia. Following World War II, Yugoslavia gained possession of the entire city. It was under Yugoslav control until Croatia became independent in 1992.

Rikkokushi, collective noun for six Japanese historical books written between 720 and 887, commissioned by the emperors during the Nara and Heian periods. Copying Chinese examples, the Rikkokushi depicts historical subjects in chronological order; they are written in Chinese. Each book deals with a period of ancient history, and begins with the era of the gods; the Rikkokushi also describes the history of the early Japanese nation and its aristocratic families.

Riley, Bridget (1931-), British painter, representative of the 'Op Art' movement. Her paintings create the illusion of moving shapes and colors that are not really there, initially using black and white dots, zigzags, or wavy lines. Later concentrated on the optical effects of color.

Riley, Terry (1935-), American composer, studied at Berkeley, worked in Paris between 1962-1964 (0RTF) and met Pandit Pran Nath in 1970, under whom he studied Hindustani music. Many of his compositions are improvisations combining electrical equipment and live music. His works include *Ear Piece* (1960), *In C* (1964), *A Rainbow in Curved Air* (1967), *Persian Surgery Dervishes* (1971), *Descending Moonshine Dervishes (1975), June Buddhas* (1991), *The Saint Adolph Ring* (1992), and *3 Requiem Quartets* (1998).

Rilke, Rainer Maria (1875-1926), German lyric poet. His complex, symbolic poetry is preoccupied with spiritual questioning about God and death, as in the *Book of Hours* (1905) and *New Poems* (1907-1908). The poems in his later *Duino Elegies* (1923) and the *Sonnets to Orpheus* (1923) are considered his finest work.

Rimbaud, Arthur (1854-1891), French poet. His vivid imagery and his 'disordering of consciousness,' reflected in such poems as 'The Drunken Boat' (1871), have had an enormous influence on modern poetry. He published *A Season in Hell* in 1873, after which he denounced his poetry and became an adventurer. His major collection, *Les Illuminations*, was published in 1886. Rimbaud was closely associated with the poet Paul Verlaine.

Rimet, Jules (1873-1956), French sports administrator, president of FIFA (world football association) from 1921 to 1954. He was strongly committed to organizing a world cup football competition for national teams, the first of which was held in 1930. The trophy of the world cup was named Coupe Jules Rimet in his honor.

Rimsky-Korsakov, Nikolai (1844-1908), Russian composer. While still a naval officer he started teaching composition at the St. Petersburg Conservatory (1871). He wrote scores for the operas *The Snow Maiden* (1882) and *The Golden Cockerel* (1909) and a colorful symphonic suite, *Scheherezade* (1888).

Rinderpest, acute virus disease of cattle, common in North Africa and South Asia.

Ring, small circular band worn on the body as decoration. It is often made of metal and sometimes engraved or set with gems. Rings are most common on the fingers and ears, but are also worn on the nose or toes. Its symbolic value has been recognized throughout the ages. Rings have been used to show position or social status, designate membership in an organization, and denote friendship.
See also: Jewelry.

Ringling brothers, five U.S. brothers who created the world's largest circus. Led by John Ringling (1866-1936), they started with a one-wagon show and became Barnum & Bailey's chief rival, buying them out in 1907. The combined Ringling Bros. and Barnum & Bailey Circus was the world's largest by 1930. It remained in the family's hands until 1967.
See also: Barnum, P(hineas) T(aylor); Circus.

Ringtail, or cacomistle, member of the raccoon family found in North and Central America. About 12-15 in (30-38 cm) long, ringtails generally have grayish brown fur and long, black-and-white striped tails. They are nocturnal and subsist mainly on rodents. North American ringtails live in the deserts and forests of the West and Southwest.

Ringworm, common fungus disease of the skin of humans and animals; it may also affect the hair and nails. Ringshaped raised lesions occur; temporary baldness is seen on hairy skin, and the nails may disintegrate. Athlete's foot is ringworm of the toes, while tinea cruris is a variety that affects the groin. Treatments include topical ointments and systemic antifungal antibiotics.

Rinser, Luise (1911-2002), German writer. Rinser studied psychology and pedagogy. Her first successful publication, a collection of short stories called *Die gläsernen Ringe* (1940), in which she describes the world as seen from the perspective of a child, led to her works being banned. Accused of high treason, she spent one year (1944-1945) in prison, the experience of which is described in *Prison Journal* (1946). From 1945-1953 she was a staff member of the Neue Zeitung in Munich. She later explored the subject of adult womanhood from a religious viewpoint in such books as *Mitte des Lebens* (1950, and the sequel *Abenteuer der Tugend*, 1957). Both novels appeared in 1961 under the title *Nina*.

Nikolai Rimsky-Korsakov, portrayed here by V.A. Serov, was a great Russian composer of the late 19th century.

R

Rio de Janeiro (pop. 5.55 million), second largest city of Brazil, on the Atlantic coast about 200 mi (322 km) east of São Paulo. Located in a picturesque setting, the city is a leading resort, as well as a center for the manufacture of clothing, furniture, glassware, and foodstuffs. The area was settled by the French (1555-1567) and then by the Portuguese. It was the Brazilian capital from 1763 to 1960, when it was supplanted by Brasília.
See also: Brazil.

The white-throated capuchin (*C. capucines*), native to Central America, is named for its black cap of fur that resembles the cowl of a Capuchin monk. It is one of the most intelligent monkeys.

Río de la Plata, estuary formed by the Paraná and Uruguay rivers, separating Argentina and Uruguay. It flows 171 miles (275 km) southeast into the Atlantic.

Rio Grande, one of the longest rivers in North America, known in Mexico as the Rio Bravo del Norte. It rises in the San Juan Mountains in southwestern Colorado and flows 1,885 (3,034 km) southeast and south to the Gulf of Mexico at Brownsville, Tex., and Matamoros, Mexico. From El Paso, Tex., to its mouth, it forms the U.S.-Mexico border.

Rio Madeira *See:* Madeira River.

Rios, Marcelo (1975-), Chilean tennis player, won his first ATP tournament in Bologna in 1995. Since then he has won various tournaments, and in 1996 became the first Chilean tennis player to appear in the Top Ten rankings. Rios reached the fourth round of all Grand Slam tournaments in 1997, and reached the quarterfinals of the Australian Open and the American Open championships. In 1998 he was beaten in the final of the Australian Open championships by Petr Korda, but in March that year he won the prestigious Key Biscayne tournament. This victory ensured him first place in the ATP rankings.

Riot, unlawful rebellion against a public authority by a group of people, involving breach of the peace, destruction of property, and/or violence. Riots are defined variously around the world, and punishment differs accordingly. Riots can be spontaneous or planned. They often break out during a protest, due to the heightened emotions of demonstrators and authorities. Although the U.S. Constitution protects the right of its citizens to group together for the purposes of peaceful dissent, such gatherings are considered riots when they involve breach of peace, destruction of property, or violence.

R

Riparian rights, privileges accruing to owners of land on the edges of streams, rivers, and lakes. These 'water rights' allow a landowner to use the water for domestic, agricultural, or commercial purposes, usually with the provision that such use should not infringe on the rights of other riparian owners.

Rip Van Winkle, folk tale by U.S. author Washington Irving from his collection, *The Sketch Book of Geoffrey Crayon, Gent.* (1819-1820). The story concerns a cheerful but unsuccessful farmer who, while hunting in the Catskill Mountains, meets some quaintly dressed men playing ninepins. After he drinks from their keg of liquor he falls asleep and wakes to find his dog gone and his gun rusted. He makes his way home and discovers that he has slept for 20 years, his children have grown, and he has become a citizen of the United States instead of a subject of King George III. He later finds that the men he encountered were the ghosts of Henry Hudson and his crew.

Rite of passage, ceremony within a community to mark an individual's achievement of a new stage in life (e.g., birth, puberty, marriage) and consequent change of role in the community.

Ritsma, Rintje (1970-), Dutch ice skater, became all-round European champion for the first time in 1994. In 1995 he won both the European and world championships. During the 1994 Winter Olympics Ritsma won bronze in the 5 km and silver in the 1500 m. He was 1500 m world record holder with a time of 1.51.60 until Johan Olaf Koss improved that time when he won the gold medal in 1994. In 1996 he became all-round world champion again. In 1977 Ritsma became 1500 m and 5 km world champion. He won his fourth all-round European title in Helsinki in 1998. In 1999 he won again both the European and world championships. During the Olympic Games in Nagano (February 1998) Ritsma won the 1500 m bronze, 5 km silver, and 10 km bronze.

Ritual *See:* Religion.

River, long channel of water. The ground beneath is called the bed; to either side are its banks. Rivers begin as headwaters overflowing from lakes or running down mountains as the snow melts, forming rills, brooks, and streams. The amount of river water depends on rainfall, since the river system provides the drainage for the surrounding land. The water runs downward to sea level, taking the shortest, steepest route; the river's upper course has the swiftest currents, as well as any waterfalls or rapids. The force of the current may erode the valleys or cut into rock, forming canyons. The river's lower course usually flows through a flat area called the flood plain until it reaches the mouth, the point where the river reaches the coast. The mouth may form a delta (a triangular deposit of sediment), or an estuary (a deep, wide mouth filled with fresh and salt waters). Rivers, important routes of transportation, can provide power for industry and help irrigate crops. At 4,145 mi (6,671 km), the Nile River in Africa is the longest in the world.

Rivera, Diego (1886-1957), Mexican mural painter. He painted large murals of social life and political themes throughout Mexico and in the United States, where his Marxist views aroused controversy.

River dolphin, any of four species of freshwater whales found in the waters of South America and Asia, belonging to the family Platanistidae. River dolphins differ from marine dolphins in that they have longer snouts, more teeth, poorer vision, and a lower level of activity. They measure up to 9 ft (2.7 m) long, and can be black, white, yellow, pink, gray, or brown in color.

River horse *See:* Hippopotamus.

Rivers, Larry (1923-2002), U.S. painter. He adapted the style of abstract expressionism to the popular imagery of well-known pictures and commercial advertisements, as in *Dutch Masters Series* (1963).

Riveting, joining of machine or structural parts, usually plates, by rivets. Rivets are headed bolts, usually made of steel, that are passed through the plates, a second head then being formed on the plain end by pressure, hammering, or an explosive charge. Large rivets are heated for satisfactory closing. Although riveting can be automated, it is slowly being displaced by arc welding.

Riviera, coastal region of the Mediterranean Sea in southeastern France and northwestern Italy. It is a major tourist center, noted for its scenery and pleasant climate. The Riviera's fashionable resorts include Cannes, Nice, and St. Tropez in France; Monte Carlo in Monaco; and Bordighera, Portofino, Rapallo, and San Remo in Italy.

Riyadh (pop. 2,5 million), Saudi Arabian city and seat of the Saudi royal family, about 240 mi (386 km) west of the Persian Gulf. It is an important commercial center and has rapidly expanded because of the oil trade. *See also:* Saudi Arabia.

Rizal, José (1861-1896), Philippine writer and patriot. His novels *The Lost Eden* (1886) and *The Subversive* (1891) denounced Spanish rule in the Philippines. His execution by the Spanish on charges of instigating insurrection led to a full-scale rebellion.

Rizzio, David (c.1533-1566), Italian musician, favorite of Mary, Queen of Scots. He became Mary's secretary in 1564. Scottish nobles, including Lord Darnley, Mary's husband, assassinated him.

RNA *See:* Nucleic acid.

Roach, fish belonging to the carp and minnow family, commonly found in the lakes and rivers of Europe. Measuring from 6 to 16 in (15 to 40 cm) in length, it is yellow-green in color, with red eyes. It is often used as bait or caught for food. The name also refers to certain varieties of North American fish, notably the golden shiner.

Roach *See:* Cockroach.

Road, surfaced or unsurfaced path over which vehicles travel. Roads include streets; local and secondary thoroughfares linking rural areas and communities; primary highways, including freeways and expressways, connecting larger communities; and in the United States the Federal Interstate Highway System, a system of freeways connecting most cities larger than 50,000. The first roads appeared around 3000 B.C., soon after the invention of the wheel. Later the Chinese and Egyptians built roads, but the Romans are generally considered the first really knowledgeable road builders. In the United States, roads remained crude, unsurfaced or covered with gravel or wood planks, until the beginning of the 20th century; the invention and growing popularity of the automo-

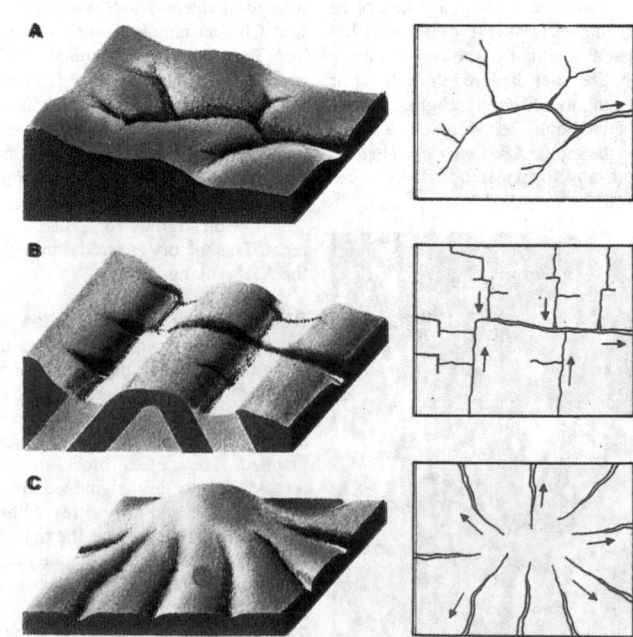

The direction in which rivers flow, depends on the nature and structure of the underlying rock layers. In an area of uniform rock erosion, a branching, tree-like drainage pattern results (A), in which all tributaries flow toward the main stream. In regions with alternating weak and strong rock strata, tributary streams form along bands of easily eroded rock, resulting in a trellislike flow pattern (B). The slope of an area also affects the stream pattern. Thus, rivers will flow down all sides of a dome or uplifted area, in a radial flow pattern (C).

bile aided road development around this time. Today, the United States has almost 4 million mi (6.5 million km) of roads.

Roadrunner (*Geococcyx californianus*), large, slenderly built bird of the cuckoo family, found in arid regions in the southwestern United States and Mexico. Roadrunners fly weakly but have strong legs and run very rapidly, up to 15 mph, catching lizards and small rodents.

Roaring Twenties, period of the 1920s in the United States identified with restlessness and social reform. After years of involvement with the war in Europe, the nation experienced a surge of economic prosperity that resulted in dramatic shifts in American attitudes and culture. This period, also called the Dollar Decade and the Jazz Age, inspired many in the arts to rebel against narrow-mindedness and traditional values. The period is often associated with bootleg liquor, short skirts, women smoking cigarettes, and sexual permissiveness.

Robbe-Grillet, Alain (1922-), French novelist, originator of the French 'new novel.' In works such as *The Voyeur* (1955), *Jealousy* (1957), and the screenplay for *Last Year at Marienbad* (1960), structure, objects, and events displace character and story.

Robber crab *See:* Hermit crab.

Robbins, Frederick Chapman (1916-), U.S. virologist who shared the 1954 Nobel Prize in physiology or medicine with J. F. Enders and T. H. Weller for their cultivation of the poliomyelitis virus in non-nerve tissues.
See also: Physiology; Poliomyelitis.

Robbins, Jerome (1918-1998), U.S. choreographer and director. He danced major roles with the American Ballet Theatre (1940-1944), where he created his first ballet, *Fancy Free* (1944). With the New York City Ballet he was associate artistic director (1950-1959), a ballet master after 1968, and from 1983 ballet master-in-chief (with Peter Martins). For motion pictures, television, and Broadway he choreographed and directed such productions as *West Side Story* (1957) and *Fiddler on the Roof* (1964).

Robert, Joël (1943-), Belgian motocross racer, became national champion several times. When Robert won his first 250 cc world title in 1964, he was the youngest world champion ever. He also became world champion from 1968 to 1972. Robert initially rode for the Czech CZ team and switched later to Suzuki.

Roberts, Kenny (1951-), American motorcycle racer, turned professional in 1970. In 1973 he became the youngest rider ever to win the AMA Grand Prix National Championship. Two years later Roberts won all five American championships with the renowned 750 cc Yamaha, and was victorious in Daytona. In 1978, 1979 and 1980 Roberts became 500 cc world champion on a Yamaha. After his active career he became a team manager.

Roberts, Sir Charles George Douglas (1860-1943), Canadian writer. His simple, descriptive poems of the Maritime provinces contributed to an emerging Canadian consciousness. Among his works are animal stories, such as *Red Fox* (1905).

R

The history of roads shows the development from ill-defined paths surfaced only by the action of tramping feet and rolling wheels, to the sophisticated robust structures of today. (A) Until Roman times, a road was—at best—a route between two places, marked only by footprints and wheel tracks and a lack of vegetation. The Romans made their routes more permanent by removing obstacles, laying foundations of gravel and surfacing their roads with paving stones, with drainage ditches at each side. They tended to be straight and ignored contours. (B) In the eighteenth century, major roads were constructed of beaten down gravel, on a foundation of large blocks. Nineteenth century roads were very much similar, but they were often raised and had a surface of beaten earth. (C) With the vast increase of traffic in the twentieth century, roads had to be made more durable. The same graded build-up of stones is used these days, but now it is topped with a hard surface of macadam or asphalt.

R

Robertson, Oscar (1938-), U.S. basketball player. Nicknamed the 'Big O' and renowned for his passing and scoring ability, Robertson played for the National Basketball Association (NBA) Cincinnati Royals (1960-1970) and Milwaukee Bucks (1971-1974). His achievements include NBA Rookie of the Year (1961), 4 Most Valuable Player awards-1 regular season (1964) and 3 All-Star (1961, 1964, 1969), and ranking fourth on the all time regular season scoring list (26,710 career points). Robertson is the only player to average a triple-double (10 or more assists, points, and rebounds per game) for an entire season (1961-1962). In 1979 he was inducted into the Basketball Hall of Fame.

Robert's Rules of Order *See:* Parliamentary procedure.

Robeson, Paul (1898-1976), U.S. singer and stage and film actor. A basso, he made his concert debut in 1925 and became known for his renditions of spirituals. Son of a former slave, his most famous song was 'Ol' Man River' from the musical *Show Boat* (1928). Robeson starred in the play and film of *Emperor Jones* (1925; 1933) and in Shakespeare's *Othello*. As a collegiate athlete Robeson was twice named an All-American end in football. He also starred in 3 other sports and was valedictorian of his class. Ostracized in the United States for his communist beliefs, he lived and sang in Europe between 1958 and 1963.

Robespierre, Maximilien Marie Isidore (1758-1794), fanatical idealist leader of the French Revolution. A lawyer, he was elected as a representative of the third estate to the States-General (1789) and rose to become leader of the radical Jacobins in the National Convention (1793). He liquidated the rival moderate Girondists and as leader of the Committee of Public Safety initiated the Reign of Terror. The National Convention rose against him, alienated by his increasing power. He was arrested, summarily tried, and executed.
See also: French Revolution.

Robin, vernacular name for various unrelated species of small birds with red breasts. They include the European robin (*Erithacus*

The American robin (*T. migratorius*) commonly eats earthworms and insects. It ranges from Guatemala to the tree line in Alaska.

rubecula), American robin (*Turdus migratorius*), Pekin robin (*Leiothrix lutea*), and Indian robin (*Saxicoloides fulicata*). Most familiar are the European robin (robin redbreast), an insectivorous thrush noted for its beautiful song, and the American robin, a common garden and woodland bird of the United States.

Robin Hood, legendary medieval English hero. He is usually depicted as an outlaw, living with his band of followers, including Little John and Friar Tuck, in Sherwood Forest in Nottinghamshire. He robbed the Norman overlords to give to the poor.

Robinson, Bill (1878-1949), popular U.S. dancer and entertainer, nicknamed 'Bojangles.' He won national and international acclaim as a musical comedy performer and was featured in numerous Broadway shows and Hollywood films, including those in which he starred with Shirley Temple. He was especially known for his 'stair tap' dance, which he claimed to have invented when he danced up a staircase to receive an award from the king of England.

Robinson, David Maurice (1965-   ), American basketball player, played countless times for the American national team and was a member of the Dream Team that won Olympic gold in 1992. Left-handed Robinson played as center with the Antonio Spurs.

Robinson, Edwin Arlington (1869-1935), U.S. poet, known for his series of terse, sometimes bitter, verse characterizations of the inhabitants of the fictitious Tilbury Town. His *Collected Poems* (1921), *The Man Who Died Twice* (1924), and *Tristam* (1927) won Pulitzer Prizes.

Robinson, Frank (1935-), U.S. baseball player and manager. Known as an excellent outfielder, Robinson won the Rookie of the Year award (1956) and was the first player to be named Most Valuable Player in both the National and American Leagues (1961 and 1966, respectively). He played for the Cincinnati Reds (1956-1965), Baltimore Orioles (1966-1971), Los Angeles Dodgers (1972), California Angels (1973-1974), and Cleveland Indians (1974-1976). Robinson became the first African-American manager of a major league baseball team, as player-manager of the Cleveland Indians (1975-1977). He also managed the San Francisco Giants (1981-1984) and Baltimore Orioles (1988). Robinson was inducted to the National Baseball Hall of Fame in 1982.

Robinson, Jackie (Jack Roosevelt Robinson; 1919-1972), U.S. baseball player. A letter-men in 4 sports at UCLA, Robinson became the first African-American to be admitted into baseball's major leagues (1947). Known for his exceptional hitting and base-stealing ability, he was named Rookie of the Year and won the National League's Most Valuable Player award once (1949). Robinson played for the Brooklyn Dodgers (1947-1956) and led them to a championship in 1955. He was inducted into the National Baseball Hall of Fame in 1962.

Robinson, James Harvey (1863-1936), U.S. historian. He was one of the founders of the 'new history,' studying the intellectual, social, and scientific development of humankind rather than only the narrow range of political events.

Robinson, Joan Violet (1903-1983), British economist, writer, and advocate of Keynesian economics. A colleague of John Maynard Keynes, she worked with him to provide a new economic model based on increased government spending as a solution to depression and unemployment. Her work helped to shape the economic policies of the 1930s and has been an important influence on economic thought.

Robinson, Mary (1944-), United Nations High Commissioner for Human Rights and former President of Ireland. Mary Robinson became a professor in criminal law soon after graduating from Trinity College, Dublin. From 1969 to 1989 she was the University of Dublin Constituency representative to the Irish Senate, and in 1990 she became the seventh President of Ireland, a post she relinquished when she accepted the appointment as High Commissioner for Human Rights. She resigned from the UN in 2002.

Robinson, Sir Robert (1886-1975), English organic chemist awarded the 1947 Nobel Prize in chemistry for his pioneering studies of the molecular structures of alkaloids and other vegetable-derived substances.
See also: Chemistry.

Robinson, Sugar Ray (Walter Smith; 1921-1989), U.S. boxer. Considered one of the greatest fighters of all time, Robinson won the world welterweight title (1946) and the middleweight title (1951). He retired in 1952, but returned in 1955 to regain the middleweight title. In 1958 Robinson won his fifth middleweight title, becoming the first boxer to win a divisional world championship 5 times. He retired in 1965.

Robot, mechanical device equipped with sensing instruments for detecting input signals or environmental conditions, with a calculating mechanism for making decisions, and with a guidance mechanism for providing control.
See also: Automation.

Rob Roy (Robert MacGregor; 1671-1734), Scottish outlaw, romanticized in Sir Walter Scott's *Rob Roy* (1818). He was outlawed for cattle theft in 1712 by the duke of Montrose, whose tenants he then plundered. Hunted for many years, he surrendered in 1722 but was pardoned in 1727.

Robusti, Jacopo *See:* Tintoretto.

Rocard, Michel Louis Leon (1930-   ), French prime minister (1988-1991). Rocard is a socialist who served as secretary to the Unified Socialist Party (1967-1973). He was elected to 2 terms in the National Assembly (1969-1973 and 1978-1981) and held several government positions. Member of the European Parliment since 1994.

R

Roche, Mazo De la *See:* De la Roche, Mazo.

Roche, Stephen (1959-), Irish cyclist, won Paris-Nice in his debut professional year in 1981. After that he had a checkered career: in 1982 and 1986 Roche won no races at all, but in 1987 he was the world's strongest cyclist, winning the Tour de France, the Giro d'Italia, and the road race world championship. He won no races in 1988 either, due to a chronic knee injury, but the following year he won the Dunkirk Four-Day race. In 1991 he won the Catalan Week. Roach was a stylish cyclist, and his strong points were climbing and time trials. After his cycling career was over he began rally riding.

Rochester (pop. 245,000), large industrial city in upstate New York, on the banks of the Genesee River, near its confluence with Lake Ontario. The community was laid out by Col. Nathaniel Rochester in 1811, and it became a commercial and industrial center within 20 years. Modern Rochester is known for the manufacture of cameras and film equipment, consumer goods, and machinery and precision instruments. The city is the home of the University of Rochester and the Eastman School of Music.
See also: New York.

Rock, hard, solid matter of the earth's crust, sometimes a combination of one or more minerals. Rock may occur close to the earth's surface or deep underground. Rocks are classified according to their origin. Igneous rock forms when magma (molten material deep within the earth) rises toward the surface and cools. Intrusive igneous rock, such as granite, results if the magma solidifies before it reaches the earth's surface. Extrusive igneous rock, such as obsidian, occurs when magma reaches the surface, as it does in a volcano eruption. Sedimentary rock, such as sandstone, gypsum, and chalky limestone, forms when sediments, or parts of other rocks, mix together and harden. These sediments can be formed by erosion, chemical action, or an accumulation of plant and animal parts. Metamorphic rock, such as marble and slate, occurs when igneous or sedimentary rocks are exposed to intensive pressure or heat and subsequently change their form. Rock is used primarily as a building material and is an important component of concrete.

Rockefeller, family of U.S. financiers and politicians. **John Davison Rockefeller** (1839-1937) entered the infant oil industry in Cleveland, Ohio, at the age of 24 and ruthlessly unified the oil industry into the Standard Oil Trust. He devoted a large part of his later life to philanthropy, creating the Rockefeller Foundation. **John Davison Rockefeller, Jr.** (1874-1960), only son of John D. Rockefeller, followed his father's business and charitable interests. He donated the land for the UN headquarters and helped found the Rockefeller Center in New York City. **John Davison Rockefeller, 3rd** (1906-1978) first son of John, Jr., helped establish New York City's Lincoln Center for the Performing Arts and the United Negro College Fund. **Nelson Aldrich Rockefeller**

(1908-1979), second son of John, Jr., governor of N.Y. 1959-1973, was appointed U.S. vice president in 1974. He sought presidential nomination in 1960, 1964, and 1968. He expanded transportation, welfare, housing, and other social services in N.Y. **Winthrop Rockefeller** (1912-1973), fourth son of John, Jr., was Republican governor of Arkansas (1967-1971). **David Rockefeller** (1915-), youngest son of John, Jr., was president of the Chase Manhattan Bank and chairman of Rockefeller University. **John Davison 'Jay' Rockefeller, 4th** (1937-), grandson of John D. Rockefeller, Jr., became Democratic governor of West Virginia in 1977 and 1980 and was elected to the U.S. Senate in 1985.

Rockefeller Foundation, U.S. philanthropic foundation. Founded in 1913 by John D. Rockefeller, it supports research in three main areas: medical and natural sciences, agricultural sciences, and the humanities and social sciences.

Rocket, form of jet-propulsion engine in which the substances (fuel and oxidizer) needed to produce the propellant gas jet are carried internally. Working by reaction, and being independent of atmospheric oxygen, rockets are used to power interplanetary space vehicles. In addition to their chief use to power missiles, rockets are also used for supersonic and assisted-takeoff airplane propulsion, and sounding rockets are used for scientific investigation of the upper atmosphere. The first rockets-of the firework type, cardboard tubes containing gunpowder-were made in 13th-century China, and the idea quickly spread to the West. Their military use was limited, guns being superior, until military rockets were developed by Sir William Congreve (1772-1828). The 20th century saw the introduction of new fu-

els and oxidants, e.g., a mixture of nitrocellulose and nitroglycerin for solid-fuel rockets, or ethanol and liquid oxygen for the more efficient liquid-fuel rockets. The first liquid-fuel rocket was made by R.H. Goddard, who also invented the multistage rocket. In World War II Germany, and afterward in the U.S., Wernher von Braun made vast improvements in rocket design. Other propulsion methods, including the use of nuclear furnaces, electrically accelerated plasmas and ion propulsion, are being developed.

Rocket, model, or space model, small-scale working replica of the kind of rocket used in military and space programs. Weighing under 1 lb (0.45 km) and measuring 8-24 in (20-61 cm), these models have fuel-burning engines that allow them to travel distances of up to 2,000 ft (610 m) at a speed of 300 mph (480 kmph). Model rocketry kits are commercially available to hobbyists. Associations, clubs, and competitions exist throughout the world.

Rocket, The, first locomotive powered by steam. It was invented by George and Robert Stephenson of Britain in 1829 to provide a railway link between the cities of Liverpool and Manchester. The name derives from a response by the Stephensons to a public jibe that the locomotive was as hazardous to ride as a space rocket. The speed of *The Rocket* reached as high as 36 mph (57.9 kmph).
See also: Locomotive.

Rock festival *See:* Rock music.

Rock music, the dominant popular music since the late 1950s. Rock music first emerged in the mid-1950s as rock 'n' roll, a hybrid evolving from a sophisticated blues style called rhythm and blues, which often

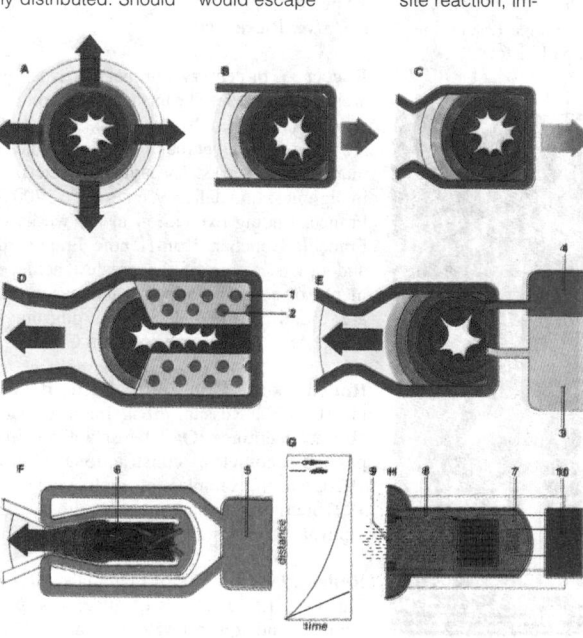

The force of an explosion in an unrestricted space (A) is evenly distributed. Should this explosion occur in a semi-enclosed chamber (B), its force would escape through the only possible exit, providing an equal and opposite reaction, impelling the chamber in the opposite direction. The chamber of a rocket engine (C) is designed to maximize the thrust as its fuel undergoes a sustained explosion. Most rockets require an oxidant for combustion. In a solid-propellant rocket (D), fuel (1) and oxidant (2) are packed together in the combustion chamber. In a liquid-propellant rocket (E), fuel (3) and oxidant (4) are pumped into the chamber and burned. A nuclear rocket (F) is fuelled by liquid hydrogen (5), which is vaporized, rather than burned, in the reactor (6). The outwardly expanding gases thus created, provide the propulsive force. Unlike an automobile, rockets accelerate constantly, while their engines are in operation (G). An ion rocket (H), because of its extended period of operation, could therefore possibly approach the speed of light. A propellant, such as cesium or mercury, is ionized in a vaporizer (7) and accelerated through an electrostatic field (8)—both powered by a nuclear reactor (10) —before exiting (9), providing the rocket's propulsive force. If the ionized particles are not neutralized, however, they will eventually cause the rocket to cease functioning.

used amplified instruments to produce a heavy beat. The first national rock 'n' roll hit-and the one that probably gave the genre its name-was 'Rock Around the Clock,' by Bill Haley and His Comets (1955). Rock 'n' roll's first superstar, Elvis Presley, hit on a riveting combination of harddriving rhythm and blues with country and western music. Other important performers includeed Chuck Berry and Buddy Holly. Rock 'n' roll, with its exciting beat and lyrics about school, cars, and love, was especially popular with adolescents. The impetus for the transformation of rock 'n' roll into rock music came from England, where, in the early 1960s, bands like the Beatles and the Rolling Stones remixed the original ingredients, adding new musical textures, forms, and rhythms and more sophisticated lyrics. The 1960s also saw the emergence of soul music, a product of rhythm and blues and gospel styles, which would add its sound to rock; folk rock, as in the later work of Bob Dylan; and acid rock, an attempt to reproduce musically the hallucinogenic drug experience. In the 1970s acid rock was followed by hard rock or heavy metal, which was louder and more repetitive and by eclectic mixtures of the rock sound with country, jazz, calypso, and other styles. Another 1970s innovation was disco, repetitive dance music with a rock beat. In the mid-1970s punk rock, an angry, harsh, sometimes violent style, emerged out of the postindustrial despair of working-class youth in England. Punk rock, also reflected young people's disillusionment with the so-called rock establishment and the overcommercialization of what had been a rebellious art form. The 1980s and 1990s were dominated by rock videos, short films that feature acting, dancing, and effects as well as music.

Rockne, Knute Kenneth (1888-1931), U.S. football coach. Known for his inspirational talks, and use of great speed and variety on the field, Rockne helped make football a more entertaining sport. While coaching for Notre Dame (1918-1930) he achieved a record of 105 wins, 12 losses, and 5 ties, giving him a winning percentage (.881) that is the best in college football history.

One of the purest examples of German Rococo, is the Amalienburg hunting lodge (1734) in the park of Nymphenburg Palace (near Munich), designed by François Cuvilliés senior (1698-1767).

Rock oil *See:* Petroleum.

Rockwell, Norman (1894-1978), U.S. illustrator, known for his realistic and humorous scenes of U.S. small town life. His work includes magazine covers for *The Saturday Evening Post* and a series of paintings of the Four Freedoms.

Rocky Mountain goat (*Oreamnos americanus*), goatlike herbivorous mammal closely related to the antelope. It is found in the coastal mountain ranges of North America. An excellent climber, it is considered to be fairly unintelligent. It has curved horns, dense whitish fur, black hoofs, and a long beard in the male of the species.

Rocky Mountain National Park, natural wild area in north central Colorado, in the heart of the Rocky Mountains. Founded in 1915, the park is dominated by Longs Peak (14,225 ft/4,345 m) and has many glaciers.

Rocky Mountains, principal range of the western region of North America. Extending from north Alaska for more than 3,000 mi (4,800 km) to New Mexico, they form the Continental Divide; rivers rising on the eastern slopes flow to the Arctic or Atlantic Ocean, and those rising on the western slopes flow toward the Pacific. Rivers originating in the Rockies include the Missouri, Rio Grande, Colorado, Columbia, and Arkansas. A relatively new system, the Rockies were formed by massive uplifting forces that began about 70 million years ago.

Rocky Mountain spotted fever, acute febrile disease caused by *Rickettsia rickettsii* and transmitted by ixodid ticks. The onset is abrupt, with severe headache, chills, and muscular pains. Fever reaches 40°C (104°F) within several days and remains high for 10 to 15 days. Untreated patients may develop pneumonia, tissue necrosis, and circulatory failure, with resulting brain and heart damage. Starting antibiotic therapy early has significantly reduced mortality, formerly about 20 percent.
See also: Rickettsia.

Rococo, 18th-century European artistic and architectural style. The term derives from *rocaille* (French, 'rock work'), whose arabesque and ingenious forms are found in many rococo works. The style, characterized by lightness and delicacy, emerged c.1700 in France, finding expression in the works of François Boucher, Jean-Honoré Fragonard, and others. Some of the greatest achievements of rococo sculpture and decoration are found in the palaces and pilgrimage churches of Austria and southern Germany.

Rodchenko, Aleksander Mihailovich (1891-1956), Russian artist. Initially made abstract paintings. Of interest are his suspended geometric constructions (1919-1920, early examples of mobiles). After 1921 he turned to photography, film, typography, and set designing.

Rodent, largest order of mammals, including some 1,500 species of mice, rats, porcupines, and squirrels. Rodents have a single pair of incisors in the upper and lower jaws that continue to grow throughout life. Behind the incisors is a gap to allow recirculation of food in chewing. The cheek skin can be drawn across the gap, in front of the molars and premolars, leaving the incisors free for gnawing. Rodents are predominantly eaters of seeds, grain, and other vegetation.

Rodeo, in the United States and Canada, contest and entertainment based on ranching techniques; it derives from late-19th-century cowboy meets held to celebrate the end of a cattle drive. It usually comprises 5 main events: calf-roping, in which a mounted cowboy must rope a calf, dismount, throw the calf, and tie 3 of its legs together; steerwrestling, in which the cowboy jumps from a galloping horse and wrestles a steer to the ground by its horns; bareback riding on an unbroken horse for 8 to 10 secs; saddlebronc riding; and bull-riding.

Rodgers, Richard (1902-1979), U.S. songwriter and composer. He collaborated with librettist Lorenz Hart on *A Connecticut Yankee* (1927), *Pal Joey* (1940), and many other Broadway musicals containing dozens of enormously popular songs. Later he teamed up with Oscar Hammerstein II on the Pulitzer Prize-winning *Oklahoma!* (1943), *South Pacific* (1949), *The King and I* (1951), and *The Sound of Music* (1959), among other shows.

Rodham Clinton, Hillary (1947-   ), American lawyer, wife of President Clinton. After receiving her degree in law at Yale University, she began her own lawyer's practice. When her husband became Governor of Arkansas she also became a national figure due to her efforts to improve the position of women, education and children's' rights. After her husband was elected president she played an active role developing his policies, particularly his attempt to reform American health care. In 2000 she became a member of the Senate of the Democratic Party in New York.

Rodin, Auguste (1840-1917), French sculptor. He rose to fame in the late 1870s and in 1880 began the never-completed *Gate of Hell*, the source of such well-known pieces as *The Thinker* (1880) and *The Kiss* (1886). His works, in stone or bronze, were characterized by energy and emotional intensity, as in *The Burghers of Calais* (1884-1894).

Rodnina, Irina (1949-), (Soviet) Russian figure skater, dominated the pairs competition for many years, as can be seen from her three Olympic titles (1972, 1976, 1980), eleven European titles, and ten world titles. She was also national champion for many years. Up until 1973 she skated together with Alexey Ulanov, and thereafter with her husband Alexandr Zaitsev.

Rodrigo Díaz *See:* Cid, El.

Roemer, Olaus (1644-1710), Danish astronomer, the first to show that light has a finite velocity. He noticed that Jupiter eclipsed its moons at times differing from

those predicted and correctly concluded that the discrepancy resulted from the finite nature of light's velocity, which he calculated as 141 mi per sec (now calculated as about 186,282 mi per sec/299,792.458 km per sec).
See also: Astronomy.

Roentgen, Wilhelm Conrad (1845-1923), German physicist, recipient (1901) of the first Nobel Prize in physics for his discovery of X rays.
See also: X ray.

Roethke, Theodore (1908-1963), U.S. poet who won a Pulitzer Prize for *The Waking* (1953) and a National Book Award for *Words for the Wind* (1958). Much of his imagery is drawn from nature.

Rogers, Carl Ransom (1902-1987), U.S. psychotherapist, who instituted the idea of the patient determining the extent and nature of his course of therapy, the therapist following the patient's lead.
See also: Psychotherapy.

Rogers, Ginger (real name, Virginia Katherine McMath; 1911-1995), American film actress and dancer, Ginger Rogers began her career as a review dancer. Her big breakthrough came in 1933 with the film *Flying Down to Rio*, in which she formed a dance pair with Fred Astaire for the first time. The famous duo performed together up until 1939 in such films as *Top Hat* (1935) and *Swing Time* (1936). Despite her attempts to lose her musical image (her dramatic role in *Kitty Foyle*, 1940, received an Oscar), she was still mainly cast in musicals. Her most famous films without Fred Astaire include *Tom, Dick and Harry* (1941), *Monkey Business* (1952), and *Harlow* (1965). She also appeared regularly on Broadway. *Ginger: My Story* (1991) contains her memoirs.

Rogers, John (1829-1904), U.S. sculptor known for realistic figural groups, such as *The Slave Auction*. His extremely popular works were often mass-produced.

Rogers, Will (William Penn Adair; 1879-1935), U.S. humorist known for his homespun philosophy and mockery of politics and other subjects previously considered 'untouchable.' Part Irish and part Cherokee, he became famous in the Ziegfeld Follies of 1916. He wrote a syndicated column that appeared in 350 newspapers.

Roget, Peter Mark (1779-1869), English scholar and physician, author of the definitive *Thesaurus of English Words and Phrases* (1852).

Rohrer, Heinrich (1933-), Swiss physicist, winner with Gerd Binnig and Ernst Ruska of West Germany of the Nobel Prize for physics (1986) for his contribution to the development of the scanning tunneling microscope (STM) that allows scientists to view individual atoms.
See also: Physics.

Roh Tae Woo (1932-), South Korean president (1988-1992), succeeded by Kim Young

Sam. Roh Tae Woo led the Defense Security Council (1979-1981) under President Chun Doo Hwan. He retired from the military (1981) and organized the Summer Olympic Games held at Seoul (1988). He was active in the Democratic Justice Party before his election.
In 1996, he was accused of corruption and sentenced to 17 year's imprisonment. However, in 1997 he was pardoned.

Roland, one of Charlemagne's commanders, hero of the *Song of Roland*. Ambushed by Basques at Roncesvalles in A.D. 778, he and his men were massacred because he was too proud to summon help.
See also: Charlemagne.

Rolland, Romain (1866-1944), French writer, who won the 1915 Nobel Prize for literature. He is best known for his biographies, including *Beethoven* (1903), his pacifist articles *Above the Battle* (1915), and the novel-cycle *Jean Christophe* (1904-1912).

Roller, species of bird belonging to the roller family. Flocks of rollers can be found in southern Europe during the warm season and northern Africa during the cold season. Standing at 10-16 in (25-40 cm), the roller resembles-but is not closely related to-the jay. Its name derives from the mating dance of the male, which consists of a series of airborne dives and tumbles.

Roller skating, popular source of sport and recreation. Traditional skates consist of four wheels fitted with ball bearings attached, 2 in front and 2 in back, to a shoe or to a steel platform that can be attached to a shoe. Clamp-on skates with metal wheels are generally worn out-of-doors while bootskates are most often used on rinks. For racing, wooden wheels are favored; for figure skating and roller hockey, wheels are usually made of plastic. In the late 1980s, a new type of skate, the roller blade, was introduced, with four wheels placed front to back to form a single line, or blade, of wheels.

Rolling Stones, influential rock band from Britain. Renowned for their hard-driving, blues-inspired, often sexually explicit songs, the band has influenced the course of popular music since the mid-1960s. Original band members include Mick Jagger (1943-), Keith Richard (1943-), Bill Wyman (1936-) and Charlie Watts (1941-). Guitarist Brian Jones left the band shortly before his death and was replaced by Mick Taylor in 1969 and then by Ron Wood in 1974. Bill Wyman left the band in 1993 and has not officially been replaced. In addition to their many recordings, the Stones are known as one of the world's most exciting performance bands.

Rölvaag, Ole Edvart (1876-1931), Norwegian-born novelist, who came to the United States in 1896 and wrote in Norwegian. His trilogy *Giants in the Earth* (1927-1931) is the story of Norwegian settlers in the United States.

Romains, Jules (Louis Farigoule; 1885-1972), French author and exponent of unan-

imism, or the collective personality. He is known for his plays and his 27-volume cycle *Men of Good Will* (1932-1946).

Roman Catholic Church, major branch of the Christian church consisting of Christians in communion with the pope. It comprises the ecclesiastical organization that remained under papal obedience at the Reformation, consisting of a hierarchy of bishops and priests, with other officers such as cardinals. Roman Catholicism stresses the authority of tradition and the church (through ecumenical councils and the papacy) to formulate doctrine and regulate moral and spiritual life. Members participate in grace, mediated through the priesthood, by means of the seven sacraments. The mass is central to Roman Catholic life and worship. Doctrinally, Roman Catholic theologians emphasize the role of the Virgin Mary and the authority and infallibility ·of the pope. Other distinctive doctrines include clerical celibacy, limbo, and purgatory. Those held in common with the orthodox churches (but rejected by Protestants) include the invocation of saints, veneration of images, acceptance of the Apocrypha, the sacramental system, and monasticism. Since the Second Vatican Council, there has been a movement toward accommodation with the modern world, cautious dealings with the ecumenical movement, and encouragement of lay participation and vernacular liturgy. There are more than a billion Roman Catholics worldwide.
See also: Christianity.

Romance, literary term identified with fiction usually depicting idealized love. Romances typically contain nonrealistic characters and plots and use elements of fantasy or adventure. The ancient Greek romance, *Daphnis and Chloë*, written C.A.D. 200, is considered to be the first great romance. The genre reached its height in the Middle Ages with the tales of King Arthur. In the 19th century, romances contained a strong element of mystery and the supernatural.

Auguste Rodin's *The Age of Bronze* (1876, Musée du Luxembourg, Paris). Initially, this lifelike statue of the first thinking man was strongly criticized.

Romance languages, one of the main groups of the Indo-European languages. It comprises those languages derived from the vernacular Latin that was spread by Roman soldiers and colonists, and that superseded local tongues. The languages include Italian, the Rhaeto-Romanic, Provençal, French, Walloon, Spanish, Catalan, Portuguese, and Romanian. The languages share a similar vocabulary and grammatical development.

Roman Circus *See:* Rome, Ancient.

Roman de la rose, French allegorical work of poetry with a didactic background. Written in Western Europe in the 13th century, it consists of two volumes; the first was written by Guillaume de Lorris (1200-1240) and is a lyrical allegory about love with the rose as the symbol of unrequited love. The second volume appeared 40 years later (1275), written by Jean de Meung (1240-1305), and is of a completely different nature. It is predominantly didactic, but also ridicules the idealized love of the first vol-

R

R

Reconstruction of the enormous abbey church of Cluny (France), the largest Roman church from medieval times. The ship (1) had two side arches (2 and 3) and two transepts (4 and 5). The larger of the two had two towers (6). More towers rose from both intercepts (7 and 8) and a western front building (9), that also had two towers (10 and 11). The abbey (12) had a corridor (13) with five radiating chapels (14). This church was finished around 1113. Due to mistakes in construction, however, part of the barrel vaults collapsed in 1125. In the rebuilding, flying buttresses (15) were used to help strengthen the structure.

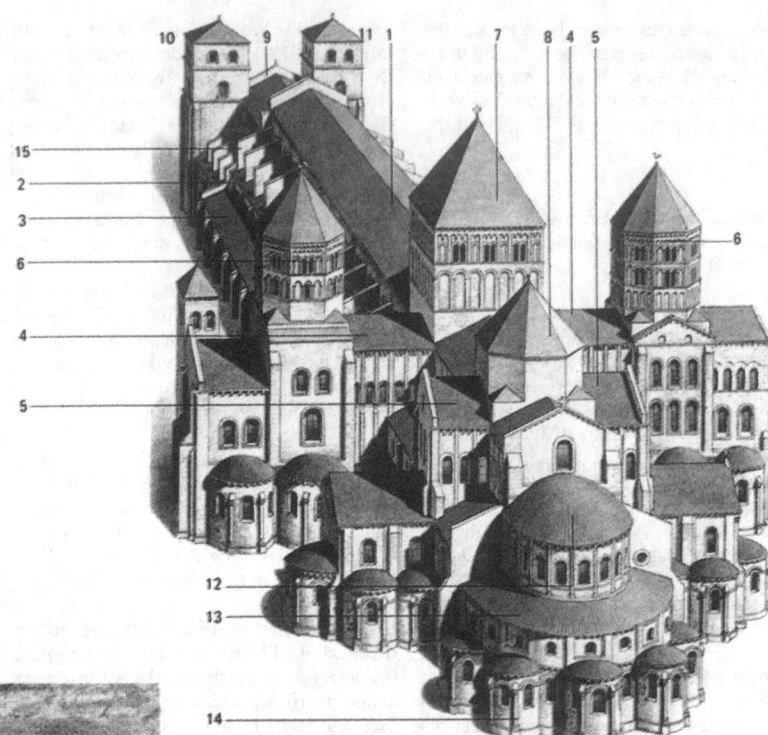

Fresco painted around 1087 in the abbey of the St. Angelo in Formis (Campania, Italy) showing the abbot Desiderius. The model in his hands shows that he is the founder of the church, and the striking square halo behind his head means that he was still alive when the fresco was painted.

Roman church in Middle Italy. A building craze started up in the 11th century, fed by the fact that there was not an apocalypse in the year 1000, thousand years after Christ had died on the cross. The 11th century Burgundian chronicler Raoul Glaber described the craze in the following way:
'In approximately the third year after the year 1000, churches were raised all over the world, especially in Italy and Gallia. This was not really necessary; they had been built fairly well to begin with. Every Christian community wanted to compete with neighboring communities in the race to possess an even more beautiful church than they did. It seemed as if the world was shaking off its old clothes and was covering itself from head to toe with a milky white cloth of churches. All Episcopal and monastic churches, dedicated to all kinds of saints, and even little village churches, were all rebuilt by Christians to be even more beautiful than ever.'

William the Conqueror (on the right) giving out orders to his messengers. Detail of a Bayeux tapestry (end of 11th century), that depicts the conquest of the Normans in England (1066). The bare, massive walls of medieval buildings were often decorated with tapestries, especially after the Crusaders had returned with examples from the Byzantine Kingdom.

Capital from the Ste.-Madeleine in Vézelay (France), with a picture of Moses and Paul with the 'mystical mill', the mill that was used to grind the corn of the Old Testament into the flour of the gospel. Unlike work from other periods, Romanesque capitals were not designed in any set style. Often times, the capital was not finished until the last phases of building, when it was decorated with religious images on the spot.

Interior of the early Romanesque Saint-Philibert in Tournus (Saône-et-Loire, mainly 11th century). Compared to the fine lines of a Gothic church, the massive, somewhat closed-off character is very apparent. The characteristic round arches preceded the Gothic arch.

R

ume. Very popular, although many consider it to be anti-clerical because of the great importance that De Meung places on science. This contradistinction was the subject of much debate well into the 15th century, which increased the influence of the *Roman* on medieval literature in Western Europe.

Roman Empire *See:* Rome, Ancient.

Romanesque art and architecture, artistic style prevalent in Christian western Europe from c.a.d. 950 to 1200. Romanesque preceded Gothic art and architecture and is so called because its forms are derived from Roman art and architecture. The architecture, based on the round Roman arch and improvised systems of vaulting, was characterized by a massive, simple, and robust style with great vitality, particularly in the case of Norman architecture. Churches had immense towers; interiors were decorated with frescoes depicting biblical scenes. The sculptural style was varied, vigorous, and expressive, with carved, sculptured scenes on column capitals, and larger reliefs and figures on exterior portals and tympanums.

Roman Forum *See:* Forum.

Roman gods *See:* Mythology.

Romania

Capital:	Bucharest
Area:	91,699 sq mi (237,500 sq km)
Population:	22,608,000
Language:	Romanian
Government:	Republic
Independent:	1878
Head of gov.:	Prime minister
Per capita:	US$ 1,600
Monetary unit:	1 Romanian leu = 100 bani

Romania, or Rumania, republic in southeastern Europe occupying the northeastern part of the Balkan Peninsula and bordering the Black Sea. Once part of the Roman Empire, its language is directly descended from Latin and closely resembles modern Italian. Although Romania was a communist country and a member of the Warsaw Pact, its foreign and economic policies were independent of those of the Soviet Union. Romania has worked to advance its own

The nave of the Early Romanesque Ste.-Philibert at Tournus (Saône-et-Loire, mainly 11th century) has remarkable pillars, which neither have a base, nor a capital, but which are covered by diagonal barrel vaulting, while the side-aisles are cross-vaulted.

agriculture and industry, seeking relations with nations of the West as well as the East. Not withstanding democratization in the early 1990s the communists still hold key positions in politics and society.

Land and climate. The Carpathian Mountains are Romania's dominant geographical feature. They cross the forested southern Bukovina region and divide Moldavia in the east from Transylvania in the west. Moldavia extends east from the mountain highlands and sheltered valleys to the Prut River, forming the Moldavian 'platform'-an unrelievedly flat plain covered by loess. Around Brasov, the Carpathians turn westward into the Transylvanian Alps, whose peaks reach heights of 8,347 ft (2,541 m). Beyond the Timis River, the mountain chain is continued by the Banat Mountains, which slope down to the fertile plains of the Tisza River Lowlands on the eastern edge of the Hungarian Plain. Within the arc of the Carpathians lies the Transylvania Plateau, a region of low hills, fertile valleys, and alluvial plains. At the western edge of the Carpathians, the Danube River flows south and east before swinging north to its delta, which is rich in wildlife. Between the Danube and the Carpathians are the fertile plains of Walachia. The only part of Romania south of the Danube is the Dobruja, a narrow, low-lying coastal strip that is marshy but fertile, extending into Bulgaria.

In general, Romania has a continental climate with cold, snowy winters. Winters are especially long and severe on the eastern plains and in the Dobruja. Summer temperatures average 70°F (20°C). Rainfall averages 25 in on the plains and 10 in in parts of the Dobruja. The high west-facing mountain slopes receive more than 60 in of rain and snow annually.

People. About 90% are Romanians, with Hungarian, Roma and German minorities. Over half of the population of Romania lives in town. The largest cities are Bucharest, Brasov, Iasi, Timisoara, Constantsa, Cluj-Napoca, and Galati. Bucharest is the capital city.

Economy. Over 60% of the land area of Romania is agricultural, but industry provides half of the national income. About 25% of the land is covered by forests. With large oil fields in the Prahova Valley, Romania is one of the largest producers of petroleum and natural gas in Europe. Copper, lead, coal, iron ore, and lead are mined. Principal industries are iron and steel, machinery, textiles, and chemicals. The main exports are oil-field equipment, furniture, agricultural machinery, and textiles.

History. Most of modern Romania was once part of ancient Dacia, thoroughly imbued with the language and culture of Rome. After the 13th century the two principalities of Moldavia and Walachia emerged, existing as dependencies of Turkey until 1829, then as Russian protectorates. United in 1861, Romania gained its independence in 1878. After World War I the Romanian-speaking province of Transylvania was acquired from Austria-Hungary. In the 1930s the country was dominated by Fascist rule; in 1941 dictator Ion Antonescu sided with the Axis powers. Overrun by the USSR in 1944, Romania became a satellite state. After King Michael's abdication in 1947 it became a republic. In the 1960s and 1970s Romania worked to establish diplomatic and economic relations with the West. In the 1980s, Nicolae Ceausescu, Romania's ruler since

Peles castle (1883), near Sinaia in the eastern Transylvanian Alps.

1965, began a 'modernization' program to industrialize urban communities. Romania's subsequent debt to Western European banks has slowed its economic growth. In December 1989, an anti-communist revolution resulted in Ceausescu's ouster and subsequent execution. On May 20, 1990 Ion Iliescu was elected president. While trying to modernize its economy, Romania has adopted harsh economic measures, which have led to continued political and social unrest. The 1996 elections ended the ex-Communists' power.

In 2002, Romania was formally invited to join the NATO, but not to join the EU. Membership of the EU is an option for 2007. The country has a great deal of work ahead of it: corruption needs to be abolished, and bureaucracy has to be taken care of in order to strengthen legislation and the economy.

Roman numerals, system of numerical representation based on symbols invented by

the ancient Romans c.500 B.C. The early Roman system-with some modification-was commonly used for simple calculations as late as the 16th century, when it was eclipsed by the Arabic system. It is used today primarily for notational and decorative purposes, and to record dates. In the Roman system, the symbols I, V, X, L, C, D, and M stand for the numbers 1, 5, 10, 50, 100, 500, and 1,000, respectively.
See also: Numeration systems.

Romanov, ruling dynasty of Russia (1613-1917). The first Romanov tsar was Michael. The last of the direct Romanov line was Peter, but succeeding tsars retained the name of Romanov, down to Nicholas II (r. 1894-1917).

Romanov, Grigoriy Vasilyevich (1923-), former USSR Communist Party official and member of the Politburo (1976-1985). He was previously a member of the Secretariat and the Presidium. Although he ostensibly quit his post for medical reasons, it is believed his removal was political.
See also: Union of Soviet Socialist Republics.

Roman Republic *See:* Rome, Ancient.

Romans, Epistle to the, New Testament book written by Saint Paul to the Christians of Rome (A.D. 58). It presents his major statement of justification by faith, and the Christian's consequent freedom from condemnation, sin, and the law. It stresses God's sovereignty and grace.
See also: New Testament.

Romanticism, 19th-century European artistic movement. Its values of emotion, intuition, imagination, and individualism were in opposition to the ideals of restraint, reason, and harmony promoted by classicism. The word 'romantic' was first applied to art by Friedrich von Schlegel in 1798. It was later used as a label for works emphasizing the subjective, spiritual, or fantastic; those concerned with wild, uncultivated nature; and those that seemed fundamentally modern rather than classical. The evocative qualities of nature inspired poets such as William Wordsworth, Samuel Taylor Coleridge, and Alphonse Lamartine, and painters such as Joseph Turner and Caspar Friedrich. William Blake and J.W. von Goethe sought to develop new spiritual values; individualism concerned artists as disparate as Walt Whitman and Francisco Goya. The lives of Lord Byron and Frédéric Chopin seemed to exemplify the romantic myth. Among the greatest romantic composers were C.M. von Weber, Hector Berlioz, Felix Mendelssohn, Franz Liszt, and Richard Wagner.

Roman walls, walls constructed by the ancient Romans in what is now Germany, Romania, and northern England. They served to protect the Romans against invasion as well as to facilitate trade and the collection of taxes. The ruins of Hadrian's Wall, built C.A.D. 120, still exist today. It was built primarily of stone and had ditches both in front of the wall and behind. Forts and watchtowers were placed along the wall at regular intervals.
See also: Rome, Ancient.

Romario (real name, Romario de Souza Faria; 1966-), Brazilian football player, appeared countless times for the national team as a forward. After he won silver with Brazil in the 1988 Olympic football tournament (Seoul), he was contracted by the Dutch football club PSV Eindhoven. He was top scorer at this club for several years. In 1993 Romario went to FC Barcelona, in 1995 to the Brazilian Fluminese, in 1996 to Valencia, and in 1998 back to Brazil (Flamengo). The high point of his career was winning the World Cup with Brazil in 1994. Romario was named best player of the tournament. What he lacked in speed, he more than compensated for with his technique and scoring ability.

Romberg, Sigmund (1887-1951), Hungarian-born U.S. composer. He wrote over 70 operettas and musicals, including *The Student Prince* (1924) and *The Desert Song* (1926). He went on to write many film scores.

ROM (computer) (Read Only Memory), memory that stores information that can only be read.

Rome (Italian: *Roma*; pop. 2,723,000), capital and largest city of Italy, located on the rolling plain of the Roman Campagna, 15 mi (24 km) from the Thyrrenian Sea. Rome has been a center of Western civilization for over 2,000 years. 'The Eternal City' was capital of the Roman Empire and is of unique religious significance as the site of the headquarters of the Roman Catholic Church in Vatican City. Administration (of the Italian government

Joseph Severn (1793-1879): *Shelley near the Baths of Caracalla* (Keats-Shelley Memorial House, Rome). Italy was an inexhaustible source of inspiration for romantic writers, both in its landscape and in its cultural wealth. A trip to Italy therefore became very fashionable indeed (Goethe, Stendhal). Several authors, such as the English poet Percy Bysshe Shelley (1792-1822), chose Italy as their permanent residence.

catacombs, and fountains. There are also many fine museums, art collections, and libraries; the Rome opera house; and the Santa Cecilia music academy, the world's oldest (1584). The University of Rome was founded in 1303.
See also: Italy.

The famous Via Appia antica, in the southern part of Rome.

as well as of Roma province and the region of Latium), religion, and tourism are the most important activities of modern Rome, which is also a center for commerce, publishing, movies, and fashion. A great transportation hub, the city has relatively little industry. The site of ancient Rome is the Seven Hills. The Tiber River flows through the city, which contains many important relics of classical Rome, such as the Forum, the Colosseum, the *Domus Aurea* (Golden House), the baths of Caracalla, and the Pantheon. Rome is famous for its squares, Renaissance palaces, churches, basilicas,

A lively Roman scene on a relief: we see a market in Ostia, the large harbour of Rome, where fowl, bread and other items were sold.

R

The ruins of the Forum Romanum in Rome. From the 1st century B.C., this square developed into the political and religious center of the Roman Empire. This is where the armies celebrated their triumphant entry to Rome after they had won a battle, where Emperors were enthroned and dethroned and important political decisions were publicized.

The medicinal baths in the English place of Bath date back to the Roman occupation in the first century A.C. This only illustrates how far Roman influences reach in Europe.

Bronze statue of Emperor Marcus Aurelius on horseback, from the 2nd century A.C. Size and finish show us some very fine die-casting indeed. Knowledge on this subject was lost during medieval times and was not rediscovered until the Renaissance. The reason the statue was not melted down in medieval ovens was that it was thought to depict the Christian Emperor Constantine the Great, instead of the persecutor of Christians, Marcus Aurelius.

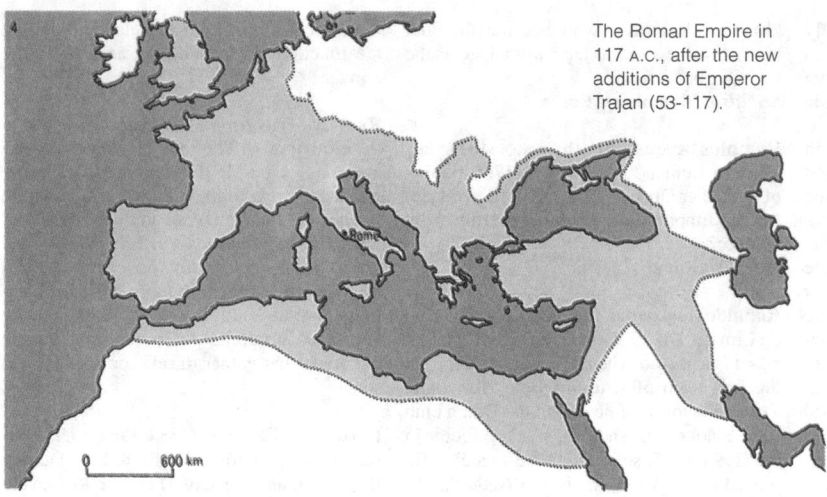

The Roman Empire in 117 A.C., after the new additions of Emperor Trajan (53-117).

Roman musicians on a floor mosaic, around 100 B.C. Mosaic flourished during Roman times and several different techniques developed. To attain larger ranges of color, they used marble, precious stones like lapis lazuli, alabaster, malachite and onyx, and even glass that was colored using metal oxides under very high temperatures.

Marble bust of Emperor Augustus (the 'Sublime'), founder and first Emperor of the Roman Empire, that came into being around the beginning of the Christian era. After a long period of civil war, Augustus managed to attain a period of relative peace in the Roman Empire, the so-called pax romana.

Mural of a still life, from around 50 B.C. Not much is left of Roman art, except the paintings in the ruins of the Italian city of Pompeii. After the Vesuvius erupted in 79 A.C., they were preserved in almost perfect condition under a thick layer of lava and ashes.

R

Rome, Ancient, city-state in central Italy that grew into a vast empire. At its height, in A.D. 117, it comprised most of the known Western world. The ancient Romans made great advances in the fields of law, civil engineering, standardization in coinage and measurement, philosophy, architecture, and literature. The region was controlled by the Etruscans until Romans established an independent republic in 500 B.C. Throughout the period of the republic (500-31 B.C.), warfare was almost continuous. Under a government controlled by consuls and the senate, Rome overran central and southern Italy and defeated Carthage. Expansion continued to Greece, Asia Minor, Syria, Palestine, and Egypt, Gaul, and England. From about 100 B.C., Rome began to move steadily toward disaster. Civil wars arose from conflicts between senatorial factions, and between rich and poor. The army leaders Pompey and Julius Caesar arose to form the first Triumverate with Crassus. After the assassination of Caesar, Caesar's nephew Octavian defeated Antony and became the first emperor of Rome, renaming himself Augustus. For more than 200 years (27 B.C.-A.D. 180) the empire flourished. The establishment of trade routes throughout the empire lead to the spread of new ideas, particularly Christianity. From about A.D. 200 the period was characterized by internal strife and barbarian raids. Under Constantine I (emperor 306-337) the capital was moved to Byzantium (renamed Constantinople), and Christianity was officially recognized. At the beginning of the fifth century, the empire was divided into East and West, and a period of barbarian invasion and vandalism followed.

Rommel, Erwin (1891-1944), German field marshal, named the 'Desert Fox' for his tactical genius as commander of the Afrika Korps (1941-1943). His advance ended with the battle of El Alamein (1942). He commanded Army Group B in northern France when the Allies landed in Normandy (1944). He was implicated in the July 1944 plot to assassinate Hitler. Given the choice of suicide or trial, he took poison.
See also: World War II.

Romney, George (1734-1802), English portrait painter, rival of Sir Joshua Reynolds in late-18th-century London. Influenced by classical sculpture, he tended to flatter his subjects, among whom was Lady Emma Hamilton.

Romulo, Carlos Pena (1901-1985), Filipino journalist and statesman. His World War II broadcasts during the Japanese occupation of the Philippines were known as 'The Voice of Freedom.' He won a Pulitzer Prize (1941) and was ambassador to the United States and president of the UN general assembly (1949-1950).
See also: Philippines.

Romulus and Remus, mythical founders of Rome (by tradition in 753 B.C.), twin sons of Rhea Silvia, descendant of Aeneas, by the god Mars. Abandoned as infants, they were suckled by a she-wolf until adopted by a herdsman. After a long rivalry, Remus was killed by Romulus, who became the first king of Rome and was later worshiped as the god Quirinus.
See also: Mythology; Rome.

Romulus Augustulus (b. C.A.D. 461), last Western Roman emperor (475-176), puppet of his father Orestes. The end of the Western Roman Empire dates from his overthrow by Odoacer.
See also: Rome, Ancient.

Ronaldo (real name, Ronaldo Luis Nazarino de Lima; 1976-), Brazilian football player, was 17 years old when he made his debut in the first team of Cruseiro Belo Horizonte. The following year he joined the Dutch club PSV Eindhoven, where he was top scorer in the 1994-1995 season with 30 goals. He played for two seasons in the Netherlands, after which he moved to FC Barcelona. After only one season he signed a long-term contract with the Italian club Inter Milan. Ronaldo is a quick, strong center forward, with a feel for goals. Thanks to his goals, Brazil won the Copa America in 1997 and 1999 (the South American championships for national teams). Ronaldo was chosen European football player of the year in 1997 and in 2002. In that same year, he transferred to Inter Milan.

Rondo, musical form in which a main theme is repeatedly stated between two contrasting sections. The rondo generally consists of five or seven parts and has a fixed pattern (ABACA or ABACABA). It was frequently used by composers of the late 18th and early 19th centuries as the last movement of a larger work. Wolfgang Amadeus Mozart and Franz Josef Haydn often concluded their symphonies with a rondo section.

Ronsard, Pierre de (1524-1585), French 'Prince of Poets,' leader of the influential group of poets called Pléiade. Best known as a lyric poet, as in *Sonnets for Hélène* (1578), he also wrote lofty *Hymns* (1556) on more public subjects and an epic, *La Franciade* (1572).

Ronstadt, Linda (1946-), U.S. singer. Ronstadt began her musical career with the rock group Stone Poneys (1967). She achieved solo success and starred as Mabel in the Broadway production and film of *The Pirates of Penzance* and sang the lead in Puccini's *La Bohème* in New York (1983). In 1993 she received a Grammy Award for best country singer.

Roof, cover for the top of a building. A roof encloses and protects a building from the elements, and helps drain water from rainfall. Large beams (often called joists), timbers, and rafters support a roof. Metal, concrete, or composite materials are used to build a roof or smaller roofing units called shingles. Flat and lean-to roofs consist of designs of one flat plane. Roofs in which the design consists of two joined flat planes are the gable roof and its inverted design, the butterfly roof. The hip, gambrel, and mansard roofs are more sophisticated designs, in which more than two flat planes are joined at various angles. The design of the roof and the choice of roofing materials are based on the function of the building as well as the climate.

Rook (*Corvus frugilegus*), European bird in the crow family. The rook is about 18 in (45 cm) long. A purple gloss on the black back, white skin next to the bill, and gray to white feathers on the face of an adult are its distinguishing features. It eats insects, worms, and grain. Some rooks native to Europe do not migrate while others in more northern locations migrate south in winter. Rookeries are enormous groupings of rooks-often in the hundreds-that gather during the mating season.

Roosevelt, Eleanor (1884-1962), U.S. humanitarian, wife of Franklin Delano Roosevelt, and niece of Theodore Roosevelt. Active in politics and social issues (notably for women and minority groups), she was a UN delegate (1945-1953, 1961) and coauthored the Universal Declaration of Human Rights. Her many books include *This Is My Story* (1937) and *On My Own* (1958).
See also: Human Rights, Declaration of.

Roosevelt, Franklin Delano (1882-1945), American Democratic politician, 32nd president of the U.S. (1933-1945). Roosevelt was particularly popular with the people and was elected president four times. His policy was more pragmatic than conservative or progressive. He tried to solve the national economic crisis with his New Deal. Internationally, he initially chose to support his allies with material aid (Lend and Lease Act), but after Pearl Harbor he brought the U.S. into WW II. Roosevelt was the driving force behind the conferences between Stalin, Churchill, and himself.

Roosevelt, Theodore (1858-1919), American Republican politician, 26th president of the U.S. (1901-1909), successor to the murdered McKinley. In 1898 he fought in the Spanish-American war as commander of the Rough Riders, an army of volunteers he had organized himself. Governor of the state of New York 1898 to 1901. As president he ended isolationism and started imperialism. To support that policy, he announced the Roosevelt Corollary in 1904, an addition to the Monroe Doctrine in which the U.S. gave itself the right to intervene in Latin America and to act as an international police force. He received the Nobel Prize for peace (1906), for his successful intervention in the Russian-Japanese war (1905).

Root, quantities that when taken a designated number of times will result in a specific quantity. Some roots are the second (square) or third (cube) time a number is designated; for example, the square of 25 is 5, because the root 5 is designated twice: $5 \times 5 = 25$. Similarly the cube of 27 is 3, because the root 3 is designated three times: $3 \times 3 \times 3 = 27$. The number of times a root is designated is called its index. In algebra, the number that may stand for x and satisfy the equation is also called a root.
See also: Algebra; Factor.

Root, part of a plant that absorbs water and

nutrients and anchors the plant. Water and nutrients enter a root through minute root hairs sited at the tip of each root. There are two main types of root systems; the taproot system, in which smaller secondary and tertiary roots branch out from a strong main root; and the fibrous root system, in which a mass of equal-sized roots are produced. In plants such as the sugar beet, the taproot may become swollen with stored food material. Adventitious roots anchor the stems of climbing plants, such as ivy. Epiphytic plants such as orchids have roots that absorb moisture from the air. The roots of parasitic plants such as mistletoe and dodder absorb food from other plants.

Root, Elihu (1845-1937), U.S. statesman. He reorganized the command structure of the army as war secretary (1899-1904) under President William McKinley, and as Theodore Roosevelt's secretary of state (1905-1909) he oversaw administration of the new possessions won from Spain. A champion of the League of Nations and the World Court, he won the 1912 Nobel Peace Prize. He was a New York Republican senator (1909-1915).

Root, John Wellborn (1850-1891), U.S. architect, member of the Chicago School. Along with the architect Daniel Hudson Burnham, he was a leader in technical innovations and design of early skyscrapers. The use of heavy, load-bearing mason walls and iron frame interior supports were used to construct the Montauk Block office building (1881-1882) and the Rookery (1885-1888). The Monadnock Building (1889-1891) is still the highest building with load-bearing walls and a steel interior frame. The Rand McNally Building (1889-1890) used a steel-frame construction, still important in modern architecture. Root also designed the tallest building in the world for its time, the 22-story Masonic Temple (1890-1892).
See also: Architecture; Burnham, Daniel Hudson.

Rope, thick, strong cord made from twisted lengths of fiber. It can be made from manila hemp, henequen, sisal, true hemp, coir (coconut palm fiber), flax, jute, and cotton. Synthetic fibers, particularly nylon and polyesters, are used for lighter and more durable rope. Other ropes, such as for suspension cables in bridge building, are made from wire.

Rorschach test, the first and most talked about projective test which measures personality characteristics. The subject is asked to interpret a number of ink-blot patterns (some colored, some black and white). The test can be carried out with subjects aged four and up. The test results are largely dependent upon the interpretation made by the subject and are therefore not valid or reliable.

Rosario (pop. 1.1 million), city in east-central Argentina on the Paraná River. The third largest city in the country, it developed as a shipping and processing center for the many food products from the Pampa, the fertile plains of Argentina, which Rosario borders to the east. Water and railway transportation make Rosario an important inland port city. Chemical, textile, and metal manufacturers as well as petroleum refiners are also located here. Founded in 1730, it became an important city in the 1800s when the Pampas began developing agricultural products.
See also: Argentina.

Rosas, Juan Manuel de (1793-1877), Argentine dictator, governor of Buenos Aires province (1835-1852), who built up a private army of *gauchos* (cowboys). Bribery, force, expansionism, and continuous revolt marked his rule, which nevertheless contributed to Argentine unification.
See also: Argentina.

Roscius, Quintus (Quintus Roscius Gallus; d. 62 B.C.), Roman actor of such renown that 'Roscius' was long a compliment for actors.

Rose, popular name for various woody shrubs and vines of the genus *Rosa*, with tough thorns and colorful flowers. There are some 100 wild rose species native to the Northern Hemisphere, but only 9 have been involved in the breeding of the hundreds of varieties now available. In many cultivated varieties the stamens become petaloid, producing double flowers. The rose family contains many important cultivated plants, including the apple, cherry, plum, and strawberry.

Rose, Pete (1941-), U.S. baseball player. Known for his aggressiveness, he earned the nickname 'Charlie Hustle.' He holds the all time major league record for hits (4,256) and was named the National League's Most Valuable Player in 1973. He played several positions while a member of the Cincinnati Reds (1963-1978), the Philadelphia Phillies (1979-1983) and the Montreal Expos (1984). In 1984, Rose returned to the Reds as a player-manager for 3 years, after which he continued to serve as manager until 1989, when he was suspended (later banned for life) from baseball for alleged gambling on baseball games.

Roseau (pop. 16,000), capital city of Dominica, one of the Windward Islands in the Caribbean Sea. It is a port city, located on a river by the same name. Its exports include spices and lime products. Before its independence (1978), Dominica was ruled by the British (1759-1978) after the original European colonization by the French (mid-17th century).
See also: Dominica.

Rose chafer, or rose bug (*Macrodactylus subspinosus*), beetle found in the eastern and central regions of the United States. The rose chafer feeds on and destroys rose, grape, and apple blossoms. It measures about 1/3 in (8 mm) long, is light brown to gray, and has long legs with tiny spines. Special cultivating techniques used by commercial growers, cloth coverings used by home gardeners, and insecticides used by both help rid plants of these beetles.

Rosefish, or Norway Haddock, important food fish of the family Scorpaenidae. The orange-to-red colored rosefish is abundant in the North Atlantic, especially between the New England coast and Greenland. It is also plentiful off the North Atlantic coast of Europe. It may grow up to 2 ft (61 cm) in length.

Rosemary (*Rosmarinus officinalis*), evergreen shrub of the mint family, found in southern Europe and western Asia. It has blue flowers and grayish leaves and produces a pungent, refreshing perfume.

Rosenberg, husband and wife, the only U.S. citizens put to death in peacetime for espionage. **Julius** (1918-1953) and **Ethel** (1915-1953) were convicted in 1951 for passing atomic secrets in World War II to the USSR, then a U.S. ally. They were electrocuted on June 19, 1953.

Rosenberg, Alfred (1893-1946), Nazi propagandist and newspaper editor, early associate of Adolf Hitler. In his *Myth of the 20th Century* (1930) he outlined a theory of Nordic racial superiority that was used to justify Nazi anti-Semitism and German world conquest. After the Nuremberg Trials, he was executed for war crimes.
See also: Nazism; Propaganda.

Rosenquist, James Albert (1933-), U.S. painter who turned his early billboard-painting career into a style of art. His gigantic images of movie stars, such as Kirk Douglas, and objects of cultural impact, such as *F-111*, put him in the vanguard of pop art.
See also: Pop art.

Rose of Jericho *See:* Resurrection plant.

Rose of Lima, Saint (1586-1617), born in Lima, Peru, first canonized saint in the New World (1671) and patron saint of South America.

The hybrid tea rose is a modern type of rose noted for its long blooming period and spicy fragrance.

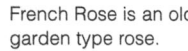

French Rose is an old garden type rose.

R

R

Rose of Sharon, or Althaea (*Hibiscus syriacus*), shrub in the mallow family. The rose of Sharon, a native of Asia, is abundant in North American gardens. It is grown indoors in pots and often transplanted to the outdoors. The late purple through white and blue blooms of September are about 3 in (8 cm) wide. This shrub often reaches a height of 12 ft (3.7 m).

Rosetta Stone, inscribed basalt slab, discovered in 1799, that provided the key to Egyptian hieroglyphics. About 4 ft (1.2 m) long and 2.5 ft (0.75 m) wide, it is inscribed with identical texts in Greek, Egyptian demotic, and Egyptian hieroglyphs. Found near Rosetta, Egypt, the stone is now in the British Museum.
See also: Hieroglyphics.

Rose window *See:* Stained glass.

Rosewood, any of a genus (*Dalbergia*) of trees in the pea family. All species are located in tropical climates. Rosewood from Honduras and Brazil, in particular, is valuable in the commercial manufacture of fine furniture and musical instruments. The color ranges from a deep brown to purple, with attractive blackish streaks and grain markings. When cut, rosewood has a scent similar to that of garden roses.

Rosh Ha-Shanah (Hebrew, 'head of the year'), Jewish New Year, observed on the 1st and 2nd days of the 7th Jewish month, Tishri (Sept.-Oct.). It is considered the Day of Judgment, when each person's fate is inscribed in the Book of Life. On Rosh Hashanah the *shofar* (ram's horn) calls Jews to 10 days of penitence ending with Yom Kippur.
See also: Yom Kippur.

Rosin, resin derived from certain pine trees from North America and Europe. A distilling process makes the resin collected from live trees usable in the manufacture of various products, from paints and paper sizing to adhesives and inks. String bows and dance shoes are treated with dried rosin to prevent

Dante Gabriel Rossetti's (1828-1882) *The bower meadow* (1872, City Art Galleries, Manchester).

slipping. Rosins range in color from black to deep red amber, and yellow. The cluster and scotch pines of Europe and the longleaf and loblolly pines of the United States produce most resins for rosin. Three main types of rosin include gum, wood, and sulfa.
See also: Resin.

Ross, Sir James Clark (1800-1862), British polar explorer who reached a point farther south (78°10'S) than any explorer until 1900. He made a number of Arctic expeditions, some with his uncle, Sir John Ross, and with William Parry. He located the north magnetic pole in 1831. In the historic 1839-1843 Antarctic expedition, he discovered the Ross Sea and Victoria Land.
See also: Antarctica.

Ross, Sir Ronald (1857-1932), British physician awarded the 1902 Nobel Prize in physiology or medicine for his investigations of the *Anopheles* mosquito in relation to the transmission of malaria.

Ross Dependency, section of Antarctica on the Ross Sea. Science personnel are located on bases here. The base established by the U.S. explorer Richard E. Byrd in 1928 is also here. This New Zealand-administered dependency covers about 160,000 sq mi (414,000 sq km) of land uninhabited except for the bases. An ice shelf takes up approximately 130,000 sq mi (337,000 sq km). McMurdo Sound is also found within its borders.
See also: Antarctica.

Rossellini, Roberto (1906-1977), Italian film director. His *Open City* (1945), partly made up of footage of the Italian resistance during World War II, established him as a leader of the neorealist movement. Among his other films are *General della Rovere* (1959), *The Rise of Louis XIV* (1966), and *Socrates* (1970).

Rossetti, two leading English artists, brother and sister. The poems of **Christina Georgina Rossetti** (1830-1894) range from fantasy (*Goblin Market*, 1862) to religious poetry. Her brother, **Dante Gabriel Rossetti** (1828-1882), was a founder of the Pre-Raphaelites. His paintings, of languid, mystical beauty, depict subjects from Dante and medieval romance. He excelled as a poet, notably in his love sonnets.

Rossi, Aldo (1931-1997), Italian architect and theoretician. Rossi, one of the leading architects of his generation, carried out interesting research in the 1960s into the structure of the European city. He made an analysis of the connection between urban form (the morphology) and the type of building from which it was made (the typology). In practice he tried to give the buildings that he abstracted from his research an elementary, pure form. This approach, which was partly based on the so-called neo-rationalism, became very influential. His most important works in Italy include the Gallaratese apartment building near Milan (1970), the elementary school in Fagnano Olona (1978), the Teatro del Mondo (1980) in Venice, and the cemetery in Modena (1982).

Rossini, Gioacchino Antonio (1792-1868), Italian composer best known for his comic operas, especially *The Barber of Seville* (1816). The dramatic grand opera *William Tell* (1829), with its famous overture, was his last opera.

Rosso, Il (Giovanni Battista di Iacopo di Gasparre; c.1495-1540), Italian painter, one of the founders of mannerism. *The Deposition* (1521) exemplifies the elongated figures, hectic color, and emotionalism of his paintings.

Rostam Shah (7th century), Persian folk hero and army commander. He beat the Arabs in 633 in the Battle at the Bridge, but suffered a humiliating defeat in 637 in the battle of Kadisjja (Qadisya, Iraq) at the hands of the Arab commander Sa'd ibn Abi Waqqas, after which the Arab armies managed to finally occupy Persia in 642. Despite this defeat, Rostam became the subject of many epic poems, in which great heroic deeds were ascribed to him.

Rostand, Edmond (1868-1918), French dramatist, best known for his play *Cyrano de Bergerac* (1897), which led a romantic revival.

Rostock (pop. 250,000), city in eastern Germany, located on the Baltic Sea and the Warnow River. It is an important port city through which ships, machinery, and supplies for the petroleum industry are transported. Founded in 1218, it became an important member of the medieval Hanseatic League. The University of Rostock (1419) is also located here.
See also: Germany.

Rostov-on-Don, or Rostov (pop. 1,025,000), important city in Russia, near the Sea of Azov on the Don River. Rostov-on-Don is known mainly for farm products, coal, and farm machinery. Founded in 1780, it is an active port and railway center, as well as an industrial city at the foot of the Caucasus Mountains. It is also the site of a World War II battle (1942) in which German forces defeated the Soviet army, until the city was retaken by the Soviets a year later.
See also: Russian Federation.

Rostropovich, Mstislav Leopoldovich (1927-), Soviet cellist, who has had works created for him by many composers. From the mid-1970s he and his wife, the soprano Galina Vishnevskaya, lived outside the USSR. He became conductor of the National Symphony Orchestra, Washington, D.C., in 1977. In 1990 he returned to Russia.

Roszak, Theodore (1907-1981), U.S. sculptor. Best known for his sinister, birdlike figures in steel and bronze, he also designed the 45-ft (14 m) spire of the Massachusetts Institute of Technology chapel.

Rot, the name given to several fungi and bacteria that destroy plants. Root rot attacks various root crops, sugarcane, and peas. Brown rot is either a cup fungus or a bacterial attack on tobacco, peas, and beans. Black rot attacks cabbages and cauliflower heads.

Rot, Dieter (real name, Karl Dietrich Roth; 1930-), German artist. Created graphics, concrete poetry, films, and designed furniture. Experimented with rotting and molding processes, for which he used perishable material such as foodstuffs. He regularly worked in Reykjavik. His work was an extension of the Dadaist tradition, and was strongly influenced by Kurt Schwitters.

Rota Romana, highest court of appeal for cases concerning the nullification of marriages (and some other court cases) in the Roman Catholic Church. The judges are priests educated in ecclesiastical and civil law.

Rotary engine, internal-combustion engine that uses rotors instead of pistons. The most important parts of this type of engine are the triangle-shaped rotor and the chamber. The movement of the rotor keeps the chamber divided into three sections in which different stages of the combustion process occur. Depending on the engine, there may be several rotors, each containing its own chambers. The rotary engine works on a four-stroke cycle of induction, compression, combustion, and exhaust. In the induction stage a mixture of air and gas enters the chamber. The mixture is then compressed in the second stroke of the cycle. The mixture is then ignited by spark plugs in the combustion stroke. This creates gases which cause the rotor to move. The exhaust stroke forces the burnt gases to leave the engine. Although it consists of fewer parts than equally-powered piston engines, it emits more pollution and burns more fuel. At low speeds, but not high speeds, it emits a loud noise. Felix Wankel of Germany created the most popular rotary engine design in the 1950s.
See also: Internal combustion engine.

Rotary International, worldwide service organization, consisting of members from various professions and businesses. The organization originally met in a rotating basis at the homes of its members in Chicago, where it was founded (1905) by Paul P. Harris. The club provides scholarships and business exchanges as well as health programs in communities around the world. It has member clubs in over 150 countries.

Rotary wing aircraft *See:* Helicopter; V/STOL; Autogiro.

Rotenone, naturally occurring insecticide. This substance is extracted from the root of the tropical derris and cube plants. Harmless to humans and other warm-blooded animals, it poisons cold-blooded animals, especially insects. Rotenone protects garden plants and vegetable crops from insect destruction and protects farm animals from certain parasites, such as fleas.
See also: Insecticide.

Roth, Joseph (1894-1939), German-language writer of Jewish descent. His first works were published while he was serving in the army (1916-1918). After WW I Roth worked as a journalist in Germany for various newspapers. In 1933 he left Germany to drift around Europe, mainly in the larger cities (Marseille, Amsterdam, Paris). He suffered from alcoholism. His earlier books reveal a strong socialist engagement. His works include *Rebellion* (1924), *The Radetzky March* (1932), *The Tale of the 1002nd Night* (1939), *Confession of a Murderer: Told in One Night* (1936) and *Right and Left: The Legend of the Holy Drinker* (1939).

Roth, Mark (1951-), U.S. professional bowler. He set the record for the highest average, 221.662, in 1979. Roth's achievements include winning a record 8 Professional Bowlers Association (PBA) titles (1978), and the U.S. Open and Touring Players Championship (1984). A member of the PBA since 1970, Roth was selected as Player of the Year 4 times (1977-1979, 1984). In 1987 he was inducted into the PBA Hall of fame.

Roth, Philip (1933-), U.S. writer. His protagonists agonize between a traditional Jewish upbringing and modern urban society. He became recognized with the novella and stories in *Goodbye Columbus* (1959). His best-known novel is *Portnoy's Complaint* (1969), a hilarious, bitter account of sexual frustration. Among his other works are the novels *The Ghost Writer* (1979), *Zuckerman Unbound* (1981), and *The Anatomy Lesson* (1983), later reissued in a single volume as *Zuckerman Bound* (1985), and an autobiography, *The Facts* (1988), *Patrimony* (1991), *Sabbath's Theater* (1995), *I Married a Communist* (1998), *The Human Stain* (2000) and *The Dying Animal* (2001). He received a Pulitzer Prize for *American Pastoral* (1998).

Rothko, Mark (1903-1970), U.S. painter, a leading abstract expressionist. On large canvases he used rich and somber colors to create designs of simple, lightly painted rectangular shapes.

Rothschild, family of European Jewish bankers who wielded considerable political influence for nearly two centuries. The founder of the house was **Mayer Amschel Rothschild** (1743-1812), who established banks at Frankfurt, Vienna, London, Naples, and Paris, with his sons as managers. The financial genius who raised the business to dominance in Europe was his son **Nathan Mayer Rothschild** (1777-1836), who handled Allied loans for the campaign against Napoleon. His son, **Baron Lionel Nathan de Rothschild** (1808-1879), was the first Jewish member of the British Parliament.

Rotifer, or wheel animal, microscopic roundworm only a fraction of an inch long. Rotifers are plentiful in fresh water, a few live in the sea, and others live in damp moss. They may be fixed in one place or able to swim. At the head end is the 'wheel organ,' a delicate ring of rapidly beating hairs that is used for movement or feeding.

Rotterdam (pop. 600,000), commercial and industrial seaport in South Holland province, second largest city in the Netherlands, and the largest harbor in the world. Site of the Europoort industrial and harbor complex, it lies at the center of an extensive canal system connecting with other parts of the Netherlands, the German Rhine ports, and the river Ruhr. Major industries include shipyards and oil refineries.
See also: Netherlands.

Rottweiler, large work dog, ancestor to the Doberman pinscher. This strong, muscular dog stands up to 27 in (69 cm) at the shoulder and weighs up to 90 lb (41 k). It is a short-haired black dog with brown markings at the legs, chest, neck, and face. In Roman times, these dogs guarded herds for the army; in medieval times, they served as guard dogs. They are named for the German town, Rottweil, in which they were developed as a breed.

Rouault, Georges (1871-1958), French artist known especially for his intense religious paintings such as *The Three Judges* (1913). Influenced by medieval stained glass work, he developed a distinctive style with the use of thick black outlines around primary colors.

Rouen (pop. 105,500), city and major port on the Seine River, industrial and commercial center, capital of historic Normandy and of today's Seine-Maritime department, northwestern France. Joan of Arc was burned at the stake here, and Champlain and La Salle sailed from Rouen to explore the New World.
See also: France.

The German rottweiler, a formidable guard dog.

R

Delfshaven, near Rotterdam, the birthplace of Piet Hein. This naval hero took as his heraldic device: 'Gold surpasses silver, virtue surpasses both.' After having captured the Spanish fleet (the 'Zilvervloot'), there was no-one who could appreciate the saying better than he himself.

Roulette, game of chance. The roulette wheel is divided into a series of small compartments, alternatively black and red, numbered 1 to 36 with an additional zero (the U.S. game sometimes has two zeros). A croupier spins the wheel and releases into it a small ivory ball. Players bet on where the ball will settle.

Roumania *See:* Romania.

Round, Dorothy (1909-1982), English tennis player whose technique was noted for its accuracy and power. She won the Wimbledon ladies' singles final in 1934 and 1937, and the mixed doubles in 1934 (with R. Miki) and in 1935 and 1936 (with Fred Parry). She also won the ladies' singles Australian championship in 1935.

Roundheads, derogatory name for Puritans in the Parliamentary forces in the English Civil War (1642-1648). Many wore their hair closely cropped, in sharp contrast to their royalist opponents, called Cavaliers. *See also:* Puritans.

Round Table, table at which the medieval King Arthur and his knights sat. The actual table is claimed as an artifact that can be seen in the remains of a castle in Winchester, England. The 15th-century author Sir Thomas Malory wrote about the Round Table knights in his book *Le Morte d'Arthur*. The Round Table knights also were mentioned in the 12th-century French history *Le Roman de Brut* by Wace of Jersey. The shape of the table (with 12 positions) supposedly allowed for equal status of all the knights. A position left purposely vacant (*Siege Perilous*) was left for the knight who would eventually recover the cup-holy grail-from which Jesus drank at the Last Supper. Sir Galahad became the occupant of that seat and, according to the legend, captured the holy grail along with Sir Bors and Sir Perceval. The knights of the Round Table included, among others, Sir Gawain, Lancelot,

Illustration for *Émile ou de l'éducation* (1762), by French writer and philosopher Jean-Jacques Rousseau (1712-1775). This work, with the basic theme 'man is by nature good, but is corrupted by his institutions', signifies an important innovation in the field of pedagogy (Bibliothèque Nationale, Paris).

Ban, Gareth, Bedevere, Ector, Launfal, Palomides, and Sagramore. One of the major figures in the legends of the knights of the Round Table was the sorcerer Merlin who, according to one legend, had the table constructed for Uther, King Arthur's father. *See also:* Arthur, King.

Roundworm, or nematode, any of more than 10,000 species of worms making up the phylum Nematoda, found in terrestrial, freshwater, and marine forms. All roundworms are long and thin, tapering at each end, and are covered with a complex cuticle. The internal organs are suspended within a fluid-filled cavity pseudocoeom. The free-living and plant-parasitic forms are usually microscopic, but animal-parasitic species may reach up to 3.5 ft (1.07 m). Rotifers, and horsehair worms are in the same phylum.

Rous, Francis Peyton (1879-1970), U.S. physician. He shared (with C.B. Huggins) the 1966 Nobel Prize in physiology or medicine for his discovery (1910) of a tumor-causing virus in chickens.

Rous, Stanley (1896-1986), British football administrator, was a referee before he was elected as secretary of the Football Association (1934). Rous was a great stimulator of youth football, and was responsible for the FA rejoining FIFA in 1946, after they had parted ways in 1928. Rous was chosen president of FIFA in 1961, and remained in that post until 1974.

Rousseau, Henri (1844-1910), self-taught French primitive painter much admired by Gauguin, Picasso, and others. Rousseau is known mainly for his portraits, landscapes, and jungle paintings, such as *The Sleeping Gypsy* (1897) and *The Hungry Lion* (1905).

Rousseau, Jean-Jacques (1712-1778), Swiss-born French writer, philosopher, and political theorist. Greatly influenced by Denis Diderot, Rousseau first gained fame from his essay *Discourse on the Sciences and the Arts* (1750), an attack on the arts as a source for the increased wealth of the rich and an instrument of propaganda. In his *Discourse on Inequality* (1755), he professed the equality and goodness of 'natural man' and asserted that the golden age of humanity occurred before the formation of society, which bred competition and the corrupting influences of property, commerce, science, and agriculture. *The Social Contract* (1762), influential during the French Revolution, claimed that when human beings formed a social contract to live in society, they delegated authority to a government; however, they retained sovereignty and the power to withdraw that authority when necessary. On education, Rousseau suggested, in his didactic novel *Emile* (1762), that rather than imparting knowledge, education should build on a child's natural interests and sympathies, gradually developing his or her potential. For the last 10-15 years of his life, Rousseau fought mental illness (persecution mania) and lived in seclusion. *Confessions* (1782), written shortly before his death, describes

Rousseau's romantic feelings of affinity with nature. He was an influential figure of the French Enlightenment and of 19th century romanticism. *See also:* Age of Reason.

Rousseau, Théodore (1812-1867), French landscape painter, a leader of the Barbizon school. His scenes of wooded landscapes at sunset include *Coming out of the Fontainebleau Woods* (c.1850). *See also:* Barbizon school.

Roussel, Albert Charles Paul Marie (1869-1937), French composer. His music was based on contrapuntal rather than tonal construction, varying in style from *The Feast of the Spider* (1912) to *Padmavati* (1918).

Rowing, propelling a boat by means of oars operated by hand. In sport there are 2 types: sculling, in which each member of the team (2, 4, or 8 people) uses 2 oars, and sweep rowing, in which each has 1. In the United States competitive team rowing is known as crew. For speed, the craft (shells) are long, narrow, and light. The team may be steered by a coxswain, who also sets the rhythm and speed for the crew's strokes. The first recorded race was held on the Thames River, London (1716). The annual Oxford-Cambridge race (England) began in 1829, and the Yale-Harvard race in 1852.

Rowlandson, Thomas (1756-1827), English caricaturist. His satirical work is a valuable record of contemporary English life. It includes *The English Dance of Death* (1815-1816) and illustrations for *The Tour of Dr. Syntax in Search of the Picturesque* (text by William Combe, 1812-1821).

Rowling, Joanne K., (1966-), British author of children's books. She became instantly famous with her novels about the magical world of sorcerers starring Harry Potter: *Harry Potter and the Sorcerer's Stone* (1997; filmed in 2001), *Harry Potter and the Chamber of Secrets* (1998; filmed in 2002), *Harry Potter and the Prisoner of Azkaban* (1999), *Harry Potter and the Goblet of Fire* (2000) and *Harry Potter and the Order of the Phoenix* (2002).

Roxas y Acuña, Manuel (1894-1948), Philippine politician. He was a member of the Japanese-sponsored Philippine puppet government in World War II while aiding the Philippine underground. He became the 1st president (1946-1948) of the Republic of the Philippines, leader of an administration marked by corruption. *See also:* Philippines.

Royal Canadian Mounted Police (RCMP), Canadian federal police force. It was formed in 1873 as the Northwest Mounted Police to bring law and order to the new Canadian territories. In 1874, the persistence and determination of the 300 men on the force became legendary: 'The Mounties always get their man.' In 1920 it absorbed the Dominion Police and received its present name and duties. The Royal Canadian Mounted Police serves as a provincial police

force in the nation's provinces (excluding Ontario and Quebec).
See also: Canada.

Royal Household of Great Britain, those who administer the private business and court life of the monarchy of Great Britain. Many of these positions, established in the Middle Ages, are hereditary. Today these offices are ceremonial. Over the centuries British monarchs have adjusted the roster of royal attendants. Among the many positions, the lord chamberlain administers ceremonial affairs and is head of the Royal Household; the lord steward governs financial matters of the Royal Household; and ladies of the bedchamber, ladies in waiting, and the mistress of the robes are the Queen's attendants.

Royal palm, tree (genus *Roystonea*) in the palm family, found in the southeastern United States, the West Indies, and Central America. Royal palms have column-shaped trunks with feathery palm fronds gathered at their tops.

Royce, Josiah (1855-1916), U.S. philosopher, a major proponent of idealism. Influenced by Hegel and Schopenhauer, his philosophy emphasized will and purpose rather than intellect, as expressed in *The World and the Individual* (2 vols., 1901-1902). Among his other major works was *The Problem of Christianity* (2 vols., 1913), in which he developed his metaphysic of interpretation and community.
See also: Idealism.

Rozeanu, Angelica (1921-   ), Romanian table tennis player, won no less than 17 world titles between 1950-1956. She was six-time singles world champion, three-time doubles champion, and three-time mixed doubles champion; she was also a member of the team that won the world championships five times. The slender Rozeanu possessed a strong defense and was extremely agile.

RSI (repetitive strain injury), number of complaints that develop when a person makes the same repetitive movements again and again. Examples are: reporters who work on word processors all day and telephone operators. There are two types of RSI: the first type is caused by muscle strain, repetitive movement causes the second type. RSI can be explained by the fact that even minor movement repeatedly contracts the same groups of muscles. However, we also have indications that the complaints can derive from deviations in the brain's reaction to signals of one's own limbs. In 1999 it was established that one in three computer workers develops RSI; mainly resulting in pains in the neck, shoulders or arms, partly caused by an overload of working pressure. The number of RSI patients in the U.S. tripled between 1986 and 1993.

Ruanda-Urundi,   Belgium-supervised United Nations territory (1946), which later became the independent nations of Rwanda and Burundi (1962). Pygmies called Twa, a Bantu people called Hutu (or Buhutu), and Watusi are the native inhabitants of this area.

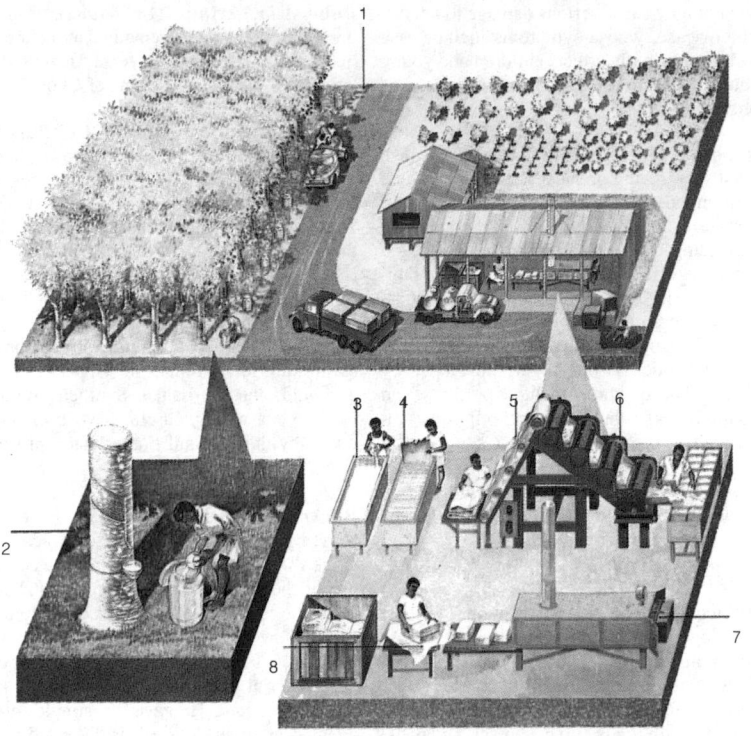

The rubber plantations (1) of Southeast Asia are the source of most of the world's natural rubber. Watery latex, or sap is tapped from the tree (2) by scoring the bark with a knife to a depth of 0.04 in (1 mm) and slanting the cut downward, to channel the sap into a cup. The latex is strained into aluminium tanks (3) to remove impurities. Acid is added to coagulate the rubber particles, which are deposited on aluminium partitions (4), rolled into sheets (5), and shredded (6). The rubber is dried and compressed into bales (7) and then wrapped for shipment (8).

The Germans laid claim to Ruanda-Urundi in the late-19th century. The Belgic gained a mandate here through the League of Nations (1923). This area is bordered by Zaïre to the west, Uganda to the north, and Tanzania to the east. Lake Tanganyika borders Burundi to the south.

Rubaiyat, collection of quatrains written by Omar Khayyám, an 11th century Persian poet, and translated to English by Edward Fitzgerald (1859). The oldest known manuscript of the original is housed at the Bodleian Library, Oxford and is dated 1460. *The Rubaiyat* views sensual pleasure as the purpose of life, and it heavily influenced post-Victorian English poetry.

Rubber, elastic substance; that is, one which quickly restores itself to its original size after it has been stretched or compressed. Natural rubber is obtained from many plants, and commercially from *Hevea brasiliensis*, a tree native to South America and cultivated also in southeast Asia and West Africa. A slanting cut is made in the bark, and the milky fluid latex, occurring in the inner bark, is tapped off. The latex-an aqueous colloid of rubber and other particles-is coagulated with dilute acid, and the rubber creped or sheeted and smoked. Natural rubber is a chain polymer of isoprene, known as caoutchouc when pure; its elasticity is due to the chains being randomly coiled but tending to straighten when the rubber is stretched. Known to have been used by the Aztecs since the 6th century A.D., and first known in Europe in the 16th century, it was a mere curiosity until Goodyear invented the process of vulcanization. Synthetic rubbers have been produced since World War II. Some latex (natural or synthetic) is used as an adhesive and for making rubber coatings, rubber thread, and

foam rubber. Most, however, is coagulated, and the rubber is treated by vulcanization and the addition of reinforcing and inert fillers and antioxidants, before being used in tires, shoes, rainwear, belts, hoses, insulation, and many other applications.

Rubber plant, any of several plants, including the Ceará tree, Pará rubber tree, and guayule, that are sources of latex, a milky fluid used to make rubber. The India rubber fig (*Ficus elastica*), a popular house plant native to India and the East Indies, was once grown for its gum, which was made into erasers.

Rubella, or German measles, contagious viral disease that presents little danger unless contracted in the first trimester of pregnancy,

The plant *Hevea brasiliensis* is grown for the production of natural rubber, which is being sapped from the stem of the plant.

R

when it may cause serious damage to a fetus. The disease, whose symptoms include rash and fever, usually affects children and young adults. Vaccination against rubella has proven effective.

Rubens, Peter Paul (1577-1640), Flemish artist, one of the greatest Baroque painters. Influenced by Tintoretto, Titian, and Veronese, he developed an exuberant style depending on a rich handling of color and sensuous effects. His workshop, an organization of skilled apprentices and talented associates, completed an impressive body of work, designed by Rubens (who also added the final touches) but largely developed by others. These works include portraits and mythological, allegorical, and religious subjects such as *Raising of the Cross (1610), Descent from the Cross* (1611), *History of Marie de Médicis* (1622-1625), *Judgment of Paris (c.1638),* and portraits of his wife. His works influenced many artists.
See also: Baroque.

Rubicon, Italian stream, famous for the crossing made by Julius Caesar in 49 B.C. As commander of Roman troops in Gaul, Caesar crossed this stream-once the border between Rome and Gaul-in reaction to the order for him to give up his power. Today the saying 'to cross the Rubicon' indicates that something irreversible has occurred. In 49 B.C. this crossing eventually led to the rule of Rome by Julius Caesar.
See also: Caesar, (Gaius) Julius.

Rubidium, chemical element, symbol Rb; for physical constants see Periodic Table. Rubidium was discovered spectroscopically by Robert Bunsen and Gustav Kirchhoff in 1861. It occurs in lepidolite and several other minerals. The element is prepared by reducing the chloride with calcium. Rubidium is a silver-white, soft, low-melting, reactive metal of the alkali metal group. It can be liquid at room temperature and ignites spontaneously in air. Rubidium and its compounds are used in ion propulsion systems, vapor turbines, thermoelectric generators, batteries, photo cells, and special glasses.

Rubinstein, Akiba (1882-1961), Polish chess grandmaster of considerable ability, and between 1907 and 1914 presumably the strongest chess player in the world. The consequences of WW I affected him so much that after 1918 he never recovered his former strength, and in 1932 had to be admitted to an institution. His last years were spent in abject poverty. Rubinstein was a chess virtuoso who has left many wonderful games behind. He was brilliant in combination play, but also understood the art of being able to slowly convert a small advantage into a victory, where he often demonstrated a flawless endgame technique.

Rubinstein, Anton Gregor (1829-1894), Russian piano virtuoso and composer. In 1862 he founded the St. Petersburg Conservatory, where he was director 1862-1867 and 1887-1891. His brother, Nicholas Grigoryevich Rubinstein (1835-1881), also a pianist, founded (1864) and served as director of the Moscow Conservatory.

Rubinstein, Arthur (1889-1982), Polish-born U.S. pianist who remained at the top of his profession for over 70 years. He was well known for his interpretations of Chopin.

Rubliov, Andrei (1360-1430), Russian painter, one of the little-known icon painters. His work shows influences of Byzantine art. Well known is his *Old Testament Trinity* (1410-1420) painted for the Trinity Sergius monastery in Zagorsk (now in the Tretyakov gallery, Moscow).

Ruby, deep-red gemstone, a variety of corundum colored by a minute proportion of chromium ions, found in Upper Burma, Thailand, and Sri Lanka. Synthetic rubies, used to make ruby lasers, have been produced by the Verneuil flame-fusion process (1902).

Rückriem, Ulrich (1938-), German artist, started work in 1959 as a masonry sculptor at the Kölner Dombauhütte (a renovated studio in the Dom, Cologne). From 1962 onwards he turned to other forms of sculpture. In 1968 he developed a simple but varied language of form in stone, iron and wood. The material itself was the most important part of his work. He gave it a simple form, which was often doubled or dissected. The craft character of his early training remained an important influence in his work.

Rudolf I (1218-1291), German king, elected in 1273, who established the Habsburg dynasty by gaining control of Austria and Styria. The Diet of Augsburg (1282) invested his two sons with these duchies.

Rudolf II (1552-1612), king of Bohemia and Hungary. He succeeded his father Maximilian II as Holy Roman Emperor (1576-1612). His religious persecutions and a Hungarian rebellion led to his replacement by his brother Matthias.
See also: Holy Roman Empire.

Rudolph, Paul (1918-1997), U.S. architect, connected with Yale University (1958-1965). He rejected the international style to experiment with externally visible ducts, a futuristic parking facility, and stacking mobile-home frames. His campus buildings include a controversial art-and-architecture building.
See also: Architecture.

Rudolph, Wilma Glodean (1940-1994), American athlete, was the star of the 1960 Olympic games. She was afflicted by scarlet fever and polio at a young age, and according to doctors would never be able to walk properly again. By playing basketball (which she was apparently very talented at) she came into contact with athletics. During the games in Rome in 1960 she won gold medals in the 100 m, the 200 m, and the relay, which earned her the nickname 'the black gazelle'. Furthermore, Rudolph was the first woman to run 100 m in 11 seconds. After her active career she dedicated herself to helping disadvantaged children through the Wilma Rudolph Foundation.

Ruff (*Philomachus pugnax*), bird in the sandpiper family. The term *ruff* refers to the male, while the term *reeve* refers to the female. The male measures about 12 in (30 cm) long and the female measures 10 in (25 cm) long. Both ruff and reeve are gray in appearance during the winter months. In spring, when courtship begins, the male displays a cluster of feathers on his head and neck of red, brown, black, and white feathers. The male uses these feathers in an elaborate courtship performance. Mostly an inhabitant of Europe and Asia, the ruff has been spotted in North America.

Ruffed grouse (*Bonasa umbellus*), bird in the grouse subfamily, Tetraoninae, in the family Phasianidae. When the grouse beats it wings in the air, a loud drumming sound is created that can be heard far away. These birds, which measure up to 17 in (43 cm) long, display a white neck collar of thick feathers on an otherwise brownish body. In winter their legs grow thick feathers for warmth, and their feet develop webs for walking on top of the snow. They reside in the forests of North America. The ruffed grouse is the state bird of Pennsylvania.

Rugby, ball game that originated (1823) at Rugby School in England during a soccer match. Somewhat similar to soccer and American football, rugby is played in two 40-minute halves on a field 75 yd (69m) wide by 160 yd (146 m) long. Goal lines are 100 yd (101 m) apart and there are 2 in-goals (equivalent to end zones in football). Each side, comprised of 15 in amateur play and 13 in Rugby league, attempts to move the oval, leather-covered ball beyond the opponents' goal; kicking, carrying, and passing the ball (to the side or rear) is permitted, as is tackling. Blocking, however, is not. Little protective equipment is worn and play is almost continuous.

Rugs and carpets, thick, heavy fabric, most often used as a floor covering. Carpet weaving with sheep's wool was first highly developed in the Near East. By A.D. 600 Persian carpets were internationally famous. Their vivid, long-lasting dyes came from natural materials, e.g., bark and roots. Persian designs influenced the 16th-and 17th-century carpets of India's Mogul courts and the beautiful Chinese carpets produced from the 14th to 17th centuries. Carpet weaving spread in the West, particularly in the 17th century, via France, Belgium, and England. Oriental carpets were woven on looms, still the basic technique of carpet making. But as of 1841, power-driven looms began to mechanize the industry. Classifications of carpets include Oriental, chenille, velvet, hooked, European handwoven, straw, and rag.

Ruhr, important coal-mining and industrial region in Germany, east of the Rhine River, between the valleys of the Ruhr and Lippe rivers. It has more than 30 large cities and towns including Düsseldorf, Essen, Gelsenkirchen, and Dortmund.
See also: Germany.

Ruhr River, river and tributary of the Rhine River in Germany. Through reservoirs and lakes created by dams, this river furnishes

The largest industrial area in Europe, the Ruhr region, extends over a length of about 62 mi (100 km). In this region, the sky is constantly blackened by smoke and fumes from the factories of the more than twenty cities that are located very close to eachother.

water for a densely populated industrial area of Westphalia. The river flows through the industrial Ruhr Valley for over 140 miles before it joins the lower Rhine.

Ruisdael, or **Ruysdael, Jacob van** (1629-1682), celebrated Dutch landscape painter and etcher. A great influence on English and French landscapists for 2 centuries, he favored a new heroic-romantic style in which small human beings were dwarfed by forests, stormy seas, and magnificent cloud-scapes. His works include *Wheatfields* and *Jewish Cemetery*.

Ruiz, Juan (1283?-1350?), Spanish poet, of whom little is known apart from the fact he was archpriest of Hita, and spent many years in the Toledo prison on the order of the local Archbishop. He wrote *Libro de buen amor* (The Book of Good Love), a highlight of medieval Spanish literature.

Ruiz Cortines, Adolfo (1891-1973), Mexican president (1952-1958). During his presidency, corruption was curbed and the March to the Sea to aid the maritime industry was initiated; in addition, the implementation of widespread irrigation boosted agricultural productivity and women were given the vote.

Rules of order *See:* Parliamentary procedure.

Rulfo, Juan (1918-1986), Mexican writer who only wrote two books, but they nonetheless ensured him international recognition: a collection of short stories *The Burning Plain and Other Stories* (1953), and a novel *Pedro Páramo* (1955). Here he impressively describes the villages and landscape of Jalisco with their closed, introverted residents, during the latter days of the revolution that broke out in 1910.

Rumania *See:* Romania.

Rumba, or **rhumba**, ballroom dance of Afro-Cuban origin popular in the 1930s and 1940s. The dancers take 3 steps to each bar, 2 fast side steps and 1 slow forward step in 4/4 time. The rumba is noted for the dancers' side-to-side hip motions with the torso erect and the knees relaxed. Rumba music is performed chiefly with percussion instruments.

Rumford, Benjamin Thompson, Count (1753-1814), U.S.-British scientist best known for his recognition of the relation between work and heat (inspired by observation of heat generated by friction during the boring of a cannon). He played a primary role in the founding of the Royal Institution (1799).

Rumi, Jalal-ed-Din, or **Jalal-ud-Din** (1207-1273), Sufi poet and mystic of Persia. His major work was the *Mathnawi*, a poetic exposition of Sufi wisdom in some 27,000 couplets.

Ruminant, any of a group of even-toed, hoofed mammals (e.g., giraffes, camels, goats, cows) that regurgitate and rechew their food after swallowing it. They feed by filling one compartment (the rumen) of a 3- or 4-chambered stomach with unmasticated food; the food is mixed with fluid which creates a soft pulp (cud or bolus), and then is regurgitated, rechewed, and sent to the other stomach chambers for digestion.

Rummy, group of card games, all of which, including gin rummy and canasta, are variants on a set of fundamental rules. Rummy is derived from the Spanish game of *conquian* and was called 'rum' (queer) poker by the English. Basic rummy was devised about 1895. The object of the game is to lay down as many sets, or melds, of cards as possible; the first player to get rid of all the cards in his hand is the winner. Melds may consist of 3 or 4 cards of the same value in different suits, or sequences of 3 or 4 cards in the same suit.

Rump Parliament, in English civil war, remaining members of Parliament after 'Pride's Purge' (led by Col. Thomas Pride) ejected all opposition to Oliver Cromwell's army (1648). These 60 members created a high court that tried King Charles I and had him executed (1649), abolished the House of Lords and monarchy, and established a ruling Council of State. The Rump Parliament itself was dissolved (1653) by Cromwell in his consolidation of power.
See also: Cromwell, Oliver.

Rumsfeld, Donald Henry (1932-), American politician. Rumsfeld obtained a degree in history at Princeton, served as a pilot for the navy and had a very diverse career in politics, business and education. In 1962 he won a seat in the House of Representatives after having been a congressional assistant twice. Rumsfeld was re-elected congressman three times. He belonged to the progressive wing of the Republican Party, was called 'a hawk' during the Cold War. He held several offices under President Richard Nixon (social economical policies), President Gerald Ford (Chief of Staff and from 1975 Secretary of State for Defense) and President Ronald Reagan (Senior Advisor for the Middle East). Rumsfeld was also the American representative for the NATO in Brussels.

Between his political offices, he taught at Northwestern University and Princeton and was CEO of G.D. Searle & Co. and of General Instruments Cop. In 2001, he was re-appointed Secretary of State for Defense under President George W. Bush. Rumsfeld advocates advanced weapon systems and flexible alliances with allies. He supports a hard line concerning Iraq.
See also: Bush, George W.; September 11, 2001; North Atlantic Treaty Organization.

Rundstedt, Karl Rudolf Gerd von (1875-1953), German field marshal. In World War II he was the leader of army groups in Poland, France, and Russia; military ruler of France and commander on D-Day (June 6, 1944) on the western front and during the Battle of the Bulge.
See also: World War II.

Runes, characters of a pre-Christian writing system used by the Teutonic tribes of northern Europe from as early as the 3rd century B.C. to as late as the 10th century A.D. and sometimes after. The three distinct types are Early, Anglo-Saxon, and Scandinavian. The Runic alphabet is sometimes known as Futhork for its first six characters.

An example of late Runic script, from the Codex Runicus (Scandinavia, end of the 13th century).

Running, pastime and popular sport since ancient times. Running can be divided into 3 basic classes: sprinting, middle-distance running, and long-distance running. Subclasses include relay racing, steeple-chasing, and cross-country running. Sprints, fueled by continuous bursts of speed, generally cover distances of 100, 220, and 440 yds (91, 201, and 402 m). At peak speed a champion sprinter may reach 26 mph (42 kmph). The mile (1.6093 km) is the traditional middle-distance race for British and U.S. runners. In long-distance running, defined as 2 miles (3.2 km) and farther, the emphasis is on endurance and pace. The marathon (26 mi, 385 yd/42.2 km) is a popular long-distance race run annually in many cities worldwide.

R

R

Runnymede, or Runnimede, meadow in Surrey, South England, on the southern bank of the Thames River. Here (or at nearby Magna Carta Island), King John conceded the barons' demands embodied in the Magna Carta (1215).
See also: Magna Carta.

Runyon, Damon (1884-1946), U.S. journalist and writer. His entertaining stories of tough-talking gangsters, Broadway actors, and the sporting underworld are written in the colorful vernacular of New York City. *Guys and Dolls* (1931), the first of several collections, became the basis for the successful musical (1950).

Rupert's Land, vast, mineral-rich region of northwest Canada granted to the Hudson's Bay Company in 1670 by Charles II. Named for Prince Rupert (first governor of the company), it comprised the basin of Hudson Bay. In 1818, the United States acquired the portion south of the 49th parallel. In 1869-1870, the remainder of the land was sold back to Canada.
See also: Hudson's Bay Company.

Rupture *See:* Hernia.

Rush, tall, grasslike plant (of various genera) in the family Juncaceae, found in marshes, on lake edges, and in paths and ditches. The green stem of the rush bears small scales, which are the leaves, and near the tip is a tuft of brownish or greenish flowers. Rushes are used for floor mats, chair seats, and baskets. The stems, when peeled of their outer covering, are used as wicks.

Rushdie, Salman (1947-), British writer and critic born in India. Rushdie has written both non-fiction and novels. His fiction often combines fantasy and folklore with realism. His works include *Grimus* (1975), *Midnight's Children* (1981), *Shame* (1983), *Jaguar Smile: A Nicaraguan Journey* (1987), and *The Satanic Verses* (1988), an allegorical novel that so offended Muslims that he was condemned to death by the Ayatollah Khomeini and forced into hiding. Rushdie has since published *Haroun and the Sea of Stories* (1990), *The Ground Beneath Her Feet* (1999), *Fury* (2001), and *Step*

Across this Line (2002). He received the Aristeion prize for *The Moor's Last Sigh<D (1992). In 1998 the Iranian government withdrew Khomeini's death sentence.*

Rushmore, Mount *See:* Mount Rushmore National Memorial.

Ruska, Ernst August Friedrich (1906-1988), German physicist and teacher, winner, with Gerd Binnig of Germany and Heinrich Rohrer of Switzerland, of the Nobel Prize (1986) for inventing the electron microscope, allowing scientists to study single atoms. He was named director of the Institute of Electron Microscopy at the Fritz Haber Institute of the Max Planck Society (1955).
See also: Microscope; Physics.

Rusk, Dean (1909-1994), U.S. politician and educator. He was secretary of state (1961-1969) in both the Kennedy and Johnson administrations, and he was outspoken against the Vietnam War. Serving the state department, he worked for the United Nations and the implementation of both the Marshall Plan and North Atlantic Treaty Organization after World War II. As an educator he has served as president of the Rockefeller Foundation (1952), a 'distinguished fellow' at that same institution, and as professor of law at the University of Georgia since 1970.

Ruskin, John (1819-1900), English art critic, writer, and social reformer. The first volume of his *Modern Painters* (1843) championed J.M.W. Turner over the old masters; the subsequent 4 volumes (1846-1860) expanded his views of the principles of true art, based on integrity and morality. He went on to apply these ideas to architecture in *The Seven Lamps of Architecture* (1849), which stimulated a Gothic revival, and *The Stones of Venice* (1851-1853). *Unto This Last* (1860), first of his 'letters' to workmen, began his attacks on laissez-faire philosophy. *Sesame and Lilies* (1865) continued to address social and political issues, offering such social reforms as nationalization of education and organization of labor that came to be widely accepted.

Russell, prominent family in British politics. The first member to gain national fame was **John Russell** (c.1486-1555), created first earl of Bedford for helping Edward VI to quell a 1549 rebellion. The family fortune, including Woburn Abbey, Bedfordshire, was acquired during this period. **Francis Russell** (1593-1641), fourth earl, built the square of Covent Garden (c.1631) and was active in Parliament's effort to contain the power held by Charles I. **William Russell** (1613-1700), fifth earl, was a parliamentary general in the Civil War. He was created first duke of Bedford in 1694, partly because of the fame, as a patriotic martyr, of his son **Lord William Russell** (1639-1683), first notable Whig in the family. The title of Lord John Russell, first earl Russell, was inherited by his grandson **Bertrand Russell. Hastings William Sackville Russell** (1883-1953), a pacifist, defended some of Adolf Hitler's policies in

World War II. **John Robert Russell** (1917-), is journalist and farmer in South Africa. In 1955 he turned his land at Woburn into a public park.

Russell, Bertrand (1872-1970), British philosopher, mathematician, and man of letters. Initially a subscriber of idealism he broke away in 1898 and eventually became an empiricist. His most important work was relating logic and mathematics. Russell endeavored to reduce all mathematics to logical principles. His results appeared in *The Principles of Mathematics* (1903) and, in collaboration with A.N. Whitehead, *Principia Mathematica* (3 vols., 1910-1913). This work particularly influenced mathematics' set theory, logical positivism, and 20th-century, symbolic logic. Russell was a vehement pacifist for much of his life, especially during World War I and after, in the 'ban the bomb' movement, and in his active opposition in Europe to U.S. involvement in Vietnam in the 1960s. His views twice earned him prison sentences (1918, 1961): during the former he wrote his *Introduction to Mathematical Philosophy* (1919). His other works include *Marriage and Morals* (1929), *Education and the Social Order* (1932), *An Inquiry into Meaning and Truth* (1940), *History of Western Philosophy (1945), and popularizations such as The ABC of Relativity* (1925), as well as his *Autobiography* (3 vols., 1967-1969). He received the 1950 Nobel Prize for literature and founded the Bertrand Russell Peace Foundation.

Russell, Bill (1934-), U.S. basketball player and coach. Known for strong rebounding and shot blocking, the 6-ft 10-in (208-cm) center is considered one of the best players of all time. Russell's achievements include winning 6 Most Valuable Player awards-5 regular season (1958, 1961-1963, 1965) and 1 All-Star (1963), and being named an All-Star 11 times. He played in the National Basketball Association (NBA) for the Boston Celtics (1956-1968) and led them to 11 NBA championships (1957, 1959-1966, 1968, 1969). Russell became the first major-league head coach of African American descent in U.S. professional sports (1966) as player-coach of the Boston Celtics. He was inducted into the Basketball Hall of Fame in 1974.

Russell, Charles Marion (1864-1926), U.S. cowboy painter, sculptor, and author. He translated his great love for the West into his many canvases of frontier life, horses, Native Americans, and cattle camps, usually set in Montana.

Russell, George William (1867-1935), Irish poet, nationalist, mystic, and painter, known by the pseudonym A.E. A theosophist, he was, with W.B. Yeats, a leader of the Celtic Renaissance and a cofounder of Dublin's Abbey Theatre.

Russell, Henry Norris (1877-1957), U.S. astronomer. His theory of stellar evolution led to the construction of the Hertzsprung-Russell diagram, work done independently of Ejnar Hertzsprung, showing the relation

Bertrand Russell (1872-1970).

between a star's brightness and color. He also determined the chemical-element content of the solar atmosphere and analyzed the spectra of various chemical elements.
See also: Astronomy.

Russell, Lillian (Helen Louise Leonard; 1861-1922), U.S. singer, actress, and flamboyant beauty of the 'Gay Nineties.' She became a star in the show *The Great Mogul* (1881). She married 4 times, but her affair with 'Diamond Jim' Brady spanned 40 years.

Russell, Lord John (1792-1878), British political figure, leader of the British reform movement. As a member of the House of Commons, he helped bring about the repeal of the Test and Corporation acts, which enabled Protestants who did not belong to the Church of England to participate in politics for the first time. He also helped extend the right to vote to more middle-class men through the Reform Bill of 1832. Russell later served as prime minister (1846-1852, 1865, 1866).
See also: United Kingdom.

Russell Cave National Monument, location of artifacts related to pre-Columbian man in northeastern Alabama. This cave offers information about ancient peoples, from a fire built about 9,000 years ago to evidence of human habitation from 3 to 4 centuries ago. As part of the National Parks System, it was made a national monument in 1961.

Russia, Slavic people were first known to live in the West as early as 2500 BC. Kiev was the first large Russian settlement (in the 9th century). It was subjected by the Tartars (a Mongolian people), who joined it in one government with several other Russian settlements in 1240. When the power of the Tartars decreased in the 15th century, the Moscowian settlement had developed into the most stable and powerful state. Czar Ivan IV the Terrible (r. 1547-1584) conquered the southeast and large parts of Siberia. Peter the Great opened the access to the Black Sea and the East Sea in 1696. He founded St. Petersburg in 1702 and introduced Western-European culture. Catherine II (r. 1762-1796) obtained parts of Poland and elevated Russia to a great power. Alexander I (r. 1801-1825) conducted the Russian-French war against Napoleon. The Crimean War (1853-1856) against the Ottoman Empire prevented the Russians from occupying Constantinople and the straits. Nicholas II (r. 1894-1917) lost the Russian-Japanese War and was forced to abdicate after the outbreak of the Russian Revolution (1917). In 1918, the Russian Soviet Federal Socialist Republic was constituted, forming the most important Union Republic in the Soviet Union (1922-1991).
See also: Russian Federation; Union of Soviet Socialist Republics.

Russian, chief official language of Russia, member of the East Slavic Indo-European languages (Byelorussian and Ukrainian diverged c.1300). Russian is written in the 33-character Cyrillic alphabet introduced in the 800s by Christian missionaries. By combining colloquialism with the formal Church Slavonic, the poet Pushkin did much to shape modern literary Russian, which is based on the Moscow dialect.

Russian Federation

Capital:	Moscow
Area:	6,592,850 sq mi (17,075,400 sq km)
Population:	145,979,000
Language:	Russian
Government:	Federal presidential republic
Independent:	1991
Head of gov.:	Prime minister
Per capita:	US$ 8,300
Monetary unit:	1 New rouble (= 1,000 old rouble) = 100 kopecks

Russian Federation, or Russia, largest country in the world. Its 6,592,850 sq mi (17,075,400 sq km) cover Asia's north and a major part of eastern Europe. The capital is Moscow. The federation consists of 21 republics, one autonomous province, 10 autonomous regions, and 55 dependent provinces. After the disintegration of the USSR in 1991 the federation replaced the Russian Federal Soviet Republic (RSFSR) and is considered to be successor to the USSR. (For history before 1991, see Union of Soviet Socialist Republics). Boris Yeltsin, who was president of the RSFSR since 1990, kept his position and replaced Gorbachev. Yeltsin faced severe economic crises and political division with respect to the future development of the country. Yeltsin's policy was one of quickly implementing measures that would establish an economy based on private enterprise, which was opposed by many members of parliament. The political division culminated in the temporary occupation of the Russian White House in 1993. After the rebellion had been suppressed, a new constitution was approved in December. In 1994 Yeltsin sent the army into the small Central Asian republic of Chechnya, which had declared independence from Russia in 1991. After a 21-month war in which more than 35,000 people were killed, the Russian army withdrew, granting the Chechens limited independence. The war was politically damaging to Yeltsin, both at home and abroad. In December 1995, the Communists, fierce critics of the Chechen war, won more than a third of the seats in the Duma. The next year Yeltsin was only narrowly reelected. In 1997 Russia signed an agreement of mutual cooperation and security with the North Atlantic Treaty Organization. The agreement paved the way for NATO to admit countries formerly allied with the Soviet Union. In December 1999, Yeltsin unexpectedly resigned. He was succeeded by Putin, who sent troops to Chechnya after terrorist bombing attacks in Moscow, ascribed to Chechen rebels. After the attacks in the U.S. on September 11, the war in Chechnya was linked to the war against terrorism. In October 2002, Chechen rebels occupied a Moscow theatre and held approximately 800 people hostage. During the ending of the siege, most of the rebels and some 120 hostages were killed. Relations with the NATO improved by the introduction of the NATO Russia Council, at which Russia and the 19 NATO partners hold equal votes in the decision-making.
See also: Union of Soviet Socialist Republics.

Russian literature, fiction, poetry, prose, and religious writings written in the Russian language. Throughout its history, Russian literature has been characterized by a deep concern for moral, religious, and philosophical problems.
Early literature. The Byzantine influence that accompanied Russia's conversion to Christianity in the late 900s A.D. also caused Church Slavonic to be adopted as the language of religion and literature. Church Slavonic was used in the Balkans and Russia as the language of secular and religious writings and served in much the same way as Latin did in the West. The earliest writings were primarily the works of clergymen and

To help rectify a serious housing shortage in Moscow, many high-rise apartment projects were constructed during the 1960s and '70s.

Alexander Pushkin (1799-1837) is considered Russia's greatest poet and the founder of modern Russian literature. His work represents the culmination of earlier Russian folk and literary traditions.

R

R

were religious in content and didactic in purpose although the *chronicles*, records of historic events attributed to the friar Nestor, were nonreligious and had some literary quality. More important than these were the *blyiny*, oral folk lays with a mixture of pagan and Christian themes, that sometimes attained the level of epic poetry. The finest piece of early Russian literature was *The Song of Igor's Campaign* (c. 1187, author unknown), describing an unsuccessful campaign by a Russian prince against an Asian tribe, the Polovtsians.

Beginning of modern Russian literature. Western influence became important in the 17th century when numerous translations appeared and the first theater in Russia was established (1662). The most notable writer of the period was the conservative priest Avvakum (martyred 1682), who opposed the changes in the ritual of the Russian Orthodox Church in the 1650s that led to the great schism. Under Tsar Peter I (the Great), European influence increased, the Russian alphabet was revised, and Russian works were printed in the vernacular. A monk, Simeon Polotsky, introduced a rigid syllabic

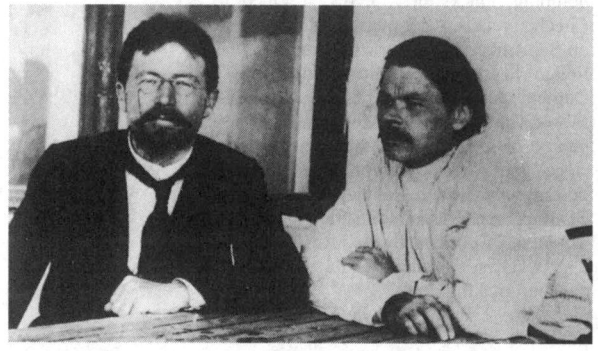

Anton Chekhov and Maxim Gorki, two of Russia's finest dramatists, photographed in Yalta (1900).

system of verse, whereby each line of poetry contained a fixed number of syllables with regularly placed pauses. Prince Antioch Kantemir (1703-1744) wrote verse satires supporting Peter the Great's reforms, using the syllabic system. Mikhail Lomonosov, a trained scientist, was a noted writer and poet. He was most noted as the founder of modern Russian literature and a precursor of classicism. In his odes, he used the new tonic form of versification (regular patterns of stressed and unstressed syllables) which was more suitable to Russian than the strict syllabic system, and he thereby changed the nature of Russian prosody.

Classicism in Russian literature. Inspired by Lomonosov and influenced by Western models, Russian writers such as Alexander Sumarokov mixed European style with Russian themes. This is especially true of his fables and his plays, which helped begin Russian drama. His *Khorev* (1747) was the first classical tragedy in Russian. The plays of Denis I. Fonzivin (1745-1792) mixed satire with more realistic concerns while the outstanding poet of the period, Gavril R. Derzhavin, wrote odes praising Catherine and ridiculing the vices of the court around her, as in his 'Ode to Felitsa' (1783). Toward the end of the 18th century, Ivan A. Krylov (1768-1844) wrote many fables, some of them adapted from Aesop and La Fontaine, but most were original.

Romanticism in Russian literature. Vasili Zhukovsky and Konstantin Batyushkov were the leading poets of the preromantic period. In the 1820s, a new group of poets introduced the Golden Age of Russian poetry. The greatest of these was Alexander Sergeyevich Pushkin (1799-1837), who wrote the remarkable historical play *Boris Godunov* in 1825. Other poets of the age included Yevgeny Baratynsky, Baron Anton Delvig, and Wilhelm Kuchelbecker. By the end of the romantic period, Russian writers turned more to social criticism, even under the strict censorship of Tsar Nicholas I. Among these were Mikhail Lermontov, whose *A Hero of Our Times* (1840) was the first psychological novel in Russian literature. The poet Fyodor Tyutchev wrote pessimistic verse, as exemplified in his 'A Vision' (1829) and 'Holy Night' (1849). The most important writer of this time was Nikolai Vasilyevich Gogol (1809-1852). He is best known for his socio-political satires, such as his famous play *The Inspector General* (1836), still performed in many countries today.

Realism in Russian literature. Around mid-19th century began the period of great Russian novels, which attempted to depict Russian life, customs, and politics in a realistic manner. Ivan Turgenev's *A Sportsman's Sketches* (1852) and *Fathers and Sons* (1862) showed his interest in social themes and particularly in character analysis, as did his gentle comedy *A Month in the Country* (completed 1850). Count Leo Tolstoy (1828-1910), one of the greatest of Russian novelists, expanded the form to include deep philosophical probing as well as realistic depictions of Russian life and people, as exemplified in his two great works *War and Peace* (1869) and *Anna Karenina* (1875-1877). The other great Russian novelist of the period, Fyodor Dostoevsky (1821-1881), wrote novels of extraordinary psychological penetration. Among his most famous works are *Crime and Punishment* (1866), *The Possessed* (1871-1872), and *The Brothers Karamazov* (1879-1880). Toward the end of the century, the playwright and short story writer Anton P. Chekhov (1860-1904) portrayed Russian life with a kind of lyric realism in such plays as *Uncle Vanya* (1899), *The Three Sisters* (1901), and *The Cherry Orchard* (1904). Prefiguring the Russian Revolution was the playwright and novelist Maxim Gorki (1868-1936) whose works depicted the terrible plight of the Russian poor and downtrodden. His most famous play is *The Lower Depths* (1902).

Russian literature in the 20th Century. The unsettled times before and during the revolution in 1917 spawned new literary trends like symbolism, as exemplified in the poets Alexander Blok and Andrey Bely. Post-symbolist poets included Anna Akmatova and Osip Mendelstam, and futurists found a strong voice in the remarkable poet Vladimir Mayakovsky. Boris L. Pasternak was also associated with the futurists, but is most known for his lyric poetry and his later novel *Doctor Zhivago* (begun 1948, published 1957) for which he won the Nobel Prize. The terrible years of Stalin's repressive rule took a toll on Russian literature, but in the 1960s a new generation of writers moved to

reassert liberal ideas. Among them are Yevgeny Yevtushenko and Andre Voznesensky (poets) and prose writers Vasily Aksyonov and Vasily Shukshin. In 1962 Aleksandr Solzhenitsyn's novel *One Day in the Life of Ivan Denisovich* was published in *Novy Mir*, a literary magazine at that time edited by the poet Aleksandr Tvardovski. It was an unprecedented exposure of the horrors of Soviet concentration camps. Within a year Solzhenitsyn's work was banned in the Soviet Union. He was awarded the Nobel Prize in 1970, and in 1974 he was exiled. Joseph Brodsky, generally regarded as the most talented poet of his generation, was expelled from the Soviet Union in 1972. He won the Nobel Prize in literature in 1987 and went on to become poet laureate of the United States. Andre Sinyavski, whose stories criticizing the Soviet regime were published abroad under the pseudoniem Abram Tertz, was allowed to emigrate in 1973 after serving six years in a labor camp. The fiction writer Vasali Aksyonov emigrated in 1980. Under the Soviet regime, it was common for writers, in order to avoid censorship, to secretly pass around their works in unpublished form. Sometimes works were smuggled out of the country, as was Boris Pasternak's novel *Doctor Zhivago* (1957). Memoirs became a popular form of literature in post-Stalin Russia. Many, like *Hope against Hope* (1970) and *Hope Abandoned* (1974), by Nadezhda Mandelstam, Osip Mandelstam's widow, had to be smuggled out of the country to be published. The giants of the early Soviet era were gradually officially recognized. A nine-volume edition of Bunin's work was published in 1965-1967. A long-suppressed novel by Mikhail Bulgakov, *The Master and Margarita*, which had appeared in a censored version in 1967, was published in full in 1974. Poems by Mandelstam, Akhmatova and Pasternak were printed in official publications. Vladimir Soloukhin and Valentin Rasputin were prominent among the many writers who took village life as their subject. Chingiz Aytmatov, a Kyrgyz, wrote both in the Kyrgyz language and in Russian. In the 1970's, Vasili Aksyonov, Yuri Trifonov, Valentin Rasputin, and Vladimir Soloukhin were among the best writers. *Pushkin House* (1978) by Andrey Bitov looks at life among the intelligentsia. 'Glasnost', Mikhail Gorbachev's domestic policy encouraging openness, greatly affected literature. Among the changes made were the rehabilitation of emigré novelist Vladimir Nabokov and the poet Vladislav Khodasevich, the publication in 1987 of Anatoly Rybakov's long-suppressed novel about the terror under Stalin, *Children of the Arbat* and in 1988 of Pasternak's longbanned *Doctor Zhivago*.

Russian Orthodox Church *See:* Union of Soviet Socialist Republics; Eastern Orthodox Church.

Russian Revolution, momentous political upheaval that changed the course of world history. It destroyed the autocratic tsarist regime and culminated in the establishment of the world's first Communist state, the Soviet Union (1922). Its roots lay in the po-

The October Revolution, also called the Bolshevik Revolution, began on Nov. 6-7, 1917, when Red Guards stormed the Winter Palace, headquarters of the provisional government, in Petrograd. Although this painting stresses martial heroism, the seizure was virtually unopposed.

litical and economic backwardness of Russia, the chronic poverty of most of the people, and rising discontent in the middle and lower classes.

The Revolution of 1905. On 'Bloody Sunday,' Jan. 22, troops fired on a workers' demonstration in St. Petersburg. Widespread disorders followed, including mutiny on the battleship *Potemkin* and a national general strike organized by the St. Petersburg *soviet* (workers' council). These events, coupled with the disastrous Russo-Japanese War, forced Nicholas II to grant civil rights and set up an elected duma (parliament) in his October Manifesto. Repression continued until late in World War I, during which Russia suffered severe reverses.

The February Revolution (1917). Food shortages and strikes provoked riots and mutiny. A provisional government under the progressive Prince Georgi Lvov was set up, and Nicholas II abdicated.

The October Revolution (1917). The Bolsheviks, led by V.I. Lenin, staged an armed coup. Moscow was seized, and the remnants of the provisional government were arrested. The constitutional assembly was dispersed by Bolshevik ('Red') troops, and the Cheka (political police) was set up. A Council of People's Commissars was established, headed by Lenin and including Leon Trotsky and Joseph Stalin. In the civil war (1918-1920), the anticommunist 'Whites,' commanded by A.I. Denikin, A.V. Kolchak, and P.N. Wrangel were defeated. Russian involvement in World War I ended with the Treaty of Brest-Litovsk. The tsar and his family were murdered at Ekaterinburg (July 1918), and the new Soviet constitution made Lenin and the Communist (formerly Bolshevik) Party all-powerful.
See also: Communism; Marxism; Lenin, V.I..

Russian wolfhound *See:* Wolfhound.

Russo-Finnish wars, conflicts during World War II. The first, the Winter War (1939-1940), arose from rejection of Russian demands for military bases in Finland, territorial concessions, and the dis-

mantling of the Mannerheim line, Finland's defense system across the Karelian Isthmus. When the Russians attacked (Nov. 30), the Finns unexpectedly threw them back. But in Feb. 1940 the Mannerheim line was broken and Finland signed the Peace of Moscow (March 12), surrendering about 10% of its territory. In the Continuation War (1941-1944), Finland fought alongside Nazi Germany, and was forced to pay reparations to the USSR and to lease it the Porkkala Peninsula (returned in 1956).
See also: World War II.

Russo-Japanese War (1904-1905), culmination of rivalry in the Far East between powers who sought expansion at the expense of the decaying Chinese empire. Russia occupied Manchuria during the Boxer Rebellion and coveted Korea, dominated the region and refused to share with Japan its position of influence. As a result, the Japanese attacked the Russian naval base of Port Arthur (now Lüshun, China), defeated the Russians at Mukden (now Shenyang) in Manchuria, and destroyed the Russian Baltic fleet in the Battle of Tsushima. Mediation by U.S. president Theodore Roosevelt ended the war in the Treaty of Portsmouth (1905). Russia ceded territory to Japan, recognized Japan's dominance in Korea, and returned Manchuria to China. Russia's disastrous defeat was one immediate cause of the 1905 Russian Revolution.

Russo-Turkish wars (1697-1878), conflicts resulting in Russian expansion into Ottoman territory. The first Russian success was the capture of Azov by Peter I (the Great) in 1696; it was subsequently recaptured (1711) by the Turks and lost again (1739). The 2 earliest major wars (1768-1774, 1787-1792), the first was declared by Sultan Mustafa III with France's encouragement, were against Catherine the Great. Allied with Austria, Russia gained the rest of the Ukraine, the Crimea, an outlet to the Black Sea, and the straits, and adopted the role of protector of Christians in the declining Ottoman Empire. Western concern over this major gain came to be known as the Western Question. Russia won Bessarabia in the war

of 1806-1812 and rose to the height of its power in the war of 1828-1829. When Russia next pressured the Turks, France and Britain intervened, defeating Russia in the Crimean War (1853-1856). The Congress of Paris, which ended that war, marked a major setback for Russia in the Middle East. The last war (1877-1878), which began with an anti-Turkish uprising (1875), brought more territory to Russia in the Treaty of San Stefano. Alarmed Western powers revised the treaty in the Congress of Berlin (1878). Russia and Turkey were opponents again in World War I.
See also: Ottoman Empire.

Rust, brownish-red substance that forms on the surface of iron or steel when exposed to oxygen in the air. Rust both corrodes and weakens metal. It is brittle and easily flakes off the metal. Rust can be prevented by coating metal objects with heavy greases or spray-on plastics.
See also: Oxidation.

Rust, in botany, fungi of the order Uredinales and the plant diseases they cause. Rusts infect their hosts by forming orange or red spots, their spore-bearing organs, on their host's leaves. Some rusts are heteroecious: they alternate between host plants of 2 different species (e.g., the cedar rust, which infects apple and cedar trees). One crucial rust fungus (*Puccinia graminis*) attacks grain crops, causing black-stem rust of wheat. Rusts also attack ornamentals, fruits, and vegetables.

The beginning of the Russo-Japanese War (1904-05) was a disaster for the Russian fleet: after Japanese torpedo attacked the fleet at Port Arthur and Vladivostok, the Russians sallied fort on 13 April, 1904, only to have their flagship, the Petropavlovsk, go down with Admiral Makarov and about 600 men on board.

Rutabaga, also called Swedish turnip, plant in the mustard family. Both its leaves and yellow root are used for food. The rutabaga root is harvested late in the autumn, when it is larger and stronger than the white turnip, a similar root vegetable. The leaves are harvested in early summer, before they become spongy and bitter.

Ruth, Babe (George Herman Ruth; 1895-1948), U.S. baseball player. Known as the first great power hitter in the major leagues, he is second on the all time home run list (714). Originally an outstanding pitcher (won 94 games, lost 46 for his career), Ruth was switched to the outfield and became a prolific hitter (.342 career average). Ruth's

The rutabaga, *B. napus*, is a large edible root that grows best in cool climates.

R

R

achievements include hitting 60 home runs in one season (1927), winning the American League Most Valuable Player award (1923), and leading the majors in home runs 11 times (1918-1921, 1923-1924, 1926-1929, 1931). He played for the Boston Red Sox (1914-1920), New York Yankees (1920-1934) and Boston Braves (1935). Known as The Bambino, he led the Yankees to 4 World Series championships (1923, 1927, 1928, 1932) and was among the first group of players inducted into the National Baseball Hall of Fame (1936).

Ruth, Book of, name of Old Testament book in the Bible. It focuses on the love and loyalty of Ruth, described as a descendant of King David and the royal family of Israel. As a widowed non-Israelite, she gave up her home in Moab to follow Naomi, her mother-in-law, to Bethlehem. There, after working to secure a life for both herself and Naomi, she married Boaz, a kinsman to Naomi. Through the sacrifice and effort of Ruth, an Israelite family line continued. This Old Testament book, completed c. 2,500 years ago, is appreciated for its vivid characterization of Ruth and for its literary qualities. *See also:* Bible; Old Testament.

Ruthenia, region in western Ukraine, southwest of the Carpathian Mountains, covering 4,940 sq mi (12,800 sq km). Formerly part of Hungary, then of Cze-choslo-vakia (from 1919), it was ceded to the USSR (1945). The region came under independent Ukrainian rule in 1991. Uzhgorod is capital of this mountainous and densely forested region. *See also:* Ukraine.

Ruthenium, chemical element, symbol Ru; for physical constants see Periodic Table. Ruthenium was discovered by Karl Klaus in 1844. It occurs in nature associated with native platinum and also with copper-nickel ores. It is obtained in commercial quantities from the mineral pentlandite. The element is prepared by the reduction with hydrogen of the oxychloride. Ruthenium is a hard, lustrous, white metal and is a member of the platinum group of elements. It is used to harden other metals and improve their wear-resistance and resistance to corrosion. It is also a versatile catalyst.

Rutherford, Ernest (1871-1937), New Zealand-born English physicist. He taught at McGill University (Montreal, 1898-1907) and the University of Manchester (1907-1919); in 1919 he became director of the Cavendish Laboratory, Cambridge. In studying uranium he discovered and named alpha and beta radiation. For his theory concerning the radioactive transformation of atoms he was awarded the 1908 Nobel prize in chemistry. In 1911 he proposed his nuclear theory of the atom, on which Bohr based his celebrated theory years later. In 1919 Rutherford announced the first artificial disintegration of an atom. His work was commemorated (1969) by the naming of rutherfordium, a chemical element. *See also:* Atom; Physics.

Rutherfordium *See:* Element 104.

Rutile, mineral (TiO_2) found in the United States, Brazil, Europe, Australia, and India. It is a red to brown or black crystal. The titanium of this titanium-oxide mineral is refined for use as pigment in white paint. Porcelain as well as coating for welding rods are also colored with rutile.

Rutin, yellow pigment used as a medicine to treat problems in the circulatory system. Found in such plants as tobacco, rue, and buckwheat, among others, rutin helps make weak capillaries strong.

Ruwenzori Range, east-central African mountain range between Uganda and Zaïre. These mountains, slightly north of the equator, rise to a snowy height of 16,763 ft (5,109 m) at Margherita Peak on Mount Stanley. The range was given its present name by the European explorer Henry Stanley (1889). In ancient times it was named Mountains of the Moon by the geographer Ptolemy. These non-volcanic mountains consist of glaciated masses of crystalline rock. The range has deep chasms and deeply carved river valleys. The rainfall and snow melt from these mountains are considered a source of the Nile River.

Ruysdael, Jacob van *See:* Ruisdael.

Rwanda

Capital:	Kigali
Area:	10,169 sq mi (26,338 sq km)
Population:	7,398,000
Language:	French, Kinyarwanda, English
Government:	Presidential republic
Independent:	1962
Head of gov.:	Prime minister
Per capita:	US$ 1,000
Monetary unit:	1 Rwandese franc = 100 centimes

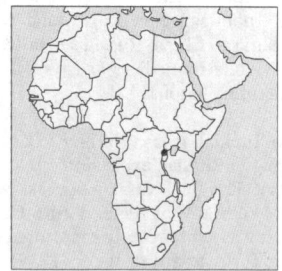

Rwanda, small independent republic in east-central Africa. It is one of the most densely populated counties in Africa.
Land and climate. The land of Rwanda is dominated by the Rift Valley Highlands. From the high volcanic Virunga Mountains in the northwest, the land falls away southeastward in a series of steeply sloping flat-ridged hills. The forests that once covered

Lake Bulera and, in the background, Muhavura volcano in northwest Rwanda. The volcano is part of a chain of volcanos in the Central-African tectonic rift system.

these hills have been largely cleared for farming. Marshy plains form the bottoms of the deep, intersecting valleys. In the west, the land rises sharply from Lake Kivu. Chief rivers include the Nyabarongo, the Kagera, the Akanyaru, and the Ruzizi. Because it lies on high plateaus, Rwanda has a cool climate.
People. The population is comprised of three main ethnic groups: 85% are Bantu farming people known as the Hutu, 14% are a pastoral people known as the Tutsi, and a small percentage are the Twa, a pygmy people who live by hunting. The people live mostly in small villages. Kigali is the capital and largest center.
Economy. Agriculture and mining provide nearly 80% of the gross national product. The chief crops are coffee, pyrethrum, and tea. Efforts are being made to expand production. Agricultural output is insufficient to provide enough food for the people.
History. The earliest inhabitants of Rwanda, the Twa pygmies, were long ago driven into the forests by the Hutu, who came from the Congo. In the 16th century the Hutu were conquered by the tall, cattle-rearing Tutsi. The Tutsi established a feudal state and remained in control until 1959, when the Hutu liberation party known as Parmehutu set up a republican regime that was later recognized by the United Nations. The country was granted full independence in 1962. An attempted invasion of Rwanda from Burundi was bloodily repulsed in 1963. Military leaders took control of the government in 1973, and Major General Juvenal Habyarimana declared himself president. While he at first filled cabinet posts with military leaders, he gradually replaced them with civilians during the 1970s. With civilian rule restored under the new constitution of 1978, Habyarimana was elected president. Habyarimana's death in 1994, resulting from an aircrash, led to a violent and bloody strife between the two ethnic groups: the Hutus turned on the Tutsis and massacred some 500,000. The Tutsi exile army then moved to rescue the Tutsis and succeeded in conquering the country. About a million Hutus were displaced, fleeing to neighboring countries as refugees. The Rwanda tribunal was established in 1995 in Tanzania. In 1996 many Hutu refugees returned to Rwanda. In 1997 Rwandan troops played an important role in the ousting of

president Mobutu of Zaire (now DR Congo). In 1998, Jean Kambanda, who served as Rwanda's Prime Minister during the 1994 massacre, was convicted of genocide by the tribunal and sentenced to life in prison.
Paul Kagame (a Tutsi) has been President since April 2000. The government presented a new flag and a new anthem to promote national unity and the reconciliation which took place on December 31, 2001.
See also: Rwanda tribunal.

Rwanda tribunal, UN's Security Council appointed international tribunal, established in 1995 in Arusha (Tanzania). It is charged to run to earth and prosecute people that have been guilty of Rwanda's genocide on Tutsis in 1994. The tribunal concentrates on the main suspects. The maximum penalty is life imprisonment.
See also: United Nations; Rwanda.

Ryan, Elisabeth (1892-1979), American tennis player, won 26 doubles championships during her twenty year long career (1914-1934). She won the Wimbledon ladies' doubles title twelve times (with Morton, Suzanne Lenglen, Mary Brown, Helen Moody-Wills, and Simone Mathieu) and the mixed doubles seven times (with Randolph Lycett). Moreover, she won three American and four French championships. Her record of 19 Wimbledon titles was still unbeaten when she died during the Wimbledon tournament of 1979. One day later, Billie Jean King-Moffitt broke her record by winning the ladies' doubles (with Martina Navratilova) and bringing her total up to 20 Wimbledon titles. Ryan's game was characterized by a powerful service and smash as well as her controlled volleys.

Ryan, Nolan (1946-), U.S. baseball player. Known for his blazing fastball (clocked at a record 100.8 mph/161.3 kmph), he is considered one of the greatest pitchers of all time. At the end of the 1990 season, Ryan had 302 career wins and held the records for career strikeouts (5,308), strikeouts in a single season (383 in 1973), and career no-hitters (6). He pitched his seventh no-hitter early in the 1991 season. Ryan played in the major leagues for the New York Mets (1966-1971), California Angels (1972-1979), Houston Astros (1980-1988), and Texas Rangers (1989-1993).

Ryder, Albert Pinkham (1847-1917), U.S. painter, noted for his darkly poetic landscapes, seascapes, and allegorical scenes such as *Toilers of the Sea* (1884), *The Flying Dutchman* (1890), and *The Race Track* (1895). Ryder's body of work (only about 160 canvases) is considered among the finest of American art.

Rye (*Secale cereale*), grain of the grass family, hardiest of all cereal crops. It can grow in poor, sandy soils in cool and temperate climates. Most rye is used for human consumption, e.g. pumpernickel and light-colored rye bread or to make gin and whiskey, but rye grain and middlings (a by-product of milling) are also fed to livestock and used for cattle pasturage. The leading producer of rye is the USSR. If rye is infected with ergot, a poisonous fungus, it becomes unsafe for use.

Rykov, Aleksei Ivanovich (1881-1938), Russian communist leader. Active in the October Revolution (1917), he was Soviet Premier (1924-1930) after Lenin's death. Opposed to Stalin's policies, he was dismissed from office until he recanted (reinstated 1931-1936). Due to involvement in an assassination plot against Stalin, he was executed after a show trial.
See also: Russian Revolution; Union of Soviet Socialist Republics.

Ryman, Robert (1930-), American painter. Made paintings that had as their subject the fundamental elements of painting: the paint, how and how much is applied, how various materials behave when used as a canvas, and the limitations of the focal plane. Used predominantly white paint, because white was more definite than color and allowed the inherent potential of painting as a medium to be revealed. Since 1976 Ryman has integrated the means by which the painting is hung on the wall into his composition. His work can be defined as fundamental painting.

Ryukyu Islands, archipelago, of approximately 1,850 sq mi (4,790 sq km), forming a 650-mi (1,050-km) arc between Japan and Taiwan. Dividing the East China and Philippine seas, the 100-plus islands comprise 3 groups: the Amami Islands in the north; the central Okinawa Islands, including Okinawa; and the Sakishima Islands in the south. Many have coral reefs and some have active volcanoes. Climate is subtropical; the economy is supported by agriculture and fishing. The Ryukyus became part of Japan in 1879; they passed to the United States after World War II. The northern islands were returned in 1953, and the remainder in 1972.

Ryun, Jim (1947-), U.S. athlete who set world records for middle-distance running. In 1966 he ran the mile in 3 minutes 51.3 seconds and 880 yards in 1 minute 44.9 seconds; in 1967 he ran 1,500 meters in 3 min-

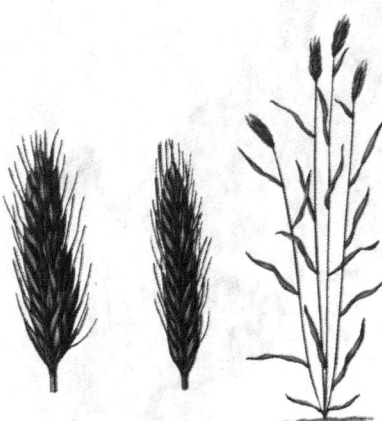

Summer rye (left) is planted in spring and grows in summer; winter rye (center) is planted in fall, lies dormant during winter and grows in spring.

utes 33.1 seconds. He also broke his own mile-run record by 0.2 seconds.

Ryzhkov, Nikolai Ivanovich (1929-), former prime minister of the USSR (1985-1991). He left office when the restructuring of the Soviet government reduced the scope of the position. After his admittance into the Communist Party (1956), he rose through the ranks of the government, becoming deputy minister of heavy machinery (1975), chairman of the Soviet economic planning commission, called Gosplan (1979), Secretariat of the Central Committee involving economic concerns (1982), then full member of the Communist Party Politburo (1985). In 1991 he was a presidential candidate but lost the elections.
See also: Union of Soviet Socialist Republics.

R/x, symbol used on medical prescriptions. It is believed to have evolved from the Latin word recipe (meaning take), or from the ancient symbol for Jupiter that when placed on a prescription became a plea for hasty remedy.

S, 19th letter in the alphabet, corresponding to the Semitic letter *sin*, meaning *tooth*, represented by a rounded W shape derived from an ancient Egyptian symbol for *tusk*. Phoenicians squared off the curves; Greeks turned the resulting sign on its side (as *sigma*); and, as the 18th letter of the Roman alphabet, S assumed its present form. S is used as an abbreviation for such words as south and sulfur.

Saadi, or **Sadi**, (1184-1292), Persian lyric poet. This Sufi writer is best known for 2 ethical works: his masterpiece *Gulistan* (*The Garden of Roses*, 1258) and *Bustan* (*The Orchard*, 1257), both blending prose and poetry.

Saadia ben Joseph (882-952), known as Saadia Gaon, leading figure in medieval Judaism. He was head of the Academy at Sura, Babylonia, and orthodox champion against the ascetic Karaites. He wrote a Hebrew grammar and lexicon, an Arabic translation of the Bible, created the *siddur*, or prayer book, and the *Book of Beliefs and Opinions* (933).
See also: Judaism.

Saar, or Saarland, state in southwest Germany, 991 sq mi (2,567 sq km), bordering France. Its capital is Saarbrücken. It is a major coal-mining, iron, and steel region whose control has historically alternated between France and Germany. After World War I, it was administered by France under the League of Nations. It was reunited with Germany after a plebiscite (1935), occupied by France after World War II, and instated as a German state in 1957.
See also: Germany.

Saarinen, 2 modern architects, father and son. **Eliel Saarinen** (1873-1950), the leading Finnish architect of his day, designed the influential Helsinki railroad station (1905-1914). In 1923 he emigrated to the United States, where he designed numerous struc-

S

Eero Saarinen's avian design for the Trans World Airline Terminal (1956-62) at Kennedy International Airport, New York City, is a magnificent exemple of the sculptural possibilities of formed concrete.

tures in the Midwest, including the Gateway Arch in St. Louis, Mo. **Eero Saarinen** (1910-1961) collaborated with his father (1938-1950). His outstanding works include the General Motors Technical Center in Warren, Mich. (1951-1955); Massachusetts Institute of Technology's circular chapel and concrete-dome auditorium (1955); and the Trans World Airline Terminal in New York City. He also designed Dulles International Airport in Chantilly, Va., which was completed posthumously.
See also: Architecture.

Saavedra Lamas, Carlos (1880-1959), Argentinian lawyer and statesman. As Argentina's foreign minister (1932-1938), he presided over the conference that ended the Chaco War (1935). He won the 1936 Nobel Peace Prize.
See also: Argentina.

Sabah, formerly North Borneo, state in the Federation of Malaysia, on the northern tip of the island of Borneo, Malay archipelago. It lies on the South China and Sulu seas, with Kalimantan (Indonesian Borneo) to the southwest and Brunei to the west. Sabah and Sarawak (also on the island of Borneo) became British protectorates in 1882 and then crown colonies in 1946. In 1963 they joined the newly formed Federation of Malaysia. Sabah's capital is Kota Kinabalu. It has a tropical climate and is largely mountainous

(highest peak, Mt. Kinabalu, 13,432 ft/4,094 m). Main exports are timber, rubber, and copra (dried coconut).
See also: Malaysia.

Sabatier, Paul (1854-1941), French chemist who shared with Victor Grignard the 1912 Nobel Prize in chemistry for his work on catalyst action in organic syntheses; especially his discovery that finely divided nickel accelerates hydrogenation.
See also: Chemistry.

Sabatini, Gabriela (1970-), Argentinean tennis player, turned professional at the age of 15. Won her first major titles in 1988: the Italian Open championship and the Masters. In 1990 she won the American Open championship, followed in 1991 by the Italian Open. She won the Masters tournament again in 1994.

Sabbath, seventh day of the Hebrew week. The Jews observe it as the day of rest laid down in the Fourth Commandment to commemorate the Creation. It starts at sunset on Friday and ends at sunset on Saturday. Christians adopted Sunday as the Sabbath to commemorate the Resurrection.
See also: Judaism.

Sabbatical year, among ancient Jews every seventh year was a year of rest for the land, ordered by the law of Moses. Crops were to be unsown and unreaped, and debtors were to be released. Today a professor's sabbatical is for rest or research.

Saber-toothed cat, either of 2 genera of extinct cats of the Cenozoic: *Smilodon* of North America and *Machairodus* of Europe and Asia. Slightly smaller than lions but similar in build, saber-toothed tigers had enormous upper canines, up to 10 in (254 mm) long, which they probably used as daggers to pierce the skin of their prey.

Sabin, Albert Bruce (1906-1993), U.S. virologist best known for developing an oral

poliomyelitis vaccine, made from live viruses (1959).
See also: Poliomyelitis.

Sabines, ancient people of the Sabine Hills (Apennines) in central Italy, northeast of Rome. The legend of the abduction of the Sabine women by the Romans is fictitious, but there were numerous Roman-Sabine wars. Though there were Sabines in Rome from the earliest times, they became Roman citizens c.268 B.C. and disappeared as a separate people.

Sable (*Martes zibellina*), carnivorous fur-bearing mammal related to the martens. Sable live on the ground of coniferous forests, now restricted to parts of North Asia. About 20 in (508 mm) long, they prey on small rodents.

Saccharides, or carbohydrates, chemical compounds composed of simple sugar or sugars in combination, including table sugar, starch, and cellulose. Saccharides, fats, and proteins are the 3 main classes of food. *Monosaccharides*, including glucose ($C_6H_{12}O_6$), are sugars that cannot be further digested to yield simpler sugar molecules. *Disaccharides*, including sucrose or table sugar ($C_{12}H_{22}O_{11}$), are composed of 2 linked monosaccharide molecules. *Polysaccharides*, including starch and cellulose, are complex molecules consisting of many linked monosaccharides.

Saccharin, calorie-free sweetening agent, much sweeter than sucrose, normally used in its soluble sodium salt form. Not absorbed by the body, it is used by diabetics and in low-calorie dietetic foods.
See also: Artificial sweetener.

Sacco-Vanzetti case, famous legal battle (1920-1921) that polarized opinion between U.S. liberal-radicals and conservatives. In 1921, Nicola Sacco and Bartolomeo Vanzetti were found guilty of murdering a paymaster and his guard in South Braintree, Mass. When arrested, they were armed and gave false statements, many say out of fear of deportation due to their alien status. By 1927, opponents of the verdict claimed that there had been insufficient evidence, and that the trial had been unduly influenced by the fact that Sacco and Vanzetti were aliens, anarchists, and draft evaders. The supreme court of Massachusetts and the governor ruled that the trial was fair. The 2 were executed on Aug. 22, 1927, preceded by demonstrations around the world. Public debate continued for years.
See also: Anarchism.

SACEUR (Supreme Allied Commander Europe); NATO's highest military commander in Europe. Because the United States is the largest contributor to the defense of Western Europe, SACEUR is always an American who also has command over American combat forces in Europe at the same time. This post was first held in 1950 by general Dwight Eisenhower, who later became American president. In the event of war, the authority of SACEUR, the so-called Allied Commander Europe (ACE),

Saber-toothed tigers, distinguished by their 8 in (20 cm) long canine teeth, were effective predators of such mammals as the mastodon and giant sloth. The saber-tooths became extinct about 10,000 years ago.

stretches from the northern tip of Norway to North Africa, and from the Atlantic Ocean to the eastern border of Turkey (including Great Britain, Spain and Portugal). His authority covers all operations on land, at sea, and in the air. In peacetime the task of SACEUR is to prepare defense plans for ACE, to organize military exercises, and to give advice about how to equip the armed forces put under NATO control in time of war. SACEUR has three subordinate commands: the Allied Forces Northern Europe West (AFNORTHWEST), Allied Forces Central Europe (AFCENT), and Allied Forces Southern Europe (AFSOUTH).

Sachs, Hans (1494-1576), most popular German poet and dramatist of his time, one of the Meistersingers, and by trade a shoemaker. His prolific output included 'The Nightingale of Wittenberg' (1523), which honors Martin Luther. Sachs was the model for a leading character by the same name in Richard Wagner's *Die Meistersinger (1868)*.

Sachs, Julius von (1832-1897), German botanist. Sachs studied plant metabolism and respiration, the role of minerals in plant nutrition, and the location of chlorophyll within plant cells. His *The Textbook of Botany* (1868) and *History of Botany* (1875) are among the most comprehensive and influential books in the field of botany.
See also: Botany.

Sachs, Nelly (1891-1970), German-born Swedish poet who fled Nazi Germany in 1940. Her poems deal with the sufferings and destiny of her Jewish people (*O the Chimneys*, 1967). She shared the 1966 Nobel Prize for literature with S. Y. Agnon of Israel.

Sackville, Thomas, 1st Earl of Dorset, (1536-1608), English statesman and poet. He was coauthor (with Thomas Norton) of the first English blank-verse tragedy, *Gorboduc* (1561). He is also noted for his poems 'Induction' and 'Complaint of Buckingham' in the collection *A Myrrovre for Magistrates* (1559-1563). Sackville was raised to peerage status in 1567 and also had the dubious distinction of announcing the death sentence to Mary, Queen of Scots (1586).

Sackville-West, Victoria Mary (1892-1962), English poet, novelist, and biographer, associated (like her husband, Sir Harold Nicolson) with the Bloomsbury Group. Her works include the poem *The Land* (1926) and the novels *The Edwardians* (1930) and *All Passion Spent* (1931).

Sacrament, in Christian theology, visible sign and pledge of invisible grace, ordained by Jesus Christ. The traditional 7 sacraments (first listed by Peter Lombard) are baptism, Holy Communion, confirmation, penance, ordination, marriage, and extreme unction, of which only the first two are accepted as sacraments by many Protestants. In Roman Catholic theology the sacraments, if validly administered, convey grace objectively to the believing recipients; Protestants stress the joining of Word and sacrament and the necessity of faith.
See also: Christianity.

Sacramento (pop. 383,000), capital city of California since 1854, and seat of Sacramento County, at the confluence of the Sacramento and American rivers in central California. Its economy is based primarily upon the business of government, military manufactures, and agriculture, for which it is a shipping, marketing, and processing center. Its history dates back to 1839, when John Sutter established a colony there on a land grant from Mexico. After the discovery of gold at nearby Sutter's Mill, Sacramento became a boom town.
See also: California.

Sacramento River, longest tributary in California, rising in the Klamath Mountains in the north, flowing southwest for about 380 mi (610 km) to join the San Joaquin River in the Central Valley, before exiting at San Francisco Bay. It is navigable for large vessels as far as Sacramento, 67 mi (108 km) upstream, the major port and largest city on the river. Shasta and Keswick are the chief dams of the Sacramento, which contributes its water to the Central Valley Project (irrigation for the southern part of the state).

Sacrifice, cultic act found in almost all religions, in which an object is consecrated and offered by a priest in worship to a deity. It often involves the killing of an animal or human being and thus the offering up of its life; sometimes a communion meal follows. Sacrifice may also be seen as the expiation of sin, the sealing of a covenant, or a gift to the god that invites blessing in return. Ancient Israel had an elaborate system of sacrifices (chief being that of Passover) that ceased when the Temple was destroyed (A.D. 70). In Christianity, Jesus' death is viewed as the one perfect and eternal sacrifice for sin.
See also: Religion.

Sadat, Anwar el- (1918-1981), president of Egypt (1970-1981). An army officer, he was active in the coup that overthrew King Farouk in 1952. As vice president, he became president on Nasser's death, expelling

Anwar el-Sadat (1918-1981) succeeded Nasser (1918-1970) as President of Egypt in 1970, after having previously fulfilled important governmental functions. Although he lacked the charisma of his predecessor, he long succeeded in maintaining his position, despite internal problems and a partial defeat in the October War against Israel in 1973.

Soviet military advisers. His war with Israel and support of an Arab oil boycott against the West (both 1973) were followed by a policy reversal. Establishing close ties with the United States, he took initiatives leading to an Egyptian-Israeli peace treaty (1979). He shared the Nobel Peace Prize with Menachem Begin in 1978. Sadat was assassinated by a group of Muslim army officers.
See also: Egypt.

Saddam Hussein *See:* Hussein, Saddam.

Saddle, seat to support a rider on the back of an animal. Most horse saddles are leather and are held in place by a girth (strap) passing underneath the horse. Two stirrup-leathers (straps) support the stirrups in which the rider places his or her feet. The English saddle is light, almost flat, and often used by jockeys and horse-show riders. The Western saddle is heavier, has a raised frontal horn to which a lariat may be attached, and is most often used by cowhands and rodeo riders.

Sadducees, Jewish sect active in Judea, Palestine, during the 1st century B.C. and active until the destruction of the Second Temple in Jerusalem, A.D. 70. The sect, associated with priests and the upper class, claimed the Old Testament alone as the source of Jewish law. With their dismissal of Jewish Oral Law they dismissed the beliefs in immortality, resurrection, and angelic beings, beliefs all held by the opposing Pharisee sect.
See also: Sanhedrin.

Sade, Marquis de (Comte Donatien Alphonse François de Sade; 1740-1814), French soldier and writer. He proposed that the existence of sexual deviation and criminal acts prove they are natural. He was charged with many sexual offenses and spent much of his life in prisons, writing sexually explicit romances, e.g., *Justine* (1791). He lived his last 11 years in Charenton lunatic asylum. The word *sadism* (infliction of pain to attain sexual pleasure) was named for him.
See also: Sadomasochism.

Sadi *See:* Saadi.

Sadomasochism, finding sexual pleasure in both inflicting pain or suffering pain. It is not clear how sadomasochistic tendencies originate. Some researchers claim that a connection between sexual satisfaction and pain in childhood can lead to sadomasochism. It is certainly true that elements of sadomasochism appear in the sexual fantasies and relationships of many people.
See also: Sade, Marquis de.

Safdie, Moshe (1938-), Israeli architect. His best known project is Habitat, a modular housing project designed for Expo '67, the 1967 Montreal exposition, and later reproduced in Israel, New York City, Puerto Rico, and the Virgin Islands. Other designs by Safdie include the Yeshivat Porat Joseph Rabbinical College in Jerusalem (1971-1979) and the National Gallery of Canada in

S

S

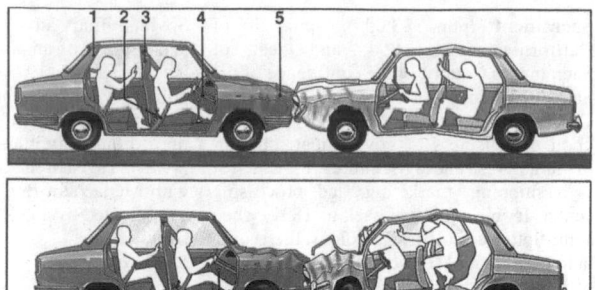

Safety devices may prevent death or severe injuries in a head-on collision. The car on the left has a rigid passenger compartment (1), seat belts (2), and headrests (3). Its engine is designed to deflect downward, collapsing its steering column (4), thus avoiding the driver. The car's front end (5) will absorb the energy of the impact. The injuries, sustained by the passengers in the unprotected car, are indicated by red dots.

Ottawa (1988). Safdie became a Canadian citizen in 1959.
See also: Architecture.

Safety, protection from harm, injury, or loss. In a modern, technological society the risks of injury or accidental death caused by machines are very high. Every year in the United States there are over 100,000 deaths from accidents and around 50 million people are injured severely enough to require medical attention. This works out to 1 accidental death every 5 minutes and an injury every 3 seconds. Apart from the immense personal suffering these figures represent, the cost to the economy is enormous. The prevention of accidents is a major concern of all governments.

Safety lamp, oil-burning lamp used in coal mines that indicates the presence of explosive methane gas without igniting it. Designed in 1815 by English chemist Sir Humphry Davy, it uses a double wire gauze cylinder to enclose the flame, preventing heat from escaping and causing an explosion. In the presence of *firedamp*, the methane-air mixture commonly released in

The Sago palm (*Metroxylon sagu*) flourishes in Southeast Asian freshwater swamps. Usually the palms are self-regenerating. Each palm flowers once in its lifetime (approximately 15 years of age), just after a build-up of starch in the trunk occurs.
Just before flowering, the palm is cut, and the pith of the trunk is ground, in order to make sago flour.

coal mining operations, the flame burns with a blue center, warning miners to leave the mine immediately. The safety electric lamps now used to light mines are designed so that if the bulb is broken the current shuts off, thus preventing ignition of firedamp. But although electric lamps are safe, they do not indicate the presence of the gas, and Davy lamps are still used to warn miners of the danger.
See also: Mining.

Safety valve, relief device that automatically opens to allow excess pressure to escape. Sealed by a compressed spring or a weight, it is held open until the pressure has fallen by a predetermined amount. Safety valves are used on all pressurized vessels (e.g., steam boilers) to prevent explosion.

Safflower, thistlelike herb (*Carthamus tinctorius*) that grows in most warm regions. Safflowers are grown by farmers for the oil and meal that can be made from the seeds. Safflower oil has uses in medicine and is used to make varnishes. The safflower's bright red flowers are used as a substitute for true saffron dye.

Saffron, purple-flowered Asian crocus (*Crocus sativus*) of the iris family; also, the yellow dye extracted from it. The orange-yellow stigmas of its pistils yield saffron powder, which is used for flavoring food and in medicine and perfume.

Saga, epic narrative, in prose or verse, of Old Norse literature (11th to mid-14th century). Subjects of sagas range from history (*Sturlungasaga*) to histories of mythical heroes (*Volsungasaga*) or families (*Njala*). One of the greatest saga authors was Snorri Sturluson, whose *Heimskringla* (1230) traced the history of the kings of Norway.

Sagan, Carl Edward (1934-1996), U.S. astronomer, educator, and popular science writer. From 1968 a professor at Cornell University, he worked on NASA space probe projects and conducted research into the possibility of extraterrestrial life. He helped popularize science through his public television series *Cosmos* (1980). Sagan's books

include the Pulitzer Prize-winning *The Dragons of Eden* (1977) and the novel *Contact* (1985).
See also: Astronomy.

Sagan, Françoise (Françoise Anne Quoirez; 1935-), French novelist best known for the precocious and highly successful *Bonjour Tristesse* (1954), written when she was 18, and *A Certain Smile* (1956), both of which deal with the disillusion of gilded youth. In 1984 her memoires *Avec Mon Meilleur Souvenir* were published.

Sage, aromatic herb or shrub of the mint family. There are several North American species, including the crimson and purple sages of California and the lyre-leaved sage of New England. Cultivated sages include bright-flowered ornamentals known by their scientific name, *salvia*. The common garden sage (*Salvia officinalis*), native to Southern Europe and Asia Minor, has grayish leaves that are used to make tea and as a seasoning.

Sagebrush, small aromatic shrub (genus *Artemisia*) of the composite family, native to the plains and mountains of western North America. These deciduous shrubs grow anywhere from 2 to 12 ft (0.6 to 3.7 m) high and have white or yellow flowers. Sagebrush is unrelated to true sage. It is the state flower of Nevada.

Sagebrush State *See:* Nevada.

Sago, starch derived from the coontie or sago palm. The starch is found in the fibrous tissue at the base of the tree's stem. Sago is used to make sago flour, one of the principal foods of East Indian people.

Saguaro, or giant cactus (*Cereus giganteus* or *Carnegiea gigantea*), large member of the cactus family native to the deserts of the U.S. Southwest and Mexico. The plant uses a shallow, wide network of roots to collect moisture, which it then stores in the ribbed, spiny trunk, 1-2.5 ft (30-76 cm) in diameter. The plant may reach the age of 150-200 years, growing to a height of nearly 40 ft (12 m) and occasionally up to 60 ft (18 m). The white night-blooming flowers form at the ends of the trunk and the large branches in late spring, attracting bats, birds, and insects. The red, egg-shaped fruit is eaten by humans and desert animals.

Saha, Meghnad (1893-1956), Indian astrophysicist, professor in Allahabad (1923) and Calcutta (1938). Carried out research into the ionization of gases and the interpretation of star spectra. 'Saha comparison': comparison whereby the gas in a star and the temperature and the relative abundance of elements in the star atmosphere can be derived from the ionization of the gas.

Sahara Desert, largest desert in the world, covering about 3,500,000 sq mi (9,065,000 sq km) of North Africa from the Atlantic Ocean to the Red Sea, about 3,000 mi (4,830 km) by 1,200 mi (1,930) north to south. The terrain includes sand hills, rocky wastes, tracts of gravel, and fertile oasis. The central plateau, about 1,000 ft (305 m) above sea level, has mountain groups (Ahagger, Aïr, and Tibesti), some of which rise well over 6,000 ft (1,829 m). Rainfall averages from less than 5 in (12.7 cm) to 10 in (25 cm) annually (dry periods may last for several years), and temperatures may soar higher than 135°F (57°C) and plunge below freezing at night. Natural resources include oil, iron ore, natural gas, and phosphates. Also underground are vast aquifers holding water thought to date from the Pleistocene epoch.

Sahel, semiarid region south of the Sahara Desert, extending across north-central Africa from Senegal in the west to Ethiopia in the east. The land supports a grazing and agricultural economy with savanna-type grassland and scrub. Rainfall is 8-16 in (20-40 cm) annually, from June to August. A severe drought (1967-1974) caused mass migration and the starvation of hundreds of thousands of people.

Saigon *See:* Ho Chi Minh City.

Sailer, Toni (1935-), Austrian skier, winner of many top-class international competitions. His most successful year was 1956, when he won the gold medal in all alpine events during the Winter Olympics of Cortina d'Ampezzo. He also won the non-Olympic alpine combination class. In 1958 he became world champion in downhill and giant slalom in Bad Gastein.

Sailfish, food and game fish of the family Istiophoridae, related to the marlin and swordfish. The sailfish has a pointed beak on the snout and a high, wide dorsal fin sail. Averaging 6 ft (180 cm) in length and 60 to 100 lb (27 to 45 kg), they feed on fish and squid and are highly prized by anglers for their fighting qualities.

Sailing, popular pastime or sport involving the navigation of a boat powered primarily by wind. The earliest known sailing vessels evolved in the Mediterranean region, particularly among the Upper Nile dwellers of ancient Egypt. These sailboats had a mast with 1 sail hung from a fixed yardarm. The Chinese developed the movable yardarm, which allowed vessels to sail with the wind across their bows as well as before the wind. In recent history, boats of varying lengths, with multiple sales and masts, gather to compete with other like vessels.
See also: America's Cup.

Saint, in Christian theology, person preeminent for holiness. The term was used in the New Testament to refer to all the faithful. It is now used to designate those recognized by a church as occupying an exalted position in heaven and being worthy of veneration due to martyrdom, holiness of life, miracles during life or after death, or a popular cult. All angels are saints, and the Virgin Mary is chief among them. Feast days in the Anglican, Orthodox, and Roman Catholic liturgies commemorate those canonized with sainthood.
See also: Christianity.

Saint Andrews (pop. 16,000), town in east-

ern Scotland on the North Sea, in the district of Fife, between the firths of Forth and Tay. The University of St. Andrews is Scotland's oldest (founded 1411). The town, known as the birthplace of golf, is home to the Royal and Ancient Golf Club (founded 1754).
See also: Scotland.

Saint Bartholomew's Day, Massacre of, the killing of French Huguenots (Protestants) by Roman Catholics, beginning in Paris on Aug. 24, 1572. Jealous of the influence of the Huguenot admiral Coligny on her son King Charles IX, Catherine de Médicis plotted to assassinate him. When this failed, Catherine, fearing Huguenot reaction, persuaded Charles to order the deaths of all leading Huguenots. On the morning of St. Bartholomew's Day thousands were slaughtered. Despite government orders to stop, the murders continued in the provinces until October. The Wars of Religion (1562-1598) resumed as a result.

Saint Bernard, breed of large, stout dog developed as a rescue dog at the Alpine monastery of St. Bernard, Switzerland, in the 17th century. It measures up to 30 in (76 cm) at the shoulder and 180 lb (82 kg), and has a white and red or white and brown coat. Its acute sense of smell has helped it locate people buried in snow and makes it a valued guide dog.

Saint Bernard Passes, routes through the Alps. The Great St. Bernard (8,100 ft/2,469 m) links Martigny, Switzerland, with Aosta, Italy. The Little St. Bernard (7,177 ft/2,188 m) connects France's Isère Valley with Aosta.
See also: Alps.

Saint Christopher *See:* Saint Kitts and Nevis.

Saint Denis, Ruth (Ruth Dennis; 1878?-1968), U.S. dancer, choreographer, and teacher, whose work strongly influenced modern dance. Deeply interested in ethnic and U.S. dances, music visualizations, and

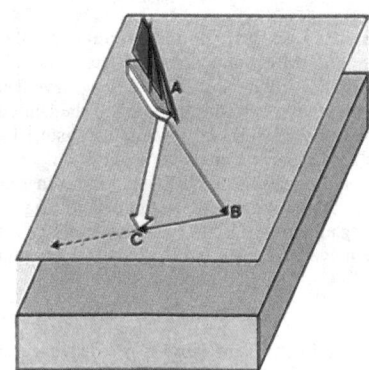

The dead reckoning method estimates a ship's approximate position by calculating how far it has traveled from the last known position (A) along a course (AB) after a given time at a known speed. Additional correction may be applied for a known or predicted ocean current in a direction (BC), to fix the final position of the ship at point (C).

Sand dunes in the Sahara.

Hindu and other Eastern philosophies, she staged her first major success, the solo *Radha*, in 1906. She and her husband, Ted Shawn, ran the influential Denishawn School and widely touring Denishawn Company (both, 1915-1932).
See also: Shawn, Ted.

Sainte-Anne-de-Beaupré, village and Roman Catholic shrine in Montmorency County, southern Quebec, Canada, on the St. Lawrence River near the mouth of the Ste.-Anne River. The village was first settled in 1650. A chapel was built there in 1658 by shipwrecked French sailors who believed they were saved from death by their prayers to Saint Anne, patron saint of sailors. There were subsequent reports of miracle cures in the area, and the village became a pilgrimage center. A basilica was built as a shrine in 1876 and rebuilt after a fire destroyed it in 1922.
See also: Quebec.

Sainte-Beuve, Charles Augustin (1804-1869), a French literary critic. He is credited with being the first to employ the biographical method of literary criticism. He believed that knowledge of an author's personality and environment is essential to a full understanding of his or her writing. Sainte-Beuve applied this theory in his most important works, which include *Literary Portraits* (1844), *Contemporary Portraits* (1846), *Monday Chats* (1851-1862), and *New Mondays* (1863-1870). A champion of the Romantic movement, Sainte-Beuve himself wrote poems and a novel in the Romantic style.
Sainte-Beuve studied medicine in Paris, but soon turned his attention to literature. He contributed to several journals and lectured at various universities. He was elected to the French Academy in 1844 and was appointed to the French Senate in 1865.

Saint Elmo's fire, glowing electrical discharge seen at the tips of tall, pointed objects-e.g., church spires, ship masts, and airplane wings-in stormy weather. The negative electrical charge of the storm clouds induces a positive charge on the prominent structures. The impressive display is named (corruptly) for St. Erasmus, patron of sailors.

Saint-Exupéry, Antoine de (1900-1944), French aviator and author. After serving in

S

S

the French Army Air Force (1921-1923), he flew commercial routes between France, West Africa, and South America. Most of his writing gives accounts of his flying experiences (*Southern Mail*, 1928) and the philosophical and spiritual meaning he found in its challenges (*Wind, Sand and Stars*, 1939). His most famous work, however, is the fantasy *The Little Prince* (1943). Saint-Exupéry flew reconnaissance missions during World War II, disappearing over Europe on one such mission in 1944.

Saint-Gaudens, Augustus (1848-1907), U.S. sculptor famed for his heroic public monuments, including Abraham Lincoln (Lincoln Park, Chicago), the Robert G. Shaw monument on the Boston Common, and the equestrian statue of General William Sherman (Central Park, N.Y.C.).

Saint George Island *See:* Pribilof Islands.

Saint George's (pop. 4,200), capital, chief port, and industrial center of Grenada, in the West Indies. Originally settled by the French in 1650 at a location near present-day St. George's, the current site was established in 1705. In 1783 control of the town, on the southwestern coast, passed to the British, who soon made it the government headquarters for all of the Windward Islands. A center of tourism, St. George's gained its independence in 1974.

Saint-Germain, Treaty of, treaty signed by the United States and other World War I Allies and the Republic of Austria in France (1919-1920), limiting Austrian powers and redistributing some of the lands of the Austro-Hungarian Empire. The treaty resulted in the complete independence of Poland, Czechoslovakia, and Hungary, and the creation of the independent state of Yugoslavia. Austria's army and war industry were restricted, and the country was required to pay reparations to the Allies. The treaty's provision prohibiting the unification of Austria and Germany was violated by Adolf Hitler in 1938.
See also: World War I.

Saint Helena, British island (47 sq mi/122 sq km) in the South Atlantic Ocean, 1,200 mi (1,931 km) west of Africa. Discovered by the Portuguese in 1502, its capital is Jamestown, where Napoleon I died in exile in 1821. With Tristan da Cunha and Ascension, it comprises the British dependency of St. Helena.

Saint Helens, Mount *See:* Mount Saint Helens.

Saint James's Palace, former royal residence (1698-1837), London, England, situated in Pall Mall. Royal gatherings are still held here and foreign ambassadors to Britain are received at its court.

Saint-John's-wort, name generally given to over 400 species of low shrubs of the family Hypericaceae, native to temperate and tropical regions. The flowers, which include both wild and cultivated varieties, are generally yellow, with 5 petals.

The Saint-John's-wort (*H. calycinum*) is a evergreen ornamental, often used as a thick ground cover in shaded areas.

Saint Kitts and Nevis

Capital:	Basseterre
Area:	101 sq mi (262 sq km)
Population:	41,000
Language:	English
Government:	Parliamentary monarchy in the British Commonwealth
Independent:	1983
Head of gov.:	Prime minister
Per capita:	US$ 5,870
Monetary unit:	1 East Caribbean dollar = 100 cents

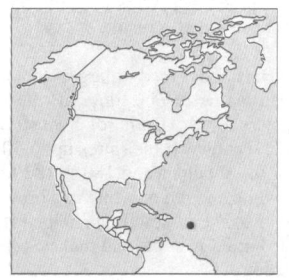

Saint Kitts and Nevis, officially Federation of Saint Kitts and Nevis. Former Caribbean island state of the British West Indies, in the Leeward Islands. The area is 101 sq mi (262 sq km); the capital is Basseterre, on Saint Kitts. Discovered (1493) by Columbus, the islands were awarded to Britain (1783) after struggles with France. Autonomy in internal affairs was granted in 1967, followed by full independence in 1983. In 1998 a referendum was held on Nevis concerning its independence, but the majority of its people voted against it. Denzil Douglas has been President since 1995. Hurricane George destroyed 85% of the buildings in 1998 and caused an economic recession.

Saint Laurent, Louis Stephen (1882-1973), prime minister of Canada (1948-1957). Internationally, St. Laurent played an important role in the founding of the United Nations (1945). As prime minister he strengthened Canada's position in the Commonwealth of Nations and was instrumental in founding the North Atlantic Treaty Organization (NATO). Domestically, he achieved the incorporation of Newfoundland as a Canadian province in 1949.
See also: Canada.

Saint Lawrence River, largest tributary in Canada, flowing 744 mi (1,197 km) northeast from Lake Ontario to the Gulf of St. Lawrence. It forms 120 mi (193 km) of the U.S./Canadian border. Canalized as part of the Saint Lawrence Seaway, it serves as the chief outlet for Great Lakes shipping (although it is closed from mid-December to mid-April due to ice).

Saint Lawrence Seaway and Great Lakes

Waterway, U.S./Canadian inland waterway for oceangoing vessels connecting the Great Lakes with the Atlantic Ocean, and comprising a system of natural waterways, canals, locks, dams, and dredged channels (including the Welland Ship Canal) 2,342 mi (3,769 km) long. A joint venture between the United States and Canada, it was completed in 1959.

Saint Louis (pop. 384,000), city in eastern Missouri, on the Mississippi River. Founded as a fur-trading post by the French in 1764, it was ceded to Spain in 1770, reverting briefly to the French before passing to the United States as part of the Louisiana Purchase in 1803. The city expanded rapidly after the War of 1812 and became a major inland port, transportation center, and market. Products include beer, machinery, chemicals, and basic metals. St. Louis' Gateway Arch (630 ft/192 m high), designed by Eero Saarinen, is the city's most famous landmark. It is also known for its symphony orchestra and Washington University.
See also: Missouri.

Saint Lucia

Capital:	Castries
Area:	238 sq mi (616 sq km)
Population:	160,000
Language:	English
Government:	Parliamentary monarchy in the British Commonwealth
Independent:	1979
Head of gov.:	Prime minister
Per capita:	US$ 4.400
Monetary unit:	1 East Caribbean dollar = 100 cents

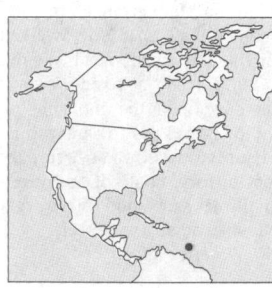

Saint Lucia, independent West Indies island nation (238 sq mi/616 sq km) in the Windward Islands in the Caribbean Sea.
Land and Climate. St. Lucia, 27 mi (43 km) long and 14 mi (23 km) wide, is of volcanic origin with 1 active volcano. The terrain is hilly, with Morne Gimie reaching 3,145 ft (959 m), and the interior is covered with tropical rain forests. The average annual temperature is 79°F (26°C).
People. Most of the inhabitants are of black African heritage. Roman Catholicism is the religion of nearly 90% of the population, and English is the official language. How-

ever, a French patois is widely spoken.

Economy. Small-scale agriculture is the principal economic activity, with bananas, coconuts, cocoa beans, oil, and citrus fruits grown for export. Industry, including food processing, electrical components, and garments, is being diversified to include an ambitious oil complex and free-trade zone. Although tourism is growing, imports exceed exports by 200%, and the country is heavily dependent upon foreign aid.
In 1998, the EU decided to reduce the import of bananas from Saint Lucia and other Windward Islands drastically, which meant a threat to the survival of the island. Saint Lucia desperately needs to diversify its economy (tourism) and to grow other export crops.

History. Though the island was probably sited by Columbus in 1501, the Carib were able to prevent several settlement attempts by the British and French from the early 17th century until 1814, when the island was ceded to Britain. St. Lucia was part of the West Indies Federation from 1958 until it was dissolved in 1962. Full independence from Britain was granted in 1979. It has a parliamentary government. Saint Lucia's aims are to reach further economical and political integration for countries in the Caribbean area within the Caribbean Community and Common Market (CARICOM). It has decided to work on a federative cooperation with the three other English-speaking Caribbean islands (Dominica, Grenada and Saint Vincent) in 1992.

Saint Mark, Basilica of, cathedral in Venice, Italy, named for the city's patron saint. Originally Romanesque, it became an outstanding example of Byzantine architecture through alterations made from the 12th century on. It is built in the form of a Greek cross surmounted by 5 large domes (1 in the center, the others on the 4 arms of the cross). The richly constructed and sculptured west façade, facing the Piazza San Marco, has Gothic additions. Its famous 4 bronze horses were taken from Constantinople in 1204.

Saint Moritz (pop. 5,000), alpine resort town in southeastern Switzerland, Graubünden (Grisons) canton. The original Roman settlement dates from 50 B.C. The town became a resort in the 19th century, and was home to the 1928 and 1948 Winter Olympics. Saint Moritz is located in the region where Romansh, an Italic language (of Latin derivation) and one of Switzerland's official languages, is spoken.

Saint Nicholas, Feast of, festival on Dec. 6 in honor of a 4th-century bishop of Asia Minor. Saint Nicholas, later known also as Santa Claus, is patron saint of children, and the festival is celebrated as a children's holiday, with rewards and punishment according to the children's behavior. Although Santa Claus became identified with Christmas, the Feast of Saint Nicholas continues to be celebrated by some on Dec. 6.

Saint Patrick's Cathedral, largest U.S. Roman Catholic cathedral, seat of the New York Archdiocese. The Gothic Revival structure was designed by James Renwick and built between 1858 and 1879. It is located on 5th Avenue and 50th Street, New York City.

Saint Patrick's Day, March 17, celebrated as the anniversary of the death (C.A.D. 461) of Patrick, Ireland's patron saint. The Irish celebrate the day by wearing leaves of shamrock (Ireland's national flower) or green-colored items of clothing and by staging colorful parades.

Saintpaulia *See:* African violet.

Saint Petersburg (pop. 248,000), city in the American State of Florida on Tampa Bay, on the Pinellas peninsula. Known as Sunshine City, because the sun shines there every day. Port exporting fruit, fish, and vegetables; electronic goods, cement, and aluminum industry. Founded (1834) by John C. Williams and Peter A. Demens, who was born in Saint Petersburg, Russia. The city is well known for its Salvador Dalí museum, which has the largest collection of this Spanish artist.
See also: Florida.

Saint Petersburg *See:* Leningrad.

Saint Peter's Church, or Saint Peter's Basilica, church in Vatican City, Rome. The world's largest Christian church, it is built over the tomb thought to hold the remains of St. Peter, the first pope. The original church was built by the emperor Constantine the Great in the 4th century A.D. but demolished by Pope Julius II in the 16th century to make way for the new building. Among the successive architects to be involved in the creation of the current church were Donato Bramante, who developed the original design on the shape of a Greek cross (from 1506); Michelangelo Buonarroti, who created the great dome (from 1547); and Carlo Maderno, who added the façade and altered the overall proportions to arrive at the shape of a Latin cross (1607-1614). The church was dedicated in 1626, but further work continued, most notably by Gian Lorenzo Bernini, who created the great elliptical piazza in front of the church (completed 1667) as well as much of the interior detail. The church measures nearly 700 ft (210 m) long and is 450 ft (137 m) at its widest. The nave (main aisle) is 150 ft (46 m) high, while the dome is over 400 ft (120 m) high.

Saint-Phalle, Niki de (1930-2002), French artist. She joined the Nouveau Réalistes in the 1960s. Above all known for her large dolls, the 'nanas': voluptuous female figures, usually made from papier-mâché and painted with bright colors.

Saint Pierre and Miquelon, groups of French islands in the Atlantic Ocean, south of Newfoundland. The capital is Saint Pierre. First visited in the 17th century by Breton and Basque fishermen, the islands' ownership was long disputed between France and England. They became France's in 1814 and are now an overseas department, electing a deputy and senator to parliament. Fisheries (for cod and others), fox- and mink-farming, and tourism are important industries.

Saint-Saëns, Camille (1835-1921), French composer. He wrote many large-scale symphonies, piano concertos, symphonic poems, operas, including *Samson et Dalila* (1877), and such short works as *La Danse Macabre* (1874), and *Carnival of the Animals* (1886).

Saint-Simon, Comte de (Claude Henri de Rouvroy; 1760-1825), French philosopher and early socialist. According to his theories, voiced in *The New Christianity* (1825) and other influential writings, all people would be treated as economic equals-no wealth would be inherited, everyone would work, and compensation would be commensurate with labor. He believed that science could be used to create a fair and harmonious society. Saint-Simon fought on the side of the colonies in the American Revolution.
See also: Socialism.

Saint Sophia *See:* Hagia Sophia.

Saint Vincent and the Grenadines

Capital:	Kingstown
Area:	150 sq mi (389 sq km)
Population:	116,400
Language:	English
Government:	Parliamentary monarchy in the British Commonwealth
Independent:	1979
Head of gov.:	Prime minister
Per capita:	US$ 2,900
Monetary unit:	1 East Caribbean dollar = 100 cents

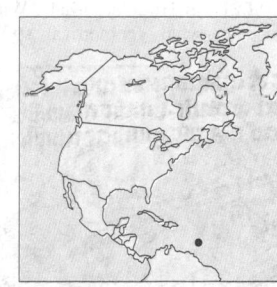

Saint Vincent and the Grenadines, island nation in the West Indies, part of the Windward Islands in the Caribbean Sea, part of the British Commonwealth.
Land and climate. The principal island, St. Vincent (133 sq mi/344 sq km), is of volcanic origin, with a forested, mountainous spine running down the center of the island. It reaches 4,000 ft (1,219 m) at Soufrière, an active volcano peak that erupted in 1979, causing extensive crop damage and the evacuation of 20,000 people. The 5 small, main islands of the Grenadines extend to the southwest. The climate is tropical.
People. The majority of the inhabitants are descendants of slaves brought from Africa.

S

Most of the population is a member of the Roman Catholic church; the official language is English.

Economy. Agriculture provides all exports, principally arrowroot and bananas, followed by spices and cacao. The small industrial sector mostly processes food crops. Tourism is also important.

In 1998 Saint Vincent suffered from the EU decision to phase out preferential treatment from the Windward Islands. Saint Vincent needs to diversify its industry.

History. St. Vincent was discovered by Christopher Columbus in 1498. Although both Britain and France subsequently contested control of the island, it was left largely to the Carib Indians until 1797 when, following a war with both the French and Caribs, the British deported most of the Indians. Full independence was achieved in 1979.

Saint Vincent agreed with Dominica, Grenada and Saint Lucia to aim for the establishment of an economic and political union in 1992. For a long period of time (1984-2001), the conservative NDP had a majority in Parliament. However, the 2001 elections meant a major victory for the ULP, the social-democratic opposition. Ralph Gonzalez became President.

Saint Vitus's dance *See:* Chorea.

Saito, Joshishige (1904-), Japanese artist. Made strange machines in the 1930s, and pop-art paintings that deliberately bordered on kitsch. In 1956 he painted an abstract demon series ('Oni'). He also made colorful plywood constructions.

Sakakura, Junzo (1904-), Japanese architect. Worked together with Le Corbusier (1929-1937). Designed the Japanese pavilion for the world's fair in Paris in 1937. He went on to design the Museum in Kamakura (1952) and the city halls in Hajima (1959), Kura (1962) and Hiraoka (1964). With his stylized, somewhat geometrical style, he

was one of the designers responsible for the renewal of Japanese architecture in the 1950s.

Sake, or saki, alcoholic drink made from fermented rice. It is Japan's national beverage and contains 12-16% by volume of ethanol.

Sakhalin (formerly Saghalien), Russian island off the coast of eastern Siberia, in the Sea of Okhotsk, north of the Japanese island of Hokkaido. It measures about 600 mi (970 km) long and 16-100 mi (26-160 km) wide, and contains coal and iron deposits and lumber. Fishing and fur trading are also important economic activities. Ownership of the island, which was originally discovered by the Dutch, was disputed by Japan and Russia-from 1905 it was divided between the 2 countries. The Ainu people were the original inhabitants; Russian colonization dates from the discovery of oil in 1931. By 1951 Japan had given up all claims to the island.

Sakharov, Andrei Dmitriyevich (1921-1990), Soviet physicist and human-rights proponent. He played a prominent part in the development of the first Soviet hydrogen bomb (1948-1956). He subsequently advocated worldwide nuclear disarmament (for which he was awarded the 1975 Nobel Peace Prize) and became a leading Soviet dissident. His subsequent banishment (1980) to the city of Gorki provoked international protest. He was pardoned in 1986. *See also:* Nuclear weapon.

Saki *See:* Munro, Hector Hugh.

Saladin (1138-1193), Muslim ruler and warrior who fought against the Crusaders. He united the Shiite and Sunnite Muslims in 1171 and thus became sultan of Egypt and Syria. In 1187 he led the capture of Jerusalem from the Christians. The Third Crusade that followed resulted in a lengthy siege of the city (1189-1191). Saladin finally surrendered to England's King Richard I and entered into a truce ceding coastal lands to the Christians and giving pilgrims access to Jerusalem. Saladin was a noted patron of learning and the arts.
See also: Crusades.

Salam, Abdus (1926-), Pakistani physicist, professor in Lahore (1951-1954) and London (since 1957). Received the Nobel Prize for physics in 1979, awarded for his contribution to the unified fields theory.

Salamander, tailed amphibian (order *Vrodela*) related to frogs and toads. Sala-

manders' weak limbs, which are not used for locomotion to any great extent, are small and can regenerate. These mostly nocturnal creatures range in size from under 6 in (15 cm) to 5 ft (1.5 m) and are abundant in damp areas of the northern temperate zone. Some species are aquatic, most are terrestrial, and a few are arboreal. Salamanders feed on insects and other invertebrates.

Salamis, or Koulouri (Greek, 'baker's crescent'), Greek island in the Saronic Gulf (arm of the Aegean Sea between Attica and the Peloponnisos), about 10 mi (16 km) west of Athens. The rocky, crescent-shaped island, 37 sq mi (95 sq km) in area, supports little agriculture, and most residents now work in the shipping industry or in businesses in Athens. In the Battle of Salamis (480 B.C.), fought at sea by the Persians and the Athenians, Themistocles led the Greeks to a decisive victory.

Salazar, António de Oliveira (1889-1970), dictator of Portugal (1932-1968). He reorganized public finances as finance minister (1926, 1928), and achieved certain modernizations as premier. Education and living standards, however, remained almost static, and political freedom was restricted, both at home and in Portugal's African colonies, where he actively suppressed revolts. A stroke in 1968 led to his replacement as premier.
See also: Portugal.

Salem witchcraft trials, trials held in Salem, Massachusetts Bay Colony, in 1692, as a result of hysteria. The accusations of innocent townspeople began when 3 young girls claimed possession by the devil. The special court sentenced 19 men and women to death by hanging and imprisoned about 150 more. The witch hunt was brought to a halt and those imprisoned were freed in 1693. Samuel Sewall, one of the 3 judges, apologized publicly, and the colony's legislature made payments to families of those who were executed.

Salerno (pop. 148,000), city and tourist center in Campania, on the Gulf of Salerno in southern Italy. Founded by Romans in 197 B.C., it was occupied by the Norman conqueror Robert Guiscard in 1076 and was the site of a fierce beach battle between the Allies and Germans in World War II. Salerno's medical school, founded in the 9th century and at its peak in the 12th, was the first of its kind, with teachings influenced by the leading Mediterranean cultures.
See also: Italy.

Sales, Saint Francis de *See:* Francis de Sales, Saint.

Christian monarchs and the Church pictured Moslem leader Saladin as an utterly cruel heathen. In reality, he was neither as bloodthirsty, nor as filled with wrath in his conquest of Jerusalem in 1187, as the Christians had been before him, in 1099. In this miniature from the *Historia Maior* by British historian Matthew Paris, Saladin pulls the holy cross away from a Crusader (Cambridge University).

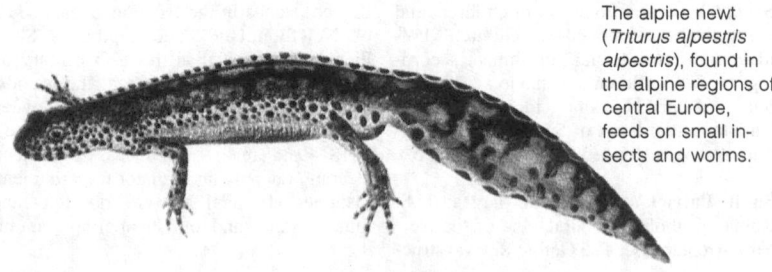

The alpine newt (*Triturus alpestris alpestris*), found in the alpine regions of central Europe, feeds on small insects and worms.

Salic law, from the 14th century, law to prevent women and those descended from female lines from inheriting the throne and other titles and offices. It was not part of the Germanic *Lex Salica* (laws regarding the penal code and succession to property), as it is sometimes mistaken to be. Salic law was used into the 19th century in France and Spain, where it was rescinded for Queen Isabella II.

Salicylic acid ($C_7H_6O_3$), white crystalline solid made from phenol and carbon dioxide. It is used in medicine against calluses and warts and to make aspirin and dyes. Its sodium salt is an analgesic and is used for rheumatism.
See also: Aspirin.

Salinas de Gortari, Carlos (1948-), president of Mexico (1988-1994). As secretary of planning and the budget in the cabinet of President Miguel de la Madrid Hurtado, Salinas managed Mexico's economy from 1982 to 1987. He was elected on the ticket of the ruling party, the Institutional Revolutionary Party (PRI), to succeed Madrid. In 1995 he left for the United States. He was suspected of being involved in political murders. In 1996, thousands of Mexican farmers blamed him for the 1994 financial crisis and wanted him imprisoned.
See also: Mexico.

Salinger, J(erome) D(avid) (1919-), U.S. author. His novel, *The Catcher in the Rye* (1951), became one of the most popular postwar books, and its adolescent hero, Holden Caulfield, was accepted as a spokesperson of his generation. Salinger's short stories include *Nine Stories* (1953), *Franny and Zooey* (1961). and *Raise high the Roof Beam, Carpenters, and Seymour: An Introduction* (1963).

Salisbury, or New Sarum (pop. 105,000), town in Wiltshire, southern England, 80 mi (130 km) southwest of London. The original town of Old Sarum was rebuilt as New Sarum when it became a bishopric in the 13th century; Salisbury's main tourist attraction, its cathedral, dates from this time. The famous prehistoric stone circle known as Stonehenge lies 7 mi (11 km) north.
See also: England.

Saliva, watery secretion of the salivary glands, partly controlled by the parasympathetic autonomic nervous system, that lubricates the mouth and chewed food and begins the breakdown of starches in the digestive process. There are 3 sets of salivary glands: the parotid, submaxillary, and sublingual. Saliva contains mucin, water, salts, some gamma globulins (proteins), and ptyalin (a starch-splitting enzyme) and is secreted in response to food in the mouth or by conditioned reflexes such as the smell or sight of food.

Salivary glands *See:* Saliva.

Salk, Jonas Edward (1914-1995), U.S. physician and microbiologist. He is best known for developing the first poliomyelitis vaccine, made from killed viruses (1952-1954). He served as director of the Salk Institute for Biological Studies at the University of California, San Diego (1963-1975). From 1986 he worked on a vaccine against AIDS.
See also: Poliomyelitis.

Sallustius Crispus, Gaius (86-34 B.C.), Roman historian. Sallustius argued that the fall of Rome was inevitable. Apart from *Bellum Iugurthinum* (40 B.C.; 'The war against Iugurtha') he also wrote *Historiae* (about the period 78-67 B.C.), of which only fragments remain.

Salmanassar I (ruled 1273-1243 B.C.), king of the Assyrian Empire. Occupied the remains of the Mitanni empire and fought against Urartu.

Salmanassar II (ruled 1031-1020 B.C.), king of the Assyrian Empire.

Salmanassar III (ruled 858-824 B.C.), king of the Assyrian Empire, his conquests (Babylonian Empire, Palestine) laid the foundation for the New Assyrian Empire. His rule saw much building activity (black obelisk of Salmannasser).

Salmanassar V (ruled 726-722 B.C.), king of the Assyrian Empire, deposed by Sargon II.

Salmon, large, silver, soft-finned game and food fish of the family Salmonidae. Salmon are born in fresh water, spend most of their lives in the ocean, and return to fresh water to breed. The most commercially important salmon is the Pacific salmon (genus *Oncorhynchus*), of which there are 5 species. The largest is the chinook, which reaches up to 100 lb (45 kg); the blueback is the source of most canned salmon. The Atlantic salmon (*Salmo salar*), endangered due to overfishing and pollution, lives in the North Atlantic and reaches only 15 lb (6.8 kg), feeding on crustaceans and small fish. All salmon return to their natal streams to breed, spawning in the sand or gravel of the stream bed.

Salmonellosis, common type of food poisoning caused by the *Salmonella* bacteria. Poultry, milk, eggs, and egg products often carry the bacteria. Salmonellosis is usually confined to the intestines, where it causes nausea, abdominal pain, diarrhea, and fever. Treatment includes rest, replacement of body fluids and, in severe cases, the use of antibiotics.
See also: Food poisoning.

Salome (fl. 1st century A.D.), daughter of Herodias and stepdaughter of Herod Antipas (governor of Galilee), described in the New Testament (Matthew 14:6-12, Mark 6:22-28). She is said to have danced for Herod, for which she was granted a wish. At the urging of her mother, Herodias, she requested the head of the imprisoned John the Baptist. Oscar Wilde's play *Salome* (1893), which gives an erotic interpretation of these events, formed the basis for Richard Strauss's opera (1905). Another biblical Salome, possibly mother of the apostles James and John, appears in Mark 15:41 and 16:1.
See also: Bible; New Testament.

Salomon, Haym (1740-1785), Polish-born

The Atlantic salmon, *Salmo salar*, spawns in freshwater. Fertile eggs (A), about 0.24 in (6 mm) in diameter, develop prominent eyes (B). A newly hatched larva (C) bears an external yolk sac, which it later absorbs (D). When about 1.6 in (4 cm) long (E), the larva, now sometimes called a parr, begins to feed independently. Its skin (F) has dark blotches that are shed as the fish matures. Now known as a smolt (G), it migrates to the sea. Sexually mature salmon (H, the hooked jaw of a male is shown here) return to freshwater to spawn.

S

S

U.S. financier, patriot, founder of the first Philadelphia synagogue. Salomon was active in the Polish independence movement before emigrating to New York in 1772. He was a major financial supporter of the American Revolution, lending large sums of money to the colonial government, giving money outright to equip troops, and making interest-free loans to Thomas Jefferson and other prominent statesmen. He was twice arrested and imprisoned for treason by the British (1776, 1778). Salomon challenged the Pennsylvania rule that civil servants swear belief in the New Testament, a rule that was later changed.

Salon, reception hall or drawing room often used for gatherings of society figures, intellectuals, politicians, or artists and their work. Salons can also be fashion establishments offering products or services to customers.

Salonika (pop. 396,000), port city in northern Greece, on the Salonika Gulf, established c.316 B.C., by the Macedonian king Cassander. Known as Thessaloniki in Greek, the city is now an industrial center producing textiles, soap, tobacco, minerals and leather products. It is also the second most important home of modern Greek culture, after Athens.
See also: Greece.

Salpiglossis *See:* Painted-tongue.

Salsify, or oyster plant (*Tragopogon porrifolius*), purple flowering plant of the composite family whose edible root has a flavor similar to oysters.

SALT *See:* Strategic Arms Limitation Talks.

Salt, common name for sodium chloride (NaCl), a chemical compound with an equal number of sodium ions (+) and chlorine ions (-). It is found in seawater and in solid deposits (rock salt, or halite). Pure salt forms colorless-to-white odorless cubic crystals. An essential in the diet of humans and animals, salt is most familiarly used to flavor food. It is also used in much larger quantities to preserve hides in leathermaking, to manufacture soap, as a food curative and preservative, to keep highways ice-free in winter, and in the manufacture of sodium, chlorine, and sodium hydroxide.

Colorful salt formations in the volcanic Danakil plain, a part of the Great East African Rift.

Salt, chemical, compound that is formed by a chemical reaction between an acid and a base. When a base totally neutralizes the acid with which it combines, a normal salt results. If neutralization is less than total, an acid salt or basic salt is produced. Table salt (sodium chloride) is a simple salt, a compound of a metal and a non-metal. When simple salts combine with other simple salts, double salts result.

Salt Lake *See:* Great Salt Lake.

Salt Lake City (pop. 160,000), capital of Utah, seat of Salt Lake County, on the Jordan River in north-central Utah, near the Great Salt Lake. Founded in 1847 by Brigham Young, who led a band of Mormons from persecution, it is the world center of the Church of Jesus Christ of Latter-Day Saints. The city surrounds the Temple (1853-1893) at its center. It is a commercial and industrial center for minerals, electronics, oil refining, and chemicals. Other sights include the State Capitol (1914) and the Brigham Young Memorial (1897).
See also: Utah.

Salton Sea, large saline lake in southeastern California. Until flooded by the Colorado River in 1905, it was a depression, known as the Salton Sink, 280 ft (85 m) below sea level. It now covers 370 sq mi (958 sq km) and is 232 ft (71 m) below sea level.

Saltpeter, or potassium nitrate (KNO_3), chemical compound occurring as a colorless crystal or white powder. It is found in limestone caves or can be produced by combining potassium chloride with sodium nitrate. It is used for explosives, matches, fertilizer, and to preserve food.
See also: Explosive.

Salts, any of various chemical salts used as agents for cleansing the intestines or as laxatives. Epsom salt, Glauber's salt, and Rochelle salt are examples.

Saluki, lean, fast-running working hound first bred c.5000 B.C. in Arabia and Egypt to hunt gazelle. The dog has long, silky ears and weighs about 60 lb (27 kg); it stands 23 to 28 in (58 to 71 cm) high at the shoulders. Its colors are light tan, white, brown, or black and tan.

Salute, formal greeting to honor another person, flag or nation, done by raising the hand to the head, by firing guns or presenting arms. Salutes can include dipping of flags, tilting of airplane wings or raising a clenched fist or outstretched palm. Salutes are used mostly in the military or to show respect to a visiting dignitary.

Salvador, or Bahia (pop. 2,900,000), third largest city in Brazil, after São Paulo and Rio de Janeiro. An Atlantic port, Salvador's main industries include food and tobacco processing, textile manufacturing, petrochemical production, and oil exploration equipment. Its exports include cacao, fruit and fruit juices, petroleum, sugar, tobacco and vegetable oils. Founded in 1549, Salvador is the home of the University of

Bahia, the Catholic University, and the city's 16th-century cathedral.
See also: Brazil.

Salvage, in maritime law, either the rescue of life and property (a ship and its cargo) from danger on water or the reward given by a court to those who effect a rescue (called *salvors*). Under the law of the sea, it is the duty of a ship's master to go to the aid of an imperiled vessel. If life or property are saved, the owner of the rescue ship, the master, and the crew share in the salvage award. These awards are generous in order to encourage sailors and shipowners to risk their lives and property in rescue operations.
See also: Flotsam, jetsam, and lagan.

Salvation Army, nonsectarian, Christian organization founded in London as the Revival Society by William Booth (1865). In 1878 the mission became the army, with Booth as general. Under strict, quasimilitary discipline, the members seek to strengthen Christianity and help the poor and destitute. The army's official journal is *War Cry*.

Salvia, any of various plants (genus *Salvia*) of the mint family, that thrive in tropical climates. Some are used as food seasonings, others for ornamental purposes. The 700 species of woody plants vary in size and height and produce flowers of many colors, including brilliant reds, blues, whites, yellows, and violets. Salvia originates in Brazil.

Salween River, or Salwin River, river in eastern Burma, originating in eastern Tibet and flowing south 1,500 mi (2,400 km) to empty into the Bay of Bengal. A gorge makes the river largely unnavigable, but the Salween is important agriculturally, providing irrigation and flowing through a fertile delta.

The saluki, one of the oldest breeds of dog, resembles a grey- hound with fringed ears, legs and tail.

Salzburg (pop. 144,000), historic city in central Austria, on the Salzbach River. The birthplace of Wolfgang Amadeus Mozart, it is world famous for its annual music festival (begun 1917).
See also: Austria.

Samara (formerly Kuybyshev; pop. 1,300,000), city in east-central European Russia, located on the Volga River. It is an important port and industrial center, where

automobiles, locomotives, and aircraft are manufactured. It is also the site of a hydro-electric power plant. Founded as Samara in 1586, renamed Kuybyshev in 1935. In 1991 the city's name was restored.
See also: Union of Soviet Socialist Republics.

Samaranch, Juan Antonio (1920-   ), Spanish diplomat and sports administrator. Samaranch originally began his career in local (Barcelona) and national government, after which he was appointed ambassador to Russia in 1977. In 1966 joined the International Olympic Committee (IOC), of which he became the vice-president in 1974. In 1980 he was chosen as president of the IOC, succeeding Michael Morris Killanin. Under his leadership the Olympic movement was greatly expanded, so that such factors as sponsorship and commercial interests began to play an important role. He was succeeded by the Belgian Jacques Rogge and was appointed honorary life President of the IOC in 2001.

Samaria, city in ancient central Palestine built by King Omri c.800 B.C. as the capital of northern Israel; also, the region surrounding the city. It fell to Assyria c.722 B.C. and to Alexander the Great in 331 B.C. John Hyrcanus destroyed Samaria in 120 B.C., but it was rebuilt by Herod the Great. Samaria is the traditional burial site of St. John the Baptist.

Samaritans, members of a religious sect residing in the ancient district of Samaria, central Palestine. Originally non-Jewish colonists from Assyria, the Samaritans intermarried with the Israelites and accepted the Jewish Torah. However, they were not socially accepted-hence the significance of the Good Samaritan in Luke's Gospel.

Samarium, chemical element, symbol Sm; for physical constants see Periodic Table. Samarium was discovered spectroscopically in 1879 by Paul Émile Lecoq de Boisbaudran in the mineral samarskite. It is found in the minerals monazite and bastnasite, which are commercial sources. It is present to the extent of 1% in misch metal. The metal is prepared by reducing the oxide with barium. Samarium is a silvery, reactive metal. Ion-exchange and solvent extraction techniques have led to much easier isolation of the so-called rare-earth elements. An alloy of samarium with cobalt is used to make a permanent magnet with the highest resistance to demagnetization of any known material. Samarium and its compounds are used in carbon-arc lighting applications, permanent magnets, special glasses, and organic catalysts and as a neutron absorber in nuclear reactors.

Samarkand (pop. 370,000), city in and former capital of Uzbekistan, central Asia. One of the world's oldest cities, Samarkand was a stopover on the ancient trade route between China and the Middle East. In 329 B.C. it was conquered by Alexander the Great. In the 8th century it was taken by the expanding Arab empire, and by the 9th century it had become a center of Asian Islamic

The 'ziggurat' of the Al-Yami Mosque in Samarra (847) is a 171 ft (52 m) tall, spiral-shaped minaret, a construction that probably harks back to the Assyrian towers. It was supposedly built by Al-Mussasim and Al-Mutawaqil.

culture. It was destroyed by Genghis Khan in 1220. Rebuilt, it became the capital of Tamerlane's empire in the 14th and 15th centuries. The Uzbeks conquered it in the 1500s, and surrendered it to the Russians in 1868. After 123 years of Russian rule government returned to Uzbekistan. Today its industries include cotton and silk goods, wine, tea, and radio and automotive parts.

Samarra (pop. 20,000), city in Iraq, on the Tigris north of Baghdad. Place of pilgrimage for the Shiites with tombstones of religious leaders. Site of a settlement in prehistoric times. The present-day city was founded by Abbasid caliphs (9th century), of which some impressive ruins still remain, including the Great Mosque and the mosque of Abu Dulaf. At the beginning of the 20th century earthenware utensils were found dating from 5000 B.C.

Samnites, ancient tribe of the mountains of southern Italy who fought 3 wars with the Romans (343-341 B.C., 316-304 B.C., 298-290 B.C.) before being conquered and almost totally destroyed. In 80 B.C. the Romans completely suppressed the remaining Samnites in the Social War, and the few survivors blended into Roman culture.

Samoa, chain of 10 islands and several islets in the South Pacific, midway between Honolulu and Sydney. Volcanic and mountainous, their total area is about 1,200 sq mi (3,108 sq km.). The people are mostly Polynesians. The soil is fertile, producing cacao, coconuts, and bananas. The climate is tropical. Savai'i (the largest), Upolu, and the other Western islands constitute the Independent State of Samoa. The capital is Apia, on Upolu. American Samoa consists of the eastern islands: Tutuila, the Manua group, and the Rose and Swains islands. The capital is Pago Pago, on Tutila. Discovered by the Dutch in 1722, Samoa was claimed by Germany, Great Britain, and the United

States in the mid-19th century, but in 1899 the United States acquired sole rights to what is now American Samoa.
See also: American Samoa; Samoa, Independent State of.

Samoa, Independent State of

Capital:	Apia
Area:	1,093 sq mi (2,831 sq km)
Population:	180,000
Language:	Samoan, English
Government:	Parliamentary monarchy in the British Commonwealth
Independent:	1962
Head of gov.:	Prime minister
Per capita:	US$ 1,170
Monetary unit:	1 Tala = 100 sene

Samoa, Independent State of, formerly known as Western Samoa, since 1997 officially Independent State of Samoa, independent state in the southwestern Pacific Ocean, comprising 2 large islands, Savai'i and Upolu, and 7 smaller islands, only 2 of which are inhabited. Its area is 1,133 sq mi (2,934 sq km).
Land and climate. Most of the islands are mountainous, volcanic, forested, fertile and fringed with coral reef. Mauga Silisili (6,128 ft/ 1, 857 m) is the highest point. The climate is rainy and tropical.
People and economy. The people are Polynesian, and the majority live in Upolu, where Apia, the capital and chief port, stands. Samoans speak probably the oldest Polynesian language in use. The economy is agricultural, the main exports being copra, bananas, and cacao. Tourism is important. The current development program, backed by foreign aid, aims to expand agriculture and encourage modest industrialization (e.g., soap, lumber).
History. The islands were probably discovered by the Dutch explorer Jacob Roggeveen (1722). Germany, Great Britain, and the United States jointly administered the islands (1889-1899), and agreed in 1899 that Samoa should be divided between the United States and Germany. In 1914 New Zealand seized German Samoa, later administering it by League of Nations mandate and, later, as a UN Trust Territory. It became independent as Western Samoa in 1962. It joined the UN in 1976. Universal suffrage

S

S

was introduced in 1990. In 1997 parliament agreed to change the country's name to Samoa, despite opposition of American Samoa.

In 2002, New Zealand formally apologized for its poor treatment of Samoan citizens from 1914 to 1962.

Sámos, one of the Sporades islands, southeastern Greece, in the Aegean Sea, separated from Turkey by the Sámos Strait. The island, 184 sq mi (476 sq km), yields crops of olives and grapes. For a time under Turkish control, it became part of Greece in 1913. It was the birthplace of the mathematician and philosopher Pythagoras and is known as the home of Aesop, the semilegendary creator of fables.

Samothrace, mountainous Greek island in the northeastern Aegean Sea. About 70 sq mi (180 sq km) in area, Samothrace has hot springs, clay deposits, and one high mountain, the Fengári, near its center. Its many

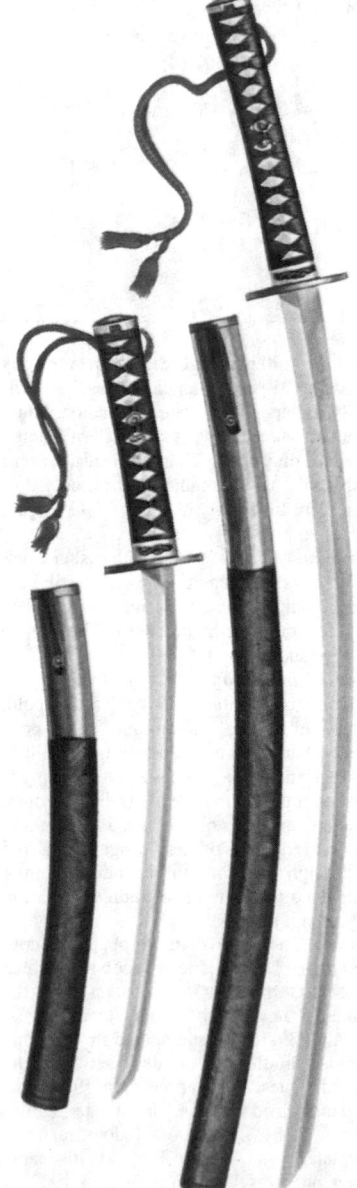

Samurai were privileged to wear two swords. The large sword was called the katana, and the small one was the waki-ayashi. The pair were known as 'daisho'.

Hellenistic artifacts and ruins date back to the 4th century B.C. Industries today include sponge fishing and sulfur production.

Samoyed, strong working dog of northern Siberia used to pull sleds and oversee reindeer herds. Its heavy white or cream colored coat protects it from severe weather and moisture. It weighs 35-65 lb (15.9-29.5 kg) and stands 19-23.5 in (48.3-59.7 cm) high at the shoulder. The Samoyed people of Siberia developed the breed thousands of years ago.

Sampras, Pete (1971-), U.S. tennis player, youngest ever to win the men's singles title in the United States Open tennis tournament (1990). He is known for his powerful serve, one-handed backhand, and serve-and-volley style of playing. In July 1998, Sampras won the Wimbledon tournament for the fifth time. Sampras was the number one on the ATP world ranking list for six consecutive years. He won the Queens tournament in 1999, followed by another Wimbledon title. In 2000, he won Wimbledon for the seventh time. After a less successful period, he came back in 2001 and won the U.S. Open (his 14th Grand Slam title), which makes him the all-time leading Grand Slam title winner.

Samson, in the Bible, hero in ancient Israel known for his extraordinary strength, which came from his long hair. During Israel's war with the Philistines, Samson killed a thousand Philistines with the jawbone of an ass. His love for a Philistine woman, Delilah, became his downfall when she learned the secret of his strength and cut his hair as he slept. Samson was captured and imprisoned. When his hair grew back, he tore down the pillars of the temple, killing both himself and the Philistines inside.
See also: Bible.

Samuel, Books of, Old Testament books (known to Catholics as 1 and 2 Kings) that tell of the statesman, general, and prophet Samuel (11th century B.C.). He united the tribes under Saul and chose David as Saul's successor.
See also: Bible; Old Testament.

Samuelson, Paul Anthony (1915-), U.S. economist, adviser to Presidents John F. Kennedy and Lyndon B. Johnson, and winner of the 1970 Nobel Prize in economics. His widely used college textbook, *Economics* (1948), has been translated into 21 languages.
See also: Economics.

Samurai, hereditary military class of Japan. From A.D. 1000 the samurai dominated Japan, though after 1600 their activities were less military than cultural. They exerted influence through bushido, a code that demanded feudal loyalty and placed honor above life. The class lost its power in the reforms of 1868.
See also: Shogun.

Sana (pop. 850,000), capital and largest city of Yemen, in southern Arabia on a high inland plain. The city, a trade center for grapes and other crops as well as the economic, political, religious, and educational center of

Yemen, is linked to the Red Sea port of Hodeida by road. Sana, which is shaped like a figure eight and surrounded by a wall 20-30 ft (6-9 m) high, is noted for the architectural splendor of the Bab al-Yaman (Yemen Gate) and the 7-story Republican Palace, as well as some 50 mosques. Originally a pre-Islamic settlement, it was subsequently ruled by the Ethiopians (6th century) and the Ottoman Turks (17th century and 1872-1918) before Yemen's independence (1918).
See also: Yemen.

San Andreas Fault, break in the earth's crust running 600 mi (965 km) from Cape Mendocino, northwestern Calif., to the Colorado desert. It was the sudden movement of land along this fault that caused the San Francisco Earthquake of 1906. The fracture, and the motion responsibile for this and other quakes, is a result of the abutment of the eastern Pacific and North American plates.
See also: Earthquake.

San Antonio (pop. 1,0 million), city in south-central Texas, seat of Bexar County, on the San Antonio River 150 mi (241 km) north of the Gulf of Mexico. Founded in 1718 by the Spanish, who built a series of missions in the area over the next 13 years, it was an important settlement in early Texan history. Captured (1835) by the Texans during the Texas Revolution, its Alamo was attacked by Mexicans in 1836. It is one of the largest military centers in the United States and the site of a major medical complex. Its manufactures include clothing, chemicals, and processed food; San Antonio is well known for its artists' colonies, museums, and historical sites.
See also: Texas.

Sánchez, Oscar Arias (1941-), Costa Rican politician, president of Costa Rica since 1986. He received the Nobel Prize for peace in 1987, awarded for his role as most important architect of the Central American peace plan.

Sanchez-Vicario, Arantxa (1972-), Spanish tennis player, became famous by winning the French Open title at the age of 17. In 1994 she won in France again, and went on to win the American Open title later that year. She also won many Grand Prix tournaments. Sanchez-Vicario plays a powerful kind of tennis, in which her fighting spirit is decisive. She ended her tennis career in 2002.

Sanchi, town in central India, in the constituent state of Madhya Pradesh, northwest of Bhopal. Location of many Buddhist monuments, of which the most important is the First of Great Stupa (begun by Ashoka in the 3rd century B.C., extended in the 2nd century), built on a round terrace. The four gateways are decorated with reliefs that represent a highlight of Ancient Indian art.

Sand, in geology, collection of rock particles with diameters in the range 0.125-2.0 mm. It can be graded according to particle size: fine, medium, coarse, and very coarse. Sands result from erosion by glaciers, winds, or ocean or other moving water. Their chief constituents are usually quartz and feldspar. Sand's uses include making bricks, cement, glass, and concrete.

Sand, George (Amandine Aurore Lucie Dupin; 1804-1876), French novelist. Her novels, at first romantic, later socially oriented, include *Indiana* (1832) and *The Haunted Pool* (1846). Her life-style-coupled with her ardent feminism-caused much controvery. Her lovers included Frédéric Chopin and Alfred de Musset. Her memoirs, *The Story of My Life* (1854-1855), provide a graceful justification of her views.

Sandalwood, any of several parasitic trees of the family Santalaceae (especially *Santalum album*), native to India, whose timber exudes a fragrant odor; also, the wood obtained from the trees. Sandalwood oil is used in perfumes and medicines.

Sandbur, or bur grass, any of several species of prickly weed (genus *Cenchrus*) that grow in wasteland. Sandbur is native to the western United States. The prickly fruits cause painful wounds when they catch onto flesh.

Sandburg, Carl (1878-1967), U.S. poet and biographer who won Pulitzer prizes for *Abraham Lincoln: The War Years* (1940) and *Complete Poems* (1951). He left school at 13 and at 20 fought in the Spanish-American war. While a journalist in Chicago, he wrote vigorous earthy free verse, as in *Chicago Poems* (1916) and *Smoke and Steel* (1920). He was also a notable folk-song anthologist.

Sand dollar (*Echinarachnius pama*), marine invertebrate animal that lives in the sand in shallow coastal waters. It has a thin circular body about 2-4 in (5-10 cm) wide. The sand dollar has tiny, movable spines that it uses to dig and crawl. It feeds on aquatic organisms that it finds in the sand.

Sanderling, shorebird (*Calidris alba*) belonging to the snipe and sandpiper family. It stands about 8 in (20 cm) high. Sanderlings breed on Arctic beaches and migrate south in winter to sandy beaches everywhere. They feed on small shellfish and insects that wash up on the shore. Their feathers are rust or gray on the upper parts and pure white underneath.

Sand fly, any of various minute, biting, 2-winged flies (families Psychodidae, Simuliidae, and Ceratopogonidae) found in the southern United States and the tropics. Sand flies are a major health hazard. They carry several diseases, including kalazar.

Sandhill crane *See:* Crane.

San Diego (pop. 2,8 million), city in southern California; seat of San Diego County, located on the Pacific Coast close to the Mexican border. A center for oceanography, culture, medicine, and research, its natural harbor houses a great navy base, a large fishing fleet, and lumber and shipbuilding yards. Its heavy industries include aircraft, missiles, and electronics; its economy is also

George Sand (pen name of Amandine Dupin) became one of the most succesful French novelists of the 19th century.

supported by tourism and convention business. San Diego was explored and claimed in 1542 by Spain, who later built (1769) the Presidio (historic fort) and the first of Father Junípero Serra's missions. It is also the site of the Cabrillo National Monument, an enormous zoo, and a well-known aquatic park. *See also:* California.

Sandinistas, leftist Nicaraguan revolutionary movement that overthrew the Somoza family dictatorship in 1979. Named after César Sandino, a Nicaraguan patriot and guerrilla leader of the 1920s, it assembled a broad coalition in the country to defeat Anastasio Somoza and his hated Civil Guard. After the revolution the Sandinista National Liberation Front (FSLN) ruled through a 5-man junta. *See also:* Nicaragua.

San Domingo *See:* Santo Domingo.

Sand painting, highly developed art form among the Navajo and Pueblo peoples of the southwestern United States, used in connection with rites of healing. Painting designs are made from crushed, colored sandstone. When the painting is completed, the person needing healing sits on it and has sand from it applied to his or her body. When the ritual is completed, the painting is destroyed.

Sandpiper, any of several small to medium-sized wading birds forming part of the family Scolopacidae and found in all parts of the world. Most are slim birds with long straight bills and dull brown, gray, or white plumage. Among the species found in North America are the spotted sandpiper (*Actitus macularia*) and the upland sandpiper (*Bartramia longicauda*).

Sandstone, sedimentary rock consisting of consolidated sand, cemented after deposition by such minerals like quartz, calcite, or hematite or set in a matrix of clay minerals. The sand grains are chiefly quartz. Sandstone beds may bear natural gas or petroleum, and they are commonly aquifers (water-bearing). Sandstone is quarried for building and crushed for use as an agglomerate.

Sandstorm, storm in which wind drives masses of coarse sand through the air a few feet above the ground. Sandstorms are powerful agents of erosion and can damage crops.

Sand verbena, low-growing summer annual plant (genus *Abronia*) native to western North America. The plants have fragrant pink, white, or yellow flowers and grow best in open, sunny places and light soils. There are about 25 species of sand verbena.

San Francisco (pop. 729,000), western California city and seaport on the Pacific coast, on a peninsula between the Pacific and San Francisco Bay. Its economy is based on shipping and shipbuilding, with exports of cotton, grain, lumber, and petroleum products. It is also the financial, cultural, and communications center for the Northwest Coast. The city, noted for its cosmopolitan charm, has many tourist attractions including cable cars, Chinatown, Fisherman's Wharf, the Nob Hill mansions, and Golden Gate Park. There are several museums, art galleries, and a famous opera house. Founded by the Spanish (as Yerba Buena) in 1776, the city passed into U.S. hands in 1846 and was named San Francisco (1847). The gold rush (1848) soon attracted thousands of settlers to the area, which grew even more during World War II when the city served as an embarkation and supply point for the Pacific theater. Parts of the city were rebuilt after the earthquake of Apr. 18-20, 1906, and more recently, the earthquake of 1989, which occurred on the 84th anniversary of the 1906 quake and measured from 3.3-5.4 on the Richter scale.

San Francisco Conference, conference (April-June 1945) to set up the UN. The conference was sponsored by the United States, Great Britain, the USSR, and China and attended by 50 nations. *See also:* United Nations.

Sanger, Frederick (1918-), British biochemist awarded the 1958 Nobel Prize in chemistry for his work on proteins, particu-

S

The purple sandpiper, *Calidris maritima* (left), about 9 in (23 cm) long, inhabits rocky coasts in much of the Northern Hemisphere. The semipalmated sandpiper, *C. pusilla* (right), which has partly webbed toes, and the spotted sandpiper, *A. macularia* (center) breed primarily in northern North America and winter from southern North America through South America.

S

larly for first determining the complete structure of bovine insulin (1955). He shared the 1980 Nobel Prize in chemistry with Paul Berg and Walter Gilbert of the United States for research on nucleic acids (DNA), the carriers of genetic traits. His work helped develop a process for analyzing the structure of DNA. Sanger is one of a handful of people to receive 2 Nobel prizes.
See also: Biochemistry; DNA.

Sanger, Margaret (1883-1966), U.S. pioneer of birth control and feminism who set up the first birth-control clinic in the United States (1916), founded the National Birth Control League (1917), and helped organize the first international birth-control conference (1927).

Sanhedrin, supreme Jewish legislative and judicial court in Roman times. Some scholars hold that there were two Sanhedrin, one religious and one political. Jesus was tried by the religious Sanhedrin while Saints Peter, John, Stephen, and Paul appeared before it on charges of religious error. It ceased to exist in Jerusalem after the Romans put down a rebellion by the Jews in A.D. 66-70.

Sanherib (Sennacherib; died 681 B.C.), king of the Assyrian Empire (704-681 B.C.), successor of Sargon II. Sanherib made Niniveh the capital and embellished the city with parklands and viaducts. He destroyed Babylon (689 B.C.). He was succeeded by Esarhaddon.

Sanitation, field of public health dealing with environmental control and the prevention and control of disease. In the United States, government agencies establish and enforce laws that promote a healthful environment. Sanitation activities include food processing and distribution, to prevent contamination of food products through various stages of handling; water and sewage treatment, to treat bacteria, viruses, etc. in water and to remove solid wastes and harmful chemicals from sewage that would contaminate the lakes, rivers, and other bodies of water (and their inhabitants) that receive it;

San José, both a national and a provincial capital, is the largest city in the Republic of Costa Rica. Founded by Spanish settlers in 1736, San José became the capital in 1823, when the administrative offices were transferred from Cartago. The city has emerged during the 20th century as the commercial and industrial center of this Central American nation.

solid waste disposal, also known as refuse disposal, to prevent environmental damage and the fostering of disease; and measures to control air pollution, rodents, and noise.

San José (pop. 300,000), capital and largest city of the Central American nation of Costa Rica. It is a center for government, industry, and finance, and is the location of the nation's largest agricultural market. San José is situated at the center of the country in a valley. It was founded by Spanish settlers in the mid-18th century.
See also: Costa Rica.

San José (pop. 801,000), western Californian city (incorporated 1850) about 50 mi (80 km) southeast of San Francisco in the Santa Clara Valley, the seat of Santa Clara County. The economy has long been centered around fruit processing; since World War II heavy industry has also been developed, including aerospace, chemical and electronics firms. San Jose State College (founded 1857) is the oldest state-run college of California. Founded in 1777, San Jose was the first state capital of California (1849-1852).
See also: California.

San Jose scale (*Aspidiotus perniciosus*), insect in the armored scale family. Although small as a pinhead, this insect causes mass destruction to a wide variety of trees and their fruit. The wind blows the scales from tree to tree, and upon arrival, they begin to eat a tree's sap. Native to China, they have been found throughout the United States and Canada since their discovery in the San Jose area of California around 1880. Oil spray and natural enemies such as the Chinese ladybird beetle help protect trees from this insect.
See also: Scale insect.

San Juan (pop. 820,000), capital and chief port of Puerto Rico on the northeastern coast of the island. Ponce de León named its bay (Puerto Rico) in the early 1500s, prior to the founding of the city in 1521. The city, which has retained its colonial atmosphere, is known for its fine beaches and exceptional harbor. It is now a trade center producing sugar, rum, metal products, textiles, and furniture, and has a strong tourist industry. Among its landmarks is El Morro castle (begun 1539).
See also: Puerto Rico.

On all three peaks of the approximately 2,461 ft (750 m) high Monte Titano, which stretches above the city of San Marino, you can find medieval fortresses which, together with the 12th-century basilica, are the oldest monuments to be found in the city.

San Juan Hill, Battle of *See:* Spanish-American War.

San Marino

Capital:	San Marino
Area:	24 sq mi (61 sq km)
Population:	27,700
Language:	Italian
Government:	Republic
Independence:	1263
Head of gov.:	President
Per capita:	US$ 34,600
Monetary unit:	1 Italian lira = 100 centesimi

San Marino, one of the world's smallest republics and possibly the oldest state in Europe, southwest of Rimini, Italy. Built on 3 peaks of Mount Titano, its townships include San Marino (the capital) and Serravalle. Tradition reports that San Marino was founded as a refuge for persecuted Christians in the 4th century A.D. The area is 24 sq mi (61 sq km). San Marino's chief sources of income are tourism and the sale of postage stamps. The republic is governed by 2 captains-regent assisted by a 60-member council of state. In 1992 San Marino joined the UN. It has access to the EU by means of a customs union with Italy.

San Martín, José de (1778-1850), Argentine patriot and hero of South American struggles for independence. Under his military leadership, Argentina fought successfully for its independence from Spain (1812).

S

San Martín also, with the aid of Bernard O'Higgins, freed Chile (1817-1818) and helped Simón Bolívar gain independence for Peru (1821-1822). San Martín was born in Argentina but raised mainly in Spain, where he was educated as a professional soldier. After the struggles for South American independence were fought and won, he went to Europe (1824).
See also: Argentina; Chile; Peru.

Sannyasi(n), Indian ascetic; person of old-age who has become a hermit, or any holy beggar, especially a follower of Shiva. The initiation rites can include a ceremonial birth. Lives alone or in groups. Like other sadhus (ascetics), they are not burned after they die, but buried in a meditating position.

San Quentin, California's oldest prison, opened in 1852. Its normal capacity is 2,700 inmates, but it has held as many as 3,900 prisoners. Located about 10 mi (16 km) from San Francisco, San Quentin is a maximum security prison for prisoners convicted of violent crimes. The prison administration provides counseling, education, and work-release programs.

San Salvador (pop. 1.5 million), capital and largest city of El Salvador, about 25 mi (40 km) from the Pacific Ocean. Because it is situated in a volcanic region, it has suffered many earthquakes. The city was founded in 1525 by Spanish explorer, Pedro de Alvarado. It is now a trade center, producing textiles, tobacco and soap.
See also: El Salvador.

Sanskrit, classical language of the Hindu peoples of India and the oldest literary language of the Indo-European family of languages. Some early texts date from 1500 B.C., including the Vedic texts. Vedic Sanskrit was prevalent roughly 1500-150 B.C., classical Sanskrit roughly 500 B.C.-A.D. 900. Sanskrit gave rise to such modern Indian languages as Hindi and Urdu and is distantly related to the Celtic, Romance, and Slavonic languages.

Santa Anna, Antonio López de (1794-1876), Mexican general and dictator who tried to suppress the Texan revolution and fought U.S. troops in the Mexican War. He helped establish Mexican independence (1821-1829) and became president (1833). When the Texan settlers revolted against his tyranny (1836), he defeated them at the Alamo but lost the battle of San Jacinto (1836), was captured, and had to resign. He gained and lost the presidency 3 further times (1841-1844, 1846-1847, 1853-1855). He spent most of his final years in exile.
See also: Mexico.

Santa Claus, Christmastide bearer of gifts to children. The jolly fat man who is transported by flying reindeer and drops presents down chimneys is a comparatively recent (19th-century) legend derived from St. Nicholas (introduced as *Sinter Klaas* to the New World by Dutch settlers), whose feast day (Dec. 6) is a children's holiday. A drawing by cartoonist Thomas Nast is believed to have helped fix the image of a rotund, white-bearded Santa Claus in the popular imagination after such a figure was described in Clement Moore's 1822 poem, 'An Account of a Visit from St. Nicholas.'
See also: Christmas.

Santa María *See:* Columbus, Christopher.

Santayana, George (1863-1952), Spanish-born U.S. philosopher, writer, and critic. He was an influential writer on aesthetics in books like *The Sense of Beauty* (1896). In *The Life of Reason* (1905-1906) he emphasized the importance of reason in understanding the world, but was skeptical of what one can really know. *Skepticism and Animal Faith* (1923) suggests a relationship between faith and knowledge.

Santiago (pop. 5,000,000), capital and principal industrial, commercial, and cultural city of Chile, on the Mapocho River. Industries include textiles, foodstuffs, and iron and steel foundries. It was founded in 1541 by Pedro de Valdivia. Numerous earthquakes destroyed most of the colonial buildings, and Santiago is now a modern city with parks and wide avenues.
See also: Chile.

Santiago de Cuba (pop. 451,000), second-largest city in Cuba, founded in 1514 by Diego de Velazquez de Cuellar, and capital of Oriente province. The center of Cuba's mining industry, Santiago is also a shipping center for iron, manganese, sugar, coffee, and tobacco. The Morro Castle is one of its landmarks.
See also: Cuba.

Santo Domingo (pop. 3,3 million), capital and chief port of the Dominican Republic, at the mouth of the Ozama River. Its official name was Ciudad Trujillo (1930-1961). Founded by Columbus's brother Bartholomew (1496), it is the oldest continuously inhabited European settlement in the Western Hemisphere, with a university dating from 1538. It was the site of the first Church in the New World.
See also: Dominican Republic.

Santo Domingo, University of, oldest university in the Western Hemisphere, located

Gen. Antonio López de Santa Anna dominated Mexican politics for 30 years. Although he captured the Alamo, he was defeated by the Texans at San Jacinto during the Texan revolution (1835-36).

in the Dominican Republic. It was established by Pope Paul III in 1538 as the Univ. of St. Thomas Aquinas. A lay institution since 1815, the university offers courses in agronomy, architecture, business, engineering, law, medicine, philosophy, and veterinary medicine. It has an enrollment of about 50,000 students.

Santos (pop. 429,000), one of Brazil's major port cities, and the world's leading coffee port. Cotton, sugar, bananas, castor oil, beef, oranges, hides, and manufactured goods are also exported. Its industries include sawmills, canneries, and the manufacture of candy, soap, soft drinks, and canvas. Santos has two airports and a railroad link to São Paulo.
See also: Brazil.

Santos, José Eduardo dos (1942-), Angolan prime minister and President (1979-). He became a member of the central committee and the political bureau of the Movimento Popular de Libertaçao de Angola (MPLA) in 1974. After Angola achieved independence (1975) he became Foreign Minister (1975-1977) and Minister of Economic Affairs (1977-1979). In 1979 he succeeded the late Agostinho Neto as President, government and party leader. From the time of independence his country was plagued by civil war between supporters of the ruling MPLA and UNITA, who wanted a multi-party system. Dos Santos received much military aid from the Soviet Union for his war effort. In 1990 the first peace talks took place. In 1991 he relinquished his position as government leader. In 1992 the first free elections were held since independence, in which both his party and Dos Santos himself were successful (he won the presidential elections). In 1994 a peace agreement was signed with UNITA, but its implementation ran into many difficulties. He was re-elected Prime Minister in 1999. After the death of UNITA leader Savimbi, he signed the official peace treaty with the guerrilla army UNITA in 2002.

Santos-Dumont, Alberto (1873-1932), aviation pioneer in both lighter-than-air and heavier-than-air machines. Born in Brazil of wealthy parents, he was educated in France, where he spent most of his life. His 'Demoiselle' (Grasshopper) monoplane was the forerunner of the modern light plane. He was awarded the Deutsch-Archdeacon Prize (1906) for the first observed power flight in Europe. Depressed over the use of aircraft in war, Santos-Dumont took his own life.
See also: Aviation.

Sanzio, Raffaello *See:* Raphael.

Saône River, waterway of eastern France. The Saône flows some 268 mi (431 km) and connects with the Rhône River at Lyon. The industrial city, Chalon-sur-Saône, lies on its banks. It is navigable for 233 mi (375 km) and has 30 locks. Barge traffic is heavy along its lower course.

São Paulo (pop. 9,481,000), largest city and industrial center of Brazil; capital of São Paulo state, it lies 225 mi (362 km) south-

S

west of Rio de Janeiro. Founded in 1554, it grew rapidly with the development of the coffee industry in the 1880s (it still sends coffee to the port of Santos), and its other industries are diverse. It is the site of 4 universities and numerous cultural institutions. *See also:* Brazil.

São Tomé and Príncipe

Capital:	São Tomé
Area:	372 sq mi (964 sq km)
Population:	135,000
Language:	Portuguese
Government:	Republic
Independent:	1975
Head of gov.:	Prime minister
Per capita:	US$ 330
Monetary unit:	1 Dobra = 100 cêntimos

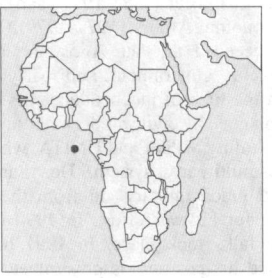

São Tomé and Príncipe, republic in the Gulf of Guinea, off the west coast of Africa, comprising 2 main islands and several islets; total area is 598 sq mi (964 sq km). The capital, São Tomé, lies 190 mi (306 km) west of Libreville, Gabon.
Land and climate. São Tomé Island accounts for almost 90% of the country's area and holds about 90% of its population. The land (volcanic rock) slopes downward to fertile volcanic soil on the east coast. Forests grow near the west shore. Príncipe is similar in land pattern. The islands have a tropical climate.
People and economy. The country depends heavily on cocoa for its income. Copra, coconuts, palm kernels, bananas, and coffee are also important exports. Most of the inhabitants are of mixed African and Portuguese ancestry. Over 90% of the people are Roman Catholic. The official language is Portuguese.
History. Discovered in the 1400s by the Portuguese, the islands achieved independence in 1975. The withdrawal of skilled Europeans after independence seriously disrupted the former plantation economy. In 1991 a multi-party system was introduced. In 1995 a group of army officers attempted a coup. After the US and France had terminated their aid and the EU had threatened to do the same, the former government returned.
In 2001 Fradique de Menezes was elected President.

Sap, in botany, the watery fluid in the stems and roots of plants. There are two kinds of sap. One consists of water and dissolved minerals and travels from the roots of the tree to the leaves, moving through a layer in the stem and trunk called the xylem. The other consists of water carrying dissolved plant foods, moving from the leaves to other parts of the plant for storage. It passes through a layer called the phloem.

Saperstein, Abraham M. (1903-1966), American sports promoter, set up a professional basketball team consisting entirely of Afro-Americans called the Harlem Globetrotters in 1927. The team, of which Saperstein directed both the technical and the financial policy, achieved many successes in the U.S., and from 1952 onwards played demonstration matches all around the world. The elements of show business and entertainment, as well as the exceptional level of skill, assured the team worldwide fame.

Sapir, Edward (1884-1939), U.S. anthropologist, poet, and linguist, whose most important work was on the relation between language and the culture of which it is a product. He suggested that one's perception of the world is dominated by the language with which one articulates it.
See also: Anthropology.

Sapodilla, evergreen tree (*Achras zapota*) found in tropical America; also, the fruit of the tree. The bark and fruits contain a milky latex (chicle) that is collected in Central America to provide the raw material for chewing gum. When ripe, the flesh of the fruit is brown and has the consistency of a pear.

Saponin *See:* Soapberry.

Sapphire, any gem variety of the mineral corundum (except those that are red, which are called ruby); blue sapphires are best known, but most other colors of the spectrum are included. The highest-quality sapphires come from Kashmir, Burma, Thailand, Sri Lanka, and Australia. Synthetic stones made by flame-fusion are used for jewel bearings, phonograph styluses, etc.

Sappho (6th century B.C.), Greek poet born in Lesbos. Surviving fragments of her work, mainly addressed to young girls, are among the finest classical love lyrics. The terms *sapphism* and *lesbianism*, meaning female homosexuality, derive from Sappho and Lesbos.

Sapporo (pop. 1,704,000), capital of Hokkaido, the northernmost island of Japan. Laid out in 1871 with wide, tree-lined boulevards intersecting each other at right angles, Sapporo serves as the island's manufacturing and cultural center, and its products include hemp cloth and rubber goods. Sapporo was the site of the Winter Olympics of 1972.
See also: Japan.

Saprophyte, plant that gets its food from dead and decaying material. Saprophytes do not carry out photosynthesis. Most fungi, including molds, mildews, and rusts, are saprophytes. Their fine threads creep over the food, secreting digestive juices and absorbing the resulting solution. Some flowering plants, such as the pinesap, are known as saprophytes, but in fact they rely on a fungus in their roots to absorb food from dead leaves.
See also: Fungi.

Sapsucker, bird of the woodpecker family. Sapsuckers drill neat rows of holes in the bark of trees and lick up the sap that oozes out, but their main food is insects, which they catch in the air or on trees. The 3 North American sapsuckers are the widely distributed yellow-bellied sapsucker (*Sphyrapicus varius*), and the red-breasted (*S. ruber*) and Williamson's sapsucker (*S. thyroideus*) of the Western and Pacific states.

Saracens, Muslims who invaded parts of the Christian world in Asia, Africa, and Europe from the 600s to the 1000s. They consisted of people of Palestine and Syria, the Arab Moors, and the Seljuks. The term *Saracen* was first used by Greek and Roman writers to describe wandering Arab tribes.
See also: Muslims.

Saragossa (pop. 840,000), industrial and trading center located in northeast Spain. The city has metalworks, sugar refineries, chemical plants, and factories that manufacture electrical equipment, farm machinery, and furniture. The city's name comes from Caesarea Augusta, the name that Roman Emperor Augustus gave it in 25 B.C.
See also: Spain.

Sarah *See:* Ishmael; Isaac.

Sarajevo (pop. 496,000), capital and cultural center of Bosnia and Hercegovina. It retains a strong Muslim character and is famous for its many Muslim mosques. Austrian Archduke Francis Ferdinand was assassinated at Sarajevo in 1914, precipitating World War I. In 1984 the Olympic Wintergames were held in Sarajevo.
During the civil war that started in the early 1990s Sarajevo was badly damaged and social and economic life virtually came to a stand still.
See also: Bosnia and Hercegovina.

View of Sarajevo, the capital of Bosnia and Hercegovina. With its many mosques, the city was strongly influenced by the Turkish occupation of the Balkans.

Saramago, José (1922-   ), Portuguese writer. He worked his way up from lathe operator to journalist. His first volume of poetry appeared in 1966, and he went on to write short stories and plays. His international fame is due to his novels, starting with the chronicle of four generations of peasants, *Levantado do Chão* (1980). Against the background of the glamour and misery of 17th-century Portugal, Saramago related the story of the building of a monastery in *Memorial do convento* (1982), his first international success. Other works include *Evangelho segundo Jesus Christo* (1992), *Ensaio sobre a cegueira* (1995) and *Todos os nomes* (1997). In 1998 Saramago was awarded the Nobel Prize for literature.

Saratov (pop. 909,000), one of the chief ports on the Volga River. Petroleum, natural gas, and power from the Balakovo hydroelectric station form the basis of oil-refining and chemical industries. Manufactures of this industrial complex include machinery, machine tools, ball bearings, flour milling, and consumer products.
See also: Union of Soviet Socialist Republics.

Sarawak, state of Malaysia on the northwestern coast of Borneo. It has a tropical climate, and much of its area, 48,050 sq mi (131,582 sq km), is covered by a primary rain forest. Sarawak became self-governing and joined Malaysia in 1963 after having been occupied by the Japanese during World War II. For 100 years prior to this, Sarawak was governed by an Englishman, James Brooke, and his heirs. The people of Sarawak are Dyaks, Malays, Melanaus, and Murits. Its products include sago palm, timber, rubber, pepper, coconuts, and camphor.
See also: Malaysia.

Sarazen, Gene (Eugene Saraceni; 1902-1999), U.S. golfer. He won the Professional Golfers Association (PGA) tournament in 1922, 1923, and 1933; the U.S. Open in 1922 and 1932; and the British Open in 1932. He also played 6 times in the Ryder Cup competition between U.S. and British players. Sarazen's outstanding 235-yd (215-m) shot helped win him the 1935 Masters tournament.

Sarcoidosis, chronic disease characterized by fibrous and inflammatory nodules principally affecting lymph glands, skin, lungs, and bones, but arising in any tissue of the body. The cause of the disease is uncertain.
See also: Lymphatic system.

Sarcoma, form of tumor derived from connective tissue, usually of mesodermal origin in embryology. It is often distinguished from cancer because its behavior and natural history may differ, although it is still a malignant tumor. It commonly arises from bone (*osteosarcoma*), fibrous tissue (*fibrosarcoma*), or cartilage (*chondrosarcoma*). Excision is required, though radiation therapy may be helpful.

Sarcophagus, stone coffin. The ancient Egyptians were probably the first to use sarcophagi for the burial of kings and important persons. Some were shaped like small houses, others like human forms with facial features. The best-known modern examples of sarcophagi include those built for George Washington in Mt. Vernon, Napoleon Bonaparte in Paris, the duke of Wellington in London, and V.I. Lenin in Moscow.

Sardine, name for the young of members of the herring family, particularly the European sardine, or pitchard (*Sardina pilchardus*). Sardines get their name from the fact that they were originally caught near Sardinia. They are usually preserved in oil and canned as food.

Sardinia, Italian island in the Mediterranean, 120 mi (193 km) to the west of mainland Italy and just south of Corsica. It is a mountainous area of 9,301 sq mi (24,090 sq km), with some agriculture on the coastal plains and upland valleys. Wheat, olives, and vines are grown, and sheep and goats raised; fish and cork are also exported. Zinc, antimony, and lead are extracted from the ancient mines, and tourism is growing in importance. The island is an autonomous region of Italy, with its capital at Cagliari.

Sardinia, Kingdom of, kingdom founded in 1720 when the Treaty of London awarded the island of Sardinia to Savoy. The kingdom included Sardinia, Savoy, Piedmont, and Nice. Napoleon annexed Sardinia to France in 1802, but it was restored after his defeat in 1815, and Genoa and Liguria were added to it. In 1861 Victor Emanuel II was proclaimed king of a united Italy that included Sardinia.

Sardis, capital of the ancient kingdom of Lydia. Its remains go back to at least 1300 B.C., but it may be even older. It was the first city to mint gold and silver coins. Destroyed by an earthquake in A.D. 17, Sardis was later rebuilt. It was destroyed and rebuilt several times until its final destruction by the Sassanian Persians c. A.D. 615.

Sardonyx, form of the mineral quartz. It is one of the less expensive gemstones. Found in Brazil, Uruguay, and India, sardonyx has bands of reddish-brown and white. It is used in rings and cameos.

Sardou, Victorien (1831-1908), a French playwright. His witty comedies and well-plotted melodramas were popular in Europe, the United States, and Japan. Critics, however, considered his plays superficial and unrealistic. Sarah Bernhardt and Sir Henry Irving were among the famous actors who appeared in Sardou's plays. Puccini's opera *Tosca* (1900) is based on Sardou's play *La Tosca* (1887). *Madame Sans-Gêne* (1893), a historical comedy, is perhaps the best of his 100 or more plays.

Sargasso Sea, oval area in the North Atlantic, of special interest as the spawning ground of American eels, many of whose offspring drift across the Atlantic to form the European eel population. Bounded on the east by the Canaries Current, on the south by the North Equatorial Current, and on the west and north by the Gulf Stream, it contains large masses of seaweed.

Sargent, John Singer (1856-1935), U.S. painter famous for his many flattering portraits of high-society figures in the United States and United Kingdom. A master of the brushstroke, he is distinctive for his treatment of texture. One of his most notable works, *Madame X* (1884), showing the alluring Parisian Madame Gautreau, created a furor that obscured the painting's brilliance.

Sargon of Akkad, king who founded the first great empire in history c. 2300 B.C. An outstanding military leader and administrator, he was the first king to maintain a permanent army. Sargon built a magnificent capital city called Akkad in central Mesopotamia. He reigned for 56 years.
See also: Mesopotamia.

Sark, one of the Channel Islands and the smallest self-governing unit in the United Kingdom. Located in the English Channel, 22 miles (35 km) off the coast of France, it has an area of 2 sq mi (5 sq km).

Saroyan, William (1908-1981), U.S. author known for combining patriotism with emotional idealism. Among his many works are *The Daring Young Man on the Flying Trapeze* (1934), a collection of short stories; the novel *The Human Comedy* (1943); and the play *The Time of Your Life* (1939). He won the Pulitzer Prize for the latter but turned it down because he disapproved of literary awards.

Sarraute, Nathalie (Nataliya Elievna Tcherniak; 1900-1999), Russian-French writer. Worked as a lawyer from 1925-1941. In her work she attempted to describe inner life, which she considered to be the driving force behind everything a person did or said; the 'monologue intérieur' (a literary technique where the 'I' character or any other main character loses himself in contemplation, and in doing so allows the reader a look into the deepest regions of his soul) was often applied. Her works include *Tropisms* (1938), *The Planetarium* (1957), *Fools Say* (1976).

Sarto, Andrea del (1486-1530), an Italian painter of the High Renaissance. He was a superb craftsman with a fine sense of color harmony and did much to advance *chiaroscuro* (the treatment of light and shade

A sarcophagus of a married couple from Cerveteri (latter half of the 6th century B.C.). (Museo Nazionale di Villa Giulia, Rome).

S

S

Jean-Paul Sartre (1905-1980) philosopher, novelist, and playwright, was a leading exponent of modern existentialism.

in painting) as in his *Portrait of a Young Man* and other works. Many of his paintings, such as Madonna del Sacco, foreshadow Mannerism, the 16th-century movement that was a revolt against the classicism of the Renaissance.

Andrea was born in Florence. His nickname del Sarto ('of the tailor') was a reference to his father's trade. Del Sarto spent most of his life in Florence, where Pontormo and Vasari were among his pupils. He was named court painter to Francis I of France in 1518, but gave up that position the next year and returned to Italy. Robert Browning's poem *Andrea del Sarto* (1855) tells of his great love for his wife.

His other works include *Madonna of the Harpies, Charity*, and *Sacrifice of Isaac*.

Sartre, Jean-Paul (1905-1980), French philosopher, novelist, and playwright, exponent of existentialism. His writings reflect his vision of the human being as master of his or her own fate, with each life defined by a person's actions: 'Existence precedes essence.' His works include *Being and Nothingness* (1943); the novels *Nausea* (1938) and *The Roads to Freedom*, a trilogy (1945-49); and the plays *The Flies* (1943) and *No Exit* (1944). Sartre founded the review *Les Temps Modernes* in 1945. A close associate of Simone de Beauvoir and a Communist who spoke eloquently for the left, his influence was international. In 1964 he refused the Nobel Prize for literature.
See also: Existentialism.

Saskatchewan (pop. 989,000), Canadian province (1905), bordered by Alberta, Northwest Territories, Manitoba and the U.S.; 251,962 sq mi (652,330 sq km) (of which 31,529 sq mi/81,631 sq km is lakes). Capital, Regina. Cold continental climate. High forested areas in the north and west with lakes and marshes, sloping down to the vast prairies in the southeast. One of the largest wheat producers in the world, as well as cattle, barley, and malt. Extraction of oil, coal, potassium carbonate, uranium, copper, helium, gold, silver, and potassium. Foodstuffs, petrochemicals, graphics and metal industry. Henry Kelsey was the first European to go there; in 1690 he scoured the region for the Hudson's Bay Company. The first settlement was established by the Hudson's Bay Company (1774). In 1869 it became a Canadian province; this created problems with the Native Americans and the métis, who revolted in 1885 under the leadership of the métis Louis Riel. Today 8% of

the population is native American. Joined the Canadian Confederacy in 1905. During the crisis years the grain farmers set up the Saskatchewan Wheat Pool, one of the largest grain marketing cooperatives in the world. *See also:* Canada.

Sassafras, tree (*Sassafras albidum*) of the laurel family, found in the eastern half of North America. In the northern states it is usually little more than a shrub, but it grows to 100 ft (30.5 m) in the south. Oil of sassafras, used to flavor foods and perfume soap, is extracted from its bark and roots. Sassafras tea is also made from the roots.

Sassoon, Siegfried (1886-1967), English poet and novelist. Decorated for bravery in World War I, he wrote bitterly satirical poetry such as *The Old Huntsman* (1917) and *Counter Attack* (1918), which shocked the public with their graphic portrayal of trench warfare, their attacks on hypocritical patriotism, and their pacifist conclusions. His novels include *Memoirs of a Fox-Hunting Man* (1928).

Satellite, in astronomy, celestial object that revolves with or around a large celestial object. In our Solar System this includes planets, comets, asteroids, and meteoroids, as well as the moons of the planets, although the term is usually restricted to this last sense. Of the dozens of known moons, the largest is Callisto (Jupiter IV); the smallest, Phobos (the inner moon of Mars). The earth's moon is the largest known satellite relative to its parent planets; indeed, the earth-moon system is often considered a double planet.
See also: Astronomy.

Satellite, artificial, object placed in orbit as a satellite. First seriously proposed in the 1920s, they were impracticable until large enough rockets were developed. The first artificial satellite, Sputnik 1, was launched by the USSR on Oct. 8, 1957, and was soon followed by a host of others, mainly from the USSR and the United States, but also from the United Kingdom, France, Canada, West Germany, Italy, Japan, and China. These satellites have many scientific, technological, and military uses. Astronomical observations (notably X-ray astronomy) can be made unobscured by the atmosphere. Studies can be made of the radiation and electromagnetic and gravitational fields in

which the earth is bathed and of the upper atmosphere. Experiments have been made on the functioning of animals and plants in space (with zero gravity and increased radiation). Artificial satellites are also used for reconnaissance, surveying, and meteorological observation, as navigational aids (position references and signal relays), and in communications for relaying television and radio signals. Manned satellites, especially the historic Soyuz and Mercury series, have paved the way for space stations, which have provided opportunities for diverse research and for developing docking techniques; the USSR Salyut and U.S. Skylab projects are notable. The basic requirements for satellite launching are determined by celestial mechanics. Launching at various velocities between that required for zero altitude and the escape velocity produces an elliptical orbit lying on a conic surface determined by the latitude and time of launch. To reach any other orbit requires considerable extra energy expenditure. Artificial satellites require a power supply-solar cells, batteries, fuel cells, or nuclear devices; scientific instruments; a communications system to return encoded data to earth; and instruments and auxiliary rockets to monitor and correct the satellite's position. Most have computers for control and data processing, thus reducing remote control to the minimum.
See also: Satellite.

Satie, Erik (Eric Alfred Leslie Satie; 1866-1925), French composer and pianist. Satie was the philosophical leader of 'Les Six,' a group of French composers including Darius Milhaud, Arthur Honneger, and Francis Poulenc who rejected the impressionist style of Claude Debussy and Maurice Ravel. He was deliberately eccentric, rejecting convention and popular acceptance. He best-known works include the ballet *Parade* (1917) and pieces for solo piano. His *Gymnopédies* (1888) for solo piano were made famous in their orchestrated version by Debussy.

Satinwood, East Indian tree (*Chloroxylon swietenia*) or shrub of the citrus family. Their wood is very hard and is used for inlays on furniture. West Indian satinwood, or yellow wood, so-called for its color, is found in Florida, as is wild lime, a close relative.

Satire, in literature or cartoons, on stage or screen, use of broad humor, parody, and irony to ridicule a subject. More serious than

Since 1962 the United States has launched 8 orbiting solar observatory (OSO) spacecraft to study the sun.

burlesque, it often contains moral or political criticism. In literature, classical satirists Aristophanes, Horace, and Juvenal were followed by such writers as Rabelais, Daniel Defoe, Jonathan Swift, Voltaire, Oscar Wilde, and Mark Twain.

Sato, Eisaku (1901-1975), prime minister of Japan (1964-1972). A Liberal-Democrat, he presided over the reemergence of Japan as a major economic power and was active in foreign affairs. He won the 1974 Nobel Peace Prize for work on deterring the proliferation of nuclear weapons.

Saturation, in chemistry and physics, term applied to a state in which further increase in a variable above a critical value produces no increase in a resultant effect. A saturated solution will dissolve no more solute, an equilibrium having been reached. Raising the temperature usually allows more to dissolve; cooling may produce supersaturation, in which sudden crystallization depositing the excess solute occurs if a seed crystal is added. In organic chemistry a saturated molecule has no double or triple bonds and so does not undergo additional reactions.

Saturn, in early Roman mythology, god of fertility and planting, eventually identified with the Greek god Cronus as father of Jupiter, Juno, Ceres, Pluto, and Neptune. In ancient Rome he was honored in the Saturnalia festival, a period of revelry and gift-giving starting Dec. 17, during which business, school, and war were suspended. *See also:* Mythology.

Saturn, second-largest planet in the Solar System, the sixth from the sun. Until the discovery of Uranus (1781), Saturn was the outermost planet known. It orbits the sun in 29.46 years at a mean distance of 886.7 million mi (1.427 billion km). Saturn has the lowest density of any planet in the Solar System, less than that of water, and may contain over 60% hydrogen by mass. Its total mass is about 95 times that of the Earth. Saturn has 17 known satellites; the largest, Titan, about the same size as Mercury, has a cold nitrogen atmosphere with traces of methane and other gases. Other major satellites include the Mimas, Enceladus, Tethys, Dione, Rhea, Iapetus, Phoebe, and Hyperion. The most striking feature of Saturn is its ring system, composed of countless tiny particles of ice and rock. Three or four major ring divisions are visible from Earth; space probes (1980, 1981) revealed the rings to consist of hundreds of narrow ringlets. The rings are about 10 mi (16 km) thick. *See also:* Planet; Solar System.

Saturnalia, in ancient Rome, festival honoring Saturn, god of fertility and planting. The annual festival, which started Dec. 17, originated as a 2-day celebration of the winter planting, but became a week-long period of feasting and gift-giving, the cessation of business and a brief time of freedom for slaves. Its observances are thought to have eventually been absorbed into the celebration of Christmas. 'Saturnalia' has become a generic term for any period of wild revelry. *See also:* Saturn.

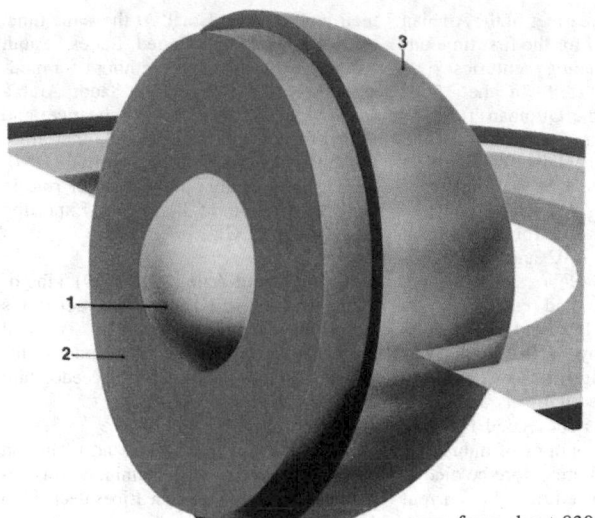

Satyr, in Greek mythology, male spirit of the forests and mountains, often shown as part man and part goat, with hooves, tail, and pointed ears. Companions of Dionysus, satyrs played an important part in his festivals. *See also:* Mythology.

Saucer, flying *See:* Unidentified flying object.

Saudi Arabia

Capital:	Riyadh
Area:	865,000 sq mi (2,240,000 sq km)
Population:	23,513,000
Language:	Arabic
Government:	Islamic absolute monarchy
Independent:	1932
Head of gov.:	King
Per capita:	less than US$ 10,600
Monetary unit:	1 Saudi riyal = 20 qurush = 100 halalah

Saudi Arabia, desert kingdom occupying most of the Arabian Peninsula of southwestern Asia.

Land and climate. Parts of the frontiers of Saudi Arabia have yet to be accurately determined. Estimates of the country's area

Saturn, the second largest planet in the solar system, has a density less than that of water and therefore must be made up mainly of the light gases hydrogen and helium. Saturn is thought to consist of a small rocky core (1), a large liquid-hydrogen layer (2), and a gaseous atmosphere (3), composed primarily of hydrogen and helium and containing small amounts of methane and frozen ammonia. A samll inner portion of the liquid-hydrogen layer is in the form of metallic hydrogen. The remainder is in the normal molecular state.

S

vary from about 830,000 sq mi (2,149,700 sq km) to 927,000 sq mi (2,400,930 sq km). It is bordered on the north by Jordan, Iraq, and Kuwait; on the east by the Persian Gulf, Qatar and the United Arab Emirates; on the south by Oman and Yemen; and on the west by the Red Sea and the Gulf of Aqaba. Most of the country is desert. Rising steeply from the narrow, barren Red Sea coastal plain are the western highlands of the Hejaz in the north and the Asir Highlands bordering Yemen in the south. Eastward sloping desert plateaus of sand and rock cover the interior of the country. The Rub al Khali (Empty Quarter) is a great, southern sand desert of some 250,000 sq mi (647,500 sq km). The An Nafud, the northern sand desert, covers almost 25,000 sq mi (64,750 sq km). In the east, the Hasa Lowlands, mostly sand or gravel, fall away gradually to the sands, lagoons, and occasional coral reefs along the Persian Gulf. There are oases where date palms, tamarisks, and acacias grow, but there are neither lakes nor rivers. The coastal regions have an oppressively humid climate. The interior deserts are hot and dry, and summer temperatures in some areas exceed 120°F (49°C). In winter, however, frosts are common on the plateaus and in the mountains. Some desert areas go without rain for several years in succession.

People. The people of Saudi Arabia are Arabic. Riyadh, the capital, the Red Sea port of Jiddah, and the Muslim holy cities of Mecca and Medina are the main centers. Islam is the state religion: 85% of the people belong to the Sunni branch of Islam.

Economy. Saudi Arabia's rich oil fields, discovered in 1938, represent nearly one-fifth of the world's known reserves, and the oil and natural gas industry dominates the economy. The Arabian American Oil Company (Aramco) is chiefly responsible for oil operations in Saudi Arabia, although other U.S. and some Japanese concerns also have concessions. Since 1974, Saudi Arabia has held 60% of the ownership of these foreign concessions. Petro dollars are used for industrial development, especially oil refining, ambitious irrigation projects, and foreign investments. Saudi Arabia also produces limestone, gypsum, and salt. Its chief crops are sorghum, dates, wheat, barley, coffee, citrus fruits, and millet.

History. In the 7th century, the formerly dis-

S

parate Semitic nomadic tribes of the Arabian Peninsula were united for the first time under Islam. In succeeding centuries rival sheikdoms rose and fell. In the 1500s Arabia came under the Ottoman Turks as part of the Ottoman empire. Between 1750 and 1800 the fundamentalist Wahabi sect led by the Saudi rulers of Dariya reconquered most of the Arabian Peninsula. Modern Saudi Arabia was founded by Ibn Saud, who, between 1902 and 1932, conquered Hijd and the Hejaz, joining them with Hasa and Asir and establishing a hereditary monarchy. Ibn Saud died in 1953 and was succeeded by Saud IV, who was deposed in 1964. King Faisal succeeded to the throne and reigned until his assassination in 1975. He was succeeded by King Khalid, who began programs of industrialization and social welfare before he died in 1982; he was followed by the current monarch, King Fahd. Saudi Arabia, through its oil wealth, has considerable political influence in the Middle East and has supported Arab countries and the Palestinians in

their conflict with Israel. At the same time, as an ally of the United States, Saudi Arabia also has been something of a moderate voice in the region. Saudi Arabia asked for U.S. military assistance and joined forces with the U.S. and other allies in the Persian Gulf War against Iraq (1990-1991). Saudi Arabia plays a major role in the Organization of Petroleum Exporting Countries (OPEC).

Saud ibn Abdul-Aziz (1902-1969), king of Saudi Arabia (1953-1964), successor to his father Ibn Saud Abdul-Aziz III. The real power, however, was in the hands of his younger brother Faisal, who succeeded him after he was deposed.

Saul, first king of Israel (1000 B.C.). The son of Kish of the tribe of Benjamin, he was annointed by Samuel after the tribes decided to unite under a king. His reign was generally successful, but he killed himself after a defeat by the Philistines. His rival, David, succeeded him. (1 Sam,10-31.)

Saura, Antonio (1930-1998), Spanish painter. Was a surrealist until the mid 1950s. Thereafter he developed a stormy, expressionistic style, similar to tachism. Made a series of crucifixions, self-portraits and imaginary portraits.

Saurischian *See:* Dinosaur.

Saussure, Ferdinand Mongin de (1857-1913), Swiss linguist, founder of structuralism with his posthumously published *Course in General Linguistics* (1916), who-

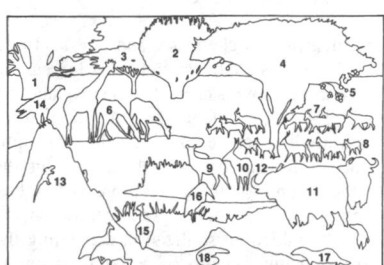

Savannas are areas within the tropics, that are covered with grass or grass with trees. The African savanna, with its characteristic flat-topped acacia trees, supports amongst other animals large herds of herbivorous mammals.
1. Baobab tree (*Adansonia digitata*)
2. Umbrella thorn (*Acacia tortilis*), may grow up to 33 ft (10 m) high
3. Candelabra tree (*Euphorbia ingens*), rarely exceeds 33 ft (10 m)
4. Whistling thorn (*Acacia dreparalobium*)
5. Weaver bird (*Quelea quelea*), nesting in an acacia tree
6. Grasses (eg. *Cynodon dactylon*, *Vossia cuspidata*, red oat grass *Themeda triandra*, *Heteropogon contortus*, or *Imperata cylindrica*)
7. Giraffe (*Giraffa camelopardalus*)
8. Topi (*Damaliscalus korrigum*)
9. Impala (*Aepyceros melampus*)
10. Waterbuck (*Kobus defassa*), male right, female left
11. Cape buffalo (*Syncercus caffer*)
12. Yellow billed oxpecker (*Buphagus africanus*)
13. Marabou stork (*Leptoptilus crumeniferus*)
14. Crested or helmeted guinea fowl (*Nimida meleagris*)
15. Tawny eagle (*Aquila rapax*)
16. Common agamid lizard (*Agama agama*)
17. Banded mongoose (*Mungos mungos*)
18. Adder (*Bitis arietans*).

se main thesis was: the study of one particular language presupposes a general concept of language, thus a general theory of language.

Savanna, tropical grassland of South America and particularly Africa, lying between equatorial forests and dry deserts.

Savings bank, financial institution that encourages saving by individual depositors, paying them interest or dividends, while providing funds to borrowers, who pay interest.

Savings bond, interest-bearing bond issued to an individual by the government in specific denominations, functioning as a loan to the government for a fixed term.

Savonarola, Girolamo (1452-1498), Italian religious reformer. A friar of the Dominican order living in Florence, he was a powerful and outspoken critic of the Church, preaching against the corruption of the court of Pope Alexander VI and predicting that the Church would be punished. When he refused the pope's order to present himself in Rome, he was forbidden to preach (1495), the violation of which order led to his excommunication (1496). Savonarola remained unrepentant, and he was tried by an ecclesiastical court and executed by civil authorities.

The burning of Dominican monk Girolama Savonarola (1452-1498) and two of his followers, at the Piazza della Signoria in Florence, on May 23, 1498. From 1494 to 1498, Savonarola headed a regime in Florence that was supposed to be democratic, but which was in fact dictatorial and inspired by religion.

Savoy, powerful dynasty of northwestern Italy that at times ruled portions of Italy, France, and Switzerland. It was founded in the 11th century by Humbert, whose holdings were in the regions of Savoy and Piedmont. Savoy holdings extended into France and Switzerland by the 15th century. Its control in Italy expanded in the 18th and 19th centuries, helping to consolidate rule of the peninsula, and a member of the family, Victor Emmanuel II, became king of Italy in 1861. Victor Emmanuel II was succeeded by his son Humbert I, who was assassinated (1900), Victor Emmanuel III, who abdicated after World War II, and Humbert II, whose brief reign ended (1946) when Italy became a republic.
See also: Italy.

Saw, cutting tool consisting of a flat blade or circular disk, having on its edge a row of sharp teeth of various designs, usually set alternately. The first true saws (copper and bronze) were used in Egypt c.4000 B.C., but only with the use of steel did they become efficient. Hand saws include the crosscut saw for cutting wood to length, the backsaw for joints, the coping saw for shaping, and the hacksaw for cutting metal. Power saws include circular saws, band saws (with a flexible endless steel band running over pulleys), and chain saws.

Sawfish, any of a family (*Pristidae*) of sharklike fish having 'saws' of cartilage set with 2 rows of teeth on their snouts. Sawfish are found in all warm seas and may swim up rivers. The common sawfish of the Gulf of Mexico swims up the Mississippi. Sawfish can grow up to 30 ft (9 m) in length. They use the saw to dig up shellfish or to kill small fish. Although they are reported to be docile, fishers treat them with considerable respect.

Sawfly, insect related to the wasps. Sawflies often have striped bodies. They are harmless to humans, although they do serious damage to plants. They have a long, tubular egg-laying organ with which they drill holes in the leaves of plants or in wood to lay their eggs. The larvae, which look like caterpillars, eat the plants' tissues.

Saw Maung (1928-), former president of the Union of Myanmar (Burma, 1988-1992). Armed forces chief of staff and a close associate of former ruler Ne Win, he led the coup that placed him in office, ousting President Maung Maung. He then abolished parliament and formed the National Unity Party. *See also:* Myanmar.

Saxifrage, any of a genus (*Saxifraga*) of small rock plants whose leaves grow in a rosette at the base of the stem and whose flowers grow in clusters at the tip of the stem. Many of them produce a small bulb at the base of each leaf. The usual place to find saxifrages is in crevices and ledges of rocky cliffs in cold and temperate regions of the Northern Hemisphere. Several species are native to the United States, including the early saxifrage (*S. virginiensis*) and the umbrella plant (*S. peltata*).

Saxons, Germanic people who, with the Angles and the Jutes, founded settlements in Britain from A.D. 450 supplanting the Celts. The 3 peoples eventually formed the Anglo-Saxon kingdom. From modern Schleswig (northern Germany) the Saxons also spread along the coast to northern France before being conquered by Charlemagne (804).

Saxony, state in eastern Germany. Saxony was established as a duchy in the late 9th century. Its size and boundaries shifted as it was broken up and then reestablished as Electoral Saxony (1356). From 1697 to 1763 the elector of Saxony was also king of Poland; during this time the state and its capital city of Dresden were an important center of culture. Saxony was made a kingdom by Napoleon I (1816), but upon his defeat half of its lands became part of Prussia. After

World War II Saxony became part of East Germany but was abolished as a political unit by the Communists. In 1990, with the reunification of Germany, Saxony was reestablished as a state.

Saxophone, brass musical instrument, classified as a woodwind since its sound is produced by blowing through a reed. Patented by the Belgian Adolphe Sax in 1846, the

Frederick III the Wise, Elector of Saxony (1486-1525), was one of the first German emperors to apply the rule of 'cuius regio, eius religio' (whose region, his religion), by granting Luther safe conduct to the Diet of the Realm at Worms, and subsequently providing him with shelter at Warburg. This principle became law in Germany in 1555, so that the Holy Roman Empire from that moment on was actually divided up into small independent Roman Catholic and Protestant principalities.

S

The saxophone, named after its 19th-century inventor Adolphe Sax, is a single reed instrument and a hybrid of the clarinet, oboe, and brass instruments. Although eight types are made, only four of them are widely used: the B-flat soprano, the E-flat alto, the B-flat tenor, and the E-flat baritone. The saxophone is used in military bands, dance bands, and orchestras, and is particularly important in jazz music. Its parts include the mouthpiece (1), reed (2), neckpiece (3), crook (4), upper stack keys (5), lower stack keys (6), bell keys (7), and bell (8).

S

saxophone exists in soprano, alto, tenor, and baritone forms; the bass is rare. Sometimes used in the symphony orchestra, the saxophone is better known for its important role in jazz, where it is a leading solo and ensemble instrument.

Sayda (pop. 35,000; Sidon), city in Lebanon on the Mediterranean. Port for oil export. In ancient times the most important Phoenician harbor; golden age 1500-1000 B.C., thereafter eclipsed by Tyre. Successively part of the Ptolemaic, Seleucid, Roman, Arab and Turkish empires.

Sayers, Dorothy (1893-1957), English writer of detective stories and creator of the popular, impeccably aristocratic and erudite Lord Peter Whimsey. He is the hero of some 16 books, beginning with *Whose Body?* (1923). Sayers also wrote religious essays and dramas.

Scabies, infectious skin disease caused by a mite (*Sarcoptes scabiei*) that burrows under the skin, often of the hands or feet; it causes an intensely itchy skin condition that is partly due to allergy to the mite. The disease is spread through contact. Treatment is with ointments.

Scale, weighing, instrument for measuring weight. *Balance scales*, which date to about 2500 B.C. and are still in use, measure an unknown quantity by balancing it against established weights. *Mechanical scales*, which date from the 18th century, use beams, springs, or pendulums to convert the measurement of weight into a precise reading on a graduated scale. For example, *spring scales*, including the ordinary bathroom scale, measure weight according to the tension created when the weight stretches or compresses a spring. *Electronic scales*, which have been in commercial use since the 1950s, convert the force exerted by the weight into an electronic signal.

Stående orange fig-urer (Standing Orange Figures) by Carl-Henning Pedersen (1913), painted in 1949. Pederson is one of the foremost Danish twentieth-century artists. His work, inspired by folk art and children's drawings, influenced the international Cobra movement (1948-51), of which he was a member, considerably. Pedersen did a number of important commissions in his own country.

Scale insect, any of various small insects of the order Homoptera (especially family Coccidae) with a flattened body covered by a layer, or 'scale,' of waxy secretion. There are more than 2,000 species. They live on plants, and many are serious pests. The *cottony cushion scale* did immense damage to the Californian orange plantations after its introduction from Australasia. The *elm scale* kills trees. Other scale insects are collected for their secretions. The dye cochineal is obtained from a scale insect, and the lac insect used to be collected by the millions-its 'scale' turned into shellac.

Scallop, bivalve mollusk (family Pectinidae) distinguished by a shell whose valves are rounded, with a series of ribs radiating across the surface in relief. Scallops are used for food. Unique among bivalves, scallops swim extremely well, propelled by jets of water expelled in snapping the shell shut. There are about 300 species. Chief among the commercial species is the common bay scallop (*Argopecten irradians*), found in North America.

Scandinavia, region of northwestern Europe. Geographically it consists of the Scandinavian peninsula (about 300,000 sq mi/777,000 sq km), occupied by Norway, Sweden, and Denmark. Because of close historical development, Finland, Iceland, and the Faeroe Islands are also covered by the term in matters of language, culture, peoples, and politics.

Scandinavian literature, literature of Scandinavia (Denmark, Norway, and Sweden) and usually including Finland and Iceland, from the end of the Viking Age (c.1100) to the present. The peoples of Scandinavia speak closely related North Germanic languages, except those of Finland, whose language is related to Hungarian. Early literature of the 12th and 13th centuries captured works of the oral tradition in writing. These included heroic ballads of Denmark and Sweden, Icelandic poetry collected in the *Poetic Edda*, and heroic *sagas* of Iceland and Norway. There followed a period during which most writing was in Latin and was technical or religious. Literature in the vernacular and about everyday life reemerged in the 18th century, including writings of Swedish poet Carl Michael Bellman and Danish playwright Johannes Ewald. The interest in folk tales shown by the romantic movement of the early 19th century is evident in the epic poem *Kalevala* (1835; derived from Finnish legend), collections of tales in Norway, and the original tales of Hans Christian Andersen in Denmark. Other writers of the romantic movement were Norway's Bjørnstjerne Bjørnson (*A Happy Boy*, 1860) and Finland's Aleksis Kivi (*Seven Brothers*, 1870). Henrik Ibsen of Norway and August Strindberg of Sweden were playwrights of the realist movement of the late 19th century who had international influence. The modern period includes writings of Knut Hamsun of Norway (*Hunger*, 1890) and Selma Lagerlöf of Sweden (*Gösta Berling's Saga*, 1891), and more recently, Isak Dinesen of Denmark (*Winter's Tales*, 1942) and Nobel Prize

winners Sigrid Undset of Norway (*Kristin Lavransdatter* trilogy, 1920-1922) and Pär Fabian Lager-kvist of Sweden (*Barabbas*, 1950).

Scandium, chemical element, symbol Sc; for physical constants see Periodic Table. Scandium was discovered in 1876 by Lars Nilson in the minerals euxenite and gadolinite. It occurs in nature in over 800 mineral species in minute amounts. Scandium is obtained from thortveitite or uranium mill tailings. It is prepared by reducing the fluoride with calcium metal. Although not a member of the rare earth series of metals, it is chemically similar and often considered with them. It is a soft, silvery, reactive metal resembling yttrium and the rare-earth metals (more than aluminum or titanium), and is often associated with tin and zirconium. It is used to produce high-intensity lights. Scandium-46 is used as a radioactive tracing agent. Scandium is the ekaboron predicted by Dmitri Mendeleev (1869).

Scapegoat, in the Old Testament (Leviticus 16:8), goat designated by the Jewish high priest on Yom Kippur (Day of Atonement) to bear the sins of the people and to be sent out into the wilderness. Similar practices existed in ancient Greece and Rome. By extension, the term also refers to a person or group unfairly blamed for the ills of others.
See also: Old Testament.

Scar, mark resulting from the healing of a wound or disease process in a tissue, especially the skin. Also called a cicatrix. The presence of excessive scar tissue is called a keloid.

Scarab, family (*Scarabaeidae*) of beetles that includes the dung beetles, chafers, and dor beetles. Most of the 20,000 species are scavengers of decaying organic matter, especially dung, or they feed on the foliage and roots of growing plants, as do the chafers, many of which may become agricultural pests.

Scarlatti, name of 2 Italian composers of the baroque period. **Alessandro Scarlatti** (1660-1725) was a leading musical scholar, teacher, and composer of hundreds of church masses, cantatas, and oratorios, as well as more than 100 operas. Although few of his works are now performed, he is important for innovations in harmony, thematic development, and the use of instruments. His son **Domenico Scarlatti** (1685-1757) also composed operas and church music but is known for his many brilliant sonatas for harpsichord. An influence upon Franz Joseph Haydn and W.A. Mozart, he is still widely played.
See also: Baroque.

Scarlet fever, infectious disease caused by certain strains of streptococcus. It is common in children and causes sore throat with tonsillitis, a characteristic skin rash, and mild systemic symptoms. Penicillin and symptomatic treatment are required. Scarlet fever occurs in epidemics; some infections are followed by rheumatic fever or nephritis.
See also: Impetigo.

Schacht, Hjalmar Horace Greeley (1877-1970), German financier and banker. He helped halt post-World War I inflation in Germany and was finance minister (1934-1937) and Reichsbank president (1923-1930; 1933-1939). Conflict with Goering and Hitler led to imprisonment in a concentration camp. He was acquitted at the Nuremberg Trials (1946).
See also: Germany.

Schaeffer, Pierre (1910-1995), French composer. During WW II developed techniques for recording sound and manipulating recorded sound. With his compositions for tape recording he was the founder of the so-called 'Musique Concrète' in 1948. This led to the Group de Recherches Musicales. From 1960 onwards Schaeffer began to specialize in new electronic developments, and from then on was only active as a theorist. He is more renowned as the inspiration for many young composers rather than for his own compositions. His published works include *A la Recherche d'une Musique Concrète* (The Search for a Concrete Music; 1952) and *Traité des Objets Musicaux* (1966).

Schally, Andrew Victor (1926-), Polish-born U.S. medical researcher who shared the 1977 Nobel Prize in physiology or medicine with Rosalyn S. Yalow and Roger C. L. Guillemin for the discovery and synthesis of hormones produced by the hypothalamus. The analysis of these hormones, which control body chemistry, had a revolutionary effect on the study of brain functioning.
See also: Hypothalamus.

Schapiro, Meyer (1904-1996), Lithuanian-born U.S. art historian and critic. One of the most highly regarded and influential art scholars in the United States, he taught for many years at Columbia Univ. Among his books are *Romanesque Art* (1977) and *Modern Art: 19th and 20th Centuries* (2 vols., 1978-9). He also wrote important essays, e.g., 'The Nature of Abstract' (1937) and 'Leonardo and Freud' (1956).

Scharoun, Hans Henry Bernard (1893-1972), German architect. As opposed to functionalism, his architecture was based on the organic relationship between human beings and the environment. One of the first examples of this theory was Siemensstadt in Berlin (1930). During the Nazi era and WW II, Scharoun did not build at all. After WW II he designed Charlottenburg-Nord in Berlin (1955-1961), the high-rise apartment complex Romeo and Juliet in Stuttgart (1955-1959) and his most important work, the Philharmonie in Berlin (1957-1963), famous for its superb acoustics. Received the Erasmus Prize in 1970.

Schawlow, Arthur (1921-), U.S. physicist who did pioneering work in the 1950s that led to the construction of the first laser. He shared the 1981 Nobel Prize in physics with Nicolass Bloembergen (of the United States) and Kai M. Siegbahn (of Sweden) for contributions to the development of laser spectroscopy.
See also: Laser.

Scheckter, Jody (1950-), South African racing car driver, made his Formula 1 debut in 1972. He became Formula 1 world champion in a Ferrari in 1979.

Scheele, Carl Wilhelm (1742-1786), Swedish pharmacist and chemist. He was the discoverer of chlorine and isolated oxygen, although credit went to English scientist Joseph Priestley, who published findings before Scheele. He also isolated many acids, and made significant discoveries regarding nitrogen and manganese, conducting his experiments in the restricted environment of the apothecaries where he was employed.
See also: Chemistry; Chlorine.

Schelde River, important navigable waterway of northwestern Europe. Rising in northwestern France, it flows 270 mi (434.5 km) north and northeast to Antwerp, Belgium, then northwest, as the East Schelde and West Schelde rivers, through the Netherlands to the North Sea. There are canal links to the Rhine and Meuse rivers.

Schelling, Friedrich Wilhelm Joseph von (1775-1854), German philosopher. Influenced by Baruch Spinoza, J.G. Fichte, and others, he developed a concept of an absolute unity of mind and matter toward which all history and nature progressed. Although once a close friend of G.W.F. Hegel, he became an opponent and rival. His view of art as the union of the natural and the spiritual influenced Samuel Taylor Coleridge, Schelling's contemporary and an English poet and philosopher.
See also: Philosophy.

Schengen, Treaty of, the treaty signed by the governments of the Benelux countries, Germany and France in Schengen in 1985 and 1990, dealing with the gradual phasing out of border controls between the countries. In 1990 Italy joined the Schengen agreement and in 1991 Spain and Portugal followed. Greece joined in 1992 . The agreement eventually became operational in March 1995.

Schenk, Adri (Ard) (1944-), Dutch ice skater. Schenk was all-round world champion in 1970, 1971 and 1972, and European champion in 1966, 1970 and 1972. During the 1972 Winter Olympics he won the 1500 m, 5000 m and 10,000 m. Schenk developed from a 500 m skater to a 10,000 m skater, and was world record holder in all distances in 1972, except for the 500 m. A short period as a professional skater failed, after which he ended his career. From then on Schenk was active as a physiotherapist and in sports administration management.

Scherzo (Italian, 'joke'), light, lively musical composition. The term most often refers to a movement in 3/4 meter (usually the third) of a sonata, symphony, or similar composition of the late 18th or 19th century; it developed from the minuet but was characterized by a much faster tempo and, frequently, a display of rhythmical humor and surprise (especially in the works of Ludwig van Beethoven). Some light vocal and instrumental compositions of the Baroque period, as well as some dramatic piano pieces

by Frederick Chopin and Johannes Brahms, were also named scherzo.

Schiele, Egon (1890-1918), Austrian artist. A leader of the Austrian expressionists, he was influenced by the French impressionists and by Austrian artist Gustav Klimt. His paintings exhibit decorative qualities and a strong sense of line, but also an eroticism and emotional intensity that the public sometimes found disturbing. He is best known for self-portraits and paintings of nude or partly clothed women.

Schiller, Johann Christoph Friedrich von (1759-1805), German playwright, poet, writer on philosophy, history, and aesthetics. Schiller's highly successful early plays, including *The Robbers* (1781) and *Don Carlos* (1787), articulated his violent opposition to tyranny. In Weimar he became professor at the Univ. of Jena (1789) and married writer Charlotte von Lengefeld. At this time he also began his important friendship with Johann Wolfgang von Goethe, with whom he shared many values and ideas. In 1787 Schiller began writing historical works, as well as works on philosophy and aesthetics, heavily influenced by Emmanuel Kant. He and Goethe also edited the literary magazines *Horen* and *Musenalmanach*. Some of his most important works were historical dramas, including *Wallenstein* (1798-1799), *Mary Stuart* (1800), and *William Tell* (1804). He also translated works of Shakespeare and Racine. Schiller is acknowledged to be a leading figure of German literature, second only to Goethe. Beethoven used Schiller's poem 'Ode to Joy' (1785) as the text for the final movement of his Ninth Symphony.

Schinkel, Karl Friedrich (1781-1841), German architect, painter, drawer, lithographer, theatre designer, and publicist. His style of building, in which classicism and romanticism were combined, was very influential in Prussia until the end of century. Of particular importance are the buildings he designed in Berlin between 1816 and 1830, such as the Neue Wache (1816-1818), the Schauspielhaus (1818-1821) and the Altes Museum (1822-1828).

Schipperke (Flemish; 'little skipper'), Belgian breed of dog once used to guard canal barges. Descended from the Leeuvenaar, a black sheep dog, it is a short, stout dog, often tailless, with a foxlike head and a

The schipperke is a small, nonsporting breed of dog that has a full black coat, short tail, and small erect ears.

S

S

thick black coat, standing 12-13 in (30.5-33 cm) and weighing about 15 lb (7 kg).

Schism, Great *See:* Pope.

Schist, common group of metamorphic rocks that have acquired a high degree of schistosity, i.e., the parallel arrangement of sheety, or prismatic, minerals resulting from regional metamorphism. Schistosity is similar in nature and origin to cleavage in slate but is coarser. The major constituents of most schists are either mica, talc, amphibole, or chlorite.

Schistosomiasis, or bilharziasis, parasitic disease caused by the schistosome, a type of flatworm. The disease is usually acquired by bathing in infected water. The schistosome larvae enter the body through the skin and live in the blood as parasites. As adults they lay eggs that cause infection and destroy the kidneys, liver, and other organs. The disease can ultimately cause death. It afflicts more than 200 million people in Africa, Asia, and Latin America.

Schizophrenia (formerly called dementia praecox), type of psychosis characterized by confusion of identity, hallucinations, delusion, and illogical thought. The 3 main types of schizophrenia are catatonia, in which the individual oscillates between excitement and stupor; paranoid schizophrenia, which is similar to paranoia except that the intellect deteriorates; and hebephrenia, which is characterized by withdrawal from reality, bizarre behavior, delusions, hallucinations, and self-neglect.
See also: Psychosis.

Schlegel, August Wilhelm von (1767-1845), German philologist and linguist, brother of Friedrich von Schlegel, with whom he often worked together. From 1804-1817 he was a friend of Mme de Staël, and became her literary mentor. Became professor in arts and literary history in Berlin in 1818, and was a founder of Ancient Indian philology. Similar to his brother, his most important works are considered to be his lit-

Oskar Schlemmer's characteristic emphasis on architectural landscape, linear design, and streamlined, statuesque figures, reflecting his association (1921-29) with the Bauhaus, is seen in *Group of Fourteen in Imaginary Architecture* (1930) in the Wallraf-Richartz Museum, Cologne.

erary studies written from a romantic point of view rather than his poetry. Also achieved lasting recognition for his translations of Dante and Shakespeare.

Schlegel, Friedrich von (1772-1829), German linguist, brother of August Wilhelm von Schlegel: leading figure and great initiator of early German romanticism. Was a staff member of various literary journals and held many readings about literature (compiled later), where he analyzed and explained aesthetic, theoretical, critical and philosophical aspects in great detail. This is where his original spirit found its fullest expression, as opposed to his poetry, which was only mediocre. His reading entitled *Vorlesungen über die Geschichte der alten und neuen Literatur* (1815) gave an impulse to modern literary history.

Schlemmer, Oskar (1888-1943), German artist; lectured at the Bauhaus in Dessau (1920-1929). In this period his work consisted mainly of rhythmically arranged concave and convex surfaces in strict color schemes. This idea was similarly expressed in his Triadic Ballet, in which the dancers moved to the music of Hindemith dressed as spheres and cylinders.

Schlesinger, name of 2 famous 20th-century U.S. historians. **Arthur Meier Schlesinger** (1888-1965) is best known for his U.S. history *The Rise of the City, 1878-1898* (1933) from the series he edited, *A History of American Life*. He stressed the cultural, social, and economic context of history. **Arthur Meier Schlesinger, Jr.** (1917-), his son, won Pulitzer prizes for both *The Age of Jackson* (1945) and *A Thousand Days* (1966), the latter written after a period as special assistant to President John F. Kennedy.

Schleswig-Holstein, state in northern Germany, 6,046 sq mi (15,660 sq km) bordering Denmark. The capital, Kiel, lies at the eastern end of the Kiel Canal, which links the North and Baltic seas. The main economic activities are dairy farming, fishing, shipbuilding, and engineering. Schleswig was a Danish fiefdom from the 12th century. Holstein came under Danish control in the 15th century. Disputes with the German states led to the Austro-Prussian War in 1864. Prussia annexed these 2 Danish duchies in 1866. North Schleswig was reunited with Denmark in 1920.

Schlieffen, Alfred von (1833-1913), German general, Marshall (1911), Count of Schliefen. He took part in the war against Austria (1866) and France (1870), and developed the 'Schlieffen Plan' in 1905, when he was head of the general staff (1891-1906): this was the German combat plan in the event of war (WW I). Fearing a war on two fronts, Germany planned a short surprise attack (Blitzkrieg), so that after a quick victory in the West they could turn against Russia. In this plan, Germany had to penetrate as far as Paris via the Oise Valley and surround the French army. This plan was eventually altered by Von Moltke.

Heinrich Schliemann, a German amateur-archeologist, as photographed in 1876 at the Lions' Gate of the citadel at Mycenae. Together with his assistant, Wilhelm Dörpfeld (above left), Schliemann dug at Mycenae for several years, and with great success: major art treasures were found in the tombs that he discovered.

Schliemann, Heinrich (1822-1890), German archeologist, best known for his discoveries of Troy (1871-1890) and Mycenae (1876-1878).
See also: Archeology.

Schlöndorff, Volker (1939-), German film director. Was assistant to Louis Malle and Alain Resnais, went on to make TV reports, and eventually received much praise for his film debut based on Robert Musil *Der junge Törless* (1966). He has since made a large number of impressive movies, often filming well-known literary works. His films include *The Lost Honour of Katharina Blum* (1975), *The Tin Drum* (1979), *Swan in Love* (1983), *Death of a Salesman* (1986), *The Handmaid's Tale* (1990), *Voyager* (1991), *The Ogre* (1996), *Palmetto* (2000), and *The Legend of Rita* (2001).

Schmalkaldic League, alliance of German Protestant states during the Reformation, formed in 1531 for defense against the Catholic Holy Roman emperor Charles V. Member states included Hesse, Saxony, Brunswick, Anhalt, Mansfeld, Magdeburg, Bremen, Strassburg, and Ulm. The Protestants were defeated in 1547 in the War of the Schmalkaldic League, but the subsequent Peace of Augsburg (1555) gave Lutheran churches the right to exist.
See also: Reformation.

Schmidt, Arno (1914-1979), German writer. Only began his literary career after WW II, and developed to become one of the most avant-garde West German authors, experimenting with montage and half tone printing. The *monologue intérieur* and Freud's psychoanalysis played an important part his work. Schmidt wrote literary essays in the form of radio plays, the so-called Funkessays, including *Nachrichten von Menschen und Büchern* (1971). His novels include *Aus dem Leben eines Fauns* (1953),

Die Gelehrtenrepublik (1957), *Kaff auch Mare Crisium* (1960), *Zettels Traum* (1970), and *Abend mit Goldrand* (1975).

Schmidt, Helmut (1918-　), chancellor of West Germany (1974-1982). A Social Democrat, he was party floor leader in the Bundestag (1962-1969), defense minister (1969-1972), and finance minister (1972-1974). He succeeded Willy Brandt as chancellor when the latter resigned amid a spy scandal. In a continent plagued with economic difficulties, Germany under Schmidt remained stable and prosperous. However, violent radical groups asserted themselves in the early 1980s, and he stepped down after losing a confidence vote in 1982. Since 1983 he is editor in chief of the German newspaper Die Zeit.

Schmidt-Rottluff, Karl (real name, Karl Schmidt; 1884-1976), German painter, sculptor and graphic artist, one of the most important German expressionists; joint founder of 'Die Brücke'. The main features of his work are heavy contours, bright colors and simplified forms. Influenced by primitive art.

Schnabel, Artur (1882-1951), an Austrian pianist, teacher, and composer. He was known for his interpretations of the works of Beethoven and other classical composers. Schnabel was born in Lipnik and studied in Vienna with Leschetizky, 1891-1897. Schnabel settled in Berlin, where he taught at the High School for Musics, 1925-1933. He then lived in the United States and Switzerland. Schnabel's compositions, marked by dissonance, include *Symphony No. 1* (1946) and *Rhapsody for Orchestra* (1948). He wrote the books *Reflections on Music* (1933), *Music and the Line of Most Resistance* (1942), and *My Life and Music* (1961).

Schnabel, Julian (1951-　), American painter. Was influenced by the new, expressionistic tendency in Europe. Painting mainly on wooden panels and on velvet. The colors he used played a subsidiary role - the emotional expression was more important. His motifs were aggression, violence, and death. He is also a sculptor and director of films such as *Basquiat* (1996) and *Before Night Falls* (2000).

Schnauzer *See:* Giant schnauzer; Miniature schnauzer; Standard schnauzer.

Schnittke, Alfred Garsievich (1934-1998), Russian composer. Taught instrumentation at the Moscow conservatory (1962-1972). His work, initially conventional, was influenced by the European avant-garde after 1962. From the 1970s onwards it featured strong eclectic and polystylistic elements. Schnittke wrote many orchestral works (including five symphonies and five concertos), chamber music (four string quartets), music dramas (including the opera *The Life of an Idiot*, 1990-1991), ballets, choral works as well as about 60 compositions for film.

Schnitzler, Arthur (1862-1931), Austrian playwright. He wrote about love and the personality basis of racism, particularly anti-Semitism, in the Vienna of Sigmund Freud. His work included *Anatol* (1893), *Playing with Love* (1896), and *Merry-Go-Round* (1897).

Schoenberg, Arnold (1874-1951), German composer, theorist, and teacher who revolutionized music by introducing serial, or 12-tone, music. His string sextet *Transfigured Night* (1899), with harmonic clashes, was followed by the declaimed songs of *Pierrot Lunaire* (1912) and experiments in wholetone and finally 12-tone music, culminating in his unfinished opera *Moses and Aaron* (1930-1951). Schoenberg emigrated to the United States in 1933.

Scholarship, grant-in-aid awarded to a student.

Scholasticism, philosophical system of medieval Church teachers, or scholastics, who applied philosophic (primarily Aristotelian) ideas to Christian doctrine. They held that although reason was always subordinate to faith, it served to increase the believer's understanding of what was believed. Typical scholastic works are the commentary on an authoritative text and the *quaestio*, in which the writer sets out opposing authorities and then reconciles them in answering a question. St. Thomas Aquinas's *Summa Theologica* consists of a systematically constructed series of *quaestiones*. The influence of Aristotle on medieval thought was enormous but was not available in the West until a Latin translation appeared in the 13th century.

Schongauer, Martin (1450?-1491), German painter and engraver. He was one of the first engravers to use copper plates, and his delicate, skillful work influenced Albrecht Dürer and other German artists. His works include the engravings *The Death of the Virgin Mary* and *Christ Bearing the Cross*, the painting *The Virgin in the Rose Arbor* (1473), and the mural in Breisach, *Last Judgment* (c.1491).

School, institution whose primary purpose is to impart knowledge. The most numerous and the most important kinds of schools are those used to educate the young, from early childhood to early adulthood, preparing them for the roles they will play in society, the economy, and in political life. Schools provide students with knowledge, from the basics of reading, writing, and reasoning, to the most sophisticated branches of the arts and sciences. Schools also reflect society and transmit its values and norms.

Before the 1800s in the West, education was reserved for a relatively privileged few. Among the Assyrians, Babylonians, and Egyptians, organized knowledge was largely dominated by priests. Much of what was known was deliberately kept secret and obscure to enhance the power and prestige of a privileged few. Masters of arts and crafts passed on their techniques directly from one generation to the next; the process of teaching and learning was more restricted, personal, and direct. The ancient Greeks marked a significant departure from this approach. Politically independent, socially mobile, free of the dominance of a priesthood, they used their own senses and reason to question what they saw and heard. The spirit of free, rational inquiry among the Greeks led to a free exchange of ideas, the growth of rival world views, the gathering of organized bodies of knowledge, the appearance of the Western world's first teachers for hire, and the first schools open to free inquiry. Education was still a privilege, but the Greeks made learning a goal in its own right and the mark of a truly free individual. The Romans were deeply influenced by Greek practice and ideals.

After the fall of the Roman Empire, education at first declined and then was revived and transformed by the Christian church. It was no longer necessary to educate citizens but to preserve and spread the faith. What little education there was took place in monasteries and was almost wholly religious. Over the centuries, bodies of knowledge accumulated and new needs had to be met. Busy with war and politics, the aristocracy could not read or write, but they needed clerks; in the early days they used men trained by the church. In time, education moved from the monastery schools to schools in the great cathedrals that developed into universities. The upper classes began to cultivate and patronize learning and schools.

In the Renaissance, from the 14th to the 16th centuries, scholars recovered and began to read the works of Greeks and Romans and aspired to their learning and level of culture. Education and the schools began to break away from the church and its priesthood. The Renaissance was followed by the Protestant Reformation and the invention of the printing press. The former challenged the authority of the Roman church, the latter made books available to all who could read, leading to profound changes in education and in schools. The modern state, modern commerce and finance, the rise of a more complex urban society dominated by the middle class and the advent of modern science and technology revolutionized education and schools. Learning was no longer a luxury, privilege, or virtue; it had become a necessity. School systems were established, theories of education were developed, and the modern profession of teaching had its beginnings.

In the United States today, in addition to preschools and kindergartens, there are elementary schools, many of them public; middle schools; junior public high schools; and public high schools. Education generally proceeds on a two-track system-vocational or academic. For higher education, students may go on to community college, three-quarters of which are public, or to one of the nation's colleges and universities. There are also many schools for advanced training and retraining of highly skilled professionals, as well as correspondence schools, night schools, and special and vocational education schools.

In the United States, schools are run by elected school boards of education or by local boards composed of parents and teachers. Schools deal with questions of curricu-

S

la, libraries and censorship, and teachers and their qualifications, as well as questions of the separation of church and state that arise over school prayer and religious instruction. Fundamental issues of conflicting moral values and public health must be addressed in dealing with drugs in the schools. In the universities, corporate and government grants providing badly needed funds for scientific research often generate controversy. In the United States, Japan, Africa, and Europe, schools and particularly colleges and universities not only are places for study and research, but also play vital roles in their relation to the leading issues in their societies.

Schopenhauer, Arthur (1788-1860), German philosopher, noted for his doctrine of the will. In *The World as Will and Idea* (1819), his main work, he argued that will is the ultimate reality, but advocated the negation of will to avoid suffering. He encouraged the contemplation of philosophy and the arts as a haven of relief from the insatiable strivings of will. Schopenhauer's ideas influenced Friedrich Nietzsche and modern existentialism.
See also: Philosophy.

Schrieffer, John Robert (1931-), U.S. physicist who shared with Leon Cooper and John Bardeen the 1972 Nobel Prize in physics for their work on superconductivity.
See also: Superconductivity.

Schröder, Gerhard Fritz Kurt (1944-), German social democratic politician. Chancellor of Germany (1998-). Schröder worked his way through evening school and a degree in law to become a lawyer. In 1963 he became a member of the Young Socialists, and was a member of the party executive from 1986 onwards. In 1989 he became a member of the SPD Presidium, and as such was responsible for economic and energy policies. At the federal state elections in 1990 he was elected Prime Minister of Lower Saxony. When the SPD became the largest party in the federal parliament after the 1998 elections, Schröder was elected Chancellor. Since 1999 he has also been President of the SPD. Schröder's intention is to create a bridge between politicians, employers, and workers (called the 'New Middle Ground') via a revitalized social democratic policy. At the 2002 elections, Schröder's coalition succeeded in maintaining the majority, and he was re-appointed as Chancellor.

Schrödinger, Erwin (1887-1961), Austrian-born Irish physicist and philosopher of science who shared with Paul Dirac the 1933 Nobel Prize in physics for his discovery of the Schrödinger wave equation, describing the wavelike behavior of electrons, which is of fundamental importance in studies of quantum mechanics. It was later shown that his theories of wave mechanics were equivalent to the matrix mechanics theories of Werner Heisenberg.
See also: Quantum mechanics.

Schubert, Franz Peter (1797-1828), Viennese composer. He wrote nine symphonies, of which the Fifth (1816), Eighth (1822), and Ninth (1828) are among the world's greatest. He is also famous for his piano pieces and chamber music (especially his string quartets), but above all for his over 600 *lieder* (songs). In addition to individual lieder such as 'The Erl King' and 'The Trout,' he wrote song cycles, among them *The Maid of the Mill* and *Winter's Journey*.

Schulz, Charles Monroe (1922-2000), U.S. cartoonist, creator of 'Peanuts.' The 'Peanuts' series, which Schulz began in 1950, is about young children but appeals to adults as well in its benign humor and insight into human foibles. The characters of the comic strip, including the insecure Charlie Brown, the bossy Lucy, and the beagle Snoopy, have become the subjects of television programs, an Off-Broadway play, and many books and greeting cards. The comic strip appeared in thousands of newspapers throughout the world.
See also: Cartoon.

Schumacher, Michael (1969-), German racing car driver, became a Formula 3 driver (German champion 1990), after winning the 1987 European carting championship. He began racing in Formula 1 in 1991 in a Jordan-Ford, but after only one Grand Prix he moved to Benetton-Ford. The following year Schumacher won his first Grand Prix. In 1993 he ended fourth in the Formula 1 drivers championship with 52 points. In 1994 he became the first German to win the Formula 1 world championship, driving a Benetton-Ford, and in 1995 he was world champion for the second time. In 1996 Schumacher moved to Ferrari, for which team he won the 2000, 2001 and 2002 world titles. His strong points are his quick reflexes and tactical insights.

Schuman, Robert (1886-1963), French politician. Prime minister (1947-1948) and foreign minister (1948-1952), he launched the Schuman Plan, which resulted in the European Coal and Steel Community, precursor of the European Economic Community.
See also: France.

Schuman, William (1910-1992), U.S. composer. His symphonies, chamber music, ballets, and operas are known for their rhythmic vivacity and their debt to jazz. His cantata *A Free Song* won the first Pulitzer Prize in music (1943). He was president of the Juilliard School of Music (1945-1962) and of Lincoln Center for the Performing Arts (1962-1969). In 1985 he was again awarded with a Pulitzer Price.

Schumann, Clara (1819-1896), German pianist and composer. The daughter of the important piano teacher Friedrich Wieck, she became a well-known soloist and the first to perform entirely from memory. She married pianist and composer Robert Schumann over strenuous objections of her father, and became one of the chief exponents of his piano compositions. After her husband's death in 1856 she continued performing widely, touring frequently to England. A close friend of Johannes Brahms, she also was one of the main interpreters of his compositions. In her later years she was active as a piano teacher, heading the piano department of the Frankfurt Conservatory (1878-1892). Her compositions include a piano concerto, smaller piano compositions, songs, and cadenzas for Beethoven's 3rd and 4th piano concertos.

Schumann, Robert (Alexander) (1810-1856), German composer and critic, a leader of the romantic movement. His early work, until 1840, comprises inspired piano pieces (e.g., *Symphonic Études*, *Papillons*). He then turned his attention to music for orchestras (e.g., *Piano Concerto in A Minor*, 1841-1845), achieving great heights of emotional intensity, and to songs, uniting voice and piano in beautiful classical compositions. He was an ardent advocate for and influence on new composers, such as Brahms and Chopin. In the 1840s he began to show signs of mental illness and, after a suicide attempt in 1854, was placed in an asylum, where he remained until he died.

Schumpeter, Joseph Alois (1883-1950), Moravian-born U.S. economist. Schumpeter emigrated to the United States in 1932, when he joined the faculty of Harvard University. His major works were on the importance of entrepreneurs (*The Theory of Economic Development*, 1911) and the inevitability of business cycles and the unequal distribution of wealth (*Capitalism, Socialism, and Democracy*, 1942) in the healthy capitalist economy.
See also: Economics.

Schütz, Heinrich (1585-1672), a German composer. He influenced the development of

An excursion of Schubertians, the group of artists that centered itself around Franz Schubert (1797-1828). The painter of this romantic scene, Leopold Kupelwieser (1796-1862), was one of Schubert's close circle of friends.

German church music by introducing the Italian dramatic Baroque style. In the *St. Matthew Passion*, the oratorio *Seven Words from the Cross*, and other works, he used Italian forms and techniques to convey the deep feeling characteristic of German music. He composed the first German opera, *Dafne* (1627), set to a German translation of an Italian libretto. The music, however, is lost. Schütz began his career as a choirboy in the court chapel at Kassel in 1599. He continued his music studies in Venice, 1609-1612. About 1615 he settled in Dresden as court conductor, but he continued to visit Italy.

Schwab, Werner (1958-1994), Austrian playwright. Schwab's plays caused a sensation in the early 1990s, especially his faeces dramas: *Die Präsidentinnen* (1990), *ÜBERGEWICHT, unwichtig: UNFORM* (1991), *Volksvernichtung oder Meine Leber ist sinnlos* (1991), and *Mein Hundemund* (1992). In these plays he raised the theme of bowel movements and opposed hypocrisy and narrow-mindedness. His plays are characterized by strong language, extreme violence, sexual excess and alcohol abuse. Other important plays written by Schwab are *Offene Gruben - offene Fenster* (1992), *Mesalliance - aber wir ficken uns prächtig* (1992), *Pornogeographie* (1993), and *Endlich tot, endlich keine Luft mehr* (1994). Schwab took his own life in 1994.

Schwartz, Delmore (1913-1966), U.S. poet admired for his rhapsodic yet philosophic style. His works include *In Dreams Begin Responsibilities* (1938), *Summer Knowledge* (1959), and *Last and Lost Poems of Delmore Schwartz* (1979). He also wrote short stories, a play, and a children's book.

Schwartz, Melvin (1932-), U.S. physicist. Schwartz, Leon Lederman, and Jack Steinberger won the 1988 Nobel Prize in physics for their work in using streams of subatomic neutrinos and their discovery of the muon neutrino. The work was conceived at Columbia Univ. in 1960 and executed at Brookhaven National Laboratory in 1962. *See also:* Neutrino.

Schwarzkopf, Elisabeth (1915-), a German operatic and concert soprano. She became known for the flexibility of her lyric voice and for her interpretation of *lieder* (art songs) by Hugo Wolf and Franz Schubert. The Marschallin in *Der Rosenkavalier* and the Countess in *The Marriage of Figaro* are among her varied operatic roles. Schwarzkopf made her operatic debut in Berlin in 1938. She then sang with the Vienna State Opera and other leading opera companies in Europe and the United States. *See also:* Opera.

Schweitzer, Albert (1875-1965), German physician, theologian, missionary, musician, and philosopher. He was an authority on Bach and a noted performer of Bach's organ music. He abandoned an academic career in theology to study medicine and became (1913) a missionary doctor in French Equatorial Africa (now Gabon). He devoted his life to the hospital he founded there. His many writings include *The Quest of the*

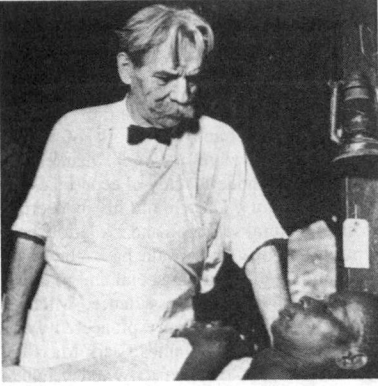

Albert Schweitzer (1875-1965), recipi- ent of the 1952 Nobel Peace Prize.

Historical Jesus (1906), and *The Decay and Restoration of Civilization* and *Civilization and Ethics* (1923), the first two volumes of his *Philosophy of Civilization*. Schweitzer won the 1952 Nobel Peace Prize for his inspiring humanitarian work.

Schwind, Moritz von (1804-1871), Austrian painter, drawer and draftsman. Important representative of the late romantic school. Painted religious and historical frescoes in Wartburg castle (1853-1855) and the Royal Opera in Vienna (1866-1868). Worked as a caricaturist and illustrator. Took his themes from fairy tales and legends. Works include *Die Hochzeitsreise* (1855; Schack Gallery, Munich).

Schwinger, Julian Seymour (1918-1994), U.S. physicist who shared with Richard P. Feynman and Japan's Shinichiro Tomonaga the 1965 Nobel Prize in physics for independent work in formulating the theory of quantum electrodynamics. *See also:* Quantum electrodynamics.

Schwitters, Kurt (1887-1948), a German painter, sculptor, and writer. He was a leader of German dadaism, which he called *Merz*. He was known especially for his fanciful collages, such as *Opened by Customs*, and for his assemblages, called, *Merzbau*. Many of his poems and stories appeared in the magazine *Der Sturm*. He also published his own magazine *Merz* (1923-1932). Schwitters studied in his native Hanover and in Dresden. He left Germany in 1937 and settled in England in 1940.

Sciatica, pain in the distribution of the sciatic nerve in the leg caused by compression or irritation of the nerve. The pain may resemble an electric shock and be associated with numbness and tingling in the skin area served by the nerve. One of the most common causes is a slipped disk in the lower lumbar spine. *See also:* Nervous system.

Science, systematic study of nature and of individual and social human behavior. Science is distinguished from other intellectual disciplines, like the arts and humanities, by several key characteristics. It is based upon observation, either by the unaided senses or with the help of instruments that increase the power of the senses, like microscopes or telescopes. Science requires the careful collection and organization of data. Above all, science employs a rigorous method of reasoning about what it observes. The scientific method relies upon logic to draw conclusions from evidence and tests its reasoning with experiments. As study progresses, a larger pattern or underlying law begins to emerge that helps explain phenomena like the formation of gases, the motion of planets, or the division of cells. Scientists attempt to state those laws or patterns in the form of theories or hypotheses, and those statements are also subjected to experiments. Some hypotheses prove useful and enduring, others are refuted or superseded by new experiments or new findings. Finally, science expresses itself mathematically, in formulas that state numerically the dynamics or relations underlying what we see. Neither the arts nor the humanities are rigorous in the way that science is; the questions they ask, the methods they use, and their findings and results are different.

The scope of science is vast. It is broken up into a great many fields and specialties. But a few major divisions are still useful for an overview. The physical sciences are, historically, probably the oldest and include astronomy, meteorology, chemistry, physics, and geology. These fields cover inanimate nature. Life and living beings are studied by the life sciences, including biology, zoology, botany, physiology, and paleontology. The social sciences study human beings as they reveal themselves in individual behavior and in society and its institutions. Such studies include political science, economics, psychology, anthropology, and sociology. To the extent that these disciplines are less successful than the natural sciences in expressing their findings mathematically, they have been criticized for lacking the rigor of pure science. Finally, although they are not themselves sciences in the strict sense, mathematics and logic are essential to science. Though in many ways the two overlap, mathematics provides science with symbols and procedures for measuring and for calculating relations. Logic discovers the ratio and procedures of accurate reasoning.

The development of science has led to an explosion of knowledge unprecedented in human history. Allied with mechanical ingenu-

S

Merzbild (1922), by the 20th-century artist Kurt Schwitters, is a dada collage construction made up of fragments of wood, metal, rubber, and paper. The geometric composition, which resembles that of a cubist painting, assembles objects from everyday life in an unpredictable and evocative structure (Burton Tremaine Collection, Meriden, Conn).

S

ity, it led to technology, the application of scientific knowledge to practical problems. The results have completely transformed the world. In partnership with modern industry, finance, and the state, science has produced a mixed legacy, creating tools that heal and destroy, that enhance life and threaten it with annihilation.

History. Science's earliest manifestation was among the Greeks who were the first people to reason logically about the natural world. Instead of accepting occult explanations for what they observed, the Greeks tried to discover intelligible laws underlying things. They developed logic and mathematics and made impressive contributions to human knowledge. In the 4th century B.C., Hippocrates laid down elementary principles for the practice of medicine. One hundred years later, Aristotle attempted an exhaustive classification of phenomena based upon logical categories and direct observation. Euclid and Archimedes were great mathematicians and Ptolemy's description of the motion of the planets would not be improved upon for nearly 1,500 years.

With the fall of the Roman Empire and the onset of the Middle Ages in the West, it was left to Islam to pursue some of the promise of the Greeks. To mention only a few great Muslim thinkers, Alhazan in optics, Aricanna in medicine, and Al-Khwarizmi in algebra made important contributions that had their greatest impact on Christian Europe in the late Middle Ages. Schooled in logical rigor by the Scholastics and with access to Islamic work and the Hindu-Arabic numerical notation, Europe was ripe for intellectual change. It came first in Italy between the 14th and 16th centuries in the Renaissance. The use of perspective in painting and architecture that explored principles laid down by the Greeks and Romans fostered a spirit of inquiry that led to detailed studies of human anatomy and innovations in mechanics and virtually every branch of human knowledge. Men like Galileo and da Vinci pointed the way for the rest of Europe. Nicolaus Copernicus, the Polish astronomer, put an end to the medieval view of the world with his theory, based upon careful telescopic observation, that the earth was not the center of the universe but only one of several planets that revolves around the sun. The Copernican revolution sent profound shock waves throughout Europe, and, combined with the impact of the discovery of the Americas, inspired the best minds of Europe to turn to science. In the 17th century, Descartes in France laid the philosophical foundations of the scientific method. In the same century, the Englishman Newton and the German Leibniz simultaneously discovered calculus, and Newton wrote the *Principia Mathematica* in which he proposed his law of universal gravitation. His countryman, William Harvey, described the circulation of blood and Robert Boyle advanced the science of chemistry.

Building upon the work of the previous century, the 18th century saw rapid advances. In chemistry came the discoveries of gases, among them chlorine, hydrogen, and carbon dioxide. Carolus Linnaeus developed a system for the classification of animals and

The impassive visage of the Roman Publius Cornelius Scipio (c. 234-c. 183), who achieved great fame for his successful defeat of Hannibal, near Zama in 202 B.C. (Museo Nazionale, Naples).

Luigi Galvani, Alessandro Volta, and Benjamin Franklin made advances in the study of electricity. In addition, the sciences had an impact outside of the laboratory in the rationalisms and skepticism of Voltaire, Hume, Diderot, and the work of Adam Smith, whose *Wealth of Nations* marked the advent of the modern study of economics. In the 19th century, Darwin did his pioneering work on natural selection and evolution, presenting theories that would have almost as profound an effect upon social and political thought as they did in science. Michael Faraday and Joseph Henry pioneered work in electromagnetism. James Clark Maxwell studied the laws of electricity and magnetism, and great advances were made in modern medicine, typified by the work and career of Louis Pasteur. Progress in medicine and in the care and treatment of the sick led to a dramatic increase in life expectancy.

Much of the early optimism felt about science began to be lost in the era of World War I, a grim demonstration of what the new knowledge and technology could do when applied to war. But the decades between World War I and World War II saw perhaps the most fertile and creative years of 20th-century science with the work of Einstein, who proposed his theory of relativity, as well as Max Planck and Nils Bohr, who deepened our understanding of the structure and mechanics of the atom. It was their work that made possible the creation of the atomic bomb, a weapon which revolutionized both war and peace.

In the latter half of the 20th century, science has become a highly complex and competitive intellectual pursuit, engaging the talents of many of the best minds throughout the world and tackling problems as diverse as the origin's of the universe to the perfecting of high-definition TV or the next generation of high-speed computers. Modern science is pursued almost entirely in the laboratories of universities, governments, or private industries, and research and development commands billions of dollars every year. But no matter how large or complex the facilities and supporting institutions, the basic work of science requires a combination of intellectual rigor, intuitive power, ambition, and a desire to know that are the characteristics of the individuals who pursue science.

Science fiction, literary genre based on speculation about scientific or social development. With the works of Jules Verne and H.G. Wells, science fiction broke from supernatural fantasy. In the United States in the 1920s 'pulp' magazines popularized but all too often debased the form. John W. Campbell's magazine *Astounding* (founded 1937, now called *Analog*) revitalized the genre through its consistently high literary standards; it nurtured writers who today lead the field, among them Isaac Asimov, Robert Heinlein, Poul Anderson, Hal Clement, and Eric Frank Russell. Many science fiction writers, such as Asimov, Arthur C. Clarke, Ray Bradbury, Kurt Vonnegut, and John Wyndham, are well known outside the field. The critical acclaim they and writers no less accomplished but less well known receive indicates that the best science fiction may be

There are many different types of periodicals: weeklies, monthlies and quarterlies. Here, we see the science-fiction magazine *Amazing Stories*, from the United States.

considered to rank with the best contemporary general fiction.

Science project, independent project in which the student studies, explores, and demonstrates principles of science. Such projects include building models of anatomical structures or machines, collecting plant or animal specimens, demonstrating chemical reactions, or conducting controlled experiments on heredity in insects. The subject of these studies is not only the area of science involved but also the scientific method itself.

Scientific creationism, belief that current forms of life did not evolve from simpler forms over millions of years but were created more or less as they exist now. According to scientific creationists, neither logic nor physical evidence (fossils) supports the ideas of differentiation and transitions between life forms that are central to the theory of evolution. The scientific creationist movement developed in the mid-20th century, particularly with the activities of Henry M. Morris, cofounder of the Creation Research Society (1963) and founder of the Institute for Creation Research (1970s).

Scientology, religio-scientific movement stressing self-redemption, which originated in the United States in the 1950s and was incorporated as a church in 1965. It was founded by L. Ron Hubbard. Based on Hubbard's theory of dianetics, a 'modern science of mental health,' scientology holds that all aspects of individual human behavior are linked and must be harmonized; it also posits a life energy in the universe at large that affects human behavior.

Scipio, Publius Cornelius (Scipio Africanus Major, Scipio the Elder; 234?-183? B.C.), Roman general. Scipio defeated the Carthaginian forces under Hannibal in the Second Punic War (218-201 B.C.), fighting in Spain and winning decisively at Zama, in North Africa (202 B.C.). In 199 B.C. he was elected to public office, serving until 184 B.C.

See also: Punic Wars.

Scissors, cutting tool made of 2 metal blades joined at a pivot point. Cutting occurs between the blades as they are brought together when the handles at one end are squeezed together. Scissors may have been invented as early as the Bronze Age. They were in use in ancient Rome, China, Japan, and Korea, and came into regular domestic use in Europe in the 16th century. Among specialized scissors are *shears* (large scissors) and *pinking shears* (sawtooth scissors that cut fabric leaving zigzag edges).

Scoliosis, curvature of the spine to one side, with twisting. It occurs as a congenital defect or may be secondary to spinal diseases. Severe scoliosis causes hunchback deformity and loss of height, and may restrict cardiac or lung function. Scoliosis becomes apparent in adolescence or earlier, and it occurs more often in girls than in boys. Severe cases may require surgery, after which a body cast is worn for several months. *See also:* Spine.

Scone, Stone of, ceremonial stone in Westminster Abbey, London, on which British monarchs are crowned. The stone originated in the village of Scone, Scotland, where it was used to crown Scottish kings. It was brought to London by Edward I of England in 1296. *See also:* Westminster Abbey.

Scopolamine, or hyoscine, alkaloid drug derived from plants of the Solenaceae (nightshade) family (especially genus *Scopolia*) and used as a depressant. Toxic unless given in very small quantities, it is administered to control tremors of Parkinson's disease and other disorders, to combat motion sickness, and in combination with morphine, as an analgesic and amnesic drug (reducing pain and inducing forgetfulness) before childbirth or surgery.

Scorpion, any of an order (*Scorpionida*) of terrestrial arachnids having two claws held in front of the head and a stinging tail curled forward over the back. All scorpions have a poisonous sting but few are dangerous to humans. The sting is usually used in defense or, with the palps, in catching prey. Scorpions are restricted to dry, warm regions of the world and feed on grasshoppers, crickets, spiders, and other arthropods.

Scorpionfly, harmless insect (family *Panorpidae*) with transparent or colored wings and long, dangling legs. Some species

are wingless. The long legs are used to trap smaller insects, which are then bitten and eaten. The caterpillar-like larvae are also flesh eaters.

Scorsese, Martin (1942-), U.S. film director. His first and somewhat experimental feature-length film, *Who's That Knocking at My Door?* (1968), was followed by the semi-autobiographical *Mean Streets* (1973), which he co-wrote. Other films include *Taxi Driver* (1976), *Raging Bull* (1980), the controversial *The Last Temptation of Christ* (1988), based on a novel by Nikos Kazantzakis, *GoodFellas* (1990), *Cape Fear* (1992), *Casino* (1995), *Kundun* (1998), *Bringing Out the Dead* (1999), and *Il mio viaggio in Italia* (2002). Scorsese received the Lifetime Achievement Award (1996).

Scotland, former kingdom now part of the United Kingdom. It is bounded by England in the south, the Atlantic Ocean in the north and west, and the North Sea in the east.
Land. Covering northern Britain and the Hebrides, Orkney, and Shetland islands, Scotland is 30,414 sq mi (78,772 sq km) in area. It is divided into 3 main land regions: the Highlands, the Central Lowlands, and the Southern Uplands. Great Britain's highest peak, Ben Nevis (4,406 ft/1,343 m) is located in the Highlands. Scotland's most important river is the River Clyde.
People. Over 50% of the population is urban; major cities include Edinburgh, the capital and cultural center; Glasgow, the industrial center; Aberdeen; and Dundee. English is spoken everywhere, but some 77,000 Scots in the northwest also speak Gaelic.
Economy. Scotland was one of the first industrialized countries; its economy rests on iron and steel, aluminum, shipbuilding, chemicals, North Sea oil, and the whiskey industry. Agriculture, mainly grain, sheep and cattle, and fishing are also important.
History. Scotland's original inhabitants were the Picts, displaced by the Scots, Britons, and Angles. United under Kenneth I MacAlpin (9th century A.D.) the country maintained an embattled independence from England, ensured by Robert the Bruce (Robert I; r. 1306-29). A brief Renaissance under James IV (r. 1488-1513) ended in disaster at Flodden Field. In the turmoil of the Reformation, James VI (James I of England) united the crowns of Scotland and England, but union of government came only in 1707. It was widely resented, and England fueled this by attacking Scottish autonomy and

prosperity; this helped incite the two Jacobite rebellions (1715 and 1745). A great cultural rebirth followed, but also the hardships of the Industrial Revolution and Highland depopulation for sheep farming. Devolution (i.e., greater autonomy) was defeated by referendum vote in 1979, although there continued to be a movement for greater autonomy. As a result of a referendum in 1997 Scotland received greater autonomy, such as a parliament and a greater say regarding the levy of taxes. In 1999 parlementary elections were held which were won by the Labour party.
See also: United Kingdom.

Scotland Yard, headquarters of the Criminal Investigation Department (CID) of the London Metropolitan Police since 1829. Its jurisdiction covers 786 sq mi (2,036 sq km) containing more than 8 million people. It also coordinates police work throughout Britain and provides national and international criminal records.

Scott, Barbara Ann (1928-), Canadian figure skater. In 1947 she became the first non-European to win a world title in figure skating, and in 1948 she won the Olympic gold medal. She then became a professional skater, featured in *Hollywood Ice Revues*, and subsequently, a competitor in equestrian events.

Scott, Dave (1954-), American triathlete, made a definitive breakthrough in 1980 with his victory in the Bud Light Ironman in Hawaii, which he later went on to win five times. The Ironman of Hawaii was considered for a long time to be the unofficial world championship for the full-distance triathlon (2.4 mile swim -112 mile bike ride -26.2 mile run (3.8 km -180 km -41.2 km re-

Roman Catholic Mary Stuart (reigned 1542-67), Queen of France and Scotland and rival of the English Queen Elizabeth I (1558-1603), visiting the battlefield after the battle of Grookstone (painting by Giovanni Fattori, 1825-1908).

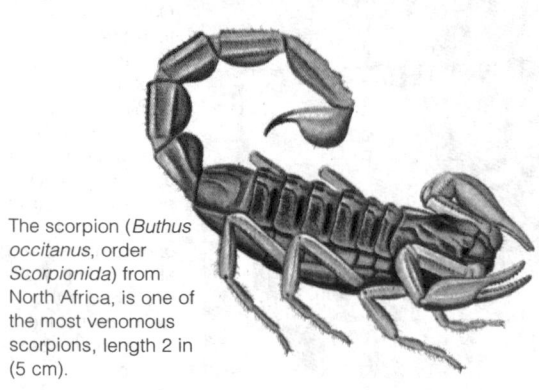

The scorpion (*Buthus occitanus*, order *Scorpionida*) from North Africa, is one of the most venomous scorpions, length 2 in (5 cm).

Scorpion flies, belonging to the insect order of *Mecoptera*, are primitive insects with a beak-like elongation of the head bearing mouthparts at its tip. Here, we see an adult male scorpionfly, *Panorpa communis*, length 0.8 in (2 cm) and a larva.

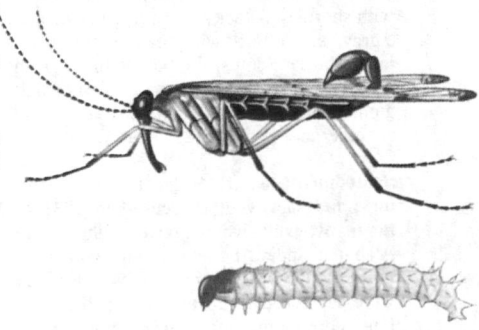

S

sp.). Scott won countless triathlon competitions of various distances.

Scott, Robert Falcon (1868-1912), English explorer remembered for his fatal attempt, on his second antarctic expedition, to be the first to reach the South Pole. In 1911 he led 4 men with sleds 950 mi (1,529 km) from the Ross Ice Shelf to the South Pole. They

Robert Scott (1868-1912) and his fellow-explorers in the Antarctic (January 18, 1912).

arrived on Jan. 18, 1912, only to discover that Roald Amundsen had reached the Pole a month before. Scurvy, frostbite, starvation, and bitter weather hampered the grueling 2-month return journey, and the last 3 survivors died in a blizzard, only 11 mi (18 km) from the next supply point.
See also: South Pole.

Scott, Sir Walter (1771-1832), Scottish poet and the foremost romantic novelist in the English language. Scott was the inventor of the historical novel, and his vivid recreations of Scotland's past were widely read throughout Europe. He started by writing popular narrative poems, including *The Lay of the Last Minstrel* (1805). After these successes he turned to fiction and completed 28 novels and many nonfiction works. His novels included *Waverly* (1814), *The Heart of Midlothian* (1818), and *Ivanhoe* (1819).

Sir Walter Scott (1771-1832).

Scottish deerhound, dog bred by the Scottish nobility since the 16th century to hunt deer. It stands 30 in (76 cm) or more and weighs 76-110 lb (34-50 kg), with a frame much like the greyhound but more heavily built. Its wiry coat is light gray to yellow brown. In the United States the breed is used to hunt wolves.

Scottish terrier, or Scottie, breed of dog with short legs, stocky body, large head, and a gray, tan, or black wiry coat. Scotties originated in the Scottish highlands in the 19th century, where they were used to hunt small game. They average 10 in (25 cm) at the shoulder and 18-22 lb (8-10 kg).

Scottsboro Cases, U.S. legal cases involving nine black youths accused in 1931 of raping two white women on a freight train in Alabama. Indicted and tried in Scottsboro, all the youths were found guilty, and eight were sentenced to death. They had no defense counsel until two lawyers volunteered

to aid them on the day of the trial. The first Scottsboro case, *Powell* v. *Alabama*, reached the U.S. Supreme Court in 1932. The court reversed the convictions on the ground that failure to provide adequate counsel for the boys violated the due process clause of the 14th Amendment. Three years later the second case, *Norris* v. *Alabama*, reached the U.S. Supreme Court; it reversed the convictions because blacks had been excluded from the grand jury that indicted the youths. By 1976 all of the youths but one (who had escaped in 1948) were released from prison.

Scotus *See:* Duns Scotus, John.

Scouring rush *See:* Horsetail.

Scout *See:* Boy Scouts; Girl Scouts and Girl Guides.

Screw, simple machine consisting of a cylindrical or conical body around which is wrapped a spiral plane or thread, and used as a fastener, propeller, and part of many more complex machines. Screws were developed by the ancient Greeks and used in presses (to extract oil or juice) and weight-lifting devices. They came into wide use as fasteners in the 1500s, with major refinements in the 1800s including the development of the sharp-tipped wood screw. Screws that modify force and motion, such as are used in vises and drilling tools, are called power screws.

Scriabin, Alexander (1872-1915), Russian composer and pianist. He wanted performances of his tone poem *Prometheus* (1911) to be accompanied by a play of colored lights corresponding to the musical tones.

Scribe (Latin *scrivere*, 'to write'), person hired to write out letters, books, and documents by hand. Scribes were particularly important in ancient times, as most people were illiterate. They were involved in legal, political, and business transactions as well as personal communication. In Europe, before the widespread use of the movable-type printing press, many books were copied out by monks, one of the most literate segments of the population. Highly trained scribes are still used to copy out Jewish sacred texts according to precise ritual standards.

Scribe, Augustin Eugène (1791-1861), French playwright and opera librettist. His 'well-made plays', realistic dramas con-

structed according to a formula including a climactic revelation that dictates consequences of the characters' actions, influenced such modern playwrights as George Bernard Shaw and Arthur Miller. Among his works are the plays *Adrienne Lecouvreur* (1849) and *The Ladies' Battle* (1851) and the opera librettos for Auber's *Fra Diavolo* and Meyerbeer's *The Huguenots*.

Scribner, family name of U.S. book publishers. **Charles Scribner** (1821-1871) co-founded the publishing company in New York City in 1846. His 3 sons served in turn as president of Charles Scribner's Sons, as the firm became known, but **Charles** (1854-1930) held the position the longest, from 1879 to 1928, during which time it published such major U.S. and British authors as Henry James, Ernest Hemingway, Ring Lardner, and Rudyard Kipling. The founder's grandson **Charles** (1890-1952) and great-grandson **Charles** (1921-) also served as company presidents.

Scrofula, tuberculosis of the lymph nodes of the neck, usually acquired by drinking infected milk. The eradication of tuberculosis in cattle and the pasteurization of milk have substantially reduced the incidence of scrofula. Treatment includes antituberculous chemotherapy.
See also: Lymphatic system; Tuberculosis.

Scruple, in the system of apothecaries' weights, unit equal to 20 grains (1.296 g). Three scruples equal 1 dram. These measures are used by pharmacists to measure drugs.

Scuba diving *See:* Diving, deep-sea; Skin diving.

Sculpin, bullhead, or sea scorpion, family of bottom-dwelling fishes (Cottidae) distinguished by a long body, large, wide head, and spiny gills and dorsal fin. Sculpins are found most often in the shallows of seas in northern regions. Bony and sometimes covered with spines, they have little food value, and sometimes steal bait and eat shrimp and young food fish. They are sometimes used as bait. The miller's thumb (*Cottus goblo*) is a common freshwater sculpin of Europe that grows to about 4 in (10 cm). The bullrout (*Myoxocephalus scorpius*) is a larger marine sculpin of Europe, North America, and the Arctic. The largest species grow to a length of 2 ft (60 cm).

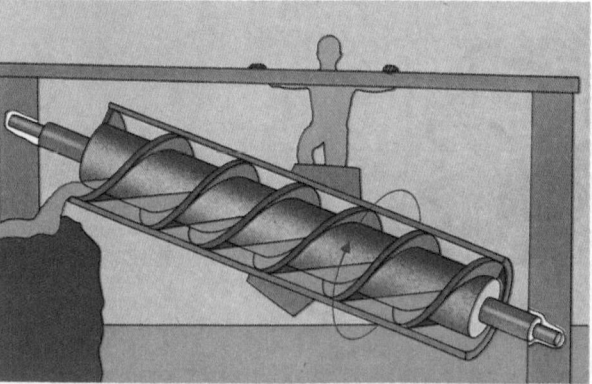

One of the inventions that was — perhaps incorrectly — attributed to Archimedes (a 3rd-century B.C. engineer and mathematician), is the screw pump. It consists of a spiral, which is open at the top and at the bottom. Water is trapped in the lowest part of the spiral, and is lifted as it rotates.

Sculpture, artistic creation of three-dimensional forms in materials such as stone, metal, wood, or even foam rubber.

High cost and durability tended to make ancient sculpture an official and conservative art form. This is evident in the monumental sculpture of Egypt, which changed little in 2,000 years. Greek sculptors aimed to portray beauty of soul as well as body, and idealized the human form. In the archaic period (about 630-480 B.C.) Egyptian influence is evident in the frontal, stylized figures, showing little movement or emotion. Greater realism led to the classical perfection of Phidias, and in the 4th century to Praxiteles, with his more sensuous forms and wider range of expression. The Hellenistic Age favored an exaggerated style, of which the *Laocoön* sculpture and the *Winged Victory of Samothrace* are fine examples. Roman sculpture was deeply indebted to Greek art but was also under Etruscan influence and excelled at realistic portraiture.

The Western tradition revived about A.D. 1000 with the elongated, stylized figures of Romanesque art leading to the more graceful and expressive sculptures of Gothic art. Renaissance sculpture, starting about 1350, was dominated by the Italians. Lorenzo Ghiberti and Donatello treated classical models in a new spirit, and Michelangelo gave to works, such as his *David*, an inner tension quite foreign to classicism. The elegant mannerism of Benvenuto Cellini and the elaborate baroque style of Gian Bernini gave way about 1800 to the neoclassical reaction of Jean-Antoine Houdon, Antonio Canova, and Bertel Thorvaldsen. The great 19th-century sculptor Auguste Rodin created a style of partially unworked figures, such as his *Balzac*, influencing Jacob Epstein. This century has seen the abstract art of Constantin Brancusi and Jean Arp, while Henry Moore and Alberto Giacometti showed interest in the human form. Outstanding U.S. sculptors are David Smith and Alexander Calder, who utilized mobiles to create movable sculpture.

Scurvy, disease caused by the gross deficiency of vitamin C. It is characterized by extreme weakness, spongy gums, and a tendency for hemorrhages to occur under the skin, membranes, and periosteum (the membrane covering the bones).

Scylla and Charybdis, in Greek mythology, perils faced by Odysseus in the Straits of Messina. Scylla was a six-headed monster who ate all within reach and Charybdis was a whirlpool. The phrase 'between Scylla and Charybdis' means a straight, narrow course between two dangers.
See also: Mythology.

Scythians, nomadic people of central Asia, settled in what is now southern Russia in approximately the 8th century B.C.. Our knowledge about the Scythians is based on burial ground remains. Excavations revealed objects richly decorated with stylized images of animals, the so-called 'animal style'; influenced by contact with the Greek world, the Greek style became dominant in the 5th and 4th century B.C. In the 2nd century B.C. the Scythians were overrun by Sarmatian horsemen.

Sea anemone, cylindrical marine polyp with a ring of tentacles, belonging to the division of the animal kingdom known as Cnideria, or Coelenterata. Anemones are related to the jellyfish. The body of the anemone consists of a hollow sac with a mouth at one end. The base of the sac is fastened to a rock and the mouth is surrounded by a ring of tentacles armed with stinging cells, or *nematocysts*. Sea anemones feed on fish and other small animals, which they catch with their tentacles and force into their mouths. While most anemones are fixed to rocks, some burrow in the sand, some can float free, and many can creep over the rocks. Certain sea anemones live on the shells of hermit crabs. Sea anemones reproduce by laying eggs that develop into minute, floating larvae. They can also split in two.

The sea anemone *Laomeda geniculata* has delicate, transparent tentacles surrounding its mouth that capture its microscopic prey.

Seaborg, Glenn Theodore (1912-   ), U.S. physicist who shared the 1951 Nobel Prize for physics with E.M. McMillan for his work in discovering several actinides: americum and curium (1944), berkelium and californium (1949). Later discoveries were einsteinium (1952), fermium (1953), mendelevium (1955), and nobelium (1957).
See also: Element; Physics.

Sea cow, any of an order (*Sirenia*) of tropical, herbivorous, aquatic mammals. Probably evolved from a marsh-dwelling ancestor related to the elephant, all serenians are completely seal-like with forelimbs modified into flippers and hindlimbs fused into the horizontal flukes of a whalelike tail. Genera include *Trichechus* (the manatee) and *Dugong* (the dugong).

Sea cucumber, any of a class (*Holothuroidea*) of sea animal of the echinoderm group, which also contains sea urchins and starfish. The leathery, flexible, cucumber-shaped animals grow up to 3 ft (1 m) in the tropics but are smaller in cooler waters. Tentacles around the mouth of the sea cucumber are used to catch food, and suction disks on the tube feet along the body provide locomotion. The animal can eject internal organs to distract attackers, regenerating these organs later.

Sea elephant *See:* Seal.

Sea fan, colony of coral animals called polyps (genus *Gorgonia*) common to shallow, warm waters of the Atlantic and Pacific oceans. The tiny, cylindrical polyps grow together in a flat, treelike form 2-24 in (5-60 cm) across. Coloration commonly ranges from yellows to reds to purples.

Sea gull *See:* Gull.

Seahorse, small marine fish of the Syngnathidae family (genus *Hippocampus*) found mostly in tropical waters, the head and forepart of which strongly resemble the head and neck of a horse. The seahorse is generally under 6 in (15 cm) long, with a body covered with bony plates and a long prehensile tail used to anchor the fish to plants. The female lays eggs in a pouch on the underside of the male, where they are fertilized and mature until they are released as live young.

George Segal (1924) placed life-sized gypsum sculptures in real-life surroundings. The contrast between reality and imitation has an alienating effect. *Restaurant Window*, 1967, Walfraff-Richartz Museum, Köln.

The seahorse (*Hippocampus*) swims in an upright position propelled by a dorsal fin, which beats about 35 times each second.

Seal, stamping device with an inscription or emblem in relief or cut into its surface, used to make impressions in wax, paper, or other materials, for certification or authentication of documents. 'Seal' also refers to the impression made, as well as to the proprietary design itself.

Seal, fin-footed mammal of the order Pinnipedia, which includes both the sea lions (family *Otariidae*) and the true seals (*Phocidae*). True seals have no external ears and have a thick coat of strong guard hairs. Seals are animals of the colder seas of both

S

S

hemispheres. Northern species (subfamily *Phocidae*) include the bearded seal, the gray seal, and the common, or harbor, seal. Southern species (subfamily *Monachinae*) include the monk seals, elephant seals, crabeater, and Weddell seals. Most seals are gregarious; all live on the open seas and many go ashore only to breed. A single, light-colored pup is born, and further mating takes place immediately afterward. Males form harems of females on the breeding grounds. Many species are now endangered, having been extensively hunted for their skins and meat.

Sea level, increase of, sea level change caused by an increasing temperature as a result of global warming, among other things. The IPCC, the Intergovernmental Panel on Climate Change, has stated that the sea level has risen 10 to 25 cm between 1900 and 2000, as a result of global warming. The rise between 2000 and 2100 is estimated to be around 50 cm.
See also: Greenhouse effect; Environmental pollution.

Sea lily, delicate, deep-sea echinoderm (class *Crinoidea*) shaped like a plant. It is related to the starfishes. Its body has a skeleton of chalk and consists of a stalk with five arms at one end. The arms branch repeatedly so that the animal has a feathery appearance and is often called the feather star. The largest star lily is 2 ft (61 cm) long, but 70-ft (21-m) fossils have been found. They used to be thought rare, but now they are sometimes dredged up by the ton.

Sealing wax, wax once used for sealing letters and still used for taking impressions from seals and for sealing bottles. Sticks of sealing wax, originally made of beeswax, turpentine, and coloring, are held over the material to be sealed and heated by a flame. The wax drips onto the paper or other surface; an impression can be made in the drops before they cool and harden.
See also: Wax.

Sea lion, fin-footed seal (family *Otariidae*) differing from the true seals in having external ears and an almost hairless body. Sea lions are found in the northern Pacific Ocean and oceans of the Southern Hemisphere.

The South American sea lion (*Otaria byronia*) lives in the ocean and along the shores of South America and the Falkland Islands.

Males may measure between 6 and 10 ft (1.8 and 3.0 m). They are active marine carnivores, feeding on fishes, squids, and other mollusks.

Sealyham terrier, short-legged dog originally bred in 19th-century Wales for hunting small burrowing animals. The terrier is of sturdy build, about 11 in (28 cm) tall and 23-25 lb (10-11 kg), with a large head and strong jaws. Its wiry coat is white, sometimes with darker markings around its head.

Sea onion *See:* Squill.

Sea otter (*Enhydra lutris*), marine mammal of the weasel family that lives near shores in the North Pacific Ocean. The animal averages 4-5 ft (1.2-1.5 m) and 60-85 lb (27-39 kg), and is covered with a thick, soft brown fur that insulates it against cold. It swims on its back, paddling with its hind feet, the pup carried on the chest of the female, sleeping in masses of kelp. Sea otters dive to a depth of 180 ft (55 m) for food, consisting of shellfish and other sea animals. They eat on their backs, breaking open shells by pounding them together. Sea otters have been hunted for their fur since the 1700s; a 1911 treaty saved them from extinction.

Search warrant, in law, court order issued to give law officers the authority to enter and search private premises for evidence, persons, contraband goods, or illegal equipment, such as counterfeiting machinery. 'Unreasonable searches and seizures' are forbidden in the Fourth Amendment to the U.S. Constitution, and the scope of such a warrant is severely limited.

A sea otter, *E. lutris*, whose diet comprises of mainly clams and mussels, cracks open a shell on a rock that it has placed on its chest.

Sea serpent, in myths and legends from many parts of the world, large, snakelike sea animal. Sea monsters of various description appear in ancient myths of the Middle East. Sightings of sea serpents, especially in the North Atlantic, have been common but have never been confirmed by material evidence. It is thought that what have appeared to be sea serpents have actually been giant squid, masses of seaweed, schools of porpoises, and other natural phenomena. The Loch Ness Monster is a similar freshwater creature thought to inhabit a lake in northern Scotland.

Seashore, land at the edge of a sea, alternately submerged and exposed by the tides. This land-water environment produces a rich variety of life forms. Tiny plankton (animals and plants floating in the tides) are the basis of shore life, both as larvae for shore animals and as food near the bottom of the food chain. The mollusks, sponges, and other animals that feed on plankton serve as food for shorebirds and other larger animals. Rocky seashores provide surface for seaweeds, mussels, sea urchins, and other organisms to attach themselves. Tide pools left by retreating tides shelter fish and other aquatic animals. Sandy shores are less hospitable, but some clams and crabs can make their home in the loose sand. Where protected bays create muddy shores and sea water mixes with fresh river water, plants thrive and crabs and turtles are common.

Season, one of several divisions of the year, characterized by cyclical changes in the predominant weather pattern. In the temperate zones there are four seasons; spring, summer, autumn (fall), and winter. These result from the constant inclination of the earth's polar axis as the earth orbits the sun: during summer in the Northern Hemisphere the North Pole is tilted toward the sun; in winter, when the solar radiation strikes the hemisphere more obliquely, it is tilted away from the sun. The summer and winter solstices (about June 21 and Dec. 22), popularly known as midsummer and midwinter, mark the beginnings of summer and winter, respectively. Spring begins on the day of the vernal equinox (about Mar. 21) and autumn at the autumnal equinox (about Sept. 23).

Sea squirt, any of a group of marine animals (class *Ascidiacea*), also known as ascidians, that squirt water when squeezed. The sea squirt's body is enclosed in a jelly-like coat; there are two openings, at the top and side, from which the water squirts. When the sea covers it, the sea squirt takes water in through one opening sieving off minute food particles. The waste water is passed out of the other opening. Sea squirts are found alone or in clusters, sometimes with individual animals joined together. Each sea squirt is both male and female; in the larval stage it looks like a tadpole.

SEATO *See:* Southeast Asia Treaty Organization (SEATO).

Seattle (pop. 520,000), largest city in Washington, situated on hills between Elliott Bay (Puget Sound) and Lake Washington; seat of King County. Seattle is the financial, cultural, commercial, industrial, and transportation center of the Pacific Northwest. Its chief industries are aerospace production, steel, shipbuilding, food processing, and chemicals. Settled in 1852, Seattle rapidly expanded with the coming of the railroad, the 1897 Alaska gold rush, and following the boom created by World War II. Its port is important in trade with Asia and serves as the main connection with Alaskan oil. This scenic city has a thriving recreational industry and is a cultural hub for theater, music and art. Seattle, host of the 1962 World's Fair, still boasts the landmark Space Needle, a 600-ft (183-m) structure built for the fair.

Sea urchin, any of a class (*Echinoidea*) of spiny marine animals related to the starfish and the sand dollar, occurring worldwide. The basic structure of the sea urchin is a sphere of 20 columns of calcareous plates, the 'test,' within which the gut, gonads, and water-vascular system are looped around the inside wall. The center of the sphere is empty. The test bears tubercles and short spines, and pedicellaria-pincer-like organs that clear the surface of detritus. Tube feet protrude through pores in the test, arranged in double rows down the sides.

Seaweed, algae found around coasts from the shore to fairly deep water. Most common are the brown algae, or wracks. Some, such as bladderwrack, clothe the rocks between tides; others live up to 40 ft (12m) deep. The large brown algae (kelps) sometimes form thick beds of long, tangled fronds, with

tough, well-anchored stems. Gulfweed is another widespread species. Delicate green and red seaweeds live mainly in rock pools. Seaweeds provide oxygen through photosynthesis. Some seaweeds also provide food and shelter for sea animals, and many are used for food, fertilizer, iodine, and gelatin.

Sebastian, Saint (d. A.D. 288), early Christian martyr. Stories about him are mostly legends. According to these legends, Sebastian joined the Roman army with the intention of helping Christians. He became popular with Emperor Diocletian, who made him a military commander. When his religious faith was discovered, Sebastian was tied to a tree and shot with arrows. Left for dead, he recovered only to be captured later and put to death in the Roman amphitheater. Scenes of his martyrdom were popular subjects of early Italian painters. His feast day is January 20.

Sebastopol *See:* Sevastopol.

Secession, the withdrawal of part of a country or state from the central government's control. The withdrawal may be carried out peacefully or violently. Political conflicts that lead to secession are usually based on economic, cultural or religious differences. In the United States history the term generally refers to the withdrawal of the Southern states from the Union in 1860-1861.

Second, measurement of time and angles in the metric system. In time, 60 seconds make up 1 minute; 60 minutes make up 1 hour. In measuring angles, 60 seconds make up 1 minute and 60 minutes make 1 degree. According to the standard established by use of an atomic clock, a second is defined as 9,192,631,770 times the vibration of radiation from a cesium atom.
See also: Metric system.

Secretary bird (*Sagittarius serpentarius*), tall bird of prey of the dry African plains. It nests in trees but is the only predatory bird to hunt on the ground, using its long legs to stalk and stamp on snakes and other prey. Standing over 40 in (1 m) tall, it is mostly

S

gray above and black below, with a red or orange face. The black feathers that stand out from the back of its head resemble quill pens, thus its name.

Secretion, complex substance produced in certain cells or glands in the body and discharged into or expelled from the body; also, the process of forming and discharging the substance. External secretions, those released through ducts from the exocrine glands onto an internal or external surface of the body, include tears, mucous, sweat, bile, saliva, and pancreatic juice. Internal secretions, or hormones, are released from the endocrine glands directly into the blood or lymph and effect processes distant from the point of origin. These include thyroxine, insulin, epinephrine, androgens, and estrogens.

Security Council *See:* United Nations.

Sedative, any of several drugs that reduce anxiety and induce relaxation without causing sleep. Many are also hypnotics, drugs that in adequate doses may induce sleep. Barbiturates, among the earlier drugs used in sedation, have fallen into disfavor because of addiction, side-effects, dangers of over-dosage, and the availability of safer alternatives. Benzodiapezines (e.g., Valium, Librium), classified as minor tranquilizers, are now used more often.
See also: Barbiturate.

Sedge, any of a family (*Cyperaceae*) of grasslike plants found in damp places worldwide in temperate regions. They have triangular, flattened or cylindrical stems, and the leaves arise from sheaths that enclose the stem. The flowers are in clusters grouped in a spikelet. True sedges have triangular stems. Some are used for making matting. Other sedges include the bulrushes (genus *Scirpus*), cotton grass (genus *Eriophorum*), and papyrus (*Cyperus papyrus*).

Sedimentary rock, one of three main rock classes of the earth's crust; the others are igneous rock and metamorphic rock. Sedimentary rocks consist of weathered fragments of rock transported usually by water and deposited in distinct strata. They may also be of organic origin, as in coal and some

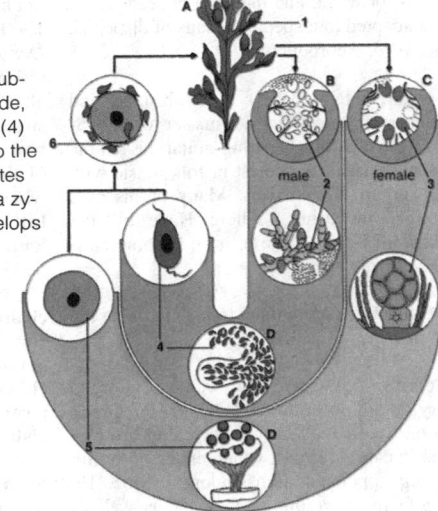

Unlike many other types of brown algae, rockweed, or Focus (A), has a life cycle that includes sexual reproduction. The reproductive organs are formed at the swollen ends of branches, within fertile areas called receptacles (1). Separate hollow chambers, or conceptacles (B, C), give rise to (2) antheridia (male) and (3) oogonia (female), which eventually burst (D) while submerged by the tide, releasing sperm (4) and eggs (5) into the water. The gametes fuse (6) to form a zygote, which develops into a new adult plant.

S

Sedimentary rocks are composed of layers of sediment, or small particles, derived from rocks. The particles are compressed by the weight of overlying materials into solid rocks. (A) A special class of rocks, called tephra, results from the compaction of ashes and rock fragments ejected by volcanoes. (B) Limestone, a second basic type of sedimentary rock, results from the deposition of eroded products (1) of coral reefs and of the shell and skeleton remains (2) of warm-seawater organisms. (C) Evaporation of seawater (3) from enclosed ocean bays results in deposits of various chemical salts, or evaporites

(4). Repeated formations of barriers and closures of basins (5) lead to a succession of such deposits. (D) Most sedimentary rocks are formed by deposition of matter from rivers, discharging into the sea along continental shelves. Coarse particles (6) are deposited first, followed by fine sand particles (7) and mud particles and clay (8).

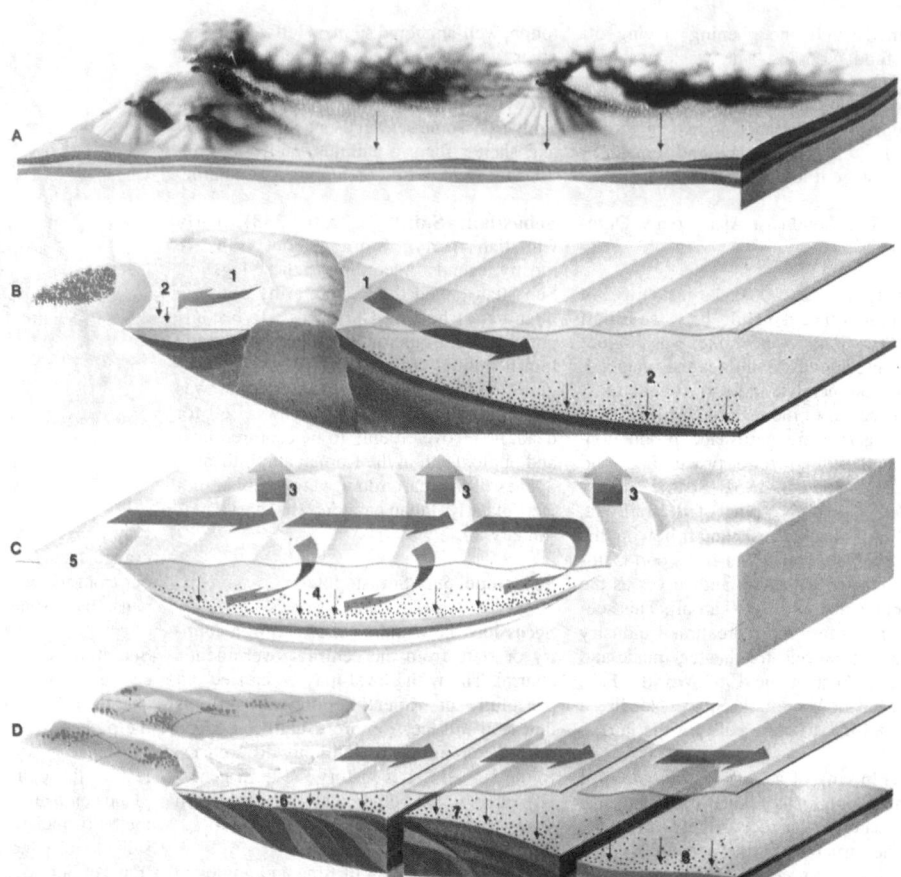

organic limestone, or they may be formed by chemical processes, as in the evaporites. About three-quarters of the earth's land area and most of the ocean floor are covered by sedimentary rock. Most common are shale, sandstone, and limestone. Sedimentary rocks frequently contain fossils as well as most of the earth's mineral resources.

Sedition, incitement of the violent overthrow of the government. During World War I Congress passed sedition and espionage acts that banned communications attacking the U.S. government. In appealing convictions under these acts to the U.S. Supreme Court, defendants claimed a violation of their freedom of speech and press. The Court paid some attention to Justice Oliver Wendell Holmes's 'clear and present danger' test but gave more weight to the 'evil intent' of the defendants and, without exception, upheld their convictions.

Sedum, genus of succulent plants of the Crassulaceae family. Sedums are native to the temperate zone and tropical mountains of the Northern Hemisphere. Low-grading sedums are planted as ground and rock cover. Sedums are also called stonecrops and live-forevers.

See, Holy *See:* Pope.

Seed, mature reproductive body of angiosperms and gymnosperms (seed-bearing plants). It also represents a resting stage that enables plants to survive through unfavorable conditions. Seeds develop from the fertilized ovule. Each seed is covered with a tough coat called a testa, and contains a young plant or embryo. In most seeds three main regions of embryo can be recognized: a radicle, which gives rise to the root; a plumule, which forms the shoot; and one or two seed leaves, or cotyledons, which may or may not be taken above ground during germination. Plants that produce one seed leaf are called monocotyledons and those that produce two, dicotyledons. The seed also contains enough stored food to support embryo growth during and after germination. It is this stored food that is of value to animals. Flowering plants produce their seeds inside a fruit, but the seeds of conifers lie naked on the scales of the cone. Distribution of seeds is usually by wind, animals, or water, and the form of seeds is often adapted to a specific means of dispersal. *See also:* Reproduction.

Seeger, Pete (1919-), U.S. folksinger and conservation activist. A master of the 5-string banjo and 12-string guitar, he led the 1950s revival of interest in folk music with his group the Weavers. Many of his own songs, including 'Where Have all the Flowers Gone?' (1961), have become classics of folk music.

Seeing Eye dog, animal trained to guide the blind.

Seferis, George (real name, Giorgos Stylianou Seferiades; 1900-1971), Greek poet. Studied law, began thereafter a diplomatic career (1924), which ended with him being appointed ambassador in 1962. He wrote many volumes of poetry as well as several long poems in which he told of his great love for his country, both the old and the new Greece, but which he hardly ever saw because he spent most of his time abroad. Became national poet. Because he openly criticized the regime of the colonels, his death was officially ignored, but his burial led to a large demonstration for freedom and democracy. In 1963 he was the first Greek ever to receive the Nobel Prize.

Segal, George (1924-2000), U.S. sculptor. He is best known for his life-size white figures, resembling plaster casts of his subjects, placed in natural settings, such as a doorway or behind a steering wheel.

Seghers, Anna (real name, Netty Reiling; 1900-1983), German writer. Her first book *Der Aufstand der Fischer von St. Barbara* (1928), about a revolt of Breton fishermen, already gave an early indication of her strong social engagement. When Hitler took power in 1933 she became an active member of the Communist Party, and fled to Paris where, as a representative of the 'Exile Literature', she worked on the emigrant journal *Neue Deutsche Blätter*. Seghers settled in East Berlin in 1947 and played a leading role in the cultural life of the GDR as chairperson of the German Writers League. Her best work is considered to be *The Seventh Cross* (1942). The novel *Transit* (1944) also became very well-known. Her postwar work is written in the style of socialist realism.

Sego lily, one of the mariposa lilies (*Calochortus nuttallii*) native to the dry areas of western North America. Its long stems (18 in/46 cm) grow from corms and bear narrow leaves and large 3-petaled flowers. The white petals are marked with yellow-green, purple, or lilac, with a purple spot at the center. The Mormon settlers in Utah used the edible corms as food. The sego lily is Utah's state flower.

Segovia (pop. 58,000), town in Spain, northwest of Madrid, capital of the province of the same name, 3,275 ft (998 m) high. (prov. 2,684 sq mi (6,949 sq km); pop. 147,200). Center of agricultural area trading in ceramics, foodstuffs and luxury goods. Town renowned for its architecture, its castle and city walls, and many remains from the Roman era and the Middle Ages, including the richly decorated Late Gothic cathedral (mid-16th century), a Roman aqueduct (119 arches), an alcazar (14th century), and many churches and palaces. Established as a military settlement by the Romans, who helped to develop Segovia with their wool trade.

Segovia, Andrés (1893-1987), Spanish classical guitarist, most celebrated of modern players. He did much to revive serious interest in the guitar, transcribing many pieces for it. Manuel de Falla, Heitor de Villa-Lobos, and others have composed works for him.

Segregation, separation of people according to race, religion, or ethnic origin. Custom or law may restrict the group's place of residence, use of public facilities and institutions, employment, movement, ownership of property, marriage, and the exercise of citizenship. Segregation has occurred throughout history and in most multiracial societies, especially those in which one group has seized or attained social, economic, and political dominance. In the United States from the early 1800s to the mid-1900s, laws required blacks and whites to use separate public facilities. This is known as *de jure* (by law) segregation. From the mid-1950s on, several Supreme Court decisions were made and federal laws passed that forbade segregation in voting, education, and the use of public facilities, and prohibited job discrimination in federally funded programs. While legal reforms and social patterns have made racial segregation less common in the world, it has not been eradicated. *De facto* segregation-segregation passed along through customs, not laws-actually increased in the mid-1900s and was one of the main causes of the race riots of the 1960s and early 1980s.

Seiche, standing wave that occurs in a lake, bay, or similar basin. A seiche is most often started by wind or a change in air pressure, and sometimes by an earthquake or ocean swell, that suddenly alters the basin's surface. While the surface regains stability, a simple harmonic wave is set in motion along the length of the basin. This wave is reflected by the basin's walls, creating interference. The repeated reflections produce a standing wave, a wave having fixed points with no vertical motion, with a wavelength equal to twice the length of the basin. Lasting a few minutes to an hour, seiches can interfere with shipping, damage property, and imperil lives.

Seifert, Jaroslav (1901-1985), Czechoslovakian poet who was awarded the 1984 Nobel Prize for literature. His early work concentrated on revolutionary themes. *City in Tears*, his first book of poems, was published when he was 20.

Seigneurial system, feudal system of landholding practiced in France and in the French colonies in eastern Canada. Beginning in the early 1600s, the French king granted land in Canada to nobles, religious groups, merchants, and military officers. The *seigneury*, often narrow strips of land touching the St. Lawrence River, generally covered 12-100 sq mi (31-259 sq km). The owners, or *seigneurs*, rented the land to farmers in return for an annual payment, a share of the harvest, and several days' free labor. The seigneurs and tenants provided the king with military service and contributed material and labor to such works as the building and maintenance of public roads. The seigneurial system at first spurred French settlement of Canada, but it later proved an impediment to industrialization and urban expansion. The system was abolished by the Canadian government in 1854.
See also: Feudalism.

Seine River, France's principal waterway. Rising on the Langres Plateau 18 mi (29 km) northwest of Dijon, it winds 475 mi (764 km) northwest to Paris, where over 30 bridges span it, through Rouen and Normandy, to the English Channel. It is the main artery of a far-reaching river system converging on Paris. Canals link it to the Loire, Rhône, Rhine, and Schelde rivers.

Seismograph, instrument used to detect and record seismic waves caused by earthquakes, nuclear explosions, etc.; the record it produces is a seismogram. The simplest

seismograph has a horizontal bar, pivoted at one end with a recording pen at the other. The bar, supported by a spring, bears a heavy weight. As the ground moves, the bar remains roughly stationary owing to the inertia of the weight, while the rest of the equipment moves. The pen traces the vibrations on a moving belt of paper. Seismographs are used in seismic prospecting.
See also: Richter scale.

Seismology, branch of geophysics concerned with the study of earthquakes, seismic waves and their propagation through the earth's interior. Seismologists use seismographs to detect the location and severity of earthquakes and to locate oil and minerals.
See also: Geophysics.

Selangor (pop. 2,289,000), Malaysian state on the mainland, bordering on the Strait of Malaya 3,073 sq mi (7,956 sq km). Capital: Shah Alam. Cultivation of pineapple, tea, cocoa, coconuts; rubber extraction. Mining: tin and coal. Became an independent state in the 18th century; British protectorate in 1874.

Selassie, Haile *See:* Haile Selassie.

Selective Service System *See:* Draft, military.

Selene, in Greek mythology, goddess of the moon, called Luna in Roman mythology. At night, her crescent-shaped crown shining gold, she drove a 2-horse chariot across the sky. She figures in magic rituals held at the full and new moons. There are few myths about her and her relationship to the other Greek gods and goddesses is unclear. Helios, the sun god, was her brother, or possibly her father. She was the daughter of Hyperion and Theia or Zeus and Leto. Some Greek writers added to the confusion by

Geologists often use seismometers to locate mineral deposits and oil and gas reservoirs. (A) A hole is bored in the ground with a special drill assembly (1), and a dynamite blast (2) is set off, creating seismic waves. The shock waves (3) are reflected from various rock layers, they travel at different speeds, and reach the seismometer, or geophone detectors (G0-G4), at different times. The geophone signals are recorded on an instrument truck (4). Graphs (B) of wave travel time and distance are plotted from velocity data (V0, V1, V2), obtained from seismometer charts (5), and are used to calculate the structure and depth of underground rock strata. Depth profile charts (6) are then drawn to yield a visual representation of subsurface rock structure.

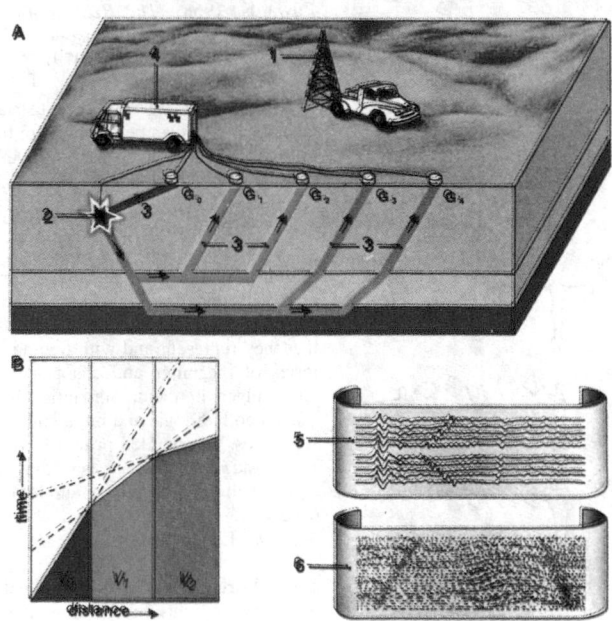

S

identifying Selene with Artemis, a goddess also associated with the moon.
See also: Mythology.

Selenga, river in Mongolia and Russia; 982 mi (1,580 km). Source in Changajn Nuruu, flowing into the Lake Baykal delta. Navigable from May to October from Süchbaatar, where it is joined by the Orkhon.

Selenium, chemical element, symbol Se; for physical constants see Periodic Table. Selenium was discovered by Jöns J. Berzelius in 1817. It occurs in nature in the minerals crooksite and clausthalite. It is obtained commercially from the anode muds left from electrolytic copper refining, from which selenium is prepared by roasting with soda or sulfuric acid. Selenium is a lustrous gray metalloid which exists in several allotropic forms. It can be amorphous or crystalline. The most stable form is the crystalline hexagonal form. Selenium is an essential trace element for humans, however selenides resemble arsenic in their extreme toxicity. Selenium and its compounds are used in photocells, light meters, solar cells, rectifiers, special glasses, and xerography.

Seles, Monica (1973-), American tennis player of Yugoslavian descent, won the French Open championship in 1990 at the age of 16, becoming the youngest winner ever of a Grand Slam tournament. She went on to win the Open championships of Italy (1990), France (1991, 1992), the U.S. (1991, 1992), and Australia (1991, 1992, 1993). She also won the Masters tournament in 1990, 1991 and 1992. The run of victories was interrupted in 1993 during a tournament in Hamburg when she was stabbed in the back by a supporter of Steffi Graf. Seles did not return to the international circuit until the second half of 1995, when she celebrat-

ed her comeback by winning the Canadian open title. The left-handed Seles is known for powerful strokes accompanied by a characteristic groaning. In 2000 she won the Open championship of the U.S..

Seleucid dynasty (312-64 B.C.), dynasty in southwestern Asia, founded by Seleucus I (c.358-354 B.C.-218 B.C.). A general under Alexander the Great, Seleucus gained control of the eastern part of the Macedonian empire following Alexander's death (323 B.C.). The Seleucids came to rule the area between what is now Turkey and India. In the 200s B.C., the Parthians overran their eastern lands. In the 100s B.C., the Romans began to take over their western regions and brought the dynasty to a close with the occupation of Syria (64 B.C.). The Seleucids helped to spread Greek culture to western Asia.

Seljuks, members of the ruling family of Ouz Turkmen tribes. The warlike and nomadic Seljuks originated in Turkestan, in central Asia, and were named for Seljuk, their first leader. The Seljuks invaded western Asia in the mid-11th century. By 1092 they controlled most of Iran and all of Mesopotamia, Syria, and Palestine. But the Seljuks' territory soon was splintered into small states, one of which, in Anatolia, gave rise to the Ottoman Turks and the modern Turkish state. During the Crusades of the 11th, 12th, and 13th centuries, the Islamic Seljuks defended the Holy Land against the European Christians.

Sellers, Peter (1925-1980), English comedian and actor, real name Richard Henry Sellers. Master of disguise, accents and caricature. Became famous for his participation in the radio program *The Goon Show*. From 1951 onwards he acted in various films, including *The Ladykillers* (Alexander MacKendrick, 1955), *The Mouse That Roared* (1959), *Lolita* (after Nabokov; Stanley Kubrick, 1962), *What's New, Pussycat?* (1965), the James Bond parody *Casino Royale* (1967), *The Party* (Blake Edwards, 1968), *The Return of the Pink Panther* (1975), *The Prisoner of Zenda* (1979), and *Being There* (1979).

Selye, Hans (1907-1982), Austrian-born Canadian physician best known for his work on the physiological effects of environmental stress, which he suggested might cause certain diseases.
See also: Physiology.

Semantics, study of meaning, concerned both with understanding the relationship of words and symbols to the ideas or objects that they represent and with tracing the histories of meanings and changes that have taken place in them. Semantics is thus a branch both of logic and linguistics. General semantics, propounded primarily by Alfred Korzybski, holds that habits of thought have lagged behind the language and logic of science.
See also: Linguistics.

Semaphore, system of visual signaling using flags or lights to represent letters and

numbers. The first such system was introduced by Claude Chappe (1763-1805) used 5-10 mi (8-16 km) apart. Semaphore is still used for signaling between ships and on some railroads.

Semarang (pop. 1,249,000), city on the Indonesian island of Java on the Java Sea, capital of the Jawa Tengah province. Port; export of sugar, copra, kapok and tobacco; shipbuilding, textile and electrical industries. The harbor is not protected from the northwest monsoon. Archbishop's seat and university; airport.

Semiconductor, solid with an electrical conductivity that lies between the high conductivity of metals and the low conductivity of insulators. A semiconductor device is an electronic element fabricated from crystalline materials, such as silicon or germanium, that in the pure state, are neither good conductors nor good insulators and are unusable for electronic purposes. When certain impurity atoms, such as phosphorus or arsenic, are diffused into the crystal structure of the pure metal, the electrical neutrality is upset, introducing positive or negative charge carriers.

Seminole, last Native American tribe to make peace with the U.S. government. Seminole formed in Florida out of an alliance including refugee Creek from Georgia, native Apalachee and runaway slaves. They fought Andrew Jackson's troops in 1817-1818 while Florida was still a Spanish territory. The major Seminole War began in 1835 when the U.S. government ordered their removal to west of the Mississippi. A fierce guerrilla war against overwhelming odds ended in 1842, after which most Seminoles were moved to Oklahoma. However, a small band held out in the Everglades until 1934, when they agreed to a settlement.

Semiramis, mythical Assyrian queen who supposedly founded the city of Babylon. Born of the union of a Syrian youth and a fish goddess, she was raised by doves. She married King Ninus of Assyria, and became queen when he died. During her long reign, she conquered Persia and Egypt. She was overthrown by her son and became a dove. Her story may be based on the life of Sammuramat, regent of Assyria (810-805 B.C.).
See also: Babylon.

Semites, in the Old Testament, the 'sons of Shem' (who was the son of Noah). The term now generally applies to speakers of Semitic languages, including ancient Akkadians, Babylonians, Assyrians, and Phoenicians and modern Arabs and Israelis.
See also: Old Testament.

Semitic languages, group of the Hamito-Semitic language family found in the Near East and North Africa. Most of the group is now extinct; extant members include Hebrew, Arabic and Maltese. A few were written in cuneiform, but most used alphabets. Most of the letters of the Latin alphabet have descended from the North Semitic al-

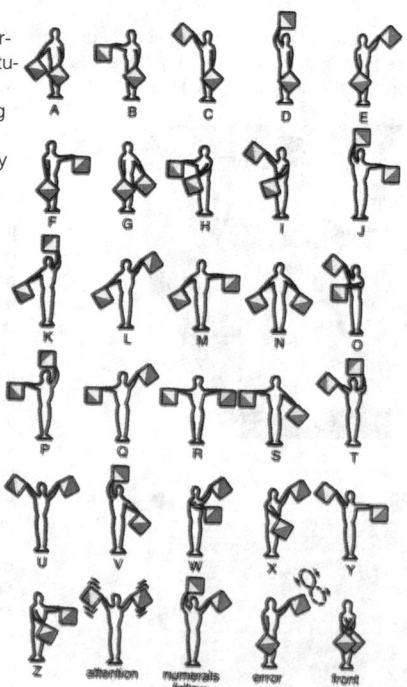

The alphabet, numerals, and basic punctuation symbol of the semaphore signaling system adopted for use by the U.S. Navy are indicated.

phabet, the first fully formed alphabetical writing system.

Semmelweis, Ignaz Philipp (1818-1865), Hungarian obstetrician. He was the first doctor to use antiseptic methods in childbirth, after his discovery that puerperal fever was transmitted by obstetricians who had failed to thoroughly clean their hands after performing autopsies on mothers who had died of the disease and then had made examinations of living mothers.
See also: Obstetrics.

Semper, Gottfried (1803-1879), German architect and architecture historian. His style changed from classicism to neo-renaissance. Considered to be the founder of modern theatre design. Most important works: the opera building in Dresden (1838-1841), rebuilt after the fire in 1869 (1871-1878) and after WW II (1945-1971); in Vienna, Burgtheater (1874-1888), Art History and Natural History Museum (1872-1881) and Neue Hofburg (1881-1908). Influential theoretician; published *Über die formelle Gesetzmässigkeit des Schmuckes und dessen Bedeutung als Kunstsymbol* (1856).

Semprun, Jorge (1923-), Spanish-French writer and Spanish minister of culture (1988-91). Writer of often autobiographical novels and of political screenplays for such well-known directors as Resnais, Costa-Gavras and Losey, in the films *La Guerre est finie* (1966), *Z* (1968), and *Les Routes du Sud* (1978) respectively. As the son of a republican diplomat, Semprun had to go into exile. He arrived in Paris in 1937 and joined the communist resistance after the Germans occupied the city. In 1943 he was sent to the Buchenwald concentration camp but survived: after the liberation he returned to Spain, where he became one of the leaders of the Communist Party. In 1964 he was forced out because of his criticism of Stalinism, and moved to Paris where he became an independent writer. His works include *The Long Voyage* (1963), *The second death of Ramon Mercadet* (1969), *What a beautiful Sunday!* (1980), and *Literature or Life* (1994).

Sen, Amartya (1933-), Indian economist. Was awarded the Nobel Prize for economics in 1998 for his contribution to the welfare economy. Currently lives in Cambridge, England. He wrote various books, including *Collective Choice and Social Welfare* (1970), *On Economic Inequality* (1973), *Poverty And Famines* (1981), and *On Ethics and Economics* (1987).

Sen, Mrinal (1923-), Indian film director. His films often deal with personal or domestic problems in a modern India divided by contradictions. A big success, also internationally, was *Mr. Shome* (1969). He also made *Night's End* (1956), *The Wedding Day* (1960), *Chorus* (1974), *The Man with the Axe* (1978), *The Ruins* (1983), and *Genesis* (1986).

Senate, the state council of ancient Rome, made up of members of the nobility and other leading families. Although predominantly an advisory body, the Senate became the leading government body during the time of the Republic. The 300 senators were elected for life to create a continuity that would counterbalance the constant change in the magistracy, magistrates being appointed for one year only. In the civil war (1st century B.C.) the Senate became less influential; in the time of the emperors the Senate had no power at all. The name Senate has since been used to describe government bodies in various countries throughout history: for example, in the Late Middle Ages all Italian city states had Senates. In modern democracies where the parliament has two chambers, it is often the name used for the chamber that is made up of notables or of representatives from constituent states (in the American Congress), or from other regional bodies or interests (e.g. in France and Belgium).
See also: Congress of the United States.

Sendak, Maurice (1928-), U.S. illustrator and author of children's books whose inventive renderings both delight and startle. His works include the Caldecott Medal winners *Where the Wild Things Are* (1963) and *In the Night Kitchen* (1970). His lively art became known to a wider public in the 1980s through his stage sets for operas, including *Così fan tutte.*

Sender Garcés, Ramón José (1902-1982), Spanish writer, one of the most important novelists of the 20th century. The theme of his work is the struggle of the solitary individual against elements that threaten to alienate him from what is most dear to him. Much of his work has an historical background. Well-known novels: *Imán* (1929), *Míster Witt en el cantón* (1935), *Contraataque* (1938), *El lugar del hombre* (1939), *Epitalamio del prieto Trinidad* (1942), and *Requiem por un campesino español* (1960).

Seneca, Native American tribe (*O-nondowanagh*, 'people of the great hill') of western New York and eastern Ohio, once the largest nation of the Iroquois League (5 tribes that banded together in the 1400s). Today most Seneca live on 3 reservations in western New York; they make up the Seneca Nation (a republic) and the Tonawanda Band of Seneca (ruled traditionally by chiefs).

Seneca, Lucius Annaeus (4 B.C.?-A.D. 65), Roman statesman, philosopher, and writer. As Nero's tutor, he restrained the worst excesses of the young emperor. Writing in highly rhetorical, epigrammatic style, Seneca advocated stoicism in his *Moral Letters*, essays, one masterly satire, and nine bloody, intense tragedies. After implication in a conspiracy, he was commanded to commit suicide.
See also: Nero; Rome, Ancient.

Senefelder, Alois (1771-1834), German lithographer. He invented the process of lithography in Munich when he inked and printed some wax crayon marks he had made on a stone slab (c.1796). He published a history of the method in 1818. Senefelder was also a playwright.
See also: Lithography.

Senegal

Capital:	Dakar
Area:	75,955 sq mi (196,722 sq km)
Population:	10,590,000
Language:	French, Wolof
Government:	Presidential republic
Independent:	1960
Head of gov.:	Prime minister
Per capita:	US$ 1,580
Monetary unit:	1 CFA franc = 100 centimes

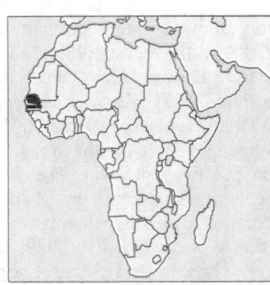

Senegal, Republic, westernmost country in Africa, formerly part of French West Africa. *Land and climate.* Bordering on the Atlantic Ocean, Senegal is flanked on the north by Mauritania, on the east by Mali, and on the south by Guinea and Guinea Bissau. The small independent country of Gambia cuts deeply into southern Senegal from the Atlantic coast, forming a long, narrow enclave along the Gambia River. Senegal has an area of 75,955 sq mi (196,722 sq km). The country is mostly plain, with the semi-desert Ferlo area in the northeast and savanna grassland elsewhere. In the north, the Senegal River has a broad flood plain which is cultivated. The south is drained by the Gambia, Casamance, Sine, and Saloum rivers. The coastline is sandy in the north and muddy in the south. Climate varies, but is relatively cool along the coast most of the year. Inland temperatures are much higher, especially in the northeast.
People. The people are black African, the most numerous ethnic groups being the Wolof, Fulani, Serer, Toucouleur, and Diola peoples. More than 90% of the people are Muslim. Dakar, the capital, is a modern port city. The official languages are French and Wolof.
Economy. The majority of the people are employed in agriculture, the mainstay of Senegal's economy. Peanuts are the major crop, and peanut processing is the leading industry. Senegal's industrial sector is growing. Limestone and phosphates are important mineral exports, and oil and natural gas deposits have yet to be exploited.
History. Parts of Senegal were within the medieval empires of Ghana, Mali, and Songhai. Under French control and part of French West Africa from 1895, Senegal became part of the Federation of Mali from 1959 to 1960, but declared independence in

S

During the 1970s, the government of Senegal greatly encouraged the growing of vegetables.

1960. Léopold S. Senghor, a leading African Nationalist, was elected president. Famine, resulting from persistent drought, marked the 1970's. At the end of 1980, Senghor resigned from the presidency and retired (he deceased in 2001). He was succeeded by Abdou Diouf, who was reelected in 1988. In 1981 Senegal helped the president of Gambia put down a coup. The following year Senegal and Gambia united in a loose confederation called Senegambia; the confederation was dissolved in 1989. In 1991 however, Gambia and Senegal signed a treaty of friendship in which they agreed on economic and military cooperation. In the 1990s Diouf had to deal with a secession movement in Casamance. In 1991 there were border conflicts between Mauritania and Senegal. But relations improved in 1992.

In 2001, a peace agreement was concluded with the separatist movement in Casamance. That same year, the first female President was elected in the history of the country; Mame Madior Boye, who was succeeded by Idrissa Seck in 2002.

Senghor, Léopold Sédar (1906-2001), Senegalese statesman and poet, Senegal's first president (1960-1980), and first black member of the French academy (1984). He became known for his philosophy of *négritude*, a concept of socialism incorporating black African values and rejected the French policy of assimilation.
See also: Senegal.

Senility, general mental and physical deterioration often (but not always) seen in the elderly. Because the term refers to several conditions and causes, experts on the elderly avoid using it. Failure of recent memory, dwelling on the past, episodic confusion, and difficulty in absorbing new information are common conditions associated with so-called senility. Permanent damage can be caused by the brain diseases multi-infarct dementia and Alzheimer's disease.
See also: Alzheimer's disease; Geriatrics.

Senna (*Cassia marilandica*), perennial plant of which the leaves are used for medicinal purposes. Senna is an effective laxative when combined with other herbs.

Senna, Ayrton (1960-1994), Brazilian racing car driver, made his debut in Formula 1 in 1984 in a Lotus, and promised to have a great career ahead of him from his very first race. In 1988 he won his first world title in a McLaren-Honda, and won again in 1990 and 1991. Senna drove in 161 Grand Prix races (of which he won 41) and was one of the most experienced drivers in Formula 1. He died when his Williams-Renault car crashed during the San Marino Grand Prix on 1 May 1994. Senna received an official state funeral that was attended by hundreds of thousands of people.

Sennacherib (d.681 B.C.; r.704-681 B.C.), Assyrian king who succeeded his father, Sargon II. Sennacherib's reign was characterized by war. He put down a revolt by the Elams and the Babylonians led by Merodach-Baladan, the former Babylonian king (703 B.C.). He defeated Egypt and, except for Jerusalem, crushed revolts in Syria and Palestine (701 B.C.). He again fought Babylon and razed the city in 689 B.C. He made Nineveh the Assyrian capital and a magnificent city. Sennacherib was murdered by his sons.

Sennett, Mack (1884-1960), Canadian-born U.S. silent movie director-producer, a pioneer of slapstick humor on the screen. After working with D.W. Griffith, he formed his own Keystone Co. and made over 1,000 short subjects ('shorts') with his Keystone Kops, Bathing Beauties, and stars like Charlie Chaplin, W.C. Fields, and Gloria Swanson.

Senses, media through which stimuli in the environment of an organism act on the organism (external senses); also, the internal senses, which report on the the internal state of the organism (through thirst, hunger, pain, etc.). The organs of sense-the eye ear, skin, etc.-contain specialized cells and nerve endings that communicate with centers in the nervous system. Sense organs may be stimulated by pressure (in touch, hearing, and balance), chemical stimulation (smell, taste), or electromagnetic radiation (vision, heat sensors).

Sensitive plant, small shrub (*Mimosa pudica*) of the pea family. Its leaves and stems curl toward the main stem when touched or exposed to fumes. The plant is native to the tropics of the Western Hemisphere and is grown in greenhouses.

Sensitivity training, technique using group discussion and interaction intended to increase one's awareness of self and others and how one behaves with others. Sensitivity training takes many forms and goes by many names: encounter group, T-group, human relations, and group dynamics training. The group has 8-20 participants. The leader, who is trained in psychotherapy, establishes a psychologically safe environment and encourages participants to speak frankly about their feelings and each other, but remains neutral and outside the discussion. The participants choose the topics and direct the discussion. They examine their reactions to each other and test new ways to communicate. The goal of sensitivity training is to develop trust and improve communication and intrapersonal behavior. The techniques of sensitivity training have been applied to education and to training businesspeople. Sensitivity training was developed at the Esalen Institute, Big Sur, Calif., and was popular in the 1960s.

Seoul (pop. 11 million), or Kyongsong, capital, largest city, and industrial and cultural center of South Korea, on the Han River, 25 mi (40 km) east of Inchon, its seaport. It was founded in 1392 as capital of the Yi dynasty, and remained so until 1910. Seoul changed hands several times in the Korean War and suffered great damage. Largely built, it has grown rapidly. The 1988 Summer Olympic Games were held in Seoul.

Separation of powers, political theory developed by Montesquieu from his studies of the British constitution, arguing that the arbitrary exercise of government power should be avoided by dividing it between distinct departments: the executive, legislature, and judiciary. This was a basic principle of the Founding Fathers in producing the U.S. Constitution; legislative powers were vested in Congress, judicial powers in the Supreme Court and subsidiary courts, and executive powers in the president and his governmental machinery. Each branch was to have its functions, duties, and authority, and in theory no branch could encroach upon another. In practice there has always been a degree of necessary overlap. The legislature can oppose and impeach members of the executive, the president can veto legislation, and the Supreme Court can adjudicate the actions of the other branches; its members, in turn, are presidential appointees subject to congressional approval. In U.S. history one branch has always tended to dominate others for long periods, but this 'checks and balances' ensures that power can and does shift between them.
See also: Montesquieu.

Separatists, in religion, English Christian congregations that sought independence from the state and Established Church, beginning in 1580 with the Norwich Brownists. John Robinson led refugee Separatists in Leyden, the Netherlands, who were later prominent among the Pilgrims.

Sepoy Rebellion, or Indian Mutiny, mutiny of Sepoys (Hindi, 'troops') in the Bengal Army of the East India Company. It began at Meerut, near Delhi, in May 1857 and spread over northern India. The immediate cause was the issuing of cartridges greased with the fat of cows (sacred to Hindus) and pigs (unclean to Muslims), but the underlying cause, years of increasing British domination, led to a general revolt that was not suppressed until Mar. 1858. As a result, the British government took over the rule of India.
See also: India.

September 11, 2001, on September 11, 2001, the United States were subjected to a number of terrorist attacks. Within a short period of time, two hijacked passenger planes crashed into the two towers of the World Trade Center in New York, which collapsed shortly after. A third passenger plane

penetrated the Pentagon in Washington, while a fourth hijacked aircraft crashed 81 miles (130 km) south of Pittsburgh. Approximately 3,100 people were killed. Although no one claimed responsibility for the attacks, Osama bin Laden, leader of al-Qaida, to whom the attacks on the American embassies in Kenya and Tanzania were also attributed, became the main suspect. President Bush declared war on international terrorism. The Taliban regime in Afghanistan was summoned to extradite Bin Laden. Almost every country (with exceptions, such as Iraq) sided with the United States and its coalition against international terrorism. Bush also gave orders to freeze all financial assets of Bin Laden and al-Qaida. On October 7, 2001, the United States and the United Kingdom started bombing the Afghan bases and military targets.
In December 2001 the Taliban regime toppled, and Bin Laden fled.
See also: New York City; Osama bin Laden; Taliban; World Trade Center; Bush, George W.

Septicemia *See:* Blood poisoning.

Septuagint, oldest Greek translation of the Hebrew Old Testament, probably from an older source than any now extant. The Pentateuch was translated in Alexandria at the behest of Ptolemy II (250 B.C.), according to legend by 70 scholars (hence the name *septuagiht*, Latin for 'seventy'). It was completed, including the Apocrypha in 130 B.C.
See also: Old Testament.

Sequoia, genus including the two largest trees, the redwood (*Sequoia sempervirens*) and the giant sequoia (*Sequoiadendron giganteum*), both found only in the Pacific Northwest of the United States. Only the bristlecone pine lives longer. The largest living organism in the world is the General Sherman giant sequoia in Sequoia National Park, which is over 270 ft (82 m) high with a circumference at the base of over 100 ft (30.5 m).

Sequoia National Park, park in south-central California (administered with the adjacent Kings Canyon National Park), established in 1890 to preserve the groves of giant sequoia. It covers 402,482 acres (162,879 hectares). Lying in the southern Sierra Nevada, it includes Mount Whitney, the highest U.S. peak outside Alaska.

Serapis, Egyptian god, worshipped also in Greece and Rome. He ruled the underworld and the universe and was lord of the Nile. He was a source of fertility and healing and gave the oracles speech. The god may have derived his traits and name from the more ancient gods Osiris and Apis. Osiris was also a fertility god, ruled the underworld, and associated with Isis. Apis was the earthly form of Osiris. The Ptolmaic rulers of Egypt (323-330 B.C.) built temples to Serapis and encouraged his worship.
See also: Mythology.

Serbia, Balkan state. The Serbs were Slavs who settled the Balkans from the 600s onward. Stephen Nemanja (r.1168-1196) created the first united kingdom, which became a great empire under Stephen Dushan (r.1331-1355), but after the battle of Kosovo (1389) Serbia remained under Turkish rule until independence was restored in 1878. After World War I occupation by Austria, it became the core of the kingdom of Yugoslavia. After 1992 it formed the Federal Republic of Yugoslavia together with Montenegro. Serbia (34,00 sq mi/88,060 sq km) is mountainous and mainly agricultural. Its capital is Belgrade.
See also: Yugoslavia, Federal Republic of.

Serbia and Montenegro *See:* Yugoslavia, Federal Republic of.

Serf, medieval peasant generally bound to the land. A serf held the lowest status in the feudal hierarchy and owed allegiance, service, and often certain payments to the lord. The serf retained a number of hereditary rights that were usually determined by local custom. With the development of a money economy and the growth of towns, many serfs escaped or purchased their freedom, and by the 18th century serfdom had largely died out. In Russia and parts of eastern Europe, however, forms of serfdom survived into the 19th century.
See also: Manorialism.

Sergeant at arms, officer who preserves order in a legislative, judicial, or social organization. The sergeant at arms has the power to execute commands, such as serving legal papers, and to require the body's members to attend meetings. Anyone who disregards the sergeant at arms is guilty of contempt. Each house of the U.S. Congress has a sergeant at arms. The office of sergeant at arms is believed to have been instituted by Richard I of England.

Series, in mathematics, sum of a sequence of terms (numbers or algebraic expressions). The terms in a sequence have a specific relationship and order based on how the terms are formed. The series may be finite (with a definite sum), or infinite. As more terms from an infinite series are added, the sum may approach a value called the limit. Series with a limit are said to converge; those without a limit diverge. Mathematicians have devised formulas and notations to express the values of a series and individual terms in a series.
See also: Mathematics.

Sermon on the Mount *See:* Beatitudes; Golden rule.

Serpentine, hydrous magnesium silicate mineral, $Mg_3(Si_2O_5)(OH)_4$, that occurs in 2 forms: chrisotile, the fibrous variety which is the primary source of asbestos, and antigorite, the flaky variety. Serpentine, usually green, may also be black, red, yellow, gray, or white. It is used as an indoor building or decorative stone or as a gemstone. Serpentine is widely distributed and is quarried in Quebec, the USSR, South Africa, and the United States.

Serum, clear yellowish fluid that separates from blood, lymph, and other body fluids when they clot. It contains water, proteins, fat, minerals, hormones, and urea. Serum therapy involves injecting serum (obtained from humans or horses) containing antibodies (globulins) that can destroy particular pathogens. Occasionally injected serum gives rise to an allergic reaction known as serum sickness; a second injection of the same serum may induce anaphylaxis (hypersensitivity).
See also: Gamma globulin; Plasma.

Serval (*Felis capensis*), large, black spotted, nocturnal wildcat of Africa. It has long legs, a small head, and pointed ears. Its prey is mainly rodents and sometimes birds, reptiles, or insects.

The serval, *F. capensis*, is a large African cat that is quick enough to catch birds that have already taken flight.

Servetus, Michael (Miguel Serveto; 1511-1553), Spanish theologian and physician whose religious work *Christianismi restitutio* (1553) contains the earliest known description of the pulmonary circulation of blood. As a theologian, Servetus antagonized Roman Catholics and Protestants alike by denying the doctrines of the trinity (*De trinitatus erroribus*, 1531), transubstantiation, and original sin. He eventually embraced pantheism, believing that a supreme intelligence orders the universe. He was tried for heresy by the Inquisition (1553) and condemned to death, but escaped from prison. Passing through Geneva, Switzerland several months later, Servetus was arrested on the orders of John Calvin, retried, and burned at the stake.
See also: Inquisition.

Serviceberry, also called shadbush, shadblow, or Juneberry, wild rose tree or shrub found in many parts of North America and in the Mediterranean region and eastern Asia. It bears clusters of small white flowers and blue fruits.

Service industries, commercial, government, or nonprofit occupations performed without involving the sale of commodities. Service industries may be classified as several types: business services, including advertising, bookkeeping, or banking; personal services which might include recreation, travel, housekeeping, and beauty or barbershops; art, including theaters and museums; the professions, including legal, medical, or educational services; and government. Economists consider service occupations an indicator of a country's economic development: the greater the growth, the more advanced the nation. In the late 1950s services accounted for 25% of the U.S. gross national product, and in the 1980s for 66%.

S

A Sunday Afternoon on the Island of La Grande Jatte (1884-86) is the most impressive of the few large paintings painstakingly executed by Georges Seurat. Seurat's theoretical system, which he called divisionism and which is also called pointillism, is seen in the small dots of pure color and the precise geometrical composition (Art Institute of Chicago).

S

Servomechanism, or feedback control system, automatic device that detects and corrects errors and maintains constant performance of a mechanism, for example an automatic pilot.
See also: Automation.

Sesame (*Sesamum indicum*), tropical plant cultivated mainly in China and India for its flat seeds; also, the seeds themselves. Sesame seeds yield an oil used as a salad or cooking oil and in margarine, cosmetics, and ointments. The residue left after oil extraction is used as a cattle feed and fertilizer.

Sesshu (1419-1506), Japanese Buddhist monk and landscape artist. Combining Chinese ink-painting technique with Japanese aesthetics, Sesshu's style is characterized by strong composition, straightforward forms, and vigorous brushstrokes. He produced his greatest works, including screens, scrolls, and religious paintings, after 1469, following a period of study in China.

Sessions, Roger (1896-1985), U.S. composer, winner of the Pulitzer Prize for music (1982). He was professor of music at the University of California, Berkeley (1945) and Princeton University (1935-1945, 1953-1965). Sessions's compositions include operas, symphonies, piano sonatas, and chorus music. He is best known for *The Black Maskers* (1923) and *Concerto for Orchestra* (1981). His written works include *The Musical Experience of Composer, Performer and Listener* (1950) and his collected essays, *Roger Sessions on Music* (1979).

Seth, or **Set**, in Egyptian mythology, god of evil, represented with an ass's head and a pig's snout. Originally a royal deity, he came to personify evil as killer of Osiris, god of goodness. Osiris's son Horus fought and killed Seth.
See also: Mythology.

Seth, Vikram (1952-), poet, novelist and travel writer. After he finished his studies in India, he attended universities in England and the U.S., and finally settled in California. He studied Chinese economy, and in 1983 was awarded the Thomas Cook Prize for his controversial *From Heaven Lake: Travels through Sinkiang and Tibet.* Poetry lovers learned to appreciate him for *The Humble Administrator's Garden* (1985), and even more for his Californian novel in verse *The Golden Gate* (1986), styled after Pushkin's *Eugene Onegin. A Suitable Boy* (1993) was a huge novel (1349 printed pages) about four families and more than 30 characters in India during the early 1950s, centered around the search for a suitable husband for a Hindu student who falls in love with a Muslim. *An Equal Music* was published in 1999. This book is about the members of a string quartet.

Seti I, Egyptian ruler of the 19th dynasty who reigned about 1303-1290 B.C. Seti I established his seat of government at Memphis and directed several military campaigns into Syria against the Hittites. He built his mortuary temple at Abydos in the Valley of the Kings and continued work on the temple of Amon at Karnak. Seti I was the father of Ramses II.

Setter, 3 breeds of long-haired dog used in bird hunting: the English, the Gordon, and the Irish setter. Classified in the United States as sporting dogs, setters are derived from the medieval setting spaniel. They have long heads and tails, silky coats, and hanging ears. A setter is trained to locate game by smell, come to a point with its nose directed toward the bird, and retrieve the game after the shot.

Set theory, branch of mathematics or symbolic (mathematical) logic in which systems are analyzed by membership in and exclusion from *sets*. A set is any specified collection of *elements* or *members*. In the notation of set theory, members of a set are enclosed in braces as, {a,b,d,x}. Alternatively, a rule defining inclusion in the set may appear in braces. The expression {xx is a U.S. state bordered by 3 or more other states} defines the set of all U.S. states bordered by 3 or more other states; this is a *finite set*, having a definite number of members. The set of all positive even numbers is an example of an *infinite set*, one with an infinite number of members. It might be represented as {2,4,6,8,...} or as {xx/2 is an integer greater than 0}. *Null sets*, those with no members (e.g., all U.S. presidents who are female, nonwhite, or non-Christian) are represented as { }. Sets that have exactly the same members (the set of all U.S. presidents who have served more than 2 terms, the set of all presidents crippled by polio) are said to be *equal sets*, while those with the same number of members but not necessarily the identical membership are *equivalent*. Set A is a *subset* of set B if all of the members of set A are contained in set B. (The set of all equal sets is thus a subset of the set of all equivalent sets, but not vice versa). The *union* of 2 sets A and B (A B) is the combined membership of those 2 sets. The *intersection* of sets A and B (A ... B) is the set of those elements belonging to both set A and set B. *Disjoint* sets have no common members and thus their intersection is a null or empty set (the set of all women, the set of all U.S. presidents). If A is a subset of B, the *complement* of A consists of all members of B not in A. Set theory, which owes much to the techniques of symbolic logic established by 19th-century English mathematician George Boole, was developed by 19th-century German mathematician Georg Cantor. It is of particular importance in representing logical relationships and approaches to algebraic solutions.
See also: Mathematics.

Seurat, Georges (1859-1891), French painter, one of a small group representing neoimpressionism or postimpressionism. Interested in color both scientifically and artistically, he invented pointillism, in which discrete points of color are placed to create patterns that are perceived at a distance as complex tones. His works include *A Sunday Afternoon on the Island of La Grande Jatte* (1884-1846).
See also: Impressionism.

Seuss, Dr. (Theodor Seuss Geisel; 1904-1991), U.S. author-illustrator of children's books. His many imaginative verse tales-*Horton Hears a Who* (1954), *How the Grinch Stole Christmas* (1957)-and humorous pictorial fantasies are tremendously popular. In 1984 he was acknowledged by the Pulitzer committee for having contributed for nearly half a century to the education and reading enjoyment of U.S. children.

Sevastopol (pop. 361,000), Black 'Sea port of the Crimea peninsula in Ukraine, southeast Europe. Now an industrial city, and railroad terminal with lumber milling and shipbuilding industries, the city suffered long sieges in the Crimean War (349 days; 1854-1855) and World War II (8 months; 1941-1942). During the Soviet period there was a major naval base. Sevastopol is situated near the site of the ancient Greek colony Chersonesus, founded in 421 B.C. It eventually became part of the Roman Empire (first century B.C.) and Byzantine Empire (4th century A.D.).

Seven Cities of Cibola *See:* Cibola, Seven Cities of.

Seven seas, archaic collective term for the world's large bodies of water. The term is usually thought to refer to the Arctic, Antarctic, North and South Atlantic, Indian, and North and South Pacific oceans.

Seventh-day Adventists, Christian religious group, organized in 1863 in both Europe and the United States, who believe that Christ will return in person. They observe the Sabbath on Saturday, the seventh day of the week. There are about 2 million members in 150 countries.
See also: Christianity.

Seven Weeks' War (Austro-Prussian War, June 16-August 23, 1866), conflict between Austria (and its German allies), led by Field Marshal Lieutenant von Benedek, and Prussia (and its Italian ally) under Helmuth Karl von Moltke, over control of the Danish duchies of Schleswig and Holstein. Austria declared war on Prussia on June 14, 1866, and the decisive battle was fought July 3 at Königgrätz in Bohemia, resulting in a Prussian victory. The war ended formally on Aug. 23 with the Treaty of Prague. It gave Prussia undisputed leadership of the new North German Confederacy, effectively ending Austrian influence in German affairs.

Seven Wonders of the Ancient World, seven magnificent structures of the ancient world, as listed by Greek scholars. The oldest and only to survive are the pyramids of Egypt. The others were the Hanging Gardens of Babylon, the 30-ft (9-m) statue of Zeus at Olympia, the great temple of Artemis at Ephesus, the mausoleum at Halicarnassus, the Colossus of Rhodes, and the Pharos lighthouse of Alexandria.

Seven Years' War (1756-1763), war between Austria, France, Russia, Saxony, Sweden (from 1757), and Spain (after 1762) on the one side and Britain, Prussia, and Hanover on the other. In the United States the struggle centered on colonial rivalry between Britain and France, and formed part of the French and Indian Wars. In Europe the main dispute was between Austria and Prussia for supremacy in Germany. Austria's Maria Theresa aimed to recover Silesia (lost in the War of the Austrian Succession). This provoked Prussia to attack Saxony and Bohemia. Although severely pressed, the Prussians avoided complete defeat. By the treaties of Hubertusberg and Paris (1763), Britain emerged as the leading colonial power and Prussia as a major European force.

Severini, Gino (1883-1966), Italian painter; joined the futurists in 1910. Later worked as a cubist, then a neoclassicist, and then again as a cubist. Wrote *Du cubisme au classicisme* (1921).

Severn, River, Britain's longest river, 220 mi (354 km) long. It rises in eastern Wales and flows east and south into the Bristol Channel. The Severn Bridge is one of the world's longest suspension bridges.

Seville (pop. 715,000), city of southwest Spain, capital of Seville province, and an important industrial center and port on the Guadalquivir River. Seville produces tobacco, machinery, and perfume, among other products, and exports wine and olives. The city is famous for its historic buildings, including the Gothic cathedral (1401-1519), and Holy Week processions. It was the birthplace of the painters Diego Velázquez and Bartolomé Murillo.
See also: Spain.

Sèvres, Treaty of (1920), peace pact between the Allies and Turkey after World War I, signed at Sèvres, France. It redistributed almost all of the Turkish Ottoman Empire, leaving only Istanbul and Anatolia under Turkish control. Though signed by the representatives of Sultan Mohammed VI, the treaty was never ratified by the Turkish National Assembly. After the overthrow of the government by Kemal Atatürk and the nationalists (1922), the Treaty of Sèvres was superseded by the Treaty of Lausanne (1923), which offered Turkey more acceptable terms.
See also: World War I.

Sewage, liquid and semisolid wastes from dwellings and offices, industrial wastes, and surface and storm waters. Sewage systems collect the sewage, transport and treat it, then discharge it into rivers, lakes, or the sea. Vaulted sewers had been developed by the Romans, but from the Middle Ages until the mid-19th century sewage flowed through the open gutters of cities, constituting a major health hazard. Later sewage was discharged into storm-water drains that were developed into sewers. Because the dumping of large amounts of untreated sewage into rivers led to a serious water pollution, modern treatment methods arose, at least for major cities. An early solution (still sometimes practiced) was sewage farming, in which raw sewage was used as fertilizer. Noting that natural watercourses can purify a moderate amount of sewage, sanitary engineers imitated natu-

ral conditions by allowing atmospheric oxidation of the organic matter by the activated-sludge process, in which compressed air is passed through a sewage tank, where the sludge is decomposed by the many microorganisms that it contains. A by-product is sludge gas, chiefly methane, burned as fuel to help power the treatment plant. Sedimentation is carried out before and after decomposition; the filtered solids are buried, incinerated, or dried for fertilizer. Dwellings not connected to the sewers have their own septic tanks.

Sewing, use of a needle and thread to attach, repair, fasten, or decorate fabric or other materials. Sewing dates from the second Stone Age period, when stone or bone needles and hair or animal ligament thread were used to stitch pieces of skin together. Sewing now may be accomplished by hand or machine. The most basic hand-sewing stitches are basting, running, slipstitch, blindstitch, overcast, and catch stitch. Isaac Merritt Singer, improving on earlier inventions, produced the first sewing machine practical for home use (1851). Singer's machine used a top thread with a bobbin thread, allowing continuous stitching. Modern machines commonly provide 3 types of stitches: straight, zigzag, and embroidery. Mechanical sergers can sew, trim, and finish straight seams in a single operation.

Sewing machine, machine for sewing cloth, leather, or books. There are two main types: chainstitch machines, using a needle and only one thread, with a hook that pulls each looped stitch through the next, and lockstitch machines, using two threads, one through the needle eye and the other interlocking with the first in the material, from a bobbin/shuttle system. Chain-stitch machines-the first to be invented, by Barthélemy Thimmonier (1793-1859)-are now used chiefly to make sacks or bags. The lockstitch machines now in general use are based on the one invented by Elias Howe

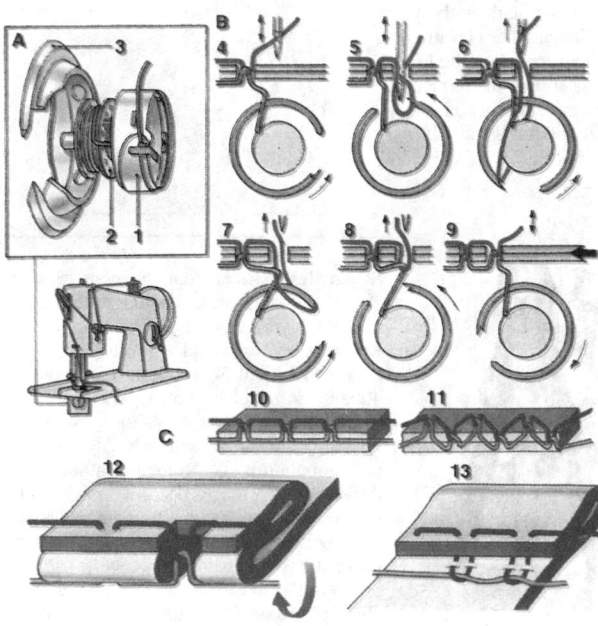

The modern sewing machine is driven by an electric motor. The movements of the needle arm and the bobbin (A) are synchronized and driven by the motor. A stitch is formed with the thread from both the needle and the bobbin. The bobbin case (1) surrounds the bobbin (2) in a housing (3) that rotates beneath the sewing table. (B) First, the needle descends (4) through the cloth, and as the needle rises, it forms a loop (5). This loop passes around the bobbin (6) and surrounds the bobbin thread (7). As the bobbin rotates, the loop slips off (8), and the stitch is tightened around the cloth by the thread take-up lever. When the needle is above the cloth, the fabric feed advances the cloth, and another stitch begins (9). (C) The lock stitch (10) and the zigzag stitch (11) are standard stitches. The hemming stitch is also shown (12 and 13).

S

(1846). Isaac M. Singer invented the foot treadle and the presser foot (1850), which holds the fabric down. Zigzag machines differ from ordinary straight-stitch machines in having variously shaped cams that move the needle from side to side. Almost all U.S. machines are electrically powered, but foot-treadle machines are common elsewhere.

Sex (sexual behavior), term covering a wide range of behavior derived from or analogous to sexuality and sexual drive. To the psychologist 'sex' and 'sexual behavior' are used in connection with human drives linked to reproduction, including fantasies, sensations, etc. To the psychoanalyst, sexual behavior has its roots in infantile sexuality as well as instinct.

Sex education, study of human sexuality and how it is acquired and expressed. Sex education begins in early childhood when children first show curiosity about their sexuality and body processes. Until the mid-20th century, satisfaction of that curiosity was solely a function of a child's parents, and information from outside the family was discouraged. Today children may receive sexual information from their peers, the media, churches, or schools and rely less on traditional sources. Sex education has generated controversy between those who believe that home sex education may be inadequate and those who believe it may encourage pre-marital sex or fail to teach moral responsibility. Many sex education curricula are available to schools and other agencies, beginning with programs for kindergarten and continuing through high school. They cover aspects of human sexuality including social, physical, and psychological aspects, rudimentary anatomy, marriage, and parenthood.

Sextant, instrument for navigation, invented in 1730, superseding the astrolabe. The sextant is named for its shape ($1/6$ of a circle). A fixed telescope is pointed at the horizon, and a radial arm bearing a mirror is moved against an arc graduated in degrees. The mirror reflects an image of a known star or the sun down the telescope to coincide with the image of the horizon. The angular elevation of the star, with the exact time, gives the latitude. The air sextant is a similar instrument, usually periscopic, designed for use in aircraft; it has an artificial horizon, generally a bubble level.
See also: Navigation.

In order to measure the angular distance between the sun and the horizon, the sextant is held in a way that the horizon can be seen through the telescope (1). The index, or movable arm (2), and the attached mirror (3) are rotated, so that the image of the sun is reflected through the darkened glass (4) into the half-silvered mirror (5), until the sun is aligned with the horizon. The angle is read on the limb, or calibrated arc (6) of the sextant.

The American poet
Anne Sexton (1928-74).

Sexton, Anne (1928-1974), U.S. poet. Her work was largely confessional and explicitly personal (*To Bedlam and Part Way Back*, 1960; *Live or Die*, 1966, Pulitzer Prize). *Transformations* (1971) is her ironic retelling of Grimms' fairytales. Sexton struggled with mental illness, ultimately committing suicide.

Seychelles

Capital:	Victoria
Area:	175 sq mi (454 sq km)
Population:	80,000
Language:	Creole
Government:	Presidential republic
Independent:	1976
Head of gov.:	President
Per capita:	US$ 7,600
Monetary unit:	1 Seychelles rupiah = 100 cents

Seychelles, African republic consisting of about 85 islands in the Indian Ocean 1000 mi (1600 km) east of Kenya. Part of the British Commonwealth. Seychelles's total area is 175 sq mi (454 sq km) scattered over 400,000 sq mi (1 million sq km) of ocean. The climate is tropical. Victoria, on Mahé Island, is the capital and only city. Most of the population is Roman Catholic, of African and French descent, and speaks Creole, a French patois. Tourism, construction, agriculture, and fishing are the primary occupations. Cinnamon, coconuts and copra, vanilla, livestock, and poultry are the chief products. Portuguese explorer Vasco

da Gama discovered Seychelles (1502), and French planters began colonizing the area in 1768. Britain controlled the islands from 1794 to 1976, when they achieved independence. In 1977 France-Albert René was elected President. He wanted to guide the economy in a more centralist and socialist direction and declared the country a single-party state. The 1980s were characterized by political instability. However, René's government managed to survive several coups. The single party government was replaced by a multi-party government in 1991. In 2001, René was re-elected for the 5th time. The Seychelles provides good health care and good education, which is rare for an African country.

Seymour, Jane (1509?-1537), third wife of England's Henry VIII (from 1536). She died soon after the birth of her son, Edward VI.

Seyss-Inquart, Arthur von (1892-1946), Austrian Nazi leader, governor of Austria (1938-1939), and deputy governor of Poland (1939-1940). As a high commissioner for the Netherlands (1940-1945), his cruelty was notorious. He was executed for war crimes.
See also: Nazism.

Shabuot *See:* Shavuot.

Shackleton, Sir Ernest Henry (1874-1922), Irish explorer who commanded 3 Antarctic expeditions (1907, 1914, 1921), the first of which came within 97 mi (156 km) of the South Pole and located the south magnetic pole. His 1914 expedition was marked by an open-boat crossing from Elephant Island to South Georgia Island and a winter traverse of that island's crest after his ship was crushed by ice. Written works include *Heart of the Antarctic* (1909), *South: The Story of Shackleton's 1914-1917 Expedition* (1919), and *Adventure* (1928).
See also: Antarctica.

Shad, deep-bodied food fish of the herring family (genus *Alosa*), which grows to about 3 lb (1.4 kg) and 2 ft (61 cm). Native to Atlantic waters from Newfoundland to Florida, the shad was successfully introduced to Pacific waters (c.1871). Characterized by bluish coloring with silver sides and a spineless upper fin, it swims up freshwater rivers to spawn. Some shad is smoked and sold as kippers.

Shadow, reduction of light on an area caused when an opaque object interrupts the light source. The shadow appears on the side of the body away from the source; the brighter the light, the darker and crisper the shadow seems. A very dark shadow, called an umbra, occurs when the light is completely obstructed. A lighter area surrounding the umbra, called the penumbra, occurs when the light source is larger than the interrupting object, allowing some light to shine beyond it.

Shadow matter, in science, term to describe a theoretical form of matter that neither reflects nor absorbs light and interacts with ordinary matter only through the force of grav-

ity. The existence of shadow matter (a type of dark matter) has not been proved, but physicists theorize that as much as 90% of the mass of the universe may be comprised of this kind of invisible particle.
See also: Dark matter.

Shaftesbury, 3 important English earls, each bearing the name **Anthony Ashley Cooper**. The **1st earl** (1621-1683) was a founder of the Whig Party and a staunch Protestant. After supporting both Cromwell and the Restoration, he became Lord Chancellor (1672) but was dismissed (1673) for supporting the Test Act. He then built up the Whig opposition to Charles II, supporting the duke of Monmouth, the pretender, and opposing James II's successor. He was acquitted of treason (1681) but fled to the Netherlands (1682). The **3rd earl** (1671-1713), grandson of the 1st, was a moral philosopher and pupil of John Locke. He aimed to found an ethical system based on an innate moral sense. The **7th earl** (1801-1885) was a politician and leading evangelical Christian who promoted legislation to improve conditions in mines and factories and supported movements for better housing and schools.

Shagari, Shehu (1925-), Nigerian politician. Shagari set up a cultural organization in 1949, out of which the Northern People's Congress (NPC) was formed in 1951. After he was elected to parliament in 1954, he occupied various government posts from 1962 to 1975. When the military took over power in 1975, Shagari temporarily retired from politics. As a candidate for the National Party of Nigeria (NPN), the successor to the NPC, Shagari won the presidential elections of 1979. In 1983 he was reelected president, and his NPN achieved an absolute majority in the Senate and the House of Representatives. However, at the end of that year his government was brought down by a military coup.

Shah (Persian, 'king'), title borne by the rulers of Middle Eastern and some Asian countries. It is used especially to refer to rulers of Iran (Persia) until 1979.

Shah Jahan (1592-1666), fifth mogul emperor of India (1628-1658), under whose rule the Moguls achieved their cultural peak. He built New Delhi and is best known for construction of lavish buildings, particularly the Taj Mahal (1632-1645) at Agra, a tomb for his wife, Mumtaz Mahall. He was deposed (1658) by his son Aurangzeb and imprisoned at Agra until his death.
See also: India.

Shah Namah *See:* Firdausi.

Shakespeare, William (1564-1616), English playwright and poet, considered the greatest dramatist ever as well as the finest English language poet.
Shakespeare was born of middle class parents in Stratford-upon-Avon where he spent his school years. At 18 years of age he married Anne Hathaway, with whom he had 3 children. In the years 1594 to 1608, Shakespeare was heavily involved in the

world of London theater as a stockholder and an actor in the Lord Chamberlain's Company-renamed the King's Men in 1603-which performed at the Globe Theater. He also wrote an average of 2 plays a year in this period, including several comedies and virtually all of his famous tragedies.
All of Shakespeare's plays have been grouped into 4 periods reflecting general phases of his artistic development. In the first period (1590-1594) he wrote comedies, histories, and tragedies. *The Comedy of Errors, Henry VI* (parts I, II, and III) *Richard III, The Taming of the Shrew, Titus Andronicus, The Two Gentlemen of Verona,* and *King John* were all written in the first period.
The second period (1595-1600) consists primarily of historical drama and romantic comedies. Included in this period are *A Midsummer Night's Dream, Richard II, Love's Labour's Lost, Romeo and Juliet, The Merchant of Venice, Henry IV* (parts I and II), *As You Like It, Julius Caesar, Much Ado About Nothing, Twelfth Night,* and *The Merry Wives of Windsor.*
Shakespeare's great tragedies were written in the third period (1601-1608). At the height of his artistry his writing now moved back and forth easily between verse and prose in portraying his characters. *Hamlet, All's Well That End's Well, Measure for Measure, Othello, King Lear, Troilus and Cressida, Macbeth, Timon of Athens, Pericles, Antony and Cleopatra,* and *Coriolanus* all were written in this period.
In the fourth and final period (1609-1613) Shakespeare wrote 3 comedies and a history. They are *Cymbeline, The Winter's Tale, The Tempest,* and *Henry VIII.*
Shakespeare began to write poems between 1592 and 1594 partly because poetry was considered to be of greater importance than drama by the Elizabethans. His 2 long narrative poems were *Venus and Adonis* (1593) and *The Rape of Lucrece* (1594).
The sonnets were probably written over a period of several years. The first 126 are addressed to a young nobleman and the next 26 to a young woman with whom Shakespeare may have been having a love affair. The common theme of the sonnets concerns the destructive effects of time, the quickness of physical decay, and the loss of beauty, vigor, and love. Although the poems celebrate life, they do so with a keen sense of death.
Shakespeare shaped and used language with great power. He invented, changed, and borrowed words from other languages and employed rhetorical devices such as alliteration and repetition to produce dramatic effect.
Shakespeare's plays and poems have been the subject of critics and scholars who have examined every aspect of the man himself, his works, and his influence. His works have long been a required component of liberal education. His brilliant portrayal of historical figures and events has caused many people to visualize the likes of Julius Caesar, Mark Antony, and Cleopatra not as they have been described in history books but as Shakespeare envisioned them.
Shakespeare was knowledgeable in a wide variety of subjects, including music, the law, the Bible, military science, the stage, art, politics, history, hunting, woodcraft, and

This engraving of Shakespeare by Martin Droeshout was the frontispiece for the First Folio edition.

S

sports. He displayed a keen sense of human nature with vivid characters, including kings, pickpockets, drunkards, generals, hired killers, and philosophers. His genius seems all the more amazing considering that as far as scholars have been able to determine, Shakespeare had no experience in any field other than theater.

Shakhlin, Boris (1932-), Russian gymnast, won his first medal (silver) in the world championships of 1954 (high bar). By the time his career had come to an end (1966) he had won a total of 19 gold, 10 silver, and 4 bronze medals at European championships, world championships and Olympic games, both in the individual competitions and in the team events. Shakhlin was always very concentrated, and was a master in practically all gymnastic events, possessing a flawless style.

Shale, fine-grained sedimentary rock formed by compaction and drying-out of mud (clay and silt). Shales are sometimes rich in fossils and are laminated (they split readily into layers, or laminae). Their metamorphism produces slate.

Shallot, edible hardy perennial (*Allium ascalonicum*) of the Liliaceae family, used in cooking. The plant has edible stems, bulbs, and leaves, and grows like garlic or onions. The bulb, composed of cloves attached to a common disk, is green, shading to lavender with a thick grayish skin. Shallots probably developed by cultivation as early as the 9th century.

Shamanism, primitive religious system centered around a shaman, or medicine man. (The word *shaman* is from the language of the Tungus of Siberia). In a trance state, he is believed to be possessed by spirits who speak and act through him; he is expected to cure the sick, protect the tribe, and foretell the future, among other mystical activities.
See also: Religion.

Shamir, Yitzhak (1915-), Prime Minister of Israel (1983-1992), successor to Menachem Begin. Born in Poland, he went to Palestine in 1935, where he joined the underground military organization Irgun Zvai Leumi and later the more radical Stern Gang in combating British rule. From 1955 to 1965 he worked for the Israel intelligence agency. As Foreign Minister (1980-1983), he was identified as a strong supporter of

S

Begin's policies. In 1984 and 1988 his Likud Party formed coalition governments with the Labour Party. Shamir was succeeded by Netanyahu. He had resigned when the Likud Party was defeated at the 1992 elections. *See also:* Israel.

Shamrock, popular name in Ireland for several leguminous plants, the trifoliate leaves of which were cited by St. Patrick as a symbol of the Christian Trinity. Among the plants called shamrock are the wood sorrel (*Oxalis acetosella*), white clover (*Trifolium repens*), and black medic (*Medicago lupulina*).

Shang dynasty, first historic Chinese dynasty, traditionally said to have lasted from 1766 to 1122 B.C. The legendary founder was T'ang. The Shang civilization was agriculturally and technically advanced and is famed for the artistic quality of its bronzes. *See also:* China.

Shanghai (pop. 13,700,000), China's largest city, in the southeastern region of Jiangsu province. It is a major seaport and a leading commercial and industrial center, producing textiles, iron and steel, ships, petroleum products, and a wide range of manufactured goods. In 1842 it was one of the first Chinese ports opened by treaty to foreign trade. Great Britain (1843), France (1849), and the United States (1862) gained concessions to develop the city, and most of it remained under foreign control until after World War II. The British and U.S. concessions were renounced in 1945. Shanghai is now China's film capital and the home of 190 research institutes, colleges, and universities. *See also:* China.

The commercial centre of Shanghai along the Winsung river.

Shankar, Uday (ca. 1900-1977), Indian dancer and choreographer. Shankar studied art at the Royal College of Art in London. In 1923 he began his dancing career with performances of Indian dance in European cities (including London, Vienna, Berlin and Budapest). For some time he was the partner of Anna Pavlova, with whom he went on tour in the U.S. Back in India he formed his own company with Indian dancers and musicians, and went on tour to cities like New York. In 1938 he founded an institute for research and teaching in ancient Indian dancing in Almora, and went on many tours with his pupils in Europe and the U.S. Shankar has contributed much to the knowledge of and interest in Indian dance.

Shannon River, chief river in Ireland and longest (240 mi/386 km) in the British Isles. It rises in northern Cavan county, Ulster, and flows south and west through several loughs (lakes) into the Atlantic Ocean. From Limerick westward, it is navigable by all but the largest vessels.

Shaped canvas, term for a painting in a shape and/or on a surface structure that is different than a traditional canvas.

Shapiro, Karl Jay (1913-), U.S. poet and literary critic. His early poetry, such as *V-Letter and Other Poems* (1944; Pulitzer Prize), shows the influence of W. H. Auden and was admired for its verbal conceits. Later work, such as *The Bourgeois Poet* (1964), became more Whitmanesque. His *Collected Poems: 1948-1978* appeared in 1978.

Shapley, Harlow (1885-1972), U.S. astronomer whose work on pulsating stars (Cepheid variables) and globular clusters established the position of the sun in the galaxy and the size of the Milky Way. Shapley discovered 2 star systems in distant galaxies and was director of the Harvard Observatory (1921-1952). Shapley's written works include *Star Clusters* (1930), *Galaxies* (1943), and *Cosmic Facts and the Human Response* (1957). *See also:* Astronomy.

Sharaku (fl. late 1700s), professional name of a Japanese woodcut artist known for color portraits of Kabuki actors, produced in 1794 and 1795. The actors, shown dressed for their roles, have enlarged heads and exaggerated expressions. The backgrounds are plain. Little is known about the artist.

Sharansky, Anatoly Borisovich (1948-), Soviet mathematician and political dissident. Jailed in 1974, he was sentenced in 1978 in Moscow to 13 years in a labor camp for anti-Soviet agitation, espionage, and treason. In 1986 he was released as part of a 'spy trade' and was welcomed in Israel as a hero. In 1996 he was appointed Minister of Industry and Trade.

Sharecropping, arrangement whereby a share of a tenant farmer's yearly land yield (usually 50%) went to the landowner in lieu of rent. The tenant provided the labor, while the landowner provided land, equipment, and often loans to buy seed. The system was notorious for its abuses.

Sharif, Nawaz (1949-), Prime Minister of Pakistan (1990-1993 and 1997-1999), President of the Islamic Democratic Alliance (IDA), a right-wing Pakistani coalition. He has shown special interest in accelerating Pakistan's economy while at the same time reducing the country's dependence on foreign aid. He served as Punjab's Finance Minister under former President Zia ul-Haq (1981). In February 1997 he was elected President for the second time. He was overthrown by a military coup and sentenced to life imprisonment on charges of hijacking and terrorism by a special court of justice in 1999.

Sharjah *See:* United Arab Emirates.

Shark, any of about 250 species of cartilaginous fishes of marine and fresh waters, order *Selachii*. Sharks, with the related rays and chimeras, have a skeleton formed entirely of cartilage rather than bone. Other distinguishing features are that the gills open externally through a series of gill slits, rather than through a single operculum, and reproduction is by internal fertilization, unlike that of bony fishes. The body is fusiform, and the upper lobe of the tail is usually better developed than the lower lobe. Sharks swim by sinuous movements of the whole body; there is no swim bladder, so they must swim constantly to avoid sinking. All are extremely fast swimmers and active predators. Despite a universal reputation for unprovoked attack, only 27 out of the 250 known species have been definitely implicated in attacks on humans.

Sharon, Ariel (1925-), Israeli soldier and prime minister (2001-). He became an officer in the army in 1948, and was chiefly concerned with combating Arab guerrillas. During the wars of 1967 and 1973 he distinguished himself by his actions at the Suez Canal. He then became active in politics and was appointed successively Minister of Agriculture (1977) and Defense (1981). Sharon is known to be a supporter of a hard line against the Arabs and is notorious for his policy of colonizing the West Bank. Sharon was held responsible for the mass murder of Palestinians in the Sabra and Chatila refugee camps in West Beirut (1982), and therefore had to resign as Minister of Defense, although he remained in the cabinet as minister without portfolio. In 1984 he became Minister of Trade and Industry, but resigned in 1990 in protest against the plans for elections in the occupied areas. In the new Shamir government he was Minister of Public Housing from 1990 to 1992. After the victory of Benjamin Netanyahu in the parliamentary elections of 1996, the right wing of the Likud party put pressure on the new Prime Minister to recall Sharon to the cabinet. Sharon joined the Netanyahu government as Minister of Infrastructure. In 1998 Sharon was appointed Minister of Defense. He became leader of the Likud party in 1999. In 2001, he became Prime Minister. The Israeli politics towards the Palestinians hardened, and it was not long before the violence escalated on both sides.

Shar-pei, dog of Chinese origin first bred from c.200 B.C. as a guard or fighting dog. The Shar-pei is characterized by a compact body, small flat ears, and a loose, wrinkled skin. It grows 16-20 in (41-51 cm) high and weighs 35-55 lb (16-25 kg). The coat is short, of a solid color, and may be tan, black, cream, or red.

Shavuot, Jewish holiday known as the Festival of Weeks, held on the sixth and sev-

enth days of the month of Sivan (May-June). Originally an agricultural celebration of the harvest, it was observed by presenting the season's first fruits and bread baked from the first wheat at the Temple in Jerusalem. Later it came to commemorate the receipt of the Ten Commandments.
See also: Passover.

Shaw, George Bernard (1856-1950), Irish dramatist, critic, and political propagandist whose witty plays contained serious philosophical and social ideas. Born in Dublin, he moved to London (after 1876), where he became a music and theater critic and a leader of the Fabian Society. He began writing his brilliantly witty, ironical, and polemical comedies in the 1890s. Success came with such plays as *Major Barbara* (1905), *Caesar and Cleopatra* (1906; written 1899), *Androcles and the Lion* (1912), and *Pygmalion* (1913; adapted as the musical *My Fair Lady*, 1956). He lost popularity for his opposition to World War I, but regained it with *Back to Methuselah* (1921). *Saint Joan* (1921), his greatest success, was followed by the 1925 Nobel Prize in literature.

Shawn, Ted (Edwin Meyers Shawn; 1891-1972), U.S. dancer, choreographer, and teacher. With his wife, Ruth St. Denis (1877-1968), he founded the Denishawn school and company. He led an all-male company of dancers (1933-1940), and in 1941 established an international dance center at Jacob's Pillow, in Massachusetts.

Shawnee, Native North Americans of the Algonquian language group. They settled in the Ohio Valley during the 18th century, hunting and cultivating maize. In 1811 the Shawnee chief Tecumseh attempted to unite the Native Americans of the region, but his plan failed when the Shawnee were defeated at Tippecanoe by Gen. William Henry Harrison's army. The Shawnee were eventually resettled in Oklahoma, where about 2,250 still live.

Shearwater, any of about 12 species of oceanic birds related to the petrel and the albatross. They are brown or dark gray, sometimes with a white belly, 10-26 in (25-66 cm) in length with long, slender wings. Shearwaters land only to reproduce, congregating in huge colonies on offshore islands and the rugged coasts of the Atlantic and Pacific oceans and the Mediterranean. They nest in burrows. The female lays one egg, and the chick is tended by both parents.

Sheeler, Charles (1883-1965), U.S. painter and photographer whose linear treatment of architectural forms, interiors, and industrial settings shows the influence of cubism. In 1913, six of Sheeler's paintings were shown at the New York Armory Show, the exhibition that first introduced European modernism to Americans. Among his paintings are *Upper Deck* (1929) and *American Interior* (1934).

Sheep, diverse genus of mammals best known in the various races of domestic sheep (*Ovis aries*), bred for both meat and wool. Wild sheep are a diverse group of mountain-dwelling forms with about 37 races alive today, divided into 2 large groups: the Asiatic sheep, which include the mouflons, urials, and argalis; and the American sheep, the thinhorns and bighorns. Asiatic sheep are long-legged, lightly built animals that prefer a gently rolling terrain. American-type sheep by comparison are heavyset and barrel-chested and characteristic of steep slopes and rocky areas, in part filling the role played in Europe and Asia by the ibex. Sheep are social animals; males usually form bands following a dominant ram, and females form separate parties following a mature ewe. The rams use their horns and the specially thickened bone of their foreheads for combat, not only when sexually excited but also in dominance struggles.

Sheepdog, type of dog bred to herd and protect sheep. The American Kennel Club lists these 9 breeds of sheepdogs: Belgian sheepdog, Briard, collie, German shepherd, Great Pyrenees, Komondor, old English sheepdog, puli, and Shetland sheepdog.

Sheffield (pop. 531,000), city in South Yorkshire, northern England. Known worldwide for its high-grade steel, metal products, cutting tools, cutlery, and silverware, Sheffield probably began as an Anglo-Saxon farming settlement in the 1000s. It grew into a center of steel production during the Industrial Revolution.
See also: England.

Sheik (more properly spelled 'sheikh'), Arabic term for the leader or elder of a family, tribe, or village, also applied to some Muslim religious leaders.

Shell, any hard external covering secreted by an invertebrate, enclosing and protecting the body. The term is used particularly for the coverings of mollusks, but it also refers to those of foraminifers and may be used loosely to describe the exoskeleton of crustaceans and insects.

Shellac, resin produced by the lac insect (*Laccifer lacca*). It softens when it is heated to about 158° F (70° C), a property that makes it useful for making sealing wax. Shellac is also used as a binder in the manufacture of mica board and stiffening materials, and to make polishes, varnishes, and insulating materials. Shellac once had many uses, including the manufacture of phonograph records, but it has mostly been superseded by plastics.

Shelley, Mary Wollstonecraft (1797-1851), English writer, daughter of philosophical radical William Godwin and Mary Wollstonecraft and wife of poet Percy Bysshe Shelley. Her best-known work is the Gothic horror story *Frankenstein* (1818). She wrote several other novels and edited her husband's works (1839-1840).

Shelley, Percy Bysshe (1792-1822), English romantic poet whose work reflects his revolutionary political idealism and his strong faith in the spiritual power of the imagination. It includes long narrative po-

Merino sheep are prominent in many countries of the world. Their heavy fleece is composed of fine fibres, which are pure white when secured. The outer appearance of the wool is often dark, due to its high natural fat content, combined with dirt.

S

The Romney is a long-wool sheep that is raised mostly for its mutton.

The white-faced Dorset Horn sheep provides both meat and wool.

The Karakul is a fur-bearing breed of sheep. Persian lamb pelts are made from the young animals.

ems, such as *Queen Mab* (1813), *The Revolt of Islam* (1818), and *Epipsychidion* (1821); the verse drama *Prometheus Unbound* (1820); and such famous lyrics as 'Ode to the West Wind' (1819) and 'To a Skylark' (1820). He was drowned in a boating accident in Italy, were he had settled with his second wife, Mary Wollstonecraft.

Shelter, structure to protect people from the weather, animals, insects, and other threats. A shelter can be a house, tent, cave, houseboat, or a lean-to. Shelters have been made from animal skins, cloth, grass, vines, timber, stones, mud, clay, brick, glass, steel, concrete, and plastic. The materials, forms, and method of construction vary worldwide.

Shenyang (pop. 5,200,000), formerly Mukden, capital of Liaoning province in northeastern China, on the Hun River. A major industrial city, its products include steel and steel products, tools, chemicals, and processed food. It is also a transportation hub. The city dates from the Middle Ages. It

S

was the capital of Manchu China and the site of the Japanese invasion of Manchuria (1931).
See also: China.

Shepard, Sam (1943-   ), U.S. actor and playwright noted for almost cinematic inventiveness in such plays as *Buried Child* (1978; Pulitzer Prize), *True West* (1980), and *Lie of the Mind* (1987). Other works are collected in *Mad Dog Blues and Other Plays* (1972). Shepard appeared in the films *Frances* (1982), *The Right Stuff* (1983), *Country* (1984), and *The Pelican Brief* (1993).

Sheraton, Thomas (1751-1806), English furniture designer. Sheraton's furniture is noted for its delicacy and simplicity of shape. It may be decorated with inlays, oval or diamond shapes, or classical motifs such as lyres and urns. Sheraton published his designs in *The Cabinet-Maker and Upholsterer's Drawing Book* (1791-1794). His style of furniture was popular in England (1790-1805) and in the United States (1795-1810).

Sheridan, Philip Henry (1831-1888), U.S. general and Union Civil War hero. After successes in the Chattanooga and Wilderness campaigns, he commanded the army that defeated Gen. Jubal Early and devastated the Shenandoah Valley (1864). In 1865 he won the Battle of Five Forks in Virginia and helped end the war by cutting off Robert E. Lee's line of retreat from Appomattox. He became commander of the U.S. Army in 1884.
See also: Civil War, U.S..

Sheridan, Richard Brinsley (1751-1816), Irish-born English dramatist and politician famous for his witty comedies of manners, including *The Rivals* (1775), *School for Scandal* (1777), and *The Critic* (1779). A Whig member of Parliament (1780-1812), he played a leading part in the impeachment trial (1787) of Warren Hastings.

Sheriff, executive officer of a county, a post that has existed in England since before 1066. Today the duties of a sheriff entail the execution of writs, the preparation of jurors, and the custody of prisoners. In the United States a sheriff functions as a peace officer in areas of a county not protected by city police. The office of sheriff is also found in Canada, Scotland, and Northern Ireland.

Sherman, brothers important in the U.S. Civil War era. **William Tecumseh Sherman** (1820-1891) was a Union commander. He fought in the battles of Bull Run (1861) and Shiloh (1862) and in the Vicksburg campaign (1862-1863). He was given command of the Army of Tennessee and took part in the Chattanooga campaign (1863). As supreme commander in the West (1864) he invaded Georgia, capturing Atlanta and marching on to Savannah. Turning north, he pushed Gen. Joseph Johnston's army before him and accepted its surrender at Durham, N.C. (1865). The destruction Sherman wrought in obliterating Confederate supplies

Northern general William Sherman (1820-1891), as portrayed by George P.A. Healy (1813-1894). Sherman was a die-hard soldier, who later summarized his war experiences as: 'War is hell' (National Portrait Gallery, Washington).

and communications and breaking civilian morale made him a hero in the North and a villain in the South. He was U.S. Army commander 1869-84. **John Sherman** (1823-1900) was a founding member of the Republican Party. A senator (1861-1877, 1881-1897) and secretary of the treasury (1877-1881), he introduced the Sherman Antitrust Act.
See also: Civil War, U.S..

Sherpas, Buddhist people of northeast Nepal, famous as Himalayan guides. Of Tibetan origin and speaking a Tibetan language, they number some 85,000 and raise cattle, grow crops, and spin wool in the high valleys of the Himalayas.

Sherrington, Sir Charles Scott (1857-1952), British neurophysiologist who shared with Edgar D. Adrian the 1932 Nobel Prize in physiology or medicine for studies of the nervous system that form the basis of our modern understanding of its action. He established the use of the word 'synapse,' explained the functions of the spinal cord, and made vital contributions to the understanding of muscles. He is the author of *The Integrative Action of the Nervous System* (1906).
See also: Nervous system.

Sherry, alcoholic beverage named for Jérez de la Frontera, Spain, where it originated. It is an aperitif wine, matured in wooden casks and fortified with brandy to bring the alcohol level to 15%-23% by volume.

Sherwood, Robert Emmet (1896-1955), U.S. playwright. His plays *Idiot's Delight* (1936), *Abe Lincoln in Illinois* (1938), and *There Shall Be No Night* (1940), and his biography *Roosevelt and Hopkins: An Intimate History* (1948) won Pulitzer Prizes for drama or biography.

Shetland Islands, archipelago of about 200 islands, covering 550 sq mi (1,425 sq km) northeast of Scotland's mainland, constituting its northernmost county. Lerwick, on Mainland Island, is the chief port and administrative center. Along with the Orkneys, the Shetlands are the center of the North Sea oil industry. Fishing and cattle and sheep raising are the main occupations of the some 18,500 Scots on the 24 inhabited islands. The Shetlands are noted for their knitted woolen goods and the Shetland pony.

Shetland pony, smallest of the ponies, probably a relic of prehistoric British and Scandinavian horses. Tiny, shaggy, and once restricted to the Shetland Islands, it has now been widely bred as a riding pony for children.

Shetland sheepdog, small dog, developed (19th century) in the Shetland Islands to herd sheep. Measuring 13-16 in (33-41.6 cm) at the shoulder and weighing about 15 lb (7 kg), the Shetland sheepdog resembles a miniature collie. Agile and hardworking, it can cover great distances without tiring and is also kept as a pet or watchdog.

Shevardnadze, Eduard Amvrolyevich (1928-   ), president of the Republic of Georgia (1992-   ). USSR foreign minister 1985-1990. He was head of the ministry of internal affairs of the Republic of Georgia, 1965-1972. He became foreign minister after being promoted to a full voting member of the Politburo in 1985. Shevardnadze was known as a liberal on friendly terms with the West. He resigned Dec. 20, 1990 over disagreements with other members of the Soviet government. In 1995 and 1998 attempts on his life were made. He survived both assaults.
See also: Georgia; Union of Soviet Socialist Republics.

Shevchenko, Taras (1814-1861), Ukrainian patriot and poet. He was also a realist painter and a publisher of Ukrainian ballads in Russian. He opposed serfdom and was active in the Ukrainian independence movement. As punishment, the Russian government sentenced him to military service in the Ural Mountains (1847-1857). His nationalistic poems include *Katerina* (1840), *Haydamaki* (1841), and *The Dream* (1844). He was born in Kiev.

Shield, defensive armor, usually carried on the left arm to leave the right arm free for fighting. The ancient Greeks and early Romans used large, circular wooden shields covered with bronze. The later Romans, for the sake of greater mobility, switched to smaller, rectangular shields that were curved to half encircle and thus protect the body more effectively. Kite-shaped shields were employed during the Middle Ages. The introduction of body armor and then firearms (requiring the use of both hands) gradually made the shield obsolete. In modern times shields have been reintroduced by riot police as protection against urban rioters.

Shih Huang-ti *See:* Shi Huangdi.

Shih Tzu, breed of toy dog. It stands 8-11 in (20-28 cm) at the shoulder and weighs 9-18 lb (4-8 kg). The dog has a broad head, a short, square muzzle, and drooping ears. The thick coat varies in color. The breed originated in Tibet and is related to the Pekingese and Lhasa apso.

Shi Huangdi (259?-210 B.C.), emperor of the first Chinese empire and founder of the Qin dynasty. He became ruler of the kingdom of Qin (246 B.C.), conquered Qin's rival states, and declared himself emperor of China (221 B.C.). He established a strong central government. He had his opponents executed and potentially inciteful books burned. He ordered the construction of roads and canals and the completion of the Great Wall of China, a defense along China's northern frontier.
See also: Qin dynasty.

Shijiazhuang (also Shihchiachuang and Shih-chia-chuang; pop. 1,700,000), China, the capital of Hebei province, about 160 mi (260 km) southwest of Beijing. Shijiazhuang is a railway junction and manufacturing center. The city was a small agricultural village until early in the 20th century, when it became the junction point of two newly constructed railways.

Shingles, or herpes zoster, viral disorder of a nerve center, characterized by pain, a vesicular rash, and later scarring of the skin of the abdomen or trunk. The disorder is caused by the same virus that causes chickenpox. Predominantly striking people past age 50, it leads to an acute skin eruption that follows the path of the nerve involved.
See also: Herpes.

Shinto (Japanese, 'way of the gods'), indigenous religion of Japan originally based on worship of nature's forms and forces. As this worship evolved, entering a stage of polytheism, its most revered deity became the sun goddess, Ama terasu-o-mi-kami, from whom it was believed the emperors descended. They were regarded as chief priests by divine right, until the disavowal of divin-

ity by Emperor Hirohito in 1946. The blending of church and state occurred in 1882, when the religion was organized into state shrines (supervised by the government) and sectarian shrines. (The imperial shrine is at Ise.) State Shinto was used by the militarists of Japan until its dismantling after World War II. Shinto beliefs, rituals, and prayers, transmitted orally before the introduction of writing by the Chinese in the 5th century, are recorded in 3 texts: the *Kojiki*, the *Nihongi*, and the *Yengishiki*. Today Shinto, influenced by Buddhism and Confucianism, is practiced through rituals and customs involving celebration of festivals, pilgrimages to shrines, and the honoring of ancestors. The practice of pure Shinto involves prayer, food offerings, and dances.
See also: Religion.

Ship, large seagoing vessel for transport of people and goods. The wooden ships of ancient times were propelled by oars, sails, or a combination of the two. In the history of ships, highlights include the triremes (warships) of the Greeks and Romans, the Viking ships of the Middle Ages, and the ships of such powers as Spain, Portugal, and England during the 1400s and 1500s. Transoceanic voyages (of Columbus and others), made possible by improved navigational instruments, and the continued use of the seas to conquer new lands and expand empires prompted a booming shipbuilding industry of a wide variety of ships. With the introduction of steel, as well as the steam engine, the steam turbine, and then the diesel engine of the 20th century, the endurance and speed of ocean craft improved markedly. Nuclear engines for ships came into use in the 1950s. Despite competition from the airplane, railroad, and truck, ships still transport the bulk of the world's freight. Half the cargo at sea is oil, carried by supertankers that can hold millions of gallons of crude oil. Luxury cruise ships continue to hold their own in the travel/vacation industry. Ships, including destroyers, cruisers, and frigates, have also maintained an important position in the defense forces of many nations.

Ship, model, small copy of a ship. Some models are built and sailed by hobbyists for pleasure. Historically, shipbuilders have made models as plans for a larger ship's construction. Ship models also are made so the hull's design can be tested in different wave conditions.

Shipworm, bivalve mollusk (*Teredo navalis*) notorious for burrowing into the timbers of piers and wooden ships. The body is long and wormlike, with the shell reduced to a tiny pair of abrasive plates at the head end. These are used for rasping into wood-at a rate sometimes exceeding 1 ft (30.5 cm) per month.

Shiraz (pop. 1,0 million), city in southern Iran, capital of the province of Fars, at an altitude of 5,250 ft (1,600 m) in the Zagros Mountains. Oil refinery; varied industry. Traditional industry; trade in the famous Shiraz carpets. Marketplace for rich agricultural area (wine). University (1948); many mosques. Ruins of the ancient Persepolis are nearby.

Shire, administrative division in Great Britain. The Anglo-Saxon shires, first organized in the A.D. 800s, were made up of smaller divisions called *hundreds*. A shire was headed by an ealdorman and a sheriff. The term *shire* was eclipsed in the 1400s by the word *county*.

Shi'te (Arabic, 'sectarian'), member of one of Islam's two great sects, the other being the orthodox Sunni. The schism arose over disagreement about Muhammad's successor. The Shi'te reject the first 3 caliphs and recognize Ali (Muhammad's son-in-law) and his descendants as rightful successors. They are concentrated principally in Iran, but also with communities in Iraq, Yemen, Pakistan, Oman, and Lebanon.
See also: Islam; Sunni.

Shiva, Hindu deity representing that aspect of the Godhead connected with the destruction necessary for renewal of life. He is sometimes depicted as an ascetic youth. In the role of re-creator he is called 'the happy one.' His phallic emblem is worshipped.
See also: Brahmanism; Hinduism.

Shock, specifically refers to the development of low blood pressure, inadequate to sustain blood circulation, usually causing cold, clammy, gray skin and extremities, faintness, mental confusion, and decreased urine production. It is caused by acute blood loss, burns with plasma loss, acute heart failure, massive pulmonary embolism, and septicemia. If untreated, death ensues. Early replacement of plasma or blood and administration of drugs to improve blood circulation are necessary to prevent permanent brain damage and acute kidney failure.

Shock absorber, any mechanism used to lessen impact in vehicles, aircraft, or stable structures. Most shock absorbers are hydraulic: They operate by forcing liquid through a small opening, an action that sets up resistance to both contraction and expansion of the spring mountings. In automobiles, shock absorbers control up-and-down vibrations and absorb impact on the car body. They are made of a piston inside an

A Torii, or 'gateway', the most typical architectural structure of the Japanese Shinto religion. It is believed that Torii were originally entrances of ancient dwelling houses. Subsequently they were refined and used specifically to mark the entrances of religious shrines.

A Brahmin (Hindu priest). As a representative of Shivaism (the cult of the god Shiva), the priest is wearing horizontal stripes on the forehead (those who practise the Vishnu cult wear vertical ones). The trident is one of Shiva's attributes. On the tree is a picture of Shiva's wife, Durga, riding a lion and reconquering heaven from the mighty demon Mahisha.

S

Ancient Egyptian ships were characterized by square sails, oars, and a curved hull similar to that of a reed boat.

The cog, a broadly built ship with bluff prow and stern, was used primarily for commercial transport from the 13th to the late 14th century.

Unlike earlier galleys, Venetian galleys of the 16th century had fewer oars and more men working each oar.

The Sea Witch, built in New York in 1846 for the China trade, was one of the earliest clippers: sleek, light ships built for speed.

The Queen Elizabeth II, built in 1967, operates as a transatlantic liner and a cruise liner.

Steam-operated paddleboats, such as John Fitch's 1786 model, were superseded by rudderboats.

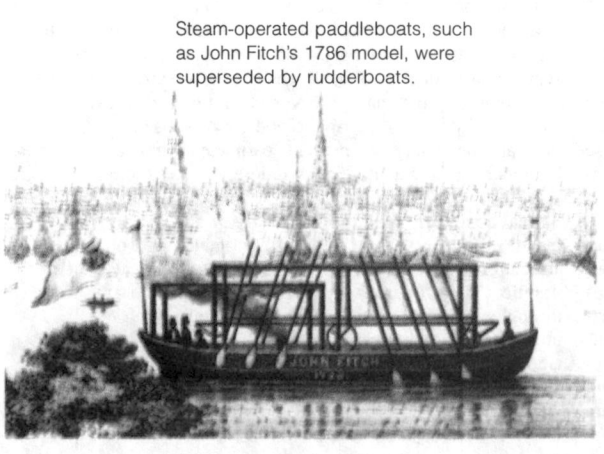

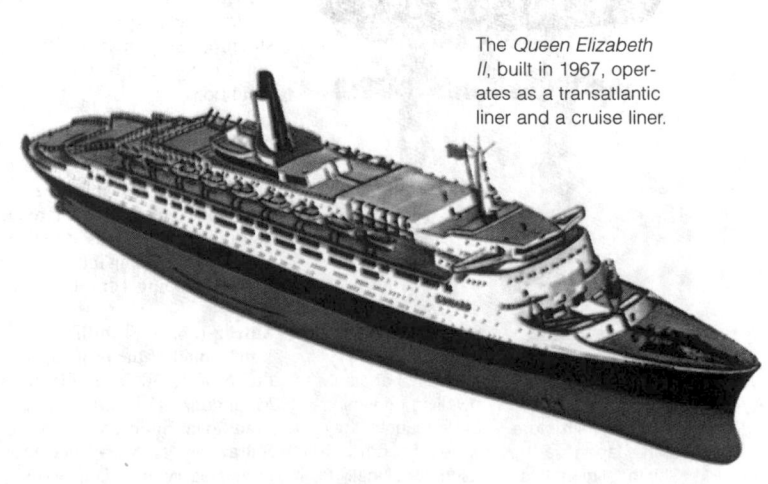

oil-filled cylinder. When the piston slides, it allows the fluid to flow through a spring-loaded valve.

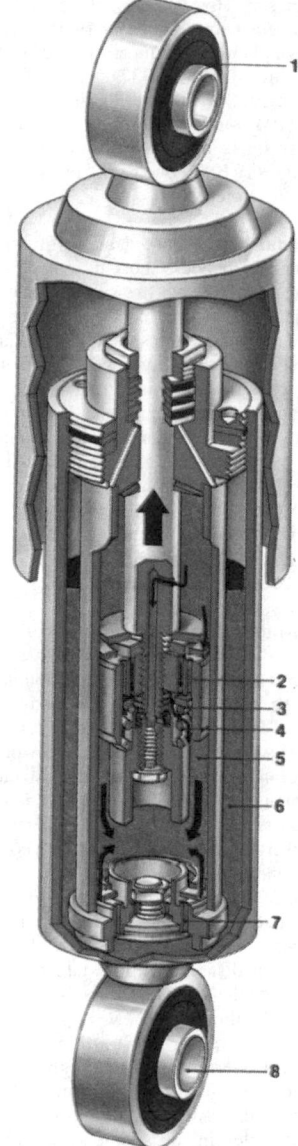

Hydraulic shock absorbers are used to reduce the bouncing motion of vehicles moving over rough roads. The telescopic shock absorber is the most common type. It comprises a double-chambered tube that is connected at its lower end to the wheel control arm by means of an eye-ring mounting (8) and fits within a larger tube attached to a chassis bracket by a mounting (1). A piston rod connects the larger tube to a piston (2) that moves in an oil-filled inner chamber (5) of the smaller tube. The piston contains a valve (3) that is normally kept closed by a spring (4). When a road shock moves the wheel and the attached lower tube upward, the piston moves down, the valve opens, and oil flows above the piston and is simultaneously forced through narrow channels (7) from the inner to the outer chamber (6). The restricted flow of fluid through the narrow gaps reduces the vertical movement.

Shockley, William (1910-1989), U.S. physicist who shared with John Bardeen and Walter H. Brattain the 1956 Nobel Prize in physics for their joint development of the transistor. He is also known for promoting the erroneous belief that black people are intellectually inferior to Caucasians.
See also: Transistor.

Shock treatment, any of several types of therapy for mental illness that involve subjecting the patient to convulsions or seizures produced by electricity. It is now generally used only for hospitalized patients who are suicidal or severely depressed. Controversial because of its negative side effects, particularly amnesia and cardiac damage, shock therapy has been widely replaced by the use of tranquilizers.

Shoe, protective covering for the foot. The various types include the boot, whose upper extends above the ankle; the clog, a simple wooden-soled shoe; the moccasin, a hunting shoe whose sole extends around and over the foot; the sandal, an open shoe whose sole is secured to the foot by straps; and the slipper, a soft indoor shoe. Shoes have been made from earliest times, the type depending mainly on the climate; clogs, sandals, and moccasins predominated until the early Middle Ages. Since then boots and typical shoes in widely varying styles have been most popular. Leather has always been the main material used, shaped on a wood or metal form (*last*) and hand sewn, the sole being nailed to the upper. In the mid-19th century the sewing machine was adapted for sewing shoes, and nailing and gluing were also mechanized, allowing mass production.

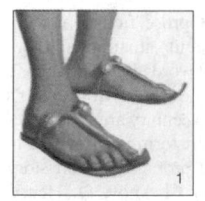

Sandals (1), worn by ancient Egyptians, were the first important style of footwear. Cothurnus (2), worn in Greek drama and adopted by the Romans, was the first evidence of a heel or platform. During the early Middle Ages, low and soft leather shoes that were cross-gartered over breeches were the general style (3). Crakows, the ankle- high, pointed shoe (4), a typical shape that was worn in the Middle Ages, was worn together with wooden 'pattens' that raised the foot above the ground.

Other materials have to some extent displaced leather: natural and synthetic rubber for the sole and heel and various plastics and synthetic fibers for the upper.

The heavy, wooden sabot (1) was worn by peasants all over Europe in the Middle Ages. By the end of the 15th century, shoes had broadened considerably (2), the leather slashed, showing puffs of satin. Hitherto, there had been little marked difference between male and female styles, but the outrageous Venetian chopines (3), a variant of the Chinese pedestal shoe (4), indicated the women's desire for heels. Small heels appeared on normal footwear (5) by the end of the 16th century. Seventeenth-century shoes were ornate and luxurious: (6) a Spanish man's shoe with leather soles and embroidered velvet, (7) wooden heels attached to slippers, very popular in France. The Spanish influence dwindled and the lace-cuffed, spurred leather boot increased in popularity (8). Women's shoes continued to be heeled and decorative (9) during the 18th century. At the turn of the century, buckles were still popular for both sexes, and the black buckled shoe (10) was very frequent. During the 19th century, women began to wear neat side-buttoned boots (11). Side buttoning was also a feature of the spats (12), worn by men at the turn of the century. In the 20th century, the Oxford (13) was one of the most influential male styles, while in the 1950's the thinnest-ever heel — the stiletto (14) — arrived, together with the return of the pointed toe.

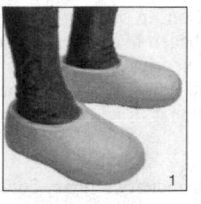

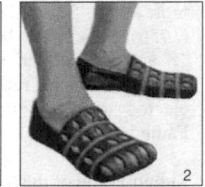

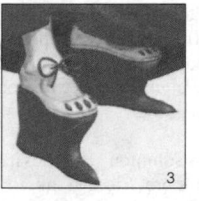

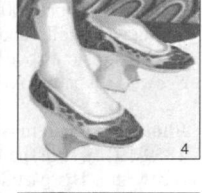

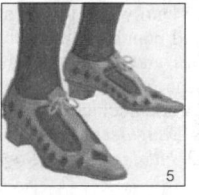

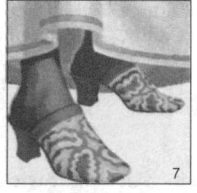

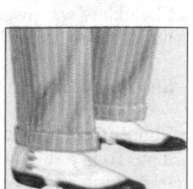

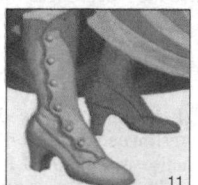

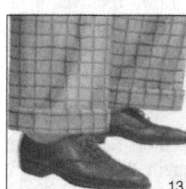

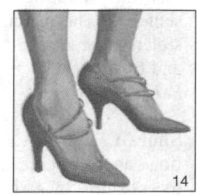

S

Shoebill, African wading bird (*Balaenicips rex*), native to the White Nile area of the Sudan. The shoebill is gray, long legged, and has a large, wide bill ending in a hook. It stands 3-4 ft (90-120 cm) high and eats small frogs and shallow-water fish. Shoebills live in pairs and nest on the ground in grass-lined reed platforms.

Shoemaker, Willie (William Lee Shoemaker, 1931-), U.S. jockey. The most successful jockey in U.S. history, he rode 4 Kentucky Derby winners (1955, 1959, 1965, 1986) and was the first jockey to win more than $2 million in a single year (1956). Shoemaker began his career at age 18 and had ridden nearly 9,000 winning mounts when he retired in 1990. He was elected to the National Racing Hall of Fame in 1958.

Shogun, title of the hereditary military commanders of Japan who usurped the power of the emperor in the 12th century and ruled the country for about 700 years. In 1867 the last Tokugawa family shogun was forced to re-sign and restore sovereignty to the emperor. *See also:* Japan; Tokugawa.

Sholem Aleichem (Solomon Rabinovitz; 1859-1916), Russian-born Yiddish humorous writer. His pseudonymous first name is Hebrew for 'Peace be unto you.' He was an immensely prolific and popular author, and his novels, short stories, and plays tell of the serious and absurd aspects of Jewish life in Eastern Europe. His works include *The Old Country* and *Tevye's Daughters* (1894; the basis for the musical *Fiddler on the Roof*, 1964).

Sholes, Christopher Latham (1819-1890), U.S. inventor (with Carlos Glidden and Samuel Soulé) of the typewriter (patented 1868). He sold his patent rights to the Remington Arms Co. in 1873. *See also:* Typewriter.

Sholokhov, Mikhail Aleksandrovich (1905-1984), Soviet Russian writer. His first book *Stories from the Don* was published in 1925. Became world-famous with *And Quiet Flows the Don* (4 volumes, 1928-1940), an epic novel set during WW I and the civil war about a Don Cossack family, written with great power. Also remarkable was his socialist realist novel about the collectivization of agriculture: *Virgin Soil Upturned* (1931). Sholokhov was awarded the Nobel Prize for literature in 1965.

Shooting star *See:* Meteor.

Shoplifting, crime of stealing displayed items from a store. It is estimated that $8 billion worth of merchandise is shoplifted in the United States annually, and that fewer than one shoplifter in 1,000 receives a jail sentence. The merchandise most frequently stolen is beauty and health aids, cigarettes, and fresh meat. *See also:* Crime.

Shoran, acronym for short-range navigation, an electronic system for establishing the position of a ship or aircraft. The craft being monitored sends a radio signal to 2 separate land stations, and the stations return the signals. Shoran calculates the distance to the craft by the time between transmission and reception of the signal. It can pinpoint the craft's position to within 1 part in 10,000. Its range is limited to 500 mi (800 km). First used during World War II, shoran has largely been replaced by more accurate systems. *See also:* Navigation.

Shorthand, or stenography, any writing system permitting the rapid transcription of speech. Most used today are Speedwriting, which uses abbreviations; (Isaac) Pitman shorthand, the first to be commercially developed (1837); and Gregg shorthand, by John Robert Gregg (published 1888). Pitman and Gregg shorthands are both phonetic, using symbols to represent recurring sounds. Shorthand is much used by secretaries, journalists, and court reporters. *See also:* Speedwriting.

Shorthand machine, any of several mechanical devices that use keyboards to record dictation. Invented (1912) by a court stenographer, Ward Stone Ireland, the shorthand machine is used chiefly to record court testimony, legislation, and speeches. The operator works by touch, typing words phonetically while watching the speaker. The keyboard is arranged to allow any number of the 21 lettered keys to be struck simultaneously, so that an entire word or phrase can be typed with 1 stroke. The shorthand machine is portable and operates silently. *See also:* Court reporter.

Short story, form of prose fiction, usually limited in character and situation and between 500 and 20,000 words long. Chaucer's *Canterbury Tales* and Boccaccio's *Decameron* of the 14th century are prototypes of short stories. The art form was revived in the 19th century, and prominent short-story writers include Anton Chekhov, O. Henry, Ernest Hemingway, Henry James, Katherine Mansfield, Guy de Maupassant, John O'Hara, Edgar Allen Poe, Jean Stafford, and Eudora Welty.

Short waves, electromagnetic (radio) waves having a wavelength from about 32 to 328 ft (10 to 100 m) and a frequency between about 3,000 and 30,000 kilohertz-shorter and of higher frequency than the wavelengths of amplitude modulation (AM) transmissions. Short waves are used to carry international broadcasting, FM (frequency modulation) radio stations, and transoceanic telephone calls. Shortwave radios that can receive and transmit signals are used by pilots, the police, and amateur and citizens band operators. *See also:* Radio, amateur.

Shoshone, group of Native North Americans originally inhabiting the territory between southeastern California and Wyoming. The Shoshone of eastern Utah and Wyoming were typical buffalo hunters of the plains. In the 18th century the Comanche split off and moved south to Texas. There are about 8,000 Shoshone on reservations.

Shostakovich, Dmitri (1906-1975), Soviet composer. His works include the opera *Lady Macbeth of Mtsensk* (1930-1932) and 15 symphonies, the most famous of which are the Fifth (1937), the Seventh-'Leningrad,' written during the siege of the city (1941)-and the Tenth (1953). Some of his music is notably patriotic. The Piano Quintet (1940) is one of his leading chamber music pieces.

Shotgun, smoothbore shoulder firearm that discharges pellets (shot) designed to disperse as they leave the gun muzzle. Used primarily in hunting small game and birds and in skeet, or trapshooting, the shotgun evolved from the early fowling guns of 16th century Europe, becoming lighter and shorter and benefitting from the addition of a choke to control the spread of the shot and from the patent of the shotgun cartridge (1831). The repeating shotgun appeared c.1880. A shotgun's caliber is measured by its gauge, the most popular U.S. gauges being 12, 16, 20, and the 410 bore. Models may be single or double barreled.

Shot-put, track-and-field competition in which a weight, generally a solid metal ball, is thrown one-handed from the shoulder, using the whole weight of the body in the heave. Dating from ancient times, when stones were used as shots, the shot-put was made an official event of the first modern Olympic Games (1896). The shot is tossed (or put) from a 7-ft (2.1-m)-diameter circle and weighs 16 lb (7.3 kg) in men's competitions and 8 lb 13 oz (4 kg) in women's. The distance of the put is measured from the inside edge of the throwing circle to the nearest edge of the shot's first ground contact. The put is disqualified if the athlete steps on or outside the circle or allows the shot to fall below shoulder level.

Shoulder, term for the area of the body between the trunk and the arm, including bones, joints, and the adjacent tissue. There are 2 bones in the shoulder: the clavicle (collarbone), which is the horizontal bone that connects to the breastbone, and the scapula (shoulderblade), the flat triangular bone of the back. The upper arm bone (humerus) fits into the socket formed by the scapula. There are several muscles in the shoulder, primarily the trapezius, which helps turn the scapula, and the deltoid, which moves the upper arm. In primates the shoulder protrudes; in other mammals, it slopes.

Shoveler (*Anas clypeata*), common duck of the family Anatidae native to marshes and lakes of North America, particularly west of the Mississippi River. The shoveler also lives in Asia and Europe and migrates to the Southern Hemisphere. The shoveler has a broad bill longer than its head. The drake has a green head and neck, a white breast, and a black tail. The female is mottled brown. The shoveler feeds in shallow water and nests on the ground. It migrates in small flocks of 5 to 10 birds.

Showa period, period in Japanese history designating the reign of Emperor Hirohito (1926-1989). During the worldwide economic crisis of 1929 the influence of the military in Japanese politics increased. Extreme nationalistic groups wanted to solve the economic problems with territorial expansion. In the 1930s this concept was expressed by the aggressive policy that Japan pursued from 1931 onwards in Manchuria, and in the rest of China from 1937 onwards. In 1936 Japan signed the Anti-Comintern Pact, replaced in 1940 with the Berlin Pact between Japan, Germany and Italy. After the outbreak of WW II Japan captured Indochina from France in 1941. After Pearl Harbor Japan captured the Philippines, Singapore and the Dutch Indies. After the Japanese defeat the country was occupied by the Americans under general Douglas MacArthur (1880-1964), from 1945 to 1952. The U.S. tried to eradicate Japanese militarism and imperialism and introduce democracy. A new constitution was written, by which Japan became a type of constitutional monarchy; the divine nature of the Emperor was abolished. The army and the navy were disbanded, voting rights for women were introduced, the freedom of the press restored, the education system reformed, and the zaibatsu (large corporations) disbanded. In 1952 Japan regained its sovereignty, and a normalization of international relations returned. Thereafter Japan grew to become an economic superpower. An end came to the Shawa (Enlightened Peace) era when Emperor Hirohito died. When Okihito became Emperor on 8 January 1989, the Heisei (Fulfilment of Peace) era began.

Shrapnel, type of antipersonnel artillery shell made of a hollow metal sphere filled with musket balls or other large shot and an explosive charge detonated by an adjustable fuse. Shrapnel was invented by Lt. Henry Shrapnel (1761-1842) and first used (1804) by British forces in the Napoleonic Wars. Since World War II, the term *shrapnel* has usually been understood to mean exploded fragments of the shell casing.
See also: Artillery.

Shrew, small, mouselike, insect-eating mammal with short legs, and long, pointed nose. Shrews have narrow skulls and sharp, rather unspecialized teeth for feeding on insects, earthworms, and small-mammal carrion. They are highly active creatures. The somewhat indigestible nature of their food combined with the high energy consumption of their constant activity means that they may eat 2-3 times their own weight of food in a day. Having a pulse rate that sometimes approaches 1,000 beats a minute, few shrews live longer than a year.

Shri (Sanskrit: prosperity, happiness, bliss), goddess of the ancient Indian Vedic religion, later a term for any important goddess, and for a holy book or a holy man.

Shrike, aggressive and predatory passerine bird of the family Laniidae that kills insects, birds, or small mammals with its hooked bill. Because shrikes store their victims impaled on thorns like the carcasses hung in a butcher's shop, they are often called butcher-

birds. They live on the edges of woods and forests worldwide.

Shrimp, decapod crustacean (suborder Natantia) that uses its abdominal limbs to swim instead of crawling like a lobster or crab. The body, more or less cylindrical and translucent, bears 5 pairs of walking legs and 2 pairs of very long antennae. The eyes are stalked. Shrimp are mostly scavengers or predators and may be found in the open ocean, near shore, in estuaries, and even in fresh water. They are fished for food worldwide.

Shroud of Turin, linen cloth bearing the image of a crucified man, believed to be Jesus' burial cloth. Stored at the Cathedral of Turin since 1578, the shroud measures 14 ft 3 in by 3 ft 7 in (434 cm by 109 cm). It received publicity in the 1970s and 1980s when it became available for scientific research. Tests proved that the negative image was not painted but did not determine how it was produced. They also showed, from pollen and dust samples, that the linen could have been in the Palestine area where Jesus died and that bloodstains on the fabric were genuine. However, radiocarbon dating (1988) seemed to prove that the cloth is no older than about 500 years. Theologians, historians, and scientists have sustained the controversy surrounding the shroud, particularly since no early accounts of an imaged burial cloth exist. Historians usually agree that the shroud's whereabouts can be traced from the 500s with a gap from 1204 to 1355. However, recent research has shown that it is in fact possible that the shroud dates from the beginning of our era. In April 1996 the shroud was saved from a fire which destroyed the chapel.

Shrove Tuesday, last day before Lent begins. It is a traditional day for Mardi Gras (Fat Tuesday) carnivals, such as those in New Orleans, Rio de Janeiro, and Nice.
See also: Lent.

Shrub, term for a woody plant that is shorter than a tree and usually has branching stems that give it a bushy appearance.

Shuffleboard, game played by 2 or 4 persons who use cues (long sticks) to slide disks down a long, narrow court, 52 x 6 ft (15.8 x 1.8 m), that has a triangular scoring area at either end. The game is generally played outdoors on pavement, a ship deck, or other smooth surface. Players try to knock their opponents' disks into the penalty section, while leaving their own disks in one of the scoring positions on the triangle.

Shultz, George Pratt (1920-), U.S. secretary of state (1982-1989). A former dean of the Graduate School of Business at the University of Chicago, in Pres. Richard Nixon's administration he was secretary of labor (1969-1970), director of the Office of Management and Budget (1970-1972), and secretary of the treasury (1972-1974). He was president of the Bechtel Corp. when Pres. Ronald Reagan appointed him to succeed Alexander Haig as secretary of state. He was awarded the 1992 Seoul Peace Prize.

Shush *See:* Susa.

Siam *See:* Thailand.

Siamese fighting fish *See:* Fightingfish.

Siamese twins, identical twins joined most commonly at the hip, chest, abdomen, buttocks, or head. Some share one internal organ, such as the heart or the liver. Originating from a single fertilized egg that has developed imperfectly, Siamese twins occur about once in every 50,000 births. Surgery in some cases can successfully separate these twins.

Sibelius, Jean (Julius Christian Sibelius, sometimes Jan; 1865-1957), Finnish composer. His best-known work is *Finlandia* (1900), which expressed his country's growing nationalist feeling. He composed several tone poems, such as *En Sagà* (1892), that evoke the physical beauty and ancient legends of Finland. He wrote 7 symphonies and many violin and piano pieces.

Siberia, vast, indefinite area of land (about 2.9 million sq km/7.5 million sq km) in northern Russia between the Ural Mountains in the west and the Pacific Ocean in the east, forming most of the Russian Federation. The landscape varies from the Arctic tundra to the great forest zone in the south and the steppes in the west. Summers are mild in most parts, winters extremely severe (as low as -90° F/-67.8° C in some parts). Most of the people are Russian or Ukrainians; Yakuts, Buryats, and Tuvans form autonomous republics. The largest cities are Novosibirsk, Omsk, Krasnoyarsk, and Novokuznetsk. Siberia has rich natural resources-farmland, forests, fisheries, natural gas, and such minerals as coal, iron ore, tungsten, and gold. Industrial centers have developed in the regions of Krasnoyarsk and Lake Baikal (the world's deepest lake), and

S

A shrimp cutter, photographed at the moment that the fishing gear (a shrimp dredge net) is still partially in the water. During the fishing, the dredge nets are pulled along, just above the bottom. If one of the nets gets hung up on the bottom, the dangerous listing of the boat can be diminished, by lowering the block on top of the gig. The tractive force will then be transferred to the gallows block at the stern of the cutter.

The taiga — the coniferous forest belt — covers the northern part of European Russia and the whole of Siberia, with the exception of the tundras. It is the largest coniferous area in the world. Exploitation is problematic, due to the climate, the vast distances and the lack of good communications. Another problem is the fact that all rivers flow from south to north and are therefore of no use for transportation.

S

one of the world's largest hydroelectric plants is near Bratsk. Siberia was inhabited in prehistoric times. Russians conquered much of Siberia by 1598. Political prisoners were first sent to Siberia in 1710 and forced-labor camps still exist. The Trans-Siberian Railroad (completed 1905) led to large-scale colonization and economic development. There are now a number of large industrial centers. A pipeline has been placed in order to transport natural gas to Western Europe. *See also:* Union of Soviet Socialist Republics.

Portrait of British writer Sir Philip Sidney (1554-1586) painted by an unknown artist.

Siberian husky, arctic working dog bred to pull sleds. The husky stands 20-23 in (51-58 cm) high at the shoulder and weighs 35-60 lb (16-27 kg). It has a dense undercoat and a smooth outercoat, of colors ranging from white through tan and gray to black. Originally raised by the Chukchi tribe of northeastern Siberia, the husky was introduced to Alaska (1909) as a sled-racing dog. It is related to the Samoyed and the malamute.

Sibyl, in Greek and Roman mythology, female prophet, usually divinely inspired and associated with a shrine or temple. There were sibyls throughout the ancient world, the most famous being the Cumaean sibyl, who accompanied Aeneas to Hades and sold the books of the Sibylline Prophecies to King Tarquin of Rome. Her caverns still exist in Mount Cuma in southern Italy. Medieval monks adapted the sibyls to Christianity, making them 12 in number and giving each a separate prophecy regarding Jesus.
See also: Mythology.

Sichuan (pop. 110 million), province in southwest China; 219,000 sq mi (567,000 sq km). Capital, Chengdu (pop. 2.8 million). Agricultural area, very important for China. The province is known for its rich culinary tradition (Sichuan kitchen). Cultivation of crops (rice, wheat, etc.). Also mining (iron ore and oil), and industry (wood processing and chemical).

Sicilies, Kingdom of the Two, name taken by the kingdoms of Sicily and Naples when they merged in 1816 under Ferdinand I. The Two Sicilies were conquered by the Italian revolutionary leader Guiseppe Garibaldi in 1860, and subsequently absorbed, by popular vote, into the kingdom of Italy.
See also: Italy.

Sicily, largest Mediterranean island (9,925 sq mi/25,706 sq km), part of Italy, but with its own parliament at the capital, Palermo. Its most notable feature is the active volcano, Mt. Etna (height varies around 10,750 ft/3,277 m). Much of the island is mountainous, but there are lowlands along the coasts. About half the population live in the coastal towns Palermo, Catania, Messina, and Siracusa. Agriculture is the mainstay of the economy, though hampered by the low rainfall and feudal land tenure system. Wheat is the staple crop; grapes, citrus fruits, and olives are also grown. Main exports, from Ragusa, are petroleum products. Sicily was the site of Greek, Phoenician, and Roman

The interior of the Cathedral of Monreale in Sicily, south of Palermo. In the 12th century, the huge space was entirely decorated with mosaics, similar to the Christ Pantocrator above the altar. Sicily had been dominated by Norman Vikings since the 11th century, but culturally it was entirely under the influence of Byzantium. Byzantine artisans often took part in building and decorating jobs in Sicily.

colonies before conquests by the Arabs, who in turn were ousted by Robert Guiscard, the Norman conqueror. The Sicilian Vespers rebellion (1282) led to Spanish rule, ended by Garibaldi (1860), when Sicily became part of the kingdom of Sardinia, then of unified Italy. In World War II, Sicily was conquered by the Allies (1943) and used as a base for attack on Italy.

Sickle-cell anemia, one of many hereditary blood diseases caused by chemically abnormal hemoglobin in the red blood cells, occurring almost exclusively among blacks. Rather than the normal disk shape, the red cells have distorted (crescent) shapes when their oxygen supply is low. It is from this unusual appearance of the red blood corpuscles that the disease and its abnormal hemoglobin derive their names, the hemoglobin being known as the sickle hemoglobin, or hemoglobin S. The disease was first described by J. B. Herrick in 1910, but it was not until 1949 that Linus Pauling and his associates demonstrated the basic defect to be in the hemoglobin molecule of the red blood cells. Since the discovery of the sickle hemoglobin, more than 100 other abnormal hemoglobins have been described. Characteristics of the disease, for which there is no cure, include fever, anemia, and pain in the joints and abdomen.

Siddhartha Gautama *See:* Buddha, Gautama.

Sidereal time, time as measured by the rotation of the earth relative to the fixed stars rather than relative to the sun. The sidereal day is the time it takes the earth to complete one rotation on its axis, such that a given star reappears on the observer's celestial meridi-

an. The sidereal day (23 hr, 56 min, 4 sec) is slightly shorter than the solar day. The difference is caused by the earth's movement around the sun.

Sidewinder, any of several species of snake, especially rattlesnakes, that exhibit a peculiar sideways looping motion when moving rapidly. The name is particularly applied to the horned rattlesnake (*Crotalus cerastes*) of the southwestern United States.

Sidney, Sir Philip (1554-1586), Elizabethan poet and courtier, a favorite with Queen Elizabeth I and a classic example of Renaissance chivalry. He had great influence on English poetry, both through his poems, of which the best known are *Arcadia* (1590) and the love sonnets *Astrophel and Stella* (1591), and through his critical work *The Defence of Poesie* (1595), all published posthumously.

Sidon, or Saida (pop. 35,000), city in southern Lebanon, on the Mediterranean Sea. Founded by the ancient Phoenicians, Sidon was prominent in shipbuilding and trade, and was famous for its bronzeware and purple dyes. The art of glassblowing probably originated in the city. Today, as a result of conflict within Israel, it has a large population of Palestinian refugees.

SIDS *See:* Sudden infant death syndrome.

Siegbahn, Karl Manne Georg (1886-1978), Swedish physicist who was awarded the 1924 Nobel Prize in physics for his pioneer work in X-ray spectroscopy. He devised a way of measuring X-ray wavelengths with great accuracy and developed an account of X-rays consistent with the Bohr theory of the atom. His son, **Kai M. Siegbahn** (1918-), also a Swedish physicist, and a professor at Uppsala University (from 1954), shared the 1981 Nobel Prize in physics with U.S. physicists Nicolass Bloembergen and Arthur Schaalow for work in developing high-resolution electron spectroscopy.

Siegfried, or Sigurd, legendary figure of Germanic mythology possessing outstanding strength and courage. He appears in both the Icelandic *Edda* and the 13th-century German *Nibelungenlied*, and is the hero of Richard Wagner's 'Ring' operas *Siegfried* and *Die Götterdämerung*.
See also: Nibelungenlied.

Siegfried Line, defensive line of fortifications built on Germany's western frontier. The first Siegfried Line was constructed in the winter of 1916-1917 and ran through northern France and Belgium. The Allies called it the Hindenburg Line and finally breached it at the end of World War I. The second line, built in the 1930s along the German-French border, was smashed by the Allies in World War II.
See also: World War II.

Siemens, German family of technologists and industrialists. **Ernst Werner von Siemens** (1816-1892) invented, among other things, an electroplating process (patented 1842), a differential governor (c.1844), and a regenerative steam engine. The principle for it was developed by his brothers **Friedrich** (1826-1904) and then **Karl Wilhelm** (1823-1883) to form the basis of the open-hearth process. Karl later became Sir Charles William Siemens after obtaining British citizenship (1859). He and Ernst both made many innovative contributions to telegraph science, culminating in the laying of the Atlantic Cable (1874) by the company Sir William owned-done from the *Faraday*, a ship he designed.

Siena (pop. 61,900), city in Tuscany, central Italy. Siena is an agricultural and tourist center and produces wine, cotton goods, marble, and chemicals. An ancient Etruscan settlement, Siena was occupied by the Gauls (c.400 B.C.) and became a free commune in the 12th century. It was attached to Tuscany after 1555. Home to the medieval Sienese school of painting (13th-14th centuries), its attractions include the public square (Piazza del Campo), the 14th-century cathedral, and the Piccolomini Library. It is the scene of 2 medieval, pageant-like horseraces, known as the Palio, held every summer.

Sienkiewicz, Henryk (1846-1916), Polish novelist awarded the 1905 Nobel Prize in literature. His greatest works are a trilogy about 17th-century Poland (*With Fire and Sword* (1883), *The Deluge* (1886), and *Pan Michael* (1887-1888)) and the internationally famous *Quo Vadis?* (1896).

Sierra Leone

Capital:	Freetown
Area:	27,699 sq mi (71,740 sq km)
Population:	5,615,000
Language:	English
Government:	Presidential republic
Independent:	1961
Head of gov.:	President
Per capita:	US$ 500
Monetary unit:	1 Leone = 100 cents

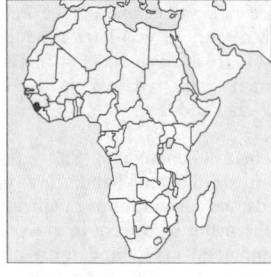

Sierra Leone, Republic; small, independent country in West Africa; a former British colony.
Land and climate. Bordering on the Atlantic Ocean and situated between the republics of Guinea, to the north and east, and Liberia, to the south, Sierra Leone has an area of 27,699 sq mi (71,740 sq km). The coastal area consists of mangrove and freshwater swamps that are gradually being transformed into rice fields. The inland plains, in places as much as 100 mi (161 km) wide, are crossed by many rivers draining westward to the Atlantic. The land to the north and northeast rises in a series of irregular steps reaching 6,390 ft (1,948 m) in Loma Mansa. The climate is tropical.
People. The population is mostly black African with the Mende people of the south and the Temne people of the north predominating. Creoles, descendants of freed slaves, mainly from the Americas, live around Freetown, the country's capital and chief port. Most of the people adhere to traditional beliefs, but there are also sizable minorities of Christians and Muslims. The official language is English. Education is not compulsory in Sierra Leone and the literacy rate is 40% (2002).
Economy. Sierra Leone's economy is heavily dependent for export revenue upon diamond mining and the production of cocoa and coffee. Rice is the chief food crop. Cattle are raised in the north, pigs and poultry in the west. Fishing and tourism also contribute to the economy.
History. Named by the Portuguese who first arrived in 1460, the coastal area of present-day Sierra Leone was long the haunt of slavers. In 1787 the English abolitionist Granville Stamp settled freed slaves there. In 1808 Sierra Leone became a British crown colony, and in the years following thousands more freed slaves settled there. Independent since 1961, Sierra Leone has seen much internal political unrest. It was declared a republic in 1971 under the presidency of Dr. Siaka Stevens, who sought to establish a one-party regime in the face of more than a decade of protest and resistance. In 1985 Maj. Gen. Joseph Saidu Momoh was elected president. Despite several initiatives the democratization process that started in 1991 progressed slowly and without real accomplishments. In 1992 Momoh was ousted by the army and the new head of state was Valentine Strasser. The latter was ousted in 1996. Since 1992 the country is plagued by a devastating civil war between the government, the Revolutionary Front and the National Patriotic Front Liberra (NPFL).

One of the rebel's main goals was to dispose of the influence of foreign companies. In 1997, a military coup resulted in the ousting of President Ahmad Tejan Kabbah. Major General Paul Koroma took over, but was ousted in 1998, after which Kabbah returned as the President.
UN troops intervened with a peace force addressed towards the guerrillas of the RUF in 1999. In January 2002, the civil war was declared over. At the elections of 2002, Kabbah won by a landslide. He asked the UN to extend its mission because of the fighting in the neighboring country Liberia.

Sierra Madre, vast mountain system of Mexico. The Sierra Madre Oriental, the eastern range, stretches 1,000 mi (1,609 km) south from the Rio Grande, forming the eastern edge of the central plateau and reaching 18,700 ft (5,700 m) in Orizaba. The Sierra Madre Occidental, running southward from Arizona and New Mexico, borders the plateau on the west, rising to over 10,000 ft (3,048 m). The Sierra Madre de Sur parallels the southwest coast.
See also: Mexico.

Sieve of Eratosthenes, mathematical process for discovering prime numbers. The ancient Greek mathematician Eratosthenes worked out this method by which whole numbers are eliminated-as if filtered through a sieve-until only prime numbers (those that can be divided evenly by themselves and 1) remain. The sieve starts as a string of consecutive whole numbers, beginning with 2. Every even number (except 2 itself) is eliminated, since each of them can be divided by 2. Next, beginning after the first untouched number after 2 (namely 3), every third number is eliminated, because they can all be divided evenly by 3. The next prime is the next untouched number. Since there is no largest prime number, the process can go on indefinitely.
See also: Eratosthenes.

Sieyès, Emmanuel Joseph (1748-1836), French revolutionary, legislator, and author. He participated in drafting such basic documents of the French revolution as the Declaration of the Rights of Man and Citizen and the Constitution (1791). His

The Cathedral of Siena. The façade is richly decorated with sculpture and mosaics, while the other sides of the building and the clock tower are constructed in two shades of marble.

S

S

pamphlet *What is the Third Estate?* (1789) helped inspire the revolution. He served in various legislative bodies throughout the changing post-revolutionary governments, and he ended his life as an exile in Brussels, Belgium, following the Bourbon restoration in France.
See also: French Revolution.

Sight *See:* Eye.

Sigismund (1368-1437), Holy Roman emperor (1433-1437), king of Germany (1410-1437), Hungary (1387-1437), and Bohemia (1419-1437). His coronation as German king was challenged by his half-brother, the former King Wenceslaus of Germany. Sigismund was an important organizer of the Council of Constance (1417), which ended the Great Schism in the Catholic church over papal elections. His coronation as king of Bohemia was contested by the Czech religious reformer John Hus. When Sigismund offered Hus safe-conduct and then went back on the pledge and had Hus executed, the Hussite Wars broke out.
See also: Holy Roman Empire; Hus, Jan.

Signac, Paul (1863-1935), French painter, leading theorist of neoimpressionism. A friend of Georges Seurat, he developed pointillism and painted many views of ports, like *Port of St. Tropez* (1916).

Signaling, any of various methods of nonverbal communication. Early visual and sound signals included smoke signals, drum calls, whistles, torch fires, and buoys. Sailors position flags in specific arrangements to communicate through the international flag code. Electrical signals are transmitted through various electronic devices, including radios, radar, computers, and telephone-operated facsimile (FAX) machines.

Sign language, any system of communication using gesture (usually of the hand and arm) rather than speech. The most comprehensive sign language in modern use is that employed by the hearing- or sight-impaired, but sophisticated sign languages are also used by many primitive peoples to communicate with one another.

Sihanouk, Norodom (1922-), Cambodian politician. King of Cambodia (1941-1955). Sihanouk won all the seats in Parliament with his People Socialist Party Sangkoem. He was Prime Minister several times and, after the title of King had been abolished in 1960, he became President. In 1970 he was

The Sikh temple of 'Darbar Sahib' (Spring of Immortality), in Amritsar. Like many other Sikh temples (Gurdwara), its roof is covered with gold leaf. There are no images at all in the temple, just the sacred book, the *Adi Granth*, which is continually read from in a lilting manner.

ousted by Lon Nol's Coup. Based in Beijing he organized the resistance, supported by the Khmer Rouge. After Lon Nol's escape, he was declared President. However, in 1976, he was forced to resign again by the Khmer Rouge. After the fall of the Khmer Rouge administration in 1979, Sihanouk opposed the Vietnamese backed Cambodian government. He returned from exile and was declared President in 1991. In 1993, he was proclaimed King again.

Sikhism, religion combining elements of Hindu and Muslim beliefs. Founded by the guru Nanak at the turn of the 16th century, Sikhism is a monotheism whose teachings are embodied in its holy book, *The Adi Granth*. The word *sikh* means 'disciple.' Among the beliefs of the Sikhs is the Hindu concept of reincarnation. Their tenth and final guru, Gobind Singh (1666-1708), led a fight against Muslim persecution, creating the warrior image with which Sikhs are still identified today. Additional characteristics are their turbans and their uncut hair. After the partition of India (1947), a war between Sikhs and Muslims resulted in the transfer of several million Sikhs from the western Punjab, which became part of Pakistan, to the eastern Punjab, in India. There the Sikhs, numbering some 14 million, have played a major role in the economy and in politics, often clashing with the central government in New Delhi. The Indian government's 1984 military occupation of the Golden Temple, the major shrine of Sikhism, has led to continuing conflict.
See also: Punjab; Ranjit Singh.

Sikkim, state in northeast India, located in the Himalaya Mountains, bordered by Tibet on the north, Nepal on the west, and Bhutan on the east. The altitude of the state ranges from sea level rain forests to Mount Kanchenjunga, at over 28,000 ft (8,530 m), the world's third tallest mountain. The capital city, Gangtok, is also the only significant town. The official religion is Buddhism, although many practice Hinduism. Major products of the country are agricultural, although there is some mining of copper, lead, and zinc. A Sikkim monarchy was established by neighboring Tibet in 1642 and lasted until Indian statehood (1975), functioning under British rule from 1861 to 1947.
See also: India.

Sikorsky, Igor Ivanovich (1889-1972), Russian-born U.S. aircraft designer best known for his invention of the first successful helicopter, flown in 1939. He also designed several airplanes, including the first to have more than one engine (1913).
See also: Helicopter.

Silanpää, Frans Eemil (1888-1964), Finnish novelist awarded the 1939 Nobel Prize in literature. His best-known works are *Meek Heritage* (1919) and *The Maid Silja* (1931).

Silesia, region of central Europe, mostly in Poland but extending to the Czech Republic and eastern Germany. Known for the mineral and coal deposits of heavily industrialized Upper Silesia, the region is heavily forested and traversed by the Oder River. The Sudetes Mountains rise in the south. The largest cities are Polish: Wroclaw and Katowice. Silesia became part of Poland in the 10th century. It was later conquered by Austria (1526) and Prussia (1742). The present borders were redrawn at the end of World Wars I and II.

Silica, chemical compound (SiO_2), properly called silicon dioxide. Sand, clay, granite, and sandstone contain forms of silica, which is also the major ingredient in glass. Quartz is an important crystalline form of silica used in optical tools and communications instruments. Opals are forms of amorphous silica polished and used in jewelry.

Silica gel, chemical substance (SiO_2) forming a noncrystalline form of silica. Silica gel absorbs moisture and this is its prime use. It was used in World War I in gas masks and now serves to dehumidify foods.

A Morse two-pole telegraph key is essentially a switch for opening and closing an electric circuit between two telegraph stations. When the transmission line (red) is not in use, the current flows from the power line (black) through a bypass line (blue). Depressing the key (1) breaks the bypass contact (2), and a current pulse is sent through the transmission-line contact (3).

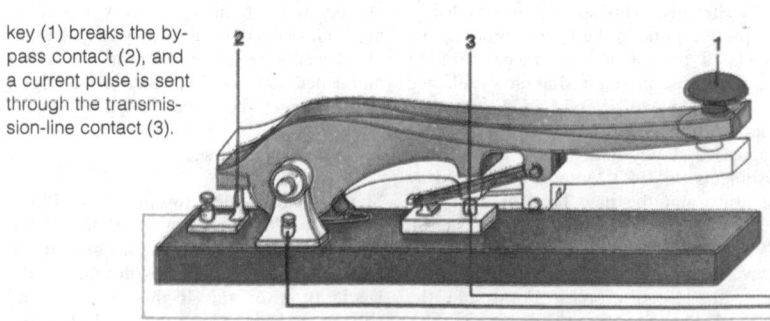

Silicate, any of various metallic compounds containing silicon and oxygen, generally with tetrahedral structures. This material makes up 95% of the earth's crust, including soil and rocks. Its basic structure consists of 4 oxygen atoms forming a pyramid-type shape with a silicon atom at the center. This structure may adhere to metals with positively charged ions.

Silicon, chemical element, symbol Si; for physical constants see Periodic Table. Silicon was isolated by Jöns J. Berzelius in 1823. It occurs in nature as sand, quartz, granite, feldspar, asbestos, and many other minerals. It is the second most abundant element and makes up 25.7% of the earth's crust by weight. Silicon is prepared by heating silicon dioxide in an electric furnace, using carbon electrodes. Silicon is a gray, lustrous, unreactive metalloid. It can be amorphous or crystalline. Silicon transmits more than 95% of all wavelengths of infrared radiation. Single crystals of silicon are used for solid-state or semiconductor devices. Silicones, a class of compounds prepared by hydrolyzing organic chlorides, are numerous with hundreds of useful properties, especially in the form of pottery, glass, and building materials. Silicon and its compounds are used in steel, as abrasives, and in lasers.

Silicone, polymer with alternate atoms of silicon and oxygen and organic groups attached to the silicon. Silicones are resistant to water and oxidation and are stable to heat. Liquid silicones are used for waterproofing, as polishes and antifoam agents. Silicone greases are high- and low-temperature lubricants, and resins are used as electrical insulators. Silicone rubbers remain flexible at low temperatures.

Silicon Valley, area around Sunnyvale, in the Santa Clara Valley, Calif., where many semiconductor manufacturers are located. More generally, it contains the greatest concentration of electronics industries in the United States. The region acquired the name because silicon is a material used in the fabrication of electronic equipment.
See also: Semiconductor.

Silicosis, form of pneumoconiosis, or fibrotic lung disease, in which long-standing inhalation of fine silica dusts in mining causes a progressive reduction in the functional capacity of the lungs. The normally thin-walled alveoli and small bronchioles become thickened with fibrous tissue, and the lungs lose their elasticity. Characteristic X-ray appearances and changes in lung function occur.

Silk, natural fiber produced by certain insects and spiders to make cocoons and webs, a glandular secretion extruded from the spinneret and hardened into a filament on exposure to air. Commercial textile silk comes from various silkworms. The cocooned pupae are killed by steam or hot air, and the cocoons are placed in hot water to soften the gum (sericin) that binds the silk. The filaments from several cocoons are then unwound together to form a single strand of 'raw silk,' which is reeled. Several strands

Already at the beginning of the Christian era, the Chinese silk industry was famous throughout the known world. There even was a special overland silkroute from China to the Roman Empire. When the Europeans established a sea trade with the Chinese during the 16th century, silk, and chinaware became the most popular items of trade. This illustration from an eighteenth-century silk album, shows women sorting out silkworms.

are twisted together (thrown) to form yarn. At this stage, or after weaving, the sericin is washed away. The thickness of the yarn is measured in denier. About 70% of all raw silk is produced in Japan.

Silk-screen printing, method of printing derived from the stencil process. A stencil is attached to a silk screen, or fine wire mesh, or formed on it by a photographic process or by drawing the design in tusche (a greasy ink). The screen is sealed with glue and then the tusche and its covering glue are washed out with an organic solvent. The framed screen is placed on the surface to be printed, and viscous ink is pressed through by a rubber squeegee. Each color requires a different screen. The process, which may be mechanized, is used for printing labels, posters, and fabrics, and on bottles and other curved surfaces. Since 1938 it has been used by painters, who call it *serigraphy*.

Silkworm, caterpillar of a moth (*Bombyx mori*) that, like many other caterpillars, spins itself a cocoon of silk in which it pupates. The cocoon is, however, especially thick and may be composed of a single thread commonly 3,000 ft (915 m) long. This is unraveled to provide commercial silk. Originally a native of China, *B. mori* has been introduced to many countries. The caterpillar, which takes about a month to develop, feeds on the leaves of the mulberry tree.

Silky terrier (formerly called Sydney Silky), breed of toy dog from Australia. Weighing up to 10 lb (4.5 kg), the silky terrier has long dark hair with tan markings. The tail is normally cut, or 'docked,' and the ears are erect and pointed. It was bred in the early 20th century from the Yorkshire and Australian terriers. Like most terriers, it is attentive and friendly.

Sillanpää, Frans Eemil (1888-1964), Finnish writer. His first novels were *Life in the Sun* (1916) and *Meek Heritage* (1919), which beautifully analyze the spiritual life of a simple Finnish peasant. The countryside and the people who live there continued to inspire him, particularly his native Hämeenkyro, and they were described in many short stories and novels in which he

chiefly wrote about the organic relationship between people and nature. He received the Nobel Prize for literature in 1939.

Silliman, Benjamin (1779-1864), U.S. chemist and geologist who founded *The American Journal of Science and Arts* (1818). The mineral sillimanite is named for him.
See also: Geology.

Sillimanite, relatively rare silicate mineral (Al_2SiO_5) found in France, Madagascar, Brazil, and the eastern United States. It is glassy in appearance, white, green, or brown in color, and often located in areas where metamorphic rock has formed under thermal pressure.

Sills, Beverly (Belle Silverman; 1929-), U.S. coloratura soprano. She made her debut at the New York City Opera in 1955, and ultimately became internationally acclaimed both as a singer and an actress in a broad variety of roles, ranging from bel canto to modern works. After retiring she was general director of the City Opera (1979-1989).
See also: Opera.

Silo, structure used on farms to preserve grasses, or silage, for livestock feed. Most silos are cylindrical and up to 50 ft (15 m) high. They are made of an air-tight material, such as glass or porcelain on the inside, and a sturdy material such as metal, brick, tile, concrete, or wood on the outside. The sweetness of certain grasses or the addition of a solution (such as sulfur dioxide) promotes fermentation, a natural process that prevents spoilage. Steady deposit and removal of silage keeps the grasses in the silo fresh for year-round feeding of livestock.

Silone, Ignazio (Secondo Tranquilli; 1900-1978), Italian writer and social reformer. Opposed to fascism, he spent 1931-1944 in exile in Switzerland. His novels include *Fontamara* (1933), *Bread and Wine* (1937), and *A Handful of Blackberries* (1952).

Silt, fine deposit, or sediment, found on river or lake bottoms. Over long periods of time, natural forces break down rock into silt, which generally has a diameter of

0.00008 to 0.002 in (0.002-0.05 mm), approximately half that of a grain of sand. During floods, silt is deposited on land, helping to make it fertile.

Silurian, third period of the Paleozoic era, which lasted between c.435 and 395 million years ago.

month of Tishri. It marks the end of the annual cycle of Sabbath readings from the Torah in the Jewish house of worship, the synagogue. The festival falls in September or October of the Roman calendar. The Saturday morning Torah readings recommence the Saturday after Simhat Torah. *See also:* Bible; Sukkot.

(apostles) of Jesus. Called Zelotes, he may have been associated with the fanatical Zealots. His feast day is Oct. 28. *See also:* Apostles.

Simon Peter *See:* Peter, Saint.

Simplon Pass and Tunnel, Alpine route, 6,590 ft (2,009 m) high and 29 mi (46.7 km) long, between Brig, Switzerland, and Isella, Italy. Napoleon I built a road across it (1800-1806).

S

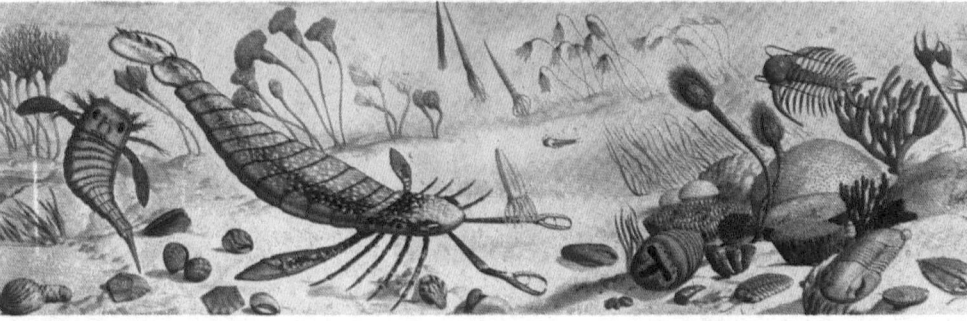

During the Silurian, the seas of the northern hemisphere teemed with animal life that included the compound corals (1) *Favosites*, (2) *Halysites* and (3) *Thamnopora*; the solitary corals (4) *Tryplasma*, (5) *Goniophyllum* and (6) *Rhabdocyclus*; the stalked echinoderms (7) *Eucalyptocrinites*, (8) *Gissocrinus*, (9) *Crotalocrinites*, (10) *Periechocrinites*, (11) *Sagenocrinites*, (12) *Leptocrinites*; the trilobites (13) *Phacops*, (14) *Dalmanites*, (15) *Bumastus* and (16) *Deiphon*; the brachiopods (17) *Rhynchotreta*, (18) *Dicoelosia*, (19) *Leptaena*, (20) *Atrypa* and (21) *Eospirifer*; the bivalve mollusk (22) *Grammysia*; the snails (23) *Tremanotus* and (24) *Platyceras*; the nautiloid (25) *Gomphoceras*; the cone-shaped shell (26) *Tentaculites*; and the eurypterids (27) *Pterygotus* and (28) *Eurypterus*.

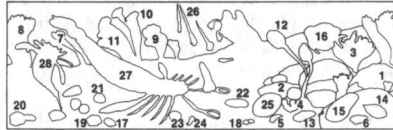

Silver, chemical element, symbol Ag; for physical constants see Periodic Table. Silver has been known and used since ancient times. It occurs in nature as argentite and horn silver, and is sometimes found uncombined. The element is produced as a byproduct from ores. It has the highest electrical and thermal conductivity of all metals. In the past silver was used as a coinage metal, but its value as bullion has driven silver coins from circulation. Silver is the best reflector of visible light known and a poor reflector of ultraviolet. Silver and its compounds are used in photography, jewelry, for mirrors and in dentistry.

Silverfish, any of various wingless insects of the order *Thysanura*. One common variety, *Lepisma saccharina*, has 2 long antennae, 3 barbed tail parts, and silver-to-gray scales. It is a pest that lives in damp areas of houses, feeding on wallpaper, books, clothes, or food.

Silver nitrate, chemical compound ($AgNO_3$) made from silver and nitric acid, used medically and industrially. As a medicine it helps prevent blindness in newborn babies and works as an antiseptic. In the form of lunar caustic, a crystalline mass, it helps cauterize wounds and ulcerations. The material called emulsion that coats photographic film is made from silver nitrate, which is also used in the manufacture of silver-plated mirrors and indelible ink.

Simenon, Georges (Georges Joseph Christian Sim; 1903-1989), Belgian-born French author of over 200 novels and thousands of short stories. He is best known for his detective novels about Inspector Maigret, works of tightly plotted suspense and psychological insight.

Simhat Torah, Jewish holiday celebrated on either the 22nd or 23rd day of the Hebrew

Simon, Claude (Eugene-Henri) (1913-), French writer. Author of *Le tricheur* (1945), *L'herb* (1958), *Tryptyque* (1973), and *L'Acacia* (1989), he won the 1985 Nobel Prize for literature as a major figure in France's *nouvelle roman* ('new novel') movement of the 1950s and 1960s. Other works include *l'Acacia* (1989), *Photographies* (1992), *Le jardin des plantes* (1997), and *Le tramway* (2001).

Simon, Neil (1927-), U.S. playwright whose career began with successful comedies such as *Come Blow Your Horn* (1961), *Barefoot in the Park* (1963), and *The Odd Couple* (1965). Many of his plays are autobiographical-including the trilogy made up of *Brighton Beach Memoirs* (1983), *Biloxi Blues* (1985), and *Broadway Bound* (1986)-and several have been made into movies. Simon has also written lyrics for Broadway musicals, such as *Sweet Charity* (1966) and *They're Playing Our Song* (1979). He received the Pulitzer Prize for *Lost in Yonkers* (1991).

Simon, Saint, one of the twelve disciples

Belgian author Georges Simenon (1903-1989).

Simpson, O.J. (Orenthal James Simpson; 1947-), U.S. football player. Known for his speed and elusive running style, he won the Heisman Trophy as the top national college player (1968). Simpson led the National Football League (NFL) in rushing 4 times (1972, 1973, 1975, 1976), and he is 6th on the alltime rushing list (11,236 career yards). He played in the NFL for the Buffalo Bills (1969-1977) and San Francisco 49ers (1978-1979) and was inducted into the Pro Football Hall of Fame (1985). In 1994 he was charged with the brutal slaying of his ex-wife, Nicole Brown Simpson, and Ronald L. Goldman. After an extensive 9-month-long trial and accompanying media frenzy, he was declared not guilty in October of 1995. However, in a civil case in 1997 he was declared guilty and sentenced to pay damages to the next of kin.

Simpson, Tom (1937-1967), British cyclist, excelled in the classics and stage races. He won the Ronde van Vlaanderen in 1961, in 1963 Bordeaux-Paris, in 1964 Milan-San Remo, and in 1965 the Giro di Lombardia. He also won the road race world championship in 1965. In 1962 he wore the yellow jersey in the Tour de France for the first time, a race which would prove fatal for him. During the climb of Mont Ventoux on 13 July, Simpson died from a combination of sunstroke, alcohol and stimulant abuse.

Simpson, Wallis Warfield *See:* Edward.

Sin, or transgression, in Judeo-Christian tradition, unethical act considered as disobedience to the revealed will of God. Sin may be viewed legally as crime-breaking God's commandments-and so deserving punishment, or as an offense that grieves God the loving Father. According to the Bible, sin entered the world in Adam's fall and all humankind became innately sinful. Both for this and for actual sins committed, people become guilty and in need of salvation. Since sin is rooted in character and will, each sinner bears personal responsibility; hence the need for repentance, confession, and absolution. Views as to what constitutes sin vary, being partly determined by church authority, social standards, and one's own conscience. The traditional '7 deadly sins' are pride, covetousness, lust, envy, gluttony, anger, and sloth. The Roman Catholic church defines a mortal sin as a serious sin committed willingly and with clear knowledge of its wrongness; a venial sin is less grave, does not wholly deprive the perpetrator of grace, and need not be individually confessed.

Sinai, in the Bible, mountain on the Sinai Peninsula where Moses received the Ten Commandments.

Sinai Peninsula, triangular desert-mountain area, nearly 150 mi (241 km) at its widest and about 230 mi (370 km) north to south, bounded by the northern arms of the Red Sea, i.e., the Gulf of Suez on the west and the Gulf of Aqaba on the east. It is believed that the Bible's Mt. Horeb, where Moses is said to have received the Ten Commandments, is one of the granitic southern peaks, either Jebel Serbal or Jebel Musa (Arabic, 'mount of Moses'; also named Mt. Sinai).

Large-scale movements of the earth's crust occurred in the Red Sea and Gulf of Aden region, and new ocean floors were formed. Africa and the Arabian Peninsula drifted apart, turning away from each other. The Sinai Peninsula (here on a satellite picture) was left: a wedge-shaped block between the two fracture systems. The system to the right (the Gulf of Eilat and the Dead Sea) can be clearly distinguished.

Sinatra, Frank (Francis Albert Sinatra; 1915-1998), U.S. singer and film star. A master of timing and communication, he achieved fame as a crooner with Tommy Dorsey's band, and then as a solo performer was a teen-age idol during World War II. He starred in several movie musicals, then became a dramatic actor of note in *From Here to Eternity* (1953), for which he received the Academy Award for best supporting actor, as well as other films. He remained one of the world's most popular vocalist-entertainers.

Sinbad, one of the folktales from the Arabian collection of stories *The Thousand and One Nights*. It consists of a preface where a poor, hard-working porter called Sinbad complains about his fate in front of the wealthy Sinbad the Sailor's large house. Sinbad the Sailor hears him and invites him to tell him about his wondrous adventures, and so a collection of stories begins within a collection of stories. The seven journeys of Sinbad the Sailor form seven separate stories, and the folktale ends with a short epilogue in which Sinbad the Sailor appoints his poor namesake as his secretary, and in so doing lets him share in his wealth.

Scheherazade begins this folktale on the 290th night, and it ends on the 315th night.

Sinclair, Upton (1878-1968), novelist and social reformer. He is best known for *The Jungle* (1906), a muckraking exposé of the horrors of the Chicago meat-packing industry, and for an 11-novel cycle, beginning with *World's End* (1940), about world events and centered on the fictional Lanny Budd. *Dragon's Teeth* (1942), the cycle's third novel, won a Pulitzer Prize.

Singapore

Capital:	Singapore
Area:	240 sq mi (648 sq km)
Population:	4,453,000
Language:	English, Malay, Chinese, Tamil
Government:	Republic
Independent:	1965
Head of gov.:	Prime minister
Per capita:	US$ 24,700
Monetary unit:	1 Singapore dollar = 100 cents

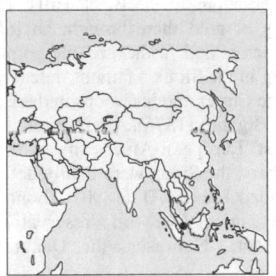

Singapore, small island republic in southeast Asia lying at the southern end of the Malay Peninsula.

Land and climate. Consisting of Singapore Island and several adjacent islets, Singapore has a total area of about 251 sq mi (648 sq km). Singapore Island is separated from the Malay Peninsula by the narrow Johore Strait crossed by a road and a railroad causeway that also has a pipeline bringing fresh water to the island. South of the island is the Singapore Strait. Mostly fringed by mangrove swamps, Singapore Island is largely low-lying, but has a central plateau bounded on the west by low hills. The climate is hot and humid and has no distinctive seasons.

People. The people of Singapore are predominantly Chinese with large Malay and Indian minorities. Principal religions are Buddhism, Islam, Christianity and Hinduism. English, Malay, Chinese, and Tamil are spoken.

Economy. The capital of the republic, Singapore City, has a fine natural harbor and is southeast Asia's foremost commercial and shipping center, conducting a flourishing international trade as a free port. It trades in textiles, rubber, petroleum, timber, and tin

and produces microelectronics, electrical goods, petroleum products, and textiles. Shipbuilding and repair are also important industries.

History. Singapore was founded as a trading port by Sir Thomas Raffles in 1819 and became part of the Straits Settlements in 1826. Occupied by the Japanese during World War II and self-governing since 1959, Singapore joined the Federation of Malaysia in 1963 but withdrew and has been independent since 1965, under the leadership of the strong prime minister (1959-1990) Lee Kuan Yew. He was succeeded by Goh Chok Tong.

Singer, Isaac Bashevis (1904-1986), Polish-born U.S. Yiddish novelist and short-story writer, known for his portrayal of European Jewish life. His work includes *The Family Moskat* (1950), *The Magician of Lublin* (1960), *The Estate* (1969), and *The Collected Short Stories of Issac Bashevis Singer* (1981). He was awarded the 1978 Nobel Prize for literature.

Singer, Isaac Merrit (1811-1875), U.S. inventor of the first viable domestic sewing machine (patented 1851). Although he lost a legal battle with the earlier inventor, Elias Howe, the Singer sewing machine soon became the most popular in the world. *See also:* Sewing machine.

Singer, Israel Joshua (1893-1944), Polish-born U.S. Yiddish novelist, playwright, and journalist, best known for his epic novel *The Brothers Ashkenazi* (1936). He was the brother of novelist Isaac Bashevis Singer.

Singh, Vishwanath Pratap (1931-), Indian politician, prime minister from 1989 to 1990. Singh was elected to the Federal Parliament in 1971 as a member of the Congress party. Under Indira Gandhi and Rajiv Gandhi, he was successively minister of commerce, finance and defense. But after the corruption scandal about the award of defense contracts to the Swedish Bofors company was made public, he was thrown out of the government and the Congress party. He returned to politics as leader of the Vanseta-Dal coalition and became prime minister. Plagued by political crises, he suffered a defeat less than a year later in a vote of no-confidence.

Singing, music created with the voice. In humans, vibrations of the vocal cords in the throat result in sounds whose mechanics are

The historic commercial district Raffles Place was named for Sir Thomas Raffles, who founded Singapore in 1819 and launched its economic development.

S

similar to those of wind instruments. The length and thickness of vocal cords as well as their tension in the throat affect the kind of sound that is made. Classifications of women's voices-from highest to lowest in pitch-are soprano, mezzo-soprano, and contralto. For men the classifications are tenor, baritone, and bass.

Singing Tower, tower in central Florida with the biggest bell chimes in the world. Located in Mountain Lake park, which also serves as a bird sanctuary, the tower, designed by Milton B. Medary with doors and railings by Samuel Yellin, stands 205 ft (62 m) high. Marble bridges cross a surrounding moat to allow access to it.

Single tax, proposed reform that tax on land value should be a government's sole revenue, stated by Henry George in *Progress and Poverty* (1879). He argued that economic rent of land results from the growth of an economy, not from an individual's effort; therefore, governments are justified in approaching all economic rents, thus eliminating the need for other taxes. The proposal was never enacted in the United States.

Sing Sing, state prison in the city of Ossining, N.Y. Built in 1925 under a program that employed inmates as laborers, the prison has been expanded with the addition of later buildings.
See also: Prison.

Sinhalese, also Singhalese or Sinhala, Indo-Aryan language derived from Sanskrit, spoken by the majority of the people of Sri Lanka. Most other Sri Lankans (or Sinhalese) speak Tamil.

Sinn Féin (Irish, 'we, ourselves'), Irish nationalist movement formed by Arthur Griffith in 1905. It secured wide support in 1916, when most of the leaders of the Easter Rebellion against English suppression were martyred. Led by Eamon De Valera, the Sinn Féin set up a separate Irish Parliament, the Dáil Éireann, which declared Irish independence (1918). Sinn Féin guerrilla activity was countered by British Black and Tans military terrorists (1920), but Irish resolve strengthened to the point of war. Britain negotiated a peace treaty with De Valera, and the result was the establishment of the Irish Free State in 1922. The treaty split the Sinn Féin into factions; civil war ensued. Eventually the majority of the Irish backed De Valera's party, the Fainna Fáil, and he became president of the Irish Free State in 1932. With independence, the Sinn Féin movement ended-except for that faction called the Irish Republican Army, which was outlawed.
Sinn Féin has been the political wing of the IRA since the 1950s; it participated in the peace talks that would lead to the Good Friday Agreement in 1998. After the direct government from London had been abolished under the condition that the IRA would decommission their weapons, Sinn Fein and the Ulster Unionist Party formed a coalition. However, when the IRA did not get rid of their weapons, the peace process reached a deadlock. In 2001, the self-government came to an end, because Sinn Féin was no longer accepted as a coalition partner. As a result, Sinn Féin put pressure on the IRA, which started to disarm in that same year. The Northern-Irish government was reconvened.
See also: De Valera, Eamon.

Sintering, process by which powdered metal is used to form solid objects. The particles of the powdered metal are heated until they adhere one to the other to form solid objects.

Sinus, body cavity, usually containing air or blood. Generally, this term refers to the large air space connected with the nose that may become infected and obstructed after upper respiratory infection and cause facial pain and fever (sinusitis). The major nasal sinuses are maxillary, frontal, ethmoid, and sphenoid.

Sioux, or Dakota, confederation of Native American peoples in the North American plains. There were 7 main Sioux tribes, including the Santee, or Dakota, of what is now Minnesota, and the Lakota, or Teton, of the western Dakotas and Nebraska. The Sioux lived in tepees, and their principal activities were buffalo hunting and raiding. Their most famous ceremony was the sun dance. However, by 1867 the Sioux had been forced to give up their lands and move to reservations in the Black Hills. The discovery of gold there brought an influx of prospectors and further trouble erupted, resulting in the Sioux's famous defeat of Gen. George Custer and his troops in the Battle of Little Bighorn (1876). After repeated revolts against European-American misrule and treachery, the Sioux were finally defeated at Wounded Knee, S.D. (1890). About 40,000 Sioux now live on reservations in Minnesota, Nebraska, the Dakotas, and Montana.

Siphon, device, usually consisting of a bent tube with 2 legs of unequal length, that utilizes atmospheric pressure to transfer liquid over the edge of one container into another at a lower level. The flowing action depends on the difference in the pressures acting on the 2 liquid surfaces and stops when these coincide.

Siqueiros, David Alfaro (1896-1974), a Mexican painter. With Rivera and Orozco he helped found the Mexican mural movement in the 1920's. A technical innovator, Siqueiros experimented with industrial and synthetic paints, spray guns, and curved surfaces in such murals as *Portrait of the Bourgeoisie*. In *The March of Humanity in Latin America* his metal sculptured relief figures add to the illusion of movement. Siqueiros was born in Chihuahua, and studied art in Mexico City and in Paris. Siqueiros served as a revolutionary soldier in his teens and remained a political activist throughout his life; he was imprisoned several times by the Mexican government.
His other murals in Mexico City include *Burial of a Worker*, National Preparatory School; *New Democracy*, National Palace of Fine Arts; *The Revolution against the Porfirian Dictatorship*, National Museum of History. His major easel paintings include *Proletarian Mother* and *Our Present Image*.

Siren, device used to create loud, shrill warning signals. Foghorns are sirens that warn of low visibility due to foggy weather conditions. Electronic devices are now often used as sirens. Older ones worked mechanically, one cylinder or disk rotating within another punctured with air holes. The motion created the sound waves.
See also: Civil defense.

Sirenian, or sea cow, any of an order (*Sirenia*) of aquatic mammals. These large, shy animals feed on plant life in shallow tropical seas. The manatee of Florida, a sirenian, is an endangered species. The name comes from the sirens, sea creatures of Greek mythology.

Sirens, in Greek mythology, sea nymphs whose irresistible singing lured sailors to their deaths on rocky coasts. Sirens appear in ancient stories, including Homer's *Odyssey*, whose hero, Odysseus, had himself tied to a mast and his men's ears plugged as they sailed past the sirens' coast in order to resist.
See also: Mythology.

Sirius, Alpha Canis Majoris (Dog Star), brightest star in the night sky. About 8.8 light years distant from the earth, it is 20 times more luminous than the sun and has an absolute magnitude of +1.4. A double star, its major component is twice the size of the sun; its major component (the Pup), the first white-dwarf star to be discovered, has a diameter only 50% greater than that of the earth but is extremely dense, its mass being just less than that of the sun.
See also: Binary star.

Sirocco, in southern Europe, warm, humid wind from the south or southeast, originating as a dry wind over the Sahara and gaining humidity from passage over the Mediterranean.

Sisal, any of various plants of the agave family, genus *Agave*. Two types of sisal, *A. sisalana*, found in eastern Africa and Brazil, and *A. fourcroydes*, found in Mexico, El Salvador, and Cuba, contain long fibers used to manufacture twine and hemp.

Sisley, Alfred (1839-1899), Anglo-French painter, a founder of impressionism. His fine landscapes and snow scenes, painted in the 1870s, often show London and Paris neighborhoods; for example, *Effet de neige* (1874). His work achieved wide recognition only after his death.
See also: Impressionism.

Sistine Chapel, papal chapel in the Vatican Palace, Rome, renowned for its magnificent frescoes by Michelangelo and other Renaissance artists like Perugino, Botticelli, and Ghirlandaio. It is named for Pope Sixtus IV, who began its construction in 1473, and is used by the College of Cardinals when it meets to elect a new pope.

Sisyphus, in Greek mythology, founder and king of the ancient city-state of Corinth. Zeus, the head of the gods, was angered at Sisyphus and condemned him to push a heavy rock to the top of a hill. When it reached the top, it rolled back down, and Sisyphus was compelled to repeat the task for all eternity.
See also: Mythology.

Sitar, Indian stringed instrument with a long neck and smallish, rounded soundbox. There are usually 7 strings-5 melody and 2 drone. These are plucked by a player seated on cushions or the floor. In 1957 the Indian sitar virtuoso Ravi Shankar made the first of several concert tours of the United States, spreading the popularity of the instrument, which was then used by several rock bands.

Sitting Bull (c.1831-1890), chief of the Teton Sioux who led the last major Native American resistance in the United States. Born in South Dakota, he became head of the Sioux nation and inspired the 1876 campaign that resulted in the massacre of Gen. George Custer and his troops at Little Bighorn.

Sitwell, Dame Edith (1887-1964), British poet and critic. A master technician of sound, rhythm, and symbol, she helped launch *Wheels* (1916), a magazine of experimental poetry, and wrote the satirical *Façade* (1922; music by William Walton).

Six, les, term coined in 1920 for a group of French composers: Georges Auric, Louis Durey, Arthur Honegger, Darius Milhaud, Francis Poulenc, and Germaine Tailleferre, inspired by the anti-impressionist work of Erik Satie. They also worked with the writer Jean Cocteau.

Sixtus, name of 5 popes. **Sixtus IV** (1414-1484) succeeded in 1471 and built the Sistine Chapel. His reign was characterized by nepotism and simony. **Sixtus V** (1521-1590) succeeded in 1585 and brought the Papal States to order and made the pope one of Europe's richest princes. His reforms of church administration were part of the Counter-Reformation.

Skagerrak, also spelled Skager-Rak and Skagerrack, arm of the North Sea that separates Denmark from Norway and Sweden. About 130 mi (209 km) long, the Skagerrak joins the North Sea and the Kattegat.
See also: North Sea.

Skate, any of various fish (genus *Raja*) similar to rays. A popular skate used for food is the little skate (*R. erinacea*), which measures up to 2 ft (61 cm) long and is caught along the U.S. and Canadian Atlantic coast. Along the Pacific coast, the big skate (*R. binoculata*), which can measure up to 8 ft (2.5 m) long, are found. The pectoral fins of skate look and act like underwater wings, spanning the length of the fish from head nearly to its rudderlike tail. The wings move up and down to move the fish along. Skates generally feed on smaller animals, such as snails.

Skateboard, small board with plastic wheels, forming a kind of surfboard to be used on land. Professional and experienced skateboard riders can turn in circles on one wheel (endovers), travel on just 2 of the 4 wheels (wheelies), and jump over a multitude of objects during a ride.

Skeet, sport in which the competitor shoots at clay disks mechanically thrown into the air. The disks are tossed to imitate the flight of certain birds. Shooters, using modified shotguns, stand at specific stations from which they shoot at the disks, which may be tossed individually or in pairs.

Skeleton, in vertebrates, framework of bones that supports and protects the soft tissues and organs of the body. It acts as an attachment for the muscles, especially those producing movement, and protects vital organs such as the brain, heart, and lungs. It is also a store of calcium, magnesium, sodium, phosphorous, and proteins, while its bone marrow is the site of red blood corpuscle formation. In the adult human body there are about 206 bones, to which more than 600 muscles are attached.
The skeleton consists of the axial skeleton (the skull, backbone, and ribcage) and the appendicular skeleton (limbs). The function of the *axial skeleton* is mainly protective. The skull consists of 29 bones, 8 being fused to form the cranium, protecting the brain. The *vertebral column*, or backbone, consists of 33 small bones (or vertebrae). The upper 25 are joined by ligaments and thick cartilaginous disks, and the lower 9 are fused. It supports the upper body and protects the spinal cord, which runs through it. The *ribcage* consists of 12 pairs of ribs forming a protective cage around the heart and lungs, and assists in breathing. The *appendicular skeleton* is primarily concerned with locomotion and consists of the arms and pectoral girdle and the legs and pelvic girdle. The limbs articulate with their girdles in ball-and-socket joints that permit the shoulder and hip great freedom of movement but that are prone to dislocation. In contrast, the elbows and knees are hinge joints that permit movement in one plane only but that are very strong.

Skepticism, philosophical attitude of doubting all claims to knowledge, chiefly on the ground that the adequacy of any proposed criterion is itself questionable. Examples of thoroughgoing skeptics, wary of dogmatism in whatever guise, were Pyrrho of Elis (*Pyrrhonism* and *skepticism* are virtual synonyms) and David Hume. Other thinkers-among them St. Augustine, Desiderius Erasmus, Michel de Montaigne, Blaise Pascal, Pierre Bayle, and Sören Kierkegaard-sought to defend faith and religion by directing skeptical arguments against the epistemological claims of rationalism and empiricism. Pragmatism and Immanuel Kant's critical philosophy repre-

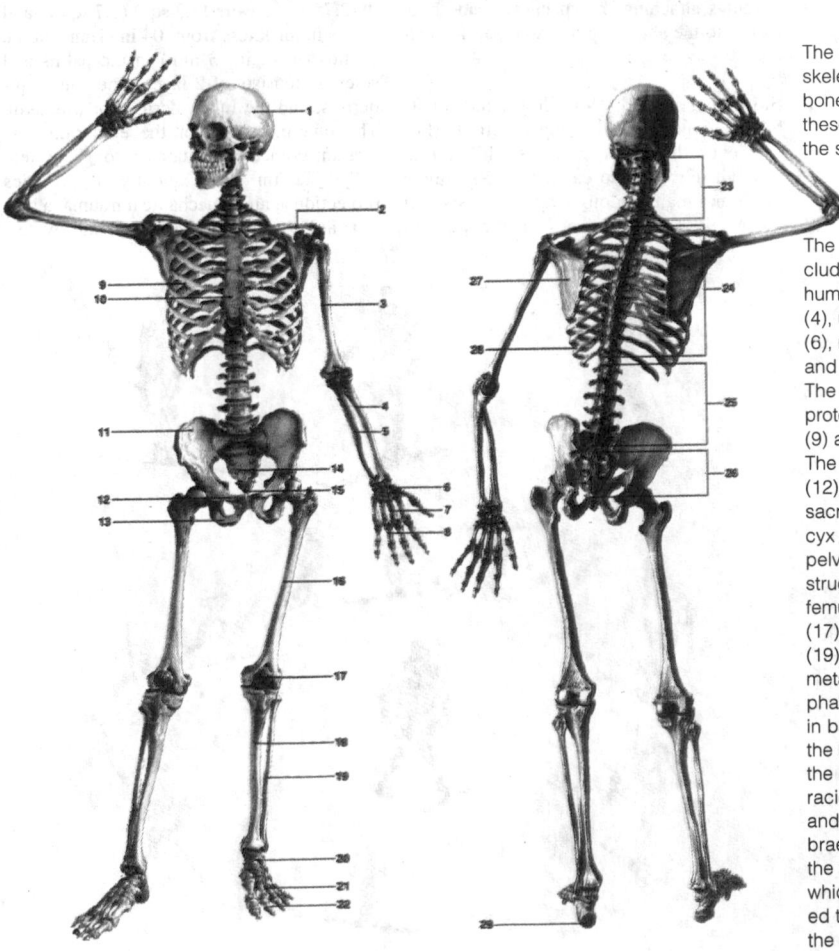

The adult human skeleton contains 206 bones. Twenty-two of these are located in the skull (1).

The arm structure includes the clavicle (2), humerus (3), radius (4), ulna (5), carpus (6), metacarpus (7), and phalanges (8). The chest organs are protected by the ribs (9) and sternum (10). The ilium (11), pubis (12), ischium (13), sacrum (14), and coccyx (15) make up the pelvic girdle. The leg structure includes the femur (16), patella (17), tibia (18), fibula (19), tarsus (20), metatarsus (21), and phalanges (22). Visible in back view (right) is the spine, consisting of the cervical (23), thoracic (24), lumbar (25) and sacral (26) vertebrae; the scapula (27); the floating ribs (28), which are not connected to the sternum; and the calcaneus (29).

S

sent two influential attempts to resolve skeptical dilemmas.
See also: Carneades; Pyrrho of Elis.

Skew line, in geometry, line that neither intersects nor runs parallel to another line in the same plane; in statistics, a line, as on a graph, indicating that the measured quantity departs from a normal distribution to the right or left of the curve.
See also: Geometry.

Skidmore, Louis (1897-1962), U.S. architect and cofounder of the firm of Skidmore, Owings and Merrill (1936), which designed such government and corporate projects as Oak Ridge, Tenn. (1943-1945), the U.S. Air Force Academy in Colorado Springs (1954-1962), and the Sears Tower in Chicago (1971-1973).
See also: Architecture.

Skiing, sport of gliding over snow on long, thin runners called skis. It began some 5,000 years ago in northern Europe as a form of transport and became a sport in the 19th century. In 1924 the Fédération Internationale de Ski was formed and the first Winter Olympics held. It has increased enormously in popularity, either for pleasure or through participation in such Olympic-style activities as Alpine downhill slaloms, giant slalom obstacle races, Nordic cross-country skiing, or ski-jumping. Skis are generally made of laminated wood, fiberglass, plastic, metal, or a combination of these. They have safety bindings attaching the specially made boot firmly to the ski; ski poles are used for balance.

Skimmer, seabird whose lower half of its bill is longer than the upper half. It flies low over the water with its bill cutting through the water to catch fish. Skimmers are found mainly along tropical coasts, but the black skimmer comes up the western

Human skin consists of two strata, the epidermis (1) and the dermis (2), supported by a layer of fat (3). The epidermis is made up of several layers. Its outer layer (4) contains scalelike dead cells that are continously shed. Granular cells in the next layer (5) produce a hard protein called keratin, which forms hair and nails. The third layer (6) consists of flattened polygonal cells. Below this is a deep layer of columnar cells (7), among which are found the melanocytes (8) — the cells that produce the pigment melanin. The dermis consists of collagen and elastin, fibrous proteins that form connective tissue (9). In this tissue are embedded nerve fibers (10), sensory nerve endings (11), capillaries (12), lymph vessels (13), sweat glands (14), and hair follicles (15). Each follicle bears a hair shaft (16) in a sheath (17); an oil gland (18), which lubricates the shaft; and an arrector pili muscle (19), which tightens in response to fear or chill.

Atlantic as far as Massachusetts. They live in flocks, and their calls sound like a pack of hounds.

Skin, tissue that forms a sensitive, elastic, protective, and waterproof covering of the body, together with its specializations (e.g., nails, hair). In the adult human it weighs 6.1 lb (2.75 kg), covers 18.3 sq ft (1.7 sq m), and varies in thickness from .04 in (1mm) in the eyelids to .12 in (3 mm) in the palms and soles. It consists of 2 layers: the outer, epidermis, and the inner, dermis, or true skin. The outermost part of the epidermis, the stratum corneum, contains a tough protein called keratin. Consequently, it provides protection against mechanical trauma, a barrier against microorganisms, and water-proofing. The epidermis also contains cells that produce the melanin responsible for skin pigmentation and that provide protection against the sun's ultraviolet rays. The unique pattern of skin folding on the soles and palms provides a gripping surface and is the basis of identification by fingerprints. The dermis is usually thicker than the epidermis and contains blood vessels, nerves, and sensory receptors, sweat glands, sebaceous glands, hair follicles, fat cells, and fibers. Temperature regulation of the body is aided by the evaporative cooling of sweat, regulation of the skin blood flow, and the erection of hairs that trap an insulating layer of air next to the skin. The rich nerve supply of the dermis is responsible for the reception of touch, pressure, pain, and temperature stimuli. Leading into the hair follicles are sebaceous glands that produce the antibacterial sebum, a fluid that keeps the hairs oiled and the skin moist. The action of sunlight on the skin initiates the formation of vitamin D, which helps prevent rickets.

Skin diving, underwater swimming and diving with or without selfcontained underwater breathing apparatus (SCUBA). The simplest apparatus is the snorkel, generally used with goggles, or mask, and flippers. An aqualung consists of compressed-air cylinders with an automatic demand regulator that supplies air at the correct pressure according to the diver's depth. 'Closed-circuit' SCUBA contains a chemical that absorbs carbon dioxide from exhaled air.

Skin grafting, application of portions of skin, either the outer layers or the full thickness, to a raw surface to promote healing or to replace a defect.
See also: Plastic surgery.

Skink, slender lizard found in many of the warmer parts of the world. Skinks are abundant in Africa and 50 species live in the Americas. Some have rough scales, but the rest have very flat scales, sometimes so

Basic ski techniques. (A) Walking on the level, in which the skis are not lifted, but pushed forward on the snow. (B) The posture for running straight downhill, with the ankles, knees and waist easily flexed. (C) The kick turn, useful for an about turn. (D) The snowplough position: a means of braking and, on gentle slopes, of coming to a stop. (E) Traversing: skiing across the slope. (F) Sideslipping, used for losing height from a traverse position. (G) The stem turn, which is a snowplough turn, from one traverse position to the opposite.

small that they are hard to see. Skinks may be aquatic or tree dwellers, and many have taken up burrowing, like the Florida sand skink. The largest skink is the 2-ft (0.61-m) giant zebra skink of the Solomon Islands, which has a prehensile tail. Skinks eat plants or small animals. Most lay eggs that are guarded by the mother; others bear live young. Young skinks often have blue tails that break off when they are attacked.

Skinner, B.F. (1904-1990), U.S. psychologist and author whose advocacy of behaviorism helped it gain acceptance in 20th-century psychology. His best-known books are *Science and Human Behavior* (1953); *Walden Two* (1961), a Utopian novel based on behaviorism; and *Beyond Freedom and Dignity* (1971).

Sklodowska, Marie *See:* Curie, Marie Sklodowska.

Skopje (pop. 444.000), the capital of the Republic of Macedonia. It lies on the Vardar River, in the northern part of the republic near its border with Yugoslavia. Skopje is an important trade and transportation center with varied industries, including food processing, metallurgy, and chemical manufacturing. The city has a university, several museums, and numerous mosques.
Skopje dates from at least the third century A.D., when it was a Roman colony. After being destroyed by an earthquake in 518, it was rebuilt and flourished as part of the Byzantine Empire. Skopje was captured by the Slavs by 695, but in the next 700 years it changed hands many times. Late in the 14th century the Ottoman Turks conquered the city. They held it until 1913, when it was granted to Serbia by the Treaty of Bucharest. After World War I, Skopje became part of the Kingdom of the Serbs, Croats, and Slovenes (Yugoslavia). It became capital of an independent country when Macedonia seceded from Yugoslavia in 1991.

Skryabin, Alexander *See:* Scriabin, Alexander.

Skua, any of various sea birds (genus *Stercorarius*) known for stealing food from other sea birds, such as gulls, terns, petrels, and penguins. The skua lives in arctic and antarctic regions. Similar in looks to a sea gull, it is normally reddish to brown, with white patches on the wings. Skuas are strong fliers who harass weaker birds, causing them to drop their prey.

Skull, bony structure of the head and face situated at the top of the vertebral column. It forms a thick, bony protection of the brain, with small apertures for blood vessels, nerves, the spinal cord, and the thinner framework of facial structure.

Skunk, carnivorous mammal of the weasel family renowned for the foul stink it produces when threatened. There are 10 species distributed throughout the Americas. All are boldly patterned in black and white. Most are nocturnal and feed on insects, mice, and eggs. For defense, a skunk can expel fine jets of foul-smelling liquid from scent glands

under the tail to a distance of 10 ft (3 m) with a remarkably accurate aim.

Skunk cabbage, either of two plant species (*Symplocarpus foetidus* or *Lysichitum americanum*), of temperate regions named for the foul smell that comes from the plant when the tissues are squeezed. Apart from the smell, the skunk cabbage is a welcome addition to the damp woods and fields of the eastern United States for its purple and green arum-type flower, which appears in late winter. The leaves appear after the flowers have died. A third species, *Veratrum californicum*, also called false hellebore or corn lily, grows in western North and Central America and is poisonous.

Sky *See:* Atmosphere.

Skydiving, popular name for sport parachuting. Skydivers reach speeds of up to 100 mph (160 kmph) after jumping out of planes at altitudes of up to 15,000 ft (4,600 m). The last 3,000 ft (920 m) or so of the fall is slowed by a parachute. Skydivers who aim for a ground target are called accuracy skydivers. Those that fall in formation with other divers are called relative work skydivers.

Skye terrier, breed of dog named after the Isle of Skye, Scotland, where it was first bred, in the 17th century. A work dog, good rat hunter, and pleasant companion, this terrier stands up to 10 in (25 cm) high at the shoulder and has a long body. Ears may be floppy or erect.

Skylab *See:* Space exploration.

Skyscraper, extremely tall building. In the mid-19th century the rising cost of land in big cities made building upward rather than outward worthwhile, and this became practicable with the development of safe electric elevators. The first skyscraper was the 130-ft (39.6 m) Equitable Life Assurance Society Building in New York (1870). A major design breakthrough was the use of a load-bearing skeletal iron frame, first used in the 10-story Home Insurance Building in Chicago (1883). The tallest skyscrapers are the Sears Tower in Chicago and the World Trade Center in New York City, with more than 110 stories.

Slag, residual material produced during the manufacture of pig iron and the smelting of metals, such as copper or lead. Slag is used in the making of concrete, road-building materials, and fertilizer. Its composition depends on the metallurgical process that produced it, though all slag contains silicates.

Slander, false statements intended to damage a person's reputation. A slanderous statement that is written or printed is called libel. The civil laws of the United States allow people to sue for libel.
See also: Libel.

Slang, informal and innovative use of language. Slang generally expresses new ideas or variations of old ones, most often in spoken speech. The particular words and expressions used tend not to remain popular

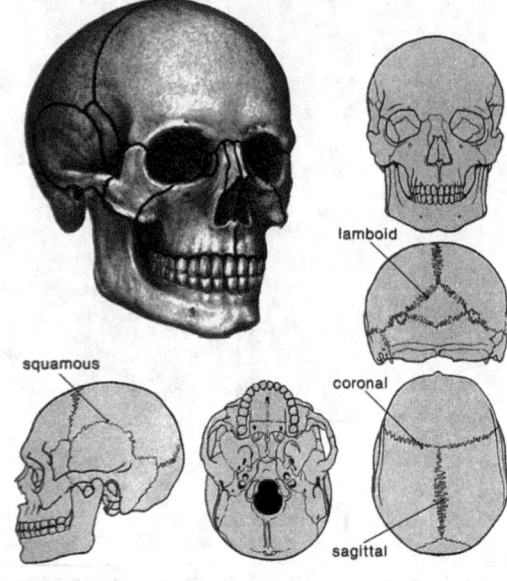

lamboid

squamous

coronal

sagittal

S

for long, and slang often changes from region to region or from one ethnic or class group to the next.

Slate, fine-grained, low-grade metamorphic rock formed by the regional metamorphism of shale. The parallel orientation of platy minerals in the rock causes it to split evenly (slaty cleavage) in a plane that is perpendicular to the direction of the compressive metamorphic stress.

Slavery, practice found at different times in most parts of the world, now condemned in the UN's Universal Declaration of Human Rights. Slavery generally means enforced servitude, along with society's recognition that the master has ownership rights over the slave and his or her labor. Some elements of slavery can be found in serfdom, as practiced during the Middle Ages and in Russia up to 1861; in debt bondage and peonage, both forms of enforced labor for the payment of debts; and in forced labor itself, exacted for punishment or for political or military reasons (examples being the 'slave' labor used by the Nazis in World War II and the Soviet labor camps). In some places a form of slavery, or bondage, is still practiced today, under the guise of exacting a bride price, or the 'adoption' of poor children by wealthier families for labor purposes. While peonage is still rampant in South America, actual slavery is reputed to exist in Africa, the Arabian Peninsula, Tibet, and elsewhere. Slavery in Saudi Arabia was officially abolished only in 1962.
Warfare was the main source of slaves in ancient times, along with enslavement for debt or as punishment and the selling of children. But there was not necessarily a distinction in race or color between master and slave. Manumission (the granting of freedom) was commonplace, and in Greece and Rome many slaves or freedmen rose to influential posts. A slave dynasty, the Mamelukes, ruled Egypt (1250-1517). Germans enslaved many Slavic people (hence *slave*) in the Dark Ages. By the 13th century feudal serfdom was widespread in Europe. Slavery in-

The skull contains seven deep bones and seven superficial bones. With the cranium bones, they house the sense organs, brain, and spinal cord. The lower jaw is attached to the cranium by a hinge; all other major skull bones are fused together by immovable joints, called sutures. Clockwise from top right: front view, back view, top view, base of the skull, showing the opening for the spinal cord, and side view.

S

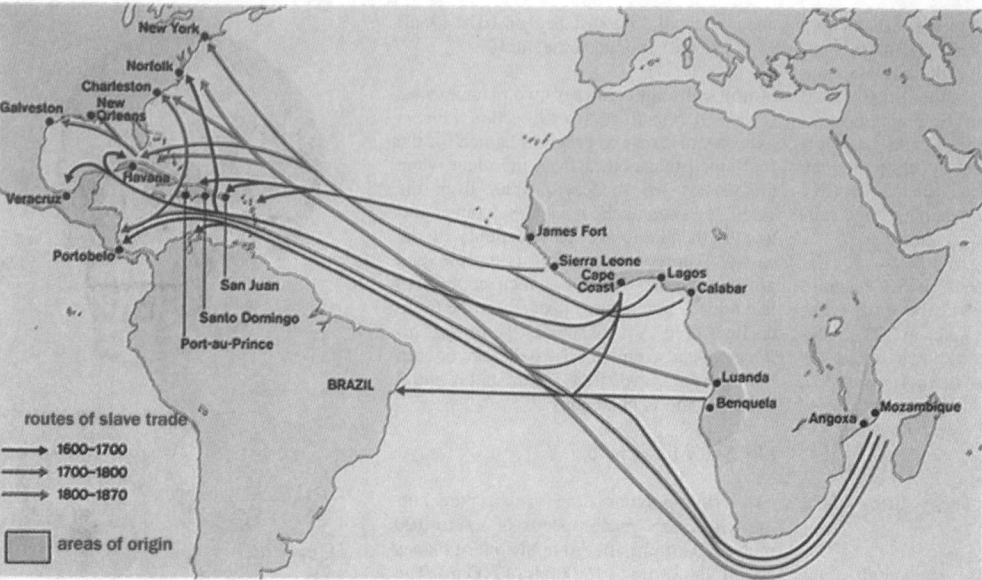

Slave routes from Africa to the New World. African slaves were transported to depots in the Caribbean or straight to Northeastern Brazil, Central America or the harbors near the Northern American cotton fields.

TO BE SOLD, on board the Ship *Bance-Island*, on tuesday the 6th of *May* next, at *Ashley-Ferry*; a choice cargo of about 250 fine healthy

NEGROES,

just arrived from the Windward & Rice Coast.
—The utmost care has already been taken, and shall be continued, to keep them free from the least danger of being infected with the SMALL-POX, no boat having been on board, and all other communication with people from *Charles-Town* prevented.

Austin, Laurens, & Appleby.

N. B. Full one Half of the above Negroes have had the SMALL-POX in their own Country.

English poster offering a load of 'niggers' for sale. Everything was done to guarantee high-quality trading.

Slave brands in Suriname. The brands were scorched into the slaves' skin, so it would always be clear who the rightful owner was.

Idyllic picture of Negro slaves on an American cotton plantation. The memoirs of Josiah Henson tell the real story of how slaves were treated. Henson was a slave who managed to escape from a plant in Maryland and founded a colony of former slaves in Canada. 'Our favorite way to sleep (in the hut) was on a plank, with our head resting on an old coat and our feet warming by the fire. The wind howled, rain and snow came through gaps in the roof and the musty earth sucked up all the water, making the floor look like one in a pig's sty. This was where we lived. This was where we were locked in at night, fed during the day; this was were our children were born and the sick – neglected.' Henson's memoirs from 1849 inspired Harriet Beecher Stowe (1811-1896) to write the book *Uncle Tom's Cabin* (1852).

Former collection point for slaves on the island of Goré, off the cost of Senegal, now a museum. The slaves left by the back way and walked straight onto the waiting ships.

Locket against slavery from 1787, made by porcelain producer Josiah Wedgwood. The locket was part of a big English anti-slavery campaign. This pressurized Britain into the abolition of slavery in the United Kingdom in 1807, and slavery itself in 1833. After that, other countries followed: France in 1848, the United States and the Netherlands in 1863, and Brazil in 1888.

Every year, the people of Suriname still celebrate the abolition of slavery on the 1st of July, like here in Rotterdam, the Netherlands, in 1998. The celebration is called Keti Koti Dey, the Day the Chain Was Broken.

Diagram of a slave ship. The slaves were transported under terrible conditions to the New World, packed together like cattle. Between 15 and 20% of them did not survive the crossing.

Store Room.

Store Room.

S

The two-toed sloth, *Choloepus* is camouflaged by its fur, on which algae are growing. The algae turn green in rainy weather and yellow during periods of drought.

creased when the Portuguese, exploring the coast of Africa, began to import slaves in 1433. With the European discovery of the Americas and the development of plantations, the need for cheap, abundant labor encouraged slave trade. The British abolished its own slave trade in 1807 and slavery in 1833. By constitutional provision, the U.S. slave trade ended in 1808, but not the practice. The abolition issue ignited the U.S. Civil War in 1861. President Lincoln's Emancipation Proclamation (1863) took full effect with the end of the war in 1865.

Slavonic, 3 groups of Indo-European languages spoken by about 440 million people in central and eastern Europe and Siberia. The groups are West Slavonic (Polish, Czech, Slovak), South Slavonic (Slovene, Serbo-Croatian, Macedonian, Bulgarian), and East Slavonic (Russian, Ukrainian, Byelorussian). Byzantine missionaries in the 9th century first developed written Slavic, using a modified Greek alphabet known as Cyrillic. Today Slavs converted by the Orthodox church use Cyrillic characters, and Slavs converted by the Roman church use the Latin alphabet.

Slavs, largest European ethnic group, living today in central and eastern Europe and Siberia, all speaking Slavic languages. About 4,000 years ago they migrated to land north of the Black Sea and later split into 3 groups: the East Slavs (Byelorussians, Russians, and Ukrainians), the West Slavs (Czechs, Poles, Slovaks, and Sorbs (Wends), and the South Slavs (Bulgarians, Macedonians, Serbs, Croats, and Slovens). By the 9th century Slavic nations were formed, but almost all were overwhelmed by Turkish or Mongol invaders. In the 15th century Russia gained national independence, but other Slavic nations did not regain their national identities until World War I.

Sled, transportation vehicle that moves over ice and snow on runners. Early sleds were made from joined logs. Some Native American tribes developed toboggans-sleds shaped like canoes. Today in Alaska and other ice-covered regions, sleds with thin, parallel runners pulled by dogs help to transport people and goods. Bobsleds are fiberglass-and-steel sleds ridden on special courses for speed.

Sleep, state of relative unconsciousness and inactivity. The need for sleep recurs periodically in all animals. If deprived of sleep, humans initially experience hallucinations and acute anxiety and become highly suggestible. Eventually coma and sometimes death result. During sleep, the body is relaxed and most bodily activity is reduced. Cortical, or higher, brain activity, is measured by the electroencephalograph; blood pressure, body temperature, and rate of heartbeat and breathing are decreased. However, certain activities, such as gastric and alimentary activity, are increased. Sleep tends to occur in daily cycles that exhibit up to 5 or 6 periods of deepness-alternating with periods of paradoxical, or rapid-eye-movement (REM), sleep, characterized by restlessness and jerky movements of the

eyes. Paradoxical sleep occurs only when we are dreaming and occupies about 20% of total sleeping time. Sleepwalking (somnambulism) occurs only during orthodox sleep, when we are not dreaming. Sleeptalking occurs mostly in orthodox sleep. Many theories have been proposed to explain sleep. Separate sleeping and waking centers in the hypothalamus cooperate with other parts of the brain in controlling sleep. Sleep as a whole-and particularly paradoxical sleep, when dreaming occurs-is essential to health and life. Consequently, the key to why animals sleep may reside in a need to dream.

Sleeping sickness, serious disease caused by protozoan parasites and transmitted by the bite of the tsetse fly. Sleeping sickness is common in many areas of Africa. Symptoms include fever, headache, skin rash, swollen lymph nodes, and lethargy. The disease is named after the comalike state that may eventually result. Early diagnosis and drug treatment can lessen the sometimes fatal effects.

Sleepwalking (somnambulism), condition in which a partly awakened sleeper performs physical activities during a period of tension or worry. It occurs during deep sleep, early in the night. Most sleepwalkers do not remember their activities upon awakening. Sleepwalking is generally harmless, although injury can occur.

Sleet, partially frozen, transparent bits of ice, falling initially as rain or melted snowflakes and freezing as they travel through parts of the atmosphere below 32°F (0°C).

Slime mold, organism classified as a fungus but that resembles an animal in its ability to move. A slime mold is a yellowish mass, like the raw white of an egg, that is found in damp, dark woods, where it oozes over rotten logs and decayed leaves. It moves like an amoeba, sweeping up particles of dead leaves and bacteria as it goes.

Sling, device used to hurl stones or other objects. In ancient slings, a stone was placed on a strap and spun quickly above the head before being let loose to fly through the air with great force. The biblical hero David killed Goliath with a stone from a sling. Soldiers from the armies of ancient Egypt through those of medieval Europe used slings in combat. Another form of sling, the bola, is tossed along with the stone. Thrown at an animal, it will entangle its legs as well as forcefully hit it.

Slipperwort, or slipper flower, any of a group of 300-400 evergreen plants belonging to the figwort family found in Mexico and South America. Its name derives from the slipperlike shape of its flowers, which are variously colored.

Sloe, or blackthorn, spiny shrub (*Prunus spinosa*) of the rose family found in some parts of North America, Asia, and Europe. Its plumlike fruits are used to make a variety of products, such as dyes, jellies, and wine.

Sloth, slow, tree-dwelling, toothless mam-

mal. There are 2 genera of modern tree sloths; 2-toed sloths (*Choloepus*) and 3-toed sloths, or ai (*Bradypus*), descending from the giant ground sloths (*Megatherium*) of the Pleistocene epoch. The arms and legs are long and the digits are bound together by tissue and terminate in long, strong claws. With these the sloth can suspend its body from branches. All sloths are South American in origin and vegetarian, feeding on fruits, shoots, and leaves.

Sloth bear, or honey bear, slow-moving mammal of the bear family found in the warm forest regions of India and Sri Lanka. Although its sense of smell is highly developed, the sloth bear has poor vision and hearing. A staple of its diet is insects, which it ferrets out with its long claws and snout, then sucks in through spaces between the teeth. It is also known to like honey. A sloth bear stands about 5 ft (1.5 m) tall and can weigh up to 250 lb (113 kg). Unlike some other bears, it does not hibernate during the winter months.

Slot machine, mechanized gambling device first developed in 1899. Coins are inserted through a slot, a handle is pulled, and a series of reels, visible through a window, spin for a while before coming to a halt. The player wins if the reels show a certain number of identical symbols.

Slovakia

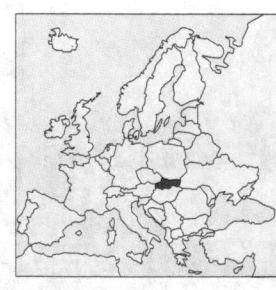

Capital:	Bratislava
Area:	18,933 sq mi (49,036 sq km)
Population:	5,422,000
Language:	Slowak
Government:	Republic
Independent:	1993
Head of gov.:	Prime minister
Per capita:	US$ 11,500
Monetary unit:	1 Koruna = 100 halierov

Slovakia, or Slovak Republic, independent country in central Europe, bordered on the north by Poland, on the east by Ukraine, on the south by Hungary, on the west by Austria, and on the northwest by the Czech republic.
Land and climate. Slovakia is mostly mountainous, but the heights slope down to plains and the Danube River in the south and

southwest. The climate is continental with warm summers and cold winters.

People. The population consists mainly of Slovaks (68%), minorities are Hungarians (11%) and Roma (gypsies). The official language is Slovak. About 60% of the population is Roman Catholic.

Economy. Slovakia has rich farmlands and mineral deposits; shipbuilding and metal processing are leading industries. The capital is a prominent Danube port.

History. Slovakia was principally under Hungarian rule from the early 10th century to 1918. Slovakia then became part of Czechoslovakia until its independence in 1993.

In 1998, a center-right government was elected to power and headed for connection to the west. Mikulás Dzurinda became Prime Minister. The government forged ahead with privatization, reforms of the government system and a better treatment of minorities. This led to a formal invitation to join the NATO and the EU (2004) at the end of 2002.

See also: Czechoslovakia.

Slovaks, Slavic people who settled in central Europe during the 5th and 6th centuries. Slovakia was dominated by Hungary from about 900 until the 1800s, when the Slovaks began a struggle for autonomy. Together with the more numerous Czechs, they formed the independent nation of Czechoslavakia in 1918.

See also: Slavs.

Slovenia

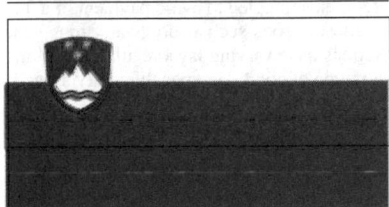

Capital:	Ljubljana
Area:	7,820 sq mi (20,253 sq km)
Population:	1,933,000
Language:	Slovene
Government:	Republic
Independent:	1991
Head of gov.:	Prime minister
Per capita:	US$ 16,000
Monetary unit:	1 Tolar = 100 stotins

Slovenia (Republic of), independent country in central Eastern Europe, bounded by the Adriatic Sea and Italy in the west, Austria in the north, Hungary in the northeast, and Croatia in the south.

Land and climate. This small country (7,819 sq mi; 20,251 sq km) is mostly mountainous, with a narrow coastal strip. The largest part has a continental climate, with an alpine climate in the mountainous north and a Mediterranean climate along the coast.

People. The population consists of Slovenes (88%), with minorities of Croats, Serbs, and Muslims. The official language is Slovene. The majority is Roman Catholic (84%).

Economy. Industries currently include chemicals, textiles, and there is an active tourist trade. As a Yugoslav republic Slovenia used to be the most prosperous one. In the 1990s prosperity diminished, but the outlook is not unfavourable.

History. From the 13th century until the end of World War I Slovenia was ruled by Austria. In 1918, it became part of Yugoslavia. In recent years Slovenia sought increasing independence from Yugoslavia and finally declared its own sovereignty in 1991. The federal Yugoslav army invaded Slovenia but was unable to defeat Slovenian forces and a cease-fire was signed. Slovenia's independence was recognized in 1992.

Slovenia's foreign policies have been internationally focused ever since. In 2002, the EU regarded Slovenia to be the most successful candidate for membership. It was formally invited to join the EU in 2004. At the end of 2002, it was also invited to join the NATO. Prime Minister Janes Drnovsek won the Presidential elections at the end of 2002.

See also: Yugoslavia.

Slug, mollusk best described as a snail without a shell or with a tiny shell inside the body. An exception is the roundback slug, which has an outside shell. Behind the head, with its 4 tentacles, is an oval shield containing a pore that leads to the lungs. Slugs creep over the ground like snails and leave a trail of slime. As they have no shell to retire into, they have to live in moist places to escape drying up. Some slugs eat fungi, others eat green plants and are garden pests.

Smallpox, acute, highly contagious viral disease, initiated by sudden severe constitutional symptoms and characterized by a progressive skin eruption that often results in permanent pits and scars. The disease is of historical interest only, for the World Health Organization declared the world free of smallpox in 1980.

See also: Jenner, Edward.

Smartweed, weed belonging to the buckwheat family and found in the lowlands and marshes of North America. It can grow up to 5 ft (1.5 m) tall. It is recognized by its small white, pink, or green flowers. The name derives from its sharp, bitter taste.

Smell, sense that enables humans and animals to perceive and identify odors. The organ of smell is the nose. Respiratory air is drawn into the nostrils and passes across a specialized receptor surface-the olfactory epithelium. Receptor cells detect the tiny concentrations of odors in the airstream and stimulate nerve impulses that pass to olfactory centers in the brain for coding and per-

ception. It is not possible to classify odors in the same way as the primary colors in vision, and it is probable that pattern recognition is more important. Certain animals depend mainly on the sense of smell, while humans are predominantly visual animals. But with training, humans can achieve sensitive detection and discrimination of odors.

Smelling salts, chemical stimulant used to alleviate faintness. It consists of a mixture of ammonium carbonate, alcohol, and fragrance. When fumes are inhaled, nasal membranes are irritated and breathing becomes more rapid, resulting in a feeling of clear-headedness.

See also: Ammonia.

Smelt, small, silvery fish that lives in large shoals in the colder waters of the Northern Hemisphere. Smelts range from 3 to 12 in (7.6 to 30.5 cm) and are an important food for other fishes. Like the related salmon and trout, they have a fleshy fin on the back. The American smelt is caught in large numbers as it ascends Atlantic Coast rivers to spawn. Pacific smelt are not often eaten because of their oily flesh.

Smelting, in metallurgy, process of extracting a metal from its ore by heating the ore in a blast furnace or reverberatory furnace (one in which a shallow hearth is heated by radiation from a low roof heated by flames from the burning fuel). A reducing agent, usually a coke, is used, and a flux is added to remove impurities.

See also: Metallurgy.

Smetana, Bedrich (1824-1884), Czech composer. Many of Smetana's compositions reflect his ardent Bohemian nationalism; best known are the comic opera *The Bartered Bride* (1866) and the symphonic poem *Má Vlast* (*My Fatherland*; 1874-1879), which contains *Vltava* (*The Moldau*).

Smilax, any of many species of woody vines (genus *Smilax*) found in temperate or tropical areas. There are about 300 different species, including the common greenbrier. Smilax typically have prickly stems, veined leaves, white or yellow-green flowers, and bluish-black or red berries.

Smith, Adam (1723-1790), Scottish economist and philosopher. The free-market system he advocated in *Inquiry into the Nature and Causes of the Wealth of Nations* (1776) came to be regarded as the classic system of economics. Smith drew on the ideas of his friends D. Hume, A. R. Turgot, F. Quesnay, and C. Montesquieu, and argued that if market forces were allowed to operate without state intervention 'an invisible hand' would guide self-interest for the well-being of all. His concept of the division of labor and the belief that value derives from productive labor were major insights. An earlier work, *Theory of Moral Sentiments* (1759), contrasts with *The Wealth of Nations* in its emphasis upon sympathy rather than self-interest as a basic force in human nature.

See also: Economics.

Smith, Bessie (1894-1937), U.S. jazz sin-

S

ger. 'The Empress of the Blues' came from a poor Tennessee home and first recorded in 1923; later she performed with many leading musicians, including Louis Armstrong and Benny Goodman.

Smith, David (1906-1965), influential U.S. sculptor, famous for his constructions of wrought iron and cut steel. His late works, like *Cubi XVIII* (1964), comprised burnished or painted cubic forms dramatically welded together.

Smith, Ian Douglas (1919-), Rhodesian prime minister (1964-1979). As leader of a white minority government, he declared unilateral independence from Great Britain and made Rhodesia a republic in 1970. Civil strife ensued. In 1978 Smith and 3 black leaders agreed to share control until power was transferred to the black majority, but guerrilla nationalists rejected the plan. A British cease-fire was accepted in 1979, and complete independence came in 1980 with the formation of a black regime in Rhodesia, renamed Zimbabwe. Under the black majority rule Smith remained active in politics until 1987.

Smith, John (1580?-1631), English soldier who helped found the first successful English colony in America, in 1607. As president of the colony-Jamestown, Va.-Smith enforced organization and discipline among the settlers. His harsh treatment of Native Americans, however, contributed to hostilities between the groups. Late in life, he wrote several books about his experiences, one of which was the source of the story of his capture by Powhatan and last-minute rescue by Pocahontas.

Smith, Joseph (1805-1844), founder of the Church of Jesus Christ of Latter-Day Saints in Fayette, N.Y., in 1830. Its doctrine and organization are derived from several texts, principally the *Book of Mormon* (1830), which is based on golden tablets inscribed with sacred writings that Smith claimed to have found and translated with miraculous help. Community opposition caused him to move his colony to the Midwest, where it flourished despite schisms. But when Smith announced his candidacy for the US presidency in 1844, non-Mormons arrested both him and his brother, Hyrum, for conspiracy and treason. Taken from jail at Carthage, Ill., by a mob, they were shot.
See also: Mormons.

Smith, Walter Bedell (1895-1961), U.S. Army chief of staff in Europe in World War II. He negotiated the surrenders of Italy (1943) and Germany (1945), was ambassador to the USSR (1946-1949), CIA director (1950-1953), and undersecretary of state (1953-1954).
See also: World War II.

Smith-Hughes Act, congressional act adopted in 1917 providing eligible states with funds for job-training programs. State proposals must be submitted and approved prior to the allocation of funds.

Smithson, Robert (1938-1973), American sculptor; initially made minimalist, abstract, geometric sculptures. However, he is mainly known for his landscape art projects.

Smithsonian Institution, world's largest museum complex, known as the 'nation's attic,' comprising 14 U.S. government-sponsored museums and the National Zoo. All of these are in Washington, D.C., except for the Cooper-Hewitt Museum in New York City, and hold perhaps 100 million artifacts illustrating both scientific and artistic culture. Founded with a bequest from James Smithson, the institution was established by Congress in 1846. The Smithsonian undertakes considerable scientific research, but is popularly known for its National Air and Space Museum, National Museum of Natural History, National Gallery of Art, National Portrait Gallery, and National Museum of American Art.

Smog, term first used in 1905 to describe the combination of smoke and thick fog that hung over London and other cities in Great Britain. London-type fog occurs when moisture in the air condenses on smoke particles produced by burning coal. Sulfur dioxide, the dangerous part of London-type smog, attacks the lungs. Petrochemical smog results from the action of sunlight on hydrocarbons and nitrogen oxides in the air that are formed by burning gasoline and petroleum products. It can irritate the eyes, nose, throat, and lungs. Smog is poisonous in heavy concentrations and can be fatal. It also destroys plant life and deteriorates building materials.
See also: Air pollution.

Smoke, vapor consisting of fine carbonaceous particles suspended in a gas, produced by the burning of fuel. Smoke can harm the lungs as well as cause damage to property and vegetation. It is used commercially in agriculture and in the preservation of meats.
See also: Air pollution.

Smoke detector, or smoke alarm, device placed in a room or floor of a building to signal the presence of smoke or fire. When smoke passes through the device, a loud, high-pitched sound is triggered. The 2 basic types are photoelectric detectors and ionization detectors.

Smoking, habit of inhaling the smoke of dried tobacco or other leaves from a pipe or a cigarette. Smoking has been practiced for centuries in various communities, often using plants with hallucinogenic or other mood-altering properties. The modern habit of smoking began in America and spread to Europe in the 16th century. Mass production of cigarettes began in the 19th century. Researchers have noted an uneqivocal association between smoking and such life-threatening diseases as lung cancer, chronic arthritis, emphysema, and diseases of the arteries and heart. Smoking appears to play a part in other forms of cancer and peptic ulcers, and is responsible for 2-2.5 million deaths each year. It is not yet clear what part of the smoke is responsible for promoting disease. Nonsmokers may be affected by environmental smoke; passive smokers are perhaps 3 times more likely to die of lung cancer than they would be otherwise. Smoking causes both physical and psychological addiction.

The health hazards resulting from the practice of smoking have generally been recognized by the public. Filter cigarettes and then low-tar and low-nicotine cigarettes have gained popular acceptance. Behavioral scientists have devoted much attention to helping people stop smoking. Although many people have successfully quit, many others have had great difficulty ending the habit. Efforts to educate the public have concentrated on presenting negative images of smoking, regulating the advertising of cigarettes, limiting the public spaces in which smoking is permitted, and increasing the cost of cigarettes by taxation. Some controversy exists between those who believe smoking is an individual choice and those who believe society has the right to act on its own behalf.

SMS (Short Message Service), a service offered by telephone companies. Short messages (with a maximum of 160 signs, including spaces) can be sent using a mobile phone or via the Internet to other mobile phones or to companies with an SMS switchboard. The digit buttons are used to compile the text. It is also possible to send a logo or a sound fragment as an SMS. Nowadays, SMS is frequently used for services including reservations, bookings and advertising.

Smuggling, unlawful conveyance of goods or individuals across a border. Legitimate goods are often smuggled to avoid payment of a duty; illegal goods-such as drugs-are smuggled. Nations have varying laws regulating the importation of goods, and penalties vary as well. In the United States, proof of intent is a necessary precondition for conviction.

Smut, fungi named for the masses of sooty spores formed on the surface of the host plant. Within the plant the smut develops a network of threads that take nutrients from it and cause stunting. Smuts attack wheat, corn, and other cereals, onions, sunflowers, and a few other plants. Smuts are hard to control because their spores can survive in the ground over the winter.

Smuts, Jan Christiaan (1870-1950), Afrikaaner soldier and politician, prime minister of South Africa (1919-1924 and 1939-1948). A general in the South African War against the British, Smuts later cooperated with them to found the Union of South Africa (1910). He was made a field marshal during World War II and participated in the British military leadership.
See also: South Africa.

Snail, herbivorous gastropod mollusk with, typically, a spirally coiled shell, found on land, in fresh water, or in the sea. The shell is secreted by the underlying mantle and houses the internal organs. The internal structure is similar in all groups, though land snails (pulmonates) have air-breathing lungs instead of gills. Nonpulmonate snails are mostly unisexual, while pulmonates are typically hermaphrodite.

Snake, legless reptile related to the lizards. There are about 2,700 species, most of which live in tropical countries, though a few survive in nearly arctic conditions. Snakes do not have legs, although the boas and pythons have the remains of a hind pair of legs. It is thought that they evolved from burrowing, legless lizards. Snakes, unlike lizards, do not have eardrums and are deaf to airborne sounds (they cannot hear the snake charmer's flute), but they can sense sounds coming through the ground by their vibrations. Locomotion is achieved by several methods. In the common serpentine movement, the body is pushed forward in S-shaped waves. In concertina movement the body is thrown forward in loops. Large snakes can push themselves along by movements of the belly scales. The sidewinder and the horned viper move over loose sand by throwing the body into S-shaped waves in side-winding locomotion.

Snakes feed on live animals or eggs. They kill their prey by constriction-preventing it from breathing but not crushing it-or by biting. Poisonous snakes inject venom through grooved or hollow fangs from modified saliva glands. Hematoxic venoms attack the blood and nervous system; and neurotoxic venoms attack the nerves. The young hatch from eggs or are born alive. The mother may look after the eggs; otherwise they are left in a nest in soil or under a log. Snakes grow throughout their lives and shed their skins every year or so.

Snakebird *See:* Anhinga; Wryneck.

Snakebite, bite of a snake that, when poisonous, can be fatal. Sometimes it may be necessary to cut and suction the wound, and many first-aid kits contain a syringe for this purpose.

Snake charming, folk art originating in northern Africa and southern Asia in which a charmer uses rhythmic body movements to encourage similar swaying movements by a snake, usually a cobra. Although snakes cannot hear, the charmer typically plays a flute while swaying.

Snake killer *See:* Roadrunner.

Snakeroot, any of a group of unrelated plants found in the prairies and wooded areas of North America and believed to be useful in curing snakebite. Black snakeroot, Virginia snakeroot, and button snakeroot were used to treat a variety of ailments. Texas snakeroot was used as an anesthetic and stimulant.

Snapdragon, plant (genus *Antirrhinum*) of the figwort family whose flowers have the upper and lower petals pressed together like an animal's jaws. Only strong insects, such as bumblebees, can force their way inside the petals to pollinate the flower, but butterflies can insert their tubular tongues between the 'lips' to suck nectar. Snapdragons came from the Mediterranean and are a favorite garden flower.

Snapper, large-headed fish with a long dorsal fin and a deep body. There are over 250 warm water species. They live in shoals and feed on almost anything edible. Many have red bodies, and several kinds are marketed as red snapper. The fish is good to eat, and some of the inshore species are caught by anglers. Snappers get their name from a habit of suddenly shutting their mouths when dying-which can be painful for someone who has a finger in the way, for they have sharp teeth.

Snead, Sam (1912-), U.S. golfer. Known for his strong drives and fluent swing, 'Slamming Sammy' won a record 84 Professional Golfers' Association (PGA) tournaments between 1936 and 1965. His achievements include winning the PGA championship (1942, 1949, 1951), the Masters Tournament (1949, 1952, 1954) and the British Open (1946). In 1953 he was elected to the PGA Hall of Fame. He wrote *Education of a Golfer* (1962).

Sneeze, explosive expiration through the nose and mouth stimulated by irritation or inflammation in the nasal epithelium. It is a reflex attempt to remove the source of irritation.

Sneezewort (*Achillea ptarmica*), perennial plant of Europe and Asia, a species of yarrow, whose leaves are used to make sneezing powder.

Snipe, long-billed bird of the family *Scolopacidae* with flexible bill tips that can be opened below ground to grasp food items. Active mainly at dawn and dusk, snipes are birds of marshy areas or open moorland with large eyes set far back on the head. Extraordinarily well camouflaged, they rise sharply if disturbed at close quarters and escape with an erratic zigzag flight. In courtship many species produce loud whistling or drumming noises by vibration of the primaries or tail coverts in rapid dives.

Sniperscope, device developed during World War II to enable soldiers to aim rifles accurately at night. The scope emits invisible infrared rays whose reflection off objects the shooter can see by looking through the scope. It had limited effectiveness and has since been replaced by the starlight scope.

Snooker *See:* Billiards.

Snoring, rough, hoarse respiration of certain persons during sleep; the noise is caused by vibration of the soft palate. It is predisposed to by the shape of the pharynx and by the sleeping position.

Snow, precipitation consisting of flakes or clumps of ice crystals. The crystals are plane hexagonal, showing an infinite variety of beautiful, branched forms; needles, columns, and irregular forms are also found. Snow forms by direct vapor-to-ice condensation from humid air below 32°F (0°C). On reaching the ground, snow crystals lose their structure and become granular. Fresh snow is very light (specific gravity about 0.1) and is a good insulator, protecting underlying plants from severe cold. In time, pressure, sublimation, melting, and refreezing lead to compaction into névé.

Snow, C(harles) P(ercy) (1905-1980), English physicist, government official, and author, many of whose works deal with the widening gap between art and technology. He is best known for his *Strangers and Brothers* series: 11 novels (1940-1970) about the English professional classes.

Snow, Edgar (1905-1972), U.S. journalist and author. The first Westerner to visit the Chinese Communists in their remote headquarters in Yanan (1936), he wrote a sympathetic account of their programs and idealism in *Red Star over China* (1937). A personal friend of Mao Zedong and Zhou Enlai, he was one of the few U.S. citizens to visit China regularly after the 1949 revolution, about which he wrote *The Other Side of the River* (1962) and *The Long Revolution* (1972).

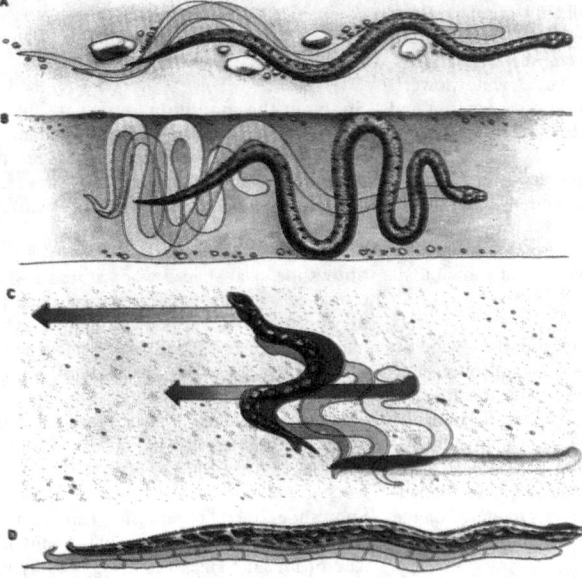

Snakes move in four main ways, all of which rely on the movement of muscles against the vertrebral column. (A) The serpentine movement, (B) concertina movement, (C) side-winding (used by rattlesnakes), and (D) rectilinear movement (used by boas).

S

S

Snowball, or European cranberry bush, any of various berry-producing shrubs (genus *Viburnum*) of the honeysuckle family native to Gelderland province, the Netherlands. They have clusters of large white flowers. When cultivated, they do not bear fruit and can grow as high as 12 ft (3.7 m).

Snow blindness, temporary loss of vision with severe pain, tears, and swelling due to excessive ultraviolet light reflected from snow. Permanent damage is rare; protective polarized glasses helps prevent snow blindness.

Snowboarding, a winter sport in which a standing person glides downhill over snow on a flat board called a snowboard. The snowboard is usually made with laminated wood and has steel edges and a polyethylene bottom. Snowboards are generally 8 to 12 inches (20 to 30 cm) wide and 39 to 78 inches (1 to 2 m) long. Bindings mounted on the snowboard hold the snowboarder's boots in place.

A snowboarder stands on the snowboard in much the same way that a surfer stands on a surfboard, facing one side of the board with feet parallel to each other. Turning and stopping are accomplished with the aid of the steel edges, which grip the snow. Snowboarding is permitted in many downhill ski areas. It became an Olympic sport in 1998.

Snow bunting, or snowflake, bird of the finch family found in Arctic regions. It resembles a sparrow except that it has a white head and breast in winter. During the coldest months, it migrates south into Canada and occasionally the United States.

Snowdrop, flowering herb (*Galanthus nivalis*) of the amaryllis family found predominantly in Eurasia. Each plant consists of a leaved stalk topped by a drooping, fragile-looking white flower resembling a snowdrop. A hardy and attractive plant, it is popular with gardeners.

Snowflake *See:* Snow; Snow bunting.

Snow leopard, or ounce, large mammal (*Felis uncia*) of the cat family found in central Asia. During the warmer months it lives high in the Tibetan plateau; in winter, it moves south into the valley. Its pale gray fur, which serves as camouflage in the snow, has been much valued by hunters and traders, and the snow leopard is now an endangered species.

Snow line, uneven line along mountain slopes marking areas of permanent snow. Since its position depends on many factors, it varies greatly from place to place. Snow lines can be used to evaluate global climatic shifts.

Snowmobile, engine-driven sled used for transport over large areas of ice and snow. An early, more cumbersome form of the vehicle was used in the 1920s. Today snowmobiling is a popular sport in many parts of North America and northern Europe. The snowmobile is also used by hunters, fishers,

rescue workers, forest rangers, and power companies. In some areas its use has been restricted because of criticisms from environmentalists.

Snow-on-the-mountain, annual plant (*Euphorbia marginata*) of the spurge family found predominantly in the central plains of the United States. Popular with gardeners and florists, it grows to about 2 ft (61 cm) in height and has small, white flowers.

Snowshoe, oval-shaped wooden frame with crosspieces strung with thongs, attached to the foot to distribute body weight so as to make it easier to walk on snow without sinking. Snowshoes were invented by Native Americans. Today they are used by loggers, hunters, and farmers. They are made of light wood and leather, and are at least 3 ft (91 cm) long and 1-1.5 ft (30-46 cm) wide.

Snowshoe hare, or varying hare, North American mammal of the rabbit family. A hare of medium size, it is recognized by its large, thickly furred hind feet, which allow it to hop effortlessly over snow. It sheds its brown coat in winter and grows a white one. It is prey for the lynx, snowy owls, and hunters.

Snowy egret *See:* Egret.

Snuff, pulverized, fermented tobacco leaves ground into a powder and inhaled, chewed, or placed in the mouth. The taking of snuff was popular in the 18th century, and decorated snuffboxes were commonly worn as jewelry. Today the practice is believed to pose substantial health risks.

Soapberry, species of trees and shrubs belonging to the soapberry family, grown in tropical and subtropical areas of the

THE HOPE OF THE WORLD

MACDONALD THE PEACEMAKER

Symbolic propaganda for the English Labour Prime Minister Ramsay MacDonald (1866-1937). The 'Hope of the World' is being watched by Germany, France, Russia, Arabia, the Netherlands and Belgium, and is led by 'Peace'.

Americas and Asia, as well as on Pacific islands. When rubbed in water, the leaves and leathery fruits, which contain saponin, produce a soapy lather.

Soap plant, herb (*Chlorogalum pomeridianum*) of the lily family, native to California. It can grow to a height of 8 ft (2.4 m). The soap plant's small, white flowers open in late afternoon or evening and close in the morning. It grows from a large bulb, which was once used by Native Americans as soap and roasted for food.

Soap sculpture, raised design or figure sculpted from a bar of soap. The design, traced in carbon on the soap, may be cut with a sharp knife and smoothed with a nail file. It may be lacquered or painted with acrylic or poster paints.

Soapstone, or steatite, metamorphic rock consisting largely of compacted talc with some serpentine and carbonates, formed by alteration of peridotite. Soft and soapy to the touch, soapstone has been used from prehistoric times for carvings and vessels. When fired it becomes hard and is used for insulators. The chief deposits are in the United States, Canada, and Norway.
See also: Talc.

Soares, Mário Alberto Nobre Lopes (1924-), Portuguese politician, premier (1976-1978 and 1983-1985) and president (1986-1996). An opponent of dictator António Salazar, he was repeatedly imprisoned and exiled. Under Soares, Portugal entered the European Community (EC) in 1986.

Sobibor, town in Poland, northeast of Lublin. Concentration camp (1942-1943), where 160,000 people died.

Sobieski, John *See:* John III Sobieski.

Soccer, national sport of most European and Latin American countries, and rapidly increasing in popularity in the United States. It is played with an inflated leather ball 27-28 in (68.6-71.1 m in circumference) on a field measuring 115 yd by 75 yd (105.2 m by 68.6 m); the goal is 8 yd (7.3 m) wide and 8 ft (2.4 m) high. Two 45-min halves make a game, supervised by 1 referee and 2 lines officials. The aim of each 11-player team is to score by kicking or heading the ball into the opponent's goal. To advance the ball, a player may dribble it (repeatedly kick it while running with it) or kick it to a teammate. The ball may not be touched with the hand or arm, except by the goalkeeper in the penalty area in front of the goal. Modern professional soccer began in the United Kingdom in 1885, in the United States in 1967. The major international competition is the World Cup, held every 4 years.

Social class, group of people with a similar social standing based on factors such as wealth, ancestry, or occupation. The different social classes recognized by members of a society form a hierarchy. This hierarchy may be an informal one, such as exists in democracies like the United States, or it may be rigidly delineated, as is the case of the caste system in India. In the United States, social class is popularly determined by income; people are grouped into upper, middle, and lower classes, with subdivisions of each main category.

Social contract, in political philosophy, concept of the formation of society in which people agree to surrender part of their 'natural' freedom to enjoy the security of the organized state. The idea, though of ancient origin, was first fully formulated in the 17th and 18th centuries by Thomas Hobbes (in *Leviathan*, 1651), John Locke, and Jean Jacques Rousseau, and was then controversial because it suggested that heads of state ruled only by their subjects' consent.

Social Darwinism, late-19th-century school of thought that held that society evolved on Darwin's biological model. Social inequalities were explained (and made to seem natural and inevitable) by the principle of 'survival of the fittest.' Its chief theorist was Herbert Spencer.
See also: Darwin, Charles Robert; Spencer, Herbert.

Socialism, economic philosophy and political movement that aims to achieve a just, classless society through the collective or governmental ownership of all property and means of manufacture and distribution of goods. Socialism was born out of the hardships of capitalism and the Industrial Revolution (late 18th-early 19th centuries). The ideas of class war, first put forth by F.N. Babeuf (and rejected by Utopian socialists such as Robert Owen and Charles Fourier), were later elaborated upon by Karl Marx and Friedrich Engels in their *Communist Manifesto* (1848). They suggested that revolution, led by the workers of the world, was inevitable. The first workers' party had already been founded by this time-in Germany in 1863 by Ferdinand Lasalle. This example was soon followed throughout Europe (1870s). Disagreement between gradualists and revolutionists soon emerged and was highlighted in 20th-century Russian socialism, eventually resulting in a split from which Bolshevism and Menshevism emerged. This was the forerunner to the worldwide break that occurred between socialism and communism after the Russian Revolution (1917). Socialism today, as well as its established place in the electoral politics of Europe, is especially active in the Third World, where its focus is on land reform and centralized economic planning.

Socialist realism, compulsory artistic doctrine since the early 1930s and until recently the dominant philosophy and style in most Communist countries. The doctrine holds that, in order to serve the people and the revolution, artistic and literary works should be realistic (representational), yet portray, with 'positive' heros, the workers' progress toward socialism.
See also: Communism.

Socialization, in psychology and sociology, process by which individuals are indoctrinated by parents, teachers, and peers into accepting and following the written and unwritten rules of conduct of a particular society.

Socialized medicine *See:* Health Insurance, National.

Social psychology, branch of psychology concerned with group processes and interactions among individuals. Subjects studied by social psychologists include conformity, altruism, interpersonal attraction, and the development of values.
See also: Psychology.

Social sciences, group of studies concerned with humanity in relation to its cultural, social, and physical environment; 1 of the 3 main divisions of human knowledge, the others being the natural sciences and the humanities. The social sciences usually include anthropology, archeology, demography, economics, political science, psychology, and sociology. Social scientists model their disciplines on the natural sciences in order to achieve a similar level of consensus, but can be frustrated by conceptual tools that are limited in relation to the complexity of their subject matter and by controlled experiments of limited scope.

Social security, government programs for protecting people from hardship due to loss of income through old age, disability, unemployment, injury, sickness, etc. State social security systems developed in Europe after 1883, when Germany started a compulsory health insurance scheme. In 1911 Great Britain adopted an unemployment insurance program. In the United States in the Depression, the Social Security Act (1935) established a federal program of old-age insurance and a federal-state program of unemployment insurance. Social security is financed by employer and employee contributions. Old-age and survivor benefits are paid to retired workers and their dependents or to survivors of workers who have died.

Social studies, elementary and secondary educational course designed to give students a knowledge of how people and institutions function in different societies and to promote understanding of both Western and non-Western cultures. The course typically is a combination of several disciplines, including history, economics, and geography.

Social work, activity of trained social workers that has as its aim the alleviation of social problems. Casework, group work, and community organization are employed. Casework involves close cooperation with individuals or families who are under mental, physical, or social handicaps. Group work developed from that in early social settlements and involves group education and recreational activities. Community organization involves the identification of community problems and the coordination of local welfare services, both public and private, in solving them. A social worker's training may include psychology, sociology, law, medicine, and criminology. The person might specialize in family service, child welfare, or medical, psychiatric, or correctional social work.

Society for the Prevention of Cruelty to Animals (SPCA), organizations promoting humane treatment of animals. These various societies aim to educate the public, introduce legislation, and assure the enforcement of laws that protect animals. Many societies maintain animal shelters and provide adoption and neutering services.

Society Islands, southern Pacific islands covering about 650 sq mi (1,684 sq km) in western French Polynesia, comprising the Windward and Leeward archipelagoes. Discovered in 1607 by the Portuguese but named for Britain's Royal Society, which explored the mountainous, volcanic, and coral islands in 1768, the 450-mi (724-km)-long chain has been France's since 1843. Most of the Polynesian population (about 100,000) live on the largest island, Tahiti, in the Windwards. Copra, sugar, and tourism are important industries.

Society of Friends *See:* Quakers.

Society of Jesus *See:* Jesuits.

Sociobiology, controversial theory that attempts to prove the influence of natural selection on human and animal behavior. The theory postulates that genes can influence behavior as well as physiology and that behavior may therefore be as subject to the laws of evolution as is the physical development of the species.

Sociology, systematic study that seeks to describe and explain collective human behavior-as manifested in cultures, societies, communities, and subgroups-by exploring the institutional relationships that hold between individuals and so sustain this behavior. Sociology shares its subject matter with anthropology, which traditionally focuses on small, relatively isolated societies, and social psychology, where the emphasis is on the study of subgroup behavior. The main emphasis in contemporary sociology is on the study of social structures and institutions and on the causes and effects of social change. Some current areas of inquiry are the family, religion, work, politics, urban life, and science.
Sociologists attempt to model their investigations on those of the physical sciences. Mainly because of the complexity of its subject matter and the political implications of social change, questions as to its proper aims and methods remain far from settled. There is little doubt, however, that sociological concepts such as internalization-the processes by which the values and norms of a particular society are learned by its members-and institutionalization-the processes by which norms are incorporated in a culture as binding rules of behavior-do often illuminate important social problems. The 2 great pioneers of modern sociology were Émile Durkheim and Max Weber.

Socrates (469-399 B.C.), Greek philosopher and mentor of Plato. Born in Athens and the son of a sculptor, Sophroniscus, Socrates became a self-appointed guide to the improvement of the intellectual and moral lives of the Athenians. His search for wisdom about

S

S

right conduct used the method of discussing virtue, justice, and piety with his many listeners. He wrote nothing, but much of his life and thought is vividly recorded in the dialogues of Plato. The exact extent of Plato's indebtedness to Socrates is uncertain-e.g., it is still disputed whether the doctrine of the forms is Socratic or Platonic; but Socrates made at least 2 fundamental contributions to Western philosophy: by shifting the focus of Greek philosophy from cosmology to ethics, and by developing the 'Socratic method' of inquiry. He argued that the good life is the life illuminated by reason and strove to clarify the ideas of his interlocutors by leading them to detect the inconsistencies in their beliefs. His doctrines are the basis of idealistic philosophy. Socrates' passion for self-consistency was evident even in his death. Ultimately condemned for 'impiety,' he decided to accept the lawful sentence-and so remain true to his principles-rather than make good an easy escape. In prison, surrounded by disciples, he drank hemlock.
See also: Philosophy.

Soda, any of a group of sodium compounds derived from common salt (NaCl). This group contains sodium carbonate (Na_2CO_3), or sal soda, a crystalline or powdered product with strong, acid-neutralizing, alkaline properties used in the production of paper and glass; sodium bicarbonate ($NaHCO_3$), or baking soda, which is used in cooking and for the relief of stomach distress; and sodium hydroxide (NaOH), or caustic soda, which is used in the manufacture of chemicals, soap, aluminum, and paper.

Soddy, Frederick (1877-1956), British chemist awarded the 1921 Nobel Prize in chemistry for his research in radioactive decay and particularly for his formulation (1913) of the theory of isotopes. His many scientific books range from *The Interpretation of Radium* (1922) to *Atomic Transmutation* (1953), and his views on technocracy and the social credit movement are found in *Money versus Man* (1933), among others.
See also: Chemistry; Isotope.

Sod house, ancient northern European type of house made from strips of turf that were used like bricks, the roof being reinforced with wood. Sod houses were also built by early settlers on the Great Plains of the United States and in western Canada.

Sodium, chemical element, symbol Na; for physical constants see Periodic Table. Sodium is the sixth most abundant element on earth. The free element was obtained by Sir Humphry Davy in 1807 by electrolysis of caustic soda (sodium hydroxide). It is found most commonly as common salt, but it occurs in many other minerals. It is obtained commercially by the electrolysis of dry fused sodium chloride. Sodium is a silvery-white, reactive metal, the most abundant of the alkali metal group. It is essential in human and animal nutrition. Sodium and its compounds are used in the paper, glass, soap, textile, petroleum, chemical, and metal industries. It is the cheapest of all metals.

Sodium chloride *See:* Salt.

Sodium hydroxide *See:* Lye; Soda.

Sodium nitrate *See:* Saltpeter.

Sodium nitrite *See:* Nitrite.

Sodium pentothal *See:* Thiopental.

Sodom and Gomorrah, in Old Testament history, cities probably in the southern region of the Dead Sea. According to Genesis, these 2 of the 5 cities on the Jordan plain were destroyed by God for their carnal wickedness. Only Lot and his family were spared, although Lot's wife turned into a pillar of salt.
See also: Old Testament.

Soeharto *See:* Suharto.

Soekarno *See:* Sukarno.

Sofia (pop. 1,221,000), capital, largest city and commercial center of Bulgaria, in west-central Bulgaria between the Balkan Mountains in the north and the Vitosa Mountains in the south. Its industry includes machinery, textiles, and electrical equipment. Landmarks include the former royal palace, the parliament building, old

mosques, churches, and synagogues. Sofia was settled by the Thracians; between the 1st and 4th centuries, Rome, Byzantium, and the first and second Bulgarian kingdoms were the ruling powers. In 1832 Turkish rule took hold until Russian's ascendance in 1878. Bulgaria achieved independence in 1879, with Sofia as its capital. Occupied by the Germans in World War II, it was taken by Soviet troops in 1944, and a Communist government was established and ruled until 1991.

Softball, type of baseball played with a softer, larger ball (12 in/30.5 cm in circumference) and a modified bat. The bases are 60 ft (18.3 m) apart and the pitcher stands 46 ft (14 m) from the home plate (40 ft/12 m in women's games). The ball is pitched underhand, and a game lasts 7 innings. Softball was developed in Chicago in 1888 by G. W. Hancock as an indoor form of baseball. Many countries, particularly in the Americas, now compete in the annual amateur world championships.
See also: Baseball.

Soft-coated wheaten terrier, sporting dog of Irish origin, used for hunting, herding, and as a guard dog. This terrier has a strong, compact body about 19 in (48 cm) high, weighs about 40 lb (30 kg), and has a shaggy coat of soft, wavy hair.

Soft drink, nonalcoholic beverage generally containing fruit acids, sweetening agents, and natural or artificial flavorings and colorings. In the early 19th century carbonated water (soda water) was developed in imitation of effervescent spa, or mineral, water; this was the antecedent of carbonated soft drinks, made by absorption of carbon dioxide under pressure. The dissolved gas gives a pleasant, slightly acid taste and acts as a preservative. Soft drinks without carbon dioxide are frozen or subjected to pasteurization.

Softwood *See:* Wood.

Soil, uppermost surface layer of the earth, in which plants grow and on which, directly or indirectly, all life on earth depends. Soil consists, in the uppermost layers, of organic material mixed with inorganic matter resultant from weathering. Soil depth (where soil exists) may reach to many meters. Between the soil and the bedrock is a layer called the subsoil. Mature (or zonal) soil may be described in terms of 4 soil horizons. The uppermost layer, containing organic components, is a continuous stream to which is added an 'active' component produced by bursts of activity on the sun's surface.

Solana Madariaga, Javier (1942-   ), Spanish politician. Solana was an adversary of the Franco regime and has been a member of the Socialist PSOE Party since 1964. After Franco's death in 1975, he became a Member of Parliament, and in 1982, Secretary of Culture in the González government. He was Secretary of Education from 1988 to 1992, and in 1992, Secretary of State. He became NATO's Secretary General in 1995, a function he relinquished in 1999 when he became

Soil profiles, or cross sections, may be divided into four layers, or horizons. Humus (A0) forms the uppermost portion of the topsoil horizon (A), which covers a mixed organic-inorganic subsoil layer (B) that lies above a partially weathered rock zone (C). Unchanged bedrock (D) forms the bottom layer. Soil types vary with the climate. Acid brown earth on sandy rock (1) and cultivated brown earth (2) are seen in temperate climates. Leached peat pedzol (3) is found in cold, wet climates. Iron-rich brown oxisol (4) is seen in warm, humid areas.

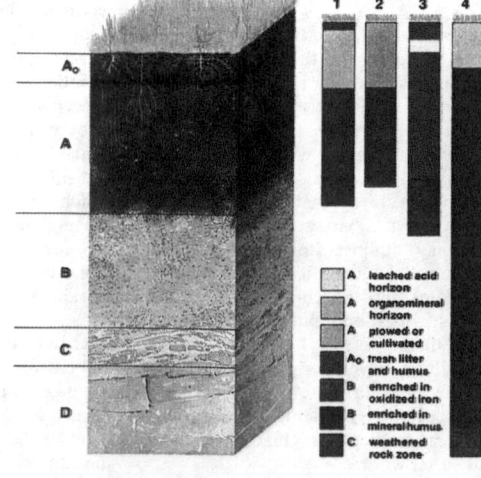

A	leached acid horizon
A	organomineral horizon
A	plowed or cultivated
A0	fresh litter and humus
B	enriched in oxidized iron
B	enriched in mineral humus
C	weathered rock zone

the EU High Representative for Common Foreign and Security Policy and Secretary-General of the Council of the European Union.

Solanum, group of herbs, shrubs, and trees belonging to the nightshade family. Solanum grows worldwide, particularly in the temperate regions of South and North America. Many of the members of this family are important for food and medicinal purposes, although all contain some amounts of poisonous alkaloids such as atropine, nicotine, and solanin. Included in this group are the potato, tomato, eggplant, tobacco, bittersweet, common nightshade, and horse nettle. The fruit may be either capsulated (tobacco) or in berry form (potato and eggplant).

Solar eclipse *See:* Eclipse.

Solar energy, power derived from the sun. Because the earth's supplies of coal, petroleum, and other fossil fuels will eventually be exhausted, while the sun's energy will not, several methods of using solar energy have been developed. One is the solar furnace, basically a huge parabolic mirror that focuses the sun's heat onto a small area. Temperatures of more than 7,232°F (4,000°C) may be produced by this method. The heat can be used to raise steam and generate electricity, or for scientific research. In the Soviet Union a solar power station has been built with a system of 1,300 moving mirrors covering an area of 5 acres (about 2

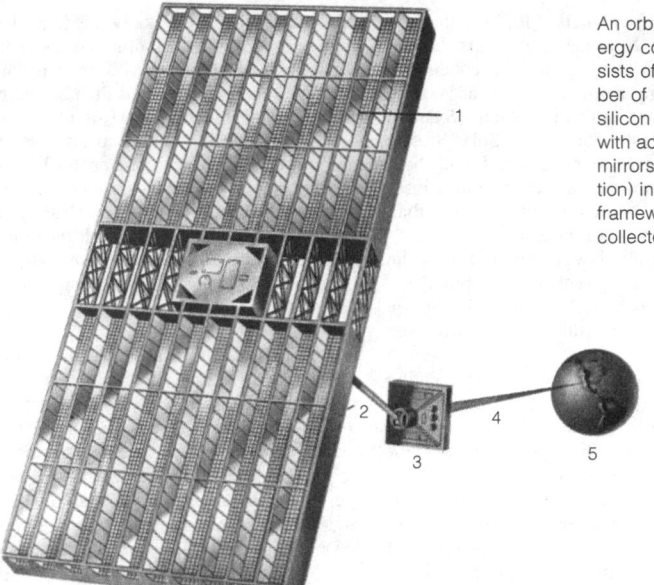

An orbiting solar energy collector consists of a large number of single-crystal silicon solar cells, with adjacent rows of mirrors (to aid collection) in a rectangular framework (1). This collector is linked through rotary joints and a 2 kilometers long electricity transmission line (2), to a control station and a microwave antenna (3). Solar cells convert the energy in the rays of the sun into electric power, which is transmitted to the microwave antenna, where it is converted into microwave radiation (4) and beamed to an earth receiving station (5). Further conversion produces direct current electricity.

S

hectares). It produces 2 1/2 million kilowatt-hours of electricity annually.

Solar energy is used increasingly for domestic heating. Heat is collected by exposing a large, darkened metal plate, covered with 1 or more layers of glass, to the sun. Water or air is passed through tubes attached to the plate and either circulated through the building or stored. Hot water is stored in insulated tanks. Hot air is passed through a tank full of rocks, which hold the heat until it is required to warm up air for circulation around the house.

Sunlight can also be converted directly into electricity in a solar cell, and there is research into the possibility of using sunlight to produce chemical energy by the same sort of reaction as photosynthesis in plants.
See also: Radiation.

Solar plexus, ganglion of nerve cells and fibers situated at the back of the abdomen that subserve the autonomic nervous system function for much of the gastrointestinal tract. A sharp blow on the abdomen over the plexus causes visceral pain and the sensation that all the 'wind' has been knocked out of the lungs.
See also: Nervous system.

Solar System, the sun and all the objects orbiting it, including the planets, asteroids, comets, and meteors. There are 9 known planets in the Solar System. Mercury, Venus, Earth, Mars, and Pluto make up the terrestri-

(A) A diagram of the solar system reveals that the four inner planets (spheres) are concentrated in nearly circular orbits (white curves) close to the sun (red), whereas the five outer planets are spread over larger distances. Of all the planets, the orbit of Pluto — the farthest known planet — is the most eccentric and the most highly inclined to the ecliptic, or the plane of the earth's orbit about the sun. Pluto's orbit periodically falls inside that of the planet Neptune. Most of the asteroids lie within a belt (dotted band) between the inner and the outer planets. Some of the asteroids (blue curves) and most of the comets (red curves) have highly inclined and eccentric orbits. (B) In a diagram of the sun (1) and the planets drawn to the same scale, the sun's size is indicated by comparing a solar prominence or jet of glowing gases (2), with the inner planets Mercury (3), Venus (4), earth (5) with its moon (6), and Mars (7) with its tiny moons Phobos (8) and Deimos (9). The asteroid belt (10) is found between Mars and the outer planet Jupiter (11), with its four largest, or Galilean satellites, Io (12), Europa (13), Ganymede (14), and Callisto (15). The other outer planets are Saturn (16), which is shown with its rings and its satellites, the largest of which is Titan (17); Uranus (18) with its five largest satellites; Neptune (19), with Triton (20), the largest of its two moons; and Pluto (21).

S

al (Earthlike) planets. Jupiter, Saturn, Uranus, and Neptune are giants largely made of gas. All but 3 planets have their own moons orbiting them. There are at least 66 known moons in the Solar System. Astronomers estimate that the Solar System contains at least 100,000 asteroids and about 100 billion comets. But the combined mass of all these bodies is little more than 1/1000th the mass of the Sun.

The Solar System is vast. Pluto, usually the outermost planet (sometimes Neptune is), moves as far as 4 1/2 billion mi (7.2 billion km) from the Sun, while comets move even farther than this.

Origin of the Solar System. From the dating of meteorites (pieces of rock from the Solar System that have hit the earth), scientists believe that the Solar System formed about 4 1/2 billion years ago. No one knows exactly how the planets originated. The first scientific theories were developed in the 18th century by the philosopher Immanuel Kant and the mathematician Pierre Simon Laplace. They believed that the Sun and planets formed together from a cloud of gas or dust. Early in the 20th century a rival theory gained favor. This suggested that a star passed close to the Sun and pulled out some of its material. Part of this material fell into orbit around the Sun, forming planets. Modern theories have returned to Laplace's idea. Astronomers now believe that stars form when giant, diffuse clouds of gas condense. As the cloud contracts, a star forms at its center. Around the rapidly spinning star is a disk of material that slowly spirals away. Most of the disk is lost into space, but at certain points the material of the disk starts to collide and build into lumps. These lumps sweep up more of the surrounding material, eventually forming planets.

Other Solar Systems. The above theory suggests that Solar Systems form naturally around most stars. Although planets are far too faint to be seen going around other stars, they will exert a slight gravitational tug on those stars. By looking at the slight movements of nearby stars, observers have found that some stars have dark companions revolving around them. Astronomers now think that Solar Systems are common in the universe and that perhaps half the stars in the sky have planets orbiting them.

Solar wind, gases in the Sun's corona that escape from its gravitational field. Made of electrically charged particles, particularly ions, and expanding under the high temperatures of the corona, about 4,000,000°F (2,200,000°C), the solar wind accelerates to a velocity of about 310 m/s (500 km/s), a speed that allows escape from the solar gravitational field. The solar wind causes deflection of the tail of Earth's magnetosphere and comet's tails away from the sun. A shock wave results when the solar wind encounters the Earth's magnetic field. The portions of the solar wind that do not encounter either the Earth or other obstacles continue to travel at supersonic velocities until they eventually lose their supersonic characteristics and pour out into galactic space.

Soldering, joining metal objects using a low-melting-point alloy, solder, as the adhe-

sive. Soft solder, commonly used in electronics to join wires and other components, is an alloy of mainly lead and tin. The parts to be joined are cleaned and then heated by applying a hot soldering iron (usually having a copper bit). A flux is used to dissolve oxides, protect the surfaces, and enable the solder to flow freely. The solder melts when applied, solidifying again to form a strong joint when the iron is withdrawn. Solder is often applied as wire with a core of noncorrosive rosin flux. Soldering at higher temperatures is termed *brazing*.

Sole, any of several species (family Soleidae) of flatfishes found in temperate seas and fresh water. Soles are commonly brown with dark patches, have flattened bodies about 10-25 in (25-66 cm) long, weigh about 1 lb (0.5 kg), and have both eyes on the right side of the head. Sole is a valued food fish, particularly the European or Dover sole and the American hogchoker.

Solenodon (genus *Solenodon*), rare, nocturnal, insect-eating mammal of Cuba and Haiti. It looks like a long-nosed rat, measuring about 2 ft (61 cm) long and 2 lb (1 kg), with long claws, a stiff tail, and short, coarse hair. Its saliva is poisonous.

Solid, one of 3 states of matter possessing the property of excluding all other bodies from the space occupied by itself; it has a definite volume and definite shape. As a result of heating, the molecules of a solid begin to vibrate more rapidly, eventually breaking out of their fixed positions (at the melting point) and becoming a liquid.

Solidarity *See:* Walesa, Lech.

Solid-state physics, branch of physics concerned with the nature and properties of solid materials, many of which arise from the association and regular arrangements of atoms or molecules in crystalline solids. The term is applied particularly to studies of semiconductors and solid-state electronic devices.
See also: Quantum mechanics.

Solitaire, or Patience, any of several card games played by 1 person. Solitaire has countless varieties, but all are played with 1 or 2 decks of 52 cards, a portion of which are laid out, some face-up, others face-down, to form a foundation (tableau) of cards, upon which the game is played. Play resumes when one card is played out onto another in a prescribed manner. The purpose of the game is to play each card out, thus successfully completing the foundations. Canfield, Klondike, Accordion, Napoleon at St. Helena, Spider, and Pyramid are a few of the games of solitaire.

Sollers, Philippe (1936-), French writer, joint founder and editor of Tel Quel (1960). Applied the new style of design that was used in this journal in such books as *Lois* (1972) and *H* (1973), in which he experimented with prosody, syntax and vocabulary. *Paradis* (1981) is a continuous 'monologue intérieur', without any punctuation at all. Sollers then went back to a more tradi-

tional storytelling technique, in such works as *Femmes* (1983), *Le portrait du joueur* (1985), and *Le coeur absolu* (1986). His later works include *Les folies françaises* (1988), *Le Lys d'or* (1989), *La fête à Venise* (1991), *Improvisations* (1991) and *Le secret* (1993).

Solomon (d. 922 B.C.), second son of David and Bathsheba. He ruled ancient Israel c.970-933 B.C. at the height of its prosperity, and gained a reputation for great wisdom. His success in establishing lucrative foreign trade and his introduction at home of taxation and forced labor enabled him to finance a massive building program that included a temple and royal palaces on an unprecedented scale of opulence. His story is told in I Kings 1-11 and II Chronicles 1-9 of the Old Testament. Biblical writings later attributed to him include Proverbs, Ecclesiastes, and the Song of Solomon.
See also: Old Testament.

Solomon Islands

Capital:	Honiara
Area:	10,639 sq mi (27,556 sq km)
Population:	495,000
Language:	English
Government:	Parliamentary monarchy in the British Commonwealth
Independent:	1978
Head of gov.:	Prime minister
Per capita:	US$ 1,700
Monetary unit:	1 Solomon Islands dollar = 100 cents

Solomon Islands, independent democracy in the British Commonwealth, extending across an ocean area of over 232,000 sq mi (600,880 sq km) in the southwestern Pacific. The land area of the islands is approximately 10,639 sq mi (27,556 sq km).
Land and climate. The mountainous Solomon Island archipelago, composed of 21 large islands and many islets, is of volcanic origin; 4 volcanoes are intermittently active. The highest peak, Mt. Makarakombou (8,028 ft/2,447 m) is on Guadalcanal, the largest island, where Honiara, the capital, is located. The Solomons are well watered and covered with dense tropical rain forests, with grasslands on the northern plains of Guadalcanal. The

climate is equatorial, and temperatures vary little during the year; rainfall, averaging 120 in (305 cm) annually, is concentrated from Nov. to Apr.

People and economy. The population is 95% Melanesian, with Polynesian, Micronesian, European, and Chinese minorities. Most follow tradition, living in small villages, fishing, and growing coconuts, taro, yams, and cassava. Exports, formerly exclusively copra, now also include fish and timber. Tourism is increasingly important.

History. In 1568 a Peruvian expedition sighted the Solomons but they were ignored by Europeans until the 19th century, when islanders were forcibly recruited to labor overseas. By 1900 Great Britain had established a protectorate over the islands. Invaded by the Japanese in 1942, the Solomons were recaptured by U.S. forces only after heavy fighting in 1945. Since independence in 1978, the Solomons have been plagued by regional disputes. In 1992 the support of the Solomon Islands to Bougainville separatists led to an attack on the Solomon Islands by Papua New Guinea government forces. The Papua New Guinea government later declared to have regretted this attack. In 1996 the Solomon Islands and Papua New Guinea reached an agreement on joint security forces.

Around 2000, civil war broke out on the islands. Lasting conflicts between ethnic groups on the different Solomon Islands resulted in a state of emergency being declared on Guadalcanal. Under pressure from Australia, a peace agreement was concluded in October 2000, which unfortunately failed to resolve the problem of violence.

Solomon Islands, island chain in the South Pacific Ocean. The islands are divided into 2 countries, one at the southern end and one at the northern end of the group. The southern portion, including Choiseul, Guadalcanal, Malaita, New Georgia, San Cristobal, Santa Isabel, and numerous smaller islands, is part of the nation of the Solomon Islands. The northern portion, including Bougainville, Buka, and various smaller islands, is part of Papua New Guinea. Together they cover a land area of about 15,700 sq mi (40,663 sq km). The Solomon Islands were the scene, during World War II (1942-1944), of numerous battles between the Japanese and the Allied forces.
See also: Papua New Guinea.

Solomon's seal, perennial plant that grows in woods and thickets. The rootstock, used for medicinal purposes, makes a good poultice for bruises, inflammations, and wounds; in a wash, it helps heal skin blemishes and counteracts the effects of poison ivy.

Solon (c.640-559 B.C.), Athenian politician and poet, and one of the Seven Wise Men of Greece (Seven Sages). Solon gained fame in 612 B.C. with his poems, which compelled the Athenians to recover the Island of Salamis. He was elected leader (archon) of the government in 594 B.C. During his leadership many political and economic reforms were initiated. They included the abolition of unfair debt laws, the institution of habeas corpus, emancipation of slaves, and reforms in the representation of the common citizens in the assembly and in courts of law.
See also: Athens; Greece, Ancient.

Solow, Robert Merton (1924-), U.S. economist. Senior economist (1961-1968) on the Council of Economic Advisors and president (1975-1980) of the Boston Federal Reserve Bank, he won the 1987 Nobel Prize in economics for work he did in the 1950s, particularly on the importance of technology in economic growth. He was an outspoken critic of 'Reagonomics,' President Ronald Reagan's economic policies.
See also: Economics.

Solstice, two times each year when the sun is on the points of the ecliptic farthest from the equator. At the summer solstice, in late June (about June 22), the sun is directly overhead at noon on the Tropic of Cancer; at winter solstice, in late December (about Dec. 22), it is overhead at noon on the Tropic of Capricorn. In the Northern Hemisphere these celestial events are used as the traditional commencement of summer and winter. They are also the days of the longest and shortest daylight hours.
See also: Equinox.

Solti, Sir Georg (1912-1997), Hungarian-born British conductor. He is noted for his recordings of works by Richard Wagner and Richard Strauss, and performances he led, usually as musical director, at London's Covent Garden (1961-1971), the Paris Opera (from 1973), the London Philharmonic (1979-1983), and the Chicago Symphony (1969-1991).

Solution, in chemistry, homogeneous molecular mixtures of 2 or more substances (solid, liquid, gas), commonly of a solid and a liquid, though solid/solid solutions also exist. The liquid component is usually termed the *solvent*; the other component (solid, liquid, or gas), which is dissolved in it, the *solute*. The solubility of a solute in a given solvent at a particular temperature is usually stated as the mass that will dissolve in 3.53 oz (100 g) of the solvent to give a saturated solution. Solubility generally increases with temperature. Two common examples of solutions include vinegar (a solution of a liquid, acetic acid, in water) and syrup (a solution of a solid, sugar, dissolved in water).

Solvent, liquid capable of dissolving a substance to form a solution. Generally 'like dissolves like'; thus a nonpolar covalent solid such as naphthalene dissolves well in a hydrocarbon solvent. Overall, the best solvents are those with polar molecules and high dielectric constant; water is the most effective known.

Solzhenitsyn, Alexander Isayevich (1918-), Russian writer. His own experience of Stalin's labor camps was described in *One Day in the Life of Ivan Denisovich* (1962), acclaimed in the USSR and abroad. But *First Circle* and *Cancer Ward* (both 1968) were officially condemned. He accepted the 1970 Nobel Prize in literature by letter. His expulsion from the USSR to West Germany in 1974 and his warnings on the moral and political fate of the West drew worldwide publicity. He has resided in the United States since 1976. Solzhenitsyn's work includes *August 1914* (1971), *The Gulag Archipelago* (1973-1975), and *October 1916* (1985).

Somalia

Capital:	Mogadishu
Area:	246,091 sq mi
	(637,541 sq km)
Population:	10,400,000
Language:	Somali
Government:	Republic
Independent:	1960
Head of gov.:	Prime minister
Per capita:	less than US$ 550
Monetary unit:	1 Somali shilling =
	100 cents

Somalia, or Somali Democratic Republic, republic occupying the horn, or northeastern tip, of Africa.

Land and climate. Covering 246,091 sq mi (637,541 sq km), Somalia is bounded on the north by the Gulf of Aden, on the west and southwest by Ethiopia and Kenya, on the east by the Indian Ocean, and on the northwest by Djibouti. In the north, a narrow, barren coastal plain is hemmed in by mountains rising to more than 8,000 ft (2,438 m) with high plateaus and dry savannas extending inland. Plateaus, plains, and valleys extend westward from a wider coastal plain bordering the Indian Ocean. Flowing southeastward from the Ethiopian highlands are Somalia's only two permanent rivers, the Wabe Shebele and the Juba. The prevailing climate is hot.

People. The population consists mainly of Somalis belonging to northern nomadic or southern farming clans. Somali, the national language, lacks a written form; Arabic, Italian, and English are the chief written languages. Sunni Islam is the country's official religion.

Economy. Most Somalis are nomadic pastoralists moving from place to place with their herds and portable wood-frame huts. Agriculture accounts for the economy's major revenues, with bananas and sugar-cane the cash crops. There is a small mining and oil-producing sector of the economy.

History. Since the 14th c. the Somali, who were converted to Islam by the Arabs, have

S

S

been moving around their current habitat. During the 15th and 16th c., the Portuguese established trade contacts. The British and the Italians colonized Somalia and established a protectorate in 1884 (Great Britain) and in 1889 (Italy). The country has been independent since 1960. Somalia lost the war against Ethiopia over the disputed territory of the Ogaden desert, mainly inhabited by

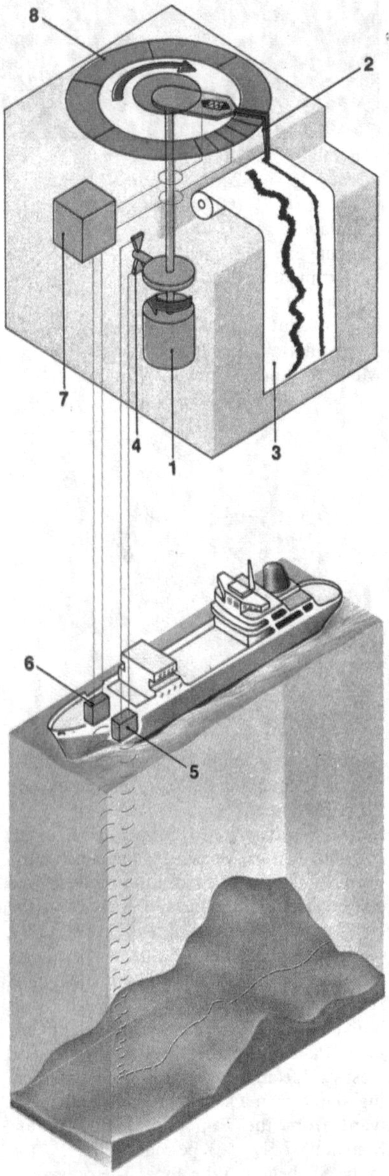

Sonar is an underwater sound-ranging system used for locating objects that are substantial and extensive enough to return an echo. The same technique is used by porpoises when they emit sounds to echolocate schools of fish. A typical sonar device has a motor (1) that drives a recording arm (2) and — through a system of gears, not shown here — a recording chart (3). A rotating contact (4) causes a transmitter (5) to emit a sound impulse once every revolution. No further impulse is sent until an echo arrives at the receiver (6) from the seafloor or from some intervening object. The echo is passed through an amplifier (7) and then activates the recording arm. A pen at the tip of the arm marks on the chart the time taken for the impulse to return. This time is given in terms of depth by a calibrated scale (8). A series of such readings is seen at the center of the chart. The steadier line at the right is the echo picked up almost immediately at the surface as the signal is transmitted.

Somali who want to join Somalia. The dictator Siad Barre was ousted in 1991. Consequently, the former British territory seceded as Somaliland and a civil war broke out between numerous clans and militias. An agreement was reached in 1992 and the U.S. led a UN operation to distribute food to the starving. The warlords, however, soon clashed again and UN troops had to resign in 1994-1995. Puntland declared independence in 1998. Social groups reached an agreement to form a government in 2000. Parliament

elected Abdiquassim Salad to be President. However, his government was not recognized by the warlords and the seceded regions.

Somaliland *See:* Djibouti.

Somerset, Edward Seymour, 1st duke of (1500-1552), protector of England (1547-1549) on the death of Henry VIII and accession of Edward VI. He used his great power to repeal heresy and treason laws and with Thomas Cranmer introduced the first *Book of Common Prayer* for the Church of England. Falsely accused of treason by his rivals, he was executed.
See also: England.

Somme River, river rising in northern France near Saint-Quentin, flowing west about 152 mi (245 km) to the English Channel. The Somme was the scene of major fighting with heavy casualties in World War I (1939-1945). The Somme's upper valley has canals to the Oise and Escaut rivers.

Somnambulism *See:* Sleepwalking.

Somoza, Nicaraguan political family, 3 members of which controlled Nicaragua from 1936 to 1979. In 1936 **Anastasio Somoza Garcia** (1896-1956) deposed his uncle, President Juan Sacasa, and became president in a nepotistic dictatorship (1937-1947; 1950-1956) ending in assassination. He was succeeded by his son **Luis Somoza Debayle** (1922-1967), who held formal office until 1963. In 1967 Anastasio's second son, **Anastasio Somoza Debayle** (1925-1980), was elected president. Replaced by a puppet triumvirate in 1972, he retained control of the army and was reelected president in 1974. His corrupt rule led to a revolt in 1977 by leftist Sandinista guerrillas, who gradually gained broad support and forced him to flee into exile in Paraguay in 1979. A year later he was assassinated in Asunción.
See also: Nicaragua.

Sonar, acronym for Sound Navigation and Ranging, technique used at sea for detecting and determining the position of underwater objects (e.g., submarines, shoals of fish) and for finding the depth of water under a ship's keel. Sonar works on the principle of echolocation. High-frequency sound pulses are beamed from the ship, and the direction of and time taken for any returning echoes are measured to give the direction and range of the reflecting objects.

Sonata, in music, term used in the 17th and early 18th centuries to describe works for various small groups of instruments, as opposed to the cantata, originally for voices only. Since the late 18th century the term has been restricted to works for piano or other solo instruments (the latter usually with keyboard accompaniment), generally in 3 movements.

Song, musical setting of words, usually a short poem, often with instrumental accompaniment. There are 2 basic kinds: songs in which each verse repeats the same tune, and

songs with a continuous thematic development. The origins of the song are lost in the history of folk music and poetry (poetry was originally sung); it became a mature art in Western cultures in opera arias, German *Lieder*-those of Schubert are supreme examples-and the French *chanson*. The song forms that have most influenced 20th-century popular music are probably the ballad and the blues.

Song dynasty (960-1279), period of Chinese rule and cultural advancement, founded by Zhao Kuangyin, who became the first emperor. The dynasty encompassed most of China. During this era of enlightenment trade, education, sculpture, painting, and literature flourished; a humane welfare system was instituted; and Confucian philosophy was organized into a cohesive doctrine. The Song dynasty was ended when it was conquered by the Mongols in 1279.
See also: China.

Songhai Empire, West African trading state created by the Songhai people of the Middle Niger. Founded in the 700s and flourishing in the 1400s, Songhai was a powerful and wealthy empire in control of trans-Saharan trade. At the height of power, during the reign of Sunni Ali (1464-1492) and that of Askia Muhammad (1493-1528), the Songhai Empire extended west to the Atlantic Ocean and encompassed roughly what is now Mali, Nigeria, and portions of Senegal. Gao, on the Niger River, was the capital. Most of the Songhai people farmed, fished, or were traders. Askia Muhammad was deposed by his 3 sons and by 1591 the empire was defeated by Moroccans at the Battle of Tondibi.

Songhua Jiang (or **Sung-hua Chiang** also **Sungari River**), a river in northeastern China, draining much of Manchuria. From its source in the Changbai Shan, a mountain range on the Korean border, the river flows northwestward to receive its principal tributary, the Nen, near Fuyu. It then turns eastnortheast, emptying into the Amur River at the Russian-Chinese border. The Songhua, navigable for much of its 1,150-mile (1,805-km) length, is a major trade artery for Manchuria's rich agricultural region. Harbin is the chief port. A dam near Jilin provides hydroelectric power and impounds a large reservoir.

Song of Roland *See:* Roland.

Song of Solomon, or Song of Songs, book of love poems in the Old Testament of the Bible. Although spoken between a man and a woman and sensual in content, the poems are usually interpreted as allegorical and dramatic descriptions of God's love for the Hebrew people.
See also: Old Testament.

Sonic boom, loud noise generated in the form of a shock-wave cone when an airplane traveling faster than the speed of sound overtakes the pressure waves it produces. Because of sonic-boom damage, supersonic planes are confined to closely defined flight paths.

Sonnet, lyric poem of 14 lines with traditional rules of structure and rhyme scheme. There are two traditional types of sonnets: The Petrarchan is comprised of an octave and sestet (rhyming scheme *abbaabba cdecde*) and the Shakespearean comprising three quatrains and a couplet (rhyming scheme *abab cdcd efef gg*). Devised in 13th-century Italy and perfected by Petrarch, it entered English literature in the 16th century and was adopted by such poets as William Shakespeare, John Milton, John Keats, and William Wordsworth as a vehicle for concentrated thought and feeling, very often of love.

Sontag, Susan (1933-), U.S. novelist, short-story writer, filmmaker, and essayist. Her best-known books include *Against Interpretation* (1966), *On Photography* (1977), *Illness as Metaphor* (1978) coupled with *AIDS and Its Metaphors* (1989), *Under the Sign of Saturn* (1980), *The volcano lover* (1992), and *In America* (1999).

Soong Ching-ling (1892-1981), deputy head of state of the Chinese Communist government (1949-1975). She also headed the Sino-Soviet Friendship Association, and was awarded the Stalin Peace Prize in 1951. Soong Ching-ling was the wife of the left-wing revolutionary leader Sun Yat-sen. When he died in 1925, she continued his work in the Kuomintang (Nationalist Party). In 1927 when Chiang Kai-Shek, then president of the Chinese Nationalist government, broke with the Chinese Communists, she went into self-exile, living in Moscow until 1937. During the Sino-Japanese War, having returned to China, Soong was the organizer of the China Defense League.

Sophist (Greek, 'wise men'), name given to certain teachers in Greece in the 5th and 4th centuries B.C., the most famous of whom were Gorgias and Protagoras. They taught rhetoric and the qualities needed for success in political life. Plato attacked them for taking fees; for teaching skepticism about law, morality, and knowledge; and for concentrating on how to win arguments regardless of truth-attacks still reflected in the modern word *sophistry*.
See also: Greece, Ancient.

Sophocles (c.496-406 B.C.), great Athenian dramatist (also, priest and general), who, together with contemporaries Aeschylus and Euripides, was one of the founders of Greek tragedy. Only 7 of about 123 plays survive, the best known being *Oedipus Rex, Oedipus at Colonus, Antigone,* and *Electra.* Sophocles, who won many dramatic competitions, introduced scene painting to the stage, expanded the size of the chorus, and added a third actor. He also chose to focus on self-contained tragedy, as opposed to the popular trilogies of his day. His plays dwell on tragic ironies of human existence, and the fate of his characters are determined more by their faults than by the gods.

Sorbonne, college founded in Paris in 1253 (named 1257) by Robert de Sorbon (1201-1274). A noted medieval theological center, it was rebuilt in the 17th century by Richelieu and, after being closed in the French Revolution, was reestablished in 1808. Its name is often used to refer to the University of Paris, into which it was incorporated in the 19th century.

Sorghum, widely cultivated cereal crop (*Sorghum vulgare*), the most important grown in Africa. It grows best in warm conditions and it is vital as a drought-resistant crop. For human food, the grain is first ground into a meal and then made into porridge, bread, or cakes. Some varieties yield molasses from the cane's juice. The grain is also used as a cattle feed and the whole plants as forage. Many types are in cultivation, including durra and kaffir.

Sorokin, Pitirim Alexandrovich (1889-1968), Russian-U.S. sociologist. He distinguished between sensate (empirical, scientific) and ideational (mystical, authoritarian) societies and wrote *Social and Cultural Dynamics* (1937-1941).
See also: Sociology.

Sorrel, plant (genus *Rumex*) of the buckwheat family. This herbaceous perennial has sour, succulent, arrow-shaped leaves and stems that are used in soups and salads. The common American sorrel (sheep sorrel or red sorrel) grows in acid soil.

SOS signal, internationally accepted emergency signal, based on an easy to recognize Morse code signal (S= ...; O= —-; S=...). Later given the meaning 'save our souls '.

Sotatsu, Tawaraya (1576-1643), Japanese painter, famous for his realistic decorative style. Painted fans, screens, and mostly emakimono (horizontal rolls).

Sotheby's (full name, Sotheby and Company), famous international auction house based in London (since 1744). Specializes in the auction of paintings, prints and books.

Soto, Jesús Rafael (1923-), Venezuelan artist, practitioner of Op Art and kinetic art. Central theme in his work is the relationship between time, space and matter. Uses very simple materials, including nylon and metal thread and small bars.

Sound, sensation produced by stimulation of the organ of hearing; instrument for insertion into a cavity to detect a foreign body or stricture; or noise, normal or abnormal, heard within the body.

Sound, in geography, any of several types of waterways, most commonly a long arm of ocean, larger than a strait or channel, that runs parallel to a mainland coast. A sound may rest between the mainland and an island or peninsula, connect an ocean and a sea, or be a fjord or lagoon.

Souphanouvong (1912-1995), Laos politician. Prince Souphanouvong, nicknamed 'The Red Prince', organized resistance against the French occupier in the Communist liberation front Pathet Lao. After Laos won its independence (1953), he was minister twice (1957-1958 and 1962-1963) in the coalition government under his half-brother Prince Souvanna Phouma. In the interim period (1958-1962) and during the Vietnam war (1963-1973) he fought with the Pathet Lao against the government, which was following a pro-Western course. After the Democratic People's Republic of Laos was proclaimed in 1975, he became president (1975-1986). In 1986 he had to step down for health reasons. In 1991 he relinquished all party positions and retired from political life.

Sour gum *See:* Tupelo.

Sourwood, or sorrel tree, ornamental deciduous tree (*Oxydendrum arboreum*) of the heath family. The sourwood is native to the

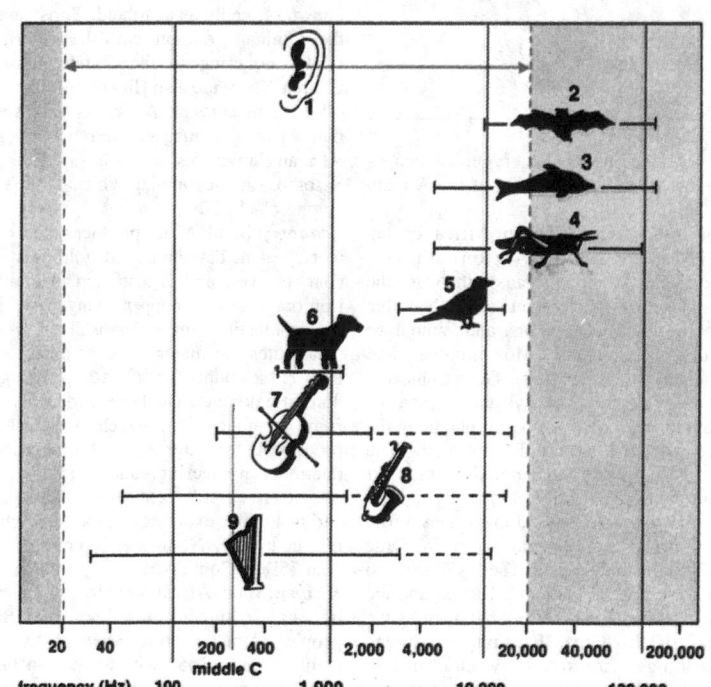

The frequency range of sounds that can be heard by human ears (1) extends from about 20 to 20,000 Hz. Bats (2), porpoises (3), and grasshoppers (4) can generate frequencies to about 100,000 Hz. Birds (5) and dogs (6) produce lower frequency sounds, all within the range of human hearing. Musical instruments, such as violins (7), saxophones (8), and harps (9), produce a range both of fundamental frequencies (solid lines) and of overtones (dashed lines) that give the different instruments their qualities. The middle C note is marked (yellow).

S

United States and grows in the woods of the southern states and in Pennsylvania, Indiana, and Ohio. The trees grow to about 75 ft (23 m) in height, have small, fragrant, white flowers, and oval, sour-tasting leaves that turn bright red in the autumn.

Sousa, John Philip (1854-1932), U.S. bandmaster and composer. He wrote many light operas but is best remembered for his military marches, including 'The Stars and Stripes Forever' and 'The Washington Post.' Sousa was leader of the U.S. Marine Band (1880-1892) before forming a world-tour band of his own.

South Africa

Capital:	Pretoria (gov.)/Cape Town (parliament)/Bloemfontein (Supreme Court)
Area:	471,320 sq mi (1,221,037 sq km)
Population:	43,648,000
Language:	Afrikaans, English, 9 African languages
Government:	Presidential republic
Independent:	1931
Head of gov.:	President
Per capita:	US$ 9,400
Monetary unit:	1 Rand = 100 cents

South Africa, independent republic occupying most of the southern tip of the African continent.
Land and climate. South Africa covers 471,320 sq mi (1,221,037 sq km). It is bordered by the Atlantic Ocean on the west, the Indian Ocean on the east and south, Namibia to the northwest, Botswana and Zimbabwe to the north, and Mozambique and Swaziland to the northeast. Geographically, South Africa is a vast system of plateaus separated from narrow coastal plains by the ranges of the Great Escarpment. The plateaus are mostly flat and undulating, their monotony occasionally varied by kopjes (low, flat-topped hills) and low ridges. From the southwestern coastal plain in Cape Province the land rises in a series of steps to the dry valleys of the Little Karroo and the plateau of the Great Karroo, bounded by the ranges of the Great Escarpment. Among these ranges are the lofty Drakensberg Mountains. Beyond the Great Escarpment is

Conical thatched roofs and earthen walls are characteris-tic of houses built by the Bantu people.

the Northern Karroo, or High Veld, the highest and most fertile of the plateaus. The westward flowing Orange River rises in the Drakensberg Mountains and drains most of the interior plateau. The South African climate is mainly subtropical with dry, sunny winters and hot summers. The country is divided into nine provinces: Eastern Cape, Gauteng, Kwazulu-Natal, Mpumalanga, Northern Cape, Limpopo, North West, Free State and Western Cape.
Its principal cities are Pretoria, the administrative capital; Cape Town, the legislative capital; Bloemfontein, the judicial capital; and Johannesburg and Durban.
People. The population of South Africa is about 76% black African, principally Zulu and Xhosa peoples, about 13% white, 8,5% of mixed white and African descent, and 2,5% Asiatics. Some two-thirds of whites are Afrikaners, descendants of Dutch settlers. Until 1993 South Africa's government and economy were dominated by whites. Blacks were excluded from the franchise, and the government ruthlessly and efficiently pursued a rigorous policy of racial segregation and systematic subjugation of black Africans known officially as apartheid. Christianity is the dominant religion, with the majority of whites adhering to the Dutch Reformed Church. There are also Hindus and Jews. The official languages are Afrikaans, English and nine African languages. The most important African languages are Xhosa, Zulu and Sesotho. Literacy among whites is 95% and among blacks 30%.
Economy. South Africa produces most of the world's gem diamonds and gold, has large coal reserves, and is also rich in uranium, iron ore, asbestos, copper, manganese, nickel, chrome, titanium, and phosphates. Mining contributes the major share of export earnings, but accounts for only 10% of the gross domestic product. The largest contribution is from manufacturing, which includes food processing, iron, steel, and oil from coal production, engineering, and textiles. South Africa is self-sufficient in food production and is a major exporter of food to neighboring countries. Nonwhites comprise more than 75% of South Africa's work force.
History. South Africa was already inhabited by San (Bushmen), Khoikhoi, and Bantu peoples from the north when white settlement began in 1652 with the establishment of a Dutch colony at Cape Town. The British

came to the area in 1795, and from 1835 to 1843 the Boers, descendants of Dutch settlers, moved inland on the Great Trek to escape British dominance. They founded the Boer republics and eventually fought the British in the Boer War (1899-1902). The bitter contest was eventually won by the British, and in 1910 the Union of South Africa was formed. During World War I, South West Africa (Namibia) was wrested from the Germans and placed under a mandate. In 1931 South Africa became independent. Since 1948 it has been ruled by the Afrikaner-led National Party and committed to the policy of apartheid. In 1961 under H.F. Verwoerd, South Africa became a republic and left the Commonwealth largely because of differences over apartheid. Succeeding governments under B.J. Vorster (1966-1978) and P.W. Botha (1978-1989) continued to enforce apartheid, and in the 1980s, met with increasingly determined and often violent resistance internally, engaged in armed conflicts in Namibia and Angola, and were subject to greater and greater international pressure and censure. As a result, the government, headed by Willem de Klerk, gradually took steps toward ending apartheid, a change of policy signalled by the release from prison of Nelson Mandela in 1990. Mandela's release triggered the democratization proces and in 1994 the white minority government was replaced by a democratically chosen black government headed by president Mandela. In October 1998 the national Commission for Truth and Reconciliation published its report on the violation of human rights during the apartheid-regime (1948-1994). The investigation and public testimonies had taken 2.5 years under supervision of bishop Desmond Tutu. In 1999 the ANC again won the elections but the party did not get enough votes to change the constitution. Thabo Mbeki succeeded Mandela as President in 1999. Mbeki's reputation was damaged by allegations of corruption and fraud in 2000. His attitude towards AIDS and HIV hampered treatment of the 4.7 million people between the ages of 15 and 49 infected with HIV or AIDS. However, 39 pharmaceutical companies were forced to withdraw their licenses for AIDS medication, to enable cheaper distribution of AIDS inhibitors and other medication.

South America, southern of the 2 continents comprising the Western Hemisphere. South America is separated from North America at the Isthmus of Panama. Covering an area of 6,880,000 sq mi (17,819,000 sq km), South America contains the 12 independent republics of Argentina, Bolivia, Brazil, Chile, Colombia, Ecuador, Guyana, Paraguay, Peru, Suriname, Uruguay, and Venezuela. There also remains one European possession on the continent, French Guiana.
Land and climate. Roughly triangular in shape, South America extends some 4,750 mi (7,640 km) north to south and, at its widest, is 3,300 mi (5,300 km) east to west. It is surrounded by the Caribbean Sea on the north, the Atlantic Ocean on the east, Drake Passage on the south, and the Pacific Ocean on the west. The continent contains 3 main river basins, the Amazon, Paraná, and

Orinoco. The Amazon, the world's most vo-luminous river, forms a basin containing the world's largest tropical rain forest. The Andes Mountains run in a nearly continuous chain from north to south. Other major top-ographical features include the grasslands of the pampas, the Gran Chaco, and the Patagonian plateau. The climate ranges from extreme cold in the high Andes to tropical heat and humidity in the lowlands and rain forests at the equator.

Economy. South America is rich in unique varieties of plant and animal life as well as mineral resources, including oil, iron ore, copper, tin, lead, zinc, manganese, gold, ni-trate, and bauxite. Much of South America's natural wealth remains to be fully devel-oped. The continent has very little coal, but considerable hydroelectric potential.

People. The peoples of South America are divisible into 4 main groups. These are Native Americans, the original inhabitants of the continent; descendants of Europeans, mostly Spanish and Portuguese; Africans, originally taken to South America as slaves; and peoples of mixed ancestry, usually di-vided into mestizos, a mixture of European and Native American, or mulattoes, a mix-ture of African and European. The total pop-ulation of the continent is about 448 million with about one-third of that number in Brazil. The chief official languages are Spanish and Portuguese, the latter spoken in Brazil. In Guyana, Suriname, and French Guiana, the official languages are, respec-tively, English, Dutch, and French. The most widely spoken of the Native American lan-guages are Guaraní in Paraguay; Quechua in Peru, Bolivia, and Ecuador; and Aymará in Bolivia. About 90% of South Americans are at least nominally Roman Catholic.

Southampton (pop. 212,000), English sea-port city, on the River Test, near the English Channel. The city is England's chief passen-ger port. Founded as a Roman settlement by A.D. 43, Southampton's modern industries include ship building and repair, construc-tion, harbor services, and tobacco process-ing. Of interest to visitors are various me-dieval structures, including Bar Gate, a por-tion of wall from the Middle Ages, and the priory of St. Denys (1124).
See also: England.

South Arabia, Federation of, previously an English protectorate of the crown colony of Aden and several Arab states including Alawi, Aqrabi, Audhali, Upper and Lower Aulaqi, Fadhli, Haushabi, Lahej, Mufhahi, Shaibi, Wahidi, and Lower Yafa. At the south-ern point of the Arabian peninsula, the feder-ation covered about 60,000 sq mi (160,000 sq km) and was controlled economically and po-litically by England. On Nov. 30, 1967, the alliance gained independence and with the is-lands of Kamaran, Perim, and Socotra, be-came the Republic of South Yemen.

South Australia, state in south-central Australia, with an area of 380,070 sq mi (984,381 sq km). Wheat, barley, wool, and wine are produced in the fertile southeast. Minerals include iron ore, opals, salt, gyp-sum, and coal. Major industries, centered in Adelaide, the capital and chief port, include

smelting, chemicals, fertilizers, engineering, and automobiles.
See also: Australia.

South Carolina (Palmetto State; pop. 3,643,000), state in the southeastern United States; bordered by North Carolina to the north, the Atlantic Ocean to the southeast, and Georgia to the southwest.
South Carolina has 3 main land regions. The Blue Ridge, a narrow region in the state's northwestern corner, is part of the Blue Ridge Mountains, which extend into the state. The Atlantic Coastal Plain, in the southeastern two-thirds of the state, has long, sandy beaches in the north; southward, it becomes increasingly swampy, with salt marshes, pine barrens, bays, and tidal rivers. South Carolina has many large rivers, the main ones being the Santee, Pee Dee, and Savannah. There are many rapids and water-falls, but no large natural lakes. Forests cover nearly two-thirds of the state. South Carolina has a warm climate, with hot summers and mild winters. Principal cities are Columbia, Charleston, and North Charleston.
South Carolina's economy is led by manu-facturing, followed by various service indus-tries, including tourism. Chief manufactured goods are textiles, chemicals, machinery, and apparel. Agriculture and mining account for minor shares of the economy. Chief farm products are tobacco, soybeans, corn, cot-ton, and peaches; chief livestock products are eggs, milk, and beef cattle. Chief mining products are granite, limestone, crushed stone, and cement.
Many Native American tribes were living in the area when the first Europeans-Spanish explorers-arrived in 1521. In 1670 the first permanent non-native settlement was estab-lished near present-day Charleston by English colonists. In 1719 the settlers revolt-ed against the colony's proprietors; the province became a royal colony in 1729. South Carolina was one of the 13 British colonies that broke from Britain and fought the American Revolution; in 1788 it became the eighth state. In 1861 South Carolina-a strong proponent of states' rights, free trade, and slavery-became the first state to secede from the Union; the war's first shots were fired at Fort Sumter. Much of the state was damaged during the Civil War. During Reconstruction, federal troops occupied the state, which suffered agricultural depression and political corruption. South Carolina was readmitted to the Union in 1868. In the late 1800s and early 1900s, industrial growth aided recovery. Today South Carolina seeks new industries as its key tobacco industry faces growing opposition to smoking.

South Dakota (Coyote State, Sunshine State; pop. 715,000), state in the U.S. bor-dered by North Dakota, Minnesota, Iowa, Nebraska, Wyoming and Montana; 77,146 sq mi (199,730 sq km). Capital, Pierre. The largest city is Sioux Falls, pop. 100,000. The state is located in the central low-lying planes of the U.S., and is divided into two by the Coteau du Missouri. It has a continental climate: in the west the average tempera-tures are -5°C in January and 22°C in July; in the east of the state: -10°C and 23°C. The economy is based on agriculture. Agricul-

tural areas spread out in the east, where mainly wheat and maize are cultivated. The most important industries are foodstuffs and electronics. Extraction of gold, sand, gravel, iron, uranium, moon stone and gypsum. Due to the lack of economic opportunities, the State is losing many younger members of the population to other parts of the U.S. Before white people came the area was pop-ulated by various Native American tribes, mostly Sioux (Dakota is another name for these people). In 1742 it was claimed by the French brothers Vérendrye. In 1803 the U.S. bought the region from France (Louisiana Purchase). In 1875 the white population was mostly fur hunters and traders; that year gold was discovered in the Black Hills, and a gold rush began. In 1889 the area was split in two, and after various wars the Native American population was mostly ousted (the Battle of Wounded Knee). In 1973 Wounded Knee was occupied by Native Americans who demanded their rights.

Southeast Asia, region of Asia south of the southernmost boundaries of China and India, including Brunei, Burma, Cambodia, Indonesia, Laos, Malaysia, the Philippines, Singapore, Thailand, and Vietnam. The area covers about 1,740,000 sq mi (4,506,600 sq km) and is comprised mostly of areas of rich agricultural lands that produce rubber, rice, tea, coffee, tobacco, pepper, and coconut oil. There are also abundant teak forests, petro-leum deposits, tin and gem mines, and fish. Southeast Asia is a land of diverse cultural backgrounds influenced in part by Europeans, who as early as the 16th century were drawn by the area's resources. Cities include Bangkok, Thailand; Ho Chi Minh City, Vietnam; Jakarta, Indonesia; Manila, the Philippines; and Singapore.
See also: Asia.

The delicate bas-re-liefs that ornament the gallery walls of Angkor Wat in Southeast Asia depict mythological and leg-endary scenes, espe-cially the events asso-ciated with Vishnu. This elegant relief sculpture, covering al-most every open space of the gallery wall, was originally painted and gilded. The city of Angkor was the capital of the Khmer empire from 880 A.D. until the 13th century.

Southeast Asia Treaty Organization (SEATO), defense treaty signed by Australia, France, Great Britain, New Zealand, Pakistan, the Philippines, Thailand, and United States after France withdrew from Indochina in 1954. Headquarters were at Bangkok, Thailand. Although there were no standing forces, its aim was to prevent Communist expansion. The treaty was in-voked by the United States in the Vietnam War (1964-1973). Pakistan withdrew in 1972. SEATO dissolved in 1977.

Southern Cross, or Crux, constellation vis-

S

ible in the Southern Hemisphere, defined by 4 stars in the shape of a cross. In ancient Babylonia and Greece it was part of the constellation Centaurus.

South Island *See:* New Zealand.

South Korea

Capital:	Seoul
Area:	38,316 sq mi (99,300 sq km)
Population:	48,324,000
Language:	Korean
Government:	Republic
Independent:	1948
Head of gov.:	Prime minister
Per capita:	US$ 18,000
Monetary unit:	1 South Korean won = 100 chon

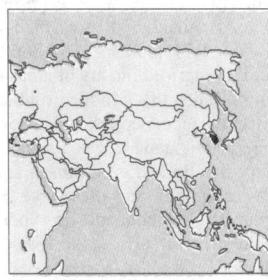

South Korea, republic in Eastern-Asia, bordered by North Korea and the Yellow Sea and the Sea of Japan on either side.
Land and climate. Two thirds of the country is woody mountain and hilly land, descending to the coastland in the west. The water from mountain streams is used to irrigate the limited agricultural land. The island Cheju is situated 31 miles (50 km) from the coast with the highest mountain in the country, Halla-san, 6,494 ft/1950 m. The country has a monsoon climate, moderated by maritime influences.
People and economy. Densely populated South Korea is one of the so-called Newly Industrialized Countries: countries that have experienced considerable economic growth for some decades, mainly because of export-led industries. Typical of the economy are the enormous conglomerates (cheabols) which are tightly connected to the government. The industrialization was combined with a fast urbanization.

Kim Dae Yung and Kim Yong II during their meeting in 2000

History. The half-legendary founder of the kingdom of Choson was Kija, who led a group of exiles from China to Korea in 1122 B.C. But there were other kingdoms on the peninsula, and Korea was not united until the 7th century A.D. Most of its early civilization was destroyed by the Mongol invasions (1231-1292), but with the establishment of the Yi dynasty (1392) Korea entered a golden age that lasted until 1592, when Japan invaded the peninsula. Although the invaders were finally driven out, the Koreans never fully recovered from the years of fighting. For 300 years, Korea, known as the Hermit Kingdom, cut itself off from the world. In the late 1800s, contact was re-established and Japan and the U.S. began trading with Korea. In 1910, Japan annexed Korea. After 35 years of Japanese exploitation, Korea was liberated in 1945 by Russia in the North and by the U.S. in the South. Despite UN intervention, no agreement was reached on a united Korea. The North became a rigidly controlled Communist state under leader Kim II Sung (r. 1958-1994). Free elections were held in the South, under UN supervision, and produced a republic under Syngman Rhee.
In 1950, the Communists of the North invaded South Korea. This was the beginning of the Korean War (1950-1953). The heavy fighting was eventually stopped by an armistice between the UN forces and the Communists, and by the establishment of the demilitarized zone (1953). Since then the uneasy peace has often been disturbed.
Since 1953, South Korea has had alternate military and civilian governments. Under President Park Chung Hee (r. 1961-1979, President for life), industrialization and economic growth took off. In 1988, democratic reforms and liberalization of the economy were initiated. The country was hit hard by the Asian crisis (1997-1998), but the economy recuperated quickly. In the course of the 1990s, the country made overtures to North Korea. In 2000, there was a historical meeting between the North and South Korean leaders Kim Yong il (since 1998) and Kim Dae Yung (since 1997) in the North Korean capital Pyongyang. Kim Dae Yung was awarded the Nobel Peace Prize in 2000 for his 'Sunshine Policy' which meant that North Korea was unconditionally supported in economic and humanitarian fields. In 2002, tension started mounting between North and South Korea again. Roh Moo Hyun was elected President in 2003.
See also: North Korea; Korean War; Kim Dae Yung; Kim Il Sung; Kim Yong Il; Park Chung Hee.

South Pole, point in Antarctica through which passes the earth's axis of rotation. It does not coincide with the earth's south magnetic pole. It was first reached by Roald Amundsen in 1911.
See also: Antarctica.

South Vietnam *See:* Vietnam.

South West Africa *See:* Namibia.

South Yemen *See:* Yemen.

Soutine, Chaim (1894-1943), a Russian-

born French painter. *Portrait of a Boy* (1928), *Side of Beef* (about 1925), and *Windy Day, Auxerre* (1939) reveal his highly personal style of Expressionism. All his paintings - landscapes, portraits, still lifes of animal carcasses - are marked by distorted forms, brilliant color, and thick, swirling brush strokes. Soutine was born near Minsk, and first studied painting in Vilnius. He went to Paris in 1913 and met Modigliani, Chagall, and other major painters of the School of Paris. Soutine lived in dire poverty until 1923, when he sold about 100 of his paintings to the American Collector Albert C. Barnes.

Sovereignty, ultimate political power in a state. In political theory, debates on sovereignty center on the role of the sovereign and on the nature of supreme power-by what rights, and by whom, it should be wielded. A sovereign state is one that is independent of control by other states. The modern theory of sovereignty was developed by Jean Bodin and Thomas Hobbes (1756), who studied the sovereignty of monarchs. The extension of their thought has been applied to the modern state.

Soviet (from Russian *sovet*, 'council'), the fundamental political unit of the former USSR. The soviets, ranging in importance from rural councils to the Supreme Soviet, the major legislative body of the Soviet Union, are elected policy-making and administrative units. The first soviets were the strike committees set up during the 1905 revolution and others developed during the 1917 revolution. Lenin institutionalized the soviet with the Bolshevik victory.

Soviet Union *See:* Union of Soviet Socialist Republics.

Sow bug *See:* Wood louse.

Soweto (South Western Township), (pop. 864,000), town in South Africa, a suburb of Johannesburg. Built after WW II as an alternative to the shantytowns which housed the non-white workforce of the rapidly expanding Johannesburg economy. During student protests in 1976 against the apartheid system, many school children were killed when police opened fire on the crowds; scene of civil unrest, 1984-1987.

Soybean (*Glycine soja* or *Glycine max*), annual legume that is one of the best sources of complete protein, as well as being a good source of calcium, phosphorus, magnesium, and virtually all other minerals, plus vitamins A, B, and C and lecithin. Most of the world's soybeans are grown in China and the United States. In Asia, the soybean seed is sometimes ground into a meal, fermented, or dried, and used as a substitute for meat. In the United States, soybeans are generally made into oil or ground for animal feed; soybeans are also used in adhesives and for waterproofing and in many industrial products.

Soyinka, Wole (1934-), Nigerian writer, first African to win a Nobel Prize in literature (1986). His works include the novel *The Interpreters* (1965) and the memoir *Ake: The Years of Childhood* (1981). He has been president of the International Theater Institute since 1985. Soyinka has been jailed for his activities on behalf of black political freedom. In 1997, the Nigerian military regime accused Soyinka-who lives in the U.S.-of high treason.

Spaak, Paul Henri (1899-1972), Belgium's first Socialist premier (1938-1939, 1946, 1947-1950), and deputy premier (1961-1965). He was the first president of the UN General Assembly (1946). He was influential in setting up the European Economic Community and was secretary-general of the North Atlantic Treaty Organization (NATO; 1957-1961).

Space *See:* Space exploration.

Spacecraft *See:* Space exploration.

Space exploration, investigation of planets, stars, and space through the use of satellites, spacecraft, and probes built by human beings. At 10:56 P.M. (E.D.T.) on July 20, 1969, Neil Armstrong stepped off Apollo 11 and became the first human to set foot on the moon. This was the climax of an intensive U.S. space program sparked by the successful launch of the Soviet artificial satellite Sputnik 1 in 1957 and accelerated by Yuri Gagarin's flight in Vostok 1, the first spacecraft flown by a human, in 1961. Later that year Alan Shepard piloted the first U.S. spacecraft, and President John F. Kennedy set the goal, to be realized within the decade, of landing astronauts on the moon and returning them safely to earth.
On Feb. 20, 1962, John Glenn orbited the earth 3 times in the first Mercury craft to be boosted by an Atlas rocket. The next Soviet mission, in June 1963, involved 2 craft. Piloting Vostok 5, Valery Bykovsky set the 1-person endurance record with a 5-day mission; and piloting Vostok 6, Valentina Tereshkova became the first woman cosmonaut. Aleksei Leonov completed the first space walk in Mar. 1965. But then it was the turn of the Gemini missions to break all records. Both countries lost men, on the ground and in space: among them Virgil Grissom, Edward White, and Roger Chaffee (in a fire on board Apollo during ground tests in 1967) and the crew of Soyuz 11, killed during reentry in 1971. Earlier Soyuz missions had docked successfully with the first space station and set new records.
Meanwhile unpiloted probes-such as Orbiter, Ranger, and Surveyor-were searching out Apollo moon-landing sites; teams preparing the Soviet Luna and Lunokhod craft were also studying the moon. In 1968 Apollo 7 carried out an 11-day earth-orbit flight, and at Christmas Apollo 8 made 10 lunar orbits. The lunar landing craft was tested on the Apollo 9 and Apollo 10 missions, opening the way for the triumphant success of Apollo 11.
Apollo 12 was equally victorious, landing only 600 yards from the lunar probe Surveyor 3, but Apollo 13's aborted mission in 1970 was a near disaster. An explosion damaged the craft on its way to the moon, and reentry was achieved only with great difficulty. Apollo 14 had no such problems in 1971, visiting the moon's Fra Mauro area

and collecting a wide range of lunar samples. Apollo 16 brought back 213 lb (96.6 kg) of moon rock, and in Dec. 1972 Apollo 17 made the last lunar landing, remaining on the moon for a record 75 hours.
In 1973 the United States launched the Skylab space station, a kind of satellite designed so that astronauts can live and work in orbit for several weeks. The station serves as a laboratory and as a base for other spacecraft.
Exploration of the planets has been carried out by unmanned probes: the Mariner series to Mars, Venus, and Mercury, and the Pioneer missions to the outer planets. There have been a number of Soviet contributions, such as the Venera soft-landing missions to Venus, the Zond bypass probe, and the Mars soft-landing craft. Results from the 2 U.S. Viking probes that soft-landed in Mars in 1976 did not show conclusively existence of life there. Voyagers 1 and 2 (1977) revealed a wealth of new information about Jupiter and Saturn.The United States launched the first reusable manned space vehicle, the space shuttle Columbia, in 1981. In 1983 Sally K. Ride, one of five crew members aboard the space shuttle Challenger, became the first U.S. woman in space. In the 25th space shuttle mission (1986), the shuttle Challenger exploded immediately after its launch, killing all seven crew members. A commission appointed by President Ronald Reagan to investigate the accident criticized NASA's decision to launch the shuttle and made several recommendations regarding safety measures to be used in future missions.The United States' Magellan space probe (launched 1989) reached Venus in 1990 and relayed to the earth clear images of Venus's surface. The Ulysses probe, launched by the United States in 1990, reaced the sun's south pole in 1994 and the north pole in 1995. Besides the U.S. and Russia also Europe, Japan and China are developing independant space programs. The space shuttle Columbia crashed shortly before landing in January, 2003. All seven crew members were killed.

Space shuttle *See:* Space exploration.

Space station the ISS – also known as Alpha of Freedom – is a space station that is being built by 16 co-operating countries, including the United States, Russia and Japan. It will have a maximum span of 100 meters and will contain six scientific laboratories. The building commenced in 1998, and if everything goes according to plan, it should be finished around 2003. The transport of materials will require 40 space missions that will have to be made by the American space shuttle and by Russian Sojoez and Proton rockets. The first part of the ISS – Zarya – was launched in November 1998, followed by the Unity and Destiny modules. The first group of permanent crewmembers (Expedition One) arrived at the ISS in November 2000.They started on scientific testing – an important part of this project. Experiments carried out in the very nearly completely zero gravity atmosphere in the space station can lead to new insights in the fields of biology, chemistry and physics. The fact that gasses and fluids have different properties under these circumstances than

they do on earth, raises the hope of discovering new technical materials and possibly even medicinal combinations. These experiments are carried out in the testing units, where the atmospheric pressure is more or less the same as the earth's, but it will also be possible to carry out experiments in space, outside the space station. This is an important breakthrough in space technology.

Space telescope *See:* Hubble Space Telescope.

Space-time, concept of the physical universe arising from Einstein's special theory of relativity. Space and time are considered as a single 4-dimensional continuum rather than as a 3-dimensional space with a separate, infinite, 1-dimensional time. Time thus becomes the 4th dimension. Events in space-time are analogous to points in space and invariant space-time intervals to distances in space.
See also: Relativity.

Spahn, Warren (1921-), U.S. baseball player. Considered one of the greatest pitchers of all time, Spahn's achievements include winning the Cy Young award (1957) and setting a record for left-handed pitching in victories (363) and shutouts (63). He played in the major leagues for the Boston (Milwaukee) Braves (1942-1964), New York Mets (1965), and San Francisco Giants (1965). Spahn was inducted to the National Baseball Hall of Fame in 1973.

Spain

Capital:	Madrid
Area:	194,898 sq mi
	(504,783 sq km)
Population:	40,077,000
Language:	Spanish (Castilian), Catalan, Galician, Basque
Government:	Parliamentary monarchy
Independent:	1492
Head of gov.:	Prime minister
Per capita:	US$ 18,900
Monetary unit:	1 Peseta = 100 céntimos

Spain, Kingdom occupying about four-fifths of the Iberian Peninsula south of the Pyrenees in southwestern Europe.
Land and climate. Including the Balearic and

S

The astronaut James S. Voss taking a walk through space, May 2000. He is safely chained to the space arm (Remote Manipulator System) that is part of the apparatus on board the space shuttle Atlantis. The following year, Voss was one of the permanent ISS crew.

The Zvezda module in the Russian Energia factories. Economic problems were one of the reasons the launch was delayed. It was held up for such a long time that the co-operation between the US and Russia was endangered. The Zvezda (that was finally coupled to the ISS halfway through 2000) helps the space station to maintain its course and position.

The astronauts James S. Voss and Jeffrey N. Williams after they had done some work on the outside of the space station in May 2000. Between the two astronauts one of the suits used for this task can be seen.

When it is completed, the ISS – a co-operative effort between 16 countries – will contain six laboratories, that have a total weight of 460 tons. Because the space station is located more or less outside the atmosphere, it is not necessary for it to be aerodynamic, which means the different modules can be linked on to it in various ways.

S

Launch of a Russian Proton rocket. These rockets were used to transport the Zvezda module.

The ISS in the early stages, when it consisted of nothing more than the modules Unity (the smallest part) and Zarya (which was launched at the end of '98).

S

Canary islands, Spain covers 194,898 sq mi (504,783 sq km). Peninsular Spain is bounded on the north by the Bay of Biscay. On the northeast, the Pyrenees mark the borders with France and Andorra. On the west, Spain is bounded by Portugal and the Atlantic Ocean, and to the east and south, by the Mediterranean Sea and the Strait of Gibraltar. About three-quarters of Spain is the great interior plateau called the Meseta, extending from the Cantabrian Mountains and the Ebro River in the north to the Sierra Morena and the Guadalquivir River in the south. In the west the plateau continues into Portugal; in the east low ranges separate it from the coastal plain. The Meseta is higher in the north than in the south, the dividing line being the central cordillera. It is traversed by the Douro, Tagus, and Guadiana rivers, which flow into the Atlantic. Except for irrigated areas and fertile valleys, the Meseta is mostly arid and large areas are barren. In the southeast, beyond the Guadalquivir River, are the Andalusian Mountains, which contain Spain's highest mountain range, the Sierra Nevada. Spain's coastal plains are mostly narrow, becoming broadest along the Gulf of Cádiz in the south. The north and northwest coasts, hemmed in by mountains, have rocky cliffs and long inlets providing good harbors and some fine beaches. The Mediterranean coast is also rocky but there are fine sand beaches north of Barcelona along the famed Costa Brava. Spain is mainly a dry country with hot summers and cool winters. But great extremes occur on the Meseta. The climate of northern Spain is more equable. Along the south and east coasts, winters are mild and summers hot.

People. The Spanish people are in many ways homogeneous, but certain traditional and ethnic differences distinguish several groups. The Basques are an ethnically distinct people and, together with the Catalonians and Galicians, have preserved their own languages. The official language is Castilian Spanish. The capital of the country is Madrid and Roman Catholicism is the established religion.

Economy. Tourism makes the most important contribution to Spain's income, followed by industry and agriculture. Mineral wealth includes mercury, iron ore, coal, pyrites, potash, and salt. Oil was found 1964. Manufacturing includes textiles, chemicals, iron and steel, paper, explosives, and armaments. Agriculture is about equally

These windmills on the Spanish plateau are still being used for the processing of various agricultural products, such as cereals.

divided between crops and livestock. Oranges, olive oil, wine, and cork are exported. Fishing is also important.

History. Present-day Spain was settled successively from prehistoric times to the 3rd century B.C. by Celts, Phoenicians, Greeks, and Carthaginians. A more enduring influence was that of the Romans, who conquered Spain in the Second Punic War in the 2nd century B.C. and remained dominant until the Vandals and Visigoths invaded in the 5th century A.D. The last invaders were the Moors, who advanced in A.D. 711. The Christian kingdoms that remained, all in the north, undertook the gradual reconquest of the peninsula, which was not completed until 1492 with the fall of Granada in the reign of Ferdinand V (Ferdinand II of Aragon) and Isabella of Castile (1474-1504). The same monarchs financed the voyages of Columbus, expelled the Jews from Spain, and sponsored the Inquisition. Within a brief period, Spain acquired a vast empire in the New World and North Africa and became rich, particularly in gold and silver from the Americas. Spain's new holdings were augmented by Habsburg lands when Charles I (1516-1556) was elected Holy Roman Emperor as Charles V. Under his son and successor, Philip II 1556-1598), Spain was at the height of its political and cultural power, as evidenced in the works of Cervantes, Lope da Vega, Velásquez, and El Greco. But Philip's reign also saw the onset of Spain's decline. The Netherlands revolted in 1568, and the Armada was defeated by the English in 1588. The War of the Spanish Succession at the beginning of the 18th century resulted in huge losses for Spain. The French, under Napoleon, invaded in 1808 and were driven out in the Peninsular War, but with revolutions in the Latin American colonies and defeat in the Spanish-American War (1898), the empire was finished. Political division in the early 20th century culminated in the Spanish Civil War (1936-1939) between leftists and Fascists, which was won by the right wing under General Francisco Franco, who subsequently became dictator. After Franco's death in 1975, Juan Carlos de Bourbon restored the Spanish monarchy and also encouraged parliamentary democracy. In 1982 socialists won the elections to lead the first leftist government in Spain since the Civil War. In 1996 the socialists were defeated by José Aznar's conservative Partido Popular. The Aznar government was unable to end the terrorist attacks committed by the Bask separatist group ETA. The ETA pursues an independent Basque State, situated partly in France and partly in Spain. In the south, the position of the British crown colony Gibraltar remains controversial since Spain wishes to obtain authority over the peninsula.

Spaniel, one of a large family of sporting dogs, probably descended from a Spanish dog, hence the name. Spaniels make good pets and companions as well as good hunters. Most spaniels have silky coats, long ears, and sturdy bodies and legs. The American Kennel Club recognizes these 10 breeds of spaniels: American water, clumber, cocker, English cocker, English springer, field, Irish water, Sussex, Welsh springer, and Brittany.

Spanish, Romance language spoken by about 341 million people, primarily in Spain and Latin America. Modern Spanish arose from the Castilian dialect centered in the town of Burgos, in north-central Spain.

Spanish-American War (1898), fought between the United States and Spain, initially over the conduct of Spanish colonial authorities in Cuba. Strong anti-Spanish feeling was fomented in the United States by stories of the cruel treatment meted out to Cuban rebels and the hardships suffered by U.S. business interests. Though President Grover Cleveland took no action, his successor, President William McKinley, had promised to recognize Cuban independence. He succeeded in obtaining limited self-government for the Cubans, but an explosion aboard the U.S. battleship *Maine* (1898), from which 260 died, was blamed on the Spanish. McKinley sent an ultimatum, some of whose terms were actually being implemented when Congress declared war on Apr. 25 (Spain had declared war the previous day). On May 1 Admiral George Dewey destroyed the Spanish fleet in Manila harbor. What remained was trapped in the harbor at Santiago, Cuba, and destroyed on July 3 by U.S. forces that had already shattered Spanish land forces in several battles, including the Battle of San Juan Hill (July 1), famed for the charge of the Rough Riders, led by Theodore Roosevelt, up Kettle Hill. Santiago surrendered on July 17. General Nelson A. Miles occupied Puerto Rico, and on Aug. 13 troops occupied Manila. The Treaty of Paris (Dec. 10, 1898) ended Spanish rule in Cuba. The United States gained the islands of Guam, Puerto Rico, and the Philippines, thus acquiring an overseas empire with accompanying world military power and responsibilities.

Spanish Armada, naval fleet from Spain that attacked England in 1588. At that time the Catholic monarchy of Spain, under King Philip II, wielded great power through its wealthy colonies in the Americas and its control over Portugal and the Netherlands in Europe. Philip wanted to invade and control England, a Protestant country under the rule of Queen Elizabeth I. Sir Francis Drake, encouraged by the Queen, successfully raided Spain and Spanish holdings, which provoked Philip II to attack England from the English Channel. The smaller, swifter ships of the English navy drove the larger Spanish boats away from the coast, sunk 2 Spanish vessels, and damaged many others. Bad weather conditions also wrecked many ships of the Armada as they fled the English coast. Only about half the ships of the Spanish Armada returned to Spain.

Spanish bayonet, plant in the agave family, of the genus *Yucca*. The Spanish bayonet (*Y. aloifolia*) is about 25 ft (8 m) in height. Its name refers to the shape of its leaves, which are like slender, pointed bayonets. This plant can be found in the United States, the West Indies in the Caribbean, and Mexico.

Spanish Civil War (1936-1939), one of the most violent and bloody conflicts in Spanish history, between the liberal second republic and conservative forces in Spain. After the bloodless overthrow of the monarchy in 1931, the democratic republican government proposed far-reaching reforms that alienated conservatives. On the election (1936) of the Popular Front, a left-wing coalition, the rightists under Gen. Francisco Franco resorted to force. Supported by Hitler and Mussolini, Franco was on the verge of shattering the republicans when the Soviet Union began to send them aid. Madrid and Barcelona fell to Franco in 1939. Over 600,000 died in the war, many of them foreign volunteers, and the country suffered massive damage. Franco's dictatorship remained in power until his death in 1975. The Luftwaffe's systematic destruction of the Basque town of Guernica, a preview of Hitler's blitzkrieg, shocked the world.

Spanish fly, beetle found mainly in southern Europe. It is the source of cantharidin, which causes blistering and bleeding of the skin and was a fashionable remedy for many diseases in the 19th century. It was also alleged to be an aphrodisiac. When taken by mouth, it is poisonous.

Spanish Inquisition *See:* Inquisition; Torquemada, Tomás de.

Spanish literature, European literature containing elements of the Western traditions of Europe and the Eastern traditions of North Africa. The heritage left behind when the Romans occupied the Spanish peninsula was the vernacular Latin, the foundation for the Romance languages, three of which became the most common Spanish dialects-Castilian, Galician-Portuguese, and Catalan. The long struggle from the A.D. 700s to 1400s between the Christians and the Muslim Moors created a religious patriotism that inspired some of the finest poetry and prose.

The Middle Ages. The first lyric poems, called *jarchas*, appeared in the A.D. 900s, expressing themes of longing for love. The epic work, *Poem of the Cid*, relates the adventures of Castilian hero, Rodrigo Díaz de Vivar. Early Spanish prose was promoted by the Castilian king Alfonso X. Two histories, *General Chronicle of Spain* and *General History*, appeared under his direction. Prose fiction first appeared about 1100 in a series of moral tales written by Pedro Alfonso entitled *Scholar's Guide*. The first distinctive prose writing was that of Don Juan Manuel who wrote on a variety of subjects; his *Count Lucanor* (1335) is a collection of moral tales. The three great poets of the 1400s were Iñigo López de Mendoza, Juan de Mena, and Jorge Manrique. López de Mendoza wrote elaborate pastoral poems called *serranillas*. Mena's allegorical work, *The Labyrinth of Fate* (1444), was inspired by Dante. Manrique eulogized his father in the *Coplas* (1476).

Printing was introduced to Spain c. 1473. The first book to set forth the rules of a European language, *Castilian Grammar*, by Antonio de Nebrija, was published in 1492. Other prose works such as Diego de San Pedro's *The Prison of Love* (1492) and a book of chivalry, *Tirant lo Blanch* (1490) appeared at this time. A novel about chivalry,

Amadís of Gaul, was the masterpiece of the period. *La Celestina*, appeared as an anonymous novel in the late 1400s; it combines medieval theology with Renaissance concern for life and love. The story, probably written by Fernando de Rojas, features a witch, Celestina, who unites two lovers, Calisto and Melibea.

The Golden Age. The two main schools of poetry were the Castilian school of Salamanca and the Andalusian school of Seville, both of which followed the style of the Italian poet Petrarch. Writers of the Salamanca school adopted a cautious use of metaphor, while the poets of the Seville school developed a formal use of language that led to the Baroque style of the 1600s. The mystic poets wrote lyrically of a union with God, while the epic poets glorified people and events in long works. The pastoral novel, glorifying the simple life, became popular during the Renaissance. The picaresque novel presented life in satiric fashion through the eyes of a rogue.

Playwriting developed more slowly during the 1500s. The actor-playwright Lope de Rueda created short, farce works called *pasos* that ridiculed the everyday life of his time.

In the 1600s the picaresque novel quickly became a tradition. Mateo Aleman's *Guzmán de Alfarache* presents a bitter, pessimistic view of life in which neither human nature nor the conditions of life can be changed. Francisco López de Beda created a female rogue in *La pícara Justina* (1605).

In contrast to the picaresque novel, Cervantes's masterpiece novel, *Don Quixote*, contrasts the ideal and the practical. His characters present universal themes and qualities that extend to all humanity.

Lope de Vega was the leading dramatist of the Golden Age, presenting love and honor as sources of conflict, especially in his two greatest dramas, *Fuenteovejuna* (1619) and *Justice Without Revenge* (1634).

Two literary examples of the Baroque (ornamental) style of writing of the 1600s were *conceptismo* and *culteranismo*. Conceptismo writers used metaphors to create complicated, original views of life. Culteranismos such as Pedro Soto de Rojas created lyric poetry in full color and imagery.

In drama, Pedro Calderon de la Barca's brilliant work *Life Is a Dream* (1635) was written in the Baroque style. He used symbolism to express in verse philosophical explorations of life and death, original sin, and free will.

Neoclassicism, romanticism, and realism. Neoclassicism, stressing the ideas of reason, proper behavior, and moral sense, became the important literary trend of the 1700s. A Benedictine monk, Benito Jerónimo Feijoo, covered almost every branch of learning in the 9-volume *Universal Theatre of Criticism* (1726-1740) and the 5-volume *Erudite and Interesting Letters* (1742-1760). In the 1800s the most accomplished writer of neoclassical comedy was Leandro Fernández de Moratín, whose most famous play was *The Maiden's Consent* (1806).

Romantic literary forms intensified after the death of King Ferdinand VII in 1833. Ángel de Saavedra's drama *Don lvaro or The Force of Destiny* (1835) was a successful romantic

A poster from Spanish anarchists, which means to send out a warning against the threat of fascism in Spain. The translation of the text is: 'Tomorrow the world, today Spain'. The anarchists formed an important group within the Republican camp, one of the contending parties in the Spanish Civil War.

tragedy. Antonio García Gutiérrez's historical tragedy *The Troubadour* (1836) was a triumph. Francisco Martínez de la Rosa and Juan Eugenio Hartzenbusch wrote plays reflecting rebellion, melancholy, and the passion of Spanish romanticism. José de Espronseda's poems *The Student from Salamanca* (1836-1839) and *Devil World*, unfinished, are rich expressions of Spanish romantic anguish and social protest. Gustavo Adolfo Bécquer's light, airy poetry contains elements of romanticism, and he is often considered the most sensitive poet of the 1800s.

Short prose sketches, called *costumbrismo*, led to the development of the realistic Spanish novel in the mid-1800s. José María de Pereda's *The Upper Cliffs* (1895) was a costumbrista novel describing life on Spain's northern coast. Emilia Pardo Bazán's *The Ulloa Estate* (1886) narrated local traditions and politics in the interior of Galicia. Vicente Blasco Ibáñez's novel *The Cabin* (1898) described life in Valencia. Ibáñez gained international popularity for his novel about the terror of World War I, *The Four Horsemen of the Apocalypse* (1916).

The 1900s. The loss of the last remnants of Spain's empire during the Spanish-American War (1898) led to a resurgence of creative genius that dominated Spanish letters in the early 1900s. Miguel de Unamuno's essay *The Tragic Sense of Life* (1913) was an expression of romantic and philosophical grief. He is often considered the forerunner of the existential movement. Antonio Machado's poetry expresses the severe spirit and landscape of Castile. Ramón María del Valle-Inclán's *Bohemian Lights* (1924) was a picture of Spain as a grotesque distortion of normalcy. Scholars also rediscovered Spain's literary past, and interpreted, edited, and published works at the Center of Historical Studies in Madrid.

The short-lived age of modernism was represented by Manuel Machado and Gregorio Martínez Sierra. It inspired poetry of unequaled quality and intensity in Spanish literature. In Spanish drama, the best-known

S

S

works are the comedy *The Bonds of Interest* (1907) and the domestic tragedy *The Passion Flower* (1913), by Jacinto Benavente.

The poets of the Generation of 1927 turned to the traditional ballad for inspiration. Their members included Pedro Salinas, Jorge Guillén, León Felipe, Gerardo Diego, Federico García Lorca, and others.

The Spanish Civil War (1936-1939) caused a disruption in Spanish literature. Some writers were killed, and others continued to work in exile. The dark novel *The Family of Pascual Duarte* (1942) by Camilo José Cela (Cela won a Nobel Prize for his work in 1989) was followed by Carmen Laforet's existential novel *Nothing* (1944).

Major novels since the mid-1950s have included *The Jarama River* (1956) by Rafael Sanchez Ferlioso, *Time of Silence* (1962) by Luis Martín Santos, and *Soldiers Cry at Night* by Ana María Matute. International renown was won by Juan Goytisolo, some of whose powerful novels, such as *Marks of Identity* (1966), were too contraversial for the Spanish authorities and had to be published outside of the country. From the late 1960's through the early 1980's Spanish literature was marked by increased experimentation and a neobaroque style. The 1980's brought a cultural flowering to Spain as Madrid resumed its pre-Civil War way of life. Juan Benet, Eduardo Mendoza, and Fernando Savater became major contributors to this literary revival.

Playwrights wrote in a variety of styles. Miguel Mihura wrote farces about everyday life. Antonio Bueno Vallejo promoted interest in serious drama with *History of a Staircase* (1949). The poets who wrote after 1939 used simpler forms of expression than the Generation of 1927. Some, including Claudio Rodríguez and Carlos Bousoño, were less interested in social realism. The newest generation of poets, called *novisimos*, reject social concerns and show interest in more personal, intimate, and intellectual concerns.

Spanish Main, former name of the north Caribbean coast of South America, from Panama to the Orinoco River in Venezuela. It was the hunting ground of the English pirates and buccaneers who attacked the Spanish treasure fleets.

Spanish moss, or Florida moss, epiphyte (*Tillandsia usneoides*) that can be found festooning trees, such as oaks and cypresses, and even telephone poles and wires in the southeastern United States. It is not a true moss. It absorbs water through scaly hairs on the leaves and stem, and is used as a substitute for horsehair stuffing and for insulation.

Spanish Succession, War of the (1701-1714), conflict between France and the Grand Alliance of England, the Netherlands, Austria, and the smaller states of the Holy Roman Empire over control of the Spanish Empire. The childless Charles II of Spain willed his kingdom and its empire to France on his deathbed. The alliance sought to prevent France from becoming the dominant European power. Though the decisive battles were fought in Europe, there were also engagements overseas, including North America. The duke of Marlborough and Prince Eugene of Savoy won remarkable victories at Blenheim (1704), Ramillies (1706), and Malplaquet (1709), but Louis XIV fought on. The accession of Charles VI as the new Holy Roman emperor removed obstacles to the recognition of Philip of Anjou as Philip V of Spain. England made a separate peace in 1712, and a general settlement of differences in the Peace of Utrecht followed in 1713.

Spark, Muriel (1918-), Scottish writer best known for her witty, often satirical novels, including *Memento Mori* (1959), *The Prime of Miss Jean Brodie* (1961; later a play and film), *The Mandelbaum Gate* (1965), *Loitering with Intent* (1981), *Curriculum Vitae* (autobiography; 1992), and *Reality and Dreams* (1996).

Sparrow, gregarious, seed-eating bird of the subfamily *Passerinae* of the weaverbird family. There are 8 genera: 5 confined to Africa, the other 3-the true sparrows, rock sparrows, and snow finches-are also found in the Palearctic. Of the true sparrows, one species, the house sparrow (*Passer domesticus*), has been successfully introduced to the Americas. Closely associated with human habitation, it is the only bird not known to occur in a 'natural' habitat but always with human beings. In the United states some small finches are called sparrows (song sparrow, tree sparrow, field sparrow, etc.).

Sparrowhawk, name for small birds of prey (genus *Accipiter*). They eat insects and small birds and mammals and often hunt by hovering. Upper feathers range from gray to rusty brown. In the United States the kestrel, a small falcon, is called the sparrow hawk.

Sparta, or Lacedaemon, city of ancient Greece, capital of Laconia in the Peloponnesus, on the Eurotas River. A center for culture and wealth, its society was divided into 3 classes: the helots (serfs bound to the land); the free perioeci (freemen allowed to take part in commerce and crafts); and the Spartiates, citizens with legal and civil rights, whose rigorous military training led to the word *Spartan*. There were 2 hereditary kings, though real power resided with the 5 annually elected ephors (magistrates). Founded in the 13th century B.C., Sparta dominated the Peloponnesus by 550 B.C. Despite alliance with Athens in the Persian Wars, Sparta fought and won the Peloponnesian War against Athens (431-404 B.C.), but a series of revolts and defeats destroyed Spartan power, and in 146 B.C. the city became subject to Roman rule. It prospered under the Romans but was destroyed by the Goths in A.D. 395.
See also: Greece, Ancient.

Spartacus (d.71 B.C.), leader of the Gladiators' War, a slave revolt against ancient Rome (73-71 B.C.). With an army of runaway slaves, Spartacus heavily defeated forces sent against him and gained control of southern Italy, but after his death in battle the revolt was quickly crushed and 6,000 slaves were crucified along the Appian Way.
See also: Rome, Ancient.

Spastic paralysis, form of paralysis due to disease of the brain (e.g., stroke) or spinal cord (e.g., multiple sclerosis), in which the affected muscles are in a state of constantly increased tone (or resting contraction). Spasticity is a segmental motor phenomenon where muscle contractions occur without voluntary control.
See also: Cerebral palsy.

Speaker, Tristram E. (1888-1958), U.S. baseball player. Known for his outstanding defense and speed, Speaker holds the American League record for putouts by an outfielder (6,794 career). He compiled a lifetime batting average of .344 and set a major league record for doubles (793). Speaker played for the Boston Red Sox (1907-1915) and Cleveland Indians (1916-1926), managing the Indians as well (1919-1926). He was inducted into the National Baseball Hall of Fame in 1937.

Spear, weapon on which a point tops a long shank. Spears have been constructed and used by humans since primitive times. The points of spears have evolved from the earliest ones made of wood to those crafted from bones, stones, bronze, and iron. Whether used in hunting or warfare, spears may be thrown toward their targets or used by their owners to stab the intended targets. In the 17th century, the bayonet took over the popular role of the spear in combat.
See also: Javelin.

Spearfishing, sport in which fish are caught underwater with the use of spears. An underwater slingshot device called a Hawaiian sling, a simple spear with a metal tip called a pole spear, and various kinds of spearguns are used to catch the fish. People spear fish from the surface or dive underwater, using breathing equipment, such as snorkels or scuba gear. In official meets, divers must breathe on their own underwater. After a fish is caught, the diver must gain control of it, with the help of a line that connects the spear to the spearing apparatus.

Spearmint, herb in the mint family. Spearmint (*Mentha spicata*), originally from Europe and Asia, is plentiful in North America. It grows to about 2 ft (61 cm) high and displays white to light purple flowers. The leaves, when dried, are used for cooking, baking, and flavoring beverages. Oil extracted from the leaves is used in perfume.

Special education, instruction designed for the special needs of certain students, both gifted and handicapped. Mainstreaming refers to the time spent by these exceptional students in a regular classroom; special instruction takes place in 'resource rooms.' Over 10% of U.S. schoolchildren need special education programs (approximately 8% are handicapped, including physical and mental impairments; 3-5% are considered gifted). Students of both average and above-average intelligence may need special education, due to learning disabilities from minor disorders. Hyperactive children also participate in special education programs. The Education for All Handicapped Children Act (1975) provides for their education.

Special effects, in cinema, technique developed to enhance visual illusion, especially important in 'disaster movies' and ambitious science fiction films, such as *Star Wars*. Most effects are produced in special studios and are added to the film after it is shot. A great many techniques are employed, including animation, the use of miniature models, and slow-speed or fast-speed photography. An important and increasingly sophisticated technique is the creation of a composite picture-using several different images superimposed within a single frame-often with the aid of electronic memories and timers to match perspectives, light, and camera angles.

Special Olympics, international sporting program designed for participation by mentally retarded people. This program is active in summer and winter sports year round through communities and schools. Like the Olympics, an international winter and summer Special Olympic event takes place every 4 years. The program develops events according to the age and ability of its participants. Headquartered in Washington, D.C., the Special Olympics were founded (1968) and are sponsored by the Joseph P. Kennedy, Jr., Foundation.

Species *See:* Classification.

Specific heat, warmth required to raise the temperature of 1 kg (2.2 lb) of a substance through 1 kelvin; measured by calorimetry. The concept was introduced in 1760 by Joseph Black (1728-1799). Subsequently, P. L. Dulong and A. T. Petit evolved a law in 1819 showing that the specific heat of elements is inversely proportional to their atomic weights, which could thus be roughly determined, and the product of the atomic weight and the specific heat is a constant for all solid elements.
See also: Black, Joseph.

Spectrometer, tool that analyzes an object through a spectrum of light. This device can be used to examine evidence at crime scenes, to determine the composition of celestial bodies, and to detect pollution in the sky or water. Spectroscopes allow a scientist to view the light spectrum of an object, which for every object is different. Sometimes photographs of the light spectrum are taken by a spectrograph. The brightness of light in an object may be determined through a spectrophotometer.

Spectrum, array of light in the form of different colors produced when a ray of plain white light passes through a prism by a process known as dispersion. The different colors of light are created by different wavelengths, which are forms of electromagnetic radiation. The short-wave lengths (low frequency) create indigo and violet on one end of the spectrum; the long-wave lengths (high frequency) produce red, orange, and yellow on the other end of the spectrum.

Speculation, practice of entering into business transactions in order to make a quick profit from an anticipated substantial price fluctuation. Speculation is also applied to investment in any undertaking when the risks and the potential profit are both high. Most speculation, however, involves the buying of commodities or stocks and bonds.
See also: Stock exchange.

Speech and speech disorders, communication through spoken words and the impairments of this ability. Speech can be subdivided into conception, or formulation, and production, or phonation and articulation.

Speech development in children starts with associating sounds with persons and objects, comprehension usually predating vocalization by some months. Nouns are developed first, often with 1 or 2 syllables only; later acquisition of verbs, adjectives, etc., allows the construction of phrases and sentences. A phase of babbling speech, where the child toys with sounds resembling speech, is probably essential for development.

Line spectra are of two fundamental types. An emission spectrum (A) is the result of light emitted by an atom when its electrons return to their original low-energy states from higher energy levels. An absorption spectrum (B) is a series of dark lines obtained as atoms absorb selective wavelengths of incident light. The lines of each spectrum occur in the same positions. An absorption spectrum is observed (C) by passing white light through a sample and then a spectograph; the absorbed wavelengths appear as black lines.

S

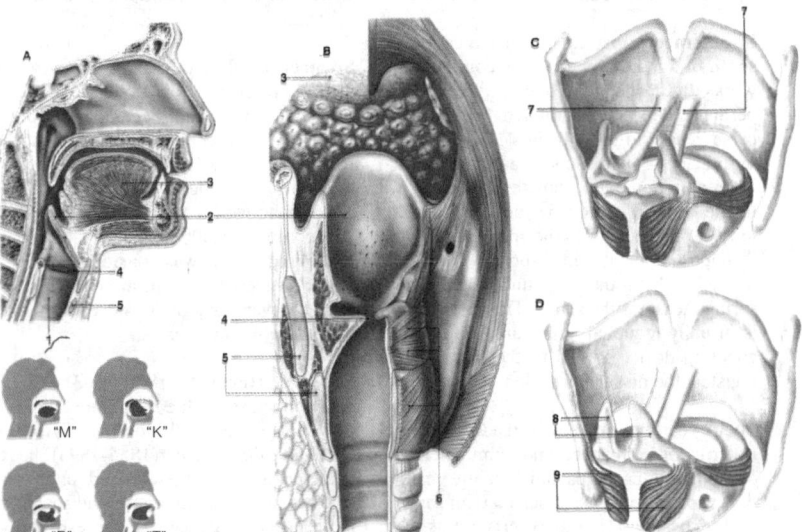

The principal speech organs, seen here in a side view (A) and back view (B), include the larynx (1), epiglottis (2), tongue (3), mouth, and lips. Air expired from the lungs and forced through the larynx, causes the vocal cords (4) to vibrate, producing a continuous tone — the voice. The pitch of the voice is regulated by the arrangement of the various cartilages (5) in the larynx, which are controlled by muscle (6) action. During breathing (C), the vocal cords (7) are held apart, forming a V-shaped opening. The voice is produced (D) when the moving cartilages (8) are drawn together by the muscles (9), forming a linear gap between the vocal cords. The cartilages tilt to regulate vocal-cord tension. Greater tension produces a higher pitch, and less tension produces a lower pitch. Loudness depends on how fast the air travels. The faster the air is forced through the gap, the louder the voice. When the voice is further modified by altering the position and shape of the other organs, speech can occur. Different vowels are produced by varying the shape of the mouth cavity. Consonants, which depend on the relative position of the lips and tongue (lower left), are produced when the air is expired suddenly or stopped sharply.

S

Reading is closely related to speech development and involves the association of auditory and visual symbols. Speech involves coordination of many aspects of brain function (hearing, vision, etc.), but 3 areas particularly concerned with aspects of speech are located in the dominant hemisphere of right-handed persons and in either hemisphere of left-handed people.

Disease of these parts of the brain leads to characteristic forms of dysphasia or aphasia alexia, etc. Development dyslexia is a childhood defect of visual pattern recognition. Stammering or stuttering, with repetition and hesitation over certain syllables, is a common disorder, in some cases representing frustrated left-handedness. Dysarthria is disordered voice production and is due to disease of the neuromuscular control of voice. In speech therapy, attempts are made to overcome or circumvent speech difficulties, which is particularly important to address in children.

Speech therapy, detection and correction of speech problems. Speech-language pathologists work with people who, for various reasons, cannot speak at all (asphasiacs), cannot speak clearly or easily, stutter or have a problem with voice pitch or volume. The most common problem dealt with in speech therapy is that of articulation, the way in which sounds are produced. Speech problems may be physical, environmental, or emotional in origin. Many speech-language professionals belong to The American Speech and Hearing Association (founded 1925).

Speed *See:* Methamphetamine.

Speedometer, instrument for indicating the speed of a motor vehicle. The common type works by magnetic induction. A circular, permanent magnet is rotated by a flexible cable geared to the transmission. The rotating magnetic field induces a magnetic field in an aluminum cup, thus tending to turn it in the same direction as the magnet. This torque, proportional to the speed of rotation, is opposed by a spiral spring. The angle through which the cup turns against the spring measures the speed. The speedometer is usually coupled with an odometer, a counting device geared to the magnet, that registers the distance traveled.

Speed reading, mastery of reading material in terms of both speed and comprehension. Mental training helps quicken the reading pace more than do exercises that improve visual focus, according to experts in this field. A combination of complete concentration, attention to a specific reading purpose (pleasure, fact-finding), and continual reading without pause (regardless of multisyllabic vocabulary or total speed comfort) often yield increased comprehension simultaneously with increased speed.

Speedwriting, writing method that uses the letters of the alphabet in a shortened form. Each letter corresponds with a sound, which in longhand often is made up of a cluster of letters. For example, the letter *a* is pronounced like the word *ate*; therefore, *fa*

would stand for *fate*, *stra* would stand for *straight*, etc. Because of fewer (though familiar) letter and sound relationships employed, a person may write what is dictated quickly. Emma B. Dearborn invented this trademarked method of shorthand writing in 1923.
See also: Shorthand.

Speer, Albert (1905-1981), German architect and Nazi leader. For his organization of slave labor for Germany during World War II, the international tribunal at Nuremberg sentenced him to 20 years' imprisonment in Spandau. After his release he wrote revealingly of the inner workings of the Nazi regime in *Inside the Third Reich* (1972).
See also: Nazism; World War II.

Speleology, scientific study of caves. The world's first speleological society was founded in France in 1895, and interest soon became worldwide. The U.S. National Speleological Society was founded in 1939. Nonacademic cave exploration is called *spelunking*.
See also: Cave.

Spelling, often referred to as orthography, manner in which letters represent words in writing. Orthographers study sound and letter relationships, base words and affixes (which include prefixes and suffixes), preferred spellings of words, spelling rules and exceptions, homophones, and word pronunciation. Individuals devise their own methods for correct spelling, which may include word visualization, spoken pronunciation, syllabic division of words, repeat writing of the word, and using the word in context.

Spencer, Freddie (1962-), American motorcycle racer, rode his first race at the age of 10. In 1983 he became one of the youngest world champions in the history of road racing, on a Honda 500 cc. Two years later he won the double: with Honda Spencer he won the world title in both the 250 cc and the 500 cc classes. Known as 'Fast Freddie', he was considered to be one of the greatest talents in motorcycle racing history, even though he never won more than three world titles.

Spencer, Herbert (1820-1903), English philosopher, social theorist, and early evolutionist. In his multivolume *System of Synthetic Philosophy* (1855-1893) he expounded a world view based on a close study of physical, biological, and social phenomena, arguing that species evolve by a process of differentiation from the simple to the complex. Spencer coined the phrase 'survival of the fittest.' His political individualism deeply influenced the growth of Social Darwinism, and, in general, U.S. social thinking.
See also: Social Darwinism.

Spender, Sir Stephen Harold (1909-1995), English poet and critic, coeditor of the literary magazine *Encounter* (1953-65). His poetry collections include *Poems* (1933), *Ruins and Visions* (1941), and *Generous Days* (1971).

Spenser, Edmund (1552?-1599), English poet. His most famous poem, *The Faerie Queene* (1590, 1596), considered a classic in English literature, is an allegory-a story in which people or personified things represent qualities and virtues in addition to their human character. Some of his other poems include *The Shepheardes Calendar* (1579), *Colin Clouts Come Home Againe* (1595), and *Amoretti* (1595)-a collection of sonnets that includes a famous poem about marriage, 'Epithalamion.'

Sperm *See:* Reproduction.

Sperm whale, family of toothed whales, with 2 species: the cachalot (*Physeter catodon*) and pigmy sperm whale (*Kogia breviceps*). They are among the best known of all whales because of their enormous, squared heads. The front of the head contains a huge reservoir of spermaceti oil, perhaps used as a lens to focus the sounds produced by the whales in echolocation. Spermaceti solidifies in cool air to form a wax once used for candles and cosmetics. Sperm whales are also the source of ambergris, a secretion in the gut produced in response to irritation by the beaks of squids, an important prey. Ambergris is used as a fixative in perfumes. Sperm whales are found in all oceans, migrating from the poles into warmer waters during the breeding season. They are deep-water whales, capable of diving to 1,650 ft (503 m) or more. Female and young form large schools of up to several hundred animals. Males tend to travel alone or in small groups.

Sphagnum moss *See:* Peat moss.

Sphalerite, also called zinc blende, zinc ore and sulfur ore. It is the major mineral ore of zinc. Sphalerite appears in a variety of colors-brown, red, black, yellow-but is always opaque and dark. When it is abraded by a sharp metal object, an orange flash appears in this ore. The sulfur content may release the scent of rotten eggs. Sphalerite is found in the United States, Mexico, northern Europe, and northern Africa.
See also: Zinc.

Sphere, surface produced by the rotation of a circle through 180° about one of its diameters. The intersection of a sphere and any plane is circular; should the plane pass through the center, the intersection is a great circle. The surface area of a sphere is $4pr^2$, where r is the radius; its volume $4/3pr^3$. If mutually perpendicular x-, y-, and z- axes are constructed such that they intersect at the center, the sphere's equation is $x^2 + y^2 + z^2 = r^2$.

Sphinx, mythical monster of the ancient Middle East, in Egypt portrayed as a lion with a human head and used as a symbol of the pharaoh. In Greek mythology the sphinx propounded a riddle to travelers on the road to Thebes: When Oedipus answered correctly the sphinx threw herself from her rocky perch.
See also: Mythology.

Sphinx moth *See:* Hawk moth.

S

Spice, one of a large number of aromatic plant products that have a distinctive flavor or aroma and are used to season food. Most spices are obtained from tropical plants and were once highly valued as a means of making poor-quality food more palatable.

Spider, any of an order (*Araneida*) of arachnids, with a body of 2 main parts, 4 pairs of legs, and 4 pairs of eyes. Unlike insects, spiders have no antennae and no larval or pupal stages. Their abdominal spinnerets produce silk thread that is used to make cocoons for their eggs and nests, to capture their prey, and as a means of travel. They are a diverse group of some 26,000 species, including jumping spiders, wolf spiders, and trapdoor spiders. They paralyze their prey with poison, which in several species (e.g., black widows) is dangerous to humans.

The bird-eating spider, *Sericopelma communis*, is about 2.4 in (6 cm) long and is found in Panama. Here, it is seen feeding on a hummingbird.

Spider monkey, slender, pot-bellied monkey found in the forests of central and northern South America. It has a prehensile tail with a naked patch at the end that is ridged like a fingerprint. Spider monkeys swing through the trees by their long forearms and tails. The 2 species, the common and the woolly spider monkeys, live in small groups and feed solely on fruit.

Spiderwort, or Job's tears, family of plants found in the tropical and temperate Americas and cultivated as house plants. Spiderworts have hairy stems that exude a sticky substance that can be drawn into a thread as fine as a spider's web. The leaves are grasslike, and the clusters of 3-petaled flowers open in the morning and die in the afternoon. Spiderwort can be found wild in woods across the country. As house plants they are usually known by their scientific name of *Tradescantia*. Wandering Jew, a house plant from Mexico, belongs to the same family.

Spielberg, Steven (1947-), U.S. film director, writer, and producer. Many of his films have been box office hits, such as *Jaws* (1975), *Close Encounters of the Third Kind* (1977), *Raiders of the Lost Ark* (1981), *E.T.: The Extra-Terrestrial* (1982), *The Color Purple* (1985), *Empire of the Sun* (1987), *Jurassic Park* (1993), *Schindler's List* (1993; seven oscars), *The Lost World* (1997), *Saving Private Ryan* (1998), *A.I. Artificial Intelligence* (2001), and *Minority Report* (2002). Brilliant technical special effects plus a romantic and heroic quality are signature characteristics of his films.

Spikenard, flowering plant in the Valerianaeceae family (*Nardostachys jatamansi*) or in the ginseng family (*Aralia racemosa*). The oriental, or 'true' spikenard, from India, has a thick stem and a root shaped like an ear of corn; it is valued for its perfume. The American spikenard, or Indian root, is an herb often used in place of sarsaparilla for flavor.

Spina bifida, congenital deformity in which a fissure in the lower part of the spine allows the spinal membranes to protrude. The condition leads to a variable degree of leg paralysis and loss of urine and feces sphincter control; it may be associated with other malformation, particularly hydrocephalus. Mild cases can be treated by surgical closure of the defect, and orthopedic procedures can be applied to balance muscle power.

Spinach (*Spinacia oleracea*), leafy annual plant widely cultivated as an edible vegetable. Spinach leaves have a relatively high content of iron and vitamins A and C.

Spinal cord and spinal nerves, that part of the central nervous system contained within the spinal column and extending from the skull to the level of the first or second lumbar vertebra; the nerve structures and nerve pathways within the vertebral canal, extending from the skull opening to the second lumbar vertebra. These nerves carry sensory information from the body to the brain, and

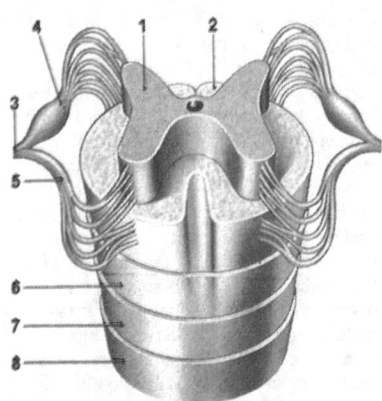

The spinal cord is the lower part of the central nervous system. It functions as a conductor of impulses between the brain and the body, and it is concerned with independent reflex actions. It is divided into grey (1) and white (2) nervous tissue, the grey giving off the dorsal (4) and ventral (5) nerve roots, which are joined, to form the spinal nerves (3). Surrounding the spinal cord, are continuations of the membranes that cover the brain: the pia mater (6) and the arachnid (7), inbetween which flows cerebro-spinal fluid, and on the outside, the dura mater (8).

then return with commands from the brain to the rest of the body.
See also: Nervous system; Spine.

Spinal tap, or lumbar puncture, procedure to remove cerebrospinal fluid (CSF) from the lumbar spinal canal using a fine needle. It is used in diagnosis of meningitis, encephalitis, multiple sclerosis, and tumors. In neurology it may be used in treatment, by reducing CSF pressure or allowing insertion of drugs.

Spine, spinal column or vertebral cord, vertical structure of bone, nerves and nerve fibers, ligaments, and cartilage that act as a skeletal support and transmission center for the nervous system in vertebrate animals. Vertebrae are the flexible, bony joints that make up the spinal column; they number 33 in humans. The spinal cord, where bundles of nerve fibers are found, is encased in the spinal column. The human spine extends from the brainstem to the tailbone region, or coccyx. Sensory impulses travel up the spinal column to the brain; in turn, the brain sends its commands down the spinal column to voluntary muscles used for motion and balance. Paralysis occurs when an injury to the spine interrupts the transmission of these messages between the brain and limbs.
See also: Skeleton.

Spinning, craft of twisting together fibers from a mass to form strong, continuous thread suitable for weaving. The earliest method was merely to roll the fibers between hand and thigh. Later 2 sticks were used: the distaff to hold the bundle of fibers, and a spindle to twist and wind the yarn. Mechanization began with the spinning wheel, which was invented in India and spread to Europe by the 14th century.

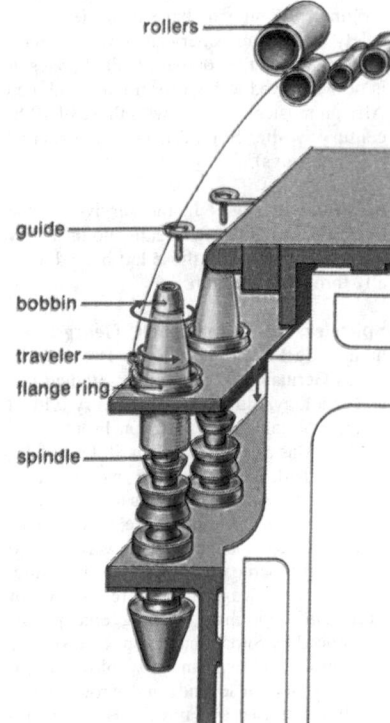

The ring frame invented (1828) by John Thorp and based on Richard Arkwright's spinning frame, is used to spin cotton. The fibers are drawn through a series of rollers and a guide down to the traveler on the flange ring. The traveler replacing the flyer, spins around the flange ring and guides the thread onto the bobbin, which is positioned on the spindle. The traveler and flange ring are located on a movable plate that rises and falls with each revolution of the spindle, distributing the tread evenly on the bobbin. The ring spinning method is the most common today.

rollers

guide

bobbin

traveler

flange ring

spindle

S

Improved weaving methods in the Industrial Revolution caused increased demand, which in turn provoked several inventions. The spinning jenny, invented by James Hargreaves (1767), spun as many as 16 threads at once. Richard Arkwright's 'water frame' (1769), so-called from being water-powered, produced strong thread. Then Samuel Crompton produced (1779) a hybrid of the two-his 'mule,' which had a movable carriage. One modern spinning machine is the ring-spinning frame (1828) in which the strands, drawn out by rollers, are twisted by a 'traveler' that revolves on a ring around the bobbin on which they are wound.

Spinoza, Baruch, or **Benedict de** (1632-1677), Dutch philosopher who held that God is nature or all that is, an interpretation that brought him expulsion from the Amsterdam Jewish community. He claimed that matter and mind are attributes of the one substance: God. His most famous work, *Ethics* (1677), contains the development of his pantheism, which is both rationalist and mystical.
See also: Philosophy.

Spiny anteater *See:* Echidna.

Spiraea, any of several shrubs with tall clusters of pink or white flowers. They grow wild in the Northern Hemisphere, and several are grown in gardens. Meadowsweet, staplebush, and queen-of-the-meadow are wild American species. The cultivated forms, of which bridal wreath is the most popular, come mainly from the Far East.

Spiritual, form of emotional, often sorrowful, religious folk song using syncopation, a variety of rhythms, and the pentatonic scale (5 whole tones). It usually consists of a number of verses for solo voice, often with biblical text, and a rhythmic choral refrain. Originally though to have been developed solely by African-American slaves and their descendants in the southern United States, it is now believed to be a form that combined African musical systems with those of 19th-century white Southerners (i.e., revival meeting songs).

Spiritualism, belief in the survival of the human personality after death and its ability to communicate with those left behind, usually through a medium.

Spitteler, Carl Friedrich Georg (real name, Carl Felix Tandem; 1845-1924), Swiss-German poet and writer. Studied law and theology, although he was very critical of the official church religion. From 1871-1879 he was a private tutor in St. Petersburg and Finland, and thereafter worked as a teacher of classical languages and as a journalist. In 1892 an inheritance gave him financial independence and he was able to completely dedicate himself to literature. Spitteler is an important representative of European symbolism, writing epic poems influenced by Shopenhauer's pessimism. He transformed biblical and mythological stories into modern legends and wrote essays, children's stories and novels. His work includes *Prometheus and Epimetheus* (1880-

1881), *Laughing Truths* (1898), *Olympian Spring* (1900-1905), *Two Little Misogynists* (1907) and *My Earliest Experiences* (1914; memoirs).

Spitz, family of dogs, distinguished by their thick, long coats, curly tails, and pointed ears. Breeds in the spitz family include small dogs, such as the Pomeranian; medium-size dogs, such as the Samoyed and chow chow; and large dogs, such as the Alaskan malamute and Akita. Spitz dogs are native to northern climates in the Americas, Europe, and Asia.

Spitz, Mark Andrew (1950-), North American swimmer, won 9 Olympic gold medals (2 in 1968, 7 in 1972) in the freestyle, butterfly, and relays. Spitz managed to set 34 world records.

Spleen, spongy vascular organ between the stomach and diaphragm on the left side of the abdomen. It eliminates foreign organisms and worn-out red blood cells, recycling their iron. Most of its functions are duplicat-

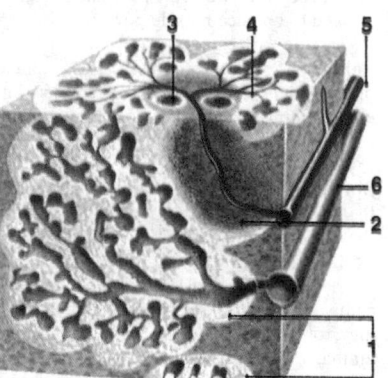

The spleen is an oval-shaped organ that is located on the left side of the abdominal cavity. As a filter for the blood, it removes damaged red blood cells and recycles the iron from the hemoglobin, as well as filtering out bacteria and debris. It also acts as a reservoir for newly matured red blood cells and produces immunologically active white blood cells. As seen in cross section, the spleen is composed of white pulp (1), consisting of sheaths of lymphatic tissue, and red pulp (2), consisting of cords of cells and bloodfilled venous sinuses. Lymphatic follicles (3) — enlargements of the lymphatic sheaths where lymphocytes are produced — are found at various locations. Small arterioles (4), branching from the trabecular arteries (5), carry blood through the white pulp into the red pulp. Blood flows from the venous sinuses to the trabecular veins (6) and is transported from the spleen.

ed by other organs.

Split (pop. 190,000), city in Croatia, in the southwestern region of Dalmatia on the Adriatic Sea; known as Spalato in Italian. The remains of the palace of the Roman emperor Diocletian (A.D. 245-313) are central to this modern port city. The tomb of the em-

peror, within the palace walls, became the Cathedral of Split (A.D. 653). Many have ruled this city, including the Byzantine Empire (mid-4th century to early 12th century), Venice (1420-1797), and Austria (1797-1918). It was part of Yugoslavia from 1918-1991. Today it supports many industries, including chemicals, plastics, aluminum, and shipbuilding.

Spock, Benjamin McLane (1903-1998), known as 'Dr. Spock,' U.S. pediatrician and pacifist noted for his best-selling *Common Sense Book of Baby and Child Care* (1946) and *Bringing Up Children in a Difficult Time* (1974). He ran for president in 1972 as candidate of the People's Party.
See also: Pediatrics.

Spode, British family of potters. **Josiah Spode I** (1733-1797) founded the Spode works at Stoke-on-Trent and introduced transfer decoration and oriental motifs. His son, **Josiah Spode II** (1754-1827), developed stone china, porcelain, and bone china. He popularized the willow pattern and gained royal patronage.
See also: Pottery and porcelain.

Spoerri, Daniel (real name, Daniel Isaac Feinstein; 1930-), Romanian-Swiss artist. Originally studied to be a missionary, and then later to be a dancer. Was the leading dancer with the Opera in Bern (1954-1959). Joined the Nouveau Réalistes (1960). Created 'tableaux-pièges': still lives of remains of meals and cutlery glued on to the surface of a table. He went on to make what he called 'eat art' (artworks made from sugar, biscuits, chocolate, etc.), whereby he questioned the 'eternal value' of art.

Spohr, Ludwig (Louis) (1784-1859), a German Romantic composer, conductor, and violinist. His music was widely performed in his lifetime, and forms a link between the Classical and Romantic styles. Spohr often experimented with new instrumental combinations, writing a concerto for string quartet, a symphony for two orchestras, and double string quartets. He was one of the first conductors to use a baton. Spohr toured Europe as a violin virtuoso and conductor before settling in Kassel as court conductor in 1822.

His compositions include 9 symphonies, 15 violin concertos, overtures, oratorios, and much chamber music. Of his 10 operas, *Jessonda* (1823) remained popular throughout the 19th century.

Sponge, primitive animal of both marine and fresh water. Sponges are true animals, although they have only a simple body wall and no specialized organ or tissue system. They may be solitary or live in colonies. They are filter-feeders, straining tiny food particles out of water drawn in through pores all over the body surface and expelled through one or more vents. The body wall is strengthened by spicules of calcite or silica, or by a meshwork of protein fibers called spongin. Sponges with spongin skeletons are fished for use as bath sponges.

Spontaneous combustion, or spontaneous

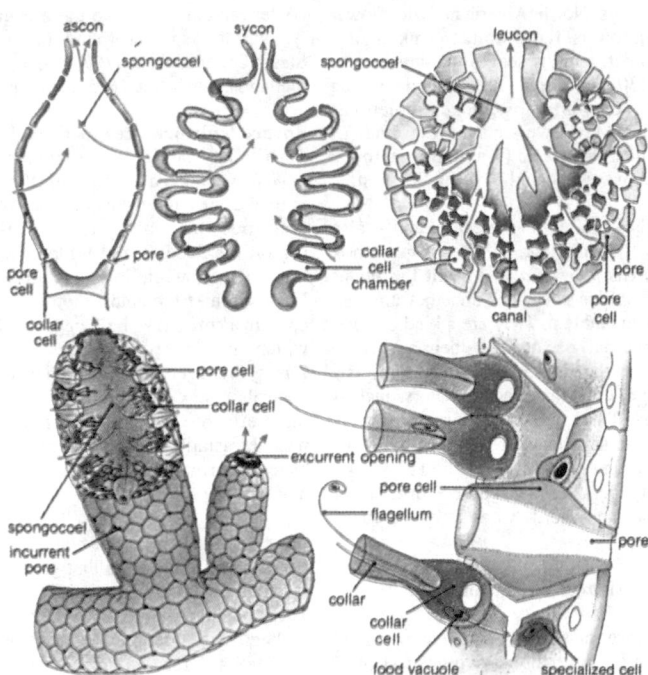

Sponges range in body structure from simple to highly complex. Their anatomy permits water (blue arrows) to flow through, into, and out of the body. The most primitive type of sponge, an ascon, has smooth walls and no canals. A sycon's body is furrowed into simple canals, where water first passes before entering the spongocoel, or body cavity. A leucon, or advanced sponge, has numerous canals and cavities and performs more specialized functions than the simpler sponges. (bottom left) Water enters through pores and passes through collar cells, where microorganisms are trapped. (detail, bottom right) A food vacuole digests the microscopic animals before transporting nutrients to a specialized cell, which supplies the body with energy.

S

ignition, phenomenon in which material suddenly bursts into flame without apparent cause but resulting from a slow build-up of heat. The chemical process of oxidation naturally produces heat. If that heat is trapped, oxidation becomes more rapid, and heat builds up quickly. A critical temperature may be reached, causing ignition.

Spontaneous generation, or abiogenesis, theory that living creatures can arise from nonliving matter. Dating from the writings of Aristotle, the idea remained current even after it had become clear that higher orders of life could not be created in this way. It was only with the work of Francesco Redi (1626-1697), showing that maggots did not appear in decaying meat protected from flies, and Louis Pasteur (1822-1895), who proved that the equivalent was true of microorganisms (i.e., bacteria), that the theory was finally discarded.

Spoonbill, bird in the ibis family. The Roseate spoonbill (*Ajaia ajaja*) lives in warm locations in the Americas. The spoonbill can grow to 32 in (80 cm) long, with rose to red coloring on its body and white on and around its head. The bill is dipped and then moved through water in search for water insects, crabs, and fish. Other kinds of spoonbills are found in southern regions on all continents.

Spore, minute single- or multicelled body produced during the process of reproduction of many plants, particularly bacteria, algae and fungi, and some protozoa. Their structures vary greatly and depend upon the means of dissemination from the parent. Some, such as the zoospores of algae, are capable of movement.

Sports, organized athletic events in which people are either participants or spectators. Some sporting activities include team play-

ing, such as baseball, football, and basketball; others engage one participant in competition against another, such as tennis and ping-pong. Other sports may not necessarily be competitive, such as jogging, swimming, and horseback riding. There are organized amateur sporting competitions, such as the Olympics, and professional leagues and associations, such as the National Football League (NFL) and the National Basketball Association (NBA).

Sports medicine, area of medical practice based on the effects of sports on the human body. Physicians who practice sports medicine develop preventive treatments, exercises, and mechanical devices for individual athletes and specific activities, as well as treatment for specific injuries. Coaches work with sports medicine professionals to maximize the output of athletes, while minimizing the physical stress experienced by those participating in sports. Sports medicine grew as a separate branch of medicine beginning in the 1970s, through the work of doctors attached to professional teams.

Spot, fish in the croaker family. The spot (*Leiostomus xanthurus*) inhabits the coastal waters of the Atlantic Ocean and the Gulf of Mexico. It is caught for sport and has a commercial value because it is edible. A dark spot at the pectoral fin, or shoulder, of this fish is its most prominent characteristic. It is 6-10 in (15-25 cm) long and weighs about 0.5 lb (0.2 kg).

Spotted fever, Rocky Mountain, *see:* Rocky Mountain spotted fever.

Sprague, Frank Julian (1857-1934), U.S. inventor and engineer of the high-speed electric elevator and the electric railroad system, including that now used in the New York City subway.
See also: Elevator; Railroad.

Sprain, injury to a ligament (which connects bone to bone in a joint). The symptoms are rapid swelling and inflammation and some initial pain and stiffness around a joint. Swelling and pain seem worse 24 to 48 hours after injury occurs. Discoloration and limitation in motion and function may also take place.

A ligament is like a rope that, when stretched beyond resting length, is susceptible to injury, and with a severe enough force it may be torn apart. This usually occurs when turning and twisting are involved, especially very quick, sudden motions that twist the joint. The disability depends on the degree of damage. It can be as minor as swelling and inflammation only, causing minimal discomfort, or as severe as a rupture of the ligament(s).

Treatment is with cold compresses (not heat) after the injury occurs and elevation of the injured joint, if possible. The joint should be immobilized and a compression wrap used. If quite painful, inflamed, or swollen, a doctor should be consulted. Some sprains resolve themselves with rest and immobility, while others require splinting, casting, or bracing. With very serious sprains, surgical repair may be required.
See also: Ligament.

Sprat (*Clupea sprattus*), small marine food fish of the herring family native to coastal waters of Europe. Sprats have a flat body and grow to 8 in (20 cm). Canned sprats are sometimes known as brisling sardines.

Spratly Islands, group of approx. 600 islands, reefs and rocks in the South China Sea, between Vietnam, Malaysia and the Philippines. The largest islands are Itu Aba and Spratly. None of the islands is permanently inhabited; most of them disappear at high tide. They are mostly populated by turtles and seabirds. According to international law, the islands belong to the country which is on the same geological continental plate. The possibility that large reserves of oil and gas are present under the seabed around the islands has meant that nearly all countries in the region claim sovereignty over the Spratly Islands: China and Vietnam claim virtually the whole area, while Brunei, Malaysia, the Philippines and Taiwan each claim a portion. Most of these countries have troops stationed on the islands. In 1988 tensions in the South China Sea led to an armed conflict between the Chinese and Vietnamese navies.

Spring, mechanical device that exhibits elasticity according to Hooke's Law. Most springs are made of steel, brass, or bronze. The most common type is the *helical spring*, a coil of stiff wire, loose wound if to be compressed, tight wound if to be extended under tension. Helical springs have many uses, including closing valves, spring balances, and accelerometers. The *spiral spring* is a wire or strip coiled in one plane, responding to torque applied to its inner end, and used to store energy, notably in clocks and watches. The *leaf spring*, used in vehicle suspension systems, consists of several steel strips of different lengths clamped on top of each other at one end. When deformed, springs store potential energy, and exert a restoring force. Hydraulic and air springs work by compression of a fluid in a cylinder.
See also: Hooke, Robert.

Spring, in geology, naturally occurring flow of water from the ground. Some are outflows from underground streams, but most often a spring occurs when an aquifer (a layer of water-bearing porous rock or sediment) intersects with the earth's surface. Such an aquifer may travel for hundreds of kilometers underground before emerging to the surface. Spring water is generally fairly clean, since it has been filtered through permeable rocks, but all spring water contains some dissolved minerals.

Spring beauty, wild flowers in the purslane family. This North American wild flower grows in forests. It has white to pink blooms and slender, lengthy leaves on stems up to 12 in (30 cm) high. The Virginia spring beauty (*Claytonia virginica*)-sometimes called the Mayflower-and the Carolina (*C. caroliniana*) are found from Canada through Georgia in the east and Texas in the west.

Springbok, animal in the cattle family, also called springbuck. The springbok (*Antidorcas marsupialis*) inhabit the plains of South Africa, for which area they are considered an emblem. They are a kind of antelope, unusual because of their ability to spring into the air 6.5-11.5 ft (2-3.5 m) as a defensive action to detract predators, such as cheetahs. These red to brown slim-legged animals stand about 32 in (80 cm) at the shoulder and weigh 73-95 lb (33-43 k). Males and females have curved horns. Their once-enormous herds were greatly reduced by hunters.

Springer spaniel *See:* Spaniel.

Springhare, or springhaas (*Pedetes capensis*), small, nocturnal, herbivorous rodent of eastern and southern Africa, resembling a rabbit with a long tail but belonging to the family Pedetidae. Springhares grow to a body length of 17 in (43 cm) and a weight of 9 lb (4 kg). Their large hind legs enable them to jump up to 10 ft (3 m). They live singly or in small families in burrows and feed on roots and bulbs.

Springsteen, Bruce (1949-), U.S. rock singer, songwriter, and guitarist, known as 'The Boss'. He has performed with his E Street Band since the early 1970s, recording such albums as *Born to Run* (1975, *Born in the U.S.A.* (1984), which sold 15 million copies, *Human Touch* (1992), and *The Ghost of Tom Joad* (1995). His lyrics are often topical and idealistic.

Spruce, evergreen coniferous tree of the genus *Picea*, with a conical form. There are some 40 species, all of which grow in the cooler regions of the Northern Hemisphere. Among the species found in the United States are the black (*P. mariana*), blue (*P. pungens*), and white (*P. glauca*) spruces.

Spruce budworm, destructive insect in the Tortricidae family. This insect (*Choristoneura fumiferana*) lives in the northern United States and Canada. It destroys evergreen trees-particularly the spruce-by feeding on the needles and pollen each spring for 3-6 years while in the caterpillar stage. Each summer the small moths that display dark markings lay their eggs in the trees, which in turn spin cocoons. Methods of forest management and other biological controls check the spread of these insects more effectively than do pesticides. In the past devastating outbreaks of these pests have occurred approximately once every half century.

Spurge family, group of plants that include herbs, shrubs, and trees that grow mainly in tropical climates throughout the world. These plants provide castor oil, cassava, and rubber; some are poinsettias. Commercial applications for waterproofing, polishes, candle waxes, and other products are derived from a species of the spurge family (*Euphorbia antisyphilitica*) native to Mexico.

Sputnik, series of unmanned satellites launched by the Soviet Union. The first was launched on Oct. 4, 1957. It circled the earth once about every 95 minutes at a speed of 18,000 mph (29,000 kmph) until it fell to earth on Jan. 4, 1958. Nine more Sputnik missions were carried out from 1957 to 1961.
See also: Space exploration.

Square dancing, popular, lively U.S. folk dance in which 4 couples formed in a square carry out steps and formations under the direction of a caller. It dates back to the quadrille dances of 15th-century Europe.

Squash, any of several edible plants in the Cucurbitaceae family. These vegetables, related to the pumpkin, are eaten cooked or raw. Different species both look and taste different from one another; they have in common a 5-pointed leaf that grows from either a bush or vine.
Summer squash (zucchini, crookneck, pattypan) are harvested when immature, about 2 months after planting.
Winter squash (Hubbard, acorn, butternut) are harvested when mature, up to 4 months after planting, and can be stored. Squash, popular with home gardeners and truck farmers, were introduced to settlers by Native Americans.

Squash, game played on a 4-walled court with a small, hard-rubber ball and 27-in (68-cm) rackets. Singles squash is played on an indoor court that measures 18.5 ft x 32 ft (5.6 m x 9.75 m); doubles squash requires a larger court. The ball may be hit against any of the 4 walls as long as it bounces on the front wall before striking the floor. The opponent must then hit the ball before it touches the floor twice.

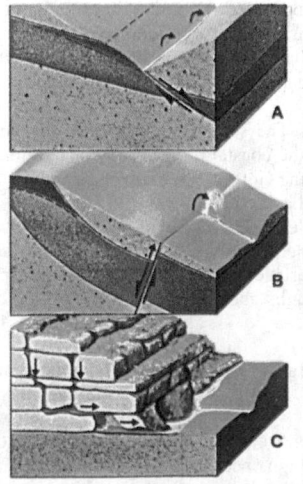
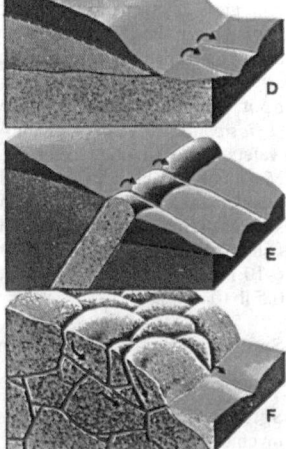

A spring is formed whenever a fault brings an aquifer, or water-bearing rock layer, to the surface (A). Artesian springs are found where an inclined aquifer, sealed between two impermeable rock layers, flows upward under its own pressure through cracks in the layer above it (B). In hilly limestone areas, water seeps down through fissures to an impermeable layer and then flows out horizontally (C). Springs also form when an aquifer emerges at the foot of a slope (D). An impermeable intrusive rock that cuts across an aquifer leads to formation of a spring along the top of the intrusion (E). Water may flow through cracks in granite until it finds a surface opening (F).

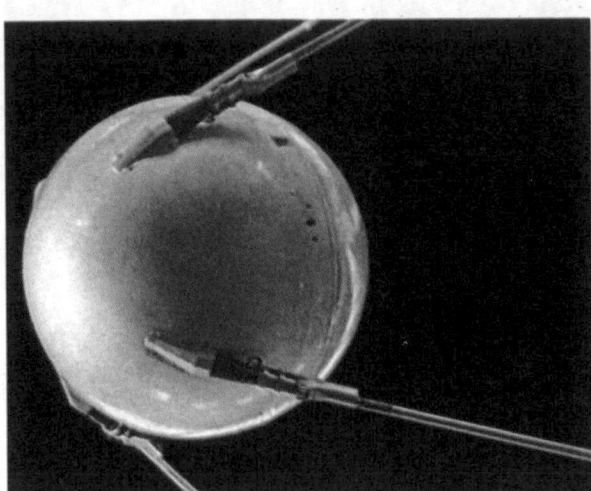

Sputnik I weighed only 183 lbs (83 kg), used chemical batteries as a source of energy and sent radio signals to earth via four antennae.

S

Squeteague *See:* Weakfish.

Squid, shell-less cephalopod mollusk, order Teuthoidea. Although a few species live in coastal waters, the majority inhabit the open ocean. The squid is a streamlined animal with 10 arms around the head, facing forward. The mantle at the rear of the body houses the gills and the openings of the excretory, sex, and digestive organs. Sudden contraction of the mantle cavity produces a blast of water that can be directed forward or backward, providing the main means of propulsion. All squid can swim very rapidly and are active predators of fish, shooting out their long arms, provided with suckers and hooks, to grab their prey.

Squill, plant in the lily family. The sea onion (*Urginea maritima*), like other squill, is a plant with a bulb root; it is used as medicine. Other species of squill ornament gardens with their clusters of tiny white to blue leafless flowers (*Scilla peruviana*).

Squire *See:* Knights and knighthood.

Squirrel, member of one of the largest families, Sciuridae, of rodents. The name commonly refers only to tree squirrels, found in most forested parts of the world. Typically they have long, bushy tails and short muzzles. They are diurnal and feed on seeds, nuts, and leaf buds, with some insect and other animal food. A number of temperate species, while not true hibernators, store food for the winter and enter deep torpor. The family includes the chipmunk, woodchuck, and prairie dog.

Squirrel monkey, primate of the New World monkey family, Cebidae. They live in the rain forests in Central and South America. Small in size, no longer than 1 ft (30 cm), they weigh no more than 2 lb (0.9 kg). They use their dark-tipped tail for balance as they travel in large groups, single file behind a leader, on paths through the forest trees. Squirrel monkeys have white fur on their undersides and faces, dark facial features, and large eyes. Their fur color ranges from black to gray or reddish brown and olive green to yellow. They are used as laboratory animals and make good pets when kept with other squirrel monkeys.

Sri Lanka

Capital:	Colombo
Area:	24,879 sq mi (65,610 sq km)
Population:	19,577,000
Language:	Sinhala Tamil, English
Government:	Socialist presidential republic
Independent:	1948
Head of gov.:	Prime minister
Per capita:	US$ 3,250
Monetary unit:	1 Sri Lanka rupee = 100 cents

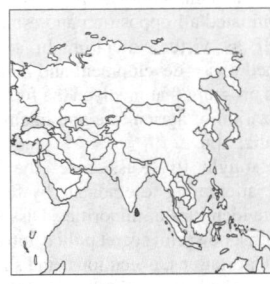

Sri Lanka, formerly Ceylon, officially the Democratic Socialist Republic of Sri Lanka, independent island republic in the Indian Ocean.

Land and climate. Sri Lanka is separated from southeastern India by the Gulf of Mannar, Palk Strait, and Adam's Bridge, a 30-mi (48-km)-chain of shoals. With an area of 24,879 sq mi (64,454 sq km), Sri Lanka extends 270 mi (435 km) north to south and 140 mi (225 km) east to west. The south-central area of the island is mountainous and its major rivers, including the Mahaweli Ganga, rise in this region, which is dominated by Mt. Pidurutalagala (8,281 ft/2,524 m) and Adam's Peak (7,360 ft/2,243 m). Around the mountains extends a coastal plain up to 100 mi (161 km) wide in the north. Originally dense with tropical forest, much of the plain has been cleared for agriculture. The climate is tropical, but due to its situation the island enjoys more equable temperatures than those prevailing in southernmost India.

People. Buddhist Sinhalese make up 75% of the population. The Hindu Tamils, people of South Indian origin living mainly in the north and east, are the principal minority, but there are also Veddah, probably the island's original inhabitants, and Burghers, Christian descendants of Dutch-Sinhalese forebears. The capital of Sri Lanka is Colombo and Sinhala (Sinhalese) is the official language, though English and Tamil are also widely spoken.

Economy. Sri Lanka produces a large proportion of the world's tea and over 100,000 tons of rubber a year. Coconuts are commercially grown for their oil, but rice, the main food crop, often has to be supplemented by imports. The country is the world's chief producer of high-grade graphite.

History. The island was settled around 550 B.C. by the Sinhalese, a people from the Indian subcontinent, who built Anuradhapura and made the island a center of Buddhist thought after the religion was introduced there in the 3rd century B.C. The Tamil people held the northern part of the island from the 12th to the 16th centuries. Lured by the spice trade, Europeans began arriving in the 16th century. They called the island Ceylon, and it was held successively by the Portuguese, who landed in 1505, the Dutch, who came after 1658, and finally the British, who came in 1796. Ceylon gained its independence in 1948, and it became a republic in 1956. In 1972 a new constitution was adopted and Ceylon was given the Sinhalese name Sri Lanka. In the late 1970s and early 1980s violence flared up between the Sinhalese and Tamil separatists.

During 1987-1990 Indian troops assisted Sri Lankan forces in a campaign against Tamil separatists. Although the campaign destroyed some Tamil strongholds, it failed to end the rebellion, and fighting continued in the 1990's. In 1993 Ranasinghe Premadasa, Sri Lanka's president, was assassinated by separatists. By 1996 about 50,000 people had been killed in the conflict between Tamil separatists and the government.

The attacks by the Tamil separatist continued until peace talks were held in Norway, December 2002. The separatists would have autonomy in the mainly Tamil-speaking north and east. UNICEF became involved in

Women harvest tea leaves on this hillside plantation in Sri Lanka. The crop is cultivated primarily in the highlands of the south central portion of the country, an area receiving abundant rainfall.

S

returning child-soldiers, who had been recruited by Tamil separatists, to their parents in 2003.

Srinagar (pop. 595,000), the summer capital and principal city of the Indian-held part of Kashmir. Srinagar lies 400 miles (640 km) northwest of Delhi, India, in the beautiful Vale of Kashmir, a high, mountain-ringed valley. The city is the center of an attractive resort area noted for its fine scenery, vacation houseboats on the Jhelum River and nearby Dal Lake, and formal gardens built by the Mogul emperors. Many centuries old, Srinagar was at various times a Hindu, Buddhist, and Muslim city. When Kashmir was divided in 1949 after fighting ended between India and Pakistan, Srinagar became capital of the Indian-held section.

Staël, Madame de (Anne Louise Germaine Necker; 1766-1817), French-Swiss novelist and critic, celebrated personality, and liberal opponent of Napoleon I's regime. A noted interpreter of German Romanticism, she maintained brilliant salons in Paris until her exile to Geneva. Her major work, *On Germany* (1810), influenced European culture. She also wrote the novels *Delphine* (1802) and *Corinne* (1807). Her memoirs, *Ten Years of Exile* (1818), is a fascinating account of her times. She had liaisons with Talleyrand and the writer Benjamin Constant.

Staffordshire bull terrier, also known as pit bull terrier, breed of dog. These muscular dogs stand up to 19 in (48 cm) and weigh up to 50 lb (23 k). They may be any color, solid in patches, or brindled. They are named after the town in which they were bred in early 19th-century England. Their original purpose was to fight other dogs-usually in pits-or bears.

Stag beetle, also called pinching bug, beetle in the Lucanidae family. These beetles are named for the jaws, or mandibles, of the males, which greatly resemble the horns of the male deer, or stag. These mandibles may be from half to the entire length of the body, which ranges from 1.5-2 in (3.8-5 cm). A bite by a toothed mandible can cause bleeding. Stag beetles feed on tree sap, and live and breed among decomposing trees.

Stained glass, pieces of colored glass held in place by a framework usually of lead strips, to form patterns or pictures in a window. The earliest Western windows date from the 5th century, but the art reached its highest development in the period of Gothic architecture (1150-1500): the series of windows made (1200-1240) for the cathedral at Chartres is a well-known example. Huge circular windows became common during this period. These windows, because of their flowerlike shape, were known as rose windows. Interest revived in the 19th and 20th centuries with the work of Edward Burne-Jones, Louis Comfort Tiffany, and John La Farge. Later masters of stained glass were the painters Henri Matisse, Fernand Léger, Georges Rouault, and Marc Chagall. The glass is colored during manufacture by mixing it with metallic oxides, then cut according to full-scale cartoons. Details may be painted onto the glass with colored enamels, which fuse to the surface when it is heated.

Stainless steel, corrosion-resistant steel containing more than 10% chromium, little carbon, and often nickel and other metals. There are 4 main types: ferritic, martensitic, austenitic, and precipitation-hardening. Stainless steel is used for cutlery and many industrial components.

Stalactite, and **stalagmite**, rocky structures found in limestone caves. Rainwater (containing atmospheric carbon dioxide) percolates through the rocks above limestone caves, dissolving some calcium carbonate, a major component of limestone. Upon reaching the cave, some of the water that drips from the roof evaporates, leaving a little of the calcium carbonate as calcite on the roof; repetition of this process forms a stalactite. The water that continues to drip to the floor leaves a small amount of calcium carbonate (as calcite) on the floor; repetition of this process forms a stalagmite. The two structures often meet to form pillars.

Stalin, Joseph (Josif Vissarionovich Dzhugashvili; 1879-1953), ruler of the Soviet Union from 1924 until his death. A Georgian village shoemaker's son intended for the priesthood, he joined the Georgian Social Democratic Party in 1901. In 1912 V. I. Lenin placed him on the Bolshevik central committee. (Around this time he took the name Stalin, 'man of steel.') After the Russian Revolution (1917) he advanced rapidly. In 1922 he was elected general secretary of the Russian Communist Party. In the struggle for the leadership after Lenin's death (1924), he eliminated all opposition and established himself as virtual dictator. In 1928 he launched a vast development and industrialization program that involved the forced collectivization of agriculture and intensive industrialization.

Stalin sought to 'Russianize' the Soviet Union, attempting to eradicate by force the separate identities of minorities. Dissent was met with a powerful secret police, informers, mass deportations, executions, and show trials. In 1935 he initiated the first of the great 'purges,' which spared neither his family nor former political associates. Equally ruthless in foreign affairs, he partitioned Poland with Germany (1939) and imposed Communist rule on the Baltic states (1940). The reversal of German fortunes on the eastern front during World War II strengthened his hand. In 1945 at Yalta he sealed the postwar fate of Eastern Europe to his satisfaction. Thereafter, he pursued Cold War policies abroad and supported rapid industrial recovery at home until his death from a brain hemorrhage. Almost immediately a process of 'destalinization' began, culminating in Nikita Khrushchev's 1956 attack on the Stalinist terror and personality cult.
See also: Union of Soviet Socialist Republics.

Stalingrad *See:* Volgograd.

Stalingrad, Battle of, decisive engagement in World War II, fought in the vicinity of Stalingrad (since 1961, Volgograd) from Aug. 1942 to Feb. 1943. The 500,000-man German 6th army surrounded the city on Sept. 14, 1942, but was itself encircled early in 1943 by a Russian army, and forced to surrender. The battle wrested the psychological initiative from the Nazis for the remainder of the war.
See also: World War II.

Stalino *See:* Donetsk.

Stallone, Sylvester (1946-), American film actor and director. Became famous for his role as a boxer in *Rocky* (1976). Directed three of the four sequels, *Rocky II* (1979), *Rocky III* (1982) and *Rocky IV* (1985), and also *Paradise Alley* (1978) and *Stayin' Alive* (1983). Other films in which he often played the role of a muscleman hero were *First Blood* (1982), *Rambo: First Blood part II* (1984), *Over The Top* (Menahem Golan, 1987), *Rambo III* (1988), *Cliffhanger* (1993), *Judge Dredd* (1995), *Assassins* (1995), *Cop Land* (1997), and *Driven* (2001).

Stamitz, Johann Wenzel Anton (1717-1757), Bohemian violinist and composer, oldest son of the organist Antonin Stamitz (d. 1756), from whom he received his first music lessons. He studied at the Jesuit school in Iglau from 1728 to 1734, and entered into the service of Karl Philipp, Prince Elector of Palatine, in 1741, and his successor Karl Theodor in 1743. Stamitz became first violin of the court orchestra in Mannheim in 1844, and in 1850 was appointed general music director. Under his leadership the orchestra became widely known, partly due to the expansion of the orchestra (with clarinets) and the introduction of many new performance techniques, such as the crescendo and decrescendo. During his life Stamitz achieved great fame as a violinist and conductor, and as a composer he was one of the founders of what is known as the Mannheim school, historically important with regard to the development of symphonies, in which Stamitz gave the minuet a permanent place. His genuine originality made him very influential: Haydn, Mozart and Beethoven all built on Stamitz's work. His oeuvre includes 70 symphonies, many concertos for violin, flute, clarinet and cello, chamber music and choral works.

Stamp Act (1765), first direct tax imposed by the English Parliament on the 13 North American colonies. All legal and commercial documents, pamphlets, playing cards, and newspapers were to carry revenue stamps, which would help finance the British army quartered in America. The colonists balked at the idea of 'taxation without representation,' and delegates from 9 colonies met in the Stamp Act Congress held in New York to protest the law. A boycott of British goods finally led Parliament to repeal the act in Mar. 1766.
See also: Taxation.

Stamp collecting, or philately, popular worldwide hobby. The first postage stamps were issued in England on May 1, 1840. The first in the United States appeared in 1847, and by 1860 most countries had adopted the prepaid postage stamp system. Today stamp catalogs list more than 200,000 items. Serious collectors, who generally specialize in particular countries, periods, or themes, make a close study of each stamp's paper, ink, printing method, perforations, cancellation, design, information content, and historical occasion. Stamps can also be a good investment; large sums of money have been paid for rare specimens.

Stamp weed *See:* Indian mallow.

Standard of living, statistical measure that attempts to rate the quality of life in a nation or a group in terms of its level of consumption of food, clothing, and other basic goods and services, including transportation, education, and medical care.

Standard schnauzer, breed of dog originally from Bavaria, Germany, in the 15th century. These dogs stand up to 19.5 in (50 cm) at the shoulder and weigh up to 40 lb (18 kg). They have short, gray to black, wiry coats, short docked ears and tail, shaggy whiskers, and bushy eyebrows. They were originally used as herders and rodent killers. Later, in the 18th century they were used as carriage and guard dogs for stables. Today they are kept as pets.

Standard time, time kept within the time zones (24 in total) of the world. The standard time in each zone lags Greenwich mean time (GMT) by 5, 6, 7, and 8 hours respectively. The zones depend on the fact that the earth takes an hour to rotate 15°. Therefore the sun rises an hour later for every 15° west. Each time zone is roughly centered on a meridian (line of longitude) 15° farther west than its predecessor.

Stanford-Binet test, adaptation of the Stanford Revision of the Binet-Simon Intelligence Tests introduced by Lewis Madison Terman (1916; 2d revision, 1937), and used primarily to determine the Intelligence Quotient (IQ) of children.
See also: Intelligence quotient.

Stanford University, leading U.S. educational and research center. Stanford was founded by Leland and Jane Lathrop Stanford in 1885 as a memorial to their son who died of typhoid fever. Located in Stanford, Calif., Stanford is a private, coeducational university that offers both undergraduate and graduate courses of study.

Stanislavski, Konstantin (Konstantin Sergeyevich Alekseyev; 1863-1938), Russian-born stage director, teacher, and author. Stanislavski and Vladmir Nemirovich-Danchencko founded the Moscow Art Theater (1898); they used a new acting technique called the *method*, in which actors drew upon personal experiences to bring out the emotions of the characters they portrayed. This technique, outlined in Stanislavski's book *An Actor Prepares* (1926), is often used by actors today.

Stanley and Livingstone, British explorers in Afica. David Livingstone (1813-1873)

traveled to southern Africa as a missionary and remained on the continent for the rest of his life. His interest in geography ignited a coast-to-coast journey in which he followed the Zambezi River (1853-1856). Victoria Falls was named by him, the first European to see it (1855). He met Henry Morton Stanley (1841-1904) while on Lake Tanganyika (1871). Stanley was a reporter employed by the *New York Herald* (1869) to find Livingstone, believed lost in the interior of Africa. Upon discovering Livingstone, Stanley, instead of returning with him to New York, joined Livingstone in a search for the source of the Nile River. After Livingstone's death, Stanley explored the Congo River (1874-1877) in a grueling journey that ended up on the Atlantic coast. He helped found the Free Congo State for the king of Belgium, recognized in 1885. He described his African experience in 2 books, *In Darkest Africa* (1890) and *Through South Africa* (1898). He served in the British Parliament (1895-1900) and was knighted (1899).

Stanley brothers, U.S. inventors and twins; **Francis Edgar Stanley** (1849-1918) and **Freeland Oscar Stanley** (1849-1940). Their first company manufactured their inventions related to the field of photography and was eventually sold to Eastman Kodak Company (1904). Their experimentation with steam engines led to building the Stanley Steamer (1897). Their Stanley Motor Carriage Company (1901) produced a steam engine that traveled 128 mph (206 km), breaking the existing speed record (1906). With the manufacture of gasoline-engine automobiles, Stanley Steamers became far less popular; they were discontinued in 1924.

Staphylococcus, bacterium responsible for numerous skin, soft tissue, and bone infections, less often causing septicemia, pneumonia, bacterial endocarditis, and enterocolitis. Boils, carbuncles, impetigo, and osteomyelitis are commonly caused by staphylococci. Treatment usually requires antibiotics and drainage of pus from abscesses.

Star, large incandescent ball of gases held together by its own gravity. The sun is a fairly normal star in its composition, parameters, and color. It is believed that stars originate as condensations out of interstellar matter. In certain circumstances a protostar will form, slowly contracting under its own gravity, part of the energy from this contraction being radiated, the remainder heating up the core; this stage may last several million years. At last the core becomes hot enough for thermonuclear reactions to be sustained and stops contracting. Eventually the star as a whole ceases contracting and radiates entirely by the thermonuclear conversion of hydrogen into helium; it is then said to be on the main sequence. When all the hydrogen in the core has been converted into helium, the now purely helium core begins to contract while the outer layers continue to 'burn' hydrogen; this contraction heats up the core and forces the outer layers outward, so that the star as a whole expands for some 100-200 million years until it becomes a red

giant star. Although the outer layers are comparatively cool, the core has become far hotter than before, and thermonuclear conversions of helium into carbon begin. The star contracts once more (though some expand still further to become supergiants) and ends its life as a white dwarf star. It is thought that more massive stars become neutron stars, whose matter is so dense that its protons and electrons are packed together to form neutrons; were the sun to become a neutron star, it would have a radius of less than 12.5 mi (20 km). Finally, when the star can no longer radiate through thermonuclear or gravitational means, it ceases to shine. At this stage some stars may undergo ultimate gravitational collapse to form black holes.

Starbuck Island, South Pacific island. This coral island, covering about 1 sq mi (2.6 sq km), claims no human population. Guano, a natural material used in fertilizer, was mined off this island until the resource was depleted (1870-1920). Starbuck Island is located 2,000 mi (3,000 km) south of Hawaii. Now part of the country of Kiribati (1979), it was formally discovered (1823) and appropriated (1866) by Britain.
See also: Kiribati.

Starch, white, odorless carbohydrate powder, essential to both plants and animals as a source of energy (it is converted to glucose when needed). It is made naturally in green plants during photosynthesis; commercially, it is made chiefly from potatoes and corn. Cornstarch is used to make corn syrup and corn sugar, both of which are used to sweeten food products. Starch is also used to size paper and textiles and to stiffen shirts and other laundered items.

S

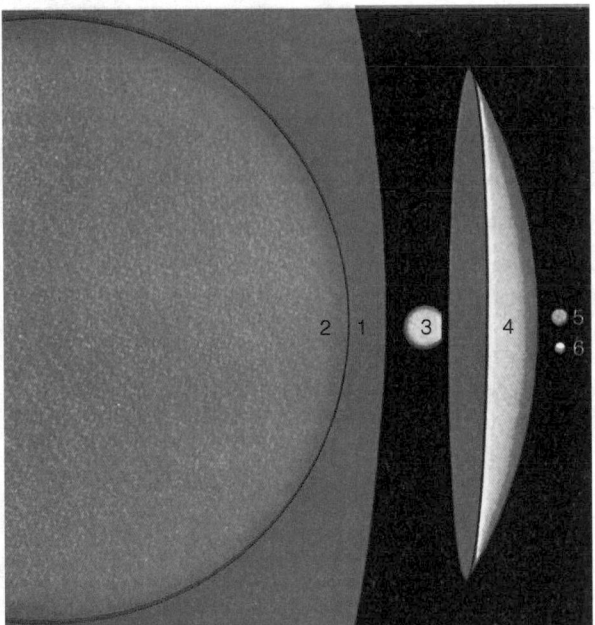

Stars range greatly in size, depending on their mass, temperature, state of matter within the star, and stage of evolution. The sun (3) is a fairly typical star, greatly exceeded in size by a giant star (2) and a red supergiant (1), such as Betelgeuse. If a segment of the sun (4) is expanded, it can be compared to the size of the earth (5) and to a white dwarf (6). Neutron stars, greatly condensed, are much smaller.

S

Star Chamber, in early English history, meeting room for the King's advisors. The room was located in Westminster Palace, London, and derives its name from the stars which decorated the ceiling of the chamber. During the 1400s these advisors evolved into a powerful council that assumed courtlike powers. It was officially set up in 1487. Operating outside common law, with no jury, it was speedy and efficient but also arbitrary and cruel, particularly under James I and Charles I. It was abolished by the Long Parliament (1641) for its abuses.
See also: United Kingdom.

Starfish, member of a class, *Asteroidea*, of star-shaped marine echinoderms, with 5-fold symmetry. A starfish consists of a central disk surrounded by 5 or more radiating arms. There is a dermal skeleton of calcite plates, and a water-vascular system gives rise to rows of tube feet on the lower surface by which the animal moves about. The mouth is on the lower surface. Most species are carnivorous or omnivorous scavengers. Starfishes can regenerate lost or damaged parts.

A

B

(A) The common sea star (*Asterias rubens*, phylum *Echinodermata*, class *Asteroidea*), diameter up to 20 in (50 cm), is capable of righting itself, when accidentally turned over. (B) Stages in righting movements: (1) The end of one arm twists, the tube feet grip the substratum; (2) The gripping arm moves backwards and the body folds in half; (3) Right orientation is achieved.

Stark, Johannes (1874-1957), German physicist who received the Nobel Prize (1919) for his discovery that light was uniquely affected by an electrical field, in that the field would cause spectral lines to split. Stark also discovered the laboratory basis (as opposed to celestial observation) of the Doppler effect in optics, in which the light frequencies of moving atoms dispensed in a gas-charged tube changed. Stark was a professor of physics at the Universities of Greifswald (1917-1920) and Wurzburg (1920-1922). He served as president of Reich Physical-Technical Institute (1933-1939). He served 4 years in a labor camp, beginning in 1947, for his Nazi participation.
See also: Relativity.

Starling, member of a family, *Sturnidae*, of more than 100 species of songbirds. They have slender bills, an upright stance, and smooth, glossy plumage. Found worldwide, they feed on insects, invertebrates, and seeds. They flock for feeding and roosting, with communal roosts of up to 500,000 birds.

Star-of-Bethlehem, flower in the lily family. This flower (*Ornithogalum umbellatum*) assumes a star shape with 6 white petals. It grows from a bulb, which is poisonous. Star-of-Bethlehem flowers have green stripes on their undersides, while the green leaves have white stripes. They bloom in May and June, often in home gardens or window boxes.

Star of David, known also as Shield of David, symbol of Judaism and the state of Israel. This star is comprised of 2 triangles, one inverted and superimposed over the other. The Hebrew title *Magen David* originates from the late A.D. 200s. Its first recorded appearance is from as long ago as 960 B.C.
See also: Judaism.

Starr, Ringo *See:* Beatles.

START *See:* Strategic Arms Limitation Talks.

Starter, device that causes the crankshaft in an engine to turn and operate. Different kinds of engines require different kinds of starters. For example, the starter in an automobile receives electric current from the battery, which, in turn, starts the starter motor: This rotates the crankshaft and ignites the spark plugs in the engine. Diesel-powered engines, including those found on many railroad cars, sometimes inject compressed air into cylinders that start the engine. The air turbine starters or jet turbine starters on airplanes use high-pressure air to start the engine; a separate device on the aircraft or ground-the auxiliary power unit (APU)-ignites the starter.
See also: Kettering, Charles Franklin.

Star Wars *See:* Strategic Defense Initiative.

State government, body that administers laws and regulations within a state. State governments have powers that are independent from those of the federal government and can set policy as long as there is no breach of constitutional law. Powers overlap in some areas, however, and it becomes necessary for the state and federal governments to work closely together.

State press, system of publishing owned and controlled by a government or dominant political party. The opposite of a free press, a state press is common in dictatorships, and is used by the state to shape popular opinion and to conceal or manipulate the flow of information to the public.

States' rights, power allowed by the U.S. Constitution to individual states, other than those rights vested in the federal government.

Static, interference in a radio or television signal caused by disturbance in the electrical charge of the receiver. The motion of charged dust particles or drops of water can result in static. More serious static may occur in the event of such natural disasters as earthquakes, volcanoes, and tornadoes.
See also: Frequency modulation.

Statics, branch of mechanics dealing with systems in equilibrium, i.e., those in which all forces are balanced and there is no motion.

Statistics, branch of mathematics that collects, tabulates, and analyzes data by a numerical system which, in turn, is used to make predictions and projections about situations that are uncertain. The process usually involves the acquisition of data from a small group that is used to make predictions about the behavior of a larger group. For example, in a presidential campaign most candidates take polls indicating their level of popularity. These polls do not survey every person in the country, but are based on a sample from a much smaller number of people. Essential to such calculations is the theory of probability, which is utilized to judge the soundness of the numerical assumptions. Statistics plays a significant role in many areas, including scientific research, business (insurance), and politics.

Statue of Liberty, colossal bronze female figure rising more than 300 ft (91 m) above the sea, on Liberty Island in New York Harbor. She bears in one hand a tablet marked 'July 4, 1776' and in the other a torch. Designed by the sculptor Frédéric Bartholdi, the statue was given to the United States by France on the 100th anniversary of U.S. independence. The U.S poet Emma Lazarus epitomized the statue's meaning in an inscription on its base, which reads in part:
'Give me your tired, your poor,
Your huddled masses yearning to breathe free,
The wretched refuse of your teeming shore.
Send these, the homeless, tempest-tost to me,
I lift my lamp beside the golden door!'

Statue of Liberty National Monument, on New York City's Ellis and Liberty islands, 58-acre (23 ha) monument. It includes the Statue of Liberty on Liberty Island, a massive copper work given to the United States by the people of France on July 4, 1884. It was created by the sculptor Frédéric-Auguste Bartholdi to commemorate the friendship between the 2 nations. Ellis Island, an immigration station until 1954, was made part of the national monument in 1965; from 1892 to 1943 it was the chief entry station for thousands of immigrants seeking a new life in the United States.
See also: Ellis Island.

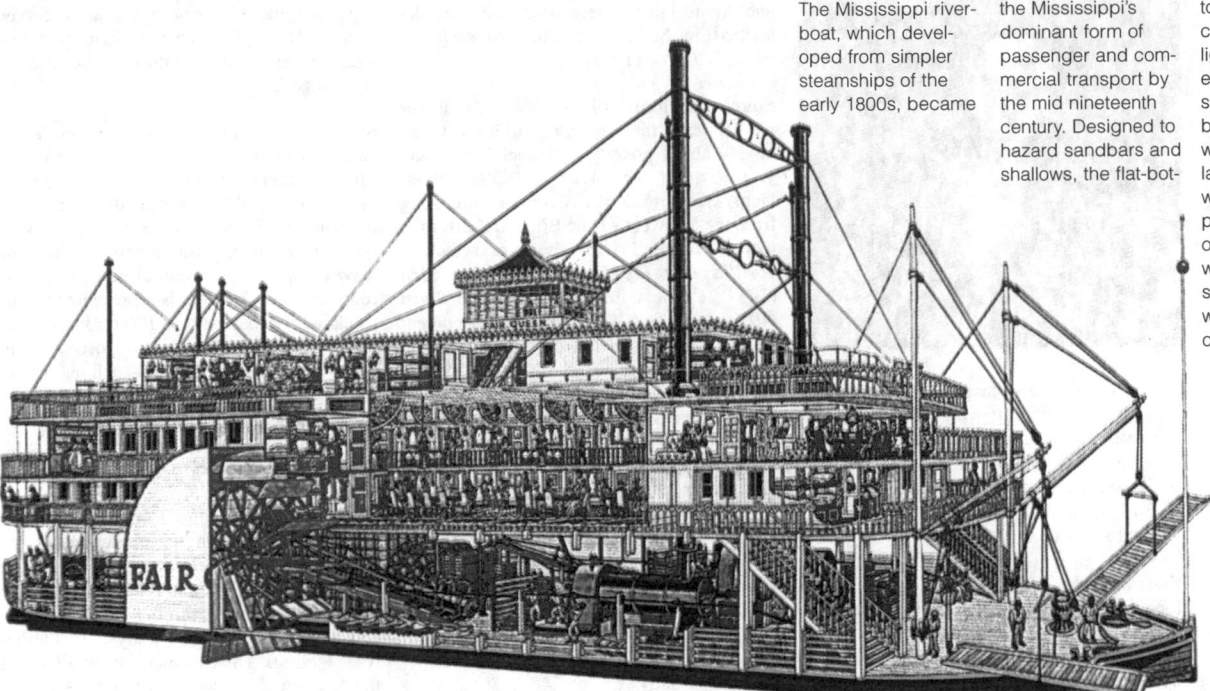

The Mississippi riverboat, which developed from simpler steamships of the early 1800s, became the Mississippi's dominant form of passenger and commercial transport by the mid nineteenth century. Designed to hazard sandbars and shallows, the flat-bottomed, shallow-hulled craft supported a light, but lofty wooden superstructure. Its steam engines burned either coal or wood, powering two large, lateral flywheels. The elegant passenger quarters of the upper decks were crowned by a small pilothouse, from which the captain could survey the river.

S

Stauffenberg, Claus Graf Schenk von (1907-1944), German officer severely injured in 1943 in Africa and transferred to Hitler's staff. There he became one of the central figures in the plot to assassinate Hitler, and on 20 July 1944 he placed a bomb in a meeting room which only managed to inflict slight injuries to Hitler. Stauffenberg was arrested and executed by a firing squad.

Staunton, Howard (1810-1874), British chess grandmaster and organizer of the first official international chess tournament (London 1851). After his victory over the strong French grandmaster Pierre Charles Fournier de Saint-Amant (1800-1872) in Paris in 1843 (+11, -6, =4), Staunton considered himself to be Labourdonnais' successor. Staunton did much for English chess. In 1841 he founded the magazine The Chess Players Chronicle, and from 1845 until his death he wrote the chess column in The Illustrated London News. He was also well-known for his knowledge of Shakespeare's works, a completely revised edition of which he published in 1857-1860. Staunton is also known as the designer of modern chess pieces.

STD *See:* Venereal disease.

Steamboat, any steam-powered sailing vessel. The term is commonly used to identify the kind of riverboat used in the United States in the 1800s, particularly along the Mississippi. The steamboat was a primary means of transportation before the advent of the railroad. The most famous of the U.S. steamboats was the *Clermont,* which sailed along the Hudson River from New York to Albany in about 30 hours in 1807.
See also: Fulton, Robert.

Steam engine, first important heat engine,

supplying the power that made the Industrial Revolution possible. It was the principal power source for industry and transport (notably railroad locomotives and steamships) until the 20th-century advent of steam turbines and internal-combustion engines. The steam engine is an external-combustion engine, the steam being raised in a boiler heated by a furnace. The first working example was that of Thomas Newcomen (1712). Steam was admitted to a cylinder as a piston moved up and was condensed by a water spray inside the cylinder, whereupon the air pressure outside forced the piston down again. James Watt radically improved Newcomen's engine (1769) by condensing the steam outside the cylinder (thus no longer having to reheat the cylinder at each stroke) and by using the steam pressure to force the piston up. Watt also invented the double-action principle-both strokes being powered by applying the steam alternately to each end of the piston-and devices for converting the piston's linear motion to rotary motion. The compound engine (1781) made more efficient use of the steam by using the exhaust steam from one cylinder to drive the piston of a second cylinder. Later developments included the use of high-pressure steam.
See also: Newcomen, Thomas; Watt, James.

Stearic acid, or octadecanoic acid, common fatty acid derived from animal or vegetable fats. A waxy, colorless solid, it has a wide variety of industrial uses, including the manufacture of soap, cosmetics, and pharmaceuticals.

Steatite *See:* Soapstone.

Steel, alloy of iron and up to 1.7% carbon, with small amounts of manganese, phosphorous, sulfur, and silicon. These are termed carbon steels; those with other metals are

termed alloy steels-low-alloy steels if they have less than 5% of the alloying metal, high-alloy steels if more than 5%. Carbon steels are far stronger than iron, and their properties can be tailored to their uses by adjusting composition and treatment. Alloy steels-including stainless steels-are used for their special properties. Steel was first mass-produced in the mid-19th century and is now basic to all industrial economies. The United States, the former USSR, and Japan are the major producers. All steelmaking processes remove the impurities in the raw materials-pig iron, scrap steel, and reduced iron ore-by oxidizing them with an air or oxygen blast. Thus most of the carbon, silicon, manganese, phosphorus, and sulfur are converted to their oxides and, together with added flux and other waste matter present, form slag. The main processes are the Bessemer process; the Linz-Donawitz, or basic oxygen, process, and the similar electric-arc process, used for highest-quality steel; and the open-hearth process. When the impurities have been removed, desired elements are added in calculated proportions. The molten steel is cast as ingots that are shaped while still red-hot in rolling mills, or it may be cast as a continuous bar (strand casting). The properties of carbon steels may be greatly improved by heat treatment: annealing, casehardening, and tempering.

Steele, Sir Richard (1672-1729), Irish-born English essayist, playwright, and poet. His first play was *The Funeral* (1701) and his last, *The Conscious Lovers* (1722). He founded a periodical *The Tatler* (1709-1711) and soon began collaborating with Joseph Addison. Together they founded the *Spectator* (1711-1712). *The Tatler* and the *Spectator* contained their essays on theater, literature, and family life.

Steen, Jan (c.1626-1679), Dutch painter, a

S

Gertrude Stein (1874-1946) painted by Pablo Picasso (1881-1973) in 1906 (Metropolitan Museum, New York).

master of color and facial expressions. His almost 900 surviving works include jovial scenes of eating, drinking, and revelry, such as *St. Nicholas' Feast* and *As the Old Sing, the Young Pipe*; portraits; landscapes, such as *The Game of Skittles*; and classical and biblical scenes.

Steenbok, or steinbok, small African antelope belonging to the family Bovidae. It lives alone in wooded areas. A distinctive feature is its ability to obtain all the water it needs from the plants it eats. It stands about 21 in (53 cm) high and is reddish in color; the male has small, pointed horns.

Steeplechasing, horse-racing over a course with such obstacles as fences, hedges, and water. It originated in England as a race from one church steeple to another. The world's most famous steeplechase is the Grand National, first run in 1839 and held annually near Liverpool, England. U.S. steeplechases are normally held at racing tracks or hunts.

Stefano, Giuseppe di (1921-), Italian singer (tenor). Di Stefano first appeared on stage in 1946 in Reggio Emilio in Massenet's opera *Manon*, and went on to sing in Barcelona, Rome, Milan, and New York (1948-1950), becoming in 1951 first tenor in La Scala in Milan. In the 1950s and 1960s he was very successful as an opera singer (including the partnership with Maria Callas) and made numerous tours.

Steffens, Lincoln (1866-1936), U.S. writer, lecturer, and political critic. Identified with a group of journalists called muckrakers, he worked to expose the corrupt connection between government and private self-interest. He later developed an interest in revolutionary politics. He wrote numerous magazine articles for *McClure's Magazine, American Magazine,* and *Everybody's Magazine,* as well as his *Autobiography* (1931).
See also: Muckraker.

Stegosaurus *See:* Dinosaur.

Stein, Gertrude (1874-1946), U.S. writer who lived in Paris from 1903. Author of short stories, long narratives, critical essays, 'cubist' poetry, and operas, her first important work was *Three Lives* (1909). Stein is best known for her experimental syntax and her influence on such figures as Pablo Picasso, Ernest Hemingway, Henri Matisse,

and André Gide. These friendships are described in Stein's *The Autobiography of Alice B. Toklas* (1933).

Steinbeck, John (1902-1968), U.S. author who came to the fore in the 1930s with his novels about poverty and social injustice. *The Grapes of Wrath* (1939), about Depression-era farm workers migrating from the Midwest's Dust Bowl to California, won a Pulitzer Prize. Other works include *Tortilla Flat* (1935), *Of Mice and Men* (1937), *Cannery Row* (1945), *East of Eden* (1952), and *The Winter of Our Discontent* (1961). He was awarded the 1962 Nobel Prize in literature.

Steinberger, Jack (1921-), U.S. physicist. Steinberger, Leon Lederman, and Melvin Schwartz won the 1988 Nobel Prize in physics for their work on the use of the subatomic particles known as neutrinos to study other subatomic particles, and their discovery of the muon neutrino. He worked at the University of California, Berkeley (1948-1950), Columbia University (1950-1971), and the European Laboratory for Particle Physics (1968-).
See also: Neutrino.

Steinbok *See:* Steenbok.

Steinem, Gloria (1934-), U.S feminist and writer. A founding editor of *New York* magazine and cofounder (1971) of the National Women's Political Caucus, she also founded (1972) and edited *Ms.* magazine. *Outrageous Acts and Everyday Rebellions* is a collection of her writings.

Steiner, Rudolf (1861-1925), Austrian founder of anthroposophy, an attempt to recapture spiritual realities ignored by modern man. He founded the Waldorf School movement and stressed music and drama as aids to self-discovery. Works include *The Philosophy of Spiritual Activity* (1922).

Steinitz, Wilhelm (1836-1900), Austrian chess grandmaster, world champion 1866-1894. He was the founder of modern chess principles, further developed by such chess players as Lasker and Tarrasch. He was both a formidable tournament and match player, and called himself world champion after his victory against Anderson in 1866 (+8, -6). Steinitz defended his title successfully on many occasions, but lost in 1894 to Lasker. Steinitz' strategic principles are still used today in a number of opening variants named after him.

Steinway, U.S. family of piano manufacturers. **Henry Engelhard Steinweg** (1797-1871), who changed his name to Steinway after emigrating from Germany to the United States in 1851, founded Steinway & Sons in 1853 in New York City. It was carried on by his sons, notably **Christian Friedrich Theodore** (1825-1889) and **William** (1835-1896).

Stella, Frank (1936-), U.S. painter. Stella developed the abstract style called minimalism in the 1960s, and he began using 3-dimensional canvases in the 1980s. His paint-

ings are usually large with angular or curved shapes. Often the canvases themselves are irregularly shaped to conform to the shape of the image in the painting.

Stem, part of a plant from which the leaves and flowers sprout. Formed by the growing tip as it emerges from the seed after germination, it may divide repeatedly to produce branches and twigs. A stem may be very short, as in low-growing plants in which the leaves appear to sprout directly from the roots. In trees the stem is represented by the trunk, which may be over 100 ft (30 m) high. Stems are responsible for support and contain strengthening tissues, such as wood. They also carry food and water between the leaves and roots. Green stems carry out photosynthesis; modified stems, such as the tuber, act as food stores.

Stendhal (Marie Henri Beyle; 1783-1842), French pioneer of the psychological novel. *The Red and the Black* (1831) and *The Charterhouse of Parma* (1839) explore the search for happiness through love and political power, with minute analysis of the heroes' feelings. His treatment of the figure of the 'outsider,' his social criticism, and brilliant ironic prose style make him one of the greatest and most 'modern' of French novelists.

The French author Stendhal (1783-1842) sought for maximum precision and conciseness in his writings.

Stengel, Casey (c.1890-1975), U.S. baseball manager. A popular and garrulous figure, he managed the Brooklyn Dodgers (1934-1936), Boston Braves (1938-43), New York Yankees (1949-1960), and New York Mets (1962-1965). Stengel led the Yankees to 7 World Series championships (1949-1953, 1956, 1958) and was inducted to the National Baseball Hall of Fame in 1966.

Stenmark, Ingemar (1956-), Swedish skier, outstanding in alpine events. Stenmark was one of the top skiers in the World Cup circuit right from his very first race in 1974. He won numerous world cups in the slalom, giant slalom, downhill, and combined events. In 1980 he won the gold medal in the slalom and giant slalom during the Winter Olympics at Lake Placid.

Stephen, name of 9 popes. **Stephen I** (reigned 254-257), who died during

Emperor Valerian's persecutions, defended the validity of the baptism of heretics, a stance St. Cyprian of Carthage denounced. **Stephen II** (reigned 752-757) was supported by Pepin the Short in his defeat of the Lombards. The Papal States were founded with land gifts from Pepin. Controversy over papal elections dominated the reign (768-772) of **Stephen III**. **Stephen IV** (reigned 816-817) crowned Louis I emperor (establishing a prerogative of the papacy) and strengthened links with the Franks. **Stephen VI** (reigned 896-897) declared void the reign of his predecessor, Formosus, but was himself imprisoned and strangled. His rule marked the papacy's lowest point. **Stephen IX** (b.1000; reigned 1057-1058) continued the reforms of Leo IX, enforcing priestly celibacy and attacking simony. But he failed to stop the rift between the Eastern and Western churches.

Stephen (c.1097-1154), king of England (1135-1154). A nephew of Henry I, he was briefly supplanted (1141) by Matilda, Henry's daughter. Though a just and generous ruler, he was not strong enough to govern the warring factions of his realm.

Stephenson, British family of inventors and railroad engineers. **George** (1781-1848) first worked on stationary steam engines. His first locomotive, the Blucher, took to the rails in 1814; it traveled at 4 mph (6.5 kmph). In 1825 his Locomotion carried 450 people at a rate of 15 mph (25 kmph), and the modern railroad was born. In 1829 the Rocket ran the 40 mi (65 km) of his new Manchester-Liverpool line at speeds up to 30 mph (48 kmph). His only son, **Robert** (1803-1859), is best known as a bridge builder, notably for the tubular bridges over the Menai Straits, North Wales (1850), and the St. Lawrence River at Montreal, Canada (1859).

Steppe, extensive temperate grasslands of Europe and Asia (equivalent to the North American prairies and South American pampas). They extend from southwest Siberia to the lower reaches of the Danube River.

Stereoscope, optical instrument that stimulates binocular vision by presenting slightly different pictures to the 2 eyes so that an apparently 3-dimensional image is produced.

Stereotyping, in printing, process in which a metal plate is made from a mold of typeface or art. The same plate is then used to print many pages. Use of this method speeds up the printing process and lowers its cost. Although largely replaced in the United States by offset lithography, stereotyping is still used in other parts of the world.
See also: Printing.

Sterility, condition of being incapable of producing offspring; freedom from germs. In human beings, the inability to reproduce can have several causes, including defects in the reproductive organs, hormonal imbalance, and surgical sterilization.

Sterilization, surgical procedure designed to prevent conception. In females, the fallopian tubes are cut and tied to prevent eggs reaching the womb, thus providing permanent contraception. The procedure is essentially irreversible. In males, sterilization may be achieved by vasectomy, an operation in which the vas deferens on each side is tied off and cut to prevent sperm from reaching the seminal vesicles. Sterilization is also the name of the process of treating medical equipment to ensure that it is not contaminated by bacteria and other microorganisms. Metal and linen objects are often sterilized by heat. Chemical disinfection is also used, and plastic equipment is exposed to gamma rays.

Stern, Isaac (1920-2001), Russian U.S. violinist. A child prodigy born in the USSR, he came to the United States as a baby, where he studied and made his debut in 1931 in San Francisco. A noted virtuoso, he has recorded extensively and concertized worldwide.

Sternberg, Joseph von (1894-1969), Austrian-born German-U.S. film director. He is most famous for the films he made with Marlene Dietrich, notably *The Blue Angel* (1930), *Morocco* (1930), and *Shanghai Express* (1932).

Sterne, Laurence (1713-1768), British clergyman who became known as a novelist, largely because of the popularity of his book *The Life and Opinions of Tristram Shandy, Gentleman* (1760-1767). In it, Sterne was thought to anticipate the work of post-Freudian stream-of-consciousness writers. Sterne drew on the ideas of philosopher John Locke to give form to this impressionistic, unconventionally structured novel about life as seen through the eyes of a young boy. Sterne also wrote a work of satire and a book about his experiences and reflections while traveling.

Steroid, hormone produced in the body from cholesterol, mainly by the adrenal glands. Cortisol is the main glucocorticoid (steroids that regulate glucose metabolism) and aldosterone, the main mineralocorticoid (regulating salt, potassium, and water balance). Increased amounts of cortisol are secreted during times of stress, such as shock, surgery, and severe infection. Sterols, mainly of the glucocorticoid type, are also given in doses above normal hormone levels to obtain other effects, e.g., the suppression of inflammation, allergy, and immunity. High-dose systemic steroids may have adverse effects if used for long periods; they may cause acne, osteoporosis, hypertension, fluid retention, altered facial appearance, and growth retardation in children.
See also: Hormone.

Stethoscope, instrument devised (1819) by René T. H. Laënnec (1781-1826) for listening to sounds within the body, especially those from the heart, lungs, abdomen, and blood vessels.

Stettin *See:* Szczecin.

Stevens, U.S. family of inventors and engineers. **John** (1749-1838) built the first steamboat with a screw propeller (1802) and the first seagoing steamboat (1809). He also built the first U.S. steam locomotive (1825). His son **Robert Livingston** (1787-1856) invented the inverted T-rail still used in modern railroads (1830). Another son, **Edwin Augustus** (1795-1868), also made contributions to railroad technology.
See also: Railroad.

Stevens, Cat (real name, Stephen Demetri Georgiou; 1947-), British pop singer of Greek descent. Became well known for such songs as *I Love My Dog* (1966) and *Matthew and Son* (1967). After a period of ill-health and contemplation he began to concentrate on folk music, and his lyrics became more personal and soul-searching. This new style brought him a whole new audience, and he had several hits, which include *Lady D'Arbanville* (1970) and *Morning Has Broken* (1972). In 1977 he converted to Islam, and in 1981 withdrew from the music world altogether.

Stevens, Wallace (1879-1955), U.S. poet. Working for a Connecticut insurance company, he achieved wide literary recognition with the 1955 Pulitzer Prize for his *Collected Poems*. Rich in imagery and vocabulary, his verse explores the use of imagination to give meaning to life.

Stevenson, family of U.S. Democratic politicians. **Adlai Ewing** (1835-1914) was elected U.S. vice president (1893-1897). His grandson **Adlai Ewing** (1900-1965) was elected governor of Illinois (1949-1953). He was chosen as his party's presidential candidate in 1952 and 1956 but lost to Dwight D. Eisenhower. He lost the 1960 nomination to John F. Kennedy. From 1961 until his death he was U.S. ambassador to the UN. His son **Adlai Ewing III** (1930-) was elected from Illinois to the U.S. Senate (1970-1981).

Stevenson, Robert Louis (1850-1894), Scottish author, essayist, and poet who was one of the most successful writers of his day. Critically acclaimed for his exceptional ability as a prose stylist, his novels of adventure and romance-among them *Treasure Island* (1883) and *The Strange Case of Dr. Jekyll and Mr. Hyde* (1886)-are known worldwide. He also wrote a popular book of children's poems, *A Child's Garden of Verses* (1885).

Steward, Julian Haynes (1902-1972), U.S. anthropologist. A major exponent of cultural evolution, he was among the first anthropologists to emphasize ecology as a determinant of culture. He edited the *Handbook of South American Indians* (7 vol., 1946-1959) and wrote *The Theory of Culture Change* (1955).
See also: Anthropology.

Stewart, James (1908-1997), U.S. popular screen actor acclaimed for his sympathetic portrayals of the American common man. He was known for his lanky build, midwestern drawl, and folksy charm. Stewart starred in several films directed by such cinematic pioneers as Frank Capra and Alfred Hitchcock. Among his most well-known

S

S

films are *It's a Wonderful Life* (1946) and *Rear Window* (1954). In 1985 he received an Academy Award for his complete works.

Stewart, John Young (Jackie) (1939-   ), British racing car driver, originally a clay pigeon shooter. In his first Formula 1 year, 1965, he drove for BRM. His racing career was threatened by an accident on the Spa circuit, and in 1967 Stewart raced for the Tyrrell Matra Team in Formula 2. He returned to Formula 1 the following year driving a Ken Tyrrell Matra with a Ford Cosworth engine, and became world champion for the first time in 1969. In 1971 and 1973 he won the Formula 1 world title again. In 1998 the Dutch racing car driver Jos Verstappen joined his team.

Stibnite *See:* Antimony.

Stickleback, small fish with spines on its back that lives in fresh and salt waters of the Northern Hemisphere. There are sticklebacks with 3, 4, and 10 spines and the marine stickleback has 15. Sticklebacks are very abundant. They feed on small animals. The male builds a nest of waterweed and entices several females to lay their eggs in it. He stays with the young and drives away enemies.

Stickseed, North American wild plant belonging to the borage family. Its name derives from the stickiness of its fruit, which adheres to clothing and animal fur. It has small white, lavender, or blue flowers.

Stieglitz, Alfred (1864-1946), U.S. photographer and founder of Photo-Secession (1902), an organization dedicated to the promotion of photography as a fine art. His magazine *Camera Work* (first published in 1903) as well as his gallery '291' helped introduce the work of many avante-garde artists, critics, and photographers. His wife was the painter Georgia O'Keeffe, a frequent subject of his photographic compositions.
See also: Photography.

Stifter, Adalbert (1805-1868), Austrian writer. Had an exceptional storytelling technique, and mostly wrote novels which were set in an imaginary harmonious world, albeit with a tragic undertone. The fact that he also painted probably explains his sensitive, picturesque descriptions of nature. Well-known novels: *Der Hagestolz* (1844) and *Bergkrystall* (1845). Also the 'Bildungsroman' *Der Nachsommer* (1857) and the long historical novel *Witiko* (1865-1867), set in 12th-century South Bohemia.

Still, Clyfford (1904-1980), one of the first abstract expressionist painters in the United States, known for his dramatic use of color. He abandoned his landscape paintings in the late 1940s and began experimenting with large jagged shapes and abstract themes. Still significantly influenced the work of younger abstract painters.
See also: Abstract expressionism.

Stilt, bird belonging to the stilt and avocet family, commonly found in warm pond areas throughout the world. It is known for its long, thin legs and bill. It measures from 14-18 in (35-45 cm) and usually has black and white feathers and pink legs. It wades in the water and feeds on the small creatures it finds there.

Stimson, Henry Lewis (1867-1950), U.S. politician, author of the Stimson Doctrine. As secretary of state (1929-1933), he declared at the time of Japan's invasion of Manchuria that the United States would not recognize any territorial changes that impaired U.S. treaty rights or were brought about by force. As secretary of war (1940-1945), he advocated development and use of the atomic bomb.

Stimulant, drug that stimulates an organ. Nervous system stimulants range from amphetamines and hallucinogenic drugs to drugs liable to induce convulsions. Cardiac stimulants such as digitalis and adrenaline are used in cardiac failure and resuscitation, respectively. Bowel stimulants have a laxa-

tive effect. Womb stimulants (oxytocin and ergometrine) are used in obstetrics to induce labor and prevent postpartum hemorrhage.
See also: Drug.

Stingray, one of 100 species of flat, disk-shaped fish belonging to the family Dasyatidae. On its tail are poisonous spines that can cause serious injury to swimmers. Although some varieties can be found in rivers, most live in saltwater. Stingrays vary in size; the largest can measure up to 14 ft (4 m).

Stink bug, shield-shaped insect belonging to the stink bug family, known for the unpleasant odor it emits when disturbed. It feeds on plants and insects. Some varieties are pests that destroy cabbage and rice crops and cause damage to certain kinds of garden plants.

Stirling engine, type of external-combustion engine invented in Scotland by the Rev. Robert Stirling in 1816. Long in disuse, the Stirling engine has recently been reinvestigated as a possible substitute for the gasoline engine, but so far has not proved practical. Different versions of the Stirling engine exist, but all involve a gas (usually air) circulating in a closed system of cylinders and pistons and deriving energy from an external source of heat.

Stoat *See:* Ermine.

Stock, group of about 50 varieties of fragrant garden flowers belonging to the family Cruciferae. Common types are the Virginia stock, the Grecian stock, and the Brampton, or common, stock. They are variously red, white, lilac, or yellow in color.

Stock, capital, ownership in a corporation. A corporation allows stockholders to purchase stock certificates to represent shares of the corporation they own. Stocks can be sold by the stockholders, often for a profit. The value of the stock fluctuates according to such factors as the success of the corporation or the general state of the economy. There are various kinds of stock; a newly formed corporation decides which kinds of stock will be issued.

Stock exchange, auction for the sale and exchange of stock, which is a certificate of ownership in a corporation. Stock markets exist in all major industrial states; stock market proceedings are published in most large daily newspapers. The price of each stock is determined each hour of the trading day, according to the laws of supply and demand. Factors that influence stock prices include the state of the economy, the public confidence in the economy, the amount of profit a company has made or is predicted to make, the rate of a company's growth or decline, and the market for a particular product. Major exchanges include those in New York, London, Paris, Frankfurt, Milan, Zurich, Amsterdam, Brussels, Buenos Aires, Sydney, Tokyo, Hong Kong, Singapore and Johannesburg.

Stockhausen, Karlheinz (1928-   ), German composer and theorist. An experimenter with a variety of avant-garde musical techniques,

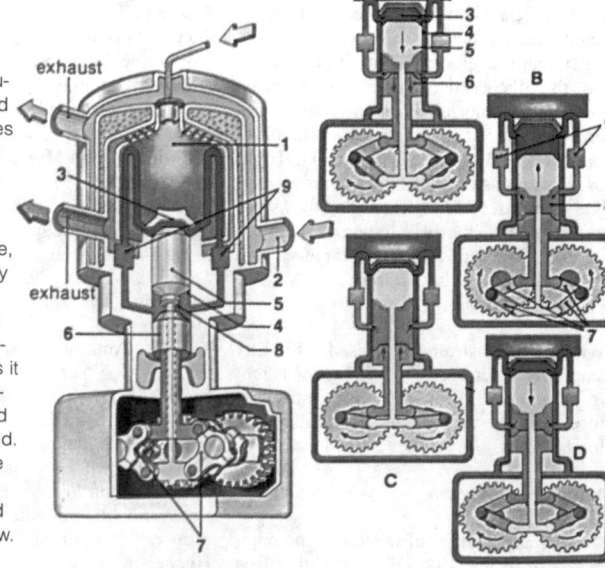

The Stirling engine (left) converts heat into mechanical energy through expansion of a fluid, usually hydrogen. Heat is transferred to the fluid from an external combustion system (1). Cooling is provided by cold-air intake pipes (2). (A) Working fluid in the hot end (3) of a cylinder (4) expands, forcing a displacer (5) and a piston (6) downward. (B) The drive linkage (7) moves the displacer upward, pushing fluid from the hot into the cold end (8). The fluid's heat is absorbed by regenerator boxes (9). (C) Fluid at the cold end is compressed by the piston. As its pressure and temperature rise, the fluid is cooled by passage through a cooling system. The compressed fluid regains stored heat as it flows through the regenerator boxes and returns to the hot end. (D) Expansion of the hot fluid pushes the displacer down, and the cycle starts anew.

including electronic, 12-tone, and aleatory music, he studied with Frank Martin, Olivier Messiaen, and Darius Milhaud, and was much influenced by Anton Webern. He has produced works like *Gruppen* (1959), in which 3 orchestras play 'groups' of sounds against each other, the electronic *Kontakte* (1959-1960), *Harlekin* (1975, for the clarinet), and the cycle *Licht* (1977-1980).

Stockholm (pop. 700,000), capital of Sweden, located on a network of islands on the country's eastern coast. It is Sweden's major commercial, industrial, cultural, and financial center, and an important port. Chief industries are machinery, paper and print, shipbuilding, chemicals, and food-stuffs. Founded in the 13th century, it was long dominated by the Hanseatic League. It became the capital in 1634.
See also: Sweden.

Stock market crash of 1929 *See:* Great Depression.

Stock ticker, teletype device for recording the buying and selling of stock. The machine prints transactions on a continuous strip of tape, with symbols to refer to the names of the corporations. First used by the New York Stock Exchange in 1867, the stock ticker became widely used during the early 20th century. It is now almost obsolete, having been largely replaced by electronic devices.

Stoicism, ancient Greek school of philosophy founded by Zeno of Citium, who taught in a stoa (portico) in Athens c.300 B.C. The Stoics believed that man should live rationally and in harmony with nature, and that virtue is the only good. In performing his duty the virtuous man should be indifferent to pleasure and misfortune, thus rising above the effects of chance and achieving spiritual freedom and conformity with the divine reason controlling all nature. Famous Stoics include Seneca, Epictetus, and Marcus Aurelius.
See also: Zeno of Citium.

Stoke-on-Trent (pop. 253,000), city in England known for its pottery, located on the River Trent. Created in 1910 by the confederation of 5 ceramic-producing towns called The Potteries, it achieved status as a city in 1925. It still exists as the pottery center of England. Its other industries include coal mining and steel and iron production.

Stoker, Bram (1847-1912), British author who won notoriety for his book *Dracula* (1897), a tale of horror about a Transylvanian vampire with supernatural abilities. He wrote a sequel, *Dracula's Guest* (1927), as well as other novels. Stoker spent many years as the manager and companion of actor Sir Henry Irving.

Stokowski, Leopold (Boleslawowicz Stanislaw Antoni; 1882-1977), U.S. conductor. He gained his early reputation as musical director of the Philadelphia Orchestra (1912-1936), which he conducted in recording the soundtrack for Walt Disney's *Fantasia* (1940). He was noted for innovative orchestrations and championing modern music in his repertoire.

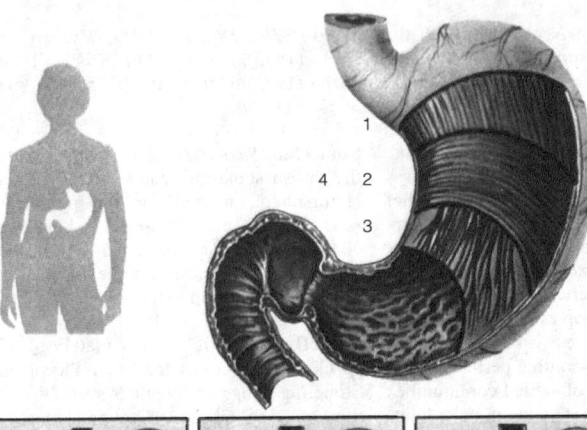
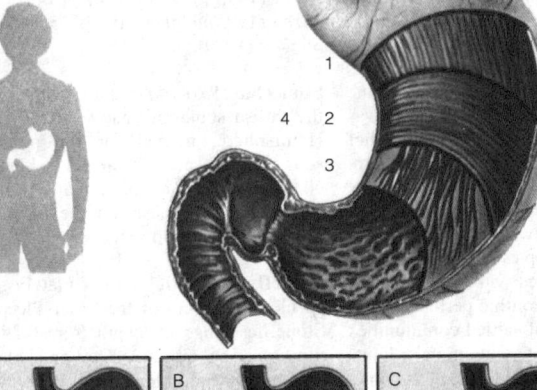

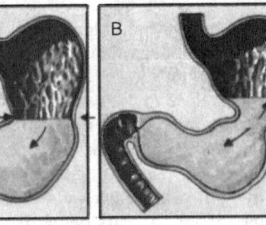
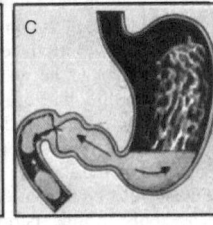

The stomach (4) is an expandable reservoir for food, located in the abdomen. Its wall has three layers of muscles: a longitudinal outer layer (1), a circular middle layer (2), and an oblique inner layer (3). These muscles churn and knead solid food, helping to convert it into a semiliquid mass, known as chyme. As the stomach fills with food, the wavelike contractions of the wall begin (A). As the waves move along the wall (B), the chyme is forced out (C), little by little, through the pyloric sphincter into the duodenum — the first part of the small intestine. The stomach empties within 4 hours after ingestion of a meal, and digestion is completed in the small intestine.

S

Stol *See:* V/STOL.

Stomach, large organ of the digestive system. It receives food from the esophagus and mixes it with hydrochloric acid and the stomach enzymes; fats are partially emulsified. After some time, the pyloric sphincter relaxes and food enters the duodenum and the rest of the gastrointestinal tract.
See also: Digestive system.

Stone, Edward Durell (1902-1978), U.S. architect whose works include the U.S. pavilion for the Brussels World's Fair (1958), the U.S. Embassy in Delhi (1958), and the Kennedy Center for the Performing Arts in Washington, D.C. (1971).
See also: Architecture.

Stone Age, stage of earliest human cultural development, preceding the Bronze Age and Iron Age. It is characterized by the nearly exclusive use of stone tools and weapons and is divided into 3 periods. The Paleolithic

An artist's reconstruction of the Mesolithic settlement at Lepenski Vir (5000-4600 B.C.), on a terrace beside the Danube River in the Iron Gates gorge in Yugoslavia. The inhabitants are believed to have been hunters and gatherers. Bones of forest-dwelling animals, such as red deer and wild pig, and many fish species, including sturgeon, have been found at the site. There is no evidence of farming of herding practices. The trapezoidal houses at Lepenski Vir were closely spaced and they all faced the river. They had wood and stone walls and red or white plastered floors. The hearths within the houses consisted of rectangular pits, lined with limestone blocks.

period, or Old Stone Age, began with the emergence of *Homo sapiens*. These nomadic hunters and gatherers lived in caves, used fire, and made tools of chipped stone (some relics have been dated at 2.5 million years old). By the end of this period, known as the Upper Paleolithic, it is believed hunting was communal, shelter was manmade, and belief in the supernatural, or magic, had been born. The Mesolithic period, or Middle Stone Age, was confined exclusively to northeastern Europe where, between 10,000 B.C. and 3000 B.C., various peoples enjoyed a culture that showed similarities with those of both the Paleolithic and Neolithic periods. There were the beginnings of settled communities and domesticated plants and animals; hunting was expanded to include use of the bow; and the making of pottery was introduced. The Neolithic, or New Stone Age, began in Asia c.8000 B.C. and spread through Europe between 6000 B.C. and 2000 B.C.; it was signaled by the development of agriculture, with a consequent increase in the stability of the population and hence elaboration of the social structure. The tools of this period were of polished stone. In addition to farming, men also worked mines. The Neolithic period merged slowly into the Early Bronze Age.

Stone, Lucy (1818-1893), U.S. reformer and feminist. A fervent abolitionist, she helped to found the American Woman Suffrage Association (1869) and edited its magazine, *Woman's Journal* (1870-1893). *See also:* Woman suffrage.

Stone, Oliver (1946-), U.S. film director and screenwriter. He won an Academy Award for direction of *Platoon* (1987), for which he also wrote the screenplay, based on his own experiences serving in the Vietnam war. He also directed *Wall Street* (1987), *Born on the Fourth of July* (1989), *JFK*

In recent years, it has become clear that some prehistoric buildings, like Stonehenge in southern England, have been built to determine the course of the sun and the moon in the sky — in other words, as a kind of calendar. In Stonehenge this became apparent from the fact that on certain days of the year, the sun and the moon will rise at fixed points within the structure of the stones. Here, we see the rising of the midsummer sun on June 20, right in the direction of the Heel Stone.

(1991), *The Doors* (1991), *Heaven and Earth* (1993), *Natural Born Killers* (1994), *Nixon* (1995), *U turn* (1997), and *Any given Sunday* (1999).

Stonechat (*Saxicola torquata*), small bird of the thrush subfamily native to the Eastern Hemisphere, named for the percussive sound of its call. The male is black and chestnut in color, the female somewhat duller. The bird nests on the ground and feeds on insects and seeds.

Stonefly, any of approximately 1,550 species of insects of the order Plecoptera. Stoneflies range in length from 0.25 in (6 mm) to 2.5 in (60 mm). Their gray, black, or brown coloration blends with their environment. Although they have 2 pairs of wings, they do not fly well, and are often found on rocks close to the water. Females drop their eggs-up to 6,000 at a time-into small bodies of water. Fish eat many of them before they have a chance to develop into stonefly nymphs, which have gills and live in the water for 1 to 4 years before becoming adults and developing wings.

Stonehenge, ruins of a megalithic monument, dating from the Stone Age and early Bronze Age, on Salisbury Plain, in southern England. Its most noticeable features are concentric rings of stones surrounding a horseshoe of upright stones, and a solitary vertical stone, the Heel Stone, to the northeast. Stonehenge was built between 1900 B.C. and 1400 B.C. in 3 distinct phases. It appears to have been both a religious center and an astronomical observatory.

Stoneware, durable kind of pottery with a variety of industrial and aesthetic applications. Because it is nonporous, it is used to store food and chemicals and to create art objects, such as statues. It is produced by subjecting a mixture of clays to temperatures as high as 2,200°F (1,200°C). The art of making stoneware was developed in China in the 5th century. The technique achieved popularity throughout Europe and was widely used by the early American colonists.
See also: Pottery and porcelain.

Stoppard, Tom (1937-), English playwright best known for *Rosencrantz and Guildenstern Are Dead* (1966), an existentialist drama centering on 2 minor characters from Shakespeare's *Hamlet*. Critics admire his scintillating dialogue in plays such as *Travesties* (1974) and *Hapgood* (1988). Other plays include *Arcadia* (1993), *Indian ink* (1995), and *The invention of love* (1997). He also wrote film scripts, among which *Empire of the Sun* (1987) and *Shakespeare in Love* (1998).

Storey, David (1933-), English playwright and novelist. *This Sporting Life*, his novel (1960) and film (1963), and the play *The Changing Room* (1971), his best-known works, are based on his years as a professional rugby player.

Stork, large, heavily built bird, family Ciconiiodae, with long legs and neck, a

long, stout bill, and usually black-and-white plumage. The stork's long legs and slightly webbed feet are adaptations for wading in shallow water, where it feeds on freshwater animals and large insects. Storks tend to be gregarious. They mainly live in the tropics, though some spend part of the year in temperate zones.

Störmer, Horst L. (1949-), German physicist. In 1998 he was awarded the Nobel Prize for physics, together with Daniel Tsui and Robert Loughlin, for the discovery and explanation of the Fractional Quantum Hall Effect (SQHE). Stömer and Tsui had discovered this phenomenon as early as 1982, but it took almost ten years before Loughlin's explanation in terms of quasi-particles was proven and accepted.

Storytelling, folk art practiced throughout the ages whose forms include the reciting of folk tales, myths, legends, epics, and fables. Some stories are handed down through the generations; others are created by an author. Storytelling has been used to transmit information about culture and history, explain the nature of existence, expand the imagination, entertain, and reinforce moral values. The earliest forms of storytelling combined narrative, music, and dance. Since the 1970s there has been a resurgence of interest in the art of storytelling.

Stoss, Veit (1440?-1533), influential German sculptor and wood carver who created dramatic, detailed religious statues in the late Gothic style. His most ambitious work, a carved and painted altar depicting the life of Mary, is located in the Church of St. Mary's in Krakow, Poland; it measures over 42 ft (13 m) high and 36 ft (11 m) wide.

Stowe, Harriet Beecher (1811-1896), U.S. writer, author of the antislavery novel *Uncle Tom's Cabin* (1852). From her home in Cincinnati, Ohio, she learned about slavery in nearby Kentucky. Her other books include the documentary *Key to Uncle Tom's Cabin* (1853) and the novels *Dred: A Tale of the Great Dismal Swamp* (1856) and *The Minister's Wooing* (1859). She was also committed to the temperance and woman suffrage movements.
See also: Abolitionism.

Strabismus, condition in which the 2 eyes do not see the identical image simultaneously; usually one eye is directed in a slightly different direction from the other. Most often this condition is the result of an eye muscle weakness (eye movement is controlled by 6 different muscles); it can also come from brain and nerve involvement. Forms of strabismus include heterotropia (squinting); esotropia (cross-eyes), where one or both eyes look inward; exotropia (walleyes), where one eye looks outward; and diplopia (double vision).

Strabo (63 B.C.?-A.D. 24?), ancient Greek geographer and historian known for his massive *Geographical Sketches*, a detailed description of the geography of the known world of his day. His work is a chief source of ancient knowledge on people and places

in Europe, Asia, and Africa. He also wrote a 47-volume work, *Historical Sketches,* which has not been recovered.
See also: Geography.

Strachey, Lytton (1880-1932), English critic and biographer who belonged to the famed circle of artists and intellectuals known as the Bloomsbury group in London. He revolutionized biographical writing with his imaginative, irreverent, and psychologically astute sketches of famous Victorian figures. He is best known for his biographies *Eminent Victorians* (1918) and *Queen Victoria* (1921).
See also: Bloomsbury group.

Stradivari, or **Stradivarius, Antonio** (1644-1737), Italian violin maker, most famous of a group of fine craftspeople who worked in Cremona. Stradivarius violins, violas, and cellos are highly prized.

Strait, narrow water channel that joins 2 larger bodies of water, such as an ocean or a sea. Major straits include the Bosporous Strait, the Strait of Magellan, and the Strait of Gibraltar. Considered strategically advantageous, they have been the focus of many of history's great battles.

Strand, Paul (1890-1976), U.S. photographer whose work helped raise photography to an art. He was best known for his photographs of modern machinery and of scenes of life in Manhattan. Later on in his life, Strand took nature photographs and worked a motion pictures.
See also: Photography.

Strasberg, Lee (1901-1981), a United States actor, director, and teacher. he developed the Method system of acting. This system, emphasizing the subjective quality in acting, is based on the theories of the Russian actor and director Konstantin Stanislavsky. Strasberg was born in Austria-Hungary. He came to the United States in 1909 and became a citizen in 1936. After holding various positions as a director and stage manager, Strasberg helped found the Group Theater in New York City in 1931 and directed it until 1937. He became the artistic director of Actors' Studio, a drama school, in 1948.

Strasbourg (pop. 258,000), commercial and industrial city in northeastern France, famed for its Gothic cathedral. A major river port linked with the Rhine and the Rhône, it has metallurgical, petroleum, heavy-machinery, and food-processing industries. Seat of the Council of Europe, it was a free imperial city until the French seized it in 1681. Strasbourg was under German rule from 1871 to 1919.

Strassmann, Fritz (1902-1980), German physical chemist who, with Otto Hahn, split the uranium atom (1938). He briefly joined the staff at the Kaiser Wilhelm Institute for Chemistry, taught inorganic and nuclear chemistry at the University of Mainz, and became the head of the Max Planck Institute for Chemistry. In 1966 the U.S. Atomic Energy Commission presented

him, Hahn, and Lise Meitner with the Fermi Award.
See also: Chemistry; Uranium.

Strategic Arms Limitation Talks (SALT), negotiations between the United States and the USSR aimed at preventing the expansion of strategic weapons in both countries. Salt I (1969-1972) achieved an antiballistic missile treaty and an interim agreement on some offensive nuclear weapons. Salt II was initiated in 1972. A treaty was signed in 1979, but ratification by the U.S. Senate was shelved (1980) after the USSR invaded Afghanistan. In 1982 the United States and USSR initiated a new series of negotiations called the Strategic Arms Reduction Talks (START). In 1991 the american president George Bush and the russian president Mikhail Gorbachev signed a treaty on the elimination of one third or their nuclear arsenal within seven years. In 1992 both parties agreed to even further reduction of nuclear weapons in START II.

Strategic Defense Initiative (SDI), controversial program developed by the U.S. government in 1983 to develop a space-based shield against nuclear missile attack. Commonly called 'Star Wars,' the program was to rely on satellites and lasers to destroy incoming missiles. Its opponents argued that it was impractical and costly. Funding for research on the project continues, although at a reduced rate. Part of the program has been replaced by GPALS, Global Protection Against Limited Strikes.

Strategic Services, Office of (OSS), U.S. government organization founded during World War II (1942) to gather intelligence. It was headed by William J. Donovan, working under the authority of the Joint Chiefs of Staff. With the end of the war the agency was dismantled, its tasks being distributed to the War Department and the Department of State. In 1947 the Central Intelligence Agency (CIA) became the successor to the OSS.
See also: Central Intelligence Agency (CIA).

Stratford-upon-Avon (pop. 24,000), market town in west-central England, home of William Shakespeare. A tourist mecca, it contains his birthplace (now a museum), his tomb, and the riverside theater where the Royal Shakespeare Company performs.
See also: England.

Stratosphere, layer of the atmosphere that extends upward from the tropopause (upper level of the troposphere) to approximately 18 mi (29 km) above the earth's surface. Its upper level is called the stratopause, which includes the ozone layer.
See also: Atmosphere.

Stratus *See:* Cloud.

Straus, Oscar (1870-1954), Austrian composer of about 50 operettas, notably *A Waltz Dream* (1907; film, 1926) and *The Chocolate Soldier* (1908; film, 1941), performed internationally. In the 1930s he wrote a half-dozen Hollywood film scores.

On November 17, 1969, the Strategic Arms Limitation Talks (SALT) started in the Finnish capital of Helsinki, between representatives of the United States and the Soviet Union. The talks achieved a certain restraint on armament with strategic rockets. Here, the Soviet representatives are sitting on the left side of the table, while the American delegation is on the right.

Strauss, Viennese composers, father and son. **Johann, the Elder** (1804-1849), achieved immense popularity and established the distinctive light style of the Viennese waltz. His son, **Johann, the Younger** (1825-1899), wrote many favorites, including the waltzes *The Blue Danube* (1866) and *Tales from the Vienna Woods* (1868), and the operetta *Die Fledermaus* (1873).

Strauss, Botho (1944-), German writer. Writes about the lost illusions of the 1960s, and offers a sobering vision of a society in which people are in danger of losing their individuality. His books include *Tumult* (1980), *The Young Man* (1984); plays include *Big and Little* (1978) and *The Park* (1983).

Strauss, Levi (1829-1902), German-born U.S. clothing manufacturer, founder of Levi Strauss & Co. (1853). The company began making denim work clothes in 1874, and was the world's first manufacturer of denim jeans.

Strauss, Richard (1864-1949), German composer and conductor, the last of the great Romantic composers. He leapt to fame with the tone poem *Don Juan* (1888). Other symphonic poems include *Till Eulenspiegel's Merry Pranks* (1895), *Thus Spake Zarathustra* (1896), *Don Quixote* (1898), and *A Hero's Life* (1898). After 1900 he concentrated on vocal music, and with Hugo von Hofmannsthal as librettist, produced brilliantly scored and popular operas, including *Salome* (1905), *Elektra* (1909), *Der Rosenkavalier* (1911), and *Die Frau ohne Schatten* (1919).

Stravinsky, Igor (1882-1971), Russian-born U.S. composer. He caused a sensation with his scores for the ballets *The Firebird* (1910), *Petrouchka* (1911), and *The Rite of Spring* (1913). Living in France from 1920, he adopted an austere neoclassical style, as in *Symphonies of Wind Instruments* (1920), the opera *Oedipus Rex* (1927), and *Symphony of Psalms* (1930). As a U.S. resident after 1939, he wrote many works, including *Symphony in*

S

S

Three Movements (1945) and the opera *The Rakes' Progress* (1951). He adopted 12-tone composition for such late pieces as *Agon* (1957) and *Threni* (1958).

Straw, dried stalks of several kinds of grain, including wheat, barley, oats, rye, and buckwheat. Straw is employed on farms for litter or bedding. It can also be used as livestock feed although it is inferior to hay in feeding value. Straw forms an important ingredient of farmyard manure and garden composts. In some parts of the world, houses are still thatched with straw.

Strawberry, fruit-bearing plant of the genus *Fragaria*, native to the Americas, Europe, and Asia. Strawberries have been cultivated locally for many centuries; most modern varieties originated in crosses between New World species.

Strawflower, any of various tall annual plants, originally grown in Australia, particularly the *Helichrysum bracteatum*, which measures up to 3 ft (91 cm). This plant produces a variously colored, paperlike flower that is commonly dried and used in winter bouquets.

Streamlining, process of contouring a body to minimize its drag as it travels through a fluid, whether liquid or gas. At subsonic speeds turbulent flow is minimized by using a rounded shape in the front of the body and tapering to a point in the rear. At supersonic

The string quartet comprises of four string instruments, usually two violins (A), a viola (B) and a cello (C).

speeds a different shape is needed, thin and pointed at both ends.
See also: Aerodynamics.

Stream of consciousness, literary technique in which a character's thoughts are presented in the jumbled, nonsequential manner of real life, apparently without the author imposing any order on them. Its best-known exponents are Marcel Proust, James Joyce, and Virginia Woolf.

Streep, Meryl (Mary Louise Streep; 1949-), U.S. actress. Streep made her New York stage debut in 1975. She has appeared in many successful films, including *The Deer Hunter* (1978), *Kramer vs. Kramer* (1979; Academy Award, best supporting actress), *Sophie's Choice* (1982; Academy Award, best actress), *Silkwood* (1983), *Out of Africa* (1985), *A Cry in the Dark* (1988), *House of the Spirits* (1992), *The River Wild* (1994), *The Bridges of Madison County* (1995), and *Music of the Heart* (1999).

Street, public road in a town or city. A street within an urban area usually has a sidewalk and buildings on one or both sides. Streets are part of a network of thoroughfares that include roads, highways, and expressways connecting communities and cities. Most modern streets are paved with tar or asphalt mixed with sand and crushed stone, although some may be paved with cobblestones, bricks, or concrete.

Streetcar, passenger vehicle that rides on rails laid in the pavements of city streets. Horse-drawn streetcars (horsecars) were first used in 1850/60. Electrified streetcars (trolley cars), developed in 1888, drew power from overhead lines by means of a trolley, a device consisting of a pole attached to a wheel that ran along the lines. Although internal combustion buses replaced streetcars during the mid-1900s, the use of streetcars may be on the increase because they are more energy-efficient and less polluting.

Streisand, Barbra (Barbara Joan Streisand; 1942-), American singer and actress. Made successful albums in the 1960s, such as *People* and *My Name Is Barbra*, also performed in musicals. After a number of acting roles in films she made a successful comeback as a singer in the 1970s. Her films include *Funny Girl* (William Wyler, 1968), *The Owl and the Pussycat* (Herbert Ross, 1970), *Hello Dolly* (Gene Kelly, 1971), *What's Up, Doc?* (Peter Bogdanovich, 1972), *The Way We Were* (Sydney Pollack, 1974), *Funny Lady* (Ross, 1975), *A Star Is Born* (Frank Pierson, 1975), *The Main Event* (1979), and *Nuts* (Martin Ritt, 1987). She also acted in and directed *Yentl* (1983), *The Prince of Tides* (1992) and *The Mirror Has Two Faces* (1996).

Strep throat, infection affecting the throat and tonsils. Its symptoms include fever and a reddening and swelling of the tonsils. The infection is caused by bacteria called *streptococci*, treatable with penicillin. Left untreated, the bacteria may spread from the throat to other parts of the body, such as the

lungs, nose, and ears, causing greater health problems.

Streptococcus, any of a genus of bacteria responsible for many common infections, including sore throat, tonsilitis, scarlet fever, and other ailments. Penicillin is the antibiotic of choice.

Streptomycin, strong antibiotic acquired from a fungus that lives in soil. Streptomycin has the ability to hinder bacteria's protein-creating process. Its discovery in 1943 led to its widespread use to treat infectious diseases, such as tuberculosis, pneumonia, typhoid fever, and spinal meningitis. However, it was found that with continued use, streptomycin loses its effectiveness and some bacteria become resistant to it. Streptomycin today has been replaced by more powerful antibiotics. *See also:* Antibiotic; Waksman, Selman Abraham.

Stress, in medicine, physical, chemical, or emotional factor that causes tension, whether physical or mental, and may result in disease or malfunction.

Strike, cessation of work by a group of employees to achieve certain goals. Reasons for a strike may include demands for higher wages, better working conditions, shorter work hours, and more benefits. Trade unions may play a role in strikes. Workers may strike to force the employer to recognize a certain union as their bargaining representative. Strikes are intended to create a financial loss for the company in goods produced or services rendered, thus prompting earnest negotiations. The first nationwide strike in the United States occurred in 1877, by railroad workers. As organized labor grew stronger in the late 19th century and strikes occurred more frequently, employers sometimes responded with harassment, engaging police or armed guards to disperse striking workers or to protect strike breakers. In Europe strikes involving all the workers of a nation or region are common.

Strindberg, Johan August (1849-1912), Swedish playwright and novelist, widely considered the leading author in the Swedish language. His biting, pessimistic plays, such as *Master Olof* (1873), *The Father* (1887), and *Miss Julie* (1888), have made a deep mark on modern drama. His novel *The Red Room* (1879), about injustice and hypocrisy, won international acclaim. Later plays, such as *The Ghost Sonata* (1907), combine dream sequences with Swedenborgian religious mysticism.

Stringed instruments, musical instruments whose sound is produced by vibrating strings or wires, the pitch being controlled by their length and tension. In the balalaika, banjo, guitar, harp, lute, mandolin, sitar, ukulele, and zither, the vibration is produced by plucking with the fingers or a plectrum. The strings of the dulcimer are struck with 2 small, light hammers. In the keyboard instruments-clavichord, harpsichord, piano, spinet, virginal-the strings are either plucked or struck by hammers operated by depressing the keys. The violin, viola, cello, and bass are played with a horsehair bow, which is drawn across the strings, or the strings are plucked.

Strip mining, technique used where ore deposits, such as coal, lie close enough to the surface to be uncovered merely by removal of the overlying material.

Stroessner, Alfredo (1912-), president of Paraguay (1954-1989). An army commander, he took power in a coup and established a totalitarian dictatorship that proved one of Latin America's most stable. He was ousted in a coup in 1989 during his eighth term as president.

Stroheim, Erich von (1885-1957), German-born U.S. film director. Working under D. W. Griffith, Stroheim became known for his realism, careful construction, and attention to detail, as in *Greed* (1924) and *The Wedding March* (1928), in which he also acted. Other distinguished screen performances were in *Grand Illusion* (1937) and *Sunset Boulevard* (1950).

Stroke, or cerebrovascular accident (CVA), sudden loss of some aspect of brain function due to lack of blood supply to a given area. Stroke may result from embolism, arteriosclerosis and thrombosis, or hemorrhage (in which case it is termed apoplexy). Areas with permanent loss of blood supply do not recover, but other areas may take over their function.

Stromboli, Italian island located in the Tyrrhenian Sea, off northeastern Sicily. It has an area of approximately 5 sq mi (13 sq km) and contains an active volcano, which is 3,031 ft (924 m) high. The volcano produces a continuous flow of lava that pours into the sea. Its volcano, as well as its climate and beaches, make Stromboli a popular tourist attraction.

Strontium, chemical element, symbol Sr; for physical constants see Periodic Table. Strontium was discovered by Adair Crawford in 1790. In nature it is found as celestite and strontianite. Strontium is prepared by electrolysis of its fused chloride mixed with potassium chloride. Strontium is a silvery-white, soft, reactive metal, a member of the alkaline earth metals. It reacts with water more vigorously than calcium, and quickly oxides in air. Strontium-90, present in nuclear fallout, is a strong, long-lived beta emitter and is of potential use in nuclear-electric power devices. Strontium and its compounds are used in fireworks, flares, glass for color television picture tubes, and optical materials.

Struve, Otto (1897-1963), U.S. astronomer. Struve studied the wavelengths of the light emitted from stars to help him draw conclusions about the stars-such as their size, and gases and elements in or surrounding them. *See also:* Astronomy; Star.

Struycken, Peter (1939-), Dutch artist. His working method is based on logical systems and coincidence. Researched the mutual relationship between shape and color; visual elements that make a structure visible. From 1968 onwards uses computers. Also produced large works, including a piece for the auditorium of the Kröller-Muller museum in Otterlo (Netherlands) (1977), and the ceiling of the Muziektheater in Amsterdam (1987).

Strychnine, poisonous alkaloid produced from the seeds of the *Strychnos nux vomica* tree, which grows in India, Sri Lanka, and Australia. It can cause violant spinal convulsions and asphyxia, which can be fatal if not treated swiftly with barbiturate sedatives.

Stuart, Charles Edward (1720-1788), pretender to the throne of England. The grandson of James II, he was known as the Young Pretender and, in Scotland, as Bonnie Prince Charlie. After the French refused to support his cause, he rallied the Highland clans to invade England, but was defeated at Culloden Moor in 1746.
See also: United Kingdom.

Stuart, Gilbert Charles (1755-1828), U.S. portrait painter, best known for the portrait of George Washington (1796) reproduced on the one-dollar bill. Praised for his use of color, technique, and psychological insight, he painted nearly 1,000 portraits and created a distinctive U.S. portrait style.

Stuart, House of, royal family of Scotland (1371-1714) and England (1603-1714). The first Stuart king, **Robert II** (r. 1371-1390) was a hereditary steward of Scotland whose father had married a daughter of Robert the Bruce. A descendant, **James IV** (r. 1488-1513), married Margaret, daughter of Henry VII of England (r. 1567-1625). Their grandson, **James VI** (r. 1603-1625), became James I of England. Between 1603 and 1714, six Stuarts ruled: James I, his son Charles I (r. 1625-1649), Charles II (r. 1660-1685), James II (deposed 1688), Mary II, wife of William III (r. 1689-1694), and Anne (1702-1714).
See also: Scotland.

Stuck, Franz von (1863-1928), German painter; studied at the Munich art academy and lectured there from 1895 onwards; taught Kandinsky, Klee and Geiger. Stuck was originally influenced by the Pre-Raphaelites. After having worked mainly as a graphic artist (illustrating the Fliegende Blätter), he turned to painting, particularly the representation of symbolic themes, including *Innocentia* (1889), *Kämpfende Faune* (1889), *Die Sünde* (1893), which are currently part of the Bavarian state collection in Munich. Stuck was the one of the founders of the Munich Secession in 1892. The house in Munich he designed and decorated himself is an example of a Jugendstil 'total artwork' (since 1936 the Stuck Museum). Stuck was one of the most important exponents of Jugendstil.

Sturgeon, fish of the north temperate zone whose eggs are eaten as caviar. Sturgeon have a row of bony plates down the side of the body and sharklike tailfins; toothless, they suck their food (mostly crayfish) from the water bottom. Most of the 2 dozen or so species are marine but breed in fresh water. The largest is the Russian sturgeon, or bellu-

ga (*Acipenser huso*), which grows to 13 ft (4 m) and can weigh 2,000 lb (908 kg). This species, which lives entirely in fresh water, provides half the world's caviar. The white sturgeon of the U.S. Pacific Northwest has been overfished and is now much reduced in number.

Sturges, Preston (1898-1959), U.S. playwright, screenwriter, and film director. His films, many of them witty satires of U.S. life and values, include *The Great McGinty* (1940), *Sullivan's Travels* (1941), and *The Miracle of Morgan's Creek* (1944).

Sturm und Drang (German, 'storm and stress'), name given to a period of literary ferment in Germany (1770-1784). Influenced by Jean Jacques Rousseau, its leading figures-Johann Gottfried von Herder, Johann Wolfgang von Goethe, and Friedrich von Schiller-espoused an antirationalist and rebellious individualism in opposition to the prevailing classicism.

Stuttering, speech impairment characterized by repeated attempts to pronounce a syllable or word.

Stuttgart (pop. 588,000), capital of Baden-Württemberg, a state in southwest Germany. Stuttgart is a major governing, industrial, and cultural center in West Germany. Once the capital of the Württemberg kingdom, Stuttgart is situated on the Neckar River, in a rich farm and vineyard region. Besides producing wines and fruits, Stuttgart manufactures automobiles, machines, precision instruments, tools, computers, musical instruments, beer, and paper. It has more than 200 publishing houses. A powerful manufacturing center, Stuttgart was severely bombed by the Allies during World War II; it has since been rebuilt. Some of the many historic buildings in Stuttgart are notable for their fine architecture. Two examples are the Old Palace, which was built in the Renaissance style, and the New Palace, which was built in the baroque and rococo styles; both were the homes of rulers of Württemberg. Stuttgart is culturally active with museums and an opera house, as well as schools for art, architecture, and music.
See also: Germany.

Stuyvesant, Peter (c.1610-1672), Dutch director-general (1647-1664) of New Netherland, Holland's North American colony, which included the city of New Amsterdam, later renamed New York. Autocratic and unpopular, he lost Dutch territory to Connecticut in 1650, conquered and annexed New Sweden in 1655, and finally surrendered New Netherland to England in 1664, after his citizens failed to support him against a surprise English attack. He retired to his farm, 'the Bouwerie,' now New York's Bowery.

Sty, infection in an eyelash follicle or in a gland in the eyelid. A sty is usually caused by staphylococcus bacteria. Sties are treated with antibiotics and, in some cases, with surgery.

Styron, William (1925-), U.S. novelist and winner of the 1968 Pulitzer Prize for *The*

S

S

Confessions of Nat Turner (1967), a first-person novelization of an 1831 slave rebellion. Other novels include *Lie Down in Darkness* (1951), *Sophie's Choice* (1979), *Darkness Visible: a Memoir of Madness* (1990), and *A Tidewater Morning* (1993).

Styx, in Greek mythology, river of the underworld. The souls of the dead had to cross the Styx to reach Hades, the underworld. For payment, the boatman Charon would ferry them across. *Styx* in Greek means 'hateful.' The Greeks abhorred death. According to the Greek poet Homer, the gods made their most important oaths in the name of the Styx. If a god lied, he or she would be punished severely by being banished to a deep pit in the underworld for nine years. The Styx was thought to begin at a waterfall in Arcadia, an ancient Greek region.
See also: Mythology.

Suárez, Francisco (1548-1617), Spanish Jesuit philosopher who represented a late flowering of Scholasticism. He was an influential political and legal theorist, attacking the divine right of kings and arguing that international law was based on custom, not natural law.
See also: Scholasticism.

Sublimation, in chemistry, act of changing a solid into a gas, or a gas into a solid, without going through a liquid stage. Some substances when heated vaporize and become a gas, without melting into a liquid first. When the gas is cooled, the substance returns directly to a solid state. Examples of such substances are dry ice and iodine crystals. Sublimation is used to purify substances: When the solid is heated, only the substance that is pure becomes a gas-the impurities remain solid. When the impurities are removed the substance becomes refined.

Submarine, ship capable of sustained underwater operation. The first working craft, built by the Dutch inventor Cornelis Drebbel (1620), was a wooden rowboat covered with greased leather that could remain submerged for as long as 15 hours. The first submarine used in warfare, designed by David Bushnell of the United States (1776), was a one-man, hand-powered, screw-driven vessel designed to attach mines to enemy ships. In the Civil War the Confederate states produced several submarines. Later (late 1800s and early 1900s) John P. Holland and his rival Simon Lake designed vessels powered by gasoline engines on the surface and by electric motors when submerged. The forerunners of modern submarines, they were armed with

torpedoes and guns. Great advances were made during World War I and World War II. German U-boats introduced snorkels to hinder detection while recharging batteries. The first nuclear-powered submarine was the USS *Nautilus* (1955), which made the first voyage under the polar ice-cap (1958). Modern submarines are streamlined vessels, generally with a double hull, the inner one a pressure hull separated from the outer one by fuel and ballast tanks. The submarine submerges by flooding the ballast tanks to displace its own weight of water. It uses hydrofoil diving planes. Besides their military applications, submarines are used for oceanographic research and exploration, salvage, and rescue.

Suburb, community that lies on the outskirts of a city. Suburbs can be residential or industrial, or a combination of both. A city may have any number of suburbs surrounding it. A suburb may be self-governing, or be governed by the city near it, or by the county in which it lies. Suburbs began in the late 19th century when railroad expansion enabled people to work in a city and commute to homes outside of it. Suburbs blossomed further with the development of automobiles and roads. Now, more people live in suburbs than in cities.

Subway, underground railroad system designed for urban and suburban passenger transport. The first subway, known as the Underground, was built in London (1860-1863) and used steam trains. From 1886 to 1890 a 3-mile section of the London subway was built using a large, cylindrical steel tube (developed by J.H. Greathead) that was forced forward through the earth by hydraulic jacks; tunnel walls were then built around it. This technique made deep tunnels possible without surface disturbance. The London 'tube' thus constructed was the first to use electrically-powered trains, which soon replaced steam trains everywhere. Many cities throughout the world then followed London's lead, notably Paris (begun 1898) and New York (begun 1900). The New York subway, using multiple-unit trains developed by Frank Sprague, is now the largest in the world. The Moscow subway (begun 1931) is noted for its palatial marble stations. Many cities have extended, improved, and automated their subway systems to reduce surface congestion. Some, such as Montreal, have introduced quieter rubber-

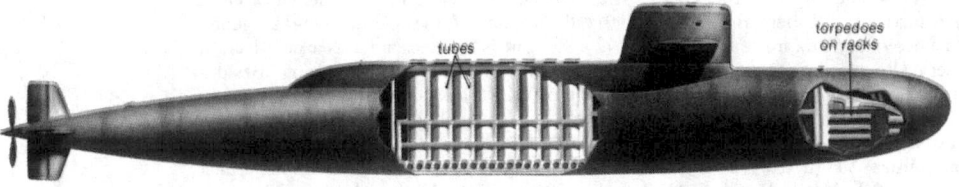

The U.S.S. *Patrick Henry*, a nuclear-powered submarine, carries 16 Polaris missiles that have a range of 1,200 mi (1,920 km). Polaris subs came into use during the 1960s and changed the role of the sub in naval warfare. Besides destroying enemy ships, they could launch nuclear missiles against inland targets without surfacing and could stay underwater for long periods of time.

The German World War II U-boat was named after the German word Unterseeboot, meaning 'submarine'. During the war, by day these boats operated in packs, to stalk convoys of Allied merchant ships crossing the Atlantic. At night, they surfaced and attacked. With these tactics, they succeeded in destroying millions of tons of Allied shipping, until the Allies used radar and air and sea escorts.

The German Class 31-37 submarine, or U-boat, cruised underwater at 11.6 mi/h (10.1 knots) and packed four torpedo launchers. Under Germany's policy of unrestricted submarine warfare, U-boats harassed Allied commercial shipping, as well as naval targets.

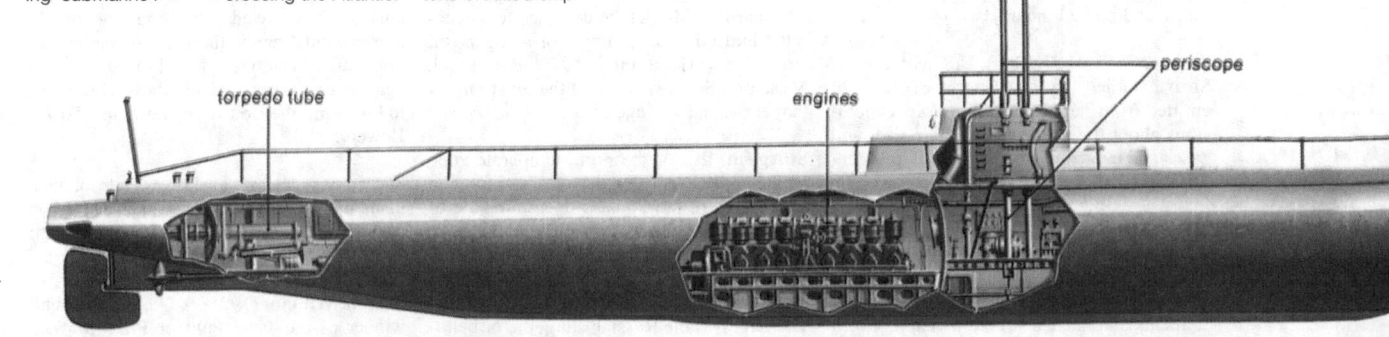

S

Passenger cars of the underground rail transit system of 6 major cities. The subway operated by the New York City Transit Authority (A), the second largest system in the world, has 231 mi (372 km) of track, and it connects Manhattan to other boroughs of the city and New Jersey. This rail system serves more than 1 billion passengers annually. The U-Bahn railway of Berlin (B), operated by the Berliner Verkehrs-Betriebe, has more than 900 cars in service, and it conveys 285 million passengers a year. Montreal's subway (C), of which construction was begun in 1962, features rubber-tired cars to provide an exceptionally smooth, quiet ride. London's subway (D), the most extensive metropolitan system in the world, was opened in 1863 and has 9 separate lines. Stockholm's subway (E), operated by AB Storstockholms Lokaltrafik, uses only motor and trailer cars that were built in Sweden. The system carries 175 million passengers annually. The Paris Métro (F), which began operating in 1900, is notable for its large number of stations (404) along the length of the system.

tired trains that run on concrete guideways. *See also:* Railroad.

Succession wars, conflicts that result from disagreements about who should inherit a throne, or who should succeed a monarch. These disputes usually arise when a monarch has no child, or son, to whom to pass the throne. Europe has experienced 4 succession wars, all during the 18th century. They were the War of Spanish Succession (1701-1714), the War of Polish Succession (1733-1738), the War of Austrian Succession (1740-1748), and the War of Bavarian Succession (1778-1779).

Succot *See:* Sukkot.

Succulent, category of plants whose leaves or stems are covered with a waxy substance that reduces water loss and enables them to live in arid regions. Cacti are the most familiar, but aloes and yuccas are other examples. Many succulents have attractive foliage and colorful flowers.

Sucker, any of various freshwater fishes (family Catostomidae) related to the minnows. Most suckers live in North America, but there are a few in Asia. They have thick lips and feed by sucking food from the bottoms of lakes and rivers. Some suck up mud and eject inedible matter, while others turn over pebbles and suck the animals attached to the underside. A few have hard lips for scraping rocks.

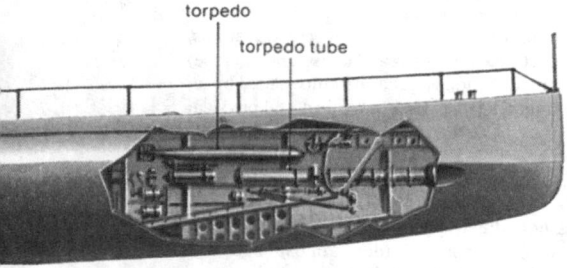
torpedo
torpedo tube

Suckling, Sir John (1609-1642), poet and playwright. Suckling belonged to a troup known as the Cavalier poets, associated with the court of the British king Charles I. Born into a wealthy family in Middlesex, he was knighted at the age of 21 and became a familiar figure at court, where he was a colorful, witty, gallant character. Suckling was a friend of the king, whom he accompanied in the war against the Scots in 1639. In 1641 Suckling fled to Paris when he was suspected of taking part in a scheme to free the earl of Strafford from prison. He died shortly thereafter, perhaps by suicide. Suckling's works include the plays *Aglaura* (1637), a tragedy, and *The Goblins* (1638), a comedy. He also wrote *A Session of Poets* (1637), an entertaining verse about famous poets much admired by his contemporaries.
See also: Navy.

Sucre (pop. 112,000), city in central Bolivia, founded as La Plata in 1538 and renamed for Antonio José de Sucre in 1839. A commercial and agricultural center and the seat of the national university and the Supreme Court, Sucre is the judicial capital of Bolivia. It is 250 mi (400 km) southeast of La Paz, which is the administrative capital of the country.
See also: Bolivia.

Sucre, Antonio José de (1795-1830), important leader in Latin American wars against Spanish rule and first president of Bolivia (1826-1828). Born in Venezuela, he joined the revolutionary army at age 15 and soon displayed great military skills. He gained the respect of the Venezuelan leader of the Latin American revolution, Simón Bolívar, who made him a general. In the course of several battles, Sucre successfully drove the Spanish from Ecuador and Bolivia. Bolívar appointed Sucre lifetime president of Bolivia (1826). Sucre agreed to serve 2 years, after which time he wanted to retire to Ecuador. Although he was a skillful executive, his attempts to set up a strong Bolivian government were thwarted by other political groups. He resigned his office in 1828 and withdrew to Ecuador when the Peruvian army invaded Bolivia. The next year he returned to drive away the Peruvian invaders. Sucre was assassinated the following year by what were believed to be opponents of Simón Bolívar. He is considered a Latin American hero. The capital of Bolivia is named after him.
See also: Bolivia.

Sucrose, white, crystalline disaccharide carbohydrate ($C_{12}H_{22}O_{11}$) commercially obtained from sugar beet, sugarcane, and sweet sorghum. Common table sugar, sucrose is composed of a glucose unit joined to a fructose unit. Sucrose is produced from juice or sap, which is evaporated to form molasses. Additional evaporation yields brown-colored sugar, which is whitened through further refining.
See also: Sugar.

Sudan

Capital:	Khartoum
Area:	966,472 sq mi
	(2,503,813 sq km)
Population:	37,090,000
Language:	Arabic
Government:	Islamic republic
Independent:	1956
Head of gov.:	President
Per capita:	less than US$ 1,360
Monetary unit:	1 Sudanese dinar = 10 pound
	= 100 piastres

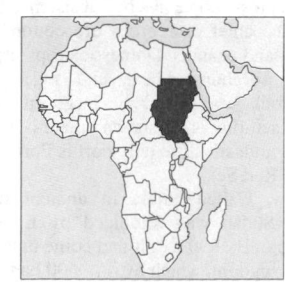

Sudan, Republic of the Sudan, largest country in Africa, located in the northeast of the continent.
Land and climate. Sudan occupies 967,494

S

Agricultural workers gather long-staple cotton from a field in the Gezira region, Sudan's principal cotton-growing area.

sq mi (2,505,813 sq km) and is bounded on the north by Egypt; on the west by Libya, Chad, the Central African Republic, and Congo; on the south by Uganda and Kenya; and on the east by Ethiopia and Eritrea. It has a 400-mi (644-km) coastline on the Red Sea. Sudan may be divided into two main regions: the barren desert region north of Khartoum, comprising about one-third of the country, and the well-watered region of the south. The Nile River enters Sudan from Uganda in the south and crosses the entire length of the country on its way to Egypt and the Mediterranean. In the far south is a region of tropical forest and to the southeast wooded grassland. Further north is the Sudd region, a great marshy area where the river is congested with floating vegetation. Between the Sudd and Khartoum, the central area of the Sudan is grasslands. At Khartoum the White Nile is joined by the Blue Nile, both branches of the Nile flowing north to form a triangle of land between them whose apex is at Khartoum, where the rivers meet. The land between them is the Gezira plain, the most fertile part of the Sudan. Beyond Khartoum to the north, the Nile flows through the Libyan and Nubian deserts. In the northeast there are mountain ranges bordering the Red Sea coastal plain. The prevailing climate of the Sudan is hot with rainfall increasing in frequency toward the south. The capital is Khartoum.

People. The people are divided into Arabic-speaking Muslims in the north and black African and Nilotic peoples of the south and west. The Muslims are 80% of the population and profess Sunni Islam. The black Africans are mainly animists and Christians. *Economy.* The Sudan is basically agricultural, and most people live by subsistence farming. The chief cash crops are cotton, gum arabic, and peanuts. Domestic crops include millet, sorghum, wheat, and sugar cane. Livestock are raised in large numbers. Manufacturing is limited and there is a small mining industry. The only port is Port Sudan on the Red Sea.

History. Called Nubia in ancient times, North Sudan was colonized by Egypt in 2000 B.C. By 800 B.C. it had come under the Cush kingdom, which by A.D. 600 had given way to independent Coptic Christian states. In the 13th to 15th centuries they collapsed under Muslim expansion, and the Muslim Funj state was established, lasting until Egypt invaded the Sudan in 1821. The nationalist Mahdi led a revolt in 1881, after

which a series of campaigns resulted in joint Anglo-Egyptian rule in 1899. Since independence in 1956, the country has been racked by civil war pitting southerners fearful of Muslim dominance against northerners. By 1972 1.5 million southerners had died in the fighting but some autonomy had been achieved for the south. Hostilities have continued and Sudan has been additionally burdened in recent years by an influx of nearly half a million refugees fleeing war and famine in neighboring countries. A 1989 coup brought to power an authoritarian Islamist government, led by General Umar Hassan Ahmad al-Bashir, just as a coalition of moderates appeared set to govern. The United Nations condemned Sudan for human rights violations (including the imposition of human slavery). In 1997 the US decided to impose harsh sanctions against Sudan due to Sudan's supposed support of international terrorism. The continuing hostilities resulted in a famine (1998).

The civil war between the government army of President Umar al-Bashir and the Sudan People Liberation Army (SPLA) ended for the time being in 2002. The parties signed a peace agreement and the leaders met. However, the US maintained several sanctions against Sudan. January 2003, the Secretaries of State from Sudan, Ethiopia and Yemen formed an alliance to fight against terrorism in the 'Horn of Africa'.

Sudan grass (*Sorghum vulgare*, variety *sudanese*), hay plant in the grass family. Native to Sudan, in northeastern Africa, this grass was brought to the United States in 1909 to be planted in dry areas because it needs very little water to grow. Farmers grow it to feed their livestock. Sudan grass, first grown in the South and Southwest, now is found throughout the United States.

Sudden infant death syndrome, sudden, unexpected death of an apparently healthy infant, also known as SIDS, crib death, or cot death. It usually occurs while the baby is asleep during the night. Victims' ages range from 2 weeks to 1 year. More crib deaths occur during cold than warm weather. SIDS strikes approximately 1 out of every 350 babies in the United States. It kills more boys than girls, and claims more children born prematurely and those born in poverty. The causes for crib death are difficult and sometimes impossible to determine. A baby dying of SIDS will first turn blue and then stop breathing. Investigation of cases has led to the belief that victims of SIDS may have a slightly defective nervous system that stops their breathing and heart.

Sudetenland, region in the north of the Czech Republic. Originally designated as the area of the Sudetes Mountains on the Bohemia-Silesia border, it came to apply to all the German-speaking Bohemian and Moravian borderlands incorporated into Czechoslovakia in 1919. The Sudetenland was ceded to Nazi Germany by the Munich Pact in 1938 and restored to Czechoslovakia in 1945.
See also: Czech Republic.

Suez (pop. 392,000), city in Egypt located at the top of the Gulf of Suez. The southern en-

tranceway into the Suez Canal, it is an important Egyptian port and major industrial center. Railways and roads connect it to Cairo, 80 mi (130 km) west. Its major industries are oil refinement and the manufacture of artificial fertilizer. Suez has been a port since ancient times. Its economy and industries blossomed with the opening of the Suez Canal in 1869. Suez's industries suffered much destruction during the Arab-Israeli War, causing the canal to be closed. Since then, the industries have been rebuilt, and the canal was reopened in 1975.
See also: Egypt.

Suez Canal, canal in Egypt linking the Gulf of Suez (an arm of the Red Sea) to the eastern Mediterranean. About 100 mi (160 km) long, the canal cut over 4,000 mi (6,400 km) from the route from Britain to India and has been a major commercial waterway since its opening in 1869. It has a minimum width of 179 ft (54 m), a dredged depth of almost 40 ft (12 m), and no locks. Work began in 1859 under Ferdinand de Lesseps. In 1875 Britain acquired the canal from the Ottoman ruler of Egypt. In 1956 it was nationalized by President Gamal Abdel Nasser, prompting an invasion by Britain, France, and Israel. After UN intervention, the canal reopened in 1957 under Egyptian control. It was closed again by the Arab-Israeli War of 1967, but cleared of wreckage in 1974 and reopened in 1975. The canal was deepened (1976-1980) to permit the passage of oil tankers up to 500,000 tons (453,600 metric tons) and 53 ft (16 m) in draft.

Suffrage *See:* Woman suffrage.

Sufism, Muslim mystical philosophical and literary movement dating from the 10th and 11th centuries. Stressing personal communion with God through ascetic practices or quietism, it has spread throughout Islam in a variety of forms, most apparently in Persia. Al-Ghazali was Sufism's greatest philosophical exponent, and among its great literary exponents are the poets Omar Khayyam and Hafiz.
See also: Omar Khayyam.

Sugai, Kumi (1919-96), Japanese painter. Studied at the academy of Osaka and moved to Paris in 1952, painted visions of dreams reduced to simple geometric forms. His later work was influenced by Op Art, where he allowed himself to be inspired by the speed of the modern age, painting images of motorways, rockets, etc.

Sugar, sweet, soluble compound of carbon, hydrogen, and oxygen. There are 3 groups of sugars. Monosaccharides (such as fructose and glucose) are called simple because they contain a single chain of carbon atoms. Disaccharides (such as lactose and sucrose) contain 2 monosaccharide units joined by an oxygen bridge. Their chemical and physical properties are similar to those of monosaccharides. Trisaccharides (such as raffinose) are composed of 3 monosaccharide units.

Sugar beet, plant (*Beta vulgaris*) whose swollen root provides almost half the world's sugar. It was first extensively grown

The root of sugar beets, *B. vulgaris*, yield a substantial amount of the world's total sugar. Beet tops and by-products of the sugar-extraction process are used as animal feed.

in Europe to replace cane sugar from the West Indies, supplies of which were cut off during the Napoleonic Wars. Sugar beet is grown in all temperate areas in which cool summers ensure good sugar formation.

Sugar cane (*Saccharum officinarum*), tall plant of the grass family. It grows in tropical and semitropical regions throughout the world. The plant is made up of a solid stalk with joints at regular intervals. Each joint has a single bud. Stalks grow to a height of 7-26 ft (2-8 m), with a diameter of 1.5-2 in (3.5-5 cm). The color of the stalk ranges from yellow to green, violet, or red, depending on the variety. Long, thin leaves grow from the stalk, which contains a juice from which sugar and syrup is made. It was grown as early as 8,000 years ago in the South Pacific. The leading producers of sugar cane are Brazil, India, and Cuba. Sugercane by-products include molasses, rum, alcohol, fuel, and livestock feed.

Sugar maple *See:* Maple.

Suharto (1921-), Indonesian statesman, president 1968-1998. A general, he defeated an attempted Communist coup in 1965, in the process overthrowing the government of Sukarno and killing as many as 500,000 people. Popular unrest and an economic crisis forced him to resign in 1998. He was brought to trial for corruption in 2000.
See also: Indonesia.

Suicide, act of voluntarily taking one's own life. In some societies (notably Japan's) suicide is accepted or even expected in the face of disgrace. Judaism, Islam, and Christianity, however, condemn it. Until 1961 the United Kingdom sought to discourage it by making it a crime, and it is still illegal in some U.S. states. Suicide attempts are often considered by psychologists implicit pleas for help and may result from extreme depression.

Sui dynasty, dynasty (ruling family) that governed China from A.D. 581-618. Its first ruler, **Yang Jian**, united North and South China, which had been involved in a lengthy civil war. After his death in 604, his son **Sui Yangdi** worked to strengthen the unified territory's government and economy. One of his most outstanding projects was the building of the Grand Canal, a waterway system over which products could be shipped between northern and southern China. Yangdi suffered military defeats, however, when he tried to overtake Korea and Manchuria, and when he fought Eastern Turks. He was overthrown and assassinated. The Sui dynasty ended with his death in 618. The T'ang dynasty, which began that same year, adopted many of the policies and systems established by the Sui dynasty.
See also: China.

Suite, musical form developed in Germany and France in the 17th and 18th centuries, originally inspired by dance. By the 19th century it had lost its connection to dance. The Baroque suite and its component movements-allemande, courante, sarabande, and gigue-is the more well-known suite form.

Sukarno (1901-1970), first president of independent Indonesia (1945-1965). A leader of the independence movement from 1927, he was instrumental in creating the republic in 1945. His flamboyant rule turned dictatorial in 1959 and in 1963 he proclaimed himself president for life. In 1965 an attempted coup by the Communist Party, which had been his ally, was crushed by Gen. Suharto who assumed de facto power from Sukarno, formally removing him from the presidency in 1966. Sukarno was placed under house arrest until his death.
See also: Indonesia.

Sukenobu, Nishikawa (1671-1751), Japanese painter, one of the most well-known Ukiyo-e artists in Kyoto. He chiefly worked with prints, sometimes signing himself with the pseudonym Yittokusai (he who understands from within). Sukenobu almost exclusively portrayed women and girls just like countless other graphic artists. He also designed kimonos and illustrated more than 300 books. His enormous output was an inexhaustible source of inspiration for later masters, including Harunobu.

Sukkot, or Feast of Tabernacles, 8-day autumn Jewish festival, during which meals are taken in a hut (sukkah) roofed with branches and fruits to symbolize the shelters used by the ancient Hebrews during their wanderings after the Exodus from Egypt.
See also: Simhat Torah.

Sulawesi (pop. 13,279,000), one of the four main islands of Indonesia, bordered by the Sulawesi Sea, the Molucca Sea, the Banda Sea and the Makassar Strait; 73,085 sq mi (189,216 sq km). Divided into Sulawesi Utara, capital Manado, and Sulawesi, capital Ujung Pandang (Makassar). Four mountainous, volcanic peninsulas; tropical monsoon climate. Populated by Makassarese, Buginese, Torajans, Minahasans, and Gerontalese. Agriculture (rice, copra), fishing, and forestry. Rich in natural resources (nickel, copper). The Portuguese were the first Westerners on the islands; they were displaced by the Dutch East India Company, who built a fort there in 1655. During WW II occupied by Japan; since 1950 part of Indonesia. From that time onwards the islands have been the scene of regular revolts against the Indonesian government (led by Andi Azis and Kahar Muzakkar; Premesta rebellion, 1958), which have been brutally repressed (e.g. aerial bombardments).

Suleiman I, or **Sulayman** (1494-1566), sultan of Ottoman Empire from 1520-1566. He was also known as The Magnificent and The Lawgiver. His reign was marked by his numerous successful military campaigns and the legal, literary, and artistic achievements of his empire. He waged ground and naval wars in parts of Europe, Asia Minor, and Africa, enlarging his territory with each successive victory. During a brief period his navy dominated the Mediterranean Sea, the Red Sea, and the Persian Gulf. He did not succeed, however, in his naval warfare against Holy Roman Emperor Charles V and Venice. His court included lawyers, artists, writers and architects, whom he engaged to help him create his vision of a magnificent and sophisticated empire.
See also: Ottoman Empire.

Sulfa drug, any of various synthetic compounds derived from sulfanilimide that inhibit the multiplication of invading bacteria, thus allowing the body's cellular defense mechanisms to suppress infection. The first sulfa drug was synthesized in 1908 and used widely as a dye before Gerhard Domagk reported its effectiveness against streptococci (1938). In recent years many sulfa drugs have been replaced by antibiotics in the treatment of bacterial infections.

Sulfate, chemical mixture containing sulfur and oxygen. Sulfates are usually formed in crystals. Epsom salt and gypsum are two common sulfates. Most sulfates are water soluble, but some, such as lead sulfates, are not. Industrial uses for sulfates include fabric printing and dying and the manufacture of medicine and varnishes.

The members of the Toraja tribe in Sulawesi decorate their houses with abstract motifs, mainly in red, blue and white.

S

Sulfide, compound of sulfur and another element or elements. The element-made up of atoms that are alike and cannot be changed chemically-may be a metal, such as silver or gold, or a gas, such as oxygen or hydrogen. Sulfides have various industrial uses. When sulfur burns, it produces a poisonous gas. A mixture of carbon and sulfur is used as an insecticide. In small doses, it is used as an anesthetic. Some sulfides are used to create color in paints.

Sulfur, chemical element, symbol S; for physical constants see Periodic Table. Sulfur has been known and used for thousands of years. It is referred to in the bible as brimstone. As a mineral, it occurs in iron pyrites, galena, sphalerite, Epsom salts, barite, and many others. It occurs free in nature in the vicinity of volcanoes and hot springs. Sulfur is also found in the atmosphere of Venus and in meteorites and interstellar clouds. It is produced commercially using the Frasch process in which heated water is used to melt underground sulfur that is then brought to the surface. Sulfur is a yellow, brittle, low melting, reactive nonmetal. It readily forms sulfides with many elements. Hydrogen sulfide is poisonous and can cause death by respiratory paralysis. Sulfur forms several allotropes amorphous and crystalline. Sulfur is essential to human and animal life. Sulfur and its compounds are used in gunpowder, in the vulcanization of rubber, as a fungicide, in making sulfite paper, as a fumigant, and in bleaching dried fruits. It is used to produce sulfuric acid, the most important manufactured chemical.

Sulfur dioxide (SO_2), colorless, poisonous gas that has a sharp smell. It is released naturally in gases emitted during volcanic eruptions. Factories or refineries that burn oil or coal also release sulfur dioxide into the atmosphere, creating the potential for human health problems. Sulfur dioxide in the atmosphere may form acid rain when it dissolves in water droplets. Acid rain is damaging to the environment, killing animals and plants. For this reason, many nations are concerned about how much sulfur dioxide their industries should be allowed to release into the air.
See also: Acid rain.

Sulfuric acid, chemical compound (H_2SO_4) that is a colorless, oily liquid that corrodes materials. Exposure to it or its fumes can damage a person's nose, lungs, and skin. Sulfuric acid has been used since the 15th century. In the 19th century it was discovered that adding sulfuric acid to soil made the soil more fertile for plant growth; this discovery led to improved methods of manufacturing sulfuric acid. Besides being used in the manufacture of fertilizer, sulfuric acid is used in steel processing, petroleum refining, and the manufacture of other acids. Because it is so strong and potentially dangerous, great caution must be taken when handling sulfuric acid.

Sulla, Lucius Cornelius (138-78 B.C.), Roman general and ruler. Sulla was born into the Roman upper class and entered politics as a praetor in 94 B.C. In 88 B.C., after fighting in the Social War, he became one of two consuls ruling Rome. As a military leader, he successfully fought armies of King Mithridates VI of Pontus that were attempting to overtake Roman territories (87-85 B.C.). After Mithridates surrendered, Sulla returned to Rome to confront his opponents, headed by Marius, who accused him of being an enemy of Rome (83 B.C.). He won the civil war against them the following year and became a dictator. Sulla initiated many reforms, such as restoring power to the Senate, but his reign was known for cruelty and illegality. He retired in 79 B.C.
See also: Marius, Gaius; Rome, Ancient.

Sullivan, Harry Stack (1892-1949), U.S. psychiatrist and head of William Alanson White Institute and Washington School of Psychiatry, who contributed to the study of schizophrenia and originated the idea that psychiatry depends on study of culture and its influence on behavior.
See also: Psychiatry.

Sullivan, John L., U.S. boxing champion. Sullivan was the last bare-knuckle heavyweight champion, winning the title from Paddy Ryan in 1882 and defending it again in 1888 and 1889. He then boxed with gloves under the Queensbury Rules, losing his title to James J. Corbett in 1892.

Sullivan, Leon Howard (1922-), Baptist minister whose numerous projects have improved economic opportunities for African Americans. In 1977 he initiated a plan for equal treatment of black Africans in South Africa.

Sullivan, Louis Henri (1856-1924), U.S. architect whose office buildings pioneered modern design. In partnership with Dankmar Adler in Chicago (1881-1895), he championed the view that a building's form should express its function. His works include the Auditorium (1889) and the Carson Pirie Scott building (1899-1904) in Chicago, and the Guaranty Building in Buffalo (1894-1895). Frank Lloyd Wright was his pupil.
See also: Architecture.

Sullivan, Sir Arthur Seymour (1842-1900), English composer. He was born in London and studied at the Royal Academy of Music. He first met with success for the music he wrote for the Shakespeare play *The Tempest* (1862). Sullivan is perhaps best known for his collaborations with the playwright Sir William Gilbert in which he produced many operettas. Gilbert and Sullivan first became a team with *Thespis* (1871), an operetta that was not very successful. Their next work, *Trial by Jury* (1875), became an instant hit. Other successful collaborations include *The Pirates of Penzance* (1880), *The Mikado* (1885), and *The Gondoliers* (1889).

Sully-Prudhomme, René François Armand (1839-1907), French Parnassian poet, winner of the first Nobel Prize in literature, in 1901. His philosophical poems include *Justice* (1878) and *Happiness* (1888).

Sulphur *See:* Sulfur.

Sultan, a title of the ruler of some Muslim countries. It is derived from the Aramaic word for 'power,' which was also used to mean 'possessor of power.' A country ruled by a sultan is called a *sultanate* It is uncertain when and where the title originated, but it was used by the Seljuk Turks as early as the 11th century A.D. The most powerful sultans were those of the Ottoman (Turkish) Empire. Turkey abolished the title in 1922, but several small countries are still ruled by sultans.

Sulu Sea, also known as the Sea of Mindoro, sea located between Borneo and the Philippine Islands. It is bounded by many other islands as well, including the Sulu Islands and the Visaya Islands, and is used for trade among them. The sea has an area of approximately 100,000 sq mi (260,000 sq km). Narrow bodies of water connect the sea to the Pacific Ocean and the South China Sea.

Sumac, common name for trees, shrubs, and vines (genus *Rhus*) with resinous, sometimes bitter sap. Members of the group include the staghorn sumac, used by Native Americans to make an acidic but pleasant drink, and the Sicilian sumac, whose bark is used for tanning leather. Sumacs, however, are often poisonous: poison oak, poison sumac, and poison ivy. They can be recognized by their white or gray berries.

Sumatra, second-largest island of Indonesia, about 183,000 sq mi (473,970 sq km) in area. Lying on the equator, with a hot, wet climate, Sumatra is heavily forested and rich in oil, bauxite, and coal; it produces 70% of Indonesia's export wealth. Crops include rubber, coffee, pepper, and tobacco. Medan and Palembang are the chief cities.
See also: Indonesia.

Sumba (pop. 355,000), Indonesian island, part of the Lesser Sunda Islands. 4,249 sq mi (11,000 sq km). Falls under the province of Nusu Tenggara Timur (East) (pop. 2,504,000; 18,492 sq mi (47,876 sq km), capital Kupang. Limestone mountains reaching a height of 4,019 ft (1,225 m). Cultivation of rice and maize on the plains; forestry.

Sumbawa (pop. 540,000), Indonesian island, part of the Lesser Sunda Islands. 5,948 sq mi (15,400 sq km). Falls under the province of Nusu Tenggara Barat (West) (pop. 2,481,000; 7,793 sq mi, 20,177 sq km), capital Mataram. Very mountainous and volcanic. Cultivation of rice, maize and coffee.

Sumer, southern region of ancient Mesopotamia (presently southern Iraq). From c.3000 B.C.-2400 B.C. it was dominated by several small kingdoms, the first civilizations in the world. The kingdoms had developed from cities founded in the fertile valley between the Tigris and Euphrates rivers, a setting ideal for farming and raising cattle. The Sumerians created an advanced civilization, building palaces and temples and constructing irrigation canals in their fields.

Their craftspeople were skilled weavers, potters, jewelers, and stonecarvers. Sumerians traded their goods with regions surrounding the Persian Gulf and promoted the practice and study of medicine, astronomy, mathematics, economy, law, and politics. One of their most noteworthy achievements was the development of the first writing system, known as cuneiform, consisting of wedge-shaped characters pressed into clay tablets. Other civilizations that took control of Sumer absorbed the knowledge and skills developed by them. *See also:* Mesopotamia.

Sumo, Japanese wrestling sport in which speed, body weight, height and strength are important. The object is to maneuver the opponent out of the ring (diameter 14 ft 9 in [4.5 m]) or onto the floor, by using one of 48 different wrestling grips. Each bout lasts approximately 10 seconds, but is preceded by a ritual that can last as long as four minutes, in which the wrestlers throw salt in the ring and try to impress each other by stamping their feet on the ground; this also acts as a balancing exercise. The wrestlers wear a simple *mawashi*: a silk loincloth or hip girdle that is wrapped around the body six times and once between the legs. The wrestlers try to increase their body weight as much as possible, especially around the navel; 330 lb (150 kg) is not exceptional. Similarly to other eastern martial arts, sumo is divided into a hierarchical classification system: sekiwakè, komusubi, ozeki, and yokozuna (great champion).

Sun, star at the center of our Solar System, a luminous sphere of gas about 865,000 mi (1.4 million km) in diameter and 93 million mi (150 million km) from earth. The sun is 332,000 times as massive as earth, and its volume is 1.3 million times greater. The temperature in its center is about 15,000,000°K. The source of its energy is a series of nuclear fusion reactions in which hydrogen is converted into helium-light, heat, and gamma rays being produced in the process. Light from the sun takes about 8 minutes to reach earth. Although the sun is entirely gaseous, its bright surface looks like a kind of skin. This outer layer is called the photosphere, whose temperature is about 6,000°K. Above the photosphere lies the chromosphere, an irregular layer of gases, sunspots, flares, and prominences visible to the naked eye only during eclipses. The corona is the sparse outer atmosphere. *See also:* Solar System.

Sunbelt and Frostbelt, popular terms designating, respectively, the southern tier of states stretching from North Carolina to California and the states of the Northeast and Midwest. The Frostbelt states, besides their more rigorous climate, are characterized by aging industrial plants and urban infrastructures, unionized labor, high rates of unemployment and poverty, static or declining populations, and the severe fiscal problems these conditions impose on state and local governments. By contrast, the Sunbelt states are usually characterized by burgeoning economic development, expanding cities, rising populations (due to migration from the Frostbelt states), and increasing political importance.

Sunbird, any of approximately 115 species of songbirds in the sunbird family. Sunbirds are found in Africa, Southeast Asia, and the Pacific islands. They range in size from 3.5-6 in (9-15 cm). Their plumage may be yellow or gray. Breeding male birds have brilliantly colored feathers of various combinations of red, blue, purple, green, and yellow. Sunbirds resemble hummingbirds, but the two are not related. Like hummingbirds, sunbirds feed on nectar. But whereas a hummingbird hovers in the air as it extracts a flower's nectar, a sunbird perches on a flower or stalk while feeding.

Sunburn, burning effect on the skin caused by exposure to ultraviolet radiation from the sun. First-degree burns may occur, but usually only minor discomfort results, with skin sensitivity. Repeated sunburns may cause skin cancer, including melanoma, the most dangerous variety.

Sun dance, religious ceremony observed by a number of Plains tribes of Native Americans during the summer. It involves eight days of fasting, self-torture (as penance), and the seeking of visions. Common during the 19th century, the ceremonies were discouraged by the U.S. government and have almost died out.

Sundar Singh, Sadhu (1889-1929?), Indian mystic, converted from Sikhism to Christianity after seeing a vision in 1904. Although he was evangelist, he led the life of an Indian acetic (sadhu). Traveled to Afghanistan and Tibet. During visits to the Far East and Europe (1918-1922) he made a great impression with his wisdom and stories about real and mystical experiences. These stories were written down in several books. Never returned from a trip to Tibet.

Sundew, any plant in the sundew family. Sundews have leaves that produce a sticky fluid enabling them to trap and digest insects. (This same fluid makes the leaves glisten like dew-hence their name.) Sundews are found throughout the world in regions with mild or tropical climates. The round-leaved sundew (genus *Drosera*) is the most common, thriving in wet marshy areas. Its thin, curving stem grows to a height of 4-10 in (10-25 cm) and has small white or pinkish flowers on top. The base of the stem has flat round leaves covered with gland-tipped hairs, which produce the sticky fluid that attracts insects. When an insect lands on the leaf, the tiny hairs curve around it and hold it while the fluid engulfs and suffocates it. Enzymes in the fluid digest the insect, after which the hairs unfold, ready to trap the next victim.

S

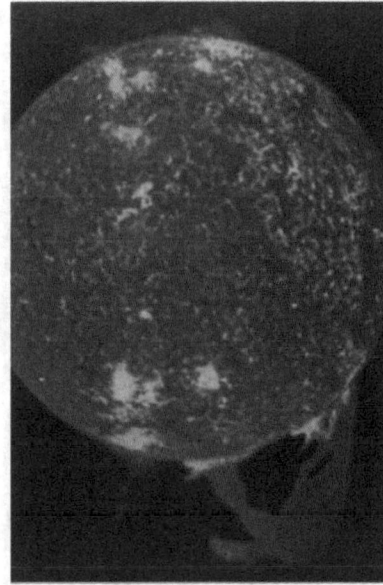

A giant eruption on the sun, photographed by the Skylab crew. A prominence like this comprises of a region with a lower temperature and a higher density than the surrounding corona. At times, the main bulk of the prominence will flow out into space at a speed of hundreds of kilometers per second.

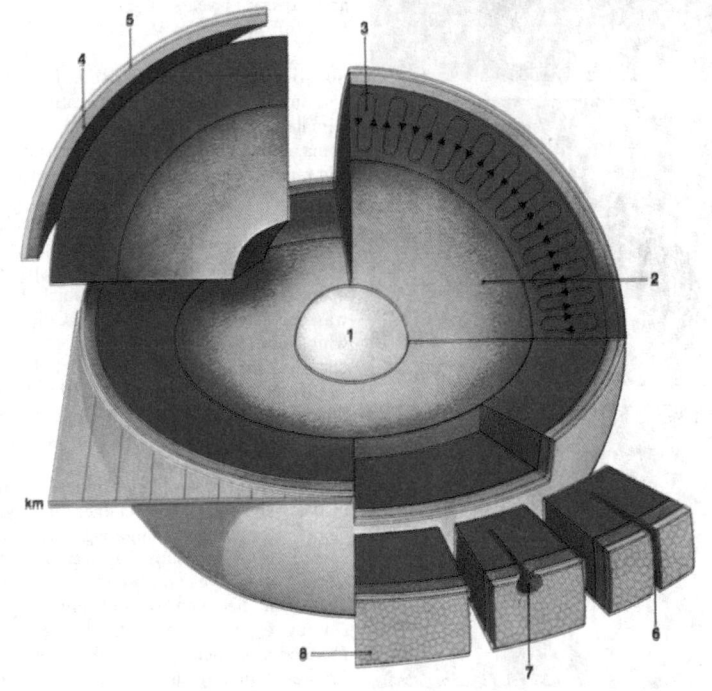

The sun's energy is produced by nuclear fusion in the central core (1). The energy is transported mainly by radiation in the surrounding region (2), and then by circulating currents of gas in the convection zone (3), a 93,150 mi (150,000 km) thick region just below the visible surface, or photosphere (4). In turn, the photosphere is surrounded by the chromosphere (5). Features such as dark filament (6) or sunspot (7) may appear on the granular-textured (8) solar surface.

S

A sundial uses the changing position of a shadow to indicate the time of day. A raised pointer or gnomon, is fixed to a horizontal plate, at an angle that is equal to the latitude of the site, pointing north (angle A). The plate is marked off in hourly segments. As the sun passes from east to west, the shadow of the gnomon will move through the divisions, indicating the hours.

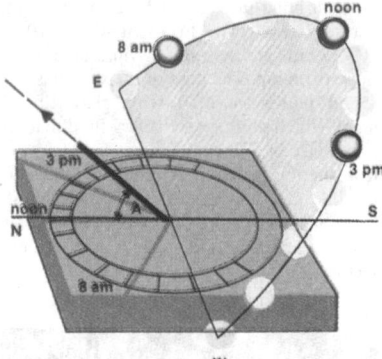

Sundial, ancient type of clock, consisting of a stylus (called a gnomon) parallel to the earth's axis that casts a shadow on a calibrated dial plate, which may be horizontal or vertical. Sundials usually show local time, but they may be calibrated to show standard time.

Upon detailed examination, a sunspot is usually found to consist of two separate regions of smaller spots. Following the direction of solar rotations, these two regions are called the preceding and following spots. The dynamic nature of these two regions, which persist for no more than a few months, is seen in this 1947 sequence of a large bipolar group of sunspots. (A) On February 11, the distinction between the two regions is unclear, but close examination of their spectra reveals their opposite polarity. The distinction between the preceding spot (1) and the following spot (2) is clearer on March 9 (B) and April 7 (C). Sunspot activity had virtually stopped in this region by May 5 (D).

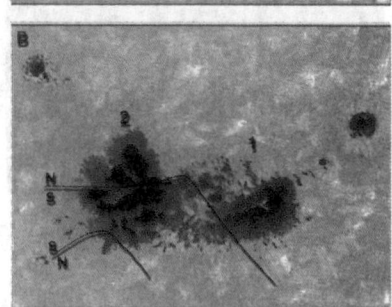

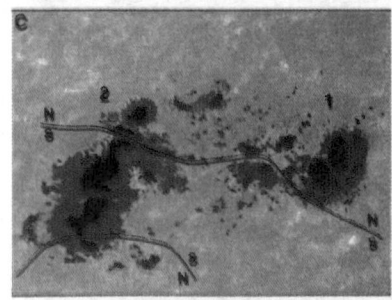

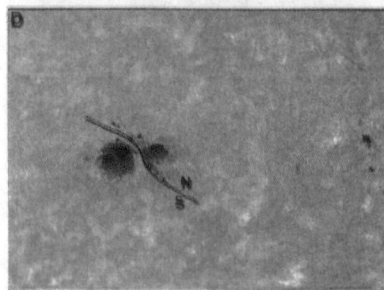

Sunfish, popular fresh water sports fish of the bass family, found in North America. The body is perchlike: deep and flattened, and with a long dorsal fin. Male sunfish dig nests in sand and guard the eggs. They feed on small animals and other fish and are active only during periods of sunshine. Ocean sunfish (*Mola mola*) are unrelated fish that live in the sea.

Sunflower, any of various tall plants (genus *Helianthus*) with large, disk-shaped yellow and brown flowers that twist to face the sun. Most of the 60 species are native to the United States. The common sunflower (*Helianthus annuus*) is cultivated in many parts of the world. The seeds yield an oil and the remainder becomes cattle feed.

Sunflower State *See:* Kansas.

Sungari *See:* Songhua Jiang.

Sung dynasty *See:* Song dynasty.

Sunni, followers of the majority branch of Islam, as distinct from the Shi'te. The term refers to the tradition (Sunna) of the prophet Muhammad. About 85% of the world's Muslims are Sunni, considered the orthodox or traditionalists. Within the Sunni currently, there are four recognized schools of Islamic law and ritual: Hamafi, Maliki, Shafi, and Hambali.
See also: Islam; Shi'te.

Sunshine State *See:* Florida; South Dakota.

Sunspot, apparent dark spot on the surface of the sun. Vortices of gas associated with strong electromagnetic activity, sunspots appear dark only by contrast with the surrounding photosphere. Single spots are known, but mostly they form in groups or pairs. They are never seen at the sun's poles or equator. Their cause is not known, but they seem cyclical, reaching a maximum about every 11 years.
See also: Sun.

Sunstroke, or heatstroke, rise in body temperature and deficiency of sweating in hot climates, often following exertion. Delirium, coma, and convulsions may occur suddenly, and rapid cooling must then be effected.

Sun worship, reverence for the sun, as for a god or goddess. Sun worship was practiced by peoples throughout the world, especially in agricultural communities in which the sun was necessary for crop growth. Cultures in which sun worship was prevalent include those of ancient Egypt, Persia, India, and Rome. Native Americans and the Aztecs, Incas, and Mayas of Central and South America also considered the sun sacred.

Sun Yat-sen (1866-1925), Chinese political leader, regarded as the 'father of modern China.' Born in the Guangdong province, he spent most of his youth in Hawaii, where he learned about Western thought and politics. He then studied medicine in Hong Kong, becoming a doctor in 1892. In 1894 Sun founded a political group and attempted his first revolution against the Manchu dynasty.

It failed and Sun left China in 1895. He traveled throughout Europe, the United States, and Japan, trying to gain support for his cause. In 1911, the Manchu dynasty was overthrown during a revolt, and Sun returned to China. He was elected temporary president and tried to unite China under a strong government. Some considered his ideas too extreme, however, and after 6 weeks he turned his presidency over to Yüan Shikai. Sun remained committed to his vision of a unified China. In 1923 he and his Kuomintang Party took control of China with assistance from the Soviet Union (Shih-kai had become increasingly dictatorial). He died 2 years later. The Communists and the Kuomintang, who eventually dissolved their partnership, both claimed his legacy to be their inheritance. *Three Principles of the People*, his writings in which he summarized his political doctrines, inspired and guided subsequent developments in China.
See also: China.

Supachai Panichpakdi (1946-   ), Thai politician. He studied Human Resource Planning and Development. Supachai started his career at the Bank of Thailand, where he worked at the international financial department. He was elected to Parliament and became Vice Chancellor for the Exchequer in 1986. As Vice Prime Minister, he was responsible for international trade politics four years later. He was also active in establishing regional trade agreements, including the Asia-Pacific Economic Cooperation (APEC), the Association of Southeast-Asian Countries (ASEAN) and the Asia Europe Meeting (ASEM). In 2002, he became general director of the World Trade Organization (WTO). He received most votes from Asian and African countries which were hoping to gain a more powerful vote in the Geneva based organization. Therefore, his first priority is to make sure that the advantages of free trade are more equally distributed, and do not only apply to developed economies.
See also: World Trade Organization.

Superconductivity, complete disappearance of resistance to electricity in a wire or other electric circuit, which allows a current to continue without any driving voltage. Superconductivity was discovered in 1911 and was long thought to be possible only in certain metals at very low temperatures (close to absolute zero, a total absence of molecular movement). This severely limited the possible applications of superconductivity. In recent years, however, researchers have made considerable progress in inducing superconductivity in some materials at the relatively 'high' temperature of about 125°K, or -243°F.
See also: Bardeen, John.

Superego, term coined by Sigmund Freud meaning the mostly subconscious dimension of personality that represents moral and cultural standards established by society. The superego (ego ideal and conscience) develops as a result of the child's identification with parental standards.
See also: Freud, Sigmund.

Superman *See:* Nietzsche, Friedrich.

Supernova, exploding star that may increase in brightness by as much as a billion times its original state in just a few days, after which it gradually fades back to less than its original brightness. It is thought that supernovas are caused by the gravitational collapse of extremely massive stars. Although many presumed remnants of supernovas have been detected, only four of these have been definitely matched to explosions that were seen and recorded in human history. These occurred in 1006, 1054, 1572, and 1604. In more recent times (since the 19th century) many supernovas have been observed by astronomers.
See also: Nova; Star.

Superstition, belief or practice that is not based on reason. Some superstitions involve the belief that an incident will have certain results, or foretell an event-for example, believing that walking under a ladder will bring bad luck. Other superstitions attribute qualities and powers to objects, such as a rabbit foot bringing luck. The origins of superstitions vary, but they have probably existed in every culture since ancient times. They arise out of uncertainty and fear and the desire to empower oneself somehow. Some superstitions are part of a cultural or religious tradition and are believed by a number of people, such as the belief that a groom should not see his bride before the ceremony on their wedding day. Other superstitions may be personal, such as having a lucky number.

Supply and demand, in economics, central concepts that explain changes in prices, production, and consumption of goods and services. Demand refers to the quantity of a product desired by consumers. Supply is the quantity available. Normally, if demand increases relative to supply, the price will rise. If supply rises relative to demand, the price will fall. Competition is the mechanism through which supply and demand tend to reach an equilibrium. In practice, however, such factors as monopolization, state interference, and other variables generally prevent this equilibrium from ever being reached.
See also: Economics.

Supply-side economics, theory of economic management that focuses on stimulating production through tax reduction, which is intended to inspire increased investment in business, leading to higher employment. The theory also calls for a cutback in government spending to achieve a balanced and much smaller budget, thus eliminating deficit spending, which causes inflation and drains funds from the private sector. Inspired by laissez-faire economic thought, the leading theorists of supply-side thinking include Milton Friedman, Arthur B. Lafter, Jack Kemp, and David Stockman. Supply-side economics dominated President Ronald Reagan's economic policies (1981-1989).
See also: Economics.

Suprematism, art movement (1913-1919) originated by the Russian-Polish painter Kasimir Malevich (1878-1935), establishing a system of nonrepresentational composition in terms of pure geometric shapes and patterns. The movement's influence on graphic design and typography has been significant.

Supreme Court of the United States, highest court of the United States, with the authority to adjudicate all cases arising under U.S. law, including treaties and constitutional matters.

Sur (pop. 23,000), port on the southern coast of Lebanon. In ancient times known as Tyre, it was the second most important Phoenician port after Sidon. Flourished in the 10th and 9th centuries B.C.. The people of Tyre established many colonies, including Carthage. The city was captured by Alexander the Great (332B.C.) but retained its independence. Successively occupied by Romans (64 B.C.), Arabs (638), Crusaders (1124) and Mamelukes (1291). The city was regularly bombed by Israel in the 1980s.

Surabaya, or Surakaja (pop. 2,473,000), city in Indonesia, located on the northeastern coast of Java at the mouth of the Mas River. Surabaya's port is the second busiest in Indonesia (Jakarta has the busiest). It exports Indonesian products, including sugar, coffee, tobacco, spices, oils,and petroleum. The port is also home to Indonesia's main naval base. Surabaya is a busy industrial center. Its industries include shipbuilding and repair, textiles, chemicals, rubber, and cigarettes. Surabaya's educational facilities include a large university and a naval college.
See also: Indonesia.

Surakarta (pop. 504,000), city in the Indonesian province of a Jawa Tengah on Java on the Solo (as Surakarta was formerly known); important administration and cultural center; trading center for agricultural region (rice, sugarcane, maize, coffee, tea, tobacco) with varied industry; some tourism, less popular than Jogyakarta. Built around the *kraton* (walled palace), residence of the former sultans. Seat of the Surakarta principality (emerged from the Mataram principality in 1755) until Indonesia's independence (1949).

Surat (pop. 1,8 million), India, a city in Gujarat state, on India's northwestern coast, about 155 miles (250 km) north of Bombay. Surat is a railway junction and a textile-milling center noted for its fine silks, cottons, and brocades. The city dates from at least the 1300's. It achieved its greatest prominence during the 17th century, when it was one of the richest trading ports in India and the headquarters of the English East India Company.

Surface tension, property that makes the surface of a liquid act as if it were an elastic film. The molecules in a liquid stay together because they are pulled towards each other equally. This force is called cohesion. The molecules at the surface of a liquid have no molecules above them to attract and pull them; these molecules are pulled only by those beside and below them. This continuous sideward and downward pull creates tension at the surface, making it act as if it were a resilient film. A razor blade placed flatly on the surface of water does not sink because the surface tension supports it. Because of surface tension some birds are able to stand on water.
See also: Capillarity; Cohesion.

Surfing, sport of riding a wooden or foam plastic surfboard on the incline of a wave. It requires balance, timing, and coordination. Surfing originated in Hawaii and is the oldest sport in the United States. With worldwide competitions organized by the International Surfing Committee, surfing has gained widespread popularity, particularly in the United States, Australia, Brazil, France, Japan, Mexico, and Peru.

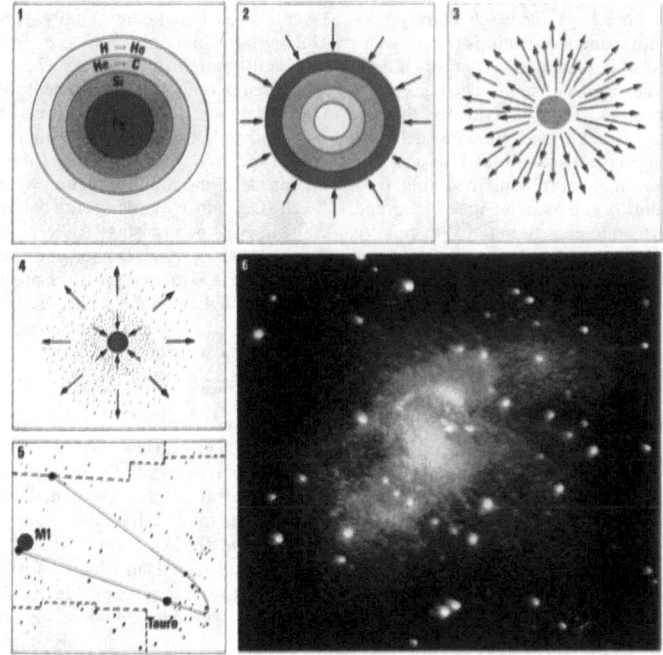

A supernova occurs when the outer, gaseous portion of a massive star explodes. According to one theory, as nuclear reactions in a star's core (1) start to produce heavy elements, such as iron, continued contraction (2) of the inner core begins to release enormous amounts of energy. The star explodes (3) and expels stellar matter. The core continues to contract, probably producing a dense neutron star (4). A supernova in the constellation Taurus (5) was observed by Chinese astronomers in 1054 A.D. Its remnants form M1, the Crab nebula (6).

S

S

Surgery, branch of medicine chiefly concerned with manual operations to remove or repair diseased, damaged, or deformed body tissues. The origins of surgery go back to ancient times, and there is evidence that the Egyptians, Greeks, and Romans achieved some impressive results. Infections and gangrene were major problems resulting from surgery during the Middle Ages in Europe, but this began to change in the 19th century. The development of techniques of sterilization and anesthetics allowed for the expansion of modern surgery under much safer conditions, and the invention of new diagnostic tools, such as X-rays and CAT scans, has made surgery more effective.

Suriname

Capital:	Paramaribo
Area:	63,251 sq mi (163,820 sq km)
Population:	436,000
Language:	Dutch
Government:	Presidential republic
Independent:	1975
Head of gov.:	Prime minister
Per capita:	US$ 3,500
Monetary unit:	1 Surinam guilder = 100 cents

Suriname, republic on the northeastern coast of South America, bordered by Guyana on the west, Brazil on the south, and French Guiana on the east.
Land and climate. The country consists largely of unexplored forested highlands and the flat Atlantic coast. The climate is tropical, with heavy rains.
People and economy. The population is about 34% East Indian, 34% Creole, and 18% Indonesian. Other groups include Europeans, Chinese, and Native Americans. The official language is Dutch, but most people speak the Creole Sranang Tongo. Hindi, Javanese, Chinese, English, French, and Spanish are also spoken. The most important product of the economy is bauxite. The main crops are rice, sugar, fruits, coffee, and bananas.
History. Columbus probably first sighted the coast in 1498. Several Indian tribes inhabited the area at the time. The Dutch colonized the country in 1667. They built tobacco and sugar plantations, cultivated by African slaves. By the time slavery was abolished,

revenues had fallen considerably. However, Hindus from India and Javanese from Java were still brought in to work. The country was given internal self-government in 1954. On November 25 1975, Suriname became independent. Desi Bouterse's military junta ousted the civil government in 1980. After opponents of the military regime were murdered (December murders), the country became internationally isolated. Even after the free elections of 1987, Bouterse remained in power, albeit in a low profile manner. His party, the NDP, won the 1996 elections, but were defeated in 2000 after economic problems. Ronald Venetiaan, leader of the opposition, became President.

Surrealism, movement in literature and art that flourished between World War I and World War II, especially in Paris; influenced by Freudianism. Writers associated with surrealism include André Breton, Louis Aregon, and Jean Cocteau; surrealist artists include Salvador Dali, Joan Miró, René Magritte, Yves Tanguy, and Max Ernst. The movement was devoted to unleashing the imagination of the unconscious minds, free of the constraints of reason. In painting and films everyday objects were often placed in dreamlike settings; apparently unrelated objects were juxtaposed, and incongruous images were dominant.

Surrey, Earl of (1517?-1547), English poet. Surrey was born into the English nobility and received a classical education in France. He was knighted in 1541 and was a member of the court of King Henry VIII.
Surrey's friendship with King Henry's illegitimate son, the duke of Richmond, created speculation that he was part of a treason plot against the king. This led to his arrest and beheading. Surrey's major achievement is his contribution of verse styles to English poetry. His translation of *The Aeneid* was the first English usage of blank verse. Together with Sir Thomas Wyatt (1503-1542), Surrey introduced to English poetry the Petrarchan sonnet form used in Italy. Surrey and Wyatt's *The Book of Songs and Sonnets* was published in 1557. Many English poets and writers subsequently wrote in blank verse and the sonnet form, creating an age of high poetic achievement in England.

Surtees, John (1934-), English motor sport racer, became both motorcycle and racing car world champion. Surtees began motorcycle racing on a Norton, but moved to MV Agusta in 1956, for whom he won seven world titles between 1956 and 1960 in both the 350 cc and 500 cc classes. In 1960 he stopped motorcycle racing to join Ferrari, with whom he won the Formula 1 world championship in 1964. In 1966 Surtees moved to Cooper-Maserati.

Surveying, process of measuring distances and features on the earth's surface for map preparation and locating boundary lines. Geodetic surveying, which covers large areas, takes the earth's curvature into account. After a base line of known length is established, the positions of other points are found by triangulation (measuring the angles of the point from each end of the base

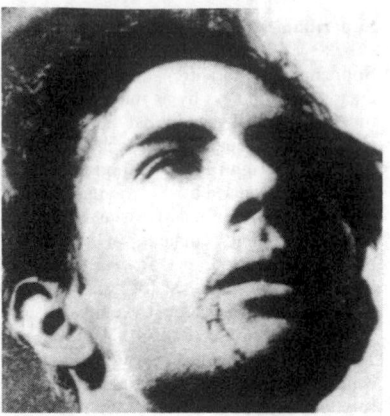

Scene from the surrealist movie *Un chien andalou* (1928), by Luis Buñuel, which he made together with Salvador Dali.

line) or by trilateration (measuring all the sides of the triangle formed by point and base line). Distances are measured by tape or by electronic means. Instruments for measuring angles are the theodolite and the alidade. Vertical elevations are determined by levels. Much modern surveying is done by photogrammetry, using the stereoscope to determine contours.

Susa (also called Shush), capital of the ancient Middle East country of Elam and later of the Persian Empire. Its ruins are located in southwestern Iran, just north of the Persian Gulf. Susa was an active community as early as biblical times. Archeological digs in the region have unearthed remains of many civilizations. Elam reached the peak of its power after 1300 B.C., after overthrowing Babylonia.
See also: Persia, Ancient.

Süskind, Patrick (1949-), German writer. After he finished his studies he began writing

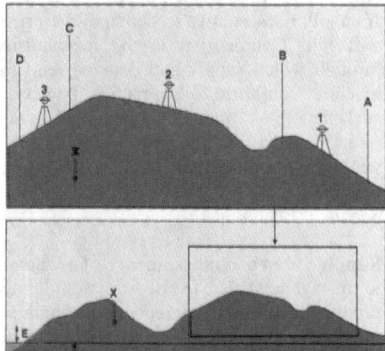

In measuring the height of a hilly area, a measuring rod is first staked at a known elevation, called the bench mark (X). A leveling instrument is positioned (1) to sight the rod at position A, and then at position B, and the difference in height is measured. The instrument is

then moved to a second bench-mark position (2), and point C is measured. At position (3), the instrument uses point C to measure point D. The heights of all these points can be related to sea level (Y), by knowing the height of the bench mark x above sea level (E).

screenplays for television. In 1984 he wrote the solo theatre piece - since performed by many star actors - *The Contrabass*, about the loves and hates of a musician. The following year he broke through as a novelist with *Perfume: The Story of a Murderer*, about an outsider, a perfumer in 18th-century Paris, who becomes a mass murderer in his search for the perfect perfume. This original idea was told in brilliant prose. In 1987 he wrote *The Pigeon*.

Suslov, Mikhail Andreyevich (1902-1982), Communist Party official in the USSR. An orthodox Stalinist during Stalin's lifetime, Suslov rose steadily through the party ranks, helping to form the Cominform in 1947 and serving as editor of the party newspaper, *Pravda* (1949-1950). A member of the ruling Politburo from 1955, he became one of its most rigid ideologues. With an instinct for survival, he at first supported Nikita Khrushchev and then helped overthrow him in 1964. He opposed any suggestion of relaxing party rule in the country.
See also: Union of Soviet Socialist Republics.

Suspension, in chemistry, mixture in which solid particles hang in a liquid or gas. The suspension is maintained by the continued movement of the molecules of the liquid or gas, which bump the molecules of the particles. Two examples of suspensions are dust (solid in a gas) and muddy water (solid in a liquid).
See also: Solution.

Suspension bridge *See:* Bridge.

Sussex spaniel, strong, short, stocky dog originally bred in Sussex, England. It weighs 35-45 lb (16-20 kg) and has a dark gold coat.

Sutermeister, Heinrich (1910-1995), Swiss composer. Sutermeister studied under Carl Orff, and influenced by the work of Verdi and Puccini he acquired a fascination for opera and its musical-dramatic potential. After the radio opera *Die schwarze Spinne* (1936) he received recognition for his opera performed in Dresden *Romeo and Juliet* (1940), in which he showed himself to be a great melodic composer with an instinct for theatre. He went on to write numerous operas including *Die Zauberinsel* (1942), *Raskolnikoff* (1948), *Titus Feuerbuchs* (1958), *Madame Bovary* (1967), *Der Flaschenteufel* (1971) and *König Bereuger I* (1985). In addition to this musical drama oeuvre, Sutermeister wrote orchestral works, ballets, three piano and two cello concertos, choral works, cantatas, songs and chamber music.

Sutherland, Dame Joan (1926-), Australian soprano, one of the foremost exponents of the art of bel canto. She made her debut in Sydney (1950), her U.S. debut in Dallas (1960), and her N.Y. Metropolitan debut (1961) in *Lucia di Lammermoor*. In 1990 she retired.
See also: Opera.

Sutherland, Graham Vivian (1903-1980), a British painter. He became known for his imaginative abstract landscapes. In such works as *Thorn Trees* he painted strange forms in brilliant colors to convey an unearthly mystical mood. A versatile artist, Sutherland also painted powerful portraits of W. Somerset Maugham, Sir Winston Churchill, and others. His other works include *The Crucifixion* for St. Matthew's Church, Northampton, and the design for the tapestry *Christ in Glory* for Coventry Cathedral.
Sutherland was born in London and attended Goldsmiths' College School of Art there. He was an etcher and teacher before he turned to painting in the 1930's.

Sutra, an aphorism (brief statement of a fundamental idea) or collection of aphorisms in Hindu and Buddhist sacred scriptures. In Sanskrit, sutra means 'thread' or 'string.' Because certain early religious teachings were very brief and therefore needed explanation, they came to be thought of as sutras, or threads, upon which to hang commentary.
Hindu sutras are practical rules for various subjects. The Dharma Sutras are concerned with the law and social obligations. The Yoga Sutras of Patanjali are a systematic presentation of yoga. The Vedanta Sutras (also called the Brahma Sutras) present various aspects of Hindu philosophy.
In Buddhism, a sutra is a text said to have been spoken by the Buddha himself. However, various Buddhist sutras are known to have originated centuries after Buddha and their source remains unknown. An example is the Lotus Sutra, in which the spiritual nature of man and the significance of the Buddha are discussed.

Suttner, Bertha von (born countess Kinsky; 1843-1914), Austrian writer and pacifist. She inspired Nobel to introduce the Nobel Prize for peace, which she herself received in 1905. She published *Lay down Your Arms* (2 volumes, 1889), translated into nearly all European languages, which gave an impulse to the modern peace movement. From 1892 to 1899 she published the magazine *Die Waffen nieder!*.

Suva (pop. 72,000), capital of Fiji, a country made up of more than 800 islands in the South Pacific. Suva is located on the southeast coast of Viti Levu, the fifth-largest Fijian island. Its harbor is the country's main port. It is also an educational center, with the University of Fiji and the Fiji School of Medicine located there.
See also: Fiji.

Suzuki, Zenko (1911-), Japanese politician. Suzuki was minister of postal services and telecommunications (1960-1964), cabinet secretary (1964-1965), minister of public health and welfare (1965-1968), and minister of agriculture (1976-1977). He also held various posts within the Liberal Democratic Party (LDP), serving as chairman of the executive organ (1968-1980). He was prime minister from 1980 to 1982. Suzuki continued to play a prominent role in Japanese politics even when he was no longer prime minister.

Suzuki method, style of musical instruction begun in the 1940s to teach very young children to play musical instruments. The method was initiated by Shinichi Suzuki, who believed that children could aquire musical skills as they do language, by listening and imitating. Parent involvement is an important component of the method.

Svalbard, or Spitsbergen, island group in the Arctic Ocean 400 mi (640 km) north of Norway and officially belonging to that country since 1920. The 5 main islands are Spitsbergen, North East Land, Edge Island, Barents Island, and Prince Charles Foreland. They were known to the Norwegians by the Middle Ages. Formerly of importance in the whaling and fur trading industries, since the 1890s they have been mined for coal, largely by companies of the former Soviet Union.

Svedberg, Theodor (1884-1971), Swedish chemist awarded the 1926 Nobel Prize in chemistry for inventing the ultracentrifuge, important in studies of colloids and large molecules.
See also: Chemistry.

Sverdlovsk *See:* Ekaterinburg.

Svevo, Italo (real name, Ettore Schmitz; 1861-1928), Italian writer from Trieste. His masterpiece *Confessions of Zeno* (1923) became world-famous, partly due to the efforts of his friend James Joyce, who held his work in great esteem. In this novel, Svevo, long before Freud was fashionable, uses his main character Zeno to make an ironical commentary on the psychoanalytical profession: this immature character continues to launch himself with undiminished enthusiasm into a series of tasks he never completes, and spends his whole life smoking his last cigarette. Svevo's ironic and intellectual style, his hypothetical view of the world, and the constant indecision of his main character led many people to consider him a modernist, although his early work definitely shows a tendency towards naturalism. Other works include *A Life* (1892) and *As a Man Grows Older* (1898).

Swahili, Bantu language of East Africa, widely spoken in Kenya, Uganda, Tanzania, and parts of Zaire. Swahili is heavily influenced by Arabic in its vocabulary, the name of the language itself coming from the Arabic word for 'coasts.'

Swallow, common name for various small birds of the family Hirundinidae. There are

The barn swallow, *Hirundo rustica*, the most common of all swallows, is found almost worldwide and in all sorts of environments. It migrates vast distances: it is not unusual for the birds to fly from Scandinavia to southern Africa, traveling up to 569 mi (960 km) in a day. However, such an extended migration also produces a high annual mortality rate (about 70%).

S

at least 78 species; all have long, sickle-shaped wings and long, forked tails. The plumage is generally dark, often with a metallic sheen. Many species have lighter underparts. The legs and feet are small and weak. Swallows can perch on wires or tree branches but are adapted to spend most of their time on the wing, feeding on insects. Many species are migratory.

Swammerdam, Jan (1637-1680), Dutch entomologist, zoologist, and anatomist, who made major contributions to research on insect metamorphosis, life cycles, and anatomy. He also studied red blood cells and the working nerves and muscles in animals, showing that muscles change their configuration but not their size when contracting. His written works include *A General History of Insects*, and the *Bible of Nature*.
See also: Entomology; Zoology.

Swamp, area of poorly drained, low-lying land saturated with water. Swamps normally covered by water are called marshes. The obstruction of drainage that causes swamps to form may result from the flatness of the land, the presence of impermeable rock beneath the surface, or the growth of dense vegetation. Lakes that are filled in by sediment may develop into swamps. When drained, swamps usually make fertile farmland. Large swamps in the United States include the Everglades (Florida), the Dismal (North Carolina), and the Okefenokee (Georgia and Florida).

Swan, any of various large, long-necked aquatic birds related to ducks and geese. There are eight species, seven within the genus *Cygnus*. Five of these are found in the Northern Hemisphere; all are white in adult plumage but have different-colored bills. The two remaining species are the black swan of Australia and the black-necked swan of South America. Most feed on vegetation.

Swanscombe man, prehistoric human dating back to the Second Interglacial Period about 350,000 years ago. Three parts of a skull were discovered 3 consecutive years (1935, 1936, 1937) in Swanscombe, England at the River Thames. A better specimen, found in Steinheim, Germany, in 1933, dates back 375,000 years.
See also: Prehistoric people.

Swansea (pop. 200,000), industrial seaport

Mbabane, the capital and largest city of Swaziland.

in Wales, originally settled in the 1000s. Its 281 acres of waterfront docks on Swansea Bay export the products of nearby oil refineries, aluminum factories, nickel and zinc refineries, and coal mines. In the 1800s the city was a major copper trading center and produced great amounts of tin plate for cans. *See also:* Wales.

SWAPO (South-West African People's Organization), Black nationalist movement in Namibia (formerly South West Africa), which under the leadership of Sam Nujoma fought a guerrilla war against the South African domination of Namibia from 1966 to 1989. In 1971 SWAPO was recognized by the United Nations as the legitimate representative of the Namibian people. After Namibia achieved its independence on 21 March 1990, SWAPO won an absolute majority in the first free general elections. Nujoma became president of Namibia.

Swastika, ancient symbol of well-being and prosperity employed by such diverse peoples as Greeks, Celts, Native Americans, and the Hindus of India, where it apparently arose. The word comes from the Sanskrit for 'good fortune.' In the 20th century the symbol became infamous as the emblem of Nazism.

Swaziland

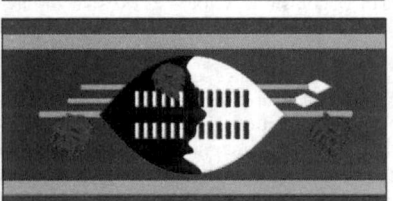

Capitals:	Mbabane, Lobamba
Area:	6,704 sq mi (17,363 sq km)
Population:	1,124,000
Language:	SiSwati, English
Government:	Monarchy
Independent:	1968
Head of gov.:	Prime minister
Per capita:	US$ 4,200
Monetary unit:	1 Lilangeni = 100 cents

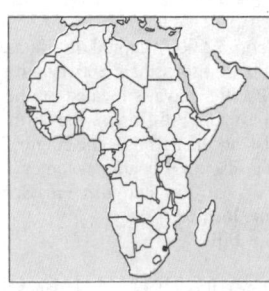

Swaziland, kingdom in southeastern Africa, bordered by Mozambique on the east and the Republic of South Africa on the other three sides.
Land and climate. There are three main regions: the mountainous High Veld in the west, the lower Middle Veld, and the Low Veld rising in the east to the narrow Lebombo range. The four major rivers, running west to east, are being developed for irrigation and could provide abundant hydroelectricity.

People and economy. Swazis and a smaller number of Zulus constitute 97% of the population. 'Coloreds' (of mixed ancestry) and Europeans make up the rest. Agriculture, including forestry, is the largest single sector in the economy. Sugar, wood pulp, asbestos, fruits, iron ore, and canned meats are the main exports. Swaziland has close communication, economic, and trade links with South Africa.
History. Settled by the Swazis, a Bantu people, and unified as a kingdom in the 1800s, Swaziland was taken over by Britain in 1903 and later fell under South African influence. The country became self-governing in 1963 and fully independent in 1968 under King Sobhuza II. Mawati III has ruled since Sobhuza's death in 1982. At the beginning of the 1990s the king announced a reform of the electoral system. A blind eye was turned to the oppositional party PUDEMA (People's United Democratic Movement). However, at the 1993 parliamentary elections the existing political parties were not allowed to select candidates.
Mswati III appropriated more power by restraining freedom of press in 2002. Meanwhile, AIDS is taking its toll; approximately 25% of the population is HIV positive.

Sweat gland *See:* Perspiration.

Sweatshop, place of work with long hours, poor pay, and bad conditions. Such places often exploit those who find difficulty in obtaining employment, such as women, unskilled laborers, newly arrived immigrants, and children. Sweatshops have been curbed by the growth of organized labor.

Sweden

Capital:	Stockholm
Area:	173,604 sq mi (449,964 sq km)
Population:	8,878,000
Language:	Swedish
Government:	Constitutional monarchy
Independent:	1917 (constitutional monarchy)
Head of gov.:	Prime minister
Per capita:	US$ 24,700
Monetary unit:	1 Swedish krona = 100 öre

Sweden, kingdom in northern Europe, occupying most of the eastern and southern portion of the Scandinavian peninsula.

Land and climate. Sweden has an area of 173,604 sq mi (449,750 sq km). It is bounded on the west and north by Norway; on the northeast by Finland; on the east and south by the Baltic Sea; and on the southwest by the Öresund, Kattegat, and Skagerrak, the narrows linking the Baltic with the North Sea. At its northernmost, it lies within the Arctic Circle and includes part of Lapland. Sweden may be divided into four main regions: Norrland, the northern two-thirds of the country; the central lowlands; southern Sweden; and Skåne. Barren heights, high lakes, peat bogs, and great forests of spruce, pine, and larch cover most of the thinly populated Norrland. Sweden's rivers and lakes make up nearly 10% of the country's area and some of the largest of its lakes are in the central lowlands. Most of the people live in this area and it is also the site of the country's two largest cities, Stockholm and Göteborg. Southern Sweden is a fertile, coastal lowland region, and Skåne is the low-lying agricultural region in the extreme south. Northern Sweden has long, cold winters and brief, cool summers. The south enjoys longer summers and milder winters. The capital of the country is Stockholm.

People. The population is almost entirely Swedish, except for a minority of Lapps in the north. The official language is Swedish, and almost everyone is Lutheran.

Economy. Sweden has extensive forests, rich deposits of iron ore, abundant hydroelectric power, and enough good farmland to be nearly self-sufficient in food production. Main exports are machinery, iron, steel, paper, wood pulp, timber, and motor vehicles. Sweden enjoys one of the highest living standards in the world with relatively low unemployment and extensive social services, including free education, retirement pensions, and comprehensive medical care. An economic downturn in the 1970s, 1980s and 1990s partly eroded Swedish prosperity, slowing economic growth and leading to unemployment, inflation and the relinquishment of some social achievements.

History. Mention of the Swedes is first recorded by the Roman historian Tacitus in the 1st century A.D. In the 9th and 10th centuries A.D., Vikings from Sweden known as Varangians pioneered trade routes through Russia as far as the Black Sea. Throughout the Middle Ages, the history of the Swedes was tied to that of Norway and Denmark. The Danes, dominant in the Kalmar Union of Denmark, Norway, and Sweden, which was founded in 1397, were driven out of Sweden in 1523. In the 17th century, Gustavus II (Gustavus Adolphus) made Sweden a leading European power, but the rise of Russia in the 18th century checked Swedish ambitions. In 1809 the monarchy became constitutional; a new constitution took effect in 1975. Sweden took no part in World War I or World War II. The Social Democrats have been the predominant political party through much of Sweden's 20th-century history, architects of the country's social welfare system and its policy of neutrality. Sweden opposed the U.S. war in Vietnam and in 1969 recognized North Vietnam, thereby marking the high point of a period of strained relations with the United States. Swedish domestic politics have been free of violence with the sole exception being the assassination of Prime Minister Olof Palme (1986), a murder that remains unsolved. The socialists were defeated in the elections of 1991 but regained power in the 1994 elections. In 1995 Sweden joined the EU, but remained outside the Euro zone. Following the elections of 2002, Prime Minister Göran Persson (governing since 1996) began his third term of office.

Swedenborgians, followers of the religious ideas of the Swedish theologian Emanuel Swedenborg (1688-1772). A scientist and engineer, Swedenborg became a Christian mystic in 1747. He believed that the Second Coming of Christ occurred in 1757. After his death, his followers founded the Church of the New Jerusalem, first organized in London in 1787 and introduced in the United States in 1792.

Swedish, one of the North Germanic or Scandinavian languages, spoken by about 9 million people in Sweden, Finland, Estonia, the United States, and Canada. Old Swedish developed from Old Norse and gave place to modern Swedish (1500) with the onset of standardization.

Sweet alyssum, vigorous, low-growing perennial herb (*Lobularia maritima*) of the mustard family, originating in the Mediterranean area. It produces sweet, mostly white but sometimes lavender or pink flowers. Plants can grow to 9 in (23 cm) high.

Sweetbrier *See:* Eglantine.

Sweet flag, tall, straight, perennial marsh herb (*Acorus calamus*) of the arum family, growing in moist areas near streams and ponds. Its fat root is edible and is also used in medicines and perfumes. Flat leaves grow 2-6 ft (61-180 cm) high from the root rather than the stem.

Sweet gum, any of various tall shade trees (genus *Liquidambar*) of the hazel family named for the sweet-smelling gummy substance they produce, called storax. Sweet gums have star-shaped leaves that turn brilliant colors in the fall. Storax is used for perfumes, adhesives, and ointments. Brown, spiny seed balls are produced as fruit and remain on the tree most of the winter.

Sweet pea, fragrant, annual garden plant (*Lathyrus odoratus*) native to Italy and thriving in numerous temperate countries where there is rich soil and abundant sunshine. Flowers grow to 2 in (5 cm) across, either individually or in small clusters.

Sweet potato, trailing creeper plant (*Ipomoea batatas*) of the morning glory family, native to tropical America. It produces a tuberous root that is sweet-tasting when cooked. In the United States an orange variety is grown, with roots rich in carotene.

Sweet William, Eurasian pink biennial (*Dianthus barbatus*), also known as New-port pink. Originating in Europe and Asia, the plant produces thick clusters of white, pink, or purple ringed flowers.

Swift, any of several highly mobile, small, insect-eating lizards (genus *Sceloporus*) found in dry temperate regions of the United States, Mexico, and Central America. Most swifts reproduce by laying eggs, while others give birth to live young.

Swift, small, fast-flying insectivorous bird, similar to a swallow but classed with the hummingbirds in the order Apodiformes. Both swifts and hummingbirds have very small feet and extremely short arm bones, the major flight feathers being attached to the extended hand bones. Entirely aerial, most species feed and even sleep on the wing.

Swift, Graham (1949-), British writer. His first book, *The Sweet Shop Owner* (1980), was followed by *Shuttlecock* (1981). *Waterland* (1983), set in the marshy Fenlands north of Cambridge, was nominated for the Booker Prize. He then wrote *Out of this World* (1988), *Ever After* (1992) and *The Light of Day* (2002). He eventually received the Booker Prize for *Last Orders* (1996). In this novel, inspired by Chaucer's *Canterbury Tales*, four men set out to perform the last wish of a friend who has recently died: to have his ashes spread at sea.

Swift, Jonathan (1667-1745), Anglo-Irish writer, journalist, poet, and prose satirist. Two of his satires were published in 1704: *The Battle of the Books* and *The Tale of a Tub*. He became a Tory in 1710, taking over *The Examiner*, the Tory journal. From 1714 he lived in Ireland, as dean of St. Patrick's, Dublin. He deplored the plight of the Irish poor in the *Drapier's Letters* (1724). His masterpiece is *Gulliver's Travels* (1726), a political and social satire that has been adapted as a children's classic.
See also: Gulliver's Travels.

Swimming and diving, popular water sports. Common swimming styles include the side stroke, a simple sidewise propulsion for distance swimming and lifesaving; the breaststroke, a froglike arm-and-leg thrust; backstroke, either overarm or, for distance endurance, an inverted breaststroke; and the crawl, the most common freestyle form, us-

Gamla Staden, the historic center of Stockholm, Sweden, covers three small islands in Lake Mälar, linked by bridges to the mainland.

S

S

ing an overarm pull and a flutter kick. The butterfly, a modified breaststroke that thrusts the head and arms up from the water and incorporates a dolphin kick, has become a popular competitive style. Distance swimming has produced many well-publicized attempts to cross the English Channel and other large bodies of water. Organized, artistic diving dates back to 17th century Sweden and Germany. Competitions include forward, backward, reverse, inward, twisting, and armstand dives in layout (extended), tuck (rolled in a ball), pike (bent at waist, legs straight), and free positions, from a platform or springboard. Various swimming and diving events are part of the Summer Olympic Games and other competitions.

Swinburne, Algernon Charles (1837-1909), English poet and literary critic. He established his reputation as a writer with the verse play *Atalanta in Calydon* (1865). Other important works were 2 volumes of *Poems and Ballads* (1866, 1878) and the long poem *Tristram of Lyonesse* (1882). His knowledge of literary works of classical Greece and Rome, Shakespeare and other Elizabethans, and French poetry informed his work. His own poetry is known both for its sensuality and its exploration of complex meters and rhyme schemes.

Swing *See:* Jazz.

Swiss chard, green leafy vegetable (*Beta vulgaris cicla*) similar to the beet but with an inedible root. Its large leaves, rich in vitamins A, B complex, and C, grow throughout the summer.

Swiss Family Robinson *See:* Wyss family.

Swiss Guard, member of the Swiss mercenary soldiers who served in various European armies from the 15th to the 19th centuries, most notably as bodyguards to the French monarch (1497-1792 and 1814-1830). The colorfully uniformed Papal Swiss Guard at the Vatican Palace in Rome dates back to the late 1400s. It is the only surviving branch of the Guard.

View of Lake Geneva.

Switzerland

Capital:	Bern
Area:	15,943 sq mi (41,294 sq km)
Population:	7,302,000
Language:	German, French, Italian
Government:	Federal republic
Independent:	1499
Head of gov.:	President (chosen each year by the Federal Council)
Per capita:	US$ 31,100
Monetary unit:	1 Swiss franc = 100 rappen

Switzerland, officially the Swiss Confederation, federal republic situated in the Alps in central Europe.

Land and climate. Switzerland covers 15,943 sq mi (41,293 sq km). It is bounded by Germany on the north, Austria and Liechtenstein on the east, Italy on the south, and France on the west. Lying almost entirely within the western Alps, Switzerland has three main regions: the Jura Mountains of the western Alps, the Swiss Foreland or Plateau, and the Swiss Alps. The parallel ranges and narrow valleys of the Jura run southwest to northeast along the Swiss-French border from Lake Geneva to the Rhine River at Basel. The long, narrow Swiss Foreland or Plateau, between the Jura Mountains and the Swiss Alps, extends from Lake Geneva to Lake Constance. The plateau is Switzerland's major agricultural area. It contains most of Switzerland's large cities and important manufacturing centers, and is home to about 60% of the population. The outer ranges of the Swiss Alps stretch from Lake Geneva to Lake Thun. They are succeeded by much higher ranges culminating in the Perrine Alps in the south where Monte Rosa soars to 15,203 ft (4,634 m) and the Matterhorn rises to 14,701 ft (4,481 m). Covering more than half of Switzerland, the region contains less than 20% of the population. There are many lakes in the Alps, and both the Rhine and the Rhône have their sources in its mountains. There are great variations of climate in Switzerland, due mainly to differences in altitude. Much of the country has a typically Central European climate. Sheltered valleys in the south have hot summers and mild winters. Elsewhere winters are cold, with heavy snowfall. Among Switzerland's major cities are Zurich, Basel, and Geneva. The capital is Bern.

People. The four official language groups are German (74%), French (20%), Italian (5%), and Romansh, a Rhaeto-Roman dialect (1%). The Latin word for Switzerland, *Helvetia*, appears on Swiss currencies and postage stamps. The Swiss are divided almost equally between Protestant and Roman Catholic.

Economy. Highly industrialized and with plentiful hydroelectric power, Switzerland exports watches, jewelry, precision tools and instruments, textiles, and chemicals. Dairy cattle are raised. Cheese and chocolate are important exports, and tourism and international banking are major industries.

History. Rome conquered the Helvetii, the native Swiss, in 58 B.C. The area subsequently came under the Alemanni, the Burgundians, the Franks, and, in the 10th century, the Holy Roman Empire. Habsburg oppression led to the Perpetual Covenant among the cantons or states of Uri, Schwyz, and Unterwald in 1291, the traditional beginning of the Swiss Confederation. Wars against Austria resulted in virtual independence in 1499. During the Protestant Reformation, the country was divided by religious civil wars, but it remained neutral throughout the Thirty Years' War and its independence was formally recognized in the Peace of Westphalia of 1648. French revolutionary armies imposed a centralized Helvetic Republic from 1798 to 1803. In 1815 the Congress of Vienna restored the Confederation. After a three-week civil war, a federal democracy was established in 1848. Switzerland remained neutral in both world wars. As presently constituted, the republic is a federation of 20 cantons and 6 semi-cantons, with Bern as the federal capital. Women have had the right to vote on federal matters since 1971. In 1997 Switzerland participated in NATO's Partnership for Peace. In the late 1990's, however, Switzerland's neutrality, a source of great pride for the Swiss people, was called into question when it was revealed that Switzerland had helped Germany profit from looted gold and other assets, including gold taken from victims of the Holocaust. In 1998, Swiss banks agreed to a $1.25 billion compensation payment. In a referendum in 2001, negotiations with the EU were voted against. A year later, however, the Swiss voted in favor of joining the UN.

Sword, ancient weapon consisting of a handle and a metal blade with a sharp point and one or two cutting edges. Leaf-shaped Bronze Age swords gave way to short, flat blades in Rome, and these to longer laminated iron (in Damascus) and tempered steel (notably in Toledo). Asian curved cutting blades (the Turkish scimitar) inspired the cavalry saber. The Japanese samurai used a longer, two-handed version. The thrust-and-parry rapier became the weapon of the duel and of fencing.

Swordfish, or broadbill, large, streamlined food and game fish (*Xiphias gladius*) of tropical seas, having a swordlike upper jaw. The maximum length is 16 ft (4.9 m); the maximum weight 1,500 lb (680 kg). Swordfish can swim extremely fast and, when hooked, will leap high out of the water. They eat fish that they kill with strokes of their swordlike jaw.

Sycamore, popular name for a number of deciduous trees. In North America the name is applied to a plane tree (*Platanus occidentalis*), the bark of which flakes off. In Europe the sycamore is a maple (*Acer pseudoplatanus*). The sycamore of ancient times is a fig (*Ficus occidentalis*) that is now seldom cultivated.

Sydenham, Thomas (1624-1689), English physician, considered a founder of modern medicine. He pioneered the use of quinine for treating malaria and of laudanum as an anesthetic. He was the author of an important treatise on gout, and first described Sydenham's chorea (St. Vitus's Dance).

Sydney (pop. 3,657,000), oldest and largest city in Australia, capital of New South Wales, in southeastern Australia on the Port Jackson inlet of the Pacific Ocean. Famous for its natural harbor, Harbour Bridge, and opera house, Sydney was founded as a penal colony in 1788, and gold rushes of the 1850 spurred its growth. It is now a major commercial, industrial, shipping, cultural, and recreational center. Manufactures include ships, textiles, chemicals, and refined petroleum.
See also: Australia.

Syllogism, in logic, term for a form of argument consisting of 3 statements: 2 premises and a conclusion. The conclusion of a valid syllogism follows logically from the premises and is true if the premises are true. Aristotle first formulated the concept of syllogistic logic that has served as the basis for logical thought in the West for more than 2,000 years.

Sylvester I, Saint (d.335), pope who reigned from 314 to 335. During his reign the Council of Nicaea declared Arius a heretic for arguing that the Son was unequal to God. Many legends associate Sylvester I with the Donation of Constantine, a document supposedly granting him control of church property. He is thought to be buried in the Cemetery of Saint Priscilla in Rome.
See also: Arianism.

Sylvester II (940-1003), first Frenchman to serve as pope (999-1003), known for his learning, his close links to the Holy Roman emperor Otto III, and his support of the Christianization of Poland and Hungary. Before being elected pope, he was superior at the monastery of Bobbio, Italy, and archbishop of Reims, France.

Symbiosis, also called mutualism, relationship between 2 dependent organisms of different species in which mutual benefit is derived by both participants. Other types of symbiotic relationships are commensalism which denotes independence of the symbiotes; parasitism, which implies potential injury to the host organism, and helotism, which denotes a master-slave relationship.

Symbolism, in literature, movement begun by a group of French poets in the late 19th century in opposition to naturalism.

Prominent poets associated with symbolism include Jules Laforgue, Stéphane Mallarmé, Paul Valéry, and Paul Verlaine. Influenced by Charles Baudelaire, the symbolists aimed to create poetic images, or symbols, that would be apprehended by the senses and reach into the preconscious world of the spirit. Though short-lived as a movement, symbolism influenced such major writers as James Joyce, Marcel Proust, R.M. Rilke, and W.B. Yeats.

Symphonic poem, or tone poem, form of orchestral music in one movement that describes a story or scene. Popular with composers c.1850-1900, the form was originated by Franz Liszt and perfected by Richard Strauss.

Symphony, major form of music for orchestra. Developed from the overture, by 1800 it had 4 movements: a fairly quick movement in sonata form; a slow movement; a minuet and trio; and a quick rondo. Haydn and Mozart played a central role in developing the classical symphony. Beethoven introduced the scherzo movement and a new range of emotion. Major symphonic composers include Schubert, Berlioz, Mendelssohn, Brahms, Bruckner, Dvořák, and Mahler in the 19th century, and Stravinsky, Prokofiev, Shostakovich, Vaughan Williams, Elgar, Sibelius, and Nielsen in the 20th century.
See also: Orchestra.

Synagogue (Greek, 'house of assembly'), Jewish place of worship. The synagogue became the center of communal and religious life after the destruction of the Temple in Jerusalem (A.D. 70) and dispersal of the Jews. Most synagogues have an ark containing the Torah, an 'eternal light,' 2 candelabra, pews, and a platform (bimah) for readings and conduct of services. Orthodox synagogues segregate women.
See also: Judaism.

Synchro-cyclotron, cylindrical-shaped particle accelerator designed to accelerate protons. A cylindrical magnet bends the particle beams into a circular path, as in a cyclotron, an electric field being applied to accelerate the protons each time they come around the circle. In the synchro-cyclotron the frequency of the electric field steadily decreases to compensate for the increasing mass acquired by the protons as they approach the speed of light.
See also: Lawrence, Ernest Orlando; Particle accelerator.

Synchrotron, type of particle accelerator in

which a doughnut-shaped ring of magnets around a vacuum produces a magnetic field that rises in intensity as the accelerated protons rise in velocity. This keeps the particles moving in circular orbits whose radii remain constant. The design, which requires no magnet in the center, allows rings to be built of several miles in diameter.
See also: Particle accelerator.

Syndicalism (French: *syndicat*, 'labor union'), revolutionary labor movement that aimed at seizing control of industry through strikes, sabotage, even violence, and, as its ultimate weapon, the general strike. It originated in late-19th-century France from the theories of Pierre Joseph Proudhon and Georges Sorel. Syndicalists agreed with Marxist class analysis but like anarchists rejected any state organization. Syndicalism was strong in France and Italy in the early 1900s and found U.S. expression in the industrial unionism of the Industrial Workers of the World. World War I and the advance of communism overtook the syndicalists; their influence lasted longest in Spain, where it was destroyed in the civil war (1936-1939).
See also: Labor movement.

Synge, John Millington (1871-1909), Irish poet and playwright. His plays often portray rural Irish life of his times. Among his best-known and most-respected works are the tragedy *Riders to the Sea* (1904) and the comedy *Playboy of the Western World* (1907). Some of his plays were produced in the Abbey Theatre, Dublin, which he and W.B. Yeats helped to found (1904).

Synod, council of bishops and/or other officials within the church of a diocese or country. In Calvinist and other Presbyterian churches, which do not have bishops, the synod is the highest body of the church in a country, with legislative powers and the authority to make decisions on matters of doctrine, the so-called synodic council.

Synoptic Gospels, in the New Testament, comprehensive view of the life of Jesus according to Matthew, Mark, and Luke, which contain a high level of agreement on subject matter and phraseology. Modern scholars commonly regard Mark as having written his gospel first and suppose that Matthew and Luke also used *Q*, a now-lost source containing the non-Marcan material common to them.
See also: New Testament.

Synthesizer, electronic musical device able

The Sphinx (also called *The Art* or *The Embrace*, 1896, Museum voor Schone Kunsten, Brussels) by Fernand Khnopff (1858-1921). It symbolizes the sometimes dangerous allure of enigmatic women and art.

S

to produce and change the timbre, quality, and frequency of sounds generated. First developed in 1955 and increasingly complex since the advent of microprocessors, the instrument has enabled composers and entertainers to create new works using isolated sounds or various sound combinations.

Synthetic, substance created by chemical processing and used as a substitute for naturally occurring substances. Synthetic fibers such as acrylic and nylon are used as substitutes for silk, cotton, linen, and wool. Plastics, which are all synthetics, replace glass, wood, metal, and other materials. Synthetics are often produced from carbon, hydrogen, oxygen, and other elements by polymerization, which creates extremely large molecules. Rayon, a synthetic fiber, results from dissolving and extruding cellulose, which is one of the main components of wood. Properties of synthesized materials can be controlled to suit their intended form and function.

Synthetic fuels, combustible matter that can replace crude oil and natural gas. Sources for synthetic fuels include plant and animal matter, coal, oil shale, and bituminous sands.

Syphilis, highly contagious venereal disease, caused by a spirochete, *Treponema pallidum*, and characterized by a variety of lesions (chancres, mucous patches, and skin ulcers) at the point of infection. If untreated, syphilis can cause degeneration of the central nervous system resulting in death. It is most often transmitted by sexual contact, but can also be passed on by transfusions of infected blood. Once a widespread cause of death, syphilis is now relatively easily treatable with penicillin, if detected before major damage to the nervous system occurs.
See also: Venereal disease.

Syracuse, city in southeastern Sicily, on the Ionian Sea. Founded by Corinthians (734 B.C.), it became a brilliant center of Greek culture, notably under Hiero I (r.478-466 B.C.) and Dionysius the Elder (r.405-367 B.C.). Syracuse was defeated by Rome in 212 B.C. Later conquerors included the Arabs (878) and Normans (1085). The modern provincial capital, a port and tourist center, has many ancient monuments.
See also: Sicily.

Syr Darya, a river in Central Asia. Including its chief headstream, the Naryn, which begins in the Tien Shan range of Kyrgyzstan, the Syr Darya is about 1,850 miles (2,980 km) long. The Syr Darya proper begins at the junction of the Naryn and Kara Darya rivers in Uzbekistan and flows some 1,370 miles (2,200 km) northeastward to the Aral Sea. Very little of the river's water reaches the Aral Sea because much of it is diverted for irrigation.
Virtually all of the river's lower course runs through the desert wastes of the Kyzyl Kum in Kazakhstan. In ancient times the river was known as the Jaxartes.

Syria

Capital:	Damascus
Area:	71,498 sq mi (185,180 sq km)
Population:	17,156,000
Language:	Arabic
Government:	Presidential republic
Independent:	1946
Head of gov.:	Prime minister
Per capita:	US$ 3,200
Monetary unit:	1 Syrian pound = 100 piastres

Syria, Arab republic in southwest Asia.
Land and climate. Syria covers about 71,498 sq mi (185,180 sq km) and is bounded by Turkey on the north, Iraq on the east and southeast, Jordan and Israel on the south, and Lebanon and the Mediterranean Sea on the west. Syria has a 100-mi (161-km)-long coastline on the Mediterranean. The coastal plain is separated from the inland reaches by a coast range, the Jebel Ansariya, part of the Lebanon Mountains. In the southwest, the border with Lebanon is marked by the Anti-Lebanon Mountains and Syria's highest peak, Mt. Hermon (9,232 ft/2,814 m). The mountains fall away to the plains of Hawran, extending from the Jebel ed Druz Mountains to the Sea of Galilee and the Jordan River valley. To the east and southeast are the arid wastes of the Syrian Desert, dominating most of the country and extending through Jordan and Iraq into Saudi Arabia. Syria's largest river, the Euphrates, flows through the desert. The coastal region has a Mediterranean climate. In the inland plains and the desert, the climate is much harsher.
People. Over 80% of the Syrian people are Arab-speaking Sunnite Muslims, but there are also Kurdish, Turkish, Armenian, and Circassian minorities. Christian Orthodox churches claim some 1,000,000 members, and there are about 250,000 Druzes. The capital is Damascus.
Economy. About 25% of the people work in agriculture. Industry includes textiles, iron and steel, and assembly of transportation and electrical equipment. Exports include cotton, fruits and vegetables, and phosphates. Most oil revenues are derived from pipe lines crossing the country, but income from oil drilled in the northeast is increasing. The large Euphrates Dam power station, completed with aid from the Soviet Union, was opened in 1978.
History. Part of the Hittite Empire in the second millennium B.C., Syria was conquered in succeeding centuries by Assyrians, Babylonians, Persians, and Greeks. Under the Seleucids in the 4th century B.C., it was incorporated into the Roman Empire by Pompey in 63 B.C. Governed by the Byzantines from the 5th to the 7th centuries A.D., Syria was conquered by the Arabs in the 7th century A.D. and, in the centuries that followed, it was governed by the Umayyad caliphs, the Seljuk Turks, the Mongols, and the Mameluks. Part of the Ottoman Empire from 1516, Syria was mandated to the French after World War I and became fully independent in 1946. It joined with Egypt in the United Arab Republic from 1958 to 1961. The ruling Baathist Party, which assumed control of the government in 1963, favored socialism and pan-Arab nationalism. Its foreign policy aligned with the (former) Soviet Union and against the state of Israel. In the early 1980s, the Baathist regime under Hafez al-Assad faced a period of growing unrest and challenge to its authority from the fundamentalist Muslim Brotherhood. As a result of its participation against Israel in the Six-Day War of 1967, Syria lost control of the Golan Heights to an Israeli occupying force. In 1981 the Israelis annexed the area and tensions between the two countries increased. In 1976 Syrian troops intervened in the Lebanese civil war in support of Palestinians, and since then

Now in ruins, Palmyra, an ancient caravan stop in central Syria, became a vital link in east-west commerce during the era of Roman rule.

Syria has retained a force in Lebanon. Syrian forces suffered serious losses when Israel invaded Lebanon in 1982. Syria continued to maintain close ties with the Soviet Union and, although the regime has been linked to international terrorist organizations, its cooperation was sought by the United States in the Persian Gulf War (1990-1991). Syrian troops were part of the international force created for the liberation of Kuwait. In the 1990s a process of economic and political liberalization took place. In 1996 peace negotiations with Israel proved unsuccessful. A major issue remains Israel's occupation of the Golan Heights since 1967. President Hafez al-Assad died in 2000 and was succeeded by his son Bashar.

Syriac, Aramaic language of the northwestern Semitic group. It was used in early Christian writings but was largely superseded by Arabic after the spread of Islam. Closely related to Hebrew, Syriac is still spoken by a few groups in the Middle East.

Syrian Desert, triangular desert plateau covering much of the Arabian Peninsula, including portions of present-day Saudi Arabia, Jordan, Syria, and Iraq. Al-Hamad, the name of the western part of the desert, is sometimes used as a name for the entire expanse. The northern portion is a flat plain, while the southern portion is rocky, with a mountainous central region. The extreme aridity has made the desert nearly uninhabitable, although there are remains of ancient oasis towns, including the caravan city of Palmyra. The desert is now crossed by 2 highways and by oil pipelines from Iraqi oilfields.

Syringa *See:* Mock orange.

Systematic art, art in which the elements of shape and color are ordered according to a particular system based on mathematical principles. This type of art was predominantly practiced in Europe after WW II by such artists as Albers, Morellet, Noland, Struycken and Vasarely.

Systems analysis, method of studying the interactions of humans, machines, and other elements engaged in activity through the creation of mathematical models. The system is a particular environment of physical and social interaction (e.g., school, factory, economy) viewed as an abstraction so that it can be translated into mathematical statements describing its operation. These are then subject to logical analysis, which can be used to improve the efficient operation of the system. The field, developed in the 1930s, now makes extensive use of computers.

Systolic pressure *See:* Blood pressure.

Szczecin (German: *Stettin*; pop. 416,400), city in northwestern Poland, capital of Szczecin province, on the Baltic Sea at the mouth of the Oder River. It is the main port for Poland, and also an important shipping center for goods in and out of Czechoslovakia, Hungary, and Germany. Szczecin was a fishing settlement by the 8th century. Its status changed a number of times between the 10th century, when it was annexed to Poland, and 1720, when it came under Prussian control. It then remained in German hands until 1945, when it was made part of post-World War II Poland. In addition to shipping, its economy is based on shipbuilding and manufacturing.

Szell, George (1897-1970), Hungarian-born U.S. conductor. He established his reputation in Germany but emigrated to the United States when the Nazis rose to power. Szell's performances and recordings with the Cleveland Orchestra (1946-1970) gained international acclaim.

Szent-Györgyi, Albert (1893-1966), Hungarian-born U.S. biochemist awarded the 1937 Nobel Prize in physiology or medicine for his work on biological oxidation processes and his discovery of ascorbic acid in the adrenal glands. He was also the first to isolate vitamin C.

Szymborska, Wisława (1923-), Polish poet. Szymborska achieved recognition with her unaffected poetry, initially showing influences of socialist realism, and later marked by a certain sense of melancholy. In 1996, this 'grand lady' of Polish poetry was awarded the Nobel Prize for literature.

T, 20th letter in the English alphabet, corresponding with the Semitic letter *taw*, meaning 'mark,' it is represented by an upright cross and is probably derived from an ancient Egyptian symbol for a check mark. The Greeks raised the horizontal cross-stroke to produce a capital *T*, which they called *tau*, and which became the 19th letter of the Roman alphabet. The small letter *t* developed from 6th century Roman script. *T* is used as an abbreviation for *testament*, *tablespoon*, and *township*, and *t* for words including *teaspoon*, *tempo*, *tense*, and *ton*.

Tabasco, southwestern state in Mexico on the Bay of Campeche of the Gulf of Mexico. The capital city is Villahermosa. Petroleum is the major resource of this flat, marshy region. Food crops, such as bananas and sugar cane, along with rubber, resins, and hardwoods constitute the important products of this state. Conflicts between native Mexicans (the Olmec) and the Spanish explorer Hernando Cortés took place here in the early 1500s.

Tabernacle, portable temple carried by the Israelis during their nomadic period. According to Exodus its design was given to Moses on Mt. Sinai. The inner chamber contained the Ark of the Covenant, which held the Ten Commandments.

Tabernacles, Feast of *See:* Sukkot.

Table tennis, or ping-pong, indoor game played with a ball, rackets ('paddles'), and a net, a miniature version of tennis. The 9-ft (3-m) table on which it is played is laid out like a tennis court, its 5-ft (150-cm) width spanned by a small net over which the players hit the hollow celluloid ball. The game is played by 2 players, one at either end, or by 4 players, as *doubles*. It originated in

England in the late 19th century and is now popular in many countries, particularly in Asia.

In a doubles match, the ball should be hit by each player in turn. It is therefore essential that the players are used to playing with each other, so that they do not literally get under each other's feet.

Taboo, or **tabu**, prohibition linked to an object, place, or person by law or social custom. The word taboo comes from the Polynesian word *tapu*, meaning something sacred, dangerous, or unclean. In Polynesia, violation of a taboo requires a ritual purification and at times may even warrant the death of the offender (to save the community from suffering ill consequences). In most western societies incest is considered taboo. This taboo was established hundreds of years ago to promote genetic and cultural exchanges between members of clans and tribes by prohibiting the intermarriage of close family relations.

Tabriz (pop. 1,170,000), city in northwestern Iran, capital of East Azerbaijan province, on the Aji Chai (Talkheh) River. Once called Tauris, it was the capital of Armenia in the 3rd century A.D. It was also briefly the capital of Iran (16th century). Tabriz is surrounded by mountains and has been repeatedly damaged by earthquakes. It produces Persian rugs and other textiles, and is a resort and trade center.
See also: Iran.

Tabularium, library of ancient Rome, used to store records. Erected in 73 B.C., . tt was located on Capitoline Hill, the historic center of ancient Rome.

Tachism (Fr.: tache = stain), movement of European art, similar to abstract expressionism. Created around 1950. Characterized by the spontaneous application of paint on the canvas without any form of composition being worked out in advance. Exponents included Jean Fautrier, Georges Mathieu and Wols.

Tachometer, instrument that measures the speed at which a wheel or shaft spins. This measurement, usually given in terms of revolutions per minute (rpm), helps gauge the efficiency and power of an engine. Tachometers are used in automobiles, ships, and aircraft.

Tachycardia, abnormally fast heartrate. Generally, anything over 100 beats per minute is considered a tachycardia.
See also: Heart.

Tachyon, subatomic particles that in theory move faster than the speed of light.

T

According to Albert Einstein's theory of relativity (1905), all matter moves slower than the speed of light (186,282 mi per sec/299,792 km per sec). Theoretically, tachyons gain energy as they slow down; it would take massive amounts of energy to slow them down to approximately the speed of light. Physicists today believe that the existence of tachyons fits into Einstein's theory, even though experiments have not as yet proved their existence.

Tacitus, Cornelius (c.A.D. 55-120), Roman historian. His most famous works are critical studies of the 1st-century empire, the *Histories* and *Annals*. A son-in-law of Agricola, of whom he wrote a biography, he rose to consul (97) and proconsul (112) of Asia. His *Germania* is the earliest study of the Germanic tribes.

Taconite, rock containing about 30% iron ore, from which iron is made. The noniron-bearing part of taconite is called chert. Because taconite is very hard, it takes a number of steps to extract the iron ore material, which is speckled throughout the chert. After the rock is initially blasted or cracked, it is broken down further and crushed. Magnets then can attract the iron ore and separate it from the pulverized chert. A large deposit of taconite is found in the Mesabi Range in Minnesota. Taconite is named after the Taconic Mountains of southern New England, where taconite is also found.

Tadpole, or polliwog, larval amphibian hatched from transparent, jellylike eggs laid on the water. Tadpoles have the physical characteristics of fish (tail and gills). Through metamorphosis (a stage that can last from 10 days to 2 years, depending on the species) legs appear, the digestive system develops, the tail begins to shrink, and lungs develop as the gills disappear. In the adult frog or toad, the tail also disappears.

Tadzhikistan *See:* Tajikistan.

Taegu (pop. 2,500,000), South Korea, the capital of North Kyongsang province. It is about 150 miles (240 km) southeast of Seoul, the national capital. Taegu serves as the market and transportation center for a large agricultural area. Chief industries include food processing and textile milling. Kungpook National University and Yeungnam University are here. During the

Korean War, Taegu was the key point in the defense of the Pusan perimeter by United Nations and South Korean forces.

Taejon (pop. 1,300,000), South Korea, the capital of South Chungchong province. It lies near the Kum River about 85 miles (137 km) southeast of Seoul, the national capital. Taejon is in the heart of a rich agricultural region where rice is the principal crop. It is a regional trade center and has foodprocessing, silk, and leather industries. In 1950, during the Korean War, Taejon suffered heavy damage when it was captured by the North Koreans.

Tae Kwon Do (tae = kick, kwon = hit with fist or hand, do = way, manner), Korean martial art based on punch and kick techniques, similar to karate. Tae Kwon Do was created out of various Korean martial arts that had been practiced since the Middle Ages, such as Tang Soo Do, Kong Soo Do, Soo Bak Gi. Each bout lasts two minutes, and competitions are divided into various weight classes. Points, from 1 to 3, are awarded based on the quality of the kicks or punches, in which technique, style and sportsmanship are important. The level of ability in Tae Kwon Do is classified according to a Dan grading system.

Taft, William Howard (1857-1930), 27th president of the United States (1909-1913). In his own time, Taft was judged one of the weakest of U.S. presidents, yet the achievements of his administration were substantial. Taft served as the first civil governor of the Philippine Islands (1901-1904), then as President Theodore Roosevelt's secretary of war. He became a valued troubleshooter, helping to reorganize the building of the Panama Canal, settle the Russo-Japanese War, and avert a revolution in Cuba. Roosevelt, who chose not to run for reelection in 1908, pushed Taft as his successor. Taft resolved to carry on 'the same old plan' of the Roosevelt administration: domestic reform, the curbing of big business, and conservation of the nation's resources. In foreign affairs, Taft was less successful. He and his secretary of state initiated 'dollar diplomacy'-a policy of using trade and commerce to enhance the nation's influence abroad. It poisoned foreign relations, particularly with Latin America, for more than a generation. Taft's tariff and conservation policies put him at odds with Republican progressives. Theodore Roosevelt ran against him in 1912, splitting the Republican vote and allowing Democrat Woodrow Wilson to win the presidency.

Tagalogs, a people living in the Philippines. A modified form of their language, called Pilipino, is the country's national language and is spoken by more than half the population. The Tagalogs are of Malayan origin and their ancestors migrated to the Philippines during the first 13 centuries A.D.

Taglioni, Italian family of ballet dancers, ballerinas and choreographers. Most important members were:
1. **Salvatore Taglioni** (1790-1868), dancer

and choreographer. Founder of the royal dance school in Naples (1812). Created more than 150 choreographies.
2. **Filippo Taglioni** (1777-1871), dancer, ballet master and choreographer, brother of Salvatore, father of Marie (1804-1884). Began his career as a dancer in Pisa (1794). Worked in Stockholm, Vienna and Paris. Developed a completely new style of choreography that encapsulated the spirit of romanticism. His first romantic ballet was *La Sylphide* (Paris, 1832, music by Jean Schneitzhöffer).
3. **Paolo Taglioni** (1804-1884). Dancer, ballet master and choreographer, son of Filippo. Began dancing in 1824. Often performed as the partner of his sister Marie. Choreography of *Don Quichotte* (1839) and *Coppélia* (1882).
4. **Marie Taglioni** (also Maria, 1833-1891) called 'the younger'. Daughter of Paolo. First performed in London (1847). Performed in Vienna (1853-1856), and from 1856 to 1866 worked at the Berlin State Opera.

Taglioni, Marie (1804-1884), Swedish-born Italian ballerina. Trained from an early age by her father, Filippo Taglioni, she gained worldwide renown for her dancing in *La Sylphide* (1832) at the Paris Opéra. Taglioni was noted for her innovative style and was considered a major figure during ballet's romantic era, which lasted until the mid-1840s.
See also: Ballet.

Tagore, Sir Rabindranath (1861-1941), Bengali Indian writer, painter, musician, and mystic who founded what is now Visva-Bharati University to blend the best in Indian and Western culture. His literary work includes many songs, poems, plays, novels, short stories, and essays. He received the 1913 Nobel Prize for literature.

Tagus River, or Tajo River, river that runs 626 mi (1,007 km) from central eastern Spain west through Portugal to the Atlantic Ocean. The mouth of the river opens into the harbor at Lisbon, Portugal.

Tahiti, largest (400 sq mi/1,036 sq km) of the Society Islands in the South Pacific, the center of French Polynesia. The island is mountainous and rich in tropical vegetation. The people are mostly Polynesians, with some French and Chinese. Papeete is the capital. Tahiti, claimed for France by

Marie and Paolo Taglione in the ballet *La Sylphide*, which was first performed in 1832.

Tahitian copra harvesters.

Bougainville in 1768, was visited by James Cook and William Bligh. Its beauty inspired the painter Paul Gauguin.

Taine, Hippolyte Adolphe (1828-1893), French writer and intellectual concerned with aesthetics-the nature of art and artistic judgments. He approached his study of art as a scientist. Taine concluded that the artist's art was determined by influences such as the artist's heredity, environment, and aesthetic training. His belief in determinism supported the French philosophical movement of Positivism-a school of thought developed in 19th and 20th century Europe. It also influenced the artistic movement of naturalism in France, of which the 19th-century novels of Emile Zola are examples. Taine's books include *History of English Literature* (1863), *Philosophy of Art* (1865-1869), and *Origins of Contemporary France* (1875-1893). He was a professor at the École de Beaux-Arts in Paris (1864-1883).
See also: Naturalism; Positivism.

Taipei (pop. 2,700,000), capital and largest city of Taiwan, lying to the north on the Tanshui River. A major industrial city, with steel plants, oil refineries and glass factories, Taipei is also the cultural and educational center of Taiwan. Founded in the early 1700s, it became capital of the Nationalist Chinese government in 1949.

Taiwan

Capital:	Taipei
Area:	13,900 sq mi (36,000 sq km)
Population:	22,548,000
Language:	Chinese (Mandarin)
Government:	Republic
Independent:	1950
Head of gov.:	Prime minister
Per capita:	US$ 17,200
Monetary unit:	1 New Taiwan dollar = 100 cents

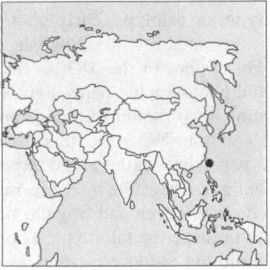

Taiwan, formerly Formosa, island in the western Pacific Ocean, formally Republic of China. Together with the Pescadores, Quemoy, and Matsu groups, it is the official seat of the Republic of China government, which claims to be the legal ruler of all China. Taiwan is separated from mainland China by the Formosa Strait, which is about 90 mi (145 km) wide.

Land and climate. With an area of 13,900 sq mi (36,000 sq km) the island of Taiwan is forested and mountainous, with extensive plains in the west. Its highest point is Yü Shan (13,113 ft/3,997 m). The monsoonal climate is tropical in the south, subtropical in the north, and makes possible 2 rice harvests a year.

People. Most of the people of Taiwan are Chinese and come largely from the Fukien province on the mainland. The major religions are Buddhism and Taoism. The official language is Chinese.

Economy. Once predominantly agricultural, Taiwan's economy has become heavily industrialized. Major industries include steel, aluminum, textiles, metals, machinery, and chemicals, but the mainstay of its manufacturing and exports is in electronics. Irrigation is vital for growing rice, sweet potatoes, soybeans, sugar, tea, fruits, and cotton; sugar and tea are exported. There are rich fisheries and the island has much timber. Its natural resources include coral, natural gas, some oil, gold, copper, and silver.

History. Named Formosa by the Portuguese, who arrived in 1590, the island came under the control of the Dutch in 1624. It subsequently fell to a Ming general in 1662 and then to the Manchus in 1683. Taiwan was ceded to Japan in 1895 as part of the settlement of the First Sino-Japanese War and remained in Japanese hands until the end of World War II. In 1949, it became a refuge and stronghold for Chiang Kai-shek's Nationalists, the Kuomintang, after they were driven from the mainland by Communist forces under Mao Zedong. The Kuomintang turned the island of Formosa into the Republic of China, and declared it the legitimate government of China under the presidency of Chiang Kai-shek. Between 1951 and 1965, Taiwan was supported with the help of substantial subsidies from the U.S. government. But eventually the United States decided to recognize Mao's government, and in 1971 Taiwan was expelled from the UN and its seat given to the government of the People's Republic of China. From 1954 to 1980, Taiwan was protected by the United States under the terms of the Mutual Defense Treaty of 1954, but in the years following U.S. recognition of the mainland government, Taiwan found itself increasingly isolated. The death of Chiang Kai-shek in 1975 dealt a further blow to Taiwan's political aspirations. Chiang was succeeded by his son, Chiang Ching-kuo, who died in 1988. From 1949 to 1987, Taiwan was under martial law, but with its suspension there arose opposition parties on the island in addition to the dominant Kuomintang of the Nationalists and their supporters. In 1990 Chiang Ching-kuo's successor, Lee Teng-hui, a native Taiwanese, was elected without opposition to a 6-year term. In 1996 the first direct presidential elections were held. They were won by Leng Teng-hui. China regarded the elections as an illegal act, and tried to intimidate Taiwan by carrying out military drills and missile tests.

Chen Shui-bian, leader of the opposition party DPP, won the 2000 Presidential elections. This ended the Kuomintang's 50-year monopoly of power. In 2001, the Kuomintang also lost their majority in Parliament. Despite China's opposition, the U.S. continued to sell arms to Taiwan. Both Taiwan and China joined the World Trade Organization in 2002.

Taiyuan (pop. 2,1 million), China, the capital of Shanxi province. It lies in the fertile Fen River valley, some 240 miles (390 km) southwest of Beijing. Coal, iron ore, and other nearby resources have helped make the city one of China's principal centers of heavy industry. Taiyuan's growth has been especially rapid since the early 1950's. Attractions include the Jin temples and gardens and the Shanxi Museum. Though of ancient origin, Taiyuan was of little importance until the eighth century A.D., when it became a fortified city. The original original walled city was destroyed during a siege in the late 10th century. Taiyuan was rebuilt near the original site and was made the capital of Shanxi province in the 15th century. From 1912 to 1947 the city was called Yangku.

Taizz (pop. 242,000), capital of the province of the same name in Yemen (province pop. 1,644,000; 4,025 sq mi [10,420 sq km]). Center of agricultural area (coffee, qat); aluminum industry. Beautiful mosques. Islamic theoretical school. International airport. The city was part of the Arab Republic of Yemen (South Yemen) until 1990.

Balloons are released in Presidential Square during Nation Day festivities in Taipei. Nation Day, also called Double Tenth Day because it is observed on each October 10, celebrates the revolution of 1911, which established the Chinese republic.

T

T

Tajikistan

Capital:	Dushanbe
Area:	55,251 sq mi (143,100 sq km)
Population:	5,927,000
Language:	Tajik
Government:	Presidential republic
Independent:	1991
Head of gov.:	Prime minister
Per capita:	US$ 340
Monetary unit:	1 Tajikistan rouble = 100 kopeks

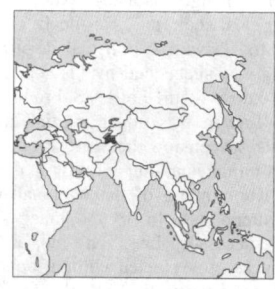

Tajikistan (Republic of), also Tadzhikistan, independent country in Central Asia, bordering China (east), Afghanistan (south), Kyrgyzstan (north), and Uzbekistan (west). *Land and climate.* Tajikistan is the smallest of the five Central Asian republics (55,300 sq mi; 143,000 sq km). The country is very mountainous, and has a continental climate. *People.* Most of its inhabitants are Tajiks (62%), a people related to Sunni Muslim Iranians. Uzbeks constitute the largest minority (24%). The official language is Tajik. The major religion is Sunni Islam. *Economy.* Farming and mining are the region's chief industries. Cotton, barley, rice, and wheat are important crops. Major products from mining include fluorite, lead, ura-

nium, zinc, and tungsten. During the civil war (1992-1997) part of the infrastructure was destroyed. *History.* In the past, the area was frequently occupied by other peoples: Macedonians (Alexander the Great), Persians, and Turks. In the seventh century the population was converted to Islam. After the Mongolian domination the country was conquered by Russia (19th century). One of the 15 constituent republics of the USSR (Soviet Union), Tajikistan became independent in 1991. The country is part of the Commonwealth of Independent States (CIS). In the spring of 1992 a coalition of forces opposed to Tajikistan's pro-Communist government rebelled. The rebels captured the capital and formed a government. By the beginning of 1993 forces loyal to the ousted government had recaptured the capital and consolidated power. Many rebels fled to Afghanistan, where they received support and from where they launched attacks into Tajikistan. In 1993 Tajikistan signed a collective security treaty with Kazakhstan, Kyrgyzstan, Russia, and Uzbekistan. Peacekeeping forces from these nations were deployed along the Tajik-Afghan border, making Tajikistan one of the few former Soviet countries where Russia is still military present. In 1994 Tajik voters approved a new constitution in a national referendum, turning the country into a parliamentary republic. A peace treaty was signed in 1997, but peace is threatened continually by fighting. Since it borders on Afghanistan, Tajikistan received a great deal of international attention after the attacks of September 11, 2001. The country supported the Northern Alliance, and therefore, the U.S. The U.S. used Tajikistan's strategic position to attack Afghanistan. Russia was concerned by the renewed U.S. presence in the region.
See also: Union of Soviet Socialist Republics.

Taj Mahal, mausoleum built by the Mogul emperor Shah Jahan for his wife Mumtaz-i-Mahal at Agra in North India. Faced in white marble, the central domed tomb stands on a square block with a minaret at each corner, surrounded by water gardens, gateways, and

walks. It took some 20,000 workers over 20 years to complete (1630-1650).
See also: Shah Jahan.

Takemitsu, Toru (1930-1996), Japanese composer. Takemitsu, who was almost completely self-taught, attempted in his compositions to achieve a synthesis between Japanese and Western music. His most well-known works, noted for their poetic style, transparency, and a permanent fluidity, include *Requiem for strings* (1957), *Textures* (1965), *November steps* (1967), *Riverrun* (1984), and *Archipelago S* (1993). He also wrote film music.

Takeshita, Noboru (1924-2000), Japanese politician, prime minister 1987-1989. He was elected to parliament in 1858, subsequently serving as chief cabinet secretary (1971-1972, 1974), construction minister (1976), and finance minister (1979-1980, 1982-1986). He became head of the Liberal-Democratic Party in 1987. In a major upheaval, Takeshita and many other high officials of the Japanese government were implicated in a stocktrading scandal, and he resigned as prime minister in 1989.
See also: Japan.

Takeuchi, Shusaku (1948-), Japanese choreographer and dancer, has worked in the Netherlands since 1973, where he combines Japanese and European dance to create a slow, captivating theatrical display full of the unexpected.

Tal, Mikhail (1936-1992), Lithuanian chess player, achieved his first major success in 1987, when he won the international grandmaster title. Two years later he won the candidate's tournament, and went on to win the world title in 1960 by beating Mikhael Botvinnik 121/2-81/2. He lost the title the very next year to Botvinnik. Tal was an obsessive chess player, who literally played the game day and night. His brilliant style led him to be called the 'wizard of Riga'. Despite his weak health, Tal became champion of the Soviet Union in 1957, 1958, 1967, 1974 and 1978, also winning numerous prestigious international tournaments. In 1979 he was second in the Elo rankings, behind Anatoly Karpov.

Talbotype, or calotype, early photographic process invented by the English scientist W.H. Fox Talbot in the 1830s. Talbot first made the photographic paper light-sensitive by treating it with sodium chloride and silver nitrate solution. When he then placed the treated paper in a camera and exposed the paper to light, a negative image formed on it, which he then developed in gallo-nitrate of silver to produce the talbotype. Though this method did not produce pictures as clear as the daguerreotype, any number of prints could be made from the talbotype negative.
See also: Photography.

Talc, [$Mg_3Si_4O_{10}(OH)_2$], hydrous magnesium silicate mineral occurring in metamorphic rocks, chiefly in the United States, USSR, France, and Japan. It has a layer structure resembling that of mica, and is extremely soft. Talc is translucent but not

The Taj Mahal (1632-53) in Agra is Shah Jahan's mausoleum for his wife, Mumtaz-i-Mahal. It is the supreme work of Moghul architects, who 'built like Titans and finished like goldsmiths'. The mausoleum of Markana marble stands on a plinth (1), of 22 ft (6.7 m) high and 313 ft (95.4 m) square, with four corner minarets (2). A central dome (3), reflecting Safavid influence, contains an inner dome and is flanked by smaller domes (4). The crypt (5) is underground.

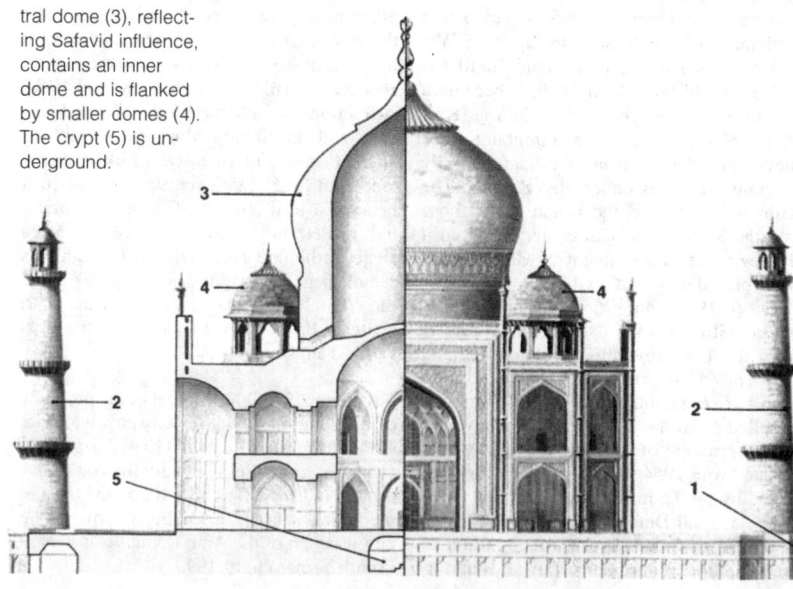

transparent. It is used in ceramics, roof insulation, cosmetics, as an insecticide carrier, and as a filler in paints, paper, and rubber. Impure, massive talc is called soapstone.

Taliban (Taleban) fundamentalist Islamic movement in Afghanistan. The word 'Talib' is Pashto for 'student of Islamic books'; Taliban is the plural form. The movement began during the 1994 civil war in the southern city of Kandahar. From there the militant movement captured virtually the whole country. In 1996 Kabul was taken. In the occupied areas they introduced a strict regime that particularly restricted the rights and freedom of movement of women. Girls were no longer allowed to go to school and women were not allowed to work, except in the health care sector. Dress code for both men and women was strict: no uncovered body parts. Many men had to grow a beard. The Taliban belong to the Pathan ethnic group (Pashto), an ethnic group in which women are traditionally protected against the outside world. This practice has been taken over by the Taliban and strictly enforced. There are several different groups within the Taliban, none of which has a permanent leadership. In 2001, the Taliban government refused to give up Osama bin Laden, following his suspected involvement in the terrorist attacks on the U.S., provoking a US-led military attack on Afghanistan, and the removal of the Taliban regime.

Tallchief, Maria (1925-), U.S. ballet dancer, of Native American and European ancestry. With her debut as a dancer for the Ballet Russe de Monte Carlo (1942), she became the first U.S. dancer of prominence in Europe-then the ballet center of the world. As a dancer with the New York City Ballet (1947-1965), she performed the female lead in many of the ballets choreographed by George Balanchine. The ballet *Firebird* (1949) became her signature role. The Chicago City Ballet was established by her (1980), and for the first 7 years she was its artistic director.
See also: Ballet.

Talleyrand (Charles Maurice de Talleyrand-Périgord; 1754-1838), French politician. A member of the clergy, he represented them in the French parliament (States-General) in 1789 and became a moderate leader and influential spokesperson for the French Revolution in its early years. A fall from favor with the new leadership in 1792 led to a 4-year exile. Appointed an adviser by Napoleon I, Talleyrand rose to the rank of foreign minister until mutual mistrust between the 2 men led to his resignation in 1807. After Napoleon's first exile (1814), Talleyrand helped restore the Bourbon monarchy and was a key negotiator at the Congress of Vienna (1815). In 1830 he helped lead the overthrow of the last Bourbon king, Charles X, and became the ambassador to England under King Louis Philippe. He helped steer the negotiations that resulted in the independence of Belgium (1830).
See also: France.

Tallinn (pop. 452,000), capital city of Estonia, on the Gulf of Finland, an arm of the Baltic Sea. Tallinn, which dates from the Middle Ages, was a member of the Hanseatic League from the late 1200s to the mid-1300s. Many churches, castles, and buildings survive from that time. From 1346 to 1710, control of Tallinn and the surrounding area passed from the Livonian Knights to Sweden and then Russia. In 1919 it became the capital of an independent Estonian republic, which was overrun in 1940 by the Soviet Union, along with the rest of Estonia and the other 2 Baltic republics, Latvia and Lithuania. Tallinn today is the capital of independent Estonia and is an important seaport and shipbuilding center.
See also: Estonia.

Tallowtree, any of several trees of the family Euphorbiaceae producing a waxy substance that can be used to produce tallow for candles. The Chinese tallowtree (*Sapium sebiferum*) has also been planted as a shade tree in the southeastern United States.

Talmud (Hebrew, 'teaching'), compilation of Jewish oral law and rabbinical teachings begun in the 5th century A.D. It has two parts: the Mishnah (oral law), written between A.D. 70 and 200, and the Gemara (commentary on the Mishnah), written between 200 and 500. In addition to commentary and debates on the details of Jewish law, the Gemara contains many traditional legends and stories. The Talmud consists of 63 sections (*tractates*), which are divided into 6 orders. Each order deals with a different subject, such as civil and criminal law and cleanliness. The study of the Talmud has been the core of Jewish education for over 1,000 years. After the Bible, the Talmud stands as the second most important and influential written work of the Jewish religion.

Tamarack *See:* Larch.

Tamarin, one of 14 monkey species belonging to the tamarin and marmoset family, native to the rain forests of Central and South America. Somewhat larger than the marmoset, it lives in groups of about 40 and uses various high-pitched calls to communicate. Tamarins are generally multicolored and grow up to 12 in (31 cm) long, excluding the tail, which may extend to 17 in (44 cm). As a result of the deforestation of the Amazon rain forest, the lion tamarin-so-called because of its long gold mane-is in danger of extinction.

Tamarind (*Tamarindus indica*), tropical tree belonging to the pea family. The fruits are made into preserves and laxative drinks.

Tambourine, percussion instrument comprising a skin stretched across a hoop fitted with bells, or 'jingles,' that rattle as it is tapped or shaken. Originating in the Middle East, it is used in folk and popular music and in some orchestral scores.

Tamerlane, or Timur the Lame (c.1336-1405), Mongol conqueror, descendant of Genghis Khan. Tamerlane succeeded to the throne of Turkestan in 1369 and from his capital at Samarkand set out on a series of conquests, including Afghanistan, Persia,

Timur, or Tamerlane, enters his capital city of Samarkand in this 14th-century Persian miniature. This conqueror, who acclaimed descent from Genghis Khan, led his Turko-Mongol armies in brilliant military campaigns against India, Persia and the Ottoman Empire. Timur's vast empire collapsed shortly after his death in 1405.

and southern portions of what was the USSR. In 1398 he invaded India and sacked Delhi, where it is believed he and his troops massacred 80,000 people. Three years later he moved against Syria and captured Baghdad. The following year (1402) his armies defeated the Ottoman Turks and captured their sultan, Beyazid I. After capturing Damascus and defeating the Egyptian army, he plotted to overrun China but died before he could implement his plans. His empire, centered in Turkestan, crumbled after his death.
See also: Mongol Empire.

Tamil, Dravidian language spoken by some 40 million people, principally in southeast India and northeast Sri Lanka. It is the main language of Tamil Nadu (formerly Madras) state. Tamil has its own script and a rich ancient literature.

Tamil Nadu (pop. 55,900,000); called Madras until 1968), constituent state in the south of India; 50,235 sq mi (130,058 sq km). Capital, Madras. Important industrial area; steel, textiles, transport, sugar and construction industries. Fertile agricultural area with rice, maize, sugarcane, cashew nuts, tobacco and rubber. Also mining and tourism. The majority of the population is Hindu.

Tan, Amy (1952-), American writer of Chinese descent. Amy Tan's first book *The Joy Luck Club* was published in 1989, and is about the lives of Chinese women who have recently emigrated to the U.S., and whose daughters are born in America. This was followed with *The Kitchen God's Wife* (1991), *The Hundred Secret Senses* (1995), and *The Bonesetter's Daughter* (2001).

Tanaka, Kakuei (1918-1993), Japanese prime minister (1972-1974). He built up a construction business, headed the Liberal Democratic Party from 1965, and held cabinet posts from 1968. He was forced to resign in 1974 because of financial misconduct and was convicted in 1983 of having accepted bribes from Lockheed Corporation.
See also: Japan.

Tanaka, Min, Japanese dancer. He began to create his own choreographies in 1973 based on improvisation, in which he appeared

T

naked. He set up his own dance group called Maijuku in 1981, and in 1982 began to work closely with Tatsumi Hijkata, founder of the modern Japanese Butóh style. Since Hijkata's death, Tanaka has been the successor and heir to this master. Tanaka often worked with visual artists, and performed regularly in museums in Paris, Basel, New York, San Francisco and Berlin. In 1987 he designed the choreography for a ballet by Karel Appel in Paris entitled *Can We Dance a Landscape?*

T

Tan, Melvyn (1956-), Singaporean pianist and harpsichord player. Tan studied piano with Vlado Perlemuter. He is mainly known as a fortepianist, but in recent years has also played the modern grand piano with Ronald Brautigam (4-hands).

Tananarive *See:* Antananarivo.

Tang dynasty, rulers of China from A.D. 618 to 907. The Tang period is regarded as the golden age of Chinese civilization by many historians. During this period, Tang rulers centralized the government and unified the country. The capital city, Chang'an (now Xian), served as a worldwide center for scholarship and the arts. During this time, the Chinese invented block printing and produced the first block-printed book (A.D. 868). Emperor Tang Taizong, who ruled for 22 years, led the rise of the Tang dynasty. He conquered foreign lands and opened trade routes that brought the country great wealth and prosperity. Empress Wu followed Emperor Taizong's rule with great skill and came to be known as the second greatest Chinese leader. An 80-year war with the Tibetans in northwestern China, coupled with years of internal fighting, weakened the Tang dynasty, and it came to an end in 907. *See also:* China.

Until the beginning of the 9th century, China was a feudal society that was entirely dominated by aristocratic landowners, who were usually also the local rulers. This drawing on paper, dating from the early T'ang period (7th century), shows one of these potentates, accompanied by his humble servant.

Tange, Kenzo (1913-), trend-setting Japanese architect. His work included elements from both the Western world and traditional Japanese culture. His first important work was the Peace Monument in Hiroshima (1956). Designed many daring concrete structures, such as sports complexes for the Olympic games in Tokyo in 1964 and the meeting hall for the World's Fair in Osaka in 1970. He was the supervising director for the whole construction complex. Was also a town planner (Bologna, 1940).

Tangelo, citrus fruit produced by crossing a tangerine with a grapefruit. The name *tange-*lo is a combination of *tangerine* and *pomelo* (another word for grapefruit). Like the tangerine, the tangelo has a thin peel and sweet pulp. The Minneola and the Orlando are North American varieties, and the Ugli is a Jamaican strain common to the West Indies.

Tangerine, fruit in the rue family, related to the orange. In shape, color, and taste the tangerine resembles the orange, but is smaller and easier to peel. Although originated in Southeast Asia, tangerines are grown in the southeast and western United States and Brazil, Italy and Spain. Clementine and Dancy are two popular varieties of tangerine.

Tangier (pop. 554,000), seaport and residential and commercial city of Morocco, facing the Strait of Gibraltar. Tangier is a major center of tourism and shipping and is considered Morocco's main passenger-vessel port. It is heavily populated by Arabs and Berbers. The city has its origins in the settlements built by the Phoenicians and Romans in ancient times. It was under Arab control in the 700s. From the 1400s to the late 1600s, when the sultan of Morocco acquired the power to guide Tangier, it was held, at different times, by France, Portugal, and England. In 1912 the city again fell under the control of Spain and France, and in 1923 it was put under international control. In 1956 Tangier became fully independent of France and Spain, gave up its international status, and came under the full control of Morocco.
See also: Morocco.

Tangshan (pop. 1,500,000) China, a city in Hebei province, about 100 miles (160 km) east-southeast of Beijing, the national capital. Tangshan lies on a main railway line to Manchuria in a rich coal-mining region. It is a center for iron and steel manufacturing and other heavy metallurgical industries. In 1976 two earthquakes nearly destroyed the city, killing several hundred thousand persons.

Tank, combat vehicle, armed with guns or missiles, and self-propelled on caterpillar treads; the chief modern conventional ground assault weapon. Tanks were first built in 1915 by Britain and used from 1916 against Germany in World War I. These early tanks were very slow, and development between the wars greatly improved speed and firepower. The Spanish Civil War and World War II showed the effectiveness of concentrated tank attacks. Amphibious and airborne tanks were developed. Heavy tanks

The Abbott Self Propelled Howitzer fires 105 mm. ammunition, over a range of up to 11 mi (17 km). It requires a five man operating crew.

proved cumbersome and were generally abandoned in favor of the more maneuverable (though more vulnerable) light and medium tanks. Improved models are now used where heavy guns are needed. Light tanks (less than 25 tons/23 metric tons) are used mainly for infantry support.
See also: Army.

Tanker, ship designed to carry liquid cargo in bulk, notably crude oil, gasoline, or natural gas. The first tanker (1886), a 300-ft (90-m) vessel, carried 3,000 tons (272 metric tons) of oil. Some tankers today hold 100 times as much: a 483,939-ton (439,029-metric ton) vessel (the *Globtik London*, 1975) has been built in Japan. Ships this size greatly reduce per-ton transport costs but cannot enter many ports; some large tankers transfer their cargo to smaller tankers offshore. In gross tonnage tankers account for over a third of all merchant shipping.

Tannhäuser (c.1200-1270), German poet and legendary character who wrote poems that were sung. A number of dance songs, love songs, and lyric songs of his still exist. He supposedly participated in the Crusades (1228-1229) and traveled widely throughout Europe. The composer Richard Wagner based his opera *Tannhäuser* on the poet's life. As legend has it, Tannhäuser lived in a mountain with the goddess Venus for 7 years. During a visit to Rome, Tannhäuser asked the pope to forgive his sins, but the pope responded that just as his staff could never blossom, never could Tannhäuser's sins be forgiven. Dejected, Tannhäuser returned to Venus. Three days later the pope's staff blossomed into flowers.

Tannic acid, or tannin ($C_{76}H_{52}O_{46}$), organic substance extracted from the bark of certain trees (e.g., oak, hemlock, and chestnut). In a process known as tanning, tannin is added to animal hides to resist decomposition. Tannin is also used to manufacture inks and is used as a fixative (mordant) for dyes. It can also be used as a medicine for treating burns and as an astringent. Most of the tannin used in the United States today is obtained from the quebracho trees of Argentina and Paraguay.

Tantalum, chemical element, symbol Ta; for physical constants see Periodic Table. Tantalum was discovered by A.G. Ekeberg in 1802. It occurs in the mineral microlite. It is obtained commercially from columbite-tantalite, a mixed oxide with niobium and iron and manganese. The element is prepared by the high-temperature reaction of tantalum (V) oxide with tantalum carbide in a vacuum. Tantalum is a gray, hard, malleable, ductile metal. It is high-melting and resistant to chemical attack. A tantalum carbide-graphite composite is one of the hardest materials ever made. Tantalum and its compounds are used in laboratory apparatus, surgical prostheses, special glasses, electrolytic capacitors, nuclear reactors, aircraft, missiles, and catalysts.

Tantalus, in Greek mythology, king of Lydia and son of Zeus and the nymph Pluto. Zeus banished him to Hades because of his cruel sacrifice of his son Pelops. Tantalus was punished by being forced to stand chin-deep in water under hanging fruit, each of which receded just beyond his reach whenever he wanted to eat or drink. The word *tantalize* is derived from his name.
See also: Mythology.

Tantrism, religious current within both Hinduism and Buddhism, originated in the 6th century in India. The particular characteristic of tantrism is the use of various rituals to achieve salvation or enlightenment: mantras, sayings only known to the initiated; mudras, ritual gestures and body postures; mandalas, diagrams which represent the sources of difference and unity in the cosmos. Tantrism makes a distinction between the male and female aspects; only through their unification can world events remain on course.

Tanzania

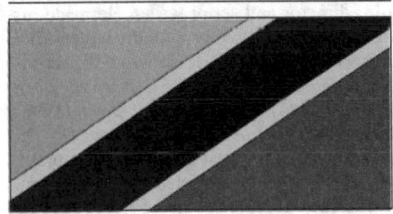

Capital:	Dodoma
Area:	364,804 sq mi (945,087 sq km)
Population:	37,188,000
Language:	Swahili, English
Government:	Federal presidential republic
Independent:	1964 (1961 Tanganyika/ 1963 Zanzibar)
Head of gov.:	Prime minister (1 of 2 Vice-Presidents)
Per capita:	US$ 610
Monetary unit:	1 Tanzanian shilling = 100 cents

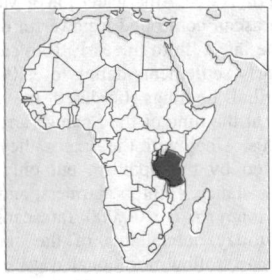

Tanzania, independent republic in East Africa consisting of the mainland, formerly Tanganyika, and the islands of Zanzibar and Pemba. The mainland of Tanzania has Mozambique, Malawi, and Zambia to its south; Congo, Burundi, and Rwanda to the west; Uganda and Kenya on the north; and the Indian Ocean to the east. Zanzibar and Pemba are separated from the mainland by the 22-mi- (35-km)-wide Zanzibar Channel.
Land and climate. Mainland Tanzania covers an area of 366,313 sq mi (945,087 sq km), including 22,888 sq mi (59,050 sq km) of inland water. The islands cover an area of 950 sq mi (2,461 sq km). A coastal belt, fringed by sand beaches, coral reefs, and mangrove swamps, leads inland to plains and plateaus 2,000 to 4,000 ft (1,219 km) above sea level with vast expanses of grasslands and open woodlands, as well as isolated hills and hill ranges. In this area is the Serengeti Plain, site of one of several national parks. To the north is Lake Victoria, and above the plateaus rise the Usambara, Pare, Kilimanjaro, and Meru mountains. Mt. Kilimanjaro (19,340 ft/5,895 m) is Africa's highest peak. The uplands extend to the south where they meet Lake Nyasa and the Ufipa Highlands. To the west lies Lake Tanganyika. Zanzibar and Pemba are coral islands and fertile. Their climate, like that of the coastal belt, is tropical. The inland climate is hot and dry for most of the year, and most humid in the highlands and along the western shore of Lake Victoria.
People. The vast majority of the people are black Africans, but there are also people of Asian, Arab, and European descent. Christianity (45%) and Islam (35%) account for more than three-quarters of the population. The rest of the people adhere to traditional beliefs. The official languages are Swahili and English.
Economy. Tanzania's economy is chiefly agricultural. Coffee and cotton are primary exports, but other important exports include cloves from Zanzibar, pyrethrum, sisal, tobacco, and tea. Manufacturing is limited principally to processing agricultural products and industry is dominated by mining. Tanzania is a producer of diamonds. A new gold mine was opened in 2001, making Tanzania Africa's third largest producer of gold.
History. Olduvai Gorge in North Tanzania is the site of the fossil remains of the earliest hominid. The remains have been dated to some 1.7 million years ago. In historical times, the coast and Zanzibar came under Arab control some time in the 8th century A.D. The Portuguese established a presence in the 16th and 17th centuries and introduced the slave trade, but were driven out by natives in 1699. Arabs from Oman established control of Zanzibar and set up on the mainland as well, conducting a flourishing trade in slaves and ivory throughout the 18th and 19th centuries. The Germans established a mainland protectorate in 1891, but, after World War I, the regions passed to Britain through a League of Nations mandate. Tanganyika gained its independence in 1961 and was joined with Zanzibar in 1964. The capital was transferred from Dar-es-Salaam to Dodoma in 1975. Tanzania was directly involved in the overthrow of the regime of Idi Amin Dada in neighboring Uganda in 1978-1979. During the 1980s, Tanzania's economic difficulties, brought about by trade deficits and debt, resulted in a decreased emphasis on a government-controlled economy. In 1985 Nyerere left office and was replaced by his recommended successor, Ali Hassan Mwinyi. Nyerere passed away in 1999. The first multiparty elections were held in 1995. Benjamin William Mkapa of the Revolutionary Party was elected president. He was re-elected in 2000. That same year, Tanzania was given the Heavily Indebted Poor Country (HIPC) status by the IMF and the World Bank. This means that a large part of it's foreign debt will be forgiven to improve the economy.

Tanzanite, zoisite mineral and semiprecious gem unearthed in Tanzania (1967). This stone is popular for use in jewelry because its polished surfaces, created through a cutting process, reflect beautiful color. When a heat process is applied to tanzanite, it reflects a blue color. Before the heat treatment, tanzanite shines purple, blue, or yellow, depending upon the way light hits it.

Taoism, or Daoism (from Chinese *tao* or *dao*, 'the way'), philosophy that originated in China (c.300 B.C.); also, a religion that had its beginnings c.100 B.C. Taoism as a philosophy is chiefly derived from 2 books: the *Lao-tzu* (renamed *Tao Te Ching, The Classic of the Way and the Virtue*), traditionally ascribed to Lao-tzu, and the *Chuang-tzu*. The *Lao-tzu* is a collection of writings by several unknown authors containing ideas that are in direct opposition to the Confucian philosophy. Confucianism stresses a life guided by definite rules of conduct, whereas Taoism emphasizes simplicity and spontaneity. Tao was considered impossible to describe save in cryptic imagery. Chinese literature and art were greatly influenced by Taoism.

Tao Te Ching *See:* Taoism.

Tape recorder, instrument for sound recording on magnetic tape and subsequent playback. A microphone changes sound to an electric current, which is in turn changed in the recording head into magnetic flux variations. The tape, consisting of small particles of iron oxides on a thin plastic film base, is wound from the supply reel to the takeup reel by a rotating capstan that controls the speed. The tape passes in turn: the erase head, which by applying an alternating field reduces the overall magnetization to zero; the recording head, which magnetizes the particles; and the playback head. Most recorders use two, four, or even more tracks

A herd of elephants forages for food along the northeastern savannas with Kilimanjaro, the tallest mountain of Africa, in the background.

T

T

A tape recorder stores sound waves on magnetic tape by electromagnetic induction. The tape (1) is coated on one side with tiny particles of iron oxide. As the tape travels between spools, it passes across the record head (2), a small electromagnet energized by the electronic signal from a microphone (3). The magnetic field produced by this signal emerges through a narrow gap in the magnet (4) and magnetizes the particles. The tape will retain this information indefinitely until erased. To play back the record sound, the tape is re-run across the record head. The magnetic field produced by the magnetized particles is channeled back

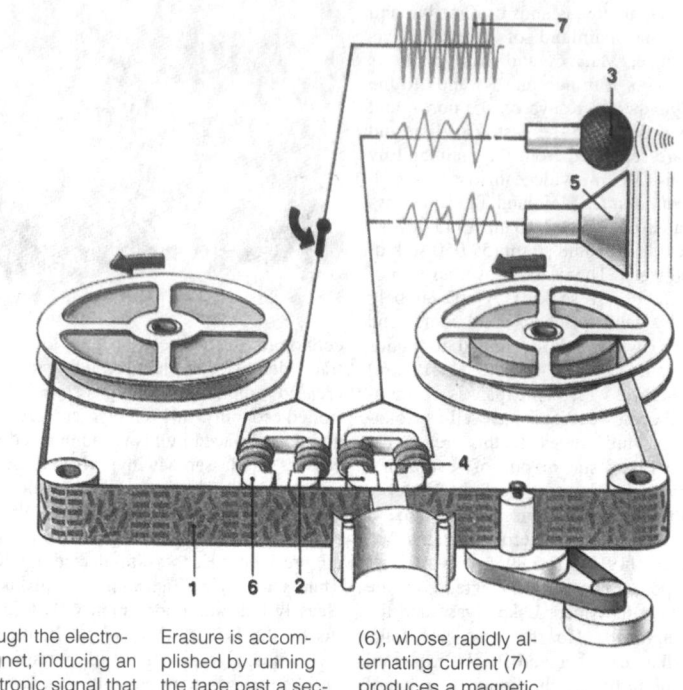

through the electromagnet, inducing an electronic signal that is amplified by a loudspeaker (5).

Erasure is accomplished by running the tape past a second electromagnet, called an erase head

(6), whose rapidly alternating current (7) produces a magnetic field that scrambles the particles.

side by side on the tape. The most common form of audio tape recorder is the cassette recorder, in which the cassette (a small plastic case) is simply snapped into a recorder and is ready to be played.

Tapestry, fabric woven with colored threads to form a design and used to cover walls and furniture. Vertical threads, which make up the warp are stretched on a loom, and horizontal threads, which make up the weft, are woven over and under them and then compacted. Tapestries were known in ancient Egypt, Syria, Persia, and China. North Europe's great era of tapestrymaking began in the 1300s, notably at Arras in Flanders. It reached a peak in the Gobelin tapestries of the 1600s. Great painters who have made tapestry designs include Raphael and Rubens. The Peter Paul Bayeux tapestry is in fact embroidery.

Tapeworm, any of numerous flatworms (class *Cestoda*) that live as parasites in the intestines of humans and other animals. Some tapeworms measure less than 1 in (2.5 cm) long, while others reach 30 ft (9 m) or more. A person can be infected by a tapeworm by eating undercooked meat or fish containing tapeworm larvae. An adult tapeworm can sometimes cause diarrhea, nausea, and other ill effects in a person. Tapeworm larvae pose a more serious threat because they can develop into young worms and spread to other organs of the host body.

Tàpies, Antoni (1923-), Spanish artist, initially influenced by Miró. Since the 1950s he has been active as a material painter, mixing thick layers of paint with gypsum, lime and sand. Creates monumental canvases with almost monochromatic surfaces in black, gray and ochre.

Lady World, detail from the Apocalypse tapestries of Angers (1374-80), that were woven in the Parisian workshop of Nicalos Bataille, after a design by Jan van Brugge. The use of a limited number of colors and the lack of perspective, give this series a particularly decorative effect (Musée des Tapisseries, Angers).

Tapir, a hoofed mammal (family *Tapiridae*) found in Central and South America, southern Mexico, and southeastern Asia. Tapirs range from 30 to 40 inches (75 cm to 1 m) in height and weigh about 500 to 650 pounds (225 to 295 kg). The animal has oval, erect ears; a short, thick tail; and a long, narrow snout covered with short, bristly hair. Tapirs hide in wooded or grassy areas near streams and emerge at night to eat leaves, vegetables, fruit, and other plant matter. There are four species of tapirs. The Malayan tapir (*Tapirus indicus*) is distinguished by its coloration; the front half and the back legs are black, while the rear half above the legs is silvery white. The Brazilian tapir (*T. terrestris*), mountain tapir (*T. pinchaque*), and Baird's tapir (*T. bairdii*) are dark brown to reddish above and paler below. The young are dark brown with yellow and white horizontal stripes interspersed with yellow and white spots. Tapirs live alone or in pairs and are good swimmers, divers, and runners. They are shy and mild-tempered but can defend themselves by biting. Due to loss of habitat, tapirs are now endangered.

Tar, thick, dark, viscous liquid obtained through distillation of organic matter, primarily coal, petroleum products, and wood. Coal tar, obtained at high temperatures and condensed from vapors given off during the manufacture of coke from bituminous (soft) coal, is used for roofing and waterproofing materials, synthetic drugs, disinfectants, dyes, perfumes, and plastics. Coal gassifier tar, a source of organic chemicals, is a byproduct of the process that converts coal into a natural gas substitute. Wood tar is made from the condensed vapors created during the wood-burning process; pine tar, the major derivative, is used to manufacture soap, disinfectants, and turpentine. Other types of coal- or petroleum-derived tar are used to seal road surfaces and produce asphalt paving material.
See also: Pitch.

Tarabulus *See:* Tripoli.

Tarantino, Quentin (1963-), American film director and script writer. He made his debut as writer/director with the violent film *Reservoir Dogs* (1992). He wrote the scripts for *True Romance* (1993), *Natural Born Killers* (1994), *From Dusk Till Dawn* (1996) and *Pulp Fiction* (1994; Palme D' Or, Academy Award best original screenplay), which he also directed. Furthermore, Tarantino directed one fourth of the Anthology *Four Rooms* (1995), *Jackie Brown* (1997) and *The Others* (2001).

Tarantula, popular name, originally of the large wolf spider (*Lycosa tarantula*), but now used for various unrelated giant spiders throughout the world. All are long and hairy and eat large insects or small vertebrates. Their venom seldom has serious effects on humans.
See also: Spider.

Tarascan, Native American tribe of Mexico. The Tarascan controlled a powerful empire from the late 14th to the early 16th century. With early settlements dating to c.500 B.C., their tribal holdings bordered the Aztec Empire at the time of the Spanish arrival in the 1520s. Along with the Aztecs, they were conquered by the Spanish, but only after great resistance. Hunters, farmers, and fishermen, many of the 60,000 Tarascans surviving today, inhabitants of the state of Michoacán, follow traditional ways of life. They are skilled craftspeople, weavers, and woodcarvers. Many still speak the Tarascan language, which bears no relationship to any other known language.

Tariff, customs duty on an export or, more commonly, an import. The aim is generally to protect home industries from foreign competition, though it may be merely to provide revenue. During the 17th and 18th centuries the European powers created tariff systems that gave their colonies preferential treatment, but Britain's tariffs, by limiting North America's trade, helped provoke the Revolutionary War. In the early 1800s the free trade movement, bolstered by the economic philosophy of laissez-faire, helped limit the spread of tariffs. However, U.S. federal tariffs imposed to aid Northern industry damaged the South and contributed to the Civil War. U.S. and European tariffs were moderate in the early 1900s but, after the Great Depression, both the United States and the United Kingdom adopted high tariffs, with a consequent decline in international trade. In 1947 the United States and 22 other nations signed the General Agreement on Tariffs and Trade (GATT), aimed at reducing trade discrimination. GATT and the Common Market have been responsible for generally lower tariffs throughout the world.
See also: Taxation.

Tarkenton, Fran (Francis Asbury Tarkenton; 1940-), U.S. football player. A quarterback known for his passing and scrambling ability, Tarkenton holds the career records for pass attempts (6,467), pass completions (3,686), touchdown passes (342), and passing yards (47,003). He played in the National Football League (NFL) for the Minnesota Vikings (1961-1966, 1972-1979) and New York Giants (1967-1971). Tarkenton was inducted into the Pro Football Hall of Fame in 1986.

Taro, plant (*Colocasia esculenta*) of the arum family whose rhizomes provide a starch food for millions of people in eastern Asia and the Pacific. Taros have to be peeled to remove a poisonous acid compound, and they do not provide an adequate diet by themselves. In Hawaii taro is fermented to make poi.

Tarot, pack of 78 playing cards used mainly for fortune-telling. There are four suits (cups, pentacles, swords, and wands), each of 14 cards and a major arcana (heavily symbolic 'picture cards') of 22 cards. There are various systems of interpretation.

The tarantula, *Aphonopelma chalcodes*, is a member of a genus of harmless tarantulas, living in North America. Its fearsome looks have given it the unfounded reputation of being poisonous.

Tarpon (*Tarpon atlanticus*), game fish that can survive in salt or fresh water. Tarpon of over 100 lb (45 kg) are often caught, and they can grow up to 840 lb (381 kg). The body bears large, silvery scales up to 2 in (5 cm) across, and the dorsal fin has a long ray protruding from the rear end. Tarpon live in warm seas from Florida to Brazil and also off West Africa. The eggs are laid in shallow water and the larvae grow up in stagnant lagoons and marshes.

Tarragon (*Artemisia dracunculus*), plant whose aromatic leaves provide a pleasant characteristic flavor to various meats, vegetables, sauces, and stuffings.

Tarrasch, Siegbert (1862-1937), German chess grandmaster and doctor. Between 1890 and 1910 he was considered to be one of the strongest players in the world. As a tireless stimulator of chess he was given the honorary title Praeceptor Germaniae. In his many theoretical works he discussed the importance of the open line, the pair of bishops, and the center. Tarrasch was a major theorist of openings, and many systems still carry his name. His principles led to two books: *Dreihundert Schachpartien* (1895) and *Die moderne Schachpartie* (1912). He won many victories, but after his defeat in the match with Lasker for the world championship in 1908 (-8, +3, =5), he never won another major tournament.

Tarsus (pop. 146,000), city in central Turkey on the Mediterranean coast. Archeological studies date the city to Neolithic times. The Assyrians built here in the early 8th century B.C. The Romans once took control of Tarsus (67 B.C.). The city claims to be the place of the first meeting of Antony and Cleopatra (41 B.C.) and the birthplace of St. Paul. Cotton and agriculture are products of the modern city and were the foundation of the ancient economy of Tarsus.

Tartan, checkered fabric of Scotland's native dress. Each clan is ascribed a particular tartan, though often in more than one variety: the hunting tartans are usually somber blues and greens, while reds generally predominate the dress tartans. The authenticity of ascriptions to clans is questioned, and some tartans are of comparatively recent origin.

Tartaric acid ($C_4H_6O_6$), naturally derived plant acid, used extensively for making jellies, jams, and carbonated drinks. There are tartaric salts-cream of tartar, Rochelle salt, and tartar emetic. The first is used in baking powder, hard candies, and for cleaning brass. Rochelle salt is used to silver mirrors and electronically cover metals with gold or silver; tartar emetic (antimony potassium tartrate) is used in medicines. Tartaric acids and their salts are solids, colorless, and water soluble.

Tartars, or **Tatars**, people of Turkish descent who live in the Russian Federation, Bulgaria, Romania, China, and Turkey. Originally a nomadic people, they turned to agriculture in the 16th century and have

since figured prominently in the history of the Russian people. Many Tarters now live in the Tatar Autonomous Soviet Socialist Republic; most are Sunni Muslims.

Tartu (German: *Dorpat*), city in eastern Estonia, lying on the Emajogi River. It was a fortified settlement in the 5th century A.D. From the 11th century it was at different times held by the Russians, Swedes, and Poles; Russian control was established in 1704. Its university, founded 1632, is now an important center for the study of botany and agriculture.
See also: Estonia.

Tashkent (pop. 2,100,000), capital of Uzbekistan, located in Chirchik Valley west of the Chatkal Mountains. One of the oldest cities in Asia, it was an important trading center for Arab, Muslim, and Mongol empires. Major products are textiles and agricultural machinery. Rebuilt after a devastating earthquake in 1966, it is an important cultural center.
See also: Uzbekistan.

Tasmania, smallest Australian state (26,383 sq mi/68,332 sq km). The 150-mi (253.5-km) Bass Strait separates Tasmania from the southeastern mainland. It includes King, Flinders, and Macquarie islands, as well as the main island. Tasmania's forests contain two unique marsupials, the Tasmanian devil and the thylacine. Chief cities are Hobart (the capital), Launceston, Burnie, and Devonport. Important industries are livestock (dairying, wool), horticulture, lumber and newsprint, mining, and mineral processing (zinc, copper, and lead).
See also: Australia.

Tasmanian devil (*Sarcophilus harrisi*), mammal of the marsupial family, native to the Australian island of Tasmania. This nocturnal, 4-legged animal measures 3-4 ft (0.9-1.2 m) long. Like other marsupials, the female gives birth to underdeveloped babies who grow to maturity in pouches on the mother's belly. Noted for their fierceness, they have been known to attack livestock and poultry, and have been hunted for that reason.

The Tasmanian devil, *Sarcophilus harrisi*, a scavenger with gaping jaws and sharp teeth, is less savage than it looks.

Tasman Sea, arm of the South Pacific Ocean, between Australia and Tasmania (east) and New Zealand (west). Named for the Dutch explorer Abel Tasman, the Tasman Sea is about 900,000 sq mi (2.3 million sq km). An underwater cable on its floor provides a key communication link between Australia and New Zealand.

TASS (Telegraph Agency of the Soviet Union), state news agency of the former USSR. Founded in 1925, it was managed by the Propaganda Department of the Communist Party's Central Committee.

Elizabeth Taylor, in one of her finest performances, played Martha opposite Richard Burton's George in the film version of *Who's afraid of Virginia Woolf?* (1966).

Tasso, Torquato (1544-1595), an Italian poet. Tasso was one of the greatest poets of the Renaissance, and his writings strongly influenced European literature for more than two centuries. His best works are *Aminta* (1573), a pastoral play, and *Jerusalem Delivered* (1581), an epic poem about the First Crusade, 1096-1099. Tasso made pastoral drama a popular literary form.
Tasso was born in Sorrento. He studied law, philosophy, and literature in Padua and Bologna. While in Padua he wrote *Rinaldo* (1563), a romantic epic that made him famous. From 1565 to 1579 he was in the service of the d'Este family, first under the patronage of Cardinal Luigi d'Este and later that of Alfonso d'Este, duke of Ferrara. In 1575 he began to show symptoms of mental disturbance. The years between 1577 and his death were spent in periods of confinement in hospitals for the insane, alternated with restless traveling from one Italian city to another.

Taste, special sense concerned with the differentiation of basic modalities of food or other substances in the mouth; receptors are distributed over the surface of the tongue and are able to distinguish sweet (generally at tip), sour, salt (along the sides), bitter (mainly at the back), and possibly water as primary tastes. Much of what is colloquially termed taste is actually smell perception of odors.

Tate, (John Orley) Allen (1899-1979), U.S. writer, critic, and teacher. He edited the literary magazine *Fugitive* (1922-1925) and later *Sewanee Review* (1944-1946) and advocated the 'New Criticism,' with its stress on a work's intrinsic qualities. His own work includes several collections of poetry and essays, biographies, and a novel.

Tatlin, Vladimir (1885-1953), Russian artist, representative of constructivism. Mainly known for his model of the *Monument for the Third International*

(1919-1920), that was designed to be 1,312 ft (400 m) high. Consisted of three rotating glazed units on top of each other, in the shape of a cube, a pyramid and a cylinder, in which the various organs of the Communist International would be located, surrounded by an enormous spiral-shaped construction. The original model was lost; it has been reconstructed many times.

Tatum, Art (1910-1956), U.S. jazz pianist. With the physical handicap of only slight vision, he became a master of piano technique and various forms of jazz. As an accompanist to jazz singers and as a member of his own jazz trio, he performed mainly in New York City nightclubs, beginning in 1932. *See also:* Jazz.

Tatum, Edward Lawrie (1909-1975), U.S. biochemist awarded the 1958 Nobel Prize for physiology or medicine, with G.W. Beadle and J. Lederberg, for work with Beadle showing that individual genes control production of particular enzymes (1937-1940) and for work with Lederberg showing genetic recombination in the bacterium *Escherichia coli* (1947). *See also:* Biochemistry; Genetics.

Taube, Henry (1916-), Canadian-born U.S. chemist who won the 1983 Nobel Prize for chemistry for his work in the mechanisms of electron transfer reactions, especially in metal complexes. *See also:* Chemistry.

Taurus Mountains, a range in southern Turkey between the Anatolian Plateau and the Mediterranean coast. It is some 250 miles (400 km) long and forms part of the great Alpine mountain system, which stretches eastward from the Alps through Eurasia. Much of the land is rugged and relatively inaccessible. The range's maximum height, in the east, is 12,828 feet (3,910 m) above sea level. The best-known pass is the Cilician Gates, used since ancient times.

Tautog *See:* Blackfish.

Tawney, Richard Henry (1880-1962), English historian and social theorist. His best-known book, *Religion and the Rise of Capitalism* (1926), connects the hard work and individualism of the Protestants of North Europe in the 16th and 17th centuries with the growth of capitalism there.

Taxation, raising of revenue to pay for government expenditure. Broadly speaking, a tax can be described as direct or indirect: income tax is paid directly to the government, but sales taxes are collected indirectly through government charges on goods or services. A tax is progressive or regressive; income tax is usually progressive (its rate rises as the taxable sum increases); sales taxes tend to be regressive (their burden decreases as the taxpayer's income increases).

Taxidermy, stuffing and mounting animal skins to make lifelike replicas. Taxidermy is now practiced mainly in large museums, though it originated in the production of hunting trophies; in modern taxidermy,

rather than stuffing, the animal's skin is streched over an artificial skeleton.

Taxonomy *See:* Classification.

Taylor, Elizabeth (1932-), English-born U.S. film actress. Beginning her career as a child actress (*Lassie Come Home*, 1943; *National Velvet*, 1944), she went on to become a major Hollywood star in such films as *Little Women* (1949), and *A Place in the Sun* (1951). She received Academy Awards for her roles in *Butterfield 8* (1960) and *Who's Afraid of Virginia Woolf?* (1966). Other films include *Secret Ceremony* (1969), *The Blue Bird* (1976), *The Mirror Crack'd* (1980), and *The Flintstones* (1994). In 1992 she received a Jean Hersholt Humanitarian Award for her dedication to the fight against AIDS.

Taylor, Lawrence (1959-), U.S. football player. A linebacker known for his quickness and powerful hits, he was the National Football League (NFL) Player of the Year (1986) and the National Football Conference (NFC) defensive player of the year 3 times (1981, 1982, and 1986). Taylor plays for the New York Giants (1981-) and has led the team to 2 Super Bowl victories (1987, 1991).

Taylor, Paul (1930-), U.S. modern dance choreographer. He debuted with Merce Cunningham in 1953 and danced with Martha Graham's company (1955-1961) before founding the Paul Taylor Dance Company in the mid-1950s. His work includes *3 Epitaphs* (1956), *Aureole* (1962), *Esplanade* (1975), and *Last Look* (1985).

Taylor, Zachary (1784-1850), war hero and 12th president of the United States (1849-1850). Taylor was a bold and resourceful general in the Mexican War and one of the most popular presidents of the period. During his 40-year army career, he did a great deal to open the West to settlement.
The Whig Party, which saw the war hero as a sure winner, nominated Taylor as its presidential candidate in 1848. Taylor and his running mate, Millard Fillmore, won the election.
In Dec. 1849, Congress was faced with California's request to enter the Union as a free state. Unexpectedly, Taylor urged Congress to accept California and New Mexico as free states. This, coming from a Southerner and slave owner, outraged militant Southerners. There was talk of secession, but Taylor declared that, if there was any rebellion, he would personally lead the army to put it down. Senator Henry Clay offered a set of bills that would admit California as a free state, with no provisions against slavery in Utah and New Mexico, and would prohibit the slave trade in the District of Columbia. To appease the South, they provided a rigorous law for the return of fugitive slaves. There was a great debate in the Senate; Taylor held firm and tensions grew. Then on July 9, 1850, Taylor died suddenly of acute gastroenteritis. He was succeeded by vice-president Millard Fillmore, who allowed the compromise bills to go through.

Tay-Sachs disease, inherited disorder that occurs primarily in Jewish people from eastern Europe. Children born with the disease have little or no active hexosaminidase enzyme, the lack of which causes fat to accumulate in the brain's ganglions (bundles of nerves). The consequences are mental retardation, paralysis, blindness, and cherry-red spots on the retina of the eye. The disorder is usually fatal before the child reaches the age of four.

TB *See:* Tuberculosis.

Tbilisi, or Tiflis (pop. 1,268,000), capital city of the Republic of Georgia, situated on the Kura River south of the Caucasus Mountains. Tbilisi, founded in the 4th century B.C., was subsequently ruled by the Persians, Arabs, Khazars, and Turks into the Middle Ages and was the capital of an independent Georgia (1096-1225). It was then conquered by the Mongols, Iranians, and Turks again before it was finally ceded to Russia in 1801. Following the Bolshevik Revolution (1917), Tbilisi again served as capital of an independent Georgia, but the Communists soon overran it and its neighboring states (1920). Much of the older section of the city remains. Today it is a center for agricultural products and manufacturing. Warm springs, for which the city is named in the Georgian language, are nearby.
See also: Georgia.

Tchaikovsky, Peter Ilich (1840-1893), Russian composer. He studied with Anton Rubinstein, became professor at Moscow Conservatory, and gave concerts of his own music in Europe and the United States. His gift for melody and brilliant orchestration, plus the drama, excitement, and emotional intensity of his music, place him among the most popular composers. Orchestral works include *Violin Concerto in D Major* (1878) and *Symphony No. 6*, or the the 'Pathétique' (1893). His ballets, *Swan Lake* (1876), *Sleeping Beauty* (1889), and *The Nutcracker* (1892), have become classics. His operas include *Eugene Onégin* (1879) and *The Queen of Spades* (1890).

Tchizhov, Aleksander (1964-), Russian checkers player, his first major success was in 1984 when he became junior world champion. Four years later he won his first senior world title by beating Ton Sijbrands. Tchizhov became world champion again in 1990, 1991, 1992, 1996 and 1998. He has also won numerous international tournaments.

Tea (*Camillia sinensis*), evergreen shrub, related to the camellia; also, the leaves of the plant and the beverage made from the leaves. The drink is prepared by pouring boiling water over dry processed tea leaves. Types of tea drunk include green, black (which is fermented), and oolong (which is partly fermented). Tea has been drunk in China since early times, but it was not until the early 1600s that the Dutch introduced it into Europe. Although expensive, it soon became fashionable. In the United Kingdom and the British colonies, the East India Company enjoyed a monopoly of the China tea trade until 1833; it was the attempt of the British government to levy a tax on tea imports into the American colonies that led to the Boston Tea Party of 1773. Today, the chief producers are India and Sri Lanka (Ceylon). Tea contains the stimulant caffeine. The term *tea* is also used to describe many other local drinks produced from the leaves of a vast array of plants.

Tea ceremony, the tea ceremony, or *cha-no-yu*, is known to have been in use in the higher circles of Japanese society since the 13th century, but its spiritual significance is linked to the development of Zen Buddhism in the 15th century: the setting of the *cha-do*. The tea ceremony is primarily about creating a friendly and happy atmosphere in which one serves green tea (*koicha*). At the same time, it is also a religious ceremony in which the actions create an aesthetic and contemplative atmosphere based on four principles: harmony, respect, purity and tranquillity. The ceremony, which must be carried out according to a lengthy protocol, takes place in a room especially set up and decorated for this purpose (*cha-shitsu*), and which leads on to a garden. This room also contains an altar, the *tokonoma*. The utensils used to make the tea play a central role in the ceremony, and are considered to be elements of sublime art: *cha-wan* (teapot), *cha-i-rè* (tea caddie), *cha-sen* (stirrer), and *cha-ku* (bamboo spoon). In modern Japan the ritual tends to have more of a social function than a ritual significance.

Teach, Edward *See:* Blackbeard.

Teaching, range of activities used to demonstrate skills, impart information, and guide individuals in learning. Informal teaching, which takes place in any setting and without any requisite structure, may come from parents, employers, colleagues, or other persons. Formal teaching generally occurs in a structured setting and is administered by professional teachers. Training in education includes general coursework in the subject areas the teacher will specialize in, special courses in educational theory and practice, and practice or student teaching in real classrooms. Both training programs and certification are particular to the grade level and the subject area. Uncertified support personnel are known as teacher aides or paraprofessionals.

Teak (*Tectona grandis*), deciduous tree whose wood is among the most valuable. Teaks grow in tropical climates from India to Malaysia. The hard, oily (thus water-resistant) wood is used for house construction, furniture, railroad ties, etc. Several other trees produce a similar hardwood also called teak.

Teal, name for various species of river ducks (genus *Anas*) related to the mallard. The blue-winged teal of North America is one of the fastest flying migratory ducks, able to travel over 3,500 mi (5,632 km) in a month. Other teal include the Cape teal of Africa and the Laysan teal, which lives only on the island of Laysan, west of Hawaii.

Tears, watery secretions of the lacrimal glands situated over the eyes, which provide continuous lubrication and protection of cornea and sclera. A constant flow runs across the surface of the eye to the nasolacrimal duct at the inner corner, where tears drain into the nose. Excess tears produced in states of high emotion or because of conjunctival or corneal irritation overflow over the lower eyelid.

Teasel, or **teazel** (*Dipsacus fullonum*), European plant found in fields in North America. The small blue flowers grow on a conical head that remains as a prickly head after they have died. It was formerly cultivated, its dead heads used to raise the nap on cloth (fuller's teasel).

Tebaldi, Renata (1922-), Italian operatic soprano. A major rival of Greek-American soprano Maria Callas, she was known for the beauty and purity of her tone. She made her operatic debut in Italy in 1944 and her U.S. debut in 1950. Tebaldi, who performed many roles in the repertoire of Italian opera, sang frequently at the Metropolitan Opera in New York from 1955 to 1973.
See also: Opera.

Technetium, chemical element, symbol Tc; for physical constants see Periodic Table. Technetium was discovered by C. Perrier and E.G. Segrè in 1937. It was the first element to be produced artificially. It was produced in the Berkeley cyclotron by bombarding molybdenum with deuterons. It is present in some stars. It has not been found in any ores on earth. Technetium is prepared by reducing the sulfide with hydrogen at 1,100°C. Technetium is a silvery-gray, reactive metal. Its chemistry is said to be similar to that of rhenium. Potassium pertechnetate is a corrosion inhibitor for steel. Technetium and its compounds have limited commercial use because of its high radioactivity.

Technology, application of science to practical human ends-particularly, to increase productivity and the availability of leisure and to improve the quality of life. Although technology includes developments since ancient times, such as occurred in the metallurgy involved in tool making, the term generally refers to industrial technology of the past 200 years. In agriculture, technology has improved crop yields and reduced the need for labor with the advent of farm machinery. Technology applied to manufacturing has made available goods in large numbers at the same time that industrial labor has become less strenuous and hazardous and work hours have been reduced. Major technological innovations of the past century have included the internal combustion engine used in automobiles and the harnessing of electricity for light, heat, and power. In the 20th century radio communication and powered flight, and more recently, the computer, laser, and atomic fusion and fission have created profound changes in many aspects of life. Technology applied to the field of medicine has greatly increased life expectancy. The extremely rapid changes caused by technology have also created serious problems. Population shifts to cities re-

T

T

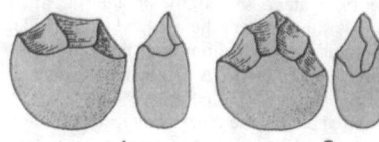

The chopping tool (1) was developed 2.5 million years ago. During the next 2 million years sharper tools with thinner edges were developed (2) and longer stones were used.

The vertical water mill was designed by Roman engineers as early as the 1st century B.C.

The era of rapid land transportation was initiated by such steam locomotives as the Rocket (1829).

sult in overcrowding. Natural resources have been depleted due to the industrial use of raw materials and the population explosions made possible by technology. Segments of the labor force are suddenly unemployed due to mechanization and automation, in a phenomenon known as technological unemployment. The assembly line that has made possible efficient production has also created boring and repetitive jobs, and the resulting loss of pride in work has created quality problems. Most seriously, technology has resulted in many forms of environmental pollution, including toxic industrial waste, air pollution from motor vehicles, noise pollution, and the destruction of ecosystems by the use of insecticides.

Tectonics, branch in geology that studies the earth's structural deformations, the forces involved, and the resulting forms. The most popular theory used to explain the origin of tectonic forces is the plate tectonic theory, developed in the 1960s. This theory holds that the movement of the rigid plates that line the surface of the earth's outer shell (either aigainst one other or away from one another) produces the crustal deformations in the earth. A second theory contends thet the earth originated from molten rock, which

cooled as it shrunk; this shrinking in turn produced the tectonic forces. A third theory maintains that the earth began as a cold mass, and as it warmed it produced forces that fractured the crust.
See also: Volcano.

Tecumseh (1768?-1813), Shawnee chief. Tecumseh and his brother Tenskwatawa (the Prophet) attempted to unite the Native American tribes of the upper Midwest in a confederacy, calling upon them to maintain their ancient culture and beliefs and to oppose all attempts by European-Americans to settle on tribal lands. At the Battle of Tippecanoe (Indiana) in 1811, they were defeated by Gen. William Henry Harrison who was elected president in 1840. Tecumseh joined the British army against the United States in the War of 1812 and was made a brigadier general. He was killed at the battle of the Thames River in Ontario.

Teeth, specialized hard structure used for biting and chewing food. The number of teeth varies from species to species and from age to age, but in most cases an immature set of teeth (milk teeth) is replaced during growth by a permanent set. In humans the latter consists of 32 teeth, comprising 8 incisors, 4 canines, 8 premolars or bicuspids, and 12 molars, of which the rearmost are the late-erupting wisdom teeth. Each tooth consists of a crown (the part above the gum line) and a root (the insertion into the bone of the jaw). The outer surface of the crown is covered by a thin layer of enamel, the hardest animal tissue. This overlies the dentine, a substance similar to bone, and in the center of each tooth is the pulp, which contains blood vessels and nerves. The incisors are developed for biting off food with a scissor action. The canines are for maintaining a hold on an object. The molars and premolars are adapted for chewing and macerating (separating) food. The most common disease of the teeth is dental decay, ot caries, in which acid produced by bacteria dissolves the tooth enamel, causing a cavity.

Tegu, or **Teju**, bold, quick and muscular South American lizard (genus *Tupinambis*). They weigh about 5 lb (2.3 kg) and grow up to 4 ft (1.2 m) in length. They have small square scales on their black-colored bodies with yellow horizontal bands over their backs.

Tegucigalpa (pop. 700,000), capital and largest city of Honduras, situated on the Choluteca River and on the slopes of Mt. Picacho in southern-central Honduras. Founded by the Spaniards in the late 1570s as a gold- and silver-mining center, in 1880 Tegucigalpa replaced Comayagua as the national capital. The 2 cities, on opposite banks of the Choluteca, merged in 1938. Today Tegucigalpa is a major manufacturing and agricultural hub, as well as the governmental center. The National University of Honduras is on the outskirts of the city.
See also: Honduras.

Teheran, or **Tehran** (pop. 6,9 million) capital and largest city of Iran. It is situated in northern Iran, south of the Elburz Mountains. It is believed that the area known today as Teheran was settled some 3,000 years ago; it began as a small town, but by the 1200s it had grown significantly. It received prominence after the Mogol destruction of nearby Ragy (1220) and became capital of Iran in 1788. Teheran is Iran's chief center of commerce and industry, employing a majority of the Iranian working population. Under Reza Shah Pahleve the city was modernized and is considered today to be one of the most modern cities in the Middle East. Teheran has two major universities.
See also: Iran.

Teheran Conference, inter-Allied conference of World War II, held in Teheran (Nov.-Dec. 1943) and attended by Soviet premier Joseph Stalin, U.S. president Franklin D. Roosevelt, and British prime minister Winston Churchill. Important items were the coordination of landings in France with a Soviet offensive against Germany from the

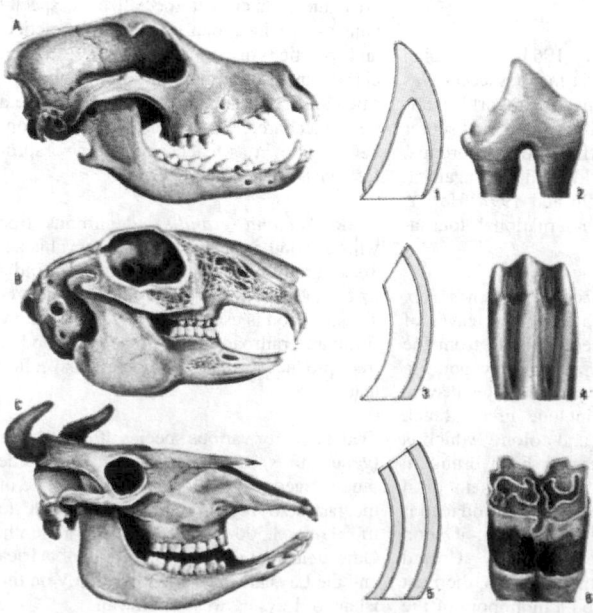

The dog (A), a carnivore, has large, sharp canine teeth (1) and special cheek teeth (2) that are specialized for shearing. Rodents (B) are herbivores with chisellike, continuously growing incisors (3) for gnawing, and cheek teeth (4) adapted for grinding. They lack canine teeth. The cow (C), a grazing ruminant, cuts vegetation with its lower incisors (5)—it lacks upper incisors—and chews it with broad, flat cheek teeth (6). Enamel (green) and dentine (yellow) are shown.

east, future Soviet entry into the war against Japan, agreement on Iran's future independence, and international cooperation after the war.

See also: World War II.

Tehuantepec, Isthmus of, a tropical lowland in southern Mexico. It is the narrowest stretch of land between the Pacific Ocean and the Gulf of Mexico. From the Bay of Campeche in Veracruz state to the Gulf of Tehuantepec in Oaxaca it is as little as 120 miles (190 km) wide. The isthmus is sparsely inhabited except along the coasts. It is crossed by a highway and a main railway line and affords a potential canal route.

Teilhard de Chardin, Pierre (1881-1955), French Jesuit, philosopher, and paleontologist. In China (1923-1946) he studied Peking Man (*Homo erectus*). *The Phenomenon of Man* (1938-1940, published 1955) attempted to reconcile Christianity and science with a theory of human evolution toward final spiritual unity. His superiors held his views to be unorthodox and warned against them; fame came to him and his ideas only posthumously.

See also: Paleontology.

Teju *See:* Tegu.

Te Kanawa, Dame Kiri (1944-), New Zealand operatic soprano. Her portrayal of the Countess in Mozart's *The Marriage of Figaro* won her international acclaim in 1971. She made her Metropolitan Opera debut in 1974 as Desdemona in Giuseppe Verdi's *Othello*. Widely recorded, she is known for her roles in works by Wolfgang Amadeus Mozart, Giuseppe Verdi, Giacomo Puccini, Georges Bizet, and Richard Strauss.

See also: Opera.

Tel Aviv-Jaffa (pop. 356,000), second-largest city in Israel, on the Mediterranean coast northwest of Jerusalem. It is a modern city-port and Israel's chief manufacturing center, as well as a tourist resort. Tel Aviv was Israel's first capital (1948-1949). Jaffa (Hebrew: *Yafo*), an ancient port, was incorporated with Tel Aviv in 1950; the city officially became Tel Aviv-Yafo, but it is generally referred to as Tel Aviv. Tel Aviv has two museums and several educational institutions, including Tel Aviv University and Bar Ilan University.

See also: Israel.

Telegraph, electrical apparatus for sending coded messages. The term was first applied in the 18th century to Claude Chappe's semaphore. Experiments began on electric telegraphs after the discovery (1819) that a magnetic needle was deflected by a current in a nearby wire. In 1837 W.F. Cooke and Charles Wheatstone patented a system using six wires and five pointers that moved in pairs to indicate letters in a diamond-shaped array. It was used on English railroads. In the same year Samuel Morse, in partnership with Alfred Vail and helped by Joseph Henry, patented a telegraph system using Morse code in the United States. The first intercity line was inaugurated in 1884. In 1858 Wheatstone invented a high-speed automat-

ic Morse telegraph, using punched paper tape in transmission; the telex system, using teletypewriters, is now most popular. In 1872 Jean-Maurice-Emil Baudot invented a multiplexing system for sharing the time on each transmission line between several operators. Telegraph signals are now transmitted not only by wires and land lines, but also by submarine cables and radio.

See also: Morse, Samuel Finley Breese; Wheatstone, Sir Charles.

Telegraph plant (*Desmodium motorium*), plant of the pea family, native to tropical Asia. It is sometimes cultivated for its unusual behavior in response to touch-the leaves droop abruptly, like the arms of a railroad semaphore signal (hence its name). The plant grows about 4 ft (1.2 m) high and bears small purple flowers.

Telemann, Georg Philipp (1681-1767), German composer. He was a prolific composer who worked well with musical forms popular in his day. He wrote operas, including *Der geduldige Socrates* (1721) and *Pimpinone* (1725); orchestral music, including *Musique de Table* (1733); concertos; and cantatas. His work was influenced by Italian opera as well as by earlier baroque composers, principally Johann Sebastian Bach. He served as musical director for the 5 churches of Hamburg (1721) and the Hamburg Opera (1722-1738).

Teleology (from Greek *telos*, 'end'), study of an action, event, or thing with reference to it's purpose or end. Plato and Aristotle argued that the purpose, perfection, and good of a thing, which Aristotle called its 'final cause,' was the ultimate explanation of the thing. The teleological view of nature has declined since the rise of science. The teleological argument, or argument 'from design,' argues that the order and perfection of nature requires the existence of a divine Creator who effected that order.

Telepathy *See:* Extrasensory perception.

Telephone, apparatus for transmission and reproduction of sound by means of frequency electric waves. The telephone was invented in 1876 by Alexander Graham Bell. Bell's transmitter worked by the voltage induced in a coil by a piece of iron attached to a vibrating diaphragm; the same apparatus, working in reverse, was used as a receiver. The carbon microphone (invented by Thomas Edison, 1878) provided a more sensitive transmitter. In 1878 the first commercial exchange was opened in New Haven, Conn.; local telephone networks spread rapidly in the United States and elsewhere. Repeaters, or amplifiers, made long-distance telephone calls possible. Today, microwave radio links, communications satellites, and optical fibers are used. Telephone subscribers are connected to a local exchange, these in turn being linked by trunk lines connecting a hierarchy of switching centers so that alternative routes may be used. When a call is dialed, each digit is coded as pulses or pairs of tones that work electromechanical or electronic switches.

In the 1980s use of carphones spread and in

the 1990s the mobile phone became popular.

See also: Bell, Alexander Graham.

Telescope, instrument used to detect or examine distant objects. It consists of a series of lenses and mirrors capable of producing a magnified image and of collecting more light than the unaided eye.

The refracting telescope (refractor) essentially consists of a tube with a lens system at each end. Light from a distant object first strikes the objective lens, which produces an inverted image at its focal point. In the terrestrial telescope the second lens system, the eyepiece, produces a magnified, erect image of the focal image, but in instruments for astronomical use, where the image is usually recorded photographically, the image is not reinverted, thus reducing light losses.

The reflecting telescope (reflector) uses a concave mirror to gather and focus the incoming light. The various types of instruments use different combinations of mirrors and lenses to view the focal image with fewer optical aberrations.

The size of a telescope is measured in terms of the diameter of its objective. Up to about 12 in (30 cm) diameter, the resolving power (the ability to distinguish finely separated points) increases with size, but for larger objectives the only gain is in light gathering. A 200-in (508-cm) telescope can thus detect much fainter sources but resolve no better than a 12-in (30-cm) instrument. Because mirrors can be supported more easily than large lenses, the largest astronomical telescopes are all reflectors.

See also: Galileo Galilei.

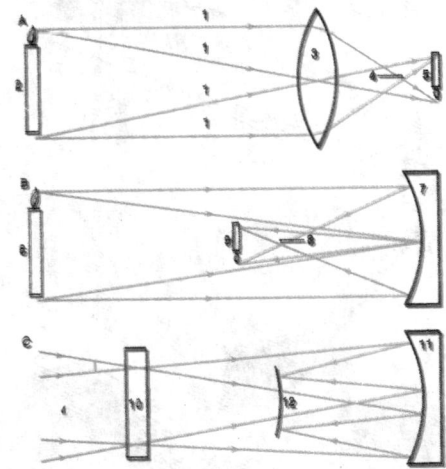

In a refracting telescope, or refractor (A), light rays (1) from an object (2) pass through a lens (3), are bent, or refracted, to a focal point (4), and form an inverted image (5). In a reflector (B), light rays from the object (6) are reflected by a concave mirror (7) to a common focus (8) and form an inverted image (9). In a Schmidt telescope, or camera (C), be- cause it is used only for photographic work, an aberration-free wide field of view is obtained by use of a spherical mirror and a correcting lens. Light from an object passes through a thin lens, or corrector plate (10), and is reflected from the spherical mirror (11) to a curved focal surface (12), which holds the photographic film.

T

T

Television, communication of moving pictures between distant points over wire or by means of electromagnetic waves. In television broadcasting, centrally prepared programs are transmitted to millions of individual receivers. Closed-circuit transmissions, which rely upon signals carried over wire rather than electromagnetic waves broadcast at large, are most often used for industrial and educational applications.

The moving picture on a television screen originates with a television camera, which forms an optical image of the scene to be transmitted and then breaks the image down into electrical signals. The signals may be amplified and transmitted directly over a ca-

Color-television cameras use dichroic mirrors (1) to split a colored image into red, green, and blue components, which are fed into separate camera tubes (2). One encoding unit (3) combines the output signals into a luminance signal (4), intended for black-and-white sets. Other encoders (5, 6) convert the signals into a chrominance signal (7), containing information for color sets. The luminance signal is then amplified (8) and combined with the color signal for transmission (9).

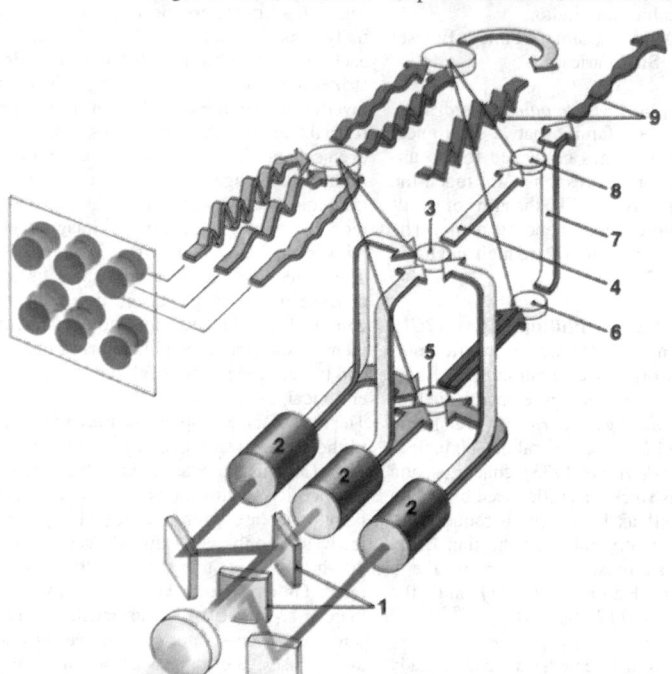

ble, or they can be converted into electromagnetic waves. As electromagnetic waves, they are transmitted by antennas, like radio waves, picked up by receiving antennas, and then conveyed to a television set equipped to reconstitute the electromagnetic waves into an optical image on the screen of a cathode-ray tube.

In the early days of television technology, most cameras used the iconoscope, but the iconoscope technology has since been replaced by orthicon or vidiscope. In order for an image to be transmitted and received electronically, it must be broken down into discrete but organized electrical signals and then reassembled or reconstructed by the receiver. The image formed by the optical lens system of a television camera is scanned as a sequence of 525 horizontal lines. As an image is scanned, variations in the light intensity along each line are converted into a fluctuating electrical signal, the brightness signal, which gives the image its gradations from light to darkness. Each scan is then repeated 30 times a second to create the illusion that the image is moving and without noticeable flicker. When reassembled on the television screen, the image appears whole and in fluid motion because of the persistence-of-vision effect of the human eye.

In color television, the image is not only resolved into brightness, but into hue and saturation as well. The light entering the camera is analyzed into red, green, and blue components, the 3 primary colors. Both hue and saturation are converted to electronic information, which is added to the brightness signal and transmitted. In the color receiver, this information is recovered and used to control 3 electron beams fired within the television set. The beams are projected through a shadow mask, a screen containing some 200,000 minute, precisely positioned holes, and they excite the mosaic of red, green, and blue phosphor dots, which reproduce the color image on the television screen.

The possibility of television was conceived in the early days of the electric telegraph, but the realization had to await several key developments. First was the discovery of the photoconductive properties of selenium, followed by the development of the cathode-ray tube in 1897 and the electron tube in 1904. Crucial to both systems and at the heart of television technology was scanning. The first practical television system, demonstrated in London in 1926 by J. L. Baird, used a mechanical scanning method devised by Paul Nipkow in 1884. Electronic scanning dates from 1923 when Vladimir Zworykin filed a patent for his iconoscope camera tube. Television broadcasting began in London in 1936 using a 405-line standard. After 1950, use of television as a mass communication means first spread in the United States, then in Europe, and gradually in the rest of the world. Recent technology, both in Japan and the United States, has led to the development of High Definition TV with greatly increased scanning capacities making possible images that are much cleaner and much larger.
See also: Videodisc; Videotape recorder.

Tell (Arab. and Hebr.: hill), artificial, sloping mound in the Middle East (and in some other areas), under which ruins of earlier cities are frequently buried. Tells come about due to continuous rebuilding on top of collapsed houses. Archaeologists can sometimes identify many eras of habitation, which can be individually analyzed, as some of these mounds are as high as 131 ft (40 m).

Tell, William, legendary 14th-century Swiss hero. Ordered by the Austrian bailiff Gessler to bow to a hat on a pole as a symbol of Austrian supremacy, he refused and was forced to shoot an apple from his son's head, using a cross-bow; in this almost impossible task he succeeded. Later he killed Gessler, starting a revolt that overthrew the bailiffs. The story was the basis of a drama by Friedrich von Schiller and an opera by Giacomo Rossini in the early 19th century.

Teller, Edward (1908-), Hungarian-born U.S. nuclear physicist who worked with Enrico Fermi on nuclear fission at the start of the Manhattan Project, but is best known for his fundamental work on, and advocacy of, the hydrogen bomb. He also helped create the Strategic Defense Initiative (SDI) program in the 1980s.
See also: Manhattan Project; Nuclear weapon.

Tellurium, chemical element, symbol Te; for physical constants see Periodic Table. Tellurium was discovered by Franz von Reichenstein in 1782. It occurs in nature as metallic tellurides. It is obtained commercially from the anode mud obtained in the electrolytic refining of copper. Tellurium is a silvery-white, brittle, reactive metalloid. It can be amorphous or crystalline and is a *p*-

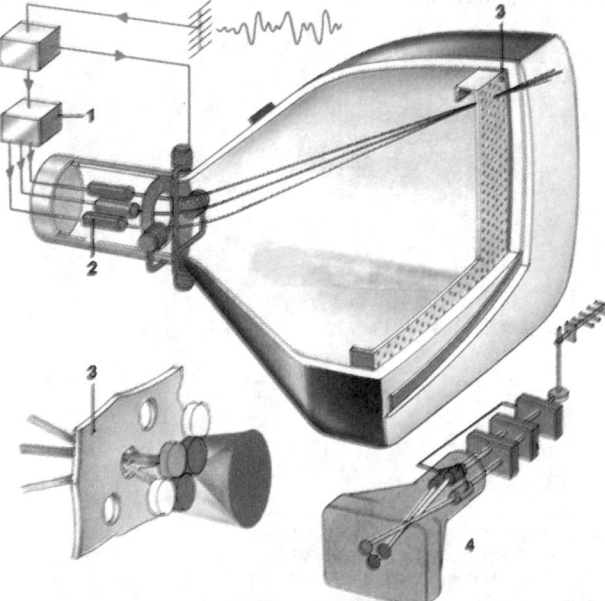

In a color-television receiver, a decoding circuit (1) is employed, to extract the original information from the incoming signal, containing red, green and blue signals from the camera tubes. These signals are then used to modulate the intensity of the beams from three electron guns (2). The front of the tube is coated with a pattern of tiny phosphor dots, arranged in threes. The dots will fluoresce with a red, green or blue glow when struck by an electron beam. Behind these tri-phosphor dots is a shadowmask (3), with thousands of holes, arranged in a way that electron beams from the green gun can only impinge on green dots, etc. Owing to the limited discrimination of the human eye, these dots make up a colored image on the screen.

type semiconductor. Tellurium and its compounds are used in alloys with copper, steel, and lead, blasting caps, ceramics, and thermoelectric devices. Tellurium and its compounds are probably toxic.

Telstar, U.S. artificial satellite, launched July 10, 1962. The first to relay television signals across the Atlantic Ocean. Telstar weighed 170 lb (77 kg). Broadcasts ended (Feb. 1963) after Van Allen belt radiation damaged some of the 1,000 transistors.

Temperature, degree of hotness or coldness, as measured quantitatively by thermometers. The various scales used are arbitrary: the Fahrenheit scale was originally based on the values 0°F for an equal ice-salt mixture, 32°F for the freezing point of water, and 96°F for normal human body temperature. There are certain primary calibration points corresponding to the boiling, freezing, or melting points of particular substances, whose values are fixed by convention. The thermodynamic, or absolute, temperature scale, is not arbitrary; starting at absolute zero, at which there is no kinetic energy, and graduated in kelvins, it is defined with respect to an ideal reversible heat engine working on a Carnot cycle between two temperatures, T_1 and T_2. If Q_1 is the heat received at the higher temperature T_1, and Q_2, the heat lost at the lower temperature T_2, then T_1/T_2 is equal to Q_1/Q_2. Absolute temperature is independent of a body's mass or nature; it is thus only indirectly related to the heat content of the body. Heat always flows from a higher temperature to a lower. On the molecular scale, temperature may be defined in terms of the statistical distribution of the kinetic energy of the molecules.

Temperature, body, measurement of body heat in animals. Warm-blooded animals (including human beings, other mammals, and birds) are able to maintain a fairly constant body temperature, which does not significantly fluctuate with the temperature of the environment. Body temperature in warm-blooded animals may change slightly over the course of a day: an adult human being's normal temperature, 98.6°F (37.0°C), may be slightly lower in the morning and slightly higher by late afternoon. In warm-blooded animals, body temperature is controlled by the hypothalamus, a part of the brain that includes autonomic regulatory centers. The workings of the hypothalamus enable warm-blooded animals to balance the amount of heat lost to the environment with the heat produced by burning food. Cold-blooded animals, including reptiles, cannot regulate body temperature this way and must use other methods to maintain it. For example, snakes lie in the sun or shade, depending on whether they need to raise or lower their body temperature.

Templars, Knights *See:* Knights Templars.

Temple, building or place dedicated to the worship of a deity. Temples have been common to most religions; they date back to c.2000 B.C. in Egypt. In Eastern Asia, temples (pagodas) are towerlike structures built with many stories, each story a symbolic represen-

Communications satellite Telstar II, weighs about 176 lbs (80 kg), and has a diameter of about 34 in (86 cm). The surface contains a total of 3600 solar cells, combined into several solar panels. The small rods that can be seen around the diameter of the satellite, are microwave antennas for the receiving and relaying of radio waves.

tation of a different level in the Buddhist religion. Worship in temples usually involves traditional ceremonies and at times may even contain sacrifices. The first of the three successive temples built by Solomon in ancient Jerusalem became the central shrine where sacrifice could be legally offered. This First Temple, destroyed in the Babylonian invasion 586 B.C., is considered the most important temple in Western history.

Temple, Shirley (1928-), U.S. child film star, later a politician. She made her movie debut at 3 and became phenomenally popular through such films as *Little Miss Marker* (1934) and *The Little Colonel* (1935). She retired from films in 1949. After working on television in the 1950s, Shirley Temple Black (her married name) took up Republican politics. She became a U.S. delegate to the United Nations (1969), ambas-

sador to Ghana (1975), and U.S. chief of protocol (1976), ambassador to the Czech and Slovak Federal Republic (1989).

Tenant farming, system by which agricultural land holders, known as landlords, rent land to farmers, known as tenants, to produce crops. Landlords may either collect an agreed-upon payment for rental of the farm land and buildings or they may share other production costs and investments, as well as the harvested crop, with the farmer. This method of farming has been especially successful in the British Isles and the United States.

Ten Commandments, or the *Decalogue*, moral laws delivered by God to Moses on Mt. Sinai, as recorded in the Bible (Ex. 20:2-17; Deut. 5:6-21). They provide the foundation for Jewish, Christian, and Muslim teaching. *See also:* Bible.

Tendon, fibrous structure at the ends of most muscles that transmits the force of contraction to the point of action (usually a bone). Tendons facilitate mechanical advantage and allow bulky power muscles to be situated away from small bones concerned with fine movements, as in forearm muscles acting on the hands. *See also:* Muscle.

Teng Hsiao-p'ing *See:* Deng Xiaoping.

Tennessee (Volunteer State; pop. 4,897,000), state in the south-central United States; bordered by Kentucky, Virginia, North Carolina, Georgia, Alabama, Mississippi, Arkansas, and Missouri.

Tennessee is drained by three major river systems: the Cumberland, Tennessee, and Mississippi. Forests cover about half of the state. Tennessee has a humid, temperate climate. Principal cities are Memphis and Nashville (capital).

Manufacturing leads Tennessee's economy, followed by wholesale and retail trade and other service industries. Chief manufactured goods are chemicals, processed foods, non-

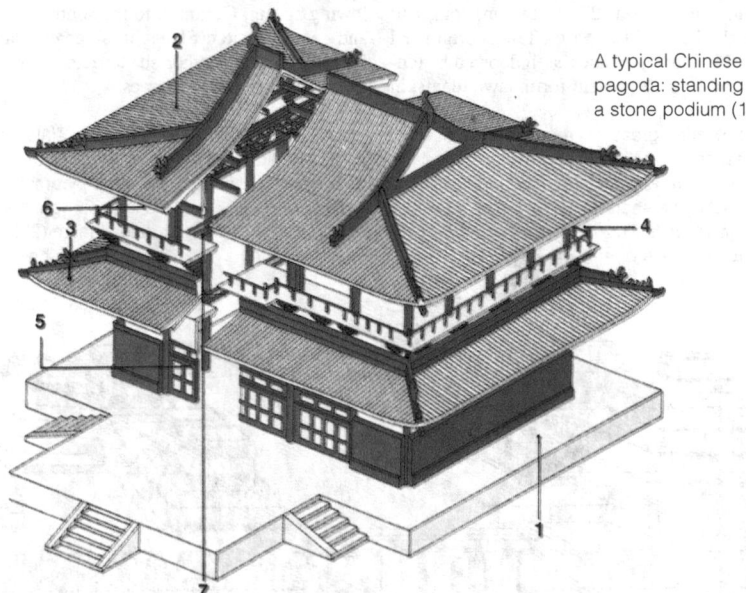

A typical Chinese pagoda: standing on a stone podium (1), the wooden hall has a two-storied elevation, covered by a single-hipped roof (2). The first story is overhung by shallow eaves (3), which are supported by bracketing, as is the balcony (4). Divided into five bays, doors occupy the center three bays (5), which are left open on the upper story (6). The fabric of the roof is wood, insulated with mud, and tiled. The interior has a gallery (7) on each story around the central wall, which is the full height of the temple.

T

electrical machinery, electric and electronic equipment, apparel, fabricated metal products, transportation equipment, and rubber and plastic products. Agriculture and mining are less important to Tennessee's economy. Chief crops are soybeans, tobacco, cotton, corn, and wheat. Chief livestock products are beef and dairy cattle and hogs. Chief mining products are coal, marble, limestone, and zinc.

When the first Europeans, Spanish explorers, arrived in 1540, it was populated by the Cherokee, Chickasaw, Shawnee, and other tribes. The area, claimed by France in 1682, was ceded to Britain in 1763. European settlers began building permanent settlements. In 1796, Tennessee became the 16th state. Bitterly divided over slavery, Tennessee was the last state to join the Confederacy (June 8, 1861) and the first readmitted to the Union (July 24, 1866).

Tennessee Valley Authority (TVA), U.S. federal agency responsible for developing the water and other resources of the Tennessee River Valley, established (1933) as one of the early measures of President Franklin D. Roosevelt's New Deal. The TVA has 26 major dams on the Tennessee River and its tributaries. The dams and reservoirs have made it possible to eliminate major flooding. Locks make the Tennessee navigable throughout, and TVA hydroelectric and steam plans provide most of the region's electricity. TVA projects have also involved conservation, agriculture, and forestry.
See also: New Deal.

Tennis, racket game played on a rectangular court by two or four players. The court, divided by painted lines into sections (78 ft-23.8 m long and 27-31.5 ft-8.2-9.6 m wide) is bisected by a net 3 1/2 ft (107 cm) high. The object is to hit the hollow ball of cloth-covered rubber, about 2 1/2 in (6.4 cm) in diameter and 2 oz (57 g) in weight, over the net into the opposite court such that the opposing player is unable to return it. The racket has a metal or laminated wood frame, with gut or nylon strings forming an oval 'head'; it is about 27 in (69 cm) long and weighs 12 oz (340-454 g). Tennis originated in 15th-century France as indoor court tennis and took its present form, lawn tennis, in

1870. It was first played in the United States in 1874. In 1877 England held the first Wimbledon Championship. Dwight Davis donated the Davis Cup in 1900. The International Lawn Tennis Federation regulates rules and play in over 80 countries.

Tenno (Jap: heavenly ruler), title of the Japanese Emperor. The 'tenno' derived his authority from the heavenly mandate he received because he was a descendant from the gods. In the 7th century it replaced the title 'mikado' (exalted gateway), although that name was still used in other countries for many years. Emperor Hirohito (reign 1926-1989) was forced to relinquish his claim to divine descent after the capitulation of Japan in 1945.

Tennyson, Alfred, Lord (1809-1892), English poet. His *Poems* (1842) established him as a major poet. His philosophic elegy *In Memoriam* (1850) became the favorite of Queen Victoria, who appointed him poet laureate. *Idylls of the King* (1842-1885) is an epic based on the legends of King Arthur. Tennyson's mastery of sound and rhythm is perhaps best seen in haunting lyrics like 'The Lotus-Eaters' and 'The Lady of Shalott,' which appear in *Poems* (1832).

Tenochtitlán, capital of the Aztecs, now in Mexico City. Founded c. 1325 on an island in Lake Texcoco, connected to the mainland by causeways, it was a rich city of brick houses, palaces, canals, aqueducts, and a great square of temple-topped pyramids. It was destroyed by Hernán Cortés in 1521.
See also: Aztecs; Cortés, Hernando.

Tenpins *See:* Bowling.

Tent caterpillar, larval stage of moths (genus *Malacosoma*) in the Lasiocampidae family. Striped, colorful, and hairy, the tent caterpillar is so-called because most of its species spin communal, tentlike webs in the forks of trees. Notorious for damaging trees in which they live, these caterpillars are capable of killing a small tree by eating all of its leaves. The female moth lays 150-350 eggs during the summer that hatch the following spring. Common to the southeastern and central United States, these caterpillars feed on oaks and other shade trees, as well as on conifers and fruit trees.

Terbium, chemical element, symbol Tb; for physical constants see Periodic Table. Terbium was discovered by C.G. Mosander in 1843. It is found in cerite, and gadolinite and is obtained commercially from monazite. The metal is prepared by reducing the anhydrous fluoride with calcium. Terbium is silvery-white, soft, malleable, ductile metal. Ion-exchange and solvent extraction techniques have led to much easier isolation of the so-called rare-earth elements. Terbium and its compounds are finding use in laser materials, solid-state devices, color TV phosphors, and fuel cells.

Terence (195?-159? B.C.), playwright of Roman comedies, written in Latin. His 6 plays, based on earlier Greek comedies, still exist: *The Woman of Andros, The Self-Tormentor, The Eunuch, Phormio, The Mother-in-Law,* and *The Brothers.* These plays display his wit and his realistic understanding of human nature. He was brought from his native Carthage as a slave to Rome, and a Roman senator secured his education.

Teresa, or **Theresa, Saint** (1515-1582), also known as Theresa of Ávila, Spanish nun and Doctor of the Church. She worked toward reforming the Carmelite order, which she believed was lacking in self-denial and austerity, and in 1562, with approval from the pope, established her own convent. She was a leading figure in the Catholic Reformation. Her writings rank among the greatest in mystical literature. St. Teresa was considered a miracle worker and was canonized in 1622. Her feast day is Oct. 15.

Teresa, Mother (1910-1997), Roman Catholic nun, Albanian parents, who worked as a missionary in Calcutta, India. For her work with the poor of India, which began in 1950, she was awarded the Nobel Peace Prize (1979). The religious order she joined (1928) sent her to India, where she at first worked as a teacher. Her convent later permitted her to work among the poor people of Calcutta (1948), and she became an Indian citizen. She has received global recognition for her work, including the Pope John XXII peace prize (1971) and the Jawaharlal Nehru award for international understanding (1972).

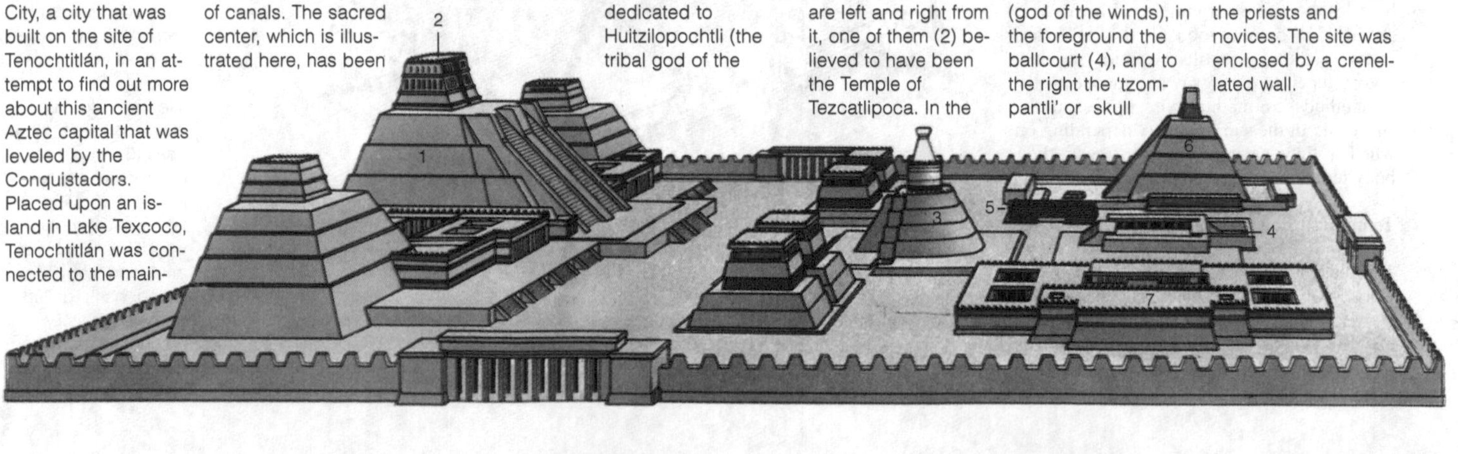

Archaeological research is still being executed in Mexico City, a city that was built on the site of Tenochtitlán, in an attempt to find out more about this ancient Aztec capital that was leveled by the Conquistadors. Placed upon an island in Lake Texcoco, Tenochtitlán was connected to the mainland by three great dykes, and was itself divided by a network of canals. The sacred center, which is illustrated here, has been reconstructed from archaeological evidence, and is still conjectural. On the great pyramid (1) are the temples that were dedicated to Huitzilopochtli (the tribal god of the Aztecs) and Tlaloc (god of the rains). The other pyramids are left and right from it, one of them (2) believed to have been the Temple of Tezcatlipoca. In the center (3), is the round temple of Quetzalqatl-Eleqatl (god of the winds), in the foreground the ballcourt (4), and to the right the 'tzompantli' or skull rack (5). (6) Is the Temple of the Sun, (7) the living quarters of the priests and novices. The site was enclosed by a crenellated wall.

Tereshkova, Valentina Vladimifouna (1937-), Soviet cosmonaut, the first woman to orbit the earth. Simultaneously with a fellow cosmonaut, Very F. Bykovsky, she circled the earth 45 times in her spacecraft *Vostok VI* (June 16-19, 1963). Her orbits, which she controlled manually, took less than 1 1/2 hours each.

Termite, or white ant, primitive insect (order Isoptera) closely related to the cockroach, found in all warm regions. Termites have a complicated social system and live in well-regulated communities, with different castes taking distinct roles. They build large nests of soil mixed with saliva, in which the colony of king, queen, workers, soldiers, and juveniles live. Soldiers and workers are sterile individuals, their development arrested at an early stage. Termites feed on wood and vegetation, digesting the food with the aid of symbiotic protozoa or bacteria in the gut.

Tern, or sea swallow, slender, graceful seabird related to, but smaller than, the gull. Terns have a bounding, butterfly-like flight and feed on small fish that they catch by diving from the air. They are found in all seas from the Arctic to the Antarctic and also on some lakes and marshes. They nest on the ground in large, noisy colonies. The Arctic tern migrates from the Arctic to the fringes of the Antarctic.

Ter-Petrosian, Levon (1945-), Armenian politician. A fervent nationalist, Ter-Petrosian was president of Armenia from 1990 to 1998. He was one of the leading figures within the Armenian National Movement, which campaigned for independence, and was also chosen as chairman of the Armenian Supreme Soviet in 1990, which made him the *de facto* president. In 1995, after the constitution was rewritten, the powers of president were considerably increased and those of the parliament curtailed. After the presidential elections of 1998 Ter-Petrosian was succeeded by the leader of the Armenian revolt in Nagorno-Karabakh, Robert Kocharian.

Terra cotta (Italian, 'baked earth'), any fired earthenware product, especially one made from coarse, porous clay, red-brown in color and unglazed. Being cheap, hard, and durable, it has been used from ancient times for building and roofing, and for molded architectural ornament and statuettes. Its use for sculpture and plaques was revived in the Renaissance and in the 18th century.

Terrapin, turtle (family Testudinidae) of fresh or brackish water, with diamond-shaped plates on its shell. It grows to 8 in (20 cm) and is found from Massachusetts to Mexico. At one time a cheap food for slaves, it became a luxury dish as *Terrapin à la Maryland*. The name is sometimes given to all brackish and freshwater turtles.

Terrier, class of dogs. Most of the 24 kinds of terrier were originally bred in England. They were developed specifically to hunt or flush out from the ground rats and burrowing animals. Terrier breeds include the fox terrier, the schnauzer, and the Scottish terrier.

Territoriality, behavioral drive causing animals to set up distinct territories defended against other members of the same species (conspecifics) for the purposes of establishing a breeding site, home range, or feeding area. It is an important factor in the spacing out of animal populations. Territoriality is shown by creatures of all kinds: birds, mammals, fish, and insects. A territory may be held by individuals, pairs, or even family groups.

Territorial waters, in international law, the belt of sea adjacent to a country and under its territorial jurisdiction. Important for control of shipping, seabeds, and fisheries, such limits used to extend 3 mi (4.8 km), and more recently 12 mi (19.3 km), from low-water mark. A 200-mi (322-km) limit has been accepted by some countries. *See also:* High seas.

Territory, in politics, area under a government's control, but with limited self-government. Territories have lower status than the states of the mother country.

Terrorism, actual or threatened violence for political ends. Although terrorim has always been part of societies, the level of terrorism increased markedly in the 1970s as antigovernment groups throughout the world turned to violent acts such as bombing, hijacking, kidnapping, and murder. Terrorism attracted increased international attention through the activities of Palestinians and their allies, who gave up hope of defeating Israel by conventional military tactics after the rout of the Arab nations in the 1967 war. The more active terrorist groups of the period included the Provisional wing of the Irish Republican Army, the Japanese Red Army (3 of the members killed 28 people and wounded 76 at Tel Aviv's Lod airport in 1972), the Palestinian Black September group (responsible for the deaths of 11 Israeli athletes at the 1972 Munich Olympics), the Baader-Meinhof Gang in Germany, the Italian Red Brigades (who kidnapped and killed the former Italian premier, Aldo Moro, in 1978), the Tupamoros in Uruguay, and the Weathermen in the United States. While receiving a great deal of publicity, terrorists are actually accountable for a relatively small number of deaths compared with other causes (nearly 10 times as many people are murdered every year by ordinary criminals in the U.S. alone). Since the 1980s, terrorism has been aimed increasingly at causing large numbers of victims: for example the attacks in Beirut against the American and French military barracks in the beginning of the 1980s; the attack on the PanAm airplane in Lockerbie (1988); the first attack on the World Trade Center in New York (1993); the attack on Tokyo's subway (1995); the attack on the Oklahoma State Building (1995); attacks on the houses of American soldiers in Saudi Arabia (1996); on the American embassies in Nairobi and Dar es- Salaam (1998); and on the American warship *Cole* in Yemen (2000), with the sad climax on 11 September 2001. Approximately 3,100 people were killed that day.

It is extremely hard to bring terrorists to justice, however. Their groups are small, tightly organized, and highly mobile.

The attacks of 11 September, have possibly started up a new trend in the fight against terrorism. After the American 'Declaration of War' on terrorism, the emphasis seems to be shifting all over the world, to criminal law and military means.

Terry, Dame Ellen Alicia (1848-1928), English actress. Throughout more than 50 years on the stage, she performed often as Sir Henry Irving's leading lady, and is remembered for her roles as Beatrice in *Much Ado About Nothing*, Juliet in *Romeo and Juliet*, and Desdemona in *Othello*.

Tertiary Period, the lower division of the Cenozoic era, extending from the end of the

Warm, humid climates characterized the Tertiary Period, about 50 million years ago. In southeastern England, a tropical or subtropical lowland met the sea, along a coastal area that supported swamps of bald cypress, *Taxodium* (1), and the trunkles nipa palm, *Nypa* (2). Crocodiles, *Crocodylus* (3), and river turtles, *Podocnemis* (4), were common in shallow water. Drier land supported forests of *Magnolia* (5) and sabal palm, *Sabal* (6), as well as a fauna of early birds and mammals. *Odontopteryx* (7), a gannetlike bird, had unusual toothlike outgrowths of bone along its jaws. A kingfisherlike bird (8) and the vulture *Lithornis* (9) are usually assigned to Oligocene and Paleocene faunas, respectively. The fox-sized eohippus, or dawn horse, *Hyracotherium* (10), browsed in Lower Eocene forests. The hippopotamuslike *Coryphodon* (11) belongs to an extinct group of hoofed mammals, the pantodonts.

T

Cretaceous to the beginning of the Quaternary, from 70,000,000 to 2,000,000 years ago. It is divided into 5 epochs: Paleocene, Eocene, Oligocene, Miocene, and Pliocene. The early Tertiary period was characterized by a large amount of mountain building (Andes, Alps, Hymalayas). In this period marsupials and placental mammals diversified and began to take a more modern appearance. Also during this time, worldwide climates began to gradually change into today's climatic zones.

Teshigahara, Sofu (1900-1979), Japanese painter, sculptor, and ikebana artist. Teshigahara learned the art of flower arranging from his father. In 1927 Teshigahara founded the Sogetsu School, a famous school for flower arranging. Flowers also play an important part in his abstract paintings and sculptures.

Tesla, Nikola (1856-1943), U.S. electrical engineer, inventor of the induction motor. His innovative motor used alternating electric current. This concept, purchased by a George Westinghouse company, was used to develop a successful commercial motor. Tesla worked on other successful inventions, including the Tesla coil, an arc-lighting system, and various generators and transformers. He was a forerunner in the field of communications with his work on wireless radio transmissions. He was born in Croatia, and moved to the United States in 1884.
See also: Electric motor.

Tessai, Tomioka (1836-1924), Japanese painter, one of the last great Nanga artists. Mainly known for his simulated Western style, in which he applied the paint in large, thick, sometimes dark layers, and for his daring color play which was reminiscent of Cézanne.

Testes *See:* Testicle.

Testicle, or testis (plural: testes), one of paired male sex glands. The testes are contained in the scrotal sac just between the legs. They have two functions. As ductless glands, they secrete testosterone, the male sex hormone. This substance is responsible for maintenance of the accessory reproductive organs and also for the secondary sexual characteristics-deep voice, strong muscles, and facial hair. Their other function is to produce the sperm needed to fertilize the female egg. Sperm is produced in a series of long coiled tubes called seminiferous tubules. In higher mammals, this process requires a temperature lower than normal body temperature, a condition provided by having the scrotal sac outside the body cavity. Mature sperm are stored in a coiled tube, the epididymis, up to 20 ft (6 m) long, which leads from the rear of the testis to the ejaculatory duct.

Testing, in education and psychology, procedures to evaluate individuals with respect to intelligence, skills, perceptions, or other parameters. Testing in the classroom is generally nonstandardized, designed by the teacher to measure the achievements of the students in assimilating subject matter.

Standardized testing in education is used to compare individuals to group norms, as in Graduate Record Examinations (GREs), or to measure them against predetermined standards, as in tests used to license professionals in law and medicine. Achievement tests measure learning in specific subject areas. Aptitude tests, which include intelligence tests that measure intelligence quotient (IQ), attempt to evaluate potential while eliminating factors of previous experience. Psychologists use a variety of personality tests, including both standardized tests that determine categories of personality profile and projective tests, like the Rorschach inkblot test, which can be evaluated only by a trained professional. Because test results are widely used to determine an individual's future in education and work, the validity of test procedures and contents must be scrutinized. Testing may inadvertently favor those of particular socioeconomic groups or otherwise express cultural biases.

Testosterone, androgen steroid produced by the testes under the control of luteinizing hormone. It is responsible for most male sexual characteristics-voice change, hair distribution, and sex organ development.
See also: Steroid.

Tetanus, or lockjaw, disease of the nervous system caused by toxins produced by the bacterium *Clostridium tetani*. The bacteria enter the body through breaks in the skin. The first symptom is often painful contraction of jaw and neck muscles; trunk muscles, including those of respiration, and muscles close to the site of injury are also frequently involved. Untreated, many cases are fatal, but artificial respiration, antiserum, and penicillin have improved the outlook. Regular vaccination and adequate wound cleansing are important in prevention.

Tet Offensive, in the Vietnam War, a coordinated cluster of attacks against cities and bases in South Vietnam by Vietcong and North Vietnamese forces, beginning on Jan. 30, 1968, the first day of the Tet (New Year) holiday. The offensive, which included a brief occupation of part of the U.S. embassy in Saigon, was costly to the enemy; nevertheless, it converted many Americans to the view that the war could not be won.
See also: Vietnam War.

Tetracycline, name for broad-spectrum antibiotics that can be given by mouth. They are useful in bronchitis and other minor infections and especially valuable in diseases due to rickettsia and related organisms; they can also be used in acne.
See also: Antibiotic.

Teutonic Knights, group of German crusaders. Founded in the Middle East at the end of the 12th century, this organization of knights worked to conquer and convert areas of central and eastern Europe to Christianity. Prussia was converted in the 1200s as were the neighboring countries of Estonia and Livonia, where the Livonian Knights were founded. Lithuania was eventually converted (1387), but with Poland later defeated the Teutonic Knights (1410). The order contin-

ued to weaken and, beginning in Prussia (1525), its various branches were eventually dissolved.
See also: Knighthood, Orders of.

Teutons, Northern European tribes that attacked the Roman empire early in the 1st century B.C. Though the Teutons, with the Cimbri, were badly beaten by the Romans under General Gaius Marius, both Caesar and the historian Tacitus wrote of the Teutons' warlike nature. As the Teutons moved south, southeast, and west, what is known as the Teutonic languages came to encompass the Scandinavian as well as Germanic languages, including Dutch, English, and Flemish.

Texas (Lone Star State; pop. 18,031,000), the second-largest state of the United States; bordered by Oklahoma, Arkansas, Louisiana, the Gulf of Mexico, the Rio Grande, and New Mexico.
Texas has a varied landscape with land regions such as the Rocky Mountains, the Prairie Plains, and the Great Plains. The Rio Grande, which forms the entire border between Texas and Mexico, is one of the largest rivers in the nation. Forests cover about 14% of the state. Texas's climate ranges from temperate in the Panhandle region to subtropical in the Rio Grande delta. Principal cities are Houston, Dallas, and San Antonio. Capital is Austin.
Texas's economy depends heavily on its oil and natural gas resources, among the richest in the world. Other mineral resources include sulfur, helium, coal, clay, salt, asphalt, limestone, gypsum, and sand and gravel. Service industries and manufacturing are also important to the economy. Chief manufactured goods are nonelectrical machinery, chemicals, processed foods, oil and coal products, electrical equipment, fabricated metal products, transportation equipment, and apparel. A leading agricultural state, Texas produces beef cattle, cotton, grain sorghum, rice, wheat, vegetables, and citrus and other fruits.
Spanish gold-seekers, the first Europeans in the area, arrived in the early 1500s. In 1685, the French explorer La Salle arrived and claimed the area, which France sold to the United States as part of the 1803 Louisiana Purchase. In 1821, Texas became part of the newly independent Empire of Mexico. But U.S. settlement in the area continued to grow; the Texas Revolution-a rebellion of U.S. settlers against Mexico-began in 1835. In 1836, after the famous battle at the Alamo, the independent Republic of Texas was formed. It became the 28th state in 1845. Texas played a major role in the expansion of the western frontier during the late 1800s. The 1901 discovery of oil near Beaumont spurred rapid industrial growth, as did World War II. During the 1960s and 1970s, growth was centered in the U.S. space program and the oil and oil-related industries. Falling oil prices during the mid-1980s dealt Texas a heavy blow; it has been working to diversify and attract new industries.

Texas Rangers, law enforcement body, part of the Texas department of public safety.

The first Rangers were 10 men employed (1823) by S.F. Austin to protect settlers from Native American and Mexican raiders. In 1935 the Rangers were merged with the state highway patrol.

Textile, fabric made from natural or synthetic fibers, whether knitted, woven, bonded, or felted. The fibers (silk, wool, cotton, linen, or synthetics) are prepared and spun into yarn, which is formed into fabric by weaving or other methods. Finished processes include bleaching, calendering, mercerizing, dyeing, brushing, sizing, fulling, and tentering. Chemical processes are used to impart crease-resistance, fireproofing, stain resistance, waterproofing, or non-shrink properties.

Thackeray, William Makepeace (1811-1863), English novelist, essayist, and illustrator. He did much to shape *Punch* and was first editor of *the Cornhill Magazine* (1860). His best-known novel is *Vanity Fair* (1848), a gentle satire of the early 19th-century middle classes. His other novels include *Barry Lyndon* (1844), *Pendennis* (1850), and *Henry Esmond* (1852).

Thailand

Capital:	Bangkok
Area:	198,115 sq mi
	(513,115 sq km)
Population:	62,354,000
Language:	Thai (Siamese)
Government:	Parliamentary monarchy
Independent:	1939
Head of gov.:	Prime minister
Per capita:	US$ 6,600
Monetary unit:	1 Thai baht = 100 satangs

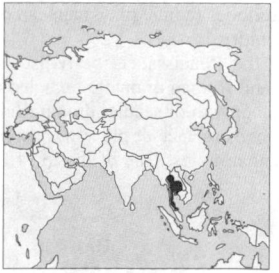

Thailand, Kingdom of Thailand, formerly Siam, constitutional monarchy in Southeast Asia. Thailand is bordered by Myanmar (Burma) to the west and northwest, Laos in the north and east, Cambodia to the southeast, and Malaysia and the Gulf of Siam to the south.
Land and climate. Thailand takes up an area of 198,115 sq mi (513,115 sq km) and is divisible into 3 main areas. The principle region is a fertile plain approximately in the center of the country. It is here that most of the people live. To the north and northeast is a region sometimes called the Khorat

The development of textile printing machines during the first half of the 19th century increased production and reduced costs over the previous method of pattern weaving. Designs were applied as fabric passed between rollers into which patterns have been engraved.

Plateau. It is a high red sandstone plateau that drains eastward to the Mekong. It has poor clay, sand soils, and scrub vegetation and is dry and dusty about half of the year. The region is thinly populated. To the south, Thailand extends into the long narrow Malay Peninsula, which it occupies with Myanmar and Malaysia. In places where it borders Myanmar, Thailand's peninsular territory is not more than 10 mi (16 km) wide. The region is mostly mountainous and forested, but has rice-producing plains and mineral deposits. The many islands along its coast include Phuket, important for its tin. The climate of Thailand is monsoonal.
People. The Thai people are of Mongol origin. Ethnic Chinese are an important minority, and there are hill peoples in the north and Malays, most of them Muslim, in the south. Hinayana Buddhism is the official religion and Thai, a Sino-Tibetan language is the official language.
Economy. Rice is the chief crop in Thailand's predominantly agricultural economy, but sugarcane, cotton, corn, coconuts, rubber, and tobacco are also cultivated. Fishing is important and forestry yields teak, oils, resins, and bamboo. Among the few manufactures is quality silk production. Thailand is one of the world's largest exporters of rice. Other exports include corn, rubber, and teak. Tourism is also important to the economy.
History. The Thai people migrated from South China c.1000 B.C. The center of their culture and civilization moved under the successive dynasties of the Sukho Thai (c.1220-1350) and Ayuthai (1350-1778). The coming of the Portuguese in the 16th century eventually led to an enduring association between the kingdom of Siam and the Western powers. The only country of Southeast Asia that has never been a colony of a European power, Siam lost territorial influence in the 1800s to the British in Burma and Malaya and to the French in Laos and Cambodia, but kept its independence. Thailand was invaded and occupied by the Japanese in World War II. In the early 1950s it sent troops to Korea and joined the South East Asia Treaty Organization (SEATO) in 1954, which is headquartered in Bangkok. Thailand supported the United States in Vietnam, providing troops as well as air bases. King Prajadhipok was forced to grant the country a constitution in 1932 and Siam became Thailand in 1939. The post-World War II years saw political instability and military coups. A new constitution was

promulgated in 1978 and general elections were held in 1979. The civilian government was brought down by a coup in 1991 and was restored in 1992. In 1997 a new constitution was adopted. Thaksin Shinawatra won the elections of 2001. He set out to deal with the narcotics problem, for which he largely held Myanmar responsible. Relations between Thailand and Myanmar worsened as a result.

Thalassemia, inherited blood disorder in which hemoglobin is not adequately produced. Without hemoglobin-the red pigment in blood that carries oxygen through the body-children become sick and, with some varieties of the disease, die. This disorder most often affects people from the Mediterranean, along with Asian and Middle Eastern people as well as Black Americans. A mild form of the disease called thalassemia minor may cause a person to transmit the disorder to the next generation. With thalassemia major, or Cooley's anemia, a child may suffer various symptoms that often become fatal by early adulthood. Thalassemia intermedia is a serious but not always fatal variation of the disorder. Although not a cure, blood transfusions may relieve symptoms if administered on a regular basis.

Thales (625?-546? B.C.), first known Greek philosopher. His ideas are known to us through the writings of others, such as the Greek philosopher Aristotle. Thales ap-

T

The Royal Chapel with its 'Emerald Buddha' is located in the eastern part of the Royal Palace. The temple with its Buddha statue (which is probably made of jade) is one of the principal shrines in the country.

T

proached subjects through what he could scrutinize and logically reason about them—an approach quite different from the Greek tradition of explanations through supernaturally directed myths. Because of this approach, he is considered the first philosopher in the Western tradition. His observations led him to the conclusion that water was the cornerstone of all things on earth. He also introduced geometry to Greece. His school of thought is called either Milesian (based on Miletus, his birth place) or Ionian (based on Ionia, city-state of Greece in which Miletus was located).
See also: Pre-Socratic philosophy.

Thalidomide, mild sedative introduced in the late 1950s and withdrawn a few years later when it was found to be responsible for congenital deformities in children born to mothers who took the drug. This was due to an effect on the embryo in early pregnancy, in particular causing defective limb bud formation. Stricter regulations for testing new drugs in the United States resulted.

Thallium, chemical element, symbol Tl; for physical constants see Periodic Table. Thallium was discovered spectroscopically by William Crookes in 1861. It occurs in crookesite, loandrite, orbaite, and other minerals. It is obtained commercially from flue dusts remaining from pyrite calcination. Thallium is a tin-white, soft, reactive metal. It is soft enough to be scratched with the finger nail. The metal oxidizes in air and should be kept covered by an inert liquid. Thallium is a suspected carcinogen. The element and it compounds are poisonous, and contact with the skin should be avoided. The sulphate has been used as an insecticide and rodenticide, but its use in the United States is now prohibited. Thallium and its compounds are used in photo cells, infrared detectors, low-temperature mercury switches, and special glasses.

An illustration of the stage setting for the mystery play *Passion de Valenciennes* (1547), by French painter Hubert Cailleau (1526-1576). In France, the settings for the various acts were placed in a row on the stage (masiones).

Thames River, England's chief waterway, winding east from the Cotswolds to its North Sea estuary. The Thames is 210 mi (338 km) long. On its banks lie Oxford, Reading, Eton, Windsor Castle, Runnymede, Hampton Court Palace, and Greenwich. Canals link it to the West and Midlands. Above London it displays fine, gentle scenery; below London it is of con-

siderable importance for shipping. It is tidal up to Teddington (10 mi/16 km west of London).
See also: England.

Thanksgiving Day, since 1863, an annual U.S. national holiday to give thanks for blessings received during the year. It is celebrated on the fourth Thursday in November with feasting and prayers. The tradition was begun by the colonists of Plymouth, Mass., in 1621, and can be traced back to the English harvest festivals. In Canada, it is celebrated on the second Monday in October.

Thant, U (1909-1974), Burmese diplomat, United Nations secretary-general (1961-1971). A cautious and unassertive negotiator, he was involved in the Cuban missile crisis (1962), and in peace negotiations in Indonesia (1962), the Congo (now Zaïre; 1963), Cyprus (1964), and the India-Pakistan war (1965).
See also: United Nations.

Thar Desert, also called the Indian Desert, located in northwest India and eastern Pakistan. This desert covers 74,000 sq mi (192,000 sq km). Even though rainfall is scarce (10 in/25 cm per year on average), the Indian government has developed the Indian Gandhi canal for irrigation (completed 1986), so that crops and people may thrive in this arid region. Nuclear power facilities of India are located within the desert in Kota.

Tharp, Twyla (1941-), U.S. choreographer and dancer. After 2 years as a dancer with the Paul Taylor Company (1963-1965), she began to create original, expressive dances for her own company (founded 1965) and later the American Ballet Theater (joined in 1988). She uses various aspects of dance genres (ballet, tap-dance, social dance) and genres of music (classical, jazz, rock and roll). Some of her well-known dances are *Re-Moves* (1966), *Deuce Coupe* (1973), *Short Stories* (1980). She has also choreographed movies, such as *Hair* (1979) and *Amadeus* (1984).

Thatcher, Margaret Hilda (1925-), English prime minister (1979-1990). She entered Parliament in 1959 and served (1970-1974) as secretary of state for education and science. In 1975 she was elected

Conservative Party leader, and in 1979, when the Conservatives won a parliamentary majority, Mrs. Thatcher became Britain's first female prime minister. To fight inflation she introduced austerity measures, but this kept unemployment high and contributed to domestic unrest. She took a firm line against the hunger strikes and terrorist tactics of the Irish Republican Army. Her vigorous defense of the Falkland Islands against Argentina in 1982 contributed to her party's solid electoral victory in 1983. She resigned in 1990 after failing to win the Conservative Party's leadership election.
See also: United Kingdom.

Theater, term used to refer to drama as an art form, as well as to the building in which it is performed. According to Aristotle, the drama of ancient Greece, the ancestor of modern European drama, grew out of the dithyramb (choral song). The form of tragedy credited to Thespis was refined successively by Aeschylus, Sophocles, and Euripides in Periclean Athens. Comedy developed separately. The plays of Aristophanes are the only remains of Greek Old Comedy (5th century B.C.), a form that was extremely licentious and close to its ritual origins. Middle and New comedy (4th and 3rd centuries B.C., respectively) became increasingly sentimental. Greek drama was performed at religious festivals in amphitheaters built into hillsides; that at Epidaurus is still used each summer.
The Roman plays of Plautus, Terence, and Seneca were influenced by Greek theater. However, mime and pantomime were the popular theatrical forms in the Roman Empire. After the fall of the Empire, theater was banned by the Church until the 9th century. Medieval drama evolved from musical elaborations of the church service. Eventually these developed into mystery plays and were moved outdoors onto play wagons. Miracle plays, based on the lives of the saints and on scripture, also developed; cycles of plays were performed at religious festivals. Morality plays (such as *Everyman*) and interludes (comic plays) appeared in the 15th century.
During the Renaissance the rediscovery of Greek and Roman dramatic texts led directly to the growth of secular drama. Buildings for the performance of plays were erected in Elizabethan times. One of the most famous

was the Globe Theatre (associated with Shakespeare), a multistory roofed building inside which the audience ranged around an open stage.

The modern form of the stage, with painted scenery and a proscenium arch across which a curtain falls between acts, was established by the 17th century. However, in the 20th century attempts have been made to eliminate the distancing of audience from the dramatic action, using such new theatrical designs as theater in the round.

Theater of the Absurd, term to describe plays in which traditional values are unable to fulfill emotional and spiritual needs. Human experience is seen as chaotic and without purpose, and people are often depicted as victims of technology and bourgeois values. Samuel Beckett, Eugéne Ionesco, Jean Genet, Edward Albee, and Harold Pinter have been identified with this genre.

Thebes, ancient Greek city located on same site as the modern-day Greek city of Thivai. It headed an alliance, or confederacy, of Greek city-states called Boeotia. As a rival of Athens-a southeastern neighbor about 30 miles away-Thebes supported an invasion of Athens by Persia (480 B.C.). Thebes also sided with Sparta against Athens in the Peloponnesian War (431-404 B.C.). After this war Thebes was dominated by Sparta until a Theban victory by Epaminondas (371 B.C.) made Boeotia powerful once again. Thebes was controlled by other city-states after the death of Epaminondas. Alexander the Great sacked Thebes (336 B.C.); the city was rebuilt 20 years later.
See also: Greece, Ancient.

Thebes, southern city in ancient Egypt, located on the Nile River; present-day city of Luxor. Temples to the god Amon-Re as well as elaborate pyramids constructed for the burial of kings from the Eighteenth Dynasty (1554-1304 B.C.) are found here. The temples of Karnak and Luxor still stand. Thebes served as the capital for many of these rulers, including Tutankhamen, whose remains were unearthed in the 20th century (1922). Remnants of tombs are still apparent in the nearby Valley of the Kings. Thebes was destroyed by the Assyrians (661 B.C.) and the Romans (29 B.C.).

Theism, philosophical system, as distinguished from deism and pantheism, that professes the existence of a personal, transcendent God who created, preserves, and governs the world. Orthodox Christian philosophy is a developed form of theism.
See also: Religion.

Themistocles (514?-449? B.C.), ancient Greek politician and military strategist of Athens. He endorsed the development of the Athenian navy, which helped bring victory to Athens in their war against Persia. Themistocles is best known for his participation in the Athenian victory against the Persians in the battle at Salamis (480 B.C.). Suspicions due to political intrigues resulted in his exile to Persia, where he died on an estate presented to him by the Persian king.
See also: Salamis.

Theocracy, government in which power and authority are seen as derived directly from God and rulers are considered either incarnations or representative of divine power. In ancient times theocracy was widespread. During the Middle Ages in Europe the pope claimed ultimate authority in governing based on his religious authority, and later kings used the 'divine right of kings' to justify their absolutist rule. Early Puritan colonies in New England like Massachusetts Bay and New Haven had leaders who claimed to derive their authority from God. While today secular and religious authority are for the most part separated in the Western democracies, their fusion in such political units as the Iranian Islamic Republic is still strong.

Theocritus (c.3rd century B.C.), poet of ancient Greece. He expressed himself through the idyll-a short, lyrical and emotional poem that describes the virtues and beauty of the countryside. This form of poetry is also called a pastoral. He worked in Alexandria, Egypt, a literary center of his time. Of his life's work, 30 written poems remain. Theocritus was influenced by the Alexandrian librarian and poet Callimachus, and in turn influenced the work of the Roman poet Vergil.

Theodorakis, Mikis (1925-), Greek composer and left-wing resistance fighter. Studied at the conservatory in Athens from 1943; was imprisoned from 1947-1949 because of his communist activities. Studied from 1954-1960 at the Paris conservatory under Messiaen. Set up the Lambrakis youth movement in Greece in 1961. During the colonels' regime he was imprisoned again (1967-1970), after which he moved to Paris, returning in 1974 to Greece, where he was welcomed as a hero. Besides symphonies he also composed ballet and chamber music, folk songs and popular songs. He achieved wide recognition for his music to the films *Elektra* (1962), *Zorba the Greek* (1964) and *Z* (1969), and for the *Mauthausen cycle* (songs, 1965). He also composed several pop oratorios, including *Canto general* (1972) with lyrics by Pablo Neruda, and the operas *Kostas Kariotakis* (1985), *Medea* (1990), and *Elektra* (1997).

Theodoric (A.D. 455?-526), conqueror of Italy, king of Ostrogoths. He inherited the crown from his father Theodemir (A.D. 471). With the help of the Byzantine emperor, Zeno, Theordoric and his barbarians defeated Odoacer, the ruling barbarian of Italy (A.D. 493). Rather than tyrannize the Italians, Theodoric respected Roman citizens and used their political and legal institutions during his peaceful rule. He allowed Catholics to practice their religion even though his Arian beliefs conflicted with the beliefs and doctrines of the church. His elaborate tomb is located in Ravenna, Italy. Theodoric was known in Germanic legends as Dietrich of Bern.
See also: Ostrogoths.

Theodosius I (A.D. 346-395), emperor of Rome. Theodosius was of Armenian descent, born in Spain. He rose through the ranks of the Roman military. Later with

Emperor Gratian he ruled Rome, becoming responsible for provinces in the east (A.D. 379). He would not allow religious practices that were not Christian, but he did allow the formation of an independent nation for the non-Christian Visigoths (A.D. 382) within the eastern provinces. He became emperor of all of Rome when he conquered the non-Christian peoples that populated the west (394 A.D.).
See also: Rome, Ancient.

Theology, science of religious knowledge; the formal analysis of what is believed by adherents of a religion, making its doctrine coherent, elucidating it logically, and relating it to secular disciplines. Most religions have no well-developed theology. The concept arose in Greek, but its elaboration took place only in Christianity. The early Church Fathers and Doctors formulated doctrine in contemporary philosophical terms, and major advances were made by resolving controversies. In the Middle Ages Scholasticism developed, partly in reaction to the influence of Neoplatonism, and divided theology into natural theology and revealed theology. From the Reformation each branch of Protestantism began to develop its own distinctive theology. From the Enlightenment rationalist theology became dominant, leading to modernism and the modern critical view of the Bible. Partly in reaction, neo-orthodoxy and the existentialist theology of Reinhold Niebuhr and Paul Tillich arose.
See also: God; Religion.

Theorell, Axel Hugo Teodor (1903-1982), Swedish biochemist awarded the 1955 Nobel Prize for physiology or medicine for his studies of enzyme action, specifically the roles of enzymes in biological oxidation and reduction processes.
See also: Biochemistry; Enzyme.

Theorem *See:* Geometry; Pythagorean theorem.

Theosophy (Greek, 'divine wisdom'), mystical system of religious philosophy claiming direct insight into the divine nature. The speculations of such philosophers as Plotinus, Jakob Boehme, and Emanuel Swedenborg are often called theosophical, as are many Eastern philosophies. The Theosophical Society was founded in 1875 by Madame Helena Petrovna Blavatsky.
See also: Besant, Annie (Wood).

Theotokopoulos, Domenikos *See:* Greco, El.

Therapy *See:* Occupational therapy; Physical therapy; Psychotherapy.

Theresa, Saint *See:* Teresa.

Thermal pollution, ecologically harmful warming of rivers, lakes, or oceans. In the past, this pollution was most often caused by heated wastewater discharged from nuclear power plants or factories into streams, rivers, or other bodies of water, resulting in elevated water temperature that endangered both plant and animal life in the water. The Environmental Protection Agency (EPA) es-

T

T

tablished regulations requiring such parties either to cool the heated wastewater before discharging it or to release small amounts of it into many different places. Both precautions are aimed at maintaining normal temperatures in rivers and lakes to protect the life in them.

Thermal springs *See:* Hot springs.

Thermocouple, electric circuit involving two junctions between different metals, or semiconductors. These junctions create a small electromotive force (emf) in the circuit (known as the Seebeck effect). Measurement of this electromotive force provides a sensitive, if approximate, temperature reading ranging from 70°K to 1,000°K. Thermocouples can be run in reverse as small refrigerators. A number of thermocouples connected in series with one set of blackened junctions form a thermopile, which measures radiation. Thermoelectricity embraces the Seebeck and other effects relating heat transfer, thermal gradients, electric fields, and currents.
See also: Electric current.

Thermodynamics, division of physics concerned with the interconversion of heat, work, and other forms of energy, and with the states of physical systems. *Classical thermodynamics* is basic to engineering, parts of geology, metallurgy, and physical chemistry. Building on earlier studies of temperature and heat, Sadi Carnot pioneered the science with his investigations of the cyclic heat engine (1824), and in 1850 Rudolf Clausius stated the first two laws. Thermodynamics was further developed by J.W. Gibbs, H.L.F. von Helmholtz, Lord Kelvin, and J.C. Maxwell.
In thermodynamics, a system is any defined collection of matter: a *closed system* is one that cannot exchange matter with its surroundings; an *isolated system* can exchange neither matter nor energy. The *state* of a system is specified by determining all its properties, such as pressure, volume, etc. A *process* is a change from one state to another, the path being specified by all the intermediate states. A *state function* is a property or function of properties that depends only on the state and not on the path by which the state was reached.
See also: Physics.

Thermography, method to measure the slightest variations in temperature of soft tissue in the body using infrared heat sensors. The technique is often used in mammography (breast examination) to detect any growth in the breast (the mass will have a different temperature from other breast tissue). Thermography can also be used on an extremity, particularly the leg, to help diagnose a thrombus (clot) in a vein. The area of the body to be tested is usually placed on a heat-detection device that reacts to specific temperatures, either by color changes or by a direct display of temperatures.

Thermometer, instrument for measuring the temperature of a substance or object. Clinical thermometers are made of a glass tube with a bulb containing liquid (usually mercury) that expands and rises in the tube as the temperature increases. A scale on the tube indicates the object's temperature by measuring how high the liquid rises. The type of thermometer used in a given application depends on the temperature range.

Thermopylae (Greek, 'hot gates'), narrow mountain pass that in ancient Greece led from the north to the south. This pass between Mt. Oeta and the Maliac Gulf was the scene of a famous battle from the Persian Wars (480 B.C.) that the Spartans lost against the invading Persian forces. Although this area is a marshy plain rather than a mountain pass, it contains hot springs as it did in ancient times.

Thermosphere, outermost layer of the earth's atmosphere, at altitudes between approximately 53 mi (85 km) and 300 mi (480 km). The heat, caused by radiation of the sun, varies from –135° (–93°C) at the lowest altitude to 2,700°F (1,500°C) and more at the highest altitude. The thermosphere is different from the layers of the atmosphere closest to earth in that the pressure is much lower (1 million times lower than at sea level) and the chemical makeup includes mostly atoms of helium and hydrogen.
See also: Atmosphere.

A clinical, or fever, thermometer consists of a bulb of mercury (1) in a glass stem (2). Body heat causes the mercury to expand through a constriction (3), into a capillary tube (4), where it is measured against a scale (5).

The shape of the glass (6) acts as a magnifying lens to facilitate reading. Surface tension at the constriction keeps the mercury at its highest reading until shaken down by hand (7).

Thermostat, device for maintaining a material or enclosure at a constant temperature by automatically regulating its heat supply, which is cut off if the temperature exceeds and reconnected if it falls below that required. A thermostat comprises a sensor whose dimensions or physical properties change with temperature and a relay device that controls a switch or valve accordingly.

Theropod *See:* Dinosaur.

Theseus, in Greek mythology, son of King Aegeus and princess Aethra, renowned for his heroism. As a youth he went to Crete with other youths to be sacrificed to the Minotaur, but instead succeeded in killing the beast. On his voyage back to Athens, he failed to fly his ship's white sails, a symbol of his safe return. Aegeus thought his son was dead and killed himself in his grief. Theseus was then declared king.
See also: Mythology.

Thespis (c. 6th century B.C.), ancient Greek actor. Among his many innovations was that of allowing a character to speak dialogue separately from the words spoken by the chorus. The use of make-up and masks is also attributed to him. Most importantly, through an innovative performance in honor of the Greek god Dionysus at an Athenian festival (c.534 B.C.), Thespis became known as the originator of tragedy. A word for actors, thespians, honors his contributions to drama.

Thessalonians, Epistles to the, books 13 and 14 of the New Testament Bible. After the founding of the church at Thessaloniki in Greece, the apostle Paul wrote a letter (c.A.D. 50) to its members, explaining the purpose of the resurrection of Christ. A second letter, attributed to Paul but more likely written by one of his followers, indicated the lengthy time that would elapse before Christ's second coming. These letters represent the first Christian writings.
See also: Bible; New Testament.

Thessaloniki *See:* Salonika.

Thessaly, northeast region of Greece in which Mount Olympus of ancient Greek legend is located. This region was the home of the legendary Achilles, hero of the Trojan War, and Jason, head of the Argonauts. Lack of cooperation among its own people kept Thessaly weak militarily. It was conquered (344 B.C.) by Philip of Macedon, father of Alexander the Great. Later rulers included the Romans (146 B.C.), the Turks (1355), and the Greeks (1878). In ancient times, Pherae, Crannon, and Larisa were its major cities. Today, its major cities are Volos and Larisa.
See also: Greece.

Thiamine *See:* Vitamin.

Thibault, Jacques A.F *See:* France, Anatole.

Thiers, Louis Adolphe (1797-1877), French author and diplomat. Among his writings are *History of the French Revolu-*

tion (1823-1827), a 10-volume study, and *History of the Consulate and the Empire* (1845-1862). He helped organize the July Revolution (1830), which opposed the rule of Charles X. He served in the government of Louis Philippe, successor of Charles X. He opposed the rule of Napoleon II in the Second Empire. Later, after the Franco-Prussian War, he served 2 years as the first president of the Third Republic of France (1871-1873).
See also: France.

Thieu, Nguyen Van (1923-2001), president of South Vietnam (1967-1975). An army officer, he helped overthrow Ngo Dinh Diem (1963), becoming premier in 1965 and president in 1967. He was re-elected (1971), but after U.S. troops were withdrawn his dictatorial regime gradually collapsed, and he resigned in April 1975. He fled to Taiwan and later to Great Britain, after South Vietnam fell to the North.
See also: Vietnam.

Thimphu (pop. 32,000), capital of the Himalayan kingdom of Bhutan in the Thimphu district. Fortified monastery built in traditional style. The city (the monastery) was founded in 1581, and was besieged at various times by conquerors from Tibet. Until the 20th century it could only be reached by mountain paths; the first road to Phuntsholing, on the Indian border, was built in 1968 (Indo-Bhutan route). Designated as the capital in 1962. Royal palace. Cultivation of rice, maize and wheat. Landing strip for airplanes.

Thiopental, drug used in general anesthesia. It is commonly known by its trade name, Pentothal or Sodium Pentothal. It was first demonstrated in 1934. Because it will not burn or explode, it is preferred over combustible anesthetics, such as ether. It is often used, usually by injection, to begin the anesthesia process. Small doses tend to release emotional inhibitions, and it is sometimes used in the treatment of psychiatric patients.
See also: Anesthesia.

Third International *See:* International, The.

Third Reich *See:* Germany; Reich.

Third World, term often applied to the non-aligned (and mostly developing) nations of Africa, Latin America, and Asia as opposed to Western and Eastern (Communist) countries.

Thirty-Nine Articles, doctrine issued by the Church of England to bridge the gap between Roman Catholic and Protestant Reformation groups in 16th-century England. The Articles, approved by Parliament in 1571, are still accepted today by the Anglican Church. Among the tenets are the condemnation of such Roman Catholic beliefs as purgatory, transubstantiation, and reverence for saints. Because the language of the Articles is intentionally vague, interpretations have been various.
See also: Anglicans.

Thirty Tyrants, or The Thirty, term used to identify the group of Athenians who ruled Athens after it fell to Sparta (404 B.C.). The oligarchy was set up by the Spartan general Lysander. Under the leadership of the Athenian politician Critias, the group terrorized the Athenian citizenry and seized their property. In 403 B.C., Sparta reinstated Athens's democratic form of government.
See also: Athens; Greece, Ancient.

Thirty Years' War, series of European wars (1618-1648). Partly a Catholic-Protestant religious conflict, they were also a political and territorial struggle by different European powers, particularly France, against its greatest rivals, the Habsburgs, rulers of the Holy Roman Empire. War began when Bohemian Protestants accused 2 government ministers of wrongdoing and threw them out a window (a customary Bohemian punishment for offending officials). This event became known as the Defenestration of Prague (from Latin *fenestra*, 'window') and triggered a civil war in Bohemia that rapidly spread to all of western Europe. The Bohemians were defeated by General Tilly (1620), who went on to subjugate the Palatinate (1623). In 1625 Denmark, fearing Habsburg power, invaded North Germany but was defeated in 1629. The emperor Ferdinand II issued the Edict of Restitution, restoring lands to the Roman Catholic Church. In 1630 the Swedish king Gustavus Adolphus led the Protestant German princes against Ferdinand. He was killed at Lützen (1632). By 1635 the Swedes had lost support in Germany, and the German states concluded the Peace of Prague. But now France, under Cardinal Richelieu, intervened. Further wars ensued, with France, Sweden, and the German Protestant states fighting in the Low Countries, Scandinavia, France, Germany, Spain, and Italy against the Holy Roman Empire, Spain (another Habsburg power), and Denmark. Peace negotiations, begun in 1640, were completed with the Peace of Westphalia (1648).

Thistle, common name for many prickly, herbaceous plants (family Compositae).

The creeping Canada thistle, *C. arvense*, is a noxious, ubiquitous, prickly perennial weed. It is able to reproduce itself from root fragments, and plowing it under, spreads rather than kills it. At times, the thistle is grown for display because of its stark natural beauty.

The treaties of Westphalia in 1648, marked the end of both the Thirty Years' War and the Eighty Years' War between Spain and the Dutch Republic. The Dutchman Gerard Terborch (1617-1681) painted this solemn declaration of peace (National Gallery, London).

They normally have purple or yellow flowers. When the seeds are ripe, they are dispersed as fluffy thistledown. Thistles normally produce a thick taproot that can be eaten or used as a coffee substitute.

Thomas à Becket *See:* Becket, Saint Thomas à.

Thomas, Dylan (1914-1953), Welsh poet who first achieved recognition with *Eighteen Poems* (1934). His prose includes the quasi-autobiographical *Portrait of the Artist as a Young Dog* (1940) and *Adventures in the Skin Trade* (1955); his poetry includes *Deaths and Entrances* (1946) and *Collected Poems* (1952). His drama *Under Milk Wood* (posthumously published, 1954) was originally a radio play.

Thomas à Kempis (Thomas Hermerken von Kempen; 1380-1471), German religious writer and Augustinian friar at Zwolle in the Netherlands. He is the probable author of *The Imitation of Christ* (c.1427), one of the most widely read works of Christian literature.

The English poet Dylan Thomas (1914-1953). Portrait by Augustus John (1878-1961) (National Museum of Wales, Cardiff).

Thomas Aquinas, Saint *See:* Aquinas, Saint Thomas.

Thomas, Saint, one of the 12 apostles, known as 'Doubting Thomas' because he would not believe Jesus' resurrection until he put his fingers in Jesus' wounds. His subsequent career and martyrdom at Madras are recounted in the apocryphal *Acts of Thomas*.
See also: Apostles.

Thompson, Daley Francis (1958-), British decathlete, completed his first decathlon at the age of 16. He was 18 when he went to his first Olympic Games (1976). Four years later, during the games in Moscow in 1980, he won the gold medal with 8495 points. He retained his Olympic title in 1984 in Los Angeles with 8797 points, just one point away from the world record. He became the decathlon world champion in 1983. Apart from his sporting achievements, Thomson also drew attention to himself by wearing T-shirts with messages intended to stimulate the public and the press.

Thomson, Sir Joseph John (1856-1940), British physicist. The Nobel Prize in physics (1906) was awarded to him for his discovery of the electron. This discovery was made as he studied rays-known as cathode rays-that occurred in a vacuum in a glass tube when electric current was introduced. Eventually he proved that this phenomenon was due to moving particles rather than light rays; those particles were later named electrons. As professor of physics at Cambridge in England, he helped develop their atomic research facilities. His son, Sir George Paget Thomson, also won the Nobel Prize for physics (1937), along with Clinton Davisson of the United States.
See also: Electron.

Thomson, Virgil (1896-1989), U.S. composer and music critic. Influenced by The Six in Paris, he became a leading 'Americanist.' His works include the operas *Four Saints in Three Acts* (1928) and *the Mother of Us All* (1947), in collaboration with Gertrude Stein, symphonies, and instrumental, chamber, and film music. He won a 1949 Pulitzer Prize for his *Louisiana Story* score.

Thon Buri (Chon Buri; pop. 600,000) City in Thailand on the Chao Phraya River, district of metropolitan Bangkok. It is a center of sawmills and rice-husking plants and an important residential area. Wat Arun temple (temple of the dawn). It was the capital of Thailand (Siam) during Takh Sin (1767-1782).

Thor, in Norse mythology, god of thunder. Son of Odin, the king of the deities, Thor is depicted as a powerful warrior with a huge appetite. The fiercest adversary of the giants, Thor's strength is symbolized by his weapon, a magical hammer called Mjollnir, which unerringly hits its target and flies back to Thor. According to Norse myth, the world will be destroyed in a great war between the giants and the gods, which will also kill Thor. Thursday is named after Thor (Thor's day).
See also: Mythology.

Thucydides (approximately 460-400 B.C.).

Thoreau, Henry David (1817-1862), U.S. writer, naturalist, and abolitionist. His book *Walden* (1854) was a philosophical essay that recounted Thoreau's experiences living close to nature in a cabin at Walden Pond, near Concord, Mass. His influential essay 'Civil Disobedience' promoted the concept of passive resistance that inspired leaders such as Mohandas K. Gandhi and Martin Luther King, Jr. Thoreau's place in literature is as a major voice among the New Transcendentalists, led by his mentor Ralph Waldo Emerson. Self-direction and an intimate understanding of nature, as found within and outside of the individual, were Thoreau's consistent themes.

Thorium, chemical element, symbol Th; for physical constants see Periodic Table.

Discovered by Jöns Jakob Berzelius in 1828. The element occurs in the minerals thorite, thorianite, orangite, yttrocrasite, and monazite and is obtained commercially from the latter. Thorium is obtained as a powder by reduction of its oxide with calcium. It is a gray-white, radioactive metal. It is pyrophoric in powder form and burns in air to form the oxide, which has the highest melting point of all oxides. It is a member of the actinide series. Thorium is used as a nuclear fuel source and for incandescent lamp mantles. It is estimated that the energy available from thorium in the earth's crust is probably greater than that from uranium and fossil fuels combined.

Thorn apple *See:* Jimsonweed.

Thorndike, Edward Lee (1874-1949), U.S. psychologist best known for devising tests to measure intelligence, learning, and aptitude. His system of psychology, *connectionism*, had a profound influence on U.S. school education techniques, especially his discovery that the learning of one skill only slightly assists in the learning of another, even if related.
See also: Psychology.

Thorpe, Jim (James Francis Thorpe; 1888-1953), U.S. athlete. Known for his all-around athletic ability, he played major league baseball (1913-1919), professional football (1915-1930), and was the first athlete to win both the decathlon and pentathlon at the Olympic Games (1912). Thorpe was stripped of his gold medals after a controversy arouse involving his amateur status; the International Olympic Committee restored these medals in 1982. Thorpe was inducted into the Pro Football Hall of Fame in 1963.

Thorvaldsen, Bertel (1770-1844), a Danish sculptor known for his Neoclassic works. *The Three Graces* and the reliefs *Night* and *Day* are typical of his restrained, graceful style. He also designed many monuments, including the *Lion of Lucerne* in Lucerne, Switzerland.
Thorvaldsen studied art in Copenhagen and Rome. In 1803 *Jason* established his reputation and Thorvaldsen opened a studio in Rome. When he returned to Copenhagen in 1838, he gave the city models of all his famous works. These and other sculptures are in Copenhagen's Thorvaldsen Museum.

Thoth, Greek name for Djhowtey, an ancient Egyptian moon god who became associated with civilization, learning, and healing. His sacred animals are the ibis and the baboon, and he is often depicted as a human with the head of an ibis or a baboon with the head of a dog. Said to be the inventor of writing, he was often considered the representative on earth and the scribe of the sun god, Re.
See also: Mythology.

Thothmes III *See:* Thutmose III.

Thousand and One Nights *See:* Arabian Nights.

Thrace, ancient region in the eastern part of the Balkan Peninsula, southeastern Europe,

bordering the Black and Aegean seas. It includes modern northeastern Greece, southern Bulgaria, and European Turkey.

Thrasher, any of 17 U.S. bird species belonging to the mockingbird family. A brownish, long-tailed bird, it is known for its raucous call. It forages on the ground for insects, worms, seeds, and fruit. The most familiar is the brown thrasher, found east of the Rocky Mountains.

Three Gorges Dam *See:* Yangtze River.

Three Mile Island, site in the Susquehanna River, near Middletown, Penn., of a nuclear reactor that, on March 28, 1979, began to emit 'puffs' of radiation as a result of malfunction of the cooling system, aggravated by problems with the computer monitors and some human error. Initial reports downplayed the crisis, but it developed that a core meltdown was a possibility and that a large, potentially explosive hydrogen bubble had formed in the reactor; also, it was learned that no workable plans existed for evacuating the area. Luckily, catastrophe was averted without fatalities or known injury.
See also: Nuclear reactor.

Three-mile limit *See:* Territorial waters.

Three Wise Men *See:* Magi.

Thrombosis, formation of a clot (thrombus) in the heart or blood vessels. It commonly occurs in the legs and is associated with varicose veins (thrombophelotist), but is more serious if it occurs in the heart or in the brain arteries. Detachments from a thrombus in the legs may be carried to the lungs as an embolus; this may have a fatal outcome if large vessels are occluded. Treatment includes anticoagulants.

Thrush, name for a family (Turdidae) of slender-billed songbirds found in most parts of the world. The plumage is often gray or red-brown, and many species have speckled or striated breasts. The tail is usually rounded or square and is held erect in some species. Birds of worldwide distribution, they feed largely on insects, worms, and snails, but many species also take fruit and berries. Species include the robin, the nightingale, the hermit thrush, and the bluebird.

Thrush, infection due to the fungus *Candida albicans*. It occurs usually in children and is characterized by small whitish spots on the tip and sides of the tongue and the lining membrane of the mouth.

Thucydides (460?-400 B.C.), historian of ancient Greece. His work *History of the Peloponnesian War* (441-404 B.C.) eloquently communicates an unbiased and accurate account of events in the first 30 years of that war. Both sides in the conflict are quoted, analyzed, and described in detail. Thucydides was an Athenian naval general who, upon failure to defeat the Spartan troops at Amphipolis in the Peloponnesian War, was exiled (424-404 B.C.).
See also: Greece, Ancient; Peloponnesian War.

Thugs, members of an Indian religious sect (13th-19th centuries) who murdered and robbed to honor the goddess Kali. All victims, usually wealthy travelers, were systematically strangled because the spilling of blood was forbidden. In 1831, British and Indian regimes collaborated to eliminate thug activities.

Thule, American air base in northwest Greenland on Baffin Bay, established in agreement with the Danish (1952). The original Thule was founded by Knud Rasmussen (1910), who undertook inland expeditions from this settlement. Pytheas of Massalia reached the ancient settlement of Thule in 325 B.C., although its exact location is not known (Iceland, Norway, Faeroe Islands).

Thulium, chemical element, symbol Tm; for physical constants see Periodic Table. Thulium was discovered in 1879 by P.T. Cleve in crude erbium oxide. It occurs in the minerals gadolinite, euxenite, ytterspar, and monazite and is obtained commercially from the latter. It is prepared by reducing the anhydrous chloride with calcium. Thulium is a silvery, soft, reactive metal belonging to the series of elements known as the rare-earth metals. Thulium salts have a characteristic absorption spectrum. Ion-exchange and solvent extraction techniques have led to much easier isolation of the rare-earth elements. Thulium and its compounds are used in carbon-arc lighting, glass, and refractory materials.

Thunberg, Clas (1893-1973), Finnish skater, in the 1920s one of the strongest skaters in the world. Thunberg won the world title in 1923, 1925, 1928, 1929 and 1931. During the Olympic Games of 1924 he won the 1500 m and the 5000 m, four years later he won the gold medal in the 500 m and the 1500 m. Thunberg was active in competitive sports until the age of 42.

Thurber, James (1894-1961), U.S. humorist and cartoonist. The sophisticated humor of his writing contrasts with the simplicity of his line drawings. Several stories, such as 'The Secret Life of Walter Mitty' (1942), were filmed. He contributed to *The New Yorker* from 1927. His collections include *My Life and Hard Times* (1933) and *The Thurber Carnival* (1945).

Thutmose III, or **Thothmes III** (d.1450 B.C.), king (c.1490-1436 B.C.) of ancient Egypt. Upon accession to the throne, his half sister and wife, Queen Hatshepsut, acted forcefully as his governing ruler. Upon her death he became sole ruler and a brilliant leader and conqueror, expanding Egypt's boundaries, increasing its wealth, improving its manpower, and building and enlarging numerous temples, including the temple at Karnak.

Thyme, pungent, aromatic herb (genus *Thymus*) of the mint family. It has pale purple flowers. *T. vulgaris* is commonly used in seasoning.

Thymus, lymphoid organ situated in humans in the chest cavity, behind the breast-bone, and extending into the neck. It reaches its maximum weight at about puberty and then undergoes involution (shrinks). It is necessary in early life for the development of immunological functions.

Thyroid gland, ductless two-lobed endocrine gland lying in front of the trachea in the neck. The principal hormones secreted by the thyroid play a crucial role in regulating the rate at which cells oxidize fuels to release energy and thus strongly influence growth. Thyroid stimulating hormones (TSH) are released by the pituitary gland. Undersecretion (hypothyroidism) in adults leads to myxedema, with mental dullness and cool, dry, puffy skin. Oversecretion (thyrotoxicosis) produces nervousness, weight loss, and increased heart rate. Goiter, an enlargement of the gland, may result when the diet is deficient in iodine. *See also:* Gland; Hormone.

Tianjin, or Tientsin (pop. 9,600,000), international port city on the Hai River in northeastern China. One of China's largest cities and Beijing's major port, it is a viable industrial center producing machinery, textiles, chemicals, and consumer products, in addition to offshore oil production. Tianjin was occupied by Western powers during the Boxer Uprising (1900) and was controlled by Japan from 1937 until the end of World War II. A major earthquake inflicted serious damage to Tianjin in 1976. *See also:* China.

Tian Shan, or Tien Shan, major mountain system of central Asia. It runs some 1,500 mi (2,410 km) through Kirghizstan and China. Its highest peak, the Pobeda Peak, stands 24,406 ft (7,439 m) above sea level.

Tiberias, Lake *See:* Galilee, Sea of.

Tiberius (Tiberius Julius Caesar Augustus; 42 B.C.-A.D. 37), Roman emperor, successor of his stepfather, Augustus, upon his death in A.D. 14. Tiberius oversaw tax collections and selected capable administrators to supervise his provinces. However, due to unpopular financial reforms and his growing tyranny, he retired to the island of Capri, where he ruled until his death. *See also:* Rome, Ancient.

Tiber River, river in central Italy, flowing 252 mi (405.5 km) from the Appenines south through Umbria and Latium and southwest through Rome to the Tyrrhenian Sea near Ostia. Ancient Rome was built on its east bank.

Tibet, autonomous region of China in central Asia, bordering Myanmar (Burma), India, Nepal, Bhutan, and Sikkim. *Land and climate.* Tibet's area is 471,662 sq mi (1,221,600 sq km), and the region averages 15,000 ft (4,570 m) in altitude. Tibet is often called the 'Roof of the World.' The tallest mountain in the world, Mt. Everest (29,028 ft/8,848 m above sea level), is in the Himalaya, the world's tallest mountain chain. The Himalaya rise along the southern end of the Plateau of Tibet. The Kunlun Mountains in the north are almost as high as the Himalayas. The Brahmaputra, Indus, and Yangtze rivers rise in Tibet. The winters are dry and intensely cold; summers, hot and humid.

People. Tibetans follow Buddhist Lamaism, headed by the Dalai Lama and the Panchen Lama. Until 1965 there were many monasteries, involving 20% of the male population as monks. After 1965, the Chinese Communists decreased emphasis on religion.

Economy. The pastoral, livestock-based economy has been affected by roadbuilding and new cement, chemical, paper, textile, and other industries. Tibet has deposits of coal and iron (exploited in the northeast) and other minerals.

History. Tibet was a powerful kingdom during the A.D. 600s, flourishing until the early eighteenth century, when it fell under Chinese control. In 1911 Tibet expelled the Chinese, but friction remained between the 2 countries until 1950, when China invaded again. An agreement signed in 1951 ended Tibetan sovereignty, but allowed self-government and freedom of religion and speech. However, Chinese rule became steadily more oppressive, and in the mid-1950s

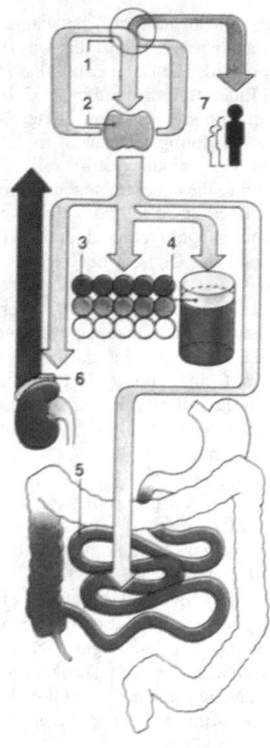

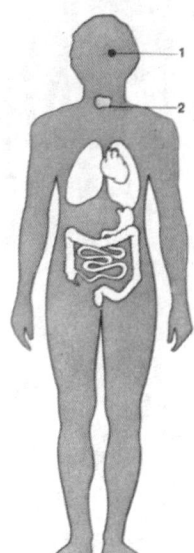

T

The thyroid gland regulates the body's use of energy. When signaled by the pituitary (1), the thyroid (2) releases hormones into the bloodstream. They are transported to the body's cells (3), stimulating them to burn more fuel. These hormones affect the blood cholesterol levels (4), the intestinal absorption of sugars (5), the adrenal medulla (6), which influences the brain, and growth hormones (7).

This is a 17th incarnate lama of the Yellow Hat (Gelugpa) sect in India. In Tibetan Buddhism, lamaist succession is based on direct reincarnation. It is believed that when a lama dies his soul passes into a newly born infant, who is then sought out by the religious community.

T

Chinese rule in eastern Tibet caused open dissent and a revolt (1959) that was ruthlessly suppressed. The Dalai Lama fled from the capital Lhasa to India, and in 1965 Tibet became an autonomous region. After 20 years of periodic rioting and unrest in Tibet, the Chinese began a policy of liberalization, decentralizing the economy and allowing a degree of freedom of religion. However, massive rioting again erupted during the late 1980s and the Chinese declared a state of matrial law and sent in troups. Unrest continues in Tibet today. In 1993 there were talks between the Chinese government and the Dalai Lama, but this did not result in a change of Chinese policy. In 1995 the persecution of the followers of the Dalai Lama increased.
See also: China.

Tick, name for a group of parasitic arthropods (order Acarina). Unlike most other arthropods, ticks have no head, and the thorax and abdomen are fused. All ticks are bloodsucking external parasites of vertebrates. They are divided into two main families: the soft ticks, Argasidae, and hard ticks, Ixodidae. Ticks transmit more diseases to humans and domestic animals than does any other arthropod group except the mosquitoes.

Tickseed *See:* Coreopsis.

Tide, periodic rise and fall of land and water on the earth. Tidal motions are primarily

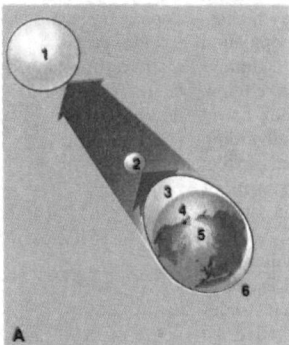
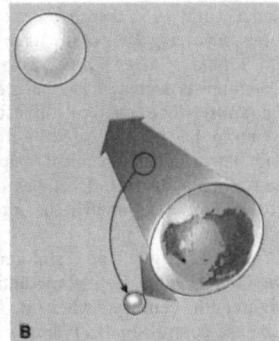
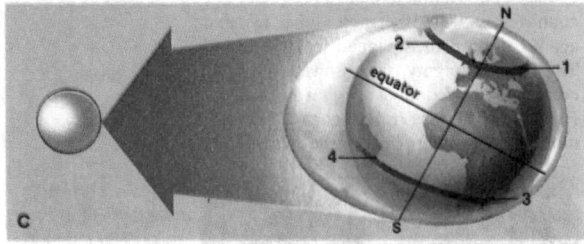

Two ocean tides occur on earth every 24 hours and 50 minutes. (A) During spring tides, a large tidal bulge (3) is produced on earth (5) by the combined effects of the sun (1) and the moon (2). A smaller and opposite tidal bulge (6) is caused simultaneously by centrifugal forces, resulting from the earth's rotation about the common center of gravity (4) of the earth-moon system. (B) Smaller neap tides occur when the sun and moon partially neutralize each other's effects. (C) Because the axis of the tidal bulges is inclined to the earth's equator, any particular location on the earth's surface will experience different tidal heights (1, 2 and 3, 4) during each daily rotation.

exhibited by water: the motion of the land is barely detectable. As the earth-moon system rotates about its center of gravity, which is within the earth, the earth bulges in the direction of the moon, as well as in exactly the opposite direction owing to the moon's gravitational attraction and the centrifugal forces resulting from the system's revolution. Since the moon orbits the earth in the same direction that the earth rotates, the bulge 'travels' round the earth each lunar day (24.83 hr); hence most points on the earth have a high tide every 12.42 hr. The sun produces a similar though smaller tidal effect. Exceptionally high high tides occur at full and new moon (spring tides), particularly if the moon is at perigee; exceptionally low high tides (neap tides), at first and third quarter. The friction of the tides causes the day to lengthen 0.001 sec per century.

Tieck, Ludwig (1773-1853), a German author. His writings form a link between the Storm and Stress literature and the Romantic movement. A main theme of Tieck's novels, folktales, and plays is the belief that the world can be redeemed through the nobility of art. His writing is characterized by irony and often portrays the presence of supernatural forces. Tieck's popular folktale *Fair Eckbert* (1796), presents a character who becomes psychologically lost in a mixture of illusions and reality. In the novel *Franz Sternbald's Wanderings* (1798), he depicts the spontaneous, carefree life and travels of a young artist. Tieck rejuvenated German drama with his satiric comedies, such as *Puss in Boots* (1797), which mocked sentimentality.
Tieck was born in Berlin. In later life he worked on translations and was less associated with Romanticism.

Tien Shan *See:* Tian Shan.

Tientsiu *See:* Tianjin.

Tiepolo, Giovanni Battista (1696-1770), most renowned Venetian painter of his time, a capable craftsman, decorator, and artist of vivid, large murals. His frescoes in Labia Palace brought him widespread recognition. As a result he was commissioned by Emperor Frederick I of Bavaria and by the Spanish royalty of Madrid, where his work included the *Apotheosis of Spain*.

The tiger, *P. tigris*, with its strong legs and sharp claws, is a fierce hunter that devoures even lions and other tigers. If a tiger starts attacking domestic cattle, it will probaby also become a man-eater.

Tierra del Fuego (Spanish, 'Land of Fire'), several small islands (28,476 sq mi/73,753 sq km) separated from the southern coast of South America by the Strait of Magellan. Named by Ferdinand Magellan in 1520, the islands belong to Chili and Argentina. The small population is supported by income from sheep and petroleum.
See also: Cape Horn.

Tiffany, Charles Lewis (1812-1902), U.S. jeweler and retailer. The stock in his first store, opened in 1839, was limited mainly to ordinary glassware and stationery, but it soon included bohemian glass, jewelry, silverware, and rare porcelain. Tiffany began manufacturing his own jewelry in 1848, and by 1870 had extended his operations to Paris and London.

Tiffany, Louis Comfort (1848-1933), U.S. artist and designer, a leader of Art Nouveau; son of jeweler Charles Tiffany. He created decorative objects of iridescent 'favrile,' or Tiffany glass.
See also: Art nouveau.

Tiflis *See:* Tbilisi.

Tiger (*Panthera tigris*), major cat of Asia with distinct races in different parts of that continent. Closely related to lions, they are the largest of all the cats. A tawny coat broken with dark, vertical stripes provides excellent camouflage against natural patterns of light and shade. Tigers do not chase after food, but prefer to stalk and spring. For the most part they are solitary animals, hunting in the cool of the day and otherwise lying in the shade to rest.

Tiger lily (*Lilium tigrinum*), plant of the lily family originating in eastern Asia and grown widely as a garden flower. The dark stem, 2-6 ft (0.6-1.8 m) tall, supports large red-orange flowers with black markings. The plant propagates by means of small, black, berrylike bulbs that form where the leaves join the stem and fall to the earth to produce new plants.

Tiglath-pileser, rulers of ancient Assyria. **Tiglath-pileser I** ruled from 1115-1077 B.C. A great military leader, he conquered territories from the Mediterranean coast to what are now Turkey and Iran. Historians know little about **Tiglath-pileser II**, who ruled from 967-935 B.C. during a seemingly stable reign. **Tiglath-pileser III**, who ruled from 744-727 B.C., founded the Assyrian Empire. He led a massive military and diplomatic campaign that extended into parts of what are now Iraq, Syria, and Turkey. In 728 B.C., he united the kingdoms of Assyria and Babylonia and declared himself king of Babylonia.

Tigris River, easternmost of the two great rivers of ancient Mesopotamia. The Tigris-Euphrates valley was the cradle of Middle East civilizations. Baghdad, city of the Abbasids, now capital of Iraq, stands on its banks. It rises in the Taurus Mountains in Turkey and flows 1,180 mi (1,900 km) southeast through Iraq to join the Euphrates at Basra.

Tijuana (pop. 1,3 million), city in Mexico, near the U.S. border. Tijuana, its name derived from the Tia Juana (Spanish, 'Aunt Jane') ranch in the area, was settled in the early 1900s. It is a popular tourist town, noted for its bullfights and racetracks.
See also: Mexico.

Tikhonov, Nikolai Aleksandrovich (1905-1985), soviet premier (1980-1985). In 1940 Tikhonov joined the Communist Party. During the 1950s-70s he rose in the Soviet government, becoming a member of the Politburo in 1979. Failing health caused him to resign in 1985.
See also: Union of Soviet Socialist Republics.

Tilden, William Tatem (1893-1953), American tennis player, was the first American to win the singles title at Wimbledon (1920), which he also won in 1921 and 1930. Tilden won 13 championships (seven singles, four doubles, two mixed doubles) in the U.S., and also won numerous other tournaments. He was a member of the teams that won the Davis Cup from 1920 to 1926, and was a formidable doubles player. He became a professional at the age of 37, and wrote history books about tennis (the best known of which is *Matchplay and of the Spin of the Ball*). His game featured a fast service and a wide variety of strokes and effects.

Tilefish, colorful ocean fish belonging to the tilefish family, found along the New England coastline. It is about 3 ft (91 cm) in length and can weigh over 30 lb (14 km). It eats mostly crabs and other fish, and is considered to be a good food fish.

Tillich, Paul Johannes (1886-1965), German-born theologian and teacher. He attempted to synthesize Christianity and classical and modern existentialist philosophy in works like *Systematic Theology* (1951-1963), *The Shaking of Foundations* (1948), and *The Courage to Be* (1948). Dismissed from Frankfurt University because of opposition to the Nazis, he taught at the Union Theological Seminary, New York (1933-1959) and at Harvard and Chicago universities (1954-1962 and 1962-1965, respectively).
See also: Theology.

Timbuktu (pop. 19,000), city in central Mali, in the southern Sahara. It was settled in the 1100s by the Tuareg and used by merchants of the 14th century as a major trading center for gold, salt, ivory, and slaves. The 15th and 16th centuries saw the rise of the Songhai Empire and Timbuktu became a center of Muslim learning. It was sacked by the Moroccans (1593), and French rule was established in 1894. Today it continues to be an important marketplace (salt, handicrafts) for the nomads of the Sahara.
See also: Mali.

Time, measure of duration, whether past, present, or future; a particular portion or part of duration; period at which any definite event occurred or person lived; prevailing state or circumstances. Absolute time is time considered without relation to bodies or their motions. Relative time is the sensible measure of any portion of duration. Astronomical time is mean solar time reckoned through the 24-hour cycle. Civil time is mean time adapted to civil uses and distinguished into years, months, days, etc. A timetable is a table or register of times, as of the hours to be observed in a school, of the departure and arrival of railroad trains, buses, etc. Time-sharing is a method of operation in which a computer facility is shared by several users for different purposes at the same time. A time quantum, in a time-sharing system, is a unit of time allotted to each user. Time slicing is the allotment of a portion of processing time to each program in a multiprogramming system to prevent the monopolization of the central processing unit by any one program.

Timisoara (Temesvár, Maria-Theresiapol; pop. 334,000), Romania, the capital of the Banat region of western Romania. It is the leading city in a rich agricultural area and is also an industrial center. Manufactured goods include processed foods and textiles. Numerous railways and highways and the Bega Canal make it a transportation hub. A polytechnic institute and a medical school are here. In the ninth century Timisoara came under Magyar rule. It was part of Hungary from 1010 until it was taken by the Turks in 1552. The Austrians captured the city in 1716. Austria (later Austria-Hungary) retained control until 1919, when the western part of the Banat was ceded to Romania as a result of World War I.

Timman, Jan Hendrik (1951-), Dutch chess grandmaster (since 1974), one of the most talented chess players that the Netherlands has produced since Max Euwe. He made his international breakthrough with his victory in the master group of the Hoogoven tournament in Wijk aan Zee in 1971, after which many tournament victories followed. Timman was one of the world's best players for many years, and was placed high in the Elo rankings.

Timmer, Marianne (1974-), Dutch skater, specialist in the middle-distance events. She won her first international title in 1997, when she became the 1000 m world champion in Warsaw. The same year she became Dutch champion in Groningen in the sprint event. During the Winter Olympics in Nagano in 1998, Timmer won the gold medal in the 1500 m with a world-record time of 1.57.58, and gold medal in the 1000 m in an Olympic record time of 1.16.51. In 1998 she became Dutch champion once more in the sprint event and in the 1000 m. The following year she retained her sprint title and became 1000 m world champion. She became a member of the commercial Sanex skating team in 1998. She skated for the DSB team and founded her own team (Team Timmer). In 2001, she joined the Spaar Select team.

Timor, largest and easternmost of the Lesser Sunda Islands, 400 mi (644 km) northwest of Australia.
Portugese settlement (1520), which later became Dutch. During the transfer of sovereignty, the western part (West Timor) became part of Indonesia (1950). The eastern part (East Timor) remained Portugese until 1975, but was occupied by Indonesian troops in 1976. The fight of the resistance organization for freedom, Fretilin, was violently suppressed by the Indonesian army. In 1995 there were talks between Indonesia and Portugal on a diplomatic level, the latter representing East Timor. In 1996 bisshop Carlos Belo and José Ramos Horta received the Nobel Peace Prize for their support of the population's struggle for autonomy. In mid-1999 a referendum was held on East Timor concerning its future as an autonomous province of Indonesia or an independant country. The majority chose for the latter. In 1999 the UN sent a peacekeeping force (INTERFET) to East Timor when violence erupted between opponents and supporters of independence. In October 1999, Indonesia's president Wahid offically handed over East Timor to UN control. On May 20, 2002, East Timor finally became independent.

Timothy, disciple of the Apostle Paul; also, 2 epistles of the New Testament addressed to Timothy. They became part of the Pastoral Epistles, providing guidelines and advice on governing a church.
See also: New Testament.

Timpani, or kettledrums, drums having a calfskin head over a hollow brass or copper hemisphere. They were first used in orchestral music in the 1600s. A set of timpani usually consists of three drums. Pitch is governed by the tension of the head, which can be adjusted. Tone may be varied by the type of stick used for play and by the region of the head struck.

Timur the Lame *See:* Tamerlane.

Tin, chemical element, symbol Sn; for physical constants see Periodic Table. Tin was known to the ancients. It occurs in cassiterite, stannite, and tealite. The element is produced by reducing the oxide with coal in a reverberatory furnace. Tin is a silver-white, soft, malleable, ductile metal. It is resistant to corrosion and is used extensively for coating other metals. Tin exists in 2 forms: alpha (gray) and beta (white). Change to the unusable gray form, called tin pest, is prevented

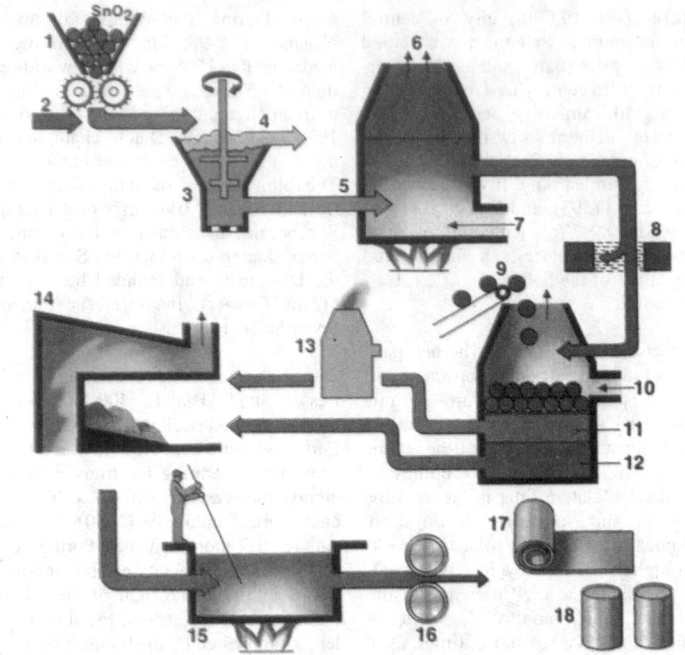

T Tin is obtained from cassiterite, a heavy oxide ore. The ore is crushed (1) and mixed with oil and water (2) in a flotation tank (3). The light parts of the ore rise and are skimmed off (4). The heavy tin oxide, which sinks to the bottom, is dried and placed in a roasting oven (5), where it is heated in air (7) to remove arsenic and sulfur as volatile oxides (6). Other impurities are removed by a chemical leaching process (8). The purified ore is heated with coke (9) and air (10) in a reverberatory oven. The tin oxide is reduced to tin (12), and the impurities collect in a floating layer (11) of molten slag.

This crude tin and additional tin recovered (13) from the slag, are first refined by a controlled melting process (14) and then by a poling process (15), in which the remaining metal impurities are removed. The refined tin is then rolled (16) into sheets for processing into tin-plate (17) and tin cans (18).

by the addition of small amounts of antimony or bismuth. Pewter, bronze, type metal, and soft solder are some important tin alloys. Stannous chloride is an important reducing agent. Tin and its compounds are used in electrically conductive coatings, dyeing, and super-conductive magnets.

Tinbergen, Jan (1903-1994), Dutch economist who in 1969 shared the first Nobel Prize for economic science with Ragnar Frisch for work in developing dynamic models (econometrics).
See also: Economics.

Tinbergen, Nikolas (1907-1988), Dutch ethologist awarded, with Konrad Lorenz and Karl von Frisch, the 1973 Nobel Prize for physiology or medicine for their individual, major contributions to the science of animal behavior.
See also: Ethology.

Tinguely, Jean (1925-1991), Swiss artist. Settled in Paris in 1951. In the 1960s he organized, together with Rauschenberg, international happenings. Tinguely was an exponent of kinetic art, and was influenced by Dadaism and the mobiles of Calder. He created metal sculptures from scrap, powered by motors, with parts that rotated and threw themselves back and forth, making grunting, stamping and gnashing noises. His self-destroying machines were huge pieces of equipment which blew themselves up, the meta-metics were ingenious drawing machines which produced abstract drawings, and the roto-zaza was a machine that spat out balls which had to be caught by the public. From the 1970s onwards he mainly worked with his wife, Niki de Saint-Phalle.

Tinnitus, sensation of sounds not derived from the outer environment, such as ringing, roars, or banging in the inner ear. It is a common symptom of most ear disorders. Tinnitus is not a severe or disabling problem, but a medical diagnosis is important in determining whether an underlying cause requires treatment.

Tintoretto (Jacopo Robusti; 1518-1594), Venetian mannerist painter of the Renaissance. His popular name, Tintoretto ('Little Dyer'), refers to his father's occupation. Influenced by Titian and Michelangelo, Tintoretto's paintings and frescoes are characterized by free brushwork, dramatic viewpoint, movement, monumental figures, and rich colors. He sought to express drama through color and light, as in *Saint Mark Rescuing a Slave* (1548), the Scuola di San Rocco *Life of Christ* (1564-1587), and his masterpiece, *The Last Supper* (1594).

Tippecanoe, Battle of *See:* Indian wars.

Tipperary (pop. 5,000), town in southern Ireland established in the late 12th century, located on the Ara River. Its chief industry is the processing of dairy products. Its name was made famous due to the popularity of the marching song 'It's a Long, Long Way to Tipperary,' sung by Allied soldiers during World War I (1914-18). Originally Tipperary was a small town encircling a castle built by the man who became King John of England.

Tiranë, or **Tirana** (pop. 427,000), capital of Albania, located about 20 mi (32 km) east of the Adriatic Sea. It was founded in the early 17th century and became the capital city in 1920. After the proclamation of Communist rule in 1946, the city grew as an industrial center. It is the home of many of Albania's cultural and educational institutions as well as the center of the country's publishing and broadcast industries. Most residents are Muslim.
See also: Albania.

Tirso de Molina (1584-1648), pen name of Spanish author and playwright, Gabriel Tellez. He is known as one of the greatest playwrights of the Golden Age of Spain. Among the hundreds of plays he wrote, 86 survive, most notably *The Deceiver of Seville* (1630), which introduced the legendary character of Don Juan. A friar and a respected theologian, he wrote plays, stories, and poetry that reflected his knowledge and understanding of history, religion, and human nature. These include *The Gardens of Toledo* (1624) and *Pleasure with Profit* (1635).

Tissue, in biology, similar cells grouped together in multicellular animals and plants. These cells are usually specialized for a single function; thus muscle cells contract but do not secrete, and nerve cells conduct impulses but have little or no powers of contraction. The cells are held together by intercellular material. Having become specialized for a single or at most a very narrow range of functions, they are dependent upon other parts of the organism for necessities like food and oxygen. Groups of tissues, each with its own functions, make up organs. Connective tissue refers to the material in which all the specialized body organs are embedded and supported.

Tissue transplant, permanent transfer of tissue or organs from one part of a body to another. It may involve transplanting tissue, such as skin or bone, within the same body (autografts); or it might involve more than one body, as when one person donates an organ to another person (allografts). Autografts are usually successful because the body normally does not reject its own tissues. Allografts, however, are often unsuccessful because the transplant recipient may reject the donor's tissue or organ. To avoid such rejections, physicians try to match donors and recipients with compatible tissues. People who have a number of similar proteins (HLA antigens) in the cells of the tissues to be exchanged are more likely to achieve a successful tissue transplant. Because HLA antigens are inherited, siblings have a higher rate of tissue transplant success.

Titanic, 46,328-ton British liner that sank in 1912 after hitting an iceberg on its maiden voyage. At least 1,500 of the 2,200 aboard drowned. After the disaster (caused mainly by excessive speed), lifeboat, radio watch, and ice patrol provisions were improved.

Titaniferous ore, blend of minerals rich in the metal titanium. The ore is black and granular and is usually composed of ilmenite and magnetite.

Titanium, chemical element, symbol Ti; for physical constants see Periodic Table. Titanium was discovered by William Gregor

T

in 1791 (named after the Titans). It occurs in the minerals rutile, ilmenite, and sphene. Titanium is the ninth most abundant element in the earth's crust. It is prepared by reducing titanium tetrachloride with magnesium. Titanium is a white, lustrous, strong, corrosion-resistant metal. It is the only element that burns in nitrogen. It is as strong as steel, but 45% lighter. Titanium and its compounds are used in heat-resistant alloys, paint pigments, and chemical smoke screens.

Titans, in Greek mythology, offspring of Uranus and Gaea, including Cronus, Hyperion, Iapetus, Oceanus, Coeus, Creus, Theia, Rhea, Mnemosyne, Phoebe, Tethys, and Themis, as well as their descendants (e.g., Atlas, Prometheus). Cronus and his siblings overthrew Uranus. In turn one of Cronus's offspring, Zeus, led the Olympians to defeat Cronus and become rulers of the universe, banishing the Titans, except for Cronus (who ruled the Isle of the Blessed) and Atlas (who held up the sky), to Tartarus. Prometheus, who aided Zeus, was also allowed to remain.
See also: Mythology.

Titi, small tree-dwelling monkey belonging to the New World monkey family Cebidae and found in Brazil's Orinoco River Basin. It lives in 2-parent family units and subsists on fruit, leaves, small birds, and insects. A characteristic of the titi is its habit, with others of its kind, of winding its tail around a tree branch when asleep or at rest.

Titian (Tiziano Vecellio; 1487-1576), Venetian painter, leading Renaissance artist. He worked for Giovanni Bellini and Giorgione, who influenced his early work, before becoming Venice's official painter (1516). His perceptive portraits, monumental altarpieces, and historical and mythological scenes are famous for their energetic composition, use of rich color, and original technique. Among his works are *La Gloria* (1554), *Rape of Europe* (1562), and *Adam and Eve* (1570).
See also: Renaissance.

Titmouse, forest bird of the family Pariclae, found mainly in the Northern Hemisphere. Related to the nuthatch and the chickadee, these small, brown-and-gray birds travel

Bridled titmouse (*Parus willweberi*). Found in mountainous areas of southwest U.S.A. Inhabits forests up to 6,562 ft (2,000 m) above sea level. Length up to 6 in (15 cm).

with other birds in flocks and are easily trained to do tricks.

Tito, Josip Broz (1892-1980), president of former Yugoslavia (1953-1980), founder of the post-World War II republic. He became a Communist while a World War I prisoner of war in Russia, and later spent several years in Yugoslav jails. General secretary of the Communist Party from 1937, Tito organized partisan resistance to the Nazis in World War II, eclipsing the Chetniks, and after the war established a Socialist republic. He served as prime minister (1945-1953) before becoming president. Tito broke with Joseph Stalin in 1948. He suppressed home opposition but worked for workers' self-management and the reconciliation of national minorities. Later years saw a substantial liberalization of his policies. On the international scene, Tito became an organizer and leading representative for Third World or neutralist countries.
See also: Yugoslavia.

Titus (Titus Flavius Sabinus Vespasianus; A.D.39-81), Roman emperor, successor (79) to his father Vespasian. A successful soldier, he captured (70) Jerusalem in the Jewish revolt (66-70). He was popular for lavish entertaining and for aiding victims of the eruption of the Vesuvius (79) and the fire at Rome (80).
See also: Rome, Ancient.

Titus, early Christian follower of St. Paul. He traveled with Paul to the Council of Jerusalem, and later went with him to Greece. Appointed by Paul as a special representative to the church in Corinth, he was later made the first archbishop of Crete. Paul's epistle to Titus, the 17th book of the New Testament, believed to have been written in A.D. 65 or 66, gave Titus instructions on how to organize the church in Crete.
See also: Paul, Saint.

TNT, or trinitrotoluene, [$CH_3C_6H_2(NO_2)_3$], pale yellow crystalline solid made by nitration of toluene. It is the most extensively used high explosive, being relatively insensitive to shock, especially when melted by steam heating and cast.
See also: Explosive.

Toad, name strictly referring only to members of the family Bufonidae, but generally distinguishing warty-skinned, tailless amphibians from smoother-skinned types, which are called frogs. Toads range in size from 1 to 7 in (2.5 to 18 cm). They are independent of water except for breeding, the larvae-tadpoles-being purely aquatic. Most toads feed nocturnally on insects.

Toadstool *See:* Mushroom.

Tobacco, plant of the nightshade family (especially genus *Nicotiana*); also, the dried and cured leaves of the plant, used for smoking and chewing and as snuff. Native to America, tobacco was introduced to Europe by the Spanish in the 16th century and from there spread to Asia and Africa. Today the United States remains the world's largest producer, followed by

China, India, and the former USSR. Consumption is increasing despite the health hazards of smoking. Tobacco is grown in alluvial or sandy soils and may be harvested after about 4 months. Cultivation is dependent on hand labor.

Tobago *See:* Trinidad and Tobago.

Tobey, Mark (1890-1976), U.S. painter. Strongly influenced by Chinese calligraphy and Zen Buddhism, he developed his 'white writing' style in the 1930s in small abstracts representing street scenes. His later, delicately colored abstracts have more intricate linear rhythms.

Tobin, James (1918-2002), U.S. economist. He won the 1981 Nobel Memorial Prize in economic science for his research in relating the effects of financial markets to consumption, prices, production, and investment, as well as his studies of government monetary policies and budgets. He had served as one of President John F. Kennedy's economics advisors.
See also: Economics.

Tobit, or **Tobias, Book of**, in the Apocrypha, account of how Tobias, son of the devout but blinded Jew Tobit (or Tobias), successfully undertook a dangerous journey, helped by the angel Raphael, to exorcise a demon from, and marry, Sara. He then helped Tobit regain his sight.
See also: Old Testament.

Toboganning, sport of riding down snow or ice slopes on a sled or toboggan. Although sleds with runners are sometimes called toboggans, the term usually refers to runnerless sleds such as were originally developed by Native American hunters. The modern toboggan is generally 6-8 ft (1.8-2.4 m) long and 1 ft (46 cm) wide, and carries 4 people,

Quality sorting of Zimbabwean tobacco. Thanks to its supply of cheap black labor, Zimbabwe became the world's second most important exporting country of tobacco. After 1965, however, the trade boycott against the country, and the closing of the Zambian and Mozambican borders took their effect. Despite these measures, in 1975 there were still enough buyers to purchase half of the amount originally produced.

T

one behind another. Artificial chutes for the initial acceleration have allowed high speeds. Bobsledding, a type of tobogganing, is a sport of the Winter Olympics.

Tocopherol *See:* Vitamin.

Tocqueville, Alexis de (1805-1859), French historian and writer best known for the 2-volume *Democracy in America*, written after visiting the United States in the early 1830s. The book made him a leading European advocate of democracy, a system he believed would eventually replace the European monarchies and aristocracies. A philosopher, Tocqueville also saw the pitfalls of democracy, warning against a 'tyranny of the majority' in which conformity would discourage individualism. He served in the French legislature (1839-1851) and was foreign minister following the Revolution of 1848.
See also: France.

Tofu, or bean curd, soft, white, cheeselike food made by treating soybean milk with coagulants and pressing the curds into cakes. It originated in China more than 1,000 years ago and is widely used in Asia. Tofu is bland, high in protein, low in salt and calories, and cholesterol-free. It has thus become popular in the West as a substitute for cheese, cream, and other animal fat products.

Toga, robe worn in ancient Rome. Originally worn by both men and women, it gradually fell out of favor with women. Made of soft wool, it was loosely draped in abundant folds over an undergarment called a tunic. Its color delineated the status, rank, or age of the wearer. Because it limited movement, it eventually came to be worn by the upper classes and politicians.

Togo

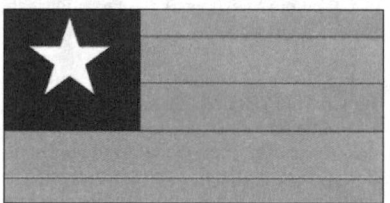

Capital:	Lomé
Area:	21,925 sq mi (56,785 sq km)
Population:	5,285,000
Language:	French
Government:	Presidential republic
Independent:	1960
Head of gov.:	Prime minister
Per capita:	US$ 1,500
Monetary unit:	1 CFA franc = 100 centimes

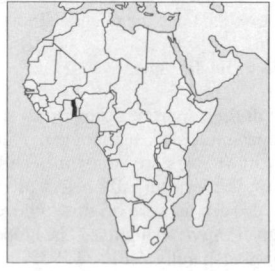

Togo, republic in West Africa. Bordered by Ghana on the west, Benin on the east, Burkina Faso on the north, and the Gulf of Guinea on the south, Togo has an area of 21,925 sq mi (56,785 sq km) and is 340 mi (547 km) long and 70 mi (113 km) wide.
Land and people. From the central Togo Mountains a grassy plateau slopes east to the Mono River and south to the sandy coastal plain. North of the mountains is the savanna of the Oti Plateau. The climate is hot and humid. The people of Togo are almost entirely black Africans of the Ewe, Ouatchi, Mina, and Kabre ethnic groups. There are Christians and Muslims, but most people follow traditional beliefs. French is the official language.
Economy. Over 70% of the people live in rural areas, mostly in the south, and the economy is primarily agricultural. The chief exports are cocoa and coffee, but cassava, corn, and cotton are also important. Large phosphate deposits discovered northeast of Lomè have proven profitable and Togo ranks high in world production.
History. Togo was settled in the 1300s by a group of Ewe-speaking people, then further populated by invaders and refugees from various wars north of the area. As the slave trade grew, Togo became an important center for the buying and selling of slaves (by the Danes for example). Germany set up a protectorate (known as Togoland) in 1884; after World War I, it was administered by the French. Togo became an independent nation in 1960 with Sylvanus Olympio as president. After a long period of political turmoil, a military coup in 1967 installed Lt. Col. Gnassingbé Eyadéma as the country's leader. He received popular support in a 1972 presidential vote and was reelected in 1979 and at the first democratic elections in 1993. In 1998 the presidential elections were won again by Eyadéma. However, the opposition and international observers challenged the outcome.
Since the 1990s, Togo has been criticized immensely over its poor human rights record, mainly due to its unreliable central government, resulting in many civilian and military victims that have been executed unlawfully.

Tojo, Hideki (1884-1948), Japanese military and political leader. He became minister of war in 1940, premier in Oct. 1941, and approved the bombing of Pearl Harbor on Dec. 7, 1941, leading Japan into World War II against the United States. Assuming totalitarian control over Japan during the early years of the war, Tojo was responsible for atrocities and the torture of Allied prisoners of war. He was forced to resign as premier in 1944 but continued to advocate a 'no surrender' policy. After the war he was captured, tried as a war criminal, and hanged on Dec. 23, 1948.
See also: World War II.

Tokugawa (also: Edo period), the family name of the dynasty that ruled Japan from 1603 to 1867. The period was the last and greatest of the *shogunates* (rule by shoguns, or military governors). As in earlier shogunates, the emperors reigned but the shoguns, through their military power, actually con-

The Nijubashi (Double Bridge) spans a moat surrounding the grounds of the Imperial Palace, residence of Japan's Emperor Akihito.

trolled Japan. Under Tokugawa Ieyasu (1542-1616), founder of the the Tokugawa shogunate, the political unification of Japan begun by preceding military dictators was completed, and the internal warfare that had plagued the country for centuries was ended. Prosperity increased art and literature flourished. Distrusting Europeans, the Tokugawa eliminated almost all contact between Japan and other nations. The rigid class system and highly formalized cultural patterns that marked Japan until the end of World War II were to a great extent the product of the Tokugawa period. In 1868 the last shogun, Keiki, was forced to relinquish ruling power to Emperor Mutsuhito.
See also: Shogun.

Tokyo (pop. 8,200,000), capital of Japan. It lies at the head of Tokyo Bay on the southeastern coast of Honshu Island and contains over 10% of Japan's population. Founded in the 12th century as Edo, it became capital of the Tokugawa shoguns in 1603; it was renamed and made imperial capital in 1868. Reconstruction after earthquake and fire (1923) and the air raids of World War II transformed much of Tokyo. It is today a center of government, industry, finance, and education. The National Diet (parliament) meets here; most of Japan's great corporations have their head offices in the Maurunochi district; Tokyo University (founded 1877) is one of hundreds of educational institutions. Tokyo has many parks, museums, and temples, the Imperial Palace, and the Kabukiza theater. Industries (with large complexes to the west) include printing, shipbuilding, metal manufactures, automobile, chemicals, and textiles. The harbor and airport are Japan's busiest.
See also: Japan.

Toledo (pop. 63,000), city in central Spain 40 mi (64 km) southwest of Madrid, seat of Toledo province, former Roman and Visgoth capital. Possessing minimal industry, Toledo produces textiles, sabers, and firearms. The entire city has been declared a national monument and contains beautiful examples of medieval and Renaissance art and architecture. Toledo's many landmarks include the Alcázar (citadel), Gothic cathedral (the archbishop is Spain's primate), and El Greco's house, which serves as a museum for several of his paintings.
See also: Spain.

Tolkien, J(ohn) R(onald) R(euel) (1892-

1973), English author and scholar, celebrated for *The Hobbit* (1937) and the trilogy *The Lord of the Rings* (1954-1956), which present a mythical world of elves and dwarfs, partly based on Anglo-Saxon and Norse folklore. Tolkien was professor of Anglo-Saxon, then of English, language and literature at Oxford University.

In 2001, the first part of *The Lord of the Rings*, *The Fellowship of the Ring* was released in the cinemas, followed by *The Two Towers* in 2002. In 2003, the last part of the trilogy will be released.

Toller, Ernst (1893-1939), a German playwright. As a leader of radical Expressionism he had a strong influence on the proletarian and revolutionary theater in Europe, especially in Russia. Typically, Toller's characters are symbolic rather than realistic, representing principles and attitudes rather than individuals. Toller served in the German army in World War I. In 1919 he took part in an unsuccesful Communist uprising in Bavaria, for which he was imprisoned for five years. He left Germany in 1932 and lived for a while in Spain. In 1936 he came to the United States. *Man and the Masses* (1921) and *The Machine Wreckers* (1922) attack capitalism in its militaristic and mechanistic aspects, but also present the dilemma of the revolutionary leader who must oppose his followers. Toller's last play, *Pastor Hall* (1939), is more realistic than his other works. It is based on the persecution of the clergyman Martin Niemöller by the Nazis.

Tolstoy, Aleksei Nikolaevich (1882-1945), Russian novelist and playwright, best known for his trilogy *The Road to Calvary* (1921-1940), the novella *Nikita's Childhood* (1922), and the novel *Peter the First* (1929-1945). A nobleman distantly related to Leo Tolstoy, he left Russia in 1917 but returned in 1922 and became a supporter of Joseph Stalin's regime.

Tolstoy, Leo (1828-1910), Russian novelist. Educated at Kazan University, he served in the army, married in 1862, and spent the next 15 years on his estate at Yasnaya Polyana near Moscow. In this period he produced his masterpieces, including *War and Peace* (1865-1869), an epic of vast imaginative scope and variety of character, telling the story of five families against the background of the Napoleonic invasion of Russia. *Anna Karenina* (1875-1877), the tragic story of an adulterous affair, is remarkable for its psychological portrayal. In later years Tolstoy experienced a spiritual crisis, recounted in his *Confession* (1882), and embraced an ascetic philosophy of Christian anarchism. His other works include *Childhood* (1852), *The Cossacks* (1863), and *Resurrection* (1899).

Toltec, Native American civilization dominant in the central Mexican highlands between the 900s and 1100s. The Toltec god was Quetzalcoatl, for whom they performed human sacrifice. The Toltecs, sophisticated builders and artisans, erected their capital at Tollán (ruins near modern Tula, 60 mi [96.5 km] north of Mexico City). The dominant group were Nahuati speakers. Aztecs and others overran the area and adopted various aspects of Toltec culture.

Toluene ($C_6H_5CH_3$), liquid hydrocarbon related to benzene. Made from treated petroleum or distilled coal tar, it is commonly used in the production of a wide range of industrial chemicals, such as the preservative benzoic acid and the explosive trinitrotoluene (TNT). Because it is toxic, federal guidelines exist to regulate its use in the workplace.
See also: Benzene.

Tomato (*Lycopersicon esculentum*), herbaceous plant of the nightshade family, native to South America but introduced to Europe in the 16th century and now cultivated worldwide; also, the fruit of the plant. Most of the crop is canned or processed to make prepared foods, a relatively small proportion being grown for salad use. In northern latitudes, tomatoes are grown under glass, but the bulk are grown as a field crop. Italy, Spain, Brazil, and Japan are among the leading producers.

Tomba, Alberto (1966-), Italian skier, nicknamed Tomba la Bomba. He won 15 World Cup victories in the giant slalom and 32 in the slalom in the period 1987-1996. In 1988 he became the Olympic champion in both the giant slalom and the slalom, but four years later he only won the giant slalom. In 1996 Tomba became world champion in the giant slalom and the slalom.

Tomonaga, Sin-Itiro (1906-1979), Japanese physicist, professor in Tokyo (1941). Winner of the 1965 Nobel Prize (with Feynman and Schwinger) for fundamental work in quantum electrodynamics in 1947-1949.

Tonegawa, Susumu (1939-), Japanese biologist. An expert in immunology, he won the 1987 Nobel Prize for physiology or medicine for his discovery of techniques to study the response of the body's immune system in order to protect against new disease agents. Formerly at the Basel Institute for Immunology in Switzerland, he has worked at the Massachusetts Institute of Technology since 1981.
See also: Biology; Immunity.

Tonga

Capital:	Nuku'alofa
Area:	289 sq mi (748 sq km)
Population:	106,000
Language:	Tongan, English
Government:	Constitutional monarchy
Independent:	1970
Head of gov.:	Prime minister
Per capita:	US$ 2,200
Monetary unit:	1 Pa'anga = 100 seniti

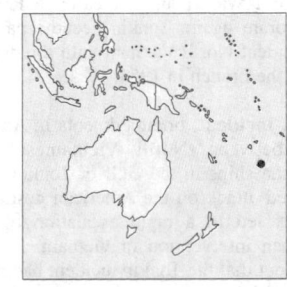

Tonga, or Friendly Islands, constitutional monarchy in the South Pacific. The kingdom comprises over 170 islands of which the chief groups are Tongatapu, Háapai, and Vaváu. The climate is tropical. The population is mainly Polynesian, with a small number of Europeans. The economy is agricultural, with copra, banana, and vanilla the chief exports. Promising petroleum deposits were located near Tongatapu in 1977. The islands were discovered in 1616 by the Dutch explorer Jacob Lemaire and later visited by Abel Tasman (1643), and James Cook (1773), who named them the Friendly Islands. The present kingdom was founded in 1875 by George Tupou I and became a British protectorate in 1900. It achieved independence in 1970. The present king (since 1965) is Taufa' ahau Tupou IV. A feudal government governed the country. The King's family members held offices in the government and members of other noble families were appointed Secretaries for life.

Leo Tolstoy (1828-1910).

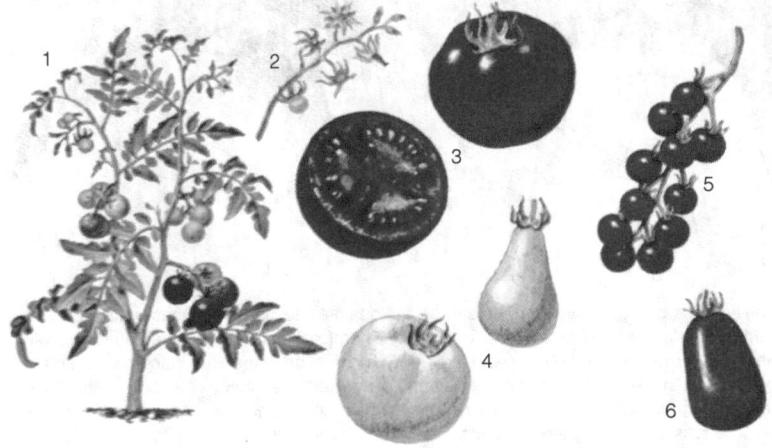

(1) Plant with large-fruited red tomatoes in various stages of ripeness; (2) flowers and newly set fruit; (3) the large-fruited red tomato, the most common variety; (4) yellow large-fruited and pear tomatoes; (5) cherry tomatoes; (6) the Italian plum tomato.

T

T

Opposition was not illegal, but was heavily repressed. However, the opposition party Human Rights and Democracy won for the first time in 2002 the elections, which reduced the King's powers.

Tongue, muscular organ in the floor of the mouth, concerned with the formation of food boluses and self-cleansing of the mouth, taste sensation and voice production. In certain animals, the tongue is used to draw food into the mouth from a distance.

Tonkin, historic region of Southeast Asia, now comprising most of northern Vietnam. It was the European name for the region around the Red River delta, which became a French protectorate in 1883, part of French Indochina. Under Japanese occupation during World War II and thereafter a French protectorate again, Tonkin became part of independent North Vietnam with the departure of the French in 1954.

Tonkin incident, bombardments in August 1964 between North Vietnamese and American ships in the Gulf of Tonkin. The supposed attack on the American destroyer Maddox led to a rapid escalation of the American intervention in Vietnam. It later turned out that the Tonkin incident had been provoked by the Americans in order to get Congress to agree to go ahead with the planned invasion of North Vietnam.
See also: Vietnam War.

Tonle Sap, a lake in central Cambodia, drained by the Tonle Sap River. During the rainy season the lake receives water from many streams, mainly the flooding Mekong River, and greatly increases in size, inundating surrounding areas. By November the floodwaters have receded. Fishing in the lake and rice cultivation along its shores are important in the Cambodian economy. North of the Tonle Sap are the ancient ruins of Angkor.

Tonsil, name for either of two small oval-shaped, fleshy bodies, situated on each side of the back of the throat (palatine tonsils). They act as filters of disease organisms. Similar lymphoid masses are the phalangeal tonsils (adenoids) between the back of the nose and throat, and the lingual tonsils, on the back of the tongue.
See also: Adenoids.

Tonsillitis, inflammation of the tonsils due to virus or bacteria infection. It may follow sore throat or other pharyngeal disease, or it may be primary tonsil disease. Sore throat and red swollen tonsils, which may exude pus or cause swallowing difficulty, are common; lymph nodes at the angle of the jaw are usually tender and swollen. Quinsy is a rare complication. Antobiotic treatment for the bacterial cause usually leads to a resolution, but removal of the tonsils is needed in few cases.

Topaz, aluminum silicate mineral of composition $Al_2SiO_4(F,OH)_2$, forming prismatic crystals (orthorhombic) that are variable and unstable in color and valued as gemstones. The best topazes come from Brazil, Siberia, and the United States.

Töpffer, Rodolphe (1799-1846), Swiss artist and writer. Became known for his very personal picture stories, and achieved lasting recognition with the ironical-farcical *Histoire de Monsieur Cryptogame* (1846).

Topology, branch of mathematics that studies properties of geometrical figures or abstract spaces that are independent of shape or distance. Point-set topology deals with ways of defining 'nearness' of elements, or points, of a set without necessarily assigning numerical distances to pairs of points. Such a definition is called 'a topology on the set,' and the set is called a topological space. The topology makes it possible to define continuous functions on the space. Algebraic topology, or combinatorial topology, uses abstract algebra to treat the ways in which geometrical figures fit together to form figures of higher dimension, disregarding shape. For example a sphere is topologically the same as a cube, but it is distinct from a torus (doughnut) because if the surfaces of the figures are divided into triangles, the algebraic relationships between the triangles will be different in the two cases.

Topor, Roland (1938-1997), Polish-French writer and artist. Topor used his writing and drawings to fervently explore excessive fantasies of barbaric cruelty, sparing nothing and nobody, especially himself. He fought against his fear (of death, of pain, of sexuality) with absurd, often terrifying means. His style of drawing was characterized by an abundant use of shading, which gave an expressive depth to the somewhat strange, awkward figures. In 1962 he set up the Arrabal de Académie Panique. He worked for such satirical journals as Bizarre and Hara-kiri, and also worked in stage and film. His most well-known novels are *Le locataire chimérique* (1964; filmed by Polanski in 1976), *Erika* (1969) and *Souvenir* (1972).

Torah (Hebrew: 'law, teaching'), the Pentateuch (first five books of the Bible) kept in the ark of every synagogue. In a wider sense it is the whole body of the oral and written teaching central to Judaism and includes the rest of the Hebrew Bible, rabbinic codes, the Talmud, and the Midrash.
See also: Bible.

Tormé, Melvin Howard (Mel) (1925-1999), American jazz singer, drummer, arranger, pianist, writer and songwriter. Went on tour with the group of the comedian and pianist Chico Marx (1942-1943); thereafter became leader of the singing group the Mel-Tones. Became known as The Velvet Fog because of his sultry, hoarse voice. Thanks to his flexible voice he was both an adventurous improvising vocalist and a singer of lyrics in the style of Frank Sinatra. His autobiography was entitled *It Wasn't All Velvet*, his compositions include *The Christmas Song*, *Country Fair*, *Stranger in Town* and *Born to Be Blue*. In his later years he wrote scripts for television and also played a number of film and TV roles. He also worked as a music critic, and published a book about Judy Garland called *The Other Side of the Rainbow* (1970).

Tornado, violent whirlwind cloud of small diameter, extending downward from a convective cloud in a severe thunderstorm, generally funnelshaped. Air rises rapidly in the outer region of the funnel, but descends in its core, which is at very low pressure. The funnel is visible owing to the formation of cloud droplets by expansional cooling in this low-pressure region. Very high winds spiral in toward the core. There is almost total devastation and often loss of life in the path of a tornado, which may move at speeds up to 656 ft (200 m) per sec. Though generally rare, tornadoes occur worldwide, especially in the United States and Australia in spring and early summer.

Toroni, Niele (1937-), Swiss artist, works in Paris. His art is of a conceptual nature.

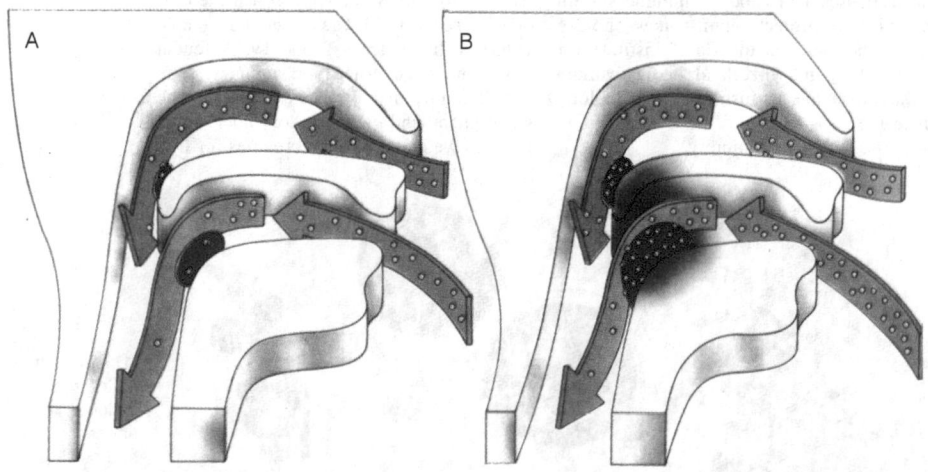

Inhaled air is partly purified of dust particles and germs by the mucosa in the nose and the throat (A). The tonsils are lymph node structures in the back of the nose and the throat, which play an important role in the defence mechanism against infections. Therefore, in case of an infection of the nose and the throat, the mucosa and the tonsils will also be easily affected. Infected tonsils will become red and swollen, with white, pus-containing dots (B).

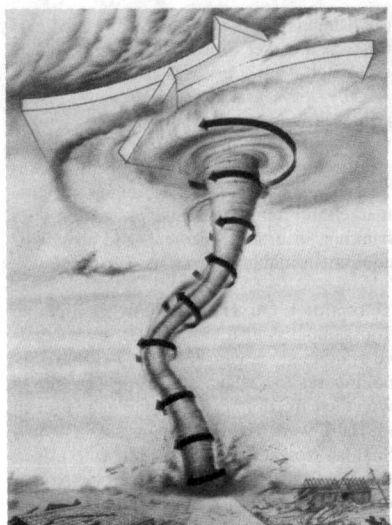

Tornadoes are dark, rapidly rotating funnel-shaped columns of air, water droplets, and dust, projecting down from cumulonimbus clouds. The smallest, but most violent of all storms, they usually originate where cold and warm air masses interact. They are always associated with severe thunderstorms. High wind speeds, ranging up to 500 mph (800 km/h), and areas of exceedingly low pressure within the tornado's vortex may cause destruction of everything in its ground path.

Makes since 1967 so-called 'interventions', in which he applies a regular pattern of pencil impressions of the same color on a canvas or wall. The important part of his work is making the impressions visible and not the spatial effect they create.

Toronto (pop. 4,445,000), capital of Ontario province and York County, second-largest city in Canada (after Montreal), on the northwestern shore of Lake Ontario. It is a major port, as well as a commercial, manufacturing, and educational center. The cultural focus of English-speaking Canada, Toronto is home to the Royal Conservatory of Music, the Canadian Music Center, the Royal Ontario Museum, and a parks system that covers 6,000 acres (2,400 hectares). Its industrial products include chemicals, machinery, electrical goods, and clothing. The French settled the area and built Fort Rouillé (1750), which was replaced by the English city of York (1793). Sacked in the War of 1812, York was renamed Toronto in 1834.
See also: Ontario.

Torpedo, flat, broad fish of the Torpedinidae family, found in tropical and temperate regions of the Atlantic and Pacific oceans. Also known as the electric ray, it emits electricity to stun fish for food and to protect itself. The shock from the torpedo is not lethal to humans but has been known to stun them.

Torpedo, self-propelled streamlined missile that travels underwater, its explosive warhead detonating when it nears or strikes its target. The torpedo was invented (1866) by Robert Whitehead, a British engineer. Torpedoes are now chiefly antisubmarine weapons.

Torquemada, Tomás de (1420-1498), Spanish Inquisition leader. A Dominican monk, he became the confessor to Queen Isabella and was named inquisitor general (1483), responsible for the executions of more than 2,000 people considered heretics (primarily Muslims and Jews). He was largely responsible for the expulsion of more than 200,000 Jews from Spain in 1492. Torquemada established rules and procedures for the Inquisition, some of which involved torture and other cruel methods of execution; his name has become synonymous with excessive cruelty.
See also: Inquisition.

Torricelli, Evangelista (1608-1647), Italian physicist and mathematician who invented the barometer in 1643. He also improved the effectiveness of the telescope and the microscope. His work in the field of pure mathematics was influential in the development of integral calculus. He was inspired by the work of his friend and mentor, Galileo.
See also: Barometer.

Torsion balance, device for measuring the force of a twisting motion. These measurements are registered on a gauge that is calibrated-readings adjusted for correct measurement. In a torsion bar, stretched fibers (usually gold, quartz, or steel) are attached to heavy noncorrosive balls (usually gold, lead, or stainless steel) that twist and turn to compensate for the introduced push-and-pull actions. A balanced zero reading is the desired result. In automobiles, a torsion bar, through torsion balance, compensates for bumps and holes experienced on the road.

Torsion bar suspension, system designed to absorb front-end shock in automobiles. There is one torsion bar for each of an automobile's 2 front wheels. One end of the torsion bar is attached to the car's frame. The other end is attached to the axle near the wheel. When the car hits a bump, the torsion

Ice skating on Nathan Philips Square in front of Toronto city hall (the two semicircular office buildings).

bar, which somewhat resembles a straightened spring, twists and then untwists. This movement absorbs the shock and makes the ride smoother.
See also: Shock absorber.

Tort (French, 'wrong'), in law, a wrongful act against a person or their property for which that person can claim damages as compensation. It is distinguished from a crime, which the state will prosecute; it is up to the injured party to sue for redress of a tort. The same wrongful act, an assault for example, may be both actionable as a tort and prosecuted as a crime. Torts range from personal injury to slander or libel; they include trespass and damage or injury arising through negligence. Wrongful breach of an agreement, however, is covered by the law of contract.

Tortoise, name for slow-moving, herbivorous, heavily armored terrestrial reptiles of the family Testudinidae, found in the tropics, subtropics, and warmer temperate regions. The body is enclosed in a boxlike shell into which the head and limbs can be withdrawn. The shell is covered with horny plates, or scutes. Toothless, the tortoise's jaws are covered to form a sharp, horny beak. There are many species, ranging from the familiar garden tortoises to the 5-ft (1.5-m) giant tortoises of the Galapagos and Seychelles.

Tory Party, popular name of the Conservative and Unionist Party, one of Britain's two chief parties. The term (originally describing Irish highwaymen) was applied in 1679 to supporters of the future James II of England. In the main, Tories became staunch royalists and supporters of the Church of England. 'Tory' was applied to Loyalist colonists in the American Revolution. Taking a reactionary stance because of the threat to authority posed by the French Revolution, the party lost its support after the Reform Bill of 1832 and became the Conservative Party.

Toscanini, Arturo (1867-1957), Italian conductor, one of the greatest of his time. He became musical director of La Scala in Milan (1898) and went on to conduct the New York Metropolitan Opera (1908-1914) and New York Philharmonic orchestras (1926-1936). The NBC Symphony Orchestra was created for him in 1937.

Totalitarianism, system of government in which the state exercises wide-ranging control over individuals within its jurisdiction. Usually, a totalitarian state has only one political party, led by a dictator, and an official ideology; dissent is suppressed. Nazi Germany epitomized the repression of totalitarian states.

Totem, object, animal, or plant toward which a tribe, clan, or other group feels a special affinity, often considering it a mythical ancestor. Killing of the totemic animal or animals by members of the group is taboo, except, with some peoples, ritually during religious ceremonies. Totem poles, on which human and animal shapes representing a particular warrior's heritage, were common among the Native Americans.

T

T

Toucan, exotic bird of the family *Ramphastidae*, native to the tropical regions of Latin America. It is noted for its huge, brightly colored bill. About forty varieties exist, ranging in size from 13-25 in (33-64 cm). It subsists on fruits, often using its saw-edged bill to tear off small pieces. It lives in small flocks and is believed to be highly social.

Touch, sensory system concerned with surface sensation, found in all external body surfaces including the skin and some mucous membranes. Functional categories of touch sensation include light touch (including movement of hairs), heat, cold, pressure, and pain sensation. Receptors for all the senses are particularly concentrated and developed over the face and hands. When the skin receptors are stimulated, they activate nerve impulses in cutaneous nerves; these pass via the spinal cord and brain stem to the brain, where coding and perception occur.
See also: Senses.

Touch-me-not, wild flower of the balsam family, related to the impaties. Its seed pods pop open when touched, hence its name. It grows in damp, shady regions of the eastern and central United States, reaches 3-5 ft (0.9-1.5m) tall, and bears pale yellow or spotted flowers. The pale yellow variety is thought to prevent poison ivy rashes when the juice from its stems and leaves are rubbed on the skin.

Toulon (pop. 172,000), port city in southeastern France. It is the administrative seat of the district of Var and an important French naval base. Historic landmarks include medieval churches and a 16th-century fish market. Toulon is the site of a Roman colony founded in the 100s B.C. Chief economic activities include shipbuilding, fishing, wine making, and chemical and machine manufacturing.
See also: France.

Toulouse (pop. 366,000), historically significant city in southwestern France, located on the Garonne River. It is the capital and administrative seat of the district of Haute-Garonne. During the Middle Ages, it served as an artistic and cultural center of Europe. Many medieval buildings, including the University of Toulouse, still stand. The city supports many economic activities, including the manufacture of electronics, aircraft, chemicals, and textiles.

Toulouse-Lautrec, Henri de (1864-1901), French painter and lithographer who portrayed Parisian nightlife. Born into an old aristocratic family, he was crippled at 15, studied art in Paris, and settled in Montmartre to paint the entertainers and circus performers who lived there, such as Jan Avril and Aristide Bruant. Influenced by Edgar Degas and by Japanese prints, his work did much to popularize the lithographic poster.

Touré, Sékou (1922-1984), president of the Republic of Guinea (1958-1984). A labor leader in French colonial times, a Marxist, and a political writer, Touré was the winner of the 1960 Lenin Peace Prize.
See also: Guinea.

Tourette syndrome, disorder of the central nervous system characterized by muscular tics, or twitches, and uncontrollable vocalizing. Symptoms first appear in childhood between 2 and 15 years and, if not treated, continue throughout the person's life, sometimes becoming more severe and other times less so. People with Tourette syndrome may also suffer from hyperactivity. Though no cure is yet known, symptoms can be alleviated by drug therapy.

Tourmaline, hard, complex silicate mineral containing such elements as boron, aluminum, and silicon. Colors include pink, green, blue, yellow, violet, red, and black. Transparent stones are considered semiprecious and are used as gems in jewelry. Tourmaline is found in granites, schists, and crystalline limestone of Brazil, Asia, the former USSR, and parts of the United States.

Tournament, or tourney, series of games; originally a combat between armored knights, usually on horseback. Popular in Europe in the Middle Ages, it provided both entertainment and training for war. In the 13th century the dangerous melée was replaced by the joust contest between only two knights, who tried to unhorse each other with lance, mace, and sword.

Tours (pop. 133,000), city in west-central France along the Loire River. Established by the Romans in 50 B.C., it served in medieval times as a center for Christian learning. The great Battle of Tours was fought nearby in 732 by the Christian Franks and Muslim armies, effectively stopping the Moorish advance in Europe. During World War II the city became the French government's headquarters. Today Tours is an important wine market and tourist and business center, with banking, insurance, medical- and electrical-equipment manufacturing industries.

Toussaint L'Ouverture (Pierre Dominique Toussaint-Bréda; c.1774-1803), emancipated Haitian slave who led the 1791 slave rebellion on the island of Haiti. The slaves won their freedom in 1793, while the French in Haiti were fighting against British and Spanish troops there. Toussaint, who joined forces with the French and forced the British to evacuate, became ruler of the island in 1799. He suppressed a mulatto uprising (1799) and resisted Napoleon's attempt to reimpose slavery on Haiti. Ultimately, Toussaint was captured and imprisoned until his death. His popular name, L'Ouverture, is French for 'The Opening.' He has remained a symbol of the struggle for freedom.
See also: Haiti.

Tower of Babel, mythical tower built in the ancient Mesopotamian city of Babylon. The myth popularly connected with it is related in the Bible (Genesis 11.1-9). According to this version the tower was built by the descendants of Noah and was intended by these peoples to reach heaven. God, however, disapproved of the tower and, as a consequence, confused the builders by causing them to speak in different languages. As a result of their confusion, the people stopped work on the tower and wandered off to various parts of the world. Many people believe today that the myth was an attempt by ancient peoples to explain the origin of different languages.

Tower of London, ancient fortress on the Thames River in the eastern part of London. Built 1078-1300, mainly by William the Conqueror and Henry III, its massive stone buildings are enclosed by high walls and a moat. It has been palace, prison, arsenal, and mint. Today it houses the crown jewels and an armor museum. Here Thomas More, Anne Boleyn, and Roger Casement were executed. Convicted Nazi war criminal Rudolf Hess was its last prisoner.

Townes, Charles Hard (1915-), U.S. physicist awarded the 1964 Nobel Prize for physics, with Nikolai Basov and Aleksander Prokhorov, for independently working out the theory of the maser and, later, the laser. He built the first maser in 1951.
See also: Laser; Maser.

Toxemia of pregnancy, or preeclampsia, disease caused by bacterial toxins or other toxic substances in the blood, usually referring to a condition that attacks women in the last stages of pregnancy or just after childbirth. It occurs in about 5% of all pregnancies and, unless treated, may lead to eclampsia (convulsions and coma) and other complications, including death of the mother and

The concentric fortifications of the Tower of London surround the White Tower (center), a Romanesque keep, built from 1078 to 1097 by William the Conqueror, to dominate the town of London. The famous Traitor's Gate, facing the Thames, was once the main entry. Structures have been added throughout the Tower's long history, during which it has served purposes ranging from royal residence and prison, to museum and repository of the Crown Jewels.

fetus. Toxemia is characterized by an increase in blood pressure, excessive protein in the urine, and swelling of the body, and can be treated by drugs if diagnosed in time.

Toxic shock syndrome (TSS), rare and sometimes fatal bacterial disease associated with the use of tampons. TSS is characterized by high fever, vomiting, and diarrhea, followed by a sharp drop in blood pressure that may bring on fatal shock. At greatest risk are women under 30 during their menstrual periods. The incidence is low, with a frequency of about 3 cases per 100,000 women annually in the United States, and the mortality rate is about 10%.

Toxic wastes *See:* Hazardous wastes.

Toxin, poisonous substance produced by a living organism. Examples of toxin-producing organisms include fungi, which secrete substances that destroy bacteria (and provide antibiotics), and poisonous spiders and snakes, which deliver their toxin via fangs. The symptoms of many infectious diseases (e.g., cholera, diphtheria, tetanus) are due to the release of toxins by the bacteria.

Toy dog, any of several small breeds of dogs kept as pets. Toy dogs are either naturally small or selectively bred to keep them small. In most cases they do not constitute a separate genus or species, but are related to larger dogs of various species. Examples include the Maltese, chihuahua, Pekingese, Pomeranian, shih tzu, toy poodle, and Yorkshire terrier.

Toynbee, Arnold Joseph (1889-1975), English historian. His principal work, *A Study of History* (12 vol., 1934-1961), divides the history of the world into 26 civilizations and analyzes their rises and falls according to a cycle of 'challenge and response.'

Trace elements, minerals that make up all human, animal, and plant life. Small quantities of trace elements are needed to ensure the normal action of enzymes and hormones. In humans, lack of essential minerals such as iron may result in conditions such as pernicious anemia and goiter. Necessary minerals can generally be obtained from a healthy diet. Requirements vary among the different human, animal, and plant species.

Trachea, conduit by which air reaches the lungs from the pharynx. Air is drawn in through the mouth or nose and passes via the larynx into the trachea, which then divides into the major bronchi. It may be seen below the Adam's apple. In a tracheostomy, it is incised to bypass any obstruction to respiration.
See also: Respiration.

Trachoma, chronic conjunctivitis caused by *Chlamydia trachomatis*. Tetracycline eye ointments are usually effective.

Track and field, athletic sports including running, walking, hurdling, jumping for distance or height, and throwing various objects. The revival of the Olympic Games in 1896 gave international and national competition an enormous boost, and in 1912 the International Amateur Athletes Federation was set up.
Track events. Distances raced vary from the 50-m sprint to the 5,0000-m run. Hurdlers and steeplechasers have to clear a set number of obstacles. In relay races a baton is passed from one runner to the next.
Field events. In high jump and pole vault the contestant who clears the greatest height with the least number of attempts wins. A long jump running or triple jump (hop, step and jump) competitor is permitted six jumps. Throwing events also permit six throws. The javelin is a spear thrown by running up to a line and releasing. The shot, a solid iron ball, is 'put' from the shoulder. The discus is a circular plate released with a sweeping sidearm action. The hammer throw consists of throwing an iron ball attached to a handle by a wire. All-around events include the 10-event decathlon and the 5-event pentathlon.

Tracy, Spencer (1900-1967), U.S. film actor. During his career he appeared in more than 70 films over 37 years and won Academy Awards for *Captains Courageous* (1937) and *Boys' Town* (1938). His pairing with Katharine Hepburn in several movies, including *Woman of the Year* (1942) and *Adam's Rib* (1949), made them one of Hollywood's most famous cinematic couples.

Trade, buying and selling of commodities. It can take place within a nation (domestic trade) or between nations (foreign or international trade). Trade occurs because the people of a particular community or country do not produce all the goods they need. As a consequence, they must purchase these goods from another community or country. They may in turn sell their products to other communities or countries that need them. Trade among early peoples and civilizations usually involved an exchange of one product or service for another. For example, one group might have traded wood to another group for grain. As populations grew and their needs became more complicated, money became the medium of exchange and the boundaries of trade expanded. During the 13th, 14th, and 15th centuries, European merchants traveled to the Middle East and China in search of exotic goods. Overseas exploration created important trade between Europe and Africa and India, and between Europe and the colonies in both North and South America. Today in many countries, including the United States, trade occurs on many levels. People exchange money for services (subway or bus rides) and for goods (food, clothes, radios, and so on). Communities and states trade among one another, which explains why people in Ohio can buy California oranges. The United States also maintains a vast and active foreign trade with countries all over the world.

Trademark, name, symbol, or other device that identifies the product of one company. Strong trademarks, such as Tonka, are words with no apparent meaning which lessen the chance of them being used by another com-

American actor Spencer Tracy (1900-67).

T

pany. Weak trademarks, such as Bubbles, are ordinary words that often communicate the main feature of the product. Trademarks do not need to be registered with the U.S. Patent and Trademark Office to protect them from being duplicated, but such registration makes it easier to sue for infringement if the trademark is copied.

Trade route, land or water route used to transport goods from one area to another. Trade routes have historically led to the development of civilizations, the growth of cities, and the interchange of ideas. They have existed since ancient times and have increased in number and importance as civilizations have grown. The search for trade routes has contributed to the exploration of new territories and the establishment of colonial empires. Today an extensive network of air, land, and water routes covers all parts of the globe.

Trade union *See:* Labor movement.

Trade winds, persistent warm moist winds that blow westward from the high pressure zones at about 30°N and °S latitude toward the doldrums (intertropical convergence zone) at the equator. They are thus northeasterlies in the Northern Hemisphere and southeasterlies in the Southern Hemisphere. They are stronger and displaced toward the equator in winter.
See also: Horse latitudes.

Trafalgar, Battle of, decisive naval engagement of the Napoleonic Wars, fought on Oct. 21, 1805. The British fleet of 27 warships under Admiral Horatio Nelson met a combined French and Spanish fleet of 33 ships off Cape Trafalgar (southwestern Spain). By attacking in an unorthodox formation, Nelson surprised the enemy, sinking or capturing 20 vessels without loss, but was himself killed.
See also: Napoleonic Wars; Nelson, Horatio.

Tragedy, form of drama originating in ancient Greece, in which exceptional characters are led, by fate and by the very qualities that make them great, to suffer calamity and often death. Aristotle, in his famous definition, spoke of purification (*catharsis*) through the rousing of the emotions of pity and fear. The great classical tragedians were Aeschylus,

T

Transformers raise or lower the voltage of an electric current. To construct a transformer (left), wire is coiled around each leg of a laminated metal core (lower right). When alternating current enters the first coil (1) a magnetic field travels through the core and induces current in the second coil (2). The ratio between the number of windings in each coil determines whether the voltage (V1, V2) will be stepped up or down. The standard diagram for a step-up transformer is seen upper right. Large transformers require cooling and are usually submerged in a tank of oil (left).

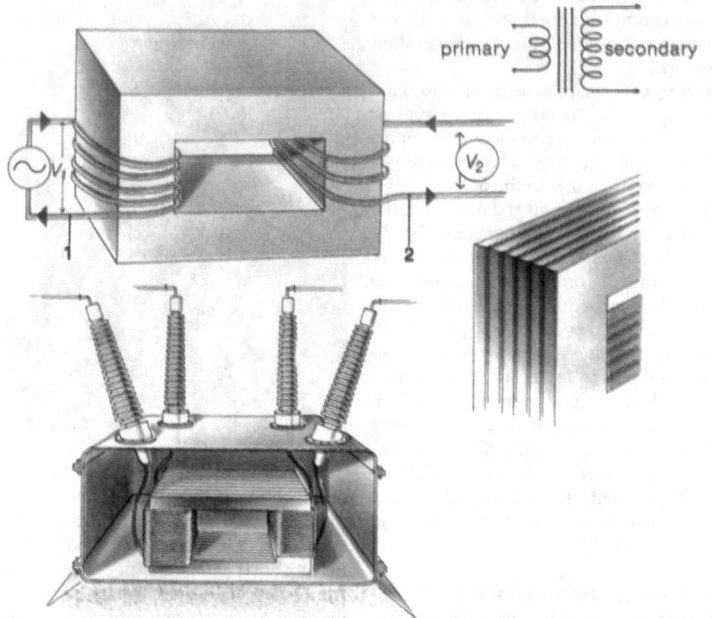

Sophocles, and Euripides. Supreme in modern times is William Shakespeare. Great tragedians include Félix Lope de Vega, Pedro Calderón de la Barca, Pierre Corneille, Jean Racine, Johann Wolfgang von Goethe, and Friedrich von Schiller. In the 19th and 20th centuries, in which the heroic dimension of tragedy is often shunned, the greatest exponents are probably Henrik Ibsen and Eugene O'Neill.

Tragopan, any of 5 species of birds in the pheasant family. These inhabitants of central and southern Asia mainly live on forested mountains. During courtship the colorful feathered folds of throat skin (the lappet) and blue fleshy horns on the sides of the head of the males enlarge for a brilliant display. Unlike many other kinds of pheasants, tragopans nest in trees rather than on the ground.

Trajan (A.D. 53-117), Roman emperor responsible for great extensions of the empire and vast building programs. He conquered Dacia (Romania) and much of Parthia and rebuilt the Roman Forum. Adopted heir by Nerva (97), he became emperor in 98. He was known as a capable administrator and a humane and tolerant ruler.
See also: Rome, Ancient.

Tranquilizer, any of the agents that induce a state of quietude in anxious or disturbed patients. Minor tranquilizers are sedatives (e.g., benzodiazepines) valuable in treating anxiety. In psychosis, especially schizophrenia and (hypo) mania, major tranquilizers are required to suppress abnormal mental activity, as well as to sedate; phenothiazines (e.g., chlorpromazine) are often used.
See also: Depressant.

Transcendentalism, philosophical and literary movement that flourished in New England c.1835-1860. Regarding rationalist Unitarianism and utilitarian philosophy as morally bankrupt and shallow, the transcen-

dentalists took their inspiration from the German idealists, notably Immanuel Kant, from Samuel Coleridge, and from Eastern mystical philosophies. They believed in the divinity and unity of humankind and nature, and in the supremacy of intuition over sense perception as well as reason as a source of knowledge. The major figures were Ralph Waldo Emerson and Margaret Fuller, who edited *The Dial* (1840-1844), Henry David Thoreau, and Amos Bronson Alcott. The movement had considerable influence on U.S. literature (Nathaniel Hawthorne, Herman Melville, Walt Whitman) and politics (abolitionism, Brook Farm).

Transcontinental treaty *See:* Adams-Onís Treaty.

Transducer, device for converting an input of energy or information of one form into an output of another. Passive transducers require only the input signal to produce the output signal; active transducers require an additional source of energy. The light bulb and the microphone are examples of transducers.

Transformer, device for moving an alternating current by increasing or decreasing the voltage. This is an easy, inexpensive way for power companies to transport electricity over long distances. Transformers work by electromagnetic induction, where a magnetic field alters the voltage of the electric current. The current goes through a step-up transformer, which increases the voltage. High voltage electricity loses very little power when transported over long distance wires. When the current reaches its destination, step-down transformers are used to decrease the voltage to the level where it can be used by customers.

Transfusion, blood *See:* Blood transfusion.

Transistor, device in electronic equipment thast regulates the flow of electricity in such equipment. It works by controlling the flow

of current between two terminals, the emitter and collector, by means of variations in the current flow between a third terminal, the base, and one of the other two. Transistors lower the voltage of the electricity to be used by a piece of electronic equipment, but keep the current strong. This provides items such as calculators, which require small voltages, with enough power to perform complex calculations. Transistor-transistor logic is a family of integrated circuits characterized by relatively high speed and low power consumption. Transistors are used in radios, television sets, and computers to control the flow of electric current.

Transkei, former independent homeland established by South Africa for the black Xhosa-speaking people. Located between the Indian Ocean and the Republic of Lesotho, it is 15,831 sq mi (41,002 sq km) and its capital is Umtata. Transkei, granted independence in 1976, was not recognized by any nation except South Africa. Many of Transkei's people are farmers and herders living in small villages, but the mining of the nation's rich mineral deposits is on the increase. With the abolishment of the apartheid policy, Transkei lost its independent status and fell under central South African rule.

Transmigration of the soul *See:* Reincarnation.

Transmission, automobile part that transmits the power generated by the engine to a driving axle. The power travels from the transmission to the drive shaft, then to the final drive. These 3 parts make up the drive train of an automobile. The transmission has several gears, which regulate the speed of the automobile by controlling the amount of power delivered to the driving axle. There are 2 types of automobile transmissions: manual, where the driver is responsible for shifting the gears, and automatic, where a device automatically shifts the gears when necessary.

Transmutation of elements, conversion of an atom of one element to an atom of another. Since atoms are identified by their atomic number (number of protons), any change in the number of protons will result in a different element. Atoms may change their number of protons by giving off or taking in atomic particles. Transmutation occurs naturally as a result of radioactive decay. Radioactive atoms are very unstable and give off atomic particles in order to become more stable. With one form of radioactive decay, alpha decay, the atom emits an alpha particle (2 protons and 2 neutrons). With beta decay the atom emits an electron, resulting in the production of a proton and the loss of a neutron. Sometimes, but less often, a positron (a positively charged electron) is emitted, so that a proton is lost and a neutron gained. Artificial transmutation may be accomplished by bombarding atoms with alpha particles so that the atom accepts an extra proton (1 of the 2 is immediately expelled). Transmutation is a by-product of fission (the splitting of nuclei) and fusion (the joining of nuclei).
See also: Radioactivity.

Above an automatic transmission passes power from the engine to the torque converter (1) and then to the various clutches (2) and epicyclic (planetary) gears (3). Different combinations of clutches and brake bands (4) automatically operated by the governor (5), select the appropriate driving gear. Gear selection depends on the vehicle's speed and engine load and on the position of the accelerator pedal, which is linked to the governor on the output shaft (6).

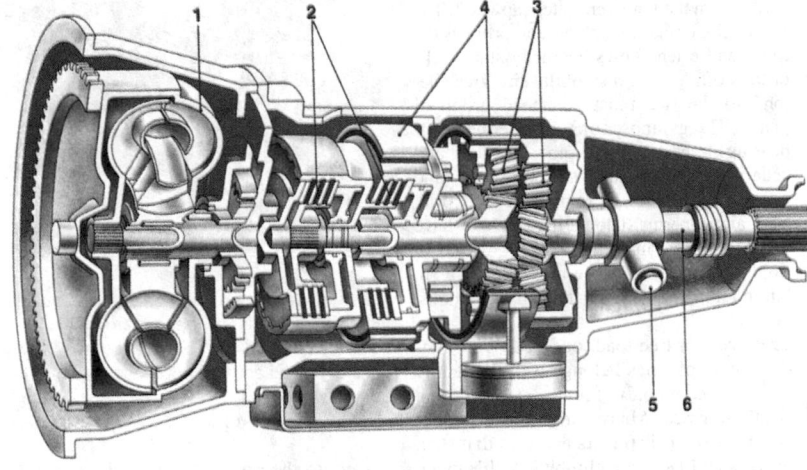

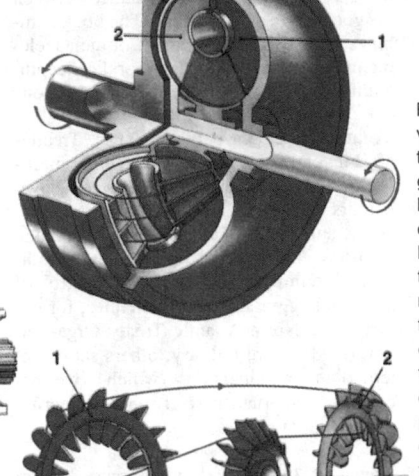

Right a torque converter, which couples the engine and the gearbox, works much like two fans facing each other: if the blades of one fan are turning, the air current created will turn the blades of the other fan. Similarly, when the torque converter's engine-driven impeller (1) turns, with oil (instead of air) as the medium (red arrows show direction of motion), the turbine blades (2) will turn.

Transpiration, loss of water by evaporation from the aerial parts of plants. Considerable quantities of water are lost in this way, far more than is needed for the upward movement of solutes and for the internal metabolism of the plant alone. Transpiration is necessary for photosynthesis: In order to obtain sufficient carbon dioxide from the air, considerable areas of the plant's wet surface have to be exposed. But as a result, much water is lost through evaporation.

Transplant, organ removed from one person and surgically implanted in another to replace a lost or diseased organ. Autotransplantation is the moving of an organ from one place to another within a person, where the original site has been affected by local disease (e.g., skin grafting). Blood transfusions between those with compatible blood groups was the first practical form of transplant. In organ transplantation, tissue compatibility typing as well as blood grouping are needed to minimize the risk of rejection. Immunosuppressive drugs are also given to block the creation of antibodies that would attack the donor tissue. The most important, and now most successful, of organ transplants is that of the kidney. A single kidney is transplanted from a live donor who is a close relative or from a person who has recently suffered sudden death. Heart transplantation has been much publicized, but is limited to a few centers, and many problems remain. Liver and lung transplants have also been attempted, but there are still numerous difficulties. In corneal grafting the cornea of the eye of a recently dead person replaces that of a person with irreversible corneal damage leading to blindness. The lack of blood vessels in the cornea reduces the problem of rejection. Grafts from nonhuman animals are occasionally used (e.g., pig skin as temporary cover in extensive burns). Both animal and human heart valves are used in cardiac surgery.

Transsexualism, condition in which a person has a psychological urge to belong to the opposite sex. People who experience this condition are called transsexuals. In most cases, therapy is not an effective treatment. Surgical techniques in conjunction with certain hormones can be used to make transsexuals physically resemble a member of the opposite sex. Transsexuality is not the same as homosexuality.

Trans-Siberian Railroad, railroad in Russia, the longest in the world, stretching 5,787 mi (9,313 km) from Moscow to Vladivostock on the Sea of Japan. Its construction (1891-1916) had a dramatic effect on the development of Siberia.

Transuranium elements, elements of atomic number above 92. All transuranic elements are radioactive and are products of artificial nuclear changes.

Transvaal, former province in the Republic of South Africa, between the Vaal and Limpopo rivers in the northeast. It is mainly high veld, 3,000-6,000 ft (914-1,829 m) above sea level. The capital is Pretoria and the largest city is Johannesburg. Mineral wealth includes gold, silver, diamonds, coal, iron ore, platinum, asbestos, and chrome. Its farmlands are noted for their cattle, corn, and tobacco. In 1993 Transvaal was divided over four provinces.
See also: South Africa.

Transylvania, province in central Romania near the Hungarian border, situated between the Transylvanian Alps and the Carpathian Mts. Transylvania has been in dispute between Romania and Hungary for several hundred years. Once part of the Roman Empire, Transylvania was conquered and ruled by the Magyars (Hungarians) from the 11th to the 16th centuries. The Ottoman Turks took control in 1526 but vied with Austria for prominence until 1711, when

Austria dominated. From 1867 to 1918, it was part of the Austro-Hungarian Empire. Transylvania was absorbed by Romania after World War I and, though a portion of it went to Hungary in 1940, Romania regained control after World War II. The province is rich in iron and other minerals and is a fertile farming, grazing, and wine-making area. It is famous as the setting of the legend of Dracula, written by English author Bram Stoker in 1897.
See also: Romania.

Trappists, members of the clan of the Reformed, or Strict, Observance, a Roman Catholic monastic order founded (1664) by Armand de Rancé, abbot of La Trappe in Normandy, France. He instituted a rigorous discipline of silence, prayer, and work. The abbot general lives in Rome.
See also: Cistercians.

Travertine, type of limestone that forms in dense layers. It is easily cut and often used in construction for decorative purposes. It is found in places where limestone is in contact with evaporated water containing calcium carbonate, and around hot springs and streams. Stalactites and stalagmites are chiefly comprised of travertine, which is mostly white or cream colored.

Treason, political offence which endangers external national security, committed by entering into communication with a foreign power, for example, with the intention of inciting it to acts of aggression against one's own nation.

Treatise of the Most High on Action and Retribution (T'ai-shang kan-ying-p'ièn, Taishang ganying pian), this has been one of the most widely read books of Chinese moralist scriptures since the 18th century. It comprises various versions and goes back to an original 11th century text. The book includes a catalogue of vices and virtues,

T

which may result in either an extension or a reduction of life. The believer is encouraged to continuously justify the balance between his good and his bad actions. The book combines Taoist, Buddhist and Confucian elements and characterizes the moral conceptual universe of the Chinese national religion.

Treaty, agreement between states. Treaties are bilateral (between two states) or multilateral (between several states), and cover matters such as trade, tariffs, taxation, economic and technical cooperation, diplomatic relations, international boundaries, extradition of criminals, defense, and control of arms and aggression. Some treaties, for example the North Atlantic Treaty Organization (NATO), are military; others set up international organizations, which have become an important part of modern international relations.

Treaty of 1783 *See:* Revolutionary War in America.

Tredici, David del (1937-   ), American composer. His large-scope *Alice in Wonderland* cycle (1968-1976), inspired by the music of Mahler and Richard Strauss, is so full of fondant harmonies that it continually balances on the edge of cliche and kitsch.

Tree, woody perennial plant with a well-defined main stem, or trunk, that either dominates the form throughout the life cycle (giving a pyramidal shape) or is dominant only

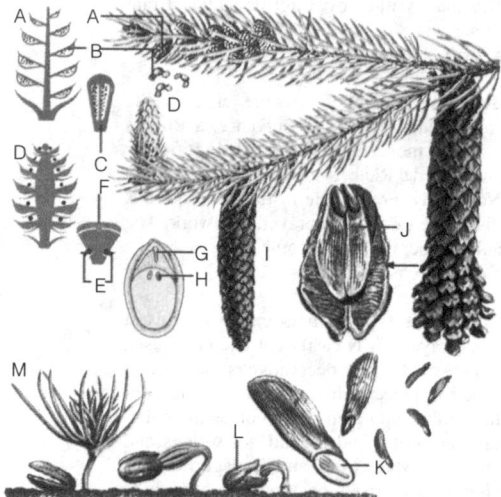

Gymnospermous trees produce seeds that are not enclosed in an ovary. The male cones (A) of the Norway spruce, *Picea abies*, shed pollen grains (B) from two sacs under each cone scale (C). Female cones (D) have two unfertilized eggs (E) per scale (F). After a pollen grain lands on a female cone, the nucleus of the grain grows down a pollen tube (G) and fuses with an egg (H), to form a seed. At maturity, the female cone (I) hangs from the branch, allowing the winged seeds (J) on each scale to be dispersed by the wind. On a suitable site, the seed embryo (K) will germinate (L) and become a spruce seedling (M).

in the early stages, later forking to form a number of equally important branches (giving a rounded or flattened form to the tree). The trunk of a tree consists almost wholly of thick-walled water-conducting cells (xylem) that are renewed every year, giving rise to annual rings. The older wood in the center of the tree (the heartwood) is much denser and harder than the younger, outer sapwood. The outer skin, or bark, insulates and protects the trunk and often shows characteristic cracks or falls off, leaving a smooth skin. Trees belong to the two most advanced group of plants. The gymnosperms include the cone-bearing trees such as pine, spruce, and cedar; they are nearly all evergreens and most live in the cooler regions of the world. The angiosperms (flowering plants) have broader leaves and much harder wood; in tropical climates they are mostly evergreen, but in temperate regions they are deciduous.

Tree frog, or tree toad, one of several hundred types of frogs belonging to the family Hylidae, commonly found in North and South America. Many varieties have adhesive pads on their fingers and toes that stick to trees and facilitate climbing and leaping. Males have a characteristic high-pitched call, which they use to attract their mates. Tree frogs are about 1-5 in (2.5-13 cm) long, eat insects, and change color.

Tree shrew, small, squirrel-like arboreal insectivore (family Tupaiidae) with a pointed snout. Tree shrews were once thought to be primates, related to the lemurs, but they are now considered a group of their own. They live in trees and bushes from India and China to the Philippines and Borneo. Except for the pen-tailed tree shrew they come out by day, and most species live in family groups. They feed on leaves, fruit, and small animals. The babies are born in a nest of leaves, and the mother visits them every two days to feed them.

Tree toad *See:* Tree frog.

Trench mouth, or Vincent's infection, disease of the mouth and throat, probably caused by bacteria, poor oral hygiene, and malnutrition. Initial symptoms include pain and bleeding of the gums and bad breath. Chewing and swallowing food is also painful. If not treated, trench mouth can lead to gum destruction and eventual tooth loss.

Trent, Council of, series of 3 conferences held in Trent, Italy, by leaders of the Roman Catholic church in the mid-16th century. Convened by Pope Paul III in 1545 to counteract the Protestant Reformation in Europe, the council did much to define Catholic doctrine and bring about a Counter-Reformation. The first council, which lasted until 1547, established the Catholic church's sole right to interpret the Scriptures and took issue with the Protestant interpretations of sin and salvation. The second council (1551-1552) defined the nature of the sacraments and reaffirmed the validity of the rituals practiced in Holy Communion. The third council (1562-1563) defended the controversial granting of pardons (indulgences) for the commission of certain sins, approved

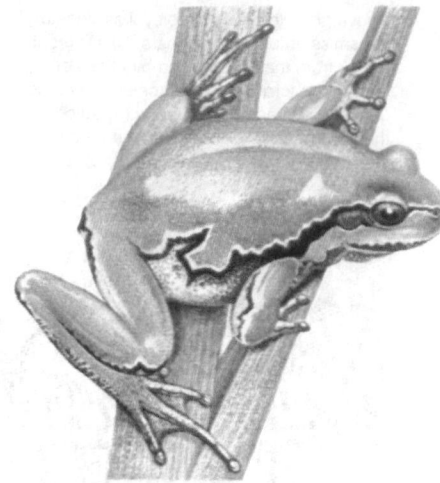

The European green tree frog has expanded discs on the ends of its digits, as an adaptation to its arboreal life. Its habitat ranges from central Europe, south of Italy and east of Central Asia.

prayers to the saints, and established seminaries for training the priesthood. The council's actions became part of the Catholic doctrine by papal confirmation in 1564. *See also:* Counter-Reformation.

Trephining, surgical removal of a small, circular piece of skull. An ancient, even prehistoric, practice, it was probably first performed to release evil spirits from a person's head. Today it is used primarily to open the way for certain brain surgeries and to relieve pressure caused by bleeding between the brain and the skull. The operation is performed with a small saw called a trephine.

Trevelyan, George Macauley (1876-1962), English historian who rejected the 'scientific' approach to history in favor of a more humanistic and literary approach. He taught at Cambridge (1927-1951) and was best known for a colorful study of Garibaldi (3 vols., 1907-1911), a one-volume *History of England* (1926), *England Under Queen Anne* (3 vols., 1903-1934), and *English Social History* (1942).

Trevor, William (1928-   ), Irish writer; wrote mainly short stories. Writes with an ironic distance and great insight, thus giving apparently unimportant events a deep emotional meaning. His collections of short stories include *The Day We Got Drunk on Cake* (1967), *The Ballroom of Romance* (1972), *Lovers of Their Time* (1978), *Other People's Worlds* (1980), *Beyond the Pale* (1981), *The News from Ireland* (1986), *Nights at the Alexandra* (1987; novella), *Reading Turgeniev* (1991), *William Trevor: the Collected Stories* (1992), *After Rain* (1996), and *The Hill Bachelors* (2000). He also wrote the novels *The Old Boys* (1964), *Fools of Fortune* (1983), *The Silence in the Garden* (1988), *Two Lives* (1991), *Felicia's Journey*, awarded the Whitbread Prize in 1994 and *The Story of Lucy Gault* (2002).

Triage (French, 'sorting'), allocation of limited medical or food resources by selecting those in need who would most benefit in the long run. During World War I (1914-1918) the word was introduced to describe the classification of wounded soldiers. Medical help was first administered to those who would survive only with immediate treatment; help was delayed or, if necessary, withheld from those who were expected to die or to recover with or without treatment. By extension, a triage system is suggested to determine what countries in need of food are to receive supplies. A system of triage also is used in hospital emergency rooms to determine the order in which patients are attended.

Trial, method of settling disagreements of determining criminal guilt. In the United states, this involves a hearing before a judge, with or without a jury. In the United States the right of an accused person to a speedy and public trial by a jury of peers is guaranteed in the Constitution. Trials in common law countries, such as the United Kingdom and United States, are 'adversary' proceedings, in which the court impartially decides between the evidence of two parties. Under civil law systems trials tend to be more 'inquisitorial,' allowing the court itself a greater role in the gathering of evidence. Under both systems the judge ensures that procedure is followed and that the rules of evidence are observed, and determines the guilty offender's sentence. Questions of fact are left to a jury, if there is one; jury trial is more expensive and time-consuming, and so it is reserved for more serious offenses.

Trial by combat, medieval method of settling disagreements. According to its tenets, the two disputing parties fought hand-to-hand combat, the belief being that God would intervene on behalf of the just participant. Nobles, women, and priests were usually represented by substitute fighters. Eventually the method was replaced by trial by jury.
See also: Divination.

Triangle, three-sided polygon. There are three main types of plane triangle: scalene, in which no side is equal in length to another; isosceles, in which two of the sides are equal in length; and equilateral, in which all three sides are equal in length. A right (or right-angled) triangle has one interior angle equal to 90° and may be either scalene or isosceles. The 'corners' of a triangle are termed vertices (singular: vertex). The sum of the angles of a plane triangle is 180°. A spherical triangle is an area of the surface of a sphere bounded by arcs of three great circles, each arc being less than 180°, each side and interior angle being termed an element. The sum of the three sides is never greater than 360°; the sum of the three angles is always in the range of 180°-540°.

Trianon, Treaty of, World War I treaty that reduced Hungary's territory by almost two-thirds as punishment for its part in the war. Signed June 4, 1920 by Hungary and the Western Allies, including the United States, the treaty forced Hungary to relinquish almost 90,000 sq mi (233,100 sq km) to Romania, Czechoslovakia, and what is now Yugoslavia. As a result, the country lost all of its seaports as well as about 12 million inhabitants.
See also: World War I.

Triassic Period, first period of the Mesozoic Era (c.225-190 million years ago).

Triathlon, an athletic contest in which each competitor takes part in three events - a swimming race, a bicycle race, and a footrace. There are no rest periods between events. The most rigorous triathlon competition, popularly called the Ironman Triathlon, consists of a 2.4-mile (3.86-km) swim, a 112-mile (180-km) bicycle race, and a marathon (a footrace of 26 miles, 385 yards [42 km, 195 m]). Top male competitors can complete the Ironman contest in less than 9 hours; top female competitors, in less than 11 hours. In lesser triathlons, the distances are reduced considerably. Most triathlons consist of a 2-kilometer swim, a 40-kilometer bicycle race, and a 15-kilometer run.
The triathlon originated in Hawaii in 1978, when two Navy men challenged each other to a test that would involve all the major muscles of the body; they were joined by 13 others in what became the first triathlon. The sport grew rapidly, and by the mid-1980's hundreds of triathlons were being conducted each year worldwide.

Tribe, people who live in a community in a particular area, sharing the same language, culture, and often kinship. The tribal system is one of the earliest forms of society and still exists in most of Africa, on many Pacific islands, and among Australian aborigines and Native Americans. Tribes may be made up of only 50 to 60 people or, like the Kikuyu of East Africa, have more than a million members. Tribal rule may be by a local chief

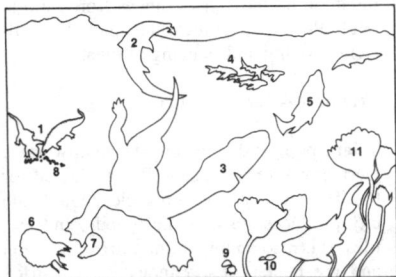

During the Triassic Period, much of Europe was covered by a shallow, limy sea. It contained a variety of reptiles, fish, ammonites, brachiopods, bivalve mollusks, and crinoids. The reptile *Placodus* (1), about 7 ft (2 m) in length, had protruding front teeth for picking shellfish from the seafloor, and large, flat side teeth for crushing them. *Mixosaurus* (2), a primitive, fish-eating ichtyosaur, probably resembled a porpoise. It possessed paddlelike limbs and a long beak. *Nothosaurus* (3), which could reach lengths of up to 10 ft (3 m), had webbed feet, a long, slender neck, and jaws with numerous sharp teeth that were adapted for catching fish. The fish included *Thoracopterus* (4), with large pectoral fins like those of a modern flying fish; and *Semionotus* (5). Ammonites, cephalopod mollusks with coiled, chambered shells, flourished during the Triassic. They included *Trachyceras* (6), with a shell marked by transverse ridges; and *Cladiscites* (7), whose shell was ribbed lengthwise. Brachipods, or lamp shells, such as *Coenothyris* (8) and *Tetractinella* (9); and bivalve mollusks, including *Myophoria* (10), lived on the seafloor. Stalked crinoids, or sea lillies, such as *Encrinites* (11), were locally abundant. Remains of these animals have been preserved in the mud of the seafloor, which eventually solidified into limestone and was later raised to form the Alps.

T

T

or, as in some large African tribes, by a king and councillors. Native American Plains tribes, such as the Arapaho and Cheyenne, were ruled by a council of chiefs. In earlier times, the kingdom of Israel united a number of Jewish tribes.
See also: Ethnic group.

Trichina, parasitic roundworm, belonging to the trichina family, that causes an infection known as trichinosis. Larval worms that infect the muscles of animals usually die by themselves; if an infected animal is eaten, however, the larvae can be set free from their cysts (sacs) to invade the intestine of the host and reproduce more larvae. The degree of infection in these cases ranges from mild to fatal. Preventative measures include sufficient cooking and freezing of meat.

Trichinosis *See:* Trichina.

Trier (pop. 100,000), city in southwestern Germany, on the Moselle River. Named for the Treveri, a people of ancient Gaul, the city produces steel, leather goods, and textiles. It is also an important railroad junction and the center of a famous wine district. Trier has been a center of Roman Catholic tradition since the Renaissance.
See also: Germany.

Trier, Lars von (1956-), Danish director and screenplay writer. Very ambitious director, uses an abundance of striking photography and editing. His films often have a sinister undertone. Von Trier started his career directing short films, which include *Orchidégartneren* (1976), *Menthe la bienheureuse* (1979) and *Nocturne* (1980). In 1984 his first feature film was released: *Forbrydelsens element*, a mixture of 'film noir' and German expressionism, in a style that shows influences of Dreyer, Andrei Tarkovski and Orson Welles. Although his next films, *Epidemic* (1987) and *Europa* (1991), have the same beautiful cinematography and are made in same style, it was not until *Breaking the Waves* (1996) that Von Trier made his international breakthrough. The film won the Grand Prix Speciale at Cannes and a César for best film. Von Trier has since made *Idioterne* (1998) and *Dancer in the Dark* (2000).

Trieste (pop. 240,000), city-seaport in northeastern Italy at the head of the Adriatic Sea, with steel, oil, and shipbuilding industries. A busy port in Roman times, it was part of Austria (1382-1919) and then of Italy. Claimed by Yugoslavia in 1945, it was made a Free Territory (1947-1954), then restored to Italy.
See also: Italy.

Triggerfish, fish belonging to the Balistidae family, found in tropical coastal waters. It measures less than 1.5 ft (46 cm) in length, is colorful, and has a round, flat body. When threatened, it uses one of its spines to 'trigger' a spinal enlargement, thus allowing it to lock itself into tight spaces.

Trigonometry, branch of geometry that deals with the ratios of the sides and angles of triangles, particularly of right-angled triangles and the applications of these ratios. Plane trigonometry deals with these relationships mapped on a plane surface. The principle ratios, when considering angle A of right-triangle ABC whose sides opposite the angles A, B, and C respectively are a, b, and c, and where c is the hypotenuse, are:

name	abbreviation	ratio
Tangent	tan A	a/b
sine	sin A	a/c
cosine	cos A	b/c

As can be seen, the cotangent is the reciprocal of the tangent, the cosecant that of the sine, and the secant that of the cosine. The basis of trigonometric calculations is Pythagoras's theorem, $a^2 + b^2 = c^2$, which in trigonometric form reads $\sin^2 A + \cos^2 A = 1$; this is true for angle A. From these ratios are derived the trigonometric functions, setting y equal to tan x, sin x, etc. These functions are termed transcendental (nonalgebraic). Of particular importance is the sine wave, in terms of which many naturally occurring wave motions, such as sound and light, are studied. Spherical trigonometry studies triangles lying on a sphere, and thus can be used to calculate distances on a globe.

Trillium, colorful wildflower (genus *Trillium*) of North American woodlands and eastern Asia. A member of the lily family, trilliums have 3 sepals, petals, and leaves on each stem. They bloom in early spring, and are also called wake-robins because their flowers appear at the same time robins return north. Colors of the more than 40 varieties include white, pink, dark red, yellow, green, or a painted variety.

Trilobite, extinct marine animal (phylum Arthropoda) from the Paleozoic Era (570-240 million years ago). Scientists have identified about 10,000 species from the fossilized remains of these small (4 in/10 cm) invertebrates. Their name (Latin, '3 lobes') refers to the 3 sections created by 2 lengthwise grooves across their soft, horny shells. The thorax contained many sections, each bearing legs that had gills, enabling the trilobites to breathe.

Trimble, David (1944-), Northern Irish politician. Leader of the Ulster Unionist Party, since 1995 a pragmatic politician. He was awarded the Nobel Prize for peace in 1998, together with John Hume, for his contribution to the peace process in Northern Ireland. Trimble became an independent Northern Ireland's first Prime Minister in 1999. However, he resigned in 2001 when the IRA still had not started to decommission. As a result, the peace process reached a deadlock. After the IRA started disarming in 2001 Trimble returned as Prime Minister.

Trinidad and Tobago

Capital:	Port of Spain
Area:	1,980 sq mi (5,128 sq km)
Population:	1,164,000
Language:	English
Government:	Presidential republic
Independent:	1962
Head of gov.:	Prime minister
Per capita:	US$ 9,000
Monetary unit:	1 Trinidad and Tobago dollar = 100 cents

Trinidad and Tobago, officially Republic of Trinidad and Tobago, independent republic in the West Indies, consisting of 2 separate islands in the Caribbean Sea north of Venezuela. The island of Trinidad is 1,864 sq mi (4,828 sq km) and Tobago is 116 sq mi (300 sq km).
Land and people. Trinidad is very fertile and mainly flat, rising to c.3,000 ft (914 m) above sea level in the north. Tobago is densely forested and is dominated by a mountain ridge some 1,800 ft (549 m) high. The climate of both islands is tropical. The majority of the people are of black African descent, but more than 40% is East Indian. The principal languages are English and a French patois.

The triggerfish has a triggerlike top fin that can be locked in a vertical position. if alarmed, a fish may retreat to a coral cavity, erect its fin, and jam itself in place. A The decorated triggerfish (*Pseudobalistes fuscus*) has its fin erect. B The clown triggerfish (*Balistoides niger*), has its fin folded.

Economy. The country is one of the more prosperous in the Caribbean, producing and exporting sugarcane, cocoa, and bananas, as well as chemicals and petroleum products. Tourism is a growing industry.

History. Trinidad was discovered by Christopher Columbus in 1498 and settled by the Spanish, but British rule was established in 1802. Tobago, once held by the Dutch and French, went to the British in 1814. Combined politically in 1889, Trinidad and Tobago joined the West Indies Federation in 1958 but left in 1962. Eric Williams was premier from independence in 1962 until his death in 1981. During this term, Trinidad and Tobago became a republic (1976). In 1990, a coup attempt against the government of Prime minister Arthur Napoleon Raymond Robinson was diffused when the government promised new elections and amnesty for the rebels. However, rebel leader Iman Yasin Abu Bakr and many of his followers were imprisoned upon their surrender. Economic troubles have recently plagued the country, and severe rioting has taken place in the capital, Port of Spain. In 1997 Robinson was elected president.

Trinitrotoluene *See:* TNT.

Trinity, central doctrine of Christian theology, that there is one God who exists in three Persons and one Substance. The definition of the doctrine, implicit in the New Testament, by the early ecumenical councils (notably Nicaea and Constantinople) was the product of violent controversy with heresies like Arianism, Monophysitism, Nestorianism, and Monarchianism. It is classically summed up in the Athanasian Creed. The three Persons-the Father, the Son (incarnated as Jesus Christ), and the Holy Spirit-are each fully God: coequal, coeternal, and consubstantial, yet distinct. The Son is 'eternally begotten' by the Father; the Holy Spirit 'proceeds' from the Father and (in Western theology) from the Son. The doctrine is a mystery, being known by revelation and being above reason (though not unreasonable). Hence it has been challenged by rationalists and by sects like the Jehovah's Witnesses and the Mormons.
See also: Christianity; Religion.

Triple Alliance, defense arrangement between Austria-Hungary, Germany, and Italy in the late 19th and early 20th centuries. In 1882 the 3 nations pledged mutual help if any of them were attacked by 2 or more other nations. Germany and Austria-Hungary signed an agreement in 1879 at the prompting of German chancellor Otto von Bismarck, and Italy joined them 3 years later. Serbia also joined in 1882 and Romania in 1883; the name remained Triple Alliance because the 2 Balkan nations were not considered major powers. The alliance was renewed several times before the outbreak of World War I in 1914, but actually broke up when the war started: Italy and Romania fought on the side of the Allies-France, Great Britain, and Russia (the Triple Entente).
See also: World War I.

Triple Entente, defense pact originally formed between France and Russia in 1890 to counterbalance the threat posed by the Triple Alliance-Germany, Austria-Hungary, and Italy-8 years earlier. In 1907 Great Britain joined. Each nation agreed to help the others if attacked by any or all of the Triple Alliance nations. After World War I broke out in 1914, the Triple Entente nations became known as the Allies; they signed the Declaration of London in which each ally agreed not to make a separate peace with the Central Powers, as the Triple Alliance nations came to be called.
See also: World War I.

Tripoli (pop. 215,000), city located in northwestern Lebanon, second largest in the country. A manufacturing center and seaport, its industries include petroleum refining, sponge fishing, textiles and the growing of citrus fruits. The name Tripoli comes from the Arabic *Tarabulus* ('Three Cities') because the city was founded in the 300s B.C. by explorers from 3 different Phoenician cities.
See also: Lebanon.

Tripoli (pop. 1,000,000), capital and largest city of Libya, located in northwest Libya on an arm of the Mediterranean Sea. Founded in the 600s B.C. by the Phoenicians, it was captured by the Romans in the 1st century B.C. Control passed to the Vandals in the 4th century A.D., the Arabs in the 7th century, the Spanish in 1510, and the Ottoman Turks in 1551. In the early 1800s, Tripoli was a stronghold for the Barbary Pirates, who attacked ships in the Mediterranean and exacted money from their captains in exchange for their freedom. The United States went to war against Tripoli (1801-1805) to end the practice. Tripoli was conquered by Italy in 1911 and remained in Italian hands until freed by the Allies during World War II. Today it is a major manufacturing center, shipping port, and oil-refining center. The city was bombed by the United States in 1986 as a result of Libya's alleged condoning of terrorist activities.
See also: Libya.

Tripura (pop. 2,760,000), Indian federal state, bordering on Bangladesh. (6,553 sq mi/ 10,486 sq km). The capital is Agartala. Agriculture: rice, burlap, cotton, and tea. Also cattle breeding and forestry. During more than 1000 years Tripura was an independent Hindu kingdom. It was part of the Mogul empire in the 17th century.

Tristan and Isolde, the hero and heroine of a romantic legend of the Middle Ages. The legend is apparently Celtic in origin, but has been translated and adapted, with numerous variations, in prose and poetry in many languages. The basic plot concerns a youth of Brittany, Tristan (also called Tristram and Tristrem), and his ill-fated love for an Irish princess, Isolde (aslo called Isolt, Iseult, and Yseult).Tristan, in the service of his uncle, King Marc of Cornwall, is sent to Ireland to ask Isolde to become Mark's bride. On the return voyage the couple drink by mistake a love potion intended for Mark and Isolde. From that moment they are bound to each other by a great love, in spite of their desire to be loyal to Mark. Finally, they both die.

One of the earliest versions of the legend is a poem by Thomas, an Anglo-Norman poet of the 12th century. In the 13th century, the story became combined with the legends of King Arthur and his court. The story is included in Sir Thomas Malory's *Le Morte d'Arthur*, printed by William Caxton in 1485. Later English versions, based on Malory, were written by Alfred Tennyson, Matthew Arnold, and Algernon Charles Swinburne. Richard Wagner based his opera *Tristan und Isolde* (1865) on an early-13th-century poem by Gottfried von Strassburg, a German poet.

Triticale (genus *Triticosecale*), hybrid grain produced by crossbreeding wheat with rye. When developed by botanists in 1876, it could not produce seeds; the development of seed-bearing triticale in the 1930s suggested commercial uses. It has a high yield and is high in protein. It can be bred for special soil and climatic conditions and resistance to disease, and may become an important food for humans and animals.

Tritium, hydrogen isotope that is 3 times heavier than ordinary hydrogen. One of 3 hydrogen isotopes (the others are protium and deuterium), tritium contains 1 proton and 2 neutrons in its nucleus. It is used in the release of nuclear energy through the fusion process. A radioactive gas and a key component of the hydrogen bomb, it is also used in luminous paints and as a tracer. Helium is formed when tritium decays.

Triton, in Greek mythology, sea god with human head and chest and a fishlike tail. Son of the sea god Poseidon and Amphitrite, he lived in a golden palace on the sea floor and stirred or calmed the seas by blowing on a conch shell. He is credited with helping Jason's Argonauts on their journey and with befriending sailors in the seas around ancient Greece. In Virgil's *Aeneid*, Triton is accused of drowning Misenus, a human trumpeter who challenged Triton's skill on the conch shell.
See also: Mythology.

Triumph, Arch of *See:* Arc de Triomphe.

Trogon, bird of the family *Trogonidae*. Male trogons have dark feathers of green, blue, or violet on their heads and backs and bright feathers of red, orange, or yellow on their undersides. Female trogons are similar but duller in color. Trogons inhabit warm regions in both the Western and Eastern hemispheres.

Trojan horse *See:* Trojan War.

Trojan War, conflict between Greece and Troy, made famous by Homer's *Iliad*. Paris, son of Priam of Troy, carried off Helen, wife of Menelaus of Sparta, and took her to Troy. The Greeks, led by Agamemnon, Menelaus, Odysseus, Achilles, and other heroes, swore to take revenge. They besieged Troy for 10 years; in seeming defeat they pretended to sail away, leaving a huge wooden horse outside the city, with Greek soldiers concealed in its belly. The Trojans took it into the city, and that night the soldiers opened the city

One of the things all Greeks had in common, wherever they lived and however politically divided they were, was the heroic tale of the Trojan War. On this relief, a number of scenes from this tale are depicted (Capitolini Museum, Rome).

T

gates to the Greek army. Most of the Trojans were killed, the city was burnt, and Helen reclaimed. The legend is thought to have been based on an actual conflict of 1250 B.C. *See also:* Greece, Ancient.

Trollope, Anthony (1815-1882), English author. His series of 6 books, known as 'the

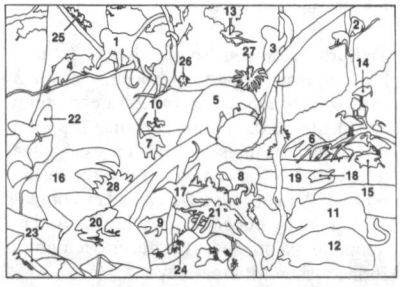

Barsetshire novels,' (1855-1867) are satires that portray the lives of ordinary people in a fictional county (Barsetshire): *The Warden, Barchester Towers, Doctor Thorne, Framley Parsonage, The Small House at Allington,* and *The Last Chronicle of Barset.* In all he wrote more than 50 books, including *The Bertrans* (1859), *The Eustace Diamonds* (1873), *The Way We Live Now* (1875), and *Cousin Henry* (1879).

Trombone, musical instrument, one of the brass wind instruments. It has a slide mechanism to alter the length of the playing tube and increase the note range. Developed from a sackbut, it was first used in a symphony by Ludwig van Beethoven in 1808. There is also a valve trombone, similar to the trumpet.

Trona, carbonate mineral found in dry regions of the world or extracted from evaporated brine. It is light-colored, has crystal formations, and is soluble in water. Trona is a source of soda ash, which is used to manufacture paper, glass, and chemicals.

Tropical fish, any of a variety of marine and freshwater fish native to the tropics, but particularly those valued for use in aquariums because they are ornamental, small, and able to reproduce quickly and easily. The tropical fish most commonly found in home aquariums are guppies and other freshwater fish of the *Poeciliidae* family, bearing live young (rather than eggs). Some other popular aquarium fish are cichlids, which are egg

bearing, and clownfish, a saltwater species. Tropical fish range in size from 1-12 in (2.5-30 cm) and generally eat food made from grains, as well as insects, fish, aquatic plants, and dried fish.

Tropical rain forest, regions of the world near the equator characterized by high levels of rainfall and humidity. Vast numbers of unique animal and bird species inhabit these regions. Vegetation includes many trees that have significant commercial value. This has resulted in extensive deforestation, especially in the Amazon rain forest region of South America. This practice endangers many plant and animal species and poses a threat to the world's climate system. The temperature in a rain forest ranges from 68°F (20°C) to 93°F (34°C).

Tropic bird, graceful seabird (genus *Phaethon*) with long, trailing tail feathers. Tropic birds are found in all tropical oceans and are often seen far out to sea. Their food is fish and squids, which they catch by diving. They nest under rocks or in crevices on islands. Plumage is generally satiny and white, with some black.

Red-billed tropic bird (*Phaethon aethereus*), tropical Pacific, Atlantic and Indian Oceans, length 30 in (75 cm).

Tropic of Cancer, imaginary line of latitude showing the northernmost point on the earth at which the sun can appear directly overhead. The sun's rays shine straight down on the Tropic of Cancer on June 20 or 21, which is the summer solstice and the first day of summer in the Northern Hemisphere. Lying 23°27' north of the equator and encircling the earth, the Tropic of Cancer also represents the northern boundary of the Tropical Zone.
See also: Latitude; Tropics.

Tropic of Capricorn, imaginary line of latitude showing the southernmost point on the earth at which the sun can appear directly overhead. The sun's rays shine straight down on the Tropic of Capricorn on December 21 or 22, which is the winter solstice and the first day of winter in the Northern Hemisphere. Lying 23°27' south of the equator and running completely around the earth, the Tropic of Capricorn also marks the southern boundary of the Tropical Zone.

Tropics, land and water 1,600 mi (2,570 km) north and south of the equator, as defined by the Tropic of Cancer (23°27' north

Animals of a South American rain forest include: black-capped capuchins (1), *Cebus appella*, and howler monkeys (2), *Alovatta seniculus*; the three-toed sloth (3), *Bradypus tricactylus*; and the opossum (4), *Didelphis marsupialis*. The tamandua (5), *Tamandua tetradacty-* la, is related to the great anteater (6), *Myrmelophaga tridactyla*. Other inhabitants are the brown coatimundi (7), *Nasua narica*, the capybara (8), *Hydrochoerus hydrochaeris*, and the paca (9), *Cuniculus paca*; and the red brocket deer (10), *Mazama americana*. A jaguar (11), *Panthera onca*, strikes its prey, a tapir (12), *Tapirus terrestris*. Birds include: the scarlet macaw (13), *Ara macao*; the scarlet ibis (14), *Eudocimus ruber*, and the roseate spoonbill (15), *A. ajaia*; the keel-billed toucan (16), *Ramphastos sulfura-* tus; and the ruby-topaz hummingbird (17), *Chrysolampis mosquitus*. Other animals are: a South American river turtle, the Arrau (18), *Podocnemis expansa*, shown on a giant lily pad (19), *Victoria amazonica*: the arrow poison frog (20), genus *Dendrobates*; the bird-eating spider (21); a rare butterfly (22), *Heliconius ethillus*; a leaf hopper (23); and leaf-cutter ants (24), genus *Atta*. Three epiphytic plants are two orchid genera, *Oncidum* (25) and *Cattleya* (26), and a bromeliad (27). *Cephaelis* (28) carpets the floor.

latitude) and the Tropic of Capricorn (23°27' south latitude). Because the sun's rays are more direct in these latitudes, the tropics generally have warm to hot climates year round with little variation in temperature, and receive sunshine for longer hours each day. Elevation, wind, and proximity to the ocean are also factors that affect weather conditions in the tropics, creating several climatic types, including tropical rain forests, steppes, deserts, and savannas.

Tropism, movement of a plant in response to external directional stimuli. If a plant is laid on its side, the stem will soon start to bend upward again; this movement (geotropism) is a response to the force of gravity. The stem is said to be negatively geotropic. Roots are generally positive geotropic and grow downward. Phototropisms are bending movements in response to the direction of light. Stems are generally positive phototropic (bend toward the light). Most roots are negatively phototropic. Some roots exhibit positive hydrotropism: They bend toward moisture. This response is more powerful than the response to gravity. Tropisms are controlled by differences in concentration of growth hormones.

Troposphere, lowermost zone of the earth's atmosphere, extending from the earth's surface up to 5-6 mi (8-9 km) over the poles and 8-10 mi (12.8-16 km) over the equator. In this zone normal lapse rates prevail, i.e., temperatures decrease with altitude. The top of the troposphere is called the tropopause. *See also:* Atmosphere.

Trotsky, Leon (Lev Davidovic Bronstein; 1879-1940), Russian revolutionary Communist, a founder of the USSR. President of the Petrograd (Leningrad) soviet in the abortive 1905 revolution, he escaped from prison to France, Spain, and New York. In 1917 he returned, went over to Bolshevism, and led the Bolshevik seizure of power in the October Russian Revolution. As commissar of foreign affairs (1917-1918) he resigned in protest over the Treaty of Brest-Litovsk and became commissar of war (1918-1925), organizing the Red Army into an effective force. After V.I. Lenin's death (1924), he lost power to Joseph Stalin and was deported (1929). Bitterly opposed to Stalin's 'socialism in one country,' he continued to advocate international revolution, founded the Fourth International, and attacked Stalinism in *The Revolution Betrayed* (1937). He was murdered in Mexico City by a Stalinist agent.
See also: Union of Soviet Socialist Republics; Russian Revolution.

Troubadour, name for courtly poet-musicians of Provence, southern France (1100-1300). Their poems, written in Provençal, mostly on the theme of love, were sung. Troubadours developed the conventions of courtly love, and influenced poetry and music in Germany, Italy, Spain, and England. Courtly poets in northern France were called *trouvéres.*

Trout, any of several relatives of the salmon, native to the Northern Hemisphere. Trouts are prized as game and food fishes. Like salmon, trout can be recognized by the fleshy, adipose fin. Some trout spend all their lives in fresh waters, favoring clear, well-aerated streams or lakes, but others live in the sea and return to river beds to breed. Various species include the brown trout, imported from Europe, the rainbow trout of western states, and the red-spotted Dolly Varden. The lake, or mackinaw, trout of deep lakes used to be netted by the ton in the Great Lakes until the arrival of lampreys.

Trout lily *See:* Dogtooth violet.

Troy, city of ancient northwestern Asia Minor, near the Dardanelles, described in Homer's *Iliad* and rediscovered by Heinrich Schliemann in 1870. The earliest site (Troy I) dates from 3000 B.C. Troy II contained an imposing fortress and had wide trade contacts. Its famous treasure of gold, copper, and bronze indicates a wealthy community. Troy VI (2000-1300 B.C.) had a citadel surrounded by huge limestone walls and large houses built on terraces; it was destroyed by earthquake. The rebuilt Troy VIIa was probably Homer's Troy. It was looted and destroyed by fire (c.1250 B.C.). Troy VIII was a small Greek village. Troy IX was the Greek and Roman city of Ilium, or Ilion. *See also:* Trojan War.

Trucial states *See:* United Arab Emirates.

Trudeau, Pierre Elliott (1919-2000), Canadian prime minister (1968-1979, 1980-1984). A law professor, he entered parliament in 1965, became minister of justice in 1967, and succeeded Lester Pearson as prime minister and Liberal Party leader (1968). He sought to promote a dialogue between the provincial and federal governments and to contain the Quebec separatist movement, giving the French language equal status with English. In 1970 he recognized the People's Republic of China. Briefly out of office (1979-1980), he returned to cope anew with the constitutional issue that resulted in the Constitution Act (1982), giving Canada its independence from Great Britain.
See also: Canada.

Truffaut, François (1932-1984), French

The rainbow trout, *S. gairdneri* (top), native to the North American Pacific coast, is stocked in lakes throughout the world as a game fish. The lake trout, *S. lasustris* (bottom), also popular among anglers, thrives in cold, deep lakes of the United States and Canada.

T

film director and critic. A leading New Wave director, he attracted attention for his series of semi-autobiographical films, including *The 400 Blows* (1959) and *Stolen Kisses* (1968). His other films include *Jules and Jim* (1961), *Day for Night* (1973), and *The Last Métro* (1980).

Truffle, underground fungus (genus *Tuber*) that has long been regarded as a delicacy. Pigs and dogs are trained to find them by scent. Some grow up to 2.2 lb (1 kg) and resemble potatoes; most are much smaller. They have not yet been cultivated on a wide scale, but there are attempts underway.

Trujillo Molina, Rafael Leonidas (1891-1961), Dominican Republic dictator (1930-1961) and president (1930-1938, 1942-1952). He introduced much material progress but savagely suppressed political opposition and feuded with neighboring countries. He was assassinated.
See also: Dominican Republic.

Truk Islands, group of islands in the western Pacific, part of the Caroline Islands. All of the major islands and many smaller ones lie within a lagoon almost 40 mi (64 km) wide surrounded by a coral reef. Nearly 40,000 people live on the islands, which were first explored by Europeans in 1825. Possession of the islands passed from Spain to Germany to Japan. After World War II, they came under U.S. control. Today, along with other Caroline Islands, they make up the Federated States of Micronesia.

Truman, Harry S. (1884-1972), American democratic politician. He was senator (1934-1944), vice-president (1944-1945), and 33rd president of the U.S. (1945-1953). At the end of WW II Truman decided to use the atom bomb against Japan. During his government both the United Nations and NATO were set up and the Korean War was fought. His behavior contributed to the worsening of U.S.-Soviet relations after 1945. His was the Truman Doctrine (1947), whereby the U.S. offered military help to preserve democracy and combat the rise of communism at the same time. In combination with the Marshall Plan (economic aid to Europe), Truman pursued an anti-Soviet policy. In the U.S. his Fair Deal program, aimed

T

at consolidating and extending the achievements of the New Deal, failed. Against all expectations, Truman was reelected in 1948; he did not put himself up for reelection in 1953.

Truman Doctrine, U.S. declaration (1947) stating the United States would 'support free peoples who are resisting attempted subjugation by armed minorities or by outside pressures.' Aimed at halting communist expansion and aggression, the Truman Doctrine provided substantial aid to Greece and Turkey, helping those nations defeat communist guerrillas.

Trumbull, John (1756-1843), U.S. painter. He studied with Benjamin West in London, where he started *The Battle of Bunker's Hill* (1786). He made 36 life-portrait studies for his best known work, *The Signing of the Declaration of Independence* (1786-1794), one of his four monumental pictures on Revolutionary themes for the U.S. Capitol rotunda (1817-1824). He is also well known for his portraits of George Washington.

Trumpet, musical instrument, one of the brass wind instruments. The modern trumpet comprises a cylindrical tube in a curved, oblong form that flares out into a bell. Three piston valves (first introduced in 1815) regulate pitch. The trumpet is a popular dance and jazz-band instrument, as well as an orchestral instrument.

Truong Chinh (1907-1988), Vietnamese writer and politician (real name, Dang Xuan

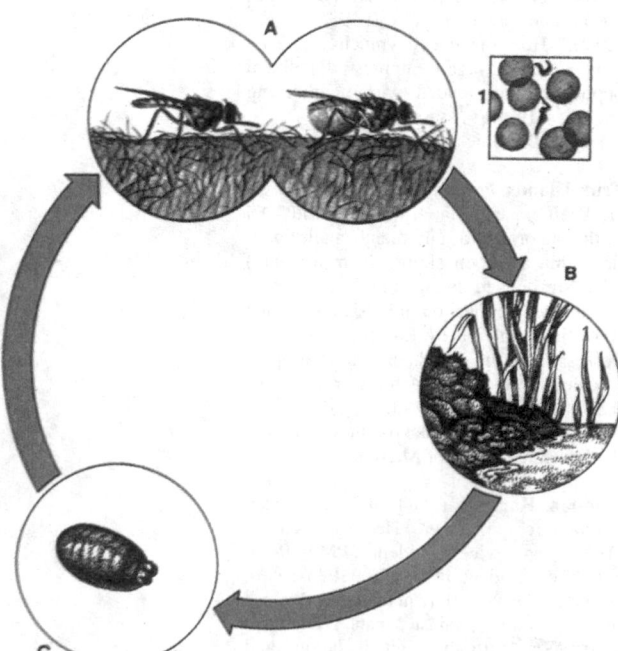

Here, we see the life cycle of a tsetse fly, *Glossina pulpatis*, body length 0.3 in (8 mm).
A. Adult tstese flies feeding on a human arm, before and after taking blood.

1. Trypanosomes, transmitted by the flies into human blood, cause sleeping sickness in man.
B. The female tsetse fly hatches her eggs internally and lays living larvae on soil

near water.
C. The larvae burrow into the soil within an hour and become pupae. In 4 weeks the pupa becomes an adult.

Khu). Together with Ho Chi Minh, Truong set up the Indochinese Communist Party in 1930. In 1951 he became the formal leader of this party (directly under Ho Chi Minh), which is now known as the Lao Dang (Labour Party). Truong was the architect of the radical agricultural reform in the north of Vietnam. The criticism of the bloody way in which this was carried out was probably the reason for his resignation in 1956. He went on to become chairman of the parliament and a party ideologue. From 1981 to 1987 Truong was president of Vietnam, chiefly a ceremonial office. In 1986 he became the leader of the Vietnamese Communist Party for a short period.
See also: Ho Chi Minh.

Trust, in law, legal relationship in which property is administered by a trustee, who has some of the powers of an owner, for the benefit of a beneficiary; the trustee is obliged to act only in the beneficiary's best interest and can derive no advantage except an agreed upon fee. The trustee may be an individual, perhaps looking after the property of a child until it comes of age, or a corporate body; banks and trust corporations often act as trustees of larger properties. Under specialized form, called corporate trust, a group of trustees may hold the stock and thus control the operations of companies that would normally be competitors. The Sherman Antitrust Act (1890) attacked such trust, but enforcement was weakened by U.S. Supreme Court decisions. Enforcement of antitrust legislation has become complicated by the growth of huge conglomerates, which control many companies in different industries.

Trust territory, formerly dependent territory administered under United Nations supervision. A trustee nation was responsible for developing the trust territory and assisting it to independence. The Trusteeship Council helped the General Assembly and Security Council supervise trust territories. Of the 11 trust territories (mostly former mandates of the League of Nations), the U.S.-administered Pacific Islands was the last to be terminated.

Truth, Sojourner (1797?-1883), U.S. abolitionist and feminist. Born into slavery in New York State as Isabella Baumfree, she escaped shortly before slavery was declared unlawful in the state (1828). In 1843, after taking the name Sojourner Truth, she became a traveling preacher. Soon after, she began to speak out against slavery, the first black woman to do so. She was known for her passionate oratorial style, her great energy, and her ready wit. In 1864 she went to Washington, D.C., to work for improved living and working conditions for the black people who settled there after fleeing the South. In the 1870s she tried unsuccessfully to convince the U.S. government to set apart undeveloped land for farms for blacks.
See also: Abolitionism.

Truth table, systematic tabulation of all the possible input/output combinations produced by a binary circuit.

Trypanosome, microscopic unicellular parasite that infests the blood plasma of animals and humans, producing disease; it is transmitted by insects. Trypanosome protozoa are responsible for trypanosomiasis of the African (Changas's disease) varieties, carried by the tsetse fly and certain other bugs. They are relatively insensitive to chemotherapy in established cases; prevention is therefore important.

Tsai Ming-liang (1957-), Taiwanese film director. Born in Malaysia of Chinese parents, he went to Taiwan to study. Once there he soon turned to writing, producing and directing experimental theatre pieces, in which he played the lead role himself. These were very successful and led to his film debut *Ching siao nien na cha* (Rebels of the Neon God; 1992), a portrait of the existential ennui in the life of young people in Taipei. His second film, *Aiqing wansui* (Vive l'amour; 1993), won a Golden Lion and the Critics Prize in Venice. Other films include *The River* (1996), *The Hole* (1998) and *What Time is it There?* (2002). He was widely praised for his innovative, stylish cinema with a hint of Antonioni.

Tsar, or czar, English spellings of the Russian word for 'emperor.' The term is used for the rulers of Russia from 1547 to 1917. The last tsar, Nicholas II, was executed in 1918, during the civil war that followed the October 1917 revolution.

Tschaikowsky, Peter Ilich *See:* Tchaikovsky, Peter Ilich.

Tsedenbal, Yumjaagiyn (Joe) (1916-1991), Mongolian politician. Tsedenbal became a member of the Central Committee of the communist Mongolian Revolutionary People's Party in 1940, and was its secretary-general from 1958-1984. From 1952-1974 he was prime minister, and from 1974-1984 president of the Mongolian People's Republic. A loyal supporter of the Soviet Union, he ruled his country with an iron fist. In 1984 he was pushed out. He spent the remainder of his life in exile in Moscow. Accused of decades of mismanagement, he was expelled from the party in 1990 and stripped of all his decorations.

Tsetse fly, name for 20 species of muscoid flies (genus *Glossina*). They are true winged flies very like houseflies, except that the mouthparts are adapted for piercing the skin of mammals and sucking blood. Widespread in tropical Africa, some species act as vectors of the trypanosomes that cause sleeping sickness.

Tshombe, Moise Kapenda (1919-1969), president (1960-1963) of the Congolese breakaway state of Katanga. Backed by Belgian interests, he unsuccessfully opposed Prime Minister Patrice Lumumba and the UN. He returned from exile to be premier (1964-1965) of the Congo (Zaïre). He died in prison in Algeria.

Tsui, Daniel C. (1939-), Chinese physicist. In 1998 he was awarded the Nobel Prize for physics, together with H. Störmer and B.

Laughlin, for the discovery and explanation of the Fractional Quantum Hall Effect (FQHE). Stömer and Tsui had discovered this phenomenon as early as 1982, but it took almost ten years before Loughlin's explanation in terms of quasi-particles was proven and accepted.

Tsunami, a term commonly applied to an unusually large ocean wave that overflows the land. A tsunami usually consists of many long waves occurring one after the other, usually at intervals of 10 minutes or more. Tsunamis are produced by undersea earthquakes, volcanic eruptions, or landslides. Tsunamis produced by undersea earthquakes are also called *seismic sea waves* and are generally the most severe. Tsunamis, which read speeds of about 450 miles per hour (725 km/h) when traveling over deep water, can inflict damage great distances from their point of origin. When a tsunami enters shallow water, its speed is greatly reduced, causing the water to pile up to great heights. Tsunamis are generally less than 3 feet (1 m) high when traveling over deep water and can attain heights of over 100 feet (6 m) or more near shore.

Tuamotu Islands, group of 75-80 small islands and atolls spanning nearly 1,000 mi (1,609 km) in the South Pacific Ocean. The first European to see the islands (1606) was Pedro Fernandes de Queivós, a Portuguese explorer in the service of Spain. Annexed by France in 1881, the islands now are part of French Polynesia. About 11,000 Polynesians inhabit the Tuamotu Islands, making their living primarily from the sale of pearls and coconut oil.

Tuareg, Berber tribe in the Sahara. Its people are fair skinned and its social system comprises noble families, a large number of vassal tribes, and black slaves. Adult men, but not women, wear a blue veil. Tuareg script is like that of the ancient Libyans.

A group of Tuareg at Ahaggar (Hoggar), the southernmost region of Algeria. Note that the colours of their robes are purely restricted to black, white and blue.

Tuatara (*Sphenodon punctatus*), reptile resembling the lizard. Inhabitants of a few small islands off the coast of New Zealand, they are the last surviving members of the order Rhynchocephalia, which lived on earth more than 200 million years ago. Green-skinned tuataras have a row of scales down their backs and tails and grow to 2 ft (60 cm) in length. Females carry their eggs for up to a year before depositing them in the ground,

where they take another year to hatch. Some tuataras live as long as 77 years.

Tuba, low-pitched brass musical wind instrument with three to five valves. It is held vertically. There are tenor, baritone, euphonium, bass, and contrabass tubas. They are included in symphony orchestras and in marching bands.

Tuber, swollen, underground stem or root that contains stored food material; they are prennial. The potato is a stem tuber, swells at the tip of a slender underground stem (stolon) and gives rise to a new plant the following year. Dahlia tubers are swollen roots.

Tuberculosis (TB), group of infectious diseases caused by the bacillus *Mycobacterium tuberculosis*, which kills some 3 million people every year throughout the world. TB may invade any organ but most commonly affects the respiratory system, where it has been called consumption or phthisis. In 1906 it killed 1 in every 500 persons in the United States, but today it leads to only 1 in 30,000 deaths because of effective drugs and better living conditions. Symptoms of pulmonary tuberculosis include fatigue, weight loss, persistent cough with green or yellow sputum and possibly with blood. Treatment is mainly by triple drug therapy, with streptomycin, para-aminosalicylic acid (PAS), and isoniazid, together with rest. Recovery takes about 2 years. The tuberculin skin test can show whether a person has some immunity to the disease, though the detection of the disease in its early stages, when it is readily curable, is difficult. Control of the disease is accomplished by preventive measures such as X-ray screening, vaccination, isolation of infectious people, and food sterilization.

Tuberose (*Polianthes tuberosa*), tropical plant of the agave family, native to Asia and America but cultivated elsewhere for its use in perfumes and other products. The tube-shaped root produces a long stem up to 3 ft (91 cm) tall, with sword-shaped leaves and waxy, white, heavily fragrant flowers.

Tubman, William Vacanarat Shadrach (1895-1971), president of Liberia (1944-1971). He made extensive economic, social, and educational reforms and extended the rights of tribespeople and women. *See also:* Liberia.

Tucholsky, Kurt (1890-1935), German writer. Received a doctorate in law (1914). His writings, mainly in the journal *Die Schaubühne* (after 1918, *Die Weltbühne*), were full of social criticism; often used the pseudonyms Peter Panter, Theobald Tiger, Ignaz Wrobel and Kaspar Hauser. Tucholsky moved to France in 1924, and in 1929 to Sweden. His fervent anti-Nazi stance cost him his German citizenship in 1933. With his incisive, poignant prose he showed himself to be a confirmed pacifist and an untiring fighter against the reactionary conservatism of the German judicial system. He also ridiculed national arrogance (*Deutschland, Deutschland über alles*, 1929). His only book was *Schloss Gripsholm* (1931). Tucholsky committed suicide in 1935.

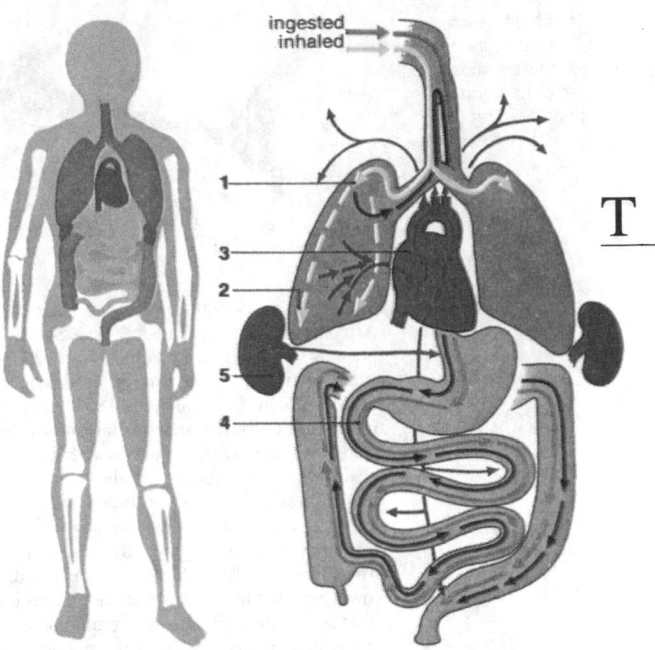

ingested
inhaled

T

Tuberculosis is a very contagious disease, caused by the bacterium *Mycobacterium tuberculosis*. Throughout the world, the disease kills 1 to 2 million people per year. Tuberculosis is most often contracted by inhalation but can also result from ingesting unpasteurized milk. In most active cases the bacteria produce lesions, known as tubercles, in the lungs (1). Occasionally, the bacteria infect the lymph nodes (2) that drain the lungs, enter the bloodstream (3), and spread to such organs as the kidneys (5), bones and joints, brain, or genital organs. Ingested tubercle bacteria may infect the throat or the intestines (4).

Tucker, Richard (1914-1975), U.S. opera singer. In 1945 Tucker, a lyric tenor, made his debut at the New York Metropolitan Opera as the lead in Amilcare Ponchielli's *La Gioconda*, and went on to sing in the leading opera houses of North America and Europe. Equally versatile in French and Italian, he was a star at the Metropolitan until his death. *See also:* Opera.

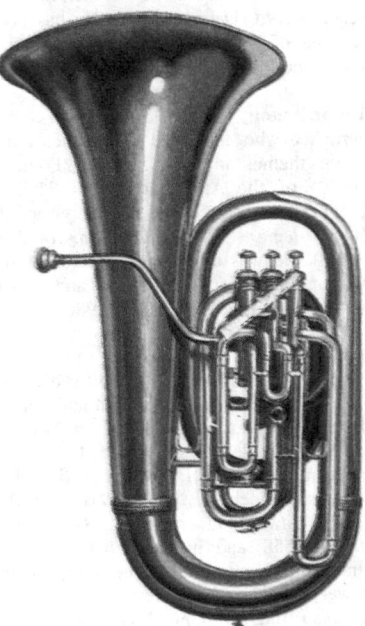

The orchestral tuba is the double bass of the brass section of the orchestra. It is often used to play quick staccato solos but can also play sustained melodies. The tuba used in military bands may have a fiberglass bell to lessen its weight when carried in marches.

The bluefin tuna, *T. thynnus*, found worldwide, mostly in temperate and sub-tropical waters, is an important food fish.

T

Tucson (pop. 449,000), city in southeast Arizona, inc. 1877. Founded as a Spanish presidio (walled military outpost) in 1776 by Juan Bautista de Anza, Tucson became part of Mexico in 1821, and, in 1853, control passed to the United States as a result of the Gadsden Purchase. A major research and educational center, Tucson is also a popular tourist destination, transportation hub, and home of the University of Arizona, several museums, and the San Xavier del Bac Mission, dating from the earliest days of the town. Situated in a valley with mountains on 3 sides, Tucson enjoys a year-round hot, dry, sunny climate that has made it a popular retirement center.
See also: Arizona.

Tudjman, Franjo (1922-1999), Croatian politician. Tudjman, president of the Croatian Republic since 1990, began his career as a soldier in the former Yugoslavia. In 1961 he left the army and began an academic career. His studies were interrupted by various arrests for his 'anticommunist' activities. In 1989 Tudjman founded the Croatian Democratic Community (HDZ), and in 1990, in the first free elections since 1945, he won with a landslide victory. His policies were aimed at the creation of a free-market economy and the territorial expansion of Croatia. Under his leadership Croatia declared itself independent in June 1991. In the ensuing conflict with Serbia, Croatia lost one third of its territory, although in May and July of 1995 it managed to recapture most of it (Western Slovenia and Krajina). Tudjman was one of the signatories of the Bosnian peace accord (Dayton, 1995). He has been accused of being responsible for Croatian war crimes during the recapture of Krajina.

Tudor, Antony (1909-1987), English choreographer who introduced dramatic, emotional themes into U.S. ballet. Founder (1939) of the American Ballet Theatre (ABT), his works for the company include *Dark Elegies* (1937) and *Pillar of Fire* (1942). He was also ballet director of the Metropolitan Opera (1957-1963) and associate director of the ABT (1974-1980).

Tudor, House of, reigning dynasty of England (1485-1603). Of Welsh descent, Henry Tudor, earl of Richmond and heir to the House of Lancaster, ended the Wars of the Roses by defeating Richard III in 1485; he became Henry VII, first Tudor king. The succession included Henry VIII (r.1509-1547), Edward VI (r.1547-1553), Mary I (r.1553-1558), and Elizabeth I (r.1558-1603). Under the Tudors England became a major power and enjoyed a flowering of the arts.
See also: England; United Kingdom.

Tuileries, former royal palace in Paris. Situated on the right bank of the River Seine, the palace was built by order of Catherine de Medici (1564) and was completed in the 1600s. Forced into use as a residence by King Louis XVI and his queen, Marie Antoinette, during the French Revolution (1789), it was also used during the 1790s by revolutionary leaders to hold session and by Napoleon, who made it his primary residence after taking power. After the Bourbon restoration (1814-1815) it once again became a royal residence before being destroyed by fire during the Paris Commune uprisings of 1871. The 75-acre (30-hectare) Tuileries Gardens remain affiliated with the Louvre museum.

Tula (pop. 540,000) City in Russia, on the Upa River, 110 miles (177 km) south of Moscow. Tula is a railway highway junction and one of Russia's oldest industrial centers. The heart of the city is a 16th-century kremlin (fortress), preserved as a park and sports grounds. Nearby is the country estate and burial place of author Leo Tolstoy. Tula has been known since the 12th century. It long served as a fortress protecting the southern routes to Moscow, especially against the invasions of the Crimean Tatars in the 16th and 17th centuries. The first Russian arms works was built in Tula in the early 18th century. In 1941, during World War II, Tula was the southern anchor of the Moscow defense line and withstood a German siege.

Tularemia, or rabbit fever, infectious disease due to bacteria (*Pasteurella tularensis*), causing fever, ulceration, lymph node enlargement, and sometimes pneumonia. It is carried by wild animals, particularly rabbits, and insects. Antibiotics are fully effective in treatment.

Tulip, name for plant (genus *Tulipa*) native to Europe and Asia, grown from bulbs. Cultivated tulips were introduced to Europe via Holland in the 16th century and have become popular spring-flowering garden and pot plants. They have deep, cup-shaped flowers; new varieties are continually being bred. Tulips come in a variety of colors and in some instances in a combination of colors.

Tuliptree *See:* Yellow poplar.

Tumbleweed, common name for several plants native to North America that grow in clumps on waste land and dry into loose balls. These break from the soil and are blown by the wind, scattering seeds. Examples are the so-called Russian thistle (*Salsola kali*) and *Amaranthus albus*.

Tumboa *See:* Welwitschia.

Tumor, or neoplasm, abnormal overgrowth of tissue. These may be benign proliferations, such as fibroid of the womb, or they may be forms of cancer (lymphoma or sarcoma), which are generally malignant. The rate of growth, the tendency to metastasize (spread locally and to distant sites via the blood vessels and lymph system), and systemic effects determine the degree of malignancy. Tumors may present as a lump, by local compression effects (especially with brain tumors), or by systemic effects, including anemia, weight loss, false hormone actions, neuritis, etc. Treatments include surgery, radiation therapy, and chemotherapy.
See also: Cancer.

Tuna, high-speed fish with rows of finlets on the tail. Also called tunnies, they live in shoals in the warmer seas of the world. The bluefin tuna (*Thunnus thynnus*) of the North Atlantic and Mediterranean grows to 14 ft (4.3 m) long and weighs up to 1,800 lb (816.5 kg). Others, such as the Pacific albacore and yellow-fin tuna, are smaller, but all are important commercial fish. They are caught by net, hook, and harpoon, and their 'white meat' is canned. Tuna feed on small fish, eating considerable amounts during the summer months in the northern parts of their ranges before migrating southwards to spawn.

Tundra, plains of the Arctic Circle. For most of the year the temperature is less than 32°F (0°C), and even during the short summer it never rises above 50°F (10°C). The soil is a thin coating over permafrost. Tundra vegetation includes lichens, mosses, and stunted shrubs. Similar regions on high mountains (but generally without permafrost) are called alpine tundra.
See also: Permafrost.

Tung Chi-Chang (1555-1636), Chinese painter and calligrapher from the later Ming period. Famous for his extremely refined landscapes.

Tungsten, or wolfram, chemical element, symbol W; for physical constants see Periodic Table. Tungsten was discovered by brothers Fausto and Juan José de Elhuyar in 1783. It occurs in wolframite, scheelite, huebnerite, and ferberite. The element is prepared by reduction of the oxide with hydrogen or carbon. It is a steel-gray, hard, ductile, unreactive metal, and has the highest melting point and lowest vapor pressure of all metals. Alloys of tungsten have many high-temperature applications. Tungsten and its compounds are used in filaments for electric lamps and television tubes, fluorescent lighting, glass-to-metal seals, and high-speed tool steels.

Tungting Lake, also **Dongting Hu** and **Dangting Hu**, a lake in Hunan province, China, just south of the Yangtze River. Except when swollen by summer floodwaters, the lake is shallow and covers an area of about 1,400 square miles (3,600 sq km). Two major rivers of southern China-the Xiang and

Yuan-flow into Tungting Lake; several channels connnect it with the Yangtze River. Rice fields in the area near the lake are among the most productive in China.

Tunguska, the name of two eastern tributaries of the Yenisey River in Russia. They are the Lower Tunguska and the Stony Tunguska. A third tributary, the Angara River, is sometimes called the Upper Tunguska.

The Lower Tunguska begins in the Central Siberian Plateau and flows northward and westward to join the Yenisey at Turukhansk; it is 1,588 miles (2,556 km) long. The Stoney Tunguska begins near the Upper Tunguska and flows generally westward 976 miles (1,571 km) to the Yenisey at the town of Podkamennaya Tunguska. The region through which the rivers flow is inhabited primarily by Evenki, a people of Ural-Altaic stock who are seminomadic herders and trappers.

Tunis (pop. 1,8 million), capital city of Tunisia, on the Lake of Tunis, in northeastern Tunisia. Probably established before Carthaginian times, the city was part of the ancient Carthaginian empire until Carthage was destroyed by the Romans in 146 B.C. Later rebuilt, Tunis became a major trading port that was captured by the Moslems in the 7th century. It was established as the country's capital by the Hafsid dynasty (13th-16th centuries) and was under Turkish rule from 1534 to 1881, when it became a center for piracy as well as trade. The French occupation of Tunisia lasted 1881-1956, after which time the country gained its independence. Today it thrives as a major port and is active in the manufacture of olive oil, textiles, and carpets. Since 1979 it has been the headquarters for the Arab League.
See also: Tunisia.

Tunisia

Capital:	Tunis
Area:	63,362 sq mi (164,150 sq km)
Population:	9,816,000
Language:	Arabic
Government:	Presidential republic
Independent:	1956
Head of gov.:	Prime minister
Per capita:	US$ 6,600
Monetary unit:	1 Tunesian dinar = 1,000 millimes

Tunisia, republic in North Africa. With an area of some 63,362 sq mi (164,150 sq km), Tunisia is bounded on the south by Libya, on the west by Algeria, and on the north and east by the Mediterranean Sea. The Cape Bon peninsula, in the extreme northeast, is only 96 mi (153 km) from Sicily.
Land. Tunisia's irregular coastline has several good harbors, among them Bizerte. In the northwest, spurs of the Atlas Mountains enter the country from Algeria. The Medjerda River, Tunisia's only permanent river, flows through the northern mountains on its way to the Gulf of Tunis. The Medjerda River valley is a major wheat-producing area. The northern highlands also have dense forests of oak and cork oak, pines, and junipers. The Tabassah Mountains rise in west-central Tunisia and include the country's highest peak, Mt. Sha'nab (5,066 ft/1,544 m). In north-central Tunisia, the dry plain of the Sahel lies between the Atlas and Tabassah mountains and gives way to Tunisia's fertile, heavily populated coastal plain. To the south of the Sahel, beyond the Chott el Djerid and other salt lakes, are the Saharan sands and date-palm oases of southern Tunisia. In coastal Tunisia, summers are generally hot and dry; winters are warm and wet. The Sahel has less than 10 in (25 cm) of rain yearly. Rainfall can be irregular and there are sometimes droughts.
People. The people of Tunisia, predominantly Berber and Arab, include small French, Italian, and Maltese minorities. Most people live in the fertile north and some 59% of the population live in towns. The people are overwhelmingly Sunni Muslim, and French is spoken, though Arabic is the official language.
Economy. Tunisia's economy is primarily agricultural. The main crops are wheat, barley, and other grains; olives, citrus fruits, dates, and wine grapes; and vegetables. Crude petroleum is the country's principal export, followed by clothing, olive oil, and phosphates. Industry has traditionally centered around food processing, but is expanding.
History. Once a colony of the Phoenicians, Tunisia was the state of the ancient city of

Carthage, center of a rich and powerful commercial empire which was conquered by the Romans in 146 B.C. After several centuries of Roman rule, Tunisia was conquered by the Vandals in 439 A.D., by the Byzantines in 533, and by the Arabs in 670. Tunisia saw its heyday as a Muslim state under the Hafsid dynasty, from the 13th to the 16th centuries. Late in the 16th century, Tunisia came under the sway of the Ottoman Turks and the Barbary States were a haven for pirates until Tunisia was made a protectorate by the French in 1883. Tunisia achieved its independence from France in 1957 and became a republic under the presidency and virtual one-man rule of Habib Bourguiba. Bourguiba's dominance was not effectively challenged until 1987, when he was replaced by Gen. Zine al-Abidine Ben Ali. Ben Ali set a period of political liberalization in motion. He increased freedom of press and introduced a multi-party system in 1988. In 1999, Ben Ali was re-elected, winning 99% of the votes. He won a referendum on constitutional changes, which made it possible for him to stay in power after his third term of Presidential office.

Tunnel, underground passageway usually designed to carry a highway or railroad, to serve as a conduit for water or sewage, or to provide access to an underground working face. Although tunnels have been built since prehistoric times, tunneling methods remained primitive and hazardous until the 19th century. Modern softground tunneling was pioneered by Marc Brunel, who invented the 'tunneling shield' (1824), a device subsequently improved (1869-1886) by James Greathead, whose shield is basically a large steel cylinder with a sharp cutting edge driven forward by hydraulic rams. Tunneling through hard rock is facilitated by an array of pneumatic drills mounted on a 'jumbo' carriage running on rails. Explosives are inserted in a pattern of holes drilled in the rock face and then detonated. Increasingly, however, automatic tunneling machines called moles, with cutting heads consisting of a rotating or oscillating wheel that digs, grinds, or chisels away the working face, are em-

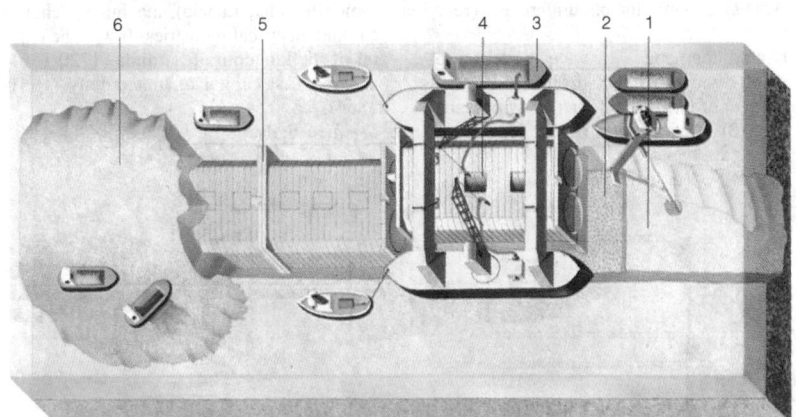

In the immersed-tube method of tunnel construction, first, an underwater trench (1) is dredged and leveled with a sand-aggregate foundation (2). Prefabricated steel or prestressed-concrete tunnel sections are then sealed with temporary bulkheads, floated into position between pontoons (3), and sunk—end to end—into the trench, by filling the ballast tanks (4) with water. Divers will bolt or weld (5) the sections together. The completed tunnel segments are then covered with earth (6), and the bulkheads are removed, to permit fitting out.

T

ployed. Another common tunnel-building method-used in constructing the New York subway-is 'cut-and-cover,' which involves excavating a trench, building the tunnel lining, and then covering it. The world's longest vehicular or railroad tunnel is the 12.3-mi (19.8-km) Simplon II in the Alps, completed in 1922.

Tunney, Gene (James Joseph Tunney; 1898-1978), U.S. world heavyweight boxing champion (1926-1928). In 1926 he beat Jack Dempsey in the controversial fight of the 'long count.' He retired in 1928, having lost only one of his professional bouts.

Tunny *See:* Tuna.

Tupelo, name of several trees belonging to the *Nyssaceae* family, found in Southeast Asia and in North America. The trees produce small white flowers and fruits, which provide food for many species of birds. The wood of the tupelo is used for making boxes, baskets, and other wooden products. The black tupelo, or Blackgum (*Nyssa sylvatica*), is found in moist areas of the United States and in parts of Canada and Mexico. It grows from 35-80 ft (11-24 m) tall. The water tupelo, or sourgum (*N. aquatica*), is found in swamps in the southeastern United States. It grows as tall as 115 ft (35 m).

Tupí-Guaraní, group of Native American tribes from central and eastern South America. The tribes inhabiting Paraguay and southern Brazil are called Guaraní; those in the Amazon Basin are of the Tupí, or Tupinabá, stock. Practitioners of ritual cannibalism in ancient times, they developed into farmers, hunters, fishers, and fruit gatherers. Guaraní is still one of the major languages spoken in Paraguay today.

Turbine, machine for directly converting the kinetic and/or thermal energy of a flowing fluid (air, hot gas, steam, or water) into useful rotational energy. The working fluid either pushes against a set of blades mounted on the drive shaft (impulse turbines) or turns the shaft by reaction when the fluid is expelled from nozzles (or nozzle-shaped vanes) around its circumference (reaction

turbines). Water turbines include the vast inward-flow reaction turbines used in the generation of hydroelectricity and the smaller-scale tangential-flow 'Pelton wheel' impulse types used when exploiting a very great head of water. In the 1800s, Charles Alernon Parsons (1854-1931), a British engineer, designed the first successful steam turbines, having realized that the efficient use of high-pressure steam demanded that its energy be extracted in a multitude of small stages. Steam turbines thus consist of a series of vanes mounted on a rotating drum with sator vanes redirecting the steam in between the moving ones. They are commonly used as marine engines and in thermal and nuclear power plants. Gas turbines are not as yet widely used except in airplanes and for peak-load electricity generation.

Turbojet *See:* Jet propulsion.

Turbot (*Psetta maxima*), large flatfish found in the North Sea and Icelandic waters. It has an almost circular body up to 3 ft (91 cm) long, with a warty upper surface. Its an important food fish in Europe. Two American Pacific flatfish are also known as turbot: the curlfin turbot and the 'C-O' sole.

Turgenev, Ivan (1818-1883), Russian writer whose realistic portrayals of the peasants and nobility of his country helped bring about social reforms and influenced later Russian writers. *A Sportsman's Sketches* (1852), one of his earliest works, is believed to have led to Czar Alexander II's emancipation of the serfs. Other major works include *Rudin* (1856), *A Nest of Gentlefolk* (1859), *On the Eve* (1860), *Fathers and Sons* (1861), *Smoke* (1867), and *Virgin Soil* (1877). Also a playwright, his best-known drama is *A Month in the Country* (1850), which influenced Anton Chekhov. A member of the landowning class who spent much of his time in Western Europe, Turgenev was one of a group of reformers who believed that Russia should adopt some of the best attributes of Western culture.

Turin (pop. 914,000), city in northwestern Italy. It is a major industrial center, with automobile (Fiat, Lancia), machinery, chemical and electrical industries. It was the capital of the kingdom of Sardinia (1720-1861) and the first capital of united Italy (1861-1864).
See also: Italy.

Turkestan, or **Turkistan**, large region in Asia covering parts of China, the former USSR, and Afghanistan. It is so-called because peoples of Turkic ancestry have inhabited this region since the 6th century A.D. From the time of Marco Polo, the area has served as an important trade link between the Asian and European continents. The region, which has no distinct boundaries, has been officially divided into Chinese, Russian, and Afghan Turkestan. Many of the region's people are Muslim.

Turkey

Capital:	Ankara
Area:	300,948 sq mi
	(779,452 sq km)
Population:	67,309,000
Language:	Turkish
Government:	Republic
Independent:	1923
Head of gov.:	Prime minister
Per capita:	US$ 6,700
Monetary unit:	1 Turkish lira or pound =
	100 kurus

Turkey, republic occupying Asia Minor and a small part of southeastern Europe. Lying between the Black and the Mediterranean seas, the Asian and European parts of Turkey are separated by the Straits, a waterway consisting of the Bosporus, the Sea of Marmara, and the Dardanelles. The Straits strategically link the Black Sea with the Mediterranean Sea. Covering 301,382 sq mi (780,574 sq km), Turkey is bounded by Iraq, Syria, and the Mediterranean Sea on the south; the Aegean Sea on the west; Greece and Bulgaria on the north; and Georgia, Armenia, Azerbaijan and Iran in the east. *Land.* Asian Turkey is mountainous inland and has an extensive semiarid plateau giving way to narrow coastal lowlands. Mt. Ararat, at 16,945 ft (5,165 m), is Turkey's highest peak, and the Tigris and Euphrates rivers rise in the east. Earthquakes are frequent. European Turkey, which is actually eastern Thrace, is fertile hill country and the site of the city of Istanbul, formerly Constantinople. The climate is Mediterranean around the coastal lowlands and the European section, but drier and subject to greater extremes inland on the Asian side, with harsh winters toward the northeast.

Here, we can see a typical turbine layout. Steam is heated in a boiler (1), channeled through a high-pressure turbine (2), reheated, then channeled through a medium-pressure turbine (3). A portion of the steam returns to heat the boiler feed water, while the remainder condenses in the low-pressure turbine (4).

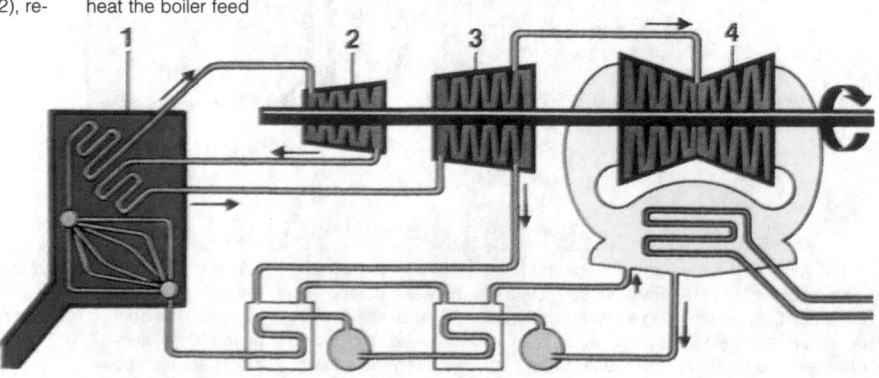

Istanbul, Turkey's largest and commercially most important city, was the capital of the Byzantine and Ottoman empires.

People. The Turks are largely descended from the Tatars, who entered Asia Minor in the 11th century A.D. There are Kurdish, and small Arab and Orthodox Christian minorities. The people are overwhelmingly Muslim (Sunny 70%). The official language is Turkish.

Economy. Agriculture is the basis of the economy. The chief crops are grains, cotton, fruits, and tobacco. Cattle are raised on the Anatolian plateau, in the western reaches of Asian Turkey. Turkish industry has been developed greatly since World War II and includes steel, iron, and textile manufacturers. There are large deposits of coal, iron, and other metals, and some oil.

History. Anatolia was the cradle of ancient civilizations, dating back to at least 7000 B.C. Its famous sites include Troy, Ephesus, and the Hittite capital of Hattusas. Turkey was, successively, part of the Hittite, Persian, Roman, Seljuk, and Ottoman empires. Its western coast was, for a time, the site of some of the most brilliant city-states of the ancient Greeks, including Halicarnassus and Miletus. The Ottoman Empire, with its center in Turkey, was founded in the 13th century and endured until it was formally dissolved after World War I. Modern Turkey was largely the work of Mustafa Kemal Atatürk, who declared the republic in 1923. Atatürk initiated an ambitious program of reform and modernization aimed at establishing Turkey as a modern nation-state on the European model. His reforms ranged from changing the alphabet to emancipating women. Atatürk died in 1938 and Turkey remained neutral for most of World War II. Afterwards, the country joined NATO and received substantial U.S. aid. Turkey has undergone 2 major military coups since the end of World War II, one in 1960 and another in 1980. Tension with Greece has almost led to war on several occasions. In 1974, Turkey invaded and occupied the northern third of the island of Cyprus. The central government has also fought intermittently with Kurds in Anatolia. Civilian rule returned to Turkey in 1983 with the election of Turgut Ozal to the presidency. In 1984 Kurdish separatists began a terrorist campaign against the government. The Turkish military launched reprisal raids throughout Kurdish regions in Turkey and, during the early 1990's, also attacked Kurdish settlements in northern Iraq. In 1996, for the first time in Turkey a Muslim

fundamentalist (Necmettin Erbakan) became prime minister. Entry into the EU became problematic, due to the unfavourable relationship between Turkey and Greece, the human rights situation in Turkey, and Turkey's poor economic situation. In 1999 Abdullah Öcalan, leader of the Turkish-Kurdish Labor Party (PKK), was arrested and sentenced to death by the Turkish government.
The liberal Ahmet Necdet Sezer became President in 2000. His relations with Prime Minister Ecevit became increasingly strained. Parliament adopted several laws, including the abolishment of capital punishment and the introduction of more rights for the Kurdish minority, in order to assist it's effeort to join the EU. Turkey will not know if they are allowed to join the EU until 2004.

Turkey, name of two species of large New World game birds, family Meleagrididae. The common turkey (*Meleagresi gallopavo*) is found in the open woodland and scrub of North America, and is the ancestor of the domestic turkey. The head and neck of both species are naked and have wattles; a fleshy caruncle overhangs the bill. The naked skin in the common turkey is red; in the ocellated turkey, blue.

Turkish, Turkic language, official language of Turkey, also spoken by minorities in eastern Europe and southwestern Asia. Evolved during the Ottoman Empire, it was written in Arabic script until Atatürk introduced a modified Latin alphabet in 1928.

Turkmenistan

Capital:	Ashkhabad
Area:	188,456 sq mi
	(488,100 sq km)
Population:	4,689,000
Language:	Turkmenian
Government:	Presidential republic
Independent:	1991
Head of gov.:	President
Per capita:	US$ 4,700
Monetary unit:	1 Turkmenian manat =
	100 tenge

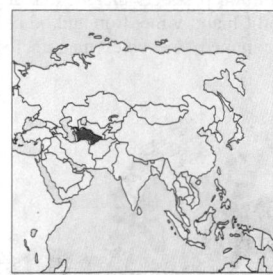

Turkmenistan (Republic of), independent country in central Asia. Covering 303,110 sq mi (488,100 sq km), Turkeminstan is bounded by Kazakhstan and Uzbekistan in the

north, Afghanistan in the southeast, Iran in the south, and the Caspian Sea in the west.
Land and climate. The Kara Kum desert covers about 90% of the landmass in this region. The country has a desert climate with hot summers and cold winters.
People. Most of the population are Muslims, who speak a Turkic language: Turkmen. Russians, Uzbeks, and Kazakhs are important minorities. The majority of the population lives in the southeast, where the capital city of Ashgabat is located.
Economy. The major products are related to their herds of Karakul sheep and Turkoman horses. In spite of the large gas and oil supplies the economy developed slowly in the 1990's.
History. In the late 19th century Turkmenistan came under Russian rule; it became part of the USSR (Soviet Union) in 1921 and a constituent republic in 1925. Turkmenistan declared its sovereignity in 1990 and became fully independent in 1991. Turkmenistan became a member of the Commonwealth of Independent States at the end of 1991. Saparmurad Niyazov became President, while the Democratic Party was the only legal party. Members of the extra-parliamentary opposition were prosecuted; freedom of press was restricted. The Democratic Party won all 50 seats in the 1999 elections. Niyazov was elected President for Life by the Parliament.
See also: Union of Soviet Socialist Republics.

Turks, family to Turkic-speaking, chiefly Muslim people extending from Sinkiang (west China) and Siberia to Turkey, Iran, and former East European USSR. They include the Tatars, Kazakhs, Uzbeks, Kirghiz, Turkmens, Vighurs, Azerbaijanis, and many others. The Turks spread through Asia from the 6th century onward and were converted to Islam in the 10th century. In the west they controlled vast lands under the Seljuks (1000s-1200s) and the Ottoman Empire (1300s-1923).

Turks and Caicos Islands, two British colonial island groups in the West Indies. They cover 166 sq mi (430 sq km) of land in the southeastern part of the Bahama Islands group. The chief economic activity is the exportation of lobster, hemp, and sponges. Many of the region's inhabitants fish for a living.

Turnbull, William (1922-   ), Scottish painter and sculptor. Studied at the Slade School of Art. Apart from his evenly painted canvases, he is chiefly known for his serial compositions and the often vertical piles of balanced convex wooden cylinders. His work, which creates a somewhat totem pole-like impression, is similar to that of Constantin Brancusi.

Turner, Frederick Jackson (1861-1932), U.S. historian. His view of the role of the frontier in shaping U.S. individualism and democracy was influential. *The Frontier in American History* (1920) reprinted earlier papers. He won a Pulitzer Prize for his study of sectionalism in the United States (1932).

Turner, John Napier (1929-), prime minister of Canada following the resignation of Prime Minister Pierre Trudeau. In 1984, after having served 2 1/2 months, Turner called a general election and lost to Progressive Conservative candidate Brian Mulroney. Turner had previously held a variety of posts in the cabinets of prime ministers Lester Pearson and Pierre Trudeau. A Liberal Party member, he was interested in developing social programs to help the nation's poor and unemployed.
See also: Canada.

Turner, J(oseph) M(allard) W(illiam) (1775-1851), English Romantic landscape painter. His work is famous for its rich treatment of light and atmosphere, in oil, watercolor, or engraving. His paintings include *The Fighting Téméraire* (1839) and *Rain, Steam and Speed* (1844).

Turner, Nat (1800-1831), U.S. slave and revolutionary. He believed that God had chosen him to free the slaves. He led what came to be known as the most serious slave rebellion in the nation's history. The militia suppressed the revolt 6 weeks later, capturing and hanging Turner and about 20 of his followers. Although the rebellion led to reprisals and stricter laws against slaves, Turner became a symbol for the abolitionist movement.

Turnip, plant (genus *Brassica*) native to Europe and Asia. It was developed into a root crop, mainly for cattle feed, in the 19th century. Its swollen, yellowish-white taproot is packed with starch and is fit for human consumption. If left in the ground over the winter, the turnip sends up a flowering stem, using food stored in the root during its first year.
See also: Starch.

Turnstone, one of two types of shore birds belonging to the sandpiper family. It characteristically uses its short bill to turn over stones in search of food. The ruddy turnstone is found in arctic regions of the world. The black turnstone is native to the Bering Sea region and migrates to southern Alaska and California for the winter.

Turtles had already developed their defensive hard shell, into which head and legs can be withdrawn, by the time of the dinosaurs. (A) The shell (1) consists of keratin plates fused to the backbone (2) and ribs (3). Ornamental tortoiseshell is obtained from the horny shell of the hawksbill turtle (*Eretmochelys imbricata*).

Turquoise, $AL_2(OH)_3PO_4H_2O+Cu$, igneous (volcanic) mineral containing aluminum, copper, and phosphorus, found in arid regions of the earth, especially Iran, the Sinai Peninsula, and the North American Southwest. Varying in color from light blue (gem quality) to greenish-gray, turquoise has been used to make jewelry for thousands of years. Native American tribes of the Southwest, especially the Navajos, became skilled in fashioning turquoise-and-silver jewelry.

Turtle, reptile (order *Chelonia*) with a shell that almost encloses the body. A land turtle is sometimes called a tortoise, and some freshwater turtles are given the name terrapin. The turtle has existed for more than 175 million years, and there are now about 230 species spread over the warmer parts of the world, 44 of them in the United States. Some species are becoming rare because they are hunted for their flesh or for their shells. The turtle's shell is made of two parts-the upper carapace and the lower plastron. The vertebrae and ribs are fused to the carapace. The shell is covered with horny plates, except in the soft-shell and the leathery turtle, where it has a leathery covering. There are five kinds of marine turtles: the leathery turtle and the green, hawksbill, loggerhead, and ridley turtles. Except for the last, all are found in North American waters. All come ashore to lay their eggs in sandy beaches: Freshly hatched turtles have to rush down to the shore after hatching to avoid predators. The green turtle is the species most used for turtle soup, and the hawksbill provides tortoise shells. The land and freshwater turtles are smaller than the marine turtles. They range from 2-in (5-cm) mud turtles to the 2-ft (61-cm) 100-lb (45-kg) alligator snapping turtle or 'stinkpot', the reptilian equivalent of the skunk. The box turtles have a hinged plastron so that they can completely shut themselves in their shells.

Turtledove, woodland bird belonging to the pigeon and dove family. It is native to Europe and parts of Asia and Africa. During the winter, it migrates south to the sub-Saharan continent. A small, shy bird, it is often recognized by its sad, cooing song.

Tuscany, region in west-central Italy, extending from the Apennine Mountains to the west coast. It is mostly mountainous, with fertile river valleys and coastal strip. Agricultural products include cereals, olive oil, and Chianti wine. Iron and other minerals are mined; the chief manufactures are textiles, chemicals, and machinery. Center of the ancient Etruscan civilization, Tuscany has many famous cities, including Florence, Lucca, Pisa, and Siena.

Tussock moth, type of moth belonging to the Lymantriidae family. Caterpillars of the species have brightly colored hair, but adults are whitish-gray in color. Some varieties, such as the gypsy moth, were brought to the United States from Europe. Tussock moths often cause extensive damage to trees and orchards.

Tutankhamen (fl.c.1350 B.C.), Egyptian pharaoh. Though he died at 18, he gained modern-day fame when his tomb was discovered in Thebes by Howard Carter and the earl of Carnarvon in 1922 with its treasures intact. His solid gold coffin, gold portrait mask, and other treasures are housed in the Cairo museum.

Tuttle, Richard (1941-), American artist. In the 1970s he made reliefs out of wood with a saw, trying to achieve the representation of a natural - albeit somewhat symbolic - state of affairs. His later work went more in the direction of the so-called 'shaped canvas', in which he preferred to present the material as irregularly and shapeless as possible. This almost 'unshaped canvas' can be considered as minimal art.

Tutu, Desmond (1931-), South African black minister, recipient of the 1984 Nobel Peace Prize. In 1957 Tutu was named the first black Anglican dean of Johannesburg. In 1978 he was appointed general secretary of the South African Council of Churches, elected bishop of Johannesburg in 1984, and archbishop of Cape Town in 1986. He has been a consistent opponent of apartheid. In 1995, he became chairman of the Commission for Truth and Reconciliation, which investigated violations of human rights during the apartheid era.

Tutuila *See:* American Samoa.

Tuur, Regilio Benito (1967-), Dutch boxer, made a first impression during the Olympic games of 1988 in Seoul, when he knocked out the reigning world champion Kelcie Banks in the first round. He then moved to New York, where he became a hardened professional. In 1993 he won his first international title: the European super featherweight championship. Two years later Tuur became the first Dutch boxer to win a world title. He beat his challenger, the American Eugene Speed, in the Ahoy sports center in Rotterdam for the World Boxing Organization world title. Tuur went on to successfully defend his title several times. His entourage of manager, trainers and attendants became known as 'Tuur on Tour'. Tuur ended his career in 1997, but made a comeback in 2001.

Tuva, republic of the Russian Federation between Siberia and Mongolia. Formerly a Russian protectorate, the region became the autonomous republic of Tannu Tuva in 1921. In 1944, it was annexed by the USSR and its name changed to Tuva. Most of the region's inhabitants are descended from Turkic-speaking peoples and raise animals for a living. Tuva exports animal hides and wool; its mineral resources include gold, asbestos, and cobalt.

See also: Union of Soviet Socialist Republics.

Tuvalu

Capital:	Vaiaku
Area:	10 sq mi (26 sq km)
Population:	11,100
Language:	Tuvaluan
Government:	Parliamentary monarchy in the British Commonwealth
Independent:	1978
Head of gov.:	Prime minister
Per capita:	US$ 1,100
Monetary unit:	1 Australian dollar = 100 cents

Tuvalu (formerly Ellice Islands), independent Commonwealth nation composed of nine small atolls spread over more than 500,000 sq mi (1,295,000 sq km) in the West Pacific. The capital is Fongafale on Funafuti. *Land and climate.* The largest island, Vaitupu, covers only 2 sq mi (5.2 sq km). No spot on these coral atolls rises more than 16 ft (4.9 m) above sea level. The soil is poor and there are no rivers and little vegetation besides coconut palms. The average annual temperature is 86°F (30°C); most of the rainfall occurs between Nov. and Feb.
People and economy. The inhabitants are Polynesian, with almost 30% living on the island of Funafuti. Copra is the only export, although the sale of postage stamps abroad also produces income.
History. The islands were largely ignored by Europeans until the 19th century, when whaling began in the area. The population was reduced from 22,000 to 3,000 between 1850 and 1875 because of disease and forcible recruitment for labor abroad. A British protectorate over both the Ellice and Gilbert (now Kiribati) islands was established in 1892. In 1974 Ellice Islanders voted for separate status, achieving independence of Tuvalu in 1978, followed by Kiribati in 1979. That same year, Tuvalu signed a friendship treaty with the U.S., who abandoned their claim to the four southern islands. Tuvalu, Kiribati and the U.S. signed

an agreement in 1983 that included the regulation of territorial waters between Kiribati and Tuvalu. The new flag was presented in 1995.

TV *See:* Television.

TVA *See:* Tennessee Valley Authority.

Twain, Mark (Samuel Langhorne Clemens; 1835-1910), U.S. author and popular humorist and lecturer. After being a printer's apprentice (1848-1853), he led a wandering life, becoming a Mississippi river pilot (1857-1861) and then a journalist, establishing a reputation with his humorous sketches. In 1869 he produced his first best-seller, *The Innocents Abroad*, followed by *The Adventures of Tom Sawyer* (1876), *The Prince and the Pauper* (1882), his masterpiece *Huckleberry Finn* (1884), and the satirical *A Connecticut Yankee in King Arthur's Court* (1889). In later life, Twain lost most of his money through speculation and suffered the loss of his wife and daughters. His works became increasingly pessimistic and bitingly satirical, as in *The Tragedy of Pudd'nhead Wilson* (1894) and *The Man Who Corrupted Hadleyburg* (1899).

Tweed River, waterway forming part of the Scotland-England border. It rises in southeastern Scotland and flows into the North Sea. In the 19th century, mills were built along the river to produce water power for local textile factories. The name of the cloth known as tweed may come from the name of the river.

Twelve Tables, Laws of the, earliest Roman code of laws. Created by decemvirs (members of a council of 10 men) who based the laws on earlier Roman customs, the Laws of the Twelve Tables were written on tablets (450 B.C.) and displayed in the forum. They contained civil, criminal, and sacred legal precepts and became revered as a prime source of law. Only fragments survive.
See also: Rome, Ancient.

Twelve-tone music, or serial music, type of music developed in the 1920s that rejects tonality as the basis for composition. Its most famous exponent, Arnold Schoenberg, laid down a method of composition that attempted to free music from the 8-note octave and its associated conventions. Twelve-tone compositions are constructed around a specific series of the twelve notes of the chromatic scale. Later 20th-century composers have used the twelve-tone construction with greater freedom. Composers of twelve-tone music include Igor Stravinsky, Roger Sessions, Walter Piston, Ernst Krenek, Domitry Shostakovich, and Schoenberg's pupils Anton von Webern and Alban Berg.

Twelve Tribes, twelve family groups into which the ancient Hebrews were divided. According to the Bible they were descended from and named for ten sons of Jacob and two sons of Joseph. Those descended from Jacob's sons were Asher, Benjamin, Dan, Gad, Issachar, Judah, Naphtali, Reuben,

Simeon, and Zebulun; the two from Joseph's sons were Ephraim and Manasseh. When the Hebrews finally reached the Promised Land, they divided the country among these twelve family groups. A thirteenth tribe, Levi, third son of Jacob, had no portion of land set aside for it.

Tyler, John (1790-1862), 10th president of the United States (1841-1845). A political conservative, Tyler believed in a narrow interpretation of the Constitution, and that the powers of the federal government should be strictly limited. When William Henry Harrison became president, Tyler was elected vice-president. Within a month after the inauguration in 1841, however, Harrison died and Tyler became president. It was the first time a U.S. vice president succeeded a president in office.
Tyler soon angered his Whig supporters. When the Whigs presented a nationalist program, including a National Bank, Tyler vetoed the bill. When he vetoed another bill in September, his entire cabinet, except Secretary of State Daniel Webster, resigned. Tyler was expelled from the Whig party and there was an unsuccessful attempt to impeach him.

Tyler, Wat (d. 1381), leader of the English Peasant's Revolt (1381), England's first popular rebellion. Protesting high taxation after the Black Death, Tyler and his Kentish followers captured Canterbury, then took the Tower of London. Richard II promised abolition of serfdom and feudal service. At a second meeting with the king, Tyler was stabbed, and the revolt was brutally crushed.

Tylor, Sir Edward Burnett (1832-1917), British anthropologist. A pioneer in the field, he was an authority on animism and primitive mentality. His books *Research into the Early History of Mankind* (1865) and *Primitive Culture* (1871) were among the earliest works on anthropology as a social science. Additional theories were expounded in *Anthropology* (1881).
See also: Anthropology.

Tyndale, William (c.1494-1536), English biblical translator. A Roman Catholic priest, he translated the New Testament from Greek and Hebrew to the English vernacular in his effort to stem church corruption, but he was unable to get his work published in England. He was strongly influenced by Martin Luther. In 1535 he was arrested by Roman Catholic authorities in Antwerp, Belgium, tried and convicted of heresy, and the following year was executed. His translations form the basis of the King James (Authorized) Version of the Bible, which is in common usage today.
See also: Bible.

Type, characters, including letters, numbers, and punctuation marks, assembled to form words and sentences in the printing of books, magazines, and newspapers. Type consists of thousands of styles, or type faces (fonts), that fall into 4 categories: Roman type, with small finishing strokes (serifs) that extend outward from the characters; sans-serif type, lacking the serifs; script type, which closely

T

resembles actual handwriting; and italic type, which is slanted to the right. Type size is measured by 'points' in North America and England. One point equals 0.012837 in (0.3514598 mm) and most type ranges from 6 to 72 points. Movable type was invented in Asia in the 11th century and was introduced to Europe by Johannes Gutenberg in the 1440s. Type was later cast in lead and set by hand or machine. Today most type is set on computers programmed for correct size, style, and line width.
See also: Printing.

Typewriter, writing machine activated manually or electrically by means of a keyboard. In the classic model, when a key is depressed, a pivoted bar bearing a type character strikes an inked ribbon against a sheet of paper carried on a cylindrical rubber 'platen.' The platen carriage then automatically moves a space to the left. In some electric models all type is carried on a single rotatable sphere that moves from left to right and strikes a fixed platen. The first efficient typewriter was developed in 1868 by C.L. Sholes.
See also: Sholes, Christopher Latham.

Typhoid fever, infectious disease due to *Salmonella typhosa*, causing fever, a characteristic rash, lymph node and spleen enlargement, gastrointestinal tract disturbance with bleeding and ulceration, and usually marked malaise or prostration. It is contracted from other cases or from disease carriers, with contaminated food and water as major vectors. Carriers must be treated with antibiotics (and have their gall bladder removed if this site is the source). Vaccination may help protect high-risk persons; antibiotics (e.g., chloramphenicol) form the treatment of choice.

Typhus, infectious disease caused by rickettsia and carried by lice, leading to a feverish illness with a rash. Severe headache typically precedes the rash, which may progress to skin hemorrhage; mild respiratory symp-toms of cough and breathlessness are common. Death ensues in a high proportion of untreated adults, usually with profound shock and kidney failure. Recurrences may occur in untreated patients who recover from their first attack, often after many years. A similar disease due to a different but related organism is carried by fleas (murine typhus). Chloramphenicol or tetracyclines provide suitable antibiotic therapy.

Tyrannosaurus *See:* Dinosaur; Prehistoric animal.

Tyre, or Sur (pop. 23,000), town in southwest Lebanon, situated on the eastern end of the Mediterranean Sea. A thriving seaport under the Phoenicians, Tyre was ruled by Egypt before 1000 B.C. From 1100 to 573 B.C. it enjoyed its most prosperous period, which included the founding of Carthage (9th century), and was a major cultural, intellectual, and commercial center, famous for its purple dye and high-quality ceramics. In 332 B.C. Alexander the Great conquered Tyre and built a causeway that connected what was then the island of Tyre to the mainland, creating a peninsula, site of the present-day city of Tyre. The city later fell under the control of the Roman and Byzantine empires and was captured by the Crusaders in 1124, before being overrun and destroyed by the Muslims in 1291. Tyre was taken by Israeli forces in 1982 during their invasion of Lebanon.

Tyrol, or Tirol, state in western Austria. Over half its original area was ceded to Italy in 1919. Austria's highest peak, Grossglockner (12,461 ft/3,798 km), is located there. Farming, lumber, and tourism are its main sources of income. The capital is Innsbruck.

Tyrrhenian Sea, part of the Mediterranean Sea bounded by the west coast of Italy and by the islands of Corsica, Sardinia, and Sicily. The Strait of Messina in the south connects it with the Ionian Sea.

Tyson, Mike (1966-), American boxer, won the heavyweight world championship at the young age of 20, knocking out Trevor Berbick. Tyson successfully defended his world title against Larry Holmes, Michael Spinks and the British Frank Bruno, but lost it to James Buster Douglas in 1990. From 1992 until 1995 Tyson served a prison sentence for rape. Several months after his release Tyson returned to the ring. While in prison he converted to Islam and now calls himself Malik Abdul Aziz. Within 89 seconds he knocked down his opponent Peter 'Hurricane' McNeely twice. In 1996 Tyson beat the WBC champion Frank Bruno by knocking him out in the third round. Later that year he lost his WBA title to Evander Holyfield. During the rematch in 1997 Tyson was disqualified because he bit off part of Holyfield's right ear. In 1999 he was imprisoned again, this time for assault.

Tzara, Tristan (1886-1963), Romanian artist, Dadaist. Known for his absurd, aggressive-destructive happenings.

U, 21st letter of the English alphabet, corresponding to the Semitic letter *waw*, meaning 'hook,' represented by a tenthook symbol and probably derived from an ancient Egyptian symbol for a pole support. The Greeks altered it to *Y*, and as the 20th letter of the Roman alphabet it became *V*, representing both *U* and *V* sounds. The use of *U* for the *U* sound dates from the Middle Ages. *U* is also the chemical symbol for the element uranium.

U-2, U.S. spy plane used during the 1950s and 1960s. The U-2 was effective because it could fly at extremely high altitudes of 70,000 ft (21,100 m) and photograph military installations on the ground. It became the focus of international attention when a U-2 was shot down while flying over the USSR in 1960, at the height of the Cold War between the United States and the USSR.
See also: Cold War.

U2, Irish rock act, founded in 1978. Members are Bono (b. Paul Hewson; lead singer), The Edge (b. Dave Evans; guitar), Adam Clayton (bass) and Larry Mullen (drums). Their debut album *Boy* (1980) contained the first of their dramatic and passionate songs which would make them one of the most successful and popular bands ever. Their next albums were traditional to begin with, but became more experimental, without losing their identity. Other important albums are *The Unforgettable Fire* (1984), *The Joshua Tree* (1987), *Achtung Baby* (1991), *Pop* (1997) and *All That You Can't Leave Behind* (2001).

U-235, any of the different forms of an isotope of the element uranium with a mass number of 235 (the number of protons and neutrons in the atom's nucleus). When found in minerals, U-235 is always combined with the isotopes U-234 and U-238. Separating the natural U-235 from the other isotopes produces a more potent form of U-235, which is used in atomic bombs and nuclear reactors because it easily undergoes fission. The use of U-235 in nuclear reactors pro-

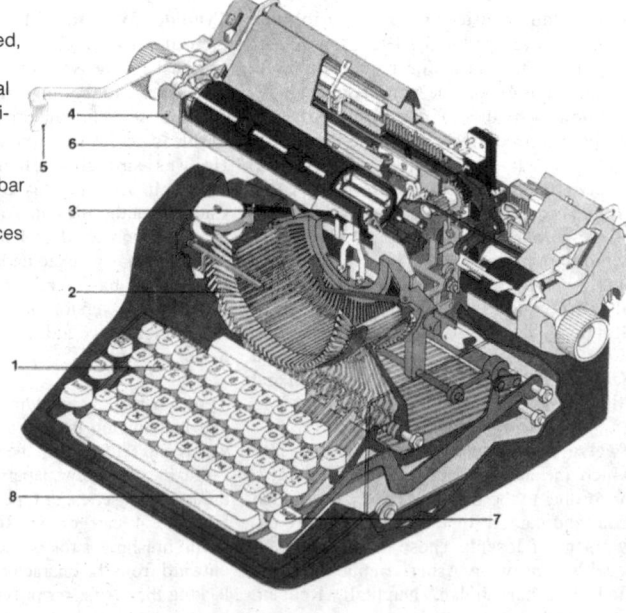

This cutaway drawing illustrates the parts of a manual typewriter. A typist depresses a key (1), which by a lever system causes a type bar (2) to lift. The type bar presses against an inked ribbon (3) to print a letter, number, or punctuation mark on a piece of paper. As a letter is typed, the carriage (4) moves to the left. At the end of the line, the typist pushes the carriage-return lever (5) to move the carriage to the right and roll the platen (6) so that a new line can be typed. When the shift key (7) is depressed, the type bars are lowered and capital letters or signs indicated above the number keys are typed. The space bar (8) moves the carriage to allow spaces between words.

duces extremely toxic isotopes of other elements, such as strontium 90. U-235 was used in the atomic bombs that the United States dropped on Hiroshima and Nagasaki, Japan, in 1945.
See also: Nuclear energy; Radioactivity.

U-238 *See:* Uranium.

U.A.R. *See:* United Arab Republic.

Ubangi River, chief northern tributary of the Zaïre (Congo) River, in central Africa. Formed by the junction of the Mbomu and Uele rivers, it flows 700 mi (1,130 km) west and south, forming part of Zaïre's northwest border with the Central African Republic.

U-boat *See:* Submarine.

Ucayali River, chief headstream of the Amazon, in northern Peru. Formed by the junction of the Urubamba and Apurímac rivers in central Peru, it flows 1,000 mi (1,600 km) north to the Marañón River southwest of Iquitos.
See also: Amazon River.

Uccello, Paolo (c.1397-1475), Florentine early Renaissance painter, noted for his use of perspective. His best-known works are the *Creation* and *Noah* scenes (1431-50) in Santa Maria Novella, Florence, and the three richly decorative panels of *The Battle of San Romano* (1455-1460).
See also: Renaissance.

Udaipur (pop. 308,000), city in the Indian state of Rajasthan, situated in the southern foothills of the Aravalli mountain range; district of the same name (pop. 2,900,000). Agricultural trading center (cotton, grain) with various industries. Situated near the artificial Pichola Lake (irrigation); many beautiful gardens, temples and palaces, including the palace of the Maharaja (1570). From 1568-1948 capital of the Udaipur principality.

Udall, Nicolas (1505-1556), English schoolmaster, scholar, and playwright. Headmaster of Eton (1534-1541) and of Westminster (1554-1556), he wrote the first known English comedy, *Ralph Roister Doister* (c. 1553).

Udmurtia (pop. 1,641,000), Russian district along the river Kama; 16,261 sq mi (42,100 sq km). Capital, Izhevsk. Heavily industrialized (machine, car, cement industries). The arms industry is also important in the republic, making SS-20 and SS-25 cruise missiles, and the Kalashnikov assault rifles. Agriculture in the south (grain, cattle). Populated by Finnish-Urgric Udmurts (34%), Tatars (10%) and Russians (56%; 1989 figures). A large part of the Udmurts has assimilated the Russian culture: they no longer speak Udmurts. In the course of the 15th and 16th centuries Russia established its control over the Udmurts. In 1920 the area became an autonomous region, and in 1934 an Autonomous Soviet Socialist Republic within the Russian part of the Soviet Union. Since 1991 Udmurtia is a republic within the Russian Federation.

Ufa (pop. 1,1 million), city in Russia in the Ural Mountains, capital of the Bashkir Republic. Oil refinery, petrochemicals, metal, electrical equipment and light industries. Nuclear power stations. University (1957). Railway junction; airport. Founded in 1574.

Uffizi Palace, 16th-century palace in Florence, Italy, built by Giorgio Vassari for Cosimo I de' Medici as a public office building. It houses one of the world's finest art collections, rich in classical, Dutch, Flemish, and Italian Renaissance paintings and sculptures.
See also: Florence.

UFO *See:* Unidentified flying object.

Uganda

Capital:	Kampala
Area:	93,070 sq mi (241,139 sq km)
Population:	24,699,000
Language:	English, Swahili
Government:	Presidential republic
Independent:	1962
Head of gov.:	Prime minister
Per capita:	US$ 1,200
Monetary unit:	1 Uganda shilling = 100 cents

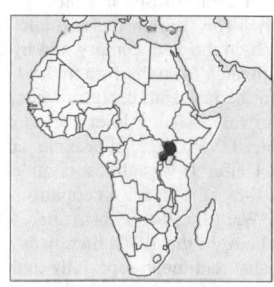

Uganda, landlocked republic in east-central Africa. Covering 93,070 sq mi (241,040 sq km), Uganda is bordered by Tanzania and Rwanda in the south, Sudan in the north, Congo in the west, and Kenya in the east.

Land and People. More than 80% of the land area of Uganda consists of a fertile plateau some 3,000 to 5,000 ft (914-1,524 m) above sea level, with highlands to the east and west. About 16,386 sq mi (42,440 sq km) of Uganda consists of freshwater lakes and swamps. At the center of the plateau that dominates the country is Lake Kyoga. Other lakes are lakes Edward, Albert, George, and Victoria. Although Uganda is a tropical country, crossed by the equator, its altitude ensures a comparatively mild climate. Almost all Ugandans are black Africans, the majority belonging to one of several Bantu-speaking groups. The Baganda people of the south are the most numerous of these. About two-third of the people are Christians, with a small minority of Muslims; the rest of the people adhere to animist beliefs. The official languages are English and Swahili.
Economy. Uganda's economy is agricultural and most farms are small, growing subsistence crops and raising livestock. Despite severe economic dislocation under Idi Amin Dada, Uganda remained one of the world's major producers of coffee, which accounts for almost all of its export earnings. Copper is the principal mineral.
History. The Bunyoro Kingdom of Bantu-speaking people that flourished in the 16th and 17th centuries and dominated Uganda was succeeded by the Buganda Kingdom, which came under the British in 1894. The British protectorate was gradually extended to other kingdoms, and by 1914 the present boundaries of Uganda became fixed. In 1962, Uganda became independent and was governed by Milton Obote until he was deposed by Maj. Gen. Idi Amin Dada in 1971. In 1972, Amin expelled Uganda's Asian population and established a brutal and bizarre reign of terror that cost some 300,000 Ugandans their lives and brought the nation to near total ruin. In 1979, Tanzania invaded Uganda and Idi Amin fled. By 1980, Milton Obote had been returned to power only to be replaced, 5 years later, by Gen. Tito Okello. Okello was overthrown by the National Resistance Army (NRA) of Yoweri Museveni, who was sworn in as president in 1986. He pursued reconciliation and national unity. At the end of the 1980s, peace was restored somewhat and there was some economical recovery. In 1996 Museveni was elected president in the country's first direct elections for that office. At

Kampala, the capital of independent Uganda, was once the capital of the kingdom of Buganda. It also served as the administrative and commercial center of Uganda during British colonial rule.

U

U

the end of the 1990s, Ugandan troops were involved in armed conflicts in southern Africa, including Sudan and Rwanda. Uganda terminated all relations with Sudan, because it supported the Lord Resistance Movement, a northern guerrilla army that fights against the Museveni movement. Relations with Rwanda worsened when Uganda became involved in the Rwandan civil war in 1992. The war spread to the south of Uganda. In 2001, Museveni was re-elected President.

Ugarit, ancient capital city of the Ugarit Kingdom of northwestern Syria, discovered in 1929 by French archeologists. Settled in the 5th millennium B.C., it flourished in the 15th and 14th centuries B.C. Numerous cuneiform tablets have revealed much information about the Ugarit language, related to biblical Hebrew.

UHF waves *See:* Ultrahigh frequency waves.

Ujung Pandang (pop. 950,000), Indonesia, the capital of South Sulawesi province, on Celebes island. It was formerly called Makassar. It is a port on the Makassar Strait, about 500 miles (800 km) east-northeast of Surabaya, Java. Coffee, copra, and spieces are exported. Hasanuddin University is here. The Dutch controlled Ujung Pandang from 1668 until 1950, except during World War II when Indonesia was occupied by the Japanese.

Ukraine

Capital:	Kiev
Area:	233,090 sq mi
	(603,700 sq km)
Population:	48,396,000
Language:	Ukrainian
Government:	Republic
Independent:	1991
Head of gov.:	Prime minister
Per capita:	US$ 4,200
Monetary unit:	1 Hryvna = 100 kopiykas

Ukraine (Republic of), independent country in Eastern Europe, bordered by Poland to the northwest; by Slovakia, Hungary, Romania, and Moldova to the southwest; by the Black Sea and the Sea of Azov to the south; by

St. Andre Church in Kiev, the capital of Ukraine.

Russia to the northeast and east; and by Belarus to the north.

Land and climate. Ukraine consists for a large part of lowlands, with mountains on the Crimean and in the west: the Carpathian Mountains. The country has a moderate continental climate, with a subtropical climate in the Crimean peninsula.

People. About 75% of the population is Ukrainian, and Russians form the largest minority. The official language is Ukrainian. The population belongs to either the Ukrainian Orthodox Church or the Greek Orthodox Church.

Economy. The economy is based on heavy industry. Principal crops are sugar beets and potatoes. Important industrial cities include Kharkov, Donetsk, and Dnepropetrovsk. The chief Black Sea port is Odessa. Ukraine owns a number of nuclear plants; the explosion in the Chernobyl plant (1986) was the biggest nuclear disaster in history.

History. The region was ruled by the Mongols in the 13th century and by Poland and Lithuania from the 14th to the 17th century. In the late 18th century it came under Russian rule. After a brief period of independence (1918-1922), it became part of the Soviet Union. It was almost completely destroyed by the Nazi occupation during World War II (1941-1944), after which it was rebuilt. In the 1980s there was a rise in nationalist sentiment, especially in the western Ukraine. Together with the collapse of communism this resulted in independence in 1991. During 1992-1994 Ukraine encountered many economic and political problems. The country suffered from a declining standard of living mainly owing to a high rate of inflation and widespread shortages of consumer goods. Relations with Russia during this period were strained because of a dispute concerning ownership of the former Soviet Black Sea fleet, which was based in Crimea. Ukraine also faced increasing political unrest, mainly among ethnic Russians in Crimea and eastern Ukraine. In 1994 relations with countries in the West were strengthened when Ukraine signed the Nuclear Nonproliferation Treaty, promising to relinquish all of its nuclear weapons. Also that year Ukraine held its first post-Soviet parliamentary elections; a plurality of seats were won by the Communist Party and parties allied with the Communists. Leonid Koetsjma was elected President. Tensions between Ukraine and Russia were eased in 1997 when both countries agreed to divide the Black Sea fleet and Ukraine agreed to

sell most of its portion to Russia. Koetsjma was re-elected President in 1999. The Ukraine has sought contact with the NATO and the EU since 2001. The NATO and the EU made it clear in 2002 that further political and economical reforms are necessary before Ukraine will be able to join the NATO or the EU.
See also: Union of Soviet Socialist Republics.

Ukranian, East Slavic language of the Slavonic group, closely related to Russian, from which it diverged c.1200. Written in a modified Cyrillic alphabet, it emerged as a literary language in the 18th century. It is the official language of the Ukraine.

Ukulele, small guitarlike instrument. Modeled after a small guitar of Portuguese origin, the ukulele became popular in Hawaii during the late 19th century. It was widely used throughout the United States and Europe in jazz bands and as accompaniment in folk songs.

Ulan Bator (pop. 753,000), capital and largest city of Mongolia. Located in the northeastern part of Mongolia along the Tuul Gol River, the city developed around a famous Buddhist monastery built in 1639. For years it served as an important trade center along a route between Russia and China. The city was known as Urga and Niislel Khureheh until it was renamed in 1924 in honor of the famous Soviet revolutionary leader Sukhe Bator. Today, Ulan Bator is Mongolia's cultural and industrial center. It is the home of the Mongolian State University and a science academy. Meat packing is an important industry along with the manufacture of furniture, textiles, and pharmaceutical products.
See also: Mongolia.

Ulanova, Galina (1910-1998), Russian prima ballerina of the Bolshoi Theater, Moscow (1944-1962). She excelled as a dramatic and lyric dancer, notably in Tchaikovsky's *Swan Lake* and Prokofiev's *Romeo and Juliet.*

Ulan Ude (pop. 359,000), city in Russia, capital of Buryatia. Foodstuffs, textile, glass and construction materials industries. Reparation of rolling stock and shipbuilding. Lies on the Trans-Siberian railway.

Ulbricht, Walter (1893-1973), leader of

post-World War II East Germany. A founding member (1918) of the German Communist Party, he spent 1933-1945 in exile in the USSR. He became first deputy premier (1949) and head of state (1960-1973) of the German Democratic Republic. An uncompromising Stalinist, he headed the Socialist Unity Party from 1950 until his replacement (1971) by Erich Honecker. He ordered the building of the Berlin Wall (1961) and had Eastern German troops participate in the invasion of Czechoslovakia, in 1968.
See also: Germany.

Ulcer, pathological defect in skin or mucous membrane caused by inflammation due to infection, loss of blood supply, failure of venous circulation, or cancer. Peptic, gastric, and duodenal ulcers may cause pain or acute hemorrhage, and may lead to perforation and peritonitis. Antacids usually provide effective treatment.

Ullrich, Jan (1973-), German cyclist, became road race amateur world champion in 1993. The following year, still as an amateur, he was third in the combined amateur-professional world championship time trials. In 1995 he joined the German Telekom professional cycling team, and the same year he became German time trial champion. His second German title was the road race championship in 1997. In the 1996 Tour de France he achieved international recognition for his second place behind team leader Bjarne Riis. In 1997 Ullrich became the first German ever to win the Tour de France. The following year he once again finished second in the Tour behind the Italian Marco Pantani. At the 2001 Olympics in Sydney, he won the gold medal for the road race. In 2001, he was runner-up in the Tour De France, after Lance Armstrong.

Ultima Thule, ancient Greek and Roman name for lands of the far north. Scholars believe that the Greek term referred to Norway, Iceland, and possibly the Shetland Islands. The Greek sailor Pytheas mentions the icy waters and long nights and days of a region he reached sometime during the 4th century B.C., but the location is not specified.

Ultrahigh frequency waves (UHF), radio waves with frequencies from 300 to 3,000 megahertz (1 megahertz equals 1 million cycles per second) and with short ranges, usually less than 50 mi (80 km). They are used primarily for television broadcasting, but are also used for air and naval navigation, for police radios, and for tracking spacecraft.
See also: Short waves.

Ultramicroscope, special microscope used for studying colloidal particles (particles in solution or suspension) too small to be seen with a regular-light microscope. A high intensity light beam originates not from the bottom of the instrument as with an ordinary microscope, but from the side. As this beam passes through the solution or suspension, the colloidal particles scatter the light, producing tiny dots of light that then can be seen against a dark background. The ultramicroscope, however, cannot provide the

viewer with any structural detail of the particles.
See also: Microscope.

Ultrasonics, science of sound waves with frequencies above those that humans can hear (above 20,000 cycles per second). Modern piezoelectric techniques generate ultrasonic waves with frequencies above 24,000 cycles per second. These exhibit the normal wave properties of reflection, refraction, and diffraction, and are used to clean fine machine parts and, in medicine, to examine internal organs non-surgically.

Ultraviolet rays, invisible light lying beyond the violet end of the spectrum. It is produced naturally by the sun and lightning. Prolonged exposure to the sun's ultraviolet rays can result in sunburn and over a period of years, can cause skin cancer. Plants and animals are partially protected from the sun's ultraviolet rays by ozone, a form of oxygen formed in the upper atmosphere. Ultraviolet rays can, however, be beneficial. They are used by physicians to destroy some bacteria and viruses and by food manufacturers to disinfect food containers. Special lamps that produce ultraviolet rays have been successfully used to treat acne and other skin disorders.

Ulysses, or Odysseus, legendary hero of ancient Greece, son and successor of King Laertes of Ithaca, and husband of Penelope. He was the crafty counselor of the Trojan War (described in Homer's *Iliad*) and the subject of Homer's *Odyssey*, a recount of 10 years of adventures and obstacles faced by Ulysses in his effort to return home after the war.

Umbilical cord, in mammals, tubelike structure linking the developing embryo, or fetus, to the placenta through most of pregnancy. It consists of blood vessels that carry blood to and from the placenta, along with a gelatinous matrix. In humans, the cord is clamped at birth to prevent blood loss. It undergoes atrophy and its remains become the navel.

Umbrellabird, any of several crowlike birds (genus *Cephalopterus*) of tropical American forests, especially *C. ornatus*, whose crest can be expanded into an 'umbrella.' It also has a lappet of feathers hanging from the throat.

UN *See:* United Nations.

Unamuno, Miguel de (1864-1936), Spanish philosopher and writer, rector of Salamanca University from 1900 to his death. Influenced by Kierkegaard, he explored the faith-reason conflict and the desire for immortality in *The Tragic Sense of Life in Men and Nations* (1913) and in essays and novels, such as *Mist* (1914). 'The Christ of Velázquez' (1920) is his best-known poem.
See also: Philosophy.

Uncle Sam, popular figure developed by 19th-century cartoonists and officially adopted as a U.S. national symbol in 1961.

Uncle Sam is the widely recognized symbol for the United States. First created by cartoonists in the 1800s, Uncle Sam changed from a character of derision to one of respectability.

He is portrayed as a white-haired, bearded gentleman dressed in the Stars and Stripes. The name possibly derives from Samuel 'Uncle Sam' Wilson, an inspector of Army supplies in Troy, N.Y., during the War of 1812.

Unconscious, in psychology, that part of the mind the individual is unable to recall at will. The concept of the unconscious, or subconscious, was developed and studied by Sigmund Freud, the founder of psychoanalysis. He believed the unconscious included instinctual drives and repressed memory and desires. To this foundation of belief, C.G. Jung added the idea that there is also a collective unconscious, universal or cultural mental patterns and acts.
See also: Freud, Sigmund.

Unctad (United Nations Conference on Trade and Development), permanent organization of the United Nations, founded to promote the economic interests of developing nations, particularly in relation to the trade in natural resources. Any decisions taken are not binding; the Unctad is more of a forum for discussion and recommendation. In general, the objectives of Unctad are in line with the New International Economic Order, which aims to achieve a restructuring of the economic system in favor of the poorer countries. The Unctad was founded in 1964. In 1993 Unctad had 187 members, who come together for a plenary session every four years. The governing body of 130 members meets every two years. Separate commissions deal with natural resources, combating poverty and international cooperation. The headquarters are in Geneva, Switzerland.

Underground, term generally used for any secret political movement that seeks to overthrow a country's existing government or military authority. Though undergrounds have operated in many nations throughout history, they came to wide public attention during World War II (1939-1945). They were especially effective in German-occupied countries such as Yugoslavia, Poland, France, and the Netherlands.
See also: Guerrilla warfare.

U

Underground Railroad, secret network that helped U.S. slaves to escape from the South to the northern states and to Canada before the Civil War. Neither underground nor railroad, it was named for its necessary secrecy and for the railroad terms used to refer to its operation. Most of the 'conductors' were slaves themselves, Harriet Tubman being one of the best known. Abolitionists, notably Quakers such as Levi Coffin, ran 'stations' providing food and shelter along the way. Some 40,000-100,000 slaves escaped in this way.
See also: Abolitionism; Slavery.

Undset, Sigrid (1882-1949), Norwegian novelist. Largely known for her epic trilogy set in medieval Norway, *Kristin Lavransdatter* (1920-1922), she won the 1928 Nobel Prize in literature. Her contemporary novels dealt with the position of women in society and with Roman Catholicism.

Undulant fever *See:* Brucellosis.

Unemployment, situation in which people who are normally part of the labor force are unable to find jobs. Seasonal layoffs occur because certain jobs are not available year round. Cyclical unemployment occurs during economic depressions or recessions, when production declines. Structural unemployment refers to permanent shifts in a nation's productive system such that certain groups become permanently unemployed.

Unemployment insurance, type of Social Security providing income to people involuntarily unemployed. Most modern industrial nations have programs of this kind, financed by the government, employers, employees, or a combination of these. In the 1800s some labor unions initiated unemployment benefits for out-of-work members. France introduced a voluntary national scheme in 1905, and Britain introduced the first compulsory insurance program in 1911. In the United States the first unemployment insurance law was passed in Wisconsin in 1932.
See also: Welfare.

UNESCO *See:* United Nations Educational, Scientific, and Cultural Organization.

Ungaretti, Giuseppe (1888-1970), Italian poet; Professor of Italian literature in São Paulo (1936-1942) and Rome (1942-1958). Great rejuvenator of Italian poetry, initially influenced by symbolism. Ignored all metric and rhythmic conventions, developing a new, original spontaneity. His works include *The Burried Harbour* (1916), *L'Allegria* (1931), *Time Feeling* (1933), *Promised Earth* (1950) and *A Cry and Landscapes* (1952).

Ungerer, Tomi (real name, Jean Thomas U.; 1931-), French graphic artist. Ungerer moved to the U.S. in 1957, where he began illustrating children's books and published cartoons in Life, Esquire, and similar magazines. He used his drawings, which he sometimes combined with photography, to express a cutting criticism of American society. A book was published about his poster design called *The Poster Art of Tomi Ungerer*. His other published work is *Fornicon* (1969), *America* (1975), and *Testament: A Collection of Satirical Drawings 1960-1980* (1985).

Ungulate, term for any mammal with hoofs. Ungulates evolved to stand on their toes, and the toenails have become solid hoofs. The odd-toed ungulates (order Perissodactyla), with one or three toes per foot, include horses, rhinoceroses, and tapirs; the even-toed ungulates (order Artiodactyla), with two or four toes, include pigs, deer, antelopes, camels, cattle, and hippopotamuses.

UNICEF *See:* United Nations Children's Fund.

Unicorn, mythical creature with the body of a horse and one horn on its forehead. Unicorns have appeared in the art and legends of India, China, the Middle East, and medieval Europe, where they were associated with the Virgin Mary and Christ.
See also: Mythology.

Unicycle, single-wheeled vehicle with pedals, a seat mounted above the wheel, and no handlebars. The rider moves it by pedalling and can change direction by pedalling backward or forward or by shifting his or her weight. Unicycles were first used in the 19th century by circus performers, who often juggled objects as they rode.

Unidentified flying object (UFO), object or light reprotedly seen in the air during day or night that cannot always be explained by conventional phenomena. Though many UFOs are found to be objects, such as weather balloons or satellites, or the result of atmospheric conditions, there are certain sightings that do not fall into any known-phenomena categories. The U.S. government continues to investigate thousands of such reports and to sponsor scientific studies on the subject.

Unification Church, religious organization of Korean origin that has became highly visible in the United States in the late 1960s. Based on the ideas of the Reverend Sun Myung Moon, who represents himself as an elect leader and seer, the organization recruits and regiments young people to dedicate their lives to the church in a highly disciplined fashion. The Unification Church has followers throughout the world.

Uniformitarianism, doctrine in geology originally opposed to Catastrophism. Originated (1785) by James Hutton and championed by Charles Lyell in the 19th century, it holds that the same geologic processes are at work today as have always existed thoughout geologic time. Uniformitarianism emphasizes the relative slowness and gradual nature of geological change.
See also: Geology.

Union, Act of, British Parliamentary act of 1840 that officially united Upper Canada and Lower Canada. Two separate Canadas had originally been established to appease the English and French inhabitants. The act not only joined the two Canadas but also stipulated that a government should be formed, consisting of a colonial governor and a legislative assembly composed of members elected by the people. Under the act, English became the official government language.
See also: Canada.

Union of South Africa *See:* South Africa.

Union of Soviet Socialist Republics (USSR) also known as the Soviet Union. Name of a union of 15 Soviet republics that existed from 1922 to 1991. The constituent republics were Armenia, Azerbaijan, Belorussia, Estonia, Georgia, Kazachstan, Kirgizstan, Latvia, Lithuania, Moldova, Russian Federation, Tadzhikistan, Turkmenistan, Ukraine and Uzbekistan. The union covered more than half of Europe and two-fifths of Asia. The capital was Moscow.
Land and People. The country comprised 15 constituent republics divided into 4 regions-European, Central Asian, Siberian, and Far Eastern. The Ural Mountains separate the European (west) sector from the Asian (east) sector. Most of the European sector is flatland, broken by the Urals, the Caucasus, and other highlands. To the east lie the great Siberian Plain and the deserts of central Asia; beyond them are the Siberian highlands and the Far Eastern mountains. Because it occupies about one-sixth of the land area of the world, the former USSR has several different climatic regions, ranging from the polar north to the subtropical south. Long, cold winters and short summers are characteristic of much of the climate. Over 100 ethnic groups and nationalities make up the people. Chief among them are Slavic-speaking peoples (Russians, Ukrainians, and Byelorussians); Turkic-speaking peoples (Uzbeks, Tatars, Kazakhs, and Azerbaijani); and the Armenians, Georgians, Lithuanians, and Moldavians. The official language is Russian. Approximately 75% of the people live in the European sector. Religion is officially discouraged, but many people still follow the Russian Orthodox church. Other religions include Roman Catholicism, Protestantism, Islam, Judaism, and Buddhism. The ban on religion may have been relaxed in the 1990s.
Economy. Under Communism, all industry was owned and operated by the government.

Mechanization has greatly increased the productivity of large-scale agricultural enterprises, such as this Russian tea plantation.

The peaks of Mount Elbrus, the highest mountain in the Caucasus Mountains.

U

Saint Basil's Cathedral, or Saint Basil the Blessed, on Moscow's Red Square, was built from 1555-60 during Ivan the Terrible's reign. Its bold departure from classic or Byzantine traditions heralded the start of a new national epoch in Russian architecture.

Agriculture was organized around state farms (*collective farms*), with some small private plots permitted to farmers. A centralized economy was a feature of the Soviet Union since 1917, but in the latter part of the 1980s, dissatisfaction with the performance of the economy led to a time of turmoil and change. The former USSR is a major producer of oil, coal, iron ore, natural gas, and timber, and it possesses a wealth of other natural resources. In the 1990s the Soviet Union began to move away from top-down, centralized management in an attempt to form a market economy. Widespread strikes and demonstrations were an early result of this transition.

History. Russia was ruled by tsars (emperors) for hundreds of years in an extremely autocratic manner. Under them the country was largely cut off from the industrially developing West. There were sporadic uprisings in the 19th and early 20th centuries against this despotic rule, and finally, due in large measure to the horrendous losses suffered by the Russians in World War I, the Russian Revolution of 1917 forced Tsar Nicolas II to abdicate. He was replaced by a provisional government, led by Alexander F. Kerensky, a Socialist. The government proved ineffective and was itself overthrown in November 1917 by the Marxist Bolsheviks led by Vladimir I. Ulyanov, who took the name of Lenin. He was helped by Leon Trotsky in organizing the takeover and in successfully prosecuting the following civil war. Lenin and the Bolsheviks set Russia on the course of state ownership of the means of production (farms, factories, mills, mines, etc.). In 1922, the Communist government established the Union of Soviet Socialist Republics (then 4 union republics) with the Russian Republic the first and the largest, which it remains to this day. Lenin died in 1924, and, after some jockeying for power among his successors, Joseph Stalin emerged in 1927 as undisputed leader. He embarked on a far-reaching policy of collectivizing the farmland and of securing total government control over all economic planning. The followers of Trotsky and many other opponents of Stalin's rule were purged in the fierce repression of the 1930s. In 1941, Germany invaded the USSR despite having signed a nonaggression pact with it

in 1939. The Great Patriotic War, as the Russians call World War II, lasted until the defeat of Germany in 1945, in which the Russian forces played a key role despite having sustained fearful losses. After World War II, the Soviet Union went on to establish Communist governments throughout eastern Europe and in Soviet-held East Germany. Friction between the Soviet Union and the United States and other West European democracies led to the Cold War, which effectively divided the world into competing East and West blocs, led by the Soviet Union and the United States, respectively. Stalin died in 1953 to be replaced by Nikita S. Khrushchev, who denounced the worst excesses of the Stalin era but who also continued the rivalry with the United States. Partly as a result of the dangerous confrontation with the United States over Soviet missiles in Cuba in 1962, where Russia was forced to turn back, Khrushchev was ousted by the party in 1964, replaced by Leonid I. Brezhnev. Relations with the West improved somewhat under Brezhnev (the period of détente), but the Soviet economy continued to stagnate and even deteriorate. The era of the old Bolsheviks, trained under Stalin, was coming to an end. Brezhnev died in 1982, to be replaced by Yuri V. Andropov. Andropov died in 1984 and was succeeded by Konstantin V. Chernenko, who died in 1985. Mikhail S. Gorbachev, at age 54, became head of the Communist Party, the first of the new generation of Soviet leaders to head the country. Faced with an unpopular war in Afghanistan, begun in the Brezhnev years, and with dire economic problems at home, Gorbachev embarked on a series of reforms

he hoped would revitalize the country. He ended the Afghan war, allowed non-Communist governments to take power in Eastern Europe, approved the reunification of Germany by relinquishing control of East Germany, and set in motion new domestic policies such as *glasnost* (openness or freedom of expression for the people) and *perestroika* (reforms designed to transform the command economy of the USSR into one more receptive to free market forces). All these changes led to turmoil, where long-simmering disputes between ethnic groups and rival republics of the union broke into the open. With non-Communist parties allowed to participate in elections, various republics clamoring for independence, ethnic strife, and challenges mounted by powerful political leaders, the future existence of the Union of Soviet Socialist Republics was threatened and the union collapsed in 1991.

Unions, labor, workers' organizations formed to improve pay, working conditions, and benefits through collective power. Modern labor unions arose out of the concentrations of workers created by the Industrial Revolution. A craft (horizontal) union organizes workers by their particular skill; an industrial (vertical) union includes all workers in an industry. Unions negotiate contracts with employers by the process of collective bargaining. A closed (or union) shop increases bargaining strength by requiring that all workers belong to a union. Some states prohibit union shops by law. A dispute with employers may be referred to arbitration, or union members may resort to strikes, slowdowns, boycotts, or, more rarely, sit-downs. Britain has a single Trades

U

Union Congress, but many countries have rival unions with differing political outlooks.

Unitarianism, current in Christianity which rejects the concept of the Trinity, together with the dogma of Jesus' divinity. Unitarianism originated shortly after the beginning of the Reformation (early in the 16th century). Its principles were spread by Michael Servetus (1511-1553), who was burnt as a heretic in Geneva by the Protestants. Unitarian churches which adhered to the moderate and tolerant teachings of the Socinians appeared in Hungary, Transylvania and Poland. In 1774 the first Unitarian community in England was founded by Theophilus Lindsey (1723-1808) and Joseph Priestley (1733-1804). The church has been active in the U.S. since 1785. In 1961 the Unitarian Universalist Association was formed in the U.S.
See also: Protestantism.

Unitas, John (1933-), U.S. football player. A quarterback known for his accurate passing, he threw at least one touchdown pass in 47 consecutive National Football League (NFL) games. His achievements include 40,239 career passing yards (third on the all time list) and 253 career touchdown passes (second on the all time list). He played for the Baltimore Colts (1956-1973), winning 2 world championships (1958, 1959) and 1 Super Bowl (1971). He finished his career with the San Diego Chargers (1974) and was inducted into the Pro Football Hall of Fame in 1979.

United Arab Emirates

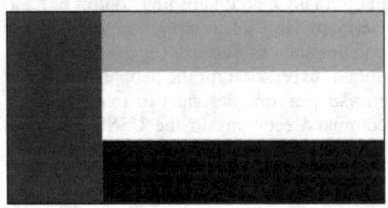

Capital:	Abu Dhabi
Area:	29,992 sq mi (77,700 sq km)
Population:	2,466,000
Language:	Arabic
Government:	Federal union of seven autonomous states
Independent:	1971
Head of gov.:	Sjeikh
Per capita:	US$ 21,100
Monetary unit:	1 UAE dirham = 100 fils

United Arab Emirates, federation of emirates in the eastern Arabian Peninsula, bordered in the north by the Persian Gulf, in

The ruins of the 14th-century fortress Dunluce Castle. Ramore Head, Ireland, where the castle is located, extends into the North Channel, which seperates Northern Ireland from Scotland.

the east by the Gulf of Oman, in the south by Oman, in the south and west by Saudi Arabia, and in the northwest by Qatar. It comprises Abu Dhabi, Ajman, Dubai, Fujairah, Ras al-Khaimah, Sharjah, and Umm al-Qaiwain. The indigenous population is Arab, and Arabic is the official language. Islam is the state religion, and most of the people are Sunni Muslim. The majority of inhabitants, however, are foreign workers, mostly from Asia. The country has a 400-mi (644-km) coastline and is mostly desert. In the east mountains rise to over 8,000 ft (2,438 m), giving way to a fertile coastal strip where dates, grains, and tobacco are cultivated. Herding, fishing, and pearling were the traditional occupations, but since the 1960s the country and its economy have been dominated by oil. The large oil income and small native population have made the Emirates one of the world's richest countries. Abu Dhabi, the largest emirate, is the site of the bulk of the oil production, but Dubai and Sharjah are significant oil exporters, too. Historically, the Emirates were dominated by Britain, to which they were bound by a formal truce (1820) that gave them the name Trucial States. After World War II, Britain granted the Trucial States autonomy. At that time they included Qatar and Bahrain, which chose separate statehood when the United Arab Emirates was formed as an independent state (1971). In 1981, the Emirates and other Gulf countries founded the Gulf Cooperation Council (GCC). During Iraq's occupation of Kuwait, the Emirates worked closely with the allied forces. In 1992, Iran confiscated 3 small islands off the coast. The Emirates received military aid from the U.S., France, and the GCC-countries. The borders of the territorial waterways of the Emirates were established in 1993. The Emirates supported the peace agreements between Israel and Palestine and terminated the indirect economic boycott of Israel (1994).

United Arab Republic (UAR), union of Egypt and Syria proclaimed in 1958 as a step toward Arab unity. Cairo was the capital, and Egyptian president Gamal Abdul Nasser was president. The UAR effectively collapsed in 1961, when Syria withdrew. A 1963 attempt to unite Egypt, Syria, and Iraq failed. Egypt was still called the UAR until 1971, when its name was changed to Egyptian Arab Republic.

United Kingdom

Capital:	London
Area:	94,251 sq mi (242,429 sq km)
Population:	59,778,000
Language:	English
Government:	Parliamentary monarchy
Independent:	1801
Head of gov.:	Prime minister
Per capita:	US$ 24,700
Monetary unit:	1 Pound sterling = 100 pence

United Kingdom, officially, United Kingdom of Great Britain and Northern Ireland, commonly known as Great Britain, constitutional monarchy consisting of most of the British Isles located off the northwestern coast of Europe. With a total area of 94,251 sq mi (244,110 sq km), the United Kingdom is entirely surrounded by water, bounded on the east by the North Sea, on the west by the North Atlantic Ocean, and on the south by the English Channel. The island of Great Britain is separated from Northern Ireland, located in the northeast part of the island of Ireland, by the North Channel and the Irish Sea. The Strait of Dover is the narrowest part of the English Channel and is a passage of 21 mi (34 km) between Great Britain and France. In addition to Great Britain and Northern Ireland, the British Isles consists of thousands of smaller islands, including the Shetland Islands, the Orkneys, the Outer Hebrides, the Isle of Man, and the Scilly Islands.
Land and People. Geographically, the island of Great Britain is divisible into 7 distinct zones. The northernmost section of the island is the Scottish Highlands, a mountainous area and the site of Britain's highest mountain, Ben Nevis, 4,408 ft (1,344 m). Most of Scotland's people and its best farmland are in the Central Lowlands, a fertile plain just south of the Highlands. The Southern Uplands are the southernmost part of Scotland. It is hilly country culminating in Cheviot Hills, which separates England from Scotland.

The hilly country continues south of the Cheviot Hills in the Pennines of England, an area that includes England's famous Lake District. Below the Pennines and extending to the Channel are the English Lowlands. It is on this undulating plain that most of England's farms, villages, mines, industries, and major cities are located. West of the Central Lowlands lies Wales, dominated in the north by the Cambrian Mountains and in the south by fertile river valleys. The Bristol Channel separates Wales from the Southwest Peninsula, an uneven plateau that ends in cliffs facing the open seas. Northern Ireland, situated at the northeast end of the island of Ireland, has fertile land somewhat similar to the Central Lowlands of Scotland. Great Britain contains many bays and inlets, several navigable rivers, and numerous lakes. Though Britain is located in a relatively high northern latitude, its climate is comparatively mild, moderated by the influence of the Gulf Stream. In addition, the island gets regular and adequate rainfall.

The people of Great Britain have a mixed ancestry of Celtic peoples and Romans, as well as Germanic, Scandinavian, and Norman peoples. Over the centuries, the population has tended toward a certain homogeneity, but clear distinctions are still discernible and are reinforced by differences in language, religion, and custom. Welsh remains a distinct Celtic language. The native Scots and Irish speak varieties of Gaelic. And even the dominant English language has strong regional variants, though they began to disappear with the advent of television. Since World War II England has also become a racially varied society, thanks to a large influx of immigrants in the 1950s and 1960s, mostly from Asia, Africa, and the West Indies. The established church in England is the Church of England, headed by Archbishop of Canterbury. In Scotland, the established church is the Church of Scotland. Both churches are Protestant, but there are sizable minorities of Roman Catholics and Jews.

The United Kingdom is governed as a constitutional monarchy. In modern times, England's monarchs have reigned, but they have not governed. The monarch's role, though almost entirely symbolic, is important to England's social and political system and to the maintenance of the traditions that are the sources of authority. Power resides in the Parliament, a representative body divided into an upper and lower house. Members of the upper house, the House of Lords, hold their seats as privileges attached to rank; they are not elected. Members of the House of Commons must be elected. Effective political power is in the House of Commons. Elections must be held at least once every five years, but are usually held more often, and can be called at any time. After an election, the head of the winning party is designated prime minister and forms a government of ministers from among the most important members of the party. These leading ministers make up the cabinet, or inner council. Although Great Britain has a constitution, it is not in the form of a single written document as it is in the United States. It is made up, in part, of certain documents, like the Magna Carta, and, more loosely, of

the vast body of Common Law, but it also consists, to a very large degree, of traditions that have continued over many generations. The British people are at liberty to reconstitute their government at any time. In addition to the monarchy and parliament, the system relies upon an independent judiciary with courts of appeal and judges who are appointed for life. It also relies upon a professional civil service to staff the government's many ministries. British civil servants hold their jobs regardless of the party in power.

Economy. Surrounded by water and with limited natural resources, England has long grown accustomed to and made a virtue of looking beyond its own borders for its economic well-being. Though not nearly as rich and powerful as it was in the 18th and 19th centuries, England remains a competitive manufacturing and trading economy. The country does not have enough arable land to meet all its farm needs: agriculture accounts for just 2% of the gross national product. It has also used up the best of its once-rich coal reserves, though since the mid-1960s it has been self-sufficient in natural gas from the North Sea, and since the late 1970s it has also been self-sufficient in petroleum, also from the North Sea wells.

Trade is critical to the British economy. Britain ranks fifth in the world in foreign trade, after the United States, Germany, Japan, and France, and trades principally in manufactured goods, though one-third of its trade volume is given to food and raw materials. Britain has one of the world's largest merchant marine fleets. The country also continues to be a leading manufacturer, producing steel, automobiles and other vehicles, heavy machinery, appliances, machine tools, products of advanced technology (including jet engines and aircraft for military and civilian use), and electronic equipment. The economy is aided by advanced scientific and technological research at its great universities. Great Britain also supplies markets in the chemical industries, pharmaceuticals, textiles and apparel, and food processing and beverages. Worldwide printing and publishing concerns are headquartered in England.

Government continues to be a strong presence in the British economy, and service industries are the major part of its economy, employing some two-thirds of its work force. The service sector includes education and the health-care system. It also includes wholesale and retail trade and the various institutions that provide financial services, including banks and insurance companies. The financial services industry contributes substantially to Great Britain's economy, and London continues to be one of the world's leading financial centers.

In 2001 a large epidemic (footh and mouth disease) broke out among the British cattle. Thousands of animals had to be killed, which dealt a heavy blow to the economy.

History. Evidence of Bronze Age civilization in England can be seen in the ruins of Stonehenge, but comparatively little is known about England before the arrival of the Romans in the 1st century B.C. The Romans were followed in the 5th century A.D. by Germanic tribes, the Angles, Saxons, and Jutes, who set up petty kingdoms. These

in turn were overrun by Vikings, chiefly Danes, in the 9th and 10th centuries. The last successful invasion of England was in 1066, under William the Conqueror, of Normandy. The political and social organization the Normans imposed upon England laid the foundations of customs and traditions that would prove remarkably durable over the centuries and contribute much to the distinctive character of the people. In the 13th century, a group of English barons won concessions from King John set forth in the Magna Carta in 1215, marking an important development in the growth of Britain's unique political institutions. The 14th century was dominated by the Hundred Years War and the final unsuccessful bid by England's monarchs to establish effective control over their French lands and vassals. The 15th century witnessed the turmoil of the Wars of the Roses, dynastic struggles, which led to the rise of the Tudors, Henry VIII and Elizabeth I, whose combined reigns embraced the 16th century. Henry VIII embodied the English Renaissance and established England's independence from the papacy by seizing all church properties and establishing the Church of England. Elizabeth presided over the England of William Shakespeare and Sir Francis Drake. England, after destroying the Spanish Armada in 1588, claimed supremacy at sea and began expanding its overseas colonies and markets, an expansion that was to lead to a great empire. This was after nearly a century of civil and religious warfare centered upon the throne and, in particular, the Stuarts. The issue was finally put to rest with the Glorious Revolution and the ac-

The town of Mevagissy is a small fishing port and tourist resort along Saint Austell Bay in southwestern Cornwall.

U

Due to the deterioration of nineteenth-century houses and the obsolescent infrastructure of Lancashire, large parts of the area do not conform to modern requirements for living conditions. On the other hand, delightful houses were built here in idyllic spots, such as here, on Bridgewater Canal in Worsley.

U

In 1917, George V changed the name of the British royal family from Saxe-Coburg-Gotha to Windsor, the latter derived from Windsor Castle, which was originally built for William the Conqueror. The castle received its present form under Henry II and Henry III (at the end of the 12th, and the beginning of the 13th centuries). Under Edward III (14th century) it became the royal residence.

Emblem of the United Nations, established in 1945.

cession of William III and Mary II in 1689, but only after bitter fighting and the Protectorate of Oliver Cromwell, leader of the Puritans. It was in the course of the conflicts of the 17th century that Parliament rose to prominence as a governing institution and the groundwork was laid for the governance of England in modern times. Modern Great Britain, with sovereignty residing in Parliament, was born with the Act of Union of 1707, which joined the formerly separate kingdoms of England and Scotland to form the United Kingdom. Through the laws of succession, the heirs to the British throne in the 18th century were German and this, as well as George III's disastrous policy leading to the loss of the American colonies, contributed to the reduction of the monarch to a symbolic head of state. Sovereignty resided in Parliament and the official leader of the government became the prime minister.

In the 18th century, Great Britain increased its power tremendously by using both the raw materials and markets of its growing empire to fuel the Industrial Revolution. Using modern technology, especially the steam engine, to build the first modern industries and turning its populace from agricultural work to industrial labor, Great Britain rapidly increased its wealth and power. At the end of the century, Great Britain faced a determined adversary in Napoleon Bonaparte of France. Defeated first at sea by Admiral Nelson in 1805 and on land by Lord Wellington at Waterloo in 1815, Napoleon, in fact, marked Britain's passage to world dominance. The 19th century also saw England's attempt to resolve the centuries' old hostilities with the Irish with the Act of Union of 1800, which created the United Kingdom of Great Britain and Ireland.

The 19th century was a period of political conflict and reform occasioned by Great Britain's wealth and power. There were bitter debates in Parliament over laws to ameliorate the harsh conditions in factories, and equally bitter disputes over the Corn Laws and the franchise. These debates would lay the foundations for the political parties that would dominate British politics throughout the 20th century, with the Whigs representing Liberal policies and the Tories conservative policies. These differences developed at the height of Britain's empire under Queen Victoria, who reigned from 1837 to 1901 and the rival views of politics were embodied in her two brilliant prime ministers, Benjamin Disraeli, the conservative, and

William Gladstone, the liberal. By the time of Queen Victoria's death, the British empire consisted of about one-quarter of the world. The 20th century proved much harder on England's fortunes. Great Britain entered World War I in 1914 against its economic rival, Germany. Great Britain helped win the war but lost 750,000 men in the fighting and did not adequately recover economically. The Irish problem continued to vex England, and in 1921 the British agreed to the independence of southern Ireland, but retained Northern Ireland. The worldwide depression hit England hard, and the 1930s saw the rise of fascism and the Nazis. Neville Chamberlain's policy of appeasing Hitler proved disastrous, and, led by Winston Churchill, England resisted Nazi ambitions. The English not only defended their own country, but in union with the United States and other allies, they destroyed the Nazis. England lost 360,000 men in World War II and its economy was in decline. In 1945, the Labour Party acceded to power and established England's welfare state with unemployment benefits, a comprehensive program of national health insurance, and the nationalization of key industries. The changes were dramatic, but the economy continued to lag. The same period saw the beginning of the breakup of Britain's empire. In 1947, India and Pakistan became independent, then in succession, one foreign policy and possession after another asserted its independence in Africa, Asia, and the Pacific.

In the 1950s Great Britain decided not to join the European Coal and Steel Community, nor would it join the European Economic Community, the Common Market. These proved costly decisions. The British economy expanded for a time but began to contract in the 1960s, and in 1963 and 1967 bids by Britain to gain admission to the Common Market were rejected, principally by France. Britain finally succeeded in joining the EEC in 1973, in the grip of the deepest economic downturn in the postwar years. In addition, the conflict in Northern Ireland turned violent. In May 1979 the Conservative Party, led by Margaret Thatcher, the first woman prime minister, came to power. The Conservatives drastically reduced government holdings, curbed the power of the unions, and strove to increase investment, all with some positive results. But after 11 years as prime minister, Mrs. Thatcher resigned in Nov. 1990 after losing Conservative Party leadership over her opposition to England's participation in European economic union, and in the late 1980s and early 1990s, the economy continued to be the major issue and challenge confronting England. Thatcher was succeeded by John Major as Conservative leader and prime minister. In 1997 the Conservative Party was defeated by Labour, led by Tony Blair. In 1998 a major breakthrough was achieved between the British and the Irish concerning the peaceprocess in Northern Ireland. An agreement (the Good Friday Agreement) was signed establishing the Northern Ireland Assembly and ending direct rule from London. The Assembly was postponed after an argument about the IRA's arms decommissioning. Scotland and Wales

were granted more autonomy by the Labour government. After the attacks of September 11, 2001, Prime Minister Blair became Bush's main ally in the war on international terrorism, supporting Operation Enduring Freedom in Afghanistan, in October and November 2001. Furthermore, Blair declared Britain would support the U.S. if they were to attack Iraq. In 2002 the inhabitants of the British colony Gibraltar voted by referendum to remain British.

United Nations (UN), international organization of the independent states founded after World War II, with the declared goals of promoting peace and international cooperation. It was launched at the 1945 San Francisco Conference prepared by the 'Big Three' Allied Powers of World War II (the United States, Britain, and the USSR), and 51 states signed the charter. Membership has grown to 189 in 2002. The headquarters are in New York City. The UN has six major organs. The General Assembly, composed of delegates from all member states, meets once a year and provides a general forum but has little actual power. The Security Council has five permanent members, (China, France, Great Britain, the United States, and the USSR), each of which has the right to veto any resolution, and ten rotating members. The Economic and Social Council, with 54 elected members, deals with 'nonpolitical' matters, coordinating the work of the specialist agencies and operating commissions, such as those on children, refugees, and human rights. The Trusteeship Council is responsible for UN Trust Territories. The International Court of Justice, in The Hague, Holland, is the UN's principal organ of international law. The Secretariat is the administrative body headed by the Secretary General. Other UN institutions include the United Nations Conference on Trade and Development, the Office of the United Nations High Commissioner for Refugees, and the United Nations Children's Fund.

Major specialized agencies affiliated with the UN include the Food and Agriculture Organization (FAO), General Agreement on Tariffs and Trade (GATT), International Atomic Energy Agency (IAEA), International Civil Aviation Organization (ICAO), International Labor Organization (ILO), International Monetary Fund (IMF), International Telecommunication Union (ITU), United Nations Educational, Scientific, and Cultural Organization (UNESCO), Universal Postal Union (UPU), World Bank (IBRD), World Health Organization (WHO), World Meteorological Organization (WMO), World Trade Organization (WTO). Initial enthusiasm regarding the role the UN would play on a global scale, has been reduced. This as a result of experiences in Somalia and Yugoslavia, where UN forces were hindered in their work and where their safety could not be guaranteed. The United Nations and their Secretary General, Kofi Annan, were awarded the Nobel Peace Prize in 2001.

Believing Iraq to still possess weapons of mass destruction, the United Nations Security Council voted unanimously on November 8th 2002 to approve Resolution 1441 that forces Iraq to disarm of face serious consequences.

United Nations Children's Fund (UNICEF), UN organization formed (1946) as the UN International Children's Emergency Fund to help in countries devastated by World War II. It became a permanent body in 1953, retaining the UNICEF acronym and specializing in child welfare, family planning, and nutrition programs in disaster areas and in many poorer countries. It is financed voluntarily. In 1965 UNICEF was awarded the Nobel Peace Prize.
See also: United Nations.

United Nations Educational, Scientific, and Cultural Organization (UNESCO), UN agency established in 1946 to promote international collaboration through scientific, educational, and cultural activities. Its policy-making general conference meets biennially at its Paris headquarters. UNESCO has helped develop education in poorer countries and arranges scientific and cultural exchanges. Both the United States and Britain withdrew from UNESCO in 1985, charging that the organization was being manipulated for political purposes with an anti-American slant.
See also: United Nations.

United Nations University, research and training institution chartered in 1973 by the United Nations (UN). It is actually an agency through which institutions coordinate educational programs. Its aims are to provide information, research, and training opportunities for scholars and organizations around the world. Projects usually focus on the management of natural resources, hunger, and developing societies. University headquarters are in Tokyo.
See also: United Nations.

United Press International (UPI), world's largest independent news agency, created by the 1958 merger of United Press (founded 1892 by Edward W. Scripps) and the International News Service (founded by William Randolph Hearst in 1906). UPI was bought and sold several times in the 1980's. In 1992 it was acquired by Middle East Broadcasting Center Ltd.

United States, government of the, the constitution of the U.S. came into effect in 1789. Three central organs of government were created by the constitution: the legislative, the executive and the judiciary. The highest judicial body is the Supreme Court. Just as important as the constitution itself are the amendments to it. In the first 10 amendments, the so-called Bill of Rights written in 1791, is a summary and declaration of the rights of the ordinary citizen, such as freedom of speech and religious conviction. E.g. the abolition of slavery was also added to the constitution in an amendment. The last amendment, no. 27, was ratified in 1992.
The U.S. is a federal republic; the 50 states and the cities have a considerable amount of autonomy. The federal government is responsible for defense, foreign policy, the monetary system, national security and the federal courts. The president, the governors of the states, county councilors, mayors, and

public officials at all levels - including local magistrates, sheriffs and many other public posts - all have to be elected. In several states it is also possible for the electorate to vote on specific proposals such as tax reform, nuclear energy and abortion. In the 'primaries' candidates are chosen for the presidential elections. The president is chosen by an electoral college every four years. The number of delegates each state sends to the electoral college is the same as the number of representatives it has in Congress. Americans are entitled to vote once they reach the age of 18.
The president is the head of state, leader of the government and supreme commander of the army; he appoints the ministers, but must have these appointments approved by Congress. The executive power is counterbalanced by the legislature (Congress) and the judiciary. Congress has two chambers: the House of Representatives with 45 members, where each state is proportionally represented according to the size of its population, and for which elections are held every two years, and the Senate, which has 100 members, two for each state. Senators are chosen for a term of six years; every two years there are elections for one third of the seats. Both the president and members of Congress can put forward proposals for legislation. Any new law has to be approved by a majority vote of both chambers as well as by the president. Thus the president has the right of veto, and can send any proposals for new legislation back to Congress. However, the president's approval is not needed if the legislation is passed by a two-thirds majority in Congress. The most important part of parliamentary political life takes place in the numerous permanent committees of the Senate and the House of Representatives. These deal with proposals for legislation in detail, listen to representatives of interest groups, and put questions to members of the government. The chairmen of these committees have considerable power.
The two dominant political parties are the Democratic Party and the Republican Party. The presidential elections of 1992 were won by Bill Clinton, the Democratic Party candidate. His term of office began in 1993. After the parliamentary elections at the end of 1994, Clinton was forced to cooperate with a Republican-dominated Congress. The Republicans won 230 seats in the House of Representatives and 53 in the Senate, while the Democrats only won 204 and 47 seats respectively. Only one seat was won by an independent candidate. Parties other than the Republicans and Democrats do exist but they seldom succeed in getting elected to Congress. Only the party with the largest number of votes in any particular district wins a seat in Congress. Thus in reality the U.S. is a two-party system, in which power is passed back and forth between the Democratic and Republican parties.

United States Congress *See:* Congress of the United States.

United States Constitution *See:* Constitution of the United States.

United States literature, literary works in English beginning in the original 13 English colonies and continuing in the present-day United States. Although the United States is a large continental country with varied influences, several strands or themes characterize its literature. The pioneer heritage of the country left its mark on later writers, primarily in their concern with individual values and liberties and a certain pervasive skepticism toward authority. Perhaps aligned with this, U.S. writers have shown a consistent tendency to break with literary traditions and strike out in new directions.
Colonial literature. The first writings in English in North America were by adventurers and colonists for readers back in England. While few of these could be called literature, some journals and accounts did manifest a lasting quality and interest. Capt. John Smith's vigorous *True Relation of Such Occurrences and Accidents...as Hath Happened in Virginia* (published in England in 1608) was the first personal account of life in the colonies. More sober histories of the period included John Winthrop's *Journal*, which described life in the Massachusetts Bay Colony from 1630 to 1649, and William Bradford's *History of Plimoth Plantation*. Religious and instructional works, however, dominated colonial writing, with sermons and religious tracts making up most of the colonists' reading matter. The first book published in the Puritan colonies was the *Bay Psalm Book* (1740). The most important of the early religious writers were Cotton Mather (a 2-volume ecclesiastical history of New England), Jonathan Edwards (sermons and books), and John Woolman (a journal reflecting on his life in the Quaker belief). Poetry in colonial times also largely reflected religious and pious themes. Among the early poets were Michael Wigglesworth, Anne Bradstreet, and Edward Taylor.
Revolutionary period literature. Not surprisingly, writing during the period of the Revolution concentrated on politics and on political philosophy. Benjamin Franklin encouraged writers by acting as a publisher and founder of newspapers. He also wrote political and satirical works, with his witty *Poor Richard's Almanac* (1733-1758), one of the period's most popular publications. Political writing during this time reached new heights as men like Thomas Paine, Thomas Jefferson, Alexander Hamilton, and John Madison examined the nature of society. A formidable female writer of the late 18th century, Mercy Otis Warren, wrote not only plays and poetry but a history of the American Revolution-one of two contemporary histories considered significant. At war's end, as the new nation struggled to discover its identity, Hamilton, Madison, and John Jay wrote a brilliant series of letters called *The Federalist* in support of the new constitution. For style and content they are scarcely rivaled in political discourse.
Literature in the New Nation. The first U.S. novel was William Hill Brown's *The Power of Sympathy* (1789). Charles Brockten Brown, the first professional U.S. novelist, modeled his work after the English gothic romances, as exemplified in *Wieland* (1798) and *Edgar*

U

Huntly (1799). Fame both in the United States and Europe was gained by Washington Irving with his *Sketch-Book* (1819-1820) and by James Fennimore Cooper with his *Leatherstocking Tales* (1823-1841). The leading poet of this time was William Cullen Bryant, who became known as the American Wordsworth for his deeply felt nature poems. Among his most important lyrics are 'Thanatopsis' (1811), 'To a Waterfowl' (1818), and 'To the Fringed Gentian' (1832). Also notable was Henry Wadsworth Longfellow (*Evangeline*, 1847). The nation's attention turned to the problem of slavery in the 1830s with William Lloyd Garrison and his newspaper, *The Liberator*, leading the antislavery movement. The most influential antislavery work was Harriet Beecher Stowe's novel *Uncle Tom's Cabin* (1851-1852), the best-selling book of the time.

Literature at mid-19th century. By the middle of the 19th century, U.S. literature had come of age. The transcendentalists were a group of New England writers who displayed in their works characteristics thought to be specifically American. They espoused a high moral seriousness and a sense that the individual was superior to tradition and social customs. They also called for a distinctly American literature, quite independent of European models. Chief among them was Ralph Waldo Emerson, who presented the group's theories in *Nature* (1836) and in his brilliant essays (e.g., 'Self-Reliance,' and 'The Over-Soul,' both 1841). Henry David Thoreau (*Walden*, 1855) was another transcendentalist who wrote observant, thought-provoking, and beautifully styled prose. Utterly American was the poet Walt Whitman (*Leave of Grass*, first edition published 1855), writing a free-form verse that broke with European models and celebrated the new country in the New World. Quite different, but equally untraditional, were the compact, emotionally intense lyrics of Emily Dickinson, almost all of which were published after her death in 1886. A darker strand in U.S. literature was evident in the eerie, haunting poetry and short stories of Edgar Allen Poe, for example, in lyrics such

as 'The Raven' (1845) and the sinister *Tales* (1840). Nathaniel Hawthorne's masterpiece *The Scarlet Letter* (1850) probed the psychological aspects of sin in the closed society of early New England Puritanism. In *Moby Dick* (1852), Herman Melville created an American epic, at once an adventure tale of the sea and a deep, enigmatic allegory.

Literature in the second half of the 19th century. After the Civil War, literature in the United States took on a national aspect in that writings of distinct regions gained a nationwide audience. The country eagerly read about the California gold rush and life in the West in the short stories of Bret Harte. Joel Chandler Harris retold the old black tales of the South. The greatest of the regionalist writers, however, Mark Twain, surpassed the genre and in *The Adventures of Tom Sawyer* (1876) and *The Adventures of Huckleberry Finn* (1884) wrote two American classics. By century's end, a new realism was taking hold in U.S. literature as was a reaching-out to European models and culture. Stephen Crane's *Red Badge of Courage* (1895), set in the Civil War, won acclaim for its realistic portrayal of warfare. Henry James went to Europe where he wrote novels of rare psychological insight about the clash of U.S. and European cultures (*The Portrait of a Lady*, 1881, and *The Golden Bowl*, 1904). William Dean Howells set out to depict the lives of average Americans (*The Rise of Silas Lapham*, 1885). Other noted realists included Frank Norris, Harold Frederick, Theodore Dreiser, Hamlin Garland, Jack London, and James T. Farrell. A group of journalists and writers known as 'muckrakers' employed realism to examine corruption and fraud in U.S. society. Among them were Lincoln Steffins, Ida M. Tarbell, and Upton Sinclair, whose novel *The Jungle* (1906) was instrumental in bringing about food and drug laws.

Literature after World War I. Disillusionment with the war stirred a generation of U.S. writers to become expatriates in Europe, in search of something to believe in. Labeled the 'lost generation' by Gertrude Stein (*The Autobiography of Alice B. Toklas*, 1933), the group included Ernest Hemingway (*The Sun Also Rises*, 1925), F. Scott Fitzgerald (*The Great Gatsby*, 1925), and John Dos Passos (*U.S.A.*, 1930-1936). One of the most powerful of U.S. novelists was William Faulkner (*The Sound and the Fury*,

1929). Social criticism continued with such writers as critic H. L. Mencken and Edmund Wilson and novelists Sherwood Anderson and Sinclair Lewis. Other novelists of the period include Willa Cather, Thomas Wolfe, and Nathanael West. The Great Depression fostered more socially aware writing, as evidenced in the works of John Steinbeck (*The Grapes of Wrath*, 1939). Notable U.S. poets of the 20th century include Edward Arlington Robinson, Edna St. Vincent Millay, Robert Frost, T.S. Eliot, Carl Sandburg, Hart Crane, Marianne Moore, Wallace Stevens, e.e. cummings, Langston Hughes, and, more recently, Robert Lowell, Elizabeth Bishop, Sylvia Plath, John Berryman, and John Ashberry. Among the most important playwrights of this period were Eugene O'Neill (*Long Day's Journey Into Night*, first produced in 1956), Elmer Rice, Maxwell Anderson, Lillian Hellman, Tennessee Williams, Arthur Miller, William Inge, and, in recent years, Edward Albee, David Rabe, Sam Shepard, and Neil Simon. Major novelists include Flannery O'Connor, Eudora Welty, J.D. Salinger, Norman Mailer, Saul Bellow, Philip Roth, Ralph Ellison, James Baldwin, Truman Capote, Mary McCarthy, Joyce Carol Oates, Thomas Pynchon, John Barth, Toni Morrison, and John Updike.

United States of America

Capital:	Washington, D.C.
Area:	3,618,770 sq mi
	(9,372,614 sq km)
Population:	280,562,000
Language:	English
Government:	Federal presidential republic
Independent:	1776
Head of gov.:	President
Per capita:	US$ 36,300
Monetary unit:	1 US Dollar = 100 cents

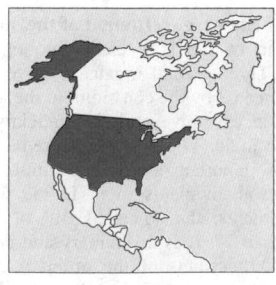

United States of America, country whose territory is principally on the continent of North America, but which includes islands of the Hawaiian archipelago in the Pacific Ocean. The United States is organized into 50 political subdivisions, or states, and the District of Columbia. In addition, the U.S. government maintains special political associations with various overseas territories including Puerto Rico and the U.S. Virgin

The snow-capped tops of Mount Deborah (highest point: 12,304 ft/3,750 m), near Alaska. At the foot of these mountains is a taiga region with low pine forests.

Islands in the Caribbean, and Guam, American Samoa and Northern Marianas, all formerly parts of the Trust Territory of the Pacific Islands. Johnson, Midway, and Wake islands, also in the Pacific, are also dependent upon the United States. The contiguous states of the United States are bounded by the Atlantic Ocean to the east, the Pacific Ocean to the west, Canada to the north, and Mexico, the Gulf of Mexico, and the Caribbean Sea to the south. Alaska is separated from the 48 contiguous states by Canada and bounded by that country as well as the Pacific and Arctic oceans. The Hawaiian islands are in the central Pacific Ocean c.2,100 mi (3,380 km) from San Francisco, Calif.

Land and People. With an area of 3,618,770 sq mi (9,372,614 sq km), the United States is geographically varied, and can be divided into approximately 6 regions. The Atlantic and Gulf Coastal Lowlands stretch south from Long Island to Florida and then west to Mexico. They extend inland an average of 200 mi (322 km) with many lagoons, sandbars, and good natural harbors. In southern Florida they include the Everglades and, on the Gulf Coast, the Mississippi River delta. The Appalachian mountain chain separates the Atlantic Lowlands from the western interior. The Appalachians run northeast to southwest from Nova Scotia in Canada to the southern United States. A low mountain system, the Appalachians include the White Mountains of New Hampshire, the Great Smoky Mountains, and the Blue Ridge Mountains of North Carolina, and give way to the Allegheny Plateau. The north-central section of the United States has the Great Lakes, among the world's largest freshwater lakes. The Great Lakes region forms a natural boundary between the eastern and western United States, and between the United States and Canada. Beyond the Alleghenies are the Central and Interior Plains, stretching to the Rocky Mountains and drained by the Mississippi-Missouri river system and its branches. Its uplands include the Ozarks in Arkansas and Missouri, and the Black Hills of South Dakota and Wyoming. The Rocky Mountains mark the western barrier of the Great Plains and are part of a mountain system extending from Alaska, through Canada and the United States and continuing down the length of South America. The highest mountain in the United States is Mt. McKinley in Alaska at 20,320 ft (6,194 m). Between the Rocky Mountains and the mountains of the Cascade and Sierra Nevada ranges farther west lies the Western Plateau and Basin, or the Intermontane Region. It contains the Great Salt Lake and Grand Canyon. Finally, beyond the western mountains, are the Pacific Coastlands extending south from Puget Sound in the state of Washington to Central Valley in California. The lowest point in the United States is Death Valley in California, one of several desert regions to be found in the southwestern United States.

Climate in the continental United States is greatly influenced by geographic position. Winter temperatures vary greatly, being relatively high along the sheltered Pacific coast, but often extremely low in the interior and the east. Summer temperatures are mainly high in most areas with the southeast becoming subtropical and humid. Tornadoes can occur in spring, especially in the Mississippi valley, and summer thunderstorms and hurricanes are frequent along the south Gulf and Atlantic coasts.

The original inhabitants of the Unites States were the Native Americans, racially distinct and consisting of various peoples of different languages and cultures. Displaced and decimated by successive waves of migration from Europe beginning in the 16th and 17th centuries, remnant populations now live for the most part on reservations, principally in the Great Plains and Western states. The majority of the people of the United States are immigrants or descendants of immigrants who came to the United States in 2 distinct groups. From 1600 to 1820, most settlers were from England and Scotland. From the 1820s to the present, newcomers arrived from Ireland, Germany, and Scandinavia before the U.S. Civil War, then from Eastern Europe, the Mediterranean, and Asia. The U.S. population also includes a significant number of citizens who are descendants of the Mexicans who originally settled what is now the U.S. Southwest. African Americans are the descendants of men and women who were brought to North America as slaves as early as 1619. An exhaustive list of the origins of all U.S. citizens would include peoples from all over the world. Despite their varied origins, they have combined sufficiently to constitute an identifiable people with a common language, culture, and outlook. There is no established religion in the United States, but a majority of the people are Christians, chiefly Protestants but also Roman Catholics. The country's language is English, though many immigrants speak their own native languages.

Economy. In 2001, the gross national product of the U.S. was in excess of $9.8 trillion dollars, making it by far the world's richest country. The United States can grow nearly all temperate and subtropical crops and is not only self-sufficient in essential foods but regularly produces surpluses. About half the land surface is given to farming, including dairy farming and the raising of livestock. The country contains valuable forests, particularly in the northwest and Alaska, and rich fisheries in the Atlantic, the Pacific, and the Gulf. Its considerable mineral wealth includes coal, iron ore, petroleum, and natural gas, but the needs of its vast economy and the consumption it generates have led to a decline in the reserves of some minerals, and the United States has increasingly become an importer of ores and of oil. Its enormous manufacturing sector produces steel, automobiles, aircraft, and aerospace technology, electronic equipment, textiles, and most kinds of consumer goods. The United States not only manufactures in quantity, but it also has long been a leader in setting standards for quality and efficiency in modern industrial production. In addition, a large sector of the economy is committed to research, development, and production in sophisticated weaponry and aerospace systems. Banking and the interrelated institutions that provide financial services and products worldwide are also major contributors to the economy.

History. The first permanent European settlement in the United States was St. Augustine, Fla., founded by the Spanish in 1565. Early English settlements were in Jamestown, Va., in 1607; Plymouth, Mass., in 1620; Maryland in 1634, Connecticut in 1636, and Pennsylvania in 1681. There were also French, Dutch, and Swedish settlements. By the 18th century, Britain was the paramount power on the new continent with prosperous, flourishing colonies in what was later to become the United States. Oppo-sition to Britain's policy toward its North American colonies led to the Revolutionary War in which the forces of the 13 colonies under the generalship of George Washing-ton, and with timely and substantial assistance from France, defeated Britain's armies. The war lasted from 1775 to 1783. Independence was declared in 1776, and after the war the separate states joined to form a federal republic with

Field of wheat in Washington State.

U

West Virginia, sheep farming in an Appalachian valley.

U

George Washington as its first president, in 1789. Expansion westward followed.

The area of the United States was doubled by the Louisiana Purchase, made in 1803. Florida was purchased from Spain in 1819. U.S. ambitions for expansion into Canada ended with the War of 1812 between Britain and the U.S. Settlers moved over the Alleghenies and west over the Great Plains. Texas was annexed in 1845 and much of the territory of the U.S. Southwest was acquired through the Treaty of Guadalupe Hidalgo, which ended the Mexican-American War of 1848. Five years later, southern New Mexico and southern Arizona were added to the United States with the Gadsden Purchase in 1853 and, at the other end of the continent, Alaska was purchased from Russia in 1867.

As the country expanded, differences deepened between the cultures and economies of the northern and southern states. The southern states eventually elected to secede from the union and the result was the Civil War (1861-1865), the bloodiest single conflict in

Even early in the Civil War, the Union foot soldier (right) was more formally equipped than his Confederate counterpart. As the war disrupted the already limited industrial capacity of the South, Confederate supplies became so scarce that some men had to march barefoot.

the nation's history. Following the war came a period known as Reconstruction (1865-1877). What was Reconstruction for the South was development and expansion for the rest of the country. The North became more and more industrialized and urbanized and the settlement of the West was hastened with the completion of the transcontinental railroad in 1869. As the nation became richer, more powerful, and more self-confident, its presence began to be felt abroad.

In 1898 Hawaii was annexed and other overseas territories came under U.S. control as a result of its victory in the Spanish-American War. The United States completed its entry into international affairs by participating

(from 1917) in World War I (1914-1918) and tipping the scales in favor of the Allies, the British and the French. Power and prosperity were soon followed by the Great Depression of the 1930s, an economic breakdown so complete that many felt the country was on the brink of revolution. Franklin D. Roosevelt became president and instituted his New Deal reforms, which halted the economic decline. Worldwide economic frustration and ambition led to World War II (1940-1945) and the Japanese attack on Pearl Harbor on Dec. 7, 1941, marked the entrance of the U.S. into the war.

The U.S. emerged from World War II a military and economic superpower, leader of the Western, or free, world, and locked in rivalry with the Communist bloc led by the Soviet Union. With an ideology of anti-communism, which it pursued relentlessly at home and abroad, and a policy of resisting and containing what it saw as the spread of communism, the U.S. committed itself to the Cold War. It participated in the Korean War (1950-1953) and, later, in the Vietnam War (1961-1973).

Domestically, the Congressional hearings and investigations of Sen. Joseph McCarthy and his staff into Communist subversion, the unofficial purges of people who had been slandered or blackballed, and the trial and execution of Ethel and Julius Rosenberg for spying for the Soviet Union dominated much of the postwar decade. In the 1960s, at the same time the country was engaged in the Vietnam War, the government pursued its war on poverty, a combination of programs meant to alleviate poverty and equalize access to equal economic opportunity. The country also faced the profound social and legal crisis generated by the civil rights movement led by the Rev. Martin Luther King, Jr. The turmoil and unrest of the period was marked at the very outset by the assassination of President John F. Kennedy and later of Dr. King, and then Robert Kennedy. Richard Nixon's election to the presidency signalled the end to the Vietnam War, but not before Cambodia had been embroiled in the widening regional disaster. Defeat in Vietnam was followed by economic recession at home. The Nixon presidency saw a major diplomatic breakthrough in its recognition of Communist China, but lost its credibility and authority with the Watergate domestic political scandal. Rather than face impeachment, Nixon resigned the presidency in disgrace. Both Gerald Ford and his Democratic successor, Jimmy Carter, worked to restore the sagging economy. The last year of Carter's presidency witnessed a further blow to the international standing of the U.S. with the ouster of the Shah of Iran by Iranian Muslim fundamentalists under the leadership of Ayatollah Khomeini, whose followers held the U.S. embassy staff in Teheran hostage for more than a year.

The Republican administration of Ronald Reagan sought to revive the economy by radically reducing governmental regulation. The policy proved stimulating in the short run, but left the nation deep in debt, with a great part of its banking system in disarray, and the gap between rich and poor wider than it was before Reagan's program was initiated. Internationally, the Reagan presi-

dency struck a more militant anti-Communist tone. Defense spending was increased and the administration was determined to regain ground from communism, particularly in Nicaragua. The result was the Iran-contra scandal, in which it was discovered that the executive branch had been selling arms to Iran to finance forces seeking to overthrow the Marxist regime in Nicaragua. The president denied knowledge of the transactions or involvement in any wrongdoing, but the hearings into the matter raised serious questions, among them, whether or not the president was competent to govern. Ronald Reagan was succeeded by George Bush, whose administration inherited the severe economic consequences of his predecessor's policies, in particular the collapse of the savings and loan institutions and the weakening of the U.S. banking system. In foreign policy, President Bush urged a continuation of normalizing relations with China despite pressure from many quarters to censure China for the Tiananmen Square massacre of dissident students and workers. In 1993 Bush was succeeded by the Democrat Bill Clinton. Clinton stood for a better social policy, but was often frustrated by the Republican majority in the Congress and Senate.

The closely fought Presidential elections of 2001 between Democrat Al (Albert) Gore and the Republican candidate George W. Bush led to Bush assuming the presidency after five weeks of complex legal argument over voting procedures. Although, Gore won the majority of popular votes, Bush succeeded in winning the number of electoral votes necessary to assume power. After the tragedy of September 11, 2001, when the U.S. was attacked by terrorists, Bush promised to hunt down and punish the offenders of the attacks, which lead to a war on international terrorism. Furthermore, Afgha-nistan was invaded since its Taliban regime and Osama Bin Laden (leader of the al-Qaida network) were held responsible for the attacks. A new government was re-instated in Afghanistan but Bin Laden could not be traced. Further to the campaign against terrorism, Bush received Congre-ssional support to take serious measures against Saddam Hussein's government in Iraq unless it disarmed itself of weapons of mass destruction. Saying the 'danger is clear' that the Iraqi regime would provide terrorists with biological, chemical or nuclear weapons, on March 17th 2003, President Bush gave the Iraqi leader, President Saddam Hussein and his sons forty eight hours to leave Iraq or face military action.

United States President *See:* President of the United States.

United States Supreme Court *See:* Supreme Court of the United States.

Universalism, the belief in the final salvation of all souls. This was first put forward by Origen (185-253), one of the greatest Christian thinkers and writers of ancient times, but who was condemned at the Second Council of Constantinople in 533. Universalism was supported by some radical currents up until the 18th century, and in mystical, apocalyptic and theosophical

groups. The optimistic and harmonious Universalism is practiced in England and mostly in America, where a Universalist church was founded in 1779.
See also: Unitarianism.

Universal language, proposed language that people of all nations could speak and understand. Since the 1600s, the idea of a universal language has attracted philosophers, educators, politicians, and businesspersons alike. Its advocates believe that it would aid both cultural and political understanding among the disparate nations of the world. Its detractors claim that the idea of such a language is impractical. Several universal languages, including Volapuk and Esperanto, have been developed and used with some success. During the Middle Ages and Renaissance, Latin almost achieved the status of a universal language as it was used as a common language by diplomats and other educated people throughout Europe. Today, English is fast becoming a universal language.

Universe, general term for all of space and everything in it.

Universities and colleges, schools that are designed for the continuation of education beyond high school and that emphasize the study of liberal arts, arts, and sciences. A university generally offers courses in many subjects, including agriculture, art, history, literature, philosophy, and science. It may be divided into different departments, or colleges. For example, a university may have a College of Education within it. A college may also be a separate school, which usually emphasizes study in one area, such as liberal arts. Most universities and colleges offer students a course of study leading to an undergraduate degree, a bachelor of arts or science degree. Most also have various graduate programs in which a student may continue to work toward a master of arts or science degree or a doctor's degree. Though the oldest university in the world is probably Al-Azhar University in Egypt (founded in A.D. 970), the prototypes for most universities today sprang up in Europe during the 12th century. These universities were usually associated with the Church, though by the 14th century, they were designed to train students in medicine and law as well as theology.

Unknown soldier, in several countries, an unidentified soldier killed in action in war whose tomb serves as a national shrine honoring all war dead. Unknown U.S. soldiers of World War I, World War II, the Korean War, and the Vietnam War are buried in the Tomb of the Unknown Soldier in Arlington National Cemetry, Arlington, Va., USA. France's Tomb of the Unknown Soldier is located beneath the Arc de Triomphe in Paris, Britain's is in Westminster Abbey.

UN Peacekeeping Forces, Peacekeeping forces are put in place when requested by the countries in conflict, with the agreement of the UN Security Council; personnel is then supplied voluntarily by UN member states. Primary areas of activity have been the Congo, Central America, and the Middle East. UN forces have been active in the Israeli-Arab conflict and in conflicts between Iran and Iraq, India and Pakistan, and parties within Cyprus, Angola, Cambodia, Somalia, and former Yugoslavia. Particularly after the failures in Somalia and Yugoslavia, the purpose of UN peacekeeping forces has been subject of discussion. Also, after the Cold War, the number of peacekeeping operations has increased and, as a result, organizational and financial problems.
See also: United Nations.

Untermeyer, Louis (1885-1977), U.S. writer and editor. Though he published many volumes of poetry and two novels, he is better recognized today as having been the editor of several poetry anthologies: *Modern American Poetry* (1919 and subsequent revision), *Modern British Poetry* (1920), and *A Treasury of Great Poems, English and American* (1942). From 1961 to 1963, he served as the poetry consultant for the Library of Congress.

Upanishads, group of philosophical treaties that make up the final part of the Veda, a collection of Hindu scriptures. They are thought to have been written from 900 to 600 B.C. Most of the existing 112 Upanishads are in dialogue form, and their speculative nature has inspired the formulation of several concepts central to the Hindu religion. One puts forth that the soul of an individual is one with the soul of the universe, or God.
See also: Hinduism; Vedas.

Upas, forest tree (genus *Antiaris*) of tropical Asia and Indonesia. Ancient tales describe this tree as yielding a juice that was used as arrow poison by ancient peoples; this accounts for a lot of the superstition and mysticism that surrounds this tree.

Updike, John (1932-), U.S. novelist, short-story writer, poet, and critic. He has dealt with the trials of contemporary life in such novels as *Rabbit, Run* (1960), *Couples* (1968), *Bech: A Book* (1970), *The Coup* (1978), *Rabbit is Rich* (1981, Pulitzer), *The Witches of Eastwick* (1984), *S.* (1988), *Rabbit at Rest* (1990; Pulitzer), *Brazil* (1994), *Toward the End of Time* (1997), *Gertrude and Claudius* (2000), and *Seek My Face* (2002). He published a book of memoirs, *Self-Consciousness*, in 1989.

Upjohn, Richard (1802-1878), English-born U.S. architect, noted for his Gothic Revival churches, such as Trinity Church, New York City (1846). He was one of the founders and the president of the American Institute of Architects (1857-1876).
See also: Architecture.

Upland sandpiper (*Bartramia longicauda*), also called upland plover, North American bird of the sandpiper family. For most of the year, it lives on the prairies and meadows of Canada and the northern United States, but it migrates for the winters to the grassy plains of Argentina and Brazil. It is usually about 12 in (30 cm) long, with dark- and light-brown feathers and a white belly. It eats locusts and other insect pests.

Upper Volta *See:* Burkina Faso.

Upshaw, Eugene, Jr. (1945-), U.S. football player. Upshaw played for the Oakland Raiders (1967-1981) and was captain of the team (1970-1981). Upon retirement as an active player, he became president of the National Football League Players' Association (1981-1983). He was appointed to executive director in 1984 and supported the players in the football strike of 1987. He was inducted into the Pro Football Hall of Fame in 1987.

Upsilon particle, unstable subatomic particle without electrical charge. With a mass almost 10 times that of a proton, it is the heaviest known subatomic particle.
See also: Quark.

Ur, ancient Sumerian city that lay in what is now southern Iraq along the Euphrates River. An important port as well as religious and trade center, Ur thrived from about 3500 B.C. until the 4th century B.C. At that time, the Euphrates River changed its course and the then useless port city was abandoned. According to the Bible, the Hebrew leader Abraham was born in Ur. Some important architectural ruins of Ur have been found in southern Iraq. These ruins include the remains of a ziggurat, an ancient pyramid-like structure.
See also: Sumer.

Ural Mountains, mountain chain about 1,500 mi (2,400 km) long in western Russia, running north-south from the Kara Sea toward the Caspian. The Urals are the traditional boundary between Europe and Asia. Mt. Narodnaya (6,214 ft/1,894 m), in the northern section, is the highest peak. The Urals are heavily forested and rich in minerals.

A typical village of wooden houses in the mixed-forest area in the Central Urals. Many of the inhabitants used to be nomads, now they earn their living by hunting, wood-cutting and agriculture.

Ural River, river in former USSR. Originating in the Ural Mountains of west-central Russia, it flows some 1,570 mi (2,527 km)

U

south to the Caspian Sea. Several important Russian cities lie along it, including Magnitogorsk, a steel-making center. It is a rich source of salmon and sturgeon.

Uranium, chemical element, symbol U; for physical constants see Periodic Table. Discovered by Martin H. Klaproth in 1789, it occurs in the minerals pitchblende, uraninite, carnotite, autunite, and uranophane, among others. It is prepared by reduction of the tetrafluoride in a Thermit type of reaction. Uranium is a silver-white, lustrous, radioactive, reactive metal, a member of the actinide series. It is pyrophoric. Uranium-235 is fissionable and is used as fuel in nuclear reactors, and in atomic and hydrogen bombs. One pound of uranium has the fuel value of 1,500 tons of coal. Uranium-238 is fertile and used to produce plutonium-239, which is fissionable in breeder reactors. Uranium and its salts are highly toxic.

Uranium-235 *See:* U-235.

Uranus, third-largest planet in the Solar System and the seventh from the sun. Physically very similar to Neptune, but rather larger, Uranus orbits the sun every 84.02 years at a mean distance of 1.78 billion mi (2,87 billion km), rotating on its axis once every 10.75 hours. Since the plane of its equator is tilted 98° to the plane of its orbit, the rotation of the planet and the revolution of its five known moons (Titania, Oberon, Ariel, Umbriel, and Mirando), which orbit closely parallel to the equator, are retrograde. In 1977 the planet was found to have five rings, like those of Saturn but

much fainter. In 1998 American and Canadian scientists discovered that Uranus has two more moons.
See also: Planet; Solar System.

Uranus, god of the sky in Greek mythology. His union with Gaea, the earth, produced a race of giants known as the Titans. Because Uranus hated and feared his offspring, he forced them to live deep within the earth. The Titan Cronus rebelled against his father's decree, attacking and emasculating Uranus, a wound that separated Uranus from Gaea. (The myth may have originated as an explanation for the separation of the sky and earth.) The function of Uranus as god of the sky was eventually taken over in Greek mythology by Zeus, a son of Cronus.
See also: Mythology.

Urban, name of eight popes. **Urban II** (c.1042-1099; r. 1088-1099) continued the struggle against the emperor Henry IV begun by his predecessor, Gregory VII. At the Council of Clermont (1095) he initiated the Crusades. **Urban III** (r. 1185-1187) was absorbed in a struggle with Emperor Frederick Barbarossa and his son Henry IV. **Urban IV** (c.1200-1264; r. 1261-1264) continued the struggle against the Hohenstaufen emperors and gave the crown of Naples and Sicily to Charles I. **Saint Urban V** (c.1310-1370; r. 1362-1370) attempted to return the papacy to Rome from Avignon and to effect a reconciliation with the Eastern Church. **Urban VI** (1318?-1389; r. 1378-1389) was involved in disputes with his cardinals that precipitated the Great Schism. **Urban VIII** (1568-1644; r. 1623-1644) played an am-

biguous role in the Thirty Years War through political opposition to the Roman Catholic Hapsburgs.

Urban renewal, removal of city slums and their replacement with improved residential or commercial facilities. Ideally, the federal government grants a city a certain amount of money to replace a slum neighborhood. The city then uses the funds to buy and demolish derelict property, relocating families and businesses to new areas. Next, the land is sold to private or public developers at a low price. Schools, parks, office centers, and so on are then to be built where the slum once stood. The program as a whole has been only moderately successful. In many cities cleared land has remained unsold and undeveloped for years. Federal funding of urban renewal has also been greatly cut, shifting the financial burden to the state and city governments.

Urdu, Indo-European language that is spoken in India and Pakistan, where it is the official language. In ancient times Urdu was the language of the Mohammedan Indians, and closely related to Hindi. Urdu has borrowed many words from Persian. Urdu literature, written in Persian-Arabic characters, flourished from the 17th to the 19th centuries.

Urea, organic compound, $CO(NH_2)_2$, that is the end product of the metabolism of nitrogen in protein in many animals. It is excreted in the urine. Urea's major uses are as a nitrogenous fertilizer and to make urea-formaldehyde resins.

Uremia, biochemical disorder often seen in cases of kidney failure, consisting of high levels of urea and other nitrogenous waste products entering the blood. Nausea, vomiting, malaise, itching, pigmentation, anemia, and acute disorders of fluid and mineral balance are common.
See also: Kidney.

Urey, Harold Clayton (1893-1981), U.S. chemist awarded the 1934 Nobel Prize in chemistry for his discovery of deuterium, an isotope of hydrogen. He was a leading theorist of the nature and origin of the moon.
See also: Deuterium.

Uribe Vélez, Alvaro (1952-), Colombian politician and President (2002-). He entered public service in 1976, as the Secretary General for the Ministry of Labor and Director of the civil aviation. He became mayor of Medellin in 1982. From 1986 to 1994, he was a senator. He was elected governor of the north east province of Antioquia in 1995. In 2002, after only one round, he became President for the period 2002-2004. His promise to end the civil war in Columbia, that has gone on for 40 years and kills three to four thousand people each year, won him the elections. He promised to be tough on the left wing guerrilla movement FARC as well as the right militia.

Urine, waste product consisting of a dilute solution of excess salts and nitrogenous material, such as urea and deaminated protein, excreted by many animals. The wastes are filtered from the blood by the kidneys or

The urinary system rids the body of liquid waste materials, including excess compounds, acids, and toxic substances. These materials are filtered out of the bloodstream in the kidneys (1), where they are combined with excess water, to form a solution called urine. The ureters (2), two narrow tubes, transmit the urine to the bladder (3), moving individual drops along by contractions of the muscular walls. The accumulated urine is passed out of the body through a third tube, the urethra (4). (A) In males, the urethra serves as a conduit for both the urinary and the reproductive systems. In addition to receiving urine from the bladder, the male urethra can receive fluids from the seminal vesicles (5), the prostate gland (6),

and Cowper's glands (7), plus sperm from the testicles (8). (B) In females, the urinary and reproductive systems are entirely separate. The bladder is located in front of the uterus (9). The urethra terminates in a small opening (10) between the head of the clitoris and the entrance of the vagina (11). In both sexes, the outflow of urine from the bladder is controlled by two sets of sphincter muscles. Pressure to urinate is felt when 24 cub in (400 cub cm) of urine have accumulated, although the bladder can stretch to hold more fluid. A cross section of the male urethra shows the gland ducts (12); a cross section of the female urethra shows its muscular wall (13).

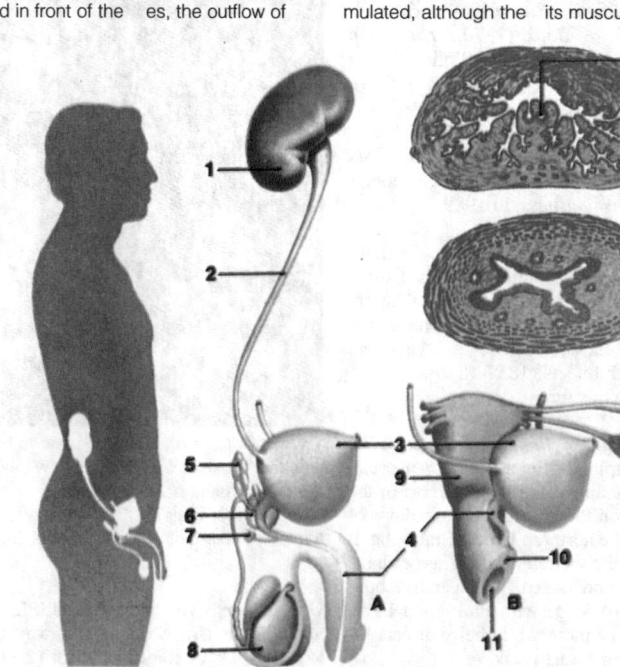

equivalent structures and stored in the bladder until excreted. The passage of urine not only serves to eliminate wastes, but also provides a mechanism for maintaining the water and salt concentrations and pH of the blood. While all mammals excrete nitrogenous wastes in urine, other animals-birds, insects, and fish-excrete them as ammonia or in solid crystals as uric acid.

Uris, Leon (1924-), U.S. author of modern historical fiction. His most famous novel, *Exodus* (1958), follows the development of the state of Israel. His first novel, *Battle Cry* (1953), is a personalized account of service in the Marine Corps during World War II. Other works include *QB VII* (1970), *Trinity* (1976), *Mitla Pass* (1988), and *A God in Ruins* (1999). Uris, in collaboration with his wife, Jill, has also written two photoessays, *Ireland: A Terrible Beauty* (1975) and *Jerusalem: Song of Songs* (1981).

Ursa Major and Ursa Minor *See:* Big and Little Dippers.

Ursulines, Roman Catholic religious order of women, the first devoted exclusively to the education of girls. The order was founded in Brescia, Italy (1535), by St. Angela Merici, with St. Ursula as patron saint. *See also:* Roman Catholic Church.

Uruguay

Capital:	Montevideo
Area:	68,037 sq mi (176,215 sq km)
Population:	3,387,000
Language:	Spanish
Government:	Presidential republic
Independent:	1828
Head of gov.:	President
Per capita:	US$ 9,200
Monetary unit:	1 Uruguay peso = 100 centesimos

Uruguay, officially the Oriental Republic of Uruguay. Covering 68,037 sq mi (176,215 sq km), which makes it the smallest republic in South America, Uruguay is bordered by Brazil to the north and northeast, the Atlantic Ocean to the east, Argentina to the west, and the Rio de la Plata to the south. The capital and chief port is Montevideo, where about 40% of the people live.

Land and People. Uruguay is a country of rolling grasslands and low hills, fringed by sands, lagoons, and bays. In the south, the Rio de la Plata estuary forms an alluvial plain called the Banda Oriental. From the narrow coastal plain the land rises gently to the Cuchilla Grande and other highlands, reaching their highest point in the Sierra de las Animas at 1,644 ft (501 m). Uruguay has a pleasantly mild climate. The people are mostly of Spanish and Italian descent with some 300,000 mestizos, persons of mixed European and Native American descent, forming a significant minority. Spanish is widely spoken, and most people are Roman Catholic.

Economy. The economy of Uruguay is based on cattle and sheep raising with meat, wool, and hides providing 80% of the country's exports. Wheat, oats, flax, oilseeds, grapes, fruit, and sugarbeets are grown. Meat packing and tanning are the chief industries. There are important fisheries, but few mineral resources. Uruguay faced economic difficulties in the 1980's, including high inflation and unemployment. By means of industrialization, the government tries to switch from exporting live animals and animal products to new export products.

History. The region was visited by the Spanish in 1516 and settled by them in 1624. Resisting Portuguese incursions, they founded Montevideo in 1726. José Artigas led the independence movement from 1808 to 1820. Uruguay was then occupied by Brazil for several years, but finally expelled the invaders and became independent in 1828. A period of prolonged political instability was followed, in the early 20th century, by government under José Battle y Ordóñez. His economic and social reforms made Uruguay one of the most developed Latin American countries with a comprehensive social welfare system and advanced labor legislation. Labor unrest and the terrorism of the leftist Tupamaro guerrillas in the late 1960s led to a military takeover in 1973. Repression in the decade following was widespread, but eventually gave way to a return to civilian government in 1985. Julio María Sanguinetti was elected President. A revised constitution was approved that same year. However, the army was still very influential behind the scenes. Luis Alberto Lacalle Herrera, the candidate of the right wing Partido Blanco became President after the elections of 1989. He received little support for his economic reform policies, which provided for the privatization of state-owned companies and cutbacks on social security services. At the elections of 1994, Sanguinetti was re-elected. The new government took measures to cut back on the government's budgetary deficit, which would reduce inflation. Jorge Batlle Ibáñez was elected President in 2000. He promised privatization, a reduced number of civil servants and he promised to find out what happened to the people who disappeared during the dictatorship in the 1970s and 1980s.

Uruguay River, southern South American river. Originating in southern Brazil, it flows for 1,000 mi (1,600 km) first west and then south before finally emptying into the Rio de la Plata, a huge estuary on the Atlantic coast. It forms part of the Argentine-Brazil border and all of the Argentine-Uruguay border.

Uruk (Erech in the Bible), classical city in Lower Mesopotamia on the left bank of the Euphrates (currently Warka, Iraq). One of the centers of Sumarian civilization. The city's Golden Age was between 3500-2900 B.C.. One of their kings was Gilgamesh. A temple of pillars designed with cones and the White Temple (3500-3000 B.C.), whose name was derived from the white-plastered outside walls, have been preserved; both can be found on a terrace, probably dedicated to Anu, the god of heaven.

U.S. *See:* United States of America.

USA *See:* United States of America.

USSR *See:* Union of Soviet Socialist Republics.

Utagawa Kuniyoshi (1797-1861), Japanese painter of landscapes, historical and mythical scenes, and actors of the Kabuki theater. He illustrated many fairy tales.

Utah (Beehive State; pop. 1,860,000), state in the U.S., bordered by Idaho, Wyoming, Colorado, Arizona, Nevada and New Mexico; 84,932 sq mi (219,889 sq km). Capital, Salt Lake City. Utah consists mainly of dry, arid regions, such as the great Salt Lake Desert, separated by the foothills of the Rocky Mountains and the equally dry Colorado plateau. The state has a fascinating erosion landscape. The climate is very dry. The warmest part of the state is in the southwest; the lowest average temperatures are in the north. There is some agriculture; since WW II industry has expanded. Extraction of copper, oil, coal, iron, uranium, gold, silver, zinc, lead, natural gas and salt.

In prehistoric times the area was inhabited by people who lived in caves around Lake Bonneville. Between 400 and 1250 the area was inhabited by Pueblo Indians, who cultivated maize. They are thought to have left the area because of the dry climate. When Europeans visited the area in the 18th and 19th centuries, they came across Shoshone. Mormons, driven out of other states and searching for an area where no one else wanted to live, founded the state of Deseret there in 1849. After the creation of the territory of Utah, a conflict between the U.S. government and the Mormons led to troops being sent to the area (1857). Only after the Mormons abolished polygamy was Utah admitted to the Union (1896).

Utamaro Kitagawa (1753-1806), Japanese graphic artist and painter. Made a name for himself with his colored wood engravings. In his realistic performances courtesans play an important role.

Uterus, or womb, female reproductive organ that is specialized for implantation of the fertilized egg and development of the embryo and fetus during pregnancy. The regular turnover of its lining under the influence of estrogen and progesterone is responsible for menstruation. *See also:* Reproduction.

U

U

U Thant *See:* Thant, U.

Utica, ancient Phoenician colony on the coast of North Africa on the Mediterranean Sea. Founded about 1100 B.C., it was an important port and helped give the Phoenicians control over sea trade on the Mediterranean. A rival of its neighbor Carthage, Utica sided with Rome against Carthage in the Third Punic War (149-146 B.C.). With the Roman victory and the destruction of Carthage, Utica became the capital of the province. It fell to the Vandals (A.D.439), was recaptured by the Byzantine Empire (534), and destroyed by the Arabs (c.700).

Utilitarianism, theory of ethics that holds that the rightness or wrongness of an action is determined by the happiness its consequences produce. The theory dates from the 18th-century thinker Jeremy Bentham, who believed that actions are motivated by pleasure and pain and that happiness can be assessed by the quantity of pleasure. His follower John Stuart Mill later argued in *Utilitarianism* (1863) that some pleasures should be sought for their intrinisic quality. He interpreted the principles of utilitarianism as a basis for the struggle for political and social reforms.
See also: Bentham, Jeremy; Mill; Watson-Watt, Sir Robert Alexander.

Utopia, term used to denote any imaginary ideal state. Based on the Greek words meaning 'no place,' it was coined by Sir Thomas More as the title of his *Utopia* (1516), in which he described a just society free of internal strife.

Utrecht (pop. 260,000), city in the central Netherlands. Built on the site of a Roman fort, it was during its early history the residence of several German emperors. Until the 15th century, it was the region's most important cultural and industrial center, a role eventually taken over by Amsterdam. In 1579, representatives from the northern provinces met in Utrecht and signed the Union of Utrecht, uniting them against Spain and setting up the eventual formation of what is now the Netherlands. Today Utrecht is an important cultural center and the site of many historical buildings, medieval churches, museums, and universities. It is also the headquarters of the Netherland's rail network. Chief industries include construction and metalworking.
See also: Netherlands.

Utrecht, Peace of (1713-1714), series of treaties among England, France, the Netherlands, Portugal, Prussia, Spain, and the Holy Roman Empire concluding the War of the Spanish Succession.
See also: Succession wars.

Utrillo, Maurice (1883-1955), French painter best known for his Paris street scenes. His finest works capture in modified cubism the atmosphere of old Montmartre, as in *Sacré Coeur de Montmartre* (1937).

Uttar Pradesh (pop. 139,112,000), Indian constituent state on the Gangetic Plain; 113,715 sq mi (294,410 sq km). Capital, Lucknow. Predominantly agricultural area with irrigated cultivation: grain, sugarcane, cotton, jute, tea. Very little industry. An area that has contributed much to Indian culture. Eighty percent of the population is Hindu.

Utzon, Jörn (1918-), Danish architect, influenced by the work of Aalto, Le Corbusier and Wright. Above all known for his design of the Sydney Opera House (1956-1973), with its distinctive roof that looks like a row of sails. Also designed a theatre in Zurich (1964), an art museum in Silkeborg (1963-1965) and the Bagsåuard church in Copenhagen (1976).

Uxmal, ancient city in Yucatán, Mexico. Built by the Mayas, it flourished c. 600-900 and has some fine examples of the late classical Mayan style of architecture.
See also: Mexico.

Uzbekistan

Capital:	Tashkent
Area:	172,740 sq mi
	(447,400 sq km)
Population:	25,563,000
Language:	Uzbek
Government:	Presidential republic
Independent:	1991
Head of gov.:	Prime minister
Per capita:	US$ 2,500
Monetary unit:	1 Som = 100 tichin

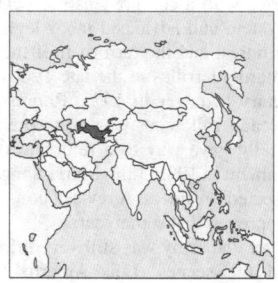

Uzbekistan (Republic of), independent country in central Asia, surrounded by Kazakhstan and the Aral Sea (north), Kyrgyzstan and Tajikistan (east), Afghanistan (south), and Turkmenistan (west).
Most of the country is flat, there are mountains only in the east. The Aral Sea diminishes every year, as a result of the fact that it no longer receives any water from rivers such as the Amudarja. The climate is continental, with little precipitation.
The inhabitants are mostly Uzbeks (74%), an Islamic people. Russians (6%), Tartars, Kazakhs and Tajiks are minorities.
Farming (especially cotton, rice and fruit), horse breeding and cattle raising are its chief industries. This country also has rich deposits of coal and oil. Tashkent is the industrial center of Central Asia.
Before the 4th century it was a province of the Persian Empire. Control of the region then shifted to the Arabs and other groups, including the Turks, until it finally fell to the Russians toward the end of the 19th century. In 1991 the country gained independence. That year, Uzbekistan also joined the Commonwealth of Independent States. In the parliamentary elections of 1995 the former Communist party won a majority of seats. Since its independence, Uzbekistan has pursued a policy of economic liberalization.
In 1998 Uzbekistan took part in a joint military exercise with NATO and the United States, and later that year the collaboration with the U.S. was further intensified with the creation of the American-Uzbekistan Commission. Its aim is to achieve close bilateral collaboration in politics, economics and defense. During that year Uzbekistan also formed a 'troika' with Russia and Tajikistan to combat radical Muslim fundamentalism. President Karimov (elected in 1990) has advocated active economic cooperation, the control of narcotics and arms smuggling and religious extremism within regional organizations like the economic cooperation organization with Kazakhstan, Kyrgyzstan and Tajikistan. Uzbekistan became a member of the Shanghai Cooperation Organization (SCO; members being: China, Russia, Kazakhstan, Kyrgystan and Tadzjikistan) in 2001. This organization stimulates regional cooperation. Parliament extended Karimov's term in 2002 by 2 years. New Presidential elections will not take place until 2007. Karimov will be allowed to seek re-election then.
See also: Union of Soviet Socialist Republics.

V, 22nd letter in the English alphabet, corresponding with the Semitic letter *waw*, meaning 'hook,' represented by a tenthook symbol probably derived from an ancient Egyptian symbol for a pole support. The Greeks altered it to *Y*, and as the 20th letter of the Roman alphabet it became a *V*, representing both *V*, and *U* sounds. The use of *V* for the *V* sound dates from the Middle Ages, though the old confusion persisted longer. *V* represents 5 in Roman numerals, and serves as an abbreviation for words including *vanadium*, *verb*, *versus*, and *volt*.

Vaccination, method of inducing immunity to infectious disease due to bacteria or virus.Early methods of inducing immunity consisted of the deliberate innoculation of material from a mild case. The vaccinated body forms antibodies and is able to produce large quantities of them rapidly thereafter. This gives protection equivalent to that induced by an attack of the disease. It is occasionally followed by a reaction resembling a mild form of the disease, rarely by the serious manifestations. Persons on steroids, with immunity disorders, or eczema may suffer severe reactions and should generally not receive vaccinations.
See also: Immunity.

Vacuum, region of space devoid of matter. Such a region will neither conduct heat nor transmit sound waves. Because all materials that surround a space have a definite vapor pressure, a perfect vacuum is an impossibility and the term is usually used to denote merely a space containing air or other gas at very low pressure.

Vacuum cleaner, electric appliance that cleans dirt from surfaces such as carpets, rugs, and bare floors by suction. The first vacuum cleaning machines were developed about 1900 by several different inventors.

Vacuum tube, glass or metal envelope that controls electronic currents that are necessary to operate electronic equipment like radios, televisions, and computers. It gets its name from the fact that almost all air is removed from the tube for it to work. Between 1920 and 1950, all electrical equipment used vacuum tubes. They have now been replaced by a newer device, the transistor, which is smaller and more reliable and consumes less power.

Vaduz (pop. 5,200), capital of Liechtenstein, a principality in the Alps between Switzerland and Austria. Many medieval buildings still stand. Within walking distance of the picturesque town is the famous castle of the Liechtenstein princes.

Vagina, female reproductive organ consisting of a tubeshaped canal leading from the external genital orifice to the uterus. It measures 4 in (10 cm). The muscular walls, which are covered with a mucous membrane, fall together to give the vagina a slit-like appearance. During sexual intercourse, the male's penis is inserted into the vagina. During birth the vagina serves as the passage through which the baby leaves the mother's body.
See also: Reproduction.

Vaginitis, inflammation of the vagina, occurring particulary in women of childbearing age. Under normal circumstances, balanced quantities of various bacteria, fungi, and protozoa are present in the vagina. When the balance of these organisms is disrupted and larger amounts of organisms are allowed to reproduce at larger and faster rates, vaginitis occurs. Vaginitis can be triggered by pregnancy, lack of sleep, and poor health and diet. Common symptoms include swelling, itching, and vaginal discharge.

Vajpayee, Behari Atal (1926-), Indian politician, Prime Minister of India (since 1998). In the period 1957-1977 he was the parliamentary leader of the Jan Sangh party, of which he was co-founder in 1951. Vajpayee was Foreign Minister at the end of the 1970s, and in 1980 was elected President of the nationalist Bharatiya Janata Party (BJP). He had been previously elected Prime Minister in 1996, but this initial term of office only lasted 13 days. After the 1999 elections, he was re-elected Prime Minister. He advocates the liberalization of the economy and after both India and Pakistan had carried out nuclear tests, he tried to normalize relations between the countries.

Valence, ability of an atom to form compounds, expressed as the number of elec-

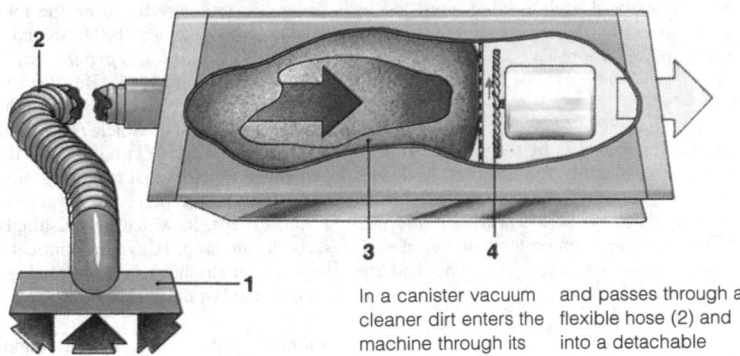

In a canister vacuum cleaner dirt enters the machine through its cleaning head (1) and passes through a flexible hose (2) and into a detachable dust bag (3). The vacuum's suction is created by an electric motor-driven fan (4).

V

trons an element gives up or accepts from other elements. The meaning of the term has undergone several changes over the past century. One of the first definitions of valence referred to the number of hydrogen atoms with which an atom of a different element could combine. The term then came to encompass the bonding capabilities of ionized (electrically charged) atoms.
See also: Bond, chemical.

Valencia (pop. 800,000), third-largest Spanish city, in eastern Spain on the Turia River. A Roman settlement (138 B.C.), it came under the rule of the Moors (750-1238). Today it is a commercial and industrial center.

Valens (A.D. 328-378), Roman emperor from 364 to 378. He was actually co-emperor, ruling the eastern part, while his brother Valentinian ruled the western part. During his reign the Visigoths, a tribe living along the empire's northern borders, rebelled against the Romans. The Visigoths met and defeated the Romans in the battle of Adrianople. Valens was killed during the fighting.
See also: Rome, Ancient.

Valentine, Saint (d.A.D. 270), Roman martyred priest. His traditional association with love probably reflects the near-coincidence of his feast day (Feb. 14) with the ancient Roman fertility festival of Lupercalia (held Feb. 15). The practice of sending Valentine cards dates from the 19th century.

Valentinian I (A.D. 321-375), Roman emperor who ruled 364-375 in conjunction with his younger brother Valens. Valentinian succeeded the Emperor Jovian and appointed his brother to rule the eastern part of the empire while he ruled the west. During his reign, he subdued the Germanic tribes threatening the western provinces and built fortifications along the Rhine.
See also: Rome, Ancient.

Valentinian III (A.D. 419-455), Roman emperor 425-455. Though declared emperor at the age of 6; he never ruled the empire in his own right, since political power was wielded in his youth by his mother, Galla Placidia, and later by the patrician Flavius Aëtius. The invasion of the Vandals and Huns occurred during his reign. Hostilities between Valentinian and Aëtius led to the murder of

Aëtius by Valentinian (454), who was himself murdered the following year.
SEE ALSO: Rome, Ancient.

Valentino, Rudolph (Rodolfo d'Antonguolla; 1895-1926), Italian-born U.S. film star, one of the greatest romantic male stars of the silent film era. Valentino's films included *The Four Horsemen of the Apocalypse* (1921), *The Sheik* (1921), and *Blood and Sand* (1922).

Valera, Eamon de *See:* De Valera, Eamon.

Valerian (d.A.D. 269), Roman emperor 253-260. In 257 he campaigned against the Persians, but was defeated and captured (260) by the Persian emperor, Shapur I, and died in captivity.
See also: Rome, Ancient.

Valéry, Paul (1871-1945), French poet, essayist, and critic. His early verse, *Album de Vers Anciens* (1920), was influenced by Stéphane Mallarmé. His best-known works are *La Jeune Parque* (1917) and *Le Cimetière Marin* (1920). He wrote on poetry in *Monsieur Tetse* (1896) and also on philosophical and critical themes.

Valhalla, in Scandinavian mythology, paradise hall of the dead where slain warriors live under the leadership of the god Odin. Valhalla is depicted as a magnificent palace built of battle shields, spears, and gold. The chosen heroes are wounded in battle daily

Plaza del Caudillo, in the centre of Valencia.

V

and are restored each evening, until led by Odin to battle the giants at the time of Ragnarok, or Doomsday.
See also: Mythology.

Valkyrie, in Scandinavian mythology, warriorlike maidens sent by Odin to escort dead heroes to Valhalla. The armored Valkyries rode on horseback to the battlefields to choose slain warriors worthy of afterlife. Valkyries were often portents of war in a supernatural or a human form who had the power to cause death.
See also: Mythology.

Valle, José Cecilio Del (1780-1834), Guatemalan political leader and author of the Central American Declaration of Independence (1821). Valle led Guatemala's fight for independence from Spain, and when the country was annexed by Mexico (1822), he was imprisoned. Although elected vice president of the Central American Confederation (1823), Valle declined to serve.
See also: Guatemala.

Valle-Inclán, Ramón María del (1866-1936), Spanish writer. He was a journalist in Mexico from 1892-1895 before moving to Madrid, where he led a bohemian lifestyle and was a friend of Darío and Azorín. In this period he wrote collections of short stories *Of Women. Six Amorous Tales* (1895) and

Sonatas, a tetralogy based on the four seasons (*Sonata de otoño*, 1902; *Sonata de estío*, 1903; *Sonata de primavera*, 1904; *Sonata de invierno*, 1905). Besides a trilogy about the Carlist Wars (1908-1909), he also wrote many plays, of which *The Cuckolding of Don Friolera* (1921) belongs to the 'esperpentos' (mirrors that create distorted images). His first esperpento novel was *The Tyrant* (1926), in which he crushingly dissects dictatorship. His more political work, largely satirical, has received growing interest over the last decades.

Valletta (pop. 9,200), seaport capital of Malta, on the northeastern coast of the island. A commercial and cultural center, Valletta is the site of the Royal Malta Library, the Royal University of Malta, and the Manoel Theatre.
See also: Malta.

Valley, long, narrow depression in the earth's surface, usually formed by glacier or river erosion. Young valleys are narrow, steep-sided, and V-shaped; mature valleys are broader, with gentler slopes. Rift valleys are the result of collapse between faults. A hanging valley, of glacial origin, is a side valley whose floor is considerably higher than that of the main valley.

Valley of the Kings, or Valley of the Tombs

of Kings, narrow canyon on the west bank of the Nile near Thebes, Egypt. It is the site of over 60 ancient tombs, including the burial places of most of the Pharaohs of the 18th, 19th, and 20th dynasties (1550-1085 B.C.). Among the tombs are those of Tutankhamen, Set I, Thutmose III, Ramses II, Ramses III, and Queen Hatshepsut.

Valois, royal house of France that ruled 1328-1589. The first Valois king was Philip VI; under his rule and that of his descendants, the Valois region of France was a Duchy held by family members. The rule of the Valois Dynasty survived the Hundred Years War (1337-1453), and other conflicts. With the death of Henry III (1589), the crown passed to the house of Bourbon.
See also: France.

Valparaíso (pop. 302,000), seaport city in central Chile, capital of Valparaíso province. The city, founded in 1536, lies on the Pacific Ocean about 70 mi (110 km) northwest of Santiago. It is a major center for manufacture. Chief products include chemicals, textiles, tobacco, sugar and machinery.

Value added by manufacture, statistical measurement of the gain in value of raw materials after being processed into a finished commodity. This is computed by subtracting the overall cost of manufacture-including materials, supplies, storage, fuel, and labor-from the value of the finished product.

Value-added tax (VAT), tax on the value added to goods or services at each stage in their production and distribution. It originated in France in 1954 and was later extended throughout the European Economic Community; it has been considered at various times in the United States. In effect, VAT is a sales tax computed on the difference between what a producer pays for a raw material or semifinished product and what he or she sells it for. The cost of the tax is borne ultimately by consumers. It is a regressive tax because it bears most heavily on low-income people, who spend more and save less than those with high incomes. For government, VAT has the advantage of being broader than most sales taxes and thus producing large revenues even at low rates. The tax is virtually self-enforcing; producers who make tax payments submit claims for credit for the taxes included in their suppliers' prices, and this tends to discourage nonpayment along the line.
See also: Taxation.

Valve, mechanical device that, by opening and closing, enables the flow of fluid in a pipe or other vessel to be controlled. Common valve types are generally named after the shape or mode of operation of the movable element-cone, or needle, valve; gate valve; globe valve; poppet valve; and rotary plug cock. In the butterfly valve a disk pivots on one of its diameters. Self-acting valves include safety valves, usually spring-loaded and designed to open at a predetermined pressure; nonreturn valves, which permit flow in one direction only; and float-operated valves, set to shut off a feeder pipe before a container overflows.

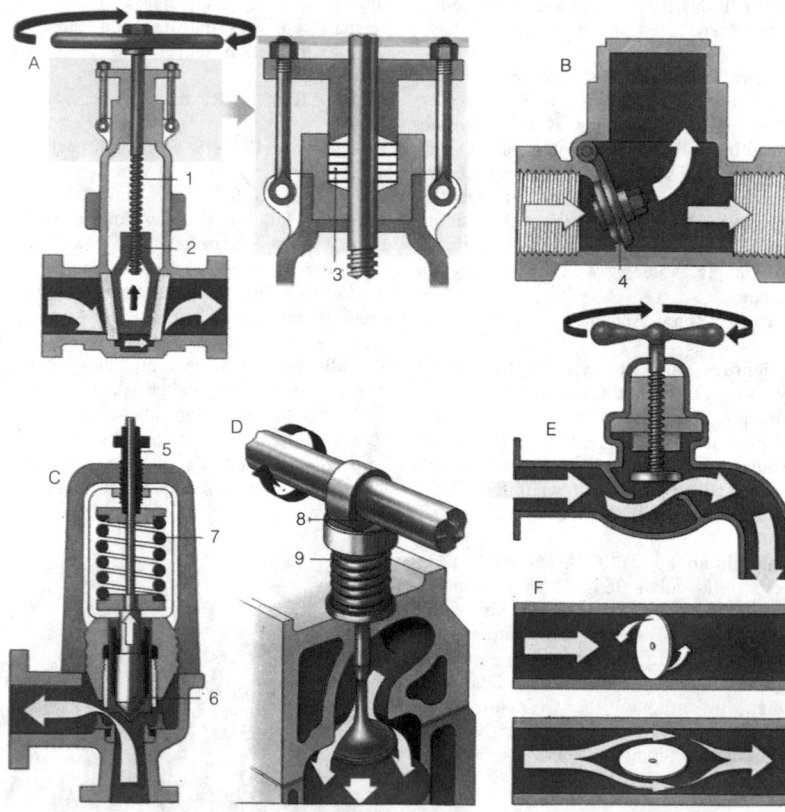

Different valves. (A) Gate valve: the gate (1) is lifted by screw thread on the stem (2), these valves are usually operated closed or wide open, the packing (3) is kept under pressure, and forms the stuffing box, which acts as a seal. (B) Swing check valve: an automatic device for preventing reverse flow. During normal flow, the disc (4) is kept horizontally, at any reversal flow, the disc drops. (C) Safety valve: used for boilers and high pressure steam, set by the adjusting screw (5), that raises (6) against a spring (7), thus relieving the pressure. (D) Poppet valve: moved by a cam (8), and returned by a spring (9). (E) An ordinary tap: a type of pipe valve, with a disc on a circular aperture. (F) Butterfly valve: used for throtling, from hydroelectric systems to car throttles.

Vampire, in folklore, spirit of the dead that leaves its grave at night to suck the blood of living persons. A victim who dies must be decapitated or buried with a stake through his or her heart, to keep from becoming a vampire.
See also: Dracula.

Vampire bat, South and Central American bat (genera *Desmodus* and *Diphylla*) that feeds on the blood of larger mammals and birds; the only parasitic mammal. The bat cuts a slit with its teeth and laps blood from the wound; anticoagulants in its saliva ensure a constant flow.

Vana, Bohumil (1920-), Czechoslovakian table tennis player, won his first singles world title at the age of 18 (the second in 1947). He went on to win 6 more world titles (three doubles and three mixed doubles), and was a member of the team that won the Swaythling Cup five times. Vana had a very attacking style of play, which left very little room for his opponents to take the initiative.

Vanadium, chemical element, symbol V; for physical constants see Periodic Table. Vanadium was discovered by A.M. del Rio in 1801. It occurs in the minerals carnotite, roscoelite, vanadinite, and patronite. It is obtained commercially from patronite, a sulfide. The element is prepared by reduction of the trichloride with magnesium. Vanadium is a bright white, soft, ductile metal, resistant to corrosion. It has a low thermal neutron cross section. It is used to bond titanium to steel. Vanadium and its compounds are used in special steels and ceramics and as catalysts and superconductive magnets. Vanadium and its compounds are toxic.

Van Allen, James Alfred (1914-), U.S. physicist and inventor who discovered two zones of radiation surrounding the earth (1958). This led to new knowledge of the effects of cosmic radiation on the earth. Van Allen developed the research rocket Aerobee. He was also instrumental in organizing the International Geophysical Year (1957-1958), a program promoting worldwide cooperation in research. With the help of the results and the instruments developed on board the Explorer 1 (1958), he deduced the existence of belts of charged particles around the earth (Van Allen radiation belts).

Van Allen belts, 2 belts of high-energy charged particles, mainly protons and electrons, surrounding the earth, named for U.S. physicist James Van Allen, who discovered them in 1958. They extend from a few hundred to about 40,000 mi (65,000 km) above the earth's surface and radiate intensely enough that astronauts must be specially protected from them. The mechanisms for their existence are similar to those involved in the production of the aurora borealis.
See also: Radiation; Van Allen, James Alfred.

Van Buren, Martin (1782-1862), eighth president of the United States (1837-1841). In 1821, he was elected to the U.S. Senate. He stood for state's rights and opposed a strong central government, and began to

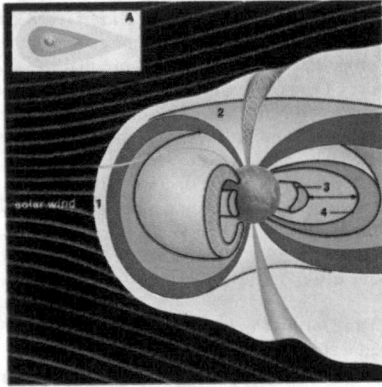

The Van Allen belts are doughnut-shaped zones of highly energetic charged particles within the earth's magnetosphere, or magnetic-field region. Solar wind (yellow lines) distorts the magnetosphere, causing it to take the form of a teardrop with its tail pointing away from the sun (A). Solar particles compress the earth's magnetic field at the shock front (1) and flow around the field's boundary, or magnetopause (2). The most intense Van Allen belts include an inner zone of protons (3), and an outer zone of electrons (4).

bring together other powerful Republicans who shared his sentiments. These 'new' Republicans became the Democratic Party. He became president Jackson's secretary of state (1829-1831), and one of the most powerful men in Washington. When Jackson won reelection in 1832, Van Buren was his running mate. In 1836, Van Buren won the presidential elections. Within days of Van Buren's inauguration, the Panic of 1837 broke. Banks and business failed, specie payments were suspended, and rents, fuel and food prices soared. The Panic had been caused by unchecked speculation in western lands, manufacturing, transportation, and banking. A firm hand was needed to control it, but Van Buren, who believed that 'the less government interferes with private pursuits the better for the general prosperity,' did almost nothing. Inevitably, he was blamed for the depression, as well as for the costly war against the Seminoles in Florida. He also antagonized the South by opposing the annexation of Texas.

Vancouver (pop. 1,890,000), largest city in British Columbia and third-largest in Canada, located on the Burrard Inlet, Strait of Georgia. Originally known as Granville, in 1886 it was renamed for the English explorer George Vancouver. It is an important Pacific port and a major manufacturing center for wood, paper, iron, steel, and chemical products. Other industries are shipbuilding, oil refining, and fish processing. After becoming the terminus of the trans-Canada railroad (1886), it rapidly expanded.
See also: British Columbia.

Vancouver, George (1757-1798), English explorer. He took part in Captain Cook's voyages (1772-1780) and in 1791-1794 led an expedition that explored the Pacific and surveyed the American coast from San Luis Obispo, Calif., to British Columbia. He made surveys of Vancouver Island and the Strait of Georgia, visited Cook's Inlet, Alaska, and failed to find a Northwest Passage. The city of Vancouver, in British Columbia, Canada, was named after him in 1886.

Vandals, ancient Germanic people. They gradually migrated from south of the Baltic to Pannonia and Dacia. In the 5th century they invaded the Roman Empire, ravaging Gaul and Spain. Under Genseric they established a strong Vandal kingdom in northern Africa (429) that extended to Sicily, and in 455 they sacked Rome. The Vandals were finally defeated by the Byzantine Belisarius, after which they disappeared as a unified people.

Van de Graaff, Robert Jemison (1901-1967), U.S. physicist and inventor of the electrostatic generator, used in nuclear research. While a student at the Sorbonne, Van de Graaff attended lectures given by Marie Curie. He formed the idea for his generator when he realized that the study of atomic behavior requires a source of energetic beams of subatomic particles. In 1946 he became a founder of the High Voltage Engineering Corporation (HVEC).

Van de Graaff generator, or electrostatic generator, device for generating a high voltage charge, important in the study of nuclear power. Invented in the 1930s by Robert Van

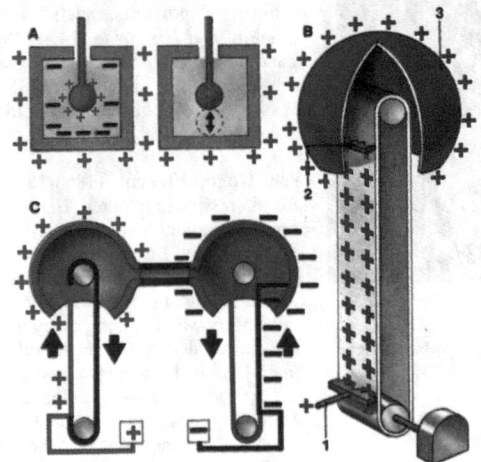

(A) A positively charged sphere induces an equal, negative charge on the interior of a metal box and hence a positive charge on the exterior (left). If the sphere touches the interior, the charges cancel out and the exterior charge remains (right). Similarly, in a Van de Graaf generator (B) a charged comb (1) induces a charge on a belt of insulating material. Through another comb (2) inside the conducting sphere (3) the charge is transferred to the sphere's exterior. Two oppositely charged generators (C) yield a large electrical potential.

A detail from the *Portinari Altarpiece* by Hugo van der Goes (1440?-82). The central panel shows the adoration of the shepherds on the left (Uffizi, Florence).

Van der Goes, Hugo (1440?-1482), Flemish painter of religious subjects. He was influenced by Jan van Eyck and Rogier van der Weyden. Among his works are the *Portinari Altarpiece* (c.1476) and *Death of the Virgin* (c.1480).

Van der Meer, Simon (1925-), Dutch physicist who shared the 1984 Nobel Prize for physics with Carlo Rubia for their leading roles in planning and executing the experiments, reported in 1983, that demonstrated the existence of the elementary particles called intermediate vector bosons. *See also:* Boson; Physics.

A portrait of Giovanni Arnolfini and his wife (1434), painted by Jan van Eyck. In this painting, a number of objects have a symbolic significance: for example, the dog, which means faithfulness. Over the mirror, an inscription reads: 'Johannes van Eyck was here, 1434'. (National Gallery, London).

Van der Waals, Johannes Diderik (1837-1923), Dutch physicist who investigated the properties of real gases. Noting that the kinetic theory of gases assumed that the molecules had neither size nor interactive forces between them, in 1873 he proposed **Van der Waals' equation**, in which allowance is made for both these factors. The weak attractive forces between molecules are therefore named Van der Waals forces. He received the 1910 Nobel Prize for physics. *See also:* Physics.

Van Doren, Carl (1885-1950), U.S. author, educator, and literary critic. Van Doren taught at Columbia University (1911-1930) and was an editor of the *Cambridge History of American Literature* (1917-1921); *The Nation* (1919-1922); and *Century Magazine* (1922-1925). He is best known for his biographies, including *Swift* (1930), *Sinclair Lewis* (1933), and *Jane Mecom* (1950). He was awarded the Pulitzer Prize in 1939 for his biography *Benjamin Franklin* (1938).

Van Doren, Mark (1894-1972), U.S. poet and critic. His *Collected Poems* (1939) earned him the Pulitzer Prize in 1940. As a critic, Van Doren began his career with a study of Henry David Thoreau in 1916. His major critical writings appear in *Private Reader* (1942) and *The Happy Critic* (1961). Van Doren was a renowned professor of English at Columbia University (1920-1959), where his students included John Berryman and Lionel Trilling. He also wrote plays, novels, and short stories.

Van Dyck, Sir Anthony (1599-1641), Flemish baroque portrait and religious painter. He was a pupil of Peter Paul Rubens, and his portrait style, influenced by Venetian art, was one of elegantly posed figures and rich but refined color and handling, particularly of materials. He painted Italian and English nobility and was court painter from 1632 to Charles I of England. *See also:* Baroque.

Van Eyck, Jan (1390-1441), Flemish painter. The first leading artist from the Netherlands, he collaborated with his older brother, Hubert (c.1370-1426), on the Ghent altarpiece. Completed in 1432, it comprises more than 250 figures in 20 panels. Van Eyck's other important works include a number of portraits, such as *Giovanni Arnolfini and His Bride* (1434). All are remarkable for realistic, closely observed details. He was the first painter to develop effects of richness, brilliance, and intensity in oil paint.

Van Gogh, Vincent (1853-1890), Dutch postimpressionist painter. His early, dark-toned work, done in the Netherlands, focuses on peasant life. Later (1886-1888), in Paris, he met Paul Gauguin and Georges Seurat. In 1888 he moved to Arles, in southern France, where—among many other paintings—he produced the brilliantly colored *Sunflowers* in a direct style and the symbolic *The Night Café*, using color suggestively. After a fit of insanity, in which he cut off his left ear (1889), he painted at the asylums of St. Rémy and Auvers. In *Portrait of Dr.*

Gachet (1890) he attempted to express ideas and emotion in and through paint. He committed suicide.

Vanilla, any of various tropical vines (genus *Vanilla*) of the orchid family; the term also refers to the extract made from the vine's pods and used for flavoring. The plants grow to about 50 ft (15.2 m) and bear yellow-green flowers that produce the pods, 5-10 in (13-25 cm) in length. Vanilla extract is obtained by a process of pulverization of the cured vanilla pods which are then heated in alcohol and water. Vanilla is widely used to flavor chocolate, candy, ice cream, baked goods, and beverages.

Van Leeuwenhoek, Anton *See:* Leeuwenhoek, Anton van.

Vanuatu

Capital:	Port Vila
Area:	4,707 sq mi (12,190 sq km)
Population:	196,000
Language:	English, French, Bislama
Government:	Republic
Independent:	1980
Head of gov.:	Prime minister
Per capita:	US$ 1,300
Monetary unit:	1 Vatu = 100 centimes

Vanuatu, officially the Republic of Vanuatu, formerly the New Hebrides, independent republic consisting of 80 small islands, situated east of Australia and extending over some 500 mi (805 km) of the South Pacific Ocean. *Land.* The overall area of the islands of Vanuatu is 4,707 sq mi (12,190 km). Espíritu Santo, the largest island, has an area of 1,542 sq mi (3,994 sq km). The capital, Port-Vila, is on the second-largest island, Efâte. The islands are of volcanic origin and there are 6 active volcanos. The rugged mountainous interiors, densely covered with tropical rain forests, give way to narrow coastal strips where most of the islands' inhabitants live. *People.* Almost all the people of Vanuatu are Melanesians. There are also small Chinese, British, and French minorities. The official languages are Bislama, English, and French. *Economy.* About 75% of the people live in rural villages and pursue traditional subsistence farming. They grow coconuts and oth-

The Van de Graaff generator, invented by Robert Jemison Van de Graaff, the machine operates by carrying electrical charges from a collection of high-voltage points on a moving belt into a hollow metal casing. A metallic brush transports the charge to the surface of the casing, and as the charge accumulates, the voltage increases. *See also:* Particle accelerator; Van de Graaff, Robert Jemison.

er fruits, yams, and taro; pigs are raised for food and ceremonial purposes. Local industries process copra, fish, and beef for export. Manganese has been mined since 1961, and (eco) tourism is increasing. Special tax laws have made Vanuatu a banking center and corporate haven.

History. There is evidence of human settlements on the islands as early as 1300 B.C., but the islands were not discovered by Europeans until the arrival of the Portuguese in 1606. The British and French explored the islands in the 18th century. During the 19th century, strife broke out between native inhabitants and British and French settlers. In 1906 a joint British-French condominium was established to rule the islands. In 1980, on the eve of independence, fighting broke out on Espíritu Santo where guerrillas were mounting an armed struggle for that island's secession. The fighting ended after British peacekeeping forces arrived. The islands of Vanuatu became independent within the British Commonwealth on July 30, 1980. George Kalkoa became President. Soldiers from Papua New Guinea substituted the French-British peace troops and put a definite stop to the separation movement Espíritu Santo. Political instability marked the years following the independence. The distribution of land among the people remained a constant point of contention.

In the 1990's Vanuatu agreed to the South Pacific Forum to destroy a number of American chemical weapons on Johnston, a remote coral island.

In 1998, it came to light that banks on Vanuatu had been lending large sums of money to politicians. The banks were also allegedly involved in the laundering of Russian and Latin American drug money. The Organization for Economic Cooperation and Development (OECD) warned they would press for sanctions.

Vanzetti, Bartolomeo *See:* Sacco-Vanzetti case.

Vapor, substance that, though present in the gaseous phase, generally exists as a liquid or solid at room temperature.
See also: Evaporation.

Varanasi (pop. 932,000), formerly Benaraš, ancient city in Uttar Pradesh State, on the Ganges River in northern India. The city is of great religious import as a center for Hindu pilgrimage, with over 1,500 temples and shrines. Varanasi has miles of riverfront ghats, or stairways, from which pilgrims may bathe in the holy Ganges River before praying. Industries include textiles and brassware. Varanasi is the site of Benaras Hindu University (1916) and the Mosque of Aurangzeb.
See also: India.

Vardhamana (5th century B.C.), the actual, historical founder of Jainism (a religion in India). Descendant from a caste of warriors, he began to lead a severely ascetic and meditative existence at the age of 28, which allowed him to free his soul from its physical confinement. This is why he came to be known as Mahavira (great hero) and Jina (victor). Preached his teachings for 30 years.

These were possibly only put down in writing as late as the 4th century A.D. (the so-called siddhanta).

Varèse, Edgard (1883-1965), French-born U.S. composer of non-traditional music and sound techniques. *Ionisation* (1931), his most famous composition, is written for numerous percussion instruments and two sirens. Other works include *Hyperprism* (1923), and *Density 21.5* (1935). After 1950 Varèse concentrated mainly on electronically produced music.

Vargas, Getúlio Dornelles (1883-1954), president of Brazil (1930-1945,1951-1954). He set up a 'New State' (1937), strongly centralized government-promoted industrial, economic, and social development. Opposition from the army during his second term led him to commit suicide.
See also: Brazil.

Vargas Llosa, Mario (1936-), Peruvian author of novels depicting modern Peruvian social and political life. His novels include *The Time of the Hero* (1962), *The Green House* (1966), *Conversations in the Cathedral* (1969), *The War of the End of the World* (1984), *Who Killed Palomino Molero?* (1987), *The Storyteller* (1989), *A Fish in the Water* (1993), and *The Feast of the Goat* (2000). Vargas Llosa was an unsuccessful candidate for the presidency of Peru in 1990. In 1994, he received the Cervantes Prize for his complete works.

Varicella *See:* Chickenpox.

Varicose vein, enlarged or twisting vein, usually occuring in the legs, resulting from incompetent or damaged valves in the veins. Unpleasant in appearance, they cause venous stagnation, with skin eczema and ulcers on the inside of the ankle, hemorrhage, and edema (swelling). Treatment includes support stockings and, in more serious cases, removal through surgery.
See also: Vein.

Varnish, solution of resin that dries to form a hard, transparent film. It is widely applied to wood, metal, and masonry to improve surface properties without changing appearance. There are two main types: spirit varnishes, consisting of natural or synthetic resins dissolved in a volatile solvent such as alcohol, and oleoresinous varnishes-more resistant to heat and weather-which are mixtures of resins and drying oils dissolved in turpentine or a petroleum oil. Lacquer, the original wood varnish, is the sap of the varnish tree.
See also: Resin.

Varying hare *See:* Snowshoe hare.

Vasarely, Victor (real name, Viktor or Gyözö Vasarhelyi; 1908-1997), Hungarian-French artist. Vasarely is considered to be one of the great pioneers of op art. In the 1950s he made experimental prints and paintings of black and white lines (often forming wavy patterns). In the 1960s he researched the optical effect of color using a systematic arrangement of geometric shapes, such as circles and squares, in dif-

ferent colors or in a progression of colors. He made three-dimensional objects which produced various optical effects as the viewer moved around them. Vasarely advocated the abolition of the unique artwork. According to his theory, an artwork had to be replicable so it could be seen by as many people as possible.

Vasari, Giorgio (1511-1574), an Italian painter, author, and architect. Vasari was born in Arezzo. At 13 he went to Florence, where he studied with Andrea del Sarto. Vasari was a prolific painter in the Mannerist style. Among his most famous works are frescoes in the Palazzo Vecchio, Florence, and in the Scala Regia in the Vatican. His most important architectural works are the Uffizi Palace, Florence; the corridor connecting the Uffizi and Pitti palaces; and the Palazzo dei Cavalieri, Pisa. His *Lives of the Most Excellent Italian Architects, Painters and Sculptors from Cimabue to the Present Time* (1550, revised and enlarged 1568) laid a foundation for later writers on the history of Italian renaissance art.

Vasco Da Gama *See:* Da Gama, Vasco.

Vasectomy, sterilization procedure for men. The vas deferens are cut to prevent sperm from reaching the seminal vesicles and hence the urethra of the penis. It does not affect ejaculation.
See also: Sterilization.

Vásquez de Coronado, Francisco *See:* Coronado, Francisco Vásquez de.

Vassal *See:* Feudalism.

Vatican City

Area:	109 acres (44 hectares)
Population:	900
Language:	Latin, Italian
Government:	Sovereign state
Independent:	1929
Head of gov.:	Pope
Monetary unit:	1 Italian lira = 100 centesimi

Vatican City, independent state, the world's smallest. It occupies 108.7 acres (44 hectares) of territory within the city of Rome, Italy. Vatican City serves as the spir-

V

itual, administrative, and political center of Roman Catholicism, and it is ruled by the pope, as head of the Roman Catholic church. It has a population of c.1,000 and its official languages are Italian and Latin.

Vatican City is dominated by Saint Peter's basilica and the Vatican Palace, one of the world's largest residential palaces. Among the city's treasures are the frescoes of the Sistine Chapel executed by Michelangelo Buonarroti as well as the paintings, sculpture, and other artifacts in the Vatican Museum collection. The Vatican Archive and Library contain many priceless manuscripts and, reputedly, the world's most extensive holdings of erotic literature, including a collection that once belonged to Benjamin Franklin.

The Vatican has its own bank, mints its own coins, and oversees the administration and investment of the church's assets worldwide. The city has no income tax and no restriction on the import or export of funds. It has its own broadcasting facilities, railroad station, and the newspaper *L'Osservatore Romano*. The Swiss Guard, the pope's personal bodyguard, are Vatican City's army. The city maintains diplomatic relations with many countries throughout the world by means of ambassadors, called nuncios, and sends apostolic delegates to other countries to represent the church's interests. As a matter of tradition and practice, the U.S. government did not post an ambassador to the papal court in the 18th and 19th centuries, nor to the Vatican City for most of the 20th century. Under President Ronald Reagan, the United States broke with this long-standing tradition and appointed an ambassador to Vatican City.

The official independence of Vatican City from Italy was established in 1929 following a long period of estrangement between the papacy and Italy over the papacy's loss of its once extensive territorial holdings, known as the Papal States, on the Italian peninsula. The issue was finally resolved in the Lateran

Treaty negotiated that year between Cardinal Pietro Gasparri for the papacy and the Fascist dictator Benito Mussolini. In 1993 official ties with Israel were established and in 1994 with Jordan. The latter step was taken in order to improve relations with the Arab world.

The year 2000 drew many Catholic pilgrims to the Vatican City to celebrate the Jubilee Holy Year.
See also: Roman Catholic Church.

Vatican Councils, the two most recent Roman Catholic ecumenical councils, held at the Vatican. Vatican Council I (1869-1870), summoned by Pius IX, restated traditional dogma against materialism, rationalism, and liberalism. It also declared the pope to be infallible when, speaking *ex cathedra*, he defines a doctrine of faith or morals. Some dissenters seceded as Old Catholics. Vatican Council II (1962-1965), summoned by John XXIII, aimed at renewal of the church, the updating of its organization and attitude to the modern world, and the ultimate reunion of all Christian churches. Protestant and Orthodox observers attended. Along with calling for a reform of the ministry and liturgy, including increased lay participation and use of vernacular languages, the council decreed that the bishops with the pope form a body ('collegiality') and that the Virgin Mary is 'Mother of the Church.'

Vatican Library, official library of the Roman Catholic Church in Vatican City. It was founded by Pope Nicholas V (r.1447-1455) as a library for handwritten manuscripts. Open to scholars, the library contains about 1 million printed books and more than 70,000 manuscripts.

Vaudeville, term for variety shows deriving from Vau de Vire, a French valley and source of 15th-century songs, or from *voix de ville*, French street songs. It was applied from the 1880s to U.S. shows with musical, comic,

dramatic, acrobatic, and juggling acts. Noted artists included Eddie Cantor, Will Rogers, and W. C. Fields. Vaudeville declined in the 1930s.

Vaughan Williams, Ralph (1872-1958), English composer famous for his use of traditional English folk music. The three *Norfolk Rhapsodies* (1906) were the first major works characteristic of his distinctive style. Other works include nine symphonies.

VD *See:* Venereal disease.

Veal, meat of young cattle or calves. The calves are fed on milk and the meat is drained of blood. As a result, veal is light in color and in flavor. Consumption in the United States averages about 4 1/2 lb (2 kg) per person yearly.

Veblen, Thorstein Bunde (1857-1929), U.S. economist and author. A social theorist known for his study of economic evolution and social change, Veblen produced sharp analyses of the wealthy classes. His *Theory of the Leisure Class* (1899), coined such terms as 'conspicuous consumption' and 'pecuniary emulation.' Other works include *The Theory of Business Enterprise* (1904), a criticism of capitalism; and *The Engineers and the Price System* (1921).
See also: Economics.

Vecellio, Tiziano *See:* Titian.

Vector *See:* Force.

Vedanta (Sanskrit, 'end of knowledge'), system of Hindu philosophy, based at first on the Upanishads (the final part of the Veda) and later on the Brahma Sutras, commentaries on the Upanishads, that date from the 1st century A.D. The Vedanta concern the relation of the individual (*atman*) to the Absolute (*Brahman*).
See also: Upanishads.

Vegetables that are commonly grown in temperate zones, include varieties of cabbage—such as brussels sprouts, cauliflower, broccoli, and kale—and spinach, which is valued for its high iron and vitamin contents. Lettuce varieties, such as romaine, as well as the herbs chicory and endive, are used as salad greens. Cooked immature flower buds of the globe artichoke are considered a delicacy. A variety of plant parts are considered edible. Pulses— plants that have leguminous pods as their fruit—include garden peas, broad beans, runner beans, French beans, and lentils. Plants whose stems are eaten as vegetables include celery, asparagus, and rhubarb. Among tubers—enlarged underground stems of plants—are the potato and the Jerusalem artichoke, the latter related to the sunflower.

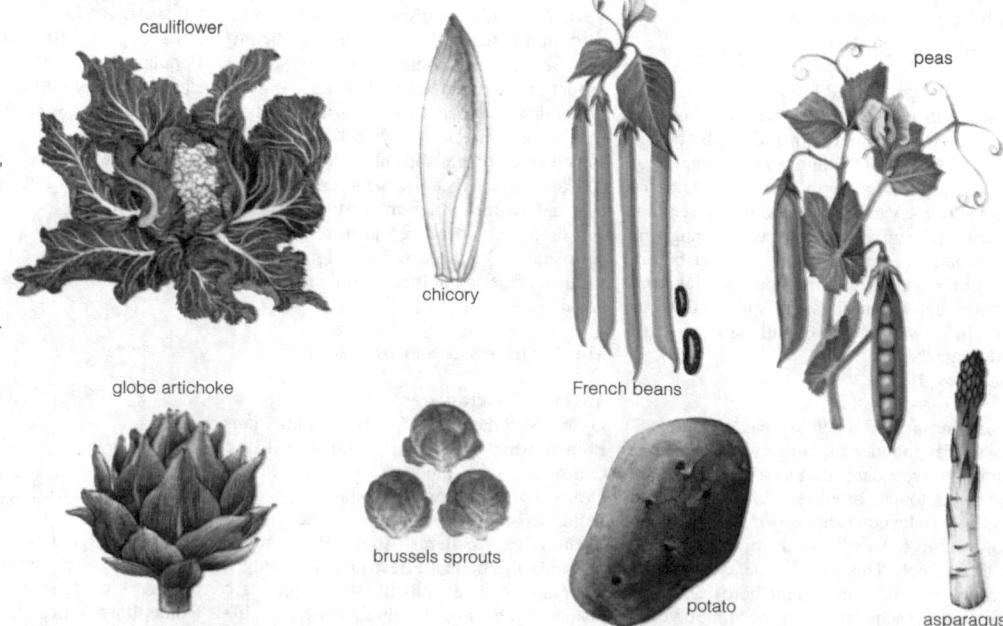

cauliflower
chicory
globe artichoke
brussels sprouts
French beans
potato
peas
asparagus

Vedas (Sanskrit, 'knowledge'), most ancient of Indian scriptures, believed to have been inspired by God and basic to Hinduism. There are 4 *Samhitas* or collections of mantras (hymns)-the *Rig, Yajur, Sama,* and *Atharva-Veda.* The oldest may date from 1500 B.C. Vedic literature consists of the Veda itself, the *Brahmanas* and *Aranyakas,* and the Upanishads.
See also: Hinduism.

Veery (*Catharus fuscescens*), brownish bird of the thrush family, found in the northeastern United States and Canada. It is about 7 in (18 cm) long and nests in the lower branches of bushes or small trees.

Vega, or Alpha Lyrae, brightest main-sequence star in the constellation Lyra in the northern hemisphere, the fourth-brightest star in the night sky. The star is surrounded by a shell of solid particles indicating that it may be a solar system in a formative state. Vega is 26 light years away and is expected to become earth's polar star c.A.D. 14,000.
See also: Star.

Vega, Lope de (1562-1635), Spanish dramatist and poet credited with founding Spain's national drama. A prolific writer, Lope produced 426 plays of which 42 short ones survive. He also wrote narrative poetry, prose romances, and a poetical essay, *The New Art of Writing Plays* (1609), that expounded his theories of drama. His main themes were the friction between the masses and a corrupt nobility and the conflicts of honor and passion.

Vegetable, general term for the edible part of a plant. Vegetables are excellent sources of vitamins, iron, and calcium. They are sometimes grouped according to the part of the plant they represent: flower clusters (e.g. cauliflower), fruits (tomatoes), leaves (spinach), roots (carrots), seeds (peas), stems (asparagus), tubers (potatoes), and bulbs (onions).

Vegetable oil, substance obtained from the seeds of plants and the fleshy part of fruits. It consists almost entirely of fat, an important part of a healthy diet. It is used in both the production and the cooking of many foods. Soybean oil is the most commonly used vegetable oil in the United States, followed by corn, cottonseed, olive, peanut, safflower, and sunflower oil. Most margarines are made with soybean or sunflower oils as the main ingredient.

Vegetarianism, restriction of one's food to substances of vegetable origin. Vegetarianism is practiced variously for health and fitness and because of ethical or religious beliefs. A vegetarian is a person who abstains from eating meat, either keeping strictly to a diet of vegetables, grains, nuts, and fruit, or including eggs, milk, butter, and cheese. The latter is called an ovo-lacto-vegetarian.

Vein, thin-walled collapsible vessel that returns blood to the heart from the tissue capillaries. Veins contain valves that prevent back-flow, especially in the legs. Blood drains from the major veins into the inferior to superior vena cava.

Velázquez, Diego (1599-1660), Spanish painter. In 1623, he became court painter to King Philip IV of Spain. His style was influenced strongly by his Flemish contemporary, Peter Paul Rubens, and also by Italian artists of the High Renaissance. His masterpieces include *The Drunkards, Christ on the Cross,* and *The Maids of Honor.*
See also: Renaissance.

Velde, Henricus Clementius (Henry) van de (1863-1957), a Belgian architect and designer. He supported functionalism, the idea that an object's design should reflect and aid its use. During the 1890's he was a leader in the style known as Art Nouveau. This style used the rhythmic, natural lines of plant forms in wood, metal, and stone, instead of the historical forms of Classical or Gothic architecture. Later, Velde came to believe that the machine would establish a style and would control the cultural pattern of the 20th century. Velde began as painter but turned to architecture in 1890 and industrial design in 1892. In 1914 he designed the Werkbund Theatre (Cologne, Germany), which had a strong influence on the design of other auditoriums.

Velde de Jonge, Willem van de (1633-1707), Dutch painter, son and pupil of Willem van de Velde the Elder (1611-1693). He also studied under Simon de Vlieger. In 1673 he went with his father to England, where he was soon appointed royal painter to the court of King Charles II. Like his father, he also painted ships and naval battles, and was one of the great masters of this genre. The fact that he had actually taken part in a number of the naval battles he painted, gives his paintings an added historical value. His most beautiful paintings are those of ships on a calm sea.

Velocity, vector quantity expressing the direction and speed of any moving object. Velocity may be uniform, in which case both speed and direction remain constant, or variable, in which case speed and/or direction change.
See also: Falling bodies, Law of.

Velvet leaf *See:* Indian mallow.

Venerable Bede, The *See:* Bede, Saint.

Venereal disease, name for infectious diseases transmitted mainly or exclusively by sexual contact. *Gonorrhea* is an acute bacterial disease that is frequently asymptomatic in females, although they may suffer mild cervicitis or urethritis. In males it may be asymptomatic also, but it usually causes a painful urethritis with urethral discharge of pus. Gonorrhea is best treated with peni-

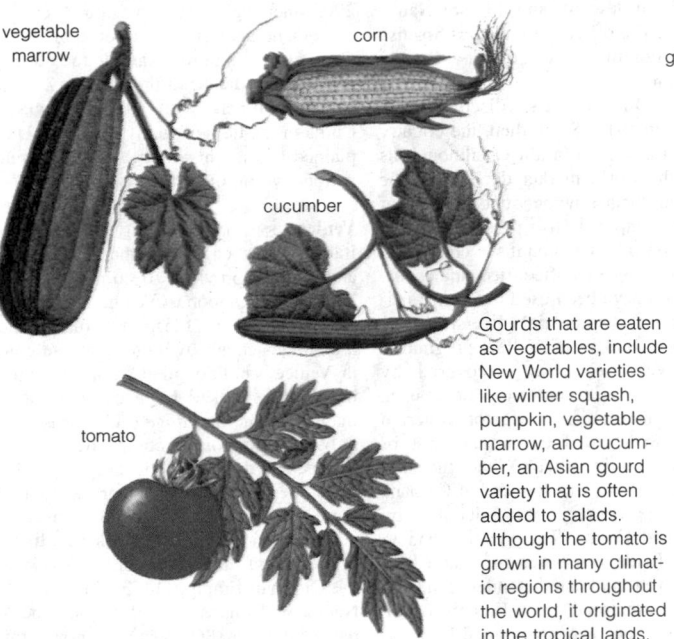

vegetable marrow

corn

cucumber

tomato

Gourds that are eaten as vegetables, include New World varieties like winter squash, pumpkin, vegetable marrow, and cucumber, an Asian gourd variety that is often added to salads. Although the tomato is grown in many climatic regions throughout the world, it originated in the tropical lands.

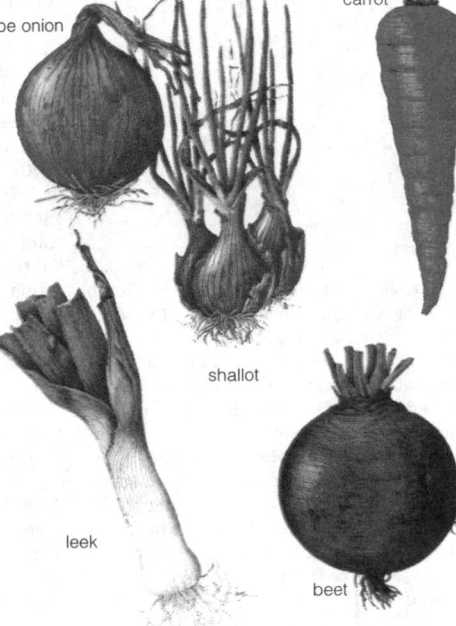

globe onion

carrot

shallot

leek

beet

Onions are bulb vegetables that are used to season salads, soups, and cooked dishes. Common varieties include the globe onion, shallot, spring onion, and the leek. Root vegetables like carrots, turnips, rutabagas, parsnips, and beets are harvested in autumn and winter; radishes are harvested in spring. The sweet potato, a tropical root vegetable, is related to the morning glory.

V

cillin. *Syphilis*, due to *Treponema pallidum*, a spirochete, is a disease with 2 stages. A painless genital ulcer, or chancre, develops in the weeks after contact. Secondary syphilis, starting weeks or months after infection, involves fever, malaise, and a characteristic rash, as well as organ disease (hepatitis, meningitis). If the disease is treated with a full course of penicillin in the early stages, its progression is prevented. Tertiary syphilis takes several forms. Gummas-chronic rubbery tumors affecting skin, epithelium, bone, or internal organs-may develop. Tertiary syphilis causes heart disease. Syphilis of the nervous system may cause tabes dorsalis, primary eye disease, chronic meningitis, or paralysis, with mental disturbance, personality change, failure of judgment, and muscular weakness. Penicillin may only partially reverse late syphilis. Other venereal diseases include Reiter's disease (in males only), genital trichomoniasis, thrush, *Herpes simplex* virus, and 'nonspecific urethritis.' Tropical venereal diseases include chancroid, lymphogranuloma vene-reum, and granuloma inguinale.

Venezuela

Capital:	Caracas
Area:	352,144 sq mi
	(912,050 sq km)
Population:	24,288,000
Language:	Spanish
Government:	Federal presidential republic
Independent:	1830
Head of gov.:	President
Per capita:	US$ 6,100
Monetary unit:	1 Bolívar = 100 céntimos

Venezuela, republic in northern South America. Covering an area of 352,134 sq mi (912,050 sq km), Venezuela extends along the Caribbean coast from Colombia in the west and southwest to Guyana in the east. It is bordered by Brazil to the south and the Caribbean Sea in the north.
Land. Venezuela may be divided into 4 contrasting geographical regions: the Venezuelan Highlands in the west and north; the coastal lowlands; the great central plain called the Llanos, dominated by the Orinoco River; and the Guyana Highlands. The Venezuelan Highlands are an extension of

The Palazzo Ducale, or Doge's Palace, served as the residence of Venice's elected rulers and contained its governmental offices during the Middle Ages.

the Andes. Entering the country in the southwest, they contain Venezuela's highest mountains, including Pico Bolivár rising to 16,411 ft (5,002 m) to dominate the Sierra Nevada de Mérida. The central highlands with their fertile valleys form the most important part of the country and contain several large cities, including the capital, Caracas. The coastal lowlands, almost completely enclosed by mountains and centered on swamp-fringed Lake Maracaibo, are known as the Maracaibo Lowlands. They constitute one of the world's great oil-producing regions. The lowlands are known for their hot and humid climate. Inland lies the great central grassland plains called the Llanos. Covering some 120,000 sq mi (310,800 sq km) and drained by many streams descending from the mountains to the Orinoco River, they are the great cattle-grazing region of Venezuela. Finally, the Guyana Highlands, south of the Orinoco River, cover about half of Venezuela and are very thinly populated. Much of the region is covered with tropical forests and parts have yet to be explored. Angel Falls, the highest falls in the world at a height of 3,212 ft (979 m), are located in the Guyana Highlands.
People. Nearly 70% of the people of Venezuela are mestizo, a mixture of whites and Native Americans. About 20% of the population is white, mostly of Spanish descent; another 10% of the people are of black African descent; and 2% are Native Americans. The official language is Spanish and the dominant religion is Roman Catholicism.
Economy. Oil was first discovered in Venezuela in 1918. Since then, the country has been a major oil producer, although its share of the world market declined in the 1970s. Venezuela now accounts for 4% of the world's output. It also produces natural gas and iron ore. The country's chief agricultural products are coffee, rice, and cocoa. Oil revenues have been used to finance irrigation projects, industrial diversification, public works, and social welfare programs.
History. Venezuela was discovered by Columbus in 1498, but may have been named by the Italian navigator Amerigo Vespucci, who sailed the north coast of South America in 1501. When the first Spanish settlement was founded at Cumaná in 1521, the country was inhabited by Arawaks and Caribs. The Spanish had to overcome fierce resistance in establishing dominion. Venezuelan independence, unsuccessfully attempted by Francisco de Miranda in 1806, was proclaimed by a na-

tional congress in 1811. Miranda became dictator in 1812, but was imprisoned by the Spanish. Simón Bolívar, who was born in Venezuela, led the independence struggle and triumphed in 1821. He made the country part of Greater Colombia, but it later broke free and became an independent republic in 1830 under José Antonio Páez. Dictatorships followed, the longest and most successful under Juan Vicente Gómez, who ruled the country from 1908 to 1935. It was under Gómez that Venezuela's oil riches were first developed and concessions granted to foreign companies. In 1958, the corrupt dictatorship of Marcos Pérez Jiménez was brought down by a military junta under Rómulo Betancourt and the country was restored to democracy. The petroleum industry was nationalized peacefully in 1976. Venezuela's economy suffered in the early 1980s with the drop in oil prices, but new discoveries of oil fields and higher oil prices brought on by the crisis in the Persian Gulf (1990) have led to a boost in oil production. Military coups staged in 1992, were quickly put down. Hugo Chávez, the former head of the army who had tried to seize power in 1992, won the presidential elections of 1998. He promised to end corruption and the inequality of incomes. He was re-elected in 2000. Laborers grew increasingly agitated in 2001: they demanded higher wages. After a number of unpopular economic reforms in 2002, their agitation grew into a resistance movement against the policies of Chávez. General strikes in for example the oil industry, severely damaged the economy. Chávez sought contacts with Russia, Cuba and China in the field of foreign politics. He explained this as 'his contribution to a multinational world order'.

Venice (pop. 330,000), city in northeastern Italy, seaport capital of the Veneto region and Venezia province. It comprises 118 islands in the Lagoon of Venice at the head of the Adriatic Sea. Transport is mainly along the famous canals by motorboat and gondola. Venice is built on piles sunk deep into the mud and is linked by a causeway to the mainland. The first *doge* (duke) was elected in 697. Venice rose to control trade between Europe and the East. At its height (15th century), Venice ruled many areas along the coast of the eastern Mediterranean, the Aegean, and parts of the Black Sea. Its power weakened during the long struggle with the Ottoman Empire (1453-1718). It fell to Napoleon Bonaparte in 1797 and became part of Italy in 1866. Venice is now a major

tourist resort, boasting unique beauty and a magnificent cultural heritage.
See also: Italy.

Venkataraman, Ramaswamy (1910-), Indian statesman and president of India (1987-1992). Venkataraman was an attorney and pro-labor advocate and social worker who was elected to parliament (1950). He served as minister of finance (1980-1984), and as minister of defense (1982-1984). He was active in the United Nations and then served as Indira Gandhi's vice president (1984-1987).
See also: India.

Ventricle *See:* Heart.

Ventris, Michael George Francis (1922-1956), English architect and cryptographer who deciphered (1953) Linear B, a semi-pictorial Minoan-Mycenaean script, and showed it to be an ancient form of Greek. Following World War II, during which he was trained as a decoder, Ventris established a Committee of Correspondents, a group of scholars worldwide. With their advice, he set about deciphering the script, discovered on a number of clay tablets at Knossos, Crete (1900-1908). Ventris used statistical analysis to plot a tentative syllabary. The results were published as 'Evidence for Greek Dialect in Mycenaean Archives' (1953) and are significant for proving the Greek world to be literate some 500 years before Homer.

Venturi, Robert (1925-), U.S. architect. A controversial critic of the purely functional and spare designs of modern orthodox architecture, he set forth his 'counterrevolutionary' views in *Complexity and Contradiction in Architecture* (1966) and *Learning from Las Vegas* (1972).
See also: Architecture.

Venus, in Roman mythology, goddess of love and beauty. Originally a minor deity associated with gardens, fruits, and flowers, Venus was adopted by Latin soldiers (c.217 B.C.) who enlarged her image to symbolize the life force. Venus was closely identified with the Greek Aphrodite. The Julii family, ancestors of Julius Caesar, were her priests.
See also: Mythology.

Venus, second planet from the sun in the solar system. Its diameter is 7,700 mi (12,392 km), slightly smaller than that of the earth. Its face is completely obscured by dense clouds containing sulfuric acid, although the USSR's spaceprobes *Venera-9* and *Venera-10* (Oct.1975) landings provided photographs of the planet's rocky surface. Venus revolves about the sun at a mean distance of 67.2 million mi (108.2 million km) in 225 days, rotating on its axis in a retrograde direction in 243 days. Its atmosphere is 97% carbon dioxide, and its surface temperature is c.850°F (455°C). Venus has no known moons and could not support life.
See also: Planet; Solar System.

Venus de Milo, armless statue of the Greek goddess Aphrodite. It was carved in marble c.150 B.C. and was discovered (1820) on the island of Melos. It is now in the Louvre in Paris.

Venus's-flytrap (*Dionaea muscipula*), insect-catching plant that lives in the sandy country of the Carolinas and neighboring states. Its leaves form a rosette against the ground, and the outer part of each forms a pad hinged in the middle. Around the edge of the pad are stiff teeth and 3 spines stick up from the middle of the pad. When an insect brushes the spines, the pad rapidly folds up so that the insect is caught behind the teeth. Secretions digest the soft parts of the insect's body. The Venus-flytrap's speed is remarkable. It has even been recorded catching a small frog.

Veracruz (pop. 330,000), port city in east central Mexico on the Gulf of Mexico. Once the site of a Native American village, Veracruz is now an important shipping center handling much of Mexico's foreign trade. It exports sugar, coffee, vanilla, chicle, and petroleum products. The city manufactures tiles, chocolate, liquor, footwear, and textiles. Gallega Island protects the harbor and is the site of the Spanish fortress of San Juan de Ulua (1565).
See also: Mexico.

Verbena, genus (*Verbena*) of the vervain family of herbaceous plants, especially several cultivated species with blue, white, crimson, purple, or striped flowers.

Verdi, Giuseppe (1813-1901), Italian opera composer. He rose to fame during the struggle for Italian unification and independence; early operas, such as *Nabucco* (1842), express these political ideals. By the time of *Rigoletto* (1851), *Il Trovatore* (1853), and *La Traviata* (1853), he had developed his powerful individual style well beyond the conventions inherited from Gioacchino Rossini, Gaetano Donizetti, and Vincenzo Bellini. *Don Carlos* (1867), *Aïda* (1871), and the *Requiem* (1874) honoring the novelist Alessandro Manzoni are works of his maturity. The 2 great Shakespearian operas of Verdi's old age, *Otello* (1887) and *Falstaff*

Up close, Venus shows nothing but her impenetrable cloud cover. The upper cloud layers are rotating extremely fast: one rotation in almost four days. These fast atmospheric currents are sometimes compared to the jetstreams on earth.

(1893), were written to libretti by Arrigo Boito.
See also: Opera.

Verdin (*Auriparus flaviceps*), songbird common in low deserts and brushlands of the U.S. Southwest and northern Mexico. The verdin is gray, with a yellow head, long tail, and sharp, black bill. It makes an oblong, thorny nest with a small side opening and the female lays 3 to 6 blue-green eggs. The verdin feeds on small insects and is usually seen singly but may travel in pairs or small family groups.

Verdun, Battle of (Feb.-Dec. 1916), major World War I engagement. The Germans launched a concentrated offensive against the fortified line of Verdun. The French logistically could not abandon this position, and the Germans hoped to exhaust France's forces during the battle. Total casualties were well over 700,000. No significant advantage was gained by either side.
See also: World War I.

Verdun, Treaty of, pact (A.D. 843) concluding the civil war between the heirs of Louis I, by which Charlemagne's empire was divided between his 3 grandchildren (Louis's sons). Lothair I kept the title emperor and received Italy and a narrow strip of land from Provence to Friesland. Louis the German received the lands between the Rhine and Elbe. Charles the Bald held the area west of the Rhine.
See also: Charlemagne.

Vergil, or **Virgil** (Publius Vergilius Maro; 70-19 B.C.), Roman poet. Maecenas became his patron and Octavian (later the Emperor Augustus) his friend. He won recognition with his *Eclogues* or *Bucolics*, pastoral poems reflecting the events of his own day. The *Georgics*, a didactic poem on farming, uses the world of the farmer as a model for the world at large. His last 10 years were spent on his epic masterpiece, the *Aeneid*, about the wanderings of the Trojan War survivor Aeneas and his struggle to found Rome.

Verlaine, Paul (1844-1896), French poet, an early and influential exponent of symbolism. While imprisoned (1873-1875) for shooting and wounding his friend and lover, the poet Arthur Rimbaud, he wrote *Romances sans Paroles* (1874), one of his finest volumes. After a period of religious piety, he returned to his life of bohemian dissipation and died in poverty.

Vermeer, Jan (1632-1675), Dutch painter who spent his entire life in Delft. His interior scenes are noted for superb control of light, precise tonality, cool harmonious coloring, and classical composition. Of the fewer than 40 works attributed to him, his masterpieces include *The Letter* and *Head of a Girl* (both 1665).

Vermiculite, foliated clay mineral formed as a change in biotite. Vermiculite is soft, yellow or brown in color, with a monoclinic crystal structure. When heated, it can expand to a lightweight, highly absorbent, fireproof material about 16 times its original volume.

V

Deposits occur in the United States, Australia, the former USSR, South Africa, and Brazil. Vermiculite is used in construction as a sound and thermal insulator, as a fireproofing element, and as a potting medium for plants.

Vermont (Green Mountain State; pop. 565,000), state in New England, the n76th-eastern region of the United States; bordered by Canada, New Hampshire, Massachusetts, New York and Lake Champlain.
In the Green Mountains region, rounded peaks run north-south through the center of the state. In the southwest lie the Taconic Mountains region, part of a mountain range running from Massachusetts into Vermont, and the Vermont Valley, a narrow region of river valleys. The Connecticut is the state's major river; others include Otter Creek and the Winooski, Missisquoi, and Lamoille rivers. Forests cover about four fifths of the state. Principal cities are Burlington and Rutland. The capital is Montpelier.
Vermont's economy is led by service industries and manufacturing. Chief manufactured goods are electrical equipment, fabricated metal products, books and other printed materials, processed foods, transportation equipment, and furniture. Agriculture and mining account for a small share of the state's economy. Chief farm products are milk and dairy products, apples, maple syrup, potatoes, corn, and hay. Granite is the chief mining product.
Several Native American tribes lived in the area before the first Europeans-an expedition led by French explorer Samuel de Champlain-arrived in 1609. The first permanent white settlement was established at present-day Brattleboro in 1724. In 1777, Vermont's settlers declared it an independent territory; it is one of 3 states (with Texas and Hawaii) that were recognized by the U.S. government as being independent republics before they joined the Union. In the second half of the 20th century, Vermont sought new industries while trying to preserve the scenic beauty that attracts tourists to the area.

Vernal equinox *See:* Equinox.

Verne, Jules (1828-1905), French novelist, pioneer of the genre of science fiction. He often incorporated genuine scientific principles in his imaginative adventure fantasies and anticipated the airplane, submarine, television, space travel, etc. His most famous novels include *Journey to the Center of the Earth* (1864), *Twenty Thousand Leagues Under the Sea* (1870), and *Around the World in Eighty Days* (1873).

Verona (pop. 256,000), Italy, the capital of Verona province in the northern region of Venetia. It is situated on the Adige River 60 miles (97 km) west of Venice. Verona is a rail and highway junction on the route leading southward from the Brenner Pass in the Alps. Manufactured products include machinery, paper, drugs, plastics, printed goods, and furniture. Verona has many medieval buildings. The cathedral, built during the 12th to 15th centuries, has an altarpiece by Titian. The Roman amphitheater, only slightly smaller than the Colosseum in Rome, can seat 27,000 and is used for opera performances. Verona was occupied by the Romans about 200 B.C. It was a leading city in the Lombard League in the 12th century and reached its peak in the 13th. Shakespeare's *Romeo and Juliet* portrays Verona in the 14th century when it was torn by strife between rival noble families. The city came under the control of Milan in 1387. It was held by Venice (1405-1797) and Austria (1797-1866) before becoming part of the kingdom of Italy. Verona was heavily bombed during World War II.

Veronese, Paolo (or **Paolo Caliari** or **Cagliari**) (1528-1588), an Italian painter of the Venetian school. He is noted for his large decorative paintings showing the colorful pageantry of 16th-century Venice. He was born in Verona, studied in Verona and Rome, and was called to Venice in 1553 to decorate the Hall of the Council of Ten in the Palace of the Doges. Veronese remained in Venice, where he competed with Titian and Tintoretto for painting commissions.
The church of St. Sebastian in Venice contains many of Veronese's pictures, including the *Martyrdom of St. Sebastian*. Veronese painted many religious narrative works, such as *Marriage at Cana* and *Rebecca at the Well*. In his *Feast in the House of Levi* (originally titled *Last Supper*) he included many figures unrelated to the Biblical event. When the Inquisition ordered him to change certain details to match Biblical descriptions more closely, Veronese changed the title of the painting.

Verrazano-Narrows Bridge, world's longest suspension bridge (4,260 ft/1,298 m), spanning the Narrows at the entrance to New York harbor, completed in 1964.

Verrocchio, Andrea del (1435-1488), Italian sculptor, painter, and architect. Verrocchio trained as a goldsmith and probably learned painting under Fra Filippo Lippi. Many of Verrocchio's sculptures survive, but only 1 or 2 paintings are positively identified as his. His works are characterized by naturalistic poses, strong forms, and careful craftsmanship. His most famous works include the bronze sculptures *Christ and Saint Thomas* and *David* and an equestrian statue, the Colleoni Monument. Leonardo da Vinci and Il Perugino were among Verrocchio's students.

Versailles (pop. 100,000), French city, residential suburb 12 mi (19 km) southwest of Paris, capital of Yveline department. It is world-famous for its magnificent Palace of Versailles, built for King Louis XIV in the mid-1600s. The seat of the French court for over 100 years, it was made a national museum in 1837, and the palace and its formal gardens are among France's greatest tourist attractions.
See also: France.

Versailles, Treaty of, agreement ending World War I, imposed on Germany by the Allies on June 28, 1919. It set up the League of Nations. Under the treaty, Germany lost all her colonies and Lorraine was given to France, Eupen-Malmédy to Belgium, and Posen and West Prussia to Poland. Gdansk became a free city, the Saar (with its coalfields) was to be under international administration for 15 years, and the Rhineland was to be demilitarized and occupied by the Allies for 15 years at German cost. Heavy reparations were imposed, and Germany's armed forces were drastically reduced. German resentment of the treaty's harshness was a factor in the rise of Nazism and the eventual outbreak of World War II.

Verstappen, Jos (1972-), Dutch racing car driver, achieved recognition for his successes in carting and by winning the German Formula 3 championship. Taken on by Benetton-Ford as a test driver, he made his debut in Formula 1 in the Brazilian Grand Prix in 1994. He was the first Dutchman to stand on the winner's podium after coming third in the Hungarian Grand Prix. That year he narrowly escaped death when his car burst into flames during a pit stop in the German Grand Prix at the Hockenheim circuit. In 1995 he became a test driver again. In 1996 Verstappen was the lead driver for the Arrows-Hart team, but with varying degrees of success; the following year he drove for Tyrrell. In 1998 he joined the team of Jackie Stewart. In December that year he signed a contract with Honda and in 2000 he signed with Arrows, who fired him in 2002. In 2003 he was contracted by the Minardi-team.

Vertebra *See:* Spine.

Vertebrate, subphylum of the chordates, containing all those classes of animals that possess a backbone-a spinal column made up of bony or cartilaginous vertebrae. The classes of vertebrates are fish, amphibians, reptiles, birds, and mammals.

Vertical take-off aircraft *See:* V/STOL.

Vertigo, disturbance in which the individual has a subjective impression of movement in space or of objects moving around him or her, usually with a loss of equilibrium. As distinguished from faintness, lightheadedness, or other forms of dizziness, vertigo results from a disturbance somewhere in the body's equilibratory apparatus, e.g., the inner ear.

Vervain *See:* Verbena.

Verwoerd, Hendrik Frensch (1901-1966), Dutch-born South African politician and premier (1958-1966). A professor of psychology from 1927, he became editor of the Afrikaans nationalist newspaper *Die Transvaaler* (1937). A senator from 1948, he was appointed minister of native affairs (1950), and enforced apartheid rigorously, stressing 'separate development' and creating the homelands. He was assassinated.

Very high frequency waves (VHF), electromagnetic radio waves falling between high frequency and ultra high frequency. VHF waves are from 30 million to 300 million cycles per second, and the wavelengths range from 1 to 10 meters. They are used for tele-

V

vision and FM (frequency modulation) radio broadcasts and by amateur radio operators. *See also:* Radio.

Vesalius, Andreas (1514-1564), Flemish biologist regarded as a father of modern anatomy. After considerable experience of dissection, he became one of the leading figures in the revolt against Galen. In his most important work, *On the Structure of the Human Body* (1543), he described several organs for the first time.
See also: Anatomy.

Vesco, Donald A. (real name, Loma Linda; 1939-), American motorcycle racer, held the world speed record for motorcycles. In 1975, on the Bonneville salt flats (U.S.), he reached a speed of 302.928 mph (487.5 km/h) in the 20 ft (6 m) long and 2 ft 8 in (81 cm) high Silver Bird 1. The machine was powered by two two-stroke Yamaha 750 cc engines.

Vespasian (Titus Flavius Vespasianus; A.D. 9-79), Roman emperor from 69. The son of a tax collector, he rose in the army under Nero and was sent in 66 to suppress a rebellion in Judaea. His reign began an era of order and prosperity. He began the building of the Colosseum.
See also: Rome, Ancient.

Vespucci, Amerigo (1454-1512), Italian navigator for whom America was named. In 2 voyages (1499-1500, 1501-1502) he explored the coast of South America and deduced that the New World must be a continent and not part of Asia. The name *America* first appeared on a map published in 1507.
See also: America.

Vessel, Blood *See:* Artery; Blood; Vein.

Vesta, in Roman mythology, goddess of the hearth and home. She was the daughter of Saturn and Ops and the sister of Jupiter and is portrayed as young and virginal. Vesta's symbol, that of fire, evolves from the Roman necessity of maintaining a perpetual fire in the home as a sacred obligation. Vesta's temple, in the Forum in Rome, housed a public flame guarded by the six vestal virgins.
See also: Mythology.

Vestal virgins, in ancient Rome, priestess, chosen very young, who served the shrine of Vesta, goddess of the domestic hearth, for 30 years. Punishment for breaking the vow of chastity was burial alive. The virgins' chief responsibility was to tend to the sacred flame in Vesta's temple.
See also: Vesta.

Vestris, Auguste (Marie Jean Augustin; 1760-1842), French dancer of Italian descent, performed at a very young age in *La Cinquantaine*, and was instantly recognized as a very exceptional talent, partly thanks to his particularly high leaps and extreme suppleness combined with a certain amount of charisma. In 1778 he danced in Gluck's *Alceste*, and in 1780 in the first production of *Les Petits Riens* (choreography, Noverre; music, Mozart). He was undoubtedly the greatest star of his age, and when he performed together with his father in London in 1781, the House of Commons suspended proceedings so that members could attend the performance. He danced in nearly all of Noverre's ballets, and later in life was a celebrated dance teacher with such pupils as Charles Louis Didelot, Jules Perrot, August Bournonville and Marie Taglioni. According to ballet historians, it was not until 1909 that a dancer of equal talent, Vaslav Nijinsky, appeared on stage.

Vestris, Gaetano Apolline Baldassare (1728-1808), Italian dancer who became famous in Paris, where he first performed at the Opera, before being promoted to first dancer in 1751 and achieving major success. He was the first dancer to perform without masks in *Médée et Jason*. He became so successful that he was called the God of Dance. From 1770 to 1776 he was the artistic director of the Paris Opera ballet, a position he gladly handed over to Noverre so he could concentrate on the career of his son Auguste, of whom he said: 'He is an even better dancer than I was, but then he had the great advantage of having had me as father, an advantage I had to do without.'

Vesuvius, a volcano in southern Italy near the eastern shore of the Bay of Naples, about eight miles (13 km) southeast of the city of Naples. The summit of the cone is 4,190 feet (1,277 m) above sea level. An extinct crater, Mount Somma (3,714 feet; 1,132 m), forms a ridge on the north slope of Vesuvius. It is separated form the newer cone by a deep valley. The lower slopes of Vesuvius are covered with vineyards, gardens, and citrus groves. There are villages on the slopes and on the plains at the foot of the mountain. A seismological observatory, built in 1845, is on the west slope. Mount Somma is believed to have been formed by an eruption that occurred more than 12,000 years ago. The first recorded eruption was in 79 A.D. In that year Somma erupted violently, creating Mount Vesuvius and destroying Pompeii, the town of Herculaneum, and Stabiae, a resort. A detailed account of the event was written by the Roman author Pliny the Younger. His uncle, Pliny the Elder, was killed at Stabiae by poison gases from the eruption.
There were more than 15 recorded eruptions of the Vesuvius before the 20th century. One of the most destructive occurred in 1631, about 21,000 people lost their lives. In 1906 the volcano again wiped out a number of villages. An eruption in 1929 was less severe. In 1944, during the Allied occupation of Naples, a violent eruption destroyed the villages of San Sebastiano and Massa. Allied soldiers prevented much loss of life by helping the people escape from their doomed villages.
Thousands of people, among them noted scientists, visit Vesuvius each year. A cable railway that took visitors to the crater was destroyed in 1944 and was replaced by a chair lift.

Vetch, climbing or trailing vine (genus *Vicia*) of the pea family. At the tip of each leaf stem is a pair of slender tendrils that curl around other plants. They have attractive flowers like those of peas, and their seeds are carried in pods. There are several native vetches in North America, but the most common ones are of European origin. In Europe they are grown as crops for hay or pasture or to hold the soil on embankments.

Veterans' organizations, groups formed to foster the spirit of comradeship developed during war and to demonstrate support for the government. The groups are politically influential due to the size of their memberships, and they lobby for legislation beneficial to veterans such as pensions, education, and services for disabled veterans.

Veterinary medicine, medical care of sick animals, sometimes including the delivery of their young. It is practiced separately from human medicine since animal diseases differ largely from those affecting humans. Veterinarians treat domestic, farm, sport, and zoo animals. General medical advances-e.g., in vaccines and antibiotics-have been aided by veterinary research.

Veto, in politics, the power of the executive to reject legislation. It is a Latin word meaning 'I forbid,' pronounced by the Roman tribunes when they exercised their right to block laws passed by the Senate. In the Security Council of the United Nations, the 5 permanent members (China, France, Great Britain, the United States, and Russia) possess a veto over proceedings.

VHF waves *See:* Very high frequency waves.

Via Dolorosa (Lat.: path of suffering), the route that Christ is supposed to have followed from the courthouse of Pontius Pilate to the place where he was crucified outside Jerusalem (Golgotha). The name dates from the 16th century. The Via Dolorosa is now a pilgrim's road, punctuated by 14 stations of the cross.

Viagra (sildenafil citrate), oral drug that is used to treat erective dysfunction by increasing the blood supply to the corpus cavernosum of the penis, which results in an erection.

Vian, Boris Paul (1920-1959), French engineer and writer; also painted, played the trumpet, was an expert in jazz, and a translator. Wrote two novels in 1943: *Trouble dans les Andains* (1966) and *Vercoquin et le plancton* (1947), became an existentialist, but soon ridiculed this philosophy in *l'Écume des jours* (1947). In 1946 his best novel, *l'Automne à Pékin*, was published, but his so-called English translation *J'irai cracher sur vos tombes* (1946) was not appreciated in some circles and he was sentenced for pornography. After the play *Les bâtisseurs d'empire* (1947), a farce, he wrote *l'Arrache-coeur* (1953), and then became a songwriter, but caused public offense once more with the lyrics of songs such as *Monsieur le président* and *Le déserteur*. Only after his death was he recognized as an innovator and a true avant-gardist.

Vibraphone, electric percussion instrument resembling a xylophone but having metal

V

rather than wooden bars. The vibraphone has 37 bars (keys), each attached to a frame above a tuned resonator that can be opened or closed to produce a vibrating note. The player uses hard or soft cloth-headed beaters to strike the keys and can control the length and loudness of the notes with a sustaining pedal. The vibraphone was invented (1921) by Hermann Winterhoff and was first used orchestrally in the opera *Lulu* (1937).

Vicente, Gil (ca.1465-ca.1536), Portuguese playwright, founder of Portuguese theatre. His work built upon the medieval form of stage play, which he enriched with elements of folklore and his own critical perceptions. Due to his keen powers of observation, his plays, of which more than 40 have survived, give a vivid portrayal of Portuguese life at that time.

Vice president of the United States, second-highest elected official. Constitutionally and politically, this office does not carry great power. The vice president was originally intended as the neutral presiding officer in the Senate and as the constitutional successor on the death or resignation of the president. Eight vice presidents have succeeded to the presidency during their time in office, taking over for presidents who have died or resigned. The increase in presidential duties with World War II has been partly responsible for giving the vice president a greater share in political and legislative matters, in particular as a member of the National Security Council. The 25th Amendment (1967) permits the president to fill a vacancy in the office of vice president, subject to the approval of Congress. The amendment permits the vice president to act as president when the president is disabled. For 8 hours in 1985, while President Reagan was in surgery, Vice President George Bush served as acting president, the first vice president to do so.

A cartoon appearing in the May 1, 1900, edition of the *New York Telegram* shows Republican senator Mark Hanna shaping the second-term ticket of William McKinley with a protesting Theodore Roosevelt as the vice-presidential candidate.

Vichy (pop. 27,000), health resort in south-central France, famous for its mineral springs. Its chief industry is bottling Vichy water. In World War II it was the seat of the Vichy government of Marshal Henri Pétain,

which was set up in unoccupied France in 1940. After Germany occupied the whole of France in 1942, the Vichy government under Pierre Laval continued to collaborate with the Nazis, until the Allies liberated France. *See also:* France.

Vicksburg, Battle of *See:* Civil War, U.S..

Victor Emmanuel, name of 3 Italian kings. **Victor Emmanuel I** (1759-1824) was king of Sardinia (1802-1821). He recovered his mainland possessions after Napoleon I's fall (1814), but his harsh rule provoked a revolt in Piedmont led by the Carbonari, and he abdicated. **Victor Emmanuel II** (1820-1878) was king of Sardinia (1849-1861) and the first king of united Italy (1861-1878). With the Conte di Cavour and Giuseppe Garibaldi he played a major part in Italy's unification. **Victor Emmanuel III** (1869-1947) was king of Italy (1900-1946), emperor of Ethiopia (1936-1943), and king of Albania (1939-1943). After appointing Benito Mussolini premier in 1922, he became a mere figurehead. His unpopular association with Fascism ultimately obliged him to abdicate.

Victoria (1819-1901), queen of Great Britain and Ireland from 1837 and empress of India from 1876. As a young queen she depended heavily on the counsel of Lord Melbourne. Her life was transformed by marriage in 1840 to Prince Albert, who became the greatest influence of her life. She mourned for the rest of her life after his death in 1861. She had strong opinions and believed in playing an active role in government, and her relations with a succession of ministers colored the political life of her reign. Her dislike of Palmerston and Gladstone and fondness for Disraeli, for example, were notorious. In old age she became immensely popular and a symbol of Britain's imperial greatness.
See also: United Kingdom.

Victoria (pop. 1,500,000), capital of the colony of Hong Kong. The city is located on the slopes of Victoria Peak on the island of Hong Kong. It is commonly referred to as the Central District or merely as Hong Kong. Victoria is the government, banking, and commercial center of the island and home to the University of Hong Kong.
See also: Hong Kong.

Victoria, state in southeast Australia, the second-smallest and most densely populated in the country. It is divided east-west by an extension of the Australian Alps, with lowlands, hills, and valleys in the south and low plains north and west. The climate is temperate. Agriculture is important: wheat, oats, barley, and grapes are grown, and cattle and sheep are raised. Automobiles, textiles, and processed foods are produced, and coal and some gold are mined. Melbourne is the capital and largest city.
See also: Australia.

Victoria Falls, waterfall on the Zambesi River in south-central Africa between Zimbabwe and Zambia, where the 1-mi- (1-km-) wide river plunges 400 ft (122 m) into

a narrow fissure. The falls were named for Britain's Queen Victoria by the explorer David Livingston in 1855.

Vicuña (*Lama vicugna*), member of the camel family living in the western High Andes at up to 16,400 ft (c.5,000 m). They are believed to be the original of the domesticated alpacas. Vicuñas are graceful animals living in family groups of a stallion and up to 20 mares, occupying a fixed territory.

Vidal, Gore (1925-), a United States author. His novels are noted for their realistic portrayal of contemporary American life. *Myra Breckenridge* (1968) is a satire on the influence of Hollywood on American society. Vidal also wrote a series of historical novels about the United States. They include *Washington, D.C.* (1967), *Burr* (1973), *1876* (1976), *Lincoln* (1984), *Empire* (1987), and *Hollywood* (1990). His novels include: *Williwaw* (1946), *Kalki* (1978), *Creation* (1981), *Live from Golgotha* (1990), *The Smithsonian Institution* (1998), and *The Last Empire. Essays 1992-2000* (2001). He also wrote essays and plays. *Palimpsest* (1995) is a memoir.

Videla, Jorge Rafael (1925-), Argentinean military leader and politician. Videla became Chief of Staff of the army in 1975, and in 1976 he was the leader of the coup which deposed President Isabel Perón. In 1978 he stepped down as supreme commander of the army, but remained President until 1981. Videla played a major role in organizing the 'dirty war', in which tens of thousands of Argentineans suspected of having links with left-wing organizations were tortured and murdered. After the restoration of civilian government, Videla was sentenced to lifelong imprisonment in 1985. In 1990 he was granted a pardon by President Menem. In 1998 he was arrested again on charges of kidnapping. In 2001 he was arrested and prosecuted for conspiring with other right-wing militia leaders to eliminate left-wing political adversaries in South America in the 1970s.

Video art, a form of art which makes use of video equipment in various ways, such as integrating moving images into installations, or recording documentation. Became common in the 1960s, and has been utilized by countless artists.

Video camera, device that converts images into electronic signals for television viewing. The first video cameras, developed in the 1930s, were used for live telecasts. Color video cameras were developed in the 1950s. By the 1970s portable video cameras were being manufactured for use in the home. In the mid-1980s the videotape recorder was small enough to be combined with a video camera in a single unit.

Video cassette recorder *See:* Videotape recorder.

Videodisc, flat, round, plastic platter on which both picture and sound are reproduced on a television set. Unlike a video cassette recorder (VCR), a videodisc cannot record television programs off the air. Videodiscs do, however, offer superior picture and sound quality. There are 2 different videodisc systems: one employs a mechanical stylus and the other a laser. Originally developed in the 1970s for use as home entertainment, videodiscs are now used widely in education and industry.

Videotape, magnetic tape used to record television programs. In order to record the vast amounts of information necessary to reconstruct a television picture, 2-in- (5-cm-) wide tape must be run through the tape heads at 15 in (38 cm) per sec. The tape heads rotate to record the track crosswise on the tape.

Videotape recorder (VTR), mechanism that records visual images and sounds on magnetic tape. The recorded picture and sound can be played back and seen on the television screen. Home videotape recorders, also known as video cassette recorders (VCRs), are used largely by a consumer population to record television programs.

Vieira, António (1608-1697), Portuguese priest and author of a vast oeuvre of sermons, letters, and theological and philosophical treatises. Spent most of his life in Bahía (Brazil), where he became well-known as a pulpit speaker, but also drew much opposition because of his support for the Indian cause. He became the court preacher in Lisbon (1641-1652). His oeuvre is typical of the Baroque style of the Iberian peninsula; all the characteristics of conceptismo are clearly defined in his work. His literary legacy is considered to be the highlight of Portuguese prose. His complete works comprise 27 volumes.

Vienna (German: *Wien*; pop. 2,1 million), capital of Austria, on the Danube River, one of the world's great cities. Associated with Josef Haydn, W. A. Mozart, Ludwig von Beethoven, and the various Strausses, it is a celebrated musical, theatrical, and cultural center and has many famous buildings and museums, including the Hofburg, Schönbrunn, and Belvedere palaces, the Cathedral of St. Stephen, the State Opera, the Art History Museum, and the City Hall. A Roman town, it became the residence of the Hapsburgs in 1282. It was besieged by the Turks in 1529 and 1683. A great period of prosperity and building began in the 18th century, and Vienna was capital of the Austro-Hungarian empire until 1918, when the modern republic of Austria was formed. In World War II it was occupied by the Nazis and bombed by the Allies. The modern city, population 1,500,000 (1987 est), is also a commercial and industrial center, producing machinery, metals, textiles, chemicals, furniture, handicrafts, and food products.
See also: Austria.

Vienna, Congress of, assembly held in Vienna (1814-1815) to reorganize Europe after the Napoleonic Wars. Effective decision making was carried out by Metternich of Austria, Tsar Alexander I of Russia,

Castlereagh and Wellington of Britain, von Humboldt of Prussia, and Talleyrand of France. Among other territorial adjustments, the Congress established the German Confederation and the kingdoms of the Netherlands and Poland (under Russian rule), and restored the Papal States and the kingdoms of Sardinia and Naples. Austria gained parts of Italy, Prussia gained parts of Austria, and Britain gained overseas territories to achieve a new balance of power, ignoring the nationalist aspirations of the peoples concerned.
See also: Napoleonic Wars.

Viennese Secession, Viennese artists' organization. Set up in 1897 at the initiative of Gustav Klimt, as a reaction to the dominant academism in the art and crafts. Proclaimed the rejuvenation of all art forms as its aim. Acquired its own exhibition gallery in 1898. The Viennese Secession made an important contribution to art nouveau: the Secession style, which emphasized symbolism and decorative elegance. After 1905 the group split up, but the Viennese Secession still remained active for some time, organizing exhibitions.

Vientiane (pop. 442,000), capital and largest city of Laos, located on the Mekong River. Vientiane is the commercial center of Laos and produces livestock, rice, cigarettes, silk and other textiles, and plastics. It is the site of the Royal School of Medicine and the Royal School of Public Administration and is noted for its many Buddhist pagodas.
See also: Laos.

Vietcong *See:* Vietnam War

Vietminh *See:* Vietnam War.

Vietnam

Capital:	Hanoi
Area:	127,512 sq mi
	(330,341 sq km)
Population:	81,098,000
Language:	Vietnamese
Government:	Socialist republic
Independent:	1954 (South Vietnam)
Head of gov.:	Prime minister
Per capita:	US$ 2,100
Monetary unit:	1 Dong = 100 xu

Vietnam, officially the Socialist Republic of Vietnam, located in southeast Asia. With an area of 127,545 sq mi (330,341 sq km), Vietnam is bordered by Cambodia, and Laos on the west; China to the north and east; and the Gulf of Tonkin, the South China Sea, and the Gulf of Thailand to the east and south.
Land and climate. Narrow and S-shaped, Vietnam is a 1,000-mi (1,609 km)-long strip on the Indo-China peninsula. The country's major cities and economic centers are located in the Red River delta in the north and the Mekong River delta in the south. More than 90% of the people live in the delta regions. Between them lies a heavily forested mountainous backbone giving way to a narrow coastal strip along the South China Sea and the Gulf of Tonkin. Vietnam has a tropical monsoon climate with high humidity and rainfall.
People. About 85% of the people are Vietnamese. There are also urban Chinese minorities, though many Chinese fled the country in 1979 when hostilities flared up between Vietnam and China. There are also several distinct peoples in the highlands, such as the Meo, also called the Hmong, who preserve their own cultures. The major cities are Hanoi, Ho Chi Minh City (formerly Saigon), Hue, Da Nang, and Haiphong. The official language is Vietnamese and the dominant religions are Buddhism and Roman Catholicism, though the Vietnamese government discourages both.
Economy. Vietnam has an agricultural economy based principally upon rice growing in the Mekong and Red River deltas. Other crops include corn, cotton, hemp, sugarcane, rubber, coffee, and tea. Fishing and forestry are locally important. Minerals, including coal, iron, tin, zinc, lead, and phosphates are found mainly in the north, where most of the country's industry, chiefly the manufacture of iron and steel, chemicals and textiles, is concentrated. There is also some manufacturing around Ho Chi Minh City. Offshore oil deposits have been found.
History. Established as a distinct people by the 2nd century B.C., the Vietnamese now occupy what were formerly the distinct regions of Tonkin in the north, Annam in the center, and Cochin China in the south of their country. Tonkin and Annam were conquered by China in 111 B.C. In the 2nd century A.D., the Champa kingdom emerged in central Vietnam. The Chinese were eventually driven out in 939. The Annam empire then grew, eventually defeating and displacing the Champas in 1471 and expanding south into Cochin China. European traders and missionaries began arriving in the 1500s. French forces captured Saigon in 1859 and in 1862 the French annexed Cochin China and merged it with present-day Cambodia to form French Indochina. During the Japanese occupation of Indochina (1941-1945), the Vietnamese resisted. After the defeat and withdrawal of the Japanese, a republic was proclaimed under Ho Chi Minh in 1945. The French attempted to reassert their authority by establishing Bao Dai as emperor and became embroiled in a war between nationalist and communist guerrillas beginning in 1946. The French were finally defeated in 1954 at Dien Bien Phu. At the Geneva Conference held that same year, the country was divided,

V

An agricultural worker tends rice plants in a paddy along the Mekong River in southern Vietnam.

pending nationwide free elections, into Communist North Vietnam under Ho Chi Minh, and non-Communist South Vietnam. The French withdrew and, with U.S. backing, the regime of Ngo Dinh Diem declared an independent republic in South Vietnam in 1955 and, in 1956, refused to hold free elections. The Vietnam war ensued with South Vietnam being aided by the United States. At the height of its involvement, the United States had committed some 550,000 ground troops to the war. Despite a major military effort, the United States were unable to contain or defeat the Viet Cong guerrillas consisting of South Vietnamese opposed to the regime and North Vietnamese guerrillas reinforced by regulars of the North Vietnamese army. Successive South Vietnamese regimes proved unable to win popular backing and to provide the necessary political and military leadership. In addition, the United States suffered substantial setbacks to its international standing as the object of widespread criticism and resistance to the war at home and abroad. A cease-fire agreement was finally signed in 1973 and U.S. troops were withdrawn, but only at the end of a prolonged bombing campaign and the invasion of Cambodia. Upon the withdrawal of U.S. troops, Communist forces launched a major offensive and by 1975 had won control of all of South Vietnam, effectively ending 35 years of fighting. The unified Socialist Republic of Vietnam was pro-

claimed in 1976. Since then, Vietnam has attempted to rebuild its society and economy but was further distracted by war with neighboring Cambodia in 1979 when its forces overthrew the regime headed by Pol Pot. Years of war and economic dislocation have resulted in harsh living conditions and a large number of refugees. In the early 1990s the economy was liberalized. The World Bank and the IMF have been supporting the country economically since 1994. The road to reform started in 1997 with the appointment of President Tran Duc Long, party leader Le Kha Phien and Prime Minister Phan Van Kai. This went hand in hand with a period of political instability (1997-2000), caused by confrontations between people who were pro or contra the reforms. Nong Duc Manh was elected party leader of Vietnam in 2001. He pursues economic development: Vietnam has to be a fully developed industrialized country in 2020.

Vietnam Veterans Memorial *See:* Washington, D.C..

Vietnam War, conflict in South Vietnam (1957-1975) between South Vietnamese government forces, backed by the United States, and Communist guerrilla insurgents, the Vietcong, backed by North Vietnam. The conflict originated in 1941 when a Vietminh guerrilla force was formed under Hi Chi Minh to fight the Japanese. After 1946 it fought the French colonial government, defeating them at Dien Bien Phu. The Geneva Conference then temporarily divided Vietnam at the 17th parallel between the Communists (North) and the Nationalists (South). Ngo Dinh Diem, the South Vietnamese premier, canceled national elections and declared the South independent in 1956. The Viet Nam Cong San (Vietnamese Communists), or Vietcong, was than formed to oppose his increasingly corrupt regime. The Vietcong fought a ferocious guerrilla campaign that led Diem to call in U.S. support forces under the U.S.-South Vietnamese military and economic aid treaty of 1961. In 1963 he was overthrown by his officers; after a period of turmoil, Nguyen Van Thieu became president in 1967. In 1965 the United States had begun bombing the North

in retaliation for the use of northern troops in the South. Increasing numbers of U.S. combat troops, many of them drafted, began to arrive in 1965 and totaled nearly 550,000 by 1968, when fruitless peace talks began in Paris. The large-scale U.S. campaign proved unable to do more than hold back the highly motivated Vietcong. Vietnamese civilians suffered terribly at the hands of both sides. The American people were sharply divided by severe uncertainties about U.S. goals and participation in the war. In November 1969 President Richard M. Nixon announced the 'Vietnamization' of the war by building up South Vietnamese forces and withdrawing U.S. combat troops, but ever mounting, sometimes violent U.S. anti-war demonstrations reached their peak later that month when 250,000 protesters marched on Washington. The war had spread to Cambodia and Laos before a cease-fire was signed in Jan. 1973, followed by the total withdrawal of U.S. troops a few months later. The South was then overrun by Vietcong and North Vietnamese forces; the war effectively ended with the fall of the South Vietnamese capital of Saigon in May 1975. In the late 1980s the government began an economic restructuring plan with the purpose of stimulating private enterprise. In 1990 the Vietnamese Foreign Minister, Nguyen Co Thach, met with U.S. Secretary of State James A. Baker III in the first high-level meeting since the 1970s. They discussed Vietnam's involvement in Cambodia and U.S. MIAs, 2 issues that have kept the countries from establishing diplomatic relations.

Vigeland, Gustav (1869-1943), a Norwegian sculptor. His freestanding and relief nude figures starkly and simply symbolize such human events as birth, love, conflict, and death. Most Vigeland's works are owned by the city of Oslo and are in the city's Frogner Park. Also in the park is the Vigeland Museum, the sculptor's studio from 1921 until his death. Vigeland studied in Paris and was influenced by Rodin.

Vigny, Alfred de (1797-1863), French writer and poet. Belonged to the literary circle of Victor Hugo. Had a pessimistic outlook on life, clouded by thoughts about pain and death. Wrote *Cinq-Mars ou une conjuration sous Louis XIII* (1826), the first genuine French historical novel, the drama *Chatterton* (1835), and the collection of poems *Les destinées, poèmes philosophiques* (1864). His diaries from 1824-1847 were published under the title *Le journal d'un poète* (1867).

Vikings, or Norsemen, Norwegian, Swedish, and Danish seafarers who raided Europe from the 9th to the 11th centuries. Expert shipbuilders and navigators, they were capable of long sea voyages, and their ferocity made them the terror of Europe. The Norwegians raided Scotland, Ireland, and France and colonized the Hebrides, Orkneys, the Faroes, Iceland, and Greenland. They may also have discovered America. The Danes raided England, France, the Netherlands, Spain, and Italy. The Swedes went down the eastern shores of

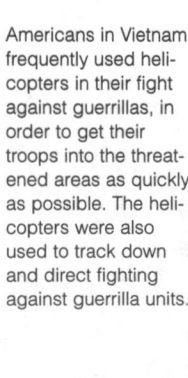

Americans in Vietnam frequently used helicopters in their fight against guerrillas, in order to get their troops into the threatened areas as quickly as possible. The helicopters were also used to track down and direct fighting against guerrilla units.

Harold I, the Norwegian king who gained control of and ruled most of western Norway during the late 9th century, is portrayed with the Viking chief Guthrum in this illustration from the Flateyar-bók, a 14th-century Norse saga collection.

V

the Baltic, through what is now western Russia, and reached the Bosporus and Byzantium. In addition to being raiders, the Vikings traded and created permanent settlements. They united the Hebrides and the Isle of Man into a kingdom. The Shetlands, the Orkneys, and Caithness became an earldom. Kingdoms were also set up in Ireland and Russia.

Villa, Pancho (Francisco Villa; 1877-1923), Mexican revolutionary leader. Originally a bandit in northern Mexico, Villa joined (1910) the insurgent forces of Francisco Madero fighting against the dictator Porfirio Díaz. After the successful campaign, he remained in the irregular army. When Madero was assassinated (1913), Villa joined forces with another revolutionary, Venustiano Carranza, and together they took Juárez (1914). Villa became governor of the state of Chihuahua and with Carranza continued his rebellion against Madero's successor, Gen. Victoriano Huerta (1914). In 1914-1915 Villa and Emiliano Zapata took control of Mexico City but were later defeated by Gen. lvaro Obregón. Competition between Villa and Carranza forced a break in their alliance, and Villa, embittered by U.S. recognition of Carranza's government, attacked and burned the town of Columbus, N.M., killing 16 people. U.S. Gen. John Pershing then led an unsuccessful 11-month expedition into northern Mexico in pursuit of Villa. The invasion strained U.S.-Mexican relations, and Pershing was recalled. When Carranza's government was overthrown (1920), Villa was awarded a grant of land. He was assassinated at his ranch (1923).
See also: Mexico.

Villa-Lobos, Heitor (1887-1959), Brazilian composer, conductor, and teacher, known for his research on and use of folk music. He composed over 2,000 works, many of which combine indigenous melodies with the counterpointing of Johann Sebastian Bach. His compositions include 9 instrumental suites called the *Bachanias Brasileiras* (1930-1945), 14 *Serestas* (1925-1941) for voice and piano, 12 symphonies, and 16 string quartets. Villa-Lobos founded the Brazilian Academy of Music (1945).

Villella, Edward Joseph (1936-), U.S. dancer who performed his first solo within a year of joining the New York City Ballet (1957). He is noted for his bravura style,

with powerful leaps. Villella's most famous performances include the title role in Balanchine's *The Prodigal Son*, and Oberon in *A Midsummer Night's Dream*.
See also: Ballet.

Villeneuve, Jacques (1971-), Canadian racing car driver, made his debut in Formula 1 in 1995 in Monza driving a Williams-Renault. Villeneuve drove in the Italian Formula 3 and the Formula 3000 before moving up to Formula 1. In 1994 he came second in the Indy 500, and the following year he became the IndyCar world champion. In 1996 Villeneuve won his first Grand Prix for Williams-Renault at the Nürburgring. In 1997 he became world champion in his Williams-Renault by beating his nearest rival Michael Schumacher in the last Grand Prix.

Villon, François (1431-1484?), a French poet. He was recognized as the foremost lyric poet of medieval France. Companion of beggars and rogues, Villon scorned the conventions observed in the artificial poems of courtly love, and found instead material in his own tempestuous life. A good example of his exquisite style is 'Ballad of Old-Time Ladies' with its wistful refrain, 'Where are the snows of yesteryear?' *The Vagabond King* (1925), an operetta with music by Rudolf Friml, was adapted from the novel and play *If I Were King* by Justin McCarthy, based on Villon's life.
Villon was born in a poor family of Pontoise, near Paris. After he was adopted by a rich churchman named Villon he changed his surname, possibly Montcorbier, to that of his patron. He received a master's degree from the University of Paris in 1452. In the meantime, he associated by choice with vagabonds and thieves in the lowest dives in Paris. He was twice sentenced to death, once for fatally stabbing a priest (1455), but somehow escaped the penalty in each case. Little is known of his later life. Most of Villon's known work is contained in two small volumes: *The Small Testament* (1456) and *The Great Testament* (1462).

Vilnius, or Vilna, capital and largest city of Lithuania (pop. 590,000). Settled in the 10th century, Vilnius was named the Lithuanian capital in 1323. The city later came under Polish rule (1569) and then was annexed by Russia (1795) which retained power until 1918. Between that year and 1938, control

was contested by Poland and Lithuania. In 1939 Lithuania recovered control, but the country (and the city) was occupied by the USSR until 1991. The Nazi occupation (1941-1945) destroyed the large Jewish population. Today Vilnius is an important trade center for grain, timber, chemicals, machinery, leather goods, paper, and textiles. It is noted for its public buildings and churches reflecting Roman, Byzantine, and Gothic influences.
See also: Lithuania.

Viña del Mar, leading resort and second largest city in Chile, located on the Pacific coast just northeast of Valparaíso. The city is noted for its pleasant climate, beaches, hotels, and nightclubs.

Vinci, Leonardo da *See:* Da Vinci, Leonardo.

Vine, general name for plants with climbing or trailing stems that cannot grow upright without support. Vines have either woody or herbaceous (nonwoody) stems. They can be evergreen or deciduous. Some have tendrils (the sweet pea, the grapevine, and the cucumber), and others have adhesive disks (the woodbine or Virginia creeper) or small roots (English ivy) to anchor them to their support. Some twine their stem around the support (the convolvulus and hop), and others simply ramble over the surrounding area, with no means of holding themselves up (the blackberry and the rambler rose). By far the most important vine economically is the grapevine, from which the wine grape is harvested.

Vinegar, sour liquid, consisting mainly of acetic acid and water, used for seasoning and preserving foods. Vinegar is produced by the action of yeast and bacteria on fruits and grains. It is made from alcoholic beverages such as wine and cider.

Vinegar eel (*Turbatrix aceti*), tiny roundworm, about 1/16 in (1.6 mm) in length, found in fermenting cider vinegar. Vinegar eels feed on fruit pulp and the bacteria that produce the vinegar from the cider. They are harmless if swallowed.

Vinland, region of eastern North America discovered A.D. 1000 by Viking explorers, probably led by Leif Ericson, and briefly settled (1004) by Thorfinn Karlsefni. Some scholars believe it was in New England, others favor Newfoundland (where Viking remains have been found). The Norse sagas describe the discovery of a fertile region where grapes grew, hence 'Vin(e)land.'

Vinyl, durable and useful plastic material used in making a variety of products. Vinyl plastics were first manufactured commercially in 1927. By 1973 the production of vinyl plastics in the United States totaled 4.6 billion lb (2.1 billion kg). One of the strongest vinyl plastics is polyvinyl chloride (PVC), produced by combining vinyl with chloride to form vinyl chloride gas, and then putting the gas through a process known as polymerization. Research in the 1970s showed that serious illness, including a form of liver cancer, can result from breathing air

V

polluted by vinyl chloride. The Environmental Protection Agency now requires that manufacturers install equipment to eliminate vinyl chloride from the air breathed by workers.

Vinyl chloride *See:* Vinyl.

Viol, forerunner (15th-17th centuries) of the violin. Viols have sloping shoulders, frets, a low bridge, and a soft, mellow tone. The 6 strings are tuned in fourths. The treble, alto, tenor, and bass (*viola da gamba*) viols are all held upright, as was the double-bass *violone,* which became today's double-bass. Interest in the viol has revived in the 20th century.

Viola, stringed musical instrument, the tenor voice of the violin family. It is 14.5-17 in (37-43 cm) long, has 4 strings, and is played with a bow. The viola originated in the 1500s. The composers Hector Berlioz, Richard Strauss, and Sir William Walton wrote for the viola as a solo instrument.

Viola, Bill (1951-), American artist. Studied at Syracuse University. Used advanced laser and video techniques in combination with everyday objects in his installations. Explored opposites such as nature-technology, peace-violence, mind-body in his work, which due to the slow motion and fade-outs often had a contemplative character. Viola was inspired by Chinese and Tibetan philosophy and archaeology.

Violet, low herbaceous plants (genus *Viola*) that produce characteristically shaped flowers on slender stalks. Most species occur in the Andes, but many are found in North America and Europe. Several species, including the pansy, are cultivated as garden

ornamentals. They grow mainly in moist woods.

Violin, smallest, most versatile member of the bowed, 4-stringed violin family (violin, viola, cello, double bass). Violins succeeded the viol in the 17th century, differing in their flexibility, range of tone and pitch, arched bridge, squarer shoulders, narrower body, and lack of frets. The violin proper, derived from the 16th-century arm viol, is tuned in fifths and ranges over 4 1/2 octaves above G below middle C. Perfected by the craftsmen of Cremona, it became a major solo instrument. The principal violinist leads the orchestra. Classical string quartets have 2 violins.

Viollet le Duc, Eugène Emmanuel (1814-1879), French architect and restorer. Made an important contribution to the development of neo-Gothic. Well known as a restorer of Gothic churches, cathedrals, palaces and town halls, including Notre Dame in Paris, the abbey in St. Denis, the cathedral of Rheims, the town hall in Narbonne, the fortifications of Carcassonne, and the castle Pierrefonds near Compiègne. His radical restorations were highly criticized, yet undoubtedly saved many irreplaceable architectural features.

Violoncello *See:* Cello.

Viper, family of snakes with highly developed venom apparatus, found in Europe, Africa, and Asia. Vipers are short, stoutly built, and typically terrestrial. One of the best-known species is the common European viper, or adder (*Vipera berus*).

Viper's bugloss, or blue thistle (*Echium vulgare*), plant found in dry areas of the eastern

United States. It has bright blue flowers and grows to about (90 cm) tall. It was once thought to be a cure for viper bites.

Virchow, Rudolf (1821-1902), Pomeranian-born German pathologist. His most important work was to apply knowledge concerning the cell to pathology. He was the first to document leukemia and embolism. He was also distinguished as an anthropologist and an archeologist.
See also: Leukemia; Pathology.

Viren, Lasse Artturi (1949-), Finnish athlete, won the gold medal in the 5000 m and the 10,000 m in both the Olympic Games of 1972 in Munich and the Olympic Games of 1976 in Montreal. He also broke several world records. Viren was accused by some people of achieving his results with blood doping.

Vireo, small, greenish, insectivorous bird (family Vireonidae) of tropical and temperate America. Vireos live in thick undergrowth except for the red-eyed vireo. This species is also noted for its rambling song. The white-eyed vireo mimics other birds. The nest is built near the ground and is anchored by cobwebs. Most species are migratory.

Virgil *See:* Vergil.

Virginal, type of small harpsichord, its strings parallel to the single keyboard. There is 1 wire per note. Encased in a small rectangular box, the virginal was popular c.1550-1650.

Virginia (Old Dominion; pop. 6,491,000), state in the southeastern United States; bordered by Maryland, the Atlantic Ocean, North Carolina, Tennessee, Kentucky, and West Virginia. The Appalachian Ridge and Valley region, covering most of western Virginia, consists of a series of parallel ridges separated by river valleys and lowlands. The rugged Appalachian Plateau, in the state's southwestern corner, contains extensive coal deposits. Virginia's major rivers are the James, Rappahannock, and Potomac. The state's largest lake, Kerr Reservoir, is artificial. Forests cover nearly two thirds of the state. Principal cities are Norfolk, Virginia Beach, and Richmond (capital).
Virginia's economy is based on service industries and manufacturing. Chief manufactured goods are chemicals, tobacco products, processed foods, electrical and transportation equipment, and textiles. Chief livestock products are beef and dairy cattle and turkeys; chief crops are tobacco, soybeans, peanuts, corn, and hay. Chief mining products are coal and crushed stone. Virginia is the nation's leading producer of kyanite.
The Virginia area was home to various Native American tribes when the first European settlers-Spanish Jesuits-arrived in 1570. In 1607, the first permanent English settlement in the New World was established at Jamestown. In 1612, John Rolfe, a Jamestown settler, began raising tobacco, which became the basis of Virginia's econo-

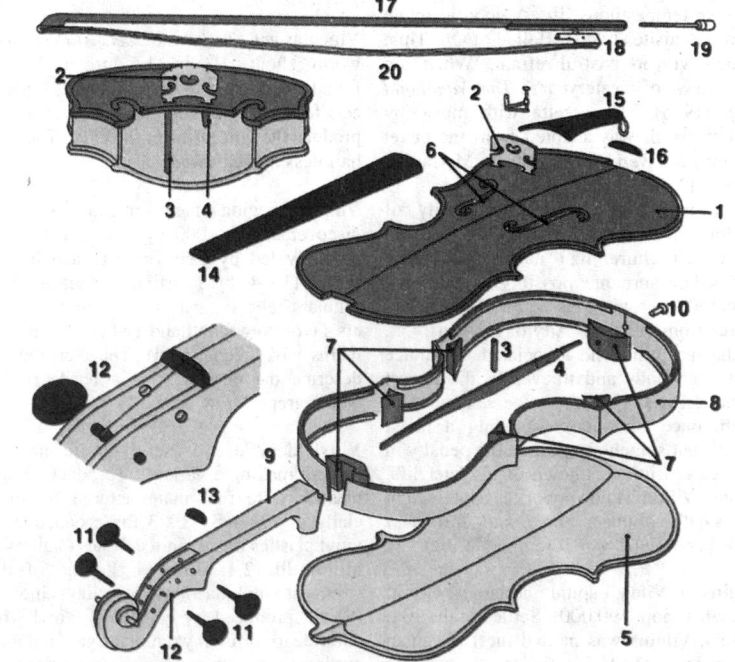

The parts of the violin are shown in this exploded view. The violin's softwood belly (1), which functions as a resonating soundboard, receives vibrations of the strings through the bridge (2). The soundpost (3) and bass bar (4), shown in cross-sectional view, carry vibrations along the belly and transmit them to the less resonant hardwood back (5). The f-shaped sound holes (6) also aid vibration. Interior blocks (7) support the ribs (8), neck (9), and button (10). The strings extend from pegs (11) in the pegbox (12) over the nut (13), fingerboard (14), and bridge to the tailpiece (15), secured over the lower nut (16) to the button. Parts of the bow include the stick (17), the nut or 'frog' (18), the screw (19), and the horsehair (20).

my. In 1776, Virginia became the first American colony to adopt a constitution and a declaration of rights.

Virginia creeper (*Parthenocissus quinque-folia*), rambling, viny plant that grows in eastern North America. A member of the vine family, it resembles poison ivy. Its leaves turn red and yellow in autumn.

Virgin Islands, westernmost group of the Lesser Antilles in the West Indies, east of Puerto Rico. The western islands belong to the United States and the eastern group to Britain. Discovered and claimed for Spain by Christopher Columbus (1493), the Virgin Islands were settled chiefly by English and Danes in the 1600s. England secured the British Virgin Islands in 1666. The Danish West Indies were acquired by the United States for strategic reasons in 1917 and became the U.S. Virgin Islands. The economy of both groups now depends on tourism, but farming (food crops, livestock) and fishing are also important. The Virgin Islands of the United States, a U.S. territory covering 133 sq mi (344.5 sq km) include St. Thomas, St. John, St. Croix, and some 65 islets. Charlotte Amalie, the capital and only city, stands on St. Thomas. The British Virgin Islands are separated from the American islands by a strait called The Narrows. Covering 59 sq mi (153 sq km), the group consists of about 30 mainly uninhabited islands. The largest island is Tortola, which has the capital and chief port, Road Town.

Virgin Mary *See:* Mary.

Viroid, class of infectious agents, causing several plant diseases. Made up of a complex chain of RNA (ribonucleic acid) molecules, they are replicated by the host cell's enzymes. Viroids affect such plants as potatoes, tomatoes, hops, and avocadoes, among others.

Virus, submicroscopic parasitic microorganism comprising a protein or protein/lipid sheath containing nucleic acid (DNA or RNA). Viruses are inert outside living cells, but within appropriate cells they can replicate (using raw material from the cell), causing viral diseases in the host organism. Various viruses infect animals, plants, and bacteria (in which case they are bacteriophages). Few drugs act specifically against viruses, although immunity can be induced against particular viruses. Various pathogenic organisms formerly regarded as large viruses are now distinguished as *bedsonia*.

Virus (computer), computer term. A short program that copies itself and secretly 'infects' (joins itself to) useful programs, usually for some malicious purpose. For example, a virus can be designed to alter data or destroy files in a computer after an infected program is run. A virus spreads from computer to computer by means of computer networks or through the use of diskettes containing programs that have been infected.

Visconti, Luchino (real name, Don

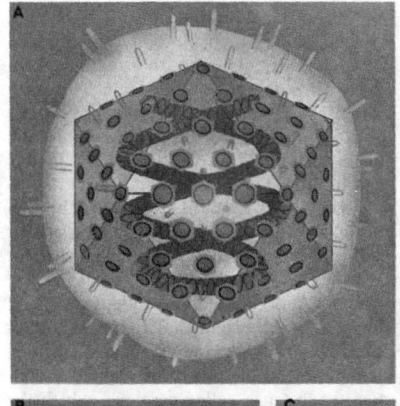
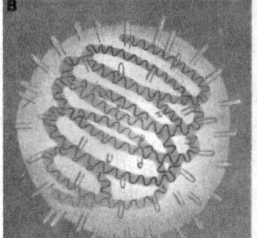

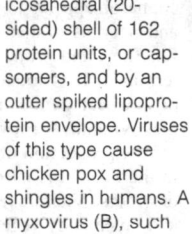
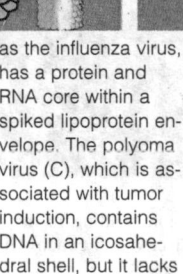
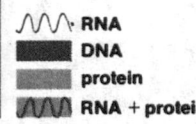

RNA
DNA
protein
RNA + protein

A complete virus particle, or virion, consists of one molecule of nucleic acid—either DNA or RNA—and a protein coat called a capsid. The DNA of a herpes virus particle (A) is enclosed by an icosahedral (20-sided) shell of 162 protein units, or capsomers, and by an outer spiked lipoprotein envelope. Viruses of this type cause chicken pox and shingles in humans. A myxovirus (B), such as the influenza virus, has a protein and RNA core within a spiked lipoprotein envelope. The polyoma virus (C), which is associated with tumor induction, contains DNA in an icosahedral shell, but it lacks an outer envelope. The tobacco mosaic virus (D) consists of a helical strand of RNA with about 2,200 protein molecules coiled around it. The bacteriophage T2 (E) has a head—composed of DNA and a bipyramidal hexagonal (6-sided) protein shell—and a protein tail—made up of a tube core, a retractable sheath, and 6 tail fibers.

V

Luchino Visconti di Modrone; 1906-1976), Italian film and theatre director. Assistant to Jean Renoir (1935) in Paris. He made *Ossessione* in 1942, considered to be the first Italian neo-realistic film. Grew to become a great director with a preference for the recent past, which he portrayed in fin-de-siècle, aesthetically attractive cinematography. The decay and fall of the aristocracy, of which he himself was a member, is the most important theme in the oeuvre of the marxist Visconti. His films include *La terra trema* (1948), *Bellissima* (with Anna Magnani; 1951), *Le notti bianche* (White Nights, after Dostoyevski; 1957), *Rocco e i suoi fratelli* (Rocco and his Brothers; 1960), *Il gattopardo* (The Leopard; after Tomaso di Lampedusa; 1963), *La caduta degli dei* (The Damned, 1969), *Morte a Venezia* (Death in Venice, after Thomas Mann; 1971), *Ludwig* (1973), *Gruppo di famiglia in un interno* (Conversation Piece; 1975), and *L'innocente* (The Innocent, after Gabriele d'Annunzio; 1976). Virtually every single actor who worked under Visconti considered him to be the best director they had ever worked for.

Viscosity, resistance of a fluid to shape change or relative motion within itself. All fluids are viscous, the viscosity arising from internal friction between molecules. The viscosity of liquids decreases as they are heated, but that of gases increases.

Vishinsky, Andrei Yanuarievich (1883-1954), Soviet diplomat and jurist. Chief state prosecutor in the purge trials of 1936-1938, he was deputy commissar (1940-1949) and commissar (1949-1953) for foreign affairs, and USSR's chief UN delegate (1953-1954).
See also: Union of Soviet Socialist Republics.

Vishnevskaya, Galina Pavlova (1926-), Russian singer (dramatic soprano), married to the cellist Mstislav Rostropovich. She first performed in Leningrad in 1944 as an opera singer, and was taken on by the Moscow Bolshoi Theatre in 1952, where she sang the title role in Beethoven's *Fidelio* and Tatiana in Tchaikovsky's *Eugene Onegin* as well as modern Russian repertoire. Towards the end of the 1950s she toured outside the Soviet Union, and sang the title role in Verdi's *Aida* at the Metropolitan Opera in New York in 1961. In 1962 she sang the part written for her in Britten's *War Requiem*. She left the Soviet Union in 1974 with her husband, and returned there in 1990. Vishnevskaya has a vibrant soprano voice, which is considered to be one of the most beautiful of her generation.

Vishnu, in Hinduism, second deity in the Trimurti (divine trinity, including Brahma, the creator, and Shiva, the destroyer), representing the preserving and protecting aspect of the godhead. The ancient *Vishnu Purana* text describes him as the primal god, as do his followers (Vaishnavas), who also worship his many avatars, such as Rama, Buddha, and Krishna. Vishnu is often repre-

V

Vishnu, one of the most important gods of Hinduism, on the back of the Garuda (half man, half vulture), a symbol for the winged man. This miniature from 1770 can be found in the Victoria and Albert Museum in London.

sented dark blue in color, holding in his 4 hands a lotus, mace, discus, and conch. His consort is Lakshmi.
See also: Hinduism.

Visigoths (West Goths), Germanic people. In the 3rd century A.D. they invaded Roman Dacia (Romania). Under Fritigern they defeated the Romans at Adrianople (378) and, led by Alaric I, they invaded Thrace and Italy, sacking Rome (410). They founded a kingdom in Gaul and Spain (419), but Alaric II lost the northern lands to Clovis, king of the Franks (507). Roderick, last Gothic king of Spain, lost his throne to the Moors (711).

Vision *See:* Eye.

Vistula River, largest (678 mi/1,091 km long) and most important river in Poland. Through a system of canals, it connects the Oder, Dmepr, and Neman rivers, all of which are navigable. It empties into the Baltic Sea. The Vistula is frozen 2 to 3 months of the year.

Vital statistics, data related to the important events, such as birth, marriage, and death, in a person's life. Registration of many such statistics, including birth dates filed on birth certificates, is required by law. The Vital Statistics Division of the National Center for Health Statistics, a division of the U.S. Dept. of Health and Human Services, analyzes and publishes U.S. data.

Vitamin, specific nutrient compounds essential for body growth or metabolism and which can be supplied by a balanced diet or, when necessary, in the form of supplements. Enzymes and coenzymes are neces-

sary for metabolism, especially the processes by which the body absorbs and utilizes nutrients. But there are certain coenzymes the body can obtain only from vitamins. Vitamins are denoted by letters and are often divided into fat-soluble and water-soluble kinds. Fat-soluble vitamins can be stored in the body's fat; water-soluble vitamins pass out of the body through urine. The A, D, E, and K vitamins are fat soluble; the B and C vitamins are water soluble.

Vitamin A, or retinol, is essential for skeletal growth, healthy epithelial tissue, and eyesight. It is found in milk, butter, and egg yolks. Green leafy or yellow vegetables contain a substance called carotene, which the body converts to Vitamin A. Vitamin A deficiency can cause skin, eye, or mucous membrane lesions. Overdoses can be harmful to the skin. Vitamin D, or calciferol, is a crucial factor in calcium metabolism, especially the growth and maintenance of bone. It is found in human skin and is activated with exposure of the skin to sunlight. Vitamin D deficiency can cause rickets or bow legs. An overdose can cause kidney damage. Vitamin E, or tocopherol, appears to play a role in blood cell and nervous system tissues, but its precise functions and properties have yet to be determined. It is found in peanuts, vegetable oils, wheat germ, and green leafy vegetables. Vitamin K provides essential cofactors for the production of certain clotting factors in the liver. It is used to treat some clotting disorders. Vitamin K is contained in liver and green leafy vegetables.

Important members of the B group include B_1 or thiamine; B_2 or riboflavin; niacin; B_6 or pyridoxine; folic acid; and B_{12} or cyanocobalamin. Thiamine acts as a coen-

zyme in carbohydrate metabolism. It occurs naturally in whole grains, yeast, nuts, and lean pork. Its deficiency, seen in rice-eating populations and alcoholics, causes beriberi. Riboflavin is also a coenzyme active in oxidation reactions. It is found in milk, green leafy vegetables, and liver and organs. A deficiency will cause lesions of the skin, mouth, or eyes. Niacin is a general term for nicotinic acid and nicotinamide, coenzymes in carbohydrate metabolism. Niacin occurs in wheat germ, lean meat, fish, and peanuts. A deficiency causes pellagra and, if the deficiency is extreme, it can cause death. Pyridoxine provides an enzyme important in energy storage and its deficiency can lead to anemia. It occurs naturally in lean meat, whole grains, milk, and egg yolks. Folic acid is an essential cofactor in the metabolism of nucleic acid and a deficiency of the vitamin, which is not uncommon in pregnancy, can cause anemia. Folic acid occurs naturally in yeast and in green leafy vegetables. Cyanocobalamin is essential for all the body's cells and a deficiency can lead to pernicious anemia. It occurs naturally in bivalves and fish, eggs and lean meat, and rigorous vegetarians are at particular risk of deficiency. Pantothenic acid, biotin, choline, inositol, and para-aminobenzoic acid are other members of the B-group. Vitamin C, another of the water-soluble vitamins, is also known as ascorbic acid and plays an important role in the healing process, blood cell formation, and bone and tissue growth. It occurs naturally in citrus fruits, cabbage, berries, peppers, and tomatoes. Deficiency leads to scurvy, and extreme and prolonged deficiency causes death. The beneficial effects of Vitamin C in the prevention and treatment of the common cold have yet to be conclusively determined.

Vivaldi, Antonio (c.1680-1741), Venetian Baroque composer. He wrote vocal music, sonatas, some 450 concertos for violin and other instruments (helping establish the 3-movement form), and *concerti grossi*, including the famous *Four Seasons*. His work has a sparkling clarity, strong rhythms, and a wealth of melody.
See also: Baroque.

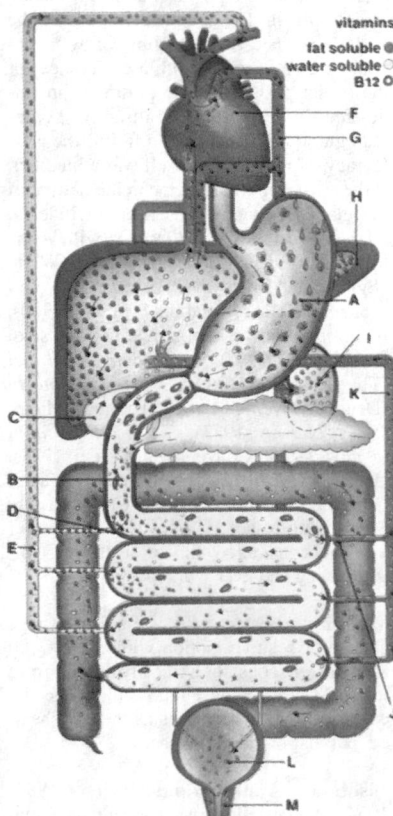

vitamins
fat soluble ●
water soluble ○
B12 ○

Vitamins are released from foods in the stomach (A). The fat-soluble vitamins, A, D, E, and K, are broken down in the small intestine (B) by bile from the gall bladder (C). The emulsified molecules pass through lymphatics (D) and veins (E) to the heart (F), which distributes them to the rest of the body through the arterial system (G). Excess fat-soluble vitamins are stored in the liver (H) and kidneys (I). The water-soluble vitamins, B-complex and C, are absorbed into the bloodstream through capillaries (J) in the small intestine. (Vitamin B_{12} cannot be absorbed, unless it mixes with a special substance found in digestive juices.) Portal veins (K) carry the vitamins to the liver, heart, and arteries. Excess water-soluble vitamins are filtered out by the kidneys to be excreted in urine (L). Undigested excess vitamins are excreted in feces (M).

Anonymous portrait of the Italian compos-er Antonio Vivaldi (1678-1741).

Vivekananda (real name, Narendra Nath Datta; 1862-1902) Indian religious leader. Introduced the Vedanta teachings of his mentor Ramakrishna to America at the International Religious Conference in Chicago in 1893. The headquarters of his movement was the Ramakrishna Mission near Calcutta, established in 1897.
See also: Ramakrishna Paramahansa.

Vivisection, dissection of living animals, usually in the course of physiological or pathological research; the use of the term is often extended to cover all animal experimentation. The practice remains the subject of considerable public controversy.

Vizsla, or Hungarian pointer, breed of hunting dog. It was probably first brought to central Europe by the Magyars about 1,000 years ago. The vizsla weighs about 50 lb (23 kg) and has a rusty or sandy yellow coat.

Vladimir I (?-1015), Russian grand duke who established Christianity as the country's official religion. Born a pagan, he converted to Christianity about 988. He built churches, schools, and libraries and promoted trade with European countries. He was declared a saint after his death.

Vladivostok (pop. 1,0 million), capital of Primorski Kray, in the eastern Russian Federation, chief Pacific naval port of Russia, on Peter the Great Bay near North Korea. Founded in 1860, it has shipbuilding, manufacturing, chemical, and fish-canning industries. It is the east terminus of the Trans-Siberian Railway.
See also: Union of Soviet Socialist Republics.

Vlaminck, Maurice de (1876-1958), French artist who, along with André Derain and Henri Matisse, was a leader of the fauvist movement. Vlaminck was strongly influenced by Vincent van Gogh and adopted his slashing brushstrokes and brilliant colors for dramatic effect. He moved gradually to a style close to that of Paul Cézanne. Notable works include *The Storm.*

Vocal cord *See:* Larynx.

Vocational education, courses of study that prepare students for a range of occupations that do not require baccalaureate or higher degrees, in areas such as agriculture, business, trades, industry, health services, home economics, and various technical fields. Instruction takes place in high schools, trade schools, community colleges, and correspondence schools and through formal apprenticeship programs and on-the-job training.

Vocational rehabilitation, service designed for persons, usually 16 years of age and older, with mental and/or physical handicaps, to become employable. The three components of vocational rehabilitation are rehabilitation counseling, vocational evaluation, and job placement. Specialists in each of these areas work as a team, matching job skills and performance against standards in a career field. Counselors in vocational rehabilitation are usually required to have a bachelor's degree and preferably a master's degree with a concentration in counseling, human relations, industrial psychology, statistics, and testing.

Vogelweide, Walther von der *See:* Walther Von der Vogelweide.

Voice, sound emitted in speech, the method of communication exclusive to *Homo sapiens.* Dependent upon the passage of air from the lungs through the trachea, larynx, pharynx, and mouth, its quality is largely determined by the shape and size of these structures and the resonance of the nose and nasal sinuses. Phonation is the sounding of the elements of speech by the action of several small muscles on the vocal cords of the larynx. Articulation consists in the modulation of sounds by the use of the tongue, teeth, and lips in different combinations. Vowels are produced mainly by phonation, while consonants derive their characteristics principally from articulation.

Voiceprint, or speech spectrogram, visual record of the sound waves of a human voice made by running a tape recording of a voice through an instrument called a sound spectrograph. The sound spectrograph was developed in the 1940s by U.S. scientists at Bell Research Laboratories. Voiceprints are used in the study of speech and hearing disorders. Police use voiceprints for evidence in the prosecution of criminal cases.

Vojvodina (pop. 2,013,000), province in the Yugoslavian republic of Serbia; 8,306 sq mi (21,505 sq km). Capital, Novi Sad. Most important agricultural area of the country (grain), cattle; agricultural industry. Extraction of oil and gas. The province contributes much to the economy of other parts of Serbia. There is a large Hungarian minority (19%). Vojvodina became part of Serbia in 1918. From 1974 onwards the region, just like Kosovo, was an autonomous province within Serbia, having its own central bank and control over its own education and judicial system; this status was withdrawn from both regions in 1989 by Serbian President Milosevic, who played into Serbian nationalist sentiments. Halfway through the 1990s thousands of ethnic Hungarians, driven from their homes by Serbs, fled the region toward Hungary. Serbia's Parliament returned autonomy to Vojvodina in 2001.

Volapük, universal language created in 1879 by Johann Martin Schleyer, a German priest. It combined elements of English, German, Latin, French, and Italian. It proved difficult to learn because of the unfamiliar appearance of the words and its grammatical complexity. Few people speak Volapük today.

Volcano, fissure or vent in a planet's crust through which magma and associated material may be extruded onto the surface. This may occur with explosive force. The extruded magma, or lava, solidifies in various forms soon after exposure to the atmosphere. In particular it does so around the vent, building up the characteristic volcanic cone, at the top of which is a crater containing the main vent. There may be secondary vents forming 'parasitic cones' in the slopes of the main cone. If the volcano is dormant or extinct, the vents may be blocked with a plug (or neck) of solidified lava. Classifying volcanoes in order of increasing violence, the main types are Hawaiian, Strombolian, Vulcanian, Vesuvian, and Peléan. Volcanoes are generally restricted to belts of seismic activity, particularly active plate margins, but some intraplate volcanic activity is also known, as in the case of Hawaii. At midocean ridges magma rises from deep in the mantle and is added to the receding edges of the plates. In mountain ranges, where plates are in collision, volatile matter ascends from the subducted edge of a plate, perhaps many kilometers below the surface, bursting through the overlying plate in a series of volcanoes. Around 500 active volcanoes are known of on earth; active volcanoes have also been found on Mars and on Jupiter's satellite Io.

Vole, mouselike member of the New World rat and mouse family, closely related to the lemming. Voles are about 5 in (13 cm) long with short, shaggy, grayish-brown fur. Most inhabit fields and meadows. There are over 40 species of vole. The most common North American species is the meadow vole (genus *Microtus*).

Volga River, chief tributary of Russia and the longest in Europe. It rises in the Valdai Hills, northwest of Moscow, and flows 2,293 mi (3,690 km) through Gorki, Kazan, Kuibyshev, Saratov, Volgograd, and Astrakhan to its Caspian Sea delta. Draining an area of some 530,000 sq mi (1,372,700 sq km) it is the main artery of the world's greatest network of commercial waterways linking the White, Baltic, Caspian, Azov, and Black seas.

Volgograd (pop. 1,007,000), important manufacturing city in Ukraine located on the west bank of the Volga River. It was founded in the 1200s as Tsaritsyn and renamed

V

V

The eruption of lava and hot ash from the ocean floor lead to the formation, in 1963, of Surtsey, a volcanic island to the south of Iceland.

According to the theory of plate tectonics, the earth's outer shell is divided into sections called plates, which move continuously. Most volcanoes occur where two plates collide. When two plates move away from each other they form an oceanic ridge; when two plates slide past each other, the dipping plane forms the subduction zone.

Key:
a. movement of plates
b. volcanoes in sub- duction zones
c. volcanoes on mid- oceanic ridges
d. mid-oceanic ridge
e. subduction zone

Before the great eruption in 1883, Krakatoa was a small volcanic island in the Sunda Strait of Indonesia consisting of three vol- canic cones: Perbuwatan (northwest), Danan (middle), and Rakata (south). At the termination of the 1883 activity, it was dis- covered that Perbuwatan, Danan, and half of Rakata had been destroyed, leaving only a sterile, ash-covered islet some 59 ft (18 m) higher than its predecessor.

Stalingrad (after Joseph Stalin) in 1925. During World War II the city was devastated by the battle between the advancing German army and the defending forces. It was completely rebuilt after the war and renamed Volgograd in 1961, after Stalin was downgraded.

Volkswagen (German, 'the people's car'), one of the world's largest producers of passenger cars. It was established by the German government in 1937 and is now owned privately. The Volkswagen beetle, designed by the Austrian engineer Ferdinand Porsche in the mid-1930s, became the most popular car ever built. Volkswagen builds over 2.5 million cars annually in countries throughout the world. In 1998 Volkswagen took over Rolls-Royce.

Volleyball, game for 2 teams of 6, who volley (using any part of the body above the waist) an inflated ball (8.25 in/21 cm in diameter) across an 8-ft (2.4-m) high net, conceding points by failing to return the ball or by hitting it out of bounds. Invented at the Holyoke (Mass.) YMCA in 1895 by W. G. Morgan, it became an Olympic event in Tokyo (1964).

Volta, River in Burkina Faso and Ghana; 709 mi (1140 km). Tributaries are the White and Black Volta in North Ghana; flows into the estuary near Ada in the Gulf of Guinea. Navigable below Akuse (60 mi; 97 km). Hydroelectric power stations. The artificial Volta Lake (3,277 sq mi; 8,485 sq km) near Akosombo has large fish stocks. The water management of the river has drastically changed since the building of the Akosombo dam.

Volta, Alessandro (1745 1827), Italian physicist. The volt was named for him. He invented (1800) the voltaic pile (the first battery) and thus provided science with its earliest source of continuous electric current. Volta's invention demonstrated that 'animal electricity' could be produced using solely inanimate materials, thus ending a long dispute with the supporters of Luigi Galvani's view that it was a special property of animal matter.
See also: Electric current.

Voltaire (François-Marie Arouet; 1694-1778), French author, philosopher, and major figure of the Enlightenment. An enemy of tyrants, he spent much of his life in exile, including 23 years at his property on the Swiss border. His *Letters Concerning the English Nation* (1733) extolled religious and political toleration and the ideas of Sir Isaac Newton and John Locke. The satire *Candide* (1759), a rational skeptic's attack on the optimism of Gottfried von Leibniz, shows Voltaire's astringent style at its best. A friend of Frederick II of Prussia, Voltaire contributed to Denis Diderot's *Encyclopedia* and wrote his own *Philosophical Dictionary* (1764).
See also: Age of Reason.

Vomiting, return of food or other substance (e.g., blood) from the stomach. It may be induced by drugs, motion sickness, infection,

uremia, or stomach or pyloric disorders. Morning vomiting may be a feature of early pregnancy. Drugs may be needed to control vomiting, along with fluid and nutrient replacement.

Vo Nguyen Giap (1912-), Vietnamese military leader and politician. Became a member of the Vietminh in 1941, and set up a well-organized guerrilla army which fought against the Japanese and the French. As chief of police and later head of the People's Army (from 1945 onwards), he was responsible for the victory over the French at Dien Bien Phu (1954), where he employed all his tactical acumen and strategic insight. He was minister of war, vice premier (1954), supreme commander of North Vietnamese troops (1967) and minister of defense (1976-1980). In 1982 he was pushed out of the Politburo.

Vonnegut, Kurt, Jr. (1922-), U.S. fiction writer. Vonnegut writes dark and humorous science-fictionalized novels of life with little purpose. His works portray societal, religious, political, and scientific systems as unavoidably destructive. His first novel, *Player Piano* (1952), is a study of technology in modern society. *Mother Night* (1961), *Cat's Cradle* (1963), and *God Bless You, Mr. Rosewater* (1965), explore the morals and social conventions in America. *Slaughterhouse Five* (1969), ruminates on the compulsion humans have to impose devastation on themselves. Other works include *Breakfast of Champions* (1973), *Deadeye Dick* (1982), *Galapagos* (1985), *Bluebeard* (1987), *Hocus Pocus* (1990), *Timequake* (1997), and *Bagombo Snuff Box* (1999).

Von Neumann, John (1903-1957), Hungarian born U.S. mathematician who put quantum mechanics on a rigorous mathematical foundation. He created game theory, and made important contributions to the theory of computers, as well as to many branches of abstract mathematics.
See also: Quantum mechanics.

Von Willebrand's disease, hereditary disease in which there is prolonged bleeding when the skin is injured. Unlike hemophilia, Von Willebrand's disease causes external

Swiss painter Jean Huber (1721-1786) mainly became known for his series of pictures depicting the domestic life of Voltaire (1694-1778, the one with his hand raised). This picture shows the collaborators that produced the *Encyclopédie* at a meal. Among others we can see Diderot (1713-1784) and d'Alembert (1717-1783).

bleeding; internal bleeding is rare. It affects both males and females and occurs most commonly in Scandinavian countries. The disease is caused by the absence of one of the clotting factors in the blood. Erik von Willebrand, a German professor of medicine, first identified the disease in 1926.

Voodoo, folk religion, chiefly of Haiti, with West African and added Roman Catholic and native West Indian elements. It involves worship of the spirits of saints and ancestors, who may 'possess' participants. Prayers, drumming, dancing, and feasts are part of the ritual. A cult group's priest or priestess is believed to act as a medium, work charms, lay curses, and recall zombies (the 'living dead').
See also: Religion.

Voronezh (pop. 1,0 million) Russia, a city on the Voronezh River, near its junction with the Don, about 290 mi (470 km) southsoutheast of Moscow. Voronezh is an important commercial, industrial, and railway center. Its industries produce synthetic rubber, tires, chemicals, processed foods, electrical appliances, and heavy machinery. Voronezh has been largely rebuilt since World War II, and it is essentially a modern city. Among the few remaining historic structures are St. Nicolas Church and the Arsenal, both dating from the 18th century. Several institutes of higher learning, including a university, are here. Voronezh was founded in 1586 as a frontier outpost to protect Moscow against invasions by the Crimean Tatars. Rapid growth began in the early 19th century, when the city became a prominent trading center. Voronezh was heavily damaged during World War II.

Vorster, Balthazar Johannes (1915 1983), South African political leader and prime minister (1966-1978). On the right of the Nationalist Party, he was in charge of education (1958-1961) and minister of justice (1961-1966), responsible for some of the most repressive of the apartheid laws. He sought later to improve relations with black Africa. Elected president in 1978, he resigned in 1979 after being accused of false testimony on expenditure of government funds.
See also: South Africa.

Voting, formal collective expression of approval or rejection of a candidate for office or a course of action. The election of officers is a basic feature of democracy, but universal adult suffrage is recent: U.S. women obtained the vote only in 1920. Sometimes voting is compulsory, as in Australia and in Communist states. In the United States, voting originally followed English parliamentary practice, with the addition of the New England town meeting. Ballot papers first appeared in Massachusetts in 1634. Most U.S. states now use voting machines to ensure secrecy, speed, and accuracy.

Voyages of discovery, the period of the great European voyages of discovery started in the 15th century. Up until then, the Europeans only sailed their ships across the Mediterranean Sea and along the coasts of

V

V

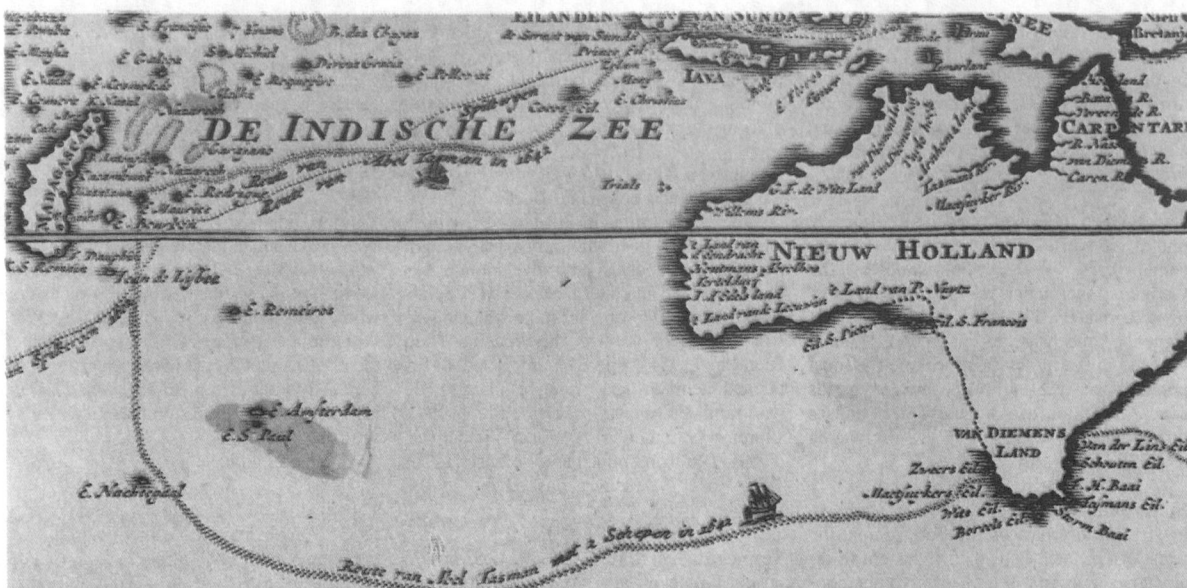

'Flat map of the whole world for Dutch travels' (producer and year unknown) depicting Abel Tasman's (1603-1659) route. While he was sailing for the VOC in 1642-43, he discovered Tasmania, which was named after him (he called it Van Diemensland), and New Zealand (which he called Stateland). Sailed round Australia in 1644, proving it was indeed an island, but found the coast 'extremely dry and infertile' and the population too 'miserable and ugly' to step ashore and 'discover' Australia properly.

Vasco da Gama's arrival in the Indian city of Calicut (now known as Kozhikode) in 1498, depicted on a Flemish tapestry from the 16th century. Once the way to India became known, numerous Portuguese sailors followed Da Gama's trail, which resulted in a great many conflicts with Indian monarchs and Arab merchants. Military force put a stop to these problems. The following competitors in the race for the lucrative luxury product trade, England, France and Holland, did not appear until the next century.

Map of the world by the Genoa Paolo dal Pozzo Toscanelli from 1457. Columbus tried to reach the Far East via a Western route with the help of these kinds of maps and his conviction that the earth was round.

The Dutch explorer Willem Barents got into trouble in 1596 whilst trying to find a Northern route to China. His ship hit an iceberg near Nova Zembla, and the crew was forced to spend the winter on the island in the 'Behouden Huys', a shelter they built. Barents's dream did not come true until 1879, when the Swede Otto Nördenskjöld (1869-1928) discovered a Northern route with his steam ship Vega.

The French explorer Jean-François La Pérouse (1741- around 1788) informing King Louis XVI of his plans. La Pérouse set out on an expedition to the Pacific Ocean in August 1785, where he explored Easter Island and Hawaii. La Pérouse discovered the strait which was named after him to the north of Japan. He sent his last journal from Botany Bay (January 1788); nothing more was heard from him after that.

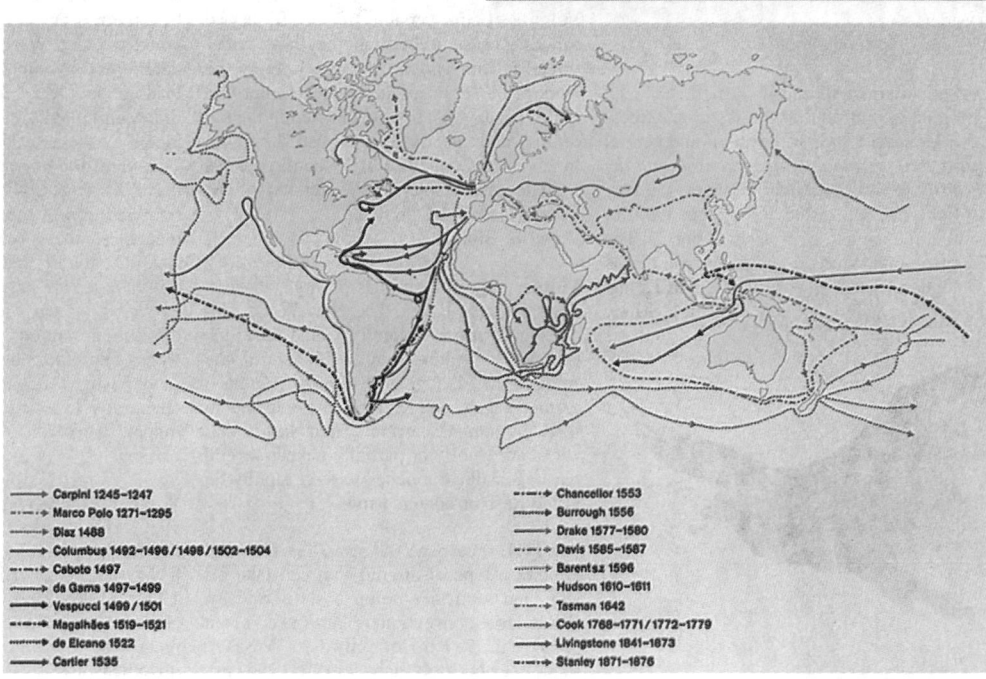

The routes used by several of the best-known explorers.

→ Carpini 1245–1247
⟶ Marco Polo 1271–1295
→ Diaz 1488
→ Columbus 1492–1496 / 1498 / 1502–1504
⟶ Caboto 1497
→ da Gama 1497–1499
→ Vespucci 1499 / 1501
→ Magalhães 1519–1521
→ de Elcano 1522
→ Cartier 1535

⟶ Chancellor 1553
⟶ Burrough 1556
⟶ Drake 1577–1580
⟶ Davis 1585–1587
⟶ Barentsz 1596
⟶ Hudson 1610–1611
⟶ Tasman 1642
⟶ Cook 1768–1771 / 1772–1779
⟶ Livingstone 1841–1873
⟶ Stanley 1871–1876

V

Western Europe and Western Africa. The exceptions were the Vikings, who reached the coast of Northern Africa in 1000. The desire to enter the lucrative trade in Asian products, up till then an Arabic monopoly, impelled the Portuguese to find a sea route to Asia in the 15th century. In 1498, after a voyage around the Cape of Good Hope, Vasco da Gama reached the Indian coast. The Italian Christopher Columbus, sailing a Spanish ship, discovered America by accident. He was convinced the earth was round, which meant he would be able to get to Asia if he crossed the Atlantic Ocean in a Westely direction. At the beginning of the 16th century, the Portuguese Fernão de Magalhães sailed via Cape Horn to Asia, returning via the Philippines and the Cape of Good Hope, thus proving that the earth was indeed round. The commercial successes attained by these voyages, in particular the colonization of newly discovered parts of the world, resulted in other countries setting out on their own voyages. The Englishman Francis Drake was the second man to sail around the world and the Dutchman Willem Barentsz reached Spits Bergen and Nova Zembla between 1594 and 1596, in an attempt to find a Northern route to Asia. In the 18th century, the voyages gained a more scientific character, like the voyages of the Englishman James Cook and the Frenchman La Pérouse and, even later, in the systematic research into the interior of Africa.

Voyager Program, two unmanned U.S. probes of the outer solar system. *Voyager 1* made close approaches to Jupiter in March 1979 and to Saturn in Nov. 1980. *Voyager 2* bypassed Jupiter in July 1979, swung around Saturn in Aug. 1981, continued to Uranus in 1986 and Neptune in 1989. The probes provided remarkable close-up views of the two giant gas planets and their satellites, revealing, among other things, the existence of a ring around Jupiter, active volcanoes on Jupiter's moon Io and a completely unexpected complexity in Saturn's ring system.
See also: Space exploration.

Vries, Adriaen de (1546?-1626), a Dutch sculptor. He introduced the restless, expressive Mannerist style to northern and central Europe. In *Virtue and Vice, Samson and the Philistine*, and other small bronzes, the play of light on body surfaces heightens the illusion of movement. De Vries was born in The Hague, and studied with Giovanni da Bologna in Florence. He worked in Rome, Copenhagen, Prague, and Augsburg. Many

This Hawker-Siddeley Harrier (1969) only needs a very short runway (STOL), and it can also take off and land completely vertically (VTOL). This is done by special fins that can bend the jetstream downwards. The Harrier is a light jet-bomber, with a maximum speed of about one mach and an operational height of approximately 5.3 mi (8.5 km).

critics consider the Mercury Fountain in Augsburg his best work.

Vuillard, Édouard (1868-1940), French painter, printmaker, and decorator who, along with his friend Pierre Bonnard, developed the intimist style of painting. His subjects were scenes from his private world, chiefly domestic scenes from his mother's home. Vuillard received commissions to do decorative works also. He painted the foyer of the Théatre des Champs-Elysées (1913) and the murals in the Palais de Chaillob (1937) and the League of Nations, Geneva (1939).

Vulcan, in Roman mythology, god of fire. He was also the blacksmith of the gods, skilled in metalworking. Vulcan is identified with the Greek god Hephaestus. He was a son of Jupiter and Juno and was married to Venus.
See also: Mythology.

Vulgate, Latin version of the Bible, so called because it became the most widespread (Latin: *vulgata*) in use. Largely the work of St. Jerome, who revised earlier Old Latin translations, it was collected in the 6th century and universally established by 800. In 1546 the Council of Trent confirmed the Vulgate as the sole official version of the Roman Catholic church.
See also: Bible.

Vulture, any of 2 families of large, soaring, diurnal birds of prey. The New World vultures are a primitive family, Cathartidae; the Old World vultures are a branch of the Accipitridae, being most closely related to certain eagles. All vultures are adapted to feed on animal carrion. Their heads and necks are wholly or partially naked; several have specialized tongues to feed rapidly on liquid flesh or bone marrow.

V/STOL (*V*ertical/ *S*hort *T*ake-*O*ff and *L*anding), type of aircraft that can take off and land vertically or on a short runway. While large conventional planes need about 5,000 ft (1,500 m) of runway, a V/STOL plane needs less than 500 ft (150 m).

V/STOLs have great military value because they can land on small airfields near the scene of battle as well as on small aircraft carriers and military ships without large flight decks. Both the United States and Great Britain have a combat V/STOL called the Harrier. There are commercial STOLS that can operate from small airports.
See also: Airplane.

W, 23rd letter of the English alphabet. Its origins have been traced to the Semitic letter *waw* (meaning 'hook'), which was a symbol resembling a tent peg or hook, itself perhaps derived from a *y*-shaped Egyptian hieroglyph. This letter reached the Roman alphabet as a *v*, though it was used both for *u* and *v*. Medieval Norman scribes began writing *vv* or *uu* ('double *u*') to represent the Anglo-Saxon *w* sound for which Norman French had no equivalent.

Wages and hours, income derived from labor, figured on the basis of the number of hours worked. Wages, the rate of which is determined by supply and demand, are the leading source of income in the United States and may be calculated for work completed by the hour, day, week, month, or by individual job or service performed. In addition to wages, workers may also receive remuneration in the form of overtime payments, bonuses, paid vacations, holidays, sick or maternity leave, and retirement benefits. Wages are categorized as either money wages or real wages. Money wages are the actual amount paid to workers; real wages represent the buying power of the money wages. Economists gauge economic change by investigating the fluctuations in money wages and making real-wage comparisons.

Wagner, Honus (John Peter Wagner; 1874-1955), U.S. baseball player. Wagner, considered to be baseball's greatest shortstop, won 8 National League batting titles (1900, 1903, 1904, 1906-1909, 1911) and holds the National League record for triples (252 career). Wagner's hit over .300 for 17 consecutive seasons (1897-1913), a major league

Red-headed turkey vulture (*Cathartes aura*, order *Falconiformes*, length about 30 in (75 cm), Southern Canada to the Magellan Strait.

record. He played for the Louisville Colonels (1897-1899) and Pittsburgh Pirates (1900-1917) and was among the first group of players inducted into the National Baseball Hall of Fame (1936).

Wagner, Otto (1841-1918), Austrian architect, originally built in a neo renaissance style. Became one of the most important representatives of the Viennese Secession (Austrian art nouveau); built the Majolika Haus (1898), and the Karlsplatz metro station (1901) in Vienna. Later became an advocate of a more functional design, as shown by the post office bank building (1904-1906, Vienna).

Wagner, Richard (1813-1883), German composer. His adventurous and influential music marks the high point of German romanticism. A conductor in provincial opera houses, he achieved his first successes as a composer with the operas *Rienzi* (1838-1840), *Der Fliegende Holländer* (1841), *Tannhäuser* (1844), and *Lohengrin* (1846-1848), in which he pioneered his new ideas in fusing music and drama. The culmination of his creative principles is found in the myth cycle, *Der Ring des Nibelungen,* comprising *Das Rheingold* (1853-1854), *Die Walküre* (1854-1856), *Siegfried* (1856-1869), and *Götterdämmerung* (1874). Involved in the 1848 Dresden revolution, Wagner fled (with the help of Franz Liszt) to Switzerland, where he wrote *Tristan und Isolde* (1857-1859) and the comic opera *Die Meistersinger von Nürnberg* (1862-1867), in addition to part of the Ring cycle. He next moved to Bavaria (1872), where Ludwig II helped him found the Bayreuth Festival. *Parsifal* (1877-1882) was his last opera. His second wife, **Cosima** (1837-1930), the daughter of Liszt, was largely responsible for the continuing success of the Bayreuth Festival.

Wagon, wheeled vehicle of primary importance to transportation and commerce. The invention of the wagon coincided with that of the wheel, over 5,000 years ago, when solid wooden wheels were fixed to a simple axle attached to a sledge. Wheeled transport vehicles, hauled by oxen, developed in Mesopotamia. The Greeks and Romans improved vehicle design until after the fall of the Roman Empire, when little was done to advance the design of wheeled conveyance. Farm carts remained the most widely used transport until the development of 4-wheeled coaches in Germany in the Middle Ages. By the 17th century, in western Europe, a period of mechanical and scientific enlightenment had begun. Spring suspension came into use permitting longer-distanced travel at higher speeds. This led to development and improvement of commercial and passenger coaches and carriages, freight-transport vehicles, and ultimately to the invention of the automobile.

Wagtail, any of several small Old World birds (family Motacillidae) related to the pipits. Wagtails have long tails that they wag up and down to keep their balance. The yellow wagtail has spread across the Bering Strait and nests in Alaska.

The Majolica House in Vienna, was built by Otto Wagner in 1898. An outstanding example of Art Nouveau. Its symmetrical design and sculptural and painted decoration had much in common with the work of Wagner's American contemporary, Louis Sullivan.

Wahid, Abdurrahman (also known as Gus Dur; 1940 -), Indonesian politician and President (1999-2001). He is reputed to be a quick-witted thinker and a moderate leader of the Islamic movement Nadhlatul Uulama. He founded the Forum Demokrasi (Democratic Forum) in 1995 to reinforce Indonesia's democracy. He was confronted with religious, political and ethnic crises (Aceh, Irian Jaya and Maluku) during his government. Furthermore, his health failed him and the Parliament increasingly openly criticized his government. Shortly after he declared the state of emergency in 2001, he was dismissed by the Parliament. Vice President Megawati Sukarnoputri, former President Sukarno's daughter, succeeded him.
See also: Megawati Sukarnoputri.

Wahoo, swift-swimming sport and food fish (*Acanthocybium solandri*), of the mackerel family. The wahoo is found worldwide in warm waters, particularly tropical areas of the Atlantic, Pacific, and Indian oceans. The wahoo has a slender, elongated body with a pointed nose, long backfin, and crescent-shaped tail. Its back is dark gray-blue, with silvery, irregularly striped sides. Wahoos may grow to 8 ft (2.4 m) in length and attain a weight of about 180 lb (82k).

Wailing Wall, part of the western wall of the ancient Temple in Jerusalem, destroyed by the Romans in A.D.70. It is held sacred by the Jews, who gather there to pray and mourn the Temple's destruction.
See also: Jews.

Waitz, Grete (real name, Grete Anderson; 1953-), Norwegian athlete, initially specializing in middle-distance running. In 1976 she broke her first world record: 8 min 45.4 sec for the 3000 m. Later concentrated on long-distance running, and won the New York marathon in 1982. The following year she won the New York marathon again. Her versatility showed itself once more when she won the cross country world title in 1983.

Wajed, Sheikh Hasin (1947-), Bengali politician. She settled in India after the Coup

in 1975. She returned as party leader of the socialist Awami-Liga in 1981. She led the opposition against the military regime, and from 1991, against the government of the Bengali Nationalist Party (BNP). The BNP won the elections in 1996, which led to massive protests led by Wajed. She declared that there had been irregularities during the elections. Prime Minister Khaleda Zia was forced to resign, after which new elections were called. Wajed became Prime Minister after the Awami-Liga won these elections. The government of Wajed was the first to remain in office the complete governmental period until 2001, when she resigned in favor of a transitional government.

Wake, tradition in which people gather at the home of a dead person before burial. This is a popular custom, especially in Western cultures. Its purpose in part is to console the family and friends of the deceased, but it is also assumed that long ago a consensus of people was needed to confirm the status of the corpse.

Abdurraham Wahid (white shirt) forced to resign in 2001

Wake-robin *See:* Trillium.

Waksman, Selman Abraham (1888-1973), U.S. microbiologist. Waksman, an authority on soil microbiology, developed a controlled system to discover antibiotics among microbes, particularly actinomycetes. Antibiotic activity was tested on about 10,000 soil microbes, leading to the discovery of the antibiotic streptomycin (1943), the first truly effective agent in the treatment of tuberculosis. Waksman was awarded the Nobel Prize in physiology or medicine in 1952.
See also: Microbiology.

Walachia (Romanian: Tara Românesca) Historical region in southern Romania between the Carpathian mountains and the Danube; 19,892 sq mi (51,500 sq km). Cultivation of maize and wheat; oil at Plusti. Part of the Roman province of Dacia (1st century A.D.). Independent principality in the 14th century; from 1460 onwards paid tax to the Ottoman Empire. In the 18th and 19th centuries occupied successively by Austria and Russia. United with with Moldavia (1859), since 1862 has the name Romania.

W

A mining town in South Wales with its monotonous rows of working-class houses.

Walata, important trade city of West Africa in the 11th-16th centuries, now the town of Oualata in Mauritania. Settled by the Muslims in the late 11th century, it was successively controlled by the Mali Empire, the Tuareg, and the Songhai Empire. Trade was conducted in copper, gold, swords, and slaves.

Walcott, Derek (1930-), a West Indian poet and playwright. Walcott was born in Castries, St. Lucia. He graduated from the University of the West Indies in Kingston, Jamaica, in 1953. He has taught in the United States and Great Britain. In 1992 he became the first Caribbean author to win the Nobel Prize in literature. His verse is noted for combining English poetry forms with rhythmic language, island imagery, and descriptions of Caribbean life. He first came to prominence with the poetry collections *In a Green Night* (1962), *The Castaway* (1965), and *The Gulf* (1969), in which he portrays a search for cultural identity. Other works include: poetry-*Another Life* (1973), *Sea Grapes* (1976), *The Star-Apple Kingdom* (1979), *Midsummer* (1984), *Omeros* (1990), and *The Bounty* (1997). Plays (with date of first performance) *TiJean and His Brothers* (1978), *Dream on Monkey Mountain* (1967), and *Pantomime* (1978).

Wald, George (1906-1997), U.S. chemist and prominent pacifist. His work on the chemistry of vision brought him a share, with Haldane K. Hartline and Roger A. Granit, of the 1967 Nobel Prize in physiology or medicine.
See also: Chemistry.

Waldenses, or Waldensians, reforming Christian sect founded by Peter Waldo in Lyons, France, in the 12th century. They preached poverty, rejected the papacy, and took the Bible as their sole authority, for which they were excommunicated (1184) and persecuted. The survivors united with the Protestants in the Reformation. The Waldensian Church still exists, with several offshoots in the United States.
See also: Protestantism.

Waldheim, Kurt (1918-), Austrian diplomat and minister of foreign affairs (1968-

1970), and secretary general of the United Nations (1972-1981). As secretary general he worked to strengthen the UN's peacekeeping role and to increase aid to poor countries. In 1986 he was elected to the Austrian presidency, up to 1992, in spite of his history as a German intelligence soldier and Nazi officer (World War II).
See also: Austria; United Nations.

Waldner, Jan-Ove (1965-), Swedish table tennis player, won his first singles world title in 1989 when he beat his fellow countryman Jorgen Persson 3-2. Three years later he won the singles title during the 1992 Olympic Games in Barcelona. In 1996 he beat Jorgen Persson again, 3-1, to win the European championship, and together they won the doubles title. Sweden also won the European title that year. In 1984, 1986, 1988, and 1989 Waldner won the European Top Twelve Tournament. He also won numerous national titles and other important tournaments.

Wales (Welsh: *Cymru*), historic principality of Great Britain, politically united with England since 1536. It is a large, roughly rectangular peninsula projecting into the Irish Sea west of England. Covering 8,016 sq mi (20,761 sq km), it is dominated by the Cambrian Mountains (Mt. Snowdon, 3,500 ft/1,085 m), and its rivers include the Severn, Wye, Usk, Taff, Dee, and Teifi. The climate is mild and wet. The majority of the population lives in the south, near the rich coalfields. Less than 20% speak both Welsh and English. The largest cities are Cardiff, the capital, and Swansea. Major industries, including coal mining, steel, oil refining, manmade fibers, and electronics, are also concentrated in the south. Agriculture, mostly cattle and sheep raising, predominates elsewhere. In a referendum in 1997 a small majority (53%) voted for the introduction of the National Assembly for Wales. The new body was granted limited powers, primarily in disbursement of the British budget for Wales. Wales maintained all its seats in the British Parliament.
See also: England.

Walesa, Lech (1943-), president of Poland (1991-1995). In 1980 he led the Polish labor

movement in its struggle to win government recognition of Solidarity (an umbrella labor group composed of about 50 trade unions)-the first time a Communist government had recognized an independent labor organization. In a 1981 military crackdown, the Polish government banned Solidarity and interned Walesa. He was released in 1982 and awarded the Nobel Peace Prize in 1983. In the upheavals of 1989, Solidarity was revived, and Walesa played a key role in establishing the new non-Communist Polish government.
See also: Poland.

Walker, Alice (1944-), U.S. author of poetry and novels examining the life experiences of African Americans. Walker was awarded the Pulitzer Prize for *The Color Purple* (1982), the story of Celie, a poor girl growing up in the rural South. Other works include *Once* (1968) and *Revolutionary Petunias and Other Poems* (1973), both volumes of poetry; a biography, *Langston Hughes, American Poet* (1974); the novels *The Third Life of Grange Copeland* (1970), *Meridian* (1976), *Possessing the Secret of Joy* (1992), and *By the Light of My Father's Smile* (1994).

Walker, Herschel, Jr. (1962-), U.S. football running back. Walker, a 3-time All-American player from the Univ. of Georgia, won the Heisman Trophy in 1982. He played for the New Jersey Generals (U.S. Football League), the Dallas Cowboys, and the Minnesota Vikings.

Walkie-talkie, portable 2-way radio frequently used by police, hunters, and others on the move to communicate over short distances (up to a few kilometers). In the United States, walkie-talkies operate on 1 or more of 23 channels lying between 26.960 MHz and 27.255 MHz.

Walking, or race-walking, competitive track-and-field sport. This form of racing utilizes a precise heel-and-toe gait: The leading foot touches the ground heel first advancing the walker quickly forward onto the toe, which provides a pushing momentum to each stride. The leg is locked in a straight position momentarily while the foot is still touching the ground. An expert race-walker can walk 1 mi (1.6 km) in about 6.5 minutes while an ordinary walker would take about 15-20 minutes to cover the same distance. Walking competitions, particularly in the Olympic Games, are held at distances of about 12-31 mi (20-50 km).

Walking stick, or stick insect, insect (*Diapheromera femorata*) that resembles a twig, camouflaging it from its enemies. There are several species of these insects of the family Phasmidae; the common walking stick has long, slender legs and a body of about 2-3 in (5-8 cm). They are usually a green or brownish color, may have sharp spines, and release a noxious scent. Walking sticks harm trees by eating the leaves; however, few survive the larval stage because the female lays her eggs where she stands and most fall to the ground.

Wallaby, rabbit-sized member of the kangaroo family (especially genus *Macropus*), native to Australia, Tasmania, and New Guinea. Like kangaroos, wallabies have large, strong hind feet and limbs and long tails. They are herbivores. All wallabies produce a single offspring, suckling it in the marsupium, or pouch.

Wallace, Alfred Russel (1823-1913), English naturalist and evolutionist. He formulated a theory of natural selection (survival of the fittest) simultaneously with, but independent of, Charles Darwin. Wallace explored at length the Malay Archipelago and the Amazon, where the idea of natural selection occurred to him, and where he formulated a basis for geographically categorizing animals. Wallace published 'On the Law Which Has Regulated the Introduction of New Species' (1855), which he shared with Darwin. Together they presented their theory before the Linnaean Society (1858). Other works include *The Malay Archipelago* (1869), *Contributions to the Theory of Natural Selection* (1870), and *The Geographical Distribution of Animals* (2 vols, 1876), a systemization of the science of biogeography.
See also: Darwin, Charles Robert.

Wallace, George Corley (1919-1998), U.S. political leader, governor of Alabama (1963-1967, 1971-1979, 1983-1986). Wallace, a segregationist, achieved notoriety in 1963 with his unsuccessful attempt to prevent racial integration at the University of Alabama. He ran for president 3 times, and in 1972 was shot and paralyzed in an attempted assassination while campaigning for the Democratic presidential nomination. Unable by Alabama law to succeed himself as governor, he had his wife, Lurleen, run for office to replace him (she won the election). He won the 1982 gubernatorial election with black support, and retired in 1986.

Wallace, Lew (Lewis Wallace; 1827-1905), U.S. military leader, lawyer, and author. Wallace is best known for his novels, particularly *Ben Hur* (1880), about the advent of Christianity in the Roman Empire. Wallace served in the Mexican War, and while a Union Army major general in the Civil War, captured Fort Donelson, Tenn. Wallace had studied law before the wars and became a practicing attorney in Indianapolis after military service. He headed courts of inquiry investigating wartime conduct of some Union and Confederate leaders, and served on the trial of Abraham Lincoln's assassins. He was appointed governor of New Mexico (1878-1881) and minister to Turkey (1881-1885).

Wall, Jeff (1946-), Canadian artist. Wall became well-known for his cibachromes in black-and-white, later in color, which were exhibited in huge light boxes like advertisements. These photographic images seemed to be natural representations of everyday situations, but were in reality carefully worked out in advance. Social behavior is subtly accentuated and critically illuminated. In the 1990s Wall manipulated his pictures in the studio using computer programs and concentrated on traditional genres such as still lives and landscapes.

Wallboard, fibrous building material made in rigid sheets and used to cover walls and ceilings for temperature and sound insulation, fire protection, and decoration. Types of wallboard include *fiberboard*, made of compressed cane or wood fibers; *hardboard*, a denser, more compressed board of similar composition; and *plasterboard*, used in building as a substitute for plaster, made of heavy paper, fiberboard, or other material bonded to a gypsum core.

Wallenberg, Raoul (1912-1947?), Swedish diplomat. While representing Sweden in Budapest during World War II, he issued Swedish passports to 20,000 Hungarian Jews to prevent their deportation into Nazi hands. Soviet authorities arrested him as a spy in 1945 and reported his death in prison in 1947. In 1981 an international association found evidence indicating he might be alive and urged the former Soviet Union to investigate (his death was never verified). In the same year the U.S. Congress declared him an honorary U.S. citizen.
See also: Sweden.

Waller, Fats (Thomas Wright Waller; 1904-1943), U.S. jazz and blues pianist, composer, and entertainer. Waller began his career working in cabarets and theaters, where he accompanied various singers. He was one of few jazz musicians to become widely popular, and by the late 1920s his music, which was often witty and animated, was heard in many Broadway revues. From 1929 to 1943 Waller recorded hundreds of songs, including 'Ain't Misbehavin`,' 'Honeysuckle Rose,' and 'Blue Turning Gray Over You.' Waller also appeared in films, including *Stormy Weather* (1943).
See also: Jazz.

Walleye *See:* Perch.

Wallflower, or gillyflower, fragrant flowering plant (*Cheiranthus cheiri*) of the mustard family. Wallflowers, native to southern Europe and now widely cultivated, are so named for their tendency to grow on walls or on the sides of cliffs. The plants are biennial or perennial, grow to about 28 in (70 cm), and have stalks bearing clusters of maroon or purple flowers. The western wallflower (*Erysimum asperum*), a perennial, produces golden, orange, or brown flowers.

Wallis en Futuna, an overseas territory of France in the Pacific Ocean between Fiji and the Samoan Islands. It consists of three major islands: Uvéa in the Wallis Islands and Futuna and Alofi in the Horn group, and several islets. The total area of the territory is 106 square miles (274 sq km). In 1982 the territory had a population of about 12,000. Two-thirds of the people lived on Uvéa, the rest on Futuna. Mata Utu, on Uvéa, is the administrative center and only sizable town. The islands were discovered in 1767 by Samuel Wallis. They came under French control in 1842.

Walloons, French-speaking people (chiefly Celtic), inhabitants of southern Belgium and adjacent areas of France. The Walloons, who make up about 40% of Belgium's population, have often been at odds with the Flemish-speaking majority, who have resented French political and cultural domination. Separate regional administrations were set up in 1974.

Wallpaper, printed, painted, or embossed wall covering used to finish interior walls. Wallpaper, which is hung with glue or paste on the undecorated side, is utilized mainly as a decorative feature, and may be from any of 5 categories: ceiling papers, border papers, scenic or panel papers, papers of imitative design, or relief-surfaced papers made of ricepaper, burlap, straw fibers, or thin wood. It is thought that wallpapers originated in Europe in the 1500s to imitate expensive tapestries. Other wallpapers evolved in China (1600s) and in France (1700s). The first U.S. wallpapers were produced in Philadelphia (1739).

The brush-tailed rock wallaby, *Petrogale penicillata*, is an adept rock climber that can leap horizontally as much as 13 ft (4 m). A marsupial, the young climbs into the mother's pouch shortly after birth, where it feeds and grows for several months.

'Blackthorn' wallpaper, designed in 1892 by Englishman William Morris (1834-1896).

W

Wall Street, financial center of the United States, located in lower Manhattan, New York City. Wall Street is the home of the New York Stock Exchange, many other commodity exchanges, and head offices of many banks and insurance and brokerage firms. The term 'Wall Street' also refers to the nation's aggregate financial interests.
See also: Stock exchange.

Walnut, deciduous tree of the genus *Juglans*, prized for its wood and nuts. In the United States the black walnut (*J. nigra*) grows to 150 ft (45.7 m), its wood being used for furniture, musical instruments, and gun stocks. The English walnut (*J. regia*), which provides edible walnuts, is naturalized throughout the world. The walnut tree is a member of the family Juglandaceae and is related to the hickory and pecan.

Walnut trees are commercially valuable for their wood and nuts. Before the fruits harden into nuts, they may be used for pickling. Once they are mature, they will burst from their green casing, after which the edible nuts can be removed from the hard outer shell.
Above: fruiting branch
Below left: nut
Below right: tree

Walpole, Sir Robert (1676-1745), English politician often described as Great Britain's first prime minister. A Whig, he held ministerial posts from 1708 to 1717. He was rewarded for his role in salvaging the government from the South Sea Bubble (a speculation scandal) with an appointment as first lord of the treasury and chancellor of the exchequer (1721), during which time he dominated Parliament and created political and financial stability. Facing opposition and unpopularity as Britain became involved in European wars from 1739, he resigned in 1742, becoming first earl of Orford.
See also: United Kingdom.

Walraff, Hans Günter (1942-), German writer of a great number of reports in book form about the lives of workers in West Germany written from a marxist perspective, such as *13 Unerwünschte Reportagen* (1969). Was able to become a reporter for the tabloid newspaper Bild by assuming a false identity. Wrote about his experiences there in *Der Aufmacher. Der Mann der bei Bild Hans Esser war* (1977), a book which created much controversy and Bild started court proceedings against him. Just as sensa-

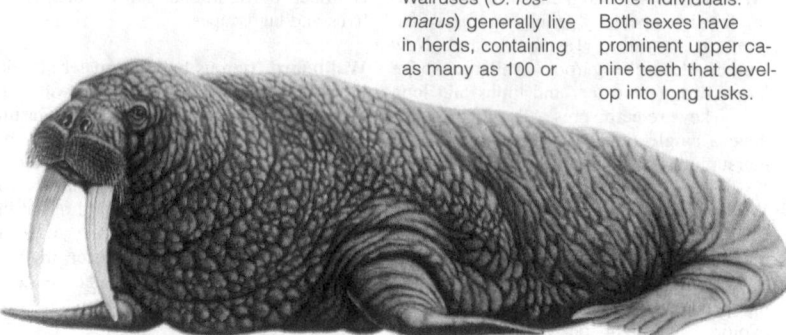

Walruses (*O. rosmarus*) generally live in herds, containing as many as 100 or more individuals. Both sexes have prominent upper canine teeth that develop into long tusks.

tional was his report about the grueling experiences he endured when disguised as a Turkish immigrant: *Ganz Unten* (1985).

Walrus, either of 2 subspecies of seal-like marine mammals (*Odobenus rosmarus*), distinguished by upper canines that extend into long tusks (up to 3.5 ft/1.1 m) and wrinkled brown hides. Adult males may weigh up to 3,000 lb (1,400 kg). Walruses are found in shallow waters around Arctic coasts, often hauling themselves out onto rocks or ice floes to bask. They feed almost exclusively on mollusks.

Walser, Martin (1927-), German writer. Studied philosophy and literature, received a doctorate in 1959 on Kafka. Published novels, stories, and plays, which were critical of society and full of irony. A particularly recurring theme was the impossibility of sustaining human relationships within marriage. His work includes *The Unicorn* (1966), *Swan Villa* (1980), *Letter to Lord Liszt* (1982), *Breakers* (1985), and *Runaway Horse* (1978; play 1985).

Walter, Bruno (Bruno Walter Schlesinger; 1876-1962), German-born U.S. conductor. He was a protégé of Gustav Mahler, but his career in Europe was cut short by the Nazis (they forced him to leave), and he lived in the United States from 1939. He was renowned for his interpretations of Mahler, Wagner, Beethoven, and Brahms with the Metropolitan Opera and the New York Philharmonic.

Walther Von der Vogelweide (c.1170-c.1230), most renowned medieval German lyric poet, or minnesinger. Walther's poetry was more politically oriented than that of other minnesingers, with about one-half of his 200 poems being moral, political, or religious in nature. These didactic poems encouraged such virtues as self-discipline, charity, and fidelity, and extolled the benefits of pilgrimage. The other half were love poems, which were fresh in their appraisal of courtly love and of the society of his time. Walther was a poet in the Viennese court of Leopold V, and later wandered from court to court until German Emperor Frederick II granted him a small fief in Wurzburg, where it is assumed that he lived out the remainder of his life.

Walton, Ernest Thomas Sinton (1903-1995), Irish nuclear physicist. He shared with John D. Cockcroft the 1951 Nobel

Prize in physics for their development of the first particle accelerator, with which they initiated the first nuclear-fission reaction applying nonradioactive substances.
See also: Cockcroft, Sir John Douglas; Particle accelerator.

Walton, Izaak (1593-1683), English writer. His famous *The Compleat Angler* (1653), written as a dialogue between a fisherman, Piscator, and a hunter, Venator, combines praise for simple living with sound advice on the sport of fishing. His biographies include *John Donne* (1640), *Sir Henry Wotton* (1651), *George Herbert* (1670), and *Bishop Sanderson* (1678).

Walton, Sir William Turner (1902-1983), English composer. He had a brilliant early success with *Façade* (1923), a chamber work set to poems by Edith Sitwell. Other works include the oratorio *Belshazzar's Feast* (1931), film scores (notably for films of Shakespeare plays), and the opera *Troilus and Cressida* (1954).

Waltz, ballroom dance in 3/4 time, probably originating from the *ländler*, a folk dance; also, music in 3/4 time. Its popularity in the 19th century was due largely to the music of the Strauss family.
See also: Strauss.

Walvis Bay, or Walvisbaai, South African exclave district within Namibia's boundaries, on the Atlantic coast. Walvis Bay has an area of about 434 sq mi (1,124 sq km) and is Namibia's only deep-water seaport. The harbor is a major one with links to most leading overseas shipping centers, and has been a point of controversy since the 1970s, with South Africa and Namibia in dispute over the area's jurisdiction. When Namibia became independent of South Africa (March 21, 1990), Walvis Bay was adjudged to remain under the dominion of South Africa. After two years of mutual administration, Walvis Bay was delegated to Namibia. Industries include fishing and fish processing.
See also: Namibia; South Africa.

Wampum, strings of shell beads and disks made by Native Americans, used as ornaments and as money in trading. Early European settlers accepted wampum as currency (a purple variety was especially valuable), but the production of counterfeit glass beads undermined their value in the early 18th century.

The wandering jew,
T. fluminensis.

Wandering Jew, or striped inch plant, any of several trailing plants that are grown indoors for their flowers and foliage. *Tradescantia fluminensis variegata* has green leaves, irregularly striped with white; *Callisia elegans* has green leaves with white pinstripes; and *Zebrina pendula* has purple, green, and silver striped leaves. They grow best in sunny windows and are extremely easy to propagate by taking cuttings and rooting them in water and wet sand.

Wandering Jew, legendary man (identified as a Jew in the 17th century) doomed to wander the earth until the Second Coming of Christ as punishment for taunting Jesus as He struggled to His Crucifixion. This tale has been chronicled several times, in the medieval tale *Flores historiarum*; in 'A Brief Description and Narration Regarding a Jew Named Ahasuerus' (1602); and in the play 'Le Juif errant' (1844-1845).

Wang Wei (699-759), Chinese poet, landscape painter, and calligrapher of the T'ang dynasty (618-907). Wang Wei is credited with the creation of the broken ink (*p'o-mo*) method of wash brushstrokes, and was a master of monochromatic landscape paintings, particularly snowscapes. The lyric poetry of Wang Wei often related nature's attributes. He was revered in later years, probably for uniting poetry, painting, and calligraphy in a single art form.

Wankel engine, internal-combustion engine that produces rotary motion directly. Invented by the German engineer Felix Wankel, who completed his first design in 1954, it is used in automobiles and airplanes. A triangular rotor with spring-loaded sealing plates at its apexes rotates eccentrically inside a cylinder, while the 3 combustion chambers formed between the sides of the rotor and the walls of the cylinder successively draw in, compress, and ignite a fuel-and-air mixture. The Wankel engine is simpler in principle, more efficient, and more powerful weight-for-weight than a conventional reciprocating engine, but it is more difficult to cool.
See also: Internal combustion engine.

Wapiti (*Cervus canadensis*), North American subspecies of the red deer, called elk in the United States. It is larger than the typical European red deer, and, unlike the red deer, the terminal points of its antlers are in the same plane as the beam and do not form a crown. Once the most abundant deer in North America, wapiti are now severely reduced in number and range.

War, organized armed conflict between groups of people or states. War is not found elsewhere in the animal kingdom. Since recorded history began, people have been involved in hostility for different aims: power, territory, wealth, ideological domination, security, or independence. Until modern times most wars were fought with limited means for limited aims, but modern weapons threaten mass destruction with their ability to eliminate whole populations, thus endangering the survival of the human race.

War aces, combat pilots with at least 5 'victories' or 'kills,' confirmed downings of enemy aircraft. Famous aces of World War I, the first air war, included Baron Manfred von Richthofen of Germany (the 'Red Baron') and Captain Eddie Rickenbacker of the United States. The leading ace of World War II was Captain Erich Hartmann of Germany (a record 352 kills); Lieutenant Colonel Heinz Bär of Germany was the first jet ace.

War Between the States *See:* Civil War, U.S..

Warble fly, also cattle warble or heel fly, large, beelike fly of the family Hypodermatidae that deposits its eggs on the legs or feet of cattle. There the larvae (cattle grub) enter the skin and migrate within the body for several months. This produces a characteristic painful lump, or warble. At maturity, the cattle grub emerges and pupates wherever it drops. The warble fly is a pest in Europe and North America, causing economic losses due to damaged hides and meat.

Warbler, small songbird native to the Americas. Warblers (family Parulidae) are seen throughout the United States and Canada during the temperate months, and migrate south to winter in South and Central America. Among the many species of warblers are the American redstart (*Setophaga ruticilla*), the yellow warbler (*Dendroica petechia*), and the hooded warbler (*Wilsonia citrina*). The feathers of warblers vary in color. The birds grow to about 3.5-10 in (9-25 cm), and they are noted for their lively movements and song. Warblers are beneficial to farmers and gardeners as they feed on harmful insects.

Warburg, Otto Heinrich (1883-1970), German biochemist. He was awarded the 1931 Nobel Prize in physiology or medicine for discovering the chemistry of cell respiration. He was director of the Kaiser Wilhelm (now Max Planck) Institute for Cell Physiology, Berlin, from 1931 to 1953. *See also:* Biochemistry; Cell.

War correspondent, news reporter who sends information from a war front to print or broadcast media, to provide accurate, up-to-date coverage. The Mexican War (1846-1848) was probably the first war to be reported on systematically by getting information immediately from the front. U.S. writers

W

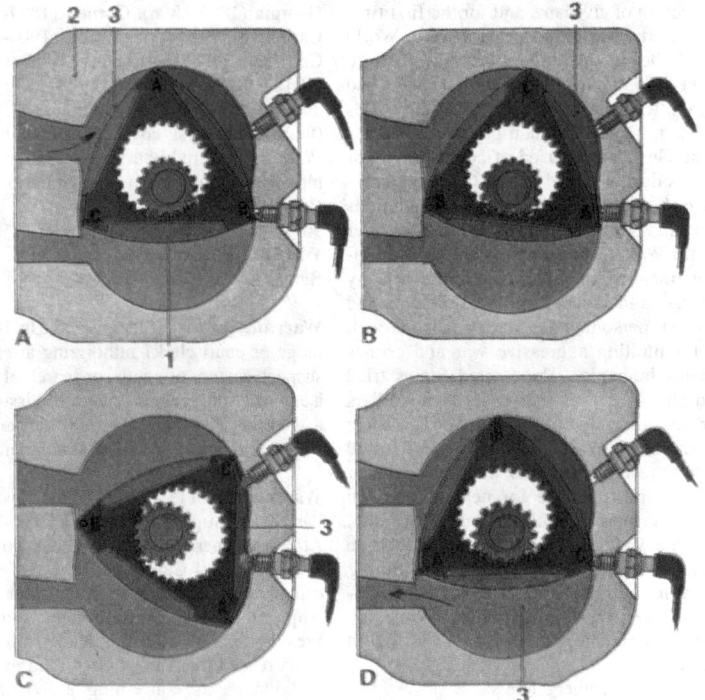

The Wankel engine (A) is an internal-combustion rotary engine. Its curved triangular rotor (1) orbits around a crankshaft inside a curved casing (2). As the rotor turns, its apexes slide along the casing, creating a series of combustion chambers constantly alternating size. Gaseous fuel enters a chamber (3) through an intake port. (B) Rotary movement decreases the size of the chamber, compressing the fuel, which is ignited (C) by a spark plug. (D) continuing movement of the rotor permits release of exhaust gases through an exit port.

W

This silk-screen portrait of filmstar Elizabeth Taylor (1964) is characteristic of the pop art nature of the work of Andy Warhol (1927-87).

who have been important war correspondents include Walt Whitman (Civil War, 1861-1865) and Stephen Crane (Spanish-American War, 1898).

War crime, wartime acts that violate the protections guaranteed to noncombatants under either the international laws of war or the military code established by a particular country. Most laws defining war crimes attempt to protect prisoners of war and unarmed civilians from hostile action by ground troops. Protection of noncombatants from air attack is less defined in law and is largely ignored in practise. The body of international law defining war crimes was formulated at several conferences held in Geneva, Switzerland, and The Hague, Netherlands. The Geneva Conventions of 1949, signed by most nations of the world, updated previous rules providing for humane treatment of prisoners of war and the protection of civilians, and for the first time forbade the use of hostages. Prior to World War I, the custom at the end of a war was to grant amnesty to all belligerents who had committed war crimes. In 1920 the Allies insisted that the German government prosecute Germans accused of committing war crimes during World War I. Germany complied, but there were very few convictions and the sentences were nominal. After World War II, the Allies established an international tribunal to try and punish many German and Japanese political leaders and military personnel for war crimes, as well as for plotting aggressive war and crimes against humanity. The United States tried and punished a number of its own soldiers for war crimes in both World War II and the Vietnamese War. In 1944 the United Nations established two international war crimes tribunals: one for persons accused of war crimes committed during the civil war in Rwanda in 1994, the other for those accused of war crimes committed during the war in the former Yugoslavia, 1991-1995. They were the first war crime tribunals established since the end of World War II.
See also: Nuremberg Trials.

Ward, Barbara (1914-1981), British writer, economist, and commentator on the relations between the Western powers and developing nations. She was foreign editor of *Economist* magazine (from 1946), governor of British Broadcasting Corp. (1946-1950), and a professor at Columbia Univ. (N.Y.C.;

1968-1973). In her writings she stressed the importance of economic aid and international cooperation in such books as *The Rich Nations and the Poor Nations* (1962), *Nationalism and Ideology* (1967), and *Progress for a Small Planet* (1979).
See also: Economics.

Warhol, Andy (1927-1987), U.S. artist and filmmaker, famous for his pop art silk-screen paintings that incorporated everyday objects (e.g., soup cans). His highly innovative, often erotic, and often lengthy films include *Chelsea Girls* (1966) and *Lonesome Cowboys* (1969).

Warm-blooded animal, or homoiotherm, animal whose body temperature is not dependent on external temperature but is maintained at a constant level by internally generated metabolic heat. This constant temperature enables the chemical processes of the body, many of them temperature dependent, to be more efficient. Mammals and birds have developed this homoiothermy, and it is now believed that pterodactyls, therapsids, and many other extinct reptiles may also have been warm-blooded.

Warner, Jack L. (1892-1978), U.S. film producer who, with his 3 brothers, founded Warner Brothers, one of the largest and most successful Hollywood film studios. Warner Brothers produced the first sound film, *The Jazz Singer* (1927), and was the first studio to produce for television.

Warner, Pop (Glenn Scobey Warner; 1871-1954), U.S. football coach. He coached at Georgia (1895-1896), Cornell (1897-1898), Carlisle (1899-1903), Cornell (1904-1906), Carlisle (1907-1914), Univ. of Pittsburgh (1915-1923), Stanford (1924-1932), and Temple (1933-1938), winning 313 games (third winningest coach in Division I-A). Warner pioneered both the single- and double-wing formation and led Standford to a Rose Bowl victory (1928).

War on Poverty *See:* Johnson, Lyndon Baines.

Warrant, judicial order (signed usually by a judge or court clerk) authorizing arrest of a suspect, seizure of goods, or search of premises. Strict procedures govern the issuing of a warrant. There are also tax warrants and warrants of attorney and of attachment.

Warren, Earl (1891-1974), chief justice of the U.S. Supreme Court (1953-1969). Attorney general (1939-1943) and governor (1943-1953) of California, he was Republican vice presidential candidate in 1948. Appointed to the Supreme Court by President Eisenhower, his leadership of the court resulted in a number of landmark liberal judgments concerning individual and civil liberties, notably *Brown* v. *Board of Education of Topeka* (1954), declaring racial segregation in schools unconstitutional. Warren also led the commission assigned to investigate Pres. John F. Kennedy's assassination.
See also: Supreme Court of the United States.

Warren, Mercy Otis (1728-1814), U.S. author of patriotic works. Warren, who knew several Revolutionary War leaders, wrote to express her own political beliefs. She encouraged pro-Revolutionary sympathy with her satirical, anti-Tory plays: *The Adulateur* (1773), *The Defeat*, and *The Group* (1775). Her major work was a history of the American Revolution titled *History of the Rise, Progress, and Termination of the American Revolution* (3 vols., 1805). Warren advocated equal rights for women and the conservation of rights of individuals.

Warren, Robert Penn (1905-1989), U.S. novelist, poet, and critic. One of the poets associated with the *Fugitive* magazine (1922-1923), Penn's poetry and novels are often set in the South and address political and moral themes. He won Pulitzer prizes for his novel *All the King's Men* (1946),and his poetry collections *Promises* (1957) and *Now and Then* (1979). In 1986 he was appointed the first U.S. poet laureate.

Warren Report, findings of the commission established (Nov. 1963) by President Lyndon Johnson to investigate the assassination of President John F. Kennedy. The commission comprised Supreme Court Chief Justice Earl Warren, U.S. Representatives Hale Boggs and Gerald Ford; U.S. Senators Richard Russell and John S. Cooper; Allen Dulles; and John J. McCloy. The report, released in Sept. 1964, concluded that neither assassin Lee Harvey Oswald nor his killer, Jack Ruby, was part of a conspiracy. It criticized the FBI and Secret Service and recommended reforms in presidential security. The work of the commission has been widely challenged since its findings were published, and in 1979 a congressional committee announced its determinations, based on acoustical evidence, that 2 gunmen had shot at Kennedy.

Warsaw (pop. 1,650,000), largest city and capital of Poland, on the Vistula River. It is a commercial, industrial, cultural, and educational center, and transportation hub. Chief products are machinery, precision instruments, motor vehicles, electrical equipment, textiles, and chemicals. Warsaw has frequently been a focal point in European history. It replaced Kraków as Poland's capital in 1596 and subsequently fell into Swedish, Russian, Prussian, and German hands. Much of the city, which was razed in World War II, has been carefully reconstructed, including Warsaw's medieval old town, Stare Miasto.
See also: Poland.

Warsaw Pact, or Warsaw Treaty Organization, mutual defense pact signed in 1955 in Warsaw by the USSR and its Communist neighbors (Albania, Bulgaria, Czechoslovakia, East Germany, Hungary, Poland, and Romania) after the formation of the North Atlantic Treaty Organization (NATO). Its unified command has headquarters in Moscow. In 1968 (when Albania formally withdrew) pact forces invaded Czechoslovakia to overthrow its independent-minded regime. In 1980-1981 the USSR used pact maneuvers and threats of intervention by

pact members to discourage labor unrest in Poland. Following the conventional arms treaty signed with NATO (1990), which drastically reduced the number of soldiers and weapons on the European continent, and the breakup of the Soviet-led Communist bloc, the Warsaw Pact was officially dissolved (1991).
See also: North Atlantic Treaty Organization.

Warship, ship armed and employed for combat. Ships have been used in battle since antiquity, when cargo carriers became warships when necessary. The oar- and sail-powered galley ships of the Romans and Greeks, and the Viking long ships attacked enemy vessels by ramming them. By the 1500s ships were larger and heavier, and when armed became floating artillery depots. Spain had such a fleet-galleons built for their explorers' long expeditions; however, when England, with lighter galleons, destroyed the Spanish Armada, heavier-armed but more maneuverable warships (called capital ships) were built and ruled the seas for the next 200 years. In the early 1800s steam-powered warships with rotating gun turrets were invented and outfitted with explosive shells, which replaced cannonballs. But ironclad ships, the precursors of modern warships, proved able to withstand their attack, as was attested in the Civil War battle between the *Monitor* and the *Merrimack* (neither lost in battle). The English ship *Dreadnought* was the first truly modern battleship, and in the early 1900s designers improved battleship capabilities using it as a model. This type of massive battleship, as well as the submarine, were the most effective of the World War I warships. By the end of World War II there were great advances in the design and capabilities of combat ships. Aircraft carriers, destroyers, cruisers, frigates, amphibious ships, and minesweep-

ers led the way into modern warfare. Advances in technology yielded further specialization, and with the advent of the *Nautilus* submarine, warships entered the nuclear age.

Wars of Succession *See:* Succession wars.

Wars of the Roses, fight between the House of Lancaster and the House of York for the English throne (1455-1485). A white rose stood for the House of York and a red rose stood for the House of Lancaster. The throne of England changed hands 5 times after the beginning of the war, at which time Henry VI, a Lancaster, ruled. When Henry Tudor, King Henry VII, took the throne (1485), he married Elizabeth, a York. This union dissolved the conflict between both houses and created a new dynasty, the House of Tudor.

Wart, scaly excrescence on the skin caused by a virus. Warts may arise without warning and disappear equally suddenly. Numerous remedies have been suggested, but local freezing or cauterization are often effective. Warts that grow on the soles of the feet, pushed inward by the weight of the body, are called verrucas.

Warta, one of the longest rivers in Poland and the main tributary of the Oder River. The Warta's source is 35 miles (56 km) northwest of Kraków. The river flows north and west for some 470 miles (756 km) through drained and cultivated marshes, and into the Odor at Kostrzyn. The Warta is joined to the Vistula River by the Notec River and the Bydgoszcz Canal. It is navigable in its lower half.

Wart hog, wild hog (genus *Phacochoerus*) distinguished by large, gristly facial warts

W

and 1-ft (30.5-cm) curling tusks. Wart hogs are found in Africa south of the Sahara. They prefer plains and open scrub and live in family groups, feeding on grass, leaves, sometimes fruit, roots, and carrion.

Warwick, Earl of (Richard Neville; 1428-1471), British soldier and influential leader, who later became known as *The Kingmaker*. He was one of the most powerful noblemen in the era of the Wars of the Roses, the prolonged struggle between the houses of York and Lancaster for the English throne. Warwick, related to both houses, at first sided with the York family. He held high offices under Henry VI of Lancaster after bringing about a compromise between the two houses. Warwick in 1461 led a march on London that resulted in Edward IV of York replacing Henry on the throne. For several years afterward Warwick was England's real ruler. A break with Edward led him to join the Lancastrians. Warwick restored Henry to the throne in 1470. Yorkists under Edward IV defeated Warwick's forces at Barnet, where Warwick was killed. Edward Bulwer-

The wart hog, *P. aethiopicus*, uses its curved tusks to dig for food and to defend itself when attacked. The male's upper tusks reach up to 25 in (63 cm) in length; the female's are smaller.

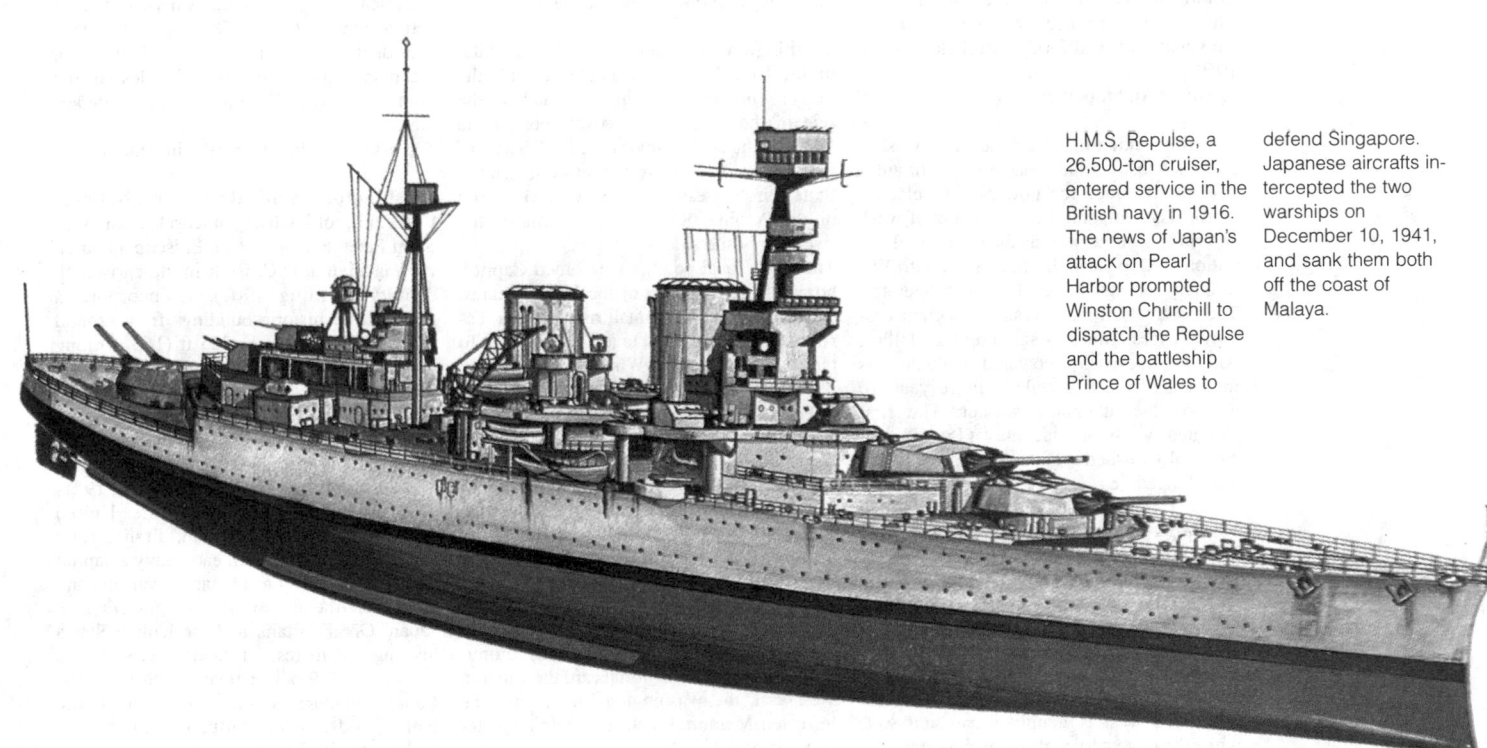

H.M.S. Repulse, a 26,500-ton cruiser, entered service in the British navy in 1916. The news of Japan's attack on Pearl Harbor prompted Winston Churchill to dispatch the Repulse and the battleship Prince of Wales to defend Singapore. Japanese aircrafts intercepted the two warships on December 10, 1941, and sank them both off the coast of Malaya.

Two of the landmarks of Washington, D.C., the capital of the United States, include the Capitol (left) and the Jefferson Memorial (right foreground), which overlooks the Tidal Basin and is adjacent to East Potomac Park.

W

Lytton's novel *The Last of the Barons* (1843) is about Warwick.
See also: United Kingdom.

Wasatch Range, part of the Rocky Mountains that stretches southward from northern Utah into southern Idaho. The range is about 140 mi (225 km) long and its height averages about 10,000 ft (3,000 m). Its highest peak is Mt. Timpanogos, at 11,750 ft (3,581 m). West of the Wasatch Range lies a lake valley in which the Great Salt Lake and Salt Lake City are located. Streams from the Wasatch Range are used to irrigate farmlands in the valley.
See also: Rocky Mountains.

Washburn, Sherwood Larned (1911-2000), U.S. anthropologist. An expert on ape behavior and anatomy, he was one of the first scientists to study apes in their natural environments. Washburn was editor of *American Journal of Physical Anthropology* (1955-1957). Previously on the faculties of Columbia University and the University of Chicago, he has been on the faculty of University of California, Berkeley, since 1959.
See also: Anthropology.

Washing machine, machine that washes clothes. Most washing machines work automatically through the power of an electric motor. The temperature and amount of wash and rinse water as well as the strength of agitation used to clean the clothes is controlled through settings selected by the operator. The last cycle of most washing machines removes excess water by spinning the clothes. Although an electric-powered machine was invented in 1910, it took 27 more years to develop the automatic washer. The first patented washing machines (1860s) mechanically pushed clothes through water by use of a paddle.

Washington (Evergreen State; pop. 5,255,000), state in the U.S., bordered by British Columbia (Canada), the Pacific Ocean, Oregon, and Idaho; 68,165 sq mi (176,479 sq km). Capital, Olympia. Largest cities are Seattle and Tacoma. The state is divided into two by the Cascade Range. The climate varies a great deal between east and west. The west is mainly warm and wet, while the east is dry and cooler. The state has

a richly varied agricultural sector; forestry is also very important. Industries include aviation, space, and wood processing. Mining of sand, gravel, coal, lead, and uranium. The region was explored in the 16th century by the English and Spanish, and colonized in the 19th century. In the 18th century Europeans were mainly interested in hunting sea otters for their valuable fur. The region was part of Oregon until 1853. Washington has been a member of the Union since 1889.

Washington, Booker T. (1856-1915), U.S. educator. Born into a Virginia slave family, he was educated and chosen in 1881 to head a new school for blacks, the Tuskegee Institute, Ala. Under his guidance the institution expanded from 2 unequipped buildings to a complex with over 100 buildings and 1,500 students. Washington urged industrial education as the way to economic independence, which he believed to be an essential prerequisite to the demand for social equality. His writings included an autobiography, *Up from Slavery* (1901).

Washington, D.C. (pop. 3,724,000), capital of the United States, coextensive with the federal District of Columbia, which is the seat of the U.S. federal government. (The 'D.C.' in the city's name stand for District of Columbia.) It lies in the eastern United States on the west-central edge of Maryland on the Potomac River, with Virginia on the river's opposite side.
The city's focal point is the domed Capitol, home of the Congress of the United States. The Capitol lies on a small rise; for this reason the area is referred to as Capitol Hill. To the northwest lies the White House, official office and residence of the President. Other important buildings are the headquarters of government departments and agencies, the U.S. Supreme Court, the Federal Bureau of Investigation (FBI), and the Library of Congress. Also a cultural and educational center, Washington, D.C., is the site of the Smithsonian Institution, the National Gallery of Art, the John F. Kennedy Center for the Performing Arts, the National Archives, and the Folger Shakespeare Library. Among the city's famous monuments, parks, and memorials are the Lincoln Memorial, the Washington Monument, the Jefferson Memorial, and the Vietnam Veterans Memorial.

Economy. The city's economy is based largely on the federal government and related services; many important organizations also have offices there. There is little industry.
Government. The city's present system of government was established in 1973 by an act of Congress and approved by the people in 1974. Washington, D.C., is run by an elected mayor and city council. However, the federal government has final authority over all the city's government concerns. The mayor serves a 4-year term. The city council consists of 13 members serving 4-year terms. Washington, D.C., is represented in the U.S. Congress by 1 nonvoting representative.
History. In 1783 the Continental Congress voted for a federal city. In 1791 President George Washington chose the present site as a compromise between North and South. Washington, D.C., is one of the few cities to be planned before being built. In 1800 Congress moved to Washington, which replaced Philadelphia as the national capital. In 1814, during the War of 1812, the government buildings were burned down by British troops; new and more splendid plans were made and carried out. Since then, the city's population has risen steadily. Washington has long served as a gateway for blacks emigrating north; since the 1950s, blacks have made up a majority of the city's population. Since the 1970s, there has been a growing call among Washingtonians for statehood for the District of Columbia, but the U.S. Congress would have to vote approval of statehood and the proposed state constitution written by a 1982 constitutional convention. As the nation's capital, Washington, D.C., is a focal point for tourism, government, and political demonstrations.

Washington, George (1732-1799), American politician, supreme commander of the American army during the American War of Independence (1775-1783), and the first president of the United States (1789-1797). He managed to maintain unity despite the conflict between Federalists and Confederates.
See also: Revolutionary War in America.

Washington Cathedral, or National Cathedral, officially, Cathedral Church of Saint Peter and Saint Paul, Episcopal church in Washington, D.C. Built in the early 20th century (starting 1907), it incorporates stones from historic buildings from around the world. It measures 525 ft (160 m) long and 275 ft (84 m) wide at the widest point of its transept.

Washington Conference, post-World War I disarmament meetings convened by Pres. Warren Harding in Washington, D.C., 1921-1922. Agreements between the United States, Great Britain, Japan, France, and Italy included a limit on each navy's capital ships, restrictions on submarine warfare, and a ban on the use of poison gas. France, Japan, Great Britain, and the United States also agreed to respect each other's Pacific territories. A 9-power treaty, with the additional signatures of Belgium, China, the Netherlands, and Portugal, guaranteed China's territorial integrity.

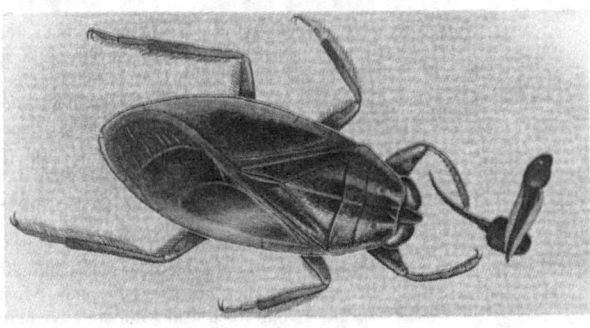

Washington Monument, stone obelisk in Washington, D.C., honoring George Washington. Begun in 1848, it was completed in 1884 and opened to the public in 1888. Faced with white marble, it is 555.5 ft (169.3 m) high. Visitors may go to the top by elevator or by climbing 898 steps.

Wasp, stinging winged insect, banded black and yellow, related to bees and ants in the order Hymenoptera. There are a number of families; most are solitary, but members of the Vespoidea are social, forming true colonies with workers, drones, and queen(s). Most of the solitary species are hunting wasps. These make nest cells in soil or decaying wood, in which they place one or more paralyzed insects before the egg is laid, to act as a living larder for the larva when it hatches. Social wasps congregate to form a permanent colony with both adults and young. The nest is usually constructed of wasp paper, a thick pulp of wood fibers and saliva. The adults feed the developing larvae on dead insects that have been killed by a bite on the neck; the sting, which in solitary wasps is used to paralyze prey, is reserved for defense. Adult wasps feed on carbohydrates: nectar, aphid honeydew, or jam.

Wasserman, August von (1866-1925), German physician and scientist. In 1906 he developed a process, known as the Wasserman test, which indicated syphilis infection through the testing of blood or spinal fluid. Earlier, Wasserman had developed inoculations against cholera, diphtheria, and tuberculosis.
See also: Venereal disease.

Waste disposal, disposal of such matter as animal excreta and the waste products of agricultural, industrial, and domestic processes, where an unacceptable level of environmental pollution would otherwise result. Where an ecological balance exists, wastes are recycled naturally or by technological means before accumulations affect the quality of life or disrupt the ecosystem. The most satisfactory waste disposal methods are therefore probably those that involve recycling, as in manuring fields with dung, reclaiming metals from scrap, or pulping waste paper for remanufacture. Recycling, however, may be inconvenient, uneconomic, or not yet technologically feasible. Many popular waste disposal methods consequently represent either an exchange of one form of environmental pollution for another less troublesome one, at least in the short term-e.g., the dumping or burying of nondegradable garbage or toxic wastes-or a reducing of the rate at which pollutants accumulate-e.g., by compacting or incinerating bulk wastes before dumping. Urban wastes are generally disposed of by means of dumping, sanitary landfill, incineration, and sewage processing. Agricultural, mining, and mineral-processing operations generate most solid wastes-and some of the most intractable waste disposal problems: the 'factory' farmer's problem of disposing of surplus organic wastes economically without resorting to incineration or dumping in rivers; the problems created by large mine dumps and open-cast excavations; and the culm dumps that result from the processing of anthracite coal. Another increasingly pressing waste disposal problem is presented by radioactive wastes. Those with a 'low' level of radioactivity can be safely packaged and buried; but high-level wastes, produced in the course of reprocessing the fuel elements of nuclear reactors, constitute a permanent hazard. Even the practice of encasing these wastes in thick concrete and dumping them on the ocean bottom is considered by many environmentalists to be an inadequate long-term solution.

Watch, small, portable timepiece. It is usually worn around the wrist, but may also be carried in a pocket or purse, or be worn as part of jewelry, such as a ring, necklace, or pin. Watches have been in use since the early 1500s when a method was discovered whereby a mainspring could be used to power a clock instead of falling weights; this made it possible to create portable clocks. Most modern watches are electronic, powered by small quartz crystals. After running a year, an electronic watch may be off fewer than 60 seconds.

Water (H_2O), transparent, odorless liquid that in liquid form and solid form (ice) covers about 74% of the earth's surface. Water is essential to life, which began in the oceans. Water is also humanity's most precious natural resource. The advent of desalination technology has made sea water, which accounts for 97% of the total water on earth, available for use as fresh water. Chemically, water is a compound of hydrogen and oxygen. It is a good solvent for many substances, especially ionic and polar compounds; it is ionizing and itself ionizes to give a low concentration of hydroxide and hydrogen ions. It is thus also a better conductor of electricity than most pure liquids. Water is a polar molecule and shows anomalies due to hydrogen bonding, including contraction when heated from 0°C to 4°C (32°F to 39.2°F). Formed when hydrogen or volatile hydrides are burned in oxygen, water oxidizes reactive metals to their ions and reduces fluorine and chlorine. It converts basic oxides to hydroxides and acidic oxides to oxyacids.

Water beetle, any of a number of families of oval insects, in the order Coleoptera, that live in or near water and propel themselves by fringed hind legs. Three of the most common water beetles are the giant water scavenger beetle (family Hydrophilidae), predaceous diving beetle (family Dytiscidae), and whirligig (family Gyrinidae). The predaceous diving beetle and water scavenger beetle feed on small fish and insects.

Water boatman *See:* Water bug.

Water buffalo, any of several oxen in the family Bovidae, most common of which is the Indian buffalo (*Bubalus bubalis*), standing 6-6.5 ft (1.5-2 m) at the shoulder. Bulls have curved horns that may measure as wide as 12 ft (3.7 m) along the curve. The fierce-tempered water buffalo feeds on grass and has very little hair on its dull, bluish-black hide. Domesticated, the water buffalo is a strong and helpful farm animal, used throughout China, southeast Asia, Egypt, Europe, and the Philippines.

Giant water bug (*Hydrocrius nanus*, order *Hemiptera*, family Belostomatidae).

Water bug, name given to a number of insects that live on or below the surface of fresh water, especially the giant water bug, which may grow up to 4 in (10 cm) long. Water bugs feed on small aquatic animals, including fish. Backswimmers, water boatmen, and water scorpions are also water bugs.

Water chestnut, name of 2 different plants that grow in subarctic and temperate wetlands. The Oriental water chestnut (*Eleocharis tuberosa*) is in the sedge family and is native to China. Some of its tubelike stems, which may grow to a height of approximately 5 ft (1.5 m), grow upward out of the soil and water. However, some of the stems grow underground and have small, round, edible bulblike swellings at the end called corms. The water caltrop (genus *Trapa*) also belongs to the water-chestnut family. It is native to tropical and subtropical areas of Africa, Europe, and Asia, and bears edible, nutlike fruits.

The backswimmer (*Notonecta glauca*, order *Hemiptera*, family Noctonectidae), length 0.6 in (16 mm), found in Europe.

Water clock, also called clepsydra, ancient instrument that measured time by the amount of water flowing from it. Used as early as the 14th century B.C. by the Egyptians, it consisted of a hollow container, such as a cylinder or a glass jar, with measuring lines. Water was poured into the container and then allowed to flow out. The lines indicated how much water had escaped, and from this it could be determined how much time had passed. Water clocks were used by Greeks and Romans as well. Among its various purposes was the timing of orators' speeches.

Watercolor, painting technique in which the pigment is mixed with water before application, such as fresco and tempera, but more particularly the aquarelle technique of thin washes. Ancient Egyptians produced watercolor paintings, and the medium was used during and after the Renaissance by, among others, Rembrandt and Van Dyck. The aquarelle technique was mastered by such English artists as John Cotman and J.M.W. Turner around 1800. Watercolor permits powerful effects of transparency, brilliance, and delicacy. Important U.S. watercolorists include Winslow Homer and John Marin.

Water dog *See:* Mudpuppy.

Waterfall, vertical fall of water formed

W

where a river flows from hard rock to an area of more easily eroded rock, or where there has been a rise of the land relative to sea level or a blockage of the river by a landslide. The power of waterfalls often provides energy for the many cities that have sprung up around them. The highest waterfall in the world is Angel Falls, Venezuela (3,212 ft/979 m).

Water flea, any of a group of small animals belonging to the class Branchiopoda. Most species live in fresh water and are anywhere from 1/125-3/4 in (0.2-18 mm) long. Their bodies are covered by a transparent shell, exposing their organs for easy viewing. Water fleas move through water by jumping in jerky motions resembling those of fleas–hence their name.

Waterford (pop. 45,000), port city in southeastern Ireland, located on the River Suir near the point where it flows into the Waterford Harbour. Waterford was first settled in the A.D. 800s by Vikings. It was captured by the English in 1170. Waterford became prominent during the latter part of the 18th century because of the well-known Waterford crystal glassware manufactured there. The city remains an important export center of locally produced items, including canned fruits and meats, beer, paper, chemicals, furniture, and electrical products. *See also:* Ireland.

Watergate, series of scandals involving Pres. Richard Nixon and his administration. On June 17, 1972, 5 men from Nixon's re-election committee were arrested as they tried to plant electronic eavesdropping equipment in the headquarters of the Democratic Party national committee in the Watergate office building, Washington, D.C. As a result of their convictions and the sus-

picions of Judge John Sirica, who tried the case, that a conspiracy was being covered up, investigations were opened that led to Nixon's inner councils. Though Nixon easily won reelection in Nov. 1972, his public support eroded as a televised U.S. Senate investigation continued. Newspaper revelations (notably by Carl Bernstein and Bob Woodward in the *Washington Post*) and testimony of Republican Party and former governmental officials clearly implicated him and his senior aides in a massive abuse of power and the obstruction of justice involving campaign contributions, the CIA, the FBI, the Internal Revenue Service, and other government agencies. The House of Representatives Judiciary Committee voted to impeach Nixon in July 1974, and his ouster from office became inevitable; on Aug. 9, 1974 he resigned the only U.S. president to do so. One month later he was granted a full pardon by Pres. Gerald Ford. Almost 60 individuals, including former U.S. Attorney General John Mitchell and senior White House staff were convicted of Watergate crimes. *See also:* Nixon, Richard Milhous.

Water glass, also known as soluble glass, colorless lump made up of sodium, silicon, and oxygen that resembles glass. Water glass is soluble in water, turning into a thick liquid. It has many industrial uses: as adhesive in fiberboard boxes, glass, and porcelain; to manufacture concrete and cement; and to fireproof and waterproof materials.

Water hyacinth, South American floating plant (*Eichhornia crassipes*). The plants, which have attractive purple or yellow flowers growing on erect stems, float on air-filled bladders, trailing their roots in the water, or in mud where the water is very shallow. Water hyacinths grow wild in South

America but have been introduced into other tropical areas. They frequently clog waterways, as in the southern United States.

Water lily, aquatic plant of the genus *Nymphaea* (unrelated to true lilies). They grow in calm, shallow fresh water, with stems rooted in the mud and floating leaves. Many hybrids are used as ornamentals in water gardens. The most well known of the species is the blue or white Egyptian lotus, Egypt's national emblem.

Waterloo, Battle of (June 18, 1815), final engagement of the Napoleonic Wars. Having escaped from exile on Elba and having reinstated himself with a new army, Napoleon returned to face a coalition of Austria, Great Britain, Prussia, and Russia. On the offensive, he advanced into Belgium to prevent an Anglo-Dutch army under Wellington from uniting with the Prussians. After separate battles with the British and Prussians on June 16, the French army, led by Marshall Ney, attacked Wellington's strongly defended position at Waterloo, south of Brussels. The intervention of a Prussian force under Blücher allowed Wellington to take the offensive. The French were routed, losing some 25,000 men. Napoleon abdicated on June 22, 1815. *See also:* Napoleon I; Napoleonic Wars.

Watermelon, plant (*Citrullus vulgaris*) and its edible fruit, with a thick rind, juicy pulp, and many seeds. A member of the gourd family native to Africa, the watermelon has been cultivated for at least 4,000 years. Watermelons, so named because more than 90% of their substance is water, may weigh from 5-40 lb (2.3-18.1 kg) or more and are rich in vitamins A and C. They grow on vines and their pulp is red to pink, yellow, or white.

A water polo team consists of 11 players, 7 of whom are permitted in the water at any one time. The players of opposing teams are distinguished by their caps (1). A play begins when the single referee (2) throws the ball into the pool at the half-distance line (3) and the players swim out from their respective goal lines (4) to retrieve the ball. While on offense, no player may pass the 7-ft (2-m) line (5) without possession of the ball. Penalty shots are awarded in case of major fouls. Such shots are attempted from a line, 13 ft (4 m) (6) from the goal.

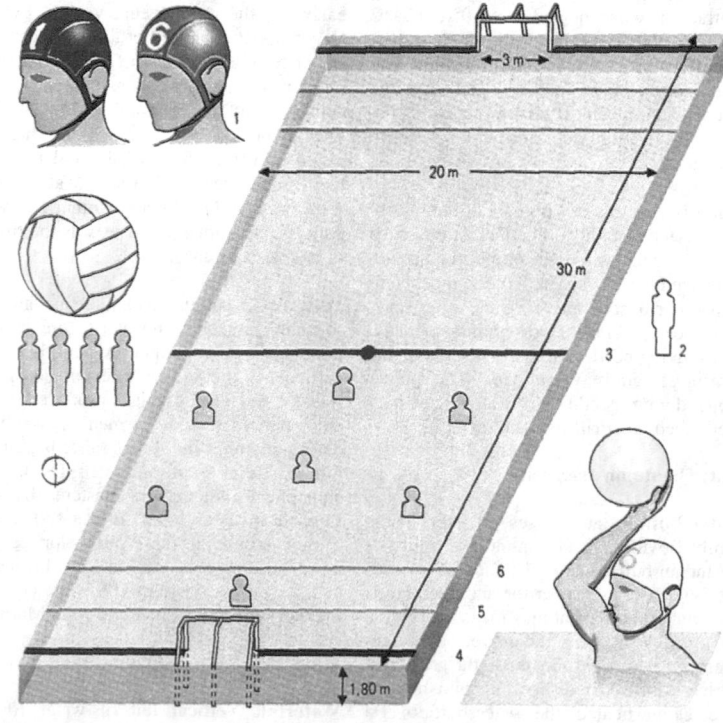

Water meter, device to measure the quantity of water flowing through a pipe or other channel. Such meters, connected with registers that display numerical readings indicating gallons, cubic feet, or other quantities, are used to measure home or business use of water from public water systems or other sources, or to monitor flow in rivers and other moving bodies of water. Quantity may be measured by the water's motion or pressure, or by using magnetism, sound waves, or other energy affected by the rate of flow.

Water moccasin, also called cottonmouth or moccasin snake, poisonous snake in the viper family. This species (*Agkistrodon piscivorus*) lives in the southeastern United States in swampy or marshy areas of rivers, streams, and lakes. It may grow between 3 1/2 ft (107 cm) and 5 ft (1.5 m) long. It is considered a pit viper because of a hollow pit located between the eye and nostril on the side of its head. Its often fatal bite may be preceded by a warning, which involves the exposure of the white, cottonlike inside of its mouth.

Water pipit *See:* Pipit.

Water plant, also called aquatic plant or hydrophyte, any of several plants classified as those that live on the surface or below the surface of water. Water lilies, sedges, and cattails are common water plants. Water bladders, or pores that contain air, are found in submerged water plants to support their upright position. Water plants most often grow in lakes and ponds.

Water pollution, contamination to water systems as a direct result of the discharge of harmful products. There are 3 main sources of water pollution: industrial waste, sewage, and chemical and agricultural wastes. Environmental concern has grown through the years, and government agencies worldwide have helped pass laws that limit the amount of wastes that may be dumped into our waters. Billions of dollars a year are spent to clean up the diseased waters, yet specialists doubt that the natural state of the waters will ever be fully restored. Water pollution has become a grave environmental problem that increasingly threatens lakes, rivers, and oceans.

Water polo, game played in a swimming pool in which 2 teams try to pass or throw a ball into the opponent's goal. The game began in England in the 1870s. Each team consists of 7 players-6 in the field and 1 goalkeeper. Fieldplayers may use head, feet, or 1 hand to manage the ball; goalkeepers may use both hands while in the goal area. The team with the ball is allowed 35 seconds to get the ball across the opponent's goal and score. If the team is unsuccessful, the ball goes to the other team. Water polo is played in an area 66-98 ft (20-30 m) long and 26-66 ft (8-20 m) wide. A men's game lasts 28 minutes, and is divided into 7-minute quarters. A women's game lasts 24 minutes and is divided into 6-minute quarters.

Water power, energy obtained from flowing or falling water used to run machinery or create electrical power. Water has been used to drive devices since ancient times, beginning with the invention of the water wheel. Streaming water flowing over the blades of a wheel caused the wheel to rotate, setting in motion other mechanisms-thus creating the energy that drove the mechanisms. Water was first used to power grinding stones that ground grains. Water power was very important during the Industrial Revolution, when it was used to operate factory machines. The most important modern use of water power is the generating of electricity. Hydroelectric power plants producing electrical energy have been built on rivers in many parts of the world. The largest U.S. power plant is the Grand Coulee on the Columbia River in Washington.
See also: Turbine.

Water-skiing, sport in which a person wearing a pair of ski-like runners glides over water while being pulled by a motorboat moving at speeds of 15-35 mph (24-56 kmph). Water skiing is done for recreation as well as for competition events, which include jumping, slalom, and trick riding. In the jumping competition, skiers ski jump off a ramp 24 ft (7.3 m) long and 6 ft (1.8 m) high in an attempt to achieve the greatest distance. In the slalom competition, a skier negotiates through a course of buoys as quickly as possible. For trick skiing, skiers perform intricate actions, such as jumps and turns.

Water snake, any of nearly 80 species of nonvenomous snakes of the genus *Natrix*, including the European grass snake. Water snakes live in fresh waters and feed on fish and amphibians.

Water softening, process of removing calcium and magnesium from hard water. These insoluble minerals, when left in water, form scale in pipes and prevent the dissolution of cleansers, such as soap. Hard water may be softened by adding soda ash and lime to it. The soda ash and lime join with the calcium and magnesium, making them settle to the bottom of the water container. Water may also be softened by filtering it through zeolites, minerals that contain sodium ions. The sodium ions change places with the calcium and magnesium ions, thereby softening the water. When the zeolites become depleted of sodium ions, a strong solution of common salt can be placed in the filter to replenish the sodium.

Waterspout, rotating column of air, or tornado, as it passes over water. A funnel-like cloud of condensed water vapor extends from a parent cumulonimbus cloud to the water surface, where it is surrounded by a sheath of spray.

Water wheel, wheel that is turned by flowing water, providing power to operate a device. The running water may come from rivers or waterfalls. Water wheels were used by ancient Romans to grind grain and in time were developed to run other devices, such as machinery. There are 2 basic types: vertical and horizontal. Vertical water wheels often have containers around the wheel. Water usually flows into a container at the top of the wheel, the weight of the water causes the container to fall, and the water flows into the next container, creating a constant motion. Horizontal water wheels have vertical blades. Water strikes the blade on one side of the wheel, causing the wheel to turn to the next blade, thus creating continual motion. Horizontal water wheels are capable of converting more water power into energy and have greater use in the modern world.
See also: Water power.

Watson, James Dewey (1928-), U.S. biochemist. He shared with Francis Crick and Maurice H.F. Wilkins the 1962 Nobel Prize in physiology or medicine for his work with Crick establishing the double-helix molecular model of DNA. His personalized account of the research, *The Double Helix* (1968), became a best-seller.
See also: Biochemistry.

Watson, John Broadus (1878-1958), U.S. psychologist who founded behaviorism, which states that a person's behavior is a result of stimuli in his or her environment. It rejects the idea of inborn emotions, with the exceptions of fear, anger, and love. While Watson's work helped lead to the development of psychology as a science, his views are not widely held today.
See also: Psychology.

Watson, Thomas John (1874-1956), U.S. business executive and philanthropist. He took over an ailing computing company (1914), changed its name to International Business Machines Corp. (IBM; 1924), and built it into one of the world's largest corporations. Under his presidency (1914-1949) and chairmanship (1949-1956), IBM became the leader in electronic data-processing equipment, with sales in 82 countries and assets of more than $600 million at the time of his death.

Watson-Watt, Sir Robert Alexander (1892-1973), Scottish scientist and inventor. His research into radio led to his creation (1935) of a radar device capable of detecting and tracing the movements of flying airplanes.

Watt, James (1736-1819), Scottish engineer and inventor. His first major invention (patented 1769) was an improved steam engine, with a separate condenser air pump, and insulated engine parts. For the manufacture of such engines he entered into partnership with John Roebuck and later (1775), more successfully, with Matthew Boulton. Between 1775 and 1800 he invented the sun-and-planet gear wheel, the double-acting engine, a throttle valve, a pressure gauge, and the centrifugal governor-as well as taking the first steps toward determining the chemical structure of water. He also coined the term *horsepower* and was a founding member of the Lunar Society.
See also: Steam engine.

James Watt at the age of 56, depicted by the German artist Carl Friedrich von Breda (1759-1818, National Portrait Gallery, London).

Watteau, Jean-Antoine (1684-1721), French draftsperson and painter, strongly influenced by Peter Paul Rubens. A masterful colorist, he specialized in small, gay paintings called *fêtes galantes* ('elegant parties') or *fêtes champêtres* ('country parties'). He also painted theater scenes. His works include

When the Académie, in 1717, accepted this painting, *L'Embarquement pour l'Île de Cythère* (Louvre, Paris) by Antoine Watteau (1684-1721), the conquest of the Rubensists over the Poussinists became reality. One year later, Watteau painted a new version of this picture (Museum Dahlem, Berlin).

The Embarkation for Cythera (1717), based upon a play of the day, and *Gilles* (c.1718). *See also:* Rococo.

Wattmeter, instrument that measures electric power in watts, kilowatts, or megawatts.

Watusi (Swahili: *Watutsi*), Tutsi people of Burundi and Rwanda in central Africa (formerly Ruanda-Urundi). The Watusi, probably originally from Ethiopia, differ ethnically from other African peoples, and many attain a height of over 7 ft (2.13 m). In the 1400s and 1500s the invading Watusi imposed a feudal system on the native Hutu, who revolted in 1959 and drove their cattle-raising rulers to what is now Burundi (the 2 parts became independent nations in 1962). The Tutsi king of Burundi was deposed in 1966. An unsuccessful Hutu rebellion in Burundi in 1972-1973 left 10,000 Tutsi and 150,000 Hutu dead. With the outbreak of vi-

olence in 1993 and 1994, some 500,000 Hutu and Tutsi were killed in Rwanda.

Waugh, name of 3 English writers, the sons and grandson of journalist and publisher Arthur Waugh (1886-1943). **Alexander Raban (Alec) Waugh** (1898-1981) wrote over 40 novels and travel books, including *Loom of Youth* (1918) and *Island in the Sun* (1956). **Evelyn Arthur St. John Waugh** (1903-1966) wrote mainly satire, both elegant and biting. His conversion to Roman Catholicism in 1930 had a deep affect on his work. His novels include *Decline and Fall* (1928), *Vile Bodies* (1930), *Put Out More Flags* (1942), *Brideshead Revisited* (1945), *The Loved One* (1948), and his World War II trilogy, *The Sword of Honour* (1952-1961). Evelyn's son **Auberon Alexander Waugh** (1939-) is a novelist whose works include *Bed of Flowers* (1972).

Wave, in physics, energy that travels in rhythmical motions. Waves may travel on a substance (waves on water), through a substance (the waves of an earthquake through the earth), or in a space devoid of matter (radio waves through space). The top of a wave is the crest, the bottom of a wave is the trough. Wavelength refers to the distance between 2 consecutive crests. There are 3 kinds of waves: transverse, standing, and longitudinal. In transverse waves the energy flows in a steady forward direction and causes the medium through which it travels to move up and down, like water waves. Standing waves are created by 2 identical waves moving in opposite directions, creating a series of loops. Longitudinal waves travel in a forward direction in a series of short back-and-forth motions, like the coils of a spring.
See also: Physics.

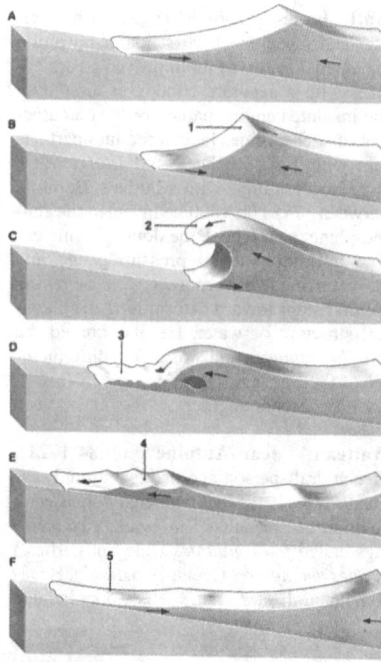

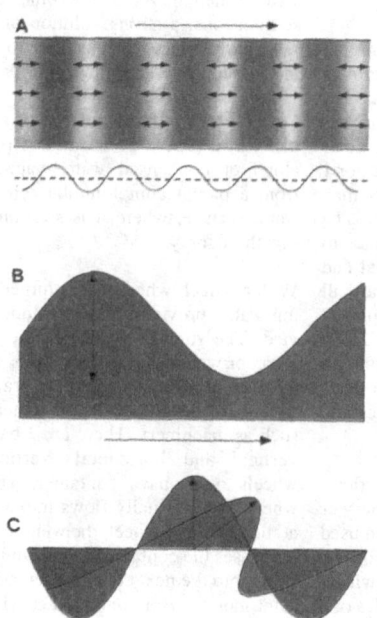

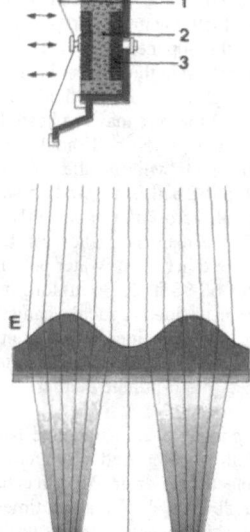

(A) When a wave passes into water that is shallower than half its wavelength, frictional interaction with the bottom will slow the waves near the shore. (B) Waves farther out then overtake those closer in and increase the wave height to a peak (1). (C) If the shore slope is steep, the crest peaks rapidly and curls over the friction-retarded lower wave portion. Because no underlying water supports the curled crest, the crest eventually breaks, or collapses, and crashes down as a plunging breaker (2). (D) After breaking, the water rushes up the beach as a swash (3). (E) It continues its forward movement as a trans-lation wave (4). (F) The water then returns down the slope as a backwash (5).

The form of a wave depends on the nature of the oscillating source and the medi-um through which the wave travels. Sound moves as longitudinal waves (A), in which particles of the medi-um—such as air or water—oscillate back and forth in the wave's direction of travel. This may be depicted as a sine wave (below), with zones of greatest compression as maxi-ma. A water wave (B) is a transverse wave, in which water parti-cles move at right an-gles to the wave's di-rection of travel. An electromagnetic wave (C) may be depicted as a transverse wave, in which electric and magnetic forces act at right angles. In or-der to measure a wave, it is usually converted to some other form of energy. For example, a micro-phone (D) may be used to intercept a sound wave. The vi-bration of the di-aphragm (1) com-presses carbon gran-ules (2) and alters the resistance between blocks (3), producing electrical pulses that correspond in ampli-tude to the sound wave. A water wave (E) may focus light on a screen, to measure amplitudes.

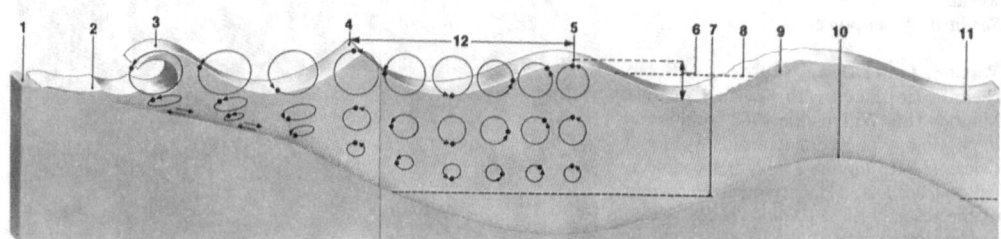

All waves may be de-scribed in terms of: a crest, or highest point (5); a trough, or low-est point (11); mid-point, or still-water level (8); a height, or crest-to-trough verti-cal distance (6); and a wavelength, or hori-zontal distance be-tween successive crests or troughs (12). Each water par-ticle in deep water moves in a circular orbit. Because of fric-tion, the particle will orbit, and the ener-gies will decrease with the water depth and become negligi-ble at the water base (7). When a wave ap-proaches the beach (1), the water particle orbits become flat-tened ellipses. If the shore slope is steep, the wave will rapidly peak (4), and a plunging breaker re-sults (3). The water moves up the shore as a translation wave (2). If the waves pass over a gently sloping sandbar (10), they will move slowly to-ward the shore, as spilling breakers (9).

Wavell, Archibald Percival, 1st earl (1883-1950), British field marshal. He was British commander-in-chief in the Middle East during World War II, defeating the Italians in North Africa (1940-1941). He served as viceroy and governor general of India from 1943 to 1947.
See also: World War II.

Wax, moldable, water-repellent solid, of which there are several entirely different kinds. *Animal waxes* were the first known: Wool wax when purified yields lanolin; beeswax, from the honeycomb, is used for some candles and as a sculpture medium (by carving or casting); spermaceti wax, from the sperm whale, is used in ointments and cosmetics. *Vegetable waxes*, like animal waxes, are mixtures of esters of long-chain alcohols and carboxylic acids. Carnauba wax, from the leaves of a Brazilian palm tree, is hard and lustrous and is used to make polishes; candelilla wax, from a wild Mexican rush, is similar but more resinous; Japan wax, the coating of sumac berries, is fatty and soft but also tough and kneadable. *Mineral waxes* include montan wax, extracted from lignite, which is bituminous and resinous; ozokerite, an absorbent hydrocarbon wax obtained from wax shales; and paraffin wax, or petroleum wax, the most important commercially, obtained from the residues of petroleum refining by solvent extraction. Some of its uses are to make candles, to coat paper products, in the electrical industry, and to waterproof leather and textiles. Various *synthetic waxes* are made for special uses.

Wax myrtle, tree in bayberry or wax myrtle family. The common wax myrtle (*Myrtca cerifera*) grows to about 35 ft (11 m) high. It has thick leaves with small brown dots and small green flowers that bloom between April and June. As an ornamental tree wax myrtle arc found along the east coast of the United States.

Waxwing, any of 3 species of starling-sized birds (genus *Bombycilla*) named for the red, waxlike marks on their wings. Found in the Northern Hemisphere, they are the Bohemian waxwing, the cedar waxwing, and the Japanese waxwing (of northeastern Asia). Waxwings feed largely on berries but feed their chicks on insects. They move their nesting grounds from place to place, and in some years migrate en masse southward in the fall.

Wayne, John (Marion Michael Morrison; 1907-1979), U.S. film actor, known mostly for his tough hero roles. He acted in low-budget westerns until his big break in 1939 in *Stagecoach*. Over the course of his career, Wayne appeared in over 175 films, including *Red River* (1948), *She Wore a Yellow Ribbon* (1949), *Sands of Iwo Jima* (1950), and *The Quiet Man* (1952). He received an Academy Award for his acting in *True Grit* (1969).

Weakfish, or squeteague, any of a genus (*Cynoscion*) of saltwater fishes used for food, measuring 1-2 ft (30-61 cm) long or more. Its name comes from the fact that it has a weak, fleshy mouth that is easily torn. It is found along the Atlantic and Gulf coasts of the United States.

Weapon, any device used to attack or defend. Throughout human history, weapons have been used to kill animals for food, to protect people in wilderness, and to wage wars. Bows and arrows, slings, swords, blowguns, rifles, guns, bombs, torpedoes, and hand grenades are examples of weapons. As technology has become more sophisticated, destructive power has increased, e.g., nuclear bombs capable of killing millions of people and destroying the planet.

Weasel, small, carnivorous mammal (*Mustela nivalis*) related to the skunk, wolverine, and mink. A slender, lithe, red-brown creature, which often kills prey many times its own size, it measures only up to 10-11 in (25.4-27.9 cm) in the male, 8 in (20.3 cm) in the female. The normal diet is mice, voles, and fledgling birds, though rabbits may be taken. The many races of weasel are distributed throughout Eurasia, Africa, and the Americas.

Weather, variations in atmospheric conditions (temperature, precipitation, wind, humidity, air pressure, and cloudiness) experienced at a given place over a short period of time. Longer periods of data fall under the term *climate*.
See also: Climate.

Weather vane, instrument used to perceive the direction in which the wind is moving. The vane is built in the form of an arrow, so as to pick up even the smallest breeze. Often the vane has electrical connections by which it can communicate the wind movement to areas that might be far from the device itself.

Weaverbird, small, seed-eating bird (family Ploceidae) of Africa and Asia. Weaverbirds

The long-tailed weasel (*Mustela frenata*) found from Canada to South America, is one of the largest weasels. Its body averages 10-12 in (25-30 cm) in length, and it has a tail 4-8 in (10-20 cm) long.

Meteorological satellites play an important role in weather forecasting. Photographs cover extensive areas (here, we see large parts of Europe and Africa) and enable the forecasters to record for example cloud patterns. By comparing the photos every few hours, one may obtain a fairly good idea of the build-up of fronts and depressions.

are related to the English sparrow and are usually drab, though during the nesting season many males develop bright plumage. They are named for their elaborate flask-shaped nests, woven from strips of palm fronds or grasses. Weavers live in flocks and are often pests when they descend on crops.

Weaving, process of making a fabric by interlacing 2 or more sets of threads. In plain, or tabby, weave, 1 set of threads (the warp) extends along the length of the fabric; the other set (the woof, or weft) is at right angles to the warp and passes alternately over and under it. Other common weaves include twill, satin, and pile. In basic twill, woof threads pass over 2-4 warp threads, producing diagonal ridges, or wales, as in denim, flannel, and gaberdine. In satin weave, a development of twill, long 'float' threads passing under 4 warp threads give the fabric its

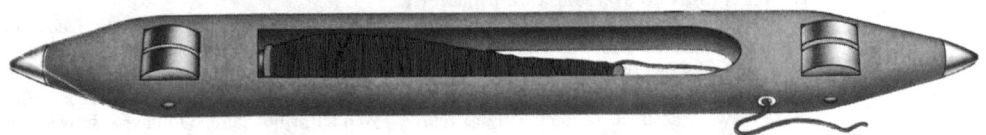

The flying shuttle was a major step toward the mechanization of looms. A spool of filling yarn was originally passed back and forth by hand through a shed of warp yarns to lay in the filling. A shuttle box is placed on each side of the loom in which a picker, or block, could slide along a wire above a shuttle, or wooden block containing a conical bobbin of yarn. When the picker was suddenly jerked by a cord, the shuttle was driven from one box to the other, unwinding the filling yarn through an eyelet.

W

Fabrics are woven by interfacing warp yarns with filling yarns. Warp ends are wound on a warp beam, or roll (1). The warp yeans are passed alternately over and under lease rods (2), through heddle eyelets (3, 5) in harness frames (4, 6), through dents in a reed (8), over a sand roll (13) and breast beam (11), and onto a cloth roll (12). As the harness frames are raised and lowered, a shed (7) is formed through which filling yarn (9) on a shuttle is passed back and forth in a trough (14). The reed—mounted on a hinged lever (15)—moves forward and beats the thread into place (10).

characteristically lustrous and smooth appearance. Pile fabrics, such as corduroy and velvet, have extra warp or weft threads woven into a ground weave in a series of loops that are then cut to produce the pile. Weaving is usually accomplished by means of a hand- or power-operated machine called a loom. Warp threads are stretched on a frame and passed through eyelet in vertical wires (heddles) supported on a frame (the harness). A space (the shed) between sets of warp threads is made by moving the heddles up or down, and a shuttle containing the woof thread is passed through the shed. A special comb (the reed) then pushes home the newly woven line.

Webb, name of 2 English social reformers and economists. **Beatrice Webb** (née Potter, 1858-1943) studied working life for her *Life and Labour of the People in London* (1891-1903). Her husband, **Sidney James Webb** (1859-1947), was a Labour member of Parliament (1922-1929) and held several cabinet posts. The couple were leading intellectuals of the Labour movement and wrote together *The History of Trade Unionism* (1894). They were Fabians and helped found the London School of Economics in 1895 and the left-wing journal *The New Statesman* in 1913.

Weber, Carl Maria von (1786-1826), German composer, pianist, and conductor who established the romantic opera and paved the way in Germany for Richard Wagner. His operas include *Der Freischütz* (*The Marksman*; 1821), *Euryanthe* (1823), and *Oberon* (1826). He wrote a number of orchestral and chamber works, notably for the piano, including the well-known *Invitation to the Dance* (1819).

Weber, Max (1881-1961), U.S. painter. He introduced European modern art movements, such as Fauvism and Cubism, to America by incorporating the styles into his own work. His works between 1912 and 1919 were abstract, becoming more representational from 1919 on. Weber was born in Russia and came to the United States when he was 10. He studied art at the Pratt Institute in Brooklyn, N.Y., at the Académie Julian in Paris, and with the renowned French artist Henri Matisse. Weber was an influential teacher at the Art Students League. Among his students there was Mark Rothko, who later became an important abstract artist.

Weber, Max (1864-1920), German economist and sociologist. His theories contributed to the formation of modern sociological theory. Weber considered bureaucracy the crucial component of society and created an ideal type method for examining different societies. His most influential work, *The Protestant Ethic and the Spirit of Capitalism* (1904-05), deals with Protestantism's economic aspects. Other works include *From Max Weber: Essays in Sociology* and *The Theory of Social and Economic Organization.*

Webern, Anton (1883-1945), Austrian composer. He studied with Arnold Schoenberg and developed 12-tone music. His works include *Five Pieces for Orchestra* (1911-1913), 2 symphonies, 3 string quartets, and a number of songs.

Webster, Daniel (1782-1852), U.S. politician, lawyer, and orator whose advocacy of strong central government earned him the name 'defender of the Constitution.'

Webster, Noah (1758-1843), U.S. lexicographer whose works-such as *The Elementary Spelling Book*, called the 'Blue-Backed Speller' (1829; earlier versions, 1783-1787)-helped standardize American spelling. He also compiled a grammar (1784) and a reader (1785). Working on dictionaries from 1803, he published *An American Dictionary of the English Language* (1812), with 70,000 entries and 12,000 new definitions. Today his name is often applied to dictionaries that are in no way based on his work.
See also: Dictionary.

Weddell Sea, arm of the Atlantic Ocean in Antarctica between Palmer Land and Coats Land. At its southern end are the Ronne and Filchner ice shelves. It was named for James Weddell, who claimed to have discovered it in 1823.
See also: Atlantic Ocean.

Wedding anniversary, celebration that takes place at the yearly return of an original wedding date. In Western society it has become common practice to commemorate this event with a characteristic gift, symbolic of the number of years a couple has been married; e.g., silver represents a 25th wedding anniversary; gold, a 50th anniversary.

Wedekind, Frank (1864-1918), German playwright and actor. His work denounced a corrupt bourgeois society that had no interest in the arts or learning, and that was stifling the freedom of individuals. His plays include *The Awakening of Spring* (1895), *Earth Spirit* (1895), and *Pandora's Box* (printed 1904). Although Wedekind was considered scandalous by many in his time, he had a strong following and inspired modern dramatists, including Bertolt Brecht.

Wedge, device with 2 or more surfaces that slope and taper to a thin edge. A wedge may be made of wood, metal, or other material and is used to split something apart. The wedge's thin edge is forced into a narrow opening of the object. The top of the wedge is hammered, driving the wedge further down, thereby piercing the object. A wedge may also be used to move a heavy object.

Wedgwood, Josiah (1730-1795), English potter, inventor of Wedgwood ware. Famous for his cream-colored queen's ware, patented in 1765, he frequently employed artists such as John Flaxman for the designs on his blue-and-white jasper ware. Wedgwood, who introduced new materials and machinery to the craft of pottery-making, was the first to acquire steam engines at his factory in Etruria, Staffordshire, and contributed much to improve the standard of living of his workers.

Wedgwood ware, fine English pottery first created by Josiah Wedgwood (1730-1795). Wedgwood comes in various styles, includ-

One of the most famous Wedgwood products is the blue Jasper with its white figures. The decoration on this vase (1785, Victoria and Albert Museum, London) refers to classic examples and clearly shows how much Josiah Wedgwood (1730-1795) had been influenced by neoclassicism.

ing a cream-colored stoneware called creamware (also called queen's ware because Queen Charlotte was so pleased with her set of creamware), a black stoneware called Egyptian black or black basalt, and colored stoneware that often had white designs or figures in relief called Jasperware. Wedgwood ware's durability and beauty made it very popular. Production of it has continued to present time, and it still has a world market.

Weed, any plant that is useless or destructive, or that grows where it is not desired. A plant that grows abundantly in an area where it is not wanted crowds out and takes nutrition, water, and space away from plants that are being cultivated. Injurious plants may be considered weeds. For example, poison ivy and oak can produce a skin rash; goldenrod and ragweed can cause hay fever; and thistles have prickly leaves that can hurt skin. Herbicides and soil cultivation are among methods developed to control the proliferation of weeds.

Weevil, any of 35,000 species of oval- or pear-shaped beetles (from the largest animal family, Curculionidae), having a greatly drawn-out head that ends in a pronounced snout. They feed on hard vegetable matter, seeds, and wood; the larvae, which develop within seeds, are legless. Weevils are pests of such important economic crops as cotton and grain and of stored peas, beans, and flour.

Weight, gravitational force experienced by an object in relation to another massive body (planet). The weight of a body (measured in newtons) is equal to the product of its mass and the local acceleration due to gravity. Weight differs from mass in being a vector quantity.
See also: Gravitation.

Weight, Atomic *See:* Atom.

Weight control, method by which a person maintains a healthy weight. The medical as well as social and emotional well-being of a person is based in part on the maintenance of proper weight. A person must take in 3,500 calories of food to gain 1 lb (0.45 kg). In turn the human body burns up calories during exercise. Therefore food intake and physical exercise are important factors in weight control. Not all weight gain is unhealthy, since exercise often encourages a gain in muscle mass and weight. However, too much weight, based on fat, can cause health problems and, in the extreme, *obesity* – a state of being extremely overweight. Some studies indicate that weight may be related to heredity. In general, underweight people are considered healthy as long as they do not have a disease or serious eating disorder and people who are somewhat overweight are also considered healthy if they maintain a balanced diet and exercise.
See also: Diet.

Weightlessness, condition that arises in the apparent absence of gravitational pull. Experienced by astronauts in space, weightlessness occurs when the centrifugal force of the astronauts and spacecraft in forward motion exactly cancels the force of gravity.

Weight lifting, bodybuilding exercise and competitive sport. As a contest, it has long been popular in Turkey, Egypt, Japan, Europe, and the former USSR, and has been a regular event in the Olympics since 1920. There are 3 basic lifts: the snatch (from the floor to over the head in a single motion); the clean-and-jerk (2 movements-first to the chest and then over the head); and the military, or 2-hand, press (similar to the clean-and-jerk but performed while maintaining a 'military' stance).

Weights and measures, units of weight, length, area, and volume commonly used in the home, in commerce, and in industry. Although, like other early peoples, the Hebrews used measures such as the foot, the cubit (the length of the human forearm), and the span, which could easily be realized in practice by using parts of the body, in commerce they also used standard containers and weights. Later, weights were based on the quantity of precious metal in coins. During and after the Middle Ages each region evolved its own system of weights and measures. In the 19th century these were standardized on a national basis, and then in turn were superseded by standards of the metric system. In the Western world, only the British Empire and the United States retained their own systems (the Imperial System and the U.S. Customary System, respectively) into the mid-20th century. With the United Kingdom's adoption of the International System of Units (SI units), the United States remains one of the few countries that does not use metric units, although, as has been the case since 1959, the U.S. customary units are now defined in terms of their metric counterparts and not on the basis of independent standards.

Weil, Simone (1909-1943), French philosopher, religious mystic, and left-wing intellectual. She was active in the Spanish Civil War and the French resistance in World War II. She converted from Judaism to Roman Catholicism in 1938. Among her books to be translated into English are *Waiting for God* (1951) and *The Need for Roots* (1952).

Weill, Kurt (1900-1950), German-born U.S. composer. His most well-known music is for the 2 satirical operas on which he collaborated with Bertolt Brecht, *The Threepenny Opera* (1928) and *The Rise and Fall of the City of Mahagonny* (1927, rev. 1930). Unpopular with the Nazis, he came to the United States in 1935 and became a successful Broadway composer, creating the music for such musicals as *Knickerbocker Holiday* (1938, with Maxwell Anderson) and *Street Scene* (1947). He was married to singer Lotte Lenya.

Weimar (pop. 63,000), city in east-central Germany, on the Ilm River. Weimar is a center for manufacturing agricultural machinery, electrical equipment, and chemicals. It was capital of the Saxe-Weimar duchy from 1547, and its court became the German cultural and intellectual center in the 18th and 19th centuries. Weimar was the site of the national assembly that established the so-called Weimar Republic in 1919. Buchenwald concentration camp was located nearby (1937-1945).

Weimaraner, hunting dog developed in the early 19th century in Weimar, Germany. First used to hunt large animals such as deer, it was later used to hunt game. The Weimaraner has a smooth, short, gray coat and amber eyes. It weighs 55-85 lb (25-39 kg), and is 23-27 in (58-69 cm) high. Weimaraners are graceful, affectionate, and obedient companions and watchdogs.

Weimar Republic, German government (1919-1933) based on the democratic republican constitution adopted at Weimar in 1919. The constitution provided for a parliament of 2 houses and a popularly elected president. President Paul von Hindenburg made Adolf Hitler chancellor in 1933, whereupon Hitler suspended the constitution.

Weinberg, Steven (1933-), U.S. physicist who shared the 1979 Nobel Prize in physics for work demonstrating that 2 of the basic forces of nature, electromagnetism and weak interaction (the cause of radioactive decay in certain atomic nuclei), are aspects of a single interaction.
See also: Physics.

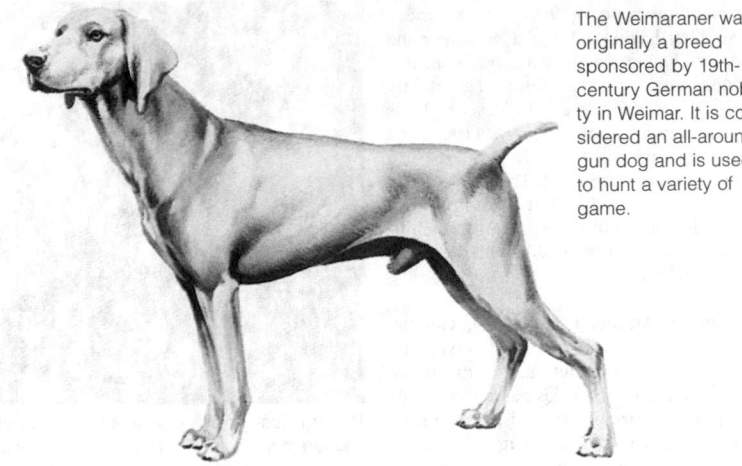

The Weimaraner was originally a breed sponsored by 19th-century German nobility in Weimar. It is considered an all-around gun dog and is used to hunt a variety of game.

W

W

Weiner, Lawrence (1940-   ), American artist. After having dabbled as a painter and sculptor, Weiner made a decision to become a conceptual artist in 1968. He mainly worked with language. He described his principles in his book *Statement* (1968): his basic ideas about art are, 1. The artist can make the work himself. 2. The work can be made by someone else. 3. It is not necessary to actually carry out the work. All possibilities are equal and compatible with the intentions of the artist.

Weismann, August (1834-1914), German biologist. He is renowned for his work on and theories about evolution. Weismann was interested in how a species passed to its offspring various traits, which traits could be inherited, and which could not. He wrote several books, the most famous being *The Germ Plasm: A Theory of Heredity* (1893). *See also:* Biology; Evolution.

Weiss, Peter (1916-1982), German-Swedish playwright, artist, and filmmaker. He fled Nazi Germany in 1934. With his innovative play *The Persecution and Assassination of Jean Paul Marat as Performed by the Inmates of the Asylum of Charenton Under the Direction of the Marquis de Sade*, or *Marat/Sade* (1964), Weiss was acclaimed the successor of Bertolt Brecht. His other dramas include *The Investigation* (1965), and *Trotsky in Exile* (1970).

Weissmuller, Johnny (Peter John Weissmuller; 1904-1984), American swimming champion and film actor. He set national and world freestyle records, and was the first person to swim the 100 m inside a minute. After he won five gold medals at the Olympic Games of 1924 and 1928 he appeared in several sport films, but became famous for his role of Tarzan in 12 Tarzan films, including *Tarzan, the Ape Man* (1932), *Tarzan and His Mate* (1934), *Tarzan Finds a Son* (1939), *Tarzan and the Amazons* (1945), and *Tarzan and the Mermaids* (1948). He then appeared in a number of Jungle Jim Films, including *Jungle Jim* (1948) and *Jungle Jim in the Forbidden Land* (1952), and several other films, including *The Phynx* (1970).

Weizmann, Chaim (1874-1952), Polish-born scientist and Zionist leader, first president of Israel (1948-1952). He emigrated to England in 1904 and became an eminent biochemist and director of the British Admiralty laboratories in 1916. He helped secure the Balfour Declaration (1917), which promised a Jewish state in Palestine. He was head of the World Zionist Organization (1920-1929) and of the Jewish Agency (1929-1931, 1935-1946). He also founded what is known today as the Weizmann Inst. of Science. *See also:* Zionism.

Welding, process of bringing pieces of metal together under conditions of heat or pressure, or both, until they coalesce at the joint. The oldest method is forge welding, in which the surfaces to be joined are heated to welding temperature and then hammered to-

The American actor and director Orson Welles appears in the title role of *Citizen Kane* (1940), an Academy Award-winning film that he also co-authored and directed.

gether on an anvil. The most widely used method today is metal-arc welding: An electric arc is struck between an electrode and the pieces to be joined, and molten metal from a 'filler rod'-usually the electrode itself-is added. Gas welding, now largely displaced by metal-arc welding, is usually accomplished by means of an oxyacetylene torch, which delivers the necessary heat by burning acetylene in a pure oxygen atmosphere. Sources of heat in other forms of welding include the electrical resistance of the joint (resistance welding), an electric arc at the joint (flash welding), a focused beam of electrons (electron-beam welding), and friction (friction welding). Some more recently applied heat sources include hot plasmas, lasers, ultrasonic vibrations, and explosive impacts. *See also:* Soldering.

Welfare, direct government aid to the needy. In the United States various programs, operated by the social security office and by state and local governments, provide aid to the handicapped, aged, poor, and unemployed. Benefits to the aged are more-or-less standardized nationally, but the form of, amount of, and qualifications for other benefits differ from state to state. Benefits fall under many programs, such as veterans' aid and workmen's compensation. All welfare programs are linked to programs that do not give direct financial assistance, such as housing, food stamps, and medical aid. The Reagan administration made significant cuts in federal welfare programs.

Well, manmade hole in the ground used to tap water, gas, or minerals from the earth. Most modern wells are drilled and fitted with a lining, usually of steel, to forestall collapse. Though wells are sunk for natural gas and petroleum oil, the most common type yields water. Such wells may be horizontal or vertical, but all have their innermost end below the water table. If it should be below the permanent water table (the lowest annual level of the water table), the well will yield water throughout the year. Most wells require pumping, but some operate under natural pressure.

Welland Ship Canal, Canadian waterway running 27.6 mi (44.4 km) from Port Colborne on Lake Erie to Port Weller on Lake Ontario to form a major link of the Saint Lawrence Seaway and Great Lakes Waterway. The canal was built 1914-1932, modernized in 1972, and has a minimum depth of about 30 ft (9.1 m). It has 8 locks to overcome the 326-ft (99.4-m) difference in height between Lakes Erie and Ontario. *See also:* Saint Lawrence Seaway and Great Lakes Waterway.

Weller, Thomas Huckle (1915-   ), U.S. bacteriologist and virologist who shared with John F. Enders and Frederick C. Robbins the 1954 Nobel Prize in physiology or medicine for their cultivation of poliomyelitis viruses on tissues of human embryos outside the body. *See also:* Poliomyelitis.

Welles, Orson (1915-1985), U.S. actor, director, and producer. In 1938 his realistic radio production of H.G. Well's *War of the Worlds* caused thousands of listeners to panic, fearing the account of the alien attack was a genuine news report. His first motion picture, of which he was director, cowriter, and star, was *Citizen Kane* (1940), loosely modeled on the life of newspaper magnate William R. Hearst. Innovative camera work and film editing continued to characterize his work in such films as *The Magnificent Ambersons* (1942), *The Lady from Shanghai* (1947), *Macbeth* (1948), and *Touch of Evil* (1962).

Wellington (pop. 162,000), capital city of New Zealand since 1865, at the southern end of North Island. Founded in 1840, it is the nation's second-largest city and an important port and transportation center. Manufactures include processed food, transportation equipment, textiles, and clothing. *See also:* New Zealand.

Wellington, Arthur Wellesley, 1st duke of (1769-1852), British general and politician, 'the Iron Duke,' who defeated Napoleon I at the Battle of Waterloo. After distinguished military service in India (1796-1805), he drove the French from Spain and Portugal in the Peninsular War and entered France in 1813. After being created duke, he led the victorious forces at Waterloo (1815). Serving the Tory government (1819-1827), he became prime minister (1828-1830), and passed the Catholic Emancipation Act; however, he opposed parliamentary reform. In 1842 he became commander-in-chief for life. *See also:* Napoleonic Wars.

Wells, Henry (1805-1878), U.S. pioneer businessperson. With William G. Fargo, he founded Wells, Fargo & Co. (1852), which carried people, freight, and mail from New York City to California. With the acquisition of Benjamin Holladay's mail and stagecoach business (1866), Wells, Fargo & Co. became the most powerful firm in the Far West.

Wells, H. G. (1866-1946), British writer and social reformer. A draper's apprentice, he

The Welsh springer spaniel has been used to hunt opland game and as a duck retriever.

The Welsh terrier has been used to hunt fox, otter, and badger, and is now primarily a show dog and pet.

studied science and became a teacher. After such early science fiction as *The Time Machine* (1895) and *The War of the Worlds* (1898), he wrote novels on the lower middle class, including *Kipps* (1905) and *The History of Mr. Polly* (1910). A founder of the Fabian society, he became a social prophet (*A Modern Utopia*, 1905). After World War I he popularized knowledge in *Outline of History* (1920) and *The Science of Life* (1931).

Wells-Barnett, Ida Bell (1862-1931), African-American reformer and journalist known for her anti-lynching efforts in the late 1800s and early 1900s. In 1909 she helped establish the National Association for the Advancement of Colored People (NAACP). She also participated in the campaign aimed at giving women the right to vote.

Welsbach, Baron von (1858-1929), Viennese chemist and inventor who worked on artificial lighting. He developed the Welsbach mantle (1885), a gas lamp that produced brighter light than previous gas lamps. A few years later, he created the filament for an incandescent lamp that led to the development of the modern light bulb. He also created a metal, called Auer's metal, which, when struck, creates a spark. It is used in modern-day cigarette lighters.
See also: Chemistry.

Welsh *See:* Wales.

Welsh corgi *See:* Cardigan Welsh corgi.

Welsh springer spaniel, breed of dog. This sporting dog can withstand long hours, poor weather, and rough terrain as a retrieving companion to a hunter. Welsh spaniels need careful training, though, because of their

tendency to roam. They stand up to 17 in (43 cm) at the shoulder and weigh from 35-45 lb (15.75-20.25 kg). Their fur, including that on their tail, legs, and chest, is white with red patches or spots.

Welsh terrier, small dog native to Wales, used to hunt foxes. The Welsh terrier has a wiry coat with black and reddish-tan markings. It weighs approximately 20 lb (9 kg) and is about 15 in (38 cm) high. The Welsh is a very lively and spirited dog.

Welty, Eudora (1909-2001), U.S. novelist and short-story writer, known for sensitive tales of Mississippi life. She superbly depicted atmosphere and characters in *The Wide Net* (1943), *The Ponder Heart* (1954), *The Optimist's Daughter* (1972; Pulitzer Prize), and others.

Welwitschia, also known as tumboa, family of desert plants (*Welwitschia mirabilis*) that grow in Africa. The Welwitschia is a large, slow-growing plant that lives 100 or more years, and may reach an age of 1,000-2,000 years. Its long main root extends into a short, cone-shaped trunk that spreads to a width of 5-6 ft (1.5-1.8 m). At the base of the trunk grow a pair of leaves 2-3 ft (61-91 cm) wide and 4-6 ft (1.2-1.8 m) long. These leaves, which grow for the entire life of the plant, are usually shredded into thinner strips by strong desert winds and sand.

Wen, or sebaceous cyst, blocked sebaceous gland, often over the scalp or forehead, that forms a cyst containing old sebum under the skin. Should it become infected, its excision is a simple procedure.

Wendlinger, Karl (1968-), Austrian racing driver, due to his success in karting, Formula Ford, and Formula Three, signed by the Sauber Mercedes motor sport team. Wendlinger made his debut in Formula One during the Japanese Grand Prix in 1991 in a Leyton House March. In 1993 he moved to Sauber Ford.

Werewolf, in folklore, a man who can supernaturally turn into a wolf and devour humans. The belief dates from Greek legend and was widespread in medieval Europe and in the 19th-century Balkans. The psychiatric condition of lycanthropy involves the belief that one is a werewolf or other beast.

Werfel, Franz (1890-1945), Austrian novelist, poet, and playwright. His early plays and poetry, such as *Der Spiegelmensch* (1920), were important works of German expressionism. He fled Nazi-occupied Austria (1938) and later settled in the United States. His novels include *Embezzled Heaven* (1939), *The Song of Bernadette* (1941), and *Jacobowsky and the Colonel* (1944).

Wergeland, Henrik Arnold (1808-1845), Norwegian writer and nationalist. He promoted Norwegian independence from Sweden and inspired Norwegians to feel pride in their own culture. He produced much poetry, drama, and prose, but it is his poetry that received the most acclaim. *Creation, Humanity, and Messiah* (1830), *Jan van Huysum's Flower Piece* (1840), and *The English Pilot* (1844) are some of his best-loved poems. He was dedicated to the causes of liberty, democracy, and international cooperation.

Wertheimer, Max (1880-1943), German psychologist who founded (with Kurt Koffka and Wolfgang Köhler) the school of Gestalt psychology. He taught at Frankfurt and Berlin and emigrated to the United States in 1933.
See also: Gestalt psychology.

Weser River, major German river whose source is the junction of the Fulda and Werra rivers at Munden. The Weser is about 273 mi (440 km) long and flows into the North Sea near Bremerhaven. About 45 mi (72 km) of the river, from its North Sea mouth to Bremen, is navigable by large ships.

Wesker, Arnold (1932-), English playwright, one of the so-called angry young men to emerge in England in 1956. His early plays, such as the trilogy *Chicken Soup with Barley* (1958), *Roots* (1959), and *I'm Talking About Jerusalem* (1960), are committed to the ideals of socialism. The later, more introspective *Chips with Everything* (1962) and *The Friends* (1970) explore themes of private pain.

Wesley, name of 2 English evangelistic preachers who, with George Whitefield, founded Methodism. **John Wesley** (1703-1791) and his brother **Charles** (1707-1788) formed an Oxford Holy Club of scholarly Christians, known as Methodists for their 'rule and methods.' In 1738 the brothers were profoundly influenced by the

John Wesley (1703-1791), whose survivalist sermons in England and America led to the formation of the Methodist church (N. Hone, 1766, National Portrait Gallery, London).

W

W

Moravian Church in Georgia and, John in particular, by Luther's *Preface to the Epistle to the Romans*. Aiming to promote 'vital, practical religion,' the Wesleys took up evangelistic work by field, or open-air, preaching. Rejected by the Church of England, they were enthusiastically received by the people, and they organized conferences of itinerant lay preachers. Charles composed some 6,500 hymns, including 'Hark! The Herald Angels Sing.'
See also: Methodists.

Wesselmann, Tom (1931-), American artist, exponent of pop art. Known for his montages and paintings, depicting such themes as communication media, advertising, wealth, and sex idols.

West, Benjamin (1738-1820), U.S.-born painter. After studying in Rome he settled in London (1763) and was appointed the official historical painter (1772) to King George III. He was also a founder of the Royal Academy of Arts. His best-known works are *Death of General Wolfe* (1771) and *Penn's Treaty with the Indians* (1776). Gilbert Stuart and J.S. Copley were among his students.

Benjamin West's (1738-1820) *The Death of General Wolfe* (1770, National Gallery of Canada, Ottawa). The poses and facial expressions of the contemporarily dressed figures, fully correspond with the Neoclassical ideal. The squatting Indian in the foreground should be seen as an indication of place: he personifies America.

West, Dame Rebecca (Cicily Isabel Fairfield; 1892-1983), British novelist, critic, and journalist. *Black Lamb and Grey Falcon; A Journey through Yugoslavia* (1941) is perhaps her finest work. Her novels include *The Return of the Soldier* (1918) and *Birds Fall Down* (1966).

West, Jerry (1938-), U.S. basketball player and coach. Known for his high scoring as well as ball-handling and defense, he scored 25,192 regular-season points in his National Basketball Association (NBA) career. His achievements include 2 Most Valuable Player awards-1 Playoff (1969) and 1 All-Star (1972)-and appearing in 13 All-Star games. West played for the Los Angeles Lakers (1960-1974), leading them to a championship (1972) and, after retiring, became the team's head coach (1976-1979) and later, general manager (1982-). He was inducted into the Basketball Hall of Fame in 1979.

West, Jessamyn (1907-1984), U.S. author. A Quaker whose writings often reflect the ideals of the Quaker religion, West's most famous book is *Friendly Persuasion* (1945), a view of life in a rural Quaker family in the 1800s (she later adapted this book for the 1956 film of the same name). Other works include *The Witch Diggers* (1951), *Cress Delahanty* (1953), and *Except For Thee and Me* (1969), which chronicles the lives of various characters in *Friendly Persuasion*.

West, Mae (1892-1980), U.S. stage and screen actress. This sultry mistress of provocative innuendo and sex symbol of Hollywood films of the 1930s was frequently at odds with the censors. She immortalized the phrase 'come up 'n' see me sometime,' and starred in such movies as *She Done Him Wrong* (1933), *I'm No Angel* (1933), and *My Little Chickadee* (1940).

West, Nathanael (Nathan Wallenstein Weinstein; 1903-1940), U.S. author. His acerbic novels about the American dream include *The Dream Life of Balso Snell* (1931); *Miss Lonelyhearts* (1933), a gloomy satire about a lovelorn columnist; *A Cool Million* (1934), a lampoon of the rags-to-riches theme; and *The Day of the Locust* (1939), a surrealistic view of life and failure in Hollywood.

West, The, western portion of the United States, formerly the region west of the Appalachian Mountains; presently, the territory west of the Mississippi River, in particular the northern part of this area. In U.S. history, the West was a region that lay at the rim of the settled land. This unsettled area was a place where unlimited land was available at a very cheap price to anyone willing to lead a life on the frontier.

West Bank, Disputed area on the west bank of the River Jordan, captured from Jordan by Israel during the six-day war in 1967. The continuous occupation of the area, inhabited by Palestinians, and the construction of Jewish settlements in the region, met with intense protest from the Palestinians. In 1987 a Palestinian uprising broke out against the Israeli occupation, called the 'intifada'. After the Oslo Accords of 1993 and 1995 (Oslo I and II), parts of the region were handed back to the Palestinians, who were able to introduce limited self rule. Jericho was handed over in 1994, Hebron in 1997. Together with the Gaza Strip these areas fall under the jurisdiction of the Palestinian National Authority, of which Arafat was chosen as president in 1996. In October 1998 an accord was reached about the withdrawal of Israeli troops from another 13% of the region. Israel and the Palestinians continued to disagree about the definitive status of the Palestinian West Bank.
See also: Palestinian National Authority.

West Bengal (pop. 80,078,000), Indian constituent state, bordering on Bangladesh; 34,280 sq mi (88,750 sq km). Capital, Calcutta. Half of the working population works in agriculture: rice, jute, and above all tea. Coal mining is also important. The state is an important center for Indian culture and education.

West Berlin *See:* Berlin.

Western Australia, largest Australian state (975,290 sq mi/2,527,633 sq km), first settled 1826-1829, covering the western third of the country. Beyond the narrow coastal strip and fertile southwest, it is mostly dry plateau with vast desert wastes. Major products are wool, wheat, and lumber, and chief minerals are gold, coal, and iron.

Western European Union (WEU), defensive, economic, social, and cultural alliance among Belgium, France, Great Britain, Italy, Luxembourg, the Netherlands, and Germany, formed in 1955. Spain and Portugal joined in 1988 and Greece in 1991. Comprising most of the members of the North Atlantic Treaty Organization (NATO), the organization works to strengthen the European part of NATO.
See also: North Atlantic Treaty Organization.

Western Isles *See:* Hebrides.

Western Samoa *See:* Samoa, Independent State of.

West Germany *See:* Germany.

West Highland white terrier, small, white Scottish dog. About 11 in (27.9 cm) high and weighing 13-20 lb (5.9-9.1 kg), its coat is thick and wiry. This terrier was once used to hunt small birds and animals.

West Indies, chain of islands extending about 2,500 mi (4,020 km) from Florida to Venezuela, separating the Caribbean Sea and the Gulf of Mexico from the Atlantic Ocean. An alternative name (excluding the Bahamas) is the Antilles. The West Indies comprises 4 main groups: the Bahamas to the northeast of Cuba and Hispaniola; the Greater Antilles (Cuba, the largest island in the West Indies, Hispaniola, Jamaica, and Puerto Rico); the Lesser Antilles (Leeward and Windward islands, Trinidad and Tobago, and Barbados); and the Netherlands Antilles (Aruba, Bonaire, Curaçao) as well as other islands off the Venezuelan coast. Many of the islands are mountainous and volcanic with lagoons and mangrove swamps on their coastlines. The climate is warm, but there are frequent hurricanes. The principal crop is sugarcane and tourism is an important industry. After Columbus reached the West Indies (1492), they were settled by the Spanish, followed by the English, French, and Dutch, who exploited the spices and sugar, using African slaves. The political status of the islands varies widely.

Westinghouse, George (1846-1914), U.S. engineer, inventor, and manufacturer. In 1869 he founded the Westinghouse Air Brake Company to develop the air brakes he had invented for railroad use. From 1883 he did pioneering work on the safe transmission of natural gas. He also pioneered the use of high-voltage AC electricity and in 1886 founded the Westinghouse Electric Company to develop AC induction motors and transmission equipment. The company was largely responsible for the acceptance of AC in preference to DC for most applica-

tions, in spite of opposition from the influential Thomas Edison.
See also: Brake.

Westminster Abbey, officially the Collegiate Church of Saint Peter, English Gothic church in London, a national shrine. The Abbey has been the traditional scene of English coronations since that of William the Conqueror, and is a burial place for English monarchs and famous subjects, including many of England's greatest poets, who lie in the Poets' Corner. The present building, begun in 1245 by Henry III, is on the site of a church built (1065) by Edward the Confessor.

Westminster, Statute of (1931), British parliamentary act abolishing Great Britain's power to legislate for its dominions. It gave the dominions complete independence in the commonwealth of nations, although they owed common allegiance to the British crown.

Westminster Hall, building that serves as an entranceway to Britain's House of Parliament (Westminster Palace) in London. Westminster Palace was the royal residence before it became the home of Parliament (16th century), and the rulers of Britain held court in its Great Hall. Westminster Hall is all that remains of the Great Hall, which was built in the late 11th century but mostly destroyed by German fire bombs during World War II. Westminster Hall measures 240 ft (73 m) long, 68 ft (21 m) wide, and 89 ft (27 m) high.
See also: Parliament.

Westmoreland, William Childs (1914-), U.S. general, army chief of staff (1968-1972). He was superintendent of West Point (1960-1963) and the U.S. commander (1964-1968) in Vietnam.

Weston, Edward (1886-1958), U.S. photographer, winner of the Guggenheim Fellowship (1937). Originally a producer of hazy, unclear pictures, popular in the late 1800s, Weston switched in the 1920s to crisp, focused photographs of simple subjects, a stlye known as straight photography. His pictures emphasized the form and texture of objects and centered predominantly on nature scenes.
See also: Photography.

Westphalia (German, 'western plain'), region in Germany, located just east of the Netherlands. Westphalia was first settled C.A.D. 700 by a group of Saxons. It came under the control of the archbishops of Cologne in 1180. During the 18th century, Prussian rulers steadily acquired the region. Napoleon transferred portions of Westphalia to his brother and to the duchy of Berg. However, the Congress of Vienna (1814-1815) reestablished Prussian rule of the region. It came under German control in 1946.

West Point, site of, and common name for, the U.S. Military Academy in southeast New York, an institute of higher education that trains officers for the regular army. Established by an Act of Congress in 1802, its training methods and traditions were set down by Col. Sylvanus Thayer, superintendent of the academy from 1817 to 1833. Candidates for entry (since 1976, of either sex) to the academy must be unmarried U.S. citizens age 17-22 and must meet minimum academic requirements. Cadets are enlisted in the regular army on entrance. Graduates are awarded a B.S. degree and a commission as second lieutenant.

West Virginia (Mountain State; pop. 1,820,000), state in the east of the U.S. bordered by Pennsylvania, Maryland, Virginia, Kentucky, and Ohio; 24,241 sq mi (62,760 sq km). Capital, Charleston. To the west the Appalachian Mountains become the Cumberland Plateau. West Virginia has a wet, continental climate: warm summers (average July temperatures 24°C), and cool to cold winters (average January temperature around freezing point). The chief industry of the state is coal mining; there is also extraction of oil, gas, sand, gravel, chalk, and sandstone. The mountainous landscape makes agriculture and the establishment of industry difficult. In the north there is some glass and metal industry. The state also has several universities. When the first Europeans (British and French) came to the region it was inhabited by Iroquois and Cherokee Indians. West Virginia was originally part of Virginia; the region was divided in 1862 when Virginia joined the Confederacy (the South during the American Civil War). West Virginia has been a member of the Union since 1863.

Westward movement, in the United States, events and conditions comprising the several major migrations by which the country was settled. The exploration and settlement of the U.S. frontier was an ongoing process that began with the first communities founded on the Atlantic seaboard in the 17th century and ended in the 1890s with the settlement of the Great Plains between the Mississippi River and the Rocky Mountains.

Wetland, area of land where the earth is continuously saturated with water. Three major types of wetlands are bogs, swamps, and marshes, each supporting a different kind of plant life. Bogs, usually located in cooler climates, have acidic soil that appears dry but is not. Bogs are dominated by mosses, which, when they decay, turn into peat. (Peat is valuable because, when dried, it can be burned as a fuel.) Swamps and marshes have mineral soils and are found mostly in warmer climates. Wetlands support a variety of valuable bird and mammal life.

Weyden, Rogier van der (Rogier de la Pasture: 1399?-1464), a Flemish painter. His religious paintings are marked with a mystical ferfor and a sure sense of pathos. He had the ability to organize realistic details into a harmonious whole. His portraits are simple and forceful, usually in bold relief. Rogier's influence on other Flemish painters was great. *The Descent from the Cross* is considered his masterpiece. Other notable works are *The Annunciation, St. Luke Painting the Virgin, Braque Triptych, Portrait of a Lady*. Little is known of Rogier's life. He was probably born in Tournai. About 1426 he settled in Brussels and in 1435 was named official painter of the city. While visiting Italy in the Holy Year of 1450, he received several commissions.

Whale, one of the order Cetacea of large, wholly aquatic mammals. All are highly adapted for life in water, with a torpedo-shaped body, front limbs reduced and modi-

sperm whale

killer whale

pilot whale

beluga

The toothed whales are predators with sharp teeth and wide throats. They include the sperm whale, *Physeter catodon*, the largest toothed whale that reaches a maximum size of about 65 ft (20 m); the beluga, or white whale, *Delphinapterus leu* cas; the pilot whale, *Globicephala*, found in schools with several hundred members; and the black-and-white killer whale, *Orcinus orca*, that co- operatively hunts in packs that number from 3 to 50

W

(A) A whale-catching ship (1), with the help of a helicopter, sights a whale and then tracks it by the sound-ranging system known as sonar. (B) To kill the whale, a harpoon gun (detail, 2) fires a harpoon (3) equipped with a grenade that explodes inside the animal. The harpoon also has expanding flukes (4) that anchor it when the whale is struck. The whale-catching ship then hauls the whale to a factory ship through a slipway (5). On the flensing deck (6) the blubber is stripped from the carcass, rendered into oil by boilers (7), and stored in tanks (8). The carcass is then dragged to the meat

deck (9), where the meat is stripped and either frozen or boiled and the bones are cut by a saw (10) and processed in pressure boilers for oil.

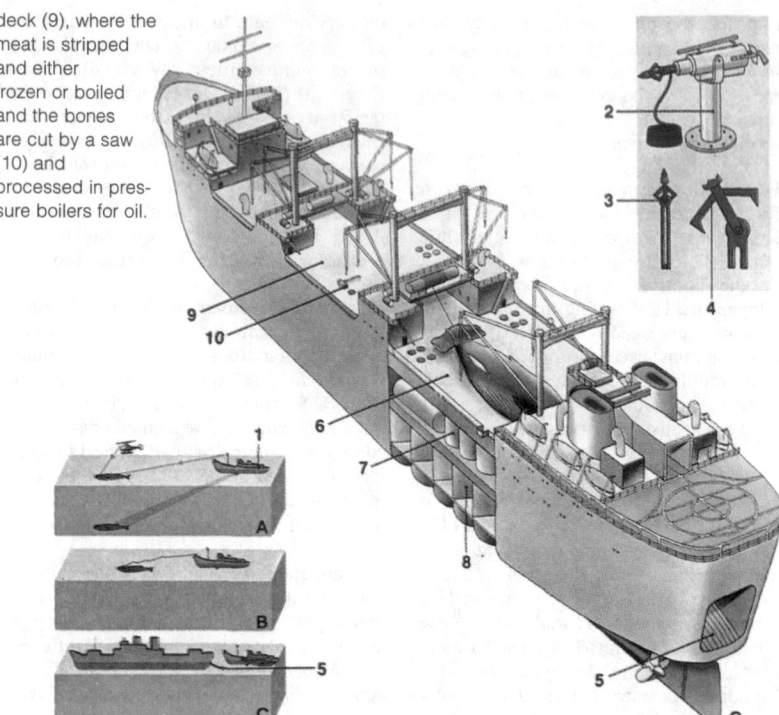

fied as steering paddles, and hind limbs absent. They have a tail of 2 transverse flukes and swim by up-and-down movements of this tail. Most species have a fleshy dorsal fin that acts as a stabilizer. The neck is short, the head flowing directly into the trunk. The body is hairless, and the smooth skin lies over a thick layer of blubber that has an insulating function but also acts to smooth out the passage of water over the body in rapid swimming. The nose, or blowhole, is at the top of the head, allowing the animal to breathe as soon as it breaks the surface of the water.

Modern whales divide into 2 suborders, the whalebone whales and the toothed whales. Whalebone whales feed on plankton, straining the enormous quantities they require from the water with special plates of whalebone, or baleen, developed from the mucus membrane of the upper jaw. Whalebone whales-the right, rorqual, and gray whales-are usually large and slow-moving. The group includes the blue whale (*Balaenoptera musulus*), the largest animal of all time (up to 100 ft/30.5 m long). Toothed whales, equipped with conical teeth, feed on fishes and squids. The group includes the dolphins and porpoises, the sperm whale (*Physeter macrocephalus*), and the narwhal (*Mmonodon monoceros*). Many species of whale are endangered.
See also: Whaling.

Whaling, Whale catching, formerly for whale oil and baleen, but nowadays for the flesh (which is mainly used as cattle fodder and as tinned pet food). Known to have been practised since the 10th century, when the Northern Right whale was hunted along the coasts of Europe. Stocks began to decline in the 19th century, so that whaling activities moved to the Antarctic, hunting the more difficult to catch Rorquals. The whaling was carried out on factory ships so that

the whales could be slaughtered, the oil cooked, and the flesh processed or frozen, and then unloaded while at sea, which meant the ships could stay at sea for a very long time. Whale stocks began to decline very quickly; an increasing number of species were even in danger of becoming extinct. An International Whaling Commission (IWC) was established in 1945, and set a quota for the number of whales that could be caught each year, but this measure turned out to be insufficient. In 1982 the whaling industry was dismantled, and from 1986 onwards an indefinite moratorium has been in place. Countries such as Japan, Russia, Norway, and Peru continue to fish whales however, for what they call 'scientific' purposes. In 1994 the IWC decided to turn the waters of the Antarctic into a whale reserve.

Wharton, Edith (1862-1937), U.S. novelist, poet, and short-story writer. She wrote subtle and acerbic accounts of society in New York, New England, and Europe, including *The House of Mirth* (1905), *Ethan*

Frome (1911), and *The Age of Innocence* (1920; Pulitzer Prize).

Wheat, cereal plant (genus *Triticum*) of the grass family, the world's main cereal crop; about 300 million tons are produced every year, mostly used to make flour for bread and pasta. Wheat has been in cultivation since at least 5000 B.C. and grows best in temperate regions of Europe, North America, China, and Australia. The USSR is the largest producer, followed by the United States and Canada. There are many varieties of wheat, and different parts of the grain are used to produce the various types of flour. Grains comprise an outer husk called bran and a central starchy germ (which is embedded in a protein known as gluten). Wheat is graded as hard or soft depending on how easily the flour can be separated from the bran. Wheat for bread is hard wheat and contains a lot of gluten. Soft wheat flours containing more starch and less protein are used for pastries. There are 2 main types of wheat; these are sown either in the fall (winter wheat) or in the spring (spring wheat). Harvesting is carried out by combine harvesters that cut and thresh the crop in one operation. Wheat is vulnerable to several diseases, including smut, rust, army worm, and Hessian fly.

Wheatstone, Sir Charles (1802-1875), British physicist and inventor. He popularized the 'Wheatstone bridge' for measuring voltages and, with W.F. Cooke, invented the electric telegraph at about the same time as U.S. inventor Samuel F.B. Morse (1837). *See also:* Telegraph.

Wheatstone bridge, electric circuit used for comparing or measuring resistance. Four resistors, including the unknown one, are connected in a square, with a battery between one pair of diagonally opposite corners and a sensitive galvanometer between the other. When no current flows through the meter, the products of opposite pairs of resistances are equal. Similar bridge circuits are used for impedance measurement.
See also: Electric circuit; Wheatstone, Sir Charles.

Wheel and axle, disklike mechanical device consisting of a wheel mounted on an axle of smaller diameter; the wheel and axle turn on the same axis. A first-class lever, it is used to

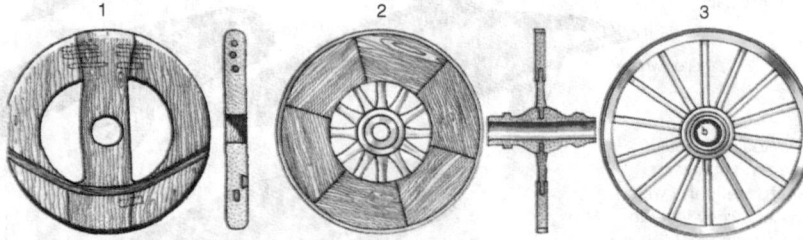

The development of the wheel with spokes in prehistoric Europe. The wheel took more than a thousand years to reach a certain level of technical perfection.
1. an early form of the wheel with spokes, from Italy, probably around 1200 BC.
2. a wheel with spokes from the Hallstatt-culture, with a bronze hub, around 500 BC.
3. a modern wheel with spokes from the Celtic La Tène-culture, with a hub that had round furrowed metal bushings, in which little bars rolled, a system that may be compared to modern-day roller bearings.

The whippoorwill (*C. vociferus*) spends the daylight hours asleep on the forest floor. Its plumage blends well with dead leaves and other undergrowth, making the bird difficult to observe.

facilitate the movement of heavy objects. The wheel and axle is one of the classic simple machines, along with the pulley and the screw.

Wheelbarrow, boxlike device used to move small loads. The load is carried in a box or tub at the front, below which there is a wheel. The box or tub is lifted and pushed by 2 handles at the rear.

Whelk, spiral-shelled sea snail found worldwide. It feeds off other mollusks and fish caught in commercial traps. The northern whelk, found in North Atlantic waters, has a shell about 3 in (8 cm) long. Most are edible.

Whetstone, natural or artificial abrasive stone used for sharpening and grinding tools. Quartz is the abrasive agent that makes whetstones effective.

Whig Party, English and U.S. political party. In England the term was applied in 1679 to Protestant opponents of the English Crown. The Whigs enjoyed a period of dominance c.1714-1760, notably under Robert Walpole. Largely out of office when led by Charles James Fox, they were increasingly associated with Nonconformism, mercantile, industrial, and reforming interests. After the Whig ministries of the 2nd earl Grey and Lord Melbourne (1830-1841), during which the Reform Bill of 1832 was passed, the Whigs helped form the Liberal Party in the mid-1800s.

The U.S. Whig Party was formed c.1836 from diverse opponents, including the National Republicans, of Andrew Jackson and the Democrats. Its leaders were Henry Clay and Daniel Webster, and a national economic policy was its principal platform. Whig President William Henry Harrison died after one month in office and was succeeded (1841) by John Tyler, who was disowned by the Whigs when he vetoed their tariff and banking bills. Clay, the next Whig candidate, lost the 1844 election. The second Whig president, Zachary Taylor, died in of-

fice (1850) after serving 1 year. He was succeeded by a loyal Whig, Millard Fillmore, but the party was by then divided by the issues of slavery and national expansion; the Compromise of 1850 did not last, and Winfield Scott was heavily defeated in the 1852 election. The party never recovered, and many of the Northern Whigs joined the new Republican Party, while the Cotton (Southern) Whigs joined the Democratic Party.

Whip, in U.S. and British politics, party member of a legislative body chosen to enforce party discipline in attendance and voting. The first U.S. whip, Republican congressperson James E. Watson, was appointed in 1899.

Whiplash, cervical sprain, or neck injury. As a result of the head accidently thrown backward then forward, the muscles and ligaments in the head, neck, and shoulder area may become strained. This strain causes pain and stiffness that may be treated with a neck brace, heat, massage, or pain medicine. It happens most often through automobile accidents, although automobile headrests and shoulder harnesses help prevent or lessen the severity of this injury.

Whippet, greyhoundlike dog possessing great speed. It can run as fast as 35 mph (56 kmph). Whippets weigh 18-23 lb (8-10 kg) and stand 18-22 in (44-57 cm) high. They

have short coats of tan, gray, or white, and are used for racing and for rabbit hunting.

Whippoorwill, nocturnal North American bird (*Caprimulgus vociferus*) known for its odd, deliberate call. They are found in southeastern Canada, the United States, Mexico, and Central America. Whippoorwills are about 10 in (25 cm) long with brown spotted feathers. They assist farmers by feeding on crop-damaging insects.

Whirligig *See:* Water beetle.

Whirlpool, rotary current in water. Permanent whirlpools may arise in the ocean from the interactions of the tides. They occur also in streams or rivers where 2 currents meet or the shape of the channel dictates. Short-lived whirlpools may be created by wind.

Whiskey, strong, distilled spirituous liquor made from grain. When from Scotland or Canada, *whiskey* is spelled without an *e* (whisky). The ingredients and preparation vary. In the United States corn and rye are commonly used: 51% corn for bourbon whiskey and 51% rye for rye whiskey. A grain mash is allowed to ferment, then distilled, diluted, and left to age. Bourbon and rye whiskey stand in oak barrels for 4 years. Irish whiskey uses barley, wheat, oats, and rye, and vessels called potstills for the distilling process. Scotch whisky is

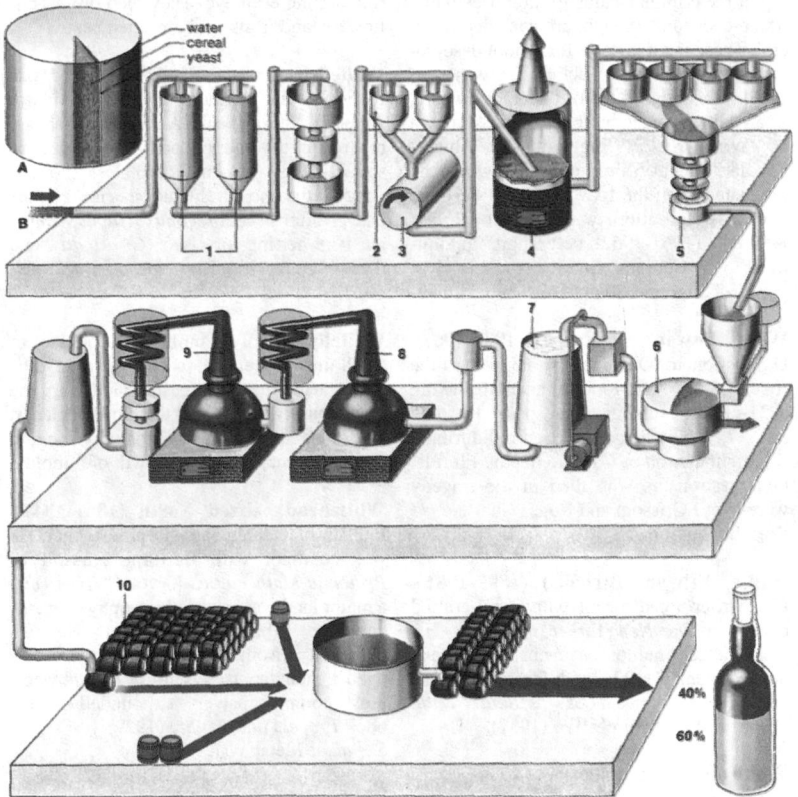

The basic constituents of whiskey are: water, cereal and yeast. The relative proportions of each are shown in (A). Manufacturing of whiskey (B) begins with the harvesting of barley, which is saturated with water (1), steeped (2), and allowed to germinate inside a rotating drum (3). Here enzyms in the barley convert its starch to the sugar maltose. The malted barley is heated in a peat furnace (4), ground (5), and mashed with water, creating a liquid called wort, from which waste material is discarded (6). Sugar in the cooled wort is changed to alcohol (fermented) by the addition of yeast (7). The mixture is distilled twice (8, 9), then diluted. Aging and flavoring take place in oak casks (10). The whiskey is blended with water at a ratio of 40 to 60, and bottled.

the finest form: the best types are pure barley malt or grain whiskies. The secret of its flavor is said to be the peat-flavored water of certain Scottish streams. Manufactured commercially since the 16th century, whiskey is one of the most popular of alcoholic beverages.

Whistle, device used for signaling, consisting of a tube with a sharp edge or lip that makes a sound when air or steam is blown through it.

Whistler, James Abbott McNeill (1834-1903), U.S. artist. Born in Lowell, Mass., in his youth he lived with his family in Russia. Later he attended the U.S. Military Academy at West Point but failed academically after 3 years. He resumed his art studies in Paris and moved to London, where he lived until his death. His best-known painting is *Arrangement in Gray and Black No. 1: Portrait of the Artist's Mother* (1872), commonly called 'Whistler's Mother.' Whistler believed paintings should be abstract responses to the artist's imagination.

White *See:* Color.

White, Byron Raymond (1917-2002), U.S. Supreme Court justice, appointed by President John F. Kennedy (1962). The majority of his decisions have leaned more toward conservatism. These include votes against a person's right to privacy, abortion, fair treatment for criminal suspects, and lifting of the criminal status for homosexuality. Some decisions, though, are considered liberal. These include votes for school desegregation and affirmative action. He was educated in his home state of Colorado (where, as an All-American halfback, he was known as 'Whizzer'), in England as a Rhodes Scholar, and at Yale University, where he graduated from the Law School (1946). He was assistant attorney general to Robert Kennedy (1961-1962) before his appointment to the Supreme Court.
See also: Supreme Court of the United States.

White, Edward Higgins, II (1930-1967), U.S. astronaut. On June 3, 1965 he was the first U.S. astronaut to leave his craft, taking a 21-minute walk in outer space. He died Jan. 27, 1967 when a fire occurred during a flight simulation at Cape Kennedy, Florida. Other astronauts who died in the tragedy were Virgil Grissom and Roger Chaffee.
See also: Astronaut.

White, E(lwyn) B(rooks) (1899-1985), U.S. writer noted for his witty, well-crafted essays in *The New Yorker* magazine. His work includes humorous poems, the satire *Is Sex Necessary?* (1929, with James Thurber), and such children's books as *Stuart Little* (1945) and *Charlotte's Web* (1952).

White ant *See:* Termite.

White, Patrick (1912-1990), Australian novelist, winner of the 1973 Nobel Prize in literature. His long novels, set mostly in Australia, include *Voss* (1957), *The Vivisector* (1970), *The Eye of the Storm* (1974), and *The Twyborn Affair* (1980).

White, Paul Dudley (1886-1973), U.S. physician, prominent cardiologist. White was an early advocate of diet and exercise for the prevention of heart attacks, and was one of the first to use electrocardiograms for diagnosis of heart disease. His book *Heart Disease* (1931), in its original and numerous revised editions, became a standard text in the field. He became well known as Dwight D. Eisenhower's cardiologist following the president's heart attack. In 1971 White visited the People's Republic of China to study medicine in that country.
See also: Cardiology.

White, Stanford (1853-1906), U.S. architect and painter in the firm of McKim, Mead & White, a renowned architectural firm. His designs include the Washington Arch (1889-1895), the Judson Memorial Church (1891), the campus of Bronx Community College (1892-1901), and the Tiffany Building (1906). Born in New York City, White was shot to death by Harry Thaw, the jealous husband of his lover, Evelyn Nesbit.
See also: Architecture.

White, T(erence) H(anbury) (1906-1964), English novelist, noted for *The Once and Future King* (4 vol., 1939-1958), a retelling of the legends of King Arthur, and *The Goshawk* (1951).

White-eye, common name for about 85 species of small birds (family Zosteropidae) of the Old World tropics that have a white ring around each eye. They feed on insects, flowers, and fruits, and are often pests.

Whitefish, important freshwater food fish found in the northern regions of North America, Europe, and Asia. Whitefish are related to the salmon and trout but have small scales and small, toothless mouths. Among the most valuable species are the lake whitefish (*Coregonus clupeaformis*), the lake herring, or cisco (*C. artedii*), and the mountain whitefish (*Prosopium williamsoni*).

Whitefly, any of a family (Aleyrodidae) of small insects related to the scale insects. Some whiteflies are pests, including the greenhouse whitefly and the citrus whitefly. The latter damages citrus plants by sucking sap and encouraging the growth of a mold.

Whitehead, Alfred North (1861-1947), English mathematician and philosopher. He was coauthor with Bertrand Russell of *Principia Mathematica* (3 vol., 1910-1913), a major landmark in the philosophy of mathematics. While teaching at Harvard University (from 1924), Whitehead developed a monumental system of metaphysics, most comprehensively expounded in his book *Process and Reality* (1929).
See also: Metaphysics.

White House, official home of the president of the United States, in Washington, D.C. It was designed in the manner of an 18th-century English gentleman's country house by James Hoban (1792). John Adams was the first president to live there. It was severely damaged by the British in 1814,

but rebuilt and extended (and painted white) by 1818. In 1824 Hoban added the semicircular south portico. The grounds were landscaped in 1850 by Andrew Downing. Major renovations, including the addition of the executive office building, were carried out in the early 20th century by the architectural firm of McKim, Mead & White. From 1948 onward the building was extensively rebuilt.
See also: President of the United States.

White House conference, extended meeting called by the U.S. president in which professional experts, community leaders, and other individuals discuss a specified topic. Similar state-level conferences may be mandated by the president. The topic of the first White House conference, called by Theodore Roosevelt in 1908, was conservation. Many of the more than 60 conferences since then have dealt with children or the aging.

Whiteman, Paul (1891-1967), U.S. orchestra leader known as the 'King of Jazz.' He introduced a personal style called 'symphonic jazz.' Whiteman encouraged George Gershwin to compose *Rhapsody in Blue* (1924). Born in Denver, Colo., he spent his later years as a popular musical conductor on radio shows.
See also: Jazz.

White paper, British government report or policy statement on an important issue. The documents are called white papers because they are hastily prepared and submitted without the blue cover used for longer documents.

White Sands Missile Range, main U.S. Army missile-testing site located in south-central New Mexico. It was established as White Sands Proving Ground in 1945 and renamed in 1958. The range extends 120 mi (193 km) from north to south and 40 mi (64 km) east to west. The first atomic bomb was exploded there in 1945.

White Sea, arm of the Arctic Ocean, called *Beloye More* in the Soviet Union. It is icebound Sept.-June, but heavy shipping is conducted on it during the summer months.
See also: Atlantic Ocean.

White-tailed deer (*Odocoileus virginianus*), North American deer named for its long white tail, raised as a danger signal when the deer is alarmed.

White walnut *See:* Butternut.

Whitman, Walt (1819-1892), major U.S. poet. His *Leaves of Grass* (1855; expanded in successive editions), one of the most influential volumes of poetry in U.S. literary history, was praised by Ralph Waldo Emerson and Henry David Thoreau, but did not achieve popular recognition at the time of its publication. Other works include *Drum-Taps* (1865), a collection of Civil War poems; *Democratic Vistas* (1871), prose studies of U.S. democracy; and the autobiographical *Specimen Days* (1882-1883). Whitman rejected regular meter and rhyme in favor of flowing free verse and celebrated erotic love, rugged individualism, democracy, and equality.

Whitney, Eli (1765-1825), U.S. inventor of the cotton gin (1793) and pioneer of mass production. In 1798 he contracted with the U.S. government to make 10,000 muskets: He took 8 years to fulfill the 2-year contract, but he showed that with unskilled labor muskets could be put together using parts that were precision-made and thus interchangeable, a benefit not only during production but also in later maintenance.
See also: Cotton gin.

Whitney, Gertrude Vanderbilt (1875-1942), U.S. sculptor. She is best known for her monuments commemorating the victims of World War I and for her fountain sculptures. The Whitney Studio Club, which she established in New York City (1918), was a center for U.S. avant-garde art and led to the founding of the Whitney Museum of American Art (1931).

Whittier, John Greenleaf (1807-1892), U.S. poet born in Haverhill, Mass., to a Quaker family. The themes of his work were the injustice of slavery and the beauty of the New England countryside. He served in the state legislature and was active in the anti-slavery movement. His political poem, 'Ichabod' (1850), attacked Daniel Webster for his role in passing the Compromise of 1850. He attacked what he saw as hypocrisy in a nation that espoused freedom but allowed slavery.

WHO *See:* World Health Organization.

Whooping cough, or pertussis, contagious bacterial disease of children causing upper respiratory symptoms, with a characteristic whoop or inspiratory noise due to inflammation of the larynx. Whooping cough is a serious disease that can lead to pneumonia, brain damage, convulsions, and collapse of the lungs. Vaccination is widely practiced to prevent it.

Whooping crane, *G. americana* (background) and the sandhill crane, *G. canadensis*, (foreground).

Whooping crane (*Grus americana*), white wading bird with a red cap on its head. The tallest bird in North America, it reaches a height of about 5 ft (1.5 m). Once widespread, whooping cranes have for several decades been close to extinction and have been preserved only by determined conservation measures.

Wichita (pop. 312,000), city in Kansas, located on the Chisholm Trail. Cowboys used to bring their herds to Wichita on their way to Texas markets. Cattle, along with the Santa Fe Railroad, made this city an important location during 19th-century westward expansion. Today there is still a strong meat industry as well as a large aviation and oil industry. McConnell Air Force Base is located here as well as the domed Century II cultural-convention center and Wichita State University. The city was founded as a trading post (1864) where European-American settlers traded with the Wichita tribespeople. The legendary western law man Wyatt Earp worked in Wichita in the 1870s.
See also: Kansas.

Wicker, material woven from flexible plant fiber or willow twigs. Furniture, especially in hot climates, has been made from wicker since the days of ancient Egypt. Wicker has been appreciated as a durable as well as comfortable and attractive material. Bamboo, rattan, reed, and cane are natural plant fibers used for wicker. Modern synthetic wickers have been developed from materials such as treated twisted paper fibers.

Wiclif, John *See:* Wycliffe, John.

Widgeon *See:* Wigeon.

Wieland, Christoph Martin (1733-1813), a German author. His verse brought a light, ironic touch to German poetry. *Oberon* (1780), the most ambitious of his verse romances, is based on an old French tale. *Agathon* (1766-1767) introduced the psychological novel into German literature. Wieland translated 11 of Shakespeare's plays into German prose. In 1722 he went to Weimar as tutor to the sons of the Duchess of Saxe-Weimar.

Wien *See:* Vienna.

Wiener, Norbert (1894-1964), U.S. mathematician noted for his contributions to computer science. He developed the theory of cybernetics. His major book is *Cybernetics: Or Control and Communication in the Animal and the Machine* (1948).
See also: Cybernetics.

Wieniawski, Henri (1835-1880), a Polish violinist and composer. His individual, impetuous style made him one of the great violin virtuosos of his time. After studying at the Paris Conservatory, he toured in Europe and America. He taught at the St. Petersburg and Brussels conservatories. *Legende* and *Concerto in D* are among his compositions that are standards in the violin repertoire.

Wiesbaden (pop. 262,000), city in southwestern Germany, capital of the German state of Hesse. The word *wiesbaden* translates as 'baths on the meadows,' and this resort, located in a valley of the Taunus Mountains, is known for its hot springs. The Romans enjoyed this area since the 1st century B.C. and considered it a spa-a resort where mineral springs are often found. People today still come to Wiesbaden for its mineral springs. Tourism is the economic base of the city.
See also: Germany.

Wiesel, Elie (1928-), Romanian-born U.S. novelist. In 1944, with other Jews, he and his family were sent to Auschwitz, where his parents and sister died. He then was sent to Buchenwald, which was liberated in 1945. Wiesel later became the leading spokesperson for survivors of Nazi concentration camps. His autobiographical novel, *Night* (1958), recaptures the horrors he encountered. Other novels include *The Jews of Silence* (1966), *Souls on Fire* (1972), *The Testament* (1980), *The Fifth Son* (1984), and *The Forgotten* (1992). His memoirs include *All Rivers run to the Sea* (1995) and *Memoir in two Voices* (1996). He won the Nobel Peace Prize in 1986.
See also: Concentration camp; Holocaust.

Wiesel, Torsten Nils (1924-), Swedish neurobiologist who shared the 1981 Nobel Prize in physiology or medicine for his research on the brain's processing of visual information.
See also: Brain.

Wiesenthal, Simon (1908-), Austrian hunter of Nazi war criminals. Having lost a large number of relatives in Nazi concentration camps during World War II, he established the Jewish Documentation Center in Vienna, Austria, through which he located more than 1,000 former Nazis accused of war crimes, including Adolf Eichmann.
See also: Holocaust.

Wig, covering for the head of real or artificial hair, worn as a cosmetic device, as a mark of rank or office, as a disguise, or for theatrical portrayals. Known since ancient times, wigs became fashionable in 17th- and 18th-century Europe, when elaborate headpieces for women and full, curled wigs for men came into wide use. The latter are still worn in British law courts. In the 1960s wigs came back into fashion for women. Small

In the past, the enormous wigs were usually powdered, as seen here on Charles II's portrait (1630-1685), that is hanging on the wall in this caricature by James Gillray (1757-1815). In times of need, however, a thrifty English family maked do without the powder. Quite a saving!

W

The wildcat (*F. silvestris*), a heavily built, fierce cat of the forest region, somewhat resembles a domestic tabby, but it cannot be tamed.

hairpieces called *toupees* are worn to conceal baldness.

Wigeon, duck in the family Anatidae. Wigeons found in the United States (*Anas americana*) and those found in northern Europe (*A. penelope*) are the same size, about 19 in (48 cm) long. The U.S. wigeon, also called the *baldpate*, is known for its call, the sound *whew* repeated a number of times. These ducks feed on water plants, using their flat, broad bills. The male heads and throats are marked with white.

Wight, Isle of, diamond-shaped island, 147 sq mi (381 sq km), off the southern coast of England. Its scenery and mild climate make it a popular resort area. Cowes, the chief port, is a well-known yachting center.

Wigman, Mary (1886-1973), a German dancer. Miss Wigman pioneered in the modern, or expressionistic, dance. She was born in Hanover. From her early studies in classical ballet, she developed disciplined technique. She then broadened the art of dancing into expressions of psychological reactions. Many of her dance creations were done to the piercing music of primitive instruments. In 1920 she founded a dance school in Dresden, Germany. After World War II, she opened a dance studio in West Berlin. She wrote *Language of the Dance* (1966).

Wigner, Eugene Paul (1902-1995), Hungarian-born U.S. physicist who worked with Enrico Fermi to produce the first nuclear chain reaction in 1942. Wigner shared the Nobel Prize in physics with J. Hans Jensen and Maria Goeppert in 1963. He was professor of mathematical physics at Princeton University.
See also: Nuclear energy.

Wigwam, kind of dwelling used by Algonquian-speaking Native Americans in the eastern part of North America. Wigwams are usually oval or round and are covered with bark. The term is sometimes used to describe any Native American home, including the conical tepee and wickiup.

Wilander, Mats (1964-), Swedish tennis player, became the youngest ever winner of the French Open tennis championship in 1982. He went on to win the Australian Open (1983, 1984, 1988), the French Open (1985, 1988), the Italian Open (1987), and the U.S. Open (1988). Wilander was also a member of the team that won the Davis Cup in 1984 and 1985.

Wilberforce, Samuel (1805-1873), English priest of the Anglican church. He held important church offices, including bishop of Oxford, dean of Westminster, and chaplain of the House of Lords. Wilberforce mediated a dispute between the Anglo-Catholic and the Evangelical factions of the church. Politically, he fought for prison reform and measures to prevent the abuse of women and children.
See also: Anglicans.

Wilbur, Richard (1921-), U.S. poet and essayist. He won a Pulitzer Prize in poetry for *Things of This World* (1957) and *New and Collected Poems* (1989). In 1987 he received an appointment as poet laureate of the United States.

Wild barley, plant in the grass family. One kind of wild barley, squirreltail (*Hordeum jubatum*), is named because of its prickly, bearded appearance. The seeds of this grass

Pesticide pollution endangers the bald eagle (*Haliaeetus leucocephalus*, 4); peregrine falcon (*Falco peregrinus*, 6); and Japanese white stork (*Ciconia ciconia boyciana*, 8). Oil spills threaten the puffin (*Fratercula arctica*, 3). Water pollution has also led to the decline of the North Atlantic salmon (*Salmo salar*, 1); Atlantic sturgeon (*Acipenser sturio*, 2); manatee (*Trichechus manatus*, 5); and black-footed, or jackass penguin (*Spheniscus demersus*, 7), of South Africa.

Superstitions endanger such animals as the aye-aye (*Daubentonia madagascariensis*, 9), which some Madagascans regard as an evil spirit. The horns of the black rhinoceros (*Diceros bicornis*, 10), and sika deer (*Cervus nippon*, 13), are thought to have aphrodisiac properties. The Japanese giant salamander (*Andrias japonicus*, 11), and Formosan serow (*Capricornis crispus swinhoei*, 12) are used for healing.

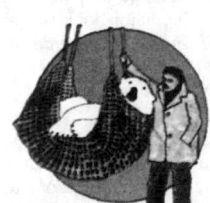
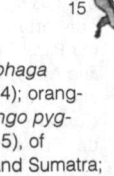
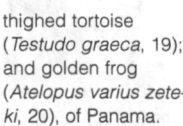

The capture and collection of animals for zoos, pets, or research threatens populations of the Philippine monkey-eating eagle (*Pithecophaga jefferyi*, 14); orangutan (*Pongo pygmaeus*, 15), of Borneo and Sumatra; golden marmoset (*Leontideus rosalia*, 16); giant anteater (*Myrmecophaga tridactyla*, 17); Texas blind salamander (*Typhlomolge rathbuni*, 18); Mediterranean spur-thighed tortoise (*Testudo graeca*, 19); and golden frog (*Atelopus varius zeteki*, 20), of Panama.

not only spread quickly and destroy other plants, they burrow through to the hide of woolly sheep and cause irritation. In addition the rest of the plant, when chewed, often causes sheep to choke.

Wild canary *See:* Goldfinch.

Wild carrot, also called Queen Anne's lace, plant (*Daucus carota*) in the parsley family. This relative of the edible carrot has a root that looks like the domesticated carrot, but it is inedible. It displays a cluster of lacy white flowers on top of a tall, thin green stalk that grows to about 3 ft (91 cm) high. It is usually a biennial plant-one that lives for 2 years.

Wildcat, name given generally to any small or medium-sized wild cat, such as the Canada lynx (*Lynx canadensis*) and bobcat (*L. rufus*), which are found in North America. The true wildcat (*Felis silvestris*) is a powerful, vicious animal found in Europe and Africa. Wildcats are longer than common house cats and have shorter tails. One type of wildcat, the Egyptian cat, is probably the ancestor of the modern domestic cat.

Wilde, Oscar (1854-1900), Irish author. He achieved celebrity with the novel *The Picture of Dorian Gray* (1891) and such witty society comedies as *Lady Windermere's Fan* (1892), *An Ideal Husband* (1895), and his masterpiece, *The Importance of Being Earnest* (1895).

Wildebeest *See:* Gnu.

Wilder, Billy (1906-2002), Austrian-born U.S. screenwriter and film director. Wilder, known for his humorous treatment of serious subject matter, often dealt with topics that had not previously been considered for entertainment purposes, including alcoholism in *The Lost Weekend* (Academy Award; 1945), a prisoner-of-war camp in *Stalag 17* (1953), the Cold War in *One, Two, Three* (1961), and prostitution in *Irma La Douce*

(1963). Other works include *Double Indemnity* (1944), *Sunset Boulevard* (Academy Award; 1950), *Some Like It Hot* (1959), *The Apartment* (Academy Award; 1960), *Fedora* (1979), and *Buddy, buddy* (1981).

Wilder, Laura Ingalls (1867-1957), U.S. children's author best known for her series of 9 popular autobiographical novels, including *Little House on the Prairie* (1935), depicting pioneer life in the Midwest.

Wilder, Thornton Niven (1897-1975), U.S. novelist and playwright. His novels include *The Bridge of San Luis Rey* (1927; Pulitzer Prize) and *The Ides of March* (1948). Wilder experimented with stylized techniques in plays such as *Our Town* (1938; Pulitzer Prize), *The Skin of Our Teeth* (1942; Pulitzer Prize), and *The Matchmaker* (1954).

Wildlife conservation, organized supervision of the environment that protects the native plant and animal life. Without good environmental management many species would become extinct (killed off) or serious-

ly endangered (greatly diminished in number). Human activities have caused the decline of native species, including hunting and clearing land for crops. Plant life has become endangered through land development and industrial pollution. U.S. National Parks, first developed by President Theodore Roosevelt, protect wilderness areas. The International Union for the Conservation of Nature and Natural Resources (IUCN) has created the *Red Data Book*, a publication that reports the status of endangered species worldwide. Conservation of plants and animals is important for many reasons: their beauty, their importance in the ecological balance of an area, their scientific and medical value, their economic value to an area.

Wild rice (*Zizania aquatica*), aquatic plant of the grass family, native to the lakes and streams of North America; also, the cereal grain harvested from the plant. Wild rice is not related to rice. The grain has long been eaten by Native Americans and is now planted to feed wildfowl.

W

Species whose numbers have been decimaled by hunting and over-exploitation include the dugong (*Dugong dugon*, 21); Bengal and Siberian tigers (*Leo Panthera tigris tigris*, 22 and *L. Tigris altaica*, 23); several subspecies of leopard (*Leo Panthera pardus*, 24); the arrau (*Podocnemis expansa*, 25), a South American river turtle; the Atlantic walrus (*Odobenus rosmarus rosmarus*, 26); the blue whale (*Balaenoptera mus-* culus, 27); the European beaver (*Castor fiber*, 28); the Nile crocodile (*Crocodylus niloticus*, 29); the green turtle (*Chelonia mydas*, 30) of tropical seas; the American alligator (*Alligator mississippiensis*, 31), which is no longer in danger of extinction; the wild yak (*Bos grunniens mutus*, 32) of Tibet; the chincilla (*Chincilla laniger*, 33) of the Chilean Andes; and the snow leopard (*Uncia uncia*, 34) of central Asia.

Wilhelm, name of 2 German emperors: **Wilhelm I** (1797-1888) and **Wilhelm II** (1859-1941). The elder became the first emperor of modern Germany-crowned king of Prussia and Wilhelm I (1861)- then kaiser of Germany (1871). With the help of the prime minister, Otto von Bismarck, Germany was unified into an empire with the success of the Franco-Prussian Wars (1870-1871). The younger was the grandson of Wilhelm I and the last emperor (kaiser) of Germany. Not only did he make Germany prosperous through growth in manufacturing, trade, and colonization of parts of Africa and the Pacific, he also developed a powerful military force. Expansion and his disruption of an alliance with Russia resulted in World War I (1914-1918). With German defeat eminent, Wilhelm II moved to the neutral Netherlands where he lived out the rest of his days in exile.
See also: Germany.

Wilhelmina (1880-1962), Queen of the Netherlands (1890-1948), having acceded to the throne after the death of her father, King William III. In 1940 she fled to London to escape the German invasion, and from there directed her country's forces against Germany and Japan. Wilhelmina returned home at the end of the war (1945), and 3 years later turned the throne over to her daughter, Juliana.
See also: Netherlands.

Wilkins, Maurice Hugh Frederick (1916-), British biophysicist. He shared the 1962 Nobel Prize in physiology or medicine with biologists James D. Watson of the United States and Francis H.C. Crick of Great Britain. His research on deoxyribonucleic acid (DNA) led to the model of the molecular structure of DNA. Wilkins also worked on the development of the atomic bomb as part of the Manhattan Project in World War II.
See also: DNA.

Will, legal document by which a person (the testator) gives instructions concerning the disposal of his or her property (bequest, or

Deforestation, wetland drainage, and other forms of habitat destruction have contributed to the decline of the white-throated wallaby (*Macropus parma*, 35); the mountain gorilla (*Gorilla gorilla beringei*, 36) of central Africa; the indri (*Indri indri*, 37), a lemurlike primate of Madagascar; several subspecies of the cutthroat trout (*Salmo clarki*, 38) in the western United States; the Komodo dragon (*Varanus komodoensis*, 39), on a few Indonesian islands; the chimpanzee (*Pan trogdolytes*, 40); the Everglade kite (*Rostrhamus socialibis plumbeus*, 41); the Hawaiian gallinule (*Gallinula chloropus sandvicensis*, 42); the Indian elephant (*Elephas maximus*, 43); the woolly spider monkey (*Brachyteles arachnoides*, 44) of Brazil; the Comanche springs pupfish (*Cyprinodon elegans*, 45) of Texas; and the British swallowtail butterfly (*Papilio machaon brittanicus*, 46).

W

legacy) after death. Wills are generally prepared by lawyers. Under most jurisdictions a will must be attested in order to be legally valid: Independent witnesses who have nothing to gain under the will must attest that the signature on the will is in fact that of the testator. Wills may be revoked during the life of the testator or altered by codicils. Wills generally appoint executors to administer the estate of the deceased and carry out his or her instructions. When a person dies intestate (without making a will), the property is normally divided among the next of kin.

Willemstad (pop. 150,000), city on the Caribbean island of Curaçao, capital of the Netherlands Antilles. Arawak tribes inhabited this area before Dutch settlers arrived (1634). The island contains the Western Hemisphere's oldest Jewish cemetery (1659) and synagogue (1732). Its harbor is used for crude oil shipment. Oil refinement as well as banking are important to the economic base of Willemstad.

Willet, bird in the sandpiper family. This gray- to white-colored shore bird measures about 16 in (40 cm) long. It has a long, thin bill and long, thin legs. It also is known for its loud call. The eastern willet (*Catoptrophorus semipalmatus*) and the western willet (*C. semipalmatus inornatus*) live in both North and South America.

William, 4 kings of England. **William I**, or **William the Conqueror** (1027?-1087), duke of Normandy from 1035, became the first Norman king in 1066 by defeating Harold in the Battle of Hastings; he suppressed all opposition by 1071. William I was a harsh but capable ruler, reorganizing England's military and land-holding systems, building many castles, and creating a strong feudal government. The Domesday Book, a survey of England, was compiled by his order (1085). His son, **William II** or **Rufus** (c.1056?-1100), succeeded him in 1087. Autocratic and brutal, William II put down a rebellion by his own barons in 1088 and invaded Scotland in 1097. He quarreled with St. Anselm over the independence of the Church. He was killed (probably deliber-

A portrait of William of Orange, by Adriaan Thomasz Key (1544-after 1589). The painting, made in 1580, can be seen in the Mauritshuis in The Hague.

ately) by an arrow while hunting. He was succeeded by his brother, Henry I. **William III**, or **William of Orange** (1650-1702), was *stadholder* (ruler) of Holland (1672-1702) and king of England (1689-1702). He married Mary, Protestant daughter of the Roman Catholic king of England, in 1677. English Protestants, unhappy with James II, invited William to invade England, which resulted in the so-called Glorious Revolution (1688). William became coruler of England with his wife after they accepted the Bill of Rights, which reduced their power (1689). William ruled alone after Mary's death (1694) and was succeeded by Queen Anne. **William IV** (1765-1837) succeeded his brother George IV in 1830. He exercised little political influence and was succeeded by his niece Victoria.
See also: United Kingdom.

William I (1772-1843), king of the Netherlands (1815-1840) and son of William V, Prince of Orange and last governor of the Dutch Republic. After the French invaded the Dutch Republic and ousted William V in 1795, William lived in England and Prussia (northern Germany) until 1812. In 1813 the Dutch successfully rebelled against French rule, and in 1815 William was named king of the Netherlands, which then included Belgium, Liege, and the Grand Duchy of Luxembourg. In 1830 the Belgians demanded independence from the Netherlands, but William I refused to accede to the separation. Due in part to public disapproval of his handling of the Belgium question, William I abdicated in 1840.
See also: Netherlands.

William I, prince of Orange (1533-1584), founder of the present dynasty of the Netherlands. Born in Germany, he supported the Spanish rule of the Netherlands, first under Charles V and then Philip II, until 1568. In that year the Protestant William led a revolt against the Catholic Philip and Spain's policies of religious and political repression in the Netherlands. He worked to unite all of the provinces of the Netherlands, and in 1579 the Dutch Republic consisting of 7 provinces was formed. He was outlawed by Philip II and subsequently assassinated.
See also: Netherlands.

William of Ockham (c.1285-1349), also spelled *Occam*, English philosopher, member of the Franciscan order. Like other great thinkers of the Middle Ages, he was a Scholastic-one who uses reason to understand faith. He broke, though, with other great Scholastics-especially the church-supported St. Thomas Aquinas. Ockham did not believe that reason could deepen understanding of faith. He did advance ideas associated with modern scientific thought in that he believed conclusions should be drawn from things observed by the senses and reasoned through logic. The saying 'less is more' describes Ockham's Razor-the belief that a problem should be stated as simply as possible and supported with appropriate evidence. Pope John XXII brought charges of false theological teaching, or heresy, to William of Ockham (1324), which resulted

in Ockham's self-imposed exile to Bavaria (1328).
See also: Scholasticism.

Williams, Betty (1943-), Northern Irish peace activist. Williams set up the Northern Irish peace movement together with Mairead Corrigan. Both housewives received the Nobel Prize for Peace in 1976 for their initiative.

Williams, Emlyn (1905-1987), Welsh actor and playwright, noted for his semiautobiographical play *The Corn is Green* (1938) and for his concert readings from the works of Dylan Thomas and Charles Dickens. He also wrote *Night Must Fall* (1935).

Williams, Ted (Theodore Samuel Williams; 1918-), U.S. baseball player. Considered one of the greatest hitters in baseball history, he was the last major leaguer to achieve a .400 season batting average (.406 in 1941), finishing with a .344 career average. Williams, an outfielder, led the American League in hitting 6 times (1941, 1942, 1947, 1948, 1957, 1958) and won the Most Valuable Player award twice (1946, 1949). He played in the major leagues for the Boston Red Sox (1939-1942; 1946-1951; 1954-1960) and was inducted into the National Baseball Hall of Fame in 1966.

Williams, Tennessee (Thomas Lanier Williams; 1911-1983), U.S. playwright. His emotionally intense plays are full of brilliant, poetic dialogue and deal with the effects of failure, loneliness, and futile obsessions on human beings. His first success, *The Glass Menagerie* (1945), was followed by *A Streetcar Named Desire* (1947) and *Cat on a Hot Tin Roof* (1955), both of which received Pulitzer Prizes. Other plays include *Sweet Bird of Youth* (1959) and *The Night of the Iguana* (1961).

Williams, Venus (1980-), American tennis player, made her debut in professional tennis at the young age of 15. Since then she has risen quickly through the rankings after reaching the quarterfinals of two ATP tournaments in 1997. In 1998 she won two tournaments and reached the quarterfinals of the French Open championship and Wimbledon. During Wimbledon she broke Brenda Schultz's record for the fastest service with a serve of 131 mph (211 km/h). She won the Grand Slam Titles of Wimbledon and the U.S. Open in 2000 and 2001. She lost the 2002 finale of Roland Garros to her sister, Serena. In 1999 Venus and Serena won the doubles title at the French Open championships. Venus was the first African-American to reach the number one ranking in either the men's or women's game.

Williams, William Carlos (1883-1963), U.S. poet. Williams was a practicing doctor and specialized in the care of children for over 40 years. He is best known for the long, reflective poem *Paterson* (1946-1958) and *Pictures from Breughel* (1963), which won a Pulitzer Prize. He also wrote plays, fiction, and essays, including *In the American Grain* (1925), a study of the American character. Williams wrote hard, clear free verse emphasizing the importance of the subject matter over literary form.

William the Conqueror *See:* William.

Will-o'-the-wisp, or jack-o-lantern, blue light caused by the natural combustion of gas from decaying matter. It is sometimes visible at night over marshes and graveyards. Also called *ignis fatuus* ('foolish fire'), it was once believed to be an evil spirit that enticed travellers with its elusive glow.

Willow, common name for about 300 species of trees of the genus *Salix*, which occur from the tropics to the Arctic. The leaves are generally swordlike, and male and female catkins are borne on separate plants. The willows of the temperate zone are large, but the dwarf willow, found beyond the tree lines of the Arctic, grows to only about 6 in (15.2 cm). The long, pliable twigs of some species are cut regularly for use in making wicker baskets and furniture. Other species are used for tannins or for their light and durable wood. The ornamental weeping willow is a native of China and southwest Asia.

Willow herb *See:* Fireweed.

Wills, Helen Newington (1906-1997), U.S. tennis player. Known for her strength and grace, she won 7 U.S. Open singles titles (1923-1925, 1927-1929, 1931), 8 Wimbledon championships (1927-1930, 1932, 1933, 1935, 1938), and 4 French Open titles (1928-1930, 1932).

Wilson, Angus (1913-1991), English novelist and short-story writer who satirizes English class attitudes and social life. His novels include *Hemlock and After* (1952), *Anglo-Saxon Attitudes* (1956), *No Laughing Matter* (1967), and *Setting the World on Fire* (1980).

Wilson, Edmund (1895-1972), U.S. critic and writer who investigated the historical, sociological, and psychological background to literature. His prolific imaginative and critical output includes *Axel's Castle* (1931), a study of symbolism; *To the Finland Station* (1940), on the intellectual sources of the Russian Revolution; *The Wound and the Bow* (1941), on neurosis and literature; the explosive novel *Memoirs of Hecate County* (1949); and *Patriotic Gore* (1962), a study of Civil War literature.

Wilson, Harold (1916-1995), prime minister of Great Britain (1964-1970, 1974-1976). An Oxford economist, he entered Parliament in 1945, became president of the Board of Trade in 1947, and became leader of the Labour Party in 1963. Identified initially with the left wing and known for his tactical skill, he preserved party unity during a period of economic crisis and division over the Common Market. He resigned in 1976 and was knighted that same year and was made a life peer in 1983.
See also: United Kingdom.

Wilson, Robert (1941-), American avant-garde theater director, originally a painter and architect. His productions are characterized by extreme slow motion, repetition techniques, and non discursive use of language, creating a stream of images and sounds without meaning. The audience is reduced to a state of consciousness that approaches a dream state. Made a big impression in Europe with *Deafman's Glance* (1970) and the opera *Einstein on the Beach* (1976, in collaboration with the minimalist composer Philip Glass). In 1983 he created the first part of the big international project *The Civil Wars*. Has since moved more in the direction of orthodox, narrative drama.

Wilson, Woodrow (1856-1924), 28th president of the United States (1913-1921). Democrat. Governor of New Jersey (1910-1912). As president, Wilson pursued a progressive national policy (New Freedom): the first legislation concerning social security, recognition of trade unions, introduction of income tax, and government regulation of banking. He detailed his desire to achieve world peace, 'the 14 points of Wilson', in a speech in 1918. He called for the right of self-determination for all people and the abolition of secret diplomacy. His points were partially used as the basic principles for the League of Nations. However, the peace accord and the U.S.'s membership of the League of Nations were not ratified by the American Senate. Wilson was awarded the Nobel Prize for Peace in 1919.

Wilson cloud chamber, instrument that makes radiation visible and measurable. This device is made out of a container, a piston, and water-concentrated gas. It works on the same principle as natural cloud formation-that is, when more than 100% humidity occurs and water cools, water droplets become apparent either in the form of a cloud in the sky or, in the case of the Wilson cloud chamber, as tracks of charged particles. Particles with an electric charge within the chamber join with molecules of the cooled gas to form the visible tracks. Alpha and beta rays emitted from radioactive materials form these visible streaks.
See also: Radiation.

William the Conquerer (right) hands over his orders to messengers. A fragment of the fa- mous Bayeux tapestry, which depicts the invasion of England by the Normans in 1066. The tapestry dates from the 11th century and is invaluable as a source of the history of the Early Middle Ages.

Wilt, condition where plants droop and wither due to lack of water in their cells. This can be caused by lack of available moisture, physiological disorders, or fungi or bacteria damaging water-conducting tissues inside roots or stems.

Wimbledon *See:* Tennis.

Winch, device facilitating the hoisting or hauling of loads. It comprises a rotatable drum around which is wound a rope or cable attached to the load. The drum is turned by means of a hand-operated crank or a motor.

Winchester (pop. 94,000), English town, site of the famous 14th-century Winchester Cathedral, the longest church (556 ft/169 m) in England. During the reign of Alfred the Great (871-899) Winchester became a center of learning. It was the seat of government for the Danish king Canute (1016-1035). Today Winchester is a prosperous religious, service, and light industry center.

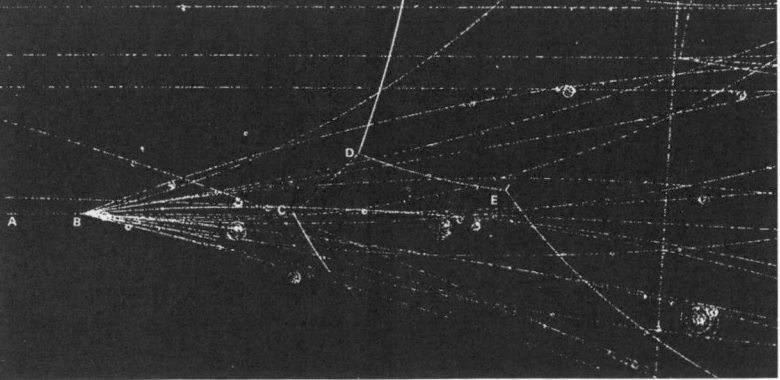

An elementary particle (A) that has entered a cloud chamber, has caused an improbable number of collisions there. The cloud tracks indicate that in (B) 15 pi- ons and one proton have been knocked loose. One of these particles, then collides three more times (C, D, and E). However, this is so unlikely, that we can be practically certain that this will never happen. Quantum mechanics, used to calculate the course of events for processes like these, is a theory that can predict the probability of a certain result. Nature can always extricate itself from this, by allowing things to happen that were thought to be extremely unlikely.

W

Johann Joachim Winckelmann (1717-1768), portrayed by Anton Raphael Mengs (1728-1799). Winckelmann is shown holding one of his favourite works, Homer's *Iliad* (Metropolitan Museum, New York).

Winckelmann, Johann Joachim (1717-1768), German scholar, founder of archeology and art history. He demonstrated that art can reveal the history of a culture just as writing does. As a youngster he studied Greek and Latin in order to read Homer and other classical writers. His principal work, *The History of Ancient Art* (1764), is still used by art historians.
See also: Archeology.

Wind, body of air moving in relation to the earth's surface. The world's major wind systems are set up to counter the equal heating of the earth's surface and are modified by the rotation of the earth.

Wind chill, index that determines the relative temperature, based on the effects of wind on exposed human flesh. An increase in wind speed increases the rate at which a person becomes chilled. Thus, the temperature will seem to be colder when there is wind than when there is not. Wind chill measurements are not exact, but they do reflect more how a person feels the cold than a thermometer reading of temperature alone.

Windermere, lake in the northwestern Cumbria section of England, better known as the Lake District. This, the largest lake in England, measures 10.5 mi (16.9 km) long and 1 mi (1.6 km) at its widest point, with a total area of 5.69 sq mi (14.7 sq km). It is a popular resort area described in the poetry of the 19th-century English romantic poets William Wordsworth and Samuel Coleridge, among others.

Windhoek (pop. 115,000), capital and largest city of Namibia, as well as its commercial, administrative, and communications center. Windhoek was originally called Aigams ('hot water')-a reference to the

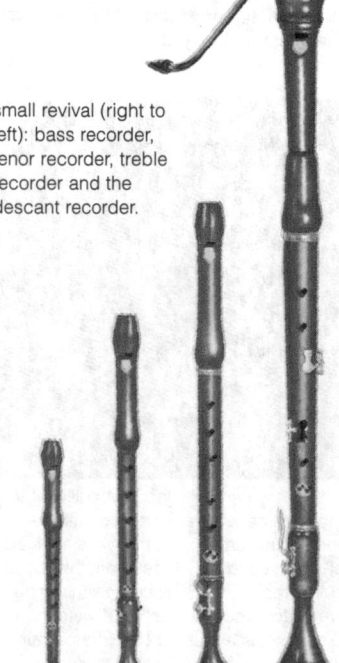

The recorders, members of the woodwind family without reeds. The sound is produced by blowing vertically into the mouthpiece. The recorder family is softer in tone than the flutes and superseded by them, though recently enjoying a small revival (right to left): bass recorder, tenor recorder, treble recorder and the descant recorder.

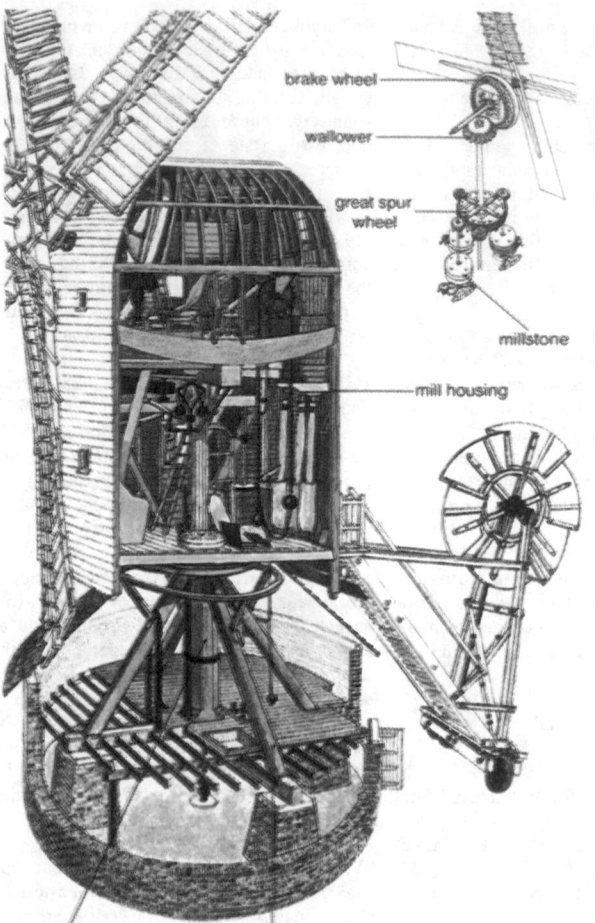

brake wheel

wallower

great spur wheel

millstone

mill housing

center post

crosstree

This traditional flour mill is supported by a vertical center post around which the entire mill revolves. The center post usually is about 31 in (80 cm) square and about 19.8 ft (6 m) high and weighs up to 3,300 lb (1.5 kg). Four posts, or crosstrees, below the mill housing support the center post. The sail mechanism (detail) of the post mill is connected to the grinding stones by means of wheels and gears. The fantail at the rear turns two vertical iron shafts that connect the two fantail wheels. When sidewinds turn the fantail, and thus the wheels, the mill is brought around so the sails face into the wind again.

area's hot springs. In the late 1880s Germany occupied the city, but it was taken over by South African forces in World War I. Until Namibia's independence in 1990, the white government of South Africa ruled Namibia, and apartheid was strictly enforced. While the population of Windhoek is mostly black, the whites controlled the politics and economy of the city until 1990.
See also: Namibia.

Wind instrument, any of the musical instruments whose sound is produced by blowing air into a tube, causing a vibration within it. In *woodwind* instruments the vibration is made either by blowing across or into a specially shaped mouthpiece, as with the flute, piccolo, recorder, and flageolet, or by blowing against a single or double reed, as in the clarinet, saxophone, oboe, English horn, and bassoon. The pitch is altered by opening and closing holes set into the tube. In *brass* instruments the vibration is made by the player's lips on the mouthpiece. The bugle and various types of posthorn have a single, unbroken tube. The cornet, French horn, trumpet, and tuba have valves to vary the effective tube length and increase the range of notes; the trombone has a slide mechanism for the same purpose.

Windlass, compound machine made from a rope or chain wound around a cylinder shape attached to a crank. This wheel and axle design is commonly used to lift water from wells. A container attached to the end of the

rope or chain collects the well water. Human power or machine power hoists up the container and line.

Windmill, machine that performs work by harnessing wind power. In the traditional windmill the power applied to a horizontal shaft by 4 large radiating sails is transmitted to milling or pumping machinery housed in a sizable supporting structure. The windmill's modern counterpart is the wind turbine, often seen in rural areas. Here a multi-bladed turbine wheel mounted on a steel derrick or mast and pointed into the wind by a fantail drives a pump or electric generator.

Window, building openings for air and light. Some windows open inward or outward from the opening, and these are called *casement* or *hinged* windows. Many windows are double-hung and are opened by lifting them up or pushing them down, and these are called *double-hung* windows. Double-hung windows were a Dutch invention (1800s). The arrangement of windows-known as *fenestration*-in a building is an important part of its overall design. Stained-glass windows, in which colored bits of glass within metal frames create a picture or pattern, were an important part of church design from the Middle Ages.

Windsor, name of the ruling dynasty of the United Kingdom of Great Britain and Northern Ireland, adopted by King George V in 1917 to replace the royal family's German

name, Saxe-Coburg-Gotha (from Albert Wettin, Queen Victoria's husband), when anti-German feeling was high.
See also: United Kingdom.

Windsor, Duke of *See:* Edward.

Windsor Castle, principal residence of British sovereigns since the 11th century. Begun by William I, it stands about 20 mi (32 km) west of London. The Round Tower, built in 1180, is the castle's center, and St. George's Chapel (1528) is a fine example of English Perpendicular architecture.

Windsurfing, water sport in which an individual rides a *sailboard*, a surfboard with a central mast to which a sail is attached. The sail is turned by the rider to steer. The *sailsurfer* uses a board up to 7 ft (2.1 m) long, riding waves as in surfing. The *sailboarder* uses a longer board (up to 12 ft/3.7 m) and depends on wind as in sailing.

Wind tunnel, structure in which a controlled stream of air is produced in order to observe the effects on scale models or full-size components of airplanes, missiles, automobiles, or such structures as bridges and skyscrapers. An important research tool in aerodynamics, the wind tunnel enables a design to be accurately tested without the risks attached to full-scale trials. Hypersonic wind tunnels, operating on an impulse principle, can simulate the frictional effects of flight at over 5 times the speed of sound.
See also: Aerodynamics.

Windward Islands, group of islands in the Lesser Antilles, West Indies, stretching toward Venezuela. They include St. Lucia, St. Vincent, the Grenadines, Grenada, and Martinique. The area is about 950 sq mi (2,461 sq km) and the islands produce bananas, cacao, limes, nutmeg, and cotton. Tourism is an important industry.

Wine, alcoholic beverage made from fermented grape juice; wines made from other fruits are always named accordingly. Table wines are red, rosé, or white in color; red wines are made from dark grapes, the skins being left in the fermenting mixture; white

wines may be made from dark or pale grapes, the skins being removed. The grapes–normally varieties of *Vitis vinifera*–are allowed to ripen until they attain suitable sugar content-18% or more-and acidity (in cool years or northern areas, sugar may have to be added). After crushing, they undergo fermentation in large tanks, during which time a small amount of sulfur dioxide is added to inhibit growth of wild yeasts and bacteria. When the alcohol and sugar content is right, the wine is cellared, racked off the lees (from which argol is obtained), clarified by filtration or fining (adding absorbent substances such as bentonite, gelatin, and isinglass), aged in the wood, and bottled. Sweet wines contain residual sugar; dry wines little or none. The alcohol content of table wines varies from 8% to 14% by volume. Sparkling wines-notably Champagne-are made by secondary fermentation under pressure, in bottles or in tanks. Fortified wines, or dessert wines-including sherry, port, and Madeira-have brandy added during or after fermentation and contain about 20% alcohol. Vermouth is a fortified wine flavored with wormwood and other herbs. Major wine-producing areas of the world include France, Germany, Spain, Portugal, Italy, and California.

Winged bull, mythic beast of ancient Assyria, frequently appearing in paintings and statues. The beast, which originated c.1000 B.C., had a man's head on a winged

bull's body. Enormous portal statues of winged bulls were used as guardians of palaces, to frighten away enemies and evil spirits.
See also: Mythology.

Winged lion, mythic beast of ancient Babylonia and Assyria, represented in paintings and statues. The beast had a man's head on a winged lion's body. Enormous winged lion statues were placed at a city's gate or the entranceway to a palace to frighten off harmful spirits or humans.
See also: Mythology.

Winged Victory, Greek sculpture dated c.180 B.C. depicting Nike, the goddess of victory, bringing a message of victory from the gods. The sculptor is unknown. In 1863 the statue, broken into 118 pieces, was discovered by a French archeologist. The statue was reconstructed; it stands today in the Louvre Museum in Paris.

Winkler, Hans Günther (1926-), West German showjumper, was successful at all major showjumping tournaments. During his long career he won one bronze medal and five gold medals (in both individual and team events) at the Olympics from 1956 to 1972, was world champion twice (1954, 1955), and European champion (1987). Winkler was most successful on the mare Halla, although this horse had originally been trained for racing.

In modern winegrowing, large machines are taking care of weeding, fertilizing, etc. Riding high over the vines, they guarantee optimal accessibility to the plants.

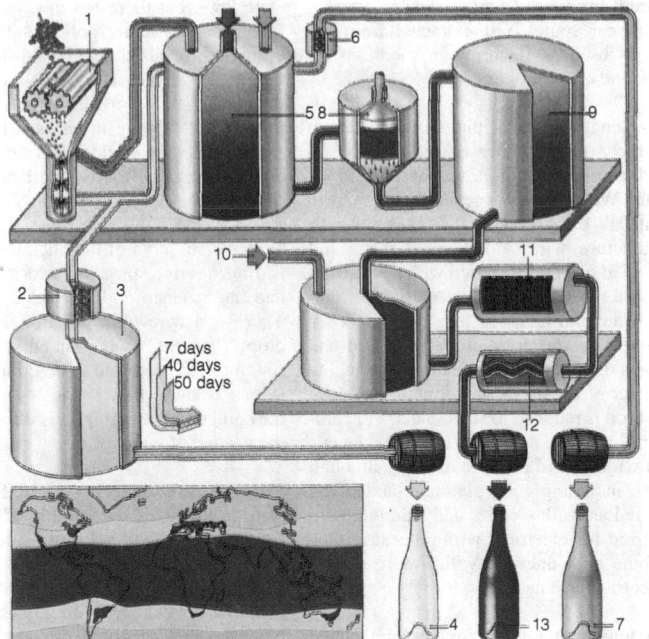

Wine manufacturing processes vary in detail with the type of wine required. The basic reaction however, involves the fermentation of grape sugar into alcohol and carbondioxide, incited by yeast. The grapes are crushed, the stalks and skin are removed (1), the pulp and juice are piped away. In order to obtain white wine, the pulp and juice mixture is being filtered (2), and the filtrate is passed into a vat (3). The type of wine indicates the duration of the fermentation process: sweet wine is being drawn off and bottled (4) after about a week, sparkling and dry wines are being bottled after 40 or 50 days, respectively. For red and rose wines, grapeskins, stalks, more yeast and sulphurdioxide are being added in the fermenting vat (5). After some time, rose wine is being drawn off, filtered (6) and bottled (7). The remainder of the fluid is drawn off through a filter press (8), for a second period of fermentation (9). When this time is complete, finings are added (10), to purify the wine, which is then filtered (11) and sometimes pasteurized (12), before being bottled (13). On the map, you can see the regions of the world where wine producing grapes are grown. Vines are extremely sensitive to the effects of humidity and temperature, and are thus restricted to these geographical zones. Purple indicates the major grape-growing areas.

W

Winnipeg (pop. 652,000), capital city of Manitoba, Canada, on the Red and Assiniboine rivers. The Canadian transcontinental railroad goes through this city in the center of the country. Along with a network of highways, this made Winnipeg an important distribution location for Canada in the past. At the time of French settlement (1738), fur trading was the base of the Winnipeg economy. Because of its location in the wheat belt, the city became home to Canada's grain market. Early in the 20th century, with cross-continental access, the population of the area grew. At the same time it developed as a major manufacturing center. Today the city is a center for culture and finance as well as trade and industry, with a symphony orchestra, theater center, art museum, and planetarium. The city was originally inhabited by Cree and Assiniboine Native Americans, and the population of Winnipeg today contains a large number of people of Native American ancestry.
See also: Manitoba.

Winterberry, shrub in the holly family. The winterberry (*Ilex verticillata*) displays red berries in November. It grows between 6 and 12 ft (2 and 4 m), usually in swampy areas in the eastern United States.

Wintergreen, plant in the heath family. This ground creeper shows pink globe-shaped flowers or bright red berries. The shiny leaves are grouped at the end of upright red-colored branches, whose leaves remain green year round. Oil extracted from the plant is used as flavoring in foods, medicines, and chewing gum.

Wire, length of metal that has been drawn out into a thread. Wire is usually flexible, circular in cross-section, and uniform in diameter. Wire diameters generally range from about 0.001 to 0.5 in (0.025-12.7 mm). To manufacture wire, a hot-rolled metal rod pointed at one end is coated with a lubricant, threaded through a tungsten, carbide, or diamond die, and attached to a drum called a *draw block*. The draw block is rotated and wire-its diameter (gauge) determined by the diameter of the die-is drawn until the entire metal rod is reduced to steel. Steel, iron, aluminum, copper, and bronze are the metals most widely used for wire making, although others, including gold, platinum, and silver, are used as well. Copper and aluminum are preferred for electrical wiring because they combine high ductility with low resistance to electric current.

Wire glass, glass with wire mesh embedded in it to provide reinforcement for use in doors and windows. Usually 1/4-3/4 in (6-18 mm) thick, it may be produced by pressing the wire between 2 sheets of glass (Appert process), by pressing the wire into a single sheet (Shuman process), or by pouring molten glass over the mesh.

Wirehaired pointing griffon, hunting dog first bred in the Netherlands in the late 1800s. A slow, deliberate hunter, it points its body toward the location of the game. The griffon stands 19-23 in (48-58 cm) high and

Witches waylaying a saint. Painting by Goya, in the Lazaro Galdiàno Museum in Madrid.

weighs 50-60 lb (23-27 kg). Its rough coat is steel gray and chestnut brown in color.

Wiretapping, interception of telephone conversations without the knowledge of those communicating. Wiretapping and the use of other 'bugging' devices by private citizens are prohibited by U.S., federal, and state laws, but there has always been argument about whether police and other government officials should be able to use wiretapping to detect crimes and collect evidence. In 1968 Congress passed a law allowing wiretapping to be used in cases involving national security and certain serious crimes, provided that a court order is first obtained.

Wireworm, larva of the click beetle, which is often a serious pest. Wireworms are brown and hardskinned and are found in the soil. There is a wireworm pest for nearly every crop: They eat newly planted seeds or burrow into the roots and underground parts of stems. Because they spend several years in the soil before pupating, it is difficult to free the ground of wireworms.

Wisconsin (Badger State; pop. 5,038,000), state in the U.S., bordered by Upper Lake, Lake Michigan, Illinois, Iowa, and Minnesota; 56,175 sq mi (145,436 sq km). Capital, Maddison. The largest city is the port of Milwaukee. Rolling landscape with many lakes. The climate is wet and continental; the summers are warm in the south, elsewhere cool. The average July temperatures are 22°C; in January the average temperatures are as low as -8°C. The state is an important producer of dairy products; there is also cultivation of maize, potatoes, tobacco, and vegetables. Heavy industry is located mainly around Milwaukee. Extraction of sand, gravel, stone, and zinc. The area was under French rule until 1763, thereafter British. Since 1783 part of the U.S.; became a member of the Union in 1848.

Wisdom of Solomon, book of the Old Testament Apocrypha, traditionally ascribed to Solomon but probably written in the 2nd or 1st century B.C. An example of wisdom literature (pre-Christian Jewish philosophical writings), it praises wisdom and outlines God's care for the Jews.
See also: Old Testament.

Wisteria, plant in the pea family. Blue- to white-colored clusters of flowers blossom on this lacy-looking vine, which may grow to more than 35 ft (11 m) long. The Chinese wisteria (*Wisteria sinensis*) is commonly found in gardens throughout the United States while other species of this vine are native to the eastern portion of the country.

Witchcraft, manipulation of supernatural forces, usually toward evil ends. It has existed in most cultures throughout history and still has its devotees in modern society. In the Christian West witchcraft developed from surviving pagan beliefs. Witches were held responsible for disease and misfortune and were believed to acquire their evil power from the devil, whom they worshiped in obscene ritual (satanism, or devil worship, is not synonymous with witchcraft). From the 14th to the 18th century a witch-hunting epidemic prevailed in Europe, and many thousands of innocent people were tortured and executed in fanatical and hysterical persecutions.

Witch hazel, low tree or shrub (genus *Hamamelis*) growing in eastern North America and eastern Asia. It produces its small, yellow flowers in the autumn, when the leaves have fallen. A year later the seeds ripen and are thrown 20 ft (6.2 m) or more when the pods dry up and contract suddenly. Extracts from its bark and leaves are used in aftershave lotions and lotions for treating bruises.

Witenagemot, group of counselors to the Anglo-Saxon king. Before the king's court (*curia regis*) was established by the Norman conquerors of England (1066), these men partook in decisions to make war, grant lands, make important appointments in the court or church, and so on. They even had the power to dethrone a king during conflicts involving various claims to the throne. *Thanes*, or followers, of the king along with earls, bishops, and abbots were members of the witenagemot, which in translation means 'a meeting of wise men.'

Witness, individual who testifies under oath in a legal proceeding or acts as a signer of a legal document. In giving testimony, a witness provides a court of law with information about persons or events relating to a particular case. A witness is criminally liable if he or she fails to appear in court or lies under oath. Certain individuals, such as children, are exempted from giving testimony.

Witt, Katarina (1966-), East German figure skater, won her first European title in 1983. In 1984 and 1988 she was world, European, and Olympic champion. In 1985 and in 1987 she also won the world and European titles. In 1986 she became

European champion, but lost her world title to the American Debi Thomas. She skated a better free program than compulsory program, helped by her elegant technique and her enthusiastic performance which led to her success. After she stopped competitive sport in 1988, she performed in the Holiday on Ice revue.

Wittgenstein, Ludwig (1889-1951), Austrian philosopher whose two chief works, *Tractatus Logico-philosophicus* (1921) and the posthumous *Philosophical Investigations* (1953), have profoundly influenced the course of much British and U.S. philosophy. The *Tractatus* dwells on the logical nature and limits of language, understood as 'picturing' reality. The *Investigations* rejects the assumption in the *Tractatus* that all representations must share a common logical form and instead relates the meanings of sentences to their uses in particular contexts: Philosophical problems are attributed to misuses of language. Wittgenstein was professor of philosophy at Cambridge University, England (1929-1947).
See also: Philosophy.

Witwatersrand, or the Rand, gold-bearing rocky ridge in southern Transvaal, South Africa. It produces one-third of the world's gold output and is South Africa's major industrial region, with Johannesburg located at its center. Soweto township also lies in the Rand.
See also: South Africa.

Wodehouse, P.G. (Sir Pelham Grenville Wodehouse; 1881-1975), English writer of humorous novels and short stories. His writings, set in the early 1900-1920s, portray life in the upper class. Wodehouse's best known novels, *Carry On Jeeves* (1925) and *The Code of the Woosters* (1938), relate the humorous predicaments of the dim-witted Bertie Wooster and his ever-sensible valet, Jeeves. Other works include *A Pelican at Blandings* (1969) and lyrics for such musical comedies as *Leave It to Jane* (1917) and *Rosalie* (1928). Wodehouse became a U.S. citizen (1955) and was knighted in England (1975).

Woden *See:* Odin.

Wöhler, Friedrich (1800-1882), German chemist, the first to synthesize an organic substance (urea) from inorganic chemicals. He isolated the element beryllium, and was the first to measure the gravity of aluminum. Along with chemist Justus von Liebig, he developed an early theory of the structure of organic compounds.
See also: Chemistry.

Wolf (*Canis lupus*), powerful carnivore ranging throughout the deciduous and coniferous forests and tundra of the Northern Hemisphere. Broad-chested, with small, pointed ears and long legs, wolves are pack hunters, preying on the huge northern moose, deer, and elk herds. In the summer, with the onset of the breeding season and with small-mammal prey more readily available, the packs break up into smaller groups.

Wolf packs have distinct territories, and within the pack there is a complex social structure under a top male and female.

Wolf, Christa (1929-), German writer. Was an important 'gesamtdeutsch' author, writing for both parts of Germany. The novel *Divided Heaven* (1963) dealt with the problem of the two Germanies. For many people Christa Wolf embodied the resistance against a socialist society in which ideology dominated all aspects of life. This caused her to be in regular conflict with the authorities. Other important works by her include *The Quest for Christa T.* (1969), *Patterns of Childhood* (1976) *No Place on Earth* (1979), *Cassandra* (1983), *On the Way to Taboo* (1994), and *Medea: a Modern Retelling* (1995).

Wolf, Hugo Philipp Jakob (1860-1903), an Austrian composer. He has been called one of the greatest composers of the German art song, or *lied*. Wolf was highly original and had a keen dramatic sense. Many of his songs are miniature music dramas. He composed more than 200 songs for poems of Mörike, Goethe, and others. Wolf studied at the Vienna Conservatory. He lived in near poverty most of his life as his works were not recognized until after his death. His works include: *Mörike Songs* (1888), *Spanish Song-Book* (1890-1891; 1896), *Italian Serenade* (1892), for orchestra.

Wolfe, James (1727-1759), British general whose capture of Quebec was the decisive victory in the last of the French and Indian Wars. He fought in the War of the Austrian Succession (1742-1745) and at Falkirk and Culloden Moor in the Jacobite rebellion (1745-1746). Second in command under Amherst (1758), he distinguished himself in the capture of Louisburg and was chosen to lead the attack on Quebec. By brilliant strategy, aided by good luck, he routed the French but died during the battle.
See also: French and Indian Wars.

Wolfe, Thomas Clayton (1900-1938), U.S. novelist whose works constitute an autobiographical epic. *Look Homeward, Angel* (1929), *Of Time and the River* (1935), and the posthumous works *The Web and the Rock* (1939) and *You Can't Go Home Again* (1940) are rich in detail and characterization and capture the author's vividly felt sense of place.

Wolfe, Tom (Thomas Kennerly Wolfe, Jr.; 1931-), a United States journalist and author. His flamboyant style of reporting is characterized by the use of slang, made-up words, and unorthodox punctuation. He was influential in the New Journalism movement. Wolfe's writings satirize American society while deftly capturing the mood of the times by portraying pop culture. *The Electric Kool-Aid Acid Test* (1968), one of his bestknown novels, records his travels with Ken Kesey and the Merry Pranksters, a group of hippies. The book describes the group's search for self-realization through psychedelic drug use, bohemian living, and cross-country travel.
Wolfe was born in Richmond, Virginia. He

received a B.A. from Washington and Lee University and a Ph.D. from Yale. Several of his books are illustrated with his own drawings.
Collections of Wolfe's essays include *The Kandy-Kolored Tangerine-Flake Streamline Baby* (1965), *The Pump House Gang* (1968), *Radical Chic and Mau-Mauing the Flak Catchers* (1970), and *In Our Time* (1980). *The Painted Word* (1975) and *From Bauhaus to Our House* (1981) are critiques of modern art and modern architecture respectively. The novels *The Right Stuff* (1979) and *The Bonfire of the Vanities* (1987) were made into motion pictures.

Wolffish, fish belonging to the Anarhichadidae family that lives in the northern Atlantic and Pacific oceans. It is known for its strong jaws and teeth, and for attacking its capturers, causing painful injury. The Atlantic wolffish measures up to 3 ft (91 cm) in length; the Pacific variety can grow to almost 8 ft (2.4 m) in length. It is a popular eating fish, and its tough skin is sometimes used for leather-type goods.

Wolfhound, family of hunting dogs consisting of three breeds. The borzoi, or Russian wolfhound, was first used by 17th-century Russian tsars to hunt wolves. The Irish wolfhound was first bred by the Celts and later imported to Ireland by the Romans. The Scottish deerhound, a descendent of the staghound, was once used for hunting deer. Wolfhounds are fiercely loyal and can make good companion dogs if they are given enough space for long, unrestricted runs.

Wolfram *See:* Tungsten.

Wolframite, brownish-black mineral derived from tungsten. It is commonly found in the veins in and around granite. Major ore deposits are located in England, the former USSR, China, and Australia. Wolframite is used commercially in the production of electronic and industrial equipment.

Wolfram von Eschenbach (1170?-1220?), a German epic poet and minnesinger. His poem *Parzival*, about the quest for the Holy Grail, is a classic of Middle High German literature and was the basis for the libretto of Wagner's opera *Parsifal*. Little is known of Wolfram's life.

Wollongong (pop. 253,000), city located in the state of New South Wales on the southeast coast of Australia. Founded in 1816, it achieved status as a city in 1942. Because of nearby coal deposits, it has become a major industrial and shipping center; its industries include coal mining, iron and steel production, chemicals, and processed foods. The city includes many examples of 19th-century Victorian and Georgian architecture.

Wollstonecraft, Mary (1759-1797), British author and feminist. Her influential book, *A Vindication of the Rights of Woman* (1792), was based on the egalitarian principles of the French Revolution and promoted the cause of equal rights for women. She also wrote other essays, translations, and stories that focused attention on the role of women in so-

W

ciety. Harshly critical of the notion that women were intellectually inferior to men, she was a strong believer in equal educational opportunities for women. She died shortly after the birth of her daughter, Mary Wollstonecraft Shelley, author of the novel *Frankenstein.*

Wolsey, Thomas (1473?-1530), Roman Catholic cardinal and politician. He became a political power during the reign of King Henry VIII, wielding great influence in both church and state matters; however, he fell into sudden disrepute due to his disapproval of Henry VIII's decision to divorce Catherine of Aragon and marry Anne Boleyn. Criticisms of his opulent way of life contributed to a growing desire for clerical reform.

Wolverine (*Gulo gulo*), large terrestrial carnivore of the weasel family, weighing up to 54 lb (24.5 kg). They live in tundra regions, the males defending a home range of up to 100 sq mi (259 sq km). Fierce animals, wolverines feed on insects, fish, small mammals, and carrion, although they have been known to attack big game, such as elk.

Wolverine State *See:* Michigan.

Woman suffrage, women's lawful right to vote. Under the U.S. Constitution, states initially gave voting rights to land-holding white men only. By 1830, although all states had abolished property requirements for white men, no state allowed women to vote. In the 19th century, as a result of changing social conditions and new ideas about equality, the movement for woman suffrage took shape; however, the efforts of such activists as Elizabeth Cady Stanton and Susan B. Anthony were strongly opposed. The 15th Amendment, which gave the vote to black men, still did not grant voting rights to women. During the early 20th century, an extensive and highly organized campaign to win congressional support for woman suffrage began. By 1920 more than half the states had granted either full or partial voting

The headquarters of the suffragettes, in the American state of Ohio, in 1912. Women's suffrage was at that time the subject of one of the amendments to the new Constitution of the state. It was not passed, however. The moderate American suffragettes tried to obtain their goals by influencing the public opinion and by distributing information.

rights to women. With the passage of the 19th Amendment in 1920, women in the United States were given full voting rights. Women in 27 countries were also granted voting rights during the period following World War I. In 1952 the United Nations Convention on the Voting Rights of Women resolved that all women be entitled to vote in all elections.
See also: Women's movement.

Wombat, heavy, stockily built, burrowing marsupial of Australia, closely related to the koala. Wombats share many anatomical features with placental, burrowing rodents. Nocturnal animals, they emerge from their holes to feed on grasses and roots.

Women's movement, Movement that campaigns for an improvement in the position of women. As an organized entity, a women's movement can be said to have existed since the second part of the 19th century. Before that time there were individual women who campaigned for the principle of equality of the sexes. The women's movement appeared in the 19th century in what is known as the first feminist wave, and campaigned for political, social, and economic rights. After women were enfranchized, the women's movement was pushed into the background by the economic crisis of the 1930s, WW II, and the economic reconstruction in the 1940s and 50s. In the second feminist wave, which started in the 1960s, the women's movement concentrated on the personal development of women in a male dominated society. The women's movement now consists of various organizations that focus on the discrimination of women, the process of awareness in women, the change of traditional role patterns, and the sexual liberation of women, for example, by legalizing abortion.
See also: Feminism.

Wonder, Stevie (Stevland Judkins, or Morris; 1950-), U.S. composer, keyboard player, and singer of popular music, leading Motown musician of the 1970s. 'Little Stevie Wonder''s first recorded hit, 'Fingertips,' became number 1 on the pop charts when he was 13. Among his many successful albums were *Songs in the Key of Life* (1976), *Hotter than July* (1980), *In square Circle* (1985), *Characters* (1987), and *Conversation Peace* (1995). His music combines elements of gospel, soul, jazz, and African and Jamaican music. Blind from an early age, he progressed from the harmonica to keyboards, to become a highly skilled performer on synthesizers. Stevie Wonder received three Grammy's for his music in 1996, amounting to a total of 19.

Wood, hard, dead tissue obtained from the trunks and branches of trees and shrubs. Woody tissue is also found in some herbaceous plants. Botanically, wood consists of xylem tissue, which is responsible for the conduction of water around the plant. A living tree trunk is composed of (beginning from the center): the pith (remains of the primary growth); wood (xylem); cambium (a band of living cells that divide to produce new wood and phloem); phloem (conducting

Woodcarving. A Kitwancool Indian village in British Columbia, with totem poles that are typical of the Indians of the northwest coast of North America.

nutrients made in the leaves); and bark. The wood nearest the cambium is termed *sapwood* because it is capable of conducting water. However, the bulk of the wood is heartwood, in which the xylem is impregnated with lignin, which gives the cells extra strength but prevents them from conducting water. In temperate regions, a tree's age can be found by counting its annual rings. Commercially, wood is divided into hardwood (from deciduous angiosperm trees) and softwood (from gymnosperms).

Wood, Grant (1891-1942), U.S. painter, exponent of the 1930s movement known as regionalism. Influenced by Gothic and Early Renaissance painting, he realistically depicted the people and places of Iowa, as in his best-known painting, *American Gothic* (1930).

Wood alcohol *See:* Methanol.

Woodcarving, old art form involving the chiseling of wood to create designs or figures. Woodcarving has played a significant role in the religious and cultural life of many of the world's great civilizations. Notable woodcarvers throughout history have achieved status as artists. Today woodcarving involves a variety of tools, including chisels of many sizes and shapes, gouges with different types of cutting edges, and parting tools for deeper cutting. Some woodcarving is done by machine on high-speed cutters.

Woodchuck, or groundhog (*Marmota monax*), familiar ground squirrel of the woodlands of North America. A large rodent, up to 2 ft (61 cm) long, with a short, bushy tail, the woodchuck is diurnal and feeds on water animals.

Woodcock, large game bird of the snipe family. One species lives in eastern North

America and another in Europe and Asia. Woodcocks are very well camouflaged and are difficult to see against the forest floor. They become active at dusk, and the males fly up and down regular routes, croaking and whistling to establish a territory. They feed mainly on earthworms that they catch by thrusting their bills into the soil, opening just the tip to seize the worm.

Woodcut and wood engraving, techniques for producing pictures by incising a design on a block of wood, inking the design, and then pressing the inked block onto paper. Those parts of the design that are to be white are cut away and not inked, leaving in relief the areas to be printed. Woodcut is the older method, originating in China and Japan, and used in Europe from the 14th century, particularly for book illustration. Eminent artists in the medium include Albrecht Dürer, Gauguin, and Maillol. In wood engraving the artist uses a tool called a *burin*, producing a design of white lines on a black background. It became popular in the 18th and 19th centuries.

Wood duck, bird belonging to the Anatidae family and found in the wet woodlands of southern Canada and the United States. It searches for seeds and insects in the shallow waters of swamps and ponds. It is about 20 in (51 cm) in length. The male of the species has bright multicolored feathers, while the female has feathers of yellowish brown.

Wooden, John (1910-), U.S. basketball player and coach. Between 1964-1975, he led the University of California at Los Angeles (UCLA) to an unprecedented 10 National Collegiate Athletic Association (NCAA) championships, including a record 7 straight titles (1967-1973) and an 88-game winning streak (1971-1974). Wooden coached at Indiana State (1947-1948) and UCLA (1949-1975), compiling 664 career wins. A former star basketball player at the University of Purdue, he was inducted into the Basketball Hall of Fame in 1960 as both a player and a coach.

Wooden horse *See:* Trojan War.

Wood ibis (*Mycteria americana*), large wading bird found in the swamps of South and Central America and the southern United States. The wood ibis is not a true ibis, but a stork. It has a curved bill and feeds on water animals.

Wood louse, land-living crustacean. It has a flattened body and 7 pairs of legs. Wood lice live in moist places, under bark or stones, and come out at night to feed. Moisture is essential to wood lice, and they often bunch together to reduce evaporation. Pill wood lice can roll into a ball for protection against spiders and other predators.

Woodpecker, one of the family Picidae of birds specialized in obtaining insects from the trunks and branches of trees. The 210 species occur worldwide, except in Australasia. All have wedge-shaped tails that may be pressed against the trunk of a tree as a prop. The bill is strong and straight,

In 1498, Albrecht Dürer (1471-1528) published a series of 15 woodcuts, called the *Apocalypse*. This *Four Horsemen of the Apocalypse* is a detail of one of them.

and the muscles and structure of head and neck are adapted for driving the bill powerfully forward into tree bark and absorbing the shock of the blow. The tongue is long and slender for picking out insects. One group, the sapsuckers, also feeds on tree sap. Woodpeckers also use the bill during courtship 'drumming' and to hack out nesting holes in tree trunks.

Wood pewee, or Eastern pewee, woodland bird belonging to the flycatcher family. It lives in southern Canada and the eastern United States in the summer and migrates to Central America for the winter. It is a small, gray-brown bird with white bars on its wings. Its name is a reference to its distinctive song, which it sings at dawn and at dusk. The pewee feeds on insects that are known to destroy plants and crops.

Wood rat, or pack rat, any of 22 rat species belonging to the Cricetidae family and found in the mountains and deserts of North and Central America. It resembles the house rat but has softer fur, longer ears, and a furry tail. Its name derives from its habit of picking up small articles of interest and carrying them back to its den. Also known as *trade rat*, it will typically drop one object in favor of a more attractive one.

Woods, Eldrick Tiger (1975-), American golfer, became the youngest winner of the prestigious Masters tournament in Augusta (U.S.) at the age of 21 in 1997. Of African American descent, was the first non white golfer to win the Masters. He began playing serious golf at a very young age. He soon became the number one on the world-ranking list. In 1999 and 2000, he won the prestigious USA PGA Championship title. In 2000 he also won the US Open. He consecutively won the US Masters in 2001 and 2002, while in 2002, he also won the US Open and the World Golf Championship.

Woods is a master of all strokes, but his strongest point is his swing, which enables him to achieve a sublime combination of both distance and positioning.

Woods Hole Oceanographic Institution, research center for marine science located at the southwest tip of Cape Cod, Mass. Its facilities include laboratories as well as deep-sea vessels. Scientists conduct research in areas such as marine biology, physics, engineering, and chemistry. Established in 1930 as a nonprofit, independent institution, it offers programs for undergraduate, doctoral, and postdoctoral students.

Wood sorrel *See:* Shamrock.

Woodward, Robert Burns (1917-1979), U.S. chemist who won the 1965 Nobel Prize for his contributions in the field of synthetic organic chemistry. His work involved developing methods for the artificial synthesis of various chemical compounds found in nature, such as quinine, cortisone, cholesterol, and vitamin B_{12}. He was a faculty member at Harvard University from 1941 to 1979. *See also:* Organic chemistry.

Woodworking, process of making objects from wood. Such objects can be of any size and may be utilitarian (houses, furniture) or purely decorative. Many wooden objects are produced at home, and woodworking is often pursued as a hobby. By the Middle Ages the status of woodworking as a profession was formalized in organizations known as craft guilds. The use of tools to work in wood dates to about 8000 B.C. The wide variety of materials and hand tools now in use includes measuring tools (rules, squares, gauges), cutting tools (saws, chisels, planes), tools for fastening (screws, glues, hammers), and finishing tools (sandpaper, paint). Modern woodworkers such as carpenters and cabinetmakers also use power drills, saws, and other electricity-driven tools. According to the requirements of a woodworking project, wood is chosen for its hardness, pliability, durability, appearance (grain, color), and availability. *See also:* Carpentry.

Wool, animal fiber that forms the fleece, or protective coat, of sheep. Coarser than most vegetable or synthetic fibers, wool fibers are wavy and vary in color from the usual white

In New South Wales, merinos are kept for wool as well as for their meat. The total stock adds up to 180 million sheep. Australia is the largest wool producer in the world.

W

to brown or black. Wool is composed of the protein keratin, whose molecules are long, coiled chains, giving wool elasticity and resilience. Reactive side groups result in good affinity for dyes and enable new, desirable properties to be chemically imparted. Wool lasts if well cared for but is liable to be damaged by some insect larvae (which eat it), by heat, sunlight, alkalis, and hot water. It chars and smolders when burned but is not inflammable. Wool strongly absorbs moisture from the air. It is weakened when wet and liable to form felt if mechanically agitated in water. Wool has been used since ancient times to make cloth. Sheep are shorn, usually annually, and the fleeces are cleaned-the wool wax removed is the source of lanolin-and sorted, blended, carded (which disentangles the fibers and removes any foreign bodies), and combed if necessary to remove shorter fibers. A rope of woolen fibers (roving) is thus produced and is spun. The woolen yarn is woven into cloth, knitted, or made into carpets or blankets. The main wool-producing countries are Australia, New Zealand, the USSR, and India. Because the supply of new (virgin) wool is inadequate, some textiles are made of reprocessed wool.

Virginia Woolf (1882-1941), one of the most distinguished novelists and critics of the first half of the 20th century.

Woolf, Virginia (1882-1941), English novelist and essayist. The daughter of Sir Leslie Stephen, she married the critic Leonard Sidney Woolf (1880-1969), and they established the Hogarth Press (1917). Their home was the center of the Bloomsbury group. Her novels *Mrs. Dalloway* (1925), *To the Lighthouse* (1927), and *The Waves* (1931) display-using the technique of stream of consciousness-her characters' thoughts and feelings about common experiences. Some of her brilliant criticism was published in *The Common Reader* (1925). She also wrote feminist tracts, including *A Room of One's Own* (1929). Subject to fits of mental instability, she drowned herself.
See also: Bloomsbury group.

Woolly monkey, or woolly spider monkey, either of two species of monkey belonging to the New World monkey family and found in the Amazon rain forest. It is a large, heavy monkey with dark, thick fur and a prehensile tail. It moves through the trees in groups of about 12, subsisting on fruit, seeds, and leaves. Its existence is threatened due to deforestation; the yellow-tailed variety is already considered very rare.

Woolworth, name of two brothers who co-founded the F.W. Woolworth Company, an extensive chain of '5-and-10-cent' stores. **Frank Winfield Woolworth** (1852-1919) was the principal founder and **Charles S. Woolworth** (1856-1947) served as vice president and later as chairman of the board. The venture, which began in Utica, N.Y., grew out of the idea that profits could be made by selling a large assortment of goods at fixed, low prices. The company later went on to operate stores in Canada, Germany, France, and Cuba.

Word processing, use of electronic equipment to write, edit, and print documents. A word processor is basically an electronic typewriter with information storage devices similar to those of a computer and a cathode-ray-tube screen on which text is displayed. This makes it possible to edit or correct the text before it is printed out; the processor 'remembers' the corrections and prints out the final version. The processor can also make the right-hand margins even (justify them) and produce documents in any desired format. The documents can be stored on magnetic disk or tape for later use. In many newspaper offices the word-processing equipment is connected directly to electronic typesetting machines.

Wordsworth, William (1770-1850), considered to be the greatest poet of the English romantic period. Known for his descriptions of nature, he derived much of his inspiration from the northern English countryside where he lived. Along with close friend and collaborator Samuel Taylor Coleridge, he believed that poetry could come out of actual experience and be written in the language of the common person. Together, they wrote *Lyrical Ballads* (1798), a collection of poems regarded as the first great works of the romantic movement. Wordsworth completed his great autobiographical poem, *The Prelude: Growth of a Poet's Mind,* in 1805, but subjected it to constant revision for the rest of his life. The author of more than 500 sonnets, he was appointed poet laureate in 1843.

Work, in physics, alternative name for energy, used particularly in discussing mechanical processes. Work of 1 joule is done when a force of 1 newton acts through a distance of 1 meter.
See also: Joule, James Prescott.

Worker's compensation, provision by employers of medical, cash, and sometimes rehabilitation benefits for workers who are injured in accidents at work.

Works Progress Administration *See:* New Deal.

World, term used in various ways to designate a comprehensive unity. The idea or concept of a world is ancient. Numerous cultures have proposed models for the unity of all things signified by the idea of a world. In its simplest form, the idea is suggested by the containment of a horizon, with a dome of sky above, and the ground of earth below. In premodern cultures, the idea of a world is never far removed from religious concerns. It is usually understood as animate and many ancient mythologies tell stories of the marriage of earth and sky. In higher cultures, animism takes on the more distinct characteristics of individual deities or spirits, gods and goddesses, and attempts are then made to explain what appears in the world, the sun and the moon, the stars, and various creatures, including humans, in terms of the workings of occult forces with which the world is understood to be infused. Another aspect of the idea of a world in its earlier forms is that it attempts to unite and explain the visible and the invisible. Most importantly, it includes a realm of the dead. In Egyptian culture, this conception took the literal form of a necropolis, or city of the dead, on the western banks of the Nile, corresponding to the city of the living on the eastern bank. Some early concepts of a world are relatively static, others dynamic and even cataclysmic. The Mayans, speculating in astronomical expanses of time, proposed the growth, fiery destruction, and birth of many worlds over the aeons. The ancient Chinese conceived of the world as the result of a ceaseless dynamic that moved according to internal laws. All of these ancient concepts of a world were graphically symbolized, many in the form of maps. Their conceptualization and elaboration was the work of many generations and inspired the arts.

The Greeks also had mythopoetic conceptions of the world peopled by gods and goddesses, but they were the first to decisively depart from the mystical and magical conceptions of the world. Greek thinkers were the first to look for reasonable answers to why the world was as it was and how things came to be. In doing so, they rejected occult explanations and put forth questions to the world, believing that the world itself was somehow reasonably organized or directed by an intelligence, resembling human intelligence. Not coincidentally, it was a Greek who worked out a reasonable approximation of the earth's circumference, and a Greek who devised star and planet charts that used to be the basis of Western astronomy until modern times. To the practical Romans, Greek concerns were too speculative. Nonetheless, the Romans further altered the content of the concept of world by conquering and organizing a vast empire. Their work as soldiers, engineers, administrators, and legislators contributed to a very practical sense of the world that was in many ways the forerunner of the modern sensibility. But the Romans were not wholly without religion; in fact, they tended to be superstitious, and as the empire aged, religion played a more and more dominant part in people's conception of the world. The most important distinction between the idea of the world in premodern times and the modern conception is that the Old World view had always to account for the visible and the invisible, this world and the next. The spiritualism and dualism that characterized the ancient view of the world in the West came to an end with Columbus and Copernicus.

Columbus's discovery of the New World radically changed people's conception of place. It wasn't only the matter of having discovered hitherto unknown continents, but the challenge this discovery posed to all previous knowledge and the demands it made to know and measure the world as it actually was. Working within Columbus's lifetime, the Polish astronomer Nicholas Copernicus (1473-1543) reported that the earth was not the center of the universe, but rather one of several planets revolving about the central sun. The very meaning of the word *world*, in its most fundamental sense for modern peoples, begins with Columbus and Copernicus. Modern science continued to add to the concept. The idea of world retained the ancient sense of unity, but with scientific skepticism and knowledge, the world and its societal ideas were radically separated from religions and spiritual concerns. The world was no longer divided between the visible and invisible, but rather between the known and the unknown. The work of science further altered the common sense of the world thanks to Darwin. His theory of natural selection offered an explanation for the variety of life on the planet, including *Homo sapiens*, that was radically different. In absorbing the new knowledge, humans had to reconsider their position in relation to other animals.

Not only modern science but modern institutions changed people's sense of the world. Modern capital and commerce made international business possible and by the 17th century, markets in Amsterdam and London could be affected by events half a world away. Nation-states changed the way people thought of the world as well. In old Europe there had been a binding force in the ideas of a common Christendom and the Holy Roman Empire. The nation-states substituted for these ideals clearly defined territorial entities measured accurately and administered with ruthless rationalism. Printing presses and the modern printed media spread information rapidly and universally, bringing people closer to one another in their calculations and concerns.

Both the Industrial Revolution and imperialism in the 18th and 19th centuries brought to people's attention for the first time certain economic forces and conditions working on a worldwide scale. The theories of Karl Marx were an attempt to formulate the laws inherent in those forces and, combined with international socialism, to promote an understanding of the world that was opposed to the limited views and interests of nation-states and nationalism. Finally, drawing upon 2 centuries of industrial and technological development, World War I and World War II gave birth to a world united by a sense of common peril, a world with the technical capacity to utterly annihilate itself.

The modern conception of world can be considered a framework or canister for holding an ever-accumulating body of data. In 1992 there were some 5 1/3 billion people on earth and, at current rates of reproduction, there are likely to be more than 6.5 billion by the year 2005. Numerous species of plants and animals have become extinct, and, as pressure increases in the competition with humans for living space and food, more and more species face extinction. Currently the world consists of 193 countries and some 45 dependencies, but boundaries are changeable and, in many places in the world, volatile. Until the early 1990s it was a common convention to divide the world's nations among the First World, consisting of the prosperous industrialized societies; the Second World, the Soviet Union; and the Third World, consisting of all the less-developed countries. Most of the Third World is concentrated in Africa, South America, and the Asian subcontinent, the southern half of the world. Some 3,000 languages are spoken the world over, though 12 are the most widely used. The 12, in order of the numbers of people who use them, are Chinese, English, Russian, Spanish, Hindi, Arabic, Bengali, Portuguese, Japanese, German, Malay-Indonesian, and French. The 8 major religions of the world are Christianity, Islam, Buddhism, Confucianism, Hinduism, Shinto, Taoism, and Judaism. The world, as a framework or container for the data that has already been accumulated and that continues to accumulate, is virtually infinite. At the same time that it has this property of never-ending expansion, it also seems incredibly small and contracted. Modern communications and media have made it possible to connect any 2 points on the globe instantly, for business or pleasure. Modern transport puts the entire planet within reasonable traveling distance. Common concerns suggest there may be a basis for a more genuine unity in coming to terms with overpopulation, shrinking resources, and the threat posed by a degraded environment. There are as many indications that divisions will deepen and multiply. Still we use the term *world* in numerous ways and continue to find it useful, in fact, indispensable, no matter how unstable the notion of unity it contains.

World Bank, officially the International Bank for Reconstruction and Development (IBRD). Specialized agency of the United Nations, founded in 1945. Its headquarters is in Washington, D.C. From capital (limited to $24 billion) it lends money to its 176 member states for investment, foreign trade, and repayment of debts. Members own shares of $100,000 and belong to the International Monetary Fund. The bank is self-sustaining and profit-making. In 1960 it set up the International Development Association.

World Council of Churches, international association of about 300 Protestant, Anglican, Eastern Orthodox, and Old Catholic churches in some 90 countries. Founded 1948, with headquarters in Geneva, it promotes Christian unity, religious liberty, missionary cooperation, interfaith doctrinal study, and service projects such as refugee relief.
See also: Christianity.

World Court *See:* International Court of Justice.

World government, theoretical organization with the authority and power to maintain law order throughout the world. The idea first began in the 1300s and the massive destruction caused by World Wars I (1914-1918) and II (1939-1945) has led to a revival of the concept. Supporters see the creation and effective leadership of the United Nations as a positive model and test case for a world government.

World Health Organization (WHO), specialized agency of the United Nations founded in 1948 and based in Geneva. Its services are available to all nations and territories. WHO advises countries on how to develop health services, combat epidemics, and promote health education and standards of nutrition. It also coordinates the standardization of drugs and health statistics and studies pollution.

World Intellectual Property Organization (WIPO), international agency, part of the United Nations (UN), that protects the legal rights of intellectual property, such as inventions, trademarks, literary and artistic works, and other original ideas. Founded in 1967, WIPO became part of the UN in 1974 and has a membership of over 110 countries. Its headquarters are located in Geneva, Switzerland.

World Jewish Congress, international body, representing Jewish organizations from over 70 countries, whose goals are to maintain Jewish unity, culture, and religion. Founded in 1936, the congress was active during World War II (1939-1945), helping Jews escape Nazi persecution, and in the 1970s, securing the release of thousands of Jews from the USSR. Its headquarters are located in New York City.
See also: Jews.

World Meteorological Organization (WMO), specialized agency of the United Nations, established in Geneva in 1951 to promote international meteorological observation and standardization.

World's fair, international exposition of science and technology, entertainment, and culture. The first such fair was the Great Exhibition of 1851 in London. World's fairs have frequently displayed new inventions and feats of engineering, such as the telephone (Philadelphia, 1876), the Eiffel Tower (Paris, 1889), the automobile (St. Louis, 1904), and television (New York, 1939). More recently, fairs have had central themes such as outer space or the oceans. World's fairs have been held all over the world.

World Trade Center, twin towers (each 110 stories) rising 1,350 ft (411 m) over lower Manhattan in New York City. Completed in 1973, they were the tallest buildings in the world until 1974, when they were surpassed by the Sears Tower in Chicago. The center was designed by Minoru Yamasaki and Emery Roth and cost $750 million to build.
See also: Skyscraper.

World Trade Organization (WTO) Organization set up in 1995 with the aim of advancing the expansion of international trade on a non discriminatory basis. The WTO mediates on request in international trade conflicts and functions as a forum for consultation about trade agreements. The WTO built on the foundations laid by the General Agreement on Tariffs and Trade (GATT). In 2002, 144 countries were members of the WTO, and the organization assessed applications from 31 countries, including China and Russia. The headquarters are in Geneva.

W

A map of Europe in 1914, drawn by W. Trier and sold for the benefit of the Red Cross. England is pictured as a Scotsman hiding a fleet under his kilt, and who is being threatened from the rear by an Irish dog. Germany and Austria-Hungary are attacking everyone in all directions. Germany is using Belgium as a defense against the retreating French soldier, while Spain is watching without interfering.

World War I, global conflict waged from 1914 to 1918 that caused more destruction and involved more participants than any other conflict up to that time. The war's spread was facilitated by an interlocking system of military alliances that Europe had forged during the previous decades, ostensibly to keep the peace. These alliances comprised the Central Powers (primarily Germany and Austria-Hungary) and the Allies (primarily Russia, France, and Great Britain). Later, other nations joined one or the other of the blocks.

Causes of the war. The underlying causes of the conflict involved the rise of nationalism in Europe, the military buildup pursued by parties of both alliances, and the competition among various European countries for colonies. The immediate cause of the war was the assassination of Austrian Crown Prince Francis Ferdinand at Sarajevo on June 28, 1914, by a Serbian nationalist. Austria, looking for a pretext to suppress Slavic nationalist aspirations in the Austro-Hungarian Empire, declared war on Serbia (July 28), with the approval of Germany.

Russia announced full mobilization (July 30), and France rejected a German demand that she declare herself neutral.

The two fronts. Germany declared war on Russia (Aug. 1) and on France (Aug. 3) and invaded neutral Belgium, the shortest route to Paris, in search of a quick victory in the west before Russia had time to muster all its forces in the east. The invasion prompted Britain to enter the war (Aug. 4) in support of Belgium and France. All the major members of the alliances were now committed to war.

The western front. German armies gained initial successes, sweeping through Belgium and into France. They were halted at the Marne River (First Battle of the Marne, Sept. 6-9, 1914) by French forces led by Gen. Joseph Joffre. This battle ended German hopes of quickly overrunning its opponents in the west, and by late Nov. 1914 war on the western front settled into a dreadful stalemate. For the next $3\frac{1}{2}$ years, terrible trench warfare raged along a 450-mile (724-km)-long front extending across Belgium and northeastern France to the Swiss border.

The eastern front. In late Aug. 1914 the Russians invaded East Prussia, but were defeated by the Germans in the battles of Tannenberg and the Masurian Lakes, suffering about 250,000 Russian casualties.

In 1914, Turkey became an ally of Germany. The title page of the *Illustrierte Zeitung* of May 18, 1916, shows a number of Turks in Damascus, preparing for battle against the British.

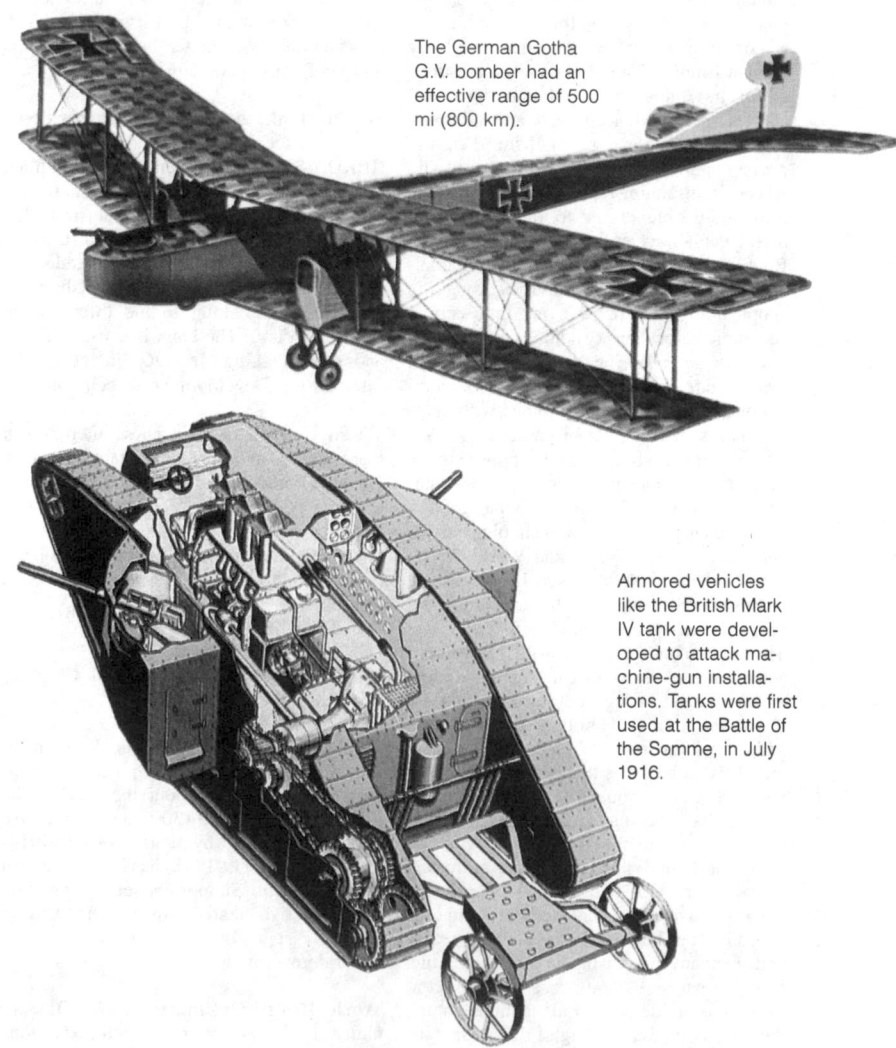

The German Gotha G.V. bomber had an effective range of 500 mi (800 km).

Armored vehicles like the British Mark IV tank were developed to attack machine-gun installations. Tanks were first used at the Battle of the Somme, in July 1916.

The Eastern Front. In May 1915, there was a breakthrough of German-Austrian troops near Luzna, in the battle near Gorlice (in Galicia). Illustration by Oscar Laske.

An English war poster from 1917, exhorting the population to be thrifty, with the slogan: 'Don't waste bread! Save two slices every day and defeat the U-boat'.

Austria-Hungary was less successful, failing to capture Serbia and losing its province of Galicia to the Russians. In Oct. 1914 Turkey joined the Central Powers against Russia. In a vain attempt to aid the Russians, the Allies in early 1915 sent a fleet to the Dardanelles and ground forces to the Gallipoli Peninsula. The thrust proved unsuccessful, and troops were evacuated in Dec. 1915 with losses of about 250,000.

Outside Europe. After the Gallipoli disaster, the Allies attacked Turkey through her empire in the Middle East, and were largely successful, leaving her in possession of little more than Anatolia. Farther afield, British, French, and South African troops overran Germany's African possessions, while the Japanese (who had entered the war in Sept. 1914) and Australasian troops captured German possessions in the Far East and the Pacific.

Attrition in the West. In 1915 Italy joined the Allies and engaged the Austrian army in the Alps. In 1916 German forces were repulsed in their attempt to take the French city of Verdun with fearful losses on both sides (about 315,000 casualties for the French and 280,000 for the Germans). Paul von Hindenburg and Erich Ludendorff, the heroic leaders of German forces in the east, took command in the west, Hindenburg as chief of general staff with Ludendorff his aide.

An Allied offensive late in the year (the Battle of the Somme), led principally by the British, was also unsuccessful, and by its end it had cost the Germans over 600,000 casualties, the British over 400,000, and the French nearly 200,000. Britain maintained a naval blockade of the continent while German submarines harassed Allied mercantile shipping. An attempt by the German fleet to lift the blockade at Jutland (May 1916) failed.

The final stages. In Mar. 1917 the Russian people, sick of the war that had cost them dearly, revolted and overthrew Tsar Nicholas II. In Apr. 1917 V.I. Lenin returned to Russia from his exile in Switzerland, and 7 months later, as head of the revolutionary Bolshevik government, sued for peace with Germany. The Germans dictated a harsh peace between the 2 nations in Mar. 1918 at Brest-Litovsk. The sinking of 3 U.S. merchant ships in Mar. 1917 together with the discovery of a German plan to try to persuade Mexico to go to war against the United States (the 'Zimmermann Telegram') caused the United States to declare war on the Central Powers in Apr. 1917. The American Expeditionary Forces, led by Gen. John J. Pershing, began arriving in France in mid-1917. Despite a massive final German offensive in 1918 that drove the Allies back to the Marne, Allied forces, boosted by U.S. contingents, eventually began to tell. In September the Hindenburg Line was breached. The Central Powers sued for peace, and an armistice went into effect on Nov. 11, 1918. The Treaty of Versailles (June 28, 1919), imposed on Germany, formalized the Allied victory. The dead on both sides totaled about 10 million.

Aftermath of the war. Europe had spent much of its economic resources on the war and was exhausted and in debt. The dissolution of old empires in Europe and Turkey spawned a host of new countries and allegiances, and the United States, unscathed in the war, emerged as the economic world power. An era of European dominance was clearly coming to an end, and a new, but very unsettled, world order was in the making.

World War II, second global conflict lasting from 1939 to 1945 that involved civilian populations on an unprecedented scale. Military deaths probably amounted to some 17 million, but civilian deaths were undoubtedly much higher because of mass bombing of cities, starvation, epidemics, massacres, and other war-related causes. The parties to the conflict involved nearly every major power in the world, divided into 2 groups: the Allies (principally Great Britain, the United States, the Soviet Union, and China) and the Axis Powers (principally Germany, Italy, and Japan). The development-and use-of the atomic bomb late in the war ushered in the nuclear age.

Causes of the war. The conflict arose because of the increasing military might of the aggressive, totalitarian regimes in Germany, Italy, and Japan following World War I. The harsh terms of the Treaty of Versailles after World War I had left Germany bitter and un-

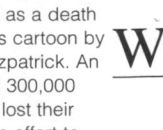

The Battle of Stalingrad (August-December 1942), during which Hitler had forbidden the surrounded German armies to withdraw, is portrayed as a death trap in this cartoon by Daniel Fitzpatrick. An estimated 300,000 Germans lost their lives in the effort to take the city.

The Messerschmitt was the most formidable German fighter in the Battle of Britain.

The Supermarine Spitfire VB became symbolic of British air power in World War II.

On Aug. 1, 1944, Polish resistance fighters led the people of Warsaw in an uprising against the German occupation forces. Unaided by the Soviet armies that were approaching the city, the Poles held out against ferocious German efforts to recover control for 63 days.

stable, and hard economic times plagued much of the world in the 1920s and 1930s. These conditions fostered fascistic dictatorships in Germany and Italy, and Japan became aggressively militaristic and expansionist in Asia. Attempts to contain the aggressive impulses of these states through the League of Nations (which the U.S. did not join) proved ineffectual. With the rise of Hitler and Nazism to power in Germany (1933), the Versailles arrangements began to crumble. Germany rearmed and, on the pretext of defending German ethnic nationals in certain neighboring countries, laid claim to some of their territories. Hitler annexed Austria in Mar. 1938 (the *Anschluss*) and obtained the Sudetenland (in Czechoslovakia) through the Munich Pact (Sept. 1938). The policy of appeasement practiced at Munich failed, however, as Germany in Mar. 1939 occupied the rest of Czechoslovakia. On Aug. 23, 1939, Germany signed a non-aggression pact with its former arch enemy the Soviet Union, clearing the way for Hitler to move westward.

Outbreak of the war. Germany invaded Poland on Sept. 1, 1939. France and Britain responded by declaring war on Germany

U.S. marines take cover as explosives shake a Japanese stronghold on the island of Iwo Jima, one of the most heavily fortified of Japan's Pacific island garrisons.

W

(Sept. 3). Germany, using the blitzkrieg strategy of speed and surprise, soon overran most of Poland, and on Sept. 17 Soviet forces invaded Poland from the east. By the end of September the Soviets had occupied the eastern third of Poland while Germany held all the rest. The Soviet Union continued with invasions of Finland and the Baltic states, as Germany went on to swift conquests of Denmark and Norway (Apr. 1940), and in May overran the Low Countries and invaded France. By June German troops had swept through France to the English Channel. British forces, almost trapped by the Germans, effected a desperate evacuation from Dunkirk back to England. France accepted an armistice on June 11, although Free French forces led by Gen. Charles de Gaulle continued the struggle. With Germany and Italy dominant on the continent, Hitler turned his sights on Britain, and attempted to bomb the nation into submission. Inspired by their leader, Winston Churchill, the British held firm and the Royal Air Force thwarted the effort in the Battle of Britain. In May 1941 Hitler broke off the massive air attack and began rebuilding his depleted air force. He continued, however, to harass British shipping with submarine warfare in the North Atlantic principally. On June 22 Germany invaded the Soviet Union, bringing that country, under its leader Joseph Stalin, into the war. Surprised, the Soviet forces initially suffered

heavy losses. However, with Moscow and Leningrad surrounded and under siege, resistance stiffened. Also, a severe winter in 1941 caused enormous hardship for the German army, and they were never able to fully capture either city. Late in 1941 Germany and Italy found a new ally in Japan, whose aggressive militarism was bent on the conquest of Eastern Asia and the Western Pacific. On Dec. 7, 1941, Japan surprised and crippled the U.S. fleet at Pearl Harbor, Hawaii. President Franklin Roosevelt asked for, and obtained, an immediate U.S. declaration of war.

Turn of the tide. Though the United States initially fared badly in the Pacific, its first major victories were recorded at Coral Sea and Midway (June 1942). In North Africa, Allied supremacy was established at the Battle of El Alamein (Oct.-Nov. 1942). On the eastern front the Germans lost an army at the siege of Stalingrad (early 1943), and Soviet forces began to push the invader back. Sicily fell to Anglo-American forces in July 1943, and the Italian dictator Benito Mussolini was driven from power.

D-Day (June 6, 1944) signaled the last phase of the war in Europe, as Allied troops stormed across the Channel and invaded Normandy. By Sept. 1944 German forces, already expelled from the Soviet Union, had been driven out of France and Belgium. The Battle of the Bulge (Dec. 1944) proved to be the final German counteroffensive. By Jan. 1945 the Allies resumed their drive into Germany; the Russians captured East Germany, and the Allies broke the Siegfried Line in March. As Russian forces at last entered Berlin, Hitler committed suicide (Apr. 30, 1945) and 8 days later all German resistance ended. The fate of conquered Europe was subsequently settled at the Yalta Conference and the Potsdam Conference, although Germany itself was not reunited into one country until 1990.

Defeat of Japan. Since 1943 Allied forces had been eroding Japanese power in the Pacific and Asia. By mid-1945 island-hopping assaults by U.S. forces, culminating in Iwo Jima and Okinawa, had largely swept Japan from the Western Pacific. The Soviet Union declared war on Japan and occupied Manchuria, and U.S. and Allied forces were massing in the Pacific for an invasion of the Japanese homeland. President Harry Truman ordered the dropping of the atomic bomb on Hiroshima and Nagasaki (Aug. 6 and 9), and on Aug. 14 Japan accepted unconditional terms of surrender.

Aftermath of the war. The stupendous destruction of World War II left much of the world in ruins, with the Soviet Union and the United States emerging as the 2 world superpowers. A struggle, known as the Cold War, soon developed between the Communist world, led by the Soviet Union, and the non-Communist world, led by the United States. Perhaps most important of all, the horror of nuclear devastation was introduced as a possibility in any future global conflict.

Worm, term used for any elongate, cylindrical invertebrate, such as the earthworm, roundworm, hairworm, or acorn worm. The word has no taxonomic validity; animals commonly referred to as worms belong to many related phyla: Chordata, Annelida, and Platyhelminthes. However, the term is sometimes restricted to the phylum Annelida.

Worms (pop. 82,000), city in southwestern Germany, situated on the Rhine River. Its main industries include the manufacture of chemicals, furniture, leather goods, and machinery. It is also a famous wine producer. Founded in 14 B.C. by Roman soldiers, Worms has a Romanesque cathedral that dates from the 1000s, and what may be Europe's oldest Jewish cemetery, also from the 1000s.

Worms, Edict of, civil decree issued at Worms, Germany, in 1521, denouncing religious reformer Martin Luther as a heretic, banning his writings, and calling for his capture. The question of whether or not to enforce the edict was a subject of great controversy until a truce was declared in 1555 with the Peace of Augsburg.
See also: Luther, Martin; Reformation.

Wormwood, group of herbs and shrubs in the composite family, found chiefly in arid regions of the Northern Hemisphere. Wormwood is grown commercially to provide an essential oil that has a variety of medicinal uses. The leaves of another type of wormwood, tarragon, is used as a seasoning. Common wormwood, or mugwort, is used in medicines and in the manufacture of absinthe.

Worsted, type of yarn known for its strength and its smooth, shiny texture. It was first produced in Worsted, England. It is made by combing the wool fibers into parallel layers before they are spun. Worsted yarns are frequently used in knitting. The term *worsted* also refers to any fabric made with worsted yarns.

Wouda, Marcel (1972-), Dutch swimmer, had his international breakthrough by breaking the 400 m medley world record on 1st February 1927 in a time of 4.05.59, which he improved himself a week later to 4.05.41. During the European championships in Seville that year, Wouda won both the 400 m and the 200 m medley gold medal, and with the relay team he won the 4 x 200 m freestyle silver medal. Wouda has since gone on to win numerous international competitions.

The Soviet T-34 tank was regarded as the most outstanding armored vehicle of World War II. It played a major role in resisting the German invasion of the USSR, in 1941. Its effectiveness caused the Germans to reevaluate the designs of their tanks.

Wouk, Herman (1915-), U.S. author of novels and plays. His work often draws on his own naval experiences during World War II. In 1952 he won the Pulitzer Prize in fiction for his war novel, *The Caine Mutiny* (1951), which was later adapted for stage and screen. Other popular novels that were adapted for the screen include *Marjorie Morningstar* (1955), *The Winds of War* (1971), and *War and Remembrance* (1978). In 1993 *The Hope* was published.

Wounded Knee, Battle of, massacre by U.S. soldiers of more than 200 Sioux men, women, and children at Wounded Knee Creek, S.D., on Dec. 29, 1890, in the last major battle of the Indian Wars. In 1973, 200 members of the American Indian Movement (AIM) occupied the Wounded Knee Reservation for 69 days, demanding a Senate investigation into the conditions of Native Americans.
See also: Indian wars.

WPA *See:* New Deal.

Wrangel Island, island belonging to Russia and located in the Arctic Ocean, about 90 miles north of Siberia. Whalers from the United States discovered the uninhabited island in 1867. Despite the claims of the United States and Canada, the USSR sent settlers there in 1926. The land is icy and barren during most of the year. Polar bears, walruses, and birds can be found there. It is inhabited by about 50 people who fish and hunt for a living.

Wren, name of several groups of small birds. The true wrens are the Troglodytidae, a family of 60 species of small perching birds. The name is also used for some 80 species (family Malurinae) of warblers of Australia and New Guinea, and the New Zealand wrens (family Xenicidae). True wrens are small, compact birds with short to long tails cocked upward. They occur in Central and North America.

Wren, Sir Christopher (1632-1723), English architect, astronomer, mathematician. Wren is best remembered as architect of St. Paul's Cathedral (1710) and over 50 other churches that were rebuilt after having been destroyed by the Great Fire of London (1666). A widely respected astronomer, he

The wren (*Troglodytes troglodytes*, order *Passeriformes*), is found throughout the northern hemisphere and has a length of up to 5 in (13 cm).

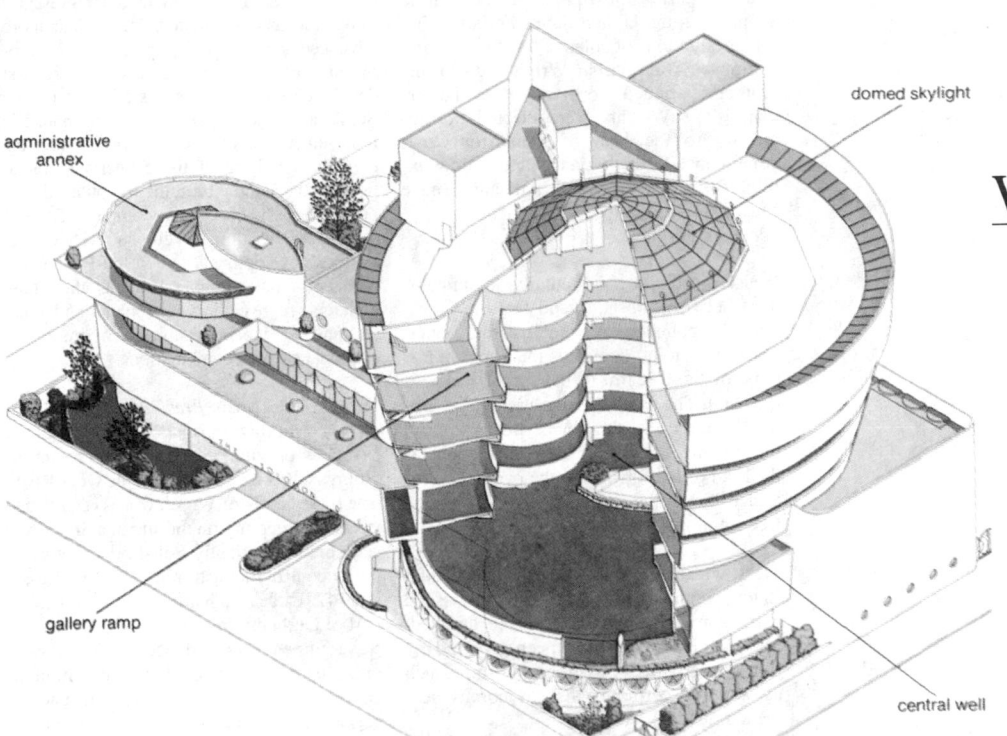

administrative annex

domed skylight

gallery ramp

central well

was appointed professor of Gresham College, London (1657), served on the faculty of Oxford University (1661-1673), and was a founder of the Royal Society (1660). *See also:* Architecture; Astronomy.

Wrestling, in the West, sport in which 2 persons grapple and try to pin one another's shoulders to the floor by means of various holds. An ancient Greek sport, wrestling became a recognized Olympic sport in 1904. In the United States the preferred form is the free-style, or catch-as-catch-can. The Greco-Roman form, popular in Europe, forbids holds below the waist. Bouts are divided into 3 periods of 3 minutes each. The match is over when a wrestler pins both his opponent's shoulders for the count of 3 (a fall). Matches can also be won on points awarded by the referee for skilled maneuvers.

Wright, Frank Lloyd (1869-1959), 20th-century U.S. architect. He studied engineering, joined the architect Louis Sullivan, and was influenced by the Arts and Crafts movement. His pioneering 'prairie style' (Robie House; 1908-1909)-strong, horizontal lines; low-pitched, hipped roofs; open plan; and change of internal levels-influenced De Stijl. He articulated massive forms clearly (Larkin Building, 1904) and, though he liked natural materials and locations, was innovative in his use of reinforced concrete, dramatic cantilevering, and screen walls (Kaufmann House, or Falling Water, 1936-1937; Johnson's Wax Building, 1936-1949; Guggenheim Museum, 1946-1959).
See also: Architecture.

Wright, Quincy (1890-1970), U.S. political scientist, an expert on international law. He was a supporter of the League of Nations and United Nations. His books include *A Study of War* (2 vol., 1942) and *The Study of International Relations* (1955).

Wright, Richard (1908-1960), U.S. novelist and social critic. His works include *Uncle Tom's Children* (1938), stories of Southern racial prejudice; *Native Son* (1940), about a victimized black in Chicago; and *Black Boy* (1945), his autobiography.

Wright brothers, name of two U.S. inventors; designers and builders of the world's first successful airplane (1903). Inspired by the work of Otto Lilienthal, who did pioneering work with gliders in the 1890s, the Wrights, **Wilbur** (1867-1912) and **Orville** (1871-1948), conducted experiments with kites and gliders (1899-1902) to develop and test theories of control and lift. Their powered airplane was first tested Dec. 17, 1903, at Kill Devil Hill, near Kitty Hawk, N.C. The machine weighed 750 lb (340 kg), with wings 40 ft (12 m) long. The Wrights con-

The Guggenheim Museum (1943-59) in New York City, one of Frank Lloyd Wright's most controversial designs, consists of an ascending spiral ramp that creates a continuous display area and defines the building's exterior form. A domed skylight over the central well illumines the interior. This design, derived from curving, organic forms, creates a startling and graceful interior space.

Wilbur Wright caused a sensation with his biplane (1909). The first powered flight with an airplane was made by the Wright Brothers in 1903.

W

tinued experimental flights, receiving little attention in the United States but arranging for production of planes in France and Germany. After Wilbur Wright's death, his brother continued work to perfect the airplane. The Wrights were elected posthumously to the Hall of Fame for Great Americans. Their original plane is now exhibited in the National Air and Space Museum, Washington, D.C.
See also: Airplane.

Wrist, or carpus, particularly in humans, joint between the hand and forearm, along with the connecting 8 small carpal bones. The wrist joint connects the long *radius* bone of the forearm to the carpal bones of the hand. The tendons and muscles that connect the arm to the finger bones control movement of the fingers. A joint connects the *ulna* of the forearm to the parallel radius rather than to the carpal bones, allowing the free rotation of the wrist.

Writ, written order of a court of law. Under English common law, a writ had to be issued before any legal action could be initiated. Most ancient writs have been replaced by summonses and declarations, but some-such as writs of certiorari, habeas corpus, and mandamus-survive.

Writing, in business, career in such diverse areas as technical writing, journalism, fiction and poetry, and screenplay and script writing. *Staff writers* have salaried jobs with newspapers and magazines, in company public relations departments, at advertising agencies, and elsewhere. However, writing services are largely provided by *freelance writers* who are hired for particular projects (e.g., computer manuals, encyclopedia articles) or who create their own articles, scripts, and so on, which they then attempt to sell to various publishers and producers. Writers, particularly those already well established, may work through a *literary agent* to place a manuscript with a buyer. Only a small percentage of fiction writers and a handful of poets actually make a living from their creative writing.

In this painting, that can be seen in the Bradford City Art Gallery, Wycliffe reads the Bible to John of Ghent.

Writing, visual representation of human language and other communication according to social convention. Early writing included marks used for counting and pictures representing situations and objects. Pictures devel-

oped into *ideographs*, symbolic representations of ideas rather than of speech. The more advanced and abstract *logographs*, which represent actual elements of speech, were first developed by the Sumerians c.3500 B.C. The Sumerians also began to develop phonetic representations, or *syllabograms*. While this *cuneiform* writing of the Sumerians spread through the Middle East, the Egyptians developed *hieroglyphics*. The complex Chinese system of writing developed c.1500 B.C. Further developments led to the Phoenician alphabet, representing consonants, the Greek alphabet, representing consonants and vowels, and the Japanese alphabet, representing consonant-vowel combinations.

Wroclaw (German: *Breslau*; pop. 645,000), city in southwestern Poland, capital of Wroclaw province; located in the region of Dolny lsk (Lower Silesia) on the Oder River. The trade center of Wroclaw was established in the 10th century on the site of a Stone Age settlement. Originally Polish, the city came under control of Austria in 1526 and Prussia in 1742. Under the name of Breslau it was a part of Germany from 1871 to 1945, when it was returned to Poland. Modern Wroclaw is an industrial, transportation, and communication center. Manufactures include machinery, electronics, textiles, and food products.
See also: Poland.

Wryneck, jynx, or snakebird (genus *Jynx*), small, gray-brown, insect-eating bird of the Eastern Hemisphere, named for the snakelike hissing and movement of its head and neck when it is threatened. The 2 species, often considered members of the woodpecker family, are the Eurasian wryneck (*J. torquilla*) and the African red-breasted wryneck (*J. ruficollis*).

WTO *See:* World Trade Organization.

Wu, Chien-shiung (1912-1997), U.S. experimental physicist. In 1957 her experiments in particle physics disproved the law of the conservation of parity, a long-held theory that the direction in which beta particles are emitted from a radioactive nucleus is not related to the direction of spin of the nucleus. Her work confirmed the theory of physicists Tsung Dao Lee and Chen Ning Yang (who shared the 1957 Nobel Prize in physics) that the direction of spin affects the predominant direction of such emissions. Her experimental work also helped confirm theoretical work of Richard P. Feynman and Murray Gell-Mann. Wu emigrated from China to study at the University of California, Berkeley. She worked at Columbia University from 1944, first in the Division of War Research and after 1957 as a professor.
See also: Parity; Physics.

Wuchang *See:* Wuhan.

Wuhan (pop. 4,300,000), city in east-central China comprised of the former cities of Hankou, Hanyang, and Wuchang. Located at the confluence of the Yangtze and Han rivers, Wuhan is a major commercial, transportation, and industrial (iron and steel production) center.
See also: China.

Wilhelm Wundt, German physiologist, philosopher and psychologist (1832- 1920), is considered the founder of experimental psychology.

Wundt, Wilhelm (1832-1920), German psychologist and philosopher. He thought that research psychologists should combine laboratory work with an examination of their own thoughts and feelings. In 1879 he started a laboratory in which his ideas on experimental psychology were practiced.
See also: Psychology.

Wyatt, Sir Thomas (1503?-1542), English poet of the early Renaissance. He and Henry Howard, earl of Surrey, translated and introduced Italian poetry and poetic forms to English literature. They are generally credited with having written the first sonnets in English. Wyatt, a lover of Anne Boleyn before her marriage, was known for his wit and charm in the court of King Henry VIII, and served his country as a diplomat to the European continent. In addition to sonnets, he wrote lyrics for lute accompaniment, epigrams, and satires. His poems were first published in Tottel's *Miscellany*, a famous early Renaissance collection.
See also: Renaissance.

Wycliffe, John (1328?-1384), British religious reformer, created first English translation of the Latin Bible. He lived during a time that saw the roles of church and state seriously questioned. Siding with the common people against both corrupt church and civil rulers, he claimed that obedience was due only to God. For his beliefs and writings on this subject, he was tried several times, unsuccessfully. Protected by England's royal family, he wrote vehement attacks against the church, fighting in large part against its hypocrisy and in favor of the rights of the poor. Subsequent religious reformers, including the Protestants of the Reformation in the 16th century, considered Wycliffe a major influence.
See also: Reformation.

Wyeth, Andrew (1917-), U.S. painter. His work depicts scenes of strange, lonely rural life in a highly detailed style that seems almost photographic. His best-known picture is *Christina's World* (1948).

Old Faithful Geyser, one of the many geothermal phenomena found in Yellowstone National Park, in northwestern Wyoming.

Wyler, William (1902-1981), U.S. film director. He won Academy Awards for *Mrs. Miniver* (1942), *The Best Years of Our Lives (1946)*, and *Ben Hur* (1958). His other films include *Wuthering Heights* (1939), *Friendly Persuasion* (1956), and *Funny Girl* (1968).

Wyoming (Equality State; pop. 470,000), state in the Rocky Mountain region of northwestern United States; bordered by Montana, South Dakota, Nebraska, Colorado, Utah, and Idaho.
A large part of the state lies in the Rocky Mountains. Three major river systems rise in the Rocky Mountains of Wyoming: the Missouri, the Colorado, and the Columbia. Forests cover about one-sixth of the state. Yellowstone National Park, in the state's northwestern corner, has the world's largest geyser, magnificent waterfalls, and deep canyons. Principal cities are Casper and Cheyenne (capital).
Mining and service industries (including tourism) lead Wyoming's economy. Chief mining products are petroleum, natural gas, coal, uranium, sodium carbonate, clays, Portland cement, and crushed stone. Ranching is the leading agricultural activity; chief livestock products are beef cattle, milk, sheep, and wool; chief crops are hay, barley, wheat, sugar beets, corn, and beans.
The Territory of Wyoming was created by Congress in 1868; in 1869 it became the first state or territory to give women the right to vote. Cattle and oil industries developed in the 1880s; in 1890 Wyoming became the 44th state.

Wyss family, authors of and models for the famous children's story *The Swiss Family Robinson*. The story of a family's life and survival alone on an island was first created and written down by **Johann David Wyss** (1743-1818) as an entertainment for his children. Many years later in 1812, one of his sons, **Johann Rudolf** (1781-1830), who was at the time a well-known Swiss editor of folklore, edited and published his father's account. The novel was an instant success and was translated into English in 1814. The book, now available in many languages, is still a popular children's book.

Wyszynski, Stefan Cardinal (1901-1981), Polish Catholic cardinal, archbishop of Warsaw, and primate of Poland. Arrested for his attacks on the Communist government's persecution of the church in 1953, he was released after Wladyslaw Gomulka's rise to power (1956). His funeral was a national event attended by Pope John Paul II.
See also: Poland.

X, 24th letter of the English alphabet, corresponding to the 21st letter of the Latin alphabet, which was itself derived from a letter of the western subdivision of the ancient Greek alphabet representing the sound 'ks.' The same letter in the eastern Greek alphabet represented 'ch' or 'kh,' and as such passed into the later Greek and Cyrillic alphabets. X represents 10 in Roman numerals, and in algebra and in the sciences it is used as the symbol for an unknown quantity.

X and Y chromosomes, or sex chromosomes, cell nuclei that determine the sex of a person (as well as carrying some genetic information not related to sex determination). Sex chromosomes are inherited in the same way as the other 22 human chromosome pairs, normal persons being either XX (female) or XY (male). The Y chromosome carries little genetic information, and it is largely the properties of the X chromosome that determine sex-linked characteristics in males. Sex-linked characteristics include hemophilia and color blindness, which are carried as recessive genes in females.
See also: Chromosome.

Xanthippus (ca. 520 B.C..), Athenian general, father of Pericles. He was partly responsible for the exiling of Miltiades in 489 B.C., a fate which he himself had to endure in 484B.C. when he was exiled by Themistocles. Called back for the Battle of Salamis as commander of the Athenian fleet, he was responsible for the victory over the Persians at Mycale in 479 B.C..

Xavier, Saint Francis (Spanish: Francisco Javier; 1506-1552), Spanish missionary. A friend of St. Ignatius of Loyola, he helped him found the order of Jesuits. In 1541 he set out as a missionary, reaching the East Indies, Goa, India, Malacca, and Ceylon. In 1549 he established a Jesuit mission in Japan and in 1552 sought to extend his work to China, but died on Shangchuan while waiting for permission to enter the country. His feast day is Dec. 3.
See also: Jesuits.

Xenakis, Yannis (1922-2001), Greek avant-garde composer who developed 'stochastic' music using computer-programmed sequences based on mathematical probability, as in *Métastaseis* (1953-1954) and *Achorripsis* (1958). Other works include *Polytope* (1967), *Rebonds* (1987-1989), and *Plektó* (1993).

Xenon, chemical element, symbol Xe; for physical constants, see Periodic Table. Xenon was discovered by Sir William Ramsay and Morris W. Travers in 1898. It occurs in the atmosphere to the extent of one part in 20 million. It is obtained from liquid air residues and from the gases evolved from certain mineral springs. Xenon is a colorless, odorless, and chemically inert gas. It is a member of the noble or 'inert' gases. The noble gases do not normally combine with other elements, but the existence of many xenon compounds has been established. Xenon difluoride, tetrafluoride, hexafluoride, and others have been prepared. It is used in special electric lamps.

Xenophanes (570-480 B.C.), Greek poet and pre-Socratic philosopher. An Ionian who emigrated to South Italy, he wrote satires and ridiculed the idea that the gods had human attributes, positing a single, all-embracing divine being. Only some 40 fragments of his works survive.
See also: Pre-Socratic philosophy.

Xenophon (431-355 B.C.), Greek soldier and author. An Athenian and admirer of Socrates, he joined the Greek expedition supporting Cyrus the Younger (401) and after its defeat led the Greeks back in a heroic 1,500-mi (2,414-km) march recounted in his famous *Anabasis*. He later fought for Sparta, whose conservative militarism he admired. Retiring to the country, he wrote his famous volumes of Greek history, memoirs of Socrates, a romanticized account of Cyrus the Great's education, and works on horsemanship and politics.
See also: Greece, Ancient.

Xerography *See:* Photocopying.

Xerxes, name of two kings of ancient Persia. **Xerxes I** (r.486-465 B.C.) continued the war against Greece started by his father, Darius I. His vast army crossed the Hellespont in 480 B.C., and despite a defeat at Thermopylae, destroyed Athens. However, his fleet was defeated at Salamis (480), and he returned to Persia, leaving his army, which was defeated at Plataea (479). He was murdered in a court intrigue. **Xerxes II**, his grandson, was murdered by his half brother, Sogdianus, in 424 B.C., after ruling for 45 days.
See also: Persia, Ancient.

Xhosa, group of related tribes (formerly called *Kafir*) predominantly living in Transkei, South Africa. Bantu-speaking, they are mainly agriculturists, though some

X

Young man in traditional Xhosa outfit. The clothes show that the man is not yet initiated.

cattle are raised. The Xhosa are organized in patrilineal clans. Many now work as migrant laborers in Johannesburg.

Xiamen (pop. 1,1 million), Hsia-men, or Amoy, port city in Fujian province, southeastern China, located on Amoy and Ku-lang islands, on the Strait of Formosa at the mouth of the Chiu-lung Chiang (river). The city has a history of contact with Western nations, beginning in 1544 with the arrival of Portuguese traders, who were soon expelled. The port was visited by Dutch, Spanish, and British ships during the 17th and 18th centuries, but foreign trade restrictions were imposed in 1757. As a result of a treaty following the Opium War of 1839-1842, Xiamen and 4 other ports were reopened to the British, and foreigners were allowed residence. During the 19th century the port was a center of the tea trade. It was held by the Japanese from 1938 to 1945. It remains a shipping center, with industries including food processing, shipbuilding, and engineering. Xiamen is now connected to the mainland by a causeway. It has had close ties with nearby Taiwan, and has a large emigrant Chinese population.
See also: China.

Xi'an (also Sian or Hsi-an; pop. 2,800,000), China, the capital of Shaanxi province. The city lies in the Wei River valley, about 570 miles (917 km) southwest of Beijing. Xi'an is a trade and transportation center on one of China's main east-west railways. It was part of the Silk Road. Industries include the manufacturing of textiles, machinery, fertilizers,

and plastics. Xi'an Jiaotong University, a provincial library, and one of China's foremost historical museums are here. Near Xi'an is the tomb of Chin Shih Huang Ti, which dates to the third century B.C. Outside the tomb are more than 7,000 terra-cotta warriors.

Inhabited since about 6,000 B.C., Xi'an is one of China's oldest settled areas. The city served as the capital of several ancient tribal states and dynasties and became prominent when the Han established their capital here in 206 B.C. The city was then known as Changan. Xi'an's greates period came under the Tang dynasty, founded in 618. For nearly 300 years the city was the political and cultural center of China, during a golden age of art and literature.

Following the end of the Tang dynasty in 907, Xi'an entered a period of decline. It revived after 1368, when it became a provincial capital under the Ming dynasty, and remained an important city under the Manchus (1644-1912).

Xi Jiang (also Hsi Chiang), longest river of southern China. Originating in the highlands of Yunnan province, it flows some 1,500 mi (2,414 km) southeast to the South China Sea. There, along with several other rivers, it forms a delta on which is located the large Chinese city of Guangzhou.

Xinjiang, large, northwestern province of China, bordered on the northwest by Kazachstan. Most of the region's inhabitants are of Middle Eastern origin, including Turkish. The main religion is Islam. The region has been under Chinese rule off and on since the Han dynasty (202 B.C.-A.D. 220). It was officially made a province by the Chinese in 1884. The region's economy is based primarily on herding (cattle, sheep, and goats) and farming (corn, cotton, wheat, and rice). Ürümqi is its capital.
See also: China.

Xochimilco *See:* Lake Xochimilco.

X ray, type of radiation of higher frequency than visible light but lower than a gamma ray. Discovered by the German physicist Wilhem Conrad Roentgen in 1895, X rays are usually produced by high-energy electrons impinging upon a metal target. X rays are often used in medicine to make radiographs (X-ray pictures) of the bones and internal organs of the body.
See also: Roentgen, Wilhelm Conrad.

Xunzi, or Hsun Tzu (340?-245? B.C.), Chinese philosopher. He is considered a follower of Kongfuzi (Confucius; 551-479 B.C.). Whereas Mengzi (Mencius), the 'Second Sage' (4th century B.C.), interpreted Kongfuzi in an optimistic light, teaching the intrinsic goodness of human nature, Xunzi taught that human nature is intrinsically evil and that morality must be taught and reinforced by society. His teachings are articulated in the book *Xunzi*.
See also: Philosophy.

Xuzhou (pop. 1.5 mln), a city in Jiangsu province, China. It is about 325 mi (523 km) northwest of Shanghai. Xuzhou is a

major railway junction and a port on the Grand Canal. It is the trading center for the surrounding agricultural area, which produces wheat, cotton, and peanuts. Industries include food processing, textile manufacturing, and metalworking. Coal and iron ore are mined nearby. Although a long-established trading center, Xuzhou remained a small city until the building of railways in the early 1900's. A major battle in the Chinese civil war was fought here in November 1948.

Xylophone, percussion instrument consisting of a series of tuned wooden blocks set in a frame and struck with special hammers. Of ancient origin, it was widespread in Asia and Africa before being introduced in Europe.

XYZ Affair, diplomatic incident that nearly led to open war between the United States and France in 1798. President John Adams sent John Marshall, Elbridge Gerry, and C. C. Pinckney to settle disputes with France following Jay's Treaty. They were met by three unnamed agents, later called X, Y, and Z, who demanded U.S. loans and bribes before opening negotiations. When this was announced in Congress, there was an uproar, but Adams averted war and reopened negotiations with Talleyrand, the French foreign minister. Later, the agents were identified as Jean Conrad Hottinguer (X), a U.S. banker in Hamburg named Bellamy (Y), and Lucien Hauteval (Z).

Y, 25th letter of the English alphabet. Like *u*, *v*, and *w*, it derives from the ancient Semitic letter *waw* (meaning 'hook'), itself adapted from an Egyptian hieroglyphic. It passed into the Greek alphabet as the letter *upsilon* and was later used in the Roman alphabet only for words of Greek origin. In Old and Middle English, *y* was often used instead of *i*, a usage that is part of our language today. In chemistry, *y* is used as the symbol for the element *yttrium*.

Yablonovyy Mountains, mountain range in Russia and northern Mongolia. The range, which extends 1,000 mi (1,600 km), is a watershed, dividing those rivers that flow into the Arctic Ocean from those that flow into the Pacific. Its highest peak is Mt. Sokhondo (8,199 ft/2,499 m). There are large tin mines in the mountains. The range is crossed by the Trans-Siberian Railroad at Yablonovo.

Yachts and yachting, popular international sport and pastime of racing or cruising in yachts. Yachting developed in the early 19th century as steam began to supplant sails in commercial vessels. It became established on an organized basis with the setting up of the New York Yacht Club in 1844. In 1851 the first race for the *America's Cup* took place, and subsequent races for the cup played a major role in the evolution of yacht design. After World War I the trend moved away from large, expensive yachts, and popular 'one-design' classes emerged, with the Bermuda rig predominating. Small-keep yachts and catboats are now raced and sailed for pleasure throughout the world. Ocean racing is also popular, and recently single-

handed transatlantic and round-the-world races have attracted enormous public attention.
See also: Sailing.

Yahweh *See:* Jehovah.

Yak (*Bos grunniens*), shaggy ox of the high plateau of Tibet. Yaks are distinguished by the long fringe of hair on shoulders, flanks, thighs, and tail, and the long in-curved horns. Wild yaks are large animals, up to 7 ft (2.1 m) at the shoulder, with black coats. Domestic yaks, kept as beasts of burden and for their milk, are smaller and may be any of several colors.

Yale, Elihu (1649-1721), American-born English merchant who made a fortune in India (1670-1699). In 1718 he made a donation to the collegiate school at New Haven, which was renamed Yale College (now Yale University).

Yale, Linus, Jr. (1821-1868), U.S. inventor and manufacturer of locks. He developed the Yale Infallible Bank Lock (1851) and other bank locks, the combination lock (1861), and the key-operated cylinder pin-tumbler lock (patents 1861 and 1865), developed from a design used in ancient Egypt and now commonly used on doors of residences. Yale and partners Henry Towne and Henry Robinson Towne founded the Yale Lock Manufacturing Company in 1868.

Yale University, U.S. university chartered in 1701 as the Collegiate School, first at Killingworth, Milford, and Saybrook, Conn., then (1716) at New Haven, Conn., its present site. Renamed Yale College in 1718 in honor of Elihu Yale (1649-1721), it expanded greatly in the 19th century, awarded the first Ph.D. in the United States in 1861, and was renamed Yale University in 1887.

Yalow, Rosalyn Sussman (1921-   ), U.S. medical researcher who shared the 1977 Nobel Prize in physiology or medicine for helping develop *radioimmunoassay*, a technique for measuring minute amounts of hormones, vitamins, or enzymes that could not be detected by other means.
See also: Physiology.

Yalta (pop. 90,000), winter and health resort on the Black Sea, in southern Crimea,

The yak, *B. grunniens*, can be domesticated and used as a pack and saddle animal. The yak also serves as a source of milk and meat.

Y

Ukraine. It was site of the 1945 Yalta Conference between U.S. president Roosevelt, British prime minister Churchill, and Soviet premier Stalin.
See also: Union of Soviet Socialist Republics.

Yalta Conference, meeting held near Yalta (Crimea, Ukraine), Feb. 4-11, 1945, between Winston Churchill, Franklin Roosevelt, and Joseph Stalin, representing the major Allied powers in World War II. Plans were drawn up for the treatment of Germany after the war, including its division into occupation zones, the elimination of its war industries, and the prosecution of war criminals. The foundation of a new Polish state was decided upon, and the creation of the United Nations was discussed. The USSR agreed to join in the war against Japan after Germany's defeat, receiving occupation areas in eastern Europe in return.
See also: World War II.

Yalu River (Chinese: *Ya-Lu Chiang*; Korean: *Amnok-Kang*), river forming most of the boundary between North Korea and Manchuria, China. It rises in the Changbai Shan (Long White Mountains) of Manchuria and flows southeast 500 mi (800 km) to Korea Bay (Yellow Sea). The crossing of the river by Chinese Communist troops to help North Korea (Oct. 1950) was an important event of the Korean War.

Yam (genus *Dioscorea*), plant of the yam family with a flowering vine and a large tu-

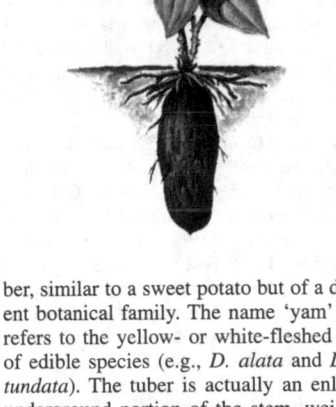

The yam is grown as food in warm climates, and the vine is grown as an ornamental in northern regions. Its tubers are eaten as a vegetable.

ber, similar to a sweet potato but of a different botanical family. The name 'yam' often refers to the yellow- or white-fleshed tuber of edible species (e.g., *D. alata* and *D. rotundata*). The tuber is actually an enlarged underground portion of the stem, weighing as much as 100 lb (45 kg), in which the plant stores starch, water, and some sugar. Some varieties contain toxic substances that can only be eliminated by cooking, and cortisone and other drugs are derived from *saponin* compounds found in certain wild yams. Yams grow in warm, moist climates, and are an important food crop in West Africa, India, Southeast Asia, and the Caribbean area.

Yamagata, Aritomo (1838-1922), Japanese statesman, Minister of Defense and head of the general staff in the 1870s and 1880s; in these positions he devoted himself to modernizing the Japanese army using a Western model. Yamagata was Prime Minister in the periods 1889-1891 and 1898-1901, and played a major part in the Russian-Japanese War (1904-1905). As Minister of War he signed the Lobonov-Yamagata Treaty between Russia and Japan in 1896. After his active political career, he became a member and the president of the Secret Council.

Yamamoto, Isoroku (1884-1943), commander of the Japanese fleet in World War

Allied leaders Winston Churchill, Franklin Delano Roosevelt, and Joseph Stalin planned the final phase of World War II at Yalta (Feb. 4-11, 1945).

Y

Qutang Gorge, one of the three Tangzi Gorges on the Yangtze River.

II. He planned and commanded the attack on Pearl Harbor (1941) and Midway Island (1941). He was reported killed in an air ambush.
See also: World War II.

Yamani, Ahmed (1930-), Saudi politician. Yamani, who was responsible for Saudi oil policy (1962-1986), was identified with OPEC for many years. He used the Saudi oil power within Opec to keep the oil price as stable as possible. He was dismissed by King Fahd in 1986, after oil prices dropped to a record low.

Yamasaki, Minoru (1912-1986), U.S. architect. The Lambert-St. Louis air terminal (1951), the McGregor Conference Center at Wayne University, Detroit (1956), and the U.S. science pavilion at the Seattle Exposition (1962) reveal his mastery of ornamental and sculptural form. He was also the architect, with Emery Roth, of the World Trade Center in New York.
See also: Architecture.

Yamashita, Tomoyuki (1885-1946), Japanese army commander in World War II. His forces overran Malaya and captured Singapore (1942). He later commanded Japanese forces in the Philippines, surrendering in 1945. He was hanged by the Allies for the atrocities committed by his troops.
See also: World War II.

Yamato period, portion of Japanese history (c.A.D. 200-646) during which the imperial center was Yamato, the area around current-day Nara, near Osaka. During this time the Japanese empire included much of central Japan and parts of southern Korea. The period was characterized by the influence of Chinese culture on Japanese arts and government, and the transmission of the Buddhist religion from China to Japan (although the primary popular religion remained Shinto).
See also: Japan.

Yam bean *See:* Jicama.

Yang, Chen Ning (1922-), Chinese-born U.S. physicist who shared with Tsung Dao Lee the 1957 Nobel Prize in physics for their studies of violations of the conservation of parity.
See also: Parity; Physics.

Yangon (pop. 4,000,000; formerly Rangoon), capital, largest city, and chief port of Myanmar (Burma), on the Rangoon River. It is a commercial and manufacturing center, with textile, sawmilling, food-processing, and petroleum industries. Its gold-domed Shwe Dagon Pagoda is the country's principal Buddhist shrine. Yangon was founded in 1753 as the Burmese capital. It was occupied by the British (1824-1826) and retaken by them in 1852, after which it developed as a modern city. During World War II Yangon was occupied by the Japanese and suffered heavy damage.

Yangtze River, or Chang River, China's longest river. It rises in the Kunlun Mountains of Tibet and flows 3,434 mi (5,526 km) into the East China Sea, draining an area (about 750,000 sq mi/1,942,500 sq km) that includes China's richest agricultural land along its lower reaches. Its main tributaries are the Min, Wu, and Han. It is navigable for oceangoing ships for some 600 mi (966 km), as far as Wuhan.

Yankee, slang term of uncertain origin, probably Dutch. Outside the United States, it refers to anyone from the United States; inside the country, it normally refers to a New Englander, especially someone descended from colonists. In the South it refers to Northerners, a tradition dating from the Civil War.

Yankee Doodle, song popular among American troops in the Revolutionary War. It probably originated among the British during the French and Indian Wars as a song making fun of the Americans, who later adopted it for themselves.

Yaoundé, or Yaunde (pop. 750,000), capital city of Cameroon, located in the south-central part of the country between the Nyong and Sanaga rivers. It was founded in 1888 by the Germans, under whom Cameroon was a protectorate. When the area was divided in 1922, the city became the capital of French East Cameroon. In 1960 it was made capital of the newly independent Republic of Cameroon. Yaoundé is a center for transportation, light industry, and education.
See also: Cameroon.

Yap Islands, in the western Pacific Ocean, part of the Caroline Islands, consisting of 4 large and 10 small islands, surrounded by a coral reef. The Micronesian population fishes and grows yams, taro, bananas, and coconuts.

Yawning, involuntary gaping of the mouth, often accompanied by involuntary stretching of the muscles and accompanied by a deep inspiration. It usually occurs during the drowsy state produced by fatigue or boredom and is often a prelude to sleep.

Yaws, disease caused by an organism related to that which causes syphilis. Common in the tropics, it occurs often in children and consists of a local lesion on the limbs; there is also mild systemic disease. Chronic, destructive lesions of skin, bone, and cartilage may develop later. When the Wassermann test is positive, that indicates the disease is present, and penicillin is the treatment of choice.

Yazdegerd I (r. 399-420), Persian Emperor of the Sasanian dynasty. He protected Christians, which caused dissent amongst the Magi priest caste. Succeeded by Bahram V.

Yeager, Chuck (Charles Elwood Yeager; 1923-), U.S. fighter pilot in World War II, test pilot, first person to fly faster than the speed of sound (Oct. 14, 1947). Yeager set a second record by flying 2 1/2 times the speed of sound, or 1,650 mph (2,655 kmph) on Dec. 12, 1953. He retired from the military as a brigadier general (1975), later serving on the presidential commission investigating the 1986 explosion of the *Challenger* space shuttle. He told his life story in *Yeager* (1985), coauthored by Leo Janos, and his exploits as a test pilot are celebrated in Tom Wolfe's *The Right Stuff* (1979).

Year, name of various units of time, all depending on the revolution of the earth about the sun. The *sidereal year* (365.256636 mean solar days) is the average time the earth takes to complete one revolution measured with respect to a fixed direction in space. The *tropical year* (365.24220 mean solar days), the year measured by the changing seasons, is that in which the mean longitude of the sun moves through 360°. The *anomalistic year* (365.25964 mean solar days) is the average interval between successive terrestrial perihelions. The *civil year* is a period of variable duration, usually 365 or 366 days (leap year), depending on the type of calendar in use.

Yeast, any of single-celled plants classified with the fungi. Some cause diseases of the skin and mucous membranes, while others, notably the strains of *Saccharomyces cerevisiae* (baker's yeast), are used in baking, brewing, and winemaking. Yeasts employ either or both of 2 metabolic processes: Fermentation involves the anaerobic decomposition of hexose sugars to yield alcohol (ethanol) and carbon dioxide; 'respiration' involves the exothermic decomposition of various sugars in the presence of oxygen to give carbon dioxide and water. Yeasts are also grown as a source of food rich in B-complex vitamins.

Yeats, William Butler (1865-1939), Irish poet and dramatist, leader of the Celtic Renaissance in Ireland and one of the world's greatest lyric poets. Nationalism was a major element in his early poetry, such as *The Wanderings of Oisin* (1889), which drew on Irish legend. Yeats cofounded (1898) Dublin's Irish Literary Theatre, later the Abbey Theatre. His mature poetic works, often symbolic and mystical, treated universal themes. They include *The Wild Swans at Coole* (1917), *The Tower* (1928), and *Last Poems* (1940). Yeats was awarded the Nobel Prize in literature in 1923.

Yeh Chien-Ying, or Ye Jianying (1899-1985), Chinese minister of defense (1971-1978). A planner of the Long March and a Central Committee member from 1945, his seniority and military connections assured his continued position within the inner circle of leadership after the death of Mao Tse-tung (Mao Zedong).
See also: China.

Yellow *See:* Color.

Yellow daisy *See:* Black-eyed Susan.

Yellow fever, infectious disease caused by a virus carried by mosquitos of the genus *Aëdes* and occurring in tropical Americas and Africa. The disease consists of fever, headache, backache, prostration, and vomiting of sudden onset. Protein loss in the urine, kidney failure, and liver disorder with jaundice are also frequent. Hemorrhage from mucous membranes, especially in the gastrointestinal tract, is also common. A moderate number of cases are fatal, but a mild form of the disease is also recognized. Vaccination to induce immunity is important and effective as no specific therapy is available; mosquito control provides a similarly important preventive measure.

Yellowhammer, or yellow-shafted flicker (*Colaptes auratus auratus*), bird of the woodpecker family, subspecies of the common flicker, native to North America; also, the yellow bunting (German: *Ammer*, 'bunting'; *Emberiza citrinella*), finch of Europe and Asia.

Yellow jacket, one of a genus (*Vespula*) of hornets, social wasps of the family Vespidae, common in North America. They usually construct an underground nest of paper, frequently in or near human habitation. Yellow jackets can inflict a painful sting.

Yellow journalism, vulgar and sensational newspaper reporting whose sole aim is to attract readers. The term originated with the 'Yellow Kid' comic strip in the Sunday supplement of Joseph Pulitzer's New York *World* (1896). This began a 'yellow journalism' circulation war in the city with William Randolph Hearst's *Journal*. It is still evident today.

Yellowlegs (genus *Tringa*), migrating shore bird of the sandpiper family, native to the Western Hemisphere and identified by dark wings, white belly and tail, and long yellow legs. The 2 species are the greater yellowlegs (*T. melanoleuca*), measuring 13-15 in (34-38 cm), and the lesser yellowlegs (*T. flavipes*), measuring about 10 in (25 cm). The birds nest in Canada and winter in the southern United States, around the Gulf of Mexico, and as far south as Chile.

Yellow poplar, or tulip tree (*Liriodendron tulipifera*), tall hardwood tree of the magnolia family, native to eastern North America. It is the tallest broadleaf tree of eastern North America, its straight trunk growing to a height of 200 ft (60 m) and a diameter of 10 ft (3 m). The light-colored wood is widely used for furniture, veneer, plywood, and crates. Nectar from its tulip-shaped yellow and green flowers is an important source of honey.

Yellow River, or Hwang Ho, river of northern China, flowing 2,903 mi (4,672 km) from the Kunlun Mountains, generally east to the Yellow Sea. It is named for its fertile yellow silt and is often nicknamed China's Sorrow because of terrible floods and destructive changes of course. In 1955 a major 50-year flood-control and hydroelectric project was begun on the river.

Yellow Sea, or Huang Hai, western arm of the Pacific Ocean between Korea and northeast China. It opens in the south into the East China Sea. The name arises from the color of its waters, which receive yellow silt from the Yellow and other rivers.
See also: Pacific Ocean.

Yellowstone National Park, oldest and largest U.S. national park, created in 1872 and covering 3,472 sq mi (8,992 sq km), mostly in northwestern Wyoming. It contains some of the most spectacular wonders in the United States, including Old Faithful geyser, thousands of hot springs and mud pools, petrified forests, black grass cliffs, and the Grand Canyon of the Yellowstone River. Wildlife abounds in the forests covering most of the park.

Yellowstone River, river flowing 671 mi (1,080 km) from northwestern Wyoming north and east through Montana to join the Missouri River at the North Dakota state line. It rises in the Rocky Mountains, flowing into Yellowstone Lake in Yellowstone National Park, emptying by a dramatic drop of over 420 ft (128 m) into Yellowstone Canyon. It then flows northeast through the Great Plains of Montana. The river system, including the tributaries Bighorn, Tongue, and Powder, drains 70,000 sq mi (181,000 sq km). The river is visited for its natural beauty and is used for irrigation.

Yellowthroat (*Geothlypis trichas*), small, migratory bird of the wood warbler family native to North America. Yellowthroats are olive-green with white and buff breasts and measure about 5 in (13 cm) long; males have black masks. They are found in the tall grasses of marshes and other wet areas.

Yeltsin, Boris Nikolayevich, (1931-), president of the Russian Federation (1990-99). He joined the Communist Party in 1961. Yeltsin was a member of the Politburo, the policy-making organ of the party, and was President Mikhail Gorbachev's chief rival. After he was elected president of the Russian republic, Yeltsin resigned from the Communist Party. In 1991, after a general election, he retained the presidency of the Russian Federation. In 1993 he suppressed a rebellion of communist and nationalist members of parliament. He tried to shake off the communist past by discontinuing a number of communist organizations. In 1995 he temporarily left politics due to health problems. However, in 1996 he won the presidential elections with an ample majority. On 31 Dec. 1999, he unexpectedly resigned from the presidency.

Yemen

Capital:	Sana'a
Area:	207,232 sq mi (536,869 sq km)
Population:	18,701,000
Language:	Arabic
Government:	Islamic presidential republic
Independent:	1918 (north)/1967 (south)/ 1990 (united)
Head of gov.:	Prime minister
Per capita:	US$ 820
Monetary unit:	1 Yemen rial = 100 fils

Yemen, officially the Republic of Yemen, formerly divided into Yemen (Sana), also known as North Yemen, and Yemen (Aden), also known as South Yemen, now united into a single republic occupying the southwest corner of the Arabian peninsula and including the islands of Kamaran, Perim, and Socotra. With a combined area of 207,232 sq mi (536,870 sq km), Yemen is bordered by Saudi Arabia to the north and northeast, the Gulf of Aden to the south, Oman to the east, and the Red Sea to the west.
Land and climate. Beyond the Red Sea

The capital of Yemen, Sana'a, is located in the central highlands and has preserved its beauty through the ages. The high brick houses that are built close to each other, are beautifully decorated. Other Yemenite towns that have long remained isolated, also consist of houses in this style.

Y

Y

coast with its coral reefs and low-lying beaches is the Tihamah, a dry coastal plain, and, farther inland, a foothill region scored by valleys, known as *wadis*. The coastal plain along the Gulf of Aden is hot and arid with palm oases. The lowlands along both shores give way to a mountainous interior with some peaks exceeding 12,000 ft (3,658 m). Among the mountains is a mosaic of plateaus, upland plains, and fertile valleys. The mountains eventually give way in the north and east to the Rub'al-Khali desert. The highlands of Yemen enjoy the best climate on the Arabian peninsula, with annual rainfall of some 16-32 in (41-81 cm).

People. The people of what was formerly South Yemen consist of various tribes of Arabs and are either farmers or nomads. The people of what was formerly Yemen are mostly south Arabians, but there are African influences in the people living along the Red Sea coast and toward the south. Though the people are Muslim, they are divided about equally between Sunni and Shi'te Muslims. The religious differences translated into significant social and political divisions in the former Yemen Arab Republic, and are now part of the United Republic of Yemen as well. The official language of Yemen is Arabic.

History. The histories of North Yemen and South Yemen have, since antiquity, sometimes blended, sometimes gone their separate ways, and at other times collided. Formerly known as Al-Yaman, the land of South Yemen was once home to the Minaean, Sabaean, and Himyarite kingdoms. Conquered by Arabs in the 8th century A.D., it became part of the Ottoman Empire during the 16th century. Known as Aden under British control from the 1830s, South Yemen became fully independent in 1967 following the collapse of the Federation of South Arabia. Governed by the Marxist National Liberation Front, it was known as the People's Democratic Republic of Yemen. Neighboring North Yemen was once part of the Sabaean kingdom and was incorporated into the Muslim caliphate in the 7th century A.D. Various foreign powers have exercised nominal suzerainty over North Yemen, including the Ottoman Turks from the 1500s to 1918. But effective power from the 9th to the 20th centuries lay in the hands of competing local imams. In 1962 an army coup led to the proclamation of a republic. In the ensuing civil war, Saudi Arabia backed the royalist tribes, while Egypt supported the republicans. The conflict ended with a mediated settlement in 1970 from which the republicans emerged in control of the fledgling Yemen Arab Republic.

In 1972 war erupted between the Yemen Arab Republic and the People's Democratic Republic of Yemen. A ceasefire was followed by an agreement to unify North Yemen and South Yemen, but hostilities flared again in 1979. Finally, on May 22, 1990, the two countries were united as the Republic of Yemen under the interim presidency of Ali Abdullah Saleh. Yemen abstained from a vote in the Arab League to condemn Saddam Hussein's invasion of Kuwait and earned the immediate enmity of its powerful neighbor, Saudi Arabia, at considerable cost to its already troubled economy. After the 1993 elections tensions between the north and the south increased. The ensuing civil war of 1994 was won by the north. In 1995 there was an armed conflict with Eritrea regarding some small islands in the strait which gives entrance to the Red Sea. The islands were divided between the two countries in 1998. In 2000, Yemen and Saudi Arabia signed the Jeddah agreement, a treaty that determined the border between both countries so the 65-year border conflicts could come to an end. That same year, terrorist attacks were carried out on the American naval vessel USS Cole and the British embassy. The reason for this was supposed to be the military cooperation between the U.S. and Yemen. Ethiopia, Sudan and Yemen established a regional alliance that will attempt to combat terrorism in the Horn of Africa in 2003.

Yenisey River, river in Russia, in Siberia; 2,566 mi (4,129 km), including the Great Yenisey. Its source is in the Sayani Mountains; the river basin is 1,003,862 sq mi (2,599,000 sq km). Beyond Krasnoyarsk it is calmer and flows through a grain-growing area, then through taigas, pine forests and tundras. The mouth is in the Yenisey Bay in the Kara Sea. The ports there are frozen up from October to June. The Tunguska and the Angara are its largest subsidiaries.

Yeoman, Middle English word denoting a king's or nobleman's retainer or officer, or a freehold farmer cultivating his own land, ranking below the gentry. Yeoman now refers to a naval petty officer performing clerical duties.

Yerevan, or Erevan (pop. 1,300,000), capital city of Armenia, on the Razdan River, in southeastern Europe, near Turkey. Archeological remains indicate a settlement on the site dating from before 2000 B.C., and a fortress from the 8th century B.C.

The city was often under siege and destroyed by rival powers, particularly, during the 15th-19th centuries, the Persians and Ottomans. It was established as capital of the Armenian republic in 1920. Hydroelectric power from the Razdan River has helped the city become a center for chemical, engineering, and other industries. It is also a center for culture and higher education.
See also: Armenia.

In this photograph, four leading Yiddish authors are gathered together. From left to right we see Mendele Mocher Sefarim (1835-1917), Sholem Aleichem (1859-1916), Mordecai Ban-Ammi (1854-1932) and Chaim Nahman Bialik (1873-1934).

Yesenin, Sergei Aleksandrovich (also Sergei Aleksandrovich Esenin; 1895-1925), Soviet-Russian lyrical poet. He is regarded as one of the 'peasant poets': it is impossible to imagine his often melancholy poetry without allusions to nature and the Russian countryside. In 1918 Yesenin joined the Imaginists, whose poetry is characterized by pessimism and licentiousness. Collections from this period include *Confessions of a Hooligan: Fifty Poems* (1921). After 1919 Yesenin grew gradually more disillusioned, seeing the industrial, proletarian revolution as a threat to the countryside. Not being capable of adjusting to the reality of the soviet and after a short and unhappy marriage to the dancer Isadora Duncan, he committed suicide.

Yevtushenko, Yevgeny (1933-   ), Russian poet who became a spokesperson for 'liberal' forces in Soviet literature in the early 1960s. His best-known poems include 'Babi-Yar' (1961), dealing with the Nazis' massacre of Soviet Jews in 1941, and 'The Heirs of Stalin' (1962), warning of the persistence of Stalinism.

Yew, any of several species of evergreen trees and shrubs of genus *Taxus* native to the Northern Hemisphere. Yews are often grown as ornamental plants. They have flat, dark-green needles and red-brown bark. Their wood, which is hard and dense, was once valued for its use in archery bows and furniture. The bark, needles, and seeds are poisonous and can be fatal to livestock. Yews native to North America include the western, or Pacific, yew (*T. brevifolia*), used for cabinetry; the Japanese yew (*T. cuspidata*), an ornamental shrub; and the American yew, or ground hemlock (*T. canadensis*), which grows along the ground.

Yiangsu (Kiangsu, Chiang-su; pop. 69.1 million), province on the east coast of China, 39,783 sq mi (103,000 sq km). The capital city is Nanying. Soochow, Wuxi, Suzhou and the port of Lianyungang are also important. It is a highly populated region and one of China' s most important agricultural areas, where rice, wheat, vegetables, cotton and silk are cultivated. Coal, phosphate and salt are mined. The industries are textile, steel, chemicals and machinery. The autonomous city province of Shanghai is situated in the southeast of the province.

Yiangxi (Kiangsi, Chiang-hsi; pop. 39.1 million), province in the east of China, 65,276 sq mi (169,000 sq km). In the north rice, tobacco and cotton are cultivated. In the southern hills mostly tea is grown. Coal is mined, and clay for porcelain. Textile and paper industries. It was an important military base for the communists from 1920 to 1934, when they began their Long March.

Yiang Zemin (1926-), Chinese President (1993-). After many years of working at the Ministry of Mechanical Engineering, Yiang became Vice Chairman of the State Committee for Import and Export and Foreign Investments in 1980. He was Minister of Industry and Mayor of Shanghai before becoming Chairman of the Party in 1989. In 1993 the National People's Congress elected him to succeed President Deng Xiaoping. Yiang is known for his liberal economic ideas, but he is not an advocate of social-political reforms.

Yiddish, language spoken by Jewish people, developed during the A.D. 900s and 1000s. Yiddish has roots in several languages, including German, Hebrew, Aramaic, French, and Italian. After World War II (1939-1945), in which the Nazis exterminated over 6 million Jews, the use of Yiddish declined considerably.

Yiddish literature, body of written works that developed in the late 1200s and remained strongly connected to Jewish religious tradition until the 1800s, when modern Jewish literature had its beginnings through a cultural literary movement called the *Haskalah* (Enlightenment). The humorist Solomon Rabinowitz, who wrote under the name Sholom Aleichem, Shalom Jacob Abramovich, whose pen name was Mendele the Bookseller, and Isaac Leibush Peretz stand out as major exponents of Yiddish literature during much of the 1800s and 1900s. Some of the common themes underlying most works of this time include the hardships involved with living in a non-Jewish world and the social conflicts within the Jewish community.
The flowering of Yiddish literature took place during the period of 1914-1918 in Poland, the Soviet Union, and the United States. During this period, Sholem Asch in Poland, David Bergelson in the Soviet Union, and Moishe Leib Halpern in the United States ranked as the most important figures in Yiddish literature. During World War II (1939-1945), many notable Yiddish writers perished along with the 6 million Jews that were exterminated by the Nazis. Isaac Bashevis Singer, a Polish-born U.S. author, became the first Yiddish writer to win the Nobel Prize in literature (1978).

Yilmaz, Mesut (1947-), Turkish politician, elected prime minister in March 1997. Cofounder of the late President Turgut Ozal's center right ANAP (Motherland Party), and its leader since 1983. Former foreign minister. Was previously prime minister for several months in 1991. The Yilmaz government lost the support of parliament in November 1998. Yilmaz was accused of corruption.

Yin and yang, two principles in Chinese philosophy, representing the passive and the active forces of the universe. Yin stands for earth, female, passive, dark, and receiving; yang, for heaven, male, active, light, and generative. All things exist through their interaction. The symbol for yin-yang is a circle divided into 2 curved forms, one dark, the other light.
See also: Philosophy.

YMCA *See:* Young Men's Christian Association (YMCA).

Yoga (Sanskrit, 'union'), forms of spiritual discipline practiced in Buddhism and Hinduism. Through these disciplines the yogi (one who follows yoga) strives to free the mind from attachment to the senses and to achieve *samadhi*-or union with *Brahma*, the deity-and fusion into oneness. In Hindu tradition there are three varieties of yoga: *karma yoga*, salvation through action; *jnana yoga*, salvation through knowledge; and *bhakti yoga*, salvation through devotion. In each the student passes through 8 levels of attainment, supervised by a guru, or teacher. The practice of *hatha yoga*, based on physical postures and control, has become increasingly popular in the West.
See also: Hinduism.

Yogurt, or yoghurt, semisolid, cultured milk food made by inoculating pasteurized milk with a culture of *Streptococcus thermophilus* and *Lactobacillus bulgaricus* and incubating until the desired acidity is achieved. Various fruits can be added.

Yogyakarta (pop. 457,000), city in Indonesia, on Central Java, capital of the autonomous district of the same name. (District pop. 2,913,000; 1,224 sq mi (3,169 sq km). Leather, tobacco, and food industry, crafts (silver smithery). Trade in the region's agricultural products (rice, sugar cane, and tobacco), one of the most fertile areas of Java. Situated on the railroad between Jakarta and Surabaya and the railroad to Semerang. Two universities. The principality of Yogyakarta was a Dutch protectorate before the Japanese occupation. The principality then joined the Indonesian Republic when it came into being in 1945. From 1945 until 1950 temporarily the capital of the Indonesian republic. The Merapi volcano is clearly visible from the city. The sultan's residence and the university are located in the *kraton* (walled palace).

Yokohama (pop. 3,300,000), city in Japan on the western shore of Tokyo Bay, a leading national seaport and part of Tokyo's industrial belt in southern Honshu Island. It is a trading center and supports large shipbuilding, iron, steel, chemical, machinery, and oil industries. It also has several universities. Yokohama was a fishing village when visited by Commodore Matthew Perry in 1854. Its growth began in 1859, when it became a foreign-trade port.
See also: Japan.

Yom Kippur, Jewish Day of Atonement, the most sacred day in the Jewish religious calendar. It falls on the 10th day after the

An Indian yogi, staring at the sun in a rather difficult position. Yogis of some trends use these kinds of exertions to induce mystic experiences.

Y

Jewish New Year (Rosh Hashanah) and is marked by repentance, prayers, and abstention from food, drink, sex, and work.
See also: Judaism.

York (pop. 174,000), city in northern England. Built on the site of a Roman fort, it emerged during the early Middle Ages as an important religious capital and trade center. Today York, with its many museums and historic buildings and churches, thrives primarily on tourism. The Cathedral of St. Peter, known as Minster Cathedral, and the National Railway Museum are of special interest. It also supports several industries, including the manufacture of precision instruments.
See also: England.

York, ruling dynasty of England (1461-1485), a branch of the Plantagenet family, whose symbol was the white rose. The three Yorkist kings were **Edward IV** (r.1461-1483), his son **Edward V** (r.April-June 1483), and **Richard III** (r.1483-1485), who was killed at the Battle of Bosworth Field by Henry Tudor (Henry VII), who established the House of Tudor as the ruling family.
See also: United Kingdom.

Yorkshire terrier, breed of toy dog developed in Yorkshire and Lancashire, England, in the mid-19th century to hunt rats. Yorkies stand 8-9 in (20-23 cm) at the shoulder and weigh 4-8 lb (2-2.3 kg). Their long, straight, silky coat is bluish gray, with tan on the head and chest.

Yorktown, Battle of *See:* Revolutionary War in America.

Yoruba, African people in southwest Nigeria, characteristically urban dwellers. Yoruba culture exists also in Cuba and Brazil because of large slave importations.

Yosemite Falls, North America's highest waterfalls, in Yosemite National Park, central California. Here Yosemite Creek descends in 2 dramatic drops: the Upper Falls (1,430 ft/436 m), and the Lower Falls (320 ft/98 m). In between the waters fall in cascades, for a total descent of 2,425 ft (739 m).

Y

Yosemite National Park, national park in eastern California, established in 1890, 1,189 sq mi (3,000 sq km) of spectacular mountain scenery formed during the last glacial period, on the western slopes of the Sierra Nevada. Its chief attractions are the Yosemite Valley; Yosemite Falls, the highest falls in North America; and the Mariposa Grove of 200 giant sequoias.

Yoshida, Shigeru (1878-1967), Japanese politician. Prime minister from 1946 to 1947, and from 1948 to 1954. As prime minister of five cabinets and foreign minister during the American occupation of Japan, he played a major role in helping to reach a peace treaty with the US and the restructuring of postwar Japan. During his last two cabinets (1952-1954), however, a small number of the reforms introduced by the Americans were reversed.

Youmans, Vincent (1898-1946), U.S. composer of popular musical comedies of the 1920s, among them *No, No, Nanette* and *Hit the Deck*. His songs included 'Tea for Two,' 'Without a Song,' and 'I Want to Be Happy.'

Young, Andrew Jackson, Jr. (1932-), U.S. clergyman and civil rights leader. He helped draft the civil rights and voting rights acts (1964, 1965) and served in the U.S. House of Representatives (1971-76). As the first black U.S. ambassador to the UN (1977-79), he stirred up frequent controversy with undiplomatic public statements. In 1981 he was elected mayor of Atlanta.
See also: Civil rights.

Andrew Jackson Young Jr.

Young, Cy (Denton True Young; 1867-1955), U.S. baseball player. Considered one of the greatest pitchers of all time, he holds the record for career wins (511) and innings pitched (7,356), he pitched no-hit games (1897 and 1908) and pitched one perfect game (May 5, 1904). Young played for the Cleveland Spiders (1890-1898), St. Louis Nationals (1898-1900), Boston Red Sox (1901-1908), Cleveland Indians (1909-1911), and Boston Braves (1911) and was inducted into the National Baseball Hall of Fame in 1937. The Cy Young Award is given each year to the leading pitcher of each league.

Young, John Watts (1930-), U.S. astronaut. Young was a U.S. Navy test pilot (1952-1962), setting 2 world altitude records, before becoming an astronaut in 1962. He made more space flights than any other astronaut. His missions included the first *Gemini* mission with Virgil I. Grissom in 1965, and the command of the 1972 *Apollo 16* flight and lunar landing. Chief of the National Aeronautics and Space Administration's (NASA's) astronaut office at Johnson Space Center, Houston, Tex., Young was the commander of the *Columbia* in 1981, the first space-shuttle flight.
See also: Astronaut.

Young, La Monte (1935-), American composer. Studied composition and ethnomusicology at the University of California, thereafter electronic music under R. Maxfield, and Hindustani music under Pandit Pran Nath. At the beginning of the 1960s he became a member of the 'Fluxus' movement, and became an exponent of minimalist music. Since the middle of the 1960s he has concentrated on improvized music and meditation. His works include *Poem for Chairs, Tables, Benches, Etc.* (1960), *The Well-Tuned Piano* (1964), and *The Tortoise, His Dreams, and Journeys* (1964), a composition that can go on for ever.

Young, Lester Willis (1909-1959), U.S. tenor saxophonist, one of the most influential jazz musicians. Young grew up in New Orleans, playing in his father's carnival band, first as drummer and then saxophonist. He was active in Kansas City jazz, playing with 'King' Oliver and other bands. Young (or 'Prez' as he became known) played with Count Basie from 1935 to 1944 and on tour with 'Jazz at the Philharmonic' in the 1940s and 1950s. He helped develop the 'cool' jazz style of the 1940s, using the saxophone to create new sounds and employing expressive silences.
See also: Jazz.

Young Men's Christian Association (YMCA), worldwide organization that seeks, through programs of sport, religious and current-affairs study groups, and summer camps, to promote a healthy way of life based on Christian ideals. It was begun in England in 1844.

Young Women's Christian Association (YWCA), international organization that promotes a Christian way of life through educational and recreational activities and social work. The movement started in the United States in 1858.

Yourcenar, Marguerite (1903-1987), pen name of Marguerite de Crayencour, Belgian-born French author who became a U.S. citizen in the 1940s. The first woman elected to the Académie Française (1980), she is best known for the historical novel *Memoirs of Hadrian* (1951) and *The Abyss* (1968).

Youth hostel, inexpensive, supervised overnight lodging, particularly for young people but generally accommodating all members of such hosteling organizations as the International Youth Hostel Federation. Hostels provide dormitory-style sleeping and a communal kitchen, but little in the way of bedding and services. Length of stay is often limited to 1-3 nights. The first hostel was founded in Westphalia, Germany, in 1910. Hostels spread rapidly in Europe after World War I.

Ypres (Flemish, 'Ieper'; pop. 35,000), city in West Flanders, western Belgium, on the Yperlee River. The city was a major textile center in the Middle Ages, and the main political power of Flanders in the 13th century. It declined in the 15th-18th centuries due to a succession of civil wars, religious strife, and military domination by the French and Dutch. It was nearly destroyed during World War I (battles of Ypres) and was again the scene of fighting in World War II. The city, with many of its medieval buildings, was rebuilt, and it is now a center for linen and lace-making and agricultural products.
See also: Belgium.

Ysaye, Eugène (1858-1931), a Belgian violinist and conductor. One of the great virtuosos of his time, Ysaye was known for his original style and interpretations. He studied at the conservatory in his native Liège, and with Wieniawski and Vieuxtemps in Brussels. While teaching violin at the Brussels Conservatory, 1885-1898, Ysaye was manager and conductor of the Ysaye Orchestral Concerts in Brussels. He went to the United States during World War I and was conductor of the Cincinnati Symphony Orchestra, 1918-1922. He made extensive tours of the United States and Europe.

Ytterbium, chemical element, symbol Yb; for physical constants, see Periodic Table. Ytterbium was discovered by Jean de Marignac in 1878. It occurs in the minerals xenotime, polycrase, gadolinite, and monazite, the principal source of the element. It is prepared by reducing the anhydrous fluoride with calcium. Ytterbium is a silvery, soft, malleable, ductile, reactive metal belonging to the series of elements known as the rare-earth metals. Ion-exchange and solvent extraction techniques have led to much easier isolation of the rare-earth elements. Ytterbium has strong magnetic properties and a characteristic spectrum. It has possible use as a stainless steel additive. Ytterbium and its compounds are used in carbon-arc lighting, glass, and ceramics. Radioactive ytterbium is used as a portable X-ray source.

Yttrium, chemical element, symbol Y; for physical constants, see Periodic Table. Yttria, an earth (oxide) containing yttrium, was discovered in 1794 by John Gadolin. Yttrium was first isolated by Friedrich Wöhler in 1828. Yttrium occurs in nature as xenotime (yttrium phosphate), and other minerals, monazite being the commercial source. It is obtained by the reduction of the fluoride with calcium metal. Yttrium is a silvery-white, soft, reactive metal. Although not a member of the rare-earth series of metals, it is chemically similar and often considered with them. Yttrium and its compounds are used in phosphors for color televisions, in yttrium aluminum garnets used in YAG-lasers, and in mantles for incandescent lamps. In 1843 Carl Gustav Mosander divided the earth yttria into three earths, which then were named yttria, erbia, and terbia.

Yüan Shih-k'ai, or Yuan Shikai (1859-1916), Chinese soldier and president of China (1912-1916). His efforts to check Japan in Korea led to the Sino-Japanese War of 1894-1895. He supported the dowager empress Tz'u Hsi and helped suppress the Boxer movement (1900). Supported by his army during the revolution of 1911, he emerged as president but was unable to attain his goal of establishing himself emperor.
See also: China.

Yucatán Peninsula, peninsula (c.70,000 sq mi/c.181,200 sq km) dividing the Gulf of Mexico from the Caribbean Sea. It is comprised of Belize, El Petén (part of Guatemala), and 3 Mexican states. The climate is hot and humid, and farming and forestry are the main activities. The northern region is the leading producer of henequen (fiber used for twine). The people are of Maya stock and Chichén Itza, a famed Mayan site, is on the peninsula.
See also: Mexico.

Yucca, genus of plants of the Lily family found in desert regions of Mexico and the southwestern United States. The Joshua tree is a small tree, but other yuccas are shrubs or low plants bearing clusters of sword-shaped leaves and white, waxy flowers. All depend on the yucca moth for pollination.

Yugoslavia, from 1929 until 1991 the Socialist Federal Republic of Yugoslavia, republic with six constituent republics: Serbia, Croatia, Bosnia and Hercegovina, Macedonia, Slovenia and Montenegro.
Land and climate. Yugoslavia was made up of four geographical areas. A mostly mountainous country, it has an Alpine region in the nortwest, but also fertile northern plains. The south rugged mountainous region and

Bled Lake in the Julian Alps, an attractive region for tourists, with its health spas and skiing facilities. Bled has long been the summer residence of the Yugoslav rulers.

there is also the island-studded Dalmatian coast. Most of Yugoslavia is drained by the Danude river, which flows southeast from the Hungarian border across the northern plains. The climate varies from being continental in the north to Mediterranean in the south.
People. Yugoslavia was a federation of many different peoples, principly Serbs, Croats, Slovenes, Macedonians and Montenegrins, but also including many minority groups. The various peoples also profess several different religions. Roman Catholics comprise some 30% of the population, and most of them are Croats and Slovenes. Members of the Eastern Orthodox Church make up about 40% of the population and they are chiefly Serbs, Macedonians, and Montenegrins. The Roman Catholics use the Roman alphabet, whereas the Eastern Orthodox use the Cyrillic alphabet. Finally some 10% of the people are Muslims. Serbs and Croats speak Serbo-Croatian. Each of the other ethnic groups has its own language. About 40% of the people live in cities, the federal capital is Belgrade.
History. In 1918 the 'Kingdom of the Serbs, Croats, and Slovenes' was created. Its name was changed to Yugoslavia in 1929, but separatist pressures were strong from the very start, particularly among Croats and Macedonians. The Germans invaded in 1941, and two rival resistance groups were organized, one the royalist Draža Mihailovic and the other the communist resistance under Josip Tito. In 1943, even before the war had ended, the rival resistance groups were fighting one another; backed by Great Britain and the USSR, Tito prevailed. In 1945 he proclaimed Yugoslavia a federal republic of six states and established a communist government. Yugoslavia was expelled from the Cominform in 1948, and relations between the Yugoslavians and Soviets were strained. President Tito charted a policy of independent 'national communism' for Yugoslavia and successfully withstood Soviet pressure. Tito's regime continued to have to deal with internal tensions, which were centered on the nationalist aspirations of the constituent republics, most notably from Croatia. The regime was also challenged on issues of intellectual freedom. Following Tito's death in 1980, a collective state presidency was established. Despite attempts to maintain the federal system and the country's unity, the collapse of communist regimes throughout eastern Europe, beginning in 1989, has had profound repercussions in Yugoslavia. Separatism could not be contained, and in 1991 Slovenia and Croatia were the first republics to claim independence. Macedonia and Bosnia Hercegovina followed, and Serbia and Montenegro amalgamated into a new Federal Republic of Yugoslavia in 1992. Not all inhabitants of the newly independent countries complied with the new situation, and many protested violently, resulting in civil wars in both Bosnia Hercegovina and Croatia. Yugoslavia ceased to exist on February 5, 2003 when the confederation of Serbia and Montenegro was declared.
See also: Tito, Josip Broz.

Yugoslavia, Federal Republic of

Capital:	Belgrade
Area:	39,499 sq mi
	(102,173 sq km)
Population:	10,657,000
Language:	Serbian
Government:	Federal republic
Independent:	1992
Head of gov.:	Prime minister
Per capita:	less than US$ 2,250
Monetary unit:	1 New dinar = 100 para

Yugoslavia, Federal Republic of, independent country in southeastern Europe, bordered by Croatia in the west and the north, Bosnia Hercegovina on the west, Hungary on the north, Romania and Bulgaria on the east, and Macedonia and Albania in the south. The Federal Republic consists of Montenegro in the south and the dominant republic Serbia in the north.
Land and climate. Serbia's landscape is varied, with fertile plains and woody hills. Montenegro is mainly mountainous. Along the coast the climate is Mediterranean, while the interior has a continental climate.
People. About two-thirds of the population is Serbian. Montenegrans constitute 5% of the population. Many Albanians live in the Kosovo province (17%). The official language is Serbian. The major religions are: the Serbian Orthodox Church (44%), the Roman Catholic Church (31%), and the Islam (12%).
Economy. Because of the wars against Croatia and in Bosnia and the UN trade boycott, the economy suffered severely. In the early 1990s tourism collapsed. Agriculture and mining are currently on the increase.
History. Although Serbia was a dominant republic in the former Socialist Federal Republic of Yugoslavia, it could not prevent the separation of the prosperous republics Slovenia and Croatia in 1991. A bloody civil war ensued. Early in 1992 the United Nations negociated a cease-fire in Croatia and peacekeeping forces were sent there. Later that year the people of Bosnia and Herzegovina voted to secede from Yugoslavia. Conflict arose in the republic between Slavic Muslims, Croats, and Serbs. The Serb-led federal army lent its support to the Serbs in Bosnia and Herzegovina and war erupted. In April 1992, Serbia and

Y

Montenegro formed a new Yugoslav federation. The new Yugoslav state continued to support Serbs fighting in Bosnia and Herzegovina, and as war in that country intensified, the United Nations sent forces to the region and imposed sanctions (including a trade embargo) on Serbia and Montenegro. Also, the UN barred the new Yugoslav state from acquiring the membership of the former Yugoslavia in that body. The civil war in Bosnia and Herzegovina raged throughout 1993 and 1994. In August, 1994, Yugoslavia agreed to cut off all supplies, except for food and medicine, to Serbs in Bosnia and Herzegovina. In response, the UN lifted some of its sanctions against Yugoslavia. The war in Bosnia and Herzegovina ended in 1995 (Dayton accord), and all remaining sanctions against Yugoslavia were lifted. In 1999, ethnic violence between Serbs and Albanians in Kosovo resulted in air attacks by NATO on Serbia's military targets. The attacks ended in June 1999, when Serbia accepted NATO's peace plan for Kosovo. President's Slobodan Milosevic's government, that had been in power since 1989, ended in 2000, pressured by the population. Milosevic is generally acknowledged to be one of the major instigators of the war. The Serbian government handed him over to the Yugoslavia tribunal in The Hague in 2001, to answer accusations of crimes against humanity. In 2002 Montenegrin and Serbian leaders decided to change the country in a confederation called Serbia and Montenegro. Both republics will be semi-independent within the confederation, working only together in the areas of defense and foreign policies.

Yukawa, Hideki (1907-1981), Japanese physicist who postulated the meson as the agent bonding the atomic nucleus. In fact, the mu-meson (now called *muon*), discovered shortly afterward (in 1936) by Carl D. Anderson, does not fulfill this role, and Yukawa had to wait until Cecil F. Powell discovered the pi-meson (now called *pion*) in 1947 for vindication of his theory. He received the 1949 Nobel Prize in physics. *See also:* Meson.

Yukawa, Hideki (1907-1981), Japanese physicist, professor in Kyoto (1939-1970), interrupted for engagements in the U.S. 1948-1953). Won the Nobel Prize for physics in 1949 for his research into the structure of the atom nucleus, which in 1935 had led to the prediction of the existence of a meson particle.

Yukon River, sixth-longest river in North America, flowing from northern British Columbia for 1,979 mi (3,185 km) through Yukon Territory into Alaska, then southwest to the Norton Sound on the Bering Sea. It is navigable for about 1,770 mi (2,848 km).

Yukon Territory, subarctic territory in northwestern Canada. Covering 207,076 sq mi (536,327 sq km), the Yukon is bordered by the Arctic Ocean to the north, the Northwest Territories to the east, British Columbia and Alaska to the south, and Alaska to the west.
The mountainous Yukon Territory includes the Rocky Mountains and, in the southwest, the St. Elias Range. The latter includes Canada's highest mountain, Mount Logan (19,850 ft/ 6,050 m). A large central basin, or plateau, is heavily forested.
The Yukon is the original home of about 2,500 Native Americans, who live principally as trappers and hunters. The majority of the territory's population is concentrated in the warmer southern and central valleys. Whitehorse, the largest city, has been the capital since 1956.
Mining, the Yukon's principal industry, centers on the production of silver, lead, gold, and zinc, and provides jobs for most of the territory's inhabitants. During the 1960s, mining operations expanded to include the production of copper and asbestos; potential reserves of oil and iron ore remain to be developed.
The Yukon territory was first explored by the fur traders Robert Campbell and John Bell of the Hudson's Bay Company between 1840 and 1848. Canada acquired the territory from the Hudson's Bay Company in 1870. In the 1860s and 1870s prospectors began mining gold in the area. In 1897 the famous Klondike gold rush began after gold was discovered in several tributaries of the Klondike River. In 1898 the Yukon achieved separate territorial status, but the mines were soon depleted and between 1901 and 1911 the population dropped. The decline of the territory was arrested during World War II. The construction of airports on the staging route to Alaska, and the Alaska Highway, brought a new influx of people to the Yukon. Since then, the expansion of mining and new transportation facilities has brought a slow but steady increase in growth to the territory. *See also:* Canada.

Yun, Isang (1917-1995), Korean-German composer. Isang Yun studied in Japan, and emigrated to the west in 1956, where he continued his studies under Boris Blacher in Berlin. In 1971 he adopted German nationality. With his *Fünf Klavierstücke* (1958) and *Musik für sieben Instrumente* (1959) he reached the most important locations that perform contemporary music. His music was a refined synthesis of eastern influences and western serial and postserial techniques. His compositions include the orchestral works *Fluktuationen* (1964), *Reak* (1966), and *Dimensionen* (1971), concertos for cello (1976), flute (1977), clarinet (1981), and violin (1981; 1983-1986), five symphonies, five string quartets, and five operas.

Yung-lo-reign (Yongle), the Yung-lo emperor, also known under his personal name of Tszu Ti (Zhudi), was the third emperor of the Chinese Ming dynasty (1368-1644). During his reign the dynasty reached its first peak. As 'Prince Yen' (Yen = the Peking district) he revolted against his cousin, the emperor, in 1399, and seized the throne upon capturing the capital city, Nanying, a few years later. His internal politics were aimed at the centralization of power and the restriction of the authority of the princes; his government was energetic and effective, partly due to the existence of a well-organized secret police force. Being interested in 'the South' from early on, from 1403 onwards he sent large fleets under the command of eunuchs even as far as Africa, to demand tribute from the southern countries. In 1406 he annexed Annam (North Vietnam). Later he turned to the North: after renovating the Great Canal, he removed the capital to Peking and pacified the Mongolian tribes.

Yunnan (pop. 39,900,000), province in southwestern China, bordering on Vietnam, Laos, and Burma; 152,182 sq mi (394,000 sq km). Capital, Kunming. Mountainous in the north and west; the economically more important east is relatively flat. Agriculture producing tea, rice, grain, tobacco, and opium. Extraction of tin, copper, gold, silver, lead, and sulfur. Fell into Chinese hands during the Yuan dynasty (1279-1368).

Ywan dynasty, Mongolian dynasty that governed China from 1279 to 1368. The Mongols had conquered parts of China from the north under Ghengis Khan (1167-1227); the Ywan completed this process by defeating the last Chinese dynasty, the Sung, in South China. On the one hand the Ywan took over the structure of the Sung government and made use of Chinese achievements (exam system, paper money), but on the other hand they discriminated against the defeated Chinese. The Mongolian rulers had a policy, opposing traditional Chinese politics, of openness towards other nations and religious tolerance; Christianity, Islam and Buddhism were tolerated next to Confucianism. The Ywan dynasty fell due to revolts of the subordinated Chinese and because of fights between brothers in the Mongolian ruling family.

YWCA *See:* Young Women's Christian Association (YWCA).

Z, 26th and last letter of the English alphabet, corresponding to the ancient Semitic letter *zayin*, meaning 'weapon.' The Greeks adopted the familiar z form for *zeta*, the sixth letter of their alphabet. The Romans used the letter only for words of Greek origin. In Old French, the letter was called *zède* or *zé*, hence the name *zed* used in Great Britain and Canada, and the name *zee* commonly used in the United States. In Old English, the z sound was represented by the letter.

Zadkine, Ossip (1890-1967), Russian-born French sculptor. Came to Paris in 1909. He was influenced by Rodin and African art. His often large works in bronze, wood, and stone include *The Destruction of Rotterdam* (1954),

Zagreb (pop. 752,000), capital of the republic of Croatia. Zagreb occupies the site of an early Roman settlement that was also home to Slavic tribes from c.A.D. 600. The present city of Zagreb grew from the merger of 2 earlier towns, Kaptol and Gradac, in the 16th century. It was part of the Austro-Hungarian Empire until 1918, when Croatia, Dalmatia, and Slovenia declared themselves independent. It is a cultural and industrial center, supplying machinery, leather, pharmaceuticals and chemicals, textiles, metal, and paper. Zagreb is characterized by parks and open squares, and is home to Zagreb University, a national theater, and various galleries and museums.
See also: Yugoslavia; Croatia.

Zaibatsu (Jap: financial cliques), large Japanese family corporations, originated in the Meiji period (1867-1912) when the Japanese government sold off state-owned businesses. After WW II, during the American occupation, they were dismantled because of the part they had played in fermenting Japanese aggression. Some prewar Zaibatsu managed to regroup, and they still exercise a great deal of influence today.

Zaire *See:* Congo (Zaïre).

Zaitsev, Aleksandr (1952-   ), Soviet Russian figure skater, became pairs national champion numerous times with his wife Irina Rodnina. In 1976 and 1980 he also won the Olympic gold medal with her, as well as six European and six world titles.

Zambezi River, river in southeast Africa, fourth-largest in Africa. Rising in northwest Zambia, it flows about 1,700 mi (about 2,736 km) south, then east along the Zambia-Zimbabwe border, through Mozambique to enter the Mozambique Channel of the Indian Ocean through a 2,500-sq mi (6,475-sq km) delta.

Zambia

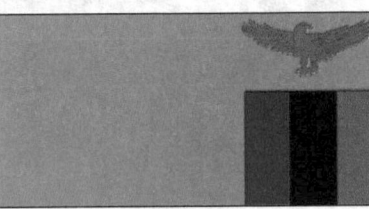

Capital:	Lusaka
Area:	290,586 sq mi (752,614 sq km)
Population:	9,215,000
Language:	English
Government:	Presidential republic
Independent:	1964
Head of gov.:	President
Per capita:	US$ 360
Monetary unit:	1 Kwacha = 100 ngwee

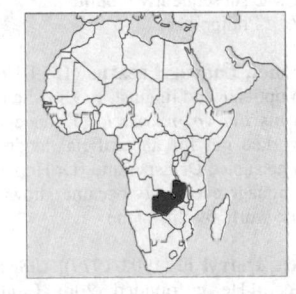

Zambia, formerly Northern Rhodesia, officially the Republic of Zambia, independent republic in south-central Africa. With an area of 290,584 sq mi (752,614 sq km), Zambia is bordered by Congo on the north; Tanzania on the northeast; Malawi and Mozambique on the east; Zimbabwe, Botswana, and Namibia on the south; and Angola on the west.

Land and climate. The country occupies a mostly flat plateau some 3,000 to 4,500 ft (914 to 1,372 m) above sea level and broken by deep valleys formed by the Luangwa and Zambezi rivers. The plateau is largely savanna and open woodland, and the course of the Zambezi includes Victoria Falls and Lake Kariba, formed by the Kariba Dam. Both Victoria Falls and Lake Kariba are on Zambia's border with Zimbabwe. In the northeast part of the country, the Muchinga Mountains rise some 7,000 ft (2,124 m). Zambia's climate is tropical, but its effects are moderated by altitude.

People. The Zambian people are black Africans, mostly Bantu peoples, with over 70 different tribes and a variety of languages. There are also European and Asian minorities. More than half the people follow animist beliefs. The balance profess Christianity, either Roman Catholicism or Protestantism. While English is the official language, many Bantu languages are also spoken. The capital of Zambia is Lusaka.

Economy. The majority of Zambia's people are engaged in subsistence farming, but the country is also one of the world's major producers of copper, which accounts for the bulk of its export earnings. Cobalt is the second-largest export earner and Zambia also supports lead, zinc, manganese, and sulfur. The agricultural sector produces cash crops, including tobacco, sugarcane, and wheat. Despite its resources, Zambia underwent considerable economic dislocation as a result of its active opposition to Southern Rhodesia in the 1960s and 1970s. In the 1980s the country faced severe food shortages principally due to drought.

History. Present-day Zambians are descendants of Bantu peoples who migrated to the region between the 16th and 18th centuries. European traders and missionaries came in the 19th century, most notably David Livingstone, who came in 1851. In 1889 Cecil Rhodes led the way for British commercial interests. As Northern Rhodesia the area became a British protectorate in 1911. Copper deposits were discovered in the 1920s, leading to rapid and lucrative development but at the expense of the native inhabitants. A nationalist movement arose in 1946, and despite its rigorous opposition to the plan, Northern Rhodesia was combined by the British into the Federation of Rhodesia and Nyasaland, which included Southern Rhodesia (now Zimbabwe) and Nyasaland (now Malawi). Northern Rhodesia and Nyasaland left the federation in 1963 and Northern Rhodesia became the independent Republic of Zambia in 1964,

View from the top of Victoria Falls. Among the many rivers, running from the western plateaus to the sea, only the Zambesi is navigable over a large distance, starting at Tete.

Z

The Rokana copper-melting works in Kitwe, one of the mining and industrial cities of Zambia's Copperbelt.

under the presidency of Kenneth Kaunda. The fledgling country protested against and eventually opposed the white regime of Ian Smith in Southern Rhodesia. Though contributing to the isolation of the Smith regime and the eventual emergence of Zimbabwe, the policy proved costly. After more than 25 years President Kaunda was defeated in democratic elections in 1991. He was succeeded by Frederick Chiluba. Chiluba was confronted with a threatening famine in 1992, a result of the worst drought in years. In 1993, the austerity policy caused political instability while the government was discredited by allegations of corruption, drug trafficking and money laundering. Levy Mwanawasa won the Presidential elections of 2001.

Emiliano Zapata (1879?-1919), guerilla fighter in the Mexican Revolution.

Zamboanga (pop. 551,000), Philippine city on the extreme western tip of Mindanao Island, capital of Zamboanga del Sur Province. Zamboanga is the major port and trade center of the Sulu Archipelago and exports hardwoods, rice, abaca, rubber, copra, fish, and sugar. Settled by Spain in 1635, much of the city was destroyed in World War II and was subsequently rebuilt.
See also: Philippines.

Zamenhof, Ludwig Lazarus (1859-1917), Polish optician and linguist. In 1887 he published his *Lingvo Internacia*, a concept he had worked out for an artificial language, which he signed Dr Esperento (Dr Hopeful). The language eventually became known all over the world by this name.

Zanuck, Darryl F. (1902-1979), U.S. film producer. He cofounded 20th Century Pictures, which merged with Fox Films (1935) to form 20th Century-Fox, was its production head (1935-1952), and its president (1962-1971).

Zanzibar, island, part of Tanzania, off eastern Africa. It was a center of an Omani Arab sultanate (1700) with extensive mainland territories. Zanzibar became a British protectorate (1890-1893), part of German East Africa (1893), an independent sultanate (1963), and a republic (1964). It then united (1964) with nearby Pemba and with Tanganyika to form Tanzania. The chief exports are cloves and copra.
See also: Tanzania.

Zapata, Emiliano (1879?-1919), Mexican revolutionary whose chief ambition was to return Mexican land to the native population. Zapata joined the successful forces of Francisco Madero against the dictatorship of President Porfirio Díaz (1910) and led the insurrectionists of Morelos, his native state. After Díaz's overthrow, Zapata refused to recognize Madero or his successor, Victoriano Huerta, for their failure to redistribute land to the people. Together with

Pancho Villa, he renewed his revolutionary endeavors. On 3 occasions (1914-1915), Zapata occupied Mexico City. He was assassinated (1919).

Zapotec, ancient native people of southeast Oaxaca, Mexico, and their descendants. They created a formative pre-Columbian culture about 2,000 years ago. Monte Alban, west of Oaxaca city, contains magnificent ruins of tombs, stelae, temples, and plazas.

Zappa, Frank (1940-1993), American musician. Zappa worked for many years together with the group The Mothers of Invention, originally set up in 1964, but whose composition changed many times over the years. The shocking performances, biting, satirical lyrics, and complex music of this group became popular with a relatively small, mostly intellectual public. In 1975 he disbanded the group, and pursued various musical directions, generally characterized by nonconformism and eclecticism. Zappa, who was both loved and hated for his improvized guitar solos, made keen use of jazz and pop music, but was also a serious composer in the tradition of Stravinsky, Cage, and Varèse. He therefore demanded a high level of discipline from the musicians who accompanied him. As a nonconformist, Zappa continually struggled against anyone who prevented him from expressing what he considered to be his right to freedom of speech, and often came into conflict with the authorities and television evangelists. In order to maintain his artistic freedom, Zappa twice set up his own record label, and released more than 60 LPs and CDs.

Zarathustra *See:* Zoroastrianism.

Zatopek, Emil (1922-2000), Czechoslovakian athlete and soldier, won the 10,000 m gold medal at the Olympic Games in 1948, and the 5000 m, 10,000 m, and marathon gold medals at the Olympic Games of 1952. Zatopek broke 18 world records and won three European titles. The tortured facial expressions he made during competition caused him to be called 'Zatopek the Terrible' and 'The Locomotive'.

Zau-tung (Jap.: Soto), Zen sect, started in China by Lin-chi (808-869), who used I-Ching diagrams in his teachings and preached a gradual path to enlightenment. The za-zen (sitting meditation) is practiced facing the wall. Brought by Dogèn (1200-1253) to Japan, where today Soto has about 15,000 monasteries and temples. The monks' lifestyle places more emphasis on tranquillity and dignity than in Rinzai-zen.

Zealots, Jewish religious and political fanatics in Palestine about the time of Jesus. Led by Judas of Galilee and Zadock the priest, they resisted Rome and its collaborator Herod the Great, but they later perished (A.D. 70) with the destruction of Jerusalem. St. Simon the Apostle may have been a Zealot.

Zebra, 3 species of striped horses (genus *Equus*) of Africa. The zebra's black-and-white striped coat makes the animal inconspicuous at long range. The 3 species-plains

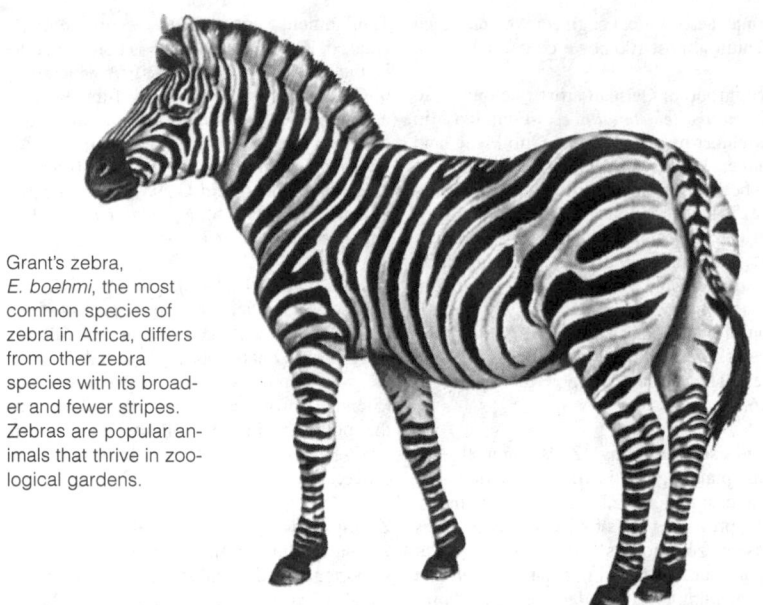

Grant's zebra, *E. boehmi*, the most common species of zebra in Africa, differs from other zebra species with its broader and fewer stripes. Zebras are popular animals that thrive in zoological gardens.

zebra, mountain zebra, and Grévy's zebra differ in stripe pattern, habitat, and behavior. Plains and mountain zebras live in permanent, nonterritorial stallion groups, but mountain zebras are adapted to life in more arid regions. Grévy's zebras, with very narrow stripes, are territorial animals.

Zebu, or Brahman ox (*Bos indicus*), ox found in India, Africa, and Asia. It has a hump on its shoulders and a dewlap under the chin. The horns are large, up to 5 ft (1.5 m) in the *ankole* cattle of Uganda. Zebus are used as draft animals and for milk and meat. They react to heat well and have been introduced to many areas with hot climates, including the southern United States, where they are immune to the Texas fever carried by cattle ticks.

Zebulun, one of the 12 tribes of Israel and one of the 10 lost tribes removed from Palestine by the conquering Assyrians (721 B.C.) and dispersed. Zebulun was part of the Northern Kingdom of Israel and occupied lands northeast of the Plain of Jezreel. The tribe name comes from the sixth son born to Jacob and Leah (Genesis 30:20).

Zechariah, Book of, Old Testament book named for 1 of the 12 minor prophets. Zechariah (or Zacharias), an associate of the prophet Haggai, prophesied from 520 B.C.–518 B.C., and, after the Jews returned to Palestine from exile, advocated rebuilding the Temple. The Book of Zechariah has 14 chapters. The first 8, attributed to Zechariah himself, record a series of visions showing hope for a new order in Jerusalem and the plans for its establishment and organization. The last 6 chapters, attributed to a later author or group of authors, elaborate on Zechariah's themes of the restoration of the Davidic royal line, the intervention of a messiah, and Jerusalem's exiles returned and forgiven.
See also: Bible; Old Testament.

Zedillo Ponce de Léon, Ernesto (1951–), Mexican politician. Studied economics in Mexico City, Great Britain, and the U.S., and worked for the Banco de Mexico and with the Ministry of Planning. He was successively Minister of Planning and Minister of Education in the government of President Salinas. After the murder of the presidential candidate Colosio, Zedillo became the candidate for the ruling PRI in the presidential elections of August 1994. After winning the elections, he became President on 1st December 1994. Vicente Fox of the conservative PAN succeeded him in 2000.

Zeeman effect, changes in the energy levels of atoms that may be observed by the splitting of spectral lines when a light source is placed in a magnetic field. The line separations are expressed as differences of frequency and increase in direct proportion to the strength of the magnetic field. They occur when an atom's electron moves from one energy level, corresponding to the concentric orbits the electron makes around the atomic nucleus, to another. The effect was discovered (1896) by Pieter Zeeman, a Dutch physicist, and was the first indication that electrons are negatively charged particles. It is used by astronomers and physicists to study the properties of nuclei, atoms, and molecules.
See also: Atom; Electron.

Zeiss, Carl (1816-1888), German optical manufacturer who founded a famous workshop at Jena in 1846. Realizing that optical technology had much to gain from scientific research, in the mid-1860s he formed a fruitful association with the physicist Ernest Abbe.
See also: Optics.

Zeman, Milos (1945–), Czech Social Democratic politician. Before the Velvet Revolution of 1989, Zeman was attached to the then famous Institute for Prognostica as an economist. Since 1994 he has been leader of the CSSD, the social democratic party. In March 1998 he was reelected as leader. He led the party to victory in the elections: the party won 74 of the 200 seats, and in so doing wiped out the majority held by the largest opposition party, the Citizen's Democratic Party (ODS) led by the former prime minister Vaclav Klaus. Zeman formed a minority cabinet, which was however tacitly supported by the ODS.

Zemlinsky, Alexander von (1871-1942), Austrian composer and conductor of Polish descent. Zemlinsky studied in Vienna, was conductor at the Carl Theatre in Vienna from 1899-1904, then at the Volksoper from 1904-1911, and then the Hofoper from 1907-1908. In 1911 he became director of the Deutches Landestheater in Prague, and from 1920 taught composition at the Deutsche Musikakademie. From 1927-1930 he conducted at the Berlin Kroll-Oper, from 1930-1933 he was guest conductor at the Berlin Staatsopera. In 1938 he emigrated to the U.S. Zemlinsky, as a conductor, had great admiration for Brahms and Mahler, and was Arnold Schönberg's teacher and friend. He wrote a number of operas (*Sarema*, 1897; *Es war einmal*, 1900; *Der Traumgörge*, 1904-1906; *Der Kreidekreis*, 1933), orchestral works (including three symphonies; *Sinfonietta*, 1934), choral works (*Frühlingsbegräbnis*, 1896; Psalm, 83, 1900; Psalm 23, 1910; Psalm 13, 1935), chamber music (including four string quartets and a string quintet, 1896), and songs.

Zem-Zem, well in Mecca near the Kaaba, where according to legend Hagar discovered water after Abraham had turned her and Ismael away. During the hadj pilgrims drink water from this well.

Zen (Chinese: *Ch'an*, meaning 'meditation'), form of Buddhism that developed in China from c.500 A.D. and spread to Japan, exerting great influence on Japanese culture. Zen differs markedly from traditional Buddhism in its abhorrance of images and ritual, scriptures and metaphysics. Rinzai Zen uses *koan* (paradoxical riddles) to shock into sudden enlightenment; Soto Zen stresses contemplation.
See also: Buddhism.

Sitting (za-zen) is a fundamental part of Zen Buddhism. For instance, a devotee of the Soto sect, will sit for hours with his face towards the wall. In the meditation hall, the zendo, meals are taken as well. Intensive Zen exercises may last several days, the sitting only being interrupted by the collective meals.

Zenith, in astronomy, point on the celestial sphere directly above an observer and exactly 90° from the celestial horizon. It is directly opposite to the nadir.
See also: Astronomy; Nadir.

Z

Zeno of Citium (335?-265? B.C.), Cypriot philosopher who founded the Stoic school of philosophy in Athens (301 B.C.). A wealthy merchant forced by shipwreck to remain in Athens, Zeno became fascinated with the life of Socrates and the writings of the Cynics, and abandoned trade for philosophy. After years of study he established his own school. Zeno saw the cosmos as the reference point for human ethics, with a divine intelligence guiding both nature and humanity toward 'the city of Zeus,' that is, toward goodness. He felt that natural law superseded civil law, and that the practice of acceptance and moderation were characteristics of a virtuous life. He defined morality as surrender to divine governance. At his death, the Athenian Assembly gave him citizenship and voted him a statue and gold crown.
See also: Stoicism.

Zeno of Elea (490?-430 B.C.), Greek philosopher who studied under Parmenides and defended his teacher's theories. Zeno used indirect argumentation to try to prove his philosophy and is considered the inventor of pre-Socratic dialectic. He based his arguments on 4 propositions: that all things belong to one unchanging reality as opposed to many; that nothing can be proved by human reason; that empty space is not real because the One fills all voids; that motion is not real because it assumes movement from someplace to empty space, which does not exist. Zeno is known for his book of about 40 paradoxes (of which 8 survive), particularly the 4 concerning motion, which were the beginnings of modern mathematical concepts of infinity and continuity.
See also: Pre-Socratic philosophy.

Zephaniah, Book of, Old Testament book written c.640-630 B.C. during the reign of Josiah (638-608 B.C.) and after the Scythian invasion of Palestine. The dominant themes of the book are condemnation of the Judeans for adopting foreign idols and customs, and a catastrophic day of judgement, the 'day of the Lord,' when only the few faithful will be saved. This element evolved into the popular notion of the judgement day prominent in Biblical prophecy.
See also: Bible; Old Testament.

Zeppelin *See:* Airship.

Zeppelin, Ferdinand von (1838-1917),

One of the many zeppelins that were built in the 1930s and 40s.

German aeronautical engineer who designed and built almost 100 powered balloons.

Zero, group of German artists, belonging to the *nouvelle tendance.* Founded in Düsseldorf by Heinz Mack, Otto Piene, and Günther Uecker in 1958. 'Zero' means a new beginning: an art without historical baggage. Their work consisted of identical geometrical shapes, in which no single component was emphasized nor any composition discernible. Only a variation in lighting or in the viewing angle resulted in any differentiation. The magazine 'Zero', in which they set out their ideas, only appeared three times. Their last exhibition took place in 1966.

Zero-base budgeting (ZBB), annual economic planning that justifies expenditure on actual cost or need rather than on increments of the previous year's budget. ZBB assumes a base of zero dollars and asks managers to prepare outlines showing expected high and low spending levels. Budgeting for the coming year is based on these outlines. Introduced in the 1960s by the electronics manufacturer, Texas Instruments, Incorporated, ZBB is used by government and business as a means of controlling spending.

Zero population growth, close approximation in numbers of births and deaths needed to stabilize a nation's population and prevent annual increases.

Zeus, supreme god of Greek mythology. His mother, Rhea, saved him from his jealous father, Cronus, and he was brother and husband of Hera. He led the Olympian gods in overthrowing Cronus and the other Titans. By lot he became god of earth and sky (Poseidon won the sea, Hades the underworld). Zeus's Roman counterpart is Jupiter.
See also: Mythology.

Zhang Yimou (1951-), Chinese film director. Zhang Yimou studied at the film academy in Peking, and was a cameraman for *Huang tudi* (Yellow Earth) (1985) by Chen Kaige. His directing debut *Hong gaoliang* (Red Sorghum) (1988) was both a national and international success. This was followed by the films *Dahong denglong gaogao guo* (Raise the Red Lantern; 1991), and *Qiu Ju da guanshi* (The Story of Qiuju; 1992), all with Gong Li in the lead role, but which were all censored. After the bloodbath of

Tian'anmen Square (1989) censorship increased. Zhang Yimou, who is considered to be the leading director of the fifth generation of Chinese film makers, makes films with an exceptional sense of color and composition. He won the jury prize at Cannes with *Huozhe* (Lifetimes) in 1994. Other films include *Shanghai Triad* (1995), *Breaking Up Is Hard to Do* (1996), *Not One Less* (1999), and *The Road Home* (2000).

Zhao Ziyang (1919-), premier of China (1980-1987), successor to Hua Kuo-feng (Hua Guofeng). Purged during the Cultural Revolution, Zhao was later 'rehabilitated.' He was appointed governor of Szechwan (Sichuan) province in 1975 and elected to the politburo in 1979. Party leader from 1987-1989. In 1989 he was removed from office.

Zhengzhou (pop. 2,0 million), city in China, capital of the province of Henan. Important textile industry; also machine, metal, electrical machinery industry. Many educational institutions. Museum of ancient history; airport. One of the oldest Chinese cities, rebuilt after being destroyed and flooded many times. City walls dating from 2100 B.C..

An old coin showing Zeus.

Zhou dynasty (also Chou), China's third and longest-ruling (1122 B.C.-256 B.C.) royal house. The Zhou people were seminomadic tribes who overturned the Shang dynasty, expanded their territory by conquering neighboring tribes, and established a feudal society of separate states ruled by a central government. Their control corresponded to the flowering of Chinese culture. Under Zhou governance, the merchant class emerged, coinage replaced trade by barter, education flourished, and the family became the focus of society. Iron implements, including the traction plow, were introduced, and irrigation improved farming. Confucius, Mencius, and Laozi lived during the Zhou dynasty, and Buddhism was introduced to China in that period.

Zhou Enlai, or **Chou En Lai** (1898-1976), Chinese Communist leader, premier and foreign minister of China (1949-1959). Zhou began his political activity (1919) when he was imprisoned for a year for demonstrating against the Treaty of Versailles. He was a

A tile from the Zhou period (1122-256 B.C.) shows a mounted archer. The artwork probably represents a member of the barbarian tribes who, through much of China's history, raided the empire from strongholds along its northern and western frontiers.

Z

leader in the labor revolts of Nanchang and Shanghai (1927) and helped establish the Red Army, of which he succeeded Mao Zedong as commissar (1932). In the 1940s he was a leader in the struggle for control of China and was instrumental in the ouster of Chiang Kai-shek. He became prime minister of the Chinese People's Republic (1949), and after his removal (1959) remained influential in Chinese foreign affairs.
See also: China.

Zhuangzi (Chuang Tsu or Chuang-Tzo; 377?-286 B.C.), Chinese scholar and Taoist philosopher, to whom the book *Zhuangzi*, the first Chinese book dealing only with spiritual matters, is attributed. Zhuangzi was a minor official who several times rejected public office. He advocated a life of simplicity, submissive to and at one with nature, and renounced government, science, and even education as of no help in understanding that unity. The *Zhuangzi*, an interpretation of the *Tao*, has as its primary theme unending and inevitable change. The work was important in the development of Zen Buddhism.
See also: Taoism.

Zhukov, Georgi Konstantinovich (1896-1974), Soviet general, hero of the battles at Stalingrad (1943) and Berlin (1945). After the death of Stalin (who had blocked his career), Zhukov was defense minister (1955-1957) and briefly a full member of the Communist Party Presidium (1957).
See also: World War II.

Zhu Rongji (1928-), Chinese politician. After the foundation of the People's Republic in 1949, Zhu Rongji became a member of the communist party. He worked for the Northeast China Ministry of Industries as deputy head of its production planning office in 1951 and became a member of the State Planning Commission in 1952. In 1957, he was convicted for participating in a movement for freedom of speech and sentenced to penal servitude. Being a dissident, he was forced to enter a political re-educational camp during the Cultural Revolution. He was politically rehabilitated by Deng Xiaoping and elected for the State Commission for Economy in 1979. From 1988 to 1991, he was Shanghai's mayor and in 1991, he had risen to the post of Deputy Prime Minister of China. Zhu Rongji became a member of the party leadership and

became head of the Central Bank in 1993. The National People's Congress elected him successor of Li Peng in 1998. He was the first prominent Chinese politician to openly admit that Chinese human rights left room for improvement.

Zia ul-Haq, Mohammad (1924-1988), Pakistani military leader and politician. Zia served in the British-Indian army, and from 1947 onwards in the Pakistani army. In 1976 he became its Chief-of-Staff. When violence swept the country during the parliamentary elections of 1977, the army took power under his leadership. Zia promised new elections, but appointed himself president instead in 1978. When a civil government took office in 1985, he remained president and leader of the army, and effectively still ran the country. Zia attempted to introduce an Islamic government in Pakistan, and managed to receive enormous amounts of economic and military aid from the US after the invasion of Afghanistan by the Soviet Union in 1979. He died when his aircraft crashed for reasons that have never become clear.

Zia ur-Rahman (1936-1981), Bengali military leader and politician, joined the Bengali independence struggle against Pakistan in 1971, and after the independence of Bangladesh in 1972 was appointed to important military posts. In 1975 he took power in a coup, but nonetheless tried to reintroduce democracy and civil government. In 1977 he became president, and in 1978 he was re-elected. The party which he set up, the Bangladesh National Party (BNP), won a two-thirds majority in parliament at the general elections in 1979. Zia died during an attempted military coup in May 1981.

Ziegfeld, Florenz (1869-1932), U.S. theatrical producer. In 1907 he launched the Ziegfeld Follies, an annual revue famous for its spectacular staging, beautiful women, and star performers; under his direction it ran for 24 years. Ziegfeld also produced musicals, including *Sally* (1920) and *Show Boat* (1927).

Ziggurat, temples built in the shape of a tower in ancient Mesopotamia; a pyramidal building of a number of stories that became progressively smaller. The floor plan was usually square or rectangular. At the top was the room of worship. This room could only

be accessed via steps that led directly up the middle of the front of the building, and via two stairways at an angle on either side of the facade. Remains of a ziggurat have been found in Elam and Urr. The tower of Babel was a ziggurat.

Zimbabwe

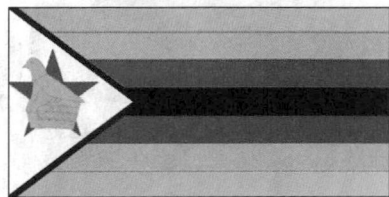

Capital:	Harare
Area:	150,873 sq mi (390,759 sq km)
Population:	11,248,000
Language:	English
Government:	Presidential republic
Independent:	1980
Head of gov.:	President
Per capita:	US$ 610
Monetary unit:	1 Zimbabwean dollar = 100 cents

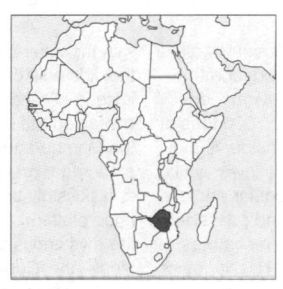

Zimbabwe, officially the Republic of Zimbabwe, formerly Southern Rhodesia under the British, and Rhodesia under Ian Smith, a landlocked republic in south central Africa. With an area of 150,873 sq mi (390,759 sq km), Zimbabwe is bordered by Zambia to the north, Mozambique to the northeast and east, and Botswana to the southwest and west.
Land and climate. Zimbabwe is situated

The ziggurat of Ur in ancient Mesopotamia is shown here in an artist's rendering as it probably looked in the 3rd millennium B.C., with a religious procession approaching the entrance. The biblical Tower of Babel may have been a structure similar to this.

Z

Zimbabwe has been occupied since the 1st millennium A.D., although what can be seen there today, was built by native African peoples between the 11th-19th centuries. On a granite hill to the west, is the ruined 'Acropolis' or Western Enclosure. In the valley below, lies the high-walled Eastern Enclosure, or 'Temple', in which lived the Mambo of the Rozwi people. The masonry here is perhaps the most spectacular achievement of man in Southern Africa: the

temple's outer wall, which is decorated with chevron, contained 15,000 tons of stone. Inside, it is divided by lower walls into irregular enclosures and passages. Its plan resembles the chief's villages of more recent times,

with the difference that it is built of stone, instead of reeds. It contained the huts of the Mambo and his entourage, granaries, and possibly an audience platform near the mysterious stone steal – the 'Conical Tower'. There are

three periods and types of wall-building. The earliest, 1000-1400, consists of untrimmed stones in irregular courses. The next, possibly dating from the 15th century and coinciding with the arrival of the Rozwi, is of fine, reg-

ular courses of dressed stone. Poorly-coursed walls with stones of all sizes were built in the 1830s, when the Rozwi had lost the secret of fine building.

astride a high plateau between the Zambezi and Limpopo rivers. The plateau is divided into three distinct zones. The High Veld is over 4,000 ft (1,219 m) above sea level and extends across the country from the southwest to the northeast. The Middle Veld is most extensive in the northwest and rises 3,000-4,000 ft (914-1,219 m) above sea level. The Low Veld occupies land near river basins in the north and south and is 3,000 ft (914 m) below sea level. In the east, the highlands include Mt. Inyangani which rises to 8,503 ft (2,592 m). Zimbabwe's climate varies with the altitude.

People. The people of Zimbabwe are overwhelmingly black Africans, principally Bantus of the Shona or Ndebele groups. Other important tribes include the Tonga, Sena, Hlengwe, Venda, and Sotho. About 5% of the population consists of whites, coloreds (descendants of whites and black Africans), and Asians. The majority of the people is Christian, about 45% follow traditional animist beliefs, and there are Hindus among the small Asian minority. English is the official language, but Shona and Ndebele are widely spoken.

Economy. Most of the people of Zimbabwe work as subsistence farmers. But the country's agricultural sector was a major food exporter to the South African region. The principal cash crop is tobacco. Zimbabwe is also rich in mineral resources. Gold is the coun-

try's major export, but other valuable minerals include iron ore, asbestos, chrome, copper, and nickel. The country also has an expanding and diversified industrial sector.

History. Bushmen paintings and tools indicate that Zimbabwe had Stone Age inhabitants. Bantu peoples settled the area about A.D. 400, and during the 15th century, the Shona civilization established an empire; the capital was called Zimbabwe. In 1889, Cecil Rhodes obtained a charter from Britain to colonize and administer the area, and in 1923 it became the self-governing British colony of Southern Rhodesia. In 1953 the British combined Southern Rhodesia with Northern Rhodesia (now Zambia) and Nyasaland (now Malawi) to form the Federation of Rhodesia and Nyasaland. The federation dissolved in 1963 and in the face of growing demands from black Africans for self-determination, white conservatives led by Prime Minister Ian Smith declared independence from Britain in 1965. Britain refused to recognize the all-white regime and white Rhodesia was beset by international pressure and an armed insurgency. Rebel forces were headed by Robert Mugabe and Joshua Nkomo. In a negotiated settlement, the country gained its independence and black majority rule in 1980, and its name was changed from Rhodesia to Zimbabwe. Rivalry between elements loyal to Robert Mugabe, who was elected president in 1987,

and Joshua Nkomo threatened the new country's unity, but by the late 1980s the worst excesses of the internal fighting seemed to be under control. In the early 1990s land reforms were carried out, intended to diminish the difference in landownership between black and white. However, there was little or no compensation for the farmers whose land had been seized and much of the land was left unfarmed precipitating the current famine in Zimbabwe. Mugabe increasingly oppressed the opposition in the lead up to the Presidential elections of 2002. Furthermore, he passed a law that made criticism of President Mugabe a serious crime, he banned foreign reporters from working in Zimbabwe and the freedom of the media was limited. This led to fierce international criticism. Mugabe won the 2002 elections. International observers labeled them as unfair.

Zimmermann, Bernd Alois (1918-1970), German composer. He studied at the Musikhochschulen in Cologne and Berlin, and thereafter followed courses at the Darmstädter Ferienkursen für Neue Musik, under Wolfgang Fortner and René Leibowitz. From 1957 onwards he became a teacher of composition (became a professor in 1961) at the Musikhochschule in Cologne, where he also taught film, radio play, and stage music. Zimmermann was originally influenced by Stravinsky, but after 1955 he became one of the avant-garde composers in Germany, who developed their own completely new methods for using serial techniques. His most famous work is the opera *Die Soldaten* (1958-1960, rewritten 1963-1964). He also wrote orchestral works (symphonies in one part, 1953; Concert for strings, 1948), ballet music (*Kontraste*, 1954; *Musique pour les soupers du roi Ubu*, 1966), concertos (for violin, 1950; for oboe 1952; for trompet, 1954; for cello, 1965-1966), choral works (*Vokal-Symfonie*, 1959; *Requiem für einen Jungen Dichter*, 1967-1969), chamber music, and electronic music.

Zinc, chemical element, symbol Zn; for physical constants, see Periodic Table. Zinc ores were used for making brass centuries before zinc was recognized as a distinct element. The metal was prepared in India in the 13th century by reducing calamine with organic substances such as wool. It occurs in nature principally as sphalerite (zinc sulfide). It is produced by reduction of the oxide with carbon. Zinc is a bluish-white, lustrous, brittle, reactive metal. It is used in many important metal alloys, including bronze, Babbitt metal, and German silver. Zinc is an essential growth element for humans and animals. The uses of the metal and its compounds are numerous, including in pigments, dry cell batteries, pharmaceuticals, and television screens.

Zinjanthropus, humanlike creature that probably lived about 1,750,000 years ago. Its skull was discovered (1959) at Olduvai Gorge, Tanzania, by Mary D. Leakey. The skull belonged to a creature about 17 years of age with a low brow and large, flat teeth. *Zinjanthropus* was probably chiefly herbivo-

rous and had a brain about one-third the size of a modern human. It may have used stone tools. It became extinct about 1 million years ago. *Zinjanthropus* was renamed (1967) *Australopithecus boisei*.
See also: Australopithecus.

Zinneman, Fred (1907-1997), film director and winner of Academy Awards for *That Mothers Might Live* (1938), *From Here to Eternity* (1953), and *A Man for All Seasons* (1966). Zinneman studied film making in France before moving to the United States in 1929. Other works include *High Noon* (1952) and *The Nun's Story* (1958). His autobiography *A Life in the Movies* was published in 1992.

Zinnia, popular garden plant of the composite family that came from Mexico and has been bred in many forms, including double-flowered varieties. It has a stiff stem, thick leaves, and a single, large flower, which can be 4 in (10.2 cm) across. It is pollinated by hummingbirds, butterflies, and moths.

Zion, in the Old Testament, ancient citadel of David, on the southeast hill of Jerusalem. In a wider sense it symbolizes the whole of Jerusalem and the Jewish people and their aspirations.

Zionism, movement to establish a Jewish national home in Palestine. After the destruction of their state in A.D. 70, the Jews retained their identity and kept alive their dream of an eventual return from exile. The dream turned into a political movement in the 19th century, largely in response to the persecution of Jews in the USSR and Austria, and Jewish farmers and artisans began to settle in Palestine. The decisive impetus came in 1897, when Theodore Herzl organized the first World Zionist Congress, after which Zionist groups were established all over the world. In 1903 the British government offered the Jews a home in Uganda, but this was rejected. Leadership of the Zionist movement was assumed by Chaim Weizmann, who was largely responsible for the Balfour Declaration (1917).
See also: Herzl, Theodor.

Zion National Park, established in 1919 and covering 147,035 acres (59,528 hectares) in southwest Utah. It is noted for its canyons and multicolored rock formations.

Z

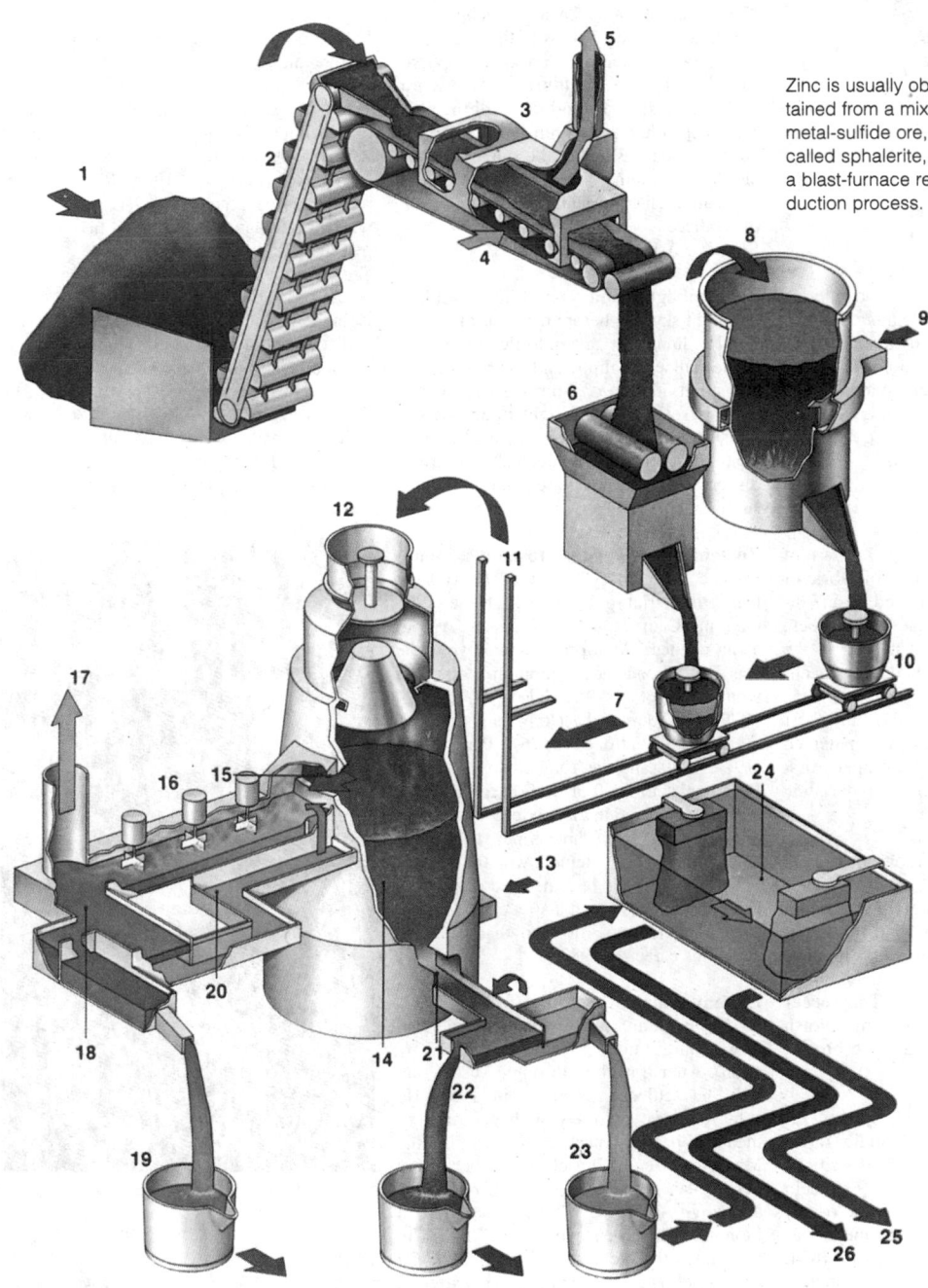

Zinc is usually obtained from a mixed metal-sulfide ore, called sphalerite, by a blast-furnace reduction process.

Ground ore (1) is transported (2) to a roasting oven (3) through which hot air (4) is blown. The heated metal sulfides are converted into oxides and sulfur dioxide, which is taken off (5) and processed into sulfuric acid. The oxides are crushed (6) and stored (7) until needed. Finely divided coke (8) is preheated with hot air (9) and loaded into a container (10). The oxides and coke are charged (11) into a blast furnace (12), which is sealed when filled and then heated. Hot air (13) is passed through the oxides-coke mixture (14). Carbon monoxide is formed and this reduces the oxides to the free metals. The temperature of the furnace is kept above the boiling point of zinc. The zinc vapors pass (15) into a chamber (16) and are condensed by a spray of molten lead. The excess carbon monoxide from the furnace is removed (17). The liquid lead and zinc are immiscible and separate into two layers (18). The upper, zinc, layer is collected (19) for commercial uses. The lower layer of lead (20) is returned to the spray chamber. In the blast furnace, the reduced molten-metal impurities (21) – mainly lead and often smaller amounts of gold and silver – collect at the bottom and are covered by a layer of liquid slag. This slag is poured out (22) and saved for later recovery of copper impurities. The molten lead is collected (23) and refined by electrolysis (24) for consumer use (25). The silver and gold build up as a sludge in the electrolyte bath and are periodically taken out and refined (26).

Z

ZIP Code, acronym for Zone Improvement Plan, a 5-digit code implemented (1963) to speed sorting and delivery of domestic mail. An optional extra 4 digits were added in 1981. The first number of the code identifies 1 of 10 large geographical areas in the United States where the mail will be delivered. The second 2 numbers indicate the metropolitan area, and the last 2 numbers represent the addressee's local post office. The ZIP code facilitates mechanical mail processing.

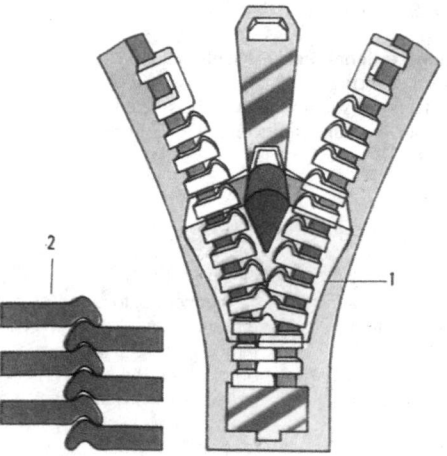

The metal zip was patented in Germany by Catharina Kuhn-Moos, in 1912. Zips are made of brass, steel, aluminium, nickel/silver and plastics. (1) The slide pulls the teeth together, to close, or pushes them apart, to open the zip. (2) Each tooth has a protrusion on top, and a recess underneath, which fit together alternately.

Zipper, slide fastener having 2 rows of coils or teeth attached to strips of fabric or other material. The slide, moved in one direction, pulls the teeth together to interlock, and unlocks the teeth when moved in the opposite direction. The original slide fastener was displayed (1893) by Whitcomb L. Judson at the Chicago World's Fair Columbian Exposition and was patented that year. The B. F. Goodrich Company first used the name zipper (1922) for the slide fastener on overshoes.

Zircon, silicate mineral, zirconium silicate ($ZrSiO_4$), used chiefly as a gemstone and as the main source of the metals zirconium and hafnium, in industry and research. Zircon crystals are widespread in igneous deposits such as granite, in some metamorphic rock, and in beach sands. They occur in Australia, Asia, Europe, and North America, and may be clear, red-brown, green, yellow, or blue.

Zirconium, chemical element, symbol Zr; for physical constants, see Periodic Table. Zirconium is mentioned in biblical writings as the mineral zircon. In 1789 Martin Heinrich Klaproth isolated the oxide of zirconium from zircon. The impure metal was first isolated by Jöns J. Berzelius in 1824. Zircon (zirconium silicate) is the principal ore of zirconium. Zirconium is produced commercially by reduction of the chloride with magnesium. It is a grayish-white, lustrous metal resistant to corrosion by acids, alkalis, sea water, and other agents. It is superconductive at low temperatures. The metal has a low absorption cross section for neutrons. Most zirconium is used in nuclear reactors. Zirconium oxide is a refractory material and is used in furnaces and in the glass and ceramic industries.

Zither, stringed instrument related to the dulcimer and psaltery. It is placed across the knees, and the strings, which stretch across a shallow sound box, are plucked. The zither is a traditional folk instrument of central Europe.

Zodiac, band of the heavens whose outer limits lie 9° on each side of the ecliptic. The 12 main constellations near the eclipse, corresponding to the 12 signs of the zodiac, are Aries; Taurus; Gemini; Cancer; Leo; Virgo; Libra; Scorpio; Sagittarius; Capricorn; Aquarius; Pisces. The orbits of all the planets except Pluto lie within the zodiac, and their positions, as that of the sun, are important in astronomy and astrology. The 12 signs are each equivalent to 30° of arc along the zodiac.
See also: Astrology.

Zodiacal light, faint cone of light visible in the night sky just before dawn or after sunset. The luminosity extends along the plane of the zodiac or ecliptic and can best be seen at a point 30° to 90° from the sun, though there is some zodiacal light in all parts of the sky. Scientists explain zodiacal light as dust particles from comets and asteroids dispersed over a vast area and reflecting sunlight.

Zoetemelk, Gerardus Josephus (Joop) (1946-), Dutch cyclist, won the 100 km team time trial gold medal at the 1968 Olympic Games, and the Tour de l'Avenir, as an amateur. As a professional cyclist he was Dutch road race champion twice, and won among others Paris-Nice (1974, 1975, 1979), the Tour of the Netherlands (1975), the Flèche Wallone (1976), Paris-Tours (1977, 1979, and the Tour of Spain (1979). He completed the Tour de France 16 times, and usually ended in the top ten; he was second six times, forth three times, fifth once, and eighth once; Zoetemelk won the Tour de France in 1980. He became road race world champion in 1985, and also won the Italian stage race Tirreno-Adriatico that year. He ended his career in 1987.

Zoffany, Johann (later John Zoffany, 1733-1810), German painter, who studied in Regensburg under Martin Speer (1702-1765). After travelling through Austria and Italy he settled in London in 1758. He achieved great notoriety with paintings of theater performances, in which his Maecenas, Derek Garrick, and other actors performed, including *The Clandestine Marriage* (Garrick Club, Londen). In Florence, where he stayed from 1772-1776, he painted the famous *Trubuna degl' Uffizi* (Windsor Castle). His paintings are extremely carefully painted and full of brightly colored detail.

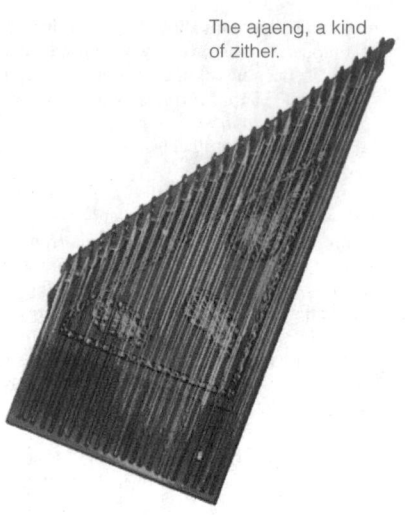

The ajaeng, a kind of zither.

Zog (Ahmedi Bey Zogu; 1895-1961), king of Albania (1928-1946). After serving in the Austrian army he was made premier (1922-1924) and president (1925-1928), whereupon he proclaimed himself king. He fled when the Italians invaded, and he spent the rest of his life in exile.
See also: Albania.

Zola, Émile (1840-1902), French novelist and founder of naturalism. His works proclaim a 'scientific' vision of life determined entirely by heredity and environment. His first success, *Thérèse Raquin* (1867), was followed by the *Rougon-Macquart* cycle (20 vol., 1871-1893), depicting, with powerful and often lurid realism, the fortunes of a contemporary family. It includes his cele-

Portrait of the French writer Émile Zola (1840-1902) by Edouard Manet (1832-1883). When Manet's paintings caused a scandal in the 1860s, Zola fiercely defended him (1868, Louvre, Paris).

brated studies of alcoholism (*The Dram Shop*, 1877), prostitution (*Nana*, 1880), and life in a mining community (*Germinal*, 1885). In 1898 Zola threw himself into the Dreyfus affair with the pamphlet 'J'accuse,' attacking the army.
See also: Naturalism.

Zone melting, technique used in industry and research to remove or distribute impurities in solid materials. Zone melting uses alternate heating and freezing provided by a row of ring-shaped heaters that pass slowly along a tube of solid substance. As the rings travel, they melt bands, or zones, of the solid matter. The resulting liquid holds and carries the impurities to the end of the tube, and the melted area is then refrozen. Subsequent repetitions of the procedure improve the purification.

Zoning, control by ordinance of the uses or character of urban land or buildings, usually accomplished by confining a specific type of development, either residential, public, commercial, or industrial, to a designated area. Zoning laws are used by city and county planning departments to regulate growth and population concentration, preserve neighborhood environments, and isolate industry and commerce. The first U.S. zoning laws were enacted in New York City (1916), and until the 1950s, U.S. zoning was used chiefly in previously developed areas. Now nearly all new urban construction is controlled by zoning.

Zoo, or zoological garden, collection of wild-animal species preserved for public education, scientific research, and the breeding of endangered species. The first modern zoo (1826) was that of the Royal Zoological Society at Regent's Park, London.

Zoogeography, study of the geographical distribution of animal species and populations. Physical barriers-such as wide oceans and mountain ranges, major climatic extremes, or intense heat or cold-may prevent the spread of a species into new areas or may separate 2 previously like populations, allowing them to develop into distinct species. The effect of these barriers on movement and interbreeding, both now and in the past, are reflected in the distributions and, later, adaptive radiations of animal species, resulting in the zoogeographical distributions we find today.

Zoology, scientific study of animal life. Originally concerned with the classification of animal groups, comparative anatomy, and physiology, the science now embraces studies of evolution, genetics, embryology, biochemistry, animal behavior, and ecology.

Zorn, John (1954-), American jazz musician. Plays the alto saxophone, is band leader, and a prodigious composer, also of 'modern-classical' works. Heavily influenced by free jazz, but also fascinated by film music and klezmer. Lives alternately in Japan and New York, where he can often be seen performing in the avant-garde Knitting Factory club. His record, *The Big Gun down* (1985), received

wide acclaim, as did his arrangements of themes from film soundtracks.

Zoroaster *See:* Zoroastrianism.

Zoroastrianism, Persian religion based on the teachings of Zoroaster (Greek form of *Zarathustra*), a sage who lived in the 6th century B.C. It was founded on the old Aryan folk religion but abolished its polytheism, establishing 2 predominant spirits: Ahura-Mazda (Ormazd), the spirit of light and good; and Ahriman, the spirit of evil and darkness. Zoroastrianism includes the belief in eternal reward or punishment after death according to man's deeds. Its scriptures are the *Zend-Avesta*. Almost wiped out in the 7th century by the Muslim conquest of Persia, Zoroastrianism survives among the Parsees (Parsis) of India.
See also: Persia, Ancient.

Zucchini (*Cucurbita pepo*), annual summer squash of the family Cucurbitaceae. Developed in Italy and first used in the United States in California, zucchini is widely and easily cultivated. It is a bush plant with large leaves. The edible blossoms are gold; the fruits are cylindrical with dark-green skins, though some varieties are pale green or gold. Zucchini is eaten raw or cooked and is a valuable source of vitamins A and C and of calcium.

Zuckmayer, Carl (1896-1977), German-American-Swiss author. After having received his high school diploma, he volunteered for the army and rose to the rank of lieutenant. After drifting for a number of years, he began to study drama in Berlin together with Brecht under Max Reinhardt in 1924, and had his first success in 1925 with the comedy *The Merry Vineyard*. In 1926 he bought a house, Wiesmühle, near Salzburg, but it was confiscated by the Gestapo in 1938 because of his antifascist views; views which also led to the performance of his plays being banned. He left the country soon thereafter, and in 1946 adopted American nationality. After WW II he lived alternately in Germany

and the U.S., but settled in Switzerland in 1958, where he became a naturalized citizen in 1966. Zuckmayer is one of the most successful playwrights of the century, initially with plays full of hilarity and the joy of life, later with socially critical satires (*The Captain of Köpenick*, 1930). His extensive oeuvre includes a variety of genres; in 1930 he wrote *The Blue Angel* (screenplay) and in 1946 the play *The Devil's General*.

Zuider Zee, formerly an inlet of the North Sea indenting the Netherlands and divided by the chain of the West Frisian Islands. Due to floods during the Middle Ages, the Zuider Zee grew enough to threaten habitations along its shores. There were many schemes to stem the encroachment of the Zuider Zee, but the first feasible plan was developed by Cornelis Lely, a Dutch engineer, and approved by the Dutch government in 1918. He proposed constructing a heavy dike between Friesland and North Holland that would shorten the coastline and discharge the salt water. Construction began in 1920 and the 19-mi (30-km) dam, the Afsluitdijk, was completed in 1932. It separated the Zuider Zee into two areas, the Waddenzee, open to the sea, and the IJsselmeer, in which large areas of land have been reclaimed for agricultural use.

Zukerman, Pinchas (1948-), Israeli-born violinist, violist, and conductor who came to New York (1962) as a protégé of Isaac Stern. He performed with orchestras throughout the world and made his conducting debut in 1974.

Zulu, South African Bantu people who settled what is now Natal Province early in the 17th century. Under King Shaka (or Chaka), the Zulus conquered neighboring tribes and expanded their domain (1818-1820). Shaka was friendly to Europeans, but his half-brother and successor, Dingaan, fought with Boer settlers (1838) in a cattle dispute. The British invaded Zulu territory (1879) and, after losing a battle at Isandhlwana, defeated the Zulus at Ulundi. There was political un-

Marken, a typical Zuider Zee village.

Z

Z

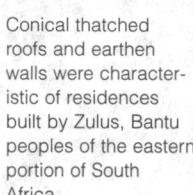

Conical thatched roofs and earthen walls were characteristic of residences built by Zulus, Bantu peoples of the eastern portion of South Africa.

rest until 1910 when the Union of South Africa absorbed the Zulu province. Traditionally cattle and grain farmers, the Zulus live in a patriarchal clan society and the clan chief is the genealogically senior male. They practice polygyny. Zulu religion was based on ancestor worship and the belief in a divine creator, though now many Zulus have adopted Christianity.

Zululand, former semi-autonomous homeland in Natal, South Africa. It borders on Mozambique, the Indian Ocean, Swaziland, and the Buffalo and Tugela rivers. It produces sugarcane, cotton, and maize. Cattle raising is the traditional occupation of the Zulus, a Bantu people who comprise most of the population. Traditionally they live in beehive-shaped huts in fenced compounds called *kraals.* Zululand was annexed by the British in 1887 after prolonged Zulu resistance to white conquest. Many Zulu men now work as migrant laborers in mines and in cities.
See also: South Africa.

Zuñi, Native Americans of the Zuñian lin-

guistic stock, in New Mexico. The Zuñi live mainly by agriculture and produce fine jewelry and sculpture. They have retained their ancient religion, which they celebrate in magnificent festivals noted for their dancing and costumes.

Zunz, Leopold (1794-1886), German Jewish scholar and historian who made the first scientific analysis of Jewish prayers and literature. Zunz was one of the founders of the Society for Jewish Culture and Science (1819), established to analyze and explore Jewish literature, culture, and history, and he was editor of the society's periodical (1820-1823). His works in German include *On Rabbinic Literature* (1818), *The Worship Sermons of the Jews, Historically Developed* (1832), and *On History and Literature* (1845).
See also: Jews.

Zurbarán, Francisco (1598-1664), Spanish painter of the Baroque period known for his religious paintings and representations of monastic life. Zurbarán's naturalistic style was stimulated by Caravaggio and Velázquez and was characterized by sculptural modeling of form created by intense contrast between shadow and light. His first known painting is dated 1616, but he produced his finest works between 1629 and 1645, including a series, *Labors of Hercules,* and *Defense of Cadiz* (1634), *Adoration of the Kings* (1638), and a number of paintings exported to Lima, Peru (1647), that influenced colonial art. His later works were more sentimental and idealized in style.
See also: Baroque.

Zürich (pop. 400,000), city in northern Switzerland, capital of Zürich canton, and the nation's financial and education center. The Romans settled Zürich c.A.D. 100 as the fortified Turicum. It joined the Swiss Confedera-tion that became modern Switzerland (1351). Zürich is a tourist and cultural center, home to the University of Zürich; the National Museum; 2 11th-century churches, the Grossmünster and the Fraumünster; and the 15th-century Wasserkirche. Industrial products include precision

machinery, textiles, food, paper, and tobacco. The world's banking and gold-trade centers are located in Zürich.
See also: Switzerland.

Zweig, Arnold (1887-1968), German novelist. He wrote an 8-volume epic that includes his best-known novel, *The Case of Sergeant Grischa* (1927), which powerfully indicted militarism in its description of World War I and its effects on German society.

Zweig, Stefan (1881-1942), Austrian biographer and novelist. He is best known for his psychological studies of such historical figures and writers as Erasmus, Mary, Queen of Scots, and Honoré Balzac. He wrote of European culture in *The Tide of Fortune* (1928).

Zwicky, Fritz (1898-1974), Swiss-born U.S. astronomer and astrophysicist best known for his studies of supernovas, which he showed to be quite distinct from, and much rarer than, novas. He also did pioneering work on jet propulsion.
See also: Astronomy; Supernova.

Zwingli, Huldreich (1484-1531), influential Swiss Protestant leader of the Reformation, originally a Roman Catholic priest. In 1523 the city of Zürich accepted his 67 articles demanding such reforms as the removal of religious images, simplification of the Mass, and the introduction of Bible readings. Zwingli was killed in the war between the Catholic and Protestant cantons.
See also: Reformation.

Zworykin, Vladimir Kosma (1889-1982), Russian-born U.S. electronic engineer regarded as the father of modern television: His kinescope (patented 1924), little adapted, is our modern picture tube; and his iconoscope, though now obsolete, represents the basis of the first practical television camera. He also made important contributions to the electron microscope.
See also: Television.

In *The Holy House of Nazareth* (c. 1630), by the Spanish baroque painter Francisco de Zurbarán, the young Christ has cut his finger on a crown of thorns, a portent to the Virgin Mary, and by extension to the viewer, of her son's Passion (Museum of Art, Cleveland, Ohio).

Huldreich Zwingli (1484-1531), a leader of Swiss Reformation.

Chemical Elements

Name	Symbol	Atomic No.	Name	Symbol	Atomic No.
Actinium	Ac	89	Molybdenum	Mo	42
Aluminum	Al	13			
Americium	Am	95	Neodymium	Nd	60
Antimony	Sb	51	Neon	Ne	10
Argon	Ar	18	Neptunium	Np	93
Arsenic	As	33	Nickel	Ni	28
Astatine	At	85	Niobium	Nb	41
			Nitrogen	N	7
Barium	Ba	56	Nobelium	No	102
Berkelium	Bk	97			
Beryllium	Be	4	Osmium	Os	76
Bismuth	Bi	83	Oxygen	O	8
Bohrium	Bh	107			
Boron	B	5	Palladium	Pd	46
Bromine	Br	35	Phosphorus	P	15
			Platinum	Pt	78
Cadmium	Cd	48	Plutonium	Pu	94
Calcium	Ca	20	Polonium	Po	84
Californium	Cf	98	Potassium	K	19
Carbon	C	6	Praseodymium	Pr	59
Cerium	Ce	58	Promethium	Pm	61
Cesium	Cs	55	Protactinium	Pa	91
Chlorine	Cl	17	Radium	Ra	88
Chromium	Cr	24	Radon	Rn	86
Cobalt	Co	27	Rhenium	Re	75
Copper (Cuprum)	Cu	29	Rhodium	Rh	45
Curium	Cm	96	Rubidium	Rb	37
			Ruthenium	Ru	44
Dubnium	Db	105	Rutherfordium	Rf	104
Dysprosium	Dy	66			
			Samarium	Sm	62
Einsteinium	Es	99	Scandium	Sc	21
Erbium	Er	68	Seaborgium	Sg	106
Europium	Eu	63	Selenium	Se	34
			Silicon	Si	14
Fermium	Fm	100	Silver (Argentum)	Ag	47
Fluorine	F	9	Sodium	Na	11
Francium	Fr	87	Strontium	Sr	38
			Sulfur	S	16
Gadolinium	Gd	64			
Gallium	Ga	31	Tentalum	Ta	73
Germanium	Ge	32	Technetium	Tc	43
Gold (Aurum)	Au	79	Tellurium	Te	52
			Terbium	Tb	65
Hafnium	Hf	72	Thallium	Tl	81
Hassium	Hs	108	Throrium	Th	90
Helium	He	2	Thulium	Tm	69
Holmium	Ho	67	Tin (Stannum)	Sn	50
Hydrogen	H	1	Titanium	Ti	22
			Tungsten (Wolfram)	W	74
Indium	In	49			
Iodine	I	53	Ununbium	Uub	112
Iridium	Ir	77	Ununhexium	Uuh	116
Iron (Ferrum)	Fe	26	Ununnilium	Uun	110
			Ununquadium	Uuq	114
Krypton	Kr	36	Unununium	Uuu	111
			Uranium	U	92
Lanthanum	La	57			
Lawrencium	Lr	103	Vanadium	V	23
Lead (Plumbum)	Pb	82			
Lithium	Li	3	Xenon	Xe	54
Lutetium	Lu	71			
			Ytterbium	Yb	70
Magnesium	Mg	12	Yttrium	Y	39
Manganese	Mn	25			
Meitnerium	Mt	109	Zinc	Zn	30
Mendelevium	Md	101	Zirconium	Zr	40
Mercury	Hg	80			

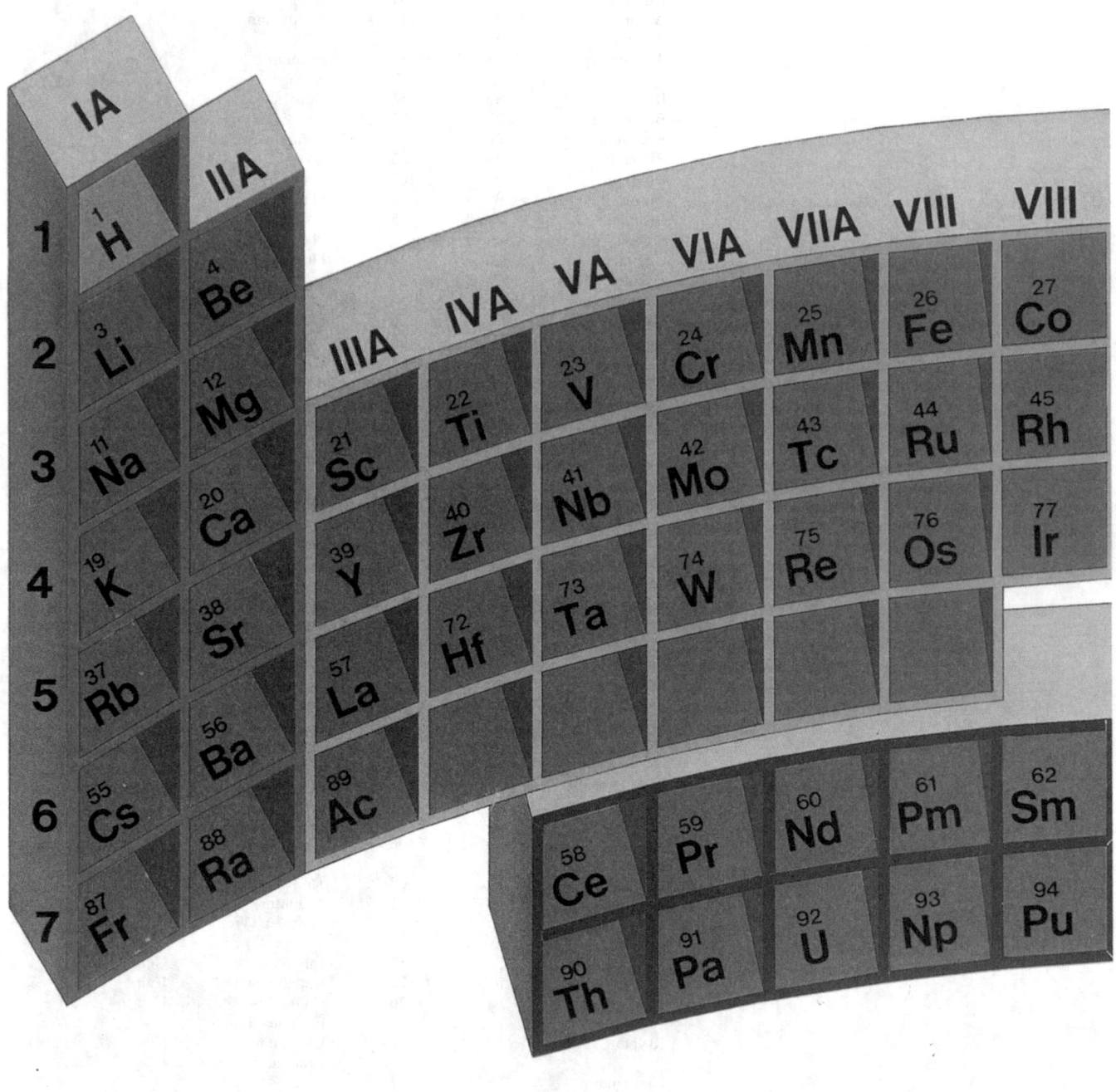

The periodic table shows an arrangement of elements according to atomic number. The vertical columns (with Roman numerals) contain elements with similar properties. The horizontal rows (with arabic numbers) relate to the build-up of the atomic constituents of each element. Metallic elements are in yellow boxes, while non-metallic are in blue. The two series of elements shown separate are the lanthanide and actinide series. The colored edges of the boxes indicate the main groups of elements: alkaline and alkaline earth (green), transition metals (yellow), and main group elements (red). Hydrogen can be considered either as a metal or as a non-metal.

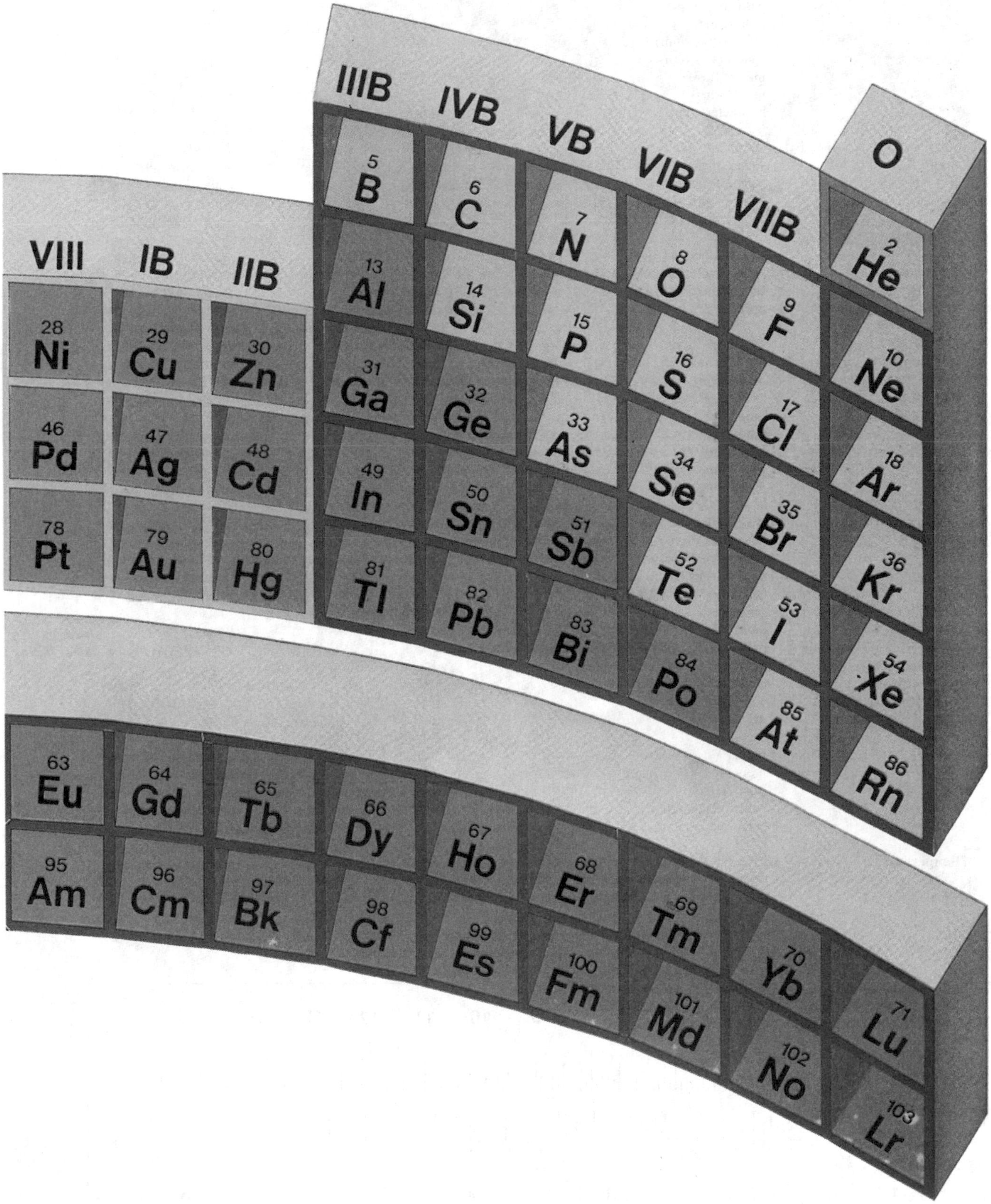
IIIB
IVB
VB
VIB
VIIB
O
VIII
IB
IIB
5 B
6 C
7 N
8 O
2 He
13 Al
14 Si
15 P
16 S
9 F
10 Ne
28 Ni
29 Cu
30 Zn
31 Ga
32 Ge
33 As
34 Se
17 Cl
18 Ar
46 Pd
47 Ag
48 Cd
49 In
50 Sn
51 Sb
52 Te
35 Br
36 Kr
78 Pt
79 Au
80 Hg
81 Tl
82 Pb
83 Bi
84 Po
53 I
54 Xe
85 At
86 Rn
63 Eu
64 Gd
65 Tb
66 Dy
67 Ho
68 Er
69 Tm
70 Yb
71 Lu
95 Am
96 Cm
97 Bk
98 Cf
99 Es
100 Fm
101 Md
102 No
103 Lr

Metric Measurement Conversions

Lenght	When you know:	Multiply by:	To find:
	inches (in)	2.54	centimeters (cm)
	feet (ft)	30	centimeters (cm)
	yards (yd)	0.9	meters (m)
	miles (mi)	1.6	kilometers (km)
	millimeters (mm)	0.04	inches (in)
	centimeters (cm)	0.4	inches (in)
	meters (m)	3.3	feet (ft)
	meters (m)	1.1	yards (yd)
	kilometers (km)	0.6	miles (mi)

Area	When you know:	Multiply by:	To find:
	square inches (sq in)	6.5	sq. centimeters (sq cm)
	square feet (sq ft)	0.09	square meters (sq m)
	square yards (sq yd)	0.8	square meters (sq m)
	square miles (sq mi)	2.6	sq. kilometers (sq km)
	acres	0.4	hectares
	sq. centimeters (sq cm)	0.16	square inches (sq in)
	square meters (sq m)	1.2	square yards (sq yd)
	sq. kilometers (sq km)	0.4	square miles (sq mi)
	hectares	2.5	acres

Weight	When you know:	Multiply by:	To find:
	ounces (oz)	28	grams (g)
	pounds (lb)	0.45	kilograms (kg)
	short tons	0.9	metric tons
	long tons	1.01	metric tons
	grams (g)	0.035	ounces (oz)
	kilograms (kg)	2.2	pounds (lb)
	metric tons	1.1	short tons
	metric tons	0.98	long tons

Volume	When you know:	Multiply by:	To find:
	teaspoons (tsp)	5	milliliters (ml)
	tablespoons (tbsp)	15	milliliters (ml)
	fluid ounces (fl oz)	30	milliliters (ml)
	cups (c)	0.24	liters (l)
	pints (pt)	0.47	liters (l)
	quarts (qt)	0.95	liters (l)
	gallons-U.S. (gal)	3.8	liters (l)
	gallons-imperial (gal)	4.5	liters (l)
	cubic feet (cu ft)	.028	cubic meters (cu m)
	cubic yards (cu yd)	0.76	cubic meters (cu m)
	milliliters (ml)	0.03	fluid ounces (fl oz)
	liters (l)	2.1	pints (pt)
	liters (l)	1.06	quarts (qt)
	liters (l)	0.26	gallons-U.S. (gal)
	liters (l)	0.22	gallons-imperial (gal)
	cubic meters (cu m)	35	cubic feet (cu ft)
	cubic meters (cu m)	1.3	cubic yards (cu yd)

Temperature

$$°C = (°F - 32) \times .555$$
$$°F = (°C \times 1.8) + 32$$

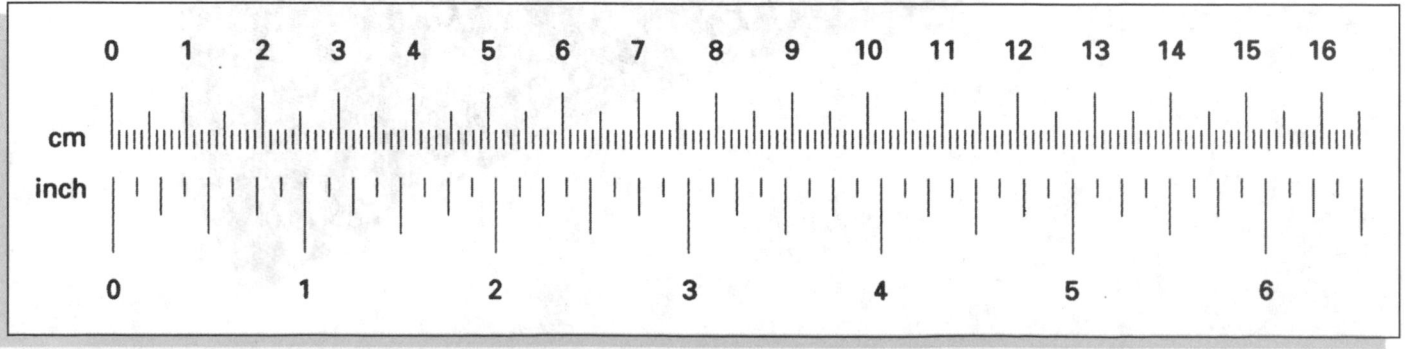

Illustrated Survey of World History

The intention of this survey is to indicate key developments which receive elaboration in text entries. Nonspecific dates -for example, Bayeux tapestry (c.1080)- denote approximate timings of the rise of important political or cultural developments, of significant events, and of individuals' major accomplishments.

10,000 - 4000 B.C.

Historic Overview: By 10,000 B.C. humans were beginning to develop agriculture and change from hunter-gatherer economies to permanent farm-based economies, which created the proper environment for the development of civilization. Between 9000 and 4000 B.C. humans had developed sophisticated farm settlements with technological advancements in the Middle East (Tigris and Euphrates rivers region), America (Mexico), and China. With the advent of agriculture human societies were transformed from egalitarian tribal societies organized by family ties into chiefdoms with hierarchical organization, which were forerunners of the ancient city-states.

Technology: Use of stone farm tools (axes, sickles, knives), pottery, weaving, and the development of craft. The construction of houses made of mud bricks and stone.

Religion and Philosophy: Spiritual beliefs based on the central importance of agriculture. Fertility celebrated in shrines to gods and goddesses; the bull as a recurrent theme in religious rituals.
Art: By 10,000 B.C. humans had been painting (rocks, cave walls), sculpting (walls), carving (figurines, amulets), and engraving for thousands of years. Much of prehistoric art had hunting as a central theme.

Neolithic stone configurations in France (6000-2000 B.C.) This was probably a holy site that had use in astronomy.

Cave paintings in North Africa (3500 B.C.)

Neolithic sickle with flint pieces inserted into wood (3000-2500 B.C.)

4000-700 B.C.

Historic Overview: Development of Sumerian culture (4000-3500 B.C.) • Rise of the city-states (400-3400 B.C.) of Uruk, Ur, Kish, Lagash, Ender, and Umna • Unification of the two kingdoms of Egypt and the rise of its civilization (3200-1200 B.C.) • Cave paintings in North America (c.3000 B.C.) • First pottery in Mexico (c.2000 B.C.) • Reign of Hammurabi in Babylon (1790-50 B.C.) • Shang dynasty in China (1600-1100 B.C.) • Development of Mycenean civilization (c.1600 B.C.) • Height of Minoan civilization on Crete (c.1500 B.C.) • Olmec civilization in Mexico (c.1500 B.C.) • Moses and Jewish people leave Egypt (c.1250 B.C.) • Height of Phoenician civilization (c.1200 B.C.) • Solomon builds the temple at Jerusalem (c.950 B.C.) • Carthage established by Phoenicians (c.814 B.C.) • Rome founded (753 B.C.)

Technology: Invention of the wheel in Mesopotamia (c.4000 B.C.) • Copper and bronze axes in Sumeria (c.3200 B.C.) • Plows in Mesopotamia and Egypt (c.3000 B.C.) • First 365-day calendar in Egypt (c.2700 B.C.) • Zoser's step pyramid (c. 2700 B.C.) and Great Pyramid and Great Sphinx (c. 2500 B.C.) in Egypt • Temple of Ur in Sumeria (c.2000 B.C.) • Iron weapons in the Middle East (c.2000 B.C.) • Minoan palace at Knossos (c.1800 B.C.) • Molten glass in Egypt (c.1500 B.C.) • Chinese bronze works (c.1500 B.C.) • Food preservation in Greece and Phoenicia (c.1200 B.C.) • Wheat, barley and cotton in the Middle East (c.750 B.C.)

The Egyptian Book of the Dead (1300 B.C.)

Religion and Philosophy: Fertility cults based on farming in Middle East (c.4000 B.C.) • Memphite theology and concept of divine kingship in Egypt (c.3000 B.C.) • Stonehenge built (c.2000 B.C.) • Canaanite religion, based on the worship of El and Baal, in Palestine (c.1900 B.C.) • Vedas of India (c.1300 B.C.) • Worship of a single god, Yahweh, instituted by Moses (c.1200 B.C.) • Shinto religion in Japan (c.900 B.C.) • Old Testament prophets (c.750 B.C.)

Art: Painted pottery in Mesopotamia (c.4000 B.C.) • Use of gold and copper in Mesopotamian decorative arts (c.2500 B.C.) • Decorative textiles in Peru (c.1800 B.C.) • Minoan pottery flourishes (c.1600 B.C.) • First known pottery in North America (c.2400 B.C.) • Use of precious materials in Egypt (c.1500 B.C.) • Bronze casting in China (c.1300 B.C.) • Pottery flourishes in Greece (c.800 B.C.) • Jade ornaments in Mexico (c.800 B.C.)

Two-handled vase from the Yangshao period in China (2500 B.C.)

Victory scene on a mosaic from Mari (c. 2500 B.C.)

Diorite stele with the laws of Hammurabi (1700 B.C.)

---

700 B.C. – A.D. 500

Historic Overview: Etruscan cities flourished in Italy (c.700 B.C.) • Dominance of Sparta (c.650 B.C.) • Persian Empire and Cyrus the Great (c.550 B.C.) • Rome as an independent republic (c.500 B.C.) • Athens under Pericles (c.450 B.C.) • Peloponnesian War (c. 400 B.C.) • Canyon de Chelly in Arizona (c.350 B.C.) • Alexander the Great (c.30 B.C.) • First Punic War (c.250 B.C.) • Hannibal (c.200 B.C.) • Great Wall of China (c.200 B.C.) • Confucianism as basis of Chinese law (c.100 B.C.) • Pompey and Julius Caesar (c.100 B.C.) • Jesus (A.D. 30) • Persecution of Christians (A.D. 200) • Constantine and founding of Constantinople (c.A.D. 300) • Mayan civilization (c.A.D. 400) • Sack of Rome (c.A.D. 400) • Huns attack Gaul (c.A.D. 450)

Technology: Greek silver coins (c.700 B.C.) • Hanging Gardens of Babylon (c.600 B.C.) • Pythagoras (c.500 B.C.) • Iron welding in Greece (c.500 B.C.) • Parthenon (c.450 B.C.) • Hippocrates (c.400 B.C.) • Aristotle (c.350 B.C.) • Euclid (c.300 B.C.) • Colossus of Rhodes (c.280 B.C.) • Archimedes (c.250 B.C.) • Pyramid of the Sun in Mexico (c.100 B.C.) • Roman aqueducts and roads (c.A.D. 60) • Paper in China (c.A.D. 100) • Ptolemy (c.A.D. 150) • Galen (c.A.D. 200) • Abacus in China (c.A.D. 200) • Mayan mathematics and astronomy (c.A.D.350) • Boethius (c.A.D. 500)

Religion and Philosophy: Taoism in China (c.600 B.C.) • Zoroastrianism in Iran (c.600 B.C.) • Confucius (c.500 B.C.) • Buddhism in India (c.500 B.C.) • Protagoras and the Greek Sophists (c.450 B.C.) • Socrates (c.450 B.C.) • Plato (c.400 B.C.) • Aristotle (c.350 B.C.) • Yogic thought codified in India (c.150 B.C.) • The gospel of St. Mark written (c.A.D. 62) • Buddhism in China (c.A.D. 250) • Mithraism (c.A.D. 250) • Council of Nicaea (A.D. 325) • St. Augustine (c.A.D. 400)

Art: Elaborate Olmec sculptures in Mexico (c.700 B.C.) • Attic black-figure pottery (c.550 B.C.) • Celtic bronzes (c.460 B.C.) • Praxiteles (c.350 B.C.) • *Venus de Milo (c.150 B.C.)* • Early Christian painting (c.A.D. 200) • Mochican art in Peru (c.A.D. 300) • Manuscript illustration (c.A.D. 500)

Temple of Zeus in Athens (2nd century B.C.)

Statue of Apollo (540 B.C.)

The Cross of Justinian (A.D. 570)

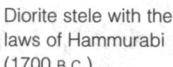

Roman aqueduct: Pont du Gard in France (C.A.D. 300)

A.D. 500 – A.D. 1500

Historic Overview: Frankish king Clovis I (c.500) • Byzantine emperor Justinian the Great (c.550) • Mayans build Palenque (c.650) • Charlemagne crowned Holy Roman Emperor (800) • Roman and Byzantine Christianity split (867) • Viking invasions of northern Europe (900-1000) • Norman conquest of England by William I; Battle of Hastings (1066) • Ottoman Empire begins (1071) • First Crusade (1096-99) • Pueblo civilizations in Americas (c.1100) • Saladin captures Jerusalem (1187) • King John signs Magna Carta (1215) • Kublai Khan establishes Yuan dynasty in China (c.1260) • Marco Polo (c.1290) • Aztecs found Tenochititlan (1325) • Hundred Years War starts (1337) • Black Death in Europe (c.1350) • Papacy split between Rome and Avignon (1378) • Rise of Moscow as political power (c.1380) • Joan of Arc leads French against English (c.1430) • Rise of the Medici (1434) • Christopher Columbus sails on first voyage (1492)

Technology: Ma'daba mosaic depicts oldest map of Holy Land (c.550) • Advancement of medical diagnosis in China (c.600) • Invention of windmill in Persia (c.640) • Mayan astronomy develops (c.740) • Jabir, father of Arabic chemistry (c.750) • Gunpowder invented in China (c.760) • Printing from relief blocks in Japan (c.800) • The word 'algebra' appears in Arabic mathematical document (c.850) • Lateen sails for ships introduced to the West (c.880) • Alembic used in distilling (c.950) • Avicenna (c.1000) • Fibonacci writes first text on algebra in West (c.1200) • Stern-mounted rudders appear on European ships (c.1250) • Roger Bacon (c.1275) • Spinning wheel and gunpowder in Europe (c.1300) • Henry the Navigator establishes school for the study of geography and navigation (1416) • Johann Gutenberg prints from moveable type (c.1450) • Leonardo da Vinci (c.1490)

Religion and Philosophy: First Benedictine monastery (c.529) • Buddhism appears in Japan (552) • Pope Gregory the Great (c.590) • Mohammed receives first call (610) • Islam reaches Spain (715) • Alcuin writes vulgate text for Bible (c.780) • Rise of Sufism (c.900) • Abbey of Cluny founded (910) • Schism between Greek church and papacy (1054) • Averroes's commentaries on Aristotle (1169) • St. Thomas Aquinas's *Summa Theologica* (1266-73) • Papacy moves to Avignon (1309) • John Wycliffe (c.1380) • Papacy returns to Rome (1420) • John Huss (c.1400) • Thomas à Kempis writes *Imitation of Christ* (c.1425) • Spanish Inquisition begins (1478) • Jews expelled from Spain (1492)

Art: Manuscript illumination of early Christian era (c.500) • Cathedral of Hagia Sophia (532-37) • Great Chalice of Antioch (c.600) • Sutton Hoo treasure (c.650) • Caedmon (c.670) • Dome of the Rock construction starts (688) • *Lindisfarne Gospels* (c.700) • 20*Venerable Bede* (c.700) • *Beowulf* (700-1000) • Construction of Great Mosque at Cordoba begins (785) • *Book of Kells* (c.790) • The *Anglo-Saxon Chronicle* begun under Alfred the Great (c.870-99) • *The Tale of Genji* (c.1000) • Troubadours appear (c.1075) • Bayeux tapestry (c.1080) • Cathedral of Notre Dame in Paris (c.1160) • Chartres Cathedral (c.1195) • *Parzival* written by Wolfram von Eschenbach (c.1210) • Polyphony in motets and madrigals (1250-1300) • Giotto (c.1300) • Dante Alighieri begins *Divina Commedia* (c.1307) • Petrarch (c.1340) • The Japanese No play (c.1380) • Geoffrey Chaucer's *Canterbury Tales* (c.1395) • Donatello (c.1440) • Sir Thomas Malory writes *Morte d'Arthur* (c.1469-70) • Sandro Botticelli (c.1480)

A mosaic of the emperor Justinian (c.A.D.600)

Mohammed (14th century illustration)

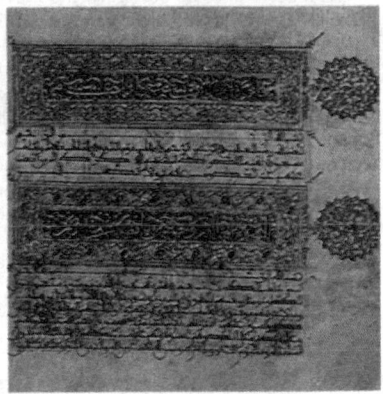

A page from the Koran (14th century)

An illustration from *La cité des dames* by Christine de Pisan (c.1341-1430)

1500 A.D. - 2003 A.D.

Historic Overview: Height of the Inca civilization (c.1500) • Amerigo Vespucci (c.1500) • African slaves introduced in the West Indies by Spain (1501) • Vasco Núñez de Balboa (1513) • Ferdinand Magellan (1520) • Hernando Cortés (1520) • Aztec Empire ends (1521) • Mogul Empire founded in India (1526) • Henry VIII (c.1530) • Suleiman the Magnificent (c.1540) • Queen Elizabeth I (c.1560) • Spanish Armada defeated (1588) • Jamestown, Va., founded (1607) • Thirty Years War begins (1618) • Pilgrims sail on *Mayflower* (1620) • English Civil War (1642-46) • Charles I of England executed (1649) • Louis XIV of France ascends to the throne (1661) • Glorious Revolution in England (1688) • Peter the Great (c.1690) • War of the Spanish Succession (1702-13) • Chinese invade Tibet (1751) • French and Indian War (1754) • Boston Tea Party (1773) • American Revolution (1775-83) • Declaration of Independence (1776) • U.S. Constitution is ratified (1788) • French Revolution begins (1789) • George Washington becomes first president of U.S. (1789) • Napoleon Bonaparte (c.1800) • Simon Bólívar (c.1810) • Holy Roman Empire ends (1806) • U.S. War of 1812 • Congress of Vienna (1814-15) • Monroe Doctrine (1823) • Battle of the Alamo (1836) • Opium Wars in China (1839) • Potato famine in Ireland (1846-47) • Gold rush in California begins (1848) • Crimean War (1854-56) • Giuseppe Garibaldi (c.1860) • U.S. Civil War (1861-65) • Karl Marx (c.1870) • Otto von Bismarck (c.1880) • All Native Americans confined to reservations (1887) • Boxer Rebellion in China (1900) • Spanish-American War (1898) • World War I (1914-18) • Russian Revolution (1917) • Chiang Kai-shek (c.1925) • Joseph Stalin begins collectivization in USSR (1929) • U.S. Wall Street crash (1929) • Mohandas Gandhi (c.1930) • Adolf Hitler made chancellor of Germany (1933) • Franklin D. Roosevelt's New Deal (1933) • World War II (1939-45) • U.N. Charter drafted (1945) • Mao Zedong establishes People's Republic of China (1949) • Korean War (1950-53) • Common Market established (1957) • Berlin Wall built (1961) • John F. Kennedy assassinated (1963) • Martin Luther King, Jr., assassinated (1968) • Height of U.S. involvement in Vietnam War (1969) • Watergate forces Richard M. Nixon to resign (1974) • Camp David Accord between Egypt and Israel (1978) • Glasnost and perestroika in USSR (1986) • Berlin Wall removed (1989) • Nelson Mandela freed in South Africa (1990) • Persian Gulf War (1991) • USSR and Eastern European Warsaw Pact dissolved (1991) • War in Chechnya (1994) • Good Friday Agreement in Northern Ireland (1998) • 2nd Intifadah (2000) • Terrorist attacks on the U.S. (2001) • War on Iraq (2003)

Technology: Cast iron produced on a large scale (c.1520) • Coal becomes a major fuel (c.1520) • Andreas Vesalius (c.1540) • Nicolaus Copernicus publishes his theory of astronomy (1543) • Decimals in mathematics (c.1585) • Telescope invented (1608) • Galileo (c.1610) • Francis Bacon (c.1620) • William Harvey discovers circulation of blood (1628) • Blaise Pascal (c.1640) • Isaac Newton postulates gravity (1664-66) • Christopher Wren (c.1675) • Single-lens microscope invented (c.1675) • Calculus developed (c.1675) • First steam engine (1696) • Classification of plants and animals by Carl Linnaeus (1735) • Benjamin Franklin investigates electricity (1752) • Carbon dioxide discovered (1756) • Antoine Lavoisier (c.1790) • Cotton gin invented (1793) • Edward Jenner discovers vaccination (1796) • First railroad locomotive (1804) • Gas lighting in Europe (c.1805) • Single-wire telegraph (1816) • Photography (c.1815) • Michael Faraday (c.1830) • Morse Code invented (1838) • Sewing machine developed (1851) • Charles Darwin's theory of evolution (1858-59) • Louis Pasteur (c.1860) • Gregor Mendel (c.1865) • Telephone invented by Alexander Graham Bell (1876) • Thomas Edison invents phonograph (1877) • Karl Benz invents automobile (1885) • X-rays discovered by Wilhelm Roentgen (1895) • Guglielmo Marconi (c.1900) • First flight by Wright brothers (1903) • Einstein publishes special (1905) and general

A perspective study by Leonardo Da Vinci

William Harvey

Martin Luther

John Locke

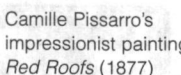
William Shakespeare

Nicolaus Copernicus

Camille Pissarro's impressionist painting *Red Roofs* (1877)

(1915) theories of relativity • Penicillin discovered by Alexander Fleming (1928) • Frank Lloyd Wright (c.1935) • First nuclear reactor built (1942) • First nuclear bombs (1945) • Structure of DNA found (1953) • Polio vaccine developed (1953-55) • Computers enter into commercial use (1955) • Sputnik launched (1957) • First manned space flight (1961) • First heart transplant (1966) • First moon landing (1969) • First test-tube baby (1978) • First artificial human heart (1982) • U.S. *Magellan* space probe reaches Venus (1990) • International Space Station (1998) • Human Genome Project 2001) • Space shuttle Columbia crashed (2003)

Religion and Philosophy: Erasmus (c.1500) • Machiavelli's *The Prince* (1513) • Martin Luther (c.1520) • Sikhism founded (c.1519) • John Calvin (c.1540) • Edict of Nantes (1598) • Hugo Grotius's *On Law* (1625) • René Descartes (c.1645) • Quakers founded in England (1652) • Thomas Hobbes's *Leviathan* (1651) • Spinoza's *Ethics* (1675) • John Locke (c.1690) • Gottfried Leibniz (c.1715) • Hasidism founded (c.1720) • Voltaire (c.1730) • David Hume (c.1735) • Methodist movement founded (c.1740) • Charles Montesquieu's *The Spirit of Laws* (1748) • Denis Diderot's *Encyclopédie* (1751) • Jean-Jacques Rousseau's *The Social Contract* (1762) • Adam Smith's *The Wealth of Nations* (1776) • Immanuel Kant's *Critique of Pure Reason* (1781) • Jeremy Bentham (c.1785) • Tom Paine's *The Rights of Man* (1791) • Mary Wollstonecraft's *Vindication of the Rights of Woman* (1792) • G.W.F. Hegel (c.1815) • Artur Schopenhauer's *The World as Will and Idea* (1819) • Alexis de Tocqueville (c.1840) • Soren Kierkegaard (c.1840) • Karl Marx and Friedrich Engels's *Communist Manifesto* (1848) • Henry David Thoreau (c.1850) • John Stewart Mill (c.1685) • Friedrich Nietzsche's *Beyond Good and Evil* (1886) • Sigmund Freud (c.1900) • Max Weber (c.1905) • Martin Heidegger (c.1930) • Jean-Paul Sartre's *Being and Nothingness* (1943) • Claude Levi-Strauss (c.1960) • John Paul II (1978) • Desmond Tutu (1984)

Art: Michelangelo's Sistine Chapel (c.1510) • Raphael (c.1515) • Titian (c.1530) • François Rabelais (c.1550) • Michel de Montaigne (c.1580) • El Greco (c.1590) • William Shakespeare (c.1600) • Miguel de Cervantes's *Don Quixote* (1605-15) • Claudio Monteverdi's *Orfeo* (1607) • Ben Jonson (c.1610) • Peter Paul Rubens (c.1620) • John Donne (c.1620) • Fugue developed (c.1630) • Molière (c.1660) • Racine (c.1670) • John Milton's *Paradise Lost* (1674) • Matsuo Basho (c.1685) • Concerto developed (c.1690) • Pianoforte invented (1709) • Jonathan Swift (c.1730) • J.S. Bach (c.1740) • George Frederick Handel (c.1740) • Joseph Haydn (c.1760) • Johann Goethe (c.1770) • W.A. Mozart (c.1785) • William Blake (c.1790) • William Wordsworth (c.1800) • Ludwig van Beethoven (c.1810) • Jane Austen (c.1810) • Percy Bysshe Shelley (c.1815) • Francisco de Goya (c.1815) • John Keats (c.1820) • James Fenimore Cooper (c.1830) • Alexander Pushkin (c.1835) • Frédéric Chopin (c.1835) • Charles Dickens (c.1845) • Herman Melville's *Moby Dick* (1851) • Walt Whitman's *Leaves of Grass* (1855) • Gustave Flaubert's *Madame Bovary* (1856) • Leo Tolstoy's *War and Peace* (1865-72) • Rise of Impressionism (1872) • Fyodor Dostoevsky (c.1875) • Richard Wagner (c.1875) • Auguste Rodin (c.1880) • Mark Twain (c.1885) • Henry James (c.1885) • Vincent van Gogh (c.1885) • Bernard Shaw (c.1900) • Pablo Picasso and Cubism (1907) • Igor Stravinsky's *The Rite of Spring* (1913) • Marcel Proust (c.1920) • James Joyce (c.1930) • Surrealism founded (c.1930) • F. Scott Fitzgerald and the Lost Generation (c.1930) • George Gershwin (c.1935) • Eugene O'Neill (c.1940) • Walt Disney (c.1940) • Orson Welles's *Citizen Kane* (1941) • Bebop emerges (c.1945) • Abstract Expressionism (c.1945) • Martha Graham (c.1950) • Beat Generation (c.1960) • Pop Art in U.S. (c.1965) • The Beatles' *Sergeant Pepper* (1967) • Gabriel Garcia Marquez (c.1970) • Michael Jackson (c.1985) • Rap music (1990s) • Pulp Fiction (1994)

The signing of the Declaration of Independence, July 4, 1776

Pre-World War I automobile plant

Nuclear explosion

Info-Spreads Index

Index

Publisher's Note:

While every effort has been made to contact the copyrightholders of illustrations, we apologize for any inadvertent omissions and offer to correct any errors in future editions.

AAA-Photo
ABC-Press
Aerophoto Schiphol bv
AGE FotoStock
Agence Internationale De Presse 'Actualit'
ANP-Foto
Ardea London Ltd
Aspect Picture Library Ltd
The Associated Press

Barnaby's Picture Library
Bavaria-Verlag Bildagentur
Bayerische Staatsbibliothek
Belgisch Instituut voor Voorlichting en Documentatie INBEL
Bettmann Archive
Bibliotheque Nationale
Bibliotheque Publique et Universitaire de Geneve
Bio-Historisch Instituut
Rob Brijker Press-Service RBP
The British Council

California Institute of Technology and Carnegie Institution of
    Washington
Centraalbureau voor Schimmelcultures
CERN European Organization For Nuclear Research
Cinematheque Fran_aise
Bruce Coleman Ltd

Documentation Fran_aise

Edimages
Mary Evans Picture Library
Explorer

Van Gelder Papier
Gemeentemuseum 's-Gravenhage
Geocom bv
Photographie Giraudon
NV IJzer- en Metaalgieterij "De Globe"

Robert Harding Picture Library Ltd
HOA-QUI
Michael Holford Photographs
Holle Bildarchiv
Peter Hunter Press Features

IBM Nederland nv
Inter Nationes
International Picture Research Office IPRO
International Visual Resource

Jacana

Kant-Gymnasium
Katholieke Universiteit Nijmegen - Faculteit der Wiskunde en
    Natuurwetenschappen
Keats-Shelley Memorial Association
Keter Publishing House
Kodak Nederland bv
Koninklijk Instituut voor de Tropen
Koninklijke Smeets Offset bv
K÷vesdi International Press & Photo Agency **KIPPA**

Los Alamos Scientific Laboratory

The Mansell Collection
The Metropolitan Museum of Art
William Morris Gallery

National Aeronautics and Space Administration NASA
National Art Gallery
The National Gallery of Canada
The National Museum of Wales
The National Portrait Gallery
The National Theatre Society
Nederlands Filmmuseum
Novosti-press

Phonogram bv
Photri
Pickthall Picture Library
Picturepoint Ltd
Polyvisie bv
Pratt & Whitney Aircraft Group - United Technology Corporation
Bildarchiv Preussischer Kulturbesitz

Agence de Presse Photographique Rapho
Rijksmuseum voor de Geschiedenis der Natuurwetenschappen
Rijksuniversiteit Leiden - Bibliotheek
Roger-Viollet

SCALA Istituto Fotografico Editoriale
Science Museum
Servizio Editoriale Fotografico SEF
Shostal Associates
Snark International
South Africain Tourist Corporation SATOUR
Bureau SoviÚtique d'Information
Spaarnestad Fotoarchief
Uitgeverij Het Spectrum B.V.

Thielska Galleriet Intendenten
European Southern Observatory
High Altitude Observatory of NCAR
National Aeronautics and Space Administration NASA
Agence Photographique Top

Ullstein Bilderdienst
United Nations Office at Geneva
Universal News Organization UNO
Universitõt Wien - Institut für die Geschichte der Medizin
Universiteits-Bibliotheek van Amsterdam
University of London - Courtauld Institute of Art

Vandaag bv
Vereniging Nederland-DDR
Vereniging Nederland-USSR
Victoria & Albert Museum

Museen der Stadt K÷ln - Wallraf Richartz Museum
Werner S÷derstr÷m Osakeyhti÷
World Photo Service International

Zentrale Farbbild Agentur GmbH ZEFA